# Chambers
# Crossword
# Dictionary

**The bestseller – over 500,000 solutions**

## Chambers

CHAMBERS
An imprint of Chambers Harrap Publishers Ltd
338 Euston Road, London, NW1 3BH

*Chambers Harrap Publishers Ltd is an Hachette UK Company*

© Chambers Harrap Publishers Ltd 2011

Chambers® is a registered trademark of Chambers Harrap Publishers Ltd

This third edition published by Chambers Harrap Publishers Ltd 2011
Previous editions published 2000 and 2006

Database right Chambers Harrap Publishers Ltd (makers)

A CIP catalogue record for this book is available from the British Library.

ISBN 978 0550 10543 1

www.chambers.co.uk

Designed by Chambers Harrap Publishers Ltd
Typeset in Arial and Optima by Sharon McTeir, Creative Publishing Services
Printed and bound in India

# Contents

# Contributors

*Chambers Editor*
Anne Robertson

*Contributors*
Derek Arthur
Katharine Coates
Kay Cullen

*Crossword Essays*
Jonathan Crowther
Don Manley
Tim Moorey

*Chambers Data Management*
David Wark
Patrick Gaherty

*Chambers Prepress Controllers*
Nicolas Echallier
Jonathan Williams

*Chambers Design*
Sharon McTeir

*Chambers Editorial Team*
Elspeth Summers
Helen Vick

*Chambers Editorial Director*
Vivian Marr


*The editor would like to thank contributors to the previous editions.*

# Preface

Solving crosswords is, by all accounts, an enjoyable pastime. Why else would so many of us devote our coffee breaks, our journeys or our lazy weekend afternoons to filling in these black-and-white grids? Yet so often crossword-solving can become a frustrating experience, accompanied by the gritting of teeth, the tearing out of hair and the grumpy tossing aside of pens as the clues prove baffling and the last few squares remain mockingly blank. *Chambers Crossword Dictionary* is a balm and a help for exactly those moments, providing a wealth of potential solutions to even the thorniest and most apparently impenetrable clues.

This new edition includes more than 500,000 possible solutions to quick and cryptic clues, arranged in more than 19,600 entries. The entries comprise not only thesaurus-style synonyms, but also more than 1,200 reference lists of encyclopedic information, from famous pirates to ancient cities, baseball terms to types of grass. A list of the headwords at which these may be found is given on pxliv.

*Chambers Crossword Dictionary* draws on material from across the authoritative Chambers reference range, and notably contains many thousands of terms from *The Chambers Dictionary*, including many of the archaic, literary and obscure words so beloved of cryptic crossword compilers. This edition also makes use of the Chambers clue database, a huge and ever-growing record of the way words are actually used in crosswords. You will find abbreviations, symbols, codes and typical crossword jargon included, such as 'AB' for sailor, or 'flower' to mean 'river'.

Also helpful is the inclusion of 'indicators' to denote words that may be used in a cryptic crossword clue to show that a word or words should be reversed, anagrammatized or otherwise manipulated. For those new to cryptic crosswords, or wishing to brush up on their understanding, an introductory article by Tim Moorey that explains how indicators are used in cryptic clues may be found on pxxvi, while lists of words that may be used as indicators are given on pxxxiii.

Additional insights into the world of cruciverbalism are given in the other introductory essays. 'The art of the crossword setter' by Jonathan Crowther offers an insight into the creation of these puzzles, while 'Crossword English' by Don Manley explains the types of clues that might be encountered and offers advice on how to approach solving cryptic crosswords. Tim Moorey writes on 'The art of the crossword clue', discussing the qualities that make for a memorable clue and offering examples of the finest clues so far devised.

We would like to thank the consultants and contributors who worked on this edition and previous editions of *Chambers Crossword Dictionary*; their expertise has greatly improved the book over the years and has been much appreciated.

*The Publishers*

In memory of Derek Arthur (1945–2010), joint editor of
*Chambers Crossword Dictionary* (2nd edition) and one
of the Chambers Crossword Consultants.

# INTRODUCTION

*Chambers Crossword Dictionary* contains more than 500,000 possible solutions to quick and cryptic crossword clues. It draws on *The Chambers Dictionary*, *The Chambers Thesaurus* and other books in the Chambers reference range; it also uses the Chambers crossword clue database.

It does not contain definitions, parts of speech, usage labels or similar material. To check the exact meaning of a word or phrase, a dictionary such as *The Chambers Dictionary* is recommended.

This Introduction contains the following information:

    Content
    Word forms
    Word length
    Organization of entries
    Expressions of ...
    Indicators
    Reference lists
    Cross-references

## Content

Entries in the *Crossword Dictionary* include both single words and phrases. Also included are abbreviations, short forms, acronyms, symbols, codes and the like, for the answers to crossword clues are often built up from these small pieces. Solvers will also find crossword jargon, such as 'tar' under 'sailor' and 'goat' under 'butter'. Anagrams, however, have not been included; so, for example, an entry for 'rotten time' would not list 'emit'.

Consideration has been given to the differing needs of various kinds of crosswords, from concise to advanced cryptics, and nothing has been excluded simply on the grounds of obscurity. Archaic, dialect, literary and uncommon words have been included, as these are often found in a variety of crosswords, not just (although undoubtedly most frequently) in advanced cryptics such as Azed in *The Observer* and *The Listener* in *The Times*. An emphasis has been placed on unusual short words with helpful letter sequences – for example 'tana' under 'police station' – as these often form the 'building blocks' which make up a cryptic solution. Variant spellings listed in *The Chambers Dictionary* have often been included. Where a usage is dubious but technically possible, as with an archaic variant of a synonym where it is unclear whether the variant is also synonymous with the headword, a degree of leniency has been employed.

The content of the *Crossword Dictionary* is broadly international in scope, with words from Australian, New Zealand, American, Anglo-Indian and other varieties of English included. Some common short foreign words sometimes found in crosswords are included too, such as 'mer' under 'sea' or 'ici' under 'here'.

Synonyms which are only loosely associated with the headword have not been included (for example 'twelfth' will not be found at 'grouse'). However, some names are included, as crossword convention allows references to people by first name or surname; for example 'Berlin' with the synonym 'Irving', 'Lincoln' for 'Abe' or 'Milne' for 'AA'. While a smattering of those most commonly found have been included, the list is not exhaustive and there will be others.

There is debate in crossword circles over what constitutes a 'sound' clue, and some crossword setters and editors do not employ particular uses of words or senses which others consider to be permissible. So as to be of maximum use to solvers of crosswords from a variety of sources, terms have been included in this book even if frowned upon by some. However, some usages considered to be especially contentious (usually as a result of word spacing and grammatical links having been ignored) have not been included, such as 'G' for 'Gateshead', 'm' for 'topmast' or 'fats' for 'breakfast'.

No attempt has been made to ensure that entries are 'symmetrical', ie that a synonym found under one headword (for example 'lucky') will also be found under another broadly synonymous entry (for example 'fortunate'). Since it is impossible to anticipate every reference a clue-writer will come up with, there are bound to be gaps. This deficiency can be mitigated by searching under different headwords, and there may be hints to be picked up from what is given. For example, the entry for 'swimmer' lists 'fish' as a cross-reference, which suggests that looking at the main entry for 'fish' may be helpful; here the intended solution, say 'eel', may be found.

Plural and inflected forms of words have generally not been given. Solvers should remember that if the wording of a cryptic clue suggests that a plural or verb form is required, they may need to pluralize or otherwise inflect a possible solution found in this *Dictionary*. Some abbreviations listed in the *Dictionary* stand for both singular and plural forms of a word (for example 'kg' can be kilogram or kilograms). For parts of cryptic solutions, plural and other forms may not be straightforward; for example, where 'duck' can conventionally be 'O', then 'ducks' in a clue may indicate 'Os' or 'OO'. This may also be encountered with the reference list of collective nouns, as setters may use 'crows', for example, for 'murder'.

This is also true for comparatives and superlatives; if a clue says 'more' or 'most', for example, it may be that an -er or -est ending needs to be added (for example 'more sensible' for 'saner' or 'most stupid' for 'dopiest'). Similarly, solvers should bear in mind that 'not' may be used in a clue to indicate the prefix 'un-' (for example 'not hidden' for 'unconcealed'), that 'again' may be used for the prefix 're-' (for example, 'publish again' for 'reissue'), and so on.

Numbers, and terms which include both numbers and letters, have been included in many instances as some – although not all – setters and editors allow the number 1 to be converted to the letter I (as in the Roman numeral). Thus, 'M1' may be rendered as part of a solution as 'MI', and '1st' as 'IST'.

## Word forms

The forms *-ize* and *-ization* are used throughout, but the alternative *-ise* or *-isation* spellings may be needed for the solutions to some crossword clues.

Similarly, the form 'your' is used in place of 'one's' in phrases such as 'put your foot down'. Solvers should remember that 'one's' may be required instead for a crossword solution. In some instances this may be reflected in the indication of word-length given in a clue: for example, 'sure of yourself' would be denoted as (4,2,8), hence listed here under **14**, whereas 'sure of oneself' would be (4,2,7), which would have been **13**.

Italics have not been used, even where conventionally a word or letter is italicized. This may be noted especially in relation to physics terms, for example, under 'Boltzmann constant' the symbol 'k' is given in roman type, whereas in *The Chambers Dictionary* it is italicized as *k*. Similarly, titles of novels and films, names of ships and other similar instances will all be found in roman type.

Where words can be hyphenated (as a noun) or unhyphenated (as a phrasal verb) both forms are usually included in synonym lists (for example 'back-up' and 'back up' at 'second').

## Word length

The words and phrases given in this dictionary contain 15 letters or fewer, reflecting the most commonly used crossword grids. However, where a list represents a closed set, that is, where a list is clearly defined and limited, then all relevant terms have been included regardless of length. For example, all of the US states and all of the plays of Shakespeare have been included, even though some of these are longer than 15 letters in length.

## Organization of entries

Within the dictionary, words have been sorted into over 19,600 one-stop alphabetical entries by meaning or subject category. Entries provide a range of words that are relevant to the headword, in two types of list:

- synonym lists, which present words with similar meanings to the headword
- reference lists, which present encyclopedic information related to the headword, such as people's names, place names and types of item

Some entries include only one type of list, whereas others include a range of synonyms plus one or more reference lists. For example:

**abbey**
**03** Abb **06** abbacy, friary, priory
**07** convent, minster, nunnery
**08** cloister, seminary **09** cathedral, monastery

*Abbeys include:*

**04** Bath, Iona
**05** Cluny, Kelso, Meaux, Roche, Royal
**06** Bolton, Byland, Hexham, Romsey, Whitby, Woburn
**07** Citeaux, Furness, Melrose, Tintern, Waltham
**08** Buckfast, Crowland, Dryburgh, Fontenay, Fonthill, Holyrood, Jedburgh, Newstead, Rievaulx
**09** Clairvaux, Fountains, Holy Cross, Kirkstall, Nightmare, Sherborne
**10** Malmesbury, Northanger
**11** Westminster

Reference lists always follow thesaurus-style lists.

Within entries, words are grouped firstly by length, that is by the total number of letters in each word or phrase, and then ordered alphabetically within these word-length sections:

**aisle**
**04** lane, path **07** gangway, passage, walkway **08** alleyway, corridor
**10** passageway **12** deambulatory

Alphabetization is strictly by letter, and some stylistic conventions have been disregarded: for example, 'Mc' will be found at 'Mc' rather than mingled with 'Mac'.

No distinction is made between parts of speech, or between homonyms (words spelled the same but with different meanings), as crossword setters play on multiple meanings and possible ambiguity in clues. For example, the entry for 'rebel' lists synonyms for the adjective, verb and noun senses:

**rebel**
◇ *anagram indicator* **04** defy, riot
**06** flinch, mutine, mutiny, oppose, recoil, resist, revolt, rise up, shrink
**07** aginner, beatnik, defiant, disobey, dissent, heretic, run riot, shy away
**08** agitator, apostate, mutineer, mutinous, pull back, recusant, revolter
**09** dissenter, guerrilla, insurgent
**10** malcontent, rebellious, schismatic
**11** disobedient, turn against
**12** malcontented, paramilitary
**13** insubordinate, nonconformist, revolutionary **14** freedom fighter
**15** insurrectionary

and the entry for 'dock' presents synonyms for what are, in fact, three separate words, one being a type of plant, another meaning a wharf or to land at a wharf and the third meaning to cut short:

> **dock**
> ◇ *tail deletion indicator* **02** dk **03** bob, cut, pen **04** clip, crop, land, moor, pier, quay, rump **05** basin, berth, jetty, put in, Rumex, tie up, wharf **06** anchor, deduct, detail, lessen, marina, reduce, remove, sorrel **07** bistort, curtail, harbour, shorten **08** boat yard, canaigre, decrease, diminish, patience, quayside, subtract, truncate, withhold **09** grapetree, polygonum **10** drop anchor, tidal basin, waterfront **12** monk's rhubarb, submarine pen **15** fitting-out basin
> • **docked** **02** in
> • **in the dock** **07** on trial

Synonym lists for idioms and phrasal verbs derived from many of the headwords are also included and are marked by •:

> **vouch**
> • **vouch for** **04** back **06** affirm, assert, assure, avouch, uphold, verify **07** certify, confirm, endorse, support, swear to, warrant **08** attest to, speak for **09** answer for, guarantee **10** asseverate

There may be more than one entry in the *Crossword Dictionary* for a word or phrasal verb. For example, 'shake up' appears as a phrasal verb at the entry for 'shake', but there is also an entry for the noun 'shake-up' as a headword in its own right.

Phrases, idioms and phrasal verbs have been located under the key headword contained and so should be found in an appropriate and intuitive place; *The Chambers Dictionary* has been followed in most instances. However, if a term cannot be found in the first place sought, solvers should try under other likely headwords.

## Expressions of ...

Interjections and similar terms related to emotions are often found in cryptic crossword clues and introduced by 'expression of...' or a similar phrase. In this *Dictionary* these are listed under the relevant headword; for example 'expression of hesitation' may require 'um' or 'er', and these can be found under the headword 'hesitation'.

If expressions relating to a particular emotion cannot be found in the first place sought, solvers should look under a likely alternative; for example, if seeking an 'expression of disapprobation' but finding nothing under 'disapprobation', solvers should then try 'disapproval'.

Lists of interjections, cries, shouts and expressions may be found at the following headwords:

| | | | | |
|---|---|---|---|---|
| admiration | disbelief | enthusiasm | misfortune | silence |
| agreement | discovery | excitement | pain | stop |
| annoyance | disdain | farewell | pleasure | stupidity |
| appreciation | disgust | frenzy | praise | success |
| approval | dismay | fright | protest | support |
| attention | dismissal | gratitude | puzzlement | surprise |
| concession | dissatisfaction | greeting | realization | sympathy |
| contempt | distaste | grief | regret | triumph |
| defiance | doubt | hesitation | relief | warning |
| derision | drinking | hunting | reproof | weariness |
| disagreement | emotion | impatience | resignation | wonder |
| disappointment | emphasis | invocation | sarcasm | worry |
| disapproval | encouragement | joy | scepticism | |

# Indicators

Terms which are often used as wordplay indicators in cryptic crossword clues are denoted with a diamond icon and the type of indicator – anagram, hidden, reversal, etc – is given:

> **adrift**
> ◇ *anagram indicator* **04** lost **05** at sea
> **07** aimless **08** drifting, goalless,
> insecure, rootless **09** off course,
> unsettled **10** anchorless, unanchored
> **11** disoriented **13** directionless,
> disorientated

Some words can be used as indicators of more than one kind of word play:

> **oddly**
> ◇ *anagram indicator* ◇ *hidden alternately
> indicator* **07** weirdly **09** curiously,
> strangely, unusually **10** abnormally,
> remarkably **11** irregularly

Indicators always follow the headword, idiom or phrasal verb. There may be instances in which an idiom or phrasal verb is followed only by an indicator, and not by synonym entries; this is because it was felt helpful to include the term for its usefulness as an indicator, but where it does not have synonyms in the usual way.

Indicators may not always appear in a cryptic clue in the way in which they appear in the *Dictionary*, but rather may be encountered in an inflected form: for example, 'digest' is marked as an anagram indicator, but solvers may be more likely to encounter it in a cryptic clue as 'digested'. While efforts have been made to denote all common indicators, the lists can never be exhaustive.

More information on the use of indicators in cryptic clues can be found on pxxvi, and lists of words that may be used as indicators are given on pxxxiii.

# Reference lists

The reference lists have been derived from *Chambers Crossword Lists* and from other authoritative Chambers reference databases. Lists are entered in the *Dictionary* at the appropriate headword; a list of the headwords at which they may be found is given on pxliv.

The reference lists are not intended to be all-inclusive, but to strike a balance between comprehensiveness and the likelihood of the words and phrases actually occurring as the solutions to crossword clues. For more comprehensive reference lists, *Chambers Crossword Lists* is recommended.

The reference lists include both historical and current information; for example, in the list of actors are not only contemporary figures like Sir Ian McKellen and Robin Williams, but also notable actors from the past like Richard Burbage and Edward Alleyn. Similarly, the lists may also contain both real and fictional or legendary items. For example, the list of heroes includes the legendary Robin Hood, the literary D'Artagnan, the historical William Wallace, the cinematic Indiana Jones and the comic strip Superman.

Reference lists have been subdivided to make finding information easier. For example, there is not one list of singers, but separate lists of classical, country and western, folk, jazz, opera, pop and other singers.

Some of the reference lists contain additional information in brackets following core information. For example, first names or nicknames are given in brackets following a surname. In such lists, the core term (the unbracketed term) is presented in bold type to make browsing easier:

---

*Pirates include:*

**03** **Tew** (Thomas)
**04** **Bart** (Jean), **Gunn** (Ben), **Hook**
(Captain), **Kidd** (William), **Otto**,
**Read** (Mary), **Smee**
**05** **Barth** (Jean), **Bones** (Billy), **Bonny**
(Anne), **Bunce** (Jack), **Drake** (Sir
Francis), **Every** (Henry), **Ewart**
(Nanty), **Flint** (Captain), **Tache**
(Edward), **Teach** (Edward)
**06** **Aubery** (Jean-Benoit), **Conrad**,
**Jonsen** (Captain), **Morgan** (Sir
Henry), **Silver** (Long John), **Thatch**
(Edward), **Walker** (William)
**07** **Dampier** (William), **Lafitte** (Jean),
**O'Malley** (Grace), **Pugwash**
(Captain), **Rackham** (John), **Roberts**
(Bartholomew), **Sparrow** (Captain
Jack), **Trumpet** (Solomon)
**08** **Altamont** (Frederick), **Black Dog**,
**Blackett** (Nancy), **Blackett** (Peggy),
**Blind Pew, Redbeard, Ringrose**
(Basil)
**09** **Black Bart, Cleveland** (Clement)
**10** **Barbarossa** (Khair-ed-din),
**Blackbeard, Calico Jack**
**14** **Long John Silver**

---

Additional bracketed information is not included in the word-length count although it may form part of the solution to some crossword clues. The regnal numbers of individual popes, queens and kings have generally been omitted.

Common generic terms have often been omitted from the names and terms presented in reference lists, to avoid unwieldy and unnecessary repetition. For example, the word 'abbey' has not been included in names in the list of abbeys, and the word 'saw' has been omitted from the list of saws. Users should be aware that these terms may form part of the solution to some crossword clues.

The reference material has been selected to be as wide-ranging in scope as possible. Solvers should note that:

- numbers may be found in solutions in some instances, as numbers may be encountered or referenced in some form in cryptic puzzles. For example, the list of films includes *2001: A Space Odyssey* and *Apollo 13*.

- some items are included under a certain headword on the grounds of usefulness, even if they are not strictly types of the headword. For example, 'Washington DC' is included in the list of US states and 'tomato' is included in the list of vegetables. Similarly, items which are related to the headword may be included; succulents in the list of cacti, for example.

- variant spellings have been included, for example 'topi' and 'topee' in the list of hats.

In some entries without a distinct reference list, both synonyms and reference-list type information may be found intermingled.

## Cross-references

*Chambers Crossword Dictionary* is extensively cross-referenced to make finding solutions easy. There are two forms of cross-reference; those at main headwords directing users elsewhere:

**lough**
*see* **lake**

and those which suggest that additional information may be found at other entries:

> **petrol**
> **03** gas, LRP **05** ethyl, juice, super
> **08** gasolene, gasoline
> *See also* **fuel**

In many of the latter instances, the cross-reference directs solvers to a relevant reference list. It may also direct solvers to a similar but longer entry with additional synonyms, or may make explicit some crossword jargon or other slang; for example, a cross-reference at 'bloomer' to 'flower', or a cross-reference at 'stir' to 'prison'.

# The art of the crossword setter

Jonathan Crowther (Azed of *The Observer*)

I am regularly asked – as often by people who habitually solve crosswords as by those who never do – how I set about compiling a puzzle, and especially what order I do things in. (The other commonly-asked question is how long each puzzle takes me, but I usually hedge when answering this one. A puzzle is best constructed over several sittings, and I have never bothered to calculate accurately the total time involved.) For most normal crosswords there are three distinct stages, each more time-consuming than the last: (i) constructing the grid pattern, (ii) filling this with words and (iii) writing the clues. The three stages demand different skills, and for this reason I often compartmentalize the first two, constructing several grid patterns at a sitting and then filling all of these with words before returning to the first grid to start the lengthier and more creative process of writing the clues. Let us now look at each stage in turn.

## Crossword grids

There is no absolute rule that crosswords should be symmetrical in design, ie with their blocked squares or bars arranged so that they look the same if the grid is turned upside down or if it is given a quarter-turn. The fact is that most are, and this is the widely-accepted norm. It is also aesthetically pleasing, by no means a negligible consideration. Most importantly, the grid design should ensure a range of entries of varying lengths and a fair distribution of unchecked letters (those which belong to only one word, across or down, and are not 'checked' by a word entered in the other direction). In general the number of unchecked letters is greater in a blocked grid than in a barred one. As a rule of thumb (though one that is regularly infringed by puzzles in a number of our national dailies), no more than half the letters of a solution should be unchecked in a blocked grid. In barred grids, like mine in *The Observer*, the solver can expect a more generous quota of cross-checked letters because such puzzles tend to use more rare and unusual words. In both types of puzzle the inclusion of consecutive unchecked letters in answers is considered bad practice and generally frowned on. It is all a question of fairness to the solver.

There is a fundamental difference in standard grid design between British-style and American-style crosswords. British crosswords, with their tradition of cryptic clues and unchecked letters, normally require the solver to solve every clue in order to complete the puzzle. In most American crosswords, whose clues are not cryptic in the British sense, there are proportionally far fewer blocked squares and they are arranged in such a way that *every* letter is cross-checked, so that, in theory at least, it is possible to complete a puzzle by solving only about half its clues.

In practice, setters of most normal blocked grids in daily or Sunday newspapers in both Britain and the US do not have to concern themselves with grid construction. Each paper uses a limited number of basic patterned grids to which the setter is restricted. In an age of ever-greater standardization this is perhaps inevitable, and it reduces the risk of error, but I still regard it as regrettable and am pleased that no such restriction is placed on me. I derive much satisfaction from exploring the many different grid designs possible within the established parameters: grid size (normally 12 x 12 in my case), number of entries (usually 36), a good spread of entry lengths, and a fair number of unchecked letters. My predecessor Derrick Macnutt (the legendary Ximenes) preferred to let his patterns grow, organically as it were, around the words he wanted to include in his puzzles, effectively merging my first two stages of crossword construction into a single process. My own routine is as I have described, since I start with no preconceptions as to the words I want to use, and this only goes to show that there is no universally prescribed method. There are also no Mosaic laws governing the *size* of crosswords. Blocked grids in daily papers are usually 15 x 15, with about 32 answers (16 across and 16 down), but recent years have seen a growth in the number of 'jumbo' puzzles (typically 27 x 27, with 76 answers), presenting new challenges to solvers and setters alike by the inclusion of longer words and multi-word phrases. In a more modest way, the Azed crossword is now sometimes 13 x 11, enabling me to include

13-letter words on a regular basis. More specialized crosswords explore other designs, including circular diagrams with entries arranged circularly and radially, but these will probably remain the exception and the domain of the seriously dedicated solver.

## Word choice

Having completed the grid, or having chosen it from the available range, the setter moves on to fill it with words. There are computer programs which can do this in the twinkling of an eye, though they are limited to the word-lists in the program's memory. The human brain takes much longer but it can select or reject words according to their suitability for cluing and its own real-world knowledge, a crucial factor in the writing of clues. Which words does one choose, and where does one start? I personally start from what seems the natural place, the top left-hand corner of the grid, extending down and across more or less at the same time while keeping a weather eye open for potential problem areas. Anything in the dictionary is fair game, and for me this means *The Chambers Dictionary*. I think the setter should be free to include non-dictionary words and phrases as well, especially topical ones, if these are sufficiently well known. Assessing what is and is not familiar enough to include here is of course a matter of fine judgement. Some newspapers have a policy of not allowing certain taboo words to be used as answers in their crosswords. In these liberated days such bowdlerization strikes me as rather old-fashioned. Crossword setters, like journalists and other writers, should be trusted to know where to draw the line.

The task of filling a grid with words is naturally easier in blocked diagrams than in barred ones, since the number of unchecked letters is significantly greater in blocked diagrams. In both types the setter develops with experience a feel for the 'shape' of words: common letter-clusters, the distribution of consonants and vowels, 'danger' letters (especially at the ends of words), helpful affixes and inflections, and so on. He or she must think ahead to avoid getting boxed into an awkward corner which will involve undoing part of the grid construction, an agonizing waste of time when deadlines are tight. Special care needs to be taken with shorter words, especially those of four or five letters. There are comparatively few of these in the language (and of these far fewer begin with vowels than with consonants), so most will have been clued many times already. Good setters try to avoid reusing old clues, however proud of them they may be, and they should also not reuse *words* too often. Guarding against this is not easy, and inevitably, there being no copyright on good ideas, similar or identical clues to the same word will recur, but I do make a conscious effort not to repeat myself and think other setters should do likewise. (As a matter of passing interest, there are more different words in the language of eight letters than of any other word length.)

Fair play between setter and solver is an important principle in grid construction. Consonants, especially the less common ones, are generally more helpful to the solver as cross-checking letters than vowels are (with obvious exceptions like I or U in final position), and the setter should recognize this. I know that as a solver I feel hard done by if faced by –A–E, one of the most frequent four-letter-word patterns, especially if the setter has made matters worse by giving the word an extra-difficult clue!

## Clues

The writing of the clues for a crossword is the last and much the most important task for the setter, for it is here that one stamps one's character and personal style on the puzzle. Seasoned solvers develop clear preferences for the style of this or that setter, and satisfied solvers usually remain loyal to a particular puzzle (even, sometimes, if they are less than happy with other aspects of the paper in which it appears). I firmly believe that an impersonal style of cluing can be boring, and there is no harm at all in letting one's own interests, sense of humour, even prejudices, emerge through one's clues, provided always that these are fair and accurate. Don Manley in his essay on 'Crossword English' describes in detail the range of different clue types regularly used by setters. As a setter myself, I follow a method which has not changed greatly over the years. I always write clues in the order in which they appear in the puzzle. Taking the more colourful words first means leaving a 'sump' of less interesting ones till last, an encouragement to treat the latter as second-class citizens and produce second-class clues as a result. I write no more than nine or ten clues at a sitting, having found that, if I try to do more, staleness sets in and pedestrian clues result. The restorative effects of even quite a short break doing other things can be truly remarkable! At the same time it is important to see the puzzle as a whole and to present a reasonable variety of clue types (not too many anagrams, for example) to ensure a balanced fare for the solver. This can be tricky when a word cries out for one particular treatment but that treatment has already been used for other words in the puzzle (or for the same word in an earlier puzzle), but the principle is sound. The aim must be to divert the solver, not to massage the setter's ego, so variety is important.

Some words are much more difficult to clue interestingly than others. Scientific terms come high on my list of unfavourite words, mainly because their meaning is very specific and does not lend itself to the sort of wordplay that is at the heart of cryptic clue-writing. A word with many meanings offers far greater scope for punning and similar red herrings to strew in the solver's path. But whichever word I am cluing I always strive (with varying success, I'm sure) for three key ingredients in a clue: accuracy, economy and wit. Every clue should lead accurately and unmistakably to its solution, saying precisely and grammatically what it means (though it may not always mean what it appears to say – taking advantage of the manifold ambiguities of our language is an essential part of cryptic clue-writing). It should do this in as few words as are consistent with fair play, avoiding all superfluous verbiage or mere padding. And it should if at all possible be enjoyable to solve, leaving successful solvers feeling both satisfied at their success and pleasurably diverted by the experience.

## About the author

Jonathan Crowther is better known to many cryptic crossword solvers as Azed of *The Observer*. He has also set puzzles under the pseudonyms Gong and Ozymandias.

# Crossword English
Don Manley (crossword setter and author of
*Chambers Crossword Manual*)

I am a monoglot, more or less. Although I studied French at school, I can't say I use it much – except when I have to on holiday, and even then it's a sort of pidgin French. But at least I feel I know English, and since (as Bernard Shaw put it) England and America are two countries divided by a common language, maybe one can be a polyglot just by watching television. Or maybe I can be a polyglot just by coming from Devon, where 'thistles' used to be called 'dashels'.

So what has this to do with crosswords? Well, in a sense Crossword English is rather like a foreign language – and it is a language that must be learnt. What may seem odd (if the cross-section of crossword setters I know is anything to go by) is that the polyglots who can speak French and English are not necessarily polyglots in the sense of knowing English and Crossword English. You're more likely to find that a crossword setter is a computer scientist, a physicist or a mathematician than a French teacher these days.

The irritating thing – to anyone who has not yet learnt Crossword English – is that it looks so like Everyday English. For the crossword which offers definitions only, this is perfectly obvious. So if the clue reads 'Cry of an ass (4),' you can write in BRAY straight away. You might have a few alternative answers for 'River (5)', and if you are living in Nottinghamshire you may be disposed to write in TRENT, but when faced with 'River in Paris (5)' you'll know that anything other than SEINE just isn't sane. So for the definition puzzle we're looking at a test of our ability to recognize synonyms, or at a quiz with questions that would crop up early on in 'Who Wants To Be A Millionaire?'. This is as far as most people get with solving crosswords – the verbal quiz solved with a little help from reference books: a dictionary, an atlas and possibly an encyclopedia. They know English but not Crossword English.

So what is Crossword English? It is the language of the cryptic crossword, a language which looks like ordinary English but which has its own strange rules of grammar and construction and which has its own vocabulary. Crossword English is a series of mini-statements, mini-pictures, and mini-stories even, but the statements, the pictures, and the stories are each designed to hide a sort of riddle. So a riddle isn't a bad place to start with as an example of a cryptic clue:

> My first is in Cornwall but isn't in Devon
>
> For my second shun Hell and start looking in Heaven
>
> My third you may find in this or in that
>
> My whole is a creature that sits on the mat

Thus in a woeful verse of thirty-nine words we have written a cryptic clue for CAT, and at each stage along the way we are spoon-fed a letter at a time. It's obviously a puzzle, even if it's a pretty heavy-handed one.

Now look at these little riddles and see what you make of them:

1. Lady I rather fancy (7)
2. There's nothing in Basildon I like (3)
3. Delightful tea with the best china (8)
4. It's best to have cold sheets (5)
5. Delicate proposal (6)
6. The clock's put back? Relax! (5)
7. Company car? (3-6)

8. It could deflect battle spear (11)

9. Writer gathers wood as something that'll burn quickly (8)

10. Marsh plant enthrals artist (6)

11. Defeat brought by bowling gaining wicket – something captain controls? (9)

12. Amuse the French after a short time (6)

13. Did he have spelling lessons? (3,9,10)

14. Who you'd expect to find at gay weddings in the Isles?! (8)

15. Female beheaded in the sultanate (4)

16. Lab in, Tory out would suit him (4,5)

17. Boyfriend tied ribbon from what we hear (4)

18. Rejected young troublemaker longed to be free (8)

19. Fool about fifty, one not altogether bright (6)

20. 014? (6,5)

Here are twenty 'portrayals' – perfectly sensible 'portrayals' in generally understandable English – though 20 looks a bit odd. All of these were written by myself at some stage over the past fifteen years or so, and as I look at them I see not only Crossword English but a certain kind of Englishness. There is romance in 1 and 17 (and perhaps 5); there is an austere and rather snooty middle-Englishness about 2, 3 and 4; a concern with cricket in 11; hints of a threatening world outside modern England in 8 and 15; and so on. There may even be a touch of humour here and there. This is English language and English culture.

There are twenty puzzles to solve, so how are these clues different from those for BRAY and SEINE? The answer is (fairly) simple, though the implications of the answer may be complicated. It is this. In each cryptic clue there will still be a definition but the clue writer will have done one of two things. He (sometimes she – and, to be honest, we could do with more 'shes') will have either wrapped up the definition in 'cryptic language' or will have provided a definition plus some indication of the letters in the answer. Sometimes the crossword setter will have done both. In most cryptic clues there will be what we call a 'definition' followed by what we call a 'subsidiary indication' (sometimes also called 'wordplay'), or a subsidiary indication followed by a definition, or even an indication and a definition rolled into one. The secret to decoding a clue lies in trying to solve the answer from either or both of these components while using any letters that are already filled in.

If that all sounds horrible, it's because I've tried to give you a grammar lesson, and (as we all know) it's really much better to start learning a language by speaking it or writing it. No one ever really taught me 'all that grammar stuff' when I was a fledgling cruciverbalist (someone who 'does' crosswords). I was lucky enough to have a father who taught me how to solve clues when I was barely out of short trousers, and the best way I can explain Crossword English is to take you through the clues one by one.

### 1. Lady I rather fancy (7)

The word 'fancy' is one of a huge set of **anagram indicators**. It tells us that the letters next to it are to be made 'fancy' or jumbled up. If you jumble up 'I rather' you get HARRIET, a lady. This clue, then is an **anagram**, perhaps the one form of cryptic clue everyone knows.

### 2. There's nothing in Basildon I like (3)

If you look carefully, you'll see that there is indeed a word meaning nothing in the sequence of letters 'Basildon I like' and it's NIL. This is a **hidden word**.

### 3. Delightful tea with the best china (8)

If you put a word for 'tea' and add it to a word for 'the best china', you will add 'char' to 'Ming' to form CHARMING, meaning 'delightful'. This is a **charade clue**.

### 4. It's best to have cold sheets (5)

As it happens, this is another charade, but this time we join an **abbreviation** 'c' (= cold) to the sheets (= ream) to form CREAM (the best). Abbreviations are common in subsidiary indications.

### 5. Delicate proposal (6)

This is a **double-definition** clue, so you can look upon one definition as the official 'definition' and the other one as the 'subsidiary indication' – or vice versa. What word means both 'delicate' and 'proposal'? Answer: TENDER.

### 6. The clock's put back? Relax! (5)

This suggests (quite rightly) that you'll get an extra hour in bed when the clocks go back. But if you put back a 'timer' you will get REMIT, which means 'relax'. This is a **reversal** clue. In down clues you may see the word 'up' suggesting a reversal. And here the definition is at the end.

### 7. Company car? (3-6)

You may be tempted to think of this as another double-definition clue and look for a word that means both 'company' and 'car'. In fact the setter is inviting you to think of 'two's company, three's none', and so the answer is TWO-SEATER. There is no indication of letters in this clue, but we have noticed that it has a **cryptic definition**.

### 8. It could deflect battle spear (11)

We're looking for an anagram of 'battle spear' and find it in BREASTPLATE, but we notice that the clue as a whole is a definition. Every word in the clue is serving as a definition and as part of the subsidiary indication. We call this an **&lit.** clue. This particular type is **anagram &lit.**

### 9. Writer gathers wood as something that'll burn quickly (8)

The word 'gathers' suggests that a word for 'wood' might be inside a writer. Put 'fir' inside 'Wilde' and you'll find WILDFIRE. This is known as a **container-and-contents** clue.

### 10. Marsh plant enthrals artist (6)

This is another container-and-contents clue. This time we have an abbreviation for artist (RA) inside a plant (moss) to give MORASS.

### 11. Defeat brought by bowling gaining wicket – something captain controls? (9)

If you solve crosswords you'll need to get used to **cricket vocabulary**. In this charade bowling is 'over', wicket is 'w', and something the captain controls is 'helm'. Put the three together to get OVERWHELM (defeat).

### 12. Amuse the French after a short time (6)

Although we're talking about Crossword English, we do allow a few **foreign words** to creep in, especially definite and indefinite articles of common European languages. In this charade a short time is 'tick' added to 'the French', which in this case is 'le', giving the answer TICKLE (amuse).

### 13. Did he take spelling lessons? (3,9,10)

The setter is tempting you to think about spelling in the sense of getting the right letters in sequence. In fact you should think about spelling in the sense of magic. The answer is THE SORCERER'S APPRENTICE, another cryptic definition, this one being set in what we call a **misleading context** occasioned by the **double-meaning** of 'spelling'. You'll find many other double meanings including 'flower' which can mean river. One of the delights of learning Crossword English is to work these out for yourself!

### 14. Who you'd expect to find at gay weddings in the Isles?! (8)

This is an outrageous charade, the answer being 'he brides' (ie HEBRIDES). No one ever seems to have taken offence. Every crossword should have at least one clue with an element of **humour**.

### 15. Female beheaded in the sultanate (4)

This is a particular type of **subtractive** clue. Take the head letter off 'woman' to give the sultanate OMAN. If you take up cryptic crosswords you will also learn about 'endless' and 'heartless'.

*16. Lab in, Tory out would suit him (4,5)*

This is another **anagram &lit.** written at a time when TONY BLAIR was in the ascendant. Note the use of 'out' as an anagram indicator.

*17. Boyfriend tied ribbon from what we hear (4)*

When you see words like 'we hear' or 'they say' you almost certainly have a **homophone** clue. Here 'tied ribbon' is 'bow' and BEAU is bow 'from what we hear', ie 'beau' and 'bow' are homophones.

*18. Rejected young troublemaker longed to be free (8)*

This is a **complex** clue in that it consists of the reverse of one word in a charade with another. A rejected troublemaker is 'Ted' backwards ('det') and longed is 'ached', which when attached makes DETACHED. Who ever calls unruly troublemakers 'teddy-boys' or 'teds' these days? Well, we do in crosswords. This is one example of **preserved obsolescence** in an area of language where we still have an extended-play record (EP) and sex appeal is still 'it'.

*19. Fool about fifty, one not altogether bright (6)*

In this container-and-contents clue we make use of our knowledge of Roman numerals. Fifty is 'L' and 'twit' about 'L,I' is TWILIT. And there's a slightly misleading context here, isn't there?

*20. 014? (6,5)*

This last clue is what one might call a **zany** or **improvised** clue – a sort of one-off cryptic definition. It depends on the solver seeing that 014 = 2 x 007. Since 007 is the agent James Bond, the answer must be DOUBLE AGENT.

With these twenty clues we have touched on all of the most important aspects of Crossword English, and maybe I have already been rather too 'English English' for some. What about other Englishes? Well, I'm writing this introduction for the publisher of a very special dictionary, *The Chambers Dictionary*. This is of course an excellent 'English English' dictionary but it also contains some excellent English words from the past and some highly unusual Scottish words. *Chambers* should be in every self-respecting crossworder's library, but its greatest treasures tend to come into play in the more difficult puzzles where Edmund (Spenser) and Jock (the archetypal Scot) make frequent appearances.

Across the Atlantic, in the USA and Canada, 'American Crossword English' is developing as cryptic puzzles, based on British puzzles, become more popular. British solvers will find one or two unfamiliar abbreviations, maybe, and the contexts will be more American – but the similarities tend to contradict Shaw's assertion mentioned earlier.

It has often been pointed out that English is ideal for the crossword because words split up so agreeably. How convenient that 'astronomer' is an anagram of 'moon-starer' and how nicely 'bestride' splits into 'best ride'. Clearly it would be difficult to imagine Crossword Urdu, and yet cryptic crosswords do exist in Hebrew, Bengali, Welsh and Dutch – and other languages too, I dare say.

It's time for a final word about the 'custodians' of Crossword English and what they are trying to do. The word 'custodian' may suggest conservatism and a grammar rule-book. There's more to it than that, of course, but there is a necessary element of grammar in crosswords which needs to be preserved. There are, after all, limits to what is acceptable in Everyday English, and it is the same in Crossword English.

In our language the strict grammarians call themselves **Ximeneans** after Ximenes, *The Observer* crossword setter who died in 1971. There is no space here for a digression into the grammar over which crossword setters and their editors argue, but there is an ongoing debate about what is acceptable and what is not. Today the tradition of Ximenes is upheld by his successor Azed, who tells us about his approach to crossword setting elsewhere in this book. Many of today's crossword setters have been competitors in Azed's clue-writing competitions, and so it is no surprise that many of the crossword setters in our national dailies are Ximenean – as are their crossword editors. Puzzles will inevitably vary in style and in level of difficulty. Crossword setters are turning Crossword English Language into Crossword English Literature and different 'readers' (solvers) will inevitably have their own favourite 'authors' (setters). But there are rules within which the custodians make sure that Crossword English operates – rules not just of grammar, but rules of taste. Practitioners of this language don't have to be absolutely politically correct, but their language is still that of the polite drawing-room, not that of the gutter. We can gently poke fun at pompous bishops and politicians (though not by name specifically!), and we can make wry comments about modern society, but we aim to entertain and not to give offence.

We want to give pleasure and intellectual challenge. Crossword English began as a sort of 20th-century poetry for all to enjoy. Long may it continue into the 21st century and beyond.

## About the author

Don Manley sets crosswords under a variety of pseudonyms (Bradman, Duck, Quixote, Pasquale and Giovanni) for many national newspapers (including *The Times*, *The Guardian*, *The Independent on Sunday*, the *Financial Times* and *The Daily Telegraph*). He is also the *Church TImes* crossword editor.

# The art of the crossword clue

Tim Moorey (Mephisto of *The Sunday Times*)

What is it that makes certain clues stay in the memory when the vast majority are forgotten as soon as their solutions are discovered? I will try to answer the question by identifying characteristics and qualities that setters strive to find and solvers tend to appreciate. Each is illustrated with my choice of clue examples based on over 50 years of crossword solving, and also with choices made by fellow setters from their own past clues and those of other setters. In addition, having had the task of selecting a 'Clue of the Week' for *The Week* magazine since its inception, I regularly have to consider what constitutes a good clue, and my focus there – and here – is on what solvers are likely to have found satisfying. To an increasing extent, it is also based on actual feedback from *The Sunday Times* and *The Week* solvers, following the introduction several years ago of invitations to respond by email.

It is fairly clear which qualities are enjoyed in favoured clues: in a nutshell, short, simple, well-crafted sentences that paint a coherent and believable but misleading picture are well regarded. If these can be supplemented with topicality and wit, so much the better. Technical soundness is taken for granted, albeit that crossword professionals sometimes heatedly debate exactly what is technically sound. Solvers, I think, are unconcerned with this aspect; if a warm glow of recognition on uncovering the answer is obtained, they will value a clue that some professionals (including this one) rate as 'unsound'.

So here are four things I look for in clue selection:

## 1   Definition
My test is whether the word or words used in the clue could be substituted for the solution in a normal English sentence.

## 2   Ease of solving
The clue answer should not be immediately apparent; and the penny should drop after not too long an interval of puzzlement.

## 3   Clue length
Anything over ten words can make for indigestibility, but I wouldn't rule out clues that are slightly longer.

## 4   Artificiality in wording
There should be no strain evident, and especially no sign that the clue-writer would ideally have preferred to use a different word or words, but was unable to do so in the interest of clueing integrity.

The clues chosen as examples for this essay include what may be regarded as 'classics', that is to say that they are spoken of and quoted still, in most cases despite having appeared some years ago. I also include more recent clues that have featured as 'Clue of the Week'. In most cases, to give readers a better chance of solving, the solutions are fairly common words.

Now for the qualities and characteristics of memorable clues, with illustrations. Hints are given in italics alongside clues, with solutions provided at the end of the essay.

## 1   Short and succinct
Cryptic definition clues fit this category best, albeit that they may have the disadvantage of not conveying a picture. However, their neatness and deviousness appeal. Ideally, there can only be a unique solution to each of these; note that the bracketed number of letters can sometimes rule out possible alternatives, as in the last of the examples.

Art master (8) *Think old English*

Stiff examination (4,6) *Think Latin*

This cylinder is jammed (5,4) *Think food*

A pound of sultanas (8) *Nothing to do with food*

Bar of soap (6,6) *Two of the three words mislead*

Double definitions – where either word could define the answer – can also be mentioned here. Perhaps the two best known are:

Let rip (4) *Ideas associated with a tear mustn't be shed here*

Driving licence (2-5) *Think of driving in the 'pushy' sense*

## 2  Well-crafted, painting a believable picture
If these qualities can be included in a totally misleading sentence, then you may have a fine clue.

Neglectful having left off dicky bow (9) *Dicky and bow mislead*

Seems a hip replacement brings about stress (9) *Anagram*

Licking for Persians is a prolonged exercise (8) *Two definitions; think ancient battles*

Amazon order mailed with shrink wrapping (6-3) *A very tough but wonderful clue for a rare word; shrink = shy*

In autumn, we're piling up the last of the leaves (8) *Partial anagram*

Tumbler, nuts, smoke, rapture! (7-5) *Anagram*

## 3  Topicality
The references in these clues, in order, are: an infamous fatwa issued against an English novelist; a disastrous attempt in 1980 to rescue US hostages from Iran; fears before the 1990 World Cup relating to unruly English soccer fans; and finally the Iraq war.

He's rued his novel (7) *Anagram*

Carter coup tails off in disarray – prepare for war? (8) *Adjusted anagram*

Trouble Italy has looming (11) *Anagram*

War's started by Bush? Completely! (6) *W is the answer's first letter*

Also topical was this prize-winning effort to celebrate puzzle number 1000 by Ximenes (or X as he was often known) in 1968; C refers to Chambers.

Up to date product of X and C (8) *Think multiplication*

## 4  Wit and humour
Undoubtedly appreciated by the solver, this is probably the category hardest for setters to achieve, and thus most rarely found. The fine first example won a prize in a Ximenes competition in *The Observer* in 1967, when the recently-coined solution word had not yet made it into the dictionary.

Abbreviations not in Chambers but should not be looked up anyway (4-6) *Think feminine clothes*

Silicone valley! (8) *Think feminine*

Roman marbles lost (3,6,6) *Think Latin*

In which three couples get together for sex (5) *Last word is the key*

Odd if no males could be found here (4,2,3) *Anagram*

Variety of *English* pastry – Dane would look down on it! (7) *Anagram*

Stiff collaring's my trade – it shows what can be done by starch (4,8) *Anagram*

## 5  Definition and secondary indications being the same ('& lit.' type clues)
Often considered as the pinnacle of the clue-writer's art, the best of this type have a conciseness of wording and do not reveal their charms too easily.

We'll get excited with Ring seat (10) *Anagram*

No fellow for mixing (4,4) *Anagram*

I rifle tubs at sea (10) *Anagram*

What you might find in Lechtal overlooking lake? (6) *Overlook here means ' ignore'*
What's tea passed round in? (5) *Tea is 'cha'*
Waitress with large bust could model as this (7-4) *Bust here means 'broken'*
Names I must jot endlessly (8) *Must here means 'in a frenzy'*
What grass is (even for a fool) (5) *Substitute one word for another*
By it 'truth' and 'lie' looked alternately interchangeable (6-5) *Anagram*

## 6   Subtlety of language
This type often requires a second, careful reading of a word or words, not necessarily prominent ones.

Lass I love moving upwards you may find well beneath this (3,3) *Down clue*
A chap could attend this celebration but never does (4,5) *Read it again*
Drink causing a problem? What if it is! (9) *An additive clue*
Item Gran arranged family slides in (5,7) *Family is 'clan'*
Shot with craft on course (9) *Golf and poetry cleverly in play*
A murder suspect, one hears (7) *Last two words especially mislead*
Dive made from upturned punts? (7) *A down clue; think Ireland*

## 7   Technical virtuosity
Long anagrams, as in the first two examples, are often quoted by solvers. This shows that work by setters (whether by computer or not) is appreciated. The third example of virtuosity is also one of the most deceptive clues ever published.

Ground with the Arsenal not getting the least bit of sympathy (5,4,4) *Ground, the past tense of grind*
Poetical scene with surprisingly chaste Lord Archer vegetating (3,3,8,12) *Brooke*
Some job at hand? We'll soon see (4,3,5) *Last word misleads*

## 8   Highly original clues not obviously fitting into any category
These typically require a leap of imagination on the part of the solver and maybe raise an especially wide smile when the penny drops. Even though the first two of the following clues are often considered 'unsound', they do get plaudits from solvers.

HIJKLMNO (5) *Chemistry; no direct definition included*
ONMLKJIH (9) *No direct definition included*
I can identify vehicles here (5) *IVR code knowledge needed*
014? (6,5) *Think spooks*
His, for example (9) *Plural answer*

The clue most suggested by fellow setters goes back to 1973. Its author, Les May, won first prize in *The Observer*'s Azed competition with this clue which could have been included in several of the above categories.

Bust down reason (9) *Solution splits into three separate words for the purposes of the secondary reading*

My own favourite is a much more recent one, in fact it appeared in *The Guardian* in November 2009 and was written by Paul.

Over fifty? Wrong! (5-4) *Such a combination of accuracy, simplicity and economy of wording is rare and was highly satisfying to solve*

# Solutions and (where known) authors
Where the clue originally appeared under a pseudonym, the pseudonym is shown in brackets after the author's real name. Where there is no pseudonym or no name at all, the clue's author is unknown to me, or it may have featured either in clue-writing competitions or in publications such as *The Times* or *The Daily Telegraph* where setters are unnamed (though in three instances where names are known to me, due credit is given below).

1     TEACHEST; POST MORTEM; SWISS ROLL     Adrian Bell *The Times*; SERAGLIO Valerie Coleman; ROVER'S RETURN; RENT; GO-AHEAD   Norman Goddard;

2     GENUFLECT; EMPHASISE     John Halpern (Mudd); MARATHON and SHIELD-MAY   Ross Beresford; FAREWELL *anag we're in fall*   H S Tribe; POSTURE-MAKER I M Raab;

3     RUSHDIE     John Grimshaw; ACCOUTRE     Tim Moorey; HOOLIGANISM     Malcolm Barley; WHOLLY   Michael Curl (Orlando); THOUSAND   Sir Jeremy Morse;

4     MINI-SKIRTS     M C Raphael; CLEAVAGE     Roy Dean *The Times*; NON COMPOS MENTIS; LATIN *three times two is six*   Brian Greer; ISLE OF MAN; YAPSTER   Paul Henderson; BODY SNATCHER   Sir Jeremy Morse;

5     WAGNERITES     Derrick Macnutt (Ximenes); LONE WOLF     Don Manley (Quixote); FILIBUSTER     A N Clark; CHALET     John Tozer; CHINA; SWEATER-GIRL     Tim Moorey (Mephisto); AMNESIAC     Kathleen Bissett; GREEN *een for ass*     Richard Morse; DOUBLE-THINK   Colin Dexter;

6     OIL RIG     Jonathan Crowther (Azed); STAG PARTY; SUPPOSING; MAGIC LANTERN     Colin Dexter; ALBATROSS; EARDRUM; NITERIE *Eire tin reversed* Roger Hooper;

7     WHITE HART LANE     Richard Palmer (Merlin); THE OLD VICARAGE GRANTCHESTER     John Graham (Araucaria); BATH AND WELLS *hidden clue* Brian Greer;

8     WATER; BACKWATER     John Grimshaw *The Times*; ITALY; DOUBLE AGENT *007* Don Manley (Quixote); GREETINGS; BRAINWASH *bra in wash*   Les May; FORTY-FIVE John Halpern (Paul) *The Guardian*.

## About the author

Tim Moorey sets crosswords as one of the three-strong Mephisto team for *The Sunday Times*, for which he occasionally contributes *The Sunday Times* crossword. He has additionally appeared as Owzat in newspapers such as *The Independent*, *The Sunday Telegraph* and *The Listener* crossword in *The Times*. He is crossword editor and setter for *The Week* and *Moneyweek* magazines, author of *How To Master The Times Crossword*, gives talks on crosswords and runs regular workshops for crossword beginners.

# Indicators in cryptic crossword clues
## Tim Moorey (Mephisto of *The Sunday Times*)

## Why do crosswords have 'indicators'?

As compared to definition-only crosswords (general knowledge, quick, easy and the like) which have clues offering only one means of arriving at each solution, cryptic crossword clues usually have two. These are a definition and a secondary way, often termed 'wordplay'. This, in effect, acts as a check on the definition, or vice versa if the solver finds the definition elusive. Wordplay relies on 'indicators', of which there are many types. In effect, an indicator shows how the setter has manipulated the solution, in that a whole word (or part) may have been subject to one or more tricks, such as the following:

| | Type of indicator |
|---|---|
| Changed into another word by a letter mix | Anagram |
| Split into parts with one part inside another | Containment/Insertion |
| Letter(s) chosen for subtraction | Deletion |
| Concealed inside the rest of the clue | Hidden |
| Considered as spoken, giving a different word | Homophone |
| Linked to other part(s) | Juxtaposition |
| Written backwards (or upwards for a Down clue) | Reversal |
| Letter(s) chosen for manipulation | Selection |

## How are indicators used?

Indicators are designed to signal to solvers:

- which type of wordplay is to be unravelled
- how to adjust a letter or letters within the clue
- how the whole clue sentence fits together

## What are the main types of indicator?

In the clue examples that follow, the indicator is denoted in bold type.

### 1 Anagram

In nearly all cryptic crosswords solvers are expected to unravel some solutions from a mix of letters, and there is a need for this wordplay to be flagged up. Hence the anagram indicator, of which there are a huge number. Most – but not all – imply some form of movement, lack of order, change, uncertainty or instability (especially in assumed mental or physical state) in their meanings, albeit often in a concealed surface reading. Anagram indicators such as 'ground' being the past tense of 'grind', and 'bananas' and 'potty' with their double meanings, show such concealment.

There are also some indicators that can only be fully justified by well-established convention. For example, the many synonyms of 'drunk' such as 'pickled', 'stoned' and the like are commonly used, it being assumed that cruciverbal tipplers are wobbly rather than flat out! Nor are setters static in their usages: a modern synonym for 'crazy' such as 'out to lunch' makes a highly misleading anagram indicator, as does 'supply' in the second example.

People seen **working** in Basra (5)

The indicator 'working' for this purpose is in the sense of 'being in action' and it signals a letter mix for the solution ARABS.

Monn (Caterers) **supply** beef and grouse (12)

Here the adverb of 'supple' meaning 'pliant' shows that the first two words must be anagrammatized into REMONSTRANCE meaning complaint, or 'beef' and 'grouse'. Note that as well as wordplay there are two definitions here, a practice often found in advanced puzzles such as Azed or Mephisto.

## 2   Containment
A solution may be split such that one part of it can be seen as being 'outside' another, duly shown by the many indicators of this type. Containment and insertion indicators have the same effect.

Opportunity to **go round** one Italian city (5)

'Opportunity' is 'turn', and when that is put outside 'I' for 'one' you get the Italian city TURIN. Here 'to go round' is the indicator and 'one' for '1' for 'I' is a common crossword convention.

Saw dog **wearing** lead (7)

This requires 'Rover' for 'dog' to be placed inside 'lead' – or rather the metal's abbreviation 'Pb' – to give PROVERB, or 'saw'.

Is **trapped in** burning lift (5)

The indicator 'trapped in' signals that 'is' has to be contained by, ie put inside, 'burning' meaning 'hot' for the solution HOIST, which defines 'lift'.

## 3   Insertion
These have the same effect as containment indicators. A solution may be split such that one part is viewed as being 'inside' another.

Disreputable type in favour of **cutting** discount (9)

If you put 'pro', meaning 'in favour of', inside (ie 'cutting') the term 'rebate' meaning 'discount', the solution REPROBATE, a 'disreputable type', appears.

Crumpet may be so to speak **in** bed (8)

Here the well-concealed definition ends at the word 'so'. The wordplay is then 'utter' meaning 'to speak' in 'bed' leading us nicely to BUTTERED. (Note that the 'to' is to be ignored, as is commonly the practice with verbs in wordplay).

## 4   Deletion
These indicators signal the deletion of a letter or letters (as in the first example), or a whole word within a clue (as in the second example).

Applause left **out** in graduation ceremony (7)

'Applause' is 'clapping' and the indicator demands that its L for 'left' be taken out to leave CAPPING, a 'graduation ceremony'.

Surgeon **fails to get** on in this swell (5)

Take 'on' from 'surgeon' to get to SURGE which is the definition for 'swell'.

Note that the word 'in' here in both deletion examples is being used not as an indicator but as common crossword shorthand, in effect for 'leading to...' or 'coming from...'.

Other specific deletion indicators are discussed in Ends deletion indicators, Head deletion indicators, Middle deletion indicators and Tail deletion indicators.

## 5   End indicators

### 5a  Ends selection

The first and last letters of a word within a clue are indicated for addition to some other letters, or to a whole word, in order to form the solution.

Urges for example, **both sides** in games (4)

The indicator 'both sides' when applied to 'games' gives two letters G and S. Put these together with 'eg', meaning 'for example', and you have EGGS as in to egg or urge someone on.

### 5b  Ends deletion

The first and last letters of a word within a clue are indicated for deletion in order to form the solution.

**Shell** prawn uncooked (3)

'Shell' in the sense of 'separate from the shell or covering' implies removing the first and last letters of 'prawn' to give RAW meaning 'uncooked'.

## 6   Head indicators

### 6a  Head selection

The first letter of a word within a clue is indicated for addition to some other letters or, as below, to a whole word to form the solution.

**Starter** with pork and mild pickle (6)

Here the indicator 'starter' is applied to 'pork' to give 'P'. Added to 'light' meaning 'mild' this provides the solution PLIGHT, or a 'pickle' – a predicament if you are in one.

### 6b  Head deletion

The first letter of a word is indicated for deletion in order to form the solution.

Colleague in Monte Carlo event **failing to start** (4)

A 'Monte Carlo event' is a 'rally' which 'fails to start', ie it loses its initial letter. This leaves the answer ALLY, meaning 'colleague'.

## 7   Middle indicators

### 7a  Middle selection

The middle letter (or letters) of a word within a clue is indicated for addition to some other letters, or to a whole word, in order to form the solution.

Plastic building toy on **centre** of floor (4)

'On' for 'leg' (as in cricket) plus the middle letter of floor, 'O', makes LEGO, the required toy.

### 7b  Middle deletion

The middle letter (or letters) of a word within a clue is indicated for deletion in order to form the solution.

Royal Artillery really **disheartened?** Seldom (6)

The central two letters 'AL' are eliminated from 'really' to give 'RELY', which put after 'RA' (an abbreviation of 'Royal Artillery') gives RARELY, 'seldom'.

## 8　Tail indicators

### 8a　Tail selection

The last letter (or letters) of a word within a clue is indicated for addition to some other letters, or to a whole word, in order to form the solution.

Dull **back** of road could be a cul-de-sac (4,3)

'Dull' is 'deaden', to which an added 'D' from 'back of road' provides DEAD END, a 'cul-de-sac'.

### 8b　Tail selection down

This is similar to that above, but this indicator is for a Down clue only (see Head indicators above for an explanation of this convention). The above Across clue could be adapted as follows, with 'bottom' as the Tail Selection Down indicator.

Dull **bottom** of road could be a cul-de-sac (4,3)

This gives a Down clue with the same solution DEAD END, a 'cul-de-sac'.

### 8c　Tail deletion

The last letter (or letters) of a word is indicated for deletion in order to form the solution.

English poet messing around **endlessly** (6)

'Messing around' is 'larking' which becomes (Philip) LARKIN, the poet, when its last letter is taken off.

### 8d　Tail deletion down

This is similar to that above, but this indicator is for a Down clue only.

**Baseless** worry for vehicle (3)

If the final letter of 'care' for 'worry' is ignored, CAR, a 'vehicle', comes out as the Down clue answer.

## 9　Hidden

### 9a　Hidden

The indicator instructs solvers to look for the solution within the clue sentence, or wholly within one of the clue's words.

**In** Amritsar it's a common habit (4)

Indicated by 'in', the challenge is to uncover a hidden but defined four-letter word. This is SARI – formed from the last three letters of 'Amritsar' and the first letter of 'it's' – a common habit with the final word in its 'dress' sense.

Sensation **concealed by** Chopin, Sand – needlessly (4,3,7)

Not quite so easy to spot, as a result of its misleading punctuation, is the hidden phrase PINS AND NEEDLES, a sensation.

### 9b　Hidden alternately

A second form of this indicator applies where every other letter has to be taken to form the solution word. The indicator will not necessarily always signal whether it's the even or odd letters to be used. For example, the indicator 'regularly' may refer to either even or odd letters.

Select **even parts** of strongest gear (4)

The instruction 'select' indicates taking the even letters in 'strongest' to form a word meaning 'gear'. Hence the solution is TOGS.

## 10  Homophone

In this type, the definition when spoken becomes another word which forms the wordplay. Sometimes with careless word placement, setters do not make clear which is the solution and which the homophone, though this may be established from the word-length. It can also be a problem for solvers as to which part of the English-speaking world, with its many differing pronunciations, is deemed to be speaking the homophone.

It's cold in a S American country **reportedly** (6)

'Reportedly' is an indicator that the solver is looking for a word that sounds like another meaning of 'cold'. 'Chile' clearly fits the bill as a homonym of CHILLY, the answer.

Check **on radio** for weather forecast? (4)

If listening to the radio, 'rein' (meaning 'check') would sound like RAIN, the solution.


## 11  Juxtaposition

### 11a  Juxtaposition

The indicator shows that the two words or parts of words need to be placed together for the solution.

Endeavour perhaps to be **alongside** learner in a scrap (6)

Morse ('Endeavour', the first name of Inspector Morse in the novels by Colin Dexter) is juxtaposed with 'L' for 'learner' to make 'scrap', a MORSEL.

### 11b  Juxtaposition down

This is similar to that above, but this indicator is for a Down clue only (see Head indicators above for an explanation of this convention).

One **above** Bishop given the answer: forgiveness (10)

'A' for 'one' put on top of 'B' for 'bishop' and 'solution' for 'answer' makes ABSOLUTION, meaning 'forgiveness'. Actually there are two juxtaposition indicators here, in that as well as 'above', the word 'given' also shows that some words are to be placed together.


## 12  Reversal

### 12a  Reversal

The whole of a solution word can sometimes be reversed to form another different word (or the same word in the case of a palindrome – see below). It's the job of reversal indicators to show this, and sometimes also reversals of only part of a word which is then subject to more wordplay, as in the second example.

Huge flans **all round** – that's the plan (9)

'Huge flans' are 'mega tarts', which when reversed gives STRATAGEM or 'plan'.

Optimistic US president admitting bad **back** (7)

Reversing 'ill' for 'bad' and putting this inside (further wordplay signalled by 'admitting') Bush gives BULLISH, or 'optimistic'.

### 12b  Reversal down

Reversal indicators used in Down clues will often be, for example, 'rising' or 'brought up' rather than those used in Across clues implying reversal horizontally such as 'all round' (as above) or as 'backwards' (see Head indicators above for further explanation of this convention). Using this in the preceding example, a Down clue could have been:

Huge flans **served up** – that's the plan (9)

It's 'served up' showing the necessary upwards movement in 'mega tarts' to lead to the same STRATAGEM solution.

### 12c  Reversal palindrome

The third type of reversal indicator applies to palindromic solutions, for which there are a small number of indicators.

This note is small **whichever way you look at it** (5)

The indicator signals that the solution is the same as its reversal, in this case MINIM, the 'small note' of the clue.

## Other indicators

In addition to the most important indicators already covered above, there are some others met in cryptic puzzles that can be mentioned briefly. They tend to be self-explanatory.

## Foreign

Many European languages, especially French, can be indicated, usually obviously but occasionally not so, as in this example:

**Nice** girl has time for a piece of beef (6)

The indicator refers to the French city of Nice, where the word for 'girl' would be 'fille'. Put next to 'T' for 'time', you have FILLET, a piece of beef.

## Archaic

Rather than use the mundane 'archaic' or 'obsolete' as indicators, setters find more interesting and misleading ways of expressing words that are no longer in general usage.

Mark **antique** articles rubbish! (2,3)

'M' for 'mark' (as in Germany before the euro), plus 'ye ye' or two archaic definite 'articles' will show as MY EYE, meaning 'rubbish!'

## Dialect

Different regional words and accents may be referred to, especially British ones such as Scottish and Cockney.

The **Yorkshire** beer in fiction (4)

The solution TALE, meaning 'fiction' in the sense of a lie, comes from 'T' for 'the' as supposedly used in 'Yorkshire' plus 'ALE' for 'beer'.

## Repetition

A small number of indicators show, nearly always self-evidently, when letters or words need to be included more than once in a solution.

The Queen **repeatedly** behind grown-up man of affairs (9)

Thus 'grown-up' is 'adult' which when preceding 'ER' (the Queen) twice gives 'ADULTERER', the 'man of affairs' being sought.

## Conclusion

In the foregoing examples there is mostly only one type of indicator used in any one example. However, it is not uncommon in advanced puzzles to find one or more indicators of the same or different type being used in one clue. For example:

Clever wordplay recalled Thomas Mann's last book about love (3,3)

Here the solver is asked to do all the following:

|  | **Indicator (and type)** |
|---|---|
| Abbreviate *Thomas* to TOM | none given |
| Take *Mann's last* as N | *last* (tail selection) |
| Abbreviate *book* to B | none given |
| Abbreviate *love* to O | none given |
| Put TOM N B outside O | *about* (containment) |
| Amongst other possibilities, this gives TOMNOB. |  |
| Reverse this to get BONMOT | *recalled* (reversal) |

And finally split it (3,3) to get BONMOT, meaning 'clever wordplay'.


Note that, as is almost always the case, abbreviations have to be identified without the aid of indicators. The clue is perhaps over-complex and you may or may not agree that it offers clever wordplay!


## About the author

Tim Moorey sets crosswords as one of the three-strong Mephisto team for *The Sunday Times*, for which he occasionally contributes *The Sunday Times* crossword. He has additionally appeared as Owzat in newspapers such as *The Independent*, *The Sunday Telegraph* and *The Listener* crossword in *The Times*. He is crossword editor and setter for *The Week* and *Moneyweek* magazines, author of *How To Master The Times Crossword*, gives talks on crosswords and runs regular workshops for crossword beginners.

# Indicator lists

The following lists show those headwords, phrasal verbs and idioms that are denoted in the *Crossword Dictionary* as being indicators of cryptic crossword clue wordplay.

The lists have been compiled on the basis of those indicators most commonly seen in crosswords. They are not, and never could be, definitive. The lists reflect the way that these words have been used in actual cryptic clues. Appearance in a list does not mean that such a usage is considered acceptable by all crossword setters and editors.

As explained in the Introduction, indicators may not appear in a cryptic clue in the way in which they appear here, but rather may be encountered in an inflected form – for example the anagram indicator 'digest' is more frequently encountered as 'digested' – or as part of a phrase, for example 'not reaching a conclusion' to indicate a tail deletion. As the lists reflect the headwords of the *Crossword Dictionary*, not every form of every indicator is included.

Additionally, there are some indicators which may be encountered in cryptic clues, but which are not denoted in the text or in the following lists. Examples of these include:

| Type | Indicator example |
| --- | --- |
| Abbreviation to be used | short |
| Colloquial usage | commonly |
| First half, second half of word selected | left half, right half |
| Insertion between letters SS | aboard ship, on board |
| Move first letter to end | brings first to last, runs down |
| Move internal letter to front | puts foremost |
| Not all letters used | not entirely |
| One of two central letters deleted | half-heartedly |
| Only limited wordplay | slightly |
| Only two, three, etc letters selected | two of, three of, etc |
| Plural word loses final S | singular |
| Proportion of letters in a word selected | half, two-thirds, etc |
| Selection of second, third, fourth, etc letter | second, third, fourth, etc |
| Selection of two letters | couple of |
| Single letter instead of double | just one |
| Substitute letters | replace, take instead, change, changing |
| Unusual homophone | drunkard says (*for a homophone that sounds slurred, eg 'mesh' for 'mess'*) |

It should also be noted that as the number of foreign word indicators is potentially unlimited – any person or place might be used – only the most general have been included here. For example, 'article from Paris' , 'day in Calais', 'Renoir's here', 'lake in Savoie' or 'of Chirac's' could all indicate that a French word is required (in these instances, 'la' or 'le', 'jour', 'ici', 'lac' and 'de' respectively).

## Anagram indicators

Anagram indicators include:

| | | | | |
|---|---|---|---|---|
| abandon | anomalous | batter | broke | component |
| abandoned | anomaly | battered | broken | compose |
| aberrant | another | batting | broth | composed |
| abnormal | anxious | batty | bruise | composition |
| abominable | anyhow | beaten | bubbly | compound |
| about | anyway | beat up | buck | compromise |
| abroad | apart | become | buckle | concerned |
| absurd | appalling | bedevil | buffeted | concoct |
| abuse | appallingly | bedlam | building | condemn |
| abysmal | appliance | befuddle | built | condemnation |
| abysmally | applied | belabour | bully | condition |
| accident | appointed | belt | bum | confection |
| accidentally | appraisal | bemuse | bumble | confound |
| acrobatics | arch | bemused | bumbling | confuse |
| acting | around | bend | bundle | confused |
| action | arousal | bendy | bungle | confusing |
| activate | arouse | bent | burst | confusion |
| active | arrange | berserk | bust | constituent |
| activity | arrangement | bespoke | bustle | construct |
| adapt | array | bewildered | bustling | construe |
| adaptable | artefact | biased | busy | contaminate |
| adaptation | artful | bizarre | butcher | contamination |
| adjust | artfully | bizarrely | Byzantine | contort |
| adjustment | articulate | blast | calamitous | contrive |
| administer | articulated | blasted | camouflage | contrived |
| adrift | askew | blazing | capricious | conversion |
| affected | assassinate | blend | career | convert |
| afflicted | assassination | blessed | careless | convertible |
| afresh | assemble | blight | carelessly | convoluted |
| after injury | assorted | blotchy | carve | convulse |
| aggrieved | astonishing | blow up | carve up | cook |
| agile | astray | blue | cast | cooked |
| agitate | at fault | blunder | cavort | cook up |
| agitated | at random | blur | change | correct |
| ague | atrocious | blurred | changeable | correction |
| alarm | at sea | body | chaotic | corrupt |
| allocate | away | bogus | chew | could be |
| allocation | awful | boil | choppy | could become |
| all over the place | awfully | boiled | chop up | crack |
| alloy | awkward | boiling | churn | cracked |
| alter | awkwardly | boisterous | circulate | crackers |
| alteration | awry | bomb | clobber | crackpot |
| alternative | bad | boozy | clumsy | crack up |
| alternatively | badly | boss | cocktail | craft |
| amazing | baffle | botch | cock up | craftily |
| amend | baffling | bother | cock-up | crafty |
| amendment | bake | bottle | code | cranky |
| amiss | bamboozle | bouncing | collapse | crash |
| amok | bananas | bouncy | collected | crazed |
| analyse | bandy | brain | collection | crazily |
| analysis | barbaric | break | combustible | crazy |
| anarchic | barbarous | break up | compilation | creation |
| anew | barge | breeze | compile | criminal |
| angrily | barking | brew | complex | crocked |
| angry | baroque | brittle | complicate | crook |
| animated | bastard | broach | complicated | crooked |
| animatedly | bats | broadcast | complication | cross |

| | | | | |
|---|---|---|---|---|
| crude | disastrous | dizzy | explosive | forced |
| crudely | disband | do | extract | foreign |
| cruel | discomfit | doctor | extraordinarily | forge |
| crumble | discompose | doddering | extraordinary | forged |
| crumbly | disconcert | doddery | extravagant | forlorn |
| crush | disconcerting | dodgy | fabricate | form |
| cuckoo | discord | done | fake | foul |
| cultivate | discordant | dotty | fall | founder |
| cure | discover | doubtfully | false | found in |
| curious | diseased | drastic | faltering | fracture |
| curiously | disfigure | drawn | fan | frantic |
| cut | disgruntled | dreadful | fanciful | frantically |
| daft | disguise | dreadfully | fancy | freak |
| damage | disguised | dress | fantastic | freak out |
| damaged | dish | dressing | fashion | free |
| dance | dishevelled | dress up | fault | freely |
| dash | dish out | drift | faulty | frenetic |
| dashing | disintegrate | drunk | fearful | frenetically |
| dazed | disintegration | drunken | ferment | frenzy |
| debris | disjointed | dubious | fettle | fresh |
| decompose | dislocate | duff | feverish | freshen |
| defective | dislocation | dynamic | fickle | freshly |
| deficient | dismantle | easily | find in | frightful |
| defile | disorder | easy | finesse | frightfully |
| deform | disordered | eccentric | finicky | frilly |
| deformed | disorderly | edit | fishy | frisky |
| delirious | disorganization | effervescent | fit | frolic |
| deliriously | disorganize | elaborate | fix | frolicsome |
| demented | disorganized | elastic | fixed | fuddled |
| demolish | disorientate | elevated | flabbergasted | fudge |
| deplorable | disorientated | embarrass | flail | full |
| deploy | disorientation | embarrassed | flake | fumble |
| deranged | dispel | embroil | flaky | funnily |
| desecrate | disperse | emend | flap | funny |
| design | dispersion | emendation | flash | furious |
| desperate | disport | emerge | flawed | fussy |
| desperately | dispose | employ | flexible | fuzzy |
| destabilize | disposed | engineer | flighty | gaffe |
| destroy | disposition | enigmatic | flit | gambol |
| destruction | disrupt | enliven | floating | garble |
| desultory | disruption | entangle | flog | garbled |
| deterioration | dissipate | entanglement | flop | generate |
| detour | dissipated | entwine | floppy | giddily |
| devastate | dissolute | err | flounder | giddy |
| devastated | dissonant | errant | flourish | ginger |
| develop | distillation | erratic | flourished | gnarled |
| deviant | distort | erratically | flourishing | go crazy |
| deviate | distorted | erring | flow | gone |
| deviation | distract | erroneous | fluctuate | go off |
| devilish | distracted | error | fluff | grim |
| devious | distraught | erupt | fluid | groggy |
| diabolical | distribute | eruption | flurried | groom |
| dicky | distribution | evolution | flurry | gross |
| different | disturb | evolve | fluster | grotesque |
| differently | disturbance | exchange | flutter | ground |
| digest | disturbed | excite | fly | hairy |
| dilapidated | disturbing | excited | fly open | ham |
| dire | dither | excruciate | fog | hammer |
| direct | diverse | exercise | foolish | hammered |
| disarrange | divert | exotic | foolishly | hammer out |
| disarray | diverting | explode | force | hamper |

| | | | | |
|---|---|---|---|---|
| haphazard | insanity | loosely | misfit | negligence |
| haphazardly | insecure | lost | misguided | negligent |
| happy | intoxicate | lousy | mishandle | negotiate |
| harass | intoxicated | ludicrous | mishap | negotiation |
| harassed | intricate | lunatic | misinterpret | nervous |
| harm | invalid | mad | mislead | nervously |
| hash | invention | madden | misleading | new |
| hatch | involve | maddening | mismanage | newly |
| havoc | involved | made-up | mismanagement | nobble |
| haywire | irregular | madly | misplace | nonsensical |
| hazy | irritated | madness | misprint | not |
| head over heels | itinerant | make | misread | novel |
| heat | jagged | make up | misrepresent | nuts |
| hectic | jangle | make-up | misrepresentation | obfuscate |
| hellish | jar | maladjusted | misshapen | oblique |
| helter-skelter | jaunty | malformed | misspell | obscure |
| hideous | jazz | malfunction | mistake | obstreperous |
| higgledy-piggledy | jerk | malleable | mistaken | odd |
| high | jerky | maltreat | mistakenly | oddball |
| hit | jig | mangle | mistreat | oddly |
| hopeless | jiggle | manic | misuse | off |
| hopelessly | jitters | manically | mix | off-colour |
| horrible | jittery | manifest | mixed | on |
| horribly | jockey | manifestation | mixed up | on the rampage |
| horrid | jog | manipulate | mix in | operate |
| horrific | jolt | manipulation | mixture | order |
| hotchpotch | jostle | manoeuvre | mix up | orderly |
| hurl | judder | manufacture | mix-up | organization |
| hurt | juggle | mar | mobile | organize |
| hybrid | jumble | marshal | mobilize | organized |
| idiotic | jumbled | mash | model | original |
| ill | jump | masquerade | modification | ornate |
| ill-assorted | junk | massage | modify | other |
| ill at ease | kick | maul | mongrel | otherwise |
| ill-bred | kind of | maybe | mortal | out |
| ill-treat | kink | mayhem | mould | outlandish |
| imbecile | kinky | maze | mouldy | out of hand |
| impair | knead | meandering | move | out of order |
| impaired | knock | meddle | movement | out of place |
| imperfect | knock over | medley | moving | out of sorts |
| implicate | knot | melange | muddle | output |
| implicated | knotty | mêlée | muddled | outrageous |
| improper | labour | melt | muddy | outré |
| improperly | laboured | mental | muff | outside |
| inaccurate | labyrinthine | merry | mushy | overthrow |
| incapable | lace | mess | muss | overturn |
| in circulation | lamentable | messy | must | painfully |
| incorrect | lark | metamorphose | musty | panic |
| indecent | launder | metamorphosis | mutate | paranormal |
| indiscriminate | lawless | mill | mutation | pastiche |
| inebriated | lax | mince | mutilate | patchy |
| inept | layout | mint | mutilation | pathetic |
| ingredient | lazily | misbehave | mutinous | peculiar |
| injure | leap | misbehaviour | mysterious | peculiarly |
| injured | liberal | mischievous | mysteriously | peddle |
| inky | light | mischievously | nastily | pell-mell |
| in motion | lit | misconduct | nasty | perform |
| inordinate | lively | misconstrue | naughty | perhaps |
| in pieces | loaded | misdirect | neaten | perplex |
| insane | loony | miserable | neglect | perturb |
| insanely | loose | miserably | neglected | perturbed |

perverse
perversely
perversion
perversity
pervert
perverted
phoney
pickle
pie
piece
plan
plastered
plastic
play
play around with
play with
ply
police
pollute
pollution
poor
poorly
pop
possible
possibly
potential
potentially
potty
prance
precarious
precariously
preparation
prepare
prepared
preposterous
problem
problematic
process
produce
production
promiscuous
protean
provide
pulverize
pummel
punish
puzzle
quaint
quake
queer
questionable
quirky
quiver
raddled
rag
rage
ragged
ramble
rambling
rampage
rampant

ramshackle
random
randomly
rare
rash
rattle
ravage
ravaged
rave
raving
react
reactionary
realign
rearrange
reassemble
rebel
rebellious
rebuild
recast
reckless
recklessly
recollect
recollection
recondition
reconfigure
reconstitute
reconstruct
recover
recreate
recycle
red
redeploy
redevelop
redevelopment
redistribute
redistribution
redraft
re-edit
reel
refashion
refine
refit
reform
reformat
reformation
refurbish
refurbishment
refuse
regenerate
regenerated
regulate
rehash
rejig
relax
relaxed
relay
remake
remarkable
remedy
remodel
render

renegade
renegotiate
renew
renovate
rent
reorder
reorganize
repackage
repair
replace
reposition
represent
representation
reprocess
reproduce
resettle
reshape
reshuffle
resolution
resolve
resort
restless
restoration
restore
re-use
revamp
reveal
revel
review
revise
revolt
revolting
revolution
revolutionary
rework
rewrite
rickety
ridiculous
ridiculously
rifle
rig
rile
riot
riotous
riotously
rip
ripple
rock
rocky
rogue
roll
rollicking
rolling
rot
rotten
rough
roughen
roughly
round
rouse
rove

rub
rubbish
rude
ruffle
ruin
ruined
rum
run
running
runny
run riot
run wild
rupture
rustic
sabotage
sack
sad
sadly
salad
scatter
scatty
scheme
scour
scraggy
scramble
scrappy
scratch
screw
screwy
scruffy
scuffle
sculpt
sculpture
scuttle
seedy
seethe
serve
set
set out
settlement
shake
shaky
sham
shape
shapeless
shatter
shattered
shell
shift
shifty
shimmer
shimmering
shiver
shock
shoddy
shot
shower
show off
shuffle
sick
signal

silliness
silly
sink
sketchy
skip
slack
slapdash
slaughtered
slide
slip
slippery
slipshod
sloppy
slosh
slovenly
slyly
smash
snarl
solution
solve
somehow
sorry
sort
soup
sozzled
spasmodic
spatter
special
specially
speech
spin
splash
splice
spoil
spongy
sport
sporting
spray
spread
spring
sprinkle
spurious
squiffy
squirm
stagger
staggered
staggering
steaming
stew
stir
stirring
storm
stormy
straighten
strange
strangely
stray
stress
structure
struggle
stumble

stupid
stupidly
style
subtle
subtly
suffer
suffering
sunk
supply
surprising
suspect
suspicious
swap
swill
swim
swimming
swing
swinging
swirl
switch
swop
synthetic
tailor
taint
tangle
tangled
tattered
tease
teeter
terrible
terribly
throb
throw
tidy
tight
tipsy
topple
topsy-turvy
torment
torn
tortuous
torture
toss
totter
tour

tragic
train
trammel
transfer
transfigure
transform
transformation
translate
translation
transmute
transport
transported
transpose
trash
travelling
treat
treatment
tremble
trembling
tremulous
trick
tricky
trip
trouble
troubled
troublesome
tumble
tumbledown
tumult
turbulence
turbulent
turmoil
turn
turning
tweak
twiddle
twinkle
twinkling
twirl
twirling
twist
twisted
twitch
type
ugly

unbalanced
uncertain
uncommon
uncommonly
uncomplicated
uncontrolled
unconventional
unco-ordinated
uncouth
undisciplined
undo
undoing
undone
unduly
uneasy
uneven
unexpected
unexpectedly
unfair
unfairly
unfamiliar
unfit
unfortunate
unfortunately
ungainly
unhappily
unhappy
unholy
unkempt
unnatural
unnaturally
unorthodox
unpredictable
unravel
unreliable
unrest
unrestrained
unrestricted
unruly
unscramble
unseemly
unsettle
unsettled
unsound
unstable

unsteady
untidy
untrue
unusual
unusually
unwind
unwise
upset
upsetting
upturn
use
used
useless
vacillate
vacillating
vacillation
vagrant
vague
vaguely
vandalize
variant
variation
varied
variegated
variety
various
vary
vault
versatile
version
vibrate
vigorous
vigorously
vile
violate
violation
violent
violently
volatile
vulnerable
wacky
wag
waggle
wander
wanton

warp
warring
waste
wasted
wave
waver
wavering
way
weave
weird
whip
whip up
whirl
whisk
wicked
wild
wildly
wind
winding
wobble
wobbly
woeful
work
working
worried
worry
wound
wrack
wreck
wreckage
wrestling
wretched
writhe
wrong
wrongly
wrought
yank
yearning
yield
yielding
zany

## Containment indicators

Containment indicators include:

| | | | | |
|---|---|---|---|---|
| about | carry | encompass | hamper | possess |
| absorb | casing | enfold | harbour | protect |
| absorbed | catch | engulf | hedge | purse |
| accept | catching | ensnare | herein | receive |
| accommodate | caught | entertain | hide | repress |
| accommodating | circle | entertaining | hiding | restrain |
| accommodation | clasp | enthral | hold | restrict |
| acquire | cleft | enthralling | host | retain |
| admit | clutch | envelop | house | round |
| adopt | collect | fence | housing | sandwich |
| around | come to grips with | flank | hug | secure |
| arrest | comprehend | found in | imbibe | see around |
| assimilate | comprise | frame | imprison | seize |
| assume | conceal | framework | include | shelter |
| astride | concealed | gather | including | snare |
| ate | consume | gathering | incorporate | squeeze |
| bag | consuming | get around | in possession | stow |
| bear | contain | get hold of | introduce | stuffing |
| bearing | cover | get round | keep | superficial |
| beset | crossing | get to grips with | limit | surround |
| besiege | custody | go about | lock up | surrounding |
| bewilder | describe | go around | net | swallow |
| bite | detectable | gobble | nurse | tackle |
| biting | drape | go round | obstruct | take in |
| box | draw in | grab | occlude | trap |
| bracket | eat | grasp | outside | trapped |
| break up | embody | grasping | over | wearing |
| bring in | embrace | grip | overshadow | welcome |
| bring round | encapsulate | gripping | pen | without |
| bury | encircle | guard | pinch | wrap |
| capture | enclose | gulp | pocket | |

## Insertion indicators

Insertion indicators include:

| | | | | |
|---|---|---|---|---|
| aboard | cut | find in | intercept | pierce |
| amid | cutting | get into | interception | piercing |
| amidst | devour | go into | interrupt | puncture |
| among | divide | half | interruption | seduce |
| at heart | don | halve | invest | set in |
| between | during | held by | involve | split |
| bisect | engage in | held in | occupy | tuck in |
| block | enter | imprisoned | part | tuck into |
| break | feed | in | parting | wear |
| cleave | fill | infuse | penetrate | within |
| collected | filling | inside | penetrating | |

## Deletion indicators

Deletion indicators include:

| | | | | |
|---|---|---|---|---|
| abandon | drop | junk | no | shed |
| absent | edit | lack | not | shun |
| cut | elude | lacking | out | skip |
| disappear | excision | leave | regardless | small |
| disappearance | excluding | left | sack | take off |
| dismiss | fail to get | lose | sacrifice | withdraw |
| dismissal | heave | missing | scratch | withhold |
| disregard | ignore | nearly | scrub | |

## Ends indicators

Ends selection indicators include:

| | | | |
|---|---|---|---|
| banks | bounds | edge | limit |
| borders of | casing | extreme | side |
| both sides | determination | fringe | |

Ends deletion indicators include:

| | | | |
|---|---|---|---|
| limited | peel | top and tail | wingless |
| limitless | shell | unlimited | |

## Head indicators

Head selection indicators include:

| | | | | |
|---|---|---|---|---|
| at first | foremost | introduction | opener | tip |
| beginner | front | lead | opening | top |
| beginning | head | leader | primarily | |
| capital | heading | leadership | start | |
| extreme | initial | leading | starter | |
| first | initially | minimum | summit | |

Head deletion indicators include:

| | | | |
|---|---|---|---|
| behead | fail to start | leaderless | topless |
| decapitate | headless | limitless | trim |
| deface | head off | tip-off | |

## Middle indicators

Middle selection indicators include:

| | | | |
|---|---|---|---|
| at heart | centre | heartily | middle |
| central | heart | innards | nucleus |

Middle deletion indicators include:

| | | |
|---|---|---|
| disembowel | empty | heartless |
| disheartened | gutless | heartlessly |

# Tail indicators

Tail selection indicators include:

| | | | | |
|---|---|---|---|---|
| at last | ending | final | last | ultimate |
| at the end of | endmost | finale | lastly | ultimately |
| back | extreme | finally | rear | |
| behind | far end | finish | tail | |
| end | far side | foundation | terminal | |

Tail selection down indicators include:

| | | |
|---|---|---|
| base of | bottom | south |

Tail deletion indicators include:

| | | | | |
|---|---|---|---|---|
| abbreviate | contract | endless | most | shortly |
| abridged | curtail | endlessly | nearly | trim |
| abrupt | curtailment | immature | reduce | unfinished |
| almost | cut short | incomplete | reduction | |
| brief | detail | limit | short | |
| briefly | detailed | limitless | shorten | |
| clip | dock | Manx | shortened | |

Tail deletion down indicators include:

baseless
bottom

# Hidden indicators

Hidden indicators include:

| | | | | |
|---|---|---|---|---|
| amid | contain | extract | immersed | sample |
| amidst | content | find in | in | show |
| among | continuous | found in | include | slice |
| apparent | continuously | fragment | in part | some |
| belonging to | cover | from | inside | stuffing |
| bit | cover up | held by | keep | within |
| bottle | deposit | held in | lock up | |
| central | discover | hidden | part | |
| characters in | embrace | hide | part of | |
| concealed | emerge | immerse | piece | |

Hidden alternately indicators include:

| | | | |
|---|---|---|---|
| alternate | evenly | ignore the odds | oddly |
| even | even parts | odd | odd parts |

# Homophone indicators

Homophone indicators include:

| | | | | |
|---|---|---|---|---|
| aloud | converse | murmur | read aloud | spoken |
| announce | ear | mutter | report | state |
| articulate | hear | narrate | reportedly | told |
| articulated | hearing | on radio | said | utter |
| audible | hearsay | on telephone | say | verbal |
| aural | inform | oral | saying | vocal |
| broadcast | list | orally | sound | |
| conversation | listen | pronounce | speak | |
| conversational | listen in | pronounced | speech | |

## Juxtaposition indicators

Juxtaposition indicators include:

| | | | | |
|---|---|---|---|---|
| abut | alongside | associated | continuous | in front of |
| add | also | at the end of | continuously | join |
| adjacent | altogether | before | first | meet |
| adjoin | and | behind | follow | take on |
| adjoining | append | beside | following | trail |
| after | approach | by | given | with |
| against | arrive | chase | go together | |
| ahead | associate | come first | in front | |

Juxtaposition down indicators include:

| | | | |
|---|---|---|---|
| above | go under | subordinate | topping |
| below | on | support | under |
| beneath | over | supporter | |

## Reversal indicators

Reversal indicators include:

| | | | | |
|---|---|---|---|---|
| about | cutback | knock back | reflection | review |
| all round | east | make a comeback | regress | revolution |
| around | fall | on the contrary | reject | revolutionary |
| back | flip | preposterous | repel | rotate |
| backfire | go around | raise | retire | round |
| backing | go back | rampant | retired | set back |
| backslide | go back on | reactionary | retiring | setback |
| backsliding | go round | rear | retreat | switch |
| backtrack | go west | rebellious | retrograde | turn |
| backward | head over heels | recall | retrogress | turn back |
| backwards | hinge | recede | retrospective | turned |
| boomerang | in retrospect | recess | return | turning |
| bring back | in return | recoil | reversal | turnover |
| capsize | inversion | recollect | reverse | volte-face |
| come back | invert | recurrent | reversion | wheel |
| contrary | keep back | reflect | revert | |

Reversal down indicators include:

| | | | | |
|---|---|---|---|---|
| arise | elevated | put up | set-up | upset |
| ascend | give rise to | raised | take up | upside down |
| ascendant | hold up | rise | turn over | upturn |
| bring up | keel over | rising | turn up | upward |
| climb | mount | send up | up | use up |
| come up | over | serve up | uplift | |
| elevate | overturn | set up | uprising | |

Palindrome indicators include:

| | | |
|---|---|---|
| back and forth | to and fro | whichever way |
| either way | up and down | you look at it |

## Foreign indicators

Foreign word indicators include:

| | | |
|---|---|---|
| European | French | local |
| foreign | in France | translate |

## Archaic indicators

Archaic indicators include:

antique
old
old-fashioned
once

## Dialect indicators

Dialect indicators include:

| American | East End | Sandy | US |
|----------|----------|-------|-----------|
| Cockney | local | Scot | Yorkshire |
| Cumbrian | New York | Scottish | |

## Repetition indicators

Repetition indicators include:

| couple | repeated | twice |
|--------|------------|-------|
| double | repeatedly | |
| repeat | repetition | |

# Reference lists

Headwords followed by one or more reference list:

abbey
aboriginal
accommodation
acid
activist
actor, actress
administrative
admiral
Africa
African
agriculture
aircraft
airline
airport
alga, algae
alphabet
America
American
American football
amino acid
amphibian
anaesthetic
analgesic
anatomy
anchor
angel
animal
anniversary
ant
antelope
anthropology
antibiotic
antique
antiseptic
ape
apocryphal
apostle
apple
Arab
arch
archaeology
archbishop
archipelago
architect
architecture
armour
army
art
arthropod
artist
Asia
Asian
asteroid
astronaut

astronomer
athlete
athletics
atmosphere
Australia
Australian football
author
aviation
aviator
award

bacteriology
bacterium
badminton
bag
ballet
baseball
basketball
bat
battle
bay
beach
bean
bear
bed
bedclothes
beer
beetle
belief
believer
berry
bet
Bible
bicycle
biochemistry
biography
biology
bird
birth
biscuit
bishop
black
blemish
blue
bomb
bomber
bone
book
bookbinding
boot
border
botany
bottle
boxer

boxing
boy
brain
bread
bridge
bridle
brown
building
bulb
bushranger
business
businessman,
  businesswoman
butterfly

cactus
cake
calendar
camera
Canada
canal
canonical
cape
captain
car
cardinal
carpet
carriage
cartoon
castle
cat
cathedral
cattle
cave
celebration
cell
cemetery
cereal
ceremony
chair
channel
charity
cheese
chef
chemical
chemist
chemistry
chess
chicken
choreography
Christmas
church
cicada
cigarette

cinema
circle
circus
city
classification
clean
cloak
clock
clothes, clothing
cloud
clown
club
coat
cocktail
coffee
coin
collar
collective
collector
college
colour
comedian
comedy
comet
comic
command
commander
commonwealth
communication
compass
competition
composer
computer
conductor
constellation
container
continent
contraceptive
cook
cookery
cosmetic
cotton
council
country
county
court
cricket
crime
criminal
crop
cross
crossword
crust
crustacean

currency
cutlery
cutter
cyclist

dagger
dairy
dam
dance
dancer
dandy
daughter
day
death
deer
deficiency
delivery
department
desert
despot
dessert
detective
device
diamond
diary
dinosaur
diocese
director
disease
district
divination
doctor
dog
doll
domestic
dress
drink
drug
duck
dwarf
dye
dynasty

ear
eat
economics
economist
educational
eel
Egyptian
electorate
electrical
element
emblem

embroidery
emperor
empire
empress
engine
engineer
entertainer
entertainment
environment
enzyme
equestrian
essayist
Europe
European
execution
exercise
explorer
explosive
eye

fable
fabric
face
fairground
fairy tale
falcon
farm
fashion
fast
fastener, fastening
fate
feminism
fencing
fern
festival
fever
fictional
fictitious
Field Marshal
fighter
figure
film
fireplace
fireworks
firth
fish
fishing
flag
flower
fly
food
fool
football
footballer
footwear
forest
fortification
fossil
Frenchman
fruit
fuel

fungus
fur
furniture
fury

galaxy
gambling
game
garden
gardener
gardening
gas
gauge
gem
genealogy
general
genetics
geography
geology
German
giant
girl
gland
glass
god, goddess
golf
golf club
golfer
government
governor
grace
grass
Greek
green
grey
grouse
gulf
gun
gymnastics

hair
hairdresser
hairstyle
hat
headdress
heart
heraldry
herb
hero
heroine
highwayman
hill
historian
historical
hobby
hockey
holiday
honour
hormone
horse
horseman,

horsewoman
hour
house
household
humour
hybrid
hydrocarbon

ice
ice hockey
ice skating
incarnation
inflammation
insect
insecticide
institute
instrument
insulator
inventor
invertebrate
Ireland
Irish
island

Japanese
jazz
jewellery
journalism
journalist
judge

karate
key
king
knife
knight
knit
knot

laboratory
lace
lake
language
Latin
law
lawyer
leaf
leather
legal
legend
letter
lettuce
lexicographer
libretto
lie
lily
liqueur
literary
literature
lizard
lock

London
lover
luggage

machinery
mammal
mania
Maori
marriage
marshal
marsupial
martial art
massacre
mathematics
meal
measurement
measuring
  instrument
meat
medical
medicine
metal
meteor
meteorology
Middle East
military
mineral
miser
missile
missionary
mollusc
monarch
monastery
monk
monkey
monster
month
monument
moon
moss
moth
mountain
mountaineering
mouth
murderer
muscle
muse
museum
mushroom
music
musical
musician
musketeer
Muslim
mythical
mythology

name
narcotic
nationality
NATO

navigation
nerve
news
newspaper
New York
New Zealand
Nobel Prize
nobility
non-fiction
note
novel
number
numeral
nurse
nut

observatory
occult
occupation
ocean
office
official
oil
Olympics
OPEC
opera
optical
orange
oratorio
orchestra
orchid
ore
organ
overture

paint
painter
painting
palace
palaeontologist
palm
pantomime
paper
parasite
Paris
park
parliament
parrot
particle
party
passage
pasta
pastry
patriarch
peninsula
people
pepper
pet
pharaoh
philosopher
philosophy

phobia
photographer
photographic
physics
physiology
pianist
picture
pig
pigment
pike
pine
pink
pirate
plague
plain
planet
plant
plastic
play
playwright
plumbing
poem
poet
poetry
poison
poisoning
poker
police
police officer
political
politician
pope
porcelain
port
potato
pottery
poultry
power
prayer
precipitation
premier
president
priest
primate
prime minister
prince
princess
printing
prison
probe
prophet,
  prophetess
prosody
protein
province
pseudonym
psychiatrist
psychology
public house
publish
punctuation

punishment
purple
puzzle

qualification
queen
quiz

rabbi
rabbit
race
racecourse
racing
radiation
radio
railway
rainbow
rank
rebel
rebellion
recording
red
refine
reformer
regiment
region
reindeer
relative
religion
religious
reptile
republic
resort
restaurant
revolution
revolutionary
rhetorical
rhyme
river
road
rock
rodent
Roman
roof
room
rope
rowing
rubber
rugby
ruler
ruminant
Russia
Russian

sage
sail
sailing
sailor
saint
salad
sale

salt
satellite
satirist
sauce
sausage
saw
Scandinavian
scanner
scarf
school
science
scientific
Scottish
scripture
sculptor
sculpture
sea
seafood
seal
season
seaweed
sect
sedative
sedge
servant
service
Seven against
  Thebes
Shakespeare
shark
sheep
ship
shipping
shop
shout
shrub
SI
siege
sight
signal
sin
singer
skier
skiing
skin
smell
snake
snow
soap
society
sofa
soldier
son
song
songwriter
sound
soup
spa
space
spaniel
speech

spider
spirits
sport
sportsperson
spread
spy
square
stadium
stamp
star
state
stationery
stick
storm
strait
study
sugar
suit
surgeon
surgery
swan
sweet
swimming
sword
symbol

table
taste
tax
tea
teacher
team
teeth
television
tennis
tense
tent
term
terrier
theatre
theatrical
theologian
theory
therapy
thief
tie
time
title
tobacco
tool
torture
tower
town
toy
train
transport
travel
treaty
tree
triangle
tribe

trophy
tumour
tunnel
twin
typeface

umbrella
uncle
underground
underwear
union
United Kingdom
United Nations
United States of
  America
university
utensil

valve
vegetable
vehicle
vein
vermin
vestment
villain
virtue
virus
vitamin
volcano

wall
war
water
waterfall
weapon
weather
weed
welsh
whale
wheel
whisky
white
wind
window
wine
wise
witch
womanizer
wonder
wood
world
worm
worship
wrestling
writer
writing

year
yellow

zodiac
zoology

# A

**a**
02 an 03 ane, one, per 05 alpha
• **a French** 02 un 03 une
• **a German** 03 ein 04 eine

**aardvark**
07 antbear 08 anteater, earth-hog
09 groundhog

**aback**
• **take aback** 04 stun 05 shock, upset
06 dismay 07 astound, set back,
stagger, startle 08 astonish, bewilder,
knock out, surprise 09 dumbfound
10 disconcert 11 flabbergast

**abalone**
04 paua, pawa

**abandon**
◊ *anagram indicator* ◊ *deletion indicator*
04 cede, drop, dump, jilt, quit, sink,
stop 05 abort, cease, chuck, ditch,
forgo, leave, let go, scrap, waive, yield
06 banish, desert, desist, escape,
forego, forhow, get out, give up, jack
in, maroon, pack in, resign, strand,
vacate 07 bail out, forsake, yield to
08 abdicate, evacuate, forswear,
jettison, jump ship, part with,
renounce, run out on, wildness
09 break away, give way to, sacrifice,
stop doing, surrender, walk out on
10 break loose, depart from, go away
from, relinquish, resign from
11 discontinue, impetuosity, leave
behind 12 be overcome by, break off
with, carelessness, dispense with, kick
the habit, leave for dead, recklessness,
withdraw from 13 break free from,
impulsiveness, leave it at that 14 break
it off with, give the elbow to, lose
yourself in 15 leave high and dry, leave
in the lurch, thoughtlessness,
uninhibitedness

**abandoned**
◊ *anagram indicator* 03 mad, old 04 left,
wild 05 crazy, empty 06 unused,
vacant, wanton, wicked 07 corrupt,
disused, forlorn, immoral 08 derelict,
deserted, desolate, forsaken, reckless
09 debauched, dissolute, neglected,
reprobate 10 profligate, unoccupied
11 uninhibited 12 unrestrained

**abandonment**
05 drift, loose 07 cession, discard,
Dunkirk, jilting, leaving, neglect,
waiving 08 ditching, dropping, giving-
up, stopping 09 cessation, desertion,
forsaking, marooning, sacrifice,
scrapping, stranding, surrender
10 abdication, decampment,
exposition 11 dereliction, reprobation,
resignation 12 renunciation, running

out on 13 leaving behind
14 discontinuance, relinquishment
15 discontinuation, resignation from

**abase**
05 crawl, lower 06 cringe, debase,
demean, humble, kowtow, malign
07 degrade, mortify, put down
08 belittle, cast down, suck up to
09 disparage, humiliate

**abasement**
08 crawling, humility 09 demeaning
10 debasement, humbleness
11 humiliation, sucking up to
13 disparagement, mortification

**abash**
03 cow 05 quell, shame 06 humble
07 astound 08 confound, face down
09 embarrass, humiliate 10 disconcert
14 discountenance

**abashed**
06 shamed 07 ashamed, floored,
humbled 08 confused 09 affronted,
mortified, perturbed, shamefast
10 bewildered, confounded,
humiliated, nonplussed, remorseful,
shamefaced, taken aback
11 discomfited, discomposed,
dumbfounded, embarrassed
12 disconcerted 15 discountenanced

**abate**
04 alay, ease, fade, faik, fall, sink,
slow, vail, wane 05 aleye, allay, allow,
appal, let up, quell, remit, slake
06 lessen, pacify, rebate, reduce,
relent, soothe, weaken 07 assuage,
decline, detract, die down, drop off,
dwindle, fall off, qualify, relieve,
slacken, subside 08 decrease,
diminish, mitigate, moderate, peter
out, pluck off, taper off 09 alleviate,
attenuate

**abatement**
04 wane 05 let-up, lysis 06 easing,
relief 07 decline 08 decrease, lowering
09 allowance, deduction, dwindling,
dying-down, lessening, reduction,
remission, weakening 10 diminution,
mitigation, moderation, palliation,
slackening, subsidence 11 alleviation,
assuagement, attenuation, dropping-
off

**abattoir**
08 butchery, shambles
14 slaughterhouse

**abbess**
03 Abb 09 prelatess

**abbey**
03 Abb 06 abbacy, friary, priory
07 convent, minster, nunnery
08 cloister, seminary 09 cathedral,
monastery

*Abbeys include:*

04 Bath, Iona
05 Cluny, Kelso, Meaux, Roche,
Royal
06 Bolton, Byland, Hexham,
Romsey, Whitby, Woburn
07 Citeaux, Furness, Melrose,
Tintern, Waltham
08 Buckfast, Crowland, Dryburgh,

Fontenay, Fonthill, Holyrood,
Jedburgh, Newstead, Rievaulx
09 Clairvaux, Fountains, Holy Cross,
Kirkstall, Nightmare, Sherborne
10 Malmesbury, Northanger
11 Westminster

**abbot**
03 Abb 07 prelate 11 commendator
13 archimandrite

**abbreviate**
◊ *tail deletion indicator* 03 cut 04 clip,
trim 06 digest, lessen, précis, reduce,
shrink 07 abridge, curtail, cut down,
shorten 08 abstract, compress,
condense, contract, truncate
09 constrict, summarize

**abbreviated**
03 cut 05 short 07 clipped, compact,
reduced, summary 08 abridged
09 condensed, shortened, truncated
10 contracted

**abbreviation**
05 short 06 digest, précis, résumé
07 acronym, summary 08 abstract,
clipping, mnemonic, synopsis
09 reduction, short form 10 initialism,
shortening, truncation 11 abridgement,
compression, contraction, curtailment
13 shortened form, summarization,
truncated form

*See also* **county; United States of
America**

**abdicate**
04 cede, quit 05 forgo, shirk, yield
06 abjure, disown, forego, give up,
reject, resign, retire 07 abandon,
forsake 08 abnegate, renounce, step
down 09 repudiate, stand down,
surrender 10 relinquish 14 turn your
back on 15 give up the throne, wash
your hands of

**abdication**
07 refusal 08 giving-up 09 disowning,
rejection, surrender 10 abjuration,
abnegation, retirement
11 abandonment, repudiation,
resignation 12 renunciation, standing-
down, stepping-down
14 relinquishment

**abdomen**
03 maw, tum 04 guts, puku, womb
05 belly, bingy, heart, pleon, tummy
06 gaster, middle, paunch, venter
07 beer gut, insides, midriff, stomach
08 pot belly 09 beer belly, ventricle
10 little Mary 11 bread-basket,
corporation, opisthosoma

**abdominal**
02 ab 05 belly 07 coeliac, gastric,
ventral 08 visceral 10 intestinal
11 ventricular

**abduct**
05 seize 06 kidnap, ravish, snatch
07 capture 08 carry off, shanghai 09 lay
hold of 10 run off with, spirit away
11 appropriate, make off with, run
away with, take by force 12 hold to
ransom 13 take as hostage 15 take
away by force

## abduction

04 rape 06 kidnap 07 capture, seizure
09 ravishing, seduction, snatching
10 enlevement, kidnapping 11 carrying
off 15 taking as hostage

## aberrant

◇ *anagram indicator* 03 odd 05 rogue,
wonky 06 quirky 07 corrupt, deviant
08 abnormal, atypical, freakish,
peculiar, straying 09 anomalous,
defective, deviating, different,
divergent, eccentric, irregular,
wandering 11 incongruous

## aberration

05 lapse 06 oddity 07 anomaly, mistake
08 delusion, straying 09 deviation,
oversight, variation, wandering
10 deliration, divergence
11 abnormality, instability, peculiarity
12 eccentricity, irregularity
13 nonconformity

## abet

03 aid 04 back, help, spur 05 egg on
06 assist, back up, incite, second
07 condone, endorse, promote,
succour, support 08 sanction
09 encourage, lend a hand 11 collude
with

## abeyance

• in abeyance 05 on ice 06 on hold
07 disused, dormant, pending, shelved
09 postponed, suspended 11 hanging
fire 12 in suspension 13 no longer in
use 14 not in operation

## abhor

04 hate, shun 05 spurn 06 detest,
loathe, reject 07 despise 08 execrate
09 abominate, shudder at 10 cannot
bear, recoil from, shrink from
11 cannot abide, cannot stand

## abhorrence

04 hate 05 odium 06 enmity, hatred,
horror, malice 07 disgust 08 aversion,
contempt, distaste, loathing
09 animosity, revulsion 10 execration,
repugnance 11 abomination,
detestation

## abhorrent

05 hated, yucky 06 horrid, odious
07 hateful, heinous 08 absonant,
detested, horrible 09 detesting,
execrable, loathsome, obnoxious,
offensive, repellent, repugnant,
repulsive, revolting 10 abominable,
detestable, disgusting, nauseating
11 distasteful

## abide

03 lie, won 04 bear, hack, last, stay,
take 05 brook, dwell, stand, thole
06 accept, endure, live on, remain,
reside 07 persist, stomach, survive
08 continue, tolerate 09 put up with
• abide by 04 obey 05 stand
06 accept, follow, fulfil, hold to, keep
to, uphold 07 agree to, observe,
respect, stand by 08 adhere to, carry
out, submit to 09 conform to, discharge
10 comply with, toe the line 11 go
along with, go by the book 15 stick to
the rules

## abiding

04 firm 05 fixed 06 stable 07 chronic,
durable, eternal, lasting 08 constant,
enduring, immortal, lifelong, long-
term, standing, unending 09 continual,
immutable, permanent 10 continuous,
persistent, persisting, unchanging
11 continuance, everlasting, long-
lasting, long-running 12 unchangeable

## ability

04 gift 05 flair, forte, knack, means,
power, savvy, skill, touch 06 genius,
powers, talent 07 calibre, faculty,
knowhow, prowess, the hang
08 aptitude, capacity, deftness, facility,
strength, the knack 09 adeptness,
dexterity, endowment, expertise,
potential, resources 10 adroitness,
capability, competence, competency,
motivation, propensity 11 proficiency,
savoir-faire, what it takes, wherewithal
12 potentiality 13 qualification

## ab initio

07 at first, firstly 09 initially, primarily
10 at the start, originally 11 to begin
with, to start with 12 from the start 14 at
the beginning

## abject

03 low 04 base, mean, vile 05 awful
06 sordid, woeful 07 debased, forlorn,
ignoble, outcast, pitiful, servile, slavish
08 degraded, hopeless, pathetic,
pitiable, shameful, wretched
09 execrable, miserable, worthless
10 degenerate, deplorable, despicable,
grovelling, submissive 11 humiliating,
ignominious 12 contemptible,
ingratiating 13 dishonourable

## abjure

04 deny, reny 05 renay, reney
06 disown, eschew, recant, reject
07 abandon, disavow, forsake, retract
08 abdicate, abnegate, disclaim,
forswear, renege on, renounce
09 repudiate 10 relinquish 12 dispense
with

## ablaze

03 lit 04 alow 05 afire, aglow, alowe,
angry, fiery, lit up 06 aflame, alight,
ardent, fuming, on fire, raging
07 aroused, blazing, burning, excited,
fervent, flaming, furious, glowing,
ignited, intense, lighted, radiant
08 flashing, frenzied, gleaming,
incensed, in flames, luminous
09 brilliant, sparkling 10 passionate,
shimmering, stimulated 11 exhilarated,
illuminated, impassioned
12 enthusiastic, incandescent

## able

03 fit 04 deft, fere 05 adept 06 adroit,
clever, expert, fitted, gifted, strong, up
to it 07 capable, clued up, skilful,
skilled 08 all there, masterly, powerful,
talented 09 competent, cut out for,
dexterous, effective, efficient,
ingenious, on the ball, practised,
qualified 10 proficient 11 experienced,
intelligent 12 accomplished
• able to 05 fit to 06 free to 09 allowed
to, capable of 10 prepared to
11 competent to, qualified to

## able-bodied

02 AB 03 fit 04 fine, hale, hardy 05 burly,
hardy, lusty, sound, stout, tough
06 hearty, robust, rugged, strong,
sturdy 07 healthy, staunch
08 powerful, stalwart, vigorous
09 strapping 12 in good health 13 hale
and hearty 14 as fit as a fiddle

## ablution

05 laver 07 bathing, rinsing, soaking,
washing 08 cleaning 09 cleansing,
scrubbing, showering

## abnegate

04 deny 06 abjure, eschew, give up,
refuse, reject 07 abandon, abstain,
disavow, forbear 08 forswear,
renounce 09 repudiate, surrender
10 relinquish

## abnegation

08 eschewal, giving-up 09 martyrdom,
surrender 10 abjuration, abstinence,
self-denial, temperance
11 forbearance, repudiation
12 renunciation 13 self-sacrifice
14 relinquishment

## abnormal

◇ *anagram indicator* 03 odd 04 para-
05 outré, queer, weird 07 curious,
deviant, erratic, oddball, strange,
uncanny, unusual, wayward
08 aberrant, atypical, peculiar,
singular, uncommon 09 anomalous,
different, divergent, eccentric,
irregular, unnatural 10 paranormal,
unexpected 11 exceptional
13 extraordinary, funny peculiar,
idiosyncratic, preternatural

## abnormality

04 flaw 06 oddity 07 anomaly
08 enormity, vitiligo 09 deformity,
deviation, exception, palilalia, water-
core 10 aberration, difference,
divergence 11 atypicality, bizarreness,
dysfunction, monstrosity,
pathography, peculiarity, singularity,
strangeness, unusualness
12 eccentricity, irregularity,
malformation, monstruosity,
uncommonness 13 unnaturalness

## abnormally

09 extremely, unusually 10 especially,
remarkably, uncommonly
12 particularly 13 exceptionally
15 extraordinarily, preternaturally

## aboard

◇ *insertion indicator* 02 in, on 04 into,
onto 07 on board 09 alongside 11 on
board ship

## abode

02 in 03 inn, pad, won 04 home, seat,
stay 05 lodge, whare 06 libken, remain
07 domicil, habitat, mansion, presage
08 domicile, dwelling, lodgings
09 residence, residency 10 habitation
11 inhabitance, inhabitancy
13 dwelling-place

## abolish

03 axe, ban, end 04 chop, dump, sink,
stop 05 annul, quash, scrap 06 cancel,
repeal, revoke 07 blot out, destroy,
expunge, nullify, rescind, subvert,

## abolition

vitiate, wipe out **08** abrogate, down with, get rid of, overturn, stamp out, suppress **09** eliminate, eradicate, overthrow, terminate **10** annihilate, do away with, invalidate, obliterate, put an end to **11** discontinue, exterminate

## abolition

**03** axe **04** chop **06** ending, repeal **07** dumping, voiding **08** chopping, quashing, stopping **09** annulment, overthrow, scrapping, vitiation **10** abrogation, extinction, rescission, revocation, subversion, withdrawal **11** blotting-out, destruction, dissolution, elimination, eradication, extirpation, rescindment, suppression, termination **12** annihilation, cancellation, invalidation, obliteration **13** doing-away-with, extermination, nullification

## abomasum

**04** read

## abominable

◇ *anagram indicator* **04** base, foul, vile **06** cursed, horrid, nefast, odious **07** hateful, heinous **08** damnable, dreadful, god-awful, horrible, terrible, wretched **09** abhorrent, appalling, atrocious, execrable, loathsome, nefandous, obnoxious, offensive, repellent, repugnant, repulsive, revolting **10** despicable, detestable, disgusting, nauseating **12** contemptible **13** reprehensible

## abominably

**07** beastly **08** horribly, odiously, terribly **09** execrably **10** dreadfully **11** appallingly, obnoxiously **12** disgustingly **13** reprehensibly

## abominate

**04** hate **05** abhor **06** detest, loathe **07** condemn, despise **08** execrate

## abomination

**04** evil, hate **05** curse, odium **06** hatred, horror, plague **07** disgust, offence, outrage, torment **08** anathema, atrocity, aversion, disgrace, distaste, loathing **09** hostility, revulsion **10** abhorrence, execration, repugnance **11** detestation

## aboriginal

**05** first, Koori, local, Murri, Nunga **06** Anangu, native, primal **07** ancient, initial, earliest, original, primeval **09** Aborigine, primaeval, primitive **10** indigenous **13** autochthonous, tangata whenua

*Aboriginal activists include:*

**04** Mabo (Eddie)
**05** Scott (Evelyn)
**06** Dodson (Mick), Dodson (Patrick), O'Shane (Pat)
**07** Bandler (Faith), Gilbert (Kevin), Pearson (Noel), Perkins (Charles)
**09** Yunupingu (Galarrwuy)
**12** Burnum Burnum

*Aboriginal tribes include:*

**03** Wik
**04** Tiwi
**05** Bardi, Yanda
**06** Aranda, Dharug
**07** Noongar, Nyungar
**08** Gurindji, Warlpiri
**09** Kuring-gai, Wiradjuri
**10** Bundjalung, Pitta Pitta, Wemba Wemba
**14** Pitjantjatjara

## aborigine

**03** gin **05** koori, Maori, myall **06** native **08** indigene **11** black-fellow **15** first inhabitant

## abort

**03** axe, end **04** fail, halt, stop **05** check **06** thwart **07** call off, nullify, suspend **08** cut short, miscarry **09** frustrate, terminate **11** come to an end, discontinue **12** bring to an end **13** pull the plug on

## abortion

**08** misbirth **09** foeticide **10** aborticide **11** miscarriage, termination

## abortive

**04** idle, vain **06** barren, failed, futile **07** misborn, sterile, useless **08** bootless, thwarted **09** fruitless **10** unavailing **11** ineffective, ineffectual **12** unproductive, unsuccessful **13** inefficacious

## abound

**04** flow, teem **05** crowd, swarm, swell **06** be full, thrive **07** bristle **08** brim over, flourish, increase, overflow **09** exuberate, luxuriate **10** be abundant **11** be plentiful, proliferate, superabound

## about

◇ *anagram indicator* ◇ *containment indicator* ◇ *reversal indicator* **01** a, c **02** ca, on, re **03** cir **04** circ, near, over **05** anent, circa, close, round **06** almost, approx, around, beside, nearby, nearly **07** all over, close by, close to, nearing, roughly **08** to and fro **09** apropos of, as regards, regarding **10** adjacent to, concerning, encircling, more or less, relating to, throughout **11** approaching, dealing with, referring to, surrounding, within reach **12** encompassing, here and there, with regard to **13** approximately, concerned with, connected with, in the matter of, in the region of, with respect to **14** on the subject of **15** in the vicinity of, with reference to

• **about to 06** all but, soon to **07** going to, ready to **08** all set to **11** intending to, preparing to **12** on the point of, on the verge of

## about-turn

**03** uey **05** U-turn **08** reversal **09** about-face, turnabout, volte-face **10** turnaround **13** enantiodromia

## above

◇ *juxtaposition down indicator* **03** sup, sur **04** atop, over, owre, upon **05** aloft, prior, sopra, super-, supra- **06** before, beyond, higher, high up, on high **07** earlier, on top of **08** immune to, overhead, previous, senior to **09** aforesaid, exceeding, foregoing, not open to, preceding **10** exempt from, higher than, in excess of, prevenient, previously, superior to, surpassing **11** above-stated, greater than, not liable to **12** not exposed to **14** above-mentioned, aforementioned

• **above all 07** chiefly, firstly, notably **09** most of all, primarily **10** first of all **15** most importantly

• **above yourself 04** smug, vain **05** cocky, proud **07** haughty, stuck-up **08** arrogant, boastful, immodest, puffed-up **09** bigheaded, conceited **10** complacent **11** egotistical, toffee-nosed **12** narcissistic, supercilious, vainglorious **13** self-important, self-satisfied, swollen-headed **14** full of yourself

• **as above 02** us **07** ut supra

## above-board

**04** open, true **05** frank, legit **06** candid, dinkum, honest, kosher, square **07** upright **08** straight, truthful **09** guileless, reputable, veracious **10** forthright, honourable, legitimate, on the level **11** trustworthy **13** fair and square **15** straightforward

## abracadabra

**05** spell **09** gibberish, magic word **10** hocus pocus, mumbo-jumbo, open sesame

## abrade

**03** rub **04** stun **05** awake, chafe, erode, grate, graze, grind, rouse, scour, start **06** scrape **07** scratch, wear off **08** wear away, wear down **10** scrape away

## abrasion

**03** cut **05** chafe, graze **06** scrape **07** chafing, erosion, grating, rubbing, scratch **08** abrading, friction, grinding, scouring, scraping **10** scratching **11** excoriation, wearing-away, wearing-down

## abrasive

**04** bort **05** boart, emery, harsh, nasty, rough, sharp **06** biting **07** brusque, caustic, chafing, erodent, erosive, grating, hurtful **08** annoying, grinding, scraping **09** corrosive, sandpaper **10** frictional, glasspaper, irritating, scratching, unpleasant **11** attritional, garnet-paper, ground glass **14** silicon carbide

## abreast

**02** up **03** hep **05** level **06** afront, au fait, well up **07** in touch **08** familiar, informed, up to date **09** au courant, on the ball **10** acquainted, conversant, side by side **11** cheek by jowl **12** in the picture **13** knowledgeable **15** beside each other, next to each other

## abridge

**03** cut, lop **04** clip **05** elide, prune **06** digest, lessen, précis, reduce **07** curtail, cut down, shorten **08** abstract, compress, condense, contract, cut short, decrease, truncate **09** epitomize, summarize, synopsize **10** abbreviate **11** concentrate **12** circumscribe

## abridged

◇ *tail deletion indicator* 03 abd, abr 05 short 06 potted 07 clipped, cut down, reduced, shorter 08 cut short, digested 10 contracted, summarized 11 abbreviated

## abridgement

03 abr 06 abrégé, digest, précis, résumé 07 compend, cutting, epitome, outline, pastime, summary 08 abstract, decrease, synopsis 09 reduction 10 compendium, conspectus, diminution, shortening, truncation 11 contraction, curtailment, diminishing, restriction 12 abbreviation, abbreviature, short version 13 concentration

## abroad

◇ *anagram indicator* ◇ *foreign word indicator* 03 out 04 away 05 about, forth 06 around, astray, widely 07 at large, current 08 offshore, overseas, publicly 10 far and wide 11 circulating, doing your OE, extensively 14 in foreign parts, to foreign parts 15 out of the country
• **go abroad** 08 emigrate

## abrogate

03 axe, end 04 chop, dump, stop 05 annul, scrap 06 cancel, repeal, revoke 07 abolish, rescind, retract, reverse, vitiate 08 disenact, dissolve 09 disaffirm, repudiate 10 do away with, invalidate 11 countermand

## abrogation

03 axe 04 chop 06 repeal 07 dumping 08 recision, reversal 09 abolition, annulment, repealing, scrapping, vitiation 10 overruling, rescinding, rescission, revocation 11 dissolution, repudiation, rescindment 12 cancellation, invalidation 14 countermanding, disaffirmation

## abrupt

◇ *tail deletion indicator* 03 off 04 bold, curt, rude, snap 05 blunt, brisk, gruff, hasty, quick, rapid, rough, sharp, sheer, short, squab, steep, swift, terse 06 direct, snappy, sudden 07 brusque, hurried, instant, offhand, prerupt, uncivil 08 dramatic, impolite, snappish, vertical 09 immediate, startling 10 dismissive, surprising, unexpected, unforeseen, unfriendly 11 declivitous, precipitate, precipitous, unannounced 12 discourteous 13 instantaneous, unceremonious

## abruptly

04 bang 05 short 06 curtly, rudely 07 bluntly, briskly, gruffly, hastily, offhand, quickly, rapidly, roughly, shortly, swiftly, tersely 08 directly, snappily, suddenly 09 brusquely, hurriedly, instantly 10 impolitely, snappishly 11 immediately 12 dismissively, unexpectedly 13 precipitately 14 discourteously 15 instantaneously, unceremoniously

## abscess

04 boil, noma, sore 05 ulcer 06 canker 07 gumboil 08 swelling 09 gathering,

impostume, infection 10 imposthume, ulceration 12 inflammation

## abscond

03 fly 04 bolt, flee, quit 05 scram 06 beat it, decamp, escape, run off, vanish 07 do a bunk, make off, run away, scarper, vamoose 08 clear off, clear out, jump bail, run for it 09 disappear, do a runner, skedaddle 12 absquatulate 15 take French leave

## absence

03 abs 04 lack, need, want 06 dearth 07 default, paucity, skiving, truancy, vacancy, vacuity 08 omission, scarcity 09 privation 10 bunking off, deficiency 11 absenteeism, abstraction, inattention 12 non-existence 13 non-appearance, non-attendance, playing hookey 14 unavailability
• **feel absence** 04 miss

## absent

◇ *deletion indicator* 01 a 03 abs, MIA, off, out 04 away, AWOL, gone 05 blank 06 dreamy, truant, vacant 07 faraway, lacking, missing, not here, unaware 08 not there 09 elsewhere, miles away, not around, oblivious, unheeding 10 distracted, in absentia, not present 11 daydreaming, inattentive, preoccupied, unavailable 12 absent-minded
• **absent yourself** 04 exit 06 depart, retire 07 back out, retreat 08 slip away, withdraw 13 take your leave

## absentee

06 no-show, truant 11 non-attender

## absently

07 blankly 08 dreamily 12 abstractedly 13 inattentively 14 absent-mindedly

## absent-minded

06 absent, dreamy, musing, scatty 07 faraway, pensive, unaware 08 absorbed, distrait, dreaming, heedless, yonderly 09 distraite, engrossed, forgetful, miles away, oblivious, unheeding, withdrawn 10 abstracted, distracted, unthinking 11 impractical, inattentive, not all there, preoccupied, unconscious 13 somewhere else, wool-gathering 14 dead to the world, scatterbrained

## absent-mindedly

07 blankly 08 absently 12 abstractedly 13 inattentively

## absolute

01 A 03 abs, set 04 dead, firm, full, meer, mere, pure, rank, sure, true 05 final, fixed, rigid, sheer, total, utter 06 entire 07 certain, decided, genuine, perfect, settled, supreme, unmixed 08 almighty, complete, decisive, definite, despotic, outright, positive, thorough 09 autarchic, boundless, downright, out-and-out, sovereign, undivided, universal, unlimited 10 autocratic, conclusive, consummate, definitive, exhaustive, high-handed, omnipotent, peremptory, tyrannical 11 autarchical, categorical, dictatorial, established, indubitable, non-variable, unalterable,

unambiguous, unequivocal, unmitigated, unqualified 12 totalitarian, unrestrained, unrestricted 13 authoritarian, non-negotiable, unadulterated, unconditional 14 unquestionable

## absolutely

03 abs, yes 04 bang, dead, just, mere, very 05 fully, quite, truly 06 fairly, purely, surely, wholly 07 clearly, exactly, finally, for sure, no doubt, plainly, quite so, totally, utterly 08 entirely, of course 09 assuredly, certainly, decidedly, doubtless, genuinely, naturally, obviously, perfectly, precisely, supremely 10 by all means, completely, decisively, definitely, in every way, infallibly, positively, separately, thoroughly, undeniably 11 à toute force, doubtlessly, undoubtedly 12 conclusively, despotically, exhaustively, high-handedly, tyrannically 13 categorically, dictatorially, unambiguously, unequivocally, without a doubt 14 autocratically, in every respect, unquestionably, wholeheartedly 15 unconditionally

## absolution

05 mercy 06 pardon, shrift 07 amnesty, freedom, release 09 acquittal, discharge, pardoning, purgation, remission 10 assoilment, letting off, liberation, redemption 11 deliverance, exculpation, exoneration, forgiveness, vindication 12 emancipation 13 justification

## absolve

04 free, quit 05 clear, loose, quite, quyte, remit 06 acquit, assoil, excuse, let off, pardon, quight 07 deliver, forgive, justify, release, set free 08 liberate 09 assoilzie, discharge, exculpate, exonerate, vindicate 10 accomplish, emancipate 11 have mercy on

## absorb

◇ *containment indicator* 04 fill, hold, soak, sorb, suck, wrap 05 eat up, mop up, use up 06 blot up, devour, digest, draw in, engage, engulf, fill up, imbibe, ingest, occupy, retain, soak up, suck up, take in, take up 07 consume, drink in, engross, enthral, involve, receive 08 sponge up 09 captivate, fascinate, integrate, preoccupy, swallow up 10 assimilate, monopolize, understand 11 incorporate

## absorbed

◇ *containment indicator* 04 rapt 07 riveted 08 involved, occupied 09 engrossed 10 captivated, enthralled, fascinated, interested, spellbound 11 preoccupied, taken up with

## absorbent

03 abs 04 dope 06 porous, spongy 07 soaking 08 bibulous, blotting, pervious 09 permeable, receptive, resorbent, retentive 10 absorptive,

spongiform **12** assimilative, sorbefacient

## absorbing
**07** amusing **08** gripping, riveting **09** diverting, enjoyable **10** compelling, compulsive, engrossing, intriguing **11** captivating, enthralling, fascinating, interesting **12** entertaining, preoccupying, spellbinding **13** unputdownable

## absorption
**07** holding, osmosis **08** monopoly, raptness, riveting, taking-in **09** devouring, drawing-in, immersion, ingestion, soaking-up **10** engagement, engrossing, intentness, occupation **11** captivating, consumption, involvement **12** assimilation **13** attentiveness, concentration, preoccupation

## abstain
**04** fast, pass, quit, shun, stop **05** avoid, forgo, spare **06** cut out, desist, eschew, forego, give up, jack in, refuse, reject, resist **07** decline, forbear, not vote, refrain **08** hold back, renounce, restrain **09** be neutral, do without, go without **11** stop short of **12** deny yourself, refuse to vote **13** sit on the fence

## abstainer
**02** TT **06** tee-tee, wowser **08** teetotal **09** Rechabite **11** teetotaller **12** water-drinker
• **abstainers 02** AA, TT

## abstemious
**02** TT **05** sober **06** frugal **07** ascetic, austere, sparing **08** moderate, teetotal **09** abstinent, temperate **10** restrained **11** disciplined, self-denying **14** self-abnegating **15** self-disciplined

## abstention
**08** celibacy **09** not voting **10** neutrality **13** refusal to vote **15** declining to vote

## abstinence
**04** fast **07** fasting, refusal **08** eschewal, giving-up, sobriety **09** avoidance, frugality, nephalism, restraint **10** abjuration, abstaining, asceticism, continence, continency, declension, desistance, moderation, refraining, self-denial, temperance, water wagon **11** forbearance, self-control, teetotalism **12** going-without, renunciation **13** non-indulgence, self-restraint **14** abstemiousness, self-discipline
See also **fast**

## abstinent
**05** sober **06** frugal **07** ascetic **08** moderate, teetotal **09** continent, temperate **10** abstaining, abstemious, forbearing, restrained **11** self-denying **12** non-indulgent **14** self-controlled, self-restrained **15** self-disciplined

## abstract
**03** abs, cut, tap **04** deep **06** arcane, detach, digest, précis, remove, résumé, subtle **07** abridge, complex, cut down, draw off, epitome, extract, general, isolate, outline, shorten,

subduce, subduct, summary, take out **08** abstruse, academic, compress, condense, discrete, ideative, notional, prescind, profound, separate, syllabus, symbolic, synopsis, take away, withdraw **09** contrived, recondite, summarize **10** abbreviate, compendium, conceptual, conspectus, dissociate, ideational, indefinite **11** abridgement, compression, generalized, non-concrete, suppositive, theoretical, unpractical, unrealistic **12** hypothetical, intellectual, metaphysical, non-realistic **13** philosophical, suppositional **14** recapitulation
• **in the abstract 07** on paper **08** in theory **09** generally **10** notionally **11** in abstracto **12** conceptually **13** theoretically **14** hypothetically **15** philosophically

## abstracted
**06** absent, dreamy, musing, scatty **07** bemused, faraway, pensive, unaware **08** absorbed, dreaming, heedless **09** engrossed, forgetful, miles away, oblivious, unheeding, withdrawn **10** distracted, unthinking **11** impractical, inattentive, inconscient, preoccupied, unconscious **12** absent-minded **13** wool-gathering **14** scatterbrained

## abstractedly
**07** blankly **08** absently **13** inattentively **14** absent-mindedly

## abstraction
**04** idea **05** dream **06** entity, notion, revery, theory **07** absence, concept, formula, removal, reverie, theorem, thought **10** isolation **10** absorption, conception, conjecture, dreaminess, extraction, generality, hypothesis, remoteness, separation, withdrawal **11** bemusedness, distraction, inattention, pensiveness **13** preoccupation **14** generalization

## abstruse
**04** deep, high, long **06** arcane, hidden, subtle **07** complex, cryptic, Delphic, obscure **08** esoteric, hermetic, profound, puzzling **09** enigmatic, exquisite, recherché, recondite **10** hermetical, mysterious, perplexing **11** inscrutable **12** unfathomable

## absurd
◊ anagram indicator **04** daft **05** crazy, funny, gonzo, inane, silly **06** stupid **07** asinine, comical, foolish, idiotic, Laputan, risible **08** cockeyed, derisory, farcical, humorous, Laputian **09** fantastic, grotesque, illogical, laughable, ludicrous, priceless, senseless, unearthly, untenable **10** irrational, ridiculous **11** harebrained, implausible, incongruous, meaningless, nonsensical, paradoxical **12** preposterous, unreasonable

## absurdity
**04** joke **05** farce, folly **06** drivel, humour, idiocy **07** charade, inanity,

paradox, rubbish, twaddle **08** claptrap, daftness, malarkey, nonsense, ridicule, solecism, travesty **09** craziness, gibberish, silliness, stupidity **10** balderdash, caricature **11** fatuousness, foolishness, incongruity **12** illogicality **13** irrationality, ludicrousness, senselessness **14** implausibility, ridiculousness **15** meaninglessness

## absurdly
**07** crazily, funnily, inanely **08** stupidly **09** comically, foolishly, laughably, untenably **10** farcically, humorously **11** idiotically, implausibly, ludicrously, senselessly **12** irrationally, ridiculously, unreasonably **13** fantastically, incongruously, meaninglessly, nonsensically, paradoxically **14** preposterously

## abundance
**04** bags, glut, load, lots **05** feast, flush, fouth, fowth, heaps, loads, piles, routh, rowth, scads, sonce, sonse, store **06** bounty, excess, masses, oodles, plenty, riches, stacks, wealth **07** bonanza, fortune, lashing, oodlins, pleroma, tallent **08** fullness, lashings, opulence, overflow, plethora, richness **09** affluence, amplitude, fertility, plenitude, profusion **10** exuberance, generosity, lavishness, luxuriance, profligacy **11** copiousness, corn in Egypt, great supply, munificence, prodigality **12** extravagance, milk and honey **13** plentifulness, rack and manger **14** stouth and routh

## abundant
**04** full, rank, rich **05** ample, hefty, large, thick **06** filled, galore, lavish, strong **07** copious, opulent, profuse, teeming **08** affluent, generous, in plenty, prolific **09** bounteous, bountiful, exuberant, luxuriant, plenteous, plentiful **11** overflowing **12** well-supplied **14** more than enough

## abundantly
**04** very, well **05** amply, jolly **06** highly, plenty, really **07** acutely, awfully, greatly, utterly **08** severely, terribly **09** copiously, decidedly, extremely, intensely, profusely, unusually **10** completely, dreadfully, remarkably, thoroughly, uncommonly **11** exceedingly, excessively, extensively, exuberantly, frightfully, in abundance, in profusion, plentifully **12** immoderately, inordinately, prolifically, terrifically, unreasonably **13** exceptionally **15** extraordinarily

## abuse
◊ anagram indicator **03** hit, mud **04** beat, harm, hurt, rail, rape, rort **05** bully, curse, libel, scold, serve, slate, smear, snash, wrong **06** batter, damage, defame, impugn, injure, injury, insult, jawing, malign, misuse, molest, oppugn, pick on, revile, tirade, verbal **07** affront, beating, calumny, censure, cruelty, cursing, exploit, insults, jobbery, miscall, offence, oppress, slag off, slander, swear at,

**abusive**
torture, upbraid, violate, vitriol **08** be rude to, bullyrag, chuck off, derision, diatribe, ill-treat, maltreat, misapply, mistreat, reproach, scolding, swearing **09** call names, castigate, contumely, denigrate, disparage, invective, misemploy, swear-word, victimize **10** calumniate, chuck off at, defamation, imposition, oppression, upbraiding, vituperate **11** castigation, clapperclaw, denigration, hurl abuse at, malediction, molestation, mud-slinging, name-calling **12** billingsgate, calumniation, exploitation, ill-treatment, interference, maltreatment, mistreatment, vilification, vituperation **13** disparagement, interfere with, misemployment, sexual assault, treat like dirt **14** harass sexually, misapplication **15** assault sexually, take advantage of

**abusive**
**04** rude **05** cruel **06** bitchy, brutal **07** harmful, hurtful, railing, satiric **08** reviling, scathing, scolding, scornful **09** injurious, insulting, invective, libellous, maligning, offensive, satirical, vilifying **10** censorious, defamatory, derogatory, pejorative, scurrilous, slanderous, upbraiding **11** blasphemous, castigating, denigrating, destructive, disparaging, opprobrious, reproachful **12** calumniating, contumelious, vituperative

**abusively**
**06** rudely **07** cruelly **08** bitchily, brutally **10** revilingly, scathingly, scoldingly, scornfully **11** injuriously, insultingly, offensively **12** calumniously, censoriously, pejoratively, scurrilously, upbraidingly **13** blasphemously, denigratingly, disparagingly, opprobriously, reproachfully **14** contumeliously, vituperatively

**abut**
◊ *juxtaposition indicator* **04** join, lean **05** touch **06** adjoin, border **07** conjoin, impinge, verge on **08** be next to

**abysmal**
◊ *anagram indicator* **05** awful, utter **06** dismal **08** complete, dreadful, shocking, terrible **09** appalling, frightful **10** bottomless **11** disgraceful **12** unfathomable

**abysmally**
◊ *anagram indicator* **07** awfully **08** terribly **10** dreadfully **11** appallingly, frightfully **13** disgracefully

**abyss**
**03** pit **04** gulf, hell, void **05** abysm, chasm, depth, gorge, gulph **06** abrupt, canyon, crater, depths, ravine **07** Avernus, fissure, swallow **08** crevasse, profound, Tartarus **09** barathrum **13** bottomless pit

**acacia**
**03** koa **05** babul, boree, mulga, myall, sally **06** bablah, gidgee, gidjee, mimosa, sallee **07** robinia, shittah **08** brigalow **09** blackwood,

doornboom, fever tree, flame-tree **10** locust tree **11** shittah tree **12** golden wattle **13** kangaroo-thorn

**academic**
**03** don **04** acca **05** smart, tutor **06** brainy, fellow, master, pedant **07** bookish, donnish, erudite, learned, scholar, serious, student, teacher, trainer **08** abstract, bookworm, educated, educator, highbrow, lecturer, literary, notional, studious, well-read **09** pedagogue, professor, scholarly **10** conceptual, instructor, irrelevant, ivory-tower, scholastic **11** conjectural, educational, impractical, pedagogical, speculative, theoretical **12** hypothetical, intellectual, man of letters, well-educated **13** instructional, suppositional **14** woman of letters

**academician**
**01** A **02** RA **03** ARA, RSA

**academy**
**01** A **02** RA **03** RAM **04** RADA **05** Forty **06** school **07** academe, college **08** immortal, seminary **09** institute **10** university **11** charm school

**acanthus**
**07** ruellia **08** many-root **10** thunbergia **11** bear's-breech, brankursine, shrimp plant

**accede**
**05** admit, agree, bow to **06** accept, assume, attain, come to, concur, give in **07** agree to, consent, inherit, succeed **08** assent to, back down, take over **09** acquiesce, consent to, succeed to **10** comply with

**accelerate**
**05** hurry, speed **06** hasten, open up, spur on, step up **07** advance, forward, further, promote, quicken, speed up **08** antedate, expedite, go faster, step on it **09** festinate, stimulate **10** facilitate **11** drive faster, gather speed, pick up speed, precipitate, put on a spurt **12** gain momentum, step on the gas **14** step on the juice **15** put your foot down

**acceleration**
**01** a, g **07** speed-up **08** momentum **09** hastening, promotion **10** expedition, forwarding, speeding-up, stepping-up **11** advancement, furtherance, stimulation **14** gathering speed, rate of increase

**accent**
**04** beat, dash, tone **05** acute, force, grave, ictus, pitch, pulse, twang **06** brogue, rhythm, stress, timbre, tittle **07** cadence, diction **08** emphasis, priority **09** diacritic, intensity, pulsation **10** circumflex, importance, inflection, intonation, modulation, prominence **11** enunciation, underlining **12** accentuation, articulation, highlighting **13** pronunciation **15** diacritical mark

**accentuate**
**06** accent, deepen, show up, stress **07** point up **08** heighten **09** emphasize,

highlight, intensify, spotlight, underline **10** strengthen, underscore **15** make great play of

**accept**
◊ *containment indicator* **03** buy, get **04** bear, gain, have, take, wear **05** abide, admit, adopt, allow, bow to, grasp, stand, trust **06** come by, credit, endure, give in, honour, jump at, obtain, pocket, secure, suffer, take on, take up **07** abide by, acquire, agree to, approve, believe, embrace, fall for, let go of, receive, stomach, swallow, welcome, yield to **08** accede to, back down, face up to, say yes to, tolerate **09** approbate, believe in, consent to, integrate, put up with, recognize, undertake **10** comply with, concur with, not say no to **11** acknowledge, acquiesce in, be certain of, go along with, take on board **12** be resigned to **13** make the best of, receive warmly **15** come to terms with

**acceptable**
**01** U **02** OK, on **04** so-so **06** not bad **07** welcome **08** adequate, all right, moderate, passable, pleasant, pleasing **09** agreeable, allowable, desirable, tolerable **10** admissible, delightful, fair enough, gratifying, reasonable **11** appreciated, appropriate, permissible **12** satisfactory, the done thing **15** unexceptionable
• **make acceptable 04** sell

**acceptably**
**08** passably, suitably **09** agreeably, desirably, tolerably **10** adequately, moderately, reasonably **13** appropriately **14** satisfactorily

**acceptance**
**02** OK **03** acc, nod **04** acpt **05** faith, trust **06** assent, belief, buying, taking **07** bearing, consent, gaining, getting, receipt, welcome **08** adoption, approval, credence, currency, giving-in, securing, taking on, taking-up **09** accepting, accession, acquiring, admission, agreement, embracing, endurance, obtaining, receiving, tolerance, welcoming **10** admittance, assumption, compliance, facing up to, falling for **11** affirmation, backing-down, concurrence, endorsement, integration, recognition, resignation, undertaking **12** acquiescence, ratification **13** putting up with, taking on board **14** going along with, seal of approval **15** acknowledgement, making the best of, stamp of approval

**accepted**
**01** a **04** taen **05** taken, usual **06** agreed, common, normal **07** correct, regular **08** admitted, approved, orthodox, ratified, received, standard **09** confirmed, customary, universal **10** acceptable, authorized, recognized, sanctioned **11** appropriate, established, traditional **12** acknowledged, conventional, time-honoured

**access**
**03** key, use **04** door, path, read, road **05** drive, entry, log on, way in

## accessibility

06 course, entrée, locate 07 gateway, ingress, passage 08 approach, driveway, entering, entrance, retrieve 09 admission 10 admittance 12 gain access to, means of entry, right of entry 13 accessibility 15 means of approach, permission to see

## accessibility

11 convenience 12 availability, ease of access 13 attainability, obtainability 15 approachability, intelligibility

## accessible

04 near, open 05 cuspy, handy, ready 06 nearby, on hand, patent 07 general 09 available, get-at-able, reachable 10 achievable, attainable, come-at-able, convenient, easy to read, obtainable, procurable 11 close at hand, close to hand, within cooee 12 approachable, easy to follow, intelligible, user-friendly 14 comprehensible, understandable

## accession

04 gain, gift 06 afflux, influx 08 addition, increase, purchase 09 affluxion, attaining 10 assumption, possession, succession, taking over 11 acquisition, inheritance

## accessorize

04 trim 05 add to, adorn 06 bedaub, set off 07 augment, bedizen, enhance 08 contrast, decorate, round off 10 complement, supplement

## accessory

03 aid 04 help 05 add-in, add-on, extra, frill 06 helper 07 abettor, adjunct, cathead, fitting, partner 08 addition, conniver, ornament, trimming 09 adornment, ancillary, appendage, assistant, associate, attribute, auxiliary, colleague, component, extension, secondary 10 accomplice, additional, attachment, complement, decoration, incidental, peripheral, subsidiary, supplement 11 confederate, subordinate 12 appurtenance, contributory, supplemental 13 embellishment, supplementary

## accident

◇ anagram indicator 03 cva, hap, RTA 04 blow, fate, luck 05 crash, fluke, freak, prang, shunt, smash, wreck 06 bingle, chance, hazard, mishap, pile-up, upcast 07 fortune, smash-up, tragedy 08 blowdown, calamity, casualty, disaster, fatality, fortuity, good luck 09 collision, mischance 10 misfortune 11 coincidence, contingency, contretemps, good fortune, serendipity 12 circumstance, happenstance, misadventure

## accidental

04 flat 05 fluky, sharp 06 casual, chance, flukey, random 07 natural, outward 08 aleatory, external 09 adventive, dividuous, haphazard, uncertain, unplanned, unwitting 10 contingent, fortuitous, incidental, unexpected, unforeseen, unintended 11 inadvertent, promiscuous, unlooked-for 12 adventitious, uncalculated 13 serendipitous,

unanticipated, unintentional 14 unpremeditated

## accidentally

◇ anagram indicator 08 bechance, by chance, randomly 09 by mistake 10 by accident 11 ex accidenti, haphazardly, unwittingly 12 fortuitously, incidentally, unexpectedly 13 inadvertently 14 adventitiously 15 serendipitously, unintentionally

## acclaim

04 clap, hail, laud 05 cheer, exalt, extol, toast, voice 06 cheers, eulogy, homage, honour, praise, salute 07 applaud, commend, fanfare, ovation, tribute, welcome 08 applause, approval, bouquets, cheering, clapping, eulogium, eulogize, plaudits, shouting 09 celebrate, extolment, laudation, publicity, rave about 10 exaltation 11 acclamation, approbation, celebration 12 commendation

## acclaimed

05 famed, great, noted 06 famous 07 admired, eminent, exalted, notable, revered 08 honoured, renowned 09 legendary, prominent 10 celebrated 11 illustrious, outstanding 13 distinguished

## acclamation

03 rap 04 wrap 05 paean 06 bravos, eulogy, homage, honour, praise 07 fanfare, ovation, tribute, welcome 08 applause, approval, cheering, clapping, shouting 09 panegyric 10 enthusiasm, exaltation, laudations 11 approbation, celebration 12 commendation 13 felicitations 15 congratulations

## acclimatization

10 adaptation, adjustment 11 acclimation, habituation, orientation 13 accommodation, acculturation 14 naturalization 15 familiarization

## acclimatize

04 salt 05 adapt, inure 06 adjust, attune 07 conform 08 accustom 09 acclimate, get used to, habituate 10 naturalize 11 accommodate, acculturate, familiarize 12 find your feet 15 get your bearings

## accolade

05 award 06 homage, honour, praise 07 dubbing, embrace, tribute 11 recognition, testimonial 12 pat on the back

## accommodate

◇ containment indicator 03 aid, fit 04 help, hold, seat, take 05 adapt, board, house, lodge, put up, serve 06 adjust, assist, attune, bestow, billet, comply, modify, oblige, settle, supply, take in 07 compose, conform, provide, quarter, shelter 08 accustom, cater for, domicile 09 fit in with, habituate, harmonize, reconcile 11 acclimatize, be helpful to, give a hand to, have room for, lend a hand to 12 have space for

## accommodating

◇ containment indicator 04 kind 07 helpful, pliable, willing 08 friendly, obliging 09 agreeable, compliant, indulgent, unselfish 10 hospitable 11 complaisant, considerate, co-operative, sympathetic

## accommodation

◇ containment indicator 04 crib, home 05 abode, board, place, rooms 07 harmony, housing, lodging, quarter, storage 08 dwelling, lodgings, quarters 09 agreement, residence 10 compromise, conformity, settlement 11 negotiation 12 negotiations 13 understanding 14 reconciliation

---

*Accommodation types include:*

03 inn, pad, pod 04 camp, digs, flat, gaff, gite, tent, yurt 05 b and b, cabin, hotel, house, igloo, lodge, motel, squat, villa 06 bedsit, billet, camper, duplex, flotel, hostel, jack-up, refuge, studio, succah, sukkah 07 caravan, cottage, dockage, floatel, lairage, parador, pension, pousada, shelter, taverna 08 barracks, berthage, crashpad, pod hotel, roomette, shipping, stabling, tenement, wharfage 09 apartment, bedsitter, bunkhouse, camper van, dormitory, full board, half board, penthouse, residence, rooming-in, timeshare 10 guardhouse, guest house, labour camp, mobile home 11 bachelor pad, bed and board, youth hostel 12 halfway house, hunting-lodge, room and board, self-catering 13 boarding-house, habitat module 14 loft conversion 15 bed and breakfast, hall of residence, married quarters

---

*See also* **building; house; tent**

## accompaniment

04 vamp 06 backup, patter 07 adjunct, backing, bourdon, descant, support 08 addition, obligato 09 accessory, obbligato, orchestra, side order 10 background, complement, supplement 11 coexistence, concomitant, tracklement
• provide accompaniment 04 la-la

## accompanist

04 comp 11 accompanier 12 backing group 15 instrumentalist

## accompany

04 back, chum 05 usher 06 assist, attend, convoy, escort, follow, go with, squire, wait on 07 coexist, conduct, consort, partner, support 08 belong to, chaperon, coincide, come with, play with, tag along, wait upon, walk with 09 associate, chaperone, companion, occur with 10 complement, supplement, travel with 11 go along with 12 tag along with 13 associate with, come along with 14 go together with, hang around with

## accomplice
04 aide, ally, mate 05 shill, stale
06 bonnet, button, helper 07 abettor,
fedarie, nobbler, partner 08 approver,
complice, copemate, federary,
foedarie, henchman, sidekick,
swagsman 09 accessory, assistant,
associate, colleague, copesmate,
federarie 11 confederate, conspirator
12 collaborator, participator,
right-hand man 14 right-hand
woman

## accomplish
02 do 06 attain, effect, finish, fulfil,
hack it, manage, obtain, wangle
07 achieve, compass, execute,
perform, produce, realize 08 bring off,
carry out, complete, complish,
conclude, engineer 09 discharge, pull
it off 10 bring about, consummate,
effectuate 15 carry into effect, deliver
the goods

## accomplished
03 ace 04 arch, done, over 05 adept
06 adroit, expert, gifted, savant,
wicked 07 learned, savante, skilful,
skilled 08 compleat, masterly,
polished, talented 09 practised
10 consummate, cultivated, proficient
11 experienced 12 professional

## accomplishment
03 act, art 04 deed, feat, gift 05 doing,
forte, knack, skill 06 stroke, talent,
virtue 07 ability, exploit, faculty,
finesse, prowess, quality, triumph
08 aptitude, exercise, fruition
09 discharge, effecting, execution,
finishing, operation 10 attainment,
capability, completion, conclusion,
fulfilling, fulfilment, futurition,
management, perfection, production
11 achievement, carrying-out,
performance, proficiency, realization
12 consummation 13 qualification
14 stroke of genius

## accord
04 deal, give, jibe, pact, sort, suit
05 agree, allow, chime, endow, grant,
match, unity, yield 06 assent, bestow,
concur, confer, extend, square, tender,
treaty 07 compact, concert, conform,
congree, consort, harmony, present
08 contract, sympathy 09 agreement,
concordat, congruity, consensus,
harmonize, unanimity, vouchsafe
10 accordance, conformity,
congruence, convention, correspond,
settlement 11 be in harmony,
concurrence 13 be in agreement
14 correspondence
• of your own accord 06 freely
09 willingly 11 voluntarily
• with one accord 09 of one mind
11 unanimously

## accordance
• in accordance with 02 by 05 after,
under 10 in line with, obedient to 12 in
relation to, in the light of 13 in concert
with, in keeping with, in the manner of
14 consistent with, in proportion to
15 in agreement with

## according
03 acc
• according to 03 per 05 after, as per
08 as said by, secundum 10 as stated
by, in line with, obedient to 11 as
claimed by, depending on 12 in
relation to, in the light of 13 in keeping
with, in the manner of, on the report of
14 consistent with, in proportion to

## accordingly
02 so 04 duly, ergo, thus 05 fitly, hence
08 properly, suitably 09 agreeably, as a
result, therefore 10 sure enough,
thereafter 12 consequently,
consistently 13 appropriately, for that
reason, in consequence
15 correspondingly

## accost
04 bord, hail, halt, stop 05 abord,
assay, board, boord, borde 06 attack,
bail up, boorde, detain, molest,
nobble, waylay 07 address, solicit
08 approach, confront 09 importune
10 buttonhole

## account
02 a/c 03 acc, tab 04 acct, bill, deem,
hold, sake, tale 05 books, count, story,
value 06 assess, behalf, detail, esteem,
import, ledger, memoir, moment,
reckon, record, regard, report, sketch,
view as 07 adjudge, believe, charges,
details, history, invoice, journal,
version, write up 08 appraise,
consider, look upon, regard as, register
09 chronicle, inventory, narration,
narrative, portrayal, statement
10 commentary, importance
11 consequence, description,
distinction, explanation
12 presentation, significance
• account for 04 give, kill 06 defeat,
make up, say why, supply 07 clear up,
destroy, explain, justify, provide
08 comprise 09 answer for, eliminate,
elucidate, represent, vindicate
10 constitute, illuminate 11 rationalize
14 give reasons for
• falsify accounts 04 cook, rort
12 cook the books
• give an account of 04 tell 06 relate
• on account of 02 o/a 03 for 04 over
05 along 07 because, owing to,
through 08 in view of 09 because of
10 by virtue of, in virtue of 11 the
reason is 12 for the sake of
• on no account 05 never, no way
12 certainly not 13 not on your life

## accountability
09 liability, reporting 10 obligation
11 amenability 13 answerability
14 responsibility

## accountable
05 bound 06 liable 07 obliged
08 amenable 09 comptable, comptible,
obligated 10 answerable, chargeable,
explicable 11 charged with,
responsible

## accountant
02 CA 03 ACA, acc, CPA 06 bookie
09 bookmaker 11 bean counter

## accoutrements
03 kit 04 gear 05 stuff 06 outfit, things
07 clobber 08 fittings, fixtures
09 caparison, equipment, trimmings
10 adornments 11 decorations,
furnishings, odds and ends
12 appointments 13 appurtenances,
bits and pieces, paraphernalia

## accredit
06 depute 07 approve, certify, endorse,
license, warrant 09 attribute,
authorize, recognize 10 commission
11 certificate

## accredited
07 deputed 08 approved, endorsed,
licensed, official 09 appointed,
certified, qualified 10 authorized,
recognized 12 certificated,
commissioned

## accretion
05 add-on 06 growth 07 build-up
08 addition, increase 09 gathering,
increment 10 collecting, cumulation,
supplement 12 accumulation,
augmentation

## accrue
05 amass, mount 07 augment, be
added, build up, collect, mount up
08 increase 10 accumulate

## accumulate
04 gain, grow, pile, pool 05 amass,
hoard, stash, store, tot up 06 accrue,
distil, garner, gather, pile up
07 acquire, augment, build up, collect,
congest, distill 08 assemble, cumulate,
increase, multiply, snowball
09 aggregate, stockpile

## accumulation
04 gain, heap, mass, pile 05 hoard,
stack, stock, store 06 growth
07 accrual, build-up, reserve
08 assembly, increase 09 accretion,
aggregate, gathering, stockpile
10 building-up, collection, cumulation
11 acquisition 12 augmentation
14 conglomeration, multiplication

## accumulative
07 growing 08 mounting 09 enlarging
10 increasing 11 multiplying,
snowballing

## accuracy
05 truth 06 verity 08 fidelity, veracity
09 closeness, exactness, precision
10 exactitude 11 carefulness,
correctness 12 authenticity,
faithfulness, scrupulosity, truthfulness,
veridicality 14 meticulousness

## accurate
04 fair, nice, true 05 close, exact, right,
sound, valid 06 bang on, dead-on, spot-
on, strict 07 correct, factual, literal,
perfect, precise 08 faithful, on target,
rigorous, truthful, unerring 09 authentic,
faultless, on the mark, veracious,
veridical, well-aimed 10 meticulous
11 word-for-word, word-perfect
12 well-directed 13 letter-perfect

## accurately
05 truly 07 closely, exactly 08 strictly
09 correctly, literally, perfectly,

precisely **10** faithfully, rigorously, truthfully, unerringly **11** faultlessly, veraciously, veridically **12** meticulously

**accursed**
**05** blest, hated **06** damned, doomed, goddam, sacred **07** blessed, goddamn, hateful **08** maledict, wretched **09** bewitched, condemned, execrable, goddamned, loathsome **10** abominable, bedevilled, despicable, detestable **13** anathematized

**accusation**
**03** tax **04** bill **05** blame, cause, libel, smear **06** charge, threap, threep **08** citation, delation, gravamen **09** challenge, complaint, invective **10** allegation, imputation, indictment **11** arraignment, crimination, impeachment, inculpation, information, prosecution **12** denunciation **13** incrimination, recrimination

**accuse**
**03** tax **04** book, cite **05** blame, frame, peach **06** allege, appeal, charge, detect, impugn, impute, indict **07** appeach, arraign, asperse, attaint, censure, impeach, reprove **08** confront, denounce **09** attribute, challenge, criminate, implicate, prosecute **10** put on trial **11** incriminate, recriminate **12** bring charges, press charges **13** inform against **14** throw the book at **15** hold responsible, make accusations, make allegations

**accustom**
**03** use **05** adapt, enure, inure, teach **06** adjust, attune **07** conform **08** occasion **09** acclimate, climatize, get used to, habituate **11** acclimatize, accommodate, familiarize **15** get familiar with

**accustomed**
**03** old **04** tame, used, wont **05** fixed, given, usual **06** at home, inured, normal, wonted **07** general, regular, routine **08** everyday, familiar, frequent, habitual, ordinary **09** customary **10** acquainted, habituated, prevailing **11** established, traditional **12** acclimatized, conventional, in the habit of **14** consuetudinary

**ace**
**01** A **03** jot, one, Tib **04** cool, neat, unit **05** basto, brill, great, whizz **06** expert, genius, grouse, master, superb, wicked, winner **07** dab hand, hotshot, maestro, perfect **08** champion, spadille, terrific, top-notch, very good, virtuoso **09** brilliant, excellent **10** first-class **11** outstanding

**acerbic**
**05** harsh, sharp, spiky **06** biting **07** caustic, mordant **08** abrasive, stinging **09** rancorous, sarcastic, trenchant, vitriolic **10** astringent **11** acrimonious

**ache**
**01** H **03** die, yen **04** hurt, itch, kill, long, pain, pang, pine, work **05** agony, aitch, crave, pound, smart, sting, throb, yearn **06** be sore, desire, hanker, hunger, play up, stound, stownd, suffer, thirst, twinge **07** agonize, anguish, craving, longing **08** pounding, smarting, soreness, stinging, yearning **09** be in agony, be painful, hankering, suffering, throbbing

**achieve**
**02** do **03** get, win **04** earn, gain **05** reach **06** attain, effect, finish, fulfil, manage, obtain, wrap up **07** acquire, execute, perform, procure, produce, realize, succeed **08** carry out, complete **09** polish off **10** accomplish, bring about, consummate, effectuate

**achievement**
**03** act **04** deed, feat **06** action, effort, stroke **07** exploit, success, triumph **08** activity, fruition **09** execution **10** attainment, chevisance, completion, fulfilment **11** acquirement, performance, procurement, realization **12** consummation, effectuation **14** accomplishment, stroke of genius

**achiever**
**04** doer **08** go-getter, live wire, whizz kid **09** high-flyer, performer, succeeder **12** success story

**Achilles' heel**
**05** fault **07** failing **08** weakness, weak spot **09** weak point **12** imperfection **15** vulnerable point

**acid**
**04** keen, sour, tart **05** catty, harsh, sharp, sugar **06** acidic, biting, bitter, morose, unkind **07** acerbic, acetous, caustic, cutting, hurtful, mordant, pungent **08** critical, incisive, stinging, vinegary **09** acidulous, corrosive, sarcastic, trenchant, vitriolic **10** astringent, ill-natured **11** unsweetened

---

*Acids include:*

**03** DHA, DNA, LSD, RNA
**04** acyl, EDTA, uric
**05** amino, boric, fatty, folic
**06** acetic, citric, formic, lactic, nitric, oxalic, phenol, tannic
**07** acrylic, benzoic, boracic, chloric, nitrous, nucleic, prussic, pyruvic, silicic, stearic
**08** abscisic, ascorbic, carbolic, carbonic, ethanoic, lysergic, palmitic, periodic, retinoic, tartaric
**09** methanoic, nicotinic, propionic, salicylic, sulphonic, sulphuric
**10** aqua fortis, barbituric, carboxylic, phosphoric, sulphurous
**11** hydrocyanic, ribonucleic
**12** hydrochloric, hydrofluoric
**13** thiosulphuric, tricarboxylic

*See also* **amino acid**
• **acid test** **02** pH
• **work with acid** **04** etch

**acknowledge**
**03** con, own **04** avow, hail, mark **05** admit, allow, grant, greet, thank **06** accede, accept, affirm, agnize, answer, avouch, honour, notice, salute, wave to **07** address, agree to, concede, confess, confirm, declare, own up to, react to, reply to **08** signal to **09** acquiesce, celebrate, recognize, respond to **10** be grateful **11** say thank you, write back to **13** give thanks for

**acknowledged**
**06** avowed **08** accepted, admitted, approved, attested, declared **09** confirmed, professed **10** accredited, recognized

**acknowledgement**
**03** nod **04** wave **05** reply, smile **06** answer, avowal, credit, homage, notice, praise, thanks **07** tribute, welcome **08** bouquets, cognovit, comeback, granting, greeting, reaction, response **09** admission, allowance, deference, gratitude **10** acceptance, confession, profession, salutation **11** declaration, recognition **12** appreciation, gratefulness, recognizance

**acme**
**04** apex, peak **05** crown, prick **06** apogee, climax, comble, height, summit, zenith **07** optimum **08** pinnacle **09** high point **11** culmination, sublimation **12** highest point

**acolyte**
**06** helper **08** adherent, altar boy, follower, hanger-on, sidekick, thurifer **09** assistant, attendant **11** acolouthite

**acorn**
**04** mast **05** glans **07** oak mast, valonea, valonia **08** racahout, vallonia **09** raccahout

**acoustic**
**05** aural, sound **06** audile **07** hearing **08** auditory

**acquaint**
**04** tell **05** brief **06** advise, inform, notify, reveal **07** apprise, divulge, let know, possess **08** accustom, announce, disclose **09** enlighten **11** familiarize, make aware of **14** make conversant **15** put in the picture

**acquaintance**
**04** mate **06** friend, pick-up **07** contact, homeboy **08** confrère, habitude, hanger-on, intimacy **09** associate, awareness, colleague, companion, knowledge **10** cognizance, connection, experience, fellowship **11** association, conversance, familiarity **12** relationship **13** companionship, social contact, understanding

**acquainted**
**05** aware **06** au fait, versed **07** abreast **08** apprised, familiar, friendly, intimate **09** au courant, cognizant, in the know, up to speed **10** conversant, well-versed **11** on good terms **13** knowledgeable

## acquiesce

15 on friendly terms
• **be acquainted with** 03 ken 04 know

## acquiesce

05 agree, allow, defer 06 accede, accept, assent, concur, give in, permit, submit 07 approve, consent 12 give the nod to

## acquiescence

03 nod 05 say-so 06 assent 07 consent, go-ahead 08 approval, thumbs-up, yielding 09 agreement, deference 10 acceptance, compliance, green-light, submission 11 concurrence, countenance

## acquiescent

07 servile 08 acceding, agreeing, amenable, obedient, yielding 09 accepting, agreeable, approving, compliant 10 concurring, consenting, submissive 11 complaisant, deferential

## acquire

◇ *containment indicator* 03 bag, buy, cop, ern, get, net, win 04 earn, gain, grab 05 amass 06 attain, collar, come by, gather, obtain, pick up, secure, snap up, take on 07 achieve, collect, procure, realize, receive, snaffle, usucapt 08 purchase 10 accumulate 11 appropriate, splash out on

## acquisition

03 buy 04 gain 05 prize 07 acquest, gaining 08 property, purchase, securing, takeover 09 accession, obtaining, usucapion 10 attainment, investment, possession, usucaption 11 achievement, procurement 13 appropriation

## acquisitive

04 avid 06 greedy 08 covetous, grasping, hoarding 09 predatory, rapacious, voracious 10 avaricious 12 accumulative

## acquisitiveness

05 greed 07 avarice, avidity 08 cupidity, rapacity, voracity 12 covetousness, graspingness 13 predatoriness

## acquit

02 do 03 act 04 bear, free 05 clear, prove, repay 06 assoil, behave, bestow, excuse, let off, settle 07 absolve, comport, conduct, deliver, dismiss, perform, release, relieve, satisfy, set free 08 liberate, reprieve, uncharge 09 discharge, exculpate, exonerate, vindicate 11 make a bad job 12 make a good job 13 let off the hook

## acquittal

06 relief 07 freeing, release 08 clearing, excusing, reprieve 09 clearance, discharge, dismissal 10 absolution, liberation 11 deliverance, exculpation, exoneration, vindication 12 compurgation

## acre

01 a 02 ac

## acrid

04 acid, sour, tart 05 harsh, nasty, sharp 06 biting, bitter 07 acerbic, burning,

caustic, cutting, mordant, pungent 08 incisive, sardonic, stinging, venomous, virulent 09 malicious, sarcastic, trenchant, vitriolic 10 astringent 11 acrimonious

## acrimonious

05 sharp 06 bitchy, biting, bitter, severe 07 abusive, acerbic, caustic, crabbed, cutting, waspish 08 petulant, spiteful, venomous, virulent 09 irascible, rancorous, splenetic, trenchant, vitriolic 10 astringent, censorious 11 atrabilious, ill-tempered

## acrimony

04 gall 05 spite, venom 06 spleen 07 ill will, rancour, sarcasm, vitriol 08 acerbity, acridity, asperity, mordancy 09 harshness, ill temper, petulance, virulence 10 bitterness, causticity, ill feeling, resentment, trenchancy 11 astringency 12 irascibility

## acrobat

05 speel 07 gymnast, speeler, tumbler 08 balancer, posturer, stuntman 09 aerialist, posturist 10 rope-dancer, rope-walker, stuntwoman, wing-walker 11 equilibrist, funambulist 12 somersaulter, trick cyclist 13 contortionist, trapeze artist 15 tightrope-walker

## acrobatics

◇ *anagram indicator* 06 stunts 09 balancing 10 gymnastics 11 equilibrity, funambulism, rope-walking, wire-walking 13 somersaulting

## across

01 a 02 ac 03 dia-, tra- 04 over, tran-05 trans- 06 thwart 07 athwart 08 à travers

## act

02 be, do 03 bit, gig, kid, law 04 bill, deal, deed, fake, feat, item, mime, move, part, play, sham, show, skit, step, turn, work 05 canon, doing, edict, enact, feign, front, mimic, put on, react, serve 06 action, affect, assume, be busy, behave, decree, number, ruling, sketch, stroke 07 episode, exploit, go about, imitate, measure, operate, perform, portray, pretend, respond, routine, section, statute 08 be active, division, feigning, function, pretence, put-up job, simulate 09 dissemble, execution, manoeuvre, operation, ordinance, represent, take steps 10 do the job of, enterprise, resolution, subsection, take action, take effect 11 achievement, affectation, counterfeit, dissimulate, impersonate, make-believe, performance, undertaking 12 characterize, dissemblance, go on the stage, have an effect, take measures 13 be efficacious, dissimulation, exert yourself 14 accomplishment, acquit yourself 15 comport yourself, conduct yourself
*See also* **law**
• **act badly** 03 ham
• **act on** 04 heed, obey, take 05 alter

06 affect, change, follow, fulfil, modify, work on 08 carry out 09 conform to, influence, transform 10 comply with
• **act the part of** 04 come
• **act up** 04 fail 06 pack up, play up 07 carry on, conk out, go kaput, go wrong, not work 09 break down, mess about, misbehave 10 give bother, muck around 11 behave badly, malfunction, stop working 12 cause trouble

## acting

◇ *anagram indicator* 01 a 03 act 04 actg 05 drama 06 action, deputy, fill-in, pro tem, relief, supply 07 interim, reserve, showbiz, stand-by, stand-in, stopgap, theatre 08 artistry, covering 09 dramatics, imitating, in place of, luvviedom, melodrama, portrayal, short-term, surrogate, temporary 10 footlights, performing, play-acting, stagecraft, substitute 11 histrionics, performance, provisional, theatricals, Thespianism 12 show business 13 impersonation, standing in for 14 performing arts

## actinium

02 Ac

## actinon

02 an

## action

◇ *anagram indicator* 03 act, pas 04 case, deed, feat, fray, move, step, suit, work 05 clash, doing, fight, force, power 06 affray, battle, combat, effect, effort, energy, events, motion, result, spirit, vigour 07 exploit, lawsuit, measure, pizzazz, process, warfare 08 activity, conflict, exercise, exertion, fighting, goings-on, movement, practice, skirmish, vitality 09 encounter, endeavour, influence, mechanism, operation 10 activities, engagement, enterprise, excitement, get-up-and-go, happenings, litigation, liveliness, proceeding 11 achievement, functioning, hostilities, performance, proceedings, prosecution, stimulation, undertaking 12 exhilaration, forcefulness 14 accomplishment, course of action
• **check action** 04 stay
• **course of action** 04 path
• **critical time of action** 04 D-day

## activate

◇ *anagram indicator* 04 fire, move, stir, trip 05 impel, put on, rouse, start 06 arouse, bestir, excite, prompt, propel, set off, turn on 07 actuate, animate, trigger 08 energize, get going, initiate, mobilize, motivate, set going, switch on 09 derepress, galvanize, kick-start, stimulate 10 trigger off 11 set in motion 12 start working 13 push the button 14 press the button, throw the switch

## active

◇ *anagram indicator* 01 a 03 act 04 at it, busy, go-go, spry 05 agile, alert, astir, manic, quick, vital, yauld, zippy 06 birkie, lively, mobile, nimble,

quiver, wimble **07** devoted, engaged, forward, in force, on the go, running, springe, vibrant, working **08** activist, animated, diligent, forceful, frenetic, involved, militant, occupied, practive, spirited, vigorous **09** committed, effectual, energetic, operative, sprightly, stirabout **11** functioning, hard-working, hyperactive, industrious, in operation, light-footed, operational **12** contributing, enterprising, enthusiastic **13** indefatigable
• **be active 02** do **03** hum

**activist**
**07** inciter, stirrer **08** agitator, fomenter, henchman, militant **09** firebrand **10** incendiary, subversive **12** troublemaker **13** revolutionary

*Activists include:*

**04** Bono, King (Martin Luther)
**05** Nader (Ralph), Parks (Rosa)
**06** Gandhi (Mahatma), Geldof (Bob)
**07** Angelou (Maya), Chomsky (Noam), Guevara (Che), Jackson (Jesse), Mandela (Nelson), Mandela (Winnie)
**08** Malcolm X, Silkwood (Karen)
**09** Pankhurst (Christabel), Pankhurst (Emmeline), Pankhurst (Sylvia)

*See also* **aboriginal**

**activity**
◊ *anagram indicator* **02** do, go **03** act, job **04** deed, life, play, stir, task, work **05** hobby **06** action, bustle, labour, motion, scheme **07** pastime, project, pursuit, venture **08** business, exercise, exertion, industry, interest, movement **09** avocation, commotion, diversion, endeavour **10** activeness, enterprise, hurly-burly, liveliness, occupation **11** distraction, undertaking **13** something to do **14** toing and froing **15** a hive of activity, a hive of industry, hustle and bustle
• **bustling activity 04** rush **06** bustle **07** beehive
• **focus of activity 03** hub
• **furious activity 04** rage
• **increase in activity 04** boom

**actor, actress**
**03** ham **04** feed, mime, mute, supe **05** buffa, buffo, comic, extra, luvvy, super, thesp **06** artist, luvvie, mummer, player, stager, stooge, walk-on **07** artiste, comique, histrio, ingénue, Roscius, starlet, support, trouper **08** comedian, epilogue, film star, histrion, juvenile, thespian **09** bit player, film actor, hamfatter, movie star, performer, play actor, principal, tragedian **10** leading man, mime artist, movie actor, understudy, utility man **11** leading lady, matinée idol, pantomimist, protagonist, straight man, tragedienne, tritagonist **12** impersonator, spear carrier **13** deuteragonist, supernumerary **14** character actor, dramatic artist, stage performer **15** strolling player

*Actors include:*

**03** Cox (Brian), Fox (James), Fox (Michael J), Fry (Stephen), Law (Jude), Lee (Bruce), Lee (Christopher), Lee (Spike), Lom (Herbert), Sim (Alastair)
**04** Cage (Nicolas), Chan (Jackie), Chow (Yun-Fat), Dean (James), Depp (Johnny), Ford (Harrison), Foxx (Jamie), Gere (Richard), Holm (Sir Ian), Hope (Bob), Hurt (John), Kaye (Danny), Kean (Edmund), Lowe (Rob), Peck (Gregory), Penn (Sean), Pitt (Brad), Reed (Oliver), Sher (Sir Antony), Tati (Jacques), Thaw (John), Tree (Sir Herbert Beerbohm), Wood (Elijah)
**05** Allen (Woody), Bacon (Kevin), Bates (Alan), Brody (Adrien), Caine (Sir Michael), Clift (Montgomery), Craig (Daniel), Crowe (Russell), Dafoe (Willem), Damon (Matt), Dance (Charles), Firth (Colin), Flynn (Errol), Fonda (Henry), Gable (Clark), Grant (Cary), Grant (Hugh), Grant (Richard E), Hanks (Tom), Hardy (Oliver), Irons (Jeremy), Kelly (Gene), Kempe (Will), Kline (Kevin), Leung (Tony), Lewis (Jerry), Lloyd (Harold), Lorre (Peter), Mason (James), Mills (Sir John), Moore (Roger), Neill (Sam), Nimoy (Leonard), Niven (David), Nolte (Nick), Price (Vincent), Quinn (Anthony), Reeve (Christopher), Robey (Sir George), Scott (George C), Sheen (Charlie), Sheen (Martin), Smith (Will), Spall (Timothy), Stamp (Terence), Sydow (Max von), Tracy (Spencer), Wayne (John)
**06** Alleyn (Edward), Beatty (Warren), Bogart (Humphrey), Brando (Marlon), Brooks (Mel), Burton (Richard), Cagney (James), Carrey (Jim), Chaney (Lon), Coburn (James), Cooper (Gary), Cruise (Tom), Curtis (Tony), De Niro (Robert), DeVito (Danny), Dillon (Matt), Finney (Albert), Gambon (Sir Michael), Gibson (Mel), Glover (Danny), Harris (Richard), Heston (Charlton), Hopper (Dennis), Howard (Trevor), Hudson (Rock), Irving (Sir Henry), Jacobi (Sir Derek), Jolson (Al), Jouvet (Louis), Keaton (Buster), Keitel (Harvey), Kemble (John Philip), Laurel (Stan), Laurie (Hugh), Ledger (Heath), Lemmon (Jack), Lugosi (Bela), Martin (Steve), Murphy (Eddie), Murray (Bill), Neeson (Liam), Newman (Paul), Oldman (Gary), O'Toole (Peter), Pacino (Al), Pearce (Guy), Phelps (Samuel), Quayle (Sir Anthony), Reagan (Ronald), Reeves (Keanu), Rooney (Mickey), Rourke (Mickey), Sharif (Omar), Sinden (Sir Donald), Slater (Christian), Spacey (Kevin), Swayze (Patrick), Walken (Christopher), Welles (Orson), Wilder (Gene), Willis (Bruce), Wolfit (Sir Donald)
**07** Astaire (Fred), Auteuil (Daniel),

Aykroyd (Dan), Benigni (Roberto), Berkoff (Steven), Bogarde (Sir Dirk), Branagh (Kenneth), Bridges (Jeff), Bridges (Lloyd), Bronson (Charles), Brosnan (Pierce), Brynner (Yul), Burbage (Richard), Carlyle (Robert), Chaplin (Charlie), Clooney (George), Connery (Sir Sean), Costner (Kevin), Crystal (Billy), Cushing (Peter), Douglas (Kirk), Douglas (Michael), Everett (Rupert), Fiennes (Joseph), Fiennes (Ralph), Forrest (Edwin), Freeman (Morgan), Garrick (David), Gielgud (Sir John), Hoffman (Dustin), Hopkins (Sir Anthony), Hordern (Sir Michael), Jackman (Hugh), Jackson (Samuel L), Karloff (Boris), Marceau (Marcel), Matthau (Walter), McQueen (Steve), Mitchum (Robert), Montand (Yves), Nielsen (Leslie), Olivier (Laurence, Lord), Phoenix (Joaquin), Poitier (Sidney), Redford (Robert), Rickman (Alan), Robbins (Tim), Robeson (Paul), Roscius, Russell (Kurt), Savalas (Telly), Selleck (Tom), Sellers (Peter), Shatner (William), Steiger (Rod), Stewart (James), Ustinov (Sir Peter)
**08** Atkinson (Rowan), Barrault (Jean-Louis), Day-Lewis (Daniel), DiCaprio (Leonardo), Dreyfuss (Richard), Eastwood (Clint), Goldblum (Jeff), Guinness (Sir Alec), Harrison (Sir Rex), Kingsley (Sir Ben), Laughton (Charles), Macready (William Charles), McGregor (Ewan), McKellen (Sir Ian), Redgrave (Sir Michael), Reynolds (Burt), Robinson (Edward G), Scofield (Paul), Stallone (Sylvester), Travolta (John), Van Cleef (Lee), Van Damme (Jean-Claude), von Sydow (Max), Whitaker (Forest), Williams (Robin), Woodward (Edward)
**09** Barrymore (Lionel), Broadbent (Jim), Broderick (Matthew), Chevalier (Maurice), Courtenay (Sir Tom), Depardieu (Gérard), Fairbanks (Douglas), Fernandel, Hawthorne (Sir Nigel), Lancaster (Burt), Malkovich (John), Nicholson (Jack), Pleasence (Donald), Strasberg (Lee), Valentino (Rudolph)
**10** Richardson (Sir Ralph), Sutherland (Donald), Sutherland (Kiefer), Washington (Denzel)
**11** Mastroianni (Marcello), Weissmuller (Johnny)
**12** Attenborough (Richard, Lord), Garcia Bernal (Gael), Stanislavsky (Konstantin)
**14** Schwarzenegger (Arnold), Seymour Hoffman (Philip)

*See also* **comedian**

*Actresses include:*

**03** Bow (Clara), Cox (Courteney), Day (Doris), Loy (Myrna)
**04** Ball (Lucille), Cruz (Penélope), Dern (Laura), Diaz (Cameron), Dors

(Diana), **Duse** (Eleonora), **Gish**
(Lillian), **Gwyn** (Nell), **Hawn**
(Goldie), **Hird** (Dame Thora), **Rigg**
(Dame Diana), **Ryan** (Meg), **West**
(Mae), **Wood** (Natalie), **York**
(Susannah)
05 **Allen** (Gracie), **Berry** (Halle),
**Bloom** (Claire), **Close** (Glenn),
**Davis** (Bette), **Davis** (Geena),
**Dench** (Dame Judi), **Derek** (Bo),
**Evans** (Dame Edith), **Fonda** (Jane),
**Gabor** (Zsa Zsa), **Garbo** (Greta),
**Jolie** (Angelina), **Kelly** (Grace),
**Lange** (Jessica), **Leigh** (Janet), **Leigh**
(Vivien), **Lopez** (Jennifer), **Loren**
(Sophia), **Mills** (Hayley), **Moore**
(Demi), **Ryder** (Winona), **Smith**
(Dame Maggie), **Stone** (Sharon),
**Swank** (Hilary), **Terry** (Dame Ellen),
**Weisz** (Rachel), **Welch** (Raquel)
06 **Adjani** (Isabelle), **Bacall** (Lauren),
**Bardot** (Brigitte), **Bisset**
(Jacqueline), **Cheung** (Maggie),
**Curtis** (Jamie Lee), **Farrow** (Mia),
**Fisher** (Carrie), **Foster** (Jodie),
**Grable** (Betty), **Hannah** (Daryl),
**Harlow** (Jean), **Hedren** (Tippi),
**Hunter** (Holly), **Huston** (Anjelica),
**Keaton** (Diane), **Kemble** (Fanny),
**Kidman** (Nicole), **Kinski**
(Nastassja), **Lamarr** (Hedy), **Lumley**
(Joanna), **Midler** (Bette), **Mirren**
(Helen), **Monroe** (Marilyn), **Moreau**
(Jeanne), **Robson** (Dame Flora),
**Rogers** (Ginger), **Spacek** (Sissy),
**Streep** (Meryl), **Suzman** (Janet),
**Tautou** (Audrey), **Taylor** (Dame
Elizabeth), **Temple** (Shirley),
**Theron** (Charlize), **Turner**
(Kathleen), **Turner** (Lana), **Ullman**
(Tracey), **Weaver** (Sigourney),
**Winger** (Debra)
07 **Andress** (Ursula), **Andrews** (Dame
Julie), **Aniston** (Jennifer), **Bergman**
(Ingrid), **Binoche** (Juliette), **Colbert**
(Claudette), **Deneuve** (Catherine),
**Gardner** (Ava), **Garland** (Judy),
**Hepburn** (Audrey), **Hepburn**
(Katharine), **Jackson** (Glenda),
**Johnson** (Dame Celia), **Langtry**
(Lillie), **Lombard** (Carole), **Paltrow**
(Gwyneth), **Roberts** (Julia), **Russell**
(Jane), **Seymour** (Jane), **Siddons**
(Sarah), **Swanson** (Gloria), **Swinton**
(Tilda), **Walters** (Julie), **Winslet**
(Kate), **Withers** (Googie)
08 **Anderson** (Dame Judith), **Ashcroft**
(Dame Peggy), **Bancroft** (Anne),
**Bankhead** (Tallulah), **Basinger**
(Kim), **Campbell** (Mrs Patrick),
**Charisse** (Cyd), **Christie** (Julie),
**Collette** (Toni), **Crawford** (Joan),
**Dietrich** (Marlene), **Fontaine** (Joan),
**Goldberg** (Whoopi), **Griffith**
(Melanie), **Hathaway** (Anne),
**Hayworth** (Rita), **MacLaine**
(Shirley), **Minnelli** (Liza), **Pfeiffer**
(Michelle), **Pickford** (Mary),
**Rampling** (Charlotte), **Redgrave**
(Vanessa), **Sarandon** (Susan),
**Shepherd** (Cybill), **Signoret**
(Simone), **Stanwyck** (Barbara),
**Thompson** (Emma)
09 **Barrymore** (Drew), **Bernhardt**

(Sarah), **Blanchett** (Cate), **Cotillard**
(Marion), **Johansson** (Scarlett),
**Knightley** (Keira), **MacDowell**
(Andie), **Mansfield** (Jayne),
**Plowright** (Dame Joan), **Streisand**
(Barbra), **Thorndike** (Dame Sybil),
**Zellweger** (Renée), **Zeta Jones**
(Catherine)
10 **Rossellini** (Isabella), **Rutherford**
(Dame Margaret)
11 **Bracegirdle** (Anne), **de Havilland**
(Olivia), **Mistinguett**, **Scott-Thomas**
(Kristin), **Witherspoon** (Reese)
12 **Bonham Carter** (Helena),
**Lollobrigida** (Gina)

---

*See also* **comedian**
• **actor's portrayal** 04 part, role
• **bad actor** 03 ham

### actors
04 cast 07 company

### actress
*see* actor

### actual
04 real, true, very 07 certain, de facto,
factual, genuine 08 absolute, bona
fide, concrete, definite, existent,
material, physical, positive, real life,
tangible, truthful, verified 09 authentic,
confirmed, realistic 10 legitimate
11 substantial 12 indisputable
14 unquestionable

### actuality
03 ens 04 fact 05 truth 07 realism,
reality 08 solidity 09 entelechy,
existence, substance 10 factuality
11 historicity, materiality
12 corporeality 14 substantiality

### actually
04 even 05 truly 06 indeed, in fact,
really 07 de facto, insooth, in truth,
soothly 09 in reality 10 absolutely 11 as
it happens 12 surprisingly 14 believe it
or not 15 as a matter of fact

### actuate
04 move, stir 05 rouse, start 06 arouse,
kindle, prompt, set off, turn on
07 animate, trigger 08 activate,
motivate, set going, switch on
09 instigate, stimulate 10 trigger off
11 set in motion 12 start working

### acumen
03 wit 05 sense 06 wisdom 07 insight
08 gumption, keenness, sagacity,
sapience 09 ingenuity, intuition,
judgement, quickness, sharpness,
smartness 10 astuteness, cleverness,
perception, shrewdness
11 discernment, penetration,
percipience, perspicuity
12 intelligence, perspicacity
13 judiciousness 14 discrimination

### acupressure
04 do-in 07 shiatsu, shiatzu 09 Jin Shin
Do®

### acute
04 dire, keen 05 canny, grave, sharp,
smart, vital 06 astute, clever, severe,
shrewd, urgent 07 crucial, cutting,
drastic, extreme, intense, sapient,
serious, violent 08 critical, decisive,

incisive, peracute, piercing, poignant
09 dangerous, judicious, observant,
sensitive 10 discerning, insightful,
perceptive, percipient, unbearable
11 distressing, penetrating, sharp-
witted 13 perspicacious

### acutely
04 very 06 keenly 07 gravely, sharply
08 markedly, severely, strongly
09 extremely, intensely, seriously

### adage
03 saw 05 axiom, gnome, maxim
06 byword, saying 07 precept, proverb
08 aphorism, paroemia
10 apophthegm, whakatauki

### adamant
03 set 04 firm, hard 05 fixed, rigid, stiff,
tough 07 diamond 08 obdurate,
resolute, stubborn 09 immovable,
insistent, lodestone, unbending
10 determined, inflexible, unshakable,
unwavering, unyielding
11 unrelenting, unshakeable
12 intransigent 14 uncompromising

### Adamson
04 Abel, Cain, Seth

### adapt
◇ *anagram indicator* 03 apt, fit 04 suit
05 alter, apply, frame, match, shape,
tally 06 adjust, change, comply,
modify, reduce, tailor 07 arrange,
conform, convert, exploit, fashion, get
used, prepare, qualify, remodel
08 attemper, settle in 09 contemper,
customize, harmonize 10 specialize
11 accommodate 13 get accustomed

### adaptable
◇ *anagram indicator* 07 open-end,
plastic, pliable 08 amenable, flexible,
variable 09 alterable, compliant, easy-
going, malleable, open-ended,
versatile 10 adjustable, changeable,
modifiable 11 conformable,
convertible

### adaptation
◇ *anagram indicator* 05 shift 06 change
07 fitting, shaping 08 matching,
revision 09 refitting, reshaping,
reworking, variation 10 adjustment,
alteration, conformity, conversion,
fashioning 11 getting used,
habituation, preparation, remodelling
12 conformation, modification,
refashioning 13 accommodation,
customization, harmonization
14 transformation 15 acclimatization,
familiarization

### add
◇ *juxtaposition indicator* 03 eik, eke, put,
sum, tot 04 go on, join, tote 05 affix,
annex, boost, count, put in, put on,
raise, top up, total, tot up 06 adjoin,
append, attach, deepen, extend, hike
up, prefix, suffix, tack on 07 augment,
build on, carry on, combine, count up,
enhance, improve, include, postfix,
summate, throw in 08 complete,
continue, heighten, increase
09 aggravate, go on to say, increment,
intensify, introduce 10 supplement
15 work out the total

**added**

• **add up** 03 fit 04 cast, make, mean 05 count, run to, spell, sum up, tally, total, tot up 06 amount, come to, reckon 07 compute, count up, include, signify, stack up 08 figure up, indicate, ring true 09 calculate, make sense 10 constitute 11 add together, be plausible 12 be consistent, be reasonable, hang together 13 stand to reason

**added**

03 new 04 more 05 extra, fresh, spare 07 adjunct, another, further 10 additional 13 supplementary

**addendum**

02 PS 03 add 05 annex 07 adjunct, allonge, codicil 08 addition, appendix 09 appendage 10 attachment, postscript, supplement 11 endorsement 12 augmentation

**addict**

03 fan 04 buff, head, hype, user 05 fiend, freak, hound, junky 06 junkie, stoner 07 devotee, druggie, fanatic, hop-head, tripper 08 adherent, coke-head, drug user, follower, snowbird 09 clay eater, crackhead, dope-fiend, drug fiend, drug taker, mainliner, smackhead 10 enthusiast 14 cruciverbalist

**addicted**

04 daft, fond, nuts, wild 05 crazy, given, potty 06 hooked 07 devoted 08 absorbed, bibulous, frequent, inclined, obsessed 09 confirmed, dedicated, dependent, fanatical, strung out 10 dissipated 13 drug-dependent

**addiction**

04 need 05 habit, mania, thing 06 monkey 07 craving 08 caffeism, opiumism, vinosity 09 cocainism, ergomania, obsession 10 caffeinism, compulsion, dependence, dependency, femininism 11 a colt's tooth, etheromania

**addictive**

09 obsessive 10 compulsive 12 habit-forming, irresistible 14 uncontrollable

**addition**

02 PS 03 eik, eke, PPS 04 also, gain, plus 05 extra, rider 06 adding, annexe 07 adjunct, codicil 08 addendum, additive, appendix, counting, increase 09 accession, accessory, accretion, appendage, extension, inclusion, increment, reckoning, summing-up, totalling, totting-up 10 annexation, attachment, increasing, postscript, supplement 11 computation, enlargement 12 afterthought, appurtenance, augmentation

• **in addition** 03 too 04 also 05 forby 06 as well, to boot, withal 07 besides, further, thereto 08 as well as, moreover 09 thereunto 11 furthermore 12 additionally, not to mention, over and above 14 for good measure, into the bargain

**additional**

03 new, odd 04 more, plus 05 added, extra, fresh, other, spare 07 another, further 09 increased 10 excrescent 12 adscititious, adventitious, supervenient, supplemental 13 supplementary

**additionally**

03 too 04 also 05 forby 06 as well, to boot, withal 07 besides, further 08 moreover 10 in addition 11 furthermore 12 over and above 14 for good measure, into the bargain

**additive**

04 MTBE 05 extra 07 E-number 08 addition 09 oxygenate, summative 10 emulsifier, stabilizer, supplement 12 preservative 13 canthaxanthin 14 canthaxanthine

**addle**

03 bad 04 daze, faze 05 empty 06 barren, muddle, putrid 07 confuse, fluster, muddled, perplex 08 befuddle, bewilder

**addled**

04 lost 05 fazed 07 mixed-up, muddled 08 confused 09 befuddled, flustered, perplexed 10 bewildered

**address**

03 add 04 call, flat, hail, home, lord, mail, post, send, talk 05 abode, greet, house, label, orate, place, remit, spiel, uncle 06 accost, convey, direct, invoke, mister, prayer, sermon, speech, talk to 07 accoast, bespeak, lecture, lodging, oration, speak to, welcome, write to 08 diatribe, dwelling, greeting, harangue, location, mistress, petition, preach to 09 apartment, designate, discourse, epirrhema, inaugural, intend for, monologue, philippic, residence, rhetorize, sermonize, situation, soliloquy 10 allocution, apostrophe, directions, invocation, salutation 11 communicate, give a talk to, inscription, make a speech, superscribe, superscript, valedictory, whereabouts 12 disquisition, dissertation 13 give a speech to, poste restante 14 deliver a speech

• **address yourself to** 06 tackle 07 focus on 08 attend to, deal with, engage in 09 undertake 10 take care of 12 buckle down to 13 concentrate on 15 apply yourself to

**adduce**

04 cite, lead, name 05 quote 06 assign, object 07 mention, present, proffer, refer to, trot out, upbraid 08 allude to, evidence, point out 10 put forward

**adept**

03 ace, don 04 able, deft, good 05 handy, sharp, swell 06 adroit, clever, deacon, expert, genius, master, nimble, versed, wicked, wizard 07 capable, dab hand, maestro, mahatma, skilled, veteran 08 hot stuff, masterly, polished 09 competent, practised 10 proficient 11 experienced, nobody's fool 12 accomplished

**adequacy**

07 ability, fitness, measure 08 fairness

10 capability, competence, mediocrity 11 passability, sufficiency, suitability 12 indifference, tolerability 13 acceptability, requisiteness, tolerableness 14 reasonableness, serviceability

**adequate**

02 OK 03 fit 04 able, enow, good 05 equal, ho-hum, valid 06 enough, patchy, will do, worthy 07 average, capable, working 08 all right, passable, suitable 09 competent, requisite, tolerable 10 acceptable, reasonable, sufficient 11 appropriate, indifferent, serviceable 12 commensurate, could be worse, run of the mill, satisfactory 13 could be better, no great shakes, unexceptional 14 fair to middling 15 undistinguished

**adequately**

08 passably, suitably 09 tolerably 10 acceptably, reasonably 12 sufficiently 13 appropriately 14 satisfactorily

**adhere**

03 fix 04 bond, glue, grip, heed, hold, join, keep, link, obey 05 cling, paste, stick 06 attach, cement, cleave, cohere, defend, fasten, follow, fulfil, solder 07 abide by, accrete, combine, espouse, observe, respect, stand by, support 08 cleave to, coalesce, hold fast 10 comply with, stick up for 11 go along with 13 stick together

**adherence**

05 cling 07 defence, respect, support 08 advocacy, fidelity 10 compliance, fulfilment, observance

**adherent**

03 bur, fan, nut 04 buff, burr, Jain, Sikh, Sofi, Sufi 05 Bahai, child, freak, Hindu, Jaina 06 Hindoo, Maoist, Sabean, votary 07 admirer, devotee, engager, Genevan, gnostic, Patarin, Sabaean, sceptic, sectary, skeptic 08 advocate, believer, catholic, disciple, follower, groupist, hanger-on, henchman, Jacobite, loyalist, partisan, partizan, Patarine, rightist, royalist, sectator, servitor, sticking, upholder, Vichyite, Wesleyan 09 Caesarean, Caesarian, Communard, Gothicist, ideologue, Oliverian, Samaritan, satellite, socialist, Spinozist, supporter, Wagnerist, Wagnerite 10 aficionado, Bourbonist, enthusiast, Protestant 12 episcopalian, hereditarian 13 sun worshipper 14 restorationist 15 hereditarianist, parliamentarian

**adhesion**

04 bond, grip 08 cohesion, purchase, sticking, synechia 09 adherence 10 attachment 12 adhesiveness 15 holding together

**adhesive**

03 gum 04 bond, glue, tape 05 glair, gluey, gummy, paste, tacky 06 Blu-tak®, cement, clammy, Cow Gum®, gummed, sticky 07 Band-aid®, Blu-tack®, holding, hot melt, stick-on 08 adherent, adhering, clinging, cohesive, fixative, goldsize, mountant,

mucilage, sticking **09** attaching, emplastic, glutinous, Sellotape®, Superglue® **10** sticky tape **11** Elastoplast®, hot-melt glue **12** mucilaginous, passe-partout, rubber cement, self-adhesive

## ad hoc
**05** ad-lib **09** extempore, makeshift **10** improvised, off the cuff, unprepared, unscripted **11** spontaneous, unrehearsed **13** spontaneously

## adieu
**03** bye **04** ciao, ta-ta **05** adios **06** bye-bye, cheers, hooray, kia ora, see you, so long **07** cheerio, goodbye, haere ra **08** au revoir, farewell, take care **10** all the best **11** arrivederci, be seeing you, leave-taking, see you later, valediction, valedictory **12** have a nice day, mind how you go, see you around **14** auf Wiedersehen

## ad infinitum
**03** aye **07** for ever **08** evermore **09** endlessly, eternally **10** at all times, constantly **11** continually, incessantly, permanently, perpetually **12** till doomsday

## adjacent
◇ *juxtaposition indicator* **04** near, next, nigh **05** close **06** beside **07** closest, nearest, vicinal **08** abutting, next-door, touching **09** adjoining, alongside, bordering, proximate **10** contiguous, coterminal, juxtaposed **11** conterminal, coterminant, coterminate, coterminous **12** conterminant, conterminate, conterminous, neighbouring

## adjective
**01** a **03** adj

## adjoin
◇ *juxtaposition indicator* **03** add **04** abut, join, link, meet **05** annex, touch, unite, verge **06** append, attach, be next, border, couple **07** combine, connect **09** juxtapose, neighbour **12** interconnect

## adjoining
◇ *juxtaposition indicator* **04** near, next **07** joining, linking, uniting, verging, vicinal **08** abutting, adjacent, next door, touching **09** bordering, combining, impinging, proximate **10** conjoining, connecting, contiguous, juxtaposed **12** neighbouring **15** interconnecting

## adjourn
**04** stay **05** defer, delay, pause **06** put off, recess, repair, retire **07** retreat, suspend **08** break off, continue, postpone, prorogue, withdraw **09** interrupt **11** discontinue **14** betake yourself **15** stop temporarily

## adjournment
**04** stay **05** break, delay, let-up, pause **06** recess **08** deferral, interval **09** deferment **10** moratorium, putting-off, suspension **11** continuance, dissolution, prorogation

**12** intermission, interruption, postponement **15** discontinuation

## adjudge
**04** aret, cide, deem, side **05** aread, arede, arett, award, judge **06** addeem, addoom, assign, decide, decree, reckon, regard **07** arreede **08** consider **09** determine

## adjudicate
**04** pass **05** award, judge **06** decide, settle, umpire **07** adjudge, referee **09** arbitrate, determine, pronounce

## adjudication
**06** decree, ruling **07** verdict **08** decision **09** judgement **10** conclusion, settlement **11** arbitration **13** determination, pronouncement

## adjudicator
**03** ref, ump **05** judge **06** umpire **07** arbiter, referee **08** mediator **10** arbitrator

## adjunct
**05** added **06** joined **07** apanage **08** addition, appanage **09** accessory, appendage, appendant **10** complement, supplement **11** concomitant **13** accompaniment

## adjust
◇ *anagram indicator* **03** fit, fix, set **04** gang, sort, suit, tram, true, tune **05** adapt, align, alter, amend, coapt, frame, shape, tweak **06** change, modify, reduce, repair, revise, settle, square, temper **07** arrange, balance, compose, concert, conform, convert, dispose, measure, rectify, remodel, reshape **08** fine-tune, modulate, register, regulate **09** get used to, harmonize, reconcile, refashion **11** accommodate **14** grow accustomed **15** make adjustments

## adjustable
**07** movable **08** flexible **09** adaptable, alterable, versatile **10** modifiable **11** convertible

## adjustment
◇ *anagram indicator* **03** adj **04** COLA **06** change, fixing, tuning **07** fitting, setting, shaping **08** ordering, revision, tweaking **09** amendment, arranging **10** adaptation, alteration, coaptation, conforming, conversion, fine-tuning, regulation, settlement, settling in **11** arrangement, habituation, orientation, rearranging, remodelling **12** modification, settling down **13** accommodation, getting used to, harmonization, rearrangement, rectification **14** naturalization, reconciliation **15** acclimatization

## adjutant
**03** adj **04** adjt **06** argala **07** marabou **08** marabout

## ad-lib
**06** freely, invent, made-up, make up, wing it **09** extempore, impromptu, improvise **10** improvised, off the cuff, unprepared **11** extemporize, impulsively, play it by ear, spontaneous, unrehearsed

**12** extemporized **13** spontaneously **14** extemporaneous, unpremeditated **15** speak off the cuff

## administer
◇ *anagram indicator* **03** run **04** drug, give, head, lead, rule **05** anele, apply, fetch, guide **06** direct, govern, impose, manage, supply **07** adhibit, conduct, control, deliver, dole out, execute, exhibit, give out, mete out, oversee, provide **08** disburse, dispense, organize, regulate **09** discharge, officiate, supervise **10** distribute, measure out **11** preside over, superintend

## administration
**05** admin **06** regime, ruling, senate **07** cabinet, command, control, council, red tape, running **08** congress, ministry **09** direction, discharge, execution, executive, governing, paperwork, provision, supplying **10** government, imposition, leadership, management, overseeing, parliament **11** application, supervision **12** directorship, dispensation, organization, powers that be, term of office **13** administering, governing body **15** superintendence

## administrative
**09** executive **10** management, managerial, regulatory **11** directorial, legislative, supervisory **12** governmental **13** authoritative, gubernatorial **14** organizational

---

*Administrative areas include:*

**04** area, city, town, ward, zila, zone **05** shire, state, theme **06** county, oblast, parish, region, sector, zillah **07** borough, commune, enclave, hundred, pargana, village **08** district, division, precinct, province, township **09** pergunnah, territory **11** conurbation **12** constituency, municipality

*See also* **borough; council; county; department; district; province; state**

---

## administrator
**04** boss, head **05** chief, elder, ruler **06** bigwig, leader, top dog **07** manager, trustee **08** big noise, chairman, director, governor, guardian, overseer **09** big cheese, commander, custodian, executive, organizer, patrician, president **10** controller, supervisor **11** dispensator **14** chief executive, judicial factor, superintendent **15** director-general, judicial trustee

## admirable
**04** cool, fine, rare **05** brill **06** choice, wicked, worthy **07** slammin' **08** laudable, masterly, slamming, superior, terrific, valuable **09** deserving, estimable, excellent, exquisite, respected, wonderful **10** creditable **11** commendable, exceptional, magnificent, meritorious

**12** praiseworthy, second to none
**14** out of this world

## admirably

**09** eminently, supremely
**11** commendably, deservingly, excellently, wonderfully
**13** exceptionally, magnificently

## admiral

**02** AF, RA, VA **03** Adm **07** capitan, navarch, vanessa

*Admirals include:*

**04** Byng (George, Viscount Torrington), Hood (Samuel, Viscount), Howe (Richard, Earl), Togo (Heihachiro, Count)
**05** Blake (Robert), Croft, Doria (Andrea), Hawke (Edward, Lord), Rooke (Sir George)
**06** Beatty (David, Earl), Benbow (John), Dönitz (Karl), Fisher (John, Lord), Grasse (François, Comte de), Halsey (William F, Jnr), Nelson (Horatio, Lord), Nimitz (Chester), Raeder (Erich), Vernon (Edward)
**07** Old Grog, Tirpitz (Alfred von), Wrangel (Ferdinand, Baron von)
**08** Cochrane (Thomas), Jellicoe (John, Earl)
**09** Artemisia
**10** Villeneuve (Pierre Charles)
**11** Collingwood (Cuthbert, Lord), Mountbatten (Louis, Earl)

## admiration

**03** yen **04** mana **05** kudos **06** esteem, fureur, praise, regard, wonder
**07** acclaim, delight, idolism, respect, worship **08** approval, pleasure, surprise **09** adoration, adulation, affection, amazement, reverence
**10** high esteem, high regard, veneration **11** approbation, hero-worship **12** appreciation, astonishment, commendation
• **expression of admiration** **01** O
**02** oh **03** man, wow **05** golly, wowee
**06** by Jove **07** caramba, gee whiz, respect

## admire

**04** laud, like **05** adore, prize, value
**06** esteem, praise, revere, wonder
**07** applaud, approve, iconize, idolize, respect, worship **08** look up to, venerate **09** approve of **10** appreciate
**11** hero-worship **12** esteem highly, like very much **13** think highly of **14** put on a pedestal **15** think the world of

## admirer

**03** fan **04** beau, buff **05** fiend, freak, lover, wooer **06** suitor **07** amateur, beloved, devotee, gallant **08** adherent, disciple, follower, idolater, idolator, idolizer **09** boyfriend, supporter
**10** aficionado, enthusiast, girlfriend, sweetheart, worshipper

## admissible

**02** OK **05** legit, licit **06** lawful
**07** allowed **08** passable **09** allowable, permitted, tolerable, tolerated
**10** acceptable, legitimate **11** justifiable, permissible

## admission

**06** access, avowal, entrée, exposé
**07** ingress, peccavi **08** entrance, granting, mea culpa **09** allowance
**10** acceptance, admittance, concession, confession, confidence, disclosure, divulgence, ordination, permission, profession, revelation
**11** affirmation, declaration, entrance fee, entry charge, recognition
**12** admission fee, asseveration, grande entrée, right of entry **13** right of access
**14** acknowledgment
**15** acknowledgement, enfranchisement

## admit

◇ *containment indicator* **03** gie, own
**04** give, take **05** adopt, agree, allow, enter, grant, let in, own up, yield
**06** accept, affirm, fess up, ordain, reveal, take in **07** adhibit, concede, confess, declare, divulge, embrace, profess, receive, swear in, welcome
**08** blurt out, disclose, initiate, intromit
**09** come clean, introduce, recognize
**10** allow entry, give access
**11** acknowledge, matriculate **12** allow to enter, eat your words **13** give admission

## admittance

**05** entry **06** access, entrée **07** ingress
**08** audience, entrance **09** admission, admitting, letting in, reception
**10** acceptance, initiation
**12** introduction, right of entry **13** right of access

## admitted

**05** given **07** confest, granted
**08** accepted, affirmed, declared
**09** confessed, confirmed, professed
**10** recognized **12** acknowledged

## admittedly

**07** granted **08** avowedly **09** allowedly, certainly **11** confessedly

## admitting

**03** tho' **06** though

## admixture

**03** mix **05** alloy, blend **06** fusion
**07** amalgam, mixture **08** compound, tincture **10** commixture
**11** combination **12** amalgamation, intermixture

## admonish

**04** warn **05** chide, scold **06** berate, exhort, rebuke, school **07** censure, correct, counsel, reprove, tell off, upbraid **09** reprimand **10** discipline
**13** tear a strip off

## admonition

**05** pi-jaw **06** advice, earful, rebuke
**07** censure, counsel, reproof, warning, wigging **08** berating, moniment, monument, scolding **09** reprimand
**10** correction, telling-off, ticking-off
**11** exhortation **12** dressing-down, reprehension

## ad nauseam

**08** boringly **09** endlessly **10** constantly
**11** continually, perpetually
**12** continuously, interminably, monotonously

## ado

**04** flap, fuss, stir, to-do **05** hoo-ha, tizzy
**06** bother, bustle, hassle **07** stashie, stishie, stushie, trouble **08** stooshie
**09** commotion **10** difficulty, hurly-burly
**11** piece of work **12** song and dance

## adolescence

**05** teens, youth **07** boyhood, puberty
**08** girlhood, minority **10** boyishness, immaturity, juvenility, pubescence
**11** development, girlishness
**12** juvenescence, teenage years, youthfulness **14** young adulthood

## adolescent

**03** ned, Ted **04** teen **05** minor, young, youth **06** boyish, neanic **07** girlish, growing, puerile, teenage **08** childish, immature, juvenile, subadult, Teddy boy, teenager, youthful **09** infantile, pubescent, Teddy girl **10** bobbysoxer, developing, young adult
**11** juvenescent, young person

## adopt

◇ *containment indicator* **04** back, take, vote **05** elect **06** accept, assume, borrow, choose, father, follow, foster, mother, ratify, select, take in, take on, take up **07** appoint, approve, embrace, endorse, espouse, support **08** arrogate, decide on, maintain, nominate, settle on **10** naturalize **11** appropriate **13** take as your own

## adoption

**04** vote **05** choice **07** backing, support
**08** approval, election, espousal, taking-in, taking-on, taking-up
**09** embracing, fostering, selection
**10** acceptance, nomination
**11** appointment, approbation, embracement, endorsement
**12** ratification **13** appropriation
**15** taking as your own

## adorable

**04** dear **05** sweet **07** darling, lovable, winning, winsome **08** charming, fetching, pleasing, precious
**09** appealing, wonderful **10** attractive, bewitching, delightful, enchanting
**11** captivating

## adoration

**04** love **06** esteem, homage, praise, regard **07** worship **08** devotion, doting on, idolatry **09** laudation, reverence
**10** admiration, cherishing, exaltation, high regard, veneration **11** idolization
**12** thanksgiving **13** glorification, magnification

## adore

**04** love **05** enjoy **06** admire, dote on, esteem, honour, relish, revere, savour
**07** cherish, worship **08** be fond of, hold dear, venerate **10** idolatrize **11** be devoted to, be partial to **12** enjoy greatly, esteem highly, like very much
**15** think the world of

## adorn

**04** deck, dink, do up, gild, trim
**05** array, begem, besee, crown, dight, dress, grace, paint **06** aguise, attire, attrap, bedeck, doll up, enrich, honour, invest, ornate, set out, tart up

**adornment**

**07** adonize, apparel, bedight, bedizen, bejewel, bestick, commend, emblaze, enhance, festoon, furbish, garnish, impearl, miniate **08** beautify, decorate, emblazon, ornament **09** bespangle, embellish **10** illustrate

**adornment**

**05** frill **06** fallal **07** decking, falbala, figgery, flounce, garnish, gilding **08** frippery, furbelow, ornament **09** accessory, fallalery, fandangle, garnishry, garniture, jewellery, trappings, trimmings **10** decorating, decoration, enrichment, ornateness, tawdry lace **11** bedizenment **13** embellishment, ornamentation **14** beautification

**adrift**

◊ *anagram indicator* **04** lost **05** at sea **07** aimless **08** drifting, goalless, insecure, rootless **09** off course, unsettled **10** anchorless, unanchored **11** disoriented **13** directionless, disorientated

**adroit**

**04** able, deft, neat, pert **05** adept, slick, trick **06** clever, expert, habile **07** skilful **08** dextrous, tactical **09** dexterous, ingenious, masterful **10** proficient **11** resourceful

**adroitly**

**04** ably **06** deftly **08** cleverly, expertly **09** skilfully **11** dexterously, masterfully **12** proficiently **13** resourcefully

**adroitness**

**05** skill **07** ability, address, finesse, mastery **08** deftness, facility **09** adeptness, dexterity, expertise **10** cleverness, competence **11** proficiency, skilfulness **15** resourcefulness

**adulation**

**06** praise **07** fawning, incense **08** flattery **10** admiration, sycophancy **11** assentation, bootlicking, hero worship, idolization **12** blandishment **13** pats on the back **15** personality cult

**adulatory**

**07** fawning, fulsome, servile **08** praising, unctuous **10** flattering, obsequious **11** blandishing, bootlicking, sycophantic **13** complimentary

**adult**

**01** A, X **03** man **04** blue, ripe **05** of age, woman **06** fruity, mature, sleazy, X-rated **07** grown-up, obscene, raunchy, ripened **08** hard-core, indecent **09** developed, full-grown **10** fully-grown **11** grown person, near the bone **12** fully-fledged, pornographic **14** near the knuckle

**adulterate**

**04** card, lime, load **05** spike, taint, water **06** debase, defile, dilute, weaken **07** corrupt, degrade, devalue, falsify, pollute, vitiate **09** attenuate, water down **10** bastardize, make impure **11** contaminate, deteriorate **12** sophisticate

**adulteration**

**08** dilution **09** pollution, vitiation, weakening **10** corruption, debasement, defilement **13** contamination, deterioration

**adulterer**

**03** cad **04** rake, roué, stud, wolf **05** flirt **06** lecher **07** Don Juan, playboy **08** Casanova, deceiver **09** avouterer, ladies' man, libertine, womanizer **10** lady-killer, profligate **11** philanderer

**adulterous**

**05** false **08** cheating, disloyal **09** deceitful, faithless, two-timing **10** inconstant, unfaithful

**adultery**

**06** affair **07** avoutry, liaison **08** cheating **09** two-timing **10** flirtation, infidelity, misconduct, unchastity **11** fornication **12** entanglement **13** a bit on the side, playing around **14** unfaithfulness **15** extramarital sex, playing the field

**advance**

**01** a **03** pay, sub **04** ante, cite, give, grow, help, lend, loan, pass, push, rise, seek, step **05** early, march, offer, prior, raise **06** adduce, allege, assist, avaunt, better, come on, credit, foster, growth, incede, move on, submit, supply, thrive **07** benefit, deposit, develop, forward, furnish, further, go ahead, headway, imprest, improve, leading, present, proceed, proffer, promote, prosper, provide, suggest, support, upgrade **08** flourish, get ahead, increase, move in on, progress, retainer, vanguard **09** go forward **10** betterment, facilitate, forge ahead, gain ground, prepayment, put forward **11** advancement, come forward, development, down payment, furtherance, improvement, make earlier, make headway, move forward, preliminary, progression, step forward **12** amelioration, breakthrough, bring forward, going forward, make progress, pay in advance, surge forward **13** expeditionary, moving forward, pay beforehand **14** onward movement **15** forward movement, marching forward
• **in advance 02** on **05** ahead, early **06** sooner **07** earlier, forward, in front, up front **09** aforehand, in the lead **10** beforehand, previously **11** ahead of time **14** in the forefront

**advanced**

**01** a **03** far **04** high, lent, shot **05** ahead, early **06** higher, hi-tech, onward **07** complex, forward, leading **08** foremost, high-tech, up-to-date **09** high-level **10** avant-garde, precocious **11** progressive, ultra-modern **13** sophisticated, state-of-the-art **14** forward-looking **15** ahead of the times

**advancement**

**04** gain, rise **06** ascent, growth **07** advance, headway **08** progress **09** evolution, promotion, upgrading **10** betterment, furthering, preferment, proceeding, upward step

**11** development, furtherance, improvement **12** kick upstairs

**advances**

**05** moves, offer **08** approach **09** addresses, overtures **10** approaches, attentions, suggestion **11** proposition

**advantage**

**02** ad **03** aid, pro, use, van **04** boon, boot, edge, gain, good, head, help, lead, odds, plus, pull, sake, sted, sway **05** asset, avail, cause, favor, fruit, prise, prize, stead, value **06** beauty, favour, ground, pay-off, profit, reward, virtue **07** account, benefit, box-seat, service, utility, vantage, welfare **08** blessing, eminence, interest, leverage, whip hand **09** dominance, emolument, good point, head start, obvention, plus point, privilege, upper hand **10** assistance, percentage, perquisite, precedence, proceeding, usefulness, whip handle **11** convenience, helpfulness, pre-eminence, superiority, weather gage **12** weather gauge **14** on the windy side

**advantageous**

**04** plus **06** useful **07** gainful, helpful **08** valuable **09** favorable, of service, opportune, rewarding **10** beneficial, convenient, favourable, profitable, propitious, worthwhile **11** furthersome, serviceable **12** of assistance, remunerative

**advent**

**03** adv **04** dawn **05** birth, onset **06** coming **07** arrival, looming **08** approach, entrance **09** accession, beginning, emergence, inception **10** appearance, occurrence **12** introduction

**adventitious**

**07** foreign **09** unplanned **10** accidental, additional, fortuitous, unexpected, unforeseen, unintended **12** uncalculated

**adventure**

**04** gest, kick, risk **05** kicks, peril, quest **06** aunter, chance, danger, hazard, thrill **07** exploit, romance, venture **08** escapade, incident **09** happening **10** enterprise, excitement, experience, occurrence **11** speculation, undertaking

**adventurer**

**04** hero **06** pirate **07** heroine, Ulysses, voyager **08** Argonaut, Odysseus, venturer, wanderer **09** daredevil, traveller **10** filibuster, speculator **11** bandeirante, enterpriser, opportunist **12** carpetbagger, swashbuckler

**adventurous**

**04** bold, rash **05** gutsy, risky **06** daring, spunky **07** dareful **08** exciting, intrepid, perilous, reckless, romantic **09** audacious, dangerous, daredevil, hazardous, impetuous **10** headstrong, precarious **11** venturesome **12** enterprising **13** swashbuckling

## adversary
03 foe 05 enemy, rival, Satan
07 opposer 08 attacker, copemate,
opponent 09 assailant, copes-mate
10 antagonist, competitor, contestant

## adverse
05 cross 06 thwart 07 awkward,
counter, harmful, hostile, hurtful,
opposed, unlucky 08 contrary,
negative, opposing, opposite,
perverse, untoward 09 injurious
10 unfriendly 11 conflicting,
detrimental, inexpedient, inopportune,
uncongenial, unfortunate
12 antagonistic, inauspicious,
unfavourable, unpropitious
15 disadvantageous

## adversely
09 harmfully, unluckily 10 negatively
12 unfavourably 13 detrimentally,
unfortunately 14 inauspiciously,
unpropitiously

## adversity
03 woe 04 hell 05 cross, trial 06 misery,
sorrow 07 bad luck, ill luck, reverse,
the pits, trouble 08 calamity, disaster,
distress, hardship, traverse 09 hard
times, suffering 10 affliction, ill fortune,
living hell, misfortune, perversity
11 catastrophe, tribulation
12 wretchedness

## advertise
04 bark, bill, hype, plug, post, puff,
push, sell, tout 05 boost, quack, trail
06 inform, market, notify, poster,
praise, talk up 07 declare, display,
promote, publish 08 announce,
proclaim 09 broadcast, make known,
publicize 10 make public, promulgate
11 merchandize

## advertisement
02 ad, PR 04 bill, hype, plug, puff
05 blurb, promo 06 advert, jingle,
notice, poster, teaser, tele-ad, want ad
07 display, handout, leaflet, placard,
trailer 08 banner ad, bulletin, circular,
handbill 09 marketing, promotion,
publicity, throwaway 10 commercial,
propaganda 12 announcement

## advice
03 tip 04 help, rede, reed, view, word
05 reede 06 notice, wisdom 07 caution,
conseil, counsel, opinion, warning
08 guidance 09 direction
10 admonition, injunction,
memorandum, suggestion
11 counselling, dos and don'ts,
information, instruction 12 notification
13 communication, encouragement
14 recommendation
• **source of advice** 03 CAB
10 counsellor

## advisability
06 wisdom 07 aptness 08 prudence
09 soundness 10 expediency
11 suitability 12 desirability
13 judiciousness, preferability
15 appropriateness

## advisable
03 apt, fit 04 best, well, wise 05 sound
06 proper, wisest 07 correct, fitting,

politic, prudent 08 sensible, suitable
09 desirable, expedient, judicious,
suggested 10 beneficial, preferable,
profitable 11 appropriate,
recommended

## advise
04 read, rede, tell, urge, vise, warn
05 guide, reede, teach, tutor 06 enjoin,
inform, notify, preach, report
07 apprise, caution, commend,
counsel, suggest 08 acquaint, fill in on,
forewarn, instruct 09 make known,
recommend 10 give notice 11 give
counsel 12 give guidance 14 give the
low-down 15 give suggestions, make
suggestions

## advisedly
06 wisely 09 carefully, prudently
10 cautiously 11 judiciously
13 intentionally

## adviser
03 IFA 04 aide, guru 05 angel, coach,
guide, tutor 06 Egeria, helper, lawyer,
mentor, minder 07 counsel, monitor,
starets, staretz, teacher 08 assessor
09 agony aunt, authority, confidant,
therapist, town clerk 10 confidante,
consultant, counsellor, instructor, law-
officer, pensionary 11 consigliere
12 amicus curiae, right-hand man
13 company doctor 14 right-hand
woman 15 Attorney-General

## advisory
03 adv 07 helping 08 advising
10 consulting 11 counselling
12 consultative, consultatory,
recommending

## advocacy
06 avowry 07 backing, defence,
pushing, support 08 adoption,
espousal, proposal 09 patronage,
promotion, upholding
11 advancement, campaigning,
championing, propagation
12 promulgation 13 encouragement,
justification 14 recommendation

## advocate
02 KC, QC 03 adv 04 back, peat, plug,
urge 05 adopt, be pro, lobby 06 advise,
back up, defend, favour, lawyer,
preach, syndic, uphold 07 counsel,
endorse, espouse, justify, pleader,
promote, propose, push for, speaker,
support 08 argue for, attorney, be
behind, champion, defender,
exponent, plead for, preacher, press
for, promoter, upholder 09 barrister,
believe in, encourage, paraclete,
patronize, prescribe, proponent,
recommend, solicitor, spokesman,
supporter 10 campaigner, evangelist,
vindicator 11 campaign for,
countenance, protagonist,
spokeswoman, subscribe to 12 King's
Counsel, spokesperson 13 Queen's
Counsel 14 sympathize with

## aegis
04 wing 06 favour 07 backing, support
08 advocacy, auspices 09 patronage
10 protection 11 sponsorship
12 championship, guardianship

## aeon
03 age, eon, era 04 span, time, year
05 epoch, years 08 duration, eternity
10 generation

## aerate
06 excite, gasify 07 lighten, perturb,
refresh 09 oxygenate, ventilate 10 put
air into 13 charge with air, charge with
gas

## aerial
04 aery, dish, yagi 05 aerie 06 dipole,
duplex, midair 07 aeolian, antenna,
booster, scanner 08 air-to-air, in the
air, radiator, receiver, squarial
13 satellite dish 14 above the ground

## aeroplane
03 bus 04 kite 05 crate
See also **aircraft**

## aesthetic
04 arty, fine 07 elegant, stylish
08 adorning, artistic, tasteful
10 decorative, ornamental
11 beautifying 12 embellishing
15 greenery-yallery

## afar
06 far off 07 far away 08 a long way
09 distantly 13 a long distance

## affability
06 warmth 08 courtesy, facility,
matiness, mildness, openness
09 benignity, geniality, palliness
10 amiability, chumminess, cordiality,
good humour, good nature, kindliness
11 amicability, benevolence,
sociability 12 congeniality,
friendliness, graciousness,
obligingness, pleasantness
15 approachability, conversableness

## affable
04 maty, mild, open, warm 05 matey,
pally, suave 06 chummy, facile, genial,
kindly 07 amiable, cordial
08 amicable, friendly, gracious,
obliging, pleasant, sociable
09 agreeable, congenial, courteous,
expansive 10 benevolent, soft-spoken
11 good-natured 12 approachable,
good-humoured

## affair
02 go 03 biz 04 gear, love, ploy, shew,
show 05 amour, cause, event, fling,
issue, thing, topic 06 effeir, effere,
matter, pidgin, pigeon 07 affaire, carry-
on, concern, episode, funeral, liaison,
pidgeon, project, romance, shebang,
subject 08 activity, amour fou,
business, hypothec, incident, interest,
intrigue, question 09 happening,
operation 10 love affair, occurrence,
proceeding 11 transaction, undertaking
12 circumstance, relationship 13 affaire
d'amour, grande passion 14 affaire de
coeur, responsibility

## affect
03 hit 04 do to, fake, faze, move, sham,
stir, sway, take 05 act on, adopt, alter,
amove, assay, feign, pinch, put on,
taint, throw, touch, up-end, upset
06 assume, attack, change, impact,
modify, regard, salute, strike 07 apply
to, concern, disturb, imitate, impress,

involve, perturb, pretend, profess, trouble **08** bear upon, come home, interest, overcome, relate to, simulate **09** influence, transform **10** do things to, take hold of **11** counterfeit, impinge upon, prevail over **14** have an effect on

## affectation
**03** act **04** airs, pose, sham, show **05** gyver **06** façade **07** charade, foppery, ladyism **08** pretence, pretense **09** affection, imitation, mannerism **10** appearance, minauderie, simulation **11** insincerity, theatricism **12** false display **13** airs and graces, artificiality **15** pretentiousness

## affected
◇ *anagram indicator* **04** camp, fake, posy, sham, twee **05** ditsy, ditzy, posey, put-on, stiff **06** chichi, la-di-da, phoney **07** assumed, feigned, foppish, mincing, minikin, pompous, stuck up, studied **08** literose, mannered, precious **09** contrived, insincere, simpering, simulated, unnatural **10** artificial, euphuistic, histrionic, hoity-toity, up yourself **11** counterfeit, highfalutin, pretentious **12** highfaluting, histrionical, niminy-piminy

## affecting
**03** sad **06** moving **07** piteous, pitiful **08** pathetic, pitiable, poignant, powerful, stirring, touching **09** troubling **10** impressive **12** heart-rending **13** heartbreaking

## affection
**03** luv **04** care, love **05** amity **06** caring, desire, favour, liking, storge, warmth **07** feeling, passion, worship **08** calf-love, devotion, fondness, goodwill, kindness, localism, penchant **10** attachment, endearment, partiality, proclivity, propensity, tenderness, topophilia **11** inclination **12** friendliness, predilection **14** predisposition

## affectionate
**04** fond, kind, warm **05** eager **06** caring, doting, loving, tender **07** adoring, amiable, cordial, devoted, fervent, fulsome **08** attached, friendly, Platonic, sisterly **09** brotherly **10** passionate **11** warm-hearted

## affectionately
**06** dearly, fondly, kindly, warmly **07** amiably **08** lovingly, tenderly **09** adoringly, cordially, devotedly

## affiliate
**04** ally, join **05** annex, merge, unite **06** team up **07** combine, conjoin, connect, filiate **09** associate, syndicate **10** amalgamate, fraternize **11** confederate, incorporate **12** band together

## affiliated
**06** allied **07** related **08** in league **09** connected **10** associated, integrated **11** amalgamated **12** incorporated **13** in partnership

## affiliation
**03** tie **04** bond, link **05** union **06** league,

merger **07** joining **08** alliance **09** coalition, filiation **10** connection, federation, membership **11** association, combination **12** amalgamation, relationship **13** confederation, incorporation

## affinity
**03** kin **04** bond **06** kinred, liking **07** analogy, empathy, kindred, kinship, rapport **08** affiance, fondness, homology, likeness, sympathy **09** chemistry, good terms **10** attraction, partiality, propensity, similarity, similitude **11** resemblance **12** relationship **13** comparability, compatibility **14** correspondence, predisposition

## affirm
**03** say **04** aver, avow **05** state, swear **06** adhere, assert, attest, avouch, ratify, uphold **07** certify, confirm, declare, endorse, support, testify, witness **08** maintain **09** predicate, pronounce **10** asseverate **11** corroborate

## affirmation
**02** ay **03** aye, yes **04** oath **06** avowal **07** protest, witness **08** averment **09** assertion, statement, testimony **10** affirmance, avouchment, deposition **11** attestation, declaration, endorsement **12** asseveration, confirmation, ratification **13** certification, corroboration, pronouncement

## affirmative
**02** ay, OK **03** aye, yea, yes **08** agreeing, dogmatic, emphatic, positive **09** agreement, approving, assenting, asserting, assertory **10** acceptance, concurring, confirming, consenting **11** concurrence, predicatory **12** acquiescence, confirmation, ratification **13** corroborative

## affix
**03** add, put, tag **04** bind, glue, join, tack **05** annex, paste, pin on, set to, stick **06** adhere, adjoin, append, attach, fasten, prefix, suffix **07** connect, subjoin **09** privative **13** frequentative

## afflict
**03** ail, try **04** harm, hurt, pain, prey **05** assay, beset, curse, gripe, smite, visit, wound **06** bother, burden, grieve, harass, plague, strain, stress, strike **07** anguish, inflict, oppress, scourge, torment, torture, trouble **08** distress, lacerate **09** persecute **12** bear hard upon

## afflicted
◇ *anagram indicator* **03** ill, sad **04** hurt, sick, sore **05** beset, woful **06** cursed, humble, pained, struck, woeful **07** injured, laid low, plagued, wounded, wracked **08** affected, bothered, burdened, harassed, strained, stricken, tortured, troubled **09** aggrieved, anguished, depressed, disturbed, miserable, oppressed, sorrowful, suffering, tormented **10** distressed, overthrown **11** traumatized **13** grief-stricken

## affliction
**03** woe **04** care, pain, sore, teen, tene, tine, tyne **05** anger, cross, curse, grief, night, teene, trial **06** misery, ordeal, plague, sorrow, unweal **07** disease, furnace, illness, languor, scourge, torment, trouble **08** calamity, disaster, distress, hardship, sickness **09** adversity, suffering **10** depression, heart-grief, misfortune, visitation **11** tribulation **12** wretchedness

## affluence
**06** inflow, plenty, riches, wealth **07** fortune, tidy sum **08** opulence, property **09** abundance, megabucks, profusion, substance **10** easy street, prosperity **11** wealthiness

## affluent
**04** rich **05** flush **06** fat-cat, loaded **07** moneyed, opulent, wealthy, well-off **08** well-to-do **09** abounding, inflowing **10** in the money, prosperous, well-heeled **11** comfortable, rolling in it **12** on easy street

## afford
**04** bear, give **05** allow, grant, offer, spare, yield **06** answer, impart, manage, pay for, supply **07** furnish, present, produce, provide, sustain **08** generate **09** stretch to **11** be able to pay **13** have enough for **15** have the money for

## affordable
**05** cheap **06** budget **07** low-cost **08** moderate **09** dirt cheap, low-priced **10** economical, manageable, reasonable **11** inexpensive, sustainable

## affray
**03** row **04** fear, feud, fray, riot **05** brawl, brush, fight, mêlée, scrap, set-to **06** fracas, tussle **07** contest, disturb, punch-up, quarrel, scuffle, startle, wrangle **08** frighten, skirmish, squabble **10** fisticuffs, free-for-all **11** disturbance

## affront
**03** vex **04** face, slur, snub **05** abuse, anger, annoy, facer, pique, wrong **06** injury, insult, offend, slight **07** incense, offence, outrage, provoke **08** confront, dishonor, irritate, rudeness, vexation **09** aspersion, dishonour, displease, indignity **10** disrespect **11** discourtesy, provocation **13** slap in the face **14** kick in the teeth

## affronted
**05** angry, vexed **06** piqued **07** annoyed, injured **08** incensed, insulted, offended, outraged, slighted **09** irritated **10** displeased

## Afghanistan
**03** AFG

## aficionado
**03** fan, nut **04** buff **05** fiend, freak **06** expert **07** admirer, devotee **09** authority **10** enthusiast, specialist **11** connoisseur

## aflame

**02** in **03** lit **05** aglow, lit up **06** ablaze, alight, bright, on fire **07** burning, ignited, lighted, radiant, shining **11** illuminated

## afloat

**05** aswim, at sea, awash, sound **06** viable **07** buoyant, solvent, unfixed **08** drifting, floating, swimming, watching **09** out of debt **10** in the black, unsinkable

## afoot

**02** up **05** about, agate, astir **06** abroad, around **07** brewing, current, going on **08** in the air **09** in the wind **10** going about **11** circulating **13** in the pipeline

## aforementioned

**04** this **07** the same **09** aforesaid **10** aforenamed

## afraid

**03** rad **04** nesh **05** adrad, adred, afear, sorry, timid **06** afeard, aghast, craven, feared, scared **07** affeard, alarmed, anxious, daunted, fearful, nervous **08** affrayed, cowardly, effraide, timorous **09** concerned, petrified, regretful, reluctant, terrified, tremulous **10** apologetic, frightened, suspicious **11** distrustful, in a blue funk, intimidated **12** apprehensive, faint-hearted, in a cold sweat **13** having kittens, panic-stricken, scared to death
• **be afraid** **05** quake

## afresh

◇ *anagram indicator* **04** anew **05** again, newly **08** once more **09** once again, over again

## Africa

*African countries include:*

**04** Chad, Mali, Togo
**05** Benin, Congo, Egypt, Gabon, Ghana, Kenya, Libya, Niger, Sudan
**06** Angola, Guinea, Malawi, Rwanda, Uganda, Zambia
**07** Algeria, Burundi, Comoros, Eritrea, Lesotho, Liberia, Morocco, Namibia, Nigeria, Senegal, Somalia, Tunisia
**08** Botswana, Cameroon, Djibouti, Ethiopia, Tanzania, Zimbabwe
**09** Cape Verde, Mauritius, Swaziland, The Gambia
**10** Madagascar, Mauritania, Mozambique, Seychelles
**11** Burkina Faso, Côte d'Ivoire, Sierra Leone, South Africa
**12** Guinea-Bissau
**13** Western Sahara
**16** Equatorial Guinea
**18** São Tomé and Príncipe
**22** Central African Republic
**28** Democratic Republic of the Congo

*African landmarks include:*

**04** Giza, Nile
**05** Congo, Luxor
**06** Karnak, Sphinx
**07** Zambezi
**08** Aswan Dam, Kalahari, Lake Chad, Okavango, Pyramids
**09** Lake Nyasa, Masai Mara, River Nile, Serengeti, Suez Canal
**10** Lake Malawi, Lake Nasser, River Congo, River Niger
**11** Drakensberg, Great Sphinx, Kilimanjaro, Luxor Temple
**12** Aswan High Dam, Great Pyramid, Lake Victoria, Sahara Desert, Zambezi River
**13** Mt Kilimanjaro, Okavango Delta, Table Mountain, Victoria Falls
**14** Atlas Mountains, Cape of Good Hope, Kalahari Desert, Lake Tanganyika
**15** Great Rift Valley

## African

*Africans include:*

**03** Ibo, Kru, Twi
**04** Boer, Efik, Igbo, Kroo, Moor, Susu, Tshi, Zulu
**05** Masai, Swazi, Temne, Tonga
**06** Griqua, Herero, Kenyan, Kikuyu, Libyan, Malian, Somali, Tuareg, Yoruba
**07** Angolan, Basotho, Chadian, Gambian, Guinean, Ivorian, Mosotho, Rwandan, Sahrawi, Swahili, Ugandan, Zambian
**08** Algerian, Batswana, Beninese, Egyptian, Eritrean, Gabonese, Ghanaian, Liberian, Malagasy, Malawian, Moroccan, Motswana, Namibian, Nigerian, Nigerien, Sahraoui, Sudanese, Togolese, Tunisian
**09** Burkinabé, Burundian, Congolese, Ethiopian, Sahrawian, Santoméan, São Toméan, Tanzanian
**10** Djiboutian, Mozambican, Sahraouian, Senegalese, Zimbabwean
**11** Cameroonian, Cape Verdean, Mauritanian
**12** South African
**13** Equatoguinean, Sierra Leonean
**14** Central African, Guinea-Bissauan

## after

◇ *juxtaposition indicator* **02** on **03** epi-, for **04** past **05** about, since **06** behind **07** chasing, owing to, wanting **09** because of, following, posterior, regarding **10** concerning, in honour of **11** as a result of, in pursuit of, on account of, trying to get **12** subsequent to, with regard to **15** in consequence of
• **after all** **08** in the end **09** most of all, primarily **10** first of all **12** nevertheless **15** most importantly
• **after that** **04** then **05** later
• **after which** **04** when
• **immediately after** **04** next
• **not after** **02** by
• **until after** **04** over

## after-effect

**06** result, upshot **07** spin-off **09** aftermath **11** consequence **12** repercussion

## aftermath

**03** end **04** rawn, wake **05** rowan **06** rawing, rowing, upshot **07** effects, fallout, outcome, results **08** backwash **10** lattermath **11** aftergrowth **12** after-effects, consequences **13** repercussions

## afternoon

**01** a **02** pm **04** arvo **06** undern **07** evening **12** postmeridian
• **pleasant Sunday afternoon** **03** PSA

## afterpiece

**03** jig **05** exode

## afterthought

**02** PS **03** PPS **05** rider **07** codicil **10** postscript

## afterwards

**03** eft **04** next, syne, then **05** later **07** later on **09** after that, thereupon **12** subsequently

## again

**02** do, re- **03** eft **04** anew, back, more, over, then **05** ditto **06** afresh, encore, iterum **07** further **08** once more, yet again **09** once again, over again **11** another time, one more time
• **again and again** **05** often **10** constantly, frequently, repeatedly **11** continually **12** time and again

## against

◇ *juxtaposition indicator* **01** v **02** on, to, vs **03** con **04** anti **06** facing, versus **07** harmful **08** abutting, fronting, in case of, opposing, touching **09** close up to, hostile to, opposed to, resisting **10** adjacent to, opposite to **11** confronting, detrimental, in the face of, prejudicial **12** in contrast to, in defiance of, unfavourable **13** in contact with **14** antagonistic to, in opposition to **15** disadvantageous

## agate

**04** onyx **05** afoot, astir, murra **06** astray, murrha, pebble **10** Mocha stone **11** chalcedonyx, dendrachate **12** Scotch pebble

## agave

**05** sisal **06** maguey **08** henequen, henequin, heniquin **12** American aloe, century plant

## age

**03** day, eon, era, yug **04** aeon, date, days, span, time, yuga **05** epoch, ripen, years **06** dotage, grow up, mature, mellow, old age, period, season, wither **07** century, decline, grow old **08** duration, maturity, senility **09** become old, come of age, seniority **10** degenerate, generation, senescence **11** decrepitude, deteriorate, elderliness **14** advancing years, declining years
*See also* **old age**

## aged

**02** ae, of **03** aet, old **04** grey **05** aging, hoary **06** ageing, mature, past it, senior **07** ancient, doddery, elderly **08** advanced, wintered **09** geriatric, getting on, senescent **11** over the hill, patriarchal **13** superannuated

**15** advanced in years, no spring chicken

**agency**
**04** firm, work **05** force, means, power **06** action, bureau, effect, medium, office **07** company, vehicle **08** activity, business, workings **09** influence, mechanism, operation **10** department **11** involvement **12** intervention, organization **15** instrumentality
See also **news; spy**

**agenda**
**04** list, menu, plan **05** diary **06** scheme **08** calendar, schedule, to-do list **09** programme, timetable **12** scheme of work

**agent**
**03** agt, Fed, rep, spy, way **04** Bond, doer, G-man, mole, narc, nark, root, spie, wait **05** cause, envoy, force, means, mover, narco, plant, proxy, route, spial, spook **06** agency, beagle, broker, deputy, engine, factor, medium, setter, shadow, source, worker **07** channel, liaison, sleeper, trustee, vehicle **08** assignee, delegate, emissary, Mata Hari, minister, mouchard, operator **09** go-between, middleman, operative, performer **10** instrument, negotiator, substitute **11** double agent, functionary **12** intermediary **14** representative
See also **publicity**

**age-old**
**03** old **04** aged **07** ancient, antique, very old **08** primeval, time-worn **09** long-lived, primaeval

**agglomeration**
**04** mass **05** stash, store **07** build-up **08** increase **09** aggregate, gathering, stockpile **10** collection **11** aggregation **12** accumulation, augmentation

**aggrandize**
**05** exalt, widen **06** enrich **07** advance, amplify, dignify, elevate, enhance, enlarge, ennoble, glorify, inflate, magnify, promote, upgrade **09** glamorize **10** exaggerate, make richer

**aggrandizement**
**09** elevation, promotion **10** exaltation **11** advancement, enhancement, enlargement **12** exaggeration **13** magnification

**aggravate**
**03** irk, try, vex **05** annoy, get at, tease **06** harass, needle, pester, wind up, worsen **07** incense, inflame, magnify, provoke **08** compound, heighten, increase, irritate **09** intensify, make worse **10** exacerbate, exaggerate, exasperate

**aggravation**
**05** aggro **06** hassle **07** teasing **08** vexation **09** annoyance **10** irritation **11** irksomeness, provocation **12** exasperation **15** thorn in the flesh

**aggregate**
**03** ore, ped, sum **04** full, mass **05** gross, total, whole **06** amount, domain, entire

**08** assemble, combined, complete, dendrite, detritus, entirety, manifold, point set, potstone, sum total, totality **09** complexus, inclusive, summation **10** collection, generality, grand total **11** accumulated, combination, total amount, whole amount **12** accumulation **13** comprehensive, hypersthenite

**aggression**
**04** rage, raid **06** attack, injury, strike **07** air rage, assault, offence **08** invasion, road rage **09** hostility, incursion, intrusion, militancy, offensive, onslaught, pugnacity **10** antagonism **11** bellicosity, provocation **12** belligerence, encroachment, forcefulness, infringement **13** combativeness **14** aggressiveness

**aggressive**
**04** bold **05** lairy, pushy **06** bad-ass, brutal, chippy, feisty, full-on, savage **07** bullish, go-ahead, hostile, kick-ass, zealous **08** forceful, invasive, ruthless, vigorous **09** assertive, bellicose, combative, cut-throat, ferocious, incursive, intrusive, in-yer-face, offensive, truculent **10** in-your-face, pugnacious **11** bareknuckle, belligerent, competitive, contentious, destructive, provocative, quarrelsome **12** bareknuckled **13** argumentative

**aggressor**
**07** invader **08** attacker, intruder, offender, provoker **09** assailant, assaulter **10** instigator

**aggrieved**
◊ anagram indicator **04** hurt, sore **05** angry, upset **06** bitter, miffed, pained, peeved **07** annoyed, ill-used, injured, unhappy, wronged **08** insulted, offended, saddened **09** resentful **10** distressed, maltreated **11** disgruntled

**aghast**
**06** amazed **07** shocked, stunned **08** appalled, dismayed, startled **09** astounded, horrified, stupefied **10** astonished, confounded **12** horror-struck **13** thunderstruck

**agile**
◊ anagram indicator **04** deft, spry **05** acute, alert, brisk, fleet, lithe, nifty, quick, sharp, swank, swift, withy **06** active, astute, clever, limber, lissom, lively, mobile, nimble, supple **07** lissome **08** athletic, flexible **09** dexterous, sprightly **11** quick-witted

**agility**
**08** deftness, mobility **09** alertness, briskness, quickness, sharpness, swiftness **10** activeness, astuteness, liveliness, nimbleness, suppleness **11** flexibility **15** quick-wittedness

**agitate**
◊ anagram indicator **03** vex **04** beat, faze, fuss, heat, poss, rile, rock, stir, toss **05** alarm, argue, blend, churn, fight, rouse, shake, upset, whisk, worry **06** arouse, battle, betoss, dither, excite,

flurry, incite, rattle, ruffle, rumble, stir up, wind up, work up **07** commove, confuse, disturb, ferment, fluster, inflame, perturb, torment, trouble, unnerve **08** campaign, convulse, disquiet, distract, kefuffle, unsettle **09** carfuffle, curfuffle, kerfuffle, stimulate **10** discompose, disconcert, perturbate

**agitated**
◊ anagram indicator **04** wild **05** het up, upset **06** heated, hectic, mobled, stormy **07** agitato, anxious, excited, nervous, ruffled, worried **08** hopped-up, in a tizzy, troubled, unnerved **09** disturbed, ebullient, flustered, in a lather, steamed up, troublous, unsettled, wrought up **10** distraught, tumultuous **11** highwrought **12** all of a dither, all of a doodah, disconcerted **14** hot and bothered

**agitation**
**04** fret **05** alarm, tweak, worry **06** battle, flurry, frenzy, jabble, lather, motion, moving, pucker, ruffle, taking **07** anxiety, beating, concern, crusade, emotion, fanteeg, ferment, fluster, flutter, shaking, tempest, tension, tossing, trouble, turning **08** blending, disquiet, distress, fantigue, fighting, kefuffle, movement, stirring, striving, struggle, whisking **09** carfuffle, commotion, curfuffle, kerfuffle **10** ebullition, excitement **11** campaigning, distraction, disturbance, jactitation, trepidation **12** perturbation, restlessness

**agitator**
**07** inciter, stirrer **08** activist, fomenter **09** Bolshevik, firebrand **10** instigator, subversive **12** rabble-rouser, troublemaker **13** revolutionary

**agnostic**
**07** doubter, sceptic **08** doubting **09** sceptical **10** questioner, unbeliever **11** questioning, unbelieving **12** disbelieving **14** doubting Thomas

**ago**
**04** back, gone, past, syne **05** since **06** before **07** earlier **09** in the past **10** previously **12** from that time

**agog**
**04** avid, keen **05** eager **07** anxious, curious, excited, pop-eyed **09** impatient **10** enthralled, in suspense **12** enthusiastic **13** on tenterhooks

**agonize**
**04** fret **05** worry **06** labour, strain, strive **07** contend, trouble, wrestle **08** struggle

**agonizing**
**07** painful, racking **08** piercing, worrying **09** harrowing, torturous **10** tormenting **11** distressing **12** excruciating, heart-rending

**agony**
**03** woe **04** hurt, pain **05** spasm **06** misery, throes **07** anguish, torment, torture **08** distress **09** suffering **10** affliction **11** tribulation **12** wretchedness

## agrarian

**06** landed **07** bucolic, farming, georgic, predial **08** geoponic, praedial **09** agronomic **10** cultivated **12** agricultural

## agree

**02** OK **03** fit, yes **04** gree, jibe, jump, okay, sort, suit **05** admit, align, aline, allow, apply, atone, chime, close, fadge, get on, grant, match, tally, yield **06** accede, accept, accord, adhere, assent, assort, attone, clinch, comply, concur, cotton, decide, go with, permit, settle, square **07** be at one, comport, concede, concord, conform, congree, congrue, consent, consort, paction **08** coincide, compound, hit it off, say yes to, strike in **09** determine, harmonize, subscribe, symbolize **10** compromise, condescend, correspond, fall in with, homologate, underwrite **11** acquiesce in, be of one mind, go along with, meet halfway, rubber-stamp, see eye to eye **12** be consistent, share the view **14** give the go-ahead, strike a bargain **15** give the thumbs-up, make concessions

## agreeable

**04** fine, kind, nice **05** jolly, sapid **07** likable, willing **08** amenable, amicable, charming, euphonic, friendly, likeable, pleasant **09** compliant, congenial, desirable, enjoyable, toothsome **10** acceptable, attractive, delightful, euphonical, euphonious **11** complaisant, conformable, good-natured, sympathetic **12** approachable **13** companionable, consentaneous

## agreeably

**09** enjoyably **10** acceptably, pleasantly, pleasingly **11** accordingly **12** attractively, delightfully

## agreement

**03** agt, FTA **04** amen, band, deal, deed, GATT, pact, repo, whiz **05** chime, covin, NAFTA, tally, union, whizz **06** accord, assent, comart, covyne, pre-nup, treaty, unison **07** analogy, bargain, closing, compact, concert, concord, consent, consort, contrat, entente, fitting, harmony, syntony **08** affinity, contract, covenant, matching, Mercosur, sortance, sponsion, sympathy **09** Ausgleich, collusion, community, concordat, consensus, indenture, unanimity **10** accordance, accordancy, compliance, conformity, congruence, congruency, consonance, convention, settlement, similarity, uniformity **11** arrangement, concordance, concurrence, consistence, consistency, respondence, supersedere, transaction **12** complaisance **13** compatibility, embellishment, understanding **14** correspondence, correspondency
*See also* **treaty**
• **expression of agreement** **01** I **02** ay, OK **03** aye, oke, olé **04** amen, done, good, okay, sure **05** right, uh-huh, wilco **06** quotha, rather, righto **07** d'accord, right-ho

## agricultural

**05** rural **06** farmed **07** bucolic, farming, georgic **08** agrarian, geoponic, pastoral, praedial **09** agronomic **10** cultivated, geoponical **11** countryside
*See also* **farm**

## agriculture

**03** agr **04** plow **06** plough **07** farming, tillage, tilling **08** agronomy **09** geoponics, husbandry **10** agronomics **11** agroscience, cultivation **12** agribusiness

*Agriculturists include:*

**04** **Coke** (Thomas William), **Tull** (Jethro)
**05** **Lawes** (Sir John Bennet), **Smith** (Maria 'Granny'), **Young** (Arthur)
**06** **Carver** (George Washington)
**07** **Borlaug** (Norman), **Burbank** (Luther)
**08** **Bakewell** (Robert)
**09** **McCormick** (Cyrus)
**12** **Boussingault** (Jean-Baptiste)

## aground

**05** stuck **06** ashore, neaped **07** beached, wrecked **08** grounded, marooned, stranded **09** foundered **10** high and dry, on the rocks

## ague

◇ *anagram indicator* **05** exies, fever **07** malaria **10** the shivers

## ah

**02** ay, la **10** alas the day **12** alas the while

## ahead

◇ *juxtaposition indicator* **02** up **05** forth **06** before, onward **07** forward, in front, leading, onwards, winning **08** advanced, forwards, headlong, superior **09** at the head, earlier on, in advance, in the lead, to the fore **13** at an advantage, in the vanguard **14** in the forefront

## aid

**04** ease, gift, hand, help, prop **05** boost, grant, serve **06** a leg up, assist, backup, favour, hasten, oblige, relief, second **07** backing, benefit, charity, funding, promote, relieve, service, speed up, subsidy, succour, support, sustain **08** donation, expedite **09** encourage, lend a hand, patronage, subsidize **10** assistance, facilitate, rally round, subvention **11** accommodate, helping hand, sponsorship **12** contribution **13** a shot in the arm, co-operate with, encouragement

## aide

**02** PA **06** minder, Sherpa **07** adviser, attaché **08** adjutant, advocate, disciple, follower **09** assistant, confidant, supporter **10** aide-de-camp, confidante **12** right-hand man **14** right-hand woman

## ail

**04** fail, pain **05** upset, worry **06** bother, sicken, weaken **07** afflict, trouble **08** distress, irritate **13** indisposition

## ailing

**03** ill **04** poor, sick, weak **05** frail, unfit **06** feeble, infirm, poorly, sickly, unwell **07** failing, invalid, unsound **08** diseased **09** deficient, insolvent, off-colour, suffering **10** foundering, inadequate, indisposed, out of sorts **11** debilitated, languishing **12** in poor health **15** under the weather

## ailment

**03** ill, pip **04** waff, worm **05** cough **06** malady **07** disease, illness, passion **08** disorder, sickness, weakness **09** complaint, infection, infirmity **10** affliction, disability **11** dog's disease **13** indisposition

## aim

**03** end, eye, try **04** bend, goal, gole, hope, mark, mean, plan, sake, seek, vizy, want, wish **05** dream, ettle, level, point, sight, telos, train, visie **06** aspire, course, design, desire, direct, intend, intent, line up, motive, object, scheme, strive, target, vizzie **07** attempt, mission, propose, purpose, resolve, shoot at, take aim **08** ambition, zero in on **09** direction, endeavour, intention, objective **10** aspiration **11** work towards **15** set your sights on

## aimless

**05** stray **06** chance, futile, random **07** erratic, wayward **08** drifting, goalless, rambling, unguided **09** haphazard, pointless, shiftless, unsettled, wandering **10** irresolute, undirected **11** purposeless, unmotivated **13** directionless, unpredictable

## air

**03** sky **04** aero-, aria, aura, ayre, lift, lilt, look, mien, puff, song, tell, tune, waft, wind **05** blast, dirge, ditty, ether, ozone, state, utter, voice, whiff **06** aerate, allure, aspect, breath, breeze, demean, effect, expose, manner, oxygen, reveal, screen, zephyr **07** arietta, bearing, canzona, canzone, declare, demaine, demayne, demeane, divulge, draught, express, feeling, freshen, heavens, publish **08** ambience, carriage, cavatina, disclose, fresh air, serenade **09** broadcast, character, circulate, demeanour, make known, publicize, ventilate **10** appearance, atmosphere, expression, give vent to, impression, make public **11** chansonette, communicate, disseminate, have your say **13** speak your mind
• **air defence** **02** AD
• **Air Transport Association** **03** ATA

## airbed

**04** Lilo®

## airborne

**02** a/b **06** flying **07** winging **08** hovering, in flight, in the air

## aircraft

*Aircraft types include:*

01 B, F
03 jet, MiG
04 Hawk, kite, Moth, STOL, VTOL
05 blimp, Comet, jumbo, Piper, plane, Stuka
06 Airbus®, Boeing, bomber, Cessna, copter, Fokker, glider, Mirage, Nimrod
07 airship, air taxi, balloon, biplane, Chinook, chopper, fighter, Halifax, Harrier, jump-jet, prop-jet, Tornado, Tristar, Typhoon
08 airliner, Blenheim, Concorde, Hercules, jumbo jet, Mosquito, seaplane, Spitfire, spy plane, superjet, triplane, turbojet, warplane, Zeppelin
09 aeroplane, amphibian, aquaplane, Boeing 747, delta-wing, dirigible, freighter, Gipsy Moth, Hurricane, Lancaster, monoplane, swing-wing, Tiger Moth, turboprop, two-seater
10 dive-bomber, hang-glider, helicopter, microlight, Sunderland, Wellington, whirlybird
11 battleplane, de Havilland, Flying Tiger, intercepter, rocket plane, Thunderbolt
12 air ambulance, single-seater, Sopwith Camel, troop-carrier
13 hot-air balloon, Messerschmitt, Stealth Bomber

*Aircraft include:*

04 R101
06 Bell X-1
07 Voyager
08 Enola Gay
09 Winnie Mae
10 Hindenburg
11 Air Force One, Lucky Lady II, Spruce Goose, Wright Flyer
12 Graf Zeppelin, Memphis Belle
15 Spirit of St Louis

*Aircraft parts include:*

03 fin, rib
04 cowl, flap, hood, skid, wing
05 cabin, radar, radio, stick
06 canopy, engine, rudder
07 aileron, ammeter, cockpit, cowling, fairing, tail fin, winglet
08 elevator, fuselage, intercom, joystick, tail boom, turbojet, wing flap
09 altimeter, nose wheel, propeller, tailplane, tail wheel
10 flight deck
11 chronometer, landing flap, landing gear, vertical fin
12 control stick, equilibrator, radio compass, rudder pedals
13 accelerometer, control column, undercarriage
14 radar altimeter
15 landing-carriage, magnetic compass

## aircraftman, aircraftwoman
02 AC 03 ACW, erk, LAC 04 LACW

## air force
03 RAF 04 RAAF, RCAF, USAF, WAAF, WRAF 05 RNZAF, WRAAF 06 RAuxAF 09 Luftwaffe 11 Flying Corps
*See also* **rank**

## airily
07 lightly, readily 08 breezily, casually, jauntily 10 flippantly 12 nonchalantly 14 light-heartedly

## airing
07 venting, voicing 08 aeration, exposure, uttering 09 broadcast, statement 10 disclosure, divulgence, expression, freshening, refreshing, revelation 11 circulation, declaration, making known, publication, ventilation 13 communication, dissemination

## airless
05 close, heavy, muggy, musty, stale 06 stuffy, sultry 08 stifling 10 breathless, oppressive 11 suffocating 12 unventilated 15 badly ventilated

## airline

*Airlines include:*

02 BA, UA
03 BEA, BMI, JAL, KLM, PIA, SAS, TWA
04 BOAC, El Al
05 Pan Am
06 Qantas
07 easyJet, Ryanair
08 Aeroflot, Alitalia
09 Aer Lingus, Air Canada, Air France, Lufthansa
13 Air New Zealand, Cathay Pacific
14 British Airways, British Midland, United Airlines, Virgin Atlantic

## airman
02 AC, AR 03 ace, erk, LAC
*See also* **rank**

## airport
05 drome 08 airfield, STOLport 09 aerodrome, vertiport

*Airports include:*

03 JFK, LAX, Zia
04 Orly
05 Luton, McCoy, O'Hare
06 Cannon, Changi, Dulles, Midway, V C Bird
07 Ataturk, Bradley, D F Malan, Entebbe, Gatwick, Hopkins, Lincoln, Lubbock, Roberts
08 Ciampino, El Dorado, G Marconi, Heathrow, Jan Smuts, La Aurora, McCarran, Mohamed V, Sangster, Schiphol, Stansted
09 Ben Gurion, Charleroi, Fiumicino, James M Cox, J F Kennedy, Jose Marti, Lindbergh, Marco Polo, Queen Alia
10 George Bush, Golden Rock, Hellenikon, John Lennon, King Khaled, Louis Botha, Sky Harbour, Will Rogers
11 Berlin-Tegel, Capodichino, Jorge Chavez, Las Americas, Ninoy Aquino, Owen Roberts, Pointe Noire, Tito Menniti
12 Benito Juarez, Eduardo Gomes, Hancock Field, Indira Gandhi, Jomo Kenyatta, Norman Manley, Queen Beatrix, Simon Bolivar
13 Château Bougon, Chiang Kai Shek, Grantley Adams, King Abdul Aziz, Mariscal Sucre, Robert Mueller
14 Galileo Galilei, Juan Santa Maria, Kingsford Smith, Lester B Pearson, Murtala Mohamed
15 Augusto C Sandino, Charles de Gaulle, General Mitchell, Hamilton Kindley, Leonardo da Vinci, Theodore Francis

## airs
05 gyver, swank 06 frills, posing 07 hauteur 09 arrogance, pomposity 10 snootiness 11 affectation, haughtiness, pretensions 12 affectedness 13 artificiality 15 pretentiousness

## airtight
06 closed, sealed 08 flawless 09 windtight 10 conclusive 11 impermeable, indubitable, irrefutable 12 impenetrable, indisputable, tight-fitting 13 beyond dispute, incontestable 14 beyond question, unquestionable

## airy
04 open 05 blowy, fresh, gusty, happy, roomy, windy 06 aerial, breezy, casual, jaunty, lively 07 offhand 08 cheerful, draughty, ethereal, etherial, flippant, spacious 09 spiritual, sprightly 10 immaterial, intangible, nonchalant, spirit-like 11 incorporeal 12 high-spirited, light-hearted 13 unsubstantial 14 well-ventilated

## aisle
04 lane, path 07 gangway, passage, walkway 08 alleyway, corridor 10 passageway 12 deambulatory

## ajar
04 agee, ajee, open 08 half open, unbolted, unclosed, unlocked 09 unlatched 10 unfastened 12 slightly open

## akin
03 sib 04 like, near, sibb 05 close, sybbe 07 related, similar 08 congener 10 comparable, equivalent 13 corresponding

## Alabama
02 AL 03 Ala

## alacrity
06 ardour 07 fervour 08 keenness 09 briskness, eagerness, readiness 10 enthusiasm, impatience, promptness 11 willingness

## alarm
◇ *anagram indicator* 03 din 04 bell, fear, horn 05 alert, daunt, larum, panic, scare, shock, siren 06 arouse, beat up, dismay, fright, horror, rattle, terror, tirrit, tocsin 07 agitate, anxiety, horrify, perturb, startle, terrify, unnerve,

**alarming**
warning, whistle **08** affright, distress, frighten, Teasmade® **09** alarm-bell **10** make afraid, smoke alarm, uneasiness **11** nervousness, trepidation **12** apprehension, danger signal, perturbation, put the wind up **13** consternation, smoke detector **14** distress signal

**alarming**
**05** scary **07** ominous **08** daunting, dreadful, shocking, worrying **09** dismaying, startling, unnerving **10** disturbing, perturbing, terrifying **11** distressing, frightening, threatening

**alarmist**
**09** doomsayer, jitterbug, pessimist **11** doomwatcher, scaremonger **12** doom-merchant **13** prophet of doom

**alas**
**02** ay **03** out **04** haro, waly **06** harrow **07** welaway **08** waesucks, welladay, wellaway **09** alack-a-day, wellanear

**Alaska**
**02** AK

**Albania**
**02** AL **03** ALB

**albatross**
**10** gooneybird, Quaker-bird

**Alberta**
**02** AB

**album**
**04** disc

**albumin**
**05** ricin **06** myogen **08** leucosin

**alchemist**
**05** adept **06** chemic **08** spagyric **09** spagyrist

**alcohol**
**03** jar **04** bowl, diol, grog, lush, slug **05** booze, drink, juice, mahua, mahwa, sauce, skink, tinct **06** fuddle, gutrot, liquor, sterol, strunt, tiddly, tipple **07** butanol, ethanol, liqueur, mannite, shebeen, spirits, xylitol **08** catechol, farnesol, geraniol, glycerin, glycerol, linalool, mannitol, methanol, propanol, stimulus **09** aqua vitae, firewater, glycerine, hard stuff, the bottle **10** intoxicant **11** jungle juice, sphingosine, strong drink, the creature, tickle-brain **12** Dutch courage, spirit of wine
See also **drink**
• **low in alcohol 04** lite

**alcoholic**
**03** sot **04** alky, hard, lush, soak, wino **05** alkie, bloat, dipso, drunk, souse, toper **06** ardent, boozer, brewed, sponge, strong **07** Bacchus, drinker, tippler, tosspot **08** drunkard, habitual **09** distilled, fermented, inebriate **10** spirituous, wine-bibber **11** dipsomaniac, hard drinker, inebriating **12** heavy drinker, intoxicating
See also **drink**
• **very alcoholic 04** hard

**alcove**
**03** bay **04** nook **05** booth, niche **06** carrel, corner, recess, shrine **07** carrell, cubicle, dinette, opening **09** cubbyhole, ingleneuk, inglenook **11** compartment

**alderman**
**02** CA **03** Ald **09** ealdorman

**Alderney**
**03** GBA

**ale**
**03** nog **04** beer, mild, nogg, purl **05** nappy, swats **06** alegar, tipper **07** morocco, October **08** heavy wet, twopenny **10** barley-bree, barley-broo **11** barley-broth

**alehouse**
see **pub**

**alert**
**04** gleg, warn, wary **05** agile, alarm, awake, brisk, quick, ready, shake, sharp **06** active, inform, lively, nimble, notice, notify, signal, sprack, tip off, tip-off **07** apprise, careful, caution, heedful, wakeful, warning **08** all there, forewarn, prepared, spirited, vigilant, watchful **09** attentive, observant, on the ball, on the spot, sharp-eyed, up to snuff, wide-awake **10** on your toes, perceptive, presential, wake-up call **11** circumspect, sharp-witted **12** notification, on the lookout, on the qui vive

**alertness**
**08** wariness **09** vigilance **10** observance **12** watchfulness **13** attentiveness, perceptiveness **15** sharp-wittedness

**alga, algae**

*Algae and lichens include:*

**05** chara, manna, usnea **06** archil, corkir, crotal, desmid, diatom, korkir, nostoc, volvox **07** crottle, cup moss, euglena, oak lump, parella, seaweed, Valonia **08** anabaena, conferva, frustule, lecanora, lungwort, pond scum, red algae, sea ivory, stonerag, stoneraw, tree moss, Ulothrix, wall moss, wartwort **09** chlorella, cup lichen, Isokontae, rock tripe, spirogyra, stonewort **10** brown algae, Conjugatae, cyanophyte, fallen star, green algae, heterocont, heterokont, rock violet, water bloom **11** blanketweed, Iceland moss, manna-lichen, Protococcus **12** Cyanophyceae, Phaeophyceae, reindeer moss, Rhodophyceae, stromatolite, water flowers **13** chlamydomonas, Protococcales, Schizophyceae, witches' butter **14** blue-green algae, cyanobacterium, dinoflagellate

*See also* **seaweed**

**Algeria**
**02** DZ **03** Alg, DZA

**alias**
**03** aka, née **06** anonym **07** allonym, moniker, pen name **08** formerly, monicker, nickname **09** false name, otherwise, pseudonym, sobriquet, stage name **10** also called, nom de plume, soubriquet **11** also known as, assumed name, nom de guerre **14** under the name of

**alibi**
**05** story **06** excuse, reason **07** cover-up, defence, pretext **11** explanation, vindication **13** justification

**alien**
**02** ET **03** LGM, odd **05** metic **06** exotic, remote **07** foreign, incomer, Martian, opposed, strange, unusual **08** contrary, forinsec, inimical, newcomer, outsider, peculiar, stranger **09** estranged, foreigner, immigrant, non-native, offensive, repugnant **10** extraneous, forinsecal, outlandish, unfamiliar **11** conflicting, incongruous **12** antagonistic, incompatible **14** little green man

**alienate**
**05** sever **06** cut off, devest **07** divorce, turn off **08** amortize, estrange, separate, turn away **09** disaffect **10** antagonize, set against **11** make hostile

**alienation**
**07** divorce, rupture **08** disunion **09** diversion, isolation, severance **10** detachment, remoteness, separation **11** turning away **12** disaffection, estrangement, indifference **14** antagonization

**alight**
**02** in **03** lit, pop **04** fall, land, rest **05** alive, avail, avale, fiery, light, lit up, perch, pitch **06** ablaze, aflame, availe, bright, debark, get off, lively, on fire, settle, strike **07** blazing, burning, descend, detrain, flaming, get down, ignited, lighted, radiant, shining **08** come down, dismount, gleaming **09** brilliant, disembark, touch down **10** come to rest, disentrain **11** illuminated

**align**
**04** ally, even, join, side, tram **05** agree, order, range, unite **06** adjust, even up, line up **07** arrange, combine **08** regulate **09** affiliate, associate, co-operate, orientate **10** co-ordinate, join forces, regularize, straighten, sympathize **12** make parallel

**alignment**
**04** line **05** order **06** lining, siding **07** ranging **08** alliance, lining up, sympathy **09** agreement **10** alineation **11** affiliation, allineation, arrangement, association, co-operation **13** straightening

**alike**
**04** akin, even **05** equal, samey **06** at once **07** cognate, equally, similar, the same, uniform **08** in common, matching, parallel **09** analogous, duplicate, identical, similarly

**10** comparable, equivalent, resembling **11** analogously, much the same **12** in the same way **13** corresponding **15** correspondingly

## alimony

**06** upkeep **07** aliment, support **08** palimony **09** allowance **11** maintenance **12** child support

## alive

**04** live, vive **05** alert, awake, brisk, quick, vital **06** active, chirpy, extant, full of, lively, living **07** alert to, animate, awake to, aware of, in force, running, vibrant, working, zestful **08** animated, existent, spirited, vigorous **09** breathing, energetic, heedful of, on the hoof, surviving, to the fore, vivacious **10** carrying on, full of life, having life, in the flesh **11** abounding in, above-ground, cognizant of, conscious of, functioning, going strong, in existence, in operation, sensitive to, teeming with **12** crawling with, swarming with, thronged with **15** overflowing with

## alkaloid

**06** emetin, harmin, theine **07** atropin, betaine, brucine, caffein, cocaine, codeine, coniine, emetine, harmine, morphia, narceen **08** atropine, caffeine, curarine, cytisine, daturine, harmalin, hyoscine, ibogaine, lobeline, mescalin, morphine, narceine, nicotine, piperine, thebaine, veratrin **09** aconitine, bebeerine, berberine, chaconine, ephedrine, gelsemine, harmaline, mescaline, muscarine, narcotine, quinidine, rhoeadine, sparteine, veratrine, yohimbine **10** apomorphia, cinchonine, colchicine, corydaline, ergotamine, papaverine, pilocarpin, strychnine **11** apomorphine, gelseminine, hyoscyamine, pilocarpine, scopolamine, theobromine, vincristine **15** castanospermine

## all

**01** a' **03** sum **04** each, even, full, just **05** every, fully, quite, total, tutti, utter, whole **06** apiece, entire, the lot, utmost, wholly **07** perfect, totally, utterly **08** complete, entirely, entirety, everyone, greatest, outright **09** aggregate, everybody, wholesale **10** altogether, completely, every bit of, every one of, everything, infinitely, the whole of **11** every single, total amount, whole amount **12** each and every, universality **13** in its entirety
• **at all** **03** any, ava, eer **04** ever **10** oughtlings **14** in the slightest

## allay

**04** calm, cool, ease, stay **05** blunt, check, quell, quiet, slake **06** alegge, allege, lessen, pacify, reduce, smooth, soften, solace, soothe, stanch, subdew, subdue **07** allegge, appease, assuage, compose, mollify, relieve, smoothe, staunch **08** decrease, diminish, moderate **09** alleviate **12** tranquillize

## allegation

**04** plea **05** claim, story **06** avowal, charge **07** surmise **08** averment, citation **09** assertion, statement, testimony **10** accusation, deposition, profession **11** affirmation, declaration **12** asseveration

## allege

**04** aver, hold, urge **05** allay, claim, plead, state, trump **06** affirm, assert, attest, insist, obtend **07** contend, declare, profess **08** maintain **09** alleviate, represent **10** asseverate, put forward

## alleged

**06** stated **07** claimed, dubious, reputed, suspect **08** declared, doubtful, inferred, putative, so-called, supposed **09** described, professed, purported **10** designated, ostensible

## allegedly

**09** dubiously **10** apparently, doubtfully, ostensibly, putatively, reportedly, supposedly **11** purportedly **13** by all accounts

## allegiance

**03** foy **04** duty **06** fealty **07** loyalty, support **08** devotion, fidelity, liegedom **09** adherence, constancy, obedience **10** friendship, obligation, solidarity **12** faithfulness

## allegorical

**06** mystic **07** typical **08** symbolic **09** parabolic **10** emblematic, figurative **11** symbolizing **12** metaphorical **13** significative **14** representative

## allegory

**04** myth, tale **05** fable, story **06** emblem, legend, symbol **07** analogy, parable **08** apologue, metaphor **09** symbolism **10** comparison

## allergic

**06** averse **07** hostile, opposed **08** affected **09** sensitive **11** disinclined, dyspathetic, susceptible **12** antagonistic **14** hypersensitive

## allergy

**08** aversion, dyspathy **09** antipathy, hostility **10** antagonism, opposition **11** sensitivity **14** disinclination, susceptibility

## alleviate

**04** alay, dull, ease, kill **05** abate, aleye, allay, check **06** alegge, allege, deaden, lessen, reduce, soften, soothe, subdue, temper **07** allegge, assuage, cushion, mollify, relieve **08** diminish, mitigate, moderate, palliate **14** take the edge off

## alleviation

**06** easing, relief **07** dulling **08** soothing **09** abatement, deadening, lessening, reduction **10** allegeance, diminution, mitigation, moderation, palliation **11** aleggeaunce, assuagement, consolation **13** mollification

## alley

**03** taw **04** gate, lane, mall, road, walk, wynd **05** close **06** ginnel, marble, street, vennel **07** dead end, passage,

pathway **08** alleyway, cul-de-sac, pall-mall, rope-walk **10** back street, passageway

## alliance

**04** axis, bloc, bond, NATO, pact **05** Anzus, guild, union **06** cartel, league, treaty **07** compact, kinship **08** marriage **09** agreement, coalition, concordat, syndicate **10** connection, consortium, federation, Warsaw Pact **11** affiliation, association, combination, confederacy, partnership **12** conglomerate, consociation, popular front **13** confederation

## allied

**03** wed **05** bound, joint **06** agnate, joined, linked, united **07** cognate, connate, coupled, kindred, married, related, unified **08** combined, in league **09** connected, federated, in cahoots **10** affiliated, associated **11** amalgamated, confederate, hand in glove **12** confederated

## allocate

**04** mete, task **05** allot, allow, issue **06** assign, budget, divide, ration **07** deal out, dole out, earmark, mete out **08** dispense, set aside, share out **09** admeasure, apportion, designate, parcel out **10** distribute

## allocation

**03** cut, lot **05** grant, quota, share, stint, whack **06** budget, ration **07** measure, portion **09** allotment, allowance, giving-out **10** sharing-out **12** distribution **13** apportionment **14** slice of the cake

## allot

**03** lot **04** aret, mete, rate, sort **05** allow, arett, grant, stint, teene **06** affect, assign, budget, divide, ration **07** dole out, earmark, mete out, portion **08** allocate, dispense, set aside, share out **09** admeasure, apportion, designate **10** distribute

## allotment

**03** cut, lot **04** land, plot **05** block, grant, quota, share, stint, whack **06** ration **07** measure, portion, section **08** division **09** allowance, partition **10** allocation, percentage, plot of land **12** distribution **13** apportionment **14** slice of the cake

## all-out

**04** full **05** total **06** utmost **07** maximum **08** complete, forceful, powerful, resolute, thorough, vigorous **09** energetic, full-scale, intensive, undivided, unlimited, unstinted, wholesale **10** determined, exhaustive, forcefully, powerfully, resolutely, thoroughly, vigorously **11** intensively, unremitting **12** determinedly, exhaustively, unrestrained **13** comprehensive, energetically, no-holds-barred, thoroughgoing, unremittingly

## allow

**02** OK **03** let, own **04** give, okay **05** admit, agree, allot, grant, spare

**06** afford, assign, beteem, enable, endure, permit, suffer **07** agree to, approve, beteeme, concede, confess, consent, earmark, provide, warrant **08** allocate, sanction, say yes to, set aside, tolerate **09** apportion, authorize, consent to, give leave, put up with **11** acknowledge **15** give your consent • **allow for 07** foresee, include, plan for **08** consider **09** budget for **10** arrange for, bear in mind, keep in mind, provide for **15** take into account

## allowable
**02** OK **04** okay **05** legal, legit, licit **06** lawful **07** rulable **08** all right, approved **09** excusable **10** acceptable, admissible, legitimate **11** appropriate, justifiable, permissible **12** sanctionable

## allowance
**03** DLA, fya, ICA, JSA, law, lot, RDA **04** diet, feed, mags, size, tare, tret **05** batta, cloff, grant, maggs, quota, ratio, share, stint **06** amount, budget, corody, income, livery, milage, ration, rebate, sequel **07** aliment, alimony, annuity, benefit, bursary, charter, corrody, dietary, leakage, mileage, payment, pension, portion, provand, provend, stipend, subsidy, windage **08** discount, expenses, latitude, pittance, proviant **09** baby bonus, deduction, reduction, risk money, salt-money, strike pay, weighting **10** allocation, assistance, concession, exhibition, husbandage, percentage, privy purse, remittance, table money, toleration **11** appointment, deferred pay, maintenance, pocket money **12** child benefit, contribution, severance pay **15** capitation grant • **make allowances 06** excuse, pardon **07** condone, forgive **08** bear with, consider, overlook **10** bear in mind, keep in mind **15** take into account

## allowed
**02** OK **03** let **04** luit, okay **05** legal, legit, licit **06** lawful **08** accepted, all right, approved **09** of warrant, permitted, tolerated **10** authorized

## alloy
◊ *anagram indicator* **04** bras **05** blend, brass, Invar®, metal, potin, terne **06** Alnico®, Babbit, billon, bronze, eureka, fusion, latten, Magnox®, occamy, ormolu, oroide, pewter, solder, tambac, tombac, tombak **07** amalgam, Babbitt, chromel, mixture, Nitinol, shakudo, similor, tinfoil, tutenag **08** cast iron, compound, electron, gunmetal, Manganin®, Nichrome®, orichalc, pot metal, zircaloy, Zircoloy® **09** admixture, bell-metal, composite, Duralumin®, Dutch gold, Dutch leaf, eutectoid, magnalium, oricalche, pinchbeck, platinoid, shibuichi, type metal **10** constantan, Dutch metal, iridosmine, iridosmium, mischmetal, Monel metal®, mosaic gold, nicrosilal **11** coalescence, combination, cupronickel, white copper **12** fusible metal, German silver, prince's metal

**13** Babbitt's metal, speculum metal **14** Britannia metal, high-speed steel, phosphor bronze **15** aluminium bronze, Corinthian brass
*See also* **metal**

## all-powerful
**05** great **07** supreme **08** absolute, almighty **10** omnipotent, pre-eminent **12** totalitarian

## all-purpose
**08** all-round, flexible **09** adaptable, versatile **12** multi-purpose **14** general-purpose

## all right
**02** OK **03** A-OK, yes **04** cool, fair, fine, okay, safe, well **05** hunky, right, sound, sweet, whole **06** agreed, indeed, secure, unhurt **07** average, healthy, no doubt **08** adequate, passable, passably, suitable, suitably, unharmed, very well **09** allowable, all serene, certainly, hunky-dory, uninjured **10** absolutely, acceptable, acceptably, adequately, definitely, good as gold, good enough, reasonable, reasonably, unimpaired, well enough **11** right as rain **12** satisfactory **13** appropriately **14** satisfactorily **15** unobjectionable, unobjectionably, without question

## allspice
**07** pimento **11** calycanthus **13** Jamaica pepper

## allude
**04** hint **05** imply, infer, refer **06** remark **07** mention, speak of, suggest, touch on **08** intimate **09** adumbrate, insinuate, touch upon

## allure
**02** it, SA **03** air, win **04** coax, draw, gait, lure, mien, pull **05** charm, decoy, tempt, train, troll **06** appeal, cajole, disarm, entice, lead on, seduce, work on **07** attract, beguile, enchant, glamour, win over **08** entrance, interest, persuade, sirenize **09** captivate, fascinate, magnetism, seduction **10** attraction, come-hither, enticement, temptation **11** captivation, enchantment, fascination **13** give the come-on

## alluring
**04** sexy **05** siren **06** taking **07** agaçant, winning **08** agaçante, arousing, engaging, enticing, fetching, inviting, sensuous, tempting, to die for **09** beguiling, desirable, glamorous, seductive **10** attractive, bewitching, come-hither, enchanting, intriguing **11** captivating, fascinating, interesting

## allusion
**04** hint **06** glance, remark **07** comment, mention **08** citation **09** quotation, reference **10** intimation, side glance, suggestion **11** implication, insinuation, observation

## ally
**03** taw **04** join, link, side **05** marry, unify, unite **06** friend, helper, league, marble, team up **07** combine, connect, consort, partner **08** co-worker, sidekick **09** accessory, affiliate, associate,

colleague, supporter **10** accomplice, amalgamate, foederatus, fraternize, join forces **11** collaborate, confederate **12** band together, collaborator

## almanac
**06** annual, Wisden **08** calendar, register, yearbook **09** ephemeris, Whitaker's

## almighty
**04** huge **05** awful, great **06** severe **07** immense, intense, supreme **08** absolute, enormous, terrible **09** desperate, very great **10** invincible, omnipotent **11** all-powerful, exceedingly, plenipotent **12** irresistible, overpowering, overwhelming

## almond
**06** comfit **07** amygdal, praline

## almost
◊ *tail deletion indicator* **03** nie, sub- **04** near, nigh **05** about, quasi- **06** all but, nearly, next to, nighly, nigh on, uneath **07** close on, close to, nearing **08** as good as, nigh-hand, not quite, well-nigh **09** just about, virtually **10** more or less, not far from, pretty much, pretty well **11** approaching, practically **12** pretty nearly **13** approximately

## alms
**05** gifts **06** awmous **07** charity **08** devotion, handouts, largesse **09** donations, endowment **13** contributions

## aloft
**02** up **04** high **05** above **06** high up **07** aheight **08** in the air, in the sky, overhead **12** off the ground

## alone
**03** sad **04** just, only, sola, sole, solo **05** apart, solus **06** lonely, simply, single, singly, solely, unique **07** forlorn, herself, himself, insular, private, unaided, unhappy **08** by itself, deserted, desolate, detached, forsaken, high-lone, isolated, lonesome, rejected, separate, solitary, uniquely **09** destitute, miserable, on your own, on your tod **10** by yourself, cloistered, unassisted, unattended, unescorted **11** exclusively, sequestered, without help **12** single-handed **13** companionless, independently, off your own bat, unaccompanied

## along
**02** on, up **04** down, near **05** ahead **06** beside, next to **07** close to, further, onwards, with you **09** alongside, as company **10** adjacent to, as a partner **11** at the side of • **all along 06** always **07** for ever **10** all the time, constantly **11** continually • **along with 09** including **12** in addition to, not to mention, over and above, together with **14** to say nothing of

## alongside
◊ *juxtaposition indicator* **02** by **04** near **05** aside **06** beside **08** adjacent

## aloof

**03** off **04** cold, cool **05** chill **06** abeigh, chilly, formal, offish, remote, skeigh **07** distant, haughty, insular, stuck-up **08** detached, reserved **09** exclusive, withdrawn **10** antisocial, forbidding, unfriendly, unsociable **11** indifferent, standoffish **12** inaccessible, supercilious, uninterested, unresponsive **13** unforthcoming, unsympathetic **14** unapproachable

## aloud

◊ *homophone indicator* **06** loudly **07** audibly, clearly, noisily, out loud, plainly **10** à haute voix, distinctly, sonorously **12** for all to hear, intelligibly, resoundingly, vociferously

## alpha

**01** A

## alphabet

**05** abcee, absey **06** script **13** criss-cross-row **14** Christ-cross-row

*Alphabets and writing systems include:*

**03** ABC, IPA, ITA
**04** Cree, kana, ogam
**05** Greek, kanji, Kufic, Latin, ogham, Roman, runic
**06** Arabic, Brahmi, finger, Glagol, Hebrew, nagari, naskhi, Pinyin, romaji
**07** Braille, futhark, futhorc, futhork, Glossic, linear A, linear B
**08** Cyrillic, Georgian, Gurmukhi, hiragana, katakana, phonetic
**09** Byzantine, cuneiform, ideograph, logograph, syllabary
**10** Chalcidian, devanagari, estrangelo, pictograph
**11** estranghelo, hieroglyphs
**14** Augmented Roman
**15** Initial Teaching

*Letters of the Arabic alphabet:*

**02** ba, fa, ha, ra, ta, ya, za
**03** ayn, dad, dai, jim, kaf, kha, lam, mim, nun, qaf, sad, sin, tha, waw, zay
**04** alif, dhai, shin
**05** ghayn

*Letters of the English alphabet:*

**01** A, B, C, D, E, F, G, H, I, J, K, L, M, N, O, P, Q, R, S, T, U, V, W, X, Y, Z
**02** ar, ay, ee, ef, el, em, en, es, ex, oh, wy
**03** bee, cee, cue, dee, eff, eks, ell, enn, ess, eye, gee, jay, kay, kew, pee, see, tee, vee, you, zed, zee
**05** aitch
**06** haitch
**07** double-u
**09** double-you

*Letters of the Greek alphabet:*

**02** mu, nu, pi, xi
**03** chi, eta, phi, psi, rho, san, tau, vau
**04** beta, iota, zeta
**05** alpha, delta, gamma, kappa, koppa, omega, sampi, sigma, theta
**06** lambda
**07** digamma, epsilon, omicron, upsilon, ypsilon
**08** episemon

*Letters of the Hebrew alphabet:*

**02** fe, he, pe
**03** bet, heh, het, kaf, mem, nun, peh, qof, sin, tav, taw, tet, vav, waw, yod
**04** alef, ayin, beth, chaf, heth, kaph, khaf, koph, qoph, resh, sade, shin, teth, yodh
**05** aleph, cheth, dalet, gimel, lamed, sadhe, tsadi, tzade, zayin
**06** daleth, lamedh, saddhe, samech, samekh

*Letters of the NATO phonetic alphabet:*

**04** echo, golf, kilo, lima, mike, papa, xray, zulu
**05** alpha, bravo, delta, hotel, india, oscar, romeo, tango
**06** juliet, quebec, sierra, victor, yankee
**07** charlie, foxtrot, uniform, whiskey
**08** november

## already

**05** by now **06** by then, so soon **07** even now, just now, so early, thus far **08** even then, hitherto **09** before now **10** beforehand, by that time, by this time, heretofore, previously **12** so soon as this

## alright

*see* **all right**

## also

◊ *juxtaposition indicator* **03** and, eke, too **04** item, plus **06** as well, to boot **07** besides, further **08** as well as, likewise, moreover **09** along with, including **10** in addition **11** furthermore **12** additionally

## alter

◊ *anagram indicator* **04** turn, vary **05** adapt, amend, emend, shift, tweak **06** adjust, bushel, change, deform, modify, recast, reform, revise, rework **07** antique, convert, disform, distort, improve, qualify, remodel, reshape **08** airbrush, innovate **09** diversify, transform, transmute, transpose **10** manipulate, metaphrase **12** metamorphose **13** make different
• **alter ego** **04** Hyde **06** Mr Hyde

## alteration

◊ *anagram indicator* **05** shift, tweak **06** change **07** massage **08** revision, variance **09** amendment, reshaping, reworking, variation **10** adaptation, adjustment, conversion, difference, emendation **11** reformation, remodelling, vicissitude **12** modification **13** metamorphosis, transmutation, transposition **14** transformation **15** diversification, transfiguration

## altercation

**03** row, wap **04** beef, miff, whid, yike **05** broil, clash, scrap, set-to **06** barney, bicker, breach, breeze, bust-up, dust-up, fracas, fratch, ruffle, square **07** brattle, discord, dispute, punch-up, quarrel, wrangle **08** argument, squabble **09** high words, logomachy **10** dependence, difference, difficulty, dissension **12** disagreement **13** slanging match

## alternate

◊ *hidden alternately indicator* **03** alt **04** vary **05** alter, other **06** change, rotate, second **07** in turns **08** rotating **09** fluctuate, oscillate, take turns **10** every other, reciprocal, substitute **11** alternating, consecutive, every second, interchange, intersperse, reciprocate **13** chop and change, interchanging, take it in turns

## alternative

◊ *anagram indicator* **02** or **05** other, wacky **06** back-up, choice, fringe, option, second **07** another, oddball, unusual **08** alterant, fall-back, recourse, uncommon **09** different, duplicate, selection, surrogate **10** preference, substitute, unorthodox **12** second string **14** nontraditional, unconventional

## alternatively

◊ *anagram indicator* **02** or **06** or else **07** instead **09** otherwise **13** as a substitute **14** on the other hand **15** as another option

## although

**03** and **04** albe, as if, when **05** while **06** albeit, even if, much as, though, whilst **07** howbeit **08** as much as **09** howsoever **10** even though **11** granted that **13** even supposing **15** notwithstanding

## altitude

**03** alt **05** depth **06** height **07** stature **08** tallness **09** elevation, loftiness

## alto

**01** a **03** alt

## altogether

◊ *juxtaposition indicator* **04** alto **05** all-to, fully, in all, joint, quite, slick, whole **06** algate, in toto, wholly **07** algates, all told, in total, overall, totally, utterly **08** all in all, all to one, entirely **09** perfectly **10** absolutely, completely, holus-bolus, thoroughly **12** first and last

## altruism

**06** unself **10** generosity **11** benevolence, disinterest, magnanimity **12** selflessness **13** self-sacrifice, unselfishness **15** considerateness

## altruistic

**06** humane **08** generous, selfless **09** unselfish **10** benevolent, charitable **11** considerate, magnanimous **12** humanitarian **13** disinterested, philanthropic **14** public-spirited **15** self-sacrificing

## aluminium
02 Al

## alumnus
02 OB 06 old boy 07 old girl

## always
02 ay 03 aye, e'er 04 ever 05 still
06 algate, semper, sempre 07 algates,
forever 08 evermore 09 endlessly,
eternally, every time, regularly 10 all
the time, constantly, habitually,
invariably, repeatedly 11 continually,
in perpetuum, perpetually,
unceasingly, unfailingly
12 consistently 13 again and again
14 on each occasion 15 on every
occasion, twenty-four-seven

## amalgam
05 alloy, blend, union 06 fusion,
merger 07 mixture 08 compound
09 admixture, aggregate, synthesis
10 commixture 11 coalescence,
combination

## amalgamate
04 ally, fuse 05 alloy, blend, merge,
unify, unite 06 mingle 07 combine
08 coalesce, compound, intermix
09 commingle, integrate
10 homogenize, synthesize
11 incorporate

## amalgamation
05 blend, union, unity 06 fusion,
merger 07 joining, merging 08 alliance,
blending, compound 09 admixture,
synthesis 11 coalescence,
combination, commingling,
integration, unification
13 incorporation 14 homogenization

## amass
04 gain, heap, pile 05 hoard, store
06 accrue, garner, gather, heap up,
pile up 07 acquire, collect, store up
08 assemble 09 aggregate
10 accumulate, foregather
11 agglomerate, agglutinate

## amateur
01 A 02 Am 03 DIY, ham 04 buff
06 layman 07 admirer, dabbler,
fancier, varment, varmint 08 armchair
09 lay person 10 aficionado,
Corinthian, dilettante, enthusiast
11 afficionado 12 do-it-yourself 15 non-
professional

## amateurish
03 lay 05 crude, hammy, inept
06 clumsy, unpaid 08 bungling,
inexpert 09 unskilful, untrained
10 blundering 11 incompetent,
unqualified 14 unprofessional 15 non-
professional

## amatory
04 fond 05 randy 06 erotic, loving,
sexual, tender 07 amorous, lesbian
10 passionate 11 impassioned
12 affectionate

## amaze
03 wow 04 daze, kill, stun 05 floor,
panic, shock 06 awhape, dazzle,
dismay 07 astound, flatten, stagger,
startle, stupefy 08 astonish, bewilder,
bowl over, confound, gobsmack,

surprise 09 dumbfound 10 disconcert,
strike dumb 11 flabbergast, knock for
six 12 blow your mind

## amazed
05 dazed 06 agazed 07 floored,
stunned 08 startled 09 astounded,
surprised 10 astonished, bewildered,
gobsmacked, speechless
11 dumbfounded, open-mouthed
13 flabbergasted, thunderstruck

## amazement
04 maze 05 shock 06 dismay, marvel,
wonder 08 surprise 09 confusion
10 admiration, perplexity, wonderment
11 incredulity 12 astonishment,
bewilderment, stupefaction
13 consternation

## amazing
◇ *anagram indicator* 06 awsome, far-out,
unreal 07 awesome 08 dazzling,
exciting, fabulous, stunning
09 thrilling, wonderful 10 astounding,
eye-popping, formidable, impressive,
incredible, marvellous, monumental,
staggering, surprising 11 astonishing,
bewildering, jaw-dropping,
magnificent, spectacular 12 awe-
inspiring, overwhelming
13 disconcerting

## amazon
06 virago 09 shield-may 10 shield-maid
12 shield-maiden

## ambassador
05 agent, elchi, envoy 06 backer,
consul, deputy, elchee, eltchi, ledger,
legate, leiger, lieger, nuncio
07 leaguer, leidger 08 advocate,
delegate, diplomat, emissary, minister
09 pronuncio, supporter
10 campaigner 14 representative
15 plenipotentiary

## ambience
03 air 04 aura, feel, mood, tone
05 tenor, vibes 06 milieu, spirit
07 climate, feeling, flavour
09 character 10 atmosphere,
impression, vibrations 11 environment
12 surroundings

## ambiguity
05 doubt 06 enigma, puzzle
07 dubiety, paradox 08 polysemy
09 confusion, obscurity, vagueness
10 double-talk, woolliness
11 ambivalence, double-speak,
dubiousness, imprecision, uncertainty,
unclearness 12 doubtfulness,
equivocality, equivocation 13 double
meaning 14 double entendre

## ambiguous
05 vague 06 double, louche, woolly
07 cryptic, dubious, obscure, unclear
08 confused, doubtful, oracular,
puzzling, two-edged 09 confusing,
enigmatic, equivocal, imprecise,
oraculous, uncertain 10 back-handed,
homonymous, indefinite, multivocal
11 double-edged, paradoxical
12 inconclusive 13 double-meaning,
indeterminate

## ambit
04 area 05 range, realm, scope, sweep

06 bounds, extent, sphere 07 breadth,
compass 08 confines

## ambition
03 aim 04 goal, hope, push, wish, zeal
05 dream, drive, graal, grail, ideal
06 design, desire, grayle, hunger,
intent, object, target, thrust 07 craving,
longing, purpose 08 striving, yearning
09 eagerness, hankering, holy grail,
objective 10 aspiration, commitment,
enterprise, get-up-and-go, initiative
11 what it takes 13 determination
15 fire in your belly

## ambitious
04 bold, hard, keen 05 eager, pushy
06 driven, intent 07 arduous, driving,
emulate, go-ahead, hopeful, zealous
08 aspirant, aspiring, desirous,
exacting, full of go, striving
09 assertive, demanding, difficult,
elaborate, energetic, go-getting,
grandiose, strenuous 10 determined,
formidable, impressive, purposeful
11 challenging, industrious, power-
hungry, pretentious 12 enterprising,
enthusiastic

## ambivalence
05 clash, doubt 08 conflict, wavering
09 confusion 10 hesitation, opposition,
unsureness 11 fluctuation, uncertainty,
vacillation 12 equivocation
13 contradiction, inconsistency
14 irresoluteness

## ambivalent
05 mixed 06 unsure 07 opposed,
warring 08 clashing, confused,
doubtful, hesitant, wavering
09 debatable, equivocal, uncertain,
undecided, unsettled 10 irresolute,
unresolved 11 conflicting, fluctuating,
vacillating 12 inconclusive,
inconsistent 13 contradictory

## amble
04 pace, walk 05 drift 06 dawdle,
ramble, stroll, toddle, wander
07 meander, saunter 09 promenade
10 mosey along, single-foot
11 perambulate

## ambulance
07 pannier 09 meat wagon 10 blood-
wagon

## ambush
04 jump, trap, wait 05 await, lurch,
snare 06 attack, entrap, turn on,
waylay 07 ensnare, forelay, lay wait
08 embusqué, lie perdu, pounce on,
surprise 09 ambuscade, bushwhack,
emboscata, lie in wait, lie perdue,
waylaying 11 lay a trap for 14 surprise
attack

## ameliorate
04 ease, mend 05 amend 06 better,
remedy 07 benefit, elevate, enhance,
improve, promote, rectify, relieve
08 mitigate 09 alleviate 10 make better

## amelioration
04 help 07 benefit 09 amendment,
bettering 10 mitigation, refinement
11 alleviation, enhancement,
improvement 13 rectification

## amenable
**04** open **06** docile **07** pliable, subject, willing **08** biddable, flexible **09** agreeable, compliant, tractable **10** responsive, submissive **11** acquiescent, complaisant, persuadable, responsible, susceptible **13** accommodating

## amend
◇ *anagram indicator* **03** fix **04** cure, heal, mend **05** alter, emend **06** adjust, better, change, modify, reform, remedy, repair, revise **07** correct, enhance, improve, qualify, recover, rectify, redress **08** emendate **10** ameliorate

## amendment
◇ *anagram indicator* **03** ERA **05** Fifth **06** change, reform, remedy **07** adjunct **08** addendum, addition, revision **10** adjustment, alteration, attachment, correction, emendation **11** corrigendum, enhancement, improvement, reformation **12** modification **13** clarification, qualification, rectification

## amends
**07** redress **08** requital **09** atonement, expiation, indemnity **10** recompense, reparation **11** restitution, restoration **12** compensation, satisfaction **15** indemnification
• **make amends** **05** atone

## amenity
**07** service, utility **08** civility, facility, resource **09** advantage **11** arrangement, convenience, opportunity

## America
**01** A **02** Am, US **03** USA **04** Amer **08** Uncle Sam
*See also* **United States of America**

*Countries of the Americas include:*

**04** Cuba, Peru
**05** Chile, Haiti
**06** Belize, Brazil, Canada, Guyana, Mexico, Panama
**07** Bolivia, Ecuador, Grenada, Jamaica, St Lucia, Uruguay
**08** Colombia, Dominica, Honduras, Paraguay, Suriname
**09** Argentina, Costa Rica, Guatemala, Nicaragua, Venezuela
**10** El Salvador, The Bahamas
**15** St Kitts and Nevis
**17** Antigua and Barbuda, Dominican Republic, Trinidad and Tobago
**21** United States of America
**25** St Vincent and the Grenadines

*South American landmarks include:*

**04** moai
**05** Andes, Colca, llano, Plata, Plate, selva
**06** Amazon, Iguaçu, Itaipu, Osorno, pampas, Paraná
**07** Atacama, Ipanema, Orinoco
**08** Cape Horn, Cotopaxi, Titicaca
**09** Aconcagua, Cartagena, Galápagos, Gran Chaco, Itaipu Dam, Patagonia
**10** Angel Falls, Copacabana, Mato

Grosso, River Plate, Salto Ángel
**11** Colca Canyon, Iguaçu Falls, Machu Picchu, Mt Aconcagua, Pico Bolívar
**12** Easter Island, Lake Titicaca, Perito Moreno, Río de la Plata
**13** Atacama Desert, Kaieteur Falls
**14** Cristo Redentor, Tierra del Fuego
**15** Guiana Highlands

• **Central America** **02** CA
• **South America** **02** SA

## American
◇ *dialect word indicator* **01** A **02** Am, US **04** Amer, Yank **06** Yankee, yanqui **08** Jonathan, Uncle Sam **09** stateside
*See also* **president; United States of America**

*Native American peoples include:*

**02** Ge
**03** Fox, Han, Mam, Ofo, Ute, Zia
**04** Adai, Coos, Cree, Crow, Erie, Hopi, Hupa, Inca, Innu, Iowa, Maya, Pomo, Suma, Tewa, Yana, Yuit, Yuma, Zuñi
**05** Aztec, Carib, Creek, Haida, Huron, Inuit, Kaska, Mayan, Olmec, Omaha, Opata, Osage, Sioux, Tache, Wappo, Wiyot, Yupik
**06** Apache, Arawak, Beaver, Bororo, Cayuga, Chiaha, Dakota, Haihai, Haisla, Iquito, Jumano, Kitsai, Konkow, Lakota, Micmac, Mixtec, Mohawk, Mojave, Nakipa, Navaho, Navajo, Nootka, Ojibwa, Oneida, Ottawa, Paipai, Paiute, Pawnee, Pueblo, Quapaw, Santee, Seneca, Toltec, Yakama, Yamana
**07** Arapaho, Atakapa, Bannock, Chibcha, Chinook, Choctaw, Hohokam, Huastec, Ingalik, Koskimo, Koyukon, Kwatami, Mahican, Miskito, Mohegan, Mohican, Nahuatl, Natchez, Secotan, Shawnee, Tlingit, Walapai, Wanapum, Zapotec
**08** Algonkin, Cherokee, Cheyenne, Comanche, Delaware, Iroquois, Kwakiutl, Menomini, Onondaga, Seminole, Shoshone, Shoshoni, Squamish, Tarascan, Yanomamo
**09** Algonquin, Blackfoot, Chickasaw, Menominee, Tuscarora, Winnebago
**10** Athabascan, Athabaskan, Potawatomi, Wallawalla

• **North American** **04** Yank
**06** Yankee **08** Canadian

## American football
*American football teams:*

**11** New York Jets, St Louis Rams
**12** Buffalo Bills, Chicago Bears, Detroit Lions
**13** Dallas Cowboys, Denver Broncos, Houston Texans, Miami Dolphins, New York Giants
**14** Atlanta Falcons, Oakland Raiders
**15** Baltimore Ravens, Cleveland Browns, Green Bay Packers,

Seattle Seahawks, Tennessee Titans
**16** Arizona Cardinals, Carolina Panthers, Kansas City Chiefs, Minnesota Vikings, New Orleans Saints, San Diego Chargers
**17** Cincinnati Bengals, Indianapolis Colts, San Francisco 49ers
**18** New England Patriots, Philadelphia Eagles, Pittsburgh Steelers, Tampa Bay Buccaneers, Washington Redskins
**19** Jacksonville Jaguars

*American-football-related terms include:*

**03** AFC, NFC, NFL
**04** down, flag, pass, play, punt, sack, snap
**05** blitz, block, drive, field, guard, sneak
**06** center, end run, fumble, huddle, pocket, punter, safety, tackle
**07** defense, end zone, lateral, lineman, offense, quarter, rushing, shotgun, time out
**08** fullback, gridiron, halfback, linesman, overtime, receiver, scramble, tailback, tight end
**09** field goal, reception, secondary, Super Bowl, touchdown
**10** completion, cornerback, extra point, linebacker, nose tackle
**11** quarterback, running back
**12** defensive end, interception, interference, special teams, wide receiver
**13** defensive back
**15** run interference

*American footballers include:*

**04** **Camp** (Walter), **Monk** (Art), **Rice** (Jerry)
**05** **Allen** (Marcus), **Baugh** (Sammy), **Brown** (Jim), **Brown** (Paul), **Craig** (Roger), **Elway** (John), **Favre** (Brett), **Fouts** (Dan), **Halas** (George), **Perry** (Joe), **Perry** (William), **Shula** (Don), **Smith** (Emmitt), **White** (Reggie)
**06** **Blanda** (Frederick), **Butkus** (Dick), **Graham** (Otto), **Grange** (Red), **Greene** (Joe), **Hutson** (Don), **Landry** (Tom), **Madden** (John), **Marino** (Dan), **Namath** (Joe), **Payton** (Walter), **Rockne** (Knute), **Sayers** (Gale), **Taylor** (Lawrence), **Thorpe** (Jim), **Unitas** (Johnny)
**07** **Lambeau** (Curly), **Montana** (Joe), **Sanders** (Barry), **Sanders** (Deion), **Simpson** (OJ)
**08** **Campbell** (Earl), **Lombardi** (Vince), **Staubach** (Roger)
**09** **Tarkenton** (Fran)

## American Samoa
**03** ASM

## americium
**02** Am

## amiability
**06** warmth **08** kindness **10** cordiality, likability **11** likeability **12** cheerfulness, friendliness, pleasantness **15** warm-heartedness

## amiable
**04** kind, maty, warm **05** matey, pally, sweet **06** chummy, genial, gentle **07** affable, cordial, likable, lovable **08** charming, cheerful, engaging, friendly, likeable, loveable, obliging, pleasant, sociable **09** agreeable, clubbable, congenial, gemütlich **11** good-natured, warm-hearted **12** approachable, good-tempered **13** companionable **15** easy to get on with

## amicable
**05** civil **07** cordial **08** friendly, peaceful **09** civilized **10** harmonious **11** good-natured

## amicably
**07** civilly **09** cordially, peaceably **12** harmoniously **13** good-naturedly

## amid, amidst
◊ *hidden indicator* ◊ *insertion indicator* **05** among, midst **06** amidst **07** amongst **12** in the midst of, in the thick of, surrounded by **13** in the middle of

## Amin
**03** Idi

## amino acid
*Amino acids include:*

**04** dopa
**06** glycin, leucin, lysine, serine, valine
**07** alanine, glycine, leucine, proline
**08** arginine, cysteine, tyrosine
**09** glutamine, histidine, ornithine, threonine
**10** asparagine, citrulline, domoic acid, isoleucine, methionine, tryptophan
**11** tryptophane
**12** aspartic acid, glutamic acid, phenylalanin
**13** phenylalanine
**14** glutaminic acid

## amiss
◊ *anagram indicator* **02** up **03** ill **04** awry, evil **05** false, wonky, wrong **06** astray, faulty **07** misdeed, wrongly **08** faultily, improper, untoward **09** defective, imperfect, incorrect **10** improperly, inaccurate, out of order, unsuitable **11** out of kilter **13** inappropriate

## amity
**05** peace **06** accord, comity **07** concord, harmony **08** goodwill, kindness, sympathy **10** cordiality, fellowship, fraternity, friendship **12** friendliness, peacefulness **13** brotherliness, understanding

## ammo
*see* **ammunition**

## ammonia
• **derivative of ammonia 05** amide, amine

## ammunition
**04** ammo, mine, shot **05** bombs, round, slugs **06** rounds, shells **07** bullets, rockets **08** grenades, missiles **09** gunpowder **10** cartridges, explosives **11** projectiles

## amnesty
**05** mercy **06** pardon **07** freedom, liberty, release **08** immunity, lenience, oblivion, reprieve **09** discharge, remission **10** absolution, indulgence **11** forgiveness **12** dispensation

## amok
◊ *anagram indicator* **05** crazy, madly **06** wildly **07** berserk **08** frenzied, insanely **09** in a frenzy, violently **12** like a lunatic, on the rampage, out of control **14** uncontrollably

## among
◊ *hidden indicator* ◊ *insertion indicator* **02** in, of **04** amid, with **05** midst **06** amidst **07** amongst, between **12** in the midst of, in the thick of, surrounded by, together with **13** in the middle of **14** in the company of

## amorous
**04** fond, warm **05** kissy, nutty, randy **06** erotic, in love, lovely, loving, sexual, tender, wanton **07** amatory, gallant, lustful **08** lovesick **10** cupidinous, passionate **11** flirtatious, impassioned **12** affectionate

## amorphous
**05** vague **08** formless, inchoate, nebulous, unformed, unshapen **09** irregular, shapeless, undefined **10** indistinct **11** featureless **12** unstructured **13** indeterminate

## amount
**03** lot, sum **04** bulk, come, mass **05** quota, total, whole **06** degree, extent, figure, number, supply, volume **07** expanse, measure, quantum **08** entirety, quantity, sum total **09** aggregate, magnitude
• **amount to 04** come, make, mean **05** equal, run to, spell, total, tot up **06** come to, number **07** add up to, run into, tot up to **09** aggregate, inventory **10** boil down to, come down to **12** correspond to **14** be equivalent to, be tantamount to
• **large amount 03** lot **04** peck, slew, slue, tons
• **small amount 03** tad **04** haet, ha'it, hate, iota, whit

## amphetamine
**04** whiz **05** benny, crank, speed, whizz **06** bomber **07** crystal **10** Benzedrine®, Methedrine®

## amphibian
**04** duck **06** weasel **07** amtrack
*See also* **animal**

*Amphibians include:*

**03** ask, eft, olm
**04** frog, hyla, newt, pipa, Rana, toad
**05** Anura
**06** Anoura, peeper
**07** axolotl, paddock, proteus, puddock, tadpole
**08** bullfrog, cane-toad, mudpuppy, platanna, tree frog, tree toad
**09** Ambystoma, caecilian, green toad, marsh frog, Nototrema, warty newt
**10** Amblystoma, common frog, common toad, edible frog, flying frog, hellbender, horned toad, natterjack, salamander, smooth newt
**11** midwife toad, painted frog, Surinam toad
**12** springkeeper, spring peeper
**14** common treefrog, fire salamander, natterjack toad
**15** arrow-poison frog, common spadefoot

## amphitheatre
**04** bowl, ring **05** arena **06** circus

## ample
**03** big **04** full, good, rich, wide **05** broad, great, large, roomy, wally **06** enough, plenty **07** copious, liberal, profuse **08** abundant, adequate, generous, handsome, spacious **09** expansive, extensive, plenteous, plentiful **10** commodious, sufficient, voluminous **11** substantial **12** considerable, unrestricted **14** more than enough

## amplification
**07** raising **08** addition, boosting, increase **09** expansion, loudening **10** supplement **11** development, elaboration, enlargement **12** augmentation, making louder **13** strengthening **15** intensification

## amplify
**05** add to, boost, raise, widen **06** deepen, expand, extend, louden **07** augment, broaden, bulk out, develop, enhance, enlarge, fill out **08** enlargen, flesh out, heighten, increase, lengthen **09** enlarge on, intensify **10** make louder, strengthen, supplement **11** elaborate on, expatiate on **13** go into details

## amplitude
**04** bulk, mass, size **05** throw, width **06** extent, volume **07** expanse **08** capacity, fullness, vastness **09** greatness, largeness, magnitude, plenitude, profusion **11** copiousness **12** spaciousness **13** capaciousness

## ampoule
**04** vial

## amputate
**03** lop **04** dock **05** sever **06** cut off, lop off, remove **07** chop off, curtail, hack off **08** dissever, separate, truncate

## amulet
**04** juju, tiki **05** charm **06** fetish, grigri, mascot, scarab **07** abraxas, periapt, sea bean **08** churinga, greegree, grisgris, pentacle, talisman **09** toadstone **10** lucky charm, phylactery

## amuse
**04** play, slay **05** charm, cheer, crack, jolly, relax, sport, swing **06** absorb, crease, divert, engage, occupy, please, popjoy, regale, tickle, trifle **07** cheer up, delight, disport, engross, enthral, gladden **08** distract, interest, recreate **09** entertain, make laugh

## amusement
**03** fun, toy **04** game, play **05** flume, hobby, mirth, R and R, sport, swing **06** solace **07** cockshy, delight, Dodgems®, pastime **08** cottabus, flip-flop, hilarity, interest, laughter, pleasure **09** big dipper, diversion, enjoyment, merriment, parish top **10** recreation **11** distraction **12** fruit machine **13** entertainment, scenic railway **15** shooting gallery

## amusing
**03** fun **04** zany **05** a hoot, drôle, droll, funny, jolly, light, witty **07** a scream, comical, jocular, killing, waggish **08** charming, humorous, pleasant **09** diverting, enjoyable, facetious, funny ha-ha, hilarious, laughable, ludicrous, quizzical **10** delightful, recreative **11** interesting **12** entertaining

## amusingly
**07** wittily **09** comically, enjoyably **10** humorously, pleasantly **11** hilariously **12** delightfully **13** interestingly **14** entertainingly

## anaconda
**04** boma **08** sucurujú, water boa

## anaemic
**03** wan **04** lame, pale, poor, tame, weak **05** ashen, bland, frail, livid, pasty, stale **06** chalky, feeble, infirm, pallid, sallow, sickly **07** insipid **09** bloodless, enervated, hackneyed, whey-faced **10** colourless, exsanguine, uninspired, unoriginal **11** ineffective, ineffectual **12** exsanguinous **13** unimaginative

## anaesthetic
**05** local **06** number, opiate, premed **07** anodyne, general **08** epidural, narcotic, sedative **09** analgesic, soporific **10** nerve block, painkiller, palliative **12** stupefacient, stupefactive **13** premedication

*Anaesthetics include:*

**03** gas, PCP
**05** ether, trike
**06** eucain, Evipan®, spinal
**07** Avertin®, cocaine, eucaine, urethan
**08** ketamine, metopryl, procaine, stovaine, urethane
**09** Fluothane®, halothane, lidocaine, Pentothal®
**10** benzocaine, chloroform, lignocaine, nerve block, orthocaine, thiopental
**11** Dutch liquid, laughing gas, thiopentone
**12** cyclopropane, hexobarbital, nitrous oxide
**13** hexobarbitone, phencyclidine
**14** methyl chloride
**15** tribromoethanol

## anaesthetize
**04** dope, drug, dull, numb **06** deaden, freeze **07** stupefy **09** cocainize **10** put to sleep **11** desensitize

## analgesic
**10** painkiller

*Analgesics include:*

**06** Calpol®
**07** aspirin, codeine, Disprin®, Disprol®, menthol, metopon, morphia, Nurofen®, Panadol®, quinine, salicin
**08** Cuprofen®, fentanyl, ketamine, morphine, salicine, stovaine
**09** Calprofen®, co-codamol, ibuprofen, pethidine
**10** diclofenac
**11** aminobutene, Distalgesic®, indometacin, paracetamol, pentazocine
**12** indomethacin, salicylamide
**13** carbamazepine, phencyclidine
**14** phenylbutazone

## analogous
**04** like **07** kindred, similar **08** agreeing, matching, parallel, relative **10** comparable, equivalent, resembling **11** correlative **13** corresponding

## analogy
**06** simile **08** likeness, metaphor, parallel, relation **09** agreement, semblance **10** comparison, similarity, similitude **11** correlation, equivalence, resemblance **14** correspondence

## analyse
◇ *anagram indicator* **04** scan, sift, test **05** assay, judge, parse, study **06** divide, reduce, review **07** dissect, examine, inquire, process, resolve **08** calendar, consider, construe, critique, estimate, evaluate, separate **09** anatomize, break down, criticize, interpret, metricize, take apart **10** scrutinize **11** investigate, phonemicize

## analysis
◇ *anagram indicator* **04** test **05** assay, check, study **06** review **07** anatomy, check-up, inquiry, opinion, sifting **08** division, scrutiny **09** blood test, breakdown, judgement, reasoning, reduction **10** dissection, estimation, evaluation, exposition, inspection, resolution, separation **11** examination, explanation, explication, navel-gazing **13** anatomization, introspection, investigation **14** interpretation

## analyst
**06** prober, tester **07** assayer, chemist **08** analyser, inquirer **09** dissector **10** researcher **12** experimenter **15** experimentalist

## analytical
**07** in-depth, logical **08** analytic, clinical, critical, detailed, rational, studious **09** inquiring, searching **10** diagnostic, dissecting, expository, methodical, systematic **11** explanatory, inquisitive, questioning **13** investigative **14** interpretative

## anarchic
◇ *anagram indicator* **07** chaotic, lawless, riotous **08** confused, mutinous, nihilist **10** disordered, rebellious, ungoverned **11** anarchistic, libertarian **12** disorganized **13** revolutionary

## anarchism
**05** chaos **07** mob-rule **08** disorder, rent-a-mob, sedition **09** mobocracy, rebellion **10** insurgency, ochlocracy, revolution **11** lawlessness **12** insurrection, racketeering

## anarchist
**05** rebel **08** nihilist **09** Bolshevik, insurgent, terrorist **11** libertarian **13** revolutionary

## anarchy
**04** riot **05** chaos **06** mutiny, unrule **07** misrule **08** disorder, nihilism **09** anarchism, confusion, rebellion **10** revolution **11** lawlessness, pandemonium **12** insurrection

## anathema
**04** bane **05** curse, taboo **07** bugbear **08** aversion **09** bête noire **10** abhorrence **11** abomination **12** proscription

## anatomy
**05** build, frame **06** make-up **07** zootomy **08** analysis, topology **09** framework, phytotomy, sarcology, structure **10** dissection **11** composition, vivisection **12** anthropotomy, constitution, construction

*Anatomical terms include:*

**04** bone, hock, limb, oral, vein, womb
**05** aorta, aural, bowel, digit, elbow, gland, groin, helix, ileum, nasal, pedal, renal, spine, uvula, volar, vulva
**06** artery, axilla, biceps, buccal, carpal, carpus, dental, dermal, dorsal, gullet, lumbar, muscle, neural, ocular, septum, tendon, thymus, uterus
**07** abdomen, alveoli, auricle, cardiac, cochlea, gastric, glottis, gristle, hepatic, jugular, mammary, membral, optical, patella, sternum, thyroid, triceps
**08** cerebral, duodenal, foreskin, gingival, ligament, mandible, pectoral, thoracic, vena cava, vertebra, voice-box, windpipe
**09** capillary, cartilage, diaphragm, epidermis, funny bone, genitalia, hamstring, lachrymal, lymph node, pulmonary, sphincter, umbilicus, ventricle
**10** cerebellum, epiglottis, nociceptor, oesophagus
**11** intercostal, solar plexus
**14** Fallopian tubes

*See also* **bone; brain; ear; eye; gland; heart; hormone; mouth; muscle; teeth; vein**

*Anatomists include:*

**04** **Baer** (Karl), **Bell** (Sir Charles), **Dart** (Raymond), **Knox** (Robert)
**05** **Clark** (Sir Wilfred le Gros), **Graaf** (Regnier de), **Monro** (Alexander)
**06** **Adrian** (Edgar, Lord), **Cowper** (William), **Cuvier** (Georges, Lord),

**Haller** (Albrecht von), **Stubbs** (George), **Tobias** (Phillip)
07 **Colombo** (Matteo Realdo), **Galvani** (Luigi)
08 **Alcmaeon**, **Malpighi** (Marcello), **Vesalius** (Andreas)
09 **Bartholin** (Caspar), **Eustachio** (Bartolomeo), **Fallopius** (Gabriel), **Zuckerman** (Solly, Lord)
10 **Herophilus**
13 **Waldeyer-Hartz** (Wilhelm)

## ancestor
04 sire 05 elder 06 father, mother, tipuna, tupuna 07 forbear 08 forebear 09 ascendant, ascendent, grandsire, precursor 10 antecedent, antecessor, forefather, forerunner, progenitor 11 predecessor 12 primogenitor 13 primogenitrix

## ancestral
06 avital, lineal 07 genetic 08 familial, parental 09 inherited 10 hereditary 12 genealogical
• **ancestral image** 04 tiki

## ancestry
04 line, race 05 blood, roots, stock 06 family, linage, lynage, origin, stirps 07 descent, lignage, lineage 08 breeding, heredity, heritage, pedigree 09 ancestors, ancientry, forebears, genealogy, offspring, parentage, whakapapa 10 derivation, extraction, family tree 11 forefathers, progenitors

## anchor
03 fix 04 hook, host, moor 05 affix, berth, tie up 06 attach, fasten 07 bulwark, compère, mooring, mudhook, recluse, support 08 backbone, linchpin, mainstay, make fast 09 anchorman, announcer, presenter 10 foundation, newsreader 11 anchorwoman 15 tower of strength

*Anchors include:*

03 car, CQR, ice, sea
04 navy, rond
05 bower, drift, kedge, sheet, waist
06 drogue, plough, stream
07 grapnel, killick, killock, stocked, weather
08 mushroom
09 admiralty, stockless, yachtsman
12 double fluked

• **lie at anchor** 04 ride

## anchorage
04 cell, road, rode 06 riding

## anchorite
04 monk 05 loner 06 anchor, hermit 07 ascetic, eremite, recluse, stylite 08 solitary 09 anchoress 10 solitarian

## ancient
03 old 04 aged 05 early, first, hoary, passé 06 age-old, antick, bygone, démodé 07 antique, archaic 08 earliest, obsolete, original, outmoded, primeval, pristine, time-worn, world-old 09 antiquary, atavistic, auld-warld, out-of-date, primaeval, primitive 10 antiquated, fossilized, immemorial, primordial

11 prehistoric 12 antediluvian, old-fashioned 13 superannuated 15 as old as the hills

*See also* **city; Egyptian; festival**

## ancillary
05 extra 07 helping 08 adjuvant 09 accessory, auxiliary, secondary 10 additional, subserving, subsidiary, supporting 11 adminicular, ministering, subordinate 12 contributory 13 supplementary

## and
◇ *juxtaposition indicator* 01 'n' 02 an' 03 too 04 also, plus, then, with 06 as well 07 ampassy, besides 08 as well as, by the way, moreover, together 09 along with, ampersand, amperzand, including, what's more 10 ampussy-and, in addition 11 furthermore 12 in addition to, together with

## andiron
03 dog 06 chenet 07 firedog

## Andorra
03 AND

## androgynous
08 bisexual 09 polygamic 10 monoecious 11 monoclinous, protogynous 12 heterogamous 13 gynodioecious, hermaphrodite, male and female 14 androdioecious

## anecdotal
08 everyday, informal 09 narrative 10 unofficial 11 reminiscing 12 storytelling, unscientific

## anecdote
04 tale, yarn 05 story 06 sketch 08 exemplum 09 narrative, urban myth 11 urban legend 12 reminiscence

## anecdotes
03 ana

## anew
◇ *anagram indicator* 05 again 06 afresh, de novo, iterum 07 freshly 08 once more 09 de integro, once again 12 all over again

## angel
03 gem 05 ideal, saint 07 darling, paragon, watcher 08 guardian, treasure 09 nonpareil 13 heavenly being 14 messenger of God 15 divine messenger

*Angels include:*

05 Ariel, Eblis, Iblis, Satan, Uriel
06 Abdiel, Arioch, Azrael, Belial, Mammon, Moloch, Zephon
07 Gabriel, Israfel, Lucifer, Michael, Raphael, Zadkiel
08 Ithuriel
09 Beelzebub

*Orders of angel include:*

05 angel, power
06 cherub, seraph, throne, virtue
08 dominion
09 archangel
10 domination
12 principality

## angelic
04 holy, pure 05 pious 06 divine, lovely 07 saintly 08 adorable, beatific, cherubic, empyrean, ethereal, heavenly, innocent, seraphic, virtuous 09 beautiful, celestial, unworldly 10 cherubical, cherubimic

## anger
03 bug, ire, irk, vex, wax 04 face, fuff, fury, gall, gram, huff, miff, mood, move, nark, pelt, rage, rile, roil, teen, tene 05 annoy, blood, flake, get at, pique, teene, wrath 06 bother, choler, dander, emboil, enrage, madden, monkey, needle, nettle, offend, ruffle, temper, wind up 07 affront, air rage, bluster, chagrin, dudgeon, incense, inflame, kippage, offence, offense, outrage, provoke, rancour 08 bad blood, drive mad, irritate, paroxysm, road rage, vexation 09 aggravate, annoyance, infuriate, make angry 10 antagonism, antagonize, bitterness, conniption, drive crazy, exasperate, fit of anger, irritation, resentment 11 displeasure, indignation 12 boiling-point, drive bananas, exasperation, irritability 13 make sparks fly 14 drive up the wall
• **show anger** 06 bridle

## angle
03 aim 04 bend, edge, face, fish, fork, hook, knee, nook, side, spin, take, tilt, turn 05 coign, crook, elbow, facet, point, quoin, slant 06 aspect, coigne, corner, crotch, direct 07 flexure, outlook 08 approach, gradient, position 09 direction, viewpoint 10 projection, standpoint 11 inclination, perspective, point of view 12 intersection
• **angle for** 03 aim 04 seek 05 go for 07 fish for 08 shoot for, try to get 11 make a bid for 12 seek to obtain
• **angle in botany** 04 axil
• **angle in mining** 04 hade
• **angle of 45°** 05 mitre
• **reflex angle** 02 in

## angler
03 rod 06 fisher, Walton 07 rodster, wide-gab 08 frogfish, monkfish, piscator 09 devilfish, fisherman, goose-fish, piscatrix, Waltonian

## Anglican
02 CE

## angling
see **fishing**

## Anglo-French
02 AF

## Angola
02 AN 03 AGO

## angrily
◇ *anagram indicator* 05 hotly 06 warmly 07 crossly, irately 08 bitterly 09 furiously, stroppily 10 wrathfully 11 indignantly, rancorously, resentfully 12 passionately

## angry
◇ *anagram indicator* 03 hot, mad 04 evil, high, warm, wild, yond 05 black, cross, het up, irate, livid,

moody, radge, ratty, spewy, wrath
**06** bitter, choked, heated, raging,
sullen, sultry **07** annoyed, berserk,
blazing, crooked, enraged, furious,
ropable, stroppy, uptight **08** burned up,
choleric, foribund, hairless, in a
paddy, incensed, moody-mad,
outraged, ropeable, seething,
steaming, up in arms, wrathful **09** in a
lather, in a temper, indignant,
infuriate, irritated, rancorous, raving
mad, resentful, seeing red, splenetic,
ticked off **10** aggravated, displeased,
hopping mad, infuriated, passionate,
stomachful, up in the air
**11** disgruntled, exasperated, fit to be
tied **12** on the rampage, on the
warpath **14** beside yourself
• **make angry 07** incense

## angst
**05** dread, worry **06** stress **07** anguish,
anxiety, tension **08** distress
**09** worriment **10** foreboding,
uneasiness **11** disquietude
**12** apprehension

## angstrom
**01** A

## Anguilla
**03** AIA

## anguish
**03** woe **04** dole, pain, pang, rack
**05** agony, dolor, grief **06** dolour,
misery, sorrow **07** anxiety, torment,
torture **08** distress **09** heartache,
suffering **10** affliction, desolation,
heartbreak **11** tribulation
**12** wretchedness

## anguished
**08** dolorous, harrowed, stressed,
stricken, tortured, wretched
**09** afflicted, desperate, miserable,
suffering, tormented **10** distressed

## angular
**04** bony, lank, lean, thin **05** gaunt,
gawky, lanky, spare **06** skinny
**07** scrawny **08** rawboned **12** sharp-
pointed

## animal
**03** pig **04** wild, zoic **05** beast, brute,
swine **06** bodily, carnal, mammal,
savage **07** bestial, brutish, critter,
fleshly, inhuman, monster, sensual
**08** animalic, creature, physical
**09** barbarian **11** furry friend, instinctive
**13** theriomorphic

*Animals include:*

**02** ai, ox, zo
**03** ape, asp, ass, bay, boa, bok, cat,
cow, dog, dso, eft, elk, ewe, ewt,
fox, gnu, hob, kob, olm, pig, ram,
rat, roe, roo, sai, wat, yak
**04** anoa, anta, arna, atoc, axis, balu,
bear, boma, bull, cavy, colt,
cony, deer, dieb, douc, emys,
euro, eyra, foal, frog, gila, goat,
hare, hart, hyen, ibex, lion, mara,
mare, mico, mink, mohr, mole,
moyl, mule, naga, newt, oont,
oryx, paca, paco, peba, pipa,
pudu, puma, quey, rana, rusa,
saki, scut, seal, seps, skug, stag,

tahr, tegu, tehr, thar, titi, toad,
unau, ursa, urus, urva, wolf
**05** adder, bison, camel, civet, coney,
eland, hippo, horse, hyena, koala,
lemur, llama, loris, moose,
mouse, otter, panda, ratel, sheep,
skunk, tiger, whale, zebra
**06** alpaca, baboon, badger, beaver,
cougar, ermine, ferret, gerbil,
gibbon, impala, jaguar, monkey,
ocelot, rabbit, racoon, walrus,
weasel, wombat
**07** buffalo, caribou, cheetah,
dolphin, gazelle, giraffe, gorilla,
hamster, leopard, opossum,
panther, polecat, sealion, wallaby
**08** aardvark, antelope, elephant,
hedgehog, kangaroo, kinkajou,
mongoose, platypus, reindeer,
sea otter, squirrel, wallaroo
**09** armadillo, orang-utan, polar bear,
wolverine
**10** camelopard, chimpanzee, giant
panda, rhinoceros
**11** grizzly bear
**12** hippopotamus

*See also* **amphibian; ape; beetle;
bird; butterfly; cat; cattle; chicken;
collective; crustacean; deer;
dinosaur; disease; dog; duck; farm;
fish; game; horse; insect;
invertebrate; lizard; mammal;
marsupial; mollusc; monkey; moth;
pig; poultry; reptile; rodent; shark;
sheep; snake; sound; spider;
whale; worm**

*Animal lairs, nests and homes
include:*

**03** den, nid, pen, sty
**04** bike, bink, byre, cage, coop,
drey, fold, form, hive, hole, holt,
nest, sett
**05** earth, eyrie, lodge, shell
**06** burrow, warren, wurley
**08** dovecote, fortress, vespiary
**09** formicary
**11** formicarium, termitarium

*Adjectives relating to animals
include:*

**05** apian, avian, avine, ovine
**06** bovine, canine, equine, feline,
hippic, larine, lupine, murine,
simian, ursine
**07** acarine, anguine, asinine,
caprine, cervine, corvine, hircine,
leonine, milvine, otarine, pardine,
phocine, piscine, porcine,
saurian, sebrine, taurine, tigrine,
turdine, vespine, vulpine
**08** anserine, aquiline, bubaline,
cameline, chthyoid, elaphine,
ichthyic, lemurine, leporine,
limacine, ophidian, pavonine,
sciurine, soricine, suilline,
viperine, vituline
**09** caballine, chelonian, colubrine,
columbine, crotaline, falconine,
hirundine, musteline, ornithoid,
viverrine, volucrine, vulturine
**10** erinaceous, psittacine, serpentine
**11** accipitrine, elephantine,
fringilline, lacertilian

**12** gallinaceous, oryctolagine
**13** rhopalocerous
**14** papilionaceous

*Animal-related terms include:*

**03** ear, egg, eye, fin, fur, leg, paw,
pet
**04** beak, bill, bite, claw, coat, crop,
dock, gill, gula, hoof, horn,
hump, jowl, loin, mane, mate,
prey, rump, tail, teat, tusk, wild,
wing, wool
**05** chine, crest, fangs, feral, moult,
pouch, scale, shell, snout, spine,
sting, trunk, udder, venom
**06** antler, barrel, dewlap, jubate,
mantle, muzzle, thorax, ungula
**07** abdomen, antenna, feather,
flehmen, flipper, gizzard, habitat,
migrate, mimicry, pallium,
segment, withers
**08** coupling, domestic, forefoot,
forewing, halteres, hindfoot,
hindwing, predator, torquate,
ungulate, whiskers
**09** marsupium, oviparous, prehallux,
proboscis, pygostyle, syndactyl,
taligrade
**10** camouflage, gressorial,
ovipositor, viviparous, webbed
feet
**11** compound eye, lateral line,
search image, swim bladder,
waggle dance
**12** forked tongue
**13** electric organ, metamorphosis
**14** startle colours
**15** prehensile thumb

*Female animals include:*

**03** cow, doe, ewe, hen, pen, ree,
sow
**04** gill, hind, jill, jomo, mare
**05** bitch, dsomo, jenny, nanny,
queen, reeve, vixen, zhomo
**06** peahen
**07** greyhen, lioness, tigress
**08** water cow
**09** dolphinet, guinea hen, turkey hen
**10** leopardess, weasel coot

*Male animals include:*

**03** cob, dog, hob, nun, ram, tom, tup
**04** boar, buck, bull, cock, hart, jack,
stag, zobo, zobu
**05** billy, drake, drone, dsobo
**06** gander, musket, old man, ramcat
**08** seecatch, stallion
**09** blackcock
**10** turkey cock
**12** throstle-cock

*Young animals include:*

**03** cub, elt, fry, kid, kit, nit
**04** brit, calf, colt, eyas, fawn, foal,
gilt, grig, joey, lamb, maid, parr,
peal, sild, slip, yelt
**05** chick, elver, owlet, piper, puppy,
scrod, shote, smolt, squab, steer,
whelp
**06** alevin, cygnet, eaglet, gimmer,
grilse, heifer, hidder, kitten,
lionet, piglet, pullet, samlet,
weaner

**07** codling, eelfare, gosling, leveret, pigling, sardine, skegger, sounder, tadpole, wolfkin
**08** brancher, duckling, goatling, nestling, pea-chick
**09** fledgling

*Animals representing years in the Chinese calendar:*

**02** ox
**03** dog, pig, rat
**04** boar, cock, goat, hare
**05** horse, sheep, snake, tiger
**06** dragon, monkey, rabbit
**07** buffalo, rooster, serpent

• **animal display** **03** zoo
**09** menagerie
• **animal's body** **04** soma
• **stock of animals** **04** team, teme
• **tame animal** **03** pet
• **unsuitable animal** **04** cull

**animate**

**04** fire, goad, live, move, spur, stir, urge, wake **05** alive, impel, quick, rouse, spark, vital **06** arouse, buck up, ensoul, excite, incite, inform, insoul, kindle, living, revive, vivify **07** enliven, inspire, quicken **08** activate, embolden, energize, inspirit, vitalize **09** breathing, conscious, encourage, galvanize, instigate, stimulate **10** invigorate, reactivate **11** bring to life

**animated**

◊ *anagram indicator* **03** hot **05** alive, brisk, eager, peppy, quick, vital, zappy **06** active, ardent, chirpy, lively **07** buoyant, chipper, excited, fervent, glowing, radiant, vibrant **08** instinct, spirited, vehement, vigorous **09** ebullient, energetic, sparkling, sprightly, vivacious **10** passionate **11** full of beans, impassioned **12** enthusiastic **15** bright and breezy

**animatedly**

◊ *anagram indicator* **05** mosso **07** briskly, eagerly **08** actively, ardently **09** excitedly, fervently, radiantly, vibrantly **10** vehemently, vigorously **11** vivaciously **12** passionately **13** energetically

**animation**

**02** go **03** pep **04** fire, heat, life, zeal, zest, zing **05** verve **06** action, energy, spirit, vigour **07** elation, fervour, passion, sparkle **08** activity, radiance, vibrancy, vitality, vivacity **10** claymation, ebullience, enthusiasm, excitement, liveliness **11** high spirits **12** exhilaration **13** sprightliness, vivaciousness

**animosity**

**04** feud, hate **05** odium, pique, spite **06** animus, enmity, hatred, malice **07** ill will, rancour **08** acrimony, friction, loathing **09** antipathy, hostility, malignity **10** abhorrence, antagonism, bitterness, ill feeling, race hatred, resentment **11** malevolence

**ankle**

**04** coot, cuit, cute, hock **05** hough, talus **06** tarsus

**annals**

**04** acta **05** fasti **07** history, memoirs, records, reports **08** accounts, archives, journals **09** registers **10** chronicles

**annex**

**03** add **04** join **05** affix, seize, unite, usurp **06** adjoin, append, attach, fasten, occupy, take in **07** acquire, connect, conquer, purloin **08** arrogate, take over **09** extension, mediatize **11** appropriate, incorporate

**annexation**

**07** seizure **08** conquest, takeover, usurping **10** arrogation, occupation **11** acquisition **13** appropriation

**annexe**

**04** wing **08** addition **09** expansion, extension **10** attachment, supplement

**annihilate**

**04** raze, rout **05** erase **06** defeat, murder, rub out, thrash **07** abolish, conquer, destroy, take out, trounce, wipe out **09** eliminate, eradicate, extirpate, liquidate **10** extinguish, obliterate **11** assassinate, exterminate

**annihilation**

**03** end **06** defeat, murder **07** erasure **09** abolition **10** extinction **11** destruction, elimination, eradication, extirpation, liquidation **12** obliteration **13** assassination, extermination

**anniversary**

**04** obit **07** jubilee **08** birthday, yahrzeit **09** centenary, millenary **10** birthnight, centennial, millennium, wedding day **11** bicentenary, bimillenary, octingenary, semi-jubilee **12** bicentennial, quinquennial, sexcentenary, tercentenary **13** novocentenary, octocentenary, quincentenary, tercentennial **14** octingentenary **15** quatercentenary, sesquicentenary

*Anniversaries include:*

**04** D-Day
**05** VE Day, VJ Day
**07** Flag Day
**08** Anzac Day
**09** Canada Day, Empire Day
**10** Burns Night, Victory Day
**11** Bastille Day, Columbus Day, Dominion Day, Oak-apple Day, Republic Day, Waitangi Day
**12** Armistice Day, Australia Day, Discovery Day, Fourth of July, Thanksgiving
**13** King's Birthday, Liberation Day, Revolution Day
**14** Guy Fawkes Night, Queen's Birthday, Remembrance Day, Unification Day
**15** Constitution Day, Emancipation Day, Independence Day

*Wedding anniversaries include:*

**03** fur, tin
**04** gold, iron, jade, lace, ruby, silk, wood, wool
**05** china, coral, fruit, glass, ivory, linen, paper, pearl, steel, sugar

**06** bronze, clocks, copper, cotton, silver, willow
**07** crystal, diamond, emerald, flowers, leather, pottery, watches
**08** desk sets, platinum, sapphire, textiles
**09** aluminium
**10** appliances, silverware
**13** gold jewellery

**annotate**

**04** note **05** gloss **07** comment, explain **09** elucidate, explicate, interpret **10** add notes to **11** marginalize

**annotation**

**04** note **05** gloss **07** comment **08** exegesis, footnote, scholion, scholium **10** commentary **11** elucidation, explanation, explication **12** commentation

**announce**

◊ *homophone indicator* **04** bill, post **05** sound, state **06** advise, blazon, notify, report, reveal **07** betoken, declare, divulge, gazette, give out, publish **08** denounce, disclose, intimate, proclaim, propound **09** advertise, broadcast, make known, preconize, publicize **10** make public, promulgate **12** blazon abroad **14** make a statement **15** issue a statement

**announcement**

**04** card **06** notice, report **07** message, release **08** bulletin, dispatch, handbill, obituary **09** broadcast, giving-out, ipse dixit, publicity, reporting, statement **10** communiqué, disclosure, divulgence, intimation, revelation **11** declaration, information, making known, publication, publicizing **12** making public, notification, proclamation, promulgation **13** advertisement **14** pronunciamento

**announcer**

**02** MC **04** host **06** anchor, herald **07** compère **09** anchorman, messenger, presenter, town crier **10** newscaster, newsreader, speakerine **11** anchorwoman, annunciator, broadcaster, commentator

**annoy**

**03** bug, din, hip, hyp, irk, nag, noy, try, vex **04** fash, gall, hump, miff, nark, ride, rile, roil **05** anger, cross, sturt, tease **06** bother, harass, hassle, hatter, hector, madden, molest, nettle, pester, plague, ruffle, tee off, wind up **07** chagrin, disturb, hack off, provoke, tick off, trouble **08** brass off, contrary, irritate **09** aggravate, cheese off, displease, drive nuts, importune **10** drive crazy, exasperate **11** get your goat **12** drive bananas **13** get on your wick, get up your nose, get your back up, make sparks fly **14** drive up the wall, get your blood up, give you the hump, take the michael **15** get on your nerves, get your dander up

**annoyance**

**04** bind, bore, drag, fash, hump, pain, pest **05** anger, sturt, tease **06** bother, injury, molest, pester, ruffle

**07** bugbear, chagrin, noyance, trouble
**08** headache, irritant, mischief, nuisance, vexation **09** bête noire
**10** harassment, irritation
**11** aggravation, displeasure, disturbance, provocation
**12** exasperation, excruciation **13** pain in the butt, pain in the neck **14** thorn in the side
• **expression of annoyance** **03** dam, dee, god, hey, tut **04** damn, drat, heck, hell, hoot, phew, rats **05** blast, blimy, damme, devil, Jesus, my God!, shoot, waugh **06** blimey, bother, Christ, dammit, shucks, zounds **07** caramba, doggone **08** honestly, hoot-toot **09** cor blimey, do you mind?, good grief, gorblimey **10** hell's bells, hell's teeth, hoots-toots **11** botheration, for God's sake, that's torn it **12** Donnerwetter, for pete's sake **13** Gordon Bennett **14** for Christ's sake, for heaven's sake **15** for goodness sake

**annoyed**
**04** sore **05** angry, cross, fed up, upset, vexed **06** bugged, hipped, miffed, narked, peeved, piqued, shirty
**07** chocker, hassled, in a huff, pig sick, stroppy **08** harassed, in a paddy, provoked **09** indignant, irritated, ticked off **10** brassed off, cheesed off, displeased, driven nuts, got the hump
**11** driven crazy, exasperated

**annoying**
**05** pesky **06** trying **07** galling, irksome, teasing **08** infernal, niggling, tiresome
**09** harassing, intrusive, maddening, offensive, provoking, unwelcome, vexatious **10** bothersome, disturbing, irritating, plaguesome **11** aggravating, importunate, infuriating, pestiferous, troublesome **12** exasperating

**annual**
**06** yearly **07** almanac **08** calendar, register, yearbook
• **annual return** **02** AR

**annul**
**04** undo, void **05** quash **06** cancel, defeat, negate, recall, reduce, repeal, revoke, vacate **07** abolish, cashier, nullify, rescind, retract, reverse, suspend, vacuate **08** abrogate, disannul, dissolve, overrule, set aside
**10** invalidate **11** countermand

**annulment**
**06** defeat, recall, repeal **07** reverse, voiding **08** negation, quashing
**09** abolition, cassation **10** abrogation, rescission, revocation, suspension
**11** countermand, dissolution, rescindment **12** cancellation, invalidation **13** nullification

**anodyne**
**04** dull **05** bland **07** neutral
**08** harmless, innocent **09** analgesic, deadening, innocuous **11** inoffensive

**anoint**
**03** oil, rub **04** balm, daub, nard, oint
**05** anele, bless, salve, smear **06** grease, hallow, ordain, pomade **08** dedicate, sanctify, set apart **09** embrocate, lubricate **10** apply oil to, consecrate

**anomalous**
◇ *anagram indicator* **03** odd **04** rare
**05** freak **07** deviant, unusual
**08** abnormal, atypical, freakish, peculiar, singular **09** eccentric, irregular **11** exceptional, incongruous
**12** inconsistent

**anomaly**
◇ *anagram indicator* **05** freak **06** misfit, oddity, rarity **09** departure, deviation, exception **10** aberration, divergence
**11** abnormality, incongruity, peculiarity **12** eccentricity, irregularity
**13** inconsistency

**anon**
**04** soon **06** coming **07** by and by, shortly **09** quite soon **10** before long
**11** immediately **14** in a little while **15** in the near future

**anonymous**
**01** a **02** an **04** anon, gray, grey
**07** unknown, unnamed **08** faceless, nameless, unsigned **09** incognito
**10** authorless, impersonal, innominate, unattested **11** nondescript, unspecified
**12** unattributed, unidentified, unremarkable **13** unexceptional
**14** unacknowledged

**anorak**
**04** nerd, nurd, spod, wonk **06** cagoul, kagool, kagoul **07** cagoule, kagoule
**11** windcheater **12** trainspotter

**another**
◇ *anagram indicator* **04** more **05** added, extra, other, spare **06** second
**07** further, variant **09** different, some other **10** additional, not the same
**11** alternative

**answer**
**01** a **03** ans, fit, get, key **04** fill, meet, pass, rein, suit **05** agree, match, react, reply, serve **06** fulfil, pick up, refute, result, retort, return **07** conform, resolve, respond, riposte, satisfy
**08** comeback, quick fix, reaction, rebuttal, rescript, response, solution
**09** correlate, get back to, match up to, rejoinder, retaliate, write back
**10** come back to, resolution
**11** acknowledge, explanation, replication, retaliation, unravelling
**12** correspond to **15** acknowledgement
• **answer back** **04** sass **05** argue, rebut **06** retort **07** dispute, riposte
**08** backchat, disagree, talk back
**09** retaliate **10** be cheeky to, contradict
• **answer for** **06** pay for **08** speak for, vouch for **09** engage for, suffer for
**11** be liable for **13** be punished for
• **answer to** **08** report to **09** work under **15** be accountable to, responsible to

**answerable**
**06** liable **07** to blame **08** suitable
**10** chargeable, equivalent
**11** accountable, blameworthy, responsible

**ant**
**05** emmet, nurse **06** ergate, nasute, neuter **07** ergates, pismire, termite

*Ants include:*

**03** red
**04** army, fire, leaf, wood
**05** black, crazy
**06** Amazon, driver, weaver
**07** bulldog, forager, pharaoh, soldier
**08** honeydew
**09** black lawn, carpenter, harvester
**10** leaf-cutter
**12** red harvester

**antagonism**
**06** enmity **07** discord, ill will, rivalry
**08** conflict, friction **09** animosity, antipathy, hostility **10** antibiosis, contention, dissension, ill feeling, opposition, oppugnancy

**antagonist**
**03** foe **04** peer **05** enemy, rival
**08** opponent **09** adversary, contender
**10** competitor, contestant

**antagonistic**
**06** averse **07** adverse, hostile, opposed
**08** opponent **10** at variance, unfriendly
**11** adversarial, belligerent, conflicting, contentious, ill-disposed
**12** incompatible

**antagonize**
**03** bug **04** miff, rile **05** anger, annoy, get at, repel **06** insult, needle, nettle, offend, wind up **07** incense, provoke
**08** alienate, drive mad, embitter, estrange, irritate **09** aggravate, disaffect
**10** drive crazy **12** drive bananas
**13** make sparks fly **14** drive up the wall

**Antarctica**
**03** ATA

**Antarctic animal**
**07** Penguin

**antbear**
**08** aardvark, tamanoir
**12** Myrmecophaga

**anteater**
**05** Manis **07** echidna, tamandu
**08** aardvark, pangolin, tamandua

**antecedent**
**04** race **05** blood, roots, stock **06** stirps, tipuna, tupuna **08** ancestor, forebear
**09** genealogy, precedent, preceding, precursor **10** extraction, forefather, forerunner, prevenient, progenitor
**11** preparatory

**antedate**
**07** precede, predate, prevene
**08** antecede, go before **10** come before

**antediluvian**
**03** old **05** early, passé **06** bygone, old hat **07** archaic **08** outmoded
**10** antiquated **11** out of the Ark **15** as old as the hills

**antelope**

*Antelopes include:*

**03** bok, doe, gnu, kid, kob
**04** kudu, oryx, puku, suni, thar, topi
**05** addax, bubal, chiru, eland, goral, nagor, nyala, oribi, sable, saiga, sasin, serow
**06** bosbok, dik-dik, duiker, duyker, dzeren, impala, inyala, koodoo,

lechwe, nilgai, nilgau, pygarg, reebok
07 blaubok, blesbok, bloubok, bubalis, chamois, chikara, gazelle, gemsbok, gerenuk, grysbok, madoqua, nylghau, sassaby
08 Antilope, bontebok, boschbok, bushbuck, palebuck, reedbuck, steenbok, tsessebe
09 blackbuck, sitatunga, situtunga, springbok, steinbock, tragelaph, waterbuck
10 Alcelaphus, hartebeest, ox-antelope, wildebeest
11 zebra duiker
12 goat-antelope, klipspringer
13 sable antelope

## antenna
04 horn 06 aerial, feeler

## anteroom
04 hall 05 foyer, lobby, porch
09 vestibule 11 antechamber, waiting-room 12 entrance hall, voiding-lobby

## anthem
04 hymn, song 05 chant, motet, paean, psalm 06 motett, waiata 07 chorale, introit 08 antiphon, canticle, isodicon
10 responsory 12 Marseillaise, song of praise

## anthology
06 digest 07 omnibus 08 treasury
09 selection, spicilege 10 collection, compendium, miscellany
11 compilation, florilegium
12 chrestomathy

## Anthony
04 Tony

## anthrax
04 sang

## anthropology
09 ethnology

*Anthropologists include:*

04 **Boas** (Franz), **Buck** (Sir Peter), **Mead** (Margaret)
05 **Hiroa** (Te Rangi), **Tylor** (Sir Edward)
06 **Frazer** (Sir J G), **Leakey** (Louis), **Marett** (R R)
07 **Métraux** (Albert)
09 **Heyerdahl** (Thor)
10 **Malinowski** (Bronislaw)
11 **Lévi-Strauss** (Claude)
14 **Radcliffe-Brown** (Alfred)

## antibiotic

*Antibiotics include:*

05 Cipro®
07 allicin
08 neomycin, nystatin
09 avoparcin, kanamycin, Neosporin®, polymyxin, quinolone
10 ampicillin, Aureomycin®, bacitracin, gramicidin, lincomycin, meticillin, penicillin, polymyxin B, rifampicin, Terramycin®, vancomycin
11 amoxicillin, amoxycillin, clindamycin, cloxacillin, cycloserine, doxorubicin,

doxycycline, fusidic acid, methicillin
12 erythromycin, griseofulvin, streptomycin, tetracycline, trimethoprim
13 cephalosporin, ciprofloxacin, co-trimoxazole, metronidazole, spectinomycin, virginiamycin
15 chloramphenicol, oxytetracycline

## antibody
03 MAB 06 reagin 10 agglutinin, amboceptor, immune body, precipitin
13 isoagglutinin

## antic
04 dido 05 caper, clown 07 buffoon
09 fantastic, grotesque 10 mountebank

## Antichrist
08 man of sin, the Beast 10 lawless one

## anticipate
05 await, guess 06 bank on, expect
07 count on, foresee, hope for, look for, obviate, precede, predict, pre-empt, prepare, prevene, prevent
08 antedate, beat to it, figure on, forecast, preclude, reckon on
09 apprehend, count upon, forestall, intercept 10 prepare for
11 preoccupate, second-guess, think likely 13 look forward to

## anticipation
04 hope, type 08 forecast 09 foretaste, intuition, prejudice, prolepsis
10 excitement, expectancy, prediction, prevention 11 bated breath, expectation, preparation
12 apprehension, presentiment

## anticlimax
06 bathos, fiasco 07 let-down
08 comedown, non-event 09 damp squib 14 disappointment

## antics
06 capers, doings, pranks, stunts, tricks
07 foolery, frolics 08 clowning, mischief 09 horseplay, silliness
10 buffoonery, shenanigan, skylarking, tomfoolery 11 playfulness, shenanigans 12 monkey-tricks

## antidote
04 cure 05 serum 06 bezoar, remedy, senega 07 theriac, treacle 08 naloxone, Orvietan, theriaca 09 antitoxin, antivenin 10 corrective, mithridate
11 contrayerva, dimercaprol, neutralizer 12 alexipharmic, counter-agent 13 counter-poison, Venice treacle 14 alexipharmakon, countermeasure

## Antigua and Barbuda
03 ATG

## antimony
02 Sb

## antipathy
04 hate 05 odium 06 animus, enmity, hatred 07 allergy, disgust, dislike, ill will 08 aversion, bad blood, distaste, dyspathy, loathing 09 animosity, hostility, repulsion 10 abhorrence, antagonism, opposition, repugnance
15 incompatibility

## antiquated
05 dated, passé 06 bygone, démodé, fogram, fossil, old hat 07 ancient, archaic, outworn 08 obsolete, outdated, outmoded 09 out-of-date, primitive 10 fossilized 11 on the way out, prehistoric 12 antediluvian, old-fashioned 13 anachronistic, prehistorical

## antique
◇ *archaic word indicator* 03 old 05 curio, relic 06 bygone, quaint, rarity
07 ancient, archaic, veteran, vintage
08 Egyptian, heirloom, obsolete, outdated 09 antiquity, curiosity
10 antiquated 11 antiquarian, museum piece, period piece 12 old-fashioned
13 object of virtu 14 collector's item

*Antiques-related terms include:*

04 Goss, Ming, ring, T'ang
05 glaze, ivory
06 barock, dealer, empire, Gothic, lustre, patina, period, rococo
07 art deco, auction, barocco, baroque, ceramic, federal, impasto, opaline, pilgrim, pottery, Tiffany
08 filigree, Georgian, Jacobean, majolica, Sheraton, trecento
09 bone china, collector, Delftware, Edwardian, porcelain, Queen Anne, soft paste, stoneware, valuation, Victorian
10 art nouveau, millefiori
11 chinoiserie, Chippendale, cinquecento, haute époque, Hepplewhite, period piece, restoration
12 antiques fair, arts and craft, blanc de Chine, blue and white, reproduction, transitional
13 willow pattern
15 churrigueresque

## antiquity
03 age, eld 06 old age 07 oldness
08 agedness 09 ancientry, olden days
10 days of yore 11 ancientness, distant past 12 ancient times 14 time immemorial

## antiseptic
04 pure 05 clean 07 aseptic, sterile
08 cleanser, germ-free, hygienic, purifier, sanitary 09 germicide, medicated, mouthwash, sanitized
10 sterilized, unpolluted 11 bactericide
12 disinfectant 14 uncontaminated

*Antiseptics include:*

03 TCP®
05 eupad, eusol
06 cresol, Dettol®, flavin, formol, phenol, Savlon®, thymol
07 benzoin, flavine
08 creasote, creosote, formalin, iodoform
09 cassareep, cassaripe, cetrimide, Germolene®, Listerine®, merbromin, zinc oxide
10 acriflavin
11 acriflavine
12 carbolic acid, methyl violet
13 chlorhexidine, crystal violet,

flowers of zinc, gentian violet, silver nitrate
14 Dakin's solution, rubbing alcohol, sodium benzoate, sodium chlorate
15 hexachlorophane, hexachlorophene

## antisocial
07 asocial, hostile, lawless 08 anarchic, reserved, retiring 09 alienated, withdrawn 10 disorderly, disruptive, rebellious, unfriendly, unsociable 11 belligerent 12 antagonistic, misanthropic, unacceptable 13 unforthcoming 14 unapproachable 15 uncommunicative

## antisubmarine
02 AS

## antithesis
07 reverse 08 contrast, converse, opposite, reversal 10 opposition 13 contradiction 15 opposite extreme

## antithetical
07 opposed 08 clashing, contrary, opposing 11 conflicting 12 incompatible, in opposition 13 contradictory 14 irreconcilable

## antler
04 horn 08 staghorn 09 hartshorn

## Antony
04 Tony

## anxiety
03 tiz 04 bogy, care, cark, fear, rack, stew 05 angst, bogey, dread, sweat, tizzy, worry 06 fantad, fantod, hang-up, nerves, strain, stress 07 anguish, bugaboo, bugbear, concern, fantads, fanteeg, fantods, jitters, tension, thought, willies 08 disquiet, distress, fantigue, suspense 09 dysthymia, misgiving, worriment 10 foreboding, impatience, solicitude, uneasiness 11 butterflies, disquietude, fretfulness, nervousness 12 apprehension, collywobbles, hypochondria, restlessness 13 consternation, heebie-jeebies 14 solicitousness
See also **phobia**
• **free from anxiety** 04 ease

## anxious
◇ *anagram indicator* 04 keen, taut, toey 05 eager, het up, hinky, tense, upset 06 afraid, uneasy 07 careful, fearful, fretful, in a stew, jittery, longing, nervous, uptight, worried 08 desirous, dismayed, in a tizzy, insecure, restless, tortured, troubled, yearning 09 concerned, desperate, disturbed, expectant, ill at ease, impatient, on the rack, tormented 10 distressed, in suspense, solicitous 11 overwrought 12 apprehensive, enthusiastic 13 grandmotherly, on tenterhooks 14 hot and bothered, valetudinarian 15 a bundle of nerves

## anxiously
07 tensely 08 uneasily 09 fearfully, fretfully, nervously 10 restlessly 11 impatiently, tormentedly 12 solicitously 14 apprehensively

## any
03 ary, one 04 a few, some 05 arrow, at all 06 a bit of 09 whichever 10 a single one, in the least 11 the least bit, to any extent 12 to some extent

## anybody
03 one

## anyhow
◇ *anagram indicator* 06 anyway 07 anyways 08 at random, untidily 09 at any rate, in any case 10 carelessly, in any event, not in order, regardless 11 at all events, haphazardly 12 nevertheless, no matter what 13 indifferently

## anyone
03 you

## anything
03 owt 05 ought

## anyway
◇ *anagram indicator* 06 anyhow 07 anyroad 09 in any case 10 in any event, regardless 11 at all events 12 nevertheless, no matter what

## apace
04 fast 07 hastily, quickly, rapidly, swiftly 08 speedily 10 at top speed 11 at full speed, double-quick 12 without delay

## apart
◇ *anagram indicator* 04 afar, away 05 alone, aloof, aside 06 beside, cut off, in bits, singly, to bits 07 asunder, distant 08 by itself, distinct, divorced, excluded, in bits, isolated, separate, to pieces 09 into parts, on your own, piecemeal, privately, separated, to one side 10 by yourself, separately 11 not together 12 individually 13 independently
• **apart from** 04 save 06 beyond, but for, except 07 besides, outside 08 excepted 09 aside from, except for, excluding 11 not counting

## apartment
03 apt, pad 04 flat, gaff, room, unit 05 bower, condo, split 06 duplex walk-up 07 chamber, mansion 08 home unit, paradise, tenement 11 condominium 12 privy chamber 13 accommodation 15 duplex apartment
See also **room**

## apathetic
04 cold, cool, numb 05 blasé, ho-hum 07 passive, unmoved 08 listless, lukewarm 09 impassive, lethargic, unfeeling 10 insouciant, uninvolved 11 emotionless, half-hearted, indifferent, unambitious, unconcerned, unemotional 12 uninterested, unresponsive

## apathy
06 acedia, torpor 07 accidie, inertia, languor 08 coldness, coolness, lethargy 09 passivity, unconcern 11 impassivity 12 indifference, listlessness, sluggishness 13 insensibility, lack of concern 14 lack of interest

## ape
04 copy, echo, mock 05 magot, mimic 06 affect, mirror, parody, parrot, send up, simian 07 imitate, take off 09 proconsul 10 anthropoid, caricature, jackanapes, troglodyte 11 counterfeit
See also **animal; monkey; primate**

Apes include:

05 chimp, drill, jocko, orang, pigmy, pongo, pygmy, satyr
06 baboon, bonobo, chacma, dog-ape, gelada, gibbon, monkey, wou-wou, wow-wow
07 gorilla, hoolock, macaque, siamang
08 hylobate, mandrill
09 hamadryad, orang-utan
10 chimpanzee, silverback
11 orang-outang
12 Cynocephalus, ourang-outang, paranthropus
13 Kenyapithecus
15 pygmy chimpanzee

## aperture
03 eye, gap 04 hole, rent, slit, slot, vent 05 chink, cleft, crack, light, mouth, space 06 breach, choana, oscule, rictus, throat, window 07 fissure, foramen, opening, orifice, osculum, passage, punctum, swallow 08 fenestra, overture, punctule 09 sight-hole 10 interstice 11 perforation 14 counter-opening

## apex
03 tip, top 04 acme, peak 05 crest, crown, point 06 apogee, climax, height, summit, vertex, zenith 08 pinnacle 09 fastigium, high point 10 apotheosis, pyramidion 11 culmination 12 consummation 13 crowning point

## aphid, aphis
06 ant cow 08 blackfly, greenfly 09 bark-louse 10 dolphin-fly, plant louse, smother-fly

## aphorism
03 saw 05 adage, axiom, gnome, maxim 06 dictum, saying 07 epigram, precept, proverb 08 sentence 09 witticism 10 apophthegm, whakatauki

## aphrodisiac
06 erotic 07 amative, amatory, philter, philtre 08 venerous 09 cantharis, erogenous, stimulant, venereous 10 love potion, Spanish fly 11 erotogenous, stimulative

## Aphrodite
05 Venus

## apiece
03 all 04 each 06 singly 07 per head 09 per capita, per person 10 separately 12 individually, respectively

## aplomb
05 poise 08 calmness, coolness 09 assurance, composure, sangfroid 10 confidence, equanimity 11 savoir-faire 13 self-assurance 14 self-

confidence, self-possession, unflappability

## apocryphal
**06** made-up **07** dubious **08** doubtful, fabulous, mythical, spurious **09** concocted, equivocal, imaginary, legendary **10** fabricated, fictitious, unverified **11** unsupported **12** questionable **15** unauthenticated, unsubstantiated

*Apocryphal books of the Bible include:*

**03** Bar, Esd, Jud, Sir, Sus, Tob
**04** Macc, Wisd
**05** Tobit (Book of)
**06** Baruch (Book of), Ecclus, Esdras (Books of), Judith (Book of)
**07** Pr of Man, Susanna (History of)
**08** Bel and Dr, Manasseh (Prayer of)
**09** Maccabees
**14** Ecclesiasticus (Book of)
**15** Bel and the Dragon, Wisdom of Solomon (Book of)

*See also* **Bible**

## apologetic
**05** sorry **06** rueful **08** contrite, penitent **09** regretful, repentant **10** excusatory, remorseful

## apologetically
**08** ruefully **10** contritely, penitently **11** regretfully, repentantly **12** remorsefully

## apologia
**07** defence **08** argument **11** explanation, explication, vindication

## apologist
**06** backer **08** advocate, defender, endorser, upholder **09** supporter **10** vindicator

## apologize
**05** plead **06** grovel, regret **07** confess, explain, justify **08** say sorry **09** ask pardon **11** acknowledge **12** be apologetic, eat humble pie, eat your words **14** ask forgiveness, say you are sorry

## apology
**04** oops, plea **05** sorry **06** excuse **07** defence, mockery, regrets **08** excuse me, pardon me, travesty **10** caricature, confession, corruption, distortion, palliation **11** explanation, saying sorry, vindication **12** poor specimen **13** justification **14** poor substitute **15** acknowledgement

## apoplectic
**03** mad **04** high **05** cross, irate, livid, moody, radge, ratty, spewy, wrath, wroth **06** bitter, choked, raging, sullen, sultry **07** annoyed, crooked, enraged, furious, ropable, stroppy, uptight **08** burned up, choleric, foribund, hairless, in a paddy, incensed, outraged, seething, up in arms, wrathful **09** in a lather, in a temper, indignant, irritated, rancorous, raving mad, resentful, seeing red, splenetic, ticked off, very angry **10** hopping mad, infuriated, passionate, up in the air

**11** disgruntled, exasperated, fit to be tied **12** on the rampage, on the warpath **14** beside yourself

## apostasy
**06** heresy **07** perfidy, rattery, ratting **09** defection, desertion, falseness, recreance, recreancy, treachery **10** disloyalty, renegation **12** renunciation **13** faithlessness **14** unfaithfulness

## apostate
**03** rat **07** heretic, traitor **08** defector, deserter, recreant, renegade, runagate, turncoat **10** recidivist **13** tergiversator

## apostle
**07** pioneer, teacher **08** advocate, champion, crusader, disciple, preacher, reformer **09** apologist, messenger, proponent, supporter **10** evangelist, missionary **12** proselytizer

*Apostles of Jesus Christ:*

**04** John
**05** James, Judas, Peter, Simon
**06** Andrew, Philip, Thomas
**07** Matthew
**08** Matthias, Thaddeus
**11** Bartholomew
**13** Judas Iscariot
**14** Simon the Zealot
**15** James of Alphaeus
**17** Simon the Canaanite

## apotheosis
**03** tip **04** acme, apex, peak **05** crest, crown, point **06** apogee, climax, height, summit, vertex, zenith **08** pinnacle **09** fastigium, high point **11** culmination, deification **12** consummation **13** crowning point, glorification

## appal
**05** alarm, daunt, scare, shock **06** dismay **07** disgust, horrify, outrage, terrify, unnerve **08** frighten **10** disconcert, intimidate

## appalling
◇ *anagram indicator* **04** dire, grim, naff, poor, ropy **05** awful, lousy, pants, ropey **06** horrid **07** ghastly, hideous, the pits, very bad **08** alarming, daunting, dreadful, hopeless, horrible, horrific, inferior, pathetic, shocking, terrible **09** atrocious, frightful, harrowing, loathsome, unnerving **10** disgusting, horrifying, inadequate, outrageous, terrifying **11** frightening, nightmarish **12** intimidating, unacceptable **14** unsatisfactory

## appallingly
◇ *anagram indicator* **07** awfully **08** horribly, terribly **09** hideously **10** dreadfully, hopelessly, shockingly **11** frightfully **12** horrifically, pathetically, unacceptably

## apparatus
**03** rig **04** bank, gear, tool **05** means, set-up, tools **06** device, gadget, outfit, system, tackle **07** machine, network **08** utensils **09** appliance, equipment, framework, implement, machinery,

materials, mechanism, structure **10** implements, instrument **11** contraption
*See also* **laboratory**

## apparel
**03** kit **04** garb, gear, tire, togs **05** besee, dress, get-up, weeds **06** attire, outfit, robing, vestry **07** clobber, clothes, costume, raiment, vesture **08** clothing, garments, wardrobe **09** garniture **11** habiliments

## apparent
◇ *hidden indicator* **02** ap **03** app **04** open **05** clear, overt, plain **06** marked, patent **07** evident, obvious, outward, seeming, visible **08** declared, distinct, manifest **10** detectable, noticeable, ostensible **11** conspicuous, perceptible, superficial **12** unmistakable **13** be standing out

## apparently
**02** ap **03** app **07** clearly, plainly **08** patently **09** evidently, obviously, outwardly, reputedly, seemingly **10** manifestly, ostensibly **12** on the surface **13** on the face of it, superficially

## apparition
**05** fetch, ghost, shape, spook, taish **06** double, spirit, taisch, vision, wraith **07** chimera, eidolon, gytrash, phantom, specter, spectre **08** illusion, manifest, phantasm, presence, visitant **09** hobgoblin, semblance **10** appearance **12** doppelgänger **13** manifestation **15** materialization

## appeal
**02** it, SA **03** ask, beg, cry, SOS, sue **04** call, draw, lure, peal, pele, plea, pray, suit **05** apply, charm, claim, oomph, plead, tempt **06** allure, ask for, avouch, beauty, call on, engage, entice, invite, invoke, orison, please, prayer, review **07** address, attract, beseech, entreat, implore, provoke, reclaim, request, retrial, solicit **08** approach, call upon, charisma, entreaty, interest, petition **09** fascinate, magnetism **10** adjuration, attraction, invocation, recusation, supplicate **11** application, conjuration, enchantment, fascination, imploration, winsomeness **12** re-evaluation, solicitation, supplication **13** re-examination **14** attractiveness **15** reconsideration
• **solemn appeal 04** oath

## appealing
**07** winning, winsome **08** alluring, charming, engaging, enticing, inviting, magnetic, pleasing, tempting **10** attractive, enchanting **11** charismatic, fascinating, interesting

## appear
◇ *homophone indicator* **03** act, eye **04** go on, look, loom, peer, play, rise, seem, shew, show, star **05** arise, bob up, break, enter, issue, kithe, kythe, occur, pop up **06** arrive, attend, cast up, co-star, crop up, emerge, figure, show up, spring, turn up **07** come out, compear, develop, front up, perform,

surface, topline, turn out **08** platform, take part **09** be on stage, be present, come along **10** be a guest in **11** be published, come to light, materialize, show signs of **12** come across as, come into view, show your face **13** become visible, come into sight **14** take the guise of **15** become available
• **begin to appear** **03** ope **04** open

**appearance**
**03** air, hew, hue **04** broo, brow, face, form, garb, look, mien, rise, show, view **05** debut, front, ghost, guise, image, looks **06** advent, aspect, coming, effair, effere, façade, figure, manner, ostent, visage **07** arrival, bearing, outward **08** exterior, illusion, presence, pretence **09** appearing, demeanour, emergence, semblance **10** apparition, attendance, complexion, expression, impression **11** outward form **12** introduction **14** coming into view
• **final appearance** **08** swansong
• **personal appearance** **02** PA

**appease**
**04** stay **05** allay, atone, quiet, still **06** aslake, attone, defray, pacify, soothe **07** mollify, placate, qualify, satisfy **08** mitigate **09** reconcile **10** conciliate, propitiate **13** make peace with

**appeasement**
**09** placation **11** peacemaking **12** conciliation, pacification, satisfaction **14** reconciliation

**appellation**
**04** name **05** title **07** epithet **08** monicker, nickname **09** most noble, sobriquet **10** soubriquet **11** description, designation **12** compellation, denomination

**append**
◇ *juxtaposition indicator* **03** add, put, tag **04** join **05** affix, annex **06** adjoin, attach, fasten, tack on **07** conjoin, subjoin **08** pickback **09** pickaback, pickapack, piggyback

**appendage**
**03** lug **04** aril **05** affix, aglet, whisk **06** aiglet, arista, barbel, cercus, stipel, uropod **07** adjunct, arillus, auricle, foretop, maxilla, stipule **08** addendum, addition, appendix, gnathite, nose-leaf, pedipalp, pedicle **09** allantois, chelicera, swimmeret, tailpiece **10** paraglossa, parapodium, supplement **11** aiguillette **12** appurtenance

**appendix**
**03** app **05** annex, rider **07** adjunct, codicil, pendant, pendent **08** addendum, addition, epilogue, schedule **09** appendage **10** postscript, supplement

**appertain**
**05** apply, refer **06** bear on, effair, effere, regard, relate **07** concern, pertain **10** be relevant **14** have a bearing on

**appetite**
**03** maw, yen **04** lust, urge, zeal, zest

**05** taste, tooth, twist **06** desire, hunger, liking, orexis, relish, thirst **07** craving, longing, malacia, passion, stomach **08** inner man, yearning **09** eagerness **10** inner woman, propensity **11** inclination **13** concupiscence
• **sharpness of appetite** **04** edge

**appetizer**
**04** meze, tapa, whet **05** bhaji, mezze, tapas **06** bhagee, bhajee, canapé, dim sum, relish **07** starter **08** antepast, apéritif, cocktail **09** antipasto **11** amuse-bouche, amuse-gueule, first course, hors d'oeuvre **13** prawn cocktail

**appetizing**
**05** tasty, yummy **06** morish **07** moreish, piquant, savoury, scrummy **08** inviting, tempting **09** appealing, delicious, palatable, succulent, toothsome **11** lip-smacking, scrumptious **13** mouthwatering

**applaud**
**03** hum **04** clap, laud, root, ruff **05** cheer, extol **06** cry aim, praise **07** acclaim, approve, commend **08** eulogize **09** clap hands **10** compliment **12** congratulate **14** cheer to the echo, give a big hand to **15** give an ovation to

**applause**
**04** hand, ruff **05** éclat, salvo, vivat **06** bravos, cheers, praise **07** acclaim, ovation, plaudit **08** a big hand, accolade, approval, cheering, clapping, encomium, plaudits **11** acclamation, Kentish fire **12** commendation **14** congratulation **15** standing ovation

**apple**
**04** pome

---

*Apples include:*

**03** Cox
**04** Cox's, crab, snow
**05** Coxes, eater
**06** biffin, codlin, cooker, eating, idared, pippin, russet
**07** Baldwin, Bramley, codling, cooking, costard, crispin, ribston, Sturmer, wine-sap
**08** Braeburn, Jonathan, McIntosh, pearmain, Pink Lady, queening, ribstone, sweeting
**09** delicious, jenneting, king-apple, nonpareil, Royal gala
**11** Granny Smith, McIntosh red, russet apple
**12** Red Delicious
**13** Ribston pippin, Sturmer Pippin
**15** Golden Delicious

---

• **apple core** **04** runt
• **big apple** **02** NY **03** NYC **07** New York **11** New York City

**appliance**
**03** use **04** iron, tool **05** gizmo, truss, value, waldo **06** device, gadget, praxis **07** machine **08** function **09** apparatus, implement, mechanism, relevance **10** fire engine, instrument

**11** application, carrying-out, contraption, contrivance
*See also* **domestic; utensil**

**applicable**
**03** apt, fit **04** live **05** valid **06** proper, suited, useful **07** fitting **08** apposite, relevant, suitable **09** pertinent **10** legitimate **11** appropriate
• **not applicable** **02** n/a

**applicant**
**06** suitor **08** aspirant, claimant, inquirer **09** candidate, postulant **10** competitor, contestant, petitioner **11** interviewee

**application**
**03** use **04** suit **05** claim, study, value **06** appeal, demand, effort, praxis **07** aptness, bearing, inquiry, program, purpose, request, rubbing **08** function, hard work, industry, keenness, petition, smearing, software **09** anointing, assiduity, diligence, putting on, relevance, spreading, treatment **10** commitment, dedication, pertinence **11** germaneness **12** perseverance, sedulousness, significance **13** attentiveness **15** industriousness
• **make application** **03** sue

**applied**
◇ *anagram indicator* **04** real **06** actual, useful **07** hands-on **08** relevant **09** practical **10** functional
• **applied to** **02** on

**apply**
**03** fit, lay, ply, put, rub, set, sue, use **04** give, suit, turn **05** brush, claim, exert, lay on, order, paint, put on, refer, smear, study, wield **06** affect, anoint, appeal, appose, ask for, assign, bestow, betake, commit, devote, direct, draw on, employ, engage, relate, resort **07** address, adhibit, execute, harness, inquire, involve, pertain, present, request, solicit, utilize **08** dedicate, exercise, petition, practise, put in for, resort to, spread on, work hard **09** appertain, cover with, implement, persevere, treat with **10** administer, be diligent, be relevant, buckle down, settle down **11** bring to bear, concentrate, knuckle down, requisition, write off for **12** make an effort, write away for **13** be industrious, be significant, bring into play **14** commit yourself, devote yourself, fill in a form for **15** put into practice
• **apply carelessly** **04** slap

**appoint**
**03** fix, set **04** cast, hire, make, name, pick, post **05** allot, co-opt, elect, limit, place, put in, voice **06** assign, charge, choose, decide, decree, depute, detail, direct, employ, engage, ordain, select, settle, take on **07** arrange, command, destine, install, present, recruit, specify, station **08** delegate, nominate **09** designate, determine, establish **10** commission, constitute **13** be shortlisted

**appointed**
◇ *anagram indicator* **03** due, set **05** fixed **06** chosen **07** decided, decreed, settled

**08** allotted, arranged, assigned, destined, ordained **09** scheduled **10** designated, determined **11** established, pre-arranged, preordained

**appointment**
**03** job **04** date, post, room **05** place, tryst **06** choice, naming, office **07** meeting **08** choosing, election, position **09** interview, selection, situation **10** delegation, engagement, nomination, rendezvous **11** arrangement, assignation **12** consultation **13** commissioning
• **keep an appointment**  **04** meet

**apportion**
**04** deal, mete **05** allot, carve, grant, share, stint, weigh **06** assign, divide, morsel, number, ration **07** deal out, dole out, hand out, mete out **08** allocate, dispense, share out **09** admeasure, ration out **10** distribute, measure out

**apportionment**
**05** grant, share **06** ration **07** dealing, handout, sharing **08** division **09** allotment, rationing **10** allocation, assignment **12** dispensation, distribution

**apposite**
**03** apt **06** suited **07** apropos, germane, in point **08** relevant, suitable **09** befitting, pertinent **10** applicable, to the point **11** appropriate **12** to the purpose

**appraisal**
◇ *anagram indicator* **05** assay, prise, prize **06** rating, review, survey **07** opinion **08** estimate, once-over **09** judgement, reckoning, valuation **10** assessment, estimation, evaluation, inspection **11** examination **12** appreciation

**appraise**
**04** rate **05** assay, judge, sum up, value **06** assess, review, size up, survey **07** examine, inspect, valuate **08** estimate, evaluate, once-over

**appreciable**
**04** vast **08** definite, sensible **10** noticeable, ponderable **11** discernible, perceptible, significant, substantial **12** considerable, recognizable

**appreciably**
**08** markedly **10** definitely, noticeably **11** perceptibly **12** considerably **13** significantly, substantially

**appreciate**
**03** see **04** gain, go up, grow, know, like, rise **05** enjoy, grasp, mount, prize, sense, thank, value **06** admire, esteem, regard, relish, savour **07** apprise, apprize, cherish, enhance, improve, inflate, realize, respect, welcome **08** increase, perceive, treasure **09** be aware of, recognize **10** comprehend, strengthen, understand **11** acknowledge **12** be indebted to, take kindly to **13** be conscious of, be grateful for, be sensitive to, give thanks

for, think highly of **14** be appreciative, sympathize with

**appreciation**
**04** gain, rise **05** grasp, sense **06** esteem, growth, liking, notice, praise, regard, relish, review, thanks **07** feeling, respect, valuing **08** analysis, critique, increase, sympathy **09** awareness, enjoyment, gratitude, inflation, judgement, knowledge, valuation **10** admiration, assessment, cognizance, commentary, escalation, estimation, evaluation, obligation, perception, respecting **11** enhancement, high opinion, improvement, realization, recognition, sensitivity **12** gratefulness, indebtedness, thankfulness **13** comprehension, understanding **14** responsiveness **15** acknowledgement
• **expression of appreciation**  **02** ta **05** merci, mercy, super **06** cheers!, phwoah, phwoar, thanks **08** thank you **10** danke schön

**appreciative**
**07** mindful, obliged, pleased **08** admiring, beholden, grateful, indebted, thankful **09** conscious, sensitive **10** perceptive, respectful, responsive, supportive **11** encouraging **12** enthusiastic **13** knowledgeable

**apprehend**
**03** nab, see **04** bust, grab, nick, take, twig **05** catch, grasp, run in, seize **06** arrest, collar, detain, pick up, pull in **07** believe, capture, realize **08** conceive, consider, perceive **09** deprehend, recognize **10** comprehend, understand

**apprehension**
**04** fear **05** alarm, doubt, dread, grasp, qualm, worry **06** arrest, belief, noesis, taking, unease, uptake **07** anxiety, capture, concern, jitters, seizure, willies **08** disquiet, mistrust **09** detention, misgiving, suspicion **10** cognizance, conception, foreboding, perception, the willies, uneasiness **11** butterflies, discernment, nervousness, realization, recognition, trepidation **12** collywobbles, intellection, perturbation **13** comprehension, heebie-jeebies, understanding

**apprehensive**
**04** toey **06** afraid, uneasy **07** alarmed, anxious, fearful, nervous, worried **08** bothered, doubtful, insecure **09** concerned **10** suspicious **11** distrustful, mistrustful **13** on tenterhooks

**apprehensively**
**08** uneasily **09** anxiously, fearfully, nervously **10** doubtfully **12** suspiciously **13** distrustfully, mistrustfully

**apprentice**
**01** L **03** app, cub **04** snob, tiro, tyro **05** cadet, maiko, pupil **06** commis, indent, intern, novice, rookie **07** flat cap, learner, recruit, starter, student,

trainee **08** beginner, improver, newcomer, prentice, servitor, turnover **11** probationer **13** printer's devil

**apprenticeship**
**09** Lehrjahre, novitiate **11** studentship, traineeship, trial period **14** training period

**apprise**
**04** tell, warn **05** brief **06** advise, inform, notify, tip off **08** acquaint, intimate **09** ascertain, enlighten **11** communicate

**approach**
◇ *juxtaposition indicator* **03** nie, way **04** cost, draw, meet, near, nigh, plea, road **05** abord, anear, angle, begin, close, coast, coste, drive, greet, knock, means, reach, run-in, slant, style, treat **06** access, accost, advent, appeal, arrive, avenue, broach, coming, gain on, go near, invite, manner, method, stance, system, tackle, talk to **07** accoast, address, advance, apply to, arrival, catch up, contact, doorway, get onto, mention, opinion, passage, request, speak to, succeed, tactics **08** advances, appeal to, attitude, bear down, border on, commence, deal with, draw near, driveway, embark on, entrance, go nearer, landfall, oncoming, overture, position, proposal, set about, sound out, strategy **09** introduce, overtures, procedure, technique, threshold, undertake, viewpoint **10** buttonhole, come closer, come nearer, come near to, coming near, invitation, launch into, standpoint, suggestion **11** application, appropinque, approximate, come close to, coming close, compare with, get closer to, move towards, perspective, point of view, proposition, suggestions **12** make advances **13** appropinquate, make overtures, modus operandi **14** advance towards, course of action, get in touch with, proceed towards

**approachable**
**04** open, warm **07** affable **08** friendly, informal, pleasant, sociable **09** agreeable, congenial, get-at-able, reachable, welcoming **10** accessible, attainable **15** easy to get on with

**approbation**
**06** esteem, favour, praise **07** respect **08** applause, approval **09** allowance, laudation **10** acceptance, well-liking **11** countenance, endorsement, good opinion, recognition **12** commendation **13** encouragement

**appropriate**
**03** apt, fit, nab **04** jump, lift, meet, nick, sink, take **05** annex, filch, pinch, right, seize, steal, swipe, usurp **06** assume, choice, pilfer, pocket, proper, seemly, spot-on, suited, thieve, timely **07** apropos, correct, fitting, germane, impound, in order, pre-empt, purloin, trouser **08** accepted, arrogate, becoming, embezzle, glom on to, knock off, liberate, peculate, property, relevant, suitable **09** befitting,

## appropriately

congruous, expedient, opportune, pertinent, well-timed **10** applicable, commandeer, confiscate, felicitous, seasonable, to the point, well-chosen **11** appurtenant, expropriate, in character, make off with, requisition **12** appertaining **14** misappropriate

## appropriately

**07** apropos **08** properly, suitably **09** correctly, fittingly **10** relevantly **12** felicitously

## approval

**02** OK **03** nod **04** okay, wink **05** favor, leave, voice **06** assent, esteem, favour, honour, liking, praise, regard **07** acclaim, approof, consent, go-ahead, licence, mandate, plaudit, respect, support **08** agrément, applause, blessing, sanction, thumbs-up **09** agreement **10** acceptance, admiration, green light, imprimatur, permission, validation **11** acclamation, approbation, concurrence, endorsement, good opinion, rubber stamp **12** appreciation, commendation, confirmation, ratification **13** authorization, certification **14** recommendation
• **expression of approval 02** ay, OK **03** aye, oke, olé, rah, yay **04** good, hear, okay, viva, vive **05** bravo, hurra, huzza, there, vivat **06** beauty, hooray, hurrah, hurray **07** attaboy, too much, top-hole, way to go! **08** attagirl, long live, zindabad **09** full marks, good on you **10** good for you, hubba hubba

## approve

**02** OK **03** buy, dig **04** amen, back, like, pass **05** adopt, allow, bless, carry **06** accept, admire, concur, esteem, favour, permit, praise, ratify, regard, second, uphold **07** acclaim, agree to, applaud, commend, confirm, endorse, mandate, support **08** accede to, assent to, hold with, sanction, validate **09** authorize, consent to, recommend **10** appreciate, homologate **11** countenance, rubber-stamp, think well of **12** give the nod to **13** be pleased with, think highly of

## approved

**03** app **06** proper **07** correct **08** accepted, favoured, official, orthodox **09** permitted, preferred **10** authorized, recognized, sanctioned **11** comme il faut, permissible, recommended **13** authoritative

## approving

**08** admiring, praising **09** laudatory **10** favourable, respectful, supportive **12** appreciative, commendatory

## approvingly

**10** admiringly, favourably **12** with pleasure **14** appreciatively

## approximate

**03** app **04** like, near, wild **05** close, loose, rough, round **06** coarse **07** guessed, inexact, similar, verge on **08** approach, ballpark, border on, relative, resemble **09** estimated, imprecise **10** come near to **11** be

similar to, come close to **14** be tantamount to

## approximately

**01** c **02** ca **03** odd, say **04** or so, some **05** about, circa **06** around, nearly **07** close to, loosely, roughly **09** just about, not far off, rounded up **10** give or take, more or less, round about **11** approaching, rounded down **13** in the region of, or thereabouts, something like **14** in round figures, in round numbers **15** in the vicinity of

## approximation

**05** guess **08** approach, estimate, likeness **09** rough idea, semblance **10** conjecture, estimation, similarity **11** guesstimate, resemblance **14** ballpark figure, correspondence

## appurtenance

**09** equipment, trappings **10** belongings **11** accessories, impedimenta **13** paraphernalia

## April

**03** Apr

## a priori

**07** deduced **08** inferred **11** conjectural, theoretical **12** hypothetical **13** suppositional

## apron

**03** bay, bib, rim **04** brat, edge, tier **05** dicky, skirt **06** border, dickey, dickie, fringe, napron, pinnie, tabard **07** placket, tablier **08** pinafore, standing **09** barm-cloth, forecourt, periphery **10** loading bay **12** hard-standing

## apropos

**02** re **03** apt **05** right **06** proper, seemly, timely **07** correct, fitting **08** accepted, becoming, relevant, suitable **09** befitting, opportune, pertinent, regarding **10** applicable, felicitous, respecting, seasonable, to the point, well-chosen **11** in respect of **12** in relation to, with regard to **13** with respect to **14** on the subject of **15** with reference to

## apse

**04** bema **06** concha, exedra **07** exhedra **09** apsidiole, prothesis

## apt

**03** fit **04** gleg **05** given, happy, prone, ready **06** liable, likely, proper, seemly, spot-on, timely, toward **07** correct, fitting, germane, subject, tending **08** accurate, apposite, disposed, inclined, relevant, suitable **10** acceptable, applicable, seasonable **11** appropriate

## aptitude

**04** bent, gift, turn **05** flair, skill **06** talent **07** ability, faculty, fitness, leaning **08** capacity, facility, tendency **09** endowment, quickness **10** capability, cleverness **11** disposition, inclination, proficiency **12** intelligence **14** natural ability

## aptly

**05** fitly **08** suitably **09** fittingly

**10** appositely, relevantly, to the point **13** appropriately

## aquatic

**03** sea **05** fluid, river, water **06** liquid, marine, watery **07** fluvial **08** maritime, nautical

## aquiline

**06** hooked **09** hooknosed

## Arab

**02** Ar

*Arab League countries:*

**03** UAE
**04** Iraq, Oman
**05** Egypt, Libya, Qatar, Sudan, Syria, Yemen
**06** Jordan, Kuwait
**07** Algeria, Bahrain, Comoros, Lebanon, Morocco, Somalia, Tunisia
**08** Djibouti
**09** Palestine
**10** Mauritania
**11** Saudi Arabia
**18** United Arab Emirates

## Arabic

**02** Ar **04** Arab
*See also* **alphabet**

## arable

**03** lay, lea, lee, ley **06** fecund **07** fertile **08** farmable, fruitful, tillable **10** cultivable, ploughable, productive
*See also* **crop**

## arachnid

*see* **spider**

## arbiter

**05** judge **06** expert, master, pundit, umpire **07** oddsman, referee **08** governor **09** authority, birlieman, byrlaw-man **10** controller **11** adjudicator

## arbitrarily

**08** by chance, randomly **11** illogically **12** irrationally, subjectively, unreasonably **14** inconsistently

## arbitrary

**06** chance, random **08** absolute, despotic, dogmatic, personal **09** illogical, imperious, whimsical **10** autocratic, capricious, dominative, high-handed, irrational, subjective, tyrannical, unreasoned **11** dictatorial, domineering, instinctive, magisterial, overbearing **12** conventional, inconsistent, unreasonable **13** discretionary

## arbitrate

**05** judge **06** decide, settle, umpire **07** mediate, referee **09** determine **10** adjudicate **13** pass judgement **14** sit in judgement

## arbitration

**08** decision **09** arbitrage, judgement, mediation **10** compromise, settlement **11** arbitrament, negotiation **12** adjudication, intervention **13** determination

## arbitrator

**03** ref, ump **05** judge **06** umpire

**07** arbiter, referee **08** mediator **09** go-between, moderator **10** negotiator **11** adjudicator **12** intermediary

**arbour**
**03** bay **05** bower **06** alcove, grotto, herbar, recess **07** pergola, retreat, shelter **09** sanctuary

**arc**
**03** bow **04** arch, bend, spin, turn **05** curve, round **06** swerve **07** rainbow **09** curvature **10** curved line, semicircle

**arcade**
**04** mall, stoa **05** plaza **06** loggia, piazza **07** gallery, portico **08** cloister, galleria, precinct **09** colonnade, peristyle, triforium **10** covered way **12** shopping mall

**arcane**
**06** hidden, occult, secret **07** cryptic, obscure **08** abstruse, esoteric, mystical, profound **09** concealed, enigmatic, recondite **10** mysterious

**arch**
◊ anagram indicator **03** arc, bow, hog, sly **04** bend, dome, hoop, span **05** chief, curve, embow, ogive, roach, vault **06** bridge, camber, diadem, girdle, invert, portal, shrewd, zygoma **07** archway, concave, cunning, playful, roguish, squinch, waggish **08** cross-rib, espiègle, platband **09** curvature, principal **10** manteltree, mysterious, semicircle **11** counterfort, mischievous **13** arc de triomphe

Arches include:

**04** keel, ogee, skew
**05** round, Tudor
**06** convex, corbel, Gothic, lancet, Norman, tented
**07** pointed, stilted, trefoil
**09** Ctesiphon, horseshoe, parabolic, segmental, triumphal
**10** four-centre, proscenium, shouldered
**11** equilateral
**12** basket handle

**archaeology**

Archaeological terms include:

**03** cup, dig, jar, jug, tor, urn
**04** adze, bowl, celt, cist, core, kist, site, tell
**05** blade, burin, cairn, ditch, flake, flask, flint, henge, hoard, mound, mummy, shard, sherd, stele, whorl
**06** barrow, Beaker, bogman, dolmen, dromos, eolith, menhir, midden, mosaic, patina, strata, trench
**07** amphora, anomaly, cave art, crannog, handaxe, Iron Age, neolith, obelisk, papyrus, rock art, sondage, stratum, tumulus
**08** artefact, artifact, cromlech, excavate, hill fort, knapping, ley lines, megalith, post hole, Stone Age
**09** arrowhead, Bronze Age, cartouche, crop-marks, earthwork, enclosure, hypocaust,

longhouse, Neolithic
**10** Anglo-Saxon, assemblage, excavation, geophysics, grave goods, inhumation, roundhouse, tear bottle
**11** burial mound, rock shelter, stone circle
**12** amphitheatre, archaeometry, carbon dating, field walking, interglacial, Palaeolithic, stratigraphy
**13** kitchen-midden, standing stone, treasure trove, wattle and daub
**14** hunter-gatherer

Archaeologists include:

**04** Uhle (Max)
**05** Clark (Grahame), Evans (Sir Arthur)
**06** Anning (Mary), Breuil (Henri), Carter (Howard), Childe (Gordon), Clarke (David L), Daniel (Glyn), Hawkes (Jacquetta), Kidder (A V), Layard (Sir Austen), Leakey (Louis), Leakey (Mary), Petrie (Sir Flinders), Putnam (Frederic Ward)
**07** Binford (Lewis), Renfrew (Colin, Lord), Thomsen (Christian), Wheeler (Sir Mortimer), Woolley (Sir Leonard), Worsaae (Jens Jacob)
**08** Breasted (J H), Cunliffe (Barry), Fiorelli (Giuseppe), Koldewey (Robert), Mallowan (Sir Max), Mariette (Auguste), Marshall (Sir John)
**09** Andersson (Johan Gunnar)
**10** Pitt-Rivers (Augustus), Schliemann (Heinrich)
**11** Champollion (Jean François)

**archaic**
**03** old **05** passé **06** bygone, old hat, quaint **07** ancient, antique **08** medieval, obsolete, outdated, outmoded **09** mediaeval, out-of-date, primitive **10** antiquated **11** obsolescent, out of the ark **12** antediluvian, old-fashioned

**archangel**
**08** hierarch **10** dead-nettle **14** garden angelica
See also angel

**archbishop**
**03** abp **07** primate **12** metropolitan
See also cardinal

Archbishops include:

**04** Gray (Gordon), Hope (David), Hume (Basil), Kemp (John), Lang (Cosmo), Laud (William), Tutu (Desmond)
**05** Beran (Josef), Carey (George), Glemp (Jozef)
**06** Anselm, Beaton (David), Becket (Thomas à), Benson (Edward White), Blanch (Stuart), Coggan (Donald), Edmund (St), Fisher (Geoffrey), Heenan (John Carmel), Hilary (of Poitiers, St), Mannix (Daniel), Morton (John), Parker (Matthew), Potter (John), Ramsay (Michael), Runcie (Robert), Temple (Frederick), Temple (William), Trench (Richard Chenevix), Ussher (James), Walter (Hubert), Warham

(William), Wolsey (Thomas)
**07** Arundel (Thomas), Cranmer (Thomas), Dunstan (St), Habgood (John), Langton (Stephen), Mendoza (Pedro Gonzalez de), Sentamu (John), Sheldon (Gilbert), Wiseman (Nicholas)
**08** Adalbert, Cuthbert, Davidson (Randall), Ethelred, Makarios, Whitgift (John), Williams (Rowan)
**09** Augustine (St), Wyszynski (Stefan)
**10** Damaskinos, Huddleston (Trevor)
**12** Hollingworth (Peter)

**archdiocese**
see diocese

**archer**
**04** Eros, Tell **05** Cupid **06** bow-boy, bowman **09** sagittary **11** Sagittarius, toxophilite

**archetypal**
**05** ideal, model, stock **07** classic, typical **08** original, standard **09** exemplary **12** paradigmatic **14** characteristic, quintessential, representative

**archetype**
**04** form, idea, type **05** ideal, model **06** entity **07** classic, epitome, pattern **08** exemplar, original, paradigm, standard **09** precursor, prototype **10** stereotype **12** quintessence, typification

**archipelago**

Archipelagoes include:

**04** Cuba, Fiji, Sulu
**05** Åland, Gulag, Japan, Malay, Malta, Tonga
**06** Arctic, Azores, Chagos, Kosrae, Tuvalu
**07** Bahamas, Mayotte, Tuamotu
**08** Bismarck, Cyclades, Kiribati, Maldives, Moluccas, Svalbard
**09** Alexander, Antarctic, Cape Verde, Catherine, Galápagos, Indonesia, Louisiade, Marquesas, North Land
**10** Ahvenanmaa, Les Iles d'Or, Seychelles, Vesterålen, West Indies
**11** Iles d'Hyères, Line Islands, Philippines, Spitsbergen, Vesteraalen
**12** Kuril Islands, Novaya Zemlya, Pearl Islands, Spice Islands, Sunda Islands
**13** Aegean Islands, Caicos Islands, Canary Islands, Ellice Islands, Ionian Islands, Tubuai Islands
**14** Austral Islands, Bijagos Islands, Channel Islands, Franz Josef Land, Gilbert Islands, Leeward Islands, Lofoten Islands, Nicholas II Land, Oki Archipelago, Papua New Guinea, Phoenix Islands, Solomon Islands, Tierra del Fuego, Visayan Islands
**15** Balearic Islands, Friendly Islands, Marshall Islands, Pitcairn Islands, Severnaya Zemlya, Wallis and Futuna, Windward Islands

## architect

**05** maker **06** author, shaper **07** creator, founder, planner **08** designer, engineer, inventor **10** instigator, mastermind, originator, prime mover **11** constructor, draughtsman **13** master builder

*Architects include:*

**04 Adam** (Robert), **Boyd** (Robin), **Drew** (Dame Jane), **Loos** (Adolf), **Nash** (John), **Shaw** (Norman), **Wren** (Sir Christopher)
**05 Aalto** (Alvar), **Barry** (Sir Charles), **Costa** (Lucio), **Dudok** (Willem), **Gaudí** (Antoni), **Gehry** (Frank), **Jones** (Inigo), **Meier** (Richard), **Nervi** (Pier Luigi), **Piano** (Renzo), **Pugin** (Augustus), **Scott** (Sir George Gilbert), **Scott** (Sir Giles Gilbert), **Soane** (Sir John), **Speer** (Albert), **Velde** (Henri van de)
**06 Casson** (Sir Hugh), **Cubitt** (Thomas), **Foster** (Sir Norman), **Giotto**, **Howard** (Sir Ebenezer), **Lescot** (Pierre), **Morris** (William), **Paxton** (Sir Joseph), **Pisano** (Giovanni), **Rogers** (Sir Richard), **Semper** (Gottfried), **Serlio** (Sebastiano), **Spence** (Sir Basil), **Wright** (Frank Lloyd)
**07 Alberti** (Leon Battista), **Asplund** (Erik Gunnar), **Behrens** (Peter), **Bernini** (Gian Lorenzo), **Gropius** (Walter), **Grounds** (Sir Roy), **Ictinus**, **Imhotep**, **Lutyens** (Sir Edwin), **Olmsted** (Frederick Law), **Vignola** (Giacomo da)
**08 Bramante** (Donato), **Jacobsen** (Arne), **Miralles** (Enric), **Niemeyer** (Oscar), **Palladio** (Andrea), **Piranesi** (Giambattista), **Saarinen** (Eero), **Sottsass** (Ettore), **Stirling** (James), **Sullivan** (Louis), **Vanbrugh** (Sir John)
**09 Borromini** (Francesco), **Haussmann** (Georges, Baron), **Hawksmoor** (Nicholas), **Libeskind** (Daniel), **Mackmurdo** (Arthur), **Vitruvius**
**10 Mackintosh** (Charles Rennie)
**11 Le Corbusier**
**12 Brunelleschi** (Filippo), **Viollet-Le-Duc** (Eugène)
**14 Mies van der Rohe** (Ludwig)
**15 Leonardo da Vinci**

## architecture

**04** form **05** frame, set-up, style **06** design, make-up, system **08** building, planning **09** designing, framework, structure **11** arrangement, composition **12** conformation, constitution, construction, organization **13** configuration **14** architectonics

*Architecture styles include:*

**04** Adam
**05** Greek, Saxon
**06** Gothic, modern, Norman, rococo
**07** barocco, baroque, Bauhaus, Italian, Lombard, mission, mudéjar
**08** baronial, high tech

---

**09** beaux arts, brutalism, Byzantine, Cape Dutch, decorated, Palladian, Queen Anne
**10** art nouveau, Corinthian, Romanesque
**11** Elizabethan, Renaissance
**13** Gothic revival, international, neoclassicism, Perpendicular, post-modernism
**15** churrigueresque

*Architectural features include:*

**03** orb, web
**04** anta, apse, arch, base, bell, boss, cove, crop, cusp, cyma, dado, drum, list, neck, ribs, vase, void
**05** antae, attic, congé, crown, flute, gable, gavel, glyph, groin, gutta, hance, helix, mould, nerve, ogive, print, pylon, quirk, scape, socle, spire, stria, talon, tenia, tondo, torus, tower, truss, vault
**06** abacus, atrium, canton, caulis, chevet, cinque, cippus, column, concha, congee, coping, corona, coving, crenel, dentil, facade, fascia, fillet, finial, flèche, fornix, frieze, haunch, impost, lierne, metope, patera, patten, pillar, podium, portal, reglet, regula, rosace, scotia, severy, striae, taenia, turret, wreath
**07** aileron, annulet, balloon, bandrol, capital, cavetti, cavetto, conchae, corbeil, cornice, crocket, diglyph, doucine, echinus, fantail, festoon, fronton, fusarol, grecque, larmier, mullion, necking, nervure, pannier, parapet, Persian, pilotis, portico, rosette, solidum, squinch, surbase, tambour, telamon, tondino
**08** abutment, accolade, apophyge, astragal, baguette, bandelet, banderol, bannerol, bellcote, buttress, canephor, cartouch, chapiter, chaptrel, ciborium, cincture, crenelle, diastyle, dipteral, dipteros, entresol, epistyle, frontoon, fusarole, gorgerin, imperial, intrados, mascaron, moulding, pediment, pilaster, prostyle, pulpitum, rockwork, sept-foil, skewback, spandrel, spandril, terminus, triglyph, tympanum, voussoir
**09** apsidiole, archivolt, balection, banderole, bolection, cartouche, crossette, cul-de-four, decastyle, embrasure, embrazure, foliation, guilloche, hypostyle, mezzanine, modillion, octastyle, octostyle, peristyle, strap work, stylobate, tierceron, triforium, water leaf
**10** acroterion, architrave, ball-flower, bratticing, cauliculus, chambranle, clearstory, clerestory, demicupola, ditriglyph, egg-and-dart, eye-catcher, feathering, jerkinhead, pendentive, quatrefoil, subarcuate, water table, weathering

---

**11** brattishing, entablature, paternoster
**12** egg-and-anchor, egg-and-tongue, frontispiece
**13** chain moulding, interpilaster, quatrefeuille, vermiculation
**14** Catherine-wheel, flying buttress

*See also* **arch**

*Architectural and building terms include:*

**04** dado, dome, jamb, roof
**05** Doric, eaves, groin, Ionic, ridge, Tudor
**06** alcove, annexe, coving, duplex, façade, fascia, fillet, finial, frieze, Gothic, lintel, Norman, pagoda, plinth, reveal, rococo, scroll, soffit, stucco, Tuscan
**07** baroque, cornice, festoon, fletton, fluting, mullion, pantile, parapet, rafters, Regency, rotunda, skywalk
**08** baluster, capstone, dogtooth, dry-stone, gargoyle, Georgian, pinnacle, sacristy, terrazzo, wainscot
**09** bas relief, classical, Edwardian, elevation, gatehouse, Queen Anne, roughcast, skybridge
**10** architrave, barge-board, Corinthian, drawbridge, flamboyant, groundplan, Romanesque, weathering
**11** coping stone, cornerstone, Elizabethan, Flemish bond
**12** Early English, frontispiece, half-timbered

## archives

**04** roll **05** deeds **06** annals, papers **07** ledgers, records **09** documents, memorials, registers **10** chronicles **11** memorabilia

## arctic

**05** polar **06** boreal, frosty, frozen **07** glacial, subzero **08** Far North, freezing, Siberian **11** far northern, hyperborean **12** bitterly cold, freezing cold
• **arctic animal 09** polar bear

## ardent

**03** hot **04** avid, keen, warm **05** eager, fiery **06** fervid, fierce, strong **07** burning, devoted, fervent, intense, mettled, zealous **08** sanguine, spirited, vehement **09** dedicated, perfervid, spiritous **10** mettlesome, passionate **11** empassioned, evangelical, impassioned, warm-blooded **12** enthusiastic **14** enthusiastical
• **be ardent 04** glow

## ardently

**05** hotly **06** avidly, warmly **07** eagerly **08** strongly **09** devotedly, fervently, intensely, zealously **10** vehemently **12** passionately

## ardour

**04** fire, heat, lust, rage, zeal, zest **05** flame, wrath **06** duende, fervor, spirit, warmth **07** avidity, fervour, passion **08** covetise, devotion, keenness **09** animation, eagerness, intensity, vehemence **10** dedication, enthusiasm **12** empressement

## arduous
**04** hard **05** chore, harsh, heavy, steep, stiff, tough **06** severe, taxing, tiring, uphill **07** be a slog, onerous **08** be murder, daunting, rigorous, toilsome, wearying **09** difficult, fatiguing, gruelling, laborious, punishing, strenuous **10** burdensome, exhausting, formidable **12** backbreaking

## are
**01** A **04** live **05** exist

## area
**01** A **04** beat, part, size, zone **05** field, manor, patch, place, range, realm, scope, tract, width, world **06** branch, domain, extent, parish, region, sector, sphere **07** breadth, compass, enclave, expanse, portion, quarter, section, stretch, terrain **08** district, environs, locality, precinct, province **09** territory **10** department **11** environment, reserve area **13** catchment area, neighbourhood
*See also* **administrative; council; county; district**

## arena
**04** area, bowl, ring **05** field, realm, scene, world **06** domain, ground, sphere **07** stadium, theatre **08** coliseum, province **10** department, hippodrome **11** battlefield **12** amphitheatre, battleground **14** area of conflict

## Ares
**04** Mars

## Argentina
**02** RA **03** ARG

## argon
**02** Ar

## argot
**04** cant **05** idiom, slang **06** jargon **08** parlance

## arguable
**04** moot **09** debatable, uncertain, undecided **10** disputable **11** contentious, open to doubt **12** questionable **14** controvertible, open to question

## arguably
**05** maybe **08** possibly, probably **10** most likely **15** in all likelihood

## argue
**03** rag, row **04** feud, hold, moot, show, spar **05** claim, fight, imply, nyaff, plead, prove **06** assert, bicker, cangle, debate, denote, haggle, hassle, reason **07** accurse, contend, declare, discuss, display, dispute, exhibit, fall out, quarrel, quibble, suggest, wrangle, wrestle **08** convince, disagree, dissuade, have a row, indicate, logicize, maintain, manifest, persuade, question, squabble **09** altercate, chop logic, have it out, have words, join issue, take issue, talk out of **10** chew the fat, chew the rag, contradict, hold a brief **11** cross swords, demonstrate,

expostulate, remonstrate **13** be evidence for, have it out with **15** be at loggerheads, have a bone to pick

## argument
**03** pro, row **04** beef, blue, case, feud, plot, spat, tiff, yike **05** claim, clash, fight, lemma, logic, run-in, set-to, theme, topic, yikes **06** barney, bust-up, contra, debate, dust-up, hassle, reason, ruckus, rumpus, tangle, thesis **07** contest, defence, dispute, fallacy, outline, polemic, quarrel, summary, wrangle **08** conflict, ding-dong, evidence, exchange, squabble, synopsis, trilemma **09** argy-bargy, assertion, enthymeme, objection, quodlibet, rationale, reasoning, syllogism **10** contention, discussion **11** altercation, controverse, controversy, declaration **12** antistrophon, disagreement **13** argumentation, demonstration, expostulation, justification, running battle, shouting-match, slanging-match **14** heated exchange

## argumentation
**04** case **05** claim, logic **06** debate **07** defence **08** argument, disproof, evidence **09** rationale, reasoning **10** contention **13** expostulation, justification

## argumentative
**06** chippy **07** stroppy **08** captious, contrary, perverse **09** litigious, polemical, truculent **11** belligerent, contentious, dissentious, opinionated, quarrelsome **12** cantankerous, disputatious

## arid
**03** dry **04** drab, dull, flat **05** baked, vapid, waste **06** barren, boring, desert, dreary, jejune, meagre, torrid **07** parched, sterile, tedious **08** lifeless **09** infertile, torrefied, waterless **10** colourless, dehydrated, desiccated, monotonous, spiritless, uninspired **12** moistureless, shrivelled up, unproductive **13** uninteresting

## aright
**02** OK **05** aptly, fitly, truly **07** exactly, rightly **08** properly, suitably **09** correctly **10** accurately

## arise
◊ *reversal down indicator* **04** come, flow, go up, lift, rise, soar, stem **05** begin, climb, ensue, get up, issue, mount, occur, start, tower **06** appear, ascend, come up, crop up, derive, emerge, follow, happen, result, rise up, spring **07** emanate, proceed, stand up **08** commence **10** be caused by **11** be a result of, come to light **12** straighten up **13** come into being, get to your feet, present itself

## aristocracy
**04** nobs, rank **05** élite, lords, peers, toffs **06** gentry, ladies **07** peerage **08** nobility, noblemen **09** gentility, optimates, top drawer **10** haute monde, noblewomen, patricians, patriciate, upper class, upper crust

**11** aristocrats, high society, ruling class **15** privileged class

## aristocrat
**03** nob **04** lady, lord, peer, toff **05** noble **06** Junker **07** grandee, high-hat, peeress **08** eupatrid, nobleman, optimate **09** patrician **10** grande dame, noblewoman **13** grand seigneur
*See also* **nobility**

## aristocratic
**01** U **05** élite, noble **06** lordly, titled **07** courtly, elegant, refined **08** highborn, well-born **09** dignified, patrician **10** upper-class, upper-crust **11** blue-blooded **12** thoroughbred

## arithmetic
**07** algebra **08** algorism, logistic **11** computation

## Arizona
**02** AZ **04** Ariz

## Arkansas
**02** AR **03** Ark

## Arkwright
**04** Noah

## arm
**03** bay, fin, rig **04** barb, cove, gird, heel, iron, limb, loch, prop, whip, wing **05** array, brace, crank, creek, equip, firth, force, index, inlet, issue, might, power, prime, rearm, steel, wiper **06** branch, outfit, sleeve, supply, weapon **07** channel, estuary, euripus, forearm, fortify, furnish, passage, prepare, protect, provide, quillon, sea loch, section **08** accoutre, brachium, division, embattle, offshoot, strength **09** appendage, authority, extension, reinforce, upper limb **10** department, detachment, projection, strengthen **12** embranchment **15** windscreen-wiper

## armada
**04** navy **05** fleet **08** flotilla, squadron **10** naval force

## armadillo
**04** peba **05** tatou **07** Dasypus, tatouay **10** pichiciego

## armaments
**04** arms, guns **06** cannon **07** weapons **08** ordnance, weaponry **09** artillery, munitions **10** ammunition

## armed
**06** fitted **07** packing **08** tooled up
• **armed man 03** gun

## armed services
*see* **air force; army; military; navy; rank**

## Armenia
**02** AM **03** ARM

## armistice
**04** pact **05** peace, truce **09** ceasefire **10** still-stand **11** peace treaty

## armour
**04** gear, gere, mail, weed **05** plate, proof, stand **06** corium, shield **07** panoply **08** armature **12** iron-cladding

*Armour includes:*

**04** cush, jack, jamb, lame, mail, suit, tace
**05** armet, brace, cuish, culet, curat, jambe, salet, tasse, visor
**06** beaver, byrnie, casque, couter, crinet, cuisse, curiet, faulds, gorget, greave, grille, gusset, helmet, jamber, morion, poleyn, rondel, salade, sallet, taslet, tasset, tonlet, tuille, voider
**07** ailette, barding, basinet, besagew, brasset, buckler, cap-à-pie, corslet, cuirass, harness, hauberk, jambeau, jambeux, jambier, lamboys, morrion, palette, placcat, placket, poitrel, puldron, sabaton, surcoat, ventail
**08** aventail, bascinet, brassard, brassart, chaffron, chamfron, chausses, corselet, gauntlet, giambeux, jambeaux, jazerant, pauldron, pectoral, placcate, pouldron, shynbald, solleret, spaulder, vambrace, ventaile, ventayle
**09** aventaile, backpiece, backplate, chain mail, chamfrain, garniture, habergeon, jesserant, mandilion, mandylion, nosepiece, rerebrace, vantbrace, vantbrass
**10** body armour, cataphract, coat-armour, coat of mail
**11** breastplate, genouillère, mentonnière, plate armour, scale armour
**12** splint armour

**armoured**
**06** plated **08** iron-clad, loricate
**09** bomb-proof, protected, toughened
**10** reinforced **11** bullet-proof, steel-plated **12** armour-plated

**armoury**
**05** depot, stock **07** arsenal **08** magazine
**09** arms depot, garderobe, stockpile
**10** repository **13** ordnance depot
**14** ammunition dump

**armpit**
**05** oxter **06** axilla

**arms**
**04** guns **05** crest **06** cannon, emblem, shield **07** weapons **08** blazonry, firearms, heraldry, insignia, missiles, ordnance, weaponry **09** armaments, artillery, munitions **10** ammunition, coat-of-arms, escutcheon
**11** projectiles **14** heraldic device

**army**
**03** mob **04** host, pack, sena **05** crowd, horde, swarm **06** throng, troops
**07** cohorts, legions, militia **08** brachial, infantry, military, soldiers, soldiery
**09** multitude **10** armed force, arrière-ban, land forces **11** thin red line

*Armies include:*

**02** AA, SA, TA
**03** AVR, GAR, IRA, USA, WLA
**04** BAOR, INLA
**05** Sally
**06** Church, Tartan
**08** New Model

**09** Eurocorps, Salvation
**10** Blue Ribbon, Women's Land
**11** Grande Armée, Territorial

*See also* **rank; regiment**
• **army corps** *see* **regiment**
• **army regulation** **02** AR

**aroma**
**04** nose **05** fumet, odour, scent, smell
**06** savour **07** bouquet, fumette, perfume **09** fragrance, redolence

**aromatic**
**05** balmy, fresh, spicy **07** pungent, savoury, scented **08** fragrant, perfumed, redolent **11** odoriferous
**12** sweet-scented **13** sweet-smelling

**around**
◇ *anagram indicator* ◇ *containment indicator* ◇ *reversal indicator* **01** c **02** ca
**04** near **05** about, circa, close, round
**06** at hand, nearby, nearly **07** all over, close by, close to, roughly **08** framed by, to and fro **09** enclosing
**10** encircling, everywhere, more or less, on all sides, throughout
**11** surrounding, within reach
**12** circumjacent, encompassing, everywhere in, here and there, on all sides of, to all parts of
**13** approximately, circumambient, on every side of **15** in all directions

**arousal**
◇ *anagram indicator* **06** firing **08** stirring
**09** agitation, evocation **10** excitement
**11** provocation, titillation **12** getting going, inflammation

**arouse**
◇ *anagram indicator* **04** fire, goad, move, spur, whet **05** alarm, cause, evoke, incur, pique, rouse, spark, tease, waken **06** awaken, beat up, bestir, excite, incite, induce, kindle, prompt, stir up, turn on, wake up, whip up **07** agitate, animate, inflame, knock up, provoke, quicken, sharpen, startle, trigger, upraise **08** get going, summon up **09** call forth, eroticize, galvanize, impassion, instigate, stimulate, suscitate, titillate
**11** disentrance

**arraign**
**06** accuse, charge, impugn, indict
**07** appoint, empeach, impeach
**09** prosecute **11** incriminate **13** call to account

**arraignment**
**04** case **05** trial **06** charge **07** summons
**10** accusation, indictment
**11** impeachment, legal action
**13** incrimination

**arrange**
◇ *anagram indicator* **02** do **03** fix, set
**04** cast, comb, file, gang, list, make, plan, sift, size, sort, stow, tidy, tile, trim
**05** adapt, agree, align, aline, array, braid, class, dress, fix up, grade, group, ink in, order, place, preen, range, score, set up, swing **06** adjust, blouse, codify, decide, design, devise, digest, fettle, format, gather, lay out, line up, make up, ordain, set out, settle
**07** address, article, blow-dry, concert,

dispose, echelon, enrange, marshal, prepare, process, project, rummage, seriate, sort out, windrow **08** alphabet, classify, conclude, contrive, embattle, engineer, enraunge, organize, pencil in, position, regulate, rustle up, settle on, stratify **09** catalogue, collocate, determine, harmonize, methodize, negotiate, serialize **10** categorize, co-ordinate, distribute, foreordain, instrument, put in order, transcribe
**11** choreograph, configurate, orchestrate, systematize
**12** chronologize

**arranged**
**03** arr

**arrangement**
◇ *anagram indicator* **03** lay **04** form, pack, plan **05** array, order, plans, score, set-up, taxis, terms **06** design, detail, fixing, format, layout, line-up, method, scheme, system **07** details, display, setting, version **08** contract, disposal, grouping, ordnance, planning, position, schedule
**09** agreement, Ausgleich, bandobast, bundobust, digestion, formation, preparing, structure **10** adaptation, compromise, groundwork, schematism, settlement **11** disposition, positioning, preparation **12** modus vivendi, organization, preparations
**13** configuration, harmonization, orchestration **14** classification, interpretation **15** instrumentation

**arranger**
**03** arr

**arrant**
**04** rank, vile **05** gross, utter **06** brazen
**07** blatant, extreme **08** absolute, complete, flagrant, infamous, outright, rascally, thorough **09** barefaced, downright, egregious, notorious, out-and-out **11** unmitigated **12** incorrigible
**13** thoroughgoing

**array**
◇ *anagram indicator* **03** set **04** deck, garb, robe, show, trim **05** adorn, align, dress, group, herse, order, range
**06** attire, attrap, clothe, draw up, effeir, effere, lay out, line up, line-up, matrix, muster, parade, plight, spread
**07** apparel, arrange, bedight, bedizen, display, dispose, exhibit, marshal, panoply **08** accoutre, assemble, decorate, position **09** formation
**10** assemblage, assortment, collection, exhibition, exposition, habilitate
**11** arrangement, disposition, marshalling

**arrears**
**04** debt **05** debts **07** balance, deficit
**10** amount owed, money owing
**11** liabilities **14** sum of money owed
• **in arrears** **04** late **05** owing
**06** behind, in debt **07** overdue
**10** behindhand **11** back-ganging, outstanding

**arrest**
◇ *containment indicator* **02** do **03** cop, lag, nab, nip, sus **04** book, bust, grab, grip, halt, hold, lift, nail, nick, slow,

## arresting

stem, stop, suss **05** block, catch, check, delay, pinch, rivet, run in, seize, stall **06** absorb, attach, collar, detain, engage, fixate, hinder, impede, nobble, pick up, pull in, retard, stasis, take up **07** attract, caption, capture, engross, inhibit, seizure, snabble, snaffle **08** intrigue, obstruct, restrain, slow down **09** apprehend, detention, epistasis, fascinate, interrupt **11** nip in the bud **12** apprehension **15** take into custody
• **under arrest 06** copped **09** in custody **11** in captivity

## arresting

**07** amazing, notable **08** engaging, riveting, striking, stunning **10** impressive, noteworthy, noticeable, remarkable, surprising **11** conspicuous, eye-catching, outstanding **13** extraordinary

## arrival

**03** arr **04** dawn **05** birth, comer, entry, guest, start **06** advent, blow-in, coming, income, origin **07** entrant, fresher, incomer, visitor **08** approach, debutant, entrance, freshman, newcomer, visitant **09** debutante, emergence, invention **10** appearance, homecoming, occurrence **11** development

## arrive

◇ *juxtaposition indicator* **03** arr, get, hit **04** come, dock, gain, land, make, show **05** enter, fetch, get to, occur, reach **06** accede, appear, attain, become, blow in, come in, come to, drop in, happen, make it, obtain, pull in, rock up, roll in, roll up, show up, swan in, swan up, turn up **07** achieve, check in, clock in, get here, pitch up, succeed, surface **08** get there **09** be present, hammer out, thrash out, touch down **10** accomplish, be a success, be produced, come to hand **11** get to the top, materialize **12** become famous **14** come on the scene **15** become available, come on the market

## arrogance

**04** side **05** nerve, pride, scorn **06** hubris, hybris, morgue, vanity **07** conceit, disdain, egotism, hauteur, opinion **08** assuming, boasting, contempt, high hand, surquedy **09** contumely, insolence, lordiness, pomposity, surquedry **11** haughtiness, presumption, superiority **12** snobbishness **13** condescension, imperiousness **14** high-handedness, self-importance

## arrogant

**04** high **05** cobby, proud, stout **06** lordly, uppity, wanton **07** haughty, stuck-up, topping **08** assuming, boastful, insolent, jumped-up, scornful, snobbish, superior **09** bigheaded, conceited, dangerous, egotistic, hubristic, imperious **10** disdainful, high-handed, hoity-toity **11** overbearing, overweening, patronizing, toffee-nosed **12** contemptuous, presumptuous,

supercilious **13** condescending, high and mighty, self-important **14** full of yourself, on the high ropes

## arrogantly

**04** high **07** proudly **09** haughtily **10** boastfully, insolently, scornfully, snobbishly **11** conceitedly, imperiously **12** disdainfully, high-handedly **13** hubristically, overbearingly, overweeningly, patronizingly **14** contemptuously, presumptuously, superciliously **15** condescendingly, self-importantly

## arrogate

**05** seize, usurp **06** assume **07** presume **08** take over **10** commandeer **11** appropriate **14** misappropriate

## arrogation

**07** seizure **10** assumption, possession, taking over **13** appropriation, commandeering

## arrow

**03** any, ary **04** bolt, dart **05** shaft **06** flight, marker, quar'le **07** dogbolt, pointer, quarrel, sagitta **08** bird-bolt **09** butt-shaft, indicator **11** swallowtail **13** grey-goose wing **14** cloth-yard shaft, grey-goose quill, grey-goose shaft

## arrowhead

**04** fork

## arrowroot

**03** pia **07** Maranta

## arsenal

**05** depot, stock **06** armory **07** armoury, weapons **08** magazine, weaponry **09** arms depot, garderobe, stockpile **10** repository **13** ordnance depot **14** ammunition dump

## arsenic

**02** As

## arson

**09** pyromania, saddlebow **11** firebombing, fire-raising **12** incendiarism

## arsonist

**05** torch **07** firebug **10** firebomber, fire-raiser, incendiary, pyromaniac

## art

**04** feat, gift **05** craft, flair, guile, knack, skill, trade **06** Arthur, deceit, design, method, talent **07** artwork, cunning, daubery, finesse, knowhow, mastery, sleight, slyness **08** aptitude, artistry, facility, strategy, trickery, wiliness **09** dexterity, expertise, ingenuity, technique **10** adroitness, artfulness, astuteness, craftiness, profession, shrewdness, virtuosity **12** creative work **13** craftsmanship **15** draughtsmanship
*See also* **Japanese; painting; sculpture**

*Arts and crafts include:*

**04** film, zari **05** batik, video **06** fresco, mosaic, saikei **07** carving, collage, crochet, drawing, etching, ikebana, origami, pottery, weaving

**08** ceramics, graphics, knitting, painting, pencraft, spinning, tapestry, tsutsumu **09** animation, cloisonné, engraving, jewellery, marquetry, metalwork, modelling, patchwork, sculpture, sketching, woodcraft **10** basketwork, caricature, embroidery, enamelling, needlework, xylography **11** calligraphy, lithography, needlecraft, oil painting, photography, portraiture, psaligraphy, stitchcraft, watercolour, woodcarving, wood cutting **12** animatronics, architecture, chalcography, illustration, stained glass **13** digital design, graphic design, wood engraving **14** relief printing, screenprinting

*See also* **picture**

*Schools, movements and styles of art include:*

**05** Nabis, Op Art, video **06** Cubism, Gothic, Pop Art, Purism, Rococo **07** Art Brut, Art Deco, Baroque, Bauhaus, Brit art, Dadaism, digital, Fauvism, folk art, Realism **08** Abstract, Barbizon, Bohemian, Futurism, Japonism, Venetian **09** Byzantine, Formalism, Mannerism, Modernism, Symbolism, Vorticism **10** arte povera, Art Nouveau, Automatism, Classicism, Florentine, Literalism, Minimal Art, Naturalism, New Realism, Romanesque, Surrealism **11** Hellenistic, Pointillism, Primitivism, Renaissance, Romanticism, Suprematism **12** Aestheticism, Magic Realism, Quattrocento, Superrealism **13** Arts and Crafts, Conceptual Art, Expressionism, Impressionism, Neoclassicism, Neo-Plasticism, Post-Modernism, Pre-Raphaelite **14** Action Painting, Constructivism

*Art materials and art-related terms include:*

**03** ink **04** term, wash **05** cameo, easel, fitch, liner, sable, smock, turps, video **06** badger, crayon, fusain, pastel, pencil, relief, sketch, tusche **07** atelier, cartoon, digital, modello, organic, palette, scumble, torchon **08** abstract, alfresco, charcoal, gumption, intaglio, Luminism, monotint, paintbox, pastille **09** lay-figure, pen and ink, stretcher **10** delineavit, from nature, paintbrush, sketchbook **11** perspective, trompe l'oeil, wash drawing **12** installation, underdrawing

## artefact

13 social realism
15 oil of turpentine

• **work of art** 06 doodle 09 Old Master

## artefact

◇ *anagram indicator* 04 item, tool
05 thing 06 object 07 neolith
09 something 10 palaeolith

## Artemis

05 Diana

## artery

02 M1 04 duct, road, tube 06 vessel
07 channel, conduit 11 blood vessel
*See also* **vein**

## artful

◇ *anagram indicator* 03 sly 04 foxy, rusé, wily 05 dodgy, sharp, smart 06 cautel, clever, crafty, shrewd, subtle, tricky 07 cunning, devious, skilful, vulpine 08 masterly, scheming 09 cautelous, deceitful, designing, dexterous, ingenious 11 resourceful

## artfully

◇ *anagram indicator* 05 slyly 08 cleverly, craftily, shrewdly 09 cunningly, deviously, skilfully 11 deceitfully, ingeniously

## arthropod

*Arthropods include:*

09 trilobite, water bear
10 tardigrade
14 bear-animalcule

*See also* **crustacean; insect; invertebrate; spider**

## Arthurian legend

*see* **knight; legend**

## article

01 a 02 an, el, il, la, le, un 03 art, ein, les, the, une 04 eine, item, part, term, unit 05 curio, essay, paper, piece, point, story, thing 06 clause, exposé, object, report, review 07 account, exhibit, feature, portion, section, whatsit, write-up 08 artefact, offprint 09 commodity, editorial, monograph, paragraph, something, thingummy 10 boondoggle, commentary, subsection 11 composition, constituent 12 thingummybob, thingummyjig 14 what-d'you-call-it

## articulate

◇ *homophone indicator* ◇ *anagram indicator* 03 say 04 talk 05 clear, frame, lucid, speak, state, utter, vocal, voice 06 fluent, tongue, verbal 07 breathe, enounce, express, jointed, realize 08 coherent, distinct, eloquent, vocalize 09 enunciate, pronounce, verbalize 10 expressive, meaningful, well-spoken 12 intelligible 13 communicative 14 comprehensible, understandable

## articulated

◇ *homophone indicator* ◇ *anagram indicator* 05 joint 06 hinged, joined, linked 07 coupled, jointed 08 attached, fastened 09 connected, segmented

10 vertebrate 11 interlocked 14 fitted together

## articulately

07 clearly, lucidly 08 fluently 10 coherently, distinctly, eloquently 12 expressively, intelligibly 14 comprehensibly

## articulation

05 joint 06 saying 07 diction, segment, talking, voicing 08 coupling, delivery, jointing, junction, speaking, tonguing 09 arthrosis, clavation, consonant, gomphosis, utterance 10 connection, expression 11 diarthrosis, enunciation 12 schindylesis, synarthrosis, vocalization 13 pronunciation, verbalization

## artifice

03 art, con, gin 04 ruse, scam, wile 05 craft, dodge, fraud, guile, reach, set-up, shift, trick 06 deceit, device, scheme, tactic 07 cunning, shuffle, slyness 08 strategy, subtlety, trickery 09 chicanery, deception, stratagem 10 artfulness, cleverness, craftiness, subterfuge 11 contrivance, deviousness 12 contrivement 14 davenport-trick

## artificial

03 art 04 fake, faux, mock, sham 05 bogus, false, paste, pseud 06 ersatz, forced, made-up, phoney, pseudo 07 assumed, feigned, man-made, plastic, studied 08 affected, mannered, specious, spurious 09 contrived, imitation, insincere, pretended, processed, simulated, synthetic, unnatural 10 non-natural 11 counterfeit 12 manufactured

## artificiality

04 sham 07 falsity 08 pretence 10 simulation 11 insincerity 12 speciousness, spuriousness 13 theatricalism, theatricality, unnaturalness

## artificially

07 falsely 10 speciously, spuriously 11 insincerely, unnaturally 13 synthetically

## artillery

02 RA 03 AAA, art, RHA 04 arty, guns 05 train 07 cannons, gunnery, weapons 08 cannonry, missiles, ordnance 09 heavy guns, munitions 12 heavy weapons

## artisan

06 expert 07 pioneer 08 mechanic 09 artificer, craftsman, operative 10 journeyman, technician 11 craftswoman 12 craftsperson 13 skilled worker 14 handicraftsman

## artist

02 RA 03 ace, ARA, pro 04 poet 05 actor, maker, maven, mavin 06 author, dancer, expert, writer 07 creator, dab hand, founder, maestro 08 Bohemian, composer, inventor, musician 09 authority, mannerist, performer 10 originator, specialist, trecentist 12 professional 13 perspectivist

*Artists, craftsmen and craftswomen include:*

06 etcher, master, potter, weaver
07 painter, printer
08 animator, designer, engraver, sculptor
09 architect, carpenter, goldsmith
10 blacksmith, cartoonist, oil painter, woodworker
11 coppersmith, draughtsman, illustrator, miniaturist, portraitist, silversmith, web designer
12 caricaturist, lithographer, photographer
13 draughtswoman, graphic artist, screenprinter
14 graffiti artist, pavement artist, watercolourist
15 graphic designer

*See also* **painter; photograph; sculpture**

• **great artist** 09 Old Master

## artiste

05 actor, comic 06 dancer, player, singer 07 actress, trouper 08 comedian, musician 09 performer 10 comedienne 11 entertainer 12 vaudevillian 13 variety artist

## artistic

04 fine 06 gifted 07 elegant, refined, skilled, stylish 08 creative, cultured, graceful, original, talented, tasteful 09 aesthetic, beautiful, exquisite, sensitive 10 attractive, cultivated, decorative, expressive, harmonious, ornamental 11 imaginative

## artistry

05 craft, flair, skill, style, touch 06 genius, talent 07 ability, finesse, mastery 08 deftness 09 expertise 10 brilliance, creativity 11 proficiency, sensitivity, workmanship 13 craftsmanship 14 accomplishment

## artless

04 open, pure, true 05 frank, naive, naked, plain 06 candid, direct, honest, simple, unwary 07 genuine, natural, sincere 08 homespun, innocent, trusting 09 childlike, guileless, ingenuous, unworldly 10 unaffected 11 undesigning 13 unpretentious 15 straightforward, unsophisticated

## artlessly

05 truly 06 openly, purely, simply 07 frankly, naively, plainly 08 candidly, directly 09 naturally, sincerely 10 innocently 11 ingenuously 15 unpretentiously

## Aruba

03 ABW

## as

02 eg, so, ut 03 als, qua 04 kame, like, when 05 being, esker, since, while 06 just as, such as, whilst 07 arsenic, because, owing to, through 09 forasmuch, similar to 10 for example, inasmuch as, seeing that 11 as a result of, for instance, in the role of, on account of 12 in the guise of 13 at the same time, functioning as, with the part of 14 simultaneously 15 at

the same time as, considering that
• **as for** 07 apropos 09 as regards
10 concerning, respecting 12 in
relation to, with regard to 13 with
respect to 14 on the subject of, with
relation to 15 with reference to
• **as it were** 05 quasi 06 in a way, kind
of, second, sort of 07 so to say 09 in
some way, so to speak 10 in some sort
11 as it might be

**asafoetida**
04 hing

**asbestos**
07 amosite 08 amiantus, rock wood
09 amianthus, earthflax 10 chrysotile
11 crocidolite 12 mountain wood

**ascend**
◊ *reversal down indicator* 03 sty 04 go up,
rise, soar, upgo 05 arise, climb, fly up,
get up, mount, scale, tower 06 climax,
come up, move up 07 float up, lift off,
take off 10 gain height 12 slope
upwards

**ascendancy**
04 edge, sway 05 power 07 command,
control, mastery 08 dominion,
hegemony, lordship, prestige
09 authority, dominance, dominancy,
influence, mobocracy, supremacy,
upper hand 10 domination, prevalence
11 pre-eminence, superiority
12 predominance

**ascendant**
◊ *reversal down indicator* 07 growing
08 dominant, powerful, superior
09 prevalent 10 developing
11 predominant 12 on the up and up
13 rising in power

**ascending**
02 up

**ascent**
04 hill, pull, ramp, rise 05 climb, slope
06 rising, uphill 07 advance, incline,
scaling 08 anabasis, climbing,
gradient, mounting, progress
09 acclivity, ascending, ascension,
elevation 10 escalation
11 advancement

**ascertain**
03 fix, see 04 twig 05 learn, prove
06 detect, locate, settle, verify
07 confirm, find out, pin down, suss
out 08 discover, identify, make sure
09 determine, establish, get to know
10 come to know, make sure of
11 make certain

**ascetic**
03 nun 04 Jain, monk, yogi 05 fakir,
harsh, Jaina, plain, sadhu, stern
06 Essene, hermit, saddhu, severe,
strict 07 austere, dervish, Jainist,
puritan, recluse, spartan, stylite
08 celibate, Nazarite, rigorous,
sannyasi, solitary 09 abstainer,
abstinent, anchorite, Montanist,
pillarist 10 abstemious 11 pillar-saint,
puritanical, self-denying 14 self-
controlled 15 self-disciplined

**asceticism**
07 ascesis 08 severity 09 austerity,

harshness 10 abstinence, self-denial
11 monasticism, self-control 14 self-
discipline

**ascidian**
08 tunicate 09 sea squirt
15 appendicularian

**ascribe**
05 apply 06 assign, charge, credit,
impute 07 put down, set down
08 accredit, arrogate 09 attribute
12 give credit to

**ash**
04 kali, kelp, kilp 05 aizle, easle,
rowan 06 embers, tephra 07 cinders,
clinker, residue, witchen 08 charcoal,
Ygdrasil 09 xanthoxyl, Yggdrasil
10 Yggdrasill 11 nuée ardente
13 toothache tree 15 Pharaoh's serpent

**ashamed**
05 loath, sorry 06 guilty, modest,
shamed 07 abashed, bashful, humbled
08 blushing, contrite, hesitant,
penitent, red-faced, sheepish
09 mortified, reluctant, unwilling
10 apologetic, distressed, humiliated,
remorseful, shamefaced 11 crestfallen,
discomfited, discomposed,
embarrassed 12 on a guilt trip 13 self-
conscious

**ashen**
03 wan 04 grey, pale 05 livid, pasty,
white 06 leaden, pallid 07 anaemic,
ghastly 08 blanched, bleached 09 pale-
faced 10 colourless

**ashore**
05 aland 11 onto the land 12 onto the
beach, onto the shore 15 towards the
shore

**Asia**

*Asian countries include:*

04 Laos
05 Burma, China, India, Japan,
Nepal
06 Bhutan, Taiwan
07 Myanmar, Vietnam
08 Cambodia, Malaysia, Maldives,
Mongolia, Pakistan, Sri Lanka,
Thailand
09 East Timor, Indonesia, Singapore
10 Bangladesh, Kazakhstan,
Kyrgyzstan, North Korea, South
Korea, Tajikistan, Uzbekistan
11 Afghanistan, Philippines
12 Turkmenistan
16 Brunei Darussalam

*Asian landmarks include:*

05 Indus
06 Ganges, Mekong, Mt Fuji
07 Everest, Yangtze
08 Krakatoa, Lake Sebu, Red River,
Taj Mahal
09 Angkor Wat, Annapurna, Great
Wall, Himalayas, Hiroshima,
Ming Tombs, Mt Everest
10 Gobi Desert, River Indus,
Sagarmatha, Sea of Japan, Thar
Desert
11 Brahmaputra, Mekong River,
Three Gorges, Yellow River

12 Golden Temple, Potala Palace,
Raffles Hotel
13 Forbidden City, Kangchenjunga
14 Jaganath Temple
15 Tiananmen Square

**Asian**

*Asians include:*

03 Han, Lao
04 Ainu, Cham, Nair, Shan, Sulu,
Thai
05 Bajau, Karen, Kazak, Nayar,
Tajik, Tamil, Uzbeg, Uzbek,
Vedda
06 Afghan, Baluch, Gurkha, Indian,
Kazakh, Kyrgyz, Manchu,
Mongol, Pathan, Tadjik, Telugu
07 Baluchi, Burmese, Chinese,
Goanese, Goorkha, Karenni,
Kirghiz, Laotian, Manchoo,
Maratha, Russian, Tadzhik,
Tagálog, Turkish, Turkmen
08 Bruneian, Canarese, Filipina,
Filipino, Japanese, Kanarese,
Mahratta, Nepalese
09 Bhutanese, Cambodian,
Malaysian, Mongolian, Pakistani,
Sri Lankan, Taiwanese
10 Indonesian, Myanmarese,
Vietnamese
11 Azerbaijani, Bangladeshi,
Kazakhstani, North Korean,
Singaporean, South Korean,
Tajikistani

**aside**
02 by 04 away 05 alone, apart
07 whisper 08 secretly 09 alongside,
departure, monologue, on one side,
privately, soliloquy, to one side
10 apostrophe, digression, separately
11 in isolation, out of the way,
parenthesis 12 obiter dictum, stage
whisper 13 cursory remark
15 notwithstanding

**asinine**
04 daft 05 crazy, inane, potty, silly
06 absurd, stupid 07 fatuous, foolish,
idiotic, moronic 08 gormless
09 imbecilic, ludicrous, senseless
10 half-witted 11 nonsensical

**ask**
03 beg, bid, eft, sue 04 evet, newt, poll,
pose, pray, pump, quiz, seek 05 crave,
grill, order, plead, posit, press, query,
speer, speir, yearn 06 appeal, demand,
desire, invite, summon 07 beseech,
bespeak, canvass, clamour, enquire,
entreat, fire off, implore, inquire,
propose, request, require, solicit,
suggest 08 approach, have over,
petition, propound, question
09 entertain, have round, interview,
postulate 10 put forward, supplicate
11 interrogate, requisition 12 cross-
examine, put on the spot 13 cross-
question 14 put a question to 15 give a
grilling to

**askance**
04 awry 07 asconce 08 sideways
09 dubiously, obliquely 10 doubtfully,
indirectly, scornfully 11 sceptically
12 disdainfully, suspiciously

**askew**

**13** distrustfully, mistrustfully **14** contemptuously, disapprovingly

**askew**

◊ *anagram indicator* **04** awry, skew **05** aglee, agley, tipsy **06** skivie, squint **07** crooked, oblique **08** lopsided, sideways **09** crookedly, obliquely, off-centre, out of line, skew-whiff **10** lopsidedly **12** asymmetrical **14** asymmetrically

**asleep**

**04** numb **05** inert **06** dozing **07** dormant, napping, resting **08** comatose, inactive, reposing, sleeping, snoozing **09** conked out, flaked out, nodded off, popped off **10** crashed out, fast asleep, sparked out **11** sound asleep, unconscious **13** out like a light **14** dead to the world, in the land of Nod, out for the count

**asparagus**

**05** sprew, sprue **06** smilax

**aspect**

**03** air **04** brow, face, look, side, view **05** angle, facet, light, phase, point, trine, visor, vizor **06** facies, factor, manner, phasis **07** bearing, contour, feature, outlook, respect, sextile **08** position, quartile, quincunx, quintile **09** dimension, direction, landscape **10** apparition, appearance, biquintile, complexion, expression, standpoint **11** conjunction, countenance, physiognomy, point of view **13** configuration

**asperity**

**08** acerbity, acrimony, severity, sourness **09** crossness, harshness, roughness, sharpness **10** bitterness, causticity **11** astringency, crabbedness, peevishness **12** abrasiveness, churlishness, irascibility, irritability

**aspersion**

**04** slur **07** calumny, slander
• **cast aspersions on 04** slur **05** knock, slate, smear **06** defame, vilify **07** censure, run down, slander **08** reproach **09** criticize, denigrate, deprecate, disparage **10** calumniate, sling mud at, throw mud at

**asphalt**

**08** uintaite **09** gilsonite, Jew's-pitch, uintahite **12** mineral pitch

**asphyxiate**

**03** gas **05** choke **06** stifle **07** smother **08** strangle, throttle **09** suffocate **11** strangulate

**asphyxiation**

**07** choking **08** stifling **10** smothering **11** suffocation **13** strangulation

**aspirant**

**06** donzel, squire **09** candidate

**aspirate**

**05** rough

**aspiration**

**03** aim, yen **04** goal, hope, wish **05** dream, ideal **06** desire, intent, object **07** craving, longing, purpose **08** ambition, yearning **09** breathing, endeavour, hankering, objective **10** pretension

**aspire**

**03** aim, yen **04** hope, long, mint, seek, wish **05** crave, dream, ettle, yearn **06** desire, hanker, intend, pursue **07** pretend, purpose **11** have as a goal, have as an aim

**aspiring**

**04** keen **05** eager **07** budding, hopeful, longing, wishful, would-be **08** aspirant, striving **09** ambitious, intending **10** optimistic **12** endeavouring, enterprising

**ass**

**03** fon, git, mug, nit, oaf, sot, yap **04** berk, cake, clot, cony, coof, dill, dope, dork, fool, geek, goop, gowk, gull, joss, moke, mule, nana, nerd, nerk, nong, pony, prat, soft, twit, yo-yo **05** burro, cluck, cuddy, dicky, dweeb, galah, hinny, idiot, Jenny, kiang, klutz, kulan, kyang, neddy, ninny, patch, schmo, snipe, sumph, twerp, wally **06** bampot, cretin, dickey, dimwit, donkey, dottle, drongo, koulan, nidget, nitwit, numpty, onager, quagga, sawney, turkey, wigeon **07** airhead, asinico, buffoon, gubbins, halfwit, jackass, jughead, lemming, muggins, natural, plonker, saphead, want-wit **08** dipstick, flathead, fondling, imbecile, innocent, lunkhead, mooncalf, numskull, omadhaun, Tom-noddy **09** blockhead, capocchia, dumb-cluck, dziggetai, lack-brain, lame brain, mumchance, schlemiel **10** nincompoop **11** jenny donkey, knuckle-head **13** Jerusalem pony, proper Charlie
*See also* **fool**

**assail**

**03** din, rag, row **04** peal, pelt, slam **05** assay, beset, go for, slate, worry **06** attack, invade, malign, plague, rattle, revile, strafe, straff, strike **07** barrage, bedevil, belabor, bestorm, bombard, disturb, lay into, perplex, rubbish, run down, set upon, slag off, torment, trouble **08** badmouth, ballyrag, belabour, bludgeon, bullyrag, maltreat, overfall, set about, tear into **09** criticize, pitch into **10** fall foul of, set against

**assailant**

**05** enemy **06** abuser, mugger **07** invader, reviler **08** assailer, attacker, onsetter, opponent **09** adversary, aggressor, assaulter

**assassin**

**04** thug **05** bravo, ninja **06** gunman, hit-man, killer, slayer **07** sworder **08** murderer **09** cut-throat **10** hatchet man, liquidator **11** contract man, executioner
*See also* **murderer**

**assassinate**

◊ *anagram indicator* **03** hit **04** do in, kill, slay **06** murder **07** bump off, execute **08** dispatch **09** eliminate, liquidate, slaughter

**assassination**

◊ *anagram indicator* **06** murder **07** killing **09** execution, slaughter, taking-off **11** termination

**assault**

**02** do **03** GBH, hit, mug **04** bash, raid, rape **05** abuse, assay, blitz, feint, go for, onset, smite, stoor, storm, stour **06** affray, attack, bash up, beat up, charge, do over, fall on, insult, invade, molest, stound, stownd, stowre, strike **07** attempt, battery, bombard, lay into, mugging, offence, offense, set upon **08** invasion, storming **09** fusillade, incursion, offensive, onslaught **10** hamesucken, violent act **11** molestation **13** interfere with **15** act of aggression, throw yourself on

**assay**

**04** test **05** check, cupel, ELISA **08** analysis **09** appraisal, judgement **10** assessment, evaluation, inspection **11** examination

**assemblage**

**04** mass **05** crowd, flock, group, rally, shoal, strew **06** galaxy, school, throng **07** montage **09** aggregate, gathering, multitude **10** collection, collective, parliament **12** accumulation

**assemble**

◊ *anagram indicator* **04** band, join, make, mass, meet **05** amass, build, flock, group, rally, relie, set up, troop **06** accoil, cobble, gather, join up, muster, relide, roll up, summon **07** collate, collect, compose, connect, convene, convoke, marshal, round up, summons **08** mobilize **09** aggregate, construct, fabricate **10** accumulate, congregate, rendezvous **11** fit together, get together, manufacture, put together **12** come together **13** bring together, piece together

**assembly**

◊ *anagram indicator* **03** hui, mob **04** body, Dáil, diet, feis, meet, moot, Sejm **05** agora, bench, court, crowd, divan, flock, gemot, group, jirga, rally, synod, thing **06** indaba, kgotla, Majlis, Mejlis, muster, plenum, throng **07** chamber, chapter, company, council, gorsedd, Knesset, Landtag, meeting, squeeze, turnout, zemstvo **08** audience, building, bun fight, conclave, congress, ecclesia, folkmoot, panegyry, presence, Sobranje, Sobranye, Storting **09** Aula Regis, concourse, frequence, gathering, multitude, Skupstina, Storthing, synagogue, synedrion, synedrium, volksraad **10** assemblage, bear garden, collection, conference, consistory, convention, Curia Regis, Donnybrook, masquerade, Oireachtas, Skupshtina **11** church court, convocation, Dáil Eireann, fabrication, manufacture, Pandemonium **12** body of people, common vestry, congregation, construction, Pandaemonium **15** piecing together, putting together

**assent**

*See also* **parliament**
• **General Assembly** 02 GA

**assent**
03 buy 05 agree, allow, grant, yield
06 accede, accept, accord, comply, concur, permit, submit 07 approve, concede, consent, go-ahead, sign off
08 approval, sanction, thumbs-up
09 accession, acquiesce, agreement, subscribe 10 acceptance, compliance, concession, green light, permission, submission 11 approbation, concurrence 12 acquiescence, capitulation 14 give the go-ahead
15 give the thumbs-up
• **expression of assent** 01 I 02 ay, OK 03 aye, oke, olé 04 done, good, okay 07 d'accord 09 I am agreed 10 I am content

**assert**
03 put, say 04 have, hold, pose
05 argue, claim, state, swear, vouch
06 affirm, attest, avouch, defend, stress, uphold 07 confirm, contend, declare, lay down, profess, protest
08 constate, insist on, maintain
09 establish, predicate, pronounce, testify to, vindicate 10 stand up for
12 crack the whip

**assertion**
03 vow 04 word 05 claim, vouch
06 avowal, threap, threep 08 averment, pretence, pretense, sentence
09 statement 10 affirmance, allegation, contention, insistence, profession
11 affirmation, attestation, declaration, jactitation, predication, testificate, vindication 12 constatation, gratis dictum 13 pronouncement

**assertive**
04 bold, firm 05 perky, pushy
07 decided, forward 08 assuming, dogmatic, dominant, emphatic, forceful, immodest, positive
09 confident, insistent 10 aggressive, determined 11 domineering, opinionated, overbearing, self-assured
12 presumptuous, strong-willed 13 self-confident 14 sure of yourself 15 feeling your oats

**assertively**
06 boldly, firmly 10 dominantly, forcefully, positively 11 confidently, insistently 12 aggressively
14 presumptuously 15 self-confidently

**assess**
03 fix, tax 04 levy, rate 05 cense, gauge, Jenny, judge, stent, sum up, teind, value, weigh 06 affeer, assize, demand, extend, impose, modify, review, size up 07 compute
08 appraise, check out, consider, estimate, evaluate 09 calculate, determine 11 jenny donkey

**assessment**
04 levy, rate, toll 05 recce, stent
06 demand, review, tariff 07 opinion, testing 09 appraisal, judgement, valuation 10 estimation, evaluation, imposition 11 computation
12 appraisement 13 consideration

**assessor**
05 judge 06 expert, gauger, umpire, valuer 07 adviser, arbiter, referee
08 examiner, measurer, recorder, reviewer, valuator 09 appraiser, estimator, inspector 10 arbitrator, consultant, counsellor 11 adjudicator
12 loss adjuster 15 average adjuster

**asset**
03 aid 04 boon, help, plus 05 funds, goods, means, money 06 estate, virtue, wealth 07 benefit, capital, savings
08 blessing, holdings, property, reserves, resource, seed corn, strength, tangible 09 advantage, liability, plus point, resources, valuables
10 securities 11 hot property, possessions, receivables, strong point

**asseverate**
04 aver, avow 05 claim, state 06 affirm, assert, attest 07 confirm, declare, profess 08 maintain

**assiduity**
08 devotion, hard work, industry, sedulity 09 constancy, diligence
10 dedication 11 persistence
12 perseverance 14 meticulousness
15 industriousness

**assiduous**
06 steady 07 careful, devoted
08 constant, diligent, sedulous, studious, thorough, untiring
09 attentive, dedicated 10 meticulous, persistent, unflagging 11 hard-working, industrious, persevering
13 conscientious, indefatigable

**assign**
03 fix, put, set 04 aret, cast, give, name, rank, sort 05 allot, allow, apply, arett, grant, range 06 affect, choose, convey, detail, impute, ordain, select
07 adjudge, appoint, ascribe, consign, endorse, hive off, indorse, install, put down, specify, station 08 accredit, allocate, arrogate, delegate, dispense, hand over, make over, nominate, relegate, transfer, transmit
09 apportion, attribute, chalk up to, designate, determine, stipulate
10 commission, distribute
11 appropriate

**assignation**
04 date 05 tryst 10 engagement, rendezvous 11 appointment, arrangement 13 secret meeting

**assignment**
03 job 04 duty, post, task 05 grant
06 charge, errand 07 project
08 position, transfer 09 selection
10 allocation, commission, conveyance, delegation, nomination, obligation 11 appointment, consignment, designation, disposition
12 distribution 14 responsibility

**assimilate**
◇ *containment indicator* 03 mix
05 adapt, blend, grasp, learn, unite
06 absorb, adjust, imbibe, mingle, pick up, take in 08 accustom 09 integrate
11 acclimatize, accommodate, incorporate, internalize

**assimilation**
07 osmosis 08 blending, grasping, learning, mixing in, taking in
09 digestion 10 absorption, adaptation, adjustment, resorption 11 integration
13 accommodation, incorporation
15 acclimatization, internalization

**assist**
03 aid 04 abet, back, help 05 serve
06 back up, enable, second
07 advance, benefit, further, pitch in, relieve, succour, support, sustain
08 expedite 09 co-operate, do your bit, encourage, give a hand, lend a hand, reinforce 10 facilitate, make easier, rally round 11 collaborate 12 give a leg up to

**assistance**
03 aid 04 hand, help 05 boost 06 a leg up, relief 07 backing, benefit, service, subsidy, succour, support 08 easement
09 adjutancy 10 friendship 11 co-operation, furtherance 12 a helping hand 13 collaboration, reinforcement

**assistant**
02 PA 03 cad, PDA 04 aide, ally, mate
05 clerk, usher 06 backer, curate, deputy, helper, intern, leg-man, nipper, second, yeoman 07 abettor, acolyte, acolyth, best boy, fireman, matross, nobbler, omnibus, partner
08 chainman, leg-woman, mud-clerk, offsider, right arm, salesman, servitor
09 accessory, ancillary, associate, auxiliary, coadjutor, colleague, land-reeve, midinette, prorector, secretary, suffragan, supporter, toad-eater, whipper-in 10 accomplice, aide-de-camp, amanuensis, copyholder, evangelist, proproctor, reading-boy, roughrider, sales clerk, saleswoman, subsidiary 11 confederate, merry-andrew, salesperson, subordinate
12 brigade major, collaborator, demonstrator, driving force, right-hand man 13 counter-jumper 14 boatswain's mate, checkout person, Common Serjeant, counter-skipper 15 second-in-command, vice-chamberlain

**associate**
◇ *juxtaposition indicator* 01 A 03 Ass, mix, pal 04 ally, band, chum, gang, herd, join, link, mate, mell, pair, peer, yoke 05 crony, haunt, unite 06 attach, couple, fellow, friend, helper, hobnob, league, mingle, relate 07 combine, company, compeer, comrade, connect, consort, goombah, hang out, partner, sociate 08 complice, confrère, co-worker, follower, identify, sidekick, sororize, yoke-mate 09 accompany, affiliate, assistant, coadjutor, colleague, companion, correlate, hang about, neighbour, socialize, syndicate
10 accomplice, amalgamate, be involved, coadjutrix, consociate, fraternize, hang around, yokefellow
11 coadjutress, confederate, keep company 12 band together, collaborator, go hand in hand, rub shoulders 15 think of together

### associated

◇ *juxtaposition indicator* **03** Ass **05** alike **06** allied, linked **07** coupled, related, similar **08** combined, in league **09** connected, consorted **10** affiliated, correlated, syndicated **11** amalgamated **12** confederated **13** corresponding, in partnership

### association

**03** Ass, tie **04** band, bond, club, gild, hunt, link **05** group, guild, tie-up, union **06** cartel, chapel, clique, league, Probus, thrift, Verein **07** combine, company, contact, job club, society **08** alliance, clanship, intimacy, relation, sodality **09** coalition, goose-club, syndicate **10** connection, consortium, craft guild, federation, fellowship, fraternity, friendship, Jockey Club, Land League, propaganda, Young Italy **11** affiliation, confederacy, corporation, correlation, familiarity, involvement, partnership, triumvirate **12** consociation, Gesellschaft, organization, relationship **13** companionship, confederation, incorporation, interrelation **14** Burschenschaft, identification, Primrose League **15** friendly society

### assorted

◇ *anagram indicator* **05** mixed **06** divers, motley, sundry, varied **07** diverse, several, various **08** manifold, sortable **09** different, differing **10** variegated **11** farraginous **12** multifarious **13** heterogeneous, miscellaneous

### assortment

**03** lot, mix **05** array, bunch, group **06** choice, jumble, medley **07** farrago, mixture, variety **08** grouping, mixed bag **09** diversity, menagerie, potpourri, selection **10** collection, miscellany, salmagundi **11** arrangement, olla-podrida, smörgåsbord **13** bits and pieces

### assuage

**04** beet, bete, calm, ease, lull **05** allay, lower, mease, slake, swage **06** lenify, lessen, pacify, quench, reduce, soften, soothe **07** appease, lighten, mollify, relieve, satisfy **08** mitigate, moderate, palliate **09** alleviate

### assume

◇ *containment indicator* **03** don **04** bear, take **05** adopt, fancy, feign, guess, infer, posit, put on, seize, think, usurp **06** accept, affect, deduce, expect, strike, take it, take on **07** acquire, believe, embrace, imagine, pre-empt, presume, pretend, suppose, surmise **08** arrogate, shoulder, simulate, take over **09** enter upon, postulate, undertake **10** come to have, commandeer, presuppose, take as read, understand **11** appropriate, counterfeit **14** take for granted

### assumed

**04** fake, sham **05** bogus, false **06** made-up, phoney **07** feigned **08** affected, borrowed, putative, supposed **09** pretended, simulated **10** fictitious

**11** counterfeit **12** adscititious, hypothetical, pseudonymous **14** supposititious

### assumption

**04** idea **05** axiom, donné, fancy, guess **06** belief, donnée, notion, theory **07** embrace, premise, seizure, surmise **08** adoption, takeover **09** inference, postulate **10** acceptance, arrogation, conclusion, conjecture, hypothesis, pre-emption, usurpation **11** embarkation, expectation, postulation, presumption, shouldering, supposition, undertaking **13** appropriation, commandeering **14** presupposition

### assurance

**03** vow **04** gall, oath, word **05** nerve, poise **06** aplomb, pledge **07** courage, promise, surance, warrant **08** audacity, boldness, security, sureness **09** assertion, certainty, guarantee **10** confidence, conviction, positivism **11** affirmation, assuredness, declaration, undertaking **12** self-reliance **13** self-assurance **14** self-confidence, unflappability

### assure

**03** vow **04** affy, hete, seal, tell **05** hecht, hight, swear **06** affirm, attest, avouch, ensure, pledge, secure, soothe **07** certify, comfort, confirm, hearten, promise, resolve, warrant **08** convince, persuade, reassure **09** ascertain, encourage, guarantee

### assured

**04** bold, calm, sure **05** fixed **06** secure **07** certain, ensured, settled **08** definite, positive, promised **09** assertive, audacious, confident, confirmed, thoughten **10** guaranteed **11** cut and dried, irrefutable, self-assured **12** indisputable **13** self-confident, self-possessed **14** sure of yourself
• **be assured of** **04** know

### assuredly

**05** pardi, pardy, perdy **06** pardie, perdie, surely **07** my certy **08** my certie **09** by my certy, certainly, of a verity **10** by my certie, definitely, for certain **12** and no mistake, indisputably, without doubt **14** unquestionably **15** without question

### astatine

**02** At

### astern

**03** aft **04** baft **05** abaft, apoop

### asteroid

**09** planetoid **11** minor planet

*Asteroids include:*

**04** Eros, Hebe, Iris, Juno
**05** Ceres, Flora, Metis, Vesta
**06** Apollo, Cybele, Davida, Europa, Hygiea, Icarus, Pallas, Psyche, Trojan
**07** Eunomia
**10** Interamnia

### astir

**05** afoot, agate **07** abroach, humming **09** in the wind

### astonish

**03** wow **04** daze, stun **05** amaze, floor, shock, stony **07** astound, flummox, stagger, startle, stupefy **08** bewilder, bowl over, confound, dumfound, gobsmack, surprise **09** dumbfound, electrify, take aback **11** flabbergast, knock for six **12** blow your mind

### astonished

**05** dazed **06** amazed **07** shocked, stunned **08** open-eyed, startled, wide-eyed **09** astounded, staggered, surprised **10** bewildered, bowled over, confounded, gobsmacked, taken aback **11** dumbfounded **12** lost for words **13** flabbergasted, knocked for six, thunderstruck

### astonishing

◇ *anagram indicator* **07** amazing **08** shocking, striking, stunning **09** startling **10** astounding, impressive, marvellous, prodigious, staggering, surprising **11** bewildering, mind-blowing **12** awe-inspiring, breathtaking, mind-boggling, unbelievable

### astonishment

**05** shock **06** dismay, marvel, wonder **08** surprise **09** amazement, confusion, disbelief **10** admiration, wonderment **12** bewilderment, stupefaction **13** consternation

### astound

**04** stun **05** abash, amaze, floor, shock **06** stound **07** flummox, startle, stupefy **08** astonish, bewilder, bowl over, surprise **09** overwhelm **11** knock for six

### astounding

**07** amazing **08** shocking, stunning **09** startling **10** staggering, stupefying, stupendous, surprising **11** astonishing, bewildering **12** breathtaking, overwhelming

### astray

◇ *anagram indicator* **04** awry, lost, miss, will, wull **05** abord, agate, amiss, wrong **06** abroad, adrift, errant, erring **07** missing **09** off course **10** miswandred, off the mark **11** off the rails

### astride

◇ *containment indicator* **08** straddle **10** en cavalier **12** colossus-wise

### astringent

**04** acid, hard, kino **05** harsh, rough, stern **06** biting, gambir, severe **07** acerbic, austere, caustic, gambier, guaraná, mordant, puckery, rhatany, styptic **08** alum-root, critical, krameria, scathing **09** obstruent, tormentil, trenchant, zinc oxide **10** astrictive, witch-hazel **11** restringent

### astrologer

**09** stargazer **10** genethliac **11** horoscopist, Nostradamus **12** figure-caster **14** archgenethliac

## astronaut

08 lunanaut, spaceman 09 cosmonaut, lunarnaut, taikonaut 10 spacewoman 14 space traveller

*Astronauts and space travellers include:*

03 **Ham**
04 **Bean** (Alan), **Ride** (Sally), **Tito** (Dennis)
05 **Foale** (Michael), **Glenn** (John), **Irwin** (James), **Laika**, **Scott** (David), **Titov** (Gherman), **White** (Edward)
06 **Aldrin** (Buzz), **Conrad** (Pete), **Leonov** (Aleksei), **Lovell** (Jim)
07 **Chaffee** (Roger), **Collins** (Michael), **Gagarin** (Yuri), **Grissom** (Gus), **Schirra** (Wally), **Sharman** (Helen), **Shepard** (Alan)
08 **Mitchell** (Edgar)
09 **Armstrong** (Neil)
10 **Tereshkova** (Valentina)

• **would-be astronaut** 10 space cadet

## astronomer

04 astr 06 astron 09 stargazer

*Astronomers and astrophysicists include:*

04 **Airy** (Sir George), **Biot** (Jean-Baptiste), **Gold** (Thomas), **Hale** (George), **Lyot** (Bernard), **Oort** (Jan), **Pond** (John), **Rees** (Sir Martin), **Ryle** (Sir Martin), **Saha** (Meghnad), **Webb** (James E)
05 **Adams** (John Couch), **Adams** (Walter S), **Baade** (Walter), **Baily** (Francis), **Bliss** (Nathaniel), **Brahe** (Tycho), **Dyson** (Sir Frank), **Gauss** (Carl Friedrich), **Hoyle** (Sir Fred), **Jeans** (Sir James), **Jones** (Sir Harold Spencer), **Moore** (Sir Patrick), **Sagan** (Carl), **Smith** (Sir Francis), **Vogel** (Hermann Carl)
06 **Bessel** (Friedrich), **Halley** (Edmond), **Hewish** (Antony), **Hubble** (Edwin), **Jansky** (Karl), **Kepler** (Johannes), **Kuiper** (Gerard), **Lovell** (Sir Bernard), **Olbers** (Heinrich), **Piazzi** (Giuseppe), **Roemer** (Olaus)
07 **Babcock** (Harold D), **Barnard** (Edward Emerson), **Bradley** (James), **Cassini** (Giovanni), **Celsius** (Anders), **Galilei** (Galileo), **Galileo** (Galileo), **Hawking** (Stephen), **Huggins** (Sir William), **Langley** (Samuel), **Laplace** (Pierre), **Lockyer** (Sir Norman), **Maunder** (E W), **Penrose** (Roger), **Penzias** (Arno), **Ptolemy**, **Russell** (Henry Norris), **Sandage** (Allan), **Schmidt** (Maarten), **Seyfert** (Carl), **Shapley** (Harlow), **Whipple** (Fred), **Woolley** (Sir Richard)
08 **Burbidge** (Geoffrey), **Burbidge** (Margaret), **Chandler** (Seth Carlo), **Christie** (Sir William), **Friedman** (Herbert), **Herschel** (Caroline), **Herschel** (Sir John), **Herschel** (Sir William), **Lemaître** (Georges), **Tombaugh** (Clyde W)
09 **Eddington** (Sir Arthur), **Fabricius** (David), **Flamsteed** (John), **Maskelyne** (Nevil), **Pickering** (Sir

William), **Sosigenes**
10 **Carrington** (Richard), **Copernicus** (Nicolas), **Hipparchos**, **Wolfendale** (Sir Arnold)
11 **Bell Burnell** (Jocelyn), **Graham-Smith** (Sir Francis), **Hertzsprung** (Ejnar), **Tsiolkovsky** (Konstantin)
12 **Schiaparelli** (Giovanni)
13 **Chandrasekhar** (Subrahmanyan), **Schwarzschild** (Karl)
14 **Galileo Galilei**

## astronomical

04 astr, huge, vast 06 astron, cosmic 07 immense, mammoth, massive, stellar 08 colossal, enormous, gigantic, heavenly, infinite, thumping, whopping 09 celestial, planetary 10 tremendous 11 substantial 12 considerable, cosmological, immeasurable, interstellar
• **astronomical model** 06 orrery

## astronomy

04 astr 06 astron 08 star-read 09 uranology

## astrophysicist

*see* **astronomer**

## astute

03 sly 04 cute, keen, sage, wide, wily, wise 05 canny, sharp 06 clever, crafty, shrewd, subtle 07 cunning, knowing, prudent 09 sagacious 10 discerning, perceptive 11 intelligent, penetrating, sharp-witted 13 perspicacious

## astutely

06 keenly, wisely 08 craftily, shrewdly 12 perceptively 13 intelligently, sharp-wittedly

## asunder

02 up 05 apart, in two 06 atwain 07 in twain 08 in pieces, to pieces

## asylum

03 bin 05 girth, grith, haven 06 bedlam, refuge 07 retreat, shelter 08 madhouse, Magdalen, nuthouse 09 dark-house, funny farm, sanctuary 10 frithsoken 11 institution 12 penitentiary, port in a storm 13 place of safety 14 mental hospital

## asymmetrical

04 awry, skew 06 uneven 07 anaxial, crooked, oblique, unequal 08 lopsided 09 distorted, irregular, malformed 10 unbalanced 13 unsymmetrical

## asymmetry

09 imbalance 10 distortion, handedness, inequality, unevenness, unsymmetry 11 crookedness 12 irregularity, lopsidedness, malformation

## at

02 in, to 08 astatine

## ate

◊ *containment indicator*

## atheism

07 impiety 08 nihilism, paganism, unbelief 09 disbelief, non-belief 10 heathenism, infidelity, irreligion, scepticism 11 godlessness, rationalism, ungodliness 12 freethinking

## atheist

05 pagan 07 heathen, heretic, infidel, sceptic 08 humanist, nihilist 10 unbeliever 11 disbeliever, freethinker, non-believer, nullifidian, rationalist

## Athene

07 Minerva

## athlete

04 jock 05 miler 06 player, runner 07 gymnast, hurdler 09 contender, sportsman 10 competitor, contestant 11 sportswoman 12 quarter-miler

*Athletes include:*

03 **Coe** (Sebastian, Lord)
04 **Bolt** (Usain), **Budd** (Zola), **Cram** (Steve), **Koch** (Marita), **Mota** (Rosa)
05 **Bubka** (Sergey), **Jones** (Marion), **Keino** (Kip), **Landy** (John), **Lewis** (Carl), **Lewis** (Denise), **Moses** (Ed), **Nurmi** (Paavo), **Ottey** (Merlene), **Ovett** (Steve), **Owens** (Jesse), **Pérec** (Marie-José), **Waitz** (Grete), **Wells** (Allan)
06 **Aouita** (Said), **Barber** (Eunice), **Beamon** (Bob), **Bekele** (Kenenisa), **Devers** (Gail), **Foster** (Brendan), **Fraser** (Shelly-Ann), **Greene** (Maurice), **Holmes** (Kelly), **Kemboi** (Ezekiel), **Mutola** (Maria), **Oerter** (Al), **Peters** (Mary), **Powell** (Asafa)
07 **Backley** (Steve), **Edwards** (Jonathan), **Fosbury** (Dick), **Freeman** (Cathy), **Gunnell** (Sally), **Jackson** (Colin), **Johnson** (Ben), **Johnson** (Michael), **Liddell** (Eric), **Morceli** (Noureddine), **Wariner** (Jeremy), **Zatopek** (Emil), **Zelezny** (Jan)
08 **Christie** (Linford), **Guerrouj** (Hicham el-), **Kipketer** (Wilson), **McColgan** (Liz), **Ohuruogu** (Christine), **Phillips** (Dwight), **Pieterse** (Zola), **Thompson** (Daley)
09 **Bannister** (Sir Roger), **O'Sullivan** (Sonia), **Radcliffe** (Paula), **Sanderson** (Tessa), **Špotáková** (Babora), **Whitbread** (Fatima)
12 **Blankers-Koen** (Fanny), **Gebrselassie** (Haile), **Grey-Thompson** (Dame Tanni)
14 **Griffith Joyner** (Florence 'Flo-Jo')

## athletic

01 A 03 fit 04 wiry 05 games, leish 06 active, brawny, muscly, robust, sinewy, sports, sporty, strong, sturdy 08 muscular, powerful, sporting, vigorous, well-knit 09 energetic, gymnastic, strapping

## athletics

05 games, races 06 sports 07 matches 08 aerobics 09 exercises 10 gymnastics 11 field events, track events 13 callisthenics
*See also* **sport**

*Athletics events include:*

04 ball, shot, walk
05 relay
06 discus, hammer, sprint
07 hurdles, javelin, shot put
08 biathlon, high jump, long jump,

marathon, tug-of-war
**09** broad jump, caber toss, decathlon, pole vault, sheaf toss, triathlon
**10** heptathlon, pentathlon, tetrathlon, triple jump
**11** discus throw, fell running, fifty metres, hammer throw, race walking
**12** cross-country, half marathon, javelin throw, steeplechase
**14** hop, step and jump
**15** tossing the caber

## athwart
**04** awry **06** across, aslant **07** asklent

## atmosphere
**03** air, atm, fug, sky **04** aura, feel, mood, tone **05** ether, miasm, tenor, vibes **06** miasma, milieu, spirit, welkin **07** climate, feeling, flavour, heavens, quality, setting **08** ambience, empyrean **09** aerospace, character, firmament **10** background **11** environment **12** surroundings **13** vault of heaven

*Atmosphere layers include:*

**09** exosphere, ionopause, mesopause
**10** ionosphere, mesosphere, ozone layer, tropopause
**11** stratopause, troposphere
**12** plasmasphere, stratosphere, thermosphere

## atom
**03** bit, jot **04** hint, iota, mite, spot, whit **05** crumb, grain, scrap, shred, speck, trace **06** morsel **08** fragment, molecule, particle **09** scintilla
*See also* **particle**

## atomic
**01** A
• **atomic mass unit** **03** amu
• **atomic number** **04** at no **06** at numb
• **atomic weight** **01** A **03** AWU **04** at wt

## atone
**03** aby **04** abye **06** offset, pay for, ransom, redeem, remedy, repent **07** appease, expiate, redress, satisfy **08** make good **09** indemnify, make right, make up for, reconcile **10** compensate, make amends, propitiate, recompense **14** make reparation

## atonement
**06** amends, ransom **07** payment, penance, redress **08** requital **09** expiation, indemnity, repayment **10** recompense, redemption, reparation **11** appeasement, eye for an eye, restitution, restoration **12** compensation, propitiation, satisfaction **13** acceptilation, reimbursement

## atrocious
◇ *anagram indicator* **05** awful, cruel, enorm **06** brutal, savage, wicked **07** ghastly, heinous, hideous, vicious **08** dreadful, enormous, fiendish, grievous, horrible, ruthless, shocking,

terrible **09** appalling, frightful, merciless, monstrous, nefarious **10** abominable, diabolical, disgusting, flagitious, horrendous

## atrociously
**07** cruelly **08** brutally, horribly, terribly, wickedly **09** heinously **10** abominably, dreadfully, fiendishly, ruthlessly, shockingly **11** appallingly, monstrously

## atrocity
**04** evil **06** horror **07** cruelty, outrage **08** enormity, savagery, vileness, villainy **09** barbarity, brutality, violation **10** wickedness **11** abomination, heinousness, hideousness, monstrosity, viciousness **13** atrociousness **14** flagitiousness

## atrophy
**04** fade **05** decay, waste **06** shrink, sweeny, tabefy, wither **07** decline, dwindle, shrivel, wasting **08** diminish, emaciate, marasmus **09** waste away, withering **10** amyotrophy, degenerate, diminution, emaciation, involution **11** deteriorate, shrivelling, tabefaction, wasting away **12** degeneration **13** deterioration

## attach
**03** add, fix, lay, pin, put, sew, tag, tie **04** ally, bind, join, link, nail, send, tack, weld **05** add on, affix, annex, cling, place, put on, snell, stick, unite **06** adhere, append, assign, belong, couple, detail, fasten, impute, limber, second, secure, solder **07** adhibit, ascribe, Blu-Tack®, connect, harness, plaster **08** allocate, relate to **09** affiliate, align with, associate, attribute, factorize, latch onto, piggyback **10** articulate, make secure **11** combine with **13** affiliate with, associate with

## attached
**04** fond **06** liking, loving, tender **07** devoted, engaged, married **08** friendly **09** affianced, appendant, spoken for **11** going steady **12** affectionate **15** in a relationship

## attachment
**03** tie **04** bond, frog, link, love **05** extra **06** fetich, fetish, liking **07** adapter, adaptor, adjunct, codicil, fetiche, fitment, fitting, fixture, loyalty **08** addition, adhesion, affinity, calf-love, devotion, fixation, fondness **09** accessory, affection, appendage, closeness, extension **10** attraction, commitment, friendship, partiality, supplement, tenderness **12** accoutrement, appurtenance **13** grande passion

## attack
**03** fit, gas, get, lam, mob, mug, pan, pin, TIA **04** bash, bomb, bout, chin, fake, flak, fork, gang, go at, jump, Mace®, nuke, prey, push, raid, rear, roll, rush, Scud, slam, tilt **05** abuse, alert, begin, blame, blast, blitz, board, brash, decry, fling, fly at, foray, glass, go for, ictus, knock, prang, sally, scrag, siege, slate, snipe, spasm, start, storm, touch **06** access, affect, ambush, assail, batter, beat up, berate, bodrag, bottle,

charge, come at, do over, duff up, extent, fall on, hold-up, impugn, infect, insult, invade, jump on, malign, molest, napalm, oppugn, pounce, rebuke, revile, rocket, savage, send in, shower, sortie, strafe, strike, stroke, tackle, tongue, vilify, wade in, waylay **07** address, aggress, air-raid, assault, attempt, battery, besiege, blister, bombard, bulldog, censure, clobber, destroy, fly upon, focus on, handbag, hiccups, inveigh, kicking, lampoon, lay into, reprove, round on, rubbish, run down, sandbag, seizure, set upon, slag off, slating, torpedo **08** attend to, camisade, camisado, commence, deal with, denounce, dive-bomb, embark on, firebomb, invasion, knocking, paroxysm, pounce on, roasting, set about, slamming, storming, strike at, tear into, tomahawk **09** broadside, cannonade, criticism, criticize, go wilding, have a go at, hiccoughs, incursion, invective, irruption, light into, obsession, offensive, onslaught, pull apart, stand upon, submarine, undertake, weigh into **10** bitch about, calumniate, chuck off at, convulsion, coup de main, crise de foi, get stuck in, hatchet job, have a pop at, impugnment, revilement, take a pop at, vituperate, weight into **11** bombardment, infestation, pick holes in **12** crise de nerfs, get started on, get stuck into, go over the top, leave for dead, Pearl Harbour, pull to pieces, put in the boot, put the boot in, tear to pieces, tear to shreds, vilification **13** feeding frenzy, find fault with **14** a warm reception, make a dead set at **15** act of aggression, apply yourself to, go for the jugular, throw yourself on

## attacker
**06** abuser, critic, mugger, raider **07** invader, reviler, striker **09** aggressor, assailant, assaulter, detractor **10** persecutor

## attain
**03** get, hit, net, win **04** earn, find, gain **05** fetch, grasp, reach, seize, touch **06** effect, fulfil, obtain, secure **07** achieve, acquire, possess, procure, realize, recover **08** arrive at, complete **10** accomplish

## attainable
**06** at hand, doable, viable **08** feasible, possible, probable **09** potential, reachable, realistic **10** accessible, achievable, imaginable, manageable, obtainable **11** conceivable, practicable, within reach

## attainment
**03** art **04** feat, gift **05** skill **06** talent **07** ability, mastery, success **08** aptitude, facility **10** capability, competence, completion, fulfilment **11** achievement, acquirement, procurement, proficiency, realization **12** consummation **14** accomplishment

## attempt
**02** go **03** aim, bid, pop, shy, try

**04** bash, burl, fand, fond, make, mint, push, seek, shot, stab, trie **05** assay, crack, essay, foray, offer, trial, whack **06** aspire, effort, set out, strive, tackle **07** have a go, pretend, venture **08** attentat, endeavour, have a try, struggle **09** endeavour, give it a go, have a bash, have a shot, have a stab, tentative, undertake **10** coup d'essai, experiment, give it a try, have a crack **11** have a stab at, try your hand, undertaking **12** give it a whirl **13** see if you can do, try your hand at **15** do your level best

## attend

**04** go to, hear, heed, help, mark, mind, note, page, show, stay, tend, wait **05** audit, await, guard, holla, nurse, serve, usher, visit, watch **06** appear, assist, be here, escort, follow, listen, notice, show up, squire, turn up **07** be there, care for, give ear, go along, observe **08** chaperon, frequent, take note, wait upon **09** accompany, chaperone, come along, look after **10** minister to, take care of, take notice, take part in **11** be present at, concentrate **12** pay attention
• **attend to 03** fix **04** heed, mind, sort, tent **05** see to, valet **06** direct, handle, manage, notice **07** control, oversee, process **08** consider, cope with, deal with, follow up, see about **09** look after, supervise **10** follow up on, take care of **11** give an eye to

## attendance

**04** duty, gate **05** crowd, house **06** escort, roll-up **07** showing, turnout **08** audience, courting, presence **09** appearing, showing up **10** appearance

## attendant

**03** man **04** aide, jack, mute, page, sice, syce **05** angel, gilly, guard, guide, jäger, saice, sowar, usher, woman **06** batman, bedral, escort, gillie, helper, jaeger, keeper, porter, varlet, verger, waiter **07** acolyte, acolyth, bedral, best man, bulldog, checker, custrel, equerry, esquire, famulus, footboy, footman, ghillie, janitor, linkboy, linkman, marshal, orderly, related, servant, snuffer, steward **08** attached, batwoman, beach boy, chaperon, chasseur, follower, footpage, handmaid, janitrix, retainer, waitress **09** assistant, auxiliary, boxkeeper, chaperone, chaprassi, chaprassy, chuprassy, companion, custodian, groomsman, janitress, kennelman, lady's-maid, observant, pew-opener, resultant, satellite **10** associated, conclavist, consequent, handmaiden, incidental, kennelmaid, led captain, lock-keeper, ministrant, pursuivant, subsequent, vivandière **11** apple-squire, body servant, concomitant, gentlewoman, loblolly-boy **12** accompanying, bottle-holder, shield-bearer **13** church officer, gillie-wetfoot **14** gentleman usher, valet de chambre **15** gillie-white-foot

## attention

**03** ear, eye **04** care, gaum, gorm, heed, help, mind, 'shun **06** notice, regard **07** concern, respect, service, therapy, thought **08** civility, courtesy, scrutiny **09** alertness, awareness, gallantry, limelight, treatment, vigilance **10** advertence, advertency, attendance, politeness **11** compliments, high profile, mindfulness, observation, recognition **13** concentration, consideration, contemplation, preoccupation
• **expressions relating to attracting or directing attention 02** hi, ho, la, lo, oi, 'st, yo **03** hem, hey, hoa, hoi, hoy, pst, say, see, why **04** ahem, ecce, ecco, here, hist, look, oyes, oyez, psst, 'shun, soho, what, yo-ho **05** cooee, cooey, hallo, hello, holla, hollo, hullo, voilà **06** behold, halloa, halloo, yo-ho-ho, yoo-hoo **07** whoa-hoa **08** whoa-ho-ho **10** view-halloo
• **pay attention 04** gaum, gorm, heed **06** listen **07** focus on, hearken, observe **10** get a load of, take notice **13** concentrate on **14** watch carefully **15** focus your mind on, listen carefully

## attentive

**04** kind **05** alert, awake, aware, civil, tenty, whist **06** polite, tentie **07** all ears, careful, devoted, dutiful, gallant, heedful, listful, mindful **08** gracious, noticing, obliging, vigilant, watchful, watching **09** advertent, adviceful, avizefull, courteous, listening, observant, on the ball, regardant **10** chivalrous, particular, thoughtful **11** advertising, considerate, punctilious **12** on the qui vive **13** accommodating, concentrating, conscientious

## attentively

**09** carefully, mindfully **10** watchfully **11** observantly **15** conscientiously

## attenuated

**04** bony, fine, slim, thin **06** narrow, skinny, slight **07** scraggy, scrawny, slender

## attest

**04** aver, show **05** prove **06** adjure, affirm, assert, depose, evince, verify **07** certify, confirm, declare, display, endorse, witness **08** evidence, manifest, proclaim, vouch for **10** asseverate **11** corroborate, demonstrate **13** bear witness to

## attic

**04** loft **06** garret **07** mansard **10** sky parlour

## attire

**04** garb, gear, suit, tire, togs, wear **05** dress, habit **06** finery, outfit, rig-out **07** apparel, clobber, clothes, costume **08** clothing, garments **10** habiliment, habilitate **11** habiliments **13** accoutrements

## attired

**05** ready **07** adorned, arrayed, clothed, dressed **09** decked out, rigged out, turned out **11** habilitated

## attitude

**04** mood, pose, song, view **05** piety, sense, stand **06** aspect, manner, stance **07** bearing, feeling, mindset, opinion, outlook, posture **08** approach, carriage, position **09** mentality, sentiment, viewpoint, world-view **10** Anschauung, deportment **11** disposition, perspective, point of view **13** way of thinking **14** Weltanschauung

## attorney

**02** AG, DA, QC **03** Att **04** Atty **05** brief **06** lawyer **07** counsel, proctor **08** advocate **09** barrister, solicitor **12** legal adviser

## attract

**04** draw, hook, lure, pull **05** charm, rivet, swing, tempt **06** allure, engage, entice, excite, induce, invite, pull in, seduce **07** bewitch, bring in, enchant, incline **08** appeal to, interest **09** captivate, fascinate, magnetize

## attraction

**02** it, SA **04** bait, bond, draw, hook, lure, pull **05** charm, sight **06** allure, appeal, favour **07** draught, feature, glamour **08** activity, affinity, building, cohesion, interest **09** box office, diversion, magnetism, seduction, sex appeal **10** enticement, inducement, invitation, temptation **11** captivation, enchantment, fascination, Ferris wheel **13** entertainment
• **centre of attraction 04** clou

## attractive

**03** bad, fit, hot **04** cute, fair, foxy, sexy, taky **05** bonny, dishy, hunky, tasty, triff **06** catchy, comely, glossy, lovely, nubile, pretty, snazzy **07** dashing, elegant, nymphic, shapely, triffic, winning, winsome **08** all right, beddable, catching, charming, engaging, enticing, epigamic, fetching, gorgeous, handsome, hot stuff, inviting, knockout, luscious, magnetic, pleasant, pleasing, striking, stunning, tempting, terrific **09** agreeable, appealing, appetible, beautiful, desirable, fanciable, glamorous, insidious, seductive, toothsome **10** adamantine, personable, photogenic, voluptuous **11** captivating, charismatic, fascinating, good-looking, interesting, picturesque **12** irresistible **13** prepossessing **14** a bit of all right

## attribute

**03** lay **04** mark, note, side, sign **05** apply, blame, facet, point, quirk, refer, trait **06** aspect, assign, charge, credit, impute, reckon, streak, symbol, virtue **07** adjunct, apanage, ascribe, feature, put down, quality, set down **08** accredit, appanage, arrogate, property **09** affection, indicator **11** peculiarity **12** idiosyncrasy **14** characteristic

## attrition

**07** chafing, erosion, rubbing **08** abrasion, friction, grinding, scraping **09** detrition, weakening **10** harassment

**attuned**

11 attenuation, wearing away, wearing down

**attuned**

03 set 05 tuned 07 adapted 08 adjusted 09 regulated 10 accustomed, harmonized 11 assimilated, co-ordinated 12 acclimatized, familiarized

**atypical**

07 deviant, unusual 08 aberrant, abnormal, freakish, uncommon 09 anomalous, divergent, eccentric, untypical 11 exceptional 13 extraordinary 14 unconventional

**aubergine**

07 brinjal 08 eggplant, mad-apple

**auburn**

04 rust 05 henna, tawny 06 copper, russet, Titian 07 dark-red 08 chestnut 12 reddish-brown

**auction**

04 cant, roup, sale 06 outcry, vendue 07 outroop 09 trade sale 11 warrant sale 12 subhastation

**auctioneer**

09 outrooper 11 rouping-wife

**audacious**

04 bold, pert, rash, rude 05 brave, fresh, lippy, nervy, risky, saucy 06 brazen, cheeky, daring, plucky 07 assured, forward, valiant 08 assuming, fearless, impudent, insolent, intrepid, reckless 09 dauntless, shameless, unabashed 10 courageous 11 adventurous, impertinent, venturesome 12 devil-may-care, enterprising, presumptuous 13 disrespectful

**audacity**

04 grit, guts, neck, risk 05 cheek, nerve, pluck 06 bottle, daring, valour 07 bravery, courage, hutzpah 08 boldness, chutzpah, defiance, forehead, pertness, rashness, rudeness, temerity 09 assurance, hardihead, hardihood, impudence, insolence 10 brazenness, effrontery, enterprise 11 forwardness, intrepidity, presumption 12 fearlessness, impertinence, recklessness 13 dauntlessness, shamelessness 15 adventurousness

**audible**

◊ homophone indicator 05 clear, heard 08 distinct, hearable 10 detectable 11 appreciable, discernible, perceptible 12 recognizable

**audience**

04 fans 05 audit, crowd, house 06 public 07 hearing, meeting, patrons, ratings, theater, theatre, turnout, viewers 08 assembly, auditory, devotees, regulars 09 followers, following, gathering, interview, listeners, onlookers, reception 10 auditorium, conference, discussion, spectators 11 bums on seats 12 congregation, consultation

**audit**

05 check 06 go over, review, survey,

verify 07 analyse, balance, examine, inspect 08 analysis, scrutiny 09 balancing, go through, statement 10 inspection, scrutinize 11 examination, investigate, work through 12 verification 13 investigation

**audition**

05 trial 07 hearing

**auditorium**

04 hall 05 front, house 07 chamber, theatre 09 playhouse, sphendone 10 opera house 11 concert hall 12 assembly room 14 conference hall

**au fait**

05 aware 06 versed 07 abreast, in touch 08 familiar, up to date 09 au courant 10 conversant 13 knowledgeable

**augment**

03 ech, ich 04 eche, eech, grow 05 add to, boost, put on, raise, swell 06 expand, extend 07 amplify, build up, enhance, enlarge, inflate, magnify 08 heighten, increase, multiply 09 intensify, reinforce 10 strengthen 11 make greater

**augmentation**

05 boost 06 growth 07 build-up 08 increase 09 expansion, extension 11 enlargement 13 amplification, magnification, strengthening 15 intensification

**augur**

04 bode, spae 06 herald 07 betoken, portend, predict, presage, promise, signify 08 forebode, foretell, prophesy 09 auspicate, be a sign of, harbinger

**augury**

04 omen, sign 05 sooth, token 06 herald 07 portent, promise, warning 08 prodrome, prophecy 09 harbinger 10 foreboding, forerunner, prediction 11 forewarning 12 ornithoscopy 13 haruspication 15 prognostication

**august**

03 Aug 05 grand, lofty, noble 06 solemn 07 exalted, stately, sublime 08 glorious, imperial, imposing, majestic 09 dignified, respected, venerable 10 impressive 11 magnificent 12 awe-inspiring 13 distinguished

**Augustines**

03 OSA

**auk**

04 roch 05 rotch 06 rotche 07 Alcidae, dovekie, penguin, rotchie, sea dove 08 garefowl 09 razorbill

**Auntie**

03 BBC 04 Beeb

**aura**

03 air 04 feel, hint, mood 05 vibes 06 nimbus 07 feeling, quality 08 ambience, mystique 09 emanation 10 atmosphere, genius loci, suggestion, vibrations

**aural**

◊ homophone indicator

**aurora**

03 Eos 11 polar lights 12 merry dancers 14 northern lights, southern lights

**auspices**

• under the auspices of 11 in the care of 13 in the charge of 15 under the aegis of

**auspicious**

04 rosy 05 happy, lucky, white 06 bright, timely 07 hopeful 08 cheerful 09 fortunate, opportune, promising 10 fair-boding, favourable, felicitous, optimistic, propitious, prosperous 11 encouraging

**austere**

04 cold, grim, hard 05 basic, bleak, grave, harsh, plain, rigid, sober, stark, stern, stoic, stoor, stour, sture 06 chaste, formal, frugal, severe, simple, solemn, sombre, stowre, strict 07 ascetic, Dantean, distant, killjoy, serious, spartan 08 exacting, rigorous 09 stringent, unadorned, unbending, unfeeling 10 abstemious, astringent, economical, forbidding, functional, inflexible, restrained, Waldensian 11 puritanical, self-denying 12 unornamented 14 self-abnegating 15 self-disciplined

**austerity**

06 rigour 07 economy 08 coldness, hardness, severity 09 formality, harshness, plainness, solemnity 10 abstinence, asceticism, puritanism, self-denial, simplicity 13 inflexibility 14 abstemiousness, self-discipline

**Australia**

01 A 02 Oz 03 AUS 04 Aust 05 Austr 09 down under

See also **electorate; governor; prime minister; state; team**

---

Australian cities and notable towns include:

05 Perth
06 Cairns, Darwin, Hobart, Sydney
08 Adelaide, Brisbane, Canberra
09 Fremantle, Melbourne
12 Alice Springs

---

Australian landmarks include:

05 Uluru
08 Lake Eyre, Shark Bay
09 Ayers Rock, Botany Bay, Pinnacles, Purnululu
10 Bondi Beach, Yarra River
11 Barrier Reef, Mt Kosciusko, Murray River
12 Darling River, Fraser Island, Gibson Desert, Hunter Valley, Rialto Towers
13 Barossa Valley, Blue Mountains, Bungle Bungles, Devil's Marbles, Dividing Range, Flinders Range, Harbour Bridge, Simpson Desert
14 Australian Alps, Nullarbor Plain, Pinnacle Desert, Snowy Mountains, Twelve Apostles, Uluru-Kata Tjuta, Victoria Desert

## Australian

**01** A **02** Oz **03** gin **05** koori, myall, ocker **06** Aussie, Strine
*See also* **aboriginal; state**

## Australian football

*Australian-football-related terms include:*

**03** AFL
**04** goal, mark, ruck, wing
**05** rover
**06** ball up, behind, centre, tackle, time on, umpire
**07** dispose, kick out, quarter, ruckman
**08** follower, free kick, full back, half back, handball, handpass, left wing, screamer, stab pass
**09** playfield, right wing, ruck rover
**10** back pocket, banana kick, behind post, centre line, goal square, goal umpire, off the boot
**11** Aussie Rules, daisy cutter, full forward, half forward
**12** boundary line, centre bounce, centre square, Magarey Medal
**13** Brownlow Medal, checkside punt, fifty-metre arc, forward pocket, half-back flank, Sandover Medal
**14** aerial pingpong, boundary umpire, centre half back
**15** chewy on your boot

*Australian football players include:*

**04** Dyer (Jack)
**05** Carey (Wayne)
**06** Ablett (Gary), Blight (Malcolm), Bunton (Haydn), Capper (Warwick), Cazaly (Roy), Farmer (Graham 'Polly')
**07** Barassi (Ron), Jackson (Mark), Lockett (Tony), Whitten (Ted)
**08** Bartlett (Kevin), Brereton (Dermot), Brownlow (Charles), Matthews (Leigh), Richards (Lou)
**10** Jesaulenko (Alex)

*Australian Football League team nicknames include:*

**04** Cats
**05** Blues, Crows, Hawks, Lions, Power, Swans
**06** Demons, Eagles, Saints, Tigers
**07** Bombers, Dockers, Magpies
**08** Bulldogs
**09** Kangaroos

## Austria

**01** A **03** AUT

## authentic

**04** echt, real, true **05** legal, valid **06** actual, dinkum, honest, kosher, lawful **07** certain, correct, factual, for real, genuine **08** accurate, attested, bona fide, credible, faithful, reliable, sterling **10** dependable, historical, legitimate, true-to-life, undisputed **11** trustworthy **12** the real McCoy, the real thing

## authentically

**04** echt **06** really **08** actually, credibly, lawfully, reliably **09** genuinely

**10** accurately, faithfully **12** historically, legitimately

## authenticate

**04** test **05** prove **06** attest, ratify, signet, verify **07** certify, confirm, endorse, warrant **08** accredit, notarize, validate, vouch for **09** authorize, guarantee **11** corroborate **12** substantiate

## authentication

**10** validation **11** attestation, endorsement **12** confirmation, ratification, verification **13** accreditation, authorization, corroboration **14** substantiation

## authenticity

**05** truth **07** honesty **08** accuracy, fidelity, legality, validity, veracity **09** certainty **10** legitimacy **11** correctness, credibility, genuineness, reliability **12** faithfulness, truthfulness **13** dependability **15** trustworthiness

## author

**03** pen **04** hand, poet **05** maker, mover **06** parent, penman, writer **07** creator, founder, planner **08** composer, designer, essayist, inventor, lyricist, novelist, penwoman, producer, reporter, volumist **09** architect, dramatist, garreteer, initiator, ink-jerker, scribbler **10** biographer, ink-slinger, journalist, librettist, originator, playwright, prime mover, songwriter, trecentist **11** contributor, hedge-writer **12** man of letters, paper-stainer, screenwriter **13** Deuteronomist, revelationist **14** woman of letters
*See also* **writer**

*Authors include:*

**03** Eco (Umberto), Kee (Robert), Lee (Harper), Lee (Laurie), Poe (Edgar Allan), Pym (Barbara), RLS, Roy (Arundhati)
**04** Amis (Kingsley), Amis (Martin), Behn (Aphra), Böll (Heinrich), Boyd (William), Buck (Pearl S), Cary (Joyce), Dahl (Roald), Dane (Clemence), Fine (Anne), Ford (Ford Madox), Gide (André), Grey (Zane), Hogg (James), Hope (Anthony), Hugo (Victor), Jane (Fred T), King (Stephen), Levi (Primo), Loos (Anita), Mann (Thomas), Okri (Ben), Puzo (Mario), Rhys (Jean), Roth (Philip), Sade (Marquis de), Saki, Sand (George), Seth (Vikram), Shah (Eddy), Snow (C P), Wain (John), West (Dame Rebecca), Wood (Mrs Henry), Zola (Emile)
**05** Adams (Douglas), Adams (Richard), Agnon (Shmuel Yosef), Banks (Iain), Banks (Lynne Reid), Bates (H E), Behan (Brendan), Benét (Stephen), Bowen (Elizabeth), Bragg (Melvyn), Brink (André), Brown (George Mackay), Bunin (Ivan), Byatt (A S), Camus (Albert), Chase (James Hadley), Craik (Dinah), Crane (Stephen), Dante, Defoe (Daniel), Desai (Anita), Doyle (Sir Arthur Conan),

Doyle (Roddy), Dumas (Alexandre, fils), Dumas (Alexandre, père), Eliot (George), Ellis (Alice Thomas), Elton (Ben), Faure (Edgar), Frayn (Michael), Genet (Jean), Gogol (Nikolai), Gorky (Maxim), Grass (Günter), Greer (Germaine), Hardy (Thomas), Hasek (Jaroslav), Hesse (Hermann), Heyer (Georgette), Horne (Donald), Innes (Hammond), James (Henry), James (P D), Joyce (James), Kafka (Franz), Keane (Molly), Kesey (Ken), Laski (Marghanita), Lewis (C S), Lewis (M G 'Monk'), Lewis (Sinclair), Lewis (Wyndham), Lodge (David), Lowry (Malcolm), Marsh (Dame Ngaio), Milne (A A), Moore (Brian), Moore (Thomas), Munro (H H), O'Hara (John), Paton (Alan), Peake (Mervyn), Plath (Sylvia), Powys (John), Queen (Ellery), Reade (Charles), Sagan (Françoise), Scott (Paul), Scott (Sir Walter), Shute (Nevil), Simon (Claude), Smith (Dodie), Smith (Stevie), Smith (Wilbur), Spark (Dame Muriel), Staël (Madame de), Steel (Danielle), Stowe (Harriet Beecher), Swift (Graham), Swift (Jonathan), Twain (Mark), Tyler (Anne), Verne (Jules), Vidal (Gore), Waugh (Auberon), Waugh (Evelyn), Wells (H G), White (Patrick), Wilde (Oscar), Wolfe (Thomas Clayton), Wolfe (Tom), Woolf (Virginia), Yates (Dornford), Yonge (Charlotte)
**06** Achebe (Chinua), Alcott (Louisa May), Aldiss (Brian), Ambler (Eric), Aragon (Louis), Archer (Jeffrey), Asimov (Isaac), Atwood (Margaret), Austen (Jane), Auster (Paul), Balzac (Honoré de), Barker (Pat), Barnes (Julian), Barrie (Sir J M), Bellow (Saul), Binchy (Maeve), Blixen (Karen, Lady), Blyton (Enid), Borges (Jorge Luis), Braine (John), Bratby (John), Brazil (Angela), Brontë (Anne), Brontë (Charlotte), Brontë (Emily), Bryson (Bill), Buchan (John), Bunyan (John), Burney (Fanny), Butler (Samuel), Capote (Truman), Carter (Angela), Cather (Willa), Chopin (Kate), Clancy (Tom), Clarke (Arthur C), Conrad (Joseph), Cooper (James Fenimore), Cooper (Jilly), Cronin (A J), Faulks (Sebastian), Fowles (John), France (Anatole), Fuller (Margaret), Gibbon (Lewis Grassic), Godden (Rumer), Godwin (William), Goethe (Johann Wolfgang von), Graham (Winston), Graves (Robert), Greene (Graham), Haddon (Mark), Hamsun (Knut), Heller (Joseph), Hilton (James), Holtby (Winifred), Hornby (Nick), Hughes (Thomas), Huxley (Aldous), Ibáñez (Vicente Blasco), Jensen (Johannes V), Jerome (Jerome K), Keller (Gottfried), Kelman (James), Laclos (Pierre Choderlos de), Larkin (Philip), Le Fanu (Sheridan), Lively (Penelope), London (Jack),

Mailer (Norman), **Malouf** (David), **Mantel** (Hilary), **McEwan** (Ian), **Miller** (Henry), **Morgan** (Charles), **Nesbit** (E), **O'Brien** (Edna), **O'Brien** (Flann), **Orwell** (George), **Porter** (Katherine Anne), **Powell** (Anthony), **Proulx** (E Annie), **Proust** (Marcel), **Rankin** (Ian), **Sapper**, **Sartre** (Jean-Paul), **Sayers** (Dorothy L), **Sewell** (Anna), **Sharpe** (Tom), **Singer** (Isaac Bashevis), **Sterne** (Laurence), **Stoker** (Bram), **Storey** (David), **Tagore** (Rabindranath), **Thomas** (Dylan), **Traven** (B), **Undset** (Sigrid), **Updike** (John), **Walker** (Alice), **Warner** (Marina), **Warren** (Robert Penn), **Weldon** (Fay), **Wesley** (Mary), **Wilder** (Thornton), **Wilson** (Sir Angus), **Wright** (Richard)

**07** **Ackroyd** (Peter), **Aksakov** (Sergei), **Angelou** (Maya), **Arrabal** (Fernando), **Baldwin** (James), **Ballard** (J G), **Beckett** (Samuel), **Bennett** (Arnold), **Bentine** (Michael), **Burgess** (Anthony), **Burnett** (Frances Hodgson), **Calvino** (Italo), **Canetti** (Elias), **Carroll** (Lewis), **Chatwin** (Bruce), **Chekhov** (Anton), **Clavell** (James), **Cleland** (John), **Cocteau** (Jean), **Coetzee** (J M), **Colette**, **Collins** (Wilkie), **Cookson** (Catherine), **Deledda** (Grazia), **Dickens** (Charles), **Diderot** (Denis), **Dinesen** (Isak), **Douglas** (Norman), **Drabble** (Margaret), **Durrell** (Gerald), **Durrell** (Lawrence), **Fleming** (Ian), **Forster** (E M), **Forster** (Margaret), **Forsyth** (Frederick), **Francis** (Dick), **Gaskell** (Mrs Elizabeth), **Gautier** (Théophile), **Gibbons** (Stella), **Gissing** (George), **Golding** (William), **Grahame** (Kenneth), **Grisham** (John), **Haggard** (Sir H Rider), **Hammett** (Dashiell), **Hartley** (L P), **Kerouac** (Jack), **Kipling** (Rudyard), **Kundera** (Milan), **Lardner** (Ring), **Laxness** (Halldór), **Le Carré** (John), **Lehmann** (Rosamond), **Lessing** (Doris), **Maclean** (Alistair), **Mahfouz** (Naguib), **Malamud** (Bernard), **Malraux** (André), **Manning** (Olivia), **Manzoni** (Alessandro), **Marryat** (Captain Frederick), **Maugham** (W Somerset), **Mauriac** (François), **Mérimée** (Prosper), **Mishima** (Yukio), **Mitford** (Nancy), **Moravia** (Alberto), **Murdoch** (Dame Iris), **Nabokov** (Vladimir), **Naipaul** (V S), **Peacock** (Thomas Love), **Prévost** (l'Abbé), **Pullman** (Philip), **Pushkin** (Alexander), **Pynchon** (Thomas), **Ransome** (Arthur), **Raphael** (Frederic), **Renault** (Mary), **Rendell** (Ruth), **Richler** (Mordecai), **Robbins** (Harold), **Rolland** (Romain), **Rowling** (J K), **Rushdie** (Salman), **Sassoon** (Siegfried), **Shelley** (Mary), **Shields** (Carol), **Simenon** (Georges), **Sitwell** (Sir Osbert), **Soyinka** (Wole), **Spender** (Sir Stephen), **Surtees** (Robert

Smith), **Theroux** (Paul), **Tolkien** (J R R), **Tolstoy** (Count Leo), **Tremain** (Rose), **Wallace** (Lewis), **Walpole** (Sir Hugh), **Wharton** (Edith), **Wyndham** (John)

**08** **Andersen** (Hans Christian), **Apuleius** (Lucius), **Asturias** (Miguel), **Banville** (John), **Barbusse** (Henri), **Beckford** (William Thomas), **Beerbohm** (Sir Max), **Björnson** (Björnstjerne), **Bradbury** (Malcolm), **Bradbury** (Ray), **Bradford** (Barbara Taylor), **Brittain** (Vera), **Brookner** (Anita), **Bulgakov** (Mikhail), **Caldwell** (Erskine), **Cartland** (Barbara), **Chandler** (Raymond), **Christie** (Dame Agatha), **Constant** (Benjamin), **Cornwell** (Patricia), **Crichton** (Michael), **Crompton** (Richmal), **Day-Lewis** (Cecil), **Deighton** (Len), **De La Mare** (Walter), **Disraeli** (Benjamin), **Donleavy** (J P), **Faulkner** (William), **Fielding** (Henry), **Flaubert** (Gustave), **Forester** (C S), **Francome** (John), **Goncourt** (Edmond de), **Gordimer** (Nadine), **Hochhuth** (Rolf), **Huysmans** (J K), **Ishiguro** (Kazuo), **Jhabvala** (Ruth Prawer), **Kawabata** (Yasunari), **Keneally** (Thomas), **Kingsley** (Charles), **Koestler** (Arthur), **Lagerlöf** (Selma), **Lawrence** (D H), **Lockhart** (John Gibson), **Macaulay** (Dame Rose), **McCarthy** (Mary), **Melville** (Herman), **Meredith** (George), **Michener** (James A), **Milligan** (Spike), **Mitchell** (Margaret), **Morrison** (Toni), **Mortimer** (John), **Murasaki** (Shikibu), **Oliphant** (Margaret), **Ondaatje** (Michael), **Remarque** (Erich Maria), **Rousseau** (Jean Jacques), **Salinger** (J D), **Sillitoe** (Alan), **Sinclair** (Upton), **Smollett** (Tobias), **Spillane** (Mickey), **Stendhal**, **Tanizaki** (Junichiro), **Trollope** (Anthony), **Trollope** (Joanna), **Turgenev** (Ivan), **Voltaire**, **Vonnegut** (Kurt, Junior)

**09** **Allingham** (Margery), **Bernières** (Louis de), **Bleasdale** (Alan), **Burroughs** (Edgar Rice), **Burroughs** (William S), **Cervantes** (Miguel de), **Charteris** (Leslie), **Chatterji** (Bankim), **D'Annunzio** (Gabriele), **Delafield** (E M), **De La Roche** (Mazo), **De Quincey** (Thomas), **Dos Passos** (John), **Du Maurier** (Dame Daphne), **Du Maurier** (George), **Edgeworth** (Maria), **Gerhardie** (William), **Goldsmith** (Oliver), **Greenwood** (Walter), **Grossmith** (George), **Grossmith** (Weedon), **Guareschi** (Giovanni), **Hauptmann** (Gerhart), **Hawthorne** (Nathaniel), **Hemingway** (Ernest), **Highsmith** (Patricia), **Hölderlin** (Friedrich), **Hopkinson** (Sir Tom), **Isherwood** (Christopher), **Lampedusa** (Giuseppe Tomasi de), **Lermontov** (Mikhail), **Linklater** (Eric), **Llewellyn** (Richard), **Mackenzie** (Sir Compton), **Mankowitz** (Wolf),

**Mansfield** (Katherine), **Marinetti** (Filippo Tommaso), **Masefield** (John), **McCullers** (Carson), **Mitchison** (Naomi), **Monsarrat** (Nicholas), **Pasternak** (Boris), **Pratchett** (Terry), **Priestley** (J B), **Radcliffe** (Ann), **Santayana** (George), **Sholokhov** (Mikhail), **Steinbeck** (John), **Stevenson** (Robert Louis), **Thackeray** (William Makepeace), **Wodehouse** (Sir P G)

**10** **Bainbridge** (Beryl), **Ballantyne** (R M), **Chesterton** (G K), **De Beauvoir** (Simone), **Dostoevsky** (Fyodor), **Fairbairns** (Zoë), **Fitzgerald** (F Scott), **Galsworthy** (John), **Lagerkvist** (Pär), **Maupassant** (Guy de), **Pirandello** (Luigi), **Richardson** (Dorothy M), **Richardson** (Samuel), **Strindberg** (August), **Van der Post** (Sir Laurens), **Waterhouse** (Keith)

**11** **Kazantzakis** (Nikos), **Sienkiewicz** (Henryk), **Vargas Llosa** (Mario)

**12** **Quiller-Couch** (Sir Arthur), **Robbe-Grillet** (Alain), **Saint-Exupéry** (Antoine de), **Solzhenitsyn** (Aleksandr)

**13** **Alain-Fournier** (Henri), **García Márquez** (Gabriel), **Sackville-West** (Vita)

**14** **Compton-Burnett** (Dame Ivy)

**15** **Somerset Maugham** (William)

*See also* **playwright; poet**

## authoritarian
**04** Nazi **05** bossy, harsh, rigid, tough **06** despot, severe, strict, tyrant **07** fascist **08** absolute, autocrat, despotic, dictator, dogmatic **09** fascistic, imperious, Orwellian **10** absolutist, autocratic, inflexible, oppressive, tyrannical, unyielding **11** dictatorial, doctrinaire, domineering, magisterial **12** totalitarian **14** disciplinarian

## authoritarianism
**06** Nazism **07** Fascism **09** autocracy, despotism **10** absolutism, oppression, repression **12** dictatorship **15** totalitarianism

## authoritative
**04** bold, true **05** crisp, sound, valid **07** factual, learned **08** accepted, accurate, approved, decisive, faithful, imposing, official, reliable, truthful **09** assertive, audacious, authentic, confident, masterful, scholarly **10** authorized, commanding, convincing, definitive, dependable, imperative, legitimate, sanctioned **11** cathedratic, magisterial, self-assured, trustworthy **13** self-confident, self-possessed **14** sure of yourself

## authoritatively
**06** boldly **08** reliably **09** factually **10** accurately, decisively, dependably, ex cathedra, faithfully **11** assertively, audaciously, confidently **12** convincingly, definitively **13** authentically **15** self-confidently

## authority
**03** bar **04** buff, mana, name, rule, sage, sway, them, they **05** adept, bible,

clout, force, leave, power, right, say-so, state **06** expert, master, muscle, permit, pundit **07** command, consent, control, council, faculty, go-ahead, licence, prelacy, royalty, scepter, sceptre, scholar, Vatican, warrant **08** dominion, lordship, sanction, thumbs-up **09** influence, provostry, supremacy, vicariate **10** domination, fatherhood, government, green light, inquirendo, management, permission, specialist **11** bureaucracy, connoisseur, credentials, imperialism, landlordism, officialdom, prerogative, sovereignty **12** carte blanche, jurisdiction, professional, protectorate **13** authorization, establishment **14** administration, patria potestas **15** the powers that be
• **emblem of authority 03** rod **04** vare, wand **05** sword **07** scepter, sceptre
• **post of authority 04** seat

## authorization

**02** OK **04** okay, pass **05** leave, stamp **06** permit **07** consent, go-ahead, licence, mandate, warrant **08** approval, passport, retainer, sanction, thumbs-up, warranty **09** authority **10** commission, empowering, green light, permission, validation, warrantise **11** credentials, entitlement, procuratory **12** confirmation, ratification **13** accreditation

## authorize

**02** OK **03** let **04** okay **05** allow **06** enable, permit, ratify **07** approve, confirm, empower, entitle, licence, license, mandate, warrant **08** accredit, legalize, sanction, validate **09** consent to, make legal, privilege **10** commission, greenlight **15** give authority to

## authorized

**05** legal, legit **06** lawful **08** approved, licensed, official **09** permitted, warranted **10** accredited, recognized **12** commissioned, under licence

## autobahn

**02** AB

## autobiography

**02** CV **05** diary **06** memoir **07** journal, memoirs **09** life story **15** story of your life

## autocracy

**07** fascism, tyranny **08** autarchy **09** despotism **10** absolutism **12** dictatorship **15** totalitarianism

## autocrat

**04** cham **06** Caesar, despot, Hitler, tyrant **08** dictator **10** absolutist, panjandrum **12** little Hitler, totalitarian **13** authoritarian

## autocratic

**08** absolute, despotic **09** autarchic, imperious **10** tyrannical **11** all-powerful, dictatorial, domineering, overbearing **12** totalitarian **13** authoritarian

## autograph

**04** mark, name, sign **07** endorse, initial **08** initials, monicker **09** signature **11** countersign, endorsement, inscription, put your mark **13** write your name

## automatic

**06** reflex **07** certain, natural, robotic, routine **08** knee-jerk, unmanned, unwilled **09** automated, necessary, Pavlovian **10** inevitable, mechanical, mechanized, programmed, push-button, self-acting, unthinking **11** inescapable, instinctive, involuntary, spontaneous, unavoidable, unconscious **12** computerized **14** self-activating, self-propelling, self-regulating, uncontrollable
*See also* **gun**

## automatically

**09** certainly, naturally, routinely **10** inevitably **11** inescapably, necessarily, robotically, unavoidably **12** mechanically, unthinkingly **13** instinctively, involuntarily, spontaneously, unconsciously **14** uncontrollably

## automobile

**03** car **05** motor **07** vehicle **08** motor car **12** motor vehicle
*See also* **car**

## autonomous

**04** free **09** sovereign **11** independent **13** self-directing, self-governing **15** self-determining

## autonomy

**07** autarky, freedom **08** free will, home rule, self-rule **11** sovereignty **12** independence **14** rangatiratanga, self-government **15** self-sufficiency

## autopsy

**08** necropsy **10** dissection, post-mortem

## autumn

**04** fall **07** back-end, harvest **08** leaf-fall

## auxiliary

**03** aid **05** extra, spare **06** aiding, backer, back-up, helper, second **07** helping, partner, reserve **09** accessory, adminicle, ancillary, assistant, assisting, emergency, secondary, supporter **10** additional, peripheral, subsidiary, substitute, supporting, supportive **11** subordinate **12** right-hand man **13** supplementary **14** right-hand woman **15** second-in-command

## avail

**03** dow, use **04** doff, vail **05** lower, serve, stead **06** accept, alight, draw on **07** bestead, prevail, succeed, utilize **08** exercise, resort to **09** make use of **15** take advantage of
• **to no avail 06** in vain, vainly **11** fruitlessly **13** ineffectually **14** unsuccessfully, without success

## available

**02** on **04** free, open **05** handy, on tap, ready, to let **06** at hand, on hand,

single, to hand, usable, vacant **07** not busy, untaken **09** at liberty **10** accessible, convenient, disposable, obtainable, procurable, unoccupied, up for grabs **11** contactable, forthcoming, off the shelf, within reach **12** up your sleeve **13** at your command **14** at your disposal

## avalanche

**04** wave **05** flood **06** deluge **07** barrage, cascade, lauwine, torrent **08** landslip, snowslip **09** landslide **10** inundation

## avant-garde

**06** far-out, modern, way-out **07** go-ahead **08** advanced, original, out there **09** inventive **10** futuristic, innovative, innovatory, pioneering **11** progressive **12** contemporary, enterprising, experimental **14** forward-looking, ground-breaking, unconventional

## avarice

**05** greed **06** misery **07** avidity **08** meanness **09** pleonexia, the gimmes **10** greediness **11** gourmandise, materialism, miserliness, selfishness **12** covetousness **15** acquisitiveness

## avaricious

**04** avid, gare, mean **06** greedy, grippy, sordid **07** griping, gripple, miserly **08** covetous, grasping **09** mercenary, rapacious **10** pleonectic **11** acquisitive **12** curmudgeonly

## avatar

*see* **incarnation**

## avenge

**05** repay, right, venge, wreak **06** punish **07** pay back, requite **09** get back at, retaliate, vindicate **11** get even with **14** get your own back, take revenge for

## avenger

**04** goel

## avenue

**02** Av **03** ave, way **04** line, road, walk **05** allée, corso, drive, grove, vista **06** dromos, method, midway, scheme, street **07** Madison, passage **08** approach, broadway **09** boulevard **10** cradlewalk **12** thoroughfare **13** modus operandi **14** course of action

## aver

**04** avow **05** state **06** affirm, attest, cattle **07** confirm, declare **08** maintain **09** make known **11** possessions

## average

**02** av **03** ave, par, run **04** fair, mean, mode, norm, rule, so-so **05** usual **06** centre, common, medial, median, medium, middle, Nikkei, normal **07** regular, routine, typical **08** Dow-Jones, everyday, mediocre, middling, mid-point, moderate, ordinary, passable, standard **09** tolerable **10** not much cop **11** indifferent, not up to much **12** intermediate, run-of-the-mill, satisfactory **13** no great shakes, unexceptional **14** common-or-garden, fair to middling, nothing special **15** undistinguished
• **on average 06** mainly, mostly **07** as a rule, chiefly, usually **08** normally

**averse**
09 generally, in the main, routinely, typically 10 by and large, on the whole, ordinarily

**averse**
05 loath 07 hostile, opposed 09 reluctant, unwilling 10 indisposed 11 disinclined, ill-disposed 12 antagonistic, antipathetic, unfavourable

**aversion**
04 hate 06 hatred, horror, phobia 07 disgust, dislike 08 distaste, loathing 09 antipathy, hostility, repulsion, revulsion 10 abhorrence, antagonism, opposition, reluctance, repugnance 11 abomination, detestation 13 unwillingness 14 disinclination
See also **phobia**

**avert**
03 wry 04 stop 05 avoid, evade, parry 07 deflect, fend off, forfend, head off, obviate, prevent, ward off 08 preclude, stave off, turn away 09 forestall, frustrate, turn aside

**aviary**
06 volary

**aviation**
06 flight, flying 11 aeronautics

_Aviation-related terms include:_

04 dive, drag, flap, taxi
05 fly-by, pilot, plane, prang
06 airway, hangar, runway, thrust
07 airline, air miss, airport, airship, captain, console, fly-past, landing, lift-off, spoiler, take-off
08 aircraft, airfield, airplane, airspace, airstrip, altitude, black box, nose dive, subsonic, windsock, wingspan
09 aeroplane, aerospace, crash dive, fixed-wing, fly-by-wire, jetstream, overshoot, parachute, sonic boom, test pilot, touchdown
10 chocks away, flight crew, Mach number, solo flight, supersonic, test flight, undershoot
11 ground speed, loop-the-loop, night-flying, vapour trail
12 control tower, crash-landing, landing strip, maiden flight, sound barrier
13 ground control, jet propulsion
14 automatic pilot, flight recorder, holding pattern

**aviator**
05 flyer, pilot 06 airman 08 airwoman 11 aircraftman 13 aircraftwoman

_Aviators include:_

04 **Byrd** (Richard Evelyn), **Rust** (Mathias), **Udet** (Ernst)
05 **Bader** (Sir Douglas), **Balbo** (Italo, Count), **Brown** (Sir Arthur Whitten), **Johns** (Captain W E), **Smith** (Sir Ross)
06 **Alcock** (Sir John), **Bonney** (Maude), **Cessna** (Clyde), **Gibson** (Guy), **Harris** (Sir Arthur 'Bomber'), **Hughes** (Howard), **Nobile** (Umberto), **Watton** (Nancy Bird), **Wright** (Orville), **Wright**

(Wilbur), **Yeager** (Chuck)
07 **Bennett** (Floyd), **Blériot** (Louis), **Branson** (Sir Richard), **Cochran** (Jacqueline), **Dornier** (Claudius), **Douglas** (Donald Wills), **Earhart** (Amelia), **Fossett** (Steve), **Giffard** (Henri), **Goering** (Hermann), **Hinkler** (Bert), **Johnson** (Amy), **Korolev** (Sergei), **Piccard** (Auguste), **Sopwith** (Sir Thomas)
08 **Brabazon** (John, Lord), **Cheshire** (Leonard, Lord), **Hargrave** (Lawrence), **Zeppelin** (Count Ferdinand von)
09 **Blanchard** (Jean Pierre), **Lindbergh** (Charles), **McDonnell** (James Smith)
10 **Lindstrand** (Per), **Richthofen** (Manfred, Baron von)
11 **Montgolfier** (Jacques), **Montgolfier** (Joseph)
12 **Saint-Exupéry** (Antoine de)
13 **Messerschmitt** (Willy)

**avid**
03 mad 04 keen 05 crazy, eager, great 06 ardent, greedy, hungry 07 athirst, devoted, earnest, fervent, intense, thirsty, zealous 08 covetous, grasping, ravenous 09 dedicated, fanatical 10 insatiable, passionate 12 enthusiastic

**avidly**
05 madly 06 keenly 07 eagerly 08 ardently, greedily, hungrily 09 devotedly, earnestly, fervently, intensely, thirstily, zealously 10 covetously, insatiably, ravenously 11 fanatically 12 passionately

**avocado**
08 aguacate 09 guacamole 13 alligator pear

**avocet**
07 awlbird, scooper

**avoid**
03 fly 04 balk, duck, miss, shun 05 avert, dodge, elude, evade, evite, hedge, shirk 06 bypass, escape, eschew 07 decline, evitate, forbear, prevent 08 get out of, get round, sidestep 09 give a miss 10 circumvent 11 abstain from, make a detour, refrain from, run away from, shy away from 12 hold back from, keep away from, stay away from, steer clear of

**avoidable**
08 eludible, evitable 09 avertible, escapable, stoppable 11 preventable

**avow**
03 vow 04 aver 05 admit, state, swear 06 assert, attest, avouch 07 confess, declare, profess 08 maintain 11 acknowledge

**avowed**
04 open 05 overt, sworn 07 confest 08 admitted, declared 09 barefaced, confessed, professed 10 professing 12 acknowledged 13 self-confessed 14 self-proclaimed

**await**
04 bide, stay 05 tarry 06 expect, remain 07 hope for, look for, wait for

10 anticipate 12 be in store for, lie in wait for 13 look forward to

**awake**
04 stir, wake 05 abray, alert, alive, aware, rouse, waken 06 abrade, abraid, arouse, awaken, wake up 07 aroused, mindful, wakeful 08 stirring, vigilant, watchful 09 attentive, conscious, observant, sensitive, wide awake 12 appreciative

**awaken**
04 stir, wake 05 awake, rouse, waken 06 abraid, excite, wake up 07 inspire 08 engender, generate 09 stimulate 11 disentrance 14 cause to realize

**awakening**
05 birth 06 waking 07 arousal, awaking, revival, rousing 08 wakening 09 animating 10 activation, enlivening 11 reanimating, revivifying, stimulation 12 vivification

**award**
03 cup 04 aret, gift, give, gong 05 allot, allow, arett, endow, grant, medal, order, prize 06 accord, addeem, addoom, adward, assign, bestow, confer, modify, reward, trophy 07 adjudge, bursary, honours, payment, present, rosette 08 accolade, allocate, bestowal, citation, decision, decorate, dispense 09 allotment, allowance, apportion, conferral, determine, endowment, judgement 10 adjudicate, decoration, distribute, palatinate, settlement, subvention 11 certificate, scholarship 12 adjudication, commendation, dispensation, presentation

_Awards and prizes include:_

02 CH, MM, OM
03 CBE, OBE
04 Brit, Emmy, Tony
05 Bafta, César, Nobel, Oscar
06 Booker, Grammy, Orange, Turner
07 Academy, Olivier
08 Palme d'Or, Pulitzer, Stirling
09 Grand Jury, Grand Prix, Man Booker, Templeton
10 Golden Bear, Golden Palm
11 Fields Medal, Golden Globe
12 Prix Goncourt

See also **honour; military**

**aware**
03 hip 05 alert, awake, sharp 06 shrewd, sussed 07 alive to, clued up, heedful, knowing, mindful 08 apprised, familiar, informed, sensible, sentient, vigilant 09 attentive, au courant, cognizant, conscient, conscious, in the know, observant, on the ball, sensitive 10 acquainted, conversant 11 enlightened, recognizant 12 appreciative 13 knowledgeable
• **aware of** 04 on to
• **be aware of** 03 ken 04 feel, know

**awareness**
03 sus 04 suss 05 grasp 06 vision 07 insight, samadhi 09 knowledge 10 cognizance, perception 11 familiarity, panesthesia,

recognition, sensitivity
**12** acquaintance, appreciation, panaesthesia **13** consciousness, sensitiveness, understanding

**awash**
**04** full **05** alive **06** packed, soaked **07** flooded, replete, teeming **08** crawling, drenched, swarming **09** inundated, saturated, submerged

**away**
◇ *anagram indicator* **02** by **03** far, fro, off, out **04** from **05** apart, aside, hence **06** abroad, absent **08** from here **09** elsewhere, from there, not at home, not at work, on holiday **10** on vacation **11** at a distance

**awe**
**04** fear **05** dread **06** honour, terror, wonder **07** respect **09** amazement, reverence **10** admiration, veneration, wonderment **12** apprehension, astonishment, stupefaction

**awed**
**06** amazed, solemn **07** fearful, stunned **09** awe-struck **10** astonished **11** reverential **12** lost for words

**awe-inspiring**
**06** moving, solemn **07** amazing, awesome, exalted, sublime **08** daunting, dazzling, fearsome, imposing, majestic, numinous, striking, stunning **09** wonderful **10** formidable, impressive, stupefying, stupendous **11** astonishing, magnificent, spectacular **12** breathtaking, intimidating, mind-boggling, overwhelming

**awesome**
**07** amazing **08** daunting, stunning **10** formidable, impressive **11** astonishing, jaw-dropping, spectacular **12** breathtaking, intimidating, mind-boggling, overwhelming **13** extraordinary

**awestruck**
**04** awed **06** amazed **09** impressed **10** astonished **12** lost for words

**awful**
◇ *anagram indicator* **03** ill **04** dire, naff, sick **05** lousy, nasty, pants, rough, seedy, spewy **06** crummy, horrid, in pain, poorly, unwell **07** abysmal, fearful, ghastly, heinous, the pits **08** alarming, dreadful, gruesome, horrible, horrific, inferior, pathetic, shocking, terrible, very poor **09** appalling, atrocious, frightful, third-rate, washed out **10** disgusting,

horrifying, inadequate, second-rate, unpleasant **11** distressing **14** a load of rubbish, unsatisfactory **15** under the weather

**awfully**
◇ *anagram indicator* **04** awfy, very **06** deeply, really **07** greatly **08** terribly **09** extremely, immensely **10** absolutely, dreadfully, remarkably **12** particularly, tremendously, unbelievably

**awhile**
**10** for a moment **11** for some time **13** for a short time

**awkward**
◇ *anagram indicator* **03** shy **04** rude **05** blate, gawky, inept, nasty **06** clumsy, clunky, fiddly, gauche, rustic, thumby, touchy, tricky, ungain **07** bashful, boorish, cubbish, loutish, prickly, stroppy, uncouth **08** annoying, bungling, clownish, delicate, handless, inexpert, lubberly, stubborn, ungainly, untoward, unwieldy **09** all thumbs, difficult, graceless, ham-fisted, ill at ease, inelegant, irritable, maladroit, obstinate, unskilful **10** cumbersome, left-handed, perplexing, ungraceful, unpleasant **11** disobliging, embarrassed, heavy-handed, obstructive, problematic, troublesome **12** bloody-minded, embarrassing, inconvenient **13** chuckle-headed, oversensitive, uncomfortable, unco-operative, unco-ordinated **15** unaccommodating

**awkwardly**
◇ *anagram indicator* **05** shyly **07** ineptly **08** clumsily, uneasily, ungainly **09** bashfully **10** inexpertly **11** gracelessly, ham-fistedly, inelegantly, maladroitly, unskilfully **12** ungracefully **13** heavy-handedly, uncomfortably

**awkwardness**
**09** confusion, gawkiness, inaptness **10** clumsiness, inaptitude, inelegance, maladdress, uneasiness **11** bashfulness **12** discomfiture, ungainliness **13** embarrassment, gracelessness, left-handiness **15** heavy-handedness

**awl**
**04** brog, prod, stob **05** elsin **06** elshin

**awn**
**05** beard

**awning**
**04** tilt **05** blind, cover, shade **06** canopy **07** shelter **08** covering, shamiana,

sunblind, sunshade, velarium
**09** shamianah

**awry**
◇ *anagram indicator* **03** cam, kam **04** skew **05** aglee, agley, amiss, askew, kamme, tipsy, wonky, wrong **06** skivie, uneven **07** askance, athwart, crooked, haywire, oblique, tortive, twisted **08** cockeyed **09** off-centre, skew-whiff **10** misaligned, out of joint **12** asymmetrical, by transverse

**axe**
**03** cut, hew **04** bill, celt, chop, fell, fire, sack **05** let go, split **06** cancel, cleave, guitar, labrys, piolet, remove, sparth **07** chopper, cleaver, cut down, dismiss, gisarme, halberd, hatchet, sparthe, twibill **08** get rid of, palstaff, palstave, partisan, throw out, tomahawk, withdraw **09** battle-axe, discharge, eliminate, saxophone, terminate **11** coup de poing, discontinue, thunderbolt **12** Jeddart staff
• **get the axe** **10** get the boot, get the chop, get the sack **11** be cancelled

**axiom**
**02** ax **05** adage, maxim, truth **06** byword, dictum, truism **07** precept **08** aphorism, petition **09** postulate, principle **11** fundamental

**axiomatic**
**05** given **06** gnomic **07** assumed, certain, granted **08** accepted, manifest **10** aphoristic, proverbial, understood **11** fundamental, indubitable, presupposed, self-evident **12** unquestioned **14** apophthegmatic, unquestionable

**axis**
**01** X, Y, Z **03** cob **04** axle **05** henge, hinge, pivot **06** chital, rachis **07** rhachis **08** backbone, modiolus, vertical **10** centre-line, horizontal **13** macrodiagonal **14** brachydiagonal
• **end of axis** **04** pole

**axle**
**03** pin, rod **04** axis **05** pivot, shaft, truck **07** mandrel, mandril, spindle **11** paddle-shaft

**Azerbaijan**
**02** AZ **03** AZE

**azure**
**04** Saxe **07** sky-blue **08** cerulean, pale blue **09** light blue **11** nattier blue **13** Cambridge blue

# B

**B**
04 beta 05 bravo

**babble**
03 gab, jaw 05 babel, prate 06 burble, cackle, gabble, gibber, gurgle, hubbub, jabber, jawing, mumble, murmur, mutter, waffle, witter 07 blabber, brabble, chatter, clamour, prattle, twaddle, twattle 08 rabbit on 09 gibberish, wittering 10 tongue-work 12 bibble-babble

**babe**
03 sis, tot 04 baby 05 child 06 infant 07 newborn, tiny tot 08 suckling 10 babe in arms 11 newborn baby

**babel**
03 din 05 chaos 06 babble, bedlam, hubbub, tumult, uproar 07 clamour, turmoil 08 disorder 09 commotion, confusion 10 hullabaloo 11 pandemonium

**baboon**
05 drill 06 chacma, dog-ape, gelada 08 mandrill 09 hamadryad 12 Cynocephalus

**baby**
03 bub, sis, tot, wee 04 babe, dear, love, mini, mite, tiny 05 bairn, bubby, child, dwarf, honey, small, sprog, teeny, weeny 06 infant, little, midget, minute 07 darling, dearest, neonate, newborn, papoose, sweetie, tiny tot, toddler 08 killcrop, pint-size, suckling 09 miniature, pint-sized, tiny weeny 10 diminutive, small-scale, sweetheart 11 newborn baby

**babyish**
04 baby, soft 05 naive, silly, sissy, young 07 foolish, puerile 08 childish, immature, juvenile 09 infantile

**Babylonian**
see **god, goddess**

**bacchanalian**
• bacchanalian expression 04 euoi, evoe, upsy 05 evhoe, evohe, upsee, upsey

**Bacchus**
08 Dionysus

**bachelor**
01 B 02 BA 04 Bach 05 batch

**bacillus**
02 TB 03 bcg 07 anthrax 08 coliform 11 micrococcus

**back**
◇ reversal indicator ◇ tail selection indicator 03 aft, ago, aid, bet, bid, end, off 04 abet, ante, away, help, hind, past, rear, risk, tail 05 boost, other, spine, stake, stern, verso, wager 06 assist, before, behind, bygone, chance, dorsum, far end, favour, former, gamble, rachis, recede, recoil, retire, second, tergum 07 bolster, confirm, earlier, elapsed, endorse, finance, promote, rear end, regress, retreat, reverse, sponsor, support, sustain, tail end, venture 08 advocate, back away, backbone, backside, be behind, champion, hindmost, hind part, obsolete, outdated, previous, sanction, side with, withdraw 09 backtrack, backwards, encourage, get behind, other side, out of date, posterior, speculate, subsidize, to the rear 10 previously, underwrite 11 countenance, countersign, go backwards, reverse side 12 hindquarters 13 move backwards
• **back and forth** ◇ palindrome indicator
• **back away** 06 recede, recoil 07 retreat 08 draw back, fall back, move back, step back, withdraw 10 give ground
• **back down** 05 yield 06 give in, submit 07 abandon, concede, retreat 08 withdraw 09 back-pedal, backtrack, climb down, surrender
• **back out** ◇ reversal indicator 06 cancel, cry off, give up, recant, resign, resile 07 abandon, call off, pull out, retreat 08 crawfish, go back on, withdraw 10 chicken out 11 get cold feet
• **back up** 03 aid 04 abet 06 assist, second, soothe, verify 07 bear out, bolster, confirm, endorse, reserve, stand by, stand to, support 08 champion, validate 09 reinforce 11 corroborate 12 substantiate
• **behind your back** 05 slyly 08 covertly, secretly, sneakily 09 furtively 11 deceitfully 15 surreptitiously
• **turn your back on** 04 quit 05 leave 06 ignore, reject 07 abandon, exclude 08 throw out 09 repudiate 15 wash your hands of

**backbiting**
05 abuse, catty, libel, slurs, spite 06 bitchy, gossip, malice 07 abusive, calumny, cattish, insults, slander 08 spiteful 09 aspersion, cattiness, criticism, libellous, malicious, vilifying 10 bitchiness, defamation, detraction, revilement, rubbishing, slanderous 11 denigration, disparaging, mud-slinging, slagging off 12 back-wounding, spitefulness, vilification, vituperation 13 disparagement

**backbone**
04 core, grit, guts 05 basis, chine, nerve, pluck, power, spine 06 bottle, mettle 07 courage, nucleus, resolve, stamina, support 08 firmness, mainstay, strength, tenacity 09 character, toughness, vertebrae, willpower 10 foundation, resolution 11 cornerstone 12 spinal column,

vertebration 13 determination, steadfastness 15 vertebral column

**backbreaking**
04 hard 05 heavy 07 arduous, killing, onerous 08 crushing, grueling 09 gruelling, laborious, punishing, strenuous 10 exhausting

**backchat**
03 lip 04 face 05 cheek, mouth, nerve, snash 08 back talk, repartee, rudeness 09 brass neck, cross-talk, impudence, insolence, sauciness 12 impertinence

**backer**
05 angel 06 friend, funder, patron, second 07 sponsor 08 advocate, champion, investor, promoter, seconder, stickler 09 supporter 10 benefactor, subscriber, subsidizer, well-wisher 11 underwriter 12 bottle-holder

**backfire**
◇ reversal indicator 04 fail, flop 06 blow up, recoil 07 explode, misfire, rebound 08 detonate, miscarry, ricochet 09 boomerang, discharge 10 strike back 12 defeat itself 14 score an own goal 15 be self-defeating, come home to roost

**backgammon**
08 tick-tack, tric-trac, verquere 10 trick-track

**background**
04 fond 05 field, scene 06 canvas, family, milieu, record, status 07 context, culture, factors, history, origins, setting 08 backdrop, breeding, surround 09 backcloth, cyclorama, education, framework, grounding, tradition 10 experience, influences, upbringing 11 credentials, environment, preparation 12 surroundings 13 circumstances 14 qualifications, social standing

**backhanded**
06 ironic 07 awkward, dubious, oblique, reverse 08 indirect, sardonic, two-edged 09 ambiguous, equivocal, insincere, sarcastic 11 double-edged

**backing**
◇ reversal indicator 03 aid 04 help, vamp 05 funds, grant 06 backup, facing, favour, lining 07 finance, funding, helpers, padding, subsidy, support 08 advocacy, approval, sanction 09 obbligato, patronage, promotion, seconding 10 assistance, stiffening 11 championing, co-operation, endorsement, interlining, sponsorship 12 commendation, moral support 13 accompaniment, encouragement, reinforcement

**backlash**
06 recoil 08 backfire, kickback, reaction, reprisal, response 09 boomerang 11 retaliation 12 repercussion 13 counteraction

**backlog**
04 heap, pile 05 hoard, stock 06 excess, supply 07 reserve

**08** mountain, reserves **09** resources
**12** accumulation

## back-pedal
**05** yield **06** give in, renege, submit
**07** abandon, concede, retract, retreat
**08** do a U-turn, go back on, take back,
withdraw **09** about-face, about-turn,
backtrack, climb down, surrender
**12** tergiversate **14** change your mind

## backslide
◇ *reversal indicator* **03** sin **04** slip
**05** lapse, stray **06** defect, desert, go
back, renege, revert **07** decline,
default, regress, relapse **08** go astray,
turn away **10** apostatize
**12** tergiversate, turn your back **13** fall
from grace

## backslider
**07** reneger **08** apostate, defector,
deserter, recreant, renegade, turncoat
**09** defaulter **10** recidivist
**13** tergiversator

## backsliding
◇ *reversal indicator* **05** lapse **07** relapse
**08** apostasy **09** defection, desertion
**10** defaulting, regression
**14** tergiversation

## backtrack
◇ *reversal indicator* **06** renege **08** do a U-
turn, go back on, withdraw **09** back-
pedal, climb down **12** tergiversate
**14** change your mind

## backup
**03** aid **04** help **07** support **10** assistance
**11** endorsement **12** confirmation
**13** encouragement, reinforcement

## backward
◇ *reversal indicator* **03** shy **04** hind, slow
**05** timid **06** arrear, averse, behind
**07** arriéré, bashful, reverse **08** hesitant,
immature, rearward, retarded, reticent,
retiring, wavering **09** reluctant,
shrinking, subnormal, to the back,
unwilling **10** hesitating, regressive,
retrograde **11** undeveloped
**13** retrogressive **14** underdeveloped
**15** unsophisticated

## backwards
◇ *reversal indicator* **05** aback, retro-
**09** rearwards, to the back
**12** regressively **15** retrogressively

## backwash
**04** flow, path, wake, wash **05** swell,
waves **06** result **07** results **08** reaction
**09** aftermath **11** after effect,
consequence **12** after effects,
consequences, repercussion
**13** repercussions **14** reverberations

## backwater
**05** bogan, scrub **06** slough **08** Woop
Woop **11** remote place **13** isolated
place

## backwoods
**04** bush **05** brush **07** outback
**08** backveld **09** backwater, the sticks
**10** back-blocks, the boonies **11** remote
place **12** back of beyond, the
boondocks **13** isolated place **15** middle
of nowhere

## bacon
**04** bard, spek **05** Roger, speck
**06** collar, gammon, lardon, rasher
**07** Francis, lardoon **08** forehock,
pancetta

## bacteria
**08** gut flora
*See also* **bacterium**

## bacteriology
*Bacteriologists include:*

**04** **Cohn** (Ferdinand), **Gram** (Hans),
   **Koch** (Robert), **Roux** (Émile)
**05** **Avery** (Oswald), **Smith** (Theobald),
   **Twort** (Frederick)
**06** **Enders** (John)
**07** **Behring** (Emil von), **Buchner**
   (Hans), **Ehrlich** (Paul), **Fleming** (Sir
   Alexander), **Löffler** (Friedrich)
**08** **Calmette** (Albert), **Kitasato**
   (Shibasaburo)
**10** **Wassermann** (August von)

*See also* **biology**

## bacterium
**03** bug, rod **04** cell, germ **06** mother,
packet, strain **07** microbe **08** parasite,
serotype, superbug **13** micro-organism

*Bacteria include:*

**03** Hib
**04** MRSA
**05** C. diff, E. coli
**06** coccus, vibrio
**07** Proteus
**08** bacillus, listeria, Shigella,
   yersinia, zoogloea
**09** Azobacter, peritrich, ray
   fungus, Rhizobium, spirillum,
   spirulina, treponema,
   treponeme
**10** gonococcus, Klebsiella,
   legionella, Leptospira,
   salmonella, saprophyte
**11** acidophilus, Actinomyces,
   Azotobacter, Bacillaceae,
   clostridium, Escherichia,
   Pasteurella, Penicillium,
   pseudomonad, pseudomonas,
   spirochaete
**12** enterococcus, helicobacter,
   pneumococcus, vinegar plant
**13** campylobacter, Eubacteriales,
   fission fungus, lactobacillus,
   Mycobacterium, streptococcus
**14** actinobacillus, Corynebacteria,
   staphylococcus, trichobacteria,
   Vibrio cholerae, Yersinia pestis
**15** Escherichia coli, intestinal flora,
   sulphur bacteria

## bad
◇ *anagram indicator* **03** hot, ill, mal-, off
**04** blue, duff, eale, edgy, evil, foul,
high, hurt, lewd, mean, naff, nice,
poor, poxy, ropy, rude, sick, sour, vile,
wack, weak **05** acute, angry, awful,
black, cross, crude, dirty, gammy,
grave, gross, harsh, humpy, juicy,
lousy, narky, nasty, onkus, pants, ratty,
sorry, testy **06** aching, coarse, crabby,
cruddy, crummy, faulty, feisty, filthy,
gallus, gloomy, grumpy, guilty, in
pain, mouldy, poorly, putrid, rancid,

rotten, severe, shirty, shoddy, sinful,
smutty, snappy, spoilt, stingy, tetchy,
unruly, unwell, vulgar, wicked
**07** abusive, adverse, ashamed, bilious,
bolshie, botched, corrupt, crabbed,
decayed, gnarled, grouchy, harmful,
hurtful, immoral, in a huff, in a sulk,
injured, intense, naughty, obscene,
painful, peppery, prickly, profane,
raunchy, ruinous, serious, stroppy,
tainted, the pits, unhappy, useless,
wayward, wounded **08** choleric,
contrite, criminal, critical, damaging,
diseased, dreadful, hopeless,
impaired, impolite, indecent, inferior,
mediocre, pathetic, petulant,
shameful, terrible **09** appalling,
atrocious, crotchety, dangerous,
defective, deficient, difficult,
dishonest, dyspeptic, fractious,
impatient, imperfect, injurious,
insulting, irascible, irritable, offensive,
querulous, reprobate, splenetic, third-
rate, unhealthy **10** apologetic,
capernoity, degenerate, deplorable,
despondent, ill-behaved, inadequate,
mismanaged, outrageous, putrescent,
refractory, remorseful, second-rate,
shamefaced, unpleasant, unsuitable
**11** a load of crap, bad-tempered,
blasphemous, carnaptious,
deleterious, destructive, detrimental,
disobedient, distressing, incompetent,
ineffective, ineffectual, mischievous,
substandard, thin-skinned,
undesirable, unfortunate,
unwholesome **12** badly-behaved,
cantankerous, contaminated,
disagreeable, discourteous,
inauspicious, inconvenient,
putrefactive, unacceptable,
unfavourable **13** inappropriate, quick-
tempered, reprehensible **14** a load of
garbage, a load of rubbish,
uncontrollable, unsatisfactory
**15** under the weather
• **not bad** **02** OK **04** fair, so-so
**07** average **08** adequate, all right,
passable **09** quite good, tolerable
**10** acceptable, reasonable
**12** satisfactory

## badge
**03** mon **04** blue, logo, mark, sign, star
**05** brand, crest, eagle, patch, stamp,
token, wings **06** button, device,
emblem, ensign, rondel, shield,
symbol **07** cockade, insigne, kikumon,
rosette **08** episemon, insignia,
numerals, vernicle **09** indicator,
trademark **10** cognizance, escutcheon,
indication **14** identification

## badger
**03** nag **04** bait, goad, ride **05** brock,
bully, harry, hound, ratel **06** chivvy, go
on at, harass, hassle, keep at, pester,
plague, teledu **07** torment **08** ballyrag,
bullyrag, keep on at **09** importune
• **badger-like animal** **05** ratel
• **badgers** **04** cete

## badinage
**05** borak, chaff **06** banter, humour
**07** mockery, ribbing, teasing, waggery
**08** dicacity, drollery, raillery, repartee,

wordplay **10** jocularity, persiflage **11** give and take

## badly
◇ *anagram indicator* **03** ill, mis-
**06** deeply, evilly, poorly **07** acutely, awfully, cruelly, gravely, greatly, ineptly, wrongly **08** bitterly, faultily, severely, sinfully, terribly, unfairly, very much, wickedly **09** adversely, crucially, extremely, immorally, intensely, painfully, seriously, unhappily, uselessly **10** carelessly, criminally, critically, enormously, improperly, shamefully **11** appallingly, dangerously, defectively, desperately, dishonestly, exceedingly, imperfectly, incorrectly, negligently, offensively **12** inadequately, pathetically, tremendously, unacceptably, unfavourably **13** incompetently, ineffectually, unfortunately **14** unsuccessfully
• **badly off** **04** poor **05** needy **06** in need

## bad-mannered
**04** rude **05** crude **06** coarse **07** boorish, cubbish, ill-bred, loutish, uncivil, uncouth **08** churlish, impolite, insolent **10** ill-behaved, unmannerly **11** ill-mannered, insensitive **12** badly-behaved, discourteous

## badminton
*Badminton-related terms include:*

**03** net, set
**04** bird, kill
**05** clear, court, drive, flick, rally, serve, smash
**06** racket
**07** doubles, racquet, singles
**08** drop shot, wood shot
**11** shuttlecock
**12** service court
**13** underarm clear

## badness
**03** sin **04** evil **07** cruelty **08** foulness, vileness **09** depravity, nastiness **10** corruption, dishonesty, immorality, wickedness **12** shamefulness **14** unpleasantness

## bad-tempered
**04** edgy, mean **05** black, cross, humpy, narky, ratty, sulky, testy, vixen **06** crabby, feisty, gnarly, grumpy, shirty, snappy, stingy, tetchy **07** bilious, crabbed, crabbit, gnarled, grouchy, in a huff, in a mood, in a sulk, peppery, prickly, stroppy, vicious, vixenly **08** choleric, petulant, scratchy, vixenish **09** crotchety, dyspeptic, fractious, impatient, irascible, irritable, querulous, splenetic **10** capernoity, ill-natured, in a bad mood **11** carnaptious, curnaptious, dyspeptical, ill-humoured, thin-skinned **12** cantankerous, curmudgeonly **13** quick-tempered

## baffle
◇ *anagram indicator* **03** bar, fox, get **04** daze, faze, foil, mate **05** block, check, elude, evade, stump, throw, upset **06** bemuse, defeat, fickle, hinder, puzzle, thwart **07** bumbaze, confuse, flummox, mystify, nonplus, perplex **08** bewilder, confound **09** bamboozle, dumbfound, frustrate **10** disconcert **13** bring to naught

## baffling
◇ *anagram indicator* **07** amazing, cryptic **08** bemusing, puzzling **09** confusing, enigmatic **10** astounding, mysterious, perplexing, stupefying, surprising **11** bewildering **12** unfathomable **13** disconcerting, extraordinary

## bag
◇ *containment indicator* **03** cod, get, net, pot, sac **04** gain, grab, kill, land, pock, poke, port, take, trap **05** catch, pouch, shoot **06** come by, corner, obtain, pocket, secure **07** acquire, capture, reserve **09** container **10** commandeer, receptacle **11** appropriate

*Bags include:*

**03** bum, jag, kit, pod
**04** caba, case, grip, hand, mail, pack, sack, tote, wash
**05** bulse, cabas, dilli, dilly, ditty, money, purse, scrip
**06** carpet, clutch, duffel, flight, sachel, saddle, tucker, valise, vanity, wallet
**07** carrier, evening, holdall, satchel, shopper, utricle
**08** backpack, carry-all, gripsack, knapsack, mailsack, meal-poke, pochette, reticule, rucksack, shopping, shoulder, suitcase, wineskin, woolpack
**09** briefcase, fanny pack, Gladstone, haversack, moneybelt, overnight
**10** sabretache
**11** attaché-case, portmanteau

## baggage
**04** bags, gear, swag **05** cases **06** things **07** clobber, dunnage, effects, luggage **08** carriage, materiel **09** equipment, suitcases, viaticals **10** belongings **11** impedimenta **13** accoutrements, paraphernalia
*See also* **prostitute; tramp**

## baggy
**05** kneed, loose, roomy, slack **06** bulged, droopy, floppy, pouchy, sloppy **07** bulging, sagging **08** oversize **09** billowing, shapeless **10** ballooning, extra large, ill-fitting **12** loose-fitting

## bagpipe
**05** gaita, pipes **07** musette, piffero **08** dulcimer, zampogna **09** cornemuse **10** small-pipes, sourdeline **12** uillean pipes **13** uilleann pipes
• **bagpipe composition** **04** port **07** pibroch

## Bahamas
**02** BS **03** BHS

## Bahrain
**03** BHR, BRN

## bail
**04** bond, hoop **05** ladle **06** pledge, surety **07** caution, custody, replevy **08** security, warranty **09** guarantee **10** collateral **12** jurisdiction

• **bail out** **03** aid **04** help, quit, save **05** eject, ladle, scoop **06** assist, escape, get out, rescue **07** back out, finance, relieve, retreat **08** get clear, withdraw

## bailiff
**04** foud **05** agent, reeve **06** beagle **07** nut-hook **08** huissier **09** bum-baylie, hundreder, hundredor **10** philistine **11** land-steward **12** shoulder knot **15** shoulder-clapper

## bait
**03** dap, irk, lug **04** chum, goad, lure, rage **05** annoy, bribe, decoy, harry, hound, leger, slate, snare, squid, taunt, tease, tie-up, troll, yabby **06** badger, berley, burley, caplin, gentle, harass, hassle, ledger, lidger, needle, plague, yabbie **07** capelin, catworm, lugworm, provoke, ragworm, torment **08** irritate **09** anchoveta, angleworm, brandling, incentive, killifish, persecute, propeller, white worm **10** allurement, attraction, enticement, incitement, inducement, temptation **11** hellgramite, refreshment **12** hellgrammite, night crawler **15** give a hard time to

## bake
◇ *anagram indicator* **03** dry **04** burn, cake, cook, fire, heat, shir **05** brown, parch, roast, shirr **06** harden, scorch, wither **07** shrivel **08** pot-roast **09** oven-roast, spit-roast **12** porcellanize

## balance
**03** bal, set **04** meet, rest, trim, tron **05** agree, level, Libra, match, pease, peaze, peise, peize, peyse, poise, pound, tally, weigh **06** adjust, aplomb, equate, equity, even up, excess, juggle, launce, make up, offset, parity, review, square, stasis, steady **07** compare, even out, librate, residue, sea legs, surplus, weigh up **08** appraise, calmness, consider, equality, equalize, estimate, evaluate, evenness, symmetry **09** assurance, composure, equipoise, remainder, sangfroid, stability, stabilize **10** correspond, counteract, difference, equanimity, neutralize, set against, steadiness, uniformity **11** equilibrate, equilibrium, equivalence, self-control **12** counterweigh **13** compensate for, equiponderate **14** cool-headedness, correspondence, counterbalance, self-possession, unflappability **15** level-headedness
• **balance sheet** **02** bs
• **in the balance** **04** iffy **06** unsure **07** unknown **08** in the air **09** knife-edge, uncertain, undecided, unsettled **10** indefinite, touch and go **12** undetermined **13** unpredictable
• **on balance** **07** overall **08** all in all **09** generally **12** in conclusion

## balanced
**04** calm, even, fair **05** equal, level, sound **06** poised **07** assured, healthy, weighed **08** complete, sensible, straight, unbiased **09** equitable, impartial, objective **10** cool-headed, even-handed **11** level-headed, well-

rounded **12** unprejudiced
**13** dispassionate, self-possessed

**balcony**
**04** gods **06** loggia **07** gallery, portico,
sundeck, terrace, veranda
**09** mezzanine **10** moucharaby
**11** upper circle **14** quarter-gallery

**bald**
**04** bare **05** bleak, blunt, naked, plain,
stark **06** barren, direct, paltry, peeled,
severe, simple, smooth **07** exposed,
obvious, pollard, trivial **08** glabrate,
glabrous, hairless, outright, straight,
tonsured, treeless **09** depilated,
downright, outspoken, unadorned,
uncovered **10** bald-headed, forthright
**11** bald as a coot, unambiguous,
undisguised, unsheltered
**15** straightforward

**balderdash**
**03** rot **04** blah, bosh, bull, bunk, guff,
jazz **05** bilge, borak, hooey, trash, tripe
**06** blague, bunkum, drivel, faddle,
havers, hot air, piffle **07** baloney,
eyewash, hogwash, rhubarb, rubbish,
twaddle **08** blethers, bulldust, claptrap,
cobblers, doggerel, malarkey,
nonsense, tommyrot **09** bull's wool,
gibberish, moonshine, poppycock
**10** codswallop, galimatias
**12** clamjamphrie

**balding**
**04** bald **08** receding **09** thin on top
**14** losing your hair

**baldmoney**
**03** meu **07** spignel

**baldness**
**07** fox-evil **08** alopecia, bareness, hair
loss, psilosis **09** calvities, madarosis,
starkness **12** glabrousness, hairlessness
**14** alopecia areata, bald-headedness

**bale**
**02** bl **04** lave, pack **05** ladle, seron,
truss **06** bundle, parcel, seroon
**07** confine, package **08** woolpack
• **bale out** **04** quit **06** escape, get out
**07** back out, retreat **08** get clear,
withdraw

**baleful**
**04** evil **05** swart **06** deadly, malign,
sullen, swarth **07** harmful, hurtful,
malefic, noxious, ominous, painful,
ruinous **08** menacing, mournful,
sinister, venomous **09** injurious,
malignant, sorrowful **10** lugubrious,
malevolent, pernicious **11** destructive,
threatening

**balefully**
**09** harmfully, hurtfully **10** menacingly
**11** dangerously **13** destructively,
detrimentally, threateningly

**balk, baulk**
**03** bar, hen, jib **04** chop, foil **05** avoid,
check, demur, dodge, evade, reest,
reist, shirk, stall **06** baffle, boggle,
defeat, eschew, flinch, hinder, ignore,
impede, pull up, recoil, refuse, resist,
shrink, thwart **07** decline, prevent
**08** hesitate, obstruct **09** discomfit,
forestall, frustrate **10** counteract,

disconcert **11** frustration
**14** disappointment

**ball**
**01** O **02** ba' **03** cop, nur, orb **04** clew,
clue, drop, knur, nurr, pill, shot, slug,
tice **05** dance, fungo, globe, Jaffa,
knurr, party **06** beamer, bullet, googly,
pellet, soirée, sphere, strike, yorker
**07** bouncer, globule, leather, long hop,
shooter, swinger **08** assembly,
carnival, Chinaman, delivery, full toss,
gazunder, leg break, off break
**09** inswinger **10** masquerade,
outswinger, projectile **11** daisy-cutter,
dinner-dance **14** conglomeration
• **high ball** **03** lob
• **play ball** **07** go along, respond
**09** co-operate, play along
**11** collaborate, reciprocate, show
willing
• **position of ball** **03** lie

**ballad**
**03** jig **04** poem, song **05** carol, ditty,
mento **06** shanty **07** ballant, calypso,
romance **08** folk-song, singsong
**09** cantilena **10** forebitter **12** Lillibullero

**ballet**
**07** dancing **11** leg-business **13** ballet-
dancing
*See also* **choreography; dance;
dancer**

*Ballets include:*

**05** Manon, Rodeo, Rooms
**06** Apollo, Boléro, Carmen, Façade,
Ondine, Onegin, Parade
**07** Giselle, La Valse, Orpheus,
Requiem
**08** Coppélia, Les Noces, Nocturne,
Swan Lake
**09** Anastasia, Les Biches, Mayerling
**10** Cinderella, Don Quixote, La
Sylphide, Petroushka, Prince Igor,
Pulcinella
**11** Billy the Kid, Las Hermanas, The
Firebird
**12** Les Sylphides, Schéhérazade
**13** Pineapple Poll, The Nutcracker
**14** Daphnis et Chloé, Romeo and
Juliet, The Prodigal Son
**15** The Rite of Spring

*Ballet-related terms include:*

**03** bar, pas
**04** jeté, plié, posé, tutu
**05** barre, battu
**06** à terre, attack, ballon, chassé,
écarté, en face, en l'air, pointe,
school, splits
**07** à pointe, bourrée, bras bas,
ciseaux, company, danseur, en
avant, fouetté, leotard, maillot,
pointes, premier
**08** attitude, batterie, cabriole,
capriole, coryphée, couronne,
danseuse, en pointe, ensemble,
fish dive, glissade, première,
stulchak
**09** arabesque, ballerina, battement,
cou de pied, elevation, entrechat,
pas de chat, pas de deux, pas de
seul, pirouette, point shoe,
promenade, régisseur

**10** ballet shoe, répétiteur
**11** Laban system, ports de bras
**12** ballet-dancer, ballet-master,
choreography, labanotation
**13** corps de ballet, five positions, sur
les pointes
**14** divertissement, maître de ballet,
petit battement, premier danseur,
prima ballerina
**15** grande battement, principal
dancer

**balloon**
**03** bag **04** soar **05** belly, bulge, swell
**06** billow, blow up, dilate, expand,
rocket **07** distend, enlarge, fumetto,
inflate, puff out **08** aerostat, escalate,
snowball **09** dirigible, skyrocket
**11** grow rapidly, montgolfier **12** ballon
d'essai **15** increase rapidly

**ballot**
**04** poll, vote **06** voting **07** polling
**08** election **10** plebiscite, referendum
• **ballot-box** **03** urn

**ballyhoo**
**04** fuss, hype, to-do **05** noise
**06** hubbub, racket, tumult **07** build-up,
clamour **09** agitation, commotion, hue
and cry, kerfuffle, promotion, publicity
**10** excitement, hullabaloo,
propaganda **11** advertising,
disturbance

**balm**
**04** nard, tolu **05** cream, salve
**06** balsam, lotion, relief **07** anodyne,
bromide, comfort, unguent
**08** curative, lenitive, ointment,
sedative **09** calmative, emollient,
opobalsam **10** palliative
**11** consolation, embrocation,
restorative

**balmy**
**04** mild, soft, warm **06** gentle
**07** clement, summery **08** pleasant,
soothing **09** temperate

**balsam**
**04** heal, Tolu **06** embalm **07** wood oil
**09** impatiens, spikenard **13** noli-me-
tangere

**Balt**
**04** Esth, Lett

**bamboozle**
◊ *anagram indicator* **03** con **04** daze,
dupe, fool, gull, rook **05** cheat, trick,
upset **06** bemuse, diddle, puzzle
**07** bumbaze, confuse, deceive,
mystify, nonplus, perplex, swindle
**08** bewilder, confound, hoodwink
**09** dumbfound **10** disconcert **14** pull a
fast one on

**ban**
**03** bar **04** band, tabu, tapu, veto
**05** black, curse, taboo **06** banish,
censor, forbid, outlaw **07** abolish,
boycott, embargo, exclude
**08** disallow, outlawry, prohibit,
restrict, stoppage, suppress
**09** ostracize, proscribe, sanctions
**10** banishment, censorship, disqualify,
injunction, moratorium **11** prohibition,
restriction, suppression

**12** anathematize, condemnation, denunciation, interdiction, proclamation, proscription

## banal
**04** dull, flat **05** bland, corny, empty, inane, stale, stock, tired, trite, vapid **06** boring, old hat **07** cliché'd, humdrum, mundane, trivial **08** clichéed, cornball, everyday, ordinary, overused **09** hackneyed **10** threadbare, unoriginal **11** commonplace, nondescript, stereotyped, wearing thin **13** unimaginative

## banality
**06** cliché, truism **07** bromide, fatuity **08** cornball, dullness, vapidity **09** emptiness, inaneness, platitude, staleness, tiredness, triteness **10** prosaicism, triviality **11** commonplace, old chestnut **12** ordinariness **13** unoriginality

## banana
**08** plantain

## bananas
◇ *anagram indicator* **03** mad **04** hand, Musa **05** bunch, crazy
• **go bananas** **04** flip **05** freak **08** freak out

## band
**02** CB **03** bar, rib, rim, tie **04** ally, belt, body, bond, club, cord, core, crew, fess, frog, gang, ging, herd, hoop, join, line, link, ring, sash, tape, team, teme, tire, tyre, welt, with, zona, zone **05** chain, crowd, fesse, flock, group, horde, merge, music, party, strap, strip, thong, troop, unite, withe **06** clique, fetter, gather, girdle, ribbon, streak, stripe, swathe, team up, throng **07** bandage, binding, company, manacle, shackle, society **08** ensemble, federate, ligature, pop group **09** affiliate, gathering, orchestra **10** amalgamate, close ranks, connection, contingent, join forces, music group **11** association, collaborate, consolidate **12** club together, musical group, pull together **13** stand together, stick together
*See also* **singer**
• **raised band** **03** rib
• **twisted band** **04** torc, with **05** withe **06** torque

## bandage
**01** T **04** bind, lint, wrap **05** cover, dress, gauze, spica **06** binder, bind up, swathe **07** Band-aid®, bandeau, plaster, scapula, swaddle **08** capeline, compress, dressing, ligature, Tubigrip® **09** capelline, suspensor **10** tourniquet **11** Elastoplast®

## bandicoot
**05** bilby **06** pig-rat **10** Malabar-rat

## bandit
**05** crook, thief **06** cowboy, dacoit, dakoit, gunman, mugger, outlaw, pirate, raider, robber **07** brigand, footpad **08** criminal, gangster, hijacker, marauder **09** buccaneer, desperado, plunderer, racketeer **10** highwayman

## bandsman
**04** wait

## bandy
◇ *anagram indicator* **04** bent, pass, swap, toss **05** bowed, fight, fling, throw, trade **06** barter, curved, spread, strive **07** chaffer, crooked **08** exchange **09** bow-legged, misshapen **11** interchange, reciprocate

## bane
**03** woe **04** evil, harm, pest, ruin **05** curse, death, trial **06** blight, burden, misery, ordeal, plague, poison **07** bugbear, scourge, torment, trouble **08** calamity, disaster, distress, downfall, mischief, nuisance, vexation **09** adversity, annoyance, bête noire **10** affliction, irritation, misfortune, pestilence **11** destruction **14** thorn in the side **15** thorn in the flesh

## baneful
**07** harmful, noxious, painful, ruinous **08** annoying **09** poisonous **10** disastrous, pernicious **11** destructive, distressing, troublesome **12** pestilential

## bang
**03** hit, pop, rap **04** bash, benj, blow, boom, bump, clap, dead, drum, echo, hard, peal, shot, slam, slap, sock, thud, wham **05** burst, clang, clash, crack, crash, knock, noise, pound, punch, right, smack, spang, stamp, thump, whack **06** blow up, hammer, report, strike, stroke, thwack, wallop **07** clatter, exactly, explode, noisily, resound, thunder **08** abruptly, bump into, cannabis, detonate, directly, headlong, slap-bang, straight, suddenly **09** collision, crash into, explosion, precisely **10** absolutely, detonation

## banger
**04** bomb, heap **05** crate **06** jalopy **07** clunker, jaloppy, sausage **09** tin lizzie

## Bangladesh
**02** BD **03** BGD

## bangle
**04** band, kara **06** anklet **07** circlet **08** bracelet, wristlet

## banish
**03** ban, bar **04** band, oust **05** debar, eject, evict, exile, expel **06** deport, dispel, forsay, outlaw, remove **07** abandon, cast out, discard, dismiss, exclude, foresay, shut out **08** dislodge, get rid of, relegate, send away, throw out **09** drive away, eliminate, eradicate, extradite, ostracize, rusticate, transport **10** disimagine, expatriate, repatriate **13** excommunicate

## banishment
**03** ban **05** exile **08** eviction, outlawry **09** exclusion, exilement, expulsion, ostracism **11** deportation, extradition **12** expatriation **14** transportation **15** excommunication

## banisters
**04** rail **07** railing **08** handrail **10** balustrade

## bank
**02** as, bk **03** bar, dam, row, tip **04** bink, brae, edge, fund, heap, keep, line, link, mass, pile, pool, rank, reef, rise, rive, save, side, sunk, tier, tilt **05** amass, array, bench, bluff, cache, drift, group, hoard, hurst, knoll, lay by, levee, mound, panel, pitch, ridge, shore, slant, slope, stack, stock, store, train **06** heap up, margin, pile up, rivage, save up, series, supply **07** deposit, hillock, incline, parados, pottery, rampart, reserve, savings, stack up **08** put aside, sequence, treasury **09** earthwork, reservoir, stash away, stockpile **10** accumulate, depository, embankment, repository, succession **11** put together, savings bank **12** accumulation, clearing bank, finance house, merchant bank **14** finance company, high-street bank **15** building society
• **banking system** **04** giro
• **bank on** **05** bet on, trust **06** rely on **07** count on **08** depend on **09** bargain on, believe in **14** pin your hopes on
• **bank rate** **02** br
• **banks** ◇ *ends selection indicator*
• **bank up** **04** hele, hill

## banker
**05** gnome **06** shroff **07** Lombard **09** exchanger
*See also* **river**

## banknote
**03** fin **04** bill, note **05** fiver, scrip **06** flimsy, greeny, single, tenner, twenty **07** greenie, iron man, sawbuck **09** greenback **10** paper money **12** treasury note

## bankrupt
**04** bung, bust, duck, ruin **05** break, broke, spent **06** beggar, bereft, broken, debtor, dyvour, failed, folded, hard up, pauper, ruined **07** cripple, lacking, wanting, without **08** beggared, depleted, deprived, in the red, lame duck **09** deficient, destitute, exhausted, gone under, insolvent, penurious, sequester **10** impoverish, on the rocks, stony broke, trade-falne **11** impecunious, trade-fallen **12** impoverished, on your uppers **13** gone to the wall, in liquidation

## bankruptcy
**04** lack, ruin **05** smash **06** penury, stumer **07** beggary, dyvoury, failure **08** disaster, ruination **10** exhaustion, insolvency **11** Carey Street, liquidation **12** indebtedness **13** financial ruin, sequestration
• **to bankruptcy** **04** scat **05** skatt

## banner
**04** flag, sign **06** burgee, ensign, fanion, pennon **07** bandrol, colours, labarum, pennant, placard **08** banderol, bannerol, gonfalon, gumphion, standard, streamer, vexillum **09** banderole, bannerall, oriflamme

## banquet
04 dine, meal 05 feast, party, treat
06 dinner, junket, spread 11 dinner
party 13 entertainment

## banter
03 kid, pun, rag, rib 04 jest, joke, josh,
mock, quiz, rail 05 borak, borax, chaff,
rally, roast, tease 06 deride, joking
07 jesting, kidding, mockery, ribbing
08 badinage, chaffing, derision,
dicacity, raillery, repartee, ridicule,
word play 09 make fun of 10 persiflage,
pleasantry

## Bantu
04 Hutu, Xosa, Zulu 05 Nguni, Sotho,
Swazi, Tonga, Tutsi, Xhosa 06 Herero,
Nyanja, Tswana 07 Basotho, Lingala,
Sesotho, Swahili 08 Congoese
09 Congolese

## baptism
05 debut 06 launch, naming
07 mersion 08 affusion 09 aspersion,
beginning, immersion, launching
10 dedication, initiation, sprinkling
11 christening, parabaptism
12 inauguration, introduction,
paedobaptism, purification

## baptize
03 dip 04 call, name, term 05 admit,
enrol, style, title 06 purify 07 cleanse,
immerse, recruit 08 christen, initiate,
sprinkle 09 introduce

## bar
01 T, Z 03 ban, fen, fid, gad, inn, pub,
rib, rod, zed, zee 04 bolt, cake, dive,
howf, hunk, lock, lump, pole, rail, risp,
rung, save, shet, shut, slab, slot, snug,
spar, stop, swee, toll 05 block, check,
chunk, court, debar, estop, grill, ingot,
joint, latch, lever, shaft, stake, stick,
table, wedge 06 batten, bistro, boozer,
but for, except, fasten, forbid, hinder,
lounge, nugget, paling, saloon, secure,
tavern 07 barrier, counsel, counter,
exclude, lawyers, padlock, prevent,
railing, suspend, taproom 08 blockade,
drawback, hostelry, obstacle, obstruct,
omitting, preclude, prohibit, restrain,
snuggery, tribunal 09 advocates, apart
from, aside from, barricade, brasserie,
deterrent, except for, excepting,
excluding, hindrance, lounge bar,
stanchion 10 barristers, beer-parlor,
crosspiece, disqualify, impediment
11 obstruction, public house
12 beverage room, watering-hole

## barb
03 dig, mow 04 gibe, harl, herl, tang,
trim 05 arrow, beard, fluke, point,
prong, ramus, scorn, shave, sneer,
spike, sting, thorn 06 insult, needle,
rebuff 07 affront, bristle, killick, killock,
prickle

## Barbados
03 BDS, BRB

## barbarian
03 Hun, oaf 04 boor, Goth, lout, wild
05 brute, crude, rough 06 coarse,
savage, vandal, vulgar 07 brutish,
loutish, ruffian, uncouth 08 hooligan
09 Hottentot, ignoramus 10 illiterate,

philistine, tramontane, uncultured,
wild person 11 Neanderthal,
uncivilized 12 uncultivated
15 unsophisticated

## barbaric
◇ *anagram indicator* 04 rude, wild
05 crude, cruel 06 brutal, coarse,
fierce, savage, vulgar 07 bestial,
brutish, foreign, inhuman, uncouth,
vicious 08 ruthless 09 barbarous,
ferocious, murderous, primitive
11 uncivilized

## barbarism
07 cruelty 08 enormity, ferocity,
rudeness, savagery, wildness
09 brutality, crudeness, vulgarity
10 bestiality, coarseness, corruption,
fierceness, heathenism 11 brutishness,
inhumanness, uncouthness,
viciousness 12 ruthlessness
13 murderousness 15 uncivilizedness

## barbarity
07 cruelty, outrage 08 atrocity,
enormity, ferocity, savagery, wildness
09 brutality 10 inhumanity, savageness
11 brutishness, viciousness
12 ruthlessness 13 barbarousness

## barbarous
◇ *anagram indicator* 04 rude, wild
05 crude, cruel, harsh, rough 06 brutal,
fierce, Gothic, savage, vulgar
07 bestial, brutish, corrupt, inhuman,
vicious 08 barbaric, ignorant, ruthless
09 barbarian, ferocious, heartless,
murderous, primitive, unrefined
10 uncultured, unlettered
11 uncivilized, unscholarly
15 unsophisticated

## barbecue
03 BBQ 04 bake, cook 05 braai, broil,
brown, grill, roast 06 barbie
07 cookout, griddle, hibachi, stir-fry
09 spit-roast 10 braaivleis

## barbed
04 acid 05 armed, catty, jaggy, nasty,
snide, spiky, spiny 06 bitchy, hooked,
jagged, spiked, tanged, thorny, unkind
07 bearded, caustic, cutting, hostile,
hurtful, pointed, prickly, pronged,
toothed 08 barbated, critical, spiteful,
wounding 09 sarcastic

## barber
04 Todd 05 shave, strap 06 Figaro,
shaver, tonsor 07 scraper
11 hairdresser, Sweeney Todd

## bard
*see* poet

## bare
04 bald, cold, hard, lewd, mere, nude,
peel, pure, very 05 basic, bleak, clear,
empty, naked, plain, sheer, stark, strip,
utter 06 barren, expose, reveal, simple,
unmask, unveil, vacant 07 denuded,
display, exposed, lay bare, uncover,
undress 08 absolute, complete,
desolate, in the nip, in the raw,
stripped, treeless, unclothe,
unwooded, woodless 09 essential, in
the buff, in the nude, in the scud,
unadorned, unclothed, uncovered,
undressed, very least 10 defoliated, no

more than, stark-naked, unforested
11 unfurnished, unsheltered 13 with
nothing on 15 straightforward

## barefaced
04 bald, bold, open 05 brash, naked
06 arrant, avowed, brazen, cheeky,
patent 07 blatant, glaring, obvious
08 flagrant, impudent, insolent,
manifest, palpable 09 audacious, bald-
faced, beardless, shameless,
unabashed 11 transparent,
unconcealed, undisguised

## barefooted
06 unshod 08 barefoot, shoeless
09 discalced

## barely
04 just, only 05 scant 06 almost, hardly,
openly, scrimp 07 halfway, nakedly,
none too, plainly 08 narrowly, no
sooner, only just, scarcely 10 by a
whisker, explicitly 12 be a near thing,
by a short head 13 be a close thing

## bargain
02 go 03 buy 04 deal, pact, sell, snip,
whiz 05 broke, cheap, steal, trade,
truck, whizz 06 barter, broker, clinch,
haggle, indent, market, pledge, settle,
treaty 07 chaffer, cheapen, good buy,
promise, special, traffic 08 beat down,
cheap buy, contract, covenant,
discount, giveaway, purchase,
transact, wanworth 09 agreement, bon
marché, concordat, dirt cheap,
negotiate, reduction 11 arrangement,
negotiation, transaction 12 special
offer 13 understanding, value for
money
• **bargain for** 06 expect 07 foresee,
imagine, include, look for, plan for
08 consider, contract, figure on,
reckon on 10 anticipate
11 contemplate 13 be prepared for
15 take into account
• **into the bargain** 04 also 06 as well
07 besides 10 in addition
11 furthermore 12 additionally

## bargaining
05 trade 06 barter, buying, dicker,
outcry 07 chaffer, dealing, selling
08 dealings, haggling 09 bartering
11 negotiation, trafficking, transaction
12 horsetrading 14 wheeler-dealing

## barge
◇ *anagram indicator* 03 hit 04 bump,
keel, pram, push, rush, scow 05 barca,
butty, casco, elbow, praam, press,
shove, smash 06 galley, hopper, jostle,
plough, push in, wherry 07 birlinn,
budgero, collide, gabbard, gabbart,
lighter, piragua, pirogue, pontoon
08 budgerow, flatboat, keelboat,
periagua 09 Bucentaur, canal-boat,
houseboat 10 narrowboat 11 galley-
foist, push your way 12 force your way
• **barge in** 05 cut in 06 butt in
07 break in, burst in, intrude
09 gatecrash, interfere, interrupt

## baritone
03 bar

## barium
02 Ba

## bark

**03** bay, cry, tan, wow, yap **04** bass, bast, bawl, cork, hide, howl, husk, kina, peel, rind, skin, snap, tapa, waff, woof, yaff, yawp, yell, yelp **05** china, cough, crust, growl, quest, quill, quina, shell, shout, snarl, suber, tappa **06** bellow, bowwow, casing, cortex **07** cascara, encrust, pereira, thunder **08** calisaya, cinchona, cinnamon, covering, simaruba, tan balls **09** bull's wool, quebracho, sassafras, simarouba, xanthoxyl **10** cascarilla, integument, quercitron **11** slippery elm **13** cascara amarga **14** cascara sagrada

## barking

◊ *anagram indicator* **03** bay, mad, odd **04** daft, nuts **05** barmy, batty, crazy, dippy, dotty, loony, loopy, nutty, potty **06** cuckoo, insane **07** bananas, bonkers **08** crackers **09** latration **10** off your nut, unbalanced **11** off your head **12** mad as a hatter, round the bend **13** off your rocker, round the twist **14** off your trolley

## barley

**04** bear, bere, bigg, malt **07** Hordeum

## barmy

**03** mad, odd **04** daft, nuts **05** batty, crazy, dippy, dotty, loony, loopy, nutty, silly **06** cuckoo, frothy, insane, stupid **07** foolish, idiotic **08** crackers **10** fermenting, off your nut, out to lunch, unbalanced **11** off your head **12** round the bend **13** off your rocker, round the twist **14** off your trolley

## barn

**06** grange **07** skipper

## barometer

**07** aneroid **09** barograph **10** statoscope **12** weather glass **13** sympiesometer

## baron

**01** B **02** Bn **04** lord, peer **05** mogul **06** bigwig, fat cat, tycoon **07** big shot, magnate **08** nobleman **09** big cheese, executive **10** aristocrat, Münchausen **12** entrepreneur **13** industrialist

## baroness

**04** lady, peer **07** baronne **10** aristocrat, noblewoman

## baronet

**02** Bt **04** Bart

## baroque

◊ *anagram indicator* **04** bold **05** showy **06** florid, ornate, rococo **07** flowery **08** fanciful, vigorous **09** decorated, elaborate, exuberant, fantastic, grotesque, whimsical **10** convoluted, flamboyant **11** embellished, extravagant, overwrought **13** overdecorated, overelaborate **15** churrigueresque

## barrack

**03** boo **04** hiss, jeer **05** taunt, tease **06** casern, heckle **07** caserne, support **09** interrupt, shout down

## barracking

**04** boos **07** hissing, jeering **08** heckling **12** interruption **13** interruptions

## barracks

**03** bks **04** camp, fort **06** billet, casern **07** lodging **08** garrison, quarters **10** encampment, glasshouse, guardhouse **11** gendarmerie **13** accommodation

## barrage

**03** dam **04** dyke, hail, mass, rain, wall **05** burst, flood, onset, salvo, storm **06** attack, deluge, shower, stream, volley **07** assault, barrier, battery, gunfire, torrent **08** shelling **09** abundance, barricade, broadside, cannonade, fusillade, onslaught, profusion **10** embankment **11** bombardment, obstruction

## barrel

**01** b **02** bl **03** bbl, but, keg, tub, tun **04** butt, cade, cask, drum, pipe, wood **05** pièce **06** clavie, firkin, runlet, tierce, tumble **07** oil drum, rundlet **08** hogshead **09** water-butt **10** Morris-tube

## barren

**03** dry **04** arid, dull, eild, flat, yeld, yell **05** addle, bleak, blunt, empty, gaunt, vapid, waste **06** desert, effete, meagre **07** hirstie, sterile, useless **08** desolate, infecund, teemless **09** childless, fruitless, infertile, pointless, unbearing, valueless **10** profitless, unfruitful, unprolific **11** purposeless, uninspiring, unrewarding **12** inhospitable, uncultivable, unproductive **13** uninformative, uninstructive, uninteresting

## barrenness

**06** dearth **07** aridity, dryness **08** dullness **09** emptiness, sterility **11** infecundity, infertility, uselessness **13** pointlessness **14** unfruitfulness

## barricade

**03** bar **04** shut **05** block, close, fence **06** defend **07** barrier, bulwark, close up, defence, fortify, protect, rampart, shut off **08** blockade, obstacle, obstruct, palisade, stockade **10** protection, strengthen **11** obstruction

## Barrie

**02** JM

## barrier

**03** bar, dam **04** bail, boom, doll, gate, ha-ha, wall **05** block, check, ditch, fence, hedge, rails, spina **06** haw-haw, hurdle **07** barrage, curtain, railing, rampart **08** blockade, boundary, bulkhead, division, drawback, frontier, handicap, obstacle, railings, stockade, tick gate, traverse, turnpike **09** barricade, enclosure, hindrance, inclosure, partition, restraint, ring-fence, roadblock **10** breakwater, difficulty, dingo fence, impediment, limitation, tariff wall **11** iron curtain, mental block, obstruction, restriction **12** glass ceiling **13** bamboo curtain, cheval-de-frise, fortification, kangaroo fence **14** stumbling-block **15** cordon sanitaire, dingo-proof fence

## barring

**02** if **03** bar **06** except, unless **09** except for

## barrister

**02** KC, QC **03** Bar **04** silk **05** brief **06** lawyer **07** counsel, Rumpole **08** advocate, attorney, recorder, serjeant **09** counselor, solicitor **10** counsellor **12** King's Counsel **13** Queen's Counsel, serjeant-at-law *See also* **lawyer**

## barrow

**03** how **04** cart, howe, tump **05** hurly, truck **07** tumulus **08** push-cart **11** horned cairn

## bartender

**06** barman **07** barkeep, barmaid **08** publican **09** barkeeper **10** mixologist

## barter

**04** chop, cope, coup, deal, sell, swap, swop **05** trade, truck **06** dicker, haggle, niffer **07** bargain, dealing, trading, traffic **08** exchange, haggling, swapping, truckage **09** negotiate **10** bargaining **11** negotiation, permutation, trafficking

## basalt

**04** trap, whin **05** wacke **07** diabase **08** basanite, traprock **09** toadstone, whinstone

## base

**01** e **02** HQ **03** bed, dog, key, low, ten **04** camp, core, evil, foot, home, mean, poor, post, prop, rest, root, seat, site, stay, vile **05** basis, build, depot, found, heart, hinge, layer, lowly, stand **06** abject, bottom, centre, depend, derive, fundus, ground, locate, origin, plinth, sordid, source, vulgar, wicked **07** bedrock, coating, corrupt, essence, immoral, install, pitiful, situate, staddle, station, support **08** backbone, covering, depraved, infamous, keystone, pedestal, position, shameful, wretched **09** component, construct, essential, establish, low-minded, miserable, principal, reprobate, thickness, valueless, worthless **10** despicable, foundation, groundwork, scandalous, settlement, substratum, underneath **11** disgraceful, fundamental, ignominious **12** contemptible, disreputable, have as a basis, headquarters, substructure, unprincipled **13** starting-point **14** understructure **15** foundation stone • **base of** ◊ *tail selection down indicator*

## baseball

*Baseball players include:*

**03** **Ott** (Mel)
**04** **Cobb** (Ty), **Mack** (Connie), **Mays** (Willie), **Ruth** (Babe), **Ryan** (Nolan)
**05** **Aaron** (Hank), **Bench** (Johnny), **Berra** (Yogi), **Paige** (Satchel), **Spahn** (Warren), **Young** (Cy)
**06** **Gehrig** (Lou), **Gibson** (Bob), **Gibson** (Josh), **Koufax** (Sandy), **Mantle** (Mickey), **Musial** (Stan), **Ripken** (Cal)
**07** **Clemens** (Roger), **Jackson** (Reggie), **McGwire** (Mark), **Stengel** (Casey)
**08** **Clemente** (Roberto), **DiMaggio** (Joe),

Robinson (Brooks), **Robinson**
(Jackie), **Williams** (Ted)
09 **Alexander** (Grover Cleveland),
**Mathewson** (Christy)

*Major league baseball teams:*

11 Chicago Cubs, New York Mets
12 Boston Red Sox, Tampa Bay Rays,
Texas Rangers
13 Atlanta Braves, Detroit Tigers,
Houston Astros
14 Cincinnati Reds, Florida Marlins,
Minnesota Twins, New York
Yankees, San Diego Padres
15 Chicago White Sox, Colorado
Rockies, Seattle Mariners,
Toronto Blue Jays
16 Baltimore Orioles, Cleveland
Indians, Kansas City Royals,
Milwaukee Brewers, Oakland
Athletics, St Louis Cardinals
17 Los Angeles Dodgers, Pittsburgh
Pirates
18 San Francisco Giants
19 Arizona Diamondbacks,
Washington Nationals
20 Philadelphia Phillies
25 Los Angeles Angels of Anaheim

*Baseball terms include:*

03 ace, ERA, hit, out, RBI, run, tag
04 balk, ball, base, bunt, cage, mitt,
safe, walk
05 alley, bench, error, mound, pitch,
plate
06 assist, batter, bottom, closer,
double, dugout, fly out, inning,
on deck, single, sinker, slider,
strike, triple, wind-up
07 all-star, base hit, battery, bull pen,
catcher, chopper, diamond, fly
ball, home run, infield, pennant,
pitcher, rundown, shutout
08 ballpark, baseline, fair ball,
fastball, foul ball, foul pole,
nightcap, no-hitter, outfield, set-
up man
09 cut-off man, earned run, first
base, gold glove, grand slam,
ground out, hit-and-run, home
plate, infielder, in the hole, left
field, line drive, sacrifice,
screwball, strike out, third base,
wild pitch
10 baserunner, batter's box, double
play, ground ball, outfielder,
passed ball, right field, second
base, strike zone
11 base on balls, basket catch,
centre field, knuckleball, left
fielder, perfect game, pinch hitter,
pinch runner, run batted in,
unearned run
12 breaking ball, double-header,
extra innings, load the bases, right
fielder, warning track
13 centre fielder, foul territory, relief
pitcher, safety squeeze
14 American League, backdoor
slider, batting average, fielder's
choice, National League, suicide
squeeze
15 starting pitcher
• **baseball statistic** 03 ERA, RBI

**baseless**
◇ *tail deletion down indicator* 04 idle
06 untrue 09 unfounded 10 fabricated,
gratuitous, groundless, ill-founded,
unattested 11 uncalled-for,
unconfirmed, unjustified, unsupported
15 unauthenticated, unsubstantiated

**basement**
05 crypt, dunny, vault 06 cellar

**bash**
02 go 03 box, hit, ram, try 04 bang,
beat, belt, biff, blow, bump, clip, dent,
rave, shot, slug, sock, stab 05 blast,
break, crack, crash, knock, party,
punch, smack, thump, whack,
whirl 06 batter, rave-up, strike, thrash,
wallop 07 attempt, clobber
11 celebration

**bashful**
03 coy, shy 05 blate, timid 06 modest
07 abashed, laithfu', nervous
08 backward, blushing, hesitant,
reserved, reticent, retiring, sheepish,
timorous 09 diffident, inhibited,
shamefast, shrinking 10 shamefaced,
sheep-faced 11 embarrassed 12 self-
effacing 13 self-conscious,
unforthcoming

**bashfully**
05 shyly 07 timidly 08 modestly
09 nervously 10 hesitantly, reticently,
sheepishly 11 diffidently 14 self-
effacingly 15 self-consciously

**bashfulness**
05 shame 07 blushes, coyness,
modesty, reserve, shyness 08 timidity
09 hesitancy, reticence 10 diffidence,
inhibition 11 nervousness
12 sheepishness 13 embarrassment,
mauvaise honte 14 self-effacement,
shamefacedness

**basic**
03 gut, key 04 bare, root 05 crude, first,
plain, stark, vital 06 simple, staple
07 austere, bedrock, central, minimal,
minimum, primary, radical, spartan
08 inherent, no-frills, standard, starting
09 essential, important, intrinsic,
necessary, primitive, unadorned
10 elementary, underlying 11 bog
standard, fundamental, lowest level,
preparatory, rudimentary 12 down-
and-dirty 13 indispensable
14 unsophisticate 15 unsophisticated

**basically**
06 mainly 07 at heart 08 at bottom 09 in
essence, in the main, primarily,
radically 10 inherently 11 essentially,
in principle, principally
13 fundamentally, intrinsically,
substantially

**basics**
03 ABC 04 core 05 abcee, absey, facts
07 bedrock 08 alphabet, elements
09 realities, rudiments 10 brass tacks,
essentials, principles, rock bottom
11 necessaries, nitty-gritty
12 fundamentals, introduction, nuts
and bolts 14 practicalities 15 first
principles

**basin**
03 bed, dip, pan, pot 04 bowl, dish,
dock, park, sink, tank 05 bidet, docks,
gully, laver, playa 06 cavity, crater,
hollow, lavabo, valley 07 channel,
piscina 08 birdbath, washbowl
09 impluvium, reservoir
10 aquamanale, aquamanile,
depression

**basis**
03 key, way 04 base, core, fond, root
05 heart, radix, terms 06 bottom,
ground, method, reason, status,
system, thrust 07 bedrock, essence,
footing, grounds, keynote, premise,
reasons, support 08 approach,
pedestal, platform 09 condition,
essential, principle, procedure,
rationale 10 conditions, essentials,
foundation, grass-roots, groundwork,
hypostasis, substratum
11 arrangement, cornerstone,
fundamental 12 fundamentals,
quintessence 13 alpha and omega,
starting-point 14 main ingredient
15 first principles

**bask**
03 lie, sun 04 laze, loll 05 bathe, enjoy,
lap up, relax, revel 06 lounge, relish,
savour, sprawl, wallow 08 apricate,
sunbathe 09 delight in, luxuriate
14 take pleasure in

**basket**
03 bin, box, cob, fan, kit, rip, van, wpb
04 case, cauf, chip, coop, corf, crib,
goal, hask, kete, kipe, leap, skep, trug
05 cabas, creel, frail, maund, scull,
skull, willy 06 gabion, hamper, holder,
junket, mocock, mocuck, murlan,
murlin, petara, pottle, punnet, willey,
wisket 07 corbeil, cresset, flasket, flax
kit, murlain, pannier, scuttle, seedlip,
shopper, trolley 08 bassinet, calathus
09 container, corbeille, fish-creel,
peat-creel 10 receptacle 12 wagger-
pagger

**basketball**

*NBA basketball teams:*

08 Utah Jazz
09 Miami Heat
11 Phoenix Suns
12 Atlanta Hawks, Chicago Bulls,
Orlando Magic
13 Boston Celtics, Denver Nuggets,
Indiana Pacers, New Jersey Nets,
New York Knicks
14 Detroit Pistons, Houston Rockets,
Milwaukee Bucks, Toronto
Raptors
15 Dallas Mavericks, Sacramento
Kings, San Antonio Spurs
16 Charlotte Bobcats, Los Angeles
Lakers, Memphis Grizzlies
17 New Orleans Hornets,
Philadelphia 76ers, Washington
Wizards
18 Cleveland Cavaliers, Los Angeles
Clippers
19 Golden State Warriors
20 Portland Trail Blazers
21 Minnesota Timberwolves

*Basketball players and associated figures include:*

**04 Bird** (Larry)
**05 Belov** (Sergei), **Cousy** (Bob), **Lemon** (Meadowlark), **Mikan** (George), **O'Neal** (Shaquille)
**06 Bryant** (Kobe), **Erving** (Julius), **Jordan** (Michael), **Malone** (Karl), **Miller** (Cheryl), **Pippen** (Scottie), **Rodman** (Dennis)
**07 Barkley** (Charles), **Bradley** (Bill), **Iverson** (Allen), **Jackson** (Phil), **Johnson** (Earvin 'Magic'), **Russell** (Bill)
**08 Auerbach** (Arnold 'Red'), **Olajuwon** (Hakeem), **Petrovic** (Drazen), **Stockton** (John)
**09 Robertson** (Oscar)
**11 Abdul-Jabbar** (Kareem), **Chamberlain** (Wilt)

*Basketball-related terms include:*

**03** key, NBA
**04** dunk, hoop, trap
**05** block, drive, guard, lay-up, pivot, steal, tap-in
**06** assist, basket, box out, centre, post up, rim out, screen, tip-off
**07** dribble, forward, foul out, kick out, low post, rebound, sky hook, time-out
**08** alley oop, bank shot, charging, fadeaway, foul lane, foul line, hang time, high post, hook shot, inbounds, jump ball, jump hook, jump shot, slam dunk, turnover
**09** backboard, chest pass, fast break, field goal, free throw, perimeter, shot clock, violation
**10** bounce pass, double pump, foul circle, point guard, transition, travelling
**11** goal-tending, pick and roll, zone defence
**12** baseball pass, power forward, small forward
**13** shooting guard

**bass**
**01** B **03** low **04** base, bast, deep, full, rich **05** fibre, grave **06** burden, phloem **07** bourdon, burthen, matting, sea dace, sea wolf **08** continuo, diapason, low-toned, resonant, sea perch, sonorous **09** deep-toned, full-toned, loup de mer, succentor **10** low-pitched **11** deep-pitched

**bast**
**04** bass **05** fibre, liber **06** phloem, raffia **07** leptome, matting

**bastard**
◊ *anagram indicator* **03** git **05** slink **06** basket, by-blow, mamzer **07** buzzard **08** sideslip, spurious **09** come-o'-will, love child **10** lucky-piece, misfortune **12** come-by-chance, illegitimate, natural child **13** filius nullius

**bastardize**
**06** debase, defile, demean **07** cheapen, corrupt, degrade, devalue, distort, pervert, vitiate **10** adulterate, degenerate, depreciate **11** contaminate

**bastion**
**04** prop, rock **06** pillar **07** bulwark, citadel, defence, lunette, moineau, redoubt, support **08** defender, fortress, mainstay **10** protection, stronghold

**bat**
**04** blow, club, lath, rate **05** fungo, lingo, speed, spree, stick **06** paddle, racket, willow **07** batsman, battery, flutter **09** battalion, rearmouse, reremouse, trap stick **10** battledoor, battledore, Scotch hand **12** flitter-mouse

*Bats include:*

**03** fox, red
**05** fruit, guano, hoary
**06** kalong, yellow
**07** leisler, mastiff, noctule, spectre, vampire
**08** big brown, big-eared, Leisler's, noctilio, serotine
**09** barbastel, flying fox, horseshoe, leaf-nosed, roussette
**10** free-tailed, frog-eating, mouse-eared
**11** barbastelle, little brown, pipistrelle
**12** false vampire
**14** Kitti's hog-nosed
**15** Mexican freetail

**batch**
**03** lot, set **04** mass, pack **05** bunch, crowd, group **06** amount, parcel **07** cluster **08** quantity **09** aggregate **10** assemblage, assortment, collection, contingent **11** consignment **12** accumulation **14** conglomeration

**bath**
**03** dip, spa, tub **04** soak, stew, wash **05** banya, bathe, clean, sauna, scrub, stove, therm **06** douche, hammam, hot tub, hummum, mikvah, mikveh, shower, therms **07** bathtub, hot pool, hummaum, Jacuzzi®, spa pool, thermae **08** aerotone, balneary **09** bain-marie, freshen up, have a bath, steam bath, steam room, take a bath, whirlpool **10** Aquae Sulis **11** slipper bath, Turkish bath

**bathe**
**03** bay, dip, tub, wet **04** bath, baye, dook, lave, soak, stew, surf, swim, wash **05** beath, clean, cover, embay, flood, rinse, steep **06** paddle **07** cleanse, embathe, imbathe, immerse, Jacuzzi®, moisten, suffuse **08** permeate, saturate, take a dip **09** encompass, skinny-dip

**bathos**
**07** let-down **08** comedown **10** anticlimax **14** disappointment

**baton**
**03** rod **05** staff, stick **06** cudgel, warder **07** scepter, sceptre **09** truncheon

**bats**
◊ *anagram indicator* **03** mad **04** nuts **05** crazy **07** Mormops **15** Megacheiroptera, Microchiroptera

**batsman**
• **first batsman** **06** opener
• **weaker batsmen** **04** tail

**battalion**
**02** bn **03** bat, mob **04** army, herd, host, mass, unit **05** crowd, force, horde **06** battle, legion, throng, troops **07** brigade, company, platoon, section **08** division, garrison, regiment, squadron **09** multitude **10** contingent, detachment

**batten**
**03** bar, fix **04** bolt **05** board, strip **06** fasten, secure **07** board up, tighten **08** nail down **09** barricade, clamp down

**batter**
◊ *anagram indicator* **03** hit, lam, ram **04** bash, beat, club, dash, hurt, lash, maul, pelt **05** abuse, erode, pound, smash, whack **06** beat up, bruise, buffet, damage, hatter, injure, mangle, pummel, strike, thrash, wallop **07** assault, bombard, destroy, lay into, rough up, wear out **08** demolish, ill-treat, maltreat, wear down **09** cannonade, disfigure **10** knock about **11** overweather
• **batter down** **04** ruin **05** smash, wreck **07** destroy **08** demolish **09** break down

**battered**
◊ *anagram indicator* **03** hit **06** abused, beaten, shabby **07** bruised, crushed, damaged, injured, run-down **09** crumbling **10** ill-treated, maltreated, ramshackle, tumbledown **11** dilapidated **13** weather-beaten

**battery**
**03** bat, row, set **04** bank, cell, guns, pram **05** array, cycle, force, group, nicad, praam **06** attack, cannon, series **07** assault, beating, mugging **08** cannonry, ordnance, sequence, striking, violence **09** artillery, thrashing **10** button cell, succession **12** emplacements

**batting**
◊ *anagram indicator* **02** in

**battle**
**02** by **03** bye, row, war **04** feud, fray, race, wage **05** argue, brawl, clash, drive, field, fight, scrap, set-to, stoor, stour **06** action, affair, attack, buffet, combat, debate, engage, stoush, stowre, strife, strive **07** agitate, clamour, contend, contest, crusade, dispute, fertile, hosting, quarrel, warfare **08** campaign, conflict, darraign, disagree, naumachy, sea-fight, skirmish, struggle **09** battalion, encounter, naumachia **10** Armageddon, engagement, free-for-all, nourishing, tournament **11** altercation, competition, controversy, final battle, hostilities, turkey-shoot **12** disagreement **13** armed conflict, confrontation
*See also* **siege; war**

*Battles include:*

**04** Jena, Loos, Mons, Neva, Nile, Zama
**05** Alamo, Anzio, Boyne, Bulge, Crécy, Issus, Liège, Maipó, Maipú, Marne, Mylae, Pavia, Rhine, Sedan, Sluys, Somme, Spurs, Valmy, Varna, Ypres
**06** Actium, Amiens, Arnhem, Cannae, Crimea, Harlaw, Kosovo, Lützen, Midway, Mohács, Mycale, Naseby, Pinkie, Quebec, Shiloh, Tobruk, Towton, Verdun, Wagram
**07** Antwerp, Britain, Bull Run, Cambrai, Cassino, Colenso, Corunna, Cowpens, Dresden, Dunkirk, Flodden, Iwo Jima, Jutland, Leipzig, Lepanto, Leuctra, Marengo, Okinawa, Plassey, Salamis, Salerno, Thapsus
**08** Atlantic, Ayacucho, Blenheim, Carabobo, Culloden, Fontenoy, Formigny, Granicus, Hastings, Mafeking, Marathon, Monmouth, Omdurman, Philippi, Poitiers, Pyramids, Saratoga, Spion Kop, St Albans, Waterloo, Yorktown
**09** Agincourt, Balaclava, Bay of Pigs, Chaeronea, El Alamein, Gallipoli, Pharsalus, Ramillies, Sedgemoor, Seven Days, Solferino, Trafalgar, Vicksburg
**10** Aboukir Bay, Adrianople, Austerlitz, Brandywine, Bunker Hill, Charleston, Cold Harbor, Copenhagen, Gettysburg, Malplaquet, Oudenaarde, River Plate, Stalingrad, Tannenberg, Tel-El-Kebir, Wilderness
**11** Bannockburn, Guadalcanal, Hohenlinden, Marston Moor, Navarino Bay, Pearl Harbor, Prestonpans, Wounded Knee
**12** Mons Graupius, Monte Cassino, Tet offensive
**13** Bosworth Field, Cape St Vincent, Killiecrankie, Little Bighorn, Magersfontein, Passchendaele
**14** Fredericksburg

**battle-axe**
**03** axe, hag **04** bill, fury, wife **05** shrew, witch **06** dragon, poleax, sparth, Tartar, virago **07** gisarme, poleaxe, sparthe **08** harridan, martinet **09** termagant **12** Jeddart staff **14** disciplinarian

**battle-cry**
**05** motto **06** banzai, slogan, war cry **07** war song **09** catchword, watchword **11** catchphrase, rallying cry **12** rallying call

**battlefield**
**05** arena, field, front, place **07** war zone **09** front line **10** Armageddon, combat zone **12** battleground **13** field of battle

**battlement**
**07** barmkin **08** bartisan, bartizan

**batty**
◊ *anagram indicator* **03** mad, odd

**04** bats, daft, nuts **05** barmy, buggy, crazy, dippy, dotty, loony, loopy, nutty, silly **06** insane, stupid **07** bonkers, foolish, idiotic **08** crackers, demented, peculiar **09** eccentric **10** off your nut, out to lunch **11** off your head **12** round the bend **13** off your rocker, round the twist

**bauble**
**03** toy **06** gewgaw, tinsel, trifle **07** bibelot, flamfew, trinket **08** gimcrack, kickshaw, ornament **09** bagatelle, plaything **10** knick-knack

**baulk**
*see* **balk, baulk**

**bawd**
**04** pimp **05** madam **08** procurer **09** panderess, procuress **13** brothel-keeper

**bawdy**
**04** blue, lewd, rude **05** adult, dirty, gross **06** coarse, erotic, ribald, risqué, smutty, vulgar, X-rated **07** lustful, obscene, raunchy **08** improper, indecent, prurient **09** lecherous, salacious **10** indecorous, indelicate, lascivious, libidinous, licentious, sculduddry, suggestive **11** sculduddery, skulduddery **12** end of the pier, pornographic **14** near the knuckle

**bawl**
**03** cry, sob **04** call, gape, howl, roar, wail, weep, yell, yowl **05** shout **06** bellow, cry out, gollar, goller, holler, scream, snivel, squall **07** blubber, call out, screech **10** vociferate
• **bawl out 05** scold **06** rebuke, yell at **07** rouse on, tell off **09** dress down, reprimand

**bay**
**03** arm, cry, vae, voe **04** bark, bawl, bell, cove, gulf, howl, loch, nook, roar, yelp, yowl **05** bathe, bight, booth, creek, firth, fleet, inlet, niche, reach, sound, stall **06** alcove, bellow, carrel, holler, lagoon, laurel, recess **07** clamour, classis, cubicle, estuary, opening **09** cubbyhole, embayment **11** compartment, indentation

*Bays include:*

**04** Acre, Clew, Daya, Kiel, Luce, Lyme, Pigs, Tees
**05** Algoa, Blind, Cloud, Enard, Evans, False, Fundy, Hawke, Shark, Table
**06** Baffin, Bantry, Bengal, Biscay, Botany, Broken, Colwyn, Dingle, Dublin, Galway, Golden, Hervey, Hudson, Lubeck, Mounts, Naples, Plenty, Tasman, Torbay, Walvis
**07** Bustard, Chaleur, Donegal, Dundalk, Fortune, Halifax, Hudson's, Montego, Moreton, Pegasus, Poverty, Prudhoe, Thunder, Trinity, Volcano
**08** Campeche, Cardigan, Delaware, Georgian, Hang-Chow, Portland, Quiberon, San Pablo, Tremadog, Weymouth

**09** Admiralty, Discovery, Encounter, Frobisher, Galveston, Geographe, Hermitage, Mackenzie, Morecambe, Notre Dame, Placentia
**10** Barnstaple, Bridgwater, Carmarthen, Chesapeake, Conception, Heligoland, Providence, Robin Hood's
**11** Port Jackson, Port Phillip, Saint Bride's, Saint Magnus
**12** Saint George's, San Francisco

• **bay with spots 04** roan

**bayonet**
**04** pike, stab **05** blade, knife, spear, spike, stick, sword **06** dagger, impale, pierce **07** poniard **08** white arm

**bazaar**
**04** fair, fête, mart, sale, souk **06** market **07** alcázar **08** exchange **10** alcaicería, jumble sale **11** bring-and-buy, marketplace **13** nearly-new sale

**BBC**
**04** Beeb **06** Auntie

**be**
**03** lie **04** form, last, live, make, stay **05** abide, arise, dwell, exist, occur, stand **06** befall, endure, happen, make up, obtain, remain, reside **07** add up to, be alive, breathe, develop, inhabit, persist, prevail, survive **08** amount to, continue **09** be located, be present, beryllium, come about, represent, take place, transpire **10** account for, be situated, come to pass, constitute

**beach**
**04** hard, land, lido, sand **05** coast, plage, sands, shore **06** ground, strand **07** machair, seaside, shingle **08** go ashore, littoral, seaboard, seashore **09** coastline, run ashore **10** be grounded, be stranded, run aground, water's edge

*Beaches include:*

**04** Gold, Juno, Long, Palm, Utah
**05** Bells, Bondi, Cable, Manly, Miami, Omaha, Sword
**06** Chesil, Malibu, Sunset, Tahiti, Venice
**07** Daytona, Glenelg, Ipanema, Pattaya, Waikiki
**08** Hotwater, St Tropez, Virginia
**09** Blackpool
**10** Copacabana, Ninety Mile
**11** Coney Island
**13** Skeleton Coast
**15** Surfers Paradise

**beachcomber**
**06** loafer **07** forager **08** loiterer, wayfarer **09** scavenger

**beacon**
**04** beam, fire, sign **05** fanal, flare, light, racon **06** pharos, rocket, signal **07** bonfire **08** bale-fire, needfire **09** watch fire **10** lighthouse, watchtower **12** danger signal, warning light

**bead**
**03** dot **04** ball, bede, blob, drip, drop,

gaud, glob, nurl, tear **05** bugle, jewel, knurl, ojime, pearl **06** bubble, pellet, prayer **07** cabling, droplet, globule **08** moulding, spheroid **10** adderstone **11** paternoster, spacer plate **13** cable-moulding

## beadle
**06** bedral, Bumble **07** bederal **09** apparitor **10** bluebottle **13** church officer

## beak
**02** JP **03** neb, nib, ram **04** bill, nose **05** becke, snout **07** rostrum **09** mandibles, proboscis, rostellum **10** magistrate **12** schoolmaster **14** schoolmistress

## beaker
**03** cup, jar, mug **05** glass **07** tankard, tumbler

## beam
**03** aim, bar, ray, RSJ, tie **04** balk, boom, emit, glow, gleam, lath, send, spar, yard **05** baulk, board, chink, flare, flash, glare, gleam, glint, joist, laugh, plank, relay, shaft, shine, smile, smirk, stock, strut, trave **06** binder, bumkin, direct, gibbet, girder, hurter, lintel, needle, pencil, purlin, rafter, solive, streak, stream, summer, timber **07** bumpkin, carling, effulge, glimmer, glitter, radiate, sleeper, sparkle, support, transom, trimmer **08** herisson, kingpost, stanchel, stancher, streamer, stringer, transmit **09** broadcast, crosshead, outrigger, principal, queen post, scantling, stanchion, weigh-bauk **10** bressummer, cantilever **12** breastsummer
• **off beam 05** wrong **08** mistaken **09** incorrect, misguided, off target **10** inaccurate **11** wrong-headed **13** wide of the mark

## bean
*Beans and pulses include:*

**03** dal, Goa, pea, soy, urd, wax **04** dahl, dhal, fava, gram, guar, jack, Lens, lima, loco, mung, navy, okra, snap, soja, soya **05** aduki, berry, black, broad, carob, dholl, green, horse, moong, pinto, sugar, tonga, tonka **06** adsuki, adzuki, butter, cherry, chilli, coffee, cowpea, French, frijol, kidney, lablab, legume, lentil, locust, runner, string, winged **07** alfalfa, Calabar, edamame, fasolia, frijole, haricot, jumping, Molucca, scarlet, snow pea, tonquin **08** black-eye, borlotti, chickpea, garbanzo, pichurim, snuffbox, split pea, sugar pea, yard-long **09** black-eyed, black gram, flageolet, green gram, jequirity, mangetout, pigeon pea, puy lentil, red kidney, red lentil **10** cannellini, golden gram, prayer bead **11** black-eye pea, garbanzo pea, green lentil

**12** asparagus pea, black-eyed pea, marrowfat pea, sassafras nut, St John's bread **13** scarlet runner

## bear
◇ *containment indicator* **02** go **03** act, hae, owe, pay, sit **04** bend, dree, hack, have, hold, hump, keep, like, move, show, take, teem, tote, turn, veer **05** abear, abide, admit, allow, beget, breed, bring, brook, carry, curve, drive, fetch, stand, thole; yield **06** accept, acquit, behave, convey, endure, foster, give up, hold up, keep up, permit, suffer, swerve, uphold **07** abrooke, cherish, comport, conduct, deliver, develop, deviate, display, diverge, endorse, exhibit, harbour, produce, stomach, support, sustain **08** engender, fructify, generate, live with, maintain, shoulder, tolerate **09** entertain, propagate, put up with, transport **10** bring forth **11** give birth to **13** grin and bear it

*Bears include:*

**03** sea, sun **04** balu, cave, Pooh, Yogi **05** baloo, black, brown, Bruin, Great, honey, koala, Nandi, polar, sloth, teddy, water, white **06** Little, native, Rupert, woolly **07** grizzly, Malayan **08** cinnamon **09** Ursa Major, Ursa Minor **10** giant panda, Paddington **13** Teddy Robinson, Winnie the Pooh

• **bear down on 08** approach, browbeat, move in on **09** advance on, close in on
• **bear in mind 04** mind, note **06** keep in **08** consider, remember **10** keep in mind **11** be mindful of **15** make a mental note, take into account
• **bear out 05** prove **06** back up, ratify, uphold, verify **07** confirm, endorse, justify, support, warrant **08** validate **09** vindicate **11** corroborate, demonstrate **12** substantiate
• **bear up 04** buoy, cope **06** endure, suffer **07** carry on, survive **09** persevere, soldier on, withstand **13** grin and bear it
• **bear with 06** endure, suffer **07** forbear **08** tolerate **09** put up with **13** be patient with

## bearable
**07** livable **08** liveable, passable, portable **09** endurable, tolerable **10** acceptable, admissible, manageable, sufferable **11** supportable, sustainable

## beard
**03** awn **04** dare, defy, face, kesh, peak, tuft, ziff **05** brave **06** beaver, goatee, oppose, pappus **07** bristle, Charley, Charlie, stubble, vandyke **08** confront, imperial, whiskers **09** challenge, moustache, sideburns **10** face-fungus,

facial hair, sideboards **11** mutton chops **12** Newgate frill **13** Newgate fringe **14** stand up against

## bearded
**05** awned, bushy, hairy **06** barbed, shaggy, tufted **07** bristly, hirsute, prickly, stubbly **08** barbated, unshaven **09** pogoniate, whiskered **11** bewhiskered

## bearer
**05** agent, owner, payee **06** holder, porter, runner **07** carrier, courier, jampani **08** chairman, conveyor, jampanee **09** consignee, messenger, possessor **11** beneficiary, transporter

## bearing
◇ *containment indicator* **01** E, N, S, W **03** aim, air, way **04** east, gait, gest, mien, port, west **05** geste, north, poise, south, track **06** aspect, course, manner **07** concern, posture, stature **08** attitude, carriage, location, portance, position, relation **09** behaviour, demeanour, direction, influence, reference, relevance, situation **10** connection, deportment, pertinence **11** comportment, orientation, whereabouts **12** significance
• **strewn with bearings 04** semé **05** semée

## beast
**03** pig **04** bête, ogre **05** brute, devil, fiend, swine **06** animal, savage, tarand **07** monster, salvage **08** behemoth, creature, opinicus **09** barbarian
*See also* **animal**
• **mark of the Beast 02** mb

## beastly
**04** foul, mean, vile **05** awful, cruel, nasty **06** brutal, horrid, rotten **07** swinish **08** horrible, terrible **09** brutishly, repulsive **10** abominably, unpleasant **11** frightfully **12** disagreeable

## beat
**02** do **03** box, gub, hit, lam, mix, pug, ram, tan, tap, way, wop **04** bang, bash, belt, best, biff, blow, cane, club, cuff, dash, ding, drub, dust, firk, flap, flay, flog, form, lash, lick, mall, maul, path, pelt, race, rout, ruin, slap, slat, stir, thud, tick, time, tund, walk, welt, wham, whip, whop, work, yerk, yirk **05** all in, birch, blend, clout, crush, excel, forge, knock, knout, metre, mould, outdo, paste, pound, pulse, punch, quake, quell, repel, rhyme, round, route, shake, shape, smack, smash, stamp, strap, swing, swipe, tempo, throb, thump, tired, whack, whisk, worst **06** accent, batter, bruise, buffet, bushed, course, cudgel, done in, exceed, fill in, granny, hammer, outrun, outwit, pooped, pummel, quiver, reject, rhythm, rounds, stress, strike, stroke, subdue, thrash, thresh, thwack, wallop, zonked **07** banging, cadence, circuit, clobber, combine, conquer, contuse, eclipse, fashion, flutter, journey, knubble, lambast, lay into, measure, outplay, pulsate,

**beaten**

surpass, tremble, trounce, vibrate, wearied, whacked, worn out **08** dead-beat, dog-tired, fatigued, jiggered, knocking, malleate, outmatch, outscore, outsmart, outstrip, overcome, pounding, rib-roast, striking, throw out, tired out, vanquish, vapulate **09** devastate, discomfit, exhausted, knackered, marmelize, overpower, overthrow, overwhelm, palpitate, pooped out, pulsation, pulverize, slaughter, subjugate, territory, transcend, vibration, zonked out **10** annihilate, clapped-out, knock about **11** palpitation, tuckered out **13** have the edge on, put to the worse, run rings round **14** get the better of **15** make mincemeat of
• **beat against the wind**   **03** ply
• **beat off**   **05** repel **07** hold off, repulse, ward off **08** beat back, fight off, overcome, push back **09** drive back, force back, keep at bay
• **beats per minute**   **03** BPM **05** pulse **09** pulse rate
• **beat up**   ◇ anagram indicator **02** do **03** mug **05** scrag **06** arouse, attack, bang up, batter, donder, do over, duff up, switch **07** assault, clobber, disturb, rough up, scare up **08** duff over, work over **10** knock about **11** knock around

**beaten**

◇ anagram indicator **04** flat, ybet **05** foamy, mixed, trite **06** forged, formed, frothy, shaped, worked **07** blended, moulded, stamped, stirred, trodden, whipped, whisked, wrought **08** foliated, hammered, trampled, well-used, well-worn **09** exhausted, fashioned, stonkered **11** well-trodden

**beatific**

**06** divine, joyful **07** angelic, blessed, exalted, sublime **08** blissful, ecstatic, glorious, heavenly, seraphic **09** rapturous

**beatification**

**10** exaltation **12** canonization **13** glorification **14** sanctification

**beatify**

**05** bless, exalt **07** glorify **08** canonize, macarize, sanctify

**beating**

**04** loss, rout, ruin, warm **05** laldy, pandy, pulse, socks **06** caning, defeat, hiding, lacing, laldie **07** battery, belting, duffing, hitting, lashing, pasting, pugging, tanning, the cane, warming **08** bruising, clubbing, conquest, downfall, drubbing, flogging, knocking, once-over, punching, slapping, smacking, the birch, the strap, thumping, whacking, whipping, whupping **09** bastinade, bastinado, battering, doing-over, duffing-up, going-over, hammering, overthrow, pulsation, pulsatory, slaughter, thrashing, trouncing, walloping **10** clobbering, loundering, outwitting, paddy-whack **11** duffing-over, outsmarting, vanquishing

**12** annihilation, chastisement, overpowering, overwhelming

**beatitude**

**07** delight, ecstasy, elation, rapture **08** macarism **09** happiness **11** blessedness **13** contentedness

**beau**

**03** fop, guy **04** buck **05** dandy, lover, spark **06** Adonis, escort, fiancé, suitor **07** admirer, coxcomb **08** muscadin, popinjay **09** boyfriend **10** sweetheart

**beautician**

**07** friseur **09** visagiste **11** cosmetician, hairdresser **12** aesthetician **15** beauty therapist

**beautiful**

**04** fair, fine **05** bonny, sheen **06** bright, comely, lovely, pretty, seemly **07** auroral, radiant, smicker **08** alluring, aurorean, becoming, charming, gorgeous, graceful, handsome, pleasing, smashing, specious, striking, stunning **09** appealing, exquisite, fair-faced, fairytale, ravishing **10** attractive, delightful, voluptuous **11** good-looking, hyacinthine, magnificent, picture-book **14** out of this world, poetry in motion **15** pulchritudinous

**beautifully**

**06** fairly, lovely **09** radiantly **10** charmingly, gracefully, pleasantly, pleasingly, strikingly, stunningly **12** attractively, delightfully

**beautify**

**04** deck, gild **05** adorn, array, grace **06** bedeck, doll up, tart up **07** enhance, garnish, improve, smarten **08** decorate, flourish, ornament, spruce up, titivate **09** embellish, glamorize, smarten up

**beauty**

**04** boon, dish, fair, form **05** asset, belle, bonus, charm, doozy, glory, grace, looks, merit, peach, pride, siren, Venus **06** allure, appeal, corker, doozer, glamor, virtue **07** benefit, charmer, cracker, delight, feature, glamour, harmony, smasher, stunner **08** blessing, dividend, Greek god, knockout, radiance, strength, symmetry **09** advantage, beau ideal, good looks, good point, good thing, plus point **10** attraction, excellence, good-looker, loveliness, prettiness, seemliness **11** femme fatale, pulchritude **12** gorgeousness, gracefulness, handsomeness **13** exquisiteness **14** attractiveness, beauté du diable

**beaver**

**04** flix **05** beard **06** castor **08** sewellel
• **beaver away**   **04** slog **06** work at **07** persist **08** plug away, work hard **09** persevere, slave away

**becalmed**

**04** idle **05** still, stuck **07** at a halt **08** marooned, stranded **10** motionless **13** at a standstill

**because**

**02** as **03** 'cos, for **05** due to, since **06** for why **07** owing to, through **08** seeing as,

thanks to **09** forasmuch **10** by reason of, by virtue of **11** as a result of, on account of
• **because of**   **02** in **07** owing to **08** what with **10** by virtue of, in virtue of **11** on account of

**beckon**

**03** nod **04** call, coax, draw, lure, pull, waft, wave **05** tempt **06** allure, entice, induce, invite, motion, signal, summon **07** attract, gesture **08** persuade **11** gesticulate

**become**

◇ anagram indicator **02** go **03** get, run, set, wax, won **04** come, fall, grow, suit, take, turn **05** befit, grace, worth **06** beseem, besort, set off **07** enhance, flatter **08** come to be, grow into, ornament, pass into **09** embellish, harmonize **10** change into, look good on, mature into **11** develop into, turn out to be **13** be changed into
• **become of**   **06** befall **08** happen to **11** be the fate of

**becoming**

**03** fit **06** comely, decent, pretty, seemly **07** elegant, fitting **08** charming, decorous, fetching, graceful, gracious, handsome, suitable, tasteful **09** befitting, besitting, congruous **10** attractive, compatible, consistent, flattering **11** appropriate

**becomingly**

**09** elegantly **10** charmingly, fetchingly, gracefully, tastefully **12** attractively

**bed**

**03** fix, hay, kip, mat, pad, pit, row, set **04** area, base, bury, doss, plot, sack **05** basis, embed, floor, found, inlay, layer, patch, plant, space, strip **06** border, bottom, garden, ground, insert, matrix, settle **07** channel, implant, stratum **09** establish **10** foundation, groundwork, substratum **11** watercourse

*Beds include:*

**01** Z
**03** box, cot, day
**04** bunk, camp, cott, crib, sofa, twin
**05** berth, couch, divan, futon, water
**06** cradle, double, litter, pallet, Put-u-up®, single
**07** folding, hammock, trestle, truckle, trundle
**08** bassinet, foldaway, king-size, mattress, platform, put-you-up
**09** couchette, king-sized, lit bateau, palliasse, queen-size, shakedown
**10** adjustable, four-poster, mid sleeper, queen-sized
**11** high sleeper
**12** chaise longue

• **bed down**   **03** kip **05** sleep **06** turn in **07** go to bed, kip down **08** doss down **09** hit the hay **10** call it a day, get some kip, hit the sack, settle down
• **dry bed**   **04** wadi, wady
• **get out of bed**   **04** rise **07** surface, turn out **08** show a leg, tumble up

**10** hit the deck **12** rise and shine
• **out of bed** **02** up **05** astir, risen

**bedaub**
**04** clag, moil **05** smear **06** parget
**07** besmear, plaster **08** slaister
**09** beslubber

**bedbug**
**01** B **05** B flat **06** chinch

**bedclothes**
**06** covers **07** bed roll, bedding **08** bed-linen

*Bedclothes include:*
**05** doona, duvet, quilt, sheet
**06** downie, pillow
**07** bedroll, blanket, bolster, valance
**08** coverlet
**09** bed canopy, bedspread, comforter, eiderdown, throwover
**10** duvet cover, pillowcase, pillow sham, pillowslip, quilt cover
**11** counterpane, fitted sheet, sleeping bag
**13** mattress cover, valanced sheet, Witney blanket
**14** patchwork quilt
**15** cellular blanket, electric blanket

**bedeck**
**04** deck, trim **05** adorn, array
**07** festoon, garnish, trick up
**08** beautify, decorate, ornament, trick out **09** embellish

**bedevil**
◇ *anagram indicator* **03** irk, vex **04** fret
**05** annoy, beset, tease, worry
**06** harass, pester, plague **07** afflict, besiege, torment, torture, trouble
**08** confound, distress, irritate
**09** frustrate

**bedfellow**
**04** ally **06** fellow, friend **07** partner
**09** associate, colleague, companion

**bedlam**
◇ *anagram indicator* **05** babel, chaos, noise **06** furore, hubbub, madman, tumult, uproar **07** anarchy, clamour, turmoil **08** madhouse **09** commotion, confusion **10** hullabaloo
**11** pandemonium

**bedraggled**
**03** wet **05** dirty, messy, muddy
**06** soaked, sodden, soiled, untidy
**07** muddied, scruffy, soaking, unkempt
**08** drenched, dripping, slovenly
**10** disordered, soaking wet
**11** dishevelled

**bedridden**
**06** bedrid, laid up **07** worn-out
**10** housebound **13** confined to bed, incapacitated **14** flat on your back

**bedrock**
**04** base, core **05** basis, heart **06** basics, bottom, reason **07** essence, footing, premise, reasons, support **09** rationale
**10** essentials, foundation, rock bottom
**12** fundamentals **13** starting-point
**15** first principles

**bedroom**
**02** br **06** dormer **07** cubicle **08** roomette
**09** bed-closet **10** bedchamber

**bee**
**01** B **04** king **05** drone, nurse, queen
**06** hummer, neuter, worker **07** royalty
**10** drumbledor, dumbledore, leaf-cutter

**beech**
**05** Fagus **06** myrtle **15** Tasmanian myrtle

**beef**
**03** gag, sey **04** moan, rump, shin
**05** bully, chuck, filet, flank, gripe, keema, mouse, round, skink, steak, T-bone **06** grouse, object, runner
**07** charqui, dispute, grumble, sirloin, surloin, topside **08** bresaola, complain, disagree, pastrami, salt-junk
**09** aitchbone, criticize, rump steak, salt horse, tournedos **10** mousepiece, silverside **11** filet mignon, sauerbraten
**12** mouse-buttock **13** Chateaubriand, Scotch collops **15** scotched collops
• **beef up** **07** build up, toughen
**08** flesh out **09** establish, reinforce, toughen up **10** invigorate, strengthen
**11** consolidate **12** substantiate **15** give new energy to

**beefeater**
**04** exon **06** ox-bird, yeoman
**07** Buphaga **08** oxpecker

**beefy**
**03** fat **05** bulky, burly, heavy, hefty, tubby **06** brawny, fleshy, robust, stocky, stolid, sturdy **07** hulking
**08** muscular, stalwart **09** corpulent

**beehive**
**03** gum **04** skep

**beer**
**04** brew, grog, half, pint **06** liquor, stingo **07** brewski **11** amber liquid

*Beers include:*
**03** ale, dry, ice, IPA, keg
**04** bock, mild, Pils, rice
**05** black, fruit, guest, heavy, honey, kvass, lager, plain, sixty, stout, wheat, white
**06** bitter, eighty, export, old ale, porter, shandy, Stella®
**07** bottled, draught, pale ale, Pilsner, real ale, seventy
**08** amber ale, brown ale, Guinness®, home brew, light ale, Pilsener, Trappist
**09** microbrew, milk stout, snakebite, wheat beer
**10** barley wine, low-alcohol, malt liquor, sweet stout, Weisse Bier
**11** black-and-tan
**12** Christmas ale, India Pale Ale
**13** sixty shilling
**14** eighty shilling
**15** cask-conditioned, seventy shilling

*See also* **glass**

**beetle**
**03** nip, run, zip **04** dash, maul, rush, tear **05** hurry, scoot **06** batler, batlet, bustle, mallet, scurry
**07** scamper
*See also* **animal; insect**

*Beetles include:*
**03** dor, may, oil
**04** bark, dorr, dung, leaf, musk, pine, rove, stag
**05** black, click, clock, shard, tiger, water
**06** carpet, chafer, dor-fly, ground, may bug, sacred, scarab, sexton, weevil
**07** burying, cadelle, carabid, carrion, goliath, hop-flea, hornbug, rose bug
**08** bum-clock, cardinal, Colorado, glow-worm, Hercules, Japanese, ladybird, longhorn, wireworm, woodworm
**09** furniture, goldsmith, longicorn, tumblebug, whirligig
**10** bombardier, cockchafer, deathwatch, rhinoceros, rose chafer, scarabaean, scarabaeid, tumbledung, turnip flea
**11** coprophagan, typographer
• **beetle-crusher** **03** cop
**09** policeman **11** infantryman

**beetling**
**07** jutting, pendent **09** poking out, prominent **10** projecting, protruding
**11** leaning over, overhanging, sticking out

**befall**
**04** fall **05** ensue, occur **06** arrive, astart, betide, chance, follow, happen, result, strike **07** fortune **08** bechance, come over, come upon, fall upon, happen to
**09** befortune, overwhelm, supervene, take place **11** materialize

**befit**
**03** set, sit **04** seem, sort, suit **05** match
**06** become, befall, behove, beseem, besort **10** complement **13** harmonize with

**befitting**
**03** apt, fit **04** like, meet **05** right
**06** decent, proper, seemly **07** correct, fitting **08** becoming, sortable, suitable
**11** appropriate **12** well-becoming
**13** well-beseeming

**before**
◇ *juxtaposition indicator* **01** a **02** an, or, to **03** bef, ere, pre, pro- **04** ante, once, onst, prae- **05** ahead **07** ahead of, already, earlier, in front, prior to
**08** formerly **09** in advance, in front of
**10** on the eve of, previously, previous to, sooner than **11** earlier than **12** in the sight of, not later than **15** in the presence of
• **as before** **02** do **05** ditto

**beforehand**
**03** pre- **04** fore-, prae- **05** afore, early
**06** before, former, sooner **07** already, earlier **08** paravant **09** aforehand, in advance, paravaunt **10** previously
**11** ahead of time **13** preliminarily

**befriend**
**03** aid **04** back, help **06** assist, defend, favour, uphold **07** benefit, comfort, protect, stand by, succour, support, sustain, welcome **09** encourage, get to know, look after **10** fall in with, stick

up for **11** keep an eye on **13** make a friend of **15** make friends with

**befuddle**
◇ *anagram indicator* **04** daze, faze **06** baffle, muddle, puzzle **07** confuse, nonplus, perplex, stupefy **08** bewilder **09** disorient

**beg**
**03** ask, bum **04** pray, prog, thig **05** cadge, crave, maund, mooch, mouch, plead **06** appeal, ask for, desire, fleech, sponge, turn to **07** beseech, beseeke, entreat, implore, intreat, maunder, request, require, schnorr, skelder, solicit **08** governor, mooch off, petition, scrounge, stand pad **09** importune, panhandle **10** supplicate **11** ask for money **13** touch for money

**beget**
**03** get **04** kind, sire **05** breed, cause, spawn **06** create, effect, father, gender, lead to **07** produce, propage **08** engender, generate, occasion, result in **09** procreate, propagate **10** bring about, give rise to

**beggar**
**03** bum **04** defy **05** randy, tramp **06** baffle, blowse, blowze, cadger, canter, craver, exceed, mumper, pauper, randie, toerag **07** bludger, jarkman, maunder, moocher, ruffler, sponger, surpass, vagrant **08** Abram-man, beadsman, bedesman, besognio, besonian, bezonian, blighter, glassman, palliard, vagabond, whipjack **09** challenge, lazzarone, mendicant, schnorrer, scrounger, sundowner, transcend **10** Abraham-man, beadswoman, down-and-out, freeloader, panhandler, supplicant, upright-man **11** gaberlunzie **12** down-and-outer, hallan-shaker

**beggarly**
**03** low **04** mean, poor **05** needy **06** abject, meagre, modest, paltry, slight, stingy **07** miserly, pitiful **08** pathetic, wretched **09** niggardly, worthless **10** despicable, inadequate **12** contemptible **13** insubstantial

**begin**
**02** go **03** gin, ope **04** open, take **05** arise, enter, found, get at, set in, set up, shoot, spark, start **06** appear, broach, come on, crop up, embark, emerge, incept, set off, set out, spring **07** actuate, do first, enter on, kick off, take off **08** activate, commence, embark on, fire away, get going, inchoate, initiate, set about, shoot off, strike up **09** enter upon, instigate, institute, introduce, originate **10** launch into **11** get cracking, give birth to, open the ball, set in motion **13** take the plunge

**beginner**
◇ *head selection indicator* **01** L **03** cub, deb **04** noob, tiro, tyro **05** pupil, rooky **06** author, newbie, novice, rookie **07** fresher, learner, new chum, recruit, starter, student, trainee **08** freshman, initiate, neophyte, newcomer

**09** fledgling, greenhorn, Johnny-raw **10** apprentice, new settler, raw recruit, tenderfoot **11** abecedarian, probationer **13** alphabetarian

**beginning**
◇ *head selection indicator* **03** ord **04** dawn, germ, rise, root, seed **05** birth, debut, get-go, intro, onset, start **06** day one, launch, origin, outset, source **07** genesis, kick-off, new leaf, opening, preface, prelude **08** exordium **09** emergence, first base, first part, inception, square one, the word go **10** conception, fresh start, inchoation, incipience, initiation **11** institution, opening part, pastures new **12** commencement, fountainhead, inauguration, introduction **13** establishment, new beginnings, starting-point
• **from beginning to end 04** over **07** through **08** exordium, from A to Z

**begone**
**04** away **05** hence **06** avaunt **10** aroint thee **11** allez-vous-en

**begrudge**
**04** envy, mind **05** covet, stint **06** grudge, resent **08** object to **11** be jealous of **13** be resentful of

**beguile**
**04** dupe, fool, gull, wile **05** amuse, blend, charm, cheat, cozen, guile, guyle, trick **06** delude, divert, occupy, seduce **07** attract, bewitch, deceive, delight, enchant, engross, mislead **08** distract, hoodwink **09** captivate, entertain

**beguiling**
**08** alluring, charming, enticing **09** appealing, diverting, seductive **10** attractive, bewitching, delightful, enchanting, intriguing **11** captivating, interesting **12** entertaining

**behalf**
**04** name, part, sake **07** account, benefit **08** interest
• **on behalf of 02** pp **03** for **06** per pro **09** acting for **11** in support of, in the name of **12** for account of, for the good of, for the sake of, representing **13** to the profit of **15** for the benefit of

**behave**
**02** be, do **03** act, use **04** bear, go on, quit, walk, work **05** abear, carry, quite, quyte, react **06** acquit, be good, demean, deport, quight **07** comport, conduct, operate, perform, respond **08** function **10** act your age **11** act politely, act properly **12** not mess about, not muck about **13** be well-behaved **14** acquit yourself **15** comport yourself, conduct yourself, mind your manners, mind your p's and q's

**behaviour**
**04** form, ways **06** action, doings, habits, manner **07** conduct, manners **08** dealings, reaction, response **09** attitudes, demeanour, operation **10** deportment **11** comportment, functioning, performance, way of acting

**behead**
◇ *head deletion indicator* **04** head, kill **07** execute **09** decollate **10** decapitate, guillotine, put to death

**behest**
• **at the behest of 11** at the hest of **12** at the order of **13** on the wishes of **14** at the bidding of, at the command of, at the request of

**behind**
◇ *juxtaposition indicator* ◇ *tail selection indicator* **03** aft, ass, bum, for **04** back, baft, butt, late, next, post, rear, rump, slow **05** abaft, after, ahind, ahint, retro-, stern **06** arrear, astern, back of, bottom, heinie, in debt **07** backing, causing, close on, delayed, overdue **08** backside, buttocks, derrière, in back of **09** at the back, at the rear, endorsing, following, in arrears, in the rear, later than, posterior **10** behindhand, explaining, initiating, supporting **11** at the back of, at the rear of, instigating, on the side of, running late **12** giving rise to, subsequently **13** accounting for, at the bottom of **14** responsible for **15** slower than usual

**behindhand**
**03** lag **04** down, late, slow **05** tardy **06** behind, remiss **07** delayed **08** backward, dilatory **09** in arrears, out of date **14** behind schedule

**behold**
**02** la, lo **03** see **04** ecce, ecco, espy, look, mark, note, scan, view **05** voici, voilà, watch **06** descry, gaze at, look at, regard, survey **07** discern, observe, witness **08** consider, perceive **11** contemplate

**beholden**
**05** bound, owing **07** obliged **08** addebted, grateful, indebted, thankful **09** obligated **12** appreciative **15** under obligation

**behove**
**05** befit **06** import, profit **07** benefit, stand on **08** be proper, be seemly **11** be essential, be necessary **13** be suitable for **14** be advantageous

**beige**
**03** tan **04** buff, ecru, fawn **05** camel, khaki, sandy, suede, taupe **06** coffee, greige, oyster **07** neutral, oatmeal **08** mushroom

**being**
**03** ens, man **04** esse, life, soul, will **05** beast, heart, human, thing, woman **06** animal, entity, living, mortal, nature, person, psyche, spirit **07** essence, reality **08** creature, emotions **09** actuality, animation, existence, haecceity, inner self, substance **10** human being, individual, inner being **11** personality **13** heart of hearts

**belabour**
◇ *anagram indicator* **03** hit **04** beat, belt, flay, flog, whip **05** sauce **06** attack, pummel, strike, thrash **07** dwell on **09** lay on load, reiterate **11** flog to

**Belarus**
death, harp on about **14** go on and on about

**Belarus**
**02** BY, SU **03** BLR

**belated**
**04** late **05** lated, tardy **07** delayed, overdue **09** benighted, out of date **10** behindhand, unpunctual **14** behind schedule

**belatedly**
**07** tardily **12** unpunctually **14** behind schedule

**belch**
**03** yex **04** boak, bock, boke, burp, emit, gush, rift, spew, vent, yesk **05** eject, eruct, issue **06** hiccup **07** give off, give out **08** disgorge, eructate **09** discharge **10** eructation **11** bring up wind

**beleaguered**
**05** beset, vexed **07** plagued, worried **08** badgered, besieged, bothered, harassed, pestered, troubled **09** blockaded, tormented **10** persecuted, surrounded, under siege

**Belgium**
**01** B **03** BEL **04** Belg

**belie**
**04** deny **06** negate, refute **07** conceal, confute, cover up, deceive, falsify, gainsay, mislead **08** disguise, disprove **10** contradict **12** misrepresent, run counter to

**belief**
**03** ism **04** idea, view **05** creed, dogma, ethic, faith, ideal, tenet, trust **06** credit, notion, theory, threap, threep **07** feeling, opinion **08** credence, doctrine, ideology, reliance, sureness, teaching **09** assurance, certainty, intuition, judgement, knowledge, principle, tradition, viewpoint **10** confidence, conviction, impression, persuasion **11** expectation, point of view, presumption

*Beliefs include:*

**06** holism, malism, racism
**07** animism, atheism, elitism
**08** demonism, feminism, hedonism, humanism, nihilism, Satanism
**09** pantheism, physicism, tritheism
**10** liberalism, Manicheism, monotheism, polytheism
**11** agnosticism, parallelism, supremacism, tetratheism
**12** Manicheanism
**13** ethnocentrism, individualism, structuralism
**14** fundamentalism, traditionalism, tripersonalism
**15** supernaturalism

*See also* **religion**

**believable**
**06** likely **07** credent **08** credible, possible, probable, reliable **09** plausible **10** acceptable, imaginable **11** conceivable, trustworthy **13** authoritative

**believe**
**03** buy, wis **04** deem, feel, hold, trow, wear, ween, wish, wist **05** faith, guess, judge, opine, think, trust **06** accept, assume, credit, figure, gather, reckon **07** fall for, imagine, suppose, swallow **08** consider, maintain, perceive **09** postulate, speculate **10** Adam and Eve, conjecture, understand **11** be certain of, take on board **13** be convinced of, be persuaded by
• **believe in 04** rate **05** trust **06** favour, follow, hold by, rely on **07** swear by **08** depend on **09** approve of, encourage, recommend **11** value highly **12** be in favour of **13** be convinced of, be persuaded by **15** set great store by
• **hard to believe 04** tall

**believer**
**06** zealot **07** convert, devotee **08** adherent, disciple, follower, upholder **09** proselyte, supporter

*Believers include:*

**03** Jew
**04** Babi, Jain, Sikh, Sofi, Sufi
**05** Babee, Hindu, Jaina
**06** holist, Muslim
**07** Alawite, animist, Bahaist, Genevan, Lollard, Scotist
**08** Arminian, Buddhist, Calixtin, Catholic, demonist, Erastian, Glassite, humanist, Lutheran, Nazarean, Nazarene, Pelagian, Salesian, Satanist, Wesleyan
**09** animalist, Calixtine, Christian, Confucian, Eutychian, Gregorian, Methodist, Nestorian, Origenist, pantheist, Sabellian, Simeonite, Wyclifite
**10** Bergsonian, Berkeleian, Cameronian, Capernaite, Holy Roller, Marcionite, polytheist, Wycliffite
**11** Sandemanian, Valentinian
**12** Apollinarian, Southcottian
**13** Hutchinsonian, Roman Catholic, Swedenborgian
**14** fundamentalist, the Oxford group
**15** supernaturalist

**belittle**
**04** slag, slam **05** abase, decry, knock, scorn, slate **06** demean, deride, do down, dump on, lessen **07** dismiss, rubbish, run down, slag off **08** diminish, minimize, play down, ridicule **09** deprecate, disparage, downgrade, sell short, underrate **10** trivialize, understate, undervalue **11** detract from, pick holes in **12** pull to pieces, tear to shreds **13** underestimate **15** do a hatchet job on

**Belize**
**02** BH, BZ **03** BLZ

**bell**
**03** tom **04** gong, horn, peal, ring **05** bleep, chime, knell, larum, siren **06** alarum, curfew, hooter, signal, tocsin, vesper **07** angelus, bleeper, tinkler, warning **08** pavilion **13** tintinnabulum
• **sound of bell, sound of bells**

**04** clam, dong, peal, ring, ting, tink, toll **05** chime, knell **06** firing, tinkle **08** ding-dong **09** ding-a-ling

**bellbird**
**08** araponga, arapunga **09** campanero

**belle**
**05** peach, siren, Venus **06** beauty, corker **07** charmer, cracker, smasher, stunner **08** knockout **10** good-looker **11** femme fatale

**bellicose**
**07** violent, warlike, warring **08** bullying, militant **09** combative **10** aggressive, pugnacious **11** belligerent, contentious, quarrelsome **12** antagonistic **13** argumentative

**belligerence**
**03** war **08** bullying, violence **09** militancy, pugnacity **10** aggression, antagonism **11** provocation **12** warmongering **13** combativeness, sabre-rattling **14** unfriendliness **15** contentiousness, quarrelsomeness

**belligerent**
**06** chippy **07** hostile, scrappy, violent, warlike, warring **08** bullying, militant **09** combative, truculent **10** aggressive, pugnacious **11** contentious, provocative, quarrelsome **12** antagonistic, disputatious, warmongering **13** argumentative, sabre-rattling

**bellow**
**03** cry **04** bawl, howl, roar, rout, yell **05** shout, troat **06** buller, holler, scream, shriek **07** clamour, thunder **14** raise your voice

**belly**
**03** gut, pot, tum, wem **04** bulk, bunt, guts, kite, kyte, puku, wame, wemb **05** gastr-, tummy, weamb **06** gastro-, paunch, venter **07** abdomen, gastero-, insides, stomach **08** pot-belly **09** beer belly **10** intestines **11** bread basket, corporation

**belong**
**02** go **03** fit **04** be in, long **05** fit in **06** go with **07** be found, be yours, pertain **08** attach to, be part of, be sorted, relate to **09** appertain, be owned by, tie up with **10** be included, be situated, link up with **11** be a member of **12** be classified **13** be categorized, have as its home **14** be affiliated to, be an adherent of, have as its place **15** be connected with, be the property of

**belonging**
**04** link **05** links **07** kinship, loyalty, rapport **08** affinity **09** closeness **10** acceptance, attachment, fellowship **11** affiliation, association **12** relationship **13** compatibility, fellow-feeling
• **belonging to** ◇ *hidden indicator*

**belongings**
**03** kit **04** gear **05** goods, stuff, traps **06** tackle, things **07** clobber, effects **08** chattels, property **11** possessions

**13** accoutrements, appurtenances, paraphernalia

**beloved**
**02** jo **03** joe, joy, pet **04** baby, bird, dear, duck, leve, lief, love, wife **05** angel, fella, honey, lieve, loved, lover, sweet **06** adored, fiancé, liking, prized, spouse, tender **07** admired, darling, dearest, fiancée, husband, partner, revered, sweetie **08** endeared, lady-love, loved one, precious, true-love **09** belamoure, betrothed, boyfriend, cherished, favourite, heart-dear, inamorata, inamorato, much loved, treasured **10** bellamoure, girlfriend, sweetheart, worshipped **12** alder-liefest **13** special friend

**below**
◊ *juxtaposition down indicator* **03** inf, sub- **04** down **05** infra, later, lower, neath, under **07** beneath **09** further on, hereunder, lower down, lower than, subject to **10** inferior to, lesser than, underneath **13** at a later place, subordinate to **15** lower in rank than

**belt**
◊ *anagram indicator* **03** box, fly, hit, tan, zip **04** area, band, bang, bash, biff, blow, cane, cord, dash, flay, flog, lash, loop, pelt, rush, sash, slap, tear, whip, zona, zone **05** apron, birch, chain, clout, girth, knock, layer, mitre, punch, slosh, smack, speed, strap, strip, swipe, thump, tract, wanty, whack **06** bruise, career, cestus, charge, corset, extent, girdle, region, sector, strike, swathe, thwack, wallop, waspie **07** baldric, bashing, clobber, harness, stretch, zonulet **08** baldrick, ceinture, cincture, cingulum, district **09** bandoleer, bandolier, hip-girdle, Sam Browne, waistband **10** cummerbund
*See also* **karate**
• **below the belt** **05** dirty **06** unfair, unjust **09** dishonest, underhand, unethical **10** out of order **11** uncalled-for, unjustified **12** unscrupulous
• **belt up** **02** sh, st **03** shh **04** hist **05** shush, whish, whist **06** shut up, whisht, wrap up **07** be quiet, wheesht **08** button up, cut it out, pipe down **10** keep shtoom, stay shtoom **12** put a sock in it, shut your face **13** button your lip, shut your mouth

**belvedere**
**06** gazebo **07** mirador

**bemoan**
**03** rue **04** moan, pity, wail **05** mourn **06** bewail, lament, regret **07** deplore, sigh, weep for **09** grieve for **10** sorrow over

**bemuse**
◊ *anagram indicator* **04** daze, faze **05** floor, throw **06** baffle, muddle, puzzle **07** confuse, perplex, stupefy **08** befuddle, bewilder **09** bamboozle

**bemused**
◊ *anagram indicator* **05** dazed, fazed, mused **07** baffled, floored, muddled, puzzled **08** confused **09** astounded, befuddled, perplexed, pixilated, stupefied **10** astonished, bamboozled, bewildered, pixillated **11** overwhelmed **12** disconcerted

**bemusement**
**04** daze **09** confusion **10** bafflement, perplexity **12** bewilderment, stupefaction **14** disorientation

**Ben**
**03** Hur

**bench**
**03** pew **04** banc, bank, bink, form, seat **05** board, court, judge, ledge, stall, table, thoft **06** banker, exedra, settle, thwart **07** counter, exhedra, tribune **08** rout-seat, tribunal **09** courtroom, judiciary, shopboard, workbench, worktable **10** judicature, knife-board, magistrate **13** judgement-seat

**benchmark**
**04** norm **05** basis, gauge, level, model, scale **07** example, pattern **08** standard **09** criterion, guideline, reference, yardstick **10** guidelines, touchstone **14** reference-point

**bend**
◊ *anagram indicator* **01** S, U, Z **02** es **03** arc, bow, ess, out, ply, sag **04** arch, curb, flex, genu, hook, hump, kink, knot, lean, loop, ramp, sway, trap, turn, veer, warp, wind **05** angle, bight, courb, crimp, crook, curve, elbow, embow, hinge, hunch, kneel, mould, ox-bow, plash, round, shape, squat, stoop, trend, twist, wring **06** affect, bought, buckle, compel, corner, crouch, cut-off, deflex, direct, dog-leg, recede, reflex, spring, swerve, wimple, zigzag **07** compass, contort, crankle, decline, deflect, deviate, dip-trap, diverge, flexion, flexure, incline, incurve, inflect, meander, recline, recurve, reflect, turning, whimple, wriggle **08** persuade, swan neck **09** curvature, genuflect, incurvate, inflexure, influence, prostrate, retroflex **10** circumflex, deflection, divergence, make curved, manipulate **11** circumflect, hairpin bend, inclination, incurvation
• **bend over** **04** lean **08** double up
• **bend over backwards** **08** go all out **10** do your best **11** try very hard **13** exert yourself **14** put yourself out **15** trouble yourself

**bendy**
◊ *anagram indicator* **08** flexible

**beneath**
◊ *juxtaposition down indicator* **03** sub **05** below, lower, neath, under **06** aneath **09** lower down, lower than **10** unbecoming, underneath, unworthy of **11** unbefitting

**Benedictines**
**03** OSB

**benediction**
**05** grace **06** favour, prayer **07** benison **08** blessing **10** invocation **11** blessedness **12** consecration, thanksgiving

**benefactor**
**05** angel, donor, giver **06** backer, friend, helper, patron **07** sponsor **08** promoter, provider **09** supporter **10** subscriber, subsidizer, well-wisher **11** contributor **14** fairy godmother, philanthropist

**beneficent**
**04** kind **06** benign **07** benefic, helpful, liberal **08** generous **09** bountiful, unselfish **10** altruistic, benevolent, charitable, munificent **12** Grandisonian **13** compassionate

**beneficial**
**04** good **06** useful **07** helpful **08** edifying, salutary, valuable **09** benignant, improving, promising, rewarding, wholesome **10** favourable, profitable, propitious, worthwhile **11** serviceable **12** advantageous
• **beneficial to** **03** for

**beneficiary**
**04** heir **05** payee **07** heiress, legatee **08** receiver **09** inheritor, recipient, successor **10** the assured

**benefit**
**03** ACC, aid, DPB, pay, use **04** boon, broo, dole, gain, good, help, perk, sake **05** asset, avail, bonus, buroo, compo, merit, serve **06** assist, behalf, behoof, better, credit, favour, income, milage, pay-off, profit, reward **07** advance, bespeak, enhance, further, improve, mileage, payment, pension, promote, service, sick pay, spin-off, support, vantage, welfare **08** blessing, dividend, do good to, interest, kindness **09** advantage, allowance, good point **10** assistance, perquisite **11** benefaction **13** be of service to, fringe benefit, income support **14** social security **15** be of advantage to

**benevolence**
**04** care, pity **05** grace, mercy **08** altruism, goodness, goodwill, kindness **09** tolerance **10** compassion, generosity, humaneness, liberality **11** magnanimity, munificence **12** friendliness, philanthropy **14** charitableness **15** considerateness, humanitarianism, kind-heartedness

**benevolent**
**04** good, guid, kind **06** benign, caring, humane, kindly **07** liberal **08** friendly, generous, gracious, merciful, tolerant **10** altruistic, charitable, munificent **11** considerate, kind-hearted, magnanimous, soft-hearted **12** humanitarian, well-disposed **13** compassionate, philanthropic **15** philanthropical

**benevolently**
**06** kindly **08** benignly, humanely **09** liberally **10** charitably, generously, graciously, mercifully, tolerantly **13** considerately, kind-heartedly, magnanimously, soft-heartedly **14** altruistically **15** compassionately

**benighted**
**07** belated, nighted **08** backward,

**benign**

ignorant **09** unknowing **10** illiterate, uncultured, uneducated, unlettered, unschooled **11** unfortunate **13** inexperienced, unenlightened

**benign**

**04** good, kind, mild, warm **05** sweet, trine **06** genial, gentle, kindly **07** affable, amiable, benefic, cordial, curable, healthy, liberal **08** benedict, friendly, generous, gracious, harmless, innocent, obliging **09** agreeable, avuncular, opportune, temperate, treatable, wholesome **10** auspicious, beneficial, benevolent, charitable, favourable, propitious, refreshing, salubrious **11** restorative, sympathetic, warm-hearted **12** advantageous, non-malignant, providential

**benignly**

**06** kindly **07** affably, amiably **08** genially **10** charitably, generously, graciously, obligingly **12** benevolently **15** sympathetically

**Benin**

**02** DY, RB **03** BEN

**bent**

◇ anagram indicator **04** curb, gift, turn **05** bowed, corbe, courb, dodgy, flair, forte, knack, wrong **06** angled, arched, curved, fiorin, folded, redtop, reflex, talent, warped **07** ability, corrupt, crooked, curvate, doubled, embowed, faculty, falcate, hunched, illegal, leaning, stooped, strepto-, twafald, twisted **08** aptitude, capacity, criminal, cup of tea, curvated, facility, falcated, fondness, inclined, inflexed, penchant, reflexed, retorted, tendency **09** contorted, dishonest, infracted, refracted, retroflex, swindling **10** fraudulent, geniculate, preference, proclivity, propensity **11** disposition, geniculated, inclination **12** predilection **13** untrustworthy **14** predisposition
• **bent on 05** set on **07** fixed on **08** intent on **10** disposed to, inclined to, resolved to **11** insistent on **12** determined to

**bequeath**

**04** give, will **05** endow, grant, leave **06** assign, bestow, commit, demise, devise, impart, pass on **07** consign, entrust **08** hand down, make over, transfer, transmit

**bequest**

**04** gift **05** trust **06** estate, legacy **07** devisal **08** bestowal, donation, heritage, pittance **09** endowment **10** bequeathal, settlement **11** inheritance **13** mortification

**berate**

**05** blast, chide, scold, slate **06** rail at, rebuke, revile **07** censure, chew out, reprove, start on, tell off, upbraid **08** chastise, give hell, reproach **09** castigate, criticize, dress down, fulminate, reprimand, start in on **10** vituperate **13** give a rocket to, tear a strip off

**bereaved**

**03** orb **04** lost **06** robbed **07** widowed **08** deprived, divested, grieving, orphaned **12** dispossessed

**bereavement**

**04** loss **05** death, grief **06** orbity, sorrow **07** passing, sadness **08** deprival **11** deprivation, passing-away **13** dispossession

**bereft**

• **bereft of 05** minus **07** lacking, wanting **08** devoid of, robbed of **10** cut off from, deprived of, parted from, stripped of **11** destitute of

**berkelium**

**02** Bk

**Berlin**

**06** Irving

**Bermuda**

**03** BMU

**berry**

**05** bacca **06** acinus

---

*Berries include:*

**04** goji
**05** lichi
**06** lichee, litchi, lychee
**07** bramble, leechee
**08** bilberry, dewberry, goosegog, mulberry, tayberry
**09** blaeberry, blueberry, cranberry, raspberry, whimberry
**10** blackberry, cloudberry, elderberry, gooseberry, loganberry, redcurrant, strawberry
**11** boysenberry, huckleberry
**12** blackcurrant, serviceberry, whitecurrant, whortleberry

---

**berserk**

◇ anagram indicator **03** mad **04** nuts, wild **05** angry, barmy, batty, berko, crazy, manic, rabid **06** crazed, insane, raging, raving **07** frantic, furious, violent **08** baresark, demented, deranged, frenzied, maniacal **10** hysterical **11** off your head **13** off the deep end, out of your mind **14** beside yourself, uncontrollable

**berth**

**03** bed **04** bunk, dock, land, moor, port, quay **05** tie up, wharf **06** anchor, billet **07** hammock, harbour, mooring, sleeper **09** anchorage, couchette **10** cast anchor, drop anchor
• **give a wide berth to 04** shun **05** avoid, dodge, evade **06** eschew **09** give a miss **12** steer clear of

**beryl**

**07** emerald **08** emeraude, heliodor **09** morganite **10** aquamarine

**beryllium**

**02** Be

**beseech**

**03** ask, beg, sue **04** pray **05** crave, plead **06** adjure, call on, desire, exhort **07** entreat, implore, intreat, solicit **08** appeal to, petition **09** deprecate, importune, obsecrate **10** supplicate

**beset**

◇ containment indicator **03** lay, rag **04** bego **05** belay, hem in, press, worry **06** assail, attack, bestad, bested, harass, hassle, obsess, pester, plague, preace, prease **07** bedevil, besiege, bestead, preasse, torment **08** bestadde, entangle, scabrous, surround **11** beleaguered

**besetting**

**08** constant, dominant, habitual **09** harassing, obsessive, prevalent, recurring **10** compulsive, inveterate, persistent **11** troublesome **12** irresistible **14** uncontrollable

**beside**

◇ juxtaposition indicator **02** by, on, to **04** near **06** next to **07** close to, upsides **08** abutting, adjacent **09** abreast of, alongside, bordering **10** next door to **11** by the side of, overlooking **12** neighbouring
• **beside yourself 03** mad **05** crazy **06** crazed, insane **07** berserk, frantic **08** demented, deranged, frenetic, frenzied, overcome, unhinged **09** delirious **10** distraught, unbalanced **13** out of your mind

**besides**

**02** by **03** too, yet **04** also, else **05** forby **06** as well, either, forbye, foreby, withal **07** au reste, further **08** as well as, moreover **09** apart from, aside from, excluding, other than, otherwise, what's more **10** in addition **11** furthermore **12** additionally, in addition to, over and above

**besiege**

◇ containment indicator **03** nag **05** belay, beset, besit, hem in, hound, worry **06** assail, badger, bother, harass, invest, obsess, pester, plague, shut in **07** assiege, confine, oppress, torment, trouble **08** blockade, encircle, surround **09** beleaguer, encompass, importune, overwhelm **10** lay siege to

**besmirch**

**04** slur, soil **05** dirty, smear, stain, sully **06** damage, defame, defile **07** besmear, blacken, slander, tarnish **08** besmutch **09** dishonour

**besom**

**03** cow, kow **05** broom

**besotted**

**03** mad **04** wild **05** crazy, potty **06** doting, sotted, stupid **07** bedazed, drunken, smitten **08** obsessed **09** bedazzled, bewitched, stupefied **10** bowled over, hypnotized, infatuated, spellbound **11** intoxicated

**bespatter**

**04** dash, drop, soil **05** bemud, dirty, smear, spray, stain **06** bedash, befoam, defame, shower, splash **07** asperse, scatter, spatter, splodge **08** splatter, sprinkle

**bespeak**

**04** show **05** imply **06** attest, denote, engage, evince, reveal **07** betoken, display, exhibit, signify, suggest

**08** evidence, indicate, proclaim, speak for **11** demonstrate

**bespoke**
◇ *anagram indicator* **09** dedicated **10** tailor-made

**best**
**02** A1 **03** ace, cap, top **04** beat, lick, most, pick, plum, rout, star, tops **05** cream, élite, first, ideal, jewel, outdo, prime, worst **06** choice, defeat, finest, flower, hammer, outwit, subdue, thrash, utmost **07** clobber, conquer, greatly, hardest, highest, largest, leading, optimal, optimum, outplay, perfect, premium, supreme, the tops, trounce **08** foremost, greatest, outsmart, overcome, peerless, ultimate, vanquish **09** damnedest, excellent, extremely, favourite, first chop, first-rate, highlight, matchless, nonpareil, number one, overpower, overwhelm, slaughter, supremely, top-drawer, worthiest **10** annihilate, first-class, pre-eminent, unbeatable, unequalled, unrivalled **11** excellently, matchlessly, outstanding, superlative, unsurpassed **12** incomparable, incomparably, second to none **13** exceptionally, have the edge on, one in a million, outstandingly, superlatively, unsurpassedly **14** crème de la crème, get the better of, greatest effort, record-breaking

**bestial**
**04** rude, vile **05** cruel, feral, gross **06** animal, brutal, carnal, savage, sordid **07** beastly, brutish, inhuman, sensual **08** barbaric, degraded, depraved **09** barbarous, unrefined

**bestiality**
**07** cruelty **08** savagery **09** barbarism **10** inhumanity, sordidness **15** animal behaviour

**bestir**
**05** exert **06** arouse, awaken, incite **07** actuate, animate **08** activate, energize, motivate **09** galvanize, stimulate

**bestow**
**02** do **04** give **05** allot, award, endow, grant, spend, wreak **06** accord, commit, confer, donate, estate, impart, lavish **07** dispose, entrust, present **08** bequeath, transmit **09** apportion **11** communicate

**bestride**
**05** cross **06** defend **07** command, protect **08** dominate, straddle **10** bestraddle, overshadow, sit astride **12** stand astride

**bestseller**
**03** hit **07** success, triumph **08** smash hit **11** blockbuster, brand leader

**bestselling**
**03** top **06** famous **07** leading, popular **08** unbeaten

**bet**
**02** go **03** bid, lay, pot, put **04** ante, back, hold, punt, risk, view **05** place, pound, stake, wager **06** be sure,

chance, choice, expect, gamble, hazard, notion, option, pledge, theory **07** feeling, flutter, lottery, opinion, venture **09** be certain, intuition, judgement, speculate, viewpoint **10** conviction, impression, prediction **11** alternative, be convinced, point of view, speculation **12** have a flutter, play for money **14** course of action, not be surprised
*See also* **gambling**

*Bets and betting systems include:*

**03** TAB
**04** tote
**06** double, parlay, roll-up, tierce, treble, triple, Yankee
**07** à cheval, each way
**08** ante-post, forecast, perfecta, quinella, trifecta
**09** on the nose, quadrella
**10** martingale, pari-mutuel, superfecta, sweepstake
**11** accumulator, daily double, totalizator
**13** double or quits, starting-price

• **accept bet 03** see

**betel**
**03** pan **04** paan, pawn, siri **05** sirih

**bête noire**
**04** bane **05** curse **07** bugbear, pet hate **08** anathema, aversion **11** abomination, pet aversion **14** thorn in the side **15** thorn in the flesh

**betide**
**05** ensue, occur **06** befall, betime, chance, happen **07** develop **08** overtake **09** supervene, take place

**betoken**
**04** bode, mark, mean, sign **05** augur, token **06** betide, denote, signal **07** bespeak, declare, portend, presage, promise, signify, suggest **08** evidence, forebode, indicate, manifest **09** represent, symbolize **13** prognosticate

**betray**
**03** dob **04** dupe, sell, shop, show, tell **05** abuse, cross, dob in, grass, peach, rat on **06** bewray, delude, desert, expose, reveal, rumble, tell on, unmask **07** abandon, confess, deceive, divulge, forsake, let down, let slip, mislead, sell out, split on, stool on **08** disclose, give away, go back on, inform on, manifest, renege on, squeal on **09** play false, walk out on **11** double-cross, turn traitor **12** be disloyal to, bring to light **13** stab in the back **14** be unfaithful to, break faith with

**betrayal**
**05** abuse **06** duping **07** perfidy, sell-out, treason **08** giveaway, trickery **09** deception, duplicity, falseness, treachery **10** disloyalty **11** double-cross **12** backstabbing **13** breaking faith, double-dealing, stab in the back **14** double-crossing, traitorousness, unfaithfulness

**betrayer**
**05** grass, Judas **07** stoolie, traitor **08** apostate, deceiver, informer, renegade, traditor, treacher **09** treachour **10** supergrass **11** backstabber, conspirator, stool pigeon **13** double-crosser, whistle-blower

**betrothal**
**03** vow **04** vows **05** troth **07** promise **08** affiance, contract, espousal, handfast **09** assurance **10** engagement **11** fiançailles, handfasting, hand-promise, subarration, trothplight **12** subarrhation

**betrothed**
**05** troth **07** assured, engaged, pledged **08** espoused, promised **09** affianced, combinate **10** contracted **11** trothplight **13** trothplighted

**better**
**03** cap, top **04** beat, best, mend, well **05** cured, finer, outdo, raise **06** bigger, enrich, exceed, fitter, healed, larger, longer, punter, reform **07** correct, enhance, forward, further, gambler, greater, improve, promote, rectify, surpass **08** improved, outstrip, overtake, restored, stronger, superior, worthier **09** a cut above, healthier, improve on, improving, on the mend, recovered **10** ameliorate, make better, preferable, recovering, speculator, surpassing **11** more fitting, progressing **12** more valuable **14** fully recovered, more acceptable **15** go one better than, of higher quality

**betterment**
**10** enrichment **11** advancement, edification, enhancement, furtherance, improvement, melioration **12** amelioration

**betting**
*see* **bet**

**between**
◇ *insertion indicator* **03** bet, mid **04** amid **05** among, inter- **06** amidst **07** amongst, halfway **11** in the middle **13** in the middle of

**bevel**
**04** bias, cant, tilt **05** angle, basil, bezel, mitre, slant, slope, splay **07** chamfer, oblique **08** diagonal

**beverage**
**04** brew **05** drink **06** liquid, liquor **07** draught, potable **08** ambrosia, potation **11** refreshment
*See also* **drink**

**bevy**
**04** band, gang, pack **05** bunch, crowd, flock, group, troop **06** gaggle, throng, troupe **07** company **08** assembly **09** gathering **10** collection

**bewail**
**03** rue **04** keen, moan **05** mourn **06** bemoan, lament, regret, repent **07** cry over, deplore **08** sigh over **10** grieve over, sorrow over **14** beat your breast

## beware

**04** cave, mind, shun, ware **05** avoid, watch **06** be wary, caveat **07** look out, mind out **08** take heed, watch out **09** be careful **10** be cautious **12** guard against, steer clear of **13** be on your guard

## bewilder

◇ *containment indicator* **04** daze, faze, lose, maze **05** amaze, floor, mix up, stump **06** baffle, bemuse, fickle, muddle, puzzle, wander, wilder **07** buffalo, bumbaze, confuse, flummox, mystify, nonplus, perplex, stupefy **08** confound **09** bamboozle, disorient, obfuscate **10** disconcert, take to town **12** tie up in knots

## bewildered

◇ *anagram indicator* **04** lost, will, wull **05** at sea, dizzy, fazed, muzzy **06** fogged, tavert **07** baffled, bemazed, bemused, floored, mixed up, muddled, pixy-led, puzzled, stunned, taivert **08** all at sea, confused, jiggered, pathless, wandered **09** flummoxed, mystified, perplexed, pixilated, surprised, trackless, uncertain **10** bamboozled, distracted, nonplussed, pixillated, speechless, taken aback **11** disoriented

## bewildering

**05** dizzy **07** amazing, cryptic **08** baffling, puzzling **09** confusing, enigmatic **10** astounding, mysterious, mystifying, perplexing, surprising **12** unfathomable

## bewilderment

**03** awe, fog **04** daze, maze **05** amaze **06** muddle, puzzle **07** mizmaze **08** surprise **09** amazement, confusion, égarement, puzzledom **10** amazedness, perplexity, puzzlement **11** uncertainty **12** stupefaction **13** disconcertion, mystification **14** disorientation

## bewitch

**03** hex, obi **04** obia, take, wish **05** charm, obeah, witch **06** allure, hoodoo, obsess, seduce, strike, voodoo, voudou **07** beguile, delight, enchant, enthral, glamour, possess **08** elf-shoot, entrance, forspeak, intrigue, overlook, sirenize, transfix **09** captivate, enrapture, ensorcell, fascinate, forespeak, hypnotize, mesmerize, spellbind, tantalize

## beyond

**04** over, past **05** above, after, ayont, trans- **08** away from **09** apart from, later than, upwards of **10** remote from **11** further than, greater than **12** out of range of, out of reach of **14** on the far side of

## Bhutan

**03** BTN

## bias

**04** bent, load, sway, warp **05** angle, cross, poise, slant, twist **06** colour, earwig, weight **07** bigotry, distort, leaning, oblique **08** diagonal, jaundice, penchant, tendency

**09** influence, parti pris, prejudice, preoccupy, slantwise **10** distortion, partiality, partialize, predispose, prepossess, proclivity, propensity, unfairness **11** favouritism, inclination, intolerance, load the dice, prejudicate **12** one-sidedness, predilection, stereotyping **13** prepossession

## biased

◇ *anagram indicator* **04** skew **06** angled, loaded, skewed, swayed, unfair, warped **07** bigoted, partial, slanted, twisted **08** one-sided, partisan, partizan, weighted **09** blinkered, distorted, jaundiced **10** influenced, interested, prejudiced, subjective, tendential **11** predisposed, prejudicate, tendencious, tendentious **12** prepossessed **14** discriminatory

## bib

**04** pout **05** Bible, blain **06** brassy, feeder

## Bible

**02** NT, OT **03** ABC, Bib, law **05** canon **06** fardel, manual, omasum, primer **07** Gospels, letters, lexicon **08** epistles, good book, handbook, holy writ, prophets, textbook, writings **09** Apocrypha, authority, companion, directory, guidebook, Holy Bible, manyplies **10** dictionary, Pentateuch, psalterium, revelation, Scriptures **12** encyclopedia, New Testament, Old Testament **13** reference book **14** holy Scriptures

*See also* **plague; scripture**

*Versions of the Bible include:*

**02** AV, EV, RV
**03** NEB, RSV
**05** Douai, Douay, Itala, Reims
**06** Geneva, Gideon, Italic, Wyclif
**07** Matthew, Peshito, Tyndale, Vulgate
**08** Breeches, Peshitta, Peshitto, Wycliffe
**09** Coverdale, King James
**10** New English, Septuagint
**14** English Version, Revised Version

*Books of the Bible:*

**02** Am, Ch, Dt, Ec, Ex, Ez, Is, Jg, Jl, Jn, Kg, Lk, Mk, Mt, Ob, Pr, Ps, Ru, Th
**03** Bar, Chr, Col, Cor, Dan, Eph, Esd, Est, Gal, Gen, Hab, Hag, Heb, Hos, Isa, Jas, Jer, Job (Book of), Jon, Jos, Jud, Lam, Lev, Mal, Mic, Nah, Neh, Num, Pet, Rev, Rom, Sam, Sir, Sus, Tim, Tit, Tob
**04** Acts, Amos (Book of), Deut, Eccl, Epis, Esth, Exod, Ezek, Ezra (Book of), Hebr, Joel (Book of), John (Gospel according to), John (Letters of), Josh, Jude (Letter of), Luke (Gospel according to), Macc, Mark (Gospel according to), Numb, Obad, Phil, Prov, Ruth (Book of), S of S, Wisd, Zech, Zeph
**05** Hosea (Book of), James (Letter of), Jonah (Book of), Kings (Books of), Levit, Micah (Book of), Nahum (Book of), Peter (Letters of), Thess,

Titus (Letter of Paul to), Tobit (Book of)
**06** Baruch (Book of), Coloss, Daniel (Book of), Eccles, Ecclus, Esdras (Books of), Esther (Book of), Exodus (Book of), Haggai (Book of), Isaiah (Book of), Joshua (Book of), Judges (Book of), Judith (Book of), Philem, Psalms (Book of), Romans (Letter of Paul to the), Samuel (Books of), Sirach (Book of)
**07** Ezekiel (Book of), Genesis (Book of), Gospels, Hebrews (Letter of Paul to the), Malachi (Book of), Matthew (Gospel according to), Numbers (Book of), Obadiah (Book of), Pr of Man, Susanna (History of), Timothy (Letters of Paul to)
**08** Bel and Dr, Habakkuk (Book of), Jeremiah (Book of), Jeremiah (Letter of), Nehemiah (Book of), Philemon (Letter of Paul to), Proverbs (Book of)
**09** Apocrypha, Ephesians (Letter of Paul to the), Galatians (Letter of Paul to the), Hexateuch, Leviticus (Book of), Maccabees, Zechariah (Book of), Zephaniah (Book of)
**10** Apocalypse, Chronicles (Books of), Colossians (Letter of Paul to the), Heptateuch, Pentateuch, Revelation
**11** Corinthians (Letters of Paul to the), Deuteronomy (Book of), Philippians (Letter of Paul to the)
**12** Ecclesiastes (Book of), Lamentations, New Testament, Old Testament
**13** Song of Solomon, Thessalonians (Letters of Paul to the)
**14** Ecclesiasticus (Book of), Pauline Letters
**15** Bel and the Dragon, Pastoral Letters, Prayer of Azariah, Wisdom of Solomon
**16** Prayer of Manasseh, Revelation of John
**17** Acts of the Apostles
**22** Song of the Three Young Men

*Biblical characters include:*

**03** Dan, Eve, Gad, Ham, Job, Lot
**04** Abel, Adam, Ahab, Amos, Anna, Baal, Cain, Esau, Ezra, Joel, John, Leah, Levi, Luke, Mark, Mary, Noah, Paul, Ruth, Saul, Seth, Shem
**05** Aaron, Abner, Asher, Caleb, David, Enoch, Hagar, Herod (the Great), Hosea, Isaac, Jacob, James, Jesus, Jonah, Judah, Judas, Magog, Micah, Moses, Nahum, Naomi, Peter, Rhoda, Sarah, Sheba (Queen of), Simon, Titus, Tobit, Uriah
**06** Andrew, Baruch, Christ, Daniel, Elijah, Elisha, Esther, Gideon, Isaiah, Joseph, Joshua, Josiah, Judith, Martha, Miriam, Nathan, Nimrod, Philip, Pilate, Rachel, Reuben, Salome, Samson, Samuel, Simeon, Thomas, Uzziah
**07** Abigail, Abraham, Absalom, Azariah, Delilah, Ephraim, Ezekiel,

Gabriel, Goliath, Ishmael, Japheth, Jezebel, Lazarus, Malachi, Matthew, Michael, Obadiah, Rebecca, Rebekah, Solomon, Stephen, Susanna, Tabitha, Timothy, Zebedee, Zebulun
08 Barabbas, Barnabas, Benjamin, Caiaphas, Habbakuk, Hezekiah, Issachar, Jeremiah, Jeroboam, Jonathan, Manasseh, Matthias, Mordecai, Naphtali, Nehemiah, Thaddeus, Zedekiah
09 Bathsheba, Beelzebub, Nathanael, Nathaniel, Nicodemus, Priscilla, Zechariah, Zephaniah
10 Adam and Eve, Bartimaeus, Belshazzar, Methuselah, Simon Magus, Simon Peter
11 Bartholomew, Gog and Magog, Jehoshaphat, Jesus Christ
12 Herod Agrippa, Herod Antipas, Queen of Sheba
13 Judas Iscariot, Mary Magdalene, Pontius Pilate, Simon of Cyrene
14 John the Baptist, Nebuchadnezzar, Simon the Zealot

*Biblical place names include:*

03 Nod
04 Eden, Gaza, Rome, Zion
05 Babel, Egypt, Judah, Sinai, Sodom
06 Ararat, Canaan, Cyrene, Israel, Jordan, Judaea, Mt Zion, Red Sea
07 Babylon, Calvary, Galilee, Jericho, Mt Sinai, Nineveh
08 Bethesda, Dalmatia, Damascus, Golgotha, Gomorrah, Mt Ararat, Nazareth
09 Bethlehem, Jerusalem, Palestine
10 Alexandria, Gethsemane
11 River Jordan
12 Garden of Eden, Sea of Galilee

*See also* **apocryphal**

## bibliography
06 record 08 book list 09 catalogue 10 bibliology 11 bibliotheca, list of books

## bicker
03 row 04 spar, spat 05 argue, clash, fight, scrap 06 patter, quiver 07 dispute, fall out, glitter, quarrel, wrangle 08 disagree, squabble 09 altercate

## bickering
06 at odds 07 arguing 08 clashing 09 scrapping 10 squabbling 11 disagreeing, quarrelling 13 at loggerheads 15 like cats and dogs

## bicycle
04 bike 05 cycle, wheel 10 pedal cycle

*Bicycles include:*

03 BMX
04 push, quad, solo
05 hobby, moped, racer
06 safety, tandem
07 chopper, Raleigh®, touring
08 draisene, draisine, exercise, kangaroo, mountain, ordinary, push-bike, tricycle, unicycle
09 recumbent
10 all-terrain, boneshaker, dandy-

horse, fairy-cycle, fixed-wheel, stationary, two-wheeler, velocipede
12 mountain bike
13 penny farthing
14 all-terrain bike

*Bicycle parts include:*

03 hub
04 bell, fork, gear, lamp, pump, tire, tyre
05 brake, chain, crank, frame, pedal, spoke, wheel
06 dynamo, fender, hanger, pulley, saddle, spokes
07 bar ends, carrier, headset, hub gear, pannier, rim tape, toe clip, tool bag, top tube
08 aero bars, cassette, chainset, crankset, crossbar, down tube, head tube, mudguard, rim brake, rod brake, seat post, seat tube, sprocket, wheel nut, wheel rim
09 brake shoe, chain link, chain ring, disc brake, drum brake, gear cable, gear lever, gearwheel, inner tube, kickstand, prop stand, reflector, seat stays, tyre valve, wheel lock
10 brake block, brake cable, brake lever, chain guard, chain guide, chain stays, chain wheel, crank lever, derailleur, drive train, handlebars, seat pillar, stabilizer, Woods® valve
11 gear shifter, lamp bracket, Presta® valve, roller chain, speedometer
12 brake caliper, coaster brake, diamond frame, spoke nipples, steering head, steering tube, stirrup guide, wheel bearing, wheel spindle
13 bottom bracket, clipless pedal, freewheel unit, handlebar stem, Schrader® valve, shock absorber, sprocket wheel
14 drop handlebars, side-pull brakes

## bid
02 go 03 ask, say, sum, try, vie 04 bode, call, pray, tell, wave, wish 05 greet, offer, order, price, put up 06 amount, charge, demand, desire, direct, effort, enjoin, invite, submit, summon, tender 07 advance, attempt, call for, command, proffer, propose, request, require, solicit, venture 08 instruct, proposal 09 endeavour 10 put forward, submission
• **no bid** 04 pass

## biddable
04 meek 08 amenable, obedient 09 compliant, easy-going, malleable, tractable 10 submitting 11 subservient

## bidding
04 call 05 order 06 behest, charge, demand, desire 07 command, request, summons 09 direction 10 injunction, invitation 11 instruction, requirement
• **bidding system** 04 Acol 06 canapé 09 blackwood

## big
02 OS 03 fat 04 huge, loud, main, mega, tall, vast 05 adult, beefy, build, bulky, burly, elder, giant, great, hefty, jumbo, large, major, obese, older, stout 06 brawny, bumper, famous, mature, pile up, valued 07 eminent, grown-up, hulking, immense, leading, mammoth, massive, pompous, radical, salient, serious, sizable, weighty 08 boastful, colossal, critical, enormous, generous, gigantic, gracious, muscular, powerful, sizeable, spacious, whopping 09 cavernous, corpulent, extensive, ginormous, humungous, important, momentous, principal, prominent, unselfish, well-built, well-known 10 benevolent, extra large, munificent, noteworthy, voluminous 11 fundamental, influential, kind-hearted, magnanimous, outstanding, pretentious, significant, substantial 12 considerable 13 distinguished

## bigheaded
04 vain 05 cocky 07 haughty, stuck-up 08 arrogant 09 conceited 11 swell-headed 12 vainglorious 13 self-important, self-satisfied, swollen-headed 14 full of yourself

## bigot
03 MCP 06 racist, sexist, zealot 07 fanatic 08 partisan 09 dogmatist, homophobe, sectarian 10 chauvinist 11 religionist

## bigoted
06 biased, closed, narrow, swayed, warped 07 partial, twisted 08 dogmatic, one-sided 09 blinkered, fanatical, hidebound, illiberal, jaundiced, obstinate 10 influenced, intolerant, prejudiced 11 opinionated 12 narrow-minded

## bigotry
04 bias 06 ageism, racism, sexism 08 jingoism 09 dogmatism, injustice, prejudice, racialism 10 chauvinism, fanaticism, homophobia, partiality, unfairness 11 intolerance, religionism 12 sectarianism 14 discrimination

## bigwig
03 nob, VIP 04 tuan 05 mogul, swell 06 big gun, honcho, worthy 07 big shot, notable 08 big noise, somebody 09 big cheese, celebrity, dignitary, personage 10 panjandrum 11 heavyweight

## bijou
03 wee 04 tiny 05 jewel, small 06 little, minute, petite, pocket 07 compact, trinket 10 diminutive

## bile
04 gall 05 anger 06 choler, spleen 07 rancour 09 bad temper, ill-humour, testiness 10 bitterness, melancholy 11 peevishness, short temper 12 irascibility, irritability

## bilge
03 rot 05 balls, trash, tripe 06 drivel, faddle, hot air, piffle 07 rubbish, twaddle 08 blethers, claptrap,

cobblers, nonsense, tommyrot
**09** gibberish, poppycock
**10** codswallop **12** clamjamphrie

**bilious**
**04** edgy, sick **05** cross, lurid, testy
**06** crabby, garish, grumpy, queasy,
sickly **07** grouchy, peevish **08** choleric
**09** crotchety, irritable, nauseated
**10** disgusting, nauseating, out of sorts
**11** bad-tempered, ill-humoured, ill-
tempered **13** short-tempered

**bilk**
**02** do **03** con **05** cheat, elude, sting,
trick **06** diddle, fleece **07** deceive,
defraud, do out of, swindle
**09** bamboozle **14** pull a fast one on

**bill**
**02** a/c, ad, ax **03** acc, act, axe, fin, IOU,
neb, nib, tab **04** acct, beak, chit, note,
post **05** check, debit, flyer, score, tally
**06** advert, charge, notice, poster
**07** account, charges, handout, invoice,
leaflet, measure, placard, promote,
rostrum, statute, William **08** announce,
banknote, bulletin, circular, handbill,
mandible, playbill, proposal
**09** advertise, list costs, programme,
reckoning, statement **10** broadsheet,
give notice **11** legislation
**12** announcement **13** advertisement,
send an account, send an invoice
**14** send a statement
• **bill of sale**  **02** bs

**billet**
**03** job **04** post **05** berth, lodge, put up,
rooms **06** casern, coupon, office
**07** caserne, housing, lodging, quarter,
station **08** barracks, position, quarters
**09** situation **10** employment,
occupation **11** accommodate
**13** accommodation **14** living quarters

**billow**
**04** mass, rise, roil, roll, rush, wave
**05** bulge, cloud, flood, heave, surge,
swell **06** expand **07** balloon, breaker,
fill out, puff out **08** undulate

**billowy**
**06** waving **07** heaving, rolling, surging,
tossing **08** rippling, swelling, swirling
**09** billowing **10** undulating

**Billy**
**06** Bunter

**bin**
**03** box **04** bing, bunk **05** chest
**06** basket, bucket, chilly, holder
**07** wheelie **09** container **10** garbage
can, receptacle, rubbish tin **11** waste
basket

**bind**
**03** oop, oup, tie, wap **04** bond, bore,
gage, gird, hold, hole, join, lash, pain,
rope, spot, tape, whip, wrap, yoke
**05** chain, clamp, cover, dress, force,
impel, leash, stick, strap, thirl, tie up,
truss, unify, unite **06** attach, compel,
embale, fasten, fetter, hamper, objure,
oblige, secure, swathe, tether
**07** astrict, bandage, combine, confine,
dilemma, embrace, impasse, require,
shackle **08** astringe, enfetter, nuisance,
quandary, restrain, restrict **09** colligate,

constrain, tight spot **10** close ranks,
difficulty, irritation **11** necessitate,
predicament **12** knit together, pull
together **13** embarrassment,
inconvenience, pain in the neck, stand
together

**binding**
**04** tape, yapp **05** cover, tight, valid
**06** border, edging, strict **07** bandage
**08** covering, ligation, rigorous,
trimming, wrapping **09** mandatory,
necessary, permanent, requisite,
stringent **10** compulsory, conclusive,
obligatory **11** irrevocable, unalterable,
unbreakable **12** indissoluble

**bindweed**
**08** bearbine, bellbind, withwind,
woodbind, woodbine **09** withywind
**11** convolvulus

**binge**
**02** do **03** jag **04** bout, orgy, sesh, toot,
tout **05** beano, blind, fling, spree
**06** bender, guzzle **07** blow-out, session

**biochemistry**

*Biochemists include:*

**04** **Abel** (John Jacob), **Cori** (Carl), **Duve**
(Christian de)
**05** **Boyer** (Herbert), **Brown** (Rachel
Fuller), **Chain** (Sir Ernst B), **Doisy**
(Edward A), **Krebs** (Sir Edwin G),
**Krebs** (Sir Hans), **Monod** (Jacques),
**Moore** (Stanford)
**06** **Asimov** (Isaac), **Beadle** (George),
**Domagk** (Gerhard), **Martin** (Archer),
**Mullis** (Kary B), **Oparin** (Alexandr),
**Perutz** (Max), **Porter** (Rodney R),
**Sanger** (Frederick)
**07** **Edelman** (Gerald M), **Fischer**
(Edmond H), **Hopkins** (Sir
Frederick), **Khorana** (Har Gobind),
**Stanley** (Wendell M), **Waksman**
(Selman), **Warburg** (Otto)
**08** **Anfinsen** (Christian B), **Chargaff**
(Erwin), **Kornberg** (Arthur),
**Meyerhof** (Otto), **Northrop** (John
H), **Weinberg** (Robert)
**09** **Bergström** (Sune), **Butenandt**
(Adolf), **Michaelis** (Leonor)
**11** **Hoppe-Seyler** (Felix)
**12** **Szent-Györgyi** (Albert von)

*See also* **biology**

**biography**
**02** CV **03** bio **04** biog, life **05** diary
**06** biopic, letter, memoir, record,
résumé **07** account, diaries, history,
journal, letters, memoirs, profile
**08** journals **09** life story **11** hagiography
**12** recollection **13** autobiography,
prosopography, recollections
**15** curriculum vitae

*Biographers include:*

**05** **Spark** (Dame Muriel), **Weems**
(Mason Locke)
**06** **Aubrey** (John), **Morley** (John,
Viscount), **Motion** (Andrew), **Napier**
(Mark), **Wilson** (Andrew Norman)
**07** **Ackroyd** (Peter), **Bedford** (Sybille),
**Bolitho** (Hector), **Boswell** (James),
**Debrett** (John), **Ellmann** (Richard),
**Holroyd** (Michael), **Lubbock**

(Percy), **Pearson** (Hesketh), **Sitwell**
(Sacheverell)
**08** **Lockhart** (John Gibson), **Plutarch**,
**Strachey** (Lytton)
**09** **Aldington** (Richard), **Kingsmill**
(Hugh), **Suetonius**

**biology**

*Biological terms include:*

**02** GM
**03** DNA, RNA
**04** cell, gene
**05** class, genus, virus
**06** coccus, enzyme, family, fossil,
tissue
**07** euploid, meiosis, microbe,
mitosis, nucleus, osmosis,
protein, species
**08** bacillus, bacteria, cultivar,
euploidy, genetics, membrane,
molecule, mutation, organism,
parasite, ribosome, stem cell
**09** amino acid, cell cycle, corpuscle,
cytoplasm, diffusion, ecosystem,
ectoplasm, evolution, food chain,
Mendelism, pollution, reticulum,
symbiosis
**10** alpha helix, chromosome,
extinction, Lamarckism,
metabolism, parasitism,
protoplasm
**11** Haeckel's law, homeostasis,
respiration
**12** conservation, mitochondria,
reproduction
**13** flora and fauna, micro-organism,
mitochondrion
**14** Golgi apparatus, photosynthesis
**15** nuclear membrane, ribonucleic
acid

*Biologists and naturalists include:*

**03** **His** (Wilhelm)
**04** **Axel** (Richard), **Baer** (Karl Ernst
von), **Berg** (Paul), **Hess** (Walter),
**Hunt** (Tim), **Katz** (Sir Bernard),
**Koch** (Ludwig), **Lyon** (Mary)
**05** **Arber** (Werner), **Bacon** (Francis,
Viscount), **Bates** (Henry Walter),
**Beebe** (William), **Bruce** (Sir David),
**Crick** (Francis), **Golgi** (Camillo),
**Lewis** (Edward B), **Luria** (Salvador),
**Lwoff** (André), **Nurse** (Sir Paul M),
**Sabin** (Albert), **Scott** (Sir Peter),
**Sharp** (Phillip), **Smith** (Hamilton),
**White** (Gilbert)
**06** **Altman** (Sidney), **Anning** (Mary),
**Bishop** (Michael), **Blobel** (Günter),
**Boveri** (Theodor), **Buffon** (George-
Louis, Comte de), **Cairns** (Hugh),
**Cannon** (Walter), **Carson** (Rachel),
**Claude** (Albert), **Darwin** (Charles),
**Friend** (Charlotte), **Huxley** (Sir
Julian), **Huxley** (T H), **Isaacs** (Alick),
**Kandel** (Eric), **Lartet** (Edouard),
**Morgan** (Thomas Hunt), **Palade**
(George), **Sloane** (Sir Hans),
**Varmus** (Harold), **Watson** (James),
**Wilson** (Edward)
**07** **Adamson** (Joy), **Agassiz** (Louis),
**Andrews** (Roy), **Beneden**
(Edouard), **Brenner** (Sydney),
**Dawkins** (Richard), **Driesch** (Hans),
**Durrell** (Gerald), **Epstein** (Sir

Anthony), **Flavell** (Richard), **Gilbert** (Walter), **Haeckel** (Ernst), **Haldane** (J B S), **Hershey** (A D), **Jackson** (Barbara, Lady), **Kendrew** (Sir John), **Lamarck** (Jean), **Lubbock** (Sir John), **Nathans** (Daniel), **Pasteur** (Louis), **Roberts** (Richard), **Steptoe** (Patrick), **Wallace** (Alfred)

**08 Cousteau** (Jacques), **Delbrück** (Max), **Flemming** (Walther), **Franklin** (Rosalind), **Hartwell** (Lee), **Humboldt** (Alexander, Baron von), **Jeffreys** (Sir Alec), **Linnaeus** (Carl), **Li Shizen**, **Margulis** (Lynn), **Meselson** (Matthew), **Milstein** (Cesar), **Purkinje** (Jan), **Sielmann** (Heinz), **Starling** (Ernest), **Tonegawa** (Susumu), **Weismann** (August)

**09 Lederberg** (Joshua), **Schaudinn** (Fritz), **Wieschaus** (Eric)

**10 Ingen-Housz** (Jan)

**11 Deisenhofer** (Johan), **Leeuwenhoek** (Antoni van), **Metchnikoff** (Elie), **Ramón y Cajal** (Santiago), **Spallanzani** (Lazaro)

**12 Attenborough** (Sir David), **Maynard Smith** (John)

**13 Du Bois-Reymond** (Emil Heinrich)

**14 Levi-Montalcini** (Rita)

**15 Nusslein-Volhard** (Christiane)

*See also* **bacteriology; biochemistry; palaeontologist; physiology**

**birch**
**03** rod **04** birk, flog, twig **05** swish
**06** Betula

**bird**
**03** jug **04** avis, babe, gaol, girl, jail, nick, quod, shop, stir, time **05** choky, clink **06** chokey, lumber, prison **07** college, slammer **10** girlfriend
*See also* **animal; chicken; duck; game; hen; poultry**

*Birds include:*

**02** ka
**03** ani, auk, bat, cob, daw, doo, emu, hae, hen, jay, kea, kia, mag, maw, mew, moa, owl, pie, tit, tui
**04** barb, chat, cirl, cobb, cock, coot, crow, dodo, dove, duck, emeu, erne, eyas, fowl, gled, guan, gull, hawk, hern, huia, ibis, jynx, kagu, kaka, kite, kiwi, knot, kora, kuku, lark, loom, loon, lory, mina, myna, nene, nyas, pavo, pern, pica, piet, pyat, pyet, pyot, rail, rhea, rook, ruff, runt, ruru, rype, shag, skua, smee, sora, swan, taha, teal, tern, tody, weka, wren, xema, yite
**05** agami, ariel, booby, capon, chick, crane, diver, eagle, egret, eider, finch, fleet, flier, galah, glede, goose, grebe, heron, hobby, hoiho, macaw, mynah, ousel, piper, pipit, pitta, potoo, quail, raven, robin, scops, snipe, solan, squab, stilt, stork, swift, tewit, twite, vireo, wader
**06** avocet, bantam, barbet, brolga, budgie, bulbul, canary, chough, condor, cuckoo, curlew, cushat, darter, dipper, drongo, dunlin, falcon, fulmar, gannet, godwit, grouse, hoopoe, houdan, jabiru, jacana, kakapo, linnet, magpie, martin, merlin, mesite, mopoke, motmot, oriole, osprey, parrot, peahen, peewit, petrel, pigeon, plover, puffin, pullet, raptor, redcap, roller, sea-mew, shrike, siskin, takahe, thrush, tom-tit, toucan, trogon, turaco, turkey, yaffle, zoozoo

**07** antbird, apteryx, babbler, barn owl, bittern, bluecap, blue jay, blue tit, bullbat, bunting, bustard, buzzard, chicken, coal-tit, cotinga, courser, cowbird, creeper, dottrel, dunnock, fantail, finfoot, goshawk, grackle, halcyon, harrier, hoatzin, jacamar, jackdaw, kestrel, lapwing, leghorn, limpkin, mallard, manakin, moorhen, mudlark, oilbird, ostrich, peacock, pelican, penguin, pintail, poultry, quetzal, redpoll, redwing, rooster, rosella, ruddock, seagull, seriema, skimmer, skylark, spadger, sparrow, sunbird, swallow, tanager, tiercel, tinamou, titlark, touraco, vulture, wagtail, warbler, waxbill, wrybill, wryneck

**08** aasvogel, accentor, adjutant, aigrette, antpitta, bee-eater, bellbird, blackcap, bobolink, cockatoo, currasow, dabchick, dotterel, fish-hawk, flamingo, gnatwren, great tit, grosbeak, hernshaw, hornbill, landrail, laverock, leafbird, lorikeet, lovebird, lyrebird, megapode, myna bird, nightjar, nuthatch, ovenbird, oxpecker, palmchat, parakeet, pheasant, puffbird, rainbird, redshank, redstart, ringtail, screamer, sea eagle, shoebill, starling, tapaculo, water-hen, whimbrel, white-eye, woodcock

**09** aepyornis, albatross, bald eagle, bergander, blackbird, blackhead, bowerbird, broadbill, bullfinch, cassowary, chaffinch, chickadee, cockatiel, cormorant, corncrake, currawong, eider duck, fairy tern, fieldfare, frogmouth, gerfalcon, gnateater, goldfinch, goosander, guillemot, jack-snipe, kittiwake, little owl, merganser, mollymawk, mousebird, mynah bird, nighthawk, ossifrage, pardalote, partridge, peregrine, phalarope, ptarmigan, razorbill, sandpiper, scrub bird, sheldrake, thornbill, trumpeter, turnstone, wind-hover

**10** budgerigar, chiff-chaff, fledgeling, flycatcher, goatsucker, gobemouche, greenfinch, greenshank, guinea fowl, hammerhead, harpy eagle, honeyeater, honey guide, kingfisher, kookaburra, nutcracker, piwakawaka, sanderling, sandgrouse, shearwater, sheathbill, song thrush, sun bittern, tropicbird, turtledove, wattlebird, woodpecker, wood pigeon

**11** butcherbird, frigate bird, golden eagle, hummingbird, mockingbird, nightingale, plantcutter, reed warbler, snow bunting, song sparrow, sparrowhawk, stone curlew, storm petrel, thunderbird, tree-creeper, woodcreeper, wood-swallow

**12** adjutant bird, cuckoo-roller, diving petrel, flowerpecker, golden plover, honey creeper, missel-thrush, mistle-thrush, sedge warbler, yellowhammer

**13** archaeopteryx, barnacle goose, oyster-catcher, secretary bird, willow warbler

**14** bird of paradise, plains wanderer

**15** blue-footed booby, passenger pigeon, peregrine falcon

*Birds of prey include:*

**03** owl
**04** erne, hawk, kite, pern
**05** eagle, hobby
**06** falcon, lanner, merlin, osprey, raptor
**07** barn owl, buzzard, goshawk, harrier, hawk owl, kestrel, red kite
**08** bateleur, berghaan, duck-hawk, eagle owl, fish-hawk, Scops owl, sea eagle, spar-hawk, tawny owl
**09** bald eagle, black kite, eagle-hawk, fish eagle, gyrfalcon, little owl, marsh hawk, peregrine, stone hawk
**10** harpy eagle, hen harrier, spotted owl, tawny eagle
**11** booted eagle, chicken hawk, Cooper's hawk, golden eagle, sparrowhawk, stone falcon
**12** great grey owl, honey buzzard, long-eared owl, marsh harrier
**13** American eagle, Iceland falcon, imperial eagle, lesser kestrel, pallid harrier, secretary bird, short-eared owl
**14** short-toed eagle
**15** Montagu's harrier, peregrine falcon, red-footed falcon

*Flightless birds include:*

**03** emu
**04** dodo, emeu, kiwi, rhea, weka
**06** kakapo, ratite, takahe
**07** ostrich, penguin
**08** great auk, notornis
**09** cassowary, owl-parrot, solitaire

*Mythical birds include:*

**03** fum, roc, rok, ruc
**04** fung, huma, rukh
**07** phoenix
**08** whistler
**09** impundulu
**11** thunderbird
**12** bird of wonder

*Seabirds include:*

03 auk, cob, maw, mew
04 cobb, guga, gull, shag, skua, tern, Xema
05 cahow, solan
06 fulmar, gannet, petrel, puffin
07 pickmaw, seagull
08 comorant
09 black tern, great skua, guillemot, kittiwake, little auk, mallemuck, razorbill, swart-back
10 Arctic skua, Arctic tern, common gull, common tern, little gull, little tern, saddleback, solan goose
11 herring gull, Iceland gull, roseate tern, Sabine's gull, storm petrel
12 glaucous gull, Leach's petrel, pomarine skua, sandwich tern
13 Bermuda petrel
14 black guillemot, long-tailed skua, Manx shearwater
15 black-backed gull, black-headed gull

*Wading birds include:*

03 ree
04 hern, ibis, knot, ruff
05 crake, crane, heron, reeve, snipe, stilt, stint, stork
06 avocet, curlew, dunlin, godwit, plover
07 bittern, bustard, lapwing
08 dotterel, flamingo, redshank, whimbrel, woodcock
09 dowitcher, grey heron, phalarope, sandpiper, turnstone
10 greenshank, sanderling
11 little stint, stone curlew
12 golden plover, great bustard, ringed plover
13 little bustard, oyster-catcher

• **birds** 04 Aves 05 ornis

**birth**

04 dawn, line, race, rise, root, seed 05 blood, house, start, stock 06 advent, family, labour, origin, source, strain 07 arrival, descent, genesis, lineage, origins 08 ancestry, breeding, delivery, nativity, pedigree 09 beginning, emergence, genealogy, parentage 10 appearance, background, childbirth, derivation, extraction 11 confinement, parturition 12 commencement, fountainhead 13 starting-point

*Birth flowers:*

04 rose
05 aster, daisy, holly, poppy
06 cosmos, violet
07 jonquil
08 hawthorn, larkspur, primrose, snowdrop, sweet pea
09 calendula, carnation, gladiolus, narcissus, water lily
10 poinsettia
11 honeysuckle
12 morning glory
13 chrysanthemum
15 lily of the valley

*Birth stones:*

04 opal, ruby
05 pearl, topaz
06 garnet, zircon
07 diamond, emerald, peridot
08 amethyst, sapphire, sardonyx
09 moonstone, turquoise
10 aquamarine, bloodstone, tourmaline
11 alexandrite

• **give birth to** 03 cub, ean, kid, lay, pig, pup 04 bear, drop, fawn, foal, have, lamb, yean 05 calve, found, throw 06 create, farrow, kitten, litter, mother 08 initiate 09 establish 10 bring forth, give rise to, inaugurate 12 cause to exist

**birthday**
03 dob 10 day of birth 11 anniversary

**birthmark**
04 mole 05 naeve, nevus, patch 06 naevus 07 blemish 10 beauty spot, mother spot 13 discoloration, port-wine stain 14 strawberry mark

**birthplace**
02 bp 03 b pl 04 home, root 05 fount, roots 06 cradle, source 08 home town 10 fatherland, incunables, incunabula, native town, provenance 12 place of birth 13 mother country, native country, place of origin

**birthright**
03 due 06 legacy 08 birthdom 09 privilege 11 inheritance, prerogative

**biscuit**
04 bake, cake 05 biccy 06 bickie

*Biscuits include:*

03 dog, nut, sea, tea
04 kiss, Nice, puff, rice, rusk, ship, snap, tack, thin, Twix®, wine
05 Anzac, Marie, ship's, wafer, water
06 cookie, hob-nob, KitKat®, parkin, perkin
07 Bourbon, brownie, cracker, fig roll, Gold Bar®, iced gem, Lincoln, oatcake, Penguin®, pretzel, ratafia, rich tea, saltine
08 biscotto, captain's, cracknel, flapjack, hardtack, macaroon, Zwieback
09 Abernethy, BreakAway®, cereal bar, chocolate, digestive, four-by-two, garibaldi, ginger nut, jaffa cake, party ring, petit four, pink wafer, shortcake
10 Bath Oliver, Blue Riband®, brandy snap, butter-bake, crispbread, dunderfunk, florentine, gingersnap, malted milk, shortbread, Wagon Wheel®
11 brown George, fly cemetery, soda cracker, squashed fly
12 cream cracker, custard cream, jammie dodger, langue de chat
14 gingerbread man

• **soften biscuit** 04 dunk

**bisect**
◊ *insertion indicator* 04 fork 05 cross, halve, split 06 divide 08 cut in two,

separate 09 bifurcate, cut in half, intersect 13 divide into two

**bisexual**
02 bi 04 AC/DC 07 epicene 11 androgynous, monoclinous 12 ambidextrous, switch hitter 13 hermaphrodite 15 gynandromorphic

**bishop**
01 B 02 Bp, DD, RR 04 abba, lord 06 exarch, magpie, primus 07 pontiff, prelate, primate 08 diocesan 09 coadjutor, patriarch, suffragan 10 archbishop, episcopant, metropolis 11 intercessor 12 metropolitan 13 spiritual peer 14 vicar-apostolic

*Bishops include:*

05 **Aidan** (St), **Peter** (St)
06 **Blaise**, **Ninian** (St), **Osmund** (St)
07 **Ambrose** (St), **Carroll** (John), **Hadrian**, **Patrick** (St)
08 **Geoffrey** (of Monmouth), **Holloway** (Richard), **Nicholas** (St), **Sheppard** (David)
11 **Elphinstone** (William), **Odo of Bayeux**

*See also* **archbishop**

**bishopric**
03 see 07 diocese, Holy See 10 episcopacy, episcopate
*See also* **diocese**

**bismuth**
02 Bi

**bison**
04 gaur 06 wisent 07 aurochs, bonassus buffalo 08 bonassus

**bit**
◊ *hidden indicator* 03 ate, dot, jot, ort, tad 04 atom, chip, curb, dash, doit, drap, drop, haet, hint, iota, lump, mite part, what, whit 05 chunk, crumb, drill flake, fleck, grain, piece, scrap, shred slice, speck, touch, trace 06 cannon, morsel, nibble, pelham, sliver, tittle 07 kenning, portion, segment, snaffle, soupçon, vestige 08 fragment, mouthful, particle 09 scintilla 10 small piece 12 small portion
• **a bit** 04 tick 05 jiffy 06 a while, fairly minute, moment, rather 07 a little, a moment, not much, not very 08 slightly 10 a short time, few minutes, few moments 12 a little while
• **bit by bit** 06 slowly 08 in stages 09 gradually, piecemeal 10 step by step 14 little by little
• **bit of** ◊ *head selection indicator*
• **last bit of** ◊ *tail selection indicator*

**bitch**
03 cat, cow, pig 04 moan, slut 05 brach, gripe, harpy, shrew, swine, trial, vixen, whine 06 ordeal, virago, whinge 07 doggess, grumble, torment 08 badmouth, complain 09 criticize, female dog, nightmare 13 find fault with 15 be spiteful about

**bitchiness**
05 spite, venom 06 malice 07 cruelty 08 meanness 09 cattiness, nastiness 13 maliciousness

## bitchy

**04** mean **05** catty, cruel, nasty, snide **07** cutting, vicious **08** shrewish, spiteful, venomous, vixenish **09** malicious, rancorous **10** backbiting, vindictive

## bite

◇ *containment indicator* **03** bit, eat, nip **04** chew, crop, gnaw, grip, hold, kick, peck, pick, rend, snap, take, tang, tear, work **05** champ, chomp, crush, force, gnash, munch, piece, pinch, power, prick, punch, seize, smart, snack, spice, sting, taste, wound **06** begnaw, crunch, effect, impact, lesion, morsel, nibble, pierce, tingle **07** morsure, remorse **08** mouthful, piquancy, puncture, pungency, smarting, strength **09** influence, light meal, masticate, sharpness, spiciness **10** impression, take effect **11** refreshment

## biting

◇ *containment indicator* **03** raw **04** acid, cold, keen, tart **05** acrid, harsh, nippy, sharp **06** bitter, severe, shrewd, toothy **07** caustic, cutting, cynical, hurtful, mordant, nipping, pointed, pungent, vicious **08** freezing, incisive, piercing, scathing, stinging **09** sarcastic, trenchant, vitriolic **10** astringent, mordacious **11** penetrating

## bitter

**03** ale, raw, sad, wry **04** acid, keen, sore, sour, tart **05** acerb, acidy, acrid, angry, aygre, cruel, eager, harsh, nippy, parky, sharp, tangy, wersh **06** arctic, biting, fierce, morose, porter, savage, severe, sullen, tragic **07** acerbic, caustic, cynical, hostile, intense, painful, pungent, unhappy **08** freezing, piercing, sardonic, scathing, spiteful, stinging, venomous, vinegary, virulent **09** aggrieved, harrowing, indignant, jaundiced, merciless, rancorous, resentful, vitriolic **10** astringent, begrudging, embittered, malevolent, vindictive, wry-mouthed **11** acrimonious, disgruntled, distressing, penetrating, unsweetened **12** freezing cold, gut-wrenching, heart-rending, vituperative **13** disappointing, heartbreaking

## bitterly

**05** wryly **06** sourly **07** angrily, cruelly **08** bitingly, morosely, savagely, severely, sullenly **09** cynically, hostilely, intensely, painfully **10** grievously, grudgingly, piercingly, scathingly, spitefully, venomously **11** acerbically, caustically, indignantly, rancorously, resentfully, with vitriol **12** begrudgingly, embitteredly, malevolently, sardonically, vindictively **13** acrimoniously, penetratingly **14** vituperatively

## bittern

**05** Ardea **06** bittor, bittur **07** bittour **08** mire-drum **10** butter-bump **11** mossbluiter **12** bull-of-the-bog

## bitterness

**04** bite, edge, fell, gall, pain **05** anger, marah, spite, venom **06** enmity, grudge, rancor, spleen **07** acidity, cruelty, iciness, rancour, rawness, sadness, tragedy, vinegar **08** acrimony, coldness, cynicism, distress, ferocity, jaundice, pungency, severity, sourness, tartness, wormwood **09** harshness, hostility, intensity, sharpness, tanginess, virulence **10** acerbicity, antagonism, chilliness, frostiness, moroseness, resentment, sullenness **11** indignation, malevolence, painfulness, penetration, unhappiness **12** embitterment, heart-rending **13** heartbreaking **14** disappointment, vindictiveness

## bitty

**06** broken, fitful **07** scrappy **09** piecemeal **10** disjointed, fragmented, incoherent **12** disconnected

## bitumen

**03** tar **05** slime **09** albertite, elaterite **11** pissasphalt

## bivalve

**06** cockle, oyster, tellen, tellin **07** geoduck, scallop, scollop **08** ark-shell **10** otter shell

## bizarre

◇ *anagram indicator* **03** odd **05** funny, gonzo, outré, queer, wacky, weird **06** way-out **07** comical, curious, deviant, oddball, offbeat, strange, surreal, unusual **08** abnormal, freakish, peculiar, uncommon **09** eccentric, fantastic, grotesque, left-field, ludicrous **10** off the wall, outlandish, ridiculous **11** extravagant, Pythonesque **13** extraordinary **14** unconventional

## bizarrely

◇ *anagram indicator* **05** oddly **07** weirdly **09** comically, curiously, strangely, unusually **10** abnormally, freakishly, peculiarly **11** ludicrously **12** outlandishly, ridiculously **13** extravagantly

## blab

**04** blat, leak, tell **05** prate **06** gossip, reveal, squeal, tattle **07** blister, divulge, let slip, tattler **08** blurt out, disclose, tattling **11** blow the gaff **15** give the game away

## blabber

**04** chat **06** babble, gabble, gossip, jabber, witter **07** blather, blether, chatter, prattle, swollen, twattle, twitter

## black

**01** B **03** bad, dim, sad **04** dark, evil, inky, sick, slae, sloe, vile **05** angry, awful, bleak, cruel, dingy, dirty, dusky, grimy, gross, gungy, muddy, raven, sooty, unlit, wrong **06** bitter, dismal, filthy, gloomy, grotty, grubby, odious, soiled, sombre, sullen, tragic, vulgar, wicked **07** cynical, demonic, heinous, immoral, satanic, stained, Stygian, subfusc, swarthy, unclean, unhappy **08** coloured, devilish, funereal, hopeless, menacing, moonless, mournful, overcast, starless **09** Cimmerian, depressed, malicious, miserable, nefarious, resentful, tasteless, tenebrous **10** depressing, diabolical, fuliginous, in bad taste, lugubrious, malevolent, melancholy, melanistic, nigrescent, pitch-black **11** black as coal, crepuscular, dark-skinned, distressing, threatening **13** unilluminated

*Blacks include:*

**03** jet
**04** blae, ebon, jeat
**05** dwale, ebony, sable
**08** jet-black
**09** coal-black

• **black and white 02** b/w **04** gray, grey **05** plain **07** brocked, brockit, on paper, piebald, printed, pyebald, written **08** clear-cut, definite, distinct, on record **11** categorical, unambiguous, unequivocal, well-defined, written down **12** monochromist **13** pepper-and-salt
• **black eye** *see* **eye**
• **black out 03** gag **05** faint **06** censor, darken **07** conceal, cover up, eclipse, pass out **08** collapse, flake out, keel over, suppress, withhold
• **in the black 03** ban, bar, hit **05** punch, taboo **06** bruise, injure **07** blacken, boycott, embargo, solvent **08** in credit **09** blacklist, out of debt **11** without debt
• **very black 02** BB **04** inky

## blackball

**03** ban, bar, pip **04** oust, pill, snub, veto **05** debar, expel **06** reject **07** drum out, exclude, shut out **08** throw out **09** blacklist, ostracize, repudiate **11** vote against

## blacken

**03** ink, tar **04** cork, soil **05** black, cloud, decry, dirty, libel, smear, smoke, stain, sully, taint **06** besmut, darken, defame, defile, impugn, malign, revile, smudge, vilify **07** detract, nigrify, run down, slander, tarnish **08** besmirch **09** denigrate, discredit, dishonour, make dirty **10** calumniate

## blackguard

**05** crook, devil, knave, rogue, sweep, swine **06** rascal, rotter, wretch **07** bleeder, bounder, scumbag, stinker, villain **08** blighter **09** miscreant, reprobate, scoundrel **10** vituperate

## blackleg

**03** leg **04** fink, scab, snob **09** knobstick

## blacklist

**03** ban, bar **04** snub, veto **05** debar, expel, taboo **06** outlaw, reject **07** boycott, exclude, shut out **08** disallow, preclude **09** ostracize, proscribe, repudiate

## blackmail

**04** milk **05** black, bleed, chout, exact, force **06** coerce, compel, demand, extort, lean on, ransom, strike **07** bribery, squeeze **08** chantage, exaction, threaten **09** extortion, greenmail, hush money, shakedown **10** pressurize **12** hold to ransom, intimidation **14** put the screws on

**blackmailer**
**07** vampire **08** hijacker **10** highbinder, highjacker **11** bloodsucker, extortioner **12** extortionist

**blackout**
**04** coma **05** faint, swoon **07** cover-up, embargo, secrecy, silence, syncope **08** brownout, oblivion, power cut **10** censorship, flaking-out, passing out **11** concealment, suppression, withholding **12** power failure **15** unconsciousness

**blacksmith**
**06** vulcan **09** hammerman, ironsmith **11** burn-the-wind

**bladder**
**04** swim **05** sound **06** vesica **07** blister, utricle, vesicle **09** cholecyst

**blade**
**03** fan, oar **04** edge, peel, vane, wash **05** float, knife, lance, razor, skate, spear, sword **06** dagger, lamina, paddle, scythe, Toledo **07** bayonet, scalpel, spatula **10** cream-slice, paperknife **11** cutting edge
*See also* **dagger; sword**

**blame**
**03** rap, tax **04** onus, wite, wyte **05** chide, decry, fault, guilt, odium, stick, thank, wight **06** accuse, berate, charge, dirdam, dirdum, finger, injury, rebuke **07** appoint, censure, condemn, pin it on, reproof, reprove, upbraid **08** admonish, berating, reproach, tear into **09** criticism, criticize, dispraise, inculpate, liability, name names, reprehend, reprimand, scapegoat **10** accusation, confounded, disapprove, discommend, find guilty, hold liable **11** culpability **12** condemnation, name and shame **13** find fault with, incrimination, recrimination **14** accountability, responsibility **15** hold accountable, hold responsible

**blameless**
**05** clear **07** perfect, sinless, upright **08** innocent, virtuous, witeless **09** faultless, guiltless, lily-white, stainless **10** impeccable, inculpable, unblamable, unreproved **11** unblemished **12** irreprovable, squeaky clean, without fault **13** above reproach, unimpeachable **14** irreproachable **15** irreprehensible

**blameworthy**
**06** guilty **07** at fault **08** culpable, shameful, unworthy **10** flagitious **11** inexcusable, responsible **12** disreputable, indefensible, reproachable **13** discreditable, reprehensible

**blanch**
**04** boil **05** scald **06** blench, whiten **07** go white, lighten **08** etiolate, grow pale, turn pale **09** turn white

**10** become pale, grow pallid **11** become white **12** become pallid

**blancmange**
**04** mold **05** mould **08** flummery

**bland**
**04** dull, flat, mild, weak **05** suave **06** boring, smooth, spammy **07** anodyne, humdrum, insipid, mundane, tedious, vanilla **08** ordinary **09** tasteless **10** antiseptic, monotonous, unexciting **11** flavourless, inoffensive, nondescript, uninspiring **13** characterless, uninteresting

**blandishments**
**05** sooth, spiel **07** blarney, coaxing, fawning, flannel, treacle **08** cajolery, flattery, lipsalve, soft soap **09** agréments, sweet talk, wheedling **10** sycophancy **11** compliments, enticements, inducements **12** ingratiation, inveiglement **14** persuasiveness

**blank**
**03** gap **04** bare, void **05** break, clean, clear, empty, plain, space, white **06** glazed, vacant, vacuum **07** deadpan, vacancy, vacuity, vacuous **08** lifeless, unfilled, unmarked **09** apathetic, emptiness, impassive, unwritten **10** empty space, poker-faced **11** emotionless, indifferent, inscrutable, nothingness **12** uninterested **14** expressionless, without feeling **15** uncomprehending

**blanket**
**04** coat, film, hide, mask **05** bluey, cloak, cloud, cover, layer, manta, quilt, sheet, total **06** afghan, carpet, deaden, global, mantle, muffle, poncho, sarape, serape, stroud **07** coating, conceal, eclipse, obscure, overall, overlay, whittle, wrapper **08** bedcover, coverage, covering, coverlet, envelope, mackinaw, suppress, surround, sweeping, wrapping **09** bedspread, eiderdown, inclusive, wholesale **11** wide-ranging **12** all-embracing, all-inclusive, underblanket **13** comprehensive **14** across-the-board, indiscriminate

**blankly**
**08** vacantly **09** vacuously **10** lifelessly **11** impassively **13** apathetically, emotionlessly, indifferently **14** uninterestedly, without feeling

**blare**
**04** boom, honk, hoot, peal, ring, roar, toot **05** blast, clang **07** boom out, clamour, resound, thunder, trumpet **08** blast out **11** sound loudly

**blarney**
**05** spiel, taffy **06** cajole, sawder **07** coaxing, flannel **08** cajolery, flattery, soft soap **09** sweet talk, wheedling **10** soft sawder, soft sowder **13** blandishments **14** persuasiveness

**blasé**
**04** cool **05** bored, jaded, weary **07** offhand, unmoved **08** lukewarm **09** apathetic, impassive, unexcited **10** nonchalant, phlegmatic, uninspired

**11** indifferent, unconcerned, unimpressed **12** uninterested

**blaspheme**
**04** cuss, damn **05** abuse, curse, swear **06** revile **07** profane **08** execrate **09** desecrate, imprecate **10** utter oaths **12** anathematize

**blasphemous**
**07** godless, impious, profane, ungodly **10** irreverent, sulphurous **11** imprecatory, irreligious **12** sacrilegious

**blasphemously**
**09** profanely **12** irreverently **14** sacrilegiously **15** disrespectfully

**blasphemy**
**05** curse, oaths **07** cursing, impiety, outrage **08** swearing **09** expletive, profanity, sacrilege, violation **10** execration, unholiness **11** desecration, impiousness, imprecation, irreverence, profaneness, ungodliness

**blast**
◇ *anagram indicator* **03** dee, wap **04** bang, blow, bomb, boom, clap, dang, drat, gale, gust, honk, hoot, parp, peal, puff, roar, ruin, rush, shot, slam, toot, tout, waff, wail, zonk **05** blare, burst, clang, crack, crash, pryse, scath, slate, sound, storm, trump, whiff, whift **06** assail, attack, bellow, berate, blow up, blow-up, flatus, flurry, jigger, rebuke, scaith, scathe, scream, shriek, skaith, squall, strike, volley, wuther **07** blaring, blatter, bluster, booming, boom out, clamour, destroy, draught, explode, gun down, reprove, roaring, shatter, tantara, tell off, tempest, thunder, upbraid, whither **08** blare out, demolish, outburst, siderate **09** criticize, discharge, explosion, reprimand, shoot down, tantarara **10** detonation, sideration **12** blow to pieces **13** thunder-stroke
• **blast off 07** lift off, take off **10** be launched

**blasted**
◇ *anagram indicator* **05** ruddy **06** cursed, damned, darned **07** flaming **08** annoying, blighted, blooming, dratting, flipping, infernal **10** confounded, unpleasant **12** planet-struck **14** planet-stricken

**blatant**
**04** bald, open **05** naked, overt, sheer **06** arrant, brazen, coarse, full-on, patent **07** glaring, obvious **08** flagrant, hard-core, manifest, outright **09** bald-faced, barefaced, clamorous, obtrusive, out-and-out, prominent, shameless, unashamed **10** pronounced **11** conspicuous, undisguised, unmitigated **12** ostentatious

**blatantly**
**06** openly **08** brazenly, patently **09** glaringly, obviously, out-and-out **10** flagrantly, manifestly **11** shamelessly, unashamedly **13** conspicuously

## blaze

03 low 04 beam, boil, burn, fire, glow, lowe, lunt, rage 05 blast, burst, erupt, flame, flare, flash, glare, gleam, light, shine, shoot 06 blow up, flames, ignite, let fly, let off, see red, seethe, set of 07 bonfire, explode, flare up, flare-up, glitter, inferno 08 be alight, be on fire, outburst, radiance 09 be radiant, catch fire, discharge, explosion, fire-storm 10 brilliance 11 be brilliant 13 conflagration 15 burst into flames

## blazing

◇ anagram indicator 05 angry 06 on fire 07 burning

## blazon

05 vaunt 06 flaunt, herald 07 trumpet 08 announce, flourish, proclaim 09 broadcast, celebrate, make known, publicize

## bleach

04 fade, pale 06 blanch, whiten 07 lighten 08 decolour, etiolate, make pale, peroxide, turn pale 09 make white, turn white 10 decolorize

## bleak

03 raw 04 arid, bare, blae, blay, bley, cold, dark, drab, dull, grim, open 05 ablet, empty, harsh, windy 06 barren, chilly, dismal, dreary, gloomy, leaden, sombre 07 exposed, joyless, spartan 08 desolate, hopeless, soulless, wretched 09 cheerless, desperate, miserable, windswept 10 depressing 11 comfortless, unpromising, unsheltered 12 discouraging, unfavourable 13 disheartening, weather-beaten

## bleakly

06 grimly 08 dismally, drearily, gloomily, sombrely 09 joylessly, miserably 10 wretchedly 11 cheerlessly 12 unfavourably 13 unpromisingly

## bleary

03 dim 05 tired 06 blurry, cloudy, drowsy, rheumy, watery 07 blurred 09 unfocused 10 bleary-eyed

## bleat

03 baa, cry, maa 04 beef, blat, bray, call, moan 05 gripe, whine 06 grouse, kvetch, whinge, suck dry, trickle 07 grumble, whicker 08 complain 09 complaint

## bleed

03 run, sap 04 flow, gush, melt, milk, ooze, seep, weep 05 blood, drain, exude, flood, glide, merge, spurt 06 extort, reduce 07 deplete, exhaust, extract, squeeze, suck dry, trickle 08 let blood 09 lose blood, shed blood 10 bleed white 11 extravasate, haemorrhage 12 exsanguinate, phlebotomize

## blemish

03 mar 04 blot, blur, flaw, mark, mote, tash, vice, want 05 botch, fault, speck, spoil, stain, sully, taint, touch 06 blotch, damage, deface, defame, defect, impair, smudge 07 tarnish 08 disgrace 09 deformity, disfigure, dishonour 10 compromise 12 imperfection 13 discoloration, disfigurement

---

*Blemishes include:*

---

03 zit 04 acne, boil, bump, corn, mole, scab, scar, spot, wart 06 bunion, callus, naevus, pimple 07 blister, freckle, pustule, verruca 08 pockmark 09 birthmark, blackhead, carbuncle, chilblain, whitehead 14 strawberry mark

## blench

03 shy 05 cower, quail, quake, start, wince 06 falter, flinch, quiver, recoil, shrink 07 shudder 08 draw back, hesitate, pull back

## blend

◇ anagram indicator 03 fit, mix 04 beat, fuse, meld, melt, stir, suit 05 admix, alloy, match, merge, union, unite, whisk 06 commix, fusion, go with, mingle, set off 07 amalgam, combine, merging, mixture, uniting 08 coalesce, compound, intermix 09 admixture, commingle, composite, contemper, harmonize, synthesis 10 amalgamate, commixture, complement, concoction, go together, go well with, homogenize, intertwine, interweave, synthesize 11 combination, portmanteau, run together 12 amalgamation

## bless

04 laud 05 exalt, extol, thank, wound 06 anoint, favour, hallow, honour, ordain, praise, thrash 07 glorify, magnify, worship 08 brandish, dedicate, sanctify 10 consecrate, lay hands on 13 be grateful for, be thankful for, give thanks for
• **bless you** 10 benedicite, Gesundheit

## blessed

◇ anagram indicator 04 glad, holy 05 happy, lucky 06 adored, divine, graced, joyful, joyous, sacred 07 endowed, revered 08 benedict, favoured, hallowed, heavenly, provided 09 benedight, contented, fortunate 10 prosperous, sanctified 11 consecrated

## blessing

02 OK 04 boon, gain, gift, help 05 grace, leave 06 bounty, favour, profit 07 backing, benefit, benison, consent, darshan, go-ahead, godsend, kiddush, service, support 08 approval, felicity, sanction, thumbs-up, windfall 09 advantage, agreement, authority, good thing 10 benedicite, dedication, green light, invocation, permission 11 approbation, benediction, concurrence, good fortune 12 commendation, consecration, thanksgiving

## blight

◇ anagram indicator 03 mar, rot, woe 04 bane, dash, evil, kill, ruin, take 05 blast, check, crush, curse, decay, spoil, wreck 06 cancer, canker, damage, fungus, injure, mildew, strike, wither 07 destroy, disease, scourge, scowder, setback, shatter, shrivel, trouble 08 calamity, scouther, scowther 09 blastment, fire-blast, frustrate, pollution, undermine 10 affliction, annihilate, corruption, disappoint, misfortune, sideration 11 infestation 13 contamination

## blimey

03 coo, lor

## blind

03 mad 04 hood, mask, rash, seal, seel, slow, trap, wild 05 blend, chick, cloak, cover, front, hasty, shade, trick 06 bisson, closed, dazzle, façade, hidden, screen 07 confuse, cover-up, curtain, deceive, eyeless, mislead, shutter, unaware, winking 08 careless, heedless, ignorant, mindless, obscured, reckless, unseeing, Venetian 09 concealed, impetuous, impulsive, make blind, oblivious, sightless, unmindful, unsighted 10 beetle-eyed, camouflage, intimidate, irrational, masquerade, neglectful, obstructed, out of sight, uncritical, unthinking, visionless 11 distraction, inattentive, indifferent, injudicious, insensitive, roller blind, smokescreen, thoughtless, unconscious, unobservant, unreasoning, window shade 12 festoon blind, imperceptive 13 Austrian blind, inconsiderate, Venetian blind 14 deprive of sight, indiscriminate 15 block your vision, deprive of vision, put the eyes out of *See also* **sight**

## blindly

05 madly 06 rashly, wildly 10 carelessly, mindlessly, recklessly, unseeingly 11 impetuously, impulsively, senselessly, sightlessly 12 incautiously, irrationally, uncritically, unthinkingly, without sight 13 thoughtlessly, without vision

## blink

04 peep, pink, wink 05 flash, gleam, shine, twink 06 glance, wapper 07 flicker, flutter, glimmer, glimpse, glitter, nictate, sparkle, twinkle 09 nictitate 11 scintillate

## blip

03 pip 04 buzz 05 bleep 06 glitch, hiccup, squeal 07 screech

## bliss

03 joy 06 heaven, utopia 07 ecstasy, elation, nirvana, rapture 08 euphoria, gladness, paradise 09 happiness 11 blessedness 12 blissfulness 13 seventh heaven

## blissful

05 happy 06 elated, joyful, joyous 07 idyllic 08 ecstatic, euphoric, seraphic 09 delighted, enchanted, rapturous 10 enraptured, seraphical

## blister

03 wen 04 blab, bleb, boil, cyst, sore 05 blain, bulla, ulcer 06 canker, papula, pimple 07 abscess, measles, papilla, pustule, vesicle 08 cold sore,

furuncle, overgall, swelling, vesicate, vesicula **09** carbuncle, phlyctena, pompholyx **10** phlyctaena

**blistering**
**03** hot **05** cruel **06** fierce, savage
**07** caustic, extreme, intense, vicious
**08** scathing, vesicant, virulent
**09** ferocious, sarcastic, scorching, withering **10** epispastic

**blithe**
**05** happy, merry **06** casual, cheery
**08** carefree, careless, cheerful, heedless, uncaring **10** unthinking, untroubled **11** thoughtless, unconcerned **12** light-hearted

**blithely**
**08** casually **10** carelessly
**12** unthinkingly **13** thoughtlessly

**blitz**
**04** raid **06** attack, effort, strike **07** airraid, attempt **08** campaign, exertion
**09** endeavour, offensive, onslaught
**10** blitzkrieg **11** bombardment **12** allout effort

**blizzard**
**05** buran, storm **06** squall **07** tempest
**08** white-out **09** snowstorm

**bloated**
**04** full **05** puffy **06** sodden **07** blown up, dilated, stuffed, swollen **08** enlarged, expanded, inflated, puffed up
**09** distended, puffed out

**blob**
**01** O **03** dab, gob **04** ball, bead, drop, duck, glob, lump, mass, pill, spot, tear
**05** pearl **06** bubble, pellet, splash
**07** droplet, globule

**bloc**
**04** axis, ring **05** block, cabal, group, union **06** cartel, clique, league
**07** entente, faction **08** alliance
**09** coalition, syndicate **10** federation
**11** association

**block**
◊ *insertion indicator* **03** bar, dam, dit, jam, let, ped **04** cake, clog, cube, halt, hunk, lump, mass, plug, seal, slab, stop **05** batch, brick, check, choke, chunk, close, dam up, delay, deter, group, piece, stimy, wedge **06** arrest, bung up, clog up, hamper, hinder, impede, scotch, series, square, stimie, stop up, stymie, thwart **07** barrier, cluster, complex, occlude, section
**08** blockage, building, drawback, obstacle, obstruct, quantity, stoppage
**09** deterrent, frustrate, hindrance, stonewall, structure **10** be in the way, impediment, resistance
**11** development, obstruction
**14** stumbling-block
• **block off** **04** seal, stop **05** close
**06** stop up **07** close up, shut off
• **block out** **04** hide, mask, veil
**06** screen **07** blot out, conceal, eclipse, obscure, repress, shut out **08** blank out, suppress **10** obliterate
• **block up** **03** ram **04** cloy

**blockade**
**03** ram **04** cloy, stop **05** block, check,

siege **06** hinder **07** barrier, besiege, choke up, closure, prevent **08** encircle, keep from, obstacle, obstruct, oppilate, stoppage, surround
**09** barricade **10** investment
**11** obstruction, restriction
**12** encirclement, prevent using
**15** prevent entering, prevent reaching

**blockage**
**03** jam **04** clot **05** block **06** log jam
**08** blocking, snifters, stoppage
**09** hindrance, occlusion **10** bottleneck, congestion, impediment **11** obstruction

**blockhead**
**03** git **04** dope, dork, fool, geek, jerk, mome, mutt, nerd, nong, prat, twit
**05** chump, dunce, goosy, idiot, ninny, twerp, wally **06** dimwit, goosey, nitwit, noodle, oxhead, tumphy **07** dizzard, jackass, log-head, plonker
**08** bonehead, clotpoll, dipstick, imbecile, jolthead, lunkhead, numskull **09** besom-head, doddipoll, doddypoll, dottipoll, numbskull, pigsconce, thickhead, thickskin
**10** bufflehead, jolterhead, loggerhead, muddle-head, nincompoop, thickskull, woodenhead **11** chuckle-head, leather-head

**bloke**
**03** boy, guy, man, oik **04** chap, male
**05** fella, joker **06** fellow **09** character
**10** individual
*See also* **boy**

**blond, blonde**
**04** fair **05** light **06** cendré, flaxen, golden **08** bleached **10** fair-haired, goldilocks **11** tow-coloured **12** goldenhaired **13** light-coloured

**blood**
**03** nut **04** Blut, gore, knut, ruby, sang
**05** birth **06** claret, family **07** descent, kindred, kinship, lineage **08** ancestry
**09** lifeblood, relations **10** extraction, vital fluid **11** descendants
**12** relationship
• **draw blood** **03** cup **05** bleed
• **mass of blood** **04** clot

**bloodcurdling**
**05** scary **06** horrid **07** fearful **08** chilling, dreadful, horrible, horrific **09** appalling
**10** horrendous, horrifying, terrifying
**11** frightening, hair-raising **13** spinechilling

**bloodgroup**
**01** A, B, O **02** AB

**bloodhound**
**04** lime, lyam, lyme **06** sleuth
**07** coondog **09** coonhound, detective, lime-hound, lyam-hound, lyme-hound
**11** sleuth-hound

**bloodless**
**03** wan **04** cold, dead, pale **05** ashen, pasty, white **06** chalky, feeble, pallid, sallow, sickly, torpid **07** anaemic, drained, insipid, languid **08** lifeless, listless, peaceful **09** unfeeling, unwarlike **10** colourless, non-violent, spiritless, strife-free **11** passionless, unemotional

**bloodshed**
**04** gore **06** murder, pogrom **07** carnage, killing, slaying **08** butchery, massacre
**09** bloodbath, slaughter **10** decimation
**12** bloodletting

**bloodsucker**
**04** flea, gnat, tick **05** lamia, leech
**06** gadfly **07** deer fly, sponger, tabanid, vampire **08** birch fly, black fly, mosquito, parasite, simulium **09** stable fly **10** horseleech, vampire bat
**11** blackmailer, buffalo gnat, extortioner **12** extortionist, sucking louse

**bloodthirsty**
**05** cruel **06** brutal, savage **07** inhuman, vicious, warlike **08** barbaric, ruthless
**09** barbarous, ferocious, homicidal, murderous **10** sanguinary

**bloody**
**03** red **04** gory, rare **05** bally, cruel, ruddy **06** bluggy, brutal, fierce, purple, savage **08** bleeding, blinking, blooming, sanguine **09** ferocious, homicidal, murderous **10** sanguinary
**11** ensanguined, sanguineous
**12** bloodstained, bloodthirsty, sanguinolent **13** ensanguinated

**bloody-minded**
**05** cruel **06** touchy **07** awkward, stroppy **08** stubborn **09** difficult, irritable, obstinate, unhelpful
**11** obstructive **13** unco-operative

**bloom**
**03** bud **04** blow, glow, grow, open
**05** blush, chill, flush, prime **06** beauty, flower, health, heyday, lustre, mature, pruina, sprout, thrive, vigour
**07** blossom, develop, prosper, red tide
**08** flourish, radiance, rosiness, strength
**09** freshness **10** perfection
**11** florescence **13** efflorescence
• **in bloom** **03** out

**bloomer**
*see* **flower; mistake**

**blooming**
**04** rosy **05** bonny, primy, ruddy
**07** healthy **09** flowering **10** blossoming, florescent

**blossom**
**03** bud, may, pip **04** blow, grow
**05** bloom **06** flower, mature, pruina, thrive **07** bloosme, burgeon, develop, prosper, succeed **08** flourish, progress
**10** effloresce **11** florescence
**13** efflorescence

**blot**
**03** dot, dry, mar **04** blur, flaw, mark, soak, spot **05** dry up, fault, smear, spawn, speck, spoil, stain, sully, taint
**06** absorb, blotch, defect, smudge, soak up **07** blacken, blemish, splodge, tarnish **08** disgrace **09** black mark, disfigure **10** tarnishing **12** imperfection, obliteration
• **blot out** **04** bury, hide **05** blank, erase **06** cancel, darken, delete, efface, screen, shadow **07** conceal, eclipse, expunge, obscure **08** black out
**10** obliterate

## blotch

04 blot, dash, mark, monk, spot
05 patch, stain 06 smudge, splash
07 blemish, pustule, splodge, splotch
08 heatspot

## blotched

06 marked, pimply, spotty 07 blotchy,
freckly, scarred, spotted, stained
09 blemished, centonate, scratched

## blotchy

◇ *anagram indicator* 06 patchy, smeary,
spotty, uneven 07 spotted 08 inflamed,
reddened 09 blemished

## blouse

05 middy, shirt, smock, tunic, waist
09 garibaldi 10 shirtwaist

## blow

03 bat, bob, bop, box, cut, dad, fan,
hit, rap, tip, wap 04 bang, bash, belt,
biff, buff, bump, butt, chop, clap, clip,
conk, coup, cuff, daud, dint, flow,
flub, fuse, gale, gust, hook, jolt, lick,
melt, oner, paik, pant, pash, pelt, pipe,
play, plug, puff, ruin, rush, scat, slap,
snot, sock, stot, swat, tear, toot, waff,
waft, welt, whop, wind, wipe, yank
05 appel, blare, blast, botch, break,
burst, carry, clout, drift, drive, fling,
float, fluff, knock, one-er, peise,
punch, shock, skiff, smack, sound,
souse, spang, split, spoil, sweep,
swipe, thump, upset, waste, whack,
whang, whirl, whisk, wreck 06 buffet,
bungle, cock up, devvel, exhale,
flurry, inhale, stream, stroke, thwack,
wallop, whammy, wunner, wuther
07 blow out, breathe, flutter, lounder,
puff out, reverse, rupture, screw up,
setback, shocker, trumpet, whample,
whirret 08 calamity, comedown,
disaster, misspend, puncture,
squander, surprise 09 bombshell,
dissipate, miss out on 10 affliction,
breathe out, concussion, exsufflate,
insufflate, misfortune 11 catastrophe,
coup de grâce, coup de poing, fritter
away, make a mess of, miss the boat,
spend freely 12 short-circuit 13 rude
awakening 14 disappointment, spend
like water 15 bolt from the blue
• **blow out** 04 tear 05 burst, snift, split
06 put out 07 rupture, smother
08 puncture, snuff out 10 extinguish
• **blow over** 03 end 04 pass 05 abate,
cease 06 finish, vanish 07 die down,
subside 08 peter out 09 disappear,
dissipate, fizzle out 10 settle down
11 be forgotten
• **blow up** ◇ *anagram indicator*
04 bomb, fill, flip, gale, go up, gust,
puff, wind 05 blast, bloat, blore, burst,
go ape, go mad, go off, scold, storm,
swell 06 dilate, expand, flurry, puff up,
pump up, squall 07 balloon, distend,
draught, enlarge, explode, fill out,
inflate, magnify, tempest 08 detonate
09 overstate 10 exaggerate, hit the roof
11 become angry, blow your top, flip
your lid, go ballistic 12 get into a rage
14 lose your temper 15 fly off the
handle
• **gentle blow** 03 tip 04 peck

• **heavy blow** 02 KO 04 bang, bash,
bump, oner, slog, slug, swat 05 douse,
dowse, one-er, slosh, souse, swash,
thump 06 lander, wallop, wunner
07 lounder 08 knockout 11 neck-
herring

## blow-out

04 bash, flat, rave 05 binge, feast, party
06 rave-up 07 knees-up 08 flat tyre,
puncture 09 beanfeast, burst tyre
11 celebration

## blowpipe

03 hod 06 sumpit 07 blowgun
08 sumpitan 09 sarbacane

## blowy

05 fresh, gusty, windy 06 breezy,
stormy 07 squally 08 blustery

## blowzy

05 messy 06 sloppy, untidy 07 tousled,
unkempt 08 slipshod, slovenly
09 ungroomed 10 bedraggled
11 dishevelled

## blubber

03 cry, sob 04 blub, spek, weep
05 speck 06 bubble, snivel 07 sniffle,
snotter, whimper 09 jellyfish

## bludgeon

03 hit, sap 04 beat, club, cosh 05 baton,
bully, force 06 badger, batter, coerce,
compel, cudgel, harass, hector, strike
07 clobber, dragoon 08 browbeat,
bulldoze 09 terrorize, truncheon
10 intimidate, pressurize

## blue

◇ *anagram indicator* 03 low, sad
04 down, glum, lewd, rude, Tory
05 adult, bawdy, dirty, fed up, saucy
06 coarse, dismal, erotic, fruity,
gloomy, morose, risqué, smutty,
steamy, vulgar, X-rated 07 obscene,
raunchy, unhappy 08 dejected,
downcast, improper, indecent
09 depressed, miserable, off-colour,
offensive 10 despondent, dispirited,
melancholy 11 downhearted, near the
bone 12 Conservative, pornographic
14 down in the dumps, near the
knuckle
*See also* **squander**

*Blues include:*

03 sky
04 anil, aqua, bice, blae, cyan, navy,
Saxe, teal
05 azure, perse, smalt
06 cerule, cobalt, haüyne, indigo
07 caerule, gentian, ice-blue,
jacinth, sea-blue, sky-blue,
watchet
08 baby blue, cerulean, dark blue,
mazarine, navy blue, Nile blue,
sapphire, Saxe blue
09 caerulean, royal blue, steel-blue,
turquoise
10 aquamarine, Berlin blue,
cornflower, kingfisher, Oxford
blue, periwinkle, petrol blue,
powder blue
11 duck-egg blue, lapis lazuli, nattier
blue, peacock-blue, ultramarine
12 air-force blue, dumortierite,

electric blue, midnight blue,
Prussian blue, Wedgwood blue
13 Cambridge blue, robin's-egg blue
15 lapis lazuli blue

## bluebottle

06 beadle 07 blawort, blewart, blowfly,
brommer 09 policeman

## blueprint

04 plan 05 draft, guide, model, pilot
06 design, scheme, sketch 07 outline,
pattern, project 08 strategy
09 archetype, cyanotype, programme,
prototype 14 representation

## blues

05 dumps, gloom 06 cafard 07 sadness
08 doldrums, glumness, miseries
09 dejection, moodiness
10 depression, gloominess,
melancholy 11 despondency,
unhappiness

## bluff

03 lie 04 bank, brow, crag, fake, fool,
open, peak, sham, show 05 blind,
blunt, cliff, feign, feint, frank, fraud,
ridge, scarp, surly, trick 06 candid,
deceit, delude, direct, escarp, genial,
hearty, height, humbug 07 affable,
bravado, deceive, leg-pull, mislead,
pretend 08 foreland, headland,
hoodwink, pretence 09 bamboozle,
deception, downright, four-flush, idle
boast, outspoken, precipice
10 blustering, escarpment,
promontory, subterfuge
11 braggadocio, good-natured, plain-
spoken 15 straightforward

## blunder

◇ *anagram indicator* 03 err 04 bish,
boob, flub, gaff, goof, slip 05 bevue,
boner, botch, break, error, fault, fluff,
gaffe 06 bêtise, booboo, bumble,
bungle, cock up, cock-up, goof up,
howler, mess up, muck up, muddle,
ricket, slip up, slip-up 07 bloomer,
clanger, faux pas, floater, go wrong,
mistake, screw up, stumble
08 flounder, get wrong, misjudge,
pratfall, solecism 09 mismanage,
oversight 10 inaccuracy 12 drop a
clanger, indiscretion, make a mistake,
miscalculate, misjudgement

## blunt

04 bald, bate, curt, dull, numb, rude,
worn 05 abate, allay, frank, stark, terse
06 abrupt, candid, dampen, deaden,
direct, honest, obtund, obtuse, rebate,
retund, soften, unedge, weaken
07 brusque, disedge, rounded,
stubbed, uncivil 08 edgeless, explicit,
hebetate, impolite, not sharp, tactless
09 alleviate, downright, outspoken,
pointless 10 forthright, point-blank
11 insensitive, plain-spoken,
unsharpened 12 anaesthetize
13 unceremonious 14 take the edge off
15 straightforward

## bluntly

06 rudely 07 frankly, roundly
08 candidly, directly 09 brusquely
10 explicitly, impolitely, point-blank,

tactlessly **12** forthrightly
**13** insensitively **15** unceremoniously

## blur
◇ *anagram indicator* **03** dim, fog **04** dull,
fuzz, haze, mask, mist, muzz, slur,
spot, veil **05** befog, blear, cloud,
mudge, smear, stain **06** blotch, darken,
mackle, muddle, smudge, soften
**07** becloud, blemish, conceal,
confuse, dimness, obscure
**09** confusion, disfigure, fuzziness,
make vague, obscurity **10** cloudiness
**14** indistinctness, make indistinct

## blurb
**04** copy, hype, puff **05** spiel
**12** commendation **13** advertisement

## blurred
◇ *anagram indicator* **03** dim **04** hazy, soft
**05** blear, faint, foggy, fuzzy, misty,
muzzy, vague, woozy **06** bleary,
cloudy **07** clouded, obscure, unclear
**08** confused **10** ill-defined, indistinct,
out of focus

## blurt
• **blurt out** **03** cry **04** blab, blat, gush,
leak, tell **05** plump, spout, utter **06** cry
out, let out, reveal **07** call out, divulge,
exclaim, let slip **08** disclose
**09** ejaculate **11** come out with **13** spill
the beans **15** give the game away

## blush
**03** red **04** glow **05** flush, go red, rouge
**06** colour, mantle, redden **07** crimson,
scarlet, turn red **08** colour up, rosiness
**09** reddening, ruddiness

## blushing
**03** red **04** rosy **06** modest **07** ashamed,
flushed, glowing, red face **08** confused
**09** rubescent **10** erubescent
**11** embarrassed **12** apple-cheeked

## bluster
**04** brag, crow, huff, rage, rant, roar
**05** bluff, boast, bully, storm, strut,
vaunt **06** hector, ruffle **07** bravado,
crowing, roister, royster, show off,
swagger, talk big **08** boasting,
harangue **11** braggadocio,
domineering, fanfaronade,
rodomontade

## blustery
**04** wild **05** gusty, windy **06** stormy
**07** squally, violent **10** boisterous,
swaggering **11** tempestuous

## boar
**03** hog **05** brawn **06** barrow, tusker
**07** sounder **08** sanglier

## board
**02** bd **04** beam, deal, food, grub, jury,
nosh, slab, slat, tray **05** catch, embus,
enter, get in, get on, meals, mount,
Ouija®, panel, plank, sheet
**06** embark, timber **07** council,
emplane, entrain, get into, rations
**08** advisers, trustees, victuals
**09** committee, directors, governors
**10** commission, head office,
management, provisions, step aboard,
sustenance **11** directorate **12** working
party **13** advisory group
• **board up** **04** seal, shut **05** close,

cover **06** shut up **07** close up, cover up
• **on board** **02** SS
• **put on board** **04** lade **06** embark
• **remove from board** **04** bear

## boarder
**02** PG **09** pensioner

## board game
*see* **game**

## boast
**03** gab, gem, joy **04** blow, brag, crow,
have, yelp **05** claim, crack, crake,
enjoy, glory, prate, pride, skite, strut,
swank, vapor, vaunt **06** avaunt,
bounce, hot air, vapour **07** big-note,
bluster, crowing, exhibit, possess,
show off, swagger, talk big, trumpet
**08** mouth off, sound off, talk tall,
treasure **09** gasconade, gasconism,
jactation, loudmouth, overstate,
vainglory **10** blustering, exaggerate,
self-praise **11** fanfaronade,
rodomontade **12** cry roast-meat
**13** overstatement **15** blow your own
horn, pride yourself on

## boastful
**03** big **04** vain **05** cocky, proud, windy
**06** hot-air, swanky **07** crowing
**08** arrogant, braggart, bragging,
glorious, immodest, puffed up
**09** bigheaded, blustrous, cock-a-hoop,
conceited, thrasonic **10** blusterous,
swaggering **11** egotistical, spread-
eagle, swell-headed, thrasonical
**12** self-glorious, vainglorious
**13** swollen-headed **14** self-flattering
• **boastful talk** **03** gas **05** mouth

## boastfully
**03** big **07** cockily, proudly
**09** crowingly **10** arrogantly
**11** conceitedly **13** egotistically
**14** vaingloriously

## boat
**03** tub
*See also* **sail; ship**

## boatman
**05** rower **06** bargee, sailor **07** oarsman
**08** ferryman, hoveller, voyageur,
waterman, water rat **09** gondolier,
oarswoman, yachtsman
**11** yachtswoman

## bob
**01** s **03** bow, dop, hod, hop, nod, tap
**04** dock, jerk, jolt, jump, leap, skip
**05** float **06** bobble, bounce, curtsy,
popple, quiver, Robert, spring, twitch,
wobble **08** shilling **09** oscillate
• **bob up** **04** rise **05** arise, pop up
**06** appear, arrive, crop up, emerge,
show up **07** surface **08** spring up
**11** materialize

## bobbin
**04** bone, pirn, reel **05** quill, spool

## bobby
*see* **police officer**

## bobsleigh run
**04** lauf

## bode
**03** bid **04** sign, warn **05** augur, dwelt,
offer **06** herald, waited **07** betoken,

endured, portend, predict, presage,
purport, signify **08** forebode, foreshow,
foretell, forewarn, indicate, intimate,
prophesy, remained, threaten
**09** adumbrate, foretoken
**10** foreshadow **13** prognosticate

## bodge
**04** flub, goof, mess, ruin **05** botch, fluff,
spoil **06** bungle, foul up, goof up, mess
up, muck up **07** blunder, louse up,
screw up **11** make a hash of

## bodice
**04** body **05** choli, gilet, jumps, waist
**06** basque, corset, halter **07** bustier,
corsage **08** camisole, jirkinet, overslip
**10** chemisette

## bodily
**04** real **05** as one, fully **06** actual,
carnal, in toto, wholly **07** en masse,
fleshly, totally **08** as a whole, concrete,
entirely, material, physical, tangible
**09** corporeal **10** altogether, completely
**11** substantial **12** collectively
*See also* **humour**

## body
◇ *anagram indicator* **03** bod, lot, mob,
nub **04** area, band, bloc, bouk, buik,
buke, bulk, clay, core, form, lich,
mass, soma **05** build, crowd, frame,
group, heart, range, shell, stiff, torso,
trunk **06** amount, cartel, casing,
corpse, extent, figure, kernel, throng,
volume, weight **07** anatomy, cadaver,
carcase, chassis, company, council,
density, essence, expanse, phalanx,
society, stretch **08** congress, dead
body, firmness, fullness, main part,
physique, quantity, richness, skeleton,
solidity **09** authority, framework,
multitude, structure, substance,
syndicate **10** collection **11** association,
central part, consistency, corporation,
largest part **12** organization
**13** confederation
• **body odour** **02** BO

## bodyguard
**02** SS **05** guard **06** minder **08** defender,
guardian **09** lifeguard, protector
**10** triggerman **11** Swiss Guards
**13** Schutzstaffel **15** praetorian guard

## boffin
**05** brain **06** expert, genius, wizard
**07** egghead, planner, thinker
**08** designer, engineer, inventor
**09** intellect, scientist **10** mastermind
**11** backroom-boy **12** intellectual

## bog
**02** WC **03** can, fen, lav, loo **04** dike,
dyke, john, kazi, mire, moss, quag,
sink, spew, spue, sump **05** dunny,
gents, karsy, karzy, khazi, lavvy,
marsh, privy, swamp, yarfa **06** carsey,
karsey, ladies', lavabo, morass,
muskeg, office, petary, slough, stodge,
throne, toilet, yarpha **07** cludgie,
latrine **08** bathroom, dunnakin,
quagmire, washroom, wetlands
**09** cloakroom, marshland, swampland
**10** facilities, quicksands
**11** convenience, water closet
**12** smallest room
• **bog down** **04** halt, mire, sink, trap

## boggle

**05** delay, stall, stick **06** deluge, hinder, hold up, impede, retard, slow up **07** set back **08** encumber, slow down **09** overwhelm
• **bog myrtle 04** gale **06** Myrica **09** sweet-gale
• **hole in bog 03** hag **04** hagg

## boggle

**03** jib **05** alarm, amaze, demur **06** bungle, marvel, wonder **07** astound, confuse, scruple, stagger, startle **08** bowl over, hesitate, surprise **09** objection, overwhelm **11** flabbergast

## boggy

**04** miry, oozy, soft **05** fenny, moory, mossy, muddy, soggy, spewy **06** marshy, quaggy, sodden, spongy, swampy **07** moorish, morassy, paludal, queachy, queechy **11** waterlogged

## bogus

◇ *anagram indicator* **03** bad **04** fake, sham **05** dummy, false, pseud, spoof **06** forged, phoney, pseudo **08** spurious **09** imitation **10** artificial, fraudulent **11** counterfeit, make-believe **13** disappointing

## bohemian

**04** arty, boho **06** exotic, hippie, way-out **07** beatnik, bizarre, drop-out, oddball, offbeat **08** artistic, original **09** eccentric **10** avant-garde, off-the-wall, unorthodox **11** alternative **12** trustafarian **13** nonconformist **14** unconventional

## bohrium

**02** Bh

## boil

◇ *anagram indicator* **03** jug **04** brew, cook, fizz, foam, fume, heat, leep, rage, rave, sore, stew **05** blain, botch, erupt, froth, steam, storm, ulcer **06** bubble, bunion, decoct, growth, gurgle, pimple, see red, seethe, simmer, tumour, wallop **07** abscess, anthrax, blister, explode, gumboil, parboil, pustule **08** furuncle, ganglion, swelling **09** blow a fuse, carbuncle, fulminate, gathering **10** effervesce, hit the roof **12** blow your top **12** fly into a rage, inflammation **13** come to the boil **14** bring to the boil **15** fly off the handle, go off the deep end
• **boil down 06** amount, digest, distil, reduce **07** abridge **08** abstract, condense **09** summarize **11** concentrate

## boiled

◇ *anagram indicator* **03** sod **06** sodden

## boiler

**06** kettle

## boiling

◇ *anagram indicator* **03** hot **05** angry, surge **06** baking, fuming, torrid **07** coction, enraged, flaming, furious **08** broiling, bubbling, gurgling, incensed, roasting, scalding, steaming **09** indignant, scorching, turbulent **10** blistering, ebullition, infuriated, sweltering **12** effervescent

## boisterous

◇ *anagram indicator* **04** loud, wild **05** noisy, randy, rough, rowdy **06** active, bouncy, lively, randie, stormy, unruly **07** laddish, riotous, romping **08** animated, roisting, roysting, spirited **09** clamorous, energetic, exuberant, goustrous, turbulent **10** disorderly, knockabout, rollicking, strepitoso, tumultuous **11** dithyrambic, hyperactive, rumbustious **12** obstreperous, rambunctious, unrestrained

## boisterously

**06** loudly, wildly **07** noisily, roughly, rowdily **08** actively **09** riotously **10** animatedly, spiritedly **11** clamorously, exuberantly, turbulently **12** tumultuously **13** energetically, hyperactively **14** obstreperously, unrestrainedly

## bold

**02** bf **04** free, loud, pert **05** brash, brave, heavy, saucy, showy, steep, thick, vivid **06** abrupt, brassy, brazen, bright, cheeky, daring, flashy, heroic, manful, plucky, strong **07** assured, defiant, forward, gallant, haughty, naughty, valiant **08** definite, distinct, fearless, impudent, insolent, intrepid, malapert, outgoing, spirited, striking, valorous **09** audacious, bald-faced, barefaced, chivalric, colourful, confident, dauntless, foolhardy, prominent, shameless, unabashed, undaunted **10** chivalrous, courageous, diastaltic, flamboyant, in-your-face, noticeable, pronounced **11** adventurous, bold as a lion, bold as brass, conspicuous, eye-catching, venturesome **12** enterprising, high-spirited, presumptuous
• **be bold 04** dare

## boldly

**06** crouse **07** bravely, vividly **08** brightly, daringly, pluckily, risoluto, strongly **09** valiantly **10** definitely, distinctly, fearlessly, heroically, intrepidly, strikingly **11** audaciously, confidently, prominently **12** courageously **13** adventurously

## Bolivia

**03** BOL

## bolshie

**04** rude **06** touchy **07** awkward, prickly, problem, stroppy **08** stubborn **09** difficult, irritable, obstinate, unhelpful **10** unpleasant **12** bloody-minded **13** oversensitive, unco-operative

## bolster

**03** aid, pad **04** help, prop, stay **05** boost, brace **06** assist, buoy up, firm up, pillow **07** augment, cushion, shore up, stiffen, support **08** buttress, maintain **09** Dutch wife, reinforce **10** invigorate, revitalize, strengthen, supplement

## bolt

**01** U **03** bar, fly, peg, pin, rat, ray, rod, run **04** cram, dart, dash, flee, gulp, lock, rush, slot, sneb, snib, stud, wolf

## bomb

**05** arrow, blaze, burst, catch, elope, flare, flash, gorge, latch, rivet, scoff, screw, shaft, shoot, spark, stuff **06** devour, escape, fasten, gobble, guzzle, hurtle, pintle, run off, secure, sperre, sprint, streak **07** abscond, run away, scarper **08** fastener, wolf down

## Boltzmann constant

**01** k

## bomb

◇ *anagram indicator* **03** egg **05** prang, speed **06** attack, blow up, device, mortar, strafe **07** bombard, destroy **09** bombshell, explosive **10** projectile

*Bombs include:*

**01** A, H
**02** V-1, V-2
**03** car
**04** aero, atom, buzz, dumb, fire, mine, MOAB, nail, pipe, time
**05** dirty, E-bomb, Mills, shell, smart, smoke, stink
**06** binary, candle, cobalt, drogue, flying, fusion, letter, parcel, petrol, radium, rocket
**07** bomblet, cluster, fission, grenade, missile, neutron, nuclear, plastic, tallboy, torpedo
**08** bouncing, firebomb, hydrogen, landmine
**09** doodlebug, Grand Slam, pineapple
**10** incendiary
**11** blockbuster, daisy-cutter, depth charge, penetration, sensor fuzed, stun grenade, thermobaric
**12** bunker buster, rifle grenade
**13** fragmentation, thermonuclear
**15** Molotov cocktail

## bombard

**04** bomb, pelt, raid **05** blast, blitz, flood, hound, pound, shell, stone, swamp **06** assail, attack, batter, bother, deluge, harass, mortar, pellet, pester, strafe, straff **07** besiege, torpedo **08** inundate **09** blackjack

## bombardment

**04** fire, flak, hail **05** blitz, salvo, stonk **06** attack **07** air raid, assault, barrage, bombing, stonker **08** hounding, pounding, shelling **09** besieging, bothering, cannonade, fusillade, harassing, onslaught, pestering, shellfire

## bombast

**03** pad **04** rant **05** stuff **06** hot air **07** bluster, fustian, heroics, inflate, padding **08** euphuism, inflated, stuffing **09** dithyramb, pomposity, verbosity, wordiness **10** sophomoric, turgidness **11** ampullosity **13** magniloquence **14** grandiloquence **15** pretentiousness

## bombastic

**04** tall **05** puffy, tumid, windy, wordy **06** turgid **07** bloated, fustian, pompous, verbose **08** affected, inflated **09** grandiose, high-flown **10** euphuistic, portentous, sophomoric **11** pretentious, spread-eagle **12** magniloquent, ostentatious, sophomorical **13** grandiloquent

## bomber
**01** B

*Bombers include:*

**03** B-10, B-17, B-19, B-52, MB-1
**04** dive
**05** Stuka
**06** Gotha G, Harris, Sukhoi
**07** Avenger, Heinkel, Junkers, stealth, suicide, Tupolev, Warthog
**08** Mitchell
**09** Lancaster, Liberator
**13** Superfortress
**14** Flying Fortress

## bona fide
**04** real, true **05** legal, valid **06** actual, dinkum, honest, kosher, lawful **07** genuine **09** authentic **10** legitimate **12** the real McCoy

## bonanza
**04** boon **07** godsend **08** blessing, windfall **12** stroke of luck, sudden wealth

## bond
**02** bd **03** gum, tie, vow **04** band, bind, cord, deal, fuse, glue, join, knot, link, pact, seal, ties, weld, word, yoke **05** chain, nexus, noose, paste, starr, stick, union, unite **06** attach, cement, copula, fasten, fetter, league, pledge, treaty **07** binding, connect, liaison, linkage, manacle, promise, rapport, shackle, statute, valence **08** affinity, contract, covenant, ligament, mateship, relation, vinculum, yearling **09** agreement, chemistry, debenture **10** attachment, connection, friendship, obligation **11** affiliation, transaction **12** relationship

## bondage
**04** yoke **06** thrall **07** serfdom, slavery **08** nativity, thraldom **09** captivity, restraint, servitude, thralldom, vassalage **10** subjection, villeinage **11** confinement, enslavement, subjugation **12** imprisonment, subservience **13** incarceration

## bone
**03** nab, tot **05** seize **06** bobbin

*Bones include:*

**01** T
**02** os
**03** hip, jaw, luz, rib
**04** back, coxa, knee, shin, ulna
**05** ankle, anvil, cheek, costa, femur, funny, hyoid, ilium, incus, jugal, pubis, skull, spine, talus, thigh, thumb, tibia, vomer, wrist
**06** breast, carpal, coccyx, collar, fibula, hammer, pecten, pelvis, radius, sacrum, saddle, stapes, tarsus
**07** cranium, ethmoid, humerus, ischium, kneecap, knuckle, malleus, ossicle, patella, phalanx, scapula, sternum, stirrup
**08** clavicle, lower jaw, mandible, parietal, scaphoid, shoulder, upper jaw, vertebra
**09** calcaneum, calcaneus, occipital, trapezium, zygomatic
**10** metacarpal, metatarsal
**12** pelvic girdle
**13** shoulder-blade

## bones
**02** Dr, GP, MO **03** doc **04** dice, ossa **06** doctor **08** skeleton

## bonfire
**04** pyre **08** bale-fire **09** feu de joie

## bonhomie
**08** sympathy **09** geniality **10** affability, amiability, good nature, tenderness **12** conviviality, friendliness **15** kind-heartedness, warm-heartedness

## bon mot
**04** quip **07** riposte **08** one-liner, repartee **09** wisecrack, witticism **10** pleasantry

## bonnet
**03** cap **04** hood, poke **06** kiss-me, toorie, tourie **08** balmoral, bongrace **11** kiss-me-quick
• **bonnet monkey** **04** zati

## bonny
**04** fair, fine **05** bonie, merry, plump **06** bonnie, cheery, comely, joyful, lovely, pretty **07** smiling **08** blooming, bouncing, cheerful, handsome **09** beautiful **10** attractive, sweetheart

## bonus
**03** tip **04** gain, gift, perk, plus **05** bribe, extra, prize **06** reward **07** benefit, handout, premium **08** dividend, gratuity **09** advantage, lagniappe **10** commission, honorarium, perquisite **14** fringe benefits

## bony
**04** lean, thin **05** drawn, gaunt, gawky, lanky **06** skinny **07** angular, osseous, scraggy, scrawny **08** gangling, rawboned, sclerous, skeletal **09** emaciated

## book
**01** b **02** bk **03** bag, lib, log, vol **04** text, tome, work **05** Bible, blame, enter, folio, order, tract **06** accuse, arrest, charge, engage, script, volume **07** arrange, booklet, charter, procure, reserve **08** accuse of, libretto, organize, schedule **09** programme **10** prearrange **11** publication

*Books include:*

**03** pad
**04** A to Z, bath, chap, cook, copy, days, hand, hymn, note, text, work, year
**05** album, atlas, audio, board, cloth, comic, diary, e-book, guide, novel, pop-up, scrap, story
**06** annual, gradus, hymnal, jotter, ledger, manual, missal, phrase, prayer, primer, sketch
**07** almanac, fiction, Filofax®, journal, lexicon, omnibus, picture, psalter
**08** exercise, grimoire, hardback, libretto, self-help, softback, thriller
**09** anthology, biography, catalogue, children's, detective, directory, gazetteer, paperback, reference, thesaurus
**10** bestseller, compendium, dictionary, large print, lectionary, manuscript
**11** coffee-table, concordance, instruction, travel guide
**12** encyclopedia
**13** penny dreadful, travel journal
**15** pocket companion

*See also* **apocryphal; Bible**
• **book in** **05** enrol **07** check in **08** register
• **book of rules** **03** pie, pye **07** ordinal **11** penitential

## bookbinding
**10** bibliopegy

*Bookbinding terms include:*

**03** aeg
**04** case, head, limp, tail, yapp
**05** bolts, hinge, spine
**06** boards, gather, jacket, lining, Linson®, sewing
**07** binding, buckram, drawn-on, flyleaf, headcap, morocco
**08** backbone, blocking, casing-in, doublure, drilling, endpaper, fore edge, hardback, headband, open-flat, shoulder, smashing, stamping, tailband
**09** backboard, book block, casebound, debossing, dust cover, embossing, full bound, half bound, loose-leaf, millboard, paperback, signature, soft-cover
**10** back lining, binder's die, front board, laminating, pasteboard, raised band, side-stitch, square back, stab-stitch, strawboard, varnishing, whole bound
**11** comb binding, ring binding, velo binding, wire binding, wiro binding
**12** all edges gilt, binder's board, binder's brass, cloth binding, flexi binding, notch binding, quarter bound, saddle-stitch, thread sewing
**13** back cornering, blind blocking, spiral binding, unsewn binding, wire stitching
**14** library binding, perfect binding
**15** adhesive binding, cloth-lined board, hot foil stamping

## booking
**11** appointment, arrangement, reservation

## bookish
**07** donnish, erudite, inkhorn, learned **08** academic, cultured, highbrow, lettered, literary, pedantic, studious, well-read **09** scholarly **10** scholastic **12** bluestocking, intellectual

## booklet
**06** folder, notice **07** handout, leaflet **08** brochure, circular, pamphlet **09** programme

## books
**02** bb, NT, OT **03** bks **07** ledgers, records **08** accounts **12** balance sheet

## boom
**03** jib **04** bang, clap, gain, grow, jump, leap, roar, roll, spar **05** blare, blast, boost, burst, crash, spurt, surge, swell **06** bellow, do well, expand, growth, rumble, thrive, upturn **07** advance, burgeon, develop, explode, prosper, resound, succeed, success, thunder, upsurge, upswing **08** escalate, flourish, increase, mushroom, progress, snowball **09** bombilate, bombinate, expansion, explosion, intensify, loud noise, resonance, skyrocket **10** escalation, strengthen **11** development, improvement, reverberate **13** reverberation

## boomerang
◇ *reversal indicator* **05** kiley, kylie **06** recoil **07** rebound, reverse **08** backfire, ricochet **10** bounce back, spring back, throw stick

## boon
**04** bene, gift, help, plus **05** bonus, grant **06** favour, jovial **07** benefit, godsend, present, request **08** blessing, gratuity, intimate, kindness, petition, windfall **09** advantage, convivial
• **boon companion** **06** cupman, Trojan **07** franion **09** confidant **10** best friend, confidante, dear friend **11** bosom friend, close friend **13** special friend

## boor
**03** hog, lob, oaf, oik, yob **04** clod, Jack, kern, lout, pleb, slob **05** chuff, clown, kerne, ocker, yahoo, yobbo, yokel **06** chough, keelie, rustic **07** Grobian, peasant **08** plebeian **09** barbarian, lager lout, vulgarian **10** clodhopper, philistine **14** country bumpkin

## boorish
**04** rude **05** borel, crass, crude, gross, gruff, ocker, rough, swain **06** borrel, coarse, jungli, lumpen, oafish, rustic, vulgar **07** borrell, ill-bred, loutish, uncouth **08** ignorant, impolite, swainish **09** unrefined **10** uneducated **11** clodhopping, ill-mannered, uncivilized

## boost
**03** aid, rap **04** boom, help, hype, lift, plug, rise, spur, wrap **05** put up, raise, steal **06** assist, expand, fillip, foster, play up, praise, talk up, uplift **07** advance, amplify, augment, bolster, develop, ego-trip, enhance, enlarge, further, improve, inspire, promote, support **08** addition, heighten, increase, maximize, shoplift, stimulus **09** advertise, encourage, expansion, increment, promotion, publicity, publicize, stimulate **10** assistance, potentiate, supplement **11** development, enhancement, enlargement, furtherance, improvement, inspiration **12** augmentation, shot in the arm **13** advertisement, amplification, encouragement

## boot
**04** kick **05** shove, trunk **06** profit **09** advantage

*Boots include:*

**03** gum, top, ugg **04** crow, half, jack, lace, moon, rock, snow **05** ankle, kamik, rugby, thigh, wader, welly **06** bootee, buskin, chukka, combat, Denver, finsko, galosh, golosh, hiking, jemima, mucluc, mukluk, riding **07** blucher, bottine, Chelsea, cracowe, finnsko, galoche, Hessian, walking **08** balmoral, bootikin, climbing, finnesko, football, high shoe, larrigan, muckluck, overshoe **09** scarpetto, Doc Marten® **10** wellington **13** beetle-crusher

• **boot out** **04** fire, sack, shed **05** eject, expel **06** lay off **07** dismiss, kick out, suspend **10** give notice **12** give the heave **13** make redundant
• **to boot** **03** too **06** as well **07** besides **10** in addition **14** into the bargain

## booth
**03** box, hut **05** crame, kiosk, stall, stand **06** bothan, carrel **07** cubicle **11** compartment, luckenbooth

## bootleg
**05** wrong **06** banned, barred, pirate **07** illegal, illicit, pirated, smuggle **08** criminal, outlawed, smuggled, unlawful **09** forbidden **10** prohibited, proscribed, black-market, interdicted **12** unauthorized **15** under-the-counter

## bootless
**04** vain **06** barren, futile **07** sterile, useless **09** fruitless, pointless **10** profitless, unavailing **11** ineffective **12** unprofitable, unsuccessful

## booty
**04** haul, loot, prey, swag **05** bribe, gains, prize, spoil **06** bottom, creach, creagh, shikar, spoils **07** pillage, plunder, profits, takings **08** pickings, purchase, winnings

## booze
**03** jar **04** grog, slug, tank **05** drink, juice, skink, tinct **06** fuddle, liquor, strunt, tiddly, tipple **07** alcohol, indulge, liqueur, spirits **08** stimulus **09** firewater, hard stuff, the bottle, the cratur **10** have a drink, intoxicant **11** jungle juice, strong drink, the creature **12** Dutch courage, hit the bottle **14** drink like a fish
*See also* **beer; cocktail; drink; liqueur; liquor; spirits; wine**

## boozer
**03** bar, inn, pub, sot **04** howf, lush, soak, wino **05** alkie, bloat, dipso, drunk, local, souse, toper **06** lounge, saloon, sponge, tavern **07** Bacchus, drinker, tippler, tosspot **08** drunkard, habitual, hostelry **09** alcoholic, inebriate, lounge bar **10** wine-bibber **11** dipsomaniac, hard drinker, public house **12** heavy drinker, watering-hole

## boozy
◇ *anagram indicator*
*See* **drunken**

## bop
**03** hop, jig **04** blow, jive, jump, leap, rock, spin, sway **05** dance, stomp, twirl, twist, whirl **06** boogie, gyrate, hoof it, strike **09** pirouette, shake a leg **11** move to music

## borage
**07** alkanet, anchusa, bugloss, comfrey, manjack, myosote **08** gromwell, lungwort, myosotis, sebesten **09** stickseed, Symphytum **10** dog's-tongue, heliotrope, Pulmonaria **11** cool-tankard, oyster plant **12** hound's-tongue, lithospermum **13** viper's bugloss

## border
**03** bed, hem, mat, rim **04** abut, bank, bord, brim, cost, curb, dado, edge, join, kerb, limb, line, list, mark, mete, orle, rand, roon, rund, side, trim, welt **05** apron, board, boord, borde, bound, brink, coast, coste, flank, frill, limit, march, skirt, swage, touch, verge **06** accost, adjoin, boorde, bounds, cotise, frieze, fringe, margin, purfle, screed, trench, weeper **07** accoast, bordure, confine, connect, cottise, enclose, engrail, impinge, marches, margent, selvage, valance, valence, wayside **08** be next to, boundary, confines, dentelle, emborder, frontier, furbelow, headland, roadside, selvedge, surround, trimming **09** cartouche, guilloche, lie next to, perimeter, periphery, state line **10** borderline, limitrophe, marchlands **11** demarcation **12** be adjacent to, circumscribe **13** circumference

*Borders and boundaries include:*

**07** Rubicon **09** Green Line **10** Berlin Wall, no-man's-land **11** Iron Curtain, Maginot Line **13** Bamboo Curtain **14** Mason-Dixon line **15** cordon sanitaire

• **border on** **07** verge on **08** approach, be almost, be nearly, resemble **13** approximate to **14** be tantamount to
• **borders of** ◇ *ends selection indicator* **08** purlieus

## borderline
**04** iffy, line **05** limit **06** divide **08** boundary, division, doubtful, marginal **09** uncertain **10** ambivalent, indecisive, indefinite **11** problematic **12** dividing-line **13** indeterminate **15** demarcation line, differentiation
*See also* **border**

## bore
**03** awl, dig, irk, sap, sat, tap, vex **04** bare, bind, drag, eger, jade, mine,

pain, sink, tire **05** annoy, drill, eager, eagre, ennui, grind, weary, worry **06** bother, burrow, dig out, hollow, jostle, pall on, pierce, tunnel **07** exhaust, fatigue, sondage, trouble, turn off, turn-off, wear out **08** headache, irritate, nuisance, puncture **09** hollow out, make tired, penetrate, perforate, terebrant, terebrate, undermine **11** be tedious to, send to sleep **13** pain in the neck **15** bore the pants off
• **enlarge bore** **04** ream, rime

**bored**
**05** fed up, tired **06** ennuyé, in a rut **07** ennuied, wearied **09** exhausted, turned off, unexcited **10** bored stiff, brassed off, browned off, cheesed off **12** bored to tears, sick and tired, uninterested

**boredom**
**05** ennui **06** acedia, apathy, tedium **07** humdrum, malaise, taedium, vapours **08** dullness, flatness, monotony, sameness **09** weariness **11** frustration, tediousness **12** listlessness **14** world-weariness

**boring**
**03** dry **04** dull, flat, slow, tedy **05** dully, ho-hum, samey, stale, trite **06** draggy, dreary, jejune, stupid, tiring **07** humdrum, insipid, mundane, prosaic, routine, tedious **08** tiresome, unvaried **10** long-winded, monotonous, uneventful, unexciting, uninspired **11** commonplace, repetitious, stultifying, uninspiring **13** unimaginative, uninteresting **14** soul-destroying
• **boring piece** **05** drill

**born**
**01** b, n **02** né **03** nat, née **05** natus

**boron**
**01** B

**borough**
**03** bor **04** area, port, town **05** borgo, burgh **06** parish **08** district **09** community **12** constituency
*See also* **London; New York**

**borrow**
**03** use **04** draw, hire, rent, take **05** adopt, cadge, lease, lever, usurp **06** derive, obtain, pledge, scunge, sponge, surety, take up **07** acquire, charter **08** scrounge, take over **10** have on loan, take on loan **11** appropriate **12** have the use of, take out a loan **14** use temporarily

**borrowing**
**03** IOU, use **04** debt, hire, loan **06** calque, rental **07** charter, leasing **08** adoption, loan-word, takeover **10** derivation **11** acquisition **12** temporary use **15** loan-translation

**Bosnia and Herzegovina**
**03** BIH

**bosom**
**03** pap, tit **04** boob, boon, bust, core, dear **05** booby, chest, close, diddy, heart, midst **06** breast, centre, desire,

loving **07** breasts, devoted, shelter **08** faithful, intimate **09** sanctuary **10** protection **12** confidential

**boss**
◇ *anagram indicator* **03** cow, don, gov, guv **04** calf, head, knob, knot, stud, umbo **05** bully, chief, empty, jewel, owner, stock **06** bigwig, gaffer, hollow, honcho, leader, manage, master, oubaas, pellet, serang, top dog, top man **07** cacique, captain, cazique, control, foreman, manager, mistake, supremo **08** browbeat, bulldoze, bull's-eye, chairman, director, dominate, domineer, employer, governor, omphalos, overseer, superior, top woman **09** big cheese, excellent, executive, top banana, tyrannize **10** chairwoman, head serang, order about, push around, supervisor **11** chairperson, head sherang, order around **12** give orders to **13** administrator, lay down the law **14** superintendent

**bossiness**
**07** tyranny **09** autocracy, despotism **13** assertiveness, imperiousness **14** high-handedness

**bossy**
**03** cow **04** calf **06** lordly **08** despotic, exacting **09** assertive, demanding, imperious, insistent **10** autocratic, dominating, high-handed, oppressive, tyrannical **11** dictatorial, domineering, overbearing **13** authoritarian

**botany**
**03** bot **09** phytology **11** phytography

*Botanists include:*

**03** **Mee** (Margaret Ursula), **Ray** (John)
**04** **Bary** (Heinrich Anton de), **Bose** (Sir Jagadis Chandra), **Cohn** (Ferdinand Julius), **Dahl** (Anders), **Gray** (Asa)
**05** **Banks** (Sir Joseph), **Brown** (Robert), **Fuchs** (Leonhart), **Hales** (Stephen), **Sachs** (Julius von), **Vries** (Hugo de)
**06** **Biffen** (Sir Rowland Harry), **Carver** (George Washington), **Haller** (Albrecht von), **Hooker** (Sir Joseph Dalton), **Hudson** (William), **Mendel** (Gregor Johann), **Nägeli** (Karl Wilhelm von), **Torrey** (John)
**07** **Bartram** (John), **Bellamy** (David), **Bentham** (George), **De Vries** (Hugo Marie), **Pfeffer** (Wilhelm), **Tansley** (Sir Arthur George), **Vavilov** (Nikolai)
**08** **Blackman** (Frederick Frost), **Candolle** (Augustin Pyrame de), **Linnaeus** (Carolus)
**09** **Boerhaave** (Hermann), **Schleiden** (Matthias Jakob)
**10** **Camerarius** (Rudolph Jacob), **Hofmeister** (Wilhelm Friedrich Benedikt), **Pringsheim** (Nathaniel)

**botch**
◇ *anagram indicator* **03** mar, mux **04** boil, flop, flub, goof, hash, mess, muff, ruin, sore **05** bodge, farce, fluff, patch, spoil **06** bungle, clatch, cock up, cock-up, foul up, goof up, mess up, muck up, muddle, pimple

**07** blemish, blunder, butcher, clamper, failure, louse up, screw up **08** shambles **09** mismanage **11** make a hash of, make a mess of, miscarriage **13** make a bad job of

**both**
**04** each **06** as well, the two **07** the pair

**bother**
◇ *anagram indicator* **03** ado, bug, irk, nag, vex **04** drat, fash, fuss, pest **05** aggro, alarm, annoy, deave, deeve, grief, grind, pains, tease, upset, worry **06** bovver, bustle, dismay, effort, flurry, harass, hassle, molest, pester, plague, put out, rumpus, shtook, shtuck, strain, unrest **07** concern, disturb, fluster, perplex, problem, schtook, schtuck, trouble **08** disorder, distress, exertion, fighting, irritate, nuisance, vexation **09** aggravate, annoyance, incommode **10** difficulty, irritation **11** disturbance **12** make an effort **13** inconvenience, make the effort, pain in the neck **14** think necessary **15** concern yourself

**bothersome**
**05** pesky **06** boring, vexing **07** brickle, irksome, tedious **08** annoying, fashious, tiresome **09** laborious, vexatious, wearisome **10** irritating **11** aggravating, distressing, infuriating, troublesome **12** exasperating, inconvenient

**Botswana**
**02** BW, RB **03** BWA

**bottle**
◇ *anagram indicator* ◇ *hidden indicator* **03** bot **04** grit, guts **05** nerve, spunk **06** daring, valour **07** bravery, courage **08** boldness **09** container **11** intrepidity **12** Dutch courage

*Bottles include:*

**03** bed, gas, ink, pig
**04** beer, case, codd, jack, junk, mick, milk, tear, vial, wash, wine
**05** bidon, cruet, cruse, dumpy, flask, gourd, Klein, phial, scent, snuff, water
**06** carafe, carboy, cutter, feeder, fiasco, flacon, flagon, hottie, inkpot, lagena, magnum, poison, pooter, siphon, stubby, syphon, Woulfe
**07** amphora, ampulla, costrel, feeding, flacket, pilgrim, pitcher, squeezy, sucking, torpedo, vinegar, washing
**08** calabash, decanter, demijohn, hip flask, hot-water, magnetic, medicine, screwtop, smelling, weighing
**09** Aristotle
**10** apothecary, lachrymary, Winchester
**11** vinaigrette, water bouget
**12** Bologna phial, lachrymatory, Thermos® flask

*See also* **wine**
• **bottle up** **04** curb, hide **06** cork up, shut in **07** conceal, confine, contain, enclose, inhibit, repress **08** disguise, hold back, keep back,

restrain, restrict, suppress **11** keep in check

## bottleneck
**05** block **06** hold-up **07** snarl-up
**08** blockage, clogging, gridlock, obstacle **09** narrowing **10** congestion, traffic jam **11** obstruction, restriction
**12** constriction

## bottom
◇ *tail selection down indicator* **03** ass, bed, bum, end **04** base, butt, coit, foot, prat, rear, rump, seat, sill, sole, tail, tush **05** basis, batty, booty, botty, floor, lower, nadir, quoit, tushy **06** behind, depths, far end, fundus, ground, heinie, lowest, plinth, seabed, tushie
**07** bedrock, staddle, support
**08** backside, buttocks, pedestal, sea floor **09** posterior, undermost, underside **10** foundation, underneath
**11** farthest end, furthest end, lowest level **12** substructure, underpinning
*See also* **buttocks**

## bottomless
◇ *tail deletion down indicator* **04** deep
**07** abysmal, abyssal **08** infinite, profound **09** boundless, depthless, limitless, subjacent, unfounded, unlimited, unplumbed **10** fathomless, unbottomed, unfathomed
**11** measureless **12** immeasurable, unfathomable **13** inexhaustible

## bough
**04** limb **06** branch **07** gallows, roughie

## bought
**04** coft

## boulder
**04** rock **05** stone **06** gibber **07** bowlder
**10** niggerhead

## boulevard
**04** Blvd, Boul, mall, road **05** drive
**06** avenue, parade, street **08** corniche, prospect **09** promenade
**12** thoroughfare

## bounce
**02** go **03** bob, dap, lie, zip **04** bang, beat, give, jump, leap, stot, thud
**05** boast, boing, boink, bound, pitch, stoit, styte, throw **06** energy, morgay, recoil, spring, vigour **07** dogfish, rebound **08** boasting, dynamism, ricochet, vitality, vivacity
**09** animation, dismissal **10** ebullience, elasticity, exaggerate, exuberance, get-up-and-go, liveliness, resilience, spring back **11** springiness
**12** spiritedness
• **bounce back** **07** improve, recover
**09** get better **13** make a comeback
**15** get back to normal

## bouncer
**03** dud **04** liar **05** bully **06** bumper
**10** chucker-out

## bouncing
◇ *anagram indicator* **05** bonny **06** hearty, lively, robust, strong **07** healthy
**08** blooming, thriving, vigorous
**09** energetic, walloping

## bouncy
◇ *anagram indicator* **04** spry **05** alive

**06** active, lively, spongy **07** dynamic, elastic, rubbery, springy **08** flexible, spirited, stretchy, vigorous
**09** energetic, resilient, sprightly, vivacious **11** full of beans

## bound
◇ *containment indicator* **02** bd **03** bob, hop, lep, off **04** curb, edge, held, jump, leap, line, mere, skip, sten, stot, sure, tied, tyde **05** brink, caper, check, dance, fated, fixed, flank, frisk, going, limit, off to, roped, scoup, scowp, skelp, skirt, sling, spang, stend, sworn, vault, verge **06** border, bounce, cavort, coming, doomed, forced, fringe, frolic, gambol, headed, hurdle, lashed, liable, limits, lollop, margin, prance, spring, tied up **07** affined, certain, chained, clamped, confine, contain, control, enclose, galumph, gambado, heading, obliged, outline, pledged, secured, trussed **08** articled, attached, bandaged, beholden, confines, definite, destined, fastened, fettered, gallumph, handfast, moderate, regulate, required, restrain, restrict, shackled, strapped, surround, tethered
**09** committed, compelled, duty-bound, extremity, perimeter, restraint
**10** borderline, covenanted, limitation, proceeding, restricted, travelling
**11** constrained, demarcation, on your way to, restriction, termination
**12** circumscribe **13** circumference
• **bound up with** **09** related to
**10** linked with, tied up with
**11** dependent on **12** involved with
**13** connected with **14** associated with, hand in hand with

## boundary
**02** IV, VI **03** six **04** edge, four, goal, gole, limb, line, list, mark, mere, mete, pale, term **05** bourn, brink, limes, limit, march, meith, score, verge **06** border, bounds, bourne, fringe, limits, margin
**07** barrier, confine, marches, Rubicon, surface **08** confines, frontier
**09** extremity, parameter, perimeter, periphery **10** borderline
**11** demarcation, termination **15** point of no return
*See also* **border**

## bounded
**05** edged **07** cramped, defined, limited
**08** bordered, confined, enclosed, hemmed in, walled in **09** delimited, encircled **10** controlled, demarcated, restrained, restricted, surrounded
**11** encompassed **13** circumscribed

## bounder
**03** cad, cur, pig, rat, roo **04** euro
**05** cheat, knave, rogue, swine
**06** hopper, jumper, rotter **07** dastard, wallaby **08** blighter, dirty dog
**09** miscreant **10** blackguard

## boundless
**04** vast **06** untold **07** endless, immense
**08** infinite, unending **09** countless, limitless, shoreless, unbounded, unlimited **10** numberless, unconfined, unflagging **11** everlasting, illimitable, innumerable, measureless, never-

ending **12** immeasurable, incalculable, interminable **13** indefatigable, inexhaustible

## bounds
◇ *ends selection indicator* **05** edges, scope **06** limits **07** borders, fringes, marches, margins **08** confines
**09** perimeter, periphery **10** boundaries, parameters **11** extremities
**12** demarcations, restrictions
**13** circumference
• **out of bounds** **02** OB **04** tapu
**05** taboo **06** banned, barred
**09** forbidden, off limits **10** disallowed, not allowed, prohibited

## bountiful
**05** ample **06** lavish **07** copious, liberal, profuse **08** abundant, generous, princely, prolific **09** boundless, bounteous, exuberant, luxuriant, plenteous, plentiful **10** munificent, open-handed, ungrudging, unstinting
**11** magnanimous, overflowing

## bounty
**03** tip **04** gift **05** bonus, grant **06** reward
**07** charity, premium, present
**08** donation, gratuity, kindness, largesse **09** allowance **10** almsgiving, generosity, liberality, recompense
**11** beneficence, magnanimity, munificence **12** philanthropy

## bouquet
**04** nose, posy **05** aroma, bunch, odour, scent, smell, spray **06** eulogy, favour, honour, praise, wreath **07** corsage, garland, nosegay, perfume, tribute
**08** accolade, approval **09** fragrance, redolence **10** buttonhole, compliment
**11** boutonnière **12** commendation, felicitation, pat on the back
**15** congratulations, odoriferousness

## bourgeois
**04** dull **05** banal, trite **06** square
**07** humdrum **08** ordinary
**09** hidebound, Pooterish **10** capitalist, conformist, pedestrian, uncreative, uncultured, uninspired, unoriginal
**11** Biedermeier, commonplace, middle-class, traditional
**12** conservative, conventional
**13** materialistic, unadventurous, unimaginative **15** money-orientated

## bout
**02** go **03** fit, jag, run **04** bend, bust, dose, fall, game, heat, lush, sesh, term, time, turn **05** binge, boose, booze, bouse, brash, burst, drunk, fight, match, round, set-to, spasm, spell, spree, stint, touch, veney, venue
**06** attack, battle, beer-up, bottle, course, fuddle, period, screed, venewe
**07** booze-up, carouse, contest, session, splurge, stretch, wassail, wrestle
**08** struggle **09** encounter
**10** engagement, makunouchi
**11** competition

## bovine
**04** dull, dumb, slow **05** dense, thick
**06** stupid **07** cowlike, doltish **09** dim-witted **10** cattlelike, slow-witted
• **bovine animals** **04** cows, neat
**06** cattle

## bow

**03** arc, bob, nod, tie, yew **04** arch, arco, beak, beck, bend, duck, eugh, head, jook, jouk, knot, loop, lout, lowt, move, prow, ring, stem **05** crook, crush, curve, defer, dicky, drail, front, slope, stick, stoop, yield **06** accede, accept, circle, comply, crouch, curtsy, dickey, dickie, give in, humble, kowtow, salaam, subdue, submit **07** bending, concede, conquer, consent, incline, namaste, rostrum, succumb **08** forepart, namaskar, vanquish **09** acquiesce, genuflect, give way to, humiliate, lavaliere, obeisance, overpower, subjugate, surrender **10** capitulate, lavallière, salutation **11** fiddlestick, genuflexion, inclination, prostration **12** dorsiflexion **13** make obeisance **15** acknowledgement

• **bow out** **04** quit **05** leave **06** defect, desert, give up, resign, retire **07** abandon, back out, pull out **08** step down, withdraw **09** stand down **10** chicken out
• **part of bow** **03** nut **04** frog, heel, luff
• **with bow** **04** arco

## bowdlerize

**03** cut **04** edit **05** purge **06** censor, excise, modify, purify **07** clean up, expunge **09** expurgate **10** blue-pencil

## bowels

**04** core, guts **05** belly, colon, heart **06** cavity, centre, depths, inside, middle **07** innards, insides, viscera **08** entrails, interior **09** entralles **10** intestines

## bower

**03** bay **05** arbor **06** alcove, arbour, grotto, recess **07** retreat, shelter **09** sanctuary

## bowl

**03** cap, cog, pan **04** caup, dish, hurl, race, roll, rush, sink, spin, wood **05** basin, cogie, fling, hurry, joram, jorum, mazer, motor, pitch, speed, tazza, throw, whirl **06** beaker, bicker, career, coggie, crater, goblet, krater, piggin, propel, rotate, vessel **07** brimmer, cage-cup, chalice, écuelle, revolve **08** jeroboam, monteith **09** container, porringer, posset cup, pottinger **10** receptacle **11** fingerglass **12** move steadily
• **bowled** **01** b
• **bowl over** **03** wow **04** fell, stun **05** amaze, floor, shock **06** topple **07** astound, stagger, startle **08** astonish, push into, surprise **09** dumbfound, knock down, overwhelm, unbalance **11** flabbergast **12** affect deeply **14** impress greatly

## bowler

**03** hat **04** skip **05** Derby **06** pot hat, seamer **07** Christy, hard hat, spinner **08** Christie

## box

◊ *containment indicator* **02** TV **03** ark, dan, hit, pew, pix, pyx, urn **04** butt, case, cuff, etui, fist, fund, inro, loge, mill, pack, slap, slug, sock, spar, tele,

wrap **05** bijou, chest, clout, fight, lodge, punch, pyxis, telly, thump, whack **06** batter, buffet, carton, casket, coffin, encase, packet, parcel, strike, wallop **07** coffret, package, present **09** baignoire, container **10** receptacle, television
• **box in** **04** cage, trap **05** hem in **06** bail up, coop up, corner, shut in **07** block in, confine, contain, enclose, fence in **08** imprison, restrain, restrict, surround **09** cordon off **12** circumscribe

## boxer

**03** ham, pug **07** cruiser, fighter **08** pugilist, southpaw **12** prizefighter **15** sparring partner

*Boxers, managers and promoters include:*

**03** **Ali** (Muhammad)
**04** **Benn** (Nigel), **Clay** (Cassius), **Haye** (David), **Khan** (Amir), **King** (Don)
**05** **Bruno** (Frank), **Duran** (Roberto), **Hamed** ('Prince' Naseem), **Lewis** (Lennox), **Louis** (Joe), **Moore** (Archie), **Tyson** (Mike)
**06** **Cooper** (Henry), **Dundee** (Angelo), **Eubank** (Chris), **Holmes** (Larry), **Liston** (Sonny), **Spinks** (Leon)
**07** **Dempsey** (Jack), **Foreman** (George), **Frazier** (Joe), **Leonard** (Sugar Ray)
**08** **Harrison** (Audley), **Marciano** (Rocky), **McGuigan** (Barry), **Robinson** (Sugar Ray)
**09** **Armstrong** (Henry), **Holyfield** (Evander), **Honeyghan** (Lloyd)
**11** **Fitzsimmons** (Bob), **Queensberry** (Sir John Sholto Douglas, Marquis of)

## boxing

◊ *hidden indicator* **04** ring **06** savate **08** fighting, pugilism, sparring **10** fisticuffs, infighting, the science **11** the noble art **13** prizefighting **15** the noble science
*See also* **sport**

*Professional boxing weight divisions include:*

**09** flyweight
**11** heavyweight, lightweight, strawweight
**12** bantamweight, middleweight, welterweight
**13** cruiserweight, featherweight, mini flyweight, minimum weight
**14** light flyweight, super flyweight
**15** junior flyweight
• **boxing match** **04** bout, mill, spar **10** glove-fight, prizefight

## boy

**03** bub, cub, kid, lad, son, tad **04** boyo, loon, lown, male, tama **05** bubby, bucko, child, gilpy, groom, knave, lowne, sprog, youth **06** chield, chokra, chummy, fellow, garçon, junior, loonie, nickum, nipper, shaver **07** galopin, gorsoon, gossoon **08** manchild, spalpeen, teenager, young man **09** dandiprat, dandyprat, Jack-a-Lent, schoolboy, stripling, youngster

**10** adolescent, knave-bairn **11** guttersnipe, kinchin-cove **14** whippersnapper

*Boys' names include:*

**02** Al, Cy, Ed, Ik, Jo
**03** Abe, Alf, Ali, Asa, Bat, Baz, Ben, Bob, Dai, Dan, Deb, Dee, Del, Den, Des, Dev, Dob, Don, Gay, Gaz, Gil, Gus, Guy, Hew, Huw, Ian, Ike, Iky, Ira, Ivo, Jay, Jem, Jim, Joe, Jon, Jos, Ken, Kim, Kit, Lal, Lee, Len, Leo, Lew, Mat, Max, Nat, Ned, Nye, Pat, Pip, Rab, Rae, Ray, Reg, Rex, Rob, Rod, Ron, Roy, Sam, Sim, Sol, Tam, Ted, Tim, Tom, Val, Vic, Viv, Wat, Wyn, Zia
**04** Adam, Adil, Alan, Alec, Aled, Alex, Algy, Alun, Amin, Andy, Anil, Arch, Arun, Bart, Bert, Bill, Bram, Bryn, Carl, Ceri, Chad, Chae, Chay, Clem, Colm, Dave, Davy, Dean, Dewi, Dick, Dirk, Doug, Drew, Eddy, Egon, Eoin, Eric, Eryl, Euan, Evan, Ewan, Ewen, Ezra, Finn, Fred, Gabi, Gary, Gaye, Gene, Glen, Glyn, Gwyn, Hani, Hank, Hari, Hope, Huey, Hugh, Hugo, Iain, Ifor, Ivan, Ivon, Ivor, Jack, Jake, Jeff, Jock, Joel, Joey, John, Josh, Joss, Jude, Jule, Karl, Kirk, Kurt, Liam, Luke, Mark, Matt, Mick, Mike, Neal, Neil, Nick, Noam, Noel, Omar, Owen, Ozzy, Paul, Pete, Phil, Rana, Ravi, Raza, René, Rhys, Rick, Rolf, Rory, Ross, Ryan, Saul, Sean, Seth, Siôn, Theo, Thos, Toby, Tony, Trev, Umar, Walt, Will, Yves, Zach, Zack
**05** Aaron, Abd-al, Abdul, Abram, Adeel, Adnan, Ahmad, Ahmed, Aidan, Aiden, Alfie, Allan, Allen, Alwin, Alwyn, Amrit, Andie, Angel, Angus, Anwar, Archy, Arran, Barry, Basil, Bazza, Benny, Billy, Bobby, Boris, Brent, Brett, Brian, Bruce, Bruno, Bryan, Bunny, Cahal, Calum, Cecil, Chaim, Chris, Chuck, Claud, Clint, Clive, Clyde, Colin, Colum, Conor, Corin, Cosmo, Craig, Cyril, Cyrus, Damon, Danny, David, Davie, Denis, Denny, Denys, Derek, Dicky, Dilip, Dipak, Donal, Duane, Dwane, Dylan, Eddie, Edgar, Edwin, Elroy, Elton, Elvis, Elwyn, Emlyn, Emrys, Enoch, Ernie, Errol, Farid, Faruq, Felix, Fionn, Floyd, Frank, Gabby, Gamal, Garry, Gavin, Geoff, Gerry, Giles, Glenn, Gopal, Hamza, Harry, Harun, Hasan, Haydn, Henry, Homer, Howel, Humph, Husni, Hywel, Idris, Ieuan, Inigo, Isaac, Jacob, Jamal, James, Jamie, Jamil, Jared, Jason, Jerry, Jesse, Jimmy, Jools, Kamal, Kasim, Keith, Kelly, Kenny, Kerry, Kevan, Kevin, Kiran, Kumar, Lance, Larry, Leigh, Lenny, Leroy, Lewie, Lewis, Linus, Lloyd, Logan, Lorne, Louie,

Louis, Lucas, Madoc, Manny,
Micky, Miles, Moray, Moses,
Moshe, Mungo, Murdo, Myles,
Neale, Neddy, Niall, Nicky,
Nicol, Nigel, Ollie, Orson, Oscar,
Ozzie, Paddy, Patsy, Percy, Perry,
Peter, Piers, Qasim, Rajiv, Ralph,
Randy, Ricky, Roald, Robin,
Roddy, Roger, Rowan, Rufus,
Sacha, Salim, Sammy, Sandy,
Sasha, Scott, Shane, Shaun,
Shawn, Silas, Simon, Solly, Steve,
Sunil, Taffy, Tariq, Teddy, Terry,
Tommy, Tudor, Ulric, Ultan,
Vijay, Vinay, Waldo, Walid,
Wally, Wasim, Wayne, Willy,
Wynne

**06** Adrian, Albert, Alexei, Alexej,
Alexis, Alfred, Andrew, Antony,
Archie, Arnold, Arthur, Ashley,
Ashraf, Aubrey, Austin, Barney,
Benjie, Bernie, Bertie, Bharat,
Billie, Blaise, Bobbie, Callum,
Calvin, Caspar, Cathal, Cedric,
Ciaran, Clancy, Claude, Clovis,
Colley, Connor, Conrad, Dafydd,
Damian, Damien, Daniel,
Darren, Declan, Deepak, Delroy,
Dennis, Denzil, Dermot, Deryck,
Devdan, Dicken, Dickie, Dickon,
Dilwyn, Dobbin, Donald,
Donnie, Dougal, Dudley,
Dugald, Duggie, Duncan, Dustin,
Eamonn, Eamunn, Edmund,
Edward, Ernest, Esmond, Eugene,
Faisal, Fareed, Faysal, Fergus,
Finbar, Fingal, Finlay, Finley,
Fintan, Freddy, Gareth, Garret,
George, Georgy, Gerald, Gerard,
Gerrie, Gideon, Gobind, Gordon,
Govind, Graeme, Graham,
Gussie, Hamish, Harold, Haroun,
Harvey, Hassan, Hayden,
Haydon, Hector, Herbie, Hervey,
Hilary, Horace, Howard, Howell,
Hubert, Hughie, Husain, Isaiah,
Iseult, Ismail, Israel, Jarvis, Jasper,
Jeremy, Jerome, Jervis, Jethro,
Jimmie, Jolyon, Jordan, Joseph,
Joshua, Julian, Julius, Justin,
Kelvin, Kennie, Kieran, Kieron,
Laurie, Lawrie, Lennie, Leslie,
Lester, Lionel, Lorcan, Lucius,
Luther, Lynsey, Magnus,
Mahmud, Marcel, Marcus,
Marlon, Martin, Martyn, Marvin,
Melvin, Melvyn, Mervyn, Milton,
Morgan, Morris, Murray, Nathan,
Neddie, Nichol, Ninian, Norman,
Oliver, Osbert, Oswald, Pascal,
Pearce, Philip, Pierce, Rajesh,
Randal, Ranulf, Reggie, Reuben,
Richie, Robbie, Robert, Rodney,
Roland, Ronald, Rudolf, Rupert,
Saleem, Samuel, Sanjay, Seamas,
Seamus, Seumas, Shamus, Sharif,
Sidney, Sorley, Steven, Stevie, St
John, Stuart, Sydney, Teddie,
Thomas, Timmie, Tobias, Trevor,
Tyrone, Vernon, Victor, Vikram,
Virgil, Vivian, Vyvian, Vyvyan,
Walter, Willie, Xavier

**07** Abraham, Alister, Ambrose,
Aneurin, Anthony, Auberon,

Barnaby, Bernard, Bertram,
Brendan, Chandra, Charles,
Charley, Charlie, Christy,
Clement, Crispin, Derrick,
Desmond, Dominic, Douglas,
Eustace, Feargal, Finbarr, Francie,
Francis, Frankie, Freddie, Gabriel,
Geordie, Georgie, Geraint,
Gervase, Gilbert, Godfrey,
Grahame, Gwillym, Herbert,
Humphry, Hussain, Hussein,
Ibrahim, Isadore, Isidore, Isodore,
Jeffrey, Johnnie, Kenneth, Killian,
Krishna, Lachlan, Leonard,
Leopold, Lindsay, Lindsey,
Ludovic, Malcolm, Matthew,
Maurice, Michael, Murdoch,
Mustafa, Neville, Nicolas,
Orlando, Patrick, Peredur, Phillip,
Quentin, Quintin, Quinton,
Randall, Randolf, Ranulph,
Raymond, Reynold, Richard,
Rowland, Rudolph, Russell,
Shankar, Shelley, Solomon,
Stanley, Stephen, Stewart,
Terence, Timothy, Torquil,
Tristan, Vaughan, Vincent,
Wilfred, Wilfrid, William,
Winston, Zachary

**08** Alasdair, Alastair, Algernon,
Alistair, Augustus, Barnabas,
Benedick, Benedict, Benjamin,
Beverley, Christie, Clarence,
Clifford, Crispian, Cuthbert,
Dominick, Emmanuel, Frederic,
Geoffrey, Humphrey, Jonathan,
Jonathon, Kimberly, Kingsley,
Lancelot, Laurence, Lawrence,
Llewelyn, Matthias, Meredith,
Mordecai, Muhammad, Nicholas,
Perceval, Percival, Randolph,
Reginald, Roderick, Ruaidhri,
Ruairidh, Ruaraidh, Rupinder,
Terrance, Theodore, Tristram

**09** Alexander, Archibald, Augustine,
Christian, Ferdinand, Frederick,
Kimberley, Launcelot, Nathaniel,
Peregrine, Sebastian, Siegfried,
Somhairle, Sylvester, Valentine

**10** Maximilian

**11** Bartholomew, Christopher

---

## boycott
**03** ban, bar **04** shun, snub **05** avoid,
black, spurn **06** eschew, ignore,
outlaw, refuse, reject **07** embargo,
exclude, refusal **08** disallow, prohibit,
spurning **09** blacklist, exclusion,
ostracism, ostracize, proscribe,
rejection **11** prohibition **12** cold-
shoulder, proscription **14** send to
Coventry

## boyfriend
**03** ami, guy, man **04** beau, date
**05** bloke, fella, lover **06** fellow, fiancé,
steady, suitor, toyboy **07** admirer, best
boy, partner, squeeze **08** young man
**09** cohabitee **10** sweetheart **11** live-in
lover **15** common-law spouse

## boyish
**05** gamin, green, young **06** gamine,
tomboy **07** puerile **08** childish,
immature, innocent, juvenile, youthful

**09** childlike **10** adolescent,
unfeminine, unmaidenly

## brace
**02** ll, PR **03** duo, tie, two **04** beam,
bend, bind, pair, prop, stay, vice
**05** clamp, nerve, shore, steel, strap,
strut, truss **06** couple, fasten, gear up,
hold up, prop up, secure, steady,
wimble **07** bandage, bolster, compose,
fortify, prepare, psych up, shore up,
shoring, support, tighten, twosome
**08** accolade, bridging, buttress,
fastener, get ready **09** reinforce,
stanchion, undergird **10** strengthen
**13** reinforcement

## bracelet
**04** band **05** armil **06** bangle **07** armilla,
circlet **08** handcuff, wristlet

## bracing
**05** brisk, crisp, fresh, tonic **07** rousing
**08** reviving, vigorous **09** energetic
**10** energizing, enlivening, fortifying,
refreshing **11** stimulating
**12** exhilarating, invigorating
**13** strengthening

## bracken
**04** tara **05** brake

## bracket
◇ *containment indicator* **03** lot **04** prop,
rest, stay **05** batch, brace, class, frame,
group **06** becket, cohort, corbel,
gusset, holder, mutule, trivet
**07** cripple, potence, support
**08** category, grouping **09** goose-neck,
modillion **10** cantilever, misericord
**11** misericorde, parenthesis
**14** classification

## brackish
**04** brak, salt **05** briny, salty **06** bitter,
saline **07** saltish **11** salsuginous

## bract
**05** glume, palea **06** spathe **08** phyllary
**10** hypsophyll

## brad
**04** nail

## brag
**03** gab **04** blow, bull, crow **05** boast,
proud, skite, vapor, vaunt **06** vapour
**07** big-note, bluster, proudly, show off,
swagger, talk big **08** mouth off **10** shoot
a line **11** hyperbolize, rodomontade
**12** cry roast-meat, lay it on thick
**15** blow your own horn

## braggart
**05** skite **06** gascon, skiter **07** bluffer,
boaster, show-off, swasher, windbag
**08** bangster, big mouth, boastful,
fanfaron, puckfist **09** blusterer, loudmouth, swaggerer **11** braggadocio
**12** rodomontader, swashbuckler

## bragging
**06** hot air **07** bluster, bravado
**08** boasting, vauntery **09** thrasonic
**10** showing-off **11** jactitation,
thrasonical **12** boastfulness,
exaggeration **13** tongue-doubtie

## braid
**04** cord, lace, tail, wind, yarn **05** plait,
pleat, queue, ravel, tress, twine, twist,

weave **06** caddis, ric-rac, sennit, sinnet, thread **07** caddice, embraid, entwine **08** reproach, rick-rack, soutache **09** interlace, passement **10** intertwine, interweave **13** scrambled eggs

**brain**
◊ *anagram indicator* **03** wit **04** head, mind, nous **05** savvy, sense **06** acumen, boffin, brains, expert, genius, pundit, reason **07** egghead, prodigy, scholar **08** brainbox, highbrow, pia mater, sagacity **09** intellect, sensorium **10** encephalon, grey matter, mastermind, shrewdness **11** cleverclogs, common sense, upper storey **12** intellectual, intelligence **13** understanding

---

*Brain parts include:*

**04** falx, lobe, lobi, pons
**06** cortex
**07** cinerea
**08** amygdala, cerebrum, meninges, midbrain, thalamus
**09** brainstem, forebrain, hindbrain, ventricle
**10** Broca's area, cerebellum, grey matter, pineal body, spinal cord
**11** frontal lobe, hippocampus, white matter
**12** hypothalamus, limbic system, parietal lobe, Purkinje cell, temporal lobe, visual cortex
**13** choroid plexus, mesencephalon, occipital lobe, olfactory bulb, optic thalamus, Wernicke's area
**14** cerebral cortex, corpus callosum, left hemisphere, pituitary gland
**15** right hemisphere, substantia nigra

---

**brainless**
**04** daft **05** crazy, inept, silly **06** stupid **07** foolish, idiotic **08** mindless **09** hen-witted, senseless **10** half-witted **11** incompetent, thoughtless **12** simple-minded

**brains**
**02** IQ **03** wit **04** loaf, nous **05** harns, savey, savvy **06** common, savvey, sconce, wisdom **08** gumption **10** grey matter

**brainteaser**
**05** poser **06** puzzle, riddle **07** problem **09** conundrum **10** mind-bender **12** brain-twister

**brainwashing**
**08** grilling **09** menticide **10** persuasion **11** mind-bending, re-education **12** conditioning, pressurizing **14** indoctrination

**brainy**
**04** wise **05** smart **06** bright, clever, gifted **07** sapient **09** brilliant **11** intelligent **12** intellectual

**brake**
**04** curb, drag, fern, halt, rein, slow, stop **05** check **06** harrow, pull up, retard **07** bracken, control, slacken, thicket **08** moderate, slow down **09** restraint **10** constraint, decelerate,

retardment **11** reduce speed, restriction
• **braking system 03** ABS

**bramble**
**05** Rubus **06** lawyer **08** dewberry **10** blackberry, cloudberry **12** Penang-lawyer

**bran**
**06** chesil, chisel, shorts **07** pollard **08** roughage

**branch**
**02** br **03** arm, cow, leg, lye **04** axis, fork, limb, lobe, loop, part, reis, rice, stem, whip, wing **05** bough, corps, prong, ramus, scrog, shoot, sprig, withy **06** agency, bureau, office **07** braunch, cladode, section **08** division, offshoot **09** affiliate, succursal, tributary **10** department, discipline, subsection, subsidiary **11** local office, phylloclade, subdivision **12** ramification **14** regional office
• **branch off 04** fork **06** divide, offset, spring **07** deviate, diverge, furcate **08** separate **09** bifurcate
• **branch out 04** vary **05** add to **06** expand, extend, ramify **07** develop, enlarge **08** increase, multiply **09** diversify, spread out, subdivide **10** broaden out **11** proliferate

**brand**
**03** tag **04** burn, chop, kind, line, logo, make, mark, sear, sere, sign, sort, type, wipe **05** class, grill, label, stain, stamp, taint **06** burn in, emblem, marque, symbol **07** censure, quality, species, variety **08** besmirch, denounce, disgrace, hallmark, typecast **09** brand-name, discredit, trademark, tradename **10** stigmatize **14** identification **15** identifying mark

**brandish**
**03** wag **04** wave **05** bless, flash, raise, shake, swing, wield **06** flaunt, hurtle, parade, waving **07** display, exhibit, vibrate, wampish **08** flourish

**brandy**
**03** dop **04** fine, marc **05** bingo, mobby, Nantz, peach, smoke **06** Cognac, grappa, mobbie **07** quetsch **08** Armagnac, Calvados, eau de vie, mahogany, slivovic **09** apple-jack, aqua vitae, Cape smoke, mirabelle, slivovica, slivovitz, slivowitz **10** ball of fire **11** aguardiente, cold-without, water of life **12** cherry bounce **13** fine Champagne

**brash**
**04** bold, rash, rude **05** cocky, crude, hasty, pushy **06** brazen, flashy **07** assured, brittle, forward **08** impudent, insolent, reckless **09** assertive, audacious, bumptious, foolhardy, heartburn, impetuous, impulsive **10** incautious, indiscreet **11** impertinent, precipitate **13** self-confident

**brashly**
**06** boldly, rashly, rudely **07** cockily, hastily, pushily **08** brazenly **09** assuredly, forwardly **10** impudently,

insolently, recklessly **11** assertively, audaciously, foolhardily, impetuously, impulsively **12** incautiously, indiscreetly **13** impertinently, precipitately **15** self-confidently

**brashness**
**08** audacity, boldness, rashness, rudeness **09** hastiness, impudence, incaution, insolence, pushiness **10** brazenness **12** impertinence, recklessness **13** assertiveness, foolhardiness **14** self-confidence

**brass**
**04** gall, loot, sass **05** cheek, money, nerve **08** latten **08** audacity, chutzpah, orichalc, rudeness, temerity **09** brass neck, impudence, insolence, necessary, oricalche **10** brass nerve, brazenness, effrontery **11** presumption **12** impertinence
• **top brass 04** VIPs

**brassy**
**04** bold, hard, loud **05** brash, cocky, harsh, noisy, pushy, sassy, saucy **06** brazen **07** blaring, forward, grating, jarring, raucous **08** insolent, jangling, piercing, strident **09** dissonant, shameless **11** loud-mouthed

**brat**
**03** get, imp, kid **04** gait, geit, gyte **05** brach, puppy **06** nipper, rascal **07** brachet, nointer **08** bantling, bratchet **09** youngster **10** jackanapes **11** guttersnipe **14** whippersnapper

**bravado**
**04** show, talk **05** boast, brave **06** parade **07** bluster, bombast, bravery, swagger **08** boasting, bragging, pretence, vaunting **09** swaggerer **10** showing-off **11** braggadocio, fanfaronade, rodomontade

**brave**
**04** bear, bold, dare, defy, face **05** bravo, bully, gutsy, hardy, manly, noble, showy **06** daring, endure, feisty, gritty, heroic, plucky, spunky, suffer **07** doughty, gallant, stoical, valiant **08** confront, face up to, fearless, handsome, intrepid, resolute, stalwart, unafraid, valorous, yeomanly **09** audacious, challenge, dauntless, excellent, put up with, stand up to, undaunted, withstand **10** courageous **11** indomitable, lion-hearted, unflinching **12** face the music, not turn a hair, stout-hearted **14** game as Ned Kelly, keep your chin up

**bravely**
**06** boldly **07** hardily **08** daringly, pluckily, yeomanly **09** doughtily, gallantly, stoically, valiantly **10** fearlessly, heroically, intrepidly, resolutely, stalwartly, valorously **11** audaciously, dauntlessly, indomitably, undauntedly **12** courageously **13** unflinchingly **14** stout-heartedly

**bravery**
**04** grit, guts **05** pluck, spunk, valor **06** daring, finery, mettle, spirit, valour **07** bravado, courage, heroism,

**bravo**

prowess **08** audacity, boldness, chivalry, tenacity, valiance **09** derring do, fortitude, gallantry, hardiness **10** derring doe, resolution **11** intrepidity **12** fearlessness, stalwartness **13** dauntlessness **14** courageousness, indomitability

**bravo**

**01** B **03** olé **04** euge **08** well done **09** excellent, spadassin

**bravura**

**04** dash, élan **06** spirit **07** sparkle **10** brilliance **12** magnificence

**brawl**

**03** row **04** dust, fray, rout **05** argue, broil, clash, fight, flite, flyte, mêlée, scold, scrap **06** affray, bundle, bust-up, dust-up, fracas, fratch, ruckus, rumpus, stoush, tussle **07** bagarre, brabble, brangle, dispute, punch-up, quarrel, scuffle, tuilyie, tuilzie, wrangle, wrestle **08** argument, disorder, skirmish, squabble **09** altercate **10** Donnybrook, fisticuffs, free-for-all, rough-house **11** altercation

**brawn**

**04** beef, boar, bulk **05** might, power **06** muscle, sinews **07** muscles **08** beefcake, strength **09** beefiness, bulkiness **10** headcheese, robustness **11** muscularity

**brawny**

**05** beefy, bulky, burly, hardy, hefty, hunky, husky, meaty, solid **06** fleshy, robust, sinewy, strong, sturdy **07** hulking, massive **08** athletic, muscular, powerful, stalwart, vigorous **09** strapping, well-built

**bray**

**04** bell, hoot, roar **05** blare, neigh **06** bellow, heehaw, whinny **07** screech, trumpet

**brazen**

**04** bold, pert **05** brash, pushy, saucy **06** brassy **07** blatant, defiant, forward **08** flagrant, immodest, impudent, insolent **09** audacious, bald-faced, barefaced, shameless, unabashed, unashamed **10** hard-boiled, in-your-face • **brazen it out** **04** defy **09** be defiant **11** be unashamed **12** be impenitent

**brazenly**

**06** boldly **09** blatantly, defiantly **10** flagrantly, immodestly, impudently, insolently **11** audaciously, shamelessly, unashamedly

**brazier**

**06** hearth, mangal **07** brasero **08** scaldino **10** fire-basket

**Brazil**

**02** BR **03** BRA **04** Braz

**breach**

**03** gap **04** gulf, hole, rift, slap **05** break, chasm, cleft, crack, lapse, space, split, unlaw **06** open up, saltus, schism **07** crevice, fissure, offence, offense, opening, parting, quarrel, rupture, violate **08** aperture, breakers, breaking, division, fraction, infringe, solution, trespass, variance **09** break open, severance, violation **10** alienation, contravene, difference, disruption, dissension, infraction, separation **12** break through, burst through, disaffection, disagreement, disobedience, dissociation, estrangement, infringement **13** contravention, transgression

**bread**

**03** fat, tin **04** cash, diet, dosh, fare, food, pane **05** dough, dumps, funds, lolly, money, sugar **06** crusts **07** shekels **08** sandwich, victuals **09** nutriment **10** livelihood, provisions, sustenance **11** necessities, nourishment, spondulicks, subsistence **12** the necessary

*Bread and rolls include:*

**03** bap, cob, nan, rye, tea
**04** azym, cake, corn, diet, farl, flat, loaf, milk, naan, pita, pone, roti, soda
**05** arepa, azyme, bagel, black, brown, cheat, fancy, horse, matza, matzo, pitta, plait, poori, ravel, white
**06** burger, damper, French, garlic, graham, hoagie, hot dog, Indian, injera, lavash, matzah, matzoh, panini, panino, simnel, stotty, wastel
**07** bannock, bloomer, brioche, brownie, buttery, challah, chapati, currant, ficelle, granary, jannock, manchet, paratha, pretzel, stollen, stottie, wheaten
**08** baguette, barm cake, chapatti, ciabatta, corn pone, focaccia, grissini, leavened, milk loaf, ravelled, ryebread, schnecke, standard, tortilla
**09** bara brith, barmbrack, batch loaf, burger bun, cornbread, croissant, flatbread, hamburger, petit pain, schnecken, shewbread, showbread, sourdough, wholemeal
**10** breadstick, bridge roll, finger roll, French loaf, multigrain, stotty cake, unleavened, vienna loaf, wholewheat
**11** cottage loaf, French stick, morning roll, potato bread, potato scone
**12** pumpernickel
**13** farmhouse loaf
**14** pain au chocolat

• **bread and butter** **11** maintenance
• **bread in milk** **03** sop

**breadbasket**

**03** tum **05** tummy **07** stomach

**breadth**

**01** b **04** beam, size, span **05** range, reach, scale, scope, sweep, width **06** extent, spread **07** compass, expanse, measure **08** latitude, vastness, wideness **09** amplitude, beaminess, broadness, dimension, magnitude, thickness **10** distension **13** extensiveness

**break**

◇ *anagram indicator* ◇ *insertion indicator*
**03** gap, vac **04** beat, bust, dash, dawn, fail, gash, halt, hole, kick, lash, luck, lull, open, part, quit, rend, rest, rift, rise, ruin, snap, stop, tame, tear, tell, vary **05** begin, cleft, crack, crash, crush, excel, flout, let-up, outdo, pause, pound, sever, smash, smoko, solve, split **06** appear, be born, better, breach, chance, change, cut off, cut out, decode, divide, emerge, exceed, falter, give up, go phut, impair, impart, inform, lessen, open up, pack up, pierce, reduce, reveal, schism, shiver, soften, strike, subdue, weaken, worsen **07** abandon, conk out, crevice, cushion, decrypt, destroy, disobey, disturb, divulge, fissure, fortune, go kaput, holiday, improve, lighten, opening, respite, rupture, shatter, smoke-ho, stammer, stumble, stutter, surpass, suspend, time off, time-out, unravel, violate, work out **08** announce, breather, decipher, demolish, diminish, disclose, enfeeble, fracture, infringe, interval, outstrip, overcome, puncture, separate, shake off, splinter, vacation **09** advantage, dishonour, figure out, interlude, interrupt, perforate, undermine **10** contravene, demoralize, relinquish, separation **11** discontinue, malfunction, opportunity, stop working **12** bring to an end, disintegrate, estrangement, go on the blink, intermission, interruption, stroke of luck **13** interfere with **14** breathing space
• **break away** **03** fly **04** flee, quit **05** leave, split, start **06** depart, detach, escape, secede **07** run away **08** separate, split off **11** part company **13** make a run for it
• **break down** **02** go **04** cark, conk, fail, kark, stop **05** crash, crock, crush, plash, smash **06** detail, go down, go phut, pack up **07** analyse, burn out, conk out, crack up, crock up, destroy, dissect, founder, give way, itemize, seize up **08** collapse, demolish, separate **09** attenuate, decompose, knock down **10** be overcome, categorize, go to pieces **11** fall through, lose control, stop working **13** come to nothing
• **break in** **03** rob **04** raid, tame, wear **05** cut in, prime, start, train **06** burgle, butt in, irrupt **07** impinge, intrude **08** accustom, encroach **09** condition, cultivate, get used to, interject, interpose, interrupt, intervene **14** enter illegally
• **break off** **03** end **04** halt, part, stop **05** cease, pause, sever **06** detach, divide, finish **07** snap off, suspend **08** dissever, separate **09** interrupt, terminate **10** disconnect **11** discontinue **12** bring to an end
• **break out** **03** rip **04** bolt, flee **05** arise, begin, erupt, occur, shout, start **06** blow up, emerge, escape, happen **07** abscond, exclaim, flare up **08** burst out, commence **09** come out

**breakable**

in, interject **13** begin suddenly
• **break through** **04** pass **06** emerge
**07** succeed **08** fracture, overcome,
progress **09** penetrate **10** gain ground
**11** leap forward, make headway
• **break up** ◊ anagram indicator
◊ containment indicator **04** part, stop
**05** sever, split, stave **06** divide, finish,
reduce, reform **07** adjourn, destroy,
disband, divorce, resolve, split up,
suspend **08** demolish, diffract,
disperse, dissolve, separate, splinter,
to-bruise **09** dismantle, dismember,
take apart, terminate **11** come to an
end, discontinue, part company
**12** bring to an end, disintegrate
• **break with** **04** drop, jilt **05** ditch
**06** reject **08** part with, renounce
**09** repudiate **10** finish with **12** separate
from

**breakable**
**05** frail **06** flimsy **07** brittle, fragile,
friable **08** delicate **09** frangible **10** jerry-
built **12** easily broken **13** insubstantial

**breakaway**
**05** rebel **06** escape, revolt **08** apostate,
renegade, seceding **09** defection,
heretical, secession **10** dissenting,
schismatic, separatist, withdrawal
**12** secessionist

**breakdown**
**07** failure **08** analysis, collapse,
stoppage **10** cracking-up, dissection
**11** itemization, malfunction
**12** interruption **13** going to pieces
**14** categorization, classification,
disintegration
• **breakdown service** **02** AA **03** RAC

**breaker**
**04** wave **06** billow, buster, roller
**10** roughrider **11** white horses

**breakfast**
**07** dejeune, disjune **08** déjeuner
**10** chota hazri **13** petit déjeuner
See also **cereal**

**break-in**
**04** raid **07** larceny, robbery **08** burglary,
invasion, trespass **09** intrusion
**13** house-breaking

**breakneck**
**05** rapid, swift **06** speedy **07** express
**08** headlong, very fast **09** very quick
**11** precipitate **13** like lightning

**breakthrough**
**04** find, gain, leap, step **07** advance,
finding, headway **08** progress
**09** discovery, invention, milestone
**10** innovation **11** development,
improvement, leap forward, quantum
leap, step forward

**break-up**
**03** end **04** rift **05** split **06** finish
**07** debacle, divorce, parting, upbreak
**09** crumbling, dispersal **10** separation
**11** dissolution, splitting-up, termination
**14** disintegration

**breakwater**
**04** dock, mole, pier, quay, spur
**05** jetty, wharf **06** groyne **07** bulwark,
sea wall

**bream**
**03** tai **05** porgy **06** braise, braize,
porgie, sargos, sargus **08** tarwhine

**breast**
**03** dug, pap, tit **04** boob, bust, stem,
teat **05** booby, bosom, chest, diddy,
front, heart, mamma, titty **06** nipple,
thorax **07** brisket, bristol, knocker
**08** breaskit

**breastplate**
**06** byrnie, thorax **07** cuirass, placket
**08** pectoral, plastron, rational

**breath**
**03** air **04** gasp, gulp, gust, hint, pant,
puff, sigh, waft, wind **05** aroma, odour,
prana, smell, whiff **06** breeze, flatus,
murmur, pneuma, spirit **07** whisper
**09** breathing, suspicion, undertone
**10** exhalation, inhalation, suggestion
**11** inspiration, respiration

**breathe**
**04** gasp, pant, puff, sigh, tell **05** imbue,
snore, utter, voice **06** exhale, expire,
impart, infuse, inhale, inject, instil,
murmur **07** express, inspire, respire,
suspire, whisper **09** embreathe,
inbreathe, transfuse **10** articulate,
insufflate

**breather**
**04** gill, halt, lung, nare, rest, walk
**05** break, pause **06** recess **07** respite
**10** relaxation **14** breathing space,
constitutional

**breathless**
**04** agog, dead **05** eager **06** pooped,
puffed, winded **07** airless, anxious,
choking, excited, gasping, panting,
puffing **08** feverish, wheezing
**09** exhausted, expectant, impatient,
pooped out, puffed out **10** in suspense
**11** open-mouthed, out of breath, short-
winded, tuckered out

**breathtaking**
**06** moving **07** amazing **08** drop-dead,
exciting, stirring, stunning **09** thrilling
**10** astounding, eye-popping,
impressive, stupendous **11** astonishing,
magnificent, spectacular **12** awe-
inspiring, overwhelming

**breathtakingly**
**09** amazingly **10** excitingly, stirringly,
stunningly **11** thrillingly
**12** impressively, stupendously
**13** astonishingly, spectacularly **14** awe-
inspiringly, overwhelmingly

**breeches**
**04** hose **05** slops **06** breeks, tights,
trouse, trunks **07** plushes, trusses
**08** chausses, jodhpurs, leathers,
trossers, trousers **09** buckskins, knee-
cords, strossers, trunk hose
**12** galligaskins, pedal pushers, small-
clothes **14** knickerbockers

**breed**
**04** bear, kind, line, make, race, rear,
sort, type **05** cause, class, hatch, raise,
stamp, stock **06** arouse, create, family,
foster, hybrid, strain **07** bring up,
calibre, develop, lineage, nourish,
nurture, produce, progeny, species,

variety **08** engender, generate,
multiply, occasion, pedigree
**09** cultivate, originate, procreate,
propagate, pullulate, reproduce
**10** bring about, bring forth, give rise to
**11** give birth to

**breeding**
**05** stock **06** polish **07** culture, lineage,
manners, nurture, raising, rearing
**08** ancestry, civility, gentrice, training,
urbanity **09** education, gentility
**10** politeness, refinement, upbringing
**11** cultivation, development, good
manners, procreation, savoir-vivre
**12** reproduction
• **breeding establishment** **04** stud

**breeding-ground**
**04** nest **06** cradle, hotbed, school
**07** nursery **08** hothouse **14** training
ground

**breeze**
◊ anagram indicator **03** air **04** flit, gust,
puff, sail, trip, waft, wind **05** glide,
hurry, sally, slant, snift, sweep
**06** breath, doctor, flurry, wander,
zephyr **07** cat's paw, draught, saunter,
snifter **08** sniffler **12** periodic wind

**breezy**
**04** airy **05** blowy, brisk, fresh, gusty,
light, windy **06** blithe, bright, casual,
jaunty, lively **07** blowing, buoyant,
relaxed, squally **08** animated, blustery,
carefree, cheerful, debonair, informal
**09** confident, easy-going, vivacious
**12** exhilarating, light-hearted

**brevity**
**07** economy, fewness **08** curtness,
laconism **09** briefness, concision,
crispness, pithiness, shortness,
terseness **10** abruptness, transience
**11** compactness, conciseness
**12** ephemerality, impermanence,
incisiveness, succinctness
**14** transitoriness

**brew**
◊ anagram indicator **04** boil, cook,
loom, make, mash, plan, plot, soak,
stew **05** blend, drink, hatch, steep
**06** devise, excite, foment, gather,
infuse, liquor, potion, scheme, seethe
**07** build up, concoct, develop,
ferment, mixture, prepare, project
**08** beverage, compound, contrive,
infusion **10** be on its way, concoction
**11** combination, preparation
**12** distillation, fermentation **13** be in
the offing **15** be in preparation

**bribe**
**03** buy, fix, sop **04** bung, dash, gift,
palm, vail, wage **05** bonus, booty,
drink, sling, spoil, touch, vails, vales
**06** boodle, buy off, carrot, grease,
hamper, nobble, pay off, pay-off,
payola, reward, square, suborn **07** buy
over, corrupt, douceur, palm-oil,
pension **08** kickback, the drink **09** hush
money, incentive, keep sweet,
lubricate, refresher, slush fund,
sweetener **10** allurement, back-hander,
enticement, inducement, palm-grease,
take care of **12** straightener
**13** gratification **15** protection money

## bribery

**05** graft **09** embracery **10** corruption, inducement, protection **11** subornation **12** malversation, palm-greasing

## bric-à-brac

**06** curios **07** baubles, gewgaws **08** antiques, bibelots, trinkets, trumpery **09** gimcracks, ornaments **10** Japanesery, rattletrap, Victoriana **11** knick-knacks, odds and ends **13** bits and pieces

## brick

**03** bar, bur, pal **04** burr, chum, lump, mass, mate, rock, slab **05** adobe, block, buddy, gault, piece, stone, wedge **06** header, rubber, rustic **07** clinker, fletton, klinker, nogging, soldier **09** briquette, firebrick, stretcher **10** real friend **11** breeze block **12** Dutch clinker
• **brick waste** **04** grog
• **piece of brick** **03** bat

## bridal

**07** marital, nuptial, wedding **08** conjugal, marriage **09** connubial **11** matrimonial

## bride

**04** wife **06** spouse **07** GI bride **08** newly-wed, war bride, wife-to-be **09** bride-to-be **11** honeymooner **15** marriage partner

## bridegroom

**05** groom **06** spouse **07** husband **08** newly-wed **11** honeymooner, husband-to-be **15** marriage partner

## bridge

**02** br **03** tie **04** bind, bond, fill, join, link, pons, rest, span **05** cross, unite **06** couple, go over **07** connect, spanner **08** traverse **10** connection **11** reach across

*Bridge types include:*

**03** air, fly
**04** arch, beam, deck, draw, foot, leaf, over, raft, road, rope, skew, toll, wire
**05** chain, pivot, swing
**06** Bailey, flying, girder
**07** bascule, flyover, lattice, lifting, pontoon, railway, through, viaduct
**08** aqueduct, causeway, floating, humpback, overpass
**09** box girder
**10** cantilever, suspension, traversing
**11** cable-stayed

*Bridges include:*

**03** Tay
**04** Skye, Tyne
**05** Forth, Sighs, Tower
**06** Bailey, Humber, Kintai, London, Rialto, Severn
**07** Bifrost, Clifton, Rainbow, Tsing Ma, Yichang
**08** Bosporus, Brooklyn, Jiangyin, Mackinac, Waterloo
**09** Evergreen, Forth Road, Kurushima, River Kwai
**10** Bosporus II, Golden Gate, Höga

Kusten, Ironbridge, Millennium, Pont du Gard, Storebaelt
**11** Brocade Sash
**12** Akashi-Kaikyo, Pont d'Avignon, Ponte Vecchio
**13** Great Belt East, Kita Bisan-Seto, Millau Viaduct, Sydney Harbour
**14** Ponte 25 de Abril, Quebec Railroad
**15** Minami Bisan-Seto

• **bridge player** **01** e, n, s, w **04** east, west **05** north, south
• **bridge support** **04** pier
• **bridge system** **04** Acol **06** canapé **09** blackwood

## bridle

**05** check **06** branks, govern, halter, master, subdue **07** bristle, contain, control, repress **08** hold back, moderate, restrain **09** hackamore, restraint **12** be offended by **15** become indignant

*Bridle parts include:*

**03** bit
**04** curb
**05** cheek
**06** musrol, pelham
**07** bridoon, eye-flap, snaffle
**08** browband, noseband
**09** headstall
**10** cheekpiece

*See also* **horse**

## brief

◊ *tail deletion indicator* **02** KC, QC
**04** case, curt, data, tell **05** blunt, breve, crisp, gen up, guide, hasty, pithy, prime, quick, remit, sharp, short, surly, swift, terse **06** abrupt, advice, advise, digest, direct, fill in, flying, inform, lawyer, orders, précis **07** brusque, compact, concise, cursory, defence, dossier, explain, laconic, limited, mandate, outline, passing, prepare, summary **08** abridged, abstract, argument, breviate, briefing, capsular, evidence, fleeting, instruct, succinct **09** barrister, condensed, directive, ephemeral, fugacious, laconical, momentary, temporary, thumbnail, tout court, transient **10** aphoristic, compressed, directions, evanescent, short-lived, transitory **11** abridgement, information **12** instructions **13** bring up to date, short and sweet **14** responsibility **15** put in the picture

## briefing

**03** gen **06** advice, orders **07** low-down, meeting, priming, run-down **08** guidance **09** filling-in **10** conference, directions, intimation **11** information, preparation **12** instructions

## briefly

◊ *tail deletion indicator* **05** in few, short **07** in a word, in brief, in short, quickly, shortly, tersely **09** concisely, cursorily, precisely, summarily **10** succinctly, to the point **11** in a few words, in a nutshell

## brigade

**03** Bde **04** band, body, crew, team, unit **05** corps, force, group, party, squad, troop **07** company **10** contingent
• **Boys' Brigade** **02** BB

## brigand

**06** bandit, haiduk, outlaw, robber **07** cateran, heyduck, ruffian **08** gangster, marauder **09** desperado, plunderer **10** bushranger, freebooter, highwayman **11** trailbaston

## bright

**03** gay, lit, net **04** fine, glad, keen, nett, rosy **05** acute, clear, happy, jolly, light, merry, quick, sharp, smart, sunny, vivid **06** astute, brainy, clever, genial, joyful, lively **07** beaming, blazing, glaring, glowing, hopeful, intense, radiant, shining **08** blinding, cheerful, dazzling, flashing, gleaming, glorious, luminous, lustrous, pleasant, splendid **09** beautiful, brilliant, cloudless, effulgent, promising, refulgent, sparkling, twinkling, unclouded, vivacious **10** auspicious, favourable, glistening, glittering, optimistic, perceptive, propitious, shimmering **11** encouraging, illuminated, illustrious, intelligent, quick-witted, resplendent **12** incandescent **15** bright as a button

## brighten

**03** rub **04** glow, jazz **05** gleam, pep up, rub up, shine **06** buck up, buoy up, jazz up, perk up, polish **07** burnish, cheer up, clear up, enhance, enliven, gladden, hearten, lighten, light up, liven up **09** encourage, irradiate, refurbish, smarten up **10** illuminate, make bright

## brightly

**06** ablaze, gladly **07** happily **08** joyfully **09** glaringly, glowingly, intensely, radiantly **10** blindingly, cheerfully, dazzlingly, splendidly **11** brilliantly, vivaciously

## brilliance

**04** tone **05** glare, glory, gloss, sheen **06** dazzle, genius, lustre, talent **07** bravura, glamour, prowess, sparkle **08** aptitude, fulgency, radiance, splendor **09** greatness, intensity, splendour, vividness **10** brightness, cleverness, effulgence, excellence, refulgence, virtuosity **11** coruscation, distinction **12** magnificence, resplendence

## brilliant

**03** ace, def **04** cool, hard, mega, neat, pear, star **05** brill, gemmy, great, quick, showy, vivid **06** astute, brainy, bright, clever, expert, famous, gifted, glossy, superb, wicked **07** blazing, crucial, erudite, fulgent, glaring, intense, lambent, radical, shining, skilful **08** dazzling, glorious, masterly, smashing, splendid, talented, terrific, top-notch **09** effulgent, excellent, fantastic, refulgent, sparkling, splendent, sunbright, wonderful **10** brightsome, celebrated, glittering, remarkable **11** exceptional, illustrious, intelligent, magnificent, outstanding, resourceful, resplendent **12** accomplished, enterprising, second to none **13** scintillating **14** out of this world

**brilliantly**
**07** vividly **08** brightly, cleverly, superbly **09** intensely, skilfully **10** dazzlingly, gloriously, splendidly **11** masterfully, wonderfully **13** magnificently, resplendently

**brim**
**03** lip, rim, top **04** edge, poke **05** brink, limit, verge **06** border, margin **09** perimeter **10** be full with **12** be filled with, overflow with **13** circumference

**brimful**
**04** full **05** abrim **06** filled, jammed **07** bulging, crammed, stuffed **09** packed out **11** chock-a-block, overflowing

**brindled**
**04** pied **05** tabby **06** dotted **07** dappled, flecked, mottled, piebald **08** speckled, stippled, streaked **10** variegated

**bring**
**03** fet, get, lay **04** bear, lead, take **05** carry, cause, fetch, force, guide, usher **06** convey, create, escort, prompt, submit **07** conduct, deliver, present, produce, provoke **08** engender, initiate, result in **09** accompany, transport **10** make happen, put forward
• **bring about**   **04** make **05** cause, frame, wreak **06** create, effect, fulfil, manage **07** achieve, compass, inspire, operate, perform, procure, produce, provoke, realize **08** contrive, generate, occasion, purchase **09** encompass, instigate **10** accomplish
• **bring back**   ◇ *reversal indicator* **05** evoke, recal **06** call up, recall, reduce, relate, remind **07** recover, reverse, suggest **13** take you back to **14** make you think of
• **bring down**   **04** drop, oust, pull, stop **05** abate, lower, shoot **06** defeat, depose, derive, embace, embase, humble, imbase, reduce, sadden, topple, unseat **07** destroy **08** decrease, dismount, vanquish **09** knock down, overthrow, shoot down **11** cause to drop, cause to fall
• **bring forward**   **05** raise **06** adduce, allege, object **07** advance, prepone, present, produce, propose, suggest, trot out **10** put forward **11** make earlier
• **bring in**   ◇ *containment indicator* **03** net **04** earn, make, wind **05** fetch, gross, set up, yield **06** accrue, import, induce, launch, return **07** pioneer, produce, realize, usher in **08** initiate **09** introduce, originate, pronounce **10** inaugurate
• **bring off**   **03** win **06** fulfil, rescue **07** achieve, execute, perform, pull off **09** discharge, put across, succeed in **10** accomplish, consummate
• **bring on**   **05** cause, infer **06** foster, induce, lead to, prompt **07** advance,

improve, inspire, nurture, provoke **08** expedite, generate, occasion **10** accelerate, give rise to, make happen **11** precipitate
• **bring out**   **05** issue, print **06** launch, stress **07** draw out, enhance, produce, publish **09** emphasize, highlight, introduce **10** accentuate
• **bring round**   ◇ *containment indicator* **04** coax **05** rouse **06** awaken, cajole, revive, wake up **07** bring to, convert, win over **08** convince, persuade **11** resuscitate
• **bring up**   ◇ *reversal down indicator* **03** cat **04** barf, form, puke, rear **05** breed, nurse, raise, teach, train, vomit **06** broach, foster, nousle, nuzzle, submit **07** care for, educate, mention, nourish, noursle, nousell, nurture, propose, throw up, touch on **09** introduce **11** regurgitate

**brink**
**03** lip, rim **04** bank, brim, edge **05** limit, marge, verge **06** border, fringe, margin **08** boundary **09** extremity, threshold

**brio**
**03** pep, zip **04** dash **05** force, gusto, oomph, verve **06** energy, spirit, vigour **08** dynamism, vivacity **09** animation **10** liveliness

**brisk**
**04** busy, cant, cold, fast, good, perk, pert, yare **05** agile, alert, cobby, crisp, fresh, kedge, kedgy, kidge, quick, rapid, sharp, smart **06** active, crouse, lively, nimble, snappy **07** allegro, bracing **08** brushing, bustling, friskful, galliard, spirited, vigorous **09** energetic, sprightly **10** no-nonsense, refreshing **11** stimulating **12** businesslike, exhilarating, invigorating

**briskly**
**04** well **06** busily, nimbly **07** allegro, con moto, quickly, rapidly, sharply **08** abruptly **09** brusquely **10** decisively, vigorously **13** energetically

**bristle**
**03** awn **04** barb, hair, rise, seta **05** birse, quill, spine, thorn **06** arista, bridle, chaeta, seethe, setule, stilet, striga, stylet **07** hum with, prickle, stubble, whisker **08** abound in, bridle at, teem with, vibrissa **09** swarm with **10** seethe with, stand on end, vibraculum **11** be thick with, horripilate **12** be incensed at **14** draw yourself up

**bristly**
**05** hairy, rough, spiky, spiny **06** hispid, thorny **07** bearded, hirsute, prickly, stubbly **08** echinate, unshaven **09** echinated, whiskered **10** barbellate

**British**
**01** B **02** Br, GB, UK **03** pom **04** Brit **05** pommy
*See also* **monarch**
• **British Columbia**   **02** BC

**brittle**
◇ *anagram indicator* **04** curt, edgy, hard **05** birsy, brash, crisp, frail, frowy, frush, harsh, nervy, sharp, short, spall,

spalt, tense **06** frowie **07** bruckle, crackly, crumbly, fragile, friable, froughy, grating, nervous, redsear, shivery **08** delicate, hot-short, redshare, redshire, redshort, shattery, unstable **09** breakable, cold-short, crumbling, frangible, irritable, sensitive **12** easily broken

**broach**
◇ *anagram indicator* **03** tap **04** open, spit **05** begin, raise **06** hint at, open up, pierce, strike **07** bring up, mention, propose, refer to, suggest **08** allude to **09** introduce

**broad**
**04** free, open, vast, wide **05** ample, clear, large, plain, roomy, vague **06** coarse, direct, marked, strong, vulgar **07** evident, general, obvious **08** catholic, eclectic, spacious, sweeping, unsubtle **09** capacious, extensive, inclusive, outspoken, universal, unlimited **10** noticeable, widespread **11** compendious, far-reaching, not detailed, unconcealed, undisguised, wide-ranging **12** all-embracing, encyclopedic, latitudinous **13** comprehensive

**broadcast**
◇ *anagram indicator* ◇ *homophone indicator* **03** air, sow **04** beam, show **05** aired, cable, relay **06** repeat, report, spread **07** network, publish, radiate, scatter, trailer, webcast **08** announce, newscast, teletext, televise, transmit **09** advertise, cablecast, circulate, make known, programme, publicize, simulcast, soap opera **10** promulgate, sportscast, telebridge **11** disseminate **12** transmission **15** access broadcast
• **outside broadcast**   **02** OB **06** remote

**broaden**
**05** widen **06** expand, extend, open up, spread **07** augment, develop, enlarge, stretch **08** increase **09** branch out, diversify

**broadly**
**05** fully **06** mainly, mostly, widely **07** as a rule, largely, usually **08** commonly, normally **09** generally **10** by and large, more or less, on the whole, thoroughly **11** extensively, in most cases, in principle **14** for the most part **15** comprehensively

**broad-minded**
**07** liberal **08** tolerant, unbiased **09** impartial, indulgent, receptive **10** forbearing, open-minded, permissive **11** enlightened, progressive **12** free-thinking, unprejudiced **13** dispassionate

**broadside**
**04** tire **05** blast, salvo, stick **06** attack, volley **07** assault, censure **08** brickbat, diatribe, harangue **09** battering, cannonade, criticism, invective, philippic **11** bombardment, fulmination **12** counterblast, denunciation

**brochure**
05 flyer 06 folder 07 booklet, handout, leaflet 08 circular, handbill, pamphlet 09 throwaway 10 broadsheet, prospectus

**broil**
03 fry 04 cook 05 grill, roast, toast 08 barbecue, stramash

**broiling**
03 hot 06 baking 07 boiling 08 roasting 09 scorching 10 blistering, sweltering

**broke**
◇ anagram indicator 04 bust, poor 05 skint, stony 06 hard up, ruined 07 bargain 08 bankrupt, indigent, strapped 09 destitute, insolvent, negotiate, penniless, penurious 10 cleaned out, stony-broke 11 impecunious 12 impoverished, on your uppers 14 on your beam ends 15 poverty-stricken, strapped for cash

**broken**
◇ anagram indicator 04 bust, down, duff, rent, weak 05 burst, ended, kaput, tamed, wonky 06 beaten, failed, faulty, feeble, fitful, pakaru 07 crushed, damaged, erratic, halting, severed, smashed, subdued 08 defeated, divorced, ruptured 09 defective, destroyed, disturbed, exhausted, faltering, fractured, gone wrong, imperfect, knackered, oppressed, separated, shattered, spasmodic 10 demolished, disjointed, dispirited, hesitating, not working, on the blink, on the fritz, out of order, stammering, vanquished 11 demoralized, fragmentary, inoperative, interrupted, out of action 12 disconnected, intermittent 13 discontinuous 14 malfunctioning
• not to be broken 04 iron

**broken-down**
03 ill 04 bust, duff 05 kaput 06 broken, faulty, ruined 07 damaged, decayed, rickety, worn-out 08 decrepit 09 collapsed, defective 10 on the blink, on the fritz, out of order, ramshackle 11 dilapidated, in disrepair, inoperative

**broken-hearted**
03 sad 04 down 07 forlorn, unhappy 08 dejected, desolate, dolorous, mournful, wretched 09 miserable, sorrowful 10 despairing, despondent, devastated, prostrated 11 crestfallen, heartbroken 12 disappointed, disconsolate, inconsolable 13 grief-stricken 14 down in the dumps

**broker**
03 job 04 deal 05 agent, agree, bania 06 banian, banyan, clinch, dealer, factor, jobber, settle 07 arrange, bargain, execute, handler, mediate 08 complete, conclude, organize 09 arbitrate, go-between, land agent, middleman, negotiate 10 negotiator 11 arbitrageur, stockbroker, stockjobber 12 intermediary

**bromide**
06 cliché, downer, opiate, truism

07 anodyne 08 banality, narcotic, sedative 09 calmative, platitude 10 stereotype 11 barbiturate, commonplace 12 sleeping pill 13 tranquillizer

**bromine**
02 Br

**bronze**
02 br 03 tan 04 rust 05 brass 06 auburn, copper, Titian 07 aeneous, vermeil 08 chestnut 09 impudence 10 horseflesh 12 reddish-brown 14 copper-coloured

**bronzed**
05 brown 06 bronze, tanned 07 browned 08 hardened, sunburnt 09 sunburned, suntanned

**brooch**
03 pin 04 clip, ouch, prop 05 badge, broch, clasp 06 fibula, tiepin 08 lapel pin 09 breastpin

**brood**
03 eye, nid, nye, sit 04 aery, clan, eyry, fret, kind, mope, muse, nest, nide, race, sulk, team 05 aerie, ayrie, breed, cleck, clock, cover, covey, eyrie, hatch, issue, spawn, sperm, tribe, young 06 chicks, clutch, family, go over, kindle, litter, ponder 07 agonize, dwell on, eelfare, progeny 08 children, clecking, incubate, meditate, mull over, rehearse, ruminate 09 bairn-team, bairn-time, fret about, household, offspring, parentage 10 extraction, worry about

**brook**
04 bear, beck, burn, gill, kill, purl, rill 05 allow, creek, fleet, ghyll, inlet, stand 06 accept, branch, endure, permit, runnel, stream 07 abrooke, channel, rivulet, stomach, support 08 tolerate 09 put up with, withstand 11 countenance, watercourse

**broom**
04 wisp 05 besom, scrub, spart 06 retama 07 cytisus, hag-weed 09 knee-holly, Turk's head 10 Jew's-myrtle 15 shepherd's myrtle

**broth**
◇ anagram indicator 04 kail, kale, soup 05 ramen 06 brewis, cullis 08 bouillon, hotchpot 09 pot liquor 10 beef-brewis, hodgepodge, hotchpotch, muslin-kale

**brothel**
03 kip 04 crib, stew 05 stews 06 bagnio, bordel 07 Corinth 08 bordello, cathouse, hothouse, red light 10 bawdy-house, flash-house, whorehouse 12 knocking-shop, leaping-house 13 sporting house, vaulting-house 14 house of ill fame, massage parlour 15 disorderly house

**brother**
02 br 03 bro, fra, pal, sib 04 bhai, brer, chum, mate, monk, sibb 05 billy, buddy, frère, friar 06 billie, fellow, friend, german 07 comrade, partner, sibling 08 relation, relative 09 associate, colleague, companion 11 full brother, half-brother, twin-

brother 12 blood-brother 13 brother-german
• **big brother** 05 prior 08 dictator

**brotherhood**
03 PRB 05 guild, union 06 clique, league 07 society 08 alliance, confrère 09 community, confrérie, Félibrige 10 fellowship, fraternity, friendship 11 association, cameraderie, comradeship, confederacy 12 fraternalism, friendliness 13 confederation, confraternity

**brotherly**
04 kind 05 loyal 06 caring, loving 08 amicable, friendly 09 fraternal 10 benevolent 11 sympathetic 12 affectionate 13 philanthropic

**brow**
03 tip, top 04 peak 05 brink, cliff, ridge, verge 06 summit 07 pit-head, temples 08 forehead

**browbeat**
05 bully, force, hound 06 coerce, hector 07 dragoon, oppress 08 bulldoze, domineer, overbear, threaten 09 tyrannize 10 intimidate

**brown**
02 br 03 fry 04 cook, fusc, seal 05 grill, singe, toast 06 tanned 07 bronzed, browned, embrown, fuscous 08 sunburnt 09 infuscate

*Browns include:*

03 bay, dun, tan
04 buff, drab, ecru, fawn, pine, rust, sand, teak
05 beige, camel, cocoa, dusky, hazel, honey, khaki, mocha, ochre, rusty, sepia, taupe, tawny, tenné, umber
06 auburn, bister, bistre, bronze, burnet, coffee, copper, ginger, russet, sorrel, walnut
07 biscuit, caramel, chamois, filemot, oatmeal, oxblood
08 brunette, chestnut, cinnamon, mahogany, mushroom, nut-brown, philamot, raw umber
09 chocolate, earth-tone
10 burnt umber, café au lait, terracotta
11 burnt sienna, orange-tawny
12 vandyke brown

**browned off**
05 bored, fed up, weary 07 annoyed 09 hacked off, irritated 10 bored stiff, brassed off, cheesed off, dispirited 11 discouraged, disgruntled, downhearted, exasperated 12 discontented, disheartened

**brownie**
03 hob, nis 05 nisse

**browse**
03 eat 04 feed, look, scan, skim, surf 05 graze 06 nibble, peruse, survey 07 dip into, pasture 09 quick read 11 leaf through 12 flick through, flick-through

**bruise**
◇ anagram indicator 04 beat, hurt, mark,

stun **05** break, clour, crush, frush, pound, spoil, upset, wound **06** damage, grieve, injure, injury, insult, intuse, lesion, offend, shiner **07** blacken, blemish, contuse, rainbow, surbate **08** black eye, to-bruise **09** contusion, discolour **10** ecchymosis **13** discoloration

## bruiser
**04** thug **05** bully, rough, tough **07** hoodlum, ruffian **08** bully boy **09** bovver boy, roughneck **12** prize-fighter

## Brunei
**03** BRN, BRU

## brunt
**05** force, shock **06** burden, impact, strain, thrust, weight **07** impetus **08** pressure **09** main force **10** full weight

## brush
**03** hog, rub **04** bush, dust, kiss, swab, wipe **05** besom, broom, clash, clean, clear, fight, fitch, flick, frith, graze, scrap, scrub, scuff, set-to, shine, sweep, touch, whisk **06** badger, bushes, caress, duster, dust-up, fracas, pallet, polish, putois, scrape, shrubs, stroke, tussle **07** burnish, contact, fox-tail, stipple, sweeper, thicket, tickler **08** argument, conflict, skirmish **09** brushwood, currycomb, encounter, pope's head, underwood **10** hair-pencil **11** ground cover, overgrainer, undergrowth **12** disagreement **13** confrontation
• **brush aside** **05** flout **06** ignore **07** dismiss **08** belittle, override, pooh-pooh **09** disregard
• **brush off** **04** snub **05** spurn **06** disown, ignore, rebuff, reject, slight **07** dismiss, repulse **09** disregard, repudiate **12** cold-shoulder
• **brush up** **04** cram, swot, tidy **05** clean, study **06** go over, read up, revise, tidy up **07** improve, refresh, relearn **08** bone up on, polish up **09** freshen up **15** clean yourself up, refresh yourself

## brush-off
**04** snub **06** rebuff, slight **07** kiss-off, refusal, repulse **09** dismissal, rejection **11** repudiation **12** cold shoulder **14** discouragement

## brushwood
**03** hag **04** hagg, reis, rice **05** bavin, firth, frith, scrub **06** jungle **07** fascine **08** mattress, ovenwood **09** chaparral **10** underscrub

## brusque
**04** curt **05** blunt, brief, gruff, sharp, short, surly, terse **06** abrupt **07** uncivil **08** impolite, tactless **09** downright **12** discourteous, undiplomatic

## brutal
**05** cruel, frank, harsh, plain, tough **06** animal, coarse, savage, severe **07** beastly, bestial, boarish, brutish, callous, doggish, inhuman, ruffian, vicious, violent **08** inhumane, pitiless, ruthless **09** barbarous, ferocious,

heartless, merciless, unfeeling, unsparing **10** Rottweiler **11** insensitive, iron-hearted, remorseless **12** bloodthirsty, down-and-dirty **15** straightforward

## brutality
**07** cruelty **08** atrocity, ferocity, savagery, violence **09** barbarism, barbarity, callosity, roughness **10** coarseness, inhumanity **11** brutishness, callousness, viciousness **12** ruthlessness

## brutalize
**03** hit **04** beat, flog **05** inure, pound **06** attack, batter, deaden, harden, thrash **07** assault, degrade **09** animalize **10** dehumanize **11** desensitize

## brutally
**07** cruelly, frankly, harshly **08** savagely, severely **09** brutishly, callously, viciously **10** inhumanely, pitilessly, ruthlessly **11** barbarously, ferociously, heartlessly, mercilessly, unfeelingly **13** insensitively

## brute
**04** bête, lout, ogre **05** beast, bully, crude, devil, fiend, gross, swine, yahoo **06** animal, bodily, carnal, coarse, sadist, savage, stupid **07** Caliban, fleshly, monster, ruffian, sensual **08** creature, depraved, mindless, physical **09** senseless **10** irrational, Rottweiler, unthinking **11** instinctive

## brutish
**05** crass, crude, cruel, feral, gross **06** animal, brutal, coarse, ferine, savage, stupid, vulgar **07** bestial, loutish, uncouth **08** barbaric **09** barbarian, barbarous **11** animalistic, uncivilized

## bubble
**04** ball, bead, bell, bleb, boil, drop, fizz, foam, head, lock, seed, suds **05** fraud, froth, gloop, spume **06** bounce, burble, dimple, gurgle, lather, mantle, seethe, trifle, vanity, wallop **07** air-bell, air-lock, blister, blubber, droplet, fantasy, globule, sparkle, vesicle **08** be elated, be filled, blowhole, delusion, fleeting, illusion, rowndell **09** ball of air, be excited, deceptive, transient **10** depression, effervesce **13** effervescence, insubstantial

## bubbly
◊ anagram indicator **04** fizz **05** fizzy, happy, merry, sudsy **06** bouncy, elated, frothy, lively **07** excited, foaming **08** animated, champers **09** champagne, ebullient, exuberant, sparkling, vivacious **10** carbonated **12** effervescent

## buccaneer
**06** pirate **07** corsair, sea wolf **08** sea rover **09** privateer, sea robber **10** filibuster, freebooter

## buck
◊ anagram indicator **03** bok **04** soar, sore **05** cheer, dandy, soare, sorel **06** buoy up, dollar, ignore, marker, oppose,

resist, sorell, sorrel **07** counter, hearten, pricket **08** reassure **09** encourage **10** contradict **13** break the rules
• **buck up** **05** cheer, gee up, hurry, rally **06** hasten, perk up **07** cheer up, enliven, hearten, hurry up, improve **08** inspirit, step on it **09** encourage, stimulate, take heart **10** get a move on **14** rattle your dags **15** get your skates on

## bucket
**03** can, dip, tub **04** bail, bale, pail **05** ladle, stoop, stope, stoup **06** dipper, kibble, situla, stoope, vessel **07** pitcher, scuttle **09** clamshell
• **bucket chain** **05** noria **12** Jacob's ladder
• **bucket down** **04** pour **08** pelt down, pour down **11** rain heavily **15** rain cats and dogs

## buckle
◊ anagram indicator **04** bend, clip, fold, hasp, hook, kink, warp **05** bulge, catch, clasp, close, hitch, twist **06** cave in, fasten, secure **07** connect, crumple, distort, wrinkle **08** collapse, fastener **10** contortion, distortion
• **buckle down** **08** go all out **11** get down to it, knuckle down **15** start to work hard

## buckler
**05** pelta **06** target **08** rondache **09** protector **10** protection

## bucolic
**05** rural **06** rustic **07** country **08** agrarian, pastoral **11** countrified **12** agricultural

## bud
**03** eye, gem **04** bulb, germ, grow, knop, knot **05** caper, clove, gemma, knosp, shoot, sprig **06** bulbel, bulbil, button, embryo, friend, sprout, turion **07** brother, burgeon, cabbage, develop, plumule **09** débutante, pullulate **11** heart of palm, palm-cabbage **12** hibernaculum

## Buddhist
**03** Zen **04** lama **05** bonze **08** talapoin **09** Dalai Lama
• **Buddhist dome** **04** tope **05** stupa **06** dagaba, dagoba

## budding
**07** growing, nascent **09** embryonic, fledgling, flowering, gemmation, germinant, incipient, potential, promising **10** burgeoning, developing **11** up-and-coming

## buddy
**03** pal **04** chum, mate **05** crony **06** cobber, friend **07** brother, comrade **09** companion **10** buddy-buddy, good friend

## budge
**03** jee **04** bend, give, move, push, roll, stir, sway **05** bodge, bouge, shift, slide, stiff, yield **06** change, give in, remove **07** give way, pompous **08** convince, dislodge, persuade **09** influence **13** not compromise **14** change your mind

## budget

**04** plan **05** allot, allow, funds, means, quota **06** afford, bouget, bowget, ration **08** allocate, estimate, finances, schedule, set aside **09** allotment, allowance, apportion, economics, resources **10** allocation **13** financial plan

## buff

**03** fan, rub, tan **04** blow, fawn **05** beige, brush, fiend, freak, khaki, maven, rub up, sandy, shine, straw **06** addict, expert, nankin, polish, smooth, stroke **07** admirer, burnish, devotee, fanatic, nankeen, natural **09** yellowish **10** aficionado, enthusiast **11** connoisseur **14** yellowish-brown
• **in the buff 04** bare, nude **05** naked **08** in the raw, starkers, stripped **09** unclothed, uncovered, undressed **10** stark-naked **12** not a stitch on **13** with nothing on **15** in the altogether

## buffalo

**04** anoa, arna **05** bison, bugle **07** Bubalus, carabao, overawe, tamarao, tamarau, timarau, zamouse **08** bewilder, water cow

## buffer

**03** pad **06** absorb, bumper, deaden, fender, lessen, pillow, reduce, screen, shield, soften **07** bulwark, cushion, protect **08** diminish, mitigate, polisher, suppress **12** intermediary **13** shock absorber

## buffet

**03** box, hit, jar, tax **04** bang, beat, blow, buff, bump, café, cuff, harm, jolt, push, slap **05** clout, knock, pound, shove, smack, thump, weigh **06** batter, battle, blight, burden, pummel, strike **07** afflict, counter, disturb, oppress, trouble **08** cold meal, distress, snackbar **09** cafeteria, cold table, weigh down **11** self-service, smorgasbord **12** help yourself

## buffeted

◇ *anagram indicator*

## buffoon

**03** wag **04** fool, mime, mome, Vice, zany **05** antic, clown, comic, droll, joker **06** antick, jester, Scogan **07** anticke, antique, farceur, Scoggin, tomfool **08** comedian, farceuse, Iniquity **09** harlequin **10** mountebank, Scaramouch **11** Jack-pudding, merry-andrew, Punchinello, Scaramouche

## buffoonery

**05** farce **07** jesting, zanyism **08** clowning, drollery, nonsense **09** pantomime, silliness **10** tomfoolery **11** waggishness **12** harlequinade, pantaloonery **13** Pantagruelism

## bug

**03** fad, irk, tap, vex, wog **04** flaw, flea, germ, mite, snag **05** annoy, craze, error, fault, mania, thing, virus **06** bother, cootie, defect, harass, insect, needle, pester, wind up **07** blemish, disease, disturb, failing, gremlin, illness, microbe, monitor, wiretap **08** irritate, listen in, phone-tap

**09** aggravate, bacterium, eavesdrop, infection, obsession **10** listen in on, listen in to **11** eavesdrop on **12** creepy-crawly, imperfection **13** micro-organism **15** listening device

## bugbear

**03** bug **04** bane, bogy **05** bogey, bogle, dread, fiend, poker **06** horror **07** pet hate, rawhead **08** anathema **09** bête noire, nightmare **10** Mumbo-jumbo

## bugle

**10** flügelhorn **11** hunting-horn

## bugle-call

**04** post, taps **07** hallali, retreat **08** last post, reveille **09** first post, lights out **15** boots and saddles

## build

**03** big, set **04** body, form, make, rear, size **05** begin, edify, erect, frame, mason, put up, raise, shape, start **06** extend, figure, timber **07** augment, develop, enlarge, fashion, upbuild **08** assemble, escalate, increase, initiate, physique, throw out **09** construct, fabricate, institute, intensify, overbuild, structure, substruct **10** constitute, inaugurate **11** put together **13** knock together
• **build up 03** add **04** grow, hype, plug, rear **05** amass, boost, mount, set up **06** expand, extend, gather **07** aggrade, amplify, augment, collect, develop, enhance, enlarge, fortify, improve, mount up, promote **08** assemble, escalate, heighten, increase, snowball **09** advertise, construct, elaborate, establish, intensify, publicize, reinforce, structure **10** accumulate, strengthen **11** put together **13** piece together

## builder

**05** jerry, mason **06** waller **08** labourer **09** craftsman **11** craftswoman **12** craftsperson, manual worker **13** skilled worker

## building

◇ *anagram indicator* **04** pile **07** edifice **08** dwelling, erection **09** structure **11** development, fabrication **12** architecture, construction
*See also* **architecture**

*Building types include:*

**03** inn, pub
**04** barn, café, fort, mews, mill, pier, riad, shed, shop, silo
**05** abbey, arena, cabin, hotel, house, store, villa
**06** castle, chapel, church, cinema, garage, gazebo, mandir, mosque, museum, pagoda, palace, prison, school, stable, temple
**07** chateau, college, cottage, factory, library, low-rise, mansion, rotunda, theatre
**08** barracks, beach hut, bungalow, dovecote, fortress, gurdwara, high-rise, hospital, monument, outhouse, pavilion, showroom, skilling, skillion, windmill
**09** apartment, boathouse, cathedral, farmhouse, gymnasium,

mausoleum, monastery, multiplex, synagogue, warehouse
**10** lighthouse, maisonette, restaurant, skyscraper, sports hall, tower block, university
**11** condominium, observatory, office block, public house, summerhouse
**12** block of flats, power station
**14** apartment house, sliver building

*See also* **accommodation; house; tent**

*Buildings include:*

**05** Duomo
**07** BT Tower, CN Tower, Kremlin, La Scala, St Paul's, UN Plaza
**08** Casa Milà, Cenotaph, Chrysler, Flatiron, Panthéon, St Peter's, Taj Mahal
**09** Acropolis, Coit Tower, Colosseum, Notre Dame, Old Bailey, Parthenon, Reichstag, St Pancras, Taipei 101, The Louvre, US Capitol
**10** Guggenheim, Sears Tower, Tate Modern, The Gherkin, Trump Tower, Versailles, White House
**11** Canary Wharf, Eden Project, Eiffel Tower, Empire State, Musée d'Orsay, Space Needle, The Alhambra, The Panthéon, The Pentagon, Tower Bridge, Tower of Pisa
**12** Globe Theatre, Great Pyramid, Mont St Michel, Telecom Tower, The Parthenon, Winter Palace
**13** Crystal Palace, Dome of the Rock, Musée du Louvre, Royal Crescent, Somerset House, Tower of London
**14** Balmoral Castle, Barbican Centre, Blenheim Palace, Centre Pompidou, Hoover Building, Millennium Dome, Petronas Towers, Pompidou Centre, Sagrada Familia, UN Headquarters, Wells Cathedral
**15** Ashmolean Museum, Banqueting House, Brandenburg Gate, Capitol Building, Edinburgh Castle, Lincoln Memorial, Post Office Tower, Royal Opera House, Statue of Liberty, Westminster Hall

*See also* **religious; tower**

*Building materials include:*

**03** MDF
**04** clay, sand, tile, wood
**05** adobe, brick, fibro, glass, grout, slate, steel, stone
**06** ashlar, cement, girder, gravel, gypsum, lintel, lumber, marble, mastic, mortar, pavior, siding, tarmac, thatch, timber
**07** asphalt, bitumen, decking, drywall, fixings, granite, lagging, plaster, plastic, plywood, sarking, shingle
**08** asbestos, cast iron, cladding, concrete, hard core, roof tile, wall tile
**09** aggregate, aluminium, chipboard,

clapboard, flagstone, floor tile, hardboard, sandstone, steel beam
**10** glass fibre, insulation, matchboard
**11** breeze block, paving stone, roofing felt
**12** plasterboard
**13** building block, wattle and daub
**14** foam insulation, stainless steel

• **building area 04** site

### build-up
**04** gain, heap, hype, load, mass, plug, puff **05** drift, stack, store **06** growth **08** increase **09** accretion, expansion, marketing, promotion, publicity, stockpile **10** escalation **11** advertising, development, enlargement **12** accumulation

### built
◊ *anagram indicator*

### built-in
**05** fixed **06** fitted **07** in-built **08** implicit, included, inherent, integral **09** essential, intrinsic, necessary **11** fundamental, inseparable **12** incorporated

### bulb
**03** set **05** globe **11** Rupert's drop

*Plants grown from bulbs and corms include:*

**04** cive, eddo, iris, ixia, lily, taro
**05** camas, chive, onion, tulip
**06** allium, camash, camass, chives, crinum, crocus, garlic, nerine, scilla, squill
**07** anemone, freesia, jonquil, muscari, peacock, quamash
**08** amarylis, bluebell, camassia, curtonis, cyclamen, daffodil, endymion, galtonia, gladioli, harebell, hyacinth, scallion, snowdrop, sparaxis
**09** amaryllis, colchicum, crocosmia, galanthus, gladiolus, heliconia, narcissus, snowflake, tiger lily, Titan arum
**10** agapanthus, chionodoxa, fritillary, giant rouge, montbretia, ranunculus, snake's head, solfaterre, wand flower
**11** acidanthera, African lily, erythronium, fritillaria, hippeastrum, lapeirousia, naked ladies, spring onion, sternbergia, tiger flower
**12** autumn crocus, ornithogalum, Solomon's seal, wild hyacinth
**13** crown imperial, grape hyacinth, lily-of-the-Nile, striped squill, winter aconite
**14** belladonna lily, chincherinchee, glory of the snow, Ithuriel's spear
**15** dog's tooth violet, lily-of-the-valley

### bulbous
**06** convex, puffed **07** bloated, bulging, rounded, swollen **08** swelling, tuberous **09** distended, puffed out, pulvinate **10** pulvinated

### Bulgaria
**02** BG **03** BGR **04** Bulg

### bulge
**03** bag, bug, sag **04** bias, bulb, bump, hump, lump, rise **05** belly, pouch, strut, surge, swell **06** billow, dilate, expand, strout **07** blister, distend, enlarge, project, puff out, upsurge **08** increase, protrude, shoulder, swelling **10** distension, projection **12** protuberance **15** intensification

### bulk
**04** body, bouk, feck, hold, hull, mass, most, size **05** cargo, great, gross **06** extent, volume, weight **07** bigness **08** majority, quantity, roughage **09** amplitude, immensity, largeness, magnitude, nearly all, substance **10** dimensions, lion's share **13** preponderance
• **bulk out, bulk up 04** fill **06** expand, extend, fill up, pad out **07** fill out **08** increase **10** make bigger

### bulky
**03** big **04** huge **05** ample, gross, heavy, hefty, large, lofty, lusty **07** awkward, hulking, immense, lumping, mammoth, massive, volumed, weighty **08** colossal, enormous, unwieldy **10** cumbersome, voluminous **11** substantial **12** unmanageable

### bull
**02** ox **03** rot **04** brag, male, mick, neat **05** micky **06** mickey, strong, Taurus **07** massive **08** nonsense **09** policeman **10** Unigenitus **11** Hibernicism **12** Hibernianism

### bulldoze
**04** push, raze **05** bully, clear, force, level **06** coerce **07** flatten **08** browbeat, demolish **09** knock down **10** intimidate **11** push through, steamroller

### bullet
**04** ball, shot, slug **06** dumdum, pellet **07** missile **08** Biscayan **09** cartouche, cartridge, lead towel, Minié ball **10** projectile, propellant

### bulletin
**06** report, update **07** leaflet, message, release **08** dispatch **09** newsflash, newspaper, news sheet, statement **10** communiqué, newsletter **12** announcement, notification **13** communication

### bullfight
**07** corrida **10** tauromachy **14** corrida de toros

### bullfighter
**07** matador, picador **08** matadore, toreador **10** rejoneador **12** banderillero

### bullish
**06** upbeat **07** buoyant, hopeful **08** cheerful, positive, sanguine **09** confident, obstinate **10** aggressive, optimistic

### bully
◊ *anagram indicator* **03** cow **04** good, haze, huff, prey, thug **05** brave, bucko, great, heavy, tough, tyran **06** coerce, cuttle, hector, pick on, tyrant

### bluster
**07** bluster, bouncer, hoodlum, killcow, oppress, ruffian, torment **08** browbeat, bulldoze, bully-boy, bullyrag, domineer, overbear **09** excellent, persecute, souteneur, terrorize, tormentor, tyrannize, victimize **10** blustering, browbeater, Drawcansir, intimidate, persecutor, push around **11** intimidator **12** swashbuckler

### bulrush
**04** tule **08** cat's-tail

### bulwark
**04** wall **05** guard **06** buffer **07** bastion, defence, outwork, rampart, redoubt, sea-wall, support **08** buttress, mainstay, security **09** partition, safeguard **10** breakwater, embankment, protection **13** fortification

### bum
◊ *anagram indicator* **03** ass, bad, beg, dud, low **04** butt, coit, duff, hobo, hurl, loaf, naff, poor, rear, rump, seat, tail, toss **05** awful, booty, cadge, false, quoit, spree, tramp, wrong **06** behind, borrow, bottom, crummy, dosser, sponge **07** adverse, gangrel, rubbish, sponger, useless, vagrant **08** backside, beach boy, buttocks, scrounge, terrible, vagabond **09** imperfect, worthless **10** despicable, inadequate, unpleasant **12** disagreeable, unacceptable **14** unsatisfactory

### bumble
◊ *anagram indicator* **05** drone, idler, lurch **06** beadle, bungle, falter, teeter, totter **07** blunder, bungler, stagger, stumble

### bumbling
◊ *anagram indicator* **05** inept **06** clumsy **07** awkward, muddled **08** botching, bungling **09** lumbering, maladroit, stumbling **10** blundering **11** incompetent, inefficient

### bump
**03** hit, jar **04** bang, blow, hump, jerk, jole, joll, jolt, jowl, knur, lump, slam, thud, whap, whop **05** barge, bulge, crash, dunch, dunsh, joule, knock, prang, shake, shock, shove, smash, thump **06** bounce, impact, injury, jostle, jounce, nodule, rattle, strike **07** collide, papilla **08** dislodge, swelling **09** collision, speed bump **10** protrusion, tumescence **11** collide with **12** irregularity, protuberance
• **bump into 04** meet **07** run into **09** encounter, light upon **10** chance upon, come across, happen upon **12** meet by chance
• **bump off 03** top **04** do in, kill **06** murder, remove, rub out **08** blow away **09** eliminate, liquidate **11** assassinate

### bumper
**03** big **04** rich **05** great, jumbo, kelty, large, rouse **06** keltie **07** bouncer, massive **08** abundant, enormous, whopping **09** excellent, ginormous, plentiful **11** exceptional **12** supernaculum

## bumpkin

03 oaf, put, yap 04 boor, hick, lout, lowt, putt, rube 05 clown, yokel 06 rustic 07 hawbuck, hayseed, peasant 08 clodpate, clodpole, clodpoll 09 hillbilly 10 clodhopper, provincial 11 bushwhacker 12 country yokel 14 country bumpkin

## bumptious

04 coxy 05 brash, cocky, pushy 06 cocksy, uppish 07 forward, pompous 08 arrogant, boastful, impudent 09 assertive, bigheaded, conceited, egotistic, officious 10 swaggering, up yourself 11 overbearing 12 presumptuous 13 over-confident, self-important 14 full of yourself

## bumpy

05 jerky, lumpy, rough 06 bouncy, choppy, knobby, uneven 07 jolting, knobbly 08 pot-holed 09 irregular

## bun

03 wad 04 chou 05 brick 06 cookie 07 Bath bun, huffkin, teacake 08 black bun, cream bun, crescent, cross bun, rock cake 09 burger bun 10 Chelsea bun, currant bun, Eccles cake 11 hot cross bun 12 mosbolletjie

## bunch

03 bob, lot, mob, wad 04 band, club, crew, gang, heap, herd, hump, lump, mass, pack, pile, posy, team, tuft, wisp 05 batch, clump, crowd, flock, group, party, sheaf, spray, stack, swarm, troop 06 bundle, gather, huddle, number, string 07 bouquet, cluster, collect, corsage, nosegay 08 assemble, boughpot, fascicle, quantity, swelling 09 fascicule, gathering, multitude 10 assortment, châtelaine, collection, congregate, fasciculus, racemation 11 concentrate 12 tussie mussie 13 agglomeration

## bundle

◇ *anagram indicator* 03 bag, box, jag, kit, set, tie, wad, wap 04 bale, bind, drum, heap, mass, pack, pile, roll, rush, swag, wisp, wrap, yelm 05 batch, bavin, bluey, brawl, bunch, group, hurry, sheaf, shook, shove, skein, stack, truss, whisk 06 bottle, carton, faggot, fasces, fasten, gather, huddle, hustle, knitch, packet, parcel, tumble 07 cluster, dorlach, fascine, package 08 fascicle, quantity, shiralee, woolpack 09 fascicule, shirralee, trousseau 10 assortment, collection, fasciculus 11 consignment, push roughly 12 accumulation

## bung

03 pay, tip 04 cork, dead, dook, plug, seal 05 bribe, purse, shive 06 spigot 07 stopper, useless 08 bankrupt, cutpurse 10 pickpocket

## bungle

◇ *anagram indicator* 03 mar 04 boob, duff, flub, goof, mash, mess, muff, mull, ruin 05 blunk, bodge, botch, fluff, fudge, spoil 06 bobble, boggle, bumble, bummle, cock up, foozle, foul up, goof up, mangle, mess up,

muck up, muddle 07 bauchle, blunder, louse up, screw up 09 misguggle, mishandle, mismanage 10 mishguggle 11 make a mess of

## bungler

04 muff 05 blunk 06 bumble, bummle, duffer, tinker 07 blunker, botcher, bumbler 08 shlemiel, botcher, schlemiel, schlemihl 11 incompetent 13 butterfingers

## bungling

05 inept, messy 06 clumsy 07 awkward 08 botching 09 ham-fisted, ham-handed, maladroit, unskilful 10 amateurish, blundering, cack-handed 11 incompetent

## bunk

04 flee 05 berth, sleep 06 humbug 08 claptrap

## bunker

03 bin 04 fuel, trap 06 hazard 07 shelter 08 sand trap

## bunkum

02 BS 03 rot 04 blah, bosh, bull, bunk 05 balls, bilge, hooey, trash, tripe 06 humbug, piffle 07 baloney, garbage, hogwash, rubbish, twaddle 08 blah-blah, bulldust, claptrap, cobblers, malarkey, nonsense, tommyrot 09 bull's wool, poppycock 10 balderdash, codswallop 12 blah-blah-blah 13 horsefeathers

## bunting

04 cirl 05 flags, junco 07 ortolan 08 longspur 09 snowflake, snowfleck, snowflick 10 dickcissel 11 decorations, reed-sparrow, yellow-ammer 12 yellowhammer 13 writing-master

## buoy

03 dan 04 rise 05 float 06 beacon, marker, signal 07 dolphin, mooring
• **buoy up**   04 lift 05 boost, cheer, raise 06 bear up 07 cheer up, hearten, support, sustain 09 encourage

## buoyancy

03 joy, pep 06 bounce, growth, vigour 07 flotage 08 floatage, gladness, optimism, strength 09 geniality, happiness, jolliness, lightness, toughness 10 brightness, confidence, enthusiasm, resilience 11 development, good spirits 12 cheerfulness, floatability

## buoyant

05 happy, hardy, light, peppy, tough 06 afloat, blithe, bouncy, bright, joyful, lively, strong 07 bullish, growing 08 animated, carefree, cheerful, debonair, floating, thriving, youthful 09 adaptable, floatable, resilient, vivacious 10 developing, optimistic, weightless 12 light-hearted

## burble

03 lap 04 purl 06 babble, gurgle, murmur, tangle 07 confuse

## burden

03 bob, tax 04 bear, care, cark, duty, lade, load, onus, task, tote, yoke 05 beare, cargo, cross, crush, drone, trial, worry 06 bother, charge, fading,

impose, lumber, monkey, saddle, sorrow, strain, stress, weight 07 anxiety, burthen, holding, oppress, present, refrain, trouble 08 carriage, encumber, handicap, incumber, land with, overbulk, overload, pressure 09 agistment, cumbrance, grievance, lie hard on, millstone, overpress, overwhelm, undersong, weigh down 10 affliction, dead-weight, imposition, lie heavy on, obligation, overburden, overextend, overstress 11 encumbrance 14 responsibility

## burdensome

05 heavy 06 taxing, trying 07 irksome, onerous, weighty 08 crushing, exacting, grievous 09 chargeful, difficult, importune, wearisome 10 chargeable, oppressive 11 importunate, troublesome

## burdock

04 gobo 05 clote 07 clotbur, hardoke 08 clotebur 09 cocklebur

## bureau

04 desk 06 agency, branch, office 07 counter, service 08 division 10 department, escritoire 11 writing-desk

## bureaucracy

07 red tape 08 city hall, ministry 09 beadledom, paperwork, the system 10 government 11 officialdom 12 civil service 13 officiousness 14 administration, the authorities

## bureaucrat

04 suit 07 officer 08 Eurocrat, mandarin, minister, official 09 chinovnik 11 apparatchik, functionary 12 civil servant, office-holder 13 administrator 15 committee member

## bureaucratic

05 rigid 08 official 10 inflexible, procedural 11 complicated, ministerial 12 governmental 14 administrative

## burgeon

04 grow 05 swell 06 expand, extend 07 develop, enlarge 08 escalate, increase, snowball 11 proliferate

## burglar

04 yegg 05 thief 06 robber 07 yeggman 08 pilferer 09 cracksman 10 cat-burglar, trespasser 12 housebreaker

## burglary

05 heist, theft 07 break-in, larceny, robbery 08 stealing, trespass 09 pilferage 13 housebreaking

## burgle

03 rob 05 screw 09 break into, burst into, steal from 10 burglarize

## burial

07 burying, funeral 08 exequies 09 committal, interment, obsequies, sepulchre 10 entombment, inhumation

## burial place

05 crypt, grave, vault 06 kurgan 07 charnel, tumulus 08 catacomb, cemetery, God's acre, Golgotha, Pantheon 09 graveyard, mausoleum,

sepulcher, sepulchre **10** churchyard, necropolis **12** potter's field
*See also* **cemetery**

**Burkina Faso**
**02** BF **03** BFA

**burlesque**
**04** mock **05** comic, spoof **06** parody, satire, send-up **07** mockery, mocking, take-off **08** derisive, farcical, ridicule, travesty **09** parodying, satirical **10** caricature, heroi-comic **11** caricatural, hudibrastic **12** heroi-comical, mickey-taking **13** Pantagruelism

**burly**
**03** big **05** beefy, heavy, hefty **06** brawny, knotty, stocky, strong, sturdy **07** buirdly, hulking **08** athletic, muscular, powerful, thickset **09** strapping, well-built

**burn**
**03** fry, gut **04** bite, bren, char, fume, glow, hurt, itch, long, plot, sear, sere **05** blaze, brand, brook, cense, chark, flame, flare, flash, grill, inure, light, parch, ploat, scald, singe, smart, smoke, sting, swale, swayl, sweal, sweel, toast, yearn **06** brenne, desire, emboil, ignite, kindle, scorch, seethe, simmer, stream, tingle **07** be eager, combust, consume, corrode, cremate, destroy, flare up, flicker, glimmer, inflame, scowder, shrivel **08** be ablaze, be on fire, burn down, scouther, scowther, smoulder **09** catch fire, cauterize, incremate, set alight, set fire to **10** be in flames, deflagrate, incinerate **11** catch ablaze, conflagrate, go up in smoke, put a match to **12** be consumed by, go up in flames **13** put to the torch **15** burst into flames

**burning**
**02** in **03** hot, lit **04** live, sear **05** acrid, acute, afire, eager, fiery, quick, seare, urent, vital **06** ablaze, aflame, alight, ardent, biting, cauter, fervid, urgent, ustion **07** blazing, caustic, cautery, crucial, earnest, fervent, flaming, frantic, glowing, intense, pungent, searing **08** flagrant, flashing, frenzied, gleaming, piercing, pressing, scalding, smarting, stinging, swealing, tingling, vehement **09** consuming, essential, important, inburning, prickling, scorching **10** passionate **11** conflagrant, illuminated, impassioned, significant, smouldering **12** incendiarism **13** conflagration

**burnish**
**04** buff **05** glaze, shine **06** lustre, polish **08** brighten, polish up

**burp**
**04** wind **05** belch **08** eructate **10** eructation **11** bring up wind

**burrow**
**03** den, dig, set **04** bury, hole, howk, lair, mine, root, sett **05** delve, earth, wroot **06** gopher, nuzzle, search, tunnel, warren **07** retreat, rummage,

shelter **08** excavate, fox-earth **09** undermine **10** rabbit hole

**bursar**
**06** purser **07** cashier **09** treasurer

**bursary**
**05** award, grant **09** endowment **10** exhibition, fellowship **11** scholarship

**burst**
◊ *anagram indicator* **03** fit, fly, pop, run **04** bang, blow, clap, dart, gush, gust, loup, part, race, rush, tear **05** barge, blaze, blitz, brash, break, crack, erupt, flash, go off, go pop, hurry, plump, salvo, spate, split, spout, spurt, start, surge **06** blow up, bounce, go bang, shiver, spring, volley **07** blow-out, dehisce, disrupt, explode, rupture, shatter, torrent **08** distrain, fragment, outbreak, outburst, puncture **09** break in on, break open, discharge, fusillade, pull apart, split open **10** outpouring **11** push your way **12** disintegrate
• **burst out** **03** cry **04** buff **05** begin, flash, start, utter **06** cry out, irrupt **07** call out, exclaim, explode **08** blurt out, commence **10** break forth

**Burundi**
**02** RU **03** BDI

**bury**
◊ *containment indicator* **04** eard, hide, sink, tomb, yerd, yird **05** cover, earth, embed, grave, inter, plant, yeard **06** absorb, burrow, engage, engulf, entomb, inhume, occupy, shroud **07** conceal, enclose, engross, immerse, implant, inearth, inherce **08** enshroud, inhearse, submerge **09** lay to rest, sepulchre **15** put six feet under

**bus**
**03** ISA, PCI, USB **05** coach, trunk **06** jitney, pirate **09** two-decker, vaporetto **10** mammy-wagon, service car **11** park-and-ride **12** double-decker, single-decker

**bush**
**03** tod **05** brush, crude, hedge, plant, scrog, scrub, shrub, todde, wilds, woods **06** busket, forest, tavern **07** bramble, outback, thicket **08** bushland **09** backwoods, makeshift, primitive, scrubland **11** uncivilized **13** rough and ready
• **not beat about the bush** **11** speak openly **12** speak plainly **14** come to the point, commit yourself

**bushbaby**
**06** galago **07** nagapie **08** night-ape

**bushel**
**02** bu **03** fou

**bushranger**
**06** outlaw **07** brigand **10** highwayman **12** backwoodsman

*Bushrangers include:*

**04** **Cash** (Martin), **Hall** (Ben), **Howe** (Michael)
**05** **Brady** (Matthew), **Kelly** (Ned)
**06** **Caesar** (John 'Black Caesar'),

**Morgan** (Dan 'Mad Dog'), **Palmer** (George)
**07** **Donohoe** (Jack), **Gilbert** (Johnny)
**08** **Flash Dan** (Daniel Charters), **Gardiner** (Frank), **Governor** (Jimmy), **Governor** (Joe), **Melville** (Frank McCallum, 'Captain'), **Moonlite** (Andrew Scott, 'Captain')
**09** **Armstrong** (George), **Starlight** (Frank Pearson, 'Captain')
**11** **Thunderbolt** (Frederick Ward, 'Captain')
**12** **Jackey Jackey** (William Westwood)

**bushy**
**04** wiry **05** bosky, fuzzy, rough, stiff, thick, woody **06** dumose, dumous, fluffy, shaggy, unruly **07** bristly **09** bristling, luxuriant, spreading **12** dasyphyllous

**busily**
**04** hard **07** briskly **08** actively, speedily **09** earnestly **10** diligently **11** assiduously, strenuously **12** purposefully **13** energetically, industriously

**business**
**02** co **03** biz, bus, job **04** baby, deal, duty, firm, gear, line, task, work **05** issue, point, topic, trade **06** affair, buying, career, matter, métier, outfit, pigeon **07** calling, company, concern, problem, selling, subject, trading, venture **08** commerce, dealings, flagship, industry, question, vocation **09** franchise, operation, syndicate **10** bargaining, consortium, employment, enterprise, occupation, profession **11** corporation, partnership **12** conglomerate, organization, transactions **13** establishment, manufacturing, merchandizing, multinational, parent company **14** holding company, responsibility

*Businesses include:*

**02** BA, BP
**03** BAA, BAE, BAT, BHS, BMW, BSB, EMI, HMV, IBM, ICI, MFI, NCP, NEC, RAC, RBS
**04** Asda, BASF, Dell, Esso, Fiat, HBOS, HSBC, Rank, Sony
**05** Abbey, Alcan, Bayer, Boots, Canon, Corus, Enron, Exxon, Heinz, Honda, Intel, Mazda, Nokia, Ricoh, Sharp, Shell, Tesco, Volvo
**06** Adecco, Arriva, Boeing, Diageo, Dixons, Du Pont, Hanson, L'Oreal, Nestlé, Nissan, Pfizer, Suzuki, Texaco, Toyota, Virgin, Wimpey
**07** Alcatel, Arcadia, Aventis, Chevron, easyJet, Fujitsu, Harrods, Hitachi, Hyundai, Lafarge, Marconi, Matalan, Minerva, Pearson, Pepsico, Peugeot, Renault, Reuters, Samsung, Siemens, Toshiba, Wal-Mart, W H Smith
**08** AXA Group, Barclays, Burberry, Centrica, Chrysler, Coca-Cola, Goodyear, JP Morgan, Michelin,

Olivetti, Rentokil, Rio Tinto, Unilever, Vodafone, Waitrose **09** Akzo Nobel, John Laing, Ladbrokes, Lloyds TSB, McDonald's, Microsoft, Morrisons, Schroders, Whitbread **10** Exxon Mobil, Greene King, J Sainsbury, Kingfisher, Mitsubishi, Nationwide, Pilkington, Prudential, Rolls-Royce, Sainsbury's, Somerfield, Stagecoach, Telefonica, Volkswagen, Walt Disney **11** AstraZeneca, Caterpillar, Isuzu Motors, Nippon Steel, Standard Oil, William Hill **12** Allied Domecq, Eastman Kodak, Hilton Hotels, Merrill Lynch, Northern Rock, Philip Morris, Philips Group, Reed Elsevier, Sears Roebuck, Total Fina Elf, Union Carbide, Union Pacific, Western Union **13** Abbey National, Anglo American, Balfour Beatty, General Motors, Harvey Nichols, Lever Brothers, Sanyo Electric, Taylor Woodrow, Travis Perkins **14** Alfred McAlpine, British Airways, Credit Agricole, Hewlett-Packard, Virgin Atlantic **15** American Express, DaimlerChrysler, Deutsche Telekom, Electrolux Group, General Electric, GlaxoSmithKline, Legal and General, Marks and Spencer, National Express, News Corporation

• **business centre 04** city
• **do business 04** deal, sell
• **go out of business 04** fold

**businesslike**
**05** slick **06** formal **07** correct, orderly, precise **08** thorough **09** efficient, organized, practical, pragmatic **10** impersonal, methodical, systematic **11** painstaking, well-ordered **12** matter-of-fact, professional

**businessman, businesswoman**
**06** trader, tycoon, wallah **07** Babbitt, magnate **08** city gent, employer, merchant **09** boxwallah, executive, financier **10** capitalist **12** entrepreneur, manufacturer **13** industrialist

*Businesspeople include:*

**04** Benz (Karl Friedrich), Bond (Alan), Boot (Sir Jesse), Cook (Thomas), Ford (Henry), Jobs (Steven), Mond (Ludwig), Shah (Eddy), Tate (Sir Henry), Wang (An) **05** Arden (Elizabeth), Astor (John, Lord), Bosch (Carl), Fayed (Mohamed al-), Forte (Charles, Lord), Gates (Bill), Getty (Jean Paul), Grade (Michael), Heinz (Henry John), Honda (Soichiro), Krupp (Friedrich), Laker (Sir Freddie), Leahy (Sir Terry), Lyons (Sir Joseph), Marks (Simon, Lord), Nobel (Alfred), Rolls (Charles),

Royce (Sir Henry), Sugar (Sir Alan), Trump (Donald), Zeiss (Carl) **06** Ansett (Sir Reg), Boeing (William Edward), Browne (John, Lord), Butlin (Billy), Conran (Sir Terence), Cunard (Sir Samuel), Dunlop (John Boyd), du Pont (Pierre Samuel), Fugger (Johannes), Gamble (Josias), Hammer (Armand), Hilton (Conrad Nicholson), Hoover (William Henry), Hughes (Howard), Mellon (Andrew William), Morgan (J Pierpont), Packer (Kerry), Turner (Ted) **07** Agnelli (Giovanni), Barclay (Robert), Branson (Sir Richard), Bugatti (Ettore), Cadbury (George), Cadbury (John), Citroën (André Gustave), Iacocca (Lee), Kennedy (Joseph P), Maxwell (Robert), Murdoch (Rupert), Onassis (Aristotle), Roddick (Anita), Sotheby (John), Tiffany (Charles Lewis) **08** Birdseye (Clarence), Carnegie (Andrew), Christie (James), Gillette (King Camp), Guinness (Sir Benjamin Lee), Michelin (André), Nuffield (William Richard Morris, Viscount), Olivetti (Adriano), Pulitzer (Joseph), Rathenau (Walther), Rowntree (Joseph), Sinclair (Sir Clive) **09** Arkwright (Sir Richard), Carothers (Wallace), Firestone (Harvey Samuel), Sainsbury (Alan John, Lord), Selfridge (Harry Gordon), Woolworth (Frank Winfield) **10** Berlusconi (Silvio), Guggenheim (Meyer), Leverhulme (William Hesketh Lever, Viscount), Pilkington (Sir Alastair), Rothschild (Meyer Amschel), Vanderbilt (Cornelius) **11** Beaverbrook (Max, Lord), Harvey-Jones (Sir John), Rockefeller (John D)

**busker**
**14** street-musician

**bust**
◇ *anagram indicator* **04** duff, head, herm, phut, raid, term **05** boobs, bosom, break, chest, crack, herma, kaput, punch, smash, spree, torso, wonky **06** arrest, breast, broken, damage, demote, faulty, ruined, statue **07** breasts, destroy, shatter **08** terminus **09** defective, penniless, sculpture **10** on the blink, on the fritz, out of order **11** out of action
• **go bust 04** fail, flop, fold **05** crash **06** go bung **07** founder **08** collapse **09** close down **11** go to the wall **14** become bankrupt **15** become insolvent

**bustle**
◇ *anagram indicator* **03** ado **04** belt, buzz, dash, fuss, rush, stir, tear, to-do, trot, whew **05** haste, hurry **06** bestir, bumble, bummle, flurry, hasten, pother, ruffle, rustle, scurry, tumult **07** fluster, scamper, the rush **08** activity, rush hour, scramble, to and

fro, tournure **09** agitation, commotion, stirabout **10** excitement, hurly-burly **11** hurry-scurry, hurry-skurry **12** rush to and fro **13** dress-improver **15** a hive of activity, hustle and bustle

**bustling**
◇ *anagram indicator* **04** busy, full **05** astir **06** active, hectic, lively **07** abustle, buzzing, crowded, humming, rushing, teeming **08** eventful, restless, stirring, swarming, thronged **09** energetic, on the trot

**busy**
◇ *anagram indicator* **04** at it, full **05** manic **06** absorb, active, bustle, eident, embusy, employ, engage, hectic, lively, occupy, red-hot, throng, tied up, tiring **07** concern, crowded, engaged, engross, flat out, frantic, go about, immerse, involve, on the go, teeming, vibrant, working **08** bustling, diligent, employed, eventful, hard at it, interest, involved, meddling, occupied, on the job, restless, sedulous, swarming, tireless **09** assiduous, detective, energetic, engrossed, on the trot, stirabout, strenuous **10** busy as a bee **11** industrious, snowed under, unavailable, up to the eyes **12** having a lot on, in conference **13** under pressure **14** fully stretched, having a lot to do, in the thick of it **15** up to the eyeballs, up to the eyebrows
• **be busy 03** hum

**busybody**
**03** pry **05** snoop **06** gossip **07** meddler, snooper **08** intruder, quidnunc **09** pragmatic **10** interferer, stickybeak **11** Nosey Parker **12** eavesdropper, troublemaker **13** mischief-maker, scandalmonger **14** pantopragmatic

**but**
**03** bar, nay, sed **04** just, only, save **06** anyway, at most, even so, except, merely, purely, simply **07** barring, besides, however **08** omitting **09** apart from, aside from, excepting, excluding, objection, other than **10** all the same, for all that, leaving out, no more than **11** just the same, nonetheless **12** nevertheless **15** notwithstanding
• **all but 04** near **06** almost

**butch**
**04** male **05** macho, tough **06** virile **07** manlike, mannish **09** masculine

**butcher**
◇ *anagram indicator* **04** kill, slay **05** botch, spoil **06** killer, slayer **07** destroy, flesher **08** massacre, murderer, mutilate **09** destroyer, liquidate, slaughter **10** meat trader **11** assassinate, exterminate, meat counter, slaughterer, supermarket **12** mass murderer, meat retailer

**butchery**
**06** murder **07** carnage, killing **08** abattoir, butcher's, massacre, shambles **09** bloodshed, meat trade, slaughter **10** mass murder **11** meat-selling **12** blood-letting **13** meat

retailing **14** slaughterhouse **15** mass destruction

**butler**
**03** RAB **08** khansama **09** khansamah, sommelier **12** bread-chipper

**butt**
**03** box, bum, but, end, hit, jab, keg, nip, nut, ram, tip, tun **04** base, bump, bunt, cask, dout, dupe, foot, haft, horn, mark, pipe, poke, prod, push, stub **05** dunch, dunsh, knock, punch, roach, shaft, shove, snipe, stock, stump **06** barrel, bottom, buffet, bumper, dog-end, fag end, firkin, handle, object, stooge, target, thrust, tierce, victim **07** butt end, remnant, rundlet, subject, tail end **08** buttocks, hogshead **09** posterior, scapegoat **10** table-sport **12** jesting-stock **13** laughing-stock
• **butt in** **05** cut in **06** horn in, meddle **07** break in, intrude **09** interfere, interject, interpose, interrupt **12** put your oar in **15** stick your nose in

**butter**
**03** ghi, ram **04** drop, ghee, goat **06** beurre **08** flattery
• **butter producer** **04** mowa, shea **05** mahua, mahwa, mowra
• **butter up** **04** coax **06** cajole, kowtow, praise **07** blarney, flatter, wheedle **08** kowtow to, pander to, soft-soap, suck up to **14** be obsequious to

**buttercup**
**06** gilcup **07** giltcup, kingcup **08** crowfoot **10** goldilocks, ranunculus

**butterfingers**
**04** muff

**butterfly**
**05** light **07** flighty **10** dilettante
See also **animal; insect; moth**

Butterflies include:

**03** map
**04** blue, wall
**05** argus, comma, elfin, heath, satyr, white
**06** apollo, copper, hermit, morpho, pierid, psyche
**07** admiral, cabbage, monarch, Papilio, peacock, ringlet, satyrid, skipper, thistle, Ulysses, vanessa
**08** birdwing, cardinal, grayling, hesperid, milk-weed
**09** brimstone, cleopatra, Hesperian, holly blue, metalmark, nymphalid, orange-tip, wall brown, wood white
**10** brown argus, common blue, fritillary, gatekeeper, hairstreak, red admiral
**11** large copper, meadow-brown, painted lady, Scotch argus, swallowtail
**12** cabbage-white, dingy skipper,

Essex skipper, marbled-white, white admiral
**13** chalkhill blue, clouded yellow, mourning cloak, purple emperor, tortoiseshell
**15** black hairstreak, brown hairstreak, green hairstreak, grizzled skipper, heath fritillary, Lulworth skipper, marsh fritillary, mountain ringlet

**buttocks**
**03** ass, bum, can, fud **04** buns, butt, coit, doup, duff, prat, rear, rump, seat, tail, tush **05** booty, fanny, nates, pratt, quoit, tushy **06** behind, bottom, breech, cheeks, heinie, tushie **07** crouper, croupon, gluteus, hurdies, keister, sit-upon **08** backside, derrière, haunches **09** fundament, hinder-end, posterior **10** hinderlans, hinderlins **11** hinderlands, hinderlings **12** hindquarters
See also **bottom**

**button**
**04** disc, frog, knob, link, stud **05** catch, clasp, lever **06** barrel, olivet, switch, toggle **08** bell push, fastener **09** fastening

**buttonhole**
**03** nab **04** grab **05** catch **06** accost, bail up, collar, corner, detain, waylay **09** importune, take aside **11** boutonnière

**buttress**
**04** pier, prop, stay **05** brace, shore, strut **06** back up, hold up, prop up **07** shore up, support, sustain, tambour **08** abutment, mainstay, underpin **09** bolster up, reinforce, stanchion **10** strengthen **11** counterfort **13** reinforcement

**buxom**
**05** ample, busty, jolly, plump, sonsy **06** bosomy, chesty, comely, lively, sonsie, zaftig **07** bucksom, elastic **08** yielding **09** Junoesque, pneumatic **10** Rubenesque, voluptuous **11** full-figured, well-endowed, well-rounded, well-stacked **12** full-breasted **13** large-breasted

**buy**
**03** fix, get, job **04** chop, coff, deal, take **05** bribe, hedge, scalp, shout, trade **06** buy off, market, nobble, obtain, pay for, pick up, redeem, snap up, suborn **07** acquire, bargain, emption, engross, overbuy, procure, shop for **08** invest in, panic-buy, purchase, underbuy **09** speculate, stock up on, subsidize **10** go shopping, shop around **11** acquisition, merchandize, splash out on **13** do the shopping

**buyer**
**06** broker, client, dealer, emptor, patron, vendee **07** shopper **08** consumer, customer **09** purchaser

**buzz**
**03** fad, hum **04** call, high, kick, purr, race, ring, zing **05** craze, drone, kicks, pulse, throb, throw, whirr **06** bustle, gossip, latest, murmur, rumour, thrill **07** buzzing, hearsay, resound, scandal **08** resonate, susurrus, tinnitus **09** bombilate, bombinate, phone call, susurrate **10** enthusiasm, excitement **11** bombilation, bombination, reverberate, stimulation, susurration **15** word on the street

**buzzard**
**04** pern **05** buteo **07** bee-kite, puttock **08** zopilote **09** gallinazo

**buzzer**
**03** bee **08** telltale **09** whisperer

**by**
◇ juxtaposition indicator **01** X **02** at, in, of, on **03** gin, per, via **04** away, near, over, past, with **05** along, aside, close, forby, handy, times, using **06** at hand, before, beside, beyond, next to **07** close by, close to, through **09** alongside, by means of **11** according to, no later than **12** in relation to **15** under the aegis of

**bygone**
**04** lost, past **05** olden **06** former **07** ancient, antique, one-time **08** departed, forepast, previous **09** erstwhile, forgotten **10** antiquated, dinosauric

**bypass**
**04** CABG, omit **05** avoid, dodge, evade, shunt, skirt **06** detour, ignore **07** neglect **08** ring road, sidestep, slip road **09** diversion, sidetrack **10** circumvent **12** steer clear of **13** find a way round

**by-product**
**06** result **07** fallout, spin-off **10** derivative, entailment, side effect **11** after-effect, concomitant, consequence **12** repercussion **13** epiphenomenon, knock-on effect

**bystander**
**07** watcher, witness **08** looker-on, observer, onlooker, passer-by, talesman **09** spectator **10** eyewitness, rubberneck

**byword**
**03** saw **05** adage, ideal, maxim, model, motto **06** ayword, dictum, saying, slogan **07** epitome, example, nayword, paragon, precept, proverb **08** aphorism, exemplar, overcome, standard **09** catchword, watchword **10** apophthegm, embodiment **14** perfect example

**Byzantine**
◇ anagram indicator **06** knotty **07** complex **08** tortuous **09** intricate **11** complicated **12** labyrinthine

# C

**C**
**03** cee, san, see **07** Charlie

**cab**
**04** taxi **05** cabin, noddy **06** drosky, fiacre, hansom **07** droshky, growler, minicab, taxicab, vettura **08** quarters **10** two-wheeler **11** compartment, four-wheeler **15** hackney carriage

**cabal**
**03** set **04** plot **05** junta, junto, party **06** clique, league **07** coterie, faction **08** conclave, intrigue, plotters **09** camarilla, coalition

**cabaret**
**04** acts, club, show **05** turns **06** comedy **07** dancing, singing, variety **09** night club **10** restaurant **11** performance **13** entertainment

**cabbage**
**04** chou, cole, gobi, kail, kale, wort **05** savoy, steal **06** greens **07** bok choy, castock, custock, pak choi, purloin **08** colewort, drumhead, kohlrabi **09** banknotes **10** choucroute, greenstuff, paper money, sauerkraut **11** cauliflower, sea colewort **13** Chinese leaves **14** Brussels sprout

**cabbage-head**
**04** loaf

**cabin**
**03** hut **04** bach, crib, room, shed **05** berth, bothy, coach, cuddy, lodge, shack **06** cabana, chalet, refuge, saloon, shanty **07** cottage, gondola, shelter **08** log-house, quarters **09** signal box, stateroom **10** roundhouse **11** compartment

**cabinet**
**04** case **05** bahut, chest, filer, store **06** closet, locker, senate, shrine **07** almirah, console, dresser **08** cupboard, vargueño **09** executive, ministers **10** chiffonier, encoignure, government, leadership, secretaire **11** chiffonnier **12** Privy Council **14** administration, official family

**cable**
**03** fax, guy **04** co-ax, cord, flex, lead, line, rope, stay, wire **05** chain, e-mail, radio **06** feeder, halser, hawser **07** coaxial **08** telegram, transmit **09** facsimile, send a wire, telegraph **11** Telemessage® **13** send a telegram **15** send by telegraph

**cache**
**04** fund, hide **05** hoard, stash, stock, store **06** garner, supply **07** reserve **09** stockpile **10** collection, repository,

storehouse **12** accumulation **13** treasure-store **14** hidden treasure

**cachet**
**06** esteem, favour, status **08** approval, eminence, prestige **10** estimation, reputation, street cred **11** distinction

**cack-handed**
**05** gawky, inept **06** clumsy **07** awkward **08** bungling **09** all thumbs, ham-fisted, unskilful **10** blundering, left-handed, ungraceful **11** heavy-handed **13** unco-ordinated

**cackle**
**04** crow **05** clack **06** gabble, gaggle, giggle, keckle, titter **07** chortle, chuckle, snigger **09** loud laugh **11** laugh loudly **15** unpleasant laugh

**cacophonous**
**04** loud **05** harsh **07** grating, jarring, raucous **08** strident **09** dissonant **10** discordant **11** horrisonant **12** inharmonious

**cacophony**
**03** din **06** racket **07** discord, jarring **09** charivari, harshness, stridency **10** disharmony, dissonance **11** raucousness **12** caterwauling

**cactus**

*Cacti include:*

**04** crab, toad, tuna
**05** dildo, nopal
**06** barrel, cereus, cholla, Easter, mescal, old man, orchid, peanut, peyote
**07** jointed, old lady, opuntia, rainbow, saguaro
**08** dumpling, gold lace, hedgehog, rat's tail, snowball, starfish, Turk's cap
**09** bunny ears, Christmas, goat's horn, gold charm, Indian fig, mistletoe, sea-urchin
**10** cotton-pole, sand dollar, silver ball, strawberry, zygocactus
**11** grizzly bear, mammillaria, prickly pear, scarlet ball, silver torch
**12** golden barrel
**13** Bristol beauty, schlumbergera
**14** drunkard's dream
**15** queen of the night, snowball cushion

**cad**
**03** oik, rat **04** heel **05** devil, knave, rogue, swine **06** rascal, rotter, wretch **07** bleeder, bounder, scumbag, stinker, villain **08** blighter, deceiver **09** miscreant, reprobate, scoundrel **10** blackguard

**cadaver**
**04** body **05** stiff **06** corpse **07** carcase, remains **08** dead body

**cadaverous**
**03** wan **04** pale, thin **05** ashen, gaunt **07** ghostly, haggard **08** skeletal **09** death-like, emaciated **10** corpse-like

**caddy**
**05** chest

**cadence**
**04** beat, fall, lilt, rate **05** close, metre,

pulse, swing, tempo, throb, trope **06** accent, euouae, evovae, rhythm, stress **07** falling, measure, pattern, sinking **09** half-close **10** inflection, intonation, modulation

**cadge**
**03** beg, bot, bum **05** mooch, mouch, ponce **06** sponge **08** scrounge

**cadmium**
**02** Cd

**cadre**
**03** set **04** band, crew, gang, team **05** corps, squad **10** small group

**caesium**
**02** Cs

**café**
**04** caff **06** bistro, buffet, pull-in **07** noshery, tea room, tea shop, wine bar **08** snackbar **09** brasserie, cafeteria, coffee bar, cybercafé, estaminet, truck stop **10** coffee shop, restaurant **11** greasy spoon

**cafeteria**
**04** café, caff **06** buffet **07** canteen **10** restaurant **15** self-service café

**cage**
**03** mew, pen **04** coop, corf, dray, drey **05** cavie, grate, hutch, pound **06** aviary, corral, keavie, lock-up **07** tumbler **09** enclosure

**caged**
**05** mewed **06** shut up **07** encaged **08** confined, cooped up, fenced in, locked up **09** impounded **10** imprisoned, restrained **12** incarcerated

**cagey**
**04** wary, wily **05** chary **06** shrewd **07** careful, guarded **08** cautious, discreet **09** secretive **11** circumspect **12** non-committal

**cahoots**
• **in cahoots  08** in league **09** colluding **10** conspiring, in alliance **11** hand in glove, in collusion **13** collaborating

**cairn**
**03** man **04** barp **05** raise

**cajole**
**04** coax, dupe, lure, wile, work **05** moody, tempt **06** beflum, chat up, diddle, entice, humbug, seduce, soothe, whilly **07** beguile, blarney, cuittle, flatter, mislead, wheedle **08** blandish, butter up, get round, inveigle, persuade, soft-soap **09** sweet-talk, whillywha **10** whillywhaw **12** work yourself

**cajolery**
**05** wiles **06** duping **07** blarney, coaxing **08** flattery, soft soap **09** sweet talk, wheedling, whillywha **10** cajolement, enticement, inducement, inveigling, misleading, persuasion, whillywhaw **11** beguilement, inducements **12** blandishment, inveiglement **13** blandishments

**cake**
**03** bar, dry, pan **04** coat, cube, farl,

loaf, lump, mass, pone, slab **05** block, chunk, cover, fancy, farle, slice **06** harden, pastry, tablet **07** congeal, encrust, plaster, thicken **08** solidify **09** coagulate **11** consolidate

---

*Cakes, pastries and puddings include:*

**03** bun, pie
**04** baba, flan, fool, plum, puri, rock, roti, tart
**05** angel, bombe, cream, crêpe, fairy, fudge, Genoa, jelly, lardy, poori, pound, queen, scone, sweet, torte
**06** banana, carrot, cheese, churro, coffee, Dundee, Eccles, éclair, gateau, ginger, girdle, junket, marble, mousse, muffin, parkin, simnel, sponge, trifle, waffle, yum-yum
**07** baklava, Banbury, bannock, Bath bun, brioche, brownie, cannoli, crumble, crumpet, cupcake, currant, fig roll, fritter, iced bun, jam roll, jam tart, Madeira, mudcake, oatcake, pancake, Pavlova, pikelet, plum pie, ratafia, rum baba, saffron, savarin, soufflé, stollen, strudel, tartlet, teacake, wedding, Yule log
**08** apple pie, birthday, black bun, doughnut, flummery, macaroon, malt loaf, meringue, mince pie, mooncake, pecan pie, sandwich, seedcake, syllabub, tiramisu, turnover, whim-wham
**09** cherry-pie, chocolate, Christmas, clafoutis, cranachan, cream horn, cream puff, drop scone, fruitcake, fruit tart, lamington, lemon tart, madeleine, panettone, Sally Lunn, shortcake, Swiss roll
**10** Battenburg, cheesecake, Chelsea bun, key lime pie, panna cotta, Pontefract, pumpkin pie, tarte tatin, upside-down
**11** baked Alaska, banana bread, banoffee pie, crème brulée, custard tart, gingerbread, hot cross bun, jam roly-poly, lady's finger, Linzertorte, plum pudding, profiterole, rice pudding, Sachertorte, sago pudding, spotted dick, treacle tart
**12** apfel strudel, Bakewell tart, chocolate log, custard slice, Danish pastry, figgy pudding, hasty pudding, pease pudding
**13** apple dumpling, apple turnover, Scotch pancake, sponge pudding, summer pudding
**14** apple charlotte, charlotte russe, steamed pudding, toasted teacake, Victoria sponge
**15** chocolate éclair, queen of puddings

---

*See also* **bun**

**calamitous**
◇ *anagram indicator* **04** dire **05** fatal **06** deadly, tragic, woeful **07** ghastly, ruinous **08** dreadful, grievous, wretched **10** disastrous **11** cataclysmic, devastating **12** catastrophic

**calamity**
**02** wo **03** wae, woe **04** blow, Jane, ruin, ruth, woes **05** trial **06** mishap **07** reverse, scourge, tragedy, trouble **08** disaster, distress, downfall **09** adversity, mischance **10** affliction, misfortune **11** catastrophe, tribulation **12** misadventure **15** sword of Damocles

**calcium**
**02** Ca

**calculate**
**03** aim **04** cast, make, plan, rate, work **05** add up, count, gauge, judge, tally, think, value, weigh **06** assess, cipher, cypher, derive, design, figure, intend, reckon **07** compute, measure, purpose, suppose, work out **08** consider, estimate, reckon up **09** determine, enumerate

**calculated**
**06** wilful **07** planned **08** computed, intended, measured, purposed, reckoned, tactical **10** considered, deliberate, purposeful, well-judged **11** intentional **12** premeditated

**calculating**
**03** sly **04** wily **05** sharp **06** crafty, shrewd **07** cunning, devious **08** scheming **09** designing **10** contriving **11** circumspect **12** manipulative **13** Machiavellian
• **calculating aid 03** log **04** abac **06** abacus **07** soroban **08** computer, isopleth, nomogram **09** nomograph, slide rule **10** calculator **12** arithmometer **14** alignment chart **15** digital computer

**calculation**
**03** sum **06** answer, result **08** estimate, figuring, forecast, logistic, planning **09** evolution, judgement, reckoning **10** alligation, arithmetic, assessment, estimation, figurework, working-out **11** computation, mensuration **12** deliberation

**calculus**
**04** lith- **06** tartar **07** urolith **08** fluxions **09** sialolith **11** quaternions

**calendar**

---

*Calendars include:*

**05** Bahà'í, Hindu, lunar, Roman, solar
**06** Coptic, Hebrew, Jewish, Julian
**07** Chinese, Islamic, Persian
**09** arbitrary, Gregorian, lunisolar
**10** republican
**13** revolutionary

---

*See also* **animal; month**

**calf**
**04** boss, dogy, veal **05** bossy, dogie, poddy, slink **06** vealer **08** maverick

**calibre**
**03** cal **04** bore, gage, size **05** gauge, gifts, merit, worth **06** league, talent **07** ability, faculty, measure, quality, stature **08** capacity, diameter, strength **09** character **10** competence, endowments, excellence **11** distinction

**California**
**02** CA **05** Calif

**californium**
**02** Cf

**call**
**02** ca', go **03** bid, caa', cap, cry, dub, mot, run **04** bawl, bell, buzz, caul, cite, hail, name, need, nemn, page, pink, plea, ring, roar, term, toll, yell **05** brand, cause, claim, cleep, clepe, cooee, cooey, hight, label, order, phone, pop in, right, shout, style, title, visit **06** appeal, ask for, bellow, call in, come by, cry out, demand, drop in, excuse, invite, market, reason, reckon, rename, ring up, scream, shriek, signal, stop by, summon, tinkle **07** baptize, command, contact, convene, enstyle, entitle, exclaim, grounds, hallali, phone up, request, send for, summons, warning **08** assemble, christen, occasion **09** call round, designate, pay a visit, telephone **10** denominate, describe as, invitation **11** ask to come in, exclamation **12** announcement **13** justification **14** ask to come round
• **call for 05** levy, need, take **05** claim, fetch, go for **06** demand, entail, pick up **07** collect, involve, justify, push for, require, solicit, suggest, warrant **08** occasion, press for **11** necessitate **13** make necessary
• **call off 04** drop **05** scrub **06** cancel, revoke, shelve **07** abandon, rescind **08** break off, withdraw **11** discontinue
• **call on 03** ask, bid, gam, put, see **04** urge **05** plead, visit **06** appeal, demand, invoke, summon, wait on **07** entreat, request **08** appeal to, go and see, look in on, press for, wait upon **10** supplicate
• **call up 04** buzz, pick, ring **05** phone, raise **06** choose, enlist, invite, ring up, select, sign up, summon, take on **07** contact, display, phone up, recruit **08** settle on **09** conscript, telephone
• **on call 05** ready **06** on duty **09** on standby **10** standing by

**called**
**03** hot **04** hote **05** nempt

**call girl**
**04** tart **05** whore **06** harlot, hooker **07** hustler **10** loose woman, prostitute **12** street-walker **14** lady of the night

**calling**
**03** job **04** line, work **05** field, trade **06** career, métier **07** mission, pursuit **08** business, province, vocation **10** employment, line of work, occupation, profession **14** line of business

**callous**
**04** cold **05** cruel, harsh, horny, stony, tough **06** seared **08** hardened, indurate, obdurate, uncaring **09** heartless, insensate, unfeeling **10** hard-bitten, hard-boiled, insensible, iron-headed **11** cold-blooded, cold-hearted, hard as nails, hard-hearted, indifferent,

# callously

insensitive **12** case-hardened, stony-hearted, thick-skinned **13** unsympathetic

# callously

**06** coldly **07** harshly **11** heartlessly, unfeelingly **13** cold-bloodedly, hard-heartedly, insensitively

# callow

**03** raw **05** green, naive **06** jejune, rookie **07** puerile, untried **08** immature, innocent, juvenile **09** fledgling, guileless, unbearded, unfledged **11** uninitiated **13** inexperienced **15** unsophisticated

# calm

**03** cam **04** alay, came, caum, cool, ease, even, hush, loun, lown, lull, mild **05** aleye, allay, lound, lownd, peace, quiet, relax, sleek, still **06** becalm, pacify, placid, poised, repose, sedate, serene, settle, smooth, soothe, steady, stilly **07** appease, assuage, compose, easeful, halcyon, mollify, placate, quieten, relaxed, reposed, restful, unmoved **08** ataraxia, calmness, composed, cool down, dead-wind, laid-back, peaceful, pipeclay, quietude, serenity, tranquil, waveless, windless **09** collected, composure, impassive, lighten up, limestone, nerveless, placidity, sangfroid, stillness, supercool, temperate, unclouded, unexcited, unruffled **10** cool-headed, equanimity, phlegmatic, settle down, simmer down, untroubled **11** contentment, impassivity, restfulness, undisturbed, unemotional, unexcitable, unflappable, unflustered, unpassioned, unperturbed **12** even-tempered, keep your head, on an even keel, peacefulness, tranquillity, tranquillize, unpassionate **13** dispassionate, impassiveness, imperturbable, self-possessed, unimpassioned **14** presence of mind, self-controlled, unapprehensive, unflappability **15** cool as a cucumber

# calmly

**08** steadily **11** impassively **12** on an even keel **13** unemotionally **14** phlegmatically **15** dispassionately

# calorie

**01** C **03** cal

# calumny

**05** abuse, libel, lying, smear **06** attack, insult, mud pie **07** obloquy, slander **09** aspersion **10** backbiting, defamation, derogation, detraction, revilement **11** denigration, slagging-off **12** vilification, vituperation **13** disparagement

# camaraderie

**08** affinity, intimacy **09** closeness **10** fellowship, friendship **11** brotherhood, comradeship, sociability **12** togetherness **13** brotherliness, companionship, esprit de corps **14** fraternization, good fellowship

# Cambodia

**01** K **03** KHM

# Cambridge University

*see* **college**

# camel

**04** oont **08** Bactrian **09** dromedare, dromedary **15** ship of the desert

# camera

*Cameras include:*

**02** TV
**03** APS, SLR, TLR
**04** CCTV, cine, disc, film, Fuji®, view
**05** Canon®, Kodak®, Leica®, Nikon®, plate, press, sound, still, video
**06** Konica®, Pentax®, reflex, Rollei®, stereo, Super 8®, Webcam
**07** bellows, compact, digital, Minolta®, obscura, Olympus®, pinhole, Yashica®
**08** dry-plate, Polaroid®, Praktica®, security, wet-plate
**09** automatic, binocular, camcorder, half-plate, miniature, panoramic, Rolliflex®, single use, Steadicam®
**10** box Brownie®, disposable, Instamatic®, sliding box
**11** large-format
**12** quarter-plate, subminiature, surveillance
**13** daguerreotype, folding reflex, point-and-press
**14** twin-lens reflex
**15** cinematographic

• **move camera 03** pan **05** track

# Cameroon

**03** CAM, CMR

# camouflage

◇ *anagram indicator* **04** hide, mask, veil **05** blind, cloak, cover, front, guise **06** façade, screen **07** conceal, cover up, cover-up, deceive, obscure **08** disguise **09** deception **10** maskirovka, masquerade **11** concealment, counterfeit

# camp

**03** set **04** duar, laer, side, tent **05** campy, crowd, douar, dowar, group, gypsy, party, tents **06** caucus, clique, encamp, laager, outlie **07** bivouac, faction, leaguer, rough it, section **08** affected, campsite, mannered **09** pitch camp, posturing, set up camp **10** artificial, effeminate, encampment, over the top, pitch tents, theatrical **11** camping-site, exaggerated **12** ostentatious **13** camping-ground, sleep outdoors

• **confined to camp 02** CC

# campaign

**03** war **04** push, work **05** blitz, drive, fight, jehad, jihad, lobby **06** attack, battle, strive **07** canvass, crusade, journey, promote **08** advocate, movement, strategy, struggle **09** offensive, operation, promotion **10** expedition **14** course of action

# campaigner

**06** zealot **07** fighter **08** activist, advocate, champion, crusader, promoter, reformer **10** enthusiast

# camp-follower

**03** boy **05** toady **06** bummer, lackey, lascar **08** hanger-on, henchman **11** leaguer-lady, leaguer-lass

# can

**03** dow, jar, jug, lav, loo, mug, tin **04** dows, jail, pail, stir **06** prison, toilet **08** canister, jerrycan, lavatory, preserve **09** container **10** chimney pot, receptacle **11** depth charge
*See also* **prison; toilet**
• **can it** *see* **quiet; shut up** *under* **shut**

# Canada

**03** CAN, CDN
*See also* **prime minister; province**

*Canadian cities and notable towns include:*

**06** Ottawa, Quebec, Regina
**07** Calgary, Halifax, Toronto
**08** Edmonton, Montreal, Victoria, Winnipeg
**09** Saskatoon, Vancouver

*Canadian landmarks include:*

**06** Mt Thor
**07** CN Tower, Mt Logan, Niagara, Rockies, Sky Dome
**08** Lake Erie
**09** Hudson Bay, Lake Huron, Mt Seymour
**10** Great Lakes, St Lawrence
**11** Lake Ontario
**12** Lake Superior, Niagara Falls
**13** Algonquin Park, Parc Olympique
**14** Horseshoe Falls, Rocky Mountains

# Canadian

**03** Can, Cdn **06** Canuck

# canal

**03** Can, gut **04** duct, foss, moat, tube **05** ditch, fosse, zanja **06** groove, trench **07** channel, enteron, passage, shipway **08** waterway **10** navigation **11** watercourse **14** digestive tract

*Canals include:*

**04** Erie, Kiel, Suez
**05** Grand
**06** Panama, Rideau
**07** Corinth, Midland, Welland
**10** Caledonian, Mittelland
**11** Welland Ship
**14** Manchester Ship

# cancel

**03** axe, nix **04** drop, kill, stop, undo, wipe **05** abort, adeem, annul, erase, quash, scrap, scrub **06** delete, offset, repeal, revoke, shelve, strike **07** abandon, abolish, call off, nullify, red-line, rescind, retract, vitiate, wash out **08** abrogate, break off, cross out, dissolve, override, postpone, suppress, withdraw, write off **09** eliminate, strike out **10** declare off, invalidate, obliterate, scrub round

## cancellation

**11** countermand, discontinue
**14** counterbalance
• **cancel out** **06** offset, redeem
**07** balance, nullify **09** make up for
**10** compensate, counteract, neutralize
**14** counterbalance

## cancellation

**06** repeal **07** erasure **08** deletion,
dropping, quashing, shelving, stopping
**09** abolition, annulment, scrubbing
**10** abandoning, calling-off, nullifying,
revocation **11** abandonment,
elimination **12** invalidation
**14** neutralization

## cancer

**03** rot **04** Big C, Crab, evil **06** blight,
canker, growth, plague, tumour
**07** disease, scourge, the Big C, the
Crab **08** cancroid, sickness
**09** carcinoma **10** corruption,
malignancy, pestilence **15** malignant
growth

## candelabrum

**07** menorah **09** lampadary
**11** candlestick

## candid

**04** fair, open **05** blunt, clear, frank,
plain, round, white **06** honest, simple
**07** liberal, shining, sincere, unposed
**08** informal, truthful, unbiased
**09** guileless, impartial, ingenuous,
outspoken **10** forthright **11** plain-
spoken, unequivocal, unrehearsed
**12** heart-to-heart **15** straightforward

## candidate

**03** PPC **06** runner, seeker **07** entrant,
nominee **08** aspirant, examinee
**09** applicant, contender, postulant,
pretender **10** competitor, contestant
**11** possibility
• **candidate list** **04** leet **06** ticket

## candidly

**06** openly, simply **07** bluntly, clearly,
frankly, plainly, roundly, up-front
**08** honestly **09** liberally, sincerely
**10** truthfully **11** guilelessly,
ingenuously, outspokenly
**12** forthrightly **13** unequivocally

## candle

**03** dip **04** slut **05** cerge, sperm, taper,
torch **06** bougie, ulicon, ulikon
**07** oolakan, oulakan, shammes,
ulichon **08** amandine, eulachan,
eulachon, luminary, oulachon,
shammash, tealight, wax light
**09** tallow dip **10** night-light **12** tallow
candle

## candour

**06** purity **07** honesty, naivety
**08** kindness, openness **09** bluntness,
franchise, frankness, plainness,
sincerity, whiteness **10** directness,
liberality, simplicity **11** artlessness,
brusqueness **12** impartiality, plain-
dealing, truthfulness **13** guilelessness,
ingenuousness, outspokenness
**14** forthrightness **15** unequivocalness

## candy

**05** glacé, kandy **06** candie, sweets
**07** cocaine, encrust, lollies, toffees

**10** chocolates **11** crystallize
**13** confectionery

## cane

**03** rod **05** crook, ratan, staff, stick,
swish, swits **06** ferule, jambee, rattan,
switch **07** tickler, whangee **09** riding
rod **10** alpenstock, supplejack
**12** swagger-stick, walking-stick

## canine

**01** c **04** tush **06** cuspid **08** dogtooth, eye
tooth
*See also* **dog**

## canker

**03** rot **04** bane, boil, evil, sore
**05** decay, ulcer **06** blight, cancer,
infect, lesion, plague **07** corrupt,
destroy, disease, pollute, scourge
**08** sickness **09** corrosion, infection
**10** cankerworm, corruption,
pestilence, ulceration

## cannabis

**03** kef, kif, pot, tea **04** benj, blow,
dope, gage, hash, hemp, kaif, leaf,
puff, punk, toke, weed **05** bhang,
blunt, ganja, gauge, grass, joint, roach,
skunk, splay **06** bifter, bomber, greens,
reefer, spliff **07** hashish **08** locoweed,
Mary Jane **09** marihuana, marijuana,
substance **10** sinsemilla, wacky baccy
**12** electric puha

## cannibal

**08** man-eater **09** Thyestean, Thyestian
**11** people-eater **15** anthropophagite

## cannibalism

**08** exophagy **09** endophagy, man-
eating **12** people-eating
**13** anthropophagy

## cannibalistic

**09** man-eating, Thyestean
**10** exophagous **11** endophagous
**12** people-eating **15** anthropophagous

## cannily

**06** subtly **07** acutely, sharply
**08** astutely, cleverly, shrewdly
**09** knowingly, skilfully

## cannon

**03** gun **05** carom, saker **06** barker, big
gun, curtal, falcon, monkey, mortar,
Quaker **07** battery, bombard, chamber,
nursery **08** basilisk, culverin, field gun,
great gun, howitzer, murderer,
oerlikon, ordnance, spitfire **09** artillery,
carambole, carronade, Quaker gun,
zumbooruk **10** fieldpiece, serpentine
**11** stern-chaser **12** demi-culverin
**14** murdering-piece

## cannonade

**05** salvo **06** volley **07** barrage
**08** pounding, shelling **09** broadside
**11** bombardment

## canny

**03** sly **04** good, nice, wice, wise
**05** acute, lucky, pawky, sharp **06** artful,
astute, clever, gentle, shrewd, subtle
**07** careful, knowing, prudent, skilful
**08** cautious, innocent **09** fortunate,
judicious, sagacious **11** circumspect,
worldly-wise **13** perspicacious

## canoe

**04** waka **05** kaiak, kayak **06** dugout
**07** piragua **08** montaria, woodskin
**09** monoxylon

## canon

**03** can, law **04** line, rota, rule **05** round,
vicar **06** priest, square, squier, squire
**07** brocard, dictate, precept, statute
**08** Mathurin, minister, reverend,
standard, vice-dean **09** clergyman,
criterion, Mathurine, principle,
yardstick **10** prebendary, regulation
**12** residentiary

## canonical

**07** regular **08** accepted, approved,
orthodox **10** authorized, recognized,
sanctioned **13** authoritative
• **canonical hours**

*Canonical hours include:*

**04** none, sext
**05** lauds, nones, prime, terce
**06** matins, tierce
**07** complin, orthros, vespers
**08** compline, evensong

## canonize

**05** bless, saint **07** beatify, besaint
**08** sanctify

## canopy

**03** sky **04** dais, tilt **05** cover, herse,
shade, state **06** awning, estate, hearse,
huppah, tester **07** chuppah, majesty,
marquee, shelter, veranda
**08** ciborium, covering, marquise,
pavilion, shamiana, sunshade,
umbrella, verandah **09** baldachin,
baldaquin, clamshell, parachute,
shamianah **10** cooker hood, tabernacle
**11** baldacchino **12** cloth of state

## cant

**04** kant, tilt **05** argot, brisk, lingo,
merry, slang, slope **06** jargon, lively,
snivel **07** snuffle **09** hypocrisy
**10** vernacular **11** insincerity, rogues'
Latin **12** thieves' Latin
**15** pretentiousness

## cantankerous

**05** cross, testy **06** crabby, crusty,
grumpy, ornery **07** crabbed, grouchy,
peevish, piggish **08** contrary, perverse,
stubborn **09** crotchety, difficult,
irascible, irritable **11** bad-tempered,
carnaptious, curnaptious, ill-
humoured, quarrelsome **13** quick-
tempered

## canteen

**04** café **05** flask, Naafi **06** buffet
**08** snackbar **09** cafeteria, refectory
**10** commissary, restaurant

## canter

**03** jog, ren, rin, run **04** lope, trot
**05** amble, titup **06** gallop, tittup
**07** jogtrot, tripple **11** false gallop

## canton

**03** can **04** Vaud **05** space **06** corner
**08** division, ordinary

## canvas

**04** tent **05** Binca®, sails, tents
**06** burlap, muslin **08** oilcloth

## canvass

04 poll, scan, sift 05 study 06 debate, survey 07 agitate, analyse, discuss, examine, explore, find out, inspect 08 campaign, evaluate 09 seek votes 10 scrutinize 11 ask for votes, electioneer, inquire into, investigate 12 solicit votes 13 drum up support

## canyon

05 abyss, cañon, chasm, gorge, gully 06 cañada, ravine, valley

## cap

03 hat, lid, mob, taj, tam, top 04 beat, bung, call, caul, coat, coif, curb, kepi, plug 05 beret, chaco, cover, crown, excel, kippa, limit, mutch, outdo, quoif, shako, tammy, toque, tuque 06 amorce, barret, berret, better, biggin, bonnet, bunnet, calpac, chapka, czapka, exceed, granny, kalpak, pileus, shacko 07 biretta, bycoket, calotte, calpack, control, eclipse, ferrule, grannie, montero, stopper, surpass 08 capeline, chaperon, gorblimy, outshine, outstrip, restrain, restrict, schapska, trencher, yarmulka, yarmulke, zuchetta, zuchetto 09 capelline, chaperone, cock's-comb, crown cork, glengarry, gorblimey, transcend, trenchard, zucchetto 10 cockernony, Kilmarnock 11 bonnet-rouge, mortarboard, Tam o' Shanter 12 cheesecutter 13 international 15 go one better than
See also **hat**

## capability

05 means, power, skill 06 talent 07 ability, faculty 08 aptitude, capacity, facility 09 potential 10 competence, efficiency 11 proficiency, skilfulness 13 qualification 14 accomplishment

## capable

04 able 05 adept, apt to, smart 06 clever, fitted, gifted, suited 07 needing, notable, skilful 08 allowing, liable to, masterly, talented 09 competent, efficient, qualified, tending to 10 disposed to, inclined to, proficient 11 experienced, intelligent 12 accomplished, businesslike 13 comprehensive

## capably

04 ably 07 adeptly 08 cleverly 09 skilfully 11 competently, efficiently 12 proficiently 13 intelligently

## capacious

03 big 04 huge, vast, wide 05 ample, broad, large, roomy, womby 07 liberal, sizable 08 generous, spacious 09 expansive, extensive 10 commodious, voluminous 11 comfortable, elephantine, substantial 13 comprehensive

## capacity

03 cap, job 04 bind, gift, post, role, room, size 05 power, range, scope, skill, space 06 extent, genius, office, talent, volume 07 ability, compass, content, faculty 08 aptitude, function, position 09 largeness, magnitude, potential, readiness, resources 10 capability, cleverness, competence, competency, dimensions, efficiency 11 appointment, proficiency, proportions, sufficience 12 intelligence
• **in the capacity of** 03 qua

## cape

01 C 03 ras 04 coat, head, naze, neck, ness, robe, scaw, skaw, wrap 05 amice, cloak, fanon, fichu, point, shawl, talma 06 almuce, domino, mantle, muleta, poncho, sontag, tippet, tongue 07 burnous, manteel, mozetta, pelisse 08 burnouse, headland, pelerine 09 peninsula 10 promontory
See also **cloak; peninsula**

Capes include:

| | |
|---|---|
| 03 | Cod |
| 04 | Fear, Horn, York |
| 05 | Wrath |
| 06 | Cretin, Orange |
| 07 | Kennedy, Leeuwin, Lookout |
| 08 | Farewell, Foulwind, Good Hope, Suckling |
| 09 | Canaveral, Carbonara, St Vincent, Trafalgar, Van Diemen |
| 10 | Finisterre, Kidnappers, Providence |
| 11 | Three Points, Tribulation |
| 12 | Hopes Advance |
| 13 | Prince of Wales |

## caper

03 hop 04 dido, jape, jest, jump, lark, leap, romp, skip 05 antic, bound, crime, dance, flisk, frisk, prank, scoup, scowp, stunt 06 affair, antics, bounce, cavort, frolic, gambol, prance, spring 07 gambado 08 business, capriole, escapade, mischief 09 high jinks 10 pigeon-wing

## Cape Verde

03 CPV

## capital

◊ head selection indicator 02 A1, uc 03 cap 04 cash, head, main, seat 05 chief, first, fonds, funds, major, means, money, prime, stock 06 assets, uncial, wealth 07 central, finance, leading, primary, savings, serious 08 cardinal, foremost, main city, property, reserves 09 excellent, important, majuscule, principal, resources 10 investment 11 block letter, investments, wherewithal 12 block capital, liquid assets 13 capital letter 15 upper-case letter
See also **city; currency**
• **small capitals** 02 sc

## capitalism

12 laissez-faire 14 free enterprise

## capitalist

05 mogul 06 banker, fat cat, tycoon 07 magnate, moneyer 08 investor, moneyman 09 bourgeois, financier, moneybags, plutocrat 12 money-spinner 13 person of means

## capitalize

• **capitalize on** 07 exploit 08 cash in on 10 profit from 13 make the most of 15 take advantage of

## capitulate

05 yield 06 give in, give up, relent, submit 07 succumb 08 back down 09 surrender 15 throw in the towel

## capitulation

08 giving-in, giving-up, yielding 09 relenting, surrender 10 submission, succumbing 11 backing-down

## caprice

03 fad 04 whim 05 fancy, freak, humor, quirk 06 humour, megrim, notion, spleen, vagary, vapour, whimsy 07 fantasy, impulse 08 humoresk, migraine, phantasy 09 capriccio 10 fickleness, fitfulness, humoresque 11 inconstancy 14 changeableness

## capricious

◊ anagram indicator 03 odd 05 freak, queer 06 fickle, fitful, kittle, quirky, wanton 07 erratic, wayward 08 fanciful, freakish, humorous, perverse, petulant, variable 09 arbitrary, fantastic, impulsive, mercurial, uncertain, whimsical 10 capernoity, changeable, humoursome, inconstant 11 capernoitie, cappernoity, fantastical 13 unpredictable

## capsize

◊ reversal indicator 04 purl 05 upset 06 invert 07 tip over, whemmle, whomble, whommle, whummle 08 keel over, overturn, roll over, turn over 10 turn turtle 11 overturning

## capsule

03 pod, urn 04 boll, pill 05 craft, jelly, probe, shell 06 bomber, caplet, cocoon, module, ovisac, sheath, tablet 07 habitat, lozenge, sandbox 08 pyxidium, spansule 09 container, poppy-head, radio pill 10 nidamentum, receptacle 11 sporogonium

## captain

03 cid 04 boss, head, lead, skip 05 chief, owner, pilot 06 direct, guider, leader, manage, master, old man, patron 07 command, control, officer, patroon, skipper 08 capitayn 09 commander, commodore, supervise 10 ritt-master, shipmaster 12 be in charge of 13 master-mariner, protospataire, whaling-master 14 protospathaire 15 protospatharius

Captains include:

| | |
|---|---|
| 04 | Ahab, **Cook** (James), **Hook**, **Kidd** (William), **Nemo** |
| 05 | **Bligh** (William), **Flint** (Jim Turner), **Johns** (W E), **Queeg**, **Smith** (John), **Swing** |
| 07 | **Corelli** (Antonio), **Marryat** (Frederick) |
| 08 | **Bobadill**, **Hastings** (Arthur), **MacHeath** |
| 09 | **Singleton** |
| 10 | **Hornblower** (Horatio) |

## caption

04 note 05 title 06 arrest, legend, titles 07 cutline, heading, wording 08 headline 09 underline 11 inscription

## captious

**07** carping, peevish **08** critical, niggling **09** quibbling **10** nit-picking, scrupulous **13** hair-splitting, hypercritical

## captivate

**03** get, win **04** lure, take **05** charm **06** allure, dazzle, seduce **07** attract, beguile, bewitch, delight, enamour, enchant, enthral **09** enrapture, fascinate, hypnotize, infatuate, mesmerize **11** take by storm

## captivating

**06** taking **07** winsome **08** alluring, catching, charming, dazzling **09** beautiful, beguiling, seductive **10** attractive, bewitching, delightful, enchanting **11** enthralling, fascinating

## captive

**03** POW **05** caged, slave **06** secure, shut up **07** caitive, convict, hostage, subject, triumph **08** confined, detained, detainee, enslaved, ensnared, interned, internee, jailbird, locked up, prisoner **09** enchained, in bondage **10** imprisoned, locked away, restrained, restricted **12** incarcerated **13** held in custody

## captivity

**05** bonds, exile **06** duress **07** bondage, custody, slavery **09** detention, endurance, restraint, servitude **10** constraint, internment **11** confinement, enslavement **12** imprisonment **13** incarceration

## captor

**05** guard **06** jailor, keeper, warder **09** custodian **12** incarcerator

## capture

◇ *containment indicator* **03** cop, nab, net, win **04** land, nick, rush, take, trap, with **05** carry, catch, mop up, seize, snare, withe **06** arrest, collar, cut out, entrap, occupy, pick up, record, secure, taking **07** embrace, ensnare, express, nabbing, nicking, run down, seizure, snabble, snaffle **08** catching, hit a blot, hunt down, imprison, surprise, trapping **09** apprehend, collaring, recapture, represent, reproduce **11** encapsulate **12** imprisonment, take prisoner **13** taking captive **14** taking prisoner
• **be captured** **04** fall

## capuchin

**03** sai **05** Cebus, sajou **07** sapajou

## car

**04** auto, cart, heap **05** motor **07** chariot, clunker, vehicle, vettura **08** motor car **09** speedster **10** automobile, rust bucket **12** motor vehicle **13** shooting brake

*Car manufacturers include:*

**02** MG, RR, VW
**03** BMW, Kia
**04** Audi, Fiat, Ford, Jeep, Lada, Mini, Saab, Seat, Yugo
**05** Buick, Dodge, Honda, Isuzu, Lexus, Lotus, Mazda, Riley, Rover, Skoda, Smart, Volvo
**06** Austin, Daewoo, Datsun, Jaguar, Lancia, Morgan, Morris, Nissan, Proton, Subaru, Talbot, Toyota
**07** Bentley, Bugatti, Citroën, Daimler, Ferrari, Hillman, Hyundai, Peugeot, Pontiac, Porsche, Reliant, Renault, Trabant, Triumph
**08** Cadillac, Chrysler, Daihatsu, De Lorean, Maserati, Mercedes, Standard, Vauxhall, Wolseley
**09** Alfa Romeo, Chevrolet, Land Rover
**10** Mitsubishi, Oldsmobile, Rolls Royce, Vanden Plas, Volkswagen
**11** Aston Martin, Lamborghini
**12** Mercedes-Benz

*Car types include:*

**02** RR
**03** cab, MPV, SUV
**04** jeep, limo, Mini®, taxi
**05** brake, break, buggy, coupé, sedan
**06** banger, Beetle®, estate, hearse, jalopy, kit-car, saloon, tourer
**07** jaloppy, minivan
**08** fastback, hot hatch, panda car, roadster, runabout, Smart car®, stock car
**09** all-roader, bubble-car, cabriolet, hatchback, Land Rover®, limousine, muscle car, off-roader, patrol car, sports car
**10** Model T Ford®, Range Rover®, Sinclair C5, subcompact, veteran car, vintage car
**11** convertible
**12** station wagon
**13** people carrier, shooting brake
**14** four-wheel drive

*Famous cars include:*

**04** FAB1
**08** Blue Bird
**09** Batmobile, Christine, Genevieve
**11** Flintmobile

*Car and motor vehicle parts include:*

**03** ABS
**04** axle, boot, door, gear, hood, horn, jack, sill, tyre, vent, wing
**05** bezel, clock, grill, shaft, trunk, wheel
**06** airbag, bonnet, bumper, clutch, dimmer, engine, fender, heater, hub-cap, roo bar, towbar
**07** battery, bull bar, chassis, fog lamp, gas tank, gearbox, kingpin, spoiler, sunroof
**08** air brake, air inlet, bodywork, brake pad, door-lock, fog light, headrest, ignition, jump lead, lift gate, oil gauge, roof rack, seat belt, silencer, solenoid, sun visor, swingarm, track rod
**09** brake drum, brake shoe, crankcase, dashboard, disc brake, drum brake, filler cap, fuel gauge, gear-lever, gearshift, gear-stick, handbrake, headlight, indicator, monocoque, overrider, prop shaft, rear light, reflector, sidelight, spare tyre, stoplight, wheel arch
**10** brake light, drive shaft, petrol tank, power brake, rev counter, side mirror, stick shift, suspension, windscreen, windshield, wing mirror
**11** accelerator, anti-roll bar, exhaust pipe, ignition key, jockey wheel, number plate, parcel shelf, speedometer
**12** licence plate, parking-light, quarterlight, transmission
**13** centre console, courtesy light, cruise control, flasher switch, pneumatic tyre, rack and pinion, radial-ply tyre, reclining seat, shock absorber, side-impact bar, steering-wheel
**14** air-conditioner, central locking, electric window, emergency light, four-wheel drive, hydraulic brake, rear-view mirror, reversing light, steering-column
**15** windscreen-wiper

*Car and motoring-related terms include:*

**02** AA
**03** dip, GPS, LRP, map, MOT, RAC, tow
**04** exit, park, skid, SORN, stop
**05** amber, brake, crash, cut up, flash, layby, on tow, prang, shunt
**06** diesel, fill up, filter, garage, hold up, hybrid, L-plate, octane, petrol, pile-up, pull in
**07** blowout, bollard, bus lane, car park, car wash, cat's-eye, give way, logbook, MOT test, neutral, pull out, reverse, road map, snarl up, tax disc, traffic
**08** accident, change up, coasting, declutch, fast lane, flat tyre, gridlock, indicate, junction, main beam, overtake, puncture, red light, road rage, services, slip road, slow lane, speeding, tailback, taxi rank, turn left, unleaded
**09** blind spot, breakdown, collision, cycle lane, fifth gear, first gear, green card, hit-and-run, radar trap, road atlas, road studs, roadworks, sixth gear, third gear, T junction, turn right, wheelspin, white line
**10** accelerate, amber light, arm signals, bottleneck, change down, change gear, change lane, contraflow, crossroads, fourth gear, green light, inside lane, middle lane, pedestrian, petrol pump, roundabout, screenwash, second gear, speed limit, stay in lane, straight on, tailgating, traffic jam, yellow line
**11** box junction, crawler lane, drink driver, driving test, hand signals, highway code, outside lane, speed camera, traffic cone, traffic cops, traffic news, zigzag lines
**12** drink-driving, hard shoulder, left-hand lane, motorway toll, one-way system, parking meter, passing place, road junction,

speeding fine, tyre pressure
**13** Belisha beacon, drink and drive, driving lesson, driving school, flashing amber, handbrake turn, jump the lights, left-hand drive, level crossing, no-claims bonus, parking ticket, pay and display, penalty points, petrol station, power steering, right-hand lane, super unleaded, traffic lights, traffic police, zebra crossing
**14** cadence braking, double declutch, driving licence, four-wheel drive, mini-roundabout, MOT certificate, motorway pile-up, overtaking lane, poor visibility, puffin crossing, right-hand drive, service station, speeding ticket, unleaded petrol
**15** pelican crossing, put your foot down, road fund licence, test certificate, traction control, warning triangle

*See also* **vehicle**

**carafe**
**03** jug **05** flask **06** bottle, flagon **07** pitcher **08** decanter

**caravan**
**02** RV **03** van **04** line **05** group, train **06** cafila, convoy, kafila **07** caffila, trailer **09** camper van, Dormobile® , motor home, Winnebago® **10** mobile home

**carbon**
**01** C **04** copy **07** diamond **08** graphite **09** buckyball
• **carbon copy** **02** cc **03** bcc **06** flimsy **08** manifold

**carbuncle**
**04** boil, bump, lump, sore **06** bunion, pimple **07** anthrax, blister **12** inflammation

**carcase, carcass**
**04** body, hulk **05** shell **06** corpse, cutter **07** cadaver, remains **08** dead body, skeleton **09** framework, structure
*See also* **meat**

**card**
**03** ace, map, mix **04** Amex, club, comb, jack, king, tose, toze **05** deuce, heart, joker, knave, queen, spade, toaze **06** domino, master, meishi **07** diamond **10** adulterate **13** carte-de-visite
*See also* **eccentric; game**
• **cards suits** **01** c, d, h, s **05** clubs **06** hearts, spades **08** diamonds
• **on the cards** **06** likely **08** possible, probable **11** looking as if, looking like **13** the chances are
• **playing cards** **04** deck, hand **11** devil's books

**cardinal**
**02** HE **03** key **04** main **05** basic, chief, first, pivot, prime **06** number, red hat **07** capital, central, highest, leading, primary **08** foremost, greatest, grosbeak **09** essential, important, paramount, principal **10** pre-eminent **11** fundamental **14** apostolic vicar
*See also* **archbishop; number**

*Cardinals include:*

**03** Sin (Jaime)
**04** Gray (Gordon), Hume (Basil), Pole (Reginald), Retz (Jean Françoise de)
**05** Chigi (Fabio)
**06** Beaton (David), Borgia (Rodrigo), Fisher (John), Heenan (John Carmel), Medici (Giovanni de'), Newman (John Henry), Rovere (Francesco della), Stuart (Henry, Duke of York), Wolsey (Thomas)
**07** Bethune (David), Langham (Simon), Langton (Stephen), Mazarin (Jules), Mendoza (Pedro Gonzalez de), Pandulf, Vaughan (Herbert), Wiseman (Nicholas), Ximenes (Francisco)
**08** Alberoni (Giulio), Aubusson (Pierre d'), Beaufort (Henry), Stepinac
**09** Richelieu (Armand Jean Duplessis, Duc de), Wyszynski (Stefan)
**10** Bellarmine (Robert), Breakspear (Nicolas), Mindszenty (József)
**13** Murphy-O'Connor (Cormac)

• **cardinal's office** **03** hat

**care**
**04** cark, fear, heed, mind, reck, reke, ward **05** kaugh, pains, worry **06** bother, burden, charge, hang-up, kiaugh, regard, strain, stress, tender **07** anxiety, caution, concern, control, custody, keeping, minding, tending, thought, trouble **08** accuracy, disquiet, distress, interest, pressure, prudence, tutelage, vexation **09** attention, give a damn, oversight, vigilance **10** affliction, attendance, protection **11** be concerned, carefulness, forethought, heedfulness, safekeeping, supervision, tribulation **12** be interested, guardianship, looking-after, watchfulness, watching-over **13** consideration **14** circumspection, meticulousness, responsibility
• **care for** **04** like, love, mind, tend, want **05** enjoy, nurse **06** attend, desire **07** cherish, protect **08** be fond of, be keen on, maintain **09** be close to, delight in, look after, watch over **10** minister to, provide for, take care of **12** be in love with
• **care of** **01** c/- **02** c/o

**career**
◇ *anagram indicator* **03** job, ren, rin, run **04** bolt, dash, life, past, race, rush, tear **05** shoot, speed, trade, whang **06** gallop, hurtle, métier **07** calling, cariere, pursuit **08** life-work, vocation **10** employment, livelihood, occupation, profession

**carefree**
**05** happy **06** blithe, breezy, cheery **07** halcyon **08** cheerful, debonair, laid-back **09** easy-going, fancy-free, unworried **10** debonnaire, insouciant, nonchalant, rollicking, untroubled **11** thoughtless, unconcerned **12** happy-go-lucky, light-hearted **13** irresponsible

**careful**
**04** mean, wary, wise **05** alert, aware, chary, close, heedy, tight **06** eyeful,

frugal, stingy **07** anxious, guarded, heedful, mindful, miserly, precise, prudent, sparing, tactful, thrifty **08** accurate, cautious, detailed, diligent, discreet, rigorous, sensible, thorough, vigilant, watchful **09** assiduous, attentive, judicious, niggardly, penny-wise **10** deliberate, economical, fast-handed, fastidious, hard-fisted, methodical, meticulous, particular, scrupulous, solicitous, systematic, thoughtful **11** circumspect, close-fisted, close-handed, painstaking, punctilious, tight-fisted **12** parsimonious, softly-softly **13** conscientious, penny-pinching

**carefully**
**05** hooly **06** warily **07** charily, closely **09** guardedly, heedfully, mindfully, precisely, prudently, tactfully **10** accurately, cautiously, diligently, discreetly, handsomely, rigorously, solicitous, thoroughly, vigilantly, watchfully **11** assiduously, attentively, judiciously **12** deliberately, fastidiously, methodically, meticulously, scrupulously, thoughtfully **13** circumspectly, painstakingly, punctiliously **14** systematically **15** conscientiously

**careless**
◇ *anagram indicator* **03** lax **04** nice **05** hasty, messy, slack **06** breezy, casual, remiss, secure, shoddy, simple, sloppy, untidy **07** artless, cursory, négligé, offhand, untenty **08** carefree, cheerful, heedless, laid-back, reckless, slapdash, slipshod, tactless, uncaring **09** easy-going, forgetful, negligent, unguarded, unmindful, unworried **10** disorderly, inaccurate, incautious, indiscreet, insouciant, neglectful, nonchalant, regardless, unthinking, untroubled **11** inattentive, perfunctory, superficial, thoughtless, unconcerned **12** absent-minded, disorganized, happy as a clam, happy-go-lucky, light-hearted **13** inconsiderate, irresponsible **15** happy as a sandboy

**carelessly**
◇ *anagram indicator* **06** anyhow **07** hastily **08** casually, remissly, shoddily, slam-bang, slapdash, sloppily **09** cursorily **10** heedlessly, recklessly, tactlessly, uncaringly **11** forgetfully, negligently, offhandedly, unguardedly, unmindfully **12** incautiously, indiscreetly, neglectingly, unthinkingly **13** inattentively, irresponsibly, perfunctorily, superficially, thoughtlessly, unconcernedly **14** absent-mindedly **15** inconsiderately

**caress**
**03** coy, hug, pat, pet, rub **04** bill, kiss **05** grope, touch **06** cuddle, feel up, fondle, nuzzle, stroke **07** embrace, petting, touch up **08** canoodle, lallygag, lollygag **10** endearment **13** butterfly kiss, slap and tickle

### caretaker
06 acting, fill-in, keeper, porter, pro tem, sexton, verger, warden 07 curator, dvornik, janitor, ostiary, shammes, stand-in, steward 08 janitrix, shammash, watchman 09 concierge, custodian, janitress, short-term, temporary 10 doorkeeper, substitute 11 provisional 14 superintendent

### careworn
04 worn 05 gaunt, tired, weary 07 anxious, haggard, worn-out, worried 08 fatigued 09 exhausted

### cargo
04 bulk, haul, last, load 05 goods 06 lading 07 baggage, fraught, freight, payload, tonnage 08 contents, deck-load, frautage, shipment 10 fraughtage 11 consignment, merchandise

### Caribbean
02 WI 10 West Indies

### caricature
04 mock 05 mimic 06 parody, satire, send up, send-up 07 cartoon, distort, lampoon, mimicry, take off, take-off 08 ridicule, satirize, travesty 09 burlesque, imitation 10 distortion, exaggerate 14 representation

### caring
04 fond, kind, warm 06 loving, tender 07 devoted, helpful 08 friendly 10 altruistic, benevolent, thoughtful 11 good-natured, kind-hearted, sympathetic 12 affectionate 13 compassionate, philanthropic, tender-hearted

### carnage
06 murder 07 killing 08 butchery, genocide, massacre 09 bloodbath, bloodshed, holocaust, slaughter 10 mass murder 15 ethnic cleansing

### carnal
04 lewd 05 belly, human 06 animal, bodily, erotic, impure, sexual 07 fleshly, lustful, natural, outward, sensual 08 physical 09 corporeal, lecherous, murderous 10 lascivious, libidinous, licentious 11 flesh-eating, unspiritual

### carnival
04 fair, fête, gala 05 carny 06 carney, fiesta 07 holiday, jubilee, revelry 08 Fasching, festival, jamboree 09 amusement, Mardi Gras, merriment 11 celebration, merrymaking

### carnivorous
10 meat-eating, zoophagous 11 creophagous, flesh-eating

### carol
04 hymn, noel, sing, song 06 carrel, chorus, strain 07 carrell, wassail 13 Christmas song

### carousal
04 upsy 05 feast, rouse, upsee, upsey

### carouse
04 birl 05 birle, booze, drink, party, quaff, revel, spree 06 bender, imbibe 07 roister, wassail 09 celebrate, make merry 11 drink freely, wassail bout

### carousing
08 drinking, partying 11 celebrating, compotation, merrymaking 13 mallemaroking

### carp
02 id 03 ide, koi, nag 04 yerk 05 gibel, knock, pinch 06 go on at, twitch 07 censure, crucian, crusian, nit-pick, quibble 08 complain, cyprinid, goldfish, reproach 09 criticize, find fault, round fish 10 find faults, silverfish 11 have a shot at 14 ultracrepidate

### carpenter
05 chips 06 chippy, joiner, Joseph, Quince, wright 10 cartwright, shipwright, woodworker 12 cabinet-maker

### carpet
03 bed, mat, rug 04 cake, coat, wrap 05 cover, dress, layer 06 clothe, encase, spread 07 blanket, matting, overlay 08 covering 10 tablecloth 13 floor-covering

*Carpets and rugs include:*

03 rag, red, rya
04 kali
05 Dutch, kelim, kilim, magic, pilch, stair, throw
06 hearth, hooked, khilim, Kirman, numdah, prayer, runner, Turkey, Wilton
07 bergama, flokati, Persian, Turkish
08 Aubusson, bergamot, Brussels, moquette
09 Axminster, prayer rug, sheepskin
10 travelling
11 Bessarabian, buffalo robe
13 Kidderminster

### carping
07 nagging, Zoilism 08 captious 09 cavilling, quibbling 10 nit-picking 11 complaining, criticizing 12 fault-finding

### carriage
03 air, car, cge, job, set 04 gait, mien, port 05 guise, poise, tenue 06 burden, clatch, manner, stance 07 baggage, bearing, conduct, freight, portage, postage, posture, turnout, vehicle, voiture 08 attitude, carrying, delivery, equipage, portance, presence, truckage 09 behaviour, demeanour, porterage, transport 10 conveyance, deportment 14 transportation

*Carriages include:*

03 cab, fly, gig
04 arba, baby, chay, drag, dray, ekka, mail, pony, pram, rath, shay, trap
05 araba, aroba, bandy, buggy, coach, coupé, dilly, ratha, stage, sulky, T-cart, wagon
06 berlin, calash, chaise, drosky, go-cart, hansom, herdic, landau, pochay, purdah, spider, spring, surrey
07 britska, britzka, cariole, caroche, chariot, dogcart, droshky, hackney, phaeton, pillbox, ricksha, tilbury, vettura, vis-à-vis

08 barouche, britzska, brougham, carriole, carryall, clarence, diligent, jump-seat, po'chaise, rickshaw, rockaway, sociable, stanhope, victoria
09 britschka, cabriolet, landaulet, wagonette
10 four-in hand, post chaise, stagecoach
11 family coach, hurly-hacket, village cart
13 désobligeante, mourning coach, spider phaeton, thoroughbrace

### carried away
04 rapt 06 enlevé, way-out
• **get carried away** 06 lose it
13 become excited
*See also* **carry**

### carrier
06 bearer, porter, runner, telfer, vector 07 airline, telpher, tranter, vehicle 08 conveyor, horseman, kurveyor 09 messenger 10 plastic bag 11 transmitter, transporter 12 roundsperson 13 dispatch rider 14 delivery-person, transport rider

### carrion
03 ket
• **carrion feeder** 04 hyen 05 hyena 06 hyaena 07 vulture 08 aardwolf 09 scavenger

### carry
◇ *containment indicator* 03 act, lug 04 bear, cart, gain, haul, have, hold, hump, lead, mean, move, pass, pipe, sell, show, take, tote, wain 05 adopt, bring, cover, drive, fetch, mount, print, reach, relay, shift, stand, stock 06 accept, acquit, behave, convey, effect, entail, hold up, lead to, pass on, ratify, retail, suffer, travel, uphold, wheech 07 approve, be heard, comport, conduct, contain, deliver, display, involve, present, publish, release, support, sustain, vote for 08 hand over, maintain, result in, sanction, shoulder, transfer, transmit, underpin 09 authorize, be audible, broadcast, transport 11 communicate, disseminate, have for sale, keep in stock 12 vote in favour 14 be infected with
• **carry away** 03 rap 04 lift 06 asport, ravish 08 bear away 09 transport
• **carry off** 03 lag, net, rob, win 04 gain, hent, land, rape 05 crack 06 abduct, kidnap, pick up, secure 07 achieve 08 complete 09 succeed in, transport 12 come away with
• **carry on** 03 ren, rin, run 04 go on, hold, keep, last, wage 06 bash on, endure, keep on, keep up, manage, play up, pursue, resume 07 conduct, operate, persist, proceed, restart 08 continue, engage in, maintain, progress, return to 09 misbehave, persevere 10 administer, be involved, mess around, play around 12 have an affair 15 behave foolishly
• **carry out** 02 do 04 fill 05 mount 06 effect, fulfil 07 achieve, conduct, deliver, execute, perform, realize

**08** bring off **09** discharge, implement, undertake **10** accomplish **12** give effect to **13** put into effect **15** deliver the goods, put into practice

**carry-on**
**04** flap, fuss, stir, to-do **05** hoo-ha **06** bother, hassle **07** trouble **09** commotion, kerfuffle

**cart**
**03** car, jag, lug **04** bear, dray, gill, haul, hump, jill, lead, move, pram, tote **05** bandy, carry, float, furby, gambo, shift, truck, wagon **06** barrow, convey, furphy, gurney **07** cariole, hackery, shandry, trailer, tumbrel, tumbril **08** carriole, democrat, handcart, transfer **09** transport **11** wheelbarrow

**cartilage**
**07** cricoid, gristle **08** chondrus, meniscus

**carton**
**03** box, tub **04** case, pack **06** packet, parcel **07** package **09** container

**cartoon**
**04** toon **05** anime, manga **06** bubble, parody, send-up, sketch **07** balloon, drawing, fumetto, lampoon, picture, take-off **09** animation, burlesque **10** caricature, comic strip **12** animated film, strip cartoon

*Cartoon characters include:*

**03** PHB, Ren, Tom
**04** Bart, Fred, Huey, Kyle, Lisa, Stan
**05** Alice, Bluto, Dewey, Dumbo, Goofy, Homer, Jerry, Kenny, Louey, Marge, Mr Men, Robin, Rocky, Snowy, Wally
**06** Batman, Beavis, Boo Boo, Calvin, Daphne, Droopy, Hobbes, Maggie, Obelix, Popeye, Shaggy, Snoopy, Stimpy, Thelma, Tintin, Top Cat
**07** Asterix, Cartman, Custard, Dilbert, Gnasher, Muttley, Penfold, Roobarb
**08** Andy Capp, Butthead, Clouseau, Garfield, Krazy Kat, Olive Oyl, Superman, Superted, Tank Girl, The Joker, Yogi Bear
**09** Betty Boop, Bugs Bunny, Chip 'n' Dale, Daffy Duck, Daisy Duck, Dastardly, Dick Tracy, Elmer Fudd, Marmaduke, Oor Wullie, Pepe le Pew, Scooby Doo, Spider Man, Sylvester, The Broons, Tweety Pie
**10** Bullwinkle, Donald Duck, Judge Dredd, Road Runner, Scrappy Doo, The Riddler
**11** Bart Simpson, Betty Rubble, Danger Mouse, Felix the Cat, Flash Gordon, Fred Bassett, Korky the Cat, Lisa Simpson, Mickey Mouse, Minnie Mouse, The Simpsons, Wile E Coyote
**12** Barney Rubble, Charlie Brown, Desperate Dan, Homer Simpson, Little Misses, Marge Simpson, Ren and Stimpy
**13** Dick Dastardly, Maggie Simpson,

Modesty Blaise, Rupert the Bear, Scrooge McDuck
**14** Bash Street Kids, Foghorn Leghorn, Fred Flintstone, Incredible Hulk, The Pink Panther
**15** Calvin and Hobbes, Dennis the Menace, Penelope Pitstop, Steamboat Willie, Wilma Flintstone

*Cartoonists include:*

**02** HB
**03** Low (Sir David)
**04** Capp (Al), Kane (Bob), Rémi (Georges)
**05** Adams (Scott), Avery (Tex), Block (Herbert L), Davis (Jim), Doyle (John), Giles, Hanna (William), Hergé, Jones (Chuck), Lantz (Walter), McCay (Winsor), Segar (Elzie), Silas
**06** Addams (Charles), Disney (Walt), Fisher (Bud), Iwerks (Ub), Larson (Gary), Scarfe (Gerald), Schulz (Charles M), Searle (Ronald), Siegel (Jerry), Smythe (Reg)
**07** Barbera (Joseph), Shuster (Joseph), Tenniel (Sir John), Trudeau (Garry), Watkins (Dudley D), Webster (Tom)
**08** Goldberg (Rube), Groening (Matt), Herblock, Herriman (George), Robinson (Heath)
**09** Baxendale (Leo), Fleischer (Max), Watterson (Bill)
**12** Bairnsfather (Bruce), Hanna-Barbera

**cartridge**
**04** case, tube **05** blank, round, shell **06** charge **07** capsule, torpedo **08** canister, cassette, cylinder, magazine, streamer **09** container **11** central fire

**caruncle**
**04** aril **08** arillode **10** strophiole

**carve**
◇ *anagram indicator* **03** cut, hew **04** chip, chop, etch, form, hack **05** cut up, kerve, mould, notch, sculp, shape, slice, write **06** chisel, entail, incise, indent, sculpt, unlace **07** engrave, entayle, fashion, insculp, whittle **09** apportion, dismember, sculpture, truncheon **10** distribute **11** insculpture
• **carve up** ◇ *anagram indicator* **05** share, split **06** divide **07** split up **08** separate, share out **09** parcel out, partition **10** distribute

**carving**
**03** cut **04** bust **05** model, round, tondo **06** statue **07** incision, knotwork, tympanum **09** scrimshaw, sculpture, statuette **10** lithoglyph, petroglyph, rosemaling **11** dendroglyph, scrimshandy **12** mezzo-relievo, mezzo-rilievo, scrimshander

**cascade**
**03** lin **04** fall, gush, linn, pour, rush **05** chute, falls, flood, pitch, spill, surge **06** deluge, plunge, shower, tumble **07** descend, torrent, trickle **08** cataract, fountain, overflow **09** avalanche,

waterfall **10** outpouring, water chute, waterworks

**case**
◇ *ends selection indicator* **03** bag, box **04** étui, sted, suit **05** cause, chest, cover, crate, crime, event, point, shell, state, stead, stede, trial, trunk **06** action, affair, carton, casing, casket, client, dative, essive, holder, jacket, sheath, valise, victim **07** attaché, cabinet, capsule, context, defence, dispute, elative, examine, example, grounds, holdall, inquiry, invalid, keister, lawsuit, patient, process, wrapper **08** abessive, ablative, adessive, allative, argument, canister, evidence, genitive, illative, incident, inessive, instance, kalamdan, locative, occasion, position, showcase, specimen, suitcase, vasculum, vocative **09** briefcase, cartridge, chrysalid, chrysalis, condition, container, flight bag, papeterie, portfolio, reasoning, situation, travel bag **10** accusative, comitative, nominative, occurrence, receptacle, subjective, vanity-case **11** attaché case, contingency, hand luggage, portmanteau, proceedings, reconnoitre, translative, writing desk **12** illustration, overnight bag **13** circumstances, investigation, particularity

**cases**
**02** ca

**cash**
**03** tin **04** cent, dime, dosh, loot **05** blunt, brass, bread, coins, dough, funds, gravy, lolly, money, notes, Oscar, ready, rhino, smash **06** change, encash, greens, moolah, stumpy **07** bullion, capital, finance, readies, realize, scratch, shekels **08** currency, exchange, greenies **09** banknotes, hard money, liquidate, megabucks, resources **10** ready money **11** legal tender, spondulicks, wherewithal **12** hard currency, turn into cash
• **cash return** **07** jackpot

**cashier**
**04** fire, sack **05** annul, break, clerk, expel **06** banker, bursar, purser, teller **07** checker, discard, dismiss, drum out, unfrock **08** get rid of, throw out **09** bank clerk, discharge, treasurer **10** accountant

**casing**
◇ *containment indicator* ◇ *ends selection indicator* **03** cup, tub **04** cast, core **05** cover, shell **06** jacket, sheath **07** covering, housing **08** binnacle, covering, envelope, pair case, trunking, wrapping **09** air-jacket, crankcase, oil string, sheathing **10** protection **11** bell-housing, junction box, steam jacket, water jacket **13** cylinder block

**cask**
**03** but, keg, pin, tub, tun, vat **04** butt, cade, pipe, wood **05** flask **06** barrel, casket, casque, firkin, octave, tierce **07** barrico, breaker, leaguer

**casket**

08 hogshead, puncheon 09 kilderkin
11 scuttlebutt

**casket**

03 box 04 case, kist 05 chest, pyxis,
shell 06 coffer, coffin, larnax
08 cassette, jewel-box 11 sarcophagus
12 pine overcoat, wooden kimono
14 wooden overcoat

**cassava**

04 yuca 05 yucca 06 manioc
07 mandioc, manihoc, tapioca
08 mandioca 09 mandiocca

**casserole**

04 stew 06 diable 07 cocotte,
stew-pan, terrine, tzimmes
08 pot-au-feu 09 Dutch oven
10 slow cooker

**cast**

◊ *anagram indicator* 03 die, lob, mew,
put, see, shy 04 drop, emit, form, hurl,
look, putt, seek, shed, slip, toss, turn,
veer, view, vote, warp 05 add up,
drive, fling, found, fusil, heave, impel,
model, mould, moult, pitch, place,
shape, shoot, sling, stamp, throw
06 actors, assign, chance, create,
direct, fusile, glance, launch, look at,
manner, record, reject, spread,
thrown, troupe 07 appoint, casting,
company, condemn, diffuse, discard,
dismiss, fashion, give off, give out,
glimpse, moulded, players, predict,
project, quality, radiate, redound,
reflect, scatter 08 covering, register,
rejected 09 calculate, formulate
10 catch sight, characters, performers
12 entertainers 13 put in jeopardy
14 mark with a cross
• **cast aside** 06 reject 07 discard, say
no to 08 get rid of, turn down
12 dispense with
• **cast down** 05 abase, crush
06 abattu, deject, sadden 07 depress
08 dejected, desolate 10 discourage,
dishearten
• **cast out** 09 ostracize

**caste**

04 race, rank 05 class, grade, group,
order 06 degree, estate, status
07 lineage, station, stratum 08 position
10 background 11 social class 14 social
standing

**castigate**

03 rap 04 slam 05 chide, emend, scold
06 berate, punish, rebuke 07 censure,
chasten, correct, reprove, upbraid
08 admonish, chastise 09 criticize,
dress down, reprimand 10 discipline
13 tear a strip off 15 give someone hell

**castle**

01 R 04 fort, keep, rook 05 tower, villa
06 kasbah, palace 07 château, citadel,
mansion, schloss 08 fastness, fortress,
garrison 10 stronghold 11 stately home
12 country house

*Castles include:*

03 Doe, Eye, Lea, Mey
04 Clun, Drum, Leap, Peel, Trim,
Ward, York
05 Black, Burgh, Corfe, Croft,

Doune, Flint, Knock, Leeds,
Skibo, White
06 Cawdor, Durham, Fraser, Glamis,
Howard, Ludlow, Maiden,
Sandal, Swords
07 Alnwick, Arundel, Braemar,
Caister, Culzean, Dunster,
Harlech, Lismore, Old Wick,
Peveril, Scotney, Warwick,
Windsor
08 Balmoral, Bamburgh, Bastille,
Broughty, Corgarff, Dunottar,
Dunvegan, Egremont, Elsinore,
Goodrich, Jedburgh, Kilkenny,
Monmouth, Pembroke, Stirling,
Stokesay, Tintagel, Urquhart
09 Beaumaris, Blackrock,
Chipchase, Dunsinane,
Edinburgh, Hermitage, Inverness,
Lancaster, Lochleven, St
Andrews, Tantallon
10 Bridgnorth, Caernarvon,
Caerphilly, Carmarthen, Jewel
Tower, Kenilworth, Montgomery,
Okehampton, Pontefract,
Rockingham
11 Castell Coch, Chillingham,
Craigmillar, Eilean Donan,
Fotheringay, Lindisfarne, Narrow
Water, Ravenscraig,
Scarborough, Tattershall,
Thirlestane
12 Conisborough
13 Carrickfergus
15 St Michael's Mount

*Castle parts include:*

04 berm, keep, moat, ward
05 ditch, fosse, motte, mound, scarp,
tower
06 bailey, chapel, corbel, crenel,
donjon, merlon, turret
07 bastion, dungeon, parados,
parapet, postern, rampart
08 approach, barbican, bartizan,
brattice, buttress, crosslet,
loophole, stockade, wall walk
09 arrow-slit, courtyard, embrasure,
gatehouse, inner wall
10 drawbridge, murder hole,
portcullis, watchtower
11 battlements, curtain wall, outer
bailey
12 crenellation, lookout tower
13 enclosure wall

• **castles** 02 O-O 03 O-O-O

**castrate**

03 cut, fix 04 geld, glib, swig 05 alter,
unman, unsex 06 doctor, neuter
07 evirate, knacker 10 emasculate

**casual**

03 odd 04 orra 05 blasé, stray
06 chance, random 07 cursory, leisure,
offhand, passing, relaxed, scratch
08 careless, informal, laid-back,
lukewarm, part-time 09 apathetic,
easy-going, irregular, negligent, short-
term, temporary, throwaway
10 accidental, fortuitous, incidental,
insouciant, nonchalant, occasional,
unexpected, unforeseen
11 comfortable, free-and-easy,
indifferent, promiscuous, provisional,

spontaneous, superficial, unconcerned
12 happy-go-lucky, intermittent
13 lackadaisical, serendipitous,
unceremonious, unintentional
14 unpremeditated

**casually**

06 overly 08 sportily 10 informally, off
the cuff 11 comfortably 12 occasionally
13 spontaneously 15 parenthetically

**casualty**

04 loss 05 death 06 caduac, injury,
victim 07 injured, missing, wounded
08 accident, fatality, sufferer 10 dead
person, misfortune 13 injured person

**casuistry**

07 sophism 09 chicanery, sophistry
12 equivocation, speciousness

**cat**

03 man, mog, tom 04 chap, puss
05 moggy, pussy, queen, rumpy
06 feline, kitten, malkin, mawkin,
mouser, neuter, tomcat 08 baudrons,
pussy cat 09 catamaran, grimalkin
*See also* **animal; vomit**

*Domestic cats include:*

03 rex
04 Manx
05 Korat, tabby
06 Angora, Bengal, Birman,
Bombay, Cymric, Havana,
LaPerm, Ocicat, Somali
07 Burmese, Persian, ragdoll,
Siamese, Tiffany
08 Balinese, Burmilla, Devon Rex,
Snowshoe, Tiffanie
09 Himalayan, Maine Coon,
Singapura, Tonkinese
10 Abyssinian, Carthusian,
chinchilla, Cornish Rex, Selkirk
Rex, Turkish Van
11 Egyptian Mau, Foreign Blue,
Russian Blue, silver tabby
12 Foreign White, Scottish Fold
13 domestic tabby, Tortoiseshell,
Turkish Angora
15 British longhair, Exotic shorthair,
Japanese Bobtail, Norwegian
Forest

*Wild and big cats include:*

03 bob
04 eyra, lion, lynx, pard, puma
05 feral, tiger
06 cougar, jaguar, kodkod, margay,
ocelot, pampas
07 cheetah, leopard
08 mountain
09 Geoffroy's
10 jaguarundi
11 snow leopard
12 mountain lion, Scottish wild
13 little spotted
14 clouded leopard

*Famous cats include:*

03 Tom
04 Bast, Jess
05 Dinah, Felix, Korky
06 Arthur, Bastet, Ginger, Kaspar,
Top Cat, Ubasti
07 Bagpuss, Custard, Simpkin

**08** Beerbohm, Garfield, Humphrey, Krazy Kat, Macavity
**09** Mehitabel, Mrs Norris, Sylvester, Thomasina, Tom Kitten
**10** El Brooshna, Heathcliff
**11** Cat in the Hat, Cheshire Cat, Crookshanks, Korky the Cat, Pink Panther, Puss in Boots
**14** Bustopher Jones, Mr Mistoffelees, Old Deuteronomy, The Cat in the Hat

**cataclysm**
**04** blow **07** debacle **08** calamity, collapse, disaster, upheaval
**10** convulsion **11** catastrophe, devastation

**cataclysmic**
**05** awful, fatal **06** tragic **08** dreadful, terrible **10** calamitous, disastrous
**11** catastrophe, devastating

**catacomb**
**04** tomb **05** crypt, vault **07** ossuary
**09** mausoleum **11** burial-vault

**catalogue**
**03** cat **04** file, list, roll **05** guide, index, table **06** litany, ragman, record, roster
**07** catalog, magalog, notitia, ragment
**08** brochure, bulletin, calendar, classify, manifest, register, schedule, tabulate **09** checklist, directory, gazetteer, inventory, make a list
**10** categorize, prospectus
**11** alphabetize, iconography, specialogue **12** compile a list
**14** classification, Durchmusterung

**catapult**
**01** Y **04** fire, hurl, toss **05** fling, pitch, shoot, sling, throw **06** hurtle, launch, propel **07** balista, bricole **08** ballista, scorpion, shanghai **09** slingshot

**cataract**
**03** lin **04** linn **05** falls, force, pearl
**06** deluge, rapids **07** cascade, torrent
**08** downpour, overfall, pearl-eye
**09** floodgate, pin and web, waterfall
**10** portcullis, waterspout

**catastrophe**
**04** blow, doom, rear, ruin **06** fiasco
**07** debacle, failure, reverse, tragedy, trouble **08** calamity, disaster, upheaval
**09** adversity, cataclysm, mischance
**10** affliction, misfortune **11** devastation

**catastrophic**
**05** awful, fatal **06** tragic **08** dreadful, terrible **10** calamitous, disastrous
**11** cataclysmic, devastating

**catcall**
**03** boo **04** gibe, hiss, jeer, jibe
**07** whistle **09** raspberry **10** barracking, Bronx cheer

**catch**
◇ *containment indicator* **03** bag, cop, get, kep, nab, net **04** bolt, clip, draw, fang, find, fish, grab, grip, hank, hasp, haul, hear, hold, hook, lock, make, nail, nick, pawl, rope, sear, snag, sneb, snib, tack, take, trap, twig **05** board, clasp, get it, get on, grasp, hitch, latch, phang, seize, snare, sneck, watch
**06** arrest, clutch, collar, corner, detect,

detent, engage, entrap, expose, fathom, follow, pick up, snatch, take in, unmask **07** attract, capture, develop, discern, ensnare, find out, make out, problem, round up, seizure, startle **08** contract, discover, drawback, fastener, holdfast, hunt down, obstacle, overtake, perceive, surprise **09** apprehend, deprehend, lay hold of, recapture, recognize, succumb to **10** comprehend, difficulty, go down with, understand **11** be in time for **12** disadvantage, get the hang of **13** become ill with, catch in the act
**14** catch red-handed
*See also* **haul; song**
• **catch on** **05** grasp **06** fathom, follow, take in **10** comprehend, understand **13** become popular
• **catch up** **06** gain on **08** overtake
**09** draw level

**catching**
◇ *containment indicator* **06** taking
**10** attractive, contagious, infectious
**11** captivating **12** communicable
**13** transmissible, transmittable

**catchphrase**
**05** motto **06** byword, jingle, saying, slogan, wheeze **07** formula
**08** password **09** catchword, parrot-cry, watchword **10** shibboleth

**catchy**
**07** melodic, popular, tuneful
**08** haunting **09** appealing, deceptive, memorable **10** attractive
**11** captivating, ear-catching
**13** unforgettable

**catechize**
**04** test **05** drill, grill **07** examine
**08** instruct, question **11** interrogate
**12** cross-examine

**categorical**
**05** clear, total, utter **06** direct
**07** express **08** absolute, definite, emphatic, explicit, positive
**09** downright **10** conclusive, unreserved **11** unequivocal, unqualified **13** unconditional

**categorically**
**07** clearly, utterly **08** directly
**09** expressly **10** absolutely, definitely, explicitly, positively **12** emphatically, unreservedly **13** unequivocally
**15** unconditionally

**categorization**
**07** listing, ranking, sorting **08** grouping, ordering **11** arrangement
**14** classification

**categorize**
**03** peg **04** list, rank, sort **05** class, grade, group, order **06** docket **07** arrange, docquet **08** classify, tabulate
**09** phenotype **10** pigeonhole, stereotype

**category**
**04** head, kind, list, rank, sort, type
**05** class, genre, grade, group, order, stirp, stuff, taxon, title **06** rubric, stirps
**07** bracket, chapter, heading, listing, section, variety **08** division, grouping

**10** department, superclass, superorder
**11** superphylum **14** classification

**cater**
**05** serve **06** pander, supply **07** furnish, indulge, provide, satisfy, victual
**09** provision

**caterwaul**
**03** cry **04** bawl, howl, wail, yowl
**05** miaow, wrawl **06** scream, shriek, squall **07** screech

**catharsis**
**07** purging, release **09** cleansing, epuration, purifying **10** abreaction, abstersion, lustration **12** purification

**cathartic**
**07** lustral, purging, release, scourer
**09** cleansing, purgative, purifying
**10** abreactive, abstersive, eccoprotic

**cathedral**
**04** dome **05** duomo **07** minster
**12** procathedral
*See also* **church**

*Cathedrals in the UK include:*

**03** Ely
**05** Derby, Isles, Leeds, Ripon, Truro, Wells
**06** Bangor, Brecon, Dundee, Durham, Exeter, Oxford
**07** Arundel, Bristol, Cardiff, Chester, Clifton, Dornoch, Glasgow, Lincoln, Newport, Norwich, Salford, St Asaph, St John's, St Mary's, St Paul's, Swansea, Wrexham
**08** Aberdeen, Bradford, Carlisle, Coventry, Hereford, Llandaff, Plymouth, St Albans, St Davids
**09** Blackburn, Brentwood, Edinburgh, Guildford, Inverness, Lancaster, Leicester, Lichfield, Liverpool, Newcastle, Rochester, Salisbury, Sheffield, Southwark, St Andrews, Wakefield, Worcester
**10** Birmingham, Canterbury, Chelmsford, Chichester, Gloucester, Manchester, Nottingham, Portsmouth, Shrewsbury, Winchester
**11** Northampton, York Minster
**12** Christ Church, Peterborough
**13** Middlesbrough, St Edmundsbury

*Cathedrals worldwide include:*

**04** Lund
**05** Milan
**06** Aachen, Rheims
**07** Cologne, Córdoba, Orvieto, St Mark's
**08** Chartres, Florence, St Basil's, St Peter's
**09** Notre-Dame
**10** Strasbourg
**11** Hagia Sophia

• **cathedral city** **03** see

**catholic**
**01** C **02** RC **04** Tory, wide **05** broad, Latin, Roman **06** global, varied
**07** diverse, general, liberal **08** eclectic, Jebusite, Romanish, Romanist, tolerant
**09** inclusive, universal **10** broad-based,

left-footer, open-minded, Tridentine, widespread **11** broad-minded, wide-ranging **12** all-embracing, all-inclusive **13** comprehensive **15** all-encompassing

**catholicism**
**04** Rome **06** popery **08** Romanism

**catmint**
**03** nep, nip **06** catnep, catnip, nepeta

**cats and dogs**
**04** rain

**cattle**
**02** ky **03** fee, kye **04** aver, cows, kine, kyne, neat, nout, nowt, oxen **05** bulls, stock **06** beasts, beeves **09** livestock
*See also* **animal**

*Cattle include:*

**02** zo
**03** dso, dzo, gir, gur, gyr, zho
**04** dzho, jomo, tuli, zebu, zobo, zobu
**05** Angus, black, Devon, dsobo, dsomo, Kerry, Luing, sanga, wagyu, white, zhomo
**06** ankole, dexter, Durham, Jersey, Salers, Sussex, watusi
**07** beefalo, brahman, brahmin, brangus, cattabu, cattalo, Latvian, red poll
**08** Alderney, Ayrshire, Chianina, Friesian, Galloway, gelbvieh, Guernsey, Hereford, Highland, Holstein, illawara, Limousin, longhorn, Shetland
**09** Afrikaner, braunvieh, Charolais, Corriente, Romagnola, shorthorn, Simmental, Teeswater, Ukrainian, white park
**10** Africander, beefmaster, Brown Swiss, Canadienne, Lincoln Red, Murray grey, Piemontese, Simmenthal, South Devon, Tarentaise, Welsh Black
**11** Belgian Blue, Chillingham, Piedmontese
**12** British White, Simmenthaler
**13** Aberdeen Angus, droughtmaster, Texas longhorn
**14** Belted Galloway, Santa Gertrudis

**catty**
**03** kin **04** kati, mean **05** katti **06** bitchy **07** vicious **08** spiteful, venomous **09** malicious, rancorous **10** backbiting, ill-natured, malevolent

**caucus**
**03** set **06** clique, parley **07** meeting, session **08** assembly, conclave **09** gathering **10** convention **11** get-together

**caught**
◊ *containment indicator* **01** c **02** ct
**03** had **04** held **06** keight, netted **11** in by the week

**cauliflower**
**04** gobi
• **head of cauliflower** **04** curd

**causative**
**04** root **07** causing, factive **09** factitive

**cause**
**03** aim, end, gar **04** call, make, root, sake **05** agent, basis, beget, begin, breed, causa, force, garre, ideal, maker, mover **06** agency, author, belief, compel, create, effect, factor, incite, induce, lead to, motive, object, origin, parent, prompt, reason, render, source, spring **07** because, creator, grounds, impulse, produce, provoke, purpose, trigger **08** generate, motivate, movement, occasion, producer, result in, stimulus **09** beginning, incentive, originate, principle, stimulate, wherefore **10** accusation, bring about, conviction, enterprise, give rise to, inducement, mainspring, make happen, motivation, originator, prime mover, trigger off **11** explanation, precipitate, undertaking **12** be the cause of **13** be at the root of, justification

**caustic**
**04** acid, keen, tart **05** snide **06** biting, bitter, severe **07** acerbic, burning, cutting, erodent, mordant, pungent **08** scathing, stinging, virulent **09** acidulent, acidulous, corroding, corrosive, sarcastic, trenchant, vitriolic **10** astringent, escharotic **11** acrimonious, destructive

**caustically**
**08** bitterly, severely **10** scathingly, virulently **11** trenchantly **13** acrimoniously, sarcastically, vitriolically

**cauterize**
**04** burn, fire, sear **05** singe **06** scorch **09** carbonize, disinfect, sterilize

**caution**
**04** bail, care, heed, urge, warn **05** alert, deter, guard **06** advice, advise, cautel, caveat, surety, tip off, tip-off **07** counsel, warning **08** admonish, prudence, security, wariness **09** alertness, reprimand, vigilance **10** admonition, discretion, injunction **11** carefulness, forethought, heedfulness, mindfulness **12** deliberation, watchfulness **14** circumspection
• **lacking caution** **04** rash

**cautious**
**04** safe, ware, wary **05** alert, cagey, chary **06** Fabian, shrewd **07** careful, guarded, heedful, prudent, tactful **08** discreet, gingerly, vigilant, watchful **09** cautelous, defensive, judicious, tentative **10** deliberate **11** circumspect **12** conservative, softly-softly **13** unadventurous

**cautiously**
**08** gingerly **09** carefully, prudently, tactfully **10** discreetly **11** defensively, judiciously, tentatively **12** deliberately **13** circumspectly **14** conservatively

**cavalcade**
**05** array, train, troop **06** parade **07** cortège, retinue, sowarry **08** sowarree **09** march-past, motorcade **10** procession

**cavalier**
**04** curt **05** lofty, spahi **06** casual, escort, knight, lordly **07** gallant, haughty, offhand, partner, warlike **08** arrogant, chasseur, horseman, insolent, Ironside, royalist, scornful **09** chevalier, gentleman, Malignant **10** cavalryman, disdainful, equestrian, incautious, swaggering **11** Bashi-Bazouk, free-and-easy, patronizing **12** devil-may-care, horse soldier, supercilious **13** condescending

**cavalry**
**05** horse **07** hussars, lancers, reiters **08** dragoons, horsemen, sabreurs, troopers **09** chasseurs, Ironsides, risaldars **10** cavalrymen, light-horse, the heavies **11** equestrians, ritt-masters **13** horse soldiers, mounted troops

**cave**
**03** den **04** grot, hole **05** antar, antre, delve **06** beware, cavern, cavity, dugout, grotto, hollow, tunnel **07** pothole **09** Domdaniel

*Caves include:*

**04** Zitu
**06** Berger, Vqerdi
**08** Badalona
**09** G E S Malaga, Snezhnaya
**10** Schneeloch
**11** Batmanhöhle, Jean Bernard
**14** Lamprechstofen, Pierre-St-Martin, Sistema Huautla

• **cave in** **04** fall, slip **05** yield **06** fal in **07** give way, subside **08** collapse

**caveat**
**05** alarm **06** notice **07** caution, proviso warning **10** admonition

**cavern**
**03** den **04** cave, cove **05** vault **06** cavity, dugout, Erebus, grotto, hollow, tunnel **07** pothole **08** catacomb, vaultage

**cavernous**
**04** dark, deep, huge, vast **05** large **06** gaping, gloomy, hollow, sunken **07** concave, echoing, immense, yawning **08** resonant, spacious **09** depressed **10** bottomless **12** unfathomable

**cavil**
**03** nag **04** carp **06** haggle **07** censure, nit-pick, quarrel, quibble **08** complain, reproach **09** criticize **10** find faults

**cavity**
**03** gap, pit, sac, vug **04** bore, cell, dent, hole, mine, tear, vein, well, womb **05** celom, crypt, druse, geode, lumen, purse, sinus, vitta **06** antrum, atrium, camera, coelom, concha, cotyle, crater, hollow, lacuna, pelvis, pocket **07** chamber, cochlea, coelome, eardrum, glenoid, orifice, vacuole, vesicle **08** aperture, brood-sac **09** ventricle, vestibule **10** acetabulum, blastocoel, brood-pouch, cavitation, excavation, hollowness, thunder-egg **11** conceptacle, haematocele, mediastinum, rhynchocoel **13** neuroblastoma, splanchnocele

## cavort

◇ *anagram indicator* **04** romp, skip **05** caper, dance, frisk, sport **06** frolic, gambol, prance

## cavy

*see* **guinea pig**

## Cayman Islands

**03** CYM

## cease

**03** die, end, lin **04** blin, fail, halt, poop, quit, stay, stop, unbe **05** abate, cesse, leave, let up, stint **06** desist, devall, finish, lay off, pack in **07** poop out, refrain, suspend **08** break off, conclude, give over, leave off, peter out, surcease **09** call a halt, cessation, fizzle out, terminate **11** come to a halt, come to an end, discontinue **12** bring to a halt, bring to an end
*See also* **stop**

## ceaseless

**07** endless, eternal, non-stop **08** constant, unending, untiring **09** continual, incessant, perpetual, unceasing **10** continuous, persistent **11** everlasting, never-ending, unremitting **12** interminable **13** uninterrupted

## ceaselessly

**07** for ever **09** endlessly, eternally **10** constantly, unendingly **11** day in day out, incessantly, unceasingly **12** continuously, interminably **13** everlastingly, unremittingly **14** for ever and ever **15** uninterruptedly

## cedar

**06** arolla, deodar **11** cryptomeria

## cede

**05** allow, grant, yield **06** convey, give up, resign **07** abandon, concede, deliver **08** abdicate, hand over, renounce, transfer, turn over **09** surrender **10** relinquish

## ceiling

**04** loft, most, roof **05** beams, limit, vault **06** awning, canopy, cupola, soffit **07** lacunar, maximum, plafond, rafters, seeling **08** overhead **09** laquearia **10** upper limit **11** cut-off point

## celebrate

**03** wet **04** hold, hymn, keep, laud, mark, rave, sing, tune **05** binge, bless, carol, chant, extol, go out, revel, sound, toast **06** besing, chaunt, honour, record, renown, repeat, shrove, sonnet **07** drink to, emblaze, have fun, maffick, observe, perform, poetize, rejoice, triumph, trumpet **08** emblazon, live it up, memorize, remember **09** have a ball, solemnize, whoop it up **10** have a party, procession **11** commemorate, throw a party **12** concelebrate **13** enjoy yourself, go on the razzle **14** go out on the town, push the boat out, put the flags out **15** paint the town red

## celebrated

**03** cel **05** famed, great, noted **06** famous **07** admired, eminent, exalted, notable, popular, revered **08** fabulous, glorious, renowned **09** acclaimed, legendary, prominent, well-known **11** illustrious, outstanding **13** distinguished

## celebration

**02** do **03** ale, jol **04** fête, gala, orgy, rave **05** beano, binge, feast, jolly, spree **06** hooley, junket, rave-up **07** jubilee, revelry, shindig **08** festival, jamboree, occasion, Olympiad **09** festivity, gaudeamus **10** observance **11** merrymaking **13** jollification
*See also* **festival**

*Celebrations include:*

**04** fête, gala
**05** feast, party
**06** May Day
**07** banquet, baptism, jubilee, name-day, reunion, tribute, wedding
**08** birthday, festival, hen night, marriage
**09** centenary, Labour Day, reception, saint's day, stag night
**10** bar mitzvah, bat mitzvah, dedication, graduation, homecoming, retirement
**11** anniversary, christening, coming-of-age, harvest-home
**12** thanksgiving
**13** commemoration
**15** harvest festival, Independence Day

## celebratory

**06** festal

## celebrity

**03** VIP **04** fame, lion, name, note, sleb, star **05** celeb **06** bigwig, esteem, legend, renown, worthy **07** A-lister, big name, big shot, notable, stardom **08** eminence, luminary, megastar **09** dignitary, greatness, notoriety, personage, superstar **10** notability, prominence, reputation **11** distinction, personality **12** famous person, living legend **13** household name **15** illustriousness

## celerity

**05** haste, speed **08** dispatch, fastness, rapidity, velocity **09** fleetness, quickness, swiftness **10** expedition, promptness

## celestial

**06** astral, divine, starry, uranic **07** angelic, Chinese, elysian, eternal, godlike, sublime **08** empyrean, ethereal, heavenly, immortal, seraphic, supernal **09** spiritual, unearthly **10** paradisaic, superlunar **11** superlunary, translunary **12** supernatural **14** transcendental

## celestially

**08** divinely **09** eternally, sublimely **10** immortally **11** angelically, spiritually **14** supernaturally

## celibacy

**06** purity **08** chastity **09** virginity **10** abnegation, abstinence, continence, maidenhood, self-denial, singleness **12** bachelorhood, spinsterhood **13** self-restraint

## celibate

**04** pure **05** unwed **06** chaste, single, virgin **08** bachelor, spinster **09** abstinent, unmarried

## cell

**03** set **04** coop, cyte, jail, room, unit **05** ascus, crowd, crypt, group, party, peter, spore **06** caucus, clique, lock-up, matrix, prison, zygote **07** battery, chamber, cubicle, dungeon, faction, nucleus, section **08** organism **09** anchorage, black hole, cytoplasm, enclosure, hermitage, reclusory **10** protoplasm, protoplast **11** compartment, electric eye

*Cells include:*

**01** B, T
**03** egg, PEC, red, rod, sex, wet
**04** cone, fuel, germ, HeLa, mast, ovum, stem
**05** blood, guard, nerve, plant, solar, sperm, water, white
**06** animal, cancer, collar, diaxon, gamete, goblet, Hadley, killer, memory, mother, neuron, oocyte, plasma, target, tumour
**07** cadmium, Daniell, gravity, helper T, initial, neurone, primary, Schwann, Sertoli, somatic, voltaic
**08** akaryote, basophil, daughter, galvanic, gonidium, gonocyte, monocyte, myoblast, neoblast, parietal, platelet, Purkinje, red blood, retinula, sclereid, selenium, tracheid, zooblast
**09** acidophil, adipocyte, antipodal, astrocyte, coenocyte, corpuscle, fibrocyte, haemocyte, hybridoma, idioblast, Leclanché, leucocyte, leukocyte, macrocyte, microcyte, myofibril, phagocyte, photocell, prokaryon, sclereide, secondary, spermatid, syncytium, thymocyte, tracheide
**10** choanocyte, cnidoblast, enterocyte, eosinophil, fibroblast, gametocyte, hepatocyte, histiocyte, histoblast, leucoblast, leukoblast, lymphocyte, macrophage, melanocyte, myeloblast, neuroblast, neutrophil, osteoblast, osteoclast, spherocyte, suppressor, thread-cell, white blood
**11** B lymphocyte, erythrocyte, granulocyte, lymphoblast, megaloblast, odontoblast, poikilocyte, thrombocyte, T lymphocyte
**12** chondroblast, erythroblast, haematoblast, red corpuscle, reticulocyte, spermatocyte, spermatozoid, spermatozoon
**13** chromatophore, natural killer, photoelectric, spermatoblast
**14** blood corpuscle, spermatogonium, white corpuscle

• **mass of cells** **05** nodus **06** morula

## cellar

**04** vaut **05** crypt, dunny, vault, vaute **08** basement, catacomb, coal hole, vaultage **09** storeroom, wine vault **10** wine cellar, wine vaults

## Celtic
*see* **mythology**

## cement
**03** fix, gum **04** bind, bond, glue, join, lime, lute, weld **05** affix, compo, grout, paste, putty, stick, trass, union, unite **06** attach, cohere, fasten, gunite, maltha, mastic, matrix, mortar, screed, slurry, solder, stucco **07** bonding, combine, mastich, plaster **08** adhesive, concrete, fixative, grouting, pointing, rice glue, solution **11** ciment fondu

## cemetery
**05** tombs **06** graves **08** boneyard, God's acre, urnfield **09** graveyard **10** burial site, campo santo, churchyard, necropolis **11** burial place **12** burial ground, charnel house

---

*Cemeteries and burial places include:*

**07** Nunhead
**08** Brompton, Highgate, Panthéon
**09** Abney Park, Arlington
**10** El Escorial, La Almudena, Montmartre, Mount Holly, San Michele, Weissensee
**11** Kensal Green, Mount Olivet, West Norwood
**12** Golders Green, Les Invalides, Montparnasse, Père Lachaise, Tower Hamlets
**13** Mount of Olives
**15** Island of the Dead

---

## censor
**03** ban, cut **04** Cato, edit **06** delete, editor **08** examiner, make cuts **09** expurgate, inspector **10** blue-pencil, bowdlerize, expurgater **11** bowdlerizer

## censorious
**06** severe **07** carping **08** captious, critical, negative **09** cavilling **10** fuddy-duddy **11** disparaging **12** condemnatory, disapproving, fault-finding, overcritical **13** hypercritical

## censoriously
**08** severely **10** captiously, critically **13** disparagingly **14** disapprovingly, overcritically **15** hypercritically

## censure
**03** rap **04** damn, Hell, slam **05** blame, chide, fault, judge, scold, strop, taunt **06** jump on, rebuke, taxing **07** appeach, condemn, obloquy, reproof, reprove, scandal, tell off, trounce, upbraid **08** admonish, denounce, reproach, scolding, sentence **09** castigate, criticism, criticize, dispraise, reprehend, reprimand, reprobate, syndicate **10** admonition, imputation, perstringe, reflection, telling-off, upbraiding **11** castigation, disapproval, remonstrate, reprobation **12** admonishment, condemnation, denunciation, disapprove of, pull to pieces, remonstrance, reprehension, vituperation **15** come down heavy on

## cent
**01** c **02** ct **03** red **05** penny

## centimes
**01** c

## centipede
**08** scutiger **11** scolopendra **12** scolopendrid, thousand-legs

## central
◊ *hidden indicator* ◊ *middle selection indicator* **03** cen, key, mid **04** cent, core, main **05** basic, chief, focal, inner, major, prime, vital **06** centre, medial, median, middle, midway **07** crucial, pivotal, primary **08** dominant, foremost, interior **09** essential, principal **11** fundamental, significant **13** most important
• **central heating** **02** ch

## Central African Republic
**03** CAF, RCA

## Central America
*see* **America; god, goddess**

## centralization
**08** focusing **11** convergence, unification **12** amalgamation, streamlining **13** concentration, consolidation, incorporation **15** rationalization

## centralize
**05** focus, unify **07** compact **08** condense, converge **10** amalgamate, streamline **11** concentrate, consolidate, incorporate, rationalize **13** bring together **14** gather together

## centre
◊ *middle selection indicator* **03** hub, mid **04** core, crux **05** arena, focus, heart, hinge, pivot **06** kernel, middle, resort **07** nucleus, revolve **08** bull's-eye, converge, linchpin, midpoint, omphalos **09** gravitate **10** focal point, metropolis, stronghold **11** concentrate
• **in centre** ◊ *hidden indicator*

## centre-forward
**02** cf

## centre-half
**02** ch

## centrepiece
**04** best, peak **05** cream **06** climax **07** epergne **08** duchesse, high spot **09** highlight, high point **13** duchesse cover

## century
**01** c **03** age, cen, ton **04** cent **09** centenary
• **half century** **01** l

## cephalopod
**05** Sepia, squid **06** cuttle, loligo **07** octopus **08** ammonite, nautilus **09** goniatite, nautiloid **10** cuttlefish **13** paper nautilus **14** pearly nautilus

## ceramics
**04** raku, ware **06** bisque **07** faience, pottery **09** ironstone, porcelain **11** earthenware

## cereal
**05** grain

---

*Cereals include:*

**03** oat, rye, tef, zea
**04** bear, bere, corn, oats, rice, sago, teff, yuca
**05** bajra, emmer, maize, spelt, wheat
**06** barley, bulgur, manioc, millet
**07** bulghur, cassava, mandioc, manihoc, oatmeal, sorghum, tapioca
**08** amaranth, amelcorn, couscous, mandioca, semolina
**09** buckwheat, mandiocca, sweetcorn, triticale
**10** guinea corn, Indian corn, Kaffir corn
**11** pearl millet
**12** common millet
**13** bulrush millet, foxtail millet, grain amaranth, Italian millet

---

*Breakfast cereals include:*

**04** bran
**05** Alpen®
**06** muesli
**07** All Bran®, granola
**08** Cheerios®, Coco Pops®, Frosties®, porridge, Ricicles®, Special K®, Weetabix®
**09** Ready Brek®, Shreddies®
**10** Bran Flakes®, cornflakes, Quaker Oats®, Sugar Puffs®
**11** Fruit'n'Fibre®, Puffed Wheat®, Sultana Bran®
**12** Country Crisp®, Rice Krispies®
**13** Fruit and Fibre®, Golden Grahams®, Honey Nut Loops®, Shredded Wheat®

---

## ceremonial
**04** rite **05** state **06** custom, formal, ritual, solemn **07** mummery, stately **08** ceremony, official, protocol **09** dignified, formality, solemnity **11** ritualistic

## ceremonially
**08** formally, ritually, solemnly **10** officially

## ceremonious
**05** civil, exact, grand, stiff **06** formal, polite, ritual, solemn **07** courtly, precise, starchy, stately **08** imposing, majestic, official **09** courteous, dignified **10** scrupulous **11** deferential, punctilious

## ceremoniously
**07** civilly, exactly, grandly, stiffly **08** formally, politely, solemnly **09** precisely, starchily **10** officially **11** courteously **12** scrupulously **13** deferentially, punctiliously **15** ritualistically

## ceremony
**04** form, gaud, pomp, rite, show **05** order **06** custom, parade, ritual **07** decorum, liturgy, service **08** exercise, festival, function, niceties, occasion, protocol **09** etiquette, formality, induction, ordinance, pageantry, propriety, punctilio, sacrament, solemnity, tradition, unveiling **10** ceremonial, coronation, dedication, graduation, initiation,

observance **11** anniversåry,
celebration, investiture
**12** circumstance, commencement,
inauguration **13** commemoration, spit
and polish

*Ceremonies include:*

**05** amrit, doseh, tangi
**06** maundy, nipter
**07** baptism, capping, chanoyu,
chuppah, matsuri, wedding
**08** marriage, nuptials
**09** committal, matrimony
**10** bar mitzvah, bat mitzvah,
corroboree, graduation, initiation
**11** christening, fire-walking
**12** confirmation
• **funeral ceremonies** **04** obit

**Ceres**
**07** Demeter

**cerium**
**02** Ce

**certain**
**04** safe, some, sure, true **05** bound,
clear, fated, fixed, plain, small
**06** doomed, siccar, sicker **07** assured,
dead set, decided, evident, express,
limited, obvious, partial, perfect,
precise, regular, settled, special
**08** absolute, definite, destined, in the
bag, positive, reliable, resolved,
specific **09** confident, convinced,
indubious, persuaded, undoubted,
unfailing **10** conclusive, convincing,
dependable, determined, home and
dry, individual, inevitable, inexorable,
particular, undeniable **11** cut and
dried, established, indubitable,
ineluctable, inescapable, irrefutable,
open-and-shut, unavoidable
**12** indisputable, no ifs and buts
**13** bound to happen, meant to happen
**14** unquestionable
• **a certain** **03** one **04** some
• **make certain** **06** ensure

**certainly**
**02** OK, yes **04** iwis, okay, sure,
ywis **06** and how!, certes, siccar,
sicker, surely, you bet **07** clearly, for
sure, no doubt, plainly **08** forsooth, of
course, to be sure **09** assuredly,
doubtless, naturally, obviously, sure
thing **10** absolutely, by all means,
definitely, in very deed, positively,
undeniably **11** beyond doubt,
doubtlessly, if you please, indubitably,
past dispute, undoubtedly **12** as sure as
a gun, bang to rights, questionless,
without doubt **13** beyond dispute,
without a doubt **14** beyond question,
unquestionably, without dispute **15** in
all conscience

**certainty**
**03** nap **04** cert, fact, lock, snip
**05** cinch, faith, moral, trust, truth
**06** banker, surety **07** natural, reality,
safe bet **08** dead cert, security,
sureness, validity **09** assurance,
constancy, sure thing **10** confidence,
conviction, positivism **11** assuredness
**12** positiveness **13** inevitability
**14** matter of course

**certificate**
**04** pass **05** award, lines, proof, scrip,
title **06** cocket, docket, patent, ticket
**07** diploma, licence, voucher, warrant
**08** aegrotat, document, navicert,
register, testamur **09** clearance,
debenture, guarantee, land-scrip
**10** securities **11** credentials,
endorsement, smart-ticket, testimonial
**12** bill of health, Tyburn-ticket
**13** authorization, certificatory,
marriage-lines, qualification

**certify**
**04** aver **05** vouch **06** assure, attest,
inform, ratify, verify **07** confirm,
declare, endorse, license, testify,
warrant, witness **08** accredit, validate
**09** authorize, guarantee, pronounce,
recognize **11** corroborate
**12** authenticate, substantiate **13** bear
witness to

**certitude**
**08** sureness **09** assurance, certainty
**10** confidence, conviction, plerophory
**11** assuredness, plerophoria
**12** positiveness **13** full assurance

**cessation**
**02** ho **03** end, hoa, hoh **04** blin, halt,
rest, stay, stop **05** break, cease, let-up,
pause, stint **06** ending, hiatus, recess
**07** ceasing, failure, halting, respite
**08** abeyance, breakoff, interval,
stoppage, stopping, surcease, suspense
**09** remission **10** conclusion,
desistance, standstill, suspension
**11** termination **12** intermission,
interruption **13** discontinuing
**14** discontinuance **15** discontinuation

**Chad**
**03** TCD, TCH

**chafe**
**03** rub, vex **04** bind, fret, gall, rasp,
wear **05** anger, annoy, grate, peeve
**06** abrade, chaufe, chauff, enrage,
scrape **07** be angry, incense, inflame,
provoke, scratch **08** irritate, wear
away, wear down **09** excoriate
**10** exasperate

**chaff**
**03** kid, rag, rib, rot **04** chip, jest, joke,
josh, mock, pods **05** cases, husks, tease
**06** banter, have-on, joking, shells
**07** jesting, kidding, ribbing, rubbish,
teasing **08** badinage, repartee **09** make
fun of

**chagrin**
**03** irk, vex **05** annoy, peeve, shame
**07** mortify **08** disquiet, irritate,
shagreen, vexation, wormwood
**09** annoyance, displease, embarrass,
humiliate **10** disappoint, dissatisfy,
exasperate, irritation **11** displeasure,
fretfulness, humiliation, indignation
**12** discomfiture, discomposure,
exasperation **13** embarrassment,
mortification **14** disappointment
**15** dissatisfaction

**chain**
**02** ch **03** row, set, tie **04** bind, bond,
boom, curb, firm, line, link, rode, seal,
team **05** group, guard, hitch, range,

slang, train, union **06** albert, catena,
fasten, fetter, secure, series, string,
tether, traces **07** company, confine,
creeper, enslave, manacle, measure,
shackle, trammel **08** coupling,
handcuff, restrain, sequence
**09** fanfarona, restraint **10** succession,
watchguard **11** progression
**13** concatenation

**chair**
**02** MC **04** lead, seat **05** emcee **06** direct
**07** convene, speaker **08** chairman,
convenor, director, moderate
**09** organizer, president, supervise
**10** chairwoman **11** chairperson,
preside over, toastmaster **13** act as
chairman, professorship **15** act as
chairwoman

*Chairs include:*

**03** arm, lug, pew
**04** Bath, camp, cane, deck, easy,
form, high, push, wing
**05** bench, elbow, king's, night, potty,
sedan, stool, wheel
**06** basket, carver, curule, dining,
estate, jampan, Morris, pouffe,
rocker, sag bag, sledge, swivel,
throne, wicker
**07** beanbag, Berbice, bergère,
commode, guérite, kitchen,
lounger, nursing, rocking,
Windsor
**08** captain's, electric, fauteuil, prie-
dieu, recliner, wainscot
**09** director's
**10** boatswain's, fiddle-back,
frithstool, ladder-back
**11** Cromwellian, gestatorial
**12** ducking-stool

*See also* **seat**

**chairman, chairwoman**
**02** MC **03** Chm **04** chmn, prof
**05** emcee **06** preses **07** praeses
**08** convenor, director **09** organizer,
president, professor, spokesman
**10** prolocutor **11** chairperson,
spokeswoman **12** spokesperson

**chalcedony**
**04** sard **05** agate **06** plasma **07** sardius
**09** hornstone, moss agate
**10** bloodstone **11** chrysoprase

**chalk**
• **chalk up** **03** log **04** gain **05** score,
tally **06** attain, charge, credit, record
**07** achieve, ascribe, put down
**08** register **09** attribute
**10** accumulate

**chalky**
**03** wan **04** pale **05** ashen, dusty, white
**06** ground, pallid **07** crushed, powdery
**10** calcareous, colourless, cretaceous,
granulated

**challenge**
**03** hen, tax, try, vie **04** call, dare, defy,
gage, risk, test **05** assay, brave, claim,
demur, query, stand, stump, trial
**06** accost, accuse, appeal, cartel,
charge, hazard, henner, hurdle, invite,
strain, summon, tackle, why-not
**07** bidding, darrain, darrayn, deraign,
dispute, problem, protest, provoke,

stretch, summons **08** champion, confront, darraign, darraine, defiance, object to, obstacle, question **09** darraigne, objection, stimulate, ultimatum **10** accusation, opposition **11** opportunity, provocation, questioning **12** disagreement, disagree with **13** confrontation, interrogation **14** call in question **15** take exception to

### challenging
**06** gnarly, taxing **07** testing **08** exacting, exciting **09** demanding **10** stretching

### chamber
**02** po **03** pot **04** hall, room, silo **05** divan, fogou, house, jerry, potty, vault **06** camera, cavern, cavity, chanty, durbar, hollow, jordan, serdab, urinal **07** bedroom, boudoir, boxroom, confine, council **08** assembly, casemate, gazunder, hypogeum, moot-hall, thalamus **09** apartment, combustor, hypogaeum, mattamore, stokehold, ventricle **10** auditorium, close-stool, parliament, souterrain, subterrain, subterrane, thunderbox **11** compartment, legislature **12** assembly room, meeting-place
*See also* **room**

### champagne
**03** fiz, pop **04** fizz **06** bubbly, simkin **07** Sillery, simpkin **08** champers, the Widow **10** gooseberry
*See also* **wine**

### champion
**02** Ch **03** ace, Cid, gun **04** back, hero, kemp **05** angel, champ, ozeki **06** backer, defend, expert, kemper, knight, patron, uphold, victor, winner **07** apostle, espouse, messiah, promote, protect, saviour, support, tribune **08** advocate, asserter, assertor, defender, douzeper, guardian, maintain, Palmerin, stand for, upholder, yokozuna **09** campeador, challenge, conqueror, deliverer, doucepere, excellent, promachos, proponent, protector, supporter **10** kempery-man, stand up for, vindicator **11** excellently, protagonist, title-holder **13** hold a brief for
*See also* **seven**

### chance
**03** hap, run, try **04** cast, fate, luck, odds, risk, show, time **05** arise, break, essay, fluke, occur, stake, wager **06** casual, crop up, fair go, flukey, follow, gamble, happen, hazard, random, result, strike, upcast **07** destiny, develop, fortune, opening, venture **08** accident, Buckley's, fortuity, occasion, prospect **09** arbitrary, come about, crapshoot, haphazard, hit-or-miss, speculate, take place **10** accidental, fortuitous, hit-and-miss, incidental, likelihood, play a hunch, providence, unexpected, unforeseen, unintended **11** bet your life, coincidence, contingency, opportunity, possibility, probability, serendipity, speculation, take a chance, inadvertent, unlooked-for **12** bet your boots, happenstance, push your luck, your best shot **13** serendipitous, unanticipated, unintentional **14** Buckley's chance, chance your luck
• **by chance** **07** happily **08** bechance, randomly **09** by mistake **10** by accident **11** haphazardly, unwittingly **12** accidentally, fortuitously, incidentally, peradventure, unexpectedly **13** inadvertently **14** adventitiously **15** serendipitously, unintentionally
• **chance on, chance upon** **04** meet **07** run into **08** bump into, discover **09** run across, stumble on **10** come across **12** find by chance
• **decision by chance** **03** lot **04** draw **07** lottery

### Chancellor of the Exchequer
**02** CE

### chancy
**04** safe **05** dicey, dodgy, lucky, risky **06** tricky **07** fraught **09** dangerous, hazardous, uncertain **11** speculative **13** problematical, unpredictable

### chandelier
**06** corona, lustre **09** girandola, girandole **11** corona lucis, electrolier

### change
◊ *anagram indicator* **02** go **03** mew **04** cash, chop, move, pass, peal, swap, turn, vary **05** adapt, alter, amend, coins, renew, shift, trade, trend, U-turn, waver **06** adjust, barter, become, evolve, modify, mutate, reform, revise, rotate, silver, switch **07** commute, connect, convert, coppers, develop, novelty, remodel, renewal, replace, shake-up, variate, variety **08** do a U-turn, exchange, movement, mutation, reversal, revision, rotation, transfer, upheaval **09** about-face, about-turn, alternate, amendment, customize, diversion, evolution, fluctuate, transform, transpose, turnabout, vacillate, variation, volte-face **10** adaptation, adjustment, alteration, conversion, difference, ebb and flow, innovation, reorganize, revolution, substitute, transition **11** alternation, development, fluctuation, interchange, remodelling, replacement, restructure, state of flux, transfigure, transmutate, vacillation, vicissitude **12** metamorphose, modification, substitution, transmogrify **13** chop and change, customization, make different, metamorphosis, restructuring, transmutation, transposition **14** reconstruction, reorganization, transformation **15** become different, make a connection, transfiguration

### changeable
◊ *anagram indicator* **05** fluid, windy **06** fickle, labile, mobile, wankle, whimsy **07** erratic, flighty, movable, mutable, Protean, various, varying, voluble, whimsey **08** moveable, shifting, skittish, unstable, unsteady, variable, volatile, wavering

**09** changeful, irregular, mercurial, uncertain, unsettled, versatile **10** capricious, inconstant, unreliable **11** chameleonic, fluctuating, vacillating **12** inconsistent **13** chameleon-like, kaleidoscopic, unpredictable **15** vicissitudinous

### changeless
**05** final, fixed **06** static **07** eternal **08** constant, timeless **09** immutable, permanent **10** invariable, unchanging **11** unalterable **12** unchangeable

### changeling
**03** auf, oaf **08** elf-child, killcrop

### channel
**02** ea **03** bed, eau, gut, sny, sow, use, way **04** duct, feed, gate, kill, lake, lane, lead, main, neck, path, race, send, snye, sure, tube **05** agent, canal, chime, ditch, drain, falaj, flume, focus, force, glyph, guide, gully, latch, letch, level, major, means, radio, rigol, route, sewer, sloot, sluit, sound, stank, trunk **06** agency, airway, artery, avenue, convey, course, cut-off, direct, furrow, gravel, groove, grough, gullet, gulley, gutter, hollow, limber, medium, narrow, rigoll, sheuch, siphon, sluice, strait, trench, trough **07** chamfer, conduct, conduit, culvert, fairway, limbers, narrows, offtake, passage, raceway, shingle, station, wireway **08** approach, aqueduct, headrace, millrace, overflow, tailrace, transmit, wash-away, waterway **11** canaliculus, concentrate, katabothron, katavothron, spill-stream, watercourse

*Channels include:*

**03** Kii
**04** Foxe
**05** Bashi, Bungo, Kaiwi, Kauai, Lamma, Minas, Minch, North
**06** Akashi, Kalohi, Manche, Queens
**07** Babuyan, Bristol, English, Jamaica, Massawa, Pailolo, Sandwip, St Lucia, Yucatán
**08** Dominica, La Manche, Nicholas, Santaren, Sicilian, St Andrew, The Minch
**09** Balintang, Capricorn, East Lamma, Geographe, Kaulakahi, Northwest, Old Bahama, Skagerrak, St George's, West Lamma
**10** Alalakeiki, Alenuihaha, McClintock, Mozambique, North Minch
**11** Little Minch
**12** Kealaikahiki, Santa Barbara

*See also* **television**
• **Channel Islands** **02** CI

*The Channel Islands:*

**04** Herm, Sark
**06** Jersey, Jethou
**07** Brechou
**08** Alderney, Guernsey
**10** the Caskets
**11** the Chauseys
**12** the Minquiers

## chant

03 cry 04 haka, sing, song, yo-ho
05 ditty, psalm, shout 06 cantus,
chorus, incant, intone, mantra,
melody, recite, slogan, warcry, yo-ho-
ho 07 refrain 09 decantate, plainsong,
yo-heave-ho 10 cantillate, intonation,
recitation 11 Hare Krishna, incantation

## chaos

◇ *anagram indicator* 04 mess, muss, riot
05 abyss, havoc, musse, snafu
06 bedlam, mayhem, tumult, uproar
07 anarchy 08 disarray, disorder,
madhouse, shambles, tohu bohu,
upheaval 09 confusion 10 disruption,
dog's dinner 11 lawlessness,
pandemonium 13 pig's breakfast
14 Rafferty's rules 15 disorganization

## chaotic

◇ *anagram indicator* 05 fubar, snafu
06 unruly 07 lawless, riotous
08 anarchic, confused, deranged
09 disrupted, orderless, shambolic
10 disordered, disorderly, topsy-turvy,
tumultuary, tumultuous
12 disorganized, uncontrolled 14 all
over the shop 15 all over the place

## chap

03 boy, cat, cod, guy, jaw, man, mun,
oik, sod 04 boyo, chop, cove, gent,
hack, sort, type 05 bloke, bucko,
cheek, crack, joker, knock, spray
06 codger, fellow, Johnny, shaver,
strike 07 Johnnie, spreaze, spreeze
08 spreathe, spreethe 09 character
10 individual, male person

## chapel

05 crypt 06 Beulah 07 chantry, galilee,
martyry, oratory 08 chauntry, feretory,
parabema, sacellum 09 bead-house,
prothesis 13 Nonconformist
15 chapelle ardente

## chaperon, chaperone

04 mind 05 guard 06 attend, duenna,
escort 07 protect 08 sheepdog,
shepherd 09 accompany, companion,
look after, matronize, safeguard,
watch over 10 take care of

## chapped

03 raw 04 sore 06 chafed 07 cracked,
sprayed

## chapter

01 c 02 ch 03 cap 04 chap, part, sura,
time 05 caput, phase, stage, surah,
topic 06 branch, clause, period
07 capital, episode, portion, section
08 division 10 department

## char

02 do 03 tea 04 burn, coal, sear
05 brown, singe, togue, woman 06 Mrs
Mop, scorch 07 blacken, Mrs Mopp,
torgoch 08 barbecue, redbelly, saibling
09 carbonize, cauterize 10 accomplish,
brook trout 11 Dolly Varden

## character

03 dag 04 aura, card, case, hair, logo,
mark, part, role, rune, sign, sort, tone,
type 05 charm, ethos, image, stamp,
style, trait, write 06 appeal, cipher,
device, emblem, figure, honour, letter,
make-up, nature, oddity, person,

psyche, status, symbol, temper
07 calibre, courage, engrave, essence,
feature, honesty, imprint, oddball,
persona, quality 08 backbone,
describe, hardcase, identity, interest,
original, position, property, strength
09 delineate, eccentric, ideograph,
integrity, reference, represent
10 attributes, hieroglyph, human
being, individual, moral fibre,
reputation 11 disposition, peculiarity,
personality, specialness, temperament,
uprightness 12 constitution
13 determination, individuality
14 attractiveness 15 characteristics,
eccentric person
*See also* **alphabet; Bible; cartoon;
fairy tale; legend; letter; literary;
mythology; opera; pantomime;
Shakespeare**
• **character part** 04 role
• **characters in** ◇ *hidden indicator*
• **proper character** 03 dag, him

## characteristic

04 mark, note 05 point, right, trait
06 factor 07 feature, quality, special,
symptom, typical 08 hallmark,
peculiar, property, specific, symbolic
09 attribute, mannerism, trademark
10 individual 11 distinctive,
peculiarity, symptomatic
12 idiosyncrasy 13 idiosyncratic
14 discriminative, distinguishing,
representative

## characteristically

09 typically 10 peculiarly
12 individually 13 distinctively

## characterization

09 depiction, portrayal 11 description
12 presentation 14 representation

## characterize

04 mark 05 brand, stamp 06 depict,
typify 07 portray, present, qualify,
specify 08 describe, identify, indicate
09 designate, represent 10 stereotype
11 distinguish
• **be characterized by** 04 have

## characterless

05 inane 12 invertebrate

## charade

04 fake, sham 05 farce 06 parody,
riddle 07 mockery 08 pretence,
travesty 09 pantomime

## charge

01 Q 03 ask, chg, due, fee, ion, rap, tax
04 bill, care, cost, debt, dues, duty, fill,
levy, load, mine, rate, rent, rush, shot,
tear, tilt, toll, ward 05 blame, debit,
exact, imbue, onset, order, price,
prime, storm, terms, trust 06 accuse,
affect, amount, ask for, assail, attack,
burden, demand, dittay, impose,
impute, indict, infuse, onrush, outlay,
rental, sortie, tariff, thrill 07 arraign,
assault, command, custody, expense,
impeach, keeping, mandate, payment,
pervade, suffuse 08 godchild, saturate,
storming 09 challenge, fix a price,
inculpate, incursion, offensive,
onslaught, overwhelm, put down to,
set a price 10 accusation, accusement,

allegation, imputation, indictment,
objuration, obligation, protection
11 arraignment, expenditure,
impeachment, incriminate, rush
forward, safekeeping 12 guardianship
13 incrimination 14 responsibility
15 ask someone to pay, demand in
payment
*See also* **heraldry**
• **clear of charges** 03 net 04 nett
• **in charge of** 02 i/c 07 leading
08 managing 09 directing, heading
up 10 overseeing 11 controlling,
supervising 12 looking after, taking
care of 14 responsible for

## charged

04 live 08 instinct

## chariot

03 car 04 biga, rath, wain 05 ratha,
wagon 06 charet, vimana, waggon
08 quadriga

## charioteer

03 Hur 04 Jehu 06 Ben-Hur 07 wagoner
08 waggoner

## charisma

04 draw, lure, pull 05 charm 06 allure,
appeal 09 magnetism 10 attraction
12 drawing-power

## charismatic

08 charming, magnetic 09 appealing,
glamorous 10 attractive 11 captivating,
fascinating 12 irresistible

## charitable

04 kind 06 benign, kindly 07 lenient,
liberal 08 generous, gracious, tolerant
09 bounteous, forgiving, indulgent
10 beneficent, benevolent, open-
handed 11 broad-minded, considerate,
magnanimous, sympathetic
12 eleemosynary, humanitarian
13 compassionate, philanthropic,
understanding
• **charitable person** 04 Lion

## charitably

06 kindly 09 liberally 10 generously,
graciously, tolerantly 11 bounteously
12 open-mindedly 13 considerately
15 compassionately, sympathetically

## charity

03 aid 04 alms, fund, gift, love 05 trust
06 relief 07 caritas, concern, funding,
handout, mission 08 altruism,
clemency, donation, goodness,
goodwill, hospital, humanity,
kindness, leniency, sympathy
09 affection, tolerance 10 almsgiving,
assistance, benignness, compassion,
foundation, generosity, indulgence
11 beneficence, benevolence,
institution, munificence
12 contribution, graciousness,
philanthropy 13 bountifulness,
confraternity, consideration,
unselfishness 14 thoughtfulness
15 considerateness, kind-heartedness

*Charities include:*

03 DEC, NCH
04 PDSA, RNIB, RNLI, RSPB, WRVS
05 CAFOD, NSPCC, Oxfam, RSPCA,
Scope

**09** ActionAid, Barnardo's
**10** Greenpeace
**11** Comic Relief, Help the Aged
**12** Christian Aid
**13** National Trust, Salvation Army, Wellcome Trust, Woodland Trust
**15** Leonard Cheshire, Save the Children, St John Ambulance

*Charity fundraising events include:*

**06** fun run, raffle
**08** telethon
**09** radiothon, swimathon
**10** jumble sale
**12** slave auction
**13** coffee morning, sponsored swim, sponsored walk
**14** charity auction
**15** bring-and-buy sale

**charlatan**
**04** fake, sham **05** cheat, fraud, quack **06** con man, humbug, phoney **08** impostor, swindler **09** pretender, trickster **10** confidence, mountebank **11** bogus caller, illywhacker **13** bogus official, confidence man

**charlie**
**01** C
*See also* **fool**

**charm**
**02** it **03** obi, win **04** draw, idol, ju-ju, mojo, obia, take, tiki **05** aroma, magic, obeah, spell, weird **06** allure, amulet, appeal, cajole, enamor, fetish, glamor, grigri, mascot, please, seduce **07** abraxas, attract, becharm, beguile, bewitch, delight, enamour, enchant, encharm, glamour, hei tiki, periapt, sorcery, trinket, windbag **08** comether, greegree, grisgris, intrigue, medicine, nephrite, ornament, prestige, talisman **09** captivate, cramp-bone, enrapture, fascinate, magnetism, mesmerize **10** allurement, attraction, night-spell, phylactery **11** abracadabra, captivation, enchantment, fascination, hand of glory, what it takes **12** desirability, porte-bonheur **14** attractiveness, delightfulness

**charming**
**04** cute, nice **05** elfin, sweet **06** lovely, pretty, quaint, smooth **07** winning, winsome **08** adorable, alluring, engaging, fetching, pleasant, pleasing, tasteful, tempting **09** appealing, disarming, glamorous, seductive **10** attractive, bewitching, delectable, delightful, enchanting, entrancing **11** captivating, fascinating **12** chocolate-box, irresistible

**charmingly**
**07** sweetly **09** winsomely **10** alluringly, delectably, pleasantly, pleasingly **11** glamorously **12** attractively, delightfully, enchantingly, irresistibly

**chart**
**02** ch **03** map **04** abac, draw, list, mark, note, plan, plot **05** draft, graph, place, table **06** follow, league, map out, record, sketch **07** diagram, monitor, observe, outline, sea card **08** bar chart,

document, isopleth, nomogram, pie chart, register **09** blueprint, delineate, flow chart, flow sheet, hit parade, modulator, nomograph, sociogram, top twenty **10** hyetograph, organogram **11** put on record **13** keep a record of

**charter**
**04** bond, deed, hire, rent **05** carta, grant, lease, right **06** charta, employ, engage, patent, permit **07** licence, license, warrant **08** contract, covenant, document, sanction **09** allowance, authority, authorize, franchise, indenture, novodamus, privilege **10** commission, concession **11** prerogative **13** accreditation, authorization

**chary**
**03** shy **04** cagy, slow, wary **05** cagey, leery **06** tender, uneasy **07** careful, guarded, heedful, prudent **08** cautious, precious **09** reluctant, unwilling **10** fastidious, suspicious **11** circumspect

**chase**
◇ *juxtaposition indicator* **03** sic **04** fall, hunt, rush, seek, sick, tail **05** chevy, chivy, drive, expel, hound, hurry, track, trail **06** chivvy, course, follow, groove, pursue, quarry, scorse, shadow **07** engrave, hot-trod, hunting, pursuit **08** coursing, run after, send away **09** give chase, prosecute **12** running after **13** hare and hounds

**chasm**
**03** gap **04** gape, gulf, rift, void, yawn **05** abyss, cleft, crack, gorge, split **06** breach, canyon, cavity, crater, hollow, ravine **07** divorce, fissure, opening, quarrel **08** crevasse **10** alienation, separation **12** disagreement, estrangement

**chassis**
**05** frame **08** bodywork, fuselage, skeleton **09** framework, structure **12** substructure **13** undercarriage

**chaste**
**03** ren, rin, run **04** bare, pure, sick **05** moral, plain, worry **06** decent, demure, graced, honest, modest, scorse, simple, single, vestal **07** austere, classic **08** celibate, innocent, virginal, virtuous **09** abstinent, continent, unadorned, undefiled, unmarried, unsullied **10** immaculate, restrained **13** unembellished

**chasten**
**04** curb, tame **06** humble, punish, purify, refine, soften, subdue, temper **07** correct, repress, reprove **08** chastise, moderate, restrain **09** castigate, humiliate **10** discipline

**chastise**
**03** fix **04** beat, cane, flog, lash, whip **05** scold, smack, spank, strap **06** berate, disple, punish, purify, refine, reform, swinge, wallop **07** censure, correct, reprove, scourge, upbraid **08** admonish, moderate, restrain

**09** castigate, dress down, reprimand **10** discipline, take to task

**chastisement**
**07** beating, censure, what for **08** flogging, scolding, smacking, spanking, whipping **09** walloping **10** admonition, correction, discipline, punishment **11** castigation **12** dressing-down

**chastity**
**05** honor **06** honour, purity, virtue **07** honesty, modesty **08** celibacy **09** innocence, virginity **10** abstinence, continence, continency, maidenhood, moderation, singleness **13** temperateness **14** immaculateness, unmarried state

**chat**
**03** gas, jaw, rap **04** coze, talk **05** crack, louse, visit, wongi **06** babble, confab, cosher, gossip, jabber, natter, rabbit, waffle, yabber **07** blather, blether, chatter, chinwag, prattle, schmooz, shmoose, shmooze **08** causerie, chitchat, converse, cosy chat, rabbit on, schmooze **09** small talk, tête-à-tête **10** chew the fat, chew the rag **11** confabulate **12** conversation, heart-to-heart, tittle-tattle **13** confabulation **14** clash-ma-clavers, shoot the breeze
• **chat up**  **03** eye **04** ogle **06** leer at **08** come on to **09** flirt with **11** make a pass at **14** make advances to **15** try to get off with

**chatter**
**03** gab, gas, jaw, mag, yap **04** chat, talk **05** clack, clash, froth, skite **06** babble, cackle, confab, gabble, gammon, gossip, jabber, jargon, natter, patter, rabbit, rattle, tattle, waffle, witter, yatter **07** blether, chinwag, chitter, chunder, chunner, chunter, clatter, earbash, gabnash, nashgab, palaver, prattle, twattle **08** chitchat, chounter, rabbit on, rattle on **09** tête-à-tête **10** talky-talky, tongue-work **12** conversation, gibble-gabble, talkee-talkee, tittle-tattle, yada yada yada **14** clitter-clatter **15** yadda yadda yadda

**chatterbox**
**06** gabber, gasbag, gasser, gossip, talker **07** babbler, gabnash, tattler, windbag **08** big mouth, jabberer, natterer **09** chatterer, gossipper, loudmouth **12** blabbermouth **13** tittle-tattler **14** telephone kiosk

**chatterer**
**03** pie **06** chewet, gabber, tatler **07** gabnash, nashgab, tattler

**chatty**
**04** glib **05** dirty, gabby, lousy, newsy **06** casual, mouthy **07** gossipy, gushing, verbose **08** effusive, familiar, friendly, informal **09** garrulous, talkative **10** colloquial, long-winded, loquacious **13** communicative **14** conversational

**chauvinism**
**04** bias **06** sexism **08** jingoism **09** prejudice **10** flag-waving

11 nationalism 12 partisanship 14 male chauvinism

## chauvinist
03 MCP 05 jingo 06 biased, sexist
08 jingoist 10 flag-waving, prejudiced
11 nationalist 14 male chauvinist

## chauvinistic
06 biased, sexist 10 jingoistic,
prejudiced 13 nationalistic

## cheap
03 low 04 mean, poor, sale 05 a snip,
tacky, tatty 06 a steal, budget, cheapo,
chintz, common, jitney, paltry,
shoddy, sordid, tawdry, two-bit, vulgar
07 bargain, chintzy, economy, low-
cost, reduced, slashed, tinhorn 08 a
good buy, cut-price, dog-cheap,
giveaway, inferior, low-price, no-frills,
sixpenny, twopenny 09 bon marché,
cheapjack, cheap-rate, dirt-cheap,
good-cheap, knock-down, rinky-dink,
tasteless, ten a penny, throwaway,
worthless 10 à bon marché, affordable,
despicable, discounted, downmarket,
economical, improvised, marked-
down, ramshackle, reasonable, rock-
bottom, second-rate 11 a dime a
dozen, gingerbread, inexpensive,
reduced-rate 12 contemptible
13 cheap and nasty, going for a song,
on a shoestring, value-for-money 14 on
special offer 15 bargain-basement

## cheapen
05 lower 06 demean 07 degrade,
devalue 08 belittle, derogate
09 denigrate, discredit, disparage,
downgrade 10 depreciate

## cheaply
09 at low cost, bon marché 10 à bon
marché, affordably, reasonably 12 at a
cheap rate, economically, with no
frills 13 inexpensively 14 at a reduced
rate, on special offer

## cheat
02 do 03 bam, bob, cog, con, fix, fob,
fox, gum, gyp, rig 04 bilk, chiz, clip,
colt, deny, dupe, fake, fool, gull, have,
jink, mump, slur, snap, swiz, take, trim
05 biter, bluff, check, chess, chizz,
cozen, crook, cully, dingo, fraud,
fudge, hocus, mulct, rogue, screw,
shark, stiff, sting, touch, trick, welsh
06 baffle, begunk, cajole, chisel,
chouse, con man, diddle, dodger, do
down, fiddle, fleece, intake, rip off,
smouch, take in, thwart 07 beguile,
cheater, cozener, deceive, defraud,
deprive, escheat, forfeit, gudgeon,
mislead, prevent, sharper, skelder,
swindle, swizzle, twister, two-time
08 deceiver, hoodwink, impostor,
picaroon, swindler 09 bamboozle,
charlatan, chiseller, cony-catch,
deception, duckshove, frustrate,
trickster, victimize 10 do a flanker
11 cony-catcher, do one over on,
double-cross, extortioner, gull-catcher,
hornswoggle, short-change 12 do the
dirty on, take for a ride 13 double-
crosser

## check
02 ch 03 bar, nip, tab 04 balk, bill,

curb, damp, foil, halt, rein, scan, slow,
sneb, snub, stem, stop, test, tick
05 audit, baulk, crush, delay, limit,
pinch, probe, punch, sneap, study,
stunt, tally, token 06 arrest, blight,
bridle, coupon, hinder, impede, look
at, police, rebuff, rebuke, rein in,
retard, screen, tartan, thwart, ticket,
verify 07 account, analyse, charges,
check-up, compare, confirm, contain,
control, examine, inhibit, inquiry,
inspect, invoice, monitor, repress,
repulse, setback, shorten, staunch
08 analysis, holdback, make sure,
obstruct, once-over, research, restrain,
scrutiny, slow down, suppress,
validate 09 going-over, go through,
reckoning, reprimand, restraint,
statement, take stock 10 cross-check,
inspection, monitoring, scrutinize
11 corroborate, counterfoil,
examination, inquire into, investigate
12 confirmation, substantiate,
verification 13 investigation, look at
closely 15 give the once-over
• **check in**  05 enrol 06 book in
08 register
• **check out**  04 case, test 05 leave,
recce, study 06 depart 07 examine,
inspect 08 look into, settle up 10 pay
the bill 11 investigate
• **check up**  04 test 05 probe 06 assess,
verify 07 analyse, confirm, examine,
inspect 08 evaluate, make sure
09 ascertain 11 inquire into, investigate
• **hold in check, keep in check**
04 curb, stop 06 arrest, bridle, hinder,
impede, rein in 07 control, prevent,
repress 08 hold back, keep back,
obstruct, restrain, suppress

## check-up
04 test 05 audit, probe 07 inquiry
08 analysis, research, scrutiny
09 appraisal 10 evaluation, inspection,
monitoring 11 examination
12 confirmation, verification
13 investigation

## cheek
03 jaw, lip 04 chap, chop, gall, gena,
jole, joll, jowl, neck, sass, wang
05 chaft, mouth, nerve, sauce
06 chafts, dimple 08 attitude, audacity,
chutzpah, temerity 09 brass neck,
impudence, insolence 10 brazenness,
disrespect, effrontery 12 impertinence

## cheekily
06 pertly 10 impudently, insolently
13 impertinently 15 disrespectfully

## cheeky
04 pert, rude 05 fresh, gobby, lippy,
sassy, saucy 06 brazen, mouthy
07 forward 08 impudent, insolent
09 audacious 11 impertinent
12 overfamiliar 13 disrespectful

## cheep
04 peep, pipe, sing 05 chirp, trill, tweet
06 warble 07 chirrup, twitter, whistle

## cheer
03 hip, joy, olé, rah 04 buck, buoy,
clap, face, fare, food, glad, hail, hoop,
warm, yell 05 bravo, elate, shout,
whoop 06 buck up, buoy up, cherry,

hurrah, perk up, salute, solace, spirit,
uplift 07 acclaim, applaud, comfort,
console, enliven, fanfare, gladden,
hearten, ovation, revelry, root for,
support, welcome 08 applause,
brighten, clapping, gladness, inspirit,
plaudits, semblant 09 celebrate,
encourage, enhearten, happiness,
merriment 10 barrack for, exhilarate,
joyfulness 11 acclamation, high spirits,
hopefulness, merrymaking
12 cheerfulness 13 entertainment
• **be cheered**  04 rise
• **cheer up**  05 liven, rally 06 buck up,
perk up 07 chirrup, comfort, console,
hearten, liven up 08 brighten
09 encourage, take heart 10 brighten
up

## cheerful
02 up 03 gay 04 glad, joco, warm
05 bonny, cadgy, canty, happy, jolly,
light, merry, riant, sunny 06 blithe,
bonnie, breezy, bright, bubbly,
cheery, chirpy, genial, hearty, jaunty,
jocund, jovial, joyful, joyous, kidgie,
lively, smiley, upbeat 07 buoyant,
chipper, holiday, smiling, winsome
08 animated, carefree, chirrupy,
eupeptic, laughing, pleasant, pleasing,
spirited, stirring 09 agreeable,
contented, exuberant, inspiring,
lightsome, sparkling 10 attractive,
comforting, delightful, heartening,
optimistic 11 encouraging
12 enthusiastic, good-humoured, high-
spirited, light-hearted 13 in good spirits

## cheerily
06 gladly 07 happily 08 brightly,
jovially 10 cheerfully 14 light-heartedly

## cheerio
03 bye 04 ta-ta 05 adieu 06 bye-bye,
cheers, hooray, hooroo, see you, so
long 07 goodbye, haere ra 08 au revoir,
farewell 11 see you later
*See also* **farewell**

## cheerless
03 sad 04 cold, dank, dark, dead, drab,
dull, grim 05 bleak, dingy 06 barren,
dismal, dreary, gloomy, lonely,
sombre, sullen, wintry 07 austere,
forlorn, joyless, sunless, unhappy,
wintery 08 dejected, desolate,
dolorous, mournful, winterly
09 miserable, sorrowful 10 depressing,
despondent, melancholy, uninviting
11 comfortless 12 disconsolate

## cheers
02 ta 03 bye 04 rivo, skol, ta-ta, tope
05 adieu, skoal 06 bye-bye, health,
hooray, prosit, see you, so long
07 cheerio, goodbye, haere ra, slàinte,
wassail 08 au revoir, bless you, chin-
chin, farewell, thank you, waes hail
09 bottoms up, drink hail 10 all the
best, here's to you, many thanks,
thanks a lot 11 much obliged, see you
later 12 down the hatch, mud in your
eye 13 happy landings 14 your good
health 15 to absent friends

## cheery
03 gay 04 glad 05 happy, jolly, merry
06 breezy, bright, chirpy, genial,

hearty, jaunty, jovial, joyful, lively
**07** buoyant, smiling **08** animated, carefree, cheerful, laughing, spirited **09** contented, exuberant, sparkling **10** optimistic **12** back-slapping, enthusiastic, light-hearted **13** in good spirits

## cheese

*Cheeses include:*

**03** ewe, Oka
**04** Brie, curd, Edam, feta, goat, hard, skyr, soft, Yarg
**05** Caboc, Carré, Derby, Gouda, quark
**06** Cantal, chèvre, Dunlop, junket, Orkney, paneer, Romano, Tilsit
**07** Boursin, Cheddar, crottin, crowdie, Fontina, Gruyère, kebbock, kebbuck, Limburg, Münster, ricotta, sapsago, Stilton®
**08** bel paese, Cheshire, Churnton, Emmental, halloumi, Huntsman, manchego, Parmesan, pecorino, raclette, Taleggio, vacherin
**09** Amsterdam, Blue Vinny, Cambozola®, Camembert, chevreton, Emmenthal, ewe-cheese, Ilchester, Jarlsberg®, Killarney, Leicester, Limburger, Lymeswold®, mouse-trap, Port Salut, processed, provolone, reblochon, Roquefort, sage Derby
**10** blue cheese, Caerphilly, curd cheese, Danish blue, dolcelatte, Emmentaler, Gloucester, Gorgonzola, hard cheese, Lancashire, mascarpone, mozzarella, Neufchâtel, Red Windsor, soft cheese, stracchino, vegetarian
**11** Coulommiers, cream cheese, Petit Suisse, Pont l'Évêque, Saint-Paulin, Wensleydale
**12** Blue Cheshire, fromage frais, Monterey Jack, Philadelphia®, Red Leicester, smoked cheese
**13** Bleu d'Auvergne, cottage cheese

• **big cheese 03** nob, VIP **04** tuan **05** mogul, swell **06** big gun, bigwig, honcho, worthy **07** big shot, notable **08** big noise, somebody **09** celebrity, dignitary, personage **10** panjandrum **11** heavyweight

## cheesed off

**05** bored, fed up **07** annoyed
**09** depressed, disgusted, hacked off
**10** brassed off, browned off
**11** disgruntled **12** disappointed, discontented, dissatisfied, sick and tired

## chef

*Chefs, restaurateurs and cookery writers include:*

**03** Hom (Ken)
**04** Gray (Rose), Roux (Albert), Roux (Michel), Spry (Constance)
**05** Allen (Betty), Blanc (Raymond René), David (Elizabeth), Delia, Floyd (Keith), Leith (Prue), Roden (Claudia), Smith (Delia), Soyer (Alexis), Stein (Rick), White (Marco Pierre)
**06** Appert (Nicolas François), Beeton (Mrs Isabella Mary), Carême (Marie Antoine), Farmer (Fannie), Lawson (Nigella), Oliver (Jamie), Ramsay (Gordon), Rhodes (Gary), Rogers (Ruth), Slater (Nigel), Wilson (David)
**07** Cradock (Fanny), Erikson (Gunn), Grigson (Jane), Grigson (Sophie), Jaffrey (Madhur), Ladenis (Nico)
**08** Dimbleby (Josceline), Grossman (Loyd), Harriott (Ainsley), Mosimann (Anton), Paterson (Jennifer)
**09** Carluccio (Antonio), Escoffier (Auguste), McCartney (Linda)
**12** Two Fat Ladies
**13** Dickson Wright (Clarissa)
**14** Brillat-Savarin (Anthelme)
**15** Worrall Thompson (Antony)

## chemical

*Chemical compounds include:*

**03** PVC
**04** alum, DEET, urea
**05** epoxy
**06** phenol
**07** ammonia, borazon, chloral, ethanol, styrene, toluene
**08** kerosene, methanol, paraffin
**10** chloramine, chloroform
**12** benzaldehyde, borosilicate
**13** carbon dioxide, chlorhexidine, chlorobromide
**14** carbon monoxide, chloral hydrate
**15** organophosphate, sodium hydroxide

*See also* **element**

## chemist

*Chemists include:*

**03** Lee (Yuan T)
**04** Abel (Sir Frederick), Davy (Sir Humphry), Hess (Germain Henri), Kuhn (Richard), Mond (Ludwig), Urey (Harold Clayton)
**05** Abegg (Richard), Black (Joseph), Boyle (Robert), Curie (Marie), Darby (Abraham), Dewar (Sir James), Haber (Fritz), Hooke (Robert), Kroto (Sir Harold), Libby (Willard Frank), Meyer (Lothar), Nobel (Alfred), Soddy (Frederick)
**06** Baeyer (Adolf von), Barton (Sir Derek), Bunsen (Robert Wilhelm), Dalton (John), Eyring (Henry), Hevesy (George Charles von), Liebig (Justus von), Miller (Stanley Lloyd), Nernst (Walther), Porter (George, Lord), Ramsay (Sir William)
**07** Abelson (Philip H), Bergius (Friedrich), Buchner (Eduard), Faraday (Michael), Fischer (Emil Hermann), Fischer (Hans), Hodgkin (Dorothy), Pasteur (Louis), Pauling (Linus Carl), Scheele (Carl Wilhelm), Seaborg (Glenn Theodore)
**08** Avogadro (Amedeo), Chevreul (Michel Eugène), Hadfield (Sir Robert Abbott), Klaproth (Martin Heinrich), Langmuir (Irving), Lonsdale (Dame Kathleen), Lovelock (James), Mulliken (Robert Sanderson), Regnault (Henri Victor), Robinson (Sir Robert), Sidgwick (Nevil Vincent), Svedberg (Theodor), Tiselius (Arne Wilhelm Kaurin)
**09** Arrhenius (Svante August), Baekeland (Leo Hendrik), Berzelius (Jöns Jacob), Cavendish (Henry), Gay-Lussac (Joseph Louis), Lavoisier (Antoine Laurent), Priestley (Joseph), Prigogine (Ilya, Vicomte)
**10** Cannizzaro (Stanislao), Mendeleyev (Dmitri)
**12** Boussingault (Jean Baptiste Joseph)

• **chemists 03** ICI, RSC **04** BASF **06** IChemE

## chemistry

*Chemistry terms include:*

**02** IR, pH
**03** cis, gas, ion
**04** acid, atom, base, bond, mass, mole, rate, salt, weak
**05** assay, block, cycle, ester, group, IUPAC, lipid, order, phase, polar, redox, shell, solid, trans, yield
**06** alkali, alkane, alkene, buffer, chiral, dalton, dilute, dipole, fusion, halide, isomer, ketone, ligand, liquid, matter, period, phenyl, pi bond, proton, strong, symbol
**07** chelate, chemist, colloid, crystal, element, entropy, fission, formula, halogen, isotope, lattice, mixture, neutral, neutron, nucleus, orbital, organic, polymer, product, racemic, reagent, soluble, solvent, valency
**08** analysis, aromatic, catalyst, compound, cracking, dialysis, electron, emulsion, end point, enthalpy, fixation, half life, inert gas, miscible, molecule, noble gas, reactant, reaction, solution
**09** aliphatic, allotrope, anhydrous, bioenergy, catalysis, corrosion, diffusion, electrode, empirical, hydroxide, indicator, inorganic, insoluble, ionic bond, oxidation, reduction, saturated, side chain, sigma bond, substance, synthesis, titration
**10** amphoteric, atomic mass, combustion, curly arrow, double bond, exothermic, free energy, hydrolysis, immiscible, ion channel, ionotropic, litmus test, reversible, single bond, suspension, triple bond, zwitterion
**11** biomolecule, crystallize, diffraction, electrolyte, endothermic, equilibrium, evaporation, free radical, ground state, hydrocarbon, litmus paper, precipitate, respiration, sublimation

## cheque

**12** atomic number, atomic radius, atomic weight, biochemistry, chemical bond, chlorination, concentrated, condensation, covalent bond, dissociation, distillation, electrolysis, fermentation, hydrogen bond, masking agent, melting point, metallic bond, spectroscopy **13** chain reaction, decomposition, fractionation, periodic table, radioactivity, stoichiometry **14** Avogadro number, Brownian motion, buffer solution, chromatography, saponification **15** atomic structure, aufbau principle, chemical element, collision theory, electrospinning, transition metal, transition state

## cheque

**03** dud **04** giro **06** stumer **07** bouncer **11** counterfoil

## chequer

**04** dice **09** interrupt, variegate **10** chessboard **13** counterchange

## chequered

**05** diced, mixed **06** checky, chequy, varied **07** checked, diverse, striped **08** eventful **10** variegated **13** multicoloured, particoloured **15** with ups and downs

## cherish

**03** hug **04** love **05** adore, brood, nurse, prize, value **06** foster, nestle, tender **07** brood on, care for, harbour, nourish, nurture, shelter, support, sustain **08** enshrine, hold dear, treasure **09** encourage, entertain, look after **10** make much of, take care of **11** have at heart, refocillate **14** take good care of

## cherished

**03** pet **08** precious

## cherry

**04** gean **05** cheer, morel, ruddy **06** cornel, mazard **07** may-duke, mazzard, morello **08** hagberry **09** Malpighia **10** blackheart

## cherub

**05** angel **06** seraph

## cherubic

**04** cute **05** sweet **06** lovely **07** angelic, lovable **08** adorable, heavenly, innocent, loveable, seraphic **09** appealing

## chess

*Chess players include:*

**03** Tal (Mikhail), Xie (Jun)
**04** Euwe (Max)
**05** Anand (Viswanathan), Short (Nigel)
**06** Karpov (Anatoli), Lasker (Emanuel), Morphy (Paul), Polgar (Judit), Polgar (Zsuzsa), Thomas (Sir George), Timman (Jan), Xie Jun
**07** Fischer (Bobby), Kramnik (Vladimir), Smyslov (Vasili), Spassky (Boris)
**08** Alekhine (Alexander), Deep Blue,

Kasparov (Garry), Korchnoi (Viktor), Philidor (François André), Steinitz (Wilhelm)
**09** Botvinnik (Mikhail), Khalifman (Alexander), Petrosian (Tigran)
**10** Capablanca (José)
**13** Chiburdanidze (Maya)

---

*Chess pieces include:*

**04** king, pawn, rook
**05** queen
**06** bishop, castle, knight

---

*Chess-related terms include:*

**01** R
**03** man, pin, row
**04** bind, FIDE, fork, move, play
**05** black, board, check, flank, march, piece, white
**06** attack, centre, double, gambit, master, patzer, square
**07** chequer, defence, endgame, en prise, j'adoube, opening, promote, retract, squeeze
**08** back rank, castling, diagonal, exchange, kingside, opponent, queening, zugzwang
**09** bad bishop, checkmate, Elo rating, en passant, fool's mate, miniature, promotion, queenside, stalemate
**10** fianchetto, good bishop, major piece, middle game, minor piece, passed pawn
**11** counterplay, grandmaster, zwischenzug
**12** backward pawn, problem child
**13** counter attack, fifty move rule
**14** perpetual check
**15** knight's progress

---

## chest

**03** ark, box, cub **04** case, kist **05** bahut, caddy, crate, hutch, trunk **06** breast, bunker, bureau, casket, coffer, girnel, larnax, scrine, shrine, thorax **07** cap-case, cassone, commode, dresser, meal-ark, sternum, tallboy **08** corn-kist, glory-box, treasury, wakahuia **09** slop-chest, strongbox **10** chiffonier

## chestnut

**02** ch **04** joke **05** favel **06** cliché, conker, favell, sorrel **07** badious, buckeye, caltrop, horn-nut, saligot **08** bean tree, Castanea **09** chincapin, chinkapin **10** chinquapin **14** Castanospermum

## chevron

**01** V **06** stripe **08** dancette

## chew

◇ *anagram indicator* **03** eat **04** bite, chaw, gnaw, quid **05** champ, chomp, grind, munch **06** crunch **07** reflect **08** meditate, ruminate **09** manducate, masticate
• **chew over** **06** muse on, ponder **07** weigh up **08** consider, mull over **10** meditate on, ruminate on **14** deliberate upon

## chic

**05** smart, style **06** chichi, dapper, modish, snazzy, trendy, with it **07** à la

mode, elegant, stylish **08** elegance **11** fashionable **13** sophisticated

## chicanery

**05** dodge, fraud, guile, wiles **08** artifice, cheating, intrigue, trickery **09** deception, duplicity, quibbling, sophistry **10** dishonesty, subterfuge **11** deviousness, hoodwinking **13** deceitfulness, double-dealing, jiggery-pokery, sharp practice **15** underhandedness

## chick

**04** bird

## chicken

**03** hen **04** poot, pout **05** biddy, chook, chuck, poule, poult, rumpy, squab **06** scared **07** broiler, chookie, chuckie, poussin **08** coq au vin, cowardly, springer, yakitori **09** howtowdie **10** frightened
*See also* **animal; cowardly; hen**

---

*Chickens include:*

**06** Ancona, bantam, Cochin, houdan, sultan
**07** Dorking, Hamburg, leghorn, Minorca
**08** Hamburgh, Langshan
**09** Orpington, Welsummer, wyandotte
**10** Andalusian, Australorp, chittagong, jungle fowl
**11** Cochin-China, Spanish fowl
**12** Plymouth Rock
**14** Rhode Island Red

---

## chickpea

**04** gram **05** chana, chich **08** garbanzo

## chide

**03** row **04** rate, twit **05** blame, dress, scold, shend **06** berate, rebuke **07** censure, lecture, quarrel, reprove, tell off, upbraid **08** admonish, chastise, reproach **09** criticize, objurgate, reprehend, reprimand

## chief

**02** Ch **03** cid, key, oba **04** arch, boss, cock, head, jarl, kaid, khan, lead, lord, main, raja, ratu **05** ariki, chair, first, grand, great, major, prime, rajah, ratoo, ruler, sheik, vital **06** big gun, gaffer, honcho, leader, master, primal, sachem, sheikh, sudder, top dog **07** cacique, captain, cazique, central, headman, highest, leading, manager, mugwump, premier, primary, supreme, supremo **08** big noise, cardinal, chairman, director, dominant, foremost, governor, intimate, overlord, sagamore, superior, suzerain **09** big cheese, chieftain, commander, directing, essential, head-woman, important, number one, paramount, pendragon, president, principal, rangatira, top banana, uppermost **10** chairwoman, coryphaeus, head bummer, pre-eminent, prevailing, ringleader **11** chairperson, controlling, outstanding, predominant, supervising **13** most important, prime minister **14** chief executive, superintendent

*See also* **emperor; empress; governor; king; president; queen; ruler**

## chiefly
**06** mainly, mostly **07** usually **09** capitally, generally, in the main, primarily **10** especially, on the whole **11** essentially, principally **13** predominantly **14** for the most part

## child
**02** ch, it **03** boy, elf, get, imp, kid, son, tot **04** babe, baby, brat, chit, dalt, gait, geit, girl, gyte, mite, puss, tama, tike, tiny, trot, tyke, waif, wean **05** bairn, chick, dault, elfin, issue, mardy, minor, scamp, slink, smout, smowt, sprog, totty, wench, youth **06** cherub, enfant, infant, kidlet, moppet, nipper, pledge, rug rat, toddle, tottie, urchin, wanton **07** bambino, dilling, gangrel, hellion, kinchin, littlin, name-son, neonate, papoose, preteen, prodigy, progeny, subteen, tiny tot, toddler, young 'un **08** adherent, bantling, Benjamin, daughter, disciple, godchild, innocent, juvenile, little 'un, littling, munchkin, suckling, tamariki, teenager, weanling, young one **09** kiddywink, littleane, little boy, little one, monthling, offspring, stepchild, underfive, youngster **10** adolescent, ankle-biter, changeling, descendant, eyas-musket, fosterling, grandchild, inhabitant, jackanapes, kiddiewink, knave-bairn, little girl, orphanmite, ragamuffin, wunderkind, young adult **11** ankle-nipper, butter-print, encumbrance, guttersnipe, olive branch, preschooler, schoolchild, weeny-bopper, young person **12** kiddiewinkie
• **only child** **02** oc

## childbirth
**05** pains **06** labour **07** lying-in, travail **08** delivery **09** maternity, pregnancy, puerperal **11** confinement, parturition **12** accouchement, child-bearing

## childhood
**05** youth **07** boyhood, infancy **08** babyhood, girlhood, minority **09** early days **10** early years, immaturity, schooldays **11** adolescence

## childish
**05** silly **06** boyish **07** babyish, foolish, girlish, puerile **08** immature, juvenile, trifling **09** frivolous, infantile **10** namby-pamby **13** irresponsible

## childishly
**09** foolishly **10** immaturely **13** irresponsibly

## childless
*see* **without issue** *under* **issue**

## childlike
**05** naive **06** docile, simple **07** artless, natural **08** innocent, trustful, trusting **09** credulous, guileless, ingenuous **10** unaffected

## children
**05** issue

## Chile
**03** CHL, RCH

## chill
**03** flu, ice, icy, nip, raw **04** bite, cold, cool, fear **05** algid, aloof, bleak, dread, fever, nippy, oorie, ourie, owrie, parky, relax, scare, sharp, virus **06** biting, chilly, dampen, dismay, freeze, frigid, frosty, shiver, wintry **07** anxiety, depress, iciness, petrify, rawness, terrify **08** coldness, cool down, coolness, freezing, frighten, make cold **09** crispness, influenza **10** become cold, depressing, discourage, dishearten, make colder, unfriendly **11** refrigerate **12** apprehension, become colder
• **chilled** **05** on ice **07** relaxed
• **chill out** **05** relax **06** unwind **08** calm down **09** have a rest **10** take it easy

## chilly
**03** icy, raw **04** cold, cool **05** aloof, bleak, brisk, crisp, fresh, gelid, nippy, parky, sharp, stony **06** biting, frigid, wintry **07** distant, hostile **08** freezing **10** unfriendly **11** unwelcoming **12** unresponsive **13** unsympathetic **14** unenthusiastic

## chime
**04** boom, ding, dong, peal, ring, tink, toll **05** agree, clang, rhyme, sound **06** accord, jingle, strike, tinkle **07** harmony, resound **11** reverberate **13** reverberation **14** tintinnabulate
• **chime in** **05** agree, blend, cut in, fit in **06** butt in, chip in **09** be similar, harmonize, interject, interpose, interrupt **10** correspond **12** be consistent

## chimera
**05** dream, fancy **07** fantasy, ratfish, spectre **08** delusion, illusion **09** idle fancy **12** will-o'-the-wisp **13** hallucination

## chimney
**03** lum **04** flue, vent **05** cleft, shaft, stack, stalk **06** funnel, tunnel **07** chimley, chumley, crevice **08** femerall **10** flare stack, smokestack **12** chimney stalk
• **chimney pot** **03** can **06** top-hat

## china
**02** Ch, RC **03** CHN, TWN **04** Chin, kina, mate **05** quina **06** dishes, plates **07** ceramic, pottery, quinine **08** crockery **09** porcelain, tableware **10** terracotta **11** earthenware **13** dinner service **14** cups and saucers, the flowery land **15** Celestial Empire, People's Republic
*See also* **friend; porcelain**

## Chinese
**02** Ch **03** Han **04** Chin, Sino- **05** Seric, Sinic **07** Cataian, Catayan, Sinaean **08** Cathaian, Cathayan
*See also* **animal; dynasty**
• **Chinese society** **04** tong

## chink
**03** cut, gap **04** gasp, rift, rima, rime, slit, slot **05** cleft, crack, money, space, split

## chip
**06** cavity, cranny, rictus **07** crevice, fissure, opening **08** aperture

## chip
**03** bit, fry **04** dent, disc, EROM, flaw, gash, nick, pare **05** break, chaff, crack, crisp, EPROM, flake, nacho, notch, piece, scrap, shard, shred, slice, snick, spale, spall, tease, token, wafer **06** chisel, damage, gallet, paring, sliver **07** blitter, counter, crumble, Pentium®, pinning, scratch, shaving, whittle **08** break off, fragment, splinter **09** French fry **10** transputer **11** fried potato **14** microprocessor
*See also* **computer**
• **chip in** **03** pay **05** cut in **06** butt in, donate **07** chime in **09** interject, interpose, interrupt, subscribe **10** contribute **12** club together **13** make a donation **14** have a whip-round **15** have a collection

## chirp
**03** pip **04** peep, pipe, sing **05** cheep, chirk, chirm, chirr, trill, tweet **06** chirre, warble **07** chirrup, chitter, twitter, whistle **10** tweet-tweet

## chirpy
**03** gay **04** glad **05** happy, jolly, merry, perky **06** blithe, bright, cheery, jaunty, lively **08** cheerful

## chisel
**03** gad **04** bran, burr **05** burin, cheat, drove, gouge **06** firmer, gravel **07** boaster, bolster, scauper, scorper, shingle **12** pitching tool
*See also* **carve; cheat; sculpt**

## chit-chat
**04** chat, talk **06** confab, gossip, natter **07** chatter, chinwag, prattle **08** cosy chat **09** small talk, tête-à-tête **10** idle gossip **12** conversation, heart-to-heart, tittle-tattle

## chivalrous
**04** bold **05** brave, noble **06** heroic, polite **07** gallant, valiant **08** gracious, knightly **09** courteous **10** courageous, honourable **11** gentlemanly **12** well-mannered

## chivalry
**06** honour **07** bravery, bushido, courage **08** boldness, courtesy, noblemen **09** gallantry, integrity **10** politeness **11** courtliness, good manners **12** graciousness, truthfulness **15** gentlemanliness

## chivvy
**03** bug, nag **04** goad, hunt, prod, urge **05** annoy, chase, hound, hurry **06** badger, harass, hassle, pester, plague **07** hurry up, pursuit, torment **08** pressure **09** importune

## chlorine
**02** Cl

## chock-a-block
**04** full **06** jammed, packed **07** brimful, chocker, crammed, crowded **08** overfull **09** congested, jam-packed **14** full to bursting

## choice
**03** try **04** best, fine, list, plum, rare, trye,

wale, will **05** prime, prize, range, taste **06** answer, dainty, finest, opting, option, select **07** Auslese, picking, special, variety **08** choosing, decision, druthers, election, precious, solution, superior, valuable **09** excellent, exclusive, exquisite, first-rate, selection **10** first-class, hand-picked, preference **11** alternative, appropriate **14** discrimination

### choke
**03** bar, dam, gag **04** clog, glut, plug, silt, stap, stop **05** block, close, cough, dam up, retch, worry **06** accloy, silt up, stifle **07** congest, occlude, smother **08** obstruct, strangle, suppress, throttle **09** constrict, overpower, overwhelm, suffocate **10** asphyxiate
• **choke back** **04** curb **05** check **07** contain, control, inhibit, repress **08** restrain, strangle, suppress **09** fight back

### chokey, choky
*see* **prison**

### choleric
**05** angry, fiery, testy **06** crabby, touchy **07** crabbed, peppery **08** petulant **09** crotchety, irascible, irritable **10** passionate **11** bad-tempered, hot-tempered, ill-tempered **12** cantankerous **13** quick-tempered

### choose
**03** opt **04** list, pick, take, wale, want, will, wish **05** adopt, chuse, elect, fix on, go for **06** decide, desire, favour, opt for, prefer, see fit, select, take up **07** appoint, espouse, extract, pick out, vote for **08** decide on, plump for, settle on **09** designate, determine, single out **10** predestine **14** make up your mind

### choosy
**05** faddy, fussy, picky **07** finicky **08** exacting **09** selective **10** fastidious, particular, pernickety **11** persnickety **14** discriminating

### chop
**02** ax **03** axe, cut, eat, hew, jaw, lop, saw **04** chap, clap, dice, fell, food, hack, hash, seal, snap **05** brand, carve, crack, cut up, mince, sever, share, slash, slice, split **06** barter, change, cleave, divide, thrust **07** dissect, fissure **08** exchange, truncate **09** côtelette
• **chop up** ◇ *anagram indicator* **03** cut **04** cube, dice **05** cut up, grate, grind, mince, shred, slice **06** divide **07** slice up **13** cut into pieces

### choppy
◇ *anagram indicator* **04** wavy **05** rough **06** broken, stormy, uneven **07** ruffled, squally **08** blustery **09** turbulent **11** tempestuous

### chore
**03** job **04** duty, task **05** truck **06** burden, errand **07** routine **11** piece of work

### choreography
*Choreographers include:*

**04** **Bolm** (Adolph), **Dean** (Laura), **Feld** (Eliot), **Kidd** (Michael)

**05** **Bruce** (Christopher), **Cohan** (Robert), **Dolin** (Anton), **Jooss** (Kurt), **Laban** (Rudolf von), **Lifar** (Serge), **North** (Robert), **Sleep** (Wayne), **Tharp** (Twyla)
**06** **Ashton** (Sir Frederick), **Béjart** (Maurice), **Blasis** (Carlo), **Bourne** (Matthew), **Clarke** (Michael), **Cranko** (John), **Davies** (Siobhan), **Duncan** (Isadora), **Fokine** (Michel), **Graham** (Martha), **Morris** (Mark), **Petipa** (Marius), **Valois** (Dame Ninette de), **Wigman** (Mary)
**07** **Darrell** (Peter), **de Mille** (Agnes George), **Joffrey** (Robert), **Massine** (Léonide)
**08** **Berkeley** (Busby), **de Valois** (Dame Ninette), **Helpmann** (Sir Robert), **Humphrey** (Doris), **Nijinska** (Bronislava), **Nijinsky** (Vaslav)
**09** **Beauchamp** (Pierre), **Macmillan** (Sir Kenneth)
**10** **Balanchine** (George), **Cunningham** (Merce)
**11** **Baryshnikov** (Mikhail)

### choristers
**05** choir

### chortle
**04** crow **05** laugh, snort **06** cackle, guffaw **07** chuckle, snigger

### chorus
**04** call **05** choir, shout **06** burden, strain **07** refrain, singers **08** ensemble, response **09** vocalists **10** choristers **11** choral group

### Christ
**01** X **02** Ch, JC, XP, Xt **03** Chr, I am **04** Lord **06** the Son **07** Holy One, Messiah, Saviour **08** Immanuel, Redeemer, Son of God, Son of Man **09** deliverer, Lamb of God, Word of God **11** King of kings, Lord of lords, the Redeemer **12** Good Shepherd **13** Prince of Peace

### christen
**03** dub **04** call, name, term **05** style, title **07** baptize, immerse **08** sprinkle **09** designate **10** begin using, inaugurate **11** give a name to

### Christian
**02** Xn **03** Chr **04** Copt, Xian **05** Xtian

### Christmas
**02** Xm **04** Noel, Xmas, Yule **05** Nowel **06** Crimbo, Nowell **08** Chrissie, Nativity, Yuletide

*Gifts for the Twelve Days of Christmas:*

**09** gold rings
**10** French hens
**11** turtle doves
**12** calling birds, geese a-laying, pipers piping
**13** ladies dancing, lords a-leaping, maids a-milking
**14** swans a-swimming
**16** drummers drumming
**20** partridge in a pear tree

*Gifts from the Three Wise Men:*

**04** gold
**05** myrrh
**12** frankincense

*See also* **wise man** *under* **wise**

### Christmas Island
**03** CXR

### Christ's-thorn
**04** nabk

### chromium
**02** Cr

### chromosome
• **part of chromosome** **02** id **07** cistron

### chronic
**04** naff, ropy **05** awful, pants **07** abysmal, the pits **08** constant, dreadful, habitual, hardened, long-term, terrible **09** appalling, atrocious, confirmed, continual, frightful, incessant, ingrained, recurring **10** deep-rooted, deep-seated, deplorable, inveterate, persistent **11** long-lasting **12** incorrigible, long-standing **14** a load of rubbish

### chronically
**08** long-term **10** constantly, habitually **11** continually, incessantly, recurrently **12** deep-rootedly, incorrigibly, inveterately, persistently

### chronicle
**04** epic, list, saga, tell **05** chron, diary, enter, story **06** annals, record, relate, report **07** account, history, journal, narrate, recount, set down **08** archives, calendar, register **09** narrative, write down **11** put on record
• **entry in chronicle** **05** annal

### chronicler
**06** scribe **07** diarist **08** annalist, narrator, recorder, reporter **09** archivist, historian **11** chronologer **13** chronographer **15** historiographer

### chronological
**06** serial **07** in order, ordered **10** historical, in sequence, sequential **11** consecutive, progressive

### chubby
**03** fat **04** full **05** fubby, fubsy, plump, podgy, round, stout, tubby **06** flabby, fleshy, portly, rotund **07** paunchy **08** roly-poly

### chuck
**03** put, shy **04** cast, dump, food, hurl, jilt, lump, quit, toss **05** chunk, fling, heave, pitch, sling, throw **06** give up, pack in, pebble, reject **07** abandon, chicken, discard, dismiss, forsake **08** get rid of, jettison **12** give the elbow **15** give the brush-off

### chuckle
**04** crow **05** laugh, snort **06** cackle, clumsy, giggle, titter **07** chortle, snigger **12** laugh quietly

### chum
**03** pal **04** mate, tosh **05** buddy, butty, crony **06** cobber, friend **07** comrade **09** accompany, associate, companion
*See also* **friend**

## chummy
**04** maty **05** close, matey, pally, thick **08** criminal, friendly, intimate, sociable **12** affectionate

## chunk
**03** nub **04** hunk, junk, lump, mass, slab **05** block, chuck, piece, wedge, wodge **06** dollop, gobbet **07** portion

## chunky
**05** broad, bulky, dumpy, heavy, large, solid, thick **06** blocky, stocky **07** awkward, weighty **08** thickset, unwieldy **09** well-built **10** cumbersome **11** substantial

## church
**02** CE, Ch **04** cult, fold, kirk, sect **05** abbey, flock **06** bethel, chapel, shrine, temple **07** chantry, minster, oratory **08** assembly, basilica, Bethesda, ecclesia, grouping **09** cathedral, community, tradition **10** fellowship, house of God, Lord's house, tabernacle **11** people of God **12** body of Christ, congregation, denomination, meeting-house, procathedral **13** bride of Christ, house of prayer **14** house of worship, place of worship, preaching-house
*See also* **cathedral**

*Church and cathedral parts include:*
**03** pew
**04** apse, arch, font, nave, rood, tomb
**05** aisle, altar, choir, crypt, porch, slype, spire, stall, stoup, tower, vault
**06** adytum, arcade, atrium, belfry, chapel, chevet, corona, parvis, portal, pulpit, sedile, shrine, squint, vestry
**07** almonry, chancel, frontal, gallery, lectern, lucarne, narthex, piscina, reredos, steeple, tambour
**08** cloister, credence, crossing, keystone, parclose, pinnacle, predella, sacellum, sacristy, transept
**09** antechoir, bell tower, sacrarium, sanctuary, sepulchre, stasidion, triforium
**10** ambulatory, baptistery, bell screen, clerestory, diaconicon, fenestella, frithstool, misericord, presbytery, retrochoir, rood screen
**12** chapterhouse, confessional, deambulatory
**14** ringing chamber, schola cantorum

## churchman
*see* **clergyman, clergywoman**

## churchyard
**05** house **07** charnel **08** boneyard, cemetery, God's acre, kirkyard **09** graveyard, kirkyaird **10** burial site, necropolis **11** burial place **12** burial ground

## churlish
**04** rude **05** harsh, rough, surly **06** morose, oafish, sullen **07** boorish, brusque, carlish, crabbed, doggish, ill-bred, loutish, uncivil **08** impolite

**10** ungracious, unmannerly, unsociable **11** bad-tempered, ill-mannered, ill-tempered **12** discourteous **13** unneighbourly **14** ill-conditioned

## churn
◇ *anagram indicator* **04** beat, boil, foam, kirn, puke, stir, toss, turn **05** froth, heave, retch, swirl, vomit **06** be sick, seethe, writhe **07** agitate, disturb, throw up **08** convulse
• **churn out** **07** knock up, pump out, turn out **13** throw together

## chute
**03** lin **04** linn, ramp **05** flume, rapid, shaft, shoot, shute, slide, slope, spout, trunk **06** funnel, gutter, runway, trough **07** channel, incline **09** parachute, waterfall **10** water shoot

## chutzpah
**03** lip **04** gall **05** cheek, mouth, nerve, sauce **08** audacity **09** brass neck, impudence, insolence **10** brazenness, disrespect, effrontery **12** impertinence

## cicada
**06** tettix **10** harvest-fly **11** balm-cricket

*Cicadas include:*
**05** Myer's
**06** red-eye
**09** Union Jack
**10** blue prince
**11** black prince, floury baker, greengrocer, green Monday, masked devil
**12** floury miller, yellow Monday
**13** double drummer

## cigarette
**03** cig, fag, tab **04** burn, weed **05** cigar, ciggy, smoke **06** ciggie, dog end, fag end, gasper **10** coffin-nail, paper-cigar **11** cancer-stick

*Cigarettes and cigars include:*
**04** bidi
**05** beedi, blunt, claro, joint, paper, roach, segar, snout, stogy, whiff
**06** beedie, biftah, bifter, bomber, concha, Havana, low-tar, manila, reefer, roll-up, spliff, stogey, stogie
**07** cheroot, high-tar, manilla, menthol, regalia
**08** king-size, long-nine, perfecto
**09** cigarillo, filter tip, panatella
**10** tailor-made
**11** corona lucis, roll-your-own

## cinch
**04** snip **06** doddle, scoosh, stroll **08** cakewalk, duck soup, pushover, walkover **09** certainty, no-brainer **10** child's play **11** piece of cake

## cinders
**04** coal, coke, slag **05** ashes **06** dander, embers **07** clinker **08** charcoal

## cinema
**05** films, scope **06** flicks, movies **07** drive-in, fleapit, theatre **08** bioscope, bughouse, pictures **09** big screen, multiplex **10** movie house **11** film theatre, nickelodeon **12** movie

theatre, picture-house, silver screen **13** picture-palace **14** motion pictures, moving pictures

*Cinema and theatre names include:*
**03** ABC, MGM, Rex, Rio, UCI, UGC
**04** Gala, IMAX, Ritz, Roxy
**05** Byron, Cameo, Forum, Grand, Kings, Lyric, Metro, Odeon, Orion, Plaza, Regal, Royal, Savoy, Scala, Tower
**06** Albany, Apollo, Cannon, Casino, Curzon, Empire, Gaiety, Lyceum, Marina, New Vic, Old Vic, Palace, Queens, Regent, Rialto, Robins, Tivoli, Virgin
**07** Adelphi, Almeida, Arcadia, Astoria, Capitol, Carlton, Central, Century, Circuit, Classic, Coronet, Embassy, Essoldo, Gaumont, Granada, La Scala, Locarno, Mayfair, Orpheum, Paragon, Phoenix, Picardy
**08** Alhambra, Broadway, Charlton, Cineplex, Citizens, Coliseum, Colonial, Dominion, Electric, Everyman, Festival, Imperial, Landmark, Majestic, Memorial, Pavilion, Windmill
**09** Alexandra, Cineworld, Filmhouse, Hollywood, Palladium, Paramount, Playhouse
**10** Ambassador, Hippodrome, Lighthouse
**11** Her Majesty's, His Majesty's, New Victoria, Ster Century
**12** Metropolitan, Picturedrome, Picturehouse, Thefilmworks
**13** Lyceum Theatre, Picture Palace, Warner Village
**14** Electric Palace
**15** Screen on the Hill

## cipher
**01** O **03** nil **04** code, null, zero **05** zilch **06** Enigma, naught, nobody, nought, yes-man **07** nothing **09** calculate, character, nonentity **10** cryptogram **11** cryptograph **12** coded message, secret system **13** secret writing

## circa
**01** c **02** ca **03** cir, odd **04** circ, some **05** about **06** around, nearly **07** close to, loosely, roughly **09** just about, not far off **10** more or less, round about **11** approaching **13** approximately, in the region of, or thereabouts, something like **15** in the vicinity of

## circle
◇ *containment indicator* **01** O **03** set **04** club, gang, gird, wind **05** crowd, group, hem in, pivot, whirl **06** clique, gyrate, rotate, swivel **07** circlet, company, coterie, cycloid, enclose, envelop, hedge in, revolve, rondure, rounder, society **08** assembly, encircle, surround **09** circulate, encompass, move round **10** fellowship, fraternity **12** circumscribe **14** circumnavigate

*Circles include:*
**03** lap, orb
**04** ball, band, belt, coil, corn, crop, curl, disc, eddy, gyre, halo, hoop,

hour, loop, oval, ring, turn, tyre
05 crown, cycle, dress, globe, grand, great, magic, mural, orbit, pitch, plate, polar, round, stone, upper, wheel
06 Arctic, circus, cordon, discus, girdle, rundle, saucer, sphere, spiral, tropic, vortex, wreath
07 annulet, annulus, circuit, compass, coronet, ellipse, equator, roundel, traffic, transit, turning, vicious
08 epicycle, gyration, meridian, rotation, roundure, striking, virtuous
09 Antarctic, perimeter, whirlpool, whirlwind
10 almacantar, almucantar, Circassian, revolution
13 circumference

- **stone circle** 08 cromlech 09 cyclolith 10 Stonehenge 11 peristalith

## circuit
02 IC 03 lap 04 area, beat, eyre, tour 05 ambit, limit, orbit, range, round, route, track 06 bounds, course, diadem, region 07 compass, rondure, rounder 08 boundary, district, progress, roundure 09 perimeter, race track 10 revolution 12 running-track 13 circumference, perambulation
- **closed circuit** 02 CC
- **logic circuit** 02 OR 03 AND, NOR, NOT, XOR 04 NAND

## circuitous
07 devious, oblique, winding 08 indirect, rambling, tortuous 09 meandrian, meandrous 10 meandering, roundabout 11 anfractuous 12 labyrinthine, periphrastic

## circular
05 flyer, orbed, round 06 folder, letter, notice 07 annular, leaflet 08 handbill, junk mail, pamphlet 09 spherical 10 disc-shaped, hoop-shaped, ring-shaped, round robin 12 announcement 13 advertisement

## circulate
◇ *anagram indicator* 04 flow, pass, walk 05 float, issue, rumor, swirl, troll, utter, whirl 06 gyrate, report, rotate, rumour, spread 07 diffuse, give out, go about, go round, publish, revolve 08 go abroad, go around, put about, transmit 09 broadcast, get around, pass round, propagate, publicize, send round 10 distribute, promulgate 11 disseminate, go the rounds, spread about 12 spread around 13 make the rounds

## circulation
04 flow 05 cycle 06 motion, spread 07 issuing 08 circling, currency, cyclosis, movement, rotation 09 blood-flow, publicity 10 readership 11 propagation, publication 12 distribution, transmission 13 dissemination
- **in circulation** ◇ *anagram indicator* 05 in use 06 afloat, around, issued

07 current, printed 09 available, published 11 distributed, spread about 12 spread around

## circumference
03 arc, rim 04 edge 05 girth, round, verge 06 border, bounds, circle, fringe, limits, margin 07 circuit, compass, outline 08 boundary, confines 09 extremity, perimeter, periphery

## circumlocution
06 ambage 08 pleonasm 09 euphemism, prolixity, tautology, verbosity, wordiness 10 periphrase, redundancy 11 convolution, diffuseness, periphrasis 12 indirectness 14 discursiveness, roundaboutness

## circumlocutory
05 wordy 06 prolix 07 diffuse, verbose 08 elliptic, indirect 09 ambagious, redundant 10 convoluted, discursive, elliptical, long-winded, pleonastic, roundabout 11 euphemistic 12 periphrastic, tautological

## circumscribe
04 trim 05 bound, hem in, limit, pen in 06 define 07 abridge, confine, curtail, delimit, enclose 08 encircle, restrain, restrict, surround 09 delineate, demarcate, encompass

## circumspect
04 wary, wise 05 canny 07 careful, guarded, politic, prudent 08 cautious, discreet, vigilant, watchful 09 attentive, judicious, observant, sagacious 10 deliberate 11 calculating 14 discriminating

## circumspection
04 care 07 caution 08 prudence, wariness 09 canniness, chariness, examining, vigilance 10 discretion 11 carefulness, guardedness 12 deliberation, watchfulness

## circumstance
03 lot 04 case, fact, fate, item, nark, this 05 event, means, state, thing 06 detail, factor, plight, status 07 element, fortune, respect, situate 08 accident, ceremony, position 09 condition, happening, lifestyle, resources, situation 10 background, occurrence, particular 11 arrangement, environment 12 lie of the land 14 how the land lies, state of affairs

## circumstantial
04 tiny 06 minute 07 deduced, hearsay 08 indirect, inferred, presumed 10 contingent, evidential, incidental 11 conjectural, inferential, presumptive, provisional

## circumvent
04 dish 05 avoid, dodge, evade 06 bypass, outwit, thwart 07 get past 08 get out of, get round, go beyond, outflank, sidestep 09 encompass 12 steer clear of

## circumvention
07 dodging, evasion 09 avoidance, bypassing, thwarting 12 sidestepping 13 steering clear

## circus
06 cirque 10 hippodrome

*Circus-related terms include:*

03 top
04 geek, ring, tent
05 clown
06 big top, pie car
07 acrobat, balloon, juggler, sawdust, trapeze, tumbler
08 carnival, conjurer, conjuror, drum roll, high wire, magician, sideshow, unicycle
09 aerialist, fire-eater, lion tamer, menagerie, safety net, strongman, tightrope
10 acrobatics, acrobatism, candy floss, custard pie, ringmaster, roustabout, somersault, trick-rider, unicyclist
11 funambulist, greasepaint
12 escape artist, roll up! roll up!, stiltwalking, trick cyclist
13 bareback rider, contortionist, trapeze artist

## cissy
03 wet 04 baby, soft, tonk, weak, wimp, wuss 05 softy 06 coward, feeble 07 crybaby, milksop, unmanly, wimpish 08 cowardly, weakling 09 mummy's boy 10 effeminate, namby-pamby

## cistern
03 vat 04 sink, tank 05 basin 08 feed-head, flush-box 09 reservoir

## citadel
04 fort, keep 05 tower 06 castle 07 bastion, kremlin 08 fortress 09 acropolis 10 stronghold 13 fortification

## citation
03 cit 05 award, quote 06 honour, source 07 cutting, excerpt, mention, passage 08 allusion, epigraph 09 quotation, reference 10 allegation 12 commendation, illustration

## cite
04 call, name 05 bring, quote, state, vouch 06 adduce, allege, summon 07 advance, bring up, convent, mention, refer to, specify 08 allude to, evidence 09 enumerate, exemplify 13 give an example

## citizen
03 cit 05 local, voter 07 burgher, denizen, freeman, oppidan, subject 08 civilian, national, resident, taxpayer, townsman, urbanite 10 inhabitant, townswoman 11 city-dweller, householder

## city
02 EC 04 seat, town 08 big smoke, downtown, precinct 09 inner city, metroplex, Weltstadt 10 city centre, cosmopolis, metropolis, micropolis, pentapolis 11 conurbation, megalopolis, urban sprawl 12 municipality 13 urban district 14 concrete jungle

---

*Ancient cities include:*

**02** Ur
**04** Acre, Axum, Ebla, Nuzi, Rome, Susa, Troy, Tula, Tyre, Uruk
**05** Aksum, Argos, Bosra, Bursa, Copán, Cuzco, Eridu, Hatra, Huari, Mitla, Moche, Petra, Saida, Sidon, Tikal, Uxmal
**06** Athens, Byblos, Cyrene, Jabneh, Jamnia, Napata, Nippur, Sardis, Shiloh, Sparta, Thebes, Ugarit
**07** Antioch, Babylon, Bukhara, Corinth, El Tajin, Ephesus, Megiddo, Miletus, Mycenae, Nineveh, Paestum, Plataea, Pompeii, Samaria, Sybaris, Vergina
**08** Carthage, Damascus, Hattusas, Hattusha, Kerkuane, Palenque, Pergamon, Pergamum, Sigiriya, Tashkent, Thysdrus
**09** Byzantium, Cartagena, Epidaurus, Sukhothai
**10** Alexandria, Angkor Thom, Carchemish, Heliopolis, Hierapolis, Monte Albán, Persepolis
**11** Chichén Itzá, Herculaneum, Machu Picchu, Polonnaruwa, Teotihuacán
**12** Anuradhapura
**13** Halicarnassus
**14** Constantinople

---

*Capital cities include:*

**04** Apia, Baku, Bern, Dili, Doha, Kiev, Lima, Lomé, Malé, Oslo, Riga, Rome, San'a, Suva
**05** Abuja, Accra, Amman, Berne, Cairo, Dacca, Dakar, Dhaka, Hanoi, Kabul, Koror, La Paz, Minsk, Paris, Praia, Quito, Rabat, Sana'a, Seoul, Sofia, Sucre, Tokyo, Tunis, Vaduz
**06** Akmola, Ankara, Asmara, Astana, Athens, Bamako, Bangui, Banjul, Beirut, Berlin, Bissau, Bogotá, Dodoma, Dublin, Harare, Havana, Kigali, Lisbon, London, Luanda, Lusaka, Madrid, Majuro, Malabo, Manama, Manila, Maputo, Maseru, Monaco, Moroni, Moscow, Muscat, Nassau, Niamey, Ottawa, Peking, Prague, Riyadh, Roseau, Skopje, T'aipei, Tarawa, Tehran, Tirana, Vienna, Warsaw, Yangon, Zagreb
**07** Abidjan, Ajaccio, Algiers, Alma-Ata, Baghdad, Bangkok, Beijing, Belfast, Bishkek, Caracas, Cardiff, Cayenne, Colombo, Conakry, Cotonou, El Aaiún, Godthab, Honiara, Jakarta, Kampala, Lobamba, Managua, Mbabane, Nairobi, Nicosia, Palikir, Papeete, Rangoon, San José, San Juan, São Tomé, St John's, Tallinn, Tbilisi, Teheran, Thimphu, Tripoli, Valetta, Vilnius, Yaoundé, Yerevan
**08** Abu Dhabi, Ashgabat, Asunción, Belgrade, Belmopan, Brasília, Brussels, Budapest, Canberra, Cape Town, Castries, Chisinau,

Damascus, Djibouti, Dushanbe, Freetown, Gaborone, Helsinki, Khartoum, Kingston, Kinshasa, Kishinev, Lilongwe, Monrovia, N'Djamena, New Delhi, Port-Vila, Pretoria, Santiago, Sarajevo, Tashkent, The Hague, Tórshavn, Valletta, Victoria, Windhoek
**09** Amsterdam, Ashkhabad, Bucharest, Bujumbura, Edinburgh, Fongafale, Islamabad, Jerusalem, Kathmandu, Kingstown, Ljubljana, Mogadishu, Nuku'alofa, Phnom Penh, Port Louis, Porto Novo, Pyongyang, Reykjavík, San Marino, Singapore, St George's, Stockholm, Ulan Bator, Vientiane
**10** Addis Ababa, Basseterre, Bratislava, Bridgetown, Copenhagen, Georgetown, Kuwait City, Libreville, Luxembourg, Mexico City, Montevideo, Nouakchott, Panama City, Paramaribo, Wellington, Willemstad
**11** Brazzaville, Buenos Aires, Kuala Lumpur, Monaco-Ville, Ouagadougou, Port Moresby, Port of Spain, San Salvador, Tegucigalpa, Vatican City
**12** Antananarivo, Bloemfontein, Fort-de-France, Port-au-Prince, Santo Domingo, Tel Aviv-Jaffa, Washington DC, Yamoussoukro
**13** Guatemala City, Yaren District
**14** Andorra la Vella

---

*Cities and towns include:*

**02** Bo, LA, NY
**03** Åbo, Ayr, Ely, Fès, Fez, Gao, Hué, Lae, Nis, NYC, Pau, Qom, Ufa, Ulm, Vac, Zug
**04** Acre, Aden, Agra, Ajme, Amoy, Bari, Bath, Bonn, Brno, Bury, Caen, Cali, Cebu, Como, Cork, Dazu, Deal, Edam, Elat, Eton, Faro, Gand, Gent, Gifu, Graz, Györ, Homs, Hove, Hull, Hutt, Iasi, Icel, Ipoh, Jima, Jixi, Kano, Kiel, Kobe, Köln, Kota, La-sa, León, Linz, Lódz, Lugo, Luik, Lund, Lvov, Metz, Mold, Mons, Naas, Naha, Nara, Nice, Nuuk, Oban, Oita, Omsk, Oran, Oulu, Pécs, Pegu, Perm, Pisa, Pula, Pune, Rand, Reno, Rhyl, Ruse, Ryde, Safi, Sale, Salt, Sfax, Sian, Sion, Soul, St-Lô, Suez, Sumy, Tema, Thun, Tula, Tyre, Umeå, Vasa, Vigo, Waco, Wick, Wien, Wuhu, Wuxi, Xi'an, York, Zibo, Zörs
**05** Adana, Ahvaz, Åland, Al Ayn, Aosta, Aqaba, Argos, Århus, Arica, Arles, Arras, Aspen, Aswan, Ávila, Baden, Banff, Baoji, Basle, Basra, Beira, Belém, Benxi, Blida, Blyth, Boise, Bondi, Borga, Bouar, Braga, Breda, Brest, Bursa, Busan, Cádiz, Canea, Cavan, Ceuta, Chiba, Chita, Colón, Conwy, Cowes, Crewe, Cuzco, Davao, Davos, Delft,

Delhi, Derby, Dijon, Dover, Duala, Dubai, Dukou, Eilat, Elche, Epsom, Essen, Eupen, Évora, Fiume, Frome, Fuxin, Genoa, Ghent, Gijón, Gomel, Gorky, Gouda, Gweru, Hagen, Haifa, Halle, Hefei, Hohot, Honan, Ichun, Ieper, Iwaki, Izmir, Jaffa, Jedda, Jilin, Jinan, Jinja, Kaédi, Kandy, Karaj, Kazan, Kelso, Kirov, Kitwe, Kochi, Konya, Köseg, Kursk, Kyoto, Lagos, Leeds, Lewes, Lhasa, Liège, Lille, Limbe, Luton, Luxor, Lyons, Mâcon, Mainz, Malmö, Masan, Mecca, Medan, Miami, Milan, Mitla, Mopti, Mosul, Namen, Namur, Nancy, Nasik, Natal, Ndola, Nîmes, Ohrid, Omagh, Omaha, Omiya, Oryol, Osaka, Otley, Oujda, Padua, Parma, Patan, Patna, Pavia, Penza, Perth, Plzen, Ponce, Poole, Poona, Pusan, Reims, Resit, Ripon, Ronda, Rouen, Rovno, Rugby, Sakai, Salem, Salta, Sebha, Ségou, Sidon, Siena, Skien, Sochi, Sopot, Split, Suita, Surat, Suwon, Taegu, Talca, Tampa, Tanga, Tanta, Tempe, Thane, Thiès, Tomar, Tomsk, Torun, Tours, Trier, Troon, Truro, Tulsa, Tunja, Turin, Turku, Tzu-po, Udine, Ulsan, Urawa, Utica, Vaasa, Varna, Vejle, Vlorë, Wells, Wigan, Worms, Wuhan, Ypres, Zadar, Zaria, Zarqa
**06** Aachen, Aarhus, Agadez, Agadir, Albany, Aleppo, Amiens, Annaba, Annecy, Anshan, Anvers, Anyang, Arezzo, Armagh, Arnhem, Arusha, Ashdod, Atbara, At Taif, Austin, Avarua, Baguio, Bangor, Baotou, Bastia, Bengpu, Bergen, Bhopal, Bilbao, Biloxi, Bitola, Bochum, Bolton, Bombay, Bootle, Boston, Bourke, Brasov, Bremen, Bruges, Brugge, Burgos, Buxton, Cairns, Calais, Callao, Calmar, Camden, Campos, Cancún, Cannes, Canton, Carlow, Casper, Chania, Chi-nan, Chonju, Cochin, Cracow, Crosby, Cuenca, Dalian, Dallas, Da Nang, Danzig, Daqing, Darhan, Darwin, Datong, Dayton, Denver, Dieppe, Douala, Dudley, Duluth, Dundee, Durban, Durham, Durrës, El Gîza, El Paso, Eugene, Evreux, Exeter, Fatima, Fresno, Frunze, Fu-chou, Fushun, Fuzhou, Galway, Gdansk, Gdynia, Geneva, Gitega, Grodno, Grozny, Guelph, Guilin, Guimar, Gujrat, Guntur, Ha'apai, Hamina, Handan, Han-kou, Harbin, Harlem, Harlow, Harrow, Hebron, Hegang, Himeji, Hobart, Howrah, Ibadan, Inchon, Indore, Jaffna, Jaipur, Jarash, Jarrow, Jeddah, Jiddah, Jilong, Juneau, Kalmar, Kaluga, Kankan, Kanpur, Kaolan, Kassel, Kaunas, Kendal, Khulna, Kirkby, Kirkuk, Kosice,

Kraków, Kumasi, Kurgan, Lahore, Lanark, Leiden, Le Mans, Leshan, Leuven, Leyden, Lübeck, Lublin, Ludlow, Lugano, Maceio, Madras, Makale, Málaga, Malang, Manaus, Mantua, Matrah, Medina, Meerut, Mekele, Meknès, Meshed, Mobile, Mukden, Multan, Muncie, Munich, Murcia, Mysore, Nablus, Nagano, Nagoya, Nagpur, Nantes, Napier, Naples, Narvik, Nelson, Newark, Ningbo, Nouméa, Odense, Odessa, Oldham, Olinda, Oporto, Örebro, Osasco, Osijek, Ostend, Oviedo, Oxford, Padang, Paphos, Phuket, Piatra, Pierre, Pilsen, Porvoo, Potosí, Poznan, Presov, Puebla, Quebec, Queluz, Quetta, Raipur, Rajkat, Ranchi, Recife, Redcar, Reggio, Regina, Rennes, Rheims, Rijeka, Ryazan, Saigon, Salala, Samara, Santos, Schwyz, Sefadu, Sendai, Shiraz, Silves, Sining, Sintra, Skikda, Sliema, Slough, Smyrna, Sokodé, Sousse, Soweto, Sparta, St Ives, St John, St Malo, St Paul, Stroud, Stuart, Suchow, Sukkur, Suzhou, Sydney, Szeged, Tabriz, Tacoma, Tadmur, Taejon, Tahoua, Tainan, Tamale, Tambov, Tarbes, Tarsus, Ta-t'ung, Teruel, Thurso, Tipasa, Tobruk, Toledo, Toluca, Topeka, Torbay, Toulon, Toyama, Toyota, Tralee, Trento, Treves, Tromsø, Troyes, Tsinan, Tubruq, Tucson, Tyumen, Urumqi, Vannes, Vargas, Venice, Verona, Viborg, Weimar, Whitby, Widnes, Woking, Xiamen, Xining, Xuzhou, Yangku, Yantai, Yeovil, Yichun, Yunnan, Zabrze, Zigong, Zinder, Zurich, Zwolle

**07** Aberfan, Airdrie, Aligarh, Alnwick, Antibes, Antioch, Antwerp, Aracaju, Atlanta, Augusta, Auxerre, Avignon, Baalbek, Badajoz, Bairiki, Banares, Banbury, Bandung, Baoding, Barnaul, Barossa, Bayamón, Bedford, Beeston, Benares, Bendigo, Berbera, Bergama, Bergamo, Bexhill, Bizerta, Blarney, Bologna, Bolzano, Boulder, Bourges, Braemar, Brescia, Bristol, Bryansk, Buffalo, Bunbury, Burnley, Cáceres, Calgary, Calicut, Cardiff, Catania, Chalcis, Changan, Cheadle, Cheddar, Chelsea, Chengde, Chengdu, Cheng-tu, Chester, Chicago, Chifeng, Chi-lung, Chongju, Chungho, Clonmel, Coblenz, Coimbra, Cologne, Concord, Córdoba, Corinth, Corinto, Corunna, Crawley, Dandong, Detroit, Devizes, Donetsk, Douglas, Dresden, Dundalk, Dunedin, Dunkirk, Durango, Entebbe, Erdenet, Esbjerg, Evesham, Exmouth, Falkirk,

Fareham, Ferrara, Foochow, Fukuoka, Funchal, Ganzhou, Geelong, Glasgow, Goiânia, Gosport, Granada, Grimsby, Guiyang, Gwalior, Gwangju, Haerbin, Halifax, Hamburg, Hamhung, Hanover, Harwich, Henzada, Heredia, Houston, Huaibai, Huainan, Ipswich, Iquique, Iquitos, Irkutsk, Isfahan, Ivanovo, Izhevsk, Jackson, Jericho, Jiamusi, Jinzhou, Jodhpur, Kaesong, Kaifeng, Kalinin, Kananga, Karachi, Kassala, Kayseri, Keelung, Kenitra, Keswick, Kharkov, Kherson, Koblenz, Kolding, Kuching, Kunming, Kutaisi, Lansing, Lanzhou, La Plata, Larnaca, Latakia, Leghorn, Le Havre, Leipzig, Lerwick, Liberia, Limoges, Lincoln, Lipetsk, Liuzhou, Livorno, Logroño, Louvain, Lucerne, Lucknow, Lugansk, Lumbini, Luoyang, Machida, Madison, Madurai, Malvern, Manzini, Maracay, Marburg, Margate, Mashhad, Massawa, Matlock, Matsudo, Melilla, Memphis, Mendoza, Mildura, Mindelo, Miskolc, Mitsiwa, Mogilev, Mombasa, Morpeth, Münster, Nanjing, Nanking, Nanning, Nantong, Newbury, Newport, Newquay, New Ross, New York, Niigata, Niterói, Norfolk, Norwich, Novi Sad, Oakland, Okayama, Okinawa, Olympia, Orlando, Orleans, Ostrava, Pahsien, Paisley, Palermo, Panshan, Pattaya, Peebles, Penrith, Perugia, Phoenix, Piraeus, Pistoia, Pitesti, Plovdiv, Poltava, Popayán, Portree, Potsdam, Preston, Prizren, Qingdao, Qiqihar, Quimper, Raleigh, Randers, Ravenna, Reading, Redwood, Reigate, Roanoke, Rosario, Rostock, Rotorua, Runcorn, Sagunto, Salamis, Salerno, Salford, Sandown, Santa Fe, São Luis, Sapporo, Saransk, Saratov, Sassari, Seattle, Segovia, Setúbal, Seville, Shannon, Shantou, Shihezi, Shikoku, Shkodër, Sialkot, Sinuiju, Songnam, Spokane, Spoleto, Staines, Stanley, St Denis, St Louis, Sudbury, Swansea, Swindon, Taiyuan, Tampere, Tampico, Tangier, Taunton, Tel Aviv, Telford, Tétouan, Tianjin, Tijuana, Tilburg, Tilbury, Toronto, Torquay, Tournai, Trenton, Trieste, Tucumán, Ulan-Ude, Uppsala, Utrecht, Ventnor, Vicenza, Vitebsk, Vitosha, Walsall, Warwick, Watford, Weifang, Wenzhou, Wexford, Wichita, Windsor, Wrexham, Wroclaw, Wuhsien, Yakeshi, Yichang, Yingkou, Yonkers, Zermatt, Zhuzhou, Zwickau

**08** Aberdeen, Acapulco, Adelaide, Akureyri, Alajuela, Albacete, Alicante, Amarillo, Amritsar, Arbroath, Arequipa, Auckland, Augsburg, Aviemore, Ayia Napa, Ballarat, Banghazi, Bareilly, Barnsley, Bathurst, Bayreuth, Beauvais, Belgorod, Benghazi, Benguela, Benidorm, Besançon, Bhadgaon, Biarritz, Bismarck, Blantyre, Bobruysk, Bordeaux, Boulogne, Bradford, Braganza, Brighton, Brindisi, Brisbane, Bulawayo, Burgundy, Cagliari, Calcutta, Campinas, Carlisle, Changsha, Chartres, Chemnitz, Chepstow, Cheyenne, Chiclayo, Chimbote, Chimkent, Ching-tao, Chongjin, Clevedon, Columbia, Columbus, Contagem, Coventry, Culiacán, Curitiba, Dartford, Dearborn, Debrecen, Djakarta, Dortmund, Drogheda, Duisburg, Dumfries, Dunhuang, Dunleary, Durgapur, Dzhambul, Ebbw Vale, Edmonton, El Kharga, Elsinore, Europort, Falmouth, Florence, Flushing, Freeport, Fribourg, Fujisawa, Fukuyama, Gaoxiong, Gisborne, Gorlovka, Grantham, Grasmere, Greenock, Grenoble, Guernica, Hachioji, Haiphong, Hakodate, Hamilton, Hangchow, Hangzhou, Hannover, Hartford, Hastings, Hengyang, Hereford, Hertford, Hirakata, Holyhead, Holywell, Hong Kong, Honolulu, Huangshi, Hunjiang, Ichikawa, Iowa City, Istanbul, Jabalpur, Jaboatoa, Kairouan, Kanazawa, Kandahar, Karlsbad, Katowice, Kawasaki, Keflavik, Kemerovo, Kilkenny, Kirkwall, Kismaayo, Klosters, Kolhapur, Konstanz, Koriyama, Kuei-yang, Kumamoto, Laâyoune, La Laguna, Las Vegas, Lausanne, Legoland, Leskovac, Liaoyang, Liaoyuan, Limassol, Limerick, Londrina, Longford, Lüderitz, Ludhiana, Lyallpur, Makassar, Mandalay, Mannheim, Marbella, Mariupal, Mariupol, Mayaguez, Mazatlán, Medellín, Mercedes, Mexicali, Montreal, Montreux, Montrose, Mufulira, Mulhouse, Murmansk, Myingyan, Nagasaki, Namangan, Nanchang, Nazareth, Newhaven, Nijmegen, Novgorod, Nuneaton, Nürnberg, Oak Ridge, Omdurman, Oostende, Orenburg, Oswestry, Pago Pago, Pamplona, Panchiao, Pasadena, Pavlodar, Penzance, Peshawar, Piacenza, Ploiesti, Plymouth, Poitiers, Portland, Portrush, Port Said, Pristina, Ramsgate, Rancagua, Randstad, Redditch, Richmond, Road Town, Rochdale, Rockford, Roskilde, Rosslare, Sabadell, Salonica, Salonika, Saltillo, Salvador, Salzburg, San Diego, Santa Ana, Santarém, São Paulo, Satu Mare,

Savannah, Schwerin, Semarang, Shanghai, Shanklin, Shaoguan, Shenyang, Shizuoka, Sholapur, Silk Road, Simbirsk, Skegness, Smolensk, Solihull, Solingen, Sorocaba, Southend, Srinagar, Stafford, St Albans, Stamford, St David's, St Gallen, St Helens, St Helier, Stirling, St Moritz, Stockton, Strabane, St-Tropez, Subotica, Suicheng, Surabaya, Swan Hill, Syracuse, Szczecin, Taganrog, Taichung, Tamworth, Tangshan, Tauranga, Teresina, Thetford, Thonburi, Tiberias, Tientsin, Timbuktu, Tolyatti, Tongeren, Toulouse, Toyohasi, Toyonaka, Trujillo, Tsingtao, Tübingen, Uleaborg, Ullapool, Vadodara, Valencia, Valletta, Varanasi, Veracruz, Vila Real, Vinnitsa, Vittoria, Vladimir, Voronezh, Wakayama, Wallasey, Wallsend, Warangal, Weymouth, Winnipeg, Worthing, Würzburg, Xiangfan, Xiangtan, Xinxiang, Yangchow, Yangquan, Yangzhou, Yinchuan, Yin-hsien, Yokohama, Yokosuko, Yorktown, Zakopane, Zanzibar, Zhitomir

**09** Adis Abeba, Ahmadabad, Alba Iulia, Albufeira, Aldershot, Algeciras, Allahabad, Amagasaki, Ambleside, Anchorage, Annapolis, Archangel, Asahikawa, Astrakhan, Audenarde, Aylesbury, Bakhtaran, Baltimore, Bangalore, Barcelona, Beersheba, Berbérati, Bethlehem, Bhavnagar, Bialystok, Blackburn, Blackpool, Bossangoa, Botany Bay, Brunswick, Bydgoszcz, Cambridge, Cartagena, Castlebar, Changchun, Changzhou, Charleroi, Charlotte, Chengchow, Cherbourg, Chernobyl, Chiang Mai, Chihuahua, Choluteca, Chongqing, Chungking, Cleveland, Colwyn Bay, Constance, Constanta, Des Moines, Doncaster, Dordrecht, Dubrovnik, Dudelange, Dumbarton, Dungannon, Dunstable, Eastleigh, Eindhoven, Eskisehir, Esztergom, Fairbanks, Famagusta, Faridabad, Fishguard, Fleetwood, Fortaleza, Fort Worth, Frankfort, Frankfurt, Fremantle, Funabashi, Galveston, Gateshead, Gaziantep, Gippsland, Gold Coast, Gorakhpur, Gravesend, Greenwich, Groningen, Guangzhou, Guarulhos, Guayaquil, Guildford, Hallstatt, Hamamatsu, Harrogate, Haslemere, Helsingør, Heraklion, Hilversum, Hiroshima, Humpty Doo, Hyderabad, Immingham, Innsbruck, Inverness, Ismailiya, Jalandhar, Jamestown, Johnstone, Jönköping, Kagoshima, Kamchatka, Kaohsiung,

Karaganda, Karlsruhe, Kawaguchi, Killarney, Kimberley, King's Lynn, Kirkcaldy, Kisangani, Kishinyov, Kitzbühel, Kórinthos, Kozhikode, Krasnodar, Krivoy Rog, Kurashiki, Kuybyshev, Kwang-chow, Lancaster, Las Cruces, Leicester, Lexington, Lichfield, Liverpool, Llangefni, Long Beach, Lowestoft, Lymington, Magdeburg, Mahajanga, Maidstone, Makeyevka, Mamoudzan, Manizales, Mansfield, Maracaibo, Maralinga, Marrakesh, Matsuyama, Melbourne, Middleton, Milwaukee, Monterrey, Moradabad, Morecambe, Mullingar, Nashville, Neuchâtel, Newcastle, Newmarket, Nikolayev, Nuremberg, Ogbomosho, Osnabrück, Palembang, Pamporovo, Perpignan, Peterhead, Pingxiang, Podgorica, Pontianak, Port Natal, Port Sudan, Pressburg, Prestwick, Princeton, Qinghai Hu, Querétaro, Riverside, Rochester, Rotherham, Rotterdam, Rovaniemi, Salisbury, Samarkand, San Miguel, Santa Cruz, Santander, Saragossa, Saskatoon, Shanchung, Sheerness, Sheffield, Sioux City, South Bend, Southport, Southwark, St Andrews, Stavanger, Stavropol, St-Étienne, Stevenage, St-Nazaire, Stockport, Stornoway, St-Quentin, Stranraer, Stuttgart, Sukhothai, Sundsvall, Surakarta, Takamatsu, Takatsuki, Tarragona, Tenkodogo, T'ien-ching, Timisoara, Toamasina, Togliatti, Toowoomba, Trondheim, Tullamore, Ulyanovsk, Vancouver, Velingrad, Vicksburg, Volgograd, Wakefield, Walvis Bay, Waterford, Wiesbaden, Wimbledon, Wolfsburg, Worcester, Wuppertal, Xiangyang, Yaroslavl, Zamboanga, Zaozhuang, Zhengzhou, Zhenjiang, Zrenjanin

**10** Alexandria, Baton Rouge, Belize City, Birkenhead, Birmingham, Bridgeport, Bridgwater, Broken Hill, Caernarvon, Caerphilly, Canterbury, Carmarthen, Carnoustie, Carson City, Casablanca, Chandigarh, Charleston, Cheboksary, Chelmsford, Cheltenham, Cheng-hsien, Chichester, Chittagong, Cienfuegos, Cincinnati, Cluj-Napoca, Coatbridge, Cochabamba, Coimbatore, Colchester, Concepción, Darjeeling, Darlington, Diyarbakir, Dorchester, Düsseldorf, Dzerzhinsk, Eastbourne, El Mansoura, Faisalabad, Felixstowe, Folkestone, Fray Bentos,

Galashiels, George Town, Gillingham, Glenrothes, Gloucester, Goose Green, Gothenburg, Gujranwala, Haddington, Harrisburg, Hartlepool, Heidelberg, Hermosillo, Hildesheim, Huntingdon, Huntsville, Jamshedpur, Jingdezhen, Joao Pessoa, Juiz de Fora, Kakopetria, Kalgoorlie, Kansas City, Kenilworth, Khabarovsk, Kilmarnock, Kita-Kyushu, Kompong Som, Lake Placid, Las Piedras, Launceston, Leeuwarden, Letchworth, Linlithgow, Little Rock, Liupanshui, Livingston, Llangollen, Los Angeles, Louisville, Lubumbashi, Luluabourg, Maastricht, Maidenhead, Manchester, Marseilles, Medjugorje, Miami Beach, Monte Carlo, Montego Bay, Montgomery, Montpelier, Mostaganem, Motherwell, Mudanjiang, New Orleans, Nottingham, Nouadhibou, Nova Iguacu, Oranjestad, Oudenaarde, Palmerston, Petersburg, Pittsburgh, Pontefract, Portishead, Portsmouth, Providence, Queenstown, Quezon City, Quinnipiac, Rawalpindi, Regensburg, Sacramento, Sagamihara, San Antonio, San Ignacio, Santa Marta, Santo André, São Gonçalo, Scunthorpe, Sebastopol, Shepparton, Shreveport, Shrewsbury, Simferapol, Sioux Falls, Södertälje, Strasbourg, Sunderland, Sverdlovsk, Talcahuano, Tammerfors, Tananarive, Thunder Bay, Townsville, Trivandrum, Trowbridge, Tsaochuang, Utsunomiya, Valladolid, Valparaíso, Vijayawada, Viña del Mar, Vlissingen, Wadi Medani, Wagga Wagga, Warrington, Washington, Whitehorse, Wilmington, Winchester, Windermere, Winterthur, Wittenberg, Wollongong, Workington, Yogyakarta, Yoshkar Ola, Zaporozhye

**11** Aberystwyth, Albuquerque, Antofagasta, Bahía Blanca, Banjarmasin, Basingstoke, Bhilai Nagar, Bognor Regis, Bournemouth, Brandenburg, Bremerhaven, Bridlington, Broadstairs, Brownsville, Bucaramanga, Campo Grande, Carcassonne, Charlestown, Chattanooga, Chelyabinsk, Cherepovets, Cirencester, Cleethorpes, Cockermouth, Coney Island, Conisbrough, Constantine, Cumbernauld, Dar es Salaam, Differdange, Downpatrick, Dunfermline, Enniskillen, Farnborough, Fort

William, Francistown, Fraserburgh, Fredericton, Glastonbury, Grangemouth, Guadalajara, Guisborough, Hälsingborg, Helsingborg, Helsingfors, High Wycombe, Johor Baharu, Juan-les-Pins, Kaliningrad, Kampong Saom, Karlovy Vary, Kompong Saom, Komsomolosk, Krasnoyarsk, Lianyungang, Londonderry, Lossiemouth, Makhachkala, Mar del Plata, Medicine Hat, Medway Towns, Minneapolis, Montpellier, Narayanganj, Newport News, New York City, Nishinomiya, Northampton, Novosibirsk, Palm Springs, Pointe-Noire, Polonnaruwa, Port Augusta, Porto Alegre, Prestonpans, Punta Arenas, Qinhuangdao, Resistencia, Rockhampton, Rostov-on-Don, Saarbrücken, Scarborough, Southampton, Spanish Town, Springfield, Stourbridge, Szombathely, Tallahassee, Trincomalee, Tselinograd, Vladivostok, Westminster, White Plains, Wu-lu-k'o-mu-shi, Yellowknife, Zhangjiakou

12 Alice Springs, Anuradhapura, Atlantic City, Barquisimeto, Barranquilla, Beverly Hills, Bloemfontein, Buenaventura, Caloocan City, Chesterfield, Christchurch, Ciudad Juárez, East Kilbride, Great Malvern, Higashiosaka, Hubli-Dharwar, Huddersfield, Indianapolis, Invercargill, Jacksonville, Johannesburg, Keetmanshoop, Kota Kinabalu, Kristianstad, Léopoldville, Lisdoonvarna, Loughborough, Luang Prabang, Ludwigshafen, Macclesfield, Magnitogorsk, Mazar-e-Sharif, Milton Keynes, New Amsterdam, Nizhniy Tagil, Novokuznetsk, Oklahoma City, Petaling Jaya, Peterborough, Philadelphia, Pingdingshan, Pointe-à-Pitre, Ponta Delgada, Port Harcourt, Puerto Cortes, Rio de Janeiro, Salt Lake City, San Cristobal, San Francisco, San Pedro Sula, San Sebastian, Santa Barbara, Schaffhausen, Shijiazhuang, Shuangyashan, Sidi bel Abbès, Skelmersdale, South Shields, Speightstown, Stanleyville, St Catherines, Stoke-on-Trent, St Petersburg, Tel Aviv-Jaffa, Tennant Creek, Thessaloníki, Trichinopoly, Ujung Pandang, Villahermosa, West Bromwich, Williamsburg, Winston-Salem

13 Aix-en-Provence, Belo Horizonte, Bobo-Dioulasso, Charlottetown, Ciudad Guayana, Duque de Caxias, Ellesmere Port, Epsom and Ewell, Great Yarmouth, Ho Chi Minh City, Jefferson City, Kidderminster, Kirkcudbright,

Kirkintilloch, Leamington Spa, Lytham St Anne's, Middlesbrough, Ordzhonikidze, Port Elizabeth, Portlaoighise, Quezaltenango, Ribeirao Preto, San Bernardino, San Luis Potosí, Semipalatinsk, Sihanoukville, Veliko Turnovo, Virginia Beach, Visakhapatnam, Wolverhampton, Yekaterinburg, Zlatni Pyasaci

14 Andorra-la-Vella, Dnepropetrovsk, Elisabethville, Feira de Santana, Hemel Hempstead, Henley-on-Thames, Louangphrabang, Santiago de Cuba, Shihchiachuang, Stockton-on-Tees, Székesfehérvár, Tunbridge Wells, Ust-Kamenogorsk, Voroshilovgrad

15 Alcalá de Henares, Angra do Heroísmo, Barrow-in-Furness, Burton-upon-Trent, Charlotte Amalie, Charlottesville, Chester-le-Street, Clermont-Ferrand, Colorado Springs, Frankfurt am Main, Netzahaulcoyotl, Nizhniy Novgorod, Palma de Mallorca, Palmerston North, Sáo Joáo de Meriti, Sekondi-Takoradi, Shoubra el-Kheima, Sutton Coldfield, Weston-super-Mare

*See also* **Australia; Canada; Ireland; New Zealand; Russia; United Kingdom; United States of America • city area** 02 EC

## civet
05 genet, rasse, zibet 07 genette, linsang, nandine, Viverra 08 mongoose, suricate, toddy cat 09 binturong, delundung, ichneumon, weasel cat 10 paradoxure

## civic
04 city, town 05 local, urban 06 public 07 borough 08 communal 09 community, municipal 12 metropolitan

## civil
03 civ, lay 04 fair, home 05 civic, local, state 06 polite, public, urbane 07 affable, courtly, refined, secular 08 civilian, communal, domestic, interior, internal, mannerly, national, obliging, polished, temporal, well-bred 09 civilized, community, compliant, courteous, municipal 10 cultivated, respectful 11 complaisant 12 well-mannered 13 accommodating, parliamentary

## civilian
03 civ 05 civvy, mufti 07 citizen, gownman 08 gownsman 12 non-combatant

## civility
04 tact 06 comity, notice 07 amenity, manners, respect 08 breeding, courtesy, urbanity 09 attention 10 affability, politeness, refinement 11 good manners 12 graciousness, pleasantness 13 courteousness

## civilization
06 Kultur, people 07 culture, customs, society 08 progress, urbanity

09 community, education 10 refinement 11 advancement, cultivation, development 12 human society 13 enlightenment 14 sophistication

## civilize
04 tame 05 edify 06 polish, refine 07 educate, improve, perfect 08 humanize, instruct 09 cultivate, enlighten, socialize 12 sophisticate

## civilized
06 polite, urbane 07 refined 08 advanced, cultured, educated, sensible, sociable 09 courteous, developed 10 cultivated, reasonable 11 enlightened 12 well-mannered 13 sophisticated

## civilly
07 courtly 08 mannerly, politely, urbanely 10 obligingly 11 courteously 12 respectfully

## clad
06 vested 07 attired, clothed, covered, dressed, wearing

## claim
03 ask, bag, own, sue 04 aver, avow, call, hold, kill, need, plea, pose, take 05 cause, clame, droit, exact, right, shout, state 06 affirm, allege, assert, assume, avowal, demand, insist 07 collect, contend, darrain, darrayn, declare, deraign, deserve, pretend, profess, purport, request, require 08 averment, darraign, darraine, maintain, petition, put in for 09 assertion, challenge, darraigne, postulate, privilege 10 allegation, contention, insistence, lay claim to, pretension, profession 11 affirmation, application, declaration, entitlement, requirement, requisition 12 asseveration, be entitled to, have a right to

## claimant
06 titler 08 litigant 09 applicant, candidate, pretender, suppliant 10 challenger, petitioner, pretendant, pretendent, supplicant

## clairvoyance
03 ESP 09 telepathy 11 second sight 13 psychic powers 14 cryptaesthesia, fortune-telling, hyperaesthesia

## clairvoyant
04 seer 05 augur 06 oracle 07 diviner, prophet, psychic 08 telepath 09 prophetic, visionary 10 prophetess, soothsayer, telepathic 12 extrasensory 13 fortune-teller

## clam
03 Mya 05 cohog 06 quahog 07 quahaug, scallop 08 tridacna 11 black quahog

## clamber
04 claw, shin 05 climb, mount, scale 06 ascend, shinny 08 scrabble, scramble, sprackle 09 spraickle

## clammy
04 damp, dank 05 close, heavy, moist, muggy, slimy 06 sticky, sweaty, viscid 08 sweating

## clamorous

**04** loud **05** lusty, noisy, vocal
**07** blaring, blatant, riotous **08** blattant, vehement **09** deafening, insistent
**10** boisterous, strepitant, tumultuous, uproarious, vociferant, vociferous
**11** open-mouthed **12** obstreperous

## clamour

**03** cry, din, hue **04** bark, rout, urge, utis **05** blare, claim, noise, raird, reird, rumor **06** demand, hubbub, insist, outcry, racket, rumour, uproar
**07** brabble, call for, outrage
**08** brouhaha, press for, shouting, stramash **09** agitation, commotion, hue and cry **10** complaints **11** vociferance
**12** katzenjammer, vociferation **13** ask for noisily

## clamp

**03** fix **04** grip, heap, hold, vice
**05** brace, clasp, press, stack, tread
**06** clench, clinch, fasten, secure
**07** bracket, squeeze **08** fastener
**09** hand-screw, pinchcock, potato pit
**10** Denver boot, immobilize
**11** immobilizer
• **clamp down on 04** stop **05** limit
**07** confine, control, prevent **08** restrain, restrict, suppress **10** put a stop to
**11** crack down on **14** come down hard on

## clampdown

**04** stop **05** limit **07** control
**09** crackdown, restraint **10** prevention
**11** restriction, suppression

## clan

**03** set **04** band, gens, hapu, line, name, race, sect, sept **05** group, horde, house, tribe **06** circle, clique, family, kinred
**07** coterie, faction, kindred, society
**10** fraternity **11** brotherhood
**13** confraternity
*See also* **Scottish**

## clandestine

**03** sly **06** closet, covert, hidden, secret, sneaky **07** furtive, private **08** backdoor, backroom, stealthy **09** concealed, underhand **10** behind-door, fraudulent, undercover
**11** underground **13** hole-and-corner, surreptitious **14** cloak-and-dagger
**15** under-the-counter

## clandestinely

**05** slyly **07** on the QT **08** covertly, secretly, sneakily **09** furtively, privately
**10** on the quiet, stealthily
**12** fraudulently **15** surreptitiously, under the counter

## clang

**04** bong, peal, ring, toll **05** chime, clank, clash, clink, clunk, klang
**06** jangle, timbre **07** clatter, resound
**11** reverberate **13** reverberation

## clanger

**04** boob, flub, goof, slip **05** boner, error, fault, gaffe **06** booboo, cock-up, howler, slip-up, stumer **07** bloomer, blunder, faux pas, mistake **08** solecism
**09** oversight **10** inaccuracy
**12** indiscretion, misjudgement

## clank

**04** ring, toll **05** clang, clash, clink, clunk **06** jangle **07** clatter, resound
**10** resounding **11** reverberate
**13** reverberation

## clannish

**06** narrow, select **07** cliquey, insular
**08** cliquish **09** exclusive, parochial, sectarian **10** unfriendly

## clap

**03** hit, pat, ray **04** bang, bolt, chop, slap **05** blaze, burst, cheer, crack, flare, flash, shaft, smack, spark, whack
**06** streak, strike, wallop **07** acclaim, applaud, ovation **08** applause, handclap, plaudite **11** thunderbolt
**15** round of applause, standing ovation

## claptrap

**03** rot **04** blah, bosh, bull, bunk, guff
**05** balls, bilge, hokum, trash, tripe
**06** bunkum, drivel, faddle, hot air, piffle **07** baloney, blarney, eyewash, hogwash, rhubarb, rubbish, twaddle
**08** blethers, buncombe, cobblers, nonsense, tommyrot **09** bull's wool, gibberish, poppycock **10** codswallop

## clarification

**05** gloss **10** definition, exposition
**11** elucidation, explanation
**12** illumination **14** interpretation, simplification

## clarify

**05** clear, gloss, purge **06** define, filter, purify, refine **07** clear up, explain, resolve **08** simplify, spell out
**09** elucidate, make clear, make plain
**10** illuminate **11** shed light on **12** throw light on

## clarity

**08** lucidity **09** chiarezza, clearness, plainness, precision, sharpness
**10** definition, simplicity, visibility
**11** obviousness **12** explicitness, transparency **15** intelligibility, unambiguousness

## clash

**03** jar, war **04** bang, feud, slam, snap
**05** brush, clang, clank, crash, fight, noise, swash **06** gossip, hurtle, jangle, rattle, scream, strike **07** chatter, clatter, collide, contend, co-occur, grapple, jarring, quarrel, warring, wrangle
**08** argument, coincide, conflict, disagree, fall foul, fighting, mismatch, not match, showdown, striking
**09** collision, not go with **10** fall foul of
**11** altercation, discordance, misalliance **12** be discordant, disagreement, irregularity
**13** confrontation, not go together **14** be incompatible, look unpleasant
**15** incompatibility

## clasp

◇ *containment indicator* **03** hug, pin
**04** clip, grip, hasp, hold, hook, tach
**05** bosom, catch, grasp, press, slide, spang, tache, unite **06** attach, brooch, buckle, clutch, cuddle, enfold, fasten, preace, prease, tassel **07** agraffe, cling to, connect, embosom, embrace, enclasp, grapple, preasse, squeeze

## class

**03** set **04** chic, form, kind, race, rank, rate, sort, type, year **05** brand, caste, genre, genus, grade, group, level, order, style, taste **06** course, league, lesson, period, phylum, reckon, sphere, status, stream **07** arrange, lecture, quality, section, seminar, species, teach-in **08** category, classify, division, elegance, grouping, standing, tutorial, workshop **09** designate
**10** background, categorize, department, pigeonhole, study group
**11** distinction, social order, stylishness
**12** denomination, pecking order, social status **14** classification, social division, social standing, sophistication
*See also* **classification**

## classic

**04** best, Oaks, true **05** Derby, great, ideal, model, prime, usual **06** finest, simple **07** abiding, ageless, elegant, lasting, regular, St Leger, The Oaks, typical, undying **08** Augustan, enduring, exemplar, immortal, masterly, standard, timeless
**09** brilliant, excellent, exemplary, first-rate, prototype **10** archetypal, consummate, definitive, first-class, masterwork **11** established, masterpiece, outstanding, traditional, undecorated, understated
**12** paradigmatic, time-honoured
**13** authoritative **14** characteristic, quintessential, representative
**15** established work, unsophisticated

## classical

**04** pure **05** Attic, Latin, plain
**06** humane, simple **07** concert, elegant, Grecian, refined, serious
**08** Hellenic **09** excellent, symphonic
**10** harmonious, restrained
**11** symmetrical, traditional **12** ancient Greek, ancient Roman
*See also* **musician; singer**

## classically

**06** purely, simply **07** as a rule, plainly, usually **08** normally **09** elegantly, typically **10** ordinarily, originally
**11** customarily **12** harmoniously, historically **13** symmetrically, traditionally

## classification

**05** group **06** method **07** grading, sorting
**08** classing, grouping, taxonomy
**10** tabulation **11** arrangement, cataloguing **12** codification, distribution **14** categorization
**15** systematization

---

*Classifications of living organisms include:*

**05** class, genus, order
**06** domain, empire, family, phylum
**07** kingdom, species
**08** division

*Kingdoms, domains and empires include:*

**05** fungi
**06** monera, plants
**07** animals, archaea
**08** bacteria, protista
**10** eubacteria, eukaryotes
**11** prokaryotes
**14** archaebacteria

*Classes include:*

**04** Aves
**07** Insecta
**08** Amphibia, Bivalvia, Mammalia
**09** Arachnida, Bryopsida, Pinopsida
**10** Gastropoda, Liliopsida
**11** Cephalopoda
**12** Malacostraca
**13** Magnoliopsida

### classify
**03** peg **04** file, rank, sort, type **05** class, grade, group, order, range **06** assort, codify, divide **07** arrange, dispose, include, sort out **08** regiment, serotype, stratify, tabulate **09** catalogue **10** categorize, distribute, pigeonhole **11** systematize

### classy
**04** fine, posh **05** grand, ritzy **06** select, smooth, swanky **07** elegant, stylish **08** gorgeous, superior, up-market **09** exclusive, expensive, exquisite, high-class **13** sophisticated

### clatter
**03** jar **04** bang **05** clang, clank, clunk, crash **06** gossip, hotter, jangle, rattle, strike **07** blatter, chatter

### clause
**04** item, part **05** point, rider, salvo **06** phrase **07** adjunct, article, chapter, heading, passage, proviso, section **08** clausula, loophole, particle, tenendum **09** condition, novodamus, paragraph, provision, reddendum **10** subsection **13** specification

### claw
**03** rip **04** clat, crab, fang, maul, nail, sere, tear **05** chela, claut, cloye, graze, griff, seize, talon **06** clutch, griffe, mangle, nipper, pincer, pounce, scrape, unguis **07** falcula, flatter, gripper, scratch **08** lacerate, scrabble **11** clapperclaw

### clay
**03** cam, pug, wax **04** bole, calm, caum, glei, gley, loam, lute, marl, pisé, slip, soil, tile, till **05** argil, blaes, brick, cloam, earth, fango **06** blaise, blaize, clunch, ground, kaolin **07** kaoline, pottery **08** ceramics, cimolite, illuvium, laterite **09** bentonite **10** lithomarge, meerschaum, plastilina
• **clay-chalk mixture** **04** malm

### clean
**03** lux, net, new, rub **04** char, even, fair, good, just, neat, nett, pure, tidy, wash, wipe **05** blank, crisp, empty, final, fresh, fully, moral, quite, rinse, scour, scrub, sweep, total, utter, whole **06** chaste, decent, emunge, hollow, honest, modest, proper, scrape,

simple, smooth, soogee, soogie, unused, washed **07** aseptic, elegant, ethical, launder, perfect, regular, sterile, totally, upright **08** clean-cut, cleansed, clear-cut, complete, decisive, directly, entirely, flawless, graceful, hygienic, innocent, pristine, purified, sanitary, smoothly, spotless, straight, unerring, unmarked, unsoiled, virtuous **09** faultless, guiltless, laundered, reputable, righteous, speckless, unspotted, unstained, unsullied, wholesome **10** above board, antiseptic, completely, conclusive, even-handed, honourable, immaculate, sterilized, unpolluted, upstanding **11** appropriate, respectable, unblemished, uncorrupted, well-defined **12** spick and span, squeaky-clean **13** unadulterated **14** clean as a new pin, decontaminated, uncontaminated

*Cleaning products include:*

**04** soap
**06** bleach, polish
**07** shampoo, solvent
**09** detergent, shower gel
**10** bubble bath, soap powder
**12** disinfectant
**13** paint-stripper, washing powder
**14** scouring powder
**15** washing-up liquid

• **clean out** **03** fay, fey
• **come clean** **05** admit, own up **06** fess up, reveal **07** confess, tell all **11** acknowledge **13** spill the beans

### clean-cut
**04** neat, tidy, trim **05** fresh, natty, smart, terse **06** spruce **07** orderly **11** uncluttered

### cleaner
**03** vac **04** char **05** daily, wiper **06** Hoover®, Mrs Mop, vacuum **07** Mrs Mopp, orderly **08** charlady **09** charwoman

### cleanliness
**06** purity **09** cleanness, freshness **10** perfection **12** spotlessness

### cleanse
**04** pure, wash **05** bathe, clean, clear, flush, porge, purge, rinse, scour **06** garble, purify **07** absolve, deterge, launder, mundify **08** absterge, lustrate, scavenge **09** disinfect, sterilize **12** make free from

### cleanser
**04** soap **07** cleaner, scourer, solvent **08** purifier **09** detergent **10** soap powder **12** disinfectant **14** scouring powder

### clear
**02** go **03** net, rid **04** earn, fair, fine, free, full, gain, jump, keen, land, make, move, neat, nett, open, pass, pure, quit, sure, tidy, void, wipe **05** allow, bring, clean, empty, erase, let go, light, lucid, overt, plain, quick, quite, sharp, sheer, shift, sunny, vault **06** acquit, bright, decode, excuse, filter, glassy, go over, limpid, liquid, loosen,

pardon, patent, permit, pocket, refine, remble, remove, serene, settle, unclog, unload, unstop, vacate, vanish, wholly **07** absolve, approve, audible, break in, bring in, certain, cleanse, evident, express, fogless, hyaline, justify, logical, obvious, plainly, precise, release, through, unblock **08** apparent, coherent, definite, distinct, evacuate, evanesce, explicit, get rid of, innocent, jump over, leap over, liberate, luculent, luminous, manifest, melt away, pellucid, positive, pregnant, sanction, sensible, take away, take home, undimmed, undulled **09** authorize, blameless, cloudless, convinced, decongest, disappear, discharge, evaporate, exculpate, exonerate, extricate, guiltless, unblocked, unclouded, unimpeded, vindicate **10** articulate, colourless, diaphonous, disengaged, in the clear, perceptive, pronounced, reasonable, see-through, unhindered, unscramble, untroubled **11** acquittance, beyond doubt, conspicuous, crystalline, disentangle, make a profit, penetrating, perceptible, translucent, transparent, unambiguous, unequivocal, well-defined **12** clear as a bell, crystal-clear, intelligible, recognizable, twenty-twenty, unmistakable, unobstructed **13** find not guilty **14** beyond question, comprehensible, give permission, give the go-ahead, having no qualms, understandable, unquestionable
• **all clear** **09** copacetic, copasetic, kopasetic
• **clear away** **03** mop
• **clear off** **04** quit **06** get out, go away **07** buzz off, gertcha, push off **08** cheese it, run along, shove off
• **clear out** **03** get **04** sort, tidy **05** empty, hop it, leave, scour **06** beat it, depart, get out, go away, tidy up, vacate **07** get lost, push off, sort out **08** clear off, shove off, throw out, withdraw
• **clear up** **03** red **04** fair, redd, sort, tidy **05** crack, order, salve, solve **06** answer, remove **07** clarify, explain, improve, iron out, resolve, sort out, unravel **08** brighten **09** elucidate, liquidate, rearrange **10** become fine, brighten up, put in order, straighten **11** become sunny, stop raining **12** straighten up **13** straighten out
• **not clear** **02** nl **09** non liquet

### clearance
**02** OK **03** gap **04** room **05** leave, say-so, space, sweep **06** margin, moving **07** consent, freeing, go-ahead, removal **08** clearing, emptying, headroom, riddance, sanction, shifting, vacating **09** allowance, cleansing, unloading **10** demolition, evacuation, green light, permission, taking-away **11** endorsement **13** authorization

### clear-cut
**05** clean, clear, plain, sharp **07** precise **08** definite, distinct, explicit, sharp-cut, specific **09** trenchant **11** cut and dried,

unambiguous, unequivocal, well-defined **13** black and white **15** straightforward

## clear-headed
**04** wise **05** sober **08** rational, sensible **09** practical, realistic **11** intelligent

## clearing
**03** gap **04** dell **05** glade, slash, space **06** assart **07** opening **08** scouring, slashing

## clearly
**04** well **05** plain **06** bright, openly **07** lucidly, plainly **08** markedly, patently **09** evidently, obviously **10** coherently, distinctly, explicitly, manifestly, undeniably **11** undoubtedly **12** indisputably, intelligibly, unmistakably, without doubt **13** conspicuously, incontestably **14** comprehensibly

## cleave
◇ *insertion indicator* **03** cut, hew **04** chop, hold, open, part, rend, rift **05** cling, crack, halve, sever, share, slice, split, stick, unite **06** adhere, attach, cohere, divide, pierce, remain, sunder **07** fissure **08** dissever, disunite, separate **09** crack open, split open

## cleft
◇ *containment indicator* **03** gap, jag **04** rent, rift, riva **05** break, chasm, chink, cloff, crack, slack, split **06** breach, cranny, parted, sexfid **07** chimney, crevice, divided, fissure, octofid, opening, pharynx **08** cleaving, crevasse, fissured, fracture, scissure **09** bisulcate, quadrifid, septemfid **13** quadripartite

## clemency
**04** pity **05** mercy **06** lenity **08** humanity, kindness, leniency, mildness, sympathy **10** compassion, generosity, indulgence, moderation, tenderness **11** forbearance, forgiveness, magnanimity **12** mercifulness **15** soft-heartedness

## clench
**04** grip, grit, hold, seal, shut **05** clasp, close, grasp, press **06** clinch, clutch, double, fasten **07** squeeze **08** double up **12** close tightly **13** press together

## clergy
**06** church **07** clerics **08** learning, ministry, the cloth **09** churchmen, clergymen, education, the church **10** holy orders, priesthood **11** churchwomen, clergywomen, spiritualty **12** spirituality

## clergyman, clergywoman
**02** DD, RR **03** Rev **04** abbé, dean, imam, papa **05** canon, clerk, padre, rabbi, vicar **06** bishop, cleric, curate, deacon, divine, father, josser, Levite, mother, mullah, parson, pastor, priest, rector **07** diocese, dominie, muezzin, prelate, secular **08** cardinal, chaplain, man of God, minister, Nonjuror, preacher, reverend, sky pilot, spintext, squarson, vartabed **09** churchman, deaconess, presbyter, rural dean **10** arch-priest, prebendary, woman of

God **11** churchwoman **12** ecclesiastic **13** man of the cloth **14** superintendent **15** woman of the cloth

## clerical
**06** filing, office, typing **08** official, pastoral, priestly, reverend **09** canonical, episcopal **10** pen-pushing, sacerdotal **11** keyboarding, ministerial, secretarial, white-collar **14** administrative, ecclesiastical
*See also* **vestment**

## clerk
**04** babu **05** baboo **06** circar, notary, priest, scribe, sircar, sirkar, teller, typist, writer **07** actuary, copyist, scholar **08** cursitor, official, Petty Bag, quillman, servitor **09** assistant, clergyman, pen-driver, pen-pusher, secretary **10** book-keeper, desk jockey **11** paper-pusher, protocolist, protonotary, quill-driver **12** prothonotary, receptionist, record-keeper, stenographer **13** account-keeper, administrator, shop-assistant

## clever
**03** apt **04** able, cute, deft, gleg, keen **05** acute, natty, quick, sharp, smart, witty **06** adroit, artful, brainy, bright, expert, gifted, pretty, shrewd, souple **07** capable, cunning, knowing, notable, sapient, skilful **08** rational, sensible, talented **09** brilliant, conceited, dexterous, ingenious, inventive, sagacious, spiritual **10** discerning, perceptive **11** intelligent, quick-witted, resourceful, sharp-witted **12** apprehensive **13** knowledgeable

## cleverly
**04** ably **07** capably **08** artfully, astutely, craftily, expertly, shrewdly **09** skilfully **11** ingeniously **12** discerningly **13** intelligently, knowledgeably, quick-wittedly

## cliché
**06** truism **07** bromide **08** banality, chestnut **09** platitude **10** stereotype **11** commonplace, old chestnut **15** hackneyed phrase

## cliché'd, clichéed
**04** dull, worn **05** banal, corny, stale, stock, tired, trite **06** common **07** routine, worn-out **08** overused, time-worn **09** hackneyed **10** overworked, pedestrian, threadbare **11** commonplace, stereotyped, wearing thin **12** run-of-the-mill **13** platitudinous, unimaginative

## click
**04** beat, snap, snip, tick, twig **05** clack, clink, forge, get on, snick **08** cotton on, get along, hit it off **09** get on well, implosive, make sense **10** understand **11** become clear, suction stop **13** fall into place, suctional stop

## client
**04** user **05** buyer **06** patron, punter, vassal **07** patient, regular, shopper **08** consumer, customer, hanger-on **09** applicant, dependant, purchaser

## clientèle
**05** trade, users **06** buyers, market

**07** clients, patrons **08** business, regulars, shoppers **09** consumers, customers, following, patronage **10** purchasers

## cliff
**03** tor **04** clef, crag, face, scar **05** bluff, cleve, scarp, scaur **06** cleeve **08** overhang, rock-face **09** precipice **10** escarpment, promontory

## climactic
**05** final **07** crucial **08** critical, decisive, exciting **09** paramount

## climate
**04** mood **05** trend **06** milieu, region, spirit, temper **07** feeling, setting, weather **08** ambience, tendency **10** atmosphere **11** disposition, environment, temperament, temperature

## climax
**03** top **04** acme, apex, head, peak **06** apogee, finale, height, summit, zenith **08** pinnacle **09** crescendo, highlight, high point **11** catastrophe, culmination

## climb
◇ *reversal down indicator* **03** sty, top **04** go up, move, ramp, rise, scan, shin, soar, stie, stir, stye **05** jumar, mount, scale, sclim, shift, sklim, speel, swarm **06** ascend, ascent, prusik, shin up **07** clamber, going up, shoot up **08** increase, scramble, surmount **11** herringbone, mountaineer, upward slope **14** uphill struggle
• **climb down** **05** yield **07** concede, descend, retract, retreat **08** back down **09** surrender **12** eat your words
• **climbing party** **04** rope

## climb-down
**07** retreat **08** yielding **09** surrender **10** concession, retraction, withdrawal

## climber
**03** ivy **04** Jack, Jill, vine **05** liana **07** speeler **10** nasturtium **11** balloon-vine, honeysuckle, Jack and Jill, mountaineer **12** kangaroo vine, morning glory **13** scarlet runner **14** Scotch attorney

## clinch
**03** pun **04** land, seal **05** clink, close, rivet **06** clench, decide, secure, settle, verify **07** confirm, embrace, grapple **08** conclude **09** determine

## cling
**03** hug **04** grip, hold **05** clasp, grasp, stick **06** adhere, attach, cleave, clutch, defend, fasten, hold on, shrink **07** embrace, shrivel, stand by, support **08** hold on to, stay true **09** adherence **10** be faithful

## clinic
**07** doctor's **08** hospital **09** infirmary **10** sanatorium **12** health centre **13** medical centre

## clinical
**04** cold **05** basic, plain, stark **06** simple **07** austere, medical, patient **08** analytic, detached, hospital **09** impassive, objective, unadorned,

**clinically**

unfeeling **10** analytical, antiseptic, impersonal, scientific, uninvolved **11** emotionless, unemotional **12** businesslike **13** disinterested, dispassionate

**clinically**
**09** medically **14** scientifically

**clink**
*see* **prison**

**clip**
◇ *tail deletion indicator* **03** box, cut, dod, fix, hit, pin **04** crop, cuff, dock, hold, mute, pare, poll, slap, snip, trim **05** cheat, clout, D-ring, graze, jumar, prune, punch, shear, smack, thump, tough, whack **06** attach, crutch, cut off, cut out, fasten, reduce, staple, strike, tingle, wallop **07** Bulldog®, curtail, cutting, embrace, excerpt, extract, passage, pollard, run into, section, shorten, snippet **08** citation, cut short, encircle, fastener, truncate **09** crash into, quotation **10** abbreviate, clothes-peg, clothes-pin, jumar clamp, overcharge **11** collide with, music holder
*See also* **cut**

**clipping**
**04** clip **05** scrow, shear, shred **06** paring **07** cutting, excerpt, extract, passage, section, snippet, topiary **08** citation, snipping, trimming **09** quotation

**clique**
**03** set **04** band, clan, club, gang, pack, ring **05** bunch, crowd, group **06** circle, set-out **07** coterie, faction, in-crowd, society **08** grouplet **10** fraternity

**cloak**
**04** cape, coat, hide, mask, pall, rail, robe, veil, wrap **05** blind, cloke, cover, front **06** mantle, screen, shield, shroud **07** conceal, obscure, pretext **08** covering, disguise **10** camouflage
*See also* **cape**

*Cloaks include:*

**04** capa
**05** amice, grego, jelab, manta, pilch, sagum, shawl, talma
**06** abolla, capote, dolman, domino, poncho, visite
**07** chlamys, galabea, galabia, jellaba, korowai, manteel, mantlet, paenula, pelisse, pluvial, rocklay, rokelay, sarafan
**08** capuchin, cardinal, djellaba, galabeah, galabiah, gallabea, gallabia, himation, mantelet, mantilla, palliate
**09** djellabah, gabardine, gaberdine, gallabeah, gallabiah, gallabieh, gallabiya
**10** gallabiyah, gallabiyeh, paludament, roquelaure
**11** buffalo robe
**12** mousquetaire, paludamentum

**clobber**
◇ *anagram indicator* **03** hit, kit, zap **04** bash, beat, belt, capa, garb, gear, lick, rout, ruin, slap, sock, togs **05** clout, crush, knock, punch, stuff,

thump, whack **06** attack, defeat, hammer, strike, tackle, things, thrash, wallop **07** baggage, conquer, trounce **08** clothing, garments **09** equipment, overpaint, overwhelm **10** belongings **11** bits and bobs, possessions **13** bits and pieces, paraphernalia

**clock**
**03** hit, sit **04** face **05** brood, cluck **06** beetle, notice **07** observe **08** ornament **10** mileometer, timekeeper **11** speedometer

*Clocks and watches include:*

**03** fob, Tim
**04** ring, stop
**05** alarm, wrist
**06** atomic, cuckoo, mantel, quartz
**07** bracket, digital, pendant, sundial
**08** analogue, carriage, longcase, speaking
**09** clepsydra, repeating
**10** travelling
**11** chronograph, chronometer, grandfather, grandmother

• **clock up** **03** log **05** reach **06** attain, record **07** achieve, archive, chalk up, notch up **08** register
• **round the clock** **10** constantly **11** ceaselessly, day and night **12** continuously **15** twenty-four seven, without stopping

**clod**
**04** hunk, lump, mass, mool, pelt, slab **05** block, chunk, clump, glebe, throw, wedge **06** ground

**clog**
**03** dam, jam, log, mud **04** ball, gaum, gorm **05** block, choke, dam up, sabot **06** accloy, ball up, bung up, burden, chopin, galosh, golosh, hamper, hinder, hobble, impede, patten, pester, stop up **07** chopine, clutter, congest, galoche, occlude **08** encumber, obstruct

**cloister**
**05** aisle **06** arcade **07** portico, walkway **08** corridor, pavement **10** ambulatory

**cloistered**
**08** confined, enclosed, hermitic, isolated, secluded, shielded **09** cloistral, insulated, protected, reclusive, sheltered, withdrawn **10** restricted **11** sequestered

**close**
**03** bar, Clo, end, row **04** best, bolt, clog, cork, dear, fail, fill, flop, fold, fuse, good, hard, join, keen, lane, like, lock, mean, mews, mure, near, plug, road, seal, shet, shut, slam, stop, true **05** block, bosom, cease, court, dense, exact, fixed, fuggy, heavy, humid, muggy, pause, place, quiet, solid, tight, union, unite **06** at hand, clinch, decide, direct, ending, fasten, finale, finish, gain on, go bust, hidden, lessen, lock up, loving, marked, narrow, nearby, nearly, not far, packed, secret, secure, settle, shut up, square, sticky, stingy, stop up, strait, street, strict, strong, stuffy, sultry, verify, wind up

**07** adjourn, airless, block up, cadence, careful, close by, compact, confirm, cramped, crowded, densely, devoted, grapple, intense, literal, miserly, occlude, padlock, precise, private, similar, terrace, tightly **08** accurate, adjacent, approach, attached, block off, collapse, complete, conclude, conflict, cul-de-sac, detailed, distinct, faithful, familiar, imminent, intimate, junction, obstruct, reserved, reticent, rigorous, round off, secluded, secretly, shut down, stifling, straight, streight, taciturn, thorough **09** adjoining, cessation, close down, close-knit, condensed, courtyard, determine, enclosure, encounter, establish, immediate, impending, niggardly, searching, secretive, terminate, winding-up **10** come closer, comparable, completion, conclusion, dénouement, go bankrupt, hard-fought, methodical, oppressive, quadrangle, sweltering **11** adjournment, approaching, catch up with, culmination, discontinue, draw to an end, get closer to, go to the wall, inseparable, in the offing, neck and neck, painstaking, suffocating, termination, well-matched **12** a stone's throw, bring to an end, concentrated, confidential, neighbouring, on the brink of, on the verge of, parsimonious, unventilated **13** corresponding, evenly matched, in the vicinity, penny-pinching, unforthcoming **14** cease operating, on your doorstep **15** cease operations, uncommunicative
*See also* **approximate**
• **close in** **04** shut **08** approach, draw near, encircle, surround **10** come nearer
• **close to** **02** on **04** near, nigh **06** fast by, nearby
• **keep close to** **03** hug

**closed**
**02** to **04** dark, shut **05** drawn **06** lucken
• **not closed** **04** agee, ajar, ajee, open

**closet**
**04** zeta **05** press, privy **06** covert, hidden, recess, secret **07** cabinet, confine, furtive, isolate, private, seclude **08** cloister, cupboard, shut away, wardrobe **10** undercover, unrevealed **11** storage room, underground **13** surreptitious

**closure**
**03** gag **05** block **07** cloture, failure, folding **08** blocking, shutdown, shutting **09** stricture, winding-up **10** bankruptcy, guillotine, stopping-up **11** closing-down, obstruction **12** laryngospasm

**clot**
**03** gel, git, mug, nit, set **04** clag, dope, dork, fool, glob, lump, mass, nerd, prat, twit **05** clump, cruor, grume, idiot, twerp, wally **06** curdle, gobbet, lapper, lopper **07** congeal, embolus, plonker, splatch, thicken **08** clotting, coalesce, imbecile, solidify, thrombus **09** blockhead, coagulate

**10** bufflehead, nincompoop, thrombosis **11** coagulation, obstruction **12** crassamentum

## cloth

**03** lap, rag **05** sails, stuff, towel **06** duster, fabric, lappie **07** flannel, textile **08** material **09** churchmen, clergymen, dishcloth, facecloth, the church, the clergy **10** floorcloth, holy orders, upholstery **11** churchwomen, clergywomen, the ministry
*See also* **fabric**
• **measure of cloth** **03** ell, end
• **piece of cloth** **03** lap, rag **04** fent, gair, pane, sash **05** clout, godet, lapje **06** lappie **07** remnant

## clothe

**03** rig **04** coat, cour, deck, gird, robe, vest, wrap **05** cover, drape, dress, endew, endue, equip, habit, indew, indue, put on **06** attire, bedeck, carpet, emboss, enrobe, fit out, invest, outfit **07** apparel, bedizen, blanket, envelop, garment, overlay, vesture **08** accoutre **09** caparison

## clothes, clothing

**03** kit **04** drag, duds, garb, gear, togs, wear, weed **05** braws, claes, dress, get-up **06** attire, outfit, rig-out **07** apparel, clobber, costume, daywear, raiment, threads, toggery, uniform, vesture **08** cast-offs, clothing, dressing, garments, glad rags, wardrobe **09** trousseau, vestiture, vestments **11** habiliments, hand-me-downs
*See also* **boot; cloak; coat; dress; footwear; hat; headdress; jacket; scarf; vestment**

*Clothes include:*

**02** gi
**03** aba, boa, bra, fur, gie, obi, PJs, tie, top
**04** 501s®, abba, belt, body, buff, capa, cape, coat, daks, furs, gown, kilt, maud, midi, mink, mitt, muff, rami, ruff, sack, sari, sash, slip, slop, sock, spat, suit, sulu, toga, toge, veil, vest, wrap
**05** abaya, burka, cloak, cords, dhoti, dress, frock, glove, hoody, ihram, jeans, kanzu, Levis®, lungi, pants, parka, ruana, scarf, shawl, shift, shirt, shrug, skirt, smock, stole, teddy, thong, tunic
**06** anorak, basque, bikini, blouse, bodice, boorka, bow tie, boxers, braces, briefs, caftan, corset, cossie, cravat, denims, dirndl, fleece, garter, girdle, hoodie, jersey, jilbab, jubbah, jumper, kaross, kimono, mitten, poncho, sacque, samfoo, sarong, shorts, slacks, tabard, tights, T-shirt
**07** catsuit, crop top, doublet, g-string, hosiery, jammies, jimjams, leotard, muffler, necktie, nightie, overall, panties, pyjamas, singlet, spattee, sweater, tank top, twinset, uniform, vest top, wet suit, yashmak, Y-fronts
**08** bathrobe, bedsocks, breeches, camisole, cardigan, culottes, earmuffs, flannels, guernsey, hipsters, hot pants, jodhpurs, jumpsuit, knickers, leggings, lingerie, negligee, pashmina, pinafore, polo neck, pullover, raincoat, swimsuit, tee-shirt, trousers
**09** balaclava, bed-jacket, brassière, coveralls, dishdasha, dress suit, Drizabone®, dungarees, hair shirt, housecoat, jazz pants, jockstrap, mini skirt, outerwear, pantihose, petticoat, plus-fours, polo shirt, salopette, separates, shahtoosh, shell suit, Sloppy Joe, stockings, tracksuit, underwear, waistcoat
**10** boiler suit, Capri pants, cummerbund, dinner-gown, drainpipes, dress shirt, flying suit, leg warmers, lounge suit, nightdress, nightshirt, romper suit, rugby shirt, string vest, suspenders, sweat-shirt, turtleneck, underpants, wife-beater
**11** bell-bottoms, board shorts, boiled shirt, boxer-shorts, leisure suit, morning suit, pencil skirt, thermal vest, trouser suit
**12** body stocking, camiknickers, divided skirt, dressing-gown, evening dress, palazzo pants, pedal-pushers, shirtwaister
**13** Bermuda shorts, cycling shorts, liberty bodice, pinafore skirt, shalwar-kameez, suspender belt
**14** bathing costume, combat trousers, double-breasted, French knickers, jogging bottoms, single-breasted, swimming trunks, three-piece suit
**15** swimming costume

• **plain clothes** **05** mufti
• **shabby clothes** **03** tat

## cloud

**03** dim, fog **04** blur, dull, mist, puff, rack, veil, weft **05** chill, cover, shade **06** billow, darken, defame, mantle, muddle, shadow, shroud **07** confuse, eclipse, obscure **08** dullness, woolpack **09** obfuscate **10** overshadow

*Clouds include:*

**06** cirrus, nimbus
**07** cumulus, stratus
**08** mammatus
**10** mare's-tails
**11** altocumulus, altostratus
**12** cirrocumulus, cirrostratus, cumulonimbus, nimbostratus
**13** fractocumulus, fractostratus, stratocumulus

## cloudless

**03** dry **04** fair, fine **05** clear, sunny **06** bright **08** pleasant **09** unclouded

## cloudy

**01** c **03** dim **04** dark, dull, grey, hazy **05** foggy, heavy, milky, misty, muddy, murky, vague **06** blurry, gloomy, leaden, opaque, sombre **07** blurred, muddled, obscure, sunless

**08** confused, lowering, nebulous, nubilous, overcast **10** indistinct

## clout

**03** box, hit **04** blow, cuff, pull, slap, slug, sock **05** patch, power, punch, smack, thump, whack **06** muscle, strike, wallop, weight **07** garment **08** prestige, standing **09** authority, influence

## cloven

**05** cleft, split **07** divided **08** bisected

## clown

**04** dork, fool, geek, jerk, jest, joke, nerd, twit, zany **05** antic, chuff, comic, idiot, joker, ninny, twerp, wally **06** antick, august, chough, dimwit, jester, joskin, nitwit, Pompey, rustic **07** anticke, antique, auguste, buffoon, bumpkin, Costard **08** comedian, dipstick, gracioso, imbecile, numskull **09** blockhead, grotesque, harlequin, muck about, patchocke, Whiteface **10** act the fool, fool around, goof around, mess around, nincompoop, patchcocke, Touchstone **11** carpet clown, merry-andrew, play the fool **12** act foolishly **13** pickle-herring

*Clowns include:*

**04** Bozo, Coco, Hobo, Joey
**05** Tramp
**07** Pierrot
**08** Grimaldi, Owl-glass, Trinculo
**09** Owle-glass
**10** Howleglass, Owlspiegle
**14** Joseph Grimaldi

## cloying

**04** icky **06** sickly **07** choking, fulsome **08** luscious **09** excessive, oversweet, sickening **10** disgusting, nauseating

## club

**03** hit, set **04** bash, beat **05** bunch, clout, group, guild, order, union **06** batter, beat up, circle, clique, fascio, league, priest, pummel, strike **07** chapter, clobber, combine, company, society, sorosis **08** hetairia **09** auxiliary **10** federation, fraternity, sisterhood **11** association, brotherhood, combination, free-and-easy **12** organization **13** life-preserver
*See also* **football; golf club**

*Clubs include:*

**03** bar, bat
**04** cosh, mace, patu, polt
**05** bandy, billy, caman, nulla, staff, stick, waddy
**06** cudgel, hurley
**07** bourdon
**08** bludgeon, trunnion
**09** blackjack, truncheon
**10** knobkerrie, nulla-nulla

*Club types include:*

**03** fan, job
**04** boat, book, glee, golf
**05** disco, field, goose, night, slate, strip, yacht, youth
**06** bridge, health, social, tennis
**07** cabaret, country, singles
**09** warehouse

**10** investment
**11** discotheque
**12** Darby and Joan

*Club names include:*

**03** MCC, RAC, Ski
**04** Arts, Turf
**05** Buck's, Naval
**06** Alpine, Cotton, Drones, Jockey, Kennel, Kitcat, Pratt's, Queen's, Reform, Rotary, Savage, Savile, United, White's
**07** Almack's, Authors', Boodle's, Brooks's, Canning, Carlton, Country, Farmers, Garrick, Groucho, Kiwanis, Leander, Railway, Variety
**08** Hell-fire, National, Oriental, Portland
**09** Athenaeum, Beefsteak, East India, Green Room, Lansdowne, Wig and Pen
**10** Caledonian, City Livery, Crockford's, Flyfishers', Hurlingham, Oddfellows, Roehampton, Travellers
**11** Army and Navy, Arts Theatre, Chelsea Arts
**12** Anglo-Belgian, City of London, London Rowing, New Cavendish, Thames Rowing
**13** Royal Air Force
**14** American Women's, City University
**15** National Liberal, Royal Automobile, Victory Services

• **club together** **06** chip in **09** give money **10** contribute, join forces **12** share the cost **14** have a whip-round
• **in the club** *see* **pregnant**

**clubhouse**
**02** ch **14** nineteenth hole

**clubs**
**01** C
• **jack of clubs** **03** pam

**clue**
**03** tip **04** hint, idea, lead, sign **05** fix up, light, trace **06** clavis, notion, thread, tip-off **07** inkling, pointer **08** evidence, signpost **09** master-key, suspicion **10** indication, intimation, suggestion

**clueless**
**04** dumb **05** dense, thick **06** stupid **08** helpless, ignorant **09** unlearned **10** uninformed, unschooled **11** not all there, uninitiated **13** inexperienced

**clump**
**03** lot, mot **04** beat, blow, clot, knot, mass, mott, plod, thud, tuft, tump **05** amass, bluff, bunch, clomp, group, motte, plump, stamp, stomp, thump, tramp **06** bundle, lumber, spinny, trudge **07** cluster, spinney, stumble, thicket, tussock **10** accumulate, collection **11** agglutinate **12** accumulation **13** agglomeration, agglutination

**clumsy**
◊ *anagram indicator* **03** ham **04** rude **05** bulky, crude, Dutch, gawky, heavy,

hulky, inept, looby, rough, squab **06** clunky, gauche, oafish, thumby, wooden **07** awkward, chuckle, hulking, ill-made, uncouth, unhandy **08** bungling, clumping, tactless, ungainly, unheppen, unwieldy **09** all thumbs, ham-fisted, ham-handed, lumbering, maladroit, shapeless, two-fisted, unskilful **10** blundering, cack-handed, cumbersome, Dutch-built, kack-handed, ungraceful, unhandsome **11** heavy-handed, insensitive **12** hippopotamic, unmanageable **13** accident-prone, chuckle-headed, hippopotamian, unco-ordinated **14** banana-fingered

**cluster**
**03** bob **04** band, knot, mass, tuft **05** batch, bunch, clump, crowd, flock, group, plump, strap, truss **06** gather, huddle, raceme **07** collect, panicle **08** assemble, assembly **09** gathering **10** assemblage, assortment, collection, congregate, racemation **11** constellate **12** come together **13** agglomeration, group together, inflorescence

**clustered**
**06** massed **07** bunched, grouped **08** gathered **09** assembled, glomerate **11** agglomerate

**clutch**
◊ *containment indicator* **03** set **04** claw, grab, grip, hold, jaws, sway **05** brood, catch, clasp, claws, grasp, gripe, group, hands, hatch, mercy, power, seize **06** clench, graple, number, snatch **07** claucht, claught, cling to, control, custody, embrace, grapple, gripper, keeping, setting, sitting **08** dominion, hang on to, hatching **09** get hold of **10** incubation, possession, take hold of

**clutter**
**04** fill, mess, stir **05** chaos, cover, noise, strew **06** jumble, litter, mess up, midden, muddle **07** scatter **08** disarray, disorder, encumber **09** confusion, make a mess **10** make untidy, untidiness **12** fill untidily

**coach**
**03** bus, cab, car, gig **04** coch, cram, drag, post, trap **05** drill, prime, teach, train, tutor, wagon **06** fiacre, hansom, landau, mentor, school **07** droshky, grinder, hackney, minibus, prepare, railbus, rattler, tally-ho, teacher, trainer **08** barouche, brougham, carriage, educator, instruct, motor-bus **09** battlebus, buffet car, cabriolet, charabanc, Cobb and Co, Greyhound **10** four-in-hand, griddle car, instructor, motor-coach, répétiteur **12** express coach
*See also* **carriage**

**coagulate**
**03** gel, ren, rin, run, set **04** cake, clot, melt **06** curdle **07** clotted, clotter, congeal, curdled, thicken **08** solidify

**coagulation**
**08** clotting **10** congealing, thickening **11** solidifying

**coal**
**03** jet, jud, nut **04** char, jeat, smut **05** dross, ember, small **06** cinder, splint **07** lignite **10** anthracite **13** black diamonds
• **coal dust** **04** coom, culm, duff
• **coal scuttle** **03** hod **09** purdonium
• **coal yard** **03** ree **04** reed

**coalesce**
**03** mix **04** fuse, join **05** blend, merge, unite **06** cohere, commix **07** combine **09** affiliate, commingle, integrate **10** amalgamate **11** consolidate, incorporate **12** join together

**coalescence**
**06** fusion, merger **07** mixture **08** blending **09** immixture **11** affiliation, combination, integration **12** amalgamation, concrescence **13** consolidation, incorporation

**coalition**
**04** bloc **05** union **06** fusion, league, merger **07** compact, joining **08** alliance **10** federation **11** affiliation, association, combination, confederacy, conjunction, integration, partnership **12** amalgamation **13** confederation

**coarse**
**03** ham **04** base, blue, rank, rude **05** bawdy, broad, brute, crass, crude, gross, hairy, harsh, lumpy, rough, rudas, scaly **06** blowsy, blowzy, brutal, common, earthy, incult, ribald, ribaud, rugged, shaggy, smutty, uneven, vulgar **07** abusive, boorish, bristly, loutish, obscene, prickly, raunchy, rybauld, uncivil **08** gorblimy, immodest, impolite, improper, indecent, inferior, porterly, unbolted **09** gorblimey, off-colour, offensive, unrefined **10** indelicate, unfinished, unpolished, unpurified **11** foul-mouthed, ill-mannered, unprocessed

**coarsely**
**06** rudely **07** bawdily, crudely, roughly **08** ruggedly, unevenly, vulgarly **09** boorishly, loutishly, obscenely **10** immodestly, impolitely, improperly, indecently **11** irregularly, offensively

**coarsen**
**04** dull **05** blunt **06** deaden, harden **07** roughen, thicken **08** indurate **11** desensitize

**coarseness**
**04** smut **06** raunch **07** crudity, hoggery **08** ribaldry **09** bawdiness, hairiness, immodesty, indecency, obscenity, roughness, vulgarism, vulgarity **10** crassitude, earthiness, indelicacy, ruggedness, smuttiness, unevenness **11** grossièreté, prickliness **12** irregularity **13** offensiveness

**coast**
**04** cost, sail, side, taxi **05** beach, coste, drift, glide, limit, shore, slide, terms **06** border, cruise, region, strand **07** footing, seaside **08** littoral, seaboard, seashore **09** coastline, direction, foreshore, freewheel
• **coast road** **04** prom

## coaster
**04** grab **05** doily, doyly, smack
**07** beermat

## coat
**04** cake, daub, film, hair, hide, mack, pave, pelt, skin, wool **05** apply, cover, glaze, layer, paint, put on, quote, sheet, skirt, smear **06** clothe, enamel, finish, mantle, spread, veneer
**07** coating, encrust, overlay, plaster, put over, varnish **08** cladding, covering, laminate, pellicle
**10** integument, lamination

*Coats include:*

**03** box, car, fur, mac
**04** baju, buff, cape, jack, jump, maxi, midi, over, pink, rain, sack, tail, warm
**05** acton, cimar, cloak, cymar, drape, dress, frock, gilet, great, grego, jupon, lammy, loden, parka, sayon, wamus
**06** achkan, Afghan, anorak, Basque, blazer, bolero, cagoul, covert, dolman, duffel, fleece, jacket, jerkin, kagool, kagoul, kirtle, lammie, poncho, reefer, riding, sacque, sports, tabard, taberd, trench, tuxedo, ulster, Zouave
**07** Barbour®, blanket, blouson, cagoule, cutaway, kagoule, Mae West, matinée, morning, overall, snorkel, surtout, swagger, vareuse, zamarra, zamarro
**08** Burberry®, camisole, gambeson, haqueton, mackinaw, sherwani
**09** bed jacket, gabardine, gaberdine, hacqueton, macintosh, Mao-jacket, newmarket, pea-jacket, petticoat, redingote, shortgown
**10** body-warmer, bumfreezer, bush jacket, carmagnole, claw-hammer, Eton jacket, flak jacket, half-kirtle, life jacket, mackintosh, mess jacket, roundabout, windjammer
**11** biker jacket, puffa jacket, shell jacket, swallowtail, Windbreaker®, windcheater
**12** bomber jacket, combat jacket, dinner jacket, donkey jacket, lumberjacket, monkey jacket, Prince Albert, pyjama jacket, safari jacket, sports jacket, straitjacket
**13** hacking jacket, matinee jacket, Norfolk jacket, reefing-jacket
**14** shooting jacket

## coating
**03** fur **04** coat, film, skin, wash **05** crust, glaze, layer, sheet **06** crusta, enamel, finish, patina, resist, slough, veneer
**07** blanket, dusting, overlay, varnish, washing **08** covering, membrane
**10** colourwash, lamination, pebbledash

## coax
**03** pet **04** draw, wile **05** carny, tempt
**06** allure, cajole, carney, entice, fleech, humour, induce, soothe
**07** beguile, cuittle, flatter, wheedle, win over **08** blandish, collogue, get

round, inveigle, persuade, soft-soap, talk into, win round **09** sweet-talk, whillywha **10** whillywhaw **11** prevail upon

## cobalt
**02** Co

## cobber
*see* **friend**

## cobble
**04** pave
• **cobble together 07** knock up
**09** improvise **11** make quickly, make roughly, put together **13** throw together **14** prepare quickly, prepare roughly, produce quickly, produce roughly

## cobbler
**04** snab, snob **05** sutor **06** cosier, cozier, soutar, souter, sowter

## cobblers
*see* **rubbish**

## cobra
**03** asp **04** naga, Naia, Naja **05** aspic
**09** hamadryad

## cocaine
**01** C **04** blow, coke, snow **05** candy, crack **07** charlie, crystal **08** freebase
**09** nose candy, ready-wash **10** white stuff

## cock
**03** dog, tap, tip **04** bend, lift, tilt
**05** capon, henny, point, raise, slant, strut **07** chicken, gobbler, incline, rooster, swagger **08** cockerel, nonsense, shake-bag **10** bubbly-jock, roadrunner **11** chanticleer, game-chicken
• **cock up** ◇ *anagram indicator* **04** hash, muff, ruin **05** bodge, farce, fluff
**06** bungle, foul up, mess up, muck up
**07** blunder, screw up **08** shambles
**11** make a hash of, make a mess of

## cockeyed
**04** awry, daft **05** askew, barmy, crazy, tipsy **06** absurd **07** crooked **08** lopsided
**09** half-baked, ludicrous, senseless, skew-whiff **11** nonsensical
**12** asymmetrical, preposterous

## cockily
**08** cheekily **10** impudently, insolently
**13** impertinently **15** disrespectfully

## Cockney
◇ *dialect indicator* **04** 'Arry **06** 'Arriet
**09** Londonese **10** pearly king **11** pearly queen

## cocksure
**04** vain **05** brash, cocky **08** arrogant
**09** conceited **10** swaggering
**11** egotistical, self-assured, swell-headed **13** overconfident, self-confident, self-important, swollen-headed

## cocktail
◇ *anagram indicator*

*Cocktails include:*

**04** Sour
**05** Bronx
**06** eggnog, Gimlet, Mai tai, mimosa, mojito, Rickey, Rob Roy

**07** Bellini, Collins, Martini®, negroni, pink gin, Sazerac®, Sidecar, Slammer, Stinger
**08** Acapulco, Brown Cow, Bullshot, Daiquiri, Pink Lady, salty dog, snowball
**09** buck's fizz, Kir Royale, long vodka, Manhattan, Margarita, pisco sour, Rusty Nail, Sea Breeze, whisky mac, White Lady
**10** Bloody Mary, blue lagoon, Caipirinha, Horse's Neck, margharita, Moscow Mule, piña colada, Tom Collins, whisky sour
**11** black velvet, gin-and-tonic, gloom raiser, grasshopper, Screwdriver
**12** Black Russian, Cosmopolitan, Old Fashioned, White Russian
**13** Planter's Punch
**14** American Beauty, Singapore Sling, tequila slammer, Tequila Sunrise
**15** Brandy Alexander

*See also* **liqueur; spirits**

## cocky
**04** pert, vain **05** brash, perky **06** bouncy
**08** arrogant, cocksure, jumped-up
**09** bumptious, conceited, hubristic
**10** swaggering **11** egotistical, self-assured **13** overconfident, self-confident, self-important, swollen-headed

## cocoon
**03** pod **04** wrap **05** cover **06** defend, dupion, swathe **07** cushion, envelop, isolate, protect **08** cloister, insulate, preserve **11** overprotect

## coddle
**03** pet **04** baby **05** spoil **06** cosher, cosset, humour, pamper **07** indulge, protect **11** mollycoddle, overprotect

## code
◇ *anagram indicator* **03** law **04** laws
**05** codex, fuero, Morse, rules, signs
**06** cipher, codify, custom, cypher, ethics, morals, system, volume **07** bar code, conduct, letters, manners, numbers, symbols, zip code
**08** morality, postcode, practice
**09** etiquette, iddy-umpty, local code, Morse code **10** convention, cryptogram, postal code, principles
**11** cryptograph, machine code, regulations **12** dialling code, national code **13** secret message, secret writing **14** secret language

## codify
**05** group, order **06** digest **07** marshal, sort out **08** classify, organize
**09** catalogue **11** systematize

## coerce
**05** bully, drive, force **06** compel, lean on **07** dragoon **08** bludgeon, browbeat, bulldoze, pressure, railroad, threaten, use force **09** constrain, pressgang, strongarm **10** intimidate, pressurize
**14** put the screws on

## coercion
**04** heat **05** force **06** duress **07** duresse, threats **08** big stick, bullying, pressure

**09** restraint **10** compulsion, constraint **11** arm-twisting, browbeating **12** direct action, intimidation

## coffee
**03** joe

---

*Coffee roasts and blends include:*

**04** Java
**05** decaf
**06** filter, ground, Kenyan
**07** Arabica, instant
**09** Colombian, dark roast
**10** Costa Rican, light roast, percolated
**11** French roast
**12** Blue Mountain
**13** decaffeinated

---

*Coffees include:*

**05** black, Irish, latte, milky, Mocha, white
**06** filter, Gaelic
**07** Turkish
**08** café noir, espresso
**09** Americano, cafetière, demitasse, macchiato
**10** café au lait, café filtre, cappuccino
**11** skinny latte

---

• **coffee house 04** cafe, caff

## coffer
**03** ark, box **04** case, cash, safe **05** chest, funds, hoard, means, money, store, trunk **06** assets, casket, wealth **07** backing, capital, coffret, finance, lacunar **08** moneybox, treasury **09** resources, strongbox **10** repository

## coffin
**03** box **04** kist **05** flask, shell **06** casket, larnax **11** sarcophagus **12** pine overcoat, wooden kimono **14** wooden overcoat

## cogency
**05** force, power **06** weight **07** potency, urgency **08** strength **09** influence **12** forcefulness, plausibility **13** effectiveness

## cogent
**06** potent, strong, urgent **07** weighty **08** forceful, forcible, powerful, pregnant **09** effective **10** compelling, conclusive, convincing, persuasive **11** influential **12** irresistible, unanswerable

## cogently
**08** forcibly, potently, strongly, urgently **10** forcefully, powerfully **11** effectively **12** compellingly, conclusively, convincingly, persuasively

## cogitate
**04** mull, muse **06** ponder **07** reflect **08** consider, meditate, mull over, ruminate **09** cerebrate **10** deliberate **11** contemplate, think deeply

## cognate
**03** cog **04** akin **05** alike **06** agnate, allied, kinred **07** kindred, related, similar **09** analogous, conjugate, connected **10** affiliated, associated,

congeneric **11** consanguine **13** corresponding

## cognition
**06** reason **07** insight **08** learning, thinking **09** awareness, knowledge, reasoning **10** perception **11** discernment, rationality **12** apprehension, intelligence **13** comprehension, consciousness, enlightenment, understanding

## cognizance
• **take cognizance of 06** accept, regard **09** recognize **11** acknowledge **12** take notice of **13** become aware of

## cognizant
**05** aware **06** versed **07** witting **08** acknowne, apprised, familiar, informed **09** conscious **10** acquainted, conversant **13** knowledgeable

## cohabit
**03** bed **06** occupy **07** company, shack up **08** live with **09** live in sin, live tally **12** live together **13** sleep together

## cohere
**04** bind, fuse, hold **05** add up, agree, cling, stick, unite **06** adhere, square **07** combine **08** coalesce **09** harmonize, make sense **10** correspond **11** consolidate **12** be consistent, hang together, hold together

## coherence
**05** sense, union, unity **07** harmony **09** agreement, congruity, connexion **10** connection, consonance, logicality **11** concordance, consistency **14** correspondence

## coherent
**05** clear, lucid **07** logical, orderly **08** joined-up, rational, reasoned, sensible **09** connected, organized **10** articulate, consistent, meaningful, systematic **11** well-planned **12** intelligible **14** comprehensible, well-structured

## cohesion
**05** sense, union, unity, whole **07** harmony **09** agreement **10** connection, solidarity **11** consistency **12** togetherness **14** correspondence

## cohesive
**05** close **06** joined, united **08** coherent, together **09** connected, tenacious **10** continuous **12** interrelated

## cohort
**03** lot, set **04** band, body, mate, unit **05** batch, buddy, class, group, squad, troop **06** column, legion **07** bracket, brigade, company, partner **08** category, division, follower, myrmidon, regiment, sidekick, squadron **09** assistant, associate, companion, supporter **10** accomplice, contingent **11** combination **14** categorization, classification

## coil
**04** clew, clue, curl, fake, fank, fuss, hank, loop, ring, roll, turn, wind **05** bight, choke, helix, noise, round, skein, snake, spire, twine, twirl, twist,

whorl, wring **06** bought, hubbub, spiral, toroid, tumult, wreath, writhe **07** entwine, primary, rouleau, wreathe **08** solenoid, volution **09** convolute, corkscrew **11** convolution

## coin
**04** bean, cash, cast, dump, mint **05** forge, money, piece, quoin, stamp **06** change, create, devise, invent, make up, silver, specie, strike **07** dream up, produce, think up **08** brockage, conceive, hard cash **09** fabricate, formulate, hard money, neologize, originate **10** lucky-piece **11** cornerstone, loose change, small change

*See also* **currency**

---

*Coins include:*

**02** as, at, xu
**03** bit, bob, cob, dam, écu, esc, fen, hao, joe, mag, mil, mna, moy, ore, pul, pya, rap, sen, sol, sou, ure, zuz
**04** anna, buck, cent, chon, dime, doit, duro, fals, fils, jane, jiao, joey, kuru, lion, lwei, maik, make, merk, mina, mite, mule, obol, para, paul, peni, quid, real, rial, ryal, sent, tael, zack
**05** angel, baisa, bodle, brock, brown, butut, conto, copec, crown, ducat, eagle, gerah, gopik, groat, khoum, kopek, laari, lepta, livre, louis, mopus, noble, obang, paolo, pence, penny, piece, pound, royal, scudo, scute, stamp, taler, thebe, unite
**06** aureus, bezant, boddle, copeck, copper, denier, dirham, dollar, double, escudo, florin, guinea, hansel, kopeck, nickel, obolus, pagoda, pesewa, satang, sequin, stater, talent, tanner, thaler
**07** austral, carolus, centavo, centime, centimo, chetrum, crusado, drachma, guilder, ha'penny, jacobus, moidore, Pfennig, piastre, pistole, pollard, quarter, sextant, solidus, spanker
**08** denarius, doubloon, ducatoon, farthing, Groschen, half anna, half mark, imperial, louis d'or, millième, napoleon, new penny, picayune, qindarka, sesterce, shilling, sixpence, solidare, stotinka, ten pence, two pence, two pound
**09** centesimo, dandiprat, five pence, gold crown, gold penny, half-crown, half groat, halfpenny, pound coin, sovereign, yellow-boy
**10** broadpiece, fifty pence, half florin, half guinea, Krugerrand, sestertius
**11** bonnet-piece, double eagle, sixpenny bit, spade guinea, twenty pence, twopenny bit
**12** antoninianus, silver dollar, two pound coin
**13** brass farthing, half sovereign, quarter dollar, sixpenny piece, ten pence piece, tenpenny piece,

threepenny bit, two pence piece, twopenny piece
**14** five pence piece
**15** fifty pence piece, threepenny piece

• **counterfeit coin** **03** rag **04** shan, slip **05** shand **06** doctor, duffer, stumer
• **material for coin** **04** flan
• **supposed coin** **03** moy

## coincide
**05** agree, clash, match, tally **06** accord, concur, square **07** coexist **09** be the same, harmonize **10** correspond **11** synchronize **14** happen together

## coincidence
**04** luck, step **05** clash, fluke **06** chance **08** accident, clashing, conflict, fortuity, synastry **11** coexistence, concurrence, conjunction, consilience, correlation, eventuality, serendipity, synchronism **12** simultaneity **13** synchronicity **14** correspondence **15** synchronization

## coincident
**04** like **05** alike, close **07** related, similar, the same **09** in harmony **10** coexisting, coinciding, comparable, concurrent, consistent, equivalent **11** coterminous, in agreement **12** conterminous, simultaneous **13** corresponding **15** contemporaneous

## coincidental
**05** lucky **06** casual, chance, flukey **09** unplanned **10** accidental, fortuitous **13** serendipitous, unintentional

## coincidentally
**07** luckily **08** by chance **12** accidentally **15** unintentionally

## coke
*see* **cocaine**

## cold
**01** c **03** ice, icy, raw **04** brrr, cool, dead, jeel, keen, numb, rimy, rume, snow **05** agued, aloof, bleak, cauld, chill, fremd, fresh, frore, frost, gelid, nippy, parky, polar, rheum, stony **06** arctic, biting, bitter, brumal, chilly, frigid, frosty, frozen, numbed, remote, winter, wintry **07** brumous, callous, catarrh, chilled, cutting, distant, glacial, hostile, ice-cold, iciness, rawness, shivery, unmoved **08** clinical, coldness, coolness, freezing, lukewarm, reserved, Siberian, uncaring, unheated **09** chillness, frigidity, heartless, repulsive, unfeeling **10** chilliness, Decemberly, impersonal, phlegmatic, spiritless, unfriendly **11** Decemberish, indifferent, insensitive, passionless, standoffish, unemotional, unexcitable **12** antagonistic, unresponsive **13** unsympathetic **15** undemonstrative
• **cold and wet** **04** sour

## cold-blooded
**05** cruel **06** brutal, savage **07** callous, inhuman **08** barbaric, pitiless, ruthless **09** barbarous, heartless, merciless, unfeeling **10** iron-headed **14** poikilothermal, poikilothermic

## cold-hearted
**04** cold **06** flinty, unkind **07** callous, inhuman **08** detached, uncaring **09** heartless, unfeeling **10** iron-headed **11** indifferent, insensitive **12** stony-hearted **13** unsympathetic **15** uncompassionate

## coldly
**09** callously **11** heartlessly, unfeelingly **13** insensitively, unemotionally

## colic
**03** bot **04** bott **05** batts **10** mulligrubs

## collaborate
**04** join **05** unite **06** assist, betray, team up **07** collude **08** conspire **09** co-operate **10** fraternize, join forces **11** participate, turn traitor, work jointly **12** work together **13** associate with, combine forces **14** work as partners

## collaboration
**05** union **08** alliance, teamwork **09** collusion **10** conspiring **11** association, co-operation, joint effort, partnership **12** fraternizing **13** participation **14** combined effort

## collaborator
**07** partner, traitor **08** betrayer, colluder, co-worker, quisling, renegade, teammate, turncoat **09** assistant, associate, colleague **10** accomplice **11** conspirator, fraternizer **12** fellow worker

## collapse
◇ *anagram indicator* **03** rot **04** blow, bust, fail, fall, flop, fold, ruin, sink **05** break, close, faint, slump, swoon **06** attack, cave in, cave-in, fall in, finish, fold up, go bung, tumble **07** burst-up, crack up, crumble, crumple, debacle, deflate, failure, founder, give way, pancake, pass out, sinking, subside **08** black out, blackout, downfall, fainting, fall down, flake out, keel over **09** break down, breakdown, come apart, fall about, fall apart, falling-in, giving way **10** concertina, foundering, go to pieces, passing-out, subsidence **11** come to an end, coming apart, falling-down, fall through, go to the wall, keeling-over, lose control **12** disintegrate, fall to pieces **13** come to nothing, loss of control **14** disintegration, falling-through, have a breakdown **15** falling to pieces

## collar
**03** bag, nab **04** band, bust, grab, nick, ring, stop **05** catch, seize **06** arrest, haul in **07** capture **08** neckband **09** apprehend

*Collars include:*

**03** dog
**04** Eton, flea, roll, ruff, wing
**05** horse, ox-bow, shawl, steel, storm, whisk
**06** bertha, choker, collet, gorget, jampot, rabato, rebato
**07** brecham, partlet, rebater, stick-up, tie-neck, vandyke
**08** carcanet, clerical, granddad,

mandarin, Peter Pan, polo neck, rabatine, turn-down
**09** holderbat, piccadell, piccadill
**10** chevesaile, piccadillo, piccadilly
**11** falling band
**12** mousquetaire

## collate
**04** edit, sort **05** order **06** gather **07** arrange, collect, compare, compile, compose **08** organize **10** put in order **11** put together

## collateral
**05** funds, rival **06** pledge, surety **07** deposit **08** security **09** assurance, guarantee **10** additional, subsidiary **12** contemporary **13** corresponding

## collation
**07** editing **08** ordering **09** gathering **11** arrangement, compilation, composition **12** organization **15** putting together

## colleague
**04** aide, ally, mate **06** helper, winger **07** comrade, partner **08** confrère, conspire, co-worker, teammate, workmate **09** assistant, associate, auxiliary, bedfellow, companion **11** confederate **12** collaborator, fellow worker

## collect
◇ *containment indicator* **03** get **04** form, heap, mass, meet, save **05** amass, fetch, hoard, rally **06** gather, make up, muster, pick up, pile up, semble, take up, uplift **07** acquire, call for, come for, compose, convene, prepare, recover, solicit **08** assemble, converge, go and get **09** aggregate, go and take, stockpile **10** accumulate, congregate, go and bring, raise money **11** ask for money **12** come together, have as a hobby **14** be interested in, gather together **15** ask people to give

## collected
◇ *anagram indicator* ◇ *insertion indicator* **04** calm, cool **06** placid, poised, serene **07** unfazed **08** composed, unshaken **09** unruffled **10** controlled **11** unflappable, unperturbed **13** imperturbable, self-possessed **14** self-controlled

## collection
◇ *anagram indicator* **03** set **04** gift, heap, mass, pack, pile, sort **05** gifts, group, hoard, plate, store **06** basket, job-lot, rickle, series **07** boiling, cluster, variety **08** assembly, caboodle, donation, jingbang, offering **09** anthology, composure, congeries, donations, gathering, offertory, selection, stockpile, whip-round **10** assemblage, assortment **11** compilation, ingathering, olla-podrida **12** accumulation, conglomerate, contribution, subscription **13** contributions **14** collected works, conglomeration, omnium-gatherum

## collective
**05** joint **06** common, moshav, shared, united **07** commune, kibbutz, kolkhoz **08** combined **09** aggregate,

community, composite, concerted, corporate, gathering, unanimous **10** assemblage, cumulative, democratic **11** congregated, co-operative **13** collaborative

*Collective nouns for animals include:*

**03** **bed** (clams, oysters), **cry** (hounds), **gam** (whales), **mob** (kangaroos), **nid** (pheasants), **nye** (pheasants), **pod** (seals, whales)
**04** **army** (caterpillars, frogs), **bale** (turtles), **band** (gorillas), **bask** (crocodiles), **bevy** (larks, pheasants, quail, swans), **cete** (badgers), **dole** (doves, turtles), **erst** (bees), **herd** (buffalo, cattle, deer, elephants, goats, horses, kangaroos, oxen, seals, whales), **hive** (bees), **pace** (asses), **pack** (dogs, grouse, hounds, wolves), **romp** (otters), **rout** (wolves), **safe** (ducks), **span** (mules), **team** (ducks), **trip** (goats, sheep), **zeal** (zebras)
**05** **bloat** (hippopotami), **brace** (ducks), **brood** (chickens, hens), **charm** (finches, goldfinches), **covey** (partridges, quail), **crash** (rhinoceros), **drift** (hogs, swine), **drove** (cattle, horses, oxen, sheep), **flock** (birds, ducks, geese, sheep), **grist** (bees), **shoal** (fish), **siege** (cranes, herons), **skein** (geese), **swarm** (ants, bees, flies, locusts), **tower** (giraffes), **tribe** (goats), **troop** (baboons, kangaroos, monkeys), **watch** (nightingales), **wedge** (swans)
**06** **ambush** (tigers), **cackle** (hyenas), **colony** (ants, bees, penguins, rats), **gaggle** (geese), **kindle** (kittens), **labour** (moles), **litter** (kittens, pigs), **murder** (crows), **muster** (peacocks, penguins), **parade** (elephants), **parcel** (penguins), **rafter** (turkeys), **school** (dolphins, fish, porpoises, whales), **string** (horses, ponies), **tiding** (magpies)
**07** **bouquet** (pheasants), **clowder** (cats), **company** (parrots), **prickle** (porcupines), **turmoil** (porpoises)
**08** **building** (rooks), **mischief** (mice), **paddling** (ducks)
**09** **intrusion** (cockroaches), **mustering** (storks), **obstinacy** (buffalo)
**10** **exaltation** (larks), **parliament** (owls, rooks), **shrewdness** (apes), **unkindness** (ravens)
**11** **convocation** (eagles), **murmuration** (starlings), **ostentation** (peacocks), **pandemonium** (parrots)
**12** **congregation** (plovers)

## collector

*Collectors and enthusiasts include:*

**05** gamer
**07** gourmet
**08** neophile, zoophile
**09** antiquary, cinephile, ex-librist, logophile, oenophile, philomath, xenophile
**10** arctophile, audiophile, cartophile, discophile, ephemerist, gastronome,

hippophile, monarchist
**11** ailurophile, balletomane, bibliophile, canophilist, etymologist, notaphilist, numismatist, oenophilist, philatelist, scripophile, technophile, toxophilite
**12** ailourophile, cartophilist, coleopterist, Dantophilist, deltiologist, entomologist, incunabulist, ophiophilist, phillumenist, stegophilist
**13** arachnologist, campanologist, chirographist, lepidopterist, ornithologist, tegestologist, timbrophilist
**14** cruciverbalist
**15** conservationist, stigmatophilist

## college

**01** c **04** coll, Eton, hall, poly, tech
**06** lyceum, prison, school **07** academy, madrasa **08** madrasah, madrassa, seminary **09** institute, madrassah, medresseh **10** high school, university
**11** polytechnic

*See also* **educational; university**

*Colleges and halls of Cambridge University:*

**05** Clare, Jesus, King's
**06** Darwin, Girton, Queens', Selwyn
**07** Christ's, Downing, New Hall, Newnham, St John's, Trinity, Wolfson
**08** Emmanuel, Homerton, Pembroke, Robinson
**09** Churchill, Clare Hall, Magdalene, St Edmund's
**10** Hughes Hall, Peterhouse
**11** Fitzwilliam, Trinity Hall
**12** Sidney Sussex, St Catharine's
**13** Corpus Christi, Lucy Cavendish
**16** Gonville and Caius

*Colleges and halls of Oxford University:*

**03** New
**05** Green, Jesus, Keble, Oriel
**06** Exeter, Merton, Queen's, Wadham
**07** Balliol, Kellogg, Linacre, Lincoln, St Anne's, St Cross, St Hugh's, St John's, Trinity, Wolfson
**08** All Souls, Hertford, Magdalen, Nuffield, Pembroke, St Hilda's, St Peter's
**09** Brasenose, Mansfield, St Antony's, Templeton, The Queen's, Worcester
**10** Somerville, University
**11** Campion Hall, Regent's Park
**12** Christ Church, St Benet's Hall, St Catherine's, St Edmund Hall, Wycliffe Hall
**13** Corpus Christi
**14** Greyfriars Hall
**15** Blackfriars Hall, St Stephen's House
**16** Harris Manchester, Lady Margaret Hall

- **at college** **02** up
- **college head** **04** dean
- **college square** **04** quad

## collide

**03** hit, war **04** bump, feud, foul
**05** clash, crash, fight, prang, smash
**06** cannon, go into **07** contend, grapple, quarrel, run into, wrangle
**08** bump into, conflict, disagree
**09** crash into, smash into **10** meet head on, plough into **12** be in conflict

## collision

**04** bump, feud **05** brush, clash, crash, fight, prang, shunt, smash, wreck
**06** impact, pile-up **07** quarrel, warring, wrangle **08** accident, clashing, conflict, disaster, fighting, showdown
**09** rencontre **10** opposition, rencounter
**12** disagreement, fender bender
**13** confrontation

## colloid

**03** gel, sol **08** emulsoid **10** suspensoid
**11** carrageenan, carrageenin
**12** carragheenin

## colloquial

**06** casual, chatty **07** demotic, popular
**08** everyday, familiar, informal
**09** idiomatic **10** vernacular
**14** conversational

## colloquially

**09** popularly **10** familiarly, informally

## collude

**04** plot **06** scheme **07** connive
**08** conspire, intrigue **09** machinate
**11** be in cahoots, collaborate

## collusion

**04** plot **06** deceit, league, scheme
**07** cahoots **08** artifice, intrigue, scheming **10** complicity, connivance, conspiracy **11** machination
**13** collaboration

## Colombia

**02** CO **03** COL

## colonist

**04** boor **05** colon **07** new chum, pioneer, planter, settler **08** colonial, emigrant, Siceliot, Sikeliot
**09** colonizer, immigrant, inhabiter
**12** Australasian

*See also* **governor**

## colonize

**05** found, plant **06** occupy, people, settle **07** pioneer **08** populate

## colonnade

**04** stoa **05** porch **06** arcade, xystus
**07** eustyle, portico **08** diastyle
**09** areostyle, cloisters, peristyle
**10** araeostyle **11** covered walk
**12** columniation

## colony

**04** hive **05** apery, group, swarm
**07** outpost **08** dominion, province
**09** coenobium, community, formicary, hydrosoma, hydrosome, polyzoary, satellite, territory **10** dependency, plantation, possession, settlement
**11** association, formicarium, polyzoarium **12** protectorate
**14** satellite state

## Colorado

**02** CO **04** Colo

## colossal
**04** huge, vast **05** great, jumbo
**07** immense, mammoth, massive
**08** enormous, gigantic, whopping
**09** herculean, monstrous
**10** gargantuan, monumental
**14** Brobdingnagian

## colossus
**04** ogre **05** giant, titan **07** Cyclops, Goliath, monster **08** Hercules

## colour
**03** dye, hew, hue, ink, kit **04** bias, flag, glow, kick, leer, life, race, sway, tint, tone, wash **05** badge, blush, flush, get-up, go red, oomph, paint, shade, slant, stain, strip, taint, tinge **06** affect, banner, crayon, emblem, ensign, reason, redden, tackle, timbre **07** distort, falsify, pervert, pigment, pizzazz, pretext, redness, turn red, variety **08** clothing, colorant, disguise, insignia, pinkness, richness, rosiness, standard, tincture **09** animation, highlight, influence, overstate, prejudice, ruddiness, vividness **10** appearance, brilliance, coloration, complexion, exaggerate, liveliness, skin colour **11** ethnic group, nationality, racial group **12** misrepresent, pigmentation, plausibility

*Colours include:*

**03** dun, jet, red, sky, tan
**04** anil, blae, blue, buff, cyan, dove, drab, ecru, fawn, gold, gray, grey, guly, hoar, jade, navy, opal, pink, plum, puce, roan, rose, rosy, ruby, rust, sage, sand, wine
**05** amber, beige, black, brown, coral, cream, ebony, flame, green, khaki, lemon, lilac, mauve, milky, ochre, peach, sepia, taupe, topaz, umber, white
**06** auburn, bottle, bronze, canary, cerise, cherry, cobalt, copper, indigo, maroon, orange, purple, salmon, silver, violet, yellow
**07** apricot, avocado, crimson, emerald, gentian, magenta, saffron, scarlet
**08** burgundy, charcoal, chestnut, cinnamon, eau de nil, lavender, magnolia, mahogany, sapphire
**09** aubergine, chocolate, nile green, tangerine, turquoise, vermilion
**10** aquamarine, chartreuse, cobalt blue, grass-green
**11** burnt sienna, lemon yellow

*See also* **black; blue; dye; green; grey; orange; pigment; pink; purple; rainbow; red; white; yellow**
• **lose colour 04** fade, pale

## coloured
**01** C **09** chromatic

## colourful
**03** gay **04** deep, rich **05** gaudy, vivid **06** bright, garish, lively **07** graphic, intense, vibrant **08** animated, exciting **09** brilliant **10** flamboyant, polychrome, variegated **11** interesting, picturesque, stimulating **12** many-

coloured **13** kaleidoscopic, multicoloured, parti-coloured

## colourfully
**08** brightly **09** intensely, vibrantly **11** brilliantly

## colourless
**03** wan **04** drab, dull, fade, grey, pale, tame **05** ashen, bleak, faded, plain, white **06** boring, dreary, sickly **07** anaemic, insipid, neutral **08** bleached **09** washed out **10** lacklustre, monochrome, uncoloured **11** transparent, unmemorable **13** characterless, uninteresting **14** complexionless **15** in black and white

## colt
**01** c **04** beat, cade, stag **05** staig **06** hogget

## Columbia
*see* **British; District of Columbia** *under* **district**

## column
**03** col, row **04** anta, file, item, line, list, pier, pole, post, rank **05** Atlas, pillar, queue, shaft, story **06** parade, pillar, string **07** article, columel, feature, obelisk, support, telamon, upright **08** caryatid, pilaster **10** procession
• **shaft of column 04** fust, tige **05** scape, trunk **06** scapus

## columnist
**06** critic, editor, writer **08** reporter, reviewer **10** journalist **11** contributor **13** correspondent

## coma
**03** PVS **05** sopor **06** stupor, torpor, trance **08** hypnosis, lethargy, oblivion **09** catalepsy **10** drowsiness, somnolence **13** insensibility **15** unconsciousness

## comatose
**03** out **05** dazed **06** drowsy, sleepy, torpid, zonked **07** in a coma, out cold, stunned **08** sluggish, soporose **09** lethargic, somnolent, stupefied **10** cataleptic, insensible **11** unconscious

## comb
**03** red **04** card, hunt, kaim, kame, kemb, rake, redd, sift, tidy, tose, toze **05** combe, coomb, crest, dress, groom, scour, sweep, tease, toaze, trawl **06** coombe, hackle, kangha, neaten, screen, search **07** arrange, explore, ransack, rummage **08** scribble, untangle **09** go through **11** disentangle **14** turn upside down

## combat
**03** war **04** agon, bout, defy, duel **05** clash, fight, lists **06** action, battle, debate, oppose, resist, strive **07** contend, contest, wage war, warfare **08** conflict, do battle, fighting, skirmish, struggle **09** encounter, monomachy, rencontre, withstand **10** engagement, rencounter, take up arms **11** hostilities
• **unarmed combat 04** judo **06** karate **07** ju-jitsu **08** jiu-jitsu

## combatant
**05** enemy **07** fighter, soldier, warrior **08** opponent **09** adversary, contender, gladiator **10** antagonist, batteilant, serviceman **11** belligerent, protagonist **12** servicewoman

## combative
**06** bantam **07** hawkish, warlike, warring **08** militant **09** agonistic, bellicose, truculent **10** aggressive, pugnacious **11** adversarial, belligerent, contentious, quarrelsome **12** antagonistic **13** argumentative

## combination
**03** mix **04** club **05** blend, cross, group, union **06** fusion, merger **07** amalgam, combine, mixture, synergy **08** alliance, clubbing, compound, junction, solution **09** coalition, composite, syndicate, synthesis **10** collection, conflation, connection, consortium, federation **11** association, coalescence, composition, confederacy, conjunction, co-operation, integration, unification **12** amalgamation, co-ordination **13** confederation

## combine
**03** mix **04** ally, bind, bond, club, fuse, join, link, meld, pool, stir, weld **05** admix, alloy, blend, marry, merge, piece, trust, unify, unite **06** mingle, team up **07** conjoin, connect **08** compound, conflate, cumulate, restrict **09** associate, coadunate, co-operate, integrate, syndicate **10** amalgamate, homogenize, join forces, synthesize **11** incorporate, put together **12** club together **13** bring together
• **combined 08** together
• **combined with 03** cum

## combustible
◇ *anagram indicator* **05** tense **06** ardent, stormy **07** charged **08** volatile **09** excitable, explosive, flammable, ignitable, sensitive **10** incendiary, phlogistic **11** inflammable

## combustion
**06** firing **07** burning **08** igniting, ignition
• **internal combustion 02** IC

## come
**02** be **04** gain, hail, near, stem, turn **05** arise, enter, issue, occur, reach, yield **06** allons, appear, arrive, attain, attend, become, climax, dawn on, evolve, follow, happen, secure, show up, strike, turn up **07** achieve, advance, barge in, burst in, develop, get here, occur to, surface, think of **08** approach, draw near, get there, pass into, remember **09** be on offer, come about, go as far as, originate, take place, transpire **10** be caused by, be produced, come to pass, evolve into, move nearer, result from **11** be a native of, be available, develop into, materialize, move forward, move towards **13** be on the market, present itself, reach an orgasm, travel towards **14** have as your home **15** come to the mind of, have as its origin,

have as its source

- **come about** 04 fall, sort 05 arise, occur 06 arrive, befall, happen, result 09 take place, transpire 10 come to pass
- **come across** 04 find, meet, seem 06 appear, notice 07 run into 08 bump into, come over, discover, meet in wi' 09 encounter 10 chance upon, happen upon, meet in with 11 communicate 12 find by chance, meet by chance 13 stumble across
- **come along** 04 mend 05 rally 06 arrive 07 advance, develop, hurry up, improve, recover 08 progress 09 get better, shake a leg 10 get a move on, recuperate 11 get cracking, make headway 12 make progress 15 get your skates on
- **come apart** 04 tear 05 break, split 07 break up, crumble 08 collapse, separate 10 fall to bits 12 disintegrate, fall to pieces
- **come back** ◇ *reversal indicator* 06 go back, remind, return 07 get back 08 come home, reappear 10 be recalled 11 be suggested 12 be remembered 13 be recollected
- **come between** 04 part 06 divide 07 split up 08 alienate, disunite, estrange, separate 09 interpose
- **come by** 03 get 05 visit 06 obtain, secure 07 acquire, procure 09 get hold of
- **come down** 04 drop, fall 05 avail, avale, light 06 availe, reduce, worsen 07 decline, descend 08 decrease, dismount 10 degenerate 11 deteriorate
- **come down on** 05 blame, chide, knock, slate 06 berate, rebuke 07 reprove, upbraid 08 admonish, tear into 09 criticize, reprehend, reprimand 13 find fault with
- **come down to** 04 mean 07 add up to 08 amount to 10 boil down to 12 correspond to 14 be equivalent to, be tantamount to
- **come down with** 03 get 05 catch 06 pick up 07 develop 08 contract 09 succumb to 10 go down with 11 fall ill with 13 become ill with
- **come forward** 05 offer 06 accede, step up 09 volunteer 11 step forward 13 offer yourself
- **come in** 05 enter 06 appear, arrive, entrez, finish, show up 07 receive
- **come in for** 03 get 04 bear 06 endure, suffer 07 receive, sustain, undergo 10 experience 13 be subjected to
- **come into** 04 heir 06 be left 07 acquire, inherit, receive 08 be heir to, contract
- **come off** 04 mend, work 05 end up, occur, rally, strip 06 appear, go well, happen, pay off, thrive 07 advance, develop, improve, proceed, recover, succeed, work out 08 progress 09 get better, take place 10 recuperate, take effect 11 be effective 12 be successful, make progress
- **come on** 03 via 04 mend 05 begin,

rally 06 allons, appear, thrive 07 advance, develop, improve, proceed, recover, succeed 08 progress 09 get better 10 recuperate 12 make progress
- **come out** 03 end 05 admit, end up, erupt, issue 06 appear, emerge, finish, result, strike 07 leak out 08 conclude 09 terminate 10 be produced, be released, be revealed 11 become known, be published, come to light 12 be made public 13 declare openly 15 become available
- **come out with** 03 say 05 state, utter 06 affirm 07 declare, divulge, exclaim 08 blurt out, disclose
- **come round** 04 veer, wake 05 agree, allow, awake, grant, occur, recur, visit, yield 06 accede, come to, happen, relent 07 concede, recover 08 reappear 09 be won over, take place 11 be persuaded 13 be converted to 14 change your mind
- **come through** 04 pass, ride 06 endure 07 achieve, prevail, ride out, succeed, survive, triumph 09 withstand 10 accomplish 11 pull through
- **come to** 04 make, stop, wake 05 awake, equal, run to, total 06 obtain 07 add up to, recover 08 amount to 09 aggregate, come round
- **come together** 03 gel 04 jell, meet 05 close, rally 07 collect, convene
- **come up** ◇ *reversal down indicator* 04 rise 05 arise, occur 06 appear, crop up, happen, turn up 13 present itself
- **come up to** 04 meet 05 equal, reach 08 approach, live up to 09 match up to 11 compare with, measure up to 12 make the grade
- **come up with** 05 offer 06 devise, submit 07 advance, dream up, present, produce, propose, suggest, think of 08 conceive 10 put forward

## comeback

05 rally 06 retort, return 07 revival 08 recovery 09 rejoinder 10 resurgence 12 reappearance 13 recrimination
- **make a comeback** ◇ *reversal indicator*

## comedian

03 wag, wit 05 clown, comic, joker 06 gagman 07 gagster 08 funny man, humorist 10 comedienne, funny woman 11 entertainer

*Comedians include:*

03 **Dee** (Jack), **Fry** (Stephen), **Lom** (Herbert), **Sim** (Alastair), **Wax** (Ruby)
04 **Cook** (Peter), **Dodd** (Ken), **Hill** (Benny), **Hill** (Harry), **Hope** (Bob), **Idle** (Eric), **Kaye** (Danny), **Marx** (Chico), **Marx** (Groucho), **Marx** (Harpo), **Marx** (Zeppo), **Sims** (Joan), **Tati** (Jacques), **Wise** (Ernie), **Wood** (Victoria)
05 **Abbot** (Russ), **Allen** (Dave), **Allen** (Woody), **Brand** (Jo), **Bruce** (Lenny), **Burns** (George), **Cosby** (Bill), **Davro** (Bobby), **Elton** (Ben), **Emery** (Dick), **Hardy** (Oliver),

**Henry** (Lenny), **Inman** (John), **James** (Sid), **Jones** (Terry), **Jones** (Griff Rhys), **Kempe** (Will), **Lewis** (Jerry), **Lloyd** (Harold), **Lucas** (Matt), **Moore** (Dudley), **Oddie** (Bill), **Palin** (Michael), **Pryor** (Richard), **Robey** (Sir George), **Sayle** (Alexei), **Smith** (Mel), **Starr** (Freddie), **Sykes** (Eric)
06 **Abbott** (Bud), **Bailey** (Bill), **Barker** (Ronnie), **Brooks** (Mel), **Cleese** (John), **Coogan** (Steve), **Cooper** (Tommy), **Dawson** (Les), **Fields** (W C), **French** (Dawn), **Garden** (Graeme), **Howerd** (Frankie), **Jordan** (Dorothy), **Keaton** (Buster), **Lauder** (Sir Harry), **Laurel** (Stan), **Laurie** (Hugh), **Martin** (Steve), **Mayall** (Rik), **Merton** (Paul), **Murphy** (Eddie), **Murray** (Bill), **Reeves** (Vic), **Ullman** (Tracey), **Wilder** (Gene), **Wisdom** (Norman)
07 **Aykroyd** (Dan), **Baddiel** (David), **Bentine** (Michael), **Bremner** (Rory), **Carrott** (Jasper), **Chaplin** (Charlie), **Chapman** (Graham), **Corbett** (Ronnie), **Deayton** (Angus), **Enfield** (Harry), **Everett** (Kenny), **Feldman** (Marty), **Gervais** (Ricky), **Hancock** (Tony), **Handley** (Tommy), **Jacques** (Hattie), **Manning** (Bernard), **Matthau** (Walter), **Newhart** (Bob), **Roscius**, **Secombe** (Harry), **Sellers** (Peter), **Tarbuck** (Jimmy), **Ustinov** (Sir Peter)
08 **Atkinson** (Rowan), **Coltrane** (Robbie), **Connolly** (Billy), **Coquelin** (Benoît Constant), **Costello** (Lou), **Grimaldi** (Joseph), **Milligan** (Spike), **Mitchell** (Warren), **Mortimer** (Bob), **Roseanne**, **Saunders** (Jennifer), **Seinfeld** (Jerry), **Sessions** (John), **The Goons**, **Walliams** (David), **Williams** (Kenneth), **Williams** (Robin)
09 **Edmondson** (Adrian), **Fernandel**, **Grossmith** (George), **Morecambe** (Eric), **Rhys Jones** (Griff), **Whitfield** (June)
10 **The Goodies**, **Whitehouse** (Paul)
11 **Monty Python**, **Terry-Thomas**
12 **Brooke-Taylor** (Tim)
14 **Laurel and Hardy**, **Little and Large**
15 **The Marx Brothers**

*See also* **actor, actress**

## comedown

04 blow 06 bathos 07 decline, descent, let-down, reverse 08 demotion, reversal 09 deflation 10 anticlimax 11 degradation, humiliation 14 disappointment

## comedy

03 com, fun 06 humour, joking 07 jesting 08 clowning, drollery, hilarity 09 funniness, pantomime 13 entertainment, facetiousness

*Comedy types include:*

03 gag, low, pun, wit
04 high, joke, sick
05 black, farce, Greek
06 modern, satire, sitcom, visual
07 musical, stand-up

## comely

**08** romantic
**09** burlesque, satirical, screwball, situation, slapstick
**10** comic opera, sketch show, television, theatrical, vaudeville
**11** alternative, Pythonesque, restoration, tragicomedy
**12** Chaplinesque, neoclassical
**13** Shakespearian
**15** comedy of humours, comedy of manners, improvisational, situation comedy

## comely

**04** fair, fine, tidy **05** ample, bonny, buxom, sonsy **06** bonnie, gainly, goodly, likely, lovely, pretty, proper, sonsie **07** sightly, winsome **08** blooming, graceful, handsome, pleasing **09** beautiful, excellent **10** attractive **11** good-looking **15** pulchritudinous

## come-on

**04** lure **10** allurement, attraction, enticement, inducement, persuasion, temptation **13** encouragement

## comet

*Comets include:*

**04** West, Wolf
**05** Cruls, Encke, Kirch, Mrkos, Tycho
**06** Donati, Halley, Lexell, Newton
**07** Bennett, Halley's, Humason, Tebbutt
**08** Daylight, Hale-Bopp, Kohoutek
**09** Hyakutake, Ikeya-Seki, Morehouse, Seki-Lines
**10** De Chéseaux, Flauergues, Great Comet
**11** Arend-Roland, Swift-Tuttle
**12** Pons-Winnecke
**13** Shoemaker-Levy
**14** Tago-Sato-Kosaka

## comeuppance

**04** dues **05** merit **06** rebuke **07** deserts **08** requital **10** chastening, punishment, recompense **11** just deserts, retribution **14** what you deserve

## comfort

**03** aid **04** cosy, cozy, ease, help, stay **05** cheer **06** luxury, plenty, relief, repose, solace, soothe **07** assuage, console, encheer, enliven, gladden, hearten, refresh, relieve, succour, support **08** cosiness, opulence, reassure, snugness **09** alleviate, empathize, encourage, enjoyment, recomfort, wellbeing **10** condolence, easy street, invigorate, relaxation, strengthen, sympathize **11** alleviation, consolation, contentment, reassurance **12** compensation, satisfaction **13** bring solace to, encouragement, Gemütlichkeit **15** freedom from pain, speak to the heart

## comfortable

**04** bein, bien, cosy, cozy, easy, lazy, safe, slow, snug, tosh, warm, well **05** comfy, cushy, happy, loose, roomy **06** at ease, couthy, gentle, homely, kindly, secure **07** couthie, opulent, relaxed, restful, well-off **08** affluent, armchair, carefree, homelike, laid-back, pleasant, relaxing, well-to-do **09** agreeable, confident, contented, enjoyable, gemütlich, leisurely, luxurious, rosewater, unhurried **10** commodious, convenient, delightful, prosperous **11** well-fitting **12** loose-fitting **13** unembarrassed
• **make yourself comfortable**
**04** cose

## comforting

**07** helpful **08** cheering, soothing **09** analeptic, consoling **10** heartening, reassuring **11** consolatory, encouraging, inspiriting **12** heartwarming

## comic

**03** wag, wit **04** card, rich, zany **05** buffo, clown, droll, funny, joker, light, witty **06** absurd, gagman, joking **07** amusing, buffoon, comical, gagster, jocular **08** comedian, farcical, funny man, humorist, humorous **09** diverting, facetious, hilarious, laughable, ludicrous, priceless **10** funny woman, ridiculous **11** entertainer **12** entertaining, knee-slapping **13** side-splitting

*Comics include:*

**03** Viz
**05** Beano, Bunty, Dandy
**08** The Beano, The Dandy, The Eagle

## comical

**05** droll, funny, witty **06** absurd **07** amusing **08** farcical, humorous **09** diverting, hilarious, laughable, ludicrous, quizzical **10** ridiculous **12** entertaining

## comically

**07** funnily, wittily **08** absurdly **09** amusingly **10** farcically, humorously **11** hilariously, ludicrously **12** ridiculously

## coming

**03** due **04** anon, dawn, near, next **05** birth **06** advent, future, rising **07** arrival, nearing **08** approach, aspiring, imminent, upcoming **09** accession, advancing, impending, promising **11** approaching, forthcoming, up-and-coming
• **coming out** **09** emergence

## command

**03** bid, get **04** fiat, gain, head, hest, lead, rule, sway, warn, will **05** edict, heast, order, power, reign **06** adjure, behest, behote, charge, compel, decree, demand, direct, enjoin, govern, heaste, impose, manage, obtain, secure **07** be given, beight, bidding, control, dictate, mandate, mastery, precept, receive, require **08** dominate, dominion, instruct, pleasure **09** authority, direction, directive, supervise **10** ascendancy, domination, government, injunction, leadership, management **11** commandment, instruction, preside over, requirement, superintend, supervision **12** be in charge of, give orders to **13** be in control of **15** superintendence

*Commands include:*

**03** hie, hup, hye
**04** easy, halt, high, mush
**05** be off, enter, gee up
**06** come by, entrez, gee hup, huddup
**07** give way
**08** eyes left
**09** eyes right, stand easy
**10** quick march
**12** be off with you
**15** stand and deliver

## commandeer

**04** take **05** press, seize, usurp **06** hijack **07** impound **08** arrogate **09** sequester **10** confiscate **11** appropriate, expropriate, requisition, sequestrate

## commander

**03** Cdr, Com **04** boss, Cmdr, comm, head **05** bloke, chief, Comdr **06** leader, master

*Commanders include:*

**03** aga, mir
**04** agha, meer
**06** sardar, sirdar
**07** admiral, captain, general, officer, prefect, warlord
**08** director, governor, hipparch, phylarch, risaldar, taxiarch, tetrarch
**09** chieftain, chiliarch, imperator, polemarch, privateer, seraskier, trierarch
**11** encomendero, turcopolier
**13** generalissimo
**14** superintendent

*See also* **admiral; Field Marshal; general**

## commanding

**05** lofty **06** strong **08** dominant, forceful, imperial, imposing, powerful, superior **09** assertive, confident, directing, strategic **10** autocratic, dominating, impressive, peremptory **11** controlling **12** advantageous **13** authoritative

## commemorate

**04** keep, mark **06** honour, salute **07** observe **08** remember **09** celebrate, recognize, solemnize **11** immortalize, memorialize **12** pay tribute to

## commemoration

**04** mind, obit **06** honour, memory, salute **07** tribute **08** ceremony **09** honouring **10** dedication, observance **11** celebration, recognition, recordation, remembrance

## commemorative

**07** marking **08** memorial, saluting **09** honouring **10** dedicatory, in honour of, in memoriam, in memory of **11** celebratory, remembering **12** as a tribute to **15** in recognition of, in remembrance of

## commence

**04** open **05** begin, start **06** launch **07** go

ahead **08** embark on, initiate
**09** originate **10** inaugurate, make a start
**14** make a beginning

## commencement
**05** onset, start **06** launch, origin, outset
**07** kick-off, opening **09** beginning
**10** initiation

## commend
**03** rap **04** give, laud, wrap **05** adorn,
extol, trust, yield **06** commit, praise, set
off **07** acclaim, applaud, approve,
confide, consign, deliver, entrust,
propose, suggest **08** advocate,
eulogize, hand over **09** recommend
**10** compliment **13** speak highly of

## commendable
**04** good **05** noble **06** pretty, worthy
**08** laudable **09** admirable, deserving,
estimable, excellent, exemplary, well-
found **10** creditable **11** meritorious
**12** praiseworthy

## commendation
**06** credit, praise **07** acclaim
**08** accolade, applause, approval,
encomion, encomium, good word
**09** panegyric **10** approvance
**11** acclamation, approbation, good
opinion, high opinion, recognition
**13** brownie points, encouragement
**14** congratulation, recommendation,
seal of approval, special mention
**15** stamp of approval

## commensurate
**03** due **05** equal **07** fitting **08** adequate
**10** acceptable, comparable,
equivalent, sufficient **11** according to
**13** appropriate to, corresponding,
proportionate **14** compatible with,
consistent with, in proportion to
**15** corresponding to

## comment
**03** say **04** note, view **05** gloss, gloze,
opine **06** remark **07** descant, explain,
mention, observe, opinion, speak to
**08** annotate, footnote, point out,
scholion, scholium, sidenote
**09** criticism, elucidate, interject,
interpose, interpret, statement
**10** annotation, commentary,
exposition **11** elucidation, explanation,
observation **12** illustration, marginal
note, obiter dictum **13** give an opinion

## commentary
**04** comm **05** notes **06** Gemara, postil,
remark, report, review **07** account
**08** analysis, Brahmana, critique,
exegesis, treatise **09** narration, voice-
over **10** annotation, exposition, play-
by-play **11** description, elucidation,
explanation **14** interpretation

## commentator
**05** hakam **06** critic **07** exegete, glosser
**08** narrator, reporter **09** annotator,
commenter, expositor, glossator,
scholiast **10** newscaster, race-caller
**11** broadcaster, interpreter
**12** sportscaster **13** correspondent
See also **cricket**

## commerce
**03** com **05** trade **07** dealing, traffic
**08** business, dealings, exchange,

industry **09** marketing, relations
**11** intercourse, trafficking
**13** merchandizing

## commercial
**02** ad **04** bill, hype, plug **05** blurb,
trade, venal **06** advert, jingle, notice,
poster, shoppy **07** display, handout,
leaflet, placard, popular, trading
**08** business, circular, handbill,
merchant, monetary, saleable, sellable
**09** financial, lucrative, marketing,
mercenary, promotion, publicity
**10** industrial, mercantile, profitable,
propaganda **11** moneymaking
**12** announcement, profit-making
**13** advertisement, materialistic,
money-spinning **15** entrepreneurial

## commiserate
**07** comfort, console, feel for
**10** sympathize, understand **12** feel
sorry for **13** offer sympathy **15** express
sympathy, send condolences

## commiseration
**04** pity **06** solace **07** comfort
**08** sympathy **10** compassion,
condolence **11** condolences,
consolation **13** consideration,
understanding

## commission
**03** cut, fee, job **04** duty, send, task,
work **05** board, order, share, trust
**06** ask for, assign, charge, depute,
employ, engage, errand, select
**07** appoint, arrange, council,
empower, mandate, mission, rake-off,
request, royalty, warrant **08** contract,
delegate, function, nominate,
poundage **09** allowance, authority,
authorize, brokerage, committee
**10** assignment, delegation, deputation,
employment, percentage
**11** appointment, piece of work
**12** advisory body, compensation
**13** advisory group **14** representative,
responsibility **15** put in an order for

## commit
**02** do **03** put, sin **04** aret, bind, give,
hete, send **05** admit, arett, enact,
enure, hecht, hight, inure, trust
**06** assign, decide, effect, engage,
pledge **07** commend, confide, confine,
consign, deliver, deposit, entrust,
execute, get up to, intrust, perform,
promise, put away **08** bequeath, carry
out, covenant, dedicate, delegate,
hand over, obligate **09** indulge in,
recommend **10** perpetrate **15** cross the
Rubicon

## commitment
**03** tie, vow **04** duty, word **06** effort,
pledge **07** loyalty, promise
**08** covenant, devotion, hard work
**09** adherence, assurance, guarantee,
liability **10** allegiance, dedication,
engagement, obligation
**11** involvement, undertaking
**12** imprisonment **14** responsibility

## committal
**06** pledge **07** sending **09** admission
**11** confinement, consignment
**12** imprisonment

## committed
**05** loyal **06** active, engagé, paid up,
red-hot **07** devoted, engaged, fervent,
sold out, zealous **08** diligent, involved,
studious **09** dedicated, sold out on
**11** evangelical, hardworking,
industrious **12** card-carrying,
enthusiastic

## committee
**03** com **05** board, table **08** delegacy
**09** Politburo **10** Propaganda
**11** Politbureau

## commodious
**05** ample, large, roomy **08** spacious,
suitable **09** capacious, expansive,
extensive **10** convenient
**11** comfortable, serviceable

## commodity
**04** item **05** goods, stock, thing, wares
**06** output, profit **07** article, produce,
product **08** material **09** advantage,
privilege **10** expediency
**11** convenience, merchandise

## common
**03** com, low **05** crude, daily, joint,
plain, sense, share, stray, usual
**06** coarse, mutual, normal, public,
shared, simple, vulgar **07** average,
general, ill-bred, loutish, popular,
regular, routine, uncouth **08** accepted,
communal, everyday, familiar,
frequent, habitual, inferior, ordinary,
plebeian, standard, tritical, workaday
**09** community, customary, prevalent,
ten a penny, two a penny, universal,
unrefined **10** collective, customable,
dime a dozen, prevailing, widespread
**11** bog standard, commonplace
**12** common as muck, conventional,
run-of-the-mill **13** unexceptional
**15** undistinguished

## commoner
**02** MP **04** pleb **07** plebean **08** plebeian

## common land
**03** tie, tye **04** mark

## commonly
**05** often, vulgo **07** as a rule, usually
**08** normally **09** generally, regularly,
routinely, typically **10** frequently **14** for
the most part

## commonplace
**05** banal, stale, stock, trite, usual
**06** boring, common, modern, ornery,
vulgar **07** humdrum, mundane,
obvious, ordinar, prosaic, routine,
worn out **08** bromidic, copybook,
everyday, exoteric, frequent, ordinary,
overused **09** hackneyed, prosaical,
quotidian **10** pedestrian, threadbare,
widespread **11** a dime a dozen
**13** unexceptional, uninteresting

## commonsense
**04** sane, wise **05** sound **06** astute,
shrewd **07** prudent **08** sensible
**09** judicious, practical, pragmatic,
realistic **10** discerning, hard-headed,
reasonable **11** down-to-earth,
experienced, level-headed **12** matter-
of-fact **14** commonsensical

### common sense
04 nous 05 savey, savvy, sense
06 brains, reason, sanity, savvey,
wisdom 07 realism 08 gumption,
prudence 09 good sense, judgement,
mother wit, soundness 10 astuteness,
experience, pragmatism, shrewdness
11 discernment, rumgumption
12 practicality, sensibleness
13 judiciousness, rumelgumption,
rumlegumption 14 hard-headedness,
rumblegumption, rummelgumption,
rummlegumption 15 level-headedness

### commonwealth
03 Com 04 weal 12 Protectorate

*Commonwealth member countries:*

04 Fiji
05 Ghana, India, Kenya, Malta,
Nauru, Samoa, Tonga
06 Belize, Brunei, Canada, Cyprus,
Guyana, Malawi, Tuvalu,
Uganda, Zambia
07 Grenada, Jamaica, Lesotho,
Namibia, Nigeria, St Lucia,
Vanuatu
08 Barbados, Botswana, Cameroon,
Dominica, Kiribati, Malaysia,
Maldives, Pakistan, Sri Lanka,
Tanzania
09 Australia, Mauritius, Singapore,
Swaziland, The Gambia
10 Bangladesh, Mozambique, New
Zealand, Seychelles, The
Bahamas
11 Sierra Leone, South Africa
13 United Kingdom
14 Papua New Guinea, Solomon
Islands
15 St Kitts and Nevis
16 Brunei Darussalam
17 Antigua and Barbuda, Trinidad
and Tobago
21 St Christopher and Nevis
24 United Republic of Tanzania
25 St Vincent and the Grenadines

*Commonwealth of Independent
States members:*

06 Russia
07 Armenia, Belarus, Georgia,
Moldova, Ukraine
10 Azerbaijan, Kazakhstan,
Kyrgyzstan, Tajikistan,
Uzbekistan
12 Turkmenistan

### commotion
03 ado, row 04 fuss, Hell, riot, stir, to-
do, toss 05 hurly, hurry, noise, steer,
stire, storm, styre, whirl 06 bustle, bust-
up, flurry, fracas, fraise, furore, hotter,
hubbub, pother, pudder, racket,
romage, ruckus, rumpus, steery,
tiswas, tizwas, tumult, uproar 07 burst-
up, clamour, ferment, rummage,
tempest, turmoil 08 ballyhoo,
brouhaha, disorder, disquiet, kefuffle,
tirrivee, tirrivie, upheaval 09 agitation,
carfuffle, confusion, curfuffle,
hurricane, kerfuffle, stirabout
10 excitement, hullabaloo, hurly-burly
11 disturbance

### communal
05 joint 06 common, public, shared
07 general 09 community 10 collective

### communally
07 jointly 08 commonly 09 community,
generally 12 collectively

### commune
03 com, mir 06 colony 07 kibbutz
08 converse 09 community, discourse
10 collective, fellowship, get close to,
get in touch, settlement
11 communicate, co-operative, feel
close to, feel in touch, make contact
12 municipality

### communicable
08 catching 09 infective 10 contagious,
conveyable, infectious, spreadable
12 transferable 13 transmissible,
transmittable

### communicate
04 talk 05 phone, reach, relay, speak,
write 06 bestow, convey, empart,
impart, inform, liaise, notify, pass on,
report, reveal, spread, unfold
07 commune, contact, declare,
deliver, diffuse, divulge, express, get
over, mediate, publish, put over
08 acquaint, announce, converse,
disclose, intimate, proclaim, transmit
09 be in touch, broadcast, get across,
make known, put across, telephone
10 correspond, get in touch
11 demonstrate, disseminate

### communication
05 touch 07 contact, message
09 telephony 10 connection,
disclosure, intimation 11 information,
intercourse 12 intelligence,
transmission 13 dissemination
14 correspondence

*Communication forms include:*

02 IM, IT, TV
03 fax, MMS, Net, PDA, SMS
04 blog, memo, Moon, news, note,
post, wire, word
05 cable, e-mail, media, pager, pay
TV, press, radar, radio, Skype®,
telex, video
06 Blu-ray®, gossip, letter, notice,
poster, report, speech, tannoy, the
net
07 bleeper, Braille, cable TV,
Digibox®, journal, leaflet,
message, podcast, Prestel®,
webcast, website
08 access TV, aerogram, brochure,
bulletin, circular, computer,
dialogue, dispatch, Intelsat,
intercom, Internet, junk mail,
magazine, mailshot, pamphlet,
postcard, telegram, teletext,
wireless
09 broadband, catalogue, digital TV,
facsimile, grapevine, mass media,
megaphone, Morse code,
newsflash, newspaper, publicity,
satellite, semaphore, statement,
telephone, voice mail
10 communiqué, dictaphone, loud-
hailer, pay-per-view, television,
typewriter

11 advertising, chain letter, satellite
TV, smoke signal, Telemessage®,
teleprinter, text message, the
Internet
12 announcement, broadcasting,
conversation, press release, sign
language, walkie-talkie, World
Wide Web
13 bush telegraph, video-on-
demand, word processor
14 correspondence, subscription TV

### communicative
04 free, open 05 frank 06 candid, chatty
07 voluble 08 friendly, outgoing,
sociable 09 expansive, extrovert,
talkative 10 unreserved
11 forthcoming, informative, intelligent

### communion
02 HC 04 Mass 05 agape, unity
06 accord 07 concord, empathy,
harmony, rapport 08 affinity, occasion,
sympathy 09 closeness, communing,
community, Eucharist, Sacrament
10 fellowship 11 intercourse, Lord's
Supper 12 togetherness
13 participation 15 sharing feelings,
sharing thoughts

### communiqué
06 report 07 message 08 bulletin,
dispatch 09 newsflash, statement
12 announcement, press release
13 communication

### communism
06 Maoism 07 Marxism, Titoism
08 Leninism 09 socialism, sovietism,
Stalinism 10 Bolshevism, Trotskyism
11 revisionism 12 collectivism
15 totalitarianism

### communist
03 com, red 04 Trot 05 commo,
commy, tanky 06 commie, Maoist,
soviet 07 comrade, leftist, Marxist
08 Leninist, Viet Cong 09 communard,
socialist, Stalinist 10 Bolshevist,
Spartacist, Spartakist, Trotskyist,
Trotskyite 11 revisionist 12 collectivist

### community
04 body, town, umma 05 biome,
group, order, state, tribe, ummah
06 ashram, colony, locale, nation,
people, public, region, sangha
07 commune, dogtown, kibbutz,
phalanx, section, society 08 district,
Greekdom, locality, populace
09 Agapemone, agreement,
coenobium, residents, sociation
10 commonness, fellowship, fraternity,
population, settlement, sisterhood
11 association, brotherhood
13 neighbourhood

### commute
05 remit 06 adjust, lessen, modify,
reduce, soften 07 curtail, journey,
lighten, shorten, shuttle 08 decrease,
exchange, mitigate 10 substitute
12 travel to work

### commuter
09 passenger, traveller 11 strap-hanger,
suburbanite

## Comoros
**03** COM

## compact
**03** ram **04** bond, cram, deal, firm, neat, pact, snug, tamp **05** brief, close, dense, pithy, short, small, solid, terse, tight, union **06** accord, league, little, pocket, settle, treaty **07** bargain, concise, entente, flatten, squeeze **08** alliance, compress, condense, contract, covenant, flapjack, pack down, smallish, succinct, well-knit **09** agreement, concordat, condensed, indenture, press down, telescope **10** compressed, settlement **11** arrangement, close-packed, consolidate, transaction **12** close-grained, close-pressed, impenetrable **13** press together, understanding **15** pressed together

## companion
**03** lad, pal **04** aide, ally, feer, fere, mate **05** buddy, crony, feare, fiere **06** cohort, co-mate, cupman, escort, fellow, friend, marrow, pheere, potman, shadow, Trojan **07** compeer, comrade, consort, convive, franion, partner **08** barnacle, beau-pere, book-mate, chaperon, compadre, copemate, Ephesian, follower, intimate, playmate, sidekick, workmate **09** assistant, associate, attendant, bon vivant, chaperone, colleague, confidant, copes-mate, pew-fellow **10** accomplice, bon vivante, compotator, confidante, goodfellow **11** compotation, confederate, inseparable, skaines mate

*See also* **boon**

## companionable
**06** genial **07** affable, amiable, cordial **08** familiar, fellowly, friendly, informal, outgoing, sociable **09** agreeable, congenial, convivial, extrovert **10** gregarious **11** neighbourly, sympathetic **12** approachable

## companionship
**07** company, rapport, society, support **08** intimacy, sympathy **09** closeness **10** fellowship, friendship **11** association, camaraderie, comradeship **12** consociation, conviviality, togetherness **13** esprit de corps

## company
**02** AG, BV, Co, SA **03** Cia, Cie, Coy, PLC, set **04** band, body, cast, core, crew, firm, gang, ging, GmbH, heap, push, sort, team **05** crowd, group, house, party, troop, trust **06** cartel, circle, guests, throng, troupe **07** callers, concern, contact, society, support **08** assembly, business, ensemble, jingbang, presence, visitors **09** closeness, community, gathering, syndicate **10** attendance, consortium, fellowship, friendship, subsidiary **11** association, comradeship, corporation, partnership **12** conglomerate, conviviality, togetherness **13** companionship,

establishment, multinational **14** holding company, limited company

*See also* **business; dance company** *under* **dance**

## comparable
**04** akin, like, near **05** alike, close, equal **07** cognate, related, similar **08** parallel **09** analogous **10** equivalent, tantamount **12** commensurate, proportional **13** corresponding, proportionate

## comparably
**07** equally **09** similarly **11** analogously **14** proportionally **15** correspondingly, proportionately

## comparative
**02** -er **03** -est **08** relative **12** by comparison, in comparison

## comparatively
**10** relatively **12** by comparison, in comparison

## compare
**02** cf, cp **03** get, vie **04** even, like, link **05** equal, liken, match, touch, weigh **06** confer, equate **07** balance, compeer, compete, measure, paragon, provide, stack up **08** confront, contrast, parallel, resemble **09** analogize, correlate, juxtapose **10** be as good as, comparison, set against **13** hold a candle to, set side by side **14** bear comparison, be comparable to **15** regard as the same
• **beyond compare** **06** superb **07** supreme **08** peerless **09** brilliant, matchless, nonpareil, unmatched **10** unequalled, unrivalled **11** superlative, unsurpassed **12** incomparable, without equal **15** without parallel

## comparison
**07** analogy, parable **08** contrast, likeness, parallel **10** similarity, similitude **11** correlation, differences, distinction, parallelism, resemblance **12** relationship **13** comparability, juxtaposition **15** differentiation

## compartment
**03** bay, box, pew, pod **04** area, cage, cell, pane, part, room, till **05** berth, booth, niche, panel, stall **06** alcove, carrel, locker, locule **07** chamber, cubicle, loculus, section, sleeper **08** carriage, casemate, category, division, traverse **09** cubbyhole, partition **10** pigeonhole **11** subdivision

## compartmentalize
**03** tag **04** file, slot, sort **05** group **08** classify **09** catalogue **10** categorize, pigeonhole **11** alphabetize **12** sectionalize

## compass
**04** area, bend, dial, plot, zone **05** ambit, curve, field, gamut, grasp, limit, range, reach, realm, round, scale, scope, space, sweep, swing **06** bounds, circle, extent, limits, obtain, realms, sphere, spread **07** achieve, circuit, enclose, pelorus, stretch, trammel **08** boundary, contrive, diapason, register, surround

**09** enclosure **10** accomplish, comprehend **13** circumference

*Compass points:*

**01** E, N, S, W
**02** NE, NW, SE, SW
**03** ENE, ESE, NNE, NNW, SSE, SSW, WNW, WSW
**04** east, E by N, E by S, N by E, N by W, S by E, S by W, W by N, W by S, west
**05** NE by E, NE by N, north, NW by N, NW by W, SE by E, SE by S, south, SW by S, SW by W
**09** north-east, north-west, south-east, south-west
**11** east by north, east by south, north by east, north by west, south by east, south by west, west by north, west by south
**13** east-north-east, east-south-east, west-north-west, west-south-west
**14** north-north-east, north-north-west, south-south-east, south-south-west
**15** north-east by east, north-west by west, south-east by east, south-west by west
**16** north-east by north, north-west by north, south-east by south, south-west by south

## compassion
**04** care, pity **05** heart, mercy **06** bowels, sorrow, ubuntu **07** concern, remorse **08** humanity, kindness, leniency, sympathy **10** condolence, gentleness, tenderness **11** benevolence **13** commiseration, consideration, fellow-feeling, understanding

## compassionate
**06** benign, caring, gentle, humane, kindly, tender **07** clement, feeling, lenient, piteous, pitiful, pitying **08** bleeding, merciful **09** forgiving **10** benevolent, charitable, forbearing, passionate, remorseful, supportive **11** kind-hearted, sympathetic, warm-hearted **12** humanitarian **13** tender-hearted, understanding

## compatibility
**05** match **07** harmony, rapport **08** sympathy **11** consistence, consistency, suitability **12** adaptability **14** like-mindedness

## compatible
**06** suited **07** similar **08** matching, suitable **09** accordant, adaptable, congruent, congruous, consonant, in harmony **10** consistent, harmonious, like-minded, well-suited **11** conformable, sympathetic, well-matched **12** reconcilable **13** having rapport

## compatriot
**10** countryman **12** countrywoman **13** fellow citizen **14** fellow national

## compel
**03** gar **04** make, urge **05** bully, coact, drive, force, garre, impel **06** coerce, hustle, lean on, oblige **07** dragoon, efforce, enforce **08** browbeat, bulldoze, compulse, insist on, pressure

## compelling

**09** constrain, press-gang, strongarm **10** intimidate, pressurize **11** necessitate **14** put the screws on

## compelling

**06** cogent, urgent **07** weighty **08** coercive, forceful, gripping, mesmeric, powerful, pressing, riveting **09** absorbing **10** compulsive, compulsory, conclusive, convincing, imperative, overriding, persuasive **11** enthralling, fascinating, irrefutable **12** irresistible, spellbinding **13** unputdownable

## compendious

**05** brief, crisp, short, terse **07** compact, concise, summary **08** complete, succinct **09** condensed **10** to the point **12** all-embracing **13** comprehensive

## compendium

**06** digest, manual, symbol **07** summary **08** abstract, breviate, handbook, synopsis **09** anthology, companion, vade-mecum **10** abridgment, collection, shortening **11** abridgement, compilation

## compensate

**05** atone, repay **06** cancel, make up, offset, recoup, redeem, refund, reward **07** balance, nullify, redress, requite, restore, satisfy **08** make good, make up to **09** indemnify, make up for, reimburse **10** balance out, counteract, make amends, neutralize, recompense, remunerate **11** countervail **12** counterpoise **14** counterbalance, make reparation

## compensation

**04** boot, bote **05** compo **06** amends, refund, return, reward **07** comfort, damages, payment, redress **08** reprisal, requital, solatium **09** atonement, demurrage, indemnity, repayment **10** blood money, correction, recompense, reparation **11** consolation, restitution, restoration **12** remuneration, satisfaction **13** reimbursement **15** conscience money, indemnification

## compère

**02** MC **04** host **05** emcee, front **06** anchor **07** present **09** anchorman, announcer, presenter **10** link person **11** anchorwoman

## compete

**03** ren, rin, run, vie **04** play, race **05** enter, fight, match, rival **06** battle, jostle, oppose, strive **07** compare, contend, contest, go in for **08** struggle, take part **09** challenge **11** participate, pit yourself

## competence

**05** power, skill **07** ability, fitness, purview **08** aptitude, capacity, facility **09** authority, expertise, technique **10** capability, efficiency, experience **11** proficiency, sufficience, sufficiency, suitability **12** jurisdiction **13** legal capacity

## competent

**03** fit **04** able, good **05** adept, equal, tight **06** expert, habile, strong, useful

**07** capable, skilful, skilled, trained **08** adequate, masterly, passable, suitable **09** efficient, qualified **10** acceptable, consummate, legitimate, proficient, reasonable, sufficient **11** appropriate, experienced, respectable **12** accomplished, satisfactory **13** well-qualified

## competition

**03** bee, cup **04** bout, game, goal, gole, meet, open, quiz, race **05** event, field, match, vying **06** rivals, strife, trials **07** contest, cook off, rivalry **08** concours, conflict, knockout, struggle **09** challenge, emulation, encounter, opponents, spelldown **10** contention, opposition, tournament **11** challengers, competitors, spelling bee **12** championship, cross-country **13** combativeness **15** competitiveness

*Sporting competitions include:*

**02** TT
**05** Ashes, Derby, FA Cup
**06** Le Mans
**07** Grey Cup, Masters, Uber Cup, UEFA Cup
**08** Rose Bowl, Ryder Cup, Speedway, World Cup
**09** Motocross, Super Bowl, Thomas Cup, World Bowl
**10** Asian Games, Formula One, Solheim Cup, Stanley Cup
**11** Admiral's Cup, America's Cup, Kinnaird Cup, World Series
**12** Iditarod Race, Olympic Games, Tour de France
**13** Grand National, Kentucky Derby, Leonard Trophy
**15** Paralympic Games
**17** Commonwealth Games

## competitive

**03** low **04** fair, just, keen **05** pushy **06** modest **07** average, cut-rate **08** moderate **09** ambitious, combative, cut-throat, dog-eat-dog **10** aggressive, reasonable **11** contentious, inexpensive **12** antagonistic **15** bargain-basement

## competitively

**03** low **06** fairly **08** modestly **10** moderately, reasonably **13** inexpensively

## competitiveness

**07** rat race, rivalry **08** ambition, keenness **09** challenge, pugnacity, pushiness **10** aggression, antagonism **13** ambitiousness, assertiveness, combativeness **14** aggressiveness **15** contentiousness

## competitor

**05** rival **06** player **07** agonist, entrant, roadman **08** corrival, emulator, Olympian, opponent, trialist **09** adversary, candidate, contender, triallist **10** antagonist, challenger, contestant, opposition **11** competition, pancratiast, participant, pentathlete

## compilation

◇ *anagram indicator* **04** opus, work **05** album, segue **06** corpus **07** omnibus **08** treasury **09** amassment, anthology,

collation, potpourri, selection, thesaurus **10** assemblage, collection, compendium, miscellany **11** arrangement, collectanea, composition, florilegium **12** accumulation, chrestomathy, organization

## compile

◇ *anagram indicator* **04** cull, edit **05** amass **06** garner, gather **07** arrange, collate, collect, compose, marshal **08** assemble, organize **09** construct **10** accumulate **11** put together
• **compiler** **01** I **02** me
• **compiler's** **04** mine

## complacency

**05** pride **07** triumph **08** gloating, pleasure, serenity, smugness **11** contentment, self-content **12** complaisance, satisfaction **13** gratification, self-assurance

## complacent

**04** smug, vain **05** proud **06** serene **07** pleased **08** gloating **09** contented, gratified, satisfied **10** triumphant **11** complaisant, self-assured, unconcerned **13** self-contented, self-righteous, self-satisfied

## complain

**03** nag **04** ache, beef, bind, carp, fuss, girn, hurt, mean, mein, mene, moan, mump **05** bitch, bleat, gripe, groan, growl, grump, meane, plain, whine **06** bemoan, bewail, endure, grouse, grutch, kvetch, lament, object, repine, snivel, squawk, squeal, whinge **07** carry on, grumble, protest, wheenge **08** be in pain, feel pain **09** bellyache, criticize, find fault, make a fuss **10** make a noise, suffer from **11** expostulate, kick up a fuss, raise a stink, remonstrate **12** moan and groan **14** file a complaint **15** have a bone to pick, lodge a complaint

## complainer

**04** nark **06** kvetch, moaner, whiner **07** bleater, fusspot, grouser, niggler, whinger **08** grumbler, kvetcher **09** nit-picker **10** bellyacher, fussbudget **11** fault-finder

## complaint

**04** beef, moan **05** bleat, gripe, groan, plain, upset **06** charge, grouch, grouse, grutch, malady, plaint, squawk, whinge **07** ailment, beefing, carping, censure, disease, grumble, illness, malaise, protest, quarrel, quibble, trouble, wheenge **08** bleating, disorder, plaining, sickness **09** annoyance, bellyache, condition, criticism, grievance, infection, objection, querimony, whingeing **10** accusation, affliction **11** bellyaching **12** fault-finding, inflammation **13** indisposition **14** representation **15** dissatisfaction
*See also* **disease; inflammation**
• **expression of complaint** **02** ah

## complaisant

**06** docile **07** amiable, willing **08** amenable, biddable, obedient, obliging **09** agreeable, compliant, tractable **10** complacent, solicitous **11** conformable, deferential **12** conciliatory **13** accommodating

## complement
**03** set, sum **05** crown, match, quota, total **06** alexin, amount, number, set off **08** addition, capacity, complete, contrast, entirety, fullness, round off, strength, totality **09** accessory, accompany, aggregate, allowance, companion **10** completion, go well with **11** counterpart **12** consummation **13** accompaniment **14** go well together **15** combine well with

## complementary
**04** twin **06** fellow **08** matching **09** companion, finishing **10** compatible, completing, harmonious, perfecting, reciprocal, supporting **11** correlative **12** interrelated **13** corresponding **14** interdependent
*See also* **medicine**

## complete
**02** do **03** all, cap, end **04** done, full, over, real **05** clean, close, crown, ended, pakka, pucca, pukka, total, utter, whole **06** answer, clinch, damned, entire, fill in, finish, fulfil, intact, make up, settle, wind up **07** achieve, execute, fill out, fulfill, perfect, perform, plenary, realize, settled **08** absolute, achieved, conclude, detailed, finalize, finished, integral, outright, round off, thorough, unbroken, unedited **09** completed, concluded, discharge, downright, finalized, integrate, out-and-out, polish off, terminate, undivided **10** accomplish, consummate, exhaustive, terminated, unabridged **11** unmitigated, unqualified, unshortened **12** accomplished, unexpurgated **13** comprehensive, thoroughgoing, unabbreviated, unconditional

## completely
**02** up **03** all, out **05** fully, quite, right, whole **06** hollow, in full, wholly **07** good and, sheerly, solidly, totally, utterly **08** entirely, outright **09** all ends up, all the way, every inch, perfectly, to the hilt, to the wide **10** absolutely, abundantly, altogether, thoroughly **11** back to front, neck and crop, up to the hilt **12** from top to toe, heart and soul, stoop and roop, stoup and roup, well and truly **13** bag and baggage, head over heels, root and branch **14** in every respect **15** down to the ground, from first to last

## completion
**03** end, sum **05** close, crown **06** finish **08** fruition **09** discharge, execution **10** attainment, conclusion, fulfilling, fulfilment, perfection, settlement **11** achievement, culmination, realization, termination **12** consummation, finalization **14** accomplishment

## complex
◊ *anagram indicator* **05** mixed, thing

**06** hang-up, phobia, scheme, system, varied **07** devious, diverse, network **08** compound, disorder, fixation, involved, multiple, neurosis, ramified, tortuous **09** Byzantine, composite, difficult, elaborate, institute, intricate, obsession, plexiform, structure **10** circuitous, complicate, convoluted **11** aggregation, complicated, development **12** organization **13** establishment, preoccupation, sophisticated

## complexion
**03** rud **04** blee, cast, kind, leer, look, skin, sort, tone, type **05** guise, light, stamp **06** aspect, colour, nature **07** texture **08** attitude **09** character, colouring **10** appearance **11** perspective **12** pigmentation

## complexity
**07** variety **09** intricacy **10** complicacy, complicity **11** convolution, deviousness, diverseness, elaboration, involvement **12** complication, entanglement, multiplicity, ramification, repercussion, tortuousness **13** compositeness **14** circuitousness **15** complicatedness

## compliance
**01** C **06** assent **07** keeping **08** yielding **09** agreement, appliance, deference, obedience, passivity **10** accordance, conformity, submission **11** application, concurrence **12** acquiescence, complaisance **14** conformability, submissiveness

## compliant
**05** civil **06** docile **07** passive, pliable **08** amenable, biddable, flexible, obedient, yielding **09** agreeable, appliable, indulgent, tractable **10** obsequious, sequacious, submissive **11** acquiescent, complaisant, conformable, deferential, subservient **13** accommodating

## complicate
◊ *anagram indicator* **05** mix up **06** jumble, muddle, puzzle, tangle **07** complex, confuse, involve, inweave, perplex **08** compound, entangle **09** elaborate **12** make involved **13** make difficult

## complicated
◊ *anagram indicator* **06** fiddly, implex, tricky **07** complex, cryptic **08** confused, involved, puzzling, tortuous **09** Byzantine, difficult, elaborate, intricate **10** convoluted, perplexing **11** problematic **12** labyrinthine

## complication
◊ *anagram indicator* **03** web **04** node, snag **05** nodus **06** tangle **07** mixture, problem **08** drawback, obstacle **09** confusion, intricacy **10** complexity, difficulty **11** complexness, convolution, elaboration **12** ramification, repercussion **13** complexedness

## complicity
**08** abetment, approval **09** agreement,

collusion, knowledge **10** complexity, connivance **11** concurrence, involvement **13** collaboration **14** being in cahoots

## compliment
**04** laud **05** extol **06** admire, eulogy, favour, homage, honour, praise, salute **07** applaud, bouquet, commend, devoirs, douceur, flatter, regards, tribute **08** accolade, approval, encomium, eulogize, flattery, respects **09** baisemain, greetings, laudation, sugarplum, trade-last **10** admiration, best wishes, felicitate, good wishes, salutation **11** speak well of **12** commendation, congratulate, felicitation, pat on the back, remembrances **13** speak highly of **15** congratulations
• **looking for compliments**
**07** angling, fishing

## complimentary
**04** free **06** gratis **07** glowing **08** admiring, courtesy, honorary **09** approving **10** eulogistic, favourable, flattering, for nothing, on the house **11** meliorative, panegyrical **12** appreciative, commendatory **14** congratulatory

## comply
**04** meet, obey **05** agree, all in, defer, yield **06** accede, accord, assent, follow, fulfil, oblige, submit **07** abide by, conform, consent, observe, perform, respect, satisfy **09** acquiesce, discharge **10** condescend **11** accommodate

## component
◊ *anagram indicator* **03** bit **04** item, part, unit **05** basic, piece **06** factor, module, widget **07** element, partial, section **08** inherent, integral **09** essential, intrinsic, spare part **10** ingredient **11** constituent **12** constitutive, integral part **15** constituent part
*See also* **electrical**

## comport
**03** act, use **04** bear **05** abear, carry **06** acquit, behave, demean, deport **07** conduct, perform

## compose
◊ *anagram indicator* **03** pen, set **04** calm, dite, form, lull, make **05** build, draft, frame, quell, quiet, still, write **06** create, devise, draw up, indite, invent, make up, pacify, settle, soothe, steady **07** arrange, assuage, collect, compile, concoct, control, fashion, produce, stickle, think of, think up **08** assemble, calm down, comprise **09** construct, reconcile **10** constitute **11** choreograph, orchestrate, put together **12** tranquillize

## composed
◊ *anagram indicator* **04** calm, cool **05** quiet **06** at ease, placid, sedate, serene **07** relaxed **08** together, tranquil **09** collected, confident, unruffled, unworried **10** calmed down, controlled **11** level-headed, unflappable **13** imperturbable, quietened down, self-possessed

14 self-controlled 15 cool as a cucumber

## composer

04 bard, poet 05 lyric, maker 06 author, master, writer 07 creator, maestro 08 arranger, melodist, musician, producer, psalmist, triadist 09 epitapher, songsmith, tunesmith 10 epitaphist, operettist, originator, songwriter, symphonist 12 balladmonger, variationist, vaudevillist 13 contrapuntist, dodecaphonist, orchestralist

---

*Composers include:*

03 **Bax** (Sir Arnold), **Sor** (Fernando) 04 **Adam** (Adolphe), **Arne** (Thomas), **Bach** (Carl Philipp Emanuel), **Bach** (Johann Christian), **Bach** (Johann Sebastian), **Berg** (Alban), **Bull** (John), **Byrd** (William), **Cage** (John), **Ives** (Charles), **Orff** (Carl), **Pärt** (Arvo), **Weir** (Judith) 05 **Adams** (John), **Auric** (Georges), **Berio** (Luciano), **Bizet** (Georges), **Bliss** (Sir Arthur), **Boito** (Arrigo), **Boyce** (William), **Bruch** (Max), **D'Indy** (Vincent), **Dufay** (Guillaume), **Dukas** (Paul), **Durey** (Louis), **Elgar** (Sir Edward), **Falla** (Manuel de), **Fauré** (Gabriel), **Glass** (Philip), **Gluck** (Christoph), **Grieg** (Edvard), **Haydn** (Joseph), **Holst** (Gustav), **Lehár** (Franz), **Liszt** (Franz), **Lully** (Jean Baptiste), **Ogdon** (John), **Parry** (Sir Hubert), **Ravel** (Maurice), **Satie** (Erik), **Verdi** (Giuseppe), **Weber** (Carl Maria von) 06 **Barber** (Samuel), **Bartók** (Béla), **Bishop** (Sir Henry Rowley), **Boulez** (Pierre), **Brahms** (Johannes), **Busoni** (Ferruccio), **Casals** (Pablo), **Chopin** (Frédéric), **Clarke** (Jeremiah), **Coates** (Eric), **Delius** (Frederick), **Dvořák** (Antonín), **Franck** (César), **German** (Sir Edward), **Glinka** (Mikhail), **Gounod** (Charles), **Gurney** (Ivor), **Handel** (George Frideric), **Kodály** (Zoltán), **Ligeti** (György), **Mahler** (Gustav), **Morley** (Thomas), **Mozart** (Wolfgang Amadeus), **Previn** (André), **Rameau** (Jean Philippe), **Rubbra** (Edmund), **Tallis** (Thomas), **Varèse** (Edgard), **Wagner** (Richard), **Walton** (Sir William), **Webern** (Anton von), **Wilbye** (John) 07 **Albéniz** (Isaac), **Allegri** (Gregorio), **Bellini** (Vincenzo), **Bennett** (Sir Richard Rodney), **Berlioz** (Hector), **Borodin** (Alexander), **Britten** (Benjamin), **Campion** (Thomas), **Copland** (Aaron), **Corelli** (Arcangelo), **Debussy** (Claude), **Delibes** (Léo), **Dowland** (John), **Duruflé** (Maurice), **Fricker** (Peter), **Gibbons** (Orlando), **Górecki** (Henryk), **Janáček** (Leos), **Menotti** (Gian-Carlo), **Milhaud** (Darius), **Nicolai** (Otto), **Nielsen** (Carl), **Poulenc** (Francis), **Puccini** (Giacomo), **Purcell** (Henry), **Rossini** (Gioacchino), **Salieri** (Antonio), **Shankar** (Ravi), **Smetana**

(Bedrich), **Strauss** (Johann), **Strauss** (Richard), **Tavener** (John), **Tippett** (Sir Michael), **Vivaldi** (Antonio), **Xenakis** (Iannis) 08 **Berkeley** (Sir Lennox), **Bruckner** (Anton), **Couperin** (François), **Goossens** (Sir Eugene), **Grainger** (Percy), **Hoffmann** (Ernst Theodor Wilhelm), **Holliger** (Heinz), **Honegger** (Arthur), **Maconchy** (Dame Elizabeth), **Mascagni** (Pietro), **Massenet** (Jules), **Messiaen** (Olivier), **Respighi** (Ottorino), **Schubert** (Franz), **Schumann** (Robert), **Scriabin** (Aleksandr), **Sibelius** (Jean), **Sondheim** (Steven), **Stanford** (Sir Charles Villiers), **Sullivan** (Sir Arthur), **Telemann** (Georg Philipp), **Victoria** (Tomás Luis de), **Williams** (John) 09 **Beethoven** (Ludwig van), **Bernstein** (Leonard), **Boulanger** (Nadia), **Buxtehude** (Diderik), **Donizetti** (Gaetano), **Hindemith** (Paul), **Meyerbeer** (Giacomo), **Offenbach** (Jacques), **Pachelbel** (Johann), **Prokofiev** (Sergei), **Scarlatti** (Alessandro), **Scarlatti** (Domenico), **Tortelier** (Paul) 10 **Birtwistle** (Sir Harrison), **Boccherini** (Luigi), **Kabalevsky** (Dmitri), **Monteverdi** (Claudio), **Mussorgsky** (Modeste), **Praetorius** (Michael), **Rubinstein** (Anton), **Saint-Saëns** (Camille), **Schoenberg** (Arnold), **Stravinsky** (Igor), **Villa-Lobos** (Heitor) 11 **Humperdinck** (Engelbert), **Leoncavallo** (Ruggiero), **Mendelssohn** (Felix), **Rachmaninov** (Sergei), **Stockhausen** (Karlheinz), **Tchaikovsky** (Piotr), **Theodorakis** (Mikis) 12 **Shostakovich** (Dmitri) 13 **Khachaturian** (Aram), **Maxwell Davies** (Sir Peter) 14 **Rimsky-Korsakov** (Nikolai) 15 **Vaughan Williams** (Ralph)

---

*See also* **libretto**

## composite

05 alloy, blend, fused, mixed 06 fusion 07 amalgam, blended, complex, mixture 08 combined, compound, pastiche 09 patchwork, synthesis 10 conflation 11 agglutinate, combination, synthesized 12 amalgamation, conglomerate 13 agglutination, heterogeneous

## composition

◇ *anagram indicator* 02 op 04 book, dite, fine, form, opus, poem, port, task, text, work 05 compo, essay, motet, novel, opera, paper, piece, story, study, thing, verse 06 design, erotic, layout, make-up, making, motett, review, satire, sonata, thesis 07 article, balance, drawing, harmony, mixture, morceau, picture, writing 08 creation, devising, exercise, oratorio, painting, pencraft, rhapsody, symmetry, symphony, treatise 09 album-leaf, arranging, capriccio, character, exaration,

formation, impromptu, invention, structure, work of art 10 adaptation, assignment, compromise, concoction, confection, consonance, mock-heroic, production, proportion, whipstitch 11 arrangement, combination, compilation, formulation 12 conformation, constitution, dissertation, organization 13 accompaniment, choral prelude, configuration 15 putting together
*See also* **musical**

## compost

04 peat 05 humus, mulch 06 manure 07 grow-bag, mixture 08 dressing, leaf-soil 09 leaf-mould 10 fertilizer, growing-bag

## composure

04 calm, ease 05 poise 06 aplomb, temper 07 dignity 08 calmness, coolness, serenity 09 assurance, character, placidity, sangfroid 10 collection, confidence, dispassion, equanimity 11 composition, impassivity, self-control, temperament 12 tranquillity 13 self-assurance 14 self-possession 15 level-headedness

## compound

◇ *anagram indicator* 03 Cpd, mix, pen 04 fold, fuse, yard 05 add to, alloy, blend, court, fused, mixed, pound, put up, unite 06 corral, fusion, hybrid, make up, medley, mingle, worsen 07 amalgam, augment, blended, combine, complex, magnify, mixture, paddock 08 coalesce, combined, dispense, heighten, increase, multiple, stockade 09 admixture, aggravate, composite, enclosure, intensify, intricate, synthesis 10 amalgamate, complicate, exacerbate, synthesize 11 combination, complicated, composition, intermingle, put together, synthesized 12 amalgamation, conglomerate
*See also* **chemical**

## comprehend

◇ *containment indicator* 03 see 04 know, twig 05 catch, cover, get it, grasp, sense 06 fathom, take in, tumble 07 catch on, compass, contain, discern, embrace, include, involve, make out, realize 08 comprise, conceive, perceive, tumble to 09 apprehend, encompass, penetrate 10 appreciate, assimilate, generalize, understand 11 make sense of 15 put your finger on

## comprehensible

05 clear, lucid, plain 06 simple 08 coherent, explicit 09 graspable 10 accessible 11 conceivable, discernible 12 intelligible 14 understandable 15 straightforward

## comprehension

03 ken 05 grasp, sense 07 insight 09 judgement, knowledge 10 conception, perception 11 discernment, realization 12 appreciation, apprehension, intelligence 13 understanding

## comprehensive

**04** full, wide **05** all-in, broad **06** global
**07** blanket, capable, general, overall
**08** complete, elliptic, sweeping,
thorough **09** extensive, inclusive,
universal **10** elliptical, exhaustive,
widespread **11** compendious **12** all-
embracing, all-inclusive,
encyclopedic **14** across-the-board,
encyclopedical

## comprehensively

**05** fully **06** widely **07** broadly
**10** completely, thoroughly,
widespread **11** extensively
**12** exhaustively

## compress

**03** jam, ram, zip **04** cram, lace, pack,
pump, tamp **05** crowd, crush, pinch,
press, screw, stuff, wedge **06** impact,
reduce, squash, strain **07** abridge,
astrict, compact, embrace, flatten,
shorten, squeeze **08** astringe,
condense, contract, shoehorn
**09** coarctate, constrict, summarize,
synopsize, telescope **10** abbreviate,
pressurize **11** concentrate, consolidate,
strangulate

## compression

**07** packing, pumping **08** pinching,
pressing, stuffing, thlipsis **09** squashing
**10** condensing, flattening
**12** constriction **13** concentration,
consolidation

## comprise

◇ *containment indicator* **04** form
**05** cover **06** embody, make up, take in
**07** compose, contain, embrace,
include, involve **09** consist of,
encompass **10** comprehend, constitute
**11** incorporate **12** be composed of

## compromise

◇ *anagram indicator* **04** deal, risk
**05** adapt, agree, shame **06** adjust,
damage, expose, settle, weaken
**07** balance, bargain, concede, imperil,
involve **08** endanger, trade-off
**09** agreement, arbitrate, discredit,
dishonour, embarrass, implicate,
mediation, middle way, negotiate,
prejudice, settle for, undermine
**10** adjustment, concession, jeopardize,
settlement **11** arbitration, composition,
co-operation, give and take, meet
halfway, negotiation, temperament
**12** bring shame to, modus vivendi
**13** accommodation, understanding
**15** make concessions

## compulsion

**04** need, urge **05** drive, force
**06** demand, desire, duress **07** duresse,
impulse, longing **08** coaction,
coercion, distress, pressure
**09** necessity, obsession **10** constraint,
insistence, obligation, temptation
**11** enforcement **13** preoccupation

## compulsive

**06** hooked, urgent **07** chronic, driving
**08** addicted, gripping, habitual,
hardened, hopeless, mesmeric,
riveting **09** absorbing, besetting,
dependent, incurable, obsessive
**10** compelling, inveterate

**11** enthralling, fascinating,
unavoidable **12** incorrigible,
irredeemable, irresistible,
overpowering, overwhelming,
pathological, spellbinding
**14** uncontrollable

## compulsively

**09** incurably **10** habitually, inevitably
**11** chronically, obsessively,
unavoidably **12** incorrigibly, irresistibly
**13** involuntarily **14** pathologically

## compulsory

**03** set **06** forced **07** binding **08** coactive,
required **09** de rigueur, essential,
mandatory, necessary, requisite
**10** compelling, imperative, obligatory,
stipulated **11** contractual

## compunction

**05** guilt, qualm, shame **06** qualms,
regret, sorrow, unease **07** remorse
**09** misgiving, penitence **10** contrition,
hesitation, misgivings, reluctance,
repentance, uneasiness

## computation

**03** sum **06** answer, result **08** estimate,
figuring, forecast **09** reckoning
**10** arithmetic, estimation, working-out
**11** calculation, forecasting

## compute

**03** sum **04** rate **05** add up, count, tally,
total **06** assess, figure, reckon **07** count
up, measure, work out **08** estimate,
evaluate **09** calculate, enumerate

## computer

**02** NC, PC **03** MPC **10** calculator
**15** electronic brain

*Computers include:*

**03** HAL, IBM, Mac®, SAL
**04** iMac®, iPad®, VIKI
**05** Eddie, ENIAC, Holly, iBook®
**06** UNIVAC
**08** Colossus, Deep Blue, Spectrum
**09** The Matrix
**11** Deep Thought
**12** Commodore Pet

*Computer scientists include:*

**04** Bell (Gordon), Bush (Vannevar),
Cray (Seymour), Hurd (Cuthbert
Corwin), Jobs (Steven), Zuse
(Konrad)
**05** Aiken (Howard Hathaway), Burks
(Arthur Walter), Gates (Bill), Olsen
(Kenneth Harry), Sugar (Alan)
**06** Amdahl (Gene Myron), Backus
(John), Comrie (Leslie John), Eckert
(John Presper), Hopper (Grace
Murray), Huskey (Harry Douglas),
Michie (Donald), Milner (Robin
Gorell), Porter (Arthur), Turing
(Alan), Wilkes (Maurice Vincent)
**07** Babbage (Charles), Kilburn (Tom),
Mauchly (John William), Shannon
(Claude Elwood), Stibitz (George
Robert), Wheeler (David John)
**08** Lovelace (Ada, Countess),
Shockley (William Bradford),
Sinclair (Sir Clive), Williams (Sir
Frederic Calland)
**09** Atanasoff (John Vincent), Forrester
(Jay Wright), Goldstine (Herman

Heine), Hollerith (Herman),
Wilkinson (James Hardy)
**10** Berners-Lee (Tim), Fairclough
(John Whitaker), Michaelson
(Sidney), Von Neumann (John)

*Computing and Internet terms
include:*

**02** CD, IT, PC, VR, XP
**03** bit, bot, bug, bus, CD-R, CPU,
CSS, DOS, DTP, DVD, FAQ, FTP,
GUI, hit, IDE, ISP, Mac®, mod,
Net, P2P, PDF, RAM, rip, ROM,
RTF, sim, URL, USB, VDU, WAN,
Web, WWW
**04** BIOS, blog, boot, byte, card, CD-
RW, cell, chip, data, disk, dump,
file, game, HTML, icon, iMac®,
ISDN, leet, menu, port, ring,
SGML, Unix®, vlog, VOIP, Wi-
Fi®, wiki, worm
**05** ASCII, BASIC, cache, CD-ROM,
cuspy, e-mail, iBook®, JANET®,
Linux, login, log on, Mac OS,
macro, modem, mouse, MS-
DOS®, pixel, shell, splog, virus,
WiMAX
**06** access, backup, binary, bitmap,
botnet, buffer, cursor, DVD-
ROM, editor, format, Google®,
laptop, log off, mash-up, memory,
moblog, plug-in, reboot, screen,
script, server, the Net, the Web,
toggle, webify, weblog, window
**07** badware, browser, crawler,
darknet, deep web, default,
dequeue, desktop, enqueue,
favicon, gigabit, hacking, hot
spot, malware, monitor, network,
palmtop, Pentium®, podcast,
pointer, printer, program, rootkit,
scanner, servlet, sidebar, sim
game, toolbar, Unicode, upgrade,
vishing, vlogger, vodcast,
webinar, webmail, Web page,
webring, Web site, webzine,
Windows®, WYSIWYG, zip disk
**08** Apple Mac®, autosave, blogring,
blogroll, bookmark, chat room,
database, e-journal, emoticon,
firewall, Firewire®, flame war,
freeware, gigabyte, graphics,
handheld, hard disk, hardware,
home page, Internet, joystick,
keyboard, kilobyte, megabyte,
mouse mat, notebook, password,
pharming, phishing, platform,
protocol, realtime, rollover,
software, template, terabyte,
terminal, user name, vlogging
**09** character, debugging, directory,
disk drive, drill down, e-business,
e-commerce, hard drive,
hyperlink, hypertext, interface,
leetspeak, mainframe, megapixel,
microsite, mouseover,
newsgroup, overclock,
permalink, Photoshop®,
podcaster, shareware, sound
card, timestamp, transcode,
utilities, video card, vodcaster,
web design, workspace
**10** aggregator, courseware, domain
name, flash drive, floppy disk,

keylogging, middleware, multimedia, netiquette, open-source, peer-to-peer, peripheral, podcasting, podcatcher, rewritable, serial port, server farm, text mining, virtualize, vodcasting **11** abandonware, application, blogosphere, compact disc, compression, console game, cut and paste, deep linking, file sharing, floppy drive, memory stick, motherboard, optical disk, podcatching, proxy server, screen saver, silicon chip, spreadsheet, Trojan horse, workstation **12** circuit board, graphics card, installation, laser printer, nanocomputer, parallel port, reverse proxy, search engine, skyscraper ad, spellchecker, subdirectory, webification, webliography, World Wide Web **13** file extension, ink-jet printer, microcomputer, millennium bug, nanocomputing, user interface **14** electronic mail, internal memory, microprocessor, read only memory, rich text format, social software, virtualization, virtual machine, virtual reality, word processing **15** denial of service, operating system, wide area network

*See also* **key; language**
• **connected computers 03** net, web **07** network

### comrade
**03** pal **04** aide, ally, mate **05** billy, buddy, butty, crony **06** billie, cobber, escort, fellow, frater, friend **07** Achates, consort, partner **08** chaperon, follower, intimate, sidekick, tovarich, tovarish **09** assistant, associate, attendant, bully-rook, chaperone, colleague, communist, companion, confidant, tovarisch **10** accomplice, confidante **11** bon camarade, confederate **12** pot companion

### comradeship
**08** affinity **09** closeness **10** fellowship, friendship, sisterhood **11** brotherhood, camaraderie, sociability **12** sisterliness, togetherness **13** brotherliness, companionship, esprit de corps

### con
**02** do **04** dupe, hoax, know, rook, scam, scan, show **05** bluff, cheat, fraud, knock, learn, teach, trick **06** fiddle, fleece, racket, rip off **07** against, deceive, defraud, mislead, swindle, tweedle **08** cheating, hoodwink, inveigle, prisoner **09** bamboozle, deception **11** acknowledge, double-cross **15** confidence trick

### concatenation
**05** chain, nexus, trail, train **06** course, series, string, thread **07** linking **08** progress, sequence **10** connection, procession, succession **11** progression **12** interlinking, interlocking

### concave
**04** arch **05** vault **06** cupped, hollow, sunken **07** invexed, scooped **08** curved in, hollowed, incurved, indented **09** depressed, excavated, incurvate **14** bending inwards

### conceal
◇ *containment indicator* ◇ *hidden indicator* **04** bury, feal, heal, heel, hele, hide, mask, sink, veil **05** cloak, cloke, cover, stash **06** closet, hush up, keep in, pocket, screen, shroud, vizard **07** cover up, obscure, secrete, smother **08** disguise, keep dark, submerge, suppress, tuck away **09** dissemble, keep quiet, overgreen, whitewash **10** camouflage, keep hidden, keep secret, subterfuge **11** dissimulate, put the lid on **14** keep out of sight, keep under wraps

### concealed
◇ *containment indicator* ◇ *hidden indicator* **05** perdu **06** covert, hidden, latent, masked, perdue, unseen **07** covered **08** screened **09** disguised, submerged **10** tucked away **11** clandestine **13** inconspicuous

### concealment
◇ *containment indicator* ◇ *hidden indicator* **04** mask, veil **05** cloak, cover, wraps **06** hiding, screen, shroud **07** cover-up, hideout, mystery, privacy, secrecy, shelter **08** disguise, hideaway **09** secretion, whitewash **10** camouflage, protection **11** keeping dark, smokescreen, suppression **13** keeping secret

### concede
**03** owe, own **04** cede **05** admit, allow, grant, own up, yield **06** accede, accept, give up **07** confess, forfeit **08** hand over **09** recognize, sacrifice, surrender **10** condescend, relinquish **11** acknowledge

### conceit
**03** ego **04** fume, wind **05** image, pride, think **06** device, simile, vanity **07** bighead, egotism, imagine, swagger, thought **08** conceive, concetto, metaphor, puppyism, self-love **09** arrogance, cockiness, immodesty, vainglory **10** comparison, narcissism **11** complacency, haughtiness **12** boastfulness **13** bigheadedness, conceitedness, understanding **14** figure of speech, self-admiration, self-assumption, self-importance

### conceited
**04** smug, vain **05** cocky, flory, proud, windy, witty **06** clever, snotty **07** haughty, stuck-up **08** arrogant, boastful, immodest, puffed up **09** bigheaded, cat-witted, egotistic, upsetting **10** complacent, toffee-nose, up yourself **11** egotistical, fantastical, overweening, swell-headed, toffee-nosed **12** narcissistic, supercilious, vainglorious **13** above yourself, self-important, self-satisfied, swelled-headed, swollen-headed **14** full of yourself

### conceivable
**06** likely **07** tenable **08** credible, possible, probable **09** cogitable, plausible, thinkable **10** believable, imaginable

### conceivably
**08** possibly, probably **09** plausibly **10** imaginably

### conceive
**03** see **04** form, take **05** brain, fancy, grasp, guess, start, think **06** create, design, devise, enwomb, invent **07** believe, conceit, develop, express, fantasy, gestate, imagine, picture, produce, realize, suppose, think of, think up **08** contrive, envisage, perceive **09** apprehend, be fertile, formulate, originate, reproduce, visualize **10** appreciate, come up with, comprehend, understand **11** get pregnant, give birth to **14** become pregnant **15** get into your head

### concentrate
**04** mind **05** amass, bunch, crowd, focus, juice, rivet, think **06** apozem, attend, centre, direct, distil, elixir, gather, reduce **07** cluster, collect, essence, extract, thicken **08** boil down, compress, condense, consider, converge **09** decoction, decocture, evaporate, intensify **10** accumulate, centralize, congregate **11** consolidate, dephlegmate, put your mind **12** distillation, keep your mind, pay attention, quintessence **13** apply yourself **15** devote attention

### concentrated
**04** conc, deep, hard, rich **05** dense **06** all-out, strong **07** intense, reduced **08** vigorous **09** concerted, condensed, distilled, intensive, strenuous, thickened, undiluted, undivided **10** compressed, evaporated

### concentration
**04** conc, heed, mass, mind **05** crowd **07** cluster **08** devotion, focusing, grouping **09** attention, denseness, intensity, reduction, thickness **10** absorption, collection **11** application, boiling-down, compression, convergence, deep thought, engrossment, evaporation **12** accumulation, close thought, congregation, distillation **13** agglomeration, consolidation **14** centralization, conglomeration

### concept
**04** idea, idée, plan, view **05** image **06** notion, theory, vision **07** picture, thought **09** dimension, intention, universal **10** conception, hypothesis, impression **11** abstraction **13** visualization

### conception
**04** clue, idea, plan, view **05** birth, image **06** design, notion, origin, outset, theory, vision **07** concept, genesis, inkling, picture, thought **09** beginning, formation, inception, intention, invention, knowledge, launching, pregnancy **10** conceiving, hypothesis, impression, initiation, perception

**conceptual**

11 abstraction, fecundation, origination 12 appreciation, impregnation, inauguration, insemination, reproduction 13 comprehension, fertilization, understanding, visualization

**conceptual**

05 ideal 08 abstract, notional, thematic 11 speculative, theoretical 12 hypothetical 14 classificatory

**concern**

03 job 04 baby, busy, care, cern, duty, firm, heed, part, reck, reke, task 05 alarm, cover, field, issue, point, stake, topic, touch, upset, worry 06 affair, affect, bear on, bother, charge, debate, devote, indaba, matter, meddle, pidgin, pigeon, reckon, regard, sorrow, strain, tender, unease 07 anguish, anxiety, apply to, be about, company, disturb, involve, lookout, perturb, pidgeon, problem, refer to, subject, thought, trouble 08 argument, business, deal with, disquiet, distress, interest, pressure, question, relate to 09 attention, pertain to, syndicate 10 enterprise, solicitude 11 appertain to, association, concernment, corporation, disturbance, involvement, make anxious, make worried, partnership 12 apprehension, have to do with, organization, perturbation 13 attentiveness, consideration, establishment 14 prey on your mind, responsibility 15 be connected with
*See also* **company; business**

**concerned**

◊ *anagram indicator* 04 kind 05 upset 06 caring, uneasy 07 anxious, helpful, related, unhappy, versant, worried 08 affected, bothered, gracious, involved, troubled 09 attentive, connected, disturbed, perturbed, sensitive, unselfish 10 altruistic, charitable, distressed, implicated, interested, solicitous, thoughtful 11 considerate 12 apprehensive
• **be concerned** 04 care, mell
• **concerned with** 02 in, re 05 about

**concerning**

02 of, on, re 04 in re, over 05 about, after, anent 07 apropos 08 to do with, touching 09 as regards, regarding 10 relating to, relevant to, respecting 11 referring to 12 with regard to 13 in the matter of, with respect to 14 on the subject of 15 with reference to

**concert**

03 gig 04 prom, show 05 quill, union 06 accord, smoker, soirée, unison 07 concord, harmony, recital 09 agreement, rendering, rendition, unanimity 10 appearance, consonance, engagement, hootenanny, jam session, production 11 concordance, co-operation, partnership, performance 12 presentation 13 collaboration, entertainment

**concerted**

05 joint 06 shared, united 07 planned

08 combined 09 organized 10 collective 11 co-operative, co-ordinated, interactive, prearranged 12 concentrated 13 collaborative

**concession**

03 cut, sop 05 grant, right 06 ceding, favour 07 forfeit 08 decrease, discount, giving-up, handover, yielding 09 admission, allowance, exception, franchise, privilege, reduction, sacrifice, surrender 10 acceptance, adjustment, compromise 11 recognition, synchoresis 12 special right 14 relinquishment 15 acknowledgement
• **expression of concession** 02 ou, ow

**conciliate**

06 disarm, pacify, soften, soothe 07 appease, mollify, placate, satisfy 09 reconcile 10 propitiate 11 disembitter

**conciliation**

09 placation 11 appeasement, peacemaking 12 pacification, propitiation 13 mollification 14 reconciliation

**conciliator**

04 dove 06 broker 08 mediator 09 go-between, middleman 10 negotiator, peacemaker, reconciler 11 intercessor 12 intermediary

**conciliatory**

06 irenic 07 pacific 09 appeasing, assuaging, disarming, peaceable, placatory 10 mollifying 11 peacemaking 12 pacificatory, propitiative, propitiatory, smooth-spoken 13 smooth-talking, smooth-tongued 14 reconciliatory

**concise**

04 curt 05 brief, crisp, pithy, short, terse, tight 07 compact, laconic, summary 08 abridged, elliptic, mutilate, succinct, synoptic 09 condensed, thumbnail 10 aphoristic, compressed, elliptical, to the point 11 abbreviated, compendious 12 epigrammatic 14 epigrammatical

**concisely**

06 curtly 07 briefly, crisply, in a word, in brief, in short, pithily, tersely 10 succinctly, to the point 11 in a nutshell, laconically

**conclave**

05 cabal 06 parley, powwow 07 cabinet, council, meeting, session 08 assembly 09 gathering 10 conference 13 confabulation, secret meeting

**conclude**

03 end 04 amen, make 05 agree, allow, cease, close, debar, infer, judge, uptie 06 assume, clinch, decide, deduce, effect, finish, gather, reason, reckon, settle, top off, wind up, wrap up 07 arrange, enclose, pull off, resolve, suppose, surmise, work out 08 bring off, complete, restrain 09 culminate, determine, establish, negotiate, polish

off, terminate 10 accomplish, conjecture, consummate 11 come to an end, discontinue, draw to an end 12 bring to an end 14 close the book on 15 close the books on

**conclusion**

◊ *tail selection indicator* 03 con, end 04 coda, fine 05 close, finis, issue, omega, point 06 answer, ending, finale, finish, result, riddle, upshot 07 come-off, finding, opinion, outcome, problem, verdict 08 decision, epilogue, explicit, illation, pirlicue, settling, solution 09 agreement, brokering, cessation, clinching, deduction, effecting, inference, judgement, punchline 10 assumption, completion, consectary, conviction, experiment, peroration, pulling-off, resolution, settlement, working-out 11 arrangement, consequence, culmination, negotiation, termination 12 consummation 13 determination, establishment 14 accomplishment, discontinuance
• **in conclusion** 04 ergo 06 in fine 07 finally, to sum up 09 in closing 10 to conclude

**conclusive**

03 net 04 nett 05 clear, final 08 decisive, definite, ultimate 10 convincing, definitive, unarguable, undeniable 11 irrefutable 12 indisputable, unanswerable, unappealable

**conclusively**

07 clearly, finally 10 decisively, definitely, ultimately, unarguably, undeniably 11 irrefutably 12 convincingly, definitively, indisputably

**concoct**

◊ *anagram indicator* 03 fix, mix 04 brew, cook, make, plan, plot 05 blend, frame, hatch 06 cook up, decoct, devise, invent, make up, mature 07 develop, dream up, prepare, think up 08 contrive, rustle up 09 fabricate, formulate 11 manufacture, put together

**concoction**

◊ *anagram indicator* 04 brew, myth 05 blend, fable, story 06 potion 07 fiction, mixture, untruth 08 compound, creation 09 hell-broth, love-juice 10 fairy story 11 combination, fabrication, preparation, witches' brew

**concomitant**

07 symptom 09 attendant, by-product, conjoined, secondary, syndromic 10 co-existent, concurrent, incidental, side effect 11 associative, synchronous 12 accompanying, coincidental, conterminous, contributing, simultaneous 13 accompaniment, complementary, epiphenomenon 15 contemporaneous

**concord**

04 pact 05 agree, amity, peace, union 06 accord, treaty, unison 07 compact, concent, entente, harmony, rapport

**concourse**

09 agreement, concentus, consensus, harmonize, unanimity 10 consonance, friendship 11 amicability

**concourse**

04 hall 05 crowd, crush, foyer, lobby, plaza, press, swarm 06 lounge, piazza, repair, resort, throng 07 meeting 08 assembly, entrance 09 gathering, multitude 10 collection, confluence

**concrete**

04 firm, real 05 béton, solid 06 actual 07 factual, genuine, Siporex®, visible 08 definite, explicit, material, physical, positive, specific, tangible 09 touchable 11 perceptible, substantial

**concubine**

05 leman, lover, madam 07 lorette, sultana 08 mistress, paramour 09 courtesan, guinea-hen, kept woman 11 apple-squire

**concupiscence**

04 lust 06 desire, libido 07 concupy, lechery 08 appetite, lewdness 09 horniness, lubricity, randiness 11 lustfulness 12 sexual desire 14 lasciviousness, libidinousness

**concupiscent**

04 lewd 05 horny, randy 07 lustful 09 lecherous 10 lascivious, libidinous, lubricious

**concur**

05 agree 06 accede, accord, assent, comply 07 approve, consent 08 coincide 09 acquiesce, co-operate, harmonize 11 be in harmony

**concurrence**

06 assent 07 consent 08 approval, syndrome 09 agreement, synchrony 10 acceptance, conspiracy 11 association, coexistence, coincidence, consilience, convergence 12 acquiescence, common ground, simultaneity 13 juxtaposition 15 contemporaneity

**concurrent**

10 coexistent, coexisting, coincident, coinciding 11 concomitant, synchronous 12 accompanying, simultaneous 15 contemporaneous

**concussion**

10 head injury 11 brain injury, water hammer 15 unconsciousness

**condemn**

◇ anagram indicator 03 ban, bar 04 cast, damn, doom, hiss, kest, slam 05 blame, decry, force, judge, knock, slate 06 berate, coerce, compel, ordain, punish, revile 07 accurse, censure, consign, convict, deplore, destine, destroy, reprove, run down, upbraid 08 demolish, denounce, reproach, sentence 09 castigate, criticize, deprecate, disparage, reprehend 10 disapprove, find guilty 12 declare unfit 13 declare unsafe, give a sentence, pass a sentence

**condemnation**

◇ anagram indicator 03 ban 04 doom 05 blame 07 censure, reproof 08 judgment, reproach, sentence 09 criticism, damnation, judgement 10 conviction, thumbs-down 11 castigation, deprecation, disapproval, reprobation 12 denunciation 13 disparagement

**condemnatory**

08 accusing, critical 09 damnatory, reprobate 10 accusatory, censorious 11 deprecatory, judgemental, reprobative, reprobatory 12 denunciatory, disapproving, discouraging, proscriptive, unfavourable 13 incriminating

**condensation**

05 steam 06 digest, précis 07 summary 08 moisture, synopsis 09 reduction 11 abridgement, boiling-down, compression, contraction, curtailment, evaporation 12 distillation, liquefaction 13 concentration, consolidation, deliquescence, precipitation

**condense**

03 cut 06 distil, précis, reduce 07 abridge, compact, curtail, cut down, shorten, thicken 08 boil down, compress, contract, solidify 09 capsulize, coagulate, epitomize, evaporate, intensify, summarize 10 abbreviate, condensate, deliquesce, inspissate 11 concentrate, encapsulate, precipitate

**condensed**

03 cut 04 rich 05 dense 06 potted, strong 07 capsule, clotted, compact, concise, cut down, reduced, summary 08 capsular 09 curtailed, shortened, thickened, undiluted 10 abstracted, coagulated, compressed, contracted, evaporated, summarized 12 concentrated

**condescend**

04 bend 05 agree, deign, grant, stoop 06 comply, see fit 07 concede, consent, decline, descend, specify 09 patronize, vouchsafe 10 talk down to 12 be snobbish to 13 lower yourself 14 demean yourself, humble yourself

**condescending**

05 lofty 06 lordly, snooty 07 haughty, stuck-up 08 gracious, snobbish, superior 09 imperious 10 disdainful 11 patronizing, toffee-nosed 12 supercilious

**condescendingly**

10 snobbishly 11 imperiously 12 disdainfully 13 patronizingly 14 superciliously

**condescension**

04 airs 05 stoop 07 disdain 09 loftiness 10 lordliness 11 haughtiness, superiority 12 snobbishness

**condiment**

04 salt 05 spice 06 ginger, pepper, relish, season 07 caraway, chutney, mustard, pickles, vinegar 08 carraway, chow-chow 09 seasoning 10 flavouring 11 horseradish, tracklement 13 French mustard 14 English mustard

**condition**

◇ anagram indicator 02 do, if 03 -dom, ply 04 case, form, nick, pass, rule, sted, tone, trim, tune 05 adapt, equip, groom, limit, mould, order, prime, set-up, shape, state, stead, stedd, stede, steed, teach, terms, train, treat 06 adjust, defect, demand, factor, fettle, health, kilter, malady, milieu, plight, revive, season, stedde, temper 07 ailment, climate, context, disease, educate, factors, fitness, illness, improve, nourish, prepare, problem, proviso, restore, setting 08 accustom, disorder, position, quandary, restrict, weakness 09 brainwash, complaint, essential, infirmity, influence, necessity, provision, situation, transform, way of life 10 atmosphere, background, limitation, obligation 11 environment, familiarize, make healthy, predicament, requirement, restriction, stipulation 12 indoctrinate, precondition, prerequisite, surroundings, working order 13 circumstances, qualification, state of health

See also **disease; psychological; skin**

• **in good condition** 02 OK 03 fit 04 okay, taut, tidy, well 05 sound 07 in flesh, in shape, thrifty 13 well-preserved

• **in perfect condition** 02 go 06 groovy 12 sound as a bell

• **in such condition** 02 so

• **in what condition** 03 how

**conditional**

04 tied 05 based 07 limited, subject 08 relative 09 dependent, provisory, qualified 10 contingent, restricted 11 provisional

**conditionally**

09 limitedly 10 relatively 11 qualifiedly 13 provisionally

**conditioning**

07 shaping 08 moulding 09 influence 10 adaptation, adjustment 11 preparation 12 transforming

**condolence**

04 pity 07 comfort, support 08 sympathy 10 compassion 11 consolation 13 commiseration

**condom**

04 safe 06 johnny, rubber, sheath 07 Femidom®, johnnie, scumbag 10 protective 12 female condom, French letter, prophylactic 13 contraceptive

**condone**

05 allow, brook 06 accept, excuse, ignore, pardon 07 forgive, let pass 08 overlook, tolerate 09 disregard 15 turn a blind eye to

**conducive**

06 aiding, useful 07 helpful, leading, tending 09 promoting 10 beneficial, favourable, productive 11 encouraging, ministerial 12 advantageous, contributing, contributory, instrumental

## conduct

**conduct**
02 do 03 act, ren, rin, run 04 bear, hold, keep, lead, show, take, ways 05 bring, carry, chair, guide, pilot, steer, usher 06 acquit, behave, convey, direct, escort, handle, manage 07 actions, bearing, comport, control, manners, operate, perform, running, solicit 08 attitude, behavior, carry out, guidance, organize, practice, regulate, transmit 09 accompany, behaviour, demeanour, direction, operation 10 administer, deportment, leadership, management 11 comportment, orchestrate, supervision 12 be in charge of, organization 14 administration

## conductance
01 G

## conductor
06 leader 07 clippie, maestro, manager 09 electrode 11 non-electric

*Conductors include:*

04 **Böhm** (Karl), **Wood** (Sir Henry)
05 **Boult** (Sir Adrian), **Bülow** (Hans von), **Davis** (Sir Andrew), **Davis** (Sir Colin), **Elgar** (Sir Edward), **Hallé** (Sir Charles), **Kempe** (Rudolf), **Solti** (Sir Georg), **Sousa** (John Philip)
06 **Abbado** (Claudio), **Boulez** (Pierre), **Casals** (Pablo), **Gibson** (Sir Alexander), **Maazel** (Lorin), **Mahler** (Gustav), **Previn** (André), **Rattle** (Sir Simon), **Walter** (Bruno)
07 **Beecham** (Sir Thomas), **Gergiev** (Valery), **Haitink** (Bernard), **Harding** (Daniel), **Jansons** (Mariss), **Karajan** (Herbert von), **Lambert** (Constant), **Nicolai** (Otto), **Richter** (Hans), **Sargent** (Sir Malcolm), **Smetana** (Bedrich), **Strauss** (Johann), **Strauss** (Richard)
08 **Goossens** (Sir Eugene)
09 **Ashkenazy** (Vladimir), **Barenboim** (Daniel), **Bernstein** (Leonard), **Boulanger** (Nadia), **Klemperer** (Otto), **Mackerras** (Sir Charles), **Stokowski** (Leopold), **Tortelier** (Paul), **Toscanini** (Arturo)
10 **Barbirolli** (Sir John), **Villa-Lobos** (Heitor)
11 **Furtwängler** (Wilhelm)
12 **Rostropovich** (Mstislav)

## conduit
04 duct, main, pipe, tube 05 canal, chute, ditch, drain, flume, trunk 06 gutter, trough, tunnel 07 channel, culvert, passage, wireway 08 fountain, penstock, waterway 10 passageway 11 watercourse

## cone
03 puy 05 spire 06 cornet, funnel 09 monticule, strobilus

## confection
◊ *anagram indicator*
*See* **dessert**

## confectionery
05 candy 06 sweets 07 bonbons, goodies, junkets, lollies, toffees 08 licorice, sweeties 09 liquorice 10 chocolates, confiserie, hokey-pokey, sweetmeats, sweet-stuff
*See also* **sweet**

## confederacy
04 band, Bund 05 junta, junto, union 06 league 07 compact 08 alliance 09 coalition 10 conspiracy, federation 11 Five Nations, partnership 13 confederation

## confederate
04 ally, band 05 cover 06 allied, friend, united 07 abettor, fedarie, federal, partner 08 combined, federary, federate, foedarie 09 accessory, assistant, associate, colleague, federarie, supporter 10 accomplice, associated 11 conspirator 12 collaborator

## confederation
04 zupa 05 union 06 league 07 compact 08 alliance 09 coalition, hermandad 10 federation 11 association, confederacy, partnership 12 amalgamation

## confer
02 cf, do 03 pay 04 give, lend, talk 05 award, grant, parle, pawaw 06 accord, bestow, debate, impart, parley, powwow 07 compare, consult, discuss, give out, present 08 converse 10 deliberate 13 exchange views

## conference
03 hui 04 diet, pear 05 forum 06 debate, huddle, indaba, parley, powwow, summit 07 meeting, palaver, seminar 08 colloquy, congress, dialogue 09 symposium 10 colloquium, convention, discussion, imparlance, pourparler 11 convocation, emparlaunce, get-together 12 consultation, council of war

## confess
03 own 04 avow, sing 05 admit, cough, grant, own up 06 affirm, agnize, assert, expose, fess up, reveal, shrive, squeak 07 concede, confide, declare, divulge, profess, tell all, unbosom 08 disclose, unburden 09 come clean, make known, recognize 11 accept blame, acknowledge 13 come out with it, spill the beans, spill your guts 15 get off your chest

## confession
06 avowal, shrift 08 exposure, owning-up 09 admission, assertion 10 disclosure, divulgence, profession, revelation, submission, unbosoming 11 affirmation, declaration, making known, short shrift, unburdening 14 acknowledgment 15 acknowledgement, amende honorable

## confidant, confidante
03 pal 04 chum, mate 05 buddy, crony 06 friend 08 alter ego, intimate 09 companion 10 best friend, bosom buddy, repository 11 bosom friend, close friend

## confide
04 affy, tell 05 admit 06 impart, reveal 07 breathe, confess, divulge, entrust, unbosom, whisper 08 disclose, intimate, unburden 11 tell a secret 15 get off your chest

## confidence
03 con, ego 04 hope 05 faith, poise, trust 06 aplomb, belief, secret 07 courage 08 boldness, calmness, credence, forehead, intimacy, reliance 09 assurance, certainty, composure 10 conviction, dependence, self-belief 11 assuredness 12 positiveness, self-reliance 13 private matter, self-assurance 14 self-confidence, self-possession
• **in confidence** 08 in secret, secretly 09 entre nous, in privacy, in private, privately 10 personally 11 just quietly 12 under the rose 14 confidentially 15 between you and me

## confident
04 bold, calm, cool, sure 05 happy, hardy 06 crouse, secure, upbeat 07 assured, certain 08 composed, definite, fearless, positive, sanguine 09 convinced, dauntless, unabashed 10 courageous, optimistic, sure-footed 11 comfortable, self-assured, self-reliant 12 unhesitating 13 self-confident, self-possessed 14 sure of yourself 15 unselfconscious

## confidential
04 pack 05 bosom, privy 06 inward, secret 07 a latere, private 08 hush-hush, intimate, man-to-man, personal 09 sensitive, tête-à-tête, top secret 10 classified, restricted 12 off-the-record, woman-to-woman

## confidentially
07 privily, sub rosa 08 in camera, in secret 09 entre nous, in privacy, in private, privately 10 on the quiet, personally 11 just quietly 12 in confidence 15 between you and me

## confidently
06 boldly, calmly, coolly, surely 09 assuredly 10 composedly, fearlessly, positively 11 comfortably 12 courageously 14 optimistically, unhesitatingly

## configuration
04 cast, face, form 05 shape 06 figure 07 contour, outline 11 arrangement, composition, disposition 12 conformation

## confine
03 fix, mew, pen 04 bail, bale, bind, cage, coop, crib, edge, gate, hold, keep, mure, shut 05 bound, cramp, emmew, enmew, immew, limit, pound, scope, stick, thirl 06 bail up, border, coop up, immure, inhoop, intern, keep in, lock up, narrow, prison, shut in, shut up 07 chamber, control, delimit, enclose, impound, inclose, inhibit, repress, shackle, trammel 08 bottle up, boundary, frontier, imprison, lock away, regulate, restrain, restrict, shut away 09 constrain, immanacle, parameter, perimeter, prescribe 10 limitation 11 hold captive, incarcerate, restriction

**confined**

12 circumscribe, hold prisoner
13 circumference, hold in custody

**confined**

04 pent, poky 05 caged, close, pokey, small 06 narrow, penned, pent-up, poking 07 captive, cramped, limited, squeezy 08 enclosed 09 chambered 10 controlled, housebound, imprisoned, restricted 11 constrained, constricted 13 circumscribed

**confinement**

05 birth 06 burden, labour 07 custody, lying-in 08 delivery, solitary 09 captivity, detention, restraint 10 childbirth, constraint, internment, prisonment 11 house arrest, parturition 12 imprisonment 13 incarceration

**confirm**

03 fix, tie 04 aver, back 05 check, prove 06 affirm, assert, assure, bishop, clinch, harden, obsign, pledge, ratify, settle, soothe, uphold, verify 07 approve, certify, endorse, fortify, gazette, promise, qualify, support, warrant 08 evidence, reassure, sanction, validate 09 authorize, establish, guarantee, obsignate, reinforce 10 asseverate, homologate, strengthen 11 corroborate, demonstrate 12 authenticate, substantiate 14 give credence to

**confirmation**

05 proof 06 assent, chrism 07 backing, support 08 approval, evidence, sanction 09 agreement, testimony 10 acceptance, affirmance, validation 11 affirmation, approbation, endorsement 12 ratification, verification 13 accreditation, corroboration 14 authentication, substantiation

**confirmed**

03 set 04 firm 05 fixed, sworn, vowed 06 inured, rooted 07 affear'd, chronic, settled 08 addicted, affeered, habitual, hardened, seasoned 09 incurable 10 double-dyed, entrenched, inveterate 11 corroborate, established 12 incorrigible, long-standing 13 dyed-in-the-wool 15 long-established

**confiscate**

05 seize 06 remove 07 escheat, forfeit, impound 08 arrogate, take away 09 forfeited, sequester 10 commandeer 11 appropriate, expropriate

**confiscation**

07 escheat, removal, seizure 08 takeover 09 distraint 10 forfeiture, impounding 12 distrainment 13 appropriation, commandeering, expropriation, sequestration

**conflagration**

04 fire 05 blaze 06 flames 07 burning, inferno 09 holocaust 12 deflagration

**conflate**

04 fuse 05 blend, merge 07 combine 08 compound 09 integrate 10 amalgamate, synthesize 11 incorporate, put together 13 bring together

**conflict**

03 jar, row, war 04 agon, camp, feud, muss 05 agony, brawl, clash, close, fight, mêlée, musse, scrap, set-to 06 battle, bust-up, combat, differ, dust-up, fracas, oppose, scrape, strife, strive, tangle, thwart, unrest 07 collide, contend, contest, discord, dispute, ill-will, quarrel, warfare 08 antinomy, be at odds, clashing, disagree, friction, skirmish, struggle, variance 09 antipathy, collision, encounter, front line, go against, hostility 10 antagonism, contention, contradict, dissension, dissonance, engagement, opposition 12 be at variance, disagreement 13 be incongruous, confrontation 14 be in opposition 15 be at loggerheads, incompatibility
*See also* **battle; war**

**conflicting**

06 at odds, off-key 08 clashing, contrary, opposing 09 competing, dissonant 10 at variance 11 incongruous 12 antithetical, incompatible, inconsistent 13 contradictory

**confluence**

05 union 06 infall 07 conflux, meeting 08 junction 09 concourse 10 watersmeet 11 concurrence, convergence 12 meeting-point

**conform**

03 fit 04 obey, suit 05 adapt, agree, match, tally 06 accord, adjust, comply, follow, square 07 abide by, observe 08 parallel, quadrate 09 be uniform, harmonize 10 comply with, correspond, fall in with, toe the line 11 accommodate 12 fall into line 13 go with the flow 14 be conventional, do the same thing, follow the crowd 15 go with the stream

**conformist**

03 Con 06 yes-man 11 rubber-stamp 13 stick-in-the-mud 14 traditionalist 15 conventionalist

**conformity**

07 harmony 08 affinity, likeness 09 agreement, congruity, obedience, orthodoxy 10 accordance, accordancy, adjustment, compliance, conformism, consonance, observance, similarity, uniformity 11 resemblance 13 accommodation 14 correspondence, traditionalism 15 conventionality

**confound**

◊ *anagram indicator* 03 mix 04 beat, dash, faze, mate, ruin, stun 05 abash, amaze, floor, knock, stump, throw, upset 06 awhape, baffle, defeat, puzzle, rabbit, thwart 07 astound, confuse, destroy, flummox, mystify, nonplus, perplex, stagger, startle, stupefy, unshape 08 astonish, bewilder, demolish, surprise 09 bamboozle, discomfit, dumbfound, frustrate, overthrow, overwhelm 10 spifflicate 11 flabbergast, spifflicate

**confront**

04 defy, face, meet, show 05 beard, brave, cross 06 accost, appose, attack, oppose, resist, tackle 07 address, affront, assault, compare, eyeball, present 08 cope with, deal with, face down, face up to 09 challenge, encounter, stand up to, withstand 10 meet head on, reckon with 11 contend with 12 face the music 15 come to grips with, come to terms with

**confrontation**

05 brush, clash, fight, set-to 06 battle 07 contest, face-off, quarrel 08 conflict, showdown 09 collision, encounter 10 engagement 12 disagreement

**confuse**

◊ *anagram indicator* 03 fog 04 faze, lose, maze 05 addle, bemud, dizzy, floor, mix up, mudge, stump, throw, upset 06 baffle, bemuse, burble, didder, dither, fickle, flurry, fuddle, garble, jumble, mess up, mingle, mither, mizzle, moider, muddle, puzzle, tangle 07 bumbaze, flummox, fluster, involve, mistake, moither, mortify, mystify, perplex 08 befuddle, bemuddle, bewilder, compound, confound, disorder, distract, dumfound, entangle, surprise 09 bamboozle, disorient, dumbfound, elaborate, embarrass, embrangle, imbrangle, obfuscate 10 complicate, disarrange, discompose, disconcert, tie in knots 12 disorientate, make involved, mingle-mangle 13 make difficult 14 muddy the waters
*See also* **baffle; tangle**

**confused**

◊ *anagram indicator* 04 hazy, lost, mazy, mixt, mixy 05 dazed, dizzy, messy, mixed, muddy 06 addled, untidy 07 baffled, bemused, chaotic, floored, in a flap, jumbled, maffled, mixed-up, muddled, puzzled 08 all at sea, flustery, mithered 09 delirious, disturbed, flummoxed, flustered, mystified, perplexed 10 bamboozled, bewildered, confounded, désorienté, disordered, disorderly, distracted, hurly-burly, indistinct, nonplussed, out of order, topsy-turvy, unbalanced, up a gumtree 11 complicated, disarranged, in a flat spin, muddy-headed 12 disconcerted, disorganized, inextricable 13 disorientated, helter-skelter, muddle-brained 15 all over the place

**confusing**

◊ *anagram indicator* 05 dizzy 07 cryptic, unclear 08 baffling, involved, muddling, puzzling, tortuous 09 ambiguous, difficult 10 misleading, perplexing 11 bewildering, complicated 12 inconclusive, inconsistent 13 contradictory

**confusion**

◊ *anagram indicator* 02 pi 03 fog, pie, pye 04 mess, muss, toss 05 chaos, lurry, mix-up, musse, shame 06 baffle, bumble, bummle, cock-up, dudder, fuddle, guddle, huddle, jumble, mess-up, muddle 07 clutter, flutter, turmoil,

## confute

whemmle, whomble, whommle, whummle 08 disarray, disorder, mishmash, shambles, upheaval
09 commotion, égarement, embroglio, imbroglio, overthrow, perdition
10 bafflement, hurly-burly, perplexity, puzzlement, topsy-turvy, untidiness
12 bewilderment, entanglement, hubble-bubble, hugger-mugger
13 disconcertion, embarrassment, indistinction, mystification
14 disarrangement 15 disorganization

## confute

05 rebut, refel 06 debunk, negate, refute 07 put down 08 disprove, redargue 09 discredit 10 contradict, controvert, prove false

## congeal

03 gel, set 04 cake, clot, fuse, geal, jeel
05 jelly 06 curdle, freeze, harden
07 pectize, stiffen, thicken 08 coalesce, solidify 09 coagulate 11 concentrate

## congenial

04 cosy 06 genial, homely, kinred
07 kindred 08 friendly, pleasant, pleasing, relaxing, suitable
09 agreeable, simpatico 10 compatible, delightful, favourable, like-minded, well-suited 11 complaisant, sympathetic, sympathique
13 companionable

## congenital

05 utter 06 inborn, inbred, innate, inured 07 chronic, connate, natural
08 complete, habitual, hardened, inherent, seasoned, thorough
09 incurable, inherited 10 compulsive, connatural, entrenched, hereditary, inveterate 12 incorrigible
14 constitutional

## congested

04 full 06 choked, jammed, packed
07 blocked, clogged, crammed, crowded, stuffed, teeming 08 engorged
11 overcharged, overcrowded, overflowing

## congestion

03 jam 07 choking, snarl-up
08 blockage, blocking, clogging, crowding, gridlock 10 bottleneck, pinchpoint, traffic jam
12 overcrowding

## conglomerate

04 firm 05 group, trust 06 cartel, merger
07 combine, company, concern
08 business, fullness 10 consortium, traffic jam 11 association, corporation, engorgement, partnership
13 establishment, multinational

## conglomeration

04 mass 06 medley 09 composite
10 assemblage, assortment, collection, hotchpotch 11 aggregation
12 accumulation 13 agglomeration

## Congo

03 COD, COG, RCB, ZRE

## congratulate

05 greet 06 praise 08 wish well
09 gratulate 10 compliment, felicitate
12 pat on the back 13 say well done to

15 wish happiness to
• **congratulate yourself** 05 plume, preen, pride 09 delight in

## congratulations

04 euge 07 bouquet 08 bouquets, congrats, mazeltov, well done 09 good on you, greetings 10 best wishes, good for you, good wishes 11 compliments
12 pat on the back 13 felicitations

## congregate

04 form, mass, meet 05 clump, crowd, flock, rally 06 gather, muster, throng
07 cluster, collect, convene
08 assemble, converge 10 accumulate, rendezvous 12 come together

## congregation

04 fold, host, mass 05 crowd, flock, group, laity 06 parish, people, throng
07 meeting 08 assembly 09 multitude
10 fellowship 12 parishioners

## congress

03 hui 04 diet 05 forum, synod
07 council, meeting 08 assembly, conclave 09 gathering 10 conference, convention, parliament
11 convocation, legislature

## congruence

05 match 07 harmony 08 identity
09 agreement 10 concinnity, conformity, consonance, similarity
11 coincidence, concurrence, consistency, parallelism, resemblance
13 compatibility 14 correspondence

## congruent

07 similar 08 parallel, suitable
09 consonant 10 compatible, concurrent, consistent, harmonious
13 corresponding

## conical

06 spired 07 pointed, tapered
08 tapering 09 pyramidal, turbinate
10 cone-shaped, fastigiate 12 funnel-shaped, infundibular 13 infundibulate, pyramid-shaped

## conifer

*see* **pine; tree**

## conjectural

07 assumed, posited 08 academic, supposed, surmised 09 tentative
10 divinatory, postulated, stochastic
11 speculative, theoretical
12 divinatorial, hypothetical
13 suppositional

## conjecture

03 aim 05 augur, fancy, guess, infer
06 assume, notion, reckon, theory
07 imagine, presume, suppose, surmise, suspect 08 estimate, theorize
09 guesswork, inference, speculate, suspicion 10 assumption, conclusion, divination, estimation, hypothesis, presuppose, projection 11 guesstimate, hypothesize, presumption, speculation, supposition
13 extrapolation 14 presupposition

## conjoin

04 join, link 05 match, unify, unite
06 concur 07 combine, connect
08 alligate 10 amalgamate, synthesize
12 join together

## conjugal

06 bridal, wedded 07 marital, married, nuptial, spousal 08 hymeneal
09 connubial 11 epithalamic, matrimonial
• **conjugal union** 03 bed

## conjunction

05 synod, union 06 syzygy 07 unition
10 alligation, connection, copulative, injunction 11 association, coexistence, coincidence, colligation, combination, concurrence, unification
12 amalgamation, co-occurrence
13 juxtaposition
• **in conjunction with** 04 with
09 alongside, along with 12 combined with, together with 13 in company with

## conjure

05 charm, evoke, raise, rouse 06 call up, compel, invoke, juggle, summon
07 bewitch, do magic 08 do tricks
09 fascinate 10 make appear
11 materialize 12 perform magic
13 perform tricks
• **conjure up** 05 evoke 06 awaken, create, excite, invoke, recall
07 produce 08 summon up 09 recollect
10 call to mind 11 bring to mind

## conjurer

06 wizard 08 magician, sorcerer
10 mystery-man 11 illusionist, thaumaturge 12 prestigiator 13 miracle-worker 15 prestidigitator
• **conjurer's skill** 11 legerdemain
13 sleight of hand
• **conjurer's words** 09 hey presto
10 hocus-pocus 11 abracadabra

## conk

04 head, nose
• **conk out** 03 die 04 fail 06 go bust, go phut, pack up 07 go kaput
08 collapse 09 break down, go haywire
12 go on the blink

## con man

04 liar 05 bunco, cheat, crook 06 rorter, usurer 07 blagger, grifter, hustler
08 deceiver, swindler, tweedler 09 con artist 11 bunco artist, illy whacker, overcharger 12 bunko-steerer, extortionist, rip-off artist

## connect

03 put, tie 04 ally, bolt, bond, fuse, join, link 05 affix, clamp, unite
06 attach, bridge, couple, equate, fasten, relate, secure 07 bracket, combine 08 identify, relate to
09 associate, correlate 10 articulate
11 compaginate, concatenate 12 hang together

## connected

04 akin, tied 06 allied, joined, linked, united 07 coupled, related, secured
08 coherent, combined, fastened
09 associate, conjugate 10 affiliated, associated

## Connecticut

02 CT 04 Conn

## connection

03 tie 04 bond, link, pons 05 clasp, joint, tie-in, tie-up 06 friend, hook-up,

**conning-tower**

link-up **07** analogy, contact, context, liaison, linkage, rapport, sponsor **08** alliance, coupling, intimacy, junction, parallel, relation, relative **09** coherence, fastening, reference, relevance **10** attachment **11** association, colligation, conjunction, correlation, intercourse **12** acquaintance, relationship **13** communication, consanguinity, interrelation **14** correspondence • **in connection with** **02** re **04** as to **05** about **07** apropos **09** as regards, regarding **10** concerning, in regard to **12** in relation to, with regard to **13** with respect to **14** on the subject of **15** with reference to

**conning-tower**
**04** sail

**connivance**
**07** consent **08** abetment, abetting **09** collusion, condoning **10** complicity, conspiracy, lenocinium

**connive**
**04** plot, wink **05** allow, brook, cabal, coact, let go **06** ignore, scheme, wink at **07** collude, complot, condone, let pass **08** conspire, intrigue, overlook, pass over, tolerate **09** disregard, gloss over **11** collaborate **15** turn a blind eye to

**conniving**
**05** nasty **07** corrupt, immoral **08** plotting, scheming **09** colluding **10** conspiring **12** manipulative, unscrupulous

**connoisseur**
**04** buff **05** judge **06** expert, pundit **07** arbiter, devotee, epicure, gourmet **08** aesthete, oenophil, virtuoso **09** authority **10** aficionado, gastronome, specialist **11** cognoscente, gastronomer, oenophilist **12** iconophilist

**connotation**
**04** hint **06** intent, nuance **08** allusion, overtone **09** colouring, undertone **10** intimation, suggestion **11** association, implication, insinuation **12** undercurrent **13** comprehension

**connote**
**05** imply **06** hint at, import **07** betoken, purport, signify, suggest **08** allude to, indicate, intimate **09** associate, connotate, insinuate

**conquer**
**03** win **04** beat, best, rout, take **05** annex, crush, debel, quell, seize, worst **06** defeat, humble, master, obtain, occupy, subdew, subdue **07** acquire, control, overrun, possess, succeed, trounce **08** overcome, suppress, surmount, vanquish **09** overpower, overthrow, rise above, subjugate **11** appropriate, prevail over, triumph over **14** get the better of

**conqueror**
**04** hero, lord, Moor **05** champ, Mogul **06** master, victor, winner **08** champion **10** subjugator, vanquisher **12** conquistador

**conquest**
**03** win **04** coup, rout **05** catch, lover **06** defeat **07** beating, captive, capture, mastery, seizing, success, triumph, victory **08** crushing, invasion **09** overthrow, trouncing **10** annexation, occupation, possession, subjection **11** acquisition, overrunning, subjugation **12** overpowering, vanquishment **13** appropriation

**conscience**
**05** inwit **06** ethics, morals, qualms **08** scruples **09** diligence, moral code, standards **10** moral sense, principles, syneidesis, synteresis **11** voice within **12** sense of right **14** scrupulousness **15** still small voice

**conscience-stricken**
**05** sorry **06** guilty **07** ashamed **08** contrite, penitent, troubled **09** disturbed, regretful, repentant **10** remorseful **11** guilt-ridden **12** compunctious, on a guilt trip

**conscientious**
**06** honest **07** careful, dutiful, upright **08** diligent, faithful, thorough **09** assiduous, attentive, dedicated **10** methodical, meticulous, particular, scrupulous **11** hard-working, industrious, painstaking, punctilious, responsible

**conscious**
**05** alert, alive, awake, aware **06** wilful **07** heedful, knowing, mindful, studied, witting **08** rational, sensible, sentient **09** cognizant, conscient, on purpose, reasoning, voluntary **10** calculated, deliberate, percipient, responsive, volitional **11** intentional, recognizant **12** premeditated **13** self-conscious • **be conscious of** **04** feel **06** savour

**consciously**
**08** wilfully **09** knowingly, on purpose **11** voluntarily **12** deliberately **13** intentionally

**consciousness**
**04** mind **06** psyche **07** thought **09** alertness, awareness, intuition, knowledge, sentience **10** being awake, cognizance, perception **11** cenesthesia, cenesthesis, realization, recognition, sensibility, wakefulness **12** apprehension **13** coenaesthesia, coenaesthesis

**conscript**
**05** draft **06** call up, enlist, induct, muster, take on **07** draftee, recruit, round up **08** enlistee, enrolled, inductee **10** registered

**conscription**
**05** draft **08** drafting

**consecrate**
**03** vow **05** bless, exalt **06** anoint, devote, hallow, ordain, revere **07** devoted **08** dedicate, make holy, sanctify, venerate **10** sanctified

**consecutive**
**06** in a row, in turn, serial **07** running, sequent, seriate **08** parallel, straight,

unbroken **09** following, on the trot **10** back to back, continuous, sequential, succeeding, successive **13** uninterrupted

**consecutively**
**06** in a row, in turn **09** on the trot **10** back to back **11** hand-running **12** continuously, sequentially, successively **15** uninterruptedly

**consensus**
**05** unity **07** concord, consent, harmony **09** agreement, unanimity **10** consension **11** concurrence **12** consentience, majority view

**consent**
**05** admit, agree, allow, grant, yield **06** accede, accept, afford, assent, comply, concur, permit, submit **07** affoord, approve, concede, go-ahead **08** approval, sanction **09** acquiesce, agreement, authorize, clearance **10** acceptance, compliance, concession, condescend, green light, homologate, permission **11** concurrence, go along with **12** acquiescence **13** authorization **14** give the go-ahead **15** give the thumbs-up

**consequence**
**03** end **04** note **05** issue, value **06** effect, import, moment, result, upshot, weight **07** concern, outcome **08** eminence, sequence **09** aftermath, inference, substance **10** importance, importancy, prominence, side effect **11** distinction, eventuality, implication **12** repercussion, significance **13** reverberation

**consequent**
**07** ensuing, sequent **09** appendant, corollary, following, resultant, resulting **10** consectary, sequential, subsequent, successive

**consequential**
**03** key **05** vital **07** crucial, ensuing, serious, weighty **08** material, relevant, valuable **09** following, important, momentous, prominent, resultant, resulting **10** noteworthy, sequential, subsequent, successive **11** far-reaching, significant, substantial

**consequently**
**04** ergo, then, thus **05** hence **06** so that **09** as a result, therefore **11** accordingly, necessarily **12** subsequently **13** inferentially **15** consequentially

**conservation**
**03** con **04** care **06** saving, upkeep **07** custody, ecology, economy, keeping **09** husbandry **10** protection **11** maintenance, safe-keeping **12** preservation, safeguarding

**conservationist**
**05** green **06** econut **07** greenie **08** ecofreak **09** ecologist **10** tree-hugger **15** preservationist • **conservationists** **02** NT **03** WWF

**conservatism**
**09** orthodoxy **14** traditionalism **15** conventionalism

## conservative
**01** C **03** Con **04** blue, cons, Tory **05** right, sober **06** hunker **07** careful, diehard, guarded, old-line **08** cautious, moderate, old-liner, orthodox, Unionist, verkramp **09** bourgeois, hidebound, right-wing **10** inflexible **11** reactionary, right-winger, traditional **12** buttoned-down, conventional **13** set in your ways, stick-in-the-mud, unprogressive **14** traditionalist **15** backward-looking, middle-of-the-road

## conservatory
**06** school **07** academy, college **08** hothouse **09** institute **10** glasshouse, greenhouse, storehouse **11** music school **12** drama college, preservative **13** conservatoire

## conserve
**03** jam **04** keep, save **05** guard, gumbo, hoard, jelly **06** retain **07** husband, protect, store up **08** keep back, maintain, preserve **09** comfiture, marmalade, safeguard **10** take care of **13** keep in reserve

## consider
**03** see **04** deem, feel, hold, muse, note, rate, view, vise **05** count, judge, study, think, weigh **06** debate, devise, esteem, ponder, regard, reward **07** believe, bethink, examine, reflect, respect, toy with, weigh up **08** chew over, cogitate, envisage, meditate, mull over, prepense, regard as, remember, ruminate, see about **09** apprehend, kick about **10** animadvert, bear in mind, deliberate, keep in mind, kick around **11** contemplate **13** give thought to **15** take into account

## considerable
**03** big, gay, gey **04** some, tidy, vast **05** ample, great, large, smart **06** lavish, marked, pretty **07** healthy, notable, serious, sizable **08** abundant, generous, sizeable **09** important, plentiful, tolerable **10** noteworthy, noticeable, reasonable **11** appreciable, influential, perceptible, respectable, significant, substantial, substantive **13** distinguished

## considerably
**03** gay, gey **04** much **07** greatly **08** markedly **10** abundantly, noticeably, remarkably **11** appreciably **13** significantly, substantially

## considerate
**04** kind **06** caring **07** helpful, tactful **08** discreet, generous, gracious, obliging, selfless **09** attentive, concerned, courteous, sensitive, unselfish **10** altruistic, charitable, deliberate, respective, solicitous, thoughtful **11** sympathetic **13** compassionate

## consideration
**04** care, fact, heed, tact **05** count, issue, point **06** factor, motive, notice, reason, regard, review **07** account, concern, payment, respect, thought **08** altruism, analysis, kindness, scrutiny, sympathy **09** attention, reckoning **10** cogitation, compassion, discretion, generosity, importance, inspection, meditation, recompense, reflection, rumination **11** examination, helpfulness, sensitivity **12** circumstance, deliberation, graciousness, selflessness **13** contemplation, unselfishness **14** thoughtfulness
• **lacking consideration 04** nude
• **take into consideration 05** study **07** plan for **08** allow for, consider **10** bear in mind, keep in mind **13** give thought to **15** take into account

## considering
**08** all in all, in view of **10** respecting **12** in the light of **13** bearing in mind

## consign
**04** seal, send, ship, sign **06** assign, banish, commit, convey, devote **07** commend, deliver, entrust **08** give over, hand over, relegate, transfer, transmit **09** recommend

## consignment
**04** load **05** batch, cargo, goods **08** delivery, shipment

## consist
**03** lie **05** exist **06** embody, inhere, reside **07** contain, embrace, include, involve, subsist **08** amount to, be formed, be made up, comprise **10** be composed **11** be contained, incorporate

## consistency
**07** density, harmony, keeping **08** cohesion, evenness, firmness, identity, sameness **09** agreement, coherence, coherency, congruity, constancy, stability, substance, thickness, viscosity **10** accordance, conformity, consonance, continuity, regularity, smoothness, steadiness, uniformity **11** persistence, reliability **12** lack of change **13** compatibility, dependability, steadfastness **14** correspondence

## consistent
**04** same **06** stable, steady **07** logical, regular, uniform **08** agreeing, coherent, constant, matching, straight **09** accordant, congruous, consonant, unfailing **10** coinciding, compatible, conforming, dependable, harmonious, persistent, unchanging **11** predictable, undeviating **13** consentaneous, corresponding **15** hanging together

## consistently
**09** regularly, uniformly **10** constantly, dependably **11** predictably, unfailingly **12** persistently

## consolation
**03** aid **04** ease, help **05** cheer **06** relief, solace **07** comfort, succour, support **08** soothing, sympathy **11** alleviation, assuagement, reassurance **12** recomforture **13** commiseration, encouragement

## console
**04** calm, help, Xbox® **05** ancon, board, cheer, dials, knobs, panel **06** levers, solace, soothe **07** buttons, comfort, hearten, relieve, succour, support **08** controls, Gamecube®, keyboard, Nintendo®, reassure, switches **09** consolate, dashboard, encourage, recomfort **11** instruments, PlayStation® **12** control panel **14** sympathize with **15** commiserate with

## consolidate
**03** pun **04** fuse, join **05** merge, unify, unite **06** cement, secure, united **07** combine, compact, fortify **09** reinforce, stabilize **10** amalgamate, make secure, make stable, make strong, strengthen **12** make stronger **14** make more secure, make more stable

## consolidation
**06** fusion, merger **07** joining, uniting **08** alliance, securing **09** cementing **10** federation **11** affiliation, association, combination, unification **12** amalgamation **13** confederation, fortification, reinforcement, stabilization, strengthening

## consonance
**07** concord, harmony **09** agreement, congruity **10** accordance, conformity **11** consistency, suitability **13** compatibility **14** correspondence

## consonant
**05** lenis, velar **06** fortis, sonant, uvular **08** agreeing, alveolar, bilabial, ejective, emphatic, suitable **09** accordant, according, congruous, implosive, in harmony **10** compatible, conforming, consistent, harmonious **11** in agreement **12** articulation, in accordance **13** correspondent

## consort
**03** mix **04** lady, maik, make, mate, wife **05** agree, troop **06** accord, escort, mingle, spouse **07** husband, partner **09** accompany, agreement, associate, companion, spend time **10** fraternize **11** keep company

## consortium
**04** bloc, bond, pact **05** guild, union **06** cartel, league, treaty **07** compact, company **08** alliance, marriage **09** agreement, coalition, syndicate **10** federation, fellowship **11** affiliation, association, combination, corporation, partnership **12** conglomerate, organization **13** confederation

## conspicuous
**05** clear, showy **06** flashy, garish, marked, patent **07** blatant, eminent, evident, glaring, obvious, shining, visible **08** apparent, flagrant, kenspeck, manifest, remarked, striking **09** prominent **10** easily seen, kenspeckle, noticeable, observable, remarkable **11** discernible, perceptible **12** ostentatious, recognizable **13** easily noticed

## conspicuously
**07** clearly, showily, visibly **08** flashily, garishly, markedly, patently **09** blatantly, evidently, glaringly, obviously **10** flagrantly, manifestly, noticeably, observably, remarkably,

**conspiracy**

strikingly **11** discernibly, perceptibly, prominently **12** recognizably **14** ostentatiously

**conspiracy**

**03** fix **04** plot **05** cabal, covin, set-up **06** covyne, league, scheme **07** complot, consult, frame-up, treason **08** intrigue **09** collusion, stratagem **10** connivance **11** concurrence, confederacy, machination **13** collaboration

**conspirator**

**05** Casca, Cinna **06** Brutus **07** Cassius, plotter, schemer, traitor **08** Catiline, colluder **09** conspirer, intriguer **10** highbinder, practisant **12** collaborator
• **group of conspirators 04** band **05** cabal

**conspire**

**04** ally, join, link, plan, plot **05** unite **06** devise, scheme **07** collude, combine, complot, conjure, connect, connive **08** intrigue **09** associate, colleague, co-operate, machinate, manoeuvre **10** hatch a plot, join forces **11** act together, collaborate **12** work together

**constable**

**02** PC, SC **03** cop, WPC **04** Dull **05** jawan, wolly **06** cotwal, harman, kotwal **09** catchpole, catchpoll **10** harman-beck **11** headborough **12** thirdborough
See also **police officer**

**constancy**

**05** truth **07** loyalty **08** devotion, fidelity, firmness, tenacity **09** certainty, fixedness, stability **10** permanence, regularity, resolution, steadiness, uniformity **11** consistency, persistence **12** faithfulness, perseverance **13** dependability, steadfastness **15** trustworthiness, unchangeability

**constant**

**01** c, G, h, k **04** even, firm, trew, true **05** daily, fixed, loyal **06** stable, stanch, steady **07** chronic, devoted, endless, eternal, non-stop, regular, staunch, uniform **08** faithful, resolute, unbroken **09** ceaseless, continual, immutable, incessant, permanent, perpetual, steadfast, unfailing, unvarying **10** changeless, consistent, continuous, dependable, invariable, persistent, relentless, unchanging, unflagging, unwavering **11** everlasting, never-ending, persevering, trustworthy, unalterable, unremitting **12** interminable, unchangeable **13** uninterrupted **14** without respite

**constantly**

**03** aye **05** daily, still **06** always **07** for ever, non-stop, on and on **09** ad nauseam, endlessly **10** all the time, invariably **11** ceaselessly, continually, day in day out, incessantly, perennially, permanently, perpetually **12** continuously, interminably, relentlessly **13** everlastingly **15** twenty-four seven

**constellation**

*Constellations include:*

**03** Ara, Cup, dog, Fly, Fox, Leo, Net, Ram
**04** Apus, Argo, Bull, Crab, Crow, Crux, Dove, Grus, Hare, Harp, Keel, Lion, Lynx, Lyra, Pavo, Swan, Vela, Wolf
**05** Altar, Aries, Arrow, Cetus, Clock, Crane, Draco, Eagle, Easel, Hydra, Indus, Lepus, Level, Libra, Lupus, Mensa, Musca, Norma, Orion, Pyxis, Sails, Table, Twins, Virgo, Whale
**06** Antlia, Aquila, Archer, Auriga, Boötes, Caelum, Cancer, Carina, Chisel, Corvus, Crater, Cygnus, Dorado, Dragon, Fishes, Fornax, Gemini, Hydrus, Indian, Lizard, Octans, Octant, Pictor, Pisces, Puppis, Scales, Scutum, Shield, Taurus, Toucan, Tucana, Virgin, Volans
**07** Air Pump, Centaur, Cepheus, Columba, Dolphin, Furnace, Giraffe, Lacerta, Peacock, Pegasus, Perseus, Phoenix, Sagitta, Sea Goat, Serpens, Serpent, Sextans, Sextant, Unicorn
**08** Aquarius, Circinus, Equuleus, Eridanus, Great Dog, Hercules, Herdsman, Leo Minor, Scorpion, Scorpius, Sculptor, Triangle
**09** Andromeda, Centaurus, Chameleon, Compasses, Delphinus, Great Bear, Little Dog, Monoceros, Ophiuchus, Reticulum, Swordfish, Telescope, Ursa Major, Ursa Minor, Vulpecula
**10** Canis Major, Canis Minor, Cassiopeia, Chamaeleon, Charioteer, Flying Fish, Horologium, Little Bear, Little Lion, Microscope, Sea Serpent, Ship's Stern, Triangulum, Water Snake
**11** Capricornus, Hunting Dogs, Little Horse, Sagittarius, Telescopium, Water Bearer, Winged Horse
**12** Microscopium, Southern Fish
**13** Berenice's Hair, Canes Venatici, Coma Berenices, Northern Crown, River Eridanus, Serpent Bearer, Southern Cross, Southern Crown
**14** Bird of Paradise, Camelopardalis, Corona Borealis
**15** Corona Australis, Mariner's Compass, Piscis Austrinus

**consternation**

**03** awe **04** fear **05** alarm, dread, panic, shock **06** dismay, fright, horror, terror **07** anxiety **08** distress **11** disquietude, trepidation **12** bewilderment, perturbation

**constipated**

**05** bound

**constituency**

**04** area, seat, ward, zone **05** burgh,

shire **06** parish, region, Riding **07** borough **08** district, division, Euroseat, marginal, precinct **09** community **10** electorate

**constituent**

◇ *anagram indicator* **03** bit **04** part, unit **05** basic, voter **06** factor **07** content, elector, element, section **08** electing, inherent, integral **09** component, essential, intrinsic, principle **10** ingredient **12** constitution **13** component part

**constitute**

**02** be **04** form, make, mean **05** found, set up **06** create, make up, strike **07** add up to, appoint, charter, compose, empower **08** amount to, comprise, initiate **09** authorize, establish, institute, represent **10** commission, inaugurate **12** be regarded as **14** be equivalent to, be tantamount to

**constitution**

**03** set **04** code, laws **05** fuero, habit, rules, state **06** health, make-up, nature, policy, polity, temper, upmake **07** charter **08** habitude, physique, statutes **09** character, condition, formation, structure **10** social code **11** codified law, composition, disposition, temperament, temperature **12** bill of rights, idiosyncrasy, organization **13** configuration **15** basic principles

**constitutional**

**04** turn, walk **05** amble, by law, legal **06** airing, lawful, stroll, vested **07** politic, saunter **08** codified, ratified **09** promenade, statutory **10** authorized, legitimate **11** legislative **12** governmental

**constrain**

**03** put **04** bind, curb, rein, urge **05** check, drive, force, impel, limit **06** coerce, compel, hinder, oblige, strain **07** confine **08** hold back, obligate, pressure, restrain, restrict **09** constrict **10** perstringe, pressurize **11** necessitate

**constrained**

**04** hard **05** stiff **06** forced, uneasy **07** awkward, guarded **08** reserved, reticent **09** compelled, inhibited, unnatural **11** embarrassed

**constraint**

**04** curb, rein **05** check, force **06** damper, demand, duress **07** duresse, shackle **08** coercion, pressure **09** hindrance, necessity, restraint, reticence, stiffness **10** compulsion, forcedness, impediment, inhibition, insistence, limitation, obligation **11** awkwardness, confinement, guardedness, restriction, self-control **13** embarrassment, unnaturalness

**constrict**

**04** bind, curb **05** check, choke, close, cramp, limit, pinch **06** hamper, hinder, impede, narrow, shrink **07** confine, inhibit, squeeze, tighten **08** compress,

**constriction**

contract, hold back, obstruct, restrict, strangle **09** constrain **10** make narrow **11** strangulate

**constriction**
**04** curb **05** check, choke, cramp
**07** isthmus **08** blockage, pressure, stenosis, thlipsis **09** hindrance, narrowing, reduction, squeezing, stegnosis, stricture, tightness
**10** constraint, impediment, limitation, tightening **11** compression, contraction, restriction
**13** constringency, incarceration

**construct**
◇ *anagram indicator* **04** form, make
**05** build, craft, erect, found, model, patch, put up, raise, set up, shape, weave **06** create, design, devise, fabric
**07** compile, compose, elevate, fashion, knock up, throw up **08** assemble, engineer **09** carpenter, establish, fabricate, formulate, structure
**11** manufacture, put together **13** knock together, throw together

**construction**
**04** form **05** model, order, shape
**06** fabric, figure, make-up, making
**07** edifice, meaning, reading
**08** assembly, building, erection
**09** deduction, elevation, formation, framework, inference, structure
**11** arrangement, composition, disposition, fabrication, manufacture
**12** organization **13** configuration, establishment **14** interpretation

**constructive**
**06** useful **07** helpful **08** inferred, positive, valuable **09** practical
**10** beneficial, productive
**12** advantageous **13** architectonic

**constructively**
**08** usefully **09** helpfully **10** positively
**11** practically **12** beneficially, productively **14** advantageously

**construe**
◇ *anagram indicator* **04** read **05** infer, see as **06** deduce, render **07** analyse, explain, expound **08** regard as
**09** interpret **10** take to mean, understand

**consul**
**03** Con **05** agent, elchi, envoy
**06** ledger, legate, nuncio **07** leaguer
**08** delegate, diplomat, emissary, minister **10** ambassador
**14** representative **15** plenipotentiary

**consult**
**03** see **04** talk, vide **06** confer, debate, look up, turn to **07** discuss, refer to
**08** question **09** ask advice
**10** deliberate, seek advice
**11** interrogate **14** ask information
**15** seek information

**consultant**
**06** expert **07** adviser **09** associate, authority **10** specialist

**consultation**
**04** talk **05** forum **07** counsel, hearing, meeting, session **08** dialogue
**09** interview **10** conference, discussion

**11** appointment, examination
**12** deliberation

**consultative**
**07** helping **08** advising, advisory
**10** consulting **11** counselling
**12** consultatory, recommending

**consume**
◇ *containment indicator* **03** eat, gut, use
**04** burn, grip, kill, pine, take, wear
**05** drain, drink, eat up, scoff, shift, snarf, spend, touch, use up, waste
**06** absorb, bezzle, burn up, damage, devour, expend, gobble, guzzle, ingest, murder, obsess, punish, ravage, tuck in **07** deplete, destroy, discuss, drink up, engross, exhaust, swallow, torment, utilize **08** demolish, dominate, lay waste, mainline, squander, wear down **09** devastate, dispose of, dissipate, go through, overwhelm, polish off, preoccupy
**10** annihilate, get through, monopolize
**11** fritter away **12** get stuck into

**consumer**
**04** user **05** buyer, mouth **06** client, patron **07** end-user, shopper
**08** customer, prosumer **09** purchaser

**consuming**
◇ *containment indicator* **07** wasting, wearing **08** gripping **09** absorbing, devouring, obsessive **10** compelling, destroying, dominating, engrossing, immoderate, tormenting
**12** monopolizing, overwhelming, preoccupying

**consummate**
**03** cap, end **05** crown, exact, total, utter **06** finish, fulfil, gifted, made up, superb **07** achieve, execute, perfect, perform, realize, skilled, supreme
**08** absolute, complete, conclude, finished, polished, superior, ultimate
**09** competent, exemplary, matchless, practised, terminate **10** accomplish, effectuate, proficient **11** replenished, unqualified **12** accomplished, transcendent **13** distinguished

**consummation**
**03** end **04** pass **06** finish **07** capping
**08** crowning **09** execution
**10** completion, conclusion, fulfilment, perfection **11** achievement, culmination, performance, realization, termination **12** effectuation
**13** actualization **14** accomplishment

**consumption**
**02** TB **05** waste **06** eating **07** decline, using-up **08** draining, drinking, guzzling, scoffing, spending
**09** depletion, devouring, expending, ingestion, tucking-in **10** absorption, exhaustion, swallowing
**11** expenditure, squandering, utilization **12** going-through, tuberculosis **14** getting-through

**contact**
**03** fax **04** call, ring, text **05** e-mail, phone, reach, touch, union **06** friend, impact, notify **07** apply to, get onto, meeting, speak to, sponsor, taction, write to **08** approach, junction,

relation, relative, tangency, touching
**09** get hold of, proximity, telephone
**10** connection, contiguity
**11** association, contingence
**12** acquaintance, get through to
**13** communication, juxtaposition
**14** get in touch with **15** communicate with
• **in contact with** **02** to **04** into

**contagion**
**06** poison **08** tainting **09** infection, pollution **10** corruption, defilement
**13** contamination

**contagious**
**07** noxious **08** catching, epidemic, pandemic **09** spreading **10** compelling, infectious **12** communicable, irresistible **13** transmissible, transmittable

**contain**
◇ *containment indicator* ◇ *hidden indicator* **04** curb, hold, seat, stop, take
**05** carry, check, limit **06** embody, enseam, enwomb, hold in, rein in, retain, stifle, take in **07** control, embrace, enclose, include, involve, repress **08** comprise, keep back, restrain, suppress **09** keep under
**10** have inside **11** accommodate, incorporate, keep in check

**container**
◇ *hidden indicator* **06** carboy, holder, vessel **10** receptacle, repository

*Containers include:*

**03** bag, bin, box, can, cup, jar, jug, keg, mug, pan, pot, tin, tub, urn, vat
**04** bowl, case, cask, dish, drum, Esky®, pack, pail, sack, silo, tank, tube, vase, vial, well
**05** basin, chest, churn, crate, crock, glass, purse, trunk
**06** barrel, basket, beaker, bottle, bucket, carton, casket, hamper, kettle, locker, packet, punnet, teapot, trough, tureen
**07** cistern, dustbin, pannier, pitcher, tumbler
**08** canister, cauldron, cylinder, lunch box, suitcase, tea caddy, tea chest, waste bin
**09** water-butt

**containment**
**04** curb **05** check **07** control **08** stifling
**09** restraint **10** limitation, repression
**11** suppression

**contaminate**
◇ *anagram indicator* **04** foul, harm, soil
**05** decay, spike, spoil, stain, sully, taint
**06** debase, defile, infect **07** corrupt, deprave, pollute, tarnish, vitiate
**10** adulterate, make impure

**contamination**
◇ *anagram indicator* **04** harm **05** decay, filth, stain, taint **07** soiling, tarnish
**08** foulness, impurity, spoiling, sullying
**09** infection, pollution, vitiation
**10** corruption, debasement, defilement, rottenness **11** desecration
**12** adulteration

## contemplate

04 muse, plan, view 05 spell, study, weigh 06 behold, design, expect, intend, look at, ponder, regard, survey 07 dwell on, examine, foresee, inspect, observe, propose, weigh up 08 cogitate, consider, envisage, meditate, mull over, ruminate 09 reflect on 10 deliberate, have in mind, have in view, scrutinize, think about 11 have an eye to 13 give thought to

## contemplation

04 muse, view 05 dwell, study 06 gazing, musing, regard, survey 07 purpose, thought, viewing 08 mind's eye, scrutiny, weighing 09 beholding, pondering, regarding 10 cogitation, inspection, meditation, reflection, rumination, weighing up 11 cerebration, examination, mulling-over, observation 12 deliberation, recollection 13 consideration

## contemplative

04 rapt 06 intent, musing 07 pensive 08 cerebral 10 meditative, reflective, ruminative, thoughtful 13 deep in thought, introspective

## contemporaneous

06 coeval 10 coetaneous, coexistent, concurrent 11 synchronous 12 simultaneous

## contemporary

02 AD 03 now 04 peer 05 equal 06 coeval, fellow, latest, modern, recent, today's, trendy, with it 07 current, partner, present, topical 08 confrère, co-worker, parallel, up-to-date 09 associate, colleague 10 avant-garde, coetaneous, coexistent, collateral, concurrent, futuristic, new-fangled, present-day 11 counterpart, fashionable, present-time, synchronous, ultra-modern 12 simultaneous 13 up-to-the-minute 14 contemporanean, fashion-forward 15 contemporaneous

## contempt

05 scorn 06 hatred 07 disdain, dislike, mockery, neglect 08 derision, despisal, disgrace, loathing, ridicule 09 contumely, dishonour, disregard 10 disrespect 11 detestation 13 condescension
• **expression of contempt** 02 ho 03 ach, aha, bah, boo, foh, gup, hoa, hoh, mew, och, pho, poh, rot, sis, yah 04 booh, nuts, phew, phoh, pish, pooh, push, quep, rats, tush, yech 05 pshaw, snoot, sucks! 06 phooey 10 sucks to you!
• **sign of contempt** 04 fico, figo 05 sneer 11 Harvey Smith
• **term of contempt** 03 cit, dog, nit 05 sprat 06 monkey 07 jive-ass 08 whipster

## contemptible

03 low 04 base, mean, vile 05 petty 06 abject, cruddy, ornery, paltry, scurvy, shabby 07 hateful, pelting, pitiful 08 pitiable, shameful, unworthy, wretched 09 loathsome, miserable,

worthless 10 degenerate, despicable, detestable, lamentable 11 ignominious
• **contemptible person** 04 crud, scut, snot, toad 05 crumb, diddy, droob, snipe, squit, twerp 06 fellow, louser 07 dirtbag, dogbolt, hangdog 08 dirty dog, scullion, whiffler

## contemptuous

05 tossy 06 snorty 07 cynical, haughty, jeering, mocking 08 arrogant, derisive, derisory, insolent, scornful, sneering 09 insulting, withering 10 despiteful, disdainful, dispiteous 12 contumelious, supercilious 13 condescending, disrespectful, high and mighty

## contend

03 vie, war 04 aver, cope, deal, face, hold, wage 05 argue, brave, claim, clash, fight, rival, state 06 affirm, allege, assert, battle, combat, debate, oppose, reckon, strive, tackle, tussle 07 address, agonize, compete, contest, declare, dispute, grapple, profess, wrestle 08 conflict, face up to, maintain, militate, struggle 09 challenge 10 asseverate, meet head on 11 come to grips, come to terms

## content

◇ *hidden indicator* 04 ease, gist, glad, load, size, text 05 happy, ideas, items, parts, peace, theme, topic 06 amount, at ease, be glad, burden, humour, matter, pacify, please, soothe, volume 07 appease, be happy, chapter, comfort, delight, essence, gratify, indulge, meaning, measure, placate, pleased, satisfy, section, subject, willing 08 capacity, cheerful, contents, division, elements, gladness, material, pleasure, serenity 09 be pleased, contented, fulfilled, happiness, satisfied, substance, unworried 10 components, equanimity, fulfilment, proportion, untroubled 11 comfortable, contentment, ingredients 12 cheerfulness, constituents, peacefulness, satisfaction, significance, things inside 13 gratification, subject matter 14 component parts 15 what is contained
• **remove contents** 03 gut 05 empty 10 disembowel

## contented

04 glad 05 happy 07 content, perfect, pleased, relaxed 08 cheerful 09 fulfilled, satisfied, unworried 10 untroubled 11 comfortable

## contention

04 bate, case, plea, toil, view 05 claim, stand, sturt, words 06 belief, debate, enmity, jangle, notion, strife, theory, thesis 07 discord, dispute, feeling, feuding, opinion, rivalry 08 argument, position, struggle 09 assertion, hostility, intuition, judgement, logomachy, viewpoint, wrangling 10 conviction, difference, differency, dissension, impression, persuasion 11 controversy, point of view 12 disagreement

## contentious

07 hostile 08 captious, disputed, doubtful, perverse 09 bellicose, bickering, debatable, polemical, querulous 10 debateable, disputable, pugnacious 11 dissentious, quarrelsome, tendentious 12 antagonistic, questionable 13 argumentative, controversial

## contentment

04 ease 05 peace 07 comfort, content 08 gladness, pleasure, serenity 09 happiness 10 equanimity, fulfilment 11 complacency 12 cheerfulness, peacefulness, satisfaction 13 contentedness, gratification

## contest

03 vie, war 04 bout, deny, game, jump, race 05 doubt, event, fight, match, pairs, set-to, vying 06 battle, combat, debate, defend, oppose, pingle, refute, strife, strive, tussle 07 brabble, compete, contend, dispute, matchup 08 argument, concours, conflict, litigate, object to, question, skirmish, struggle 09 challenge, emulation, encounter, try to beat 10 tournament 11 competition, controversy 12 argue against, championship, contestation
• **in contest against** 04 with
• **part of contest** 03 leg

## contestant

05 rival 06 player, prizer 07 entrant 08 aspirant, opponent 09 adversary, candidate, contender, disputant 10 competitor 11 participant

## context

07 factors, setting 08 position 09 connexion, framework, situation 10 background, conditions, connection 12 surroundings 13 circumstances 14 state of affairs

## contiguous

04 near, next 05 close 06 beside 07 vicinal 08 abutting, adjacent, touching 09 adjoining, bordering 10 coadjacent, conjoining, juxtaposed, tangential 12 conterminous, neighbouring 15 juxtapositional

## continent

08 mainland, virtuous 09 temperate 10 terra firma

*Continents:*

04 Asia
06 Africa, Europe
07 Oceania
10 Antarctica
11 Australasia
12 North America, South America

## contingency

05 event 06 chance 07 contact 08 accident, fortuity, incident, juncture 09 emergency, happening 10 incidental, randomness 11 chance event, eventuality, possibility, uncertainty 13 arbitrariness

## contingent

03 set 04 band, body 05 based, batch, group, party, quota, share 07 company, mission, section, subject

**08** division, relative **09** dependant, dependent **10** accidental, complement, delegation, deputation, detachment **11** conditional **15** representatives

**continual**
**05** still **07** abiding, eternal, regular **08** constant, frequent, repeated **09** incessant, perpetual, recurrent, unceasing **10** persistent, repetitive **11** everlasting **12** interminable

**continually**
**03** e'er **04** ever **06** always **07** forever, non-stop, on and on **09** endlessly, eternally, regularly **10** all the time, constantly, frequently, habitually, repeatedly **11** ceaselessly, incessantly, perpetually, recurrently **12** interminably, persistently **13** everlastingly

**continuance**
**04** stay, term **06** period **07** abiding, durance **08** duration, dwelling, standing **09** endurance **10** permanence **11** adjournment, maintenance, persistence, protraction **12** continuation

**continuation**
**06** return, sequel **07** renewal **08** addition, progress **09** extension **10** carrying-on, resumption, supplement **11** development, furtherance, lengthening, maintenance, persistence, protraction **12** prolongation **13** starting again **14** recommencement
• **in continuance** **02** on

**continue**
**02** on **04** dure, go on, hold, keep, last, rest, stay **05** abide, renew **06** endure, extend, hold on, keep on, keep up, move on, pursue, remain, resume **07** adjourn, carry on, hold out, not stop, persist, press on, proceed, project, prolong, stick at, subsist, survive, sustain **08** lengthen, maintain, progress **09** keep going, persevere, persist in, soldier on **10** begin again, keep moving, keep on with, press ahead, recommence, start again **11** keep walking, persevere in, take up again **12** proceed again **14** keep travelling

**continuity**
**04** flow **07** linkage **08** cohesion, sequence, synaphea **09** synapheia **10** connection, succession **11** progression **14** continuousness

**continuous**
◇ hidden indicator ◇ juxtaposition indicator **05** solid **07** endless, flowing, lasting, non-stop, running **08** constant, extended, seamless, unbroken, unending **09** ceaseless, continued, prolonged, unceasing **10** persistent, relentless **11** consecutive, never-ending, not stopping, unremitting, with no let-up **12** interminable **13** uninterrupted, without a break

**continuously**
◇ hidden indicator ◇ juxtaposition

indicator **04** away **08** together **09** endlessly **10** all the time, at a stretch, constantly **11** ceaselessly **12** interminably, persistently, relentlessly **13** consecutively, unremittingly **15** twenty-four seven, uninterruptedly

**contort**
◇ anagram indicator **03** wry **04** knot, warp **05** gnarl, twist **06** deform, squirm, wrench, writhe **07** distort, screw up, wreathe, wriggle **08** misshape **09** convolute, disfigure **14** bend out of shape

**contortionist**
**07** acrobat, gymnast, tumbler **08** balancer, stuntman **09** aerialist **10** rope-dancer, rope-walker, stuntwoman **11** equilibrist, funambulist **12** posture-maker, somersaulter **13** posture-master, trapeze artist

**contour**
**04** form **05** curve, lines, shape **06** aspect, figure, relief **07** isobase, isobath, outline, profile, surface **08** contorno, tournure **09** character **10** silhouette

**contraband**
**08** hot goods, smuggled **09** smuggling **10** prohibited **11** banned goods, bootlegging **13** unlawful goods **14** illegal traffic **15** prohibited goods, proscribed goods

**contraceptive**

_Contraceptives include:_

**03** cap, IUD, IVD
**04** coil, IUCD, loop, pill, safe
**06** condom, johnny, rubber, sheath, Vimule®
**07** Femidom®, johnnie, the pill
**08** Dutch cap, minipill
**09** birth pill, diaphragm, prolactin
**10** Lippes loop, protective
**11** Depo-Provera®
**12** female condom, French letter, prophylactic

**contract**
◇ tail deletion indicator **03** get **04** bond, deal, knit, make, pact **05** agree, catch, purse, tense **06** draw in, engage, lessen, narrow, pick up, pledge, reduce, settle, shrink, take in, treaty **07** abridge, appalto, arrange, bargain, betroth, compact, curtail, develop, promise, shorten, shrivel, tighten, wrinkle **08** compress, condense, covenant, decrease, diminish, handfast **09** agreement, betrothal, champerty, concordat, constrict, indenture, negotiate, stipulate, succumb to, undertake **10** abbreviate, agree terms, commitment, constringe, convention, engagement, go down with, settlement **11** arrangement, make shorter, make smaller, stipulation, transaction **12** come down with **13** become ill with, become shorter, become smaller, understanding **14** be taken ill with
• **contract out** **06** get out **07** drop out, farm out **08** delegate, withdraw

**09** outsource **11** subcontract **12** give to others, pass to others

**contraction**
**06** shrink **07** systole, tensing **09** drawing-in, lessening, narrowing, reduction, shrinkage **10** abridgment, shortening, tightening **11** abridgement, astringency, compression, curtailment, shrivelling **12** abbreviation, constriction **13** shortened form

**contradict**
**03** nay **04** deny **05** argue, belie, rebut **06** impugn, naysay, negate, oppose, refute, threap, threep **07** confute, counter, dispute, gainsay, outface, sublate **08** contrary, traverse **09** argue with, challenge, clash with, disaffirm, go against **12** be at odds with, conflict with, contrast with, disagree with **14** fly in the face of

**contradiction**
**04** odds **05** clash **06** denial **07** démenti, dispute, paradox **08** antilogy, antinomy, conflict, negation, rebuttal, traverse, variance **09** challenge **10** antithesis, opposition, refutation **11** confutation, incongruity **12** disagreement **13** disaffirmance, inconsistency **14** disaffirmation **15** counter-argument

**contradictory**
**07** opposed **08** clashing, contrary, opposing, opposite **09** dissonant, repugnant **10** discordant, discrepant **11** conflicting, dissentient, incongruous, paradoxical **12** antagonistic, antithetical, incompatible, inconsistent **14** irreconcilable

**contralto**
**01** c **04** alto

**contraption**
**03** rig **05** gizmo, waldo **06** device, doodad, doodah, doofer, gadget, widget **07** machine **08** thingamy **09** apparatus, invention, mechanism **11** contrivance, thingamybob, thingamyjig **12** what's-its-name

**contrary**
◇ reversal indicator **05** annoy **06** oppose **07** adverse, awkward, counter, hostile, opposed, reverse, stroppy, wayward **08** clashing, converse, opposing, opposite, perverse, stubborn **09** difficult, obstinate **10** antipathic, antithesis, discrepant, headstrong, overthwart, refractory **11** conflicting, disobliging, intractable **12** antagonistic, cantankerous, cross-grained, incompatible, inconsistent **13** unco-operative **14** irreconcilable
• **contrary to** **10** at odds with **14** at variance with, in conflict with, in opposition to
• **on the contrary** ◇ reversal indicator **08** not at all **09** far from it, per contra **10** conversely, e contrario **11** al contrario, au contraire **14** just the reverse **15** just the opposite, quite the reverse, tout au contraire

## contrast

**04** foil **05** clash **06** differ, oppose, relief, set-off **07** compare **08** be at odds, chiasmus, conflict, disagree, opposite **09** disparity, go against **10** antithesis, comparison, contradict, difference, divergence, opposition **11** counterview, distinction, distinguish **12** be at variance, be in conflict, discriminate **13** counterchange, differentiate, dissimilarity, dissimilitude **14** contraposition **15** differentiation
• **in contrast to** **09** as against, opposed to **10** rather than **14** in opposition to

## contravene

**04** defy **05** break, flout **06** breach, oppose **07** disobey, violate **08** infringe **10** transgress

## contravention

**06** breach **08** breaking **09** violation **11** dereliction **12** infringement **13** transgression

## contretemps

**04** tiff **05** brush, clash, hitch **06** mishap **08** accident, argument, squabble **10** difficulty, misfortune **11** predicament **12** disagreement, misadventure

## contribute

**04** edit, give, help, make **05** add to, cause, endow, grant, write **06** bestow, chip in, create, donate, kick in, lead to, submit, supply **07** chuck in, compile, compose, conduce, furnish, prepare, present, produce, promote, provide **08** generate, occasion, result in **09** originate, subscribe **10** bring about, give rise to, make happen **11** be a factor in, play a part in **13** give a donation

## contribution

**03** tax **04** gift, item, koha, levy, mite, shot **05** grant, input, paper, piece, story **06** column, report, review **07** article, feature, handout, present **08** addition, bestowal, donation, gratuity, offering **09** endowment **10** feuilleton, proportion, submission **11** Peter's pence **12** subscription **14** superannuation

## contributor

**05** donor, giver **06** author, backer, critic, patron, writer **07** sponsor **08** compiler, reporter, reviewer **09** columnist, freelance, supporter **10** benefactor, journalist, subscriber **13** correspondent

## contrite

**05** sorry **06** humble **07** ashamed **08** penitent, red-faced **09** chastened, regretful, repentant **10** remorseful **11** guilt-ridden, penitential

## contrition

**05** shame **06** regret, sorrow **07** remorse **09** penitence **10** repentance **11** compunction, humiliation **12** self-reproach

## contrivance

**03** art, gin **04** gear, plan, plot, ploy, ruse, tool **05** dodge, gizmo, shift, trick **06** design, device, doodad, doodah, doofer, engine, gadget, scheme, tactic, widget **07** machine, project **08** artifice, intrigue, thingamy **09** apparatus, appliance, equipment, expedient, implement, invention, mechanism, stratagem **10** compassing **11** contraption, imagination, machination, thingamybob, thingamyjig **12** excogitation, what's-its-name

## contrive

◇ *anagram indicator* **04** brew, cook, form, plan, plot, work **05** frame, set up, spend, weave **06** create, cut out, design, devise, effect, engine, invent, manage, scheme, tamper, wangle **07** arrange, compass, concoct, imagine, succeed **08** conceive, engineer, find a way **09** construct, fabricate, manoeuvre **10** bring about, understand **11** orchestrate, stage-manage

## contrived

◇ *anagram indicator* **05** false, hokey, set-up **06** forced **08** laboured, mannered, overdone, strained **09** elaborate, unnatural **10** artificial, factitious

## control

**03** ren, rin, run **04** curb, dial, head, keep, knob, lead, rein, ride, rule, sway, work **05** brake, check, lever, limit, power, reign **06** adjust, button, charge, direct, govern, make go, manage, reduce, subdue, switch, verify **07** command, contain, mastery, monitor, operate, oversee, repress **08** dominate, guidance, hold back, modulate, regulate, restrain, restrict **09** authority, be the boss, constrain, constrict, direction, dominance, hindrance, influence, oversight, reduction, restraint, supervise, supremacy **10** constraint, discipline, government, impediment, instrument, limitation, management, perstringe, regulation, repression, run the show **11** call the tune, keep in check, preside over, restriction, self-control, superintend, supervision **12** be in charge of, call the shots, jurisdiction, rule the roost **13** be in the saddle, self-restraint **14** pull the strings, put the brakes on, self-discipline **15** superintendence, wear the trousers
• **lose control** **04** slip, spaz **05** spazz **07** flip out
• **numerical control** **02** NC

## controversial

**04** moot **07** at issue, eristic, polemic **08** disputed, doubtful **09** debatable, polemical **10** disputable **11** contentious, tendentious **12** questionable **13** argumentative

## controversy

**06** debate, strife **07** discord, dispute, polemic, quarrel, wrangle **08** argument, friction, squabble **10** contention, debatement, discussion, dissension, war of words **11** altercation **12** cause célèbre, disagreement

## contusion

**04** bump, lump, mark **05** knock **06** bruise, injury **07** blemish **08** swelling **10** ecchymosis **13** discoloration

## conundrum

**05** guess, poser **06** enigma, puzzle, riddle, teaser **07** anagram, problem **08** quandary, word game **10** difficulty **11** brainteaser **12** brain-twister

## conurbation

**04** city, town **06** ghetto **08** big smoke, downtown, precinct, suburbia **09** inner city, metroplex, urban area **10** city centre, cosmopolis, metropolis, micropolis, pentapolis **11** megalopolis, urban sprawl **12** municipality **13** urban district **14** concrete jungle

## convalesce

**05** rally **06** pick up, revive **07** get well, improve, recover **09** get better **10** recuperate **11** get stronger, pull through

## convalescence

**08** recovery **09** anastasis **11** improvement, restoration **12** recuperation **13** getting better **14** rehabilitation

## convene

**04** call, meet **05** bring, rally **06** gather, muster, summon **07** collect, convoke **08** assemble **10** congregate **12** call together, come together **13** bring together

## convenience

**03** bog, lav, loo, use **04** help **06** behoof, device, gadget, toilet **07** amenity, benefit, fitness, service, utility **08** facility, lavatory, resource **09** advantage, appliance, commodity, ease of use, handiness, usability **10** expediency, usefulness **11** propinquity, suitability, water closet **12** availability **13** accessibility, accommodation, opportuneness **14** propitiousness, serviceability **15** appropriateness
*See also* **toilet**

## convenient

**03** fit **04** easy, gain, hend **05** handy **06** at hand, fitted, nearby, suited, timely, useful **07** adapted, favored, fitting, helpful **08** favoured, handsome, suitable **09** available, expedient, opportune, well-timed **10** accessible, beneficial, commodious, near at hand **11** appropriate, close at hand, within reach **12** labour-saving **13** advantageable **14** at your disposal

## conveniently

**04** well **05** patly **06** at hand, nearby **08** suitably, usefully **09** helpfully **10** accessibly, near at hand **11** close at hand, within reach **13** appropriately

## convent

**04** cite **05** abbey, house **06** fratry, friary, priory, summon **07** convene, fratery, nunnery **08** cloister **09** monastery
*See also* **monastery**

## convention

**03** use **04** bond, code, deal, pact

**05** ethos, mores, synod, usage
**06** accord, custom, treaty **07** bargain, compact, council, fashion, meeting
**08** assembly, ceremony, conclave, congress, contract, covenant, practice, protocol **09** agreement, Blackwood, concordat, delegates, etiquette, formality, gathering, propriety, punctilio, tradition **10** commitment, conference, engagement, settlement
**11** arrangement, convocation, transaction **12** matter of form
**13** understanding **15** representatives

**conventional**
**04** lame **05** nomic, trite, usual
**06** common, formal, normal, proper, ritual **07** correct, pompier, regular, routine, uptight **08** accepted, copybook, expected, ordinary, orthodox, received, standard, straight
**09** bourgeois, customary, hidebound, prevalent **10** conformist, mainstream, pedestrian, prevailing, unoriginal
**11** commonplace, respectable, stereotyped, traditional
**12** conservative, run-of-the-mill
**14** common-or-garden

**conventionally**
**07** usually **08** commonly, formally, normally **09** regularly, routinely
**10** ordinarily **13** traditionally

**converge**
**04** form, join, mass, meet **05** focus, merge, unite **06** gather **07** close in, combine **08** approach, coincide
**09** intersect **11** concentrate, move towards **12** come together

**convergence**
**05** union **07** meeting, merging
**08** approach, blending, junction
**10** confluence **11** coincidence, combination **12** intersection
**13** concentration

**conversant**
• **conversant with**  **08** versed in
**09** skilled in **10** apprised of, au fait with
**11** practised in **12** familiar with, proficient in **13** experienced in, informed about **14** acquainted with

**conversation**
◇ *homophone indicator* **03** rap **04** chat, talk **05** board, convo, crack, craic, wongi **06** confab, gossip, natter, yabber **07** chinwag, purpose
**08** chitchat, colloquy, cosy chat, dialogue, exchange, parlance, question, speaking **09** discourse, small talk, table talk, tête-à-tête
**10** discussion, pillow talk **12** heart-to-heart **13** communication, interlocution

**conversational**
◇ *homophone indicator* **06** casual, chatty **07** relaxed **08** informal
**09** talkative **10** colloquial
**13** communicative

**converse**
◇ *homophone indicator* **04** chat, talk
**05** speak, wongi **06** confer, dialog, gossip, natter, reason, relate **07** chatter, commune, counter, discuss, obverse, propose, purpose, reverse **08** chitchat,

collogue, colloquy, contrary, dialogue, opposing, opposite, question, reversed **09** discourse
**10** antithesis, chew the fat, chew the rag, colloquize, transposed
**11** communicate **12** antithetical
**13** other way round

**conversely**
**09** e converso, obversely **10** contrarily
**12** contrariwise **13** on the contrary
**14** antithetically, on the other hand

**conversion**
◇ *anagram indicator* **05** theft **06** change, switch **07** rebirth, turning **08** exchange, metanoia, mutation **09** preaching, reshaping **10** adaptation, adjustment, alteration, conviction, persuasion
**11** proselytism, reformation, remodelling, translation
**12** modification, regeneration, substitution **13** customization, metamorphosis, transmutation
**14** evangelization, reconstruction, reorganization, transformation
**15** proselytization, transfiguration

**convert**
◇ *anagram indicator* **03** put **04** goal, make, turn **05** adapt, alter, steal
**06** adjust, change, modify, mutate, reform, revise, switch **07** rebuild, remodel, reshape, restyle, win over
**08** adherent, believer, convince, disciple, exchange, go over to, move over, neophyte, persuade, transfer, turn into **09** bring over, customize, new person, proselyte, refashion, transform, transmute **10** evangelize, reorganize, substitute, switch from
**11** jump the dyke, loup the dyke, proselytize, reconstruct, restructure, transfigure **12** metamorphose
**13** change beliefs, changed person
**14** change religion

**convertible**
◇ *anagram indicator* **06** ragtop **07** soft top **09** adaptable, landaulet
**10** adjustable, changeable, modifiable, permutable **11** landaulette
**12** exchangeable **15** interchangeable

**convex**
**04** nowy **05** bombé **07** bulging, gibbous, rounded **08** swelling
**09** curved out **10** bow-fronted
**11** protuberant **15** bending outwards

**convey**
**03** put, tip **04** bear, have, lead, move, pipe, send, take, tell, wain **05** bring, carry, drive, fetch, guide, shift, steal
**06** hand on, impart, import, pass on, relate, reveal **07** channel, conduct, deliver, express, forward, mediate, present **08** announce, disclose, transfer, transmit **09** make known, transport **11** communicate

**conveyance**
**03** bus, cab, car, sac, ute, van **04** cart, taxi **05** coach, grant, lorry, truck, wagon **06** ceding **07** bicycle, caravan, express, transit, vehicle **08** carriage, delivery, granting, mortgage, movement, transfer **09** motor home, transport **10** bequeathal, motorcycle

**11** consignment **12** transference, transmission **13** transportance
**14** transportation
*See also* **aircraft; bicycle; car; carriage; ship**

**convict**
**03** con, lag **05** crime, crook, felon, judge **06** canary, forçat, inmate
**07** approve, attaint, condemn, culprit, old hand, reprove, villain **08** criminal, imprison, jailbird, offender, prisoner, sentence, yardbird **09** wrongdoer
**10** canary-bird, emancipist, find guilty, lawbreaker

**conviction**
**04** view **05** creed, faith, prior, tenet
**06** belief **07** fervour, opinion
**08** firmness, sentence **09** assurance, certainty, certitude, judgement, principle **10** confidence, persuasion, plerophory **11** earnestness, plerophoria
**12** condemnation, imprisonment, satisfaction

**convince**
**04** sell, sway **06** assure, induce, prompt
**07** prove to, resolve, satisfy, win over
**08** persuade, perswade, talk into, talk over **09** bring home, influence **10** bring round **11** prevail upon

**convincing**
**06** cogent, likely **07** certain, telling
**08** credible, forceful, luculent, positive, powerful, pregnant, probable
**09** plausible **10** compelling, conclusive, conclusory, impressive, persuasive **12** satisfactory

**convincingly**
**08** cogently, credibly **09** all ends up, plausibly, tellingly **10** forcefully, powerfully **12** compellingly, conclusively, impressively, persuasively

**convivial**
**04** boon **05** jolly, merry **06** genial, hearty, jovial, lively, social **07** affable, cordial, festive **08** cheerful, friendly, sociable **09** fun-loving **11** Anacreontic

**conviviality**
**03** fun **05** cheer, mirth **06** gaiety
**07** jollity **08** bonhomie **09** festivity, geniality, joviality **10** cordiality, liveliness **11** good feeling, merrymaking, sociability
**12** friendliness **14** goodfellowship

**convocation**
**04** diet **05** forum, synod **07** council, meeting **08** assembly, conclave, congress **10** assemblage, conference, convention **12** congregation, forgathering

**convoluted**
◇ *anagram indicator* **04** mazy
**07** complex, unclear, winding, writhen, wrythen **08** involved, tortuous, twisting **09** convolute, intricate, Vitruvian **10** meandering
**11** complicated

**convolution**
**04** coil, fold, loop, turn **05** gyrus, helix, twist, whorl **06** spiral **07** coiling,

winding **08** curlicue **09** intricacy, sinuosity **10** complexity **11** involvement, sinuousness **12** complication, entanglement, tortuousness

**convoy**
**04** line **05** fleet, group, guard, train **06** escort **07** company **10** attendance, protection

**convulse**
◇ *anagram indicator* **04** jerk **05** seize **07** disturb, shudder **08** unsettle **10** suffer a fit **14** shake violently, suffer a seizure

**convulsion**
**03** fit, tic **05** cramp, ictus, spasm **06** attack, furore, tremor, tumult, unrest **07** seizure, turmoil **08** disorder, eruption, laughter, outburst, paroxysm, upheaval **09** agitation, commotion **10** turbulence **11** contraction, disturbance **13** electric shock

**convulsive**
**05** jerky **06** fitful **07** violent **08** sporadic **09** spasmodic **11** spasmodical **12** uncontrolled
• **convulsive disorder 03** DTs **15** delirium tremens

**cook**
◇ *anagram indicator* **02** do **03** pan **04** burn, chef, fake, heat, make, peep, ruin, warm **05** fryer, put on, spoil **06** doctor, greasy, overdo **07** babbler, concoct, falsify, prepare, scare up, underdo **08** overcook, rustle up **09** cuisinier, improvise, undercook **11** put together **13** throw together
*See also* **chef**

*Cooking methods include:*

**03** fry
**04** bake, boil, sear, stew
**05** broil, brown, curry, grill, poach, roast, sauté, steam, toast
**06** braise, coddle, flambé, pan-fry, simmer
**07** deep-fry, parboil, stir-fry
**08** barbecue, pot-roast, scramble
**09** casserole, char-grill, fricassee, microwave, oven-roast, spit-roast
**10** flame-grill

• **cook up** ◇ *anagram indicator* **04** brew, edit, plan, plot **06** devise, invent, make up, scheme **07** concoct, falsify, prepare **08** contrive **09** fabricate

**cooked**
◇ *anagram indicator*
• **lightly cooked 04** rare, rear

**cookery**

*Cookery styles include:*

**04** Thai
**05** Greek, halal, Irish, mezze, rural, tapas, vegan, Welsh
**06** French, fusion, German, Indian, kosher, Tex-Mex
**07** African, British, Chinese, Eastern, English, Italian, Mexican, seafood, Spanish, Turkish
**08** American, fast food, Japanese, Scottish

**09** Cantonese, Caribbean, Malaysian, Provençal
**10** cordon bleu, Far Eastern, gluten-free, Indonesian, Pacific Rim, vegetarian
**11** home cooking, lean cuisine
**12** haute cuisine
**13** Mediterranean, Middle Eastern
**14** cuisine minceur
**15** nouvelle cuisine

*Cookery-related terms include:*

**03** Aga, dip, gut, hob, ice
**04** chef, chop, cook, cure, dice, mash, oven, rise, whip
**05** baste, brown, carve, chill, chump, curry, daube, devil, dress, glaze, grate, knead, mince, mould, press, purée, score, shave, smoke, steep, stuff, whisk
**06** batter, blanch, de-bone, entrée, fillet, fondue, infuse, kosher, leaven, recipe, reduce, season, spread
**07** deglaze, garnish, nibbles, proving, starter, tandoor, topping
**08** cookbook, devilled, marinade, marinate, preserve
**09** antipasto, percolate, reduction, tenderize
**10** caramelize
**11** hors d'oeuvre

**Cook Islands**
**03** COK

**cool**
**03** ace, fan, ice **04** calm, chic, cold, iced, keel, mega, neat **05** abate, allay, aloof, brill, chill, crisp, fresh, great, nervy, nippy, parky, poise, quiet, smart, tepid **06** breeze, breezy, caller, chilly, dampen, freeze, frigid, frosty, lessen, placid, poised, quench, reduce, sedate, temper, trendy, wicked **07** assuage, bracing, chilled, control, distant, draught, elegant, get cold, ice-cold, relaxed, stylish, subside, unmoved **08** calmness, coldness, composed, coolness, diminish, draughty, impudent, laid-back, lukewarm, make cold, moderate, reserved, smashing, terrific, turn cold **09** admirable, apathetic, collected, composure, crispness, excellent, fantastic, freshness, get colder, impassive, nippiness, sangfroid, unexcited, unruffled, wonderful **10** acceptable, become cold, chilliness, make colder, marvellous, refreshing, streetwise, turn colder, unfriendly, untroubled **11** fashionable, half-hearted, indifferent, level-headed, refrigerate, self-control, standoffish, undisturbed, unemotional, unexcitable, unflappable, unflustered, unperturbed, unwelcoming **12** air-condition, become colder, second to none, uninterested, unresponsive **13** collectedness, defervescence, defervescency, disinterested, dispassionate, imperturbable, self-possessed, sophisticated **14** out of this world, self-discipline, self-possession, unapprehensive, unenthusiastic

**15** cool as a cucumber, uncommunicative, undemonstrative

**cooler**
*see* **jail, gaol**

**cooling**
**08** chilling, freezing **10** refreshing **11** refrigerant, ventilation **13** defervescence, defervescency, refrigeration, refrigerative, refrigeratory **15** air-conditioning

**coolly**
**06** calmly, coldly **07** quietly **08** frostily, placidly, sedately **09** distantly **10** composedly, impudently, reservedly **11** collectedly, impassively, unexcitably, unexcitedly **13** apathetically, half-heartedly, imperturbably, indifferently, level-headedly, standoffishly, unemotionally **14** uninterestedly, unresponsively **15** dispassionately

**coop**
**03** box, mew, pen, ren, rin, rip, run **04** cage **05** cavie, hutch, pound **06** keavie **09** enclosure
• **coop up 03** pen **04** cage, shut **06** bail up, immure, keep in, lock up, shut in, shut up **07** close in, confine, enclose, impound **08** imprison, lock away **11** incarcerate

**Cooper**
**04** Gary

**co-operate**
**03** aid **04** ally, help, play, pool **05** share, unite **06** assist, team up **07** combine, pitch in **08** conspire, play ball **09** play along **10** contribute, join forces **11** collaborate, participate, string along **12** band together, pull together, work together **14** pull your weight, work side by side

**co-operation**
**03** aid **04** help **05** unity **08** teamwork **10** assistance, team spirit **11** give-and-take, helpfulness, helping hand, joint action **12** contribution, co-ordination **13** collaboration, esprit de corps, participation **15** concerted action, concerted effort, working together

**co-operative**
**05** joint **06** shared, united **07** helpful, helping, willing **08** coactive, combined, obliging **09** assisting, compliant, concerted **10** collective, responsive, supportive **11** co-ordinated **13** accommodating, collaborative **15** working together

**co-ordinate**
**01** x, y, z **02** go **04** mesh **05** adapt, blend, match, order **06** go well, join up **07** absciss, arrange, blend in **08** abscissa, abscisse, ordinate, organize, regulate, tabulate **09** co-operate, correlate, harmonize, integrate, mix 'n' match **10** complement, go together **11** collaborate, synchronize, systematize **12** be compatible, work together **14** make compatible

## co-ordination
**07** harmony **08** blending, matching, ordering **10** ordonnance **11** arrangement, co-operation, integration **12** organization **13** collaboration, compatibility **15** complementation

## cop
**02** PC **03** get, pig, top **04** bull, head, nark **05** bizzy, bobby, catch **06** arrest, copper, obtain, rozzer **07** acquire, capture, officer **08** flatfoot **09** constable, policeman **10** bluebottle **11** policewoman **13** police officer
*See also* **police officer**
• **cop out 04** balk, duck, shun **05** avert, avoid, dodge, elude, evade, hedge, shirk **06** bypass, escape **07** prevent **08** get out of, get round, sidestep **09** give a miss **11** abstain from, make a detour, run away from, shy away from **12** hold back from, keep away from, stay away from, steer clear of

## cope
**04** meet **05** get by, match **06** barter, make do, manage **07** carry on, chlamys, contend, pluvial, subsist, succeed, survive **08** exchange **09** encounter **10** get through
• **cope with 04** hack **05** touch, treat **06** endure, handle, manage, take up **07** weather **08** deal with **09** encounter **11** contend with, grapple with, wrestle with **12** struggle with

## coping
**04** skew

## copious
**04** full, huge, rich **05** ample, great, large **06** bags of, lavish, plenty **07** fulsome, liberal, profuse, teeming **08** abundant, generous, numerous **09** abounding, bounteous, bountiful, extensive, luxuriant, plenteous, plentiful, redundant **11** overflowing **13** inexhaustible

## cop-out
**05** alibi, dodge, fraud **06** excuse, get-out **07** evasion, pretext **08** pretence, shirking **14** passing the buck

## copper
**01** p **02** Cu
*See also* **coin; police officer**

## cops
*see* **police**

## copse
**04** bush, carr, wood **05** brush, grove **06** spinny, spring **07** coppice, spinney, thicket

## copulate
**03** tup **04** mate **07** have sex **08** make love **10** fool around, get off with, make it with **11** go all the way, go to bed with

## copulation
**03** sex **06** coitus, mating **07** coition **08** congress, coupling, embraces, intimacy **09** relations **10** commixtion, love-making **15** carnal knowledge

## copy
**02** cc **03** ape, bcc, CRC, fax **04** crib, echo, fake, scan **05** clone, forge, image, issue, mimic, model, print, Roneo®, stuff, trace, Xerox® **06** borrow, carbon, ectype, follow, mirror, parrot, pirate, repeat, sample **07** emulate, estreat, example, forgery, imitate, pattern, replica, tracing, vidimus **08** apograph, knock-off, likeness, manifold, simulate, specimen **09** archetype, borrowing, duplicate, facsimile, imitation, photocopy, Photostat®, polygraph, replicate, reproduce, semblance **10** carbon copy, mimeograph, plagiarism, plagiarize, transcribe, transcript, triplicate **11** counterfeit, counterpart, engrossment, impersonate, replication **12** reproduction **13** transcription **14** representation **15** exemplification

## coquettish
**06** flirty **07** amorous, flighty, teasing, vampish **08** dallying, inviting **09** seductive **10** come-hither **11** flirtatious, provocative

## cord
**03** guy, tie **04** bond, flex, lace, line, link, rope **05** cable, match, twine, twist **06** bobbin, myelon, ribbon, strand, string, tendon, thread **07** funicle, service **08** bell pull, chenille **09** funiculus **10** connection, draw-string **11** navel-string **12** spinal marrow

## cordial
**04** warm **05** shrub **06** genial, hearty **07** affable, cardiac, earnest, persico, ratafia, rosolio, sincere **08** amicable, anisette, cheerful, friendly, persicot, pleasant, rosoglio, sociable **09** agreeable, heartfelt, hippocras, rosa-solis, welcoming **10** pousse-café **11** Benedictine, stimulating, warm-hearted **12** affectionate, invigorating, wholehearted **13** aqua caelestis, aurum potabile

## cordiality
**05** heart **06** warmth **07** earnest, welcome **09** affection, geniality, sincerity **10** affability, heartiness **11** sociability **12** cheerfulness, friendliness **13** agreeableness

## cordially
**06** warmly **07** affably **08** amicably, genially, sociably **10** cheerfully, pleasantly **13** warm-heartedly **14** wholeheartedly

## cordon
**04** line, ring **05** chain, fence, plant **06** column, ribbon **07** barrier
• **cordon off 07** enclose, isolate, seal off **08** close off, encircle, fence off, separate, surround

## core
**03** key, nub **04** crux, gang, gist, lead, main, nife, runt **05** basic, heart, shift, vital **06** centre, innate, kernel, middle **07** campana, central, company, corncob, crucial, essence, nucleus, typical **08** inherent, interior **09** essential, intrinsic, principal, substance **10** barysphere, definitive,

## copy
underlying **11** constituent, fundamental, nitty-gritty **12** axis cylinder, quintessence **14** characteristic

## cork
**03** lid **04** bung, plug, seal, stop **05** cover, shive, suber **07** phellem, stopper

## corm
*see* **bulb**

## cormorant
**04** shag **05** scart, skart **06** duiker, duyker, scarth, skarth **07** sea crow

## corn
**03** mow, rye, Zea **04** oats **05** grain, maize, wheat **06** barley, cereal, farina, kernel, pinole **10** arable crop, cereal crop, intoxicate

## corner
**03** cor, fix, hog, jam **04** bend, fork, hole, nook, trap, tree **05** angle, catch, crook, curve, joint, niche **06** bail up, cantle, cavity, cranny, cut off, dièdre, pickle, plight, recess, scrape **07** confine, control, crevice, hideout, retreat, straits, turning **08** block off, dominate, hardship, hideaway, hunt down, junction **09** ingleneuk, inglenook, situation, tight spot **10** monopolize, run to earth **11** predicament **12** intersection **13** nowhere to turn **15** force into a place
• **around the corner 04** near **05** close, local **06** at hand, coming, nearby **07** close by, looming **08** imminent, in the air **09** impending **10** accessible, convenient **11** approaching, within range, within reach **12** a stone's throw, neighbouring **13** about to happen
• **cut corners 05** skimp

## cornerstone
**03** key **04** base, coin, core **05** basis, heart, quoin **06** thrust **07** bedrock, essence, keyhole, skew-put, support **08** keystone, mainstay **09** essential, principle, skew-table **10** essentials, groundwork, skew-corbel **11** fundamental **12** fundamentals **13** alpha and omega, starting-point **14** basic principle, main ingredient **15** first principles

## Cornwall
**02** SW

## corny
**04** dull **05** banal, horny, stale, trite **06** feeble, spammy **07** buckeye, cliché'd, maudlin, mawkish **08** clichéed, overused **09** hackneyed **11** commonplace, Mickey Mouse, sentimental, stereotyped **12** old-fashioned **13** platitudinous

## corollary
**05** rider **06** porism, result, upshot **08** function, illation **09** deduction, induction, inference **10** conclusion, consectary, consequent **11** consequence **13** supplementary

## coronation
**08** crowning **12** enthronement

## coronet
**05** crown, tiara **06** cornet, diadem, wreath **07** circlet, crownet, garland

## corporal
**03** Cpl, NCO, Nym **04** corp, naik, pall **06** actual, bodily, carnal **07** fleshly, somatic **08** concrete, material, physical, tangible **09** brigadier, corporeal **10** anatomical **11** substantial **13** lance sergeant

## corporate
**05** joint **06** allied, common, merged, pooled, shared, united **08** combined, communal **09** concerted **10** collective, collegiate **11** amalgamated **13** collaborative

## corporation
**04** firm, gild **05** belly, guild, house, trust **06** cartel, paunch **07** commune, company, concern, council, guildry **08** business, industry, pot-belly, township **09** authority, beer belly, syndicate **10** consortium **11** association, authorities, City Company, partnership **12** conglomerate, organization **13** burgh of barony, establishment, governing body, multinational **14** holding company
See also **paunch; stomach**

## corporeal
**05** human, hylic **06** actual, bodily, carnal, mortal **07** fleshly **08** concrete, corporal, material, physical, tangible **11** substantial

## corps
**01** C **02** CD **03** RAC **04** band, body, crew, team, unit **05** squad **07** brigade, company **08** division, regiment, squadron **10** contingent, detachment

## corpse
**04** body, like, mort **05** corse, mummy, relic, stiff, zombi **06** deader, relics, zombie **07** cadaver, carcase, carcass, remains **08** dead body, skeleton **09** flatliner

## corpulent
**03** fat **05** beefy, bulky, burly, large, obese, plump, poddy, podgy, stout, tubby **06** fleshy, portly, rotund **07** adipose, fattish **08** roly-poly **10** overweight, pot-bellied, well-padded **11** Falstaffian

## corpus
**04** body **05** whole **08** entirety **10** collection **11** aggregation, compilation

## corral
**03** sty **04** coop, fold **05** kraal, pound, stall **09** enclosure

## correct
◇ anagram indicator **02** OK **03** fix **04** cure, edit, jake, just, mend, okay, real, sort, true **05** amend, debug, emend, exact, right, scold, tweak **06** actual, adjust, bang on, proper, punish, rebuke, reform, remedy, revise, seemly, spot-on, strict **07** fitting, improve, precise, rectify, redress, regular, reprove, right-on, sort out **08** accepted, accurate, admonish, disabuse, faithful, flawless, put right, regulate, set right, standard, suitable, truthful, unerring **09** faultless, reprimand **10** acceptable, ameliorate, blue-pencil, discipline **11** appropriate, comme il faut, put straight, put to rights, set to rights, word-perfect **12** conventional, rehabilitate **14** counterbalance

## correction
◇ anagram indicator **05** tweak **06** rebuke, reform **07** reproof **08** equation, grafting, scolding **09** amendment, reduction, remedying, reprimand **10** adjustment, admonition, alteration, diorthosis, discipline, emendation, punishment **11** improvement, reformation **12** amelioration, chastisement, compensation, modification **13** rectification **14** rehabilitation

## corrective
**05** penal **08** curative, punitive, remedial **09** corrigent, medicinal **10** amendatory, emendatory, palliative **11** reformatory, restorative, therapeutic **12** disciplinary **14** rehabilitative

## correctly
◇ anagram indicator **02** OK **04** okay **05** right **07** exactly, rightly **08** actually, properly, suitably **09** about east, fittingly, precisely **10** acceptably, accurately, flawlessly, unerringly **11** faultlessly **13** appropriately **14** conventionally

## correlate
**04** link **05** agree, tally, tie in **06** equate, relate **07** compare, connect **08** analogue, interact, parallel **09** associate **10** co-ordinate, correspond **15** show a connection

## correlation
**03** fit **04** link **10** connection **11** association, equivalence, interaction, interchange, reciprocity **12** relationship **14** correspondence **15** interdependence

## correspond
**03** fit, pen **05** agree, match, rhyme, tally, write **06** accord, answer, concur, square **07** balance, conform, match up **08** assonate, coincide, dovetail, register **09** be similar, correlate, harmonize, represent **10** complement, sympathize **11** be analogous, communicate, fit together, keep in touch **12** be consistent, be equivalent **13** be in agreement **15** exchange letters

## correspondence
**03** fit **04** mail, post **05** e-mail, match **07** analogy, harmony, letters, writing **08** relation **09** agreement, assonance, congruity **10** comparison, conformity, consonance, similarity **11** coincidence, concurrence, correlation, equivalence, resemblance, suitability **13** communication, comparability
See also **letter**

## correspondent
**06** keypal, pen pal, writer **08** agreeing, reporter, suitable **09** answering, columnist, pen friend **10** journalist, responsive **11** contributor, responsible **12** letter-writer

## corresponding
**04** like **07** similar, suiting **08** agreeing, matching, parallel, relative **09** accordant, analogous, answering, congruent, facsimile, identical **10** collateral, comparable, equivalent, reciprocal **12** commensurate, interrelated **13** complementary

## corridor
**04** hall **05** aisle, lobby **07** gallery, gangway, hallway, passage **08** alleyway **09** penthouse **10** passageway

## corroborate
**05** prove **06** attest, back up, ratify, uphold, verify **07** bear out, certify, confirm, endorse, support, sustain **08** document, evidence, underpin, validate **09** confirmed **12** authenticate, substantiate

## corroboration
**10** validation **11** attestation, endorsement **12** confirmation, ratification, verification **14** authentication, substantiation

## corroborative
**09** endorsing, verifying **10** confirming, evidential, supporting, supportive, validating **11** evidentiary **12** confirmative, confirmatory, verificatory **14** substantiating

## corrode
**03** eat, rot **04** burn, etch, fret, rust **05** eat in, erode, waste **06** abrade, impair **07** consume, crumble, destroy, eat away, eat into, oxidize, tarnish **08** wear away **11** deteriorate **12** disintegrate

## corrosion
**03** rot **04** rust **07** burning, erosion, rotting, rusting, wasting **08** abrasion **09** prerosion **10** tarnishing **13** deterioration **14** disintegration

## corrosive
**04** acid **07** caustic, cutting, erosive, wasting, wearing **08** abrasive **09** consuming, corroding **11** destructive

## corrugated
**06** fluted, folded, ridged **07** creased, grooved, rumpled, striate **08** crinkled, furrowed, wrinkled **10** channelled

## corrupt
◇ anagram indicator **03** buy, mar, rot **04** bent, evil, lure, warp **05** bribe, decay, shady, spoil, taint, venal **06** blight, bribed, buy off, canker, debase, defile, doctor, impure, infect, poison, putrid, rotten, seduce, sleazy, suborn, wicked **07** abusive, crooked, debauch, defiled, deprave, falsify, immoral, obscene, pervert, pollute, putrefy, subvert, tainted, vitiate **08** bribable, depraved, empoison **09** barbarize, barbarous, debauched, dishonest, dissolute, inquinate,

## corruption

unethical **10** adulterate, bastardize, degenerate, demoralize, fraudulent, lead astray, tamper with **11** contaminate **12** contaminated, unprincipled, unscrupulous **13** untrustworthy **15** be a bad influence

## corruption

**03** rot **04** evil, vice **05** abuse, bobol, fraud, graft, taint **06** sleaze **07** bribery, leprosy **08** impurity, iniquity, villainy **09** depravity, extortion, pollution, shadiness **10** adaptation, alteration, debauchery, dishonesty, distortion, immorality, perversion, rottenness, subversion, wickedness **11** criminality, crookedness, degradation, subornation **12** degeneration, modification **13** contamination, sharp practice

## corset

**04** belt, busk **05** stays **06** bodice, girdle, roll-on, shaper, waspie **08** corselet **11** panty girdle

## cortège

**05** suite, train **06** column, parade **07** retinue **09** cavalcade, entourage **10** procession

## cosh

see **weapon**

## cosily

**06** safely, snugly, warmly **08** securely **10** intimately **11** comfortably

## cosmetic

**04** fard **05** minor **06** beauty, make-up, slight **07** shallow, surface, trivial **08** external, skin-deep **10** maquillage, peripheral **11** beautifying, superficial

*Cosmetics include:*

**05** rouge, toner
**07** blusher, bronzer, mascara, perfume
**08** cleanser, eyeliner, face mask, face pack, lip gloss, lip liner, lipstick, panstick
**09** concealer, eye shadow, face cream, lightener
**10** face powder, foundation, kohl pencil, nail polish
**11** greasepaint, moisturizer, nail varnish
**13** eyebrow pencil, pressed powder

## cosmic

**04** huge, mega, vast **05** large **07** immense, in space, massive, mundane, orderly, seismic **08** colossal, enormous, infinite **09** from space, grandiose, limitless, universal, worldwide **11** measureless, significant **12** immeasurable

## cosmonaut

**08** lunanaut, spaceman **09** astronaut, lunarnaut, taikonaut **10** spacewoman **14** space traveller

## cosmopolitan

**06** urbane **07** worldly **08** cultured **09** universal **11** broad-minded, multiracial, worldly-wise **12** unprejudiced **13** international, multicultural, sophisticated, well-travelled

## cosmos

**06** galaxy, nature, system, worlds **08** creation, universe

## cosset

**03** pet **04** baby **05** spoil **06** coddle, cuddle, fondle, pamper **07** cherish, indulge **08** mollycoddle, overindulge

## cost

**03** fee, pay, tab **04** exes, harm, hurt, levy, loss, rate, take, toll **05** coast, fetch, go for, price, quote, value, worth **06** amount, ask for, budget, buy for, charge, come to, damage, figure, injure, injury, outlay, tariff **07** be worth, cost out, deprive, destroy, expense, payment, penalty, sell for, set back, stand in, work out **08** amount to, estimate, expenses, retail at, spending **09** calculate, cause harm, detriment, knock back, outgoings, overheads, quotation, sacrifice, suffering, valuation **10** be priced at, be valued at **11** asking price, cause injury, deprivation, expenditure **12** disbursement, selling price **13** disbursements **14** cause the loss of

## Costa Rica

**02** CR **03** CRI

## costly

**04** dear, posh, rich, salt **05** steep **06** lavish, pricey **07** harmful, premium, ruinous, sky-high **08** damaging, high-cost, precious, splendid, valuable **09** big-ticket, chargeful, excessive, expensive, priceless, sumptuous **10** disastrous, exorbitant, high-priced, loss-making, overpriced **11** deleterious, destructive, detrimental **12** catastrophic, costing a bomb, extortionate **15** costing the earth, daylight robbery

## costume

**02** gi **03** gie, tog **04** garb, suit **05** dress, get-up, habit, robes **06** attire, bather, bikini, cossie, judogi, livery, outfit, rig-out, toilet **07** apparel, clobber, clothes, fashion, threads, uniform **08** clothing, ensemble, garments **09** gala-dress, vestments **10** diving suit, fancy dress **11** diving dress **12** style of dress
*See also* **clothes, clothing**

## cosy

**04** cosh, safe, snug, warm **05** comfy **06** homely, intime, secure **08** intimate **09** congenial, gemütlich, sheltered **11** comfortable

## Côte d'Ivoire

**02** CI **03** CIV

## coterie

**03** set **04** camp, club, gang **05** cabal, group **06** caucus, circle, clique **07** cenacle, faction **09** camarilla, community **11** association

## cottage

**03** cot, hut **04** bach, crib, gite **05** bothy, cabin, dacha, lodge, shack, villa **06** bothie, chalet, shanty **08** bungalow **09** home-croft

## cotton

**04** lint **05** ceiba

*Cotton fabrics include:*

**04** aida, duck, jean
**05** chino, denim, dhoti, drill, jaspé, jeans, kanga, piqué, surat, toile
**06** Bengal, calico, canvas, chintz, coutil, dhooti, diaper, dimity, humhum, jersey, khanga, madras, moreen, muslin, nankin, Oxford, pongee, sateen, T-cloth
**07** batiste, buckram, challis, duvetyn, fustian, galatea, gingham, jaconet, kitenge, Mexican, nankeen, percale, printer, silesia
**08** chambray, corduroy, coutille, cretonne, drilling, frocking, lambskin, marcella, nainsook, organdie, osnaburg, shantung, thickset
**09** cottonade, huckaback, longcloth, percaline, sailcloth, satin jean, swans-down, velveteen
**10** Balbriggan, candlewick, monk's cloth, seersucker, winceyette
**11** cheesecloth, flannelette, mutton cloth, nettle-cloth, Oxford cloth, sponge cloth
**13** casement cloth

## • foreign particle in cotton

**04** moit, mote

## couch

**03** bed, set **04** bear, sofa, word **05** divan, frame, quick, utter **06** cradle, day bed, litter, pallet, phrase, quitch, scutch, settee, twitch **07** express, lounger, ottoman, quicken, sofa bed, support, vis-à-vis **08** dog-grass, dog-wheat **10** quack grass, quick grass, triclinium **11** quitch grass, scutch grass, twitch grass **12** chaise-longue, chesterfield

## cough

**03** hem, ugh **04** ahem, bark, hack, hawk, kink, rasp **05** croak, hoast **06** tisick, tussis **07** hawking **08** kink-host **09** chincough, kink-cough, pertussis **15** clear your throat
• **cough up 03** pay **04** give **05** pay up **06** ante up, pay out **07** fork out, stump up **08** hand over, shell out

## could

• **could be, could become**
◊ *anagram indicator*

## council

**04** body, diet, duma, jury **05** board, boule, cabal, crowd, divan, douma, flock, forum, group, jirga, junta, panel, rally, shura, synod, witan **06** senate, soviet, throng **07** cabinet, chamber, company, conseil, consult, meeting **08** advisers, assembly, congress, ministry, trustees **09** committee, directors, executive, gathering, governors, Landsting, Loya Jirga, multitude, panchayat, Sanhedrim, Sanhedrin, syndicate **10** commission, conference, convention, focus group, government, Landsthing, management, parliament, presidency

## councillor

**11** city fathers, convocation, corporation, directorate, witenagemot **12** advisory body, ayuntamiento, body of people, congregation, working party **13** advisory group, governing body **14** administration, local authority

*Council areas of Scotland:*

**04** Fife
**05** Angus, Moray
**06** Dundee
**07** Falkirk
**08** Aberdeen, Highland, Stirling
**10** Dundee City, Eilean Siar, Inverclyde, Midlothian
**11** East Lothian, Glasgow City, West Lothian
**12** Aberdeen City, East Ayrshire, Renfrewshire
**13** Aberdeenshire, Argyll and Bute, North Ayrshire, Orkney Islands, South Ayrshire
**15** City of Edinburgh, Perth and Kinross, Scottish Borders, Shetland Islands
**16** Clackmannanshire, East Renfrewshire, North Lanarkshire, South Lanarkshire
**18** East Dunbartonshire, West Dunbartonshire
**19** Dumfries and Galloway

*Council areas of Wales:*

**05** Conwy, Powys
**07** Cardiff, Gwynedd, Newport, Swansea, Torfaen, Wrexham
**08** Bridgend
**10** Caerphilly, Ceredigion, Flintshire
**12** Blaenau Gwent, Denbighshire
**13** Merthyr Tydfil, Monmouthshire, Pembrokeshire
**14** Isle of Anglesey
**15** Carmarthenshire, Neath Port Talbot, Vale of Glamorgan
**16** Rhondda Cynon Taff

## councillor

**02** CC, Cr, PC **04** Cllr **05** vezir, vizir **06** induna, visier, vizier, wizier **07** burgess, provost **08** decurion

## counsel

**02** KC, QC **04** read, rede, silk, urge, warn **05** aread, arede, guide, teach **06** advice, advise, direct, exhort, lawyer **07** arreede, caution, opinion, suggest **08** admonish, advising, advocate, attorney, guidance, instruct, moralism **09** barrister, direction, recommend, solicitor, viewpoint **10** admonition, advisement, conference, conferring, suggestion **11** exhortation, forethought, information **12** amicus curiae, consultation, deliberation, give guidance **13** consideration **14** recommendation **15** give your opinion

## counsellor

**04** guru **05** coach, guide, tutor **06** mentor, Nestor **07** teacher **08** director **09** authority, barrister, confidant, directrix, therapist **10** Achitophel, Ahithophel, confidante, consultant, directress, instructor

## count

**03** add, Ory, sum **04** deem, feel, Graf, hold, list, poll, tell **05** add up, check, compt, Fosco, grave, judge, noble, score, sum up, tally, think, total, tot up, whole **06** census, county, esteem, matter, number, reckon, regard **07** account, compute, Dracula, include, qualify, signify **08** allow for, consider, look upon **09** calculate, enumerate, landgrave, numbering, palsgrave, reckoning, totting-up **10** cut some ice, full amount, Rhinegrave **11** be important, calculation, carry weight, computation, enumeration **13** mean something, take account of **15** make a difference, take into account

*See also* **nobility**
• **count in** **05** put in **06** rope in **07** include, involve, let in on **08** allow for **09** introduce
• **count on** **05** trust **06** bank on, expect, lean on, rely on **07** bargain, believe, swear by **08** depend on, reckon on **10** bargain for
• **count out** **04** omit, tell **06** ignore **07** exclude **08** leave out, pass over **09** disregard, eliminate **10** include out

## countenance

**04** back, face, look, mien **05** agree, allow, brook **06** endure, favour, permit, uphold, visage **07** approve, condone, endorse **08** features, sanction, semblant, stand for, tolerate **09** patronage, put up with **10** appearance, expression **11** approbation, physiognomy **12** acquiescence

## counter

**03** bar **04** buck, chip, coin, desk, disc, dump, fish, meet **05** merel, meril, parry, piece, stand, table, token **06** answer, buffet, combat, marker, merell, offset, oppose, resist, retort, return **07** adverse, against, dispute, opposed, respond, surface, worktop **08** contrary, opposing, opposite **09** hit back, at, retaliate, shopboard **10** contradict, conversely **11** conflicting, contrasting, work surface **12** in opposition **13** contradictory

## counteract

**04** foil, undo **05** annul, check **06** defeat, hinder, negate, offset, oppose, remedy, resist, thwart **07** prevent **09** frustrate **10** act against, invalidate, neutralize **11** countervail **14** counterbalance

## counterbalance

**04** undo **05** poise **06** cancel, offset, set-off **07** balance, correct, requite **08** equalize **09** make up for **10** compensate, neutralize **11** countervail **12** counterpoise **13** compensate for

## counterfeit

**03** dud **04** base, copy, fake, sham **05** bogus, dummy, faked, false, feign, forge, fraud, phony, pseud, queer, snide **06** copied, forged, phoney, pirate, pseudo **07** falsify, feigned, forgery, imitate, pretend, simular **08** borrowed, disguise, phantasm, postiche, simulate, spurious **09** brummagem, fabricate, imitation, pretended, reproduce, simulated **10** artificial, camouflage, fraudulent **11** impersonate **12** reproduction

*See also* **counterfeit coin** *under* **coin**

## countermand

**05** annul, quash **06** cancel, repeal, revoke **07** rescind, reverse, unorder **08** abrogate, override, overturn **10** revocation

## counterpart

**04** copy, mate, peer, twin **05** equal, match, moral, tally **06** double, fellow **07** obverse **08** parallel **09** duplicate **10** complement, equivalent, supplement **14** opposite number

## counterpoint

**04** foil **06** relief, set off, set-off **07** descant, enhance **08** contrast, faburden, heighten, opposite **09** intensify **10** complement **11** counterpane **13** differentiate **15** differentiation, throw into relief

## countless

**06** legion, myriad, untold **07** endless, umpteen **08** infinite **09** boundless, limitless **10** numberless, unnumbered, without end **11** innumerable, measureless **12** immeasurable, incalculable **13** inexhaustible

## countrified

**04** hick **05** rural **06** rustic **07** bucolic, idyllic, outback **08** agrarian, pastoral **10** provincial **12** agricultural

## country

**04** area, bush, land, pays, soil **05** power, realm, rural, state, wilds **06** landed, nation, people, public, region, rustic, sticks, voters **07** bucolic, idyllic, kingdom, outback, terrain **08** agrarian, citizens, district, electors, farmland, locality, moorland, pastoral, populace, republic **09** backwater, backwoods, community, green belt, provinces, residents, rural area, territory **10** backblocks, never-never, population, provincial **11** countryside, inhabitants **12** agricultural, back of beyond, principality **13** neighbourhood **15** middle of nowhere

*Countries:*

**02** UK
**03** PRC, UAE, USA
**04** Chad, Cuba, Fiji, Iran, Iraq, Laos, Mali, Oman, Peru, Togo
**05** Benin, Chile, China, Congo, Egypt, Gabon, Ghana, Haiti, India, Italy, Japan, Kenya, Libya, Malta, Nauru, Nepal, Niger, Palau, Qatar, Samoa, Spain, Sudan, Syria, Tonga, Wales, Yemen
**06** Angola, Belize, Bhutan, Brazil, Canada, Cyprus, France, Greece, Guinea, Guyana, Israel, Jordan, Kosovo, Kuwait, Latvia, Malawi,

Mexico, Monaco, Norway, Panama, Poland, Russia, Rwanda, Serbia, Sweden, Taiwan, Turkey, Tuvalu, Uganda, Zambia
**07** Albania, Algeria, Andorra, Armenia, Austria, Bahrain, Belarus, Belgium, Bolivia, Burundi, Comoros, Croatia, Denmark, Ecuador, England, Eritrea, Estonia, Finland, Georgia, Germany, Grenada, Holland, Hungary, Iceland, Ireland, Jamaica, Lebanon, Lesotho, Liberia, Moldova, Morocco, Myanmar, Namibia, Nigeria, Romania, Senegal, Somalia, St Lucia, Tunisia, Ukraine, Uruguay, Vanuatu, Vatican, Vietnam
**08** Barbados, Botswana, Bulgaria, Cambodia, Cameroon, Colombia, Djibouti, Dominica, Ethiopia, Honduras, Kiribati, Malaysia, Maldives, Mongolia, Pakistan, Paraguay, Portugal, Scotland, Slovakia, Slovenia, Sri Lanka, Suriname, Tanzania, Thailand, Zimbabwe
**09** Argentina, Australia, Cape Verde, Costa Rica, East Timor, Guatemala, Indonesia, Lithuania, Macedonia, Mauritius, Nicaragua, San Marino, Singapore, Swaziland, The Gambia, Venezuela
**10** Azerbaijan, Bangladesh, El Salvador, Kazakhstan, Kyrgyzstan, Luxembourg, Madagascar, Mauritania, Montenegro, Mozambique, New Zealand, North Korea, Seychelles, South Korea, Tajikistan, The Bahamas, Uzbekistan
**11** Afghanistan, Burkina Faso, Côte d'Ivoire, Philippines, Saudi Arabia, Sierra Leone, South Africa, Switzerland, Vatican City
**12** Guinea-Bissau, Turkmenistan, United States
**13** Czech Republic, Liechtenstein, United Kingdom, Western Sahara
**14** Papua New Guinea, Solomon Islands, The Netherlands
**15** Marshall Islands, Northern Ireland, St Kitts and Nevis
**16** Brunei Darussalam, Equatorial Guinea
**17** Antigua and Barbuda, Dominican Republic, Trinidad and Tobago
**18** São Tomé and Príncipe, United Arab Emirates
**20** Bosnia and Herzegovina
**21** United States of America
**22** Central African Republic
**25** St Vincent and the Grenadines
**27** Federated States of Micronesia
**28** Democratic Republic of the Congo

---

*Country codes include:*

**03** ABW, AFG, AGO, AIA, ALB, AND, ANT, ARE, ARG, ARM, ASM, ATA, ATF, ATG, AUS, AUT, AZE, BDI, BEL, BEN, BFA, BGD,

BGR, BHR, BHS, BIH, BLR, BLZ, BMU, BOL, BRA, BRB, BRN, BTN, BVT, BWA, CAF, CAN, CCK, CHE, CHL, CHN, CIV, CMR, COD, COG, COK, COL, COM, CPV, CRI, CUB, CXR, CYM, CYP, CZE, DEU, DJI, DMA, DNK, DOM, DZA, ECU, EGY, ERI, ESH, ESP, EST, ETH, FIN, FJI, FLK, FRA, FRO, FSM, GAB, GBR, GEO, GHA, GIB, GIN, GLP, GMB, GNB, GNQ, GRC, GRD, GRL, GTM, GUF, GUM, GUY, HGK, HMD, HND, HRV, HTI, HUN, IDN, IMN, IND, IOT, IRL, IRN, IRQ, ISL, ISR, ITA, JAM, JOR, JPN, KAZ, KEN, KGZ, KHM, KIR, KNA, KOR, KWT, LAO, LBN, LBR, LBY, LCA, LIE, LKA, LSO, LTU, LUX, LVA, MAC, MAR, MCO, MDA, MDG, MDV, MEX, MHL, MKD, MLI, MLT, MMR, MNE, MNG, MNP, MOZ, MRT, MSR, MTQ, MUS, MWI, MYS, MYT, NAM, NCL, NER, NFK, NGA, NIC, NIU, NLD, NOR, NPL, NRU, NZL, OMN, PAK, PAN, PCN, PER, PHL, PLW, PNG, POL, PRI, PRK, PRT, PRY, PYF, QAT, REU, ROU, RUS, RWA, SAU, SDN, SEN, SGP, SHN, SJM, SLB, SLE, SLV, SMR, SOM, SPM, SRB, STP, SUR, SVK, SVN, SWE, SWZ, SYC, SYR, TCA, TCD, TGO, THA, TJK, TKL, TKM, TLS, TON, TTO, TUN, TUR, TUV, TWN, TZA, UGA, UKR, URY, USA, UZB, VAT, VCT, VEN, VGB, VIR, VNM, VUT, WLF, WSM, YEM, YUG, ZAF, ZMB, ZWE

---

*Former country names include:*

**04** Siam, USSR
**05** Burma, Zaire
**06** Bengal, Ceylon, Persia, Urundi
**07** Dahomey, Formosa
**08** Rhodesia
**09** Abyssinia, Indochina, Kampuchea, Nyasaland
**10** Basutoland, Ivory Coast, Senegambia, Tanganyika, Upper Volta, Yugoslavia
**11** Dutch Guiana, French Sudan, New Hebrides, Ubangi Shari
**12** Bechuanaland, French Guinea, Ruanda-Urundi
**13** British Guiana, Ellice Islands, Khmer Republic, Spanish Guinea, Spanish Sahara, Trucial States
**14** Czechoslovakia, French Togoland, Gilbert Islands
**15** British Honduras, British Togoland, Dutch East Indies, South West Africa

• **open country** **03** lay, lea, lee, ley **04** moor, veld, wold **05** field, heath, plain, range, veldt, weald
*See also* **Africa; America; Arab; Asia; commonwealth; Europe; Middle East**

**countryman, countrywoman**
**03** hob **04** boor, hick, hind **05** Hodge,

yokel **06** farmer, rustic, yeoman **07** bumpkin, hayseed, landman, peasant **09** hillbilly **10** clodhopper, compatriot, provincial **11** bushwhacker **12** backwoodsman **13** fellow citizen **14** fellow national

**countryside**
**06** nature **07** country, scenery **08** farmland, moorland, outdoors **09** green belt, landscape, rural area

**countrywoman**
*see* **countryman, countrywoman**

**county**
**02** Co **04** area **05** count, shire, state **06** parish, region **08** district, province **09** comitatus, territory **10** department
*See also* **council; district; province**

---

*Counties and administrative areas of England:*

**04** Kent, York
**05** Derby, Devon, Essex, Luton, Poole
**06** Dorset, Durham, Halton, London, Medway, Slough, Surrey, Torbay
**07** Cumbria, Norfolk, Reading, Rutland, Suffolk, Swindon
**08** Cheshire, Plymouth, Somerset, Thurrock
**09** Blackpool, Hampshire, Leicester, Wiltshire, Wokingham
**10** Darlington, Derbyshire, East Sussex, Hartlepool, Lancashire, Merseyside, Nottingham, Portsmouth, Shropshire, Warrington, West Sussex
**11** Bournemouth, Isle of Wight, Oxfordshire, Southampton, Tyne and Wear
**12** Bedfordshire, Lincolnshire, Milton Keynes, Peterborough, Stoke-on-Trent, Warwickshire, West Midlands
**13** City of Bristol, Herefordshire, Hertfordshire, Middlesbrough, North Somerset, Southend-on-Sea, Staffordshire, West Berkshire, West Yorkshire
**14** Cambridgeshire, Leicestershire, Northumberland, North Yorkshire, South Yorkshire, Stockton-on-Tees, Worcestershire
**15** Bracknell Forest, Brighton and Hove, Buckinghamshire, Gloucestershire, Nottinghamshire
**16** Northamptonshire, Telford and Wrekin
**17** Greater Manchester, North Lincolnshire
**18** Redcar and Cleveland
**19** Blackburn with Darwen
**20** South Gloucestershire, Windsor and Maidenhead
**21** East Riding of Yorkshire, North East Lincolnshire
**22** City of Kingston upon Hull
**24** Bath and North East Somerset, Cornwall and Isles of Scilly

---

*County abbreviations include:*

**02** Mx
**03** Dev, Dur, Ess, Mon, Som, Sur, War

04 Beds, Camb, Ches, Corn, Cumb, Dors, Glos, Mont, Oxon, Suff
05 Berks, Bucks, Cambs, Cards, Derby, E Suss, Hants, Herts, Lancs, Leics, Lincs, Middx, Notts, Wilts, Worcs, Yorks
06 Caerns, Shrops, Staffs
08 Northumb
09 Northants

_Counties of Ireland:_

04 Cork, Leix, Mayo
05 Cavan, Clare, Kerry, Laois, Louth, Meath, Sligo
06 Carlow, Dublin, Galway, Offaly
07 Donegal, Kildare, Leitrim, Wexford, Wicklow
08 Kilkenny, Laoighis, Limerick, Longford, Monaghan
09 Roscommon, Tipperary, Waterford, Westmeath

• **county town** _see_ **town**
• **home counties** 02 SE

## coup
04 blow, deed, feat 05 stunt, upset
06 action, barter, putsch, revolt, stroke
07 exploit, success, triumph
08 exchange, overturn, takeover, uprising 09 coup d'état, manoeuvre, overthrow, rebellion 10 revolution
11 tour de force 12 insurrection, masterstroke 14 accomplishment

## coup de grâce
04 kill 06 kibosh 07 quietus 08 clincher
09 death blow 11 kiss of death
13 finishing blow

## coup d'état
04 coup 06 putsch, revolt 08 takeover, uprising 09 overthrow, rebellion
10 revolution 12 insurrection

## couple
◇ _repetition indicator_ 03 duo, two, wed
04 ally, bind, join, link, mate, meng, ming, pair, tway, yoke 05 brace, clasp, hitch, marry, match, menge, twain, unite 06 attach, buckle, fasten, lovers, marrow 07 combine, conjoin, connect, diarchy, shackle, twosome 08 double up, partners 09 accompany, associate, integrate, newlyweds 12 Darby and Joan 14 husband and wife

## coupon
04 chit, form, slip, stub 05 check, token
06 billet, docket, ticket 07 voucher
11 certificate, counterfoil

## courage
04 grit, guts 05 balls, heart, metal, moxie, nerve, pluck, spunk, valor
06 bottle, daring, mettle, spirit, valour
07 bravery, cojones, heroism, stomach
08 audacity, backbone, boldness, coraggio, gumption 09 fortitude, gallantry 10 resolution 11 intrepidity
12 fearlessness 13 dauntlessness, determination

## courageous
04 bold, game 05 brave, gutsy, hardy, wight 06 ballsy, daring, feisty, heroic, manful, plucky, spunky 07 gallant, valiant 08 fearless, generous, intrepid, resolute, valorous 09 audacious,

dauntless 10 determined, stomachous
11 adventurous, full-hearted, high-hearted, indomitable, lion-hearted
12 stout-hearted
• **courageous person** 04 hero, lion

## courageously
06 boldly 07 bravely 09 gallantly, valiantly 10 fearlessly, heroically, intrepidly, resolutely 11 audaciously, dauntlessly, indomitably
13 adventurously

## courier
03 rep 05 envoy, Fed-Ex, guide
06 bearer, escort, herald, legate, nuncio, runner 07 carrier, postman
08 emissary 09 estafette, messenger, tour guide 10 pursuivant 11 travel guide 13 dispatch rider
14 representative

## course
03 ren, rin, run, way 04 beat, dash, dish, flow, gush, hunt, lane, line, mess, mode, move, part, path, plan, pour, race, rise, road, rota, span, tack, term, time 05 ambit, chase, lapse, march, orbit, order, route, spell, stage, surge, sweet, track, trail 06 entrée, follow, ground, manner, method, period, policy, pursue, remove, series, stream, system, voyage 07 advance, channel, circuit, classes, current, dessert, lessons, passage, passing, process, pudding, regimen, starter, studies
08 approach, duration, lectures, movement, progress, run after, schedule, sequence, syllabus
09 appetizer, direction, entremets, procedure, programme, racetrack, unfolding 10 curriculum, flight path, golf course, main course, racecourse, succession, trajectory 11 development, furtherance, hors d'oeuvre, progression

_See also_ **compass; golf; race; racecourse**
• **alter course** 04 gybe, jibe, tack, wear
• **deviate from course** 03 bag, yaw
• **direct course** 03 aim 04 head
• **fixed course** 03 rut 04 race
• **in due course** 02 so 06 in time
07 finally 09 in due time
10 eventually 13 all in good time, sooner or later
• **of course** 02 ay 03 aye 04 sure
05 natch 06 surely 07 no doubt 08 to be sure 09 certainly, naturally 10 by all means, definitely 11 bien entendu, doubtlessly, indubitably, undoubtedly 12 indisputably
13 needless to say, without a doubt
14 not unnaturally
• **part of course** 03 leg

## court
02 ct 03 bar, Hof, see, sew, sue, woo, wow 04 date, quad, ring, risk, seek, yard 05 alley, arena, bench, chase, green, patio, plaza, suite, track, train
06 castle, go with, ground, incite, invite, palace, piazza, prompt, pursue, square 07 attract, cortège, flatter, provoke, retinue, solicit 08 cloister,

game area, go steady, pander to, try to win 09 courtyard, cultivate, curtilage, enclosure, entourage, esplanade, forecourt, go out with, household, judiciary, peristyle 10 attendants, cozy up with, judicatory, judicature, praetorium, quadrangle
11 conservancy, go round with, playing area 12 go around with
13 spheristerion 14 royal residence
15 curry favour with

_Courts include:_

03 ICC, law
04 eyre, Fehm, high, leet, Lyon, moot, open, Vehm
05 burgh, civil, crown, curia, prize, trial, World, youth
06 appeal, Arches, church, claims, county, family, Honour, police, record
07 appeals, assizes, borough, circuit, Diplock, divorce, federal, justice, Probate, Session, sheriff, Supreme
08 chancery, coroner's, criminal, district, juvenile, kangaroo, Requests, superior, tribunal
09 children's, Exchequer, Faculties, municipal, Old Bailey, Piepowder, Sanhedrim, Sanhedrin, the Arches
10 Commercial, commissary, consistory, Divisional, Piepowders, Protection
11 Arbitration, Common Bench, Common Pleas, High Justice, magistrates', police-court, Prerogative, small claims
12 Aulic Council, court-martial, House of Lords, Privy Council
13 first instance
14 Criminal Appeal, High Commission, High Justiciary
15 Central Criminal, European Justice, Lord Chancellor's

• **bring to court** 04 file
• **court case** 04 suit 05 trial
06 action 07 lawsuit
• **court house** 02 ch
• **in court** 02 up 08 at the bar
• **right to hold court** 03 sac, soc
• **take to court** 03 law, sue

## courteous
04 hend, kind 05 civil 06 polite, urbane
07 affable, courtly, gallant, refined, tactful 08 debonair, gracious, ladylike, mannerly, obliging, polished, well-bred 09 attentive 10 chivalrous, debonnaire, diplomatic, respectful, well-spoken 11 considerate, deferential, gentlemanly 12 well-mannered

## courteously
06 kindly 07 civilly 08 politely, urbanely 09 gallantly, refinedly, tactfully 10 graciously, obligingly
11 attentively 12 chivalrously, respectfully 13 considerately, deferentially 14 diplomatically

## courtesy
04 tact 06 comity, curtsy, devoir, favour, gentry 07 manners, respect
08 breeding, chivalry, civility,

**courtier**

kindness, urbanity **09** attention, deference, etiquette, gallantry, gentility **10** generosity, gentilesse, politeness, refinement **11** good manners **12** good breeding, graciousness **13** consideration

**courtier**

**04** lady, lord, page **05** noble, toady **07** steward, subject **08** follower, liegeman, nobleman **09** attendant, cup-bearer, flatterer, sycophant **11** train-bearer **13** lady-in-waiting

**courtly**

**05** aulic, civil **06** formal, lordly, polite **07** elegant, gallant, refined, stately **08** decorous, gracious, high-bred, obliging, polished **09** dignified **10** chivalrous, flattering **11** ceremonious **12** aristocratic

**courtship**

**04** suit **05** spoon **06** affair, dating, wooing **07** chasing, pursuit, romance **08** courting, going-out, love-suit **10** attentions, lovemaking **11** going steady

**courtyard**

**04** area, quad, ward, yard **05** court, garth, marae, patio, plaza **06** atrium, square **07** cortile **08** cloister **09** enclosure, esplanade, forecourt **10** quadrangle

**cove**

**03** bay, man **04** chap **05** bight, creek, fiord, firth, inlet **06** cavern **07** estuary

**covenant**

**03** vow **04** bond, deed, pact **05** agree, trust **06** engage, pledge, treaty **07** compact, promise **08** contract, warranty **09** agreement, concordat, indenture, stipulate, testament, undertake **10** commitment, convention, engagement **11** arrangement, stipulation, undertaking **12** dispensation

**cover**

◇ *containment indicator* ◇ *hidden indicator* **02** do, go **03** cap, cup, hap, hat, lay, lep, lid, set, top **04** bury, cake, case, coat, cour, cowl, daub, deck, film, heal, heel, hele, hide, hood, leap, mask, pall, skin, tell, tilt, veil, vele, wrap **05** apron, brood, cloak, cloke, coure, cross, dress, duvet, front, guard, layer, paten, quoit, throw, treat **06** attire, be over, canopy, carpet, clothe, defend, embody, encase, extend, façade, incase, insure, jacket, mantle, pay for, refuge, report, review, screen, shield, shroud, sleeve, spread, survey, take in, toilet, travel **07** analyse, bedding, binding, blanket, coating, conceal, contain, cover-up, defence, embrace, envelop, examine, garment, include, involve, journey, measure, narrate, obscure, overlay, package, plaster, present, pretext, protect, put over, relieve, replace, shelter, stretch, swaddle, wrapper, wreathe **08** accoutre, bedcover, bespread, blankets, clothing, comprise, consider, continue, covering, deal with, deputize,

describe, disguise, enshroud, envelope, go across, overveil, pretence, security, traverse **09** assurance, bedspread, encompass, fill in for, indemnify, indemnity, insurance, make up for, place over, safeguard, sanctuary, talk about, whitewash **10** balance out, bedclothes, camouflage, complicity, conspiracy, extend over, overspread, protection, provide for, recompense, stand in for, travel over, underwrite, write about **11** be enough for, concealment, confederate, hiding-place, incorporate, investigate, pinch-hit for, smokescreen **12** compensation, take over from **13** compensate for, give details of **14** counterbalance **15** give an account of, indemnification
• **cover up** ◇ *hidden indicator* **03** hap **04** hide **05** blank, fudge **06** hush up **07** conceal, repress **08** enshroud, hoodwink, keep dark, suppress **09** dissemble, gloss over, whitewash **10** keep secret
• **original cover** **02** OC

**coverage**

**04** item **05** story **06** report **07** account, blanket, reports **08** analysis **09** reportage, reporting **11** description **13** investigation

**covering**

**03** cap, lag, rug, top **04** aril, cape, case, coat, cope, film, hood, husk, mask, pall, roof, skin **05** armor, cloak, cloke, cover, crust, layer, shell **06** armour, awning, carpet, casing, sheath, tegmen, veneer **07** blanket, coating, housing, overlay, roofing, shelter **08** clothing, pavilion, sheeting, wrapping **09** tarpaulin **10** encasement, incasement, integument, overlaying, protection **11** descriptive, explanatory **12** accompanying, introductory

**covert**

**06** hidden, secret, sneaky, veiled **07** furtive, private, shelter **08** sidelong, stealthy, ulterior **09** concealed, disguised, underhand **10** dissembled **11** clandestine, unsuspected **13** subreptitious, surreptitious, under the table

**covertly**

**08** secretly **09** furtively, privately **15** surreptitiously

**cover-up**

**05** front **06** façade, screen **08** pretence **09** deception, whitewash **10** complicity, conspiracy **11** concealment, smokescreen

**covet**

**04** envy, want **05** crave, fancy **06** desire **07** long for **08** begrudge, yearn for **09** hanker for, hunger for, lust after, thirst for

**covetous**

**06** greedy **07** craving, envious, jealous, longing, wanting **08** desirous, grasping, yearning **09** hankering, hungering, rapacious, thirsting **10** avaricious, insatiable **11** acquisitive, close-fisted, close-handed

**covey**

**03** nid, set **04** band, bevy **05** brood, flock, group, hatch, party, skein **06** flight **07** cluster, company

**cow**

**02** ox **03** mog **04** boss, mart, neat, quey, runt **05** besom, bossy, bully, daunt, doddy, moggy, mooly, muley, scare, stirk **06** crummy, dismay, hawkey, hawkie, heifer, humlie, Jersey, milker, moggie, mulley, rattle, rother, subdue **07** kouprey, overawe, unnerve **08** Alderney, browbeat, domineer, Friesian, frighten, springer **09** terrorize **10** discourage, dishearten, intimidate

**coward**

**03** cat **04** Noel, sook, wimp, wuss **05** dingo, sissy **06** craven **07** chicken, cowherd, crybaby, dastard, hilding, nithing, viliaco, viliago **08** cowheard, deserter, poltroon, recreant, renegade, villagio, villiaco, villiago, weakling **10** faint-heart, poultroone, Scaramouch, scaredy-cat **11** Scaramouche, yellow-belly

**cowardice**

**08** timidity **11** fearfulness **12** cowardliness, timorousness **13** pusillanimity, spinelessness **14** spiritlessness

**cowardly**

**04** nesh, soft, weak **05** faint, mangy, timid **06** coward, cowish, craven, mangey, maungy, scared, yellow **07** chicken, dastard, fearful, gutless, hilding, jittery, meacock, nithing, unmanly, wimpish **08** timorous, unheroic **09** dastardly, spineless, weak-kneed **10** spiritless **11** lily-livered, milk-livered **12** faint-hearted, weak-spirited, white-livered **13** pusillanimous, yellow-bellied **14** chicken-hearted, chicken-livered

**cowboy**

**05** cheat, rogue, waddy **06** drover, gaucho, herder, rascal, waddie **07** bungler, cowhand, cowpoke, herdboy, rancher, vaquero **08** buckaroo, buckayro, buckeroo, herdsman, ranchero, stockman, swindler, wrangler **09** cattleman, fraudster, scoundrel **10** cowpuncher **11** incompetent **12** bronco-buster, cattleherder

**cower**

**04** ruck **05** quail, quake, shake, skulk, wince **06** cringe, crouch, flinch, grovel, recoil, shiver, shrink **07** croodle, tremble **08** draw back

**cowhouse**

**04** byre **07** shippen, shippon

**co-worker**

**04** aide, ally **06** helper **07** comrade, partner **08** confrère, teammate, workmate **09** assistant, associate, auxiliary, colleague, companion **11** confederate **12** collaborator, fellow worker

**cows**

**02** ky **03** kye **04** kine, neat

## coxcomb

**03** fop **04** head, prig **07** princox **08** popinjay, princock

## coy

**03** shy **04** arch, nice, prim **05** squab, timid **06** caress, demure, modest, skeigh **07** bashful, disdain, evasive, prudish **08** backward, reserved, retiring, skittish **09** diffident, kittenish, reticence, shrinking, squeamish, withdrawn **10** coquettish **11** flirtatious **12** self-effacing

## coyly

**06** primly **07** timidly **08** demurely, modestly **09** bashfully, evasively, prudishly **11** diffidently **12** coquettishly **13** flirtatiously **14** self-effacingly

## crab

**04** claw, cock **05** decry, scrog, wreck **06** Cancer, hermit, partan, scrawl **07** fiddler, limulus, pagurid, souring, wilding **08** horseman, obstruct, ochidore, pagurian **09** criticize, frustrate, scrog-bush, scrog-buss, soft-shell **12** saucepan-fish

## crabbed, crabby

**04** sour, tart **05** acrid, cross, harsh, surly, testy, tough **06** cranky, morose, snappy **07** awkward, cankery, fretful, grouchy, iracund, prickly **08** cankered, captious, churlish, perverse, petulant, snappish **09** crotchety, difficult, fractious, irascible, irritable, splenetic **10** ill-natured **11** acrimonious, bad-tempered, ill-tempered **12** cantankerous, iracundulous, misanthropic

## crack

◇ *anagram indicator* **02** go **03** ace, dig, gag, gap, hit, pop, try **04** bang, bash, beat, blow, boom, bump, chap, chat, chip, chop, clap, dope, dunt, fent, flaw, gibe, jest, joke, leak, line, quip, rent, rift, rima, rock, shot, slap, snap, stab, star **05** boast, break, burst, check, chink, cleft, clout, craic, crash, craze, joint, shake, slash, smack, solve, split, whack, whirl **06** breach, cave in, cavity, choice, cleave, cranny, decode, effort, expert, go bang, gossip, report, spring, strike, wallop **07** attempt, cocaine, crackle, crevice, decrypt, dope out, explode, fissure, resolve, rupture, shatter, skilful, skilled, unravel, work out **08** collapse, crevasse, decipher, detonate, fracture, fragment, one-liner, repartee, splinter, superior, top-notch **09** break down, brilliant, excellent, explosion, figure out, first-rate, ready-wash, wisecrack, witticism **10** detonation, first-class, go to pieces, hand-picked **11** lose control, outstanding **15** find the answer to
• **crack down on** **03** end **04** stop **05** check, crush, limit **07** confine, control, repress **08** restrict, suppress **10** act against, get tough on, put a stop to **11** clamp down on
• **crack up** ◇ *anagram indicator* **05** go mad, laugh **06** praise **07** go crazy **08** collapse **09** break down, fall about,

fall apart **10** go to pieces **11** go ballistic, lose control **14** split your sides

## crackdown

**03** end **04** stop **05** check **08** crushing **09** clampdown **10** repression **11** suppression

## cracked

◇ *anagram indicator* **03** mad **04** bats, daft, nuts, torn **05** barmy, batty, crazy, harsh, loony, nutty, split **06** broken, crazed, faulty, flawed, insane **07** chapped, chipped, damaged, foolish, idiotic, starred **08** crackpot, deranged, dingbats, fissured **09** defective, imperfect **12** crackbrained, round the bend **13** off your rocker, out of your tree

## crackers

◇ *anagram indicator* **03** mad **04** daft, nuts **05** batty, crazy, loony, matza, matzo, nutty **06** matzah, matzoh **07** cracked, foolish, idiotic **08** crackpot **10** unbalanced **12** crackbrained, round the bend

## crackle

**04** snap **05** crack, money **06** rustle, sizzle **08** crepitus **09** banknotes, crepitate **10** paper money **11** crepitation, decrepitate **13** decrepitation

## crackpot

◇ *anagram indicator* **04** fool **05** freak, idiot, loony **06** nutter, weirdo **07** nutcase, oddball **10** basket case

## cradle

**03** bed, cot **04** base, crib, hold, lull, prop, rest, rock, tend **05** fount, frame, mount, nurse, stand **06** holder, nestle, origin, rocker, source, spring **07** berceau, infancy, nurture, shelter, support **08** bassinet, carry-cot, cunabula, mounting **09** beginning, framework, travel-cot **10** birthplace, gold-washer, incunabula, wellspring **11** Moses basket **12** fountain-head **13** starting-point

## craft

◇ *anagram indicator* **03** art, job **04** boat, line, ship, work **05** flair, guile, knack, skill, trade, wiles **06** deceit, talent, vessel **07** ability, calling, cunning, finesse, foxship, mastery, pursuit, sleight, slyness **08** activity, aircraft, aptitude, artistry, business, deftness, subtlety, trickery, vocation **09** dexterity, expertise, handiwork, ingenuity, sharpness, spaceship, technique **10** adroitness, artfulness, astuteness, cleverness, craftiness, employment, expertness, handicraft, occupation, shrewdness, spacecraft **11** cunningness, deviousness, skilfulness, workmanship **12** fiendishness, landing craft **13** deceitfulness, inventiveness **15** imaginativeness, resourcefulness
*See also* **art; ship**

## craftily

◇ *anagram indicator* **05** slyly **08** artfully, astutely, shrewdly **09** cunningly,

deviously **10** guilefully **11** deceitfully **12** fraudulently

## craftsman, craftswoman

**05** maker, smith **06** artist, expert, master, wright **07** artisan, artsman, workman **08** mechanic **09** artificer, tradesman **10** technician **11** tradeswoman **12** craftsperson, tradesperson **13** skilled worker
*See also* **artist**

## craftsmanship

**05** skill **07** mastery **08** artistry **09** dexterity, expertise, technique **11** skilfulness, workmanship

## craftswoman

*see* **craftsman, craftswoman**

## crafty

◇ *anagram indicator* **03** sly **04** foxy, slim, wily **05** canny, loopy, sharp **06** artful, astute, knacky, shrewd, subtle **07** crooked, cunning, devious, tricksy, versute **08** guileful, knackish, scheming **09** conniving, deceitful, designing, subdolous **10** fraudulent **11** calculating, duplicitous **12** disingenuous **13** Machiavellian

## crag

**03** tor **04** neck, noup, peak, rock **05** bluff, cliff, craig, heuch, heugh, ridge, scarp, stoss **06** throat **08** pinnacle **10** escarpment

## craggy

**05** rocky, rough, stony **06** cliffy, jagged, marked, rugged, uneven **07** cliffed, cragged **09** rough-hewn **11** precipitous **13** weather-beaten

## cram

**03** bag, jam, lie, ram **04** fill, glut, pack, pang, stap, stop, swot, tuck **05** crowd, crush, farce, force, frank, gorge, grind, mug up, press, prime, stuff **06** fill up, revise, stodge **07** compact, squeeze **08** bone up on, compress, overfeed, overfill **09** overcrowd, study hard

## cramp

**03** tie **04** ache, pain, pang, rein **05** check, crick, limit, spasm **06** arrest, bridle, hamper, hinder, impede, narrow, stitch, stymie, thwart, twinge **07** confine, cramped, inhibit, shackle **08** handicap, obstruct, restrain, restrict **09** constrain, constrict, frustrate, hamstring, restraint, stiffness **10** convulsion **11** contraction **14** pins and needles **15** overuse syndrome, scrivener's palsy

## cramped

**04** full, poky **05** small, tight **06** narrow, packed **07** bounded, crabbed, crowded, squeezy **08** closed in, confined, hemmed in, niggling, overfull, squashed, squeezed **09** congested, jam-packed **10** compressed, restricted **11** constricted, overcrowded **12** incommodious **13** uncomfortable

## crane

**05** davit, hoist, Jenny, sarus, winch **06** brolga, hooper, jigger, tackle **07** cranium, derrick, whooper

**crank**

08 adjutant 10 demoiselle 12 adjutant bird, cherry picker 14 block and tackle 15 native companion

**crank**

04 kook, whim 05 freak, idiot, loony, wince, winch 06 madman, nutter, weirdo 07 oddball 08 crackpot 09 character, eccentric 11 amphetamine
• **crank up** 05 add to 06 hike up, step up 07 build up, further 08 increase 09 intensify 10 strengthen

**cranky**

◇ *anagram indicator* 03 fey, odd 04 tart 05 cross, dotty, harsh, queer, shaky, surly, testy, wacky 06 crabby, Fifish, screwy, snappy 07 awkward, bizarre, crabbed, grouchy, prickly, strange 08 freakish, peculiar, unsteady 09 crotchety, difficult, eccentric, irritable 11 bad-tempered, ill-tempered 12 cantankerous 13 idiosyncratic 14 unconventional

**cranny**

03 gap 04 hole, nook, rent, slit 05 chink, cleft, crack 07 crevice, fissure, opening 08 cleavage 10 interstice

**crash**

◇ *anagram indicator* 03 din, hit, ram 04 bang, bash, boom, bump, clap, dash, fail, fall, fold, rack, ruin, thud, wham 05 break, clang, clank, clash, ditch, frush, knock, pitch, pound, prang, rapid, shunt, smash, thump, wreck 06 batter, bingle, cut out, fold up, fragor, go bust, go into, go phut, pack up, pile-up, plunge, racket, shiver, topple, urgent 07 clatter, collide, failure, founder, go kaput, go under, run into, shatter, smash-up, thunder 08 accident, collapse, downfall, fracture, fragment, meltdown, splinter 09 break down, collision, drive into, emergency, explosion, immediate, intensive, smash into 10 bankruptcy, depression, plough into, telescoped 11 accelerated, black Monday, come a gutser, go to the wall, malfunction, stop working, thunderclap 12 concentrated, disintegrate, go on the blink 13 round-the-clock

**crass**

04 naff, rude 05 crude, dense, gross, ocker 06 clumsy, coarse, oafish, obtuse, stupid 07 boorish, witless 08 tactless, unsubtle 09 tasteless, unrefined 10 blundering, indelicate 11 insensitive 15 unsophisticated

**crassly**

06 rudely 07 crudely 08 clumsily, coarsely, stupidly 10 tactlessly 11 tastelessly 12 indelicately 13 insensitively

**crate**

03 box, car 04 case, kist 05 chest, plane, seron 06 seroon 08 tea chest 09 container 10 packing-box 11 packing-case

**crater**

03 dip, pit 04 bowl, hole, maar 05 abyss, basin, chasm 06 cavity, hollow 07 caldera 09 shell-hole 10 depression

**cravat**

05 scarf, stock 06 choker, o'erlay 07 overlay, owrelay, soubise 09 neckcloth, steenkirk, steinkirk

**crave**

03 beg 04 need, want, wish 05 claim, covet, fancy 06 desire, hunger 07 dream of, long for, longing, pant for, pine for, require, sigh for 08 yearn for 09 hunger for, lust after, thirst for 10 be dying for 11 hanker after

**craven**

04 soft, weak 05 timid 06 afraid, coward, scared, yellow 07 chicken, fearful, gutless 08 cowardly, poltroon, recreant, timorous, unheroic 09 spineless, weak-kneed 10 spiritless 11 lily-livered 12 faint-hearted, mean-spirited, weak-spirited, white-livered 13 pusillanimous 14 chicken-hearted, chicken-livered

**craving**

04 lust, need, pica, urge, wish 06 desire, greedy, hunger, pining, thirst 07 longing, malacia, panting, sighing 08 appetent, appetite, yearning 09 hankering 10 dipsomania, hydromania, methomania 11 toxicomania 13 morphinomania

**crawl**

04 drag, edge, fawn, inch, knee, swim, teem 05 creep, snail, swarm, toady 06 cringe, grovel, kowtow, seethe, squirm, suck up, writhe 07 bristle, flatter, slither, wriggle 08 be full of 09 be all over, freestyle 10 move slowly 11 curry favour 12 bow and scrape, go on all fours 13 advance slowly 14 be obsequious to
• **crawler** 06 insect

**crayfish**

05 yabby 06 gilgie, jilgie, marron, yabbie

**craze**

03 bug, fad 04 buzz, flaw, mode, rage, ramp, whim 05 crack, mania, thing, trend, vogue 06 frenzy, furore, impair, weaken 07 fashion, novelty, passion 08 insanity 09 melomania, obsession, the latest, typomania 10 anglomania, anthomania, enthusiasm 11 acronymania, infatuation, tulipomania 12 orchidomania, potichomania, theatromania 13 preoccupation

**crazed**

◇ *anagram indicator* 03 mad 04 nuts, wild 05 berko, crazy, loony 06 insane 07 berserk, lunatic 08 demented, deranged, unhinged 09 up the pole 10 moonstruck, unbalanced 12 moon-stricken, round the bend 13 off your rocker, out of your mind, round the twist

**crazily**

◇ *anagram indicator* 05 madly 06 wildly

08 insanely 09 manically 11 frantically 12 frenetically

**crazy**

◇ *anagram indicator* 03 mad, odd, wet 04 avid, bats, daft, fond, gaga, gyte, keen, loco, nuts, wild, zany 05 barmy, batty, buggy, daffy, dippy, dotty, flaky, gonzo, loony, loopy, manic, nutty, potty, silly, wacko, wacky, wiggy 06 absurd, ardent, crazed, cuckoo, dottle, fruity, insane, maniac, mental, raving, screwy, stupid, unwise 07 bananas, barking, berserk, bonkers, cracked, devoted, dottled, foolish, frantic, haywire, idiotic, lunatic, meshuga, rickety, smitten, strange, zealous 08 crackers, crackpot, demented, deranged, dingbats, doolally, frenetic, peculiar, unhinged 09 disturbed, enamoured, fanatical, foolhardy, half-baked, imprudent, infuriate, ludicrous, lymphatic, pixilated, senseless, up the wall 10 bestraught, distracted, distraught, frantic-mad, infatuated, off the wall, off your nut, outrageous, out to lunch, passionate, pixillated, ridiculous, unbalanced 11 hare-brained, impractical, nonsensical, not all there, off the rails, off your head, unrealistic 12 crackbrained, enthusiastic, mad as a hatter, off your chump, preposterous, round the bend 13 impracticable, irresponsible, off your rocker, out of your head, out of your mind, out of your tree, round the twist 14 off your trolley, wrong in the head
• **go crazy** ◇ *anagram indicator* 04 flip 05 go ape, go mad 06 blow up, wig out 09 go bananas 11 flip your lid, go ballistic 15 lose your marbles

**creak**

04 rasp 05 grate, grind, groan 06 scrape, screak, squeak, squeal 07 scratch, screech

**creaky**

05 rusty 07 grating, rasping, squeaky, unoiled 08 grinding, groaning, scraping 09 squeaking, squealing 10 scratching, screeching

**cream**

03 oil 04 best, pale, pick, ream, skim 05 creme, élite, ivory, milky, paste, pasty, prime, salve, sweet 06 finest, flower, lotion, thrash 07 unguent 08 cleanser, cosmetic, emulsion, liniment, off-white, ointment 09 emollient 10 choice part, select part 11 application, preparation 13 whitish-yellow 14 crème de la crème, pick of the bunch, yellowish-white

**creamy**

04 oily, pale, rich 05 ivory, milky, pasty, reamy, thick 06 smooth 07 buttery, velvety 08 off-white 13 cream-coloured, whitish-yellow 14 yellowish-white

**crease**

04 fold, kris, line, ruck, tuck 05 crimp, pleat, ridge 06 creese, furrow, groove, kreese, pucker, ruckle, rumple, runkle 07 crinkle, crumple, wreathe, wrinkle

## create

**09** corrugate **10** line of life
**11** corrugation
• **crease up** **05** amuse **09** make laugh

## create

**04** coin, form, make **05** build, cause, erect, found, frame, hatch, mould, set up, shape **06** design, devise, invent, invest, lead to, ordain **07** appoint, compose, concoct, develop, install, produce **08** engender, generate, initiate, occasion, result in **09** construct, establish, fabricate, formulate, institute, originate **10** bring about, give rise to, inaugurate **13** cause to happen **14** bring into being

## creation

◇ *anagram indicator* **04** life, work **05** birth, world **06** cosmos, design, making, nature, origin **07** concept, genesis, product **08** universe **09** formation, handiwork, handywork, invention, work of art **10** biopoiesis, brainchild, conception, concoction, everything, foundation, generation, initiation, innovation, production **11** achievement, chef d'oeuvre, composition, development, fabrication, institution, masterpiece, origination, procreation **12** constitution, construction **13** establishment

## creative

**06** clever, gifted **07** fertile **08** artistic, inspired, naturing, original, talented **09** forgetive, ingenious, intuitive, inventive, visionary **10** innovative, productive **11** full of ideas, imaginative, resourceful

## creativity

**04** gift **06** talent, vision **08** artistry **09** fertility, ingenuity **10** cleverness **11** imagination, inspiration, originality **13** inventiveness **14** productiveness **15** imaginativeness, resourcefulness

## creator

**03** God **05** maker **06** author, Brahma, father, mother, Ormazd, Ormuzd **07** builder, founder **08** composer, demiurge, designer, inventor, producer **09** architect, Artificer, demiurgus, initiator **10** Ahura Mazda, first cause, originator, prime mover

## creature

**03** man **04** bird, body, fish, soul, zoon **05** beast, being, human, thing, wight, woman **06** animal, cratur, insect, mortal, person, wretch **07** crathur, critter, crittur **08** organism **10** human being, individual **11** living thing
*See also* **animal; mythical; poison**

## credence

**05** faith, trust **06** belief, credit **07** support **08** reliance **09** sideboard **10** acceptance, confidence, dependence **11** credibility

## credentials

**04** deed **05** title **06** papers, permit **07** diploma, licence, warrant **08** passport **09** documents, reference **11** certificate, testimonial **12** identity card **13** accreditation, authorization

## credibility

**04** cred **09** integrity **10** likelihood **11** probability, reliability **12** plausibility **14** reasonableness **15** trustworthiness

## credible

**06** honest, likely **07** credent, sincere, tenable **08** possible, probable, reliable **09** plausible, thinkable **10** believable, convincing, dependable, imaginable, persuasive, reasonable **11** conceivable, trustworthy

## credibly

**08** honestly, possibly, reliably **09** plausibly, sincerely, thinkably **10** believably, dependably, imaginably, reasonably **11** conceivably **12** convincingly, persuasively **13** trustworthily

## credit

**02** cr, HP **03** buy **04** fame, tick **05** asset, boast, faith, glory, kudos, mense, pride, strap, tally, trust **06** accept, assign, belief, charge, esteem, honour, impute, praise, rely on, thanks **07** acclaim, ascribe, believe, put down, swallow, tribute **08** accredit, approval, credence, plaudits, prestige **09** attribute, have faith, laudation **10** confidence, estimation, reputation **11** distinction, pride and joy, recognition, subscribe to **12** commendation **15** acknowledgement
• **in credit** **07** solvent **10** beforehand, in the black
• **on credit** **06** on tick **07** on lay-by, on trust **08** on the tab **09** on account **10** on the slate **12** on the knocker **13** by instalments **14** on hire purchase **15** on the never-never

## creditable

**04** good **06** worthy **08** laudable **09** admirable, deserving, estimable, excellent, exemplary, reputable **10** honourable **11** commendable, meritorious, respectable, trustworthy **12** praiseworthy

## creditably

**04** well **09** admirably **10** honourably **11** commendably, excellently, respectably

## creditor

**02** cr **06** debtee, lender **07** Shylock **08** apprizer **09** loan shark **11** moneylender

## credulity

**07** naivety **09** silliness, stupidity **10** dupability, simplicity **11** gullibility **13** credulousness **14** uncriticalness

## credulous

**04** fond **05** naive **06** simple **07** credent, dupable **08** gullable, gullible, trusting, wide-eyed **10** uncritical **12** overtrusting, unsuspecting

## creed

**05** canon, credo, dogma, faith **06** belief, Ophism, symbol, tenets **08** articles, doctrine, ideology,

standard, teaching **09** catechism, the belief **10** persuasion, principles

## creek

**03** bay, geo, gio, goe, pow, voe **04** cove, wick **05** bight, brook, crick, fiord, firth, fjord, fleet, inlet **06** slough, stream **07** estuary

## creep

**04** edge, fawn, fear, geek, grew, grue, inch, worm **05** alarm, crawl, slink, snake, sneak, steal, toady **06** cringe, fawner, grovel, horror, squirm, terror, tiptoe, unease, writhe, yes-man **07** shudder, slither, wriggle **08** disquiet **09** revulsion, sycophant **10** bootlicker **13** move unnoticed

## creeper

**04** vine **05** liana, plant **06** runner **07** climber, rambler, trailer **08** trailing, woodbind, woodbine **09** Boston ivy **10** ampelopsis, monkey rope, tropaeolum **13** climbing plant, trailing plant
*See also* **snake**

## creepy

**05** eerie, scary, weird **06** crawly, spooky **07** macabre, ominous **08** gruesome, horrible, horrific, menacing, sinister **10** disturbing, horrifying, mysterious, terrifying, unpleasant **11** frightening, hair-raising, nightmarish, threatening **13** bloodcurdling, spine-chilling

## crescent

**04** Cres **06** waxing **07** growing **09** croissant **10** increasing

## crescent-shaped

**05** moony **06** lunate **07** falcate, lunated, lunular **08** falcated **09** bow-shaped, falciform **12** sickle-shaped

## crest

**03** mon, top **04** apex, comb, edge, head, knap, mane, peak, tuft **05** badge, chine, crown, plume, ridge **06** cimier, copple, crista, device, emblem, summit, symbol, tassel **07** cornice, feather, panache, regalia, topknot **08** aigrette, caruncle, insignia, pinnacle, surmount **09** cockscomb **10** coat of arms

## crestfallen

**03** sad **08** dejected, downcast **09** depressed, miserable **10** cheesed off, despondent, dispirited **11** discouraged, downhearted **12** disappointed, disconsolate, disheartened **13** in the doldrums **14** down in the dumps

## cretin

**03** ass, mug, nit **04** clot, dolt, dope, dork, fool, geek, jerk, prat, twit **05** chump, dumbo, dunce, idiot, moron, ninny, schmo, twerp, wally **06** dimwit, nitwit, sucker **07** fathead, halfwit, jughead, pillock, plonker, schmuck **08** imbecile **09** birdbrain, blockhead, ignoramus, simpleton **10** bufflehead, nincompoop

## crevasse

03 gap 05 abyss, chasm, cleft, crack, split 07 fissure 11 bergschrund

## crevice

03 gap 04 hole, rift, slit 05 break, chink, cleft, crack, split 06 cranny 07 fissure, opening 10 interstice

## crew

03 lot, man, mob, set 04 band, crue, gang, pack, ship, team, unit 05 bunch, corps, crowd, eight, force, group, party, squad, troop 06 torpid 07 company 09 lower deck 10 complement

## crew member

see sailor; ship

## crib

03 bed, cot, key 04 bach, copy, lift, pony, putz, trot 05 cheat, horse, pinch, shack, stall, steal 06 cradle, cratch, pirate 07 brothel, cottage, purloin 08 bassinet, carry-cot, cribbage 09 reproduce, travel-cot 10 plagiarize 11 Moses basket

## crick

04 kink, pain, rick 05 cramp, creek, spasm 06 twinge 09 stiffness 10 convulsion

## cricket

04 grig 05 stool 09 churr-worm

*Cricket teams include:*

04 Kent
05 Essex
06 Durham, Surrey, Sussex
08 Somerset, Tasmania, Victoria
09 Glamorgan, Hampshire, Middlesex, Yorkshire
10 Derbyshire, Lancashire, Queensland
12 Warwickshire
13 New South Wales
14 Leicestershire, South Australia, Worcestershire
15 Gloucestershire, Nottinghamshire

*Cricket terms include:*

01 b, c, M, w
02 by, CC, in, lb, nb, no, on, ro
03 bat, box, bye, CCC, cut, ECB, ICC, lbw, leg, MCC, net, ODI, off, pad, peg, run, six, ton
04 bail, ball, blob, bowl, deep, draw, duck, edge, four, go in, grub, hook, Oval, over, pair, poke, pull, slip, tail, test, tice, walk, wide
05 Ashes, break, c and b, catch, cover, dolly, drive, extra, glide, gully, knock, Lords, mid-on, pitch, plumb, point, silly, skyer, snick, stump
06 appeal, beamer, bowled, bowler, caught, crease, doosra, eleven, glance, googly, ground, howzat, leg bye, long on, maiden, middle, mid-off, no-ball, not out, opener, play on, runner, run out, single, square, stumps, the leg, umpire, whites, wicket, yorker
07 batsman, batting, bouncer, century, declare, dismiss, fielder, grubber, infield, innings, last

man, leg side, leg slip, leg spin, long hop, long leg, long off, off spin, on the up, paceman, spinner, striker, stumped, wrong'un
08 bodyline, boundary, chinaman, delivery, fielding, flannels, follow-on, full toss, how's that, leg guard, long slip, long stop, misfield, off break, off drive, off guard, one-dayer, outfield, pavilion, short leg, sledging, stumping, the Ashes, third man
09 batswoman, deep field, fieldsman, hit wicket, inswinger, leg before, leg theory, long field, mid-wicket, overpitch, powerplay, short slip, square leg, test match, tip and run
10 all-rounder, cover drive, draw stumps, fast bowler, golden duck, leg spinner, maiden over, pace bowler, right guard, scoreboard, seam bowler, silly mid-on, skittle out, spin bowler, twelfth man
11 clean bowled, daisy-cutter, diamond duck, fast bowling, fieldswoman, grass-cutter, ground staff, half-century, limited-over, net practice, one-day match, pace-bowling, seam bowling, sight screen, silly mid-off, spin bowling
12 carry your bat, twenty-twenty, wicketkeeper
13 break your duck, county cricket, keep your end up, maiden century, night-watchman, popping crease
14 off the back foot
15 bowl a maiden over, caught and bowled, leather on willow, leg before wicket, square leg umpire

*See also* **delivery**

*Cricketers, commentators and umpires include:*

03 **Fry** (Charles Burgess)
04 **Ames** (Leslie), **Bedi** (Bishen), **Bird** (Dicky), **Hall** (Wesley), **Hick** (Graeme), **Khan** (Imran), **Lara** (Brian), **Lock** (Tony), **Lord** (Thomas)
05 **Abbas** (Zaheer), **Akram** (Wasim), **Allen** (Sir Gubby), **Amiss** (Dennis), **Crowe** (Martin), **Evans** (Godfrey), **Gibbs** (Lance), **Gooch** (Graham), **Gough** (Darren), **Gower** (David), **Grace** (W G), **Greig** (Tony), **Healy** (Ian), **Hobbs** (Sir Jack), **Knott** (Alan), **Laker** (Jim), **Lawry** (William), **Lloyd** (Clive), **Marsh** (Rodney), **Pilch** (Fuller), **Walsh** (Courtney), **Warne** (Shane), **Waugh** (Mark), **Waugh** (Steve)
06 **Arlott** (John), **Bailey** (Trevor), **Benaud** (Richie), **Border** (Allan), **Botham** (Ian), **Cronje** (Hansie), **Dexter** (Ted), **Donald** (Allan), **Dravid** (Rahul), **Edrich** (Bill), **Edrich** (John), **Garner** (Joel), **Hadlee** (Sir Richard), **Haynes** (Desmond), **Hughes** (Merv), **Hutton** (Len), **Jessop** (Gilbert), **Lillee** (Dennis), **Miller** (Keith), **Rhodes** (Wilfred),

**Sobers** (Sir Garfield), **Thorpe** (Graham), **Titmus** (Fred), **Turner** (Glenn), **Warner** (Sir Pelham 'Plum')
07 **Ambrose** (Curtley), **Boycott** (Geoffrey), **Bradman** (Sir Donald), **Compton** (Denis), **Cowdrey** (Colin, Lord), **Denness** (Michael), **De Silva** (Aravinda), **Gatting** (Mike), **Holding** (Michael), **Hussain** (Nasser), **Jardine** (Douglas), **Larwood** (Harold), **Miandad** (Javed), **Pollock** (Graeme), **Simpson** (Robert), **Stewart** (Alec), **Thomson** (Jeff), **Trueman** (Fred), **Tufnell** (Philip)
08 **Atherton** (Michael), **Chappell** (Greg), **Chappell** (Ian), **Chappell** (Trevor), **Flintoff** (Andrew), **Gavaskar** (Sunil), **Kapil Dev** (Nikhanj), **Richards** (Barry), **Richards** (Vivian), **Sheppard** (David)
09 **deFreitas** (Phillip), **D'Oliveira** (Basil), **Greenidge** (Gordon), **Pietersen** (Kevin), **Ranatunga** (Arjuna)
10 **Azharuddin** (Mohammad), **Barrington** (Ken), **Lillywhite** (William)
11 **Heyhoe Flint** (Rachel), **Illingworth** (Raymond), **Trescothick** (Marcus)

## crier

06 beadle, herald 07 bellman 09 announcer, messenger, outrooper, town crier 10 proclaimer 15 bearer of tidings

## crime

03 rap, sin 04 evil, fact, vice 06 crimen, felony 07 misdeed, offence, offense, outrage, villany 08 atrocity, enormity, iniquity, thievery, villainy 09 violation 10 illegal act, misconduct, wickedness, wrongdoing 11 delinquency, lawbreaking, lawlessness, malefaction, malfeasance, unlawful act 12 misdemeanour 13 transgression

*Crimes include:*

03 ABH, GBH
04 rape
05 arson, fraud, theft
06 hijack, murder, piracy
07 assault, battery, bribery, forgery, larceny, mugging, perjury, robbery, treason
08 burglary, filicide, homicide, poaching, sabotage, stalking
09 blackmail, extortion, hate crime, joy-riding, matricide, parricide, patricide, pilfering, terrorism, uxoricide, vandalism
10 corruption, cybercrime, fratricide, kidnapping, sororicide
11 drug dealing, hooliganism, infanticide, shoplifting, trespassing
12 drink-driving, embezzlement, manslaughter
13 assassination, drug smuggling, housebreaking
14 counterfeiting, insider dealing, insider trading
15 computer hacking

## criminal

◇ *anagram indicator* **03** con **04** bent, crim, evil, perp **05** felon, tough, wrong **06** chummy, guilty, outlaw, wicked **07** convict, corrupt, crooked, culprit, illegal, illicit, lawless, obscene, villain **08** crimeful, culpable, infamous, offender, prisoner, shameful, unlawful **09** dishonest, felonious, miscreant, nefarious, wrongdoer **10** delinquent, deplorable, disgusting, indictable, iniquitous, lawbreaker, malefactor, outrageous, scandalous, villainous **11** disgraceful, lawbreaking **12** preposterous **13** reprehensible

Criminal types include:

**03** dip, lag
**04** hood, thug, yegg
**05** crook, thief
**06** bandit, forger, gunman, killer, mugger, pirate, rapist, robber, vandal
**07** abactor, brigand, burglar, filcher, hoodlum, mobster, poacher, prigger, rustler, stalker, tea leaf, yeggman
**08** arsonist, assassin, batterer, bigamist, car-thief, gangster, hijacker, jailbird, joyrider, murderer, pederast, perjurer, receiver, saboteur, smuggler, swindler
**09** buccaneer, cracksman, embezzler, kidnapper, larcenist, racketeer, ram-raider, strangler, terrorist
**10** bootlegger, cat burglar, dope pusher, drug dealer, fire-raiser, highwayman, paedophile, pickpocket, shoplifter, trespasser
**11** armed robber, blackmailer, bogus caller, drink-driver, kerb-crawler, safecracker, war criminal
**12** drug smuggler, extortionist, housebreaker, serial killer, sexual abuser
**13** counterfeiter

Criminals include:

**03** **Ray** (James Earl)
**04** **Aram** (Eugene), **Hare** (William), **Hood** (Robin), **Kray** (Reginald), **Kray** (Ronnie), **Rais** (Gilles de), **Todd** (Sweeney), **West** (Frederick), **West** (Rosemary)
**05** **Biggs** (Ronald), **Blood** (Thomas), **Booth** (John Wilkes), **Brady** (Ian), **Burke** (William), **Ellis** (Ruth), **James** (Jesse), **Kelly** (Ned), **Lucan** (Richard John Bingham, Lord)
**06** **Barrow** (Clyde), **Bonney** (William H), **Borden** (Lizzie), **Capone** (Al), **Corday** (Charlotte), **Meehan** (Patrick), **Nilsen** (Dennis), **Oswald** (Lee Harvey), **Parker** (Bonnie), **Rob Roy**, **Sirhan** (Sirhan), **Turpin** (Dick)
**07** **Bathori** (Elizabeth), **Chapman** (Mark), **Crippen** (Hawley), **Hindley** (Myra), **Huntley** (Ian), **Ireland** (William), **Luciano** (Charles 'Lucky'), **Shipman** (Harold), **Winters** (Larry)
**08** **Barabbas**, **Christie** (John), **Hanratty**

(James), **Sheppard** (Jack), **Son of Sam**
**09** **Berkowitz** (David), **Dillinger** (John), **Sutcliffe** (Peter)
**11** **Billy the Kid**
**13** **Jack the Ripper**
**14** **Moors Murderers**
**15** **Yorkshire Ripper**

*See also* **highwayman; pirate**

## crimp

**04** bend, curl, fold, pote, tuck, wave **05** flute, pleat, quill, ridge **06** crease, furrow, gather, goffer, groove, hinder, pucker, rumple, thwart **07** crinkle, crumple, gauffer, wrinkle **09** corrugate

## cringe

**03** bow, shy **04** bend, duck, fawn **05** cower, crawl, creep, quail, sneak, start, stoop, toady, wince **06** blench, crouch, flinch, grovel, kowtow, quiver, recoil, shrink, suck up **07** flatter, tremble **08** draw back **09** be all over **11** curry favour **12** bow and scrape **14** tug the forelock

## crinkle

**04** curl, fold, line, ruck, tuck, wave **05** crimp, money, pleat, ridge, twist **06** crease, furrow, groove, pucker, ruffle, rumple **07** crumple, wrinkle **09** corrugate **10** paper money **11** corrugation

## crinkly

**05** curly, kinky, money **06** fluted, folded, frizzy, ridged, tucked **07** creased, crimped, grooved, pleated, rumpled, wrinkly **08** crinkled, crumpled, furrowed, gathered, puckered, wrinkled **10** corrugated, paper money

## cripple

**04** lame, maim, ruin **05** spoil **06** damage, hamper, impair, impede, injure, weaken **07** destroy, disable, lameter, lamiger, lamiter, vitiate **08** handicap, lammiger, mutilate, paralyse, sabotage **09** hamstring, undermine **10** debilitate, immobilize **12** incapacitate

## crippled

**04** halt, lame, maim **08** deformed, disabled **09** paralysed **11** handicapped **13** incapacitated

## crisis

**03** fit, fix, jam **04** acme, hole, mess, stew, turn **05** brunt, crise **06** crunch, pickle, scrape **07** dilemma, problem, trouble **08** calamity, disaster, exigency, hot water, quandary, solution **09** emergency, extremity **10** crossroads, difficulty **11** catastrophe, predicament **12** turning-point

## crisp

**04** chip, cool, firm, hard, neat **05** brief, brisk, clear, crump, fresh, pithy, short, terse **06** chilly, crispy, crumpy, snappy **07** bracing, brittle, chippie, concise, crackly, crumbly, crunchy, friable **08** decisive, incisive, succinct **09** breakable **10** refreshing **12** invigorating **13** authoritative

## criterion

**03** law **04** norm, rule, test **05** basis, canon, gauge, model, scale **06** square **07** measure **08** exemplar, standard **09** benchmark, principle, yardstick **10** shibboleth, touchstone

## critic

**05** judge **06** carper, censor, expert, pundit **07** analyst, knocker, monitor, Zoilist **08** attacker, censurer, observer, overseer, reviewer **09** Aristarch, authority, backbiter, find-fault, nit-picker **11** commentator, fault-finder

*See also* **literary**

## critical

**04** crit, nice **05** fatal, grave, major, vital **06** severe, urgent **07** carping, crucial, exigent, fateful, gingery, pivotal, probing, serious **08** captious, deciding, decisive, historic, niggling, perilous, pressing, scathing, venomous **09** cavilling, dangerous, essential, important, momentous, quibbling, vitriolic **10** analytical, censorious, compelling, derogatory, diagnostic, discerning, evaluative, expository, nit-picking, perceptive, precarious **11** climacteric, disparaging, explanatory, judgemental, penetrating, significant **12** all-important, condemnatory, disapproving, fault-finding, hypercorrect, life-and-death, sharp-tongued, vituperative **13** hypercritical **14** disapprobative, interpretative **15** uncomplimentary
• **critical position 04** pass

## critically

**07** acutely, gravely, vitally **08** urgently **09** crucially, seriously **10** captiously, decisively, perilously **11** dangerously **12** analytically **13** disparagingly, significantly **14** diagnostically, disapprovingly **15** hypercritically

## criticism

**04** flak **05** blame, snipe, stick, strop **06** attack, niggle, review **07** censure, comment, reproof, ripping, slating, write-up, Zoilism **08** analysis, bad press, brickbat, critique, knocking, niggling, slamming **09** appraisal, judgement, stricture **10** assessment, commentary, evaluation, exposition, nit-picking, textualism **11** disapproval, explanation, explication **12** appreciation, condemnation, fault-finding **13** animadversion, disparagement **14** interpretation

## criticize

**03** bag, nag, pan, rip **04** carp, crab, flay, slag, slam, zing **05** blame, cut up, decry, judge, knock, roast, score, slash, slate, snipe, trash **06** assess, attack, hammer, impugn, niggle, peck at, review, tilt at **07** analyse, canvass, censure, condemn, dissect, explain, nit-pick, rip into, rubbish, run down, scarify, slag off, snipe at **08** appraise, badmouth, denounce, evaluate, wade into **09** castigate, denigrate, disparage, excoriate, have a go at, interpret, pull apart, slaughter, take apart, tear apart **10** animadvert, come down on, go to town on, have a pop at, speak ill of, take a pop at, vituperate **11** have a shot at, pick holes in **12** disapprove of, pick to pieces, pull to pieces, put the boot in, tear to shreds **13** find fault with, tear a strip off **14** cast aspersions, ultracrepidate **15** do a hatchet job on, pass judgement on

## critique
**05** essay **06** review **07** write-up **08** analysis **09** appraisal, criticism, judgement **10** assessment, commentary, evaluation, exposition **11** explanation, explication **12** appreciation **14** interpretation

## croak
**03** caw, die **04** crow, gasp, kill, rasp **05** crake, croup, grunt **06** squawk, wheeze **07** grumble **12** speak harshly

## Croatia
**02** HR **03** HRV

## crock
**03** jar, pig, pot, urn **04** dirt, smut **06** vessel **07** disable **08** potsherd **09** break down

## crocked
◇ *anagram indicator*
See **drunk**

## crockery
**05** china **06** dishes **07** pottery **08** brockage **09** porcelain, stoneware, tableware **11** earthenware **12** breakfast-set

## crocodile
**04** croc **06** caiman, cayman, garial, gavial, mugger **07** gharial **09** leviathan, teleosaur **11** river-dragon, Teleosaurus

## croft
**04** farm, plot **07** pightle **08** farmland **12** smallholding

## Cronus
**06** Saturn

## crony
**03** pal **04** ally, chum, mate **05** buddy **06** friend **07** comrade **08** familiar, follower, intimate, sidekick **09** associate, colleague, companion, confidant **10** accomplice, confidante

## crook
◇ *anagram indicator* **03** bow, ill **04** bend, flex, hook, kink, sick, tilt, warp **05** angle, angry, cheat, cromb, crome, cross, curve, fraud, nasty, rogue, shark, slant, thief, twist, wrong **06** con man, deform, gibbet, kebbie, robber, unfair, unwell **07** crosier, crozier, distort, dubious, villain **08** criminal, crummack, crummock, inferior, offender, operator, swindler **09** card sharp, dishonest, embezzler, sheep-hook **10** distortion, lawbreaker, unpleasant **13** pastoral staff

## crooked
◇ *anagram indicator* **04** awry, bent **05** askew, bowed, shady, wrong **06** angled, camsho, curved, hooked, shifty, thrawn, tilted, uneven, warped, zigzag **07** buckled, corrupt, illegal, illicit, sinuous, twisted, winding

**08** camshoch, criminal, deformed, lopsided, slanting, thraward, thrawart, tortuous, unlawful **09** camsheugh, contorted, deceitful, dishonest, distorted, irregular, misshapen, nefarious, off-centre, skew-whiff, underhand, unethical **10** asymmetric, fraudulent **11** anfractuous, treacherous **12** unprincipled, unscrupulous

## crookedly
**04** agee, ajee, awry **05** askew **08** unevenly **09** off-centre **10** lopsidedly **14** asymmetrically

## croon
**03** hum **04** lilt, sing **06** warble **08** vocalize
• **crooner 04** Bing
See also **singer**

## crop
**03** cut, lop, lot, mow, rod, set **04** clip, craw, pare, poll, reap, snip, stow, trim **05** batch, gorge, group, prune, shear, stand, yield **06** finial, fruits, gather, growth, reduce **07** curtail, harvest, produce, reaping, shorten, vintage **08** cut short, gleaning, wool clip **09** gathering, ingluvies **10** collection

---

*Arable crops include:*

**03** pea, rye, yam
**04** bean, corn, flax, hemp, kale, milo, oats, rape, rice
**05** colza, maize, swede, wheat
**06** barley, kharif, millet, potato, turnip
**07** alfalfa, cassava, linseed, lucerne, oilseed, popcorn, sorghum, soy bean
**08** mung bean, soya bean, teosinte
**09** milo maize, sugar beet, sugar cane, sunflower, sweetcorn, triticale
**11** oilseed rape, sweet potato
**12** mangel wurzel

• **crop up 05** arise, occur **06** appear, arrive, come up, emerge, happen, turn up **09** take place **10** come to pass **13** present itself

## cross
◇ *anagram indicator* **01** X **03** cut, ill, irk, mix, woe, wry **04** arch, crux, defy, edgy, foil, ford, join, lace, load, meet, pain, sign, sore, span, vext, wade **05** angry, annoy, blend, block, check, grief, harsh, irate, short, surly, thraw, trial, vexed, worry **06** bridge, burden, crabby, franzy, grumpy, hamper, hinder, hybrid, impede, misery, oppose, peeved, put out, resist, shirty, snappy, sullen, thwart **07** adverse, amalgam, annoyed, awkward, fretful, grouchy, mixture, mongrel, oblique, peevish, prickly, trouble **08** bestride, confront, converge, diagonal, disaster, go across, obstruct, opposite, pass over, snappish, traverse, walk over **09** adversity, balancing, crosswise, crotchety, decussate, difficult, dishonest, fractious, frustrate, hybridize, impatient, intersect, irascible, irritable, splenetic, suffering **10** affliction, criss-cross, crossbreed,

displeased, interbreed, intertwine, interweave, misfortune, mixed breed, mongrelize, overthwart, reciprocal, transverse **11** bad-tempered, catastrophe, combination, ill-tempered, tribulation **12** cantankerous, disagreeable, interchanged, intersecting, neutralizing, travel across **14** cross-fertilize, cross-pollinate
See also **hybrid**

---

*Crosses include:*

---

**01** T
**03** Red, tau
**04** ankh, high, Iron, ring, rood, rose, rosy
**05** fiery, Greek, Latin, papal, Rouen
**06** ansate, botoné, Celtic, fleury, fylfot, Geneva, George, market, moline, potent, Y-cross
**07** Avelian, Calvary, capital, Cornish, Maltese, Russian, saltire, Weeping
**08** Buddhist, capuchin, cardinal, crosslet, crucifix, holy-rood, Lorraine, military, pectoral, quadrate, rood-tree, Southern, St Peter's, swastika, Victoria
**09** encolpion, encolpium, Jerusalem, preaching, St Andrew's, St George's
**10** St Anthony's
**11** patriarchal
**13** Constantinian, crux decussata
**14** archiepiscopal

• **cross out 06** cancel, cut out, delete, remove, rub out **07** edit out **09** strike out **10** blue-pencil, obliterate
• **make cross 04** vote
• **make sign of cross over 04** sain

## cross-examination
**04** quiz **08** grilling, quizzing **11** examination, questioning **13** interrogation **14** the third degree

## cross-examine
**04** pump, quiz **05** grill, targe **07** examine **08** question **11** interrogate **13** cross-question

## crossing
◇ *containment indicator* **04** ford, trip **06** voyage **07** journey, passage, traject **08** junction, traverse **09** crosswalk, overgoing **10** crossroads, trajection **12** intersection **13** zebra crossing **14** Toucan crossing **15** grade separation, pelican crossing

## crossover value
**03** COV

## crosswise
**04** awry, over **06** across, aslant, thwart **07** athwart **08** sideways **09** crossways, obliquely **10** crisscross, diagonally, overthwart, transverse **11** catercorner **12** transversely **13** catercornered

## crossword
*Crosswords and crossword setters include:*

---

**03** Phi
**04** Apex, Azed, Duck, Mass, Monk, Paul, Shed

**05** Afrit, Owzat, Rufus, Wynne (Arthur)
**06** Aelred, Crispa, Custos, Gemini, Merlin, Portia
**07** Columba, Cyclops, Fidelio, Quixote, Spurius, Ximenes
**08** Everyman, Giovanni, Mephisto, Pasquale
**09** Araucaria, Beelzebub, Bunthorne, Cinephile, Virgilius
**10** Enigmatist, Torquemada

## crotch
**04** fork **05** groin **06** crutch **08** genitals **11** bifurcation

## crotchet
**03** toy **04** whim **11** quarter note

## crotchety
**05** cross, surly, testy **06** crabby, crusty, grumpy **07** awkward, crabbed, grouchy, iracund, maggoty, peevish, prickly **08** contrary, petulant **09** difficult, fractious, irascible, irritable, whimsical **11** bad-tempered, ill-tempered **12** cantankerous, disagreeable, iracundulous, obstreperous **13** short-tempered

## crouch
**03** bow **04** bend, dare, duck, fawn, ruck **05** cower, hunch, kneel, squat, stoop **06** cringe

## crow
**03** daw, jay **04** brag, rook **05** boast, crake, exult, gloat, raven, skite, vaunt **06** chough, corbie, corvid, hoodie **07** bluster, jackdaw, rejoice, show off, talk big, triumph **08** flourish **09** flute-bird **10** nutcracker, saddleback **12** cry roast-meat **13** Cornish chough **14** cock-a-doodle-doo **15** blow your own horn

## crowd
**03** jam, lot, mob, set **04** army, band, cram, gate, herd, host, mass, mong, pack, pile, push, raft, rout **05** bunch, crush, crwth, drove, elbow, flock, group, horde, house, meiny, press, shove, stuff, surge, swarm, three **06** bundle, circle, clique, gather, huddle, hustle, jostle, masses, meiney, meinie, menyie, muster, people, public, rabble, roll-up, squash, stream, throng, thrust **07** cluster, company, congest, scrooge, scrouge, squeeze, the many, turnout, viewers **08** assembly, audience, caboodle, compress, converge, frequent, overflow, populace, riff-raff, scrowdge, varletry, watchers **09** frequence, gathering, listeners, multitude, revel-rout **10** attendance, collection, congregate, fraternity, spectators **12** grex venalium

## crowded
**04** busy, full, pang **05** close, thick **06** filled, jammed, mobbed, packed, throng **07** chocker, crammed, cramped, crushed, teeming **08** frequent, overfull, swarming, thronged **09** congested, jam-packed **11** chock-a-block, overcrowded, overflowing **13** overpopulated **14** full to bursting

## crown
**02** cr **03** cap, taj, tip, top **04** acme, apex, bays, king, noll, pate, peak, tiar **05** adorn, award, crest, glory, kudos, prize, queen, ruler, tiara, title **06** anoint, cantle, climax, corona, diadem, empire, fulfil, height, honour, induct, invest, krantz, reward, sconce, summit, trophy, vertex, wreath **07** aureola, aureole, circlet, coronal, coronet, dignify, emperor, empress, festoon, foretop, garland, install, laurels, monarch, perfect, pschent, royalty, thick'un **08** complete, enthrone, finalize, kingship, laureate, monarchy, pinnacle, round off **09** sovereign **10** consummate **11** culmination, distinction, sovereignty **13** ultimus haeres

## crowning
**03** top **05** final **07** highest, perfect, supreme **08** greatest, ultimate **09** climactic, paramount, sovereign, unmatched **10** consummate, coronation **11** culminating, investiture, unsurpassed **12** enthronement, inauguration, incoronation, installation

## crucial
**03** key **05** major, vital **06** trying, urgent **07** central, pivotal, testing **08** critical, deciding, decisive, historic, pressing **09** essential, important, momentous, searching **10** compelling **12** all-important

## crucially
**07** vitally **09** centrally **10** critically, decisively **11** essentially, importantly, momentously

## crucify
**04** mock, rack, slam **05** knock, slate **06** punish **07** execute, rubbish, run down, torment, torture **08** ridicule **09** criticize, denigrate, excoriate, persecute **10** put to death **12** pull to pieces, tear to pieces, tear to shreds **14** kill on the cross

## crude
◇ *anagram indicator* **03** hot, raw **04** blue, lewd, rude **05** basic, bawdy, brash, brute, dirty, gross, juicy, rough **06** coarse, earthy, risqué, simple, smutty, vulgar **07** natural, obscene, raunchy, uncouth **08** immature, indecent **09** half-baked, makeshift, offensive, primitive, unrefined, untreated **10** inartistic, undigested, unfinished, unpolished, unprepared **11** barrelhouse, rudimentary, unconcocted, undeveloped, unprocessed **12** down-and-dirty **13** rough and ready

## crudely
◇ *anagram indicator* **06** rudely, simply **07** roughly **08** coarsely **09** basically, obscenely **10** indecently **11** offensively, primitively

## cruel
◇ *anagram indicator* **03** raw **04** evil, fell, grim, mean **05** felon, nasty **06** bitter, bloody, brutal, fierce, flinty, immane, savage, severe, unkind, wanton,

wicked **07** callous, cutting, hellish, inhuman, painful, vicious **08** barbaric, diabolic, felonous, fiendish, indurate, inhumane, Neronian, pitiless, ruthless, sadistic, spiteful, vengeful **09** atrocious, barbarous, butcherly, ferocious, heartless, malicious, merciless, murderous, truculent, unfeeling **10** blistering, heathenish, implacable, inexorable, iron-headed, malevolent **11** cold-blooded, hard-hearted, remorseless, unrelenting **12** bloodthirsty, bloody-minded, excruciating, stony-hearted **13** marble-hearted **14** marble-breasted

## cruelly
**08** brutally, fiercely, immanely, savagely, unkindly **09** callously, inhumanly, painfully, viciously **10** implacably, inhumanely, pitilessly, ruthlessly, spitefully **11** ferociously, heartlessly, maliciously, mercilessly, truculently **13** cold-bloodedly, hard-heartedly, remorselessly

## cruelty
**05** abuse, spite, venom **06** malice, sadism **07** tyranny **08** bullying, ferocity immanity, meanness, savagery, severity, violence **09** barbarity, brutality, harshness **10** bestiality, inhumanity, unkindness **11** callousness, viciousness **12** ruthlessness **13** heartlessness, mercilessness, murderousness **15** hard heartedness

## cruise
**04** busk, sail, taxi, trip **05** coast, drift, glide, slide **06** travel, voyage **07** holiday, journey **09** freewheel

## crumb
**03** bit, jot **04** atom, iota, mite, nirl **05** flake, grain, piece, scrap, shred, speck **06** morsel, sliver, titbit **07** granule, snippet, soupçon **08** fragment, particle

## crumble
◇ *anagram indicator* **03** rot **04** fail, mull, murl **05** crush, decay, grind, pound **06** powder **07** break up, moulder **08** collapse, come away, fragment **09** break down, decompose, fall apart, pulverize **10** degenerate **11** deteriorate **12** disintegrate, fall to pieces

## crumbly
◇ *anagram indicator* **04** nesh **05** frush, short **07** brittle, friable, powdery **11** pulverulent

## crummy
**04** poor, weak **05** cheap **06** grotty, rotten, shoddy, trashy **07** useless **08** inferior, pathetic, rubbishy **09** half-baked, miserable, third-rate, worthless **10** second-rate, unpleasant **11** substandard **12** contemptible

## crumpet
**04** head **05** woman, women **06** muffin **07** pikelet

## crumple
**04** fall, fold **05** crush **06** crease, pucker, raffle, rumple **07** crinkle, wrinkle **08** collapse, scrumple

## crunch

**04** bite, chew, crux, test **05** champ, chomp, crush, grind, munch, pinch, sit-up, smash **06** crisis **07** graunch, scranch, scrunch **09** emergency, masticate **13** critical point, moment of truth

## crusade

**03** war **04** push, work **05** cause, drive, fight, jihad **06** attack, battle, strive **07** holy war, promote **08** advocate, campaign, movement, strategy, struggle **09** offensive **10** expedition **11** undertaking

## crusader

**06** zealot **07** battler, fighter **08** activist, advocate, champion, promoter, reformer **10** campaigner, enthusiast, missionary

## crush

◇ *anagram indicator* **03** jam **04** cram, love, mash, mill, mush, pack, pash, pulp, ruin **05** abash, break, chack, champ, check, crowd, grind, horde, pinch, pound, press, quash, quell, shame, smash, stamp, tread, upset **06** bruise, crease, crunch, defeat, liking, mangle, rumple, squash, squish, step on, subdue, throng **07** break up, conquer, contuse, crinkle, crumble, crumple, mortify, oppress, passion, put down, screw up, scrunch, shatter, squeeze, squelch, thrutch, wrinkle **08** compress, demolish, overcome, scrumple, squabash, suppress, vanquish **09** break down, comminute, devastate, humiliate, obsession, overpower, overwhelm, pulverize, telescope, triturate **10** annihilate **11** infatuation, steam-roller
• **crush down** **03** bow

## crust

**03** fur, reh **04** coat, film, husk, rind, scab, skin **05** argol, layer, shell, skull **06** caking, casing, gratin, pastry **07** caliche, capping, clinker, coating, outside, salband, surface, topping **08** beeswing, covering, exterior **09** wine-stone **10** concretion, livelihood **11** lithosphere **12** encrustation, impertinence, incrustation **13** efflorescence

*Parts of the earth's crust include:*

**03** sal
**04** sial, sima
**06** craton, mantle

## crustacean

*Crustaceans include:*

**04** crab
**05** koura, krill, prawn, yabby
**06** gilgie, hermit, jilgie, marron, partan, scampi, scrawl, shrimp, squill, yabbie
**07** camaron, copepod, daphnia, dog-crab, fiddler, limulus, lobster, pagurid, pea-crab, pill bug
**08** barnacle, blue crab, crawfish, crayfish, crevette, king crab, land crab, ochidore, pagurian

**09** centipede, devil-crab, fish louse, ghost crab, king prawn, langouste, millipede, phyllopod, schizopod, sea slater, shore crab, soft-shell, stone crab, water flea, woodlouse
**10** acorn-shell, Balmain bug, edible crab, hermit crab, mitten-crab, robber crab, sandhopper, seed shrimp, spider crab, stomatopod, tiger prawn, velvet-crab, velvet worm, whale louse
**11** brine shrimp, calling-crab, coconut crab, common prawn, Dublin prawn, fairy shrimp, fiddler crab, langoustine, rock lobster, soldier crab, spectre crab, tiger shrimp
**12** common shrimp, mantis shrimp, mussel shrimp, saucepan-fish, sentinel crab, spiny lobster, squat lobster
**13** acorn-barnacle, common lobster, goose barnacle, horseshoe crab, Moreton Bay bug, noble crayfish, Norway lobster, opossum shrimp, spectre shrimp, tadpole shrimp, velvet-fiddler
**14** Dublin Bay prawn, skeleton shrimp, woolly-hand crab

*See also* **animal**

## crusty

**04** firm, hard **05** baked, cross, gruff, surly, testy **06** crabby, crispy, grumpy, snappy, touchy **07** awkward, brittle, brusque, crabbed, crumbly, crunchy, friable, grouchy, peevish, prickly **08** contrary, petulant, well-done **09** breakable, difficult, fractious, irascible, irritable, splenetic, well-baked **11** bad-tempered **12** cantankerous, disagreeable, obstreperous **13** short-tempered

## crux

**03** nub **04** core **05** cross, heart **06** centre, kernel, puzzle **07** essence, nucleus **13** the bottom line
*See also* **cross**

## cry

**03** caw, mew, sab, sob **04** bawl, blub, call, gowl, hoop, hoot, howl, keen, mewl, pipe, plea, rivo, roar, wail, weep, word, yawp, yell, yelp, yowl **05** bleat, chevy, chivy, clock, greet, havoc, mouth, neigh, pewit, shout, skirl, tears, whine, whoop **06** bellow, bubble, chivvy, lament, peewee, peewit, prayer, report, rumour, scream, shriek, slogan, snivel, squawk, squeal, yoicks **07** bawling, blubber, call out, clamour, exclaim, screech, tantivy, vagitus, whimper **08** peesweep, proclaim **09** alalagmos, be in tears, peaseweep, shed tears, watchword **11** ejaculation, exclamation, lamentation **14** burst into tears, cry your eyes out
*See also* **shout; war cry** *under* **war**
• **cry off** **06** cancel **07** back out **08** withdraw **13** decide against **14** change your mind, excuse yourself
• **cry out for** **04** need, want

**06** demand **07** call for, require **11** necessitate
• **cry up** **04** sell **06** praise

## crypt

**04** tomb **05** vault **08** catacomb **09** mausoleum **10** undercroft **13** burial chamber

## cryptic

**04** dark **06** hidden, occult, secret, unseen, veiled **07** bizarre, obscure, strange **08** abstruse, esoteric, puzzling **09** ambiguous, enigmatic, equivocal **10** mysterious, perplexing

## cryptically

**08** secretly **09** bizarrely, obscurely, strangely **11** ambiguously **12** mysteriously **13** enigmatically

## crystal

**04** spar **05** macle, table **06** needle, raphis **07** cocaine, raphide, rhaphis, spicule **08** cut glass, rhaphide **09** microlite **10** watchglass **11** amphetamine, seeing stone

## crystallize

**04** form **05** candy, shoot **06** appear, emerge, harden **07** clarify **08** solidify **09** make clear **11** become clear, materialize **12** make definite **13** become clearer **14** become definite

## cub

**03** pup **04** baby, tiro **05** chest, puppy, whelp, young, youth **06** newbie, novice, rookie **07** fresher, learner, recruit, starter, student, trainee **08** beginner, freshman, initiate, neophyte **09** fledgling, greenhorn, offspring, youngster **10** apprentice, raw recruit, tenderfoot **11** probationer

## Cuba

**01** C **02** CU **03** CUB

## cubbyhole

**03** den **04** hole, slot **05** booth, niche **06** recess **07** cubicle **08** hideaway, tiny room **10** pigeonhole **11** compartment

## cube

**03** die **04** dice **05** block, solid **06** cuboid **10** hexahedron, triplicate

## cuckoo

◇ *anagram indicator* **03** ani, mad **04** daft, gouk, gowk, koel, loco, nuts **05** batty, crazy, loony, nutty, silly **07** cracked, foolish, idiotic **08** crackpot, rainbird **12** crackbrained, round the bend **13** chaparral cock **14** brain-fever bird
*See also* **fool; foolish**

## cucumber

**05** choko, wolly **07** gherkin **10** dill pickle **11** bitter-apple

## cuddle

**03** hug, pet **04** hold, neck, snog **05** clasp, nurse **06** caress, enfold, fondle, nestle, smooch **07** embrace, smuggle, snuggle **08** canoodle

## cuddly

**04** cosy, soft, warm **05** plump **07** lovable **08** huggable, loveable **10** cuddlesome

## cudgel

**03** bat, hit **04** bash, beat, club, cosh,

## cue

mace, patu, rung **05** clout, plant, pound, shrub, stick, towel **06** alpeen, ballow, batter, souple, strike, thwack, waster **07** clobber **08** bludgeon **09** bastinado, crabstick, fustigate, truncheon **10** shillelagh **12** an oaken towel

## cue

**01** Q **03** nod, rod **04** hint, mace, sign **06** prompt, signal **08** feed-line, half-butt, reminder, stimulus **09** catchword, incentive **10** indication, intimation, suggestion

## cuff

**03** box, hit **04** beat, belt, biff, clip, gowf, slap **05** clout, knock, scuff, smack, thump, whack **06** buffet, scruff, strike **07** armband, clobber, manacle **08** bracelet, gauntlet, handcuff, snitcher, wristlet **09** muffettee
• **off the cuff 05** ad lib **09** extempore, impromptu **10** improvised, off the wall, unprepared, unscripted **11** unrehearsed **13** spontaneously

## cuisine

**07** cookery, cooking **10** cordon bleu **12** haute cuisine **15** nouvelle cuisine

## cul-de-sac

**04** loke **05** close **06** no exit **07** dead end **10** blind alley **13** no through road

## cull

**04** dupe, kill, pick, sift, thin **05** amass, glean, pluck **06** choose, gather, select **07** collect, destroy, pick out, thin out **09** slaughter

## culminate

**03** end **04** peak **05** close, crest, end up **06** climax, finish, wind up **08** conclude **09** terminate **10** consummate **11** come to a head **13** come to a climax

## culmination

**03** sum, top **04** acme, apex, head, peak, roof, turn **05** crown, point **06** apogee, climax, finale, height, heyday, summit, zenith **08** meridian, pinnacle **09** high point **10** completion, conclusion, perfection, perihelion **12** consummation

## culpability

**05** blame, fault, guilt **09** liability **13** answerability **14** accountability, responsibility **15** blameworthiness

## culpable

**05** wrong **06** faulty, guilty, liable, sinful **07** at fault, peccant, to blame **08** blamable, criminal **09** blameable, offending **10** answerable, censurable, in the wrong **11** blameworthy, responsible **13** reprehensible

## culprit

**05** felon **07** convict, villain **08** criminal, offender **09** miscreant, wrongdoer **10** delinquent, lawbreaker **11** guilty party

## cult

**03** fad **04** sect **05** craze, faith, mania, party, trend, vogue, Wicca **06** belief, cultus, school, Shinto **07** faction, fashion, in-thing, macumba **08** fixation, movement, navalism,

religion **09** obsession **11** affiliation **12** denomination, macrobiotics

## cultivate

◇ *anagram indicator* **03** aid, dig, sow, woo **04** back, farm, grow, help, tend, till, work **05** court, fancy, groom, plant, raise, train **06** assist, enrich, foster, garden, labour, manure, plough, polish, pursue, refine, work on **07** advance, bring on, cherish, culture, develop, enhance, forward, further, harvest, husband, improve, nurture, prepare, produce, promote, support **08** civilize **09** encourage, enlighten, fertilize

## cultivated

**04** tame **06** polite, sative, urbane **07** genteel, refined **08** advanced, cultured, educated, highbrow, polished, well-read **09** civilized, scholarly **10** discerning **11** enlightened **12** well-informed **13** sophisticated **14** discriminating

## cultivation

**05** tilth **06** sowing **07** backing, culture, farming, growing, nurture, support, tilling, working **08** planting **09** advancing, fostering, manurance, nurturing **10** assistance, cherishing, forwarding, furthering, harvesting, refinement **11** agriculture, development, improvement, preparation **12** civilization **13** encouragement

## cultural

**04** folk **06** ethnic, tribal **07** liberal **08** artistic, communal, edifying, national, societal **09** aesthetic, educative, elevating, enriching, improving **10** broadening, civilizing, humanizing **11** educational, traditional **12** enlightening **13** developmental **15** anthropological

## culture

**04** arts, crop **05** mores, music **06** growth, habits **07** customs, history, society, the arts **08** heritage, learning, painting **09** behaviour, cultivate, education, lifestyle, nurturing, tendering, way of life **10** humanities, literature, philosophy, production, refinement, traditions **11** cultivation **12** civilization

## cultured

**04** arty **06** polite, urbane **07** erudite, genteel, learned, refined **08** advanced, artistic, educated, highbrow, polished, tasteful, well-bred, well-read **09** arty-farty, civilized, scholarly **10** cultivated **11** enlightened **12** intellectual, well-educated, well-informed **13** sophisticated

## culvert

**04** duct **05** drain, flume, sewer **06** gutter **07** channel, conduit, ponceau **11** watercourse

## cumbersome

**04** slow **05** bulky, heavy **07** awkward, complex, onerous, weighty **08** cumbrous, involved, unwieldy, wasteful **09** difficult **10** burdensome

**11** complicated, inefficient **12** incommodious, inconvenient, unmanageable **14** badly organized

## Cumbrian

◇ *dialect indicator*

## cumulative

**07** growing **08** mounting **09** enlarging **10** collective, increasing **11** multiplying, progressive, snowballing

## cunning

**03** art, fly, sly **04** arch, deep, deft, foxy, rusé, slee, wily **05** canny, carny, craft, guile, guyle, leery, sharp, skill, wiles **06** artful, astute, carney, cautel, clever, crafty, dainty, deceit, knacky, policy, quaint, shifty, shrewd, slight, sneaky, subtle, tricky **07** crabbit, devious, finesse, knowing, practic, skilful, sleekit, sleight, slyness, varment, varmint, vulpine **08** artifice, deftness, fiendish, guileful, knackish, slippery, subtlety, trickery **09** deceitful, dexterous, ingenious, ingenuity, insidious, inventive, knowledge, sharpness **10** adroitness, artfulness, astuteness, cleverness, craftiness, shrewdness **11** cunningness, deviousness, imaginative, resourceful **12** fiendishness, manipulative **13** cunning as a fox, deceitfulness, inventiveness **15** imaginativeness, resourcefulness

## cup

**03** mug, nut, pot, tig, tot **04** bowl, tass, wine **05** award, bidon, calix, cruse, medal, plate, prize, punch **06** beaker, bumper, cotyle, goblet, hollow, noggin, quaich, quaigh, reward, rhyton, tassie, trophy **07** chalice, cyathus, scyphus, tankard, tumbler **08** pannikin **09** cantharus, gripe's egg **11** doch-an-doris **12** deuch-an-doris, doch-an-dorach **13** deoch-an-doruis
*See also* **drinking**

## cupbearer

**04** Hebe **08** Ganymede

## cupboard

**05** ambry, awmry, chest, press, store **06** almery, aumbry, awmrie, closet, locker, pantry **07** almirah, armoire, cabinet, dresser, tallboy **08** cellaret, hot press, meat safe, wardrobe **09** sideboard **12** clothes-press, Welsh dresser **14** Coolgardie safe

## Cupid

**04** Eros

## cupidity

**05** greed **06** hunger **07** avarice, avidity, itching, longing **08** rapacity, voracity, yearning **09** eagerness, hankering **10** greediness **12** covetousness, graspingness **13** rapaciousness **14** avariciousness **15** acquisitiveness

## curable

**08** operable **09** medicable, reparable, treatable **10** reformable, remediable **11** rectifiable

## curative

**05** tonic **07** healing **08** medcinal,

**curator**

remedial, salutary **09** healthful, medicinal, vulnerary **10** corrective, febrifugal **11** alleviative, restorative, therapeutic **12** health-giving

**curator**
**06** keeper, warden, warder **07** steward **08** guardian **09** attendant, caretaker, custodian **11** conservator

**curb**
**03** bit **04** bend, bent, rein **05** brake, check, corbe, courb **06** bridle, damper, hamper, hinder, impede, muzzle, rebuff, reduce, retard, subdue **07** contain, control, inhibit, refrain, repress **08** hold back, keep back, moderate, restrain, restrict, suppress **09** constrain, deterrent, hindrance, kerbstone, restraint, retardant **10** constraint, impediment, limitation, repression, unofficial **11** holding-back, keep in check, restriction, suppression

**curd, curds**
**04** skyr **06** junket
• **bean curd** **04** tofu

**curdle**
**03** run **04** clot, earn, grew, grue, sour, turn, whig **05** yearn **06** lapper, lopper, posset **07** congeal, cruddle, ferment, thicken **08** solidify, turn sour **09** coagulate

**cure**
◇ *anagram indicator* **03** dry, dun, fix **04** ease, heal, help, mend, salt **05** amend, break, reast, reest, reist, smoke, treat **06** elixir, hobday, kipper, pickle, remedy, repair **07** correct, cureall, dry-salt, healing, panacea, recover, rectify, relieve, restore, therapy **08** antidote, barbecue, make well, medicine, preserve, recovery, smokedry, solution, specific, unpoison **09** alleviate, treatment **10** corrective, make better **11** alleviation, restorative **12** fever therapy

**cure-all**
**06** elixir **07** nostrum, panacea **10** catholicon **12** panpharmacon **13** diacatholicon **15** universal remedy

**curfew**
**04** gate

**curie**
**02** Ci

**curio**
**06** bygone **07** antique, bibelot, trinket **09** curiosity, objet d'art **10** knick-knack **12** objet de vertu **13** object of virtu **14** article of virtu

**curiosity**
**05** curio, freak **06** bygone, gabion, marvel, oddity, prying, rarity, search, wonder **07** antique, exotica, inquiry, novelty, trinket **08** interest, nosiness, querying, snooping **09** objet d'art, spectacle **10** knick-knack, phenomenon **11** peculiarity, questioning **12** interference **15** inquisitiveness

**curious**
◇ *anagram indicator* **03** odd **04** agog, nosy, rare **05** funny, nosey, novel,

queer, weird **06** exotic, prying, quaint, unique **07** bizarre, strange, unusual **08** freakish, meddling, peculiar, puzzling, querying, singular, snooping **09** inquiring, intrigued, searching **10** fascinated, interested, keen to know, meddlesome, mysterious, remarkable, unorthodox **11** inquisitive, interfering, questioning **13** extraordinary **14** unconventional, wanting to learn
• **be curious** **03** pry

**curiously**
◇ *anagram indicator* **05** oddly **08** quaintly **09** bizarrely, strangely, unusually **10** peculiarly, remarkably **11** inquiringly **12** meddlesomely, mysteriously **13** inquisitively, interferingly, questioningly

**curium**
**02** Cm

**curl**
**04** bend, coil, eddy, friz, kink, loop, purl, ring, roll, tong, turn, wave, wind **05** crimp, curve, dildo, frizz, helix, pinch, snake, swirl, twine, twirl, twist, whorl **06** becurl, ripple, scroll, spiral, wreath, writhe **07** crimple, crinkle, earlock, frizzle, frounce, meander, ringlet, wreathe **08** curlicue, kiss-curl, lovelock **09** corkscrew, favourite **12** heartbreaker **13** permanent wave

**curly**
**04** wavy **05** fuzzy, kinky **06** curled, frizzy, permed **07** coiling, crimped, curling, looping, turning, winding **08** twirling, twisting **09** corkscrew, spiralled, wreathing **10** spiralling **11** problematic

**currant**
**05** Ribes **06** rizard, rizzar, rizzer **07** rizzart

**currency**
**03** tin **04** cash **05** bills, brass, coins, money, notes, vogue **07** coinage **08** exposure **09** publicity **10** acceptance, popularity, prevalence **11** circulation, legal tender **13** dissemination

*Currencies include:*

**02** nu
**03** ecu, kip, lat, lei, lek, leu, lev, som, sum, won, yen
**04** baht, birr, cedi, dong, dram, euro, kina, kuna, kyat, lari, lats, lira, loti, mark, peso, pula, punt, rand, real, rial, riel, taka, tala, vatu, yuan
**05** colón, denar, dinar, dobra, franc, frank, krona, krone, kroon, kunar, leone, litas, manat, marka, naira, nakfa, pence, pound, riyal, rupee, sucre, tenge, tolar, zaïre, zloty
**06** ariary, balboa, dalasi, dirham, dollar, escudo, forint, gourde, gulden, hryvna, koruna, kwacha, kwanza, maloti, markka, new sol, pa'anga, pataca, peseta, rouble, rupiah, shekel, somoni, tugrik, tugrug
**07** afghani, bolivar, cordoba,

drachma, guarani, guilder, hyrvnia, lempira, metical, new peso, ouguiya, quetzal, ringgit, rufiyaa
**08** new dinar, ngultrum, nuevo sol, renminbi, shilling, sterling, US dollar
**09** boliviano, lilangeni, new dollar, schilling
**10** emalangeni, Swiss franc
**11** Deutschmark, French franc, karbovanets, Turkish lira
**12** Belgian franc, Deutsche mark, renminbi yuan
**14** Canadian dollar

*See also* **coin**

*Former currencies include:*

**01** m
**02** DM
**03** pie
**04** inti, lira, mark, pice, punt, reis
**05** belga, franc, krone, sucre, zaïre
**06** décime, ekuele, escudo, gilder, lepton, markka, peseta
**07** austral, cruzado, drachma, guilder, milreis
**08** cruzeiro, groschen
**09** schilling
**11** Deutschmark

**current**
**01** I **02** AC, DC, in **03** amp, cur, ebb, jet, now **04** curt, eddy, flow, live, mood, race, rife, rill, soom, swim, tide **05** drift, going, juice, swirl, tenor, trend, valid **06** abroad, common, course, extant, modern, outset, stream, trendy **07** backset, bombora, draught, exhaust, feeling, flowing, general, indraft, instant, in vogue, ongoing, outflow, popular, present, running, thermal, topical **08** accepted, backwash, existing, movement, progress, reigning, tendency, tide race, up-to-date **09** direction, indraught, in fashion, prevalent **10** mainstream, present-day, prevailing, widespread **11** back-draught, fashionable, going around, present-time **12** contemporary, undercurrent **13** in circulation, up-to-the-minute

**currently**
**03** now **05** today **07** just now **08** right now **09** at present, presently, these days **10** at this time **11** at the moment **15** for the time being

**curriculum**
**06** course, module **07** program **08** subjects, syllabus **09** programme, timetable **10** discipline **13** course of study **14** core curriculum **15** course of studies

**curry**
**04** beat **06** quarry **07** cuittle, scratch

**curse**
**02** wo **03** ban, eff, hex, moz, pox, woe **04** bane, blow, cuss, damn, evil, harm, jinx, mozz, oath, ruin **05** beset, blast, blind, shrew, spell, swear, weary, winze **06** berate, blight, maugre, ordeal, plague **07** accurse, afflict, beshrew, condemn, malison, scourge,

## cursed

torment, trouble 08 anathema, calamity, cussword, denounce, disaster, execrate, maledict 09 blaspheme, blasphemy, curse-word, expletive, fulminate, imprecate, obscenity, profanity, swear-word, vengeance 10 affliction, execration, Indian sign, misfortune, put a jinx on 11 bad language, eff and blind, imprecation, malediction, tribulation 12 anathematize, damn and blast 13 excommunicate 14 four-letter word, use bad language

## cursed

04 vile 05 curst 06 bloody, cussed, damned, darned, dashed, odious 07 blasted, flaming, hateful, unlucky 08 annoying, blinking, blooming, dratting, fiendish, flipping, infamous, infernal 09 execrable, loathsome 10 abominable, confounded, detestable, pernicious, unpleasant

## cursory

05 brief, hasty, quick, rapid 06 casual, slight 07 hurried, offhand, passing, summary 08 careless, fleeting, slapdash 09 desultory 10 dismissive 11 perfunctory, superficial

## curt

04 rude, tart 05 blunt, brief, gruff, pithy, sharp, short, squab, terse 06 abrupt 07 brittle, brusque, concise, laconic, offhand, summary, uncivil 08 snappish, succinct 10 ungracious 11 short-spoken 13 short and sweet, unceremonious

## curtail

◇ tail deletion indicator 03 cut 04 clip, dock, pare, slim, trim 05 abate, limit, prune 06 hamper, lessen, reduce, shrink 07 abridge, cut back, cut down, shorten 08 cut short, decrease, pare back, pare down, restrict, truncate 09 cut back on 10 abbreviate, guillotine 12 circumscribe

## curtailment

◇ tail deletion indicator 03 cut 06 paring 07 cutback, docking, pruning 08 decrease, slimming, trimming 09 lessening, reduction, shrinkage 10 abridgment, guillotine, limitation, shortening, truncation 11 abridgement, contraction, restriction 12 abbreviation, retrenchment

## curtain

04 pall, swag, vail, veil 05 blind, cover, drape, scene 06 purdah, screen 07 drapery, hanging, shutter, vitrage 08 backdrop, portière, tapestry, traverse 10 net curtain 13 window hanging
• theatre curtain 03 tab 04 drop, iron 05 cloth

## curtly

05 short 06 rudely 07 bluntly, briefly, gruffly, pithily, sharply, shortly, tersely 08 abruptly 09 brusquely, concisely, uncivilly 10 succinctly 11 laconically 12 ungraciously 15 unceremoniously

## curtsy

03 bob, bow, dop 06 kowtow, salaam 08 courtesy 09 genuflect

## curvaceous

05 buxom, curvy 06 bosomy, comely 07 shapely 09 curvesome 10 voluptuous 11 well-rounded, well-stacked

## curve

03 arc, bow 04 arch, bend, coil, hook, kink, loop, ogee, turn, wind 05 bulge, crook, graph, helix, rhumb, round, swell, twist 06 bought, camber, circle, record, spiral, spiric, swerve 07 caustic, cissoid, compass, flexure, incurve, quadric, quartic, winding 08 apophyge, catenary, conchoid, crescent, envelope, liquidus, parabola, sinusoid, trochoid 09 curvature, loxodrome 10 epicycloid, isoseismal, meandering, trajectory 11 catacaustic, harmonogram 12 hypotrochoid 15 brachistochrone, Lissajous figure

## curved

04 bent 05 bowed, wrong 06 arched, convex, cupped, humped, warped 07 arcuate, bending, bulging, concave, crooked, rounded, scooped, sinuous, twisted 08 sweeping, swelling, tortuous 09 curviform, incurvate 10 incurvated, serpentine

## cushion

03 cod, mat, pad 04 bank, tyre 05 squab 06 absorb, buffer, dampen, deaden, lessen, muffle, pillow, prop up, reduce, soften, stifle 07 beanbag, bolster, bum roll, hassock, kneeler, padding, pillion, protect, sandbag, support 08 buttress, diminish, headrest, mitigate, pulvinus, suppress 09 pulvillus, upholster 10 lace-pillow, protection 11 booster seat 13 shock absorber 14 vegetable sheep

## cushy

04 easy, plum, soft 05 jammy 11 comfortable, undemanding

## cusp

04 horn 05 point 07 spinode

## custard

04 flam 05 flamm, flawn 06 flaune 07 sabayon 08 zabaione 10 zabaglione

## custodian

05 guard 06 custos, keeper, warden, warder 07 curator 08 claviger, guardian, overseer, watchdog, watchman 09 caretaker, castellan, protector 11 conservator 12 conservatrix 14 superintendent

## custody

◇ containment indicator 04 bail, care, hand, hold, ward 05 hands 06 arrest, charge, prison 07 keeping 08 guarding, guidance, handfast, security, wardship, watching 09 captivity, detention, retention 10 possession, protection 11 confinement, safekeeping, supervision, trusteeship 12 guardianship, imprisonment, preservation 13 custodianship, incarceration 14 responsibility

## custom

03 use, way, won 04 form, rite, thew, wont 05 ethos, habit, mores, style, trade, usage 06 manner, policy, ritual 07 fashion, routine 08 business, ceremony, practice 09 etiquette, formality, patronage, procedure, rusticism, sacred cow, tradition 10 consuetude, convention, observance 11 institution 13 way of behaving

## customarily

07 as a rule, usually 08 commonly, normally 09 generally, popularly, regularly, routinely 10 habitually, ordinarily 11 fashionably 13 traditionally 14 conventionally

## customary

03 set 04 used 05 nomic, usual 06 common, normal, vulgar, wonted 07 general, popular, regular, routine 08 accepted, everyday, familiar, habitual, ordinary 10 obligatory, prevailing 11 established, fashionable, traditional 12 conventional, prescriptive 14 consuetudinary

## customer

05 buyer, trick 06 client, patron, punter 07 regular, shopper 08 consumer, prospect 09 purchaser, shillaber

## customize

03 fit 04 suit 05 adapt, alter, tweak 06 adjust, modify, tailor 07 convert 08 fine-tune 09 transform 11 personalize

## customs

04 dues 05 mores, taxes 06 duties, excise, impost, levies 07 tariffs 08 protocol

## cut

◇ anagram indicator ◇ deletion indicator
◇ insertion indicator ◇ tail deletion indicator 02 ax 03 axe, bit, end, hew, lop, mow, rip, saw 04 blow, burn, chop, clip, crop, curb, dash, dice, dock, edit, form, gash, hack, halt, kerf, make, nick, omit, pare, part, race, rase, raze, reap, sawn, shun, skip, slit, sned, snee, snip, snub, stab, stop, tape, trim 05 avoid, blank, block, break, carve, cross, fault, grate, joint, knife, lance, lower, mince, notch, piece, prune, quota, scalp, score, scorn, sever, shape, share, shave, shear, shred, slash, slice, slish, sneck, snick, split, spurn, style, whack, wound 06 chisel, chop up, cleave, delete, design, dilute, divide, excise, ignore, incise, insult, lessen, pierce, précis, ration, rebuff, record, reduce, saving, slight, stroke, trench 07 abridge, curtail, cutback, cut dead, diluted, dissect, economy, engrave, failure, fashion, incised, portion, profile, rake-off, scratch, section, shorten, suspend 08 break off, castrate, cleaving, condense, decrease, diminish, dividing, excision, incision, lacerate, lowering, obstruct, renounce, stoppage 09 breakdown, expurgate, intercept, interrupt, intersect, lessening, reduction, summarize, videotape 10 abbreviate,

adulterate, allocation, cutting-out, diminution, disconnect, laceration, proportion, tape-record **11** adulterated, discontinue, make shorter **12** breaking-down, bring to an end, cold-shoulder, retrenchment **14** malfunctioning, send to Coventry, slice of the cake **15** pretend not to see

*See also* **hairstyle; meat**

• **cut across 08** go beyond, surmount **09** intersect, rise above, transcend **11** leave behind

• **cut and dried 05** clear, fixed **06** sewn up **07** certain, decided, settled **08** definite **09** automatic, organized **11** prearranged **13** predetermined

• **cut back 03** lop **04** crop, curb, trim **05** check, lower, prune, slash **06** lessen, reduce **07** coppice, curtail **08** decrease, downsize, retrench **09** economize, scale down

• **cut down 02** ax **03** axe, hew, lop, mow, saw **04** curb, fell, kill, maim, raze, reap **05** level, lower, prune, slash **06** lessen, reduce **07** curtail **08** chop down, decrease, diminish

• **cut in 05** nip in **06** butt in **07** barge in, break in, intrude **09** interject, interpose, interrupt, intervene

• **cut off 03** end **04** clip, halt, nick, stop **05** block, sever, shred **06** detach, excide, remove, unhook **07** abscind, chop off, exscind, handsel, isolate, seclude, shelter, suspend, take off, tear off **08** amputate, break off, insulate, obstruct, prescind, retrench, separate, smite off **09** intercept, interrupt, keep apart **10** disconnect, interclude, stormbound **11** discontinue **12** bring to an end

• **cut out 04** clip, drop, edit, fail, omit, quit, stop **05** block, cease, debar, shape, sneck, snick **06** delete, desist, excise, exsect, go phut, lay off, pack in, pack up, remove **07** conk out, eclipse, exclude, extract, go kaput, go wrong, refrain, ride out, take out, tear out **08** carve out, contrive, knock off, leave off, leave out, separate, supplant **09** break down **11** discontinue, malfunction, stop working **12** go on the blink

• **cut out for 04** good, made **05** right **06** suited **08** suitable **09** qualified **11** appropriate

• **cut short** ◊ *tail deletion indicator* **04** crop, dock, snub **05** roach **07** abridge, bobtail, chapped, concise, curtail **08** prescind, truncate **10** detruncate

• **cut slantwise 04** bias

• **cut square across 03** bob **04** bang

• **cut up 04** chop, dice, hurt **05** break, carve, het up, mince, slash, slice, upset **06** chop up, divide, put out **07** annoyed, dissect, slice up, unhappy **08** bothered, saddened, tomahawk, troubled, worked up **09** dismember **10** distressed

## cutback

◊ *reversal indicator* **03** cut **06** saving **07** economy **08** decrease, lowering, slashing **09** lessening, reduction **11** curtailment **12** retrenchment

## cute

**04** twee **05** ankle, sweet **06** astute, clever, lovely, pretty **07** lovable **08** adorable, charming, loveable **09** appealing, endearing **10** attractive, delightful

## cutlery

**06** silver **07** canteen **08** flatware

*Cutlery items include:*

**04** fork
**05** knife, ladle, spoon, spork
**08** fish fork, teaspoon
**09** fish knife, fish slice, salt spoon, soupspoon
**10** bread knife, caddy spoon, cake server, chopsticks, pickle fork, steak knife, sugar tongs, tablespoon
**11** butter knife, carving fork, cheese knife, corn holders
**12** apostle spoon, carving knife, dessertspoon, salad servers
**14** vegetable knife

## cutlet

**04** chop **09** côtelette, schnitzel **15** Wiener schnitzel

## cut-price

**04** sale **05** cheap **07** bargain, cut-rate, reduced **08** discount **09** low-priced **10** marked-down

## cutpurse

**03** nip **04** bung **06** nipper **10** pickpocket

## cutter

**04** pone **05** axman **06** axeman **08** lapidary

*Cutters include:*

**03** axe, fox, saw, sax
**04** adze, bill, celt
**05** bilbo, blade, brand, knife, mower, plane, razor, saber, sabre, sword
**06** chisel, colter, culter, dagger, ice axe, jigsaw, labrys, lopper, meat-ax, piolet, poleax, rapier, scythe, shears, sickle, sparth
**07** chopper, cleaver, coulter, cutlass, fretsaw, gisarme, hacksaw, halberd, hatchet, meat-axe, poleaxe, poll-axe, sparthe, twibill
**08** battle-ax, billhook, chainsaw, claymore, clippers, palstaff, palstave, partisan, scimitar, scissors, shredder, stone axe, Strimmer®, tomahawk
**09** battle-axe, double-axe, Excalibur, holing-axe, lawnmower, secateurs
**10** broadsword, coal-cutter, cork-cutter, guillotine, putty-knife, spokeshave
**11** chaff-cutter, coup de poing, glass-cutter, grass-cutter, Lochaber axe, paper-cutter, straw-cutter
**12** cookie-cutter, hedgetrimmer,

Jeddart staff, marble-cutter **13** mowing machine, pinking shears

*See also* **dagger; knife; saw; weapon**

## cut-throat

**04** keen, thug **05** cruel, razor **06** brutal, cutter, fierce **07** ruffian, sworder **08** assassin, pitiless, ruthless **09** dog-eat-dog, merciless, murderous **10** relentless **15** keenly contested

## cutting

◊ *insertion indicator* **03** raw **04** acid, clip, keen, sect, sien, slip, syen **05** chill, piece, plant, scion, scrap, sharp, snide **06** bitchy, biting, bitter, secant **07** caustic, coupure, excerpt, extract, gingery, hurtful, mordant, pointed **08** clipping, incision, incisive, piercing, quickset, scathing, scission, scissure, stinging, wounding **09** malicious, sarcastic, trenchand, trenchant **11** penetrating

## cuttle-bone

**03** pen **06** pounce, sepium

## cycle

**03** age, eon, era, orb **04** aeon, bike, rota **05** epoch, order, phase, round, trike **06** circle, period, rhythm, series **07** pattern **08** go-around, rotation, sequence **09** biorhythm, body clock **10** revolution, succession **11** oscillation

## cyclical

**06** cyclic **07** regular **08** repeated **09** recurrent, recurring **10** repetitive

## cyclist

*Cyclists include:*

**03** Hoy (Sir Chris)
**04** Gaul (Charly)
**05** Binda (Alfredo), Bobet (Louison), Coppi (Fausto), Kelly (Sean), Moser (Francesco), Zabel (Erik)
**06** Boonen (Thomas), Burton (Beryl), Fignon (Laurent), Harris (Reg), LeMond (Greg), Merckx (Eddy)
**07** Bartali (Gino), Hinault (Bernard), Museeuw (Johan), Pantani (Marco), Queally (Jason), Simpson (Tom), Ullrich (Jan), Van Looy (Rik)
**08** Anquetil (Jacques), Boardman (Chris), Indurain (Miguel), Maertens (Freddy), Opperman (Sir Hubert), Poulidor (Raymond), Virenque (Richard)
**09** Armstrong (Lance), Zoetemelk (Joop)
**10** Bahamontes (Federico), van Moorsel (Leontien Ziljaard-)
**11** De Vlaeminck (Roger)
**13** Longo-Ciprelli (Jeannie)

## cyclone

**05** storm **07** monsoon, tempest, tornado, twister, typhoon **09** hurricane, whirlwind, windstorm **10** cockeye bob, depression, willy-willy **11** cockeyed bob **13** tropical storm

## cylinder

**04** drum, reel, roll **05** spool **06** barrel, bobbin, column, roller **07** spindle

## cymbal
03 zel 07 symbole

## cynic
05 surly 07 doubter, killjoy, knocker, sceptic, scoffer 08 Diogenes, snarling 09 pessimist 10 spoilsport 11 misanthrope

## cynical
05 surly 06 bitter, ironic 07 mocking 08 critical, derisive, Diogenic, doubtful, doubting, negative, sardonic, scoffing, scornful, snarling, sneering 09 hardnosed, sarcastic, sceptical 10 embittered, hard-boiled, streetwise, suspicious 11 distrustful, pessimistic, worldly-wise 12 contemptuous, disenchanted 13 disillusioned, unsentimental 14 Mephistophelic 15 Mephistophelean, Mephistophelian

## cynically
08 bitterly 09 mockingly 10 critically, derisively, negatively, scornfully 11 sceptically 12 suspiciously 13 distrustfully 14 contemptuously 15 pessimistically

## cynicism
05 doubt, irony, scorn 07 mocking, sarcasm 08 contempt, distrust, scoffing, sneering 09 disbelief, pessimism, surliness, suspicion 10 scepticism 11 misanthropy 13 heartlessness 14 disenchantment 15 disillusionment

## Cyprus
02 CY 03 CYP

## cyst
03 sac, wen 04 bleb 06 growth, ranula 07 abscess, bladder, blister, capelet, dermoid, hydatid, utricle, vesicle 08 atheroma, capellet, steatoma 09 chalazion

## Czech Republic
02 CZ 03 CZE

# D

**D**
03 dee 05 delta

## dab
03 bit, mop, pat, tad, tap 04 blot, dash, daub, drop, peck, spot, swab, wipe 05 fleck, press, smear, speck, tinge, touch, trace 06 dollop, smudge, splash, stroke 07 smidgen, trickle 08 sprinkle 09 lemon sole 10 sandsucker
• **dab hand** 03 ace 05 adept 06 expert, wizard

## dabble
03 dip, toy, wet 04 play 05 dally, flirt, plash 06 clatch, dampen, fiddle, guddle, muddle, paddle, potter, putter, splash, tinker, trifle 07 immerse, moisten, plotter, plouter, plowter, smatter 08 splatter, sprinkle

## dabbler
07 amateur, dallier, trifler 08 tinkerer 09 lay person, literator 10 dilettante

## dad
see **father**

## daemon
04 deva 05 demon, devil, force, geist 06 animus, genius, spirit 09 cacodemon 10 evil spirit, genius loci, good spirit

## daft
◇ *anagram indicator* 03 dim, mad, odd 04 avid, dull, dumb, fond, keen, nuts, slow, wild 05 barmy, batty, crazy, daffy, dense, dopey, dotty, inane, loony, loopy, nutty, potty, silly, sweet, thick, wacky 06 absurd, ardent, crazed, insane, mental, simple, stupid, unwise 07 berserk, bonkers, devoted, fatuous, foolish, glaiket, glaikit, idiotic, lunatic, smitten, touched, zealous 08 crackpot, demented, deranged, dingbats, farcical, gormless, obsessed, peculiar, unhinged 09 dim-witted, disturbed, enamoured, fanatical, foolhardy, half-baked, imprudent, laughable, ludicrous, senseless 10 infatuated, irrational, outrageous, passionate, ridiculous, slow-witted, unbalanced 11 hare-brained, nonsensical, unrealistic 12 addle-brained, crackbrained, enthusiastic, preposterous, round the bend, simple-minded 13 impracticable, irresponsible, off your rocker, out of your mind, round the twist, thick as a plank

## dagger
05 blade, knife 06 obelus

### Daggers include:
04 dirk, kris
05 kukri, skean, skene
06 anlace, bodkin, crease, creese, hanjar, kirpan, kreese
07 anelace, dudgeon, handjar, jambiya, khanjar, poniard, yatagan
08 baselard, jambiyah, puncheon, skean-dhu, skene-dhu, stiletto, yataghan
10 bowie knife, misericord, skene-occle
11 misericorde

*See also* **knife; sword**

## Dáil member
02 TD

## daily
04 char 05 adays 06 common 07 cleaner, diurnal, journal, per diem, regular, routine 08 charlady, constant, day by day, day-to-day, everyday, habitual, ordinary 09 charwoman, circadian, customary, quotidian, regularly 10 constantly 11 commonplace, day after day
*See also* **newspaper**

## dainty
04 cate, fine, neat, nice, trim 05 dinky, faddy, fancy, fussy, genty, juicy, small, tasty 06 bonbon, choice, choosy, friand, little, luxury, mignon, morsel, petite, pretty, sunket, titbit 07 cunning, elegant, finicky, friande, genteel, minikin, refined, savoury 08 charming, delicacy, delicate, graceful, luscious, mignonne, tasteful 09 delicious, enjoyable, exquisite, lickerish, liquorish, succulent, sweetmeat 10 appetizing, delectable, delightful, fastidious, particular, scrupulous 11 bonne-bouche 12 hard to please 14 discriminating

## dairy

### Dairy produce includes:
04 ghee, milk, whey
05 cream, curds, quark
06 beurre, butter, cheese, yogurt
07 UHT milk, yoghurt
08 ice cream, yoghourt
09 butter oil, goat's milk, milk shake, sour cream, whole milk
10 buttermilk, milk powder
11 double cream, semi-skimmed, single cream, skimmed milk, soured cream
12 clotted cream, crème fraîche, fromage frais, long-life milk, powdered milk
13 condensed milk, full cream milk, low-fat yoghurt, whipping cream
14 evaporated milk, sterilized milk, unsalted butter
15 clarified butter, homogenized milk, semi-skimmed milk

## dairymaid
03 dey 08 dey-woman

## dais
05 stage, stand 06 estate, podium

07 haut pas, rostrum, staging
08 footpace, platform

## daisy
05 gowan, ox-eye 07 felicia, guayule 08 feverfew, ox-tongue 10 cupid's dart, horse-gowan, marguerite, moonflower 14 hen-and-chickens

## dale
03 cwm, den, ria 04 dean, dell, dene, gill, glen, vale 05 coomb, griff, grike, gulch, heuch, slade 06 dingle, strath, valley

## dalliance
04 play 05 delay, sport 06 toying 07 playing 08 dawdling, flirting, sporting, tarrying, trifling 09 loitering, pottering

## dally
03 toy 04 play 05 delay, flirt, tarry 06 coquet, dawdle, frivol, linger, loiter, pingle, trifle 07 carry on 08 coquette 10 tick and toy 12 take your time 13 procrastinate

## dam
03 pen 04 bund, stem, sudd, wall, wear, weir 05 block, cauld, check, stank 06 anicut, mother 07 annicut, barrage, barrier, confine, staunch 08 blockage, obstruct, restrict 09 barricade, decametre, hindrance, restraint 10 draughtsman, embankment, millstream 11 obstruction

### Dams include:
04 Guri, Hume, Kiev, Mica
05 Aswan, Ertan, Nurek, Rogun
06 Beaver, Bratsk, Hoover, Inguri, Itaipu, Kariba, Vaiont
07 Benmore, Boulder, Tarbela
08 Akosombo, Chapetón, Gezhouba, Wyangala
09 Aswan High, Mauvoisin, Owen Falls
10 Glen Canyon, Warragamba
11 Afsluitdijk, Grand Coulee, La Esmeralda, Three Gorges
13 Alberto Lleras, Alvaro Obregon, Grande Dixence, Manuel M Torres
14 Afsluitdijk Sea
15 Sayano-Shushensk

## damage
◇ *anagram indicator* 03 mar, rip 04 cost, dent, fine, harm, hurt, loss, ruin 05 abuse, havoc, price, spoil, wreck, wrong 06 charge, deface, impair, injure, injury, weaken 07 blemish, destroy, empeach, expense, impeach, vitiate 08 decimate, mischief, mutilate, sabotage 09 desecrate, detriment, disprofit, indemnity, suffering, vandalism, vandalize 10 defacement, defilement, impairment, mutilation, recompense, reparation, tamper with 11 depredation, desecration, destruction, devastation, restitution 12 compensation, disadvantage, incapacitate, satisfaction 13 play havoc with, reimbursement, vandalization 14 wreak havoc with 15 indemnification

## damaged

◇ *anagram indicator* **04** mard
**07** cracked, unsound **08** impaired

## damaging

**03** bad **07** harmful, hurtful, ruinous
**09** injurious **10** pernicious
**11** deleterious, destructive,
detrimental, prejudicial
**12** unfavourable **15** disadvantageous

## dame

**03** DBE, DCB **04** Edna, lady **05** broad,
woman **06** female, matron, mother
**07** dowager, peeress **08** baroness
**10** aristocrat, noblewoman

## damn

**01** d **03** dee, jot, pan **04** dang, darn,
dash, doom, hang, hoot, iota, sink,
slag, slam, toss **05** blank, blast, curse,
decry, knock, slate, swear **06** attack,
berate, jigger, revile **07** accurse,
censure, condemn, inveigh, monkey's,
run down, slag off **08** denounce,
execrate, maledict, two hoots
**09** blaspheme, castigate, criticize,
denigrate, excoriate, fulminate,
imprecate **10** come down on,
denunciate **11** pick holes in, tinker's
cuss **12** anathematize, pull to pieces,
tear to shreds **13** brass farthing **14** use
bad language

## damnable

**06** cursed, damned, wicked **07** hateful,
hellish **08** horrible, infernal
**09** atrocious, execrable, offensive
**10** abominable, despicable, detestable,
diabolical, iniquitous, pernicious,
unpleasant **12** disagreeable
**13** objectionable

## damnation

**04** doom, hell **08** anathema, hell-fire
**09** perdition **12** condemnation,
denunciation, proscription
**15** excommunication

## damned

**04** lost, very, vile **05** pocky **06** blamed,
bloody, cursed, darned, dashed,
deuced, doomed, effing, odious
**07** blasted, flaming, hateful
**08** accursed, annoying, blinking,
blooming, complete, dratting, fiendish,
flipping, infernal, jiggered, thorough
**09** condemned, execrable, execrated,
loathsome, reprobate **10** abominable,
confounded, despicable, detestable,
pernicious, unpleasant **11** exceedingly
**13** anathematized, blankety-blank
**14** blankety-blanky

## damning

**09** damnatory **10** condemning
**11** implicating, implicative,
inculpatory **12** accusatorial,
condemnatory **13** incriminating

## damp

**03** dew, fog, wet **04** dank, dewy, dull,
mist, rain **05** check, foggy, gloom,
humid, misty, mochy, moist, muggy,
rainy, soggy **06** clammy, fousty,
mochie, moisty, rheumy, vapour
**07** drizzle, drizzly, wetness, wettish
**08** dampness, dankness, humidity,
moisture, vaporous **09** moistened

**10** clamminess, discourage
**14** discouragement, unenthusiastic
• **damp down 04** calm, dull **05** check
**06** deaden, lessen, quench, reduce
**08** decrease, diminish, moderate,
restrain

## dampen

**03** wet **04** damp, dash, dull **05** check,
deter, spray **06** deaden, dismay, lessen,
muffle, reduce, stifle **07** depress,
inhibit, moisten, smother **08** damp
down, decrease, diminish, moderate,
restrain **10** discourage, dishearten
**12** put a damper on

## damper

**04** mute **07** sordino **10** wet blanket
**13** register-plate
• **put a damper on 04** dash, dull
**05** check, deter **06** deaden, dismay,
lessen, muffle, reduce, stifle, subdue
**07** depress, inhibit, smother **08** damp
down, decrease, diminish, moderate,
restrain **10** discourage, dishearten

## dampness

**03** dew, fog, wet **04** damp, mist, rain
**06** vapour **07** drizzle, wetness
**08** dankness, humidity, moisture
**09** mugginess **10** clamminess

## damsel

**04** girl, lass **06** lassie, maiden **09** young
lady **10** young woman

## dance

◇ *anagram indicator* **04** juke, jump, leap,
play, rock, skip, spin, sway **05** caper,
flash, frisk, swing, twirl, waver, whirl
**06** bounce, cavort, frolic, gambol,
gyrate, hoof it, prance, ripple, spring
**07** flicker, shimmer, sparkle, twinkle
**09** pirouette, shake a leg **11** move
lightly, move to music **13** tread a
measure
*See also* **ballet**

*Dances include:*

**03** bop, hay, hey, jig, war
**04** dump, fado, giga, haka, hula, jive,
jota, juba, kolo, nach, polo, reel,
shag
**05** conga, gigue, mambo, natch,
polka, rumba, salsa, samba,
skank, stomp, sword, tango, twist,
waltz
**06** Balboa, bolero, can-can, cha-cha,
hustle, minuet, morris, valeta,
veleta
**07** beguine, coranto, courant,
csárdás, foxtrot, gavotte, hoedown, lancers, mazurka, morrice,
musette, one-step, tordion
**08** boogaloo, cakewalk, courante,
excuse-me, fandango, flamenco,
galliard, hay-de-guy, hey-de-guy,
hornpipe, hula-hula, kantikoy,
lindy hop, marinera, Playford, poi
dance, the twist
**09** bossa nova, cha-cha-cha,
clogdance, écossaise, jitterbug,
paso doble, passepied, Paul
Jones, quadrille, quickstep, rock
'n' roll, roundelay
**10** charleston, corroboree, hokey-
cokey, slow rhythm, turkey-trot

**11** black bottom, Lambeth Walk,
morris dance, schottische,
varsovienne
**12** boogie-woogie, mashed potato
**13** Highland fling, Viennese waltz
**15** military two-step

*Dance types include:*

**03** tap
**04** clog, folk, jazz, line
**05** belly, break, crunk, disco, Irish,
krunk, limbo, salsa, swing
**06** ballet, hip-hop, modern, morris,
square
**07** bogling, country, morrice, old-
time
**08** ballroom, flamenco, Highland,
krumping, robotics, skanking
**10** belly dance, breakdance
**12** contemporary
**13** Latin-American

*Dance functions include:*

**02** ba'
**03** hop
**04** ball, prom, rave
**05** disco
**06** social
**07** ceilidh, knees-up, shindig
**08** hunt ball, tea dance
**09** barn dance
**10** thé dansant
**11** charity ball, dinner dance
**14** fancy dress ball

*Dance steps include:*

**03** dig, dip, fan, pas, set
**04** buck, chop, chug, clip, comb,
dame, drag, draw, drop, ocho,
riff, spin, turn, vine, whip
**05** abajo, brush, catch, corté, cramp,
flare, galop, glide, grind, hitch,
pivot, scuff, seven, spike, stamp,
stomp, strut, Suzi-Q, three, twist,
whisk
**06** aerial, breaks, bronco, chassé,
circle, jockey, paddle, riffle,
shimmy, uprock
**07** box step, fan kick, feather, jig
step, locking, lollies, popping,
pop turn, rocking, scuffle, shuffle,
six-step, swivels, toprock, twinkle
**08** back step, crab walk, flat step,
four-step, hair comb, headspin,
heel pull, heel turn, hook turn,
neck wrap, pas-de-bas, push spin,
rock step, shedding, spot turn,
swingout, throwout, time step,
windmill
**09** allemagne, applejack, crazy legs,
cross over, cross turn, dile que no,
grapevine, lindy turn, pas de
deux, poussette, promenade,
quick stop, sugarfoot, sugarpush
**10** ball-change, chainé turn, change
step, charleston, chassé turn,
come-around, Cuban walks,
cucarachas, inside turn,
jackhammer, rubber legs, spiral
turn, texas tommy, triple step
**11** alemana turn, impetus turn,
natural turn, outside turn, pas de
basque, quarter turn, reverse turn,
setting step

**12** last shedding, shake and turn, under-arm turn
**13** double-shuffle, fall off the log, first shedding
**14** change of places, kick-ball-change, transition step, travelling step

• **dance company** 03 set

*Dance companies include:*

**10** Ballet West
**11** Kirov Ballet, Royal Ballet
**12** Sadler's Wells
**13** Ballet Rambert, Ballets Russes, Bolshoi Ballet, Joffrey Ballet
**14** National Ballet

## dancer

**04** alma, alme **05** almah, almeh **06** bopper, exotic, hoofer **07** baladin, danseur, kachina, morisco, skipper, slammer, waltzer **08** coryphee, danseuse, figurant, joncanoe, junkanoo, matachin, première, showgirl **09** ballerina, figurante, John Canoe, John Kanoo, tap-dancer **10** pyrrhicist **11** belly-dancer, comprimario **12** ballet dancer **13** terpsichorean **14** Jack-in-the-green

*Dancers include:*

**03** Lee (Gypsy Rose)
**04** Bull (Deborah), Edur (Thomas), Oaks (Agnes), Rowe (Marilyn)
**05** Ailey (Alvin, Jnr), Baker (Josephine), Clark (Michael), Cohan (Robert), Dolin (Anton), Kelly (Gene), Laban (Rudolf von), Lifar (Serge), Perón (Isabelita), Sleep (Wayne), Tharp (Twyla)
**06** Ashton (Sir Frederick), Béjart (Maurice), Blasis (Carlo), Childs (Lucinda), Cooper (Adam), Davies (Siobhan), Dowell (Anthony), Duncan (Isadora), Fokine (Michel), Graham (Martha), Paxton (Steve), Petipa (Marius), Rogers (Ginger), Sibley (Antoinette), Wigman (Mary)
**07** Astaire (Fred), Bussell (Darcey), Durante (Viviana), Edwards (Leslie), Fonteyn (Dame Margot), Guillem (Sylvie), Markova (Dame Alicia), Massine (Léonide), Nureyev (Rudolf), Pavlova (Anna), Rambert (Dame Marie), Seymour (Lynn), Ulanova (Galina)
**08** Danilova (Alexandra), De Valois (Dame Ninette), Hayworth (Rita), Helpmann (Sir Robert), Humphrey (Doris), Nijinska (Bronislava), Nijinsky (Vaslav)
**09** Diaghilev (Sergei), Macmillan (Sir Kenneth)
**10** Balanchine (George), Cunningham (Merce), Mukhamedov (Irek)
**11** Baryshnikov (Mikhail), Mistinguett

*See also* **ballet**

## dandelion

**09** kok-saghyz, taraxacum

## dandle

**03** pet **04** toss **05** dance **06** bounce, cradle, cuddle, doodle, fondle, jiggle

## dandy

**03** fop **04** beau, buck, dude, fine, lair, posh, toff **05** blade, blood, great, smart, swell **06** Adonis, masher **07** capital, coxcomb, jessamy, musk-cat, peacock, princox **08** macaroni, muscadin, popinjay, splendid **09** excellent, exquisite, fantastic, first-rate **10** beau garçon, dapperling, fantastico **12** man about town **13** puss-gentleman

*Dandies include:*

**04** Nash (Richard 'Beau')
**05** Crisp (Quentin), Wilde (Oscar)
**06** Coward (Noel)
**08** Beerbohm (Max), Brummell (George 'Beau')
**12** Yankee Doodle

## danger

**04** risk **05** nasty, peril, power **06** hazard, menace, risque, threat **07** pitfall **08** jeopardy **09** liability **10** insecurity **11** imperilment **12** endangerment, perilousness **13** vulnerability **14** precariousness **15** snake in the grass
• **danger signal** 03 red 08 red light
• **hidden danger** 04 trap 07 pitfall

## dangerous

**03** hot **05** dicey, dodgy, grave, hairy, nasty, risky, tight **06** chancy, daring, severe, unsafe **07** exposed, no' canny, ominous, serious **08** alarming, arrogant, critical, high-risk, insecure, menacing, perilous, reckless, unchancy **09** breakneck, hazardous, minacious, mischancy **10** jeopardous, periculous, precarious, vulnerable **11** defenceless, stand-offish, susceptible, threatening, treacherous

## dangerously

**07** acutely, gravely **08** severely **09** seriously **10** alarmingly, critically, menacingly, perilously **12** precariously **13** threateningly

## dangle

**03** sag **04** fall, flap, hang, loll, lure, sway, wave **05** droop, offer, swing, tempt, trail **06** entice, flaunt, seduce **07** hold out **08** flourish **09** tantalize

## dank

**03** wet **04** damp, dewy **05** madid, moist, musty, slimy, soggy **06** chilly, clammy, sticky

## Daphne

**08** lacebark, mezereon, mezereum **09** eaglewood, widow wail **12** spurge laurel

## dapper

**04** chic, neat, spry, tidy, trim **05** brisk, natty, smart **06** active, dainty, nimble, spruce **07** stylish **08** debonair, sprauncy **11** well-dressed, well-groomed **13** well-turned-out

## dappled

**04** pied **06** dotted **07** blotchy, flecked, mottled, piebald, spotted **08** blotched, freckled, speckled, stippled, streaked **09** chequered **10** bespeckled, variegated

## dare

**04** dace, dart, daze, defy, doze, face, goad, lurk, risk **05** brave, flout, stake, stare, stump, taunt **06** crouch, gamble, hazard, invite, resist, shrink **07** daunton, presume, provoke, venture **08** boldness, confront, endanger, frighten, gauntlet **09** adventure, challenge, go so far as, stand up to, ultimatum **11** provocation **12** be bold enough **13** be brave enough, go out on a limb **14** have the courage

## daredevil

**04** bold, rash **05** brave, hasty **06** daring, madcap, plucky **07** hothead, valiant **08** fearless, intrepid, reckless, stuntman **09** audacious, dauntless, desperado, hotheaded, impetuous, impulsive **10** adventurer **11** adventurous **12** swashbuckler

## daring

**04** bold, gall, grit, guts, rash, wild **05** brave, hardy, moxie, nerve, pluck, spunk **06** bottle, plucky, spirit, valour **07** bravery, courage, gallows, prowess, valiant **08** audacity, boldness, defiance, fearless, intrepid, rashness, reckless, shocking, ventrous, wildness **09** audacious, dauntless, foolhardy, impulsive, undaunted, venturous **10** courageous, jeopardous **11** adventurous, intrepidity, venturesome **12** fearlessness, high-spirited, recklessness **13** foolhardiness **15** adventurousness

## daringly

**06** boldly **07** bravely **10** fearlessly **11** audaciously **12** courageously **13** adventurously

## dark

**02** dk **03** bad, dim, fog, sad, wan **04** base, drab, dusk, evil, foul, grim, mirk, mist, murk, vile **05** awful, black, bleak, blind, brown, dingy, dirty, dusky, foggy, gloom, misty, moody, murky, night, olive, sable, shade, shady, tawny, unlit, wrong **06** arcane, auburn, cloudy, dismal, gloomy, hidden, morose, opaque, secret, sombre, tanned, tragic, veiled, wicked **07** bronzed, crooked, cryptic, dimness, evening, immoral, joyless, mystery, obscure, ominous, pit-mirk, privacy, secrecy, shadows, shadowy, sunless, swarthy **08** abstruse, badly lit, brunette, chestnut, darkness, dejected, dimly lit, esoteric, hopeless, horrible, menacing, mournful, overcast, puzzling, sinister, twilight, worrying **09** blackness, cheerless, concealed, enigmatic, half-light, ignorance, intricate, murkiness, nightfall, night-time, obscurity, poorly lit, recondite, shadiness, suntanned, tenebrity, tenebrose, tenebrous **10** caliginous, cloudiness, dark-haired, despicable, disastrous, forbidding, gloominess, iniquitous, mysterious, tenebrious, unpleasant **11** concealment, crepuscular, dark-skinned, distressing, frightening, inscrutable, sunlessness, tenebrosity

**12** crepusculous **13** unenlightened, unilluminated **14** unintelligible

### darken
**03** dim, fog **04** fade **05** blind, cloud, colly, frown, sable, shade, sully **06** deject, sadden, shadow **07** benight, blacken, depress, eclipse, embrown, imbrown, obscure **08** cast down **09** cloud over, grow angry, look angry, obfuscate, overshade, weigh down **10** grow darker, make gloomy, obnubilate, overshadow, sclerotize **11** become angry **12** become darker **13** disilluminate

### darkly
**05** dimly **06** glumly **07** at night, blackly, by night **08** dismally, gloomily, sullenly **09** obscurely **11** cryptically, inscrutably **12** in the shadows, mysteriously **13** enigmatically

### darkness
*see* **dark**

### darling
**03** hon, luv, pet **04** dear, duck, hero, idol, love, peat **05** angel, hinny, honey, loved, sugar, sweet **06** adored, dautie, dawtie, minion, poppet, prized **07** acushla, asthore, beloved, dearest, dilling, minikin, sweetie **08** dearling, precious, sweeting, treasure **09** celebrity, cherished, favourite, treasured **10** delightful, mavourneen, sweetheart **11** blue-eyed boy, teacher's pet, white-haired **13** fair-haired boy **14** apple of your eye

### darmstadtium
**02** Ds

### darn
**03** sew **04** drat, mend **05** patch, sew up **06** cobble, repair, stitch

### dart
**03** fly, run **04** barb, bolt, cast, cook, dace, dare, dash, flit, hurl, leap, plan, race, rush, send, skit, tear, toss **05** arrow, bound, flash, fling, lance, lanch, scoot, shaft, shoot, sling, start, throw **06** endart, flight, glance, launch, pounce, propel, scheme, scurry, spring, sprint, strike, wheech **07** feather, harpoon, project **08** spiculum **09** fléchette, love-arrow, love-shaft **10** banderilla

### dash
◇ *anagram indicator* **03** bit, cut, dad, dah, fly, hie, jaw, nip, pop, run, tad, zip **04** bang, beat, bolt, brio, dart, daud, ding, dive, drop, élan, hint, hurl, lash, life, pash, race, ramp, rash, ruin, rule, rush, slam, spot, tear, toss **05** blank, blash, bound, break, bribe, crash, crush, fling, force, grain, gusto, hurry, pinch, plash, pound, scart, shine, smash, souse, spang, speck, speed, spoil, spurt, swash, swill, throw, tinge, touch, trace, verve, wreck **06** blight, dampen, energy, hurtle, jabble, little, relish, sadden, sluice, spirit, splash, sprint, streak, strike, stroke, thwart, vigour, wheech **07** depress, destroy, fervour, flavour, let down, passion, pizzazz, scuttle,

shatter, smidgen, soupçon, sparkle, viretot **08** confound, gratuity, scramble, vitality, vivacity **09** animation, devastate, frustrate **10** disappoint, discourage, dishearten, enthusiasm, liveliness, suggestion
• **dash off** **06** scrawl **07** jot down **08** scribble

### dashing
◇ *anagram indicator* **04** bold **05** doggy, showy, smart **06** dapper, daring, lively, plucky, rakish **07** elegant, gallant, go-ahead, raffish, stylish, varment, varmint **08** animated, debonair, slap-bang, slashing, smashing, spirited, vigorous **09** energetic, exuberant **10** attractive, flamboyant **11** fashionable

### dastard
**06** coward **07** hilding

### dastardly
**03** low **04** base, evil, mean, vile **06** craven, wicked **07** nithing **08** cowardly, fiendish **09** underhand **10** despicable, diabolical, iniquitous **11** lily-livered **12** contemptible, faint-hearted

### data
**04** info **05** facts, input **07** details, figures **08** features, material, research **09** documents **10** statistics **11** information, particulars
• **collection of data** **04** file

### date
**01** d **03** age, day, era **04** ides, time, week, year **05** court, epoch, go out, month, stage, tryst **06** belong, decade, epocha, escort, friend, go back, go with, period, steady **07** century, meeting, partner, take out **08** come from, young man **09** boyfriend, exist from, go out with, man friend, obsolesce, originate, young lady **10** be together, engagement, girlfriend, go out of use, lady friend, millennium, rendezvous, show its age **11** appointment, assignation, woman friend **12** go steady with **14** become obsolete, be involved with
• **to date** **03** yet **05** as yet, so far **07** up to now **08** until now **14** up to the present
• **without date** **02** sa, sd

### dated
**05** passé **06** old hat, square **07** archaic **08** obsolete, outdated, outmoded **09** out-of-date, unstylish **10** antiquated, superseded **11** obsolescent **12** old-fashioned **13** unfashionable

### daub
**03** dab **04** blot, coat, gaum, gorm, spot, teer **05** cover, paint, slake, smalm, smarm, smear, stain, sully **06** bedaub, blotch, clatch, smirch, smudge, splash **07** plaster, slubber, spatter, splodge, splotch **08** splatter **09** beplaster, bespatter **10** blottesque

### daughter
**01** d **03** dau **04** girl, lass **05** child, fille **06** lassie **08** disciple **09** offspring **10** descendant, inhabitant

*Daughters include:*

**04** **Anne** (Princess), **Hero**, **Kate**, **Page** (Anne)
**05** **Freud** (Anna), **Lloyd** (Emily), **Mills** (Hayley), **O'Neal** (Tatum), **Regan**
**06** **Bhutto** (Benazir), **Bianca**, **Fatima**, **Fisher** (Carrie), **Forbes** (Emma), **Gandhi** (Indira), **Imogen**, **Juliet**, **Marina**
**07** **Electra**, **Forsyte** (Fleur), **Goneril**, **Jessica**, **Lavinia**, **Miranda**, **Ophelia**, **Perdita**, **Presley** (Lisa Marie)
**08** **Cordelia**, **Lovelace** (Ada), **Minnelli** (Liza), **Williams** (Shirley)
**09** **Cassandra**, **du Maurier** (Daphne), **Katharina**, **McCartney** (Stella), **Pankhurst** (Christabel)
**10** **Beckinsale** (Kate), **Richardson** (Joely), **Richardson** (Natasha), **Rossellini** (Isabella)
**13** **Princess Royal**

### daunt
**03** cow **04** adaw, faze, pall **05** abash, alarm, amate, deter, quail, scare, shake **06** dismay, put off, rattle, ruffle, subdue **07** overawe, unnerve **08** dispirit, frighten **09** take aback **10** demoralize, disconcert, discourage, dishearten, intimidate **11** disillusion

### daunted
**04** mate **05** quayd

### daunting
**05** scary **08** alarming **09** unnerving **11** dispiriting, frightening **12** demoralizing, discouraging, intimidating **13** disconcerting, disheartening

### dauntingly
**07** scarily **10** alarmingly **11** unnervingly **13** dispiritingly, frighteningly **14** demoralizingly, discouragingly, intimidatingly **15** disconcertingly, dishearteningly

### dauntless
**04** bold **05** brave, stout **06** daring, plucky **07** doughty, valiant **08** fearless, intrepid, resolute **09** undaunted **10** courageous, determined **11** indomitable

### dawdle
**03** lag **05** dally, delay, drawl, tarry, trail **06** diddle, linger, loiter, potter, putter **07** saunter **08** go slowly **09** faff about, hang about **10** dilly-dally **11** take too long **12** drag your feet, take your time

### dawn
**04** open, rise **05** begin, birth, break, gleam, onset, start, sun-up **06** advent, appear, arrive, Aurora, be born, emerge, origin, spring **07** arrival, day-peep, develop, genesis, glimmer, lighten, morning, sunrise **08** brighten, cock-crow, commence, daybreak, daylight **09** beginning, dayspring, emergence, grow light, inception, originate **10** break of day, first light **11** become light, crack of dawn **12** commencement **13** come into being
• **dawn on** **03** hit **05** click **06** sink in, strike **07** occur to, realize **12** register with

## day

**01** d **03** age, era **04** date, dies, Ides, jour, peak, time **05** bloom, epoch, flush, Nones, prime **06** heyday, period **07** calends, daytime, kalends **08** daylight **09** golden age **10** generation **13** daylight hours

*Days of the week:*

**03** Fri, Mon, Sat, Sun, Thu, Tue, Wed
**04** Thur, Tues, Weds
**05** Thurs
**06** Friday, Monday, Sunday
**07** Tuesday
**08** Saturday, Thursday
**09** Wednesday

*French day names:*

**05** jeudi, lundi, mardi
**06** samedi
**08** dimanche, mercredi, vendredi

*German day names:*

**06** Montag
**07** Freitag, Samstag, Sonntag
**08** Dienstag, Mittwoch
**09** Sonnabend
**10** Donnerstag

*Italian day names:*

**06** lunedì, sabato
**07** giovedì, martedì, venerdì
**08** domenica
**09** mercoledì

*Latin day names:*

**09** Jovis dies, Lunae dies, Solis dies
**10** Martis dies
**11** Saturni dies, Veneris dies
**12** Mercurii dies

*Spanish day names:*

**05** lunes
**06** jueves, martes, sàbado
**07** domingo, viernes
**09** miércoles

*Named days include:*

**02** VE, VJ
**09** Fig Sunday, Low Sunday, Red Friday, Red Letter
**10** Good Friday, Holy Friday, Palm Sunday, Whit Sunday
**11** Bible Sunday, Black Friday, Black Monday, Egg Saturday, Fat Thursday
**12** Advent Sunday, Ash Wednesday, Black Tuesday, Bloody Monday, Bloody Sunday, Easter Monday, Easter Sunday, Golden Friday, Stir-up Sunday
**13** Passion Sunday, Shrove Tuesday, Trinity Sunday
**14** Easter Saturday, Maundy Thursday, Pancake Tuesday, Rogation Sunday
**15** Mothering Sunday

*See also* **Christmas**
• **day after day** **09** endlessly, regularly **10** repeatedly
**11** continually, perpetually
**12** monotonously, persistently, relentlessly, time and again **13** again and again
• **day by day** **08** steadily
**09** gradually **13** progressively
**15** slowly but surely
• **day in, day out** **08** every day
**09** endlessly, regularly **10** repeatedly
**11** continually **12** monotonously, persistently, time and again **13** again and again
• **day's end** **03** e'en, ene, eve
**04** even **07** evening
• **have had its day** **08** be past it
**11** be out of date
• **number of days** **04** week, year
**05** month **07** weekend **09** fortnight
• **these days** **02** AD
• **three times a day** **03** tid
• **time of day** **04** seal, seel, seil, sele

## daybreak

**04** dawn, morn **05** sun-up **06** Aurora
**07** morning, sunrise **08** cock-crow, daylight **10** break of day, first light
**11** crack of dawn **12** skreigh of day

## daydream

**04** muse, wish **05** dream, fancy
**06** musing, trance, vision **07** fantasy, figment, imagine, reverie, zone out
**09** fantasize, imagining, pipe dream, switch off **11** inattention **13** be lost in space, woolgathering **14** stare into space **15** be in a brown study, castles in the air, not pay attention

## daydreamer

**06** rêveur **07** dreamer, rêveuse
**08** idealist, romantic **09** fantasist, visionary **10** Don Quixote, fantasizer
**11** Walter Mitty

## daylight

**03** day **04** dawn **05** light, sun-up
**07** daytime, high day, morning, sunrise
**08** broad day, cock-crow, daybreak, sunlight **10** break of day, first light
**11** crack of dawn **12** natural light

## daze

**04** dare, numb, spin, stun **05** amaze, blind, gally, knock, shock, whirl
**06** baffle, dazzle, stupor, trance
**07** astound, confuse, perplex, stagger, startle, stupefy **08** astonish, bewilder, blow away, bowl over, knock out, numbness, paralyse, surprise
**09** confusion, dumbfound, take aback
**11** distraction, flabbergast, knock for six **12** bewilderment

## dazed

◇ *anagram indicator* **03** out **05** muzzy, silly, totty, woozy **06** amazed, groggy, numbed, punchy **07** baffled, dazzled, shocked, stunned **08** confused, startled
**09** astounded, blown away, paralysed, perplexed, staggered, stupefied, surprised **10** astonished, bewildered, bowled over, punch-drunk, speechless, taken aback
**11** dumbfounded, unconscious
**13** flabbergasted

## dazzle

**03** awe, wow **04** blur, daze **05** amaze, blaze, blend, blind, flare, flash, glare, gleam **06** bedaze, strike **07** bewitch, confuse, glitter, impress, overawe, sparkle, stupefy **08** astonish, bedazzle, bowl over, knock out **09** dumbfound, fascinate, hypnotize, overpower, overwhelm, splendour **10** brightness, brilliance, razzmatazz **11** scintillate
**12** magnificence **13** scintillation

## dazzling

**05** glaik, grand **06** bright, superb
**07** glaring, radiant, shining **08** blinding, glorious, splendid, stunning
**09** brilliant, ravishing, sparkling
**10** foudroyant, glittering, impressive
**11** psychedelic, sensational, spectacular **12** awe-inspiring, breathtaking **13** scintillating

## dazzlingly

**08** brightly, superbly **09** glaringly, radiantly **10** blindingly, gloriously
**11** brilliantly **12** impressively
**13** sensationally, spectacularly
**14** breathtakingly

## deactivate

**04** stop **07** disable **08** paralyse
**10** immobilize **14** put out of action

## dead

**01** d **03** dec **04** bang, bung, bust, cold, dull, flat, gone, late, numb, very
**05** dated, exact, inert, kaput, napoo, passé, quiet, quite, smack, stiff, tired, total, utter, waned **06** asleep, barren, benumb, boring, broken, deaden, entire, frigid, no more, old hat, really, sleepy, torpid **07** awfully, defunct, disused, exactly, expired, extinct, humdrum, perfect, tedious, utterly, worn out **08** absolute, ad patres, benumbed, complete, dead beat, deceased, departed, directly, inactive, lifeless, lukewarm, obsolete, outright, passed on, perished, straight, terribly, thorough, tired out, unerring
**09** apathetic, bloodless, conked out, deathlike, downright, exanimate, exhausted, extremely, inanimate, inelastic, insensate, knackered, out of date, paralysed, thanatoid, unfeeling
**10** absolutely, breathless, broken-down, brown bread, completely, insentient, not working, on the blink, on the fritz, out of order, passed away, spiritless, unexciting **11** dead as a dodo, emotionless, gone to sleep, immediately, indifferent, ineffective, insensitive, off the hooks, ready to drop, unemotional, unqualified
**12** discontinued, six feet under, unresponsive **13** exceptionally, uninteresting, unsympathetic **14** no longer spoken **15** dead as a doornail

## deaden

**04** dull, hush, mute, numb **05** abate, allay, blunt, check, slake **06** benumb, dampen, harden, lessen, muffle, obtund, reduce, soothe, stifle, subdue, weaken **07** assuage, mortify, quieten, smother **08** diminish, mitigate, moderate, paralyse, suppress
**09** alleviate **11** desensitize
**12** anaesthetize **14** take the edge off
**15** make insensitive

## deadline

**04** term, time **06** time up **08** timeline **09** time limit **10** target date

## deadlock

**04** halt **05** stale **06** log jam **07** dead end, impasse **08** stand-off, stoppage **09** checkmate, stalemate **10** standstill

## deadly

**04** dull, fell, grim, sure, true **05** fatal, feral, great, hated, quite, toxic **06** bitter, boring, fierce, funest, lethal, marked, mortal, savage **07** deathly, extreme, humdrum, intense, killing, noxious, perfect, precise, serious, tedious, totally, utterly **08** accurate, deathful, entirely, flawless, mortific, unerring, venomous **09** dangerous, deathlike, effective, extremely, malignant, murderous, perfectly, pestilent, thanatoid, unfailing **10** absolutely, completely, dreadfully, implacable, monotonous, pernicious, thoroughly, unexciting **11** destructive, internecine, intercine **12** death-dealing **13** uninteresting **14** irreconcilable **15** life-threatening

## deadpan

**05** blank, empty **09** impassive **10** poker-faced **11** emotionless, inscrutable **12** inexpressive, unexpressive **13** dispassionate, straight-faced **14** expressionless

## deaf

**04** surd **05** dunny **07** unmoved **08** heedless **09** oblivious, stone-deaf, unmindful, untouched **10** cloth-eared, impervious, unaffected **11** deaf as a post, inattentive, indifferent, unconcerned **13** hard of hearing **15** hearing-impaired

## deafening

**07** booming, ringing, roaring **08** piercing, very loud **09** very noisy **10** resounding, thundering, thunderous **11** ear-piercing **12** ear-splitting, overwhelming **13** reverberating

## deal

**02** go **03** act, buy, lot **04** flog, hand, load, mart, mete, pact, push, vend **05** allot, reach, round, serve, share, stock, trade, treat **06** amount, assign, bestow, degree, direct, divide, export, extent, handle, market, strike **07** bargain, deliver, dish out, dole out, give out, inflict, mete out, operate, portion, traffic **08** contract, covenant, dispense, quantity **09** agreement, apportion, negotiate, treatment **10** administer, buy and sell, distribute, do business **11** arrangement, transaction **12** distribution **13** understanding
• **deal out** **04** dole, help **06** divide **08** dispense **10** distribute
• **deal with** **04** cope, sort **05** cover, see to, touch, treat **06** handle, manage, tackle **07** be about, concern, process, sort out **08** attend to, consider, cope with **09** look after **10** take care of **12** have to do with **14** get to grips with
• **good deal** **07** bargain
• **great deal** **03** lot **04** heap, mort,

much, some **05** heaps, power, sight, world

## dealer

**03** dlr **04** tout **05** agent, coper **06** broker, couper, hawker, monger, pedlar, pusher, seller, totter, trader, vendor **07** chapman, fripper **08** marketer, merchant, retailer, salesman, supplier **09** brinjarry, fripperer **10** saleswoman, trafficker, wholesaler **11** distributor, salesperson **12** merchandizer

## dealing, dealings

**05** trade, truck **07** trading, traffic **08** business, commerce **09** marketing, operation, relations **10** chevisance, operations **11** association, connections, intercourse, merchandise, trafficking, transaction **12** negotiations, transactions **13** communication

## dean

**03** den **04** dell, dene, head **05** doyen, slade, Swift **08** director **09** principal, rural dean **11** chapter head, vicar-forane **12** Very Reverend **13** head of faculty **14** cardinal-bishop
• **rural dean** **02** RD **10** arch-priest **11** vicar-forane

## dear

**03** joy, pet **04** cher, chou, high, lamb, leve, lief, love, posh, salt **05** angel, chère, close, honey, lieve, loved, steep, sugar, sweet **06** adored, costly, pricey, scarce, valued **07** beloved, darling, earnest, machree, sky-high, sweetie **08** esteemed, familiar, favoured, grievous, high-cost, intimate, loved one, not cheap, precious, treasure **09** big-ticket, chargeful, cherished, endearing, excessive, expensive, favourite, respected, treasured **10** exorbitant, high-priced, mavourneen, overpriced, sweetheart **11** well-beloved **12** au poids de l'or, costing a bomb, extortionate **15** costing the earth, daylight robbery

## dearer

**04** loor

## dearly

**06** deeply, fondly **07** greatly **08** lovingly, tenderly, very much **09** adoringly, devotedly, earnestly, extremely **10** a great deal, intimately, profoundly, with favour **11** with respect **12** at a great cost, at a high price **13** with affection, with great loss **14** affectionately

## dearth

**04** lack, need, want **06** famine **07** absence, paucity, poverty **08** dearness, scarcity, shortage, sparsity **10** barrenness, deficiency, inadequacy, meagreness, scantiness **12** exiguousness **13** insufficiency

## death

**03** end **04** loss, ruin **06** finish **07** decease, undoing **08** curtains, downfall, the grave **09** cessation, departure, mortality, perishing

**10** defunction, expiration, extinction **11** destruction, dissolution, eradication, extirpation, termination **12** annihilation, obliteration **13** extermination

*Death-related terms include:*

**03** DOA, RIP, urn **04** bier, cist, mort, obit, pall, pyre, sati, soul, toll, tomb, wake, will **05** ashes, bardo, cairn, dirge, elegy, éloge, elogy, grave, mourn, shiva, tangi, vigil, widow **06** Azrael, bedral, burial, chadar, coffin, corpse, demise, entomb, eulogy, exequy, fossor, grieve, hearse, lament, lethal, martyr, monody, mortal, orphan, rosary, shibah, shivah, shroud, suttee, wreath **07** autopsy, bederal, bereave, coroner, cortège, cremate, crucify, elogium, epitaph, funeral, inquest, karoshi, keening, mastaba, mourner, passing, quietus, requiem, widower **08** casualty, cemetery, cenotaph, deathbed, death row, deceased, disinter, dispatch, eulogium, fatality, grieving, hara-kiri, interred, last post, long home, mortbell, mortuary, mourning, necropsy, necrosis, obituary, yahrzeit **09** committal, cremation, dead march, death mask, graveside, graveyard, headstone, interment, last rites, mass grave, mausoleum, mortician, obsequies, passing on, sacrifice, sepulchre, testament, tombstone, year's mind **10** death knell, euthanasia, grim reaper, necropolis, obituarist, pall-bearer, posthumous, predecease, strae death, undertaker **11** bereavement, crematorium, eternal rest, funeral home, gravedigger, last honours, passing away, passing bell, requiem mass, rest in peace, rigor mortis, sarcophagus, suicide pact **12** burial ground, debt of nature, disinterment, last farewell, mercy killing, resting place, the other side **13** burial society, natural causes **14** extreme unction, funeral parlour **15** funeral director, resurrectionist
• **after death** **02** PM **10** posthumous, post-mortem
• **approach of death** **03** fit
• **by reason of death** **02** cm
• **put to death** **03** gas **04** do in, hang, kill **05** lynch, press, shoot, waste **06** behead, martyr, rub out **07** bump off, crucify, execute, take out **08** blow away, despatch, dispatch, knock off **09** transport **10** decapitate, guillotine **11** electrocute, exterminate
• **repose of death** **04** rest

## deathless

**07** eternal, undying **08** immortal,

timeless **09** memorable **10** ever-living **11** everlasting, never-ending **12** imperishable **13** incorruptible, ` unforgettable

## deathly
**03** wan **04** grim, pale **05** ashen, fatal, white **06** deadly, mortal, pallid, utmost **07** extreme, ghastly, ghostly, haggard, harmful, intense **08** terrible **09** deathlike, ghost-like, thanatoid **10** cadaverous, colourless

## debacle
**04** hash, rout, ruin **05** farce, havoc **06** cock-up, defeat, fiasco, foul-up **07** failure, screw-up, turmoil, washout **08** collapse, disaster, downfall, reversal, stampede **09** cataclysm, overthrow, ruination **11** catastrophe, devastation **14** disintegration

## debar
**03** ban, bar **04** deny, stop **05** eject, expel **06** cut out, forbid, hamper, hinder **07** exclude, keep out, prevent, shut out, suspend **08** conclude, obstruct, preclude, prohibit, restrain **09** blackball, proscribe, segregate **10** disqualify

## debarred
**03** out

## debase
**05** abase, allay, alloy, lower, shame, taint **06** bemean, defile, demean, dilute, embace, embase, humble, imbase, reduce **07** cheapen, corrupt, degrade, devalue, pollute, vitiate **08** disgrace **09** discredit, dishonour, humiliate **10** adulterate, bastardize, sensualize **11** contaminate

## debased
**03** low **04** base, vile **05** hedge **06** abased, fallen, impure, shamed, sinful, sordid, vulgar **07** corrupt, defiled, humbled, immoral, tainted **08** degraded, devalued, polluted, reversed **09** cheapened, debauched, disgraced, perverted **10** degenerate, humiliated, prostitute **11** adulterated, discredited, dishonoured **12** contaminated

## debasement
**05** shame **08** disgrace **09** abasement, dishonour, pollution **10** cheapening, corruption, defilement, perversion **11** degradation, depravation, devaluation, humiliation **12** adulteration, degeneration **13** contamination

## debatable
**04** moot **06** unsure **07** dubious, unclear **08** arguable, doubtful **09** uncertain, undecided, unsettled **10** disputable **11** contentious, contestable **12** questionable **13** controversial, problematical **14** open to question

## debate
**05** argue, fight, flyte, forum, weigh **06** combat, ponder, powwow, reason **07** contend, contest, discept, discuss, dispute, flyting, polemic, reflect, teach-in, wrangle, wrestle **08** argument, cogitate, consider, mull

over, polemics, talk over **09** altercate, forensics, kick about, talk about, talkathon, think over, thrash out **10** contention, deliberate, discussion, kick around, knock about, meditate on, reflection **11** altercation, controversy, disputation, knock around, talk through **12** cut and thrust, deliberation **13** consideration **15** exchange of views

## debauch
**03** wet **04** ruin **05** whore **06** debosh, ravish, seduce **07** corrupt, deprave, pervert, pollute, subvert, violate, vitiate **10** lead astray **11** over-indulge

## debauched
**04** lewd **06** wanton **07** corrupt, debased, immoral, riotous **08** decadent, degraded, depraved, rakehell **09** abandoned, carousing, corrupted, dissolute, excessive, perverted **10** degenerate, dissipated, licentious, profligate **11** hellraising, intemperate, promiscuous **13** overindulgent

## debauchery
**04** lust, orgy, riot **05** revel **06** excess **07** licence, license **08** carousal, lewdness **09** decadence, depravity **10** corruption, degeneracy, immorality, rakishness, wantonness **11** degradation, dissipation, hellraising, libertinage, libertinism **12** intemperance **13** dissoluteness **14** licentiousness, overindulgence
• **place of debauchery** **03** sty

## debenture
**04** bond

## debilitate
**03** sap **04** tire **05** drain **06** impair, weaken **07** cripple, exhaust, fatigue, wear out **08** enervate, enfeeble **09** undermine **10** devitalize **12** incapacitate

## debilitating
**06** tiring **09** crippling, fatiguing, impairing, weakening **10** enervating, enervative, enfeebling, exhausting, wearing out **11** undermining **14** incapacitating

## debility
**05** atony **07** fatigue, frailty, languor, malaise **08** asthenia, weakness **09** atonicity, faintness, infirmity, tiredness, weariness **10** enervation, exhaustion, feebleness, incapacity, myasthenia **11** decrepitude **12** enfeeblement, lack of energy, neurasthenia **14** lack of vitality

## debit
• **direct debit** **02** DD

## debonair
**05** suave **06** breezy, jaunty, smooth, urbane **07** affable, buoyant, dashing, elegant, refined, stylish **08** carefree, charming, cheerful, cultured, well-bred **09** courteous, dignified **12** light-hearted **13** sophisticated

## debrief
**05** grill **07** examine **08** question

**09** interview **11** interrogate **12** cross-examine **13** cross-question

## debris
◊ *anagram indicator* **04** bits, muck **05** drift, dross, ruins, scrap, trash, waste, wreck **06** bahada, bajada, litter, pieces, refuse, rubble, tephra **07** eluvium, remains, rubbish **08** detritus, wreckage **09** fragments, sweepings **12** pyroclastics
• **pile of debris** **03** tel **04** tell

## debt
**03** dew, due, IOU, sin **04** bill, duty, hock **05** claim, debit, score **06** charge **07** account, arrears **08** money due **09** amount due, liability, overdraft **10** aes alienum, commitment, money owing, obligation **11** amount owing **12** indebtedness
• **in debt** **06** in hock **08** in the red **09** gone under, in arrears, insolvent **10** owing money **11** in overdraft **13** gone to the wall, in Queer Street
• **indication of debt** **03** red
• **in someone's debt** **07** obliged **08** beholden, indebted, thankful **11** honour-bound **12** appreciative

## debtor
**02** Dr **07** debitor **08** bankrupt, borrower, deadbeat **09** defaulter, insolvent, mortgagor **10** abbey-laird, fly-by-night

## debunk
**04** mock **05** quash **06** expose, show up **07** deflate, explode, lampoon **08** disprove, puncture, ridicule **13** cut down to size

## debut, début
**05** start **06** launch **08** entrance, première **09** beginning, coming-out, first time, launching **10** first night, initiation **12** inauguration, introduction, presentation **14** first recording **15** first appearance

## debutante, débutante
**03** bud, deb **05** debby

## decadence
**04** fall **05** decay **07** decline **09** depravity **10** corruption, debasement, debauchery, degeneracy, immorality, perversion **11** dissipation, dissolution **12** degeneration **13** deterioration, retrogression **14** degenerateness, licentiousness, self-indulgence

## decadent
**06** effete **07** corrupt, debased, immoral **08** decaying, degraded, depraved **09** debauched, declining, dissolute, symbolist **10** Babylonian, degenerate, dissipated, licentious **12** degenerating, unprincipled **13** deteriorating, self-indulgent

## decamp
**03** fly, guy **04** bolt, flee, flit **05** lam it, scrap, slide, slope, split **06** desert, escape, hook it, levant, mizzle, run off **07** abscond, do a bunk, make off, run away, scamper, scarper, take off, vamoose **08** light out, slope off, up sticks **09** do a runner, skedaddle

**10** hightail it, make tracks
**12** absquatulate **14** take in on the lam

**decant**
**03** tap **05** drain **07** draw off, pour out
**08** transfer **09** siphon off

**decapitate**
◇ *head deletion indicator* **06** behead,
unhead **07** execute **10** guillotine

**decay**
**03** rot **04** blet, doat, dote, fail, ruin, rust,
sink **05** faint, go bad, go off, mould,
spoil, waste **06** blight, canker, caries,
dry rot, empare, fading, fester, fungus,
impair, mildew, perish, weaken, wet
rot, wither **07** atrophy, corrode,
crumble, decline, dwindle, empaire,
empayre, failing, failure, forfair, go to
pot, putrefy, rotting, shrivel, wasting
**08** collapse, downfall, foxiness, going
bad, wear away **09** crumbling,
decadence, decadency, decompose,
perishing, putridity, waste away,
weakening, withering **10** debasement,
declension, decompound, degenerate,
go downhill **11** deteriorate, go to the
dogs, labefaction, putrescence
**12** degeneration, disintegrate,
putrefaction **13** consenescence,
consenescency, decomposition,
deterioration, labefactation
**14** disintegration

**decayed**
**03** bad, off **04** rank, sour **05** druxy, stale
**06** addled, failed, mouldy, putrid,
rotten, sleepy, wasted **07** carious,
carrion, doddard, rotting, ruinous,
spoiled **08** corroded, doddered,
mildewed, perished, withered
**09** putrefied **10** decomposed, dirt-
rotten, putrescent **12** impoverished

**decease**
**03** die, end **04** rest **05** death, dying
**06** demise **07** passing **09** departure,
passing on **10** expiration
**11** dissolution, passing away

**deceased**
**03** dec **04** dead, gone, late, lost
**06** asleep, former, no more **07** defunct,
expired, extinct **08** departed, finished
**12** six feet under **15** dead as a doornail

**deceit**
**03** con **04** fake, game, ruse, sham, wile
**05** abuse, dodge, feint, fraud, guile,
guyle **06** barrat **07** cunning, forgery,
glozing, slenter, slinter, slyness,
swindle **08** artifice, cheating, coquetry,
cozenage, pretence, trickery, wiliness
**09** chicanery, deception, duplicity,
falseness, gold brick, hypocrisy,
invention, malengine, phenakism,
stratagem, treachery **10** craftiness,
imposition, subterfuge **11** fraudulence
**13** double-dealing **14** monkey business
**15** underhandedness

**deceitful**
**03** sly **04** foxy, jive, rusé **05** false, lying,
Punic, sharp **06** braide, crafty, double,
forked, shifty, sneaky, tricky
**07** crooked, cunning, devious, elusory,
knavish **08** coloured, guileful, illusory,
'two-faced **09** deceiving, deceptive,

designing, dishonest, insincere,
underhand **10** deceptious, fraudulent,
Janus-faced, mendacious, perfidious,
untruthful **11** counterfeit, dissembling,
duplicitous, prestigious, treacherous
**12** false-hearted, hypocritical
**13** double-dealing, double-tongued,
untrustworthy

**deceitfully**
**05** slyly **06** double **07** falsely **08** craftily,
sneakily **09** cunningly **11** deceivingly,
deceptively, dishonestly, insincerely
**12** fraudulently, mendaciously,
perfidiously, untruthfully
**13** duplicitously, treacherously,
underhandedly **14** hypocritically

**deceive**
**02** do **03** cog, con, gag, kid, lie **04** bite,
do in, dupe, flam, fool, gull, hoax,
mock **05** abuse, blind, bluff, cheat,
false, put on, trick, trump **06** befool,
betray, delude, entrap, have on,
humbug, lead on, misuse, outwit,
seduce, slip up **07** beguile, cheat on,
chicane, defraud, ensnare, mislead,
swindle, two-time **08** hoodwink,
misguide, outsmart **09** bamboozle,
dissemble, mislippen **10** camouflage,
disappoint, impose upon **11** double-
cross, hornswoggle, set a trap for,
string along **12** put one over on, take
for a ride **13** put a cheat upon **14** pull a
fast one on

**deceiver**
**04** fake **05** cheat, crook, fraud
**06** abuser, con man, falser, guiler,
guyler, hoaxer **07** deluder, diddler,
seducer **08** betrayer, impostor,
swindler, treacher **09** charlatan,
hypocrite, inveigler, treachour,
tregetour, trickster **10** dissembler,
mountebank **11** treachetour **12** double-
dealer

**decelerate**
**04** slow **05** brake **06** retard **08** slow
down **11** reduce speed **12** go more
slowly **14** put the brakes on

**December**
**03** Dec

**decency**
**07** decorum, fitness, modesty
**08** civility, courtesy, fairness
**09** etiquette, good taste, integrity,
propriety **10** politeness, seemliness
**11** correctness, helpfulness,
uprightness **14** respectability

**decent**
**02** OK **03** fit **04** fair, kind, nice, pure
**05** civil **06** chaste, honest, modest,
polite, proper, seemly, worthy
**07** correct, ethical, fitting, gradely,
helpful, upright **08** adequate,
becoming, decorous, generous,
gracious, graithly, moderate, obliging,
passable, pleasant, suitable, tasteful,
virtuous, wise-like **09** befitting,
competent, courteous, dignified,
tolerable **10** acceptable, dependable,
reasonable, salubrious, sufficient,
thoughtful **11** appropriate, presentable,
respectable, trustworthy **12** satisfactory
**13** accommodating

**decently**
**06** fairly, nicely **08** honestly, politely,
properly, suitably **09** correctly,
ethically, helpfully, tolerably
**10** acceptably, adequately,
becomingly, decorously, generously,
graciously, obligingly, reasonably
**11** courteously, presentably,
respectably **12** sufficiently,
thoughtfully **13** appropriately
**14** satisfactorily

**decentralize**
**07** devolve **08** delegate, localize
**11** regionalize **13** deconcentrate
**14** spread outwards **15** spread
downwards

**deception**
**03** cog, con, fib, kid, lie **04** hoax, hype,
ruse, scam, sell, sham, wile **05** bluff,
cheat, fraud, glaik, guile, kiddy,
moody, set-up, snare, sting, trick
**06** deceit, have-on, humbug, take-in
**07** abusion, cunning, eyewash, fallacy,
fubbery, gullery, leg-pull, swindle
**08** artifice, cheating, flim-flam,
illusion, nonsense, pretence, put-up
job, trickery **09** chicanery, chicaning,
duplicity, hypocrisy, imposture,
stratagem, treachery **10** craftiness,
hocus-pocus, maskirovka, pious fraud,
subterfuge **11** dissembling,
fraudulence, insincerity, supercherie
**13** deceptiveness, double-dealing,
funny business, jiggery-pokery **14** false
pretences **15** smoke and mirrors,
underhandedness

**deceptive**
**03** sly **04** fake, foxy, mock, sham
**05** bogus, false, sharp **06** bubble,
catchy, crafty, hollow **07** amusive,
crooked, cunning, elusive **08** cheating,
delusive, delusory, fraudful, illusive,
illusory, imposing, specious, spurious
**09** ambiguous, dishonest, faithless,
underhand **10** fallacious, fraudulent,
misleading, unreliable **11** dissembling,
duplicitous

**deceptively**
**07** falsely **10** illusively, speciously,
spuriously **11** ambiguously,
dishonestly **12** fraudulently,
misleadingly

**decibel**
**02** dB

**decide**
**03** end, fix, opt **04** pick, rule, seal
**05** aread, arede, go for, judge, opt in
**06** choose, clinch, define, make up,
opt for, select, settle, wrap up
**07** adjudge, arreede, darrain, darrayn,
deraign, discuss, resolve, work out
**08** conclude, darraign, darraine,
plump for **09** arbitrate, darraigne,
determine, establish **10** adjudicate,
dijudicate **11** give a ruling **12** turn the
scale **13** make a decision **14** commit
yourself, give a judgement, make up
your mind, reach a decision **15** come
to a decision

**decided**
**04** ared, firm **05** clear **06** marked
**07** certain, express, obvious

## decidedly

**08** absolute, clear-cut, decisive, definite, distinct, emphatic, positive, resolute **10** deliberate, determined, forthright, pronounced, purposeful, undeniable, undisputed, unswerving, unwavering, well-marked **11** categorical, unambiguous, unequivocal **12** indisputable, unhesitating, unmistakable **14** unquestionable

## decidedly

**04** very **05** quite **07** clearly **08** markedly **09** certainly, downright, obviously **10** absolutely, decisively, definitely, distinctly, noticeably, positively **12** unmistakably **13** unequivocally **14** unquestionably

## decider

**08** clincher **10** determiner **11** coup de grâce

## deciding

**03** key **05** chief, final, prime **06** crunch **07** crucial, supreme **08** critical, decisive **09** principal **10** conclusive **11** determining, influential, significant

## decimate

**05** tithe, tythe **07** destroy, flatten **09** devastate, eliminate, eradicate **10** annihilate, obliterate

## decipher

**04** dope **05** break, crack, solve **06** decode, detect, reveal **07** dope out, make out, suss out, unravel, work out **08** construe **09** figure out, interpret, translate **10** descramble, understand, unscramble **11** make sense of **13** transliterate

## decision

**05** arrêt, award, parti **06** decree, firman, result, ruling **07** finding, opinion, outcome, purpose, resolve, verdict **08** firmness, last word, sentence **09** judgement **10** conclusion, resolution, settlement **11** arbitration **12** adjudication, decisiveness, forcefulness **13** determination, pronouncement **14** recommendation

## decisive

**03** key **04** firm **05** crisp, fatal, final, prime **06** strong **07** crucial, decided, fateful **08** absolute, critical, deciding, definite, forceful, positive, resolute **09** effectual, momentous, principal **10** conclusive, definitive, determined, forthright, purposeful, unswerving, unwavering **11** determinate, determining, influential, significant **12** single-minded, strong-minded

## decisively

**06** firmly **08** strongly **09** crucially, fatefully **10** absolutely, critically, forcefully, positively, resolutely **11** momentously **12** conclusively, definitively, determinedly, forthrightly, purposefully, unswervingly, unwaveringly **13** influentially, significantly **14** single-mindedly

## deck

**02** dk **03** rig, tog **04** pack, prim, trap, trim **05** adorn, array, cover, grace **06** bedeck, betrim, clothe, enrich, ground, tart up **07** festoon, garland, garnish, trick up **08** beautify, covering, decorate, ornament, platform, prettify, trick out **09** embellish

• **deck out 03** rig, tog **04** do up, garb, robe **05** adorn, array, dress, get up, prick **06** clothe, doll up, tart up **07** dress up **08** decorate

## declaim

**04** rant **05** mouth, orate, spiel, spout **06** recite **07** bespout, elocute, lecture **08** disclaim, harangue, perorate, proclaim, sound of **09** hold forth, pronounce, sermonize **11** expostulate, speak boldly

## declamation

**04** rant **06** sermon, speech, tirade **07** address, lecture, oration **08** harangue **10** recitation **12** speechifying

## declamatory

**04** bold **05** stagy **07** fustian, orotund, pompous, stilted **08** dramatic, inflated, parlando **09** bombastic, grandiose, high-flown, overblown **10** discursive, oratorical, rhetorical, theatrical **12** magniloquent **13** grandiloquent

## declaration

**03** dec **04** call, dick, word **05** edict **06** avowal, decree **08** averment **09** affidavit, assertion, assurance, broadcast, manifesto, outgiving, statement, testimony **10** confession, deposition, disclosure, profession, revelation **11** affirmation, attestation, certificate, enunciation **12** announcement, asseveration, confirmation, denunciation, notification, proclamation, promulgation, protestation **13** communication, pronouncement **15** acknowledgement

## declare

**02** go **03** say, vie **04** aver, avow, read, show **05** aread, arede, claim, speak, state, swear **06** affirm, assert, attest, decree, notify, reveal **07** arreede, certify, confess, confirm, discuss, exclaim, express, profess, protest, publish, signify, testify, witness **08** announce, disclose, maintain, manifest, proclaim, set forth, validate **09** broadcast, make known, pronounce **10** asseverate, promulgate **11** communicate

## declared

**04** ared **06** avowed, stated **07** confest **09** confessed, professed

## decline

**03** dip, ebb, rot, sag, set **04** balk, deny, drop, fade, fail, fall, flag, hill, nill, sink, slip, wane, welk **05** abate, avoid, baulk, decay, droop, forgo, lapse, quail, slant, slide, slope, slump, stoop, traik **06** devall, forego, go down, lessen, plunge, recede, reduce, refuse, reject, sunset, waning, weaken, wither, worsen **07** descend, descent, deviate, drop-off, dwindle, evening, failing, failure, fall off, get less, go to pot, incline, plummet, regress, say no to, subside, tail off **08** come down,

decrease, diminish, downturn, fall away, lowering, nosedive, peter out, turn down **09** abatement, catabasis, decadence, decadency, declivity, deviation, downswing, dwindling, lessening, recession, reduction, repudiate, weakening, worsening **10** become less, condescend, de-escalate, degenerate, diminution, divergence, falling-off, go downhill, go to pieces, sunsetting **11** declination, dégringoler, deteriorate **12** de-escalation, degeneration **13** deterioration, retrogression

## decode

**04** dope **05** clear, crack **07** decrypt, dope out, make out, unravel, work out **08** construe, decipher, uncipher **09** figure out, interpret, translate **10** understand, unscramble **13** transliterate

## decomposable

**10** degradable **12** destructible **13** biodegradable **14** decompoundable

## decompose

◊ *anagram indicator* **03** rot **05** decay, go bad, go off, spoil **06** fester **07** break up, crumble, degrade, putrefy **08** dissolve, fragment, pyrolyse, separate **09** break down **10** decompound **12** depolymerize, disintegrate

## decomposition

**03** rot **05** decay **07** rotting **08** going bad, going off **09** perishing, putridity, pyrolysis **10** corruption, hydrolysis, photolysis, radiolysis **11** degradation, dissolution, putrescence **12** electrolysis, fermentation, putrefaction **14** disintegration

## decontaminate

**05** clean, purge **06** purify **07** cleanse **08** fumigate, sanitize **09** disinfect, sterilize

## décor

**07** scenery **10** decoration **11** furnishings **12** colour scheme **13** ornamentation

## decorate

**03** ice **04** cite, deck, do up, hang, pink, trim **05** adorn, array, chase, crown, grace, paint, paper **06** bedaub, bedeck, colour, daiker, enrich, fangle, honour, parget, reward, tart up **07** bedizen, bemedal, deck out, embrave, festoon, furbish, garland, garnish, smarten, trick up **08** beautify, damaskin, ornament, prettify, renovate, spruce up, trick out **09** damascene, damaskeen, damasquin, embellish, guilloche, refurbish, scrimshaw, wallpaper **10** damasceene **12** give a medal to **13** give an award to **14** give an honour to

## decoration

**04** paua, star **05** award, badge, cross, crown, décor, frill, honor, medal, mural, order, title **06** bauble, doodad, doodah, emblem, honour, laurel, parget, ribbon, scroll, wreath **07** bunting, colours, garland, garnish, trinket **08** diamanté, flourish, frou-frou, insignia, ornament, parament, trimming **09** adornment **10** enrichment, Japanesery, knick-knack **11** elaboration, enhancement, furnishings **12** colour scheme **13** embellishment, ornamentation **14** beautification

*See also* **honour; military**

**decorative**
**05** fancy **06** flashy, ornate, pretty, rococo **08** adorning **09** elaborate, enhancing **10** ornamental **11** beautifying, prettifying **12** embellishing **13** non-functional

**decorous**
**03** fit **05** staid **06** comely, decent, modest, polite, proper, sedate, seemly **07** correct, courtly, refined **08** becoming, mannerly, menseful, suitable **09** befitting, dignified **11** appropriate, comme il faut, well-behaved **13** parliamentary

**decorum**
**05** grace **07** decency, dignity, honesty, modesty **08** breeding, courtesy, good form, protocol **09** behaviour, etiquette, propriety, restraint **10** conformity, deportment, politeness, seemliness **11** good manners **14** respectability

**decoy**
**04** bait, draw, lead, lure, tice, tole, toll, trap **05** dummy, piper, roper, shill, snare, stale, stall, tempt **06** allure, bonnet, button, entice, entrap, seduce, trepan **07** attract, deceive, ensnare, pitfall, roper-in **08** inveigle, pretence **09** diversion **10** allurement, attraction, enticement, inducement, red herring, temptation **11** ensnarement, stool pigeon, tame cheater

**decrease**
**03** ebb **04** drop, ease, fall, loss, slim, trim, wane **05** abate, decay, let up, lower, slide, taper, wanze **06** decrew, go down, lessen, plunge, reduce, shrink **07** curtail, cut back, cutback, cut down, decline, dwindle, fall off, plummet, slacken, subside **08** come down, contract, diminish, downturn, lowering, make less, peter out, rollback, slim down, step-down, taper off **09** abatement, decrement, dwindling, lessening, reduction, scale down, shrinkage **10** become less, de-escalate, degression, diminution, falling-off, subsidence **11** contraction **12** de-escalation

**decree**
**03** act, law, saw **04** fiat, rule, will **05** edict, enact, grace, irade, novel, order, ukase, write **06** decern, decide, direct, enjoin, firman, modify, ordain, ruling **07** command, dictate, lay down, mandate, novelle, precept, statute **08** proclaim, psephism, rescript **09** determine, directive, enactment, indiction, interdict, judgement, manifesto, ordinance, prescribe, pronounce, testament **10** regulation **11** hatti-sherif **12** interlocutor, proclamation, promulgation **13** interlocution **14** senatus consult

**decrepit**
**03** old **04** aged, weak **05** frail, warby **06** feeble, infirm, past it **07** elderly, rickety, run-down, worn-out **08** battered, spavined **09** crumbling, doddering, enfeebled, getting on, senescent, tottering **10** broken-down, clapped-out, in bad shape, ramshackle, tumbledown **11** dilapidated, over the hill **12** falling apart **13** falling to bits **14** in bad condition **15** falling to pieces

**decrepitude**
**04** ruin **05** decay **06** dotage, old age **08** debility, senility, weakness **09** infirmity **10** disability, feebleness, incapacity, senescence **11** ricketiness **12** degeneration, dilapidation **13** deterioration **14** incapacitation

**decriminalize**
**05** allow **06** permit, ratify **07** approve, license, warrant **08** legalize, sanction, validate **09** authorize **10** legitimize

**decry**
**03** pan **04** carp, crab, slam **05** blame, knock, slate, snipe **06** attack **07** censure, condemn, devalue, nit-pick, run down, traduce **08** belittle, denounce, derogate **09** criticize, denigrate, disparage, excoriate, underrate **10** animadvert, come down on, depreciate, preach down, undervalue **12** disapprove of, pull to pieces, tear to shreds **13** find fault with, tear a strip off **14** declaim against, inveigh against **15** do a hatchet job on

**dedicate**
**04** bind, give, name, open **05** bless, offer **06** assign, commit, devote, hallow, pledge **07** address, devoted, present **08** inscribe, make holy, sanctify, set apart **09** sacrifice, surrender **10** consecrate, give over to, inaugurate

**dedicated**
**06** oblate **07** bespoke, devoted, sold out, staunch, zealous **08** diligent **09** committed, sold out on **10** customized, purposeful **11** custom-built, given over to, hard working, industrious **12** card-carrying, enthusiastic, single-minded, wholehearted **13** dyed-in-the-wool, single-hearted

**dedication**
**04** wake, zeal **07** address, loyalty **08** blessing, devotion **09** adherence, hallowing **10** allegiance, attachment, commitment, enthusiasm **11** benediction, inscription **12** consecration, faithfulness, presentation **13** self-sacrifice **14** sanctification

**deduce**
**04** dope, draw, suss **05** glean, infer **06** derive, gather, reason **07** dope out, surmise, work out **08** conclude **09** figure out, syllogize **10** understand

**deduct**
**04** dock **06** deduce, reduce, remove, weaken **07** take off **08** knock off, reduce by, separate, subtract, take away, take from, withdraw **09** strike off **10** decrease by

**deduction**
**04** dock **06** result **07** finding, removal, reprise **08** decrease, discount **09** abatement, allowance, corollary, inference, reasoning, reduction, surmising, taking off **10** assumption, conclusion, consectary, diminution, hypothesis, taking away, withdrawal **11** consequence, presumption, subtraction **12** off-reckoning
• **clear of deductions 03** net **04** nett

**deed**
**03** act **04** fact, feat, work **05** issue, starr, title, truth **06** action, escrow, factum, record **07** charter, exploit, reality **08** activity, contract, document, mortgage, valiance, valiancy **09** actuality, agreement, endeavour, indenture, quitclaim, specialty **10** attainment, backletter, bill of sale **11** achievement, disposition, enfeoffment, infeudation, performance, transaction, undertaking **14** accomplishment

**deem**
**03** see **04** hold **05** judge, think **06** esteem, reckon, regard **07** account, adjudge, believe, imagine, opinion, suppose **08** conceive, consider, estimate

**deep**
**03** far, low, sea **04** bass, dark, full, lost, main, rapt, rich, warm, wise **05** briny, grave, ocean, quiet, sound, thick, vivid **06** arcane, ardent, astute, clever, gaping, intent, severe, strong **07** abysmal, abyssal, booming, cunning, earnest, extreme, faraway, fervent, glowing, intense, learned, obscure, serious, yawning **08** absorbed, abstruse, a long way, esoteric, high seas, immersed, powerful, profound, reserved, resonant, sonorous, the drink, vigorous **09** brilliant, cavernous, difficult, engrossed, excessive, full-toned, heart-felt, intensely, recondite, sagacious, unplumbed, very great **10** bottomless, discerning, fathomless, low-pitched, mysterious, passionate, perceptive, profoundly, resounding, unfathomed **11** deep as a well, impassioned, preoccupied, uncrossable **12** immeasurable, intellectual, wholehearted **13** knowledgeable, perspicacious **14** a great distance

**deepen**
**04** grow **06** bump up, dig out, extend, hike up, hollow, step up, worsen **07** build up, magnify **08** excavate, get worse, heighten, increase, mushroom, scoop out **09** intensify, reinforce, scrape out **10** strengthen **11** deteriorate

**deeply**
**04** upsy **05** sadly, upsee, upsey **06** keenly **07** acutely, gravely, greatly, sharply **08** ardently, movingly, severely, strongly, very much **09** earnestly, extremely, feelingly,

fervently, intensely, seriously
**10** completely, mournfully,
profoundly, thoroughly, to the quick,
vigorously **12** passionately
**13** distressingly

## deep-seated

**04** deep **05** fixed **07** chronic, settled
**08** intimate, Plutonic, profound
**09** confirmed, ingrained **10** deep-
rooted, entrenched **11** fundamental

## deer

**03** doe **04** buck, fawn, hart, hind, spay,
stag **05** Bambi, spade, spayd **06** cervid,
rascal, spayad **07** pricket, spitter
**08** staggard

*Deer include:*

**03** elk, hog, red, roe
**04** axis, mule, musk, pudu, rusa, sika
**05** moose, water
**06** chital, fallow, forest, sambar,
   sambur, tufted, wapiti
**07** barking, brocket, caribou,
   jumping, muntjac, muntjak
**08** cariacou, carjacou, Irish elk,
   reindeer, Virginia
**09** barasinga
**10** barasingha, chevrotain, Père
   David's
**11** black-tailed, white-tailed
**12** Chinese water, Indian sambar
**13** Indian muntjac

## deface

◊ *head deletion indicator* **03** mar **04** ruin
**05** spoil, sully **06** damage, defame,
deform, impair, injure **07** blemish,
destroy, tarnish **08** mutilate
**09** disfigure, vandalize **10** disfeature,
obliterate

## de facto

**04** real **06** actual, in fact, really
**08** actually, existing, in effect **10** in
practice

## defamation

**04** slur **05** libel, smear **07** calumny,
obloquy, scandal, slander
**08** innuendo, slamming **09** aspersion
**10** backbiting, derogation, opprobrium
**11** badmouthing, denigration,
malediction, mud-slinging, slagging-
off, traducement **12** vilification
**13** disparagement, smear campaign

## defamatory

**09** aspersory, injurious, insulting,
libellous, vilifying **10** calumnious,
derogatory, pejorative, scandalous,
scurrilous, slanderous **11** denigrating,
disparaging, maledictory, mud-
slinging **12** contumelious

## defame

**04** slag, slam **05** cloud, libel, smear
**06** deface, infame, infamy, malign,
vilify **07** asperse, blacken, blemish,
detract, run down, scandal, slag off,
slander, traduce **08** badmouth,
besmirch, disgrace, infamize
**09** bespatter, denigrate, discredit,
dishonour, disparage **10** calumniate,
sling mud at, stigmatize, throw mud at,
vituperate **11** speak evil of **14** cast
aspersions

## default

**04** fail, lack, loss, want **05** dodge,
evade, fault, lapse **06** defect
**07** absence, defraud, failing, failure,
neglect, offence, swindle **08** omission
**09** backslide **10** deficiency,
negligence, non-payment
**11** dereliction

## defaulter

**04** duck **08** absentee, lame duck, non-
payer, offender **11** non-appearer

## defeat

**03** gub, lam, war **04** balk, beat, best,
drub, foil, kill, lick, loss, rout, ruin,
tank, tonk, undo, whip **05** annul,
block, crush, excel, paste, quell, repel,
smash, stump, throw, thump, worst
**06** baffle, granny, hammer, outwit,
puzzle, reject, subdue, thrash, thwart
**07** beating, clobber, conquer, debacle,
eclipse, failure, inch out, outplay,
pasting, perplex, reverse, setback,
surpass, tanking, trounce **08** confound,
conquest, crushing, downfall,
drubbing, obstruct, outmatch,
outscore, outsmart, overcome,
squabash, throw out, vanquish,
Waterloo, whipping, whupping
**09** breakdown, checkmate, defeature,
devastate, discomfit, disfigure,
frustrate, marmelize, overmatch,
overpower, overthrow, overwhelm,
pulverize, rejection, repulsion, shoot
down, slaughter, smackdown,
subjugate, thrashing, thwarting,
trouncing **10** annihilate, defeasance,
disappoint, disconcert, overcoming
**11** frustration, subjugation
**12** annihilation, pip at the post,
vanquishment **13** have the edge on,
put to the worse, run rings round
**14** disappointment, get the better of
**15** make mincemeat of

## defeatist

**06** gloomy **07** quitter, yielder
**08** helpless, hopeless, negative,
resigned **09** doomsayer, pessimist
**10** despairing, despondent, fatalistic
**11** doomwatcher, pessimistic
**13** prophet of doom

## defecate

**03** poo **04** mute, plop, poop **05** egest
**07** excrete, scumber, skummer
**08** evacuate **11** do number two, pass a
motion **12** cover the feet, ease yourself
**13** void excrement **14** do your
business, move your bowels **15** empty
your bowels, relieve yourself

## defect

**03** bug **04** flaw, lack, snag, spot, want
**05** craze, error, fault, rebel, taint
**06** desert, hiatus, renege, revolt,
wreath **07** abandon, abscond,
absence, blemish, default, demerit,
failing, frailty, mistake **08** hamartia,
omission, psellism, weakness, weak
spot **09** deformity, shortfall
**10** apostatize, break faith, deficience,
deficiency, inadequacy **11** change
sides, jump the dyke, loup the dyke,
shortcoming, turn traitor
**12** imperfection, tergiversate

## defection

**06** mutiny, revolt **07** perfidy, treason
**08** apostasy, betrayal **09** breakaway,
desertion, rebellion **10** absconding,
disloyalty, renegation
**11** abandonment, backsliding,
defalcation, dereliction
**14** tergiversation

## defective

◊ *anagram indicator* **04** bust, duff
**05** kaput, trick, wrong **06** broken,
faulty, flawed **08** abnormal
**09** deficient, imperfect **10** on the blink,
on the fritz, out of order **11** in disrepair
**12** insufficient **14** malfunctioning

## defector

**03** rat **05** Judas, rebel **07** traitor
**08** apostate, betrayer, deserter,
mutineer, quisling, recreant, renegade,
turncoat **10** backslider **13** tergiversator

## defence

**04** army, case, keep, navy, plea, wall
**05** alibi, cover, guard **06** excuse,
screen, shield, troops **07** apology,
bastion, bulwark, outpost, rampart,
shelter, weapons **08** advocacy, air
force, apologia, argument, buttress,
fortress, garrison, immunity, military,
munition, pleading, security, soldiers,
weaponry **09** armaments, barricade,
deterrent, safeguard, testimony
**10** apologetic, deterrence, munifience,
protection, resistance, stronghold
**11** armed forces, exoneration,
explanation, explication, extenuation,
vindication **12** propugnation
**13** fortification, justification
• **air defence** **02** AD
*See also* **fortification**

## defenceless

**04** weak **05** naked, silly **07** exposed,
unarmed **08** helpless, impotent
**09** guardless, powerless, unguarded
**10** undefended, vulnerable
**11** susceptible, unprotected **12** open to
attack

## defend

**04** back, fend, hold **05** cover, deter,
guard, plead **06** assert, forbid, oppose,
resist, screen, secure, shield, uphold
**07** bolster, bulwark, contest, endorse,
enguard, explain, fortify, justify,
protect, shelter, stand by, support,
warrant **08** argue for, bestride, buttress,
champion, garrison, maintain,
preserve, prohibit **09** barricade,
exonerate, safeguard, vindicate, watch
over, withstand **10** go to bat for, speak
up for, stand up for, stick up for
**12** keep from harm, make a case for
**15** fight your corner, stand your corner

## defendant

**03** def, dft **07** accused **08** litigant,
offender, prisoner **09** appellant
**10** respondent

## defender

**04** back **05** guard **06** backer, keeper,
patron **07** bastion, counsel, sponsor,
warrant **08** advocate, asserter, assertor,
champion, endorser, guardian,
upholder **09** apologist, bodyguard,

**defensible**

defendant, preserver, promachos, protector, supporter **10** vindicator

**defensible**

**04** safe **05** valid **06** secure **07** tenable **08** arguable **09** plausible **10** pardonable, vindicable **11** impregnable, justifiable, permissible **12** maintainable, unassailable

**defensive**

**04** wary **08** cautious, opposing, watchful **09** defending **10** apologetic, protecting, protective **12** safeguarding **13** Maginot-minded, oversensitive, self-defensive **14** self-justifying
• **defensive ring 04** laer **06** corral, laager

**defer**

**03** bow **05** delay, kotow, waive, yield **06** accede, comply, give in, kowtow, put off, shelve, submit **07** adjourn, give way, put back, rejourn, respect, suspend **08** hold over, postpone, prorogue, protract, put on ice, roll over **09** acquiesce, surrender **10** capitulate **13** procrastinate

**deference**

**04** duty **06** esteem, honour, regard **07** respect **08** civility, courtesy, yielding **09** obedience, reverence, servility **10** compliance, politeness, submission **12** acquiescence **13** attentiveness, consideration **14** respectfulness, submissiveness, thoughtfulness

**deferential**

**05** civil **06** humble, polite **07** dutiful **08** obeisant, reverent **09** attentive, courteous, regardful **10** morigerous, obsequious, respectful **11** complaisant, reverential **12** ingratiating

**deferment**

**04** stay **05** delay **07** waiving **08** deferral, shelving **10** moratorium, putting-off, suspension **11** adjournment, holding-over, prorogation **12** postponement **15** procrastination

**defiance**

**08** contempt **09** challenge, contumacy, disregard, insolence **10** opposition, resistance, truculence **12** disobedience **13** confrontation, recalcitrance **14** rebelliousness **15** insubordination
• **expression of defiance 03** yah **04** nuts **05** ya-boo **06** yah-boo **10** ya-boo sucks **11** yah-boo sucks

**defiant**

**04** bold **08** insolent, militant, roisting, roysting, scornful **09** obstinate, resistant, truculent **10** aggressive, rebellious, refractory **11** challenging, disobedient, provocative **12** antagonistic, contemptuous, contumacious, intransigent, recalcitrant **13** insubordinate, unco-operative

**defiantly**

**05** acock **06** boldly **10** insolently, militantly, scornfully **11** obstinately, truculently **12** aggressively, rebelliously **13** disobediently, provocatively **14** contemptuously,

contumaciously, intransigently, recalcitrantly **15** insubordinately, unco-operatively

**deficiency**

**04** flaw, lack, want **05** fault, minus **06** dearth, defect, shorts **07** absence, deficit, failing, frailty, poverty, wantage **08** scarcity, shortage, weakness **10** inadequacy, scantiness **11** shortcoming **12** imperfection **13** insufficiency

---

*Deficiencies include:*

---

**07** acapnia, amentia, hypoxia **09** cytopenia, hypinosis, hypoxemia, oligaemia, spanaemia **10** hypoxaemia **11** hypospadias, sideropenia **14** leucocytopenia, oligocythaemia

**deficient**

◇ *anagram indicator* **03** low **04** poor, weak **05** minus, scant, short **06** meagre, scanty, scarce, skimpy **07** lacking, wanting **08** bankrupt, exiguous, inferior **09** imperfect **10** defectible, inadequate, incomplete **12** insufficient **14** unsatisfactory

**deficit**

**04** lack, loss **07** arrears, default **08** shortage **09** shortfall **10** deficiency

**defile**

◇ *anagram indicator* **03** col, ray **04** file, gate, moil, pass, soil **05** dirty, gorge, gully, halse, hause, hawse, spoil, stain, sully, taint **06** debase, defame, defoul, enseam, infect, ravine, valley **07** blacken, corrupt, degrade, passage, pollute, profane, tarnish, violate, vitiate **08** disgrace, maculate **09** denigrate, desecrate, dishonour, inquinate **10** make impure **11** contaminate, make unclean

**defilement**

**04** moil **08** foulness, impurity, staining, sullying, tainting, tainture **09** pollution, profanity, violation **10** debasement, defamation, tarnishing **11** degradation, denigration, desecration **13** conspurcation, contamination

**definable**

**05** exact, fixed **07** precise **08** definite, specific **10** explicable **11** describable, perceptible **12** determinable, identifiable **13** ascertainable

**define**

**03** fix **05** bound, limit **06** decide, detail **07** clarify, delimit, explain, expound, mark out, pin down, specify **08** describe, pinpoint, spell out **09** delineate, demarcate, designate, determine, elucidate, establish, interpret **12** characterize, circumscribe

**definite**

**04** firm, hard, sure **05** clear, exact, fixed **06** marked **07** assured, certain, decided, obvious, precise, settled **08** clear-cut, distinct, explicit, positive, specific **10** determined, guaranteed, noticeable, particular **12** unmistakable

**definitely**

**06** easily, I'll say!, indeed, surely **07** clearly, for sure, plainly **09** certainly, doubtless, expressly, no denying, obviously, out-and-out **10** absolutely, distinctly, in terminis, positively, undeniably **11** indubitably, undoubtedly **12** unmistakably, without doubt **13** categorically, determinately, unmistakeably **14** unquestionably **15** without question

**definition**

**03** def **05** focus, sense **07** clarity, diorism, meaning **08** contrast **09** clearness, precision, sharpness **10** denotation, exposition, visibility **11** description, elucidation, explanation **12** distinctness, significance **13** clarification, determination **14** interpretation

**definitive**

**05** exact, final **07** classic, correct, perfect **08** absolute, complete, decisive, positive, reliable, standard, ultimate **09** classical **10** conclusive, exhaustive **11** categorical, terminative **13** authoritative

**definitively**

**07** finally **10** absolutely, completely, decisively **12** conclusively **13** categorically **15** authoritatively

**deflate**

**04** dash, slow, void **05** empty, lower **06** debunk, humble, lessen, reduce, shrink, squash, subdue **07** chasten, depress, devalue, exhaust, flatten, let down, mortify, put down, squeeze **08** collapse, contract, decrease, diminish, dispirit, puncture, slow down **09** humiliate **10** depreciate, disappoint, disconcert

**deflect**

**04** bend, draw, turn, veer, wind **05** avert, drift, snick, twist **06** glance, swerve **07** deviate, diverge, head off, refract **08** ricochet, withdraw **09** glance off, sidetrack, turn aside **12** change course

**deflection**

**04** bend, veer **05** drift, snick, throw **06** swerve **07** turning **08** ricochet, twisting **09** deviation, diversion **10** aberration, divergence, refraction **11** glancing-off **12** sidetracking, turning aside **14** changing course

**deflower**

**03** mar **04** harm, rape, ruin **05** force, spoil **06** defile, molest, ravish, seduce **07** assault, despoil, violate **09** deflorate, desecrate

**deform**

◇ *anagram indicator* **03** mar **04** maim, ruin, warp **05** spoil, twist **06** buckle, damage, deface **07** contort, distort, hideous, malform, pervert **08** misshape, mutilate **09** disfigure, unshapely

**deformation**

**04** bend, warp **05** curve, twist **06** buckle **08** twisting **10** cataclasis, contortion, defacement, distortion,

mutilation **11** compression
**12** diastrophism, malformation
**13** disfiguration, misshapenness

**deformed**
◇ *anagram indicator* **04** bent **06** camsho,
inform, maimed, marred, ruined,
warped **07** buckled, crooked, defaced,
dismayd, gnarled, mangled, misborn,
mishapt, twisted **08** camshoch,
crippled **09** camsheugh, contorted,
corrupted, distorted, malformed,
miscreate, misshaped, misshapen,
mutilated, perverted **10** disfigured,
miscreated, out of shape

**deformity**
**06** defect **08** claw-foot, misshape,
ugliness, vileness **09** grossness
**10** corruption, defacement, distortion,
misfeature, perversion **11** abnormality,
contracture, crookedness, monstrosity
**12** imperfection, irregularity,
malformation **13** disfigurement,
misproportion, misshapenness

**defraud**
**02** do **03** con, rob **04** dupe, fool, nick,
rook, rush, swiz **05** cheat, cozen,
lurch, mulct, screw, sting, trick, wrong
**06** delude, diddle, fiddle, fleece,
outwit, rip off **07** beguile, deceive,
mislead, swindle, swizzle
**08** embezzle, hoodwink

**defray**
**03** pay **04** meet **05** cover, repay
**06** refund, settle, square **07** appease,
satisfy **09** discharge, reimburse
**10** recompense

**defrost**
**04** melt, thaw **08** defreeze

**deft**
**04** able, feat, neat **05** adept, agile,
handy, natty, nifty, quick **06** adroit,
clever, expert, nimble **07** skilful
**09** dexterous **10** proficient

**deftly**
**04** ably **05** slick **06** neatly, nimbly
**07** adeptly **08** cleverly, expertly
**09** skilfully **12** proficiently

**defunct**
**04** dead, gone **05** passé **06** bygone,
unused **07** disused, expired, extinct,
invalid **08** deceased, departed,
finished, obsolete, outmoded
**11** inoperative

**defuse**
◇ *anagram indicator* **04** calm, cool
**06** disarm **07** disable, quieten, relieve
**08** calm down, cool down, disorder
**09** alleviate **10** deactivate, immobilize
**11** clear the air

**defy**
**04** dare, face, foil, mock **05** avoid,
beard, brave, elude, flout, repel, scorn,
spurn **06** baffle, defeat, ignore, resist,
slight, thwart **07** despise, discard,
dislike, disobey, outdare, provoke
**08** confront **09** challenge, disregard,
frustrate, stand up to, withstand
**10** disrespect **12** rebel against **14** fly in
the face of

**degeneracy**
**08** vileness **09** decadence
**10** corruption, debasement,
debauchery, effeteness, fallenness,
immorality, perversion, sinfulness,
wickedness **11** degradation,
depravation **12** degeneration
**13** deterioration, dissoluteness

**degenerate**
**03** low, rot **04** base, fail, mean, rake,
roué, sink, slip, vile **05** decay, knave,
lapse, rogue, scamp **06** effete, fallen,
rascal, recoil, sinful, sinner, wicked,
worsen, wretch **07** corrupt, dastard,
debased, decline, fall off, go to pot,
ignoble, immoral, regress, villain
**08** criminal, decadent, decrease,
degender, degraded, depraved,
derogate, evildoer, vagabond
**09** abandoned, debauched, dissolute,
miscreant, perverted, reprobate,
scallywag, scoundrel, wrongdoer
**10** bastardize, go downhill, ne'er-do-
well, profligate **11** degenerated,
deteriorate, off the rails
**12** deteriorated, troublemaker
**13** mischief-maker **14** go down the
tubes

**degeneration**
**03** rot **04** drop, slip **05** decay, lapse,
slide **06** dry rot **07** atrophy, decline,
failure, sinking **08** decrease
**09** caseation, steatosis, worsening
**10** debasement, falling-off, involution,
regression, retrogress **11** degradation
**13** deterioration

**degradation**
**05** shame **07** decline **08** comedown,
demotion, disgrace, ignominy,
vileness **09** abasement, decadence,
demission, dishonour **10** corruption,
culvertage, debasement, debauchery,
degeneracy, fallenness, immorality,
perversion, sinfulness, wickedness
**11** depravation, downgrading,
humiliation **12** degeneration,
immiseration **13** decomposition,
deterioration, dissoluteness,
mortification **14** immiserization

**degrade**
**04** sink **05** abase, erode, lower, shame,
sully **06** debase, defile, demean,
demote, depose, embace, embase,
humble, imbase, impair, reduce,
unseat, weaken **07** cashier, cheapen,
corrupt, declass, deprive, devalue,
drum out, embrute, imbrute, mortify,
pervert, put down **08** belittle, diminish,
disgrace, dishonor, relegate
**09** brutalize, decompose, discredit,
dishonour, downgrade, humiliate
**10** adulterate, disennoble, prostitute
**11** deteriorate, lower in rank **12** reduce
in rank

**degrading**
**04** base **07** ignoble **08** debasing,
lowering, shameful, unworthy
**09** demeaning **10** belittling,
cheapening, mortifying **11** disgraceful,
humiliating, undignified
**12** contemptible, discrediting
**13** dishonourable

**degree**
**01** d **02** BA, MA **03** deg, pin **04** mark,
rank, rate, rung, step, unit **05** class,
first, grade, level, limit, order, point,
range, stage, third **06** amount, extent,
second, status **07** Desmond, measure
**08** position, standard, standing,
strength **09** intensity **11** double first
**13** baccalaureate
*See also* **qualification**
• **in a high degree** **02** so **03** far
**04** much, very **05** great
• **in a lower degree** **04** less
• **in whatever degree** **02** as

**dehydrate**
**03** dry **05** drain, dry up, parch **06** dry
out **09** desiccate, evaporate, exsiccate,
lose water **10** effloresce

**dehydration**
**06** drying **08** parching **11** desiccation,
evaporation **13** dehumidifying
• **treatment for dehydration** **03** ORT

**deification**
**07** worship **08** revering **09** elevation,
extolling, reverence **10** apotheosis,
exaltation, veneration
**11** ennoblement, idolization
**12** divinization, idealization
**13** glorification **14** divinification
**15** immortalization

**deify**
**03** god **05** exalt, extol **06** revere
**07** elevate, ennoble, glorify, idolize,
worship **08** idealize, venerate
**10** aggrandize **11** immortalize

**deign**
**05** daine, stoop **07** consent
**10** condescend **13** lower yourself
**14** demean yourself

**deity**
**03** god **04** idol **05** numen, power
**06** avatar, heaven, spirit **07** demigod,
eternal, goddess, godhead, godhood
**08** divinity, immortal, numinous
**10** genius loci **11** divine being
**12** supreme being
*See also* **God; god, goddess**

**dejected**
**03** low, sad **04** blue, down, flat, glum
**05** amort **06** abattu, bummed, dismal,
gloomy, morose **07** alamort, crushed,
doleful, subdued **08** cast down,
downcast, wretched **09** depressed,
jaw-fallen, miserable, sorrowful
**10** chopfallen, despondent, dispirited,
melancholy, spiritless **11** crestfallen,
demoralized, discouraged,
downhearted, melancholic
**12** disconsolate, disheartened **14** down
in the dumps

**dejectedly**
**05** sadly **06** glumly **08** dismally,
gloomily, morosely **09** miserably
**10** wretchedly **12** despondently
**14** disconsolately

**dejection**
**04** crab **05** blues, dumps, gloom
**06** misery, sorrow **07** despair, sadness
**09** faintness **10** depression, gloominess,
low spirits, melancholy, moroseness
**11** despondence, despondency,

**de jure**

dolefulness, melancholia, unhappiness **12** wretchedness **14** disconsolation, discouragement, dispiritedness **15** downheartedness

**de jure**
**05** legal **07** legally **08** rightful **10** rightfully

**Delaware**
**02** DE **03** Del

**delay**
**03** lag, let **04** halt, keep, lull, mora, slow, stay, stop, wait **05** check, dally, defer, frist, sit on, stall, stave, tarry **06** dawdle, detain, dilute, dither, hamper, hang on, hinder, hold up, hold-up, impede, linger, loiter, put off, retard, shelve, temper, weaken **07** adjourn, forsloe, forslow, put back, respite, set back, setback, suspend, waiving **08** dawdling, foreslow, hang fire, hesitate, hold back, hold over, interval, obstruct, postpone, put on ice, reprieve, restrain, shelving, stalling, stoppage, tarrying **09** dalliance, deferment, demurrage, detaining, detention, faff about, hesitance, hesitancy, hindrance, lag behind, lingering, loitering, stonewall, tarriance **10** cunctation, dilly-dally, filibuster, hesitation, impediment, moratorium, putting-off, suspension **11** adjournment, holding-over, obstruction, retardation **12** interruption, postponement **13** dilly-dallying, procrastinate **15** procrastination

**delayed**
**04** late **08** retarded

**delectable**
**05** tasty, yummy **06** dainty, lovely **07** savoury **08** adorable, charming, engaging, exciting, luscious, pleasant, pleasing **09** agreeable, beautiful, delicious, palatable, succulent **10** appetizing, attractive, delightful, enchanting **11** flavoursome, scrumptious **13** mouthwatering

**delectation**
**06** relish **07** comfort, delight **08** pleasure **09** amusement, diversion, enjoyment, happiness **11** contentment, refreshment **12** satisfaction **13** entertainment, gratification

**delegate**
**03** del **04** give, name **05** agent, envoy, leave, proxy, vicar **06** assign, charge, commit, depute, deputy, legate, ordain, pass on, second, syndic **07** appoint, consign, deputed, devolve, empower, entrust **08** emissary, hand over, nominate, pass over **09** authorize, designate, messenger, secondary, spokesman **10** ambassador, amphictyon, commission, substitute **11** spokeswoman **12** commissioner, spokesperson **14** representative

**delegation**
**07** embassy, mission **08** legation **09** committal, passing on **10** assignment, commission, contingent, deputation, devolution,

entrusting **11** consignment, empowerment, passing over **12** substitution, transference **15** representatives

**delete**
**01** d **03** cut **04** dele, edit **05** erase **06** cancel, cut out, efface, excise, remove, rub out, strike **07** blot out, destroy, edit out, expunge, scratch, take out **08** cross out, white out **09** strike out **10** blue-pencil, obliterate

**deleterious**
**03** bad **07** harmful, hurtful, noxious, ruinous **08** damaging **09** injurious, poisonous, predatory **10** pernicious **11** destructive, detrimental, prejudicial

**deliberate**
**03** set **04** muse, slow **05** think, voulu, weigh **06** advise, debate, ponder, steady, wilful, willed **07** advised, careful, consult, discuss, heedful, knowing, planned, prudent, reflect, studied, weigh up, willful, witting **08** cautious, cogitate, consider, designed, evaluate, measured, meditate, mull over, propense, resolute, ruminate, studious, volitive **09** conscious, leisurely, ponderous, think over, unhurried **10** calculated, considered, excogitate, methodical, preplanned, think about, thoughtful, unwavering **11** circumspect, considerate, intentional, prearranged **12** preconceived, premeditated, professional, unhesitating

**deliberately**
**06** slowly **08** by design, steadily, wilfully **09** carefully, knowingly, on purpose, pointedly, prudently, wittingly **10** cautiously, studiously **11** consciously, in cold blood, ponderously, unhurriedly **12** methodically, thoughtfully **13** calculatingly, circumspectly, coldbloodedly, intentionally

**deliberation**
**04** care **05** study **06** debate, musing **07** caution, counsel, mulling, thought **08** brooding, calmness, coolness, prudence, slowness **09** pondering **10** advisement, cogitation, conferring, discussion, evaluation, excogitate, meditation, reflection, rumination, steadiness, weighing-up **11** calculation, carefulness, forethought **12** consultation **13** consideration, unhurriedness **14** circumspection, thoughtfulness

**delicacy**
**04** care, cate, tact **05** goody, taste, treat **06** dainty, delice, junket, luxury, nicety, relish, sunket, tidbit, titbit **07** finesse, savoury, trinket **08** elegance, fineness, kickshaw, niceness, subtlety, weakness **09** diplomacy, fragility, kickshaws, lightness, precision, sweetmeat **10** daintiness, discretion, morbidezza, refinement, speciality, tenderness **11** bonne-bouche, sensitivity **12** niminy-piminy **13** consideration,

exquisiteness, luxuriousness **14** discrimination

**delicate**
**04** fine, mild, nesh, nice, pale, soft, weak **05** bland, dorty, elfin, exact, faint, fairy, frail, light, muted **06** ailing, dainty, flimsy, friand, gentle, incony, infirm, luxury, pastel, polite, sickly, slight, subtle, tender, touchy, tricky, unwell **07** awkward, band-box, brittle, careful, elegant, fragile, friande, inconie, precise, subdued, tactful **08** accurate, critical, delicacy, discreet, graceful, hothouse, kid-glove, ladylike **09** airy-fairy, breakable, difficult, exquisite, fairylike, fingertip, frangible, luxurious, precision, sensitive **10** diaphanous, diplomatic, fastidious **11** considerate, debilitated, problematic **12** easily broken, in poor health, niminy-piminy, softly-softly **13** controversial, easily damaged, insubstantial

**delicately**
**06** finely, gently, mildly, palely, softly, subtly **07** blandly, faintly **08** daintily **09** carefully, elegantly, tactfully **10** critically, gracefully **11** exquisitely, sensitively **14** diplomatically

**delicious**
**04** good **05** juicy, tasty, yummy **06** choice, delish, morish **07** moreish, savoury, scrummy **08** charming, pleasant, pleasing, tempting **09** agreeable, ambrosial, enjoyable, exquisite, palatable, succulent, toothsome **10** appetizing, delectable, delightful, enchanting, goloptious, goluptious, gratifying, nectareous **11** captivating, fascinating, lip-smacking, pleasurable, scrumptious **12** entertaining **13** mouth-watering

**delight**
**03** joy **04** fain, glee, like, love, rape **05** amuse, bliss, charm, cheer, enjoy, feast, mirth **06** delice, excite, please, ravish, relish, savour, thrill, tickle **07** boast of, ecstasy, elation, enchant, gladden, glory in, gratify, rapture, revel in **08** bowl over, entrance, euphoria, felicity, gladness, pleasure, wallow in **09** amusement, captivate, enjoyment, enrapture, entertain, happiness, transport **10** appreciate, exultation, jubilation, tickle pink **11** contentment, delectation, take pride in **13** entertainment, gratification **14** take pleasure in **15** give enjoyment to

**delighted**
**04** glad **05** happy **06** elated, joyful, joyous, made up, stoked **07** charmed, excited, gleeful, pleased **08** ecstatic, euphoric, jubilant, thrilled **09** enchanted, entranced, gratified, overjoyed **10** captivated, enraptured **11** over the moon, tickled pink **12** happy as Larry **14** pleased as Punch **15** happy as a sandboy

**delightful**
**03** ace **04** nice **05** great, magic, super, sweet **06** divine, groovy, lovely, wizard **07** amusing, darling, the tops

**08** charming, engaging, exciting, glorious, luscious, pleasant, pleasing **09** agreeable, appealing, beautiful, diverting, enjoyable, ravishing, thrilling **10** attractive, delectable, enchanting, entrancing, felicitous, gratifying **11** captivating, fascinating, pleasurable, scrumptious **12** entertaining **14** out of this world
• **something delightful 03** gas

**delimit**
**03** fix, set **04** mark **05** bound **06** define **09** demarcate, determine, establish

**delineate**
**03** fix **04** draw, line, mark **05** bound, chart, stell, trace **06** define, depict, design, render, sketch **07** outline, portray **08** describe, set forth **09** determine, establish, represent

**delineation**
**06** sketch **07** tracing **09** depiction, portrayal, rendering **11** description, presentment **14** representation

**delinquency**
**05** crime, fault **07** misdeed, offence **10** misconduct, wrongdoing **11** criminality, lawbreaking **12** misbehaviour, misdemeanour **13** transgression

**delinquent**
**03** ned, ted **06** bodgie, guilty, remiss, vandal, widgie **07** culprit, lawless, ruffian **08** criminal, culpable, hooligan, offender **09** miscreant, negligent, offending, wrongdoer **10** lawbreaker, malefactor **11** Halbstarker, lawbreaking **13** young offender

**delirious**
◇ anagram indicator **03** mad **04** gone, wild **05** crazy, light **06** elated, insane, raving **07** frantic **08** babbling, demented, deranged, ecstatic, euphoric, frenetic, frenzied, jubilant, rambling, unhinged **09** overjoyed, phrenetic, rapturous, spaced out, wandering **10** hysterical, incoherent, irrational **11** carried away, light-headed, over the moon **13** out of your mind **14** beside yourself

**deliriously**
◇ anagram indicator **10** jubilantly **11** rapturously **12** ecstatically, hysterically

**delirium**
**03** joy **05** fever **06** frenzy, lunacy, raving **07** ecstasy, elation, jimjams, madness, passion, rapture **08** dementia, euphoria, hysteria, insanity, wildness **09** craziness, phrenesis **10** excitement, jubilation **11** derangement, incoherence **13** hallucination, irrationality
• **delirium tremens 03** DTs **05** jumps **07** jimjams **09** Joe Blakes **10** the horrors **11** the dingbats

**deliver**
**02** do **03** aim, rid **04** bowl, cede, deal, free, give, hand, make, save, send, take **05** bring, carry, grant, serve, speak, utter, voice, yield **06** commit, convey, direct, fulfil, launch, nimble,

ransom, redeem, render, rescue, strike, supply **07** declare, entrust, express, give out, inflict, manumit, present, provide, release, set free **08** announce, carry out, dispatch, hand over, liberate, live up to, proclaim, transfer, turn over **09** enunciate, implement, pronounce, surrender **10** administer, distribute, emancipate, relinquish **11** give voice to **15** help give birth to

**deliverance**
**06** escape, ransom, rescue **07** freedom, release **08** riddance **09** salvation **10** liberation, redemption **11** extrication **12** emancipation

**deliveries**
**04** over

**delivery**
**04** ball, dlvy, load **05** batch, birth **06** labour, speech, supply **07** travail **08** carriage, dispatch, shipment, transfer **09** elocution, transport, utterance **10** childbirth, conveyance, intonation **11** confinement, consignment, enunciation, parturition **12** accouchement, articulation, distribution, transmission **13** pronunciation **14** transportation

*Cricket deliveries include:*

**06** doosra, googly, teesra, yorker **07** bouncer, swinger **08** Chinaman, fastball, leg break, off break **09** inswinger, leg-cutter, off-cutter **10** outswinger **11** daisy-cutter

• **deliveries 04** over

**dell**
**04** dale, dean, hole, vale **05** slade, trull **06** dargle, dimble, dingle, hollow, valley **10** prostitute

**delta**
**01** D

**delude**
**03** kid **04** dupe, fool, hoax **05** blend, cheat, elude, kiddy, trick **06** cajole, have on, lead on, take in **07** beguile, deceive, mislead, two-time **08** hoodwink, misguide **09** bamboozle, misinform **11** double-cross **12** take for a ride **14** pull a fast one on, put the change on

**deluge**
**04** rush, soak, wave **05** drown, flood, spate, swamp **06** drench, engulf **07** barrage, torrent **08** downpour, inundate, submerge **09** avalanche, overwhelm, snow under **10** inundation **11** overflowing

**delusion**
**05** error, fancy **07** fallacy **08** illusion, tricking **09** deception, misbelief **11** false belief **13** hallucination, misconception **14** misinformation **15** false impression, misapprehension

**de luxe, deluxe**
**04** fine, rich **05** grand, plush, pluty, swish **06** choice, costly, lavish, luxury, select **07** elegant, opulent, quality,

special **08** palatial, splendid, superior **09** exclusive, expensive, luxurious, sumptuous

**delve**
**04** cave, hole, poke, root **05** probe **06** burrow, go into, hollow, hunt in, search **07** dig into, examine, explore, ransack, rummage **08** look into, research, scrabble **10** depression **11** hunt through, investigate

**demagogue**
**06** orator **07** speaker **08** agitator **09** firebrand, haranguer **10** tub-thumper **12** rabble-rouser **13** public speaker

**demand**
**03** ask, run **04** call, need, plea, sale, take, tell, urge, want **05** claim, draft, exact, order **06** ask for, desire, market **07** call for, clamour, command, dictate, inquire, inquiry, involve, request, require, solicit **08** exaction, exigency, insist on, petition, press for, pressure, question **09** cry out for, necessity, stipulate, ultimatum **10** hold out for, insistence **11** interrogate, necessitate, requirement **13** interrogation
• **in demand 02** in **03** big **06** trendy **07** desired, popular **08** asked for **09** requested **11** fashionable, of the moment, sought after

**demanding**
**04** hard **05** tough **06** taxing, trying, urgent **07** exigent, nagging, testing, wearing **08** exacting, pressing **09** difficult, harassing, insistent **10** a tall order, exhausting **11** challenging **12** back-breaking

**demarcate**
**03** fix **04** mark **05** bound, limit **06** define, divide **07** delimit, mark off, mark out **08** separate **09** determine, establish

**demarcation**
**04** line **05** bound, limit **06** fixing, margin **08** boundary, division **09** enclosure **10** definition, marking off, marking out, separation **11** distinction **12** delimitation **13** determination, establishment **15** differentiation

**demean**
**03** air **04** bear **05** abase, lower, stoop, treat **06** behave, debase, demote, humble **07** bearing, conduct, degrade, descend **08** belittle, ill-treat **09** deprecate, humiliate, treatment **10** condescend

**demeaning**
**04** base **07** ignoble **08** debasing, shameful, unworthy **09** degrading **10** belittling, cheapening, mortifying **11** disgraceful, humiliating, undignified **12** contemptible, discrediting **13** dishonourable

**demeanour**
**03** air **04** mien, port **06** manner **07** bearing, conduct **08** carriage, semblant **09** behaviour **10** deportment **11** comportment, countenance

## demented

◇ *anagram indicator* **03** ape, mad **04** bats, gyte, loco, nuts, wild **05** barmy, batty, buggy, crazy, daffy, dippy, dotty, flaky, gonzo, loony, loopy, nutty, potty, wacko, wacky, wiggy **06** cuckoo, fruity, insane, maniac, mental, raving, screwy **07** bananas, barking, berserk, bonkers, cracked, frantic, lunatic, meshuga **08** crackers, deranged, dingbats, doolally, frenetic, unhinged **09** disturbed, infuriate, lymphatic, up the wall **10** bestraught, distracted, distraught, frantic-mad, off the wall, off your nut, out to lunch, unbalanced **11** not all there, off the rails, off your head **12** mad as a hatter, off your chump, round the bend **13** off your rocker, out of your head, out of your mind, out of your tree, round the twist **14** off your trolley, wrong in the head

## Demeter

**05** Ceres

## demigod

**04** aitu, hero **05** pagod **06** garuda, pagoda

## demise

**03** end **04** fall, ruin **05** death, dying **07** decease, failure, passing **08** collapse, downfall **09** cessation, departure **10** expiration **11** termination **14** disintegration

## demobilize

**05** demob **07** break up, disband, dismiss **08** disperse

## democracy

**08** autonomy, republic **12** commonwealth **14** self-government

## democratic

**01** D **04** left **07** elected, popular **08** populist **10** autonomous, republican **11** egalitarian **12** Jeffersonian **13** self-governing **14** representative

## Democratic Republic of the Congo

**03** COD, ZRE

## demolish

◇ *anagram indicator* **04** beat, lick, rase, raze, rout, ruin, undo **05** abate, crush, excel, level, quash, quell, repel, wreck **06** hammer, subdue, thrash **07** break up, conquer, destroy, flatten, ruinate, surpass, unbuild **08** bulldoze, knock out, lay waste, massacre, overcome, overturn, pull down, take down, tear down, vanquish **09** break down, devastate, dismantle, knock down, overpower, overthrow, overwhelm, pulverize, slaughter, subjugate, throw down **10** annihilate **14** get the better of

## demolition

**04** rout, ruin **06** razing **07** beating, licking **08** massacre **09** hammering, levelling, overthrow, slaughter, thrashing **10** breaking-up, clobbering, flattening, surpassing **11** destruction, dismantling, pulling-down, tearing-down **12** annihilation, knocking-down, overpowering, overwhelming

## demon

**03** ace, imp **04** atua, buff, ogre, Rahu **05** afrit, beast, brute, devil, fiend, freak, ghoul, rogue, satyr **06** addict, afreet, daemon, duende, nicker, savage, wizard **07** dab hand, fanatic, incubus, monster, rakshas, villain, warlock **08** familiar, succubus **09** blue devil, cacodemon **10** evil spirit **11** fallen angel

*See also* **goblin; spirit**

## demonic

**03** mad **05** manic **06** crazed **07** frantic, furious, hellish, satanic **08** devilish, fiendish, frenetic, frenzied, infernal, maniacal **09** possessed **10** diabolical

## demonstrable

**05** clear **07** certain, evident, obvious **08** arguable, positive, provable **09** evincible **10** attestable, verifiable **11** self-evident

## demonstrate

**04** show **05** march, prove, rally, sit in, teach **06** betray, evince, parade, picket, verify **07** approve, bespeak, betoken, display, exhibit, explain, expound, express, protest **08** describe, indicate, manifest, register, validate **09** determine, establish, make clear, testify to **10** illustrate **11** communicate, remonstrate **12** substantiate **13** bear witness to

## demonstration

**04** demo, show, test **05** march, proof, rally, sit-in, trial **06** morcha, muster, parade, picket **07** display, protest **08** evidence **09** événement, mass rally, testimony **10** evincement, exhibition, exposition, expression, indication, validation **11** affirmation, description, elucidation, explanation, hunger march **12** confirmation, illustration, presentation, verification **13** communication, manifestation **14** substantiation

## demonstrative

**04** open, warm **06** loving **07** gushing **08** effusive **09** emotional, expansive, extrovert **10** expressive, scientific, unreserved **12** affectionate

## demonstratively

**06** openly, warmly **08** lovingly **11** emotionally **12** expressively **14** affectionately

## demonstrator

**06** shower

## demoralize

**05** crush, daunt, lower **06** debase, defile, deject, weaken **07** corrupt, deprave, depress, pervert **08** cast down, dispirit **09** undermine **10** disconcert, discourage, dishearten **11** contaminate **14** make despondent

## demoralizing

**08** daunting **09** weakening **10** depressing **11** dispiriting **12** discouraging **13** disconcerting, disheartening

## demote

**04** bust **05** break **06** humble **07** cashier,

degrade **08** relegate **09** downgrade **12** reduce in rank

## demotic

**06** vulgar **07** popular **08** enchoric **09** enchorial **10** colloquial, vernacular

## demotion

**09** degrading **10** relegation **11** downgrading

## demur

**04** balk, stop **05** cavil, doubt, pause, qualm **06** boggle, object, refuse **07** dispute, dissent, protest, scruple **08** demurral, disagree, hesitate, question **09** misgiving, objection **10** hesitation **11** be unwilling, compunction, reservation **12** disagreement, make question **13** express doubts, take exception

## demure

**03** coy, mim, shy **04** prim **05** grave, mimsy, quiet, sober, staid, timid **06** chaste, mimsey, modest, prissy **07** primsie, prudish, serious **08** reserved, reticent, retiring **10** unassuming **11** strait-laced

## demurely

**05** coyly, shyly **06** primly **07** quietly, staidly, timidly **08** modestly **09** seriously **10** reticently **12** unassumingly

## den

**04** dive, Hell, hole, home, lair, lare, nest **05** haunt, joint, patch, pitch, study **06** bothan, hollow, hotbed, studio **07** hideout, retreat, shelter, spieler **08** hideaway **09** Domdaniel, rock house, sanctuary **12** meeting-place

## denial

**02** no **03** nay **04** veto **05** denay **06** rebuff **07** démenti, dissent, gainsay, refusal **08** negation, rebuttal, traverse **09** disavowal, dismissal, disowning, forsaking, rejection **10** abjuration, denegation, disclaimer, opposition, refutation **11** prohibition, repudiation **12** disagreement, renunciation **13** contradiction **14** disaffirmation

## denigrate

**03** bag **05** abuse, decry **06** assail, defame, impugn, malign, revile, vilify **07** blacken, run down, slander **08** belittle, besmirch, fling mud, sling mud, talk down, throw mud, vilipend **09** blackened, criticize, deprecate, disparage **10** calumniate **11** pick holes in

## denigration

**05** abuse **07** calumny, slander **10** belittling **11** degradation, deprecation **12** vilification **13** disparagement

## denizen

**07** citizen, dweller, habitué, inhabit **08** habitant, occupant, resident, townsman **10** inhabitant, townswoman

## Denmark

**02** DK **03** DNK

## denomination

**04** cult, kind, sect, sort, unit **05** class,

**denote**

creed, faith, grade, order, value, worth
**06** belief, Church, parish, school
**08** religion **09** communion, face value,
tradition **10** persuasion **11** designation
**12** constituency **13** religious body
**14** religious group

**denote**

**04** mark, mean, note, show **05** imply
**06** typify **07** betoken, express, refer to,
signify, suggest **08** indicate, stand for
**09** be a sign of, designate, represent,
symbolize

**dénouement**

**05** close, event **06** climax, finale, finish,
pay-off, upshot **07** last act, outcome
**08** solution **10** conclusion, resolution
**11** culmination, unravelling
**13** clarification

**denounce**

**04** post, slag **05** decry, knock, slate
**06** accuse, attack, betray, impugn,
indict, revile, vilify **07** arraign, censure,
condemn, declaim, deplore, rubbish,
run down, slag off, thunder, trumpet
**08** announce, badmouth, execrate,
proclaim **09** castigate, criticize,
fulminate, inculpate, pronounce,
proscribe **10** denunciate, stigmatize
**11** pick holes in **12** pull to pieces, put
the boot in, tear to pieces **13** inform
against

**dense**

**03** dim **04** dull, dumb, rank, slow
**05** close, dopey, heavy, solid, stiff,
thick **06** obtuse, opaque, packed,
stupid **07** compact, crammed,
crowded, intense **08** gormless **09** close-
knit, condensed, dim-witted
**10** compressed, slow-witted **11** close-
packed **12** concentrated, impenetrable
**13** tightly packed **14** jammed together

**densely**

**05** close **06** firmly **07** closely, heavily,
solidly, thickly, tightly **09** compactly

**density**

**01** d **04** body, bulk, mass **08** solidity
**09** closeness, denseness, solidness,
thickness, tightness **10** spissitude
**11** compactness, consistency
**15** impenetrability
• **of little density** **04** thin

**dent**

**03** cut, dip, pit **04** bash, dint, drop, fall
**05** gouge **06** crater, damage, dimple,
hollow, indent, lessen, push in,
reduce, weaken **07** depress
**08** diminish **09** concavity, deduction,
lessening, reduction **10** depression
**11** indentation

**dentist**

**03** BDS, DDS, LDS, MDS **06** doctor
**08** odontist **09** gum-digger **13** dental
surgeon

**denude**

**04** bare **05** clear, strip **06** divest, expose
**07** uncover **08** deforest **09** defoliate

**denunciation**

**03** ban **06** attack, threat **07** censure,
decrial, obloquy, thunder **09** criticism,
invective **10** accusation **11** castigation,

commination, fulmination
**12** condemnation, counterblast,
denouncement **13** incrimination

**deny**

**03** nay **04** nick, reny, veto **05** denay,
rebut, renay, reney, renig, unget
**06** abjure, disown, forbid, naysay,
negate, oppose, rebuff, recant, refuse,
refute, reject, renege **07** decline,
disavow, dismiss, gainsay, nullify,
renague, renegue, sublate
**08** abnegate, disallow, disclaim,
disprove, forswear, prohibit, renounce,
traverse, turn down, withhold
**09** disaffirm, repudiate **10** contradict
**12** disagree with **14** turn your back on

**deodorant**

**05** scent **06** roll-on **08** fumigant
**09** fumigator **10** deodorizer **12** air-
freshener, disinfectant **14** anti-
perspirant

**deodorize**

**06** aerate, purify **07** freshen, refresh,
sweeten **08** fumigate **09** disinfect,
ventilate

**depart**

**02** go **03** dep, die, off **04** blow, exit,
fork, part, quit, scat, vade, vary, veer,
walk, wend **05** go off, lam it, leave,
quite, quyte, scoot, scram, skive, split
**06** avaunt, decamp, differ, divide,
egress, escape, go away, quight,
remove, retire, set off, set out, swerve,
vamose, vanish **07** bunk off, deviate,
digress, diverge, do a bunk, drop off,
make off, migrate, pull out, push off,
retreat, scarper, swan off, take off, tear
off, vamoose, walk off **08** check out,
clear off, drop away, get going, make
wing, separate, shove off, start out,
take wing, turn away, up sticks,
withdraw **09** branch off, disappear, do
a runner, evaporate, push along,
skedaddle, turn aside **10** hightail it, hit
the road, make tracks **11** hit the trail,
take the road **12** shoot through **13** sling
your hook, take your leave **14** absent
yourself, make a bolt for it, rattle
your dags, take it on the lam
**15** make a break for it, take to your
heels

**departed**

**04** dead, gone, late, lost, went
**07** expired **08** deceased **10** passed
away

**department**

**01** D **03** Dep, dpt **04** area, Dept, line,
nome, part, unit, wing **05** field, realm
**06** agency, branch, bureau, domain,
office, region, sector, sphere
**07** concern, section, station **08** district,
division, function, interest, province
**10** cost centre, speciality
**11** subdivision **12** organization
**14** responsibility

*Départements of France:*

**03** Ain, Lot, Var
**04** Aube, Aude, Cher, Eure, Gard,
Gers, Jura, Nord, Oise, Orne,
Tarn
**05** Aisne, Doubs, Drôme, Indre,

Isère, Loire, Marne, Meuse, Paris,
Rhône, Somme, Yonne
**06** Allier, Ariège, Cantal, Creuse,
Landes, Loiret, Lozère, Manche,
Nièvre, Sarthe, Savoie, Vendée,
Vienne, Vosges
**07** Ardèche, Aveyron, Bas-Rhin,
Corrèze, Côte-d'Or, Essonne,
Gironde, Hérault, Mayenne,
Moselle
**08** Ardennes, Calvados, Charente,
Dordogne, Haut-Rhin, Morbihan,
Val-d'Oise, Vaucluse, Yvelines
**09** Finistère, Puy-de-Dôme
**10** Corse-du-Sud, Deux-Sèvres,
Haute-Corse, Haute-Loire, Haute-
Marne, Haute-Saône, Loir-et-
Cher, Val-de-Marne
**11** Côtes-d'Armor, Eure-et-Loire,
Hautes-Alpes, Haute-Savoie,
Haute-Vienne, Pas-de-Calais
**12** Haute-Garonne, Hauts-de-Seine,
Indre-et-Loire, Lot-et-Garonne,
Maine-et-Loire, Saône-et-Loire,
Seine-et-Marne, Ville de Paris
**13** Ille-et-Vilaine, Seine-Maritime,
Tarn-et-Garonne
**14** Alpes-Maritimes, Bouches-du-
Rhône, Hautes-Pyrénées
**15** Loire-Atlantique, Seine-Saint-
Denis
**16** Charente-Maritime, Meurthe-et-
Moselle
**18** Pyrénées-Orientales
**19** Pyrénées-Atlantiques, Territoire
de Belfort
**20** Alpes-de-Haute-Provence

**departs**

**01** d **03** dep

**departure**

**03** dep **04** exit **05** going, lucky, shift
**06** change, egress, escape, exodus
**07** forking, leaving, removal, retreat,
veering **08** farewell, going off
**09** branching, decession, deviation,
egression, going away, variation
**10** difference, digression, divergence,
innovation, retirement, setting-off,
setting-out, withdrawal **11** leave-taking
**12** branching out

**depend**

**03** lie **04** need, rely, turn **06** bank on,
expect, hang on, lean on, lippen, rely
on, rest on, ride on, turn on **07** cling to,
count on, hinge on, trust in **08** reckon
on **09** be based on, build upon **11** be
decided by, be subject to, calculate on
**13** be dependent on, revolve around
**14** be contingent on, be determined by

**dependable**

**04** go-to, sure **06** honest, stable, steady,
trusty **07** certain **08** faithful, reliable
**09** rock-solid, steadfast, unfailing
**11** responsible, trustworthy
**13** conscientious **14** tried and tested

**dependant**

**04** ward **05** child, minor **06** charge,
client, feeder, minion, vassal
**07** protégé, relying **08** creature, hanger-
on, henchman, parasite, relative,
retainer **09** pensioner **10** contingent
**11** subordinate

## dependence

04 need 05 abuse, faith, trust
08 reliance 09 addiction, vassalage
10 attachment, confidence,
dependency 11 expectation
12 helplessness, subservience
13 subordination

## dependency

05 abuse, habit 06 colony 07 support
08 dominion, pendicle, province,
reliance, weakness 09 addiction,
satellite, territory 10 attachment,
immaturity 12 helplessness,
protectorate, subservience
13 subordination 14 submissiveness

## dependent

04 weak 05 based 07 decided, leaning,
reliant, relying, subject 08 dictated,
helpless, immature, relative
09 adjective, supported, sustained
10 contingent, controlled, determined,
influenced, vulnerable 11 conditional,
subordinate

## depict

04 draw, show 05 paint, trace 06 detail,
devise, record, render, sketch
07 depaint, impaint, outline, picture,
portray, present, recount 08 describe,
resemble 09 delineate, represent,
reproduce 10 illustrate 12 characterize

## depiction

05 image 06 sketch 07 drawing,
outline, picture 08 likeness
09 detailing, portrayal, rendering
10 caricature 11 delineation,
description 12 illustration
14 representation

## deplete

05 drain, empty, erode, spend, use up
06 expend, lessen, reduce, weaken
07 consume, eat into, exhaust, run
down 08 bankrupt, decrease, diminish,
evacuate 09 attenuate 10 impoverish
11 whittle away

## depletion

07 using-up 08 decrease, lowering
09 dwindling, lessening, reduction,
shrinkage, weakening 10 deficiency,
diminution, evacuation, exhaustion
11 attenuation, consumption,
expenditure 14 impoverishment

## deplorable

◇ *anagram indicator* 03 sad 04 dire
05 woful 06 rueful, woeful 07 abysmal,
chronic, ghastly 08 criminal, grievous,
pitiable, shameful, wretched
09 appalling, miserable
10 abominable, despicable, disastrous,
lamentable, melancholy, outrageous,
scandalous 11 blameworthy,
disgraceful, distressing, regrettable,
unfortunate 12 disreputable
13 dishonourable, heartbreaking,
reprehensible

## deplorably

08 shocking 09 miserably
10 abominably, despicably,
lamentably, shamefully 11 appallingly
12 outrageously, scandalously
13 disgracefully, unfortunately

## deplore

03 cry, rue 04 pine, slam, weep
05 blame, mourn, slate 06 bemoan,
berate, bewail, lament, regret, revile
07 censure, condemn, reprove,
upbraid 08 denounce, reproach
09 castigate, criticize, deprecate,
disparage, grieve for, reprehend, shed
tears 12 disapprove of

## deploy

◇ *anagram indicator* 03 use 04 open
06 extend, lay out, unfold 07 arrange,
dispose, scatter, station, utilize
08 position 09 make use of, spread out
10 distribute

## depopulate

05 empty 08 unpeople 09 dispeople

## deport

03 act 04 bear, hold, oust 05 carry,
exile, expel 06 acquit, banish, behave,
manage 07 comport, conduct, perform
09 extradite, ostracize, transport
10 repatriate

## deportation

05 exile 07 ousting 09 expulsion,
ostracism 10 banishment 11 extradition
12 repatriation 14 transportation

## deportment

03 air 04 gait, mien, port, pose
06 aspect, manner, stance 07 address,
bearing, conduct, manners, posture
08 behavior, carriage 09 behaviour,
demeanour, etiquette 10 appearance
11 comportment

## depose

04 fire, oust, sack 05 swear 06 attest,
demote, remove, topple, unseat
07 degrade, dismiss, unfrock
08 dethrone, displace, down with
09 discharge, downgrade, overthrow
12 disestablish

## deposit

◇ *hidden indicator* 03 bed, dep, dew,
fan, lay, put, set, sit 04 bank, bung,
drop, dump, file, gage, land, lees,
park, save, silt, soot, stow, ware, warp
05 amass, dregs, hoard, lay-by, lodge,
pay in, place, plant, put by, stake,
store 06 depone, locate, margin,
pledge, settle, tophus 07 consign,
earnest, entrust, fall-out, lay down, put
away, put down, reposit, saburra, set
down, sublime 08 alluvium, oviposit,
retainer, security, sediment, stratify
10 deposition, hypostasis, instalment
11 down payment, part payment,
precipitate 12 accumulation

## deposition

07 ousting, removal 08 evidence,
sediment, toppling 09 affidavit,
dismissal, overthrow, statement,
testimony, unseating 11 attestation,
declaration, illuviation, information
12 dethronement, displacement
13 sedimentation

## depository

05 cache, depot, store 07 arsenal
09 warehouse 10 repository,
storehouse 15 bonded warehouse

## depot

04 camp 05 cache, store 06 garage
07 arsenal, station 08 terminal,
terminus 09 barracoon, warehouse
10 depository, repository, storehouse
14 receiving-house

## deprave

04 warp 06 debase, defile, infect,
seduce 07 corrupt, debauch, degrade,
pervert, pollute, subvert, viciate, vitiate
10 demoralize, lead astray
11 contaminate

## depraved

04 base, evil, vile 06 sinful, warped,
wicked 07 bestial, corrupt, debased,
immoral, obscene, vicious 08 criminal
09 debauched, dissolute, felonious,
graceless, perverted, reprobate,
shameless 10 degenerate, iniquitous,
licentious

## depravity

04 evil, vice 08 baseness, iniquity,
vileness 09 reprobacy, turpitude
10 corruption, debasement,
debauchery, degeneracy, immorality,
perversion, sinfulness, wickedness
13 dissoluteness

## deprecate

04 slam 05 blame, knock, slate
06 berate, reject, revile 07 censure,
condemn, deplore, reprove, rubbish,
run down, upbraid 08 denounce,
object to, reproach 09 castigate,
criticize, disparage, protest at,
reprehend 12 disapprove of

## deprecatory

09 regretful 10 apologetic, censorious,
dismissive, protesting 11 reproachful
12 condemnatory, disapproving

## depreciate

04 drop, fall 05 lower, slump
06 defame, lessen, malign, reduce,
revile, slight 07 decline, deflate,
devalue, disable, run down 08 belittle
09 denigrate, disparage, downgrade,
underrate 10 undervalue 11 fall in
value, make light of 13 go down in
value, underestimate 15 decrease in
value

## depreciation

04 fall 05 slump 08 mark-down,
ridicule 09 deflation 10 cheapening,
depression, derogation, detraction
11 denigration, devaluation
12 belittlement 13 disparagement
15 underestimation

## depredation

04 prey 05 theft 06 damage 07 looting,
pillage, plunder, raiding, robbery
08 hardship, harrying, ravaging
09 marauding 10 denudation,
desolation, despoiling, plundering,
ransacking 11 destruction, devastation
laying waste

## depress

03 cut, sap 04 down, push, tire
05 daunt, drain, level, lower, press,
slash, upset, weary 06 burden, deject,
hammer, humble, impair, lessen,
reduce, sadden, weaken 07 cheapen,
devalue, exhaust, get down, make sad

**depressant**

oppress **08** cast down, enervate, hold down, push down **09** bring down, press down, undermine, weigh down **10** debilitate, depreciate, discourage, dishearten, overburden

**depressant**

**06** downer **07** calmant **08** relaxant, sedative **09** calmative **13** tranquillizer

**depressed**

**03** low, sad **04** blue, down, glum, poor **05** cowed, doomy, fed up, moody, needy **06** dented, gloomy, hollow, moping, morose, sunken **07** accablé, concave, dumpish, humbled, lowered, run-down, unhappy **08** cast down, dejected, deprived, downbeat, downcast, indented, pushed in, recessed **09** destitute, exanimate, flattened, heartsick, jaw-fallen, miserable **10** a peg too low, despondent, dispirited, distressed, emarginate, melancholy **11** crestfallen, discouraged, downhearted, low-spirited, pessimistic **12** disheartened, low in spirits, out of spirits, under hatches **13** broken-hearted, disadvantaged **14** down in the dumps **15** poverty-stricken

**depressing**

**03** sad **04** grey, grim **05** black, bleak, doomy, grave **06** dismal, dreary, gloomy, leaden, sombre **07** unhappy **08** daunting, downbeat, hopeless **09** cheerless, dejecting, saddening, upsetting **10** melancholy **11** dispiriting, distressing **12** discouraging **13** disheartening, heartbreaking

**depressingly**

**05** sadly **07** bleakly **08** drearily, gloomily **09** unhappily **10** dauntingly **11** cheerlessly **13** dispiritingly, distressingly **14** discouragingly **15** dishearteningly, heartbreakingly

**depression**

**03** col, dip, pit, PND **04** bowl, dent, dint, dish, glen, hole, sink, slot, swag **05** basin, blues, crash, delve, dumps, fossa, gloom, slump **06** cafard, cavity, dimple, downer, hollow, recess, trough, valley **07** cyclone, decline, despair, foveola, foveole, megrims, sadness, sinkage, sinking **08** black dog, doldrums, glumness, lowering, slowdown **09** baby blues, concavity, dejection, demission, hard times, pessimism, recession, umbilicus **10** desolation, excavation, gloominess, impression, inactivity, low spirits, melancholy, scrobicule, stagnation, standstill, the horrors **11** despondency, indentation, melancholia, unhappiness **12** hopelessness **14** discouragement **15** downheartedness

**deprivation**

**04** lack, loss, need, want **06** denial, penury **07** poverty, removal **08** hardship **09** privation **10** withdrawal **11** bereavement, destitution, withholding **12** disadvantage **13** dispossession **14** impoverishment

**deprive**

**03** rob **04** deny, geld, twin **05** spoil, strip, twine **06** amerce, denude, divest, refuse **07** bereave **08** take away, withhold **09** destitute **10** confiscate, dispossess **11** expropriate

**deprived**

**04** gelt, poor **05** needy **06** bereft, in need **07** lacking **09** destitute **12** impoverished **13** disadvantaged **15** underprivileged
• **be deprived of** **04** lose

**depth**

**01** d **03** bed **04** deep, drop, glow, gulf **05** abyss, floor, midst, range, scope **06** acumen, amount, bottom, extent, middle, vigour, warmth, wisdom **07** fervour, gravity, insight, measure, passion **08** darkness, deepness, richness, severity, strength **09** awareness, intensity, intuition, vividness **10** astuteness, brilliance, cleverness, perception, profundity, shrewdness **11** discernment, earnestness, penetration, seriousness **12** profoundness, remotest area, thoroughness **13** extensiveness **14** third dimension
• **depth charge** **03** can
• **in depth** **08** in detail, thorough **09** extensive **10** thoroughly **11** extensively **12** exhaustively **13** comprehensive **15** comprehensively

**deputation**

**07** embassy, mission **08** legation **09** committee **10** commission, delegation **15** representatives

**depute**

**06** charge, second **07** appoint, consign, empower, entrust, mandate **08** accredit, delegate, hand over, nominate **09** authorize, designate **10** commission

**deputize**

**05** cover **06** act for, double, sub for **07** relieve, replace **08** take over **09** fill in for, represent **10** stand in for, substitute, understudy **11** pinch-hit for **14** take the place of

**deputy**

**02** TD **03** Dep **04** Dept, mate, vice- **05** agent, envoy, locum, nawab, prior, proxy, vicar **06** commis, -depute, legate, second, vidame **07** stand-in **08** delegate, official, prioress, sidekick, sidesman, Tanaiste, vicaress, viscount **09** alternate, assistant, secondary, surrogate **10** ambassador, commissary, lieutenant, subchanter, substitute, vice-consul, vice-regent **11** locum tenens, subordinate **12** commissioner, spokesperson, under-sheriff, vice-chairman, vice-governor **13** pro-chancellor, sheriff depute, vice-president **14** representative **15** second-in-command, vice-chairperson, vice-chamberlain

**derail**

**05** ditch, upset **06** impede **07** disrupt, disturb, prevent **08** displace, hold back, obstruct **14** throw off course

**deranged**

◇ *anagram indicator* **03** ape, fey, mad **04** bats, loco, nuts, wild **05** barmy, batty, buggy, crazy, daffy, dippy, dotty, flaky, gonzo, loony, loopy, manic, nutty, potty, wacko, wacky, wiggy **06** crazed, cuckoo, fruity, insane, maniac, mental, raving, screwy, skivie **07** bananas, barking, berserk, bonkers, cracked, frantic, lunatic, meshuga **08** confused, crackers, demented, dingbats, doolally, frenetic, frenzied, maniacal, unhinged, unstable **09** brainsick, delirious, disturbed, lymphatic, psychotic, unsettled, up the wall **10** bestraught, disordered, distracted, distraught, frantic-mad, irrational, off the wall, off your nut, out to lunch, unbalanced **11** not all there, off the rails, off your head **12** mad as a hatter, off your chump, round the bend **13** off your rocker, of unsound mind, out of your head, out of your mind, out of your tree, round the twist **14** off your trolley, wrong in the head **15** non compos mentis, out of your senses

**derangement**

**05** mania **06** frenzy, lunacy **07** madness **08** delirium, dementia, disarray, disorder, insanity, neurosis **09** agitation, confusion **10** aberration **11** dislocation, distraction, disturbance **13** hallucination

**Derek**

**02** Bo **03** Del

**derelict**

**04** hobo **05** jakey, tramp **06** beggar, dosser, no-good, ruined, wretch **07** drifter, no-hoper, outcast, run-down, swagman, vagrant **08** deserted, desolate, forsaken, vagabond **09** abandoned, discarded, neglected **10** down-and-out, ne'er-do-well, ramshackle, tumbledown **11** dilapidated, in disrepair **12** down-and-outer **14** good-for-nothing **15** falling to pieces

**dereliction**

**04** ruin **05** ruins **07** evasion, failure, neglect **08** apostasy, betrayal **09** desertion, disrepair, forsaking **10** abdication, desolation, negligence, remissness, renegation **11** abandonment **12** dilapidation, renunciation **13** faithlessness **14** relinquishment

**deride**

**03** rag **04** gibe, jeer, mock, slag **05** knock, laugh, scorn, taunt, tease **06** bemock, chiack, chyack, insult, jeer at **07** disdain, laugh at, scoff at, slag off, sneer at **08** belittle, pooh-pooh, ridicule, satirize **09** disparage, make fun of

**de rigueur**

**04** done **05** right **06** decent, proper **07** correct, fitting **08** decorous, expected, required **09** necessary **10** compulsory **11** fashionable **12** conventional, the done thing

## derision
**05** scorn **06** insult, satire **07** disdain, hissing, mockery, ragging, teasing **08** contempt, ridicule, scoffing, sneering, taunting **10** disrespect **13** disparagement
• **expression of derision 02** ho **03** gup, hoa, hoh, mew, yah **05** sucks!, te-hee, ya-boo **06** tee-hee, yah-boo **07** so there **10** get knotted!, sucks to you!, ya-boo sucks **11** yah-boo sucks

## derisive
**06** ribald **07** jeering, mocking **08** irrisory, scoffing, scornful, taunting **09** insulting **10** disdainful, irreverent **12** contemptuous **13** disrespectful

## derisively
**10** scornfully **12** disdainfully, irreverently **14** contemptuously **15** disrespectfully

## derisory
**04** tiny **05** small **06** absurd, paltry **07** risible **08** pathetic, scoffing **09** insulting, laughable, ludicrous **10** inadequate, outrageous, ridiculous **12** contemptible, insufficient, preposterous

## derivation
**03** der **04** root **05** basis, deriv **06** origin, source **07** descent **08** ancestry, pedigree **09** beginning, deduction, etymology, genealogy, inference **10** extraction, foundation **13** parasynthesis

## derivative
**03** der **05** deriv, trite **06** branch, copied **07** cribbed, derived, product, spin-off **08** acquired, borrowed, obtained, offshoot, rehashed **09** by-product, formative, hackneyed, imitative, outgrowth, secondary **10** derivation, descendant, second-hand, unoriginal **11** development, plagiarized

## derive
**03** get **04** draw, flow, gain, reap, stem, take **05** arise, fetch, infer, issue **06** borrow, deduce, evolve, follow, obtain, spring **07** acquire, descend, develop, emanate, extract, proceed, procure, receive **09** originate **14** have its roots in **15** have as the source, have its origin in
• **derived from 02** of

## derogatory
**05** snide **06** snidey **08** critical **09** injurious, insulting, offensive, slighting, vilifying **10** belittling, defamatory, detracting, detractive, detractory, pejorative **11** denigratory, disparaging **12** depreciative, disapproving, unfavourable **15** uncomplimentary

## descend
**03** dip **04** dive, drop, fall, sink, stem **05** deign, issue, pitch, slope, stoop, storm, swoop **06** alight, arrive, derive, go down, invade, plunge, spring, tumble **07** decline, emanate, go to pot, incline, pancake, plummet, proceed, subside **08** come down, dismount, move down, take over **09** originate,

parachute **10** condescend, degenerate, go downhill **11** dégringoler, deteriorate, go to the dogs **13** lower yourself **14** arrive suddenly

## descendant
**03** son **04** cion, sien, slip, syen **05** child, niece, scion **06** nephew, sprout **08** daughter
• **descendant of 01** O'

## descendants
**04** line, race, seed **05** heirs, issue **06** family, scions **07** descent, lineage, progeny **08** children, mokopuna **09** offspring, posterior, posterity **10** generation, posteriors, successors

## descended
**04** alit

## descent
**03** dip **04** dive, down, drop, fall, line, raid **05** blood, pitch, slant, slope, stock, stoop **06** origin, plunge **07** decline, incline, lineage, sinking **08** ancestry, comedown, gradient, heredity, invasion, pedigree **09** decadence, declivity, genealogy, going-down, parentage, subsiding **10** debasement, declension, degeneracy, extraction, family tree **11** degradation **12** degeneration, dégringolade **13** deterioration

## describe
◊ *containment indicator* **04** call, draw, hail, talk, tell **05** brand, label, style, sweep, think, trace, write **06** define, depict, detail, relate, report, scrive, sketch, strike **07** explain, express, mark out, narrate, outline, portray, present, recount, scrieve, specify **08** consider, descrive **09** character, delineate, designate, elucidate, represent **10** illustrate **12** characterize **13** give details of

## description
**04** kind, make, sort, type **05** brand, breed, class, order, style **06** report, sketch **07** account, outline, picture, profile, variety **08** category, portrait **09** chronicle, depiction, narration, portrayal, statement **10** commentary, definement, exposition **11** delineation, designation, elucidation, explanation, portraiture **12** presentation **13** particularism, specification **14** representation

## descriptive
**05** vivid **07** graphic **08** detailed, striking **09** colourful, pictorial **10** blottesque, expressive **11** elucidatory, explanatory **12** illustrative

## descry
**03** get, see **04** espy, mark, spot **06** detect, notice, reveal **07** discern, glimpse, make out, observe **08** discover, perceive **09** discovery, recognize **11** distinguish **12** catch sight of

## desecrate
◊ *anagram indicator* **05** abuse **06** damage, debase, defile, insult **07** pervert, pollute, profane, violate **09** blaspheme, dishallow, dishonour,

vandalize **10** unsanctify **11** contaminate

## desecration
**06** damage, insult **07** impiety **09** blasphemy, pollution, sacrilege, violation **10** debasement, defilement **11** profanation **12** dishonouring

## desegregate
**04** join **05** blend, merge **08** intermix **09** harmonize, integrate **10** assimilate **11** incorporate

## desert
◊ *deletion indicator* **03** dry, due, fly, rat **04** arid, bare, deny, fail, flee, jilt, quit, void, wild **05** empty, leave, merit, rat on, right, waste, wilds, worth **06** barren, betray, bug out, decamp, defect, forhow, give up, go AWOL, lonely, maroon, recant, return, reward, strand, virtue **07** abandon, abscond, cast off, demerit, deserts, dried up, forsake, parched, payment, run away, sterile **08** desolate, dust bowl, renounce, run out on, solitary, solitude **09** infertile, throw over, walk out on, wasteland **10** apostasize, barrenness, chicken out, recompense, relinquish, wilderness **11** change sides, comeuppance, retribution, uninhabited **12** moistureless, remuneration, tergiversate, uncultivated, unproductive **14** turn your back on, what you deserve **15** leave high and dry, leave in the lurch

*Deserts include:*

**04** Gobi, Thar
**05** Kavir, Namib, Ordos, Sturt
**06** Gibson, Mojave, Nubian, Sahara, Syrian, Ust'-Urt
**07** Alashan, Arabian, Atacama, Kara Kum, Simpson, Sonoran
**08** Kalahari, Kyzyl Kum
**09** Dzungaria
**10** Bet-Pak-Dala, Chihuahuan, Great Basin, Great Sandy, Patagonian, Takla Makan
**13** Great Victoria
**14** Bolson de Mapimi

## deserted
**01** d **04** left, lorn, void **05** empty **06** bereft, lonely, vacant **08** betrayed, derelict, desolate, forsaken, isolated, solitary, stranded **09** abandoned, neglected **10** unoccupied **11** god-forsaken, uninhabited **14** underpopulated

## deserter
**03** rat **06** bug-out, truant **07** escapee, runaway, traitor **08** apostate, betrayer, defector, fugitive, renegade, turncoat **09** absconder **10** backslider, delinquent

## desertion
**06** bug-out, denial, flight, give up **07** jilting, leaving, truancy **08** apostasy, betrayal, giving-up, quitting **09** decamping, defection, forsaking, going AWOL **10** absconding, casting-off, renegation **11** abandonment, dereliction, running-away

**12** renunciation **14** relinquishment, tergiversation

**deserve**
**03** win **04** earn, rate **05** incur, merit **07** justify, warrant **10** be worthy of **12** be entitled to, have a right to, have it coming

**deserved**
**03** apt, due **04** fair, just, meet **05** right **06** earned, proper **07** condign, fitting, merited **08** apposite, rightful, suitable **09** justified, warranted **10** legitimate, well-earned **11** appropriate, justifiable

**deservedly**
**04** duly **06** fairly, justly **07** rightly **08** by rights, properly, suitably **09** fittingly **10** rightfully **11** justifiably **13** appropriately

**deserving**
**05** worth **06** worthy **07** upright **08** laudable, virtuous **09** admirable, estimable, exemplary, righteous **11** commendable, meritorious **12** praiseworthy

**desiccated**
**03** dry **04** arid, dead **05** dried **07** drained, dried up, parched, sterile **08** lifeless, powdered **10** dehydrated, exsiccated

**desiccation**
**07** aridity, dryness **08** parching, xeransis **09** sterility **11** dehydration, exsiccation

**desideratum**
**04** must, need, want **09** essential, necessity, requisite **10** sine qua non **11** requirement **12** prerequisite

**design**
◊ *anagram indicator* **03** aim, end, lay, map **04** draw, etch, form, gear, goal, hope, logo, make, mean, plan, plot, seal, tatu, tool, wish **05** draft, dream, guide, hatch, model, motif, point, shape, style, think **06** cipher, create, desire, device, devise, draw up, emblem, figure, format, intend, intent, invent, make-up, object, scheme, sketch, slight, tailor, target, tattoo **07** destine, develop, diagram, drawing, fashion, meaning, outline, pattern, project, propose, purpose, sleight, think up, thought **08** conceive, contrive, indicate, monogram **09** blueprint, construct, delineate, fabricate, intention, objective, originate, prototype, structure **10** assignment, compassing, enterprise **11** arrangement, composition, delineation, destination, undertaking **12** construction, contrivement, organization
• **by design 08** wilfully **09** knowingly, on purpose, pointedly, wittingly **11** consciously **12** deliberately **13** calculatingly, intentionally

**designate**
**03** dub **04** call, name, show, term **05** class, elect, style, title **06** assign, choose, define, denote, select **07** appoint, earmark, entitle, express, specify **08** christen, classify, describe,

indicate, nominate, set aside **09** stipulate

**designation**
**03** tag **04** name, term, type **05** label, style, title **07** epithet, marking **08** category, denoting, election, nickname **09** selection, sobriquet **10** definition, indication, nomination **11** appellation, appellative, appointment, description, stipulation **12** denomination **13** specification **14** classification

**designer**
**05** maker **06** author, deccie **07** creator, deviser, planner, plotter, stylist **08** inventor, producer **09** architect, contriver, couturier, fashioner **10** originator **11** draughtsman
*See also* **fashion**

**designing**
**03** sly **04** wily **05** sharp **06** artful, crafty, shrewd, tricky **07** couture, cunning, devious **08** guileful, plotting, scheming **09** deceitful, underhand **10** conspiring, intriguing **11** calculating

**desirability**
**05** merit, worth **06** allure, appeal, profit **07** benefit **08** sexiness **09** advantage **10** attraction, excellence, popularity, preference, usefulness **12** advisability **13** seductiveness **14** attractiveness

**desirable**
**03** fit, hot **04** good, sexy **06** plummy **07** popular, wishful **08** alluring, beddable, eligible, fetching, in demand, pleasant, pleasing, sensible, tempting **09** advisable, agreeable, appetible, expedient, seductive **10** attractive, beneficial, preferable, profitable, worthwhile **11** appropriate, sought-after, tantalizing **12** advantageous

**desire**
**03** ask, yen **04** Cama, earn, envy, erne, fain, itch, Kama, lech, like, list, lust, need, salt, urge, vote, want, will, wish **05** bosom, covet, crave, fancy, greed, mania, yearn **06** ardour, besoin, demand, libido, take to **07** avidity, burn for, craving, erotism, gasp for, long for, longing, passion, wish for **08** appetite, covetise, feel like, sex drive, yearn for, yearning **09** cacoëthes, hankering, hunger for, lust after, sexuality **10** aphrodisia, aspiration, be dying for, desiderate, preference, proclivity, sensuality **11** hanker after **12** be crazy about, ephebophilia, have a crush on, predilection, take a shine to **13** concupiscence, have designs on **14** have the hots for, have your eyes on, lasciviousness, predisposition, set your heart on **15** give the world for

**desired**
**05** exact, right **06** proper, wanted **07** correct, fitting **08** accurate, expected, in demand, required **09** necessary **10** particular **11** appropriate **13** in great demand

**desirous**
**04** avid, keen **05** eager, ready **06** fervid, hoping, hungry **07** anxious, burning, craving, fervent, hopeful, itching, longing, wanting, willing, wishful, wishing **08** aspiring, yearning **09** ambitious, desirable **10** cupidinous **12** enthusiastic

**desist**
**03** end **04** halt, stay, stop **05** cease, leave, pause, remit, stash **06** give up **07** abstain, forbear, refrain, suspend **08** break off, have done, leave off, peter out **09** supersede **11** discontinue

**desk**
**04** ambo **05** desse, table **06** bureau, carrel, pulpit **07** carrell, lectern, lecturn, lettern, rolltop **08** prie-dieu, vargueño **09** davenport, faldstool, secretary **10** escritoire, secretaire **11** litany-stool, reading-desk **12** writing-table **13** bonheur-du-jour

**desolate**
**03** sad **04** arid, bare, wild **05** bleak, floor, gaunt, upset, waste **06** barren, bereft, desert, dismal, dreary, gloomy, gousty, lonely **07** forlorn, get down, nonplus, shatter, unhappy **08** confound, dejected, deserted, downcast, forsaken, isolated, solitary, unpeeled, wasteful, wretched **09** abandoned, depressed, devastate, discomfit, miserable, overwhelm, take aback, wasteland **10** depressing, despondent, disconcert, distressed, drearisome, melancholy, unoccupied **11** comfortless, god-forsaken, heartbroken, uninhabited **12** disheartened, god-forgotten, unfrequented **13** broken-hearted

**desolation**
**04** ruin **05** gloom, grief, waste **06** misery, sorrow **07** anguish, despair, ravages, sadness **08** distress, solitude, wildness **09** bleakness, dejection, emptiness, isolation **10** barrenness, depression, loneliness, melancholy, remoteness, wilderness **11** despondency, destruction, devastation, forlornness, laying waste, unhappiness **12** wretchedness

**despair**
**05** gloom **06** give in, give up, misery **07** anguish, wanhope **08** collapse, distress, lose hope **09** dejection, dysthymia, lose heart, pessimism, surrender **10** depression, melancholy **11** desperation, despondency **12** be despondent, hopelessness, wretchedness **13** discouraged, hit rock bottom **15** throw in the towel

**despairing**
**08** dejected, desolate, dismayed, downcast, hopeless, suicidal, wretched **09** anguished, depressed, desperate, miserable, sorrowful **10** despondent, distraught **11** au désespoir, desperation, discouraged, heartbroken, pessimistic **12** disconsolate, disheartened, inconsolable **13** grief-stricken

**despatch**
*see* **dispatch, despatch**

**desperado**
**04** thug **06** badman, bandit, gunman, mugger, outlaw **07** brigand, hoodlum, ruffian **08** criminal, gangster **09** cutthroat, terrorist **10** lawbreaker

**desperate**
◊ *anagram indicator* **04** bold, dire, rash, wild **05** acute, dying, grave, great, hasty, risky **06** daring, severe, urgent **07** acharné, crucial, do-or-die, extreme, frantic, furious, lawless, serious, violent **08** critical, dejected, desolate, dismayed, downcast, frenzied, hairless, hopeless, pressing, reckless, suicidal, wretched **09** abandoned, anguished, audacious, dangerous, depressed, foolhardy, hazardous, impetuous, miserable, sorrowful **10** compelling, despondent, determined, distraught, incautious, on the ropes **11** discouraged, heartbroken, in great need, pessimistic, precipitate **12** at rock-bottom, crying out for, disconsolate, disheartened, inconsolable **13** grief-stricken **15** needing very much, wanting very much

**desperately**
◊ *anagram indicator* **05** badly **07** acutely, gravely, greatly **08** severely, urgently **09** extremely, fearfully, seriously **10** critically, dreadfully, hopelessly **11** à corps perdu, dangerously, frightfully

**desperation**
**04** fury, pain **05** agony, gloom, worry **06** misery, sorrow **07** anguish, anxiety, despair, trouble **08** distress **10** depression, despairing **11** despondency **12** hopelessness, recklessness, wretchedness

**despicable**
**03** bum, low **04** base, mean, vile **05** dirty, spewy **07** caitiff, lowdown, pitiful **08** dwarfish, shameful, wretched **09** dastardly, degrading, loathsome, reprobate, worthless **10** abominable, detestable, disgusting **11** disgraceful **12** contemptible, disreputable **13** reprehensible **15** beneath contempt

**despise**
**04** hate, mock, shun **05** abhor, scorn, sneer, spurn **06** deride, detest, forhow, loathe, revile, slight **07** condemn, conspue, contemn, deplore, disdain, dislike **08** vilipend **10** look down on, undervalue **11** set at naught, set at nought **14** hold in contempt

**despite**
**07** against, defying **09** in spite of **11** in the face of **12** regardless of, undeterred by **15** notwithstanding

**despoil**
**03** rob **04** loot, rape **05** pluck, rifle, spoil, strip, wreck **06** bezzle, denude, divest, maraud, ravage **07** bereave, deprive, destroy, pillage, plunder, ransack **08** spoliate **09** depredate,

devastate, vandalize **10** disgarnish, dispossess, untreasure

**despondency**
**04** hump **05** blues, gloom, grief **06** misery, sorrow **07** despair, sadness **08** distress, glumness **09** dejection, heartache, pessimism **10** depression, melancholy **11** desperation, melancholia **12** hopelessness, wretchedness **14** discouragement, dispiritedness **15** downheartedness, inconsolability

**despondent**
**03** low, sad **04** blue, down, glum **06** gloomy **07** doleful **08** dejected, downcast, mournful, wretched **09** depressed, heartsick, miserable, sorrowful **10** despairing, distressed, melancholy **11** discouraged, heartbroken **12** disheartened, inconsolable **14** down in the dumps

**despot**
**04** boss, czar, tsar, tzar **06** sultan, tyrant **08** autocrat, dictator **09** oppressor **10** absolutist **13** absolute ruler

---
*Despots include:*

**03** Idi
**04** **Amin** (Idi), **Tito** (Josip Broz)
**05** **Timur**
**06** **Caesar** (Julius), **Franco** (Francisco), **Führer, Hitler** (Adolf), **Stalin** (Joseph)
**07** **Papa Doc**
**08** **Duvalier** (François)
**09** **Ceauşescu** (Nicolae), **Mao Zedong, Mussolini** (Benito), **Tamerlane**
**10** **Mao Tse-tung**
**11** **Robespierre** (Maximilien de), **Tamburlaine**
**13** **Saddam Hussein**
**15** **Ivan the Terrible**
---

**despotic**
**08** absolute, arrogant **09** arbitrary, imperious, tyrannous **10** autocratic, high-handed, oppressive, tyrannical **11** dictatorial, domineering, overbearing **13** authoritarian

**despotism**
**07** tyranny **09** autocracy **10** absolutism, oppression, repression **11** stratocracy **12** dictatorship **15** totalitarianism

**dessert**
**03** pud **05** sweet **06** afters **07** pudding **09** sweet dish **11** aftersupper, sweet course

---
*Desserts and puddings include:*

**03** ice, pie
**04** duff, flan, fool, sago, tart
**05** bombe, jelly, kugel, kulfi
**06** mousse, mud pie, sorbet, sundae, trifle, yogurt
**07** baklava, choc ice, cobbler, compote, crumble, parfait, pavlova, soufflé, tapioca, tartufo, yoghurt
**08** Eton mess, ice cream, pandowdy, plum-duff, syllabub, tiramisu, vacherin, yoghourt
**09** clafoutis, cranachan

**10** blancmange, Brown Betty, cheesecake, egg custard, frangipane, fruit salad, panna cotta, peach Melba, zabaglione
**11** baked Alaska, banana split, banoffee pie, crème brûlée, Eve's pudding, milk pudding, plum pudding, rice pudding, spotted dick
**12** crème caramel, crêpe suzette, fruit crumble, profiteroles
**13** fruit cocktail, marrons glacés, millefeuilles, summer pudding
**14** charlotte russe
**15** clootie dumpling, queen of puddings, roly-poly pudding
---

*See also* **cake**

**destabilize**
◊ *anagram indicator* **05** upset **08** unsettle

**destination**
**03** aim, end **04** fate, goal, gole, list, stop **06** design, object, target **07** purpose, station **08** ambition, terminus **09** intention, objective **10** aspiration **11** journey's end **12** end of the line, landing place **15** final port of call, jumping-off place

**destined**
**04** born **05** bound, fatal, fated, meant **06** booked, doomed, headed, marked, routed **07** certain, en route, heading **08** assigned, designed, directed, intended, ordained, set apart **09** appointed, scheduled **10** inevitable **11** inescapable, preordained, unavoidable **12** foreordained **13** predetermined

**destiny**
**03** lot **04** doom, fate, luck **05** karma, Moera, Moira **06** future, kismet **07** fortune, portion **09** necessity **10** predestiny **14** predestination

**destitute**
**04** poor **05** broke, needy, skint **06** bereft, hard up, rooked **07** lacking, wanting **08** badly off, bankrupt, depleted, deprived, devoid of, dirt-poor, forsaken, helpless, indigent **09** deficient, penniless, penurious **10** cleaned out, distressed, down-and-out, friendless, innocent of, stony-broke **11** impecunious, necessitous, on the street **12** impoverished **14** on the breadline, on your beam-ends **15** poverty-stricken, strapped for cash

**destitution**
**06** penury **07** beggary, poverty, straits **08** distress **09** indigence, pauperdom **10** bankruptcy, starvation **13** penbefore-lessness **14** impoverishment **15** impecuniousness

**destroy**
◊ *anagram indicator* **03** eat, end, gut, zap **04** kill, raze, ruin, slay, undo **05** break, crush, erase, fordo, harry, level, smash, spoil, waste, wreck **06** banjax, canker, defeat, delete, finish, perish, quench, ravage, subdue, thwart, wither **07** attrite, deep-six, flatten, handbag, kill off, nullify, put down, ransack, ruinate, scuttle,

shatter, stonker, torpedo, unshape, vitiate **08** decimate, demolish, dispatch, knock out, lay waste, overturn, pull down, sabotage, stamp out, tear down **09** devastate, dismantle, eliminate, eradicate, extirpate, knock down, marmelize, overthrow, pulverize, slaughter, undermine **10** annihilate, do away with, extinguish, obliterate, put to sleep, spiflicate **11** spifflicate

**destroyer**
**06** locust, vandal **07** flivver, ravager, stew-can, wrecker **08** Apollyon **09** desolater, despoiler, ransacker **10** demolisher, destructor **11** annihilator, kiss of death

**destruction**
◇ *anagram indicator* **03** end **04** bane, loss, rack, ruin **05** death, havoc, stroy, waste, wrack, wreck **06** defeat, murder, razing **07** killing, undoing, wastage **08** crushing, downfall, massacre, sabotage, smashing, wreckage **09** levelling, overthrow, ruination, shipwreck, slaughter, vandalism **10** demolition, desolation, extinction, killing-off, ravagement, shattering **11** depredation, devastation, dismantling, elimination, eradication, extirpation, liquidation, pulling-down, tearing-down **12** annihilation, depopulation, knocking-down, obliteration **13** extermination, nullification

**destructive**
**05** fatal **06** deadly, lethal **07** adverse, baneful, harmful, hostile, hurtful, killing, noxious, ruinous, vicious **08** contrary, damaging, deathful, negative **09** injurious, malignant, withering **10** derogatory, disastrous, disruptive, nullifying, pernicious, subversive, unfriendly **11** deleterious, denigrating, detrimental, devastating, disparaging, mischievous, undermining **12** antagonistic, catastrophic, discouraging, pestilential, slaughterous, unfavourable

**destructively**
**08** lethally **09** harmfully, hurtfully **12** disastrously **13** detrimentally

**desultorily**
**07** loosely **08** casually, fitfully **09** aimlessly **11** erratically **13** half-heartedly

**desultory**
◇ *anagram indicator* **05** hasty, loose **06** casual, fitful, random **07** aimless, chaotic, erratic **08** rambling **09** haphazard, irregular, spasmodic **10** capricious, discursive, disorderly, undirected **11** half-hearted **12** disconnected, inconsistent, unmethodical, unsystematic **13** unco-ordinated

**detach**
**04** free, undo **05** calve, draft, sever, split, unfix **06** cut off, divide, loosen, remove, unglue **07** disjoin, divorce, isolate, take off, tear off, unhitch,

unloose, unrivet **08** break off, disunite, estrange, separate, take away, uncouple, unfasten, unloosen, withdraw **09** disengage, segregate **10** disconnect, dissociate **11** disentangle

**detachable**
**07** movable **08** moveable **09** removable, separable **10** eradicable, removeable **12** transferable

**detached**
**04** cold, free **05** aloof, loose **06** remote **07** divided, neutral, severed **08** clinical, discreet, discrete, outlying, separate **09** impartial, objective, uncoupled, withdrawn **10** disengaged, impersonal, unattached, undivested, unfastened **11** dissociated, independent, indifferent, unconcerned, unconnected, unemotional **12** disconnected **13** disinterested, dispassionate

**detachment**
**04** unit **05** corps, force, party, squad **06** detail, patrol **07** brigade, removal, reserve, undoing **08** coolness, disunion, fairness, squadron **09** aloofness, isolation, loosening, severance, task force, unconcern **10** dispassion, lack of bias, neutrality, remoteness, separation, uncoupling, withdrawal **11** impassivity, objectivity, unfastening **12** impartiality, indifference, provost guard **13** disconnection, disengagement, disentangling, lack of emotion

**detail**
◇ *tail deletion indicator* **04** fact, item, list, unit **05** corps, force, point, squad **06** aspect, assign, charge, choose, depict, factor, nicety, patrol, relate, set out **07** appoint, brigade, element, feature, itemize, portray, present, recount, respect, specify **08** allocate, delegate, describe, minutiae, point out, rehearse, specific, spell out, tabulate **09** attribute, catalogue, component, delineate, enumerate, intricacy, precision, task force **10** commission, complexity, ingredient, ins and outs, particular, refinement, triviality **11** elaboration, nitty-gritty **12** circumstance, complication, nuts and bolts, technicality, thoroughness **13** particularity, specification **14** characteristic, meticulousness
• **in detail 05** fully **07** in depth **08** at length **09** carefully, piecemeal **10** item by item, thoroughly **12** exhaustively, in particular, particularly, point by point **15** comprehensively

**detailed**
◇ *tail deletion indicator* **04** full **05** close, exact **06** minute, narrow **07** complex, in-depth, precise, special **08** complete, itemized, specific, thorough **09** elaborate, intricate **10** blow-by-blow, convoluted, exhaustive, meticulous, particular **11** complicated, descriptive **13** comprehensive

**detain**
**04** hold, keep, slow, stay, stop **05** check, delay **06** arrest, hinder, hold up, impede, intern, lock up, retard **07** confine, inhibit **08** hold back, imprison, keep back, make late, restrain, withhold **09** detention **11** incarcerate, put in prison **13** hold in custody, keep in custody **15** take into custody

**detainee**
**03** POW

**detect**
**03** spy **04** find, nose, note, spot, take **05** catch, sense, sight, trace **06** accuse, expose, notice, reveal, turn up, unmask **07** discern, find out, make out, nose out, observe, uncover, unearth **08** decipher, disclose, discover, identify, perceive **09** ascertain, deprehend, recognize, track down **11** distinguish **12** bring to light **13** become aware of

**detectable**
◇ *containment indicator* **05** clear **07** visible **08** apparent, distinct **10** noticeable **11** discernible, perceivable, perceptible **12** discoverable, identifiable, recognizable **14** before your eyes

**detection**
**04** note **06** exposé **08** exposure, noticing, sighting **09** discovery, unmasking **10** disclosure, perception, revelation, uncovering, unearthing **11** discernment, observation, recognition, smelling-out, sniffing-out **12** ascertaining, tracking-down **14** distinguishing, identification

**detective**
**02** DC, DI, DS, PI **03** Det, eye, 'tec **04** busy, dick, jack, tail **05** plant **06** shadow, shamus, sleuth **07** gumshoe **08** prodnose, sherlock **09** operative **10** bloodhound, private eye, thief-taker **11** sleuth-hound **12** investigator, thief-catcher **13** police officer

*Detectives include:*

**03** **Zen** (Aurelio)
**04** **Bony** (Napoleon Bonaparte), **Chan** (Charlie), **Cuff** (Richard), **Dean** (Sam), **Gray** (Cordelia), **Vane** (Harriet)
**05** **Brown** (Father), **Drake** (Paul), **Duffy** (Nicholas), **Dupin** (C Auguste), **Frost** (Inspector Jack), **Ghote** (Inspector Ganesh), **Grant** (Alan), **Lewis** (Sergeant Robbie), **Mason** (Perry), **Morse** (Inspector Endeavour), **Queen** (Ellery), **Rebus** (John), **Spade** (Sam), **Vance** (Philo), **Wolfe** (Nero)
**06** **Alleyn** (Roderick), **Archer** (Lew), **Essrog** (Lionel), **Hanaud** (Inspector), **Holmes** (Sherlock), **Marple** (Miss Jane), **Pascoe** (Peter), **Poirot** (Hercule), **Silver** (Miss Maude), **Vidocq** (Eugène Françoise), **Watson** (Dr John), **Wimsey** (Lord Peter)

**07** **Appleby** (John), **Cadfael** (Brother), **Campion** (Albert), **Charles** (Nick), **Columbo** (Lieutenant), **Dalziel** (Andy), **Fansler** (Kate), **Laidlaw** (Jack), **Maigret** (Inspector), **Marlowe** (Philip), **Milhone** (Kinsey), **Moseley** (Hoke), **Taggart** (Jim), **Wexford** (Reginald)
**08** **Bergerac** (Jim), **Lestrade** (Inspector), **Ramotswe** (Precious)
**09** **Bonaparte** (Napoleon), **Dalgliesh** (Adam), **Hawksmoor** (Nicholas), **Pinkerton** (Allan), **Scarpetta** (Kay)
**10** **Van Der Valk** (Piet), **Warshawski** (V I)
**13** **Continental Op**

• **detectives** **03** CID, FBI

**detention**
**05** delay **07** custody, jankers
**09** captivity, hindrance, restraint, slowing-up **10** constraint, detainment, internment, punishment, quarantine
**11** confinement, holding-back
**12** imprisonment **13** incarceration

**deter**
**04** stop, warn **05** check, daunt
**06** hinder, put off **07** caution, inhibit, prevent, turn off **08** dissuade, frighten, prohibit, restrain, scare off **09** talk out of **10** discourage, disincline, intimidate

**detergent**
**04** soap **07** cleaner **08** cleanser
**09** cetrimide, detersive **10** abstergent, surfactant **13** washing powder
**15** washing-up liquid

**deteriorate**
**03** ebb **04** drop, fade, fail, slip, wane
**05** decay, go bad, go off, lapse, slide, spoil **06** go down, starve, weaken, worsen **07** break up, decline, degrade, fall off, go to pot, relapse, tail off **08** get worse, go to seed, tail away
**09** decompose, fall apart, grow worse, run to seed **10** degenerate, depreciate, go downhill, retrograde, retrogress
**11** become worse **12** disintegrate, fall to pieces **13** go down the tube

**deterioration**
◊ *anagram indicator* **03** ebb **04** drop
**05** decay, lapse, slide **06** waning
**07** atrophy, decline, failure, relapse
**08** downturn, senility, slipping
**09** corrosion, worsening
**10** debasement, falling-off, pejoration
**11** degradation, dégringoler
**12** degeneration, exacerbation
**13** retrogression **14** disintegration

**determinate**
**05** fixed **07** certain, decided, defined, express, limited, precise, settled
**08** absolute, clear-cut, decisive, definite, distinct, explicit, positive, specific **09** specified **10** conclusive, definitive, quantified **11** established

**determination**
◊ *ends selection indicator* **03** end **04** grit, guts, push, will **05** assay, drive, value
**06** decree, ruling, thrust **07** opinion, purpose, resolve, stamina, verdict
**08** backbone, decision, firmness, sentence, tenacity **09** fortitude,

judgement, willpower **10** conclusion, conviction, dedication, insistence, resolution, settlement **11** arbitrament, arbitrement, persistence
**12** perseverance, resoluteness
**13** steadfastness

**determine**
**03** fix, set **04** rule **05** check, elect, fix on, guide, hight, impel, learn, limit, point, shape **06** affect, assign, choose, clinch, decide, define, detect, direct, finish, govern, ordain, prompt, settle, verify **07** agree on, control, dictate, find out, purpose, resolve **08** conclude, discover, identify, regulate
**09** ascertain, condition, establish, influence **12** turn the scale **14** make up your mind

**determined**
**03** out, set **04** bent, dour, firm **05** fixed
**06** dogged, gritty, intent, single, strong
**07** certain, dead set, decided **08** hell-bent, resolute, resolved, stubborn
**09** convinced, dedicated, insistent, steadfast, tenacious **10** iron-willed, persistent, purposeful, unwavering
**11** ascertained, persevering, tough-minded, unflinching, well-defined
**12** single-minded, strong-minded, strong-willed **14** uncompromising

**determinedly**
**06** firmly **08** strongly **09** decidedly
**10** resolutely, stubbornly **11** insistently, steadfastly, tenaciously **12** persistently, purposefully **13** unflinchingly
**14** single-mindedly, strong-mindedly

**deterrence**
**09** avoidance, hindrance, obviation
**10** dissuasion, heading-off, prevention, warding-off **11** elimination

**deterrent**
**03** bar **04** curb **05** block, check
**07** barrier **08** obstacle **09** hindrance, repellent, restraint **10** difficulty, impediment **11** obstruction
**12** disincentive **14** discouragement

**detest**
**04** hate **05** abhor **06** loathe **07** deplore, despise, dislike **08** execrate
**09** abominate, can't stand **10** recoil from

**detestable**
**04** vile **06** horrid, odious, sordid
**07** hateful, heinous **08** accursed, horrible, shocking **09** abhorrent, execrable, loathsome, obnoxious, offensive, repellent, repugnant, repulsive, revolting, villanous
**10** abominable, despicable, disgusting, villainous **11** abhominable, distasteful
**12** contemptible, insufferable, pestilential **13** reprehensible

**detestation**
**04** hate **05** odium **06** hatred **07** dislike
**08** anathema, aversion, loathing
**09** animosity, antipathy, hostility, revulsion **10** abhorrence, execration, repugnance **11** abomination

**dethrone**
**04** oust **06** depose, topple, unseat
**07** uncrown **08** unthrone

**detonate**
**04** pink **05** blast, go off, knock, shoot
**06** blow up, ignite, kindle, let off, set off **07** explode **08** spark off
**09** discharge, fulminate

**detonation**
**04** bang, boom **05** blast, burst **06** blow-up, report **08** igniting, ignition
**09** blowing-up, discharge, explosion
**11** fulmination

**detour**
◊ *anagram indicator* **05** byway
**06** bypass, bypath, byroad
**09** deviation, diversion **10** digression
**11** scenic route **13** indirect route
**15** circuitous route, roundabout route

**detract**
**03** mar **04** take **05** abate, lower, spoil
**06** defame, lessen, reduce **08** belittle, derogate, diminish, distract, take away
**09** devaluate, disparage **10** depreciate
**12** subtract from, take away from

**detractor**
**05** enemy **06** critic **07** defamer, reviler
**08** traducer, vilifier **09** backbiter, belittler, muck-raker, slanderer
**10** denigrator, disparager **11** substractor
**13** scandalmonger

**detriment**
**03** ill **04** evil, harm, hurt, loss **05** wrong
**06** damage, injury **07** empeach, impeach **08** mischief **09** prejudice
**10** diminution, disservice, impairment
**12** disadvantage

**detrimental**
**07** adverse, harmful, hurtful
**08** damaging, inimical, scathing
**09** injurious **10** pernicious
**11** deleterious, destructive, mischievous, prejudicial
**15** disadvantageous

**detritus**
**04** junk, scum **05** waste **06** debris, litter, rubble **07** garbage, remains, rubbish
**08** wreckage **09** fragments

**devalue**
**04** slag, slam **05** knock, lower, slate
**06** demean, reduce **07** deflate, dismiss, run down, slag off **08** decrease, minimize, play down **09** devaluate, disparage, underrate **10** devalorize, undervalue **11** make light of **12** pull to pieces, tear to pieces

**devastate**
◊ *anagram indicator* **04** raze, ruin, sack
**05** floor, level, shock, spoil, waste, wreck **06** ravage **07** despoil, destroy, flatten, nonplus, perturb, pillage, plunder, ransack, shatter **08** confound, demolish, desolate, lay waste, overcome, populate **09** discomfit, overwhelm, take aback
**10** discompose, disconcert, traumatize

**devastated**
◊ *anagram indicator* **05** upset, waste
**06** gutted **07** crushed, shocked, stunned **08** appalled, desolate, overcome **09** horrified, in anguish
**10** distressed, taken aback

**11** heartbroken, overwhelmed, traumatized **13** knocked for six

## devastating

**05** great **06** lovely **07** harmful, ruinous, wasting **08** crushing, damaging, dazzling, fabulous, gorgeous, incisive, ravaging, shocking, smashing, striking, stunning **09** brilliant, effective, wonderful **10** disastrous, impressive, marvellous, remarkable, shattering, staggering **11** destructive, magnificent, spectacular **12** catastrophic, overwhelming, traumatizing **13** extraordinary

## devastation

**04** ruin, sack **05** havoc, ruins, waste, wrack **06** damage, ravage **07** pillage, plunder, ravages **08** wreckage **09** wasteness **10** demolition, desolation, spoliation **11** destruction **12** annihilation, fire and sword

## develop

◇ *anagram indicator* **03** get **04** grow **05** arise, begin, catch, educe, ensue, found, hatch, ripen, shape, start **06** create, evolve, expand, follow, foster, happen, invent, mature, pick up, result, set off, spread, unfold **07** acquire, advance, amplify, enhance, enlarge, improve, nurture, open out, produce, prosper, shape up, work out **08** argument, commence, contract, dilate on, disclose, expand on, fetch out, flourish, generate, initiate, progress, set about **09** branch out, come about, elaborate, establish, institute, originate, succumb to **10** go down with **11** fall ill with, materialize, set in motion **13** become ill with

## development

◇ *anagram indicator* **04** area, land **05** block, event, issue **06** centre, change, estate, growth, result, spread **07** advance, complex, outcome **08** genetics, incident, increase, maturing, maturity, progress, upgrowth **09** evolution, expansion, extension, happening, promotion, situation, unfolding **10** blossoming, occurrence, phenomenon, prosperity, refinement, upbuilding **11** elaboration, enlargement, flourishing, furtherance, improvement, progression **12** circumstance, turn of events
• **stage of development** **04** pupa

## deviance

**07** anomaly **08** variance **09** disparity **10** aberration, divergence, perversion **11** abnormality **12** eccentricity, irregularity

## deviant

◇ *anagram indicator* **04** bent, geek, goof, kook **05** crank, freak, kinky **06** misfit, oddity, quirky, weirdo **07** bizarre, dropout, oddball, odd sort, pervert, twisted, variant, wayward **08** aberrant, abnormal, freakish, perverse **09** anomalous, disparate, divergent, eccentric, irregular, perverted **13** nonconformist **15** with a screw loose

## deviate

◇ *anagram indicator* **03** bag, err, yaw **04** part, seam, turn, vary, veer **05** drift, sheer, sport, stray **06** change, depart, differ, swerve, wander **07** decline, deflect, digress, diverge, incline, oblique, turn off **08** aberrate, go astray, turn away **09** turn aside **11** prevaricate **13** go off the rails

## deviation

◇ *anagram indicator* **03** yaw **05** break, drift, error, freak, quirk, sheer, shift **06** change, detour, swerve **07** anomaly, decline, turning **08** variance **09** deflexion, deflexure, departure, disparity, excursion, inflexion, variation **10** aberration, alteration, deflection, difference, digression, divergence, inflection **11** abnormality, declination, discrepancy, fluctuation, inclination **12** eccentricity, inordination, irregularity, turning-aside **13** inconsistency, prevarication

## device

**04** bomb, logo, plan, plot, ploy, ruse, seal, sign, tool, wile **05** badge, crest, dodge, gizmo, motif, motto, stunt, token, trick, waldo **06** design, emblem, gadget, gambit, masque, scheme, shield, symbol, tactic **07** conceit, machine, slinter, utensil **08** artifice, colophon, insignia, strategy **09** apparatus, appliance, implement, manoeuvre, mechanism, stratagem **10** coat of arms, instrument **11** contraption, contrivance, machination

---

*Devices include:*

**04** iPod®, Xbox®
**05** clock, Dyson®, phone, razor, torch, watch
**06** juicer, scales, shaver
**07** Game Boy®, lighter, stapler, Walkman®
**08** CD player, egg timer, Gamecube®, nail file, scissors, tweezers
**09** can opener, cell phone, corkscrew, hairdryer, hole punch, magnifier, MP3 player, pedometer, staple gun, stopwatch, telephone, tin opener
**10** calculator, coin sorter, data logger, fax machine, ice scraper, wine cooler
**11** answerphone, baby monitor, camera phone, electric fan, manicure set, mobile phone, PlayStation®, thermometer
**12** bottle opener, curling tongs, games console, kitchen timer, nail clippers
**13** remote control, smoke detector, staple remover
**14** personal stereo, Swiss army knife

---

*See also* **electrical; optical; rhetorical**

## devil

**03** div, imp, Pug **04** bogy, fend, Nick, ogre **05** beast, bogey, brute, demon, deuce, fiend, fient, rogue, Satan, sorra, worry **06** Belial, Cloots, daemon, daimon, drudge, Hornie, Mahoun, Old One, pester, ragman, rascal, savage, sorrow, terror, wretch **07** bogyman, Clootie, dickens, Evil One, goodman, incubus, Lucifer, Mahound, monster, Old Nick, Scratch, succuba, the deil **08** Apollyon, bogeyman, firework, goodyear, man of sin, Mephisto, mischief, Old Harry, Old Poker, succubus, the enemy, wirricow, worricow, worricowe **09** Adversary, arch-fiend, Beelzebub, cacodemon, Davy Jones, goodyears, Nickie-ben, yoke-devil **10** cacodaemon, evil spirit, Old Scratch, Ragamuffin, the evil one, the Tempter **11** arch-traitor, the old enemy **12** the wicked one **14** Mephistopheles, Mephistophilis, Mephostophilus

## devilish

◇ *anagram indicator* **04** evil, very, vile **05** cruel, jolly **06** highly, knotty, really, thorny, tricky, wicked **07** awfully, awkward, demonic, greatly, hellish, satanic **08** accursed, damnable, delicate, diabolic, dreadful, fiendish, infernal, severely, shocking, terribly, ticklish **09** atrocious, difficult, execrable, extremely, intensely, malignant, nefarious, sensitive, unusually **10** diabolical, disastrous, dreadfully, outrageous, remarkably, thoroughly, uncommonly **11** complicated, exceedingly, excessively, frightfully, problematic **12** excruciating, immoderately, unreasonably **13** exceptionally **15** extraordinarily

## devil-may-care

**04** rash **06** casual **08** careless, cavalier, flippant, heedless, reckless **09** audacious, easy-going, frivolous, unworried **10** insouciant, nonchalant, swaggering **11** unconcerned **12** happy-go-lucky **13** swashbuckling

## devilry

**03** sin **04** evil **07** impiety **08** atrocity, enormity, foulness, iniquity, vileness **09** amorality, depravity, diabolism, reprobacy **10** corruption, immorality, sinfulness, wickedness **11** abomination, corruptness, heinousness **12** fiendishness, shamefulness **13** dissoluteness **15** unrighteousness

## devious

◇ *anagram indicator* **03** sly **04** wily **06** artful, crafty, erring, subtle, tricky **07** crooked, cunning, erratic, evasive, winding **08** indirect, rambling, scheming, slippery, tortuous **09** deceitful, designing, deviating, dishonest, insidious, insincere, underhand, wandering **10** circuitous, misleading, roundabout **11** calculating, treacherous **12** disingenuous, unscrupulous **13** double-dealing, surreptitious

## devise

**02** do **04** cast, form, plan, plot, talk, will **05** forge, frame, guess, hatch, hit on, shape, study **06** cook up, create,

**devoid**

decoct, depict, design, invent, scheme **07** arrange, compose, concoct, dream up, hit upon, imagine, project, purpose, suppose, think up, work out **08** bequeath, conceive, consider, conspire, contrive, describe, meditate **09** construct, fabricate, formulate, originate **10** come up with **11** put together

**devoid**

**04** bare, free, vain, void **05** empty **06** barren, bereft, vacant **07** lacking, wanting, without **08** deprived **09** deficient, destitute

**devolution**

**09** dispersal **12** distribution

**devolve**

**06** convey, depute, fall to, pass on **07** consign, deliver, entrust, succeed **08** delegate, hand down, pass down, rest with, transfer **10** commission

**Devon**

**02** SW

**devote**

**04** doom, give **05** allot, apply, offer, put in **06** assign, commit, pledge **07** appoint, consign, reserve **08** allocate, dedicate, enshrine, set apart, set aside **09** sacrifice, surrender **10** consecrate **11** appropriate **12** give yourself

**devoted**

**04** fond, true **05** loyal **06** ardent, caring, devout, doomed, loving, sacred **07** staunch, zealous **08** constant, dedicate, faithful, tireless **09** attentive, committed, concerned, dedicated, steadfast **10** unswerving

**devotedly**

**06** fondly **07** loyally **08** ardently, caringly, devoutly, lovingly **09** staunchly **10** faithfully, tirelessly **11** attentively, committedly, dedicatedly, steadfastly **12** unswervingly

**devotee**

**03** bum, fan **04** buff **05** fiend, freak, hound, lover **06** addict, votary, voteen, zealot **07** admirer, fanatic **08** adherent, disciple, follower, merchant **09** supporter **10** aficionado, enthusiast

**devotion**

**04** alms, love, zeal **05** faith, piety **06** ardour, prayer, regard **07** fervour, loyalty, passion, support, worship **08** fidelity, fondness, holiness, sanctity, trueness, warmness **09** adherence, adoration, affection, closeness, constancy, godliness, reverence **10** admiration, allegiance, attachment, commitment, dedication, devoutness, observance, solidarity **11** earnestness, schwärmerei, staunchness **12** consecration, faithfulness, heart-service, spirituality **13** religiousness, steadfastness
• **object of devotion 03** god **09** Jugannath **10** Juggernaut

**devotional**

**04** holy **05** pious **06** devout, sacred, solemn **07** dutiful **09** pietistic, religious, spiritual **11** reverential

**devour**

◊ *insertion indicator* **03** eat **04** bolt, cram, gulp **05** eat up, enjoy, gorge, raven, scarf, scoff, skoff, snarf, stuff, worry **06** absorb, engulf, gobble, guzzle, ravage, relish, take in **07** consume, destroy, drink in, engorge, envelop, feast on, put away, revel in, swallow **08** chow down, dispatch, lay waste, tuck into, wolf down **09** depredate, devastate, finish off, knock back, polish off **10** appreciate, gormandize **11** gourmandize **13** be engrossed in

**devout**

**04** deep, holy **05** godly, pious **06** ardent, solemn **07** devoted, earnest, fervent, genuine, intense, saintly, serious, sincere, staunch, zealous **08** constant, faithful, orthodox, profound, reverent, vehement **09** committed, dedicated, heartfelt, prayerful, religious, steadfast **10** passionate, practising, unswerving **11** church-going **12** wholehearted

**devoutly**

**06** deeply **07** piously **08** ardently **09** earnestly, fervently, sincerely, staunchly, zealously **10** faithfully, reverently **11** prayerfully, religiously, steadfastly **12** passionately **14** wholeheartedly

**dewy**

**05** roral, roric, rorid **06** roscid **07** bedewed **08** blooming, innocent, youthful **10** starry-eyed

**dexterity**

**03** art **05** craft, knack, skill **06** slight **07** ability, address, agility, finesse, mastery, sleight **08** aptitude, artistry, deftness, facility **09** adeptness, expertise, handiness, ingenuity, readiness **10** adroitness, expertness, nimbleness **11** legerdemain, proficiency, skilfulness **14** effortlessness **15** right-handedness

**dexterous**

**04** able, deft **05** adept, agile, handy, nifty, nippy, ready **06** adroit, artful, clever, expert, facile, habile, nimble, subtle, wieldy **07** featous, skilful **08** feateous, featuous **10** neat-handed, proficient **11** right-handed **12** accomplished **14** nimble-fingered

**diabolical**

◊ *anagram indicator* **04** evil, vile **05** nasty **06** sinful, wicked **07** demonic, hellish, satanic **08** absolute, complete, damnable, devilish, dreadful, fiendish, infernal, shocking **09** appalling, atrocious, execrable, monstrous **10** disastrous, outrageous **12** excruciating

**diacritic**

**05** acute, breve, grave, haček, tilde **06** accent, macron, umlaut **07** cedilla **08** dieresis, modifier

**diadem**

**05** crown, mitre, round, tiara **07** circlet, circuit, coronet **08** headband

**diagnose**

**06** detect **07** analyse, explain, isolate **08** identify, pinpoint **09** determine, interpret, recognize **11** distinguish, investigate

**diagnosis**

**06** answer **07** opinion, verdict **08** analysis, scrutiny **09** detection, judgement **10** conclusion **11** diagnostics, examination, explanation, recognition **13** investigation **14** identification, interpretation

**diagnostic**

**10** analytical, indicative **11** symptomatic **12** interpretive, recognizable **13** demonstrative **14** distinguishing, interpretative **15** differentiating

**diagonal**

**05** cater, cross **06** angled **07** crooked, oblique, sloping **08** crossing, slanting **09** crosswise **10** cornerways **11** catercorner, catty-corner **13** catercornered, catty-cornered, kitty-cornered

**diagonally**

**05** cater **06** aslant **08** bendwise **09** at an angle, crossways, crosswise, obliquely, on the bias, slantwise **10** cornerways, cornerwise, on the cross, on the slant **11** catercorner, catty-corner **13** catercornered, catty-cornered, kitty-cornered

**diagram**

**03** key **04** abac, plan, plat, tree **05** chart, draft, graph, table **06** figure, layout, schema, scheme, sketch **07** cutaway, drawing, outline, picture **08** bar chart, isopleth, nomogram, pie chart, run chart **09** floor plan, flow chart, indicator, nomograph, schematic **10** family tree, stereogram **11** delineation **12** exploded view, illustration **14** alignment chart, representation

**diagrammatic**

**07** graphic, tabular **09** schematic **12** illustrative **14** diagrammatical

**dial**

**03** map, pan **04** bass, call, disc, face, mush, ring **05** clock, phone, tuner, watch **06** call up, circle, treble **07** control **09** give a bell, give a buzz, hourplate, telephone
• **compass dial 04** card

**dialect**

**03** Twi **04** Norn **05** argot, idiom, lingo **06** accent, jargon, patois, speech **07** diction, variety **08** language, localism **10** vernacular **11** regionalism **13** provincialism
• **dialect society 03** EDS

**dialectic**

**05** logic **06** debate **07** logical **08** analysis, logistic, polemics, rational **09** deduction, deductive, induction,

**dialogue**

inductive, polemical, rationale, reasoning **10** analytical, contention, dialectics, discussion **11** dialectical, disputation **12** disputatious **13** argumentation, argumentative, ratiocination, rationalistic

**dialogue**

**04** chat, talk **05** lazzo, lines **06** debate, gossip, script **08** colloquy, converse, exchange **09** discourse, tête-à-tête **10** conference, discussion **11** interchange, pastourelle **12** conversation, stichomythia **13** communication, interlocution

**diameter**

**01** d **03** dia **04** diam

**diametrically**

**07** utterly **08** directly **10** absolutely, completely **14** antithetically

**diamond**

**04** bort, pick, rock **05** boart, spark **06** carbon, lasque **07** adamant, paragon, rhombus **08** sparkler **09** brilliant, solitaire **10** Rhinestone

*Diamonds include:*

**04** Hope
**05** Orlov, Sancy
**06** Orloff, Regent
**07** Tiffany
**08** Blue Hope, Cullinan, Idol's Eye, Koh-I-Noor
**09** Centenary, Excelsior, Hortensia
**10** Florentine, Great Mogul
**12** Star of Africa, Taylor-Burton

• **diamonds 01** D **03** ice

**Diana**

**02** Di **07** Artemis

**diaphanous**

**04** fine, thin **05** clear, filmy, gauzy, light, sheer, veily **08** chiffony, cobwebby, delicate, gossamer, pellucid **09** gossamery **10** see-through **11** translucent, transparent

**diarrhoea**

**05** scour **06** scours **07** the runs **08** lientery, the trots, wood-evil **09** dysentery, looseness **10** Delhi belly, gippy tummy, gyppy tummy **12** Aztec two-step, holiday tummy, Spanish tummy, weaning brash

**diary**

**03** log **06** memoir **07** day-book, diurnal, Filofax®, journal, logbook **08** year-book **09** chronicle **13** journal intime **14** engagement book **15** appointment book

*Diarists include:*

**03 Lee** (Lorelei)
**04 Byrd** (William), **Gide** (André), **Mole** (Adrian), **Ooka** (Shohei)
**05 Birde** (William), **Frank** (Anne), **Grant** (Elizabeth), **Jones** (Bridget), **Pasek** (Jan Chryzostom), **Pepys** (Samuel), **Reyes** (Alfonso), **Scott** (Robert Falcon), **Torga** (Miguel)
**06 Burney** (Fanny), **Evelyn** (John), **Pooter** (Charles)
**07 Andrews** (Pamela), **Carlyle** (Jane Welsh), **Chesnut** (Mary), **Creevey**

(Thomas), **Kilvert** (Francis), **Régnier** (Paule)
**08 Greville** (Charles Cavendish Fulke), **Melville** (James), **Robinson** (Henry Crabb)
**09 Schreiber** (Lady Charlotte Elizabeth), **Slaveykov** (Petko)
**10 Ooka Shohei**
**11 Lichtenberg** (Georg Christoph), **Thermopolis** (Mia)
**12 Bashkirtseva** (Marya)

---

**diatribe**

**05** abuse **06** attack, insult, rebuke, tirade **07** reproof, slating **08** harangue, knocking, reviling, slamming **09** criticism, invective, onslaught, philippic, reprimand **10** upbraiding **11** running-down **12** denunciation, vituperation

**dice**

**04** bale **05** bones **09** astragals **11** devil's bones

• **spot on dice 03** pip **04** peep **05** peepe

**dicey**

**04** iffy **05** dodgy, hairy, risky **06** chancy, tricky **07** dubious **09** dangerous, difficult, uncertain **11** problematic **13** unpredictable

**dichotomy**

**08** conflict, division, variance **09** deviation, disparity, variation **10** difference, divergence, opposition **11** discrepancy **13** dissimilarity **15** differentiation

**dicky**

◇ *anagram indicator* **03** ass **04** weak **05** frail, shaky **06** ailing, infirm **07** unsound **08** unsteady

**dictate**

**03** law, say **04** dite, read, rule, word **05** edict, order, speak, utter **06** behest, charge, decree, demand, direct, impose, indite, insist, ruling **07** bidding, command, lay down, mandate, precept, read out, set down, statute **08** announce, instruct, transmit **09** direction, ordinance, prescribe, principle, pronounce, read aloud, ultimatum **10** injunction, promulgate **11** requirement **12** give orders to, promulgation

**dictator**

**04** dict, duce **06** despot, tyrant **07** supremo **08** autocrat **09** oppressor **10** autarchist, Big Brother **12** little Hitler **13** absolute ruler
*See also* **despot**

**dictatorial**

**05** bossy **08** absolute, despotic, dogmatic **09** arbitrary, autarchic, imperious, unlimited **10** autocratic, omnipotent, oppressive, peremptory, repressive, tyrannical **11** all powerful, domineering, magisterial, overbearing **12** totalitarian, unrestricted **13** authoritarian, authoritative

**dictatorship**

**07** fascism, tyranny **09** autocracy, despotism, Hitlerism **11** police state

**12** absolute rule **13** reign of terror **15** totalitarianism

**diction**

**05** lexis, style **06** saying, speech **07** fluency **08** delivery, language, locution, phrasing, speaking **09** elocution **10** expression, inflection, intonation **11** enunciation **12** articulation **13** pronunciation

**dictionary**

**03** DNB, OED, TCD **04** dict **06** gradus **07** alveary, lexicon **08** Chambers, glossary, wordbook **09** gazetteer, thesaurus **10** vocabulary **11** concordance, onomasticon, synonymicon **12** encyclopedia, etymologicon, etymologicum

**dictum**

**04** fiat **05** axiom, edict, maxim, order **06** decree, ruling, saying **07** command, dictate, precept, proverb **08** aphorism **09** direction, ipse dixit, utterance **12** proclamation **13** pronouncement

**did**

**01** 'd

**didactic**

**05** moral **08** pedantic **09** educative, pedagogic **10** didascalic, moralizing, preceptive, protreptic **11** educational, informative, instructive **12** prescriptive

**die**

**02** go **03** dee, ebb, end, pip **04** ache, cark, exit, fade, fail, kark, long, pass, pine, sink, stop, wane, wilt **05** be mad, choke, croak, decay, drown, go off, lapse, merge, punch, quell, swelt, yearn **06** be nuts, be wild, cark it, cut out, depart, desire, expire, famish, finish, go bung, go west, pass on, peg out, perish, pip out, pop off, starve, sterve, vanish, wither **07** be crazy, conk out, decease, decline, dwindle, kick off, kiss off, long for, pass out, pine for, snuff it, subside, succumb **08** be raring, decrease, dissolve, flatline, intaglio, melt away, pass away, pass over, peter out, spark out **09** break down, disappear, go belly up, have had it, lose power **10** buy the farm, hop the twig **11** be desperate, bite the dust, come to an end **12** lose your life, pop your clogs, slip the cable **13** close your eyes, kick the bucket, meet your maker, push up daisies **14** depart this life, give up the ghost, turn up your toes **15** breathe your last, cash in your chips, join the majority
• **die away 04** fade, fall **07** evanish, fall off **09** disappear **10** become weak **11** become faint
• **die down 04** drop, stop **05** abate, slake **06** quench **07** decline, quieten, subside **08** blow over, decrease
• **die out 06** vanish **08** peter out **09** disappear **10** extinguish **11** become rarer
• **soon to die 03** fay, fey, fie **05** fated

**died**

**01** d **02** ob **05** obiit

**diehard**

**05** blimp **06** zealot **07** fanatic

**08** hardline, old fogey, rightist **09** fanatical, hardliner **11** reactionary **12** conservative, intransigent **13** dyed-in-the-wool, stick-in-the-mud **14** traditionalist

**diet**
**04** bant, fare, fast, food, slim, VLCD **06** reduce, regime, viands **07** abstain, cut down, Landtag, rations, regimen **08** fishmeal, victuals **09** nutrition **10** abstinence, conference, foodstuffs, lose weight, provisions, sustenance **11** comestibles, subsistence, weight-watch

**differ**
**04** vary **05** argue, clash **06** debate, oppose **07** contend, deviate, dispute, dissent, diverge, fall out, quarrel **08** be unlike, conflict, contrast, disagree **09** altercate, take issue **10** contradict, depart from, disconsent **11** deviate from **12** be at odds with, be at variance, be dissimilar **14** not see eye to eye

**difference**
**03** row **04** rest, spat, tiff **05** clash, set-to **07** balance, dispute, quarrel, residue, variety **08** argument, conflict, contrast, variance **09** deviation, dichotomy, disparity, diversity, exception, remainder, variation **10** antithesis, contention, divergence, inequality, unlikeness **11** altercation, controversy, discrepancy, disputation, distinction, incongruity, singularity **12** disagreement, distinctness **13** dissimilarity, dissimilitude **14** discrimination **15** differentiation

**different**
◊ *anagram indicator* **03** new, odd **04** allo-, many, rare **05** novel, other **06** at odds, sundry, unique, unlike, varied **07** a far cry, another, awkward, bizarre, diverse, opposed, several, special, strange, unusual, variant, various, varying **08** assorted, clashing, discrete, distinct, ill-timed, mixed bag, numerous, original, peculiar, separate, untimely **09** anomalous, deviating, disparate, divergent, otherwise **10** at variance, dissimilar, individual, poles apart, remarkable, unsuitable **11** contrasting, distinctive, inopportune, worlds apart **12** heterologous, inconsistent, inconvenient, poles asunder, streets apart, unfavourable, unmanageable **13** extraordinary, miscellaneous **14** unconventional

**differential**
**03** gap **08** contrast, separate, variance **09** different, disparate, disparity, divergent **10** difference, divergence **11** contrasting, discrepancy, distinctive **14** discriminating

**differentiate**
**06** modify **07** mark off **08** contrast, separate **09** diversify, tell apart **10** specialize **11** distinguish **12** discriminate **13** individualize, particularize

**differentiation**
**08** contrast **10** separation **11** demarcation, distinction **12** modification **14** discrimination, distinguishing

**differently**
◊ *anagram indicator* **06** at odds **07** a far cry **09** diversely **10** at variance, poles apart **11** worlds apart **12** dissimilarly, incompatibly **13** contrastingly **14** inconsistently

**difficult**
**03** ill **04** dark, hard, high **05** rough, steep, stiff, tough **06** arcane, Augean, badass, gnarly, knotty, thorny, tiring, tricky, trying, uneath, uphill **07** arduous, awkward, complex, Gordian, obscure, onerous, testing **08** abstract, abstruse, badassed, baffling, esoteric, exacting, involved, perverse, puzzling, stubborn, ticklish, tiresome **09** demanding, difficile, gruelling, intricate, laborious, obstinate, recondite, strenuous, wearisome **10** burdensome, exhausting, formidable, perplexing, refractory **11** complicated, intractable, troublesome **12** back-breaking, bloody-minded, hard to please, recalcitrant, unmanageable **13** problematical, unco-operative

**difficulty**
**03** ado, fix, ill, jam, net, rub **04** hole, knot, mess, node, snag, spot, stew **05** bitch, block, devil, nodus, trial **06** aporia, bother, hang-up, hassle, hiccup, hobble, hurdle, labour, pickle, plight, strain, strait **07** barrier, dilemma, nonplus, perplex, pitfall, problem, quarrel, scruple, straits, trouble **08** distress, exigency, hardship, hot water, obstacle, quandary, struggle **09** deep water, hindrance, how-d'you-do, Lob's pound, nineholes, objection, tall order, tight spot **10** cleft stick, disability, impediment, opposition, perplexity, pretty pass, struggling **11** arduousness, awkwardness, dire straits, obstruction, painfulness, predicament, tribulation **12** complication **13** embarrassment, laboriousness, strenuousness **14** stumbling-block
• **get through difficulty** **04** pass
• **in difficulties** **06** in a fix, in a jam **07** in a hole, in a mess, in a stew, stumped, up a tree **08** bunkered **09** in a scrape, in the soup, in trouble **10** hard-pushed, in hot water, up the creek **11** hard-pressed, in deep water, up against it **12** in a tight spot **13** in dire straits **14** having problems, out of your depth
• **with difficulty** **03** ill **04** hard **06** hardly, scarce, uneath **10** at a stretch

**diffidence**
**07** modesty, reserve, shyness **08** humility, meekness, timidity **09** hesitancy, self-doubt **10** inhibition, insecurity, reluctance **11** bashfulness

**12** backwardness, self-distrust **14** self-effacement **15** unassertiveness

**diffident**
**03** shy **04** meek **05** timid **06** modest, unsure **07** abashed, bashful, nervous **08** hesitant, insecure, reserved, sheepish **09** inhibited, reluctant, shrinking, tentative, unassured, withdrawn **10** shamefaced **11** distrusting, unassertive **12** self-effacing **13** self-conscious

**diffuse**
**03** ren, rin, run **05** large, vague, wordy **06** prolix, spread, winnow **07** profuse, publish, scatter, send out, verbose **08** diffused, dispense, disperse, permeate, rambling, waffling **09** circulate, dispersed, dissipate, imprecise, propagate, scattered **10** discursive, distribute, long-winded, loquacious, promulgate **11** disseminate **12** disconnected, periphrastic **14** circumlocutory, unconcentrated

**diffusion**
**07** osmosis **08** bleeding **09** dispersal, extension, spreading **10** permeation, scattering **11** circulation, dissipation, propagation **12** distribution, promulgation **13** dissemination

**dig**
**03** get, jab **04** cast, fork, gibe, gird, grub, howk, jeer, mine, poke, prod, spit, spud, till, twig, work **05** click, crack, delve, ditch, gouge, graft, grasp, grave, lodge, probe, punch, scoop, sneer, spade, taunt **06** burrow, follow, go into, grub up, harrow, hollow, insult, pierce, plough, quarry, search, take in, thrust, trench, tunnel **07** approve, break up, channel, fossick, grub out, realize, scratch, unearth **08** disinter, entrench, excavate, research, turn over **09** cultivate, figure out, make a hole, penetrate, undermine, wisecrack **10** appreciate, compliment, excavation, understand **11** insinuation, investigate **12** get the hang of
• **dig up** **04** find **06** exhume, expose **07** root out, uncover, unearth **08** discover, disinter, excavate, retrieve **09** extricate, track down **12** bring to light
• **digging implement** **02** ko **04** spud **05** spade

**digest**
◊ *anagram indicator* **04** code **05** endew, endue, grasp, indew, indue, study **06** absorb, codify, ponder, précis, reduce, résumé, take in **07** abridge, process, shorten, stomach, summary **08** abstract, canon law, compress, condense, consider, dissolve, macerate, meditate, mull over, synopsis **09** break down, reduction, summarize **10** assimilate, compendium, comprehend, understand **11** abridgement, compression, contemplate, incorporate **12** abbreviation

**digestion**
**08** eupepsia **09** ingestion

**10** absorption, maceration
**12** assimilation, breaking-down
**14** transformation

## digit

**03** toe **05** index, thumb **06** dactyl,
figure, finger, hallux, number
**07** integer, numeral **10** forefinger, ring
finger **12** little finger, middle finger

## dignified

**04** high **05** grand, grave, lofty, manly,
noble **06** august, formal, lordly, sedate,
solemn **07** courtly, exalted, stately
**08** decorous, handsome, imposing,
majestic, reserved **10** honourable,
impressive **11** ceremonious
**13** distinguished

## dignify

**05** adorn, crown, exalt, grace, raise
**06** honour **07** advance, elevate,
enhance, ennoble, glorify, promote
**10** aggrandize **11** apotheosize,
distinguish

## dignitary

**03** VIP **04** dean, name **05** canon **06** big
gun, bigwig, high-up, worthy **07** big
name, big shot, grandee, notable,
provost **08** alderman, luminary,
somebody, top brass **09** personage
**10** archdeacon

## dignity

**05** poise, pride, state **06** honour, status
**07** decorum, majesty, worship
**08** cathedra, eminence, grandeur,
nobility, standing **09** elevation,
greatness, loftiness, nobleness,
propriety, solemnity **10** excellence,
importance, preferment, self-esteem
**11** courtliness, self-respect, stateliness
**13** honourability **14** respectability, self-
importance, self-possession

## digress

**05** drift, stray **06** depart, ramble,
wander **07** deviate, diverge, excurse
**08** divagate **09** turn aside **13** be
sidetracked **15** go off at a tangent, go
off the subject

## digression

**05** aside **06** ecbole, flight, vagary
**08** excursus, footnote, straying
**09** departure, deviation, diversion,
evagation, excursion, wandering
**10** apostrophe, divagation, divergence
**11** parenthesis **12** extravagance, obiter
dictum

## digs

**03** pad **05** place, rooms **06** billet
**08** lodgings, quarters
**13** accommodation, boarding-house

## dilapidated

◇ *anagram indicator* **05** shaky **06** beat-
up, ruined, shabby **07** decayed, in
ruins, rickety, run-down, worn-out
**08** decaying, decrepit **09** crumbling,
neglected **10** broken-down,
ramshackle, tumbledown, uncared-for
**12** falling apart

## dilapidation

**04** ruin **05** decay, waste **08** collapse
**09** disrepair **10** demolition

**11** destruction **13** deterioration
**14** disintegration

## dilate

**04** tent **05** bloat, swell, widen
**06** expand, extend, spread **07** broaden,
distend, enlarge, inflate, stretch
**08** increase **09** spread out

## dilatory

**04** lazy, slow **05** slack, tardy
**08** dawdling, delaying, sluggish,
stalling, tarrying **09** lingering, loitering,
snail-like **10** postponing, prolixious
**11** time-wasting **13** lackadaisical
**15** procrastinating

## dilemma

**03** fix **04** mess, spot **06** plight, puzzle,
why-not **07** problem **08** conflict,
quandary **10** cleft stick, difficulty,
double bind, perplexity
**11** predicament, tight corner
**13** embarrassment, vicious circle
**14** no-win situation

## dilettante

**07** amateur, dabbler, trifler **08** aesthete,
potterer, sciolist **15** non-professional

## diligence

**04** care **08** industry **09** assiduity,
attention, constancy **10** conscience,
dedication, intentness **11** application,
earnestness, painstaking, pertinacity
**12** perseverance, sedulousness,
thoroughness **13** assiduousness,
attentiveness, laboriousness

## diligent

**04** busy **06** eident **07** careful, earnest
**08** constant, sedulous, studious,
thorough, tireless **09** assiduous,
attentive, dedicated **10** meticulous,
persistent **11** hard-working,
industrious, painstaking, persevering
**13** conscientious

## dilly-dally

**05** dally, delay, hover, tarry, waver
**06** dawdle, dither, falter, linger, loiter,
potter, trifle **08** hesitate **09** faff about,
vacillate, waste time **12** shilly-shally,
take your time **13** procrastinate

## dilute

**03** cut, dil **04** kill, thin **05** allay, delay,
lower, small, water **06** lessen, reduce,
temper, weaken **07** diffuse, thin out
**08** decrease, diminish, mitigate,
moderate, tone down, waterish
**09** attenuate, water down
**10** adulterate, attenuated, make
weaker **11** make thinner

## diluted

**03** cut **04** weak **06** watery **07** thinned
**10** thinned out, wishy-washy
**11** watered down

## dim

**04** blur, dark, dull, dumb, dusk, fade,
grey, hazy, pale, paly, slow, weak
**05** appal, bedim, blear, cloud, dense,
dingy, dopey, dusky, faint, foggy,
fuzzy, misty, shade, thick, unlit, vague
**06** bleary, cloudy, darken, feeble,
gloomy, leaden, obtuse, simple,
sombre, stupid **07** adverse, becloud,
blurred, doltish, obscure, shadowy,

tarnish, unclear **08** clouding, confused,
gormless, overcast **09** dim-witted,
imperfect, make faint, tenebrous
**10** caliginous, ill-defined, indistinct,
lacklustre, obfuscated, slow-witted
**11** become faint, crepuscular, make
blurred, unpromising **12** crepusculous,
discouraging, inauspicious, simple-
minded, unfavourable **13** become
blurred

## dimension

**01** D **03** dim **04** area, bulk, mass, side,
size **05** depth, facet, range, scale,
scope, width **06** aspect, extent, factor,
height, length, volume **07** breadth,
element, feature, measure **08** capacity
**09** greatness, largeness, magnitude
**10** importance **11** measurement,
proportions

## diminish

**03** cut, ebb **04** bate, damp, drop, fade,
pare, sink, wane **05** abate, lower,
mince **06** defame, die out, impair,
lessen, minify, minish, rebate, recede,
reduce, shrink, vilify, weaken
**07** assuage, attrite, decline, deflate,
degrade, detract, devalue, die away,
drop off, dwindle, slacken, subside,
tail off, whittle **08** belittle, contract,
decrease, derogate, grow less,
minimize, pare down, peter out,
retrench, taper off, wear down
**09** denigrate, deprecate, disparage
**10** become less, deactivate, grow
weaker **11** whittle away, whittle down
**12** become weaker **14** take the edge off

## diminuendo

**03** dim **04** fade **11** decrescendo

## diminution

**03** cut, ebb **04** loss **05** decay, taper
**07** atrophy, cutback, decline
**08** decrease, drawdown **09** abatement,
deduction, detriment, lessening,
reduction, shrinkage, weakening
**10** shortening, subsidence
**11** contraction, curtailment,
defalcation **12** retrenchment

## diminutive

**03** dim, wee **04** mini, tiny **05** dinky,
elfin, pigmy, pygmy, small, teeny
**06** little, midget, minute, petite, pocket,
tottie **07** compact, minikin **08** dwarfish,
pint-size **09** miniature, pint-sized
**10** contracted, homuncular,
hypocorism, small-scale, teeny-
weeny, undersized **11** hypocorisma,
Lilliputian, microscopic, pocket-sized
**13** infinitesimal

## dimly

**05** dully **06** darkly, feebly, hazily,
weakly **07** dingily, faintly, mistily
**08** gloomily, sombrely **09** obscurely,
unclearly **12** indistinctly

## dimness

**04** dusk, mist **06** caligo **08** darkness,
dullness, greyness, twilight
**09** dinginess, half-light **10** cloudiness,
crepuscule **12** caliginosity

## dimple

**04** dint **05** fovea **06** hollow

**09** concavity, umbilicus **10** depression
**11** indentation

## dimwit

**03** git **04** berk, clot, dope, dork, fool,
geek, nong, prat, twit **05** dumbo,
dunce, dweeb, idiot **06** nitwit
**07** dullard, halfwit, plonker
**08** bonehead, numskull **09** blockhead,
ignoramus **10** dunderhead **11** knuckle-
head
*See also* **fool**

## din

**03** row **04** deen, reel, utis **05** alarm,
chirm, clash, crash, noise, noyes,
raird, reird, shout **06** babble, hubbub,
outcry, racket, randan, stound,
stownd, tumult, uproar **07** clamour,
clatter, yelling **08** brouhaha, clangour,
shouting **09** charivari, commotion,
loud noise **10** hullabaloo
**11** pandemonium

## dine

**03** eat, sup **04** feed, mess **05** feast,
lunch **06** dinner **07** banquet **10** have
dinner

## dingy

**03** dim, dun **04** dark, drab, dull, fusc,
worn **05** dirty, dusky, faded, grimy,
murky, oorie, ourie, owrie, seedy
**06** dismal, dreary, gloomy, isabel,
shabby, soiled, sombre **07** fuscous,
obscure, run-down, squalid **08** isabella
**09** cheerless **10** colourless, isabelline
**11** discoloured **12** disreputable

## dinky

**04** fine, mini, neat, trim **05** natty, small
**06** dainty, little, petite **07** trivial
**09** miniature **13** insignificant

## dinner

**03** tea **04** dine, hall, kail, kale, meal
**05** feast **06** repast, spread, supper
**07** banquet, blow-out **08** main meal
**09** beanfeast, refection, wasegoose,
wayzgoose **11** evening meal
• **dinner time** **07** evening

## dinosaur

*Dinosaurs include:*

**04** T Rex
**06** raptor
**08** coelurus, sauropod, theropod
**09** hadrosaur, iguanodon, oviraptor
**10** allosaurus, anatotitan,
    barosaurus, diplodocus,
    megalosaur, ophiacodon,
    torosaurus, utahraptor
**11** apatosaurus, ceteosaurus,
    coelophysis, coelurosaur,
    deinonychus, dromaeosaur,
    Microraptor, polacanthus,
    prosauropod, saurischian,
    stegosaurus, triceratops,
    tyrannosaur
**12** ankylosaurus, brontosaurus,
    camptosaurus, ceratosaurus,
    megalosaurus, ornithischia,
    ornithomimus, plateosaurus,
    psittacosaur, titanosaurus,
    velociraptor
**13** atlantosaurus, brachiosaurus,
    compsognathus, corythosaurus,
    dwarf allosaur, edmontosaurus,

herrerasaurus, ornitholestes,
styracosaurus, tyrannosaurus
**14** leaellynasaura, psittacosaurus
**15** cryolophosaurus,
    parasaurolophus

## dint

**04** blow, dent **05** force **06** hollow,
indent, stroke **09** concavity
**10** depression, impression
**11** indentation
• **by dint of** **09** by means of **10** by
virtue of **13** by the agency of

## diocese

**03** see **04** Ebor, Exon, Oxon **06** Cantab,
Dunelm **07** Cantuar, eparchy
**09** bishopric, eparchate

*Dioceses and archdioceses of the
UK:*

**03** Ely
**04** York
**05** Derby, Derry, Leeds, Truro
**06** Armagh, Bangor, Connor,
    Durham, Exeter, Hallam, London,
    Oxford
**07** Brechin, Bristol, Cardiff, Chester,
    Clifton, Clogher, Dromore,
    Dunkeld, Glasgow, Kilmore,
    Lincoln, Menevia, Norwich,
    Paisley, Salford, St Asaph,
    Wrexham
**08** Aberdeen, Bradford, Carlisle,
    Coventry, Galloway, Hereford,
    Llandaff, Monmouth, Plymouth,
    St Albans, St Davids
**09** Blackburn, Brentwood,
    Edinburgh, Guildford, Lancaster,
    Leicester, Lichfield, Liverpool,
    Newcastle, Rochester, Salisbury,
    Sheffield, Southwark, Southwell,
    Wakefield, Worcester
**10** Birmingham, Canterbury,
    Chelmsford, Chichester, East
    Anglia, Gloucester, Manchester,
    Motherwell, Nottingham,
    Portsmouth, Shrewsbury,
    Winchester
**11** Northampton, Sodor and Man,
    Westminster
**12** Bath and Wells, Peterborough
**13** Down and Connor,
    Middlesbrough, Ripon and Leeds
**14** Derry and Raphoe, Down and
    Dromore
**16** Swansea and Brecon
**17** Aberdeen and Orkney, Argyll and
    the Isles
**18** Arundel and Brighton, Glasgow
    and Galloway, Hexham and
    Newcastle
**21** Moray, Ross and Caithness, St
    Andrews and Edinburgh
**23** St Edmundsbury and Ipswich
**27** St Andrews, Dunkeld and
    Dunblane

## Dionysus

**07** Bacchus **10** Liber Pater

## dip

**03** dap, dib, dim, dop, nod, sag
**04** bath, dent, dive, drop, duck, dunk,
fall, hole, pawn, plot, sink, soak, swim
**05** basin, bathe, cream, delve, douse,

lower, merge, ploat, sauce, slope,
slump, souse **06** dibble, go down,
hollow, plunge, relish **07** baptize,
decline, descend, descent, ducking,
immerge, immerse, incline, moisten,
sloping, soaking, subside, suffuse
**08** decrease, dressing, infusion,
lowering, mortgage, submerge
**09** concavity, drenching, immersion,
lessening, reduction **10** depression,
pickpocket **11** indentation
• **dip into** ◇ *insertion indicator* **03** use
**04** skim **05** spend **06** browse, draw on,
look at **10** run through **11** leaf through,
look through **12** flick through, thumb
through

## diplomacy

**04** tact **05** craft, skill **07** finesse
**08** delicacy, politics, prudence,
subtlety **10** cleverness, discretion,
statecraft **11** manoeuvring, negotiation,
savoir-faire, sensitivity, tactfulness
**12** negotiations **13** judiciousness,
statesmanship

## diplomat

**02** CD, HE **05** envoy **06** consul, legate
**07** attaché **08** emissary, mediator
**09** go-between, moderator, statesman
**10** ambassador, arbitrator, negotiator,
peacemaker, politician **11** conciliator
**12** ambassadress **15** plenipotentiary

## diplomatic

**06** clever, subtle **07** politic, prudent,
skilful, tactful **08** consular, discreet
**09** judicious, sensitive
**13** ambassadorial
• **diplomatic corps** **02** CD
• **period of diplomatic service**
**04** tour

## diplomatically

**09** prudently, skilfully, tactfully
**10** discreetly **11** judiciously, politically,
sensitively **13** by negotiation, with
diplomacy **14** conciliatorily

## dipsomaniac

**03** sot **04** lush, soak, wino **05** alkie,
bloat, dipso, drunk, souse, toper
**06** boozer, sponge **07** Bacchus,
drinker, tippler, tosspot **08** drunkard,
habitual **09** alcoholic, inebriate
**10** wine-bibber **11** hard drinker
**12** heavy drinker

## dire

◇ *anagram indicator* **04** fell **05** awful,
grave, vital **06** urgent **07** crucial,
drastic, extreme, ominous **08** alarming,
dreadful, horrible, pressing, shocking,
terrible **09** appalling, atrocious,
desperate, frightful **10** calamitous,
disastrous, portentous **11** distressing
**12** catastrophic

## direct

◇ *anagram indicator* **03** aim, con, run,
set **04** airt, conn, hold, lead, mean,
near, show, tell, turn **05** apply, bluff,
blunt, focus, frank, guide, level, order,
point, ready, right, shape, steer, teach,
train, usher **06** adjure, candid, charge,
escort, govern, handle, honest, intend,
manage, market, target **07** address,
command, conduct, control, incline,

non-stop, oversee, primary, sincere, through, up-front **08** directly, explicit, instruct, organize, personal, regulate, straight, unbroken **09** first-hand, immediate, outspoken, supervise **10** administer, face-to-face, forthright, give orders, mastermind, point-blank, show the way, unswerving **11** be the boss of, plainspoken, point the way, preside over, superintend, unambiguous, undeviating, unequivocal **12** be in charge of, call the shots **13** be in control of, uninterrupted **15** straightforward, uninterruptedly

- **directed towards** **02** on
- **direct from** **02** ex

## direction

**01** E, N, S, W **03** set, way **04** airt, goal, lead, line, path, plan, road **05** brief, drift, route, rules, tenor, track, trend **06** course, orders **07** bearing, command, control, running **08** briefing, guidance, handling, tendency **10** current aim, government, guidelines, indication, leadership, management, overseeing, regulation **11** inclination, information, orientation, regulations, supervision **12** instructions **14** administration **15** recommendations, superintendency

*See also* **compass**

- **directions** **06** recipe
- **general direction** **03** ren, rin, run
- **in the direction of** **02** on, to **03** for **07** towards
- **in the wrong direction** **03** wry
- **sharp change in direction** **03** zig
- **take a different direction** **07** diverge
- **take a direction** **02** go **04** chop **06** strike

## directive

**04** fiat **05** edict, order **06** charge, decree, notice, ruling **07** bidding, command, concern, dictate, mandate **09** direction, ordinance, speech act **10** imperative, injunction, regulation **11** instruction

## directly

**03** due **04** bang, dead, full, just, slap, soon **05** plumb, right, smack **06** at once, pronto, square **07** bluntly, clearly, exactly, frankly, plainly, quickly **08** candidly, honestly, outright, promptly, slap-bang, speedily, squarely, straight **09** forthwith, instantly, precisely, presently, right away, sincerely **10** explicitly, point-blank, straightly **11** immediately, straight out, straightway **12** straightaway, straightways, unswervingly, without delay **13** unambiguously, unequivocally **15** instantaneously

## directness

**07** honesty **09** bluntness, frankness, immediacy **10** candidness **13** immediateness, outspokenness **14** forthrightness **15** plainspokenness

## director

**01** D **03** Dir **04** boss, head **05** chair,

chief **06** auteur, leader, top dog **07** manager **08** chairman, governor, overseer, Pole Star, producer **09** conductor, corrector, executive, film-maker, intendant, organizer, president, principal, régisseur, top banana **10** chairwoman, controller, counsellor, supervisor **11** agonothetes, chairperson, choirmaster, symposiarch **12** chapel master, chorus master, contributory, manufacturer **13** administrator, kapellmeister **14** chief executive, superintendent **15** Astronomer Royal

---

*Film and theatre directors and producers include:*

**03** Cox (Brian), Lee (Ang), Lee (Spike), May (Elaine), Ozu (Yasujiro), Ray (Satyajit), Woo (John)

**04** Alda (Alan), Axel (Gabriel), Bond (Edward), Coen (Ethan), Coen (Joel), Eyre (Sir Richard), Ford (John), Gray (Simon), Hall (Sir Peter), Hare (David), Hart (Moss), Hill (George Roy), Lang (Fritz), Lean (Sir David), Nunn (Trevor), Reed (Sir Carol), Roeg (Nicolas), Tati (Jacques), Todd (Mike), Weir (Peter), Wise (Robert)

**05** Allen (Woody), Barba (Eugenio), Boyle (Danny), Brook (Peter), Capra (Frank), Carné (Marcel), Clair (René), Craig (Gordon), Cukor (George Dewey), Dante (Joe), Demme (Jonathan), Fosse (Bob), Gance (Abel), Hands (Terry), Hawks (Howard), Ivory (James), Kazan (Elia), Kelly (Gene), Korda (Sir Alexander), Leigh (Mike), Leone (Sergio), Losey (Joseph), Lucas (George), Lumet (Sidney), Lynch (David), Malle (Louis), Mamet (David), Marsh (Dame Ngaio), Mayer (Louis B), Miles (Bernard, Lord), Noble (Adrian), Pabst (Georg Wilhelm), Perry (Antoinette), Roach (Hal), Scott (Ridley), Stein (Peter), Stone (Oliver), Vadim (Roger), Varda (Agnès), Verdy (Violette), Vidor (King), Wajda (Andrzej), Wells (John), Wolfe (George C), Wyler (William)

**06** Abbott (George), Altman (Robert), Ang Lee, Artaud (Antonin), Arzner (Dorothy), August (Bille), Badham (John), Barton (John), Beatty (Warren), Besson (Luc), Brecht (Bertolt), Brooks (Mel), Bryden (Bill), Buñuel (Luis), Burton (Tim), Callow (Simon), Cooney (Ray), Copeau (Jacques), Corman (Roger), Curtiz (Michael), Cusack (Cyril), Daldry (Stephen), Davies (Howard), Davies (Terence), De Sica (Vittorio), Devine (George), Dexter (John), Disney (Walt), Donner (Richard), Dunlop (Frank), Dybwad (Johanne), Ephron (Nora), Forbes (Bryan), Forman (Milos), Frears (Stephen), Fugard (Athol), Gibson (Mel), Godard (Jean-Luc), Godber (John), Haydee (Marcia), Herzog (Werner), Hopper (Dennis), Howard (Ron), Hughes (Howard), Huston (John),

Hytner (Nicholas), Jarman (Derek), Jordan (Neil), Jouvet (Louis), Kantor (Tadeusz), Kasdan (Lawrence), Landis (John), Lupino (Ida), Mendes (Sam), Miller (George), Miller (Jonathan), Moreau (Jeanne), Murnau (F W), Ophuls (Max), Parker (Alan), Powell (Michael), Prince (Hal), Prowse (Philip), Quayle (Sir Anthony), Reiner (Carl), Renoir (Jean), Siegal (Don), Tairov (Aleksandr), Usigli (Rodolfo), Warhol (Andy), Warner (Deborah), Warner (Jack), Welles (Orson), Wilder (Billy), Wilson (Robert), Zanuck (Darryl)

**07** Akerman (Chantal), Aldrich (Robert), Asquith (Anthony), Belasco (David), Benigni (Roberto), Bennett (Alan), Bennett (Michael), Bergman (Ingmar), Berkoff (Steven), Bigelow (Kathryn), Boorman (John), Branagh (Kenneth), Bresson (Robert), Cameron (James), Campion (Jane), Chabrol (Claude), Chaikin (Joseph), Chaplin (Charlie), Clavell (James), Clooney (George), Clurman (Harold), Cocteau (Jean), Coppola (Francis Ford), Costner (Kevin), De Mille (Cecil Blount), De Palma (Brian), Douglas (Bill), Douglas (Michael), Fellini (Federico), Fleming (Tom), Fleming (Victor), Forsyth (Bill), Gaumont (Léon), Gilliam (Terry), Goldwyn (Samuel), Guthrie (Sir Tyrone), Hartley (Hal), Heiberg (Gunnar), Holland (Agnieszka), Jackson (Peter), Joffrey (Robert), Kaufman (George S), Kaufman (Philip), Kubrick (Stanley), McBride (Jim), McGrath (John), Nichols (Mike), Olivier (Sir Laurence), Poitier (Sidney), Pollack (Sydney), Redford (Robert), Resnais (Alain), Robbins (Tim), Russell (Ken), Sellars (Peter), Sennett (Mack), Stiller (Mauritz), Sturges (Preston), Webster (Margaret), Wenders (Wim)

**08** Anderson (Lindsay), Barrault (Jean-Louis), Berkeley (Busby), Björnson (Björnstjerne), Bogdanov (Michael), Brustein (Robert), Carrière (Jean-Claude), Clements (Sir John), Crawford (Cheryl), Eastwood (Clint), Friedkin (William), Griffith (David Wark), Houseman (John), Jarmusch (Jim), Kurosawa (Akira), Levinson (Barry), Lubitsch (Ernst), Luhrmann (Baz), Lyubimov (Yuri), Marshall (Penny), Merchant (Ismail), Minnelli (Vincente), Mitchell (Arthur), Miyazaki (Hayao), Ninagawa (Yukio), Pasolini (Pier Paulo), Piscator (Erwin), Polanski (Roman), Pudovkin (Vsevolod), Schepisi (Fred), Scorsese (Martin), Selznick (David Oliver), Sjöström (Victor), Stroheim (Erich von), Truffaut (François), Visconti (Luchino), von Trier (Lars), Zemeckis (Robert)

**09** Alexander (Bill), Almodóvar (Pedro), Antonioni (Michelangelo),

**Armstrong** (Gillian), **Carpenter** (John), **Chen Kaige**, **Fernández** (Emilio), **Greenaway** (Peter), **Grotowski** (Jerzy), **Hitchcock** (Sir Alfred), **Malkovich** (John), **Meyerhold** (Vsevolod), **Minghella** (Anthony), **Mizoguchi** (Kenji), **Mountford** (Charles P), **Peckinpah** (Sam), **Plowright** (Joan), **Preminger** (Otto), **Spielberg** (Steven), **Stevenson** (Robert), **Strasberg** (Lee), **Streisand** (Barbra), **Tarantino** (Quentin), **Tavernier** (Bertrand), **Von Trotta** (Margarethe), **Wanamaker** (Sam), **Zinnemann** (Fred)
**10** **Bertolucci** (Bernardo), **Cronenberg** (David), **Eisenstein** (Sergei), **Fassbinder** (Rainer Werner), **Kaurismäki** (Aki), **Kiarostami** (Abbas), **Kieslowski** (Krzystof), **Littlewood** (Joan), **Makhmalbaf** (Mohsen), **Mankiewicz** (Joseph L), **Mnouchkine** (Ariane), **Rossellini** (Roberto), **Saint-Denis** (Michel), **Soderbergh** (Steven), **Sucksdorff** (Arne E), **Vakhtangov** (Evgeny), **Wertmuller** (Lina), **Zeffirelli** (Franco), **Zetterling** (Mai), **Zhang Yimou**
**11** **Bogdanovich** (Peter), **Dingelstedt** (Franz von), **Mackendrick** (Alexander), **Pressburger** (Emeric), **Riefenstahl** (Leni), **Roddenberry** (Gene), **Schlesinger** (John)
**12** **Attenborough** (Richard, Lord), **Espert Romero** (Nuria), **Stanislavsky** (Konstantin), **Von Sternberg** (Josef)
**13** **Aguilera Malta** (Demetrio), **Gutiérrez Alea** (Tomás), **Stafford-Clark** (Max)

- **directors** **05** board
- **managing director** **02** MD
**06** Man Dir

**directory**
**04** list **05** guide, index **06** folder **07** listing, red book, who's who **09** catalogue, inventory **10** court guide **11** Yellow Pages®

**dirge**
**05** elegy **06** dirige, lament, monody **07** requiem **08** coronach, threnody **09** dead-march **11** funeral song

**dirk**
**07** whinger **08** skean-dhu, skene-dhu, whiniard, whinyard **10** skene-occle

**dirt**
**03** mud **04** clay, crud, dust, grot, gunk, loam, mess, mire, muck, pick, smut, soil, soot, yuck **05** bilge, clart, crock, earth, filth, grime, gunge, scuzz, slime, stain **06** clarts, grunge, ordure, scunge, sleaze, sludge, smudge **07** gutters, rubbish, tarnish **08** impurity, lewdness **09** excrement, indecency, obscenity, pollution **10** sordidness **11** pornography **13** salaciousness

**dirty**
**03** bad, mud, ray **04** blue, dark, dull, foul, lewd, mean, mess, miry, poxy, soil, soss **05** bawdy, black, clart, dusty, grimy, manky, messy, mucky, muddy, nasty, slimy, smear, sooty, spoil, stain, sully, yucky **06** assoil, chatty, clarty,

cloudy, coarse, cruddy, defile, filthy, greasy, grotty, grubby, grungy, mess up, mingin', muck up, ribald, risqué, scungy, shabby, skanky, sleazy, smirch, smudge, smutty, soiled, sordid, splash, stormy, unfair, vulgar, X-rated **07** begrime, blacken, clouded, corrupt, defiled, draggle, grufted, immoral, minging, obscene, piggish, pollute, raunchy, scruffy, squalid, stained, sullied, tarnish, unclean **08** bedaggle, besmirch, discolor, enormous, improper, indecent, polluted, unwashed **09** bedraggle, deceitful, discolour, dishonest, salacious, tarnished **10** adulterate, despicable, flea-bitten, insanitary, suggestive, unhygienic, unpleasant **11** contaminate, treacherous, undesirable **12** contaminated, contemptible, pornographic, unscrupulous

**disability**
**04** maim **06** defect, malady **07** ailment, illness **08** disorder, handicap, weakness **09** complaint, inability, infirmity, unfitness **10** affliction, difficulty, impairment, incapacity **11** disablement **12** incapability

**disable**
**04** lame, maim, stop **05** crock, wreck **06** damage, defuse, impair, weaken **07** cripple, invalid **08** enfeeble, handicap, knock out, paralyse **09** disparage, hamstring, make unfit, prostrate **10** deactivate, debilitate, depreciate, disqualify, immobilize, invalidate, undervalue **12** incapacitate **14** put out of action

**disabled**
**04** lame, weak **05** unfit **06** infirm, maimed **07** invalid, wrecked **08** crippled, impaired, weakened **09** bed-ridden, enfeebled, paralysed **10** indisposed **11** debilitated, handicapped, immobilized, out of action **12** hors de combat **13** incapacitated

**disabuse**
**09** enlighten, undeceive **10** disappoint, disenchant **11** disillusion

**disadvantage**
**03** out **04** flaw, harm, hurt, lack, loss, snag **05** catch, minus **06** damage, defect, hang-up, injury **07** own goal, penalty, trouble **08** downside, drawback, handicap, hardship, nuisance, weakness **09** detriment, hindrance, liability, prejudice, privation, weak point **10** disamenity, disbenefit, disservice, disutility, impediment, limitation **11** disinterest **12** Achilles heel **13** inconvenience

**disadvantaged**
**04** poor **06** in need, in want **08** deprived **10** in distress, struggling **11** handicapped **12** impoverished **15** poverty-stricken, underprivileged

**disadvantageous**
**07** adverse, hapless, harmful, hurtful, unlucky **08** damaging, ill-timed **09** injurious **11** deleterious,

detrimental, inexpedient, inopportune, prejudicial, unfortunate **12** inconvenient, unfavourable

**disaffected**
**07** hostile **08** disloyal, mutinous **09** alienated, estranged, malignant, seditious **10** rebellious, unfriendly **11** disgruntled, ill-disposed **12** antagonistic, discontented, dissatisfied

**disaffection**
**07** discord, dislike, ill-will **08** aversion, coolness **09** animosity, hostility **10** alienation, antagonism, disharmony, disloyalty, resentment **12** disagreement, estrangement **14** discontentment, disgruntlement, unfriendliness **15** dissatisfaction

**disagree**
**04** vary **05** argue, clash, fight, upset **06** bicker, differ, object, oppose, sicken **07** contend, contest, discord, dispute, dissent, diverge, fall out, quarrel, wrangle **08** conflict, nauseate, squabble **09** be against, disaccord, take issue **10** contradict, make unwell, think wrong **11** beg to differ **12** argue against, be at odds with, cause illness, disapprove of **13** agree to differ, take issue with

**disagreeable**
**03** bad **04** evil, rude, sour **05** cross, nasty, surly **07** awkward, beastly, brusque, grouchy, peevish **08** churlish, contrary, dreadful, horrible, impolite **09** difficult, irritable, obnoxious, offensive, repellent, repugnant, repulsive, unhelpful, unsavoury **10** abominable, disgusting, ill-natured, unfriendly, ungrateful, unpleasant **11** bad-tempered, disobliging, displeasing, distasteful, ill-humoured, unpalatable **13** objectionable

**disagreeably**
**07** nastily **08** horribly **10** dreadfully **11** obnoxiously, offensively, repulsively **12** disgustingly, unpleasantly **13** objectionably

**disagreement**
**03** row **04** flak, tiff **05** clash, fight **06** bust-up, strife **07** discord, dispute, dissent, quarrel, wrangle **08** argument, clashing, conflict, disunion, friction, squabble, variance **09** deviation, disparity, dissensus, diversity **10** conformity, contention, difference, disharmony, dissension, dissidence, dissonance, divergence, falling-out, unlikeness **11** altercation, contretemps, discrepancy, disputation, incongruity **13** dissimilarity, dissimilitude, inconsistency **14** unpleasantness, unsuitableness **15** incompatibility
- **expression of disagreement** **02** ah, h'm **03** boo, gup, hmm, hum, nah, naw, rot **04** booh, quep, uh-uh **05** arrah **06** hardly **08** nonsense **09** do you mind?

**disallow**
**03** ban **04** veto **05** debar **06** abjure, cancel, disown, forbid, rebuff, refuse, reject **07** disavow, dismiss, embargo,

exclude, say no to **08** disclaim, overrule, prohibit **09** disaffirm, dispraise, interdict, proscribe, repudiate, surcharge

## disappear

◇ *deletion indicator* **02** go **03** ebb, end, fly **04** exit, fade, flee, hide, melt, pass, walk, wane **05** cease, ghost, slope **06** depart, die out, escape, expire, go cold, perish, recede, retire, vanish **07** die away, drop off, drop out, get lost, pass off, scarper, vamoose **08** dissolve, drop away, evanesce, melt away, peter out, withdraw **09** dissipate, evaporate, go missing **10** make tracks, take flight **12** go out of sight **13** become extinct, dematerialize, pass from sight **14** go like hot cakes **15** take French leave

## disappearance

◇ *deletion indicator* **03** end **04** exit, loss **05** going **06** expiry, fading, flight **07** passing **08** dying-out, fade-away **09** departure, desertion, immersion, vanishing **10** extinction, karyolysis, resolution, withdrawal **11** evanescence, evaporation, melting away

## disappoint

**03** vex **04** fail, foil, mock **06** baffle, betray, defeat, delude, dismay, hamper, hinder, sadden, slip up, thwart **07** deceive, depress, let down **08** dispirit, mistryst **09** devastate, frustrate, mislippen **10** disconcert, discourage, disenchant, disgruntle, dishearten, dissatisfy **11** disillusion, make a fool of

## disappointed

**04** sick **05** upset, vexed **06** balked, bummed, choked, gutted, miffed **07** letdown **08** betrayed, cast down, deflated, saddened, thwarted **09** depressed **10** despondent, devastated, dischuffed, distressed, frustrated, unequipped **11** discouraged, disgruntled, downhearted, ill-equipped **12** disconsolate, disenchanted, disheartened, dissatisfied **13** disillusioned, sick as a parrot

## disappointing

**03** sad **05** bogus, sorry **07** unhappy **08** inferior, pathetic, unworthy **10** depressing, inadequate **12** disagreeable, discouraging, insufficient **13** anticlimactic, disconcerting, underwhelming **14** unsatisfactory

## disappointment

**04** balk, blow, sell, swiz **05** baulk, frost, lemon **06** bummer, fiasco, fizzer, regret, suck-in, take-in **07** chagrin, failure, let-down, sadness, setback, swizzle, washout, wipeout **08** calamity, comedown, disaster, distress, non-event **09** damp squib **10** anticlimax, bitter pill, discontent, misfortune **11** cold comfort, despondency, displeasure, frustration **14** discouragement, disenchantment, dispiritedness **15** disillusionment, dissatisfaction

• **expression of disappointment** **02** aw **04** nuts, pity **05** shoot **06** shucks

## disapprobation

**05** blame **07** censure, dislike, mislike, reproof **08** reproach **09** criticism, disfavour, exception, objection **11** disapproval, displeasure **12** condemnation, denunciation **13** disparagement, remonstration **14** discountenance **15** dissatisfaction

## disapproval

**04** veto **05** blame **06** rebuke **07** censure, disgust, dislike, reproof **08** reproach **09** criticism, exception, misliking, objection, rejection **11** displeasure **12** condemnation, denunciation, disallowance **13** disparagement, remonstration, the thumbs-down **14** disapprobation **15** dissatisfaction

• **expression of disapproval** **01** O **02** oh **03** boo, fie, tut **04** booh, toot, tuts, umph, what **05** humph, toots **06** tut-tut **07** fie upon **10** hoity-toity

• **indication of disapproval** **03** boo **04** booh, hiss **05** frown **07** catcall, walk out **09** dirty look, raspberry **10** Bronx cheer, thumbs down **12** slow handclap **13** shake your head

## disapprove

**04** veto **05** blame, spurn **06** reject **07** censure, condemn, deplore, dislike, frown on, mislike **08** denounce, disallow, disfavor, disprove, harrumph, object to **09** be against, deprecate, disesteem, disfavour, disparage, disproove, reprobate **10** animadvert, look down on **11** not hold with **12** think badly of **13** think little of **14** discountenance, hold in contempt, take a dim view of **15** take exception to

## disapproving

**04** prim **07** killjoy **08** critical, frowning **09** reproving **10** censorious, derogatory, pejorative **11** deprecatory, disparaging, improbative, improbatory, reproachful **12** condemnatory **14** disapprobative, disapprobatory

## disarm

**05** charm, unarm **07** appease, disable, disband, mollify, placate, unsteel, win over **08** persuade, unweapon **10** conciliate, deactivate, demobilize, immobilize **11** lay down arms **12** demilitarize **13** make powerless **14** lay down weapons, put out of action

## disarmament

**11** arms control **12** deactivation **13** arms reduction **14** arms limitation, demobilization

## disarming

**07** winning **08** charming, likeable **10** mollifying, persuasive **12** conciliatory, irresistible

## disarmingly

**10** charmingly, pleasantly **12** irresistibly, persuasively

## disarrange

◇ *anagram indicator* **04** mess, muss

**05** musse **06** jumble, tousle, touzle, untidy **07** confuse, derange, disturb, shuffle **08** dishevel, disorder, displace, unsettle **09** dislocate **10** discompose **11** disorganize **13** put out of place

## disarray

◇ *anagram indicator* **04** mess, tash **05** chaos, rifle, upset **06** jumble, muddle, tangle **07** clutter, undress **08** disorder, shambles **09** confusion **10** unruliness, untidiness **11** derangement **12** dishevelment, indiscipline **13** unsettledness **15** disorganization

## disassemble

**08** separate **09** dismantle, pull apart, take apart **12** pull to pieces, take to pieces

## disassociate

**05** break **06** cut off, remove **08** separate, withdraw **10** disconnect, dissociate

## disaster

**04** blow, flop, ruin **06** fiasco, mishap, mucker, stroke **07** debacle, failure, reverse, screw-up, setback, tragedy, trouble, washout, wipeout **08** accident, act of God, calamity, reversal **09** adversity, cataclysm, holocaust, mischance, ruination, shipwreck, sticky end **10** misfortune, providence **11** catastrophe, horror story **12** misadventure

## disastrous

◇ *anagram indicator* **04** dire **05** fatal **06** gloomy, tragic **07** adverse, harmful, ruinous, unlucky **08** dreadful, ill-fated, ravaging, shocking, terrible, tragical **09** appalling, injurious, miserable **10** calamitous, ill-starred **11** cataclysmic, destructive, devastating, unfortunate **12** catastrophic

## disavow

**04** deny **06** abjure, disown, reject **08** disvouch, renounce **09** disaffirm, disavouch, repudiate **10** contradict **15** wash your hands of

## disavowal

**06** denial **07** dissent **09** rejection **10** abjuration, disclaimer **11** repudiation **12** disclamation, renunciation **13** contradiction **14** disaffirmation

## disband

◇ *anagram indicator* **05** demob **06** disarm, reduce, reform **07** break up, dismiss, scatter **08** disperse, dissolve, separate **10** demobilize **11** part company **14** go separate ways

## disbelief

**05** doubt **07** atheism, dubiety, scruple **08** acosmism, distrust, mistrust, unbelief **09** discredit, rejection, suspicion **10** infidelity, scepticism **11** incredulity, questioning

• **expression of disbelief** **03** huh, tut **04** as if!, hoot **05** hoots **06** heaven, indeed, phooey, Walker **07** get away, says you **08** honestly, hoot-toot **09** away you go! **11** away with you,

Betty Martin **12** Hookey Walker
**13** what do you know?

### disbelieve
**05** doubt **06** reject **07** suspect
**08** discount, distrust, mistrust, question
**09** discredit, miscredit, repudiate **13** be unconvinced

### disbeliever
**07** atheist, doubter, sceptic, scoffer
**08** agnostic **10** questioner, unbeliever
**11** non-believer, nullifidian
**14** doubting Thomas

### disbelieving
**07** cynical, infidel **08** doubtful,
doubting **09** sceptical, uncertain
**10** suspicious **11** distrustful,
incredulous, unbelieving,
unconvinced

### disburse
**05** spend **06** expend, lay out, pay out
**07** cough up, dish out, fork out **08** shell out

### disbursement
**06** outlay **07** payment **08** disposal,
spending **09** disbursal, outgiving
**11** expenditure

### disc
**01** O **02** CD, EP, LP **03** DVD **04** disk,
face, gong, ring **05** album, CD-ROM,
elpee, paten, plate, round, vinyl,
wheel **06** button, circle, discus, record,
saucer **07** counter, rosette, roundel
**08** diskette, hard disk, roundlet
**10** floppy disk **11** compact disk,
microfloppy

### discard
**03** bin **04** cast, defy, drop, dump, jilt,
junk, kill, shed **05** ditch, scrap, trash
**06** reject, remove **07** abandon, cashier,
cast off, dismiss, forsake, lay away,
toss out **08** chuck out, get rid of,
jettison, lay aside, throw out **09** cast
aside, chuck away, discharge,
dismissal, dispose of, repudiate,
supersede, throw away, throw over
**10** pension off, relinquish
**11** abandonment **12** dispense with

### discards
**04** crib

### discern
**03** get, see, wit **04** spot, tell **05** judge
**06** descry, detect, notice, scerne
**07** make out, observe, pick out
**08** discover, perceive, tell from
**09** ascertain, determine, recognize
**11** distinguish **12** discriminate
**13** differentiate

### discernible
**05** clear, plain **06** patent **07** obvious,
visible **08** apparent, distinct, manifest
**10** detectable, noticeable, observable
**11** appreciable, conspicuous,
perceptible **12** discoverable,
recognizable **15** distinguishable

### discerning
**04** wise **05** acute, quick, sharp, sound
**06** astute, clever, seeing, shrewd,
subtle **07** prudent, sapient, trained
**08** critical, piercing, tasteful **09** clear-
eyed, eagle-eyed, ingenious,

judicious, sagacious, selective,
sensitive **10** perceptive, percipient
**11** intelligent, penetrating **12** clear-
sighted, eagle-sighted
**13** perspicacious, understanding
**14** discriminating

### discernment
**05** flair, sense, taste **06** acumen,
wisdom **07** insight **08** keenness,
sagacity, sapience **09** acuteness,
awareness, good taste, ingenuity,
judgement, sharpness **10** cleverness,
perception, shrewdness
**11** penetration, percipience
**12** intelligence, perspicacity
**13** ascertainment, understanding
**14** discrimination, perceptiveness

### discharge
**02** do **03** arc, axe, pay, pus, ren, rin,
run **04** emit, fire, flow, free, gush, leak,
meet, ooze, oust, pass, pour, sack,
vent, void **05** clear, congé, demob,
doing, drain, egest, eject, empty,
expel, exude, issue, let go, loose,
rheum, salvo, shoot, spout **06** acquit,
congee, firing, forbid, fulfil, honour, let
fly, let off, let out, pardon, remove,
sanies, set off, settle, unload
**07** absolve, boot out, discard, dismiss,
excrete, explode, exuding, fire off,
fluxion, give off, ousting, outflow,
payment, perform, release, relieve,
removal, sacking, satisfy, send out, set
free, the boot, the sack, turf out
**08** carry out, detonate, disgorge,
dispense, displode, ejection, emission,
evacuate, get rid of, liberate, settling,
the elbow, turn away **09** acquittal,
bowler-hat, broadside, clearance,
colluvies, disburden, dismissal,
excretion, exculpate, execution,
exonerate, expulsion, honouring,
quitclaim, repayment, secretion,
unfraught, unloading **10** absolution,
cashiering, disburthen, disembogue,
fulfilment, liberation, the heave-ho
**11** achievement, carrying-out,
exculpation, exoneration,
performance, suppuration **12** give the
elbow **13** give the boot to
**14** accomplishment

### disciple
**03** son **05** chela, child, pupil **06** votary
**07** apostle, convert, devotee, learner,
scholar, student **08** adherent, believer,
follower, upholder **09** proselyte,
supporter
*See also* **apostle**

### disciplinarian
**06** despot, ramrod, tyrant **08** autocrat,
martinet, stickler **10** taskmaster
**13** authoritarian **14** hard taskmaster

### discipline
**04** bull, curb, judo **05** check, drill,
inure, limit, order, teach, train, tutor
**06** branch, disple, govern, ground,
moguls, punish, rebuke, school
**07** break in, chasten, control, correct,
educate, regimen, reprove, routine,
subject **08** chastise, dressage, exercise,
feng shui, instruct, mathesis, penalize,
practice, regulate, restrain, restrict,

training **09** castigate, direction,
inculcate, reprimand, restraint,
schooling **10** correction, punishment,
regulation, speciality, strictness **11** area
of study, castigation, keep in check,
orderliness, self-control
**12** chastisement, field of study
**13** course of study, mortification, self-
restraint **14** self-discipline **15** make an
example of

### disclaim
**04** deny **06** abjure, disown, refuse,
reject **07** abandon, declaim, decline,
disavow **08** renounce **09** repudiate
**15** wash your hands of

### disclaimer
**06** denial **09** disavowal, rejection
**10** abjuration, abnegation,
disownment, retraction **11** repudiation
**12** renunciation **13** contradiction
**14** disaffirmation

### disclose
**04** blab, leak, open, show, tell
**05** hatch, let on, unrip **06** betray,
evolve, expose, impart, open up,
relate, reveal, squeal, unfold, unheal,
unhele, unlock, unveil **07** confess,
develop, divulge, exhibit, lay bare, let
drop, let slip, open out, propale,
publish, unclose, uncover **08** blurt out,
develope, discover **09** broadcast, make
known, tell a tale **10** disclosure, make
public **11** blow the gaff, communicate
**12** bring to light **13** spill the beans
**14** blow the whistle **15** give the game
away, take the wraps off

### disclosure
**04** leak **06** exposé **08** exposure,
overture **09** admission, broadcast,
discovery **10** apocalypse, confession,
divulgence, laying bare, revelation,
uncovering **11** declaration, publication
**12** announcement
**15** acknowledgement, bringing to light

### discoloration
**04** blot, mark, spot **05** patch, stain
**06** blotch, foxing, streak **07** blemish,
blue-rot, pink-eye, splotch, tarnish
**08** cyanosis, dyschroa, foxiness
**09** dyschroia, melanosis **10** ecchymosis
**12** acrocyanosis, weather stain
**13** xanthochromia

### discolour
**03** fox, mar **04** fade, mark, rust, soil
**05** dirty, stain, tinge **06** bruise, streak
**07** tarnish, weather **09** disfigure

### discomfit
◊ *anagram indicator* **04** balk, faze, rout
**05** abash, shend, throw **06** baffle,
defeat, outwit, rattle, ruffle, thwart
**07** confuse, fluster, perplex, perturb
**08** confound, unsettle **09** embarrass,
frustrate **10** demoralize, discompose,
disconcert

### discomfiture
**05** lurch **06** unease **07** chagrin
**09** abashment, confusion
**10** uneasiness **11** frustration,
humiliation **12** discomposure
**13** embarrassment **14** demoralization,
disappointment

## discomfort

04 ache, hell, hurt, pain, pang 05 worry 06 bother, hassle, jet lag, misery, twinge, unease 07 malaise, trouble 08 disquiet, distress, drawback, hardship, nuisance, soreness, vexation 09 annoyance, purgatory 12 cardialgia, difficulty, irritation, tenderness, uneasiness 12 apprehension, disadvantage, restlessness, unpleasantry 13 embarrassment, inconvenience

## discompose

◇ anagram indicator 06 ruffle 07 agitate, disturb 08 disorder 10 disarrange

## discomposure

05 upset 06 unease 07 anxiety, fluster 09 agitation, annoyance 10 inquietude, irritation, uneasiness 11 disquietude, disturbance 12 perturbation, restlessness

## disconcert

◇ anagram indicator 04 faze 05 abash, alarm, blank, quell, shake, tease, throw, upset 06 baffle, defeat, dismay, put off, put out, rattle, ruffle 07 break up, confuse, disturb, fluster, nonplus, perplex, perturb, startle, stumble, unnerve 08 bewilder, disunion, surprise, throw off, throw out, unsettle 09 discomfit, embarrass, frustrate, knock back, take aback 14 discomboberate, discombobulate 15 throw off balance

## disconcerting

◇ anagram indicator 07 awkward 08 alarming, baffling, daunting 09 confusing, dismaying, unnerving, upsetting 10 bothersome, disturbing, off-putting, perplexing, perturbing, unsettling 11 bewildering, distracting 12 embarrassing

## disconnect

04 part, undo 05 loose, sever, split 06 cut off, detach, divide, ungear, unhook, unplug 07 disjoin, unhitch 08 disjoint, separate, uncouple 09 disengage 10 de-energize

## disconnected

05 loose 06 abrupt 07 garbled, jumbled, mixed-up, scrappy 08 confused, rambling, staccato 09 illogical, separated, wandering 10 disjointed, incoherent, irrational 12 inconsequent 13 unco-ordinated 14 unintelligible

## disconnection

07 undoing 08 division 09 severance 10 detachment, separation, uncoupling, unplugging 13 disengagement

## disconsolate

03 low, sad 04 down 06 gloomy 07 crushed, forlorn, unhappy 08 dejected, desolate, downcast, hopeless, wretched 09 depressed, miserable 10 despondent, dispirited, melancholy 11 heartbroken, low-spirited 12 heavy-hearted, inconsolable 13 grief-stricken 14 down in the dumps

## disconsolately

05 sadly 09 miserably, unhappily 10 dejectedly, desolately, wretchedly 12 despondently, inconsolably 14 heavy-heartedly

## discontent

06 misery, regret, unrest 08 disquiet, vexation 09 fed-upness 10 impatience, uneasiness 11 displeasure, fretfulness, unhappiness 12 disaffection, dissatisfied, heartburning, restlessness, wretchedness 15 dissatisfaction

## discontented

05 fed up 07 unhappy 08 restless, wretched 09 impatient, miserable 10 browned off, cheesed off, displeased, malcontent 11 complaining, disaffected, disgruntled, exasperated 12 dissatisfied

## discontinue

03 end 04 drop, halt, quit, stop 05 cease, scrap 06 cancel, finish 07 abandon, abolish, refrain, suspend 08 break off, knock off, withdraw 09 interrupt, terminate 10 do away with 11 come to an end, come to a stop

## discontinued

03 dis, off 07 at an end

## discontinuity

05 break, comma 06 breach 07 rupture 08 disunion 09 nickpoint 10 disruption, knickpoint 11 incoherence 12 interruption 13 disconnection 14 disjointedness

## discontinuous

06 broken, fitful 08 discrete, periodic, sporadic 09 irregular, separated, spasmodic 10 punctuated 11 interrupted 12 disconnected, intermittent

## discord

◇ anagram indicator 03 row 05 split 06 jangle, strife 07 dispute, dissent, jarring 08 argument, clashing, conflict, disagree, disunity, division, friction, jangling 09 cacophony, disaccord, harshness, wrangling 10 contention, difference, disharmony, dissension, dissonance, opposition, suspension 11 discordance 12 disagreement 13 inharmonicity 15 discord of sounds, incompatibility

## discordant

◇ anagram indicator 04 flat 05 harsh, sharp 06 at odds, atonal, hoarse, off-key 07 grating, hostile, jarring 08 absonant, clashing, jangling, opposing, strident 09 differing, dissonant 10 at variance, dissenting 11 cacophonous, conflicting, disagreeing, disharmonic, incongruous, unagreeable 12 incompatible, inconsistent, inharmonious 13 contradictory

## discount

03 cut 04 agio 05 slash 06 deduct, ignore, rebate, reduce 07 dismiss, take off 08 cut price, knock off, mark down, mark-down, overlook, pass over, pooh-pooh 09 allowance, deduction, disregard, gloss over, reduction 10 concession, disbelieve, rebatement

## discourage

04 damp 05 chill, daunt, deter 06 dampen, deject, dismay, hinder, put off 07 depress, prevent, unnerve 08 cast down, choke off, dispirit, dissuade, hold back, restrain 09 talk out of 10 demoralize, disappoint, dishearten 12 put a damper on 13 advise against 14 discountenance 15 pour cold water on

## discouraged

04 glum 06 dashed 07 daunted, let down 08 deflated, dejected, dismayed, downcast 09 depressed 10 dispirited 11 crestfallen, demoralized, pessimistic 12 disheartened 14 down in the dumps

## discouragement

04 curb, damp 05 gloom 06 damper, dismay, rebuff 07 barrier, despair, setback 08 obstacle 09 dejection, deterrent, hindrance, pessimism, restraint 10 depression, impediment, opposition 11 despondency 12 disincentive, hopelessness 14 disappointment 15 downheartedness

## discouraging

08 daunting 09 dampening 10 depressing, dissuasive, dissuasory, off-putting 11 dehortatory, dispiriting 12 demoralizing, inauspicious, unfavourable, unpropitious 13 disappointing, disheartening

## discourse

04 chat, tale, talk 05 essay, speak, spell 06 confer, debate, homily, preach, reason, sermon, speech, tongue 07 address, discuss, lecture, oration 08 chit-chat, colloquy, converse, dialogue, exercise, treatise 09 discursus, hold forth, rigmarole 10 discussion, exposition, meditation, preachment 11 exhortation, highfalutin 12 conversation, disquisition, dissertation, exercitation, highfaluting 13 communication, confabulation

## discourteous

04 curt, rude 05 gruff, short 06 abrupt 07 boorish, brusque, ill-bred, offhand, uncivil, uncouth 08 ignorant, impolite, impudent, insolent 09 offensive, truculent 10 ungracious, unmannerly, unpleasant 11 bad-mannered, ill-mannered, impertinent 13 disrespectful, unceremonious

## discourteously

06 curtly, rudely 07 gruffly 08 abruptly 09 brusquely, uncivilly 10 impolitely, impudently, insolently 11 offensively, offhandedly 12 ungraciously, unpleasantly 13 impertinently 15 disrespectfully, unceremoniously

## discourtesy

04 snub 06 insult, rebuff, slight 07 affront 08 curtness, rudeness 09 indecorum, insolence 10 bad manners, disrespect, incivility 11 brusqueness, ill-breeding 12 impertinence, impoliteness

**14** indecorousness, ungraciousness, unmannerliness

### discover

◇ *anagram indicator* ◇ *hidden indicator*
**03** see, spy, sus **04** espy, find, spot, suss, twig **05** dig up, hit on, learn, trace **06** create, descry, detect, devise, fathom, invent, locate, notice, reveal, rumble, sus out, turn up, unmask **07** analyse, compose, discern, discure, exhibit, find out, get onto, hit upon, light on, make out, pioneer, realize, suss out, uncover, unearth, work out **08** disclose, discoure, perceive, smoke out, sound out **09** ascertain, determine, establish, fathom out, ferret out, get wind of, get wise to, originate, recognize, stumble on **10** come across, come to know, excogitate, fossick out **11** come to light **12** find out about **13** stumble across

### discoverer

**05** scout **06** author, finder **07** creator, deviser, founder, pioneer **08** explorer, informer, inventor **09** fossicker, initiator **10** originator

### discovery

**04** find **06** descry, eureka **07** finding, heureka **08** devising, findings, learning, location, research **09** detection, invention **10** disclosure, innovation, pioneering, revelation **11** discernment, exploration, origination, realization, recognition **12** breakthrough, introduction **13** determination
• **expression of discovery 05** bingo, hallo, hello, hullo **06** eureka **07** heureka

### discredit

**04** deny, slag, slur **05** blame, doubt, shame, slate, smear **06** damage, debunk, defame, infamy, refute, reject, stigma, vilify **07** censure, degrade, discard, explode, rubbish, run down, scandal, slag off, slander, tarnish **08** badmouth, belittle, disgrace, disprove, distrust, ignominy, mistrust, question, reproach **09** aspersion, challenge, dishonour, disparage, disrepute, ill-repute, reflect on **10** disbelieve, invalidate, opprobrium **11** humiliation **14** put in a bad light, reflect badly on

### discreditable

**06** shabby **08** improper, infamous, shameful, unworthy **09** degrading **10** scandalous **11** blameworthy, disgraceful **12** disreputable **13** dishonourable, reprehensible

### discreet

**04** wary, wise **05** witty **06** modest **07** careful, guarded, politic, prudent, tactful **08** cautious, delicate, detached, reserved, sensible, separate **09** judicious **10** diplomatic **11** circumspect, considerate **13** unpretentious

### discreetly

**06** wisely **08** sensibly **09** carefully, prudently, tactfully **10** cautiously, delicately **11** judiciously

**13** circumspectly, considerately **14** diplomatically

### discrepancy

**08** conflict, variance **09** deviation, disparity, variation **10** difference, divergence, inequality **11** discordance, incongruity **12** disagreement **13** contradiction, dissimilarity, inconsistency

### discrete

**08** abstract, detached, disjunct, distinct, separate **09** disjoined **10** individual, unattached **12** disconnected **13** discontinuous

### discretion

**04** care, tact, will, wish **06** choice, desire, wisdom **07** caution, freedom, reserve **08** prudence, volition, wariness **09** diplomacy, good sense, judgement **10** preference **11** carefulness, discernment, guardedness, inclination **12** predilection **13** consideration, judiciousness **14** circumspection

### discretionary

**04** open **08** elective, optional **09** voluntary **12** unrestricted

### discriminate

**06** secern **07** discern **08** be biased, separate **09** segregate, tell apart, victimize **11** distinguish **12** be intolerant, be prejudiced **13** differentiate, show prejudice, treat unfairly

### discriminating

**04** keen **05** acute **06** astute, nasute, shrewd **08** critical, delicate, tasteful **09** invidious, selective, sensitive **10** cultivated, discerning, fastidious, particular, perceptive, respective **12** differential, preferential

### discrimination

**04** bias **05** skill, taste **06** acumen, ageism, racism, sexism, sizism **07** ableism, bigotry, fattism, insight, Jim Crow, lookism, sizeism **08** classism, inequity, judgment, keenness, subtlety **09** acuteness, colour bar, judgement, prejudice **10** astuteness, difference, differency, homophobia, perception, refinement, shrewdness, unfairness **11** discernment, distinction, favouritism, intolerance, penetration, segregation, sensitivity **12** heterosexism, perspicacity **14** male chauvinism

### discriminatory

**06** biased, loaded, unfair, unjust **07** partial **08** one-sided, partisan, weighted **09** favouring **10** prejudiced **11** inequitable, prejudicial **12** preferential **14** discriminative

### discursive

**05** wordy **06** prolix **07** diffuse, verbose **08** rambling **09** wandering **10** circuitous, digressing, long-winded, meandering **11** wide-ranging

### discuss

**03** vex **04** sift, toss **05** argue, study, treat **06** confer, debate, decide, dispel, go into, handle, parley, reason, review,

settle, take up **07** agitate, analyse, belabor, beprose, canvass, consult, declare, examine, speak to, weigh up **08** belabour, consider, converse, critique, deal with, question, talk over **09** discourse, kick about, pro and con, talk about, thrash out **10** deliberate, interplead, kick around, knock about, politicize **11** confabulate, expostulate, knock around **12** go into detail **15** exchange views on

### discussion

**03** rap **04** chat, conf, moot, talk **05** forum, study, talks **06** debate, korero, parley, powwow, review, talk-in **07** gabfest, palaver, seminar **08** analysis, argument, dialogue, exchange, question, scrutiny, speaking, talkfest **09** discourse, symposium, talkathon **10** colloquium, conference, rap session **11** examination **12** consultation, conversation, deliberation, negotiations **13** consideration

### disdain

**03** coy **04** snub **05** scorn, sdayn, sdein, spurn **06** deride, ignore, rebuff, reject, sdaine, sdeign, slight **07** contemn, despise, disavow, dislike, sdeigne, sneer at **08** belittle, contempt, derision, pooh-pooh, sneering, turn down **09** arrogance, contumely, disregard **10** look down on, sour grapes, undervalue **11** deprecation, haughtiness **12** cold shoulder, snobbishness, think scorn of **13** disparagement
• **expression of disdain 04** pooh, tush **06** powwaw
• **show disdain 04** geck

### disdainful

**05** aloof, proud, saucy **07** haughty, pompous **08** arrogant, derisive, insolent, scornful, sneering, superior **09** slighting **11** disparaging **12** contemptuous, supercilious

### disease

**03** bug, pox **05** virus **06** malady **07** ailment, illness **08** disorder, epidemic, sickness **09** complaint, condition, contagion, ill-health, infection, infirmity **10** affliction, disability, uneasiness **13** indisposition, unhealthiness

*Diseases and medical conditions include:*

**02** CF, ME, MS, TB
**03** CFS, CJD, DVT, flu, FMS, IBS, PID, PKU, PVS, tic, TSS
**04** AIDS, ARDS, clap, cold, coma, gout, kuru, LQTS, Lyme, mono, rash, SARS, yaws
**05** colic, croup, favus, lupus, mumps, polio, Weil's
**06** angina, apnoea, asthma, autism, cancer, chorea, Crohn's, dengue, dropsy, eczema, emesis, goitre, Grave's, hernia, herpes, oedema, otitis, Paget's, quinsy, rabies, scurvy, stroke, thrush, tumour, typhus
**07** abscess, allergy, anaemia,

anthrax, anxiety, atrophy, Batten's, bird flu, Bright's, bulimia, cholera, coeliac, kissing, leprosy, lockjaw, malaria, Marburg, measles, myalgia, mycosis, rickets, rubella, sarcoma, scabies, tetanus, typhoid, vertigo

08 Addison's, alopecia, aneurism, anorexia, avian flu, beriberi, botulism, bursitis, cachexia, coxalgia, Cushing's, cynanche, cystitis, dementia, diabetes, embolism, epilepsy, fibroids, gangrene, glaucoma, Hodgkin's, impetigo, jaundice, kala-azar, listeria, lymphoma, melanoma, Ménière's, migraine, necrosis, orchitis, pyelitis, Raynaud's, rhinitis, ringworm, sciatica, shingles, smallpox, stenosis, syphilis, tapeworm, Tay-Sachs, tinnitus, trachoma, venereal, viraemia

09 arthritis, arthrosis, bilharzia, chlamydia, chlorosis, cirrhosis, cri du chat, distemper, dysentery, eclampsia, emphysema, enteritis, Fujian flu, hepatitis, influenza, ketonuria, leukaemia, neoplasia, nephritis, nephrosis, neuralgia, paralysis, parotitis, pertussis, pneumonia, psoriasis, pyorrhoea, silicosis, sinusitis, sunstroke, Sydenham's, toothache, urticaria, varicella

10 acromegaly, Alzheimer's, amoebiasis, asbestosis, Bell's palsy, Black Death, bronchitis, chickenpox, common cold, depression, diphtheria, gingivitis, gonorrhoea, laryngitis, Lassa fever, meningitis, Parkinson's, rhinorrhea, thrombosis

11 anaphylaxis, brucellosis, cholestasis, consumption, dehydration, dengue fever, farmer's lung, green monkey, haemophilia, haemorrhage, heart attack, Huntington's, hydrophobia, hyperplasia, hypertrophy, hypotension, listeriosis, mastoiditis, motor neuron, myocarditis, peritonitis, pharyngitis, pneumonitis, proteinuria, psittacosis, sarcoidosis, septicaemia, septic shock, spina bifida, tonsillitis, trench fever, yellow fever

12 appendicitis, athlete's foot, cor pulmonale, encephalitis, endocarditis, fibromyalgia, foot-and-mouth, heart failure, Legionnaires', liver failure, osteoporosis, pericarditis, scarlet fever, tuberculosis

13 acoustic shock, bronchiolitis, bubonic plague, cerebral palsy, coronary heart, Down's syndrome, elephantiasis, endometriosis, gastroparesis, German measles, kidney failure, leishmaniasis, microfracture, mononucleosis, osteomyelitis,

poliomyelitis, Rett's syndrome, Reye's syndrome, schizophrenia, toxoplasmosis, varicose veins, West Nile virus, whooping cough

14 angina pectoris, break-bone fever, conjunctivitis, cystic fibrosis, glandular fever, long QT syndrome, Marfan syndrome, osteoarthritis, pneumoconiosis, rheumatic fever, river blindness, sleepy sickness, thyrotoxicosis

15 anorexia nervosa, atherosclerosis, bipolar disorder, gastro-enteritis, Gulf War syndrome, manic depression, phenylketonuria, schistosomiasis

*See also* **skin**

*Animal diseases include:*

03 BSE, FMD, gid, orf
04 gape, gout, loco, roup, wind
05 bloat, braxy, farcy, frush, hoove, pearl, surra, vives
06 canker, Johne's, mad cow, Marek's, nagana, rabies, spavie, spavin, sturdy
07 anthrax, blue ear, dourine, hard pad, measles, mooneye, moorill, murrain, roaring, rubbers, scrapie, yellows
08 bovine TB, fowl-pest, glanders, pullorum, scaly-leg, seedy-toe, sheep-pox, staggers, swayback, swine-pox, wildfire, wire-heel
09 Aujeszky's, blackhead, distemper, Newcastle, scratches, sheep scab, spauld-ill, St Hubert's, strangles
10 blue tongue, louping-ill, ornithosis, rinderpest, sallenders, swamp fever, swine fever, Texas fever, water-brain
11 blood-spavin, brucellosis, mad staggers, myxomatosis, parrot fever, psittacosis
12 black-quarter, bush sickness, cattle-plague, foot-and-mouth, furunculosis, gall-sickness
13 grass sickness, grass staggers, leptospirosis
14 sleepy staggers
15 Rift Valley fever, stomach staggers

*Plant diseases include:*

04 bunt, curl, rust, smut
05 ergot
06 blight, blotch, canker, mildew, mosaic, red rot
07 ferrugo, oak wilt, ring rot, rosette, soft rot, yellows
08 blackleg, black rot, clubroot, crown rot, Dutch elm, leaf curl, loose-cut, wheat eel, white rot
09 crown gall, potato rot, tulip root
10 fire-blight, leaf mosaic, silver leaf, sooty mould, vine-mildew
11 anthracnose, wheat mildew
12 finger-and-toe, peach-yellows, potato blight
13 powdery mildew
14 psyllid yellows, sudden oak death

*Disease symptoms include:*

04 pain, rash
05 cramp, fever, hives, sniff
06 aching, lesion, tremor
07 anxiety, fatigue, fitting, itching
08 bruising, coughing, deafness, fainting, headache, insomnia, numbness, sickness, sneezing, swelling, tingling, vomiting, weakness
09 blindness, diarrhoea, dizziness, heartburn, impotence, lassitude, nosebleed, paralysis, stiffness, twitching
10 congestion, depression, flatulence, irritation, sore throat, tenderness
11 convulsions, indigestion, loss of voice, trapped wind
12 constipation, incontinence, inflammation, irritability, loss of libido, muscle cramps
13 loss of hearing, stomach cramps, swollen glands
14 loss of appetite, pins and needles
15 high temperature, loss of sensation

• **abatement of disease** 05 lysis
• **infectious diseases** 02 ID

**diseased**
◊ *anagram indicator* 03 ill 04 poxy, sick 05 crook 06 ailing, infirm, unwell 07 unsound 08 blighted, infected, soul-sick 09 unhealthy 12 contaminated, distemperate

**disembark**
04 land 05 leave 06 alight, arrive, debark, get off 07 deplane, detrain, disbark, step off 08 dismount

**disembarkation**
07 arrival, landing 09 alighting

**disembodied**
07 ghostly, phantom 08 bodiless, spectral 09 spiritual 10 discarnate, immaterial, intangible 11 incorporeal 12 discorporate

**disembowel**
◊ *middle deletion indicator* 03 gut 04 draw 06 paunch 07 embowel 08 disbowel, gralloch 09 viscerate 10 eviscerate, exenterate

**disenchanted**
05 blasé, fed up 06 soured 07 cynical, let down 09 jaundiced 11 discouraged, indifferent 12 disappointed, dissatisfied 13 disillusioned

**disenchantment**
08 cynicism 09 fed-upness, revulsion 11 disillusion 14 disappointment 15 disillusionment, dissatisfaction

**disengage**
04 free, slip, undo 05 untie 06 detach, loosen, remove, unhook 07 release, unhitch 08 disunite, liberate, separate, throw off, uncouple, unfasten, withdraw 09 extricate 10 disconnect 11 disentangle

**disengaged**
04 free 05 clear, freed, loose 08 detached, released, separate

**09** liberated, separated, unhitched **10** unattached, unoccupied **11** unconnected **12** disentangled

**disengagement**
**07** release, removal, retreat **09** loosening, releasing **10** detachment, retirement, separating, taking away, withdrawal **13** disconnection **15** disentanglement

**disentangle**
**03** red **04** free, redd, undo **05** loose, ravel **06** detach, unfold, unknot, unwind **07** clarify, release, resolve, unravel, unsnarl, untwist **08** distance, ravel out, separate, simplify, unfasten, untangle **09** debarrass, disengage, extricate **10** disconnect, disinvolve, straighten **11** distinguish **13** straighten out

**disfavour**
**06** oppose **07** disgust, dislike **08** distaste, ignominy **09** discredit, disesteem, disregard, disrepute, hostility **10** disapprove, low opinion, opprobrium **11** disapproval, displeasure **12** unpopularity **14** disapprobation **15** dissatisfaction

**disfigure**
◇ *anagram indicator* **03** mar **04** blad, blur, flaw, maim, ruin, scar, tash **05** blaud, spoil **06** agrise, agrize, agryze, beweep, damage, deface, defeat, deform, injure, mangle **07** blemish, distort **08** discolor, make ugly, mutilate **09** defeature, discolour

**disfigurement**
**04** scar, spot, wart **05** stain **06** blotch, defect, injury **07** blemish **08** disgrace **09** defeature, deformity **10** defacement, distortion, impairment, mutilation **12** uglification

**disgorge**
**04** hawk, spew **05** belch, eject, empty, expel, spout, vomit **06** effuse **07** pour out, throw up **09** discharge **11** regurgitate

**disgrace**
**04** blot, slur **05** abase, atimy, blame, shame, shend, smear, stain, sully, taint **06** baffle, debase, defame, ignomy, infamy, stigma **07** attaint, degrade, obloquy, reproof, scandal, villany **08** belittle, contempt, dishonor, ignominy, reproach, ugliness, villainy **09** attainder, black mark, denigrate, discredit, disfavour, dishonour, disparage, disrepute, humiliate, indignify, indignity **10** debasement, defamation, disrespect, disworship, loss of face, opprobrium, put to shame, scandalize, stigmatize **11** degradation, humiliation **12** bring shame on **13** disfigurement **14** disapprobation **15** cause to lose face

**disgraced**
**06** shamed **07** branded **08** degraded **10** humiliated **11** discredited, dishonoured, stigmatized, under a cloud **13** in the doghouse

**disgraceful**
**05** awful **06** indign **08** culpable, dreadful, infamous, shameful,

shocking, terrible, unworthy **09** appalling, degrading **10** despicable, inglorious, outrageous, scandalled, scandalous **11** blameworthy, ignominious, opprobrious, reproachful **12** contemptible, dishonorable, disreputable **13** discreditable, dishonourable, reprehensible

**disgracefully**
**07** awfully **08** terribly **10** despicably, dreadfully, shamefully, shockingly **11** appallingly **12** contemptibly, disreputably, outrageously, scandalously **13** dishonourably, ignominiously, reprehensibly

**disgruntled**
◇ *anagram indicator* **05** fed up, sulky, testy, vexed **06** grumpy, peeved, put out, sullen **07** annoyed, chuffed, peevish **08** hosed off, petulant **09** hacked off, irritated, resentful **10** brassed off, browned off, cheesed off, displeased, malcontent **11** exasperated **12** discontented, dissatisfied

**disguise**
◇ *anagram indicator* **04** face, fake, hide, mask, ring, veil **05** cloak, cloke, color, cover, feign, front, fudge, visor, vizor **06** colour, façade, immask, mantle, screen, shroud, veneer, vizard **07** conceal, costume, cover up, deceive, dress up, falsify, pretend, repress **08** palliate, pretence, suppress, travesty **09** coverture, deception, dissemble, gloss over, whitewash **10** camouflage, masquerade **11** concealment, dissimulate, impersonate **12** be under cover, cook the books, false picture, misrepresent **15** put on a brave face

**disguised**
◇ *anagram indicator* **04** fake **05** false **06** covert, hidden, made up, masked, veiled **07** cloaked, feigned **09** incognito **10** under cover **11** camouflaged **14** unrecognizable

**disgust**
**03** irk, pip **04** cloy **05** repel, shock **06** hatred, nausea, offend, put off, revolt, sicken, turn up **07** outrage, scunner, turn off **08** aversion, distaste, gross out, loathing, nauseate, scomfish **09** disfavour, displease, disrelish, repulsion, revulsion **10** abhorrence, repugnance **11** detestation, disapproval, displeasure **15** turn your stomach
• **expression of disgust 02** aw, fy **03** bah, fie, foh, huh, pah, paw, pho, sis, ugh, wow, yah, yuk **04** damn, phoh, pooh, tush, whow, yech, yuck **05** faugh, shoot, wowee **06** powwaw **11** for God's sake **14** for heaven's sake

**disgusted**
**04** sick **06** put off **08** appalled, offended, outraged, repelled, repulsed, revolted, sickened, up in arms **10** cheesed off

**disgusting**
**03** bad **04** foul, vile **05** grody, gross,

nasty, slimy, yucky, yukky **06** odious, putrid, ugsome **07** mawkish, noisome, obscene **08** nauseous, shocking **09** appalling, offensive, repellent, repugnant, repulsive, revolting, sickening **10** abominable, detestable, nauseating, off-putting, outrageous, unpleasant **11** disgraceful, distasteful, rebarbative, unpalatable **12** unappetizing **13** objectionable

**dish**
◇ *anagram indicator* **04** bowl, fare, food, ruin, tray **05** plate **06** course, recipe, tureen **07** platter **08** delicacy **10** speciality
*See also* **food**
• **dish out** ◇ *anagram indicator* **07** dole out, give out, hand out, inflict, mete out **08** allocate, dispense, share out **09** hand round, pass round **10** distribute
• **dish up 05** ladle, offer, scoop, serve, spoon **07** present **08** dispense

**disharmony**
**05** clash **06** strife **07** discord, dissent **08** conflict, friction **09** disaccord **10** dissonance **11** discordance, incongruity **12** disagreement **15** incompatibility

**dishearten**
**04** dash **05** chill, crush, daunt, deter **06** dampen, deject, dismay **07** depress, unheart **08** cast down, dispirit **09** disparage, weigh down **10** demoralize, disappoint, discourage **12** put a damper on **13** make depressed

**disheartened**
◇ *middle deletion indicator* **04** down **07** crushed, daunted **08** dejected, dismayed, downcast **09** depressed **10** dispirited **11** crestfallen, demoralized, discouraged, downhearted **12** disappointed

**dishevelled**
◇ *anagram indicator* **04** wild **05** daggy, messy **06** blowsy, blowzy, untidy **07** in a mess, ruffled, rumpled, scruffy, tousled, unkempt **08** slovenly, uncombed **09** windswept **10** bedraggled, disordered **11** disarranged

**dishonest**
**03** sly **04** bent, iffy **05** crook, cross, dirty, dodgy, false, fishy, lying, shady, snide **06** crafty, shifty, untrue **07** corrupt, crooked, cunning, devious, knavish **08** cheating, unchaste **09** deceitful, deceptive, insincere, irregular, swindling **10** fraudulent, mendacious, perfidious, untruthful **11** duplicitous, treacherous **12** disreputable, unprincipled, unscrupulous **13** dishonourable, double-dealing, untrustworthy

**dishonestly**
**05** false **07** falsely **09** corruptly, deviously **10** on the cross **11** deceitfully, deceptively **12** disreputably, fraudulently, perfidiously **13** dishonourably, treacherously **14** unscrupulously

## dishonesty

**05** fraud **06** deceit **07** falsity, knavery, perfidy **08** cheating, trickery **09** chicanery, duplicity, falsehood, improbity, shadiness, treachery **10** corruption, dirty trick **11** criminality, crookedness, fraudulence, insincerity **12** irregularity **13** double-dealing, sharp practice **14** untruthfulness

## dishonour

**04** slur **05** abuse, shame, stain, sully, wrong **06** debase, defame, defile, demean, ignomy, infamy, insult, offend, refuse, reject, seduce, slight, stigma **07** affront, debauch, degrade, offence, outrage, scandal **08** disgrace, ignominy, reproach, turn down **09** abasement, aspersion, discredit, disfavour, disparage, disrepute, humiliate, indignity **10** debasement, disworship, opprobrium **11** degradation, discourtesy, humiliation

## dishonourable

**05** shady **07** corrupt, disleal, ignoble, low-down **08** infamous, shameful, unhonest, unworthy **09** shameless, unethical **10** despicable, perfidious, scandalous **11** disgraceful, ignominious, treacherous **12** contemptible, disreputable, unprincipled, unscrupulous **13** discreditable, untrustworthy

## dishy

**04** sexy **05** hunky **08** charming, gorgeous, handsome **10** attractive **11** good-looking

## disillusion

**08** disabuse **09** undeceive **10** disappoint, disenchant **14** disappointment, disenchantment **15** disillusionment

## disillusioned

**07** let-down **09** disabused **10** undeceived **12** disappointed, disenchanted

## disincentive

**06** damper **07** barrier, turn-off **08** obstacle **09** determent, deterrent, hindrance, repellent **10** constraint, dissuasion, impediment **11** restriction **14** discouragement

## disinclination

**07** dislike **08** aversion **09** antipathy, loathness, objection **10** alienation, averseness, hesitation, opposition, reluctance, repugnance, resistance **13** indisposition, unwillingness

## disinclined

**05** loath **06** averse **07** opposed **08** hesitant **09** reluctant, resistant, unwilling **10** indisposed, undisposed **14** unenthusiastic

## disinfect

**05** clean, purge **06** bleach, purify **07** cleanse **08** fumigate, sanitize **09** sterilize **13** decontaminate

## disinfectant

**05** lysol **06** cineol, cresol, phenol **07** cineole **08** fumigant, sheep-dip,

terebene **09** germicide, sanitizer **10** antiseptic, sterilizer **11** bactericide **12** methyl violet **13** decontaminant **14** glutaraldehyde

## disingenuous

**03** sly **04** wily **06** artful, crafty, shifty **07** cunning, devious, feigned **08** guileful, two-faced, uncandid **09** deceitful, designing, dishonest, insidious, insincere **11** duplicitous

## disingenuously

**05** slyly **08** artfully **09** cunningly, deviously **11** deceitfully, dishonestly, insidiously, insincerely

## disinherit

**06** cut off, reject **07** abandon **08** renounce **09** repudiate **10** dispossess, exheredate, impoverish **14** turn your back on

## disintegrate

◊ *anagram indicator* **03** rot **05** decay, smash **06** reduce **07** break up, crumble, moulder, shatter **08** separate, splinter **09** decompose, fall apart **10** break apart **12** fall to pieces, self-destruct

## disintegration

◊ *anagram indicator* **03** rot **05** decay **07** breakup **08** biolysis, decaying **09** breakdown, crumbling **10** karyolysis, separation, shattering **11** dissolution **12** falling-apart **13** decomposition, radioactivity, spondylolysis

## disinter

**05** dig up **06** exhume, expose, reveal, unbury **07** uncover, unearth **08** excavate, exhumate **09** disentomb, disinhume, resurrect **12** bring to light

## disinterest

**08** fairness **09** unconcern **10** detachment, neutrality **12** disadvantage, impartiality, unbiasedness

## disinterested

**04** cool, fair, just **07** neutral **08** detached, generous, unbiased **09** equitable, impartial, objective, unselfish **10** even-handed, open-minded, uninvolved **12** unprejudiced **13** dispassionate

## disjointed

◊ *anagram indicator* **05** bitty, loose, split **06** abrupt, broken, fitful **07** aimless, divided **08** confused, rambling **09** displaced, disunited, separated, spasmodic, wandering **10** dislocated, disordered, incoherent **11** unconnected **12** disconnected **13** directionless **14** disarticulated

## dislike

**04** defy, down, hate, lump, mind, shun **05** abhor, derry, scorn, thing **06** animus, detest, enmity, hatred, loathe, needle **07** allergy, despise, disgust, mislike **08** aversion, disfavor, distaste, dyspathy, execrate, loathing, object to **09** abominate, animosity, antipathy, disesteem, disfavour, disrelish, hostility, objection **10** antagonism, disapprove,

repugnance, resentment **11** detestation, disapproval, displeasure, take against **12** have a derry on **14** disapprobation, disinclination, take a scunner to

## dislocate

◊ *anagram indicator* **04** do in, pull, slip **05** shift, twist **06** luxate, put out, sprain, strain **07** confuse, disrupt, disturb **08** disjoint, disorder, displace, disunite, misplace **09** disengage **10** disconnect **11** disorganize **13** put out of joint, put out of place

## dislocation

◊ *anagram indicator* **04** slip **05** fault **08** disarray, disorder, luxation **10** disruption **11** disturbance **12** displacement **15** disorganization

## dislodge

**04** bump, move, oust, tuft **05** eject, shift **06** remove, uproot **08** displace, force out, untenant **09** extricate

## disloyal

**05** false **06** untrue **07** disleal **08** apostate, two-faced **09** deceitful, faithless **10** perfidious, traitorous, un-American, unfaithful **11** treacherous, unpatriotic **13** double-dealing

## disloyalty

**06** deceit **07** falsity, perfidy, treason **08** adultery, apostasy, betrayal, sedition **09** falseness, treachery **10** infidelity **11** inconstancy, waka-jumping **12** disaffection **13** breach of trust, double-dealing **14** perfidiousness, unfaithfulness

## dismal

**03** bad, sad **04** blue, dark, drab, dull, glum, gray, grey, grim, naff, poor, ropy **05** awful, black, bleak, dingy, dowie, lousy, morne, trist, wormy **06** crummy, dreary, dreich, gloomy, somber, sombre, sullen, triste **07** forlorn, useless **08** desolate, dolesome, dreadful, funereal, ghastful, hopeless, terrible **09** cheerless, frightful, ghastfull, long-faced, miserable, sorrowful **10** depressing, despondent, grimlooked, lugubrious, melancholy, sepulchral **11** low-spirited **12** discouraging, unsuccessful

## dismally

**05** badly, sadly **06** darkly, drably **08** drearily, gloomily, terribly **09** miserably **10** dreadfully **11** frightfully **12** despondently **14** unsuccessfully

## dismantle

◊ *anagram indicator* **05** derig, strip **06** strike **08** demolish, pull down, separate, take down **09** pull apart, strip down, take apart **11** disassemble **12** take to pieces

## dismay

**04** fear **05** alarm, amate, appal, daunt, dread, scare, shake, shock, upset, worry **06** bother, fright, horror, put off, terror **07** concern, depress, disturb, horrify, perturb, unnerve **08** cast down, dispirit, distress, frighten, unsettle **09** agitation, take aback **10** disappoint, disconcert, discourage, dishearten

11 consternate, disillusion, heart-strike, trepidation 12 apprehension 13 consternation 14 disappointment, discouragement
• **expression of dismay** 02 ha 03 hah 04 argh, heck, hell, oops, whew 05 aargh 06 crumbs, dear me, heaven, oh dear!, wheugh 07 cravens, crivens, deary me, heavens 08 crivvens, dearie me 09 good grief 11 that's done it, that's torn it

### dismember
04 limb 05 sever 06 divide 07 break up, disject, dislimb, dissect, quarter 08 amputate, disjoint, mutilate, separate 09 dislocate, piecemeal, pull apart

### dismemberment
07 breakup 08 division 10 amputation, dissection, mutilation, separation

### dismiss
◇ *deletion indicator* 04 boot, daff, drop, fire, free, sack 05 chuck, dooce, eject, expel, lay by, let go, spurn 06 banish, bounce, chassé, lay off, reject, remove, shelve 07 boot out, cashier, discord, fall out, kick out, kiss off, put away, release, send off, suspend, turn off 08 brush off, discount, dispatch, dissolve, relegate, send away, set aside 09 bowler-hat, discharge, disregard, repudiate 10 brush aside, give notice, give the air, pension off 11 send packing 13 give the bucket, make redundant 15 pour cold water on

### dismissal
◇ *deletion indicator* 01 b, c 02 ax, hw, ro, st 03 axe, lbw 04 bird, boot, push, road, sack 05 chuck, congé, elbow 06 avaunt, bounce, bowled, caught, congee, firing, mitten, notice, papers, run-out 07 discard, heave-ho, kiss-off, removal, sacking, stumped 08 brush-off, bum's rush, despatch, dispatch, mittimus 09 discharge, expulsion, hit wicket, laying-off 10 cashiering, redundancy 11 cashierment 12 golden bowler 13 walking-orders, walking papers, walking-ticket 14 marching-orders 15 leg before wicket
• **expression of dismissal** 03 och, out, via 04 pooh, tush 06 avaunt, begone, powwaw 07 voetsak

### dismissed
03 out

### dismissive
07 off-hand 08 scornful, sneering 10 disdainful, dismissory 12 contemptuous 13 disrespectful, inconsiderate

### dismissively
10 scornfully, sneeringly 11 off-handedly 12 disdainfully 14 contemptuously

### dismount
04 lite 05 light 06 alight, get off 07 descend, get down, unmount 09 disembark

### disobedience
06 mutiny, revolt 08 defiance 09 contumacy, rebellion 10 infraction,

unruliness, wilfulness 11 contumacity, waywardness 12 contrariness, indiscipline 13 recalcitrance 15 insubordination

### disobedient
06 unruly, wilful 07 defiant, froward, naughty, wayward 08 contrary, recusant 10 disorderly, rebellious, refractory 11 intractable, mischievous 12 contumacious, obstreperous, recalcitrant 13 insubordinate

### disobey
04 defy 05 flout, rebel 06 ignore, resist 07 violate 08 infringe, overstep 09 disregard 10 contravene, transgress 13 step out of line

### disobliging
04 rude 06 unkind 07 awkward, uncivil 09 unhelpful, unwilling 11 inofficious 12 bloody-minded, disagreeable, discourteous 13 unco-operative 15 unaccommodating

### disorder
◇ *anagram indicator* 03 ADD, OCD, SAD 04 ADHD, mess, muss, PMDD, PTSD, riot, rout 05 brawl, chaos, deray, fight, mêlée, musse 06 defuse, fracas, jumble, malady, muddle, ruffle, rumple, rumpus, tumble, tumult, unrest, uproar 07 ailment, anarchy, clamour, clutter, confuse, derange, disease, flutter, garboil, illness, misrule, overset, quarrel 08 brouhaha, confound, disarray, pell-mell, shambles, sickness 09 commotion, complaint, condition, confusion, mistemper 10 affliction, disability, disarrange, discompose, disruption, untidiness 11 derangement, disturbance 12 confusedness 14 disorderliness 15 disorganization

### disordered
◇ *anagram indicator* 03 mad 04 wild 05 messy, mussy, oncus, onkus, upset 06 turbid, untidy 07 jumbled, muddled, unkempt 08 confused, deranged, madbrain, troubled 09 betumbled, cluttered, disturbed 10 madbrained, out of joint, unbalanced, upside-down 11 distempered, maladjusted 12 disorganized, disreputable

### disorderly
◇ *anagram indicator* 04 wild 05 messy, rough, rowdy 06 ragtag, unruly, untidy 07 chaotic, jumbled, lawless 08 confused 09 cluttered, irregular, turbulent 10 boisterous, confusedly, in disarray, ragmatical, rebellious, refractory, tumultuous 11 disobedient 12 disorganized, hugger-mugger, obstreperous, unmanageable 13 undisciplined 14 uncontrollable

### disorganization
◇ *anagram indicator* 05 chaos 06 muddle 08 disarray, disorder, shambles 09 confusion 10 disruption, untidiness 11 dislocation

### disorganize
◇ *anagram indicator* 05 mix up, upset 06 jumble, mess up, muddle 07 break up, confuse, destroy, disrupt, disturb

08 disorder, unsettle, unstring 09 dislocate 10 disarrange, discompose 11 unmechanize 12 play hell with 13 play havoc with

### disorganized
◇ *anagram indicator* 07 chaotic, jumbled, muddled 08 careless, confused, unsorted 09 haphazard, shambolic 10 disordered, topsy-turvy, untogether 11 unorganized 12 unmethodical, unstructured, unsystematic 13 undisciplined 14 unsystematized

### disorientate
◇ *anagram indicator* 04 faze 05 upset 06 muddle, puzzle 07 confuse, mislead, perplex 09 disorient

### disorientated
◇ *anagram indicator* 04 lost 05 at sea, upset 06 adrift, astray 07 mixed up, muddled, puzzled 08 all at sea, confused 09 perplexed, unsettled 10 bewildered, unbalanced 11 disoriented

### disorientation
◇ *anagram indicator* 06 muddle 08 lostness 09 confusion 10 perplexity, puzzlement 12 bewilderment

### disown
04 deny 05 unget 06 reject 07 abandon, cast off, disavow, forsake 08 abnegate, disallow, disclaim, renounce 09 reprobate, repudiate 14 disacknowledge, turn your back on

### disparage
04 mock, slag, slam, slur 05 decry, knock, scorn, slate 06 defame, deride, lessen, malign, vilify 07 cry down, degrade, disable, disdain, dismiss, empeach, impeach, rubbish, run down, slag off, slander, traduce 08 belittle, derogate, disvalue, minimize, ridicule, vilipend 09 criticize, denigrate, deprecate, discredit, dishonour, sell short, talk smack, underrate 10 calumniate, depreciate, dishearten, undervalue 11 detract from 13 underestimate

### disparagement
04 slur 05 scorn 07 decrial, disdain, slander 08 contempt, decrying, derision, ridicule 09 aspersion, contumely, criticism, discredit 10 debasement, derogation, detraction 11 degradation, deprecation 12 belittlement, condemnation, denunciation, depreciation, vilification 15 underestimation

### disparaging
05 snide 07 mocking 08 critical, derisive, knocking, scornful 09 insulting 10 derogatory, dismissive, pejorative 11 deprecating, deprecatory

### disparate
06 unlike 07 diverse, unequal 08 contrary, distinct 09 different 10 discrepant, dissimilar 11 contrasting

### disparity
03 gap 04 bias, gulf 08 contrast, inequity 09 imbalance 10 difference,

inequality, unevenness, unfairness, unlikeness **11** discrepancy, distinction, incongruity **13** disproportion, dissimilarity, dissimilitude, inconsistency

## dispassionate
**04** calm, cool, fair **07** neutral **08** composed, detached, unbiased **09** equitable, impartial, objective, unexcited **10** impersonal **11** unemotional **12** unprejudiced **13** disinterested, self-possessed **14** self-controlled

## dispassionately
**06** coolly, fairly **09** equitably **11** impartially, objectively, unexcitedly **12** impersonally **13** unemotionally **15** disinterestedly

## dispatch, despatch
**04** do in, item, kill, mail, news, post, send, ship **05** haste, piece, remit, speed **06** convey, finish, letter, murder, report, settle **07** account, article, bump off, consign, dépêche, dismiss, execute, express, forward, mailing, message, perform, posting, sending, send off, special **08** alacrity, bulletin, celerity, conclude, deal with, expedite, knock off, rapidity, transmit **09** discharge, dismissal, dispose of, slaughter, swiftness **10** accelerate, communiqué, expedience, expedition, forwarding, promptness, put to death **11** assassinate, consignment, promptitude, transmittal **13** communication

## dispel
◇ *anagram indicator* **03** rid **04** rout **05** allay, expel **06** assoil, banish **07** discuss, dismiss, scatter **08** disperse, get rid of, melt away **09** chase away, dissipate, drive away, eliminate **11** disseminate

## dispensable
**07** useless **08** needless **10** disposable, expendable, gratuitous, pardonable **11** inessential, replaceable, superfluous, unnecessary **12** non-essential

## dispensation
**04** plan **05** issue, order **06** relief, scheme, system **07** economy, licence, release **08** bestowal, covenant, immunity, reprieve **09** allotment, authority, direction, discharge, endowment, exception, exemption, provision, remission **10** allocation, handing out, permission, sharing out **11** application, arrangement **12** distribution, organization **13** apportionment **14** administration

## dispense
**05** allot, apply, issue, share **06** assign, bestow, confer **07** deal out, deliver, dole out, enforce, execute, expense, give out, hand out, mete out, operate **08** allocate, carry out, compound, share out, supplies **09** apportion, discharge, divide out, implement, pass round **10** administer, distribute, effectuate **11** expenditure **12** dispensation

• **dispense with** **02** ax **03** axe **04** omit, want **05** forgo, waive **06** cancel, forego, give up, ignore, revoke **07** abolish, discard, not need, rescind **08** get rid of, renounce **09** dispose of, disregard, do without **10** do away with, relinquish

## dispersal
**07** breakup **09** dismissal **10** breaking-up, disbanding, scattering, separation **11** segregation **12** distribution

## disperse
◇ *anagram indicator* **04** melt, shed **05** break, scail, scale, skail **06** dispel, spread, vanish **07** break up, diffuse, disband, dismiss, resolve, scatter, split up, thin out **08** dissolve, melt away, separate, squander **09** dissipate **10** distribute **11** disseminate

## dispersion
◇ *anagram indicator* **07** scatter **08** diaspora **09** broadcast, diffusion, dispersal, spreading **10** scattering **11** circulation, dissipation **12** distribution **13** dissemination

## dispirit
**04** damp, dash **05** deter **06** dampen, deject, sadden **07** depress **10** demoralize, discourage, dishearten **12** put a damper on

## dispirited
**03** low, sad **04** down, glum **05** fed up **06** feeble, gloomy, morose **08** cast down, dejected, downcast, sackless **09** depressed **10** brassed off, browned off, cheesed off, despondent, spiritless **11** crestfallen, demoralized, discouraged, pale-hearted **12** disheartened **14** down in the dumps

## displace
**04** move, oust **05** eject, evict, expel, heave, shift **06** depose, luxate, remove **07** boot out, dismiss, disturb, replace, succeed, turf out **08** dislodge, force out, misplace, relocate, supplant **09** discharge, dislocate, supersede **10** disarrange

## displacement
**03** jee **04** warp **05** heave, hitch, shift, throw **06** ectopy, moving, ptosis **07** ectopia, upthrow **08** shifting **09** proptosis **10** aberration, compliance, dislodging **11** dislocation, disturbance, heterotaxis, heterotopia, subluxation, superseding, supplanting **12** misplacement, retroversion **14** Chandler wobble, disarrangement **15** Chandler's wobble

## display
**03** air, HUD, LCD **04** expo, pomp, shaw, show, wear **05** array, boast, state **06** betray, blazon, evince, expose, flaunt, layout, muster, parade, reveal, set out, splash, unfold, unfurl, unveil **07** airshow, bravura, breathe, étalage, exhibit, pageant, parafle, present, promote, show off, splurge **08** disclose, evidence, flourish, manifest, paraffle, put forth, set forth, showcase **09** advertise, pageantry, publicize, put on show, spectacle, spread out,

unfolding **10** disclosure, displaying, evincement, exhibition, exposition, revelation, tournament **11** demonstrate **12** presentation **13** demonstration, manifestation

## displease
**03** bug, irk, vex **05** anger, annoy, upset **06** offend, put out **07** dislike, disturb, incense, mislike, perturb, provoke **08** irritate **09** aggravate, infuriate, misplease **10** discompose, disgruntle, dissatisfy, exasperate **11** displeasure

## displeased
**05** angry, cross, upset, vexed **06** peeved, piqued, put out **07** annoyed, furious **08** offended **09** irritated **10** aggravated, dischuffed, infuriated **11** disgruntled, exasperated, out of humour

## displeasure
**03** ire **05** anger, pique, wrath **07** chagrin, disgust, offence, offense **08** distaste **09** annoyance, disfavour **10** irritation, resentment **11** disapproval, indignation **12** exasperation, perturbation **14** disapprobation, discontentment, disgruntlement **15** dissatisfaction

## disport
◇ *anagram indicator* **04** play, romp **05** amuse, cheer, frisk, revel, sport **06** cavort, divert, frolic, gambol **07** delight, get down **09** entertain

## disposable
**09** throwaway **10** expendable **11** replaceable **13** biodegradable, non-returnable

## disposal
**05** order **07** command, control, liberty, removal, service **08** bestowal, grouping, ordering, riddance **09** clearance, direction, scrapping **10** deployment, discarding, management **11** arrangement, jettisoning, positioning **12** getting rid of, throwing-away
• **at someone's disposal** **05** on tap, ready **06** at hand, to hand **09** available **10** obtainable

## dispose
◇ *anagram indicator* **03** put, set **04** do in, dump, kill, plot, shed, sort **05** align, group, order, place, posit, scrap, see to, sew up, tempt **06** battle, decide, finish, handle, line up, murder, settle, tackle, wrap up **07** arrange, bump off, destroy, discard, dismiss, dispone, incline, situate, sort out **08** attend to, chuck out, clear out, deal with, dispatch, get rid of, jettison, organize, position, throw out **09** clear away, determine, get shot of, look after, polish off, throw away **10** distribute, do away with, put to death, take care of **15** make short work of
• **try to dispose of** **04** hawk

## disposed
◇ *anagram indicator* **03** apt **04** bent **05** dight, eager, prone, ready **06** liable, likely, minded **07** subject, willing

**08** inclined, pregnant, prepared **11** affectioned, predisposed

## disposition

◊ *anagram indicator* **03** lay, lie **04** bent, make, mood, trim **05** cheer, habit, humor, order **06** humour, kidney, layout, line-up, make-up, nature, spirit, system, talent, temper **07** leaning, pattern, placing, stomach **08** disposal, grouping, ordnance, position, sequence, tendency, transfer **09** affection, alignment, character, proneness **10** allocation, conveyance, deployment, giving-over, proclivity, propension, propensity **11** arrangement, inclination, personality, positioning, temperament **12** constitution, distribution, ministration, predilection, propenseness **14** predisposition

## dispossess

**03** rob **04** oust **05** eject, evict, expel, strip **06** divest **07** deprive **08** dislodge, take away **11** expropriate

## disproportion

**09** asymmetry, disparity, imbalance **10** inadequacy, inequality, unevenness **11** discrepancy **12** lopsidedness **13** insufficiency

## disproportionate

**06** uneven **07** unequal **09** excessive **10** inordinate, unbalanced **12** unreasonable **14** incommensurate **15** incommensurable, out of proportion

## disproportionately

**08** unevenly **11** excessively **12** inordinately, unreasonably

## disprove

**04** deny **05** rebut, refel **06** debunk, expose, negate, refute **07** confute, reprove **08** blow away **09** discredit **10** contradict, controvert, invalidate, prove false **12** give the lie to

## disputable

**04** moot **07** dubious **08** arguable, doubtful **09** debatable, litigious, uncertain **12** questionable **13** controversial

## disputation

**03** act **06** debate **07** dispute, schools **08** argument, diatribe, exercise, polemics **09** quodlibet **10** apposition, discussion, dissension **11** controversy **12** deliberation, kilfud-yoking **13** argumentation

## disputatious

**08** captious **09** litigious, polemical **10** pugnacious **11** contentious, quarrelsome **12** cantankerous **13** argumentative

## dispute

**03** row **04** deny, feud, moot, odds, plea, spar, spat, tilt **05** argue, clash, doubt **06** bicker, cangle, debate, differ, strife, threap **07** contend, contest, discept, discuss, gainsay, quarrel, turf war, wrangle, wrestle **08** argument, conflict, litigate, question, squabble, traverse, variance **09** altercate,

challenge, have words, tug-of-love **10** contention, contradict, controvert, litigation **11** altercation, controverse, controversy, cross swords **12** disagreement, disceptation

## disqualification

**03** ban, bar **04** veto **10** disability, incapacity, preclusion **11** elimination, prohibition **13** ineligibility **14** disentitlement

## disqualified

**06** banned **08** debarred **09** incapable, precluded, struck off **10** eliminated, ineligible **11** disentitled

## disqualify

**03** ban, bar **05** debar, unfit **06** impair **07** disable, rule out, suspend **08** handicap, preclude, prohibit **09** eliminate, strike off **10** debilitate, disentitle, immobilize, invalidate **12** incapacitate **13** dishabilitate

## disquiet

**03** vex **04** faze, fear, fret **05** alarm, annoy, dread, shake, upset, worry **06** bother, harass, hassle, pester, plague, ruffle, unease, uneasy, unrest **07** agitate, anguish, anxiety, concern, disturb, perturb, trouble, turmoil, unnerve **08** distress, restless, unsettle **09** agitation, incommode **10** discompose, foreboding, inquietude, make uneasy, uneasiness **11** disquietude, disturbance, fretfulness, make anxious, nervousness **12** perturbation, restlessness

## disquieting

**04** ugly **06** trying **07** anxious **08** worrying **09** unnerving, upsetting **10** disturbing, nail-biting, perturbing, unsettling **11** distressing, troublesome

## disquisition

**05** essay, paper **06** sermon, thesis **07** descant **08** treatise **09** discourse, monograph **10** exposition **11** explanation **12** dissertation

## disregard

◊ *deletion indicator* **04** bend, omit, pass, shun, snub **05** flout, waive **06** ignore, insult, offend, slight **07** affront, despise, disdain, disobey, neglect, oversee, smile at **08** brush-off, contempt, discount, laugh off, overlook, pass over, set aside **09** denigrate, disesteem, disoblige, disparage, gloss over, oversight, sacrilege **10** brush aside, disrespect, negligence **11** denigration, desperation, inattention, make light of, set at naught, walk all over **12** carelessness, cold shoulder, cold-shoulder, dispense with, indifference **13** give the go-by to, non-regardance, put out of court **14** rule out of court, take no notice of **15** close your eyes to, turn a blind eye to

## disrepair

**04** ruin **05** decay **08** collapse **10** shabbiness **11** rack and ruin **12** dilapidation **13** deterioration

## disreputable

**03** low **04** base, mean **05** dodgy, seamy, seedy, shady **06** louche,

shabby, shifty, untidy **07** corrupt, dubious, scruffy, unkempt **08** infamous, shameful, shocking, slovenly, unworthy **09** notorious, unsavoury **10** outrageous, scandalous, suspicious **11** disgraceful, dishevelled, ignominious, opprobrious **12** contemptible, unprincipled **13** discreditable, dishonourable, unrespectable

## disrepute

**05** shame **06** infamy **07** ill fame, obloquy **08** disgrace, ignominy **09** discredit, disesteem, disfavour, dishonour **13** disreputation

## disrespect

**05** cheek, scorn **08** contempt, rudeness **09** dishonour, disregard, impudence, insolence, misesteem **10** incivility **11** discourtesy, irreverence **12** impertinence, impoliteness

## disrespectful

**04** rude **05** sassy **06** cheeky **07** uncivil **08** flippant, impolite, impudent, insolent **09** insulting **10** dismissive, irreverent, unmannerly **11** impertinent **12** contemptuous, discourteous **13** inconsiderate

## disrespectfully

**06** rudely **08** cheekily **09** uncivilly **10** impolitely, impudently, insolently **11** insultingly **12** irreverently **13** impertinently **14** contemptuously, discourteously

## disrobe

**04** bare, shed **05** strip **06** denude, divest, remove **07** take off, uncover, undress **08** unclothe **10** disapparel

## disrupt

◊ *anagram indicator* **05** burst, split, upset **06** butt in, hamper, impede **07** blemish, break up, confuse, disturb, intrude, screw up **08** sabotage, unsettle **09** dislocate, interrupt **10** disarrange **11** disorganize **13** interfere with

## disruption

◊ *anagram indicator* **05** upset **06** bust-up **07** burst-up, turmoil **08** disarray, disorder, stoppage, upheaval **09** cataclasm, confusion **11** disordering, disturbance **12** interference, interruption **14** disorderliness **15** disorganization

## disruptive

**05** noisy, rogue **06** unruly **09** turbulent, upsetting **10** boisterous, disorderly, disturbing, unsettling **11** distracting, troublesome **12** obstreperous **13** troublemaking, undisciplined

## dissatisfaction

**05** anger **06** regret **07** chagrin, dislike **08** vexation **09** annoyance **10** discomfort, discontent, irritation, resentment, uneasiness **11** disapproval, displeasure, frustration, unhappiness **12** disaffection, exasperation, restlessness **14** disappointment, disapprobation

• **expression of dissatisfaction 02** oh **03** boo, huh, tut **04** booh, umph, whow **05** humph

### dissatisfied

**05** angry, fed up **07** annoyed, unhappy
**09** irritated **10** brassed off, browned
off, cheesed off, discontent,
displeased, frustrated, malcontent
**11** disaffected, disgruntled,
exasperated, unfulfilled, unsatisfied
**12** disappointed, discontented,
disenchanted, malcontented
**13** disillusioned

### dissatisfy

**03** vex **05** anger, annoy **06** put out
**07** let down **08** irritate **09** displease,
frustrate **10** disappoint, discontent,
disgruntle, exasperate

### dissect

**05** cut up, probe, study **07** analyse,
examine, explore, inspect **08** pore
over, vivisect **09** anatomize, break
down, dismember **10** scrutinize
**11** investigate

### dissection

**05** probe, study **07** anatomy, autopsy,
zootomy **08** analysis, necropsy,
scrutiny **09** breakdown, cutting up,
necrotomy **10** inspection
**11** cephalotomy, examination,
exploration, vivisection
**13** dismemberment, encephalotomy,
investigation

### dissemble

**04** fain, fake, hide, mask, sham
**05** cloak, faine, fayne, feign **06** affect
**07** conceal, cover up, falsify, pretend
**08** disguise, simulate **10** camouflage,
play possum **11** counterfeit,
dissimulate

### dissembler

**04** fake, liar **05** fraud **06** con man
**07** feigner **08** deceiver, impostor
**09** charlatan, hypocrite, pretender,
trickster **12** dissimulator **15** whited
sepulchre

### disseminate

**03** sow **05** scale **06** spread **07** diffuse,
publish, scatter **08** disperse, proclaim
**09** broadcast, circulate, propagate,
publicize, scattered **10** distribute,
promulgate

### dissemination

**06** spread **09** broadcast, diffusion,
spreading **10** dispersion, publishing
**11** circulation, propagation,
publication **12** broadcasting,
distribution, promulgation

### dissension

**04** flak **06** square, strife **07** discord,
dispute, dissent, faction, quarrel
**08** argument, conflict, dispeace,
disunion, disunity, friction, variance
**10** contention **12** disagreement

### dissent

**05** demur **06** differ, object, refuse
**07** discord, dispute, protest, quibble
**08** disagree, friction **09** objection
**10** difference, disconsent, disharmony,
dissension, opposition, resistance
**11** controversy **12** disagreement

### dissenter

**05** rebel **07** heretic, sectary **08** objector,
recusant **09** disputant, dissident,
protester, Raskolnik **10** dissident,
schismatic, separatist **11** dissentient,
Old Believer **12** demonstrator
**13** nonconformist, revolutionary

### dissentient

**08** opposing, recusant **09** differing,
dissident, heretical **10** dissenting,
protesting, rebellious **11** conflicting,
disagreeing **13** nonconformist,
revolutionary

### dissertation

**05** essay, paper **06** thesis **08** critique,
excursus, treatise **09** discourse,
monograph **10** exposition
**11** prolegomena **12** disquisition,
propaedeutic

### disservice

**04** harm, hurt **05** wrong **06** injury
**07** bad turn **08** con trick, mischief
**09** disfavour, injustice **10** dirty trick,
unkindness **13** sharp practice **14** kick in
the teeth

### dissidence

**04** feud **06** schism **07** dispute, dissent,
rupture **08** variance **09** recusancy
**11** discordance **12** disagreement

### dissident

**05** rebel **07** heretic **08** agitator,
frondeur, objector, opposing, recusant,
refusnik **09** differing, dissenter,
heretical, heterodox, protester,
refusenik **10** discordant, dissenting,
protesting, rebellious, schismatic
**11** conflicting, disagreeing
**13** nonconformist, revolutionary

### dissimilar

**06** unlike **07** diverse, unalike, various,
varying **08** bifacial, distinct
**09** deviating, different, disparate,
divergent, unrelated **10** mismatched
**11** contrasting, hemimorphic
**12** incompatible **13** heterogeneous

### dissimilarity

**07** variety **08** contrast **09** disparity,
diversity **10** difference, differency,
divergence, inequality, unlikeness
**11** discrepancy, distinction
**13** dissimilitude, heterogeneity,
unrelatedness **15** incomparability,
incompatibility

### dissimulate

**03** lie **04** fake, hide, mask **05** cloak,
feign **06** affect **07** conceal, cover up,
pretend **08** disguise **09** dissemble
**10** camouflage

### dissipate

◇ *anagram indicator* **04** blow **05** drain,
spend, use up, waste **06** burn up,
dispel, expend, lavish, vanish, wanton
**07** break up, consume, deplete,
diffuse, exhaust, resolve, scatter,
splurge **08** disperse, dissolve, melt
away, squander **09** disappear, drive
away, evaporate **10** get through, run
through **11** fritter away

### dissipated

◇ *anagram indicator* **03** gay **04** wild
**06** rakish, wasted **07** corrupt, drunken
**08** depraved **09** abandoned,

debauched, dissolute **10** degenerate,
licentious, profligate **11** intemperate
**13** self-indulgent

• **be dissipated** **04** melt **08** peter out

### dissipation

**06** excess, racket **07** licence
**08** pleasure **09** depletion, depravity,
diffusion, dispersal **10** corruption,
debauchery, immorality
**11** abandonment, consumption,
evaporation, expenditure, prodigality,
squandering **12** extravagance,
intemperance **13** disappearance
**14** licentiousness, self-indulgence

### dissociate

**04** quit **05** sever **06** cut off, detach,
secede **07** break up, disband, disrupt,
divorce, isolate **08** break off, distance,
disunite, separate, set apart, withdraw
**09** disengage, segregate, separated
**10** disconnect **12** disassociate

### dissociation

**05** break, split **07** divorce **08** disunion,
division, severing **09** isolation,
severance **10** cutting-off, detachment,
distancing, separation **11** dissevering,
segregation **12** setting apart
**13** disconnection, disengagement
**14** disassociation

### dissolute

◇ *anagram indicator* **04** fast, lewd, wild
**05** loose **06** rakish, wanton **07** corrupt,
immoral, outward **08** depraved
**09** abandoned, debauched
**10** Corinthian, degenerate, dissipated,
licentious, profligate **11** Falstaffian,
intemperate **12** unrestrained **13** self-
indulgent

### dissolution

**06** ending, Repeal **07** break-up,
divorce, melting **08** collapse, dialysis,
disposal, division **09** annulment,
cessation, loosening, overthrow
**10** conclusion, karyolysis, separation,
suspension **11** destruction,
evaporation, termination, thermolysis
**13** decomposition, disappearance
**14** disintegration **15** discontinuation

### dissolve

**03** end **04** melt **05** annul, begin, break,
burst, solve, start **06** digest, finish,
revoke, vanish, wind up **07** break up,
crumble, disband, dismiss, divorce,
dwindle, liquefy, nullify, rescind,
solvate, unmarry **08** collapse,
discandy, disperse, evanesce, melt
away, separate **09** disappear,
discandie, dissipate, evaporate,
terminate **10** deliquesce, invalidate
**11** discontinue, lose control **12** bring to
an end, disintegrate **14** be overcome
with, go into solution

### dissonance

**03** jar **04** wolf **05** clash **06** jangle
**07** discord, grating, jarring **08** variance
**09** cacophony, disparity, harshness,
stridency **10** difference, disharmony,
dissension **11** discordance,
discrepancy, incongruity
**12** disagreement **13** inconsistency
**15** incompatibility

## dissonant

◊ *anagram indicator* **05** harsh **07** grating, jarring, raucous **08** clashing, jangling, strident, tuneless **09** anomalous, differing, irregular, unmusical **10** discordant **11** cacophonous, conflicting, disagreeing, incongruous, unmelodious **12** incompatible, inconsistent, inharmonious **13** contradictory **14** irreconcilable

## dissuade

**04** stop **05** deter **06** dehort, nobble, put off **07** prevent **09** talk out of **10** discounsel, discourage, disincline **13** persuade not to

## dissuasion

**07** caution **09** deterring **10** deterrence **11** dehortation **12** remonstrance **13** expostulation, remonstration **14** discouragement

## distance

**03** gap, way **04** span, step **05** break, depth, lunar, piece, range, reach, space, width **06** cut off, detach, extent, height, length, remove, secede **07** breadth, faraway, farness, reserve, stretch **08** coldness, coolness, interval, separate, throw out, withdraw **09** aloofness, formality, stiffness **10** detachment, dissociate, opposition, remoteness, separation **11** mountenance **12** disassociate, mountenaunce **13** codeclination **14** unfriendliness **15** inaccessibility, standoffishness
*See also* **measurement**
• **at a distance** **04** afar, wide **06** afield **12** at arm's length
• **short distance** **03** wee **06** bittie **11** stone's-throw

## distant

**03** far, icy **04** cold, cool, deep **05** aloof, blank, stiff **06** abroad, dreamy, far-off, formal, remote, slight, vacant **07** faraway, glacial **08** detached, far-flung, indirect, isolated, not close, outlying, reserved **09** dispersed, withdrawn **10** antisocial, distracted, indistinct, restrained, unfriendly **11** daydreaming, out-of-the-way, preoccupied, stand-offish, up the Boohai **12** absent-minded, back of beyond, in the wop-wops, unresponsive **14** unapproachable **15** uncommunicative

## distantly

**05** dimly, miles **06** coldly, coolly **07** faintly, far away, stiffly, vaguely **08** a long way, formally, remotely, slightly, vacantly **10** not closely **11** imprecisely **12** some distance **13** great distance, unemotionally **14** unresponsively

## distaste

**06** dégoût, horror, offend **07** disgust, dislike, offence **08** aversion, loathing **09** antipathy, disfavour, disrelish, revulsion **10** abhorrence, repugnance **11** displeasure
• **expression of distaste** **03** ugh, wow, yuk **04** whow, yech, yuck **05** wowee

## distasteful

**04** gory, icky **08** god-awful **09** abhorrent, loathsome, obnoxious, offensive, repellant, repellent, repugnant, repulsive, revolting, unsavoury **10** detestable, disgusting, uninviting, unpleasant **11** displeasing, undesirable, unpalatable **12** disagreeable **13** objectionable

## distend

**04** puff **05** bloat, bulge, swell, widen **06** dilate, expand **07** balloon, enlarge, fill out, inflate, stretch **09** intumesce **10** exaggerate

## distended

**05** puffy **06** astrut, puffed **07** bloated, dilated, distent, swollen **08** enlarged, expanded, inflated, varicose **09** puffed-out, stretched, tumescent **10** ventricose, ventricous **13** emphysematous

## distension

**05** swell **06** spread **07** breadth **08** bloating, dilation, swelling **09** emphysema, expansion, extension **10** flatulence, flatulency, tumescence, tympanites, wind dropsy **11** enlargement, turgescence **12** intumescence **14** hydronephrosis

## distil

**04** drip, flow, leak **05** still **06** derive, purify, refine **07** draw out, express, extract, rectify, trickle **08** condense, press out, vaporize **09** evaporate, sublimate

## distillation

◊ *anagram indicator* **06** spirit **07** essence, extract **10** extraction **11** evaporation **12** condensation, purification

## distinct

**05** clear, plain, sharp **06** marked **07** defined, diverse, evident, obvious, several **08** apparent, clear-cut, definite, detached, discrete, manifest, separate **09** different, disparate, trenchant **10** dissimilar, individual, noticeable, variegated **11** unambiguous, unconnected, well-defined **12** recognizable, unassociated, unmistakable **13** distinguished **14** differentiated

## distinction

**04** fame, mark, note **05** éclat, honor, merit, siege, worth **06** credit, honour, luster, lustre, renown, repute **07** diorism, feature, quality **08** contrast, division, eminence, prestige **09** celebrity, greatness **10** difference, excellence, importance, prominence, reputation, separation **11** consequence, discernment, peculiarity, superiority **12** distinctness, significance **13** dissimilarity, dissimilitude, individuality **14** characteristic, discrimination **15** differentiation, distinguishment
*See also* **honour**

## distinctive

**06** unique **07** special, typical **08** original, peculiar, singular **09** different **10** individual, noteworthy, particular **13** extraordinary, idiosyncratic **14** characteristic, distinguishing

## distinctiveness

**10** uniqueness **11** originality, peculiarity, singularity **12** idiosyncrasy **13** individuality **14** noteworthiness

## distinctly

**05** plain **07** clearly, plainly **08** markedly **09** decidedly, evidently, obviously **10** definitely, manifestly, noticeably **12** unmistakably **13** unambiguously, unmistakeably

## distinguish

**03** see **04** dist, mark **05** excel, judge, stamp **06** descry, detect, divide, do well, notice, pick up, secern, typify **07** dignify, discern, ennoble, glorify, make out, mark off, pick out **08** classify, identify, perceive, set apart, tell from **09** ascertain, determine, recognize, signalize, single out, tell apart **10** categorize **11** bring fame to **12** characterize, discriminate **13** bring honour to, differentiate, particularize **14** bring acclaim to

## distinguishable

**05** clear, plain **07** evident, obvious **08** dividant, manifest **10** noticeable, observable **11** appreciable, conspicuous, discernible, perceptible, plainly seen **12** recognizable

## distinguished

**04** fine **05** famed, noble, noted **06** famous, marked, of note **07** eminent, notable, refined, shining **08** distinct, especial, esteemed, eximious, honoured, identify, renowned, striking **09** acclaimed, egregious, prominent, well-known **10** celebrated, nameworthy **11** conspicuous, illustrious, outstanding **12** aristocratic **13** extraordinary

## distinguishing

**06** marked, unique **07** typical **08** peculiar, singular **09** diacritic, different **10** diagnostic, episematic, individual **11** diacritical, distinctive **14** characteristic, discriminative, discriminatory **15** differentiating, differentiation, individualistic

## distort

◊ *anagram indicator* **04** bend, bias, rack, skew, warp **05** color, fudge, slant, thraw, twist, wrest, wring **06** buckle, colour, deform, detort, garble, hamper, jumble, mangle, wrench, writhe **07** contort, falsify, pervert, screw up, torment, torture **08** misshape **09** disfigure, pull about **10** tamper with **12** cook the books, misrepresent

## distorted

◊ *anagram indicator* **03** wry **04** awry, bent, skew **05** false, thraw **06** biased, skewed, thrawn, warped **07** twisted **08** deformed, tortured **09** falsified, misshapen, perverted **10** disfigured, out of shape **14** misrepresented

## distortion

**04** bend, bias, skew, warp **05** slant,

## distract

twist **06** buckle **07** warping **08** cinching, garbling, twisting **09** colouring, deformity **10** contortion, perversion **11** crookedness **13** falsification

## distract

◊ *anagram indicator* **05** amuse **06** divert, harass, madden, occupy, put off, puzzle **07** confuse, deflect, detract, disturb, embroil, engross, fluster, perplex **08** bewilder, confound, draw away, forhaile, throw out, turn away **09** entertain, sidetrack, turn aside **10** discompose, disconcert

## distracted

◊ *anagram indicator* **03** mad **04** wild **05** crazy, upset **06** éperdu, raving **07** anxious, éperdue, frantic, madding **08** agitated, confused, diverted, dreaming, frenetic, harassed, maddened, worked up **09** miles away, not with it, scattered, up the wall, wandering **10** abstracted, bestraught, bewildered, distraught, distressed, hysterical **11** inattentive, overwrought, preoccupied **12** absent-minded **13** grief-stricken **14** beside yourself

## distracting

**07** diverse **08** annoying **09** confusing **10** disturbing, irritating, off-putting, perturbing, unsettling **11** bewildering **13** disconcerting

## distraction

**04** game **05** hobby, sport **07** madness, pastime **09** agitation, amusement, avocation, confusion, diversion **10** perplexity, recreation, relaxation **11** derangement, disturbance, interrupted **12** interference **13** entertainment **14** divertissement
• **drive to distraction** **05** anger, annoy, upset **06** madden **10** drive crazy, exasperate

## distraint

**03** nam **04** naam **06** stress

## distraught

◊ *anagram indicator* **03** mad **04** wild **05** crazy, elvan, elven, het up, upset **06** elfish, elvish, raving **07** anxious, frantic, worried **08** agitated, in a state, worked up, wretched **09** perplexed **10** distracted, distressed, hysterical **11** overwrought **14** beside yourself

## distress

**03** irk, vex, woe **04** hurt, need, pain, prey **05** agony, cut up, grief, peril, trial, upset, worry **06** danger, grieve, harass, harrow, misery, penury, sadden, sorrow, unease **07** afflict, agonize, anguish, anxiety, disturb, misease, oppress, perturb, poverty, put to it, sadness, torment, torture, trouble **08** aggrieve, calamity, distrain, exigence, exigency, hardship, straiten **09** adversity, extremity, heartache, indigence, privation, suffering **10** affliction, compulsion, desolation, difficulty, discomfort, exhaustion, misfortune **11** destitution, make anxious, tribulation **12** deforciation, difficulties, perturbation, wretchedness **13** make miserable

## distressed

**03** ill **04** hurt, sore **05** upset **06** pained, put out **07** uptight, worried **08** bothered, dismayed, in a state, perished, troubled, worked up **09** aggrieved, disturbed, heart-sore, on the rack, perturbed, strung out, unsettled **11** discomposed **12** impoverished

## distressing

**05** sorry **06** crying, tragic, trying, uneath **07** painful **08** alarming, tragical, worrying **09** harrowing, startling, upsetting **10** afflicting, disturbing, off-putting, perturbing, unsettling **11** frightening **13** disconcerting

## distribute

◊ *anagram indicator* **04** deal, dish, part **05** allot, carve, issue, ladle, share **06** assort, digest, divide, spread, supply **07** deal out, deliver, diffuse, dish out, dispose, dole out, give out, hand out, mete out, pass out, prorate, scatter **08** allocate, dispense, disperse, ladle out, serve out, transmit **09** apportion, circulate, discharge, pass round **10** measure out, reticulate **11** disseminate

## distribution

◊ *anagram indicator* **05** range **06** supply **07** dealing, sharing **08** delivery, division, grouping, handling, position **09** allotment, diffusion, dispersal, giving-out, placement, proration, spreading, transport **10** allocation, conveyance, handing-out, scattering **11** arrangement, circulation, disposition, repartition **12** organization **13** apportionment, dissemination **14** classification, transportation

## district

**03** gau, way **04** area, belt, hunt, land, leet, pale, ride, side, soke, walk, ward, zila, zone **05** block, patch, place, shire **06** barrio, bounds, circar, county, domain, locale, parish, region, riding, sector, sircar, sirkar, suburb **07** circuit, quarter, section **08** faubourg, highland, locality, precinct, province, quartier, stannary, vicinity **09** community, territory **12** constituency, municipality, neighborhood **13** neighbourhood **15** circumscription

*Districts of Northern Ireland:*

**04** Ards, Down
**05** Derry, Larne, Moyle, Omagh
**06** Antrim, Armagh
**07** Belfast, Lisburn
**08** Limavady, Strabane
**09** Ballymena, Banbridge, Coleraine, Cookstown, Craigavon, Dungannon, Fermanagh, North Down
**10** Ballymoney
**11** Castlereagh, Magherafelt
**12** Newtownabbey
**13** Carrickfergus
**14** Newry and Mourne

*See also* **county; London; New York; Paris**
• **District of Columbia** **02** DC

• **outer district** **03** end
• **squalid district** **04** slum

## distrust

**05** doubt, qualm **07** suspect **08** be wary of, misfaith, mistrust, question, wariness **09** chariness, disbelief, discredit, misgiving, mislippen, suspicion **10** disbelieve, scepticism **11** questioning **12** doubtfulness **14** be suspicious of **15** have doubts about

## distrustful

**04** wary **05** chary **06** uneasy **07** cynical, dubious **08** doubtful, doubting **09** sceptical **10** suspicious, untrustful, untrusting **11** distrusting, mistrustful **12** disbelieving

## disturb

◊ *anagram indicator* **03** jee, vex **04** fret, stir **05** annoy, rouse, shake, sturt, touch, upset, worry **06** affray, beat up, bother, dismay, hassle, infest, muddle, pester, put off, racket, ruffle, tumult, turn up **07** agitate, commove, concern, concuss, confuse, disrupt, fluster, inquiet, mismake, perturb, trouble **08** butt in on, disorder, disquiet, distract, distress, unsettle **09** discomfit, dislocate, interrupt **10** disarrange, discompose, disconcert, distrouble, perturbate **11** disorganize, make anxious

## disturbance

◊ *anagram indicator* **03** row **04** dust, fray, muss, riot, rout **05** brawl, broil, musse, sturt, upset **06** bother, cangle, fracas, hassle, hoop-la, kick-up, muddle, racket, ruckus, rumble, rumpus, shindy, tumult, turn-up, unrest, uproar, upturn **07** illness, ruction, stashie, stishie, stushie, trouble, turmoil **08** disorder, neurosis, outbreak, sickness, stooshie, stramash, upheaval, williwaw **09** agitation, annoyance, commotion, complaint, confusion, hindrance, intrusion **10** convulsion, disruption, hullabaloo, inquietude, perplexity, rough-house **11** derangement, distraction, embroilment, molestation **12** interference, interruption **13** collieshangie **14** distemperature
• **freedom from disturbance** **04** ease

## disturbed

◊ *anagram indicator* **04** vext **05** upset, vexed **06** hung-up, uneasy **07** anxious, inquiet, unquiet, worried **08** bothered, confused, neurotic, paranoid, troubled, unstable **09** concerned, flustered, psychotic, screwed-up, turbulent **10** mistrysted, unbalanced **11** discomposed, maladjusted, mentally ill **12** apprehensive **13** dysfunctional

## disturbing

◊ *anagram indicator* **08** alarming, worrying **09** agitating, confusing, dismaying, startling, troubling, troublous, upsetting **10** disturbant, perturbing, unsettling **11** bewildering, disquieting, distressing, frightening, threatening **12** discouraging, disturbative **13** disconcerting

## disunited
**05** split **07** divided **09** alienated, disrupted, estranged, separated **10** dissevered

## disunity
**05** split **06** breach, schism, strife **07** discord, dissent, rupture **08** conflict, division **10** alienation, dissension **11** discordance **12** disagreement, estrangement

## disuse
**05** decay **07** neglect **09** desuetude **11** abandonment, inusitation **14** discontinuance

## disused
**04** idle **06** unused **07** decayed **08** obsolete **09** abandoned, neglected **12** discontinued

## ditch
**04** delf, dike, drop, dump, dyke, foss, grip, ha-ha, lode, moat, rean, reen, sike, syke **05** canal, chuck, delph, drain, fosse, graft, gripe, gully, level, rhine, rhyne, scrap, stank **06** derail, furrow, gulley, gutter, haw-haw, sheuch, sheugh, the sea, trench, trough **07** abandon, channel, discard, euripus **08** get rid of, jettison, throw out **09** dispose of, sunk fence, throw away **11** watercourse

## dither
◇ *anagram indicator* **04** faff, flap, stew, tizz **05** delay, panic, quake, tizzy, waver **06** bother, dicker, falter, pother, shiver **07** agitate, confuse, fluster, flutter, perturb, tremble **08** hang back, hesitate **09** faff about, vacillate **10** dilly-dally, indecision **12** be in two minds, perturbation, shilly-shally, take your time

## ditto
**02** do

## divan
**04** sofa **05** couch, dewan **06** day bed, lounge, settee **07** council, lounger, ottoman, sofa bed **08** assembly **12** chaise-longue, chesterfield

## dive
**03** bar, dip, fly, ken, pub **04** bolt, club, dart, dash, drop, duck, dump, fall, hole, jump, leap, rush, tear **05** hurry, joint, lunge, pitch, sound, swoop **06** go down, header, plunge, refuge, saloon, spring, subway **07** descend, go under, plummet **08** nose-dive, submerge, tailspin **09** belly-flop, jackknife, nightclub **11** move quickly

## diver
**04** loom, loon **05** grebe **08** aquanaut, urinator **09** guillemot **10** pickpocket
*See also* **swimmer**

## diverge
**04** fork, part, vary **05** clash, drift, split, stray **06** branch, depart, differ, divide, spread, wander **07** deflect, deviate, digress, dissent, radiate **08** conflict, disagree, divagate, separate **09** bifurcate, branch off, spread out, subdivide **10** contradict, divaricate **12** be at variance

## divergence
**03** gap **05** clash, slant **07** parting **08** conflict **09** departure, deviation, dichotomy, disparity, variation **10** deflection, difference, digression, separation **12** branching-out, disagreement, divarication

## divergent
**07** diverse, variant, varying **08** separate **09** deviating, different, differing, diverging **10** dissimilar, divaricate, tangential **11** conflicting, disagreeing

## divers
**04** many, some **06** sundry, varied **07** several, various, varying **08** manifold, numerous **09** different **12** multifarious **13** miscellaneous

## diverse
◇ *anagram indicator* **05** mixed **06** sundry, unlike, varied **07** several, various, varying **08** assorted, discrete, distinct, manifold, separate **09** different, differing, multiform **10** all means of, dissimilar **11** contrasting, distracting **13** heterogeneous, miscellaneous

## diversification
**09** extension, variation **10** alteration **11** variegation **12** branching-out, modification, spreading-out

## diversify
**03** mix **04** vary **05** alter, paint, spice **06** assort, change, expand, extend, modify **08** sprinkle **09** branch out, spread out, variegate **11** intersperse **13** differentiate **14** bring variety to

## diversion
◇ *anagram indicator* **03** fun **04** game, play **05** hobby, sport **06** change, detour **07** pastime **09** amusement, avocation, deviation, switching **10** alteration, recreation, relaxation, rerouteing **11** distraction, redirection **13** divertisement, entertainment **14** divertissement

## diversionary
**09** divertive **10** deflecting **11** distracting

## diversity
**05** range **06** medley **07** mixture, variety **08** variance **09** pluralism **10** assortment, difference, embroidery, miscellany **11** variegation **12** biodiversity **13** dissimilarity, dissimilitude, heterogeneity **15** diversification

## divert
◇ *anagram indicator* **04** sway **05** amuse, avert **06** absorb, baffle, occupy, put off, siphon, switch, syphon **07** deflect, delight, engross, hive off, pervert, reroute, turn off **08** call away, distract, draw away, estrange, interest, intrigue, redirect, turn away **09** entertain, sidetrack

## diverting
◇ *anagram indicator* **03** fun **05** funny, witty **07** amusing **08** humorous, pleasant **09** enjoyable **11** pleasurable **12** entertaining

## divest
**04** doff **05** strip **06** denude, remove

**07** deprive, despoil, disrobe, undress **08** unclothe **09** disentail **10** dispossess

## divide
◇ *insertion indicator* **03** cut, div, gap **04** deal, divi, fork, gulf, part, rank, rift, sort **05** allot, break, cut up, grade, group, order, sever, share, split **06** bisect, branch, breach, cantle, cleave, depart, detach **07** arrange, break up, carve up, deal out, discide, dispart, diverge, dole out, fissure, furcate, hand out, opening, sort out, split up **08** alienate, allocate, classify, dispense, disunite, division, estrange, polarize, separate, share out **09** apportion, break down, segregate, watershed **10** categorize, disconnect, distribute, divergence, drive apart, measure out, separation **11** come between, distinguish
• **divide up 05** allot, share **07** dole out **08** allocate, share out **09** apportion, dismember, parcel out **10** measure out

## dividend
**03** cut, div, FID **04** divi, gain, perk, plus **05** bonus, divvy, extra, share, whack **07** benefit, portion, surplus **09** advantage **10** percentage, perquisite

## divination
**05** -mancy **06** augury **07** presage **08** divining, prophecy **10** conjecture, prediction **11** foretelling, hariolation, second sight, soothsaying **14** fortune-telling **15** prognostication

*Divination and fortune-telling techniques include:*

**04** dice
**05** runes, tarot
**06** I Ching, sortes
**07** dowsing, scrying
**08** geomancy, myomancy, taghairm, zoomancy
**09** aeromancy, astrology, belomancy, ceromancy, gyromancy, oenomancy, palmistry, pyromancy, sortilege, tea leaves, theomancy
**10** axinomancy, capnomancy, cartomancy, chiromancy, cleromancy, dukkeripen, hieromancy, hydromancy, lithomancy, numerology, spodomancy
**11** bibliomancy, botanomancy, crithomancy, gastromancy, hepatoscopy, oneiromancy, onychomancy, rhabdomancy, tephromancy
**12** clairvoyance, coscinomancy, lampadomancy, omphalomancy, ornithomancy, radiesthesia, scapulomancy
**13** Book of Changes, crystal gazing, dactyliomancy, fortune cookie, omoplatoscopy
**14** crystallomancy

## divine
**04** holy, spae **05** godly, guess, infer **06** cleric, deduce, intuit, lovely, parson, pastor, priest, sacred **07** angelic, exalted, godlike, prelate, saintly, suppose, supreme, surmise,

**divinely**

suspect **08** charming, foretell, glorious, heavenly, minister, mystical, perceive, reverend, seraphic, splendid **09** apprehend, beautiful, celestial, churchman, clergyman, excellent, prescient, religious, spiritual, wonderful **10** conjecture, delightful, sanctified, superhuman, theologian, understand **11** churchwoman, clergywoman, consecrated **12** ecclesiastic, supernatural, transcendent **13** prognosticate *See also* **clergyman, clergywoman; religious**

**divinely**

**08** heavenly **10** charmingly, gloriously, mystically **11** angelically, celestially, excellently, spiritually, wonderfully **12** delightfully **14** supernaturally

**diviner**

**04** seer **05** augur, sibyl **06** dowser, oracle **07** prophet **08** haruspex **09** divinator, visionary **10** astrologer, soothsayer **11** clairvoyant, conjecturer, water-finder **12** crystal-gazer

**diving**

*see* **swimming**

**divinity**

**02** RE, RI **03** god **05** deity **06** spirit **07** goddess, godhead, godship **08** holiness, numinous, religion, sanctity, theology **09** godliness **10** divineness *See also* **God; god, goddess**

**division**

**03** arm, div **04** feud, part, rift, side **05** class, group, limit, share, split, tribe, tuath, world **06** border, branch, breach, divide, region, schism, sector **07** barrier, cutting, discord, parting, portion, rupture, scruple, section, segment, sharing **08** boundary, category, conflict, disunion, disunity, dividing, frontier, scission, scissure, townland **09** allotment, cutting up, detaching, partition, severance **10** alienation, allocation, department, digitation, dividing up, separation, sharing out, subsection **11** compartment, distinction **12** disagreement, distribution, dividing-line, estrangement **13** apportionment **15** demarcation line

**divisive**

**08** damaging **09** injurious **10** alienating, discordant, disruptive, estranging, schismatic **11** troublesome **12** inharmonious **13** troublemaking

**divorce**

**03** div **04** part **05** annul, sever, split, talak, talaq **06** breach, bust up, detach, divide **07** break up, break-up, isolate, put away, rupture, split up, split-up **08** dissolve, disunion, disunite, division, separate **09** annulment, partition, repudiate, severance **10** disconnect, dissociate, separation **11** dissolution, divorcement **13** diffarreation

**divorced**

**03** div

**divorcee**

**02** ex

**divulge**

**04** leak, talk, tell **05** let on, split **06** babble, betray, bewray, expose, impart, repeat, reveal **07** confess, declare, let slip, publish, uncover **08** disclose, evulgate, proclaim **09** broadcast, make known, unconfine **10** promulgate **11** blow the gaff, communicate **12** break the news **13** spill the beans

**dizziness**

**06** megrim **07** megrims, vertigo **09** faintness, giddiness, mirligoes, wooziness **10** scotodinia **15** light-headedness, vertiginousness

**dizzy**

◊ *anagram indicator* **04** mazy **05** dazed, ditsy, faint, giddy, shaky, silly, woozy **06** wobbly **07** confuse, extreme, foolish, muddled, reeling **08** confused, Disraeli **09** airheaded, confusing, Gillespie **10** bewildered, off-balance **11** addle-headed, bewildering, light-headed, vertiginous **13** irresponsible, rattle-brained **14** feather-brained, scatterbrained, weak at the knees

**Djibouti**

**03** DJI

**do**

◊ *anagram indicator* **02** ut **03** act, con, dae, end, fix, put, rob **04** bash, char, comb, cook, dope, do up, dupe, fare, fuss, go at, have, hoax, make, raid, read, take, tidy, tour, wash, work **05** brush, cause, cheat, clean, crack, event, feast, get on, learn, mimic, offer, party, place, put on, reach, serve, solve, study, style, treat, trick, visit **06** adjust, affair, beat up, behave, bestow, come on, confer, create, finish, fleece, fulfil, manage, master, rave-up, render, rip off, soirée, supply, tackle, tart up, thrash, thrive, tidy up, work as, work at, work on **07** achieve, arrange, assault, clean up, deceive, defraud, develop, dope out, execute, exhaust, explore, furnish, go round, knees-up, major in, perform, prepare, present, proceed, produce, provide, resolve, satisfy, sort out, suffice, swindle, work out **08** activity, be enough, carry out, complete, conclude, deal with, decorate, function, get along, get ready, hoodwink, occasion, organize, progress, sightsee, travel at **09** come along, discharge, figure out, gathering, implement, look after, overreach, prosecute, puzzle out, reception, undertake **10** accomplish, be adequate, effectuate, fit the bill, have as a job, take care of, try to solve **11** celebration, impersonate, travel round **12** be employed as, be in charge of, be sufficient, take for a ride **13** earn a living as, make a bad job of **14** acquit yourself, be satisfactory, make a good job of **15** comport yourself, conduct yourself, find the answer to, put into practice

• **do away with** **04** do in, kill, slay **05** annul, scrap **06** murder, remove **07** abolish, bump off, destroy, discard, nullify **08** get rid of, knock off **09** dispose of, eliminate, finish off, liquidate, slaughter **10** put to death **11** assassinate, discontinue, exterminate

• **do down** **04** slag, slam **05** blame, cheat **06** dump on, subdue **07** censure, condemn, put down, rubbish, slag off **08** badmouth, belittle **09** criticize, disparage **13** find fault with

• **do in** **04** kill, ruin, slay **06** murder **07** bump off, deceive, exhaust **08** knock off **09** slaughter **10** put to death **11** assassinate, exterminate

• **do out of** **06** fleece **08** con out of **09** deprive of **10** cheat out of, trick out of **11** diddle out of **12** swindle out of

• **dos and don'ts** **04** code **05** rules **07** customs **09** etiquette, standards **11** regulations **12** instructions

• **do up** **03** tie **04** lace, pack **05** tie up, zip up **06** button, fasten, repair **07** arrange, restore **08** decorate, renovate **09** modernize, refurbish **10** redecorate **11** recondition

• **do without** **04** miss, want **05** forgo, spare **06** eschew, forego, give up **07** refrain **09** go without **10** relinquish **11** abstain from **12** deny yourself, dispense with **13** manage without

• **that will do** **02** so **03** sae

**docile**

**04** meek **07** dutiful, willing **08** amenable, flexible, obedient, obliging, yielding **09** childlike, compliant, tractable **10** controlled, manageable, submissive **11** co-operative **12** controllable

**docilely**

**08** amenably **09** dutifully, willingly **10** obediently, obligingly **11** compliantly **13** co-operatively

**docility**

**07** pliancy **08** meekness **09** ductility, obedience **10** compliance, pliability **11** amenability **12** biddableness, complaisance, tractability **13** manageability **14** submissiveness

**dock**

◊ *tail deletion indicator* **02** dk **03** bob, cut, pen **04** clip, crop, land, moor, pier, quay, rump **05** basin, berth, jetty, put in, Rumex, tie up, wharf **06** anchor, deduct, detail, lessen, marina, reduce, remove, sorrel **07** bistort, curtail, harbour, shorten **08** boat yard, canaigre, decrease, diminish, patience, quayside, subtract, truncate, withhold **09** grapetree, polygonum **10** drop anchor, tidal basin, waterfront **12** monk's rhubarb, submarine pen **15** fitting-out basin

• **docked** **02** in

• **in the dock** **07** on trial

**docker**

**04** ship **06** lumper **08** labourer **09** stevedore **11** farmer's wife **12** longshoreman

## docket

**03** tab, tag **04** bill, chit, file, mark **05** index, label, tally **06** chitty, coupon, record, ticket **07** receipt, voucher **08** document, register **09** catalogue, paperwork **10** categorize **11** certificate, counterfoil **13** documentation

## doctor

◇ *anagram indicator* **02** Dr **03** doc **04** cook, drug, fake, lace, load, pill, spay **05** alter, bones, medic, quack, spike **06** change, crocus, dilute, fiddle, mganga, neuter, repair, weaken **07** falsify, massage, pervert, sangoma **08** castrate, disguise, marabout, medicate, medicine, sawbones **09** body-curer, clinician, physician, sterilize **10** add drugs to, adulterate, manipulate, tamper with **11** add poison to, contaminate, witch-finder **12** misrepresent, sophisticate **13** interfere with

*Doctor types include:*

**02** BM, GP, MB, MD, MO
**03** vet
**05** locum
**06** intern
**07** dentist, surgeon
**08** houseman, resident
**09** registrar
**10** consultant
**12** family doctor
**14** hospital doctor, medical officer

*See also* **medical**

*Doctors include:*

**03** Who
**04** Bell (Sir Charles), Koch (Robert), Lind (James), Mayo (Charles), Razi (ar-), Reed (Walter), Ross (Sir Ronald)
**05** Broca (Paul Pierre), Bruce (Sir David), Galen, Lower (Richard), Osler (Sir William), Paget (Sir James), Remak (Robert), Steno (Nicolaus)
**06** Bichat (Marie), Bright (Richard), Carrel (Alexis), Celsus (Aulus), Cooper (Sir Astley) (Sir John), Fernel (Jean), Finsen (Niels), Florey (Sir Howard), Garrod (Sir Archibald), Harvey (William), Hunter (John), Jekyll, Jenner (Edward), Lister (Joseph, Lord), Manson (Sir Patrick), Mesmer (Franz), Watson (John), Willis (Thomas)
**07** Addison (Thomas), Barnard (Christiaan), Beddoes (Thomas), Burkitt (Denis), Cushing (Harvey) (Peter), Eijkman (Christiaan), Gilbert (William), Hodgkin (Thomas), Laënnec (René), Laveran (Charles), Linacre (Thomas), MacEwen (Sir William), McIndoe (Sir Archibald), Nicolle (Charles), Winston (Robert, Lord)
**08** Anderson (Elizabeth Garrett), Barnardo (Thomas), Beaumont (William), Billroth (Theodor), Charnley (Sir John), Duchenne (Guillaume), Magendie (François), Morgagni (Giovanni Battista),

Sydenham (Thomas), Tournier (Paul)
**09** Bartholin (Erasmus), Boerhaave (Hermann), Dutrochet (Henri), Fabricius (Johannes), Hahnemann (Samuel), Mackenzie (Sir James), Parkinson (James)
**10** Fracastoro (Girolamo), Paracelsus, Sanctorius
**11** Hippocrates, Ramón y Cajal (Santiago)
**12** Erasistratus

*See also* **surgeon**

## doctrinaire

**05** rigid **06** biased **08** armchair, dogmatic, pedantic **09** fanatical, insistent **10** inflexible **11** impractical, opinionated, theoretical

## doctrine

**03** ism **04** lore **05** canon, credo, creed, dogma, tenet **06** belief **07** esotery, mystery, opinion, precept **08** teaching **09** principle **10** conviction

*See also* **philosophy**

## document

**04** chop, cite, deed, form, list, roll, writ **05** chart, paper, proof, prove **06** back up, billet, detail, patent, record, report, verify **07** charter, support, warning, write up **08** evidence, register, validate **09** affidavit, chronicle, write down **10** chirograph, commission, instrument **11** certificate, corroborate, instruction, put on record **12** command paper, commit to film, give weight to, keep on record, substantiate **13** commit to paper

## documentary

**07** charted, factual, written **08** detailed, recorded **09** reportage **10** chronicled, documented, featurette

## documentation

**06** papers, record **08** evidence **09** authority, paperwork **12** verification **14** qualifications

## doddering

◇ *anagram indicator* **04** aged, weak **05** frail **06** feeble, infirm, senile **07** elderly **08** decrepit **09** tottering

## doddery

◇ *anagram indicator* **04** aged, weak **05** shaky **06** feeble, infirm **07** tottery **08** unsteady **09** doddering, faltering, tottering **10** staggering

## dodge

**03** tip **04** bolt, dart, dash, dive, duck, fake, jink, jook, jouk, lurk, ploy, ruse, rush, shun, veer, wile **05** avoid, elude, evade, fudge, shift, shirk, skive, trick **06** bypass, device, racket, scheme, swerve **07** evasion, fend off, quibble, shuffle, slinter, wrinkle **08** fakement, get out of, get round, gimcrack, jimcrack, jump away, side-step **09** deception, manoeuvre, stratagem **10** subterfuge **11** contrivance, machination **12** move suddenly, steer clear of **13** sharp practice

## dodger

**06** evader, skiver **07** avoider, dreamer,

goof-off, shirker, slacker **08** layabout, slyboots **09** lazybones, trickster **11** goldbricker, lead-swinger

## dodgy

◇ *anagram indicator* **04** iffy **05** crook, dicey, fishy, risky **06** artful, chancy, tricky, unsafe **07** dubious, fraught, suspect **08** doubtful, unstable **09** dangerous, dishonest, uncertain **10** unreliable **12** disreputable **13** problematical

## doer

**04** hand **05** agent **06** dynamo, factor, worker **07** bustler **08** achiever, activist, executor, go-getter, live wire **09** organizer **10** powerhouse **12** accomplisher **14** mover and shaker

## doff

**03** tip **04** lift, shed, vail **05** avail, avale, raise, strip, touch **06** availe, lay off, remove **07** discard, take off, undight **08** throw off

## dog

**03** cur, pup, tag **04** cock, Fido, mutt, stag, tail, tike, tyke **05** bitch, harry, haunt, hound, piper, pooch, puppy, rogue, Rover, stalk, track, trail, worry **06** barker, bitser, canine, follow, infest, plague, pursue, rascal, shadow, touser, towser, wretch, yapper **07** andiron, mongrel, traitor, trouble, villain, whiffet, yapster **08** informer **09** scoundrel **10** tripehound **11** Montmorency, trendle-tail, trindle-tail, trundle-tail

*See also* **animal**

*Dogs include:*

**03** gun, lab, Pom, pug
**04** chow, kuri, Peke, tosa
**05** akita, boxer, corgi, dhole, dingo, husky, hyena, laika, spitz
**06** badger, bandog, basset, beagle, bitser, borzoi, briard, collie, gun dog, kelpie, moppet, poodle, saluki, Scotty, setter, vizsla, Westie
**07** basenji, bouvier, bulldog, bush dog, coondog, griffon, lurcher, Maltese, mastiff, pitbull, pointer, Samoyed, Scottie, Shar-Pei, sheltie, shih tzu, sloughi, spaniel, terrier, volpino, whippet
**08** Airedale, Alsatian, chow-chow, coach dog, Doberman, elkhound, foxhound, keeshond, komondor, Labrador, malamute, papillon, Pekinese, Sealyham, sheepdog, warrigal
**09** boar-hound, chihuahua, coonhound, dachshund, Dalmatian, Eskimo dog, Great Dane, greyhound, Kerry blue, Lhasa Apso, Pekingese, red setter, retriever, schnauzer, St Bernard, wolfhound
**10** bloodhound, blue heeler, fox terrier, Iceland-dog, Maltese dog, otter hound, Pomeranian, raccoon dog, Rottweiler, sausage dog, spotted dog, St Bernard's
**11** Afghan hound, basset-hound, bichon frise, bull-mastiff, bull

terrier, carriage dog, Irish setter, Jack Russell, kangaroo dog, wishtonwish

12 Border collie, cairn terrier, Irish terrier, Japanese tosa, Newfoundland, Welsh terrier
13 affenpinscher, bearded collie, Boston terrier, cocker spaniel, Dandie Dinmont, Scotch terrier, Sussex spaniel
14 English terrier, German shepherd, Irish wolfhound, Norfolk terrier, pit bull terrier, Tibetan terrier
15 golden retriever, Scottish terrier, springer spaniel

*See also* **spaniel; terrier**

*Dog types include:*

02 pi
03 gun, hot, lap, pet, pie, pye, sea, top, toy, war
04 corn, rach, wild
05 guard, guide, house, pooch, rache, ratch, sheep, under, watch, water, zorro
06 kennet, pariah, police, ranger, ratter, sleeve, yellow
07 harrier, hearing, leading, mongrel, tracker, truffle
08 huntaway, turnspit
09 retriever
10 sheep-biter, shin-barker
11 sleuth-hound

*Famous dogs include:*

03 Lad
04 Lucy, Nana, Odie, Shep, Spot, Toby, Toto
05 Balto, Butch, Flush, Goofy, Laika, Petra, Pluto, Pongo, Sadie, Snowy, Timmy
06 Buster, Droopy, Gelert, Gromit, Hector, Lassie, Missis, Nipper, Sirius, Snoopy
07 Charley, Gnasher, Perdita, Roobarb
08 Bullseye, Cerberus, Dogmatix
09 Rin Tin Tin, Scooby Doo
10 Deputy Dawg, Fred Basset
12 Real Huntsman
13 Master McGrath, Mick the Miller
15 Greyfriars Bobby, The Littlest Hobo

• **dog's breakfast, dog's dinner**
04 mess
• **reproof to dog** 04 rate

**dogged**
04 firm 06 intent, steady, sullen
07 staunch 08 obdurate, resolute, stubborn, tireless 09 obstinate, steadfast, tenacious 10 determined, persistent, relentless, unflagging, unshakable, unyielding
11 indomitable, persevering, unfaltering, unshakeable
12 pertinacious, single-minded
13 indefatigable

**doggedly**
06 firmly 09 staunchly 10 resolutely, stubbornly, tirelessly, unshakably
11 obstinately, steadfastly, tenaciously, unshakeably 12 persistently,

relentlessly 13 indefatigably 14 single-mindedly

**doggedness**
08 firmness, tenacity 09 endurance, obstinacy 10 resolution, steadiness
11 persistence, pertinacity
12 perseverance, stubbornness
13 determination, steadfastness, tenaciousness 14 indomitability, relentlessness

**doggerel**
03 jig 08 nonsense, rat-rhyme
11 cramboclink 12 crambo-jingle

**dogma**
04 code 05 credo, creed, maxim, tenet
06 belief 07 article, opinion, precept
08 doctrine, teaching 09 principle
10 conviction 12 code of belief
14 article of faith

**dogmatic**
08 arrogant, emphatic, pontific, positive 09 arbitrary, assertive, canonical, doctrinal, imperious, insistent 10 ex cathedra, intolerant, peremptory, pontifical 11 affirmative, categorical, dictatorial, doctrinaire, domineering, opinionated, overbearing, pragmatical
13 authoritarian, authoritative
14 unquestionable 15 unchallengeable

**dogmatically**
10 arrogantly 11 assertively, imperiously, insistently
12 emphatically, intolerantly
13 categorically, dictatorially, domineeringly 15 authoritatively

**dogmatism**
07 bigotry 11 presumption
12 positiveness 13 arbitrariness, assertiveness, imperiousness
14 peremptoriness 15 dictatorialness, opinionatedness

**dogsbody**
05 gofer, slave 06 drudge, lackey, menial, skivvy 07 doormat 08 factotum
11 galley-slave 12 bottle-washer, man-of-all-work 13 maid-of-all-work

**doings**
04 acts, work 05 deeds, feats 06 events
07 actions, affairs 08 concerns, dealings, exploits, goings-on
09 handiwork 10 activities, adventures, happenings 11 enterprises, proceedings 12 achievements, transactions

**doldrums**
05 blues, dumps, ennui, gloom
06 acedia, apathy, tedium, torpor
07 boredom, inertia, malaise, megrims
08 dullness 09 dejection, lassitude
10 depression, melancholy, stagnation
12 listlessness, sluggishness
15 downheartedness, low-spiritedness

**dole**
03 JSA 04 broo, pain, vail 05 grief, guile, share, vails, vales 06 credit, income 07 benefit, payment, support
08 pittance 09 allowance 12 state benefit 14 social security
• **dole out** 04 deal 05 allot, issue,

share 06 assign, divide, ration 07 deal out, dish out, give out, hand out, mete out 08 allocate, dispense, divide up, share out 09 apportion 10 administer, distribute

**doleful**
03 sad 04 blue 06 dismal, dreary, gloomy, rueful, sombre, woeful
07 forlorn, painful, pitiful 08 dolorous, mournful, pathetic, wretched
09 cheerless, miserable, sorrowful, woebegone 10 depressing, lugubrious, melancholy 11 distressing
12 disconsolate 14 down in the dumps

**dolefully**
05 sadly 08 dismally, gloomily
09 forlornly, miserably, unhappily
10 mournfully, wretchedly
12 pathetically 14 disconsolately

**doll**
03 toy 04 babe 05 dolly 06 figure
08 figurine 09 plaything

*Dolls include:*

03 kid, rag, wax
04 baby
05 China, cloth, Dutch, metal, paper, Paris, Sindy®
06 artist, Barbie®, bisque, blow-up, ethnic, fabric, Hamble, kewpie, modern, moppet, poppet, puppet, voodoo, wooden
07 fashion, jointed, kachina, kokeshi, nesting, rag baby, Russian
08 golliwog, gollywog
09 miniature, porcelain, tachibina, Tiny Tears®
10 bobblehead, marionette, matryoshka, Raggedy Ann, topsy-turvy
11 composition, papier-mâché, Polly Pocket®
12 reproduction
15 Cabbage Patch Kid®, frozen Charlotte

• **doll up** 05 preen, primp 06 tart up
07 deck out, dress up, trick up
08 titivate, trick out

**dollar**
03 cob, dol 04 buck, peso 05 scrip, wheel 06 loonie, single 07 iron man, Mexican, smacker 09 greenback
• **eighth of a dollar** 04 real
• **five dollars** 03 fin 04 spin 05 fiver

**dollop**
03 gob 04 ball, blob, glob, lump
05 bunch, clump 06 gobbet, slairg

**dolly**
05 peggy 06 maiden, Parton, Varden

**dolorous**
03 sad 06 rueful, sombre, woeful
07 doleful, painful 08 grievous, mournful, wretched 09 anguished, harrowing, miserable, sorrowful, woebegone 10 lugubrious, melancholy
11 distressing 12 heart-rending

**dolour**
04 pain 05 grief 06 misery, sorrow
07 anguish, sadness 08 distress,

**dolphin**
mourning 09 heartache, suffering 10 heartbreak 11 lamentation

**dolphin**
06 sea-pig 07 grampus 08 porpoise 09 coryphene, Delphinus, mere swine 10 bottle-nose

**dolt**
03 ass, git, oaf 04 clot, dope, dork, fool, geek, nerd, nong, twit 05 chump, clunk, golem, idiot, ninny, twerp, wally 06 dimwit, nitwit 07 nutcase, plonker 08 dipstick, imbecile, mooncalf, numskull 09 blockhead, simpleton 10 clodhopper, nincompoop, sheep's-head 11 chuckle-head

**domain**
04 area, park 05 arena, bourn, field, lands, realm, reame, reign, world 06 bourne, empire, estate, region, sphere 07 concern, demesne, kingdom, section 08 dominion, province, seignory, universe 09 ownership, seigneury, seigniory, territory 10 department, discipline, seigneurie, speciality 12 jurisdiction
*See also* **classification**

**dome**
04 tope 05 igloo, mound, stupa, vault 06 bubble, cupola, dagaba, dagoba, tholus 07 rotunda 09 astrodome, macrodome 10 brachydome, hemisphere

**domestic**
03 dom, pet 04 char, cook, esne, help, home, maid, tame 05 daily, house, local, tamed 06 au pair, broken, family, homely, native 07 cleaner, private, servant 08 broken in, char lady, familiar, fireside, home-bred, home help, internal, national, personal 09 charwoman, daily help, household 10 home-loving, indigenous, stay-at-home 11 domiciliary 12 domesticated, domestic help, housekeeping, house-trained

---

*Domestic appliances include:*

03 Aga®, hob, Vax®
04 iron, oven, spit
05 grill, mixer, radio, stove
06 cooker, fridge, Hoover®, juicer, kettle, washer
07 blender, fan oven, freezer, griddle, ionizer, toaster
08 barbecue, gas stove, hotplate, wireless
09 deep fryer, Dutch oven, DVD player, steam iron
10 coffee mill, deep-freeze, dishwasher, humidifier, liquidizer, percolator, rotisserie, slow cooker, steam press, television, waffle iron
11 tumble-drier, washer-drier
12 kitchen range, refrigerator, stereo system, trouser press
13 carpet sweeper, electric grill, floor polisher, food processor, fridge-freezer, ice-cream maker, microwave oven, sandwich maker, vacuum cleaner,

video recorder
14 electric cooker, juice extractor, upright cleaner, washing machine
15 carpet shampooer, cylinder cleaner

---

**domestically**
06 at home 07 locally 08 near home 09 in private 10 internally, nationally

**domesticate**
04 tame 05 break, train 07 break in 08 accustom 09 habituate 10 assimilate, house-train, naturalize 11 acclimatize, familiarize

**domesticated**
03 pet 04 tame 05 tamed 06 broken, homely 08 broken in, domestic 10 home-loving, house-proud 11 housewifely, naturalized 12 house-trained

**domestication**
06 taming 08 training 10 breaking-in 11 habituation 12 assimilation 13 house-training 14 naturalization

**domesticity**
09 homecraft 10 homemaking, housecraft 12 housekeeping 13 domestication, home economics 15 domestic science

**domicile**
04 home, live 05 abode, house 06 settle 07 lodging, mansion 08 dwelling, lodgings, quarters 09 establish, residence, residency 10 habitation, settlement 12 make your home, put down roots 15 take up residence

**dominance**
04 rule, sway 05 power 07 command, control, mastery 08 hegemony 09 authority, supremacy 10 ascendancy, centrality, domination, government, leadership 11 paramountcy, pre-eminence, superiority

**dominant**
03 key 04 main 05 chief, major, prime 06 ruling, strong 07 central, leading, primary, supreme 08 powerful 09 assertive, besetting, governing, important, paramount, presiding, prevalent, principal, prominent 10 commanding, overriding, pre-eminent, prevailing 11 all-powerful, controlling, influential, outstanding, predominant 13 authoritative, most important

**dominate**
04 lead, rule 05 dwarf 06 direct, govern, master, rule OK 07 command, control, eclipse, preside, prevail 08 domineer, overbear, overgang, overlook, overrule 09 mesmerize, tower over, tyrannize 10 intimidate, monopolize, overmaster, overshadow, run the show 11 have on toast, predominate 12 hold the floor 15 have over a barrel, wear the trousers

**dominating**
06 strong 08 dominant, powerful, superior 09 assertive, confident, directing 10 commanding, overruling

11 controlling 12 advantageous 13 authoritative

**domination**
04 rule, sway 05 power 07 bossism, command, control, mastery, tyranny 09 authority, despotism, influence, prelatism, supremacy 10 ascendancy, government, leadership, militarism, oppression, repression, subjection 11 pre-eminence, superiority, suppression 12 dictatorship, predominance 13 subordination

**domineer**
04 boss, ride 07 henpeck 08 jackboot

**domineering**
05 bossy, pushy 07 haughty, kick-ass 08 arrogant, coercive, despotic, forceful, managing 09 imperious, masterful, tyrannous 10 aggressive, autocratic, high-handed, iron-handed, oppressive, peremptory, tyrannical 11 dictatorial, overbearing 13 authoritarian

**Dominica**
02 WD 03 DJI, DMA

**Dominican**
03 Dom

**Dominican Republic**
03 DOM

**Dominicans**
02 OP

**dominion**
03 Dom 04 rule, sway 05 power, realm 06 colony, domain, empire 07 command, control, country, kingdom, mastery 08 lordship, province 09 authority, direction, supremacy, territory 10 ascendancy, dependency, domination, government 11 sovereignty 12 jurisdiction, protectorate 14 rangatiratanga

**don**
◊ *insertion indicator* 04 Juan 05 adept, put on, swell, tutor 06 assume, expert, fellow, reader 07 address, dress in, get into, scholar, teacher 08 academic, Giovanni, lecturer, slip into 09 professor

**donate**
03 gie 04 gift, give 06 bestow, chip in, confer, pledge 07 cough up, fork out, present 08 bequeath, give away, shell out 09 make a gift, subscribe 10 contribute 12 club together 13 make a donation

**donation**
04 alms, gift, koha, wakf, waqf 05 grant 07 bequest, charity, largess, present 08 gratuity, largesse, memorial, offering 11 benefaction 12 contribution, presentation, subscription

**done**
◊ *anagram indicator* 02 OK 04 over 05 baked, crisp, ended, fried, ready, right 06 agreed, boiled, cooked, proper, seemly, stewed, tender 07 browned, correct, decided, fitting, roasted, settled 08 accepted, arranged,

complete, decorous, executed,
finished, prepared, realized, suitable,
well-done **09** completed, concluded,
fulfilled **10** absolutely, acceptable,
terminated **11** appropriate,
consummated **12** accomplished,
conventional
• **done for** **04** lost **06** beaten, broken,
dashed, doomed, foiled, ruined,
undone **07** wrecked **08** defeated,
finished, spitcher, washed-up
**09** destroyed **10** vanquished **14** for the
high jump
• **done in** **04** dead **05** all in, weary
**06** bushed, pooped, zonked
**07** whacked, worn out **08** dead beat,
dog-tired, fatigued, tired out
**09** exhausted, fagged out, fit to drop,
flaked out, knackered, pooped out,
shattered, stonkered **11** bushwhacked,
tuckered out **14** on your last legs, worn
to a frazzle
• **have done with** **04** stop **05** cease
**06** desist, give up **08** over with **09** throw
over **10** finish with, thrash with
**12** finished with **13** be through with
**15** over and done with, wash your
hands of

### Don Juan
**04** rake **05** lover, romeo **06** gigolo
**08** Casanova **09** ladies' man, philander,
womanizer **10** lady-killer
**11** philanderer

### donkey
**03** ass **04** moke, mule **05** burro, cuddy,
genet, hinny, jenny, neddy **06** cuddie,
gennet, jennet **07** jackass
**11** cardophagus **13** Jerusalem pony

### donnish
**07** bookish, erudite, learned, serious
**08** academic, pedantic, studious
**09** pedagogic, scholarly **10** scholastic
**11** formalistic **12** intellectual

### donor
**05** angel, giver **06** backer **07** donator
**08** provider **09** supporter **10** benefactor
**11** contributor **14** fairy godmother,
philanthropist

### doom
**03** lot **04** damn, date, dome, fate, ruin
**05** death, judge, weird **06** decree,
devote **07** condemn, consign, destine,
destiny, fortune, portion, verdict
**08** disaster, downfall, judgment,
sentence **09** destinate, judgement,
pronounce, ruination **10** death-knell,
predestine **11** catastrophe, destruction,
rack and ruin **12** condemnation
**13** pronouncement

### doomed
**03** fay, fey, fie **05** fated **06** cursed,
damned, marked, ruined **07** accurst,
devoted, unlucky **08** accursed,
destined, hopeless, ill-fated, luckless
**09** condemned, ill-omened
**10** bedevilled, ill-starred **11** star-
crossed

### door
**03** way **04** exit, haik, hake, heck, road,
vett **05** entry, hatch, route, way in
**06** access, portal **07** doorway, gateway,

opening, postern **08** entrance, open
door **11** opportunity
• **guard door** **04** tile

### doorkeeper
**05** tiler, tyler, usher **06** porter
**07** doorman, janitor, ostiary **08** huissier
**09** caretaker, concierge **10** gatekeeper
**14** commissionaire

### doorpost
**04** dern, durn

### dope
**01** E **03** gen, git, LSD, oaf, pot, tea
**04** acid, berk, clot, coke, dolt, dork,
drug, fool, geek, hash, info, lace, prat,
twit, weed **05** crack, drugs, dunce,
facts, grass, idiot, ninny, opium, speed,
spike, twerp **06** dimwit, doctor, heroin,
inject, nitwit, opiate, sedate
**07** buffoon, details, Ecstasy, halfwit,
low-down, plonker, stupefy
**08** cannabis, knock out, medicate,
narcotic **09** absorbent, blockhead,
marijuana, narcotize, simpleton,
specifics **10** nincompoop
**11** amphetamine, barbiturate,
information, particulars
**12** anaesthetize, hallucinogen
*See also* **fool; recreational drugs**
*under* **drug**

### dopey
**04** daft, dozy **05** silly **06** drowsy,
groggy, simple, sleepy, stupid, torpid
**07** foolish, muddled, nodding
**08** confused, narcotic **09** lethargic,
somnolent, stupefied **12** addle-brained
**14** not the full quid

### dormancy
**04** rest **05** sleep **07** latency, slumber
**09** inertness **10** estivation, inactivity
**11** aestivation, hibernation

### dormant
**05** inert, joist **06** asleep, fallow, latent,
torpid **07** resting **08** comatose, inactive,
latitant, sleeping, sluggish
**09** crossbeam, lethargic, potential,
quiescent **10** slumbering, unrealized
**11** hibernating, undeveloped,
undisclosed

### dormouse
**04** loir

### dosage
**04** dose **06** amount **07** measure, portion
**08** quantity

### dose
**03** fix, hit **04** pill, shot **05** bolus, treat
**06** amount, dosage, drench, potion,
powder **07** booster, draught, measure,
portion **08** dispense, medicate,
quantity **09** prescribe **10** administer
**11** horse-drench **12** prescription
• **lethal dose** **02** LD

### dosh
*see* **money**

### dossier
**04** case, data, file **05** brief, notes
**06** folder, papers, report **09** documents,
portfolio **11** information

### dot
**03** dab, dit, hit, jot, set **04** atom, iota,

limp, mark, spot, stud, tick **05** fleck,
point, prick, speck **06** bullet, circle,
pepper, stigme, tittle **07** punctum,
scatter, speckle, stipple **08** full stop,
particle, pin-point, punctule, sprinkle
**09** punctuate **11** bullet point
**12** decimal point
• **on the dot** **05** sharp **06** on time
**07** exactly **08** promptly **09** precisely
**10** punctually **13** exactly on time

### dotage
**06** old age **07** anility **08** agedness,
senility, weakness **09** infirmity
**10** feebleness, imbecility
**11** decrepitude, elderliness **12** autumn
of life **13** evening of life **15** second
childhood

### dote
• **dote on** **04** love **05** adore, spoil
**06** admire, pamper **07** idolize, indulge,
worship **08** hold dear, treasure

### doting
**04** fond, soft **06** loving, tender
**07** adoring, devoted **09** indulgent
**12** affectionate

### dotty
◇ *anagram indicator* **03** ape **04** bats,
loco, nuts **05** barmy, batty, buggy,
crazy, daffy, dippy, flaky, gonzo,
loony, loopy, nutty, potty, wacko,
wacky, weird, wiggy **06** cuckoo, fruity,
mental, raving, screwy **07** bananas,
barking, bonkers, cracked, meshuga,
touched **08** crackers, demented,
dingbats, doolally, peculiar, unsteady
**09** eccentric, lymphatic, up the wall
**10** bestraught, frantic-mad, off the wall,
off your nut, out to lunch **11** not all
there, off the rails, off your head
**12** feeble-minded, mad as a hatter, off
your chump, round the bend **13** off
your rocker, out of your head, out of
your tree, round the twist **14** off your
trolley, wrong in the head

### double
◇ *repetition indicator* **02** bi-, di- **03** dbl,
twi-, twy- **04** copy, dual, fold, twin
**05** clone, duple, image, match, trick,
twice **06** binate, clench, do also,
duplex, fill in, paired, repeat, ringer,
two-ply **07** coupled, doubled, enlarge,
magnify, replica, stand in, twofold
**08** geminate, geminous, increase, turn
down, two-edged **09** ambiguous,
bifarious, deceitful, duplicate,
equivocal, facsimile, insincere,
lookalike **10** ambivalent, substitute,
understudy **11** counterpart, deceitfully,
double-edged, paradoxical,
reduplicate **12** doppelgänger,
hypocritical, impersonator **13** double-
meaning, have a dual role, multiply by
two, spitting image **14** be an
understudy, have a second job **15** have
a second role
• **at the double** **06** at once **07** quickly
**09** right away **11** at full speed,
immediately **12** straight away, without
delay
• **double back** **04** loop **05** dodge,
evade **06** circle, return **07** reverse
**09** backtrack

## double-cross

**03** con **05** cheat, trick **06** betray
**07** defraud, mislead, swindle, two-time
**08** hoodwink **12** take for a ride **14** pull
a fast one on

## double-dealing

**07** perfidy **08** betrayal, cheating,
tricking **09** duplicity, mendacity,
swindling, treachery, two-timing
**10** defrauding, misleading
**11** crookedness, dissembling,
hoodwinking **12** ambidextrous, two-
facedness

## double entendre

**03** pun **08** innuendo, wordplay
**09** ambiguity **11** play on words
**13** double meaning **14** suggestiveness

## doubling

**04** fold, loop **05** plait, trick **08** mantling
**10** gemination **11** duplicature
**12** diplogenesis **13** reduplication

## doubly

**03** bis **05** again, extra, twice **07** twofold
**10** especially

## doubt

**04** fear **05** demur, qualm, query, waver
**06** aporia, danger, mammer, wonder
**07** dilemma, dubiety, impeach,
problem, scepsis, scruple, skepsis,
suspect **08** distrust, dubitate, hesitate,
misdoubt, mistrust, quandary,
question, wavering **09** ambiguity, be
dubious, confusion, hesitance,
hesitancy, misgiving, suspicion,
vacillate **10** difficulty, disbelieve,
hesitation, indecision, perplexity,
scepticism, skepticism, uneasiness
**11** be uncertain, be undecided,
incredulity, reservation, uncertainty
**12** apprehension, be suspicious, mixed
feeling **14** call in question **15** have
qualms about
• **expression of doubt 02** ha, h'm,
um **03** erm, hah, hmm, hum **05** humph
• **in doubt 04** moot **08** doubtful
**09** ambiguous, debatable, uncertain,
undecided **10** in question, unreliable,
unresolved, up in the air **12** open to
debate, questionable **14** open to
question
• **no doubt 04** iwis, ywis **06** surely
**08** of course, probably **09** certainly,
doubtless, no denying **10** definitely,
most likely, presumably, sure enough
**11** undoubtedly **12** bang to rights,
without doubt **13** in anyone's book
**14** unquestionably

## doubter

**05** cynic **06** Thomas **07** sceptic, scoffer
**08** agnostic **10** questioner, unbeliever
**11** disbeliever, non-believer,
questionist **14** doubting Thomas

## doubtful

**04** iffy **05** crook, fishy, shady, vague
**06** uneasy, unsure **07** dubious, in
doubt, obscure, suspect, unclear
**08** hesitant, insecure, unlikely,
wavering **09** ambiguous, debatable,
sceptical, skeptical, tentative,
uncertain, undecided **10** improbable,
in two minds, irresolute, suspicious,

touch and go **11** distrustful, vacillating
**12** apprehensive, inconclusive,
questionable **14** open to question

## doubtfully

◇ *anagram indicator* **08** uneasily
**10** hesitantly **11** sceptically, uncertainly
**12** irresolutely **14** apprehensively

## doubtless

**04** sure **05** truly **06** surely **07** clearly, no
doubt **08** of course, probably
**09** assuredly, certainly, dreadless,
precisely, seemingly **10** most likely,
presumably, supposedly
**11** indubitably, undoubtedly **12** bang
to rights, indisputably, without doubt
**13** in anyone's book **14** unquestionably

## dough

**04** cake, duff, masa **05** knish, money,
pasta, paste **08** kreplach **09** hush
puppy
*See also* **money**

## doughnut

**05** torus **06** sinker **07** olycook, olykoek
**09** friedcake

## doughty

**04** able, bold, fell, tall **05** brave, gutsy
**06** daring, gritty, heroic, plucky,
spunky, strong **07** gallant, valiant
**08** fearless, intrepid, unafraid, valorous
**09** confident, dauntless, unabashed,
undaunted **10** courageous, unblinking
**11** indomitable, lion-hearted,
unblenching, unflinching
**14** unapprehensive

## doughy

**03** sad **04** soft **05** heavy, pasty **06** pallid,
sodden

## dour

**04** grim, hard, sour **05** gruff, harsh,
rigid, stern **06** dismal, dreary, gloomy,
morose, severe, strict, sullen **07** austere
**08** churlish, rigorous **09** obstinate,
unsmiling **10** determined, forbidding,
inflexible, unfriendly, unyielding

## douse, dowse

**03** dip, wet **04** duck, dunk, soak
**05** flood, snuff, souse, steep **06** deluge,
drench, plunge, put out, quench,
splash, strike **07** blow out, immerge,
immerse, smother **08** saturate,
submerge **10** extinguish **13** pour water
over

## dove

**03** doo **06** culver, pigeon, rocker, turtle
**07** rockier **10** rock pigeon

## dovetail

**04** join, link **05** agree, match, tally
**06** accord **07** conform **08** coincide
**09** harmonize, interlock **10** correspond
**11** fit together

## dowdy

**04** drab **05** dingy, mopsy, tacky, tatty
**06** frowsy, frumpy, shabby
**08** frumpish, slovenly **10** ill-dressed
**12** old-fashioned **13** unfashionable

## down

**01** d **02** dn **03** ill, low, nap, sad **04** à
bas, blue, bust, fell, flue, fuzz, gulp,
oose, ooze, pile, shag, swig, wool

**05** along, bloom, drink, floor, floss,
fluff, kaput, swill, throw, wonky
**06** pappus, topple **07** consume,
crashed, depress, descent, floccus, put
away, swallow, toss off, unhappy
**08** dejected, downcast, feathers, fine
hair, gulp down, wretched **09** bring
down, conked out, depressed, knock
back, knock down, miserable,
overthrow, prostrate, southward
**10** behindhand, dispirited,
melancholy, not working, on the blink,
on the fritz, out of order, to the floor
**11** downhearted, inoperative, out of
action, to the bottom, to the ground
**12** soft feathers **13** to a lower level
**14** down in the dumps, malfunctioning
• **down with 03** hip **04** à bas
**06** depose **07** abolish, put down,
swallow **08** away with, get rid of **10** in
tune with
• **set down 03** lay **04** drop, dump,
land, snub, take **05** judge, state
**06** depose, esteem, record, regard
**07** ascribe, deposit, detrain
**09** attribute, discharge **10** disentrain

## down-and-out

**03** bum **04** hobo, wino **05** caird, jakey,
loser, piker, rogue, tramp **06** dosser,
ruined, toerag, truant, vagrom, walker
**07** dingbat, floater, gangrel, tinkler,
vagrant **08** clochard, cursitor,
deadbeat, derelict, homeless, straggle
stroller, vagabond **09** destitute,
landloper, penniless, sundowner
**11** rinthereout, scatterling, Weary
Willie **12** down-and-outer, hallan-
shaker, impoverished, on your uppers
**15** knight of the road

## down-at-heel

**04** drab, poor **05** dingy, dowdy, seedy,
tacky, tatty **06** frayed, frowsy, ragged,
shabby **07** run-down **08** slovenly,
tattered **09** neglected **10** ill-dressed,
ramshackle, tumbledown, uncared for
**11** dilapidated, in disrepair

## downbeat

**03** low **04** calm **06** casual, gloomy
**07** cynical, relaxed **08** downcast,
informal, laid-back, negative
**09** cheerless, depressed, easy-going,
unhurried, unworried **10** despondent,
insouciant, nonchalant **11** pessimistic
**15** fearing the worst

## downcast

**03** low, sad **04** blue, down, dull, glum
**05** fed up **06** gloomy **07** daunted,
hanging, unhappy **08** dejected,
dismayed, wretched **09** depressed,
miserable **10** despondent, dispirited,
downlooked **11** crestfallen,
discouraged, downhearted, low-
spirited **12** disappointed, disconsolate,
disheartened

## downfall

**04** fall, ruin **05** decay **07** debacle,
failure, undoing **08** collapse, disgrace
**09** overthrow **10** debasement
**11** degradation, destruction,
humiliation

## downgrade

**05** decry, lower **06** defame, demote,

## downhearted

depose, do down, humble **07** deflate, degrade, run down **08** belittle, minimize, relegate **09** denigrate, disparage, sell short, underrate **11** lower in rank, make light of **12** reduce in rank

## downhearted

**03** sad **04** glum **06** gloomy **07** daunted, unhappy **08** dejected, dismayed, downcast **09** depressed **10** browned off, despondent, dispirited **11** discouraged, low-spirited **12** disappointed, disconsolate, disheartened

## down-market

**04** poor, sale **05** cheap, tacky, tatty **06** budget, cheapo, common, shoddy, tawdry **07** bargain, economy, low-cost, reduced **08** cut-price, giveaway, inferior, low-price, no-frills **09** cheapjack, cheap-rate, knock-down, throwaway, worthless **10** affordable, discounted, economical, marked-down, ramshackle, rock-bottom, second-rate **11** inexpensive **15** bargain-basement

## downpour

**04** pelt, rain **05** flood, plash **06** deluge **07** torrent **09** rainstorm **10** cloudburst, inundation, waterspout

## downright

**04** flat **05** clear, plain, plump, sheer, total, utter **06** arrant, direct, simply **07** brusque, clearly, plainly, totally, utterly **08** absolute, complete, even-down, outright, positive, straight, thorough **09** out-and-out, up-and-down, wholesale **10** absolutely, completely, forthright, positively, thoroughly **11** categorical, plain-spoken, unequivocal, unqualified **13** categorically

## downside

**04** flaw, snag **05** minus **06** defect **07** penalty, trouble **08** drawback, nuisance, weakness **09** liability, weak point **10** impediment, limitation **12** Achilles heel, disadvantage **13** inconvenience

## downsize

**04** slim **06** reduce, shrink **08** contract, diminish, minimize, moderate **11** make smaller

## down-to-earth

**04** sane **07** mundane **08** sensible **09** practical, realistic **10** hard-headed, no-nonsense **11** commonsense, plain-spoken **12** matter-of-fact **13** plain-speaking, unsentimental **14** commonsensical

## downtrodden

**06** abused **07** bullied **08** burdened, helpless **09** exploited, oppressed, powerless **10** subjugated, trampled on, tyrannized, victimized **11** overwhelmed, subservient, weighed-down

## down under

**02** Oz **09** Australia

## downward

**07** sliding **08** downhill, slipping **09** declining, going down **10** descending, moving down

## downy

**04** fine, soft **05** fuzzy, nappy **06** fleecy, fluffy, smooth, woolly **07** cottony, dowlney, knowing, pappose, pappous, velvety **08** feathery **09** plumulate **10** lanuginose, lanuginous

## dowry

**03** dot **04** gift **05** share **06** legacy, talent, tocher **07** faculty, portion **09** endowment, provision **11** inheritance **12** wedding-dower **15** marriage portion

## dowse

see **douse, dowse**

## doxology

**04** hymn, song **05** chant, psalm **06** anthem, gloria, praise **07** chorale **08** response **11** recessional **12** hymn of praise, song of praise **13** glorification

## doze

**03** kip, nap **04** dare, zizz **05** dover, go off, sleep **06** catnap, drowse, nod off, siesta, snooze **07** drop off, shut-eye **08** drift off, take a nap **10** forty winks
• **doze off   06** catnap, nod off, snooze **08** drift off **10** fall asleep **14** have forty winks

## dozen

**02** dz **03** doz, XII **04** twal **06** twelve **07** stupefy

## dozy

**04** daft **05** dopey, silly, tired, weary **06** dreamy, drowsy, simple, sleepy, stupid, torpid **07** foolish, nodding, yawning **09** somnolent **10** half-asleep

## drab

**04** dull, flat, grey **05** dingy, whore **06** boring, dismal, dreary, gloomy, isabel, shabby, sombre **07** tedious **08** isabella, lifeless **09** cheerless **10** colourless, isabelline, lacklustre **11** featureless **12** Quaker-colour **13** uninteresting

## drabness

**05** gloom **08** dullness, greyness **09** dinginess **10** dreariness, shabbiness, sombreness **12** lifelessness **13** cheerlessness **14** colourlessness

## Draconian

**04** grim, hard **05** cruel, harsh, stern **06** brutal, savage, severe, strict **07** inhuman **08** abrasive, pitiless, ruthless **09** merciless, unfeeling **10** iron-fisted, iron-handed **13** unsympathetic

## draft

**03** dft **04** bill, draw, plan **05** essay, rough **06** cheque, design, detach, draw up, scroll, sketch **07** compose, drawing, ébauche, outline, paste-up **08** abstract, bank-bill, protocol **09** blueprint, delineate, formulate, treatment **10** money order **11** delineation, postal order, rough sketch **14** bill of exchange, letter of credit

## drag

**03** lag, lug, tow, tug **04** bind, bore, draw, hale, harl, haul, pain, pest, pull, rash, shoe, sled, snig, trek, tump, yank **05** crawl, creep, shlep, snake, sweep, trail, train **06** bother, drogue, schlep, wear on **07** schlepp, skidpan, trouble **08** go slowly, headache, nuisance **09** annoyance, go on and on, influence **11** go on for ever **12** become boring **13** become tedious, pain in the neck
• **drag on   04** go on **05** run on **07** persist **08** continue **09** be lengthy **14** be long-drawn-out
• **drag out   06** extend, hang on **07** draw out, persist, prolong, spin out **08** lengthen, protract
• **drag up   05** raise **06** rake up, remind, revive **07** bring up, mention **09** introduce

## dragon

**04** worm **05** Draco, drake **08** lindworm **09** firedrake **12** flying lizard

## dragonfly

**05** naiad, nymph **07** Odonata **10** demoiselle

## dragoon

**05** bully, drive, force, impel **06** coerce, compel, harass **08** browbeat, pressure **09** constrain, press-gang, strongarm **10** intimidate, pressurize

## drain

**02** ea **03** dry, eau, pot, sap, sew, tap, tax **04** buzz, delf, duct, grip, leak, milk, nala, ooze, pipe, pour, sink, suck, tile, void **05** bleed, cundy, ditch, drink, empty, exude, fleet, gripe, gully, ladle, leach, leech, nalla, nulla, quaff, sewer, siver, sough, stank, syver, use up **06** condie, effuse, emulge, filter, gutter, nallah, nullah, outlet, remove, sheuch, sheugh, sluice, sponge, strain, trench **07** channel, conduit, consume, culvert, cunette, deplete, dewater, draw off, drink up, exhaust, extract, flow out, piscina, pump off, seep out, swallow, trickle, unwater **08** bleed dry, evacuate, withdraw **09** depletion, discharge, lickpenny **10** bleed white, exhaustion, underdrain **11** common-shore, consumption, watercourse **12** exsanguinate
• **drained   05** tired

## dram

**02** dr **03** tot, wet **04** shot, suck, tiff, tift **06** chasse, drachm **07** caulker, morning, nobbler, snifter, tickler **08** chota peg, meridian **10** stirrup cup
See also **drink**

## drama

**02** no **03** noh **04** auto, play, show **05** opera, piece, scene **06** acting, azione, comedy, crisis, kabuki, thrill **07** dilemma, tension, theater, theatre, tragedy, turmoil **08** operetta **09** dramatics, melodrama, sensation, spectacle **10** dramaturgy, excitement, stagecraft **11** histrionics
See also **play**
• **drama students   04** RADA

## dramatic

**05** stage, tense, vivid **06** abrupt, marked, sudden **07** drastic, graphic **08** distinct, exciting, stirring, striking, Thespian **09** effective, thrilling **10** artificial, expressive, flamboyant, histrionic, impressive, noticeable, theatrical, unexpected **11** exaggerated, personative, sensational, significant, spectacular, substantial **12** considerable, melodramatic

## dramatically

**07** vividly **08** abruptly, suddenly **10** noticeably, strikingly **12** considerably, expressively, impressively **13** significantly, spectacularly, substantially

## dramatist

**06** writer **08** comedian **09** tragedian **10** dramaturge, playwright, play-writer **12** dramaturgist, screen writer, scriptwriter
*See also* **playwright**

## dramatization

**07** staging **10** adaptation **11** arrangement **12** presentation

## dramatize

**03** act, ham **05** adapt, ham up, put on, stage **06** overdo **07** play-act **09** overstate **10** arrange for, exaggerate **12** do a Hollywood, lay it on thick **14** present as a film, present as a play **15** make a big thing of

## drape

◇ *containment indicator* **04** drop, fold, hang, veil, vest, wrap **05** adorn, cloak, cover, droop **06** shroud **07** arrange, envelop, overlay, suspend **08** decorate

## drapery

**05** arras, blind, cloth **06** blinds **07** curtain, hanging, valance, valence **08** backdrop, covering, curtains, hangings, mantling, tapestry **09** coverings **10** jardinière, lambrequin

## drastic

◇ *anagram indicator* **03** bad **04** dire **05** harsh **06** severe, strong **07** extreme, radical, serious, violent **08** dramatic, forceful, forcible, rigorous **09** desperate, Draconian, swingeing **10** unpleasant **11** far-reaching

## drastically

**07** greatly **08** severely, strongly **09** extremely, radically, seriously **10** forcefully, rigorously

## draught

**03** cup **04** flow, gulp, puff, pull, rush, swig **05** draft, drink, privy, quaff, swill **06** breath, drench, influx, potion, waucht, waught **07** current, drawing, pulling, swallow **08** cesspool, dragging, movement, potation, quantity, quencher, traction **10** attraction **12** williewaught

## draw

**02** go **03** get, lug, tap, tie, tow, tug **04** bait, come, drag, haul, limn, lure, milk, move, pick, pull, pump, suck, take, walk **05** chart, drain, drive, frame, go for, infer, paint, sweep, trace, trail

**06** allure, appeal, be even, choose, come to, deduce, depict, design, doodle, elicit, entice, gather, infuse, inhale, map out, obtain, pencil, prompt, raffle, reason, remove, resort, select, siphon, sketch, travel **07** advance, attract, be equal, bring in, extract, inspire, lottery, outline, portray, proceed, procure, produce, pull out, receive, respire, take out, tombola **08** approach, bring out, conclude, dead heat, decide on, describe, interest, lengthen, persuade, plump for, progress, scribble, withdraw **09** breathe in, delineate, influence, magnetism, represent, stalemate, unsheathe **10** attraction, enticement, eviscerate, sweepstake **11** be all square

• **draw back**   **04** cock, funk **05** wince **06** boggle, flinch, recoil, retire, shrink **07** fall off, retract, retreat **08** withdraw **09** start back **10** disadvance

• **draw in**   ◇ *containment indicator* **04** pull, suck **05** hunch, rough **06** absorb, inhale **07** involve, retract **08** contract

• **draw near**   **04** come, nigh **08** approach

• **draw on**   **03** use **05** apply, train **06** allure, call on, employ, induce, lead on, quarry, rely on **07** exploit, utilize **08** approach, put to use **09** make use of **14** have recourse to

• **draw out**   **04** make, spin, tose, toze **05** educe, evoke, leave, start, toaze **06** depart, extend, set out **07** drag out, extract, move out, prolong, pull out, spin out, stretch **08** continue, elongate, lengthen, protract **09** put at ease **12** induce to talk **13** induce to speak **15** encourage to talk

• **draw together**   **04** knit **06** gather **07** close up **08** astringe, contract **10** constringe

• **draw up**   **04** halt, stop **05** draft, frame, run in **06** pull up **07** compile, compose, make out, prepare **08** write out **09** formulate **12** put in writing

• **goalless draw**   **02** 0-0

## drawback

**03** out **04** flaw, snag **05** catch, fault, hitch **06** damper, defect, hurdle **07** barrier, problem, take-off, trouble **08** handicap, nuisance, obstacle, pullback, weak spot **09** hindrance, liability **10** deficiency, difficulty, disamenity, disbenefit, disutility, impediment, limitation **12** disadvantage, imperfection **14** discouragement, stumbling-block

## drawer

**02** dr **04** till **07** shottle, shuttle
• **bottom drawer**   **08** glory box **09** hope chest

## drawing

**04** plot **05** study **06** pencil, pin-man, sketch **07** cartoon, diagram, graphic, outline, picture **08** graffito, portrait, scribble **09** attrahent, depiction, pen-and-ink, portrayal **11** composition,

delineation, scenography **12** illustration **14** representation

## drawl

**03** haw **05** drant, drone, twang **06** dawdle, draunt, haw-haw **08** protract **09** say slowly **11** speak slowly

## drawn

◇ *anagram indicator* **04** taut, worn **05** gaunt, tense, tired **06** closed, sapped **07** fraught, haggard, hassled, pinched **08** fatigued, harassed, strained, stressed **09** etiolated, washed out **10** unsheathed **11** eviscerated

## dread

**03** awe, shy **04** dire, fear, funk, fury **05** alarm, awful, quail, qualm, worry **06** dismay, feared, flinch, fright, grisly, horror, terror **07** dreaded, ghastly, shudder, tremble **08** alarming, blue funk, cringe at, disquiet, dreadful, frighten, gastness, gruesome, horrible, terrible **09** cold sweat, frightful, gastnesse, ghastness, misgiving **10** be afraid of, be scared of, blind panic, shrink from, terrifying **11** fit of terror, frightening, trepidation **12** apprehension, awe-inspiring, perturbation **13** be terrified by **14** be anxious about, be frightened by, be worried about
*See also* **phobia**

## dreadful

◇ *anagram indicator* **04** dern, dire, grim **05** awful, dearn, nasty **06** awsome, tragic **07** awesome, ghastly, heinous, hideous **08** alarming, grievous, horrible, horrific, shocking, terrible, terrific **09** appalling, frightful **10** abortional, calamitous, horrendous, outrageous, terrifying, tremendous, unpleasant **11** frightening

## dreadfully

◇ *anagram indicator* **04** very **07** awfully **08** terribly **09** extremely **10** shockingly **11** appallingly, atrociously, exceedingly, frightfully **12** horrendously

## dream

**03** aim, joy **04** dwam, goal, hope, long, mare, muse, plan, wish **05** crave, dwalm, dwaum, fancy, ideal, mirth, model, music, sound, yearn **06** beauty, design, desire, marvel, superb, sweven, trance, vision **07** aisling, delight, fantasy, imagine, perfect, phantom, reverie, supreme **08** ambition, daydream, delusion, envisage, illusion, somniate, yearning **09** excellent, fantasize, nightmare, pipe dream, switch off, wonderful **10** aspiration, minstrelsy, perfection **11** expectation, hallucinate, imagination, inattention, speculation **12** want very much **13** be lost in space, hallucination **14** phantasmagoria, stare into space **15** castles in the air, not pay attention

• **dream up**   **04** spin **05** hatch **06** create, devise, invent **07** concoct, imagine, think up **08** conceive, contrive **09** conjure up, fabricate

• **not dream of** 08 not think 10 not imagine 11 not conceive, not consider

**dreamer**
07 Utopian 08 idealist, romancer, romantic 09 fantasist, stargazer, theorizer, visionary 10 daydreamer, fantasizer

**dreamily**
06 gently, softly 08 absently 10 peacefully, pleasantly 12 romantically

**dreamlike**
06 unreal 07 phantom, surreal 08 ethereal, illusory 09 fantastic, visionary 10 chimerical, trance-like 13 hallucinatory, insubstantial, unsubstantial 14 phantasmagoric

**dreamy**
03 dim 04 hazy, soft 05 faint, misty, moony, spacy, vague 06 absent, gentle, lovely, musing, spacey, unreal 07 calming, faraway, lulling, pensive, shadowy, unclear 08 ethereal, fanciful, relaxing, romantic, soothing 09 fantastic, imaginary, visionary 10 abstracted, idealistic, indistinct, thoughtful 11 daydreaming, fantasizing, impractical, preoccupied 12 absent-minded 13 wool-gathering

**drearily**
08 boringly, dismally 09 routinely, tediously 11 monstrously 12 depressingly

**dreary**
03 sad 04 dark, drab, dull, glum 05 bleak, oorie, ourie, owrie 06 boring, dismal, dreich, gloomy, gousty, sombre 07 humdrum, routine, tedious 08 desolate, ghastful, lifeless, mournful, overcast, unvaried 09 cheerless, ghastfull, wearisome 10 colourless, depressing, monotonous, uneventful 11 commonplace, featureless 12 run-of-the-mill 13 uninteresting

**dredge**
• **dredge up** 05 dig up, raise 06 drag up, draw up, fish up, rake up 07 scoop up, uncover, unearth 08 discover

**dregs**
04 lags, lees, scum 05 draff, dross, legge, trash, waste 06 bottom, dunder, faeces, fecula, graves, mother, rabble, tramps, ullage 07 bottoms, deposit, dossers, greaves, grounds, residue, taplash 08 detritus, outcasts, residuum, riff-raff, sediment, tailings, vagrants 09 excrement, scourings, sublimate 10 faex populi 11 down-and-outs, precipitate

**drench**
03 wet 04 duck, soak 05 douse, drook, drouk, drown, flood, imbue, souse, steep, swamp 06 embrue, imbrue, sluice 07 embrewe, immerse 08 inundate, permeate, saturate 09 milk shake 13 soak to the skin

**dress**
◇ anagram indicator 02 do 03 don, fig, fit, ray, rig, tog 04 boun, busk, comb, deck, doll, draw, garb, gear, gown, rail, robe, tend, tidy, tiff, tift, tire, togs, trim, wear 05 adorn, array, bowne, chide, clean, cover, drape, erect, frock, get-up, groom, guise, habit, preen, primp, put on, style, treat 06 adjust, attire, betrim, bind up, clothe, finish, fit out, graith, manure, outfit, smooth, swathe, thrash 07 apparel, arrange, bandage, bravery, clobber, clothes, costume, deck out, dispose, flatten, garment, garnish, get into, prepare, throw on, turn out 08 accoutre, clothing, decorate, ensemble, garments, get ready, slip into 10 habiliment, straighten 13 put a plaster on 14 wearing-apparel
See also **clothes, clothing**

*Dresses include:*

03 mob
04 ball, coat, maxi, sack, sari, tent
05 shift, shirt, smock, tasar
06 caftan, dirndl, jumper, kaftan, kimono, muu-muu, sheath, tusser
07 bathing, chemise, evening, gym slip, kitenge, matinee, matinée, tussore, wedding
08 ball-gown, cocktail, gym tunic, negligée, pinafore, princess, sundress
09 cheongsam, farandine, going-away, minidress, slammakin, trollopee
10 dinner-gown, empire-line, farrandine, slammerkin, wraparound
11 décolletage, Dolly Varden, riding habit
12 shirtwaister

• **dress down** 05 chide, scold 06 berate, carpet, rebuke, thrash 07 reprove, rouse on, tell off, tick off, upbraid 09 castigate, reprimand 13 dress casually, give a rocket to, tear off a strip, tear strips off 15 dress informally
• **dress up** ◇ anagram indicator 04 deck, gild, perk 05 adorn, dizen, tog up 06 buck up, doll up, dude up, jazz up, tart up 07 dandify, improve 08 beautify, decorate, disguise, ornament 09 embellish 10 masquerade 12 dress smartly 13 dress formally

**dresser**
• **showy dresser** 03 cat 04 beau
• **special dresser** 03 Mod

**dressing**
◇ anagram indicator 03 jus, pad 04 lint 05 gauze, patch, sauce, spica 06 coulis, relish 07 bandage, Band-aid®, clothes, plaster 08 compress, ligature, poultice 09 condiment 10 tourniquet 11 Elastoplast®, vinaigrette
See also **salad**

**dressmaker**
06 tailor 07 modiste 09 couturier, midinette, tailoress 10 couturière, seamstress 11 mantua-maker, needlewoman, sewing woman 12 garment-maker

**dressy**
05 natty, ritzy, sharp, showy, smart, swish 06 classy, formal, ornate 07 elegant, stylish 09 elaborate

**dribble**
03 run 04 drib, drip, drop, foam, leak, ooze, seep, spit 05 drool, exude, froth, gloop 06 drivel, saliva, slaver 07 droplet, seepage, slobber, trickle 10 sprinkling

**dried**
04 arid, sear, sere 06 wilted 07 drained, parched, wizened 08 withered 09 mummified 10 dehydrated, desiccated, exsiccated, shrivelled

**drier**
04 oast 07 tumbler

**drift**
◇ anagram indicator 03 aim, sag 04 bank, core, crab, flow, ford, gist, heap, hull, mass, pile, rack, roam, rove, rush, vein, waft, wisp 05 amass, coast, drive, drove, float, mound, point, scope, shift, stray, sweep, tenor, trend 06 course, design, gather, heap up, import, leeway, pierce, pile up, stream, thrust, tunnel, wander, wreath 07 current, driving, essence, meaning, purport 08 movement, tendency 09 direction, freewheel, intention, substance, variation 10 accumulate, digression 11 implication 12 accumulation, significance 14 be carried along 15 go with the stream

**drifter**
04 hobo 05 nomad, rover, tramp 06 drover 07 swagger, swagman, vagrant 08 vagabond, wanderer 09 itinerant, sundowner, traveller 11 beachcomber 12 rolling stone

**drill**
02 PE, PT 03 awl, bit 04 bore 05 borer, coach, prick, punch, teach, train 06 gimlet, ground, jumper, manual, pierce, reamer, school, seeder 07 routine, tuition, wildcat 08 coaching, exercise, instruct, practice, practise, puncture, rehearse, training 09 exercises, grounding, inculcate, penetrate, perforate, procedure 10 discipline, jackhammer, repetition 11 counterbore, inculcation, instruction, make a hole in, preparation 13 square-bashing 14 indoctrination, manual exercise

**drink**
03 bib, cup, jar, lap, nip, one, peg, sea, sip, sup, tot 04 brew, down, dram, grog, gulp, have, lush, neck, pint, pull, shot, suck, swig, tass, tiff, tift, tope, toss 05 booze, drain, hooch, juice, plonk, quaff, revel, sauce, smoke, swill, tinct, toast 06 absorb, grog on, guzzle, hootch, imbibe, liquid, liquor, noggin, potion, rotgut, salute, swally, tank up, tiddly, tipple 07 alcohol, carouse, draught, drink to, indulge, shicker, spirits, swallow 08 aperitif, beverage, get drunk, infusion, potation 09 firewater, hard stuff, knock back, overdrink, partake of, polish off, soft drink, stiffener, the bottle, throw back

**10** amber fluid **11** have too much, jungle juice, refreshment, strong drink, the creature, tickle-brain **12** Dutch courage, go on the shout, hit the bottle **13** knock back a few **14** be a hard drinker, drink like a fish, have one too many, thirst-quencher **15** be a heavy drinker, propose a toast to
*See also* **glass**

*Alcoholic drinks include:*

**02** it
**03** ale, dop, gin, kir, mum, nog, rum, rye, tay
**04** arak, beer, bull, fine, flip, grog, hock, mead, nipa, ouzo, pils, port, purl, sake, saki, sour, sura, vino, wine
**05** cider, G and T, lager, perry, Pimm's®, plonk, stout, vodka
**06** arrack, bishop, brandy, bubbly, Cognac, eggnog, grappa, mimosa, porter, poteen, Scotch, shandy, sherry, whisky
**07** alcopop, aquavit, Bacardi®, bourbon, Campari, Gordon's®, liqueur, Marsala, Martell®, martini, oloroso, pink gin, red wine, retsina, sangria, sloe gin, spirits, tequila, vin rosé, whiskey
**08** advocaat, Armagnac, Calvados, cold duck, Guinness®, hot toddy, schnapps, Smirnoff®, vermouth, vin blanc, vin rouge
**09** badminton, Beefeater®, champagne, cocktails, Laphroaig®, snakebite, white wine, Wincarnis®
**10** ginger wine, Remy Martin®
**11** black-and-tan, boilermaker, Courvoisier®, gin-and-tonic, Glenfiddich®, Irish coffee, Jack Daniel's®
**12** Famous Grouse®, Glenmorangie®, malternative
**13** peach schnapps, Scotch and soda
**14** Bombay Sapphire®

*See also* **beer; cocktail; liqueur; spirits; wine**

*Non-alcoholic drinks include:*

**03** cha, pop, tea
**04** Coke®, cola, kola, milk, soda
**05** assai, Assam, cocoa, float, julep, latte, mixer, Pepsi®, tonic, water
**06** coffee, Indian, Irn-Bru®, Ribena®, squash, tisane
**07** beef tea, cordial, limeade, Perrier®, seltzer
**08** café noir, China tea, Coca-Cola®, Earl Grey, espresso, expresso, fruit tea, green tea, Horlicks®, lemonade, lemon tea, Lucozade®, Ovaltine®, root beer, smoothie
**09** Aqua Libra®, ayahuasco, Canada Dry®, cherryade, cream soda, ginger ale, herbal tea, milk shake, mint-julep, orangeade, soda water
**10** café au lait, café filtre, cappuccino, fizzy drink, fruit juice, ginger beer, rosehip tea,

still water, tonic water, Vichy water
**11** barley water, bitter lemon, camomile tea
**12** hot chocolate, mineral water, sarsaparilla
**13** peppermint tea, Turkish coffee
**14** sparkling water
**15** lapsang souchong

*Drinks of the gods include:*

**06** amrita, nectar
**08** ambrosia

*Special drinks include:*

**03** ava
**04** kava, soma
**05** haoma
**09** ayahuasca, ayahuasco

• **drink hard** **04** bend, tank
**06** bezzle
• **drink in** **05** grasp **06** absorb, digest, imbibe, take in **07** inhaust, realize **10** appreciate

**drinkable**
**04** safe **05** clean **07** potable **10** fit to drink

**drinker**
**03** sot **04** lush, soak, wino **05** alkie, dipso, drunk, toper **06** barfly, boozer, sponge, sucker **07** imbiber, pint-pot, tippler, tosspot **08** drunkard **09** fuddle-cap, inebriate **10** winebibber **11** dipsomaniac, froth-blower, hard drinker **12** heavy drinker **14** serious drinker
• **reformed drinkers** **02** AA

**drinking**
◊ *insertion indicator*
• **drinking cup** **03** nut, tig, tot
**04** bowl, tass **05** cylix, kylix **06** cotyle, goblet, quaich, quaigh, rhyton
**07** chalice, scyphus **09** cantharus
**10** parting-cup
• **drinking session** **03** bat, bum
**04** bend, bevy, bout, bust, lush, sesh
**05** bevvy, binge, blind, booze, drunk, spree **06** beer-up, bender, bottle, fuddle, grog-on, grog-up, razzle, screed **07** blinder, booze-up, carouse, session, wassail
• **expressions relating to drinking**
**04** evoe, rivo, skol **05** evhoe, evohe, skoal **06** cheers, prosit **07** slàinte
**08** chin-chin **10** good health **12** mud in your eye
• **given to drinking** **03** wet

**drip**
**02** IV **03** wet **04** bead, bore, drop, leak, ooze, plop, tear, weed, weep, wimp
**05** gloop, ninny, sissy, softy **06** filter, splash **07** dewdrop, dribble, drizzle, trickle **08** sprinkle, weakling
**09** percolate **10** stillicide
• **dripping** **03** fat

**drive**
**02** ca', Dr, go **03** caa', dig, put, ram, ren, rin, run, tax, vim, zip **04** bear, come, dash, firk, goad, herd, hunt, hurl, lash, lead, move, need, prod, push, rack, rate, ride, road, send, sink,

spin, spur, take, trip, turn, urge, will
**05** carry, chase, drift, fight, force, guide, impel, jaunt, knock, motor, pilot, power, press, screw, steer, surge, thump, verve **06** action, appeal, avenue, battle, burden, coerce, compel, convey, desire, direct, effort, energy, hammer, handle, incite, manage, oblige, outing, pizazz, plunge, prompt, propel, spirit, strike, thrust, travel, vigour **07** actuate, control, crusade, dragoon, enforce, go by car, impulse, journey, operate, overtax, provoke, resolve, roadway, round up **08** ambition, appetite, approach, campaign, driveway, instinct, motivate, movement, overdo it, overwork, persuade, pressure, struggle, tenacity **09** chauffeur, come by car, constrain, excursion, transport
**10** enterprise, get-up-and-go, initiative, motivation, overburden, pressurize, propulsion **11** give a lift to, travel by car, work too hard **12** be at the wheel, kill yourself, transmission
**13** determination **14** propeller shaft
**15** be at the controls
• **drive at** **04** hint, mean **05** aim at, get at, imply **06** intend **07** refer to, signify, suggest **08** allude to, indicate, intimate
**09** insinuate **10** have in mind
• **drive away** **04** hunt, shoo **05** chase
**06** banish, dispel **07** repulse
**08** exorcize
• **drive down** **03** ram
• **drive fast** **04** race **05** speed
• **drive inconsiderately** **03** hog
• **drive out** **04** fire **05** expel, wreak
**07** turn out **11** exterminate
• **prepare to drive** **03** tee

**drivel**
**03** rot **04** blah, bull, drip, guff **05** balls, bilge, drool, hooey, slush, tripe
**06** bunkum, slaver, waffle **07** baloney, dribble, eyewash, garbage, hogwash, maunder, rhubarb, rubbish, slabber, twaddle **08** claptrap, malarkey, nonsense **09** bull's wool, gibberish, poppycock **10** balderdash, mumbo-jumbo **12** gobbledygook

**driver**
**02** Dr **04** Jehu, whip **05** bikie, mizen, rider **06** cabbie, jarvey, jarvie, mizzen
**07** locoman, taximan, trucker, truckie
**08** bullocky, motorist, muleteer, roadsman, truckman **09** chauffeur
**12** motorcyclist **15** knight of the road
*See also* **racing**
• **new driver** **01** L

**drivers**
**02** AA **03** RAC

**driving**
**05** heavy **07** dynamic, violent
**08** forceful, sweeping, vigorous
**09** energetic **10** compelling, forthright

**drizzle**
**04** drip, drop, mist, pour, rain, smir, smur, spit, spot **05** smirr, spray
**06** mizzle, shower **07** dribble, scowder, skiffle, trickle **08** fine rain, scouther, scowther, sprinkle **09** light rain **10** rain finely, Scotch mist **11** rain lightly

## droll
**03** odd, rum **04** jest, zany **05** comic, funny, queer, witty **06** jester **07** amusing, bizarre, comical, jocular, risible, waggish **08** clownish, farcical, humorous, peculiar **09** diverting, eccentric, laughable, ludicrous, whimsical **10** ridiculous **12** entertaining

## drone
**03** dor, hum **04** buzz, dorr, purr **05** chant, drant, drawl, idler, leech, thrum, whirr **06** bumble, bummle, dog-bee, doodle, draunt, intone, loafer **07** bourdon, dreamer, goof-off, slacker, sponger, vibrate **08** hanger-on, layabout, parasite, whirring **09** bombilate, bombinate, go on and on, lazybones, murmuring, scrounger, vibration **10** lazy person **11** goldbricker

## drool
**04** dote, gush **05** gloat **06** drivel, slaver **07** dribble, enthuse, slobber **08** salivate **11** slobber over **15** water at the mouth

## droop
**03** bow, lob, nod, sag **04** bend, drop, fade, flag, peak, sink, weep, wilt **05** faint, slink, slump, stoop **06** dangle, falter, nutate, slouch, wither **07** decline **08** fall down, hang down, languish, pendency **09** lose heart

## droopy
**03** lax **04** lank, limp, weak **05** loose, saggy, slack **06** feeble, floppy **07** falling, sagging **08** drooping, dropping

## drop
◇ *deletion indicator* **02** gt **03** bit, can, dab, end, lay, nip, sip, tad, tot **04** bead, blob, cast, dash, dive, drib, drip, fall, fire, glob, gout, jilt, land, leak, omit, plop, quit, sack, shed, sink, spat, spot, stop, take, tear **05** abyss, bring, candy, carry, cease, chasm, chuck, cliff, ditch, droop, forgo, gutta, lapse, let go, lower, pinch, slope, slump, sweet, trace **06** bonbon, bubble, desert, disown, dragée, drappy, finish, forego, give up, goutte, humbug, lessen, little, plunge, put off, reject, splash, tumble, weaken **07** abandon, boot out, cutback, decline, deliver, descend, descent, dismiss, drappie, dribble, driblet, droplet, dwindle, exclude, fall off, forsake, globule, let fall, let go of, lozenge, miss out, modicum, pendant, plummet, smidgen, sweetie, trickle, turf out **08** decrease, diminish, downturn, dribblet, globulet, leave out, lowering, mouthful, pastille, renounce, run out on, spheroid, sprinkle **09** bespatter, declivity, discharge, precipice, reduction, repudiate, terminate, throw over, transport, walk out on **10** falling-off, finish with, relinquish, slacken off **11** devaluation, discontinue **12** depreciation, dispense with **13** deterioration, make redundant
• **drop back**   **03** lag **07** retreat **08** fall back **09** lag behind **10** fall behind
• **drop in**   **04** call **05** pop in, visit

**06** call by, come by, instil **07** instill **08** come over **09** call round, come round
• **drop off**   **04** doze, sink **05** go off **06** catnap, depart, hand in, lessen, nod off, plunge, snooze, unload **07** decline, deliver, deposit, doze off, dwindle, fall off, plummet, set down **08** decrease, diminish, drift off **09** disappear **10** fall asleep, slacken off **14** have forty winks
• **drop out**   **04** quit **05** leave **06** cry off, give up **07** abandon, back out, forsake **08** renounce, withdraw
• **drop out of**   **04** quit **05** leave **06** opt out, renege **07** abandon, pull out **08** opt out of, renege on, renounce **09** back out of **10** cry off from **12** withdraw from

## dropout
**05** loner, rebel **06** hippie **07** beatnik, deviant **08** Bohemian, renegade **09** dissenter **10** malcontent **11** dissentient **13** nonconformist

## droppings
**04** dung, scat, skat **06** egesta, faeces, manure, ordure, stools **07** excreta, spraint **09** excrement

## dross
**04** junk, lees, rust, scum, slag **05** dregs, lucre, slack, trash, waste **06** debris, refuse, scoria **07** remains, rubbish **08** impurity **09** recrement

## drought
**04** want **06** drouth, thirst **07** aridity, dryness **08** shortage **11** dehydration, desiccation, parchedness

## drove
**03** mob **04** herd, host, pack **05** crowd, crush, drift, flock, horde, press, swarm **06** string, throng **07** company **09** gathering, multitude

## drown
**02** go **03** die **04** sink **05** flood, swamp **06** deluge, drench, engulf, perish **07** founder, go under, howl out, immerse, silence, wipe out **08** drown out, inundate, outvoice, overcome, submerge **09** overpower, overwhelm **10** extinguish **12** lose your life

## drowsily
**06** dopily, dozily **07** wearily **08** sleepily **10** sluggishly **13** lethargically

## drowsiness
**06** torpor **08** dopiness, doziness, lethargy, narcosis **09** oscitancy, tiredness, weariness **10** grogginess, sleepiness, somnolence, somnolency **12** sluggishness

## drowsy
**04** dozy, dull **05** dopey, dozed, heavy, tired, weary **06** bleary, dozing, dreamy, sleepy, torpid **07** nodding, slumbry, yawning **08** comatose, slumbery **09** lethargic, somnolent **10** half-asleep **11** heavy-headed

## drubbing
**06** defeat **07** beating, licking **08** flogging, pounding, whipping **09** hammering, thrashing, trouncing,

walloping **10** clobbering, cudgelling, pummelling **11** shellacking

## drudge
**04** drug, hack, moil, plod, toil, work **05** devil, droil, grind, grunt, scrub, slave, snake, sweat **06** beaver, labour, lackey, menial, skivvy, slavey, stooge, toiler, worker **07** servant **08** dogsbody, factotum, labourer, plug away, slog away, trauchle **09** packhorse **10** after-guard, Cinderella **11** galley-slave

## drudgery
**03** fag **04** slog, toil **05** chore, graft, grind, sweat, yakka **06** labour, yacker, yakker **07** faggery, slavery **08** hackwork, trauchle **09** grunt work, skivvying, slaistery, spadework, treadmill **10** collar-work, donkey-work, menial work **13** sweated labour

## drug
**04** cure, dose, numb **06** deaden, drudge, potion, remedy, sedate **07** stupefy **08** knock out, medicate, medicine, shanghai **09** stimulant **10** medication **12** anaesthetize, tranquillize **15** make unconscious
*See also* **medicine**

*Medicinal drugs include:*

**03** AZT
**04** Soma®
**05** Intal®, NSAID, salep, Taxol®, Zyban®
**06** opiate, Prozac®, statin, sulpha, Valium®, Viagra®, Zantac®
**07** antacid, aspirin, codeine, heparin, insulin, Nurofen®, quinine, Relenza®, Ritalin®, Seroxat®, steroid, Tamiflu®, triptan
**08** Antabuse®, diazepam, diuretic, hyoscine, methadon, morphine, narcotic, neomycin, orlistat, Rohypnol®, sedative, warfarin
**09** aciclovir, acyclovir, analgesic, co-codamol, cortisone, digitalis, Herceptin®, ibuprofen, macrolide, methadone, oestrogen, stimulant, tamoxifen, temazepam
**10** antibiotic, anxiolytic, chloroform, chloroquin, dimorphine, interferon, penicillin, ranitidine, salbutamol
**11** allopurinol, amoxycillin, amyl nitrate, anaesthetic, beta-blocker, chloroquine, cyclosporin, haloperidol, ipecacuanha, neuroleptic, paracetamol, propranolol, vasodilator
**12** ACE-inhibitor, chlorambucil, methotrexate, progesterone, sleeping pill, streptomycin, sulphonamide, tetracycline
**13** antibacterial, anticoagulant, antihistamine, streptokinase, tranquillizer
**14** anticonvulsant, antidepressant, antiretroviral, azidothymidine, bronchodilator, corticosteroid, erythropoietin, hallucinogenic, hydrocortisone
**15** chloramphenicol, vasoconstrictor

## drug addict

*Recreational drugs include:*

**01** C, E, H
**03** hop, ice, kef, kif, LSD, PCP, pot, tab
**04** acid, bang, barb, blow, coca, coke, dope, dove, gage, hash, hemp, junk, kaif, meth, NRG-1, pill, scag, skag, snow, Tina, weed
**05** bhang, crack, crank, dagga, horse, jelly, opium, shmek, smack, speed, sugar, upper
**06** basuco, charas, downer, heroin, mescal, peyote, pituri, popper
**07** charlie, churrus, cocaine, crystal, ecstasy, fantasy, guaraná, pep pill, roofies, schmeck
**08** cannabis, freebase, ketamine, laudanum, meconium, mescalin, methadon, moonrock, morphine, nepenthe, Rohypnol®, snowball, Special K
**09** angel dust, dance drug, marijuana, mescaline, methadone, nose candy, peace pill, ready-wash, speedball, temazepam
**10** mephedrone, white stuff
**11** amphetamine, barbiturate, purple heart
**12** date-rape drug
**13** phencyclidine

*See also* **cannabis; cocaine; heroin**
• **drug dose** **03** fix **05** bolus
• **drug experience** **04** trip

## drug addict
**04** head, hype, user **05** freak **06** junkie
**07** druggie, hop-head, tripper **08** coke-head, snowbird **09** dope-fiend, mainliner

## drugged
**04** high **05** doped **06** ripped, stoned, wasted, zonked **07** on a trip
**08** comatose, hopped-up, turned on
**09** spaced out, stupefied **10** knocked out

## drum
**03** rap, tap **04** beat, dhol, reel, swag
**05** bongo, conga, daiko, house, knock, naker, ridge, tabor, taiko, throb, thrum
**06** atabal, barrel, bundle, cannon, kettle, rigger, tabour, tabret, tam-tam, tattoo, timbal, tom-tom, tum-tum, tymbal **07** bodhrán, drumlin, mridang, pulsate, tambour, timpano, tympano
**08** mridanga, tympanum
**09** mridamgam, mridangam
**11** reverberate
• **drum into** **06** hammer, harp on, instil **07** din into **09** drive home, inculcate, reiterate
• **drum out** **05** expel **07** dismiss
**08** throw out **09** discharge
• **drum up** **03** get **06** gather, obtain, summon **07** attract, canvass, collect, round up, solicit **08** petition

## drumbeat
**04** flam, roll, ruff, touk, tuck **05** hurry
**06** rafale, rappel, rattan, tattoo
**08** assembly **10** paradiddle

## drummer
**02** Dr **07** swagman **09** timpanist, tympanist

## drunk
◇ *anagram indicator* **03** fap, fou, lit, sot, wat, wet **04** full, high, inky, lush, paid, para, soak, wino **05** alkie, blind, dipso, foxed, happy, inked, lit up, merry, moppy, slued, tight, tipsy, toper, woozy **06** blotto, bombed, boozer, canned, corked, in wine, jagged, jarred, juiced, loaded, mashed, mellow, mortal, ratted, ripped, slewed, soused, sponge, stewed, stinko, stoned, tanked, tiddly, wasted
**07** bevvied, bonkers, bottled, crocked, drinker, drunken, ebriose, fairish, half-cut, legless, maggoty, pickled, pie-eyed, shicker, sloshed, smashed, sozzled, squiffy, tiddled, tiddley, tippler, toasted, tosspot, trashed, wrecked **08** bibulous, drunkard, footless, hammered, in liquor, juiced up, liquored, maggoted, moon-eyed, overseen, overshot, sow-drunk, stocious, stotious, tanked up, whiffled, whistled **09** alcoholic, blootered, crapulent, incapable, inebriate, inebrious, paralytic, plastered, saturated, shickered, stonkered, trolleyed, up the pole, well-oiled
**10** blind drunk, capernoity, inebriated, in your cups, obfuscated
**11** capernoitie, cappernoity, dipsomaniac, full as a boot, full as a goog, full as a tick, hard drinker, high as a kite, intoxicated, off your face, on the tiddly, slaughtered **12** drunk as a lord, drunk as a newt, heavy drinker, roaring drunk **13** drunk as a piper, drunk as a skunk, having had a few, under the table **14** Brahms and Liszt
**15** a sheet in the wind, one over the eight, the worse for wear, under the weather
• **getting drunk** **02** on **12** half-seas-over **13** mops and brooms
• **make drunk** **03** cup **05** sew up, souse **07** tipsify **09** inebriate
**10** intoxicate

## drunkard
**03** sot **04** lush, soak, wino **05** alkie, bloat, dipso, drunk, souse, toper
**06** boozer, sponge **07** bloater, drinker, fuddler, hophead, shicker, tippler, tosspot **08** bacchant, habitual
**09** alcoholic, inebriate **10** wine-bibber
**11** dipsomaniac, hard drinker **12** heavy drinker

## drunken
◇ *anagram indicator* **03** wat **05** boozy, drunk, happy, lit up, merry, tight, tipsy
**06** bombed, boozey, loaded, spongy, stoned, tiddly **07** Bacchic, drucken, riotous, sloshed **08** Bacchian, besotted
**09** crapulent, debauched, inebriate, worthless **10** dissipated
**11** baccanalian, intemperate, intoxicated

## drunkenness
**07** ebriety, ivresse **08** methysis
**09** ebriosity, inebriety, temulence, tipsiness **10** alcoholism, crapulence,

debauchery, dipsomania, insobriety
**11** inebriation **12** bibulousness, hard drinking, intemperance, intoxication
**13** St Martin's evil **15** serious drinking

## dry
**02** TT **03** air, sec, xer- **04** arid, brut, dull, fair, flat, kiln, sear, seco, sere, welt, wilt, wipe, xero- **05** baked, drain, droll, husky, parch, secco, witty, xeric
**06** barren, boring, clever, dreary, formal, frigid, ironic, low-key, rizzar, rizzer, rizzor, scorch, subtle, torrid, wilted, wither **07** cutting, cynical, deadpan, drouthy, gasping, hirstie, laconic, make dry, parched, precise, shrivel, tedious, thirsty, trocken
**08** droughty, rainless, scorched, teetotal, withered **09** abstinent, become dry, dehydrate, desiccate, dry as dust, sarcastic, temperate, unwatered, waterless, wearisome
**10** abstemious, dehumidify, dehydrated, desiccated, dry as a bone, monotonous, on the wagon, shrivelled, unbuttered, unexciting
**11** alcohol-free **12** moistureless
**13** uninteresting **14** prohibitionist
• **dry up** **04** fade, fail, sear, stop, wane
**05** arefy **06** die out, ensear, scorch, shut up **07** dwindle **09** desiccate, disappear, exsiccate **11** come to an end, stop talking **15** forget your lines

## dryness
**06** drouth, thirst **07** aridity, drought, siccity, xerasia, xerosis **08** aridness
**09** xerostoma **10** barrenness, xerostomia **11** dehydration, thirstiness

## dual
**04** twin **06** binary, double, duplex, paired **07** coupled, matched, twofold
**08** combined, two-piece **09** duplicate

## duality
**07** twoness **09** duplicity **10** doubleness, opposition, separation
**11** combination, duplication
**12** polarization

## dub
**03** tag **04** call, name, term, trim
**05** label, style **06** bestow, confer, puddle **07** entitle **08** christen, nickname **09** designate

## dubiety
**05** doubt, qualm **08** mistrust
**09** misgiving, suspicion **10** hesitation, indecision, scepticism **11** incertitude, uncertainty **12** doubtfulness

## dubious
◇ *anagram indicator* **04** iffy **05** crook, fishy, shady **06** shifty, unsure
**07** obscure, suspect **08** doubtful, elliptic, hesitant, wavering
**09** ambiguous, debatable, sceptical, uncertain, undecided, unsettled
**10** backhanded, elliptical, irresolute, left-handed, suspicious, unreliable
**11** vacillating **12** questionable
**13** untrustworthy

## dubiously
**09** debatably **10** hesitantly
**11** ambiguously, uncertainly,

undecidedly **12** questionably, suspiciously

## dubnium
**02** Db

## duchy
**07** dukedom

## duck
**01** O **03** bob, dip, wet **04** bend, dive, dook, drop, dunk, jook, jouk, shun, zero **05** avoid, dodge, douse, drake, elude, evade, lower, shirk, skive, souse, squat, stoop, yield **06** cringe, crouch, plunge **07** bow down, darling, immerse **08** bankrupt, sidestep, submerge **09** defaulter **10** hit the deck, sweetheart **12** steer clear of, wriggle out of
*See also* **animal**

---

*Ducks include:*

**04** blue, musk, smee, smew, surf, teal, wood
**05** eider, Pekin, ruddy, scaup
**06** burrow, hareld, herald, magpie, pateke, Peking, runner, scoter, smeath, smeeth, spirit, tufted, velvet, wigeon
**07** crested, gadwall, mallard, moulard, muscovy, old wife, pintail, pochard, steamer
**08** garganey, hookbill, mandarin, old squaw, shelduck
**09** Cuthbert's, goldeneye, goosander, harlequin, merganser, sheldrake, shielduck, shoveller
**10** bufflehead, canvasback, long-tailed, ring-necked
**11** ferruginous, St Cuthbert's, white-headed
**12** common scoter, Indian runner, velvet scoter
**13** ruddy shelduck

---

• **string of ducks** **04** sord, team
• **two ducks** **02** OO **04** pair

## duct
**03** vas **04** pipe, tube **05** canal **06** funnel, ureter, vessel **07** channel, conduit, fistula, passage, Venturi, wireway **08** deferent, diffuser **09** emunctory, excretory **11** Venturi tube

## ductile
**06** pliant **07** plastic, pliable **08** amenable, biddable, flexible, tractile, yielding **09** compliant, malleable, tractable **10** manageable **11** manipulable

## dud
**03** bum **04** bust, duff, flop **05** kaput **06** broken, failed, faulty, stumer **07** failure, let-down, washout **08** bum steer, nugatory **09** conked out, valueless, worthless **11** counterfeit, inoperative **14** disappointment

## dude
**03** cat, fop, Roy **04** buck, lair **05** dandy

## dudgeon
**04** hilt **05** pique **10** resentment

## due
**03** fee, fit, lot **04** dead, just, levy, owed, toll **05** ample, owing, right **06** charge, direct, earned, enough, merits, proper, rights, unpaid **07** awaited, charges, correct, deserts, dewfull, exactly, fitting, merited, payable, tribute **08** adequate, deserved, directly, expected, plenty of, required, rightful, straight, suitable **09** appointed, in arrears, justified, precisely, privilege, repayable, requisite, scheduled **10** birthright, sufficient **11** anticipated, appropriate, comeuppance, just deserts, long-awaited, outstanding, prerogative **12** contribution, subscription **13** membership fee
• **due to** **07** owing to **08** caused by **09** because of **11** as a result of

## duel
**04** tilt **05** clash, fight **06** battle, combat, duello **07** contest, rivalry **08** struggle **09** encounter, monomachy **10** dependence, engagement, monomachia **11** competition **14** affair of honour **15** affaire d'honneur

## duff
◊ *anagram indicator* **03** bad **04** naff, poor, poxy, ropy, rump, weak **05** awful, dough, lousy, pants **06** broken, bungle, crummy, faulty **07** botched, the pits, useless **08** buttocks, hopeless, inferior, mediocre, pathetic, terrible **09** defective, deficient, imperfect, third-rate **10** inadequate, mismanaged, second-rate **11** incompetent, ineffective, poor-quality, substandard **12** unacceptable **14** a load of garbage, a load of rubbish, unsatisfactory

## duffer
**03** git, oaf **04** clod, clot, dill, dolt, dork, fool, geek, muff, prat **05** fogey, idiot **06** dimwit, old man **07** bungler, halfwit, plonker, rustler **08** bonehead **09** blunderer, ignoramus **11** cattle-thief

## dugong
**06** sea cow, sea-pig **08** halicore, sirenian

## duke
**01** D **04** fist, lord

## dulcet
**04** soft **05** sweet **06** gentle, mellow **08** pleasant, soothing **09** agreeable, melodious **10** harmonious **11** mellifluous **13** sweet-sounding

## dulcimer
**06** santir, santur **07** cembalo, cymbalo, santoor, santour **08** cimbalom **09** pantaleon

## dull
**03** dim, dry, mat, sad **04** blah, damp, dark, dead, dowf, dozy, drab, drug, dumb, fade, flat, gray, grey, idle, logy, matt, mild, mull, numb, slow, soft, tame, weak **05** allay, bland, blunt, cloud, corny, dense, dingy, dopey, dowdy, dowie, dusty, faint, gross, heavy, ho-hum, inert, lower, matte, murky, muted, plain, prose, prosy, quiet, rusty, slack, thick, vapid **06** barren, boring, bovine, cloudy, dampen, darken, deaden, deject, dismal, dreary, drowsy, feeble, gloomy, leaden, lessen, mopish, obtund, obtuse, opaque, opiate, rebate, reduce, sadden, sleepy, soften, sombre, sopite, stodgy, stupid, subdue, sullen, torpid, wooden **07** assuage, blacken, depress, disedge, doltish, humdrum, insipid, insulse, lumpish, muffled, mumpish, obscure, prosaic, relieve, stupefy, tedious, wash out **08** blockish, Boeotian, decrease, diminish, downcast, edgeless, hebetate, inactive, lifeless, mitigate, moderate, overcast, paralyse, sluggish, tiresome, tone down, toneless, workaday **09** alleviate, cheerless, dead-alive, dimwitted, inanimate, lethargic, ponderous, prosaical, wearisome **10** discourage, dishearten, indistinct, insensible, lackluster, lacklustre, monochrome, monotonous, pedestrian, perstringe, uneventful, unexciting **11** birdbrained, blunt-witted, desensitize, distressing, heavy-headed, stereotyped, stultifying, thick-witted, troublesome, unsharpened **12** dead-and-alive, thick-skulled, tranquillize **13** uncomfortable, unimaginative, unintelligent, uninteresting **15** slow on the uptake
• **become dull** **04** rust **05** blunt **07** tarnish **08** hebetate

## dullard
**03** git, oaf, owl **04** clod, clot, dolt, dope, dork, prat **05** chump, dumbo, dunce, idiot, moron **06** dimwit, nitwit **07** plonker **08** bonehead, imbecile, numskull **09** blockhead, ignoramus, simpleton **10** bufflehead, dunderhead
*See also* **fool**

## dullness
**04** drab, yawn **05** cloud **06** fadeur, tedium, torpor **07** dryness, vacuity **08** flatness, monotony, slowness, vapidity **09** emptiness, plainness **10** dreariness, oppression **12** sluggishness

## duly
**05** fitly **08** properly, suitably **09** correctly, fittingly **10** decorously, deservedly, rightfully, sure enough **11** accordingly, befittingly **13** appropriately

## dumb
**03** mum **04** dozy, mute **05** dense, dopey, shtum, stumm, thick **06** shtoom, shtumm, silent, stupid **07** foolish, schtoom **08** gormless **09** brainless, dim-witted, soundless **10** speechless, tongue-tied **12** inarticulate, lost for words **13** unintelligent, without speech **15** at a loss for words
• **dumb down** **07** deskill **08** simplify

## dumbfound
**03** wow **04** daze, stun **05** amaze, floor, shock **07** astound, flummox, stagger, startle, stupefy **08** astonish, bewilder, bowl over, confound, gobsmack, surprise **09** take aback **11** flabbergast, knock for six **12** blow your mind **15** knock all of a heap

## dumbfounded

**04** dumb **06** amazed, thrown
**07** baffled, floored, stunned, stupent
**08** confused, overcome, startled
**09** astounded, paralysed, staggered
**10** astonished, bewildered, bowled
over, confounded, gobsmacked,
nonplussed, speechless, taken aback
**11** overwhelmed **12** lost for words
**13** flabbergasted, knocked for six

## dumbly

**06** mutely **08** silently **11** soundlessly
**12** speechlessly **14** inarticulately

## dumbo

*see* **fool**

## dumbstruck

**03** mum **04** dumb, mute **06** aghast,
amazed, silent **07** shocked
**09** astounded **10** speechless, tongue-
tied **11** dumbfounded, obmutescent
**12** inarticulate **13** thunderstruck

## dummy

**03** git, oaf **04** clot, copy, dork, fake,
fool, form, mock, prat, sham, teat
**05** bogus, chump, false, idiot, model,
trial **06** dimwit, figure, mock-up, nitwit,
phoney, sample, silent **07** feigned,
plonker, soother **08** imbecile,
numskull, pacifier, practice
**09** blockhead, comforter, duplicate,
imitation, lay-figure, mannequin,
simulated **10** artificial, bufflehead,
substitute **11** counterfeit
**12** reproduction **14** representation
*See also* **fool**

## dump

**03** tip **04** bung, drop, hole, jilt, mess,
park, pool, slum **05** chuck, ditch,
hovel, joint, leave, place, plonk, scrap,
shack, shoot, store **06** desert, marble,
midden, pigpen, pigsty, shanty, tip out,
unload **07** abandon, counter, deposit,
discard, forsake, lay down, let fall,
offload, pour out, put down, set down
**08** empty out, get rid of, jettison,
junkyard, throw out **09** chuck away,
discharge, dispose of, fling down,
scrapyard, throw away, throw down,
walk out on **10** rubbish tip **11** rubbish
heap **14** give the elbow to
• **down in the dumps 03** low, sad
**04** blue **07** unhappy **08** dejected,
downcast **09** depressed, miserable
**10** dispirited, melancholy
**11** downhearted
• **dumps 08** doldrums

## dumpling

**06** dim sum, perogi, pirogi, won ton
**07** gnocchi, knaidel, kneidel, pierogi
**08** doughboy, quenelle **09** doughball,
matzo ball **10** corn dodger

## dumpster

**04** skip

## dumpy

**05** plump, podgy, pudgy, short, squab,
squat, stout, tubby **06** chubby, chunky,
stubby

## dun

**04** dull, hill **05** dingy, dusky **06** harass,
pester, plague **11** mud-coloured
**12** greyish-brown **13** mouse-coloured

## dunce

**01** d **03** git **04** dork, fool, nerd, prat, twit
**05** idiot, ninny, twerp, wally **06** dimwit,
nitwit **07** dullard, plonker
**08** bonehead, dipstick, imbecile,
numskull **09** blockhead **10** bufflehead,
loggerhead, nincompoop

## dune

*see* **sand dune, sand dunes** *under*
**sand**

## dung

**04** chip, cock, dirt, muck, soil, tath
**05** argol, dreck, guano, mulch, shard,
sharn, siege **06** cowpat, doo-doo,
faeces, fumets, manure, ordure
**07** buttons, fewmets, scumber,
skummer, spraint **08** spraints
**09** droppings, excrement, spawn cake
**10** spawn brick **11** animal waste
**12** album Graecum, buffalo chips
• **devil's dung 04** hing
• **dog's dung 04** pure
• **plaster with dung 04** leep

## dung-beetle

**03** dor **04** dorr **06** scarab
**11** coprophagan

## dungeon

**04** cage, cell, gaol, jail, keep **05** vault
**06** lock-up, prison **09** oubliette

## dupe

**03** con, gum, mug **04** cony, cull, flat,
fool, geck, gull, hoax, pawn **05** cheat,
coney, cully, shaft, trick **06** chouse,
delude, diddle, outwit, plover, puppet,
rip off, sitter, stooge, sucker, take in,
victim **07** deceive, defraud, dottrel, fall
guy, swindle **08** dotterel, hoodwink,
pushover, soft mark **09** bamboozle,
goldbrick, simpleton **10** instrument
**11** make a fool of

## duplicate

**03** dup, fax **04** copy, echo, fold, like,
mate, twin **05** clone, ditto, match,
model, Roneo®, spare, Xerox®
**06** carbon, double, paired, repeat,
ringer **07** do again, forgery, matched,
replica, twofold **08** matching
**09** facsimile, identical, imitation,
lookalike, photocopy, Photostat®,
replicate, reproduce **10** carbon copy,
dead ringer, equivalent, transcript
**11** alternative, counterpart
**12** reproduction **13** corresponding,
spitting image

## duplication

**04** copy **05** clone **07** cloning, copying
**08** doubling **09** photocopy
**10** gemination, repetition
**11** dittography, replication
**12** photocopying, reproduction

## duplicity

**05** fraud, guile **06** deceit **07** perfidy
**08** artifice, betrayal **09** chicanery,
deception, falsehood, hypocrisy,
mendacity, treachery **10** dishonesty,
doubleness **11** insincerity
**13** deceitfulness, dissimulation,
double-dealing

## durability

**04** wear **07** durance, wearing
**08** strength **09** constancy, endurance,

longevity, stability **10** permanence
**11** durableness, lastingness,
persistence **15** imperishability

## durable

**04** fast, firm **05** fixed, hardy, pakka,
pucka, pukka, solid, sound, tough
**06** robust, stable, strong, sturdy
**07** abiding, lasting **08** constant,
enduring, reliable, unfading **09** heavy-
duty, permanent, resistant
**10** dependable, persistent, persisting,
reinforced, unchanging **11** hard-
wearing, long-lasting, serviceable,
substantial

## duration

**04** span, term, time **05** spell **06** extent,
length, period **07** stretch **08** fullness,
standing, time span **09** endurance,
time scale **10** protension
**11** continuance, persistence,
persistency, running time
**12** continuation, length of time,
perpetuation, prolongation

## duress

**05** force **06** threat **08** coercion,
exaction, pressure **09** restraint
**10** compulsion, constraint **11** arm-
twisting, enforcement **12** imprisonment

## during

◇ *insertion indicator* **02** in, of **03** dia-, for
**04** over **07** pending **10** throughout
**11** all the while, at the time of, in the
time of **12** for the time of **13** in the
course of, in the middle of

## dusk

**03** dim, eve **04** dark **05** gloom, shade
**06** sunset **07** darkish, evening,
shadows, sundown **08** darkness,
gloaming, owl-light, twilight
**09** nightfall **10** crepuscule
**11** candlelight

## dusky

**03** dim, dun, sad **04** dark, hazy
**05** black, brown, foggy, misty, murky,
swart, tawny **06** cloudy, gloomy,
phaeic, swarth, twilit **07** shadowy,
subfusc, subfusk, swarthy, umbrose
**09** tenebrous **10** fuliginous
**11** crepuscular, dark-skinned **12** dark-
coloured

## dust

**03** ash, mop **04** bort, clay, coom, culm,
dirt, duff, fuzz, grit, mote, seed, smut,
soil, soot, wipe **05** ashes, boart, brawl,
brush, clean, cover, earth, grime,
lemel, money, smoke, spray, stour
**06** bedust, ground, limail, polish,
pother, powder, pudder, spread
**07** burnish, fallout, scatter, smother,
turmoil **08** bulldust, sprinkle, stardust
**09** particles, pozzolana **10** cryoconite,
haemoconia **11** disturbance **13** meteor
streams **14** micro-meteorite
• **dust storm 05** devil **06** calima
**07** Shaitan

## dust-up

**05** brawl, brush, fight, scrap, set-to
**06** barney, bust-up, fracas, stoush,
tussle **07** punch-up, quarrel, scuffle
**08** argument, conflict, skirmish

**dusty**

**09** argy-bargy, commotion, encounter **11** disturbance **12** disagreement

**dusty**

**03** bad **04** dull **05** dirty, grimy, sandy, sooty **06** chalky, filthy, grubby, stoury **07** crumbly, friable, powdery **08** granular, lifeless **09** pulverous **11** dust-covered **12** contemptible, old-fashioned

**Dutch**

**01** D **02** Du
• **Cape Dutch** **04** Taal

**dutiful**

**05** pious **06** filial **07** devoted **08** obedient **09** compliant, officious **10** obsequious, respectful, submissive, thoughtful **11** considerate, deferential, reverential **13** conscientious

**duty**

**03** job, tax **04** debt, dues, levy, onus, part, role, task, toll, work **05** chore **06** burden, charge, excise, office, tariff **07** calling, customs, loyalty, mission, respect, service **08** business, fidelity, function **09** deference, obedience **10** allegiance, assignment, attendance, commission, obligation **11** requirement **12** faithfulness **14** responsibility
• **active duty** **02** AD
• **duty list** **04** rota
• **off duty** **03** off **04** free **07** off work, resting **08** inactive **09** at leisure, not at work, on holiday **10** not working
• **on duty** **04** busy **06** active, at work, on call, tied up **07** engaged, working **08** occupied

**dwarf**

**03** elf, toy **04** baby, Mime, mini, tiny, trow **05** check, gnome, pigmy, pygmy, small, stunt, troll **06** arrest, droich, durgan, goblin, little, midget, minute, petite, pocket, shrimp **07** atrophy, manikin, stunted **08** Alberich, dominate, homuncle, mannikin, Tom Thumb **09** homuncule, miniature, tower over **10** diminutive, homunculus, overshadow, undersized **11** Lilliputian

*Snow White's dwarfs:*

**03** Doc
**05** Dopey, Happy
**06** Grumpy, Sleepy, Sneezy
**07** Bashful

**dwell**

**03** won **04** bide, home, live, rest, stay **05** abide, lodge, stall **06** people, remain, reside, settle, tenant **07** hang out, inhabit, sojourn **08** populate **11** be domiciled
• **dwell on** **06** harp on **07** brood on **08** mull over **09** elaborate, emphasize, expatiate, reflect on **10** linger over, meditate on, ruminate on, think about

**dweller**

**07** denizen **08** occupant, occupier, resident **10** inhabitant

**dwelling**

**03** cot, dug, hut, won **04** flat, home, roof, tent, tipi, weem, woon **05** abode, bothy, bower, donga, gundy, house, hovel, humpy, lodge, place, tepee **06** grange, gunyah, mia-mia, pondok, shanty, teepee, wurley **07** bark hut, cottage, doghole, lodging **08** domicile, messuage, quarters, tenement **09** apartment, penthouse, residence, single-end **10** habitation, pied-à-terre **11** continuance **13** dwelling-house, establishment

*See also* **accommodation; house**

**dwindle**

**03** ebb **04** fade, fail, fall, wane **06** die out, lessen, reduce, shrink, vanish, weaken, wither **07** decline, shrivel, subside, tail off **08** decrease, diminish, fall away, grow less, peter out, taper off **09** disappear, waste away **10** become less
• **dwindle away** **05** peter

**dye**

**03** hew, hue **04** tint, wash **05** agent, imbue, shade, stain, tinct, tinge **06** colour, embrue, imbrue **07** embrewe, pigment **09** colouring

*See also* **colour; pigment**

*Dyes include:*

**04** anil, Saxe, wald, weld, woad
**05** chica, eosin, henna, mauve
**06** anatto, archil, corkir, flavin, fustic, indigo, kamala, korkir, madder, mauvin, orcein, orchel, orchil
**07** alkanet, annatto, azurine, cudbear, flavine, magenta, mauvein, mauvine, para-red, ponceau, saffron
**08** amaranth, fuchsine, mauveine, orchella, orchilla, safranin, turnsole
**09** cochineal, nigrosine, primuline, safranine, Saxon blue, Turkey red, Tyrian red
**10** carthamine, Saxony blue, tartrazine
**12** Tyrian purple

• **dyeing technique** **04** ikat
• **source of dye** **04** chay

**dyed-in-the-wool**

**05** fixed **07** diehard, settled **08** complete, hard-core, hardened, thorough **09** confirmed **10** deep-rooted, entrenched, inflexible, inveterate, unshakable **11** established, unshakeable **12** card-carrying, long-standing, unchangeable **14** uncompromising

**dying**

**04** last **05** final, going, waned **06** ebbing, ending, fading, mortal **07** closing, failing, passing **08** expiring, moribund **09** declining, finishing, perishing, vanishing **10** concluding **11** near to death **12** at death's door, close to death **14** on your deathbed, on your last legs

**dynamic**

◇ *anagram indicator* **05** vital **06** active, causal, lively, potent, strong **07** driving, go-ahead **08** forceful, powerful, spirited, vigorous **09** effective, energetic, go-getting **11** high-powered **12** full of energy, self-starting

**dynamically**

**07** vitally **08** actively, strongly **10** forcefully, powerfully, vigorously **11** effectively **13** energetically

**dynamism**

**02** go **03** pep, vim, zap, zip **04** push **05** drive **06** energy, spirit, vigour **07** pizzazz **10** enterprise, get-up-and-go, initiative, liveliness **12** forcefulness

**dynasty**

**04** line, rule **05** house **06** empire, regime **07** lineage **08** dominion **09** authority **10** government, succession **11** sovereignty **12** jurisdiction

*Dynasties include:*

**02** Yi
**03** Jin, Qin, Sui
**04** Asen, Avis, Chin, Lodi, Ming, Qing, Song, Sung, Tang, Vasa, Yuan, Zhou
**05** Ch'ing, Piast, Qajar, Shang
**06** Chakri, Sayyid, Valois, Wettin, Zangid
**07** 'Abbasid, Ayyubid, Chakkri, Fatimid, Romanov, Safavid, Tughlaq
**08** Capetian, Habsburg, Ilkhanid
**09** Jagiellon
**10** Qarakhanid
**11** Plantagenet
**12** Hohenstaufen, Hohenzollern
**14** Petrovic-Njegos

**dyspepsia**

**07** acidity, pyrosis **08** dyspepsy **09** heartburn **10** cardialgia, water-brash

**dyspeptic**

**04** edgy **05** humpy, ratty, testy **06** crabby, feisty, gloomy, shirty, touchy **07** crabbed, grouchy, in a huff, in a sulk, peevish, stroppy **08** snappish **09** crotchety, irritable **10** indigested **11** bad-tempered, cacogastric, indigestive **13** short-tempered

**dysprosium**

**02** Dy

# E

**E**
04 echo 07 epsilon

**each**
02 ea 03 ilk, per 05 every 06 apiece, singly 07 each one, per head 09 per capita, per person 10 separately 11 every single 12 individually, respectively 15 each and every one, every individual
• **for each** 03 per

**eager**
04 agog, avid, bore, fain, keen, rath, toey 05 antsy, dying, frack, hasty, prone, rathe, sharp 06 ardent, greedy, gung-ho, hungry, intent, raring, watery 07 anxious, earnest, fervent, longing, thirsty, up for it, willing, wishful, wishing, zealous 08 desirous, diligent, empressé, yearning 09 desperate, impatient, perfervid 12 affectionate, enthusiastic, wholehearted

**eagerly**
04 sore 06 avidly, keenly 08 ardently, greedily, intently 09 earnestly, fervently, zealously 11 impatiently 14 wholeheartedly

**eagerness**
03 yen 04 lust, zeal 05 ardor, greed 06 ardour, hunger, thirst 07 avidity, fervour, longing 08 fainness, fervency, keenness, yearning 09 fervidity 10 enthusiasm, greediness, impatience, intentness 11 earnestness, impetuosity

**eagle**
04 erne 05 harpy 06 Aquila 07 alerion, lectern 08 allerion, bateleur, berghaan 11 king of birds

**ear**
◊ *homophone indicator* 03 ere, lug 04 heed, till 05 skill, souse, taste 06 notice, plough, regard 07 ability, earhole, hearing, lughole 09 attention, shell-like 10 perception 11 sensitivity 12 appreciation 13 attentiveness 14 discrimination

*Ear parts include:*

04 drum, lobe
05 anvil, helix, incus, pinna, scala
06 concha, cupola, hammer, stapes, tragus
07 alveary, auricle, cochlea, eardrum, ear lobe, malleus, saccule, stirrup, utricle
08 pavilion, sacculus, tympanum
09 columella, endolymph, labyrinth, perilymph, vestibule
10 oval window
11 Corti's organ, round window
12 organ of Corti
13 auditory canal, auditory nerve
14 columella auris, Eustachian tube
15 vestibular nerve
• **of the ear** 04 otic
• **play it by ear** 05 ad-lib 06 busk it, wing it 09 improvise 11 extemporize 15 think on your feet

**earlier**
02 ex 06 before 07 already, prior to 08 formerly, previous 10 previously

**early**
02 am 04 auld, rare, rath, rear, soon 05 first 06 at dawn 07 advance, ancient, forward, initial, morning, opening, too soon 08 advanced, primeval, untimely 09 in advance, premature, primaeval, primitive 10 at daybreak, beforehand, in good time, precocious, primordial 11 ahead of time, prematurely, undeveloped 12 in the morning 13 autochthonous 15 ahead of schedule, with time to spare

**earmark**
03 tag 05 label 07 mark out, reserve 08 allocate, keep back, lay aside, put aside, set aside 09 designate

**earn**
03 ern, get, net, win 04 draw, gain, make, rate, reap 05 clear, gross, merit 06 attain, be owed, be paid, curdle, obtain, pocket, pull in, rake in, secure 07 achieve, acquire, bring in, collect, deserve, get paid, realize, receive, warrant 08 take home

**earnest**
03 sad 04 dear, firm, keen 05 arles, eager, fixed, grave, token, truth 06 ardent, devout, intent, pledge, solemn, steady, urgent 07 deposit, devoted, fervent, forward, intense, promise, serious, sincere, wistful, zealous 08 diligent, resolute, security 09 assiduous, assurance, committed, dedicated, guarantee, heartfelt, sincerity 10 persistent, press-money, resolution, thoughtful 11 down payment, impassioned, seriousness 12 earnest-penny, enthusiastic 13 conscientious, determination
• **in earnest** 07 genuine, serious, sincere, stand-up 08 ardently, intently, steadily 09 not joking, seriously, zealously 10 resolutely 12 passionately, purposefully 14 wholeheartedly 15 conscientiously

**earnestly**
04 hard 06 dearly, firmly, keenly, warmly, wistly 07 eagerly 08 intently 09 fervently, seriously, sincerely, zealously 10 resolutely

**earnestness**
04 zeal 06 ardour, warmth 07 fervour, gravity, passion 08 devotion, fervency, keenness 09 eagerness, sincerity, vehemence 10 enthusiasm, intentness, resolution 11 seriousness 13 determination 14 purposefulness

**earnings**
03 fee, pay 04 gain 05 wages 06 income, net pay, return, reward, salary 07 profits, revenue, stipend 08 gross pay, proceeds, receipts 09 emolument 10 honorarium 11 take home pay 12 remuneration

**earring**
04 drop, hoop, snap, stud 06 clip-on 07 pendant, pendent, sleeper

**earshot**
04 hail 05 sound 07 hearing
• **beyond earshot** 10 out of range

**earth**
01 E 02 Ge 03 orb, sod 04 clay, dirt, dust, eard, Gaea, Gaia, land, loam, mold, soil, turf, yerd, yird 05 globe, humus, mould, world 06 ground, planet, sphere 07 topsoil
• **rammed earth** 04 pisé

**earthenware**
03 pig, pot 04 delf, pots, waly 05 cloam, delft, delph, wally 07 faience, pottery 08 ceramics, crockery, figuline, maiolica, majolica 09 creamware, ironstone, porcelain, stoneware 10 Samian ware, terracotta 14 terra sigillata

**earthly**
04 vile 05 human 06 likely, mortal 07 fleshly, mundane, profane, secular, sensual, terrene, worldly 08 feasible, material, physical, possible, sublunar, telluric, temporal 09 slightest, sublunary, tellurian 10 imaginable 11 conceivable, terrestrial 13 materialistic

**earthquake**
05 quake, seism, shake, shock 06 tremor 07 temblor 08 trembler, upheaval 10 aftershock, convulsion 11 earth-tremor

**earthwork**
04 berm, ring 06 cursus, sconce 07 parados 10 breastwork, embankment, roundabout 12 entrenchment, intrenchment, maiden castle

**earthy**
04 blue, rude 05 bawdy, crude, gross, rough 06 cloddy, coarse, direct, ribald, simple, vulgar 07 natural, raunchy, terrene 08 claylike, dirtlike, soil-like 09 earthlike, unrefined 10 indecorous 11 down to earth, uninhibited 15 unsophisticated

**ease**
04 calm, edge, inch, rest 05 abate, allay, guide, peace, quiet, relax, salve, slide, steer 06 lessen, reduce, relent, repose, smooth, soothe, wealth 07 assuage, comfort, leisure, lighten, quieten, relieve 08 deftness, diminish, facility, grow less, mitigate, moderate, opulence, otiosity, palliate 09 affluence, alleviate, dexterity, enjoyment, happiness, manoeuvre 10 adroitness, ameliorate, become less, bed of roses, cleverness, easy street, facilitate, otioseness, prosperity, relaxation 11 contentment, lap of luxury, life of Riley, naturalness, skilfulness 12 peacefulness 14 effortlessness

## easily

- **at ease** 04 calm 06 secure
07 natural, relaxed 08 composed, sans
gêne 11 comfortable
- **ease off** 04 wane 05 abate 06 relent
07 die away, die down, slacken,
subside 08 decrease, diminish,
moderate, slack off 10 become less,
slacken off

## easily

◇ *anagram indicator* 04 eath, ethe, well
05 by far, eathe 06 simply, surely
07 clearly, readily 08 fluently, probably
09 certainly, readily 08 definitely, far and
away, undeniably 11 comfortably,
doubtlessly, undoubtedly
12 effortlessly, indisputably, without
doubt
- **easily handled** 04 yare

## east

01 E 04 Asia 06 Levant, Orient
07 sunrise 08 Old World 09 sunrising
11 morning-land
- **East End** ◇ *dialect indicator*
- **from the east, goes east** ◇ *reversal
indicator*

## Easter

04 Pace 05 Pasch

## eastern

01 E 06 exotic, Levant, Orient
08 Oriental

## East German

*see* **German**

## East Timor

03 TLS

## easy

◇ *anagram indicator* 04 calm, eath, ethe,
glib, soft 05 cushy, eathe 06 a cinch,
casual, dégagé, facile, simple, smooth
07 a doddle, natural, relaxed, running
08 carefree, homelike, informal, laid-
back, painless, unforced 09 a
cakewalk, a pushover, easy as ABC,
easy as pie, easy-going, easy-peasy,
foolproof, leisurely, unstudied
10 child's play, effortless, manageable,
unlaboured 11 comfortable,
undemanding 12 a piece of cake
13 uncomplicated 14 a walk in the
park 15 straightforward
- **easy thing** 03 pie 08 pushover
- **take it easy** 04 loll 05 relax

## easy-going

04 calm 06 placid, serene 07 equable,
lenient, relaxed 08 amenable, carefree,
indolent, laid-back, tolerant
10 insouciant, nonchalant
11 undemanding 12 even-tempered,
happy-go-lucky 13 imperturbable

## eat

◇ *containment indicator* 02 go 03 hog,
pig, rot, sup 04 bite, chew, chop, cram,
dine, feed, fret, grub, guts, mess, nosh,
peck, pick, take 05 binge, decay,
erode, feast, graze, hog it, lunch,
munch, scarf, scoff, snack, snarf, taste,
twist, upset, worry 06 begnaw, devour,
gobble, guttle, ingest, pig out, slairg,
predate, put away, swallow 08 bite
into, bolt down, chow down,

demolish, dissolve, gulp down, irritate,
tuck into, wear away, wolf down
09 breakfast, have a bite, knock back,
manducate, partake of, polish off,
undermine 10 gormandize, have a
snack

*Eating places include:*

04 hall, mess
06 frater, fratry
07 canteen
08 takeaway
09 refectory
10 commissary, dining-hall
11 frater-house

*See also* **restaurant**
- **eat away** 04 etch, gnaw 05 erode
06 begnaw 07 corrode
- **eat quickly** 04 bolt, cram, gulp

## eatable

04 good 06 edible 08 esculent
09 palatable, wholesome
10 comestible, digestible

## eavesdrop

03 bug, spy, tap 05 snoop 06 earwig
07 monitor 08 listen in, overhear
10 stillicide

## eavesdropper

03 spy 05 snoop 07 monitor, snooper
08 listener

## ebb

04 drop, fall, flag, sink, wane 05 abate,
decay, go out 06 lessen, recede,
reflow, reflux, shrink, waning, weaken
07 decline, dwindle, ebb tide, lagging,
low tide, retreat, slacken, subside
08 decrease, diminish, fade away, fall
back, flow back, going-out, low water,
peter out, receding 09 abatement,
dwindling, lessening, refluence,
retrocede, subsiding, weakening
10 degenerate, slackening, subsidence
11 deteriorate, flowing-back
12 degeneration 13 deterioration

## ebony

03 jet 04 dark, inky 05 black, heben,
jetty, sable, sooty 08 jet-black
09 cocuswood 10 calamander,
coromandel

## ebullience

04 zest 07 elation 08 buoyancy,
vivacity 10 breeziness, brightness,
bubbliness, chirpiness, enthusiasm,
excitement, exuberance 11 high spirits
12 effusiveness, exhilaration

## ebullient

06 breezy, bright, bubbly, chirpy,
elated 07 buoyant, excited, gushing,
zestful 08 agitated, effusive
09 exuberant, vivacious 11 exhilarated
12 effervescent, enthusiastic
13 irrepressible

## eccentric

◇ *anagram indicator* 03 cam, dag, fay,
fey, fie, nut, odd, off 04 card, case,
cure, ditz, geek, kook, loon, wack,
zany 05 crank, ditsy, ditzy, dotty, flake,
flaky, freak, geeky, kinky, kooky,
loony, loopy, nutty, queer, spacy,
wacko, wacky, weird 06 cranky,
kookie, nutjob, nutter, oddity, quirky,

screwy, spacey, way-out, weirdo,
whacko 07 bizarre, cupcake, dingbat,
erratic, nutcase, oddball, odd fish, offbeat, strange, weirdie 08 aberrant,
abnormal, crackpot, freakish,
maverick, peculiar, singular
09 character, ding-a-ling, screwball
10 loony tunes, off the wall, outlandish
13 idiosyncratic, nonconformist 14 fish
out of water, unconventional

## eccentricity

01 e 05 quirk 06 oddity 07 anomaly
09 weirdness 10 aberration, quirkiness,
screwiness 11 abnormality,
bizarreness, peculiarity, singularity,
strangeness, unorthodoxy
12 freakishness, idiosyncrasy
13 nonconformity 14 capriciousness

## ecclesiastic

04 abbé, dean 05 canon, padre, vicar
06 bishop, cleric, curate, deacon,
father, lector, parson, pastor, priest,
rector 08 chaplain, man of God,
minister, preacher, reverend
09 churchman, clergyman, deaconess,
presbyter 10 archbishop, woman of
God 11 churchwoman, clergywoman
13 man of the cloth 15 woman of the
cloth

*See also* **clergyman, clergywoman**

## ecclesiastical

04 holy 06 church, divine 07 canonic
08 churchly, clerical, pastoral, priestly
09 canonical, religious, spiritual
10 sacerdotal 11 ministerial

## echelon

03 ech 04 rank, rung, tier 05 grade,
level, place 06 degree, status
08 position

## echinoderm

07 crinoid, cystoid, sea-lily, trepang
08 starfish 09 sea-urchin 10 bêche-de-
mer 11 brittlestar, sea-cucumber

## echo

01 E 04 copy, hint, ring 05 angel, clone,
ditto, image, mimic, reply, trace
06 answer, memory, mirror, parrot,
repeat, report 07 imitate, rebound,
redound, reflect, remains, resound,
respeak, ringing, vestige 08 allusion,
imitator, parallel, rebellow, reminder,
resemble 09 duplicate, evocation,
flashback, imitation, reiterate,
repercuss, reproduce 10 reflection,
repetition, resounding 11 mirror image,
reiteration, remembrance, replication,
reverberate 12 reproduction
13 reverberation

## éclat

04 fame, show 05 glory, style 06 effect,
lustre, renown 07 acclaim, display,
success 08 applause, approval,
plaudits 09 celebrity, splendour
10 brilliance 11 acclamation,
distinction, flamboyance, ostentation,
stylishness

## eclectic

04 wide 05 broad 06 varied 07 diverse,
general, liberal 08 catholic 09 many-
sided, selective 11 diversified, wide-

## eclipse

ranging **12** all-embracing, multifarious **13** comprehensive, heterogeneous

## eclipse

**03** dim, ebb **04** fall, loss, veil **05** block, cloud, cover, decay, dwarf, excel, outdo **06** darken, exceed, shroud **07** blot out, conceal, decline, dimming, failure, obscure, shading, surpass, veiling **08** covering, darkness, outshine **09** darkening, deliquium, transcend, weakening **10** concealing, overshadow **11** blotting-out, obscuration **13** overshadowing **14** run rings around **15** cast a shadow over, put into the shade

## economic

**05** cheap, trade **06** fiscal, viable **08** business, monetary **09** budgetary, financial, pecuniary, rewarding **10** commercial, industrial, productive, profitable **11** moneymaking **12** profit-making, remunerative **13** cost-effective

## economical

**05** cheap, tight **06** budget, frugal, modest, saving **07** careful, low-cost, prudent, sparing, thrifty **08** low-price, skimping **09** efficient, low-budget, low-priced, provident, scrimping **10** reasonable **11** inexpensive **12** parsimonious **13** cost-effective **15** bargain-basement

## economics

*Economics theories and schools include:*

**07** Marxian
**09** Keynesian
**10** game theory
**11** physiocracy
**12** mercantilism, neo-classical, neo-Keynesian, neo-Ricardian, new classical
**13** Chicago school, post-Keynesian
**14** Austrian school
**15** classical school

*Economic problems include:*

**08** scarcity
**09** deflation, inflation, skills gap
**10** depression
**12** credit crunch, debt overhang, trade barrier, trade deficit, unemployment
**13** budget deficit

## economist

**10** chrematist

*Economists include:*

**03** Say (Jean-Baptiste), **Sen** (Amartya)
**04** Nash (John), **Ward** (Dame Barbara), **Webb** (Sidney)
**05** Arrow (Kenneth J), **Hayek** (Friedrich), **Laski** (Harold), **Meade** (James Edward), **North** (Douglass C), **Petty** (Sir William), **Smith** (Adam), **Solow** (Robert Merton), **Stone** (Sir Richard), **Tobin** (James)
**06** Allais (Maurice), **Cobden** (Richard), **Cripps** (Sir Stafford), **Debreu** (Gerard), **Erhard** (Ludwig), **Frisch** (Ragnar), **Horner** (Francis), **Keynes** (John Maynard), **Myrdal** (Gunnar),

**Tawney** (Richard Henry)
**07** Bagehot (Walter), **Kuznets** (Simon), **Malthus** (Thomas Robert), **Ricardo** (David), **Robbins** (Lionel, Lord), **Scholes** (Myron), **Stigler** (George Joseph), **Toynbee** (Arnold), **Vickrey** (William)
**08** Buchanan (James McGill), **Friedman** (Milton), **Leontief** (Wassily), **Marshall** (Alfred), **Mirrlees** (James), **Robinson** (Joan Violet), **Schiller** (Karl), **Shatalin** (Stanislav), **Youngson** (Alexander John)
**09** Beveridge (William, Lord), **Galbraith** (John Kenneth), **Greenspan** (Alan), **Tinbergen** (Jan)
**10** Modigliani (Franco)
**11** Kantorovich (Leonid)

## economize

**03** eke **04** save **06** budget **07** cut back, use less **08** cut costs, retrench **10** buy cheaply, cut corners **12** be economical **13** keep down costs, scrimp and save **14** cut expenditure, live on the cheap **15** tighten your belt

## economy

**04** care **06** saving, thrift, wealth **08** prudence, skimping **09** frugality, husbandry, parsimony, plutology, plutonomy, restraint, scrimping **10** providence **11** carefulness **12** catallactics, retrenchment **13** chrematistics **14** financial state, system of wealth **15** financial system

## ecstasy

**01** E **03** joy, tab **04** dove **05** bliss **06** frenzy **07** delight, elation, fervour, rapture **08** euphoria, pleasure **09** transport **10** exultation, jubilation **11** sublimation **12** disco biscuit
• **rouse to ecstasy 04** send

## ecstatic

**04** rapt, sent **06** elated, joyful, Pythic **07** fervent **08** blissful, euphoric, frenzied, jubilant **09** delirious, overjoyed, rapturous, rhapsodic **10** blissed-out, enraptured, in raptures **11** high as a kite, on cloud nine, over the moon, tickled pink **13** jumping for joy **15** in seventh heaven

## Ecuador

**02** EC **03** ECU

## ecumenical

**07** general **08** catholic **09** universal **10** broad-based **12** all-embracing, nonsectarian

## eddy

**04** curl, pirl, purl, reel, roll, spin, turn, weal, weel, well **05** rotor, swirl, swish, twirl, twist, whirl **06** vortex **07** backset **08** swirling **09** maelstrom, whirlpool, whirlwind

## edge

◊ *ends selection indicator* ◊ *head selection indicator* **03** hem, lip, rim **04** bite, brim, ease, head, inch, kerb, lead, line, side, worm, zest **05** brink, crawl, creep, elbow, force, limit, sidle, steal, sting, verge **06** border, fringe, margin **07** outline **08** acerbity,

boundary, frontier, keenness, pungency, severity, whip-hand **09** acuteness, advantage, dominance, extremity, perimeter, periphery, sharpness, threshold, upper hand **10** ascendancy, causticity, outer limit, trenchancy **11** pick your way, superiority **12** incisiveness
• **on edge 04** edgy, toey **05** jumpy, nervy, tense **06** touchy **07** anxious, keyed-up, nervous, twitchy, uptight **09** ill at ease, irritable **12** apprehensive, highly-strung
• **rough edge 03** bur **04** burr
• **straight edge 04** lute, rule

## edgy

**05** nervy, tense **06** on edge, touchy **07** anxious, brittle, keyed-up, nervous, uptight **09** ill at ease, irritable **12** highly-strung

## edible

**04** good **07** eatable **08** esculent, fit to eat, harmless **09** palatable, safe to eat, wholesome **10** comestible, digestible
• **edible shoots 03** udo

## edict

**03** act, law **04** bull, fiat, rule **05** order, ukase **06** decree, ruling **07** command, mandate, process, statute **08** decretal, rescript **09** forbiddal, manifesto, pragmatic **10** golden bull, injunction, regulation **11** forbiddance **12** proclamation **13** pronouncement **14** pronunciamento

## edification

**07** tuition **08** coaching, guidance, teaching **09** education, elevation, uplifting **10** upbuilding **11** improvement, instruction **13** enlightenment

## edifice

**08** building, erection **09** structure **12** construction

## edify

**05** build, coach, guide, teach, tutor **06** inform, school, uplift **07** build up, educate, elevate, improve, nurture **08** instruct **09** enlighten, establish

## edit

◊ *anagram indicator* ◊ *deletion indicator* **04** head **05** adapt, amend, check, emend **06** censor, choose, direct, garble, gather, head up, modify, polish, redact, revise, reword, select **07** arrange, collect, compile, correct, reorder, rewrite, subedit **08** annotate, assemble, copy-edit, organize, rephrase **09** proofread, rearrange **10** blue-pencil, bowdlerize **11** put together **12** be in charge of

## edition

**02** ed **04** Aufl, copy, edit **05** extra, issue, print **06** number, urtext, volume **07** hexapla, omnibus, reprint, version **08** printing, tetrapla, variorum **10** impression **11** publication **12** extra-special, reproduction
• **limited edition 04** Aufl

## editor

**02** ed **04** hack **06** journo, writer **07** amender, checker, newsman,

**editorial**

reviser **08** director, overseer, reporter, reviewer, rewriter **09** corrector, newswoman, publisher, subeditor **10** copy editor, desk editor, journalist, newscaster, undertaker **11** factchecker, proofreader **12** newspaperman **13** correspondent **14** newspaperwoman
*See also* **journalist**
• **assistant editor** **03** sub

**editorial**
**06** column

**educable**
**09** teachable, trainable **12** instructible

**educate**
**05** coach, drill, edify, prime, teach, train, tutor **06** inform, school **07** bring up, develop, improve, nourish, nurture, prepare, train up, uptrain **08** hothouse, instruct **09** cultivate, enlighten, inculcate, institute **10** discipline, take in hand **12** indoctrinate

**educated**
**02** ed **04** wise **06** brainy, taught **07** erudite, learned, refined, trained, tutored **08** all there, cultured, informed, lettered, literate, schooled, well-bred, well-read **09** civilized, sagacious **10** cultivated, instructed **11** enlightened **12** clever-clever **13** knowledgeable

**education**
**02** ed **07** culture, letters, nurture, tuition **08** coaching, drilling, guidance, learning, teaching, training, tutoring **09** fostering, informing, knowledge, schooling **10** upbringing **11** cultivation, development, edification, improvement, inculcation, instruction, preparation, scholarship **13** enlightenment **14** indoctrination
• **basic education** **03** RRR
• **education journal** **03** TES
• **further education** **02** FE
• **higher education** **02** HE

**educational**
**08** academic, cultural, didactic, edifying, learning, teaching **09** educative, improving, pedagogic **10** scholastic **11** informative, instructive, pedagogical **12** enlightening **13** instructional **14** institutionary

*Educational establishments include:*

**03** CFE, CTC, uni
**04** poly, tech
**07** academy, college
**08** seminary
**10** high school, playschool, prep school, university
**11** city academy, faith school, polytechnic, upper school
**12** beacon school, infant school, junior school, kindergarten, middle school, public school, summer school, Sunday school
**13** comprehensive, convent school, grammar school, nursery school, primary school, private school
**14** boarding school, business school,

combined school, flagship school
**15** community school, finishing school, grant-maintained, secondary modern, secondary school, voluntary school

**educative**
**08** didactic, edifying **09** improving **10** catechetic **11** catechismal, catechistic, educational, informative, instructive **12** enlightening **13** catechistical

**educator**
**05** coach, tutor **06** master, mentor **07** teacher, trainer **08** academic, lecturer, mistress **09** pedagogue, professor, schoolman **10** instructor **11** headteacher **12** schoolmaster **13** schoolteacher **14** educationalist, schoolmistress

**educe**
**05** infer **06** elicit **07** develop, draw out, extract

**Edward**
**02** Ed **03** Ted

**eel**

*Eels and similar fish include:*

**03** hag, sea
**04** grig, lant, sand, snig, tuna
**05** elver, lance, moray, murry, siren, snake, wheat
**06** conger, gulper, gunnel, launce, murena, murray, murrey
**07** hagfish, muraena
**08** Anguilla, electric, sandling
**09** sand lance, wheatworm
**10** spitchcock

• **bait for eel** **03** bob

**eerie**
**05** scary, unked, unket, unkid, weird **06** creepy, spooky **07** ghostly, scaring, strange, uncanny **08** eldritch, sinister, timorous **09** unearthly, unnatural **10** mysterious **11** frightening **13** bloodcurdling, spine-chilling

**eerily**
**07** weirdly **09** strangely, uncannily **11** unnaturally **12** mysteriously

**efface**
**04** dele **05** erase **06** cancel, delete, excise, remove, rub out **07** blot out, destroy, dislimn, expunct, expunge, wipe out **08** blank out, cross out, wear away **09** eliminate, eradicate, extirpate, strike out **10** obliterate

**effect**
**03** win **04** gear, make **05** carry, cause, drift, force, fruit, goods, issue, power, sense, stuff, tenor **06** action, create, fulfil, impact, import, result, things, thread, upshot **07** achieve, baggage, clobber, execute, luggage, meaning, outcome, perform, produce, purport **08** carry out, chattels, complete, contrive, efficacy, generate, initiate, movables, property, strength **09** aftermath, influence, moveables, repulsion, trappings **10** accomplish, belongings, bring about, conclusion, effectuate, give rise to, impression

**11** consequence, possessions **12** significance **13** accoutrements, paraphernalia
• **in effect** **06** in fact, really **07** en effet, in truth **08** actually **09** in reality, virtually **10** in practice **11** effectively, essentially **12** in actual fact **13** substantially **14** produce results
• **produce an effect** **03** act
• **special effects** **02** FX **03** SFX
• **take effect** **04** bite, take, talk, vest, work **05** begin **06** kick in **07** come off, succeed **08** function **09** become law **11** become valid, be effective **13** be implemented, come into force **14** produce results **15** become operative, come into service

**effective**
**04** home, neat **05** legal, valid **06** active, actual, cogent, potent, superb, useful **07** capable, current, helpful, in force, operant, telling, virtual **08** adequate, exciting, forceful, fruitful, in effect, powerful, striking **09** efficient, energetic, essential, operative, practical **10** attractive, compelling, convincing, impressive, persuasive, prevailing, productive, successful, sufficient, worthwhile **11** devastating, efficacious, energetical, functioning, implemental, in operation, serviceable

**effectively**
**04** home, well **06** in fact, really **07** in truth **08** actually, in effect **09** in reality, virtually **10** fruitfully, in practice **11** efficiently, essentially **12** in actual fact, productively, successfully

**effectiveness**
**03** use **05** clout, force, power **06** vigour, weight **07** ability, cogency, potence, potency, success **08** efficacy, strength, validity **09** influence **10** capability, efficacity, efficiency, usefulness **12** fruitfulness **14** productiveness **15** efficaciousness

**effectual**
**05** legal, sound, valid **06** lawful, proper, useful **07** binding, capable **08** decisive, forcible, powerful **09** authentic, effective, magistral, operative **10** perficient, productive, successful **11** influential, serviceable **13** authoritative

**effeminate**
**04** soft **05** cissy, minty, sissy **06** prissy, queeny **07** epicene, meacock, unmanly, wimpish, womanly **08** delicate, feminine, womanish **11** limp-wristed

**effervesce**
**04** boil, fizz, foam **05** froth **06** bubble **07** ferment, sparkle **08** be lively **10** be animated **11** be ebullient, be vivacious **13** be exhilarated

**effervescence**
**03** gas, vim, zip **04** fizz, foam, zing **05** froth **07** bubbles, ferment, foaming, sparkle **08** bubbling, buoyancy, frothing, vitality, vivacity **09** animation, fizziness, gassiness **10** ebullience, enthusiasm, excitement,

## effervescent

exuberance, liveliness **11** excitedness, high spirits **12** exhilaration, fermentation

## effervescent

◇ *anagram indicator* **05** fizzy, gassy, vital **06** bubbly, frothy, lively **07** aerated, buoyant, excited, fizzing, foaming **08** animated, bubbling **09** ebullient, exuberant, sparkling, vivacious **10** carbonated, fermenting **11** exhilarated **12** enthusiastic **13** irrepressible

## effete

**04** weak **05** spent **06** barren, feeble, used up, wasted **07** corrupt, debased, decayed, drained, shotten, spoiled, sterile, worn out **08** decadent, decrepit, infecund, tired out **09** enervated, enfeebled, exhausted, fruitless, played out **10** degenerate, unfruitful, unprolific **11** debilitated, ineffectual **12** unproductive

## efficacious

**06** active, potent, strong, useful **07** capable **08** adequate, powerful **09** competent, effective, effectual, operative, potential, sovereign **10** productive, successful, sufficient

## efficacy

**03** use **04** feck **05** force, power, value **06** effect, energy, virtue **07** ability, potency, success **08** strength **09** influence **10** capability, competence, usefulness **13** effectiveness **14** successfulness

## efficiency

**05** order, skill **07** ability **09** expertise **10** capability, competence, competency **11** orderliness, proficiency, skilfulness **12** organization, productivity **13** effectiveness

## efficient

**04** able **05** smart **06** expert, strong **07** capable, skilful, well-run **08** powerful **09** competent, effective, organized, practical **10** methodical, productive, proficient, systematic **11** streamlined, well-ordered, workmanlike **12** businesslike, rationalized **13** well-conducted, well-organized

## effigy

**03** guy **04** icon, idol, sign **05** dummy, image **06** figure, statue **07** carving, picture **08** likeness, portrait **09** Jack-straw **14** representation

## efflorescence

**03** reh

## effluent

**05** waste **06** efflux, sewage **07** outflow **08** emission **09** discharge, effluence, effluvium, emanation, pollutant, pollution **10** exhalation **11** liquid waste

## effort

**02** go **03** try **04** bash, beef, deed, feat, opus, push, shot, stab, toil, work **05** crack, essay, force, nisus, pains, power, sweat, whirl **06** energy, labour, result, strain, stress **07** attempt, exploit,

muscles, product, travail, trouble **08** creation, exertion, hard work, striving, struggle **09** endeavour **10** attainment, production **11** achievement, application, elbow-grease, muscle power **14** accomplishment **15** sweat of your brow

• **calling for effort** **02** yo
• **sudden effort** **03** fit
• **utmost efforts** **03** all

## effortless

**04** easy **06** facile, simple, smooth **07** passive **08** painless **10** unexacting **11** undemanding **13** uncomplicated **15** straightforward

## effrontery

**03** lip **04** face, gall, hide, sass **05** brass, cheek, nerve **07** hutzpah **08** audacity, boldness, brazenry, chutzpah, temerity **09** arrogance, brashness, brass neck, impudence, insolence **10** brazenness, cheekiness, disrespect **11** presumption **12** impertinence **13** shamelessness

## effulgent

**07** glowing, radiant, shining **08** glorious, splendid **09** brilliant, refulgent **11** resplendent **12** incandescent

## effusion

**04** gush **06** efflux, stream **07** outflow **08** emission, outburst, shedding, voidance **09** discharge, effluence **10** outpouring

## effusive

**03** OTT **05** gabby, gassy, gushy **06** lavish **07** fulsome, gushing, lyrical, profuse, voluble **08** all mouth **09** ebullient, expansive, exuberant, rhapsodic, talkative **10** big-mouthed, over the top, unreserved **11** extravagant, overflowing **12** enthusiastic, unrestrained **13** demonstrative

## eg

**02** as, zB **03** say **06** such as **10** for example, par exemple **11** zum Beispiel **13** exempli gratia

## egalitarian

**04** fair, just **07** sharing **09** equitable **10** democratic **12** equalitarian

## egg

**01** O **03** nit **04** blow, bomb, mine, ovum **05** berry, ovule **06** oocyte **08** oosphere

• **egg on** **03** set, tar **04** abet, coax, edge, goad, prod, push, spur, urge **05** drive, prick **06** excite, exhort, incite, prompt, urge on **08** talk into **09** encourage, stimulate
• **egg-supplier** *see* bird
• **lower half of egg** **04** doup, dowp
• **spot on egg** **03** eye

## egghead

**03** don **05** brain **06** boffin, genius **07** know-all, scholar, thinker **08** academic, bookworm, brainbox, Einstein **09** intellect, know-it-all **12** intellectual

## eggs

**02** OO **03** ova, roe **06** clutch, graine **11** pullet-sperm

## ego

**01** I **03** sel **04** self, soul **07** egotism **08** identity **09** self-image, self-worth **10** self-esteem **14** self-confidence, self-importance **15** sense of identity

## egocentric

**07** selfish **09** egotistic **11** egotistical, self-centred, self-seeking, self-serving **12** narcissistic, self-absorbed **14** self-interested

## egoism

**07** egotism **08** egomania, self-love **10** narcissism, self-regard **11** amour-propre, selfishness, self-seeking **12** self-interest **13** egocentricity **14** self-absorption, self-importance **15** self-centredness

## egoist

**07** egotist **09** egomaniac **10** narcissist, self-seeker

## egoistic

**09** egotistic **10** egocentric, egoistical **11** egomaniacal, egotistical, self-centred, self-seeking **12** narcissistic, self-absorbed, self-involved, self-pleasing **13** self-important

## egotism

**03** ego **05** pride, swank **06** egoism, vanity **08** egomania, self-love, selfness, snobbery **10** narcissism, self-regard **11** braggadocio, self-conceit, selfishness, superiority **12** boastfulness **13** bigheadedness, conceitedness, egocentricity **14** self-admiration, self-importance **15** self-centredness

## egotist

**06** egoist **07** bighead, bluffer, boaster, show-off **08** big mouth, braggart **09** egomaniac, smart alec, swaggerer **10** clever dick **11** braggadocio, clever clogs, self-admirer

## egotistic

**04** vain **05** proud **07** selfish **08** boasting, bragging, egoistic, superior **09** bigheaded, conceited **10** egocentric **11** self-centred, swell-headed **12** narcissistic, self-admiring **13** self-important, swollen-headed

## egregious

**04** fine, rank **05** gross **06** arrant **07** glaring, heinous **08** flagrant, grievous, infamous, precious, shocking **09** appalling, monstrous, notorious, prominent **10** outrageous, scandalous **11** intolerable **12** insufferable **13** distinguished

## egress

**04** exit, vent **05** issue **06** depart, escape, exodus, outlet, way out **07** leaving **09** departure, emergence **11** escape route

## Egypt

**02** ET **03** EGY

## Egyptian
**07** Thebaic

*Ancient Egyptian rulers include:*

**05** Khufu
**06** Ahmose, Cheops
**07** Ptolemy, Rameses
**08** Berenice, Thutmose
**09** Akhenaten, Amenhotep, Cleopatra, Nefertiti, Sesostris, Tuthmosis
**10** Hatshepsut
**11** Tut'ankhamun

*See also* **god, goddess; pharaoh**

## eight
**04** VIII **05** octad, octet **06** octave, octett, ogdoad **07** octette **08** octonary

## eighteen
**05** XVIII

## eighty
**04** LXXX

## einsteinium
**02** Es

## ejaculate
**03** cry **04** call, come, emit, yell **05** blurt, eject, expel, shout, spurt, utter **06** cry out, scream **07** call out, exclaim, release **08** blurt out, shout out **09** discharge

## ejaculation
**03** cry **04** call, yell **05** shout, spurt **06** climax, coming, scream **07** release **08** ejection, emission **09** discharge, expulsion, utterance **11** exclamation **12** interjection

## eject
**04** emit, fire, oust, sack, spew, spit **05** belch, degas, evict, exile, expel, exude, spout, vomit **06** banish, bounce, deport, get out, propel, remove **07** bail out, boot out, dismiss, exclude, excrete, expulse, kick out, release, turf out, turn out **08** chuck out, disgorge, drive out, evacuate, get rid of, splutter, throw out **09** discharge, ejaculate, thrust out **11** expectorate

## ejection
**05** exile **06** firing, ouster, outing **07** ousting, removal, sacking, the boot, the sack **08** eviction, vomiting **09** discharge, dismissal, exclusion, expulsion **10** banishment **11** deportation, ejaculation

## eke
• **eke out** **03** ech, ich **04** eche, eech **05** add to, get by **06** scrape **07** fill out, help out, husband, scratch, spin out, stretch, survive **08** increase, piece out **10** go easy with, supplement **11** economize on **12** feel the pinch **13** scrimp and save

## elaborate
◊ *anagram indicator* **05** exact, fancy, fussy, showy **06** devise, minute, ornate, polish, quaint, refine, rococo, work up **07** amplify, careful, complex, develop, enhance, explain, improve, precise, studied, work out **08** detailed, develope, expand on, flesh out, involved, laboured, thorough

**09** decorated, enlarge on, expatiate, extensive, intricate, perfected, storiated **10** ornamental **11** complicated, extravagant, highwrought, historiated, overwrought, painstaking **12** ostentatious

## élan
**04** brio, dash, zest **05** flair, oomph, style, verve **06** esprit, pizazz, spirit, vigour **07** panache, pizzazz **08** flourish, vivacity **09** animation **10** confidence, liveliness **11** impetuosity, stylishness

## elapse
**02** go **03** ren, rin, run **04** go by, go on, pass **05** lapse **06** go past, slip by **07** passing **08** overpass, pass away, slip away

## elastic
◊ *anagram indicator* **04** easy **05** buxom, fluid **06** bouncy, pliant, supple **07** buoyant, plastic, pliable, rubbery, springy **08** flexible, stretchy, tolerant, yielding **09** adaptable, compliant, resilient **10** adjustable **11** elasticated, stretchable **13** accommodating

## elasticity
**04** give, play **05** tonus **06** bounce, spring **07** stretch **08** buoyancy **09** tolerance **10** plasticity, pliability, resilience, suppleness **11** flexibility, springiness **12** adaptability, stretchiness **13** adjustability

## elated
**04** high **05** happy **06** joyful, joyous **07** excited **08** blissful, ecstatic, euphoric, exultant, glorious, jubilant, thrilled **09** delighted, overjoyed, rapturous, rhapsodic **11** exhilarated, on cloud nine, over the moon

## elation
**03** joy **04** glee, lift, ruff **05** bliss, ruffe **06** thrill **07** delight, ecstasy, rapture **08** euphoria **09** happiness **10** exaltation, exultation, joyfulness, joyousness, jubilation **11** high spirits **12** exhilaration, intoxication

## elbow
**04** bump, push **05** ancon, barge, crowd, force, knock, nudge, shove **06** jostle, justle **08** shoulder

## elbow-grease
**04** beef **06** effort, energy **07** muscles **08** exertion, hard work, strength **11** muscle power **15** sweat of your brow

## elbow-room
**04** play, room **05** scope, space **06** leeway **07** freedom **08** latitude **10** Lebensraum **14** breathing space

## elder
**03** OAP **04** aîné, sire **05** aînée, older, oldie **06** deacon, father, leader, senior **07** ancient, wise man **08** ancestor, boortree, bountree, bourtree, kaumatua **09** first-born, old person, pensioner, presbyter **11** older person

## elderly
**03** old **04** aged, OAPs **05** aging, hoary

**06** ageing, mature, oldies, past it, senile, silver **07** fossils **08** badgerly, has-beens **09** old people, senescent, wrinklies **10** grey-haired, pensioners **11** golden agers, older adults, over the hill **13** retired people **14** long in the tooth, senior citizens **15** older generation

## eldest
**05** first **06** oldest **09** first-born **13** first-begotten

## elect
**03** opt **04** pick, -to-be, vote **05** adopt, co-opt, élite, voice **06** choose, chosen, future, opt for, picked, prefer, return, select, vote in **07** appoint, vote for **08** decide on, nominate, plump for, selected **09** cast a vote, chosen few, designate, determine, preferred **10** hand-picked **11** prospective **12** go to the polls

## elected
**02** in

## election
**04** poll, vote **06** ballot, choice, return, voting **07** picking, primary **08** choosing, decision, free will, hustings **09** rectorial, selection **10** preference, referendum **11** appointment **13** determination

## electioneering
**08** fighting, hustings, lobbying **09** crusading, promotion **10** canvassing, struggling **11** campaigning, championing **13** mainstreeting

## elector
**05** voter **08** selector **10** electorate **11** constituent

## electorate
*Australian electorates:*

**04** Bass, Cook, Grey, Holt, Hume, Indi, Lowe, Lyne, Mayo, Page, Reid, Ryan, Swan
**05** Aston, Banks, Blair, Brand, Bruce, Casey, Corio, Cowan, Forde, Groom, Lalor, Lyons, Makin, Moore, Oxley, Perth, Sturt, Wills
**06** Barker, Barton, Batman, Bonner, Bowman, Calare, Cowper, Curtin, Dawson, Deakin, Dobell, Fadden, Farrer, Fisher, Fowler, Fraser, Gorton, Gwydir, Hotham, Hughes, Hunter, Isaacs, Lilley, Mallee, McEwan, Murray, Parkes, Pearce, Petrie, Rankin, Sydney, Wannon, Watson
**07** Bendigo, Berowra, Boothby, Braddon, Calwell, Canning, Chifley, Denison, Dickson, Dunkley, Fairfax, Forrest, Gilmore, Hasluck, Herbert, Higgins, Hinkler, Kennedy, Kooyong, La Trobe, Lindsay, Longman, Maranoa, Menzies, Moreton, O'Conner, Scullin, Solomon, Tangney, Throsby, Werriwa, Wide Bay
**08** Adelaide, Ballarat, Blaxland, Brisbane, Canberra, Charlton, Chisholm, Flinders, Franklin,

Greenway, Griffith, Jagajaga,
Kingston, Lingiari, McMillan,
Mitchell, Paterson, Prospect,
Richmond, Riverina, Stirling
09 Bennelong, Bradfield, Fremantle,
Gippsland, Goldstein, Grayndler,
Hindmarsh, Macarthur,
Mackellar, Macquarie,
McPherson, Melbourne,
Moncrieff, Newcastle, Robertson,
Shortland, Wakefield, Warringah,
Wentworth
10 Cunningham, Eden-Monaro,
Gellibrand, Kalgoorlie,
Leichhardt, New England,
Parramatta
11 Capricornia, Corangamite,
Maribyrnong, North Sydney
12 Port Adelaide
14 Kingsford Smith, Melbourne Ports

*New Zealand electorates:*

04 Ilam, Mana
05 Epsom, Otago, Otaki, Piako,
Taupo
06 Aoraki, Napier, Nelson, Rakaia,
Rodney, Tainui, Tamaki, Wigram
07 Mangere, New Lynn, Rotorua, Te
Atatu
08 Clevedon, Manurewa, Mt Albert,
Rimutaka, Rongotai, Tauranga,
Tukituki, Waiariki
09 East Coast, Hutt South, Mt Roskill,
Northcote, Northland,
Pakuranga, Wairarapa,
Waitakere, Whanganui,
Whangarei
10 Coromandel, North Shore,
Rangitikei, Te Tai Tonga
11 Bay of Plenty, Helensville,
Manukau East, New Plymouth,
Port Waikato, Waimakariri
12 Dunedin North, Dunedin South,
Hamilton East, Hamilton West,
Invercargill, Maungakiekie, Te
Tai Hauauru, Te Tai Tokerau
13 East Coast Bays, Ikaora-Rawhiti,
Ohariu-Belmont
14 Banks Peninsula, Tamaki
Makaurau
15 Auckland Central, Clutha-
Southland, Palmerston North,
West Coast-Tasman
16 Christchurch East
17 Wellington Central
19 Christchurch Central, Taranaki-
King Country

**electric**
04 live 05 tense 07 charged, dynamic,
powered, rousing 08 cordless, exciting,
stirring 09 startling, thrilling
11 stimulating 12 electrifying,
rechargeable 13 mains-operated
15 battery-operated, electric-
powered
• **electric fluid** 04 vril

**electrical**

*Electrical components and devices
include:*

04 fuse
05 cable
06 socket

07 adaptor, ammeter, battery,
conduit, fusebox
08 armature, neon lamp, test lamp
09 light bulb
10 lampholder, multimeter,
transducer, two-pin plug
11 ceiling rose, earthed plug, fuse
carrier, transformer
12 dimmer switch, three-pin plug
13 extension lead
14 bayonet fitting, circuit breaker,
dry-cell battery, insulating tape,
three-core cable, voltage doubler
15 copper conductor, fluorescent
tube

**electrify**
04 fire, jolt, stir 05 amaze, rouse, shock
06 charge, excite, thrill 07 animate,
astound, stagger 08 astonish
09 electrize, galvanize, stimulate
10 invigorate

**elegance**
04 chic 05 grace, poise, style, taste
06 beauty, luxury, polish 07 dignity
08 grandeur 09 gentility, propriety,
smartness 10 concinnity, politeness,
refinement 11 discernment, distinction,
stylishness 12 gracefulness,
tastefulness 13 exquisiteness,
sumptuousness 14 sophistication
15 fashionableness

**elegant**
04 chic, fine, jimp, neat 05 bijou, ritzy,
smart 06 dainty, humane, la-di-da,
lovely, modish, smooth, snazzy,
swanky, urbane 07 genteel, refined,
stylish 08 artistic, charming, cultured,
debonair, delicate, graceful, gracious,
handsome, lah-di-dah, polished,
tasteful 09 beautiful, excellent,
exquisite 10 concinnous, cultivated,
debonnaire 11 fashionable
13 sophisticated

**elegiac**
03 sad 07 doleful, keening 08 funereal,
mournful 09 epicedial, epicedian,
lamenting, plaintive, threnetic,
threnodic 10 threnodial
11 melancholic, threnetical,
valedictory

**elegy**
05 dirge 06 lament, plaint 07 requiem
08 threnode, threnody 10 burial hymn
11 funeral poem, funeral song

**element**
03 set 04 hint, part 05 grain, group,
haunt, niche, party, piece, touch, trace
06 basics, clique, factor, member,
storms, strand 07 climate, faction,
feature, habitat, soupçon, weather
08 filament, fragment 09 component,
electrode, rudiments, suspicion,
territory 10 essentials, individual,
ingredient, principles 11 constituent,
foundations, individuals, small
amount, wind and rain
12 fundamentals 15 first principles

*Elements and their symbols include:*

01 B (boron), C (carbon), F (fluorine),
H (hydrogen), I (iodine), K
(potassium), N (nitrogen), O

(oxygen), P (phosphorus), S
(sulphur), U (uranium), V
(vanadium), W (tungsten), Y
(yttrium)
02 Ac (actinium), Ag (silver), Al
(aluminium), Am (americium), Ar
(argon), As (arsenic), At (astatine),
Au (gold), Ba (barium), Be
(beryllium), Bh (bohrium), Bi
(bismuth), Bk (berkelium), Br
(bromine), Ca (calcium), Cd
(cadmium), Ce (cerium), Cf
(californium), Cl (chlorine), Cm
(curium), Co (cobalt), Cr
(chromium), Cs (caesium), Cu
(copper), Db (dubnium), Ds
(darmstadtium), Dy (dysprosium),
Er (erbium), Es (einsteinium), Eu
(europium), Fe (iron), Fm
(fermium), Fr (francium), Ga
(gallium), Gd (gadolinium), Ge
(germanium), Ha (hahnium), He
(helium), Hf (hafnium), Hg
(mercury), Ho (holmium), Hs
(hassium), In (indium), Ir (iridium),
Kr (krypton), La (lanthanum), Li
(lithium), Lr (lawrencium), Lu
(lutetium), Lw (lawrencium), Md
(mendelevium), Mg (magnesium),
Mn (manganese), Mo
(molybdenum), Mt (meitnerium),
Na (sodium), Nb (niobium), Nd
(neodymium), Ne (neon), Ni
(nickel), No (nobelium), Np
(neptunium), Os (osmium), Pa
(protactinium), Pb (lead), Pd
(palladium), Pm (promethium), Po
(polonium), Pr (praseodymium), Pt
(platinum), Pu (plutonium), Ra
(radium), Rb (rubidium), Re
(rhenium), Rf (rutherfordium), Rg
(roentgenium), Rh (rhodium), Rn
(radon), Ru (ruthenium), Sb
(antimony), Sc (scandium), Se
(selenium), Sg (seaborgium), Si
(silicon), Sm (samarium), Sn (tin),
Sr (strontium), Ta (tantalum), Tb
(terbium), Tc (technetium), Te
(tellurium), Th (thorium), Ti
(titanium), Tl (thallium), Tm
(thulium), Xe (xenon), Yb
(ytterbium), Zn (zinc), Zr
(zirconium)
03 tin (Sn)
04 gold (Au), iron (Fe), lead (Pb), neon
(Ne), zinc (Zn)
05 argon (Ar), boron (B), radon (Rn),
xenon (Xe)
06 barium (Ba), carbon (C), cerium
(Ce), cobalt (Co), copper (Cu),
curium (Cm), erbium (Er), helium
(He), indium (In), iodine (I), nickel
(Ni), osmium (Os), oxygen (O),
radium (Ra), silver (Ag), sodium
(Na)
07 arsenic (As), bismuth (Bi), bohrium
(Bh), bromine (Br), cadmium (Cd),
caesium (Cs), calcium (Ca),
dubnium (Db), fermium (Fm),
gallium (Ga), hafnium (Hf),
hahnium (Ha), hassium (Hs),
holmium (Ho), iridium (Ir), krypton
(Kr), lithium (Li), mercury (Hg),
niobium (Nb), rhenium (Re),

**rhodium** (Rh), **silicon** (Si), **sulphur** (S), **terbium** (Tb), **thorium** (Th), **thulium** (Tm), **uranium** (U), **yttrium** (Y)

08 **actinium** (Ac), **antimony** (Sb), **astatine** (At), **chlorine** (Cl), **chromium** (Cr), **europium** (Eu), **fluorine** (F), **francium** (Fr), **hydrogen** (H), **lutetium** (Lu), **nitrogen** (N), **nobelium** (No), **platinum** (Pt), **polonium** (Po), **rubidium** (Rb), **samarium** (Sm), **scandium** (Sc), **selenium** (Se), **tantalum** (Ta), **thallium** (Tl), **titanium** (Ti), **tungsten** (W), **vanadium** (V)

09 **aluminium** (Al), **americium** (Am), **berkelium** (Bk), **beryllium** (Be), **germanium** (Ge), **lanthanum** (La), **magnesium** (Mg), **manganese** (Mn), **neodymium** (Nd), **neptunium** (Np), **palladium** (Pd), **plutonium** (Pu), **potassium** (K), **ruthenium** (Ru), **strontium** (Sr), **tellurium** (Te), **ytterbium** (Yb), **zirconium** (Zr)

10 **dysprosium** (Dy), **gadolinium** (Gd), **lawrencium** (Lr, Lw), **meitnerium** (Mt), **molybdenum** (Mo), **phosphorus** (P), **promethium** (Pm), **seaborgium** (Sg), **technetium** (Tc)

11 **californium** (Cf), **einsteinium** (Es), **mendelevium** (Md), **roentgenium** (Rg)

12 **darmstadtium** (Ds), **praseodymium** (Pr), **protactinium** (Pa)

13 **rutherfordium** (Rf)

• **old element** 03 air 04 fire 05 earth, water

**elemental**
05 basic 07 immense, natural, primary, radical 08 forceful, powerful
09 primitive, principal 11 fundamental, rudimentary 12 uncontrolled

**elementary**
04 easy 05 basic, clear 06 simple
07 primary 09 principal 10 principial
11 fundamental, rudimentary
12 introductory, uncompounded
13 uncomplicated 15 straightforward

**elephant**
05 Babar, jumbo, rogue 07 mammoth
08 oliphant 09 pachyderm
13 megaherbivore 14 megavertebrate
• **elephant carrier** 03 roc, rok, ruc
04 rukh

**elephantine**
04 huge, vast 05 bulky, great, heavy, large 06 clumsy 07 awkward, hulking, immense, mammoth, massive, weighty 08 enormous 09 lumbering

**elevate**
◊ *reversal down indicator* 04 lift 05 boost, cheer, exalt, hoist, raise, rouse 06 buoy up, hike up, refine, uplift 07 advance, ennoble, gladden, magnify, promote, upgrade 08 brighten, heighten
09 intensify, sublimate 10 aggrandize, exhilarate 11 give a lift to 12 kick upstairs 14 put on a pedestal 15 move up the ladder

**elevated**
◊ *anagram indicator* ◊ *reversal down*

*indicator* 04 high 05 grand, great, lofty, moral, noble 06 aerial, lifted, raised, rising 07 exalted, hoisted, stilted, sublime, uplying 08 advanced, lifted up, towering, uplifted 09 dignified, high-flown, high-toned, important
10 high-raised, high-reared
11 exhilarated

**elevation**
04 back, face, hill, rise, side 05 agger, arsis, front, leg-up, mound, mount, ridge 06 aspect, façade, height, random, uplift 07 dignity, majesty, upright 08 altitude, eminence, foothill, grandeur, monticle, nobility, tallness, upheaval 09 go-getting, loftiness, monticule, promotion, sublimity, upgrading 10 exaltation, monticulus, preferment 11 advancement, sublimation 14 aggrandizement 15 step up the ladder

**elevator**
04 jack, lift

**eleven**
02 XI

**elf**
03 imp 04 peri, puck 05 dwarf, fairy, gnome, pigmy, pixie, pygmy, troll
06 goblin, sprite, urchin 07 banshee, brownie 08 entangle 09 hobgoblin
10 leprechaun
• **elf's child** 03 auf

**elfin**
03 fay, fey, fie 05 small 06 dainty, elfish, impish, petite 07 elflike, playful, puckish 08 charming, delicate
09 sprightly 10 frolicsome
11 mischievous

**elicit**
04 pump, tose, toze 05 cause, educe, evoke, exact, sweep, toaze, wrest
06 derive, extort, obtain 07 draw out, extract, mole out, worm out 08 bring out, outlearn 09 call forth

**eligibility**
09 allowance, condition
11 entitlement, suitability
12 desirability 13 acceptability, qualification

**eligible**
03 fit 06 proper, worthy 07 fitting
08 entitled, suitable 09 desirable, qualified 10 acceptable 11 appropriate

**eliminate**
03 ice, rid 04 beat, cure, do in, drop, kill, lick, omit, wipe 05 expel, whack
06 cancel, cut out, defeat, delete, hammer, murder, reject, remove, rub out, thrash 07 abolish, bump off, conquer, deep-six, exclude, take out, wipe out 08 get rid of, knock out, preclude, stamp out 09 cancel out, dispose of, disregard, eradicate, liquidate, overwhelm 10 annihilate, do away with, extinguish, put an end to, put a stop to 11 exterminate
12 dispense with

**elimination**
07 quietus, removal 08 deletion, disposal, omission 09 abolition,

exclusion, expulsion, rejection
11 eradication

**élite**
04 best, pick 05 cream, elect, noble
06 choice, gentry, jet set 08 nobility, selected 09 exclusive 10 first-class, upper-class 11 aristocracy, high society 12 aristocratic, upper classes
13 establishment 14 crème de la crème, pick of the bunch

**elixir**
04 pith 05 daffy, syrup, tinct 06 potion, remedy 07 arcanum, cure-all, essence, extract, mixture, nostrum, panacea
08 medicine, solution, tincture
09 principle 11 concentrate
12 quintessence

**elliptical**
04 oval 05 ovoid, terse 07 concise, cryptic, dubious, laconic, oblique, obscure, oviform, ovoidal 08 abstruse, succinct 09 ambiguous, condensed, egg-shaped, recondite
12 concentrated, unfathomable
13 comprehensive

**elocution**
06 speech 07 diction, oratory
08 delivery, phrasing, rhetoric
09 eloquence, utterance
11 enunciation 12 articulation
13 pronunciation 15 voice production

**elongate**
06 extend 07 draw out, prolong, stretch
08 lengthen, protract 10 make longer, stretch out

**elongated**
04 long, shot 08 extended
09 prolonged, stretched 10 lengthened, protracted

**elope**
04 bolt, flee 05 leave 06 decamp, escape, run off 07 abscond, do a bunk, make off, run away, scarper, vamoose
08 slip away 09 disappear, do a runner, skedaddle, steal away 10 hightail it, hit the road 11 hit the trail 14 make a bolt for it 15 make a break for it

**eloquence**
07 blarney, diction, fluency, oratory
08 facility, rhetoric 09 elocution, facundity, gassiness 10 expression
11 flow of words 12 forcefulness, gift of the gab 14 articulateness, expressiveness, persuasiveness

**eloquent**
04 glib 05 vivid, vocal 06 fluent, moving 07 voluble 08 forceful, graceful, stirring 09 effective, Mercurial, plausible 10 articulate, Ciceronian, expressive, persuasive, well-spoken 11 Demosthenic
12 honey-tongued 13 silver-tongued, well-expressed

**El Salvador**
02 ES 03 SLV

**elsewhere**
06 abroad, absent 07 not here, removed
10 otherwhere 13 somewhere else 14 in another place, to another place
• **and elsewhere** 04 et al 07 et alibi

## elucidate
**06** fill in, unfold **07** clarify, clear up, explain, expound **08** simplify, spell out **09** exemplify, explicate, interpret, make clear **10** dilucidate, illuminate, illustrate **11** shed light on, state simply **12** throw light on **13** give an example

## elucidation
**05** gloss **07** comment **08** footnote **10** annotation, commentary, exposition, marginalia **11** explanation, explication **12** illumination, illustration **13** clarification **14** interpretation

## elude
◇ *deletion indicator* **04** bilk, duck, flee, foil, jink, slip **05** avoid, dodge, evade, shirk, stump **06** baffle, delude, escape, puzzle, thwart **08** confound, shake off **09** frustrate **10** circumvent **11** get away from

## elusive
**05** dodgy **06** shifty, slippy, subtle, tricky **07** evasive **08** baffling, puzzling, slippery **09** deceptive, transient **10** intangible, misleading, transitory **11** hard to catch, indefinable **12** unanalysable **15** difficult to find

## elusiveness
**06** puzzle **08** subtlety **10** transience **11** evasiveness **13** intangibility **14** indefinability, transitoriness

## emaciated
**04** bony, lean, thin **05** drawn, gaunt **06** meagre, skinny, wasted **07** haggard, pinched, scrawny **08** anorexic, skeletal **10** attenuated, cadaverous, wanthriven **11** thin as a rake **14** all skin and bone

## emaciation
**07** atrophy **08** boniness, leanness, thinness **09** gauntness, symptosis **11** haggardness, scrawniness, tabefaction

## emanate
**04** come, emit, flow, stem **05** arise, exude, issue **06** derive, emerge, exhale, spring, vanish **07** give off, give out, proceed, radiate, send out **09** discharge, originate

## emanation
**04** aura, flow **06** efflux **08** effluent, effusion, emission **09** discharge, effluence, effluvium, effluxion, radiation **10** exhalation

## emancipate
**04** free **05** loose, untie **06** unyoke **07** deliver, manumit, release, set free, unchain **08** liberate, set loose, unfetter **09** discharge, unshackle **11** enfranchise **14** forisfamiliate

## emancipation
**07** freedom, freeing, liberty, release **09** discharge, unbinding **10** liberation, unchaining **11** deliverance, manumission, setting free, unfettering **15** enfranchisement

## emasculate
**04** geld, spay **06** neuter, soften, weaken **07** cripple **08** castrate, enervate **10** debilitate, impoverish

## emasculation
**09** abatement, lessening, reduction, weakening **10** moderation **12** debilitation, diminishment **14** impoverishment

## embalm
**04** balm **05** store **06** balsam, lay out **07** cherish, mummify **08** conserve, enshrine, preserve, treasure **10** consecrate

## embankment
**03** dam **04** bank, bund **05** levee, mound **06** staith **07** banking, rampart, remblai, seabank, staithe **08** causeway, stopbank **09** earthwork

## embargo
**03** ban, bar **04** stop, tapu **05** block, check, seize **06** impede **07** barrier, seizure **08** blockage, obstruct, prohibit, restrain, restrict, stoppage **09** hindrance, interdict, proscribe, restraint **10** impediment **11** obstruction, prohibition, restriction **12** interdiction, proscription

## embark
**04** ship **05** board **06** inship **08** go aboard, take ship **09** board ship
• **embark on** **05** begin, enter, start **06** engage **07** enter on **08** commence, initiate, set about **09** undertake **10** launch into **11** venture into

## embarkation
**06** vessel **08** boarding, entrance, mounting **09** embussing, emplaning, getting-on **11** entrainment

## embarrass
◇ *anagram indicator* **05** shame, upset **06** show up **07** chagrin, confuse, fluster, mortify, perplex **08** distress, encumber, incumber **09** discomfit, humiliate **10** discompose, disconcert **11** make ashamed, make awkward **14** discountenance

## embarrassed
◇ *anagram indicator* **03** red **05** upset **06** guilty, shamed, uneasy **07** abashed, ashamed, awkward, shown up **08** confused, sheepish **09** ill at ease, mortified, perplexed, unnatural **10** distressed, humiliated **11** constrained, discomfited **12** disconcerted **13** self-conscious, uncomfortable

## embarrassing
**06** touchy, tricky **07** awkward, painful, shaming **08** shameful **09** sensitive, upsetting **10** indelicate, mortifying **11** distressing, humiliating **12** compromising, cringe-making, cringeworthy, discomfiting **13** disconcerting, uncomfortable

## embarrassment
**03** fix, jam **04** gene, mess **05** guilt, shame **06** excess, pickle, plight, scrape, unease **07** chagrin, dilemma, surplus **08** distress, embarras **09** abundance, confusion, profusion **10** constraint, difficulty, perplexity, uneasiness **11** awkwardness, bashfulness, humiliation, predicament **12** difficulties, discomfiture,

discomposure, sheepishness **13** mortification, overabundance **14** superabundance

## embassy
**07** mission **08** legation, ministry **09** consulate, embassade, embassage **10** commission, delegation, deputation

## embed
**03** bed, fix, lay, set **04** dock, nest, root, sink **05** drive, inlay, plant **06** hammer, insert **07** implant

## embellish
**03** pan **04** deck, gild, trim, vary **05** adorn, grace, sex up **06** bedeck, enrich **07** dress up, enhance, festoon, garnish **08** beautify, decorate, ornament **09** bespangle, elaborate, embroider **10** exaggerate

## embellishment
**07** garnish, gilding **08** ornament, trimming, vignette **09** adornment, agreement **10** decoration, embroidery, enrichment **11** elaboration, enhancement **13** ornamentation
• **musical embellishment** **04** turn **07** melisma, roulade **09** fioritura, grace note

## embers
**05** ashes, coals **06** gleeds **07** cinders, clinker, residue **08** charcoal **09** live coals

## embezzle
**03** nab, rob **04** nick **05** filch, pinch, steal **06** impair, pilfer, rip off **07** purloin, swindle **08** peculate, shoulder **09** defalcate **11** appropriate **14** misappropriate

## embezzlement
**05** fraud, theft **07** nabbing, nicking, swindle, swizzle **08** filching, stealing **09** pilfering **10** peculation **11** defalcation **13** appropriation

## embezzler
**05** cheat, crook, fraud, thief **06** con man, robber **07** diddler **08** swindler **09** peculator **10** defalcator

## embittered
**04** sour **05** angry **06** bitter, piqued, soured **07** rankled **08** enfested **09** rancorous, resentful **11** disaffected, discouraged, exasperated **12** disenchanted, disheartened **13** disillusioned

## emblazon
**04** laud **05** adorn, extol, paint **06** blazon, colour, depict, praise **07** display, glorify, publish, trumpet **08** decorate, ornament, proclaim **09** celebrate, embellish, publicize **10** illuminate

## emblem
**04** flag, logo, mark, sign, type **05** badge, crest, image, token, totem **06** device, figure, symbol **08** colophon, insignia **09** symbolize, trademark **11** service mark **14** representation
See also **emblem of authority** under **authority**

*Floral and plant emblems include:*

04 rose
06 wattle
07 thistle, waratah
08 daffodil, shamrock
09 maple leaf, maple tree
10 fleur-de-lis, fleur-de-lys, silver fern
11 common heath, kangaroo paw
12 golden wattle
13 royal bluebell
14 Cooktown orchid
15 Sturt's desert pea
16 Sturt's desert rose, Tasmanian blue gum

**emblematic**
07 typical 08 symbolic 10 figurative, symbolical 11 allegorical
12 emblematical, representing
14 representative

**embodiment**
04 soul, type 05 model 06 vessel
07 epitome, example 10 expression
11 incarnation, realization
12 quintessence 13 concentration, incorporation, manifestation
14 representation, representative
15 exemplification, personification

**embody**
◊ *containment indicator* 05 shape
06 take in, typify 07 collect, combine, contain, express, include 08 manifest, organize, stand for 09 corporify, exemplify, incarnate, integrate, personify, represent, symbolize
10 assimilate, synonymize
11 encarnalize, impersonate, incorporate 12 substantiate 13 bring together

**embolden**
04 fire, stir 05 cheer, nerve, rouse
07 animate, hearten, inflame, inspire
08 make bold, reassure, vitalize
09 encourage, make brave, stimulate
10 invigorate, strengthen 13 give courage to

**embrace**
◊ *containment indicator* ◊ *hidden indicator* 03 hug 04 bind, clip, coll, fold, hold, lock, neck, pash, snog, span, wrap 05 admit, adopt, bosom, brace, clasp, cover, grasp, halse, hause, hawse, inarm 06 abrazo, accept, clinch, cuddle, enfold, enlace, fasten, inclip, infold, inlace, smooch, strain, take in, take up 07 colling, contain, espouse, include, involve, necking, receive, squeeze, welcome
08 accolade, canoodle, complect, compress, comprise 09 embrasure, encompass 10 tangle with
11 incorporate, take on board 13 slap and tickle 14 receive eagerly

**embrocation**
03 rub 05 cream, salve 06 lotion
07 epithem 08 liniment, ointment

**embroider**
03 sew 04 darn, purl, work 05 sprig
06 colour, enrich, stitch 07 dress up, enhance, garnish, tambour

08 decorate 09 elaborate, embellish, hemstitch 10 exaggerate 11 cross-stitch

**embroidery**
04 work 05 braid 06 crewel, sewing
07 apparel, cutwork, orphrey, sampler, tambour, tatting 08 braiding, fagoting, tapestry 09 faggoting, fancywork, stump work 10 canvas-work, needlework 11 needlecraft, needlepoint 13 embellishment, ornamentation

*Embroidery stitches include:*

04 back, long, moss, stem, tent
05 chain, cross, queen, satin
07 blanket, bullion, chevron, feather, running
08 couching, fishbone, straight, wheat-ear
09 gros point, half-cross, honeycomb, lazy daisy
10 French knot, longstitch
11 herringbone
12 long-and-short, Swiss darning

**embroil**
◊ *anagram indicator* 05 mix up
06 enmesh 07 involve 08 distract, draw into, entangle 09 catch up in, implicate
11 incriminate

**embryo**
04 germ, root, seed 06 basics, foetus
07 nucleus 08 gastrula, plantule
09 beginning, rudiments 11 unborn child
• **embryo transfer** 02 ET

**embryonic**
05 early 07 primary 08 emerging, germinal, immature, inchoate, unformed 09 beginning, fledgling, incipient 10 elementary
11 rudimentary, undeveloped

**emend**
◊ *anagram indicator* 03 fix 04 edit
05 alter, amend 06 polish, redact, refine, repair, revise 07 correct, improve, rectify, rewrite 09 castigate

**emendation**
◊ *anagram indicator* 07 editing
08 revision 09 amendment, redaction, rewriting 10 alteration, correction, refinement 11 corrigendum, improvement 13 rectification

**emerald**
07 smaragd

**emerge**
◊ *anagram indicator* ◊ *hidden indicator* 03 out 04 rise 05 arise, issue 06 appear, cast up, crop up, turn up 07 come out, debouch, develop, emanate, outcrop, proceed, surface, turn out 09 come forth, transpire 10 be revealed
11 become known, come to light, materialize 12 come into view
14 become apparent

**emergence**
04 dawn, rise 05 issue 06 advent, coming 07 arrival, outcrop 08 disclose, eclosion 09 unfolding 10 appearance, disclosure 11 development, springing-up

**emergency**
03 fix 04 mess 05 extra, pinch, spare
06 back-up, crisis, crunch, danger, pickle, plight, scrape, strait, urgent
07 dilemma, reserve 08 accident, calamity, disaster, exigence, exigency, fall-back, hot water, quandary
09 extremity, immediate 10 difficulty, substitute 11 alternative, catastrophe, predicament, top-priority
13 extraordinary

**emergent**
06 coming, rising 07 budding
08 emerging 09 coming out, embryonic, fledgling 10 burgeoning, developing 11 independent

**emetic**
04 puke 05 puker, vomit 06 emetin, ipecac 07 emetine 08 emetical, vomitary, vomitive, vomitory
11 ipecacuanha, sanguinaria

**emigrate**
04 move 06 depart 07 migrate
08 relocate, resettle 10 move abroad
13 leave your home

**emigration**
06 exodus 07 journey, removal
09 departure, migration 10 relocation
12 expatriation, moving abroad

**eminence**
03 tor 04 berg, fame, hill, knob, note, rank 05 ridge 06 esteem, height, renown 07 dignity, hilltop, stature
08 altitude, majority, prestige
09 advantage, celebrity, greatness, prelation 10 importance, notability, prominence, promontory, reputation, trochanter 11 distinction, pre-eminence, sovereignty, superiority
14 honourableness 15 illustriousness

**eminent**
04 high 05 first, grand, great, noted
06 famous 07 notable 08 elevated, esteemed, renowned, superior
09 important, prominent, respected, well-known 10 celebrated, noteworthy, pre-eminent
11 conspicuous, high-ranking, illustrious, outstanding, prestigious, superlative 13 distinguished

**eminently**
04 high, most, very, well 06 highly
07 greatly, notably 08 signally
09 extremely, obviously
10 remarkably, strikingly
11 exceedingly, prominently
12 surpassingly 13 conspicuously, exceptionally, outstandingly, par excellence

**emissary**
03 spy 05 agent, envoy, scout
06 deputy, herald 07 courier
08 delegate, diplomat, outgoing 09 go-between, messenger 10 ambassador
12 intermediary 14 representative

**emission**
04 vent 05 issue 06 escape 07 release
08 effusion, ejection 09 diffusion, discharge, emanation, exudation, giving-off, giving-out, radiation

**emit** (continued)

10 exhalation, outpouring, production 11 ejaculation 12 transmission

**emit**

03 ren, rin, run, say 04 boak, bock, boke, leak, ooze, pass, shed, spew, vent, void 05 eject, eruct, exude, issue, sound, speak, throw, utter, voice 06 exhale, expire, let out 07 diffuse, emanate, excrete, express, give off, give out, pour out, produce, radiate, release, send out 08 eructate, throw out, vocalize 09 discharge, give forth, send forth, verbalize

**emollient**

03 oil 04 balm 05 cream, salve 06 lotion 07 calming, lenient, unguent 08 balsamic, lenitive, liniment, ointment, poultice, soap-ball, soothing 09 appeasing, assuaging, assuasive, demulcent, placatory, softening 10 mitigative, mollifying, palliative 11 moisturizer 12 conciliatory, moisturizing, propitiatory

**emolument**

03 fee, pay 04 gain, hire 05 wages 06 charge, profit, return, reward, salary 07 benefit, payment, profits, stipend 08 earnings 09 advantage, allowance 10 honorarium, recompense 12 compensation, remuneration

**emotion**

03 ire, joy 04 envy, fear, hate, pang, turn 05 anger, dread, grief, sense, shock, spasm, whirl 06 affect, ardour, motion, sorrow, spirit, thrill, warmth 07 anoesis, despair, ecstasy, feeling, fervour, passion, sadness, upsurge 08 movement, reaction, surprise 09 affection, happiness, reverence, sensation, sentiment, sublimity, transport, vehemence 10 excitement 11 sensibility
• **expression of emotion** 01 O 02 ha, oh 03 hah, hoo, wow 05 arrah, hoo-oo, wowee
• **sign of emotion** 04 tear

**emotional**

04 warm 05 fiery, moved, soppy 06 ardent, fervid, heated, loving, moving, red-hot, roused, tender 07 emotive, feeling, fervent, glowing, gushing, radiant, soulful, tearful, zealous 08 effusive, exciting, hysteric, pathetic, poignant, stirring, swelling, touching, white-hot 09 excitable, schmaltzy, sensitive, thrilling 10 hot-blooded, hysterical, passionate, responsive 11 full-hearted, impassioned, overcharged, sentimental, susceptible, tear-jerking, tempestuous 12 enthusiastic, gut-wrenching, heartwarming, soul-stirring 13 demonstrative, psychological, temperamental

**emotionally**

06 warmly 07 tensely 08 ardently, lovingly, tenderly 09 awkwardly, fervently, nervously, zealously 10 delicately, poignantly, touchingly 11 sensitively 12 passionately 13 sentimental, under pressure 14 heartwarmingly 15 controversially, demonstratively, psychologically, temperamentally

**emotionless**

04 cold, cool 05 blank 06 frigid, remote 07 deadpan, distant, glacial, unmoved 08 clinical, cold-fish, detached, toneless 09 impassive, unfeeling 10 antiseptic, impassible, insensible, phlegmatic, stone-faced, stony-faced, unaffected, unblinking 11 cold-blooded, indifferent, unemotional 13 imperturbable 15 undemonstrative

**emotive**

06 touchy 07 awkward 08 delicate 09 emotional, sensitive 12 inflammatory 13 controversial

**empathize**

05 share 07 comfort, feel for, support 10 understand 12 have a rapport, identify with

**emperor**

03 Emp, Imp 04 czar, Inca, king, tsar 05 kesar, tenno 06 kaiser, keasar, mikado, purple, shogun 08 imperial, padishah 09 imperator, sovereign 12 kaisar-i-Hindi

*Emperors include:*

03 Leo
04 John, Nero, Otho, Otto, Paul, Pu Yi
05 Akbar (the Great), Babur, Basil, Boris, Galba, Henry, Louis, Murad, Nerva, Pedro, Peter, Selim, Titus
06 Caesar (Julius), Conrad, Joseph, Jovian, Julian, Justin, Mehmet, Philip (the Arab), Rudolf, Trajan
07 Agustín (de Itúrbide), Akihito, Alamgir, Alexius, Baldwin, Charles (the Fat), Charles (the Bald), Francis, Gordian, Hadrian, Leopold, Lothair, Marcian, Michael, Severus, William
08 Augustus, Aurelius, Caligula, Claudius, Commodus, Constans, Domitian, Galerius, Hirohito, Honorius, Jahangir, Licinius, Matthias, Maximian, Napoleon, Nicholas, Süleyman, Tiberius, Valerian
09 Alexander, Antoninus, Atahualpa, Aurangzeb, Caracalla, Carausius, Ferdinand, Frederick, Gallienus, Heraclius, Justinian, Maxentius, Montezuma, Mutsuhito, Shah Jahan, Sigismund, Vespasian, Vitellius, Yoshihito
10 Andronicus, Augustulus, Diocletian, Elagabalus, Kublai Khan, Maximilian, Meiji Tenno, Theodosius
11 Charlemagne, Constantine, Constantius, Jean Jacques, Valentinian
12 Chandragupta, Heliogabalus, John Comnenus, Samudragupta
13 Antoninus Pius, Francis Joseph, Haile Selassie
14 Marcus Aurelius
15 Alexius Comnenus

*See also* **Roman**

**emphasis**

04 birr, mark 05 focus, force, power 06 accent, moment, stress, weight 07 urgency 08 priority, strength 09 attention, intensity 10 importance, insistence, prominence 11 pre-eminence 12 accentuation, positiveness, significance, underscoring
• **expression of emphasis** 04 Jeez 05 Jeeze 07 you know

**emphasize**

06 accent, play up, stress, weight 07 dwell on, enforce, feature, point up 08 heighten, insist on 09 highlight, intensify, press home, punctuate, spotlight, underline 10 accentuate, foreground, strengthen 11 put stress on 14 bring to the fore 15 call attention to, draw attention to

**emphatic**

04 firm 05 vivid 06 direct, marked, strong 07 certain, decided, earnest, marcato, telling 08 absolute, decisive, definite, distinct, forceful, forcible, positive, powerful, striking, vehement, vigorous 09 energetic, important, insistent, momentous 10 conclusive, expressive, impressive, pronounced, punctuated 11 categorical, distinctive, significant, unequivocal 12 unmistakable 13 unmistakeable

**emphatically**

06 firmly 08 in spades, strongly 09 certainly 10 absolutely, definitely, forcefully, vehemently, vigorously 11 insistently 13 categorically, distinctively, unequivocally

**empire**

03 Emp 04 firm, rule, sway 05 power, realm 06 domain, empery 07 command, company, control, kingdom 08 business, dominion, province 09 authority, supremacy, territory 10 consortium, government 11 corporation, sovereignty 12 commonwealth, conglomerate, jurisdiction, organization 13 multinational

*Empires and kingdoms include:*

04 Cush, Kush, Moab
05 Akkad, Alban, Media, Mogul, Roman
06 Naples
07 Argolis, Assyria, Bohemia, British, Chinese, Galicia, Ottoman, Persian
08 Dalriada, Lombardy, Sardinia
09 Abyssinia, Byzantine, Holy Roman
10 New Kingdom, Old Kingdom
11 Northumbria
13 Middle Kingdom
15 Austro-Hungarian

*See also* **classification**
• **part of empire** 04 land

**empirical**

08 observed 09 practical, pragmatic 11 a posteriori 12 experiential, experimental

**empirically**

11 practically 13 pragmatically 14 experientially, experimentally

## employ

**03** ply, use **04** fill, hire **05** apply, exert, spend **06** bestow, draw on, engage, enlist, expend, occupy, retain, sign up, take on, take up **07** appoint, exploit, recruit, service, utilize **08** exercise, put to use **09** make use of **10** apprentice, commission **11** bring to bear **13** bring into play **15** put on the payroll, take advantage of

## employed

**04** busy, used **05** hired **06** active, in work **07** earning, engaged, working **08** occupied, with a job **11** preoccupied **12** in employment

## employee

**03** cog, man **04** hand, help **05** gofer, woman **06** casual, worker **08** labourer, munchkin **09** assistant, job-holder, operative, rainmaker **10** wage-earner, waterclerk, working man **12** working woman **13** member of staff, working person

## employer

**03** guv **04** boss, firm, head, user **05** malik, melik, owner **06** gaffer, master, old man **07** company, manager, padrone, skipper **08** business, director, governor, mistress **09** executive **10** management, proprietor, taskmaster, workmaster **12** entrepreneur, organization, taskmistress, workmistress **13** establishment

## employment

**03** job, use **04** hire, line, ploy, post, work **05** craft, place, trade **06** employ, hiring, métier **07** calling, pursuit, service **08** business, position, taking-on, vocation **09** signing-up, situation **10** engagement, enlistment, livelihood, occupation, profession **11** application, recruitment **12** exercitation **14** apprenticeship

## emporium

**04** fair, mart, shop **05** store **06** bazaar, market **08** boutique **11** market-place **13** establishment **15** department store

## empower

**05** equip **06** enable, permit **07** certify, entitle, license, qualify, set free, warrant **08** accredit, delegate, sanction **09** authorize **10** commission **11** give means to, give power to

## empress

**03** Emp, Imp **05** queen, ruler **07** czarina, tsarina **08** czaritsa, imperial, kaiserin, tsaritsa **09** imperator, sovereign

*Empresses include:*

**02** Lü, Wu
**03** Zoë
**04** Anna, Cixi
**05** Irene, Livia
**06** Helena (St), Tz'u Hsi, Wu Chao, Wu Zhao
**07** Eugénie, Wu Zhaov
**08** Adelaide (St), Cunegund (St), Faustina, Nur Jahan, Theodora, Victoria
**09** Agrippina (the Younger),
Alexandra, Catherine, Catherine (the Great), Elizabeth, Joséphine, Kunigunde (St), Messalina, Old Buddha, Theophano
**11** Marie Louise
**12** Anna Ivanovna, Maria Theresa
**13** Livia Drusilla

## emptiness

**04** void **05** blank **06** hiatus, hollow, hunger, vacuum **07** inanity, vacancy, vacuity **08** bareness, futility, voidness **09** unreality **10** barrenness, desolation, flatulence, hollowness, vacantness **11** aimlessness, uselessness **13** senselessness, worthlessness **15** ineffectiveness, meaninglessness, purposelessness

## empty

◇ *middle deletion indicator* **03** gut **04** bare, boss, free, idle, lade, pump, teem, toom, vain, void **05** addle, blank, clear, drain, go out, inane, issue, leave, strip, use up, waste **06** barren, devoid, frothy, futile, gousty, hollow, hot-air, hungry, unload, unpack, unreal, vacant, vacate **07** aimless, deadpan, deplete, exhaust, flow out, pour out, trivial, turn out, useless, vacuate, vacuous, viduous **08** clear out, deserted, desolate, evacuate, soulless, unfilled **09** available, discharge, fruitless, insincere, pointless, senseless, worthless **10** unoccupied **11** ineffective, ineffectual, meaningless, purposeless, unfurnished, uninhabited **13** insubstantial **14** expressionless, unsatisfactory **15** with nothing in it

## empty-headed

**04** daft, vain **05** batty, dippy, ditsy, ditzy, dopey, dotty, inane, silly **06** scatty, stupid **07** foolish, vacuous **09** frivolous **13** rattle-brained, unintelligent **14** feather-brained, scatter-brained

## emulate

**04** copy, echo **05** emule, match, mimic, rival **06** aemule, follow **07** imitate, vie with **09** ambitious, reproduce **11** compete with, contend with **15** model yourself on

## emulation

**06** strife **07** contest, copying, echoing, mimicry, paragon, rivalry **08** matching **09** challenge, following, imitation, rivalship **10** contention **11** competition **12** contestation

## enable

**03** fit, let **04** able, help **05** allow, endue, equip **06** permit **07** empower, entitle, further, license, prepare, qualify, warrant **08** accredit, sanction, validate **09** authorize **10** commission, facilitate, make easier **12** make possible **13** pave the way for **14** clear the way for

## enact

**04** pass, play, rule **05** order **06** act out, decree, depict, ordain, ratify **07** approve, command, make law, perform, portray **08** appear as, sanction

**09** authorize, establish, legislate, represent

## enactment

**03** act, law **04** bill, play, rule **05** edict, order **06** acting, decree **07** command, measure, passing, playing, purview, staging, statute **08** approval, sanction **09** ordinance, portrayal **10** performing, regulation **11** commandment, institution, legislation, performance **12** ratification **13** authorization **14** representation

## enamoured

**03** mad **04** fond, keen, wild **05** taken **07** charmed, smitten **08** besotted **09** bewitched, enchanted, entranced **10** captivated, enthralled, fascinated, infatuated, in love with

## en bloc

**05** as one **07** en masse, in a body **08** as a group, as a whole, ensemble **09** all at once, wholesale **11** all together

## encampment

**04** base, camp, duar, laer **05** douar, dowar, tents **06** laager **07** bivouac, hutment, manyata **08** barracks, campsite, manyatta, quarters **13** camping-ground

## encapsulate

◇ *containment indicator* **03** pot **05** sum up **06** digest, précis, take in, typify **07** abridge, capture, contain, include **08** compress, condense **09** epitomize, exemplify, represent, summarize

## encapsulation

**06** digest, précis **07** summary **10** expression **14** representation **15** exemplification

## encase

**04** line, wrap **05** bound, cover, frame **07** confine, enclose, envelop **08** surround

## enchant

**05** charm, spell **06** allure, appeal, thrill **07** attract, becharm, beguile, bewitch, delight, enamour, enthral, glamour **08** entrance, sirenize **09** captivate, enrapture, fascinate, hypnotize, mesmerize, spellbind

## enchanter

**05** magus, witch **06** wizard **07** warlock **08** conjurer, magician, sorcerer **09** archimage, mesmerist **10** reim-kennar **11** necromancer, spellbinder

## enchanting

**06** lovely **07** magical, winsome **08** alluring, charming, pleasant **09** appealing, endearing, ravishing, wonderful **10** attractive, bewitching, delightful, entrancing **11** captivating, fascinating, mesmerizing **12** irresistible

## enchantment

**05** bliss, charm, magic, spell **06** allure, appeal, glamor **07** delight, ecstasy, glamour, gramary, rapture, sorcery **08** gramarye, malefice, witching, wizardry **09** hypnotism, mesmerism **10** allurement, necromancy, witchcraft **11** conjuration, fascination, incantation **14** attractiveness

## enchantress
**04** vamp **05** Circe, fairy, lamia, siren, witch **07** charmer **08** conjurer, magician **09** sorceress **10** seductress **11** femme fatale, necromancer, spellbinder

## encircle
◇ *containment indicator* **04** belt, clip, gird, hoop, pale, ring, wind **05** crowd, girth, hem in, inorb, orbit, twine, wheel **06** circle, embail, enfold, engird, enlace, enring, girdle, inlace, stemme **07** close in, compass, enclose, envelop, environ, enwheel **08** surround **09** encompass **12** circumscribe

## enclose
◇ *containment indicator* **02** in **03** box, pen, pin **04** cage, case, coop, hold, ring, seal, tine, womb, wrap **05** bound, bower, clasp, cover, fence, frame, hedge, hem in, pound, put in **06** circle, cocoon, corral, embale, emboss, encase, enfold, enlock, girdle, immure, incase, infold, inhoop, insert, pocket, prison, shut in, take in **07** close in, compass, confine, contain, embound, embowel, embrace, enchase, envelop, include, seclude **08** conclude, encircle, send with, surround **09** encompass, ring-fence **10** comprehend, interclude **12** circumscribe

## enclosed
**03** enc **04** encl, pend, pent **07** bosomed, recluse **08** included

## enclosure
**03** box, enc, haw, pen, pit, ree, ren, rin, run, sty **04** area, bawn, boma, cage, camp, encl, fank, fold, hope, lair, pale, peel, pele, reed, ring, town, yard **05** arena, close, court, garth, kraal, pound, sekos, stell **06** corral, runway **07** enclave, fencing, haining, paddock, parrock, pightle, pinfold **08** addition, cloister, compound, enceinte, seraglio, stockade, townland **09** inclusion, insertion **10** encincture

## encode
**05** ravel **06** cipher, garble **07** encrypt, obscure **08** disguise, encipher, scramble **11** put into code **14** make mysterious

## encompass
◇ *containment indicator* **04** gird, hold, ring, span **05** admit, bathe, brace, cover, hem in **06** begird, circle, embody, enfold, infold, shut in, sphere, take in **07** close in, confine, contain, embrace, enclose, envelop, include, involve, procure **08** cincture, comprise, encircle, surround **10** circumvent, comprehend **11** incorporate **12** circumscribe

## encore
**03** bis **06** ancora, repeat, replay **10** repetition

## encounter
**04** cope, face, meet, tilt **05** brush, clash, close, fight, joust, match, run-in, set-to **06** action, battle, combat, engage, oppose, ruffle, strive, tackle, tussle **07** contact, contend, contest, dispute, meeting, run into **08** bump into, conflict, confront, cope with, deal with, happen on, skirmish, struggle **09** clash with, collision, rencontre, run across **10** chance upon, come across, engagement, experience, rencounter, rendezvous **11** be faced with, be up against, compete with, grapple with **12** do battle with **13** come up against, confrontation, passage of arms, stumble across **15** cross swords with

## encourage
**03** aid **04** abet, back, coax, fuel, help, lift, root, spur, stir, sway, urge **05** boost, cheer, egg on, gee up, jolly, pep up, rally, rouse **06** assist, buck up, buoy up, exhort, favour, foster, incite, induce, prompt, second, spirit, spur on, stroke **07** advance, animate, cheer on, cherish, comfort, console, forward, further, hearten, inspire, promote, support, sustain, upcheer, win over **08** accorage, advocate, convince, embolden, inspirit, motivate, persuade, reassure, talk into **09** accourage, enhearten, influence, stimulate **10** barrack for, strengthen **14** be supportive to

## encouragement
**03** aid **04** help **05** boost, cheer **06** come-on, urging **07** backing, coaxing, comfort, pep talk, succour, support **08** cheering, stimulus **09** incentive, promotion **10** assistance, heartening, incitement, motivation, persuasion **11** consolation, endorsement, exhortation, furtherance, inspiration, reassurance, stimulation **12** shot in the arm
• **expression of encouragement**
**02** ha, on **03** hah, olé, via, yay **04** come, sa sa **05** heigh, hollo, there **06** giddap, now now **07** attaboy, come now **08** attagirl, come come **09** ups-a-daisy, upsy-daisy

## encouraging
**04** rosy **06** bright **07** hopeful **08** cheerful, cheering **09** hortative, hortatory, incentive, inspiring, promising, uplifting **10** auspicious, comforting, heartening, protreptic, reassuring, supportive **11** cohortative, stimulating **12** satisfactory **14** proceleusmatic

## encroach
**03** jet **05** pinch, usurp **06** invade, trench **07** impinge, intrude, overrun **08** entrench, infringe, intrench, overstep, trespass **10** infiltrate, muscle in on **11** make inroads

## encroachment
**06** inroad **08** invasion, trespass **09** incursion, intrusion **11** purpresture, trespassing **12** entrenchment, infiltration, infringement, intrenchment, overstepping

## encrypt
**05** ravel **06** cipher, encode, garble **07** obscure **08** disguise, encipher,

scramble **11** put into code **14** make mysterious

## encumber
**03** jam **04** cram, load, pack **05** block, check, cramp, stuff **06** accloy, burden, hamper, hinder, impede, retard, saddle, strain, stress **07** bog down, burthen, congest, oppress, overlay, prevent **08** handicap, obstruct, overload, restrain, slow down **09** constrain, embarrass, weigh down **13** inconvenience

## encumbrance
**04** load **05** cross **06** burden, strain, stress, weight **08** handicap, obstacle **09** albatross, cumbrance, hindrance, liability, millstone, restraint **10** constraint, difficulty, impediment, obligation **11** obstruction **13** inconvenience **14** responsibility

## encyclopedia
**04** ency **05** encyc

## encyclopedic
**04** vast **05** broad **07** in-depth **08** complete, thorough **09** universal **10** exhaustive **11** compendious, wide-ranging **12** all-embracing, all-inclusive **13** comprehensive, thoroughgoing **15** all-encompassing

## end
◇ *tail selection indicator* **01** Z **03** aim, tip **04** abut, area, butt, doom, edge, fine, goal, part, ruin, side, stop, stub, tail, term **05** cease, close, death, dying, field, issue, limit, omega, point, scrap **06** aspect, be over, border, branch, demise, design, die out, ending, expire, finale, finish, intent, margin, motive, object, period, reason, region, result, run out, target, upshot, wind up **07** abolish, destroy, outcome, purpose, remnant, section, vestige **08** boundary, break off, complete, conclude, dissolve, downfall, epilogue, fade away, fragment, round off **09** cessation, checkmate, culminate, extremity, intention, leftovers, objective, remainder, terminate **10** annihilate, completion, conclusion, dénouement, department, extinction, extinguish **11** come to an end, consequence, culmination, destruction, discontinue, dissolution, exterminate, termination **12** bring to an end **13** extermination
• **at an end** **02** up **03** oer **04** over
• **at the end of** ◇ *juxtaposition indicator* ◇ *tail selection indicator*
• **at the far end** **03** out
• **east end** **04** apse
• **ends** ◇ *ends selection indicator*
• **nearly at an end** **04** late
• **the end** **06** enough **07** too much **08** the limit, the worst **10** unbearable **11** intolerable, unendurable **12** insufferable, the final blow, the last straw **15** beyond endurance

## endanger
**04** risk **06** expose, hazard, risque **07** imperil **08** threaten **09** prejudice, put at risk **10** compromise, jeopardize

11 periclitate, put in danger 13 put in jeopardy

## endearing
04 cute 05 sweet 07 lovable, winsome 08 adorable, charming, engaging, loveable 09 appealing 10 attractive, delightful, enchanting 11 captivating

## endearment
04 love 07 pet-name 08 fondness 09 affection, sweet talk 10 attachment, diminutive, hypocorism 12 sweet nothing 15 term of affection
• **term of endearment** 03 bud, hon, luv, pet, pug 04 burd, cony, dear, dove, fool, love, peat 05 chick, chuck, coney, ducks, ducky, heart, hinny, honey, jarta, lovey, mopsy, mouse, popsy, puggy, sugar, yarta, yarto 06 flower, monkey, moppet, pigsny 07 alannah, chuckie, cupcake, pigsney, pigsnie, princox 08 honeybun, precious, princock, treasure 09 pillicock, sugarplum 10 honeybunch, honey-chile, sweetie-pie 11 chick-a-biddy 12 chick-a-diddle

## endeavour
02 go 03 aim, try 04 bash, seek, shot, stab 05 assay, crack, Morse 06 aspire, effort, labour, strive 07 attempt, venture, working 08 striving, struggle 09 take pains, undertake 10 do your best, enterprise 11 undertaking 13 try your hand at

## ended
02 up 04 over, past

## ending
◊ tail selection indicator 03 end 04 last 05 close, death, dying 06 climax, finale, finish 07 closing, closure 08 epilogue, terminal 09 cessation, desinence, extremity, finishing 10 completing, completion, concluding, conclusion, dénouement, resolution 11 culmination, termination 12 consummation

## endless
◊ ends deletion indicator ◊ tail deletion indicator 05 whole 06 boring, entire 07 eternal, undying 08 constant, fineless, infinite, termless, unbroken, unending 09 boundless, ceaseless, continual, incessant, limitless, perpetual, Sisyphean, unlimited 10 continuous, monotonous, objectless, without end 11 everlasting, measureless 12 interminable 13 inexhaustible, uninterrupted

## endlessly
◊ tail deletion indicator 09 eternally 10 constantly, infinitely, unendingly, without end 11 ceaselessly, continually, day after day, day in day out, limitlessly, perpetually 12 continuously, interminably 15 uninterruptedly, without stopping

## endmost
◊ tail selection indicator 04 last 07 extreme 08 farthest, hindmost

## endorse
02 OK 04 back, okay, sign 05 adopt 06 affirm, endoss, favour, ratify, uphold 07 approve, confirm, initial, support, sustain, warrant 08 advocate, be behind, sanction, vouch for 09 authorize, get behind, recommend 11 countersign, subscribe to 15 sign on the back of

## endorsement
02 OK 04 okay, visa, visé 07 backing, support, warrant 08 advocacy, approval, sanction, thumbs-up 09 signature 10 green light 11 affirmation, approbation, initialling, testimonial 12 commendation, confirmation, ratification, subscription 13 authorization 14 recommendation, seal of approval

## endow
04 fund, gift, give, have, vest, will 05 award, boast, dower, endew, enjoy, found, grant, leave, state 06 bestow, confer, donate, pay for, supply 07 finance, furnish, possess, present, provide, support 08 bequeath, make over 12 be endued with 13 be blessed with

## endowment
04 fund, gift, wakf, waqf 05 award, dower, dowry, flair, grant, power 06 genius, income, legacy, talent 07 ability, bequest, faculty, finance, funding, present, quality, revenue 08 aptitude, bestowal, capacity, donation, dotation 09 attribute, character, provision 10 capability, fellowship, settlement 11 benefaction, studentship 13 qualification

## endurable
07 lasting 08 bearable, portable 09 tolerable 10 manageable, sufferable 11 supportable, sustainable 13 withstandable

## endurance
04 guts, stay 05 spunk 06 bottle 07 lasting, stamina 08 backbone, duration, patience, stoicism, strength, tenacity 09 captivity, fortitude, stability, tolerance 10 durability, resolution, sufferance, toleration 11 continuance, persistence, resignation 12 perseverance, staying power, stickability 13 long-suffering

## endure
03 aby 04 abye, bear, bide, dree, dure, face, have, hold, keep, last, live, lump, meet, stay, take, wear 05 abear, abide, allow, brave, brook, stand, stick, thole 06 harden, hold up, permit, remain, suffer 07 abrooke, hold out, perdure, persist, prevail, stick it, stomach, support, survive, sustain, swallow, undergo, weather 08 continue, cope with, outstand, stand for, submit to, tolerate 09 encounter, go through, put up with, withstand 10 experience, sweat it out, tough it out

## enduring
04 firm 05 stout 06 stable, steady 07 abiding, chronic, durable, dureful, eternal, lasting 08 immortal, livelong, patience, tolerant 09 permanent, perpetual, remaining, steadfast, surviving 10 continuing, persistent, persisting, prevailing, undergoing, unwavering 11 long-lasting, substantial, unfaltering 12 imperishable, long-standing

## enemy
03 foe 04 time 05 Devil, rival 06 foeman 07 anemone, hostile, opposer 08 opponent 09 adversary, other side 10 antagonist, competitor, philistine 13 the opposition 14 the competition

## energetic
04 wick 05 brisk, pithy, vital, zappy, zippy 06 active, lively, potent, punchy, strong 07 dynamic, go-ahead, rackety, slammin', zestful 08 animated, bouncing, forceful, forcible, powerful, slamming, spirited, tireless, vigorous 09 effective, go-getting, strenuous 10 boisterous 11 full of beans, high-powered, throughgaun 12 through-going 13 indefatigable

## energize
04 stir 05 liven, pep up 06 arouse, excite, fire up, vivify 07 animate, enliven, quicken 08 activate, motivate, vitalize 09 electrify, galvanize, stimulate 10 invigorate

## energy
01 E 02 go 03 pep, vim, zip 04 brio, fire, fuel, gism, head, jism, life, push, zeal, zest, zing 05 drive, force, might, power, verve 06 ardour, spirit, vigour 07 pizzazz, potency, sparkle, stamina 08 activity, dynamism, exertion, strength, vitality, vivacity 09 animation, intensity 10 efficiency, enthusiasm, get-up-and-go, liveliness, propellant 11 motive power 12 forcefulness 13 effectiveness, effervescence, kinetic energy 15 potential energy
• **lacking energy** 04 nesh, poky 05 pokey 09 out of curl
• **lose energy** 04 flag, wilt
• **primitive energy** 02 id
• **renewable energy department** 04 ETSU

## enervated
04 limp, weak 05 spent, tired 06 beaten, done in, effete, feeble, pooped, sapped 07 run-down, worn out 08 fatigued, unmanned, unnerved, weakened 09 enfeebled, exhausted, paralysed, pooped out, washed-out 10 undermined 11 debilitated, devitalized, tuckered out 13 incapacitated

## enervating
04 hard 05 tough 06 taxing, tiring 07 arduous 08 draining, exacting, relaxing, wearying 09 demanding, difficult, fatiguing, laborious, strenuous, wearisome 10 exhausting

## enfeeble
03 sap 04 geld 05 waste 06 reduce, weaken 07 deplete, exhaust, fatigue, unhinge, unnerve, wear out 08 diminish, enervate 09 undermine 10 debilitate, devitalize

### enfold
◇ *containment indicator* **03** hug, lap **04** fold, hold, wind, wrap **05** clasp, imply **06** clutch, enwrap, inclip, inwrap, plight, shroud, swathe, wimple, wrap up **07** embrace, enclose, envelop, whimple **08** encircle **09** encompass, implicate

### enforce
**04** urge **05** apply, drive, exact, force **06** coerce, compel, fulfil, impose, lean on, oblige, strive **07** execute, impress, require **08** carry out, insist on, pressure **09** constrain, discharge, emphasize, implement, prosecute, reinforce **10** administer, pressurize **11** necessitate **14** put the screws on

### enforced
**06** forced **07** binding, imposed, obliged **08** dictated, ordained, required **09** compelled, mandatory, necessary **10** compulsory, obligatory, prescribed **11** constrained, involuntary, unavoidable

### enforcement
**08** coaction, coercion, pressure **09** discharge, execution **10** compulsion, constraint, fulfilment, imposition, insistence, obligation **11** application, prosecution, requirement **14** administration, implementation

### enfranchise
**04** free **07** manumit, release **08** liberate **10** emancipate **13** give the vote to **14** give suffrage to

### enfranchisement
**07** freedom, freeing, release **08** suffrage **10** liberating, liberation **11** manumission **12** emancipation, voting rights

### engage
**02** do **03** win **04** book, busy, draw, fill, gain, grip, hire, hold, join, lock, mesh, take **05** catch, charm, enrol, fight, share, tie up **06** absorb, allure, assail, attach, attack, combat, employ, enlist, enmesh, fasten, occupy, pledge, sign on, sign up, take on, take up **07** appoint, attract, betroth, capture, engross, involve, recruit, reserve **08** contract, embark on, entangle, interact, intrigue, practise, take part **09** captivate, clash with, encounter, enter into, guarantee, interlock, partake of, preoccupy, undertake **10** battle with, commission **11** fit together, participate, wage war with **12** interconnect **15** put on the payroll
• **engage in** ◇ *insertion indicator* **04** play, wage **05** enter **07** enter on **08** voutsafe **09** enter upon, prosecute, undertake, vouchsafe

### engaged
**04** busy **05** in use, taken **06** active, in mesh, tied up **07** pledged **08** absorbed, employed, espoused, immersed, involved, occupied, plighted, promised **09** affianced, betrothed, committed, engrossed, intrigued, spoken for **11** preoccupied, unavailable **12** in conference

### engagement
**03** gig, vow, war **04** bond, date, snap **05** clash, fight, troth **06** action, attack, battle, combat, pledge, plight, strife **07** assault, booking, contest, fixture, meeting, promise, sharing **08** conflict, contract, espousal, struggle **09** agreement, assurance, betrothal, encounter, interview, offensive, partaking **10** commitment, employment, obligation, rendezvous, taking part **11** appointment, arrangement, assignation, betrothment, hand-promise, involvement, reservation, undertaking **13** confrontation, participation

### engaging
**05** sweet **07** likable, lovable, winning, winsome **08** adorable, charming, fetching, likeable, loveable, pleasant, pleasing **09** agreeable, appealing **10** attractive, delightful, enchanting **11** captivating, fascinating

### engender
**04** bear **05** beget, breed, cause **06** arouse, create, effect, excite, incite, induce, kindle, lead to **07** inspire, nurture, produce, provoke **08** generate, occasion **09** encourage, instigate, procreate, propagate **10** bring about, give rise to

### engine
**03** way **04** tool **05** agent, cause, means, motor, snare, trick **06** device, dynamo, factor, genius, medium, source **07** ability, channel, machine, vehicle **09** apparatus, appliance, generator, implement, ingenuity, machinery, mechanism **10** instrument, locomotive **11** contraption, contrivance

*Engines include:*

**03** air, gas, ion, jet, oil **04** aero, beam, heat **05** motor, steam, water **06** diesel, donkey, petrol, Petter, radial, rocket, rotary, Wankel **07** orbital, turbine, V-engine **08** compound, Stirling, traction, turbojet **09** aerospike, turboprop **10** stationary **11** atmospheric, sleeve-valve **13** fuel-injection, reciprocating **15** linear aerospike

*Engine parts include:*

**04** pump, sump **05** choke **06** con-rod, gasket, piston, tappet **07** fan belt, oil pump, oil seal, push-rod **08** camshaft, flywheel, radiator, rotor arm, scramjet **09** air filter, drive belt, oil filter, rocker arm, spark plug **10** alternator, cooling fan, crankshaft, inlet valve, petrol pump, piston ring, thermostat, timing belt **11** carburettor, rocker cover **12** cylinder head, exhaust valve, fuel injector, ignition coil, starter motor, timing pulley, turbocharger **13** camshaft cover, connecting rod, cylinder block, inlet manifold, power-steering **15** exhaust manifold

### engineer
◇ *anagram indicator* **02** BE, CE, ME **03** BAI, eng, rig **04** plan, plot **05** cause **06** create, devise, direct, driver, effect, manage, sapper, scheme **07** arrange, builder, control, deviser, greaser, handler, planner **08** contrive, designer, inventor, mechanic, operator **09** architect, machinist, manoeuvre, originate **10** bring about, controller, manipulate, mastermind, originator, technician **11** orchestrate, stage-manage **12** engine driver **13** civil engineer, sound engineer

*Engineers include:*

**03** Fox (Sir Charles) **04** Bell (Alexander Graham), Benz (Karl), Eads (James Buchanan), Ford (Henry), Otto (Nikolaus August), Page (Sir Frederick Handley), Watt (James) **05** Baird (John Logie), Baker (Sir Benjamin), Braun (Wernher von), Dodge (Grenville), Gooch (Sir Daniel), Grove (Sir George), Locke (Joseph), Maxim (Sir Hiram Stevens), Reber (Grote), Rolls (Charles Stewart), Royce (Sir Henry), Ruska (Ernst August Friedrich), Smith (William), Tesla (Nikola) **06** Brunel (Isambard Kingdom), Brunel (Sir Marc Isambard), Carnot (Sadi), Cayley (Sir George), Claude (Georges), Cugnot (Nicolas Joseph), Diesel (Rudolf Christian Karl), Donkin (Bryan), Eckert (John Presper), Edison (Thomas Alva), Eiffel (Gustave), Fokker (Anthony Herman Gerard), Fuller (Buckminster), Fulton (Robert), Jansky (Karl Guthe), Jessop (William), Lenoir (Jean Joseph Étienne), McAdam (John Loudon), Napier (Robert), Nipkow (Paul), Rennie (John), Savery (Thomas), Séguin (Marc), Sperry (Elmer Ambrose), Taylor (Frederick Winslow), Vauban (Sebastien le Prestre de), Wallis (Sir Barnes Neville), Wankel (Felix), Wright (Orville), Wright (Wilbur) **07** Balfour (George), Boulton (Matthew), Carlson (Chester Floyd), Citroën (André Gustave), Daimler (Gottlieb), Dornier (Claude), Eastman (George), Fleming (Sir John Ambrose), Giffard (Henri), Goddard (Robert Hutchings), Gresley (Sir Nigel), Heinkel (Ernst), Houston (Edwin J), Junkers (Hugo), Keldysh (Mstislav), Lesseps (Ferdinand Marie, Vicomte de), Nasmyth (James), Parsons (Sir Charles Algernon), Porsche (Ferdinand), Rankine (William John Macquorn), Siemens (Sir William),

**Siemens** (Werner von), **Smeaton** (John), **Sopwith** (Sir Thomas Octave Murdoch), **Telford** (Thomas), **Thomson** (Elihu), **Tupolev** (Andrei), **Whittle** (Sir Frank)
**08** **Bertrand** (Henri Gratien, Comte), **Bessemer** (Sir Henry), **Brindley** (James), **De Forest** (Lee), **Ericsson** (John), **Ferranti** (Sebastian Ziani de), **Huntsman** (Benjamin), **Ilyushin** (Sergei), **Kennelly** (Arthur Edwin), **Korolyov** (Sergei), **Leonardo** (da Vinci), **Maudslay** (Henry), **Mitchell** (Reginald Joseph), **Poncelet** (Jean Victor), **Reynolds** (Osborne), **Roebling** (John Augustus), **Sikorsky** (Igor), **Sinclair** (Sir Clive), **Zeppelin** (Ferdinand, Graf von)
**09** **Armstrong** (Edwin Howard), **Clapeyron** (Emile), **Cockerell** (Sir Christopher Sydney), **Fairbairn** (Sir William), **Fessenden** (Reginald Aubrey), **Issigonis** (Sir Alec), **Trésaguet** (Pierre Marie Jerome), **Whitworth** (Sir Joseph)
**10** **Bazalgette** (Sir Joseph William), **Freyssinet** (Marie Eugène Léon), **Hounsfield** (Sir Godfrey Newbold), **Lilienthal** (Otto), **Stephenson** (George), **Stephenson** (Robert), **Trevithick** (Richard)
**11** **De Havilland** (Sir Geoffrey), **Montgolfier** (Joseph Michel)
**12** **Westinghouse** (George)
**13** **Messerschmitt** (Willy)
**15** **Leonardo da Vinci**

**engineers**
**02** RE, SE **04** REME **07** sappers

**England**
**03** Eng
*See also* **county; town**

**English**
**01** E **03** Eng **04** side
*See also* **alphabet; monarch**
• **early English 02** EE
• **English as a second language**
**03** ESL
• **English language teaching**
**03** ELT
• **in English 03** Ang **07** Anglice

**engorged**
**04** full **05** puffy **07** swollen **08** enlarged, expanded, inflated, overfull

**engrave**
**03** cut, fix, set **04** etch, mark **05** brand, carve, chase, embed, inter, lodge, print, scalp, sculp, stamp, write **06** chisel, incise **07** enchase, engrain, impress, imprint, insculp **08** inscribe **09** character, mezzotint

**engraving**
**03** cut, eng **04** mark **05** block, plate, print, steel **06** niello **07** carving, cutting, etching, imprint, woodcut **08** cerotype, dry-point, glyptics, intaglio **09** headpiece, mezzotint, sculpture, tailpiece **10** chiselling, heliograph, impression, lithoglyph, photoglyph, xylography **11** inscription, stylography, zincography **12** glyptography, heliogravure, photo-

etching, photogravure **15** photoxylography

**engross**
**04** grip, hold **05** rivet **06** absorb, arrest, engage, enwrap, inwrap, occupy, take up, wrap in **07** enthral, immerse, involve **08** interest, intrigue **09** captivate, fascinate, preoccupy **10** monopolize

**engrossed**
**04** deep, lost, rapt **06** intent **07** engaged, fixated, gripped, riveted, taken up, wrapped **08** absorbed, caught up, immersed, occupied **09** intrigued **10** captivated, enthralled, fascinated, mesmerized **11** preoccupied **13** up to the elbows

**engrossing**
**08** gripping, riveting **09** absorbing, consuming **10** compelling, intriguing **11** captivating, enthralling, fascinating, interesting, suspenseful **12** monopolizing **13** unputdownable

**engulf**
◊ *containment indicator* **04** bury **05** drown, flood, gulph, swamp **06** absorb, deluge, devour, plunge, suck in **07** consume, engross, envelop, immerse, overrun, swallow **08** inundate, overtake, submerge **09** overwhelm, swallow up

**enhance**
**04** lift **05** add to, boost, exalt, raise, sex up, swell **06** enrich, stress **07** augment, elevate, improve, magnify, upgrade **08** heighten, increase **09** embellish, emphasize, intensify, reinforce **10** strengthen

**enhancement**
**05** boost **06** stress **08** emphasis, increase **09** elevation **10** enrichment **11** heightening, improvement **12** augmentation **13** magnification, reinforcement **15** intensification

**enigma**
**04** egma **05** poser **06** puzzle, riddle **07** dilemma, mystery, paradox, problem **08** quandary **09** conundrum **11** brain-teaser **12** brain-twister

**enigmatic**
◊ *anagram indicator* **06** arcane **07** cryptic, obscure, strange **08** baffling, esoteric, puzzling, riddling **09** recondite **10** mysterious, mystifying, perplexing, sphinxlike **11** inscrutable, paradoxical **12** inexplicable, unfathomable

**enjoin**
**03** ban, bar **04** urge **05** order **06** advise, charge, decree, demand, direct, forbid, impose, ordain **07** command, require **08** disallow, encharge, instruct, prohibit **09** encourage, interdict, prescribe, proscribe

**enjoy**
**03** joy **04** have, like, love **05** fancy, go for, taste, wield **06** relish, savour **07** possess, revel in, undergo **08** be fond of **09** delight in, partake of, rejoice in **10** appreciate **11** benefit

from, go a bundle on **12** have the use of **13** be blessed with, be endowed with, get a buzz out of, get a kick out of **14** be favoured with, take pleasure in
• **enjoy yourself 03** jol **04** ball, rage **05** party, sport **07** have fun, large it **08** live it up **09** have a ball, make merry **10** have a blast **11** have it large **12** get your kicks **13** have a good time **14** get your jollies **15** let your hair down, paint the town red

**enjoyable**
**03** ace, bad, fab, fun **04** cool, fine, good, mega, neat, nice, wild **05** brill, rorty, super, triff **06** lekker, lovely, wicked, wizard **07** amusing, gustful, kicking, radical, triffic **08** fabulous, glorious, pleasant, pleasing, smashing, terrific **09** agreeable, beautiful, brilliant, delicious, fantastic **10** delectable, delightful, gratifying, satisfying **11** pleasurable **12** entertaining

**enjoyment**
**03** fun, joy, use **04** glee, zest **05** gusto **06** favour, relish **07** benefit, comfort, delight **08** blessing, fruition, gladness, pleasant, pleasure **09** advantage, amusement, diversion, happiness, pleasance, privilege **10** indulgence, possession, recreation, suffisance **11** delectation **12** satisfaction **13** entertainment, gratification

**enlarge**
**03** pan **04** ream, zoom **05** add to, piece, swell, widen **06** blow up, dilate, expand, extend, let out **07** amplify, augment, broaden, develop, distend, inflate, magnify, stretch **08** dilate on, elongate, expand on, heighten, increase, jumboize, lengthen, multiply **09** expatiate, intumesce **10** make bigger, make larger, supplement **11** elaborate on, expatiate on **12** become bigger, become larger **13** go into details

**enlargement**
**05** swell, tumor **06** blow-up, bouton, goiter, goitre, growth, oedema, spavin, tumour **07** release **08** aneurism, aneurysm, dilation, increase, root-knot **09** exostosis, expansion, extension **10** ampliation, distension, stretching, varicocele **11** countersink, development **12** augmentation, cardiomegaly, hepatomegaly, intumescence, splenomegaly **13** amplification, magnification **14** multiplication

**enlighten**
**05** edify, teach, tutor **06** advise, inform, notify **07** apprise, counsel, educate **08** civilize, instruct **09** cultivate, make aware **10** illuminate, illustrate **12** open your eyes

**enlightened**
**03** lit **04** wise **05** aware **07** erudite, learned, liberal, refined **08** cultured, educated, informed, literate **09** civilized **10** conversant, cultivated, illuminate, Illuminati, open-minded,

reasonable **11** broad-minded
**12** intellectual **13** knowledgeable,
sophisticated

## enlightenment
**05** light **06** satori, wisdom **07** insight
**08** learning, literacy, sapience,
teaching **09** awareness, education,
erudition, eye-opener, knowledge
**10** Aufklärung, refinement
**11** cultivation, edification, information,
instruction **12** civilization, illumination
**13** comprehension, understanding
**14** open-mindedness, sophistication
**15** broad-mindedness

## enlist
**03** get, win **04** hire, join, list **05** enrol,
enter, prest **06** employ, engage, enroll,
gather, induct, join up, muster, obtain,
rope in, secure, sign up, take on
**07** procure, recruit **08** register
**09** conscribe, conscript, volunteer
**14** join the colours

## enliven
◇ *anagram indicator* **04** fire, jazz
**05** cheer, juice, liven, pep up, rouse,
spark **06** buoy up, excite, ginger, jazz
up, kindle, perk up, soup up, vivify,
wake up **07** animate, cheer up,
gladden, hearten, inspire, juice up,
liven up, quicken **08** brighten, ginger
up **09** stimulate **10** brighten up,
exhilarate, invigorate, revitalize
**11** give a lift to

## en masse
**05** as one **06** en bloc, in sort **07** in a
body **08** as a group, as a whole, as one
man, ensemble, together **09** all at
once, wholesale **10** in the quill **11** all
together

## enmeshed
**07** mixed up **08** caught up, involved
**09** concerned, entangled **10** associated

## enmity
**04** feud, hate **05** venom **06** hatred,
malice, needle, rancor, strife
**07** discord, ill-will, rancour
**08** acrimony, aversion, bad blood, ill
blood **09** animosity, antipathy, hostility
**10** antagonism, bitterness, ill feeling
**11** malevolence **14** unfriendliness

## ennoble
**05** exalt, raise **06** gentle, honour, uplift
**07** dignify, elevate, enhance, glorify,
magnify **10** aggrandize, nobilitate
**11** distinguish

## ennui
**04** bore **05** weary **06** acedia, tedium
**07** accidie, boredom, languor, malaise
**09** lassitude, tiredness **11** the doldrums
**12** listlessness **15** dissatisfaction

## enormity
**04** evil **05** crime **06** horror **07** outrage
**08** atrocity, evilness, iniquity, vastness,
vileness **09** depravity, violation
**10** wickedness **11** abnormality,
abomination, immenseness,
monstrosity, viciousness
**13** atrociousness **14** outrageousness

## enormous
**04** huge, mega, vast **05** dirty, giant,

gross, jumbo **07** immense, mammoth,
massive, monster, Titanic, whaling
**08** colossal, gigantic, great big,
plonking, whacking, whopping
**09** abounding, atrocious, ginormous,
humongous, humungous, monstrous,
walloping **10** astronomic, gargantuan,
hellacious, large-scale, monstruous,
outrageous, prodigious, stupendous,
tremendous **11** God-almighty
**12** considerable, hulking great

## enormously
**04** dead, very, well **05** jolly **06** hugely
**08** devilish, terribly **09** extremely,
immensely, massively **10** especially
**11** exceedingly, God-almighty
**12** tremendously **13** exceptionally, to a
huge extent, to a vast extent
**15** extraordinarily

## enormousness
**07** expanse **08** hugeness, vastness
**09** greatness, immensity, largeness,
magnitude **11** immenseness,
massiveness **13** extensiveness

## enough
**04** anow, enow, nuff **05** ample, amply,
basta, belay **06** fairly, no more, plenty
**08** abundant, adequacy, adequate,
passably **09** abundance, amplitude,
tolerably **10** adequately, moderately,
reasonably, satisfying, sufficient
**11** ample supply, sufficience,
sufficiency **12** sufficiently
**14** satisfactorily

## en passant
**02** ep **08** by the way **09** cursorily, in
passing **12** incidentally
**15** parenthetically

## enquire, enquirer, enquiring, enquiringly, enquiry
*see* **inquire; inquirer; inquiring; inquiringly; inquiry**

## enrage
**03** bug, irk, vex **04** rile **05** anger, annoy
**06** incite, madden, needle, wind up
**07** agitate, hack off, incense, inflame,
provoke **08** irritate **09** enranckle,
infuriate, make angry **10** exasperate,
push too far

## enraged
**03** mad **04** wild **05** angry, irate, livid
**06** fuming, raging **07** angered,
annoyed, furious, horn-mad
**08** incensed, inflamed, seething,
storming **09** infuriate, irritated
**10** aggravated, infuriated
**11** exasperated

## enrapture
**05** charm **06** ravish, thrill **07** beguile,
bewitch, delight, enchant, enthral
**08** enravish, entrance **09** captivate,
fascinate, spellbind, translate,
transport **10** emparadise, imparadise
**13** please greatly

## enrich
**04** gild, lard **05** add to, adorn, endow,
grace **06** fatten, manure, refine
**07** augment, develop, enhance, fortify,
garnish, improve **08** beautify, decorate,
ornament, treasure **09** cultivate,

embellish, fertilize **10** aggrandize,
ameliorate, supplement

## enrol
**03** tax **04** list, note **05** admit, enter
**06** attest, engage, enlist, enwrap, join
up, muster, record, sign on, sign up
**07** go in for, put down, recruit
**08** inscribe, muster in, register
**10** enregister **15** put your name down

## enrolment
**04** list **09** admission, enlisting, joining
up, signing on, signing up
**10** acceptance, enlistment
**11** recruitment **12** conscription,
registration

## en route
**05** march **08** on the way **09** in transit,
on the move, on the road **12** on the
journey

## ensconce
**03** put **05** lodge, niche, place **06** locate,
nestle, screen, settle, shield **07** install,
protect, shelter **08** entrench
**09** establish

## ensemble
**03** set, sum **04** band, cast, suit, unit
**05** get-up, group, total, whole
**06** chorus, circle, entity, outfit, rig-out,
troupe **07** company, costume
**08** entirety **09** aggregate, orchestra
**10** collection, whole shoot **11** coordinates **12** accumulation **13** corps de
ballet, whole caboodle **14** whole bang
shoot

## enshrine
**05** exalt, guard **06** embalm, hallow,
revere, shield **07** cherish, enchase,
idolize, lay down, protect, set down
**08** dedicate, preserve, sanctify,
treasure **10** consecrate **11** apotheosize,
immortalize

## enshroud
**04** hide, pall, veil, wrap **05** cloak,
cloud, cover **06** enfold, enwrap,
shroud **07** conceal, enclose, envelop,
obscure

## ensign
**03** Ens **04** flag, jack, mark, sign, waft
**05** badge, color, crest **06** banner,
colors, colour, pennon, shield
**07** ancient, colours, pennant
**08** gonfalon, pavilion, standard **10** coat
of arms

## enslave
**04** bind, trap, yoke **05** thirl **06** thrall
**07** enchain, subject **08** bethrall,
dominate **09** subjugate
**14** disenfranchise

## enslavement
**07** bondage, dulosis, serfdom, slavery
**08** thraldom **09** captivity, servitude,
vassalage **10** oppression, repression,
subjection **11** enthralment, subjugation

## ensnare
◇ *containment indicator* **03** net **04** hook,
lime, trap **05** benet, catch, snare, snarl
**06** enmesh, entoil, entrap, trepan
**07** capture, embroil **08** entangle
**09** mousetrap **10** illaqueate

**ensue**
04 flow, stem 05 arise, issue, occur
06 befall, derive, follow, happen, result
07 develop, proceed, succeed, turn out
08 come next 09 transpire

**ensure**
05 guard 06 effect, secure 07 betroth,
certify, protect, warrant 08 make safe,
make sure 09 guarantee, safeguard
11 make certain

**entail**
03 cut 04 need 05 carve, cause, infer
06 demand, lead to, tailye 07 call for,
fashion, involve, produce, require,
taillie, tailzie 08 occasion, result in
10 bring about, give rise to
11 necessitate

**entangle**
◇ anagram indicator 03 elf 04 ball, knot,
wrap 05 catch, mix up, ravel, snare,
twist 06 emmesh, engage, enlace,
enmesh, enroot, entoil, entrap, fankle,
immesh, inlace, inmesh, jumble,
muddle, puzzle, taigle, tangle
07 confuse, embroil, ensnare, ensnarl,
involve, perplex, trammel 08 quagmire
09 implicate, interlace 10 complicate,
intertwine

**entanglement**
◇ anagram indicator 03 tie 04 knot,
mesh, mess, trap 05 mix-up, snare, tie-
up 06 affair, jumble, muddle, tangle
07 entrail, liaison, snarl-up
09 confusion 10 difficulty, entrapment,
perplexity 11 ensnarement,
involvement, predicament
12 complication, relationship
13 embarrassment

**entente**
04 deal, pact 06 treaty 07 compact,
rapport 09 agreement 10 friendship
11 arrangement 13 understanding
15 entente cordiale

**enter**
◇ insertion indicator 03 log, ren, rin, run
04 come, go in, join, list, note
05 begin, board, enrol, get in, input,
lodge, pop in, start 06 arrive, come in,
enlist, go in to, insert, occupy, pierce,
record, sign up, submit, take up
07 break in, burst in, get in to, go in for,
put down, set down, sneak in 08 come
in to, commence, embark on, engage
in, inscribe, register, set about, take
down, take part 09 introduce,
penetrate, undertake, write down
10 embark upon, infiltrate, launch into
11 participate, put on record 12 gain
access to 13 get involved in, worm
your way in 15 become a member of

**enterprise**
03 SME 04 firm, plan, push, show, task
05 drive, oomph 06 design, effort,
energy, scheme, spirit, voyage
07 company, concern, courage,
emprise, project, venture 08 ambition,
boldness, business, campaign,
gumption, industry, vitality
09 adventure, endeavour, operation,
programme, undertake 10 assignment,
designment, enthusiasm, expedience,
get-up-and-go, initiative

11 imagination, undertaking
13 establishment, strong feeling
15 adventurousness, resourcefulness

**enterprising**
04 bold, goey, keen 05 eager, pushy
06 active, daring 07 go-ahead, pushful,
pushing, zealous 08 aspiring, spirited,
vigorous 09 ambitious, energetic,
ingenious 11 adventurous,
imaginative, resourceful, self-reliant,
undertaking, venturesome
12 enthusiastic 13 self-motivated
14 self-motivating 15 entrepreneurial

**entertain**
◇ containment indicator 04 fête, have,
host, meet, wine 05 amuse, charm,
cheer, put up, treat 06 divert, engage,
foster, harbor, junket, occupy, please,
regale 07 accourt, ask over, cherish,
delight, engross, harbour, imagine,
nurture, receive 08 ask round,
conceive, consider, distract, interest,
maintain 09 captivate, flirt with, have
round 10 experience, have guests,
invite over, play host to, think about
11 accommodate, contemplate,
countenance, invite round

**entertainer**
04 host 06 diseur 07 diseuse, hostess
09 top banana 10 Amphitryon
See also **actor, actress; comedian;
musician; singer**

Entertainers include:

02 DJ
04 bard, fool, Joey, mime
05 actor, clown, comic, mimic
06 artist, august, busker, cowboy,
dancer, jester, mummer, player,
singer
07 acrobat, actress, artiste, auguste,
juggler, Pierrot
08 comedian, conjuror, go-go girl,
gracioso, jongleur, magician,
minstrel, musician, showgirl,
stripper
09 bunny girl, chanteuse, ecdysiast,
fire-eater, harlequin, hypnotist,
ice-skater, lap dancer, lion tamer,
performer, pierrette, poi dancer,
presenter, puppeteer, strong man
10 comedienne, disc jockey, go-go
dancer, knockabout, mime artist,
mind-reader, pole dancer,
ringmaster, rope-walker,
unicyclist, wire-dancer
12 chat-show host, escapologist,
exotic dancer, game-show host,
impersonator, snake charmer,
stand-up comic, street singer,
trick cyclist, vaudevillean,
vaudevillian
13 contortionist, impressionist,
thimblerigger, trapeze artist,
ventriloquist
14 pavement artist, sword-swallower
15 jerry-come-tumble, song-and-
dance act, tightrope walker

**entertaining**
◇ containment indicator 03 fun 05 funny,
jolly, witty 07 amusing, amusive,
comical 08 humorous, pleasant,
pleasing 09 diverting, enjoyable

10 delightful 11 interesting, pleasurable
12 recreational

**entertainment**
03 fun 04 boff, olio, show 05 cheer,
drama, hobby, sport, table 07 leisure,
pastime, variety 08 activity, pleasure,
semblant 09 amusement, diversion,
enjoyment, honky-tonk, spectacle
10 confection, recreation
11 distraction, merrymaking,
performance 12 extravaganza,
presentation 14 divertissement

Entertainments include:

03 BBQ, DVD, gig
04 fête, film, play, show
05 dance, disco, opera, radio, revue,
rodeo, video
06 circus, fleadh
07 airshow, cabaret, concert,
karaoke, musical, pageant,
recital, showbiz
08 barbecue, carnival, festival,
gymkhana, waxworks
09 burlesque, fireworks, floor show,
magic show, music hall,
nightclub, pantomime, video
game
10 puppet show, television,
vaudeville
11 discothèque, variety show
12 computer game, Punch-and-Judy,
show business
13 firework party
14 laser-light show
15 greyhound racing

See also **television; theatrical**

Entertainment places include:

03 pub, zoo
04 club, dogs, fair, hall
05 arena, disco
06 big top, casino, cinema, circus,
museum, nitery
07 cabaret, funfair, gallery, hot spot,
ice rink, marquee, niterie,
stadium, theatre
08 ballroom, carnival, dog track,
flesh pot
09 bandstand, bingo hall, dance hall,
music hall, nightclub, strip club
10 auditorium, fairground, opera
house, restaurant, social club
11 boîte de nuit, concert hall,
discothèque, public house,
skating rink
12 amphitheatre, bowling alley,
cattle market
13 leisure centre
15 amusement arcade

• **entertainment industry** 12 show
business
• **undemanding entertainment**
03 pap

**enthral**
◇ containment indicator 04 grip
05 charm, rivet 06 absorb, thrill
07 beguile, bewitch, delight, enchant,
engross 08 entrance, intrigue
09 captivate, enrapture, fascinate,
hypnotize, mesmerize, spellbind

## enthralling
◊ *containment indicator* **08** charming, gripping, mesmeric, riveting **09** beguiling, thrilling **10** compelling, compulsive, enchanting, entrancing, intriguing **11** captivating, fascinating, hypnotizing, mesmerizing **12** spellbinding

## enthuse
**04** fire, gush, rave **05** drool **06** excite, fire up, praise **07** inspire **08** motivate **10** bubble over, effervesce, wax lyrical **14** go into raptures

## enthusiasm
**04** brio, buzz, fire, hype, rage, zeal, zest **05** ardor, craze, estro, furor, hobby, mania, oomph, thing, verve **06** ardour, frenzy, furore, relish, spirit, warmth **07** ecstasy, fervour, passion, pastime **08** appetite, delirium, devotion, interest, keenness **09** eagerness, vehemence **10** commitment, ebullience, ebulliency, excitement, fanaticism **11** acclamation, earnestness, schwärmerei **12** entraînement **13** preoccupation
• **expression of enthusiasm 03** boy, gee **04** Jeez **05** Jeeze, oh boy!, whack **06** whacko **10** hubba hubba
• **lose enthusiasm 04** cool **08** languish

## enthusiast
**03** bug, fan, nut **04** buff, zeal **05** fiend, freak, lover **06** maniac, zealot **07** admirer, amateur, devotee, fanatic **08** follower **09** supporter **10** aficionado **11** eager beaver
*See also* **collector**

## enthusiastic
**03** mad **04** avid, daft, into, keen, nuts, rave, warm, wild **05** crazy, eager, potty **06** ardent, gung-ho, hearty, mad for **07** devoted, earnest, excited, fervent, intense, up for it, zealous **08** empressé, gaga over, mad about, spirited, vehement, vigorous **09** committed, ebullient, exuberant, fanatical, gaga about **10** passionate **11** rhapsodical **12** rootin'-tootin', wholehearted **13** keen as mustard, self-motivated

## entice
**04** coax, draw, lure, tice, tole **05** tempt **06** allure, cajole, induce, lead on, seduce **07** attempt, attract, beguile, wheedle **08** inveigle, persuade **09** sweet-talk, tantalize

## enticement
**04** bait, lure, tice **05** decoy **06** allure, carrot, come-on **07** coaxing **08** cajolery **09** seduction, sweet-talk **10** allurement, attraction, inducement, invitation, persuasion, temptation **11** beguilement **12** inveiglement **13** blandishments

## enticing
**08** alluring, charming, inviting, tempting **09** appealing, seductive **10** attractive **11** captivating **12** irresistible

## entire
**04** full, meer **05** round, sound, total, utter, whole **06** intact, within **07** genuine, plenary, untired **08** absolute, complete, integral, livelong, outright, stallion, thorough **09** sincerely, unmingled **10** unimpaired **11** unmitigated, unqualified **12** completeness

## entirely
**03** all **04** inly, only, tout **05** clean, fully, quite **06** in toto, merely, purely, quight, solely, wholly **07** all over, totally, utterly **08** every bit, properly **09** every inch, every whit, perfectly, tout à fait **10** absolutely, altogether, completely, in every way, thoroughly **11** exclusively **12** unreservedly **14** in every respect

## entirety
**03** all, sum **05** total, whole **08** fullness, totality **09** wholeness **12** completeness

## entitle
**03** dub **04** call, name, term **05** allow, label, style, title **06** enable, know as, permit **07** empower, ennoble, license, qualify, warrant **08** accredit, christen, sanction **09** authorize, designate **12** give the title, make eligible
• **to be entitled to 04** bear **07** deserve

## entitlement
**03** due **05** claim, right, title **07** warrant **09** authority, privilege **11** opportunity, prerogative

## entity
**03** ens, Tao **04** body **05** being, thing **06** object, tensor **08** creature, organism **09** existence, substance **10** individual

## entomb
**04** bury, tomb **05** inter, inurn, plant **06** inhume, shroud, wall up **07** inearth **09** lay to rest, sepulcher, sepulchre, sepulture **15** put six feet under

## entombment
**06** burial **09** interment, sepulture **10** inhumation **12** laying to rest

## entourage
**04** gang **05** court, posse, staff, suite, train **06** escort **07** company, cortège, coterie, retinue **09** followers, following, hangers-on, retainers **10** associates, attendants, companions

## entrails
**04** guts **05** offal, tripe **06** bowels, haslet, inside, quarry, umbles **07** giblets, harslet, humbles, innards, insides, inwards, numbles, pudding, viscera **08** chawdron, gralloch, puddings **10** intestines **11** vital organs **14** internal organs

## entrance
**03** eye **04** adit, door, gate, hall, ingo, pend, pipe **05** charm, debut, drive, entry, foyer, gorge, inlet, lobby, mouth, porch, start, way in **06** access, atrium, avenue, dromos, entrée, income, infare, ingate, portal, ravish **07** arrival, Avernus, beguile, bewitch, cat-flap, delight, doorway, enchant, enthral, gateway, hallway, ingoing, ingress, jawhole, opening **08** anteroom, approach, driveway **09** admission, captivate, closehead, enrapture, fascinate, hypnotize, introitus, mesmerize, spellbind, threshold, transport, vestibule **10** admittance, appearance, initiation, passageway **12** introduction, porte-cochère, right of entry
• **narrow entrance 04** jaws **06** throat

## entranced
**04** rapt **10** spellbound

## entrancing
**06** lovely **07** winsome **08** alluring, charming, pleasant **09** appealing, endearing, ravishing, wonderful **10** attractive, bewitching, delightful, enchanting **11** captivating, fascinating, mesmerizing **12** irresistible

## entrant
**05** entry, pupil, rival **06** novice, player **07** convert, fresher, learner, starter, student, trainee **08** beginner, freshman, initiate, newcomer, opponent **09** applicant, candidate, contender **10** apprentice, competitor, contestant, new arrival **11** participant, probationer

## entrap
**03** net **04** lure, trap **05** catch, decoy, snare, tempt, trick **06** allure, ambush, delude, enmesh, entice, seduce **07** beguile, capture, deceive, embroil, ensnare **08** entangle, inveigle **09** crossbite, implicate, underfong

## entreat
**03** ask, beg, sew, sue **04** pray, prig **05** crave **06** induce, invoke, objure **07** beseech, beseeke, implore, request, solicit **08** appeal to, petition **09** flagitate, importune, plead with **10** supplicate

## entreaty
**03** cry **04** plea, suit **06** appeal, prayer **07** beseech, request **08** petition, pleading **09** exoration **10** cri de coeur, invocation **11** conjuration **12** solicitation, supplication

## entrée
**05** entry **06** access **07** ingress, prelude, starter **08** main dish **09** admission, appetizer **10** admittance, main course **11** first course **12** introduction, right of entry

## entrench
**03** fix, set **04** root, seat **05** dig in, embed, lodge, plant, wound **06** anchor, sconce, settle **07** ingrain, install **08** ensconce, stop a gap **09** establish **14** take up position

## entrenched
**03** set **04** firm **05** fixed **06** inbred, rooted **07** diehard **09** implanted, indelible, ingrained **10** deep-rooted, deep-seated, inflexible, unshakable **11** established, unshakeable **12** ineradicable, intransigent **13** dyed-in-the-wool, stick-in-the-mud **15** well-established

## entrepreneur
**05** agent **06** broker, dealer, tycoon **07** magnate, manager **08** promoter **09** financier, middleman **10** contractor,

impresario, moneymaker, speculator, undertaker **11** businessman, enterpriser **13** businesswoman, industrialist

**entrepreneurial**
**05** trade **08** business, economic, monetary **09** budgetary, financial **10** commercial, industrial, managerial **11** contractual **12** professional

**entrust**
**04** aret **05** arett, endow, trust **06** assign, charge, commit, depute, invest, resign **07** commend, confide, consign, deliver, deposit **08** delegate, encharge, hand over, turn over **09** authorize **11** put in charge

**entry**
**04** door, gate, hall, item, note **05** annal, foyer, lobby, porch, rival, way in **06** access, entrée, minute, player, record **07** account, arrival, doorway, entrant, gateway, ingress, listing, opening, passage **08** anteroom, approach, entrance, opponent, register, registry **09** admission, applicant, candidate, contender, statement, threshold, vestibule **10** admittance, appearance, competitor, contestant, memorandum **11** description, participant **12** introduction, right of entry

**entwine**
◇ *anagram indicator* **04** coil, knit, knot, mesh, warp, wind **05** braid, plait, ravel, twine, twist, weave **06** enlace, inlace **07** embroil, entrail, intwine, wreathe **08** entangle **09** implicate, interlace, interlink **10** intertwine, intervolve, interweave

**enumerate**
**04** cite, list, name, tell **05** count, quote, score **06** detail, number, recite, reckon, relate **07** compute, itemize, mention, recount, specify **08** rehearse, spell out **09** calculate, catalogue **13** particularize

**enunciate**
**03** say **05** sound, speak, state, utter, voice **06** affirm **07** declare, enounce, express, propose **08** announce, proclaim, propound, vocalize **09** pronounce **10** articulate, promulgate, put forward

**enunciation**
**05** sound **06** speech **07** diction **08** sounding **09** statement, utterance **10** expression **11** affirmation, declaration, proposition **12** announcement, articulation, proclamation, promulgation, vocalization **13** pronunciation

**envelop**
◇ *containment indicator* **04** hide, pack, veil, wrap **05** cloak, cover **06** encase, enfold, engulf, enwrap, muffle, shroud, swathe, wrap up **07** blanket, conceal, enclose, obscure, smother **08** encircle, enshroud, surround **09** encompass, enwreathe, inwreathe

**envelope**
**03** sae **04** case, skin, wrap **05** cover, frank, shell **06** casing, entire, gasbag, holder, jacket, sachet, sheath, sleeve

**07** coating, utricle, wrapper **08** covering, Jiffy bag®, wrapping **09** involucre

**enviable**
**04** fine **05** lucky **07** blessed **08** favoured **09** desirable, excellent, fortunate, invidious **10** attractive, privileged **11** sought-after **12** advantageous

**envious**
**05** green **07** jealous **08** covetous, grudging, spiteful **09** green-eyed, jaundiced, resentful **10** begrudging **12** dissatisfied **13** green with envy

**enviously**
**08** with envy **09** jealously **10** covetously, desirously, grudgingly **11** resentfully **12** begrudgingly

**environment**
**04** Gaia, mood **05** earth, scene, world **06** domain, locale, medium, milieu, nature **07** climate, context, element, habitat, setting **08** ambiance, ambience, creation **09** situation, territory **10** atmosphere, background, conditions, influences **11** mother earth **12** mother nature, natural world, surroundings **13** circumstances **15** the lie of the land

*Environmental problems include:*

**06** litter
**07** drought
**08** acid rain, landfill, oil slick, oil spill
**09** pollution
**10** extinction, fossil fuel, toxic waste
**11** soil erosion
**12** air pollution, nuclear waste
**13** climate change, deforestation, global dimming, global warming, water shortage
**14** light pollution, ozone depletion, water pollution
**15** desertification, greenhouse gases

**environmentalist**
**05** green **06** econut **07** greenie **08** ecofreak **09** ecologist **10** tree-hugger **15** conservationist, preservationist
• **environmentalists 03** FOE **10** Green Party

**environs**
**07** suburbs **08** district, locality, purlieus, vicinage, vicinity **09** outskirts, precincts **12** surroundings **13** neighbourhood **15** circumjacencies, surrounding area

**envisage**
**03** see **05** image **07** foresee, imagine, picture, predict, think of **08** envision **09** see coming, visualize **10** anticipate, conceive of **11** contemplate, preconceive

**envision**
**03** see **07** imagine, picture, think of **08** envisage **09** see coming, visualize **11** contemplate

**envoy**
**05** agent **06** consul, deputy, legate **07** attaché, courier, plenipo **08** delegate, diplomat, emissary,

mediator, minister **09** go-between, messenger **10** ambassador **12** intermediary **14** representative **15** plenipotentiary

**envy**
**05** covet, crave, spite **06** desire, grudge, malice, resent **07** ill-will **08** begrudge, jealousy **09** hostility **10** resentment **12** covetousness **13** resentfulness **15** dissatisfaction

**enzyme**

*Enzymes include:*

**05** DNase, lyase, renin, RNase
**06** cytase, kinase, ligase, lipase, papain, pepsin, rennin, zymase
**07** amylase, emulsin, erepsin, inulase, lactase, maltase, oxidase, pepsine, plasmin, trypsin, uricase
**08** bromelin, catalase, ceramide, elastase, esterase, lysozyme, nuclease, permease, protease, thrombin
**09** amylopsin, aromatase, bromelain, cellulase, coagulase, hydrolase, invertase, isomerase, peptidase, reductase, urokinase
**10** insulinase, luciferase, peroxidase, polymerase, sulphatase, telomerase, tyrosinase
**11** collagenase, glutaminase, histaminase, hydrogenase, lecithinase, nitrogenase, phosphatase, transferase, transposase
**12** alpha amylase, asparaginase, chymotrypsin, endonuclease, fibrinolysin, ribonuclease, transaminase
**13** decarboxylase, dehydrogenase, DNA polymerase, neuraminidase, penicillinase, phosphorylase, RNA polymerase, streptokinase, thrombokinase, transcriptase
**14** cholinesterase, thromboplastin

**Eos**
**06** Aurora

**ephemeral**
**05** brief, short **07** fungous, passing **08** fleeting, flitting **09** fugacious, momentary, temporary, transient **10** evanescent, short-lived, transitory **11** impermanent

**epic**
**04** epos, huge, long, myth, saga, vast **05** grand, great, Iliad, large, lofty **06** epopee, heroic, legend **07** Dunciad, exalted, history, Homeric, Odyssey, romance, sublime **08** colossal, elevated, epopoeia, imposing, Kalevala, long poem, majestic, Ramayana, rhapsody **09** ambitious, colubriad, long story, narrative **10** heroic poem, impressive, large-scale **13** grandiloquent

**epicure**
**06** friand **07** friande, glutton, gourmet **08** gourmand, hedonist, Sybarite **09** bon vivant, bon viveur, epicurean **10** gastronome, sensualist, voluptuary **11** connoisseur, gastronomer

## epicurean
**04** lush **07** gourmet, sensual **08** luscious
**09** libertine, luxurious, Sybaritic
**10** gluttonous, hedonistic, sensualist,
voluptuous **11** gastronomic
**12** gormandizing, unrestrained **13** self-
indulgent

## epidemic
**04** pest, rash, rife, rise, wave **05** spate
**06** growth, plague, spread **07** endemic,
rampant, scourge, upsurge **08** increase,
outbreak, pandemia, pandemic,
sweeping **09** extensive, pervasive,
prevalent **10** prevailing, widespread
**11** wide-ranging

## epigram
**03** pun **04** quip **05** gnome, maxim
**06** bon mot, saying **07** proverb
**08** aphorism **09** witticism
**10** apophthegm **11** old chestnut, play
on words

## epigrammatic
**05** brief, pithy, sharp, short, terse, witty
**06** ironic **07** concise, laconic, piquant,
pointed, pungent **08** incisive, succinct
**10** aphoristic

## epilepsy
**08** eclampsy, grand mal, petit mal
**09** eclampsia **15** falling sickness
• **sensation before epilepsy** **04** aura

## epilogue
**02** PS **04** coda **08** appendix, swan song
**09** afterword **10** conclusion, postscript

## episcopate
**03** see

## episode
**03** fit **04** bout, part **05** event, scene,
spasm, spell **06** affair, attack, matter,
period **07** chapter, passage, section
**08** business, incident, occasion
**09** adventure, happening
**10** experience, instalment, occurrence
**12** circumstance

## episodic
**08** periodic, sporadic **09** anecdotal,
irregular, spasmodic **10** digressive,
disjointed, occasional, picaresque
**12** disconnected, intermittent

## epistle
**02** Ep **04** Epis, line, note **06** letter
**07** message, missive, preface
**08** bulletin **10** encyclical
**13** communication **14** correspondence

## epitaph
**03** RIP **05** elegy **08** obituary
**11** inscription, rest in peace
**13** commemoration **14** funeral oration

## epithet
**03** tag **04** name, term **05** title **06** byname, to-name **08** cognomen,
nickname **09** apathaton, sobriquet
**10** expression **11** appellation,
description, designation
**12** denomination

## epitome
**04** type **05** model **06** digest, précis,
résumé **07** essence, example, outline,
summary **08** abstract, exemplar,
synopsis **09** archetype, prototype

**10** abridgment, embodiment
**11** abridgement **12** quintessence
**14** representation **15** personification

## epitomize
**03** cut, pot **05** sum up **06** embody,
précis, reduce, typify **07** abridge,
curtail, shorten **08** abstract, compress,
condense, contract **09** exemplify,
incarnate, personify, represent,
summarize, symbolize **10** abbreviate,
illustrate **11** encapsulate, incorporate

## epoch
**03** age, era **04** date, span, time
**06** period

*See also* **geology**

## equable
**04** calm, even **05** equal **06** placid,
serene, smooth, stable, steady
**07** regular, unfazed, uniform
**08** composed, constant, laid-back,
moderate, tranquil **09** easy-going,
temperate, unvarying **10** consistent,
even-minded, unchanging **11** level-
headed, unexcitable, unflappable
**12** even-tempered **13** imperturbable

## equably
**06** calmly **08** placidly, serenely
**10** tranquilly **11** unexcitably **13** level-
headedly

## equal
**02** eq **03** fit, par **04** able, egal, even,
fair, fear, feer, fere, just, like, maik,
make, mate, peer, twin, view **05** alike,
feare, fiere, level, match, reach, rival,
total **06** fellow, pheere, strong, suited
**07** add up to, balance, capable,
coequal, compeer, contend, emulate,
matched, neutral, peregal, regular, the
same, uniform **08** adequate, amount
to, balanced, come up to, constant,
corrival, equalize, parallel, suitable,
unbiased **09** competent, identical,
impartial, match up to, semblable,
tally with, unvarying **10** be as good as,
comparable, equate with, equivalent,
even-steven, fifty-fifty, keep up with,
square with, sufficient, unchanging
**11** be a match for, be level with, be the
same as, compare with, counterpart,
even-stevens, measure up to, neck and
neck, non-partisan, symmetrical **12** be
on a par with, coincide with,
commensurate, correspond to, well
balanced **13** corresponding, evenly
matched **14** be equivalent to

## equality
**03** par, tie **05** match **06** owelty, parage,
parity **07** balance, egality, justice
**08** evenness, fairness, identity,
likeness, rivality, sameness, symmetry
**10** neutrality, proportion, similarity,
uniformity **11** equal rights,
equivalence, parallelism
**12** impartiality, partisanship
**13** comparability **14** correspondence,
egalitarianism

## equalization
**08** matching **09** balancing, levelling
**10** evening-out **12** compensation
**15** standardization

## equalize
**05** equal, level, match **06** equate, even
up, smooth, square **07** balance, even
out **08** keep pace, make even **09** draw
level **10** compensate, regularize
**11** standardize

## equally
**02** as **05** alike **06** evenly, fairly, just as,
justly **07** ex aequo **08** likewise
**09** similarly, uniformly **11** as important
**12** in like manner, in the same way, on
equal terms **14** by the same token,
proportionally **15** correspondingly,
proportionately

## equanimity
**04** calm, ease **05** poise **06** aplomb
**07** dignity **08** calmness, coolness,
serenity **09** assurance, composure,
placidity, sangfroid **10** confidence
**11** impassivity, self-control
**12** tranquillity **13** self-assurance **14** self-
possession, unflappability **15** level-
headedness

## equate
**06** offset **07** balance, be equal,
compare, liken to **08** equalize, link
with, pair with, parallel **09** agree with,
compare to, match with, tally with
**10** square with **11** compare with,
connect with **12** correspond to,
identify with **13** juxtapose with
**14** correspond with **15** bracket
together, regard as the same

## equation
**02** eq **05** cubic, match **07** pairing
**08** equality, identity, likeness,
matching, parallel **09** agreement,
balancing, quadratic **10** comparison,
similarity **11** calculation, equivalence
**13** juxtaposition **14** correspondence,
identification

## equator
**07** the line **11** aclinic line
• **near the equator** **03** low

## Equatorial Guinea
**03** GNQ

## equestrian
**05** rider **06** cowboy, equine, herder,
hussar, jockey, knight, riding
**07** courier, cowgirl, mounted, rancher,
trooper **08** cavalier, horseman
**10** cavalryman, horse-rider,
horsewoman **11** horse-riding

*Equestrians and showjumpers
include:*

**03** Hoy (Andrew), Hoy (Bettina)
**04** Anne (Princess), Leng (Virginia),
Tait (Blyth), Todd (Mark)
**05** Green (Lucinda), Meade (Richard),
Smith (Harvey)
**06** Astley (Philip), Broome (David),
D'Inzeo (Raimondo), Klimke
(Reiner), Smythe (Pat)
**07** Winkler (Hans-Günther)
**08** Phillips (Mark), Whitaker (John),
Whitaker (Michael)

*See also* **horseman, horsewoman**

## equilibrium
**05** poise **06** aplomb, stasis **07** balance,
dignity **08** calmness, coolness,

evenness, serenity, symmetry
**09** assurance, composure, equipoise, sangfroid, stability **10** confidence, equanimity, steadiness **11** self-control **12** counterpoise, tranquillity **13** self-assurance **14** self-possession, unflappability **15** level-headedness

### equip
**03** arm, fit, rig **04** tool **05** array, dight, dress, endow, fit up, issue, rig up, stock **06** aguise, aguize, clothe, fit out, kit out, outfit, supply **07** apparel, appoint, bedight, deck out, furnish, prepare, provide **08** accouter, accoutre, equipage **10** accomplish

### equipment
**03** kit, rig **04** gear **05** stock, stuff, tools **06** doings, graith, outfit, rig-out, tackle, things **07** baggage, battery, clobber, fixings, luggage **08** articles, hardware, material, materiel, supplies **09** apparatus, furniture, inventory **10** appliances **11** accessories, apparelment, furnishings **12** appointments **13** accoutrements, paraphernalia
*See also* **farm; gardening; laboratory; medical; office; photographic; plumbing; sport**

### equipoise
**05** poise **07** balance, ballast **08** evenness, symmetry **09** libration, stability **10** steadiness **11** equibalance, equilibrium **12** counterpoise **13** counter-weight **14** counterbalance, equiponderance

### equitable
**03** due **04** fair, just **05** equal, right **06** honest, proper, square **07** ethical **08** rightful, unbiased **09** impartial, objective **10** even-handed, legitimate, reasonable **12** unprejudiced **13** disinterested, dispassionate, fair-and-square

### equitably
**06** fairly, justly **07** ex aequo **08** honestly **09** ethically **10** reasonably, rightfully **11** impartially **12** even-handedly **15** disinterestedly, dispassionately

### equity
**05** right **06** square **07** honesty, justice **08** fairness, fair play, justness **09** integrity, rectitude **11** objectivity, uprightness **12** impartiality **13** equitableness, righteousness **14** even-handedness, fair-mindedness, reasonableness

### equivalence
**06** amount, parity **08** equality, identity, likeness, parallel, sameness **09** agreement **10** conformity, similarity **11** correlation **13** comparability, identicalness **14** correspondence

### equivalent
**02** eq **04** even, like, peer, same, twin **05** alike, equal, match, value **06** double, fellow **07** similar **08** parallel **09** homologue, identical **10** comparable, homologous, tantamount **11** alternative, correlative, counterpart, equipollent

**12** commensurate **13** correspondent, corresponding, substitutable **14** opposite number **15** interchangeable

### equivocal
**05** fishy, vague **07** dubious, evasive, oblique, obscure **08** oracular **09** ambiguous, confusing, oraculous, uncertain **10** ambivalent, homonymous, indefinite, misleading, suspicious **12** questionable

### equivocate
**05** dodge, evade, fence, hedge, mudge **06** boggle, palter, waffle, weasel **07** mislead **09** pussyfoot, vacillate **11** prevaricate **12** shilly-shally, tergiversate **13** chop and change, hedge your bets **14** change your mind, change your tune

### equivocation
**06** waffle **07** evasion, flannel, hedging **08** shifting **09** quibbling, shuffling **10** double talk **11** weasel words **12** pussyfooting **13** prevarication **14** tergiversation **15** dodging the issue

### era
**03** age, day **04** aeon, date, days, time **05** cycle, epoch, stage, times **06** period, season **07** century **10** generation
*See also* **geology**
• **bygone era 02** BC
• **common era 02** CE
• **current era 02** AD

### eradicate
**04** root, wipe **05** erase **06** efface, remove, uproot **07** abolish, destroy, expunge, root out, weed out, wipe out **08** get rid of, stamp out, suppress **09** eliminate, extirpate **10** annihilate, do away with, extinguish, obliterate **11** crack down on, exterminate

### eradication
**07** removal **08** riddance **09** abolition **10** effacement, expunction, extinction **11** destruction, elimination, extirpation, suppression **12** annihilation, deracination, obliteration **13** extermination

### erasable
**08** washable **09** removable **10** effaceable, eradicable

### erase
**03** rub, zap **04** race, rase, raze **06** cancel, delete, efface, excise, remove, rub off, rub out, scrape **07** blot out, destroy, expunge, rub away, scratch, wipe out **08** get rid of **09** eradicate **10** obliterate, scratch out

### erasure
**06** rasure, razure **07** removal **08** deletion **09** cleansing, erasement, wiping-out **10** effacement, expunction, rubbing-out **11** blotting-out, elimination, eradication **12** cancellation, obliteration

### erbium
**02** Er

### erect
**04** firm, form, hard, lift, rear **05** build,

dress, found, mount, on end, pitch, prick, put up, raise, right, rigid, set up, stiff **06** create, raised **07** elevate, prick up, stand-up, upright **08** assemble, initiate, organize, standing, straight, vertical **09** construct, displayed, establish, institute, tumescent **10** upstanding **11** orthostatic, put together **13** perpendicular, straight-pight

### erection
**04** pile **07** edifice, raising **08** assembly, building, creation, priapism, rigidity **09** elevation, stiffness, structure **10** tumescence **11** fabrication, manufacture **12** construction **13** establishment

### ergo
**02** so **04** then, thus **05** argal, hence **09** therefore **11** accordingly **12** consequently **13** for this reason, in consequence

### Erica
**04** ling **07** heather

### Eritrea
**03** ERI

### erode
**05** spoil **06** abrade **07** consume, corrode, degrade, deplete, destroy, eat away, eat into **08** fragment, wear away, wear down **09** excoriate, grind down, undermine **11** deteriorate **12** disintegrate

### Eros
**05** Cupid

### erosion
**04** wash, wear **07** wash-out **08** abrasion, scouring, wash-away **09** attrition, corrosion **10** denudation **11** degradation, destruction, excoriation, undermining, wearing away **13** deterioration **14** disintegration

### erotic
**03** hot **04** blue, go-go, sexy **05** adult, dirty, horny **06** carnal, steamy **07** amatory, amorous, lustful, raunchy, sensual **08** erogenic, venereal **09** erogenous, seductive **10** lascivious, suggestive, voluptuous **11** Anacreontic, aphrodisiac, stimulating, titillating **12** pornographic

### erotically
**08** steamily **09** raunchily, sensually **10** explicitly **11** seductively **12** suggestively **15** anacreontically

### err
◇ *anagram indicator* **03** sin **04** boob, flub, goof **05** fluff **06** cock up, duff it, goof up, mess up, offend, slip up, wander **07** be wrong, blunder, deviate, do wrong, louse up, mistake, screw up, stumble **08** go astray, misjudge **09** make a slip, misbehave **10** transgress **11** be incorrect, make a booboo, misconstrue **12** come a cropper, drop a clanger, make a mistake, miscalculate **13** fall from grace, misunderstand **15** put your foot in it

## errand

**03** job **04** duty, task **05** chore **06** charge **07** message, mission **10** assignment, commission **11** undertaking
• **person who runs errands** **03** cad **05** caddy, cadee, cadie **06** caddie **07** express, galopin **10** message-boy **11** message-girl **13** printer's devil

## errant

◇ *anagram indicator* **05** loose, stray, wrong **06** erring, roving, sinful **07** deviant, lawless, nomadic, peccant, roaming, sinning, wayward **08** aberrant, criminal, quixotic, rambling, straying, thorough **09** itinerant, offending, wandering **10** journeying **11** disobedient, peripatetic

## erratic

◇ *anagram indicator* **06** fitful **07** vagrant, varying **08** aberrant, abnormal, shifting, sporadic, unstable, unsteady, variable, volatile **09** desultory, eccentric, irregular, planetary, unsettled, wandering **10** capricious, changeable, inconstant, meandering, unbalanced, unreliable **11** fluctuating **12** inconsistent, intermittent **13** unpredictable

## erratically

◇ *anagram indicator* **08** fitfully, variably **10** changeably, unreliably **11** irregularly **12** inconstantly, sporadically **13** unpredictably **14** inconsistently, intermittently

## erring

◇ *anagram indicator* **05** loose, stray, wrong **06** errant, guilty, sinful **07** deviant, devious, lawless, peccant, sinning, wayward **08** criminal, culpable, straying **09** misguided, offending, wandering **11** disobedient

## erroneous

◇ *anagram indicator* **05** false, wrong **06** erring, faulty, flawed, untrue **07** inexact, invalid **08** mistaken, specious, spurious, straying **09** illogical, incorrect, misguided, misplaced, unfounded, wandering **10** fallacious, inaccurate

## error

◇ *anagram indicator* **04** boob, flaw, flub, goof, miss, slip, typo **05** fault, fluff, gaffe, lapse, mix-up, wrong **06** booboo, cock-up, foul-up, glitch, hickey, howler, slip-up **07** blooper, blunder, clanger, erratum, fallacy, faux pas, jeofail, literal, miscopy, mistake, own goal, stuff-up **08** delusion, mesprize, misprint, omission, solecism **09** oversight **10** aberration, inaccuracy **11** misjudgment **12** misjudgement **13** misconception **14** miscalculation **15** misapprehension, slip of the tongue, spelling mistake
• **errors excepted** **02** EE
• **in error** **03** out **07** falsely, wrongly **08** unfairly, unjustly **09** by mistake **10** mistakenly **11** erroneously, incorrectly, misguidedly **12** fallaciously, inaccurately

**15** inappropriately
• **sign of error** **01** X

## ersatz

**04** fake, sham **05** bogus **06** phoney **07** man-made **09** imitation, simulated, synthetic **10** artificial, substitute **11** counterfeit

## erstwhile

**02** ex **03** old **04** late, once, past **06** bygone, former **07** one-time **08** previous, sometime

## erudite

**04** wise **06** brainy **07** learned **08** academic, cultured, educated, highbrow, lettered, literate, profound, well-read **09** scholarly **12** intellectual, well-educated **13** knowledgeable

## erudition

**05** facts **06** wisdom **07** culture, letters **08** learning **09** education, knowledge **10** profundity **11** learnedness, scholarship **13** reconditeness, scholarliness

## erupt

◇ *anagram indicator* **04** emit, gush, spew, vent **05** belch, burst, eject, expel, spout **06** blow up **07** come out, explode, flare up **08** break out, emit lava **09** burst open, discharge, pour forth **13** discharge lava, pour forth lava

## eruption

◇ *anagram indicator* **04** rash, spot **06** blow-up, eczema, lichen, red gum, tetter **07** ecthyma, flare-up, morphew, prurigo, Purpura, venting **08** ejection, emission, empyesis, exanthem, malander, outbreak, outburst, rose drop **09** discharge, emphlysis, exanthema, explosion, mallander, mallender, pompholyx, salt rheum **12** inflammation

## erysipelas

**04** rose **10** sideration **14** St Anthony's fire

## escalate

**04** grow, rise, soar **05** climb, mount, raise **06** ascend, expand, extend, rocket, spiral, step up **07** amplify, develop, enlarge, magnify, shoot up **08** heighten, increase, mushroom **09** intensify **10** accelerate, hit the roof

## escalation

**04** rise **06** growth **07** soaring **08** increase **09** expansion, extension **11** development, heightening, mushrooming **12** acceleration **13** magnification **15** intensification

## escalator

**04** lift **08** elevator **10** travelator, travolator **13** moving walkway **15** moving staircase

## escapable

**08** eludible, evadable **09** avertible, avoidable

## escapade

**04** hoot, lark, ploy, romp **05** antic, caper, fling, prank, scape, spree, stunt, trick **06** escape, frolic, scheme, splore **07** exploit **08** escapado, fredaine

**09** adventure, excursion **10** skylarking **11** monkey shine

## escape

**03** esc, fly, lam, out **04** bolt, bunk, duck, flee, flit, flow, go-by, gush, hole, leak, ooze, pass, scat, seep, shun, skip, slip, vent **05** avoid, break, ditch, dodge, drain, elope, elude, evade, issue, lam it, leg it, prank, sally, scape, scoot, scram, spurt **06** blower, decamp, efflux, flight, forget, get off, outlet **07** abscond, bail out, do a bunk, dodging, ducking, evasion, fantasy, get away, getaway, leakage, not know, outflow, outpour, overrun, pastime, pour out, run away, scarper, seepage, trickle, wilding **08** break out, breakout, dreaming, emission, escapism, loophole, not place, run for it, shake off, sidestep, slip away **09** avoidance, breakaway, break free, cut and run, discharge, diversion, do a runner, emanation, jailbreak, pour forth **10** absconding, break loose, circumvent, decampment, have it away, hop the twig, Houdini act, recreation, relaxation **11** distraction, fantasizing, safety-valve **12** steer clear of **13** circumvention, extravasation, not be recalled, transgression **14** make a bolt for it, make your escape, run for your life, take it on the lam, take to the boats **15** make a break for it, make your getaway, not be remembered, take to your heels, wishful thinking
• **allow to escape** **03** let **04** vent
• **means of escape** **04** hole, loop **08** loophole
• **way of escape** **03** out **04** mews, muse **05** meuse **06** get-out **08** bolthole

## escapee

**06** truant **07** escaper, refugee, runaway **08** defector, deserter, fugitive **09** absconder **11** jailbreaker

## escapism

**07** fantasy, pastime **08** dreaming **09** diversion **10** recreation, relaxation **11** distraction, fantasizing, pie in the sky, safety-valve **15** castles in the air, wishful thinking

## escapist

**07** dreamer, ostrich **09** Billy Liar **10** daydreamer, Don Quixote, fantasizer, non-realist **11** Walter Mitty **14** wishful thinker

## eschew

**04** shun **05** avoid, forgo, spurn **06** abjure, forego, give up **07** abandon, disdain **08** forswear, renounce **09** repudiate **11** abstain from, keep clear of, refrain from

## escort

**03** see, set **04** aide, beau, date, hand, lead, take, tend, wait, walk **05** bring, guard, guide, suite, train, usher **06** convoy, defend, gigolo, squire **07** company, conduct, cortège, esquire, janizar, partner, protect, retinue, take out **08** arm candy, attend on, chaperon, come with, defender, janizary, shepherd, take down **09** accompany, attendant, bodyguard, chaperone, companion, entourage, janissary, protector **10** attendance, attendants, javelin-man **13** come along with, guard of honour

## esoteric

**05** inner **06** arcane, hidden, inside, mystic, occult, Orphic, secret **07** cryptic, obscure, private **08** abstruse, mystical, rarefied **09** recondite **10** acroamatic, mysterious **11** inscrutable **12** acroamatical, confidential

## esparto grass

**04** alfa **05** halfa

## especial

**06** marked, signal, unique **07** express, notable, special, unusual **08** peculiar, singular, specific, striking, uncommon **09** exclusive, principal **10** noteworthy, particular, pre-eminent, remarkable **11** distinctive, exceptional, outstanding **13** distinguished, extraordinary

## especially

**03** esp **04** very **05** espec **06** mainly, mostly, namely **07** chiefly, largely, notably **08** above all, markedly, uniquely **09** expressly, in special, most of all, primarily, specially, supremely, unusually **10** remarkably, strikingly, uncommonly **11** exclusively, principally **12** in particular, particularly, pre-eminently **13** exceptionally, outstandingly **15** extraordinarily

## espionage

**05** scout **06** spying **07** bugging, probing **08** snooping **10** tradecraft **11** fifth column, penetration, wiretapping **12** infiltration, intelligence, intercepting, surveillance **13** investigation, secret service **14** reconnaissance, undercover work

## espousal

**06** choice **07** backing, defence, support, wedding **08** adoption, advocacy, taking-up **09** embracing, promotion **11** championing, maintenance **12** championship

## espouse

**04** back **05** adopt **06** choose, defend, opt for, take up **07** embrace, support **08** advocate, champion, maintain **09** patronize **10** stand up for

## esprit de corps

**10** team spirit **12** group loyalty, mutal respect, public spirit **13** mutual feeling

## espy

**03** see, spy **04** spot **05** sight, watch **06** behold, descry, detect, notice **07** discern, glimpse, make out, observe **08** discover, perceive **11** distinguish **12** catch sight of

## essay

**02** go **03** try **04** bash, push, shot, stab, test **05** assay, crack, go for, offer, paper, piece, study, theme, tract, trial **06** leader, review, sketch, strain, strive, tackle, take on, thesis **07** article, attempt, have a go, venture **08** causerie, critique, struggle, treatise

**09** discourse, endeavour, have a bash, have a stab, prolusion, undertake **10** assignment, commentary, experiment, have a crack **11** composition **12** disquisition, dissertation

## essayist

*Essayists include:*

**04** Greg (William Rathbone), Hunt (Leigh), Lamb (Charles), Lynd (Robert), Rodó (José Enrique)
**05** Bacon (Francis), Gould (Stephen Jay), Lucas (Edward Verrall), Pater (Walter Horatio), Smith (Sydney), White (E B)
**06** Borges (Jorge Luis), Breton (André), Orwell (George), Ruskin (John), Steele (Sir Richard)
**07** Addison (Joseph), Calvino (Italo), Carlyle (Thomas), Chapone (Hester), Emerson (Ralph Waldo), Hayward (Abraham), Hazlitt (William), Lazarus (Emma), Meynell (Alice Christiana Gertrude), Montagu (Lady Mary Wortley), Thoreau (Henry David)
**08** Beerbohm (Sir Max), Macaulay (Thomas Babington, Lord)
**09** De Quincey (Thomas), Dickinson (Goldsworthy Lowes), Montaigne (Michel Eyquem de)
**10** Chesterton (G K), Crèvecoeur (Michel Guillaume Jean de)
**12** Quiller-Couch (Sir Arthur)

## essence

**03** nub **04** alma, core, crux, esse, life, otto, pith, soul **05** being, heart, juice, point, stuff **06** centre, entity, kernel, marrow, nature, spirit **07** alcohol, extract, meaning, quality, quiddit, ratafia, reality, spirits **08** bergamot, quiddity, whatness **09** actuality, character, principle, substance **10** attributes, distillate, heart-blood, hypostasis, ylang-ylang **11** concentrate, heart's-blood **12** distillation, quintessence, significance **13** concentration, individuation, ylang-ylang oil **15** characteristics, sum and substance
• **in essence 07** in grain **08** at bottom **09** basically **11** essentially **13** fundamentally, substantially
• **of the essence 05** vital **06** needed **07** crucial **08** required **09** essential, important, necessary, requisite **13** indispensable

## essential

**03** key **04** gist, main, must, pure **05** basic, vital **06** formal, innate, needed **07** central, crucial, typical **08** inherent, key point, required, rudiment **09** important, intrinsic, key points, main point, necessary, necessity, principal, principle, requisite **10** definitive, imperative, main points, sine qua non, underlying **11** constituent, fundamental, requirement, substantial **12** all-important, constitutive, prerequisite **13** indispensable **14** characteristic

## essentially

**05** per se **07** at heart **08** deep down **09** basically, in essence, primarily **10** inherently **13** fundamentally, intrinsically

## establish

**03** fix **04** base, form, haft, make, open, seat, show **05** begin, build, edify, erect, found, lodge, pitch, plant, prove, raise, set up, start, state, stell **06** affirm, attest, create, ordain, ratify, secure, settle, verify **07** certify, confirm, install, start up **08** nail down, organize, validate **09** institute, introduce **10** constitute, inaugurate **11** corroborate, demonstrate **12** authenticate, substantiate **14** bring into being

## established

**03** est, set **05** fixed **06** proved, proven, rooted, secure, stable, stated **07** settled **08** accepted, radicate, ratified, standing **09** ensconced, radicated, respected, steadfast **10** entrenched **11** experienced, traditional **12** conventional **14** tried and tested
• **to be established 04** root **06** obtain

## establishment

**02** CE **03** fix **04** firm, shop, them **05** store **07** company, concern, forming **08** business, creation, founding **09** formation, inception, institute, setting up, the system **10** enterprise, foundation **11** corporation, down-sitting, institution, ruling class **12** inauguration, installation, organization **13** the government **14** the authorities **15** the powers that be

## estate

**03** pen **04** alod, area, land, odal, park, rank, site, udal **05** allod, class, goods, lands, manor, place, state, taluk, tract, trust **06** assets, centre, domain, entail, having, realty, region, status **07** demesne, effects, grounds, havings **08** allodium, executry, hacienda, holdings, position, property, standing **09** condition, patrimony, princedom, situation **10** belongings, latifundia, personalty, plantation, real estate **11** development, landholding, possessions **14** conditional fee

## estate agent

**07** realtor **09** land agent **13** property agent **15** real-estate agent

## esteem

**03** way **04** deem, have, hold, love, pass, rate, view **05** compt, count, favor, izzat, judge, prise, prize, set by, store, think, value **06** admire, credit, favour, honour, make of, reckon, regard, revere **07** account, adjudge, believe, cherish, respect, set down **08** consider, judgment, treasure, venerate **09** judgement, reckoning, reverence **10** admiration, estimation, veneration **11** approbation, good opinion **12** appreciation, regard highly **13** consideration, put a premium on

## esteemed

**06** prized, valued, worthy **07** admired, revered **08** favorite, honoured, precious **09** admirable, excellent, favourite, of warrant, reputable, respected, treasured, venerated **10** honourable **11** prestigious, respectable **13** distinguished, of good warrant, well-respected, well-thought-of **14** highly regarded

**estimable**
**04** good **06** valued, worthy **07** notable **08** esteemed, laudable, valuable **09** admirable, excellent, reputable, respected **10** creditable, honourable, noteworthy, worthwhile **11** commendable, meritorious, respectable, warrantable **12** praiseworthy **13** distinguished

**estimate**
**03** aim **04** cost, gage, rate, view **05** carat, gauge, guess, judge, level, value, weigh **06** assess, belief, carrat, reckon, strike **07** compute, opinion **08** appraise, evaluate, judgment, thinking **09** calculate, guesswork, judgement, quotation, reckoning, valuation **10** appreciate, assessment, conclusion, conjecture, estimation, evaluation, reputation, rough guess **11** calculation, computation, guesstimate **13** approximation, consideration **14** ballpark figure **15** approximate cost

**estimated**
**03** est

**estimation**
**04** rate, view **05** guess, honor, sight, stock **06** belief, credit, esteem, honour, regard **07** account, feeling, opinion, respect **08** estimate, judgment, thinking **09** judgement, reckoning, valuation **10** assessment, conception, conclusion, conjecture, evaluation, importance, reputation, rough guess **11** calculation, computation **12** appreciation **13** consideration, way of thinking **15** approximate cost

**Estonia**
**03** EST

**estrange**
**04** part **05** alien, sever **06** cut off, divide, remove **07** break up, divorce, split up **08** alienate, disunite, separate, withdraw, withhold **09** disaffect **10** antagonize, drive apart, set against **13** set at variance

**estranged**
**05** alien, apart, fraim, fremd **06** fremit **07** aliened, divided **08** alienate, divorced, separate **09** alienated, separated **11** antagonized, disaffected

**estrangement**
**05** split **06** breach **07** break-up, parting **08** disunion, disunity, division **09** antipathy, hostility, severance **10** alienation, antagonism, separation, withdrawal **11** withholding **12** disaffection, dissociation **14** unfriendliness

**estuary**
**03** arm, bay, Est **04** cove **05** creek, fiord, firth, fjord, inlet, mouth **07** sea-loch

**et cetera**
**03** etc **04** et al **07** and so on **10** and all that, and so forth, and the like, and the rest, or whatever **11** and suchlike, and whatever **14** and what have you

**etch**
**03** cut, dig **04** bite, burn **05** carve, eat in, stamp **06** furrow, groove, incise **07** corrode, eat away, engrave, impress, imprint, ingrain **08** inscribe

**etching**
**03** cut **05** print **06** sketch **07** carving, imprint **08** aquatint **09** aquatinta, engraving **10** aqua fortis, impression **11** inscription

**eternal**
**07** abiding, aeonian, endless, lasting, non-stop, undying **08** constant, enduring, immortal, infinite, timeless, unending **09** ceaseless, deathless, eviternal, incessant, limitless, perennial, perpetual **10** continuous, persistent, relentless, unchanging **11** everlasting, never-ending, remorseless, unremitting **12** imperishable, interminable, unchangeable **14** indestructible

**eternally**
**04** ever **06** always **07** for ever **09** endlessly, lastingly **10** constantly **11** ceaselessly, continually, incessantly, permanently, perpetually **12** interminably **13** everlastingly **14** indestructibly

**eternity**
**03** age, eon **04** aeon, ages **05** yonks **06** heaven **07** forever **08** Ewigkeit, infinity, long time, paradise **09** after-life, hereafter, next world **10** perpetuity **11** ages and ages, endlessness, everlasting, immortality, world to come **12** donkey's years, immutability, timelessness **13** deathlessness **15** everlasting life, everlastingness, imperishability, world without end

**ethereal**
**04** airy, fine **05** light **06** dainty, subtle **07** refined, tenuous **08** delicate, empyreal, empyrean, gossamer, heavenly, rarefied **09** airy-fairy, celestial, elemental, exquisite, spiritual, unearthly, unworldly **10** diaphanous, immaterial, impalpable, intangible **13** insubstantial

**ethical**
**04** fair, good, just **05** moral, noble, right **06** decent, honest, proper, seemly **07** correct, fitting, upright **08** decorous, virtuous **09** righteous **10** high-minded, honourable, principled **11** commendable, responsible **13** above reproach

**ethically**
**05** nobly **06** justly **07** morally, rightly **08** honestly **09** reputably **10** honourably, virtuously **11** responsibly **12** high-mindedly, respectfully **13** ideologically **14** moralistically

**ethics**
**04** code **05** rules **06** equity, morals,

values **07** beliefs **08** morality **09** moral code, propriety, standards **10** conscience, deontology, principles **11** moral values **13** descriptivism, moral theology **14** moral standards **15** moral philosophy, moral principles

**Ethiopia**
**03** ETH

**ethnic**
**04** folk **06** exotic, native, racial, tribal **07** foreign **08** cultural, national, societal **10** aboriginal, indigenous **11** traditional **12** ethnological **13** autochthonous **15** anthropological

**ethnically**
**08** racially, socially, tribally **10** culturally, societally **13** traditionally **14** humanistically

**ethos**
**04** code **05** tenor **06** ethics, spirit **07** beliefs, flavour, manners **08** attitude, morality **09** character, rationale, standards **10** atmosphere, principles **11** disposition

**etiquette**
**04** code, form, kawa **05** rules **07** customs, decency, decorum, manners **08** ceremony, civility, courtesy, good form, protocol **09** propriety, standards **10** politeness **11** convenances, conventions, correctness, formalities, good manners **12** unwritten law **13** code of conduct **14** code of practice **15** code of behaviour

**etymology**
**03** ety **06** origin, source **08** word-lore **09** philology, semantics **10** derivation, lexicology **11** linguistics, word history, word origins

**eucalyptus**
**03** box, gum **05** karri, marri, sally, tuart **06** jarrah, mallee, red gum, sallee, tewart, tooart, wandoo **07** blue gum, gum tree **08** coolabah, coolibah, coolibar, ghost gum, ironbark, sugar gum **09** black butt, bloodwood, fever tree **10** tallow wood, woollybutt **11** mountain ash

**eulogize**
**04** hype, laud, plug **05** exalt, extol **06** honour, praise **07** acclaim, applaud, approve, commend, glorify, magnify **09** celebrate, rave about **10** compliment, panegyrize, wax lyrical **12** congratulate

**eulogy**
**04** laud **05** paean **06** praise **07** acclaim, plaudit, tribute **08** accolade, applause, encomion, encomium **09** laudation, laudative, laudatory, panegyric **10** compliment, exaltation **11** acclamation **12** commendation **13** glorification

**euphemism**
**07** evasion **09** softening **10** genteelism, politeness, polite term, substitute **12** substitution **14** understatement **15** mild alternative
*See also* **oath**

## euphemistic

04 mild 05 vague 06 polite 07 evasive, genteel, neutral 08 indirect 09 soft-toned 10 substitute 11 understated

## euphonious

04 soft 05 clear, sweet 06 dulcet, mellow 07 melodic, musical, silvery, tuneful 08 canorous, euphonic, pleasant 09 consonant, melodious 10 harmonious, sweet-toned 11 dulcifluous, mellifluous, symphonious 12 dulciloquent 13 sweet-sounding

## euphoria

03 joy 04 glee, high, rush 05 bliss 07 ecstasy, elation, rapture 08 buoyancy 09 happiness, transport, wellbeing 10 enthusiasm, exaltation, exultation, jubilation 11 high spirits 12 cheerfulness, exhilaration, intoxication

## euphoric

04 high 05 happy 06 elated, joyful, joyous 07 buoyant, exulted, gleeful 08 blissful, cheerful, ecstatic, exultant, jubilant 09 rapturous 10 enraptured 11 exhilarated, intoxicated 12 enthusiastic

## Europe

*European countries include:*

02 UK
05 Italy, Malta, Spain
06 Cyprus, France, Greece, Latvia, Monaco, Norway, Poland, Russia, Serbia, Sweden, Turkey
07 Albania, Andorra, Austria, Belarus, Belgium, Croatia, Denmark, Estonia, Finland, Georgia, Germany, Hungary, Iceland, Ireland, Moldova, Romania, Ukraine
08 Bulgaria, Portugal, Slovakia, Slovenia
09 Lithuania, Macedonia, San Marino
10 Luxembourg, Montenegro
11 Switzerland, Vatican City
13 Czech Republic, Liechtenstein, United Kingdom
14 The Netherlands
20 Bosnia and Herzegovina

*European landmarks include:*

02 Po
04 Alps, Arno, Como, Etna, Lido, Main, Oder
05 Delos, Eiger, Garda, Loire, Prado, Rhine, Rhône, Seine, Somme, Tiber, Urals, Volga
06 Azores, Dachau, Danube, Delphi, Fátima, Geysir, Liffey, Rhodes, Tatras, Tivoli
07 Algarve, Kremlin, Lapland, La Scala, Madeira, Moselle, Pompeii, Shannon, Siberia
08 Alhambra, Ardennes, Auvergne, Canaries, Caucasus, Dordogne, Jungfrau, Lake Como, Legoland, Oude Kerk, Pantheon, Provence, Pyrenees, St Peter's, Strokkur, Tenerife, Vesuvius
09 Acropolis, Balearics, Bantry Bay,

Campanile, Colosseum, Connemara, Dolomites, Dublin Bay, Keukenhof, Lake Garda, Lanzarote, Menin Gate, Mont Blanc, Mount Etna, Notre Dame, Parc Güell, Parthenon, Red Square, Reichstag, Temple Bar, Zuider Zee
10 Bran Castle, Grand Canal, IJsselmeer, Interlaken, Julian Alps, Lake Geneva, Lenin's tomb, Matterhorn, Nieuwe Kerk, Pont du Gard, Rubenshuis, Schönbrunn, Versailles, Wienerwald
11 Afsluitdijk, Black Forest, Eiffel Tower, Königsplatz, Manneken Pis, Mount Elbrus, Rijksmuseum, Simplon Pass, Vatican City, Vienna Woods
12 Abbey Theatre, Bavarian Alps, Blarney Stone, Frauenkirche, Lake Maggiore, Leaning Tower, Mont St Michel, Mount Olympus, Mozart's House, Ponte Vecchio, Rialto Bridge, Rubens's House, Summer Palace, Tower of Belém, Winter Palace
13 Anne Frank Huis, Arc de Triomphe, Bridge of Sighs, Canary Islands, Ha'penny Bridge, Lake Constance, Little Mermaid, Massif Central, Millau Viaduct, Mount Vesuvius, Museo del Prado, Oresund Bridge, Sistine Chapel, St Mark's Square, Uffizi Gallery, Ural Mountains, Vatican Palace
14 Bolshoi Theatre, Mount Parnassus, O'Connell Street, Palazzo Vecchio, Piazza San Marco, Potsdamer Platz, Sagrada Familia, Trinity College
15 Anne Frank's house, Balearic Islands, Brandenburg Gate, Dingle Peninsula, Hermitage Museum, Rock of Gibraltar, Stedelijk Museum

## European

◇ *foreign word indicator* 01 E 03 Eur 04 Euro

*Europeans include:*

04 Balt, Brit, Dane, Esth, Finn, Flem, Lapp, Pict, Pole, Scot, Serb, Slav, Turk
05 Angle, Croat, Czech, Greek, Latin, Swede, Swiss, Vlach
06 Almain, Basque, Briton, German, Nordic, Sabine, Salian, Teuton, Zyrian
07 Belgian, Bosnian, Cypriot, Fleming, Iberian, Italian, Latvian, Lombard, Maltese, Manxman, Monacan, Russian, Samnite, Serbian, Walloon
08 Albanian, Andorran, Austrian, Croatian, Dutchman, Estonian, Irishman, Moldovan, Romanian, Scotsman, Siberian, Silurian, Spaniard, Welshman
09 Britisher, Bulgarian, Englander, Englisher, Frenchman, Hungarian, Icelander,

Manxwoman, Norwegian, Sardinian, Slovakian, Slovenian, Ukrainian
10 Anglo-Saxon, Belarusian, Dutchwoman, Englishman, Irishwoman, Lithuanian, Macedonian, Monégasque, Portuguese, Welshwoman
11 Belarussian, Frenchwoman, Montenegrin, Sammarinese
12 Luxembourger, Scandinavian
13 Herzegovinian
15 Liechtensteiner

• **European Union** 02 EU

*European Union member countries include:*

05 Italy, Malta, Spain
06 Cyprus, France, Greece, Latvia, Poland, Sweden
07 Austria, Belgium, Denmark, Estonia, Finland, Germany, Hungary, Ireland, Romania
08 Bulgaria, Portugal, Slovakia, Slovenia
09 Lithuania
10 Luxembourg
13 Czech Republic, United Kingdom
14 The Netherlands

## europium

02 Eu

## euthanasia

07 quietus, release 12 happy release, mercy killing 15 assisted suicide, merciful release

## evacuate

04 ease, quit, void 05 clear, eject, empty, expel, leave, purge, stool 06 decamp, depart, desert, getter, remove, vacate 07 abandon, excrete, forsake, nullify, relieve, retreat, vacate 08 clear out, defecate, withdraw 09 discharge, eliminate, make empty, move out of, pull out of 10 go away from, relinquish, retire from, stercorate

## evacuation

06 exodus, flight 07 Dunkirk, leaving, purging, removal, retreat 08 ejection, emptying, quitting, vacating 09 clearance, departure, desertion, discharge, expulsion, forsaking, gettering, urination, vacuation 10 defecation, retirement, withdrawal 11 abandonment, elimination 14 relinquishment

## evade

04 balk, duck, shun 05 avoid, blink, burke, dodge, elude, fence, fudge, hedge, parry, sheer, shift, shirk, skive, waive 06 baffle, bludge, bypass, cop out, escape 07 fend off, quibble, shuffle, wriggle 08 get round, sidestep, skive off 09 back out of, duckshove, gold brick, weasel out 10 chicken out, circumvent, equivocate, scrimshank, skrimshank 11 prevaricate 12 steer clear of, wriggle out of

## evaluate

04 rank, rate 05 gauge, judge, value, weigh 06 assess, reckon, size up

**evaluation**
07 compute, measure 08 appraise, estimate 09 calculate, determine 15 get the measure of

**evaluation**
05 audit 06 rating 07 opinion 08 estimate, judgment 09 appraisal, judgement, reckoning, valuation 10 assessment, estimation 11 calculation, computation 13 determination

**evanescent**
05 brief 06 fading 07 passing 08 fleeting, unstable 09 ephemeral, momentary, temporary, transient, vanishing 10 perishable, short-lived, transitory 11 evaporating, impermanent 12 disappearing 13 insubstantial

**evangelical**
03 Sim 06 Marist 07 zealous 08 biblical, orthodox, Stundist 09 crusading, High-flier, High-flyer, Simeonite 10 converting, missionary, Morisonian, scriptural 11 campaigning 12 Bible-bashing, enthusiastic, evangelistic, propagandist 13 Bible-punching, Bible-thumping, proselytizing 14 Bible-believing, fundamentalist, propagandizing
• **Evangelical Union** 02 EU

**evangelist**
04 John, Luke, Mark 07 Matthew 08 crusader, preacher 09 gospeller, missioner 10 campaigner, missionary, revivalist 12 hot gospeller, proselytizer 13 televangelist

**evangelize**
06 preach 07 baptize, convert, crusade 08 campaign 09 gospelize 10 missionize 11 proselytize 12 missionarize, propagandize 13 spread the word

**evaporate**
03 dry, end 04 fade, melt 05 steme, vapor 06 depart, dispel, distil, exhale, vanish, vapour 08 boil away, disperse, dissolve, evanesce, melt away, vaporize 09 dehydrate, desiccate, disappear, dissipate 10 volatilize 13 dematerialize

**evaporation**
06 drying, fading 07 melting 09 vanishing 10 exhalation 11 dehydration, desiccation, dissolution 12 condensation, distillation, vaporization

**evasion**
04 go-by 05 dodge, fudge, quirk 06 cop-out, deceit, escape, excuse, put-off 07 dodging, ducking, elusion, fencing, fig leaf, fudging, hedging, quibble, shuffle, skiving 08 go-around, shirking, shunning, trickery 09 avoidance, deception, quibbling, shuffling 10 scrimshank, skrimshank, subterfuge 12 equivocation 13 circumvention, prevarication 14 tergiversation 15 steering clear of

**evasive**
03 coy 05 cagey, vague 06 shifty, slippy, tricky 07 cunning, devious, elusive, elusory, fudging, oblique 08 indirect, slippery, waffling 09 deceitful, deceptive, quibbling, secretive, shuffling 10 misleading 12 equivocating 13 prevaricating, unforthcoming

**evasiveness**
06 deceit 07 cunning, fudging, secrecy 08 caginess 09 quibbling, vagueness 12 equivocation, indirectness 13 deceptiveness, prevarication

**eve**
03 e'en 04 edge 05 brink, verge, vigil 09 day before, threshold 10 time before 12 period before

**even**
◊ *hidden alternately indicator* 03 all, e'en, too, yet 04 also, calm, cool, eevn, fair, flat, just, like, more, same, true 05 align, alike, at all, clean, drawn, eeven, equal, exact, flush, level, match, oddly, plain, plane, quits, still 06 as well, hardly, indeed, in fact, nearly, placid, serene, smooth, square, stable, steady 07 balance, compare, eevning, equable, exactly, flatten, neutral, regular, similar, uniform 08 actually, balanced, composed, constant, equalize, likewise, matching, parallel, scarcely, so much as, straight, tranquil 09 equitable, identical, impartial, make equal, stabilize, still more, unexcited, unruffled, unusually, unvarying 10 all the more, balance out, consistent, even-handed, fifty-fifty, horizontal, regularize, side by side, straighten, unchanging, unwavering 11 even-stevens, make uniform, more exactly, neck and neck, non-partisan, symmetrical, unexcitable, unflappable 12 even-tempered, surprisingly, unexpectedly 13 evenly matched, more precisely, unperturbable 14 strike a balance
• **even so** 03 but, yet 05 still 07 however 10 all the same 11 despite that, nonetheless 12 nevertheless 13 in spite of that
• **get even** 05 repay 06 avenge 07 pay back, requite 11 have revenge, reciprocate 12 settle a score 14 get your own back 15 revenge yourself, take your revenge
• **not even** 03 odd 06 uneven

**even-handed**
04 fair, just 06 square 07 neutral 08 balanced, unbiased 09 equitable, impartial 10 reasonable 12 unprejudiced 13 disinterested, dispassionate, fair and square

**evening**
03 e'en, ene, eve 04 dusk, eevn, even 05 eeven, night 06 sunset, vesper 07 eevning, sundown 08 eventide, twilight 09 forenight, nightfall 10 close of day

**evenly**
◊ *hidden alternately indicator* 04 flat 06 calmly, square, stably 07 equally 08 placidly, serenely, steadily 09 regularly, similarly, uniformly 10 constantly, tranquilly 12 consistently 13 evenly matched, symmetrically

**event**
03 end 04 case, fact, fate, gala, game, item, meet, pass, race 05 issue, match, round 06 affair, effect, matter, result, upshot 07 contest, episode, fixture, fortune, meeting, ongoing, outcome 08 business, incident, occasion 09 adventure, aftermath, happening, milestone 10 conclusion, engagement, experience, occurrence, proceeding, tournament 11 competition, consequence, eventuality, possibility, termination 12 circumstance
• **in any event** 06 anyhow, anyway 09 in any case 11 whether or no 12 no matter what, whether or not 15 whatever happens

**even-tempered**
04 calm, cool 06 placid, serene, stable, steady 07 equable, unfazed 08 composed, laid-back, peaceful, tranquil 09 peaceable 11 level-headed, unflappable 13 imperturbable

**eventful**
04 busy, full 06 active, lively 07 crucial, notable 08 critical, exciting, historic 09 checkered, chequered, important, memorable, momentous 10 noteworthy, remarkable 11 interesting, ripsnorting, significant 12 action-packed 13 unforgettable

**eventual**
04 last 05 final, later 06 future 07 closing, ensuing, planned 08 ultimate 09 impending, projected, resulting 10 concluding, subsequent 11 prospective

**eventuality**
04 case 05 event 06 chance, crisis, mishap 07 outcome 09 emergency, happening, incidence 10 likelihood, occurrence 11 contingency, possibility, probability 12 circumstance, happenstance

**eventually**
06 at last, in time 07 finally 08 after all, at length, in the end 10 ultimately 11 in due course 12 in the long run, subsequently 13 sooner or later

**ever**
02 ay 03 aye, e'er 05 at all 06 always 07 for ever 08 evermore 09 at any time, endlessly, eternally, in any case 10 at all times, constantly 11 continually, incessantly, permanently, perpetually 12 on any account, till doomsday 13 on any occasion
• **ever so** 04 very 05 jolly 06 really 07 awfully 08 terribly, very much 09 extremely, immensely 11 exceedingly, frightfully 12 tremendously 13 exceptionally

**evergreen**
*see* **pine**; **tree**

**everlasting**
07 endless, eternal, non-stop, undying 08 cat's-foot, constant, immortal, infinite, timeless, unending

**evermore**

09 continual, deathless, incessant, permanent, perpetual, unceasing 10 continuous, immortelle, perdurable, persistent, relentless 11 Helichrysum, never-ending, remorseless, sempiternal, strawflower, unremitting, xeranthemum 12 imperishable, interminable 14 indestructible

**evermore**

04 ever 06 always 07 for ever 09 eternally, ever after, hereafter 10 henceforth 11 in perpetuum, unceasingly 12 in perpetuity, till doomsday 14 for ever and a day, for ever and ever, to the end of time

**every**

03 all, per 04 each, full, tout 05 total 06 entire 08 complete 11 all possible, every single 15 every individual

**everybody**

03 all 05 a'body 07 each one 08 everyman, everyone 09 one and all 10 each person 11 all the world, every person, tout le monde 12 all and sundry, every man Jack 13 the whole world

**everyday**

05 basic, daily, plain, stock, usual 06 common, folksy, modern, normal, simple 07 average, regular, routine 08 day-to-day, familiar, frequent, habitual, informal, ordinary, standard, workaday 09 customary, quotidian 10 accustomed, monotonous 11 commonplace 12 conventional, run-of-the-mill 13 unimaginative 14 common-or-garden

**everyone**

03 all 07 each one 08 universe 09 allcomers, everybody, one and all 10 each person 11 every person 12 all and sundry, every man Jack 13 the whole world

**everything**

03 all 04 lock 06 a'thing, the lot, the sum 08 the total, the works 09 all things, each thing 11 all the world, the entirety, the whole lot 12 the aggregate 14 stock and barrel 15 the whole shebang

**everywhere**

04 left 06 a'where, passim, ubique 07 all over 09 all around, eachwhere 10 every place, far and near, far and wide, high and low, near and far, throughout, ubiquitous 11 at every turn, in all places, in each place, to all places, to each place 12 the world over 14 right and centre

**evict**

04 oust 05 eject, expel 06 put out, remove 07 cast out, kick out, turf out, turn out 08 chuck out, dislodge, force out, throw out 10 dispossess 11 expropriate 12 force to leave

**eviction**

07 removal, the boot, the push 08 ejection, the elbow 09 clearance, expulsion 11 the bum's rush 12 dislodgement 13 dispossession, expropriation 14 defenestration

**evidence**

04 data, deed, hint, mark, show, sign, test 05 proof, prove, stamp, title, token, trace, vouch 06 affirm, assert, attest, avouch, betray, denote, evince, reveal 07 bespeak, confirm, display, exhibit, grounds, signify, support, symptom, witness 08 argument, document, indicate, instance, manifest, surrebut, warranty 09 adminicle, affidavit, establish, guarantee, testimony 10 indication, smoking gun, suggestion 11 affirmation, attestation, credentials, declaration, demonstrate 12 compurgation, confirmation, precognition, verification 13 corroboration, demonstration, documentation, manifestation 14 substantiation
• **in evidence** 05 clear, plain 06 patent 07 obvious, visible 08 apparent, clear-cut 10 noticeable 11 conspicuous 12 unmistakable

**evident**

05 clear, naked, overt, plain 06 patent 07 confest, obvious, visible 08 apparent, clear-cut, distinct, manifest, sensible, tangible 09 confessed, undoubted 10 noticeable 11 conspicuous, discernible, perceptible, transparent 12 indisputable, unmistakable 13 incontestable

**evidently**

07 clearly, plainly, visibly 08 patently 09 doubtless, obviously, outwardly, seemingly, so it seems 10 apparently, manifestly, ostensibly 11 doubtlessly, so it appears, undoubtedly 12 indisputably 13 as it would seem, on the face of it 15 as it would appear

**evil**

03 bad, ill, sin, woe 04 bale, base, blow, dire, eale, foul, harm, hurt, pain, ruin, vice, vile 05 amiss, black, cruel, curse, hydra, nasty, wrong 06 deadly, injury, misery, sinful, sorrow, wicked 07 adverse, badness, corrupt, demonic, disease, harmful, heinous, hurtful, illness, immoral, noisome, noxious, ruinous, unlucky, vicious 08 baseness, calamity, depraved, devilish, diabolic, disaster, distress, iniquity, mischief, sinister, stinking, vileness 09 adversity, depravity, injurious, malicious, malignant, malignity, nefarious, offensive, poisonous, suffering 10 affliction, calamitous, corruption, disastrous, immorality, iniquitous, malevolent, misconduct, misfortune, pernicious, sinfulness, wickedness, wrongdoing 11 catastrophe, deleterious, destructive, detrimental, heinousness, mischievous, unfortunate, viciousness 12 catastrophic, devilishness, inauspicious, unfavourable, unpropitious 13 reprehensible

**evildoer**

05 rogue 06 sinner 07 badmash, budmash, villain 08 criminal, offender 09 bad person, miscreant, reprobate,

scoundrel, wrongdoer 10 delinquent, malefactor 12 transgressor

**evildoing**

03 sin 07 badness, cruelty 08 iniquity, vileness 09 depravity, nastiness 10 corruption, immorality, sinfulness, wickedness 11 malefaction, malfeasance

**evince**

04 show 06 attest, betray, reveal 07 bespeak, betoken, confess, declare, display, exhibit, express, signify, witness 08 evidence, indicate, manifest, overcome 09 establish, make clear, overpower 11 demonstrate

**eviscerate**

03 gut 04 draw 06 paunch 08 gralloch 10 disembowel, exenterate

**evocation**

04 echo 06 recall 07 arousal, calling 08 inducing, kindling, stirring 10 activation, excitation, invocation, suggestion 11 elicitation, stimulation, summoning-up

**evocative**

05 vivid 07 graphic 08 redolent 09 memorable 10 expressive, indicative, suggestive 11 reminiscent

**evoke**

04 call, draw, stir 05 cause, raise, waken 06 arouse, awaken, call up, elicit, excite, induce, invoke, kindle, recall, summon 07 provoke 08 summon up 09 call forth, conjure up, stimulate 10 bring about, call to mind 11 bring to mind

**evolution**

◊ *anagram indicator* 06 growth 07 biogeny, descent 08 increase, progress, ripening 09 expansion, phytogeny, unfolding, unrolling 10 derivation, noogenesis, opening-out, working-out 11 development, progression, unravelling 12 cladogenesis, Neo-Darwinism, orthogenesis, phytogenesis, transformism

**evolve**

◊ *anagram indicator* 04 grow 06 derive, emerge, expand, mature, result, unfold, unroll 07 advance, descend, develop, enlarge, open out, unravel, work out 08 develope, disclose, generate, increase, progress 09 elaborate

**ewe**

03 keb, yow 04 yowe 05 crone, yowie 06 gimmer, lamber, theave

**ex**

01 X 03 old 04 dead, late 06 former 07 outside, without

**exacerbate**

03 vex 06 deepen, enrage, worsen 07 inflame, provoke, sharpen 08 embitter, heighten, increase, irritate 09 aggravate, infuriate, intensify, make worse 10 exaggerate, exasperate 12 fan the flames 15 make things worse

## exacerbation
**09** worsening **10** irritation
**11** aggravation **12** embitterment,
exaggeration, exasperation
**15** intensification

## exact
**04** even, flat, just, milk, true **05** bleed,
claim, close, force, right, wrest, wring
**06** bang on, compel, dead on,
demand, extort, impose, insist, minute,
spot on, square, strict **07** call for,
careful, command, correct, estreat,
express, extract, factual, literal,
orderly, perfect, precise, require,
squeeze **08** accurate, definite,
detailed, exacting, explicit, faithful,
finished, flawless, insist on, punctual,
rigorous, specific, thorough, unerring
**09** faultless, identical, on the nail,
religious, veracious **10** blow-by-blow,
consummate, methodical, meticulous,
on the money, particular, scrupulous
**11** on the button, painstaking, point-
device, point-devise, punctilious,
word-perfect

## exacting
**04** firm, hard **05** harsh, stern, tough
**06** severe, strict, taxing, tiring
**07** arduous, exigent, onerous
**08** exigeant, rigorous **09** demanding,
difficult, exigeante, laborious,
stringent, unsparing **10** fastidious,
unyielding **11** challenging, painstaking

## exactitude
**04** care **05** print **06** detail, rigour
**08** accuracy **09** exactness, precision
**10** strictness **11** carefulness,
correctness, orderliness
**12** rigorousness, thoroughness
**13** faultlessness, perfectionism
**14** meticulousness, scrupulousness
**15** painstakingness

## exactly
**02** on **03** due, e'en, yes **04** dead, even,
flat, jump, just, to a T, true **05** plumb,
quite, right, smash, spang, truly
**06** agreed, bang on, dead on, indeed,
just so, spot on, to a tee **07** quite so, to
a hair **08** of course, on the dot, strictly,
verbatim, you got it **09** carefully,
certainly, correctly, expressly, literally,
on the nail, precisely **10** absolutely,
accurately, definitely, explicitly,
faithfully, rigorously, that's right,
unerringly **11** faultlessly, on the button,
religiously, to the letter, veraciously
**12** methodically, particularly,
scrupulously, specifically, without
error **13** point for point, unequivocally
• **exactly what's looked for** **02** it

## exactness
**04** care **06** nicety, rigour **08** accuracy,
justness **09** precision **10** exactitude,
strictness **11** carefulness, correctness,
orderliness **12** rigorousness,
thoroughness **13** faultlessness
**14** meticulousness, scrupulousness

## exaggerate
**05** color, sex up **06** bounce, colour,
overdo, stress **07** amplify, distend,
enhance, enlarge, lay it on, magnify,
stretch **08** overdo it, overdraw,

overplay, oversell, pile it on
**09** dramatize, embellish, embroider,
emphasize, intensify, overstate
**10** aggrandize, goliathize, shoot a line
**11** overstretch **12** come it strong, lay it
on thick, overdo things **13** make too
much of, overdramatize,
overemphasize, pile it on thick
**15** stretch the truth

## exaggerated
**03** OTT **04** camp, tall **05** steep
**07** exalted **08** inflated, overdone
**09** amplified, bombastic, excessive,
overblown **10** burlesqued, cartoonish,
euphuistic, hyperbolic, overstated,
over-the-top, theatrical **11** caricatured,
embellished, extravagant,
overcharged, pretentious
**12** overstrained **13** overestimated
**14** larger than life

## exaggeration
**06** excess, parody **07** stretch
**08** emphasis **09** burlesque, hyperbole,
stretcher **10** caricature **11** enlargement
**12** extravagance, overemphasis
**13** amplification, embellishment,
magnification, overstatement
**14** overestimation **15** pretentiousness

## exalt
**04** laud **05** adore, bless, deify, elate,
erect, extol, honor, raise, set up
**06** excite, honour, praise, prefer,
refine, revere, throne, uplift
**07** acclaim, advance, applaud, delight,
dignify, elevate, enliven, glorify,
magnify, overjoy, promote, sublime,
upgrade, upraise, worship
**08** enthrone, eulogize, venerate
**09** reverence, subtilize, transport
**10** aggrandize, enthronize, exhilarate

## exaltation
**03** joy **05** bliss, glory, larks **06** eulogy,
honour, praise **07** acclaim, ecstasy,
elation, raising, rapture, worship
**08** erection **09** adoration, elevation,
promotion, rejoicing, reverence
**10** enthusiasm, excitement, jubilation,
veneration **11** advancement, high
spirits **12** exhilaration **13** glorification
**14** aggrandizement

## exalted
**04** haut, high **05** elate, grand, happy,
hault, lofty, moral, noble, regal
**06** elated, haught, joyful, lordly
**07** eminent, stately, sublime **08** blissful,
ecstatic, elevated, exultant, jubilant,
magnific, supernal, virtuous
**09** dignified, rapturous **10** idealistic,
magnifical **11** exaggerated **13** high and
mighty, in high spirits **15** in seventh
heaven

## exam, examination
**02** ex **03** bac, CSE, GCE, MOT, mug
**04** exam, GCSE, mods, oral, quiz,
scan, test, viva **05** audit, check, final,
paper, probe, study, trial **06** Abitur, A
level, biopsy, Greats, higher, O level,
prelim, review, search, survey
**07** canvass, check-up, great go,
inquiry, perusal **08** analysis, concours,
critique, little go, necropsy, once-over,
research, scrutiny, viva voce

**09** appraisal, exercises, going-over,
practical, questions **10** agrégation,
assessment, inspection, post-mortem
**11** exploration, inquisition,
observation, preliminary, questioning
**13** baccalaureate, interrogation,
investigation
• **reject at examination** **04** fail, plow,
spin **06** plough

## examine
**03** eye, pry, try, vet **04** case, jerk, palp,
pump, quiz, scan, seek, sift, test, view,
viva **05** assay, audit, check, grill,
probe, quote, study **06** appose, assess,
depose, go into, go over, jerque, look
at, peruse, ponder, reason, review,
revise, search, survey **07** analyse,
canvass, check up, collate, discuss,
dissect, explore, eyeball, inquire,
inspect, observe, palpate, process,
weigh up **08** appraise, check out,
cognosce, consider, look into, look
over, overhale, overhaul, pore over,
question, research, traverse, viva voce,
work over **09** catechize, check over,
check up on, overhaile, speculate
**10** go to town on, scrutinize
**11** interrogate, investigate **12** cross-
examine **13** cross-question **14** put the
screws on

## examinee
**07** entrant **09** applicant, candidate
**10** competitor, contestant
**11** interviewee

## examiner
**05** judge, juror **06** censor, critic,
marker, reader, tester **07** analyst,
arbiter, assayer, auditor **08** assessor,
external, reviewer **09** examinant,
inspector, moderator, scrutator
**10** questioner, scrutineer
**11** adjudicator, interviewer, scrutinizer
**12** interlocutor

## example
**02** ex **04** case, lead, type **05** guide,
ideal, model, peach, pearl, piece,
thing **06** corker, lesson, mirror, muster,
sample **07** caution, epitome, exemple,
pattern, warning **08** ensample,
exemplar, exemplum, exponent,
instance, monument, paradigm,
specimen, standard **09** archetype,
criterion, exemplify, footsteps,
precedent, prototype, role model
**10** admonition, apotheosis, assay-
piece, peacherino, punishment **11** case
in point, typical case **12** illustration
**14** representative **15** exemplification
• **for example** **02** as, eg, zb **03** say
**04** like **06** such as **10** par exemple **11** as
an example, for instance, zum Beispiel
**12** as an instance, to illustrate
**13** exempli gratia

## exasperate
**03** bug, irk, vex **04** bait, gall, goad, rile
**05** anger, annoy, get to, rouse
**06** enrage, madden, needle, rankle,
wind up **07** incense, provoke **08** irritate
**09** aggravate, infuriate, irritated
**14** drive up the wall

## exasperated
**05** angry, fed up, irked, riled, vexed

**06** bugged, galled, goaded, peeved, piqued **07** angered, annoyed, needled, nettled **08** incensed, maddened, provoked **09** indignant, irritated **10** aggravated, infuriated

**exasperating**
**06** vexing **07** galling, irksome **08** annoying, infernal **09** maddening, provoking, vexatious **10** bothersome, confounded, irritating, pernicious **11** aggravating, infuriating, troublesome **12** disagreeable

**exasperation**
**04** fury, rage **05** anger **07** chagrin **09** annoyance **10** discontent, irritation **11** aggravation, indignation, stroppiness **12** exulceration **14** disgruntlement

**excavate**
**03** cut, dig **04** mine, sink **05** delve, dig up, drive, gouge, navvy, scoop, stope **06** burrow, dig out, exhume, hollow, quarry, reveal, tunnel **07** uncover, unearth **08** disinter **09** hollow out

**excavation**
**03** cut, dig, pit **04** delf, hole, mine **05** delph, ditch, drift, graft, heuch, heugh, shaft, stope **06** burrow, cavity, crater, dugout, hollow, mining, quarry, trench, trough **07** cutting, digging, sondage **08** catacomb, colliery, diggings, open-cast **09** burrowing, glory hole, hollowing **10** digging out, exhumation, tunnelling, unearthing **11** countermine, side cutting **12** hollowing out

**exceed**
**03** cap, top **04** beat, pass **05** excel, outdo **06** better, go over, outrun, overdo, overgo **07** eclipse, o'ergang, outrace, overtop, surpass **08** go beyond, outreach, outshine, outstrip, outweigh, overgang, overpass, overstep, overtake **09** outnumber, overshoot, transcend **10** be more than, transgress **12** be larger than, be superior to **13** be greater than

**exceedingly**
**04** main, very **05** amain, dooms **06** damned, highly, hugely, proper, vastly **07** greatly, not half, passing **08** almighty, devilish, heavenly, powerful, very much, wondrous **09** amazingly, extremely, immensely, monstrous, unusually, vengeance **10** consumedly, enormously, especially **11** excessively **12** inordinately, out of all nick, surpassingly **13** astonishingly, exceptionally, superlatively **14** with a vengeance **15** extraordinarily, unprecedentedly

**excel**
**03** war **04** beat, ring **05** outdo, shine **06** better, exceed, outtop, overdo **07** eclipse, outpeer, outrank, succeed, surpass **08** outclass, outrival, overpeer, stand out **09** be skilful **10** outperform **11** be excellent, go one better, predominate **12** be better than, be pre-eminent, be superior to **13** be outstanding **15** go one better than

**excellence**
**05** merit, skill, value, worth **06** purity, virtue, worthy **07** quality **08** eminence, fineness, goodness, nobility **09** greatness, supremacy **10** choiceness, perfection **11** distinction, high quality, pre-eminence, superiority **13** transcendence

**excellent**
**02** A1, ME **03** ace, def, exc, fab, rad **04** best, boss, cool, fine, good, high, mean, mega, neat, pure, rare, tops **05** beaut, boffo, brave, bravo, brill, bully, crack, dicty, dilly, great, hunky, jammy, lummy, noble, noted, prime, socko, triff, wally **06** badass, beauty, beezer, bonzer, castor, cushty, dickty, divine, famous, goodly, groovy, grouse, peachy, purler, ripper, select, spot-on, superb, way-out, whizzo, whizzy, wicked, worthy **07** capital, classic, corking, cracker, crucial, elegant, eminent, kicking, notable, perfect, radical, ripping, shining, stellar, supreme, tipping, top-hole, topping, triffic, trimmer, Utopian **08** champion, clinking, cracking, eximious, fabulous, flawless, heavenly, inspired, jim-dandy, knockout, smashing, spiffing, splendid, sterling, stonking, stunning, superior, terrific, top-notch, very good, whizbang **09** admirable, brilliant, copacetic, copasetic, exemplary, fantastic, faultless, first-rate, hunky-dory, kopasetic, matchless, righteous, top-drawer, whizz-bang, wonderful **10** first-class, marvellous, noteworthy, not half bad, pre-eminent, remarkable, surpassing, unequalled **11** commendable, exceptional, high-quality, magnificent, outstanding, sensational, superlative **12** praiseworthy, second to none, the bee's knees, unparalleled **13** above reproach, distinguished **14** out of this world **15** unexceptionable

**excellently**
**04** well **06** goodly **08** champion, divinely, superbly **09** admirably, capitally, eminently, first-rate, perfectly **10** remarkably, splendidly **11** brilliantly, commendably, wonderfully **12** marvellously, terrifically **13** exceptionally, fantastically, sensationally, superlatively

**except**
**02** ex, sa' **03** bar, but, exc **04** less, omit, only, save, than **05** minus **06** bating, but for, nobbut, reject **07** barring, besides, exclude, outtake, rule out, short of, without **08** leave out, omitting, pass over **09** apart from, aside from, except for, excepting, excluding, other than, outside of **10** leaving out **11** not counting

**exception**
**02** ex **03** exc **05** freak, quirk **06** oddity, rarity **07** anomaly, offence **09** departure, deviation, exclusion, objection **11** abnormality, peculiarity,

special case **12** irregularity **13** inconsistency
• **take exception 05** argue, demur, rebut **06** object, oppose, refuse, resist **07** protest **08** complain **09** challenge, repudiate, take issue, withstand **10** disapprove **11** beg to differ, expostulate, remonstrate
• **with the exception of 03** bar, but **04** less, save **05** minus **07** barring, besides **08** omitting **09** apart from, except for, excepting, excluding, other than **10** leaving out **11** not counting

**exceptionable**
**09** abhorrent, offensive, repugnant **10** deplorable, disgusting, unpleasant **12** disagreeable, unacceptable **13** objectionable

**exceptional**
**03** odd **04** rare **06** way-out **07** notable, special, strange, unusual **08** aberrant, abnormal, atypical, peculiar, singular, superior, uncommon **09** anomalous, brilliant, excellent, irregular **10** marvellous, noteworthy, phenomenal, prodigious, remarkable, unequalled **11** outstanding **13** extraordinary, one in a million **14** one in a thousand

**exceptionally**
**05** extra **06** rarely **07** notably **09** amazingly, extremely, unusually **10** abnormally, especially, remarkably, uncommonly **11** irregularly, wonderfully **13** outstandingly **15** extraordinarily

**excerpt**
**04** clip, part **05** piece, quote, scrap **07** cutting, extract, passage, portion, section **08** citation, clipping, fragment, pericope **09** quotation, selection

**excess**
**04** glut, rest **05** extra, spare **06** gutful, spilth **07** backlog, nimiety, o'ercome, residue, surfeit, surplus, too much **08** bellyful, left-over, overcome, overflow, overkill, owrecome, plethora, residual **09** leftovers, redundant, remainder, remaining **10** additional, debauchery, oversupply **11** dissipation, exorbitance, exorbitancy, prodigality, superfluity, superfluous, unrestraint **12** extravagance, immoderation, intemperance **13** dissoluteness, overabundance, supernumerary **14** immoderateness, more than enough, overindulgence, superabundance
• **in excess of 04** over **05** above **08** more than

**excessive**
**03** OTT **04** deep, over, rank **05** steep, stiff, undue **06** de trop, lavish **07** burning, extreme, fulsome, too much **08** needless, overdone, unneeded **09** exceeding, overblown **10** exorbitant, immoderate, inordinate, over the top **11** extravagant, superfluous, uncalled-for, unnecessary, unwarranted

**12** overabundant, unreasonable
**13** superabundant

**excessively**
**06** overly, troppo, unduly **07** too much
**08** overmuch, to a fault, woundily
**09** extremely **10** needlessly **11** God-almighty **12** exorbitantly, immoderately, inordinately, out of all cess, unreasonably **13** beyond measure, exaggeratedly, extravagantly, intemperately, superfluously, unnecessarily

**exchange**
◊ *anagram indicator* **02** ex **04** chat, chop, cope, exch, swap, swop
**05** bandy, bazar, swits, trade, trock, troke, truck **06** barter, bazaar, change, excamb, market, niffer, scorse, switch **07** bargain, commute, convert, dealing, replace, traffic **08** argument, commerce, dialogue, trade-off
**09** transpose **10** discussion, stand in for, substitute **11** give and take, interchange, reciprocate, reciprocity, replacement **12** conversation, substitution

**excise**
**03** cut, GST, tax, VAT **04** duty, levy, toll
**05** erase **06** cut off, cut out, delete, impost, remove, tariff **07** customs, destroy, expunge, extract, rescind
**09** eradicate, expurgate, extirpate, surcharge **11** exterminate

**excision**
◊ *deletion indicator* **03** cut **07** removal
**08** deletion **10** expunction
**11** destruction, eradication, expurgation, extirpation
**13** extermination

**excitable**
**04** edgy **05** fiery, hasty, nappy, nervy
**06** feisty **07** nervous, rackety
**08** choleric, volatile **09** emotional, hot-headed, irascible, mercurial, sensitive
**10** passionate **11** combustible, hot-tempered, susceptible **12** highly-strung
**13** quick-tempered, temperamental

**excite**
◊ *anagram indicator* **04** fire, move, stir, sway, urge, wake, warm, whet, yerk
**05** evoke, flush, hop up, impel, rouse, steer, stire, styre, touch, upset, waken
**06** accite, aerate, arouse, awaken, emmove, enmove, fire up, ignite, incite, induce, kindle, stir up, thrill, tickle, turn on, wind up, work up
**07** agitate, animate, commove, disturb, enliven, ferment, impress, inflame, inspire, provoke, upraise **08** blow away, energize, engender, enkindle, generate, irritate, motivate **09** electrify, galvanize, instigate, sensitize, set on edge, stimulate, suscitate, titillate
**10** bring about, intoxicate

**excited**
◊ *anagram indicator* **02** up **03** het, hot
**04** high, warm, wild **05** amped, antsy, astir, crunk, eager, hyper, krunk, moved, nervy, proud, radge, randy
**06** elated, juiced, pumped, randie, roused **07** aroused, crunked, fevered, fired up, flushed, frantic, hyped up,

krunked, sexed-up, stirred, uptight
**08** agitated, animated, frenzied, hopped-up, restless, revved-up, thrilled, turned on, worked up
**09** delirious, red-headed, wrought-up
**10** corybantic, stimulated, up in the air
**11** exhilarated, overwrought
**12** enthusiastic **13** in high spirits, on tenterhooks **14** beside yourself, thrilled to bits

**excitement**
**03** ado, rut, tew **04** fume, fuss, kick, ruff, spin, stir **05** fever, furor, kicks, pride, ruffe **06** action, didder, dither, flurry, furore, hoop-la, thrill, tumult, unrest **07** arousal, elation, emotion, ferment, passion **08** activity, brouhaha, delirium, erethism, flat spin, hilarity, pleasure **09** adventure, agitation, animation, commotion, eagerness, fleshment, rousement, sensation
**10** enthusiasm, salutation **11** fun and games, stimulation **12** discomposure, exhilaration, Hobson-Jobson, intoxication, perturbation, restlessness
• **expression of excitement 04** whee **05** yahoo **06** yippee **07** way to go!
**08** hey-go-mad
• **seeking excitement 04** fast
• **state of excitement 10** fever pitch

**exciting**
**03** hot **04** sexy **05** heady, magic
**06** moving **07** rousing **08** dramatic, excitant, gripping, stirring, striking
**09** inspiring, thrilling **10** nail-biting
**11** aphrodisiac, enthralling, hair-raising, interesting, provocative, sensational, stimulating **12** action-packed, breathtaking, cliff-hanging, electrifying, exhilarating, intoxicating
**13** edge-of-the-seat, swashbuckling
• **something exciting 03** gas

**exclaim**
**03** cry **04** call, roar, yell **05** blurt, shout, utter **06** bellow, cry out, outcry, shriek
**07** declare **08** blurt out, proclaim
**09** ejaculate, interject **10** vociferate
**11** come out with, exclamation

**exclamation**
**02** ho, wo **03** boo, cry, fen, hip, olé, pah, tut, ugh, woe, wow, yah, yay
**04** call, go on, hech, I say!, oops, phew, pish, poof, pooh, push, roar, sa sa, shoo, skol, upsy, when, yell
**05** bingo, fancy, house, hurra, my hat!, shout, skoal, upsee, upsey, yahoo
**06** banzai, bellow, by Jove, hooray, hurrah, hurray, outcry, phooey, shriek, shucks, walker, whoops, zounds
**07** bless me!, crivens, good egg, good-now, heigh-ho, hosanna, right on, whoopee **08** crivvens, hear hear!, here goes!, man alive, stroll on!
**09** expletive, fancy that, good grief, unberufen, utterance **10** ecphonesis, epiphonema, Great Scott!, hoity-toity, how dare you!, upon my soul! **11** bless my soul!, bumpsadaisy, ejaculation, good heavens, marry come up
**12** boomps-a-daisy, Hookey Walker, interjection, strike a light! **15** shiver my timbers

• **exclamation mark 05** pling
**06** shriek **08** screamer

**exclude**
**03** ban, bar **04** drop, omit, skip, veto
**05** debar, eject, evict, expel, hatch
**06** delete, except, forbid, ice out, ignore, refuse, reject, remove **07** boot out, boycott, keep out, kick out, lock out, miss out, push out, rule out, shut off, shut out, turf out **08** count out, disallow, leave out, preclude, prohibit, throw out **09** blacklist, eliminate, freeze out, interdict, ostracize
**10** include out **13** excommunicate
**14** send to Coventry

**excluding**
◊ *deletion indicator* **06** except **07** barring
**08** omitting **09** debarring, except for, excepting, ruling out **10** leaving out
**11** exclusive of, not counting **12** not including

**exclusion**
**03** ban, bar **04** veto **07** boycott, embargo, refusal, removal **08** ejection, eviction, omission **09** exception, expulsion, interdict, rejection, ruling out **10** preclusion **11** elimination, prohibition, repudiation
**12** proscription

**exclusive**
**03** few **04** chic, coup, only, posh, sole
**05** plush, ritzy, scoop, swish, total, whole **06** choice, classy, cliquy, closed, clubby, exposé, narrow, select, single, snazzy, unique **07** cliquey, elegant, limited, private **08** boutique, cliquish, complete, peculiar, rarefied, snobbish, unshared, up-market
**09** high-class, sectarian, sensation, undivided **10** individual, restricted, revelation, upper-crust **11** fashionable, inside story, restrictive
**12** incompatible **14** discriminative
• **exclusive of 06** except **07** barring
**08** omitting **09** debarring, except for, excepting, excluding, ruling out
**10** leaving out **11** not counting **12** not including

**excommunicate**
**03** ban, bar **05** curse, debar, eject, expel **06** banish, outlaw, remove
**07** exclude **08** denounce, execrate, unchurch **09** blacklist, proscribe, repudiate **12** anathematize
**13** disfellowship

**excommunication**
**07** banning, barring **08** ejection
**09** exclusion, expulsion, outlawing
**10** banishment **11** unchurching
**12** denunciation **13** disfellowship

**excoriate**
**03** nag **04** carp, slam **05** blame, decry, knock, slate, snipe **06** attack
**07** censure, condemn, nit-pick, run down **08** denounce **09** denigrate, disparage **10** animadvert, come down on, vituperate **12** disapprove of **13** find fault with

**excrement**
**03** poo **04** crud, dung, flux, mess, poop
**05** frass, guano, scats, stool **06** doo-

doo, egesta, faeces, ordure
**09** biosolids, droppings, excretion
**11** waste matter **12** rejectamenta, sir-
reverence

## excrescence
**03** bur, pin **04** blot, boil, bump, burr,
knob, lump, moss, nail, nurl, wart,
wolf **05** knurl **06** cancer, growth,
tumour, wattle **07** eyesore, rat-tail,
sarcoma, twitter **08** rat's-tail, swelling
**09** appendage, carnosity, misgrowth,
outgrowth **10** projection, prominence,
proud flesh **11** monstrosity, twitter-
bone **12** intumescence, protuberance
**13** disfigurement

## excrete
**03** poo **04** pass, void **05** eject, expel,
exude **07** secrete, urinate **08** defecate,
evacuate **09** discharge

## excretion
**03** poo **04** dung **05** stool **06** faeces,
ordure **07** excreta **09** discharge,
droppings, excrement, urination
**10** defecation, evacuation
**12** perspiration

## excruciate
◊ *anagram indicator* **04** rack **07** torture
**08** irritate

## excruciating
**05** acute, sharp **06** bitter, savage,
severe **07** burning, extreme, intense,
painful, racking **08** piercing
**09** agonizing, atrocious, harrowing,
torturing **10** tormenting, unbearable
**11** intolerable **12** cringe-making,
cringeworthy, insufferable

## excruciatingly
**07** acutely **08** severely **09** extremely,
intensely, painfully **10** unbearably
**11** atrociously, intolerably

## exculpate
**04** free **05** clear **06** acquit, excuse, let
off, pardon **07** absolve, deliver, forgive,
justify, release **09** discharge,
exonerate, vindicate

## excursion
**02** ex **03** exc **04** raid, ride, tour, trip,
walk **05** drive, jaunt, jolly, sally, visit
**06** airing, detour, junket, outing,
picnic, ramble, sashay, sortie, vagary
**07** day trip, journey, outleap
**08** breather, escapade, straying
**09** departure, diversion, wandering
**10** digression, expedition **11** mystery
tour **12** pleasure trip

## excusable
**05** minor **06** slight, venial **09** allowable
**10** defensible, forgivable, pardonable
**11** explainable, justifiable, permissible
**14** understandable

## excuse
**04** faik, free, hook, plea **05** alibi, front,
salvo, scuse, shift, spare **06** acquit,
cop-out, defend, essoin, exempt, get-
out, ignore, let off, pardon, reason
**07** absolve, apology, condone, cover-
up, defence, essoyne, evasion,
explain, forgive, grounds, indulge,
justify, pretext, release, relieve
**08** liberate, mitigate, occasion,

overlook, palliate, pretence, tolerate
**09** allowance, discharge, exculpate,
exonerate, vindicate **10** indulgence,
mitigation, substitute **11** exoneration,
explanation, forgiveness, vindication
**12** apologize for **13** justification
**14** whittie-whattie

## execrable
**04** foul, vile **05** awful **06** odious
**07** hateful, heinous **08** accursed,
damnable, dreadful, horrible,
nauseous, shocking **09** abhorrent,
appalling, atrocious, loathsome,
obnoxious, offensive, repulsive,
revolting **10** abominable, deplorable,
despicable, detestable, disgusting

## execrate
**04** damn, hate **05** abhor, blast, curse
**06** detest, loathe, revile, vilify
**07** condemn, deplore, despise
**08** denounce **09** abominate, excoriate,
fulminate, imprecate **10** denunciate
**12** anathematize **14** inveigh against

## execute
**02** do **03** cut, fry, run **04** hang, kill, take
**05** dance, enact, serve, shoot, stage,
throw **06** behead, effect, finish, fulfil,
render **07** achieve, crucify, deliver,
enforce, garotte, garrote, perform,
produce, realize **08** bring off, carry out,
complete, despatch, dispatch,
engineer, expedite, garrotte, validate
**09** discharge, implement, liquidate
**10** accomplish, administer,
consummate, decapitate, guillotine,
perpetrate, put to death **11** electrocute
**13** put into effect **15** put into practice

## execution
**03** run **04** mode **05** style **06** effect,
manner **07** killing, staging **08** delivery,
dispatch **09** discharge, effecting,
enactment, operation, rendering,
rendition, technique **10** completion,
fulfilment **11** achievement, carrying-
out, enforcement, performance,
realization **12** consummation, death
penalty, presentation **13** death
sentence **14** accomplishment,
administration, implementation,
putting to death

---

*Execution methods include:*

**06** noyade
**07** burning, gassing, hanging,
stoning
**08** lynching, shooting
**09** beheading
**10** garrotting
**11** crucifixion, firing squad, stringing
up
**12** decapitation, guillotining
**13** electric chair, electrocution
**15** lethal injection

---

## executioner
**06** axeman, hit man, killer, slayer
**07** hangman **08** assassin, carnifex,
headsman, murderer **09** deathsman,
Jack Ketch, tormenter, tormentor
**10** liquidator **11** firing squad
**12** exterminator **15** Monsieur de Paris

## executive
**02** ex **04** exec, suit **06** leader **07** big

guns, guiding, leading, manager **08** big
shots, chairman, director, governor,
official, superior, top brass
**09** directing, governing, hierarchy,
lawmaking, organizer **10** chairwoman,
controller, government, leadership,
management, managerial, organizing,
regulating **11** chairperson, controlling,
directorial, ministerial, supervisory
**13** administrator **14** administration,
administrative, decision-making,
organizational, superintendent

## exegesis
**09** opening-up **10** exposition,
expounding **11** explanation,
explication **13** clarification
**14** interpretation

## exemplar
**04** copy, type **05** ideal, model
**07** epitome, example, paragon,
pattern, sampler **08** instance,
paradigm, specimen, standard
**09** archetype, criterion, prototype,
yardstick **10** embodiment
**12** illustration **15** exemplification

## exemplary
**04** good **05** ideal, model **06** worthy
**07** correct, perfect, warning
**08** flawless, laudable **09** admirable,
estimable, excellent, faultless
**10** admonitory, cautionary,
honourable **11** commendable,
meritorious **12** praiseworthy

## exemplify
**03** sum **04** cite, show, type **06** depict,
embody, typify **07** display, example,
exhibit **08** instance, manifest
**09** epitomize, personify, represent
**10** illustrate, synonymize
**11** demonstrate **12** characterize **13** be
an example of

## exempt
**04** free **05** clear, exeem, exeme, spare,
waive **06** excuse, immune, let off,
spared **07** absolve, dismiss, exclude,
excused, release, relieve **08** absolved,
excluded, liberate, released
**09** discharge, dismissed, exonerate,
liberated, not liable **10** discharged, not
subject **11** grandfather **15** grant
immunity to, make an exception

## exemption
**07** freedom, release **08** immunity,
variance **09** discharge, exception,
exclusion, indemnity, privilege
**10** absolution, indulgence, indulgency,
overslaugh **11** exoneration
**12** dispensation

## exercise
◊ *anagram indicator* **02** PE, PT **03** gym,
jog, try, use, vex **04** task, work
**05** annoy, apply, drill, exert, sport,
theme, train, upset, wield, worry
**06** burden, effort, employ, labour,
lesson, sports, warm up, warm-up
**07** afflict, agitate, concern, disturb,
exploit, perturb, problem, project,
running, trouble, utilize, work out,
workout **08** activity, ceremony,
distress, exertion, movement, practice,
practise, pump iron, training, warm
down, warm-down **09** discharge,

discourse, implement, make use of, operation, preoccupy, quodlibet **10** assignment, discipline, employment, fulfilment, gymnastics, isometrics **11** application, bring to bear, do exercises, piece of work, utilization **12** exercitation **13** bring into play, exert yourself **14** accomplishment, implementation

*Exercises include:*

**04** yoga
**05** Medau, Tae-Bo®
**06** cardio, chin-up, qigong, t'ai chi
**07** aquafit, chi kung, jogging, keep fit, Pilates, press-up
**08** aerobics
**09** boxercise, hatha yoga, Yogalates®
**10** aquarobics, daily dozen, dancercise
**11** Callanetics, eurhythmics
**12** body-building, calisthenics, step aerobics
**13** callisthenics, cross-training, physical jerks
**15** circuit training

**exert**
**02** do **03** use **05** apply, spend, wield **06** employ, expend, extend, put out **07** utilize **08** exercise, put forth **11** bring to bear **13** bring into play
• **exert yourself** **04** hump, pull, toil, work **05** sweat **06** labour, pingle, strain, strive **07** try hard **08** go all out, slog away, struggle **09** endeavour, take pains **10** do your best **11** give your all **12** do your utmost **13** apply yourself **15** make every effort

**exertion**
**03** use **04** toil, work **05** graft, pains, trial **06** action, effort, labour, pingle, strain, stress **07** attempt, travail, trouble **08** endeavor, exercise, industry, striving, struggle **09** diligence, endeavour, hard graft, operation **10** employment **11** application, utilization **12** perseverance **13** assiduousness

**exhalation**
**04** mist **06** meteor, vapour **08** emission, fumosity, mephitis **09** discharge, effluvium, emanation, expulsion **10** expiration **11** evaporation, respiration **12** breathing-out

**exhale**
**04** blow, emit, reek **05** expel, issue, smoke, steam **06** expire, vanish **07** blow out, breathe, emanate, give off, respire **08** perspire **09** discharge, evaporate, transpire **10** breathe out

**exhaust**
**02** do **03** beg, dry, sap, tax **04** do in, jade, kill, poop, suck, tire, wear **05** drain, empty, fordo, fumes, smoke, spend, steam, use up, waste, weary, whack **06** expend, fag out, finish, strain, vapour, weaken **07** consume, deplete, fatigue, knacker, overrun, overtax, play out, tire out, wash out, wear out, work out **08** bankrupt, emission, enervate, forspend,

forswink, knock out, overlive, override, overteem, overtire, overwork, squander, weary out **09** discharge, dissipate, emanation, forespend, overshoot, overspend, overweary, overwrite, tucker out **10** almost kill, exhalation, impoverish, nearly kill, run through **11** take it out of

**exhausted**
**03** dry **04** done, mate, shot, void, weak, worn **05** all in, empty, jaded, spent, tired, weary **06** all out, beaten, bushed, done in, effete, pooped, used up, wabbit, wasted, zonked **07** at an end, drained, emptied, euchred, fainted, fordone, puggled, shagged, shotten, waygone, whacked, worn out **08** a cot case, burnt out, consumed, dead-beat, depleted, dog-tired, fatigued, finished, forfairn, half-dead, jiggered, tired out, wiped out **09** burned out, dead tired, enervated, enfeebled, fagged out, knackered, played-out, pooped out, prostrate, shattered, stonkered, washed-out, zonked out **10** clapped-out, euchred out, forfeuchen, forfoughen, shagged out **11** bush whacked, forfoughten, ready to drop, stressed-out, tuckered out

**exhausting**
**04** hard **06** severe, taxing, tiring **07** arduous, killing, testing, wearing **08** draining, grueling, wearying **09** depletion, gruelling, laborious, punishing, strenuous **10** enervating, formidable **12** backbreaking, debilitating

**exhaustion**
**06** jet-lag **07** fatigue **08** distress, lethargy, weakness **09** tiredness, weariness **10** enervation, feebleness

**exhaustive**
**04** full **05** total **06** all-out **07** in-depth **08** complete, detailed, sweeping, thorough **09** extensive, full-scale, intensive **10** definitive **11** far-reaching **12** all-embracing, all-inclusive, encyclopedic **13** comprehensive

**exhaustively**
**05** fully **07** totally **10** completely, thoroughly **11** extensively, intensively **12** definitively **14** all-inclusively **15** comprehensively

**exhibit**
**03** air **04** hang, shew, show, wear **05** array, exude, model, offer, sport **06** expose, flaunt, parade, reveal, set out, unveil **07** display, express, present, propose, showing **08** disclose, discover, indicate, manifest, set forth, showcase **09** make clear, make plain, showpiece **10** exhibition **11** demonstrate **12** illustration, presentation, put on display **13** demonstration

**exhibition**
**04** demo, expo, fair, gift, show **05** grant, rodeo, Salon, simul **06** airing **07** academy, diorama, display, exhibit, ice show, preview, showing **08** aquacade, pavilion, showcase, sideshow, waxworks **09** allowance,

spectacle **10** cattle show, disclosure, exposition, expression, flower show, indication, panopticon, puppet show, revelation **11** performance **12** presentation, simultaneous **13** cinematograph, demonstration, manifestation, retrospective **14** representation

**exhibitionism**
**09** dramatics, flaunting, staginess **10** overacting, showing-off **11** flamboyance, histrionics, self-display **12** boastfulness

**exhibitionist**
**05** poser **06** poseur **07** show-off **09** extrovert **14** self-advertiser

**exhilarate**
**04** lift **05** cheer, elate **06** excite, perk up, thrill **07** animate, cheer up, delight, elevate, enliven, gladden **08** brighten, vitalize **09** inebriate, make happy, stimulate **10** intoxicate, invigorate, revitalize **11** make excited

**exhilarating**
**05** heady, sapid **06** breezy **08** cheerful, cheering, exciting **09** heartsome, thrilling **10** delightful, enlivening, gladdening **11** mind-blowing, stimulating **12** breathtaking, intoxicating, invigorating, revitalizing **13** heart-stirring

**exhilaration**
**03** joy **04** dash, élan, glee, zeal **05** gusto, mirth **06** ardour, gaiety, thrill **07** delight, elation **08** euphoria, gladness, hilarity, vivacity **09** animation, happiness **10** enthusiasm, exaltation, excitement, joyfulness, joyousness, liveliness **11** high spirits, stimulation **12** cheerfulness, invigoration **14** revitalization

**exhort**
**03** bid **04** goad, spur, urge, warn **05** press **06** advise, call on, enjoin, incite, prompt **07** beseech, caution, counsel, entreat, implore, inflame, inspire **08** admonish, call upon, persuade **09** encourage, instigate

**exhortation**
**04** call **06** advice, appeal, sermon, urging **07** bidding, caution, counsel, goading, lecture, warning **08** entreaty **09** enjoinder, parenesis **10** admonition, allocution, beseeching, incitement, injunction, invitation, paraenesis, persuasion, protreptic **13** encouragement

**exhumation**
**10** excavation, unearthing **12** disinterment **13** disentombment

**exhume**
**05** dig up **06** unbury **07** unearth **08** disinter, excavate **09** disentomb, disinhume, resurrect

**exigency**
**04** need, turn **06** crisis, demand, plight, stress **07** urgency **08** distress, pressure, quandary **09** emergency, necessity **10** difficulty **11** predicament,

**exigent**
requirement **12** criticalness
**14** imperativeness

**exigent**
**06** urgent **07** crucial **08** critical,
exacting, pressing **09** demanding,
extremity, insistent, necessary,
stringent

**exiguous**
**04** bare, slim **05** scant **06** meagre,
scanty, slight, sparse **07** slender
**10** inadequate, negligible
**12** insufficient

**exile**
**03** ban, bar **04** exul, oust **05** eject,
expat, expel, Galut **06** banish, deport,
émigré, Galuth, outlaw, pariah,
uproot, wretch **07** Babylon, cast out,
outcast, refugee **08** deportee,
Diaspora, drive out, fugitive, separate
**09** expulsion, extradite, ostracism,
ostracize, uprooting **10** banishment,
expatriate, repatriate, separating,
separation **11** deportation
**12** expatriation **13** excommunicate
**14** transportation **15** displaced person

**exist**
**02** be **04** last, live **05** abide, occur,
stand **06** endure, happen, remain **07** be
alive, be found, breathe, consist,
persist, prevail, subsist, survive
**08** continue, have life **09** be present,
have being **10** have breath **11** be
available **13** eke out a living, have
existence

**existence**
**03** ens **04** esse, fact, life **05** being, thing
**06** breath, entity, living **07** inbeing,
reality **08** creation, creature, survival,
the world **09** actuality, endurance,
lifestyle, way of life **11** continuance,
subsistence, way of living
**12** continuation, mode of living
**13** individuation
• **loss of independent existence**
**03** LIE

**existent**
**04** real **05** alive **06** actual, around,
extant, living **07** abiding, current,
present **08** enduring, existing, standing
**09** obtaining, remaining, surviving
**10** prevailing **11** in existence

**exit**
**02** go **03** die **04** door, gate, vent
**05** death, going, go out, issue, leave
**06** depart, egress, exodus, flight, log
off, log out, outlet, retire, way out
**07** doorway, leaving, off-ramp,
outgate, retreat **08** farewell, withdraw
**09** departure **10** going forth, retirement,
withdrawal **11** leave-taking **13** take
your leave

**exodus**
**02** Ex **04** exit, Exod **06** escape, flight,
hegira **07** fleeing, leaving, retreat
**09** departure, long march, migration
**10** evacuation, retirement, withdrawal
**13** mass departure **14** mass evacuation

**exonerate**
**04** free **05** clear, spare **06** acquit,
excuse, exempt, let off, pardon
**07** absolve, justify, release, relieve

**08** liberate **09** discharge, exculpate,
vindicate **15** declare innocent

**exoneration**
**06** pardon, relief **07** amnesty, freeing,
release **08** clearing, excusing,
immunity **09** acquittal, discharge,
dismissal, exemption, indemnity
**10** absolution, liberation
**11** exculpation, vindication
**13** justification

**exorbitant**
**05** steep, undue **07** a rip-off
**08** enormous **09** excessive, monstrous
**10** immoderate, inordinate
**11** extravagant, unwarranted
**12** extortionate, preposterous,
unreasonable **15** daylight robbery

**exorbitantly**
**06** unduly **11** excessively
**12** immoderately, inordinately,
unreasonably **13** extravagantly
**14** extortionately, through the nose

**exorcism**
**07** freeing **09** expulsion **10** adjuration,
casting out **11** deliverance
**12** exsufflation, insufflation,
purification

**exorcize**
**03** lay **04** free **05** expel **06** adjure, purify
**07** cast out **08** drive out **10** exsufflate,
insufflate

**exotic**
◇ *anagram indicator* **05** alien **06** ethnic,
way-out **07** bizarre, curious, foreign,
strange, unusual **08** external, imported,
peculiar, striking, tropical **09** colourful,
different, glamorous, non-native,
recherché **10** impressive, introduced,
outlandish, outrageous, remarkable,
unfamiliar **11** extravagant, fascinating,
sensational **13** extraordinary

**exotically**
**09** curiously, strangely, unusually
**10** remarkably, strikingly, tropically
**12** impressively, outlandishly
**13** sensationally **15** extraordinarily

**expand**
**03** pad **04** grow **05** swell, widen
**06** blow up, dilate, extend, fatten,
intend, put out, spread, unfold, unfurl,
work up **07** amplify, broaden, develop,
distend, enlarge, fill out, inflate,
magnify, open out, puff out, stretch,
thicken **08** dispread, enlargen,
escalate, increase, lengthen, multiply,
mushroom **09** branch out, diversify,
globalize, intensify, intumesce
**10** decompress, make bigger, make
larger **12** become bigger, become
larger
• **expand on** **08** dilate on, flesh out
**09** embroider, enlarge on **11** elaborate
on, expatiate on **13** go into details

**expanse**
**03** sea **04** area, main, mass, moor,
muir, vast **05** field, ocean, plain, range,
sheet, space, sweep, tract, vague,
waste **06** extent, region, spread
**07** breadth, stretch **08** vastness
**09** champaign, immensity, outspread
**11** immenseness **13** extensiveness

**expansion**
**04** boom **06** growth, spread **07** expanse
**08** dilation, increase, swelling
**09** diffusion, explosion, extension,
inflation, unfolding, unfurling
**10** broadening, dilatation, distension,
thickening **11** development,
enlargement, lengthening
**12** augmentation **13** amplification,
decompression, magnification
**14** multiplication **15** diversification

**expansive**
**04** open, warm, wide **05** broad
**06** genial **07** affable, growing
**08** effusive, friendly, outgoing,
sociable, sweeping, thorough
**09** diffusive, enlarging, expanding,
extensive, talkative **10** developing,
increasing, loquacious, magnifying,
widespread **11** expatiative, expatiatory,
forthcoming, multiplying, uninhibited,
wide-ranging **12** all-embracing,
diversifying **13** communicative,
comprehensive

**expatiate**
**06** dilate, expand **07** amplify, develop,
dwell on, enlarge, expound
**08** enlargen **09** elaborate, embellish,
give forth **11** hold forth on

**expatriate**
**04** oust **05** exile, expat, expel
**06** banish, deport, émigré, exiled,
uproot **07** outcast, refugee
**08** banished, deported, drive out,
emigrant, expelled, uprooted
**09** extradite, ostracize, proscribe
**10** repatriate **15** displaced person

**expect**
**04** hope, look, wait, want, ween, wish
**05** await, guess, think, trust **06** ask for,
assume, bank on, demand, lippen,
look to, reckon, rely on **07** believe, call
for, count on, foresee, hope for,
imagine, look for, predict, presume,
project, require, suppose, surmise
**08** envisage, figure on, forecast, insist
on, think for, watch for **09** bargain on,
look after **10** anticipate, bargain for,
conjecture **11** contemplate **13** look
forward to

**expectancy**
**04** hope **07** waiting **08** suspense
**09** curiosity, eagerness **10** conjecture
**11** expectation **12** anticipation

**expectant**
**05** eager, great, quick, ready **06** gravid
**07** anxious, curious, excited, hopeful
**08** awaiting, carrying, enceinte,
preggers, pregnant, watchful
**09** expecting, in the club, in trouble,
with child **10** big-bellied, in suspense
**11** open-mouthed **12** anticipating,
apprehensive **13** on tenterhooks **14** in
the family way, looking forward
**15** with bated breath

**expectantly**
**07** eagerly **09** hopefully **10** in suspense
**11** expectingly **14** apprehensively, in
anticipation, optimistically

**expectation**
**04** hope, view, want, wish **05** trust

**06** belief, demand **07** outlook, promise, suppose, surmise **08** forecast, optimism, prospect, reliance, suspense, tendance **09** assurance, eagerness **10** assumption, confidence, conjecture, insistence, looking-for, prediction, projection **11** calculation, possibility, presumption, probability, requirement, supposition **12** anticipation

**expecting**
**05** great, quick **06** gravid **08** carrying, enceinte, preggers, pregnant **09** expectant, in the club, in trouble, with child **10** big-bellied **14** in the family way

**expedience**
**05** haste **07** aptness, benefit, fitness, utility **08** despatch, dispatch, prudence **09** advantage, propriety **10** enterprise, expediency, pragmatism, properness, usefulness **11** convenience, helpfulness, suitability **12** advisability, desirability, practicality **13** effectiveness, judiciousness, profitability **14** profitableness, utilitarianism **15** appropriateness

**expedient**
**04** plan, ploy **05** dodge, means, salvo, shift, trick **06** device, method, scheme, tactic, useful **07** fitting, measure, politic, prudent, stopgap **08** artifice, resource, sensible, suitable, tactical **09** advisable, manoeuvre, opportune, practical, pragmatic, stratagem **10** beneficial, convenient, profitable **11** appropriate, contrivance, expeditious **12** advantageous

**expedite**
**05** hurry, press, quick **06** assist, hasten, prompt, step up **07** further, promote, quicken, speed up **08** despatch, dispatch **09** discharge **10** accelerate, facilitate **11** precipitate **12** hurry through, unencumbered

**expedition**
**03** dig **04** crew, hike, raid, sail, team, tour, trek, trip **05** group, haste, party, quest, shoot, speed **06** outing, ramble, safari, voyage **07** company, crusade, hosting, journey, mission, project, warpath **08** alacrity, campaign **09** adventure, excursion, field trip, swiftness **10** enterprise, pilgrimage, promptness **11** exploration, undertaking

**expeditious**
**04** fast **05** alert, brisk, hasty, quick, rapid, ready, swift **06** active, prompt, speedy **07** express, instant **08** diligent, meteoric **09** efficient, expedient, immediate

**expel**
**03** ban, bar, rid **04** hoof, oust, void **05** belch, eject, evict, exile **06** banish, deport, let out, outlaw, put out, reject **07** boot out, cast out, dismiss, drum out, expulse, extrude, fire out, kick out, read out, spew out, turn out **08** chuck out, drive out, evacuate, send down, sideline, throw out

**09** discharge, eliminate, proscribe, turn forth **10** expatriate

**expend**
**03** buy, pay, sap, use **04** blow **05** drain, empty, spend, use up, waste **06** afford, employ, lay out, outlay, pay out **07** consume, deplete, dispend, exhaust, fork out, fritter, procure, utilize **08** disburse, purchase, shell out, squander **09** dissipate, go through, overspend, splash out **10** get through

**expendable**
**09** throwaway **10** disposable **11** dispensable, inessential, replaceable, unimportant, unnecessary **12** non-essential

**expenditure**
**03** use **04** mise **05** costs, outgo, waste **06** outlay, output **07** expense, payment, sapping **08** dispense, draining, expenses, outgoing, spending **09** goings-out, outgoings **10** employment **11** application, consumption, dissipation, squandering, utilization **12** disbursement
• **reduction of expenditure** **02** ax **03** axe **06** saving **11** economizing

**expense, expenses**
**03** fee **04** cost, harm, loss, rate **05** costs, price **06** charge, outlay **07** payment **08** spending **09** detriment, outgoings, overheads, paying-out, sacrifice **11** expenditure, incidentals **12** disadvantage, disbursement
• **share of expense** **03** law

**expensive**
**04** dear, posh, salt **05** fancy, pricy, steep **06** costly, lavish, pricey **07** sky-high **08** high-cost, splendid **09** big-ticket, chargeful, excessive, executive **10** exorbitant, high-priced, overpriced **11** costing a lot, extravagant **12** costing a bomb, extortionate **15** costing the earth, daylight robbery

**experience**
**03** see, try **04** case, face, feel, find, have, know, meet, pass, spin **05** event, skill, taste **06** affair, endure, expert, ordeal, suffer **07** contact, episode, knowhow, receive, sustain, undergo **08** exposure, incident, learning, perceive, practice, training **09** adventure, encounter, go through, happening, knowledge **10** occurrence **11** familiarity, involvement, live through, observation, pass through **12** circumstance **13** participate in, participation, understanding
• **cause to experience** **04** lead
• **irritating experience** **03** rub **06** rubber
• **lacking experience** **05** green, naive
• **painful experience** **03** fit

**experienced**
**03** old **04** wise **05** adept, suave, tried **06** around, au fait, expert, mature **07** capable, skilful, skilled, trained, veteran, weighed **08** familiar, schooled, seasoned, traveled **09** au courant, competent, practised,

qualified, travailed, travelled **10** proficient, streetwise, well-versed **11** worldly wise **12** accomplished, experimented, professional **13** knowledgeable, sophisticated

**experiment**
**03** exp, try **04** test **05** assay, essay, proof, trial **06** dry run, sample, try out, try-out, verify **07** attempt, examine, explore, inquiry, observe, testing, venture **08** analysis, dummy run, piloting, research, trial run **09** procedure **10** conclusion, experience, pilot study **11** examination, investigate, observation **13** carry out tests, demonstration, investigation, trial and error **15** experimentation

**experimental**
**03** exp **04** test **05** pilot, trial **09** empirical, peirastic, tentative **10** scientific **11** exploratory, preliminary, provisional, speculative **13** investigative, observational, trial-and-error **15** at the trial stage

**experimentally**
**11** empirically, tentatively **12** innovatively, provisionally **13** by rule of thumb, speculatively **14** scientifically **15** by trial and error, investigatively

**experimentation**
**07** zoopery **08** research **10** empiricism, pragmatism **11** exploration, rule of thumb **12** verification **13** inventiveness, investigation

**expert**
**03** ace, dab, don, gun, pro, sly **04** able, buff, nark, oner, up on **05** adept, crack, fundi, maven, mavin, one-er, whizz **06** boffin, master, pundit, wunner **07** dab hand, egghead, hotshot, maestro, old hand, skilful, skilled, wise guy **08** dextrous, masterly, top-notch, virtuoso, well up on **09** authority, brilliant, dexterous, excellent, old master, practised, qualified **10** experience, past master, proficient, specialist **11** cognoscente, connoisseur, experienced **12** accomplished, practitioner, professional **13** knowledgeable

**expertise**
**05** knack, skill **07** ability, command, finesse, knowhow, mastery **08** deftness, facility **09** dexterity, knowledge **10** cleverness, expertness, tradecraft, virtuosity **11** proficiency, savoir-faire, skilfulness **13** understanding **15** professionalism

**expertly**
**04** ably **07** capably **08** masterly **09** skilfully **11** competently, efficiently, excellently **12** proficiently **14** professionally

**expiate**
**05** atone, purge **06** attone, pay for **07** redress, work out **08** atone for **09** make up for **12** do penance for **13** make amends for

## expiation
**06** amends, ransom, shrift **07** penance, redress **09** atonement **10** recompense, redemption, reparation

## expire
**03** die, end **04** emit, stop **05** cease, close, lapse **06** depart, finish, pass on, peg out, perish, pop off, run out **07** decease, snuff it **08** conclude, pass away, pass over **09** have had it, terminate **11** bite the dust, come to an end, discontinue **12** lose your life, pop your clogs **13** kick the bucket, meet your maker **14** depart this life, give up the ghost **15** be no longer valid, breathe your last, cash in your chips

## expiry
**03** end, exp, ish **05** close, lapse **06** finish **09** cessation **10** conclusion, expiration **11** termination **15** discontinuation

## explain
**04** tell **05** gloze, solve, teach **06** decode, defend, define, excuse, open up, set out, unfold **07** clarify, expound, justify, resolve, unravel **08** decipher, describe, disclose, simplify, spell out, untangle **09** delineate, elaborate, elucidate, enucleate, explicate, interpret, lie behind, make clear, translate, vindicate **10** account for, illustrate **11** demonstrate, explain away, rationalize, shed light on **12** throw light on **14** give a reason for

## explanation
**04** note **05** alibi, gloss **06** answer, excuse, motive, reason, report **07** account, comment, defence, meaning, warrant **08** apologia, decoding, exegesis, footnote, solution **09** unfolding **10** annotation, commentary, definition, exposition, expounding **11** deciphering, delineation, description, elucidation, explication, vindication **12** illustration **13** clarification, demonstration, justification **14** interpretation, reconciliation, simplification **15** éclaircissement, rationalization

## explanatory
**08** exegetic **10** exegetical, expositive, expository, justifying **11** declaratory, descriptive, elucidative, elucidatory, explicative **12** illustrative, interpretive **13** demonstrative **14** interpretative

## expletive
**04** cuss, oath **05** curse **08** anathema, cussword **09** blasphemy, obscenity, profanity, swear-word **10** execration **11** bad language, imprecation **14** four-letter word

## explicable
**08** solvable **09** definable, exponible **10** resolvable **11** accountable, explainable, justifiable **12** determinable, intelligible **13** interpretable **14** understandable

## explicate
**06** define, unfold **07** clarify, develop, explain, expound, unravel, work out

**08** describe, set forth, spell out, untangle **09** elucidate, interpret, make clear **10** illustrate **11** demonstrate

## explication
**10** exposition **11** description, elucidation, explanation **12** illustration **13** clarification **14** interpretation

## explicit
**04** open **05** adult, bawdy, clear, dirty, exact, frank, plain **06** candid, direct, filthy, full-on, smutty, stated, X-rated **07** certain, express, obscene, pointed, precise **08** absolute, declared, definite, detailed, distinct, hard-core, positive, shocking, specific **09** offensive, outspoken **10** forthright, uncensored, unreserved **11** categorical, near the bone, plain-spoken, unambiguous, unequivocal, uninhibited **12** pornographic, unrestrained **14** near the knuckle **15** straightforward

## explicitly
**06** barely **07** clearly, in terms, overtly, plainly **08** directly **09** expressly **10** definitely **12** specifically **13** in so many words, unambiguously, unequivocally

## explode
◇ *anagram indicator* **04** blow, boom, go up, leap **05** blast, burst, erupt, go off, rebut, surge **06** blow up, debunk, go bang, refute, rocket, see red, set off, spring **07** flare up **08** boil over, burst out, detonate, displode, disprove, escalate, mushroom **09** blow a fuse, discharge, discredit, do your nut, fulminate, repudiate **10** accelerate, hit the roof, invalidate **11** blow your top, go up the wall, grow rapidly, lose your rag **12** blow your cool, fly into a rage, give the lie to, lose your cool **13** hit the ceiling **14** lose your temper **15** fly off the handle, go off the deep end
• **cause to explode 04** fire **06** spring **08** detonate **09** fulminate

## exploit
**03** act, tap, use **04** deed, feat, gest, milk, mine **05** abuse, apply, bleed, geste, stunt **06** action, draw on, employ, fleece, misuse, rip off **07** oppress, utilize **08** activity, cash in on, ill-treat, impose on, profit by **09** adventure, make use of, profiteer, victimize **10** attainment, manipulate **11** achievement, walk all over **12** capitalize on, put to good use, take for a ride **13** take liberties, turn to account **14** accomplishment, play off against, pull a fast one on **15** take advantage of

## exploitation
**03** use **05** abuse **06** misuse, rip-off **07** milking **08** bleeding, fleecing **10** employment, oppression **11** application, cashing in on, making use of, utilization **12** manipulation **14** taking for a ride **15** taking advantage

## exploration
**04** tour, trip **05** probe, study **06** safari, search, survey, travel, voyage **07** inquiry **08** analysis, research,

scrutiny **10** expedition, inspection **11** examination, observation **13** investigation **14** reconnaissance

## exploratory
**05** pilot, trial **07** probing, wildcat **08** analytic **09** searching, tentative **11** fact-finding **12** experimental **13** investigative

## explore
**02** do **04** feel, palp, tour **05** probe, scout, study **06** review, search, survey, travel **07** analyse, examine, inspect **08** consider, look into, prospect, research, traverse **10** scrutinize **11** inquire into, investigate, reconnoitre, see the world

## explorer
**05** scout **06** tourer **08** surveyor **09** navigator, traveller **10** discoverer, prospector **11** bandeirante **12** reconnoitrer

*Explorers and pioneers include:*

**03 Cam, Caõ, Rae** (John)
**04 Byrd** (Richard Evelyn), **Cano** (Juan Sebastian del), **Cook** (James), **Diaz** (Bartolomeu), **Eyre** (Edward John), **Gama** (Vasco da), **Park** (Mungo), **Polo** (Marco), **Ross** (Sir James Clark), **Soto** (Fernando de), **Soto** (Hernando de)
**05 Barth** (Heinrich), **Beebe** (Charles William), **Boone** (Daniel), **Bruce** (James), **Cabot** (John), **Clark** (William), **Drake** (Francis), **Fuchs** (Sir Vivian Ernest), **Hanno, Lewis** (Meriwether), **Newby** (Eric), **Oates** (Lawrence), **Peary** (Robert Edwin), **Scott** (Robert Falcon), **Speke** (John Hanning)
**06 Baffin** (William), **Balboa** (Vasco Núñez de), **Bering** (Vitus), **Burton** (Sir Richard), **Cabral** (Pedro Alvares), **Carson** (Kit), **Nansen** (Fridtjof), **Tasman** (Abel Janszoon), **Torres** (Luis de)
**07 Andrews** (Roy Chapman), **Fiennes** (Sir Ranulph), **Fleming** (Peter), **Hillary** (Sir Edmund), **La Salle** (Robert Cavelier, Sieur de), **Pytheas, Raleigh** (Sir Walter), **Stanley** (Sir Henry Morton)
**08 Amundsen** (Roald), **Columbus** (Christopher), **Cousteau** (Jacques), **Flinders** (Matthew), **Franklin** (Sir John), **Linnaeus** (Carolus), **Magellan** (Ferdinand), **Standish** (Myles), **Thesiger** (Sir Wilfred), **Vespucci** (Amerigo), **Williams** (Roger)
**09 Emin Pasha, Frobisher** (Sir Martin), **Heyerdahl** (Thor), **Rasmussen** (Knud), **Vancouver** (George)
**10 Erik the Red, Oglethorpe** (James Edward), **Shackleton** (Sir Ernest Henry), **Van der Post** (Sir Laurens)
**11 Livingstone** (David)
**12 Leif Eriksson, Younghusband** (Sir Francis)
**14 Bellingshausen** (Fabian Gottlieb von), **Blashford-Snell** (Colonel John), **Hanbury-Tenison** (Robin Airling)

## explosion
**03** fit, pop **04** bang, boom, chug, clap, leap, rage, roll **05** blast, burst, crack, pluff, surge **06** blow-up, report, rumble **07** Big Bang, flare-up, tantrum, thunder **08** airburst, eruption, outbreak, outburst, paroxysm **09** discharge **10** detonation, displosion **14** dramatic growth, sudden increase

## explosive
◇ *anagram indicator* **02** HE **04** bomb, mine, wild **05** angry, fiery, jelly, rapid, tense **06** abrupt, raging, stormy, sudden, touchy **07** charged, fraught, violent **08** critical, dramatic, meteoric, perilous, powerful, unstable, volatile, volcanic, worked-up **09** dangerous, fulminant, hazardous, initiator, plastique, rocketing, sensitive **10** burgeoning, propellant, unexpected **11** exponential, mushrooming, overwrought **12** nerve-racking, unrestrained

*Explosives include:*

**03** RDX, TNT
**04** ANFO, TATP
**06** amatol, dualin, Semtex®, tonite
**07** ammonal, cordite, dunnite, lyddite, plastic
**08** cheddite, dynamite, melinite, roburite, xyloidin
**09** cyclonite, gelignite, guncotton, gunpowder, xyloidine
**11** nitrocotton
**14** nitrocellulose, nitroglycerine, trinitrotoluol
**15** trinitrotoluene

## explosively
**06** wildly **07** angrily, fierily, rapidly, tensely **08** suddenly, unstably **09** violently **10** critically, powerfully **11** dangerously, hazardously **12** dramatically, unexpectedly, volcanically **13** destructively, exponentially

## exponent
**05** adept, index, power **06** backer, expert, master, player **08** adherent, advocate, champion, defender, promoter, upholder **09** performer, proponent, spokesman, supporter **10** specialist **11** spokeswoman **12** practitioner, spokesperson

## export
**02** ex **03** exp **05** trade **08** deal with, Klondike, Klondyke, re-export, transfer **09** traffic in, transport **10** sell abroad **12** foreign trade, sell overseas **13** exported goods **15** exported product

## expose
**03** ope **04** open, risk, show **05** flash, strip **06** betray, detect, hazard, reveal, show up, unmask, unveil **07** display, divulge, exhibit, imperil, lay bare, lay open, present, uncover, unearth **08** denounce, disclose, endanger, manifest **09** lay open to, make known, put at risk, subject to **10** jeopardize **11** introduce to, present with **12** acquaint with, bring to light **13** put in jeopardy, take the lid off **14** blow the whistle, make vulnerable **15** familiarize with

## exposé
**07** account, article **08** exposure **10** disclosure, divulgence, revelation, uncovering

## exposed
**03** out **04** bare, open **05** naked, shown **06** object, on show, on view **07** subject **08** laid bare, revealed **09** exhibited, in the open, on display **10** vulnerable **11** susceptible, unprotected

## exposition
**04** expo, fair, show **05** moral, paper, study **06** aperçu, exposé, theory, thesis **07** account, display, exposal, Midrash, working **08** analysis, critique, exegesis **09** discourse, monograph, unfolding **10** commentary, enarration, exhibition **11** description, elucidation, explanation, explication **12** illumination, illustration, presentation **13** clarification, demonstration **14** interpretation

## expository
**08** exegetic **11** declaratory, descriptive, elucidative, explanatory, explicatory, hermeneutic **12** illustrative, interpretive **14** interpretative

## expostulate
**05** argue, claim, plead **06** reason **07** protest **08** disagree, dissuade **11** remonstrate

## exposure
**03** air **04** hype, plug, risk **05** flash **06** airing, danger, exposé, hazard **07** contact, display, exposal, showing **08** jeopardy **09** awareness, detection, discovery, exposure, knowledge, notoriety, promotion, publicity, unmasking, unveiling **10** disclosure, divulgence, exhibition, experience, revelation, uncovering **11** advertising, familiarity **12** acquaintance, denunciation, presentation **13** manifestation, vulnerability **14** susceptibility **15** public attention

## expound
**04** open, read, rede **06** open up, preach, set out, unbolt, unfold **07** analyse, clarify, dissect, explain, unravel **08** describe, prophesy, set forth, spell out, untangle **09** comment on, elucidate, explicate, interpret, sermonize **10** illuminate, illustrate **11** demonstrate

## express
**02** ex **03** air, exp, put, say **04** emit, fast, have, show, sole, tell, vent, word **05** brisk, clear, couch, exact, plain, quick, rapid, speak, state, swift, utter, voice **06** assert, convey, denote, depict, embody, intend, report, reveal, speedy, stated, strain **07** certain, declare, divulge, exhibit, get over, non-stop, precise, put over, signify, special, testify **08** announce, clear-cut, conceive, definite, disclose, distinct, explicit, indicate, intimate, manifest, point out, positive, register, specific, stand for **09** designate, enunciate,

estafette, formulate, high-speed, pronounce, put across, represent, specially, symbolize, ventilate, verbalize **10** articulate, particular **11** categorical, communicate, demonstrate, expeditious, give voice to, unambiguous, unequivocal, well-defined **12** put into words

## expression
◇ *homophone indicator* **03** air **04** look, mien, show, sign, term, tone, word **05** adage, axiom, depth, force, idiom, maxim, power, scowl, style, voice **06** aspect, phrase, saying, speech, symbol, vigour **07** diction, emotion, feeling, gesture, grimace, passion, proverb, voicing, wording **08** aphorism, artistry, delivery, language, locution, phrasing **09** assertion, intensity, set phrase, statement, utterance, verbalism, vividness **10** appearance, creativity, embodiment, exhibition, indication, intimation, intonation, modulation **11** countenance, declaration, enunciation, imagination **12** announcement, articulation, illustration, proclamation, turn of phrase, vocalization **13** communication, demonstration, manifestation, pronouncement, verbalization **14** representation
• **prevent free expression 03** gag

## expressionless
**04** dull **05** blank, empty **06** glassy, glazed **07** deadpan, vacuous **08** toneless **09** impassive, unmeaning **10** poker-faced **11** emotionless, inscrutable, meaningless **13** straight-faced

## expressive
**05** vivid **06** lively, moving **07** showing, telling **08** animated, eloquent, emphatic, forceful, poignant, striking **09** evocative, revealing, speechful **10** articulate, indicative, meaningful, suggesting, suggestive, thoughtful **11** informative, significant, sympathetic **13** communicative, demonstrating, demonstrative

## expressively
**07** vividly **09** meaningly **10** eloquently, espressivo **11** evocatively **12** emphatically, meaningfully, suggestively **13** informatively **15** demonstratively

## expressiveness
**09** poignancy, vividness **10** articulacy **13** evocativeness **14** articulateness, meaningfulness

## expressly
◇ *homophone indicator* **06** solely **07** clearly, exactly, plainly **09** decidedly, on purpose, pointedly, precisely, purposely, specially **10** absolutely, definitely, distinctly, especially, explicitly, manifestly **12** particularly, specifically **13** categorically, intentionally, unambiguously, unequivocally

## expropriate
**04** take **05** annex, seize, usurp

## expropriation

06 assume 07 impound, unhouse
08 arrogate, disseise, take away
09 sequester 10 commandeer,
confiscate, dispossess 11 appropriate,
requisition

## expropriation

07 seizure 10 arrogation, impounding,
taking-away 12 confiscation
13 appropriation, dispossession,
sequestration

## expulsion

05 exile, purge 07 removal, sacking,
the boot, the sack, voiding
08 belching, ejection, eviction
09 discharge, dismissal, ejectment,
exclusion, excretion, extrusion,
ostracism, rejection 10 banishment,
evacuation 11 throwing out

## expunge

04 raze 05 annul, erase 06 cancel,
delete, efface, remove, rub out
07 abolish, blot out, destroy, wipe out
08 cross out, get rid of 09 eradicate,
extirpate 10 annihilate, extinguish,
obliterate 11 exterminate

## expurgate

03 cut 04 geld 05 emend, purge
06 censor, purify 07 clean up
08 sanitize 10 blue-pencil, bowdlerize

## exquisite

04 fine, keen, pink, rare 05 acute, sharp
06 choice, dainty, lovely, picked,
pretty, too-too 07 elegant, fragile,
intense, perfect, refined 08 abstruse,
charming, cultured, delicate, flawless,
piercing, pleasing, poignant, precious
09 beautiful, delicious, excellent,
sensitive 10 attractive, cultivated,
delightful, discerning, far-fetched,
fastidious, impeccable, meticulous
11 outstanding 14 discriminating

## exquisitely

06 finely 08 daintily 09 elegantly
10 charmingly, delicately, pleasingly
11 beautifully 12 attractively,
delightfully

## ex-serviceman

03 vet 07 veteran

## extant

05 alive 06 living 08 existent, existing
09 remaining, surviving 10 subsistent,
subsisting 11 in existence 13 still
existing

## extempore

05 ad-lib 07 offhand 08 suddenly 09 ad
libitum, impromptu, unplanned
10 improvised, off the cuff,
unprepared, unscripted
11 spontaneous, unrehearsed
13 spontaneously 14 extemporaneous

## extemporize

04 pong 05 ad-lib 06 make up, wing it
09 improvise 11 play it by ear 15 speak
off the cuff, think on your feet

## extend

02 go 03 lap, run 04 draw, give, grow,
last, pass, span 05 cover, grant, offer,
range, reach, renew, seize, value,
widen 06 assess, bestow, come to,
confer, deploy, expand, go up to,

impart, intend, put out, spread, step
up, take in, unfold, unwind 07 amplify,
augment, broaden, carry on, develop,
drag out, draw out, embrace, enlarge,
hold out, include, involve, present,
produce, proffer, prolong, spin out,
stretch 08 come up to, continue,
elongate, go down to, increase,
lengthen, protract, put forth, reach out
09 go as far as, intensify 10 come down
to, comprehend

## extendable

07 elastic 08 stretchy 09 dilatable,
extensive 10 expandable
11 enlargeable, magnifiable,
stretchable

## extended

04 long, wide 06 spread 07 distent,
lengthy 08 at length, enlarged,
expanded 09 amplified, continued,
developed, expansive, increased,
prolonged 10 diastaltic, lengthened

## extension

03 ext 04 wing 05 add-on, delay
06 annexe 07 adjunct, stretch
08 addendum, addition, appendix,
deferral, increase, more time,
protense, quantity, widening
09 diffusion, expansion 10 broadening,
elongation, production, stretching,
supplement 11 development,
enhancement, enlargement,
lengthening, protraction
12 continuation, postponement,
prolongation 13 proliferation
14 additional time

## extensive

04 huge, long, main, vast, wide
05 broad, large, roomy 07 general, in
depth, lengthy 08 complete, extended,
far-flung, sizeable, spacious, thorough
09 boundless, capacious, fair-sized,
pervasive, prevalent, universal,
unlimited, wholesale 10 commodious,
large-scale, voluminous, widespread
11 far-reaching, substantial, wide-
ranging 12 all-inclusive
13 comprehensive

## extensively

06 widely 07 greatly, largely
09 generally, wholesale 10 completely,
thoroughly 11 boundlessly
13 substantially 15 comprehensively

## extent

04 area, bulk, play, size, span, term,
time 05 level, limit, range, reach,
scope, sweep, width 06 amount,
attack, bounds, degree, length, sphere,
spread, volume 07 breadth, compass,
expanse, lengths, measure, seizure,
stretch 08 coverage, duration, quantity
09 dimension, magnitude
10 dimensions
• **to full extent**  04 hard, much
• **to some extent**  ◇ hidden indicator
• **to that extent**  02 as
• **to the extent of**  02 by 03 for

## extenuate

06 excuse, lessen, modify, soften
07 qualify 08 diminish, minimize,
mitigate, palliate

## extenuating

08 excusing 09 lessening, modifying,
softening 10 justifying, minimizing,
mitigating, moderating, palliating,
palliative, qualifying 11 diminishing,
exculpatory, extenuative, extenuatory

## exterior

03 ext 04 face, skin 05 glaze, outer,
shell 06 façade, finish 07 coating,
foreign, outside, outward, surface
08 covering, external 09 externals,
extrinsic, objective, outermost
10 appearance, peripheral
11 superficial, surrounding 12 outer
surface 15 external surface

## exterminate

04 do in, kill 06 kill up 07 abolish,
bump off, destroy, kill off, wipe out
08 knock off, massacre 09 eliminate,
eradicate, extirpate, liquidate,
slaughter 10 annihilate, do away with

## extermination

07 killing 08 genocide, massacre
09 ethnocide 11 destruction,
elimination, eradication, extirpation
12 annihilation

## external

03 ext, out 05 outer 07 foreign, outside,
outward, surface, visible 08 apparent,
cortical, exterior, visiting 09 extrinsic,
outermost 10 accidental, extramural,
extraneous, peripheral
11 independent, non-resident,
superficial

## externally

◇ containment indicator 03 ext 07 visibly
09 outwardly 10 apparently
12 extraneously, peripherally
13 superficially

## extinct

03 ext, old, out 04 dead, gone, lost
05 ended, passé 06 bygone, former
07 defunct, died out, expired, invalid
08 burnt out, inactive, obsolete,
outmoded, quenched, squashed,
vanished, wiped out 09 abolished
10 antiquated, terminated 11 non-
existent 12 exterminated, extinguished

## extinction

05 death 07 quietus 08 dying-out,
excision 09 abolition, vanishing
11 destruction, eradication,
termination 12 annihilation,
obliteration 13 disappearance,
extermination

## extinguish

03 end 04 dout, kill 05 choke, douse,
dowse, drown, erase, quash, quell,
slake 06 die out, put out, quench,
remove, rub out, sloken 07 stifle
07 abolish, blow out, destroy,
expunge, slocken, smother, stub out
08 snuff out, suppress 09 eliminate,
eradicate, extirpate 10 annihilate,
dampen down 11 exterminate

## extirpate

04 root 05 erase 06 cut out, remove,
uproot 07 abolish, destroy, expunge,
root out, weed out, wipe out 08 stamp
out 09 eliminate, eradicate

**extol**

10 annihilate, deracinate, extinguish
11 exterminate

**extol**

04 laud, puff 05 exalt, raise 06 lift up,
praise 07 acclaim, advance, applaud,
commend, glorify, magnify
08 eulogize 09 celebrate
10 rhapsodize, wax lyrical

**extort**

04 milk, rack 05 bleed, bully, exact,
force, screw, wrest, wring 06 coerce
07 extract, squeeze 08 get out of,
outwrest 09 blackmail, shake down

**extortion**

05 chout, force 06 demand 07 milking
08 chantage, coercion, exaction
09 blackmail 10 oppression
12 malversation, racketeering

**extortionate**

04 hard 05 harsh 06 severe 08 exacting,
grasping, grinding 09 excessive,
rapacious 10 exorbitant, immoderate,
inordinate, oppressive, outrageous
12 preposterous, unreasonable

**extortionist**

05 screw, shark 06 yakuza 07 bleeder,
exacter, exactor, menacer
09 exactress, exploiter, profiteer,
racketeer 11 blackmailer, bloodsucker,
extortioner

**extra**

01 w 02 ex, lb, nb 03 bye, ext, new,
odd, too 04 also, gash, more, over,
wide 05 added, bonus, fresh, other,
spare, super- 06 as well, excess, leg
bye, no ball, unused, walk-on
07 adjunct, and so on, another,
besides, further, reserve, surplus
08 addendum, addition, additive,
buckshee, left-over, let alone,
unneeded 09 accessory, along with,
ancillary, appendage, auxiliary, bit
player, excessive, extension,
extremely, minor role, redundant,
unusually 10 additional, attachment,
complement, especially, in addition,
remarkably, subsidiary, supplement,
uncommonly, walk-on part
11 superfluous, unnecessary
12 additionally, not to mention,
particularly, spear-carrier, together
with 13 exceptionally, extraordinary,
not forgetting, supernumerary,
supplementary 14 above and beyond,
into the bargain 15 extraordinarily

**extract**

◇ anagram indicator ◇ hidden indicator
03 ext, get, gut, try 04 cite, clip, copy,
cull, draw, grog, milk, pick, pull, suck,
worm 05 educe, exact, glean, juice,
pluck, prise, quote, wrest, wring
06 choose, cut out, decoct, derive,
distil, elicit, extort, gather, get out,
gobbet, obtain, quarry, remove,
render, select, uproot, wrench
07 cutting, derived, draw out, essence,
estreat, excerpt, extrait, logwood,
passage, pull out, recover, spirits, take
out 08 abstract, boil down, citation,
clipping, euonymin, pericope,
tincture, withdraw 09 decoction,
enucleate, quotation, reproduce,

selection 10 deracinate, distillate
11 concentrate 12 distillation

**extraction**

04 race 05 birth, blood, brood, stock
06 family, origin 07 descent, drawing,
extreat, lineage, pulling, removal
08 ancestry, pedigree 09 obtaining,
parentage, retrieval, taking-out,
uprooting 10 derivation, drawing-out,
separation, withdrawal

**extradite**

05 exile, expel 06 banish, deport
08 hand over, send back, send home
10 repatriate

**extradition**

05 exile 08 handover 09 expulsion
10 banishment 11 deportation, sending
back 12 repatriation

**extraneous**

05 alien, extra, inapt 07 foreign, strange
08 exterior, external, needless,
unneeded 09 extrinsic, redundant,
unrelated 10 additional, immaterial,
inapposite, incidental, irrelevant,
peripheral, tangential 11 inessential,
superfluous, unconnected,
unessential, unnecessary
12 inapplicable, non-essential
13 inappropriate, supplementary

**extraordinarily**

◇ anagram indicator 05 oddly 07 notably
08 uniquely 09 amazingly, bizarrely,
curiously, specially, strangely,
unusually 10 remarkably,
uncommonly 12 astoundingly,
particularly, unexpectedly
13 exceptionally, significantly

**extraordinary**

◇ anagram indicator 03 odd 04 rare
06 unique 07 amazing, bizarre,
curious, notable, special, strange,
unusual 08 peculiar, singular,
uncommon 09 by-ordinar, emergency,
fantastic, wonderful 10 astounding,
marvellous, noteworthy, particular,
portentous, remarkable, surprising,
tremendous, unexpected
11 astonishing, exceptional,
outstanding, significant
13 unprecedented 14 out of this world,
unconventional

**extrapolate**

04 plan 05 gauge 06 expect, reckon,
sample 07 project 08 estimate
09 calculate 11 approximate

**extraterrestrial**

02 ET 05 alien

**extravagance**

05 extra, folly, treat, waste 06 excess,
luxury, vanity 07 riotise, splurge
08 wildness 09 profusion 10 digression,
enthusiasm, imprudence, lavishness,
ornateness, profligacy 11 dissipation,
ostentation, prodigality, squandering
12 exaggeration, immoderation,
improvidence, overspending,
recklessness, wastefulness
13 excessiveness 14 outrageousness,
thriftlessness 15 pretentiousness

**extravagant**

◇ anagram indicator 03 OTT 04 dear,
wild 05 outré, steep 06 costly, flashy,
lavish, ornate, pricey, rococo
07 baroque, bizarre, profuse, sky-high
08 fanciful, prodigal, reckless,
romantic, wasteful 09 excessive,
expensive, fanatical, fantastic, high-
flown, imprudent, irregular, wasterful
10 exorbitant, extra modum,
flamboyant, high-flying, immoderate,
outrageous, overpriced, over the top,
profligate, thriftless 11 exaggerated,
improvident, pretentious, spendthrift,
squandering 12 costing a bomb,
extortionate, ostentatious,
preposterous, unrestrained
15 churrigueresque, costing the earth,
daylight robbery

**extravaganza**

04 show 06 féerie 07 display, pageant
09 spectacle 11 spectacular

**extreme**

◇ head selection indicator ◇ tail selection
indicator ◇ ends selection indicator
03 end, top 04 acme, apex, dire, edge,
last, line, mark, peak, pink, pole, wack
05 acute, depth, final, great, gross,
harsh, limit, rigid, stern, ultra, utter
06 climax, excess, far-off, height, red-
hot, severe, strict, utmost, zenith
07 distant, drastic, endmost, faraway,
highest, intense, maximum, outside,
radical, serious, supreme, zealous
08 farthest, greatest, hardline, outlying,
pinnacle, remotest, terminal, ultimate
09 desperate, downright, Draconian,
excessive, extremist, extremity,
fanatical, out-and-out, outermost,
stringent, uttermost 10 immoderate,
inordinate, iron-fisted, iron-handed,
most remote, pre-eminent,
remarkable, unyielding 11 exceptional,
termination, unrelenting
12 unreasonable 13 extraordinary
14 uncompromising
• **in the extreme** 04 very 06 highly
07 awfully, greatly, utterly 08 terribly
09 intensely 10 dreadfully, remarkably,
uncommonly 11 exceedingly,
excessively, frightfully
12 immoderately, inordinately,
terrifically 13 exceptionally
15 extraordinarily
• **opposite extreme** 04 pole

**extremely**

◇ ends selection indicator 03 too 04 awfy,
high, mega, very 05 jolly 06 deuced,
highly, mighty, mortal, pretty, really
07 acutely, awfully, greatly, majorly,
only too, parlous, utterly 08 deucedly,
severely, terribly 09 decidedly,
intensely, seriously, unusually
10 dreadfully, remarkably, thoroughly,
uncommonly 11 exceedingly,
excessively, frightfully
12 immoderately, inordinately,
terrifically, tremendously,
unreasonably 13 exceptionally
15 extraordinarily

**extremism**

04 zeal 08 zealotry 09 terrorism

**extremist**
**10** fanaticism, radicalism
**13** excessiveness

**extremist**
**05** ultra **06** zealot **07** diehard, fanatic, Jacobin, radical **08** militant
**09** hardliner, terrorist **11** merveilleux
**12** merveilleuse **14** fundamentalist

**extremity**
**03** arm, end, fix, jam, leg, tip, toe, top
**04** acme, apex, edge, foot, hand, hole, limb, mess, peak, pole, spot, tail
**05** bound, brink, depth, limit, point, verge **06** apogee, border, crisis, danger, ending, excess, finger, height, margin, pickle, plight, zenith
**07** exigent, extreme, maximum, minimum, trouble **08** boundary, exigency, frontier, hardship, outrance, pinnacle, terminal, terminus, ultimate
**09** adversity, emergency, indigence, periphery, tight spot, utterance
**10** misfortune **11** dire straits, termination

**extricate**
**04** free **05** clear **06** detach, get out, remove, rescue **07** deliver, extract, outwind, release, relieve, set free **08** let loose, liberate, withdraw **09** disengage
**11** disentangle

**extrinsic**
**05** alien **06** exotic **07** foreign, outside
**08** exterior, external, imported
**10** extraneous, forinsecal

**extrovert**
**03** lad **05** mixer **06** joiner **07** mingler
**08** outgoing **10** socializer **14** outgoing person, sociable person

**extroverted**
**06** hearty **07** amiable **08** amicable, friendly, outgoing, sociable
**09** exuberant **13** demonstrative
**14** outward-looking

**extrude**
**05** expel, mould **08** force out, press out, protrude, put forth **09** thrust out
**10** squeeze out

**exuberance**
**04** life, zest **05** pride **06** energy, vigour
**07** elation, pizzazz **08** buoyancy, lushness, outburst, rankness, richness, vitality, vivacity **09** abundance, animation, eagerness, plenitude, profusion **10** ebullience, enthusiasm, excitement, lavishness, liveliness, luxuriance, luxuriancy, redundancy
**11** copiousness, fulsomeness, high spirits, joie de vivre, prodigality
**12** cheerfulness, effusiveness, exaggeration, exhilaration
**13** effervescence, excessiveness
**14** superabundance

**exuberant**
**03** mad **04** lush, rank, rich **06** elated, lavish, lively, skippy **07** buoyant, excited, fulsome, profuse, zestful
**08** abundant, animated, cheerful, effusive, spirited, thriving, vigorous
**09** ebullient, energetic, luxuriant, luxurious, plenteous, plentiful, sparkling, vivacious **10** boisterous, full of life **11** exaggerated, exhilarated, overflowing **12** effervescent, enthusiastic, high-spirited, rambunctious, unrestrained
**13** irrepressible **15** on top of the world

**exude**
**03** gum **04** emit, leak, ooze, seep, show, weep, well **05** bleed, issue, still, sweat, swelt **07** display, emanate, excrete, exhibit, flow out, give off, give out, guttate, radiate, secrete, swelter, trickle **08** manifest, perspire
**09** discharge

**exult**
**03** joy **04** crow **05** gloat, glory, revel
**06** relish **07** delight, rejoice, triumph
**08** be joyful, jubilate **09** celebrate
**10** tripudiate **11** be delighted **13** be over the moon

**exultant**
**06** elated, joyful, joyous **07** gleeful
**08** exulting, jubilant, thrilled **09** cock-a-hoop, delighted, overjoyed, rejoicing, revelling **10** enraptured, triumphant **11** on cloud nine, over the moon **12** transporting **15** in seventh heaven

**exultation**
**03** joy **04** glee, pean **05** glory, paean
**06** eulogy **07** crowing, delight, elation, triumph **08** gloating, glorying
**09** jubilance, jubilancy, merriness, rejoicing, revelling, transport
**10** joyfulness, joyousness, jubilation
**11** celebration

**eye**
**02** ee **03** aim, orb, see **04** glim, glom, lamp, mind, ogle, peep, scan, view
**05** brood, light, optic, sight, study, taste, watch **06** appear, assess, belief, gaze at, keeker, look at, notice, ocular, peeper, peruse, regard, survey, vision, winker **07** blinker, examine, goggler, inspect, lookout, observe, ocellus, opinion, pigsney, stare at **08** eyesight, glance at, ommateum **09** attention, awareness, judgement, viewpoint, vigilance, water pump **10** estimation, perception, scrutinize **11** contemplate, discernment, observation, point of view, recognition, sensitivity
**12** appreciation, surveillance, watchfulness **13** look up and down, power of seeing, way of thinking
**14** discrimination, faculty of sight

*Eye parts include:*

**03** rod
**04** cone, irid, iris, lens, uvea
**05** fovea, pupil, white
**06** areola, cornea, eyelid, retina, sclera
**07** choroid, eyeball, eyelash, papilla, vitreum
**08** chorioid, tear duct
**09** blind spot, optic disc
**10** optic nerve
**11** ciliary body, conjunctiva, lower eyelid, upper eyelid
**12** chorioid coat, lacrimal duct, ocular muscle
**13** aqueous humour, lachrymal duct, sclerotic coat
**14** lachrymal gland, vitreous humour
**15** anterior chamber, crystalline lens, hyaloid membrane

• **black eye** **05** mouse **06** keeker, shiner
• **keep an eye on** **04** mind
**07** monitor **08** attend to **09** look after
**10** keep tabs on, take care of
**12** watch closely
• **reflection in eye** **04** baby
• **see eye to eye** **05** agree
**06** concur, go with **07** be at one **11** be of one mind, go along with
• **set eyes on** **03** see **04** meet
**06** behold, notice **07** observe
**08** come upon **09** encounter, lay eyes on **10** clap eyes on, come across
• **up to your eyes** **04** busy **06** tied up **08** involved, occupied
**09** engrossed, inundated
**11** overwhelmed, snowed under
**13** overstretched **14** fully stretched

**eyebrow**
**04** bree

**eye-catching**
**05** showy **08** gorgeous, imposing, striking, stunning **09** arresting, beautiful, prominent **10** attractive, impressive, noticeable **11** captivating, conspicuous, spectacular

**eye-opener**
**06** wonder **10** disclosure, revelation
**14** quite something, surprising fact
**15** surprising thing

**eyes**
**03** een **04** eine, eyne

**eyeshadow**
**04** kohl

**eyesight**
**04** view **05** sight **06** vision
**10** perception **11** observation **13** power of seeing **14** faculty of sight

**eyesore**
**03** sty **04** blot, mess, scar, stye
**06** blight, horror **07** blemish **08** atrocity, disgrace, ugliness **09** carbuncle
**10** defacement **11** monstrosity
**13** disfigurement

**eyewitness**
**06** viewer **07** watcher, witness
**08** looker-on, observer, onlooker, passer-by **09** bystander, spectator

**F**
02 ef 07 foxtrot

## fable
03 lie 04 epic, myth, saga, tale, yarn
05 feign, story 06 invent, legend
07 fiction, Märchen, parable, untruth
08 allegory, apologue 09 falsehood,
invention, moral tale, tall story
11 fabrication 12 old wives' tale

*Fable writers include:*

03 **Ade** (George), **Fay** (András), **Gay**
(John)
04 **Esop**, **Ruiz** (Juan)
05 **Aesop**, **Boner** (Ulrich), **Torga**
(Miguel)
06 **Bidpai**, **Dryden** (John), **Halévy**
(Léon), **Krylov** (Ivan), **Ramsay**
(Allan), **Tessin** (Carl-Gustaf)
07 **Arreola** (Juan José), **Babrius**,
**Fénelon** (François de Salignac de la
Mothe), **Gellert** (Christian
Fürchtegott), **Iriarte** (Tomás de),
**Kipling** (Rudyard), **Sologub**
(Fyodor)
08 **Andersen** (Hans Christian), **de**
**France** (Marie), **Phaedrus**,
**Saltykov** (Michail)
09 **Furetière** (Antoine)
10 **La Fontaine** (Jean de)
15 **Iriarte y Oropesa** (Tomás de)

## fabled
05 famed 06 famous 07 feigned
08 mythical, renowned 09 legendary
10 celebrated, remarkable

## fabric
03 web 05 cloth, frame, stuff 06 make-
up 07 textile, texture 08 material
09 construct, framework, structure
10 contexture 11 foundations
12 constitution, construction,
organization 14 infrastructure

*Fabrics include:*

03 aba, abb, kid, net, rep, rug, say,
tat
04 abba, aida, baft, buff, cord,
drab, duck, ecru, felt, harn, ikat,
jean, kelt, lace, lamé, lawn, leno,
line, lyne, mull, nude, pall, piña,
puke, repp, reps, roan, silk, wool
05 abaya, baize, batik, beige, braid,
camel, chino, crape, crash, crêpe,
denim, dhoti, doily, doyly, drill,
duroy, foulé, gauze, gazar,
gunny, jaspé, kente, khaki, linen,
lisle, llama, loden, Lurex®,
Lycra®, moire, ninon, nylon,
Orlon®, panne, piqué, plaid,
plush, rayon, satin, scrim, serge,
suede, surah, tabby, tamin,

tammy, terry, Tibet, toile, tulle,
tweed, twill, voile, wigan
06 alpaca, angora, armure, barège,
Bengal, bouclé, broché, burlap,
burnet, burrel, byssus, calico,
camlet, canvas, chintz, cloqué,
coburg, cotton, coutil, cubica,
Dacron®, damask, dévoré,
dimity, dowlas, doyley, Dralon®,
duffel, durant, durrie, faille,
fleece, frieze, gloria, harden,
jersey, kersey, kincob, linsey,
madras, merino, mohair, moreen,
muslin, Oxford, plissé, poplin,
rateen, ratine, russet, samite,
satara, sateen, saxony, sendal,
shoddy, sindon, Tactel®, tamine,
tartan, Thibet, tissue, tricot, tusser,
velour, velvet, vicuña, wadmal,
wincey, winsey
07 alepine, baracan, batiste,
brocade, buckram, bunting,
cambric, camelot, caracul,
challis, chamois, Cheviot,
chiffon, cramesy, cypress,
doeskin, dornick, drabbet,
droguet, drugget, duvetyn,
façonné, fake fur, flannel, foulard,
fustian, gingham, Gore-Tex®,
grogram, hessian, holland,
hopsack, jaconet, karakul,
khaddar, kidskin, leather,
lockram, Mexican, mockado,
morocco, nacarat, nankeen, oil
silk, organza, orleans, paisley,
percale, rabanna, raschel, raw
silk, sagathy, scarlet, schappe,
seating, silesia, Spandex®,
stammel, suiting, tabaret, taffeta,
ticking, veiling, Viyella®,
webbing, woolsey, worsted
08 barathea, barracan, bayadère,
box-cloth, buckskin, cashmere,
casimere, chambray, chenille,
corduroy, coutille, cramoisy,
cretonne, diamanté, drilling,
frocking, gambroon, gossamer,
homespun, jacquard, lambskin,
marcella, mazarine, moleskin,
oilcloth, organdie, osnaburg,
pashmina, plaiding, pleather,
quilting, sarsenet, shagreen,
shalloon, shantung, sheeting,
shirting, spun silk, suedette,
swanskin, Terylene®, toilinet,
waxcloth, whipcord
09 astrakhan, baldachin, bombasine,
calamanco, carmelite, cassimere,
Chantilly, Crimplene®, crinoline,
farandine, folk-weave, fur fabric,
gaberdine, georgette, grenadine,
grosgrain, haircloth, horsehair,
huckaback, interlock, kalamkari,
macintosh, matelassé,
Moygashel®, open-weave,
organzine, paramatta, petersham,
pinstripe, polyester, raven-duck,
sackcloth, sailcloth, satinette,
sharkskin, sheepskin, stockinet,
swans-down, tarpaulin, velveteen
10 Balbriggan, broadcloth,
brocatelle, candlewick,
farrandine, florentine, grass cloth,
habit-cloth, hop-sacking,

kerseymere, mackintosh,
microfibre, monk's cloth,
mousseline, mummy-cloth,
needlecord, paper-cloth, peau de
soie, pilot cloth, polycotton,
seersucker, sicilienne, Tattersall,
toilinette, winceyette
11 cheesecloth, flannelette, Harris
tweed®, interfacing, Kendal
green, leatherette, marquisette,
mutton cloth, nettle-cloth,
sempiternum, stockinette
12 bolting cloth, Brussels lace,
butter-muslin, cavalry twill,
crêpe-de-chine, leather-cloth,
Lincoln green, Shetland wool
13 boulting cloth, casement cloth,
foundation-net, linsey-woolsey
14 heather mixture, terry towelling

*See also* **cotton**

## fabricate
◊ *anagram indicator* 04 coin, fake, form,
make 05 build, erect, forge, frame,
hatch, shape, weave 06 cook up,
create, devise, invent, make up
07 concoct, falsify, fashion, produce,
trump up 08 assemble 09 construct
11 counterfeit, manufacture, put
together

## fabrication
03 fib, lie, web 04 fake, myth 05 fable,
story 06 mock-up 07 coinage, fiction,
figment, forgery, untruth 08 assembly,
building, erection 09 falsehood,
invention 10 assemblage, concoction,
fairy story, production 11 manufacture
12 construction

## fabulous
03 def, fab, rad 04 cool, mean, mega,
neat 05 false, great, magic, super, triff
06 divine, fabled, grouse, made-up,
mythic, superb, unreal, way-out,
wicked 07 amazing, cracker, crucial,
feigned, immense, radical
08 heavenly, invented, mythical,
stonking, top-notch 09 excellent,
fantastic, fictional, imaginary,
legendary, wonderful 10 apocryphal,
astounding, fictitious, incredible,
marvellous, mythologic, not half bad,
phenomenal, remarkable, tremendous
11 astonishing, sensational,
spectacular 12 breathtaking,
mythological, unbelievable,
unimaginable 13 inconceivable 14 out
of this world

## façade
04 face, mask, show, veil 05 cloak,
cover, front, guise 06 veneer 07 frontal
08 disguise, exterior, frontage,
pretence 09 semblance 10 appearance,
storefront

## face
◊ *head selection indicator* 03 air, jib,
mug, pan 04 clad, coat, dare, defy,
dial, form, head, line, look, meet,
mien, moue, name, phiz, pout, puss,
side, trim 05 anger, brave, clock,
cover, dress, flank, front, frown, looks,
pitch, scowl 06 aspect, esteem, façade,
favour, honour, kisser, nature, oppose,
polish, resist, smooth, tackle, veneer,

## facelift

visage **07** affront, grimace, outside, overlay, profile, respect, surface **08** boldness, confront, cope with, deal with, exterior, face up to, features, frontage, give on to, look onto, overlook, presence, prestige, standing **09** demeanour, encounter, look out on, withstand **10** admiration, appearance, be opposite, effrontery, experience, expression, reputation **11** countenance, look towards, physiognomy **13** come up against

*Face parts include:*

**03** ear, eye, gum, jaw, lip
**04** brow, chin, hair, iris, jowl, lips, neck, nose, skin
**05** beard, cheek, mouth, pupil, teeth
**06** eyelid, sclera, septum, temple, tongue
**07** earlobe, eyeball, eyebrow, eyelash, freckle, jawbone, nostril, unibrow, wrinkle
**08** monobrow, philtrum
**09** cheekbone, moustache
**10** complexion, double chin

*See also* **hair**
• **face to face** **06** facing **07** vis-à-vis **08** eye to eye, in person, opposite **09** confronté, tête-à-tête **11** confronting **12** a quattr'occhi **14** across-the-table **15** in confrontation
• **face up to** **04** nose **06** accept **08** confront, cope with, deal with **09** recognize, stand up to **10** meet head-on **11** acknowledge **15** come to terms with
• **flat face** **04** pane
• **fly in the face of** **04** defy **05** clash **06** insult, oppose **08** be at odds, conflict, contrast, disagree **09** go against **10** contradict **12** be at variance, be in conflict
• **on the face of it** **07** clearly, plainly **08** patently **09** obviously, outwardly, reputedly, seemingly **10** apparently, manifestly, ostensibly **12** on the surface **13** superficially
• **pull a face** **03** moe, mow **04** girn, gurn, lour, pout, sulk **05** fleer, frown, scowl **06** glower **07** grimace **13** knit your brows
• **tilted face** **04** cant

## facelift

**05** refit **08** makeover **10** renovation **11** restoration **12** redecoration, rhytidectomy **13** refurbishment **14** plastic surgery, transformation **15** cosmetic surgery

## facet

**04** face, side **05** angle, plane, point, slant **06** aspect, factor **07** element, feature, surface **10** ommatidium **14** characteristic

## facetious

**04** glib **05** comic, droll, funny, witty **06** jocose, joking **07** amusing, comical, jesting, jocular, playful, waggish **08** flippant, humorous **09** frivolous **12** light-hearted **13** tongue-in-cheek

## facile

**04** easy, glib **05** hasty, light, quick, ready, slick **06** fluent, simple, smooth **07** affable, shallow **08** yielding **09** plausible **10** simplistic **11** superficial **13** uncomplicated

## facilitate

**04** ease, help **06** assist, grease, smooth **07** advance, forward, further, promote, speed up **08** expedite **09** encourage, lubricate **10** accelerate, make easier **12** smooth the way

## facilitation

**07** helping **09** promotion **10** assistance, expediting, forwarding, furthering **12** acceleration **13** encouragement

## facility

**03** aid **04** ease, gift **05** knack, means, skill **06** mod con, talent **07** ability, amenity, feature, fluency, pliancy, service, utility **08** aptitude, resource **09** advantage, appliance, dexterity, eloquence, equipment, provision, quickness, readiness **10** affability **11** convenience, opportunity, proficiency, skilfulness **12** prerequisite **14** articulateness, effortlessness

## facing

**06** façade, lining, veneer **07** coating, overlay, surface **08** cladding, covering, dressing, trimming **09** revetment **10** false front **13** reinforcement

## facsimile

**03** fax **04** copy **05** image, print, repro, Xerox® **06** carbon **07** replica, telefax **09** duplicate, imitation, photocopy, Photostat®, reproduce **10** carbon copy, mimeograph, transcript **11** electrotype **12** reproduction **13** telefacsimile

## fact

**03** act, gen **04** deed, info, item, poop **05** datum, event, point, score, thing, truth **06** detail, factor **07** element, feature, low-down, reality **08** incident, specific **09** actuality, certainty, component, happening **10** factuality, ins and outs, occurrence, particular **11** information **12** circumstance, fait accompli
• **in fact** **03** e'en, nay, yes **04** even **05** truly **06** indeed, really **07** de facto, en effet, in truth **08** actually **09** in reality **10** come to that, in practice **12** in actual fact **13** in point of fact **15** as a matter of fact

## faction

**03** set **04** band, camp, ring, side **05** cabal, group, junta, junto, lobby, party **06** caucus, clique, sector, strife **07** coterie, discord, section, trouble **08** argument, conflict, division, fraction, friction, grouplet, minority, quarrels, tendency **10** contention, contingent, disharmony, dissension, infighting **11** ginger group **12** disagreement **13** pressure group, splinter group

## factious

**05** rival, split **06** at odds **07** divided, warring **08** clashing, divisive,

mutinous, partisan **09** dissident, sectarian, seditious, turbulent **10** discordant, rebellious, refractory, tumultuous **11** conflicting, contentious, quarrelling, quarrelsome **12** disputatious **13** at loggerheads, troublemaking **15** insurrectionary

## factitious

**04** made, sham **05** bogus, false **09** contrived, imitation, pretended, unnatural **10** artificial, fabricated **11** counterfeit

## factor

**04** fact, gene, item, part **05** cause, facet, point **06** aspect, detail **07** divisor, element, feature **09** component, influence **10** ingredient **11** constituent, contingency, determinant, submultiple **12** circumstance **13** consideration **14** characteristic
• **unknown factor** **01** x, y, z

## factory

**04** mill, yard **05** plant, works **07** foundry **08** workshop **09** shop floor **11** manufactory **12** assembly line, assembly shop

## factotum

**05** do-all **06** circar, sircar, sirkar **07** famulus **08** handyman **09** Man Friday, odd-jobman **10** Girl Friday **12** bottle-washer **13** maid-of-all-work **15** jack-of-all-trades

## facts

**04** data, poop **05** truth **09** bare bones

## factual

**04** real, true **05** close, exact **06** actual, strict **07** correct, genuine, literal, precise **08** accurate, detailed, faithful, truthful, unbiased **09** authentic, objective, realistic **10** historical, true-to-life **12** unprejudiced

## factually

**05** truly **06** really **08** actually **09** genuinely, in reality **10** truthfully **12** historically

## faculties

**04** wits **06** powers, reason, senses **12** capabilities, intelligence

## faculty

**03** ear, wit **04** bent, bump, gift, nose **05** flair, knack, power, sight, skill, taste **06** school, talent **07** ability, licence, section **08** aptitude, capacity, division, facility, function **10** capability, department **11** proficiency **12** organization

## fad

**04** buzz, cult, mode, rage, whim **05** craze, fancy, mania, trend, vogue **06** maggot **07** fashion **10** enthusiasm **11** affectation **14** passing fashion

## faddy

**05** exact, fussy, picky **06** choosy **07** finicky **10** fastidious, nit-picking, particular, pernickety **11** persnickety **12** hard-to-please

## fade

**03** die, dim, ebb **04** dull, fail, fall, flag, melt, miff, pale, vade, wane, weak,

## faeces

wilt **05** appal, droop, faint **06** blanch, bleach, blench, die out, perish, recede, vanish, wallow, weaken, whiten, wither **07** decline, die away, dwindle, ebb away, shrivel, wash out **08** diminish, dissolve, etiolate, evanesce, grow pale, melt away, peter out, tone down, wear away **09** disappear, discolour, fizzle out, waste away **10** become pale, lose colour **11** become paler **12** become weaker

## faeces

**04** crap, crud, dung, flux, mute, poop, pure **05** frass, guano, scats, stool **06** doo-doo, egesta, ordure, stools **07** excreta, motions **09** body waste, droppings, excrement, number two **11** waste matter **12** rejectamenta, sir-reverence

## fag

**03** cig, tab **04** bind, bore, drag, pest, slog **05** chore, ciggy, grind, joint, smoke, weary, whiff **06** bother, ciggie, dog end, fag end, gasper, low-tar, roll-up **07** high-tar **08** drudgery, king-size, nuisance **09** cigarette, filter-tip **10** coffin-nail, irritation **11** cancer-stick, roll-your-own **13** inconvenience

## fagged

**04** beat, done **05** all in, jaded, weary **06** beaten, bushed, done in, pooped, wasted, zonked **07** euchred, whacked, worn out **08** burnt out, dead-beat, dog-tired, fatigued, jiggered **09** exhausted, knackered, pooped out **10** euchred out **11** ready to drop, tuckered out **14** on your last legs

## fail

**02** go **03** die, ebb, mis, sod **04** bomb, fade, feal, flag, flop, fold, lose, miss, omit, plow, sink, stop, turf, wane **05** abort, crash, decay, droop, flunk, fudge, leave, smash **06** blow it, cut out, desert, falter, forget, go bung, go bust, go phut, pack up, play up, plough, weaken **07** abandon, conk out, crap out, deceive, decline, dwindle, forsake, founder, go broke, go kaput, go under, go wrong, let down, misluck, neglect, not work **08** bottle it, collapse, diminish, fall down, fall flat, miscarry, not start **09** break down, come short, fall apart, fizzle out, go belly-up, not make it **10** come undone, disappoint, draw a blank, get nowhere, go bankrupt, not come off **11** bite the dust, come a gutser, come to grief, come unglued, come unstuck, dégringoler, deteriorate, fall through, go to the wall, malfunction **12** come a cropper, come to naught, go into the red, go on the blink, go on the fritz, underachieve **13** come to nothing **14** be unsuccessful, not do something, score an own goal **15** become insolvent, blow your chances
• **without fail 08** reliably **09** regularly **10** constantly, dependably, faithfully, punctually **11** predictably, religiously, unfailingly **13** like clockwork **15** conscientiously

## failing

**03** sin **04** flat, flaw **05** error, fault, lapse **06** defect, foible **07** blemish, default, failure, lacking, wanting, without **08** drawback, on the ebb, weakness, weak spot **10** deficiency **11** in default of, shortcoming **12** imperfection **14** in the absence of

## failure

**03** dud **04** flop, hash, mess, miss, no go, no-no, ruin **05** botch, crash, decay, flunk, loser **06** cock-up, defeat, demise, ebbing, fading, fiasco, misfit, reject, slip-up, victim, waning **07** also-ran, burst-up, debacle, decline, default, dropout, flivver, folding, has-been, let-down, neglect, no-hoper, screw-up, sinking, washout, wipeout **08** abortion, calamity, collapse, dead loss, disaster, downfall, flagging, meltdown, omission, shambles, shutdown, stalling, stopping, write-off **09** born loser, breakdown, disregard, oversight, packing-up, unsuccess, weakening **10** bankruptcy, conking-out, cutting-out, foundering, going under, ill success, insolvency, misfortune, negligence, non-starter, remissness **11** dereliction, frustration, malfunction, miscarriage **12** waste of space **13** deterioration, forgetfulness, lack of success **14** disappointment, going to the wall, malfunctioning **15** coming to nothing

## faint

**03** dim, low, wan **04** drop, dull, fade, gone, hazy, mild, pale, soft, weak **05** decay, dizzy, droop, faded, giddy, light, muted, queer, quiet, sound, swarf, swelt, swerf, swoon, swoun, vague, woozy **06** feeble, hushed, slight, stanck, swarve, swerve, swound, vanish **07** blurred, ghostly, languid, muffled, obscure, pass out, subdued, syncope, unclear **08** black out, blackout, bleached, collapse, flake out, keel over, unsteady **09** exhausted **10** indistinct, oppressive **11** half-hearted, lightheaded **14** unenthusiastic **15** unconsciousness

## faint-hearted

**04** soft, weak **05** timid, wussy **06** craven, scared, yellow **07** chicken, fearful, gutless, jittery, wimpish **08** cowardly, timorous **09** diffident, spineless, weak-kneed **10** hen-hearted, irresolute, spiritless **11** half-hearted, lily-livered **12** weak-spirited, white-livered **13** pusillanimous, yellow-bellied **14** chicken-hearted, chicken-livered

## faintly

**04** a bit **06** feebly, softly, weakly **07** a little, vaguely **08** slightly, somewhat

## fair

**02** OK **03** dry **04** even, expo, fete, fine, full, gaff, gala, good, just, mela, open, pale, pure, show, so-so, warm **05** blond, civil, clean, clear, cream, ivory, legit, light, quite, right, sunny, tryst, white, woman **06** bazaar, beauty, blonde, bright, decent, flaxen, golden,

honest, kosher, lawful, likely, market, modest, not bad, proper, square, yellow **07** upright **08** adequate, all right, carnival, detached, directly, exchange, festival, handsome, mediocre, middling, moderate, passable, pleasing, specious, sporting, unbiased **09** beautiful, cloudless, craft fair, equitable, impartial, objective, out-and-out, plausible, tolerable, trade fair, unclouded, veritable **10** above board, acceptable, even-handed, exhibition, exposition, fair-haired, fair-headed, favourable, honourable, legitimate, on the level, prosperous, reasonable, straight up, sufficient **11** light-haired, respectable, trustworthy **12** satisfactory, unobstructed, unprejudiced **13** disinterested, dispassionate, done by the book **14** going by the book **15** played by the book

## fairground

• **fairground attraction 04** ride

*Fairground attractions include:*

**06** hoop-la
**07** Dodgems®
**08** carousel, waltzers
**10** bumper cars, coconut shy, ghost train, swing boats
**11** Ferris wheel, wall of death
**12** bouncy castle, chair-o-planes, merry-go-round, tunnel of love
**13** helter-skelter, rollercoaster

## fairly

**03** gay, gey **05** fully, quite **06** enough, gently, justly, neatly, pretty, quight, rather, really, square **07** legally, plainly **08** honestly, lawfully, middling, passably, properly, somewhat **09** equitably, neutrally, tolerably, veritably **10** absolutely, adequately, moderately, positively, reasonably, unbiasedly **11** beautifully, impartially, objectively

## fair-minded

**04** fair, just **05** right **06** honest, proper, square **07** upright **08** detached, unbiased **09** equitable, impartial, objective **10** even-handed, honourable, on the level, straight up **11** trustworthy **12** unprejudiced **13** disinterested, dispassionate

## fairness

**06** equity, square **07** decency, justice **09** rightness **10** legitimacy **11** uprightness **12** impartiality, rightfulness, unbiasedness **13** equitableness **14** even-handedness, honourableness, legitimateness

## fairy

**03** elf, fay, fée, hob, imp **04** peri, pixy **05** faery, nymph, pisky, pixie, pouke **06** faerie, sprite **07** brownie, rusalka, sandman **08** delicate, fanciful **09** hobgoblin, whimsical **10** leprechaun **11** enchantress

## fairy tale

**03** fib, lie **04** myth **07** fantasy, fiction, romance, untruth **08** folk-tale

09 invention, tall story 10 fairy story
11 fabrication

*Fairy tales include:*

07 Aladdin, Ali Baba, The Bell
08 Momo Taro, Peter Pan, Rapunzel, Snowdrop, The Angel, The Daisy, The Raven, Tom Thumb
09 Ashputtel, Bluebeard, Briar Rose, Pinocchio, Snow White, The Shadow, The Storks
10 Cinderella, Clever Hans, Goldilocks, Hans in Luck, The Fir Tree, The Rose-Elf, Thumbelina
11 Clever Elsie, Hop o' my Thumb, Little Thumb, Mother Elder, Mother Goose, Puss in Boots, The Old House, The Red Shoes
12 Holger Danske, Little Red-Cap, The Elderbush, The Goose Girl, The Pied Piper, The Snow Queen, The Tinderbox, The Wild Swans, Urashima Taro
13 Chicken Licken, Red Riding Hood, The Frog Prince, The Golden Bird, The Neighbours, The Tin Soldier, The White Snake, The Wizard of Oz
14 Babes in the Wood, Sleeping Beauty, The Flying Trunk, The Golden Goose, The Juniper Tree, The Nightingale, The Seven Ravens, The Water of Life
15 Dick Whittington, Hansel and Gretel, Rumpelstiltskin, The Elfin Hillock, The Little Lovers, The Ugly Duckling, Three Little Pigs

*Fairy tale characters include:*

03 Cat, Dog
04 Duck, Jack, John, Liza, Nana, Nibs
05 Beast, Curly, Wendy
06 Beauty, Conrad, Donkey, Falada, Gretel, Hansel
07 Michael, Rooster, Rose Red, The King, The Ogre, The Wolf, Tootles
08 Baby Bear, Foxy Loxy, Geppetto, Peter Pan, Rapunzel, Slightly, The Elves, The Giant, The Queen, The Troll, The Twins, Tom Thumb
09 Briar Rose, Daddy Bear, Good Fairy, Mummy Bear, Pinocchio, Snow White, The Miller, The Mirror, The Prince
10 Cinderella, Ducky Lucky, Goldilocks, Henny Penny, Stepmother, The Emperor, Thumbelina, Tinker Bell
11 Captain Hook, Grandmother, Pedlar Woman, Puss in Boots, The Huntsman, The Lost Boys, The Princess, Ugly Sisters, Wicked Fairy, Wicked Witch
12 Goosey Loosey, The Goose Girl, The Shoemaker
13 Band of Robbers, Chicken Licken, Red Riding Hood
14 Fairy Godmother, The Golden Goose, The Seven Dwarfs
15 Alice Fitzwarren, Billy Goats Gruff, Dick Whittington, Fairy Godmothers, Mr and Mrs Darling,

Rumpelstiltskin, The Little Red Hen, The Rich Merchant, The Ugly Duckling, Three Little Pigs

**faith**
03 fay, lay 04 faix, sect 05 creed, dogma, fides, troth, trust 06 belief, church, credit, fealty, honour, indeed 07 believe, honesty, loyalty 08 credence, devotion, doctrine, fidelity, reliance, religion, teaching 09 assurance, obedience, sincerity 10 allegiance, commitment, confidence, conviction, dedication, dependence, persuasion 12 denomination, faithfulness, truthfulness
• in faith 04 fegs

**faithful**
04 feal, leal, true 05 afald, close, exact, loyal 06 aefald, afawld, strict, trusty 07 aefauld, devoted, precise, staunch 08 accurate, brethren, constant, obedient, reliable, soothful, truthful 09 adherents, believers, believing, committed, dedicated, followers, soothfast, steadfast 10 dependable, supporters, unflagging, unswerving, unwavering 11 true-hearted, trustworthy 12 communicants, congregation

**faithfully**
04 true 05 truly 06 firmly 07 closely, exactly, loyally 08 reliably, solemnly, strictly 09 devotedly, precisely, staunchly 10 accurately, constantly, dependably 11 steadfastly

**faithfulness**
05 truth 06 fealty 07 loyalty 08 accuracy, devotion, fidelity 09 closeness, constancy, exactness 10 allegiance, commitment, dedication, strictness 11 reliability, staunchness 13 dependability, steadfastness 14 scrupulousness 15 trustworthiness

**faithless**
05 false 06 fickle, untrue 08 agnostic, disloyal, doubting 09 atheistic, deceptive 10 adulterous, inconstant, perfidious, traitorous, unfaithful, unreliable, untruthful 11 nullifidian, treacherous, unbelieving 12 disbelieving, false-hearted 13 untrustworthy

**faithlessness**
06 deceit 07 perfidy 08 adultery, apostasy, betrayal 09 treachery 10 disloyalty, fickleness, infidelity 11 inconstancy 14 unfaithfulness

**fake**
◇ *anagram indicator* 03 rob 04 coil, cook, copy, faux, fold, hoax, mock, sham 05 bogus, dodge, false, feign, filch, flake, forge, fraud, fudge, phony, pseud, put on, quack 06 affect, assume, attack, bodgie, doctor, ersatz, forged, phoney, pirate, pseudo 07 assumed, forgery, hyped-up, imitate, pretend, replica, swindle 08 affected, impostor, simulate, spurious 09 charlatan, fabricate,

imitation, simulated 10 artificial, fraudulent, mountebank, simulation 11 counterfeit 12 reproduction

**falcon**

*Falcons include:*

05 hobby, saker
06 gentle, lanner, merlin
07 Iceland, kestrel
08 duck-hawk
09 gerfalcon, gyrfalcon, jerfalcon, peregrine, stone hawk
11 tassell-gent
12 falcon-gentil, falcon-gentle, tassel-gentle, tercel-gentle, tercel-jerkin

**Falkland Islands**
03 FLK

**fall**
◇ *anagram indicator* ◇ *reversal indicator* 02 fa 03 cut, die, ebb, get, lot, sin 04 dive, drip, drop, grow, hang, purl, rain, ruin, rush, sink, slip, soss, trap, trip, turn 05 abate, chute, crash, falls, lapse, occur, onset, pitch, slant, slide, slope, slump, souse, spill, yield 06 alight, autumn, become, be lost, chance, dangle, defeat, demise, give in, go down, gutzer, happen, lessen, perish, plunge, purler, recede, revert, shower, submit, topple, tumble 07 be slain, be taken, cadence, capture, cascade, decline, descend, descent, dwindle, failure, fall off, fall-off, fortune, impinge, incline, offence, plummet, stumble, subside, torrent 08 be killed, cataract, collapse, come down, come to be, conquest, decrease, diminish, down-come, downfall, fall down, giving-in, grow into, keel over, nose-dive, yielding 09 come about, declivity, dwindling, lessening, overthrow, reduction, surrender, take place, terminate, waterfall 10 be defeated, capitulate, plummeting, submission, topple over, wrongdoing 11 be conquered, come a gutser, destruction, keeling-over, lose control, original sin, precipitate, resignation 12 be vanquished, capitulation, come a cropper, disobedience, lose your life, pitch forward, precipitance, precipitancy 13 loss of control, transgression
• fall apart 03 rot 04 fail 05 break, decay 06 divide 07 break up, crack up, crumble, shatter 08 collapse, come away, dissolve, disunite, go to bits 09 break down, decompose 10 fall to bits, go to pieces 11 lose control 12 come to pieces, disintegrate, fall to pieces 15 break into pieces
• fall asleep 04 doze 06 get off, nod off, pop off 07 doze off, drop off 08 crash out, drift off, flake out, spark out 13 pass into sleep 15 go out like a light
• fall away 04 drop, fail 05 lapse 06 go down, revolt 07 decline, drop off, dwindle, relapse 08 drop away, languish 09 slope away, slope down
• fall back 06 depart, recoil, recule, revert 07 back off, give way, recoyle,

recuile, relapse, retreat **08** draw back, pull back, withdraw **09** disengage **10** give ground, lose ground
• **fall back on**   **03** use **06** call on, employ, look to, turn to **08** resort to **09** make use of **12** call into play **14** have recourse to
• **fall behind**   **03** lag **05** trail **08** drop back, straggle **09** lag behind, not keep up
• **fall down**   **04** fail, flop **07** founder **08** collapse **09** break down **11** come unglued, come unstuck **12** come a cropper **13** come to nothing **14** be unsuccessful
• **fall for**   **03** buy **05** fancy **06** accept, desire, take to **07** swallow **10** be fooled by **11** be taken in by **12** be attached to, be crazy about, be deceived by, have a crush on **14** fall in love with
• **fall in**   **04** sink **05** array, crash **06** cave in, line up, revert **07** give way, subside **08** collapse, come down **11** stand in line **14** get in formation
• **fall in with**   **06** accept **07** support **08** assent to, hang with **09** agree with **10** comply with **11** go along with, hang out with **12** go around with **13** co-operate with, hang about with **14** hang around with **15** get involved with
• **fall off**   **04** drop, shed, slow **05** crash, slump **06** lessen, perish, worsen **07** decline, die away, drop off, slacken, slip off **08** decrease, draw back **11** deteriorate
• **fall on**   **04** meet **06** assail, attack, snatch **07** assault, lay into, set upon **08** pounce on **09** descend on
• **fall out**   **03** row **05** argue, clash, fight **06** bicker, differ, happen **07** dismiss, quarrel **08** disagree, squabble
• **fall slightly**   **04** ease
• **fall through**   **04** fail **05** abort **07** founder, go wrong **08** collapse, miscarry **11** come to grief **13** come to nothing
• **fall to**   **05** begin, set to, start **07** stand to **08** commence, set about **10** get stuck in **11** be the duty of, be the task of **13** apply yourself

## fallacious
**05** false, wrong **06** untrue **07** inexact **08** delusive, delusory, illusory, mistaken, spurious **09** deceptive, erroneous, illogical, incorrect, sophistic **10** fictitious, inaccurate, misleading **11** casuistical, sophistical

## fallacy
**04** flaw, myth **05** error **06** idolon, idolum **07** idolism, mistake, sophism **08** delusion, illusion **09** deception, falsehood, false idea, sophistry **12** equivocation, misjudgement **13** deceitfulness, inconsistency, misconception **14** miscalculation, mistaken belief **15** misapprehension

## fallen
**04** dead, died, lost **05** loose, slain **06** killed, ruined, shamed **07** immoral, seduced **08** murdered, perished **09** disgraced **10** degenerate,

overthrown **11** promiscuous, slaughtered

## fallibility
**07** failing **08** weakness **09** mortality **10** inaccuracy **12** imperfection **13** unreliability

## fallible
**04** weak **05** frail, human **06** errant, erring, flawed, mortal **08** ignorant **09** imperfect, uncertain **10** unreliable

## fallow
**03** lay, lea, ley **04** idle **06** barren, unsown, unused **07** dormant, resting **08** inactive **09** unplanted **10** unploughed **11** undeveloped **12** uncultivated, unproductive

## false
◇ *anagram indicator* **03** bum **04** fake, faux, mock, sham **05** bogus, lying, pseud, wrong **06** faulty, forged, phoney, pseudo, untrue **07** assumed, feigned, inexact, invalid, pretend **08** disloyal, fabulous, illusive, illusory, invented, mistaken, postiche, pseudish, recreant, spurious, strumpet, two-faced **09** deceitful, dishonest, erroneous, faithless, imitation, incorrect, insincere, pretended, simulated, synthetic, trumped-up **10** artificial, fabricated, fallacious, fictitious, fraudulent, inaccurate, misleading, perfidious, traitorous, unfaithful, ungrounded, unreliable **11** counterfeit, double-faced, duplicitous, treacherous **12** hypocritical **13** double-dealing, untrustworthy

## falsehood
**03** fib, lie **04** flam **05** fable, porky, story **06** deceit **07** fiction, leasing, perfidy, perjury, untruth, whopper **09** deception, duplicity, hypocrisy, invention, mendacity, tall story, treachery **10** dishonesty, fairy story **11** fabrication, insincerity **12** two-facedness **13** deceitfulness, double dealing **14** untruthfulness
*See also* **lie**

## falsely
**07** in error, untruly, wrongly **09** by mistake, deviously **10** mistakenly, wrongfully **11** deceitfully, dishonestly, erroneously, incorrectly, insincerely **12** artificially, fallaciously, fraudulently **13** counterfeitly, treacherously **14** hypocritically

## falsetto
**04** alto **08** high note **09** high pitch, high voice **10** shrillness **12** head register

## falsification
**06** change, deceit **07** forgery **08** adultery **09** tampering **10** alteration, distortion, perversion **12** adulteration **13** dissimulation

## falsify
◇ *anagram indicator* **03** lie, rig **04** cook, fake, rort **05** alter, belie, false, feign, forge, twist **06** diddle, doctor, fiddle, garble, wangle **07** distort, massage, pervert **08** misstate **10** adulterate,

manipulate, tamper with **11** counterfeit **12** misrepresent, sophisticate

## falter
**04** fail, flag **05** delay, quail, shake, waver **06** flinch, hiccup, totter **07** be shaky, stammer, stoiter, stumble, stutter, tremble **08** hesitate, hiccough **09** vacillate **10** be unsteady, dilly-dally **12** be in two minds, drag your feet, shilly-shally, take your time, unsteadiness **13** sit on the fence **14** fluff your lines

## faltering
◇ *anagram indicator* **04** weak **05** timid **06** broken **07** failing **08** flagging, hesitant, unsteady **09** stumbling, tentative, uncertain **10** irresolute, stammering

## fame
**04** name, note **05** glory, kudos **06** esteem, honour, renown, report, repute, rumour **07** stardom **08** eminence **09** celebrity, greatness **10** importance, notability, prominence, reputation **11** distinction **15** illustriousness

## famed
**05** noted **06** famous **08** esteemed, renowned **09** acclaimed, prominent, well-known **10** celebrated, recognized **11** widely known

## familiar
**03** fam, old **04** bold, dear, easy, free, maty, near, open **05** aware, close, known, matey, pally, privy, usual **06** au fait, casual, chummy, common, homely, smarmy, versed, well up **07** abreast, clued up, forward, natural, relaxed, routine **08** everyday, fireside, frequent, friendly, genned up, habitual, homelike, informal, intimate, ordinary, repeated, sociable **09** au courant, customary, household, up to speed, well-known **10** accustomed, acquainted, conversant, recognized, unreserved **11** comfortable, commonplace, free-and-easy, impertinent **12** confidential, conventional, over-familiar, over-friendly, presumptuous, recognizable, run-of-the-mill, unmistakable **13** disrespectful, knowledgeable, unceremonious

## familiarity
**04** ease **05** grasp, habit, skill **07** liberty, mastery **08** boldness, intimacy, nearness, openness **09** awareness, closeness, impudence, knowledge, liberties, palliness, pushiness **10** casualness, chumminess, consuetude, disrespect, experience, inwardness **11** conversance, conversancy, forwardness, informality, naturalness, presumption, sociability **12** acquaintance, friendliness, impertinence **13** comprehension, intrusiveness, understanding **15** over-familiarity

## familiarize
**05** brief, coach, gen up, prime, teach, train **06** clue up, school **08** accustom, acquaint, instruct **09** habituate, make

aware **11** acclimatize **12** get up to speed, indoctrinate, make familiar **13** keep up to speed **14** make acquainted

## family
**03** fam, kin **04** clan, folk, gens, kids, kind, line, name, race, stem, type **05** birth, blood, brood, class, flesh, genus, group, house, issue, order, stock, tribe **06** kinred, people, scions, stirps, strain, whanau **07** descent, dynasty, kiddies, kindred, kinsmen, lineage, parents, progeny, species **08** ancestry, children, kinsfolk, pedigree, subclass **09** ancestors, forebears, household, next of kin, offspring, parentage, relations, relatives **10** extraction, generation, little ones **11** descendants, you and yours **13** nuclear family **14** classification, extended family **15** one-parent family
• **member of family 08** relation, relative
*See also* **relative**
• **family tree 04** line **06** stemma **07** descent, lineage **08** ancestry, pedigree **09** genealogy, whakapapa **10** background, extraction

## famine
**04** lack, want **05** death **06** dearth, hunger **08** scarcity **10** starvation **11** deprivation, destitution **12** exiguousness, malnutrition **14** shortage of food

## famished
**06** hungry **07** starved **08** ravenous, starving **09** famishing, voracious **14** undernourished

## famous
**04** name **05** A-list, famed, great, noted **06** legend, signal **07** eminent, notable, popular **08** esteemed, glorious, honoured, infamous, renowned **09** acclaimed, celebrity, excellent, legendary, notorious, prominent, respected, venerable, well-famed, well-known **10** celebrated, remarkable **11** illustrious, world-famous **13** distinguished

## famously
**04** well **07** greatly, happily, notably **08** superbly **09** eminently, popularly **10** infamously, splendidly, swimmingly **11** brilliantly, notoriously, prominently, wonderfully **13** conspicuously

## fan
◇ *anagram indicator* **03** air, nut **04** blow, buff, cone, cool, vane, wing **05** fiend, freak, lover, punka, rouse **06** addict, aerate, arouse, backer, blower, Colmar, cooler, excite, groupy, ignite, incite, kindle, punkah, stir up, whip up, winnow, work up **07** admirer, agitate, air-cool, devotee, flutter, freshen, groupie, provoke, refresh **08** adherent, follower, increase **09** air cooler, extractor, flabellum, instigate, intensify, propeller, rhipidion, stimulate, supporter, ventilate **10** aficionado, enthusiast, ventilator **11** afficionado **12** air-condition,

extractor fan **14** air-conditioner
• **fan out 04** open **06** spread, unfold, unfurl **07** move out, open out **09** spread out

## fanatic
**03** nut **05** bigot, fiend, freak **06** addict, maniac, zealot **07** devotee, radical **08** activist, militant **09** extremist, visionary **10** enthusiast **14** fundamentalist

## fanatical
**03** mad **04** wild **05** rabid **07** bigoted, burning, extreme, fervent, radical, zealous **08** activist, dogmatic, frenzied, militant **09** extremist, obsessive **10** immoderate, passionate **11** extravagant **12** narrow-minded, single-minded **14** fundamentalist

## fanaticism
**04** zeal **06** frenzy **07** bigotry, fervour, madness **08** activism, wildness, zealotry **09** dogmatism, extremism, militancy, monomania **10** dedication, enthusiasm **11** infatuation, schwärmerei **13** obsessiveness **14** fundamentalism

## fancier
**03** fan **05** fiend, freak **06** keeper **07** breeder, devotee **08** follower **10** enthusiast

## fanciful
◇ *anagram indicator* **04** wild **05** fairy **06** exotic, ornate, quaint, unreal **07** curious, flighty **08** chimeric, creative, fabulous, illusory, mythical, notional, romantic, vaporous **09** airy-fairy, decorated, elaborate, fairytale, fantastic, imaginary, legendary, visionary, whimsical **10** chimerical **11** extravagant, fantastical, imaginative, make-believe, unrealistic **12** metaphysical

## fancy
◇ *anagram indicator* **03** yen **04** flam, idea, itch, like, love, urge, want, ween, whim, wish **05** covet, dream, go for, guess, humor, showy, taste, think **06** desire, fangle, favour, humour, lavish, liking, notion, ornate, prefer, raving, reckon, rococo, take to, vision **07** adorned, baroque, believe, caprice, chimera, conceit, dream of, elegant, fantasy, imagine, impulse, long for, longing, not mind, opinion, picture, suppose, surmise, thought, wish for **08** chimaera, conceive, crotchet, delusion, fanciful, fantasia, feel like, fondness, illusion, penchant, phantasy, superior, yearn for, yearning **09** decorated, elaborate, expensive, fantastic, lust after **10** be mad about, conception, conjecture, creativity, far-fetched, have in mind, impression, not say no to, ornamented, preference **11** be wild about, embellished, extravagant, have eyes for, imagination, inclination **12** be crazy about, have a crush on, ostentatious, predilection, take a shine to **13** be attracted to, particoloured, take a liking to **14** be interested in, find

attractive, have the hots for **15** think the world of

## fanfare
**04** fuss, show **05** trump **06** parade, sennet, tucket **07** display **08** flourish **09** fanfarade, pageantry, publicity, tarantara **11** flamboyance, ostentation, taratantara, trumpet call

## fang
**04** claw, grip, tang, tusk **05** catch, prong, talon, tooth **10** venom-tooth

## fantasize
**05** dream **06** invent **07** imagine, romance **08** daydream **11** hallucinate **12** live in a dream

## fantastic
◇ *anagram indicator* **03** ace, odd **04** cool, mega, neat, wild **05** antic, brill, fancy, great, magic, outré, super, weird **06** absurd, antick, exotic, superb, unreal, wicked **07** amazing, anticke, antique, bizarre, extreme, foppish, radical, strange **08** enormous, fabulous, fanciful, illusory, romantic, smashing, terrific, top-notch **09** brilliant, eccentric, excellent, first-rate, grotesque, imaginary, storybook, visionary, whimsical, wonderful **10** capricious, impressive, incredible, marvellous, outlandish, phenomenal, remarkable, tremendous **11** extravagant, imaginative, sensational **12** overwhelming, transcendent, unbelievable **14** out of this world

## fantastically
**09** amazingly, extremely **10** incredibly **12** phenomenally, terrifically, tremendously, unbelievably

## fantasy
**03** GBH, GHB **04** idol, love, myth **05** dream, fancy **06** mirage, vision, whimsy **07** caprice, reverie, whimsey **08** daydream, delusion, fantasia, illusion **09** fantasque, invention, moonshine, nightmare, pipe dream, unreality **10** apparition, creativity **11** imagination, inspiration, originality, pie in the sky, speculation **12** fancifulness **13** flight of fancy, hallucination, inventiveness, misconception **15** cloud-cuckoo-land, imaginativeness, resourcefulness

## far
**03** way **04** away, much **05** miles, other **06** far-off, remote **07** distant, faraway, further, greatly, removed **08** a good way, a long way, far-flung, markedly, opposite, outlying, secluded, very much **09** decidedly, distantly, extremely **10** far-removed **11** back o' Bourke, godforsaken, nowhere near, out-of-the-way, up the Boohai **12** considerably, immeasurably, inaccessible, incomparably, in the boonies, in the wop-wops, some distance **13** great distance, significantly, the black stump **14** in the boondocks
• **as far as 02** to, up **04** up to
• **far and wide 06** widely **07** broadly

**faraway**
08 all about 09 worldwide
10 everywhere, far and near
11 extensively, in all places 13 from all places
• **far end, far side** ◇ *tail selection indicator*
• **far out** 05 weird 06 exotic, way out
07 bizarre, extreme, radical, strange, unusual 10 outlandish, unorthodox
14 unconventional
• **go far** 05 get on 06 arrive 07 succeed
08 go places 12 be successful, make your mark 14 achieve success 15 get on in the world
• **not far** 02 nl
• **so far** 02 as 03 als 06 to date 07 thus far, till now, up to now 08 hitherto
12 to some extent, within limits 13 up to this point

**faraway**
03 far 04 lost 06 absent, dreamy, far-off, remote 07 distant 08 far-flung, outlying
10 abstracted 11 preoccupied
12 absent-minded

**farce**
03 jig 04 cram, joke, mime, sham
05 exode, lazzo, stuff 06 comedy, parody, satire 07 mockery 08 burletta, nonsense, shambles, stuffing, travesty
09 absurdity, burlesque, forcemeat, pantomime, slapstick 10 buffoonery
11 opera bouffe 14 ridiculousness

**farcical**
05 comic, silly 06 absurd, stupid
08 derisory 09 diverting, laughable, ludicrous 10 ridiculous 11 nonsensical
12 preposterous

**fare**
02 be, do, go 03 fee 04 cost, diet, eats, food, go on, menu, nosh, tack, what
05 board, cheer, get on, meals, price, speed, table 06 charge, course, happen, manage, ticket, travel, viands
07 make out, passage, proceed, prosper, rations, succeed, turn out
08 eatables, get along, progress, victuals 09 nutriment, passenger
10 provisions, sustenance
11 nourishment 12 passage-money

**farewell**
02 BV 03 bye 04 ciao, ta-ta, vale
05 adieu, adios, aloha, later, leave
06 bye-bye, cheers, see you, so long, valete 07 cheerio, goodbye 08 au revoir, take care 10 all the best
11 arrivederci, be seeing you, leave-taking, see you later, valediction, valedictory 12 have a nice day, mind how you go, see you around 14 auf Wiedersehen
• **expression of farewell** 03 bye
04 ciao, ta-ta, vale 05 addio, adieu, adiós, aloha, later 06 hooray, hooroo, see you, shalom, sheers, so long
07 cheerio, goodbye 08 au revoir, chin-chin, sayonara, toodle-oo
11 arrivederci, be seeing you, see you later 14 auf Wiedersehen, shalom aleichem

**far-fetched**
05 crazy 06 forced 07 dubious

08 fanciful, unlikely 09 exquisite, fantastic, recherché, unnatural
10 improbable, incredible
11 implausible, unrealistic
12 preposterous, unbelievable, unconvincing

**farm**
03 mas 04 ferm, land, sted, till 05 acres, mains, plant, ranch 06 bowery, grange, plough, shamba 07 acreage, holding, mailing, operate, station 08 farmland, hacienda, property 09 cultivate, farmstead, homestead 11 co-operative, work the land

*Farms and farming types include:*

03 dry, ley, pig
04 deer, fish, hill, stud, wind
05 croft, dairy, mixed, store, trash, trout
06 arable, estate, salmon, turkey
07 factory, organic, ostrich, poultry
09 extensive, free-range, intensive
10 collective, plantation
11 cattle ranch, monoculture, subsistence
12 sheep station, smallholding, stock station

*Farm animals include:*

02 ox
03 ass, cow, ewe, hen, pig, ram, sow
04 bull, calf, cock, duck, foal, goat, lamb, mare, mule
05 goose, horse, sheep
06 cattle, donkey, piglet, rabbit, turkey
07 chicken, rooster
08 cockerel, stallion
09 billy goat

*Farming equipment includes:*

03 ard, ATV, axe, hoe, saw
04 fork, plow, rake, wain
05 baler, drill, flail, gambo, mower, share, spade
06 harrow, plough, ricker, ripple, scythe, shovel, sickle, tanker, tedder
07 combine, draw hoe, grubber, hayfork, hayrake, mattock, scuffle, sprayer, tractor, trailer
08 buckrake, chainsaw, hay knife, haymaker, scuffler, spreader
09 corn drill, drop-drill, harvester, irrigator, pitchfork, power lift, rotary hoe, Rotavator®, Rotovator®, scarifier, seed drill, whetstone
10 cropduster, cultivator, disc harrow, disc plough, earth-board, flail mower, seed-harrow
11 bale wrapper, broadcaster, chaff-cutter, chaff-engine, drill-harrow, hedgecutter, mole drainer, reaping hook, wheelbarrow, wheel plough
12 muckspreader, slurry tanker
13 fork-lift truck, potato planter, slurry sprayer
14 field sprinkler, front end loader, milking machine

• **farm out** 08 delegate 09 outsource
11 contract out, subcontract 12 give to others, pass to others
• **farm worker** 03 dey 04 peon
06 sheepo 07 orra man 08 farmhand
• **healthy farm animal** 04 doer

**farmer**
04 Boer, ryot 05 cocky, colon, gebur
06 cockie, mailer, raiyat, yeoman
07 crofter, grazier, métayer, rancher
08 cockatoo 09 campesino, cow-cockie, sodbuster 10 agronomist, estanciero, husbandman 11 flock-master, share-milker, smallholder, stock-farmer, store farmer
12 sharecropper 13 agriculturist
15 agriculturalist

**farming**
06 arable 07 tilling 08 agronomy, crofting 09 geoponics, husbandry
11 agriculture, agroscience, cultivation
12 agribusiness, share-milking

**Faroe Islands**
02 FO 03 FRO

**far-off**
03 far 06 remote 07 distant, faraway
08 far-flung, outlying

**farrago**
04 hash 06 jumble, medley
07 mélange, mixture 08 mishmash
09 pot-pourri 10 dog's dinner, hodgepodge, hotchpotch, miscellany, salmagundi 11 gallimaufry 13 dog's breakfast

**far-reaching**
04 wide 05 broad 06 global
08 profound, sweeping, thorough
09 extensive, important, momentous
10 widespread 11 significant, wide-ranging 13 comprehensive

**far-sighted**
04 wise 05 acute, canny 06 shrewd
07 politic, prudent 08 cautious 09 far-seeing, judicious, prescient, provident
10 discerning 11 circumspect
14 forward-looking

**farther**
07 further, remoter 11 more distant, more extreme

**farthest**
08 furthest, remotest 11 most distant, most extreme

**farthing**
01 f 03 rag 06 farden 07 farding

**fascia**
04 band, sign 05 board, front, panel
06 fillet 07 console 08 platband
09 dashboard 15 instrument panel

**fascinate**
04 draw, lure 05 charm, rivet, witch
06 absorb, allure, entice 07 attract, beguile, bewitch, delight, enchant, engross, enthral 08 intrigue, transfix
09 captivate, enrapture, hypnotize, mesmerize, spellbind

**fascinated**
06 hooked 07 charmed, curious, enticed, smitten 08 absorbed, beguiled
09 bewitched, delighted, engrossed,

entranced, intrigued **10** captivated, enthralled, hypnotized, infatuated, mesmerized, spellbound

**fascinating**
**04** sexy **07** killing **08** alluring, charming, engaging, enticing, exciting, fetching, gripping, riveting, tempting, witching **09** absorbing, seductive **10** bewitching, compelling, compulsive, delightful, enchanting, engrossing, intriguing **11** captivating, interesting, mesmerizing, stimulating **12** irresistible

**fascination**
**04** draw, lure, pull **05** charm, magic, spell **06** allure, appeal **07** delight, sorcery **08** interest, witchery **09** magnetism **10** attraction, compulsion **11** captivation, enchantment **13** preoccupation

**fascism**
**09** autocracy, Falangism, Hitlerism **10** absolutism, Sinarchism **12** dictatorship **15** totalitarianism

**fascist**
**04** duce, Nazi **08** autocrat **09** Falangist, Hitlerist, Hitlerite **10** absolutist, autocratic, Blackshirt, Brownshirt, sinarchist **12** totalitarian **13** authoritarian

**fashion**
◊ *anagram indicator* **03** cut, fad, fit, ton, way **04** fain, feat, form, kind, line, look, make, mode, rage, sort, suit, turn, twig, type, wear, work **05** adapt, alter, build, craze, faine, fayne, feign, model, mould, shape, smith, style, trend, vogue **06** adjust, aguise, aguize, create, custom, design, entail, latest, manner, method, system, tailor **07** clothes, couture, entayle, in thing, pattern **08** approach, practice, rag trade, tendency **09** construct **10** appearance, convention **11** high fashion, manufacture **12** haute couture **13** designer label **15** clothes industry, fashion business

*Fashion designers include:*

**04** **Choo** (Jimmy), **Dior** (Christian), **Erté, Lang** (Helmut), **Muir** (Jean)
**05** **Amies** (Sir Hardy), **Dolce** (Domenico), **Farhi** (Nicole), **Karan** (Donna), **Kenzo** (Takada), **Klein** (Calvin), **Ozbek** (Rifat), **Patou** (Jean), **Pucci** (Emilio), **Quant** (Mary), **Ricci** (Nina), **Smith** (Sir Paul)
**06** **Armani** (Giorgio), **Ashley** (Laura), **Cardin** (Pierre), **Chanel** (Coco), **Conran** (Jasper), **Davies** (Betty), **Lauren** (Ralph), **Miyake** (Issey), **Rhodes** (Zandra), **Ungaro** (Emanuel)
**07** **Balmain** (Pierre), **Fassett** (Kaffe), **Gabbana** (Stefano), **Hamnett** (Katharine), **Lacroix** (Christian), **Laroche** (Guy), **McQueen** (Alexander), **Missoni** (Tai Otavio), **Versace** (Gianni)
**08** **Galliano** (John), **Gaultier** (Jean-Paul), **Givenchy** (Hubert James

Marcel Taffin de), **Hartnell** (Sir Norman), **Hilfiger** (Tommy), **Molyneux** (Edward), **Oldfield** (Bruce), **Richmond** (John), **Westwood** (Dame Vivienne), **Yamamoto** (Yohji)
**09** **Claiborne** (Liz), **Courrèges** (André), **Lagerfeld** (Karl), **McCartney** (Stella), **Valentino**
**10** **Balenciaga** (Cristobal), **Mainbocher, Vanderbilt** (Gloria)
**12** **Saint Laurent** (Yves), **Schiaparelli** (Elsa)

• **after a fashion** **07** somehow **08** in a sense **11** not very well **12** to some extent
• **current fashion** **02** go
• **out of fashion** **03** out **05** dated, passé **06** démodé, old hat, square **08** dismoded, obsolete, outmoded **09** out of date, unpopular **10** antiquated **12** old-fashioned **13** unfashionable

**fashionable**
**02** in **03** fly, hip, hot **04** chic, cool, tony **05** culty, flash, funky, natty, ritzy, smart, toney, vogue **06** chichi, glitzy, latest, modern, modish, snappy, snazzy, swanky, trendy, with it **07** à la mode, cultish, current, elegant, genteel, in vogue, mondain, on-trend, popular, stylish, swagger **08** all the go, designer, fantoosh, mondaine, swinging, up-to-date **09** exclusive, happening, high-toned **10** all the rage, prevailing **11** in the groove **12** contemporary **13** up-to-the-minute **14** fashion-forward

**fast**
**03** pdq **04** diet, firm, pacy, rash, shut, slim, wild **05** apace, brisk, faced, fiery, fixed, fleet, fully, hasty, nippy, pacey, quick, rapid, sound, swift, thick, tight **06** closed, deeply, firmly, flying, presto, secure, speedy, starve **07** abstain, express, fasting, fixedly, hastily, hurried, immoral, like mad, quickly, rapidly, refrain, riotous, swiftly, tightly **08** cracking, doggedly, exciting, fastened, go hungry, immobile, in a hurry, securely, speedily **09** breakneck, dissolute, fortified, high-speed, hurriedly, immovable, immovably, indelible, like a shot, like crazy, permanent, shameless, thrilling, turbulent **10** abstinence, blistering, boisterous, dissipated, like a flash, resolutely, starvation, stubbornly **11** accelerated, double-quick, lickety-spit, like the wind, ripsnorting **12** action-packed, deny yourself, dissipatedly, exhilarating, hunger strike, like the devil **13** extravagantly, like lightning, self-indulgent, unflinchingly **14** at a rate of knots, hell for leather **15** like the clappers

*Fast-days and fasting periods include:*

**04** Lent
**06** Ashura
**07** Ramadan

**08** Moharram, Muharram, Muharrem, Ramadhan, Tisha Bov
**09** Ember-days, Tisha Baav, Tisha be'Ab, Tisha Be'Av, Tishah b'Ab, Tishah B'Av, Yom Kippur
**10** Holy Friday
**12** Golden Friday

**fasten**
**03** aim, bar, fix, pin, tag, tie **04** bind, bolt, clip, do up, grip, join, lace, link, lock, moor, nail, seal, shut, spar, tack, zero **05** affix, chain, clamp, close, focus, hitch, latch, point, rivet, steek, unite, zip up **06** anchor, attach, buckle, button, direct, secure, take up, tether **07** connect **09** interlock **11** concentrate

**fastened**
**02** to **05** bound

**fastener, fastening**

*Fasteners include:*

**03** bar, fly, pin, tie, zip
**04** bond, clip, frog, hasp, hook, knot, lace, link, lock, loop, nail, stud, tach, tack
**05** catch, clasp, hinge, latch, morse, rivet, screw, tache
**06** buckle, button, clinch, cotter, eyelet, holder, staple, stitch, tassel, toggle, Velcro®, zipper
**07** padlock, tacking
**08** cufflink, shoelace, split pin
**09** paperclip, press stud, strapping
**10** collar stud, hook-and-eye
**11** bulldog clip, Chelsea clip, treasury tag
**12** espagnolette
**13** alligator clip, crocodile clip

**fast food**
*see* **food; restaurant**

**fastidious**
**04** nice **05** chary, faddy, fussy, picky **06** choosy, dainty, quaint, queasy, queazy, spruce **07** choosey, finicky, precise **08** delicate, overnice, precious **09** difficult, exquisite, niff-naffy, squeamish, superfine **10** meticulous, niffy-naffy, particular, pernickety, scrupulous **11** persnickety, punctilious **12** hard-to-please **13** hypercritical **14** discriminating

**fat**
**02** OS **03** big, ghi, oil, pot, wax **04** bard, bulk, flab, fozy, ghee, lard, oily, rich, spek, suet, wide **05** beefy, broad, buxom, cream, dumpy, fatty, gross, heavy, keech, large, money, obese, plump, podgy, porky, pursy, round, solid, sonsy, speck, squab, stout, thick, tubby **06** butter, cheese, chubby, creesh, degras, flabby, fleshy, grease, greasy, lipoid, paunch, portly, rotund, tallow **07** adipose, blubber, fatness, fleshed, fulsome, in flesh, lanolin, obesity, paunchy, pinguid, sizable, tubbish **08** dripping, fruitful, generous, handsome, palmitin, pot belly, sizeable **09** animal fat, corpulent, fat as a pig, margarine, plumpness, sebaceous, solidness, spare tyre,

**fatal**

stoutness **10** chubbiness, corpulence, deutoplasm, gor-bellied, kitchen-fee, oleaginous, overweight, pot-bellied, profitable **11** chylomicron, lipomatosis, substantial, well-endowed **12** considerable, saturated fat, steatopygous, vegetable fat **15** well-upholstered

**fatal**
**05** final, vital **06** deadly, lethal, mortal **07** fateful, killing **08** critical, decisive, destined, terminal **09** incurable, malignant **10** calamitous, disastrous **11** destructive, mortiferous, unavoidable **12** catastrophic

**fatalism**
**08** stoicism **09** endurance, passivity **10** acceptance **11** resignation

**fatalistic**
**07** passive, patient, stoical **08** resigned, yielding **09** defeatist **10** reconciled, submissive **11** acquiescent **13** long-suffering, philosophical

**fatality**
**04** dead, loss **05** death **08** casualty, disaster **09** lethality, mortality **10** deadliness **11** catastrophe

**fate**
**03** end, lot **04** doom, joss, luck, Norn, ruin **05** cavel, death, event, issue, karma, Moera, Moira, Norna, stars, weird **06** chance, defeat, future, kismet **07** destiny, fortune, outcome **08** disaster, God's will **09** horoscope **10** ill-fortune, predestiny, providence **11** catastrophe, destruction **14** predestination

*The Greek Fates:*

**06** Clotho
**07** Atropos
**08** Lachesis

*The Norse Fates:*

**03** Urd
**05** Skuld
**08** Verdande

**fated**
**03** fay, fey, fie **04** sure **06** doomed **07** certain **08** destined **09** enchanted **10** inevitable **11** ineluctable, inescapable, predestined, preordained, unavoidable **12** foreordained, predestinate

**fateful**
**05** fatal **07** crucial, pivotal **08** critical, decisive **09** important, momentous, prophetic **10** portentous **11** significant

**fatefully**
**09** crucially **10** critically, decisively **11** importantly, momentously **13** significantly

**father**
**02** da, Fr, pa **03** dad, gov, guv, pop **04** abba, abbé, bapu, curé, male, papa, père, pops, sire **05** adopt, beget, daddy, elder, maker, padre, pappy, pater **06** author, invent, leader, old man, parent, parson, pastor, patron, priest **07** creator, founder, genitor,

produce **08** ancestor, beau-pere, begetter, engender, forebear, governor, inventor, minister **09** architect, clergyman, initiator, originate, patriarch, procreate **10** forefather, give life to, originator, prime mover, procreator, progenitor **11** birth father, predecessor **12** guiding light **13** paterfamilias

**Father Christmas**
**05** Santa **06** St Nick **10** Santa Claus **11** Kris Kringle **12** Kriss Kringle
*See also* **reindeer**

**fatherland**
**04** home **08** homeland **10** motherland, native land, old country **13** mother-country **15** land of your birth

**fatherly**
**04** kind **06** benign, kindly, tender **08** paternal **09** avuncular, indulgent **10** benevolent, forbearing, protective, supportive **11** patriarchal **12** affectionate

**fathom**
**01** f **02** fm **03** fth, get, see **04** fthm, twig **05** gauge, grasp, plumb, probe, sound **06** rumble **07** measure, plummet, suss out, work out **08** estimate, perceive **09** interpret, latch onto, penetrate, search out **10** comprehend, understand **12** get the hang of

**fathomless**
**04** deep **07** complex, endless **08** infinite **09** enigmatic, intricate **10** bottomless, mysterious **11** complicated **12** immeasurable, impenetrable

**fatigue**
**02** ME **03** CFS, sap, tax **04** do up, PVFS, tire, toil **05** drain, weary **06** overdo, weaken **07** exhaust, wear out **08** debility, enervate, lethargy, overwork, weakness **09** lassitude, tiredness, weariness, yuppie flu **10** debilitate, enervation, exhaustion **11** take it out of **12** listlessness **13** wearisomeness

**fatigued**
**04** beat **05** all in, jaded, tired, weary **06** beaten, bushed, done in, fagged, pooped, swink't, wasted, zonked **07** euchred, swinked, wappend, whacked **08** dead-beat, jiggered, tired out **09** exhausted, fagged out, knackered, overspent, overtired, pooped out **10** euchred out **11** tuckered out

**fatness**
**04** bulk, flab **06** grease **07** obesity **08** richness **09** bulkiness, fertility, grossness, heaviness, largeness, plumpness, podginess, rotundity, stoutness, tubbiness **10** corpulence, corpulency, overweight, pinguidity, pinguitude, portliness

**fatten**
**04** cram, feed, lard, soil **05** bloat, flesh, frank, stuff, swell, widen **06** batten, battle, enrich, expand, feed up, spread **07** broaden, build up, engross, fill out, nourish, nurture, thicken **08** overfeed, pinguefy, saginate **09** stall-feed

**fatty**
**03** fat **04** oily, waxy **05** oleic, suety **06** creamy, fleshy, greasy, lipoid, suetty **07** adipose, buttery, pinguid **08** unctuous **09** aliphatic, sebaceous **10** oleaginous

**fatuous**
**04** daft, gaga **05** dense, inane, moony, silly **06** absurd, stupid **07** asinine, foolish, idiotic, lunatic, moronic, puerile, vacuous, witless **08** imbecile, mindless **09** brainless, ludicrous **10** ridiculous, weak-minded

**fault**
◇ *anagram indicator* **03** bug, nag, sin **04** beam, boob, carp, flaw, flub, gall, goof, slam, slip, trap, vice **05** blame, error, fluff, hitch, judge, knock, lapse, pinch, scold, slate, wrong **06** booboo, defect, foible, glitch, impugn, nibble, slip-up **07** blemish, blunder, censure, default, demerit, failing, impeach, misdeed, mistake, offence, quarrel **08** omission, weakness **09** criticize, inculpate, liability, oversight, reprehend, weak point **10** culpa levis, deficiency, negligence, peccadillo, wrongdoing **11** culpability, delinquency, pick holes in, shortcoming **12** imperfection, indiscretion, misdemeanour, pull to pieces **13** answerability, call to account, find fault with **14** accountability, responsibility **15** blameworthiness
• **at fault** ◇ *anagram indicator* **03** out **05** wrong **06** guilty **07** at a loss, to blame **08** culpable **10** in the wrong **11** accountable, blameworthy, responsible
• **to a fault** **06** unduly **07** too much **09** extremely **10** over the top, to extremes **11** excessively **12** immoderately, inordinately, in the extreme **13** unnecessarily

**fault-finding**
**04** crab **07** carping, nagging **08** captious, critical, niggling **09** cavilling, complaint, criticism, grumbling, querulous, quibbling **10** censorious, nit-picking **11** complaining **12** captiousness, pettifogging **13** hair-splitting, hypercritical **14** finger-pointing, hypercriticism

**faultless**
**04** pure **05** model **07** correct, perfect **08** accurate, flawless, spotless **09** blameless, exemplary, lily-white, unsullied **10** immaculate, impeccable **11** unblemished **13** unimpeachable **14** irreproachable, without blemish

**faulty**
◇ *anagram indicator* **03** bad **04** bust, duff, weak **05** kaput, wonky, wrong **06** broken, flawed **07** damaged, invalid, vicious **08** culpable **09** casuistic, conked out, defective, erroneous, illogical, imperfect, incorrect, playing up **10** fallacious, inaccurate, not working, on the blink,

out of order **11** inoperative, out of action **14** malfunctioning

## Faunas
**03** Pan

## faux pas
**04** boob, goof **05** error, gaffe **06** booboo, howler, slip-up **07** blunder, clanger, mistake **08** solecism **11** impropriety **12** indiscretion

## favour
**03** aid **04** back, boon, gree, help, like, pick **05** go for, grace, spoil **06** assist, choose, esteem, opt for, pamper, prefer, select **07** aggrace, approve, backing, benefit, endorse, indulge, make for, promote, service, succour, support **08** advocate, approval, befriend, champion, courtesy, good deed, good turn, goodwill, kindness, plump for, resemble, sanction, sympathy **09** advantage, encourage, patronage, recommend **10** acceptance, act of grace, assistance, attraction, indulgence, obligation, partiality, preference **11** approbation, countenance, favouritism **12** commendation, friendliness, take kindly to **13** act of kindness
• **in favour of** **03** for, pro **06** all for, behind **07** backing **10** supporting **11** on the side of
• **obtain favour** **03** win

## favourable
**04** fair, good, kind **05** white **06** benign, toward **08** amicable, Favonian, friendly, pleasing, positive, suitable, towardly **09** agreeable, approving, benignant, effective, opportune, promising **10** auspicious, beneficial, convenient, heartening, propitious, reassuring **11** appropriate, encouraging, meliorative, sympathetic **12** advantageous, enthusiastic, well-disposed **13** complimentary, understanding

## favourably
**04** well **09** agreeably, helpfully **10** in good part, positively, profitably **11** approvingly, fortunately, opportunely **12** auspiciously, conveniently, propitiously **14** advantageously **15** sympathetically

## favoured
**05** élite, fa'ard, faurd **06** chosen, graced **07** blessed, fancied **08** selected **09** favourite, predilect, preferred **10** advantaged, privileged **11** predilected, recommended

## favourite
**03** nap, pet **04** fave, idol, peat, pick **05** great **06** choice, chosen, minion, odds-on, winger **07** beloved, best boy, darling, dearest, nostrum, special **08** Benjamin, best girl, esteemed, favoured, gracioso, white boy **09** best-loved, boyfriend, certainty, form horse, golden boy, most-liked, number one, preferred, treasured **10** girlfriend, particular, preference **11** blue-eyed boy, first choice, teacher's pet **12** likely winner **13** fair-haired boy **14** apple of

your eye, white-headed boy **15** odds-on favourite

## favouritism
**04** bias **08** inequity, nepotism **09** injustice, prejudice **10** inequality, partiality, preference, unfairness **12** one-sidedness, partisanship

## fawn
**04** buff, claw **05** beige, court, crawl, creep, khaki, kotow, sandy, smalm, smarm, toady **06** cosy up, cozy up, cringe, crouch, grovel, kowtow **07** adulate, cervine, flatter, spaniel **08** bootlick, butter up, cosy up to, pay court, soft-soap, suck up to **09** pale brown **10** cozy up with **11** curry favour **12** bow and scrape, sand-coloured **14** be obsequious to, yellowish-brown

## fawning
**06** abject, supple **07** servile, spaniel **08** crawling, cringing, toadying, toadyish, unctuous **10** flattering, grovelling, obsequious, oleaginous **11** bootlicking, deferential, sycophantic **12** ingratiating, knee-crooking

## fay
see **fairy**

## faze
**03** rub **04** beat, rush, stun **05** drive, shake, shock, worry **06** dismay, put off, put out, puzzle, rattle **07** disturb, fluster, perturb, startle, unnerve **08** disquiet, drive off, surprise, unsettle **09** dumbfound, take aback **10** disconcert **12** perturbation

## FBI member
**03** Fed **04** G-man

## fear
**03** awe **04** risk **05** alarm, doubt, dread, panic, scope, worry **06** adread, affray, chance, dismay, expect, fright, honour, horror, phobia, qualms, regret, revere, terror, unease, wonder **07** anxiety, concern, foresee, phobism, redoubt, respect, shaking, suspect, terrify **08** aversion, be afraid, disquiet, distress, freak out, prospect, venerate, wonder at **09** agitation, bête noire, fear of God, nightmare, quivering, reverence, shudder at, suspicion, tremble at, trembling **10** anticipate, be afraid of, be scared of, foreboding, heart-quake, likelihood, likeliness, misgivings, shrink from, solicitude, tremble for, uneasiness, veneration **11** expectation, fearfulness, pantophobia, possibility, probability, trepidation **12** affrightment, apprehension, get the wind up, stand in awe of, take fright at **13** be in a blue funk, be uneasy about, consternation, have a horror of, lose your nerve **14** be anxious about, be in a cold sweat, lose your bottle, your heart melts **15** have qualms about, hold in reverence
• **for fear that** **04** lest

## fearful
**04** dire, grim **05** adred, afear, awful, ferly, nervy, tense, timid **06** afraid, aghast, hunted, scared, uneasy, yellow

**07** alarmed, anxious, ghastly, hideous, in dread, nervous, panicky, shaking **08** affrayed, agitated, dreadful, effraide, fearsome, gruesome, hesitant, horrible, horrific, shocking, terrible, timorous **09** appalling, atrocious, frightful, harrowing, monstrous, petrified, quivering, spineless, trembling, tremulous **10** frightened **11** distressing, in a blue funk **12** apprehensive, faint-hearted, in a cold sweat **13** having kittens, scared to death

## fearfully
**04** most, very, well **05** jolly **06** highly **07** awfully, timidly **08** terribly, uneasily **09** anxiously, extremely, intensely, nervously, unusually **10** dreadfully, hesitantly, incredibly **11** exceedingly, frightfully **12** terrifically, unbelievably **13** exceptionally **14** apprehensively

## fearless
**04** bold, game **05** brave, gutsy, proud **06** ballsy, daring, feisty, gritty, heroic, plucky, spunky **07** aweless, doughty, gallant, impavid, valiant **08** intrepid, unafraid, valorous **09** confident, dauntless, unabashed, undaunted **10** courageous, unblinking **11** indomitable, lion-hearted, unblenching, unflinching **14** unapprehensive

## fearsome
**04** unco **05** awful **07** awesome, dreaded **08** alarming, daunting, horrible, horrific, menacing, terrible **09** appalling, dismaying, frightful, unnerving **10** formidable, horrendous, horrifying, terrifying **11** frightening, hair-raising **12** awe-inspiring

## feasibility
**09** viability **10** expedience **11** possibility, workability **12** practicality **13** achievability **14** practicability, reasonableness

## feasible
**02** on **06** doable, likely, viable **08** possible, probable, workable **09** expedient, practical, realistic **10** achievable, attainable, realizable, reasonable **11** practicable **14** accomplishable

## feast
**02** do **03** ale, pig **04** fest, fete, gala, luau, wake, Yule **05** agape, beano, binge, gaudy, gorge, hangi, Purim, revel, treat **06** bridal, dinner, double, Isodia, junket, kaikai, Lammas, pig out, regale, repast, revels, spread, Sukkot, wealth **07** banquet, blow-out, convive, holiday, holy day, lamb-ale, name day, potlach, Rood Day, Shavuot, Sukkoth **08** carnival, carousal, feast day, festival, Id al-Adha, Id al-Fitr, Passover, potlatch, Shabuoth, Shavuoth, Shevuoth **09** abundance, Eid al-Adha, Eid al-Fitr, entertain, epulation, Hallowmas, indulge in, junketing, love-feast, Martinmas, Martlemas, partake of, Pentecost, profusion, saint's day **10** cornucopia, jour de fête, Roodmas

Day, slap-up meal **11** celebration, eat your fill, festivities, Holy-rood Day, wine and dine **13** All-hallowmass

## feat
**03** act, art **04** deed **05** point, skill **06** action, henner, splits, stroke **07** exploit **08** hat trick, shanghai **09** keepy-uppy **10** attainment, Houdini act **11** achievement, performance, tour de force, undertaking **14** accomplishment

## feather
**03** pen **04** down, tuft **05** crest, egret, penna, pinna, plume, quill, wedge **06** covert, fletch, hackle, manual, pinion, sickle **07** plumage, plumula, plumule, primary, rectrix, tectrix **08** aigrette, standard, tertiary, vibrissa **09** condition, filoplume, secondary, semiplume
• **coil of feathers 03** boa
• **part of feather 04** harl, herl

## feathery
**04** soft **05** downy, light, plumy, wispy **06** fledgy, fleecy, flimsy, fluffy, plumed **07** plumate, plumose, plumous **08** delicate **09** feathered, penniform **10** pennaceous **11** featherlike

## feature
**03** act, mug, pan **04** chin, dial, face, form, item, mark, nose, phiz, show, side, star **05** clock, facet, focus, looks, piece, point, shape, story, trait **06** appear, aspect, beauty, column, factor, figure, kisser, phizog, play up, report, visage **07** article, comment, perform, phantom, present, promote, quality **08** hallmark, property **09** attribute, character, emphasize, highlight, lineament, spotlight **10** accentuate, attraction, focal point, lineaments, speciality **11** centrepiece, countenance, participate, peculiarity, physiognomy **14** characteristic **15** call attention to, draw attention to

## featureless
**04** dull **05** bland, blank, plain, vague **07** anaemic, insipid, vanilla **08** ordinary **11** commonplace, nondescript, uninspiring **12** cookie cutter, run of the mill, unattractive, unclassified, unremarkable **13** indeterminate, undistinctive, unexceptional, uninteresting **14** common or garden **15** undistinguished

## febrile
**03** hot **05** fiery **07** burning, fevered, flushed, pyretic **08** feverish, inflamed **09** delirious

## February
**03** Feb

## feckless
**03** wet **04** weak **06** feeble, futile, no-good **07** aimless, useless, wimpish **08** helpless, hopeless **09** shiftless, worthless **11** incompetent, ineffectual **13** irresponsible

## fecund
**07** fertile, teeming **08** fruitful, prolific

**09** feracious, fructuous **10** productive **12** fructiferous

## fecundity
**08** feracity **09** fertility **12** fruitfulness **14** productiveness

## federal
**03** Fed **06** allied, united **07** unified **08** combined, in league **10** associated, integrated **11** amalgamated **12** confederated

## federate
**04** ally **05** unify, unite **06** league **07** combine **09** associate, integrate, syndicate **10** amalgamate **11** confederate **12** confederated, join together

## federation
**05** union **06** league **08** alliance, federacy **09** coalition, syndicate **11** association, combination, confederacy **12** amalgamation **13** confederation, copartnership

## fed up
**03** ate **04** blue, down, glum, jack **05** bored, jaded, sated, tired, weary **06** dismal, gloomy **07** annoyed, chocker, pig sick **09** depressed, hacked off **10** brassed off, browned off, cheesed off **11** disgruntled **12** discontented, dissatisfied, sick and tired **13** have had enough

## fee
**03** due, pay, sub **04** bill, cost, fine, hire, rent, toll, wage **05** money, price, terms, tithe, tythe **06** cattle, charge, hirage, mouter, reward, salary, towage **07** account, faldage, footing, hireage, moorage, multure, payment, premium, service, tuition **08** chummage, pilotage, property, retainer **09** emolument, livestock, obvention, ownership, refresher, vassalage **10** bell-siller, honorarium, possession, recompense **11** inheritance **12** remuneration, subscription **15** appearance money

## feeble
**03** wet **04** lame, poor, puny, tame, thin, weak **05** faint, frail, silly, sober, washy, wersh, wimpy, wussy **06** ailing, debile, effete, flabby, flimsy, futile, infirm, sickly, slight, weakly **07** failing, rickety, wastrel, wearish, wimpish **08** daidling, decrepit, delicate, feckless, helpless, lustless, pathetic, sackless **09** enervated, exhausted, graspless, powerless, weak-kneed **10** dispirited, fizzenless, foisonless, impuissant, inadequate, indecisive, namby-pamby, spiritless, wishy-washy **11** debilitated, fushionless, incompetent, ineffective, ineffectual, vacillating **12** unconvincing, unsuccessful

## feeble-minded
**04** dumb **05** dotty, silly **06** simple, stupid **07** idiotic, moronic **08** imbecile, retarded **09** deficient, dim-witted, imbecilic **10** half-witted, indecisive, slow-witted, weak-minded **11** not all there **13** soft in the head **14** mouth

breathing, not the full quid **15** slow on the uptake

## feebly
**06** lamely, sickly, weakly **07** faintly **08** slightly **10** helplessly **11** powerlessly **12** dispiritedly, indecisively, pathetically **13** ineffectively

## feed
◊ *insertion indicator* **03** eat, put **04** crop, dine, food, fuel, give, paid, slip, soil, tire **05** graze, slide **06** battle, browse, dine on, fodder, forage, foster, insert, repast, silage, stooge, suckle, supply, take in, tuck-in **07** consume, deliver, fortify, gratify, nourish, nurture, pasture, provide, support, victual **08** cater for, ruminate **09** encourage, foodstuff, introduce, partake of, provender **10** give food to, provide for, strengthen

## feedback
**05** reply **06** answer **08** comeback, response **11** respondence

## feel
**02** be **03** air, paw, rub **04** aura, bear, bent, deem, gift, hand, hold, know, look, maul, mood, palp, poke, seem **05** enjoy, flair, grasp, grope, judge, knack, nurse, sense, skill, think, touch, vibes **06** appear, caress, clutch, detect, endure, finger, finish, fondle, fumble, handle, notice, reckon, stroke, suffer, talent **07** ability, believe, contact, discern, faculty, feeling, harbour, massage, observe, quality, realize, surface, texture, undergo **08** ambience, aptitude, consider, instinct, perceive **09** be aware of, give way to, go through **10** atmosphere, experience, impression, manipulate, understand **11** consistency, live through **12** be overcome by **15** feel in your bones
• **feel for 04** pity **07** weep for **09** be moved by, grieve for **10** be sorry for, sympathize **11** commiserate **13** empathize with **14** sympathize with **15** commiserate with
• **feel like 04** want, wish **05** fancy **06** desire **09** would like

## feeler
**04** horn, palp **05** probe **06** palpus **07** advance, antenna **08** approach, overture, tentacle **09** overtures **10** sense organ **12** ballon d'essai, trial balloon

## feeling
**03** air, ego **04** aura, bent, care, feel, gift, idea, love, mood, pity, view **05** flair, hunch, knack, sense, skill, touch, vibes **06** ardour, belief, motion, notion, spirit, talent, theory, warmth **07** ability, concern, emotion, fervour, inkling, opinion, passion, pitying, quality, thought **08** aptitude, emotions, esthesia, fondness, instinct, passions, sympathy **09** aesthesia, aesthesis, affection, intensity, intuition, sensation, sentience, sentiment, suspicion **10** affections, atmosphere, compassion, Empfindung, impression, perception, self-esteem, tenderness **11** point of view, sensibility, sensitivity,

sympathetic **12** appreciation
**13** compassionate, sensibilities,
sensitivities, understanding, way of
thinking **14** natural ability,
sentimentality, susceptibility
• **show feeling 05** emote
• **with no feeling 04** numb

**feign**
**03** act **04** fain, fake, sham **05** fable,
faine, false, fayne, forge, put on, shape
**06** affect, assume, gammon, invent,
make up **07** falsify, fashion, imagine,
imitate, pretend, put it on **08** misfeign,
simulate **09** dissemble, fabricate
**11** counterfeit, dissimulate, make a
show of, make believe

**feint**
**04** play, ruse, sham, wile **05** blind,
bluff, dodge, dummy **06** gambit
**08** artifice, pretence **09** deception,
expedient, manoeuvre, stratagem
**10** subterfuge **11** distraction, make-
believe, mock-assault **12** dissemblance

**feisty**
**04** bold **05** brave, gutsy, tough **06** gritty,
lively, plucky, spunky, touchy
**08** spirited **09** excitable, irritable
**10** courageous, determined

**feldspar, felspar**
**06** albite **08** adularia, andesine,
sanidine, sunstone **09** anorthite,
moonstone **10** hyalophane, oligoclase,
orthoclase **11** anorthosite, labradorite,
peristerite, plagioclase

**felicitous**
**03** apt **05** happy **06** timely **07** apropos,
fitting **08** apposite, inspired, suitable
**09** fortunate, opportune, well-timed
**10** delightful, propitious, prosperous,
well-chosen, well-turned
**11** appropriate **12** advantageous

**felicity**
**03** joy **05** bliss **07** aptness, delight,
ecstasy, rapture **08** blessing, euphoria
**09** eloquence, happiness, propriety
**11** delectation, suitability
**12** suitableness **13** applicability
**15** appropriateness

**feline**
**03** cat, tom **04** eyra, puss **05** catty, felid,
manul, moggy, ounce, pussy, queen,
quoll, rumpy, sleek, tabby **06** kitten,
malkin, mouser, ocelot, serval, slinky,
smooth, Tibert, tomcat **07** catlike,
cattish, leonine, sensual, sinuous,
wildcat **08** alleycat, baudrons,
graceful, stealthy **09** grimalkin,
sealpoint, seductive **10** jaguarundi
*See also* **cat**

**fell**
**02** ax, KO **03** axe, hew, lit, log **04** alit,
dire, gall, hide, hill, keen, moor, pelt,
raze, skin, very **05** cruel, felon, floor,
great, level **06** deadly, fierce, lay low,
mighty, poleax **07** cut down, doughty,
flatten, poleaxe, pungent **08** chop
down, demolish, felonous, membrane,
ruthless **09** knock down, overthrow,
prostrate **10** bitterness, strike down
**15** raze to the ground

**fellow**
**01** F, m **02** bo, co-, he **03** boy, bud, cat,
cod, don, guy, Joe, lad, man, pal, sod,
wag **04** bozo, chap, chum, cove, dean,
dude, gent, like, male, mate, oppo,
peer, twin **05** bloke, buddy, crony,
devil, equal, joker, match **06** buffer,
callan, double, friend, person, rascal,
sister **07** callant, compeer, comrade,
partner, related, similar **08** confrère,
co-worker **09** associate, boyfriend,
character, colleague, companion,
semblable **10** associated, compatriot,
individual **11** counterpart
**12** contemporary
*See also* **boy**
• **little fellow 03** elf, imp

**fellow feeling**
**04** care **07** empathy, feeling
**08** sympathy **10** compassion
**13** commiseration, understanding

**fellowship**
**04** club **05** guild, order, union
**06** league **07** society **08** intimacy,
matiness, sodality, sorority
**09** communion, palliness **10** affability,
amiability, chumminess, consortium,
fraternity, friendship, sisterhood
**11** affiliation, association, brotherhood,
camaraderie, comradeship, familiarity,
sociability **13** companionship,
compatibility

**felon**
*see* **criminal**

**felspar**
*see* **feldspar, felspar**

**felt**
**03** bat **04** batt

**female**
**01** f **03** doe, -ess, gal, hen, her, pen, rib,
she **04** bird, girl, hind, miss **05** woman
**06** maiden **07** girlish, womanly
**08** feminine, ladylike, womanish
**09** petticoat **10** carpellate, pistillate
*See also* **animal; girl**

**feminine**
**01** f **03** fem **04** weak **05** cissy, girly
**06** female, gentle, pretty, tender
**07** girlish, unmanly, wimpish,
womanly **08** delicate, graceful,
ladylike, womanish **09** petticoat
**10** effeminate

**femininity**
**08** delicacy **09** sissiness, womanhood
**10** effeminacy, gentleness, muliebrity,
prettiness, tenderness **11** girlishness,
womanliness **12** feminineness,
gracefulness, womanishness

**feminism**
**08** womanism **09** women's lib
**12** women's rights **14** women's
movement

*Feminists include:*

**04** Daly (Mary), Hite (Shere), **Mott**
(Lucretia), **Shaw** (Anna Howard),
**Wolf** (Naomi)
**05** Abzug (Bella), **Astor** (Nancy),
**Beale** (Dorothea), **Greer**
(Germaine), **Stone** (Lucy)
**06** Callil (Carmen), **Cixous** (Hélène),
Faludi (Susan), **Friday** (Nancy),
**Fuller** (Margaret), **Gilman** (Charlotte
Perkins), **Grimké** (Sarah Moore),
**Orbach** (Susie), **Rankin** (Jeannette),
**Stopes** (Marie), **Weldon** (Fay)
**07** Anthony (Susan B), **Davison**
(Emily), **Dworkin** (Andrea), **Egerton**
(Sarah), **Fawcett** (Dame Millicent),
**Friedan** (Betty), **Goldman** (Emma),
**Kennedy** (Helena, Baroness),
**Lenclos** (Ninon de), **Steinem**
(Gloria), **Tennant** (Emma)
**08** Beauvoir (Simone de), **Brittain**
(Vera), **MacPhail** (Agnes), **Rathbone**
(Eleanor)
**09** Blackwell (Elizabeth), **Pankhurst**
(Adela), **Pankhurst** (Christabel),
**Pankhurst** (Emmeline), **Pankhurst**
(Sylvia)
**11** Burgos Seguí (Carmen de)
**14** Wollstonecraft (Mary)

**femme fatale**
**04** vamp **05** Circe, siren **06** Sirens
**07** charmer, Delilah, Lorelei **08** Mata
Hari **09** temptress **10** seductress
**11** enchantress

**fen**
**03** bog **04** moss, quag, wash **05** marsh,
swamp **06** morass, slough
**08** quagmire

**fence**
◇ *containment indicator* **03** hay, pen
**04** coop, oxer, pale, rail, wall, wear,
weir, wire **05** bound, dodge, evade,
guard, hedge, parry **06** defend, fraise,
paling, pusher, rasper, rustic, secure,
shield, shut in **07** barrier, confine,
defence, enclose, fortify, inclose,
protect, quibble, railing, rampart
**08** encircle, palisade, palisado, restrict,
separate, sepiment, stockade,
surround **09** barricade, enclosure,
pussyfoot, stonewall, vacillate,
windbreak **10** digladiate, equivocate,
trafficker **11** prevaricate
**12** circumscribe, shilly-shally,
tergiversate
• **sit on the fence 06** dither **08** be
unsure **09** vacillate **11** be uncertain, be
undecided **12** be irresolute, shilly-
shally **13** be uncommitted **14** blow hot
and cold

**fencing**
**07** railing **08** guarding **09** defending,
swordplay

*Fencing terms include:*

**03** bib, cut, hit
**04** bout, épée, foil, pass, pink, volt,
ward
**05** allez, appel, carte, feint, forte,
lunge, parry, piste, prime, punto,
sabre, sixte, touch, volte
**06** attack, button, come in, doigté,
faible, flèche, foible, octave,
parade, puncto, quarte, quinte,
remise, thrust, tierce, touché
**07** barrage, counter, en garde, on
guard, passado, reprise, riposte,
seconde, septime, stop hit
**08** back edge, balestra, coquille,
plastron, tac-au-tac, traverse
**09** disengage, repechage

**fend**

**10** flanconade, imbroccata, time-thrust
**11** corps à corps, punto dritto
**12** colichemarde, counter-parry, punto reverso
**14** counter-riposte

**fend**

**05** avert, parry, repel **06** defend, divert, resist **07** beat off, deflect, head off, keep off, provide, repulse, shut out, support, sustain, ward off **08** maintain, stave off **09** hold at bay, look after, turn aside **10** take care of

**feral**

**04** wild **06** animal, brutal, deadly, fierce, savage **07** bestial, brutish, untamed, vicious **08** funereal, unbroken **09** ferocious **12** uncultivated **14** undomesticated

**ferment**

◇ *anagram indicator* **04** boil, brew, foam, fret, fuss, heat, rise, stew, stir, work, zyme **05** cause, fever, froth, mould, rouse, yeast **06** arouse, bubble, enzyme, excite, fester, foment, frenzy, furore, hubbub, incite, leaven, seethe, stir up, tumult, unrest, uproar, work up **07** agitate, inflame, provoke, ptyalin, turmoil **08** bacteria, brouhaha, smoulder **09** agitation, commotion, confusion **10** disruption, effervesce, excitement, turbulence

**fermium**

**02** Fm

**fern**

*Ferns include:*

**03** oak
**04** hard, lady, male, tree
**05** beech, brake, chain, crown, holly, marsh, royal, sword, water
**06** Boston, ribbon, shield, silver, tongue
**07** bladder, bracken, buckler, Dickie's, elkhorn, Goldie's, leather, ostrich, parsley, rockcap, wall rue, woodsia
**08** aspidium, cinnamon, climbing, hairy lip, licorice, moonwort, pillwort, polypody, staghorn
**09** asparagus, asplenium, bird's nest, hare's foot, rusty-back, sensitive
**10** Asian chain, Korean rock, maidenhair, soft shield, spleenwort
**11** hart's tongue, rabbit's foot
**12** broad buckler, elephant's ear, resurrection
**13** crested ribbon, Japanese holly, scolopendrium, squirrel's foot
**14** brittle bladder
**15** Japanese painted

**ferocious**

**04** deep, grim, wild **05** cruel, feral **06** bitter, brutal, fierce, savage, severe, strong **07** extreme, inhuman, intense, salvage, untamed, vicious, violent **08** barbaric, pitiless, ruthless, sadistic, Tartarly, vigorous **09** barbarous, merciless, murderous **12** bloodthirsty, catamountain, cat o' mountain

**ferocity**

**06** sadism **07** cruelty **08** savagery, severity, violence, wildness **09** barbarity, brutality, extremity, intensity **10** fierceness, inhumanity **11** viciousness **12** ruthlessness

**ferret**

**03** hob **04** gill, hunt, jill **05** rifle, scour **06** forage, search **07** rummage **09** go through
• **ferret out** **04** find **05** dig up, trace **06** elicit **07** extract, nose out, root out, suss out, unearth, worm out **08** discover, hunt down **09** search out, track down **10** fossick out, run to earth

**ferry**

**03** ply, run **04** boat, move, pont, ro-ro, ship, take, taxi **05** carry, drive, shift **06** convey, packet, ponton, vessel **07** passage, pontoon, shuttle, traject, tranect **08** car ferry **09** ferry-boat, transport **10** packet boat **12** flying bridge **13** Interislander®, roll-on roll-off

**fertile**

**04** rich **06** arable, battle, broody, fecund, potent, virile **08** abundant, creative, fruitful, inspired, pregnant, prolific **09** ingenious, inventive, luxuriant, visionary **10** generative, productive **11** imaginative, resourceful **12** reproductive

**fertility**

**07** fatness, potency **08** richness, virility **09** abundance, fecundity **10** luxuriance **12** fruitfulness, prolificness **14** generativeness, productiveness

**fertilization**

**03** IVF **04** GIFT, ICSI **07** selfing **10** conception **11** fecundation, pollination, procreation, propagation, siphonogamy **12** implantation, impregnation, insemination **13** palmification, superfetation

**fertilize**

**04** dung, feed, self **05** dress, mulch **06** enrich, manure **07** compost **08** fructify, top-dress **09** fecundate, pollinate, procreate **10** impregnate, inseminate **12** make fruitful, make pregnant

**fertilizer**

**04** dung, marl **05** guano, humus, mulch **06** manure **07** compost, humogen, kainite, nitrate, tankage **08** bone meal, dressing **09** cyanamide, plant food, soda nitre **10** fish-manure **11** top-dressing **13** sodium nitrate **14** superphosphate **15** ammonium nitrate

**fervent**

**03** hot **04** warm **05** eager, fiery **06** ardent, devout **07** earnest, excited, intense, sincere, zealous **08** spirited, vehement, vigorous **09** emotional, energetic, heartfelt **10** passionate **11** full-blooded, impassioned **12** enthusiastic, wholehearted

**fervently**

**07** eagerly **08** ardently **09** earnestly, excitedly, intensely, sincerely

**10** vigorously **11** emotionally **12** passionately **13** energetically **14** wholeheartedly

**fervour**

**04** fire, heat, hwyl, zeal **05** verve **06** ardour, energy, spirit, vigour, warmth **07** emotion, passion **09** animation, eagerness, intensity, sincerity, vehemence **10** enthusiasm, excitement **11** earnestness

**fester**

**03** irk, rot **04** brew, gall **05** anger, annoy, chafe, decay, go bad **06** gather, infect, perish, rankle **07** moulder, putrefy **08** maturate, smoulder, ulcerate **09** decompose, discharge, suppurate

**festival**

**03** ale **04** fair, fete, gala, play, tide, wake **05** feast, festa, party, revel **06** double, fiesta, pardon **07** gala day, high day, holiday, jubilee **08** carnival, high tide, panegyry **10** merry-night, semi-double **11** anniversary, celebration, festivities, merrymaking **13** commemoration, entertainment
*See also* **celebration; service**

*Ancient festivals and celebrations include:*

**03** Bon, Mod
**04** feis, Lots, Yule
**05** Litha, Mabon, Purim, Saman, Weeks, Wesak
**06** Advent, Diwali, Easter, Floria, Imbolc, Imbolg, Lammas, May Day, Oimelc, Opalia, Pesach, Plebii
**07** Beltane, Equiria, Feralia, Fugalia, holy-ale, Lady Day, Lemuria, Lugnasa, Mop Fair, Navrati, Palilia, Parilia, Ramadan, Samhain, Sukkoth, Sullani, Theseia, Vinalia
**08** Agonalia, Beltaine, Cerealia, Fasching, Faunalia, Floralia, Hanukkah, Hogmanay, Homstrom, Hull Fair, Id ul-Adha, Id ul-Fitr, Lucia Day, Lughnasa, Lugnasad, Mahayana, Matralia, Nit de foc, Passover, Samhuinn, Setsubun, Shabuoth, Stow Fair, Tanabata, Vestalia
**09** Baishakhi, Bealtaine, Boxing Day, Christmas, church-ale, Floralies, Goose Fair, Hallowe'en, Hallowmas, Ides of Mar, Liberalia, Ludi Magni, Lughnasad, Lugnasadh, Magalesia, Magha-puja, Mardi Gras, Martinmas, Nemoralia, Paganalia, Pentecost, Puanepsia, Robigalia, Thargelia, Ullambana, Up-Helly-Aa, Wakes Week, Yom Kippur
**10** Allhallows, Ambarvalia, Barnet Fair, Fordicidia, Fornicalia, Good Friday, Larentalia, La Tomatina, Lee Gap Fair, Ludi Romani, Lughnasadh, Lupercalia, Matronalia, Mother's Day, Neptunalia, Palm Sunday, Pancake Day, Parentalia, Portunalia, Quirinalia, Regifugium, Saturnalia, Swan Upping, Terminalia, Volcanalia

**11** Acension Day, All Fools' Day, All Souls' Day, Bacchanalia, Carmentalia, Epulum Jovis, Hina Matsuri, Lady Luck Day, Oktoberfest, Oskhophoria, Panathenaea, Quinquatrus, Semo Sanctus, St David's Day, Tabernacles

**12** All Saints' Day, Annunciation, Armilustrium, Ash Wednesday, Barranquilla, Day of the Dead, Doll Festival, Holy Wells Day, Kanda Matsuri, Ludi Merceruy, Mahashivrati, Meditrinalia, Moon Festival, Nutters Dance, Rosh Hashanah, St Andrew's Day, St George's Day, Thanksgiving, Tubilustrium, Twelfth Night, Well-dressing

**13** Allhallows Eve, April Fool's Day, Haxey Hood Game, Ludi Consualia, Ludi Martiales, Midsummer's Eve, Raksha Bandhan, Shrove Tuesday, St Patrick's Day, The Furry Dance, Water Festival, Widecombe Fair

**14** Chinese New Year, Maundy Thursday, St Nicholas's Day, Vinalia Rustica, Walpurgis Night

**15** Festival of Light, Harvest Festival, Lares Praestites, Ludi Apollinares, Mahavira Jayanti, Mothering Sunday, Priddy Sheep Fair, St Valentine's Day

---

*Modern festivals and celebrations include:*

---

**05** VE Day, VJ Day, WOMAD
**08** Anzac Day, Earth Day, Labor Day
**09** Canada Day, Labour Day
**10** Burns Night, Eisteddfod
**11** Bastille Day, Cinco de Mayo, Glastonbury, Republic Day, Waitangi Day
**12** Armistice Day, Australia Day, Bonfire Night, Glyndebourne, Groundhog Day
**13** New Zealand Day
**14** Guy Fawkes' Night, Remembrance Day
**15** Edinburgh Fringe, Edinburgh Tattoo, Independence Day

---

*Religious festivals include:*

---

**02** Id
**03** Eid
**04** Holi, Lent, Lots, mela, Obon, Oram, puja, Yule
**05** Litha, Pesah, Purim
**06** Advent, Bakrid, Basant, Dhamma, Divali, Diwali, Easter, Imbolc, Lammas, Mawlid, Pesach, Sukkot
**07** Baisaki, Beltane, holy day, matsuri, New Year, Ramadan, Samhain, Shavuot, Sukkoth
**08** All Souls, Baisakhi, Dipavali, Dusserah, Epiphany, feast day, Hanukkah, Id-al-Adha, Id al-Fitr, Id-ul-Zuha, Muharram, Passover
**09** All Saints, Ascension, Candlemas, Christmas, Deepavali, Dolayatra, Durga-puja, Easter Day, Eid-al-Adha, Eid al-Fitr, Mardi Gras, Navaratri, Oshogatsu, Pentecost, Up-Helly-Aa, Yom Kippur

**10** All Hallows, Assumption, Good Friday, Lughnasadh, Lupercalia, Michaelmas, Palm Sunday, Ramanavami, Rathayatra, Saturnalia, Vulcanalia, Whit Sunday
**11** All Souls' Day, Bacchanalia, Lakshmi-puja, Milad-un-Nabi, Panathenaea, Rosh Hashana
**12** All Saints' Day, Annunciation, Ascension Day, Ash Wednesday, Christmas Day, Easter Sunday, Holy Saturday, Holy Thursday, Night of Power, Ohinamatsuri, Prakash Utsav, Rosh Hashanah, Simchat Torah, Star Festival, Tango no Sekku
**13** Buddha Purnima, Corpus Christi, Holy Innocents, Night of Ascent, Passion Sunday, spring equinox, Trinity Sunday, vernal equinox
**14** Chinese New Year, Day of Atonement, Easter Saturday, Maundy Thursday, summer solstice, winter solstice
**15** autumnal equinox, Lantern Festival, Tanabata Matsuri, Transfiguration

- **day before a festival** **03** eve
- **octave of a festival** **04** utas

**festive**
**04** gala **05** happy, jolly, merry **06** cheery, festal, hearty, jovial, joyful, joyous **07** cordial, holiday **08** carnival, cheerful, feastful, jubilant **09** convivial **11** celebratory **12** light-hearted

**festivity**
**03** fun, rag **04** gala, gaud **05** party, revel, sport **06** fiesta, gaiety, let-off **07** jollity, joyance, revelry, triumph **08** carousal, feasting, festival, pleasure **09** amusement, enjoyment, joviality, junketing, merriment **10** banqueting, cheeriness, joyfulness, jubilation **11** celebration, fun and games, merrymaking **12** cheerfulness, conviviality **13** entertainment, glorification, jollification

**festoon**
**04** deck, hang, swag **05** adorn, array, drape **06** bedeck, swathe, wreath **07** bedizen, chaplet, garland, garnish, wreathe **08** decorate, encarpus, ornament

**fetch**
**03** fet, get **04** earn, fett, make, take **05** bring, carry, ghost, go for, reach, yield **06** arrive, attain, convey, derive, double, escort **07** bring in, collect, conduct, deliver, realize, sell for **08** go and get **09** stratagem, transport **10** apparition
- **fetch up** **05** end up, vomit **06** arrive, show up, turn up, wind up **07** recover **08** finish up **11** materialize

**fetching**
**04** cute **05** sweet **06** pretty **07** winsome **08** adorable, alluring, charming **09** appealing **10** attractive, enchanting **11** captivating, fascinating

**fête, fete**
**04** fair, gala **05** treat **06** bazaar, honour,

regale **07** holiday, lionize, welcome **08** carnival, festival **09** entertain **10** sale of work **11** garden party

**fetid, foetid**
**04** foul, rank **05** pongy **06** filthy, rancid, sickly, smelly, whiffy **07** humming, noisome, noxious, odorous, reeking **08** mephitic, stinking **09** offensive **10** disgusting, graveolent, malodorous, nauseating

**fetish**
**03** obi **04** idol, ju-ju, obia **05** charm, image, mania, obeah, thing, totem **06** amulet **08** fixation, idée fixe, talisman **09** obsession **10** cult object

**fetter**
**03** tie **04** bind, curb, gyve, iron **05** chain, tie up, truss **06** hamper, hinder, hobble, impede **07** confine, hopples, leg-iron, manacle, shackle **08** encumber, obstruct, restrain, restrict **09** constrain, entrammel, hamstring **10** hamshackle

**fetters**
**05** bands, bonds, curbs, irons **06** chains, checks, slangs **07** bondage **08** manacles, shackles **09** bracelets, captivity, handcuffs **10** hindrances, restraints **11** constraints, inhibitions **12** obstructions, restrictions

**fettle**
◇ *anagram indicator*
- **in fine fettle** **03** fit **04** trim **05** sound **06** on form, strong **07** healthy, in shape **09** shipshape **10** in fine form, in good nick **11** in good shape **12** in good health **13** hale and hearty **15** in good condition

**feud**
**03** row, war **04** duel, food **05** argue, brawl, clash, fight **06** bicker, enmity, strife **07** contend, discord, dispute, ill will, quarrel, rivalry, wrangle **08** argument, bad blood, be at odds, conflict, squabble, vendetta **09** altercate, animosity, bickering, hostility **10** antagonism, bitterness **12** disagreement

**fever**
**04** heat **06** frenzy, unrest **07** ecstasy, ferment, passion, pyrexia, turmoil **08** delirium **09** agitation, calenture **10** excitement **11** temperature **12** feverishness, restlessness **15** high temperature

---

*Fevers include:*

---

**01** Q
**03** hay, tap
**04** ague, camp, gaol, gold, jail, Rock, ship, tick, worm
**05** brain, cabin, dandy, Lassa, Malta, marsh, stage, swamp, swine, Texas
**06** dengue, dumdum, hectic, jungle, parrot, plague, rabbit, spring, trench, typhus, valley, yellow
**07** biliary, enteric, gastric, malaria, measles, ratbite, sandfly, scarlet, splenic, spotted, typhoid, verruga
**08** childbed, kala-azar, undulant
**09** breakbone, calenture, East Coast,

glandular, phrenitis, puerperal, relapsing, remittent, rheumatic
**10** blackwater, Rift Valley, scarlatina, yellow Jack
**12** African coast
**13** cerebrospinal, leptospirosis, Mediterranean
**14** kissing disease
**15** acute rheumatism

**fevered**
**03** hot, red **07** burning, excited, febrile, flushed, frantic, nervous **08** feverish, frenzied, restless, worked up
**09** impatient **10** passionate

**feverish**
◇ *anagram indicator* **03** hot, red **05** hasty **06** hectic, rushed **07** burning, excited, febrile, flushed, frantic, hurried, in a tizz, nervous **08** agitated, bothered, febrific, frenzied, in a tizzy, restless, troubled, worked up **09** delirious, flustered, impatient, in a dither **10** passionate **11** overwrought **12** in a kerfuffle **14** hot and bothered

**few**
**04** rare, some, thin **05** scant, wheen **06** meagre, scanty, scarce, sparse **07** a couple, handful, not many, several **08** one or two, sporadic, uncommon **09** a minority, exclusive, hardly any **10** inadequate, infrequent, negligible, scattering, sprinkling, two or three **11** scarcely any **12** insufficient **13** in short supply **14** a small number of, inconsiderable **15** thin on the ground

**fey**
**03** fay, fie, odd, shy **05** dotty, droll, elfin, funny, weird **06** doomed, quaint, quirky **07** curious, playful, unusual **08** childish, fanciful, peculiar **09** eccentric, impulsive, whimsical **10** capricious **11** mischievous **12** supernatural **13** unpredictable

**fiancé, fiancée**
**08** intended, wife-to-be **09** betrothed, bride-to-be **10** future wife **11** husband-to-be **13** future husband **14** bridegroom-to-be **15** prospective wife

**fiasco**
**04** bomb, flop, mess, rout, ruin **05** flask **06** bottle, fizzer, lash-up **07** cropper, debacle, failure, screw-up, washout **08** calamity, collapse, disaster **09** damp squib **11** catastrophe

**fiat**
**02** OK **05** edict, order **06** decree, dictum, diktat **07** command, dictate, mandate, precept, warrant **08** sanction **09** directive, ordinance **10** injunction, permission **12** proclamation **13** authorization

**fib**
**03** gag, lie **04** tale, yarn **05** evade, fable, porky, punch, story **06** invent, pummel **07** evasion, falsify, fantasy, fiction, untruth, whopper **08** sidestep, white lie **09** dissemble, fabricate, falsehood, fantasize, invention **10** concoction, taradiddle **11** prevaricate, tarradiddle **13** prevarication

**fibre**
**04** coir, hair, pile, pita, silk **05** cloth, nerve, sinew, stuff, viver **06** fibril, make-up, nature, strand, thread **07** calibre, courage, funicle, resolve, stamina, tendril, texture **08** backbone, filament, firmness, material, roughage, strength **09** character, substance, toughness, willpower **10** resolution **11** disposition, temperament **12** resoluteness **13** determination

**fibres**
**03** tow **04** pons

**fickle**
◇ *anagram indicator* **06** kittle, labile, volage **07** flighty, mutable **08** disloyal, unstable, unsteady, variable, volatile **09** choiceful, faithless, mercurial, volageous **10** capricious, changeable, inconstant, irresolute, unfaithful, unreliable **11** treacherous, vacillating **12** inconsistent, wind-changing **13** unpredictable
• **be fickle** **04** turn

**fickleness**
**06** change, levity **09** treachery **10** disloyalty, fitfulness, mutability, volatility **11** flightiness, inconstancy, instability **12** unsteadiness **13** changeability, faithlessness, unreliability **14** capriciousness, changeableness, unfaithfulness

**fiction**
**03** fib, lie **04** myth, pulp, tale, yarn **05** fable, story **06** legend, novels **07** fantasy, parable, romance, stories, untruth **08** chick lit, noveldom, pretence **09** falsehood, invention, tall story **10** concoction **11** fabrication **12** splatterpunk, storytelling **15** creative writing
*See also* **literature; non-fiction**
• **science fiction** **02** SF **05** sci-fi **09** cyberpunk

**fictional**
**06** made-up, unreal **08** fabulous, invented, literary, mythical **09** imaginary, legendary **11** make-believe, non-existent **12** mythological
*See also* **literary; novel**

*Fictional places include:*

**02** Ix, Oz
**04** Alph, Rhun
**05** Arnor, Holby, Moria, Rohan
**06** Canley, Dibley, Gondor, Laputa, Leonia, Lorien, Mordor, Narnia, Titipu, Utopia, Vulcan, Wessex, Xanadu
**07** Avonlea, Bedrock, Camelot, Erewhon, Eriador, Eurasia, Midwich, Mole End, Prydain, Sun Hill, Toyland, Walford
**08** Ambridge, Blefuscu, Borduria, Calormen, Earthsea, Flatland, Hobbiton, Islandia, Lilliput, Llaregyb, Meccania, Mirkwood, New Crete, Polyglot, Ragnarok, Stepford, Syldavia, Sylvania, Tartarus, The Shire, Toad Hall
**09** Barataria, Brigadoon, Discworld, Emmerdale, Freedonia,

Hollyoaks, Llareggub, Ringworld, Rivendell, River Alph, Ruritania, Shangri-La, Summer Bay, Venusberg, Westworld
**10** Archenland, Barchester, Borchester, Moominland, Shieldinch, Vanity Fair, Wonderland
**11** Airstrip One, Ankh-Morpork, Barsetshire, Borsetshire, Brobdingnag, Diagon Alley, Emerald City, Gormenghast, Middle-Earth, Orbitsville, Skull Island, The Wild Wood
**12** Albert Square, Celesteville, Erinsborough, Glubbdubdrib, Jurassic Park, Ramsay Street, Sleepy Hollow, Tralfamadore, Weatherfield
**13** Celestial City, Christminster, Montego Street
**14** Brookside Close, Doubting-Castle, Hogwarts School, Never-Never Land, Nightmare Abbey, Treasure Island
**15** Baskerville Hall

**fictitious**
**04** fake, sham **05** bogus, false **06** made-up, mythic, untrue **07** assumed, feigned, fictive **08** invented, mythical, romantic, spurious, supposed **09** concocted, imaginary **10** apocryphal, artificial, fabricated, improvised **11** counterfeit, non-existent

*Fictitious places include:*

**07** Speewah
**08** Woop Woop
**10** Snake Gully
**11** Bandywallop
**12** Bullamakanka, Oodnagalahbi, Waikikamukau
**13** the black stump

**fiddle**
**02** do, gu **03** con, fix, gju, gue, kit, toy **04** fuss, play, rasp, rote, scam **05** cheat, fraud, graft, viola **06** diddle, fidget, juggle, meddle, racket, rip-off, scrape, tamper, tinker, trifle, violin **07** falsify, sultana, swindle **09** gold brick, interfere, manoeuvre, racketeer **10** fool around, mess around **12** cook the books **13** sharp practice

**fiddling**
**05** petty **06** fiddly, paltry **07** trivial **08** trifling **10** negligible **13** insignificant

**fidelity**
**05** faith, fides, troth, trust **07** honesty, loyalty **08** accuracy, devotion **09** adherence, closeness, constancy, exactness, precision **10** allegiance, strictness **11** devotedness, reliability **12** authenticity, faithfulness **13** dependability **15** trustworthiness

**fidget**
**03** toy **04** fike, fret, fuss, jerk, jump **05** hotch **06** bustle, fiddle, footer, hirsle, jiggle, niggle, squirm, tamper, tinker, trifle, twitch, writhe **07** shuffle, twiddle, wriggle **09** mess about **10** play around **11** toss and turn **12** restlessness

**fidgety**
05 jumpy 06 on edge, uneasy
07 excited, jittery, nervous, restive, twitchy, uptight 08 agitated, restless
09 impatient

**field**
03 lea, ley 04 area, lawn, line, mead, play, slip, stop 05 catch, champ, close, forte, glebe, green, parry, pitch, put up, range, sawah, scene, scope, sward
06 answer, bounds, domain, ground, handle, lea-rig, limits, meadow, padang, pick up, regime, return, select, sphere 07 deflect, paddock, pasture, present, runners, send out, stubble 08 ball park, confines, cope with, deal with, entrants, province, retrieve 09 grassland, opponents, possibles, territory 10 applicants, candidates, contenders, department, discipline, opposition, speciality
11 competition, competitors, contestants, environment 12 choose to play, participants, playing-field
*See also* **athletics; cricket**
• **stubble field** 05 arish 06 arrish

**Field Marshal**
02 FM 13 velt-mareschal

*Field Marshals include:*

04 **Haig** (Douglas, Earl)
05 **Lucan** (George Bingham, Earl of), **Monty**
06 **French** (Sir John), **Raglan** (Fitzroy Somerset, Lord)
07 **Allenby** (Edmund Hynman, Viscount), **Roberts** (Frederick, Earl)
08 **Ironside** (William, Lord), **Wolseley** (Garnet Joseph, Viscount)
09 **Robertson** (Sir William)
10 **Alanbrooke** (Alan Francis Brooke, Viscount), **Auchinleck** (Sir Claude John Eyre), **Kesselring** (Albert), **Montgomery** (Bernard, Viscount)

**fiend**
03 fan, nut 04 buff, ogre 05 beast, brute, demon, devil, fient, freak, ghoul
06 addict, savage 07 devotee, fanatic, monster 10 aficionado, enthusiast, evil spirit

**fiendish**
05 cruel 06 brutal, clever, savage, wicked 07 complex, cunning, inhuman, obscure, vicious 08 barbaric, devilish, infernal, involved, ruthless
09 difficult, ferocious, ingenious, intricate, monstrous 10 aggressive, diabolical, horrendous, malevolent
11 challenging, complicated, imaginative, resourceful, unspeakable
12 bloodthirsty 14 Mephistophelic
15 Mephistophelean, Mephistophelian

**fierce**
03 hot, wud 04 fell, grim, keen, wild, wood 05 angry, breem, breme, cruel, felon, grave, stern, stout 06 brutal, raging, savage, severe, strong, wrathy
07 furious, intense, rampant, vicious, violent 08 menacing, powerful, ruthless, terrible, walleyed 09 cut-throat, dangerous, ferocious, merciless, murderous, truculent

10 aggressive, passionate, relentless
11 frightening, tempestuous, threatening 12 bloodthirsty, uncontrolled

**fiercely**
06 keenly, wildly 07 cruelly, sternly
08 bitterly, brutally, savagely, severely, strongly, terribly 09 furiously, intensely, viciously, violently
10 implacably, menacingly, powerfully, ruthlessly 11 dangerously, fanatically, ferociously, mercilessly, murderously 12 aggressively, passionately, relentlessly, tooth and nail 13 tempestuously, threateningly

**fiery**
03 hot 05 afire, aglow, sharp, spicy
06 ablaze, aflame, ardent, fierce, heated, red-hot, spiced, spunky, sultry, torrid 07 blazing, burning, fervent, flaming, flushed, frampal, glowing, piquant, pungent, violent 08 frampold, inflamed, seasoned 09 excitable, hot-headed, impatient, impetuous, impulsive, irritable 10 passionate, phlogistic, sulphurous
11 empassioned, high-mettled, impassioned

**fiesta**
04 gala 05 feast, party 07 holiday, jubilee 08 carnival, festival 09 festivity
11 celebration, merrymaking

**fifteen**
02 XV

**fifty**
01 L
• **fifty per cent** 02 so

**fight**
03 box, hit, row, wap, war 04 blue, bout, camp, curb, defy, duel, feud, fray, grit, guts, mill, riot, rout, ruck, spar, stem, yike 05 aggro, argue, bandy, brawl, brush, clash, drive, fence, joust, mêlée, mix-in, pluck, punch, rammy, scrap, set-to, spunk, yikes 06 action, attack, barney, battle, bicker, bottle, bovver, bundle, combat, debate, dust-up, engage, fracas, meddle, medley, oppose, repugn, resist, ruckus, ruffle, rumble, scrape, shindy, spirit, stifle, stoush, strike, strive, take on, thwart, tussle
07 bashing, be at war, contend, contest, crusade, discord, dispute, fall out, grapple, lay into, make war, pasting, punch-up, quarrel, repress, resolve, ruction, scuffle, smother, tuilyie, tuilzie, wage war, warfare, wrangle, wrestle 08 argument, be at odds, bottle up, campaign, champion, conflict, ding-dong, do battle, dogfight, exchange, firmness, gunfight, have a row, hold back, keep back, militate, movement, object to, pell-mell, restrain, set about, skirmish, squabble, struggle, suppress, tenacity 09 altercate, bloodshed, cockfight, duke it out, encounter, force back, monomachy, skiamachy, stand up to, weigh into, willpower, withstand
10 aggression, bandy words, digladiate, dissension, Donnybrook,

engagement, fisticuffs, free-for-all, graplement, will to live 11 altercation, come to blows, cross swords, disturbance, hostilities, snickersnee, work against 12 disagreement, resoluteness 13 confrontation, determination, measure swords, take issue with 14 hold out against
15 campaign against, do battle against, struggle against
• **fight back** 04 curb 05 check, reply
06 resist, retort 07 contain, control, repress 08 bottle up, hold back, restrain, suppress 09 force back, retaliate 11 put up a fight 13 counter-attack 14 defend yourself, hold out against
• **fight off** 04 rout 05 repel 06 rebuff, resist 07 beat off, hold off, ward off
08 stave off 09 hold at bay, keep at bay
11 put to flight
• **incite to fight** 03 tar 05 tarre

**fighter**
01 F 03 EFA, MiG 05 rival 07 bruiser, chetnik, fechter, jump jet, soldier, trouper, warrior 08 attacker, hired gun, opponent 09 adversary, combatant, contender, disputant, man-at-arms, mercenary 10 antagonist, contestant
11 bushwhacker 13 Messerschmitt
15 sparring partner

*Fighters include:*

05 boxer, pugil
06 fencer, hitman, knight
07 matador, picador, sworder
08 pugilist, toreador, wrestler
09 gladiator, kick boxer, spadassin, swordsman
10 rejoneador
11 bullfighter, cage fighter, digladiator
12 banderillero, prizefighter

*See also* **aeroplane**

**figment**
• **figment of your imagination**
05 fable, fancy 07 fiction 08 delusion, illusion 09 deception, falsehood, invention 10 concoction 11 fabrication
13 improvisation

**figurative**
03 fig 07 typical 08 symbolic, tropical
09 parabolic, pictorial 10 emblematic
11 allegorical, descriptive
12 metaphorical, naturalistic
14 representative

**figure**
03 fig, sum 04 body, form, icon, idol, ikon, sign, sums 05 build, digit, frame, guess, image, judge, maths, price, shape, think, torso, total, value
06 amount, appear, crop up, design, emblem, leader, number, person, reckon, sketch, symbol, worthy
07 believe, diagram, drawing, feature, integer, notable, numeral, outline, passage, pattern, picture, suppose
08 conclude, consider, estimate, foreshow, physique 09 authority, celebrity, character, dignitary, horoscope, personage, symbolize
10 appearance, silhouette, statistics
11 mathematics, personality 12 be

included in, calculations, illustration **13** be mentioned in **14** representation

*Figures include:*

**04** cone, cube, kite, oval
**05** prism
**06** circle, cuboid, oblong, sector, sphere, square
**07** decagon, diamond, ellipse, hexagon, nonagon, octagon, polygon, pyramid, rhombus
**08** crescent, cylinder, heptagon, pentagon, quadrant, tetragon, triangle
**09** chiliagon, dodecagon, rectangle, trapezium, undecagon
**10** hemisphere, hendecagon, octahedron, polyhedron, quadrangle, semicircle
**11** pentahedron, tetrahedron
**13** parallelogram, quadrilateral
**15** scalene triangle

*See also* **circle; triangle**
• **figure of speech** **05** image, trope
**06** flower, simile, zeugma
**07** imagery, meiosis **08** diallage, metaphor, oxymoron **09** prolepsis
**10** abscission, antithesis, hyperbaton, synecdoche **11** parenthesis
**12** antimetabole, turn of phrase
• **figure on** **04** plan **06** expect
**07** plan for **08** depend on, reckon on
**10** bargain for **13** be prepared for
**15** take into account
• **figure out** **03** see **04** dope, make, twig **05** count **06** fathom, reason, reckon **07** compute, dope out, make out, resolve, work out **08** decipher, estimate, tumble to **09** calculate, latch onto, puzzle out **10** understand
**13** get the picture

**figurehead**
**04** bust, name **05** dummy, image, token **06** figure, puppet **07** carving
**08** front man **10** man of straw, mouthpiece **11** nominal head, titular head

**Fiji**
**03** FJI

**filament**
**04** cord, hair, pile, wire **05** cable, fiber, fibre, seton **06** cirrus, elater, sleave, strand, string, thread **07** fimbria, tendril, whisker **08** fibrilla, tentacle
**09** microwire, protonema
**10** paraphysis **11** gonimoblast

**filch**
**03** nab, rob **04** crib, drib, fake, lift, nick, palm, prig, take **05** lurch, pinch, steal, swipe **06** nobble, pilfer, rip off, smouch, snitch, thieve **07** purloin, snaffle **08** embezzle, knock off, peculate **09** knock down
**14** misappropriate

**file**
**03** ask, box, row, rub **04** case, data, hone, line, list, make, note, rake, rasp, risp, roll, sand, text, whet **05** apply, enter, grate, march, plane, put in, queue, scour, shape, shave, store, trail, train, troop **06** abrade, binder, column, folder, format, papers, parade, polish,

record, scrape, smooth, stream, string, submit, thread **07** box file, cortège, data set, details, dossier, pollute, process, program, Rolodex®, rub down **08** classify, document, organize, register **09** catalogue, crocodile, lever arch, portfolio **10** categorize, pickpocket, pigeonhole, procession, put in place, walk in line
**11** information, particulars

**filial**
**04** fond **05** loyal **06** loving **07** devoted, dutiful **10** daughterly, respectful
**12** affectionate

**filibuster**
**05** delay, stall **06** hinder, impede, pirate, put off **07** prevent **08** obstruct, perorate **09** buccaneer, hindrance, speechify, waste time **10** impediment, peroration **11** obstruction
**12** postponement, speechifying
**13** procrastinate **15** delaying tactics, procrastination

**filigree**
**04** lace **07** lattice, tracery **08** fretwork, lacework, wirework **09** interlace
**10** scrollwork **11** latticework

**fill**
◊ *insertion indicator* **04** brim, bung, clog, cork, cram, glut, hold, line, pack, plug, seal, soak, stop **05** ample, block, close, crowd, imbue, prime, stack, stock, stuff **06** bishop, charge, englut, enough, fulfil, occupy, plenty, riddle, stop up, supply, take up **07** congest, furnish, implete, perform, pervade, provide, satisfy, suffuse **08** complete, make full, permeate, saturate
**09** abundance, replenish **10** all you want, impregnate, sufficient
**11** sufficiency **13** all you can take
**14** more than enough
• **fill in** **05** brief, write **06** act for, advise, answer, inform **07** cover in, fill out, replace, stand in **08** acquaint, complete, deputize **09** represent
**10** substitute, understudy **11** pinch-hit for **13** bring up to date
• **fill out** **06** answer, fill in
**08** complete **10** gain weight, grow fatter **11** put on weight **12** become fatter **13** become plumper **14** become chubbier

**fillet**
**04** list **05** label **06** anadem, fascia, reglet, regula **07** annulet, cloison
**09** sphendone, tournedos

**filling**
◊ *insertion indicator* **03** big **04** full, rich
**05** ample, heavy, large, solid **06** filler, hearty, inside, square, stodgy
**07** padding, wadding **08** contents, generous, stuffing **09** impletion, substance **10** nutritious, satisfying
**11** substantial

**fillip**
**04** goad, prod, push, spur **05** boost, flick, shove **06** incite, snitch **07** impetus
**08** stimulus **09** incentive, stimulant, stimulate **10** inducement, motivation
**11** stimulation **13** encouragement

**film**
**03** cel, ISO, pic, web **04** cell, cine-, coat, epic, haze, kell, mist, reel, skin, veil, weft **05** cloud, cover, flick, glaze, layer, movie, sheet, shoot, short, spool, video **06** cinema, deepie, screen, silent, tissue **07** blanket, coating, dusting, feature, footage, picture **08** cassette, covering, membrane, pellicle, televise **09** blue movie, cartridge, mistiness, skinflick, videogram, videotape **10** featurette, horse opera, photograph, screenplay, video nasty **11** documentary, feature film **12** record on film **13** motion picture, video cassette
*See also* **director**

*Films include:*

**02** ET, If...
**03** Big, JFK, Kes, Ran
**04** Antz, Babe, Dr No, Gigi, Heat, Jaws, MASH, Milk, Reds
**05** Alfie, Alien, Bambi, Bugsy, Crash, Dumbo, Fargo, Ghost, Giant, Rocky, Shine, Shrek
**06** Aliens, Amélie, Batman, Ben-Hur, Blow-Up, Casino, Gandhi, Grease, Heimat, Lolita, Mad Max, Misery, Psycho, Sirens, The Fly, Top Gun, Top Hat
**07** Amadeus, Big Fish, Cabaret, Das Boot, Die Hard, Dracula, Rain Man, Rebecca, Robocop, Titanic, Tootsie, Traffic, Vertigo
**08** Apollo 13, Body Heat, Born Free, Cape Fear, Chocolat, Duck Soup, Fantasia, High Noon, Insomnia, Key Largo, Kill Bill, King Kong, Mamma Mia, Scarface, Star Wars, The Birds, The Piano, The Sting, The Thing, The Tramp, Toy Story
**09** 12 Monkeys, A Bug's Life, Annie Hall, Betty Blue, Cat Ballou, Chinatown, City of God, Easy Rider, Excalibur, Funny Girl, Gallipoli, Get Shorty, Gladiator, GoldenEye, Home Alone, Local Hero, Manhattan, Moonraker, Nosferatu, Octopussy, Pinocchio, Rio Grande, Spartacus, Spider-Man, Stand by Me, The Castle, The Reader, Vera Drake
**10** Blue Velvet, Braveheart, Casablanca, Chicken Run, Cry Freedom, Dirty Harry, East of Eden, Goldfinger, GoodFellas, Grand Hotel, High Sierra, Men in Black, Metropolis, My Fair Lady, My Left Foot, Now, Voyager, Paris, Texas, Raging Bull, Rear Window, Stagecoach, Taxi Driver, The Big Easy, The Hustler, The Postman, The Shining, The Wild One, Unforgiven, Wall Street
**11** A Few Good Men, All About Eve, American Pie, Beetlejuice, Blade Runner, Citizen Kane, Deliverance, Don't Look Now, Finding Nemo, Forrest Gump, Gosford Park, Heaven's Gate, La Dolce Vita, Mary Poppins, Mean Streets, Monsters Inc, Mystic River, Notting Hill, Out of Africa,

Pretty Woman, Public Enemy, Pulp Fiction, The 400 Blows, The Big Sleep, The Evil Dead, The Exorcist, The Fugitive, The Gold Rush, The Graduate, The Lion King, The Red Shoes, The Third Man, Thunderball, Wayne's World, Wild at Heart

12 A View to a Kill, Brighton Rock, Casino Royale, Cool Hand Luke, Eyes Wide Shut, Frankenstein, Ghostbusters, Gregory's Girl, Groundhog Day, Jurassic Park, Lethal Weapon, Philadelphia, Prizzi's Honor, Roman Holiday, Rome Open City, Salaam Bombay!, Seven Samurai, Sleepy Hollow, The Apartment, The Godfather, The Searchers, The Two Towers, The Wicker Man, The Wild Bunch, Whisky Galore!, Withnail and I

13 Apocalypse Now, Basic Instinct, Batman Forever, Batman Returns, Burnt by the Sun, Death in Venice, Die Another Day, Doctor Zhivago, Dr Strangelove, Educating Rita, Eight and a Half, His Girl Friday, Licence to Kill, Live and Let Die, Mildred Pierce, Raining Stones, Reservoir Dogs, Scent of a Woman, Some Like It Hot, The Crying Game, The Dam Busters, The Dark Knight, The Deer Hunter, The Dirty Dozen, The Fisher King, The Jazz Singer, The Jungle Book, The Right Stuff, The Terminator, To Catch a Thief, Trainspotting, West Side Story, Wings of Desire, Zorba the Greek

14 A Day at the Races, American Beauty, American Psycho, As Good as it Gets, Blazing Saddles, Bonnie and Clyde, Brief Encounter, Bringing Up Baby, Central Station, Chariots of Fire, Cinema Paradiso, Dial M for Murder, Empire of the Sun, Enter the Dragon, Erin Brockovich, Five Easy Pieces, Gangs of New York, Goodbye Mr Chips, Jean de Florette, LA Confidential, Lord of the Rings, Midnight Cowboy, Minority Report, Muriel's Wedding, Schindler's List, Secrets and Lies, The Big Lebowski, The Commitments, The Elephant Man, The Great Escape, The Ladykillers, The Last Emperor, The Life of Brian, The Lost Weekend, The Mask of Zorro, The Music Lovers, The Seventh Seal, Un Chien Andalou

15 Annie Get Your Gun, A Passage to India, Back to the Future, Crocodile Dundee, Dog Day Afternoon, Do the Right Thing, Fatal Attraction, For Your Eyes Only, Full Metal Jacket, Gone With the Wind, Good Will Hunting, Heart of Darkness, Independence Day, Life Is Beautiful, Manon des Sources, Meet Me in St Louis, On the

Waterfront, Quantum of Solace, Return of the Jedi, Road to Perdition, Singin' in the Rain, Sunset Boulevard, Tarzan the Ape Man, The African Queen, The Bicycle Thief, Thelma and Louise, The Piano Teacher, The Seven Samurai, The Sound of Music, Thirty-nine Steps

---

*Film types include:*

03 spy, war
04 blue, cult, epic, noir
05 adult, anime, buddy, crime, farce, heist, short, spoof, vogue, weepy, wuxia
06 action, auteur, biopic, B-movie, comedy, Disney, erotic, family, horror, murder, police, remake, rom-com, silent, weepie
07 Carry-on, cartoon, classic, diorama, dramedy, fantasy, musical, neo-noir, new wave, passion, realist, robbery, slasher, telepic, tragedy, war hero, western
08 animated, disaster, escapist, film noir, gangster, newsreel, romantic, space-age, thriller
09 adventure, Bollywood, burlesque, chopsocky, detective, film à clef, flashback, Hitchcock, Hollywood, James Bond, love story, low-budget, machinima, melodrama, political, road movie, satirical, skin flick, Spielberg, whodunnit
10 avant-garde, bonkbuster, chick-flick, gay-lesbian, neo-realist, period epic, snuff movie, surrealist, tear-jerker, travelogue
11 black comedy, blockbuster, cliff-hanger, documentary, kitchen sink, period drama, tragicomedy, underground
12 cinéma-vérité, Ealing comedy, ethnographic, fly-on-the-wall, mockumentary, pornographic, rockumentary, social comedy
13 comic-book hero, expressionist, multiple-story, murder mystery, nouvelle vague, sexploitation, sexual fantasy, social problem
14 blaxploitation, Charlie Chaplin, comedy thriller, police thriller, rites of passage, romantic comedy, science-fiction, sword-and-sandal
15 animated cartoon, cowboy and Indian, romantic tragedy, screwball comedy

---

• **film classification** 01 A, U, X
02 AA, PG
• **film company** 05 indie 06 studio
• **film over** 03 fog 04 blur, dull
05 glaze 08 mist over 09 cloud over
13 become blurred
• **horror film** *see* **horror**
• **part of film** 04 reel

**filmy**
04 fine, thin 05 gauzy, light, sheer
06 flimsy, floaty 07 clouded, fragile
08 chiffony, cobwebby, delicate,

gossamer 09 gossamery
10 diaphanous, see-through, shimmering 11 translucent, transparent
13 insubstantial

**filter**
04 leak, mesh, ooze, seep, sift 05 drain, gauze, leach, sieve 06 purify, refine, riddle, screen, sifter, strain 07 clarify, dribble, netting, trickle 08 colander, filtrate, membrane, strainer
09 percolate

**filth**
03 mud 04 crud, dirt, dung, gore, grot, gunk, mire, muck, porn, smut, soil, yuck 05 addle, bilge, dreck, dross, grime, gunge, slime, trash 06 faeces, grunge, manure, refuse, sewage, sleaze, sludge, wallow 07 garbage, rubbish, squalor, sullage 08 effluent, foulness, hard porn, impurity 09 blue films, colluvies, excrement, indecency, obscenity, pollution, vulgarity 10 coarseness, corruption, defilement, dirty books, sordidness
11 pornography, putrescence, raunchiness, uncleanness
12 putrefaction 13 contamination, sexploitation

**filthy**
03 bad, low, wet 04 base, blue, foul, lewd, mean, vile, wild 05 adult, angry, bawdy, black, cross, dirty, grimy, gross, manky, mucky, muddy, nasty, rainy, ratty, rough, slimy, sooty, yucky 06 Augean, coarse, crabby, cruddy, faecal, grubby, impure, putrid, rotten, shirty, smutty, soiled, sordid, stormy, vulgar, X-rated 07 corrupt, obscene, raunchy, squalid, stroppy, swinish, unclean 08 decaying, depraved, explicit, indecent, polluted, unwashed, wretched 09 irritable, offensive, worthless 10 despicable, putrefying, suggestive 11 bad-tempered, foul-mouthed
12 contaminated, contemptible, disagreeable, pornographic

**fin**
03 arm 04 hand, skeg, tail, vane
05 fiver, pinna, skegg 06 dorsal
07 Finland, ventral 08 pectoral

**final**
◇ *tail selection indicator* 03 end, net
04 last, nett 05 dying 06 latest
07 closing, settled, supreme
08 decisive, definite, eventual, farewell, terminal, ultimate 09 finishing
10 concluding, conclusive, conclusory, definitive, last-minute, peremptory 11 determinate, irrefutable, irrevocable, terminating, unalterable 12 indisputable
• **final word** 04 amen

**finale**
◇ *tail selection indicator* 03 end 05 close
06 climax, ending 07 curtain
08 epilogue, final act 10 conclusion, dénouement 11 culmination
13 crowning glory

**finality**
08 firmness, ultimacy 09 certitude
10 conviction, resolution

**11** decidedness **12** decisiveness, definiteness **13** inevitability **14** conclusiveness, inevitableness, irrevocability, unavoidability **15** irreversibility

**finalize**
**03** end **05** agree, close, sew up **06** clinch, decide, finish, settle, wrap up **07** resolve, work out **08** complete, conclude, round off

**finally**
◇ *tail selection indicator* **04** last **06** at last, in fine, lastly **07** for ever, for good **08** at length, in the end **10** decisively, definitely, eventually, to conclude, ultimately **11** irrevocably, permanently **12** conclusively, in conclusion, irreversibly **13** for good and all, once and for all

**finance**
**04** back, cash, fund **05** float, funds, means, money, set up, trade **06** assets, budget, income, pay for, wealth **07** affairs, banking, capital, funding, revenue, savings, sponsor, subsidy, support **08** accounts, bankroll, business, commerce **09** economics, guarantee, liquidity, resources, subsidize **10** accounting, capitalize, habilitate, investment, underwrite **11** bank account, sponsorship, stock market, wherewithal **15** money management

**financial**
**05** money **06** fiscal **08** economic, monetary **09** budgetary, pecuniary **10** commercial **15** entrepreneurial
• **financial expert** **09** economist **10** monetarist

**financier**
**05** bania, gnome **06** banian, banker, banyan, trader **07** swindle **08** investor **10** moneymaker, speculator **11** stockbroker, white knight **12** financialist, Wall-Streeter **13** industrialist

**finch**
**05** spink, twite **06** canary, linnet, siskin, towhee, whidah, whydah **07** bunting, chewink, manikin, redbird, waxbill **08** grosbeak, mannikin, snowbird, wheatear **09** brambling, crossbill, grassquit **10** fallow-chat, indigo bird, marsh-robin, weaver bird, whidah bird, whydah bird **11** green linnet, tree sparrow **12** cardinal-bird **13** indigo bunting

**find**
**02** be **03** get, try, win **04** boon, coup, deem, earn, gain, meet, rate, rule, spot **05** asset, catch, exist, gauge, judge, learn, occur, reach, think, trace **06** attain, come by, decree, detect, dig out, expose, locate, notice, obtain, regain, reveal, review, secure, turn up, umpire **07** achieve, acquire, adjudge, bargain, believe, declare, examine, get back, godsend, good buy, mediate, observe, procure, realize, recover, referee, uncover, unearth **08** come upon, consider, discover, perceive, retrieve, sentence **09** arbitrate, be

present, discovery, encounter, recognize, stumble on, track down **10** adjudicate, chance upon, come across, experience, happen upon, lay hands on, run to earth, trouvaille **11** acquisition **12** bring to light, pass sentence **13** give a sentence, stumble across **14** sit in judgement **15** deliver a verdict
• **find in** ◇ *anagram indicator* ◇ *hidden indicator* ◇ *insertion indicator*
• **find out** **03** see, sus **04** note, suss, take, twig **05** catch, get at, learn **06** detect, expose, gather, reveal, rumble, show up, unmask **07** extract, lay bare, observe, realize, suss out, uncover **08** disclose, discover, identify, perceive, pinpoint, tumble to **09** ascertain, establish, expiscate, get wind of **10** cotton on to, understand **11** make certain **12** bring to light **13** make certain of

**finding**
**04** find **05** award, order **06** decree **07** verdict **08** decision, judgment **09** discovery, judgement **10** conclusion, innovation **12** breakthrough **13** pronouncement **14** recommendation

**fine**
**01** F **02** A1, OK **03** A-OK, dry, end, fit, log, oke, yes **04** braw, eric, fair, good, jake, keen, mooi, nice, pawn, phat, pure, safe, slim, thin, well **05** beaut, bonny, clear, dandy, exact, gauzy, great, light, mulct, nifty, right, sharp, sheer, showy, smart, sound, sting, sunny, unlaw **06** agreed, amerce, assess, bonnie, bright, choice, dainty, flimsy, goodly, ground, incony, lovely, minute, narrow, on form, pledge, punish, purify, refine, sconce, select, slight, strong, subtle **07** clement, crushed, damages, elegant, forfeit, fragile, gradely, healthy, immense, inconie, in shape, penalty, powdery, precise, radical, refined, slender, stylish **08** accurate, all right, critical, delicate, gossamer, graithly, handsome, jim-dandy, narrowly, penalize, precious, properly, splendid, striking, superior, very good, very well, vigorous **09** admirable, agreeable, beautiful, brilliant, cloudless, correctly, egregious, excellent, expensive, exquisite, first-rate, sensitive, shipshape, temperate **10** acceptable, acceptably, amercement, attractive, diaphanous, discerning, first-class, forfeiture, punishment, remarkable, tickety-boo **11** amerciament, exceptional, fashionable, fine-grained, flourishing, in good shape, lightweight, magnificent, outstanding, pretentious, tickettyboo, up to scratch **12** in good health, satisfactory, successfully **13** distinguished, hair-splitting, hale and hearty **14** satisfactorily **15** in good condition

**fine-looking**
**04** waly **05** wally

**finely**
**05** wally **06** nicely, subtly, thinly **07** exactly, lightly, sharply **08** minutely **09** admirably, precisely **10** critically, delicately, splendidly **11** brilliantly, excellently **12** attractively **13** magnificently

**finery**
**07** bravery, gaudery, regalia, wallies **08** frippery, glad rags **09** jewellery, ornaments, showiness, splendour, trappings **10** rattletrap, Sunday best **11** bedizenment, best clothes, decorations

**finesse**
◇ *anagram indicator* **04** tact **05** bluff, evade, flair, skill, trick **06** polish **07** knowhow **08** deftness, delicacy, elegance, neatness, strategy, subtlety **09** adeptness, diplomacy, expertise, manoeuvre, quickness **10** adroitness, cleverness, discretion, manipulate, refinement **11** savoir-faire, tactfulness **12** gracefulness **14** sophistication

**finger**
**03** paw **04** feel, name **05** pinky, share, talon, touch **06** agency, caress, fondle, handle, medius, paddle, pilfer, pinkie, stroke **07** annular, toy with **08** interest, virginal **09** prepollex **10** fiddle with, manipulate, meddle with **13** play about with
• **put your finger on** **05** place **06** locate, recall **07** find out, hit upon, isolate, pin down **08** discover, identify, indicate, pinpoint, remember

**fingerhole**
**04** lill, lilt, stop **07** ventage, ventige

**finial**
**03** tee **04** crop **06** pommel **09** pineapple, poppy-head

**finicky**
◇ *anagram indicator* **05** faddy, fussy, picky **06** choosy, fiddly, tricky **08** critical, delicate **09** difficult, finickety, intricate, selective **10** fastidious, meticulous, nit-picking, particular, pernickety, scrupulous **11** persnickety **13** hypercritical **14** discriminating

**finish**
◇ *tail selection indicator* **02** do **03** eat, end, use **04** coat, coda, down, rout, ruin, stop **05** apply, cease, close, crush, drain, drink, empty, glaze, gloss, grain, scoff, sew up, shine, use up **06** attain, be over, defeat, devour, ending, expend, finale, fulfil, guzzle, lustre, pack in, polish, settle, topple, veneer, wind up, wind-up, wrap up **07** absolve, achieve, coating, conquer, consume, deplete, destroy, exhaust, lacquer, outwork, perfect, surface, texture, varnish, wipe out **08** carry out, complete, conclude, curtains, deal with, get rid of, overcome, round off, run out of **09** be through, bring down, cessation, culminate, discharge, get shot of, overpower, overthrow, overwhelm, polish off, put paid to, terminate, winding-up **10** accomplish, annihilate, appearance, be done with,

call it a day, completion, conclusion, consummate, do away with, fulfilment, get through, lamination, perfection, smoothness **11** achievement, come to an end, culmination, destruction, discontinue, exterminate, termination **12** bring to an end **14** accomplishment, get the better of
• **finish off 03** end, ice, top **04** do in, slay **05** drain, mop-up, quash, quell, still, use up **06** defeat, murder **07** bump off, destroy, execute, put down, wipe out **08** despatch, dispatch, knock off **09** dispose of, eliminate, eradicate, liquidate, polish off, slaughter **10** annihilate, do away with, extinguish, put an end to, put to death, put to sleep **11** assassinate, exterminate

### finished
**02** up **04** arch, dead, done, lost, neat, over, past, ripe **05** empty, exact, spent **06** doomed, expert, made up, ruined, sewn up, undone, urbane, zonked **07** all done, at an end, defunct, done for, drained, perfect, refined, rounded, through, useless **08** complete, defeated, flawless, masterly, polished, unwanted, virtuoso **09** completed, concluded, dealt with, exhausted, faultless, played out, unpopular, wrapped up **10** consummate, impeccable, proficient **11** all over with, consummated **12** accomplished, professional **13** sophisticated **15** over and done with
• **before it is finished 03** yet

### finite
**05** fixed **07** bounded, limited **08** numbered **09** countable, definable **10** calculable, demarcated, measurable, restricted, terminable

### Finland
**03** FIN

### fire
**03** axe, can, fan **04** bake, flak, heat, hurl, kiln, life, sack, stir, whet, zeal **05** blame, blaze, eject, let go, light, rouse, salvo, shoot, start, stick, torch, verve **06** ardour, arouse, attack, energy, excite, firing, flames, heater, ignite, incite, kindle, launch, let off, set off, spirit, stir up, vigour **07** animate, barrage, bombing, bonfire, boot out, burning, censure, dismiss, enliven, explode, feeling, fervour, gunfire, inferno, inflame, inspire, kick out, passion, reproof, slating, sniping, sparkle, trigger **08** brickbat, detonate, dynamism, get rid of, knocking, motivate, radiance, radiator, shelling, slamming, spark off, vivacity **09** animation, cannonade, cauterize, convector, criticism, discharge, eagerness, electrify, fusillade, galvanize, holocaust, intensity, lightning, set ablaze, set alight, set fire to, set on fire, stimulate **10** combustion, creativity, enthusiasm, excitement, liveliness, trigger off **11** bombardment, disapproval, put a match to **12** condemnation, fault-finding **13** conflagration,

disparagement, inventiveness
• **fire up 06** arouse
• **on fire 03** lit **05** eager, fiery **06** ablaze, aflame, alight, ardent **07** blazing, burning, excited, flaming, ignited **08** creative, in flames, inspired **09** energetic, inventive, sparkling **10** passionate **12** enthusiastic

### firearm
**03** gun **04** heat **05** rifle **06** musket, pistol, weapon **07** handgun, shotgun **08** revolver **09** automatic **10** self-cocker **12** breech-loader, muzzle-loader, shooting iron, single-action **13** semi-automatic
*See also* **gun; weapon**

### firebrand
**05** rebel **07** fanatic, radical **08** agitator, militant **09** extremist, insurgent **10** incendiary **12** rabble-rouser, troublemaker **13** revolutionary **15** insurrectionist

### fireplace
*Fireplaces include:*

**04** kiln, oven
**05** forge, grate, ingle, range, stove
**06** boiler, hearth
**07** bonfire, brazier, firebox, furnace, gas fire
**08** campfire, open fire
**09** wood stove
**10** backboiler
**11** incinerator
**12** electric fire
**13** paraffin stove

### firepower
**04** ammo

### fireproof
**10** flameproof **12** non-flammable **13** fire-resistant, incombustible **14** flame-resistant, non-inflammable

### fireside
*see* **fireplace**

### firewater
*see* **drink**

### fireworks
**03** fit **04** rage, rows **05** storm **06** frenzy, sparks, temper, uproar **07** trouble **08** outburst **09** hysterics **10** explosions **12** pyrotechnics **13** feux d'artifice, illuminations

*Fireworks include:*

**04** cake, mine, pioy
**05** devil, flare, gerbe, peeoy, pioye, shell, squib, wheel
**06** banger, fisgig, fizgig, maroon, petard, rocket
**07** cracker, serpent, volcano
**08** flip-flop, fountain, pinwheel, slap-bang, sparkler, whizbang
**09** firedrake, girandola, girandole, sky-rocket, throw-down, waterfall, whizz-bang
**10** golden rain, Indian fire, tourbillon
**11** firecracker, firewriting, jumping-jack, roman candle, tourbillion
**14** Catherine wheel, Chinese cracker, indoor firework

**15** Pharaoh's serpent, Waterloo cracker

### firm
**02** Co, OK **03** Cie, oke, set **04** boon, fast, good, hard, oaky, sure, true **05** close, crisp, dense, fixed, house, rigid, solid, stiff, tight **06** dogged, secure, siccar, sicker, stable, stanch, steady, steeve, stieve, strict, strong, sturdy, trusty **07** adamant, compact, company, concern, decided, riveted, secured, settled, staunch, unmoved **08** anchored, business, constant, definite, embedded, fastened, forceful, hardened, obdurate, resolute, resolved, stubborn, unshaken, vigorous **09** committed, immovable, inelastic, obstinate, rock-solid, sclerotic, steadfast, syndicate, tenacious **10** compressed, dependable, determined, enterprise, inflexible, motionless, solidified, stationary, unchanging, unshakable, unswerving, unwavering, unyielding **11** association, corporation, established, institution, long-lasting, partnership, substantial, substantive, unalterable, unfaltering, unflinching, unshakeable **12** close-grained, concentrated, conglomerate, long-standing, organization, unchangeable **13** establishment

### firmament
**03** sky **05** ether, skies, space **06** heaven, welkin **07** expanse, heavens, the blue **08** empyrean **10** atmosphere

### firmly
**04** fast **06** fastly, stably, steeve, stieve, surely **07** tightly **08** doggedly, robustly, securely, steadily, strictly, strongly, sturdily **09** immovably, staunchly **10** decisively, definitely, enduringly, inflexibly, resolutely, unshakably **11** steadfastly, unalterably **12** determinedly, unchangeably, unwaveringly **13** unflinchingly

### firmness
**06** fixity, fixure **07** density, resolve, tension **08** fixation, hardness, obduracy, rigidity, solidity, strength, sureness, tautness **09** constancy, stability, stiffness, tightness, willpower **10** conviction, doggedness, resistance, resolution, steadiness, strictness **11** compactness, reliability, staunchness **12** immovability, inelasticity **13** dependability, determination, inflexibility, steadfastness **14** changelessness, indomitability, strength of will
• **body firmness 04** tone

### first
◊ *head selection indicator* ◊ *juxtaposition indicator* **01** A **03** 1st, key, one, top **04** arch-, best, head, main **05** basic, chief, prima, prime, primo, prior, proto-, start **06** eldest, oldest, origin, outset, primal, rather, ruling, senior **07** at first, earlier, firstly, highest, initial, leading, opening, origins, premier, primary, supreme **08** cardinal, champion, earliest, foremost, greatest, original, paravant,

## first-born (continued)

première, primeval **09** beginning, inaugural, inception, initially, paramount, paravaunt, primaeval, primitive, principal, prototype, sovereign, square one, the word go, unveiling, uppermost **10** beforehand, elementary, first of all, originally, pre-eminent, primordial **11** at the outset, fundamental, predominant, preliminary, rudimentary, to begin with, to start with **12** commencement, in preference, introduction, introductory **14** at the beginning **15** in the first place
• **at first** ◇ *head selection indicator*
**04** erst **07** at first **09** initially **10** first of all **11** at the outset, to begin with, to start with **15** in the first place
• **come first** ◇ *juxtaposition indicator*
**04** lead **05** outdo **07** precede
• **first lady** **03** Eve

## first-born

**04** aîné **05** aînée, eigne, elder, older **06** eldest, oldest, senior **10** primogenit **12** primogenital **13** primogenitary, primogenitive

## first-class

**01** A **02** A1 **03** ace, top **04** cool, fine, mean, mega **05** crack, prime, super **06** slap-up, superb, way-out, wicked **07** crucial, leading, premier, radical, supreme, top-hole **08** fabulous, peerless, splendid, superior, top-notch **09** admirable, excellent, first-rate, matchless, top-flight **11** exceptional, outstanding, superlative **12** second-to-none **14** out of this world

## firsthand

**06** direct **07** hands-on, primary **08** directly, on the job, personal **09** immediate, in service **10** personally **11** immediately

## firstly

**04** once **07** at first **09** initially **10** first of all **11** at the outset, to begin with, to start with **15** in the first place

## first name

**08** forename **09** given name **13** baptismal name, Christian name

## first-rate

**01** A **02** A1 **03** ace, top **04** cool, fine, jake, mean, mega **05** crack, prime, super **06** superb, way-out, wicked **07** crucial, leading, premier, radical, supreme **08** fabulous, peerless, splendid, superior, top-notch **09** admirable, excellent, matchless, top-flight **10** first-class **11** excellently, exceptional, outstanding, superlative **12** second-to-none **14** out of this world

## firth

*Firths include:*

**03** Tay
**04** Lorn, Wide
**05** Clyde, Forth, Lorne, Moray
**06** Beauly, Solway, Thames
**07** Dornoch, Westray

---

**08** Cromarty, Pentland, Stronsay, Szczecin
**09** Inverness
**14** North Ronaldsay

## fiscal

**03** tax **05** money **06** bursal **07** capital **08** economic, monetary, treasury **09** budgetary, financial, pecuniary, treasurer
• **procurator fiscal** **02** PF

## fiscally

**09** moneywise **11** financially, pecuniarily **12** economically

## fish

**03** ask, bob, dap, dib, dip, fry, jig, net **04** harl, hunt, look, sean, seek, spin, trot **05** angle, catch, delve, grope, otter, seine, spoon, trawl, troll, whiff **06** guddle, ledger, search **07** counter, ransack, skitter, snigger, sniggle **08** hand line, try to get **09** go fishing **11** try to obtain
*See also* **animal**

---

*Fish, crustaceans and shellfish include:*

**02** ai, id
**03** aua, ayu, bar, bib, cod, dab, eel, gar, ged, hag, ide, lax, par, ray, sar, sei, tai
**04** barb, bass, blay, bley, brit, carp, chad, char, chub, chum, clam, coho, crab, cray, cusk, dace, dare, dart, dory, fugu, gade, goby, hake, hoki, huso, huss, kelt, keta, kina, lant, ling, luce, lump, moki, opah, orfe, parr, paua, pawa, peal, peel, pike, pipi, pope, pout, pupu, rudd, scad, scar, scat, scup, seer, shad, sild, slip, snig, sole, spot, tang, tope, tuna, tusk
**05** ablet, allis, basse, bleak, bream, brill, bully, cohoe, coley, danio, elver, fluke, guppy, koura, lance, loach, molly, perch, platy, porgy, prawn, roach, shark, skate, smelt, sprat, squid, tench, tetra, torsk, trout, tunny, whelk, yabby, zebra
**06** allice, angler, barbel, blenny, braise, braize, burbot, cockle, doctor, dorado, gadoid, grilse, groper, hapuku, jilgie, kipper, kokopu, launce, marlin, marron, minnow, mullet, mussel, oyster, piraña, plaice, porgie, puffer, red cod, red-eye, salmon, saurel, shrimp, tailor, tarpon, turbot, wrasse
**07** abalone, anchovy, bloater, blue cod, candiru, catfish, cavalla, cavally, cichlid, cobbler, codfish, cowfish, dhufish, dogfish, garfish, gourami, grouper, gurnard, haddock, halibut, herring, kahawai, lamprey, lobster, morwong, mudfish, octopus, piranha, sardine, scallop, sea bass, snapper, toheroa, warehou, whiting
**08** albacore, albicore, blowfish, blue crab, bluefish, bluenose, brisling, calamari, characid, crawfish, crayfish, dragonet, flathead,

---

flounder, goldfish, grayling, ichthyic, John Dory, kingfish, luderick, mackerel, monkfish, Moray eel, pilchard, pipefish, rockfish, sailfish, scuppaug, sea bream, seahorse, skipjack, stingray, sturgeon, tarakihi, toadfish, trevally, tuna fish
**09** allis shad, angel-fish, barracuda, conger eel, Dover sole, greenling, grenadier, king prawn, lemonfish, lemon sole, Murray cod, neon tetra, red mullet, sea urchin, stonefish, swordfish, trumpeter, tunnyfish, whitebait, wobbegong, zebrafish
**10** angler fish, Balmain bug, barracouta, barramundi, bluebottle, Bombay duck, brown trout, butterfish, cuttlefish, damsel fish, flying fish, grey mullet, gummy shark, jellied eel, mossbunker, parrot-fish, puffer fish, red snapper, rock salmon, tommy rough
**11** electric eel, rock lobster, stickleback
**12** jellyblubber, orange roughy, rainbow trout, scorpion fish, skipjack tuna
**13** butterfly fish, horse mackerel, leatherjacket, Moreton Bay bug, sergeant-major
**14** Arbroath smokie

---

*See also* **crustacean; mollusc; seafood; shark**
• **fish out** **04** find **07** extract, haul out, produce, pull out, take out **08** dredge up, retrieve **10** come up with
• **fish tank** **04** stew **08** aquarium
• **queer fish** **04** cure

## fisherman

**03** rod **05** liner **06** angler, banker, codder, fisher, rodman, Walton **07** crabber, drag-man, drifter, rodsman, rodster **08** peter-man, piscator, shareman **09** cockleman, rodfisher, sharesman, Waltonian **10** trawlerman **11** piscatorian

## fishing

**07** angling **08** trawling **09** piscatory **11** piscatorial **12** catching fish

---

*Fishing- and angling-related terms include:*

**03** fly, net, rod, tag, tie
**04** bait, barb, bite, cast, drag, gimp, hook, lead, line, lure, reel, sean, weel, weir, whip
**05** angle, baker, catch, clean, creel, seine, snell, troll
**06** angler, bob-fly, coarse, dry-fly, fly-rod, leader, sagene, sinker, tackle, waders, wet-fly
**07** angling, bycatch, drifter, dropper, flyline, fly reel, harpoon, keepnet, piscary, setline, spinner
**08** backcast, drift net, roll cast, trotline
**09** brandling, drabbling, false cast, hairy Mary, halieutic, indicator, leger line, night-line, piscatory

**10** bait bucket, casting arc, casting-net, fly casting, fly fishing, halieutics, landing net, ledger bait, ledger line, net-fishing, sea-fishing, weigh sling
**11** forward cast, game fishing, line-fishing, paternoster
**12** drift fishing, night crawler, night-fishery, shooting line
**13** bottom-fishing, coarse fishing
**15** catch-and-release

*See also* **fly**

**fishy**
◊ *anagram indicator* **03** odd **05** funny, queer, shady **06** unsafe **07** dubious, piscine, suspect **08** doubtful, fish-like **09** equivocal, irregular, piscatory **10** improbable, suspicious **11** implausible, piscatorial **12** questionable

**fission**
**06** schism **07** parting, rending, rupture **08** breaking, cleavage, cleaving, division, scission **09** severance, splitting

**fissure**
**03** gap **04** chop, gape, gash, hole, rent, rift, rime, slit, vein **05** break, chasm, chink, cleft, crack, fault, grike, gryke, porta, shake, split, zygon **06** breach, cleave, cranny, divide, groove, sulcus **07** crevice, foramen, opening, rupture **08** cleavage, crevasse, fracture, scissure, sink hole **10** interstice **11** swallow hole

**fist**
**03** paw, pud **04** dook, duke, hand, mitt, neif, nief, palm **05** index, neafe, neive, nieve, puddy **06** neaffe **08** knuckles **11** handwriting **12** bunch of fives, clenched hand

**fit**
◊ *anagram indicator* **02** A1, go **03** apt, arm, cry, due, fix, gee, jag, pet, rig, sit **04** able, ague, bout, hard, huff, join, lune, mate, meet, song, sort, suit, well **05** adapt, agree, alter, burst, canto, coach, equal, equip, exies, flaky, gapes, groom, hardy, ictus, match, place, prime, put in, queme, ready, right, shape, sharp, sound, spasm, spell, surge, tally, train **06** access, adjust, attach, attack, belong, change, concur, crisis, didder, dither, dueful, follow, habile, insert, in trim, modify, passus, proper, robust, seemly, square, strong, sturdy, tailor, worthy **07** arrange, be right, capable, chipper, conform, connect, correct, debauch, dewfull, fashion, fitting, get into, gradely, healthy, in shape, install, prepare, provide, qualify, seizure, tantrum, trained **08** decorous, dovetail, eligible, equipped, eruption, graithly, outbreak, outburst, paroxysm, position, prepared, regulate, suitable, vigorous **09** agreement, befitting, competent, condition, explosion, harmonize, interlock, make ready, pertinent, qualified **10** able-bodied, be a good fit, be suitable, conformity, conniption, convenient, convulsion,

correspond, good enough, in good form, put in place, the shivers **11** accommodate, appropriate, be consonant, concurrence, correlation, equivalence, flourishing, in good shape, put together **12** be consistent, in good health, make suitable, relationship **13** be appropriate, fit like a glove, hale and hearty, put in position **14** correspondence **15** in good condition
• **fit for use 04** ripe
• **fit in** ◊ *insertion indicator* **04** slot **05** agree, match **06** accord, belong, concur, square **07** conform, squeeze **10** correspond
• **fit out, fit up 03** arm, rig **04** trim **05** equip, frame **06** kit out, outfit, rig out, supply **07** furnish, prepare, provide **08** accoutre
• **fit together 04** nest
• **in fits and starts 08** brokenly, fitfully, off and on, unevenly **11** erratically, irregularly **12** occasionally, sporadically **13** spasmodically **14** intermittently

**fitful**
**06** broken, catchy, patchy, uneven **07** erratic **08** sporadic **09** disturbed, haphazard, irregular, spasmodic **10** occasional **12** disconnected, intermittent

**fitfully**
**08** unevenly **11** erratically, haphazardly, irregularly **12** occasionally, sporadically **13** spasmodically **14** intermittently **15** by fits and starts, in fits and starts

**fitness**
**04** trim **05** shape **06** health, vigour **07** aptness **08** adequacy, aptitude, haleness, property, strength **09** condition, edibility, readiness **10** capability, competence, competency, edibleness, good health, pertinence, robustness **11** eligibility, healthiness, opportunity, suitability **12** preparedness **13** applicability **14** qualifications **15** appropriateness
• **condition of fitness 04** form

**fitted**
**03** fit **05** armed, fixed, right **06** cut out, shaped, suited **07** built-in **08** equipped, integral, prepared, provided, suitable, tailored **09** appointed, furnished, permanent, qualified, rigged out **10** integrated

**fitting**
**03** apt, fit **04** meet, part, unit **05** piece, right **06** extras, liable, proper, seemly, square **07** condign, correct, fitment, fixture **08** decorous, deserved, fitments, fixtures, suitable, wise-like **09** accessory, component, desirable, equipment, furniture **10** attachment, connection, convenable **11** accessories, appropriate, furnishings **12** appointments **13** accoutrements, installations

**fittings**
**04** trim **09** trimmings **11** furnishings

**five**
**01** V **06** pentad **07** quinary, quintet **08** quintett **09** quintette **10** quintuplet
• **one of five 04** quin

**five hundred**
**01** D

**fix**
◊ *anagram indicator* **02** do **03** aim, hit, jam, pin, rig, set, tie **04** bang, bind, comb, cook, dose, draw, fake, glue, hang, hold, hole, join, link, make, mend, mess, nail, name, root, scam, seat, shoo, shot, slug, sort, spay, spot, tidy, turn **05** affix, clamp, dress, embed, emend, focus, groom, level, lodge, order, plant, point, rivet, score, screw, see to, set up, set-up, stell, stick **06** adjust, anchor, answer, assign, attach, cement, corner, couple, decide, define, direct, fasten, fiddle, freeze, harden, locate, muddle, neaten, pickle, plight, remedy, repair, scrape, secure, settle, strike, way out **07** agree on, appoint, arrange, attract, connect, correct, destine, dilemma, falsify, implant, install, knock up, patch up, prepare, rectify, resolve, restore, rigging, situate, specify, station, stiffen, the soup **08** arrive at, castrate, chastise, finalize, get ready, position, put right, quandary, solidify, solution, valorize **09** destinate, determine, establish, injection, manoeuvre, stabilize, tight spot **10** difficulty, manipulate, put in order, resolution, straighten, tamper with **11** concentrate, predicament, put together **12** manipulation **13** throw together
• **fix up 04** clew, clue, plan **05** equip, lay on, plant **06** settle, supply **07** agree on, arrange, furnish, produce, provide, sort out **08** organize **10** bring about

**fixated**
**03** set **06** phobic **07** gripped **08** hung up on, neurotic, obsessed **09** dominated **10** compulsive, infatuated **11** preoccupied **12** pathological

**fixation**
**05** mania, thing **06** fetich, fetish, hang-up, phobia **07** complex, fetiche, setting **08** firmness, idée fixe, neurosis **09** obsession **10** compulsion, steadiness **11** infatuation **13** preoccupation

**fixed**
◊ *anagram indicator* **03** set **04** fake, fast, firm **05** false, rigid, tight **06** phoney, rooted, secure, steady **07** decided, lasting, planned, pretend, settled, well-set **08** arranged, constant, definite, immobile, standing **09** appointed, insincere, permanent, pretended **10** determined, entrenched, inflexible, persistent, set in stone, stationary **11** cast in stone, determinate, established

**fixedly**
**04** hard **07** closely **08** intently, steadily **09** staringly **10** watchfully **11** attentively, searchingly

**fixity**
09 constancy, fixedness, stability
10 permanence, steadiness
11 persistence 12 immutability

**fixture**
04 game, race, unit 05 event, match, round 06 fixing 07 contest, fitting, meeting 09 equipment, furniture
11 competition, furnishings
13 installations

**fizz**
03 gas, vim, zip 04 foam, hiss, zing
05 froth 06 bubble, fizzle 07 bubbles, ferment, foaming, sparkle 08 bubbling, buoyancy, frothing, vitality, vivacity
09 animation, champagne, fizziness, gassiness 10 effervesce, enthusiasm, excitement, exuberance, liveliness
11 excitedness, high spirits
12 exhilaration, fermentation
13 effervescence

**fizzle**
• fizzle out   04 fail, flop, fold, stop
07 die away, die down, subside
08 collapse, peter out, taper off
09 disappear, dissipate, evaporate
11 come to grief, fall through 13 come to nothing

**fizzy**
05 gassy 06 bubbly, frothy 07 aerated, foaming 08 bubbling 09 sparkling
10 carbonated 12 effervescent

**flab**
03 fat, pot 04 bulk 06 paunch
07 blubber, fatness, obesity 08 pot belly 09 plumpness, solidness, spare tyre, stoutness 10 chubbiness, corpulence, overweight

**flabbergasted**
◊ anagram indicator 05 dazed
06 amazed 07 stunned 08 overcome
09 astounded, blown away, staggered
10 astonished, bowled over, confounded, gobsmacked, nonplussed, speechless
11 dumbfounded, overwhelmed
13 knocked for six

**flabby**
03 fat, lax 04 limp, soft 05 loose, plump, slack 06 feeble, flaggy, fleshy, floppy, sloppy 07 flaccid, hanging, sagging 08 drooping, wasteful, yielding
09 lymphatic, nerveless 10 overweight
11 inefficient 12 disorganized, uneconomical

**flaccid**
03 lax 04 lank, limp, soft, weak
05 loose, slack 06 clammy, droopy, flabby, floppy 07 relaxed, sagging
08 drooping, toneless 09 nerveless

**flag**
03 die, ebb, rag, sag, tag 04 fade, fail, fall, flop, hail, iris, jade, mark, note, sink, slow, tire, waft, wane, wave, wilt
05 abate, color, droop, faint, label, slump, weary 06 Acorus, colors, colour, falter, lessen, marker, motion, salute, weaken 07 calamus, decline, dwindle, fall off, slacken, subside
08 diminish, hang down, indicate, languish, peter out, taper off, wave

down 09 grow tired, reed-grass
12 signal to stop

*Flags include:*

05 Union
07 Saltier, Saltire
08 Crescent, Old Glory, Red Cross
09 Blue Peter, dannebrog, Red Dragon, Red Duster, Red Ensign, Rising Sun, Tricolour, Union Jack
10 Blue Ensign, Jolly Roger, Yellow Jack
11 Olympic Flag, Red Crescent, White Ensign
12 Stars and Bars
15 Cross of St George, Hammer and Sickle, Stars and Stripes

*Flag types include:*

03 red
04 blue, fane, jack, sick
05 black, house, peter, pilot, union, whiff, whift, white
06 banner, burgee, cornet, ensign, fanion, pennon, prayer, signal, yellow
07 ancient, bunting, colours, pennant
08 banderol, gonfalon, pavilion, penoncel, standard, streamer, tricolor, vexillum
09 blackjack, chequered, oriflamme, pennoncel, pilot jack, tricolour
10 penoncelle, quarantine
11 pennoncelle, swallow tail
13 defaced ensign

• flags   07 bunting

**flagellation**
07 beating, flaying, lashing, whaling
08 flogging, whipping 09 scourging, thrashing 10 vapulation 11 castigation, verberation, vice anglais
12 chastisement

**flagging**
06 ebbing, fading, tiring, waning
07 abating, failing, languid, sagging, sinking, slowing, wilting 08 drooping, pavement 09 declining, dwindling, faltering, lessening, subsiding, weakening 10 decreasing
11 diminishing

**flagon**
03 jug 04 ewer 05 flask, half-g, peter
06 bottle, carafe, vessel 07 pitcher
08 decanter 09 container

**flagrant**
04 bold, open, rank 05 gross, naked, overt 06 arrant, brazen, raging
07 blatant, burning, glaring, heinous
08 blattant, dreadful, enormous, infamous 09 atrocious, audacious, barefaced, egregious, notorious, shameless, unashamed 10 outrageous, scandalous 11 conspicuous, disgraceful, undisguised
12 ostentatious

**flagstaff**
03 pin

**flail**
◊ anagram indicator 04 beat, whip

06 batter, strike, thrash, thresh
08 threshel, thresher 11 swing wildly

**flair**
04 bent, feel, gift, nose 05 knack, skill, style, taste 06 acumen, genius, talent
07 ability, faculty, mastery, panache
08 aptitude, elegance, facility
11 discernment, stylishness 14 natural ability

**flak**
02 AA 05 abuse, blame, stick
07 censure, panning 08 bad press, knocking 09 brickbats, criticism, hostility, invective 10 aspersions, complaints, opposition 11 disapproval
12 condemnation, fault-finding
13 disparagement 14 animadversions, disapprobation

**flake**
◊ anagram indicator 03 bit 04 chip, flaw, peel, smut 05 flash, scale, scurf, shark, spark, wafer 06 furfur, paring, shiver, sliver, squama 07 blister, flaught, peeling, shaving, spangle 08 fragment, particle, splinter 09 eccentric, exfoliate, flocculus 10 desquamate
11 exfoliation 12 desquamation
• flake out   04 drop 05 faint 07 pass out 08 collapse, keel over 10 fall asleep
15 relax completely

**flaky**
◊ anagram indicator 03 dry 05 crazy, inept, scaly 06 scurfy, stupid
07 laminar, layered 08 scabrous, squamate, squamose, squamous
09 eccentric 10 flocculent
11 exfoliative, incompetent
12 desquamative, desquamatory, furfuraceous

**flamboyance**
04 dash, élan 05 style 06 colour
07 glamour, panache, pizzazz
09 showiness 10 brilliance
11 ostentation 12 extravagance
13 theatricality

**flamboyant**
04 rich 05 gaudy, lairy, showy
06 bright, flashy, florid, ornate, rococo
07 baroque, dashing 08 dazzling, exciting, striking 09 brilliant, colourful, elaborate, glamorous 10 theatrical
11 extravagant 12 ostentatious

**flame**
03 low 04 beam, burn, fire, glow, heat, lowe, lunt, rage, zeal 05 blaze, flake, flare, flash, flush, glare, gleam, go red, light, lover, shine 06 ardour, redden, warmth 07 fervour, partner, passion, radiate, sparkle, turn red 08 fervency, flammule, keenness, radiance
09 become red, boyfriend, catch fire, eagerness, intensity 10 brightness, enthusiasm, excitement, girlfriend, sweetheart 13 conflagration 15 burst into flames
• in flames   06 ablaze, aflame, alight, on fire 07 blazing, burning, flaming, ignited
• old flame   02 ex

**flameproof**
09 fireproof 12 non-flammable 13 fire-

resistant, incombustible **14** flame-resistant, non-inflammable

**flaming**
**03** mad **04** vile **05** angry, fiery, gaudy, vivid **06** aflame, alight, bloody, bright, cursed, damned, darned, dashed, odious, on fire, raging, red-hot **07** blasted, blazing, burning, enraged, furious, glowing, hateful, intense, violent **08** annoying, blinking, blooming, dratting, fiendish, flipping, incensed, infamous, infernal, in flames, wretched **09** brilliant, execrable, loathsome **10** abominable, confounded, detestable, infuriated, pernicious, unpleasant **11** smouldering **13** scintillating

**flammable**
**08** burnable **09** ignitable **11** combustible, inflammable

**flank**
◇ containment indicator **03** hip **04** edge, line, lisk, loin, side, wall, wing **05** bound, skirt, thigh **06** border, fringe, haunch, screen **07** confine, quarter

**flannel**
**03** rot **05** spiel **06** waffle **07** blarney, flatter, rubbish, washrag **08** flattery, nonsense, soft soap **09** facecloth, sweet talk, washcloth **10** smooth talk **13** blandishments

**flap**
◇ anagram indicator **03** fly, lap, lug, tab, tag, wag, wap **04** beat, fall, flag, flip, fold, fuss, loma, slat, stew, sway, tail, waff, wave **05** apron, flaff, lapel, panic, shake, skirt, state, swing, swish, tizzy, tuner, visor **06** dither, elevon, lappet, thrash, thresh, tiswas, tizwas, tongue, waggle, wallop, winnow **07** agitate, aileron, flacker, fluster, flutter, overlap, tent-fly, vibrate **08** aventail, barn-door, covering, epiploon, overhang **09** agitation, aventaile, commotion **10** clack valve, epiglottis, fluttering **12** great omentum **13** move up and down

**flare**
**04** beam, burn, glow, Very **05** blaze, burst, erupt, flame, flash, glare, gleam, light, splay, torch, widen **06** beacon, dazzle, flanch, rocket, signal, spread **07** broaden, explode, flaunch, flicker, glimmer, glitter, sparkle **08** flare out, widening **09** spread out, Very light **10** broadening, Verey light **13** warning signal **14** distress signal
• **flare out 04** bell
• **flare up 05** blaze, erupt, go ape, go mad **06** blow up, let rip **07** explode **08** boil over, break out, burst out, freak out **09** blow a fuse, do your nut, go berserk **10** go to market, hit the roof **11** blow your top, do your block, flip your lid, go ballistic, go up the wall, lose control, lose your rag **12** fly into a rage, lose your cool, throw a wobbly **14** foam at the mouth, lose your temper **15** fly off the handle, go off the deep end

**flare-up**
**04** rash **07** venting **08** ejection, emission, eruption, outbreak, outburst **09** discharge, explosion **12** inflammation

**flash**
◇ anagram indicator **02** mo **03** fly, ray **04** beam, bolt, dart, dash, fork, pond, pool, race, rush, show, tear, zoom **05** blaze, blink, bound, burst, dance, flake, flare, gaudy, glaik, glare, gleam, glint, quick, shaft, shine, shoot, showy, smart, spark, speed **06** career, flaunt, glaiks, glance, kitsch, moment, streak, strobe, sudden, vulgar **07** bluette, display, flaught, flicker, glimmer, glisten, glitter, instant, lighten, light up, shimmer, show off, sparkle, twinkle **08** brandish, concetto, fire-flag, flourish, green ray, outbreak, outburst **09** coruscate, expensive, fulgurate, fulminate, glamorous, lightning **10** exhibition **11** coruscation, fashionable, fire-flaught, fulguration, pretentious, scintillate **12** ostentatious **13** scintillation **14** expose yourself
• **in a flash 03** pdq **06** pronto **08** in a jiffy, in a trice, in no time **09** in a moment, instantly **11** in an instant **12** in a twinkling **13** in no time at all **14** in a split second

**flashy**
**04** bold, loud **05** brash, cheap, flash, gaudy, jazzy, lairy, showy, tacky, vapid **06** blingy, garish, glitzy, kitsch, snazzy, tawdry, vulgar **07** buckeye, raffish, tigrish **08** tigerish **09** glamorous, tasteless **10** bling-bling, flamboyant **11** pretentious **12** meretricious, ostentatious
• **flashy person 04** lair, raff

**flask**
**04** cask, mick **05** dewar, micky **06** bottle, carafe, coffin, fiasco, flagon, mickey, retort, vessel **07** ampulla, balloon, canteen, costrel, flacket, matrass, Thermos® **08** decanter, lekythos **09** aryballos, container, livery pot **10** powder horn **12** pocket-pistol

**flat**
**03** low, OYO, pad, set **04** bust, dead, down, duff, dull, even, firm, flew, flue, fool, slow, tame, true, unit, weak **05** banal, bland, burst, empty, exact, final, fixed, haugh, kaput, level, plain, plane, prone, quiet, rigid, rooms, sheer, slack, stale, still, stock, suite, total, utter, vapid **06** bedsit, boring, callow, direct, evenly, planar, sleepy, smooth, supine, used up, watery **07** exactly, flatlet, insipid, not deep, not tall, plainly, planned, regular, shallow, tedious, totally, uniform, utterly **08** absolute, arranged, blown-out, complete, defeated, definite, deflated, dejected, directly, downcast, entirely, explicit, finished, home unit, inactive, levelled, lifeless, not thick, outright, positive, ruptured, sluggish, stagnant, standard, straight, tenement, toneless, unbroken **09** apartment, bedsitter, collapsed, depressed, downright, miserable, out-and-out,

penthouse, pointless, precisely, prostrate, punctured, reclining, recumbent, unvarying **10** absolutely, completely, despondent, homaloidal, horizontal, lacklustre, maisonette, monotonous, point-blank, spiritless, unexciting **11** categorical, discouraged, maisonnette, unequivocal, unqualified **12** outstretched, spread-eagled **13** categorically, no longer fizzy, unconditional, uninteresting **14** flat as a pancake
• **flat out 04** hard **06** all out **10** at top speed **11** at full speed
• **flat place 04** plat

**flatly**
**10** absolutely, completely, point-blank, positively **12** peremptorily **13** categorically **14** unhesitatingly **15** unconditionally

**flatness**
**06** tedium **07** boredom, languor **08** dullness, evenness, monotony, vapidity **09** emptiness, levelness, platitude, staleness **10** insipidity, smoothness, uniformity **13** horizontality, tastelessness

**flatten**
**02** KO **04** fell, iron, raze, roll **05** amaze, crush, dress, floor, level, plane, press **06** defeat, smooth, squash, subdue **07** even out, planish **08** compress, demolish, knock out, make even, make flat, tear down **09** knock down, overwhelm, prostrate

**flatter**
**04** claw, coax, fawn, soap, suit, word **05** befit, court, creep, gloze, grace, toady **06** become, butter, cozy up, cringe, fleech, humour, kowtow, phrase, praise, sawder, smooth, soothe, stroke **07** adulate, enhance, flannel, gratify, lay it on, palaver, show off, soother, wheedle **08** beslaver, blandish, butter up, collogue, eulogize, inveigle, make up to, play up to, smooth it, soft-soap, suck up to **09** beslobber, embellish, sweet-talk **10** bear in hand, compliment, cozy up with, look good on, overpraise, pay court to, soft sawder, soft sowder **12** sycophantize **14** tickle the ear of **15** curry favour with, make fair weather, show to advantage

**flatterer**
**05** carny, creep, toady **06** carney, earwig, fawner, lackey, minion, yes-man **07** crawler, creeper, proneur **08** adulator, incenser, incensor, smoother **09** encomiast, eulogizer, groveller, sycophant **10** bootlicker, foot-licker **11** lickspittle **12** court-dresser **13** back-scratcher

**flattering**
**04** kind **06** honied, sugary **07** candied, fawning, fulsome, honeyed, servile, sugared **08** becoming, effusive, unctuous **09** adulatory, enhancing, gnathonic, laudatory **10** favourable, gratifying, obsequious **11** gnathonical, soft-soaping, sycophantic **12** honey-

tongued, ingratiating, smooth-spoken, sweet-talking **13** complimentary, smooth-talking, smooth-tongued

**flattery**
**04** fawn, soap **05** carny, sugar, taffy **06** butter, carney, eulogy, praise, sawder **07** blarney, fawning, flannel, glozing, mamaguy **08** cajolery, soft soap, toadyism **09** adulation, fair words, fleeching, laudation, servility, sweet talk **10** cajolement, flapdoodle, fleechment, soft sawder, soft sowder, sycophancy **11** compliments, fulsomeness **12** blandishment, ingratiation **13** blandishments **14** back scratching, court holy water

**flatulence**
**03** gas **04** wind **06** flatus **07** farting **09** gassiness, ventosity, windiness **10** eructation **11** borborygmus

**flatulent**
**05** gassy, windy **07** ventose

**flaunt**
**03** air **05** boast, flash, skyre, sport, strut, vaunt, wield **06** dangle, parade, strout **07** display, disport, exhibit, show off **08** brandish, flourish

**flavour**
**03** hop **04** feel, gust, hint, lace, race, soul, tack, tang, tone, zest, zing **05** aroma, flava, imbue, lemon, odour, sapor, savor, smack, spice, style, taste, tinge, touch, twang **06** aspect, infuse, nature, palate, pepper, relish, savour, season, spirit **07** essence, feeling, liqueur, quality, spice up **08** ginger up, piquancy, property **09** character **10** atmosphere, impression, indication, suggestion

**flavouring**
**04** hops, miso, sage, tang, zest, zing **05** caper, shoyu, spice **06** borage, Bovril®, cassis, cloves, relish, savory **07** bay leaf, bitters, caramel, essence, extract, flavour, ratafia, saffron, vanilla **08** additive, costmary, piquancy, rosemary, tarragon **09** coriander, fenugreek, pistachio, seasoning, spearmint **10** peach-water **11** citronellal, malt-extract, wintergreen **12** bouquet garni, butterscotch
*See also* **herb**

**flaw**
**04** chip, gall, mark, rent, rift, slip, spot, tear **05** brack, break, cleft, crack, craze, error, fault, flake, lapse, speck, split, thief **06** defect, foible, uproar **07** blemish, crevice, failing, fallacy, fissure, mistake **08** fracture, fragment, hamartia, splinter, weakness, weak spot **09** windshake **11** shortcoming **12** Achilles' heel, imperfection

**flawed**
◊ *anagram indicator* **06** broken, faulty, marked, marred, spoilt **07** chipped, cracked, damaged, unsound **09** blemished, defective, erroneous, imperfect **10** fallacious

**flawless**
**05** sound, whole **06** intact **07** perfect

**08** spotless, unbroken **09** faultless, stainless, undamaged **10** immaculate, impeccable, unimpaired **11** unblemished **12** indefectible **14** without blemish

**flax**
**03** tow **04** harl, herl, line, lint **05** hards, hurds **06** byssus **07** allseed **08** Phormium **12** mill-mountain

**flay**
**03** pan **04** flog, skin, slam **05** knock, slate **06** attack, flench, flense, flinch, revile, uncase **07** condemn, lambast, run down, scourge, upbraid **08** denounce, execrate, frighten **09** castigate, criticize, excoriate, pull apart, skin alive, tear apart **12** pull to pieces **13** find fault with, tear a strip off

**flea**
**05** Pulex **06** chigoe, chigre, jigger **07** chigger, Daphnia, daphnid **09** turnip fly **11** Aphaniptera **12** Siphonaptera

**fleck**
**03** dot **04** dust, mark, spot **05** point, speck, stain **06** dapple, mottle, streak **07** freckle, spatter, speckle, stipple **08** sprinkle

**fledgling**
**03** new **04** tiro **05** squab **06** coming, novice, rising, rookie **07** budding, learner, nascent, recruit, trainee **08** beginner, emergent, emerging, neophyte, newcomer **09** coming out, embryonic, greenhorn, novitiate **10** apprentice, burgeoning, developing, tenderfoot **11** independent

**flee**
**03** fly, lam, ren, rin, run **04** bolt, bunk, loup, quit, rush, scat **05** lam it, leave, scoot, scram, skive, split **06** decamp, depart, escape, get out, vanish **07** abscond, bunk off, do a bunk, get away, make off, push off, retreat, run away, scarper, take off, vamoose **08** clear off, shove off, up sticks, withdraw **09** cut and run, disappear, do a runner, push along, skedaddle **10** hightail it, hit the road, make tracks, take flight **11** hit the trail **13** sling your hook **14** make a bolt for it **15** make a break for it, take to your heels

**fleece**
**02** do **03** con, jib, rob, teg **04** bilk, coat, down, gull, plot, rook, skin, tegg, wool **05** bleed, cheat, mulct, ploat, pluck, shave, shear, steal, sting **06** diddle, fiddle, rip off, toison **07** defraud, plunder, squeeze, swindle **08** fetch off **09** shearling, toison d'or **10** overcharge **11** string along **12** pull a fast one, put one over on, take for a ride **13** have someone on

**fleecy**
**04** soft **05** downy, hairy, nappy **06** fluffy, pilose, shaggy, woolly **07** velvety **08** floccose **10** flocculate, lanuginose **11** eriophorous

**fleet**
**02** RN **04** fast, flit, flow, navy **05** agile, flitt, float, flota, quick, rapid, swift

**06** armada, flying, marine, nimble, speedy, winged **07** caravan **08** flotilla, meteoric, navarchy, squadron **09** mercurial, task force, transient **10** naval force **11** expeditious, light-footed

**fleeting**
**04** flit **05** brief, flitt, quick, short **06** bubble, flying, hollow, rushed, sudden **07** passing **08** fugitive, volatile **09** ephemeral, fugacious, momentary, temporary, transient **10** evanescent, short-lived, transitory

**fleetingly**
**07** briefly, quickly **08** casually **10** for a moment, for a second **11** momentarily **12** for an instant

**flesh**
**03** fat **04** boar, body, meat, pith, pulp, skin **05** brawn, braxy, stuff **06** matter, muscle, tissue, weight **08** solidity **09** carnality, sexuality, substance **10** sensuality **11** human nature, physicality **12** carnal nature, corporeality, significance, sinful nature **14** physical nature
• **flesh and blood** **03** kin **04** rels **05** folks **06** family **07** kindred, rellies **08** relative **09** relations
• **flesh out** **08** expand on **09** elaborate **10** add details **11** elaborate on, give details **12** make complete
• **flesh round jaw** **04** gill
• **in the flesh** **05** alive **06** bodily **08** in person **09** incarnate **10** in real life **12** in actual life

**fleshly**
**05** human **06** animal, bodily, carnal, earthy, erotic, sexual **07** bestial, brutish, earthly, lustful, sensual, worldly **08** corporal, material, physical **09** corporeal

**fleshy**
**03** fat **05** ample, beefy, hefty, meaty, obese, plump, podgy, pulpy, stout, tubby **06** brawny, chubby, chunky, flabby, portly, rotund **07** carnose, paunchy **08** carneous **09** corpulent, succulent **10** overweight, well-padded

**flex**
**03** bow, ply **04** bend, cord, lead, wire **05** angle, cable, crook, curve **07** stretch, tighten **08** contract, double up

**flexibility**
**04** give **06** spring **07** flexion, pliancy **09** tensility **10** elasticity, pliability, resilience, suppleness **11** amenability, bendability, springiness **12** adaptability, agreeability, complaisance **13** adjustability

**flexible**
◊ *anagram indicator* **04** open **05** agile, bendy, lithe, withy **06** docile, floppy, limber, lissom, mobile, pliant, supple **07** elastic, flexile, lissome, plastic, pliable, springy, willowy **08** amenable, bendable, stretchy, variable, yielding **09** adaptable, compliant, complying, malleable, mouldable, open-ended,

tractable **10** adjustable, changeable, manageable **13** accommodating, double-jointed

## flick

**03** dab, hit, rap, tap **04** flip, jerk, lash, lick, snap, whip **05** click, flirt, swish, touch **06** fillip, strike
• **flick through** **04** scan, skim, skip **08** glance at **10** glance over, run through **11** flip through, leaf through **12** thumb through **13** browse through

## flicker

**03** bat **04** atom, drop, iota, jump, lick, play, wink **05** blink, flare, flash, gleam, glint, spark, trace, waver **06** gutter, quiver, yucker **07** flaught, flutter, glimmer, glitter, shimmer, sparkle, twinkle, vibrate **08** lambency **09** flaughter **10** indication

## flier

**02** FO, PO **07** handout, leaflet **08** brochure, bulletin, circular, pamphlet **09** statement **10** literature **12** press release
*See also* **bird**
• **expert flier** **03** ace
• **non-flier** *see* **flightless birds** *under* **bird**

## fliers

**03** RAF

## flight

**03** fly, guy, lam, set **04** exit, pair, rout, rush, trap, trip, wing **05** steps **06** escape, exodus, flying, roding, stairs, voyage **07** fleeing, getaway, journey, retreat, roading, runaway, shuttle, soaring **08** aviation, stairway **09** air travel, breakaway, departure, skedaddle, staircase **10** absconding, exaltation, running off, volitation, withdrawal **11** aeronautics, running away **12** air transport **13** globetrotting
• **take flight** **03** fly, run **04** bolt, flee, quit, rush, scat **05** lam it, leave, leg it, scoot, scram, skive, split **06** decamp, depart, escape, vanish **07** abscond, bunk off, do a bunk, get away, make off, push off, retreat, run away, scarper, take off, vamoose **08** clear off, shove off, up sticks, withdraw **09** cut and run, disappear, do a runner, push along, skedaddle **10** hightail it, hit the road, make tracks **11** hit the trail **13** sling your hook **14** make a bolt for it, take it on the lam **15** make a break for it, take to your heels

## flighty

◊ *anagram indicator* **04** wild **05** giddy, silly, swift **06** fickle, volage **07** erratic, flyaway **08** fanciful, hellicat, skipping, skittish, unstable, unsteady, volatile **09** butterfly, frivolous, impetuous, impulsive, mercurial, volageous **10** bird-witted, capricious, changeable, inconstant, unbalanced, unreliable **11** birdbrained, flirtatious, hare-brained, lightheaded, loup-the-dyke, thoughtless, unballasted **12** bubble-headed, rattle-headed, whisky-frisky **13** irresponsible, rattle-brained, weather-headed

**14** scatterbrained
• **flighty type** **04** bird

## flimsy

**04** fine, poor, thin, weak **05** filmy, light, shaky, sheer, wispy **06** feeble, meagre, slight, slimsy **07** band-box, fragile, rickety, shallow, trivial **08** banknote, delicate, ethereal, gossamer, trifling, vaporous **09** airy-fairy, cardboard, gossamery, makeshift, paper-thin **10** inadequate, jerry-built, ramshackle **11** implausible, lightweight, superficial **12** unconvincing **13** insubstantial

## flinch

**04** balk, duck, flay, flee, funk **05** avoid, cower, dodge, quail, quake, shake, shirk, start, wince **06** blench, cringe, crouch, falter, recoil, shiver, shrink **07** retreat, shudder, shy away, tremble **08** draw back, pull back, withdraw **10** shrink back

## fling

**02** go **03** lob, shy, try **04** cast, dart, dash, hurl, jerk, jibe, rush, send, shot, toss, turn **05** amour, binge, chuck, crack, heave, lance, lanch, pitch, sling, spang, spree, taunt, throw, trial, whirl **06** affair, gamble, launce, launch, let fly, propel **07** affaire, attempt, carry-on, flounce, liaison, romance, venture **08** catapult, good time, intrigue, spanghew, throw out **10** indulgence, love affair, send flying **12** relationship **13** affaire d'amour, grande passion

## flinty

**03** icy **04** cold, hard **05** blank, cruel, stern, stony **06** chilly, frigid, frosty, severe, steely **07** adamant, callous, deadpan, hostile **08** obdurate, pitiless **09** heartless, merciless, unfeeling **10** inexorable, poker-faced **11** emotionless, indifferent, unforgiving **12** unresponsive **14** expressionless

## flip

◊ *reversal indicator* **04** cast, flap, jerk, pert, snap, spin, toss, turn **05** click, flick, pitch, throw, twirl, twist **09** pitch-pole, pitch-poll
• **flip through** **04** scan, skim, skip **08** glance at **10** glance over **11** leaf through **12** flick through, thumb through **13** browse through

## flippancy

**05** cheek **06** levity **08** glibness, pertness **09** frivolity, sauciness **10** cheekiness, disrespect, persiflage **11** irreverence, shallowness **12** impertinence **13** facetiousness **14** superficiality **15** thoughtlessness

## flippant

**04** flip, glib, pert, rude **05** saucy **06** cheeky, nimble **07** offhand, playful, shallow **08** impudent **09** facetious, frivolous **10** insouciant, irreverent **11** impertinent, superficial, thoughtless **12** light-hearted **13** disrespectful, irresponsible

## flippantly

**06** glibly, rudely **11** facetiously, frivolously **12** irreverently

**13** impertinently, irresponsibly, superficially, thoughtlessly **14** light-heartedly **15** disrespectfully

## flipping

**06** cursed, damned, darned, dashed **07** blasted **08** annoying, blinking, blooming, dratting, fiendish, infernal, wretched **10** confounded, unpleasant

## flirt

**03** rap, toy **04** jerk, mash, ogle, vamp **05** dally, eye up, flick, hussy, tease **06** chat up, chippy, coquet, gillet, lead on, masher, wanton **07** carry on, pickeer, trifler **08** coquette, make up to **09** gillflirt, philander **10** make eyes at **11** make a pass at, philanderer **12** heart-breaker
• **flirt with** **03** try **04** mash **05** hit on **06** coquet **07** carry on, hit upon, toy with **08** consider, coquette, dabble in, play with **09** entertain **10** trifle with

## flirtation

**05** amour, sport **06** affair, come-on, lumber, toying **07** teasing **08** coquetry, dallying, intrigue, trifling **09** dalliance **10** chatting up **12** philandering

## flirtatious

**05** loose **06** come-on, flirty, wanton **07** amorous, flighty, teasing **08** flirtish, sportive **10** come-hither, coquettish **11** promiscuous, provocative

## flit

◊ *anagram indicator* **03** bob, fly **04** dart, dash, pass, rush, skim, skip, slip, wing **05** dance, flash, fleet, light, speed, whisk **07** flitter, flutter **08** fleeting

## float

**03** bob **04** cart, cork, hang, hull, pram, sail, swim, waft **05** balsa, camel, drift, fleet, glide, hover, quill, set up, slide, table **06** bobber, launch, smooth, submit, wander **07** oropesa, pontoon, present, promote, propose, suggest, suspend **08** get going, initiate, levitate, lifebuoy **09** be buoyant, establish, recommend **10** come up with, put forward, stay afloat **13** pneumatophore **15** get off the ground

## floating

◊ *anagram indicator* **04** free **06** afloat, natant **07** bobbing, buoyant, movable, sailing, wafting **08** drifting, hovering, swimming, variable **09** migratory, unsettled, wandering **10** indecisive, transitory, unattached, unsinkable **11** fluctuating, uncommitted

## flock

**03** mob **04** band, bevy, fold, game, herd, host, mass, mill, pack, rout, sord, trip, tuft, walk, wing, wisp, wool **05** bunch, charm, chirm, covey, crowd, drove, flush, group, shoal, skein, swarm, troop, watch **06** flight, gaggle, gather, huddle, school, spring, throng **07** cluster, collect, company, dopping **08** assemble, assembly, converge, paddling **09** flocculus, gathering, multitude **10** collection, congregate, unkindness **11** murmuration **12** come together, congregation

## flog

◇ *anagram indicator* **03** tan, tat, taw **04** beat, belt, cane, drub, flay, hawk, hide, lash, sell, whip **05** birch, knout, strap, swish, trade, whack, whang **06** breech, deal in, handle, larrup, peddle, punish, strike, thrash, wallop **07** scourge, sjambok **08** chastise, urticate, vapulate **09** horsewhip **10** flagellate **12** offer for sale, put up for sale

## flogging

**06** caning, hiding **07** beating, belting, flaying, lashing **08** birching, whacking, whipping **09** scourging, strapping, thrashing, walloping **10** vapulation **12** flagellation **13** horsewhipping, whipping-cheer

## flood

**04** bore, eger, fill, flow, glut, gush, pour, rage, rush, soak, tide **05** drown, eager, eagre, spate, speat, surge, swamp, swell **06** deluge, drench, engulf, excess, series, stream **07** debacle, freshet, immerse, smother, torrent **08** alluvion, brim over, diluvion, diluvium, downpour, inundate, overflow, plethora, saturate, submerge **09** abundance, cataclysm, overwhelm, profusion **10** flash flood, inundation, outpouring, spring tide, succession, transgress **11** superfluity **13** Ogygian deluge

## floor

**02** fl, KO **04** area, base, beat, dais, deck, fell, loft, tier **05** attic, basis, étage, level, stage, stump, throw **06** baffle, defeat, ground, planch, puzzle, storey **07** flummox, landing, nonplus, perplex **08** basement, bel étage, bewilder, confound, entresol, flooring, platform **09** discomfit, dumbfound, frustrate, knock down, overwhelm, prostrate **10** disconcert, downstairs, strike down **11** piano nobile
• **first floor** **11** ground level
• **floor material** **04** lino, pisé, rung

## floozy

*see* **tart**

## flop

◇ *anagram indicator* **03** sag **04** bomb, drop, fail, fall, fold, hang, sink, swap, swop **05** crash, droop, flump, slump **06** dangle, fiasco, go bust, pack up, slip-up, topple, tumble **07** also-ran, debacle, failure, founder, go broke, has-been, misfire, no-hoper, washout **08** collapse, disaster, fall flat, lay an egg, shambles **10** non-starter **11** go to the wall **12** come a cropper, go into the red **14** be unsuccessful
• **flop down** **03** wop **04** whap, whop **05** plump

## floppy

◇ *anagram indicator* **04** disk, limp, soft **05** baggy, loose **06** droopy, flabby **07** flaccid, hanging, sagging **08** dangling, diskette, flexible **12** flexible disk

## flora

**06** botany, Cybele, plants **07** herbage **08** plantage **09** plant life **10** vegetation

## floral emblem

*see* **emblem**

## florid

**03** red **04** high **05** Asian, fussy, ruddy **06** ornate, purple, rococo **07** baroque, flowery, flushed, pompous, reddish, taffeta, verbose **08** beetroot, blushing, figurate, red-faced, rubicund, sanguine, taffetas **09** bombastic, elaborate, high-flown **10** coloratura, flamboyant, melismatic **11** embellished, extravagant **12** high-sounding **13** grandiloquent, overelaborate

## Florida

**02** FL **03** Fla

## flotsam

**04** junk **05** dreck **06** debris, jetsam **07** flotage, rubbish **08** detritus, floatage, oddments, wreckage **11** odds and ends

## flounce

**03** bob **04** jerk, toss **05** fling, frill, stamp, storm, throw, twist **06** bounce, fringe, ruffle, spring **07** falbala, valance **08** furbelow, trimming

## flounder

◇ *anagram indicator* **05** fluke, grope, slosh **06** dither, falter, fumble, jumble, tolter, wallop, wallow **07** blunder, go under, stagger, stumble **08** struggle **10** be confused, flail about **11** thresh about **12** lose the place

## flour

**04** meal **06** red-dog **07** cribble, pollard **08** tailings **09** wheatmeal **11** strong wheat

## flourish

◇ *anagram indicator* **03** wag, wax **04** boom, élan, grow, lick, mort, show, wave **05** bloom, get on, serif, shake, swash, sweep, swing, swirl, swish, twirl, twist, vaunt, wield **06** do well, flaunt, flower, parade, paraph, rubric, swinge, thrive, tucket **07** blossom, burgeon, cadenza, develop, display, exhibit, fanfare, gesture, panache, pizzazz, prosper, show off, succeed, wampish **08** be strong, brandish, curlicue, increase, ornament, progress **09** bear fruit **10** decoration

## flourished

◇ *anagram indicator* **02** fl **04** flor

## flourishing

◇ *anagram indicator* **04** pert **05** green, palmy **06** bloomy **07** booming **08** blooming, thriving **10** blossoming, burgeoning, prosperous, successful **11** going strong

## flout

**04** defy, gibe, jibe, lout, lowt, mock **05** break, scorn, scout, spurn **06** jeer at, reject **07** disdain, disobey, laugh at, scoff at, sneer at, violate **08** ridicule **09** disregard, go against **11** set at nought **15** show contempt for

## flow

◇ *anagram indicator* **02** go **03** jet, ren, rin, run **04** drip, flux, gush, leak, make, melt, move, ooze, pour, rail, roll, rush, seep, slip, spew, stem, teem, tide, well, wend **05** arise, drift, flood, glide, issue, raile, rayle, slide, spate, spill, spout, spurt, surge, sweep, swirl, whirl **06** babble, bubble, course, deluge, derive, emerge, gurgle, morass, plenty, result, ripple, spring, squirt, stream **07** cascade, current, emanate, passage, proceed, trickle **08** effusion, movement, overflow, plethora, recourse **09** abundance, circulate, originate, quicksand **10** outpouring

## flower

**03** bud **04** acme, best, grow, open, peak, pick **05** bloom, cream, élite, prime **06** choice, finest, floret, height, heyday, mature, select, sprout, thrive, zenith **07** blossom, burgeon, come out, develop, prosper, succeed **08** best part, flourish, floweret, maturity, pinnacle **10** perfection **11** culmination, florescence **13** efflorescence, inflorescence **14** crème de la crème
*See also* **birth; river**

---

*Flower parts include:*

**05** calyx, ovary, ovule, petal, sepal, spike, stalk, style, torus, umbel **06** anther, carpel, corymb, pistil, raceme, spadix, stamen, stigma **07** corolla, nectary, panicle, pedicel **08** filament, thalamus **09** capitulum, dichasium, gynoecium **10** receptacle **11** monochasium

---

*Garden flowers include:*

**03** lis **04** aloe, daff, flag, glad, iris, lily, pink, rose, sego **05** aster, daisy, lotus, lupin, pansy, phlox, poppy, stock, tulip, viola **06** allium, azalea, crocus, dahlia, orchid, salvia, squill, violet, zinnia **07** alyssum, anemone, begonia, campion, day-lily, freesia, fuchsia, lobelia, nemesia, nigella, petunia, primula, verbena, waratah **08** arum lily, asphodel, bluebell, cyclamen, daffodil, dianthus, foxglove, gardenia, geranium, gladioli, hyacinth, marigold, pond lily, primrose, snowdrop, sweet pea **09** amaryllis, aubrietia, calendula, candytuft, carnation, digitalis, gladiolus, hollyhock, narcissus, nicotiana, regal lily, sunflower, tiger lily, torch lily **10** agapanthus, busy lizzie, cornflower, delphinium, Easter lily, fleur-de-lis, fleur-de-lys, fritillary, nasturtium, poinsettia, polyanthus, ragged-lady, snake's head, snapdragon, wallflower **11** African lily, antirrhinum, forget-me-not, gillyflower, kangaroo

paw, love-in-a-mist, Madonna-lily, naked ladies, red-hot poker, tiger flower
12 devil-in-a-bush, flower of Jove, golden wattle, rose geranium, Solomon's seal, sweet william, wild hyacinth, Zantedeschia
13 African violet, butcher's broom, chrysanthemum, grape hyacinth, lily of the Nile, winter aconite
14 belladonna lily, glory of the snow, Ithuriel's spear
15 dog's tooth violet, lily of the valley, star of Bethlehem, Sturt's desert pea

*See also* **lily**

*Wild flowers include:*

03 kex, meu
04 daff, geum, ling, nard, woad
05 clary, daisy, gowan, laser, poppy
06 clover, oxslip, teasel, violet, yarrow
07 ale hoof, bistort, campion, comfrey, cowslip, dog rose, goldcup, heather, spignel
08 bluebell, crowfoot, dog daisy, foxglove, harebell, lungwort, primrose, rock rose, self-heal, spicknel, toadflax, wild iris
09 Aaron's rod, baldmoney, birth-wort, broomrape, buttercup, celandine, columbine, edelweiss, goldenrod, horsetail, moneywort, stonecrop, water lily, wild pansy
10 crane's bill, goatsbeard, heartsease, lady's smock, marguerite, masterwort, oxeye daisy, pennyroyal, wild endive, wild orchid
11 ragged robin, wild chicory, wood anemone
12 common mallow, cuckoo flower, great mullein, lady's slipper, solomon's seal, spider orchid, white campion, yellow rocket
13 butter-and-eggs, field cow-wheat, shepherd's club, wild gladiolus
14 black-eyed susan, bladder campion, common toadflax, multiflora rose
15 bachelor's button, New England aster

• **garland of flowers** 03 lei 05 toran 06 torana
• **mass of flowers** 04 head

## flowery
05 fancy 06 bloomy, floral, florid, ornate 07 baroque, chintzy, pompous, verbose 08 blossomy 09 bombastic, elaborate, high-flown 10 euphuistic, rhetorical 12 efflorescent 13 grandiloquent

## flowing
04 easy, flux 05 loose 06 floppy, fluent, liquid, moving, oozing, smooth 07 current, cursive, falling, flaccid, gushing, hanging, natural, pouring, rolling, running, rushing, seeping, surging, welling 08 bubbling, sweeping, unbroken 09 cascading, streaming 10 continuous, effortless 11 loose-bodied, overflowing

12 hanging loose 13 hanging freely, uninterrupted

## fluctuate
◊ *anagram indicator* 04 sway, trim, vary, yo-yo 05 alter, float, range, shift, swing, waver 06 change, differ, seesaw 07 balance 08 hesitate, undulate 09 alternate, come and go, oscillate, vacillate 10 ebb and flow 11 go up and down, rise and fall 13 chop and change

## fluctuation
05 range, shift, swing 06 change, seiche 08 floating, nutation, wavering 09 variation 10 fickleness 11 alternation, ambivalence, inconstancy, instability, oscillation, vacillation, variability 12 irresolution, unsteadiness 14 capriciousness

## flue
03 fur 04 duct, flat, pipe, vent 05 shaft, tewel 06 flared, tunnel, uptake 07 channel, chimney, passage, shallow, splayed 08 fluework 09 influenza

## fluency
04 ease, flow 07 command, control 08 facility, glibness 09 assurance, eloquence, facundity, flippancy, readiness, slickness 10 outpouring, smoothness, volubility 12 flippantness 13 copia verborum 14 articulateness

## fluent
04 easy, glib 05 fluid, ready, slick 06 facile, smooth 07 elegant, flowing, natural, voluble 08 eloquent, graceful 10 articulate, effortless 11 free-flowing, mellifluous 13 silver-tongued

## fluently
03 pat 05 patly 06 easily, glibly 08 smoothly 09 elegantly, naturally 10 eloquently, gracefully 12 articulately, effortlessly

## fluff
◊ *anagram indicator* 03 fug, nap 04 blow, boob, dowl, down, dust, flue, fuzz, lint, muff, oose, ooze, pile 05 botch, dowle, flosh, floss, spoil 06 bungle, cock up, foul up, fumble, mess up, muck up, muddle 07 do badly, screw up 09 dust bunny, mismanage 11 make a mess of 13 make a bad job of 15 put your foot in it

## fluffy
04 soft 05 downy, furry, fuzzy, hairy, silky 06 fleecy, pluffy, shaggy, woolly 07 velvety 08 feathery

## fluid
◊ *anagram indicator* 02 fl 03 gas 04 easy, open 05 chyle, grume, juice, runny 06 liquid, liquor, melted, mobile, molten, smooth, vapour, watery 07 aqueous, elegant, flowing, natural, protean, running 08 atrament, flexible, graceful, shifting, solution, unstable, unsteady, variable 09 adaptable, diffluent, liquefied, unsettled 10 adjustable, changeable, effortless, inconstant, karyolymph 11 fluctuating, free-flowing 12 unsolidified

## fluke
03 fan 04 barb, worm 05 break, freak, quirk 06 chance, stroke, upcast 07 killick, killock, scratch 08 accident, blessing, flounder, fortuity, windfall 09 trematode 10 lucky break 11 coincidence, serendipity 12 stroke of luck

## fluky
05 jammy, lucky 06 chance 08 freakish 09 fortunate, uncertain 10 accidental, fortuitous 12 coincidental, incalculable 13 serendipitous

## flummox
03 fox 04 faze 05 floor, stump 06 baffle, defeat, puzzle, stymie 07 confuse, mystify, nonplus, perplex 08 bewilder, confound 09 bamboozle

## flummoxed
05 at sea, fazed, foxed 07 at a loss, baffled, floored, puzzled, stumped, stymied 08 confused 09 mystified, perplexed 10 bamboozled, bewildered, confounded, nonplussed

## flunk
04 bomb, fail, flop, fold 06 blow it 07 failure, founder 08 fall flat 09 not make it 10 come undone, not come off 11 bite the dust, come to grief, come unglued, come unstuck 12 come a cropper 14 be unsuccessful 15 blow your chances

## flunkey
05 slave, toady, valet 06 drudge, Jeames, lackey, menial, minion, yes-man 07 cringer, footman, servant, steward 08 hanger-on, retainer 09 assistant, underling 10 bootlicker, manservant

## fluorine
01 F

## flurried
◊ *anagram indicator* 05 fazed, upset 07 in a flap, in a tizzy, rattled 08 in a tizzy, unnerved 09 disturbed, flustered, perturbed, unsettled 12 all of a lather 13 having kittens

## flurry
◊ *anagram indicator* 04 bout, flap, fuss, gust, stir, to-do 05 blast, burst, hurry, spell, spurt, swirl, upset, whirl 06 bother, bustle, hassle, hubbub, hustle, rattle, ruffle, scurry, shower, squall, tumult 07 agitate, confuse, disturb, fluster, flutter, perturb, swither 08 bewilder, outbreak, unsettle 09 agitation, commotion 10 disconcert, excitement 11 disturbance 12 perturbation 14 discountenance

## flush
03 rud 04 burn, even, flat, full, gild, glow, hose, rich, swab, true, wash 05 bloom, blush, clear, eject, elate, empty, expel, flame, go red, level, plane, rinse, rouse, scour, start 06 colour, hectic, heyday, lavish, puddle, redden, sluice, smooth, square, vigour 07 cleanse, crimson, disturb, moneyed, redness, replete, suffuse, turn red, uncover, wealthy, well-off 08 abundant, colour up,

## flushed

discover, drive out, evacuate, force out, generous, rosiness, well-to-do **09** abounding, abundance, freshness, reddening, ruddiness **10** prosperous, run to earth, well-heeled **11** overflowing

## flushed

**03** hot, red **04** pink, rosy **05** aglow, rosed, ruddy **06** ablaze, aflame, blowsy, blowzy, elated, florid, hectic **07** aroused, burning, crimson, excited, glowing, scarlet **08** animated, blushing, enthused, exultant, inspired, rubicund, sanguine, thrilled **11** embarrassed, exhilarated, intoxicated

## fluster

◊ *anagram indicator* **04** faze, flap, heat, tizz **05** panic, state, tizzy, upset **06** bother, bustle, dither, flurry, pother, pudder, put off, rattle, ruffle **07** agitate, confuse, disturb, perturb, turmoil, unnerve **08** confound, distract, hurrying, unsettle **09** agitation, commotion, confusion, embarrass, flustrate **10** discompose, disconcert **11** disturbance, flustration, make nervous **12** perturbation **13** embarrassment

## flute

**04** fife **05** quena, tibia **06** poogye, zufolo **07** chamfer, piccolo, poogyee, zuffolo **08** recorder **09** flageolet **10** shakuhachi

## fluted

**06** ribbed, ridged **07** grooved **08** furrowed **10** channelled, corrugated

## flutter

◊ *anagram indicator* **03** bat, bet, fan, fly **04** beat, flap, play, punt, risk, toss, waff, wave **05** dance, flaff, hover, shake, wager, waver **06** gamble, quiver, ripple, ruffle, shiver, tremor, twitch, winnow **07** agitate, flacker, flaffer, flicker, flitter, pulsate, shudder, tremble, twitter, vibrate **08** flapping, flichter, volitate **09** agitation, confusion, flaughter, fluctuate, palpitate, vibration **11** palpitation, speculation

## flux

**04** flow, fuse, melt **05** issue **06** change, motion, unrest **08** fluidity, movement, mutation **10** alteration, transition **11** development, fluctuation, instability **12** modification **13** changeability
• **electric flux displacement** **01** D
• **magnetic flux density** **01** B

## fly

◊ *anagram indicator* **03** jet, run, sly **04** bolt, dart, dash, flap, flee, flit, quit, race, rise, rush, scat, show, soar, tear, wave, wily, wing, zoom **05** alert, canny, float, glide, guide, hover, hurry, leave, mount, pilot, scoot, scram, sharp, shoot, skive, smart, speed, split, steer **06** artful, ascend, astute, career, decamp, depart, escape, flight, get out, hasten, reveal, shrewd, slip by, sprint, stream, vanish, winnow **07** abscond, careful, control, cunning, display, do a bunk, exhibit, flutter, get away, go by

air, make off, operate, present, prudent, push off, retreat, run away, scarper, stylish, take off, vamoose **08** clear off, shove off, volitate, withdraw **09** cut and run, disappear, do a runner, golden-eye, go quickly, manoeuvre, on the ball, push along, sagacious, skedaddle **10** hit the road, make tracks, take flight **11** fashionable, hit the trail, nobody's fool, pass quickly, travel by air **14** make a bolt for it **15** make a break for it, take to your heels

---

*Flies include:*

**03** bee, bot, day, dor, gad, hop, ked, may, med
**04** beet, blow, boat, bulb, bush, cleg, corn, deer, dung, fire, frit, gnat, gout, kade, lamp, meat, pium, sand
**05** alder, birch, black, crane, drone, flesh, froth, fruit, horse, house, hover, march, midge, onion, sedge, snake, snipe, water, wheat
**06** blowie, caddis, carrot, cuckoo, forest, motuca, muscid, mutuca, pomace, robber, stable, tipula, tsetse, turnip, tzetse, tzetze, warble
**07** blister, brommer, cabbage, cluster, diptera, dolphin, harvest, Hessian, lantern, sciarid, smother, Spanish, vinegar
**08** glossina, ruby-tail, scorpion, sheep ked, simulium, tachinid
**09** cantharis, ichneumon, screw-worm
**10** bluebottle, Cecidomyia, drosophila, spittle bug
**11** biting midge, buffalo gnat, cabbage-root, greenbottle
**12** cheesehopper
**13** cheese skipper, spittle insect

---

*Fishing flies include:*

**03** bob
**04** harl, herl, tail
**05** sedge
**06** doctor, hackle, palmer, salmon
**07** watchet
**09** hairy Mary, Jock Scott
**10** cock-a-bondy

• **fly at** **03** hit **05** go for **06** attack, charge, let fly, strike **07** assault, lay into **08** fall upon **09** have a go at, lash out at
• **fly open** ◊ *anagram indicator*
**05** burst **15** burst at the seams

## fly-by-night

**05** shady **06** cowboy **07** dubious **09** ephemeral **10** short-lived, unreliable **12** disreputable, questionable, undependable **13** discreditable, irresponsible, untrustworthy

## flyer

*see* **flier**

## flying

**04** fast **05** brief, hasty, rapid **06** mobile, rushed, speedy, volant, winged **07** gliding, hurried, soaring, winging **08** airborne, flapping, fleeting, flighted, floating, hovering, volitant **09** on the

wing, wind-borne **10** fluttering, volitation **11** upon the wing, whistle-stop

## foam

**03** fry **04** boil, fizz, head, scum, suds, surf **05** froth, spume, yeast **06** befoam, bubble, lather, mousse, seethe **07** aerogel, bubbles **08** sea froth **10** effervesce **13** effervescence

## foamy

**05** spumy, sudsy **06** bubbly, frothy, yeasty **07** foaming, lathery **10** spumescent

## fob

• **fob off** **04** dump **05** foist **06** impose, put off, unload **07** deceive, inflict, palm off, pass off **08** get rid of

## focus

**03** aim, fix, hub **04** axis, core, crux, join, meet, turn **05** heart, hinge, pivot **06** accent, center, centre, direct, home in, kernel, stress, target, weight, zero in, zoom in **07** nucleus **08** converge, emphasis, linchpin, pinpoint, priority **09** attention, spotlight **10** focal point, importance, metropolis, prominence **11** concentrate, pre-eminence **12** accentuation, significance, underscoring **13** concentration **14** bring into focus
• **in focus** **05** clear, crisp, sharp **08** distinct **11** well-defined
• **out of focus** **04** hazy **05** fuzzy, muzzy **06** blurry **07** blurred **10** ill-defined, indistinct

## fodder

**02** ti **03** hay **04** feed, food, milo **05** grass, vetch **06** eatage, forage, fother, lucern, luzern, silage, stover **07** alfalfa, lucerne, pabulum, provand, provend, rations, soilage, timothy **08** browsing, goat's-rue, oat grass, proviant, rye grass, sainfoin, teosinte **09** foodstuff, milk vetch, milo maize, provender, sago grass, saintfoin **10** cow parsnip, serradella, serradilla, Sudan grass **11** nourishment, white clover **12** meadow fescue, timothy grass **13** kangaroo grass

## foe

**05** enemy, rival **08** opponent, wrangler **09** adversary, combatant, ill-wisher **10** antagonist

## foetid

*see* **fetid, foetid**

## foetus

**06** embryo **10** unborn baby **11** unborn child

## fog

◊ *anagram indicator* **03** dim **04** blur, daze, dull, haar, haze, mist, moss, smog **05** befog, brume, cloud, gloom, smoke **06** baffle, darken, muddle, stupor, trance **07** aerosol, confuse, obscure, pea-soup, perplex, sea fret, steam up **08** bewilder, haziness **09** confusion, mistiness, murkiness, obfuscate, obscurity, pease-soup, pea-souper, vagueness **10** bafflement, perplexity, puzzlement **12** bewilderment **14** disorientation

## foggy

**03** dim **04** damp, dark, grey, hazy **05** misty, muggy, murky, thick, vague **06** cloudy, gloomy, smoggy, stupid **07** brumous, clouded, muddled, obscure, shadowy, unclear **08** overcast **10** indistinct

## foible

**05** fault, habit, quirk **06** defect, faible, oddity **07** failing, oddness **08** penchant, weakness **09** weak point **11** peculiarity, shortcoming, strangeness **12** eccentricity, idiosyncrasy, imperfection

## foil

**03** pip **04** balk, stop **05** baulk, block, chaff, check, elude, foyle, stump **06** baffle, defeat, hamper, hinder, outwit, relief, set-off, thwart, window **07** balance, counter, fleuret, nullify, paillon, prevent, repulse, scupper, scuttle, setting **08** contrast, obstruct **09** frustrate **10** antithesis, background, beauty spot, circumvent, complement **11** frustration, silver paper

## foist

**03** fob **05** force **06** fob off, impose, saddle, thrust, unload, wish on **07** palm off, pass off **08** get rid of **09** introduce

## fold

**03** hug, lap, pen, ply **04** bend, cuff, dart, fail, fake, flop, hood, line, lirk, purl, ring, ruck, tuck, turn, wrap, yard **05** clasp, close, court, crash, crimp, flock, kraal, layer, paper, pleat, plica, pouch, pound, prank, quill, quire **06** church, crease, crista, diapir, dog-ear, double, enfold, furrow, gather, go bust, mantle, middle, pack up, pleach, plight, pranck, pucker, ruffle, rumple, wimple, wrap up **07** company, crinkle, crumple, dog's-ear, embrace, enclose, entwine, envelop, flexion, folding, go broke, go under, omentum, overlap, paddock, prancke, squeeze, whimple, wrinkle **08** assembly, collapse, compound, doubling, patagium, shut down, stockade, syncline, turn down, turn over **09** community, duplicate, enclosure, gathering, gill cover, inflexure, knife-edge, mesentery, monocline, plication, plicature, replicate, turn under **10** epicanthus, fellowship, go bankrupt, intertwine **11** convolution, corrugation, duplicature, go to the wall **12** congregation, parishioners **14** hospital corner **15** go out of business

## folder

**04** file **05** folio **06** binder, holder, jacket, pocket, wallet **08** envelope **09** directory, matchbook, portfolio **13** lever arch file

## foliage

**06** canopy, leaves **07** boscage, boskage, leafage, verdure **08** greenery **09** foliation, foliature, vernation **10** vegetation **12** frondescence

## folio

**01** f **02** fo **03** fol

## folios

**02** ff

## folk

**03** kin, men **04** clan, race **05** tribe **06** ethnic, family, humans, nation, native, people, public, tribal, tupuna **07** kindred, parents, persons, popular, society **08** kinsfolk, national **09** ancestral, relations, relatives **10** indigenous, population **11** ethnic group, traditional
*See also* **singer**

## folklore

**04** lore **05** myths, tales **06** fables **07** beliefs, customs, legends, stories **09** folktales, mythology, tradition **13** superstitions

## folksy

**04** fond, kind, maty, warm **05** basic, close, crude, matey, pally, plain, thick, tight **06** chummy, genial, kindly, rustic, simple **07** affable, amiable, cordial, helpful, natural **08** amicable, everyday, familiar, friendly, intimate, ordinary, outgoing, sociable **09** comradely, convivial, receptive **10** hospitable **11** good-natured, inseparable, neighbourly, sympathetic, traditional **12** affectionate, approachable, time-honoured **13** companionable **15** unsophisticated

## follow

◇ *juxtaposition indicator* **03** ape, dog, ren, rin, run, sew, sue, use **04** copy, flow, heed, heel, hunt, mind, note, obey, stag, suss, tail, twig **05** arise, catch, chase, ensue, grasp, hound, issue, mimic, stalk, track, trail, watch **06** accept, attend, escort, fathom, go with, pursue, repeat, result, second, shadow, spring, take in **07** develop, emanate, emulate, go after, imitate, observe, proceed, replace, stick to, succeed, support, suss out, yield to **08** adhere to, be a fan of, carry out, come next, go behind, practise, run after, supplant, tag along **09** accompany, come after, conform to, give chase, latch onto, supersede **10** appreciate, come behind, comply with, comprehend, keep up with, understand, walk behind **11** be devoted to, go along with, tread behind **14** be a supporter of, be interested in, take the place of **15** take your cue from
• **follow slavishly 04** echo
• **follow through 06** finish, fulfil, pursue **08** complete, conclude, continue **09** implement **10** see through
• **follow up 06** pursue **07** succeed **08** check out, continue, look into, research **09** prosecute, reinforce **11** consolidate, investigate

## follower

**03** fan, man **04** buff **05** freak, pupil **06** backer, cohort, escort, helper, lackey, voteen **07** acolyte, acolyth, admirer, Anthony, apostle, convert, devotee, janizar, lacquey, sectary **08** adherent, believer, disciple, emulator, hanger-on, imitator, janizary, retainer, sidekick **09** attendant, companion, janissary, poodle-dog, satellite, supporter **10** aficionado, enthusiast, pursuivant, running dog **11** afficionado

## following

◇ *juxtaposition indicator* **01** f **03** fol **04** fans, next **05** later, suite **06** circle, public **07** backers, backing, coterie, ensuing, patrons, retinue, sequent, support **08** admirers, audience, secundum **09** adherents, clientèle, entourage, favorable, followers, hereunder, patronage, resulting **10** consequent, favourable, subsequent, succeeding, succession, successive, supporters **13** body of support
• **following pages 02** ff

## folly

**03** sin **04** whim **05** folie, moria, tower **06** gazebo, idiocy, lunacy, vanity **07** foolery, foppery, idiotcy, inanity, madness **08** insanity, monument, nonsense, rashness **09** absurdity, belvedere, craziness, silliness, stupidity **10** imbecility, imprudence **11** fatuousness, foolishness **12** illogicality, indiscretion, recklessness **13** foolhardiness, ludicrousness, senselessness **14** ridiculousness

## foment

**04** brew, goad, spur **05** raise, rouse **06** arouse, excite, foster, incite, kindle, prompt, stir up, whip up, work up **07** agitate, promote, provoke, quicken **08** activate, incubate **09** encourage, instigate, stimulate

## fond

**03** hot, try **04** daft, dote, vain, warm **05** basis, naive **06** absurd, caring, doting, keen on, liking, loving, nuts on, spoony, tender **07** adoring, amatory, amorous, attempt, deluded, devoted, foolish, proceed **08** hooked on, mad about **09** credulous, daft about, indulgent, nuts about, partial to **10** addicted to, attached to, background, crazy about, dotty about, foundation **11** enamoured of, impractical **12** affectionate **14** over-optimistic

## fondle

**03** hug, pat, pet **05** grope **06** caress, cocker, cosset, cuddle, dandle, stroke **07** smuggle, touch up

## fondly

**06** warmly **08** lovingly, tenderly **09** amorously **14** affectionately
• **speak fondly 03** coo **04** bill

## fondness

**04** love **05** fancy, taste **06** dotage, liking, tender, tendre **07** leaning **08** devotion, kindness, penchant, soft spot, weakness **09** affection, engoûment, tendresse **10** attachment, engouement, enthusiasm, partiality, preference, tenderness, well-liking **11** inclination **12** predilection **14** susceptibility

## font
**08** bénitier, delubrum

## food
**03** kai **04** chow, diet, dish, eats, fare, feed, feud, grub, meal, menu, nosh, tack, tuck **05** board, meals, scoff, scran, table **06** edible, fodder, kaikai, staple, stores, tucker, viands **07** aliment, cooking, cuisine, edibles, pabulum, pasture, rations **08** delicacy, eatables, victuals **09** nutriment, nutrition, provender, repasture **10** bush tucker, foodstuffs, provisions, speciality, sustenance **11** comestibles, nourishment, subsistence **12** refreshments

---

*Foods include:*

**03** dal, dip, ham, pie, poi, veg
**04** dhal, eddo, flan, fool, hash, luau, mash, olio, olla, pâté, rice, soss, soup, stew, taco, tart, tofu, wrap
**05** balti, bhaji, boxty, brose, broth, champ, chips, crêpe, curry, daube, dolma, grits, gumbo, jelly, kebab, kofta, laksa, latke, pasta, pasty, pesto, pilau, pizza, Quorn®, roast, salad, salmi, salsa, satay, sauce, sushi, tapas, tikka, toast
**06** bhajee, borsch, burger, canapé, caviar, cheese, cookie, damper, faggot, fajita, fondue, fu yung, gratin, haggis, hotpot, hummus, kipper, mousse, paella, pakora, panini, pastry, pilaff, quiche, ragout, samosa, scampi, sorbet, tagine, tahina, tajine, tamale, trifle, waffle
**07** biryani, biscuit, borscht, burrito, chowder, chutney, cobbler, compote, cracker, crowdie, crumble, fajitas, falafel, felafel, fritter, friture, galette, gnocchi, goulash, gravlax, lasagne, oatcake, pancake, pavlova, polenta, pudding, rarebit, risotto, rissole, sashimi, sausage, seafood, soufflé, stir fry, stovies, tempura, terrine, timbale, tostada
**08** barbecue, biriyani, calamari, chop suey, chow mein, cocktail, coleslaw, consommé, coq au vin, couscous, dolmades, dumpling, fast food, fishcake, fricasee, gado-gado, gazpacho, ice cream, kedgeree, meringue, moussaka, nut roast, omelette, porridge, pot-roast, raclette, sandwich, souvlaki, syllabub, tandoori, teriyaki, tortilla, turnover, tzatziki, Vegemite, vindaloo, yakitori
**09** casserole, cassoulet, charlotte, colcannon, croquette, enchilada, fricassée, galantine, gravadlax, guacamole, Irish stew, jambalaya, macedoine, meatballs, nut cutlet, souvlakia, succotash, tabbouleh
**10** blancmange, cannelloni, cheesecake, corned beef, cottage pie, enchiladas, fish-finger, fruit salad, Greek salad, green salad, minestrone, mixed grill, peperonata, quesadilla,

salmagundi, salmagundy, sauerkraut, spring roll, stroganoff
**11** baba ganoush, caesar salad, cockaleekie, French fries, fritto misto, gefilte fish, potato salad, ratatouille, rumblethump, smorgasbord, vichyssoise, winter salad
**12** eggs Benedict, fish and chips, mulligatawny, pease pudding, rumblethumps, Russian salad, shepherd's pie, taramasalata, Waldorf salad, welsh rarebit
**13** bouillabaisse, colonial goose, fisherman's pie, prawn cocktail, rumbledethump, salade niçoise, toad-in-the-hole, witchetty grub
**14** chilli con carne, macaroni cheese, pickled herring, rumbledethumps
**15** bubble and squeak, Wiener schnitzel

---

*See also* **bean; biscuit; bread; cake; cheese; fruit; herb; meat; mushroom; nut; pasta; pastry; sauce; sausage; sweet; vegetable**

*Fast food includes:*

**03** KFC®
**04** taco, wrap
**05** bagel, chips, donut, fries, kebab, pizza
**06** Big Mac®, burger, hot dog, nachos
**07** burrito, chalupa, falafel, noodles, shwarma, Whopper®
**08** doughnut, sandwich
**09** bacon roll, chip butty, hamburger, Happy Meal®, milkshake
**10** beanburger, beefburger, doner kebab, fish 'n' chips, fish supper, onion rings, shish kebab
**11** bacon burger, baked potato, French fries, sausage roll
**12** cheeseburger, chicken wings, club sandwich, fish and chips, tortilla wrap, veggie burger
**13** chicken burger, sausage supper
**14** chicken nuggets, quarter pounder

---

*See also* **restaurant**
• **provide food** **05** cater

## fool
**04** goof, hoax, jest, joke **05** bluff, cheat, feign, tease, trick **06** delude, diddle, have on, play up, take in, trifle **07** beguile, carry on, deceive, mislead, pretend, swindle **08** bonehead, hoodwink **09** bamboozle, lark about, mess about, play about **10** mess around, play around, play tricks **11** horse around, monkey about, string along **12** monkey around, put one over on

---

*Fools include:*

**02** bf
**03** ass, auf, con, fon, git, kid, mug, nit, nut, oik, sap, sot, yap
**04** berk, bête, bozo, burk, butt, cake, calf, clot, cony, coof, coot, cuif, dill, dope, dork, dupe, geek, goat, goof, goon, goop, gouk, gowk, gull, gump, hash, jerk, kook,

loon, lump, lunk, muck, mutt, nana, nerd, nerk, nong, ouph, poop, prat, punk, putz, sham, shmo, simp, soft, tony, twit, yo-yo
**05** chump, clown, cluck, comic, coney, divvy, droll, dumbo, dunce, dweeb, eejit, galah, idiot, moron, neddy, nelly, ninny, patch, patsy, purée, schmo, shlub, snipe, softy, twerp, wally
**06** bampot, bauble, cretin, dimwit, donkey, doofus, dottle, drongo, dum-dum, jester, josser, madcap, monkey, motley, muppet, nitwit, nutter, sawney, schlub, schmoe, stooge, sucker, turkey, wallie, wigeon, Yorick
**07** airhead, barmpot, bourder, buffoon, Charley, Charlie, dingbat, fat-head, God's ape, gubbins, halfwit, haverel, jackass, jughead, lemming, muggins, pillock, plonker, saphead, tomfool, want-wit, wazzock, widgeon
**08** boofhead, dipstick, flathead, fondling, Fred Nerk, imbecile, Jack-fool, lunkhead, merryman, mooncalf, omadhaun, shlemiel, Tom-noddy, Trinculo
**09** April fool, birdbrain, blockhead, capocchia, chipochia, cloth head, court fool, dumb-cluck, ignoramus, joculator, lack-brain, lamebrain, mumchance, philander, schlemiel, schlemihl, simpleton
**10** head-banger, nincompoop, silly-billy, Touchstone
**11** chowderhead, knuckle-head
**13** laughing-stock, poisson d'avril, proper Charlie

---

• **play the fool** **03** fon **04** daff **07** act dido **09** fool about, mess about, muck about **10** act the fool, act the goat, fool around, mess around, muck around **11** clown around, horse around **12** monkey around

## foolery
**05** farce, folly, larks **06** antics, capers, pranks **07** carry-on, daffing, fooling, waggery, zanyism **08** clowning, drollery, mischief, nonsense, trumpery **09** high jinks, horseplay, silliness **10** buffoonery, tomfoolery **11** shenanigans **12** childishness, monkey tricks **14** practical jokes

## foolhardiness
**08** boldness, rashness **10** imprudence **12** recklessness **13** impulsiveness

## foolhardy
**04** bold, rash **06** daring **08** kamikaze, reckless **09** daredevil, imprudent, impulsive **10** ill-advised, incautious **11** temerarious **13** irresponsible

## foolish
◊ *anagram indicator* **03** mad, twp **04** daft, dumb, fond, fool **05** barmy, batty, crazy, dilly, divvy, doilt, dotty, glaik, goofy, inane, inept, nutty, potty, seely, silly, wacky **06** absurd, doiled, dottle, insane, paltry, simple, stupid,

unwise **07** dottled, étourdi, fatuous, glaiket, glaikit, goatish, gudgeon, idiotic, moronic, peevish, risible, sottish, tomfool, unwitty, vacuous **08** étourdie, gormless, ignorant, imbecile, overfond **09** half-baked, idiotical, ill-judged, ludicrous, pointless, senseless **10** half-witted, idle-headed, ill-advised, pea-brained, ridiculous **11** hare-brained, injudicious, nonsensical **12** crack-brained, short-sighted, simple-minded, unreasonable **13** cockle-brained, ill-considered, out of your mind, rattle-brained, unintelligent

### foolishly

◊ *anagram indicator* **05** fonly, madly **06** daftly **07** crazily, ineptly, wackily **08** absurdly, stupidly, unwisely **09** fatuously, shallowly **10** mistakenly **11** idiotically, imprudently, senselessly **12** ill-advisedly, incautiously, indiscreetly, ridiculously **13** injudiciously **14** short-sightedly

### foolishness

**03** rot **04** bunk **05** balls, bilge, folly **06** bunkum, idiocy, lunacy, piffle **07** baloney, foolery, hogwash, inanity, madness, rubbish **08** claptrap, cobblers, daftness, nonsense, unreason, unwisdom, weakness **09** absurdity, craziness, incaution, meshugaas, mishegaas, niaiserie, poppycock, silliness, stupidity **10** imprudence, ineptitude **12** indiscretion **13** senselessness

### foolproof

**04** safe, sure **07** certain **08** fail-safe, sure-fire **09** unfailing **10** dependable, guaranteed, idiot-proof, infallible **11** trustworthy

### foot

**01** f **02** ft **03** end, leg, pad, paw, pes, toe **04** base, heel, hoof, kick, sole **05** dance, limit, paeon **06** border, bottom, dactyl, far end, iambus, tarsus **07** anapest, paeonic, pyrrhic, spondee, tootsie, trochee, trotter **08** anapaest, bacchius, choriamb, dochmius, molossus, tribrach **09** extremity **10** amphibrach, amphimacer, choriambus, foundation **12** antibacchius, tootsy-wootsy
• **discomfort of foot 04** corn
• **division of foot 04** inch
• **model of foot 04** last
• **part of foot 03** toe **04** arch, vola **06** instep

### football

**02** RL, RU **04** camp **06** soccer
*See also* **American football; Australian football**

*English league football teams:*

**03** QPR
**04** Bury
**06** Barnet, Fulham, Yeovil
**07** Arsenal, Burnley, Chelsea, Everton, Reading, Walsall, Watford, Wrexham
**08** Barnsley, Hull City, Millwall, Port Vale, Rochdale

**09** Blackpool, Brentford, Liverpool, Luton Town, Stoke City
**10** Aston Villa, Darlington, Gillingham, Portsmouth, Sunderland
**11** Bournemouth, Bristol City, Cardiff City, Chester City, Derby County, Grimsby Town, Ipswich Town, Leeds United, Lincoln City, Norwich City, Notts County, Southampton, Swansea City, Swindon Town
**12** Boston United, Bradford City, Chesterfield, Coventry City, Leyton Orient
**13** Bristol Rovers, Crystal Palace, Leicester City, Mansfield Town, Middlesbrough, Torquay United, West Ham United, Wigan Athletic
**14** Birmingham City, Carlisle United, Cheltenham Town, Crewe Alexandra, Hereford United, Manchester City, Oldham Athletic, Plymouth Argyle, Shrewsbury Town, Southend United, Tranmere Rovers
**15** Blackburn Rovers, Bolton Wanderers, Doncaster Rovers, Newcastle United, Northampton Town, Preston North End, Rotherham United, Sheffield United, Stockport County
**16** Charlton Athletic, Colchester United, Hartlepool United, Huddersfield Town, Macclesfield Town, Manchester United, Milton Keynes Dons, Nottingham Forest, Scunthorpe United, Tottenham Hotspur, Wycombe Wanderers
**17** Accrington Stanley, Queen's Park Rangers
**18** Peterborough United, Sheffield Wednesday, West Bromwich Albion
**21** Brighton and Hove Albion
**22** Wolverhampton Wanderers

*Scottish league football teams:*

**04** Hibs
**05** Clyde
**06** Celtic, Dundee, Gretna, Hearts
**07** Falkirk, Rangers
**08** Aberdeen, Arbroath, East Fife, Montrose, St Mirren
**09** Ayr United, Dumbarton, Elgin City, Hibernian, Peterhead, Stranraer
**10** Kilmarnock, Livingston, Motherwell, Queen's Park, Ross County
**11** Brechin City, Cowdenbeath, Raith Rovers, St Johnstone
**12** Albion Rovers, Dundee United
**13** Airdrie United, Alloa Athletic, Stenhousemuir
**14** Berwick Rangers, Forfar Athletic, Greenock Morton, Partick Thistle, Stirling Albion
**15** Queen of the South
**17** East Stirlingshire, Heart of Midlothian
**18** Hamilton Academical

**19** Dunfermline Athletic
**26** Inverness Caledonian Thistle

*European football teams include:*

**04** Ajax
**05** Lazio, Malmö, Parma, Porto
**06** Alavés, AS Roma, Bastia, Monaco, Napoli, Torino
**07** AC Milan, Antwerp, Benfica, Cologne, Español, FC Porto, Hamburg, Schalke
**08** Bordeaux, Juventus, Mallorca, Mechelen, Salzburg, Tom Tomsk, Valencia
**09** Barcelona, Feyenoord, FK Austria, Marseille, Sampdoria, St Etienne, Stuttgart, SV Hamburg, TSV Munich
**10** Anderlecht, Bellinzona, Club Bruges, Club Brugge, Dynamo Kiev, Fiorentina, Inter Milan, Real Madrid
**11** Bate Borisov, FC Magdeburg, Ferencvaros, Galatasaray, Hajduk Split, Litex Lovech, MTK Budapest, Rapid Vienna, Ujpest Dozsa, Wisla Krakow
**12** Banik Ostrava, Bayern Munich, Dinamo Zagreb, Gornik Zabrze, Moscow Dynamo, PSV Eindhoven, Real Zaragoza, Stade de Reims, Valenciennes, Werder Bremen
**13** Carl Zeiss Jena, Dynamo Tbilisi, IFK Gothenburg, Nordsjaelland, Panathinaikos, Standard Liège
**14** Athletic Bilbao, Atletico Madrid, Paris St Germain, Sporting Lisbon, Twente Enschede
**15** Bayer Leverkusen, Red Bull Salzburg, Red Star Belgrade, Shakhtar Donetsk, Steaua Bucharest

*Football club nicknames include:*

**02** O's, R's, U's
**03** Ton
**04** Bees, Boro, City, Dale, Dons, Gers, Jags, Owls, Pars, Pool, Posh, Rams, Reds, Sons, Well
**05** Arabs, Bhoys, Binos, Blues, Foxes, Gills, Gulls, Hoops, Irons, Lions, Loons, Shire, Spurs, Stags, Swans, Villa, Wasps
**06** Accies, Albion, Bairns, Blades, County, Eagles, Fifers, Hibees, Jambos, Killie, Latics, Pompey, Robins, Rovers, Royals, Saints, Tigers, United, Whites, Wolves
**07** Addicks, Baggies, Bantams, Buddies, Clarets, Glovers, Gunners, Hammers, Hatters, Hornets, Magpies, Pirates, Potters, Quakers, Red Imps, Shakers, Silkmen, Spiders, Terrors, Toffees, Villans
**08** Blue Toon, Bully Wee, Canaries, Cherries, Citizens, Cobblers, Diamonds, Filberts, Harriers, Jam Tarts, Mariners, Pilgrims, Saddlers, Seagulls, Sky Blues, Terriers, Trotters, Valiants, Villains, Warriors
**09** Black Cats, Bluebirds, Borderers,

Chairboys, Cottagers, Cumbrians, Dark Blues, Honest Men, Red Devils, Seasiders, Shrimpers, Spireites, Throstles, Toffeemen, Wee Rovers

**10** Blue Brazil, Doonhamers, Light Blues, Lilywhites, Livvy Lions, Minstermen, Railwaymen, Tangerines, Teddy Bears

**11** Gable Endies, Red Lichties, Tractor Boys

**12** Caley Thistle, Merry Millers

**13** Blue and Whites

**14** Black and Whites

---

*Football-related terms include:*

**03** box, cap, lob, net

**04** back, chip, dive, foul, goal, half, head, hole, loan, mark, pass, post, save, shot, trap, wall, wing

**05** bench, chest, cross, pitch

**06** assist, corner, double, futsal, goalie, handle, header, keeper, libero, nutmeg, one-two, onside, soccer, tackle, treble, volley, winger

**07** booking, caution, dribble, far post, forward, kick-off, offside, own goal, penalty, red card, referee, stopper, striker, sweeper, throw-in, whistle

**08** back heel, crossbar, dead ball, defender, free kick, friendly, full back, goal kick, goal line, half time, hand ball, hat-trick, left back, linesman, midfield, near post, outfield, play-offs, set piece, transfer, wall pass, wingback

**09** extra time, five-a-side, formation, give-and-go, goalmouth, kickabout, promotion, right back, touchline

**10** centre back, centre half, centre spot, corner flag, corner kick, goalkeeper, goalscorer, golden goal, half volley, injury time, man marking, midfielder, off-the-ball, penalty box, possession, relegation, sending off, silver goal, substitute, suspension, yellow card

**11** bicycle kick, goalkeeping, half-way line, keepie-uppie, obstruction, offside trap, penalty area, penalty kick, penalty spot, six-yard area, straight red, time wasting

**12** back-pass rule, Bosman ruling, centre circle, overhead kick, stoppage time

**13** centre forward, dangerous play, technical area

**14** fourth official, goal difference, relegation zone

**15** eighteen-yard box

## footballer

*Footballers and associated figures include:*

**03** Fry (Charles Burgess), **Law** (Denis)

**04** Best (George), **Dean** (Dixie), **Didi**, **Figo** (Luis), **Hall** (Sir John), **Owen** (Michael), **Pelé**, **Rush** (Ian), **Zico**, **Zoff** (Dino), **Zola** (Gianfranco)

**05** Adams (Tony), **Banks** (Gordon), **Busby** (Sir Matt), **Carey** (Johnny), **Giggs** (Ryan), **Greig** (John), **Henry** (Thierry), **Hurst** (Sir Geoff), **James** (Alex), **James** (David), **Messi** (Lionel), **Moore** (Bobby), **Revie** (Don), **Rimet** (Jules), **Rossi** (Paolo), **Stein** (Jock), **Young** (George)

**06** Baggio (Roberto), **Baresi** (Franco), **Barnes** (John), **Baxter** (Jim), **Bosman** (Jean-Marc), **Clough** (Brian), **Cruyff** (Johann), **Finney** (Sir Tom), **Ginola** (David), **Graham** (George), **Gullit** (Ruud), **Haynes** (Johnny), **Hoddle** (Glenn), **Keegan** (Kevin), **Lawton** (Tommy), **McColl** (Robert Smyth), **McStay** (Paul), **Mercer** (Joe), **Morton** (Alan Lauder), **Müller** (Gerd), **Puskas** (Ferenc), **Ramsey** (Sir Alf), **Robson** (Sir Bobby), **Robson** (Bryan), **Rooney** (Wayne), **Seaman** (David), **Stiles** (Nobby), **St John** (Ian), **Walker** (Tommy), **Wenger** (Arsene), **Wright** (Billy), **Wright** (Ian), **Yashin** (Lev), **Zidane** (Zinedine)

**07** Ardiles (Osvaldo), **Beckham** (David), **Bremner** (Billy), **Butcher** (Terry), **Cantona** (Eric), **Capello** (Fabio), **Charles** (John), **DiCanio** (Paolo), **Eastham** (George), **Edwards** (Duncan), **Eusebio** (Silva), **Greaves** (Jimmy), **Lampard** (Frank), **Lineker** (Gary), **Macleod** (Ally), **Mannion** (Wilfred), **McCoist** (Ally), **McNeill** (Billy), **Paisley** (Bob), **Platini** (Michel), **Rivaldo**, **Ronaldo**, **Ronaldo** (Cristiano), **Shankly** (Bill), **Shearer** (Alan), **Shilton** (Peter), **Souness** (Graeme), **Toshack** (John), **Waddell** (Willie), **Walcott** (Theo)

**08** Bergkamp (Dennis), **Charlton** (Sir Bobby), **Charlton** (Jack), **Dalglish** (Kenny), **Docherty** (Tommy), **Eriksson** (Sven-Göran), **Ferguson** (Sir Alex), **Fontaine** (Just), **Harkness** (Jack), **Jennings** (Pat), **Johnston** (Maurice), **Maradona** (Diego), **Matthaus** (Lothar), **Matthews** (Sir Stanley), **Mourinho** (José), **Nicholls** (Sir Douglas Ralph), **Rivelino** (Roberto)

**09** Batistuta (Gabriel), **Collymore** (Stan), **Di Stefano** (Alfredo), **Garrincha**, **Gascoigne** (Paul 'Gazza'), **Greenwood** (Ron), **Johnstone** (Jimmy), **Klinsmann** (Jurgen), **Lofthouse** (Nat), **Van Basten** (Marco)

**10** Schmeichel (Peter)

**11** Beckenbauer (Franz)

**12** Blanchflower (Danny)

---

• **footballers** **02** FA **03** SFA

## footing

**04** base, cost, grip, rank, trod **05** basis, coast, coste, dance, grade, state, terms, track, tread, troad, trode **06** ground, status, troade **07** balance, support, surface, toehold **08** foothold, position, roothold, standing **09** relations **10** conditions, foundation **12** relationship

## footling

**05** minor, petty **06** paltry **07** trivial **08** piffling, trifling **10** irrelevant **13** insignificant

## footloose

**04** free **09** available, fancy-free **10** unattached, uninvolved **11** uncommitted

## footnote

**04** note **05** gloss **07** comment, subtext **08** scholium **10** annotation, commentary, marginalia **12** marginal note

## footnotes

**04** note **05** gloss **07** scholia **10** annotation, commentary, marginalia **12** marginal note

## footprint

**03** pad, pug **04** mark, seal, step **05** prick, spoor, trace, track, trail, tread **07** ichnite, vestige **08** footmark, footstep **09** ichnolite **13** ornithichnite

## footprints

**04** slot

## footstep

**04** plod, step **05** track, tramp, tread **06** trudge **08** footfall, footmark

## footwear

---

*Footwear includes:*

**03** dap, tie

**04** boot, clog, geta, mule, pump, shoe, vibs

**05** jelly, sabot, tacky, thong, wader, welly

**06** bootee, brogue, casual, galosh, lace-up, loafer, Oxford, patten, sandal, slip-on, thongs

**07** gumboot, slipper, sneaker, tap shoe, trainer

**08** boat shoe, deck shoe, flip-flop, jazz shoe, Mary Jane, moccasin, overshoe, pantofle, plimsoll, rock boot, rock shoe, sandshoe

**09** court shoe, Derry boot, rugby boot, slingback, wedge heel

**10** ballet shoe, combat boot, Doc Martens®, espadrille, hiking-boot, riding boot, rubber boot, tennis shoe

**11** bowling shoe, Chelsea boot, Hush Puppies®, running shoe, walking boot, wellingtons

**12** climbing boot, football boot, platform heel, stiletto heel, winklepicker

**13** beetle-crusher

**14** beetle-crushers, brothel creeper, wellington boot

**15** brothel-creepers

---

*See also* **boot; clothes, clothing**

## fop

**04** beau, dude, toff **05** dandy, swell **07** coxcomb, peacock **08** muscadin, popinjay, skipjack **09** exquisite, fantastic **10** Jack-a-dandy **11** petit maître **12** barber-monger

## foppish

**04** vain **05** apish, natty **06** dainty, dapper, dressy, fallal, la-di-da, spruce

**for**
07 fangled, finical 08 affected, dandyish, preening, swellish 09 coxcombic, dandified, fantastic 10 coxcomical 11 coxcombical, fantastical, overdressed

**for**
03 pro

**forage**
04 feed, food, guar, hunt, loot, prog, raid, seek 05 étape, foray, scour 06 fodder, invade, ladino, ravage, search 07 assault, pickeer, plunder, ransack, rummage, scratch 08 mung bean, scavenge 09 cast about, gama grass, pasturage, provender 10 foodstuffs, provisions

**foray**
04 raid 05 sally, swoop 06 attack, creach, creagh, forray, inroad, ravage, sortie 07 assault, attempt, journey, spreagh, venture 08 invasion 09 incursion, offensive 14 reconnaissance

**forbear**
04 hold, omit, stay, stop 05 avoid, cease, pause 06 desist, eschew 07 abstain, decline, refrain 08 ancestor, hesitate, hold back, keep from, withhold

**forbearance**
05 mercy 06 pardon 08 clemency, leniency, mildness, patience 09 avoidance, endurance, restraint, tolerance 10 abstinence, indulgence, indulgency, moderation, refraining, self-denial, sufferance, temperance, toleration 11 longanimity, resignation, self-control 13 long-suffering

**forbearing**
04 easy, mild 07 clement, lenient, patient 08 merciful, moderate, tolerant 09 forgiving, indulgent 10 restrained 13 long-suffering 14 self-controlled

**forbid**
03 ban, bar 04 deny, tabu, veto, warn 05 block, debar, taboo 06 defend, enjoin, forsay, hinder, not let, outlaw, refuse 07 exclude, foresay, forwarn, inhibit, prevent, rule out 08 disallow, forewarn, forspeak, not allow, preclude, prohibit, restrain 09 blacklist, discharge, forespeak, interdict, proscribe 13 excommunicate 14 contraindicate

**forbidden**
02 nl 04 tabu, tapu, tref 05 not on, taboo, trefa, treif 06 banned, vetoed 07 illicit, profane 08 debarred, defended, excluded, outlawed, unlawful, verboten 10 contraband, prohibited, proscribed, restrained 11 out of bounds

**forbidding**
04 grim 05 harsh, stern 06 severe 07 awesome, hostile, ominous 08 daunting, menacing, sinister 09 repulsive 10 Acherontic, foreboding, formidable, off-putting, unfriendly, uninviting 11 frightening, hard-grained, prohibitory, threatening 15 unprepossessing

**force**
◇ *anagram indicator* 01 F 02 od 03 put, vis, zap 04 army, body, care, cops, dint, gist, make, odyl, pull, push, sway, unit, urge 05 blast, bully, corps, crack, drive, exact, group, impel, might, odyle, power, press, prise, sense, squad, stuff, troop, wrest, wring 06 coerce, compel, duress, dynamo, effort, energy, extort, impose, lean on, muscle, oblige, patrol, propel, ravish, stress, strive, thrust, vigour, wrench 07 cogency, essence, extract, impetus, impulse, inflict, meaning, passion, platoon, stamina 08 armament, bulldoze, coercion, division, dynamism, emphasis, exertion, momentum, pressure, railroad, regiment, squadron, strength, validity, vehement, violence, vitality 09 battalion, break open, constrain, force open, influence, intensity, necessity, pressgang, substance, the screws, vehemence, waterfall 10 aggression, compulsion, constraint, detachment, pressurize 11 arm-twisting, enforcement 12 significance 13 determination, effectiveness, put pressure on 14 persuasiveness, put the screws on, the third degree

*See also* **army; police**
• **in force** 05 valid 07 binding, current, working 08 in crowds, in droves, in flocks 09 effective, operative 10 in strength 11 functioning, in operation 14 in great numbers, in large numbers

**forced**
◇ *anagram indicator* 02 sf 03 sfz 05 false, stiff 06 wooden 07 binding, feigned, stilted 08 affected, enforced, laboured, overdone, sforzato, strained 09 compelled, contrived, excessive, insincere, mandatory, sforzando, unnatural 10 artificial, compulsory, far-fetched, non-natural, obligatory 11 constrained, involuntary

**forceful**
05 gutty, valid 06 cogent, mighty, potent, strong, urgent 07 dynamic, telling, weighty 08 emphatic, forcible, powerful, vehement, vigorous 09 assertive, effective, energetic 10 compelling, convincing, impressive, persuasive 11 high-powered 12 high-pressure

**forcefully**
07 con brio 08 strongly 10 powerfully, vehemently, vigorously 11 assertively, effectively 12 convincingly, emphatically, persuasively 13 energetically

**forcible**
04 vive 05 pithy 06 cogent, forced, mighty, potent, strong 07 by force, drastic, marrowy, telling, violent, weighty 08 coercive, forceful, powerful, vehement 09 effective, energetic 10 aggressive, compelling, compulsory, impressive, using force 11 energetical

**forcibly**
03 out 04 hard 07 by force 09 vi et armis, violently 10 using force, vehemently, vigorously, willy-nilly 11 under duress 12 compulsorily, emphatically, obligatorily 15 against your will, under compulsion

**ford**
04 rack, wade 05 drift 06 Model T 08 causeway, crossing 09 tin lizzie 11 Irish bridge 13 crossing place

**forebear**
06 father, tupuna 08 ancestor 10 antecedent, forefather, forerunner, progenitor 11 predecessor 12 primogenitor

**foreboding**
04 fear, omen, sign 05 dread, token, worry 06 hoodoo 07 anxiety, feeling, presage, warning 09 abodement, intuition, misgiving, suspicion 10 prediction, sixth sense 11 premonition 12 apprehension, presentiment 15 prognostication

**forecast**
03 tip 04 omen, perm 05 augur, guess 06 augury, divine, expect, tip off 07 foresee, metcast, outlook, portend, predict, presage, project 08 estimate, foretell, forewarn, prophecy, prophesy 09 calculate, prognosis 10 anticipate, conjecture, prediction, projection 11 calculation, expectation, extrapolate, forewarning, guesstimate, permutation, second-guess, speculation 13 extrapolation, prognosticate, weather report 15 prognostication
*See also* **shipping**

**forefather**
06 father 08 ancestor, forebear 10 ancestress, antecedent, forerunner, progenitor 11 predecessor 12 primogenitor

**forefront**
03 van 04 fore, head, lead 05 front 06 vaward 08 vanguard 09 front line, spearhead 10 avant-garde, firing line 11 leading edge 15 leading position

**forego, forgo**
05 leave, waive, yield 06 abjure, eschew, give up, pass up, resign 07 abandon, forfeit, precede 08 renounce 09 do without, go without, sacrifice, surrender 10 relinquish 11 abstain from, refrain from

**foregoing**
05 above, prior 06 former 07 earlier 08 previous 09 aforesaid, precedent, preceding 10 antecedent 14 aforementioned

**foregone**
• **foregone conclusion** 04 fact 09 certainty, sure thing 10 inevitable 13 inevitability

**foreground**
04 fore 05 front 06 centre 09 forefront, limelight 10 prominence 15 leading position

## forehead
**04** brow **05** front **06** metope, temple
**07** temples **08** audacity **10** confidence

## foreign
◊ *anagram indicator* ◊ *foreign word
indicator* **03** odd **05** alien, fraim, fremd
**06** ethnic, exotic, forane, forren, fremit
**07** distant, faraway, migrant, outside,
strange, unknown **08** borrowed,
étranger, exterior, external, imported,
overseas, peculiar **09** barbarian,
étrangère, extrinsic, immigrant
**10** extraneous, forinsecal, outlandish,
tramontane, unfamiliar
**11** unconnected **12** adventitious
**13** international
*See also* **nationality**

## foreigner
**05** alien **06** gaijin, taipan **07** incomer,
migrant, visitor **08** étranger,
newcomer, outsider, stranger
**09** Ausländer, barbarian, étrangère,
immigrant, outlander, uitlander
**10** tramontane

## foreknowledge
**09** foresight, prevision **10** prescience
**11** forewarning, premonition, second
sight **12** clairvoyance, precognition
**15** prognostication

## foreleg
**04** gamb

## foreman
**04** bo's'n, boss **05** bosun **06** gaffer,
ganger, honcho, induna, leader
**07** manager, overman, steward,
topsman **08** gangsman, overseer
**09** boatswain, straw boss
**10** chancellor, charge hand, supervisor
**14** superintendent

## foremost
◊ *head selection indicator* **03** top, van
**04** main **05** chief, first, front, prime
**07** central, highest, leading, premier,
primary, supreme, up front
**08** advanced, cardinal, vanguard
**09** paramount, principal, uppermost
**10** pre-eminent **13** most important

## foreordained
**05** fated **08** destined **09** appointed,
predevote **10** foredoomed
**11** prearranged, predestined,
preordained **12** predestinate
**13** predetermined

## forerunner
**04** omen, sign **05** envoy, token
**06** herald **07** pioneer **08** ancestor
**09** harbinger, messenger, precurrer,
precursor **10** antecedent, forefather
**11** forewarning, predecessor **12** vaunt-
courier
• **be a forerunner** **04** lead, pace

## foresee
**06** divine, expect, prevue **07** predict,
preview, previse **08** envisage,
forebode, forecast, foreknow, foretell,
prophesy **10** anticipate
**13** prognosticate

## foreshadow
**04** bode, mean, type **05** augur **06** signal
**07** portend, predict, presage, promise,

signify, suggest **08** indicate, prophesy
**09** adumbrate, forepoint, prefigure
**13** prognosticate

## foreshore
**04** hard

## foresight
**04** care **06** vision **07** caution
**08** forecast, planning, prudence
**09** prevision, provision, readiness
**10** precaution, prescience, providence
**11** discernment, forethought,
prospection **12** anticipation,
perspicacity, preparedness
**13** judiciousness **14** circumspection,
discrimination, far-sightedness
**15** forward planning

## forest
**04** bosk, wood **05** Arden, trees, woods
**06** rustic, sylvan, timber **07** boscage
**08** Sherwood, tree farm, woodland
**09** backwoods

---

*Forests and woods include:*

---

| | |
|---|---|
| **04** | bush, gapó |
| **05** | brush, igapó, monte, selva, taiga, urman |
| **06** | boreal, jungle, mallee, maquis, pinery |
| **07** | coastal, garigue, lowland, macchie, wetland |
| **08** | caatinga, garrigue, littoral, mangrove |
| **09** | broadleaf, chaparral, deciduous, evergreen, greenwood, temperate |
| **10** | coniferous, equatorial, peat forest, plantation, rainforest |
| **11** | cloud forest, heath forest, lignum-scrub, lignum-swamp, mallee scrub, moist forest |
| **12** | várzea forest |
| **13** | ancient forest, gallery forest, mangrove swamp, savanna forest |
| **14** | moist evergreen |

---

## forestall
**03** bar **04** balk, beat, stop **05** avert,
lurch, parry **06** hinder, impede, thwart
**07** head off, obviate, pre-empt,
prevent, ward off **08** obstruct,
preclude, stave off **09** frustrate,
intercept **10** anticipate, get ahead of
**11** second-guess

## forested
**05** bosky **06** wooded **12** reafforested

## forester
**06** foster, walker **08** woodsman

## forestry
**09** woodcraft **10** dendrology
**11** forestation, woodmanship
**12** silviculture, sylviculture
**13** afforestation, arboriculture

## foretaste
**05** whiff **06** prevue, sample, taster
**07** earnest, example, pre-echo,
preview, trailer, warning **08** antepast,
specimen **09** appetizer, avant-goût,
foretoken **10** anticipate, indication
**11** forewarning, prelibation,
premonition **12** anticipation,
pregustation

## foretell
**04** bode, spae **05** augur, write **06** divine
**07** bespeak, foresay, foresee, predict,
presage, signify **08** forebode, forecast,
foreread, forewarn, indicate, prophesy,
soothsay **10** foreshadow
**13** prognosticate

## forethought
**07** caution **08** planning, prudence
**09** foresight, provision **10** precaution
**11** discernment, preparation
**12** anticipation, perspicacity
**13** judiciousness **14** circumspection,
far-sightedness **15** forward planning

## forever
**02** ay **03** aye **04** ever **06** always **07** à
jamais, for good **08** evermore
**09** endlessly, eternally **10** all the time,
constantly, for all time **11** continually,
incessantly, permanently, perpetually
**12** interminably, persistently, till
doomsday **13** everlastingly **15** till
kingdom come

## forewarn
**04** warn **05** alert, weird **06** advise,
forbid, tip off **07** apprise, caution,
previse **08** admonish, dissuade **10** give
notice, precaution **11** preadmonish

## forewarning
**06** tip-off **10** forerunner **11** premonition
**12** early warning **13** advance notice
**14** advance warning

## foreword
**07** preface, prelims **08** prologue
**11** frontmatter **12** introduction,
prolegomenon

## forfeit
**04** fine, lose, loss **05** cheat, forgo
**06** forego, give up, pass up, sconce
**07** abandon, damages, penalty **08** hand
over, renounce **09** sacrifice, surrender
**10** amercement, confiscate, relinquish,
rue-bargain **12** confiscation
**13** sequestration **14** relinquishment

## forfeiture
**04** loss **07** escheat **08** forgoing, giving
up **09** attainder, déchéance, foregoing,
sacrifice, surrender **12** confiscation
**13** sequestration **14** relinquishment

## forge
◊ *anagram indicator* **04** cast, copy, fake,
form, make, tilt, work **05** build, feign,
found, frame, mould, shape, smith
**06** create, devise, invent, smithy, stithy
**07** beat out, falsify, fashion, imitate,
stiddie **08** simulate **09** construct,
hammer out **11** counterfeit, put
together, rivet hearth **13** beat into
shape
• **forge ahead** **07** advance
**08** progress **09** go forward **11** make
headway, move forward, push forward
**12** make progress, move steadily

## forged
◊ *anagram indicator* **04** fake, sham
**05** bogus, faked, false, pseud, snide
**06** copied, phoney, pirate, pseudo
**07** feigned, simular **08** borrowed,
spurious **09** imitation, pretended,
simulated **10** artificial, fraudulent
**11** counterfect, counterfeit

**forger**
05 faker 06 coiner, framer 09 contriver, falsifier 10 fabricator 13 counterfeiter

**forgery**
03 dud 04 copy, fake, sham 05 fraud 06 deceit, faking, phoney 07 replica 09 imitation 11 counterfeit, falsi crimen 12 reproduction 13 falsification 14 counterfeiting 15 counterfeisance, counterfesaunce

**forget**
04 fail, omit, wipe 05 dry up 06 corpse, ignore 07 dismiss, let slip, neglect, unlearn 08 not place, overlook, put aside 09 disregard 11 disremember, leave behind, lose sight of, misremember 12 put behind you 13 think no more of 14 fail to remember
• **forget yourself** 09 be naughty, misbehave 11 behave badly

**forgetful**
03 lax 06 dreamy, remiss 08 careless, heedless 09 negligent, oblivious, unheeding 10 abstracted, distracted, neglectful 11 inattentive, not all there, preoccupied 12 absent-minded 14 scatterbrained

**forgetfulness**
05 lapse 07 amnesia, laxness, neglect 08 oblivion 10 dreaminess 11 abstraction, inattention 12 carelessness, heedlessness, obliviscence 13 obliviousness, wool-gathering

**forgivable**
05 minor, petty 06 slight, venial 08 innocent, trifling 09 excusable 10 condonable, pardonable

**forgive**
05 clear, remit, spare 06 acquit, excuse, let off, pardon 07 absolve, condone, let it go 08 overlook 09 exculpate, exonerate, shake on it 10 shake hands 13 think no more of 14 bury the hatchet

**forgiveness**
05 mercy 06 excuse, pardon 07 amnesty 08 clemency, leniency, oblivion 09 acquittal, remission 10 absolution, misericord 11 condonation, exoneration, misericorde

**forgiving**
04 kind, mild 06 humane 07 clement, lenient, pitying 08 merciful, placable, tolerant 09 indulgent, remissive 10 forbearing 11 magnanimous, soft-hearted 13 compassionate

**forgo**
see **forego, forgo**

**forgotten**
04 gone, lost, past 06 buried, bygone 07 ignored, omitted 09 neglected, oblivious, out of mind 10 blotted out, in the shade, left behind, overlooked, past recall, unrecalled 11 disregarded, obliterated, unretrieved 12 unremembered 13 irrecoverable, irretrievable 15 in the wilderness

**fork**
01 Y 04 part 05 grain, graip, prong, spear, split, twist 06 branch, crotch, divide 07 diverge, furcate, toaster 08 division, junction, separate 09 bifurcate, branching, branch off, furcation, tormenter, tormentor 10 divaricate, divergence, separation 11 bifurcation 12 divarication, intersection, toasting iron 14 go separate ways
• **fork out** 03 pay 04 give 05 pay up 06 pony up 07 cough up, stump up 08 shell out

**forked**
05 split, tined 06 furcal 07 divided, furcate, pronged, Y-shaped 08 biramous, branched, furcated, furcular 09 bifurcate, branching, deceitful, forficate, insincere, separated 10 trifurcate 11 divaricated

**forlorn**
◇ anagram indicator 03 sad 04 lost 06 bereft, lonely 07 unhappy 08 deserted, desolate, forsaken, helpless, homeless, hopeless, pathetic, pitiable, wretched 09 abandoned, cheerless, desperate, destitute, forgotten, miserable, neglected 10 despairing, drearisome, friendless, uncared-for 12 disconsolate

**forlornly**
05 sadly 06 in vain 09 miserably, to no avail, unhappily 10 hopelessly 11 desperately, pointlessly 12 despondently 14 unsuccessfully

**form**
◇ anagram indicator 03 cut, set 04 cast, face, grow, kind, make, mode, rite, sort, trim, turn, type, year 05 bench, build, class, forge, found, frame, genre, genus, grade, guise, model, mould, order, paper, set up, shape, sheet, style, usage 06 appear, beauty, create, custom, design, devise, draw up, fettle, figure, format, health, line up, make up, manner, nature, ritual, show up, stream, system 07 acquire, arrange, compose, develop, fashion, fitness, manners, outline, pattern, produce, serve as, species, spirits, variety 08 assemble, ceremony, comprise, conceive, contrive, document, organize, planning, protocol 09 be a part of, behaviour, character, condition, construct, establish, etiquette, formation, formulate, framework, structure, take shape 10 appearance, constitute, convention, regularity, silhouette 11 application, arrangement, crystallize, description, disposition, manufacture, materialize, put together 12 construction, organization, the done thing 13 become visible, configuration, manifestation, questionnaire 15 application form, correct practice, polite behaviour

**formal**
03 dry, set 04 prim, sane 05 aloof, exact, fixed, rigid, stiff 06 proper, pusser, remote, ritual, solemn, starch, strict 07 correct, ordered, orderly, outward, precise, regular, starchy, stately, stilted 08 academic, approved, arranged, black tie, literary, methodic, official, orthodox, reserved, standard 09 customary, essential, organized, unbending 10 ceremonial, controlled, inflexible, methodical, prescribed 11 ceremonious, established, perfunctory, punctilious, ritualistic, strait-laced, symmetrical, traditional 12 conventional

**formality**
03 ice 04 form, rite, rule 06 custom, ritual, starch 07 decorum, red tape, wiggery 08 ceremony, pedantry, protocol 09 etiquette, procedure, propriety, punctilio, sociality, stiffness 10 convention, politeness 11 bureaucracy, correctness 12 matter of form 13 spit and polish 15 ceremoniousness, conventionality

**formalization**
08 ordering 09 arranging 11 arrangement, structuring 12 arrangements, confirmation, organization 15 standardization, systematization

**formalize**
03 fix, set 05 order 06 affirm, ordain, ratify 07 arrange, confirm, stylize 08 organize 09 ritualize, structure 10 make formal, regularize 11 standardize, systematize 12 make official

**formally**
06 primly 07 exactly, rigidly 08 properly, ritually, solemnly 09 correctly, precisely 10 formaliter, inflexibly, officially 12 ceremonially, methodically 13 punctiliously 14 conventionally

**format**
03 GIF, PDF, PNG, RTF, ZIP 04 form, JPEG, look, plan, TIFF, type 05 order, shape, style 06 design, layout, make-up 07 pattern, tabloid 08 portrait 09 landscape, letterbox, structure 10 appearance, dimensions, widescreen 11 arrangement 12 construction, presentation 13 configuration

**formation**
04 make 05 order 06 design, figure, format, layout, make-up, making, series 07 pattern, phalanx, shaping 08 building, creation, founding, grouping, starting 09 emergence, structure 10 appearance, generation, production 11 arrangement, composition, development, disposition, institution, manufacture 12 constitution, construction, inauguration, organization 13 configuration, establishment

**formative**
06 creant, pliant 07 growing, guiding, plastic, shaping 08 dominant, moulding 09 malleable, mouldable, sensitive, teachable 11 controlling, determining, influential, susceptible

**13** determinative, developmental **14** impressionable

**former**
**02** ex- **03** old **04** auld, fore, late, once, onst, past **05** above, first, olden, prior **06** bygone, of yore, whilom **07** ancient, earlier, long ago, old-time, one-time, quondam **08** ci-devant, departed, long-gone, previous, pristine, sometime **09** erstwhile, foregoing, preceding **10** antecedent, historical **14** first-mentioned

**formerly**
**04** erst, once, onst **05** as was, earst, of old **06** before **07** earlier, whilere **08** ci-devant, erewhile, hitherto, sometime, while-ere **09** at one time, erstwhile, in the past, yesterday **10** heretofore, previously **12** historically **15** at an earlier time

**formidable**
**04** huge **05** great, scary, stiff, stoor, stour, sture **06** gorgon, no mean, shrewd, spooky, stowre **07** awesome, fearful, mammoth, onerous **08** alarming, colossal, daunting, dreadful, horrific, menacing, powerful, terrific **09** frightful, leviathan **10** horrifying, impressive, prodigious, staggering, terrifying, tremendous **11** challenging, frightening, mind-blowing, redoubtable, threatening **12** intimidating, overwhelming

**formidably**
**07** awfully **09** fearfully **10** dreadfully, menacingly, shockingly **11** frightfully **12** horrifically, tremendously **14** overwhelmingly

**formless**
**05** vague **06** inform **07** chaotic **08** confused, inchoate, indigest, nebulous, unformed, unshaped **09** amorphous, shapeless **10** incoherent, indefinite **12** disorganized, invertebrate **13** indeterminate

**formula**
**03** mix, way **04** code, form, rule **05** spell **06** method, recipe, rubric **07** precept, wording **08** equation, exorcism, fog index, proposal, protocol **09** blueprint, principle, procedure, technique **10** convention **12** prescription **13** set expression **15** fixed expression
• **Formula One** *see* **racing**

**formulate**
**04** cast, form, plan **05** found, frame, state **06** create, define, design, detail, devise, draw up, evolve, invent, map out **07** compose, develop, express, formate, itemize, lay down, prepare, propose, put down, set down, specify, think up, work out **08** conceive **09** originate, symbolize **10** articulate

**formulation**
**07** formula, framing, product **08** creating, devising **10** conception, definition, expression, production **11** composition, development, preparation **13** specification

**fornication**
**06** affair **07** avoutry, liaison **08** adultery, cheating, idolatry **09** two-timing **10** flirtation, infidelity, unchastity **12** entanglement **13** a bit on the side, playing around **14** unfaithfulness **15** extramarital sex, playing the field

**forsake**
**04** jilt, quit **05** chuck, ditch, forgo, leave, waive **06** desert, disown, forego, give up, reject **07** abandon, cast off, discard, forlese **08** jettison, renounce, set aside **09** destitute, repudiate, surrender, throw over **10** relinquish **12** have done with **14** turn your back on **15** leave in the lurch

**forsaken**
**04** lorn **06** dreary, jilted, lonely, remote **07** cast off, forlorn, ignored, outcast, shunned **08** derelict, deserted, desolate, disowned, isolated, lasslorn, lovelorn, marooned, rejected, solitary **09** abandoned, destitute, discarded, neglected **10** friendless **11** godforsaken **14** left in the lurch

**forswear**
**03** lie **04** deny, drop, reny **05** forgo, renay, reney **06** abjure, cut out, disown, forego, give up, jack in, pack in, recant, reject, renege **07** abandon, disavow, forsake, retract **08** disclaim, renounce **09** do without, repudiate **15** perjure yourself

**fort**
**02** Ft, pa **03** pah **04** camp, keep, rath **05** tower **06** castle, donjon, turret **07** citadel, parapet, redoubt, station **08** fortress, garrison, martello, pentagon **09** castellum **10** blockhouse, stronghold, watchtower **11** battlements **13** fortification, martello tower

**forte**
**01** f **04** bent, gift, loud **05** skill **06** métier, talent **08** aptitude, strength **10** speciality **11** strong point

**forth**
**02** on **03** off, out **04** away **05** furth **06** abroad, onward **07** forward, onwards, outside **08** forwards, into view **13** into existence

**forthcoming**
**04** open **05** frank, on tap, ready **06** chatty, coming, direct, future **07** voluble **08** expected, friendly, imminent, sociable, upcoming **09** available, expansive, impending, projected, talkative **10** accessible, loquacious, obtainable, up for grabs **11** approaching, informative, in the offing, prospective **13** communicative **14** at your disposal, conversational

**forthright**
**04** bold, open **05** blunt, frank, plain **06** at once, candid, direct, honest **07** up-front **09** outspoken, trenchand, trenchant **10** four-square **11** plain-spoken **15** straightforward

**forthwith**
**03** eft **04** asap, away **06** at once, pronto **07** quickly **08** directly, eftsoons **09** instantly, right away **11** immediately

**12** straightaway, there and then, without delay

**fortification**
**08** munition **09** munitions **10** munifience, protection, stronghold **12** embattlement, entrenchment **13** reinforcement, strengthening

---

*Fortifications include:*

---

**02** pa
**03** pah
**04** bawn, fort, gate, keep, laer, moat, wall
**05** ditch, fence, hedge, limes, tower
**06** abatis, castle, glacis, laager, sconce, trench, Vauban
**07** barrier, bastion, bulwark, citadel, defence, flanker, moineau, outwork, parapet, pillbox, rampart, redoubt, sandbag
**08** buttress, cavalier, fortress, outworks, palisade, stockade
**09** barricade, earthwork, fieldwork, fortalice, gabionade, gatehouse, razor wire
**10** barbed wire, bridgehead, fieldworks, trou de loup
**11** battlements, buttressing, crémaillère
**13** cheval-de-frise, Martello tower
**14** motte-and-bailey
**15** circumvallation, contravallation

**fortify**
**04** fort, load, wall **05** boost, brace, cheer, cover, fence, guard, mound **06** buoy up, castle, defend, munify, munite, revive, secure **07** bulwark, hearten, protect, rampart, shore up, support, sustain **08** buttress, embattle, energize, entrench, garrison, intrench, reassure **09** encourage, reinforce **10** invigorate, strengthen

**fortitude**
**04** grit, guts **05** nerve, pluck, spine **06** mettle, valour **07** bravery, courage **08** backbone, firmness, patience, stoicism, strength, tenacity **09** endurance, hardihood, willpower **10** resolution **11** forbearance **12** perseverance **13** determination **14** strength of mind

**fortress**
**04** burg, fort, keep **05** guard, place, tower **06** casbah, castle, kasbah **07** alcázar, citadel, defence **08** bastille, fastness, garrison **09** fortalice **10** stronghold **11** battlements **13** fortification

**fortuitous**
**05** fluky, lucky **06** casual, chance, random **09** arbitrary, fortunate, haphazard, unplanned **10** accidental, incidental, unexpected, unforeseen **12** providential **13** unintentional

**fortuitously**
**07** luckily **08** at random, by chance, casually, randomly **11** arbitrarily, fortunately, haphazardly **12** accidentally, incidentally, unexpectedly **13** inadvertently **15** unintentionally

## Fortuna
**05** Tyche

## fortunate
**04** rich, well **05** canny, happy, lucky, seely **06** timely **07** blessed, well-off **08** favoured **09** fairytale, opportune, promising, well-timed **10** auspicious, convenient, favourable, felicitous, fortuitous, profitable, propitious, prosperous, successful **11** encouraging, flourishing **12** advantageous, providential

## fortunately
**07** happily, luckily **10** thankfully **12** conveniently **13** encouragingly **14** providentially

## fortune
**03** cup, hap, lot **04** bomb, doom, fall, fate, life, luck, mint, pile, seal, seel, seil, sele **05** means, speed **06** assets, befall, bundle, chance, estate, future, income, packet, riches, wealth **07** destiny, heiress, history, portion, success **08** accident, big bucks, opulence, position, property, treasure **09** affluence, condition, megabucks, situation, substance **10** experience, prosperity, providence **11** coincidence, possessions, serendipity **13** circumstances **14** state of affairs
• **loss of fortune** **04** ruin **05** decay
• **sudden good fortune** **08** windfall

## fortune-teller
**04** seer **05** augur, sibyl **06** oracle **07** diviner, prophet, psychic **08** telepath **09** visionary **10** astrologer, prophetess, soothsayer **11** clairvoyant

## fortune-telling
*see* **divination**

## forty
**02** XL
• **forty winks** **03** nap **04** rest **05** sleep

## forum
**03** BBS **05** arena, stage **06** caucus, debate **07** meeting, rostrum **08** assembly **09** gathering, symposium **10** conference, discussion **12** meeting-place

## forward
**02** on, to **03** aid, out **04** back, bold, fore, head, help, mail, pert, post, send, ship **05** ahead, brash, cocky, early, first, forth, fresh, front, hurry, pushy, ready, speed **06** assist, avanti, brazen, cheeky, favour, foster, future, hasten, onward, pass on, send on, step up **07** advance, deliver, earnest, frontal, further, go-ahead, leading, onwards, promote, speed up, support **08** advanced, dispatch, expedite, familiar, foremost, forwards, impudent, into view, long-term, redirect **09** advancing, assertive, audacious, barefaced, confident, encourage, long-range, officious, premature, presuming, readdress, thrusting, transport **10** accelerate, aggressive, facilitate, medium-term, precocious **11** impertinent, into the open, medium-range, progressing, progressive, prospective

**12** enterprising, overfamiliar, presumptuous, well-advanced **13** over-assertive, over-confident, progressively, well-developed **14** forward-looking

## forward-looking
**04** goey **06** modern **07** dynamic, go-ahead, liberal **09** go-getting, reforming **10** avant-garde, far-sighted, innovative **11** enlightened, progressive **12** enterprising

## forwardness
**04** neck **05** cheek **08** audacity, boldness, pertness **09** brashness, brass neck, impudence, pushiness **10** brazenness, cheekiness, confidence **11** presumption **12** forth-putting, impertinence **14** aggressiveness, over-confidence

## forwards
**02** on **03** out **04** pack **05** ahead, forth **06** onward **07** forward, onwards **13** progressively

## fossil
**05** relic **07** remains, remnant **09** reliquiae **10** antiquated

*Fossils include:*

**04** bone, cast
**05** amber, shell
**06** burrow
**07** bivalve, crinoid
**08** ammonite, baculite, dinosaur, echinoid, nautilus, skeleton
**09** belemnite, coccolith, coprolite, fish teeth, steinkern, trilobite
**10** cast fossil, gastrolith, graptolite, snakestone
**11** ichnofossil, microfossil, mould fossil, resin fossil, sharks' teeth, trace fossil
**12** Burgess shale, stromatolite

## fossilized
**04** dead **05** passé, stony **07** archaic, extinct **08** hardened, obsolete, ossified, outmoded **09** out of date, petrified **10** antiquated **11** prehistoric **12** antediluvian, old-fashioned **13** anachronistic

## foster
**03** aid **04** back, feed, help, hold, rear **05** boost, nurse, raise **06** assist, foment, mother, nousle, nuzzle, uphold **07** advance, bring up, care for, cherish, further, harbour, nourish, noursle, nousell, nurture, promote, support, sustain **08** forester, incubate **09** cultivate, encourage, entertain, look after, stimulate **10** make much of, take care of

## foster-child
**04** dalt **05** dault

## foul
◇ *anagram indicator* **03** bad, jam, low, paw, wet **04** base, blue, clog, edgy, lewd, mean, rank, soil, ugly, vile, wild **05** angry, black, block, catch, choke, cross, dirty, fetid, gross, humpy, mucky, muddy, narky, nasty, putid, rainy, ratty, reeky, rough, snarl, stain, sully, taint, testy, twist **06** coarse,

crabby, defile, dreggy, feisty, filthy, foetid, foul up, grumpy, impure, odious, pawpaw, putrid, reekie, ribald, rotten, shirty, smelly, smutty, snappy, soiled, stingy, stormy, tangle, tetchy, unfair, untidy, virose, vulgar, wicked **07** abusive, bilious, blacken, collide, crabbed, decayed, defiled, ensnare, gnarled, grouchy, heinous, obscene, peppery, pollute, prickly, profane, rotting, squalid, squally, stroppy, tainted, unclean, vicious **08** blustery, choleric, entangle, feculent, harlotry, horrible, indecent, infected, mephitic, obstruct, polluted, shameful, stagnant, stinking **09** abhorrent, crotchety, dyspeptic, entangled, execrable, fractious, impatient, inclement, irritable, loathsome, nefarious, off-colour, offensive, repellent, repulsive, revolting, sickening, splenetic, technical **10** abominable, capernoity, despicable, detestable, disfigured, disgusting, indelicate, iniquitous, nauseating, putrescent, unpleasant **11** bad-tempered, blasphemous, carnaptious, contaminate, disgraceful **12** contaminated, contemptible, disagreeable, foul-smelling, putrefactive, unfavourable **13** quick-tempered
• **foul play** **05** crime **06** murder **08** violence **09** deception, dirty work **13** double-dealing, funny business, sharp practice **15** unfair behaviour

## foul-mouthed
**06** coarse, ribald, ribaud, sweary **07** abusive, obscene, profane, rybauld **09** offensive **10** foul-spoken **11** blasphemous

## foul-smelling stuff
**04** hing **10** asafoetida

## found
**03** fix, met, set **04** base, cast, rest, root **05** build, endow, erect, merit, plant, raise, set up, start **06** bottom, create, ground, locate, settle **07** develop **08** initiate, organize, position **09** construct, establish, institute, originate **10** constitute, inaugurate **14** bring into being
• **found in** ◇ *anagram indicator* ◇ *containment indicator* ◇ *hidden indicator*

## foundation
◇ *tail selection indicator* **03** key **04** base, call, core, crib, fond, foot, fund, rock, root **05** basis, cause, heart, score **06** bottom, excuse, ground, motive, reason, rip-rap, thrust **07** account, bedrock, charity, essence, footing, grounds, keynote, premise, reasons, roadbed, support **08** argument, creation, cribwork, founding, grillage, occasion, pitching **09** endowment, essential, grounding, institute, principle, rationale, setting-up, substance **10** essentials, grass-roots, groundwork, hypostasis, inducement, initiation, stereobate, substratum **11** fundamental, institution, vindication **12** constitution, fundamentals, inauguration,

organization, quintessence, substructure, underpinning **13** alpha and omega, establishment, justification, starting-point **14** main ingredient, understructure **15** first principles

## founder
◇ *anagram indicator* **04** fail, fall, sink **05** abort, maker **06** author, father, go down, mother, oecist, oikist **07** builder, capsize, creator, endower, go wrong, misfire, stumble, subside **08** belleter, collapse, designer, inventor, miscarry, submerge **09** architect, break down, developer, initiator, organizer, patriarch **10** benefactor, discoverer, institutor, originator, prime mover, progenitor **11** come to grief, constructor, establisher, fall through **13** come to nothing, go to the bottom **14** be unsuccessful

## foundling
**04** waif **05** stray **06** orphan, urchin **07** outcast **12** enfant trouvé **15** abandoned infant

## fount
**04** font, rise, well **05** birth, cause **06** origin, source, spring **08** wellhead **09** beginning, inception **10** mainspring **12** commencement, fountainhead

## fountain
**03** jet **04** fons, font, pant, rise, well **05** birth, cause, fount, gerbe, laver, spout, spray, spurt **06** origin, source, spring **07** bubbler, conduit, jet d'eau **08** Aganippe, wellhead **09** beginning, Castalian, inception, reservoir **10** Hippocrene, mainspring, waterworks, wellspring **11** Aonian fount, scuttlebutt, scuttle cask **12** commencement, fountainhead

## four
**02** IV **04** IIII, mess **06** tetrad **07** quartet **08** quartett **09** quartette **10** quaternary, quaternion, quaternity
• **one of four** **04** quad

## four-square
**05** frank **06** firmly, honest **07** frankly, solidly **08** honestly, squarely **10** forthright, resolutely

## fourteen
**03** XIV

## fowl
**03** hen **04** bird, cock, coot, duck **05** chook, goose, poult **06** bantam, boiler, Brahma, houdan, rumkin, sultan, turkey **07** chicken, Hamburg, leghorn, pintado, poultry **08** Hamburgh, pheasant, rose comb, wildfowl **09** wyandotte **10** chittagong, spatchcock **11** brissel-cock **14** Rhode Island red

## fox
**03** pug, tod **05** cheat, puggy, vixen, zerda, zorro **06** baffle, corsac, fennec, Lowrie **07** Charley, Charlie, deceive, Reynard **09** Lowrie-tod, Tod-lowrie **10** Basil Brush

## foxglove
**09** digitalis **13** dead-men's bells **14** witches' thimble

## foxtrot
**01** F

## foxy
**03** fly, sly **04** wily **05** canny, sharp **06** artful, astute, crafty, shrewd, tricky **07** cunning, devious, knowing, vulpine **08** guileful

## foyer
**04** hall **05** lobby **07** hallway **08** anteroom **09** reception, vestibule **11** antechamber **12** entrance hall

## fracas
**03** row **04** riot, rout, spat **05** aggro, brawl, fight, mêlée, scrap, set-to **06** affray, barney, bust-up, dust-up, ruckus, ruffle, rumpus, shindy, uproar **07** quarrel, ruction, scuffle, trouble **10** Donnybrook, free-for-all **11** disturbance

## fraction
**03** bit **04** half, part **05** ratio, third **06** amount **07** decimal, ligroin, quarter **08** repeater, tailings **10** proportion, sexagenary **11** sexagesimal, subdivision

## fractional
**04** tiny **05** small **06** little, minute, slight, subtle **07** partial **10** negligible **13** imperceptible, insignificant, insubstantial

## fractious
**05** cross, testy **06** crabby, grumpy, touchy, unruly **07** awkward, fretful, grouchy, peevish, stroppy **08** captious, choleric, petulant **09** crotchety, irritable, querulous **10** refractory **11** bad-tempered, quarrelsome **12** recalcitrant

## fracture
◇ *anagram indicator* **03** gap **04** chip, rent, rift, slit, snap **05** break, cleft, crack, fault, split **06** breach, schism **07** fissure, opening, rupture **08** aperture, breakage, breaking, splinter **09** splitting **10** microcrack

## fragile
**04** fine, weak **05** frail **06** dainty, feeble, flimsy, infirm, slight, tender **07** brittle **08** delicate, unstable **09** breakable, frangible **13** insubstantial

## fragility
**07** frailty **08** delicacy, weakness **09** infirmity **10** feebleness **11** brittleness **12** frangibility **13** breakableness

## fragment
◇ *hidden indicator* **02** fr **03** bit, end, ort **04** blad, chip, flaw, mite, part, rift, snip, spar **05** blaud, break, chink, crumb, frust, patch, piece, scrap, shard, shred, split **06** cinder, divide, morsel, sheave, shiver, sliver, snatch **07** break up, cantlet, crumble, flinder, flitter, fritter, morceau, portion, remains, remnant, shatter, snippet, split up **08** disunite, fraction, particle, potshard, potshare, potsherd, quantity, skerrick, splinter, xenolith **09** come apart, remainder

## fragmentary
**05** bitty **06** broken, snippy, uneven **07** partial, scrappy, sketchy **08** separate, snippety **09** piecemeal, scattered **10** disjointed, incoherent, incomplete **11** fractionary **12** disconnected **13** discontinuous

## fragmentation
**07** break-up **08** division **09** crumbling, splitting **10** separation, shattering **11** atomization, splitting-up **13** decomposition **14** disintegration

## fragmented
**06** broken, in bits **07** divided **08** in pieces, separate **09** disunited **10** disjointed, incomplete **13** disintegrated

## fragrance
**04** balm, otto **05** aroma, attar, odour, scent, smell **07** bouquet, perfume **09** redolence **10** sweet smell

## fragrant
**04** nosy **05** balmy, nosey, spicy, sweet **07** balsamy, odorous, savoury, scented **08** aromatic, perfumed, redolent **09** ambrosial **10** suaveolent **11** odoriferous **12** sweet-scented **13** sweet-smelling

## frail
**04** puny, rush, weak **05** shaky **06** feeble, flimsy, infirm, slight, slimsy, unwell **07** brittle, fragile, unsound **08** delicate **09** breakable, frangible **10** vulnerable **11** susceptible **12** easily broken **13** insubstantial

## frailty
**04** flaw **05** fault **06** defect, foible **07** blemish, failing **08** delicacy, weakness **09** fragility, infirmity, weak point **10** deficiency **11** brittleness, fallibility, shortcoming **12** imperfection **13** vulnerability **14** susceptibility

## frame
◇ *containment indicator* ◇ *ends selection indicator* **03** set **04** body, case, draw, edge, form, husk, loom, make, plan, plot, sash, size, tent, trap **05** adapt, box in, build, draft, erect, fit up, forge, model, mould, mount, pin on, plant, set up, shape, shell **06** adjust, border, casing, cook up, create, devise, draw up, encase, fabric, figure, map out, redact, sketch **07** carcase, chassis, compose, concoct, enclose, fashion, monture, pretend, setting, support, taboret **08** assemble, bodywork, conceive, contrive, mounting, physique, skeleton, stitch up, surround, tabouret **09** construct, establish, fabricate, formulate, framework, structure **10** articulate, foundation **11** incriminate, manufacture, put together, scaffolding **12** construction, substructure **13** cook up a charge
• **frame of mind** **04** mood, tune **05** state **06** humour, spirit, temper

**07** outlook **08** attitude **09** condition **11** disposition, state of mind

### frame-up
**03** fix **04** plot, trap **05** fit-up **08** put-up job **10** conspiracy **11** fabrication **15** trumped-up charge

### framework
◇ *containment indicator* **04** grid, plan, rack **05** frame, shell **06** casing, cradle, fabric, scheme **07** lattice, outline, tressel, trestle **08** scaffold, skeleton **09** bare bones, structure **10** foundation, groundwork, parameters **11** constraints, trestlework **12** substructure

### France
**01** F **02** Fr **03** FRA **04** Gaul
*See also* **department**
• **in France** ◇ *foreign word indicator*
• **South of France** **04** Midi
**07** Riviera **09** Côte d'Azur

### franchise
**05** right **07** candour, charter, consent, freedom, liberty, licence, warrant **08** immunity, suffrage **09** exemption, frankness, privilege **10** concession, permission **11** prerogative **13** authorization **15** enfranchisement

### francium
**02** Fr

### frank
**04** free, mark, open **05** bluff, blunt, plain, stamp **06** cancel, candid, direct, honest, pigsty **07** genuine, liberal, sincere, up-front **08** explicit, postmark, straight, truthful **09** downright, ingenuous, outspoken, Ripuarian **10** forthright, four-square **11** hard-hitting, open-hearted, plain-spoken, transparent, undisguised **12** unrestrained **13** simple-hearted **15** straightforward

### frankincense
**04** thus **08** olibanum

### frankly
**06** freely, openly **07** bluntly, in truth, plainly **08** candidly, directly, eye to eye, honestly, straight **09** to be blunt, to be frank **10** explicitly, to be honest, truthfully **11** straight out **14** without reserve

### frankness
**06** candor **07** candour, freedom, honesty **08** openness **09** bluntness, franchise, sincerity **10** directness **12** truthfulness **13** ingenuousness, outspokenness, plain speaking **14** forthrightness

### frantic
◇ *anagram indicator* **03** mad **04** wild **06** hectic, raging, raving **07** berserk, fraught, furious **08** agitated, frenetic, frenzied **09** desperate **10** distracted, distraught, distressed **11** overwrought **12** out of control **13** at your wits' end, panic-stricken **14** beside yourself

### frantically
◇ *anagram indicator* **05** madly **06** wildly **09** furiously **10** frenziedly **11** desperately **12** hysterically, out of

control **13** at your wits' end **14** beside yourself

### fraternity
**03** set **04** clan, club **05** guild, order, union **06** circle, fratry, league **07** company, fratery, kinship, society **08** sodality **10** fellowship **11** association, brotherhood, camaraderie, comradeship **13** companionship

### fraternize
**03** mix **04** move **05** unite **06** hobnob, mingle **07** consort **08** go around **09** affiliate, associate, forgather, hang about, pal up with, socialize **10** cordialize, foregather, gang up with, sympathize **11** keep company **12** rub shoulders

### fraud
**03** con, fix **04** fake, hoax, scam, sham, swiz **05** cheat, guile, phony, quack, snare, trick **06** con man, deceit, diddle, hoaxer, humbug, hustle, phoney, racket, riddle, rip-off, take-in **07** bluffer, forgery, roguery, swindle, swizzle **08** cheating, fraus pia, impostor, pia fraus, swindler, trickery **09** charlatan, chicanery, deception, duplicity, embezzler, fraudster, gold brick, imposture, pretender, swindling, trickster **10** mountebank **11** counterfeit, fraudulence, stellionate, supercherie **12** double-dealer, embezzlement **13** double-dealing, sharp practice **15** salami technique

### fraudulent
**04** sham **05** bogus, cronk, false, quack, shady **06** phoney **07** crooked, knavish **08** cheating, covinous, criminal **09** deceitful, deceptive, dishonest, shameless, swindling **11** counterfeit, duplicitous **12** exploitative, unscrupulous **13** double-dealing, surreptitious

### fraudulently
**07** falsely **09** corruptly, illegally **11** deceitfully, dishonestly, shamelessly **14** unscrupulously

### fraught
**04** full, load **05** cargo, laden, tense **06** filled **07** anxious, charged, freight, replete, uptight, worried **08** agitated, attended **09** abounding, bristling, freighted **10** distraught, distressed **11** accompanied, overwrought, stressed out, under stress

### fray
**03** rag, row, tax, vex **04** riot, wear **05** aggro, brawl, clash, fight, scrap, set-to **06** affray, battle, bovver, combat, dust-up, fridge, rumpus, scrape, strain, stress **07** bashing, frazzle, overtax, pasting, punch-up, quarrel, scuffle, unravel, wear out **08** conflict, frighten, irritate, wear thin **09** challenge, make tense, put on edge **10** excitement, free-for-all, push too far **11** disturbance, make nervous **12** become ragged **14** wigs on the green

### frayed
**04** thin, worn **06** ragged **08** tattered, worn thin **10** threadbare, unravelled

### freak
◇ *anagram indicator* **03** fan, nut, odd **04** buff, geek, turn, whim **05** fiend, fluky, quirk, twist **06** addict, chance, mutant, oddity, vagary, weirdo **07** anomaly, bizarre, caprice, devotee, erratic, fanatic, monster, oddball, unusual **08** aberrant, abnormal, atypical, mutation, surprise **09** curiosity, deformity, eccentric **10** aberration, aficionado, capricious, enthusiast, fortuitous, unexpected **11** abnormality, exceptional, monstrosity **12** irregularity, lusus naturae, malformation **13** freak of nature, unpredictable
• **freak out** ◇ *anagram indicator* **06** go wild, wig out **07** explode, go crazy **09** go bananas, go berserk **11** lose control **12** throw a wobbly **15** go off the deep end, go out of your mind

### freakish
**03** odd **05** weird **06** fitful, freaky **07** erratic, strange, unusual **08** aberrant, abnormal, fanciful, peculiar **09** arbitrary, fantastic, grotesque, malformed, monstrous, whimsical **10** capricious, changeable, outlandish **13** unpredictable **14** unconventional

### freckle
**04** spot **07** ephelis, lentigo **08** heatspot **09** fernticle **10** fernticle, ferntickle, fernytickle **11** fairniticle, fairnyticle, fernticle, fernytickle **12** fairniticle, fairnytickle

### free
◇ *anagram indicator* ◇ *deletion indicator* **03** ope, out, rid **04** bold, easy, idle, open, quit, save **05** broad, clear, empty, fluid, let go, loose, rough, spare, unmew, untie, vague **06** acquit, casual, except, excuse, exempt, freely, giving, gratis, lavish, let out, ransom, redeem, rescue, smooth, solute, svelte, unbind, vacant **07** absolve, acquite, at large, clear of, deliver, for free, for love, general, inexact, lacking, liberal, natural, off duty, relaxed, release, relieve, set free, unbowed, unchain, unleash, untaken, without **08** acquight, at no cost, buckshee, devoid of, generous, immune to, indecent, laid-back, lavishly, liberate, safe from, set loose, unburden **09** at liberty, autarchic, available, copiously, debarrass, disburden, discharge, disengage, easy-going, extricate, imprecise, liberally, liberated, sovereign, turn loose, unblocked, unimpeded, unsecured, voluntary **10** abundantly, autonomous, charitable, democratic, disburthen, emancipate, exempt from, for nothing, generously, hospitable, munificent, on the house, on the loose, open-handed, self-ruling, unattached, unconfined, unemployed, unfastened, unhampered, unoccupied, unstinting **11** Anacreontic, disentangle,

emancipated, free as a bird, independent, requiteless, spontaneous, uninhibited **12** free of charge, unaffected by, unobstructed, unrestrained, unrestricted **13** at no extra cost, complimentary, extravagantly, make available, self-governing, without charge **15** with compliments
• **free and easy** **06** casual **07** relaxed **08** carefree, informal, laid-back, tolerant **09** easy-going **11** spontaneous **12** happy-go-lucky **13** unconstrained
• **free hand** **05** power, scope **07** freedom, liberty, licence **08** free rein, latitude **09** authority **10** discretion, permission **12** carte blanche
• **setting free** **03** lib **07** release **09** unbinding **10** liberation

**freebooter**
**07** cateran, pindari **08** pindaree **09** snaphance **10** snaphaunce, snaphaunch

**freedom**
**04** ease, play **05** power, range, right, scope **06** leeway, margin **07** liberty, licence, release **08** autarchy, autonomy, free hand, free rein, home rule, immunity, impunity, latitude **09** democracy, exemption, frankness, privilege **10** separation **11** deliverance, flexibility, open slather, opportunity, prerogative, sovereignty **12** emancipation, independence **13** outspokenness **14** self-government

**free-for-all**
**03** row **04** fray **05** brawl, broil, clash, fight, mêlée, rammy, scrap **06** affray, bust-up, dust-up, fracas, fratch, ruckus, rumpus, stoush **07** bagarre, brabble, brangle, dispute, punch-up, quarrel, scuffle, tuilyie **08** argument, disorder, skirmish, squabble **10** Donnybrook, fisticuffs **11** altercation, open slather

**freely**
◇ *anagram indicator* **05** ad-lib, amply **06** easily, openly **07** bluntly, frankly, loosely, plainly, readily **08** candidly, lavishly, smoothly **09** liberally, naturally, willingly **10** abundantly, generously **11** voluntarily **12** unreservedly **13** extravagantly, spontaneously **14** frictionlessly, without jerking **15** in all directions

**freeman**
**05** ceorl, thete **07** burgess, burgher, citizen **09** liveryman

**freethinker**
**05** deist **07** doubter, infidel, sceptic **08** agnostic **09** libertine **10** esprit fort, unbeliever **11** independent, rationalist **13** nonconformist **14** doubting Thomas

**freethinking**
**07** liberal **08** agnostic **09** sceptical **10** open-minded **11** broad-minded, independent, rationalist **13** nonconformist **14** unconventional

**free will**
**07** autarky, freedom, liberty **08** autonomy, election, volition

**11** spontaneity **12** independence **15** self-sufficiency
• **of your own free will** **06** freely **08** by choice **09** purposely, willingly **11** consciously, voluntarily **12** deliberately **13** intentionally, spontaneously **15** of your own accord

**freeze**
**03** fix, ice, peg, set **04** cool, halt, hold, stay, stop, take **05** chill, frost, ice up **06** fixing, harden, quiver, shiver **07** congeal, embargo, get cold, ice over, stiffen, suspend **08** cold snap, enfreeze, freeze-up, glaciate, preserve, shutdown, solidify, stoppage **09** freeze-dry, stabilize **10** deep-freeze, immobilize, moratorium, stand still, standstill, suspension **11** catch a chill, refrigerate **12** anaesthetize, interruption, postponement **15** become paralysed
• **freeze out** **03** cut **04** snub **05** eject, evict, expel **06** ice out, ignore, remove **07** boot out, boycott, exclude, kick out, lock out, turf out **08** brush off, throw out **09** ostracize **13** excommunicate **14** send to Coventry

**freezing**
**03** icy, raw **04** cold, numb **05** polar **06** arctic, baltic, biting, bitter, chilly, frosty, wintry **07** cutting, glacial, numbing **08** piercing, Siberian, stinging **09** perishing **10** frigorific **11** penetrating **12** bitterly cold, brass monkeys

**freight**
**04** hire, load **05** cargo, goods **06** lading, let out **07** fraught, haulage, payload, portage **08** carriage, contents, shipment **10** conveyance, freightage **11** consignment, merchandise **14** transportation

**French**
◇ *foreign word indicator* **02** Fr
See also **day; month; number; shop**
• **Old French** **02** OF

**French Guiana**
**03** GUF

**Frenchman**
**01** M

*French boys' names include:*

**03** Luc
**04** Jean, Léon, Rémi, Rémy, René, Yves
**05** Alain, André, Denis, Émile, Henri, Jules, Louis, Serge
**06** Claude, Didier, Gaston, Gérard, Honoré, Jérôme, Marcel, Michel, Pascal, Pierre, Xavier
**07** Antoine, Édouard, Étienne, Georges, Gustave, Jacques, Laurent, Olivier, Patrice, Thibaut, Thierry, Vincent
**08** Frédéric, Matthieu, Philippe, Stéphane, Thibault
**09** Guillaume

**French Revolutionary Calendar**
*see* **month**

**frenetic**
◇ *anagram indicator* **03** mad **04** wild **05** manic **06** hectic, insane, madman **07** berserk, excited, frantic **08** demented, frenzied, maniacal **09** delirious, obsessive **10** distracted, distraught, hysterical, unbalanced **11** hyperactive, overwrought

**frenetically**
◇ *anagram indicator* **05** madly **06** wildly **09** excitedly, intensely, manically **10** hectically **11** frantically **12** hysterically

**frenzied**
**03** mad **04** amok, wild **05** manic **06** crazed, hectic, raving **07** berserk, frantic, furious **08** demented, feverish, frenetic **09** desperate, obsessive, phrenetic, raving mad **10** distracted, distraught, hysterical **11** overwrought **12** out of control, uncontrolled **13** at your wits' end, panic-stricken **14** beside yourself

**frenzy**
◇ *anagram indicator* **03** fit **04** bout, fury, must, rage **05** burst, fever, mania, musth, spasm **06** lunacy **07** madness, oestrum, oestrus, passion, seizure, turmoil **08** delirium, hysteria, insanity, outburst, paroxysm, tailspin, wildness **09** agitation, phrenesis, transport **10** convulsion **11** derangement, distraction, nympholepsy **13** furor poeticus
• **expression of frenzy** **04** euoi, evoe **05** evhoe, evohe, yahoo

**frequency**
**01** f **06** resort **09** constancy, incidence, oftenness **10** commonness, prevalence, recurrence, repetition **11** commonality, periodicity **12** frequentness

**frequent**
**05** daily, haunt, lobby, often, thick, usual, visit **06** attend, common, hourly, normal, weekly **07** crowded, regular **08** addicted, constant, everyday, familiar, habitual, numerous, practise, repeated **09** continual, countless, customary, habituate, hang out at, incessant, patronize, prevalent, recurrent, recurring **10** accustomed, persistent, prevailing, visit often **11** commonplace, hang about at, predominant **13** associate with, go to regularly **14** go to frequently, happening often

**frequenter**
**06** client, patron **07** habitué, haunter, regular **08** customer, resorter **14** regular visitor

**frequently**
**02** fr **03** oft **04** much **05** daily, often, thick **06** hourly, weekly **08** commonly **09** many a time, many times, regularly **10** habitually, oftentimes, repeatedly **11** continually, customarily, half the time, over and over **12** persistently

**fresh**
◇ *anagram indicator* **03** hot, new, raw **04** bold, cool, fair, firm, just, keen,

## freshen

more, pert, pink, pure, rosy, span, warm **05** alert, brisk, clean, clear, cocky, crisp, crude, extra, green, newly, novel, other, right, sassy, saucy, spick, sweet, vital, windy **06** afresh, brazen, bright, caller, cheeky, chilly, direct, latest, lively, maiden, modern, recent, rested **07** bracing, forward, freshly, further, glowing, healthy, natural, renewed, revived, span new, uncured, undried, unfaded, unusual, vibrant **08** blooming, bouncing, brand-new, dewy-eyed, exciting, familiar, impudent, insolent, original, pristine, restored, straight, up-to-date, vigorous, youthful **09** different, energetic, refreshed, virescent **10** additional, a new person, innovative, new-fangled, raring to go, refreshing, stimulated, unpolluted **11** impertinent, invigorated, unpreserved, unprocessed **12** enthusiastic, invigorating, overfamiliar, presumptuous, ready for more **13** disrespectful, fresh as a daisy, inexperienced, revolutionary, supplementary, yourself again **14** healthy-looking, unconventional
• **remain fresh** **04** keep, last

## freshen

◇ *anagram indicator* **03** air **05** clean, clear, liven, rouse **06** purify, refill, revive, tart up **07** enliven, liven up, refresh, restore **09** deodorize, stimulate, ventilate, vernalize **10** revitalize **12** reinvigorate
• **freshen up** **09** get washed, have a wash **12** get spruced up, wash yourself **14** tidy yourself up

## freshly

◇ *anagram indicator* **04** anew, just **05** newly **06** barely, lately, of late **08** recently **10** not long ago **13** a short time ago

## freshman

**05** bajan, frosh **06** bejant, pennal **07** fresher **08** newcomer **09** first-year **13** underclassman

## freshness

**04** glow **05** bloom, flush, shine **06** vigour, youths **07** May-morn, newness, novelty, sparkle, verdure **09** cleanness, clearness, fraîcheur, immediacy, vernality **10** brightness, May-morning **11** originality **13** wholesomeness
• **early freshness** **03** dew

## fret

**03** rub, vex **04** mope, pine, rile, stop **05** anger, annoy, brood, chafe, grate, worry **06** bother, nettle, ripple **07** agonize, anguish, be upset, concern, corrode, disturb, torment, trouble, whittle **08** irritate **09** be anxious, infuriate, make a fuss, variegate **10** exasperate **12** be distressed **15** concern yourself

## fretful

**04** edgy **05** tense, upset **06** uneasy **07** anxious, fearful, peevish, unhappy, uptight, worried **08** restless, troubled **09** disturbed, impatient **10** distressed

## fretfully

**06** edgily **07** tensely **08** uneasily **09** anxiously, fearfully, worriedly **10** restlessly

## friable

**05** crisp, crump **07** brittle, crumbly, powdery **12** pulverizable

## friar

**02** Fr **03** fra **04** monk **05** abbot, frate, frier, minim, prior **06** frater **07** brother, limiter **08** Capuchin, récollet **09** Carmelite, Cordelier, Dominican, mendicant, Observant, predicant, recollect, religieux, religious **10** Franciscan, religioner **12** Observantine **13** Redemptionist

## friction

**06** strife **07** arguing, chafing, discord, dispute, erosion, gnawing, grating, jarring, rasping, rivalry, rubbing **08** abrading, abrasion, bad blood, clashing, conflict, disunity, scraping, traction **09** animosity, attrition, hostility **10** antagonism, bad feeling, disharmony, dissension, ill feeling, irritation, opposition, resentment, resistance **11** disputation, excoriation, quarrelling, wearing away, xerotripsis **12** disagreement

## Friday

**02** Fr **03** Fri

## fridge

**03** rub **04** fray, frig **06** cooler, icebox **07** minibar **12** refrigerator **13** refrigeratory

## friend

**03** ami, bud, pal **04** ally, amie, chum, ehoa, mate, tosh **05** amigo, buddy, crony, homey, homie, ingle, lover **06** backer, belamy, bon ami, cobber, co-mate, gal pal, gossib, gossip, inward, mucker, patron **07** best boy, comrade, goombah, homeboy, paisano, partner, privado, sponsor **08** alter ego, best girl, compadre, familiar, intimate, playmate, sidekick, soul mate **09** associate, belle amie, bonne amie, boyfriend, companion, confidant, confident, paranymph, pen friend, supporter **10** back-friend, benefactor, best friend, better half, buddy-buddy, confidante, girlfriend, good friend, subscriber, well-wisher **11** bosom friend, cater-cousin, close friend, condisciple **12** acquaintance, fidus Achates, schoolfriend **15** sparring partner
• **man's best friend** **03** dog

## friendless

**05** alone **06** lonely **07** forlorn, shunned, unloved **08** deserted, forsaken, isolated, lonesome, solitary **09** abandoned, destitute, unbeloved, unpopular **10** by yourself, ostracized, unattached **11** lonely-heart **12** unbefriended **13** companionless **14** cold-shouldered

## friendliness

**06** warmth **08** bonhomie, kindness, matiness **09** geniality, palliness **10** affability, amiability, chumminess, kindliness **11** sociability **12** congeniality, conviviality **13** Gemütlichkeit **15** approachability, neighbourliness

## friendly

**04** fond, kind, maty, nice, tosh, warm **05** close, matey, pally, thick, tight **06** chummy, couthy, folksy, genial, kindly **07** affable, amiable, cordial, couthie, helpful **08** amicable, down-home, familiar, informal, intimate, outgoing, pleasant, sociable **09** agreeable, comradely, congenial, convivial, favorable, peaceable, receptive, welcoming **10** favourable, hospitable **11** forthcoming, good-natured, inseparable, neighbourly, sympathetic **12** affectionate, approachable, well-disposed **13** companionable

## friendship

**04** love **05** amity, amour **06** warmth **07** company, concord, harmony, rapport **08** affinity, alliance, fondness, goodwill, intimacy, mateship **09** affection, closeness **10** amiability, attachment, fellowship, kindliness **11** camaraderie, comradeship, familiarity **12** friendliness **13** companionship, confraternity, understanding

## fright

**04** fear, fleg, funk **05** alarm, dread, gliff, glift, panic, scare, shock, skrik **06** creeps, dismay, horror, terror, tirrit **07** jitters, shivers, willies **08** affright, blue funk, disquiet **09** bombshell, cold sweat **10** blind panic **11** fearfulness, trepidation **12** affrightment, apprehension, perturbation **13** consternation, heebie-jeebies, knocking knees **15** bolt from the blue
• **expression of fright** **03** eek **04** yike **05** yikes

## frighten

**03** awe **04** dare, flay, fleg, fley, fray, gast, shoo **05** afear, alarm, appal, daunt, dread, ghast, panic, scare, shock, spook, unman **06** affear, affray, boggle, dismay, gallow, rattle **07** affeare, horrify, petrify, scarify, startle, terrify, unnerve **08** affright **09** terrorize **10** affrighten, intimidate, scare silly, scare stiff **12** put the wind up

## frightened

**04** frit **05** cowed, feart, windy **06** afraid, frozen, scared **07** alarmed, chicken, panicky, quivery, trembly **08** dismayed, startled, unnerved **09** petrified, terrified **10** terrorized **11** in a blue funk, scared stiff **13** having kittens, panic-stricken, scared to death **14** terror-stricken

## frightening

**04** eery, grim **05** eerie, hairy, scary **06** creepy, scarey, spooky **08** alarming, daunting, fearsome, terrific **09** traumatic **10** forbidding, formidable, petrifying, terrifying **11** hair-raising **12** white-knuckle **13** bloodcurdling, spine-chilling

**frightful**
◇ *anagram indicator* **04** dire, grim, huge, ugly **05** awful, great, nasty **06** grisly, horrid, odious **07** fearful, ghastly, hideous, macabre, very bad **08** alarming, dreadful, fearsome, gruesome, horrible, horrific, shocking, terrible **09** abhorrent, appalling, harrowing, loathsome, repulsive, revolting **10** frightsome, horrendous, unbearable, unpleasant **11** affrightful, schrecklich, unspeakable **12** disagreeable

**frightfully**
◇ *anagram indicator* **04** much, very **07** awfully, beastly, greatly **08** terribly **09** decidedly, extremely **10** dreadfully, ghastfully, thoroughly **11** desperately, exceedingly

**frigid**
**03** dry, icy **04** cold, cool **05** aloof, chill, polar, stiff, stony **06** arctic, bitter, chilly, formal, frosty, frozen, remote, wintry **07** distant, glacial, passive, unmoved **08** clinical, freezing, lifeless, reserved, Siberian, unloving, very cold **09** unfeeling **10** impersonal, unanimated **11** indifferent, passionless, standoffish, unemotional, unexcitable **12** unresponsive **13** unsympathetic

**frigidity**
**05** chill **07** iciness **08** coldness **09** aloofness, passivity, stiffness **10** chilliness, frostiness **11** impassivity **12** lifelessness **15** cold-heartedness

**frill**
**04** fold, ruff, tuck **05** extra, jabot, ruche **06** finery, fringe, purfle, ruffle **07** armilla, flounce, orphrey, ruching, valance **08** addition, frippery, furbelow, trimming **09** accessory, fanciness, fandangle, gathering, trimmings **10** decoration, frilliness **11** chitterling, ostentation, superfluity **13** embellishment, ornamentation

**frilly**
◇ *anagram indicator* **04** lacy **05** fancy **06** ornate **07** crimped, frilled, ruffled, trimmed **08** flounced, gathered

**fringe**
◇ *ends selection indicator* **03** hem, rim **04** bang, edge, fall, loma, purl, trim **05** bangs, frill, limit, skirt, thrum, verge **06** border, edging, margin, pelmet, tassel **07** bullion, enclose, fimbria, macramé, macrami, off-beat, valance **08** frisette, surround, trimming **09** left-field, outskirts, perimeter, periphery, peristome **10** avant-garde, borderline, unofficial, unorthodox **11** alternative **12** experimental **14** unconventional

**fringed**
**05** edged **06** fringy, hemmed **07** trimmed **08** bordered, tasselly **09** fimbriate, tasselled **10** fimbriated

**frippery**
**05** froth **06** finery, frills, trivia **07** baubles, foppery, gewgaws, trifles, useless **08** glad rags, nonsense, trifling, trinkets **09** fanciness, fussiness, gaudiness, nick-nacks, ornaments, showiness **10** adornments, fandangles, flashiness, frilliness, tawdriness, triviality **11** decorations, knick-knacks, ostentation **15** pretentiousness

**frisk**
**03** hop **04** fisk, jump, leap, play, romp, skip, trip **05** caper, check, dance, sport **06** bounce, cavort, curvet, frolic, gambol, prance, search **07** inspect **09** shake down **10** body-search

**friskily**
**08** actively **09** playfully **10** spiritedly **11** exuberantly

**frisky**
◇ *anagram indicator* **04** high **05** hyper **06** active, bouncy, lively, wanton **07** buckish, coltish, dashing, playful, romping **08** skittish, spirited **09** exuberant **10** frolicsome, rollicking **11** full of beans **12** high-spirited **13** in high spirits **15** alive and kicking

**fritter**
**04** blow, idle **05** waste **06** misuse **07** beignet, friture **08** fragment, misspend, squander **09** dissipate, go through, overspend **10** get through **14** spend like water

**frivolity**
**03** fun **04** jest **05** folly, froth **06** gaiety, levity **07** inanity **08** nonsense **09** flippancy, pettiness, silliness **10** triviality **11** foolishness **13** facetiousness, senselessness **14** superficiality

**frivolous**
**04** idle, vain **05** inane, light, petty, silly **06** futile **07** étourdi, foolish, jocular, puerile, shallow, trivial **08** étourdie, flippant, juvenile, skittish, trifling **09** airheaded, facetious, pointless, senseless **11** empty-headed, giddy-headed, light-minded, superficial, unimportant **12** bubble-headed, light-hearted **13** irresponsible **14** featherbrained
• **frivolous person 09** butterfly

**frivolously**
**04** idly **06** vainly **09** foolishly, jocularly **11** pointlessly, senselessly, whimsically **13** irresponsibly **14** light-heartedly

**frizzle**
**03** fry **04** bend, coil, curl, hiss, kink, loop, purl, roll, spit, tong, turn, wave, wind **05** crimp, curve, frizz, twine, twirl, twist **06** becurl, scorch, scroll, sizzle, spiral **07** crackle, crimple, crinkle, sputter, wreathe

**frizzy**
**04** wiry **05** crisp, curly **06** curled **07** crimped, frizzed **10** corrugated

**frock**
**04** gown, robe **05** dress
*See also* **dress**

**frog**
**04** hyla, Rana **05** frush **06** peeper **07** paddock, puddock **08** platanna, tree toad **12** spring peeper **15** Cape nightingale

**frolic**
◇ *anagram indicator* **03** fun, hop, rig **04** game, lark, leap, play, rant, romp, skip **05** caper, dance, frisk, merry, mirth, prank, revel, sport, spree **06** antics, bounce, buster, cavort, curvet, gaiety, gambol, prance, pranky, razzle, splore, wanton **07** disport, gambado, gammock, jollity, May-game, rollick, skylark, stashie, stishie, stushie **08** escapade, stooshie **09** amusement, galravage, gilravage, high jinks, make merry, merriment **10** galravitch, gillravage, gilravitch, lark around **11** fun and games, gillravitch, merrymaking **12** razzle-dazzle **13** barnsbreaking

**frolicsome**
◇ *anagram indicator* **03** gay **05** ludic, merry **06** frisky, lively, skippy **07** coltish, kitteny, playful **08** skittish, sportive **09** kittenish, sprightly **10** rollicking

**from**
◇ *anagram indicator* ◇ *hidden indicator* **01** à **02** ab-, ex, of, on **03** fae, fro, off, out **04** frae **05** out of, since

**front**
◇ *head selection indicator* **03** air, bow, top, van **04** face, fore, head, lead, look, mask, meet, prow, show **05** blind, cover, first **06** aspect, façade, facing, manner, oppose, vaward **07** cover-up, leading, obverse, outside, pretext **08** confront, disguise, exterior, foremost, forepart, frontage, look over, overlook, pretence, vanguard **09** forefront, front line, look out on **10** appearance, battle zone, expression, firing line, foreground **11** countenance
• **in front** ◇ *juxtaposition indicator* **04** fore **05** ahead, first **06** before, en face **07** leading **08** anterior, paravant **09** in advance, paravaunt, preceding, to the fore
• **in front of** ◇ *juxtaposition indicator* **06** before, facing **07** ahead of **11** in advance of **14** under the nose of **15** in the presence of

**frontier**
**04** edge **05** limit, verge **06** border, bounds **07** marches **08** boundary, confines **09** bordering, partition, perimeter **10** borderline

**front-runner**
**03** nap **07** top seed **08** finalist **09** certainty, favourite, form horse **12** likely winner **15** odds-on favourite

**frost**
**03** ice, mat **04** rime **06** freeze **08** coldness, freeze-up **09** hoar-frost, Jack Frost

**frostily**
**06** coldly, coolly **07** stiffly

**frosty**
**03** icy **04** cold, cool, rimy **05** aloof, chill, frore, frorn, nippy, parky, polar, stiff **06** arctic, chilly, frigid, froren, frorne, frozen, wintry **07** glacial, hostile **08** freezing, Siberian

### froth

**10** unfriendly **11** standoffish, unwelcoming **12** bitterly cold, discouraging

### froth

**03** pap **04** barm, fizz, foam, head, mill, ream, scum, suds **05** spume, yeast **06** bubble, lather, mantle, trivia **07** bubbles, chatter, ferment, sea foam, trifles **10** cuckoo-spit, effervesce **12** trivialities **13** cuckoo-spittle, effervescence, irrelevancies

### frothy

**04** vain **05** barmy, empty, fizzy, foamy, light, nappy, reamy, spumy, sudsy **06** bubbly, slight, yeasty **07** foaming, spumous, trivial **08** bubbling, trifling **09** frivolous **10** spumescent **11** lightweight **13** insubstantial

### frown

**03** mow **04** lour, moue, pout **05** glare, scowl **06** glower **07** frounce, grimace **09** dirty look **12** knit your brow **13** look daggers at, raised eyebrow
• **frown on** **05** glare, scowl **06** glower **07** dislike, grimace **08** object to **10** discourage **12** disapprove of, think badly of **14** take a dim view of **15** not take kindly to

### frowsty

**05** fuggy, fusty, musty **06** stuffy **07** airless **12** unventilated

### frowsy

**05** dirty, fusty, messy **06** frumpy, sloppy, stuffy, untidy **07** scruffy, unkempt **08** frumpish, slovenly, sluttish, unwashed **09** offensive, ungroomed **10** slatternly **11** dishevelled

### frozen

**03** icy, raw **04** hard, iced, numb **05** fixed, frore, frorn, glacé, polar, rigid, stiff **06** arctic, frigid, froren, frorne, frosty **07** chilled, frosted, glacial, ice-cold **08** freezing, icebound, Siberian **10** ice-covered, solidified **11** frozen-stiff **12** bitterly cold

### frugal

**05** spare **06** meagre, paltry, saving, scanty, stingy **07** careful, miserly, prudent, sparing, spartan, thrifty **09** husbandly, niggardly, penny-wise, provident **10** economical, inadequate **12** parsimonious **13** penny-pinching

### frugality

**06** saving, thrift **07** economy **08** prudence **09** husbandry, parsimony **11** carefulness **12** conservation

### frugally

**05** spare **08** meagrely, scantily **09** carefully, prudently, thriftily **12** economically, inadequately **14** parsimoniously

### fruit

**03** haw, hep, hip, nut, pod **04** crop **05** acorn, berry, yield **06** effect, profit, result, return, reward **07** benefit, harvest, outcome, produce, product, rosehip **08** fruitage **09** advantage **11** consequence

---

*Fruits include:*

**03** bel, Cox, fig
**04** açaí, bael, bhel, Cox's, date, gage, kaki, lime, noni, pear, plum, sloe, Ugli®, yuzu
**05** apple, carob, galia, grape, guava, Jaffa, lemon, mango, melon, olive, peach, prune
**06** banana, cherry, citron, damson, litchi, loquat, lychee, medlar, orange, papaya, pawpaw, pippin, pitaya, pomelo, quince, raisin, russet, tomato, wampee
**07** acerola, apricot, avocado, bramble, Bramley, chayote, kumquat, mineola, rhubarb, satsuma, Seville, soursop, tangelo, William
**08** bilberry, Braeburn, date plum, goosegog, honeydew, kalumpit, mandarin, minneola, mulberry, muscatel, physalis, Pink Lady, pitahaya, rambutan, sebesten, sunberry, tamarind
**09** beach plum, blueberry, cantaloup, carambola, cherimoya, crab apple, cranberry, goji berry, greengage, Juneberry, kiwi fruit, nectarine, persimmon, pineapple, raspberry, rose apple, sapodilla, saskatoon, shadberry, star-apple, star fruit, tamarillo, tangerine, ugli® fruit, wineberry
**10** blackberry, breadfruit, cantaloupe, clementine, Conference, damask plum, elderberry, gooseberry, granadilla, grapefruit, loganberry, mangosteen, redcurrant, salal berry, sour cherry, spiceberry, strawberry, watermelon
**11** blood orange, boysenberry, dragon fruit, eating apple, Granny Smith, Jaffa orange, navel orange, pomegranate, sallal berry, sharon fruit, sweet cherry
**12** blackcurrant, buffalo-berry, cooking apple, costard apple, custard apple, passion fruit, Red Delicious, serviceberry, victoria plum, whitecurrant, winter cherry
**13** kangaroo-apple, morello cherry, sapodilla plum, Seville orange
**14** Cape gooseberry, pink grapefruit
**15** Golden Delicious

---

• **fruit juice** **03** oil **05** mobby **06** mobbie
• **fruit refuse** **04** marc
• **fruit stone** **03** pip, pit **06** pyrene **07** putamen
• **fruit syrup** **03** rob

### fruitful

**03** fat **04** rich **06** fecund, useful **07** fertile, teeming **08** abundant, fructive, pregnant, prolific **09** effective, effectual, feracious, fructuous, plenteous, plentiful, rewarding, well-spent **10** beneficial, productive, profitable, successful, worthwhile **11** conceptious, efficacious, increaseful **12** advantageous, fruit-bearing

### fruitfully

**08** usefully **10** profitably **11** effectively **12** beneficially, productively, successfully **14** advantageously

### fruitfulness

**06** uberty **08** feracity **09** fecundity, fertility **10** usefulness **11** fecundation **13** profitability **14** productiveness

### fruition

**07** success **08** maturity, ripeness **09** enjoyment **10** attainment, completion, fulfilment, maturation, perfection **11** achievement, realization **12** consummation **13** actualization

### fruitless

**04** idle, vain **06** barren, futile **07** sterile, useless **08** abortive, hopeless **09** pointless, worthless **11** ineffectual, infructuous **12** unproductive, unsuccessful

### fruitlessly

**06** in vain, vainly **09** uselessly **10** hopelessly **11** pointlessly **14** unproductively, unsuccessfully

### fruity

**03** low **04** blue, deep, full, racy, rich, sexy **05** bawdy, crazy, juicy, saucy, spicy **06** mellow, risqué, smutty, vulgar **07** naughty **08** indecent, resonant **09** salacious **10** indelicate, suggestive **11** titillating

### frumpy

**04** drab **05** dated, dingy, dowdy **06** dreary **08** frumpish **09** out of date **10** ill-dressed **12** badly dressed

### frustrate

**03** bug **04** balk, beat, crab, dash, foil, miff, nark, rile, stop **05** anger, annoy, baulk, block, check, get at, spike, stimy **06** baffle, balked, blight, defeat, hamper, hinder, hogtie, impede, needle, nobble, scotch, stimie, stymie, thwart, wind up **07** counter, depress, inhibit, nullify, scupper, useless **08** drive mad, embitter, irritate, obstruct **09** aggravate, forestall, infuriate **10** disappoint, disconcert, discourage, dishearten, dissatisfy, drive crazy, exasperate, neutralize **11** ineffectual

### frustrated

**05** angry **06** dished **07** annoyed **08** blighted, thwarted **09** repressed, resentful **10** embittered **11** discouraged **12** disappointed, discontented, disheartened, dissatisfied

### frustrating

**08** annoying **09** maddening **10** irritating **11** infuriating **12** discouraging, exasperating **13** disappointing, disheartening

### frustration

**04** balk, foil **05** anger, baulk **06** defeat, thwart **07** balking, curbing, failure, foiling **08** blocking, vexation **09** annoyance, thwarting **10** irritation, resentment **11** obstruction **12** exasperation **13** circumvention, contravention, non-fulfilment

**14** disappointment, discouragement
**15** dissatisfaction
• **expression of frustration 11** for God's sake **12** for pete's sake **14** for Christ's sake, for heaven's sake **15** for goodness sake

**fry**
**04** burn, foam **05** sauté, spawn **06** scorch, sizzle **07** frizzle, skegger **09** whitebait

**frying-pan**
**03** wok **06** spider **07** skillet

**fuddled**
◊ *anagram indicator* **03** fap **04** hazy **05** drunk, mused, muzzy, tipsy, woozy **06** addled, groggy, swipey, tavert **07** bemused, muddled, sozzled, taivert **08** confused **09** overtaken, stupefied **10** inebriated, tossicated, tosticated **11** intoxicated

**fuddy-duddy**
**04** prim **06** fossil, square, stuffy **07** carping **08** old fogey **10** back number, censorious, conformist **11** museum piece, old-fogeyish **12** buttoned-down, conservative, old-fashioned, stuffed shirt **13** stick-in-the-mud **14** traditionalist

**fudge**
◊ *anagram indicator* **03** fix **04** cook, fail, fake **05** avoid, cheat, dodge, evade, hedge, stall, stuff **06** fiddle, humbug **07** distort, evasion, falsify, shuffle **08** nonsense **10** distortion, equivocate **12** misrepresent

**fuel**
**03** fan **04** feed, fire **05** boost **06** incite **07** goading, inflame, nourish, stoke up, sustain **08** material, stimulus **09** encourage, incentive, stimulate **10** ammunition, incitement, propellant **11** combustible, motive power, provocation **13** encouragement

*Fuels include:*

**03** gas, LNG, LPG, MOX, oil, RDF
**04** coal, coke, derv, logs, peat, slug, SURF, wood
**05** argol, eldin, fagot, vraic
**06** benzol, billet, borane, butane, diesel, elding, faggot, gas oil, hydyne, petrol, smudge, Sterno®
**07** astatki, benzine, benzole, biofuel, Coalite®, eilding, gasahol, gasohol, mesquit, methane, propane, uranium
**08** calor gas®, charcoal, firewood, flex-fuel, gasoline, kerosene, kerosine, kindling, mesquite, paraffin, tan balls, triptane
**09** acetylene, biodiesel, Campingaz®, cane-trash, diesel oil, hydrazine, plutonium, red diesel
**10** anthracite, atomic fuel, bioethanol, fossil fuel, natural gas, Orimulsion®
**11** electricity, North Sea gas, nuclear fuel
**12** buffalo chips, nitromethane, nuclear power, vegetable oil

**13** smokeless fuel
**14** aviation spirit

*See also* **petrol**

**fug**
**04** reek **05** stink **09** fetidness, fustiness, staleness **10** foetidness, stuffiness **11** frowstiness

**fuggy**
**04** foul **05** close, fetid, fusty, stale **06** foetid, stuffy **07** airless, frowsty, noisome, noxious **11** suffocating **12** unventilated

**fugitive**
**04** AWOL **05** brief, exile, short **06** flying, maroon, runner **07** elusive, escapee, fleeing, passing, refugee, runaway **08** deserter, fleeting, hideaway, runagate **09** ephemeral, fugacious, momentary, temporary, transient **10** evanescent, short-lived, transitory

**fulfil**
**04** fill, keep, meet, obey **05** honor **06** answer, effect, finish, honour **07** achieve, act up to, execute, live out, observe, perfect, perform, qualify, realize, satisfy **08** carry out, complete, conclude, live up to, make good **09** conform to, discharge, implement, stand up to **10** accomplish, comply with, consummate **15** come up to scratch

**fulfilled**
**05** happy **07** content, pleased **09** gratified, satisfied

**fulfilling**
**08** pleasing **10** comforting, completion, completory, gratifying, satisfying **12** satisfactory **14** accomplishment

**fulfilment**
**04** pass **07** success **08** enacture, fruition **09** discharge, execution, impletion **10** completion, observance, perfection **11** achievement, performance, realization **12** consummation, satisfaction **14** accomplishment, implementation

**full**
◊ *anagram indicator* **03** fat, fed, top **04** bang, busy, deep, loud, rich, vast, walk, warm, wauk, wide **05** ample, baggy, broad, buxom, clear, drunk, flush, laden, large, loose, obese, plump, quite, right, round, sated, smack, stout, total, truly, waulk, whole **06** active, chubby, entire, filled, fruity, gorged, hectic, intact, jammed, lively, loaded, packed, rotund, strong, tiring, utmost **07** bulging, chocker, copious, crammed, crowded, exactly, filling, frantic, highest, intense, maximum, perfect, profuse, replete, rounded, shapely, stuffed, swelled, vibrant, well fed **08** abundant, bursting, chockers, chockful, complete, detailed, directly, distinct, eventful, exciting, generous, greatest, resonant, satiated, sonorous, squarely, straight, thorough **09** abounding, chock-full, corpulent, extensive, packed out, plentiful, satisfied **10** exhaustive, full-bodied,

overweight, sufficient, thoroughly, unabridged, voluminous **11** chock-a-block, overflowing, protuberant, well-rounded, well-stocked **12** all-inclusive, loose-fitting, unexpurgated **13** comprehensive, full to the brim
• **be full 04** teem
• **in full 05** fully, uncut **06** wholly **07** at large, in pleno, in total **08** at length, in detail **10** completely **13** in its entirety
• **to the full 05** fully **07** utterly **08** entirely **10** completely, thoroughly **11** to the utmost

**full-blooded**
**06** hearty **07** devoted **08** thorough, vigorous **09** committed, dedicated, out-and-out **11** sanguineous **12** enthusiastic, wholehearted

**full-blown**
**04** full **05** major, total **06** all-out **07** intense **08** complete, thorough **09** full-scale, out-and-out **11** full-fledged

**full-bodied**
**03** fat **04** deep, full, rich **06** fruity, strong **07** amoroso, intense

**full-frontal**
**05** total **06** direct, strong **08** absolute, complete, forceful, thorough **09** out-and-out **12** unexpurgated, unrestrained

**full-grown**
**04** ripe **05** adult, of age **06** mature, seeded **07** grown-up **09** developed, full-blown, full-scale **10** fully grown **12** fully fledged **14** fully developed

**fullness**
**04** body, fill, glut **05** depth, force, power, width **06** growth, plenty, wealth **07** breadth, fatness, pleroma, satiety **08** dilation, loudness, plethora, richness, solidity, strength, swelling, totality, vastness **09** abundance, ampleness, greatness, impletion, intensity, largeness, plenitude, plumpness, profusion, repletion, resonance, satedness, satiation, wholeness **10** complement, congestion, tumescence **11** enlargement, repleteness, shapeliness **12** completeness, inflammation, satisfaction, thoroughness **13** extensiveness **14** curvaceousness, voluptuousness
• **in the fullness of time 06** in time **07** finally **08** in the end **10** eventually, ultimately **11** in due course

**full-scale**
**05** major **06** all-out **07** in-depth **08** complete, sweeping, thorough **09** extensive, intensive **10** exhaustive **11** wide-ranging **13** comprehensive, thoroughgoing **15** all-encompassing

**fully**
**02** up **05** quite **06** fairly, wholly **07** totally, utterly **08** entirely **09** perfectly **10** altogether, completely, positively, thoroughly, to the nines **12** sufficiently, unreservedly **13** in all respects **14** satisfactorily, without reserve

## fully fledged

**06** mature, senior **07** trained
**08** graduate **09** full-blown, qualified
**10** proficient **11** experienced
**12** professional **14** fully developed

## fulminate

**04** fume, rage, rail, slam **05** curse,
decry, flash, slate **07** bluster, condemn,
declaim, inveigh, protest, thunder
**08** denounce, detonate **09** criticize
**10** animadvert, vituperate

## fulmination

**06** tirade **07** decrial, obloquy, slating
**08** brickbat, diatribe **09** criticism,
invective, philippic **10** detonation,
thundering **11** thunderbolt
**12** condemnation, denunciation

## fulsome

**03** fat, OTT **05** gross, slimy **06** smarmy
**07** buttery, cloying, fawning
**08** effusive, luscious, nauseous,
overdone, unctuous **09** adulatory,
excessive, insincere, offensive,
sickening **10** immoderate, inordinate,
nauseating, obsequious, over the top,
saccharine **11** extravagant,
sycophantic, well-rounded
**12** enthusiastic, ingratiating **13** well-
developed

## fulsomely

**10** effusively, over the top
**11** excessively, insincerely, sickeningly
**12** immoderately, inordinately,
nauseatingly **13** extravagantly

## fumble

◇ *anagram indicator* **04** faff, feel
**05** botch, grope, spoil **06** bobble,
bungle, huddle, mumble **07** blunder
**08** flounder, scrabble **09** faff about, feel
about, mishandle, mismanage

## fume

**04** boil, rage, rant, rave, reek, stum
**05** go mad, nidor, smoke, steam,
storm, vapor **06** blow up, seethe,
vapour **07** be livid, explode **08** boil
over, smoulder **09** be furious **10** hit the
roof **11** blow your top, lose your rag,
rant and rave **12** blow your cool, fly
into a rage, lose your cool **15** fly off the
handle, go off the deep end

## fumes

**03** fog, gas **04** haze, reek, smog
**05** gases, smell, smoke, stink **06** stench,
vapour **07** exhaust, vapours
**09** pollution **10** exhalation

## fumigate

**05** smoke **06** purify, smudge
**07** cleanse, incense, perfume
**08** sanitize **09** deodorize, disinfect,
sterilize

## fumigation

**09** cleansing, purifying **12** disinfecting,
purification, sanitization
**13** sterilization

## fuming

**03** mad **05** angry, livid **06** raging
**07** boiling, enraged, furious, smoking,
uptight **08** incensed, seething, up in
arms **09** in a lather, raving mad, seeing
red, steamed up, ticked off **10** hopping
mad **11** disgruntled

## fun

**03** gig, joy **04** game, hoax, jest, joke,
lark, play, romp **05** bourd, crack, craic,
mirth, music, sport, trick, witty
**06** joking, laughs, lekker, lively
**07** amusing, foolery, gammock,
jesting, jollity **08** gladness, hilarity,
laughter, pleasure **09** amusement,
diversion, diverting, enjoyable,
enjoyment, frivolity, horseplay,
merriment **10** buffoonery, delightful,
jocularity, recreation, relaxation,
skylarking, tomfoolery **11** celebration,
distraction, merrymaking, pleasurable
**12** cheerfulness, entertaining,
recreational **13** entertainment
• **for fun** **08** for kicks **09** for a laugh
**12** for enjoyment **14** for the hell of it
• **in fun** **06** in jest **07** as a joke, playful,
to tease **09** for a laugh, jokingly,
playfully, teasingly **11** mischievous
**13** mischievously, tongue in cheek
• **make fun of** **03** cod, guy, rib
**04** goof, jeer, joke, mock **05** get at,
jolly, sport, taunt, tease **06** banter,
deride, jeer at, send up **07** laugh at,
scoff at, sneer at **08** ridicule
**09** humiliate, poke fun at **11** have a
shot at, poke borak at **13** take the
mickey **15** pull someone's leg

## function

**02** do, go **03** act, cos, cot, job, log, run,
sec, sin, tan, use **04** cosh, coth, duty,
part, post, role, sech, sine, sinh, tanh,
task, work **05** chore, cosec, party,
serve **06** affair, behave, charge,
cosech, cosine, dinner, office, result,
upshot **07** concern, mission, operate,
perform, purpose, tangent **08** activity,
business, capacity, luncheon
**09** corollary, deduction, gathering,
induction, inference, reception,
situation **10** conclusion, employment,
occupation **11** concomitant,
consequence, social event **12** have the
job of **13** play the part of
**14** responsibility
*See also* **dance**

## functional

**05** plain **06** useful **07** running, utility,
working **08** clinical **09** operative,
practical **11** hard-wearing, operational,
serviceable, utilitarian

## functionally

**08** usefully **11** efficiently, practically
**13** operationally

## functionary

**07** officer **08** employee, official
**09** dignitary **10** bureaucrat **12** office-
bearer, office-holder

## fund

**03** box, IMF **04** back, bank, cash, dosh,
gelt, loot, mine, pool, well **05** brass,
bread, cache, dough, endow, float,
fonds, grant, gravy, hoard, kitty, lolly,
means, money, rhino, stack, stock,
store **06** assets, greens, moolah, pay
for, source, supply, wealth **07** backing,
capital, finance, jackpot, promote,
readies, reserve, savings, shekels,
sponsor, support, tracker **08** treasury
**09** endowment, megabucks, reservoir,
resources, slate club, subsidize
**10** capitalize, collection, foundation,
investment, repository, storehouse,
underwrite **11** spondulicks
**12** accumulation, the necessary
**14** community chest
• **reserve fund** **04** rest
• **transfer funds** **04** vire

## fundamental

**03** key **04** main, root **05** basal, basic,
chief, first, prime, vital **06** bottom,
primal **07** bedrock, central, crucial,
initial, organic, primary, radical
**08** cardinal, integral, original,
profound, ultimate **09** elemental,
essential, important, necessary,
primitive, principal **10** elementary,
underlying **11** rudimentary
**12** foundational **13** indispensable

## fundamentalist

**05** fundy, rigid, Talib **06** fundie, strict
**08** orthodox, rigorous
**14** uncompromising

## fundamentally

**05** à fond **06** deeply **07** acutely, at heart
**08** at bottom, deep down **09** basically,
crucially, in essence, primarily,
radically **10** cardinally, critically,
inherently, profoundly **11** essentially
**13** intrinsically, substantially

## fundamentals

**04** laws **05** facts, rules **06** basics
**09** rudiments **10** brass tacks, essentials
**11** necessaries, nitty-gritty **12** nuts and
bolts **14** practicalities **15** first principles

## fundraising

*see* **charity**

## funeral

**04** obit, wake **05** tangi **06** burial
**08** exequies **09** cremation, interment,
obsequies **10** entombment,
inhumation

## funereal

**03** sad **04** dark **05** feral, grave
**06** dismal, dreary, gloomy, solemn,
sombre, woeful **07** serious **08** exequial,
funebral, mournful **09** deathlike,
funebrial, lamenting **10** depressing,
lugubrious, sepulchral

## fungus

**11** thallophyte

*Fungi include:*

**04** rust, scab, smut
**05** ergot, yeast
**06** blight
**07** candida, chytrid
**08** botritis, brown rot, fusarium,
mushroom
**09** black spot, grey mould, toadstool
**10** saprophyte, slime mould, sooty
mould
**11** downy mildew, penicillium,
slime fungus
**12** brewer's yeast, potato blight
**13** powdery mildew

*See also* **mushroom**

**funk**
**04** fear, flap, fuss, stew **05** alarm, dodge, panic, spark, state, tizzy **06** balk at, blench, cop out, dither, flinch, frenzy, fright, terror, tiswas, tizwas **07** fluster **08** blue funk **09** agitation, cold sweat, commotion, duck out of, shirk from, touchwood **10** flinch from, recoil from **12** chicken out of

**funnel**
**02** go **04** flue, horn, move, pass, pipe, pour, tube, vent **05** guide, shaft, stack **06** choana, convey, direct, drogue, filter, siphon **07** channel, chimney, tun-dish **08** sink hole, transfer, windsail **10** smokestack **11** swallow hole **12** infundibulum

**funnily**
◇ anagram indicator **09** amazingly **10** incredibly, remarkably **12** surprisingly **13** astonishingly

**funny**
◇ anagram indicator **03** odd, rum **04** rich **05** a hoot, comic, corny, droll, queer, shady, silly, wacky, weird, witty **06** absurd, way-out **07** amusing, a scream, bizarre, comical, curious, dubious, killing, oddball, off-beat, riotous, risible, strange, unusual **08** farcical, humorous, peculiar, puzzling **09** diverting, facetious, hilarious, laughable **10** hysterical, mysterious, perplexing, remarkable, ridiculous, suspicious, uproarious **12** entertaining, knee-slapping **13** side-splitting
• **something funny** **04** hoot, yell

**fur**
**03** boa **04** coat, down, fell, flue, hair, hide, mane, muff, pane, pean, pelt, skin, wool **06** fleece, pelage **07** necklet

*Furs include:*

**03** fox
**04** flix, gris, mink, vair
**05** budge, civet, fitch, genet, grise, otter, sable, skunk
**06** beaver, ermine, marten, nutria, ocelot, rabbit, racoon, zorino
**07** blue fox, caracal, caracul, crimmer, fitchet, fitchew, genette, karakul, krimmer, minever, miniver, muskrat, opossum, raccoon
**08** cony-wool, kolinsky, moleskin, musquash, ponyskin, sealskin, sea otter, zibeline
**09** broadtail, silver fox, wolverene, wolverine, zibelline
**10** chinchilla
**11** beech marten, Persian lamb, stone marten

**furbish**
**04** do up **05** refit, renew **06** polish, purify, reform, repair, revamp **07** improve, remodel, restore **08** overhaul, renovate **09** modernize, refurbish **10** redecorate **11** recondition **12** rehabilitate **15** give a facelift to

**furious**
◇ anagram indicator **03** mad, wud

**04** wild, wood, yond **05** angry, irate, livid **06** fierce, fuming, raging, savage, stormy **07** acharné, blazing, boiling, enraged, flaming, frantic, in a huff, in a stew, intense, ropable, salvage, violent **08** brainish, frenzied, in a paddy, incensed, inflamed, maenadic, seething, sizzling, up in arms, vehement, vigorous **09** desperate, in a lather, indignant **10** boisterous, hopping mad, infuriated, outrageous **11** tempestuous **12** incandescent **14** purple with rage

**furiously**
**05** madly **06** wildly **07** angrily, crossly, in anger, irately, like mad **08** fiercely, in a paddy, stormily, up in arms **09** intensely, seeing red, violently **10** like blazes, vehemently, vigorously **11** indignantly **12** passionately **13** infuriatingly, tempestuously **15** avec acharnement

**furnace**
*see* **oven**

**furnish**
**03** fit, rig **04** gird, give, suit **05** besee, endue, equip, grant, offer, plant, stock, stuff, yield **06** afford, bestow, fit out, kit out, purvey, supply **07** appoint, bedight, garnish, present, provide **08** decorate, minister

**furniture**
**06** things **07** effects **08** fitments, fittings, movables **09** equipment, moveables **10** appliances **11** accessories, furnishings, possessions **12** appointments **14** household goods

*Furniture items include:*

**03** bed, cot
**04** bunk, desk, sofa
**05** chair, chest, couch, divan, stool, suite, table, trunk, wagon
**06** buffet, bureau, carver, coffer, cradle, daybed, fender, lowboy, mirror, pouffe, settee, waggon
**07** armoire, beanbag, bunkbed, cabinet, camp-bed, commode, dresser, ottoman, sofa bed, tallboy, whatnot
**08** armchair, bar chair, bedstead, bookcase, cupboard, end table, hatstand, recliner, toy chest, tub chair, wall unit, wardrobe, water bed
**09** bed-settee, card table, coatstand, easy chair, fireplace, footstool, hallstand, high-chair, lamp table, sideboard, side table, step-stool, washstand, wine table
**10** blanket box, chiffonier, dumb-waiter, encoignure, escritoire, firescreen, four-poster, secretaire, truckle bed, vanity unit
**11** coffee table, dining chair, dining table, mantelpiece, room-divider, swivel chair
**12** bedside table, chaise-longue, chesterfield, china cabinet, computer desk, folding table, gateleg table, kitchen chair, kitchen table, magazine rack,

nest of tables, rocking chair, Welsh dresser
**13** dressing table, four-poster bed, umbrella stand
**14** chest of drawers, display cabinet, extending table, refectory table
**15** bathroom cabinet, butcher's trolley, occasional chair, occasional table

*See also* **office**

*Furniture styles include:*

**04** Adam, buhl
**06** boulle, Empire, Gothic, rococo, Shaker
**07** Art Deco, Baroque, Regency, Windsor
**08** Colonial, Georgian, Sheraton
**09** Charles II, Edwardian, Queen Anne, Shibayama, Victorian, William IV
**10** Art Nouveau, Mackintosh, provincial
**11** Anglo-Indian, Biedermeier, Chippendale, Cromwellian, Hepplewhite, Louis-Quinze, Restoration
**12** Gainsborough, Transitional, Vernis Martin
**13** Anglo-Colonial, Arts and Crafts, Dutch Colonial, Louis Philippe, Louis-Quatorze
**14** William and Mary

**furore**
**04** flap, fury, fuss, rage, stir, to-do **05** craze, stink, storm **06** frenzy, outcry, tumult, uproar **08** outburst **09** commotion **10** excitement, hullabaloo **11** disturbance

**furrow**
**03** fur, rut **04** furr, knit, line, list, mill, plow, rill, seam **05** flute, gouge, stria, track **06** crease, feerin, groove, gutter, hollow, plough, sulcus, trench, trough **07** chamfer, channel, crinkle, feering, wrinkle **08** engroove, ingroove **09** corrugate, crow's foot, vallecula **11** caniculus, lister ridge **12** draw together
• **draw first furrow** **04** feer

**furry**
**04** soft **05** downy, fuzzy, hairy **06** fleecy, fluffy, woolly

**further**
**03** aid, als, new, too **04** agen, also, ease, help, more, push **05** again, extra, fresh, other, speed **06** assist, as well, foster, hasten **07** advance, besides, develop, farther, forward, promote, remoter, speed up **08** champion, expedite, moreover **09** encourage, what's more **10** accelerate, additional, facilitate, in addition **11** furthermore, more distant, more extreme **12** additionally **13** supplementary

**furtherance**
**04** help **07** backing, pursuit **08** advocacy, boosting, speeding **09** advancing, promoting, promotion **10** preferment **11** advancement, carrying-out, championing **12** facilitation **13** encouragement

**furthermore**
03 too 04 also 06 as well 07 besides, further 08 moreover 09 what's more 10 in addition 12 additionally 14 into the bargain

**furthermost**
06 utmost 07 extreme, outmost 08 farthest, furthest, remotest, ultimate 09 outermost, uttermost

**furthest**
06 utmost 07 extreme, outmost 08 farthest, remotest, ultimate 09 outermost, uttermost 11 furthermost

**furtive**
03 sly 06 covert, hidden, secret, shifty, sneaky, veiled 07 cloaked 08 stealthy, thievish, weaselly 09 secretive, underhand 11 clandestine 13 surreptitious

**furtively**
05 slyly 08 covertly, secretly 11 secretively 15 surreptitiously

**fury**
03 ire 04 rage 05 anger, dread, force, furor, power, wrath 06 Erinys, frenzy 07 madness, passion 08 ferocity, severity, violence, wildness 09 Eumenides, intensity, vehemence 10 fierceness, turbulence 11 desperation

*The Furies:*
06 Alecto, Megara
07 Megaera
09 Tisiphone

**furze**
04 whin 05 gorse

**fuse**
03 ren, rin, run 04 flux, join, meld, melt, weld 05 blend, fusee, fuzee, merge, smelt, unite 06 mingle, solder 07 combine 08 ankylose, coalesce, conflate, intermix 09 anchylose, commingle, integrate, interfuse 10 amalgamate, colliquate, synthesize 11 agglutinate, intermingle, put together

**fusillade**
04 fire, hail 05 burst, salvo 06 volley 07 barrage 08 outburst 09 broadside, discharge

**fusion**
05 blend, union 06 merger 07 melting, running, welding 08 blending, smelting 09 ankylosis, synthesis 10 anchylosis, conflation, federation 11 coalescence, integration 12 amalgamation, colliquation

**fuss**
02 do 03 ado, row 04 coil, faff, flap, fret, futz, rout, song, stir, to-do, work 05 hoo-ha, hurry, panic, tizzy, upset, worry 06 bother, bustle, chichi, create, fidget, fikery, flurry, furore, hassle, hoo-hah, pother, pudder, racket 07 agitate, carry-on, fluster, grumble, palaver, parafle, stashie, stishie, stushie, tamasha, trouble 08 ballyhoo, brouhaha, complain, paraffle, squabble, stooshie 09 agitation, be all over, commotion, confusion, kerfuffle, pantomime, take pains 10 be in a tizzy, excitement, make a thing 11 piece of work 13 a song and dance 14 storm in a teacup

**fussiness**
08 busyness, niceness, niggling 09 finicking 10 choosiness, finicality 11 finicalness 13 particularity, perfectionism 14 meticulousness, pernicketiness

**fusspot**
06 fantod, fidget 07 old maid, worrier 08 old woman, stickler 09 nit-picker 10 fussbudget 11 hypercritic 13 perfectionist

**fussy**
◇ *anagram indicator* 04 busy 05 faddy, fancy, picky, tatty 06 chichi, choosy, ornate, prissy, rococo, spoffy 07 baroque, finical, finicky 08 niggling, pedantic, spoffish 09 cluttered, demanding, difficult, elaborate, quibbling, selective 10 fastidious, nit-picking, old-maidish, particular, pernickety, scrupulous 11 old-womanish, persnickety 12 fiddle-faddle, hard to please, pettifogging 13 grandmotherly, overdecorated 14 discriminating

**fusty**
04 damp, dank, rank 05 fuggy, musty, passé, stale 06 fousty, frowsy, frowzy, mouldy, stuffy 07 airless, archaic, frowsty 08 outdated 09 out-of-date 10 antiquated, malodorous, mouldering 11 ill-smelling, old-fogeyish 12 old-fashioned, unventilated

**futile**
04 idle, no go, vain 05 empty, inept 06 barren, hollow, in vain, no good, otiose, wasted 07 forlorn, useless 08 abortive, feckless, nugatory, tattling, trifling 09 fruitless, pointless, to no avail, worthless 10 profitless, sleeveless, unavailing 11 ineffective, ineffectual, meaningless 12 unproductive, unprofitable, unsuccessful

**futility**
05 waste 06 vanity 07 mockery 08 vainesse 09 emptiness 10 barrenness, hollowness 11 aimlessness, uselessness 12 nugatoriness 13 fruitlessness, pointlessness, worthlessness 15 ineffectiveness, meaninglessness

**future**
03 fut 04 next, to be 05 fated, later 06 avenir, coming, to come, unborn 07 by-and-by, outlook, planned 08 destined, eventual, expected, imminent, tomorrow 09 designate, hereafter, impending, prospects 10 subsequent, time to come 11 approaching, coming times, forthcoming, in the offing, prospective 12 expectations
• **in future** 04 once 05 hence 09 after this, from now on, hereafter 10 henceforth 11 hereinafter 12 henceforward 13 from this day on 14 from this time on

**fuzz**
03 fug, nap 04 blur, down, hair, lint, pile 05 fibre, flock, floss, fluff 06 police

**fuzzy**
◇ *anagram indicator* 04 hazy 05 downy, faint, foggy, furry, linty, muzzy, vague 06 fleecy, fluffy, frizzy, napped, woolly 07 blurred, fuddled, muffled, shadowy, unclear, velvety 08 confused 09 distorted, unfocused 10 ill-defined, indefinite, indistinct

# G

**G**
03 gee 04 golf

**gab**
03 jaw, yak 04 blab, brag, buzz, chat, jest, talk 05 boast, prate, vaunt 06 babble, drivel, gossip, jabber, tattle 07 blabber, blarney, blather, blether, chatter, mockery, prattle 08 chitchat 09 loquacity, prattling, small talk 10 blethering, yackety-yak 12 conversation, tittle-tattle 13 tongue-wagging

**gabble**
04 blab 05 prate, spout 06 babble, cackle, drivel, gaggle, gibber, jabber, patter, rabble, rattle, waffle 07 blabber, blether, chatter, prattle, sputter, twaddle 08 cackling, nonsense, splutter 09 gibberish 10 blethering 12 gibble-gabble, ribble-rabble

**Gabon**
01 G 03 GAB

**gad**
• **gad about** 04 fisk, roam, rove 05 jaunt, range, stray 06 ramble, travel, wander 07 traipse 08 dot about 09 flit about, gallivant, run around

**gadabout**
05 rover 07 rambler 08 runabout, wanderer 10 stravaiger 11 gallivanter 14 pleasure-seeker

**gadget**
03 toy 04 tool 05 gismo, gizmo, thing, waldo 06 device, doodad, doodah, hickey, jimjam, widget 07 gimmick, gubbins, novelty, whatnot, whatsit 08 thingamy 09 apparatus, appliance, doodackie, doohickey, implement, invention, jigamaree, jiggumbob, mechanism, thingummy 10 instrument 11 contraption, contrivance, thingamybob 12 executive toy, thingummyjig 14 what-d'you-call-it

**gadolinium**
02 Gd

**Gaelic**
04 Erse

**gaffe**
◇ *anagram indicator* 04 boob, flub, goof, slip 05 brick, error 06 boo-boo, howler, slip-up 07 bloomer, blunder, clanger, faux pas, mistake 08 solecism 09 gaucherie 12 indiscretion

**gaffer**
03 gov, guv 04 boss 06 bigwig, ganger, honcho 07 foreman, manager, overman 08 overseer 09 big cheese 10 supervisor 14 superintendent

**gag**
03 pun 04 clog, curb, hoax, jest, joke, plug, pong, quip 05 block, check, choke, crack, funny, heave, quiet, retch, still 06 muffle, muzzle, stifle, wheeze 07 deceive, silence, smother 08 one-liner, restrain, suppress, throttle 09 put a gag on, wisecrack, witticism 11 nearly vomit

**gaga**
03 mad 04 nuts 05 barmy, batty, crazy, dotty, loony, loopy, potty 06 cuckoo, insane, raving 07 fatuous 08 demented, deranged, doolally, unhinged 09 disturbed 10 distracted, unbalanced 11 not all there, off the rails 12 mad as a hatter 13 off your rocker 14 wrong in the head

**Gaia**
05 Terra

**gaiety**
03 fun, joy 04 glee, show 05 mirth 06 colour, frolic, racket 07 daffing, delight, frolics, gayness, glitter, jollity, joyance, revelry, sparkle 08 buoyancy, gladness, hilarity, pleasure, vivacity 09 festivity, happiness, joviality, merriment, showiness 10 blitheness, brightness, brilliance, exuberance, good humour, liveliness 11 celebration, galliardise, high spirits, joie de vivre, merrymaking 12 cheerfulness 13 colourfulness

**gaily**
07 happily, merrily 08 blithely, brightly, joyfully 10 cheerfully 11 brilliantly, colourfully 12 flamboyantly 14 light-heartedly

**gain**
03 add, ern, get, nab, net, win 04 earn, make, near, nett, reap, rise 05 bunce, carry, clear, get to, gross, put on, reach, yield 06 attain, collar, come to, gather, growth, income, obtain, pick up, profit, rake in, return, reward, secure 07 achieve, acquire, advance, benefit, bring in, capture, collect, harvest, headway, improve, procure, produce, realize, revenue, takings 08 addition, arrive at, dividend, earnings, increase, interest, pickings, proceeds, progress, straight, winnings 09 accretion, advantage, emolument, increment 10 attainment, chevisance, convenient 11 achievement, acquisition, advancement, improvement 12 augmentation
• **gain on** 07 catch up 08 approach, overtake 09 catch up on, close in on, close with, level with 11 catch up with, get closer to, get nearer to, outdistance 12 narrow the gap
• **gain time** 05 delay, stall 09 temporize 10 dilly-dally 11 play for time 12 drag your feet 13 procrastinate
• **seek to gain** 03 woo 09 cultivate

**gainful**
04 paid 06 paying, useful 08 fruitful 09 fructuous, lucrative, rewarding 10 beneficial, productive, profitable, worthwhile 11 moneymaking 12 advantageous, remunerative

**gainfully**
08 usefully 10 profitably 11 lucratively 12 beneficially, productively 14 advantageously

**gainsay**
04 deny 06 oppose 07 dispute 09 challenge, disaffirm 10 contradict, contravene, controvert 12 disagree with

**gait**
03 get 04 brat, gyte, pace, step, walk 05 child, going, tread 06 allure, manner, stride 07 bearing 08 carriage 10 deportment

**gaiter**
04 spat 06 hogger 07 cutikin, spattee 08 cootikin, cuitikin 11 spatterdash

**gala**
04 fair, fete 05 party 07 jubilee, pageant 08 carnival, festival, jamboree 09 festivity 10 procession 11 celebration

**galaxy**
04 host, mass 05 array, stars 06 blazar, nebula 07 cluster 09 gathering, multitude 10 collection, star system 11 solar system 13 constellation, group assembly

---

*Galaxies include:*

---

03 Leo
04 Arp's, Lost, Mice
05 Bode's, Helix, Malin
06 Baade's, Carafe, Hydra A, Maffei, Spider, Virgo A, Zwicky
07 Cannon's, Cygnus A, Pancake, Sextans, Spindle, The Eyes
08 Antennae, Barnard's, Bear's Paw, Black Eye, Milky Way, Papillon, Perseus A, Pinwheel, Seashell, Sombrero
09 Andromeda, Bear's Claw, Cartwheel, Centaurus, Hercules A, Sunflower, Whirlpool
10 Draco Dwarf, Silver Coin, The Garland, Triangulum
11 Carina Dwarf, Hardcastle's, Pisces Cloud, Pisces Dwarf, The Ringtail
12 Atom For Peace, Integral Sign, Pegasus Dwarf, Siamese Twins, Virgo Cluster
13 Aquarius Dwarf, Sculptor Dwarf, Serpens Sextet, Virgo Pinwheel
14 Capricorn Dwarf, Copeland Septet, Reticulum Dwarf, Ursa Minor Dwarf
15 Exclamation Mark, Horologium Dwarf, Magellanic Cloud, Miniature Spiral

---

**gale**
03 fit 04 wind 05 blast, burst, storm 06 Myrica, squall, wester 07 cyclone, norther, sea turn, snorter, souther, tornado, typhoon 08 eruption, outbreak, outburst 09 bog myrtle, explosion, hurricane, sou'wester 10 ripsnorter 11 equinoctial, sweet willow

**gall**
03 irk, nag, vex 04 bile, dyke, fell, flaw,

neck, rile **05** annoy, brass, cheek, fault, get to, nerve, peeve, scoff, spite, venom **06** animus, bother, enmity, harass, malice, nettle, oak-nut, pester, plague, rankle, ruffle **07** ill-will, provoke, rancour **08** acrimony, bedeguar, chutzpah, irritate, oak apple, sourness, tacahout **09** aggravate, animosity, antipathy, assurance, brass neck, hostility, impudence, insolence, sage apple, sauciness, virulence **10** bitterness, brazenness, effrontery, exasperate **11** malevolence, presumption **12** impertinence, mycodomatium **13** get on your wick, get up your nose, get your back up, put your back up

## gallant
**03** fop, gay **04** beau, bold **05** brave, dandy, lover, manly, noble **06** daring, heroic, plucky, polite **07** amorous, courtly, dashing, valiant **08** cavalier, cicisbeo, fearless, gracious, intrepid, splendid **09** attentive, audacious, chamberer, chevalier, chivalric, courteous, dauntless **10** chivalrous, courageous, honourable, thoughtful **11** considerate, gentlemanly, magnificent

## gallantly
**05** nobly **07** bravely **08** politely **09** valiantly **10** fearlessly, graciously, heroically, honourably, intrepidly **11** audaciously, courteously, dauntlessly **12** chivalrously, courageously, thoughtfully **13** considerately

## gallantry
**04** game **05** pluck **06** daring, honour, spirit, valour **07** bravery, courage, heroism **08** audacity, boldness, chivalry, courtesy, nobility, valiance **09** manliness **10** politeness **11** courtliness, intrepidity **12** fearlessness, graciousness **13** attentiveness, consideration, courteousness, dauntlessness **14** courageousness, thoughtfulness **15** gentlemanliness

## gallery
**04** brow, gods, loft, mine, pawn, walk **05** alure, level **06** arcade, circle, dedans, museum **07** balcony, passage, terrace, veranda **08** bartisan, bartizan, brattice, brattish, brettice, casemate, rood loft, traverse, verandah **09** choir loft, triforium **10** art gallery, earth-house, hall of fame, pinakothek, scaffolage, spectators **11** display room, dress circle, pinacotheca, scaffoldage **14** exhibition area
*See also* **museum**

## galley
*see* **ship**

## galling
**06** bitter, vexing **07** irksome **08** annoying, nettling, plaguing, rankling **09** harassing, provoking, vexatious **10** bothersome, irritating **11** aggravating, embittering, humiliating, infuriating **12** exasperating

## gallium
**02** Ga

## gallivant
**04** roam, rove **05** range, stray **06** ramble, travel, wander **07** traipse **08** dot about, gad about, stravaig **09** flit about, run around

## gallon
**01** g **03** gal **04** cong, gall **07** congius

## gallop
**03** fly, run **04** bolt, dart, dash, race, rush, tear, zoom **05** burst, hurry, shoot, speed **06** canter, career, hasten, scurry, sprint, wallop **07** cariere

## gallows
**03** nub **04** tree, wild **05** bough, cheat, perky, saucy **06** daring, gallus, gibbet, plucky, woodie **07** stifler, the rope **08** damnably, dule-tree, impudent, scaffold, spirited, tiresome **09** sprightly **10** Tyburn-tree, villainous **11** mischievous **12** confoundedly, nubbing-cheat, unmanageable

## galore
**06** lots of, plenty, tons of **07** aplenty, heaps of, to spare **08** stacks of **09** in numbers **10** everywhere, millions of **11** in abundance, in profusion

## galvanize
**04** fire, jolt, move, prod, spur, stir, urge, zinc **05** rouse, shock **06** arouse, awaken, excite **07** animate, enliven, inspire, provoke, quicken, startle **08** energize, vitalize **09** electrify, stimulate **10** invigorate

## Gambia
**03** GMB, WAG

## gambit
**04** move, play, ploy, ruse, wile **05** trick **06** device, tactic **07** tactics **08** artifice **09** manoeuvre, stratagem **11** machination

## gamble
**03** bet **04** back, dice, gaff, game, jeff, play, punt, risk, spec **05** stake, wager **06** chance, hazard, plunge, toss-up **07** flutter, lottery, pot luck, venture **08** chance it **09** speculate, take a risk **10** put money on **11** speculation, take a chance, try your luck **12** have a flutter, play for money **13** leap in the dark, play the horses

## gambler
**06** better, punter **07** plunger, tinhorn, tipster **08** gamester **09** bookmaker, daredevil, desperado, risk-taker, throwster **14** turf accountant

## gambling
**04** play **07** betting **10** risk-taking **11** speculation **15** playing for money

---

*Gambling-related terms include:*

**03** hit, lay, pot
**04** back, bust, dice, hold, odds, punt, shoe, tout
**05** bingo, cards, craps, jeton, lotto, motza, poker, pools, stake, stick, wager, welsh
**06** bookie, casino, chip in, fan-tan, fulham, gaming, jetton, lay off, motser, punter

---

**07** flutter, lottery, tipster
**08** levanter, long shot, outsider, roulette, teetotum
**09** blackjack, bookmaker, card shark, dog racing, favourite, place a bet, vingt-et-un
**10** put-and-take, put money on, sweepstake
**11** card-sharper, find the lady, go one better, horse racing, numbers game, rouge-et-noir, slot machine
**12** break the bank, card counting, debt of honour, pitch-and-toss, scoop the pool
**13** hedge your bets, shoot the works, spread betting
**14** shove-halfpenny, three-card trick, wheel of fortune
**15** cash in your chips, disorderly house, greyhound racing, make a clean sweep

---

*See also* **bet**
• **gambling place** **04** hell **06** arcade, casino

## gambol
◇ *anagram indicator* **03** hop **04** jump, leap, romp, skip **05** bound, caper, dance, frisk **06** bounce, cavort, frolic, prance, spring **07** disport **09** cut a caper, cut capers **15** kick up your heels

## game
**03** bag, fun, jeu, pit, tie **04** ball, bold, bout, jest, joke, lame, meat, meet, play, prey, romp **05** brave, eager, event, flesh, match, prank, ready, round, sport, trick, up for **06** daring, frolic, gamble, plucky, quarry, spoils **07** contest, gallant, meeting, pastime, valiant, willing **08** activity, business, desirous, fearless, inclined, intrepid, prepared, resolute, spirited, wild fowl **09** amusement, diversion, gallantry, merriment, operation **10** courageous, interested, recreation, tournament **11** competition, distraction, lion-hearted, unflinching **12** enthusiastic **13** entertainment, practical joke

---

*Game animals and birds include:*

**03** elk, fox
**04** bear, boar, coot, deer, duck, guan, hare, lion, stag, teal, wolf
**05** bison, goose, hyena, moose, quail, scaup, snipe, tiger, zebra
**06** curlew, grouse, plover, rabbit, wigeon
**07** buffalo, caribou, giraffe, mallard, moorhen, muntjac, pintail, pochard, red deer, roe deer, widgeon
**08** antelope, elephant, kangaroo, pheasant, sika deer, squirrel, wild boar, woodcock
**09** blackcock, blackgame, crocodile, partridge, ptarmigan, waterfowl
**10** fallow deer, guinea fowl, tufted duck, wild turkey, wood grouse, woodpigeon
**11** Canada goose
**12** capercaillie, capercailzie, hippopotamus, mountain lion

*See also* **poultry**

*Games include:*

**03** loo, nap, tag, tig
**04** brag, crib, dice, faro, I-spy, ludo, pool, snap
**05** bingo, bowls, chess, clubs, craps, darts, halma, jacks, Jenga®, poker, rummy, whist
**06** bridge, Cluedo®, quinze
**07** bezique, bowling, canasta, conkers, fusball, hangman, mahjong, marbles, old maid, picquet, pinball, pontoon, snooker, tombola
**08** baccarat, card game, charades, checkers, cribbage, dominoes, draughts, foosball, forfeits, fussball, gin rummy, Kim's game, Monopoly®, napoleon, patience, ping pong, reversis, roulette, sardines, Scrabble®
**09** air hockey, bagatelle, billiards, blackjack, board game, draw poker, hopscotch, newmarket, Pelmanism, Simon says, solitaire, solo whist, stud poker, tic-tac-toe, twenty-one, vingt-et-un
**10** backgammon, Balderdash®, fivestones, jackstraws, Pictionary®, spillikins
**11** battleships, beetle drive, chemin de fer, hide-and-seek, table tennis, tiddlywinks
**12** consequences, partner whist, shove ha'penny
**13** blindman's buff, clock patience, happy families, musical chairs, pass the parcel, postman's knock, spin the bottle, table football, ten-pin bowling
**14** contract bridge, follow-my-leader, hunt-the-thimble, nine men's morris, Trivial Pursuit®
**15** Chinese checkers, Chinese whispers, duplicate bridge

*Board games include:*

**02** go
**04** ludo, Risk®, siga
**05** chess, darts, goose, halma, lurch, marls, nyout, senet, shogi, Sorry®
**06** Boggle®, Cluedo®, gobang, gomuku, merels, merils, morals, morris, tables, tabula, uckers
**07** Cranium®, mah-jong, mancala, marrels, merells, pachisi, petteia, reverse, reversi, Yahtzee®
**08** checkers, chequers, cribbage, Dingbats®, draughts, miracles, Monopoly®, parchesi, Rummikub®, Scrabble®
**09** bagatelle, Buccaneer®, Operation®, Parcheesi®, solitaire, tic-tac-toe
**10** backgammon, Go for Broke®, latrunculi, Mastermind®, Pictionary®
**11** Battleships®, fox and geese, Frustration®
**12** pente grammai
**13** Concentration®, table skittles, The Game of Life®
**14** nine men's morris, Trivial Pursuit®
**15** Chinese checkers, Chinese

chequers, duodecim scripta, fivepenny morris, ninepenny morris, three men's morris

*See also* **sport**

*Card games include:*

**03** don, nap, pig, war
**04** brag, bust, faro, fish, golf, king, loba, may I?, phat, pits, push, rook, scat, skat, snap, solo, spit, tunk, tute, ugly
**05** blitz, cheat, cinch, crash, flush, knack, nerts, pairs, pedro, pitch, poker, ronda, rummy, samba, shoot, speed, tarok, tarot, whist
**06** big two, boodle, bridge, casino, church, crates, cuckoo, dakota, deuces, écarté, euchre, fan tan, five up, go fish, hearts, henway, kaiser, knaves, oh hell!, palace, pepper, piquet, pounce, red dog, sevens, spades, spoons, squeal, stitch, switch, tarock, taroky, trumps, turtle, valets
**07** auction, authors, bezique, bone ace, canasta, clabber, last one, mah jong, old maid, pontoon, quartet, setback, spitzer, whipsaw
**08** ace-deuce, all fives, all fours, anaconda, baccarat, bid whist, blackout, carousel, cribbage, drunkard, elevator, gin rummy, high five, Michigan, napoleon, patience, pinochle, Pope Joan, sequence, shanghai, Welsh don
**09** abyssinia, bid euchre, blackjack, catch five, golden ten, king pedro, king rummy, let it ride, newmarket, Pelmanism, poker bull, president, quadrille, racehorse, solitaire, solo whist, stud poker, tic-tac-toe, tile rummy, vingt-et-un
**10** black maria, buck euchre, capitalism, Chinese ten, cincinnati, crazy nines, dirty clubs, German solo, parliament, preference, ride the bus, sheepshead, strip poker, three in one, Wall Street
**11** cat and mouse, chase the ace, chemin de fer, chicken foot, crazy eights, English stud, find the lady, French tarot, French whist, German whist, high-low-jack, Indian poker, Mexican stud, nine-card don, Oklahoma gin, racing demon, Russian bank, six-card brag, speculation, Texas hold 'em
**12** Chinese poker, devil's bridge, draw dominoes, five-card brag, five-card draw, four-card brag, high-card pool, kings corners, Mexican sweat, Mexican train, nine-card brag, one and thirty, pick a partner, ruff and trump, Russian poker, shoot pontoon
**13** concentration, contract rummy, contract whist, happy families, knockout whist, lame-brain Pete, Michigan rummy, Romanian whist, sergeant major, seven-card brag, Shanghai rummy, three-card brag

**14** Caribbean poker, contract bridge, five hundred rum, fives and threes, follow the queen, good, better, best, jack the shifter, Liverpool rummy, Minnesota whist, rich man, poor man, ruff and honours, second hand high, spite and malice, spit in the ocean, three-card monte, trust-don't trust
**15** back alley bridge, cut-throat euchre, double solitaire, nomination whist, railroad canasta, stealing bundles

• **end to game 04** draw, mate
**09** checkmate, stalemate
• **point out game 03** set
• **preliminary to game 04** toss
• **right to begin game 04** pose

**gamekeeper**
**06** keeper, warden **07** venerer

**gamely**
**06** boldly **07** bravely **09** valiantly
**10** fearlessly, intrepidly, resolutely
**12** courageously **13** unflinchingly

**gamut**
**04** area **05** field, gamme, range, scale, scope, sweep **06** series **07** compass, variety **08** sequence, spectrum

**gang**
**02** go **03** lot, mob, set **04** band, club, core, crew, crue, ging, herd, nest, pack, push, ring, team **05** coven, crowd, group, horde, party, posse, shift, squad **06** circle, clique, coffle, outfit, troupe **07** company, coterie, massive, ratpack **09** gathering
**11** tribulation
• **gang up on, gang up against**
**12** unite against **13** team up against
**15** conspire against

**gangling**
**04** bony, tall **05** gawky, lanky, rangy
**06** gangly, gauche, skinny **07** angular, awkward, spindly **08** raw-boned, ungainly **12** loose-jointed

**gangrene**
**07** mortify **08** necrosis **09** phagedena
**10** phagedaena, thanatosis

**gangster**
**02** Al **04** hood, thug **05** crook, heavy, rough, tough **06** bandit, Capone, robber, yakuza, Yardie **07** brigand, gangsta, goombah, greaser, hoodlum, mobster, ruffian, steamer, tumbler, wise guy **08** criminal, enforcer
**09** desperado, goodfella, racketeer, terrorist

**gangway**
**04** brow **05** aisle **07** passage, walkway
**08** corridor **10** passageway

**gannet**
**04** guga **05** booby, solan **10** solan goose

**gaol, gaoler**
*see* **jail; jailer**

**gap**
**04** gulf, hole, lack, leap, lull, rent, rift, rima, slap, void **05** blank, break,

chasm, chink, cleft, crack, gorge, musit, notch, pause, shard, sherd, space **06** breach, bunker, cavity, cranny, divide, hiatus, lacuna, recess, spread, street, window **07** crevice, fissure, opening, orifice, passage, saw gate, saw kerf, vacancy, vacuity **08** aperture, distance, fontanel, fracture, interval, sliprail **09** disparity, interlude **10** difference, divergence, fontanelle, interstice, separation **11** interregnum **12** intermission, interruption **13** discontinuity, node of Ranvier **14** expansion joint

## gape
**04** bawl, gaup, gawk, gawp, gaze, open, part, yawn **05** crack, gerne, split, stare **06** goggle, rictus, wonder **07** dehisce **10** rubberneck

## gaper
**03** Mya **06** comber

## gaping
**04** open, vast, wide **05** broad, hiant **06** rictus **07** ringent, yawning **09** cavernous, fatiscent, interrupt **11** open-mouthed **12** fissirostral

## garage
**04** barn **06** lock-up **07** car port **10** gas station **11** muffler shop **13** petrol station **14** service station

## garb
**03** rig **04** form, gear, look, robe, togs, vest, wear **05** array, cover, dress, get-up, guise, robes, style **06** aspect, attire, clothe, livery, outfit, rig out, rig-out **07** apparel, clobber, clothes, costume, fashion, garment, raiment, regalia, uniform, vesture **08** clothing **09** semblance, vestiment, vestments **10** appearance, habiliment, habilitate

## garbage
**03** rot **04** blah, bosh, bull, bunk, guff, junk, muck **05** balls, bilge, dross, filth, hooey, slops, swill, trash, tripe, waste **06** bunkum, debris, drivel, hot air, litter, piffle, refuse, scraps **07** baloney, eyewash, hogwash, remains, rhubarb, rubbish, twaddle **08** claptrap, cobblers, detritus, malarkey, nonsense, tommyrot **09** gibberish, leftovers, moonshine, poppycock, scourings, sweepings **10** codswallop **11** odds and ends **13** bits and pieces

## garble
◇ *anagram indicator* **04** edit, sift, warp **05** mix up, slant, twist **06** doctor, jumble, mangle, muddle **07** cleanse, confuse, corrupt, distort, falsify, pervert **08** mutilate, scramble **10** tamper with **12** misinterpret, misrepresent

## garbled
◇ *anagram indicator* **07** jumbled, mixed-up, muddled **08** confused **09** scrambled **14** undecipherable, unintelligible

## garden
**03** erf **04** bagh, park, plot, yard **05** garth **06** herbar **07** section **08** backyard, paradise **09** curtilage

*Gardens include:*

**03** Kew
**04** Eden, Ness
**05** Stowe
**06** Het Loo, Monet's, Suzhou, Tivoli, Wisley
**07** Alnwick, Bodnant, Boxwood, Giverny, Heligan, Kane'ohe, Motsuji, Urakuen
**08** Alhambra, Biltmore, Blenheim, Claymont, Ermitage, Hopewood, Hyde Hall, Inverewe, Longwood, Mt Vernon, Nanzenji, Pleasure, Rikugien, Rosedown, Rosemoor, Sankeien
**09** Bagatelle, Claremont, Lingering, Lion Grove, Stourhead, Tuileries
**10** Capel Manor, Chatsworth, Harlow Carr, Kensington, Levens Hall, Schönbrunn, Versailles
**11** Chanticleer, Eden Project, Ji Chang Yuan
**12** Castle Howard, Hampton Court, Hidcote Manor, Jingshan Park, Katsura Rikyu, Royal Botanic, Sissinghurst, Studley Royal
**13** Dumbarton Oaks, Harewood House, Orange Botanic, Vaux le Vicomte
**14** Biddulph Grange, Drummond Castle, Hua Ching Palace, Stone Lion Grove
**15** Arnold Arboretum

*Garden types include:*

**03** tea
**04** beer, herb, knot, lawn, rock, roof, rose
**05** arbor, fruit, water
**06** alpine, arbour, border, flower, herbar, indoor, market, physic, rosary, rosery, sunken, walled, winter
**07** cottage, hanging, Italian, kitchen, olitory, orchard, rockery, rose bed
**08** chinampa, Japanese, kailyard, rosarium
**09** allotment, arboretum, botanical, cole-garth, flower bed, kailyaird, raised bed, shrubbery, terrarium, truck-farm, window box
**10** ornamental, rose arbour
**13** plantie-cruive, vegetable plot

## gardener
**03** Eve **04** Adam, mali **06** mallee **07** trucker

*Gardeners include:*

**03** **Don** (Monty)
**04** **Kent** (William), **Page** (Russell)
**05** **Brown** (Lancelot 'Capability'), **Gavin** (Diarmuid), **Lloyd** (Christopher), **Monet** (Claude), **Wilde** (Kim)
**06** **Gilpin** (William Sawrey), **Ingram** (Collingwood 'Cherry'), **Jekyll** (Gertrude), **Paxton** (Sir Joseph), **Repton** (Humphry)
**07** **Clusius** (Carolus), **Dimmock** (Charlie), **Le Nôtre** (André), **Thrower** (Percy)
**08** **Hamilton** (Geoff), **Jellicoe** (Sir Geoffrey), **Robinson** (William)
**10** **Titchmarsh** (Alan), **Tradescant** (John, the Elder), **Tradescant** (John, the Younger)
**13** **Sackville-West** (Vita)

## garden flower
*see* **flower**

## gardening
**12** horticulture

*Gardening tools include:*

**03** axe, hoe
**04** fork, pots, rake
**05** Flymo®, spade
**06** cloche, gloves, scythe, shears, trowel
**07** fan rake, hatchet, kneeler, loppers, netting, pruners, trellis, wellies
**08** chainsaw, clippers, hosepipe, shredder, strimmer
**09** cold frame, fruit cage, garden saw, lawn edger, lawnmower, lawn raker, secateurs, sprinkler, water butt
**10** compost bin, cultivator, fertilizer, garden cart, greenhouse, lawn roller, soil tester, weedkiller
**11** incinerator, watering can, wheelbarrow
**12** hedge trimmer, potting table
**13** garden sprayer, lawn scarifier
**14** rotary spreader

*Gardening-related terms include:*

**03** bed
**04** bulb, clay, loam, plot, seed, soil, tree, weed
**05** bower, graft, hedge, mulch, plant, shrub
**06** annual, hoeing, hybrid, manure, raking
**07** climber, compost, cutting, digging, growing, organic, produce, pruning, staking, topiary, topsoil, weeding
**08** gardener, layering, planting, thinning, watering
**09** deciduous, germinate, leaf-mould, perennial, pesticide
**10** coniferous, fertilizer, hardy plant
**11** cultivation, green manure, ground cover, hydroponics, potting shed, propagation
**12** bedding plant, conservatory, horticulture, hybrid vigour
**13** double digging, growing season, transplanting
**15** window gardening

## Gardner
**03** Ava

## gargantuan
**03** big **04** huge, vast **05** giant, large **07** immense, mammoth, massive, titanic **08** colossal, enormous, gigantic, towering **09** ginormous, humongous, humungous, leviathan, monstrous **10** monumental, prodigious, tremendous **11** elephantine **14** Brobdingnagian

## garish
**04** heal, loud, rory **05** cheap, flash, gaudy, jazzy, lurid, roary, rorie, showy

## garishly
**06** criant, flashy, glitzy, roarie, tawdry, vulgar **07** glaring, raffish **08** luminous, tinselly **09** flaunting, tasteless **10** glittering **12** meretricious

## garishly
**06** loudly **07** gaudily, jazzily, luridly **08** glitzily **09** glaringly **11** tastelessly

## garland
**03** lei **04** bays, deck **05** adorn, crown, glory, toran **06** crants, stemma, torana, wreath **07** chaplet, coronal, coronet, festoon, flowers, girlond, honours, laurels, wreathe **08** decorate, headband, ornament **09** engarland **10** decoration, naval crown

## garments
**04** garb, gear, togs, wear **05** dress, get-up **06** attire, outfit **07** apparel, clothes, costume, uniform **08** clothing, menswear
*See also* **clothes, clothing**

## garner
**04** cull, heap, save **05** amass, hoard, lay up, put by, store **06** gather, pile up **07** collect, deposit, granary, harvest, husband, reserve, stack up **08** assemble, stow away, treasure **09** stockpile **10** accumulate

## garnet
**06** pyrope **08** melanite **09** almandine, andradite, carbuncle, demantoid, grossular, pyreneite, rhodolite, uvarovite **10** alabandine, topazolite **11** schorlomite, spessartine, spessartite **12** grossularite **13** cinnamon stone **14** Uralian emerald

## garnish
**04** deck, lard, trim **05** adorn, grace **06** kit out, relish, set off, supply **07** deck out, enhance, festoon, furnish **08** beautify, decorate, ornament, trimming **09** adornment, embellish, gremolata **10** decoration **11** enhancement **13** embellishment, ornamentation

## garret
**04** loft **05** attic, roost, solar **06** turret **07** mansard **09** roof space **10** watchtower

## garrison
**03** man **04** base, camp, fort, post, unit **05** guard, mount, place, stuff **06** assign, casern, defend, occupy, troops, zareba **07** command, furnish, protect, station **08** barracks, fortress, position **10** armed force, detachment, encampment, engarrison, stronghold **13** fortification

## garrulous
**04** glib **05** gabby, gassy, windy, wordy **06** chatty, mouthy, prolix **07** gushing, prating, verbose, voluble, wordish **08** babbling, effusive, gaggling **09** gossiping, prattling, talkative, yabbering **10** chattering, long-winded, loquacious

## garrulousness
**09** loquacity, prolixity, verbosity **10** mouthiness, volubility **11** verboseness, wordiness

**13** talkativeness **14** long-windedness, loquaciousness

## gas
*Gases include:*

**02** CS
**03** air, LNG, LPG
**04** neon, tear, town
**05** ether, marsh, nerve, niton, ozone, radon, xenon
**06** butane, helium, ketene, nitrox
**07** ammonia, krypton, methane, mustard, natural, propane
**08** cyanogen, ethylene, firedamp, laughing
**09** acetylene, black damp, chokedamp
**10** chloroform
**12** nitrous oxide
**13** carbon dioxide, dimethylamine
**14** carbon monoxide

*See also* **talk**

## gash
**03** cut **04** hack, nick, rend, rent, slit, tear **05** extra, gouge, score, slash, spare, split, wound **06** incise, scotch, tattle **07** ghastly, hideous **08** incision, lacerate **09** talkative **10** laceration

## gasp
**04** blow, gulp, kink, pant, puff **05** chink, choke, heave **06** breath, wheeze **07** breathe **11** exclamation **15** catch your breath

## gassy
**06** bubbly, frothy **07** aerated, foaming, gaseous, verbose **08** bubbling **09** sparkling **10** carbonated **12** effervescent

## gastric
**07** coeliac, enteric, stomach **09** abdominal, stomachic **10** intestinal

## gastropod
*see* **mollusc**

## gate
**03** way **04** door, exit, goat, path, port, yate, yett **05** hatch, koker **06** access, portal, street, vimana, wicket **07** barrier, caisson, channel, doorway, gateway, opening, passage, pontoon, postern, shutter **08** aboideau, aboiteau, entrance, sliprail
*See also* **circuit**

## gatecrash
**04** sorn

## gateway
**04** arch, port **05** pylon, toran, torii **06** torana **08** propylon **09** sallyport **10** propylaeum

## gather
◇ *containment indicator* **02** in **03** add, **04** camp, club, crop, cull, draw, fold, gain, grow, heap, hear, mass, meet, pick, pull, rake, reap, tuck **05** amass, build, crowd, flock, get in, glean, group, hoard, infer, learn, pleat, pluck, rally, shirr **06** assume, deduce, garner, muster, pick up, pile up, pucker, pull in, rake in, roll up, ruffle, select, summon, throng **07** accrete, advance, attract, believe, build up, cluster,

collect, convene, develop, harvest, hoard up, improve, marshal, round up, surmise **08** assemble, conclude, converge, increase, progress **09** stash away, stockpile, suppurate **10** accumulate, congregate, understand **12** come together **13** bring together

## gathering
◇ *containment indicator* **03** bee, hui, lek, mob **04** band, feis, fest, mass, meet, rave, rout, ruck, shir **05** coven, crowd, flock, group, hangi, horde, party, rally, salon, shirr, spree **06** huddle, love-in, muster, rabble, social, throng **07** company, gabfest, husking, Kommers, meeting, reunion, round-up, turnout **08** assembly, conclave, function, jamboree, musicale, singsong, tea party **09** wapenshaw, wapinshaw **10** assemblage, collective, convention, corroboree, logrolling, wapenschaw, wapinschaw, wappenschaw **11** convocation, gallimaufry, get-together, wappenschaw **12** congregation **14** belle assemblée

## gauche
**03** shy **05** gawky, inept **06** clumsy **07** awkward, ill-bred **08** farouche, ignorant, tactless, ungainly **09** graceless, inelegant, maladroit **10** uncultured, ungraceful, unpolished **11** ill-mannered, insensitive **15** unsophisticated

## gaudiness
**08** loudness **09** harshness, showiness **10** brightness, brilliance, flashiness, garishness, tawdriness **11** raffishness **13** tastelessness

## gaudy
**03** gay **04** loud **05** flash, harsh, merry, showy, stark, tacky **06** bright, flashy, garish, glitzy, kitsch, snazzy, tawdry, tinsel, vulgar **07** flaming, glaring, raffish **08** tinselly **09** brilliant, colourful, flaunting, shrieking, tasteless, too bright **12** meretricious, ostentatious **13** multicoloured

## gauge
**04** area, bore, norm, rate, rule, size, span, test **05** basic, check, count, depth, guess, guide, judge, meter, model, scale, scope, sizer, value, weigh, width **06** assess, degree, extent, figure, height, reckon, sample **07** apprise, calibre, compute, example, measure, pattern, scantle **08** capacity, estimate, evaluate, exemplar, standard **09** ascertain, benchmark, calculate, criterion, determine, guideline, indicator, magnitude, marijuana, scantling, thickness, yardstick **11** guesstimate

*Gauges include:*

**03** oil
**04** rain, ring, snap, tide, tyre, wind
**05** drill, paper, steam, taper, water
**06** feeler, radius, strain, vacuum
**07** Bourdon, cutting, loading, marking, mortise

**08** gauge rod, pressure, udometer
**09** Nilometer
**10** anemometer, gauge glass, gauge wheel, hyetograph, hyetometer, micrometer, ombrometer, planometer, touchstone
**11** pluviometer
**15** hyetometrograph

## gaunt
**04** bare, bony, grim, lank, lean, thin, yawn **05** bleak, harsh, stark **06** barren, dismal, dreary, skinny, wasted **07** angular, forlorn, haggard, rawbone, scraggy, scrawny, spindly **08** desolate, rawboned, skeletal **09** emaciated **10** cadaverous, forbidding, hollow-eyed **12** skin and bones

## Gauss
**01** G **02** gs

## gauze
**04** film **07** tiffany **08** illusion
**11** cheesecloth

## gauzy
**04** thin **05** filmy, light, sheer **06** flimsy **08** delicate, gossamer **10** diaphanous, see-through **11** transparent
**13** insubstantial, unsubstantial

## gawk
**04** gape, gawp, gaze, look, ogle
**05** stare **06** goggle

## gawky
**05** inept, lanky **06** clumsy, gauche, oafish **07** awkward, loutish
**08** gangling, ungainly **09** graceless, lumbering, maladroit **13** unco-ordinated

## gawp
**04** gape, gawk, gaze, look, ogle
**05** stare **06** goggle

## gay
**04** camp, pink, rich **05** gaudy, happy, jolly, merry, nitid, riant, showy, sunny, vivid **06** blithe, bright, flashy, garish, joyful, lively, wanton **07** festive, gallant, lesbian, playful, sapphic, spotted **08** animated, bisexual, carefree, cheerful, debonair, speckled **09** brilliant, colourful, exuberant, fun-loving, homophile, sparkling, sprightly, vivacious **10** dissipated, flamboyant, homosexual **12** light-hearted **13** in good spirits, in high spirits **15** pleasure-seeking

## gaze
**03** eye **04** gape, gawk, look, moon, muse, pore, view **05** stare, watch **06** goggle, regard, wonder **08** aftereye, gazement, outstare, wait upon **09** fixed look, moon about **10** moon around **11** contemplate **12** look vacantly, stare fixedly **13** stare intently

## gazebo
**03** hut **07** shelter **08** pavilion
**09** belvedere **11** summerhouse

## gazelle
**03** goa **04** mohr **05** ariel, mhorr
**07** chikara **08** chinkara

## gazette
**03** gaz **05** organ, paper **06** notice

---

**07** journal, tabloid **08** despatch, dispatch, magazine **09** newspaper, news-sheet **10** broadsheet, periodical

## gear
**03** cog, fit, kit, low, top **04** garb, togs **05** adapt, dress, drugs, first, get-up, shift, stuff, third, tools, works **06** affair, armour, attire, design, devise, doings, matter, outfit, second, tackle, tailor, things **07** apparel, baggage, clobber, clothes, effects, gearing, harness, luggage, prepare, ratchet, reverse, threads **08** business, clothing, cogwheel, garments, organize, supplies, utensils **09** apparatus, engrenage, equipment, gearwheel, machinery, mechanism **10** appliances, belongings, implements, link-motion, tooth-wheel, underdrive
**11** accessories, instruments, possessions, synchromesh
**12** contrivances, toothed wheel
**13** accoutrements, paraphernalia
*See also* **clothes, clothing; garments**

## geegee
**02** GG
*See also* **horse**

## geezer
**03** man **04** chap, cove **05** bloke
**06** fellow

## gel, jell
**03** set **04** form **06** harden **07** congeal, stiffen, thicken **08** finalize, solidify **09** coagulate, take shape **11** crystallize, materialize **12** come together

## gelatinous
**05** gluey, gooey, gummy **06** sticky, viscid **07** jellied, rubbery, viscous
**09** congealed, glutinous, jelly-like
**12** mucilaginous

## geld
**03** cut, lib, tax **04** sort, spay **05** unman, unsex **06** neuter **07** deprive **08** castrate, enfeeble **09** expurgate **10** emasculate

## gem
**03** bud **04** rose **05** cameo, jewel, prize, stone **06** scarab **08** gemstone, marquise, sparkler, treasure
**09** bespangle, brilliant, scaraboid
**11** masterpiece, pride and joy **12** the bee's knees **13** precious stone
**14** crème de la crème

*Gemstones include:*

**03** jet
**04** jade, onyx, opal, ruby
**05** agate, amber, beryl, coral, pearl, topaz
**06** garnet, jasper, zircon
**07** cat's eye, citrine, crystal, diamond, emerald, peridot
**08** amethyst, fire opal, sapphire, sunstone
**09** cairngorm, carbuncle, carnelian, cornelian, demantoid, malachite, marcasite, moonstone, morganite, soapstone, tiger's eye, turquoise, uvarovite
**10** aquamarine, bloodstone, chalcedony, chrysolite, greenstone, rhinestone, rose

---

quartz, serpentine, spinel ruby, tourmaline
**11** alexandrite, chrysoberyl, chrysoprase, lapis lazuli, spessartite
**13** cubic zirconia, mother-of-pearl, white sapphire

## gen
**04** data, dope, info **05** facts **07** details, low-down **09** knowledge
**10** background **11** information
• **gen up on** **05** study **08** bone up on, read up on, research, swot up on
**09** brush up on **12** find out about

## gene
*see* **genetics**

## genealogy
**04** line **05** birth **06** family **07** dynasty
**08** breeding **09** parentage, whakapapa
**10** derivation, extraction
**11** generations **13** family history

*Genealogy-related terms include:*

**03** DSP, IGI, née
**04** AGRA, clan, deed, heir, late, race, will
**05** issue, trace, widow
**06** census, degree, estate, legacy, relict
**07** archive, bastard, bequest, consort, descent, divorce, epitaph, kinship, lineage, peerage, probate, progeny, removed, surname, testate, trustee, widower, witness
**08** ancestor, ancestry, bachelor, bequeath, canon law, deceased, decedent, emigrant, forebear, maternal, paternal, pedigree, relation, spinster
**09** ascendant, given name, immigrant, indenture, intestate, necrology, offspring, sine prole, testament
**10** ahnentafel, descendant, family name, family tree, forefather, generation, maiden name, onomastics, progenitor, succession
**11** beneficiary, genealogist, record agent
**12** burial record, census record, cousin-german, Domesday Book, illegitimate, primogenitor, vital records
**13** Christian name, consanguinity, pedigree chart, primogeniture
**14** cemetery record, common ancestor, marriage record
**15** vital statistics

---

## general
**05** broad, loose, mixed, rough, total, usual, vague **06** common, global, normal, public, varied **07** blanket, diverse, inexact, overall, popular, regular, typical **08** accepted, all-round, assorted, everyday, habitual, ordinary, standard, sweeping **09** customary, extensive, imprecise, panoramic, prevalent, universal **10** ill-defined, indefinite, prevailing, unspecific, variegated, widespread

11 approximate, wide-ranging 12 all-inclusive, conventional
13 comprehensive, heterogeneous, miscellaneous 14 across-the-board

*Generals include:*

03 **Doe** (Samuel K), **Ike**, **Lee** (Robert E), **Ney** (Michel)
04 **Alba** (Ferdinand Alvarez de Toledo, Duke of), **Alva** (Ferdinand Alvarez de Toledo, Duke of), **Asad** (Hafez al-), **Dyer** (Reginald), **Haig** (Alexander), **Prem** (Tinsulanonda)
05 **Assad** (Hafez al-), **Booth** (William), **Clive** (Robert, Lord), **Gates** (Horatio), **Grant** (Ulysses S), **Scott** (Winfield), **Soult** (Nicolas Jean de Dieu), **Wolfe** (James)
06 **Anders** (Wladyslaw), **Caesar** (Julius), **Custer** (George Armstrong), **Franco** (Francisco), **Moreau** (Jean Victor), **Napier** (Sir Charles), **Powell** (Colin), **Rommel** (Erwin), **Scipio** (the Younger), **Sharon** (Ariel), **Zhukov** (Georgi)
07 **Agrippa** (Marcus Vipsanius), **Atatürk** (Mustapha Kemal), **Fairfax** (Thomas, Lord), **Masséna** (André), **Spínola** (António de)
08 **Agricola** (Gnaeus Julius), **Badoglio** (Pietro), **Brisbane** (Sir Thomas Makdougall), **Camillus** (Marcus Furius), **Cardigan** (James Thomas Brudenell, Earl of), **de Gaulle** (Charles), **Hamilton** (Sir Ian Standish Monteith), **Hannibal**, **Lysander**, **Montrose** (James Graham, Marquis of)
09 **Antigonus**, **Aristides**, **Boulanger** (Georges), **MacArthur** (Douglas), **Omar Pasha**, **Santander** (Francisco de Paula), **Townshend** (George, Viscount and Marquess), **Townshend** (Sir Charles Vere Ferrers)
10 **Abercromby** (Sir Ralph), **Eisenhower** (Dwight D 'Ike'), **Oglethorpe** (James Edward), **Timoshenko** (Semyon)
11 **Baden-Powell** (Robert, Lord), **Jiang Jieshi**, **Schwarzkopf** (H Norman)
12 **Clive of India**
13 **Chiang Kai-shek**
14 **Osman Nuri Pasha**

## General Electric
02 GE 03 GEC

## generality
03 run 04 bulk, many, most 07 breadth, the many 08 majority 09 broadness, looseness, nearly all, vagueness 10 commonness, larger part, popularity, prevalence 11 catholicity, ecumenicity, greater part, inexactness 12 more than half, universality 13 extensiveness, impreciseness, miscellaneity 14 generalization, indefiniteness 15 approximateness

## generalization
09 looseness, vagueness 11 inexactness 12 axioma medium, inexactitude 13 impreciseness 14 indefiniteness 15 approximateness

## generalize
05 infer 06 assume, deduce 08 conclude, theorize 11 standardize

## generally
06 mainly, mostly 07 as a rule, at large, broadly, chiefly, largely, overall, usually 08 commonly, normally 09 in general 10 by and large, habitually, more or less, on the whole, ordinarily 11 customarily, in most cases, universally 13 predominantly 14 for the most part

## generate
◇ *anagram indicator* 04 form, make 05 breed, cause, spawn 06 arouse, create, evolve, gender, whip up 07 produce 08 engender, initiate, occasion 09 originate, procreate, propagate 10 bring about, give rise to 11 give birth to 14 bring into being

## generation
03 age, era 04 days, kind, race, time 05 class, epoch 06 family, period 07 descent, genesis, progeny 08 age group, breeding, creation 09 engendure, formation, offspring 10 engendrure, production 11 engendering, origination, procreation, propagation 12 reproduction

## generic
04 wide 06 common 07 blanket, general 08 superior, sweeping 09 inclusive, unbranded, universal 10 collective 12 all-inclusive 13 comprehensive, non-registered, untrademarked 14 non-proprietary, non-trademarked 15 all-encompassing

## generically
08 commonly 09 generally 11 inclusively, universally 14 all-inclusively 15 comprehensively

## generosity
06 bounty 07 charity, largess 08 goodness, kindness, largesse 10 lavishness, liberality 11 benevolence, magnanimity, munificence 12 philanthropy, selflessness 13 unselfishness 14 big-heartedness, open-handedness

## generous
03 big 04 free, full, good, kind, rich 05 ample, large, lofty, noble, plump, roomy 06 giving, lavish 07 copious, liberal 08 abundant, handsome, menseful, selfless, sporting 09 bounteous, bountiful, plentiful, unselfish, unsparing 10 altruistic, beneficent, benevolent, big-hearted, charitable, courageous, free-handed, high-minded, munificent, open-handed, unstinting 11 gentlemanly, magnanimous, open-hearted, overflowing, soft-hearted, warm-hearted 12 large-hearted, wholehearted 13 disinterested, philanthropic 14 public-spirited

## generously
05 amply, fully, nobly 06 freely, richly 08 lavishly 09 copiously, liberally 10 abundantly, charitably,

handsomely, selflessly 11 bountifully, plentifully, unselfishly 12 open-handedly 13 magnanimously

## genesis
03 Gen 04 dawn, root 05 birth, start 06 origin, outset, source 08 creation, founding 09 beginning, formation, inception 10 foundation, generation, initiation, production 11 development, engendering, propagation 12 commencement

## genetic
07 genomic 09 inherited 10 biological, hereditary 11 chromosomal

## genetics
06 origin 11 development

*Geneticists include:*

05 **Brown** (Michael S), **Jones** (Steve), **Leder** (Philip), **Ochoa** (Severo), **Sager** (Ruth), **Snell** (George Davis)
06 **Beadle** (George Wells), **Biffen** (Sir Rowland Harry), **Bodmer** (Sir Walter), **Boveri** (Theodor Heinrich), **Cantor** (Charles), **Fisher** (Sir Ronald Aylmer), **Galton** (Sir Francis), **Gurdon** (Sir John), **Morgan** (Thomas Hunt), **Müller** (Hermann Joseph), **Zinder** (Norton David)
07 **Bateson** (William), **Correns** (Carl), **De Vries** (Hugo Marie), **Gehring** (Walter), **Hopwood** (Sir David), **Lysenko** (Trofim)
08 **Auerbach** (Charlotte), **Lewontin** (Richard), **Yanofsky** (Charles)
09 **Baltimore** (David), **Goldstein** (Joseph), **Lederberg** (Joshua)
10 **Darlington** (Cyril Dean), **Dobzhansky** (Theodosius), **Kettlewell** (Henry Bernard David), **McClintock** (Barbara), **Sturtevant** (Alfred Henry), **Waddington** (C H), **Weatherall** (Sir David)
12 **Maynard Smith** (John)

*Genetics-related terms include:*

02 GM
03 DNA, PCR, RNA
04 base, gene
05 allel, clone, codon, helix, sperm
06 allele, gamete, genome, hybrid, intron, vector, zygote
07 diploid, meiosis, mitosis
08 autosome, dominant, heredity, mutation, promoter, sequence
09 amino acid, haplotype, homologue, inversion, karyotype, offspring, paralogue, recessive, repressor, transgene, variation
10 adaptation, chromosome, generation, geneticist, homozygous, nucleosome, nucleotide, orthologue, polymerase, speciation
11 double helix, epigenetics, genetic code, inheritance, nucleic acid, polypeptide, X-chromosome, Y-chromosome
12 cell division, heterozygous, reproduction
13 DNA sequencing, fertilization, recombination, transcription, translocation

## genial
**04** kind, maty, mild, warm **05** happy, human, jolly, matey, pally, sunny **06** chummy, hearty, jovial, kindly, mellow **07** affable, amiable, cordial **08** amicable, cheerful, cheering, friendly, pleasant, sociable, sunshiny **09** agreeable, convivial, easy-going, healthful **11** good-natured, sympathetic, warm-hearted **12** good-humoured

## geniality
**06** warmth **07** jollity **08** bonhomie, gladness, kindness, sunshine **09** happiness, joviality **10** affability, amiability, cheeriness, cordiality, good nature, kindliness **12** cheerfulness, conviviality, friendliness, pleasantness **13** agreeableness, congenialness **15** warm-heartedness

## genially
**06** warmly **07** affably, amiably **08** amicably, heartily **09** cordially **10** cheerfully, pleasantly **13** warm-heartedly

## genie
**04** jann **05** demon, fairy, jinni **06** djinni, jinnee, spirit

## genitals
**08** privates **09** genitalia **12** private parts, sexual organs

## genius
**04** bent, gift, nous, sage **05** adept, brain, demon, flair, knack **06** boffin, brains, daemon, daimon, engine, expert, ingine, master, talent, wisdom, wizard **07** ability, egghead, faculty, maestro, prodigy **08** aptitude, capacity, fine mind, ingenium, virtuoso **09** bel esprit, intellect **10** brightness, brilliance, cleverness, grey matter, mastermind, past master, propensity, time spirit **11** inclination **12** intellectual, intelligence **15** little grey cells

## genocide
**08** massacre **09** ethnocide, slaughter **13** extermination **15** ethnic cleansing

## genre
**04** epic, form, kind, sort, type **05** brand, class, conte, genus, group, novel, sci-fi, style **06** comedy, satire, school, strain **07** fantasy, fashion, romance, variety **08** category, intimism, pastoral, prog rock **09** character, chopsocky, cyberpunk, reality TV **10** rare groove, whodunitry **11** fête galante, pastourelle, tragicomedy, whodunnitry **12** splatterpunk **13** fête champêtre **14** science fiction **15** progressive rock

## gent
*see* **gentleman**

## genteel
**05** civil **06** dainty, formal, polite, urbane **07** courtly, elegant, refined, stylish **08** cultured, graceful, ladylike, mannerly, polished, well-bred **09** courteous **10** cultivated **11** comme il faut, fashionable, gentlemanly, respectable **12** aristocratic, well-mannered

## gentile
**03** goy **06** ethnic **13** uncircumcised

## gentility
**04** rank **05** élite **06** gentry, nobles **07** culture, decorum, manners **08** breeding, civility, courtesy, elegance, nobility, poshness, urbanity **09** blue blood, etiquette, formality, high birth, propriety **10** good family, politeness, refinement, upper class **11** aristocracy, courtliness, gentle birth **12** mannerliness **14** respectability

## gentle
**04** calm, easy, gent, kind, meek, mild, slow, soft, tame **05** balmy, bland, canny, light, milky, quiet, sweet **06** benign, humane, kindly, placid, serene, slight, smooth, tender **07** amiable, clement, ennoble, gradual, lenient **08** delicate, lamb-like, maidenly, mansuete, merciful, moderate, peaceful, pleasant, soothing, tranquil, well-born **10** charitable, low-pitched **11** soft-hearted, sympathetic **13** compassionate, imperceptible, tender-hearted

## gentleman
**02** Mr **03** rye, sir **04** gent **05** Señor **06** gemman, knight, Signor, squire, stalko, yeoman **07** esquire, hidalgo, Signior, Signore, younker **08** cavalier **09** caballero, Signorino **10** duniwassal, pukka sahib **11** duniewassal, gentilhomme **12** dunniewassal **13** grand seigneur

## gentlemanly
**04** gent **05** civil, janty, noble, suave **06** jantee, jaunty, polite, urbane **07** gallant, genteel, jauntee, refined **08** generous, mannerly, obliging, polished, well-bred **09** civilized, courteous, reputable **10** chivalrous, cultivated, honourable **12** well-mannered **13** gentlemanlike

## gentleness
**05** mercy **06** warmth **08** calmness, kindness, meekness, mildness, softness, sympathy **09** sweetness **10** compassion, humaneness, tenderness

## gently
**01** p **04** soft **05** small **06** calmly, fairly, mildly, slowly, stilly, warmly **07** lightly **08** serenely, slightly, tenderly **09** gradually **10** charitably, moderately, pleasantly, sordomena, tranquilly **14** hooly and fairly **15** compassionately, sympathetically

## gentry
**05** élite **06** nobles **08** nobility, squirage **09** gentility, squireage, top drawer **10** upper class, upper crust **11** aristocracy

## gents
*see* **toilet**

## genuflect
**03** bow **05** kneel **11** bend the knee **12** pay obeisance **13** make obeisance **14** humble yourself **15** pay your respects

## genuine
**04** echt, good, open, pure, real, true **05** frank, legal, pakka, pucca, pukka, right, sound **06** actual, candid, dinkum, entire, honest, kosher, lawful, native, pusser **07** dinki-di, dinky-di, earnest, factual, natural, sincere **08** bona fide, dinky-die, original, sterling, true blue, truthful, unartful **09** authentic, intrinsic, real McCoy, simon-pure, undoubted, veritable **10** fair dinkum, legitimate, ridgy-didge, sure-enough **11** honest-to-God, intrinsical **12** unadulterate **13** unadulterated, with integrity **14** unsophisticate **15** unsophisticated

## genuinely
**04** echt **06** dinkum, really **07** dinky-di **08** actually, dinky-die, honestly **09** earnestly, sincerely

## genus
**03** set **04** kind, race, sort, type **05** breed, class, genre, group, order, taxon **07** species **08** category, division **11** subdivision

## geography
*Geographical regions include:*

**04** veld
**05** basin, coast, heath, plain, polar, veldt
**06** Arctic, desert, forest, jungle, orient, pampas, steppe, tundra
**07** outback, prairie, riviera, savanna, seaside, tropics
**08** lowlands, midlands, occident, savannah, woodland
**09** Antarctic, grassland, green belt, marshland, scrubland, wasteland
**10** Third World, wilderness
**11** countryside
**13** Mediterranean, rural district, urban district
**14** developed world
**15** developing world

*Geography terms include:*

**03** bay, col, cwm
**04** arid, cape, crag, gulf, mesa, tail, veld, wadi, wady
**05** bight, butte, delta, shott, taiga, veldt
**06** canyon, cirque, corrie, desert, strait, tundra, valley
**07** aggrade, caldera, equator, glacial, hachure, isthmus, tropics, volcano
**08** alluvium, altitude, landmass, landslip, latitude, meridian, prograde
**09** accretion, antipodes, base level, billabong, deviation, ethnology, landslide, longitude, metroplex, relief map
**10** co-ordinate, demography, glaciation, landlocked, topography
**11** archipelago, cartography, chorography, conurbation, demographic, hydrography, triangulate, vulcanology

**13** hanging valley, Ordnance Datum, shield volcano
**14** plate tectonics, roche moutonnée

*Geographers include:*

**03 Dee** (John)
**04 Cary** (John), **Mela** (Pomponius)
**05 Barth** (Heinrich), **Cabot** (Sebastian), **Darby** (Clifford), **Guyot** (Arnold), **Hedin** (Sven), **Penck** (Albrecht), **Sauer** (Carl), **Stamp** (Sir Lawrence Dudley)
**06 Batuta, Behaim** (Martin), **Bowman** (Isaiah), **Clüver** (Phillip), **Gmelin** (Johann Georg), **Harvey** (David), **Idrisi, Ritter** (Karl), **Strabo**
**07 Haggett** (Peter), **Hakluyt** (Richard), **Markham** (Sir Clements), **Ogilvie** (Alan), **Ptolemy**
**08 Büsching** (Anton Friedrich), **Filchner** (Wilhelm), **Humboldt** (Alexander, Baron von), **Mercator** (Gerhardus), **Ortelius** (Abraham Ortel), **Robinson** (Arthur)
**09 Kropotkin** (Pyotr), **Mackinder** (Sir Halford John), **Muqaddasi, Pausanias**
**10 Hartshorne** (Richard), **Huntington** (Ellsworth), **Richthofen** (Ferdinand Baron von), **Wooldridge** (Sydney)
**11 Christaller** (Walter), **Hägerstrand** (Torsten), **Kingdon-Ward** (Frank)
**12 Eratosthenes, Leo Africanus**
**15 Eudoxus of Cnidus, Vidal de la Blache** (Paul)

## geology

*Geological time periods include:*

**06 Eocene** (Epoch)
**07 Miocene** (Epoch), **Permian** (Period)
**08 Cambrian** (Period), **Cenozoic** (Era), **Devonian** (Period), **Holocene** (Epoch), **Jurassic** (Period), **Mesozoic** (Era), **Pliocene** (Epoch), **Silurian** (Period), **Tertiary** (Period), **Triassic** (Period)
**09 Oligocene** (Epoch)
**10 Cretaceous** (Period), **Ordovician** (Period), **Palaeocene** (Epoch), **Palaeozoic** (Era), **Quaternary** (Period)
**11 Phanerozoic** (Eon), **Pleistocene** (Epoch), **Precambrian** (Era), **Proterozoic** (Eon)
**13 Carboniferous** (Period), **Mississippian** (Epoch), **Pennsylvanian** (Epoch)

*Geology-related terms include:*

**02** aa
**03** bar, cwm, mya, ore
**04** clay, dome, dune, fold, lava, limb, lode, Moho, Riss, till, trap, tuff, vein, wadi
**05** agate, atoll, basin, butte, chert, delta, epoch, esker, fault, fiord, fjord, focus, gorge, gully, guyot, horst, joint, Karst, lahar, levee, magma, plain, P-wave, ridge, S-wave, talus
**06** albite, arkose, arroyo, basalt, bolson, canyon, cirque, corrie, debris, gabbro, geyser, gneiss,

graben, mantle, oolite, quartz, runoff, schist, scoria, stress, tephra, trench, uplift
**07** aquifer, barchan, bauxite, bedload, blowout, breccia, caldera, drumlin, glacier, granite, hogback, igneous, isograd, lapilli, meander, mineral, moraine, orogeny, outwash, plateau, pothole, vesicle, volcano
**08** A-horizon, alluvium, backwash, basement, B-horizon, C-horizon, feldspar, fumarole, isostasy, leaching, lopolith, monolith, mountain, obsidian, oilfield, oil shale, pahoehoe, pediment, regolith, rhyolite, syncline, xenolith
**09** alabaster, batholith, carbonate, deflation, epicentre, flood tide, hot spring, intrusion, laccolith, landslide, limestone, Mohs scale, monadnock, monocline, oxidation, peneplain, rock cycle, rockslide, sandstone, slip fault, striation, tableland, viscosity, volcanism
**10** anthracite, astrobleme, block fault, cinder cone, deposition, depression, earthquake, flood plain, kettle hole, mineralogy, rift valley, subsidence, topography, travertine, water table, weathering
**11** alluvial fan, central vent, exfoliation, geosyncline, groundwater, maar volcano, metamorphic, normal fault, sublimation, swallow hole, thrust fault, volcanic ash
**12** artesian well, coastal plain, fringing reef, magma chamber, pyroclastics, stratigraphy, unconformity, volcanic bomb, volcanic cone, volcanic dome, volcanic pipe
**13** angle of repose, barrier island, drainage basin, geomorphology, hanging valley, recumbent fold, shield volcano, stratovolcano, U-shaped valley, V-shaped valley
**14** bituminous coal, eustatic change, lateral moraine, longshore drift, stratification, subduction zone, transform fault, wave-cut terrace
**15** million years ago, sedimentary rock, strike-slip fault, terminal moraine

## Georgia
**02** GA, GE **03** GEO

## germ
**03** bud, bug, wog **04** root, seed, zyme
**05** cause, shoot, spark, start, virus
**06** embryo, origin, source, sprout
**07** microbe, nucleus **08** bacillus, fountain, rudiment **09** bacterium, beginning, inception, swarm-cell
**10** seminality, swarm-spore
**12** commencement **13** micro-organism

## German
◊ *foreign word indicator* **01** G **03** Ger, Hun **04** Jute, Ossi **05** boche, Gerry,

Jerry, Wessi **06** Almain, bosche, Teuton

*German boys' names include:*

**03** Jan, Max, Uwe
**04** Dirk, Eric, Erik, Jens, Jörg, Ralf, Sven, Swen
**05** Bernd, Erich, Fritz, Jonas, Klaus, Lukas, Ralph
**06** Dieter, Jürgen, Markus, Niklas, Stefan, Tobias, Ulrich
**07** Andreas, Dominik, Mathias, Steffen, Stephan, Torsten
**08** Kristian, Matthias, Thorsten, Wolfgang

*See also* **day; month; number**
• **East German 03** Ost

## germane
**03** apt **04** akin **06** allied, proper
**07** apropos, fitting, related **08** apposite, material, relevant, suitable
**09** connected, pertinent **10** applicable
**11** appropriate

## germanium
**02** Ge

## Germany
**01** D **03** DDR, DEU, FDR, FRG, GDR, Ger **05** Reich **06** Almany **07** Almaine
**08** Alemaine
• **in Germany** ◊ *foreign word indicator*

## germinal
**07** seminal **09** embryonic
**10** developing, generative
**11** preliminary, rudimentary, undeveloped

## germinate
**03** bud **04** grow **05** shoot, swell
**06** sprout **07** burgeon, develop
**08** spring up, take root **09** originate

## gestation
**08** drafting, planning, ripening
**09** evolution, pregnancy
**10** conception, incubation, maturation
**11** development

## gesticulate
**04** sign, wave **06** motion, signal
**07** gesture **08** indicate **09** make a sign

## gesticulation
**04** sign, wave **06** motion, signal
**07** gesture **08** movement **09** chironomy
**10** indication **12** body language

## gesture
**03** act **04** geck, gest, mint, sign, wave
**05** geste, point, snook **06** action, beckon, motion, signal **08** dumbshow, indicate, movement **09** beau geste, behaviour, chirology, reverence
**10** indication **11** gesticulate
**13** gesticulation

## get
◊ *juxtaposition indicator* **02** go **03** bug, buy, cop, fix, hit, nab, see, vex, wax, win **04** brat, bust, coax, come, cook, earn, gain, grab, grow, have, hear, kill, land, make, move, nick, rile, suss, sway, take, trap, turn, twig, urge
**05** annoy, bring, catch, child, clear, fetch, get it, go for, grasp, learn, reach, seize, snare **06** answer, arrest, arrive, attain, baffle, become, bother, collar,

come by, descry, fathom, follow, induce, manage, obtain, pick up, secure, take in, travel, wangle, wind up, work it **07** achieve, acquire, arrange, be given, bring in, capture, collect, develop, discern, make out, prepare, procure, provoke, realize, receive, succeed, suss out, win over, work out **08** come to be, contract, convince, find a way, get ready, hunt down, irritate, organize, persuade, purchase, rustle up, talk into **09** aggravate, apprehend, figure out, influence, infuriate, lay hold of, recognize, succumb to **10** comprehend, drive crazy, exasperate, go down with, understand **11** get the point, prevail upon, put together **12** come down with, get the hang of **13** be afflicted by
• **get about** **02** go **06** travel **08** go widely **09** move about **10** move around **12** travel widely
• **get across** **06** convey, impart **07** explain, express, get over, put over **08** transmit **09** make clear, put across **11** bring home to, communicate
• **get ahead** **05** get on **06** do well, make it, thrive **07** advance, prosper, succeed **08** flourish, get there, go places, make good, progress **11** go great guns **12** get somewhere, make your mark **14** go up in the world, make the big time
• **get along** **04** cope, fare **05** agree, get by, get on **06** giddap, giddup, manage, relate **07** develop, giddy-up, make out, survive **08** hit it off, progress, rub along **09** harmonize
• **get around** ◊ *containment indicator* **04** coax, move, sway **05** avoid, evade **06** bypass, cajole, induce, travel **07** win over **08** persuade **09** talk round **10** circumvent **11** prevail upon
• **get at** **04** find, hint, mean, slam **05** begin, bribe, imply, knock, reach, slate, touch **06** areach, attack, attain, intend, nobble, obtain, pick on, suborn **07** corrupt, suggest **08** discover **09** criticize, influence, insinuate, make fun of **11** pick holes in **12** gain access to **13** find fault with
• **get away** **04** flee, scat **05** be off, leave, never!, scoot, scram **06** begone, depart, escape, get out **07** do a bunk, run away, scarper **08** break out, run for it **09** break away, break free, do a runner **13** sling your hook **14** make a bolt for it, run for your life **15** make a break for it, take to your heels
• **get back** **06** go back, go home, recoup, recure, redeem, regain, return **07** pay back, recover **08** come back, come home, retrieve **09** repossess, retaliate **11** get even with **13** take revenge on **15** take vengeance on
• **get by** **04** cope, fare **05** exist **06** hang on, manage **07** subsist, survive **08** get along **12** make ends meet, see it through **13** scrape through **15** weather the storm
• **get down** **06** alight, get off, sadden **07** depress, descend, make sad

**08** dismount, dispirit **09** disembark **10** dishearten
• **get in** ◊ *insertion indicator* **04** come, land **05** enter **06** arrive, embark **09** penetrate **10** infiltrate
• **get into** ◊ *insertion indicator* **05** enjoy, enter, put on **06** arrive **09** penetrate **10** infiltrate
• **get off** **04** shed **05** learn, leave **06** alight, detach, escape, get out, remove **07** descend, get down **08** climb off, dismount, get out of, memorize, separate **09** disembark **10** alight from
• **get on** **03** age **04** cope, fare **05** agree, board, get in, mount, shift **06** ascend, embark, manage, relate, thrive **07** advance, climb on, get into, make out, press on, proceed, prosper, succeed **08** continue, get along, hit it off, progress **09** harmonize **12** hit it off with
• **get on well** **03** gee
• **get out** **04** away, flee, quit, scat **05** leave, scoot, scram **06** depart, escape, spread, vacate **07** come out, do a bunk, extract, leak out, produce, scarper, take out **08** be leaked, break out, clear off, clear out, evacuate, run for it, withdraw **09** circulate, do a runner **11** become known **12** become public, free yourself **14** make a bolt for it, run for your life **15** make a break for it, take to your heels
• **get out of** **05** avoid, dodge, evade, shirk, skive **06** escape, outwin **07** goof off **09** gold-brick
• **get over** **06** convey, defeat, impart, master **07** explain, get well, put over, survive **08** complete, deal with, get round, overcome, shake off, surmount **09** get across, get better, make clear **10** be restored **11** communicate, pull through, recover from **14** recuperate from
• **get ready** **04** boun **05** bowne, fix up, ready **06** set out **07** arrange, prepare **08** rehearse
• **get round** ◊ *containment indicator* **04** coax, move, sway **05** avoid, evade **06** bypass, cajole, induce, travel **07** win over **08** persuade **09** talk round **10** circumvent **11** prevail upon
• **get there** **06** arrive, make it **07** advance, prosper, succeed **08** go places, make good
• **get through** **04** pass
• **get together** **04** join, meet **05** rally, unite **06** finish, gather **07** collect **08** assemble, organize **10** congregate **11** collaborate
• **get up** **03** fig **04** rise, stir **05** arise, climb, mount, scale, stand **06** ascend, huddup **07** stand up **08** show a leg **11** get out of bed

**getaway**
**05** break, start **06** escape, flight **08** breakout **10** absconding, decampment

**get-together**
**02** do **04** bash **05** party, rally **06** social, soirée **07** meeting, reunion

**08** assembly, function, sing-sing **09** gathering, reception

**get-up**
**03** kit, set **04** gear, togs **06** make-up, outfit, rig-out **07** clobber, clothes, threads, turnout **08** clothing, garments **09** equipment

**Ghana**
**02** GH **03** GHA

**ghastliness**
**08** grimness **09** awfulness, nastiness **11** hideousness **12** dreadfulness, gruesomeness **13** frightfulness

**ghastly**
**03** bad, ill **04** gash, grim, ropy, sick **05** awful, grave, lousy, lurid, nasty, ropey **06** grisly, horrid, poorly, rotten, unwell **07** greisly, griesly, hideous, macabre, serious **08** critical, dreadful, gruesome, horrible, shocking, terrible **09** appalling, dangerous, deathlike, frightful, loathsome, off colour, repellent **10** deplorable, horrendous, terrifying **11** frightening **12** unrepeatable **15** under the weather

**ghost**
**04** hint, soul, waff **05** duppy, fetch, haunt, jumby, larva, lemur, shade, spook, trace, umbra **06** duende, jumbie, shadow, spirit, wraith **07** gytrash, phantom, specter, spectre **08** manifest, presence, revenant, visitant **09** semblance **10** apparition, astral body, impression, suggestion **11** poltergeist

**ghostly**
**05** eerie, faint, spook, weird **06** creepy, spooky **07** phantom, shadowy **08** chthonic, illusory, spectral **09** chthonian, ghostlike, religious, spiritual, sprightly, unearthly **10** wraith-like **12** supernatural

**ghoulish**
**04** sick **06** grisly, morbid **07** macabre **08** gruesome **09** revolting, unhealthy **11** unwholesome

**giant**
**04** eten, huge, ogre, vast **05** ettin, jotun, jumbo, large, titan, troll **06** jötunn, ogress **07** immense, mammoth, massive, monster, titanic **08** behemoth, Briarean, colossal, colossus, cyclopic, enormous, gigantic, great big, king-size, titaness, whopping **09** cyclopean, cyclopian, ginormous, humongous, humungous, leviathan, rounceval **10** gargantuan, monumental, Patagonian, prodigious, tremendous **11** gigantesque **14** Brobdingnagian

*Giants include:*

**03** Gog
**04** Gaia, Gerd, Grid, Loki, Rhea, Ymir
**05** Aegir, Arges, Argus, Atlas, Grawp, Hymir, Jotun, Magog, Orion, Pan Gu, Skadi, Theia, Thrym
**06** Albion, Bestla, Cronus, Hagrid, Phoebe, Tethys, Themis, Thiazi, Titans
**07** Cyclops, Geirrod, Goliath,

Iapetus, Oceanus, Suttung

**08** Angrboda, Cyclopes, Gigantes, Gogmagog, Hrungnir, Hyperion, Jarnsaxa, Morgante, Nephilim, Panoptes, Steropes
**09** Angerboda, Bergelmir, Enceladus, Gandareva, Gargantua, Mnemosyne, Olentzero
**10** Angerbotha, Epimetheus, Paul Bunyan, Prometheus
**11** Finn MacCool, Galligantus, Gog and Magog, Utgardaloki
**12** Giant Despair, Vafthruthnir
**15** Cerne Abbas Giant, Fionn MacCumhail

**gibber**
**04** blab, cant **05** stone **06** babble, cackle, gabble, jabber **07** blabber, blather, boulder, chatter, prattle

**gibberish**
**04** blah, bosh, guff **05** hooey **06** bunkum, drivel, jargon, linsey, yammer **07** baloney, eyewash, hogwash, prattle, ravings, rhubarb, rubbish, twaddle **08** cobblers, malarkey, nonsense, tommyrot **09** moonshine, poppycock **10** balderdash, codswallop, jabberwock, mumbo-jumbo **11** abracadabra, jabberwocky **12** gobbledygook **13** linsey-woolsey

**gibbet**
**05** crook, cross **07** gallows, potence

**gibbon**
**06** wou-wou, wow-wow **07** hoolock, siamang **08** hylobate

**gibe, jibe**
**03** bob, dig, shy **04** gird, goof, jeer, mock, poke, quip, wipe, yerk **05** crack, fleer, fling, flout, gleek, scoff, slant, sneer, taunt, tease **06** deride **07** brocard, mockery, sarcasm, teasing **08** derision, outfling, ridicule **09** make fun of, wisecrack, witticism

**Gibraltar**
**03** GBZ, GIB

**giddily**
◊ *anagram indicator* **06** wildly **07** dizzily, woozily **09** excitedly **10** restlessly, unsteadily **11** frantically **12** euphorically **13** lightheadedly

**giddiness**
**06** frenzy, nausea, thrill **07** vertigo **08** staggers **09** animation, dizziness, faintness, wooziness **10** excitement, wobbliness **11** glaikitness **12** exhilaration **15** lightheadedness

**giddy**
◊ *anagram indicator* **04** high, wild **05** dizzy, faint, light, queer, silly, woozy **06** elated, sturdy, volage **07** excited, flighty, glaiket, glaikit, reeling, stirred **08** frenzied, hellicat, skipping, thrilled, unsteady **09** volageous **10** capernoity, hoity-toity, stimulated **11** capernoitie, cappernoity, exhilarated, hair-brained, hare-brained, lightheaded, vertiginous

**gift**
**03** foy, tip **04** bent, boon, give, koha, turn **05** bonus, bribe, flair, grant, knack, offer, power, skill **06** befana, bestow, bounty, confer, donate, genius, hansel, legacy, talent **07** ability, aptness, beffana, bequest, cumshaw, étrenne, faculty, fairing, freebie, handsel, minding, present, pressie, prezzie, propine **08** aptitude, capacity, donation, donative, facility, gratuity, largesse, offering, thankyou **09** attribute, book token, endowment **10** capability, contribute, exhibition **11** beneficence, inheritance, proficiency **12** Christmas box, contribution
*See also* **Christmas**

**gifted**
**04** able **05** adept, sharp, smart **06** bright, clever, expert **07** capable, endowed, skilful, skilled **08** masterly, talented **09** brilliant **10** proficient **11** intelligent **12** accomplished

**gig**
**03** fun **04** moze **05** buggy, sport **06** dennet, whisky **07** whiskey **11** hurly-hacket

**gigantic**
**04** huge, mega, vast **05** giant, jumbo **07** immense, mammoth, massive, monster, titanic **08** colossal, enormous, great big, king-size, whopping **09** Atlantean, ginormous, Herculean, humongous, humungous, leviathan, rounceval **10** Babylonian, gargantuan, monumental, Patagonian **14** Brobdingnagian

**giggle**
**05** laugh **06** titter **07** chortle, chuckle, snicker, snigger

**gilbert**
**02** Gb
• **Gilbert and Sullivan 05** G and S

**gild**
**04** coat, deck, trim **05** adorn, array, grace, paint **06** bedeck, enrich, golden **07** dress up, enhance, festoon, garnish **08** beautify, brighten, ornament **09** elaborate, embellish, embroider

**gilded**
**04** gilt, gold **06** golden **07** aureate **08** inaurate **10** gold-plated **11** gold-layered

**gill**
**04** glen **05** brook **06** noggin, ravine **08** branchia **09** ctenidium

**gilt**
**03** elt

**gimcrack**
**05** cheap, dodge, tacky, trick **06** fisgig, fizgig, shoddy, tawdry, trashy **08** rubbishy, trumpery **10** jerry-built

**gimmick**
**04** hype, ploy, ruse **05** dodge, stunt, trick **06** device, gadget, scheme **07** novelty **09** publicity, stratagem **10** attraction **11** contrivance

**gimmickry**
**07** novelty **09** modernity **10** innovation

**gin**
**02** by, if **03** max **04** ruin, trap **05** snare **06** geneva, Old Tom, scheme, spring **07** schnaps, springe, twankay **08** artifice, blue ruin, Hollands, schiedam, schnapps **10** square-face **11** contrivance, mother's ruin
• **gin and tonic 02** gt **05** g and t

**ginger**
◊ *anagram indicator* **03** pop **04** race, rase, raze **05** bluey, sandy **06** amomum, asarum, mettle **07** curcuma, enliven, reddish **08** cardamom, cardamon, cardamum, turmeric, zingiber **09** galingale **10** cassumunar **11** stimulation

**gingerbread**
**05** parly **06** parkin, parley, perkin **10** parliament, pepper-cake **14** parliament-cake

**gingerly**
**06** warily **07** charily **09** carefully, prudently **10** cautiously, delicately, hesitantly, watchfully **11** attentively, judiciously, tentatively, with caution

**Gipsy**
*see* **Gypsy, Gipsy**

**gird**
**03** pen **04** belt, bind, girr, hoop, ring **05** brace, hem in, ready, steel, taunt **06** enfold, fasten, girdle **07** accinge, enclose, fortify, prepare **08** cincture, encircle, get ready, surround **09** encompass

**girder**
**04** beam, spar **05** H-beam, I-beam **06** rafter **07** box beam

**girdle**
**03** hem **04** band, belt, bind, gird, ring, sash, zona, zone **05** bound, mitre, waist **06** cestos, cestus, circle, corset **07** enclose, go round, griddle, zonulet **08** ceinture, cincture, cingulum, encircle, surround **09** encompass, surcingle, waistband **10** cummerbund, encincture **15** cingulum Veneris

**girl**
**03** bit, cub, gal, gel, gig, hen, her, kid, mor **04** babe, baby, bint, bird, chit, dell, gill, jill, Judy, lass, maid, mawr, minx, miss, peat, puss, romp **05** belle, chick, child, cutie, cutty, dolly, fille, filly, flirt, gerle, gilpy, hussy, madam, peach, popsy, quean, randy, tabby, wench **06** au pair, blowze, chokri, cummer, damsel, female, fizgig, gamine, geisha, giglet, kimmer, lassie, maiden, moppet, mousmé, nipper, number, pigeon, sheila, shiksa, tawpie, tomboy, tottie **07** blushet, chapess, chicken, colleen, flapper, mauther, mawther, mousmee, nymphet **08** chappess, daughter, grisette, jail-bait, princess, teenager **09** backfisch, dolly bird, maid-child, young lady, youngster **10** adolescent, bit of fluff, bit of skirt, bit of stuff, bobbysoxer, Cinderella, girlfriend, jeune fille, schoolgirl, sweetheart,

young woman **11** beauty queen, kinchin-mort, maidservant, teeny-bopper **12** bachelorette, bobby-dazzler

---

*Girls' names include:*

**02** Di, Jo, Mo, Vi

**03** Ada, Ali, Amy, Ann, Ava, Bab, Bea, Bee, Bel, Bet, Cis, Con, Deb, Dee, Die, Dot, Edy, Emm, Ena, Eva, Eve, Fay, Flo, Gay, Ida, Ina, Isa, Ivy, Jan, Jay, Jen, Joe, Joy, Kay, Kim, Kit, Lea, Lee, Liv, Liz, Lou, Mae, Mag, Mat, May, Meg, Mia, Nan, Pam, Pat, Peg, Pen, Pia, Pru, Rae, Ray, Ria, Ros, Roz, Sal, Sue, Una, Val, Viv, Win, Zoë

**04** Abby, Addy, Afra, Aggy, Alex, Ally, Alma, Alme, Angy, Anna, Anne, Asma, Babs, Bell, Bess, Beth, Cara, Caro, Cass, Ceri, Cher, Cleo, Cora, Dana, Dawn, Dian, Dora, Edel, Edie, Edna, Ella, Elma, Elsa, Elva, Emma, Emmy, Enid, Erin, Evie, Faye, Floy, Fred, Gabi, Gaea, Gaia, Gail, Gale, Gaye, Gene, Gert, Gill, Gina, Gita, Gwen, Hope, Ibby, Ines, Inez, Inga, Inge, Iona, Iris, Irma, Isla, Jade, Jane, Jean, Jess, Jill, Joan, Jodi, Jody, Joey, Joni, Joss, Jozy, Jude, Judy, June, Kate, Kath, Katy, Kaye, Lara, Leah, Lena, Lian, Lily, Lina, Lisa, Lise, Livy, Liza, Lois, Lola, Lucy, Lynn, Maev, Mary, Maud, Meta, Mina, Moll, Mona, Myra, Nell, Nina, Nita, Noel, Nola, Nona, Nora, Olga, Page, Phyl, Poll, Prue, Rana, Rene, Rita, Rona, Rosa, Rose, Ruby, Ruth, Sara, Sian, Sìne, Siri, Suke, Suky, Susy, Suzy, Tess, Thea, Tina, Toni, Trix, Vera, Vita, Zara, Zena, Zola

**05** Addie, Adela, Adèle, Aggie, Agnes, Ailie, Ailsa, Aisha, Alexa, Alice, Allie, Amber, Amina, Anaïs, Angel, Angie, Anila, Anita, Annie, Annis, Annot, Aphra, April, Areta, Aruna, Avril, Aysha, Becky, Bella, Belle, Beryl, Bessy, Betsy, Betty, Biddy, Bride, Brona, Bunny, Bunty, Candy, Carla, Carly, Carol, Carys, Cathy, Celia, Cerys, Chère, Chloe, Chris, Ciara, Cindy, Cissy, Clara, Clare, Coral, Daisy, Debby, Debra, Delia, Della, Diana, Diane, Dilys, Dinah, Dolly, Donna, Doris, Edith, Effie, Eliza, Ellen, Ellie, Elsie, Emily, Emmie, Erica, Essie, Ethel, Ethna, Ethne, Faith, Fanny, Farah, Ffion, Fiona, Fleur, Flora, Freda, Freya, Gabby, Gauri, Gayle, Geeta, Gemma, Gerda, Ginny, Golda, Golde, Grace, Greta, Haley, Hatty, Hazel, Heidi, Helen, Helga, Hetty, Hilda, Holly, Honor, Ilana, Ilona, Irena, Irene, Isbel, Isold, Ivana, Jaime, Jamie, Janet, Janis, Jemma, Jenna, Jenny, Jessy, Jinny, Jodie, Joely, Josie, Joyce, Judie, Julia, Julie, Kanta, Karen, Karin, Karla, Kathy, Katie, Katya, Kelly, Kenna, Kerry, Kiera, Kitty, Kylie, Lalla, Lally, Laura, Leigh, Leila, Leona, Letty, Liana, Libby, Linda, Lindy, Lorna,

Lorne, Louie, Lubna, Lucia, Lydia, Lynda, Lynne, Mabel, Madge, Maeve, Magda, Máire, Màiri, Mamie, Mandy, Margo, Maria, Marie, Matty, Maude, Maura, Mavis, Meena, Megan, Mercy, Meryl, Moira, Molly, Morag, Morna, Moyra, Myrna, Nabby, Nadia, Nance, Nancy, Nelly, Nerys, Nessa, Nesta, Netta, Netty, Ngaio, Niamh, Nicky, Noele, Norah, Norma, Nuala, Olive, Olwen, Olwin, Olwyn, Onora, Oprah, Paddy, Padma, Paige, Pansy, Patsy, Patty, Paula, Pearl, Peggy, Penny, Petra, Pippa, Polly, Priya, Raine, Rajni, Renée, Rhian, Rhoda, Rhona, Robin, Robyn, Rosie, Sacha, Sadie, Sally, Sarah, Sasha, Senga, Shona, Shula, Sibyl, Sindy, Sonia, Sonya, Sophy, Stacy, Sukie, Susan, Susie, Sybil, Tamar, Tammy, Tania, Tanya, Terry, Tessa, Thora, Tibby, Tilda, Tilly, Tracy, Trina, Trish, Trixy, Trudy, Unity, Viola, Wanda, Wendy, Wilma, Zahra, Zelda, Zowie

**06** Adella, Agatha, Aileen, Alexia, Alexis, Alicia, Alison, Althea, Amabel, Amanda, Amelia, Andrea, Angela, Anneka, Annika, Anthea, Aphrah, Aretha, Ashley, Astrid, Audrey, Auriel, Auriol, Aurora, Aurore, Averil, Ayesha, Babbie, Barbie, Beatty, Bertha, Bertie, Bessie, Bianca, Biddie, Blanch, Bonnie, Brenda, Bridie, Brigid, Brigit, Briony, Bryony, Bunnie, Caddie, Candia, Carina, Carlie, Carmel, Carmen, Carola, Carole, Carrie, Cassie, Cathie, Cecily, Celina, Cherie, Cherry, Cheryl, Cicely, Cissie, Claire, Connie, Daphne, Davina, Deanna, Deanne, Debbie, Delyth, Denise, Dervla, Dianne, Dionne, Dolina, Doreen, Dorrie, Dottie, Dulcie, Dympna, Eartha, Edwina, Eileen, Eilidh, Eirian, Eirlys, Eithna, Eithne, Elaine, Elinor, Eloisa, Eloise, Elspet, Eluned, Elvira, Esther, Eunice, Evadne, Evelyn, Evonne, Fatima, Fedora, Felice, Finola, Flavia, Freddy, Frieda, Gaynor, Gertie, Gladys, Glenda, Glenys, Gloria, Glynis, Goldie, Gracie, Grania, Granya, Gudrun, Gwenda, Hannah, Hattie, Hayley, Helena, Hermia, Hester, Hilary, Honora, Honour, Imelda, Imogen, Indira, Ingrid, Isabel, Iseult, Ishbel, Isobel, Isolda, Isolde, Jamila, Jancis, Janice, Janina, Janine, Jeanie, Jemima, Jennie, Jessie, Joanie, Joanna, Joanne, Joelle, Joleen, Jolene, Judith, Juliet, Kamala, Karena, Karina, Kathie, Kirsty, Kittie, Kumari, Lalage, Lalita, Lallie, Laurel, Lauren, Laurie, Leanne, Leonie, Lesley, Lettie, Lianna, Lianne, Lilian, Lilias, Linnet, Lisbet, Lizzie, Lolita, Lottie, Louisa, Louise, Lynsey, Madhur, Maggie, Maisie, Marcia,

Marian, Marina, Marion, Marsha, Martha, Mattie, Maxine, Melody, Meriel, Millie, Minnie, Miriam, Monica, Morven, Muriel, Myriam, Myrtle, Nabila, Nadine, Nellie, Nessie, Nettie, Nicola, Nicole, Noelle, Noreen, Odette, Olivia, Olwyne, Paloma, Pamela, Pattie, Petula, Phemie, Phoebe, Rachel, Rajani, Raquel, Regina, Renata, Rhonda, Robina, Rodney, Roisin, Roshan, Rosina, Rowena, Roxana, Roxane, Rubina, Sabina, Sabine, Salome, Sandra, Saskia, Selina, Seonag, Serena, Sharon, Shashi, Sheela, Sheena, Sheila, Sherry, Sheryl, Silvia, Simone, Sinéad, Sophia, Sophie, Stacey, Stella, Suhair, Sydney, Sylvia, Tamara, Tammie, Tamsin, Teenie, Teresa, Thelma, Tibbie, Tracey, Tricia, Trisha, Trixie, Ulrica, Ursula, Vanora, Verity, Vijaya, Vinaya, Violet, Vivian, Vivien, Vyvian, Vyvyan, Winnie, Winona, Wynona, Xanthe, Yasmin, Yvette, Yvonne, Zainab, Zaynab

**07** Abigail, Aisling, Allegra, Allison, Andrina, Annabel, Annette, Antonia, Anushka, Ariadne, Augusta, Barbara, Beatrix, Belinda, Bernice, Bethany, Bettina, Bharati, Blanche, Bridget, Bronach, Bronagh, Bronwen, Caitlín, Camilla, Candace, Candice, Candida, Carolyn, Cecilia, Chandra, Chantal, Charity, Charley, Chelsea, Christy, Clarice, Claudia, Colette, Colleen, Corinna, Corinne, Crystal, Cynthia, Daniela, Deborah, Deirdre, Désirée, Dolores, Dorothy, Eleanor, Elspeth, Emerald, Estella, Estelle, Eugenia, Eugénie, Felicia, Fenella, Floella, Florrie, Flossie, Frances, Francie, Frankie, Freddie, Georgia, Georgie, Gillian, Giselle, Gwennie, Gwenyth, Gwyneth, Harriet, Heather, Heloise, Isadora, Isidora, Jacinta, Jacinth, Janetta, Janette, Jasmine, Jeannie, Jessica, Jillian, Jocasta, Jocelin, Jocelyn, Johanna, Jonquil, Josette, Juliana, Justina, Justine, Kathryn, Katrina, Katrine, Kirstie, Kirstin, Lakshmi, Lavinia, Leonora, Letitia, Lettice, Lillian, Lillias, Lindsay, Lindsey, Linette, Lisbeth, Lisette, Lizbeth, Loretta, Lucilla, Lucille, Lucinda, Lynette, Madonna, Margery, Marilyn, Marjory, Marlene, Martina, Martine, Matilda, Maureen, Melanie, Melissa, Mildred, Miranda, Myfanwy, Nanette, Natalia, Natalie, Natasha, Nichola, Nigella, Ninette, Ophelia, Pandora, Parvati, Pascale, Paulina, Pauline, Phyllis, Queenie, Rachael, Rebecca, Roberta, Rosabel, Rosalie, Rosanna, Rosetta, Roxanne, Sabrina, Saffron, Sharifa, Shelagh, Shelley, Shirley, Sidonie,

Silvana, Siobhán, Surayya, Susanna, Sybilla, Tabitha, Theresa, Tiffany, Valerie, Vanessa, Venetia, Yolanda, Zuleika
**08** Adelaide, Adrianne, Adrienne, Angelica, Angelina, Angharad, Arabella, Ashleigh, Beatrice, Berenice, Beverley, Caroline, Catriona, Charlene, Charmian, Chrissie, Clarinda, Clarissa, Claudine, Cordelia, Cornelia, Courtney, Cressida, Daniella, Danielle, Dorothea, Eleanore, Emmeline, Euphemia, Felicity, Florence, Francine, Georgina, Germaine, Gertrude, Griselda, Grizelda, Gurinder, Hermione, Isabella, Jacintha, Jacinthe, Jeanette, Jennifer, Joceline, Joscelin, Katerina, Kathleen, Kimberly, Kirsteen, Lauretta, Lorraine, Madeline, Magdalen, Margaret, Marigold, Marjorie, Mathilda, Meredith, Michaela, Michelle, Morwenna, Ottoline, Patience, Patricia, Paulette, Penelope, Philippa, Primrose, Prudence, Prunella, Rhiannon, Rosalind, Rosamond, Rosamund, Roseanna, Roseanne, Rosemary, Samantha, Scarlett, Susannah, Theodora, Tomasina, Veronica, Victoria, Virginia, Winifred
**09** Albertina, Alexandra, Anastasia, Annabella, Annabelle, Cassandra, Catharine, Catherina, Catherine, Charlotte, Charmaine, Christina, Christine, Claudette, Cleopatra, Constance, Elisabeth, Elizabeth, Frederica, Gabrielle, Genevieve, Georgette, Georgiana, Geraldine, Ghislaine, Guinevere, Gwendolen, Henrietta, Jaqueline, Jeannette, Josephine, Katharine, Katherine, Kimberley, Madeleine, Magdalene, Mélisande, Millicent, Nicolette, Parminder, Priscilla, Rosemarie, Sigourney, Silvestra, Stephanie, Sylvestra, Thomasina, Valentine
**10** Antoinette, Bernadette, Christabel, Clementina, Clementine, Jacqueline, Shakuntula, Wilhelmina

---

• **society girl 03** deb **09** débutante

**girlfriend**
**03** mot **04** babe, baby, bint, bird, date, girl, lady, lass, moll **05** chick, lover, woman **06** steady **07** fiancée, partner, squeeze **08** best girl, mistress, old flame **09** cohabitee, young lady **10** sweetheart **11** live-in lover **15** common-law spouse

**girlish**
**08** childish, immature, innocent, youthful **09** childlike **10** adolescent **11** unmasculine

**girth**
**04** band, bulk, size **05** strap **06** asylum **07** compass, measure **08** encircle **09** perimeter, sanctuary, surcingle **13** circumference

**gist**
**03** nub **04** core, crux, idea, pith **05** drift, point, sense **06** import, marrow, matter, thrust **07** essence, keynote, meaning, nucleus, purport **09** direction, substance **12** quintessence, significance **15** sum and substance

**give**
◇ *juxtaposition indicator* **02** do **03** aim, gie **04** bend, cede, fall, gift, have, lead, lend, make, move, play, show, sink, slip, tell, turn, will, yeve **05** admit, allow, award, break, cause, endow, focus, grant, lay on, leave, offer, put on, slack, throw, utter, yield **06** accord, afford, bestow, buckle, commit, confer, convey, create, devote, direct, donate, fetter, give up, impart, induce, permit, prompt, render, reveal, supply **07** arrange, concede, declare, deliver, display, dispose, entrust, exhibit, furnish, give way, incline, perform, present, produce, proffer, provide, publish, shackle, stretch **08** announce, bequeath, carry out, collapse, estimate, hand over, indicate, make over, manifest, occasion, organize, set forth, transfer, transmit, turn over, yielding **09** break down, fall apart, pronounce, surrender **10** administer, contribute, distribute, elasticity, give rise to **11** cause to have, communicate, concentrate, springiness **12** stretchiness, take charge of **14** cause to undergo, let someone have

• **give away 04** leak, shed, tell **06** betray, expose, let out, reveal **07** concede, divulge, let slip, uncover **08** disclose, inform on
• **give in 04** quit **05** yield **06** give up, jack in, submit **07** chuck up, concede, give way, succumb **08** pack it in **09** chuck it in, surrender **10** call it a day, capitulate, knock under **11** admit defeat **12** knuckle under **13** concede defeat **15** throw in the cards, throw in the towel, throw up the cards
• **give off 04** emit, fume, vent **05** exude **06** evolve, exhale **07** give out, pour out, produce, release, send out **08** liberate, throw out **09** discharge
• **give on to 06** lead to **08** open on to, overlook
• **give out 04** deal, emit, vent **05** allot, exude, yield **06** exhale, impart, notify, pack up, report, run out **07** conk out, declare, dish out, dole out, give off, hand out, mete out, pour out, produce, publish, release, send out **08** announce, depleted, disperse, share out, throw out, transmit **09** advertise, be mixed up, break down, broadcast, circulate, discharge, make known **10** be depleted, distribute, pass around, relinquish **11** be exhausted, come to an end, communicate, disseminate, stop working **12** be all mixed up
• **give over 03** lin **07** chuck it **08** transfer

• **give up 03** cut **04** cede, quit, stop **05** cease, forgo, remit, waive **06** cut out, forego, give in, render, resign, turn in **07** abandon, chuck in, chuck up, concede, crap out, deliver, forbear, forgive, lay down, put down, respite, throw up **08** abdicate, forswear, leave off, renounce **09** sacrifice, surrender **10** capitulate, relinquish **11** admit defeat, discontinue **13** concede defeat **14** drop your bundle **15** throw in the towel

**give-and-take**
**08** goodwill **10** compliance, compromise **11** co-operation, flexibility, negotiation, willingness **12** adaptability

**given**
**05** prone **06** liable, likely, stated **08** assuming, definite, disposed, distinct, inclined, in view of, specific **09** specified **10** individual, particular **11** considering **12** in the light of **13** bearing in mind

**giver**
**05** angel, donor **06** backer, friend, helper, patron **07** sponsor **08** promoter, provider **09** supporter **10** benefactor, subscriber, subsidizer, well-wisher **11** contributor **14** fairy godmother, philanthropist

**glacial**
**03** icy, raw **04** cold **05** chill, gelid, polar, stiff **06** arctic, biting, bitter, chilly, frigid, frosty, frozen, wintry **07** brumous, distant, hostile **08** freezing, inimical, piercing, Siberian **10** unfriendly **12** antagonistic

**glaciation stage**
**04** Günz, Riss, Würm **06** Mindel

**glad**
**04** fain, keen **05** eager, happy, merry, ready **06** bright, cheery, elated, joyful **07** chuffed, gleeful, pleased, welcome, willing **08** cheerful, disposed, gladsome, inclined, prepared, thrilled **09** contented, delighted, gratified, overjoyed, satisfied **11** over the moon, tickled pink

**gladden**
**05** cheer, elate **06** buck up, please **07** delight, enliven, gratify, hearten, rejoice **08** brighten **09** encourage **10** exhilarate

**glade**
**03** gap **04** dell, land **05** laund, space **07** opening **08** clearing **09** cock-shoot

**gladiator**
**07** Samnite, sworder **09** retiarius, Spartacus

**gladly**
**04** fain, lief **06** fainly, freely **07** happily, readily **09** willingly **10** cheerfully, gladsomely **12** with pleasure **13** with good grace

**gladness**
**03** joy **04** glee **05** mirth **06** gaiety **07** delight, jollity **08** felicity, hilarity, pleasure **09** happiness **10** brightness,

joyousness **11** high spirits
**12** cheerfulness

## glamorous
**04** glam **05** ritzy, smart **06** exotic,
flashy, glammy, glitzy, glossy, lovely
**07** elegant **08** alluring, charming,
dazzling, exciting, gorgeous
**09** appealing, beautiful, colourful,
thrilling **10** attractive, bewitching,
enchanting, glittering **11** captivating,
fascinating, well-dressed

## glamour
**02** it, SA **04** gilt, Ritz **05** charm, magic
**06** allure, appeal, beauty, thrill
**07** glitter **08** elegance, prestige,
witchery **09** magnetism, sex appeal
**10** attraction, excitement
**11** captivation, enchantment,
fascination **14** attractiveness
• **sentimental glamour 04** halo

## glance
**03** dip, ray **04** flip, leaf, leer, look, ogle,
peek, peep, scan, skim, view **05** blink,
dekko, eliad, flash, flick, glide, slant,
squiz, thumb, tweer, twire **06** amoret,
aspect, browse, eyliad, gander, gledge,
illiad, shufti, shufty, skelly, squint,
vision **07** deflect, eye-beam, eyeliad,
eyeshot, eye-wink, glimpse, skellie
**08** butcher's, oeillade, ricochet **09** brief
look, quick look **10** redruthite **13** look
briefly at, look quickly at **15** catch a
glimpse of
• **at first glance 09** outwardly,
seemingly **10** apparently, ostensibly,
prima facie **12** at first sight, on the
surface **13** on the face of it,
superficially
• **glance off 07** rebound **08** ricochet
**09** bounce off **10** spring back

## gland

*Glands include:*

**05** lymph, ovary
**06** cortex, pineal, thymus
**07** adrenal, eccrine, mammary,
   medulla, parotid, thyroid
**08** apocrine, exocrine, pancreas,
   prostate, testicle
**09** endocrine, holocrine, lachrymal,
   lymph node, merocrine, pituitary,
   sebaceous
**11** parathyroid

## glare
**04** beam, glow, look, lour **05** blaze,
flame, flare, frown, lower, scowl,
shine, stare **06** dazzle, glassy, glower
**07** daggers, reflect **08** iceblink **09** black
look, dirty look, limelight, look frown,
spotlight **10** brightness, brilliance

## glaring
**04** open **05** glary, gross, lurid, overt
**06** garish, patent **07** blatant, obvious
**08** flagrant, manifest, walleyed
**10** outrageous **11** conspicuous

## glaringly
**06** openly **07** overtly **08** patently
**09** blatantly, obviously **10** flagrantly,
manifestly **13** conspicuously

## glass
**04** lens, opal, pony **05** loupe, poney,

specs **06** beaker, copita, cullet, goblet,
mirror, psyche, rummer **07** brimmer,
crystal, monocle, opaline, sleever,
tumbler, vitrail, vitrics **08** pince-nez
**09** barometer, glassware, lorgnette
**10** avanturine, aventurine, dildo-glass,
eyeglasses, spectacles **12** opera-
glasses, supernaculum **13** contact
lenses

*Glass sizes include:*

**03** pot, six, ten
**04** pint
**05** bobby, middy, seven
**06** handle
**07** butcher, sleever
**08** half pint, schooner

• **flaw in glass 04** tear
• **substitute for glass 04** mica

## glassy
**03** icy **04** cold, dull **05** blank, clear,
dazed, empty, fixed, glare, shiny
**06** glazed, glazen, glossy, smooth,
vacant **07** deadpan, hyaline, vacuous
**08** lifeless, polished, slippery,
unmoving, vitreous **09** glasslike
**10** mirrorlike **11** transparent **12** crystal
clear **14** expressionless

## glaze
**04** ciré, coat **05** aspic, cover, glass,
gloss, shine, smear **06** enamel, finish,
luster, lustre, polish, sancai **07** burnish,
celadon, coating, eggwash, lacquer,
varnish **08** tiger eye **09** peach-blow,
tiger's eye

## gleam
**03** ray **04** beam, glow, leam, leme
**05** blink, flame, flare, flash, glint, gloss,
light, shaft, sheen, shine **06** glance,
lustre **07** flicker, glimmer, glimpse,
glisten, glitter, radiate, shimmer,
sparkle **08** sun-blink **10** brightness,
shimmering **11** scintillate

## glean
**04** cull, pick, reap **05** amass, learn,
lease **06** garner, gather, pick up, select
**07** collect, find out, harvest
**10** accumulate

## glee
**03** fun, joy **04** gley **05** mirth, verve
**06** gaiety, squint **07** delight, elation,
jollity, triumph **08** gladness, hilarity,
pleasure **09** joviality, merriment
**10** exuberance, exultation, jocularity,
joyfulness, joyousness, liveliness
**12** cheerfulness, exhilaration
**13** gratification

## gleeful
**05** happy, merry **06** elated, jovial,
joyful, joyous **07** pleased **08** cheerful,
exultant, jubilant, mirthful **09** cock-a-
hoop, delighted, exuberant, gratified,
overjoyed **10** triumphant **11** over the
moon **14** beside yourself

## gleefully
**07** happily, merrily **08** joyfully,
joyously **10** cheerfully, jubilantly
**11** exuberantly **12** triumphantly

## glen
**03** cwm **04** gill **05** ghyll **10** depression

## glib
**04** easy **05** gabby, gassy, quick, ready,
slick, suave **06** facile, fluent, smooth
**07** voluble **08** castrate **09** insincere,
plausible, talkative **10** loquacious
**13** silver-tongued, smooth-talking,
smooth-tongued

## glibly
**05** patly, slick **06** easily **07** quickly,
slickly **08** fluently, smoothly
**11** insincerely

## glide
**03** fly, run **04** cost, flow, pass, roll, sail,
skim, slip, slur, soar, swan, swim
**05** coast, coste, drift, float, lapse, skate,
sleek, slide **06** vanish **07** scrieve
**08** volplane **10** portamento **12** move
smoothly

## glimmer
**03** ray **04** glow, hint, wink **05** blink,
flash, gleam, glint, grain, shine, stime,
styme, trace **07** flicker, glimpse,
glisten, glitter, inkling, shimmer,
sparkle, twinkle **10** suggestion

## glimmering
**04** clue, hint, idea, sign **06** notion
**07** inkling, pointer, whisper
**08** allusion, faintest, foggiest, innuendo
**09** suspicion **10** indication, intimation,
suggestion **11** insinuation

## glimpse
**03** spy **04** espy, glim, look, peek, peep,
spot, view, waff **05** blink, flash, gliff,
glift, glisk, sight, stime, styme, whiff
**06** aperçu, glance, gledge, squint
**08** sighting **09** brief look, foregleam,
quick look **12** catch sight of

## glint
**05** flash, gleam, shine **07** glimmer,
glisten, glitter, reflect, shimmer,
sparkle, twinkle **10** glistening,
reflection **11** scintillate

## glisten
**05** flash, gleam, glint, shine **07** flicker,
glimmer, glitter, shimmer, sparkle,
twinkle **09** coruscate

## glitch
**04** snag **05** block, catch, check, delay
**06** hiccup, hold-up, mishap **07** barrier,
problem, setback, trouble
**08** drawback, obstacle **09** hindrance
**10** difficulty, impediment
**11** obstruction

## glitter
**04** gilt, glee **05** flare, flash, gleam, glint,
glitz, sheen, shine **06** bicker, dazzle,
lustre, tinsel **07** flicker, glamour,
glimmer, glisten, glister, shimmer,
spangle, sparkle, twinkle **08** radiance
**09** coruscate, showiness, splendour
**10** brightness, brilliance, flashiness,
razzmatazz **11** coruscation, scintillate
**12** razzle-dazzle **13** scintillation

## glitz
**05** swank **07** glitter, pizzazz
**09** gaudiness, showiness **10** flashiness,
garishness, razzmatazz
**11** flamboyance, ostentation **12** razzle-
dazzle **13** tastelessness
**14** attractiveness **15** pretentiousness

## glitzy

04 loud, posh 05 cheap, fancy, flash, gaudy, ritzy, showy, vivid 06 flashy, garish, ornate, swanky, tawdry
07 pompous 09 brilliant, tasteless
10 flamboyant, glittering 11 pretentious 12 ostentatious

## gloat

04 crow 05 boast, exult, glory, vaunt 06 relish 07 rejoice, revel in, rub it in, triumph 09 delight in

## global

05 total 07 general 08 thorough
09 spherical, universal, worldwide
10 exhaustive 11 wide-ranging 12 all-inclusive, encyclopedic
13 comprehensive, encyclopaedic, international 15 all-encompassing

## globally

09 generally, worldwide
10 everywhere 11 in every land, under the sun, universally 12 in every place 14 in every country 15 internationally

## globe

03 orb 04 ball, pome 05 earth, round, world 06 planet, sphere 08 roundure

## globular

05 round 07 globate 08 spheroid
09 orbicular, spherical
10 ball-shaped

## globule

04 ball, bead, blob, drop, pill 05 pearl 06 bubble, pellet 07 droplet, vesicle 08 globulet, particle, vesicula

## gloom

03 woe 04 damp, dark, dusk, mirk, mood, murk 05 cloud, drere, grief, scowl, shade 06 dreare, misery, shadow, sorrow 07 despair, dimness, sadness 08 darkness, dullness, glumness, the blues, twilight
09 blackness, dejection, murkiness, obscurity, pessimism 10 cloudiness, depression, desolation, low spirits, melancholy, sullenness
11 despondency, unhappiness
12 hopelessness
14 discouragement

## gloomily

05 sadly 06 glumly 08 dismally, drearily, morosely 09 miserably
11 cheerlessly 12 depressingly, despondently 13 downheartedly
15 pessimistically

## gloomy

03 dim, low, sad, wan 04 dark, down, dull, glum, grim, mirk, murk 05 dingy, drear, dusky, heavy, morne, murky, sable, unlit 06 cloudy, dismal, dreary, drumly, morose, somber, sombre
07 obscure, shadowy, Stygian, subfusc 08 darksome, dejected, desolate, downbeat, downcast, frowning, overcast 09 cheerless, Cimmerian, depressed, dyspeptic, miserable, saturnine, sorrowful, tenebrose, tenebrous 10 Acherontic, depressing, despondent, disastrous, dispirited, downlooked, melancholy, sepulchral, tenebrious 11 crepuscular, downhearted, dyspeptical, pessimistic

12 disconsolate, in low spirits 14 down in the dumps
• **gloomy appearance** 04 lour

## glorification

06 avatar, praise 07 lauding, worship 08 doxology, thanking 09 adoration, extolling, gratitude, honouring, reverence 10 apotheosis, veneration
11 celebration, idolization, lionization 13 magnification 15 romanticization, transfiguration

## glorify

04 hail, laud 05 adore, bless, exalt, extol, thank 06 honour, praise, revere 07 elevate, heroize, idolize, lionize, magnify, worship 08 emblazon, enshrine, eulogize, sanctify, venerate 09 celebrate 10 panegyrize
11 immortalize, romanticize, transfigure

## glorious

04 fine 05 famed, grand, great, noble, noted, super, tipsy 06 bright, elated, famous, superb 07 eminent, perfect, radiant, shining, supreme 08 boastful, dazzling, gorgeous, heavenly, honoured, majestic, renowned, splendid, terrific 09 beautiful, brilliant, excellent, wonderful 10 celebrated, delightful, marvellous, triumphant, victorious 11 illustrious, magnificent 13 distinguished

## glory

03 sun 04 crow, fame, halo, pomp 05 boast, crown, exult, gloat, kudos, revel, strut 06 beauty, diadem, gloire, gloria, homage, honour, praise, relish, renown, wallow 07 acclaim, aureola, delight, dignity, garland, majesty, preface, rejoice, tribute, triumph, worship 08 accolade, blessing, doxology, eminence, gloriole, grandeur, prestige, radiance
09 adoration, celebrity, gratitude, greatness, splendour 10 brightness, brilliance, exaltation, veneration
11 distinction, recognition
12 magnificence, resplendence, thanksgiving 13 pride yourself
14 impressiveness 15 illustriousness

## gloss

04 mask, note, show, veil 05 front, gleam, sheen, shine 06 define, façade, luster, lustre, polish, postil, veneer 07 comment, explain, shimmer, sparkle, surface, varnish 08 annotate, construe, disguise, footnote, scholion 09 elucidate, interpret, semblance, translate 10 annotation, appearance, brightness, brilliance, camouflage, commentary, definition 11 elucidation, explanation, explication, translation 12 add glosses to 14 interpretation, window-dressing
• **gloss over** 04 fard, gild, hide, mask, veil 05 avoid, evade 06 ignore, soothe 07 conceal, cover up
08 disguise 09 whitewash
10 camouflage, double-gild, smooth over 11 explain away 13 draw a veil over 15 deal with quickly

## glossary

05 index 06 clavis 07 lexicon
08 wordbook, word list 09 thesaurus
10 dictionary 11 concordance

## glossy

05 glacé, shiny, silky, sleek, slick
06 bright, glassy, glazed, polite, sheeny, silken, smooth 07 shining, wet-look 08 gleaming, lustrous, polished 09 brilliant, burnished, enamelled, sparkling 10 shimmering

## glove

03 kid 04 gage, left, mitt 05 right
06 beaver, cestus, mitten, muffle
07 caestus, chevron 08 cheveron, gauntlet 09 oven glove

## glow

04 burn, leam, leme, rose 05 bloom, blush, flush, gleam, glory, light, shine 06 ardour, colour, redden, warmth
07 burning, fervour, glimmer, passion, radiate, redness, sunglow 08 grow pink, look pink, outflush, pinkness, radiance, richness, rosiness, smoulder 09 afterglow, corposant, happiness, intensity, reddening, splendour, vividness 10 brightness, brilliance, enthusiasm, excitement, luminosity
11 gegenschein, St Elmo's fire
12 satisfaction 13 incandescence
15 phosphorescence

## glower

04 look 05 frown, glare, scowl, stare
09 black look, dirty look 11 look daggers

## glowing

03 red 04 rave, rich, warm 05 ruddy, vivid 06 bright, fervid 07 candent, flaming, flushed, lambent, radiant, vibrant 08 ecstatic, luminous, rutilant 09 laudatory, rhapsodic 10 candescent, eulogistic, favourable 11 noctilucent, noctilucous, panegyrical, smouldering 12 enthusiastic, incandescent
13 complimentary 14 phosphorescent

## glue

03 fix, gum 04 bond, grip, seal, size 05 affix, epoxy, paste, rivet, stick
06 absorb, cement, compel, engage, mortar 07 engross, gelatin 08 adhesive, Araldite®, fixative, gelatine, propolis 09 hypnotize, mesmerize
11 agglutinate 12 conglutinate, ichthyocolla 14 impact adhesive

## gluey

05 gummy 06 sticky, viscid 07 viscous 08 adhesive 09 glutinous

## glum

03 low, sad 04 down, sour 05 gruff, moody, sulky, surly 06 gloomy, grumpy, morose, solemn, sullen
07 crabbed, doleful, forlorn, unhappy 08 churlish, dejected 09 depressed, miserable 10 despondent
11 crestfallen, ill-humoured, pessimistic 14 down in the dumps

## glumly

05 sadly 06 sourly 08 gloomily, gruffily, grumpily, morosely, sullenly
09 forlornly, miserably, unhappily
10 dejectedly 12 despondently

## glut

**04** clog, cram, fill, sate **05** choke, flood, gorge, stuff **06** deluge, excess **07** engorge, satiate, surfeit, surplus **08** inundate, overfeed, overflow, overload, saturate **10** oversupply, saturation **11** superfluity **13** overabundance **14** superabundance

## glutinous

**04** limy, ropy **05** gluey, gummy, ropey **06** mucous, sticky, viscid **07** viscous **08** adhesive, cohesive **09** emplastic **12** mucilaginous

• **glutinous formation 04** rope

## glutton

**03** pig **06** gorger, gutser, gutzer **07** gobbler, guzzler, lurcher **08** belly-god, carcajou, gourmand **09** cormorant, free-liver, wolverine **10** greedy guts **11** gormandizer

## gluttonous

**05** gutsy **06** greedy **07** hoggish, piggish **08** edacious, esurient, gourmand, ravenous **09** rapacious, voracious **10** gluttonish, insatiable, omnivorous **12** gormandizing

## gluttony

**05** greed **07** edacity, surfeit **08** gulosity, voracity **09** esurience **10** gormandise, greediness **11** gourmandism, piggishness **13** insatiability

## G-man

**03** fed

## gnarled

◇ *anagram indicator* **05** bumpy, lumpy, rough **06** gnarly, knotty, knurly, rugged **07** gnarred, knarred, knotted, twisted **08** leathery, wrinkled **09** contorted, distorted **13** weather-beaten

## gnash

**04** grit **05** grate, grind **06** scrape

## gnaw

**03** eat, nag **04** bite, chew, fret, prey, wear **05** erode, harry, haunt, munch, worry **06** crunch, devour, harass, nibble, niggle, plague **07** consume, eat away, torment, trouble **09** masticate

## gnome

**03** saw **05** adage, dwarf, maxim, motto **06** goblin, kobold, saying **07** proverb **08** aphorism **09** financier

## go

**03** act, bet, bid, die, fit, gae, gee, get, pep, run, say, try, zip **04** bash, bout, cark, deal, emit, fail, fare, gang, go by, grow, hark, head, kark, lead, life, move, pass, push, quit, scat, shot, span, stab, suit, turn, walk, work, yead, yede, yeed, zing **05** begin, blend, crack, croak, drive, drown, end up, fit in, force, lapse, leave, match, occur, oomph, reach, ready, scoot, scram, sound, spell, stake, start, whirl **06** accord, affair, beat it, be axed, become, be kept, belong, cark it, depart, effort, elapse, energy, expire, extend, go away, kark it, manage, matter, pan out, pass by, pass on, peg out, perish, pop off, repair, result, roll on, set off, set out, slip by, spirit, spread, starve, travel, unfold, vanish, vigour **07** advance, attempt, bargain, be fired, be found, be given, be spent, carry on, decease, develop, give off, journey, make for, operate, perform, pizzazz, proceed, release, retreat, send out, snuff it, stretch, success, turn out, urinate, work out **08** activity, be sacked, be used up, clear off, come to be, continue, dynamism, function, get rid of, melt away, pass away, progress, slip away, tick away, vitality, withdraw **09** animation, be donated, be given to, be located, be pledged, be spent on, disappear, endeavour, eventuate, harmonize **10** be consumed, be finished, be situated, complement, co-ordinate, correspond, get-up-and-go, go together, make a sound, make tracks **11** be awarded to, be discarded, be dismissed, be exhausted, be presented, bite the dust **12** be allotted to, be assigned to, be thrown away, lose your life, pop your clogs, shoot through **13** be changed into, close your eyes, kick the bucket, push up daisies, take your leave **14** be given the push, be given the sack, be shown the door, depart this life, give up the ghost **15** be made redundant, breathe your last, cash in your chips, go with each other

• **go about** ◇ *containment indicator* **02** do **04** stir **05** begin **06** tackle **07** address, perform **08** approach, attend to, embark on, engage in, set about **09** undertake

• **go ahead 04** move **05** begin **07** advance, carry on, precede, proceed **08** continue, fire away, progress **12** make progress

• **go along with 04** obey **06** accept, follow **07** abide by, support **09** accompany, agree with **10** comply with, concur with, fall in with

• **go and get 03** fet **05** fetch

• **go around, go round** ◇ *anagram indicator* ◇ *containment indicator* ◇ *reversal indicator* **04** reel, spin, turn **05** swirl, twirl, twist, wheel, whirl, whirr **06** bypass, circle, gyrate, rotate, swivel **07** go about, revolve **09** circulate, pirouette, turn round **13** be passed round, be talked about **14** be spread around

• **go at 05** argue, blame **06** attack, tackle **08** set about **09** criticize

• **go away 04** scat **05** choof, hence, hop it, imshi, imshy, leave, scoot, scram, swith **06** begone, depart, vanish **07** abscond, do a bunk, gertcha, nick off, rack off, retreat **08** choof off, run for it, withdraw **09** disappear, do a runner **10** get knotted **13** sling your hook **14** make a bolt for it, run for your life **15** make a break for it, take to your heels

• **go back** ◇ *reversal indicator* **06** return, revert **07** regress, retreat **09** backslide

• **go back on** ◇ *reversal indicator* **04** deny **05** break **08** renege on **09** default on

• **go by 04** flow, heed, obey, pass **05** lapse **06** elapse, follow **07** observe **10** comply with

• **go down 03** dip, set **04** drop, fail, fall, fold, lose, sink **07** decline, descend, founder, go under, sustain **08** be beaten, collapse, decrease, fall down **09** be met with, be reduced **10** be defeated, be honoured, be received, be recorded, degenerate **11** be reacted to, be submerged, deteriorate **12** be recognized, be remembered, come a cropper, suffer defeat **15** have as a response

• **go down with 05** catch **06** pick up **07** develop **08** contract **09** succumb to **12** come down with **13** be afflicted by

• **go for 04** like **05** enjoy **06** admire, aim for, assail, attack, choose, favour, prefer, rush at, select **07** assault, lunge at **08** set about

• **go forward 03** rip

• **go freely 03** run

• **go in for 05** adopt, enter **06** follow, go into, pursue, take up **07** embrace, espouse **08** engage in, practise **09** undertake **10** take part in **13** participate in

• **go into** ◇ *anagram indicator* ◇ *insertion indicator* **05** probe, study **06** review **07** analyse, discuss, dissect, examine **08** check out, consider, look into, research **09** delve into **10** scrutinize **11** inquire into, investigate

• **go off** ◇ *anagram indicator* **03** rot **04** quit, sour, turn **05** blast, burst, go bad, leave **06** blow up, depart, go bang, set out, vanish **07** abscond, be fired, explode, go stale **08** detonate **09** disappear **11** deteriorate **12** be discharged

• **go on 03** gab, gas, hup **04** last, stay **05** occur **06** endure, happen, natter, rabbit, remain, witter **07** carry on, chatter, persist, proceed **08** continue, ramble on **09** take place

• **go out 03** ebb **04** date, exit **05** court, leave **06** depart, go with **07** go round **08** go around, go steady, withdraw **11** be turned off **12** see each other **13** be switched off **14** be extinguished

• **go over 04** list, read, scan **05** check, study **06** peruse, repeat, review, revise **07** discuss, examine, inspect **08** look over, rehearse **10** think about

• **go quickly 03** cut, run, zap **04** hare, race, spin

• **go round 04** ring, turn **06** rotate

• **go slow 04** lose

• **go through 04** bear, face, hunt **05** check, spend, stand, use up **06** endure, search, suffer **07** consume, examine, exhaust, explore, undergo **08** be passed, be signed, rehearse, squander, tolerate **09** be adopted, be carried, withstand **10** be accepted, be approved, experience, get through **11** be confirmed, investigate, look through **12** be authorized **13** be subjected to

• **go together** ◇ *juxtaposition indicator* **03** fit **04** suit **05** blend, match **06** accord

**09** harmonize **10** complement, co-ordinate
• **go under** ◇ *juxtaposition down indicator* **03** die **04** fail, flop, fold, sink **05** drown **06** go bust, go down **07** default, founder, succumb **08** collapse, submerge **09** close down **10** go bankrupt **11** go to the wall **15** go out of business
• **go with** **03** fit **04** suit, take **05** blend, match, usher **06** escort **09** accompany, harmonize **10** complement, co-ordinate, correspond
• **go without** **04** lack, want **05** forgo **06** forego **07** abstain **09** do without **12** deny yourself **13** manage without
• **tell to go** **04** send

**goad**
**03** gad, nag, vex **04** brod, jolt, prod, push, spur, urge **05** ankus, annoy, drive, hound, impel, prick, sound, sting, taunt **06** arouse, harass, incite, induce, needle, prompt **07** inspire, provoke **08** irritate, motivate **09** instigate, stimulate **10** cattle prod, pressurize

**go-ahead**
**02** OK **05** pushy **06** assent, the nod **07** consent, dashing, dynamic, forward **08** approval, sanction, thumbs-up, vigorous, warranty **09** agreement, ambitious, clearance, energetic, go-getting **10** aggressive, green light, permission, pioneering **11** opportunist, progressive, resourceful, up-and-coming **12** confirmation, enterprising **13** authorization **14** forward-looking

**goal**
**03** aim, end **04** cage, dool, dule, hail, home, mark, race **05** bourn, grail, ideal, limit **06** bourne, design, object, target **07** purpose **08** ambition, boundary, terminus **09** direction, equalizer, intention, objective **10** aspiration **11** competition, destination
• **prevent goal** **04** save

**goat**
**03** bok, kid **04** gate, ibex, tahr, tehr, thar **05** nanny **06** Angora, butter, caprid, lecher, Saanen **07** bucardo, markhor **09** Capricorn

**goat-antelope**
**05** goral, serow **07** chamois

**goatsucker**
**06** evejar **07** bullbat, dorhawk, fern-owl **08** churn-owl, nightjar, poorwill **09** nighthawk **10** moth-hunter, night-churr **11** screech-hawk **12** mosquito hawk, whippoorwill **15** chuck-will's-widow

**gobble**
◇ *containment indicator* **04** bolt, cram, gulp, wolf **05** gorge, scoff, snarf, stuff **06** devour, guzzle **07** consume, put away, slabber, slubber, swallow **08** chow down **10** eat quickly

**gobbledygook**
**06** drivel, jargon **07** prattle, rubbish, twaddle **08** nonsense **09** buzz words, gibberish **10** balderdash, double-talk,

journalese **11** computerese, officialese **12** psychobabble

**go-between**
**05** agent **06** broker, dealer, factor, medium **07** contact, liaison **08** mediator **09** messenger, middleman **10** love-broker **11** ring-carrier **12** intermediary

**goblet**
**03** cup **05** glass, hanap **06** beaker **07** chalice, stem cup, tumbler

**goblin**
**03** elf, imp, nis, pug **04** bogy, puck **05** bogey, bogle, demon, fiend, gnome, nisse, nixie, pooka, pouke, troll **06** bodach, duende, Empusa, kelpie, kobold, redcap, spirit, sprite **07** bargest, brownie, gremlin, knocker, red-cowl **08** barghest **09** barghaist, gobbeline, hobgoblin **10** leprechaun, shellycoat **11** lubber fiend **12** esprit follet

**gobsmacked**
**04** dumb **06** amazed, thrown **07** baffled, floored, shocked, stunned **08** confused, overcome, startled **09** astounded, paralysed, staggered **10** astonished, bewildered, bowled over, confounded, nonplussed, speechless, taken aback **11** dumbfounded, overwhelmed **12** lost for words **13** flabbergasted, knocked for six

**God**
**01** D **02** od **03** dod, dog, gad, Gog, gum, Jah, odd **04** Dieu, gosh, King, Lord, Zeus **05** Allah, Deity, Judge, Maker, monad **06** Brahma, Elohim, Father, Yahweh **07** all-seer, Bhagwan, Creator, Eternal, Godhead, Holy One, Jehovah, Saviour **08** all-giver, Almighty, gracious, infinite **09** All-father **11** first cause, prime mover, Providence **11** Divine Being, Everlasting, king of kings **12** Supreme Being
• **God willing** **02** DV **09** inshallah **10** Deo volente, volente Deo

**god, goddess**
**02** as **04** aitu, cock, deus, deva, Fate, faun, icon, idol, kami, Muse, Norn **05** deify, deity, Grace, Norna, power **06** spirit, sylvan **08** divinity **09** promachos **11** divine being, graven image

*Babylonian gods include:*
**02** Ea
**03** Anu, Bel, Sin
**04** Adad, Apsu, Baal, Enki, Nabu
**05** Ellil, Enlil, Hadad, Mummu
**06** Anshar, Dumuzi, Marduk, Nergal, Tammuz
**07** Ninurta, Shamash, Thammuz

*Babylonian goddesses include:*
**03** Aja
**04** Antu
**05** Antum, Belit, Nintu
**06** Ishtar, Kishar, Ningal, Ninlil, Nintur, Tiamat
**07** Anunitu, Damkina
**10** Ereshkigal

*Central and South American gods include:*
**04** Chac, Inti
**06** Tlaloc
**07** Huang-ti, Hunab Ku, Itzamma
**08** Catequil, Kukulkan
**09** the Bacabs, Viracocha, Xipe Totec
**10** Apu Punchau, Manco Capac, Pachacamac, Xochipilli
**12** Quetzalcoatl, Tezcatlipoca, Xiuhtecuhtli
**15** Huitzilopochtil

*Central and South American goddesses include:*
**05** Aknah
**06** Ixchel
**09** Coatlicue, Ixazaluoh, Mama Oella, Pachamama
**10** Mama Quilla
**11** Tlazolteotl
**12** Xochiquetzal
**15** Chalchiuhtlicue

*Egyptian gods include:*
**02** Ra, Re
**03** Bes, Geb, Nut
**04** Apis, Aten, Atum, Ptah, Seth
**05** Horus, Thoth
**06** Amun-Re, Anubis, Osiris
**07** Khonsou, Sarapis, Serapis

*Egyptian goddesses include:*
**03** Nut
**04** Isis, Maat
**05** Khnum
**06** Hathor, Sakmet, Sekmet
**07** Nepthys, Sakhmet, Sekhmet
**08** Nephthys

*Greek gods include:*
**03** Pan
**04** Ares, Atys, Eros, Zeus
**05** Atlas, Attis, Hades
**06** Adonis, Aeolus, Apollo, Boreas, Cronus, Helios, Hermes, Hypnos, Nereus
**07** Oceanus
**08** Dionysus, Ganymede, Morpheus, Poseidon, Thanatos
**09** Asclepius
**10** Hephaestus
**11** Aesculapius

*Greek goddesses include:*
**03** Ate, Eos, Nyx
**04** Gaea, Gaia, Hebe, Hera, Iris, Nike, Rhea
**05** Tyche
**06** Athene, Cybele, Hecate, Hestia, Hygeia, Selene, Themis, Thetis
**07** Alphito, Artemis, Demeter, Erinyes, Nemesis
**08** Arethusa, the Fates, the Horae, the Muses
**09** Aphrodite, the Furies, the Graces
**10** Persephone

*Hindu gods include:*
**04** Agni, Kama, Rama, Siva, Soma, Yama
**05** Indra, Kurma, Radha, Rudra,

Shani, Shiva, Surya
**06** Brahma, Ganesa, Ganesh, Garuda, Iswara, Narada, Pushan, Ravana, Skanda, Varuna, Vishnu
**07** Ganesha, Hanuman, Krishna, Savitri
**08** Ganapati, Nataraja
**09** Kartikeya, Lakshmana, Narasimha, Prajapati
**10** Jagannatha

*Hindu goddesses include:*

**03** Uma
**04** Devi, Kali, Maya, Sita
**05** Aditi, Durga, Gauri, Radha, Sakti
**06** Shakti
**07** Lakshmi, Parvati
**09** Sarasvati

*Maori gods include:*

**02** Tu
**03** Uru
**04** Maui, Tane
**05** Rangi, Rongo
**06** Haumia
**07** Tawhiri
**08** Ranginui, Ruaumoko, Tangaroa
**10** Tane Mahuta
**11** Rongomatane, Tumatauenga
**12** Tawhiri Matea

*Maori goddesses include:*

**04** Papa
**10** Hinetitama
**11** Hinenuitepo, Papatuanuku

*Norse gods include:*

**03** Bor, Otr, Tyr, Ull
**04** Frey, Logi, Loki, Odin, Thor
**05** Aegir, Aesir, Alcis, Bragi, Donar, Freyr, Hoder, Mimir, Njord, Vanir, Vidar, Woden, Wotan
**06** Balder, Fafnir, Hermod, Hoenir, Kvasir, Weland
**07** Volundr, Wayland, Weiland
**08** Heimdall

*Norse goddesses include:*

**03** Hel, Ran, Sif
**04** Hela
**05** Frigg, Idunn, Nanna, Norns, Sigyn
**06** Freyja, Gefion
**07** Nerthus
**08** Fjorgynn
**09** Valkyries
**10** Nehallenia

*Roman gods include:*

**04** Mars
**05** Cupid, Fides, Janus, Lares, Orcus, Picus, Pluto
**06** Apollo, Consus, Faunus, Genius, Mithra, Saturn, Vulcan
**07** Bacchus, Jupiter, Mercury, Mithras, Neptune, Penates
**08** Portunus, Silvanus
**09** Vertumnus
**10** Liber Pater

*Roman goddesses include:*

**03** Ops
**04** Juno, Luna, Maia
**05** Ceres, Diana, Epona, Fauna,

Flora, Pales, Venus, Vesta
**06** Aurora, Pomona, Rumina
**07** Bellona, Egreria, Feronia, Fortuna, Minerva, Veritas
**08** Libitina, Victoria
**10** Proserpina

*Gods and goddesses of other regions and cultures include:*

**03** Rod, Wak
**04** Amma, Kane, Tane
**05** Epona, Pan Gu, Perun
**06** Guan Di, Inanna, Kuan Ti, Mithra, Modimo, Moloch, Shango, Svarog, Tengri, Teshub, Vahagn
**07** Anahita, Astarte, Kumarbi, Taranis, Triglav, Zanhary
**08** Rosmerta, Skyamsen, Sucellus, Teutates
**09** Amaterasu, Sventovit
**10** Ahura Mazda
**11** Thunderbird
**15** Izanagi no Mikoto, Izanami no Mikoto

**god-forsaken**
**05** bleak **06** dismal, dreary, gloomy, lonely, remote **07** forlorn **08** deserted, desolate, isolated, wretched
**09** abandoned, miserable
**10** depressing

**godless**
**03** bad **04** evil **05** pagan **06** sinful, unholy, wicked **07** atheous, heathen, immoral, impious, profane, ungodly
**08** agnostic **09** atheistic, faithless
**10** irreverent **11** irreligious, nullifidian, unrighteous **12** sacrilegious

**godlessness**
**07** atheism, impiety **08** paganism
**10** irreligion, wickedness
**11** agnosticism, irreverence, ungodliness **13** faithlessness
**14** unfaithfulness

**godlike**
**04** holy **06** divine, sacred **07** deiform, exalted, perfect, saintly, sublime
**08** heavenly, Olympian **09** celestial
**10** superhuman **11** theomorphic
**12** transcendent

**godliness**
**05** piety **06** belief, purity **08** holiness, morality, religion, sanctity
**10** devoutness **13** righteousness

**godly**
**04** good, holy, pure, wise **05** moral, pious **06** devout **07** saintly **08** innocent, virtuous **09** believing, religious, righteous **10** God-fearing

**godsend**
**04** boon **07** bonanza, miracle
**08** blessing, windfall **11** benediction
**12** stroke of luck

**goggle**
**04** gawk, gawp, gaze, ogle **05** stare
**06** wonder **08** protrude

**going-over**
**03** row **05** check, study **06** attack, rebuke, review, survey **07** beating, check-up, chiding, pasting **08** analysis,

scolding, scrutiny, whipping
**09** criticism, reprimand, thrashing, trouncing **10** inspection
**11** castigation, examination
**12** chastisement, dressing-down
**13** investigation

**goings-on**
**06** events, scenes **07** affairs **08** business, mischief **09** behaviour **10** activities, happenings **11** occurrences
**12** misbehaviour **13** funny business

**gold**
**02** Au, or **03** bar, Sol **04** gool, gule, leaf
**05** goold, ingot **06** nugget, riches, yellow **07** bullion **12** king of metals
**13** precious metal
• **yield gold 03** pan

**golden**
**03** red **04** fair, gilt, gold, rosy **05** blond, happy, sunny **06** blonde, bright, flaxen, gilded, gilden, gylden, joyful, yellow
**07** aureate, goldish, luteous, shining
**08** aurelian, dazzling, gleaming, glorious, inaurate, lustrous, precious
**09** brilliant, excellent, promising, rewarding, Saturnian, treasured
**10** auspicious, delightful, favourable, millennial, propitious, prosperous, successful **11** flourishing, hyacinthine, resplendent **12** gold-coloured

**goldfinch**
**06** redcap **09** goldspink, gowdspink
**10** yellowbird

**golf**
**01** G **04** gowf

*Golf courses include:*

**04** Deal, Eden
**05** Troon
**06** Manito, Merion, Skokie
**07** Balgove, Buffalo, Hoylake, Jubilee, Medinah, Newport, Oak Hill, Oakmont, Oak Tree, Prince's, Sahalee
**08** Bethesda, Birkdale, Blue Hill, Glen View, Portland, Sandwich, Valhalla
**09** Aronimink, Baltimore, Baltusrol, Bellerive, Brookline, Englewood, Hazeltine, Inverness, Minikahda, Muirfield, New Course, Old Course, Onwentsia, Pinehurst, Prestwick, St Andrews, The Belfry, Turnberry
**10** Canterbury, Carnoustie, Garden City, Gleneagles, Royal Troon, Shoal Creek, Tanglewood, Winged Foot
**11** Cherry Hills, Kemper Lakes, Miami Valley, Musselburgh, Olympic Club, Pebble Beach, Strathtyrum
**12** Crooked Stick, Laurel Valley, Oakland Hills
**13** Northwood Club, Olympia Fields, Royal Birkdale, Royal Portrush, Southern Hills
**14** Keller Golf Club, Myopia Hunt Club, NCR Country Club, Pelham Golf Club
**15** Augusta National, Chicago Golf Club, Shinnecock Hills

## golf club

*Golf clubs include:*

**04** iron, wood
**05** baffy, blade, cleek, mashy, spoon, wedge
**06** brassy, bulger, driver, jigger, mashie, putter
**07** blaster, brassie, midiron, niblick
**08** long iron
**09** midmashie, sand wedge, short iron
**10** mashie iron
**11** belly putter, driving iron, fairway wood, spade mashie
**12** putting-cleek
**13** mashie-niblick, pitching wedge, two-ball putter
**15** pitching niblick

## golfer

**06** gowfer, yipper

*Golfers include:*

**03** Els (Ernie)
**04** Lyle (Sandy), Webb (Karrie)
**05** Braid (James), Brown (Ken), Duval (David), Faldo (Nick), Floyd (Raymond), Hagen (Walter), Hogan (Ben), Jones (Bobby), Locke (Bobby), Lopez (Nancy), Singh (Vijay), Snead (Sam), Woods (Tiger)
**06** Alliss (Peter), Cotton (Sir Henry), Davies (Laura), Garcia (Sergio), Langer (Bernhard), Nelson (Byron), Norman (Greg), O'Meara (Mark), Palmer (Arnold), Player (Gary), Taylor (John), Vardon (Harry), Watson (Tom)
**07** Charles (Bob), Couples (Fred), Jacklin (Tony), Sarazen (Gene), Stewart (Payne), Strange (Curtis), Thomson (Peter), Trevino (Lee), Woosnam (Ian), Zoeller (Fuzzy)
**08** Crenshaw (Ben), Hamilton (Todd), Nicklaus (Jack), Olazábal (Jose Maria), Torrance (Sam), Westwood (Lee), Zaharias (Babe)
**09** Mickelson (Phil), Sorenstam (Annika), Whitworth (Kathy)
**11** Ballesteros (Severiano), Montgomerie (Colin)

## gone

◇ *anagram indicator* **03** ago, ygo
**04** away, dead, done, gane, lost, over, past, used, ygoe **05** agone, spent
**06** absent, astray **07** defunct, elapsed, extinct, missing, worn-out **08** departed, finished, vanished **11** disappeared
**15** over and done with

## goo

**03** mud **04** crud, grot, gunk, mire, muck, ooze, scum, slop, yuck
**05** gloop, grime, gunge, slime, slush
**06** grease, grunge, matter, sludge
**10** stickiness **14** sentimentality

## good

**01** g **02** OK **03** bad, bon, fab, fit, rum, top, use **04** able, best, dear, fair, fine, gain, kind, mega, neat, nice, safe, sake, true, well **05** adept, avail, beaut, bewdy, bonne, bosom, brill, bully, close, great, large, lucky, merit, moral, nasty, noble, pakka, pious, pucka, pukka, right, sound, super, valid, whole, worth **06** agreed, behalf, bonzer, bosker, castor, clever, corker, cushty, ethics, expert, gifted, honest, honour, indeed, just so, loving, morals, polite, profit, ripper, strong, superb, useful, virtue, wicked, worthy **07** awesome, benefit, capable, ethical, fitting, genuine, healthy, helpful, honesty, perfect, purpose, service, sizable, skilful, skilled, upright, welfare **08** adequate, all right, budgeree, cheerful, complete, cracking, fabulous, faithful, friendly, goodness, gracious, interest, intimate, morality, obedient, passable, pleasant, pleasing, reliable, sensible, sizeable, smashing, suitable, superior, talented, terrific, thorough, very well, vigorous, virtuous **09** admirable, advantage, agreeable, bodacious, brilliant, competent, compliant, desirable, dexterous, efficient, enjoyable, excellent, exemplary, fantastic, first-rate, fortunate, integrity, in the pink, rectitude, righteous, tolerable, wellbeing, wonderful **10** acceptable, altruistic, auspicious, beneficial, benevolent, charitable, convenient, convincing, dependable, favourable, first-class, good as gold, honourable, marvellous, persuasive, proficient, profitable, propitious, prosperity, reasonable, respectful, satisfying, sufficient, thoughtful, usefulness, worthwhile **11** appropriate, commendable, considerate, convenience, exceptional, kind-hearted, pleasurable, serviceable, substantial, sympathetic, trustworthy, uprightness, well-behaved **12** accomplished, advantageous, bewdy bottler, considerable, fit as a fiddle, professional, satisfactory, under control, well-disposed, well-mannered **13** hale and hearty, philanthropic, righteousness **14** salt of the earth
• **for good** **04** ever **06** always **07** for ever **08** evermore, for keeps **09** eternally **10** for all time **11** irrevocably, permanently **15** till kingdom come
• **make good** **02** do **04** abet **05** go far **06** arrive, effect, fulfil, make it, recoup, repair, supply **07** justify, perform, restore, succeed, support **08** carry out, get ahead, live up to, progress, put right, retrieve **09** establish **10** compensate **12** be successful **13** compensate for, make amends for, put into action **15** get on in the world
• **neither good nor bad** **04** so-so **14** comme ci comme ça
• **no good** **02** ng **03** bad, bum **04** duff **06** futile, no chop **07** useless **09** worthless
• **pretty good** **04** fair, tidy **06** decent, not bad **08** middling **09** tolerable **14** fair to middling
• **unusually good** **04** gear **10** incredible
• **very good** **02** OK, so, vg **03** sae, top

**04** keen, mega **05** bonza, grand
**06** bangin', beezer, bonzer, boshta, bosker, grouse, peachy **07** banging, boshter, crucial, immense, ripping
**08** all right, cracking, terrific
**09** brilliant **10** marvellous, tremendous

## goodbye

**03** bye **04** ciao, ta-ta **05** addio, adieu, adiós, later **06** bye-bye, cheers, hooray, hooroo, kia ora, see you, so long, valete **07** bonsoir, cheerio, good-day, good-den, good-e'en, haere ra, parting **08** au revoir, chin-chin, farewell, good-even, sayonara, swan song, take care, toodle-oo **09** bon voyage, good night, toodle-pip **10** all the best, a rivederci, good morrow
**11** arrivederci, be seeing you, good evening, good morning, leave-taking, see you later, valediction, valedictory
**12** have a nice day, mind how you go, see you around **13** good afternoon
**14** auf Wiedersehen

*See also* **farewell**

## good-for-nothing

**03** bum **04** idle, lazy **05** idler, lorel, losel, stiff **06** donnat, donnot, loafer, lozell, no-good, skiver, waster
**07** bludger, lorrell, sculpin, slacker, useless, vaurien, wastrel **08** feckless, indolent, layabout, scalawag
**09** lazybones, reprobate, scallawag, scallywag, worthless **10** black sheep, ne'er-do-weel, ne'er-do-well, profligate **11** scant-o'-grace
**13** irresponsible

## good-humoured

**05** happy **06** genial, jovial **07** affable, amiable **08** cheerful, friendly, pleasant
**09** congenial **12** approachable, good-tempered

## good-looking

**04** fair **05** dishy **06** comely, goodly, lovely, pretty **08** handsome, weel-far'd, weel-far'r **09** beautiful, weel-faird, weel-faur'd, weel-faurt **10** attractive, personable **11** presentable **12** well-favoured

## goodly

**04** fine, good, tidy **05** ample, large
**06** comely, proper **07** sizable
**08** sizeable **09** excellent **10** sufficient
**11** good-looking, significant, substantial **12** considerable

## good-natured

**04** kind, nice **05** sonsy **06** clever, gentle, kindly, sonsie **07** amiable, helpful, patient **08** friendly, generous, tolerant **10** benevolent **11** kind-hearted, neighbourly, sympathetic, warm-hearted **12** approachable, good-tempered

## goodness

**02** my **03** boy, law, wow **05** mercy, value **07** virtue **08** benefit, honesty, probity **08** altruism, goodwill, kindness
**09** integrity, rectitude **10** compassion, excellence, generosity **11** beneficence, benevolence, helpfulness, uprightness
**12** friendliness, graciousness

**goods**

**13** righteousness, unselfishness, wholesomeness

**goods**

**04** bona, gear **05** lines, stock, stuff, wares **06** taonga, things **07** effects, freight **08** chattels, products, property **10** belongings **11** commodities, merchandise, possessions **13** accoutrements, appurtenances, paraphernalia
• **package of goods** **04** bale, wrap

**good-tempered**

**04** kind **06** gentle, kindly **07** helpful, patient **08** friendly, generous, tolerant **10** benevolent **11** good-natured, kind-hearted, neighbourly, sympathetic, warm-hearted **12** approachable

**goodwill**

**04** gree, zeal **05** amity, favor **06** favour **08** kindness **10** compassion, friendship, generosity **11** benevolence, well-wishing **12** friendliness

**goody-goody**

**04** prig **05** pious **06** wowser **08** priggish, unctuous **09** wowserish **13** sanctimonious, self-righteous, ultra-virtuous

**gooey**

**04** soft **05** gluey, gucky, gungy, gunky, tacky, thick **06** gloopy, sickly, sloppy, slushy, sticky, syrupy, viscid **07** cloying, maudlin, mawkish, squidgy, viscous **09** glutinous **10** nauseating **11** sentimental **12** mucilaginous

**goose**

**04** wavy **05** roger, wavey **06** gander, goslet **07** gosling
*See also* **fool**
• **goose's lungs** **04** soul

**gooseberry**

**06** groser, groset **07** grosert **08** goosegob, goosegog, grossart **09** honey-blob **14** worcesterberry

**goosefoot**

**04** beet **05** blite, orach **06** fat hen, kochia, orache, quinoa, saxaul **07** pigweed, saksaul **08** saltbush, saltwort, seablite **10** greasewood, Mexican tea **13** good-King-Henry

**gore**

**02** Al **04** cloy, gair, horn, stab **05** blood, cruor, filth, grume, skirt, spear, stick, wound **06** engore, impale, pierce **07** carnage **08** butchery **09** bloodshed, penetrate, slaughter **10** bloodiness

**gorge**

**03** gap **04** bolt, cram, feed, fill, glut, gulp, pass, rift, sate, wolf **05** abyss, cañon, chasm, cleft, gully, stuff **06** canyon, defile, devour, gobble, guzzle, ravine, stodge **07** crevice, fissure, overeat, surfeit, swallow **08** barranca
*See also* **ravine**

**gorgeous**

**04** fine, good, rich, sexy **05** grand, showy, sweet **06** lovely, pretty, superb **07** opulent **08** dazzling, glorious, handsome, pleasing, splendid,

stunning **09** beautiful, brilliant, enjoyable, glamorous, luxurious, ravishing, splendent, sumptuous, wonderful **10** attractive, delightful, impressive, marvellous **11** good-looking, magnificent, resplendent **15** pulchritudinous

**gorgeously**

**06** richly **08** superbly **10** gloriously, splendidly **11** brilliantly, luxuriously, sumptuously, wonderfully **12** delightfully, impressively, marvellously **13** magnificently

**gorilla**

**04** thug **05** pongo **08** King Kong **10** silverback

**gorse**

**04** ulex, whin **05** furze, gosse

**gory**

**05** goary **06** bloody, brutal, grisly, savage **07** violent **09** murderous **10** sanguinary **11** blood-soaked, distasteful **12** bloodstained

**gospel**

**04** fact, John, Luke, Mark **05** credo, creed, truth **06** verity **07** evangel, kerygma, Matthew **08** doctrine, good news, teaching **09** certainty **12** life of Christ, New Testament **14** Protevangelium **15** message of Christ
*See also* **Bible**

**gossamer**

**04** airy, fine, thin **05** gauzy, light, sheer, silky **06** flimsy **08** cobwebby, delicate **10** diaphanous, see-through, shimmering **11** translucent, transparent **13** insubstantial

**gossip**

**03** ana, gab, gas, gup, jaw **04** aunt, buzz, chat, dirt, goss, talk **05** clash, crack, rumor, yenta **06** babble, claver, cummer, gabble, jabber, kimmer, natter, rabbit, report, rumour, tatler, tattle, tittle, waffle **07** babbler, blather, blether, chatter, chinwag, clatter, hearsay, prattle, scandal, shmooze, shmooze, tattler, whisper **08** busybody, causerie, chitchat, clatters, idle talk, prattler, rabbit on, schmooze, tell-tale **09** reportage, tell tales, whisperer **10** chatterbox, chew the fat, chew the rag, clish-clash, newsmonger, talebearer **11** mud-slinging, Nosey Parker, scuttlebutt, sweetie-wife **12** gossip-monger, spread gossip, tittle-tattle **13** bush telegraph, clishmaclaver, scandal-bearer, scandalmonger, smear campaign, spread a rumour **14** clash-ma-clavers

**gouge**

**03** cut, dig **04** claw, gash, hack **05** scoop, score, slash, wench **06** chisel, groove, hollow, incise **07** extract, scratch, swindle

**gourd**

**05** guiro, loofa, luffa **06** bryony, cacoon, loofah **07** pumpkin **08** calabash **11** white bryony **12** Hercules' club

**Gourde**

**01** G **03** Gde

**gourmand**

**03** hog, pig **06** gorger **07** glutton, guzzler **08** omnivore **09** voracious **10** gluttonous **11** gormandizer

**gourmet**

**06** foodie **07** epicure **09** bon vivant, epicurean **10** gastronome **11** connoisseur

**gout**

**04** drop, spot **05** taste **06** relish **07** podagra **08** chiragra **09** arthritis **10** cephalagra **12** hamarthritis

**govern**

**03** run **04** curb, head, lead, rein, rule, sway, tame **05** check, guide, order, pilot, quell, reign, steer **06** bridle, direct, manage, master, rein in, subdue **07** command, conduct, contain, control, oversee, preside **08** dominate, hold back, keep back, regulate, restrain **09** be in power, constrain, determine, influence, supervise **10** administer, discipline, hold office **11** keep in check, superintend **12** be in charge of

**governess**

**05** guide **06** duenna, mentor **07** teacher, tutress **08** fräulein, tutoress **09** companion **11** gouvernante **12** instructress, mademoiselle

**governing**

**06** ruling **07** guiding, leading, supreme **08** dominant, reigning **09** kingcraft, uppermost **10** commanding, dominative, overriding, prevailing, regulatory **11** controlling, predominant **12** transcendent

**government**

**01** g **03** Gov, HMG, raj **04** Govt, rule, sway **05** power, state **06** charge, circar, papacy, policy, régime, sircar, sirkar **07** cabinet, command, conduct, control, council, regence, regency, regimen, serkali **08** congress, dominion, guidance, ministry, politics, steerage **09** archology, authority, direction, executive, restraint **10** domination, governance, leadership, management, parliament, regulation **11** authorities, sovereignty, supervision **12** powers that be, surveillance **13** Establishment **14** administration **15** superintendence

*Government systems include:*

**05** junta
**06** empire
**07** kingdom
**08** monarchy, republic
**09** autocracy, communism, democracy, despotism, theocracy
**10** absolutism, federation, hierocracy, plutocracy
**11** triumvirate
**12** commonwealth, dictatorship

• **member of government** **02** in

**governor**

**02** Pa **03** Ban, beg, bey, Dad, dey, gov, guv **04** boss, head, khan, naik, vali,

**wali 05** chief, guide, hakim, mudir, pilot, ruler, tutor **06** eparch, exarch, grieve, leader, legate, master, Pilate, rector, satrap, tuchun, warden **07** alcaide, alcayde, catapan, harmost, manager, nomarch, podestà, rectrix, subadar, vaivode, viceroy, voivode **08** alderman, burgrave, director, ethnarch, gospodar, hospodar, kaimakam, overseer, pentarch, provodor, providor, resident, subahdar **09** beglerbeg, castellan, commander, corrector, directrix, dominator, executive, governess, intendant, president, proconsul, provedore, regulator **10** adelantado, controller, directress, gubernator, Lord Warden, proveditor, stadholder, supervisor **11** proveditore, stadtholder **12** commissioner **13** administrator **14** chief executive, superintendent

*Colonial governors of New South Wales:*

**04 King** (Captain Philip Gidley)
**05 Bligh** (Captain William), **Gipps** (Sir George)
**06 Bourke** (Major-General Richard), **Hunter** (Captain John)
**07 Darling** (Lieutenant-General Ralph), **Denison** (Sir William), **FitzRoy** (Sir Charles), **Phillip** (Captain Arthur)
**08 Brisbane** (Sir Thomas)
**09 Macquarie** (Colonel Lachlan)

*Governors-general of Australia:*

**04 Kerr** (Sir John), **Slim** (Field-Marshal Sir William)
**05 Casey** (Richard Gardiner, Baron), **Cowen** (Sir Zelman), **Deane** (Sir William)
**06 Denman** (Thomas, Baron), **Dudley** (William Humble Ward, Earl of), **Gowrie** (Alexander Hore-Ruthven, Baron), **Hayden** (William), **Isaacs** (Sir Isaac), **McKell** (Sir William)
**07 De L'Isle** (William, Viscount), **Forster** (Henry William, Baron), **Hasluck** (Sir Paul), **Stephen** (Sir Ninian)
**08 Hopetoun** (John Adrian Louis Hope, Earl of), **Tennyson** (Hallam, Baron)
**09 Dunrossil** (William, Viscount), **Northcote** (Henry, Baron)
**10 Gloucester** (Prince Henry, Duke of), **Stonehaven** (Sir John Lawrence Baird, Baron)
**12 Hollingworth** (Dr Peter)
**13 Munro-Ferguson** (Sir Ronald)

*Governors-general of New Zealand:*

**06 Cobham** (Charles George Lyttleton), **Galway** (Earl of), **Newall** (Cyril Louis Norton), **Norrie** (Lord), **Reeves** (Paul Alfred), **Tizard** (Catherine)
**07 Beattie** (David Stuart), **Porritt** (Arthur Espie)
**08 Blundell** (Edward Denis), **Freyberg** (Bernard Cyril), **Holyoake** (Sir Keith Jacka), **Jellicoe** (John Henry Rushworth)

**09 Bledisloe** (Charles Bathurst), **Fergusson** (Bernard), **Fergusson** (Charles), **Liverpool** (Earl of)
**10 Hardie Boys** (Sir Michael)

*Governors of New Zealand:*

**04 Grey** (George), **Weld** (Frederick Aloysius)
**05 Bowen** (George Ferguson)
**06 Browne** (Thomas Robert Gore), **Gordon** (Arthur Hamilton), **Hobson** (William), **Onslow** (Earl of), **Onslow** (William Hillier)
**07 FitzRoy** (Robert), **Glasgow** (Earl of), **Jervois** (William Francis Drummond), **Plunket** (Lord)
**08 Normanby** (Marquess of), **Ranfurly** (Earl of), **Robinson** (Hercules George Robert)
**09 Fergusson** (James), **Islington** (Lord), **Liverpool** (Earl of)

**gown**
**04** garb, robe, sack, silk **05** bania, dress, frock, habit, manto, shift, stole **06** banian, banyan, kirtle, mantua, sacque **07** costume, garment, manteau, negligé **08** mazarine, negligee, peignoir **09** sack dress, slammakin **10** slammerkin **12** bearing cloth, dressing-gown **13** Mother Hubbard

**grab**
◇ *containment indicator* **03** bag, nab, rap **04** grip, nail, take **05** annex, catch, grasp, pluck, seize, swipe, usurp **06** arrest, clutch, collar, nobble, snap up, snatch **07** capture, impress **08** interest **09** lay hold of **10** commandeer, take hold of **11** appropriate, catch hold of
*See also* **steal**
• **up for grabs 06** at hand **07** to be had **09** available **10** obtainable **12** for the asking

**grace**
**04** ease, trim **05** adorn, charm, honor, mense, mercy, poise, Venus **06** beauty, become, enrich, favour, honour, pardon, polish, prayer, set off, virtue **07** aggrace, charity, decency, decorum, dignify, enhance, finesse, fluency, garnish, manners, quarter, unction **08** beautify, blessing, breeding, clemency, courtesy, decorate, elegance, goodness, goodwill, kindness, leniency, ornament, reprieve **09** bethankit, embellish, etiquette, good taste, propriety **10** benedicite, comeliness, compassion, generosity, indulgence, kindliness, loveliness, refinement, smoothness **11** benediction, beneficence, benevolence, cultivation, distinguish, forgiveness, shapeliness **12** gracefulness, mercifulness, tastefulness, thanksgiving **13** consideration **14** attractiveness, prayer of thanks

*The Three Graces:*

**06** Aglaia, Thalia
**10** Euphrosyne

**graceful**
**04** deft, easy, fine, kind **05** agile, fluid, genty, suave **06** comely, fluent, gainly, nimble, polite, smooth, supple, svelte **07** elegant, flowing, genteel, natural, refined, slender, tactful, willowy **08** charming, cheerful, cultured, generous, gracious, grazioso, pleasant, polished, sylphine, sylphish, tasteful **09** agreeable, appealing, beautiful, courteous, sylphlike **10** attractive, cultivated, diplomatic, respectful

**gracefully**
**06** deftly, nimbly **08** grazioso, politely, smoothly **09** agreeably, elegantly, naturally, tactfully **10** cheerfully, generously, graciously, pleasantly, tastefully **11** beautifully, courteously **12** attractively, respectfully **14** diplomatically

**graceless**
**04** rude **05** crude, gawky, rough **06** clumsy, coarse, forced, gauche, vulgar **07** awkward, uncouth **08** impolite, improper, ungainly **09** barbarous, inelegant, menseless, shameless **10** indecorous, ungraceful, unmannerly **11** ill-mannered **12** unattractive **15** unsophisticated

**gracelessly**
**06** rudely **07** roughly **08** clumsily **09** awkwardly **10** impolitely **11** inelegantly **12** ungracefully

**gracious**
**04** hend, kind, mild **05** sweet **06** benign, kindly, polite **07** affable, clement, elegant, lenient, refined **08** friendly, generous, handsome, menseful, merciful, obliging, pleasant, tasteful **09** benignant, courteous, forgiving, indulgent, luxurious, sumptuous **10** acceptable, beneficent, benevolent, charitable, favourable, hospitable **11** comfortable, considerate, kind-hearted, magnanimous **12** well-mannered **13** accommodating, compassionate, condescending

**graciously**
**06** goodly, kindly **07** civilly **08** politely **09** tactfully **10** handsomely, pleasantly **11** courteously **12** respectfully **14** diplomatically

**gradation**
**04** mark, rank, step **05** array, cline, level, stage **06** ablaut, change, degree, series **07** grading, shading, sorting **08** ordering, progress, sequence **10** succession **11** arrangement, progression

**grade**
**03** gon **04** mark, rank, rate, rung, size, sort, step, type **05** brand, class, group, label, level, notch, order, place, range, stage, value **06** assess, degree, rating, status **07** arrange, echelon, quality, station **08** category, classify, evaluate, position, standard, standing **09** condition **10** categorize, pigeonhole **14** classification
• **equivalent grade 02** EG
• **first grade 05** alpha

## gradient

- **fourth grade** 05 delta
- **make the grade** 04 pass 07 succeed
10 win through 11 come through 13 cut
the mustard 15 come up to scratch
- **second grade** 04 beta
- **third grade** 05 gamma

## gradient

04 bank, hill, rise 05 grade, lapse, slope
07 incline 09 acclivity, declivity

## gradual

04 easy, even, slow 05 grail 06 gentle,
steady 07 regular 08 measured,
moderate 09 leisurely, unhurried
10 continuous, step-by-step
11 progressive

## gradually

06 evenly, gently, slowly 08 bit by bit,
gingerly, steadily 09 by degrees,
piecemeal, regularly 10 cautiously,
inch by inch, moderately, step by step
11 unhurriedly 12 continuously,
successively 13 imperceptibly,
progressively 14 little by little

## graduate

02 BA, MA 03 cap 04 grad, pass, rank,
sort 05 grade, group, order, ovate,
range 06 alumna, doctor, expert,
fellow, master, member, move up
07 advance, alumnus, arrange, go
ahead, mark off, qualify 08 bachelor,
classify, graduand, progress, whizz kid
09 calibrate 10 be promoted,
categorize, consultant, forge ahead,
licentiate, measure out, proportion,
specialist 11 make headway, move
forward 12 professional 13 skilled
person, valedictorian 15 complete
studies, qualified person

*See also* **qualification**

## graft

03 bud, dig, imp 04 join, scam, slog,
take, toil 05 affix, ditch, graff, plant,
scion, shoot, sting 06 branch, effort,
growth, inarch, insert, labour, rip-off,
sleaze, splice, sprout, sucker
07 bribery, cuckold, engraft, implant
08 exertion, hard work 09 allograft,
autograft, con tricks, extortion,
homograft, inoculate, xenograft
10 corruption, dishonesty, excavation,
transplant 11 dirty tricks, heterograft
12 implantation 13 dirty dealings,
shady business 14 sharp practices
15 sweat of your brow

## grain

02 gr 03 bit, jot, nap, rye 04 atom, corn,
curn, fork, hint, iota, mite, oats, ragi,
rice, seed 05 berry, crumb, emmer,
fibre, grits, maize, minim, piece,
prong, scrap, speck, trace, weave,
wheat 06 barley, branch, fabric, groats,
kernel, maslin, morsel 07 cereals,
graddan, granule, marking, mashlam,
mashlim, mashlin, mashlum,
modicum, pattern, soupçon, surface,
texture 08 fragment, mashloch,
molecule, particle 09 scintilla
10 suggestion
- **soften grain** 04 cree

## gram

01 g 02 gm, gr 03 urd 05 anger, grief,
pulse 07 trouble 08 chickpea

## grammar

05 Donat, Donet, style, usage
06 syntax 11 good English 14 correct
English 15 linguistic rules
*See also* **speech**

## grammatical

07 correct 09 syntactic 10 acceptable,
linguistic, structural, well-formed
11 appropriate, syntactical 14 well-
structured
*See also* **tense**

## grand

01 G 03 fab 04 arch, cool, fine, head,
main, mega 05 chief, final, great, large,
lofty, noble, regal, showy, super 06 in
full, lavish, lordly, pretty, senior,
superb, wicked 07 exalted, highest,
leading, opulent, pompous, stately,
sublime, supreme 08 complete,
exalting, glorious, imposing, majestic,
palatial, precious, smashing, splendid,
striking, terrific, thousand
09 ambitious, dignified, enjoyable,
excellent, fantastic, first-rate,
grandiose, inclusive, luxurious,
mausolean, principal, sumptuous,
wonderful 10 delightful, impressive,
marvellous, monumental, pre-eminent
11 illustrious, magnificent,
outstanding, pretentious 12 all-
inclusive, ostentatious
13 comprehensive

## grandchild

02 oe, oy 03 oye 08 grandkid

## grandeur

04 fame, pomp 05 state 06 renown
07 dignity, majesty 08 eminence,
nobility, opulence, vastness
09 greatness, splendour 10 importance,
lavishness, prominence 11 stateliness
12 magnificence 13 luxuriousness
14 impressiveness 15 illustriousness,
pretentiousness

## grandfather

04 oupa, papa 06 gramps, granda
07 grandad, grandpa, granfer, gutcher
08 goodsire, granddad, gudesire
09 grandaddy, grandpapa, grandsire,
luckie-dad 10 granddaddy
11 grandparent

## grandiloquent

06 rotund, turgid 07 flowery, fustian,
orotund, pompous, swollen 08 inflated
09 bombastic, high-flown, ororotund
10 euphuistic, rhetorical
11 exaggerated, pretentious 12 high-
sounding, magniloquent
13 grandiloquously

## grandiose

04 long 05 grand, lofty, showy
07 pompous, stately 08 imposing,
majestic, splendid, striking
09 ambitious, bombastic, high-flown,
mausolean 10 flamboyant, impressive,
monumental, over-the-top
11 extravagant, magnificent,
pretentious 12 high-sounding,
magniloquent, ostentatious

## grandly

07 regally 09 pompously 10 gloriously,
strikingly 11 excellently
12 impressively, majestically
13 magnificently, pretentiously

## grandmother

03 nan 04 gran, nana, ouma 05 nanna,
nanny 06 beldam, granny 07 beldame,
grandam, grandma, grannam, grannie
08 babushka, good-dame, gude-dame
09 grandmama 10 grandmamma
11 grandparent

## grandparental

04 aval 06 avital

## granite

07 greisen 08 resolute 09 pegmatite,
protogine 10 china stone, unyielding
11 luxulianite, luxulyanite
12 luxullianite

## grant

03 aid, fee, feu, let 04 Cary, gift, give,
lend, send 05 admit, allot, allow,
award, feoff, yield 06 accept, accord,
assign, bestow, beteem, confer,
donate, impart, permit, supply
07 agree to, annuity, appoint, bequest,
beteeme, bursary, charter, concede,
consent, furnish, licence, license,
pension, present, provide, subsidy
08 accede to, allocate, dispense,
donation, granting, transmit
09 allowance, apportion, consent to,
endowment, vouchsafe 10 concession,
condescend, contribute, exhibition,
honorarium, subvention
11 acknowledge, benefaction,
expectative, scholarship
12 contribution
- **granted** 06 agreed

## granular

04 corn 05 curny, lumpy, rough, sandy
06 curney, grainy, gritty 07 crumbly,
friable 10 granulated

## granule

03 jot 04 atom, bead, iota, seed
05 crumb, grain, pearl, piece, scrap,
speck 06 pellet 07 plastid 08 bioblast,
fragment, molecule, particle
09 chondrule, microsome

## grape

03 uva
*See also* **wine**

## grapefruit

06 pomelo 07 pompelo
10 pompelmous, pumple-nose
11 pampelmoose, pampelmouse,
pompelmoose, pompelmouse

## grapeskins

04 marc

## graph

04 grid, plot 05 chart, curve, ogive,
table 07 diagram, profile 08 bar chart,
bar graph, nomogram, pie chart,
waveform 09 histogram, nomograph,
waveshape 10 carpet plot 11 demand
curve, supply curve 13 learning curve
14 scatter diagram

## graphic

05 clear, drawn, lucid, vivid 06 cogent,
lively, visual 07 telling 08 detailed,

explicit, specific, striking, symbolic
**09** effective, pictorial, realistic
**10** blow-by-blow, expressive
**11** delineative, descriptive, well-defined **12** diagrammatic, illustrative

**graphically**
**07** clearly, vividly **10** explicitly, strikingly **12** expressively
**13** descriptively, realistically

**graphite**
**04** kish, lead **08** plumbago
**09** blacklead, pencil-ore **10** pencil-lead

**grapple**
**04** face, grab, grip, hold, lock **05** clash, clasp, close, fight, grasp, seize
**06** battle, clinch, clutch, combat, craple, engage, snatch, tackle, tussle
**07** address, contend, wrestle
**08** confront, cope with, deal with, struggle **09** encounter, lay hold of
**14** get to grips with

**grasp**
◇ containment indicator **03** get, see
**04** clat, grab, grip, have, hend, hent, hold, holt, rule **05** catch, clamp, clasp, claut, gripe, power, seize, sense
**06** clench, clutch, follow, graple, griple, master, rumble, snatch, strain, take in **07** catch on, command, compass, control, embrace, grapple, gripple, mastery, prehend, realize, squeeze **08** clutches, conceive, dominion, handgrip, perceive
**09** apprehend, awareness, knowledge, latch onto, lay hold of **10** comprehend, perception, possession, understand
**11** familiarity **12** apprehension, get a handle on, get the hang of
**13** comprehension, understanding

**grasping**
◇ containment indicator **04** mean
**06** grabby, greedy, griple, stingy
**07** griping, gripple, miserly, seizing, selfish **08** covetous **09** mercenary, niggardly, rapacious **10** avaricious
**11** acquisitive, close-fisted, large-handed, tight-fisted **12** parsimonious
**13** money-grubbing

**grass**
**03** fog, hay, lea, pot, rat, rip **04** blab, lawn, mead, nark, shop, tell, turf, veld
**05** dob in, downs, field, green, rough, split, sward, veldt **06** betray, common, inform, snitch, squeal, steppe, tell on
**07** foggage, pasture, prairie, savanna, stool on **08** denounce, informer, stitch up **09** incriminate
**11** incriminate
See also **cannabis**

Grasses include:

**03** nit, nut, oat, poa, rye, sea, seg, tef
**04** alfa, bent, cane, cord, corn, crab, dari, diss, doob, dura, gama, holy, kans, knot, lyme, moor, nard, oats, ragi, reed, rice, rusa, sago, sand, star, tape, tath, teff
**05** alang, arrow, beard, brome, bunch, canna, chess, China, couch, doura, float, grama, halfa, lemon, maize, melic, paddy, panic, plume, quack, quick,

ragee, raggy, roosa, spear, spike, starr, stipa, Sudan, wheat
**06** bamboo, barley, canary, cotton, darnel, dhurra, fescue, finger, fiorin, guinea, kikuyu, lalang, marram, marrum, meadow, melick, millet, pampas, panick, quitch, raggee, rattan, redtop, rescue, scutch, sesame, switch, twitch, vernal
**07** Bermuda, bristle, buffalo, cannach, esparto, feather, pannick, papyrus, quaking, sacaton, sorghum, timothy, wild oat
**08** cat's-tail, cockspur, dog's-tail, Flinders, kangaroo, moss-crop, ryegrass, spinifex, teosinte
**09** bent grass, bluegrass, buckwheat, cocksfoot, danthonia, hare's-tail, marijuana, porcupine, sugar cane
**10** citronella, cutty grass
**12** creeping bent, Kentucky blue, squirrel-tail
**13** meadow foxtail
**15** English ryegrass, Italian ryegrass

• **grass after hay** **03** fog **07** foggage
• **handful of grass** **03** rip **04** ripp
• **stem of grass** **04** cane, culm

**grasshopper**
**04** grig, weta **09** wart-biter

**grate**
**03** irk, jar, rub, vex **04** bray, cage, gall, grid, grit, rasp, risp **05** annoy, chirk, creak, gride, grind, gryde, mince, peeve, shred, stove **06** rankle, scrape, squeak **07** scratch, screech **08** irritate
**09** aggravate, pulverize, triturate
**10** exasperate **12** kitchen-range **15** get on your nerves

**grateful**
**07** obliged, pleased **08** beholden, indebted, thankful **09** obligated
**12** appreciative

**gratefully**
**10** thankfully **13** with gratitude
**14** appreciatively

**gratification**
**03** joy, tip **04** glee, gust **05** bribe, feast, kicks **06** relish, thrill **07** delight, elation
**08** easement, pleasure **09** enjoyment
**10** indulgence, indulgency, recompense **11** contentment
**12** satisfaction

**gratify**
**03** pay **05** charm, cheer, flesh, humor, spoil **06** arride, cosset, favour, fulfil, humour, pamper, please, thrill
**07** aggrate, delight, flatter, gladden, indulge, placate, satiate, satisfy
**08** pander to, recreate **09** make happy

**grating**
**04** grid, hack, haik, hake, heck, iron, rack **05** frame, grate, grill, harsh, siver, syver **06** grille **07** braying, galling, grizzly, irksome, jarring, lattice, rasping, raucous, squeaky, trellis
**08** annoying, cancelli, creaking, grinding, gritting, mort-safe, scrannel, scraping, scratchy, strident **09** fire-grate, graticule, offensive

**10** discordant, irritating, portcullis, scratching, screeching, unpleasant
**12** disagreeable, exasperating

**gratis**
**04** free **08** at no cost, buckshee **10** for nothing, on the house **12** free of charge
**13** complimentary, without charge

**gratitude**
**06** thanks **10** obligation **11** recognition
**12** appreciation, gratefulness, indebtedness, thankfulness
**15** acknowledgement
• **expression of gratitude** **02** ta
**06** thanks **07** thankee **08** bless you!, gramercy, thank you **09** God-a-mercy
**10** grand merci **11** God bless you!

**gratuitous**
**04** free **06** gratis, unpaid, wanton
**08** buckshee, needless **09** unfounded, unmerited, voluntary **10** for nothing, groundless, unasked-for, undeserved, unprovoked, unrewarded
**11** superfluous, uncalled-for, unjustified, unnecessary, unsolicited, unwarranted **12** free of charge
**13** complimentary, without reason

**gratuitously**
**10** needlessly **12** undeservedly
**13** unjustifiably, unnecessarily

**gratuity**
**03** tip **04** boon, dash, gift, mags, perk
**05** bonus, maggs **06** bounty, reward
**07** bansela, cumshaw, present, primage **08** bonsella, donation, donative, lagnappe, largesse
**09** backshish, bakhshish, baksheesh, beer-money, lagniappe, pourboire
**10** backsheesh, drink-money, glove-money, gratillity, perquisite, recompense

**grave**
**03** dig, pit, sad **04** bass, bury, dust, grim, high, lair, loss, tomb **05** acute, cairn, count, crypt, death, graff, heavy, mouls, quiet, sober, staid, vault, vital
**06** barrow, demise, gloomy, moulds, sedate, severe, solemn, sombre, urgent
**07** austere, crucial, decease, earnest, exigent, passing, pensive, prefect, serious, subdued, tumulus, weighty
**08** Catonian, critical, curtains, fatality, long home, matronal, menacing, perilous, pressing, reserved
**09** dangerous, departure, dignified, hazardous, important, long-faced, mausoleum, momentous, plague-pit, saturnine, sepulchre **10** burial site, expiration, loss of life, restrained, thoughtful **11** bed of honour, burial mound, burial place, destruction, passing away, significant, threatening
**12** last farewell

**gravel**
**04** grit **05** grail **06** chesil, chisel, graile, grayle, hoggin, murram, stones
**07** channel, channer, hogging, pebbles, shingle
• **layer of gravel** **04** hard

**gravelly**
**05** gruff, harsh, rough, thick **06** grainy, gritty, hoarse, pebbly **07** grating,

shingly, throaty **08** glareous, granular, guttural, sabulose, sabulous

**gravely**
**07** acutely, quietly **08** gloomily, severely, solemnly, urgently **09** crucially, earnestly, pensively, seriously **10** critically **11** dangerously, importantly **12** thoughtfully **13** significantly

**gravestone**
**05** stone, table **08** memorial **09** headstone, tombstone

**graveyard**
**08** cemetery, God's acre **10** burial site, churchyard, necropolis **11** burial place **12** burial ground, charnel house **13** burying ground

**gravitas**
**06** weight **07** gravity **09** solemnity **10** importance **11** earnestness, seriousness

**gravitate**
**04** drop, fall, lean, move, sink, tend **05** drift **06** settle **07** descend, head for, incline **09** be drawn to **11** precipitate **12** be attached to

**gravity**
**01** g **04** pull **05** peril, state **06** danger, hazard, weight **07** dignity, reserve, urgency **08** exigency, grimness, severity, sobriety **09** acuteness, graveness, heaviness, restraint, soberness, solemnity **10** attraction, gloominess, importance, sombreness **11** consequence, earnestness, gravitation, seriousness, weightiness **12** significance **13** momentousness **14** thoughtfulness

**gray**
**02** Gy
*See also* **grey**

**graze**
**03** rub **04** crop, feed, kiss, rake, rase, raze, skim, skin **05** brush, chafe, gride, gryde, scuff, shave, touch **06** abrade, browse, bruise, crease, fodder, scrape **07** pasture, scratch **08** abrasion, ruminate **09** depasture, glance off

**grease**
**03** fat, oil **04** dope, lard, seam **05** bribe, seame, smear **06** creesh, dubbin, enlard, enseam, tallow **07** dubbing **08** dripping **09** lubricate **10** facilitate **11** lubrication

**greasy**
**04** oily, waxy **05** fatty, lardy, oleic, slimy **06** smeary, smooth **07** adipose, buttery, obscene, shearer **08** slippery, unctuous **09** sebaceous **10** oleaginous **12** ingratiating
• **greasy substance** **04** glit

**great**
**02** gt **03** ace, big, fit, gay, gey **04** able, bulk, cool, fell, fine, gran, huge, main, mass, mega, neat, tall, unco, up on, vast, well **05** adept, brill, chief, crack, eager, famed, grand, jumbo, large, major, noted, stoor, stour, sture, super, titan, vital, whole **06** august, awsome, bangin', cushty, expert, famous,

grouse, lively, mickle, muckle, stowre, superb, wicked **07** awesome, banging, crucial, eminent, extreme, healthy, immense, leading, mammoth, massive, notable, primary, rousing, salient, serious, sizable, skilful, skilled, sublime, tearing, teeming, weighty **08** colossal, cracking, critical, dextrous, enormous, fabulous, gigantic, glorious, great big, habitual, imposing, masterly, powerful, pregnant, renowned, sizeable, smashing, spacious, splendid, terrific, top-notch, virtuoso, well up on, whopping **09** admirable, boundless, brilliant, dexterous, energetic, essential, excellent, excessive, extensive, fantastic, favourite, first-rate, ginormous, humongous, humungous, important, momentous, paramount, practised, principal, prominent, qualified, swingeing, wholesale, wonderful **10** celebrated, impressive, inordinate, marvellous, noteworthy, proficient, pronounced, remarkable, specialist, successful, tremendous **11** experienced, illustrious, magnificent, outstanding, significant, substantial **12** accomplished, considerable, enthusiastic, professional **13** distinguished, knowledgeable

**Great Britain**
**02** GB, UK **03** GBR

**greatly**
**04** much **06** highly, hugely, sorely, vastly **07** big-time, majorly, notably **08** markedly, mightily, very much **09** extremely, immensely **10** abundantly, enormously, noticeably, powerfully, remarkably **11** exceedingly **12** considerably, impressively, tremendously **13** significantly, substantially

**greatness**
**04** fame, note **05** glory, power **06** genius, renown, weight **07** heroism, success **08** eminence, grandeur, muchness **09** intensity, magnitude **10** excellence, excellency, importance, mightiness **11** distinction, seriousness **12** significance **13** momentousness **14** successfulness **15** illustriousness

**Greece**
**02** GR **03** GRC

**greed**
**06** desire, hunger **07** avarice, avidity, craving, edacity, longing **08** bingeing, cupidity, gluttony, rapacity, voracity **09** eagerness, esurience, pleonexia **10** impatience **11** gourmandise, gourmandism, hoggishness, itching palm, piggishness, selfishness **12** covetousness, ravenousness **13** insatiability **15** acquisitiveness

**greedily**
**06** avidly **07** eagerly **09** selfishly **10** esuriently, ravenously **11** impatiently, rapaciously **12** avariciously

**greedy**
**04** avid, gare **05** eager **06** grabby, griple, having, hungry **07** craving, gripple, hoggish, piggish, selfish **08** covetous, desirous, edacious, esurient, grabbing, grasping, ravenous, starving **09** impatient, on the make, rapacious, voracious **10** avaricious, cupidinous, gluttonous, insatiable, omnivorous, pleonectic **11** acquisitive, itchy-palmed, open-mouthed **12** gormandizing **13** money-grubbing

**Greek**
**02** Gk, Gr **07** Hellene

*Greeks include:*

**04** Esop
**05** Aesop, Galen, Homer, Plato
**06** Euclid, Lucian, Pindar, Sappho, Thales
**07** Hypatia, Pytheas (of Marseilles)
**08** Damocles, Epicurus, Plotinus, Plutarch, Polybius, Socrates, Xenophon
**09** Aeschylus, Aristotle, Euripides, Herodotus, Sophocles
**10** Archimedes, Democritus, Empedocles, Heraclitus, Hipparchos, Hipparchus, Praxiteles, Protagoras, Pythagoras, Theocritus, Thucydides, Xenophanes
**11** Hippocrates
**12** Aristophanes, Theophrastus

*See also* **alphabet; god, goddess; muse; mythology; seven**

**green**
**03** eco-, lea, new, raw **04** lawn, long, lush, pine, sage, turf **05** field, fresh, grass, leafy, naive, sward, virid, yearn, young **06** common, grassy, meadow, recent, simple, tender, unripe, virent **07** budding, envious, growing, healthy, jealous, pasture, undried, verdant **08** blooming, covetous, glaucous, grudging, gullible, ignorant, immature, inexpert, unversed, vigorous **09** grassland, resentful, untrained, verdurous, virescent **10** ecological, olivaceous, porraceous, smaragdine, unseasoned **11** eco-friendly, flourishing, unqualified, viridescent **13** environmental, inexperienced **15** conservationist, preservationist, unsophisticated

*Greens include:*

**04** jade, lime, teal, vert
**05** lovat, olive
**06** reseda, sludge
**07** avocado, celadon, corbeau, emerald
**08** eau de Nil, pea-green, sap-green, sea green
**09** moss green, Nile green, pistachio, sage green, turquoise
**10** apple-green, aquamarine, chartreuse, rifle green
**11** bottle green
**12** Lincoln green
**14** turquoise-green

**greenery**
**04** vert **07** foliage, verdure **08** verdancy,

## greenhorn

viridity **09** greenness **10** vegetation, virescence **12** viridescence

## greenhorn

**03** put **04** putt, tiro **06** newbie, novice, rookie **07** learner, recruit **08** beginner, initiate, neophyte, newcomer **09** fledgling, Johnny-raw **10** apprentice, tenderfoot

## greenhouse

**06** vinery **08** hothouse, orangery, pavilion **09** coldhouse, coolhouse **10** glasshouse **12** conservatory

## Greenland

**03** GRL

## greet

**03** bid, bow **04** hail, kiss, meet, weep, wish **05** halse, hongi, nod to **06** accost, salute, wave to **07** address, receive, regreet, weeping, welcome **08** congreet, remember **10** say hello to, shake hands, tip your hat **11** acknowledge, doff your hat **14** shake hands with **15** give someone five

## greeting

**03** bow, nod **04** kiss, wave **05** hongi **06** abrazo, accost, salute **07** accoast, address, air kiss, namaste **08** glad hand, high five, namaskar **09** handshake, reception, time of day **10** how-do-you-do, salutation **12** the time of day **15** acknowledgement
• **expression of greeting 02** hi, yo **03** ave, how **04** ciao, g'day, hail, heil!, hiya **05** aloha, chimo, hallo, hello, holla, howdy, hullo, jambo, salve, skoal **06** salaam, shalom, wotcha **07** all-hail, bonjour, bonsoir, good-day, good-den, good-e'en, salaams, salvete, save you, welcome, well met, wotcher **08** chin-chin, good-even, haeremai **09** how are you?, son of a gun, what cheer? **10** benedicite, good-morrow, how do you do? **11** good-evening, good-morning **13** good-afternoon **14** shalom aleichem

## greetings

**04** love **05** salve **07** regards, regreet, salaams **08** regreets, respects **10** best wishes, good wishes **11** compliments, kind regards, salutations, warm regards **12** remembrances **15** congratulations

## gregarious

**04** warm **06** social **07** affable, cordial **08** friendly, outgoing, sociable **09** convivial, extrovert **10** hospitable **13** companionable

## Grenada

**02** WG **03** GRD

## grenade

**09** Mills bomb, pineapple **15** Molotov cocktail

## grey

**02** gr **03** dim, old, wan **04** dark, dull, gris, pale **05** ashen, bleak, foggy, grise, grisy, misty, murky **06** cloudy, dismal, dreary, gloomy, gryesy, leaden, mature, pallid **07** griesie, neutral, unclear **08** bloncket, doubtful, griseous, grizzled, overcast **09** ambiguous, anonymous, canescent, cheerless, cinereous, debatable, uncertain **10** colourless, depressing, dove-colour **13** uninteresting **14** open to question

*Greys include:*

**03** ash
**04** drab
**05** liard, liart, lyart, perse, stone, taupe
**06** isabel, pewter, silver
**07** grizzle
**08** charcoal, dove grey, feldgrau, graphite, gridelin, platinum
**09** field grey, pearl-grey, slate-grey, steel-grey
**10** dapple-grey, dove-colour

• **greyish-brown 03** dun **04** ecru **05** mousy **06** mousey **07** chamois
• **greyish-white 04** hoar, hore

## greyhound

**04** grew **07** lurcher, sapling, whippet **08** long-tail **09** deerhound, grewhound

## grid

**05** frame, grate, grill **06** grille **07** grating, lattice, network, trellis **08** gridiron **09** framework, graticule

## grief

**02** wo **03** vex, woe **04** dole, dool, gram, pain, sore, teen, tene **05** agony, dolor, doole, grame, teene **06** bother, dolour, misery, regret, sorrow, tsuris **07** anguish, despair, remorse, sadness, thought, trouble, tsouris, wayment **08** distress, mourning **09** bemoaning, dejection, grievance, heartache, suffering, tristesse **10** affliction, depression, desiderium, desolation, heartbreak **11** bereavement, despondency, lamentation, tribulation, unhappiness **12** dolorousness
• **come to grief 04** bomb, flop, fold **05** crash, spill **06** mucker **07** founder, go wrong, miswend **08** collapse, fall down, fall flat **09** break down **10** not come off **11** bite the dust, come unglued, come unstuck, fall through **12** come a cropper **13** come to nothing **14** be unsuccessful
• **emblem of grief 03** yew
• **expression of grief 02** io, oh **03** wow **04** alas **05** ohone, waugh, wowee **06** dear me, ochone, oh dear! **07** deary me **08** dearie me
• **feel grief 04** earn **05** yearn

## grief-stricken

**03** sad **06** broken **07** crushed, unhappy **08** dejected, desolate, grieving, mourning, overcome, troubled, wretched **09** afflicted, anguished, depressed, sorrowful, sorrowing, woebegone **10** despairing, despondent, devastated, distressed **11** heartbroken, overwhelmed **12** disconsolate, inconsolable **13** broken-hearted

## grievance

**04** beef, moan **05** grief, gripe, peeve, score, trial, wrong **06** charge, damage, grouse, injury **07** grumble, offence, protest, trouble **08** distress, gravamen, hardship **09** complaint, injustice, objection **10** affliction, bone to pick, resentment, unfairness **11** tribulation

## grieve

**03** cry, rue, sob, vex **04** ache, hone, hurt, mope, pain, wail, weep **05** brood, crush, mourn, shock, upset, wound **06** bemoan, dismay, lament, offend, sadden, sorrow, suffer **07** afflict, condole, horrify, sheriff, wayment **08** distress, engrieve, governor, pine away

## grievous

**04** dear, sore **05** deare, deere, grave, heavy **06** noyous, severe, strong, tragic **07** careful, glaring, harmful, hurtful, painful **08** damaging, dolorous, dreadful, flagrant, shameful, shocking, wounding **09** appalling, atrocious, dolorific, injurious, monstrous, plightful, sorrowful **10** afflicting, burdensome, calamitous, deplorable, outrageous, unbearable **11** devastating, distressing, intolerable **12** doloriferous, overwhelming

## grievously

**04** sore **06** dernly **07** dearnly **08** severely **10** dolorously, dreadfully, shockingly, tragically, unbearably **11** appallingly, intolerably **12** outrageously

## grill

**04** cook, grid, heat, pump **05** bar-b-q, broil, frame, roast, toast **06** grille, wicket **07** grating, lattice, scallop **08** barbecue, barbeque, gridiron **09** charbroil **10** flame-grill

## grim

◇ *anagram indicator* **03** ill **04** dire, dour **05** awful, grisy, gurly, harsh, stern, surly **06** dismal, dogged, fierce, gloomy, griesy, grisly, grysie, horrid, morose, severe, sullen **07** ghastly **08** dreadful, fearsome, gruesome, horrible, menacing, obdurate, resolute, shocking, sinister, stubborn, terrible **09** appalling, ferocious, harrowing, repellent, tenacious **10** depressing, determined, forbidding, formidable, horrendous, inexorable, persistent, unpleasant, unshakable, unyielding **11** frightening, threatening, unappealing, unshakeable, unspeakable **12** unattractive

## grimace

**03** moe, mop, mou, mow, mug **04** face, girn, moue, mump, pout **05** frown, mouth, scowl, smirk, sneer **07** murgeon **09** make a face, pull a face **12** fit of the face

## grime

**03** mud **04** coom, crud, dirt, dust, grot, muck, soot, yuck **05** filth, gunge **06** grunge, smutch

## grimly

**07** harshly, sternly **08** fiercely, gloomily, morosely, sullenly

## grimy

**05** dirty, dusty, mucky, muddy, sooty **06** filthy, grubby, rechie, reechy,

**grin**

smudgy, smutty, soiled **07** reechie, stained **10** besmirched

**grin**
**04** beam, girn, gren, leer, trap **05** gerne, laugh, risus, smile, smirk, snare, sneer **06** giggle, titter **07** chuckle, snigger

**grind**
**03** pug, rub **04** bray, chew, file, grit, meal, mill, rasp, sand, task, toil, whet **05** chore, crush, gnash, grate, pound, round, slime, stamp, sweat **06** abrade, crunch, kibble, labour, polish, powder, scrape, smooth **07** chamfer, crumble, graunch, routine, sharpen, slavery **08** drudgery, exertion, levigate **09** comminute, granulate, masticate, pulverize, triturate
• **grind down** **05** crush, harry, hound **06** harass, plague **07** afflict, oppress, torment, trouble **08** wear down **09** persecute, tyrannize

**grip**
◇ containment indicator **03** bag, get, hug **04** bite, case, fang, grab, hold, vice, vise **05** catch, clasp, cling, ditch, drain, grasp, power, rivet, sally, seize **06** absorb, clench, clutch, compel, engage, graple, griple, kitbag, strain, thrill, trench, valise **07** command, control, embrace, engross, enthral, fingers, grapple, gripple, holdall, involve, mastery **08** clutches, entrance, foothold, handfast, suitcase, traction **09** fascinate, get hold of, hypnotize, influence, latch onto, mesmerize, spellbind **10** domination, grab hold of **11** catch hold of, shoulder bag **12** overnight bag **13** travelling bag
• **come to grips with, get to grips with** ◇ containment indicator **05** grasp **06** handle, tackle, take on **08** confront, cope with, deal with, face up to **09** encounter, look after **10** take care of

**gripe**
**03** nag **04** beef, carp, moan **05** bitch, ditch, drain, groan, whine **06** grouch, grouse, trench, whinge **07** griffin, griping, grumble, protest, vulture **08** complain **09** bellyache, complaint, grievance, objection **15** have a bone to pick

**gripping**
◇ containment indicator **06** griple **07** gripple **08** exciting, riveting **09** absorbing, thrilling **10** compelling, compulsive, enchanting, engrossing, entrancing **11** enthralling, fascinating, suspenseful **12** spellbinding **13** edge-of-the-seat, unputdownable
• **gripping instrument** **04** grip, vice, vise **05** clamp **08** tweezers

**grisly**
**04** gory, grim **05** awful, grisy, griesy, grysie, horrid **07** awesome, ghastly, hideous, macabre **08** dreadful, gruesome, horrible, shocking, terrible **09** abhorrent, appalling, frightful, loathsome, repulsive, revolting **10** abominable, disgusting, horrifying

**gristly**
**04** hard **05** chewy, tough **06** sinewy

**07** fibrous, rubbery, stringy **08** leathery **13** cartilaginous

**grit**
**04** dust, guts, rasp, sand **05** gnash, grate, great, grind, swarf **06** clench, gravel, mettle, scrape **07** bravery, courage, pebbles, resolve, shingle **08** backbone, hardness, strength, tenacity **09** endurance, toughness **10** doggedness, resolution **12** perseverance **13** determination, steadfastness

**gritty**
**05** brave, dusty, gutsy, gutty, hardy, rough, sandy, tough **06** dogged, feisty, grainy, pebbly, plucky, spunky **07** powdery, shingly **08** abrasive, granular, gravelly, resolute, sabuline, sabulose, sabulous, spirited **09** steadfast, tenacious **10** courageous, determined, mettlesome **14** uncompromising

**grizzle**
**03** cry **04** fret, moan **05** whine **06** snivel, whinge **07** grumble, sniffle, snuffle, whimper **08** complain

**grizzled**
**04** grey, hoar **05** hoary **07** greying **08** griseous **09** canescent **10** grey-haired, grey-headed **13** pepper-and-salt

**groan**
**03** cry **04** beef, moan, sigh, wail **05** whine **06** grouch, grouse, lament, object, outcry, whinge **07** griping, grumble, protest, whimper **08** complain **09** bellyache, complaint, grievance, objection

**grocer**
**06** dealer **07** épicier **08** pepperer, purveyor, supplier **10** victualler **11** greengrocer, storekeeper, supermarket

**groggy**
◇ anagram indicator **04** weak **05** dazed, dizzy, dopey, faint, muzzy, shaky, woozy **06** wobbly, zonked **07** reeling, stunned **08** confused, unsteady **09** befuddled, stupefied **10** bewildered, punch-drunk, staggering

**groin**
**04** lisk **05** growl, grunt **06** crotch, crutch **07** grumble **08** genitals

**groom**
◇ anagram indicator **02** do **03** fix **04** sice, syce, tidy **05** brush, clean, coach, curry, dress, drill, preen, prime, prink, saice, teach, train, tutor **06** adjust, neaten, school, smooth, spouse, tidy up **07** arrange, educate, husband, prepare, smarten, turn out **08** coistrel, coistril, instruct, newly-wed, spruce up, strapper **09** make ready, stableboy, stable lad, stableman **10** bridegroom, palfrenier, put in order, stable hand, stable lass **11** honeymooner, husband-to-be **15** marriage partner

**groove**
**03** cut, pod, rut **04** kerf, mark, oche, race, sipe, slot **05** canal, chase, croze,

ditch, flute, gouge, quirk, ridge, rigol, score, slide, track **06** cullis, furrow, gutter, hollow, keyway, rabbet, raggle, rebate, riffle, scrobe, sulcus, throat, trench, trough **07** chamfer, channel, diglyph, fissure, fossula, key-seat **09** cannelure, vallecula **11** indentation

**grooved**
**06** fluted, rutted, scored, sulcal **07** exarate, sulcate **08** furrowed, rabbeted, sulcated **09** chamfered **10** channelled **12** canaliculate, scrobiculate **13** canaliculated

**grope**
**04** feel, fish, hunt, pick, poke, ripe **05** abuse, probe, touch **06** feel up, fondle, fumble, molest, search **07** grabble, touch up **08** flounder, scrabble **09** cast about **13** abuse sexually, interfere with

**gross**
◇ anagram indicator **02** gr **03** big, fat **04** blue, dull, earn, foul, huge, lewd, make, rank, rude, slow, take **05** bawdy, bulky, crass, crude, dirty, heavy, large, nasty, obese, plain, sheer, solid, thick, total, utter, whole, yucky **06** coarse, earthy, entire, filthy, odious, pull in, rake in, ribald, risqué, smutty, strong, stupid, vulgar **07** blatant, boorish, bring in, extreme, glaring, hulking, immense, lumpish, massive, obscene, obvious, sensual, serious **08** colossal, complete, enormous, flagrant, grievous, improper, indecent, manifest, material, nauseous, outright, palpable, shameful, shocking **09** aggregate, before tax, corpulent, egregious, inclusive, offensive, repugnant, repulsive, revolting, sickening, tasteless, unrefined **10** accumulate, disgusting, earthbound, nauseating, off-putting, outrageous, overweight, salt-butter, uncultured, unpleasant **11** disgraceful, distasteful, insensitive, unpalatable **12** all-inclusive, pornographic, unappetizing, unrepeatable **13** coarse-grained, comprehensive **15** unsophisticated

**grossly**
**04** very **05** fatly **06** highly, really **07** acutely, awfully, greatly, utterly **08** severely, terribly **09** decidedly, extremely, intensely, unusually **10** dreadfully, remarkably, thoroughly, uncommonly **11** exceedingly, excessively, frightfully **12** immoderately, inordinately, terrifically, unreasonably **13** exceptionally **15** extraordinarily

**grotesque**
◇ anagram indicator **03** odd **04** ugly **05** antic, black, weird **06** absurd, antick, Gothic, rococo **07** anticke, antique, bizarre, hideous, macabre, strange, surreal, twisted **08** deformed, fanciful, freakish, peculiar **09** distorted, fantastic, ludicrous, malformed, misshapen, monstrous, unnatural, unsightly, whimsical **10** outlandish, ridiculous **11** extravagant

## grotesquely
**09** bizarrely, hideously, strangely **11** unnaturally **12** outlandishly, unpleasantly

## grotto
**04** cave, grot **05** speos **06** cavern **07** chamber **08** catacomb, Lupercal **09** Mithraeum, nymphaeum **10** subterrane

## grotty
**03** ill **04** sick, ugly **05** dirty, grody, mangy, rough, seedy, tatty **06** ailing, crummy, groggy, poorly, shabby, sleazy, untidy, unwell **07** run-down, scruffy, squalid **08** decaying **09** off-colour **10** out of sorts **11** dilapidated **15** under the weather

## grouch
**04** moan **05** gripe, grump, sulks **06** griper, grouse, kvetch, moaner, sulker, whiner, whinge **07** grouser, grumble, whinger **08** grumbler, kvetcher, murmurer, mutterer, sourpuss **09** complaint, grievance, objection **10** bellyacher, complainer, crosspatch, malcontent **11** fault-finder

## grouchy
**05** cross, sulky, surly, testy **06** grumpy **07** peevish **08** captious, churlish, petulant **09** crotchety, grumbling, irascible, irritable, querulous, truculent, whingeing **11** bad-tempered, complaining, ill-tempered **12** cantankerous, discontented, dissatisfied

## ground
◇ *anagram indicator* **03** fix, set, sod **04** base, call, clay, dirt, dust, eard, land, lees, loam, marl, park, plot, soil, yerd, yird **05** acres, arena, basis, cause, coach, dregs, drill, earth, field, found, lawns, pitch, score, teach, terra, train, tutor, yeard **06** bottom, campus, domain, estate, excuse, fields, inform, motive, reason, settle **07** account, deposit, dry land, educate, gardens, holding, prepare, residue, stadium, surface, terrain **08** argument, initiate, instruct, occasion, position, property, sediment **09** advantage, establish, introduce, principle, scourings, territory **10** background, foundation, inducement, terra firma **11** precipitate, vindication **12** acquaint with, surroundings **13** justification **15** familiarize with
*See also* **stadium**
• **leave the ground** **04** yump
• **patch of ground** **03** lot, tee **04** area
• **run along ground** **04** taxi

## groundbait
**04** chum **06** berley, burley

## groundless
**05** empty, false **08** baseless, illusory **09** imaginary, unfounded **10** unprovoked **11** uncalled-for, unjustified, unsupported, unwarranted **13** without reason **15** unsubstantiated

## grounds
**04** lees **05** dregs

## groundwork
**04** base **05** basis **06** bottom **07** footing **08** homework, research **09** spadework **10** essentials, foundation, metaphysic **11** cornerstone, preparation **12** fundamentals **13** preliminaries, underpinnings

## group
**03** lot, mob, set **04** band, body, club, crew, gang, knot, link, mass, pack, pool, rank, sort, team, unit **05** batch, bunch, class, clump, crowd, flock, genus, grade, guild, order, party, range, squad, troop, unite **06** caucus, circle, clique, cohort, family, gather, huddle, league, line up, school **07** arrange, bracket, cluster, collect, company, coterie, element, faction, marshal, society, species **08** assemble, assembly, category, classify, grouping, organize **09** associate, formation, gathering, syndicate **10** categorize, collection, congregate, contingent, detachment **11** association, combination **12** congregation, organization **14** classification, conglomeration
*See also* **singer**
• **group of women** **02** WI **05** coven
• **unit group** **04** cell

## grouse
**04** beef, carp, good, moan, neat **05** bitch, gripe, groan, peeve, whine **06** grouch, whinge **07** grumble, protest **08** complain **09** bellyache, complaint, excellent, find fault, grievance, objection

*Grouse include:*

**03** red
**04** sage, sand
**05** black, hazel
**06** ruffed, willow
**07** gorcock, greyhen, pintail, prairie, red game
**08** hazel hen, heath-hen, moorcock, moorfowl, moor-poot, moor-pout, muir-poot, muir-pout, pheasant, sage cock
**09** blackcock, blackgame, heathbird, heathcock, heath-fowl, partridge, ptarmigan
**10** heath-poult, prairie hen
**11** prairie fowl, sharp-tailed
**12** capercaillie, capercailzie
**14** prairie chicken

*See also* **game**
• **grouse-shooters' lair** **04** butt

## grove
**03** Gro **04** tope, wood **05** copse, hurst **06** arbour, avenue, covert, lyceum **07** coppice, spinney, thicket **08** woodland **10** plantation

## grovel
**04** fawn **05** cower, crawl, creep, defer, kneel, kotow, stoop, toady **06** cheese, cringe, crouch, kowtow, lie low, suck up **07** bow down, flatter, lie down **08** kiss up to **12** bow and scrape **14** demean yourself **15** butter someone up, fall on your knees

## grow
**02** go **03** bud, get, sow, wax **04** farm, rise, stem, turn **05** arise, breed, issue, plant, raise, shoot, swell, widen **06** become, change, deepen, expand, extend, flower, mature, spread, spring, sprout, thrive **07** advance, broaden, burgeon, develop, enlarge, fill out, harvest, improve, produce, prosper, stretch, succeed, thicken **08** bourgeon, come to be, elongate, escalate, flourish, increase, lengthen, multiply, mushroom, progress **09** cultivate, germinate, get bigger, get taller, originate, propagate **11** make headway, proliferate **12** become bigger, become larger, become taller **14** increase in size
• **grow up** **03** age **06** mature

## growl
**03** yap **04** bark, gnar, gurl, howl, roar, roin, snap, snar, yelp **05** groin, royne, snarl **06** rumble **07** grumble

## grown-up
**03** big, man **05** adult, of age, woman **06** mature **09** full-grown **10** fully grown **12** fully fledged **14** fully developed

## growth
**04** crop, gall, lump, rise, wart **05** plant **06** antler, flower, spread, tumour **07** advance, budding, flowers, headway, success **08** greenery, increase, progress, shooting, swelling **09** deepening, evolution, expansion, extension, flowering, outgrowth, springing, sprouting **10** burgeoning, maturation, prosperity **11** development, enlargement, excrescence, germination, improvement **12** augmentation, intumescence, protuberance **13** amplification, magnification, proliferation **14** aggrandizement, multiplication
• **halt growth** **03** nip

## grub
**03** dig, eat, wog **04** eats, food, hunt, nosh, pupa, root, rout, stub, tuck, worm **05** delve, grout, larva, meals, probe, scour, wroot **06** burrow, ferret, forage, gru-gru, maggot, muddle, rootle, search, tucker **07** explore, rummage, snuzzle, uncover, unearth **08** bookworm, excavate, flag-worm, groo-groo, muck-worm **09** chrysalis, nutrition, provision, witchetty **10** gru-gru worm, sustenance **11** caterpillar, refreshment **12** refreshments **13** leatherjacket

## grubby
**05** dirty, grimy, messy, mucky, seedy **06** filthy, shabby, soiled, thumby **07** scruffy, squalid **08** unwashed

## grudge
**04** envy, hate, mind **05** covet, pique, score, spite, venom **06** animus, enmity, grutch, hatred, malice, malign, murmur, repine, resent **07** dislike, ill-will, rancour **08** aversion, begrudge, jealousy, object to **09** animosity, antipathy, grievance **10** antagonism, bitterness, resentment **11** be jealous of,

malevolence **12** hard feelings **15** take exception to

**grudging**
**07** envious, jealous **08** hesitant **09** reluctant, resentful, unwilling **11** half-hearted **12** heartburning **14** unenthusiastic

**gruel**
**05** kasha **06** congee, conjee, skilly **07** brochan **08** loblolly **10** punishment **11** skilligalee, skilligolee

**gruelling**
**04** hard **05** harsh, tough **06** severe, taxing, tiring, trying **07** arduous **08** crushing, draining, grinding **09** demanding, difficult, laborious, punishing, strenuous **10** exhausting **12** backbreaking

**gruesome**
**04** grim, sick **05** awful **06** grisly, grooly, horrid **07** ghastly, hideous, macabre **08** dreadful, horrible, horrific, shocking, terrible **09** abhorrent, appalling, frightful, loathsome, monstrous, repellent, repugnant, repulsive, revolting, sickening **10** abominable, disgusting

**gruesomely**
**06** grimly **08** horribly, terribly **09** hideously **10** dreadfully **11** frightfully, monstrously, repulsively

**gruff**
**04** curt, rude, sour **05** blunt, harsh, husky, rough, surly, testy, thick **06** abrupt, grumpy, hoarse, sullen, tetchy **07** brusque, crabbed, rasping, throaty **08** churlish, croaking, guttural, impolite **09** crotchety **10** unfriendly **11** bad-tempered **12** discourteous

**gruffly**
**06** curtly, rudely **07** harshly, huskily, roughly **08** abruptly, hoarsely **09** brusquely **10** gutturally, impolitely **14** discourteously

**grumble**
**04** beef, carp, moan, mump, nark, roar **05** bitch, bleat, croak, gripe, groin, growl, grump, whine **06** grouch, grouse, gurgle, mumble, murmur, mutter, object, rumble, whinge **07** chunder, chunner, chunter, grizzle, maunder, protest **08** chounter, complain **09** bellyache, complaint, find fault, grievance, muttering, objection

**grumbler**
**04** moan **06** grouch, moaner, whiner **07** croaker, fusspot, grouser, niggler, whinger **09** nit-picker **10** bellyacher, complainer, fussbudget **11** fault-finder

**grumpily**
**07** crossly, in a huff, in a sulk, sulkily **08** sullenly **09** grouchily **10** churlishly

**grumpy**
**05** cross, moany, ratty, sulky, surly **06** crabby, snappy, sullen, tetchy **07** crabbed, grouchy, in a huff, in a sulk **08** churlish, grumpish, petulant **09** crotchety, irritable **11** bad-

tempered, ill-tempered **12** cantankerous, discontented

**grunt**
**03** ugh **04** oink, rasp **05** cough, croak, grate, groin, power, snore, snort **06** drudge, grumph **07** pig-fish, soldier **08** labourer

**Guadeloupe**
**03** GLP

**Guam**
**03** GUM

**guarantee**
**04** back, bond, gage, oath **05** swear, token **06** assure, avouch, engage, ensure, insure, pledge, secure, surety **07** certify, earnest, endorse, promise, protect, sponsor, support, warrant **08** contract, covenant, guaranty, make sure, security, vouch for, warranty **09** answer for, assurance, insurance, stipulate, undertake, vouchsafe **10** collateral, underwrite, warrandice, warrantise **11** endorsement, make certain, testimonial **12** word of honour **15** give an assurance

**guarantor**
**05** angel **06** backer, surety **07** referee, sponsor, voucher **08** bailsman, bondsman **09** guarantee, supporter, warrantor **10** covenantor **11** underwriter

**guard**
◊ *containment indicator* **03** pad **04** care, keep, mind, rail, save, wait, wall, ward, wear, weir **05** check, cover, fence, garda, hedge, scout, visor, watch **06** beware, buffer, bumper, captor, charge, defend, escort, fender, keeper, minder, patrol, picket, police, screen, secure, sentry, shield, warden, warder **07** barrier, be alert, control, cushion, defence, enguard, look out, lookout, oversee, protect, shelter, watcher **08** bostangi, defender, fortress, guardian, preserve, savegard, scrutiny, security, sentinel, splasher, take care, watchman **09** bodyguard, conductor, custodian, direction, keep watch, protector, safeguard, supervise, vigilance **10** inspection, monitoring, protection, regulation **11** observation, stewardship, supervision **12** guardianship, surveillance **15** superintendence
• **officer of the Guard** **04** exon
• **off your guard** **06** unwary **07** napping, unaware, unready **08** careless, unawares **09** red-handed, surprised **10** unprepared **11** inattentive **12** unsuspecting
• **on your guard** **04** wary **05** alert, ready **07** careful **08** cautious, excubant, prepared, vigilant, watchful **09** attentive, wide awake **10** on the alert **11** circumspect **12** on the lookout

**guarded**
**04** wary **05** cagey, chary **07** careful, striped, trimmed **08** cautious, defended, discreet, reserved, reticent, watchful **09** reluctant, secretive

**10** restrained **11** circumspect **12** non-committal

**guardedly**
**06** warily **07** charily **09** carefully **10** cautiously **11** reluctantly, secretively **13** circumspectly **14** non-committally

**guardian**
**05** angel, guard, Janus, tutor **06** custos, escort, gryfon, keeper, patron, warden, warder **07** curator, Granthi, griffin, griffon, gryphon, steward, trustee, tutelar **08** Cerberus, champion, curatrix, defender, tutelary **09** attendant, caretaker, chaperone, custodian, preserver, protector **10** depositary, depository, protecting **11** conservator **12** conservatrix
• **guardian of women** **04** Juno

**guardianship**
**04** care, ward **05** aegis, guard, hands, trust **07** custody, defence, keeping, tuition **08** guidance, tutelage, wardenry, wardship **09** patronage **10** attendance, protection, wardenship **11** curatorship, safekeeping, stewardship, trusteeship **12** preservation, protectorate **13** custodianship

**Guatemala**
**03** GCA, GTM

**Guernsey**
**03** GBG

**guerrilla**
**03** Che **06** haiduk, maquis, sniper **07** chetnik, fedayee, heyduck **08** komitaji, partisan, Viet Cong **09** irregular, terrorist, Zapatista **10** Tamil tiger **11** bushwhacker, franctireur, guerrillero **14** freedom fighter

**guess**
**03** aim, bet **04** feel, idea, shot **05** aread, arede, augur, fancy, hunch, judge, level, think **06** assume, belief, devise, divine, notion, reckon, theory **07** arreede, believe, feeling, imagine, opinion, predict, suppose, surmise, suspect, work out **08** consider, estimate **09** guesswork, intuition, judgement, postulate, reckoning, speculate, suspicion **10** assumption, conjecture, hypothesis, make a guess, prediction **11** guesstimate, hypothesize, speculation, supposition **13** shot in the dark **14** a shot in the dark, a stab in the dark, ballpark figure, put something at

**guessing-game**
**04** mora **05** morra

**guesstimate**
**05** guess **09** judgement, quotation, reckoning, valuation **10** assessment, estimation, evaluation, rough guess **11** computation **13** approximation **14** ballpark figure **15** approximate cost

**guesswork**
**06** theory **07** surmise **09** intuition, reckoning **10** assumption, conjecture, estimation, hypothesis, prediction **11** guesstimate, speculation, supposition

## guest
**02** PG **05** umbra **06** caller, lodger, patron **07** boarder, invitee, regular, visitor **08** manuhiri, resident, symphile, visitant **09** synoecete, synoekete

## guesthouse
**03** inn **05** hotel **06** hostel **07** Gasthof, hospice, pension, taverna **08** Gasthaus, hostelry, minshuku **11** xenodochium **12** rooming-house **13** boarding-house **15** bed-and-breakfast

## guff
**03** rot **04** blah, bosh, bull, bunk **05** balls, bilge, hooey, smell, stink, trash, tripe **06** bunkum, drivel, hot air, humbug, piffle **07** baloney, eyewash, hogwash, rhubarb, rubbish, twaddle **08** claptrap, cobblers, malarkey, nonsense, tommyrot **09** gibberish, moonshine, poppycock **10** codswallop

## guffaw
**04** hoot, roar **05** laugh, whoop **06** bellow, cackle, haw-haw, shriek **09** loud laugh **11** laugh loudly

## guidance
**03** tip **04** help, hint, lead, rule, tips **05** hints **06** advice, charge **07** conduct, control, counsel, leading, pointer **08** pointers, teaching **09** direction **10** assistance, directions, guidelines, indication, leadership, management, suggestion **11** counselling, indications, information, instruction, suggestions **12** instructions **14** recommendation **15** recommendations
• **Parental Guidance 02** PG

## guide
**03** ABC, key **04** guru, lead, mark, norm, rule, show, sign, wise **05** abcee, absey, gauge, maxim, model, pilot, point, steer, teach, train, tutor, usher, weise, weize **06** advise, attend, beacon, direct, escort, govern, leader, manage, manual, marker, mentor, ranger, signal **07** adviser, command, conduct, control, counsel, courier, educate, example, inspire, labarum, measure, oversee, pattern, pointer, red book, shikari, teacher, waymark **08** Bradshaw, chaperon, cicerone, cynosure, director, engineer, exemplar, Good Food, handbook, helmsman, instruct, landmark, navigate, Pole Star, regulate, road book, shikaree, signpost, standard **09** accompany, archetype, attendant, benchmark, catalogue, chaperone, companion, conductor, criterion, directory, guidebook, guideline, influence, manoeuvre, navigator, sightsman, steersman, supervise, tombstone, yardstick **10** counsellor, indication, instructor, show the way **11** preside over, superintend **12** be in charge of, valet de place **14** Tyrian cynosure
• **weaver's guide 04** card

## guidebook
**03** ABC **04** A to Z® **05** guide **06** manual **08** Baedeker, handbook **09** companion **10** prospectus **15** instruction book

## guideline
**04** rule **05** terms **06** advice **07** measure, road map **08** standard **09** benchmark, criterion, direction, framework, parameter, principle, procedure, yardstick **10** constraint, indication, regulation, suggestion, touchstone **11** information, instruction **14** recommendation

## guild
**03** WAG **04** club, tong **05** artel, lodge, order, union **06** chapel, league **07** basoche, company, mistery, mystery, society **08** alliance, sorority **10** federation, fellowship, fraternity **11** association, brotherhood, corporation **12** organization **13** incorporation

## guile
**04** dole, ruse **05** craft, fraud, trick **06** deceit **07** cunning, knavery, slyness **08** artifice, trickery, wiliness **09** deception, duplicity, stratagem, treachery **10** artfulness, cleverness, craftiness, trickiness **11** deviousness **12** gamesmanship **13** double-dealing

## guileless
**04** open **05** frank, naive **06** candid, direct, honest, simple **07** artless, genuine, natural, sincere **08** innocent, sackless, straight, trusting, truthful **09** ingenuous, unworldly **10** unreserved **11** transparent **13** simple-hearted **15** straightforward, unsophisticated

## guilt
**03** sin **05** blame, shame, wrong **06** regret **07** remorse **08** disgrace **09** dishonour, guilt trip, penitence **10** blood-guilt, conscience, contrition, misconduct, repentance, sinfulness, wrongdoing **11** compunction, criminality, culpability **12** self-reproach, unlawfulness **14** responsibility, self-accusation **15** blameworthiness

## guiltily
**07** at fault, to blame, wrongly **09** illegally, illicitly **10** contritely, shamefully, unlawfully, with sorrow **11** regretfully, responsibly **12** remorsefully, unforgivably **13** penitentially, reprehensibly, without excuse **14** caught in the act **15** caught red-handed

## guiltless
**04** free, pure **05** clean, clear **07** sinless **08** innocent, spotless **09** blameless, faultless, stainless, undefiled, unspotted, unsullied, untainted **10** immaculate, impeccable, inculpable, unblamable **11** untarnished **13** above reproach, unimpeachable **14** irreproachable

## guilty
**03** bad **04** evil **05** sorry, wrong **06** faulty, nocent, sinful, wicked **07** ashamed, at fault, illegal, illicit, to blame **08** blamable, contrite, criminal, culpable, infamous, penitent, sheepish, unlawful **09** condemned, convicted, offending, regretful,

repentant **10** delinquent, flagitious, remorseful, shamefaced **11** blameworthy, guilt-ridden, responsible **12** bloodstained, compunctious

## guinea
**02** Ls, RG **03** GIN **04** quid **06** canary, George **07** Geordie
• **guineas 02** gs

## Guinea-Bissau
**03** GNB, RGB

## guinea pig
**04** cavy, paca **05** aguti **06** agouti, agouty **08** capybara **09** do-nothing, triallist

## Guinness
**04** Alec

## guise
**03** air **04** face, form, mask, show **05** dress, front, shape **06** aspect, custom, façade, manner **07** purport **08** disguise, features, likeness, pretence **09** behaviour, demeanour, semblance **10** appearance

## guitar
**02** ax **03** axe, uke **04** bass **05** Dobro®, sanko **06** sancho **07** gittern, samisen, ukulele **08** shamisen **09** humbucker
• **play guitar 05** strum

## gulf
**03** bay, gap, maw **04** cove, hole, rift, void **05** abyss, basin, bight, chasm, cleft, gorge, inlet, split **06** breach, canyon, divide, hollow, ravine, vorago **07** crevice, fissure, opening **08** division **09** whirlpool **10** separation

*Gulfs include:*

**04** Aden, Huon, Lion, Moro, Oman, Riga, Siam, Suez
**05** Ancud, Aqaba, Càdiz, Davao, Dulce, Gabes, Gaeta, Genoa, Kutch, Lions, Maine, Panay, Papua, Penas, Ragay, Saros, Sidra, Sirte, Tunis
**06** Aegina, Alaska, Cambay, Chania, Darien, Gdansk, Guinea, Kavala, Mannar, Mexico, Naples, Nicoya, Orosei, Panama, Parita, Patras, St Malo, Tonkin, Triste, Venice
**07** Almeria, Arabian, Asinara, Boothia, Bothnia, Cazones, Corinth, Edremit, Exmouth, Finland, Fonseca, Hauraki, Kachchh, Lepanto, Obskaya, Persian, Salerno, San Blas, Saronic, Spencer, Taranto, The Gulf, Trieste, Udskaya
**08** Amundsen, Batabano, Cagliari, Campeche, Chiriqui, Honduras, Khambhat, Liaotung, Lingayen, Martaban, Mosquito, Oristano, Papagayo, San Jorge, Taganrog, Thailand, Valencia
**09** Buor-Khaya, Corcovado, Dvinskaya, Guayaquil, Queen Maud, San Matias, San Miguel, St Florent, St Vincent, Van Diemen, Venezuela
**10** California, Chaunskaya, Cheshskaya, Coronation, Kyparissia, Policastro, St

Lawrence, Tazovskaya,
Thermaikos
**11** Carpentaria, Guacanayabo,
Manfredonia, Pechorskaya,
Strymonikos, Tehuantepec
**12** los Mosquitos, Penzhinskaya
**13** Baydaratskaya, Santa Catalina
**15** Joseph Bonaparte

## gull
**04** dupe, fool, hoax **05** cheat
**07** deceive
*See also* **bird; fool**

## gullet
**03** maw **04** craw, crop, gula **06** throat
**07** Red Lane, weasand **09** esophagus
**10** oesophagus

## gullibility
**07** naivety **09** credulity, innocence
**10** simplicity **11** foolishness
**12** trustfulness

## gullible
**05** green, naive **07** foolish, verdant
**08** innocent, trustful, trusting
**09** credulous, ingenuous **11** suggestible
**12** overtrusting, unsuspecting
**13** inexperienced **14** easily deceived,
impressionable **15** unsophisticated

## gully
**03** geo, gio, goe **05** ditch, donga,
gorge, gulch **06** canyon, grough,
gutter, ravine, valley **07** channel,
couloir **11** watercourse
*See also* **ravine**

## gulp
◊ *containment indicator* **04** bolt, slug,
swig, wolf **05** gulch, quaff, stuff, swill,
swipe **06** devour, gobble, gollop,
guzzle **07** draught, swallow
**08** mouthful, tuck into **09** knock back

## gum
**03** fix, God, jaw **04** clog, dupe, glue,
guar, seal **05** affix, cheat, myrrh, paste,
resin, stick **06** acajou, angico, balata,
cement, chewie, chicle, chuddy,
humbug, mastic **07** benzoin, deceive,
dextrin, gamboge, mastich
**08** adhesive, bdellium, benjamin,
dextrine, fixative, galbanum,
mucilage, nonsense, olibanum,
opopanax, scammony **09** courbaril,
insolence, sagapenum, tacamahac,
tacmahack **10** ammoniacum,
asafoetida, caoutchouc, euphorbium,
sarcocolla, tragacanth
• **gum tree** **04** arar **05** karri **06** tupelo
**08** sandarac **10** eucalyptus
• **gum up** **04** clog **05** choke **06** hinder,
impede **08** obstruct

## gummy
**05** gluey, gooey, tacky **06** sticky, viscid
**07** viscous **08** adhesive **09** toothless

## gumption
**03** wit **04** nous **05** savvy, sense
**06** acumen **07** ability, courage
**08** sagacity **09** acuteness **10** astuteness,
cleverness, enterprise, initiative,
shrewdness **11** common sense,
discernment **15** resourcefulness

## gumshoe
*see* **detective**

## gun
**03** rod **05** piece, shoot **06** expert,
heater, weapon **07** firearm, shooter
**10** pre-eminent **12** shooting iron

*Guns include:*

**02** MG
**03** air, dag, gas, gat, ray, six, Uzi
**04** AK-47, Bren, burp, Colt®, hand,
pump, punt, shot, sten, stun
**05** baton, field, fusil, Lewis, Maxim,
rifle, siege, spear, tommy
**06** airgun, Archie, Bofors, cannon,
mortar, musket, needle, pistol,
pom-pom, Purdey®, Quaker,
turret
**07** bazooka, carbine, chopper,
gatling, Long Tom, machine,
pounder, scatter
**08** air rifle, arquebus, elephant,
falconet, firelock, howitzer,
pederero, revolver, starting,
Sterling
**09** Archibald, Big Bertha, flintlock,
harquebus
**10** black Maria, demi-cannon, six-
shooter, submachine,
Winchester®
**11** blunderbuss, four-pounder, half-
pounder, Kalashnikov
**12** fowling-piece, mitrailleuse, three-
pounder

• **gun's catch** **04** sear
• **row of guns** **04** tier

## gunfire
**04** flak **05** salvo **06** firing **08** gunshots,
pounding, shelling, shooting
**09** cannonade **11** bombardment

## gunman
**04** thug **05** bravo **06** bandit, gunsel, hit
man, killer, sniper **07** mobster
**08** assassin, gangster, murderer,
shootist **09** desperado, terrorist
**10** gunslinger, hatchet man **11** armed
robber

## gurgle
**03** lap **04** crow **05** brawl, clunk, plash
**06** babble, bubble, buller, burble,
guggle, murmur, ripple, ruckle, splash
**08** bubbling

## guru
**04** sage **05** swami, tutor **06** expert,
gooroo, leader, master, mentor, pundit
**07** Bhagwan, teacher, tohunga
**08** luminary, Svengali **09** authority,
maharishi **10** instructor **12** guiding light

## gush
**03** goo, jet, run **04** boak, bock, boke,
emit, flow, fuss, go on, pour, rail, rave,
rush, tide, well **05** burst, flood, issue,
raile, rayle, slush, spate, spout, spurt,
surge **06** babble, drivel, effuse, jabber,
stream **07** blather, cascade, chatter,
enthuse, outflow, regorge, torrent
**08** fountain, outburst **10** bubble over,
effervesce, outpouring **11** regurgitate
**12** effusiveness **14** sentimentality

## gushing
**05** gushy **06** sickly, too-too **07** cloying,
fulsome, mawkish **08** effusive
**09** emotional, excessive **10** saccharine,
scaturient **11** sentimental

## gust
**03** fit **04** blow, flaw, gale, puff, rush,
scud, wind **05** blast, blore, burst, erupt,
storm, surge **06** breeze, flurry, relish,
squall **07** bluster, flaught, flavour
**08** burst out, eruption, outbreak,
outburst, williwaw **13** gratification

## gustily
**06** wildly **07** windily **08** breezily,
stormily **13** tempestuously

## gusto
**04** élan, zeal, zest **05** verve **06** energy,
relish **07** delight, fervour, unction
**08** pleasure **09** enjoyment
**10** enthusiasm, exuberance
**12** appreciation, exhilaration

## gusty
**05** blowy, windy **06** breezy, stormy
**07** savoury, squally **08** blustery
**10** blustering **11** tempestuous

## gut
◊ *middle deletion indicator* **03** rob
**04** draw, gill, grit, lane, loot, sack
**05** balls, basic, belly, clean, clear,
dress, empty, nerve, pluck, rifle,
spunk, strip **06** bottle, bowels, innate,
mettle, paunch, ravage, strong
**07** bravery, courage, destroy, enteron,
innards, insides, natural, plunder,
ransack, stomach, viscera **08** audacity,
backbone, boldness, clean out, clear
out, entrails, tenacity **09** devastate,
emotional, fortitude, heartfelt, intuitive
**10** deep-seated, disembowel,
eviscerate, exenterate, intestines,
mesenteron, unthinking
**11** archenteron, instinctive,
involuntary, spontaneous, vital organs
**14** internal organs

## gutless
◊ *middle deletion indicator* **04** nesh,
weak **05** timid **06** abject, craven, feeble
**07** chicken **08** cowardly **09** spineless
**10** irresolute **11** lily-livered **12** faint-
hearted **14** chicken-hearted, chicken-
livered

## gutsily
**06** boldly **07** bravely **08** spunkily
**10** resolutely, staunchily
**11** indomitably **12** courageously,
passionately

## gutsy
**04** bold, game **05** brave, gutty, lusty
**06** ballsy, plucky, spunky **07** gallant,
staunch **08** resolute, spirited
**10** courageous, determined,
gluttonous, mettlesome, passionate
**11** indomitable

## gutter
**04** duct, grip, pipe, roan, rone, tube
**05** ditch, drain, gripe, gully, rhone,
rigol, sewer, swale, swayl, sweal,
sweel **06** cullis, gulley, kennel, rigoll,
runnel, sluice, strand, trench, trough
**07** channel, conduit, culvert, passage
**08** downpipe, roanpipe, ronepipe
**09** guttering

## guttersnipe
**04** waif **05** gamin **06** urchin **07** mudlark
**10** ragamuffin **14** tatterdemalion

## guttural

**03** low **04** deep **05** gruff, harsh, husky, rough, thick **06** hoarse **07** grating, rasping, throaty **08** croaking, gravelly

## guy

**02** bo **03** boy, lad, man **04** boyo, chap, cove, dude, joke, lark, stay, vang **05** bloke, bucko, fella, joker, youth **06** decamp, Fawkes, fellow, flight, geezer, person **09** character, decamping **10** individual

## Guyana

**03** GUY

## guzzle

**04** bolt, cram, gulp, soak, swig, wolf **05** quaff, scoff, stuff, swill **06** devour, gobble **07** put away, swallow **08** tuck into **09** knock back, polish off **10** gormandize

## gymnastics

**02** PE, PT **03** gym

*Gymnastics disciplines include:*

**04** ball, beam, hoop
**05** clubs, floor, rings, vault
**06** ribbon
**07** high bar
**08** tumbling
**10** horse vault, uneven bars
**11** balance beam, pommel horse

**12** parallel bars, trampolining
**13** horizontal bar
**14** asymmetric bars, floor exercises, side horse vault, sports aerobics

*Gymnastics-related terms include:*

**04** beam, pike, tuck
**05** cross, floor, giant, rings, salto, stick, twist, vault
**06** aerial, bridge, layout
**07** element, flyaway, Gaylord
**08** dismount, flic-flac, rotation, round-off, straddle, walkover, whip back
**09** all-around, apparatus, cartwheel, execution, handstand, Yurchenko
**10** double back, handspring, somersault, uneven bars
**11** balance beam, double twist, pommel horse, Swedish fall
**12** compulsories, parallel bars
**13** horizontal bar, inverted cross
**14** asymmetric bars

*Gymnasts include:*

**03** Kim (Nellie), Ono (Takashi)
**06** Korbut (Olga Valentinovna), Miller (Shannon), Retton (Mary Lou)
**07** Scherbo (Vitaly), Tweddle (Beth)
**08** Comaneci (Nadia), Ditiatin (Aleksandr), Latynina (Larissa

Semyonovna), Shakhlin (Boris Anfiyanovich)
**09** Andrianov (Nikolai Yefimovich), Cáslavská (Vera)
**10** Boginskaya (Svetlana), Turischeva (Lyudmila Ivanovna)

## gym shoe

**03** dap **08** plimsole, plimsoll, sandshoe

## Gypsy, Gipsy

**03** chi, faw, rom, rye **04** chai, chal, Roma **05** caird, nomad, rover **06** gipsen, gitana, gitano, hawker, roamer, Romani, Romany, tinker **07** rambler, Rommany, tinkler, tsigane, tzigany, Zincala, Zincalo, Zingana, Zingano, Zingara, Zingaro **08** Bohemian, diddicoy, Egyptian, huckster, wanderer, Zigeuner **09** out-of-door, traveller **14** unconventional

## gyrate

**04** gyre, spin, turn **05** swirl, twirl, wheel, whirl **06** circle, rotate, spiral, swivel **07** revolve **09** pirouette

## gyration

**04** spin, turn **05** swirl, twirl, twist, whirl, whorl **06** circle, spiral, swivel **08** rotation, spinning, wheeling, whirling **09** pirouette **10** revolution **11** convolution

**H**
**05** aitch, hotel **07** hydrant

**habit**
**03** way, won **04** bent, cowl, gear, mode, robe, rule, togs, ways, wont **05** dress, ethos, get-up, knack, quirk, trick, usage **06** custom, manner, monkey, outfit, policy **07** costume, garment, leaning, routine, uniform **08** clothing, fixation, practice, tendency, vestment, weakness **09** addiction, assuetude, mannerism, obsession, procedure **10** dependence, proclivity, propensity **11** familiarity, inclination **12** second nature **14** accustomedness, matter of course
*See also* **clothes, clothing**
• **bad habit** **04** vice **09** cacoethes

**habitable**
**07** livable **08** liveable **09** livable in **10** liveable in **11** fit to live in, inhabitable

**habitat**
**04** home **05** abode, niche **06** domain **07** element, station, terrain **08** dwelling, locality **09** territory **10** metropolis **11** environment **12** surroundings

**habitation**
**03** hut, pad **04** digs, flat, gaff, home **05** abode, house, joint **06** biding **07** cottage, housing, lodging, mansion, tenancy **08** domicile, dwelling, quarters, tenement **09** apartment, occupancy, residence, residency **10** occupation **11** inhabitance, inhabitancy **12** inhabitation **13** accommodation, dwelling-place **14** living quarters

**habitual**
**03** set **05** fixed, great, usual **06** common, normal, wonted **07** chronic, natural, regular, routine **08** addicted, constant, familiar, hardened, ordinary, standard **09** confirmed, customary, dependent, obsessive, recurrent **10** accustomed, inveterate, persistent, systematic **11** established, intemperate, traditional **12** pathological, systematical

**habitually**
**06** mainly, mostly **07** as a rule, chiefly, usually **08** commonly, normally **09** generally, in the main, on average, regularly, routinely, typically **10** by and large, on the whole, ordinarily **13** traditionally **14** for the most part

**habituate**
**03** use **04** tame **05** adapt, break, enure,

inure, train **06** harden, school, season, settle **07** break in **08** accustom, make used, settle in **09** condition **10** discipline **11** acclimatize, familiarize

**habitué**
**06** patron **07** denizen, regular **10** frequenter **15** frequent visitor, regular customer

**hack**
**03** cut, hag, hew, saw **04** chop, fell, gash, hash, kick, pick, rack **05** clear, cough, hired, notch, slash, slave **06** drudge, mangle, writer **07** grating, hackney, mattock **08** lacerate, mediocre, mutilate, reporter, tomahawk **09** hackneyed, mercenary, scribbler **10** journalist **11** hedge-writer, penny-a-liner
*See also* **horse**
• **hack it** **04** cope **05** get by, get on **06** manage **07** carry on, make out **08** get along **10** get through **13** muddle through

**hackle**
• **make someone's hackles rise**
**03** bug, irk, vex **04** gall, miff, nark, rile **05** anger, annoy, get at **06** bother, enrage, hassle, heckle, madden, needle, nettle, offend, ruffle, wind up **07** affront, hatchel, incense, outrage, provoke **08** flax-comb, irritate **09** aggravate, infuriate, make angry **10** antagonize, exasperate **13** make sparks fly **15** get on your nerves

**hackneyed**
**03** old **04** hack, worn **05** banal, corny, hoary, stale, stock, tired, trite **06** common **07** cliché'd, percoct, worn-out **08** clichéed, overused, time-worn **09** twice-told **10** overworked, pedestrian, prostitute, threadbare, uninspired, unoriginal, yawn-making **11** commonplace, stereotyped, wearing thin **12** cliché-ridden, run-of-the-mill **13** platitudinous, unimaginative

**had**
**01** 'd

**haddock**
**05** capon, scrod, smoky **06** finnan, rizzar, rizzer, rizzor, smokie **07** findram, speldin **08** spelding, speldrin **09** speldring **14** Arbroath smokie

**Hades**
**04** hell **05** Pluto **10** underworld

**hafnium**
**02** Hf

**haft**
**04** grip, hilt, knob **05** shaft, stock **06** handle **07** dudgeon **08** handgrip

**hag**
**03** hew **04** fury, hack **05** crone, harpy, rudas, shrew, vixen, witch **06** beldam, gorgon, virago **07** beldame, hellcat **08** harridan **09** battle-axe, termagant

**haggard**
**03** wan **04** lean, pale, thin **05** drawn, gaunt, Rider **06** pallid, wasted

**07** drained, ghastly, pinched, untamed **08** careworn, shrunken **10** cadaverous **11** intractable **13** hollow-cheeked

**haggle**
**04** prig **05** cavil **06** barter, bicker, dicker, higgle, mangle, niffer, palter **07** bargain, chaffer, dispute, quarrel, quibble, wrangle **08** beat down, huckster, squabble **09** negotiate

**hahnium**
**02** Ha

**hail**
**03** ave **04** ahoy, beat, come, goal, hale, heil, laud, pelt, rain, skol **05** cheer, exalt, greet, hello, nod to, salve, score, skoal, sleet, sound, speak, storm **06** accost, assail, attack, batter, health, honour, praise, salute, shower, volley, wave to, what ho **07** acclaim, address, applaud, barrage, bombard, earshot, torrent, welcome **08** be born in, flag down, greeting, signal to, wave down, whoa-ho-ho **09** call out to, frozen ice, hail-storm, originate, whoa-ho-hoa **10** frozen rain, hailstones, say hello to **11** acknowledge, bombardment, communicate **13** precipitation **14** have your home in **15** have your roots in

**hail-fellow-well-met**
**05** jolly, merry **06** genial, hearty, jovial, lively **07** affable, cordial, festive **08** cheerful, friendly, sociable **09** convivial, fun-loving

**hair**
**03** fur, mop **04** coat, hide, pelt, pile, type, wool **05** fibre, locks, pilus, shock **06** fibril, fleece, lanugo, thatch, villus **07** bristle, tresses **08** strammel, strummel **09** character

---

*Hair-related terms include:*

**03** bob, cue, cut, dod, dye, gel, wax, wig

**04** bald, body, clip, coif, comb, crop, curl, down, fine, grip, hank, kesh, lank, lice, lock, mane, perm, pouf, tête, tint, tong, trim, tuft, wavy, wiry

**05** bangs, black, blond, bluey, braid, brown, brush, crimp, curly, frizz, henna, layer, moult, mousy, queue, quiff, rinse, roots, sandy, serum, shade, shaft, shine, short, slick, slide, snood, tease, thick, tress

**06** auburn, barber, barnet, blonde, bobble, brunet, coarse, colour, crinal, fillet, flaxen, fringe, frizzy, ginger, greasy, hairdo, kangha, mousey, mousse, peruke, pomade, pompom, pompon, pouffe, ribbon, roller, silver, styler, tangle, titian

**07** balding, bandeau, blow-dry, cowlick, crinate, flyaway, frizzle, greying, haircut, hair gel, hair net, hair oil, hirsute, keratin, lacquer, parting, periwig, pin curl, rat-tail, redhead, ringlet, shampoo, streaks, stylist, tonsure, topknot, tow-head, tressed, wet-look, xerasia

**08** alopecia, ash-blond, back-comb, baldpate, barrette, bar slide, bouffant, brunette, canities, chestnut, clippers, coiffeur, coiffure, combover, cow's lick, crinated, dandruff, diffuser, elflocks, fixature, follicle, forelock, grizzled, hair band, hairless, hairline, headring, kisscurl, lovelock, peroxide, rat's-tail, receding, roulette, scrunchy, side comb, sidelock, split end, straight

**09** Alice band, ash-blonde, bandoline, blue rinse, Brylcreem®, capillary, chevelure, coiffeuse, colourant, curlpaper, finger-dry, fright wig, hairbrush, hairdryer, hairpiece, hair slide, hairspray, hairstyle, headdress, Kirbigrip®, lowlights, madarosis, mop-headed, papillote, redheaded, scalp lock, scrunchie, tow-headed, trichosis, water wave

**10** bad hair day, bald-headed, detangling, extensions, fair-haired, fair-headed, finger wave, hair-powder, highlights, leiotrichy, long-haired, perruquier, piliferous, pocket-comb, scrunch-dry, trichology, widow's peak

**11** conditioner, flame-haired, hairdresser, hairstylist, side-parting, tow-coloured, white-haired, white-headed

**12** bottle-blonde, brilliantine, Cain-coloured, close-cropped, curling tongs, cymotrichous, hair restorer, leiotrichous, straightener, trichologist

**13** centre-parting, corkscrew curl, Judas-coloured, lissotrichous, pepper-and-salt, permanent wave, platinum-blond

**14** shoulder-length

**15** strawberry blond, styling products

*Facial-hair-related terms include:*

**05** beard, pluck, razor
**06** goatee, tweeze, waxing
**07** epilate, eyelash, goateed, shaving, stubble
**08** bumfluff, depilate, stubbled, sugaring, tweezers
**09** depilator, moustache, sideburns
**10** aftershave, depilation, depilatory, face-fungus, pogonotomy, shaving gel
**11** clean-shaven, shaving foam, shaving-soap
**12** electrolysis, shaving-brush, shaving-stick, side whiskers
**13** eyebrow pencil, eyelash curler
**15** designer stubble

• **let your hair down** **05** relax
**08** chill out, loosen up **09** hang loose
**13** have a good time, let yourself go
**15** let it all hang out
• **make someone's hair stand on end** **03** jar **04** daze, jolt, numb, stun
**05** amaze, appal, repel, shake,

shock, upset **06** dismay, revolt
**07** agitate, astound, disgust, horrify, outrage, perturb, stagger, startle, stupefy, terrify, unnerve **08** bewilder, confound, disquiet, distress, frighten, paralyse, unsettle **09** dumbfound, take aback **10** scandalize, traumatize
• **not turn a hair** **04** calm **06** stay cool **10** remain calm **11** see it coming **12** keep your cool **14** not bat an eyelid, remain composed
• **piece of hair** **03** cue **04** lock **05** tress
• **split hairs** **05** cavil **07** nit-pick, quibble **08** pettifog **09** find fault **10** over-refine

**haircut, hairdo**
*see* **hairstyle**

**hairdresser**
**06** barber **07** crimper, friseur, stylist **08** coiffeur **09** coiffeuse **11** hairstylist **12** trichologist

*Hairdressers include:*

**06** **Clarke** (Nicky), **Sorbie** (Trevor)
**07** **Grateau** (Marcel), **Sassoon** (Vidal)
**08** **Collinge** (Andrew), **Mitchell** (Paul)
**10** **Teazy Weazy, Toni and Guy**
**11** **Worthington** (Charles)

**hairless**
**04** bald **05** shorn **06** shaven, smooth **08** glabrate, glabrous, tonsured **09** beardless, desperate **10** bald-headed **11** clean-shaven

**hairpiece**
**03** jiz, rug, tie, wig **04** gizz, jasy, jazy **05** caxon, jasey, major, syrup **06** bagwig, bobwig, Brutus, merkin, peruke, tie-wig, toupee, toupet **07** buzz-wig, periwig, Ramilie, scratch, spencer **08** postiche, Ramilies, Ramillie **09** fright wig, Ramillies **10** full-bottom, scratch-wig **12** Gregorian wig **14** transformation

**hair-raising**
**05** eerie, scary **06** creepy **08** alarming, exciting, shocking **09** startling, thrilling **10** horrifying, petrifying, terrifying **11** frightening **13** bloodcurdling, spine-chilling

**hair's-breadth**
**03** jot **04** hair, inch **07** whisker **08** fraction

**hairstyle**
**03** cut, set **05** style **06** barnet, hairdo **07** haircut **08** coiffure

*Hairstyles include:*

**02** DA
**03** bob, bun, wig
**04** Afro, crop, perm, shed, updo
**05** bangs, braid, plait, quiff, weave
**06** curled, dreads, fringe, mullet, pouffe, toupee
**07** beehive, bunches, chignon, cowlick, crewcut, crimped, Mohican, pageboy, pigtail, shingle, tonsure, topknot
**08** bouffant, combover, corn rows, Eton crop, frizette, ponytail, ringlets, skinhead, undercut

**09** duck's arse, hair-piece, Hoxton fin, number one, pompadour, sideburns
**10** backcombed, dreadlocks, extensions, French roll, Marcel wave, sideboards
**11** French pleat
**13** hair extension

**hairy**
◇ *anagram indicator* **05** bushy, dicey, dodgy, furry, fuzzy, grave, nasty, risky **06** chancy, daring, fleecy, pilose, pilous, severe, shaggy, unsafe, woolly **07** bearded, crinite, crinose, exposed, hirsute, ominous, serious **08** alarming, critical, high-risk, insecure, menacing, perilous, reckless, unshaven **09** breakneck, dangerous, hazardous **10** precarious, vulnerable **11** crinigerous, frightening, susceptible, threatening, treacherous
• **hairy person** **04** Esau

**Haiti**
**02** RH **03** HTI

**halcyon**
**04** calm, mild **05** balmy, happy, quiet, still **06** gentle, golden, placid, serene **07** pacific **09** carefree, peaceful, tranquil **10** kingfisher, prosperous **11** flourishing, undisturbed

**hale**
**03** fit **04** drag, hail, well **05** sound **06** hearty, raucle, robust, strong **07** healthy **08** athletic, blooming, vigorous, youthful **09** in the pink **10** able-bodied **11** flourishing **12** in fine fettle

**half**
◇ *deletion indicator* ◇ *insertion indicator* **02** hf **04** demi-, hemi-, part, semi- **05** share **06** barely, halved, moiety, partly, slight **07** à moitié, divided, limited, partial, portion, section, segment **08** bisected, fraction, moderate, slightly **09** bisection, equal part, partially **10** equal share, fractional, hemisphere, incomplete, moderately, semicircle **11** imperfectly **12** divided in two, fifty per cent, inadequately, incompletely **13** hemispherical **14** insufficiently
• **by half** **03** too **04** very **11** excessively **12** considerably
• **by halves** **05** à demi **07** à moitié **11** imperfectly **12** inadequately, incompletely **14** insufficiently
• **not half** **04** very **06** indeed, really **08** not at all, very much **09** not nearly **11** exceedingly
• **other half** **04** wife **06** spouse **07** husband, partner **08** alter ego
• **too ... by half** **03** too **04** over **06** unduly **11** excessively **12** immoderately, inordinately, unreasonably **13** unjustifiably, unnecessarily

**half-baked**
**05** crazy, crude, silly **06** stupid **07** foolish **08** crackpot, immature **09** ill-judged, senseless, underdone, unplanned **10** half-witted, incomplete

**half-caste**

**11** harebrained, impractical, undeveloped **12** ill-conceived, short-sighted

**half-caste**

**05** griff, metif, Métis **06** Creole, griffe, mestee **07** mestiza, mestizo, Métisse, mongrel, mulatta, mulatto **08** miscegen, quadroon **09** miscegene, miscegine, quintroon **10** mulattress, quarteroon **12** quarter-blood

**half-cough**

**03** hem

**half-hearted**

◇ *middle deletion indicator* **04** cool, weak **05** tepid **06** feeble **07** neutral, passive **08** listless, lukewarm **09** apathetic, Laodicean **10** lacklustre **11** indifferent, unconcerned **12** uninterested **14** unenthusiastic

**half-heartedly**

◇ *middle deletion indicator* **06** feebly **09** neutrally **10** listlessly **13** apathetically

**half-moon**

**04** lune **08** demilune

**halfpenny**

**03** mag, meg, rap **04** maik, mail, make, posh **05** maile **06** bawbee, magpie, obolus **07** patrick **10** portcullis

**halfway**

**03** mid **04** mean **06** barely, median, middle, midway **07** central **08** slightly **09** centrally **11** equidistant, imperfectly, in the middle, to the middle **12** intermediate
• **meet someone halfway** **09** make a deal, negotiate **10** compromise **11** give and take **15** make concessions

**halfwit**

**03** ass, git, mug, nit **04** berk, butt, clot, dill, dope, dork, dupe, fool, geek, nerk, nong, prat, twit **05** chump, clown, comic, dumbo, dunce, eejit, galah, idiot, moron, ninny, twerp, wally **06** cretin, dimwit, doofus, jester, nitwit, numpty, stooge, sucker **07** airhead, buffoon, fat-head, pillock, plonker **08** imbecile **09** birdbrain, blockhead, ignoramus, simpleton **10** nincompoop **13** laughing-stock

**half-witted**

**04** dull, dumb **05** barmy, batty, crazy, dotty, nutty, potty, silly, wacky **06** simple, stupid **07** foolish, idiotic, moronic **08** crackpot **09** dim-witted **12** crack-brained, feeble-minded, simple-minded **14** not the full quid

**hall**

**02** ha' **04** aula, gild **05** foyer, guild, lobby, odeon, salle **06** atrium, exedra **07** apadana, chamber, citadel, commons, exhedra, hallway, megaron, passage **08** basilica, corridor **09** concourse, Domdaniel, longhouse, vestibule **10** auditorium, passageway **11** concert hall **12** assembly hall, assembly room, entrance-hall **14** conference hall
*See also* **college**

**hallmark**

**04** mark, sign **05** badge, stamp **06** device, emblem, symbol **09** brand-name, indicator, platemark, trademark **10** indication **12** official mark **13** official stamp **14** typical quality

**hallo**

**02** hi **04** g'day **05** chimo, hello, hillo, hullo **06** holloa **07** welcome **09** greetings **11** good evening, good morning **13** good afternoon

**hallowed**

**04** holy, tapu **06** age-old, sacred **07** blessed, revered **08** honoured **09** dedicated, venerable **10** inviolable, sacrosanct, sanctified **11** consecrated, established

**hallucinate**

**04** trip **05** dream **07** imagine **08** daydream, freak out **09** fantasize, see things **10** see visions **13** imagine things

**hallucination**

**04** trip **05** dream **06** mirage, vision **07** fantasy, figment **08** daydream, delirium, delusion, freak-out, illusion **09** autoscopy **10** apparition **14** phantasmagoria **15** hypnagogic image, hypnogogic image

**halo**

**01** O **04** aura, ring **05** crown, glory **06** corona, gloria, nimbus **07** aureola, aureole **08** gloriole, halation, radiance **12** vesica piscis **13** circle of light

**halt**

**03** alt, end **04** curb, lame, limp, quit, rest, stem, stop, wait **05** block, break, cease, check, close, crush, pause **06** arrest, desist, draw up, finish, impede, pull up **07** limping, respite **08** break off, crippled, deadlock, full stop, hold back, interval, obstruct, stoppage **09** cessation, stalemate, terminate, vacillate **10** call it a day, come to rest, desistance, put an end to, standstill **11** come to a rest, come to a stop, discontinue, termination **12** bring to a stop, draw to a close, interruption **13** bring to a close **14** breathing space, discontinuance **15** discontinuation

**halting**

**06** broken **07** awkward **08** hesitant, laboured, unsteady **09** faltering, imperfect, stumbling, uncertain **10** stammering, stuttering

**halve**

◇ *insertion indicator* **05** sever, share, split **06** bisect, divide, lessen, reduce **07** cut down **09** cut in half **10** split in two **11** dichotomize **13** divide equally

**halved**

**03** cut **05** split **06** shared **07** divided **08** bisected **09** dimidiate

**ham**

◇ *anagram indicator* **04** hock **05** hough **06** clumsy, coarse **07** amateur, overact, pigmeat **08** inexpert **10** prosciutto

**ham-fisted**

**03** ham **05** gawky, inept **06** clumsy, thumby **07** awkward, unhandy

**08** bungling **09** all thumbs, lumbering, maladroit, two-fisted, unskilful **10** blundering, cack-handed **11** heavy-handed **13** accident-prone, unco-ordinated

**hamlet**

**05** aldea, thorp **06** thorpe

**hammer**

◇ *anagram indicator* **02** ax **03** axe, din, hit **04** bang, bash, beat, drum, form, lick, make, mall, maul, pane, pean, peen, pein, pene, pick, plug, rout, slam, slap, slog **05** blame, bully, decry, dolly, drive, force, forge, gavel, grind, knock, madge, mould, pound, rivet, shape, slate **06** attack, batter, beetle, defeat, drudge, instil, keep on, labour, mallet, martel, monkey, oliver, plexor, sledge, strike, thrash **07** censure, clobber, condemn, dog-head, fashion, malleus, Mjölnir, outplay, persist, plessor, run down, trounce **08** malleate, Mjöllnir, overcome, trouncer, work away **09** criticize, denigrate, drive home, overwhelm, percussor, persevere, reiterate, slaughter **10** annihilate, claw hammer, sheep's-foot, tack hammer, tilt-hammer, trip hammer **11** about-sledge, steam hammer, stone hammer, walk all over, water hammer **12** sledgehammer **13** run rings round, tear a strip off **14** knapping-hammer **15** make mincemeat of
• **hammer out**   ◇ *anagram indicator* **06** finish, settle **07** produce, resolve, sort out, work out **08** complete **09** negotiate, thrash out **10** accomplish, bring about **12** carry through

**hammered**

◇ *anagram indicator* **06** incuse **07** excudit

**hammerhead**

**04** pane, pean, peen, pein, pene **05** umbre **07** Zygaena **08** umbrette **09** umber-bird

**hammock support**

**04** clew, clue

**hamper**

◇ *anagram indicator* ◇ *containment indicator* **03** box, pad, ped **04** curb, foil, stop, tuck **05** baulk, block, bribe, cabin, check, cramp, creel, pinch, seron **06** basket, bridle, fetter, hinder, hobble, hold up, impede, retard, seroon, stymie, tangle, thwart **07** curtail, distort, inhibit, pannier, prevent, shackle **08** encumber, handicap, incumber, obstruct, restrain, restrict, slow down **09** container, frustrate, hamstring

**hamstring**

**03** hox **04** foil, hock, stop **05** baulk, block, check, cramp, hough **06** hinder, hold up, impede, stymie, thwart **07** cripple, disable **08** encumber, handicap, paralyse, restrain, restrict **09** frustrate **12** incapacitate

**hand**

**03** aid, fin, paw, pud **04** care, doer, fist, give, help, hond, mitt, palm, part, pass,

## handbag

side **05** arrow, manus, offer, power, skill, style, touch, yield **06** author, charge, convey, marker, needle, pledge, script, stroke, submit, worker **07** acclaim, command, conduct, control, custody, deliver, ovation, pointer, present, quarter, succour, support, workman, writing **08** applause, cheering, clapping, clutches, employee, farm-hand, handclap, hand over, hireling, labourer, producer, transmit **09** authority, direction, handiwork, indicator, influence, operative, performer, signature, workwoman **10** assistance, management, penmanship, possession **11** calligraphy, handwriting, helping hand, supervision **12** manual worker **13** participation **14** responsibility **15** instrumentality, round of applause
• **at hand** **04** near, nigh **05** close, handy, ready **06** to hand, toward **08** imminent **09** available, to the fore **10** accessible **11** forthcoming, in the offing **13** about to happen
• **by hand** **07** à la main **08** manually **13** with your hands **14** using your hands
• **from hand to mouth** **09** in poverty **10** insecurely **11** dangerously, uncertainly **12** au jour le jour, from day to day, precariously **14** on the breadline
• **hand down** **04** give, will **05** grant, leave **06** pass on **07** devolve **08** bequeath, pass down, transfer
• **hand in glove** **09** in cahoots **11** very closely
• **hand in hand** **12** holding hands **13** with hands held **14** closely related **15** closely together, with hands joined
• **hand on** **04** give **06** pass on, supply **08** transfer, transmit **09** surrender **14** let someone have
• **hand out** **04** dole **07** deal out, dish out, give out, mete out, pass out **08** dispense, share out **10** distribute **11** disseminate
• **hand over** **04** give, pass, turn **05** yield **06** donate, give up, render **07** consign, deliver, present, release **08** transfer, turn over **09** surrender **10** relinquish
• **hollow of hand** **04** vola
• **in hand** **05** put by, ready, spare **07** à la main **08** under way **09** available, in reserve **10** attended to, considered **12** under control **14** being dealt with
• **on the other hand** **03** but **04** then **05** again **12** contrariwise
• **out of hand** ◇ *anagram indicator* **06** at once **11** immediately **12** out of control
• **to hand** **04** near **05** close, handy, ready **06** at hand, nearby **07** ad manum **08** imminent **09** available **10** accessible **13** about to happen
• **try your hand** **03** try **04** seek **06** strive **07** attempt, have a go **09** have a shot, have a stab **10** have a crack **13** see if you can do
• **win hands down** **09** win easily

**15** win effortlessly
• **winning hand** **04** post

## handbag

**04** caba, grip **05** cabas, purse **07** holdall **08** handgrip, reticule **09** clutch bag, flight bag, vanity bag **10** pocketbook **11** shoulder bag

## handbill

**05** flier **06** dodger, letter, notice **07** leaflet **08** circular, flysheet, pamphlet **09** throwaway **12** announcement **13** advertisement

## handbook

**03** ABC **05** guide **06** manual **08** Baedeker **09** companion, guidebook, vade-mecum **10** prospectus **11** enchiridion **12** encheiridion **15** instruction book

## handcuff

**03** tie **04** cuff **06** fasten, fetter, secure **07** manacle, shackle **08** bracelet, snitcher, wristlet

## handcuffs

**05** cuffs, snaps **07** darbies, fetters, mittens, nippers **08** manacles, shackles, snippers **09** bracelets, snitchers, wristlets

## handful

**03** few, rip **04** hank, pain, pest, ripp **05** bunch, pugil **06** bother, little **07** fistful, loolful **08** nieveful, nuisance **10** scattering, smattering, sprinkling **11** small amount, small number **13** pain in the neck **15** thorn in the flesh

## handgun

**03** gat, gun, rod **04** iron **05** piece **06** pistol **07** sidearm **08** culverin, revolver **09** derringer **10** six-shooter **11** blunderbuss
*See also* **gun**

## handicap

**03** hcp **04** curb **05** block, check, limit **06** bridle, burden, defect, hamper, hinder, impair, impede, retard **07** barrier, disable, half-one, penalty **08** drawback, encumber, hold back, obstacle, obstruct, restrict **09** hindrance **10** constraint, disability, impairment, impediment, limitation **11** abnormality, encumbrance, obstruction, restriction, shortcoming **12** disadvantage **14** stumbling-block
• **concede as handicap** **03** owe
• **with adverse handicap** **04** plus
• **with a handicap of** **03** off

## handicapped

**08** disabled **10** challenged **13** disadvantaged, incapacitated

## handicraft

**03** art **05** craft, skill **08** artifice, handwork **09** craftwork, handiwork, scrimshaw **11** scrimshandy, workmanship **12** scrimshander **13** craftsmanship

## handily

**06** at hand, nearly, to hand **07** adeptly, readily **08** adroitly, cleverly, usefully **09** helpfully, skilfully **10** accessibly **11** practically, within reach **12** conveniently

## handiwork

**03** art **04** hand, work **05** craft, doing, skill **06** action, design, result **07** product **08** creation **09** craftwork, invention **10** handicraft, production **11** achievement, artisanship, workmanship **13** craftsmanship **14** responsibility

## handkerchief

**03** rag **04** wipe **05** blind, fogle, hanky, romal, rumal **06** hankie, napkin, tissue **07** bandana, foulard, Kleenex®, nose-rag, orarium, snotrag **08** kerchief, monteith, mouchoir **09** muckender
• **keep in a handkerchief** **04** mail

## handle

**03** bow, lug, paw **04** bail, feel, grip, haft, hilt, hold, knob, name, work **05** brake, drive, grasp, shaft, staff, stale, steal, steel, steer, steil, stele, stock, sweep, touch, treat, wield **06** behave, deal in, finger, fondle, manage, market, pick up, steale, tackle **07** control, discuss, operate, trade in, traffic **08** cope with, deal with, handgrip **09** handstaff, supervise **10** manipulate, plough-tree, take care of **11** plough-stilt **12** be in charge of, do business in

## handling

**07** conduct, running **08** approach, managing **09** direction, operation, treatment **10** discussion, management **11** transaction **12** manipulation **14** administration

## handout

**04** alms, dole **05** gifts, issue, share **07** charity, freebie, leaflet **08** brochure, bulletin, circular, largesse, pamphlet **09** statement **10** free sample, literature **12** press release

## handover

**04** move **05** shift **06** change **07** removal **08** transfer **10** assignment, changeover, conveyance, relocation **12** displacement, transference, transmission **13** transposition

## hand-picked

**05** elect, élite **06** choice, chosen, picked, select **08** screened, selected **09** recherché

## hands

**02** hh

## handsome

**04** fair, fine **05** ample, brave, dishy, hunky, large, noble **06** comely, lavish, seemly **07** elegant, featous, liberal, sizable, stately **08** abundant, becoming, feateous, featuous, generous, gorgeous, gracious, sizeable, suitable **09** bountiful, dignified, featurely, goodfaced, plentiful, unsparing **10** attractive, convenient, personable, unstinting **11** good-looking, magnanimous **12** considerable

## handsomely

**05** amply **06** richly **08** lavishly **09** carefully, liberally **10** abundantly, generously, graciously **11** bountifully, plentifully, unsparingly

**12** munificently, unstintingly
**13** magnanimously

## handwriting
**03** paw **04** fist, hand **05** Neski
**06** Naskhi, Neskhi, niggle, scrawl, script **07** writing **08** half-text, join-hand, printing, scribble **09** autograph, character, court hand, scripture
**10** penmanship **11** calligraphy, chirography, copperplate, running hand **13** secretary hand **15** Lombardic script

## handy
**04** deft, near **05** adept, gemmy, jemmy, ready **06** adroit, at hand, clever, expert, nearly, nimble, to hand, useful **07** helpful, skilful, skilled **08** handsome **09** available, dexterous, practical **10** accessible, convenient, functional, proficient **11** practicable, within reach

## handyman
**05** DIYer **08** factotum **09** odd-jobber, odd-jobman **10** bluejacket **15** Jack-of-all-trades

## hang
**03** fix, nub, sag **04** bend, damn, drop, flit, flop, glue, kill, kilt, lean, loll, pend **05** affix, cling, drape, drift, droop, float, hover, lynch, paste, put up, run up, scrag, stick, strap, swing, trail, truss **06** append, attach, cement, dangle, fasten, impend, linger, remain, string **07** execute, flutter, justify, meaning, stretch, suspend, turn off **08** hang down, string up **09** declivity **10** put to death **11** be suspended
**13** suspercollate **15** send to the gibbet
• **get the hang of** **04** twig **05** grasp, learn **06** fathom, master **08** cotton on **10** comprehend, understand **13** get the knack of
• **hang about** **04** lime, mike, stay **05** haunt **06** dawdle, linger, loiter, remain **07** hang out, persist **08** frequent **09** waste time **10** hang around **13** associate with **15** keep company with
• **hang back** **05** demur, stall **06** recoil **07** shy away **08** hesitate, hold back **10** shrink back, stay behind **11** be reluctant
• **hang down loosely** **03** lop
• **hang fire** **04** stop, wait **05** delay, stall, stick **06** hold on **08** hang back, hesitate, hold back **09** vacillate **13** procrastinate
• **hang on** **04** grip, wait **05** cling, grasp **06** append, clutch, endure, hold on, remain, rest on, turn on **07** carry on, hinge on, hold out, persist **08** continue, depend on, hold fast **09** persevere **14** be contingent on, be determined by **15** be conditional on
• **hang over** **04** loom **06** impend, menace **08** approach, threaten **10** be imminent, overshadow

## hangdog
**05** cowed **06** abject, guilty **07** furtive **08** cringing, defeated, downcast, sneaking, wretched **09** miserable **10** browbeaten, shamefaced

## hanger-on
**05** toady **06** client, lackey, minion, sponge **07** flunkey, sponger **08** follower, henchman, parasite **09** courtling, dependant, dependent, sycophant **10** freeloader

## hanging
**04** drop **05** drape, loose, tapis **06** dossal, dossel, floppy **07** curtain, drapery, draping, frontal, pendant, pendent, pending, pensile, valance **08** dangling, downcast, drooping, flapping, flopping, parament, swinging **09** drop-scene, pendulous, suspended **10** suspending, unattached **11** antependium, unsupported

## hangman
**07** lockman, topsman **08** rascally **09** Jack Ketch **11** nubbing-cove

## hang-out
**03** den **04** dive, home **05** haunt, joint, local, patch **12** meeting-place, watering-hole **14** stamping-ground

## hangover
**08** survival **10** crapulence **12** after-effects, katzenjammer, morning after

## hang-up
**05** block, thing **06** phobia **07** problem **08** fixation, idée fixe, neurosis **09** obsession **10** difficulty, inhibition **11** mental block **13** preoccupation

## hank
**04** coil, fank, loop, roll, tuft **05** catch, piece, skein, twist **06** length **07** handful **08** selvagee

## hanker
**06** linger
• **hanker after, hanker for** **04** want **05** covet, crave **06** desire **07** itch for, long for, pine for, wish for **08** yearn for **09** hunger for, thirst for **10** be dying for **14** set your heart on

## hankering
**04** ache, itch, urge, wish **06** desire, hunger, pining, thirst **07** craving, longing **08** yearning

## hankie, hanky
see **handkerchief**

## hanky-panky
**05** fling **06** affair, tricks **07** carry-on, devilry **08** adultery, cheating, mischief, nonsense, trickery **09** chicanery, deception **10** dishonesty, subterfuge **11** shenanigans **12** bit on the side, machinations **13** fooling around, funny business, jiggery-pokery, slap and tickle **14** how's-your-father, monkey business

## haphazard
◇ *anagram indicator* **04** wild **06** casual, chance, random, randon **07** aimless, wildcat **08** careless, slapdash, slipshod **09** arbitrary, hit-or-miss, irregular, orderless, unplanned **10** disorderly, hitty-missy, tumultuary, willy-nilly **11** promiscuous **12** disorganized, unmethodical, unsystematic **14** indiscriminate, rough-and-tumble

## haphazardly
◇ *anagram indicator* **06** wildly **08** by chance, randomly **10** carelessly, willy-nilly **11** arbitrarily, irregularly **14** unmethodically

## hapless
**06** cursed, jinxed **07** unhappy, unlucky **08** ill-fated, luckless, wretched **09** miserable **10** ill-starred **11** star-crossed, unfortunate

## happen
**02** be **03** hap **04** come, fall, find, go on, pass, tide **05** arise, ensue, hit on, occur, worth **06** appear, arrive, befall, betide, chance, crop up, follow, result, turn up **07** develop, light on, perhaps, turn out **08** become of, bump into, chance on, come true, discover **09** come about, eventuate, run across, stumble on, supervene, take place, transpire **10** come across, come to pass **11** be the fate of, eventualize, materialize **13** come into being, present itself

## happening
**04** case **05** event, scene, thing, weird **06** action, affair, chance **07** episode **08** accident, business, incident, occasion **09** adventure, événement, occurrent **10** experience, occurrence, phenomenon **11** eventuality, fashionable, proceedings **12** circumstance

## happily
**04** lief **06** gladly **07** luckily, merrily, perhaps **08** by chance, heartily, joyfully, joyously **09** agreeably, feliciter, fittingly, gleefully, willingly **10** cheerfully **11** contentedly, delightedly, fortunately, opportunely **12** auspiciously, propitiously **14** providentially

## happiness
**03** joy **04** glee, life, seal, seel, seil, sele **05** bliss **06** gaiety, heaven **07** delight, ecstasy, elation **08** delirium, euphoria, felicity, gladness, pleasure **09** beatitude, enjoyment, eudaemony, hog heaven, merriment, merriness **10** blitheness, cheeriness, eudaemonia, exuberance, joyfulness **11** contentment, good spirits, high spirits **12** cheerfulness

## happy
◇ *anagram indicator* **03** apt, gay **04** glad **05** blest, jolly, lucky, merry, seely **06** blithe, elated, golden, jovial, joyful, joyous, proper **07** blessed, chuffed, content, exalted, fitting, gleeful, halcyon, helpful, pleased, radiant, smiling **08** apposite, carefree, cheerful, ecstatic, euphoric, gruntled, thrilled **09** cock-a-hoop, confident, contented, delighted, delirious, exuberant, fortunate, gratified, high-blest, opportune, overjoyed, rapturous, satisfied, unworried **10** auspicious, beneficial, convenient, favourable, felicitous, propitious, starry-eyed, untroubled **11** appropriate, in a good mood, on cloud nine, over the moon, tickled pink, unconcerned

**12** advantageous, happy as a clam, happy as Larry, light-hearted, walking on air **13** floating on air, in good spirits, in high spirits **15** happy as a sandboy, in seventh heaven, on top of the world • **be happy** **03** ave

**happy-go-lucky**
**06** blithe, casual **08** carefree, cheerful, heedless, laid back, reckless **09** easygoing, unworried **10** insouciant, nonchalant, untroubled **11** improvident, unconcerned **12** devil-may-care, light-hearted **13** irresponsible

**harangue**
**05** orate, spout **06** lay off, preach, sermon, speech, spruik, tirade **07** address, declaim, lecture, oration **08** diatribe, perorate **09** hold forth, speechify **10** peroration, talky-talky **11** exhortation, paternoster **12** talkee-talkee

**harass**
◇ *anagram indicator* **03** dun, nag, vex **04** bait, cark, fret, tire **05** annoy, chevy, chivy, grind, harry, hound, pinch, press, trash, weary, worry **06** argufy, badger, bother, chivvy, harrow, hassle, infest, overdo, pester, pingle, plague, pursue, stress **07** afflict, disturb, dragoon, exhaust, fatigue, provoke, torment, trouble, trounce, turmoil, wear out **08** distract, distress, irritate **09** beleaguer, importune, persecute **10** antagonize, exasperate **11** have it in for **12** put the wind up

**harassed**
◇ *anagram indicator* **05** vexed **06** hunted **07** harried, hassled, hounded, plagued, uptight, worried **08** careworn, pestered, strained, stressed, troubled **09** pressured, tormented **10** distracted, distraught, distressed **11** pressurized, stressed-out, under stress **13** under pressure

**harassment**
**05** grief **06** bother, hassle, molest **07** mobbing, torment, trouble **08** distress, nuisance, vexation **09** annoyance, badgering, pestering **10** irritation, pressuring **11** aggravation, bedevilment, molestation, persecution

**harbinger**
**04** host, omen, sign **06** herald **07** pioneer, portent, warning **09** foretoken, messenger, precursor **10** forerunner, indication **12** avant-courier

**harbour**
◇ *containment indicator* **04** bear, dock, herd, hide, hold, keep, mole, port, quay **05** basin, haven, house, lodge, nurse, reset, wharf **06** foster, marina, refuge, retain, shield, take in **07** believe, cherish, cling to, conceal, imagine, lodging, mooring, nurture, protect, receive, shelter **08** maintain **09** anchorage, entertain

**hard**
**01** H **03** bad, raw, set **04** bony, busy, cold, firm, grim, keen, live, near, real,
sore, true **05** badly, close, cruel, dense, flint, harsh, heavy, horny, irony, rigid, sharp, solid, stern, stiff, stony, tough **06** actual, bitter, busily, crusty, deeply, flinty, keenly, knotty, marble, potent, severe, stingy, strict, strong, tiring, wooden **07** acutely, arduous, austere, callous, certain, closely, compact, complex, eagerly, harmful, harshly, heavily, hornish, intense, onerous, painful, sharply, violent, zealous **08** baffling, definite, diligent, exacting, forceful, forcibly, freezing, intently, involved, narcotic, obdurate, pitiless, powerful, puzzling, reliable, rigorous, ruthless, scleroid, sedulous, severely, steadily, strongly, toilsome, uneasily, verified, vigorous **09** addictive, arduously, assiduous, carefully, compacted, condensed, difficult, earnestly, energetic, intensely, intricate, laborious, merciless, niggardly, resistant, strenuous, unfeeling, unpliable, unsparing, violently **10** compressed, critically, diligently, exhausting, forcefully, hard as iron, hard as rock, implacable, inflexible, oppressive, perplexing, powerfully, tyrannical, undeniable, unpleasant, unyielding, vigorously **11** assiduously, attentively, bewildering, cold-hearted, complicated, constrained, distressing, hard as flint, hard as stone, hard-hearted, hard-working, industrious, insensitive, intractable, laboriously, strenuously, troublesome, unrelenting **12** backbreaking, disagreeable, enthusiastic, habit-forming, impenetrable, indisputable **13** conscientious, energetically, industriously, reverberating, uncomfortable, unsympathetic **14** after a struggle, unquestionable, with difficulty **15** conscientiously • **hard and fast** **03** set **05** fixed, rigid **06** strict **07** binding **08** definite **09** immutable, stringent **10** inflexible, invariable, unchanging **11** unalterable **12** unchangeable **14** uncompromising • **hard black** **02** HB • **hard up** **04** bust, poor, puir **05** broke, short, skint **07** boracic, lacking **08** bankrupt, dirt-poor, in the red, strapped **09** penniless **10** cleaned out, stony broke **11** impecunious, near the bone **12** impoverished, on your uppers **14** on your beam ends **15** strapped for cash • **very hard** **02** HH

**hard-bitten**
**05** tough **06** inured, shrewd **07** callous, cynical **08** ruthless **09** hard-nosed, practical, realistic, toughened **10** hard-boiled, hard-headed **11** down-to-earth **12** case-hardened, matter-of-fact **13** unsentimental

**hard-boiled**
**05** tough **06** brazen **07** callous, cynical **09** practical **10** hard-headed **11** down-to-earth **13** unsentimental

**hard-core**
**05** rigid **07** blatant, diehard, extreme,
staunch **08** explicit **09** dedicated, obstinate, steadfast **12** intransigent **13** dyed-in-the-wool

**harden**
**03** set **04** bake, cake, geal, gird **05** brace, chill, enure, flesh, inure, nerve, steel, train **06** anneal, bronze, deaden, endure, freeze, ossify, season, temper **07** calcify, congeal, fortify, petrify, stiffen, toughen **08** accustom, buttress, concrete, indurate, sclerose, solidify **09** habituate, reinforce, vulcanize **10** case-harden, sclerotize, strengthen, work-harden

**hardened**
**03** set **06** inured **07** bronzed, callous, chilled, chronic, coctile, steeled **08** habitual, obdurate, scleroid, seasoned **09** reprobate, shameless, toughened, unfeeling **10** accustomed, habituated, inveterate **12** incorrigible, irredeemable

**hard-headed**
**05** sharp, tough **06** astute, shrewd **08** pitiless, rational, sensible **09** hard-nosed, practical, pragmatic, realistic **10** cool-headed, hard-bitten, hard-boiled **11** down-to-earth, level-headed, tough-minded **12** businesslike **13** clear-thinking, unsentimental

**hard-hearted**
**04** cold, hard **05** cruel, stony **06** unkind **07** callous, inhuman **08** pitiless, uncaring **09** heartless, merciless, unfeeling **10** flint-heart **11** cold-blooded, unconcerned **12** stony-hearted **13** unsympathetic **14** marble-breasted

**hard-hitting**
**04** bold **05** blunt, frank, tough **06** direct **08** critical, forceful, straight, vigorous **09** unsparing **10** forthright **12** condemnatory **13** no-holds-barred **14** uncompromising

**hardihood**
**04** grit, guts, risk **05** pluck **06** bottle, daring, valour **07** bravery, courage **08** audacity, boldness, rashness **10** enterprise, robustness **11** intrepidity **12** fearlessness, recklessness **13** dauntlessness **15** adventurousness

**hardiness**
**06** valour **07** courage **08** boldness **09** fortitude, toughness **10** resilience, resolution, robustness, ruggedness, sturdiness **11** intrepidity

**hardline**
**05** tough **06** strict **07** extreme **08** militant **10** immoderate, inflexible, unyielding **11** undeviating **12** intransigent **14** uncompromising

**hardly**
**04** jimp, just **06** barely, jimply, uneath **07** harshly, none too **08** not at all, not quite, only just, scarcely, severely **09** almost not, by no means **14** with difficulty

**hardness**
**06** rigour **07** granite **08** coldness, firmness, rigidity, severity

**hard-nosed**
**09** harshness, sternness, toughness
**10** difficulty, inhumanity **12** pitilessness
**13** insensitivity, laboriousness

**hard-nosed**
**05** tough **08** ruthless **09** practical,
realistic **10** hard-bitten, hard-boiled,
hard-headed, no-nonsense
**13** unsentimental

**hard-pressed**
**06** pushed, strait **07** hard put, harried
**08** cornered, harassed **09** in a corner,
overtaxed **10** hard-pushed **11** under
stress, up against it **12** in a tight spot,
overburdened **13** under pressure

**hardship**
**04** need, pain, want **05** trial **06** misery,
murder, rigour, strait, stress
**07** burdens, penance, poverty, trouble
**08** distress **09** adversity, austerity,
grievance, privation, suffering
**10** affliction, difficulty, misfortune
**11** depredation, deprivation,
destitution, tribulation **12** depredations

**hardware**
**03** kit **04** gear **05** stuff, tools **06** outfit,
rig-out, tackle, things **08** articles,
supplies **09** apparatus, equipment,
furniture **10** appliances **11** accessories,
apparelment, ironmongery
**13** accoutrements, paraphernalia

**hard-wearing**
**05** stout, tough **06** rugged, strong,
sturdy **07** durable, lasting **08** well-made
**09** resilient **10** made to last **11** built to
last

**hard-working**
**04** busy, keen **07** zealous **08** diligent,
sedulous **09** assiduous, energetic
**11** industrious **12** enthusiastic
**13** conscientious

**hardy**
**03** fit **04** bold, Olly **05** brave, sound,
stout, tough **06** daring, heroic, plucky,
robust, strong, sturdy, trusty
**07** durable, healthy, spartan, stoical
**08** fearless, impudent, indurate,
intrepid, resolute, stalwart, vigorous
**09** confident, heavy-duty, indurated,
iron-sided, undaunted **10** courageous
**11** indomitable **12** stout-hearted

**hare**
**03** doe, wat **04** baud, bawd, buck,
mara, pika, puss, scut **06** hasten,
malkin, mawkin **07** leveret
**08** baudrons **10** Dolichotis, jack rabbit,
sage rabbit, springhaas **14** snowshoe
rabbit
See also **rabbit**

**hare-brained**
**04** daft, rash, wild **05** giddy, inane, silly
**06** scatty, stupid **07** foolish **08** careless,
crackpot, headlong, heedless, reckless
**09** half-baked **12** ill-conceived
**14** scatterbrained
See also **stupid**

**harem**
**05** serai **06** zenana **08** seraglio
• **room in a harem** **03** oda

**hark**
**04** hear, mark, note **06** listen, notice

**07** give ear, hearken, pay heed,
whisper **12** pay attention
• **hark back** **06** go back, hoicks,
recall, revert **07** regress, try back
**08** remember, turn back **09** recollect

**harlequin**
**04** fool, zany **05** clown, comic, joker
**06** jester **07** buffoon **10** variegated

**harlot**
**03** pro **04** base, lewd, loon, lown, slag,
tart **05** hussy, lowne, tramp, whore
**06** hooker **07** slapper, trollop, wagtail
**08** callgirl, scrubber, strumpet **10** loose
woman, prostitute **11** fallen woman,
working girl **12** streetwalker

**harm**
◇ anagram indicator **03** ill, mar **04** bane,
evil, hurt, loss, pain, ruin **05** abuse,
annoy, scath, spoil, touch, wound,
wreak, wrong **06** damage, impair,
injure, injury, misuse, molest, scathe
**07** blemish, destroy **08** ill-treat,
maltreat **09** adversity, detriment,
prejudice, suffering, vengeance
**10** disserve, impairment, misfortune
**11** destruction, work against **12** do
violence to **15** be detrimental to

**harmful**
**03** bad, ill **04** evil **05** toxic **06** wicked
**07** hurtful, noxious **08** damaging,
wounding **09** dangerous, hazardous,
injurious, poisonous, unhealthy
**10** pernicious **11** deleterious,
destructive, detrimental,
unwholesome

**harmless**
**04** mild, safe **05** silly **06** gentle
**07** anodyne **08** -friendly, hurtless,
innocent, non-toxic **09** blameless,
innocuous, woundless **11** inoffensive

**harmonious**
**06** dulcet, in sync, mellow **07** amiable,
cordial, in synch, musical, tuneful
**08** amicable, balanced, friendly,
matching, peaceful, pleasant,
rhythmic **09** according, agreeable,
congruous, consonant, consonous,
melodious, peaceable **10** Apollonian,
compatible, concinnous, concordant,
concordial, consistent, euphonious,
like-minded **11** co-ordinated,
harmonizing, mellifluous,
sympathetic, symphonious **13** sweet-
sounding

**harmoniously**
**08** amicably **09** agreeably, cordially
**10** compatibly, peacefully
**11** congruously **12** consistently
**13** symmetrically **14** in a balanced way
**15** sympathetically

**harmonization**
**08** matching **09** agreement, balancing
**10** adaptation **11** arrangement **12** co-
ordination **13** accommodation
**14** correspondence, reconciliation

**harmonize**
**02** go **03** mix **04** mesh, rime, suit, tone
**05** adapt, agree, atone, blend, fit in,
match, rhyme, salve **06** accord, attone
**07** arrange, balance, compose,
concord **08** coincide **09** get on with,

reconcile **10** co-ordinate, correspond,
go together **11** accommodate, be
congruent, be congruous

**harmony**
**04** tone, tune **05** amity, chime, music,
peace, unity **06** accord, assent,
melody, unison **07** balance, chiming,
concent, concert, concord, euphony,
keeping, oneness, rapport **08** blending,
diapason, eurythmy, faburden,
goodwill, symmetry, sympathy,
symphony **09** agreement, concentus,
eurhythmy, unanimity **10** concinnity,
conformity, consonance, consonancy
**11** amicability, concurrence,
consistence, consistency, co-
operation, tunefulness **12** co-
ordination, friendliness, thorough bass
**13** compatibility, melodiousness,
understanding **14** correspondence,
correspondency, like-mindedness
**15** mellifluousness
• **in harmony** **08** together **15** never a
cross word
• **out of harmony** **04** ajar

**harness**
**03** use **04** gear, tack, team **05** apply,
hitch, put to, trace **06** employ, straps,
tackle **07** channel, control, exploit,
gearing, hitch up, utilize **08** mobilize,
tackling **09** equipment, make use of
**10** baby-jumper **11** baby-bouncer
**13** accoutrements
• **in harness** **04** busy **06** active, at
work **07** working **08** employed,
together **11** co-operating
**13** collaborating, in co-operation

**harp**
**04** kora, lyre **05** nebel **06** trigon
**07** sambuca **08** clarsach **09** harmonica
**10** mouth organ
• **harp on** **03** nag **05** grind, press,
renew **06** labour, repeat **07** dwell on
**09** go on about, reiterate **11** flog to
death, keep on about **14** go on and on
about

**harpoon**
**03** peg **04** barb, dart **05** arrow, spear
**06** fisgig, fizgig, grains **07** fishgig,
trident **10** toggle iron

**harpsichord**
**06** spinet **07** cembalo, spinnet
**08** clavecin, spinette, virginal
**09** virginals **12** clavicembalo **15** pair of
virginals

**harridan**
**03** hag, nag **04** fury **05** harpy, scold,
shrew, vixen, witch **06** dragon, gorgon,
tartar, virago **07** hell-cat **08** battle-axe,
termagant, Xanthippe

**harried**
**05** beset **07** anxious, hassled, plagued,
ravaged, worried **08** agitated,
bothered, harassed, troubled
**09** pressured, tormented **10** distressed
**11** hard-pressed, pressurized

**harrow**
**04** drag, haro **05** brake, herse, wring
**09** pitch-pole, pitch-poll
• **point of harrow** **04** tine

## harrowing
**05** rough **08** alarming, daunting, lacerant **09** agonizing, traumatic, upsetting **10** disturbing, perturbing, terrifying, tormenting **11** distressing, frightening **12** excruciating, heart-rending, nerve-racking

## harry
**03** nag, vex **05** annoy, hound, worry **06** badger, bother, chivvy, harass, hassle, molest, pester, plague, ravage **07** destroy, disturb, oppress, plunder, torment, trouble **09** persecute **10** pressurize

## harsh
**03** raw **04** bold, grim, hard, iron, rude, wild **05** asper, bleak, cruel, gaudy, gruff, lurid, rough, sharp, showy, stark, stern, stoor, stour, sture **06** barren, bitter, bright, brutal, coarse, flashy, garish, hoarse, savage, severe, shrill, stowre, strict, unkind **07** acerbic, austere, cracked, glaring, grating, hostile, inhuman, jarring, rasping, raucous, spartan **08** abrasive, croaking, dazzling, desolate, gravelly, grinding, guttural, jangling, metallic, pitiless, rigorous, ruthless, scabrous, strident **09** barbarian, barbarous, dissonant, Draconian, inclement, merciless, unfeeling, untunable **10** discordant, unpleasant, untuneable **11** comfortless, ear-piercing **12** inhospitable **13** unsympathetic

## harshly
**04** hard **06** grimly, hardly **07** cruelly, gruffly, roughly, sharply, sternly **08** brutally, hoarsely, severely, unkindly **10** pitilessly, ruthlessly, stridently **11** mercilessly **12** discordantly, unpleasantly

## harshness
**06** rigour **07** tyranny **08** acerbity, acrimony, asperity, hardness, severity, sourness **09** austerity, brutality, ill-temper, roughness, starkness, sternness **10** bitterness, coarseness, strictness **12** abrasiveness

## harum-scarum
**04** rash, wild **05** hasty **06** scatty **07** erratic **08** careless, reckless **09** haphazard, impetuous, imprudent **11** hare-brained, precipitate **12** disorganized **13** ill-considered, irresponsible **14** scatterbrained

## harvest
**02** in **03** mow **04** crop, gain, kirn, pick, rabi, reap **05** amass, glean, horde, pluck, stock, store, strip, yield **06** autumn, effect, fruits, garner, gather, hairst, hockey, obtain, result, return, secure, silage, supply **07** acquire, collect, hopping, produce, product, reaping, returns **08** gather in, ingather, Spätlese, vendange **10** accumulate, collection, harvesting **11** consequence, harvest-home, harvest-time, ingathering **12** accumulation **13** tattie-howking, tattie-lifting

## has
◊ *juxtaposition indicator* **01** 's **04** hath
• **has not, hasn't** **03** an't **04** ain't

## hash
◊ *anagram indicator* **04** hack, mash, mess, stew **05** botch, mince, mix-up **06** bungle, hachis, hotpot, jumble, muddle, scouse **07** goulash, hashish **08** mishmash **09** confusion, lobscouse, pound sign **10** hotchpotch, lob's course **13** mismanagement

## hashish
**03** pot **04** dope, hash, hemp, weed **05** bhang, ganja, grass **08** cannabis **09** marijuana **12** electric puha

## hassium
**02** Hs

## hassle
**03** bug **04** fuss **05** aggro, annoy, fight, harry, hound, trial, upset **06** badger, bother, chivvy, harass, mither, moider, pester, strife **07** dispute, moither, problem, quarrel, trouble, wrangle **08** argument, nuisance, squabble, struggle **09** bickering **10** difficulty **11** altercation **12** disagreement **13** inconvenience

## hassled
**05** vexed **07** harried, hounded, plagued, uptight, worried **08** careworn, harassed, pestered, strained, stressed, troubled **09** pressured, tormented **10** distraught, distressed **11** pressurized, stressed-out, under stress **13** under pressure

## hassock
**04** pouf **06** pouffe **07** kneeler **09** footstool

## haste
**03** hie **04** post, rush **05** hurry, speed **06** bustle, hasten, hustle, scurry **07** urgency **08** alacrity, celerity, despatch, dispatch, fastness, rapidity, rashness, velocity **09** briskness, quickness, swiftness **10** expedience **11** impetuosity **12** carelessness, precipitance, precipitancy, recklessness **13** foolhardiness, impulsiveness, precipitation **15** expeditiousness
• **in haste** **04** fast, rash **05** apace **06** subito **07** hotfoot, quickly, rapidly **08** in a hurry, promptly, speedily **12** straightaway

## hasten
**03** aid, fly, hie, ren, rin, run **04** bolt, dash, help, race, rush, spur, tear, urge **05** boost, hurry, press, speed **06** assist, bustle, go fast, hustle, sprint, step up **07** advance, be quick, forward, hurry up, quicken, speed up **08** despatch, dispatch, expedite, step on it **09** go quickly, hotfoot it, make haste **10** accelerate, get a move on **11** precipitate, push forward **12** step on the gas **15** put your foot down

## hastily
**04** fast **05** apace **06** rashly **07** quickly, rapidly **08** chop-chop, promptly, speedily **09** hurriedly **10** heedlessly, recklessly **11** double-quick, impetuously, impulsively **12** straightaway **13** precipitately

## hasty
**04** fast, rash **05** brief, brisk, eager, quick, rapid, short, swift **06** prompt, rushed, speedy, sudden **07** cursory, hurried, running **08** careless, fleeting, headlong, heedless, reckless **09** desultory, festinate, hotheaded, impatient, impetuous, impulsive, irritable **10** transitory **11** expeditious, perfunctory, precipitant, precipitate, subitaneous, thoughtless

## hat
**03** lid, nab **04** tile **06** titfer **09** headpiece **10** upper crust

---

*Hats include:*

**03** cap, fez, sun, taj, tam, tin, top, toy
**04** doek, hard, hood, kepi, poke, tall
**05** beret, Bronx, busby, derby, mitre, mutch, opera, shako, snood, straw, tammy, toque, tuque
**06** beanie, beaver, biggin, boater, bobble, bonnet, bowler, chapka, cloche, fedora, helmet, kalpak, mob-cap, panama, pileus, sailor, topper, trilby, turban
**07** bicorne, biretta, bycoket, Cossack, flat-cap, Homburg, leghorn, montero, picture, pill-box, pork-pie, stetson, tarbush, tricorn
**08** balmoral, bearskin, chaperon, fool's cap, nightcap, skullcap, sombrero, tarboosh, tricorne, yarmulka
**09** Balaclava, cock's-comb, dunce's cap, forage cap, glengarry, jockey cap, muffin-cap, peaked cap, school cap, sou'wester, stovepipe, sun bonnet, ten-gallon, wideawake
**10** cockernony, college cap, hunting-cap, Kilmarnock, pith helmet, poke-bonnet
**11** baseball cap, crash helmet, deerstalker, mortar-board, tam-o'-shanter, trencher cap
**12** cheesecutter, hummle bonnet, Scotch bonnet

*See also* **straw hat** *under* **straw**
• **shade attached to hat** **04** ugly

## hatch
◊ *anagram indicator* **04** plan, plot **05** breed, brood, cleck, covey, sit on **06** clutch, design, devise, invent, scheme **07** concoct, develop, dream up, exclude, guichet, project, think up **08** conceive, contrive, disclose, incubate **09** formulate, originate

## hatchet
**03** axe **07** chopper, cleaver, machete, mattock, pickaxe **08** tomahawk **09** battle-axe, hedgebill **11** hedging-bill

## hate
**02** ug **04** whit **05** abhor, spite **06** detest, enmity, grudge, hatred, loathe, regret **07** be loath, be sorry, despise, dislike, ill-will, rancour **08** aversion, execrate, loathing, not stand **09** abominate, animosity, apologize, hostility **10** abhorrence, antagonism, bitterness, recoil from, resentment

## hateful

**11** abomination, be reluctant, be unwilling **15** feel revulsion at
• **pet hate** **04** bane, bogy **05** bogle, dread, fiend, poker **06** horror **07** bugbear, rawhead **08** anathema **09** bête noire, nightmare

## hateful

**04** evil, foul, loth, vile **05** loath, nasty **06** cursed, damned, goddam, horrid, odious **07** goddamn, heinous **08** damnable, horrible **09** abhorrent, execrable, goddamned, loathsome, obnoxious, offensive, repellent, repugnant, repulsive, revolting **10** abominable, despicable, detestable, disgusting, unpleasant **11** abhominable **12** contemptible, disagreeable

## hating

**04** miso-

## hatred

**04** hate **05** odium, spite **06** animus, enmity, grudge, phobia **07** despite, disgust, dislike, ill-will, phobism, rancour **08** aversion, bad blood, haterent, loathing **09** animosity, antipathy, hostility, malignity, revulsion **10** abhorrence, antagonism, bitterness, execration, repugnance, resentment **11** abomination, detestation

## haughtily

**07** proudly **08** snootily **10** arrogantly, cavalierly, scornfully **11** imperiously **12** disdainfully **14** contemptuously, superciliously

## haughtiness

**04** airs **05** pride **06** hubris, morgue **07** conceit, disdain, hauteur **08** contempt **09** aloofness, arrogance, insolence, loftiness, pomposity **10** hogen-mogen, snootiness **12** snobbishness

## haughty

**04** bold, haut, high, vain **05** aloof, hault, lofty, proud, surly **06** haught, lordly, snooty, superb, uppish, uppity **07** paughty, stuck-up **08** arrogant, assuming, cavalier, fastuous, orgulous, scornful, snobbish, stomachy, superior, toplofty **09** bigheaded, conceited, imperious, orgillous **10** disdainful, hoity-toity, stomachful, stomachous **11** cavalierish, egotistical, overbearing, patronizing, stiff-necked, toploftical **12** contemptuous, supercilious **13** condescending, high and mighty, self-important, swollen-headed **14** proud-stomached **15** on your high horse

## haul

**03** lug, rug, tow, tug **04** cart, drag, draw, find, gain, harl, hump, loot, mess, move, pull, push, ship, swag, wind **05** booty, bouse, bowse, brail, carry, catch, heave, scoop, slack, touse, touze, towse, towze, trail, trice, wince, winch, yield **06** convey, convoy, spoils **07** plunder, takings **09** transport

## haunches

**04** hips, rump **05** hucks, nates **06** thighs

**07** huckles, hunkers, rear end **08** buttocks

## haunt

**03** den **04** houf, howf, walk **05** beset, curse, ghost, harry, houff, howff, local, recur, spook, visit, worry **06** burden, obsess, plague, prey on, resort, show up **07** disturb, hangout, inhabit, oppress, possess, spright, torment, trouble **08** frequent **09** honky-tonk, patronize **10** rendezvous **11** hang about in, materialize, spend time in **12** hang around in, meeting-place **13** appear often in, favourite spot **14** stamping-ground, visit regularly

## haunted

**05** eerie **06** cursed, jinxed, spooky **07** ghostly, plagued, worried **08** infested, obsessed, troubled **09** hag-ridden, possessed, tormented **10** frequented **11** preoccupied

## haunting

**08** poignant **09** evocative, memorable, nostalgic, recurrent **10** persistent **11** atmospheric **13** unforgettable

## hauteur

**04** airs **05** pride **06** hubris **07** conceit, disdain **08** contempt **09** aloofness, arrogance, insolence, loftiness, pomposity **10** snootiness **11** haughtiness **12** snobbishness

## have

**02** ha', 've **03** ask, bid, con, eat, get, hae, han, own, put, use **04** bear, down, dupe, feel, find, fool, gain, gulp, hold, keep, know, make, meet, must, show, take, tell **05** abide, allow, beget, brook, cheat, drink, enjoy, force, order, ought, stand, trick **06** accept, assert, coerce, compel, devour, diddle, embody, endure, enjoin, esteem, guzzle, oblige, obtain, permit, secure, should, suffer, take in **07** acquire, arrange, be given, cause to, command, consume, contain, deceive, develop, display, embrace, exhibit, express, include, possess, procure, put away, receive, request, require, swallow, swindle, undergo **08** be forced, comprise, contract, manifest, organize, persuade, submit to, talk into, tolerate, tuck into, wolf down **09** be obliged, consist of, encounter, go through, knock back, partake of, put up with, succumb to **10** be required, bring forth, comprehend, experience, suffer from, take part in **11** be compelled, demonstrate, give birth to, incorporate, prevail upon **13** be delivered of, be subjected to, participate in
• **have had it** **06** be lost **10** be defeated, have no hope **11** be exhausted, be in trouble, bite the dust
• **have on** **03** kid, rag **04** hoax, wear **05** chaff, tease, trick **11** be clothed in, be dressed in, have planned, play a joke on **12** have arranged, take for a ride **13** wind someone up **15** pull someone's leg

## haven

**03** bay **04** dock, port **05** basin, hithe, oasis **06** asylum, harbor, refuge

**07** harbour, retreat, shelter **09** anchorage, sanctuary

## haversack

**06** kitbag **08** backpack, knapsack, rucksack

## havoc

◊ anagram indicator **04** Hell, ruin **05** chaos, waste, wreck **06** damage, mayhem **08** disorder, ravaging, shambles, wreckage **09** confusion, ruination **10** desolation, disruption **11** destruction, devastation, rack and ruin **12** depopulation, despoliation

## Hawaii

**02** HI

## hawk

**03** cry **04** bark, eyas, kite, nyas, sell, soar, sore, tout, vend **05** offer, soare, trant **06** falcon, keelie, market, peddle, tarcel, tarsal, tarsel, tassel, tercel **07** buzzard, goshawk, haggard, harrier, tassell, tiercel **08** brancher, huckster **10** eyas-musket **11** sparrowhawk **12** honey buzzard, offer for sale
• **accustom hawk to handling** **03** man

## hawker

**04** spiv **05** crier **06** auceps, cadger, coster, dealer, mugger, pedlar, seller, sutler, trader, vendor **07** camelot, chapman, slanger, tranter **08** huckster **09** barrow-boy, cheap-jack, cheap John **10** colporteur **11** speech-crier **12** costermonger
• **hawker's round** **04** walk

## hawseholes

**04** eyes

## hawthorn

**05** quick, thorn **07** may tree **08** cockspur **09** albespine, albespyne, mayflower, thornbush, thorntree **10** quickthorn, whitethorn

## hay

• **bundle of hay** **03** wad, wap **04** wise, wisp **06** bottle
• **pile of hay** **03** mow **04** cock, rick **05** stack **07** haycock **08** haystack

## haywire

◊ anagram indicator **03** mad **04** wild **05** crazy, wrong **07** chaotic, tangled **08** confused **10** disordered, topsy-turvy **12** disorganized, out of control

## hazard

**04** jump, luck, risk, wage **05** offer, peril, stake, wager **06** bunker, chance, danger, gamble, menace, niffer, risque, submit, threat **07** pitfall, suggest, venture **08** accident, endanger, jeopardy **09** deathtrap, hazardize, put at risk, speculate **10** jeopardize, put forward **12** endangerment **13** put in jeopardy **14** expose to danger

## hazardous

**04** nice **05** hairy, risky **06** chancy, queasy, queazy, tricky, unsafe **07** chancey **08** insecure, menacing, perilous **09** dangerous, difficult, uncertain **10** jeopardous, precarious **11** threatening **13** unpredictable

## hazardously
**07** riskily **10** insecurely, perilously
**11** dangerously, uncertainly
**12** jeopardously, precariously
**13** unpredictably

## haze
**03** fog, rag **04** blur, daze, film, mist,
smog **05** bully, cloud, steam
**06** muddle, vapour **07** dimness
**09** confusion, fogginess, mistiness,
obscurity, smokiness, vagueness
**10** cloudiness **11** uncertainty
**12** bewilderment **14** indistinctness

## hazelnut
**03** cob **06** cobnut **07** filberd, filbert
**12** Barcelona nut

## hazy
◇ *anagram indicator* **03** dim **05** faint,
foggy, fuzzy, milky, misty, muzzy,
smoky, vague **06** cloudy, veiled,
woolly **07** blurred, clouded, misting,
obscure, unclear **08** confused,
nebulous, overcast **09** uncertain **10** ill-
defined, indefinite, indistinct

## head
◇ *head selection indicator* **03** cop, nab,
nob, nut, pow, ras, ren, rin, run, tip,
top, van, wit **04** apex, bean, bent, boss,
cape, conk, face, fizz, foam, fore, gift,
lead, loaf, main, mind, ness, pash,
pate, peak, poll, rise, rule, suds, tête,
wits **05** bonce, brain, caput, chair,
chief, crest, crown, first, flair, fount,
front, froth, guide, knack, onion,
power, prime, ruler, sense, skill, skull,
steer, title **06** bigwig, brains, charge,
climax, crisis, crunch, direct, genius,
govern, height, lather, leader, manage,
mazard, napper, noddle, noggin,
noodle, origin, source, spring, summit,
talent, vertex, wisdom **07** ability,
aptness, bubbles, captain, command,
control, cranium, crumpet, dilemma,
faculty, go first, heading, headway,
highest, leading, manager, obverse,
oversee, premier, supreme, thought,
topknot, topmost **08** aptitude,
calamity, capacity, chairman,
controls, director, dominant, facility,
foremost, governor, headland,
pressure, strength, vanguard, wellhead
**09** attribute, be first in, big cheese,
capitulum, commander, emergency,
endowment, forefront, intellect,
mentality, president, principal,
reasoning, supervise, top banana
**10** administer, capability, chairwoman,
controller, grey matter, headmaster,
leadership, management, pre-eminent,
supervisor, upper crust, upperworks,
wellspring **11** catastrophe,
chairperson, common sense, head
teacher, proficiency, superintend,
supervision, upper storey **12** be in
charge of, directorship, headmistress,
intelligence **13** administrator, be in
control of, critical point,
understanding **14** be at the front of,
superintendent **15** little grey cells,
mental abilities
*See also* **toilet**
• **fox's head** **04** mask
• **go to your head** **06** puff up

**08** befuddle **09** inebriate, make
dizzy, make drunk, make proud,
make woozy **10** intoxicate **12** make
arrogant **13** make conceited
• **head for** **06** aim for **07** make for,
point to, turn for **08** steer for **09** go
towards **11** move towards **13** direct
towards, travel towards
• **head off** ◇ *head deletion indicator*
**04** stop **05** avert **06** cut off, divert
**07** deflect, fend off, prevent, ward off
**09** forestall, intercept, interpose,
intervene, turn aside
• **head over heels** ◇ *reversal down
indicator* **06** wildly **07** utterly
**08** headlong **09** intensely
**10** completely, recklessly, thoroughly
**14** uncontrollably, wholeheartedly
• **head up** **04** lead **06** direct,
manage **12** be in charge of, take
charge of
• **keep your head** **08** keep calm
**12** keep your cool
• **lose your head** ◇ *head deletion
indicator* **04** flap **05** panic **08** freak out
**12** lose your cool
• **muffle head** **03** mob
• **top of head** **04** nole, noll, noul,
nowl **05** noule

## headache
**04** bane, head, pest **05** worry **06** bother,
hassle **07** problem, trouble
**08** migraine, nuisance, splitter,
vexation **09** neuralgia **10** hemicrania
**11** cephalalgia **13** inconvenience, pain
in the neck

## headdress
*Headdresses include:*

**03** cap, taj
**04** coif, head, kell, tête, tire
**05** mitre, tower
**06** cornet, modius, pinner, turban
**07** commode, coronet, kufiyah
**08** coiffure, fontange, fool's cap,
 head-tire, joncanoe, junkanoo,
 kaffiyeh, keffiyeh, ship-tire,
 stephane
**09** John Canoe, John Kanoo,
 porrenger, porringer, war bonnet
**10** lappet-head
**11** tire-valiant
**13** feather-bonnet

*See also* **hat; helmet; scarf**

## headgear
**03** hat, jiz, lid, wig **04** call, caul, gizz,
hood, tiar **05** crown, tiara **07** coronet
**08** silly-how
*See also* **hat; helmet; scarf**

## heading
◇ *head selection indicator* **04** head,
name, text **05** class, point, title
**06** header, rubric **07** bearing, caption,
section, subject **08** category, division,
headline **09** direction **10** capitulary,
descriptor, letterhead **14** classification
*See also* **compass**

## headland
**03** ras **04** cape, head, naze, ness, noup,
scaw, skaw, spit **05** morro, point
**07** headrig **08** foreland **10** promontory

## headless
◇ *head deletion indicator* **07** trunked
**10** acephalous, leaderless
**11** decapitated

## headlong
**04** rash **05** ahead, hasty, steep
**06** rashly, wildly **07** hastily, ramstam,
tantivy **08** careless, full tilt, pell-mell,
proclive, reckless **09** breakneck,
dangerous, head first, hurriedly,
impetuous, impulsive **10** carelessly,
heedlessly, recklessly **11** hair-brained,
hare-brained, impetuously,
impulsively, precipitate, prematurely
**12** hand over head **13** precipitately,
thoughtlessly **15** without thinking

## headman
**05** chief, ruler **06** ataman, leader,
sachem **07** captain **08** caboceer,
mocuddum, mokaddam, muqaddam,
starosta **09** chieftain

## head-on
**06** direct **08** straight **10** straight-on
**11** full-frontal

## headquarters
**02** HQ **04** base, hall **05** depot, SHAPE
**06** armory, Temple **07** station **08** base
camp, Pentagon **10** head office, main
office, officialty, praetorium
**11** command post, nerve centre,
officiality

## headstone
**06** plaque **08** memorial **09** tombstone
**10** gravestone **11** cornerstone

## headstrong
**06** unruly, wilful **07** wayward, willful
**08** contrary, obdurate, perverse,
stubborn **09** obstinate, pigheaded
**10** refractory, self-willed **11** intractable
**12** intransigent, recalcitrant,
ungovernable

## headway
**03** way **06** ground **07** advance
**08** distance, movement, progress
**11** development, improvement

## headwear
*see* **headgear**

## heady
**04** rash **05** nappy **06** potent, strong
**07** huff-cap, rousing, violent
**08** ecstatic, euphoric, exciting,
inflamed **09** thrilling **11** stimulating
**12** exhilarating, intoxicating,
invigorating, overpowering

## heal
**04** cure, hide, mend, sain **05** cover,
salve, treat **06** balsam, garish, physic,
recure, remedy, settle, soothe
**07** assuage, comfort, conceal, guarish,
improve, patch up, restore **08** make
good, make well, palliate, put right, set
right **09** cicatrize, incarnate, reconcile
**10** make better **12** conglutinate

## healer
**03** Asa
*See also* **doctor**

## health
**04** form, heal, tone, trim **05** shape,
state, toast **06** fettle, sanity, vigour

**07** fitness, welfare **08** strength
**09** condition, good shape, soundness,
wellbeing **10** robustness **11** healthiness
**12** constitution **13** good condition
• **good health 04** tope **06** cheers, kia-
ora **07** cheerio, slàinte, wassail
**08** chin-chin, waes hail **09** bene vobis,
drink hail **10** Gesundheit **12** mud in
your eye

**healthily**
**04** well **07** soundly **08** robustly,
strongly **10** vigorously **11** in condition,
in good shape **12** in fine fettle

**healthy**
**03** fit **04** fine, good, hale, well, wise
**05** hardy, jolly, lusty, sound **06** robust,
strong, sturdy **07** bracing, lustick,
prudent **08** blooming, lustique,
sensible, thriving, vigorous
**09** healthful, in the pink, judicious,
wholesome **10** able-bodied, beneficial,
hartie-hale, healthsome, nourishing,
nutritious, refreshing, salubrious,
successful **11** flourishing, in condition,
in good shape, right as rain,
stimulating **12** considerable, fit as a
fiddle, in fine fettle, invigorating, well-
disposed **13** hale and hearty

**heap**
**03** lot, mow, pit, pot **04** a lot, bank,
bing, bulk, cock, load, lots, mass, pile,
pots, raff, raft, rick, ruck, ruin, tass,
tons **05** amass, build, cairn, clamp,
drift, hoard, loads, mound, stack, store
**06** bestow, bundle, burden, confer,
gather, lavish, lumber, midden,
oodles, pile up, plenty, quarry, rickle,
scores, shower, stacks, supply, toorie
**07** collect, company, congest,
cumulus, store up, uphoard
**08** assemble, cumulate, dunghill,
lashings, millions, molehill, mountain
**09** abundance, congeries, embroglio,
great deal, imbroglio, stockpile
**10** accumulate, acervation,
assemblage, coacervate, collection,
quantities **12** accumulation
**13** agglomeration, kitchen midden
**14** clearance cairn

**hear**
◇ *homophone indicator* **03** get, try
**04** heed **05** catch, judge, learn **06** be
told, gather, listen, pick up, take in
**07** examine, find out, inquire, make
out **08** consider, discover, overhear,
perceive **09** ascertain, eavesdrop, latch
onto **10** adjudicate, be informed,
understand **11** investigate **12** pay
attention **13** be in touch with, pass
judgement
• **hearer 03** ear

**hearing**
◇ *homophone indicator* **03** ear **04** case,
news, oyer **05** audit, range, reach,
sound, trial **06** review **07** earshot,
inquest, inquiry **08** audience, audition,
scolding **09** interview, judgement
**10** perception **11** examination,
inquisition **12** adjudication **13** chance
to speak, investigation **15** hearing
distance

**hearsay**
◇ *homophone indicator* **04** buzz, talk
**05** on-dit, rumor, say-so **06** gossip,
report, rumour **10** common talk
**11** word of mouth **12** tittle-tattle
**15** common knowledge

**heart**
◇ *middle selection indicator* **03** hub, nub
**04** core, crux, guts, love, mind, pith,
pity, soul **05** bosom, pluck, spunk
**06** bottle, centre, kernel, marrow,
middle, nature, spirit, vigour, warmth
**07** bravery, concern, courage,
emotion, essence, feeling, heroism,
nucleus, passion, stomach
**08** boldness, keenness, kindness,
sympathy **09** affection, character,
eagerness, fortitude, sentiment,
substance **10** compassion, cordiality,
enthusiasm, resolution, tenderness
**11** disposition, intrepidity,
temperament **12** fearlessness,
quintessence **13** determination,
essential part **14** responsiveness

---

*Heart parts include:*

**04** vein
**05** aorta, valve
**06** artery, atrium, AV node, muscle,
SA node
**07** auricle
**08** vena cava
**09** sinus node, ventricle
**10** epicardium, left atrium,
myocardium
**11** aortic valve, endocardium,
mitral valve, pericardium,
right atrium
**13** bicuspid valve, carotid artery,
left ventricle
**14** ascending aorta, pulmonary
valve, Purkinje fibres, right
ventricle, sino-atrial node,
tricuspid valve
**15** papillary muscle

---

• **at heart** ◇ *insertion indicator*
◇ *middle selection indicator* **06** really
**08** at bottom **09** basically, in essence
**11** essentially **13** fundamentally
• **by heart 03** pat **06** by rote, off pat
**08** verbatim **09** memoriter **10** from
memory **11** word for word **13** parrot-
fashion
• **change of heart 07** rethink
**12** change of mind **14** second
thoughts
• **from the bottom of your heart**
**06** deeply **08** devoutly **09** earnestly,
fervently, sincerely **10** profoundly
**12** passionately
• **heart and soul 06** gladly
**07** eagerly **08** entirely, heartily
**09** devotedly **10** absolutely,
completely **12** unreservedly
**14** wholeheartedly
• **hearts 01** H **10** black Maria
• **lose heart** ◇ *middle deletion
indicator* **08** collapse **13** be
discouraged
• **set your heart on 05** crave, yearn
**06** desire **07** long for, wish for
• **take heart 05** rally **06** buck up,
perk up, revive **07** cheer up

**10** brighten up **12** be encouraged
• **take to heart 09** be moved by, be
upset by **12** be affected by **13** be
disturbed by

**heartache**
**04** pain **05** agony, grief, worry
**06** sorrow **07** anguish, anxiety, despair,
remorse, torment, torture **08** distress
**09** dejection, suffering **10** affliction,
bitterness, heartbreak **11** despondency

**heartbreak**
**04** pain **05** agony, grief **06** misery,
sorrow **07** anguish, despair, sadness
**08** distress **09** dejection, suffering
**10** crève-coeur, desolation

**heartbreaking**
**03** sad **05** cruel, harsh **06** bitter, crying,
tragic **07** painful, pitiful **08** grievous,
poignant **09** agonizing, harrowing
**11** distressing **12** excruciating, heart-
rending **13** disappointing

**heartbroken**
**03** sad **07** crushed, grieved **08** dejected,
desolate, downcast **09** anguished,
miserable, sorrowful, suffering
**10** despondent, dispirited **11** crestfallen
**12** disappointed, disheartened, in low
spirits **13** broken-hearted

**heartburn**
**05** brash **07** pyrosis **09** cardialgy,
dyspepsia **10** cardialgia **11** indigestion

**hearten**
**05** boost, cheer, pep up, rouse **06** buck
up **07** animate, cheer up, comfort,
console, inspire **08** energize, reassure
**09** encourage, stimulate **10** invigorate,
revitalize

**heartening**
**06** moving **08** cheering, pleasing,
touching **09** affecting, rewarding,
uplifting **10** gladdening, gratifying,
satisfying **11** encouraging
**12** heartwarming

**heartfelt**
**04** deep, warm **06** ardent, devout,
honest **07** earnest, fervent, genuine,
sincere **08** profound **09** unfeigned
**12** wholehearted **13** compassionate

**heartily**
◇ *middle selection indicator* **04** upsy,
very **05** agood, upsee, upsey
**06** deeply, gladly, warmly **07** cheerly,
eagerly, hartely, lustily, totally **08** con
amore, entirely **09** cordially, earnestly,
extremely, feelingly, genuinely,
sincerely, staunchly, zealously
**10** absolutely, completely, profoundly,
resolutely, thoroughly, upsey Dutch,
vigorously **11** unfeignedly, upsey
Friese **12** upsey English **13** warm-
heartedly

**heartless**
◇ *middle deletion indicator* **04** cold, hard
**05** cruel, harsh **06** brutal, unkind
**07** callous, inhuman, unmoved
**08** pitiless, ruthless, sardonic, uncaring
**09** merciless, unfeeling **11** cold-
blooded, cold-hearted, hard-hearted
**13** inconsiderate, unsympathetic

## heartlessly

◇ *middle deletion indicator* **06** coldly **07** cruelly, harshly **08** brutally **09** callously **10** pitilessly **11** mercilessly **13** cold-heartedly, hard-heartedly

## heart-rending

**03** sad **06** moving, tragic **07** piteous, pitiful **08** pathetic, poignant **09** affecting, agonizing, harrowing **11** distressing **13** heartbreaking

## heartsick

**03** sad **04** glum **08** dejected, downcast **09** depressed **10** despondent, melancholy **12** disappointed, heavy-hearted

## heart-throb

**04** hunk, idol, star **05** pin-up **09** dreamboat

## heart-to-heart

**08** cosy chat **09** tête-à-tête **10** honest talk **12** friendly talk

## heartwarming

**06** moving **08** cheering, pleasing, touching **09** affecting, rewarding, uplifting **10** gladdening, gratifying, heartening, satisfying **11** encouraging

## hearty

**04** maty, warm **05** ample, bluff, eager, hardy, large, lusty, matey, solid, sound **06** blokey, jovial, robust, stanch, strong **07** affable, cordial, filling, genuine, healthy, sincere, sizable, staunch **08** abundant, blokeish, bouncing, cheerful, effusive, friendly, generous, sizeable, stalwart, vigorous **09** ebullient, energetic, exuberant, heartfelt, unfeigned **10** boisterous, nourishing, nutritious, unreserved **11** substantial, warm-hearted **12** enthusiastic, unrestrained, wholehearted

## heat

◇ *anagram indicator* **03** hot **04** bake, boil, cook, fire, fury, glow, race, rost, stir, warm, zeal **05** anger, annoy, beath, fever, flush, roast, rouse, toast **06** ardour, arouse, calefy, enrage, excite, fervor, reheat, sizzle, warmth, warm up **07** agitate, animate, fervour, firearm, hotness, inflame, passion, swelter, trouble **08** fervency **09** closeness, eagerness, fieriness, heaviness, intensity, microwave, stimulate, vehemence **10** enthusiasm, excitement, sultriness, torridness **11** calefaction, earnestness, impetuosity **12** feverishness **15** high temperature
• **dead heat** **03** tie **04** draw

## heated

**05** angry, fiery, fired **06** bitter, fierce, raging, roused, stormy **07** enraged, excited, furious, intense, stirred, violent **08** animated, frenzied, inflamed, vehement, worked-up **10** passionate, stimulated **11** impassioned, tempestuous

## heatedly

**07** angrily **08** bitterly, fiercely **09** excitedly, furiously, intensely, violently **10** vehemently **12** passionately

## heater

**03** gun **04** fire **06** boiler, pistol **08** Califont®, radiator **09** convector, fan heater, gas heater, immersion **11** solar heater **12** electric fire **13** storage heater **14** central heating, electric heater **15** immersion heater

## heath

**03** Ted **04** bent, fell, ling, moor, muir **05** briar, brier, erica **06** kalmia, manoao, upland **07** arbutus, heather **08** moorland **09** andromeda, bearberry **10** gaultheria

## heathen

**05** pagan **06** ethnic, paynim, savage **07** Gentile, godless, infidel, nations **08** barbaric, idolater **09** barbarian **10** idolatress, idolatrous, philistine, unbeliever **11** irreligious, nullifidian, unbelieving, uncivilized **13** unenlightened

## heather

**04** ling **05** erica **07** calluna **08** foxberry **11** Labrador tea

## heave

◇ *deletion indicator* **03** cat, gag, tug **04** barf, boke, cast, drag, give, haul, honk, hump, hurl, lift, puke, pull, rise, send, sigh, spew, toss **05** chuck, fling, heeze, hitch, hoist, lever, pitch, raise, retch, sling, surge, swell, throw, utter, vomit **06** be sick, let fly, let out, popple, sick up, wallow **07** breathe, bring up, chuck up, chunder, cough up, express, fetch up, throw up, upchuck **08** disgorge, parbreak, swelling **10** egurgitate

## heaven

**03** joy, sky **04** Zion **05** bliss, ether, glory, skies **06** Asgard, on high, Svarga, Swarga, Swerga, utopia, welkin **07** delight, ecstasy, Elysium, nirvana, Olympus, rapture, the blue, up there **08** empyrean, holy city, paradise, Valhalla **09** afterlife, firmament, happiness, hereafter, home of God, next world, Shangri-La **10** abode of God, life to come **12** Land o' the Leal, New Jerusalem, promised land, upper regions **13** elysian fields, fiddler's green, seventh heaven, vault of heaven
*See also* **paradise**
• **the heavens** **03** sky **04** pole **06** region **08** empyrean **12** upper regions

## heavenly

**04** holy, pure **06** cosmic, divine, lovely **07** angelic, blessed, godlike, perfect, sublime, Uranian **08** beatific, blissful, cherubic, empyreal, empyrean, ethereal, etherial, glorious, immortal, seraphic **09** ambrosial, beautiful, celestial, enjoyable, excellent, exquisite, rapturous, spiritual, unearthly, wonderful **10** delightful, enchanting, marvellous **12** other-worldly, supernatural **14** out of this world

## heaven-sent

**05** happy **06** bright, timely **09** fortunate, opportune **10** auspicious, favourable

## heavily

**04** hard, upsy **05** thick, upsee, upsey **06** slowly **07** closely, densely, roundly, solidly, soundly, thickly, too much, utterly **08** clumsily, to excess, woodenly **09** awkwardly, compactly, copiously, painfully, weightily **10** abundantly, completely, decisively, sluggishly, thoroughly, upsey Dutch **11** excessively, laboriously, ponderously, upsey Friese **12** immoderately, upsey English **14** with difficulty

## heaviness

**04** bulk **05** depth, gloom **06** weight **07** density, languor, sadness **08** deadness, severity, solidity **09** dejection, greatness, heftiness, intensity, lassitude, thickness **10** depression, drowsiness, gloominess, melancholy, oppression, sleepiness, somnolence **11** despondency, onerousness, seriousness, weightiness **12** sluggishness **13** ponderousness **14** burdensomeness, oppressiveness

## heavy

**03** big, dry, sad **04** dark, deep, dowf, dull, full, grey, hard, rich, sour, thug **05** bulky, close, dense, Dutch, grave, great, harsh, hefty, humid, laden, large, muggy, sharp, solid, tense, thick, tough **06** clammy, cloudy, clumpy, doughy, drowsy, gloomy, hearty, leaden, loaded, severe, sombre, steamy, sticky, stodgy, strong, sultry, taxing, trying, wooden **07** arduous, awkward, crushed, extreme, filling, hulking, intense, irksome, lumping, lumpish, massive, onerous, pesante, pompous, serious, starchy, tedious, violent, weighty **08** burdened, crushing, downcast, exacting, forceful, grievous, groaning, highbrow, overcast, pedantic, powerful, profound, strained **09** abounding, burdenous, demanding, depressed, difficult, emotional, excessive, important, laborious, miserable, ponderous, sorrowful, squabbish, strenuous, wearisome **10** burdensome, cumbersome, despondent, encumbered, immoderate, inordinate, oppressive, unbearable **11** discouraged, heavy as lead, intemperate, intolerable, substantial, troublesome, weighed down **12** considerable, indigestible, sodden-witted, weighing a ton **13** overindulgent, uninteresting

## heavy-duty

**02** HD **05** solid, sound, tough **06** robust, strong, sturdy **07** abiding, durable, lasting **08** enduring **09** resistant **10** reinforced **11** hard-wearing, long-lasting, substantial

## heavy-handed

**05** harsh, inept, stern **06** clumsy, severe **07** awkward **08** bungling, despotic, forceful, tactless, unsubtle **09** ham-fisted, maladroit **10** autocratic, blundering, cack-handed, oppressive **11** domineering, insensitive, overbearing, thoughtless

**heavy-hearted**
**03** sad **04** glum **06** gloomy, morose **07** crushed, forlorn **08** downcast, mournful **09** depressed, heartsick, miserable, sorrowful **10** despondent, melancholy **11** discouraged, downhearted **12** disappointed, disheartened

**Hebe**
**08** Juventas

**Hebrew**
**03** Heb, Jew
*See also* **alphabet**

**Hebrew alphabet**
*see* **alphabet**

**Hecate**
**06** Trivia

**heckle**
**04** bait, gibe, jeer **05** taunt **06** needle, pester **07** barrack, catcall, disrupt **09** interrupt, shout down

**hectare**
**02** ha

**hectic**
◇ *anagram indicator* **03** mad **04** avid, busy, fast, wild **05** manic **06** heated, rushed **07** chaotic, excited, flushed, frantic, furious **08** agitated, bustling, feverish, frenetic, frenzied **09** turbulent **10** tumultuous **11** consumptive

**hector**
**03** nag **04** huff **05** annoy, bully, worry **06** badger, chivvy, harass, menace **07** bluster, provoke **08** browbeat, bulldoze, bullyrag, threaten **09** blusterer **10** intimidate

**hedge**
◇ *containment indicator* **03** haw, hay, low **04** duck, dyke, edge **05** cover, dodge, evade, fence, guard, hem in, limit, mound, stall **06** insure, lay off, raddle, screen, shield, waffle, zareba, zariba, zereba, zeriba **07** barrier, confine, debased, enclose, fortify, ox-fence, protect, quibble, shuffle, wayside, zareeba **08** boundary, encircle, hedgerow, obstruct, quickset, restrict, sepiment, sidestep, surround **09** safeguard, temporize, windbreak **10** equivocate, protection **11** prevaricate **13** sit on the fence
• **escape through hedge** **04** mews, muse **05** meuse

**hedgehog**
**06** urchin **08** herisson **11** tiggywinkle

**hedonism**
**09** dolce vita, epicurism **10** sensualism, sensuality, sybaritism **12** Epicureanism **13** gratification, luxuriousness **14** self-indulgence, voluptuousness **15** pleasure-seeking

**hedonist**
**07** epicure **08** sybarite **09** bon vivant,

bon viveur, epicurean **10** sensualist, voluptuary **14** pleasure-seeker

**hedonistic**
**09** epicurean, luxurious, sybaritic **10** voluptuous **13** self-indulgent **15** pleasure-seeking

**heed**
**03** ear **04** care, gaum, gorm, mark, mind, note, obey, reak, reck, tent **06** follow, listen, notice, regard **07** caution, hearken, observe, respect, thought **08** attend to, consider **09** attention **10** bear in mind, observance, take note of **11** heedfulness **12** take notice of, watchfulness **13** animadversion, consideration **14** pay attention to **15** take into account

**heedful**
**04** wary **05** chary **07** careful, jealous, mindful, prudent **08** cautious, vigilant, watchful **09** advertent, attentive, observant, regardful **10** respective **11** circumspect

**heedless**
**04** rash **06** blithe, remiss, unwary **08** careless, reckless, tactless, uncaring **09** foolhardy, forgetful, negligent, oblivious, unguarded, unmindful **10** incautious, indiscreet, insouciant, regardless, unthinking **11** hair-brained, hare-brained, inattentive, inobservant, precipitate, thoughtless, unconcerned, unobservant **12** absent-minded **13** inconsiderate, irresponsible

**heedlessly**
**06** rashly **09** blindfold **10** carelessly, recklessly **11** negligently **12** neglectingly, unthinkingly **13** inattentively, thoughtlessly

**heel**
**03** cad, cow, rat, tip **04** bank, hele, hide, knob, lean, list, puke, seel, spur, sway, tilt **05** angle, cover, slant, slope **06** ratbag, toerag, wretch **07** conceal, incline, ratfink **08** lean over, stiletto

**hefty**
**03** big **04** hard, huge, very **05** ample, beefy, bulky, burly, heavy, large, solid, stout **06** brawny, robust, strong **07** awkward, hulking, immense, massive, sizable, violent, weighty **08** abundant, colossal, forceful, generous, muscular, powerful, sizeable, unwieldy, vigorous **09** strapping **11** substantial **12** considerable

**Hegira**
• **in the year of Hegira** **02** AH

**heifer**
**04** quey

**height**
**01** H **02** ht **03** alp, sum, top, tor **04** apex, hill, peak, torr **05** crest, crown, level, limit, pitch **06** apogee, climax, summit, vertex, zenith **07** ceiling, hill top, maximum, stature **08** altitude, eminence, highness, pinnacle, tallness, ultimate **09** elevation, extremity, loftiness,

uttermost **10** perfection **11** culmination, mountain top, sublimation

**heighten**
**04** lift **05** add to, boost, elate, exalt, raise **07** amplify, augment, build up, elevate, enhance, improve, magnify, sharpen **08** increase **09** intensify **10** strengthen

**heinous**
**04** evil **05** awful, grave **06** odious, wicked **07** hateful, hideous, vicious **08** flagrant, infamous, shocking **09** abhorrent, atrocious, execrable, loathsome, monstrous, nefarious, revolting, unnatural **10** abominable, despicable, detestable, facinorous, iniquitous, outrageous, villainous **11** unspeakable **12** contemptible

**heir, heiress**
**03** her **05** scion **06** co-heir, tanist **07** fortune, legatee **08** apparent, atheling, parcener **09** inheritor, successor **10** cesarevich, cesarewich, coparcener, fellow-heir, inheritrix, next in line, substitute **11** beneficiary, cesarevitch, cesarewitch, coinheritor, crown prince, inheritress, tsesarevich, tsesarewich **12** tsesarevitch, tsesarewitch **13** crown princess

**heist**
*see* **robbery**

**held**
• **held by, held in** ◇ *insertion indicator* ◇ *hidden indicator*

**helicopter**
**05** hover **06** copter **07** chopper, medevac **08** sikorsky **09** egg beater **10** rotorcraft, rotor plane, whirlybird **12** air ambulance

**Helios**
**03** Sol

**helium**
**02** He

**helix**
**04** coil, curl, loop **05** screw, twist, whorl **06** spiral, volute **07** wreathe **08** curlicue **09** corkscrew

**hell**
**03** Dis, pit **04** Ades, fire, heck, hele, ruin **05** abyss, agony, below, Hades, havoc, Sheol **06** Erebus, misery, ordeal, Tophet, uproar **07** Abaddon, Acheron, anguish, Gehenna, inferno, the heck, torment, torture **08** Tartarus, the deuce **09** commotion, down there, Malebolge, nightmare, perdition, suffering, the blazes **10** other place, the dickens, underworld **11** netherworld, tribulation **12** lower regions, wretchedness **13** bottomless pit, nether regions **15** abode of the devil, infernal regions
• **give someone hell** **03** vex **04** beat, flog **05** annoy, scold **06** harass, pester, punish **07** tell off, torment, trouble **08** chastise **09** criticize **13** tear off a strip
• **hell for leather** **06** rashly, wildly **07** quickly, rapidly, swiftly **08** very fast **09** hurriedly, like crazy, post-haste

**hell-bent**

10 recklessly 11 very quickly
13 precipitately 15 like the clappers
• **raise hell** 07 run riot 09 be furious
10 hit the roof 11 be very angry, make
trouble 13 object noisily, protest loudly
15 cause a commotion

**hell-bent**

03 set 04 bent 05 fixed 06 dogged,
intent 07 settled 08 obdurate, resolved
09 tenacious 10 determined, inflexible,
unwavering 12 intransigent,
unhesitating

**hellish**

◊ *anagram indicator* 04 very 05 cruel,
nasty 06 savage, wicked 07 awfully,
demonic, satanic, Stygian 08 accursed,
barbaric, damnable, devilish, dreadful,
fiendish, infernal 09 atrocious,
execrable, extremely, immensely,
intensely, monstrous, nefarious
10 abominable, diabolical, dreadfully,
unpleasant 12 disagreeable,
unpleasantly 13 exceptionally

**hello**

02 hi, yo 04 g'day, hiya 05 hallo, hillo,
howdy, hullo 06 holloa 07 bonjour,
welcome 08 chin-chin 09 greetings
10 buon giorno 11 good evening, good
morning 13 good afternoon

**helm**

05 steer, stern, timon, wheel 06 direct,
helmet, rudder, tiller
• **at the helm** 07 leading 08 in charge
09 directing, in command, in control
11 in the saddle 15 holding the reins

**helmet**

03 pot, top 04 topi 05 armet, salet,
topee 06 basnet, casque, heaume,
morion, murren, murrin, sallet, tin hat
07 basinet, hard hat, morrion, murrion,
pith hat, skid lid, sola hat 08 burganet,
burgonet, knapscal, sola topi
09 Balaclava, headpiece, knapscull,
knapskull, sola topee 11 pickelhaube

**helmsman**

03 cox 08 coxswain, timoneer
09 cockswain, steersman 10 steersmate

**help**

03 aid, use 04 back, balm, cure, ease,
heal 05 avail, boost, guide, nurse,
salve, serve, stead 06 advice, assist,
backup, helper, kick in, Mrs Mop,
oblige, relief, remedy, soothe, worker
07 assuage, backing, benefit, be of use,
bestead, charity, cleaner, further,
healing, improve, promote, relieve,
service, stand by, succour, support,
utility 08 adjuvant, employee,
guidance, home help, mitigate
09 advantage, alleviate, charwoman,
co-operate, do your bit, encourage,
lend a hand, moderator 10 ameliorate,
assistance, contribute, facilitate,
mitigation, rally round 11 alleviation,
collaborate, co-operation, helping
hand, improvement, restorative
12 amelioration, contribute to, give a
boost to, shot in the arm
13 collaboration, encouragement 14 be
of assistance, do something for
15 tower of strength

• **call for help** 03 SOS 06 mayday
09 au secours 14 distress signal
• **cannot help** 14 be unable to stop

**helper**

02 PA 03 aid 04 aide, ally, maid, mate
06 deputy, second, worker 07 partner,
servant 08 adjutant, co-worker,
employee, helpmate, treasure
09 assistant, associate, attendant,
auxiliary, colleague, man Friday,
paraclete, supporter 10 accomplice,
girl Friday, subsidiary 11 subordinate
12 collaborator, right-hand man
14 right-hand woman 15 second-in-
command

**helpful**

04 kind 05 of use 06 caring, second,
useful 08 friendly, obliging, valuable
09 of service, practical 10 beneficial,
benevolent, charitable, profitable,
supportive, worthwhile 11 considerate,
co-operative, furthersome,
neighbourly, sympathetic
12 advantageous, constructive,
instrumental 13 accommodating

**helpfully**

06 kindly 08 usefully 10 obligingly
12 conveniently, reassuringly
13 considerately 15 sympathetically

**helping**

05 order, piece, share 06 aidant,
amount, dollop, ration 07 bowlful,
portion, serving 08 adjuvant, plateful,
spoonful 09 assistant, auxiliary
12 contributive

**helpless**

04 weak 06 feeble, infirm 07 exposed,
forlorn 08 clueless, desolate, disabled,
feckless, impotent 09 abandoned,
dependent, destitute, incapable,
paralysed, powerless 10 friendless,
high and dry, vulnerable
11 debilitated, defenceless,
incompetent, unprotected

**helplessly**

06 feebly, weakly 10 desolately,
impotently, vulnerably 11 powerlessly
13 defencelessly

**helpmate**

04 wife 06 helper, spouse 07 consort,
husband, partner, support 08 helpmeet
09 assistant, associate, companion,
other half 10 better half

**helter-skelter**

◊ *anagram indicator* 06 random, rashly,
wildly 07 hastily, jumbled, muddled
08 confused, headlong, pell-mell
09 haphazard, hit-or-miss, hurriedly
10 carelessly, confusedly, disordered,
recklessly, topsy-turvy 11 impulsively
12 disorganized, like hey-go-mad,
tumultuously, unsystematic

**hem**

04 bind, edge, fold, trim 05 frill, skirt
06 border, edging, fringe, margin
07 fimbria, flounce, valance
08 trimming 09 fimbriate
• **hem in** 04 trap 05 box in, limit, pen
in 06 pocket, shut in 07 close in,
confine, enclose, hedge in 08 restrict,
surround 09 constrain

**hemispherical**

04 domy 07 rose-cut

**hemlock**

05 Tsuga 07 cowbane 10 insane root
13 water dropwort

**hemp**

03 tow 04 pita, sida, sunn 05 abaca,
bhang, dagga, ganja, hards, hurds,
murva 06 fimble, moorva 07 boneset,
hashish 08 agrimony, cannabis,
hasheesh, henequen, henequin,
heniquin, love-drug, neckweed
09 marihuana, marijuana, true dagga
10 crotalaria 13 Pantagruelion
*See also* **cannabis**

**hen**

04 balk 05 biddy, chook, layer, poule
06 Cochin, eirack, female, pullet
07 chookie, clocker, Partlet, poulard
08 Langshan 09 incubator
10 Australorp 11 Cochin-China,
Spanish fowl
*See also* **chicken**

**hence**

04 away!, ergo, thus 06 begone!
09 therefore 11 accordingly
12 consequently 13 for this reason
14 as a consequence

**henceforth**

05 hence 09 from now on, hereafter
11 hereinafter, in the future
12 henceforward 14 from this time on

**henchman, henchwoman**

04 aide, page 05 crony, heavy 06 hit
man, lackey, minder, minion
07 servant 08 follower, sidekick
09 associate, attendant, bodyguard,
supporter, underling 10 hatchet man,
led captain 11 subordinate 12 right-
hand man 14 right-hand woman

**henna**

08 camphire

**henpecked**

04 meek 05 timid 07 bullied
08 badgered, harassed, pestered
09 dominated, hag-ridden, tormented
10 browbeaten, criticized, subjugated,
woman-tired 11 intimidated

**Henry**

01 H, O 03 Hal

**Hephaestus**

06 Vulcan

**her**

04 elle

**Hera**

04 Juno

**herald**

04 Lyon, omen, show, sign 05 augur,
crier, token, usher 06 augury, Hermes,
signal 07 courier, fanfare, portend,
portent, precede, presage, promise,
trumpet, usher in 08 announce,
blazoner, indicate, Lord Lyon,
proclaim 09 advertise, announcer,
broadcast, harbinger, make known,
messenger, precursor, publicize
10 forerunner, foreshadow, indication,
king-at-arms, king-of-arms, Lyon-at-
arms, make public, pave the way,

proclaimer, promulgate **14** Lyon King of arms

## heraldry

*Heraldry terms include:*

**02** or
**04** arms, fess, lion, orle, pall, pile, semé, urdé, vert
**05** azure, badge, crest, eagle, eisen, fesse, field, gules, motto, sable, tawny, tenné, undee
**06** argent, bezant, blazon, canton, centre, charge, dexter, emblem, ensign, helmet, impale, mullet, murrey, sejant, shield, volant, wivern
**07** annulet, bordure, cendreé, chevron, dormant, griffin, gyronny, lozenge, martlet, passant, phoenix, quarter, rampant, regalia, roundel, saltire, statant, tierced, unicorn, urinant
**08** addorsed, antelope, cabother, couchant, insignia, mantling, sanguine, sinister, tincture
**09** carnation, displayed, hatchment
**10** camelopard, cinquefoil, coat of arms, cockatrice, emblazonry, escutcheon, fleur-de-lis, quatrefoil, supporters
**11** bleu celeste, compartment
**15** regaliamantling

## herb

**04** forb, weed, wort **07** olitory

*Herbs and spices include:*

**03** bay, nep, nip
**04** balm, dill, mace, mint, sage
**05** anise, basil, cumin, curry, thyme
**06** borage, cassia, chilli, chives, cloves, fennel, garlic, ginger, hyssop, lovage, nutmeg, pepper, savory, sesame, sorrel
**07** catmint, cayenne, chervil, comfrey, mustard, oregano, paprika, parsley, pimento, saffron, vanilla
**08** allspice, angelica, bergamot, camomile, cardamom, cardamum, cinnamon, lavender, marjoram, rosemary, tarragon, turmeric
**09** chamomile, coriander, fenugreek, hypericum, lemon balm
**10** gaillardia
**12** caraway seeds
**13** cayenne pepper

• **magic herb 04** moly
**13** Pantagruelion

## herbal tea

*see* tea

## herbicide

**06** diquat **08** paraquat, simazine
**10** glyphosate **11** glufosinate, graminicide

## herculean

**04** hard, huge **05** great, heavy, large, tough **06** strong **07** arduous, mammoth, massive, onerous **08** colossal, daunting, enormous, exacting, gigantic, powerful, toilsome
**09** demanding, difficult, gruelling,

laborious, strenuous **10** exhausting, formidable, tremendous

## herd

**03** mob **04** band, goad, host, lead, mass, pack, race, rout, tail, urge
**05** crowd, crush, drive, drove, flock, force, guide, horde, meiny, plebs, press, rally, swarm, troop **06** gather, huddle, meiney, meinie, menyie, muster, proles, rabble, throng
**07** collect, round up, sounder, wrangle
**08** assemble, riff-raff, shepherd **09** look after, multitude, the masses
**10** congregate, take care of **11** get together

## herdsman

**06** cowman, drover **07** cowherd, grazier, vaquero **08** shepherd, stockman, wrangler **10** stock rider

## here

**02** in **03** ici, now **05** adsum **06** around
**07** present **10** at this time **11** at this place, at this point, at this stage, in this place, to this place
• **here is 04** ecco

## hereabouts

**04** here **08** near here **10** around here
**11** in this place **12** in these parts

## hereafter

**05** hence, later **06** beyond, heaven
**08** paradise **09** afterlife, from now on, next world **10** eventually, henceforth, life to come **11** in the future
**12** henceforward **13** elysian fields
**14** life after death

## here and there

**05** about, among **06** thinly **08** to and fro
**11** irregularly **12** sporadically **15** in various places

## hereditary

**04** left **06** family, inborn, inbred, innate, willed **07** genetic, natural
**08** inherent **09** ancestral, inherited
**10** bequeathed, congenital, handed down **11** transferred **13** transmissible
• **hereditary factor 02** id **04** gene

## heredity

**03** DNA **04** gene **05** genes **08** genetics
**11** chromosomes, inheritance
**13** genetic make-up

## herein

◊ *containment indicator* **06** within
**11** contained in **13** in this respect

## heresy

**05** error **06** schism **07** atheism, dissent
**08** apostasy, Docetism, unbelief
**09** blasphemy, Montanism, recusance
**10** dissension, dissidence, heterodoxy, scepticism, separatism **11** agnosticism, revisionism, unorthodoxy **12** free-thinking, sectarianism
**13** nonconformity

## heretic

**06** zendik **07** atheist, sceptic
**08** agnostic, apostate, recusant, renegade **09** dissenter, dissident, miscreant, sectarian **10** schismatic, separatist, unbeliever **11** free-thinker, revisionist **13** nonconformist

## heretical

**07** impious **08** agnostic, recusant, renegade **09** atheistic, dissident, heterodox, sceptical, sectarian
**10** dissenting, irreverent, schismatic, separatist, unorthodox
**11** blasphemous, revisionist, unbelieving **12** free-thinking, iconoclastic **13** rationalistic

## heritage

**03** due, lot **04** past **05** share **06** estate, family, legacy **07** bequest, culture, descent, dynasty, history, lineage, portion **08** ancestry, cultural
**09** endowment, tradition
**10** background, birthright, extraction, traditions **11** inheritance
*See also* **world**

## hermaphrodite

**08** bisexual **09** androgyne, polygamic
**10** monoecious **11** androgynous, monoclinous, protogynous
**12** heterogamous **13** gynodioecious, male and female **14** androdioecious

## Hermes

**07** Mercury

## hermetic

**04** shut **06** sealed **07** magical, obscure
**08** abstruse, airtight **10** hermetical, watertight

## hermit

**04** monk **05** loner, Peter **07** ancress, ascetic, eremite, pagurid, recluse, stylite **08** beadsman, marabout, pagurian, sannyasi, solitary
**09** anchoress, anchorite, pillarist
**10** robber crab, solitarian
**11** Hieronymite, pillar-saint, soldier crab

## hermitage

**05** haven **06** ashram, asylum, refuge
**07** hideout, retreat, shelter **08** cloister, hideaway **09** sanctuary **11** hiding-place

## hero

**03** cid, god **04** idol, lead, lion, star
**05** ideal, pin-up, sheik **06** eponym, sheikh, victor **07** demigod, good guy, paragon **08** cavalier, champion, male lead **09** celebrity, conqueror, lead actor, superstar **10** heart-throb **11** brave person, demigoddess, protagonist
**12** leading actor **15** leading male part, leading male role, person of courage

*Heroes include:*

**04** Ajax, **Bond** (James), **Dare** (Dan), **Hood** (Robin)
**05** Bruce (Robert), **El Cid**, **Jason**, **Jones** (Indiana), **Kelly** (Ned), **Zorro**
**06** Arthur, **Barton** (Dick), **Batman**, **Brutus** (Lucius Junius), **Rogers** (Buck), **Sharpe** (Richard), **Tarzan**
**07** Beowulf, **Biggles**, **Glyn Dwr** (Owain), **Ivanhoe**, **Perseus**, **Theseus**, **Wallace** (William)
**08** Achilles, **Heracles**, **Hercules**, **Lancelot**, **Odysseus**, **Superman**
**09** Churchill (Sir Winston), **D'Artagnan**, **Glendower** (Owain), **MacGregor** (Rob Roy), **Schindler** (Oskar), **Spiderman**
**10** Coriolanus, **Cú Chulainn**,

Hornblower (Horatio), **Little John**, **Lone Ranger**, **Richthofen** (Manfred von 'the Red Baron')

11 **Bellerophon**, **Finn MacCool**, **Wilberforce** (William)

14 **Finn MacCumhail**, **Robert the Bruce**

15 **Three Musketeers**

## heroic
04 bold, epic 05 brave, noble 06 daring 07 doughty, gallant, Homeric, valiant 08 fearless, intrepid, selfless, valorous 09 dauntless, undaunted 10 chivalrous, courageous, determined 11 adventurous, lion-hearted 12 stout-hearted

## heroically
05 nobly 06 boldly 07 bravely 09 valiantly 10 fearlessly, selflessly 11 dauntlessly 12 courageously

## heroin
01 H 04 junk, scag, skag, snow 05 horse, shmek, smack, sugar 07 schmeck 10 white stuff 11 diamorphine

## heroine
04 diva, idol, lead, star 05 ideal, pin-up 06 Amazon, victor 07 goddess, paragon 08 champion 09 celebrity, conqueror, lead actor, superstar 10 brave woman, female lead, prima donna 11 leading lady, protagonist 14 leading actress, prima ballerina, woman of courage

*Heroines include:*

04 **Lane** (Lois)
05 **Croft** (Lara), **Szabo** (Violette)
06 **Cavell** (Edith), **Judith**, **Ripley** (Ellen)
07 **Ariadne**, **Darling** (Grace), **Deirdre**
08 **Antigone**, **Atalanta**, **Boadicea**, **Boudicca**, **Penelope**
09 **Cassandra**, **Joan of Arc**, **Macdonald** (Flora), **Snow White**
10 **Cinderella**
11 **Helen of Troy**, **Nightingale** (Florence), **Wonderwoman**

## heroism
06 daring, valour 07 bravery, courage, prowess 08 boldness, chivalry 09 fortitude, gallantry 11 doughtiness, intrepidity 12 fearlessness, selflessness 13 dauntlessness, determination 14 courageousness 15 lion-heartedness

## heron
04 hern 05 Ardea, egret 07 bittern, squacco 08 boatbill, hernshaw, heronsew 09 heronshaw

## hero-worship
07 worship 09 adoration, adulation 10 admiration, exaltation, veneration 11 deification, idolization 12 idealization 13 glorification

## herring
04 brit, sild 05 capon 06 kipper, matjes, mattie 07 anchovy, bloater, clupeid, maatjes, rollmop, soldier 08 buckling, clupeoid, menhaden, sea stick 09 gaspereau 10 mossbunker 12 Norfolk capon

• **measure of herring** 04 cran, maze, warp 05 maise, maize, mease

## hesitancy
05 delay, demur, doubt, qualm 08 scruples, wavering 09 misgiving 10 indecision, reluctance, stammering 11 reservation, uncertainty 12 doubtfulness, irresolution 13 unwillingness 14 disinclination

## hesitant
03 shy 04 wary 05 timid 06 unsure 07 dubious, halting 08 delaying, doubtful, stalling, wavering 09 demurring, reluctant, sceptical, tentative, uncertain, unwilling 10 hesitating, indecisive, irresolute, stammering, stuttering 11 disinclined, half-hearted, vacillating

## hesitate
04 halt, wait 05 delay, demur, doubt, pause, stall, waver 06 boggle, dicker, dither, falter, mammer, tarrow, teeter 07 balance, scruple, stammer, stumble, stutter, swither, um and ah 08 dubitate, hang back, hang fire, hold back 09 hum and haw, vacillate 10 dilly-dally, shrink from, think twice 11 be reluctant, be uncertain, be unwilling 12 shilly-shally 13 be disinclined

## hesitation
05 delay, demur, doubt, dwell, pause, qualm 06 demure, qualms 07 scruple, waiting 08 misdoubt, scruples, stalling, wavering 09 faltering, hesitance, stumbling 10 cunctation, indecision, misgivings, reluctance, scepticism, stammering, stuttering, unsureness 11 hanging-back, holding-back, uncertainty, vacillation 12 doubtfulness, irresolution 13 dilly-dallying, unwillingness 14 disinclination, second thoughts 15 shilly-shallying

• **expression of hesitation** 02 er, ha, um, ur 03 erm, hah 04 well

## Hestia
05 Vesta

## heterodox
07 unsound 09 dissident, heretical 10 dissenting, schismatic, unorthodox 11 revisionist 12 free-thinking, iconoclastic

## heterogeneous
05 mixed 06 motley, unlike, varied 07 diverse, opposed, piebald, pyebald 08 assorted, catholic, contrary 09 different, disparate, divergent, multiform, unrelated 10 contrasted, discrepant, dissimilar 11 diversified, incongruous, polymorphic 13 miscellaneous

## heterogeneously
09 diversely 10 contrarily 11 differently, disparately, divergently 12 dissimilarly 13 incongruously

## heterosexual
03 het 06 hetero 07 breeder 08 straight

## het up
05 angry, tense, upset 07 anxious, in a rage, uptight, worried, wound up

08 agitated, offended, stressed, worked up 09 indignant, resentful 11 stressed-out 14 beside yourself

## hew
03 axe, cut, dye, hag, hue, lop, saw 04 chip, chop, fell, form, hack, make, tint, trim 05 carve, model, prune, sever, shape, split 06 chisel, colour, hammer, sculpt 07 fashion, whittle 09 sculpture 10 appearance

## heyday
04 peak 05 bloom, flush, prime 06 summer 08 boom time, pinnacle 09 flowering, golden age 11 culmination

## hiatus
03 gap 04 lull, rest, rift, void 05 blank, break, chasm, lapse, pause, space 06 breach, defect, lacuna 07 opening 08 aperture, interval 10 suspension 12 interruption 13 discontinuity 14 discontinuance

## hibernate
06 winter

## hibernating
06 torpid 07 dormant 08 latitant

## hibiscus
04 okra 07 roselle, rozelle 10 cotton tree, rose mallow 12 rose of Sharon

## hiccup
03 hic, yex 04 snag, yesk 05 block, catch, check, delay, hitch 06 glitch, hold-up, mishap 07 barrier, problem, setback, trouble 08 drawback, obstacle 09 hindrance 10 difficulty, impediment 11 obstruction

## hick
*see* **bumpkin**

## hickory
05 pecan 08 shagbark 09 scaly-bark, shellbark

## hidden
◇ *hidden indicator* 04 dark, dern 05 close, dearn 06 arcane, covert, latent, masked, occult, secret, unseen, veiled 07 covered, cryptic, obscure, unknown 08 abstruse, mystical, shrouded, ulterior 09 concealed, disguised, invisible, recondite 10 indistinct, mysterious, out of sight, under wraps 11 camouflaged, clandestine 12 subterranean, under hatches

## hide
◇ *containment indicator* ◇ *hidden indicator* 03 fur 04 buff, bury, coat, fell, flog, heal, heel, hele, hell, lurk, mask, pell, pelt, robe, skin, stow, veil, whip, wrap 05 cache, cloak, cloud, cover, earth, slink, store 06 darken, encave, fleece, hole up, incave, lie low, screen, shadow, shroud, spetch 07 abscond, conceal, eclipse, envelop, flaught, leather, obscure, secrete, shelter, tappice 08 bottle up, disguise, keep dark, lie doggo, lock away, obstruct, suppress, withhold 09 dissemble, stash away, take cover 10 camouflage, go to ground, keep secret 12 go into hiding 13 draw a veil

**hideaway**

over, put out of sight **14** keep out of sight, keep under wraps, lay a false scent **15** conceal yourself, cover your tracks, keep a low profile

**hideaway**
**03** den **04** hole, lair, nest **05** haven **06** refuge **07** hideout, retreat, shelter **08** cloister, fugitive **09** hermitage, sanctuary **11** hiding-place

**hidebound**
**03** set **05** fixed, rigid **06** narrow **07** bigoted **08** stubborn **09** obstinate **10** entrenched, intolerant **11** Biedermeier, intractable, reactionary, strait-laced **12** conventional, narrow-minded **14** uncompromising

**hideous**
◇ *anagram indicator* **04** gash, grim, huge, ugly **05** awful **06** deform, horrid, ugsome **07** ghastly, loathly, macabre **08** dreadful, gruesome, horrible, shocking, terrible **09** appalling, frightful, grotesque, monstrous, repellent, repulsive, revolting, unsightly **10** abominable, disgusting, horrendous, horrifying, monstruous, outrageous, terrifying

**hideously**
**08** horribly, horridly, terribly **10** abominably, dreadfully, gruesomely, shockingly **11** frightfully, grotesquely, repulsively **12** disgustingly, horrendously, outrageously, terrifyingly

**hideout**
**03** den **04** hole, lair, nest **05** haven **06** refuge **07** retreat, shelter **08** cloister, hideaway **09** hermitage, sanctuary **11** hiding-place

**hiding**
◇ *containment indicator* **04** dern, mask, veil **05** cover, dearn **06** caning, shroud **07** beating, belting, licking, tanning, veiling **08** disguise, drubbing, flogging, spanking, whacking, whipping **09** battering, screening, thrashing, walloping **10** camouflage **11** concealment

**hiding-place**
**03** den, mew **04** hide, hole, lair, nest **05** cache, cover, haven, stash **06** refuge **07** hideout, hidling, hidlins, retreat, shelter **08** bolthole, cloister, hideaway, hidlings, hidy-hole **09** glory hole, hidey-hole, sanctuary

**hierarchy**
**05** scale **06** ladder, series, strata, system **07** grading, ranking **08** echelons **09** structure **12** pecking order

**hieroglyphics**
**04** code **05** runes, signs **06** cipher **07** scratch, symbols **08** scrabble, scribble, squiggle **10** bad writing, cacography, pictograms **13** secret symbols **14** picture writing

**higgledy-piggledy**
◇ *anagram indicator* **06** anyhow, untidy **07** jumbled, muddled **08** confused, pell-mell, untidily **09** any old how,

haphazard **10** confusedly, disorderly, topsy-turvy **11** haphazardly **12** disorganized, through-other **14** indiscriminate

**high**
◇ *anagram indicator* **02** up **03** bad, off, top **04** dear, fine, gamy, good, haut, loud, peak, tall, trip **05** acute, aloft, angry, chief, doped, drunk, great, gusty, lofty, moral, nervy, noble, sharp, steep, tinny, wired **06** bombed, choice, classy, costly, de luxe, elated, height, loaded, piping, putrid, rancid, record, select, senior, severe, shrill, smelly, stoned, stormy, strong, summit, tiptop, treble, turn-on, wasted, worthy, zenith, zonked **07** blasted, blitzed, complex, decayed, eminent, ethical, exalted, extreme, haughty, intense, leading, notable, on a trip, out of it, perfect, quality, rotting, shrilly, soaring, soprano, squally, upright, violent **08** abstruse, admiring, advanced, arrogant, blue-chip, blustery, elevated, falsetto, forceful, freak-out, high-tech, inflated, piercing, positive, powerful, smelling, superior, top-class, towering, turned on, vigorous, virtuous **09** admirable, agreeable, approving, difficult, dignified, elaborate, eminently, excellent, excessive, exemplary, expensive, extremely, first-rate, gilt-edged, high-level, important, luxurious, principal, prominent, spaced out **10** arrogantly, exorbitant, favourable, first-class, freaked out, honourable, inebriated, noteworthy, powerfully, surpassing, unequalled **11** anticyclone, commendable, high-pitched, high-ranking, inebriation, influential, intoxicated, luxuriously, outstanding, penetrating, progressive, superlative, tempestuous, ultra-modern **12** altitudinous, appreciative, extortionate, intoxication, unparalleled, unreasonable, well-disposed **13** complimentary, distinguished, hallucinating, hallucination, high-frequency
• **high and dry 06** bereft, dumped **07** ditched **08** helpless, marooned, stranded **09** abandoned, destitute
• **high and low 07** all over **09** all around **10** every place, everywhere, far and near, throughout **11** in all places, in each place **12** in every place
• **high and mighty 05** proud **06** swanky **07** exalted, haughty, stuck-up **08** arrogant, cavalier, snobbish, superior, toplofty **09** conceited, egotistic, imperious **10** disdainful, hogen-mogen **11** overbearing, overweening, patronizing, toploftical **13** condescending, self-important
• **hit high 03** lob, sky
• **on high 02** up **05** ahigh, aloft **07** aheight **08** supernal **10** in excelsis

**high-born**
**05** noble **08** well-born **09** patrician **11** blue-blooded **12** aristocratic, thoroughbred

**highbrow**
**04** deep **05** heavy **06** boffin, brains, brainy, genius **07** bookish, egghead, scholar, serious **08** academic, brainbox, cultured, long-hair, profound **09** classical, know-it-all, scholarly **10** cultivated, long-haired, mastermind **11** clever clogs **12** intellectual **13** sophisticated **14** third-programme

**high-class**
**01** U **04** posh **05** dicty, élite, pakka, pucka, pukka, super **06** choice, classy, de luxe, dickty, select **07** elegant, quality **08** superior, top-class **09** excellent, exclusive, first-rate, luxurious, top-flight **10** upper-class **11** high-quality

**highest**
**03** top **04** best **05** chief **07** supreme, topmost **08** crowning **09** uppermost

**highfalutin, highfaluting**
**05** lofty **06** la-di-da, swanky **07** pompous **08** affected **09** bombastic, grandiose, high-flown **11** pretentious **12** high-sounding, magniloquent, supercilious

**high-flown**
**05** lofty **06** florid, la-di-da, ornate, turgid **07** pompous, stilted **08** affected, elevated **09** bombastic, elaborate, grandiose **10** artificial, flamboyant **11** exaggerated, extravagant, highfalutin, pretentious **12** high-sounding, ostentatious, supercilious **13** grandiloquent, grand-sounding

**high-handed**
**05** bossy **07** haughty **08** arrogant, despotic **09** arbitrary, imperious **10** autocratic, oppressive, peremptory, tyrannical **11** dictatorial, domineering, overbearing

**high-handedness**
**09** arrogance, bossiness **13** arbitrariness, imperiousness, inflexibility **14** peremptoriness

**high jinks**
**06** antics, capers, pranks **07** foolery, fooling, jollity **08** clowning **09** horseplay **10** buffoonery, skylarking, tomfoolery **11** fun and games **13** fooling around **14** monkey business, practical jokes, rough-and-tumble

**highland**
**04** hill, rise **05** mound, mount, ridge **06** height, upland **07** plateau **08** mountain **09** elevation

**Highlander**
**04** Gael **06** Gadhel, Goidel **07** nainsel' **08** nainsell, plaidman, teuchter **09** Irish Scot

**highlight**
**04** best, peak **05** cream, focus **06** accent, climax, play up, set off, show up, stress **07** feature, focus on, point up **08** high spot **09** emphasize, high point, spotlight, underline **10** accentuate, illuminate **11** main feature **13** put emphasis on **15** call attention to

### highly
**04** most, very, well **06** hugely, really, thrice, vastly, warmly **07** greatly **08** very much **09** certainly, decidedly, extremely, immensely **10** favourably, thoroughly **11** approvingly **12** considerably, tremendously **13** exceptionally **14** appreciatively **15** extraordinarily

### highly-strung
**04** edgy **05** jumpy, nervy, tense **06** on edge **07** nervous, uptight, wound up **08** neurotic, restless, stressed **09** excitable, sensitive **11** easily upset, overwrought **13** temperamental

### high-minded
**04** fair, good, pure **05** lofty, moral, noble **06** worthy **07** ethical, upright **08** elevated, virtuous **09** righteous **10** honourable, idealistic, principled **14** high-principled

### high-pitched
**05** acute, sharp, steep, tinny **06** piping, plinky, shrill, treble **07** orthian, soprano **08** falsetto, piercing **11** penetrating

### high-powered
**05** pushy, valid **06** mighty, potent, strong, urgent **07** dynamic, go-ahead, telling, weighty **08** emphatic, forceful, forcible, powerful, vehement, vigorous **09** assertive, effective, energetic **10** compelling, convincing, impressive, persuasive

### high-priced
**04** dear, high **05** steep, stiff **06** costly, pricey **09** excessive, expensive **10** exorbitant **12** extortionate, unreasonable

### high-sounding
**06** florid **07** orotund, pompous, stilted **08** affected, imposing, strained **09** bombastic, grandiose, high-flown, overblown, ponderous **10** altisonant, artificial, flamboyant **11** extravagant, pretentious **12** magniloquent, ostentatious **13** grandiloquent

### high-speed
**05** brisk, fleet, hasty, quick, rapid, swift **06** flying, speedy **07** express, hurried **11** accelerated

### high-spirited
**04** bold **05** proud **06** active, bouncy, daring, lively **07** dashing, dynamic, mettled, playful, rampant, vibrant **08** animated, cheerful, spirited, vigorous **09** ebullient, energetic, exuberant, sparkling, vivacious **10** boisterous, frolicsome, hot-blooded, mettlesome **11** full of beans, high-mettled **12** effervescent, great-hearted, thoroughbred

### high spirits
**06** bounce, capers, energy, heyday, spirit **07** elation, sparkle **08** boldness, buoyancy, hilarity, vivacity **09** animation, good cheer, high jinks **10** ebullience, exuberance, liveliness **11** high feather, joie de vivre **12** exhilaration **14** boisterousness

### highway
**04** road, rode **05** grove, route **06** avenue, bypass **07** flyover, freeway, roadway, tollway **08** Autobahn, broadway, clearway, main road, motorway, ring road, toll road, turnpike **09** autoroute, boulevard, trunk road **10** autostrada, camino real, expressway, high street, interstate **11** carriageway **12** arterial road, primary route, thoroughfare **15** dual carriageway

### highwayman
**03** pad **05** scamp **06** bandit, hold-up, robber **07** footpad **08** hijacker **09** bandolero, rank-rider, road agent **10** bushranger, highjacker, land-pirate **15** knight of the road

*Highwaymen include:*

**04 King** (Tom)
**05 Duval** (Claude)
**06 Turpin** (Dick)
**07 Brennan** (Willie), **Nevison** (John/William)
**08 MacHeath**
**09 Abershawe** (Jerry), **Swift Nick**
**12 Mack the Knife**

### hijack
**05** seize **07** carjack, skyjack **08** take over **10** commandeer **11** expropriate

### hike
**03** tug **04** jack, jerk, lift, plod, pull, ramp, trek, walk, yank **05** hitch, hoist, march, put up, raise, tramp **06** jack up, pull up, push up, ramble, trudge, wander **08** bushwalk, increase

### hilarious
**05** funny, jolly, merry, noisy **06** jovial **07** amusing, a scream, comical, killing, riotous, risible **08** farcical, humorous **09** laughable **10** boisterous, hysterical, rollicking, uproarious **12** entertaining **13** side-splitting

### hilariously
**09** comically, laughably **10** farcically, humorously **12** boisterously, hysterically, uproariously

### hilarity
**03** fun **05** mirth **06** comedy, gaiety, levity **07** jollity **08** laughter **09** amusement, frivolity, merriment **10** exuberance **11** high spirits **12** conviviality, exhilaration **14** boisterousness

### hill
**03** dod, dun, how, kip, kop, law, low, man, pap, tel, tor **04** berg, cone, down, drop, dune, fell, holt, howe, knot, loma, mesa, pike, ramp, rise, tell, toot, torr **05** butte, coast, jebel, knoll, kopje, morro, mound, mount, slope **06** ascent, barrow, cuesta, djebel, height, koppie, pimple, rising **07** descent, hillock, hilltop, hummock, incline, mamelon **08** eminence, foothill, gradient, mountain **09** acclivity, declivity, elevation, monadnock, monticule, sugarloaf **10** prominence, saddleback **12** rising ground

*Rome's seven hills:*

**07** Caelian, Viminal
**08** Aventine, Palatine, Quirinal
**09** Esquiline
**10** Capitoline

• **over the hill**   **03** old **04** gone **06** past it **09** getting on **13** past your prime

### hillbilly
**03** oaf **04** boor, hick, lout **06** rustic **07** bumpkin, hawbuck, hayseed, hoedown, peasant **08** clodpoll **10** clodhopper, provincial **11** bushwhacker **12** country yokel **14** country bumpkin

### hill fort
**04** rath

### hillock
**04** dune, knap, knob, toft, tump **05** knoll, knowe, mound **06** barrow **07** hommock, hummock **08** monticle **10** monticulus
*See also* **hill**

### hill-slope
**04** brae

### hilltop
**03** dod, nab **05** crest

### hilt
**04** grip, haft, heft **05** helve, shaft **06** basket, handle **08** coquille, handgrip

• **to the hilt**   **05** fully **06** wholly **07** utterly **08** entirely, to the end **09** all the way, to the full **10** completely, thoroughly **14** in every respect **15** from first to last

### him
**02** un

### hind
**04** back, rear, rump, tail **05** after, stern **06** caudal, hinder **09** posterior

### hinder
**03** bar, let **04** balk, curb, foil, halt, hind, last, rear, stay, stop **05** block, check, crimp, debar, delay, deter, dwarf, embar, estop, imbar, stunt **06** arrest, cumber, hamper, hold up, impede, oppose, resist, retard, stymie, taigle, thwart **07** empeach, forelay, impeach, inhibit, keep off, porlock, prevent, set back, trammel **08** encumber, handicap, hold back, obstruct, preclude, slow down **09** forestall, frustrate, hamstring, interrupt, throw back, withstand **10** overslaugh **13** interfere with

### hindmost
**03** lag **04** last, tail **05** final **07** aftmost, endmost **08** furthest, rearmost, remotest, terminal, trailing, ultimate **09** aftermost **10** concluding **12** furthest back **14** farthest behind

### hindrance
**03** bar, let **04** curb, drag, foil, snag, stop **05** block, check, delay, hitch **06** hold-up, thwart **07** barrier, empeach, impeach, shackle **08** drawback, handicap, obstacle, pullback, stoppage **09** cumbrance, deterrent,

**hindsight**

impedance, restraint, thwarting
**10** difficulty, impediment, limitation,
prevention **11** encumbrance,
obstruction, obstructive, restriction
**12** disadvantage, interference,
interruption **13** inconvenience
**14** stumbling-block

**hindsight**
**06** review, survey **10** reflection,
retrospect **11** remembrance
**12** afterthought, recollection, thinking
back **13** re-examination

**Hindu**
*see* god, goddess; month

**Hindustani**
**04** Hind, Urdu **05** Hindi

**hinge**
◇ *reversal indicator* **04** hang, rest, turn
**05** gemel, pivot **06** centre, depend,
garnet **07** revolve **09** ginglymus
**11** cross-garnet **12** be contingent

**hint**
**03** cue, tip **04** clue, dash, help, mint,
note, sign, tang, wind, wink, word
**05** hunch, imply, light, point, savor,
speck, taste, tinge, touch, trace, whiff
**06** advice, allude, moment, nuance,
office, prevue, prompt, savour, signal,
squint, tip off, tip-off **07** glimmer,
inkling, let fall, mention, pointer,
preview, soupçon, suggest, thought,
whisper, wrinkle **08** allusion, indicate,
innuendo, intimate, reminder
**09** insinuate, scintilla, suspicion
**10** indication, intimation, sprinkling,
suggestion **11** implication, insinuation,
opportunity, subindicate

**hinterland**
**08** backveld, interior **10** back-blocks,
hinderland **11** back-country

**hip**
**02** in **03** hep **04** cool, huck, loin, rump
**05** croup, funky, thigh **06** dog-hep,
dog-hip, groovy, haunch, huckle,
modish, pelvis, trendy, with it
**07** stylish, voguish **08** buttocks
**09** happening, posterior **10** all the rage
**11** fashionable **12** hindquarters,
hypochondria **13** up to the minute
• **hip bone** **04** coxa **10** huckle-bone
**14** innominate bone

**hippie, hippy**
**05** loner, rebel **07** beatnik, deviant,
dropout **08** bohemian **10** long-haired
**11** flower child

**hire**
**03** fee, job, let, pay **04** book, cost, lend,
rent, wage **05** lease, price **06** charge,
employ, engage, enlist, rental, retain,
salary, sign on, sign up, take on
**07** appoint, charter, freight, reserve
**10** commission

**hire-purchase**
**02** HP **05** lay-by **09** easy terms
**10** never-never **14** instalment plan

**hirsute**
**05** hairy, rough **06** crinal, hispid,
shaggy **07** bearded, bristly, crinate,
crinite, crinose **08** unshaven, whiskery

**09** whiskered **11** bewhiskered,
crinigerous

**hiss**
**03** boo **04** buzz, hish, hizz, hoot, jeer,
mock **05** goose, scorn, taunt, whiss,
whizz **06** deride, fizzle, shrill, siffle,
sizzle **07** catcall, hissing, mockery,
scoff at, the bird, whistle **08** contempt,
derision, ridicule, scoffing, sibilant,
sibilate, taunting **09** raspberry, shout
down, sibilance **10** assibilate,
effervesce, sibilation **15** blow
raspberries

**historian**
**07** diarist **08** annalist, narrator, recorder
**09** archivist **10** chronicler
**11** chronologer **15** historiographer

*Historians include:*

**04** Bede (St, 'The Venerable'), Bois
(William Edward Burghardt du),
Livy, Read (Sir Herbert Edward),
Webb (Sidney)
**05** Barth (Heinrich), Blunt (Anthony
Frederick), Clark (Kenneth, Lord),
Ensor (Sir Robert), Gates (Henry
Louis, Jnr), Henry (of Huntingdon),
Lodge (Henry Cabot), Nepos
(Cornelius), Paris (Matthew),
Ranke (Leopold von), Renan
(Ernest), Stone (Norman)
**06** Arrian, Berlin (Sir Isaiah), Bolton
(Geoffrey), Briggs (Lord Asa),
Eliade (Mircea), Froude (James
Anthony), Gibbon (Edward), Guizot
(François), Irving (David), Namier
(Sir Lewis), O'Brien (Conor Cruise),
Schama (Simon), Strabo, Strong
(Sir Roy), Tabari (Abu Jafar
Mohammed Ben Jarir al-), Tawney
(Richard Henry), Taylor (AJP),
Terkel (Studs), Thiers (Adolphe),
Vasari (Giorgio)
**07** Barbour (John), Bullock (Alan,
Lord), Carlyle (Thomas), Comines
(Philippe de), Mommsen (Theodor),
Pevsner (Sir Nikolaus Bernhard),
Sallust, Severin (Timothy), Starkey
(David), Tacitus, Toynbee (Arnold),
William (of Malmesbury), William
(of Tyre)
**08** Foucault (Michel), Geoffrey (of
Monmouth), Gombrich (Sir Ernst
Hans Josef), Josephus (Flavius),
Las Casas (Emmanuel), Macaulay
(Thomas Babington, Lord), Michelet
(Jules), Palgrave (Sir Francis),
Panofsky (Erwin), Plutarch,
Polybius, Wedgwood (Dame
Cicely), Xenophon
**09** Dionysius (of Halicarnassus),
Froissart (Jean), Herodotus,
Holinshed (Raphael), Pausanias,
Plekhanov (Giorgiy), Procopius,
Rowbotham (Sheila), Suetonius,
Trevelyan (George Macaulay)
**10** Baldinucci (Filippo), Burckhardt
(Jacob Christopher), Dio Cassius,
Thucydides
**11** Schlesinger (Arthur Meier),
Tocqueville (Alexis de), Trevor-
Roper (Hugh Redwald)
**12** Guicciardini (Francesco)
**15** Diodorus Siculus

**historic**
**05** famed **06** famous **07** notable
**08** renowned **09** important,
memorable, momentous, red-letter
**10** celebrated, remarkable **11** epoch-
making, outstanding, significant
**13** consequential, extraordinary

**historical**
**03** old **04** past, real **05** prior **06** actual,
bygone, former, of yore **07** ancient,
factual **08** attested, recorded, verified
**09** authentic, confirmed **10** chronicled,
documented, verifiable

*Historical periods include:*

**05** Bruce, Tudor
**06** Norman, Stuart
**07** Angevin, Cold War, post-war,
Regency, Stewart, Yorkist
**08** Civil War, Dark Ages, Medieval
**09** Edwardian, Mediaeval, Modern
Age, Victorian
**10** Anglo-Saxon, Hanoverian,
Middle Ages
**11** Interbellum, Interregnum,
Lancastrian, Plantagenet,
Reformation, Renaissance,
Restoration, Roman Empire,
Romanticism
**13** British Empire, Enlightenment,
Ottoman Empire
**15** Byzantine Empire

**historically**
**04** once **07** long ago **08** formerly **09** in
the past, yesterday **10** originally
**11** some time ago **13** in former times, in
years gone by

**history**
**04** life, saga, tale **05** story, study
**06** annals, family, record, report
**07** account, memoirs, records, reports,
the past **08** archives **09** antiquity,
biography, chronicle, days of old,
education, narrative, olden days,
yesterday **10** background, bygone
days, chronology, days of yore,
experience, the old days, yesteryear
**11** credentials, former times
**13** autobiography, circumstances
**14** qualifications, the good old days

**histrionic**
**03** ham **05** bogus, stagy **06** forced
**08** affected, dramatic, operatic
**09** insincere, unnatural **10** artificial,
theatrical **11** exaggerated, sensational
**12** hypocritical, melodramatic

**histrionics**
**05** scene **08** tantrums **09** dramatics,
melodrama, staginess, theatrics
**10** overacting **11** affectation,
insincerity, performance
**13** artificiality, theatricality,
unnaturalness **14** sensationalism

**hit**
◇ *anagram indicator* **03** bat, bop, box,
cue, dod, dot, fit, get, hay, pat, tap, tip,
wow, zap **04** bang, bash, beat, belt,
biff, blow, boff, bonk, bump, clip,
club, cuff, daud, dawd, dong, harm,
hurt, move, polt, shot, skit, slap, slew,
slog, sock, suit, swap, swat, tonk
**05** catch, clonk, clout, crash, knock,

pound, prang, punch, smack, smash, smite, swipe, thump, touch, upset, whack **06** affect, batter, buffet, come to, damage, dawn on, impact, pommel, pummel, strike, stroke, thrash, wallop, winner **07** beating, clobber, disturb, occur to, perturb, run into, success, triumph, trouble **08** knockout **09** collision, crash into, devastate, overwhelm, smash into, thrashing **10** clobbering, come to mind, meet head-on, plough into **11** be thought of, blockbuster, collide with, knock for six **12** be remembered **13** enter your mind **14** have an effect on
*See also* **kill**
• **hit back** **06** return **07** respond **09** retaliate **10** strike back **11** reciprocate **13** counter-attack
• **hit it off** **05** agree, click, fadge **06** warm to **09** get on with **10** grow to like **12** get along with **13** become friends, get on well with **14** be friendly with
• **hit on** **05** guess **06** invent **07** light on, realize, think of, uncover **08** arrive at, chance on, discover **09** stumble on
• **hit out** **04** rail **05** flail **06** assail, attack, strike, vilify **07** condemn, inveigh, lash out **08** denounce **09** criticize, strike out

### hitch
**03** rub, tie, tug **04** bind, hike, hook, jerk, join, limp, pull, snag, yank, yoke **05** block, catch, check, delay, heave, hoist, hotch, stick, unite **06** attach, couple, fasten, glitch, hiccup, hike up, hobble, hold-up, mishap, tether **07** barrier, cat's-paw, connect, harness, problem, setback, trouble **08** drawback, obstacle **09** hindrance **10** difficulty, impediment **11** contretemps, obstruction

### hitherto
**03** yet **05** so far **07** thus far, till now, up to now **08** formerly, until now **10** beforehand, heretofore, previously

### hitman
**03** gun **06** ice man **08** assassin

### hit-or-miss
**06** casual, hobnob, random, uneven **07** aimless, cursory, offhand **08** careless **09** apathetic, haphazard, unplanned **10** undirected **11** perfunctory **12** disorganized **13** lackadaisical, trial-and-error **14** indiscriminate

### hive
**03** gum **04** skep **07** alveary, bee-skep

### hoard
**04** fund, heap, keep, mass, pile, pose, save **05** amass, buy up, cache, hoord, hutch, lay in, lay up, plant, put by, spare, stash, store, uplay **06** coffer, gather, heap up, mucker, pile up, supply **07** collect, put away, reserve, stack up, stock up, uphoard **08** hoarding, salt away, set aside, squirrel, treasure **09** reservoir, stash away, stockpile **10** accumulate,

collection **11** aggregation **12** accumulation, squirrel away **13** treasure-trove **14** conglomeration

### hoarder
**05** miser, saver **06** magpie **07** niggard **08** gatherer, squirrel **09** collector

### hoarse
**05** gruff, harsh, husky, raspy, roopy, rough **06** croaky, roopit **07** grating, rasping, raucous, throaty **08** croaking, gravelly, growling, guttural **10** discordant

### hoarsely
**07** gruffly, harshly, huskily, roughly **08** croakily **09** raucously **10** gutturally

### hoarseness
**04** roop, roup

### hoary
**03** old **04** aged, grey **05** banal, trite, white **06** old-hat **07** ancient, antique, archaic, cliché'd, silvery **08** clichéed, familiar, grizzled **09** canescent, senescent, venerable **10** antiquated, grey-haired **11** predictable, white-haired **12** overfamiliar

### hoax
**02** do **03** bam, cod, con, fun, gag, hum, kid **04** dupe, fake, fool, gull, jest, joke, josh, quiz, ruse, scam, sham, skit **05** bluff, cheat, fraud, kiddy, prank, put-on, spoof, stuff, trick **06** canard, delude, gammon, have on, humbug, pigeon, string, take in **07** deceive, fast one, frame-up, leg-pull, mystify, swindle, two-time **08** hoodwink, put-up job **09** April-fish, April fool, bamboozle, deception, gold brick **10** huntiegowk **11** double-cross, hunt-the-gowk, supercherie **12** take for a ride **13** practical joke **14** pull a fast one on

### hoaxer
**05** joker **06** humbug **07** sharper, spoofer **08** jokester **09** mystifier, prankster, trickster **10** bamboozler, hoodwinker **14** practical joker

### hobble
**04** clog, limp, reel **05** hilch, hitch **06** dodder, falter, fetter, hamper, scrape, totter **07** pastern, perplex, shackle, shuffle, spancel, stagger, stumble, trammel **10** walk lamely **13** walk awkwardly, walk with a limp

### hobbling
**04** game, lame **06** lamish

### hobby
**03** fad **04** game **05** sport **07** pastime, pursuit **08** interest, play-mare, sideline **09** amusement, avocation, diversion **10** recreation, relaxation **13** entertainment **14** divertissement, leisure pursuit **15** leisure activity

*Hobbies and pastimes include:*

**05** batik, chess
**06** acting, baking, bonsai, hiking, poetry, raffia
**07** camping, CB radio, collage, cookery, crochet, dancing, drawing, macramé, mosaics,

origami, pottery, quizzes, reading, singing, tatting, topiary, weaving, writing
**08** basketry, cat shows, dog shows, draughts, feng shui, knitting, knotting, lacework, lapidary, marbling, painting, quilling, quilting, spinning, tapestry
**09** astrology, astronomy, decoupage, gardening, genealogy, marquetry, millinary, model cars, philately, rug-making, sketching, strawwork, toy-making, train sets
**10** beekeeping, board games, crosswords, doll-making, embroidery, kite-flying, lace-making, pub quizzes, pyrography, renovating, upholstery, wine-making
**11** archaeology, beadworking, bell-ringing, book-binding, calligraphy, card playing, cat breeding, cross-stitch, dog breeding, dressmaking, home brewing, model-making, model trains, needlepoint, numismatics, ornithology, paper crafts, papier-mâché, photography, wine-tasting, woodcarving, woodworking
**12** amateur radio, basketmaking, candle-making, games playing, phillumenism
**13** bungee jumping, egg decorating, toy collecting
**14** book collecting, coin collecting, cruciverbalism, doll collecting, flower pressing, herpetoculture, metal detecting
**15** aquarium keeping, ballroom dancing, flower arranging, jewellery making, model aeroplanes, stamp collecting

### hobgoblin
**03** elf, imp **05** bogey, dwarf, gnome **06** buggan, buggin, goblin, spirit, sprite **07** bugaboo, bugbear, buggane, spectre **08** wirricow, worricow, worrycow **10** apparition, bull-beggar, evil spirit

### hobnob
**03** mix **06** mingle **07** consort **08** go around **09** associate, hang about, hit-or-miss, pal around, socialize **10** fraternize **11** keep company

### hock
**03** ham, hox **04** pawn **07** gambrel, Rhenish **09** Rhine wine **11** Rhenish wine
*See also* **pawn**

### hockey
*Hockey-related terms include:*

**01** D
**03** hit
**04** ball, feet, goal, push
**05** flick, scoop
**06** aerial, tackle
**07** dribble, free hit, red card, striker, sweeper
**08** back line, bully-off, left back, left half, left wing
**09** corner hit, drag flick, field goal,

green card, right back, right half, right wing
**10** centre half, centre pass, goal circle, goalkeeper, inside left, long corner, yellow card
**11** field player, hockey stick, inside right, obstruction, short corner
**12** penalty flick, reverse stick
**13** centre forward, penalty corner, penalty stroke
**14** shooting circle, striking circle

## hocus-pocus
**04** cant, hoax **05** cheat, spell **06** deceit, humbug, jargon, juggle **07** juggler, swindle **08** artifice, delusion, hoky-poky, nonsense, trickery **09** chicanery, conjuring, deception, gibberish, imposture, rigmarole **10** hokey-pokey, magic words, mumbo-jumbo
**11** abracadabra, legerdemain, trompe-l'oeil **12** gobbledygook **13** sleight of hand

## hodgepodge
**03** mix **04** mess **06** jumble, medley
**07** melange, mixture **08** mishmash
**09** confusion **10** collection, hotchpotch, miscellany

## hoe
**04** clat **05** claut **06** pecker **07** scuffle
**10** promontory

## hog
**03** pig **04** boar **05** swine **06** corner, porker **07** control, grunter **08** babirusa, dominate, shilling, take over, wild boar **09** babirussa **10** babiroussa, monopolize **14** keep to yourself

## hogshead
**04** muid
• **two hogsheads** **04** pipe

## hogwash
**03** rot **04** blah, bosh, bunk, guff, tosh
**05** balls, bilge, hooey, swill, trash, tripe
**06** bunkum, drivel, hot air, piffle
**07** baloney, eyewash, rubbish, twaddle
**08** claptrap, cobblers, malarkey, nonsense, tommyrot **09** gibberish, moonshine, poppycock **10** balderdash

## hoi polloi
**07** the herd **08** riff-raff, the plebs, varletry **09** the masses, the proles, the rabble **11** the peasants, the populace
**14** the proletariat, the third estate
**15** the common people

## hoist
**04** jack, lift, rear, sway, wind **05** crane, erect, heave, hoise, raise, steal, wince, winch **06** jack up, pulley, tackle, teagle, uplift, wind up **07** capstan, elevate, winch up **08** elevator, windlass

## hoity-toity
**05** giddy, huffy, lofty, noisy, proud
**06** snooty, uppity **07** haughty, pompous, stuck-up **08** arrogant, scornful, snobbish **09** conceited
**10** disdainful **11** overweening, toffee-nosed **12** supercilious **13** high and mighty

## hold
◇ containment indicator **02** ho **03** aim, bet, hoa, hoh, hug, own, ren, rin, run
**04** bear, bind, bulk, call, curb, deem, fill, go on, grip, have, holt, hook, keep, last, soft, stay, stop, sway, take, view
**05** apply, belay, brace, carry, catch, check, clasp, cling, clout, grasp, gripe, judge, power, rivet, seize, stick, think, treat **06** absorb, adhere, arrest, assume, clutch, detain, direct, endure, enfold, engage, esteem, fulfil, handle, hold up, keep up, lock up, nelson, occupy, prop up, reckon, regard, remain, retain, summon, suplex, take up
**07** adjudge, armlock, bear hug, believe, carry on, claucht, claught, cling to, conduct, confine, contain, control, convene, custody, embrace, enclose, engross, enthral, holding, impound, mastery, observe, persist, possess, presume, reserve, soft you, support, suppose, sustain, toehold
**08** assemble, buttress, consider, continue, dominion, headlock, hold down, imprison, leverage, maintain, organize, purchase, restrain, scissors, tenacity **09** authority, be in force, captivate, celebrate, dominance, fascinate, influence **10** Boston crab, compromise, full nelson, half nelson, hammerlock, monopolize, remain true, stronghold **11** accommodate, backbreaker, have room for, incarcerate, preside over, remain valid, scissor hold **12** have space for, stranglehold **13** be in operation, hold in custody, remain in force **14** have in your hand **15** have a capacity of, have in your hands
*See also* **wrestling**
• **get hold of** ◇ containment indicator
**03** get **05** reach **06** obtain **07** acquire, contact, speak to **12** get through to
**14** get in touch with, get your hands on **15** communicate with
• **hold back** **03** bar **04** curb, hang, pull, stop **05** check, delay, pause
**06** desist, impede, refuse, retain, retard, shrink, stifle **07** contain, control, forbear, inhibit, prevent, refrain, repress **08** hesitate, keep back, obstruct, restrain, strangle, suppress, withhold
• **hold down** **03** pin **04** have, keep
**06** occupy **07** oppress **08** dominate, keep down, restrain, suppress
**09** tyrannize **10** continue in
• **hold fast** **03** pin **04** clip, nail
**05** avast, stick **07** enchain, pin down
• **hold forth** **04** show, talk **05** orate, speak, spout **06** preach **07** declaim, lecture **08** harangue **09** discourse
**12** talk at length **13** speak at length
• **hold off** **04** wait **05** avoid, defer, delay, repel **06** put off, rebuff, resist
**07** fend off, hang off, keep off, ward off **08** fight off, postpone, stave off
**09** keep at bay
• **hold on** **04** grip, stop, wait
**05** clasp, cling, grasp, seize
**06** clutch, endure, hang on, remain
**07** carry on, cling to, survive
**08** continue **09** keep going, persevere
• **hold out** **04** give, last, stay
**05** offer, reach **06** endure, extend, hang on, resist **07** carry on, last out, persist, present, proffer, protend, subsist **08** continue **09** persevere, stand fast, stand firm, withstand
• **hold over** **05** defer, delay **06** put off, shelve **07** adjourn, put back, suspend **08** postpone
• **hold up** ◇ reversal down indicator
**03** mug, rob **04** bear, lift, rear, show, slow, stay **05** apply, brace, carry, delay, raise **06** burgle, detain, endure, hinder, impede, nobble, prop up, remain, retard, upbear, uphold **07** bolster, display, exhibit, present, put back, set back, shore up, stick up, support, sustain **08** hold high, knock off, obstruct **09** be in force, break into, knock over, steal from **10** burglarize, remain true **11** remain valid **13** be in operation, remain in force
• **hold with** **06** accept **07** support
**09** agree with, approve of
**11** countenance, go along with, subscribe to
• **hold your own** **06** resist **07** survive
**09** stand fast, stand firm, withstand
**15** stand your ground
• **put on hold** **05** defer, delay **06** put off **07** hold off **08** postpone

## holder
**04** case, rest **05** cover, haver, owner, stand **06** bearer, casing, keeper, sheath
**07** housing **08** occupant **09** container, custodian, incumbent, possessor, purchaser **10** proprietor, receptacle

## holdings
**04** land **05** bonds **06** assets, estate, shares, stocks, tenure **08** property
**09** resources **10** real estate, securities
**11** investments, possessions

## hold-up
**03** jam **04** raid, snag, wait **05** delay, heist, hitch, theft **07** break-in, mugging, problem, robbery, setback, stick-up, trouble **08** burglary, stoppage
**10** bottleneck, difficulty, stick-up job, traffic jam **11** obstruction

## hole
**03** cup, den, eye, fix, gap, jam, pit, set, tip **04** bind, bore, cave, dent, drop, dump, flaw, gash, geat, lair, mess, mine, nest, pore, rent, rift, slit, slot, slum, snag, spot, stab, stew, tear, vent
**05** break, chasm, crack, delve, error, fault, hovel, notch, scoop, shack, shaft, space, spike, split, thirl, whole
**06** breach, burrow, cavern, cavity, corner, covert, crater, defect, dimple, eyelet, hollow, outlet, pickle, pierce, pigpen, pigsty, plight, pocket, recess, scrape **07** chamber, fissure, mistake, opening, orifice, pothole **08** aperture, hot water, loophole, puncture, quandary, weakness **09** deep water, perforate **10** depression, difficulty, excavation, pretty pass, subterfuge
**11** discrepancy, perforation, predicament **13** inconsistency
*See also* **fingerhole**
• **hole in one** **03** ace
• **hole up** **04** hide **06** lie low **09** take

cover **10** go to ground **12** go into hiding **15** conceal yourself
• **pick holes in 04** slag **05** slate **07** nit-pick, run down, slag off **09** criticize **12** pull to pieces **13** find fault with

**hole-and-corner**
**06** covert, secret, sneaky **07** furtive **08** back-door, hush-hush, stealthy **09** secretive, underhand **10** backstairs **11** clandestine **13** surreptitious **15** under-the-counter

**holiday**
**03** vac **04** fete, play, rest, trip, wake **05** break, festa, leave, wakes **06** day off, fiesta, recess **07** awayday, half-day, high day, holy day, leisure, play-day, time off **08** duvet day, feast day, festival, fly-drive, furlough, half-term, vacation **09** honeymoon, minibreak, saint's day **10** staycation **11** anniversary, bank holiday, celebration, package tour **12** legal holiday, long vacation **14** leave of absence

*National holidays include:*
**05** UN Day
**07** Flag Day
**08** Anzac Day, Unity Day
**09** Labour Day, Women's Day
**10** Culture Day, Father's Day, Freedom Day, Martyrs' Day, Mother's Day, Victory Day
**11** Bastille Day, National Day, Republic Day
**12** Armistice Day, Australia Day, Children's Day, Discovery Day, Thanksgiving
**13** King's Birthday, Liberation Day, Revolution Day
**14** Armed Forces Day, Queen's Birthday, Remembrance Day, Unification Day
**15** Constitution Day, Emancipation Day, Independence Day

**holier-than-thou**
**04** smug **05** pious **08** priggish, unctuous **09** pietistic, religiose **10** complacent, goody-goody **13** sanctimonious, self-approving, self-righteous, self-satisfied

**holiness**
**05** piety **06** purity **07** halidom **08** divinity, goodness, sanctity **09** godliness **10** dedication, devoutness, perfection, sacredness, sanctimony **11** blessedness, saintliness, sinlessness **12** consecration, spirituality, virtuousness **13** religiousness, righteousness

**holler**
**03** cry **04** bawl, call, howl, roar, yell, yelp, yowl **05** cheer, shout, whoop **06** bellow, shriek **07** clamour

**hollow**
**03** cup, dig, dip, how, lap, low, pan, pit **04** boss, bowl, cave, comb, dale, deaf, deep, dell, dent, dish, dull, flat, glen, hole, howe, khud, nook, sham, vain, vale, void, vola, well **05** basin, chasm, clean, combe, coomb, delve, empty, false, gorge, gouge, niche,

scoop, womby **06** burrow, cavern, cavity, cirque, coombe, cranny, crater, dimple, dingle, furrow, futile, groove, indent, ravine, recess, sunken, trough, tunnel, unreal, vacant, valley **07** caved-in, channel, concave, deep-set, dishing, echoing, muffled, Pyrrhic, unsound, useless, vacuity **08** coreless, excavate, fleeting, fossette, indented, inflated, rumbling, unfilled **09** cavernous, concavity, deceitful, deceptive, depressed, emptiness, fruitless, incurvate, insincere, of no avail, pointless, pretended, valueless, worthless **10** artificial, completely, depression, excavation, profitless, semicirque, unavailing **11** indentation, meaningless, reverberant **12** hypocritical
• **beat someone hollow 04** lick, rout **05** crash **06** hammer, thrash **07** clobber, trounce **09** devastate, overwhelm, slaughter **10** annihilate **13** defeat soundly

**holly**
**04** holm, ilex, mate **06** yaupon **13** Aquifoliaceae

**holmium**
**02** Ho

**holocaust**
**05** Shoah **06** flames, pogrom **07** carnage, inferno **08** disaster, genocide, hecatomb, massacre **09** cataclysm, sacrifice, slaughter **10** extinction, immolation, mass murder **11** catastrophe, destruction, devastation **12** annihilation **13** conflagration, extermination **15** ethnic cleansing

**holy**
**02** pi **04** good, pure **05** godly, moral, pious, saint **06** devout, divine, sacred **07** blessed, perfect, revered, saintly, sinless **08** faithful, hallowed, virtuous **09** dedicated, pietistic, religious, righteous, spiritual, venerated **10** God-fearing, sacrosanct, sanctified **11** consecrated **13** sanctimonious
• **holy book** *see* **Bible**

**holy of holies**
**05** altar **06** shrine **07** sanctum **12** inner sanctum **13** most holy place

**homage**
**03** awe **06** esteem, honour, manred, praise, regard **07** incense, manrent, respect, service, tribute, worship **08** devotion **09** adoration, adulation, deference, reverence **10** admiration, veneration **11** knee-tribute, recognition **15** acknowledgement

**home**
**02** in **03** den, pad **04** base, digs, flat, goal, nest, semi **05** abode, fount, house, local, place, roots, villa **06** asylum, centre, cradle, family, hostel, inland, libken, native, refuge, source **07** address, blighty, cottage, element, habitat, retreat **08** bungalow, domestic, domicile, dwelling, fireside, homeland, home town, interior, internal, national **09** apartment, effective, household, residence, safe

place, searching **10** birthplace, fatherland, habitation, motherland, native town **11** effectively, institution, nursing home **13** children's home, dwelling-place, mother country, native country, place of origin **14** old people's home, retirement home **15** country of origin, residential home, somewhere to live
*See also* **animal**
• **at home 02** in **06** at ease, well up, within **07** relaxed, skilled **08** familiar **09** competent, confident **10** conversant **11** comfortable, experienced **13** knowledgeable
• **at home of 04** chez
• **bring home 05** prove **06** instil **07** impress **08** convince **09** emphasize, inculcate
• **home improvements 03** DIY
• **home in on 03** aim **05** focus **06** direct **08** pinpoint, zero in on, zoom in on **11** concentrate
• **not at home 04** out **04** away
• **nothing to write home about 02** OK **04** drab, dull **06** boring **08** inferior, mediocre, ordinary **11** not exciting, predictable **13** no great shakes **14** not interesting

**homecoming**
**06** return **07** arrival **10** coming-back, return home **13** arrival at home

**homeland**
**04** home **10** fatherland, motherland, native land **13** mother country, native country **15** country of origin

**homeless**
**06** exiled, tramps **07** dossers, dossing, evicted, nomadic, outcast, vagrant **08** forsaken, rootless, vagrants **09** abandoned, derelicts, destitute, displaced, itinerant, squatters, unsettled, vagabonds, wandering **10** down-and-out, travellers, travelling **11** down-and-outs, on the street **12** dispossessed, on the streets **13** on the pavement, sleeping rough **14** of no fixed abode
• **homeless person 04** hobo, waif **05** skell

**homelessness**
**07** dossing **08** vagrancy **11** abandonment, destitution **12** displacement, no fixed abode, rootlessness **13** sleeping rough

**homely**
**04** cosy, homy, snug, ugly **05** homey, mumsy, plain **06** folksy, modest, russet, simple **07** natural, relaxed **08** cheerful, domestic, everyday, familiar, friendly, homelike, homespun, informal, intimate, ordinary, unlovely **09** welcoming **10** hospitable, unassuming **11** comfortable **12** unattractive **13** unpretentious **15** not much to look at, unprepossessing, unsophisticated

**homer**
**03** cor **09** Maeonides

**homespun**
**04** rude **05** crude, plain, rough

## homestead

**06** coarse, folksy, homely, russet, rustic, simple **07** artless, raploch **08** home-made **09** inelegant, unadorned, unrefined **10** amateurish, unpolished **13** uncomplicated **15** unsophisticated

## homestead

**04** toft

## homework

**04** prep **09** spadework **10** groundwork **11** preparation

## homey

**04** cosy, snug **07** relaxed **08** cheerful, familiar, friendly, homelike, informal, intimate **09** welcoming **10** hospitable **11** comfortable

## homicidal

**06** bloody, deadly, lethal, mortal **07** violent **08** maniacal **09** murderous **10** sanguinary **12** bloodthirsty, death-dealing

## homicide

**06** murder **07** killing, slaying **09** bloodshed, slaughter **12** chance-medley, manslaughter **13** assassination

## homily

**04** talk **05** prone, spiel **06** postil, sermon, speech **07** address, lecture, oration **08** harangue **09** discourse, preaching

## homogeneity

**07** oneness **08** likeness, sameness **09** agreement **10** consonancy, similarity, similitude, uniformity **11** consistency, resemblance **13** analogousness, comparability, identicalness **14** correspondence

## homogeneous

**04** akin **05** alike **07** cognate, kindred, similar, the same, uniform **08** of a piece, unvaried **09** analogous, identical, unvarying **10** all the same, comparable, compatible, consistent, harmonious, indiscrete **11** all of a piece, correlative **13** corresponding, of the same kind

## homogeneously

**07** the same **09** similarly, uniformly **10** all the same **11** all of a piece, identically **12** consistently **13** of the same kind **15** correspondingly

## homogenize

**04** fuse **05** blend, merge, unite **07** combine **08** coalesce **10** amalgamate **11** make similar, make uniform

## homologous

**04** like **07** related, similar **08** matching, parallel **09** analogous **10** comparable, equivalent **13** correspondent, corresponding

## homosexual

**03** gay **04** pink **07** lesbian, same-sex **08** bisexual
*See also* **gay**

## Honduras

**02** HN **03** HND

## hone

**04** edge, file, whet **05** grind, point **06** polish **07** develop, sharpen

## honest

**04** fair, jake, just, open, real, true **05** afald, blunt, clean, frank, legal, moral, plain, round, white **06** aefald, afawld, candid, chaste, dinkum, direct, lawful, seemly, simple, single, square, trusty **07** aefauld, dinki-di, dinky-di, ethical, genuine, sincere, up-front, upright **08** bona fide, dinky-die, even-down, outright, reliable, soothful, straight, truthful, virtuous, yeomanly **09** equitable, impartial, ingenuous, objective, outspoken, reputable, righteous, soothfast **10** above-board, dependable, fair dinkum, forthright, four-square, high-minded, honourable, law-abiding, legitimate, on the level, principled, scrupulous, upstanding **11** respectable, right-minded, trustworthy **12** on the up and up, plain-hearted **13** fair and square, incorruptible, plain-speaking, unpretentious **14** straight as a die **15** straightforward

## honestly

**04** true **05** truly **06** dinkum, direct, fairly, justly, really, simply, square **07** dinky-di, frankly, legally, morally, plainly, up-front, upright **08** dinky-die, directly, lawfully, straight **09** equitably, ethically, no messing, sincerely, uprightly **10** above board, honourably, on the level, straight up, to be honest, truthfully **11** impartially, in good faith, objectively, on the square **12** legitimately **13** fair and square

## honesty

**05** faith **06** equity, ethics, honour, lunary, morals, square, virtue **07** balance, candour, decorum, probity, realtie **08** chastity, fairness, fidelity, justness, legality, moonwort, morality, openness, veracity **09** bluntness, frankness, integrity, rectitude, sincerity **10** legitimacy, principles **11** genuineness, objectivity, uprightness **12** explicitness, impartiality, truthfulness **13** outspokenness, plain-speaking, righteousness **14** even-handedness, forthrightness, scrupulousness **15** trustworthiness

## honey

**03** hon, mel, sis **04** babe **05** sweet **06** nectar **07** sweeten
• **honey buzzard** **04** pern **07** bee-kite
• **honey guide** **03** tui
• **honey possum** **04** tait **08** Tarsipes

## honeyed

**04** cute, dear, kind **05** sweet **06** lovely, pretty, tender **07** winning **08** charming, engaging, pleasant, pleasing, precious, unctuous **09** agreeable, appealing, beautiful, seductive **10** attractive, delightful, flattering **11** mellifluous **12** affectionate

## honeysuckle

**06** abelia **08** Lonicera, rewarewa, suckling, woodbind, woodbine

**09** anthemion, caprifoil, caprifole, eglantine, snowberry, wolfberry **14** Caprifoliaceae

## Hong Kong

**02** HK **03** HGK

## honorarium

**03** fee, pay **06** reward, salary **07** payment **09** emolument **10** recompense **12** remuneration

## honorary

**03** Hon **06** formal, unpaid **07** nominal, titular **09** ex officio, honorific **10** in name only, unofficial

## honour

**01** A, J, K, Q **03** pay **04** fame, keep, take **05** adorn, award, clear, crown, exalt, glory, izzat, pride, prize, title, value **06** accept, admire, credit, esteem, ethics, favour, fulfil, homage, laurel, morals, praise, purity, regard, renown, repute, revere, reward, trophy, virtue, worthy **07** acclaim, applaud, commend, decency, dignity, execute, glorify, honesty, modesty, observe, perform, probity, respect, tribute, worship **08** accolade, applause, be true to, carry out, celibacy, chastity, decorate, good name, goodness, morality, remember, venerate **09** adoration, celebrate, discharge, innocence, integrity, privilege, recognize, rectitude, reverence, virginity **10** abstinence, admiration, compliment, continence, continency, decoration, estimation, maidenhood, principles, reputation, singleness, veneration **11** acclamation, acknowledge, commemorate, distinction, pay homage to, recognition, self-respect, uprightness **12** commendation, pay tribute to, truthfulness **13** righteousness, temperateness **14** immaculateness, unmarried state **15** acknowledgement, trustworthiness

---

*Honours include:*

**02** GC, KG, OM, VC
**03** CBE, CGC, DBE, DSC, DSO, GBE, KBE, MBE, OBE
**09** Iron Cross
**10** Bronze Star, Grand Cross, knighthood, Silver Star
**11** George Cross, Purple Heart
**12** Order of Merit
**13** Croix de Guerre, Legion of Merit, Medal for Merit, Victoria Cross, Victoria Medal
**14** Légion d'Honneur

---

• **in honour of** **02** to **05** after **11** celebrating

## honourable

**03** Hon **04** fair, good, just, true **05** great, moral, noble, noted, right, white **06** decent, family, famous, honest, trusty, worthy **07** eminent, ethical, notable, sincere, upright **08** reliable, renowned, straight, truthful, virtuous, worthful **09** admirable, ingenuous, reputable, respected, righteous **10** dependable, high-minded, principled, upstanding **11** illustrious,

prestigious, respectable, trustworthy
**13** distinguished **14** high-principled

**honourably**
**04** well **05** nobly, truly **07** morally
**08** decently, honestly, worthily
**09** ethically, reputably, sincerely
**10** virtuously **11** respectably

**hood**
**02** Al **04** cowl **05** amice, blind, Robin,
scarf, snood, visor, vizor **06** almuce,
biggin, bonnet, calash, domino,
mantle **07** bashlik, capouch, capuche,
hoodlum, surtout **08** calyptra,
capeline, capuccio, chaperon, trot-
cozy **09** calyptera, capelline,
chaperone, condition, Nithsdale, trot-
cosey

**hoodlum**
**03** yob **04** hood, lout, thug **05** brute,
felon, rowdy, tough **06** gunman,
mugger, vandal **07** mobster, ruffian
**08** criminal, gangster, hooligan,
larrikin, offender **09** bovver boy
**10** lawbreaker **11** armed robber

**hoodoo**
**04** jinx **05** magic, spell **06** voodoo
**07** bewitch, sorcery **08** wizardry
**09** occultism, the occult **10** black
magic, divination, necromancy,
witchcraft **11** conjuration,
enchantment, incantation, the black
art

**hoodwink**
**03** con **04** dupe, fool, gull, hide, hoax,
rook, seel **05** blear, cheat, trick
**06** baffle, delude, have on, outwit, take
in **07** deceive, defraud, mislead,
swindle **09** bamboozle, blindfold
**12** take for a ride **14** get the better of,
pull a fast one on

**hoof**
**04** foot, kick **05** cloot, expel **06** ungula
**07** trotter **10** cloven hoof

**hoofed**
**08** ungulate **10** horn-footed
**11** unguligrade **12** cloven-footed,
cloven-hoofed

**hook**
**03** arc, bag, bow, box, dog, fix, hit,
peg, rap **04** barb, bend, blow, clip,
cuff, curl, gaff, grab, hasp, loop, snig,
trap **05** angle, catch, chape, clasp,
cleek, clout, crome, crook, curve,
elbow, hinge, hitch, knock, punch,
snare, thump, uncus **06** attach, becket,
enmesh, entrap, excuse, fasten, griple,
scythe, secure, sickle, strike, stroke,
tenter, wallop **07** attract, cantdog,
capture, ensnare, gripple, hamulus,
pretext, sniggle **08** crotchet,
crummock, entangle, fastener
**09** goose-neck, tenaculum
**10** tenterhook **13** grappling-iron
• **by hook or by crook 07** somehow
**10** by any means **11** by some means,
come what may **15** one way or another
• **hook, line and sinker 05** fully,
quite **06** in full, wholly **07** solidly,
totally, utterly **08** entirely **09** every
inch, perfectly **10** absolutely,
altogether, completely, thoroughly

**12** heart and soul **13** root and branch
**14** in every respect **15** from first to last
• **off the hook 07** cleared **08** scot free
**09** acquitted, ready-made
**10** exonerated, in the clear, vindicated

**hookah**
**06** kalian **07** chillum, nargile, nargily
**08** narghile, narghily, nargileh, nargilly
**09** narghilly, water pipe **12** hubble-
bubble

**hooked**
**04** bent **05** adunc, beaky **06** barbed,
beaked, curled, curved, hamate,
hamose, hamous, uncate **07** devoted,
falcate, hamular **08** addicted,
aduncate, aduncous, aquiline,
hamulate, obsessed, unciform,
uncinate **09** aduncated, dependent,
enamoured **10** enthralled **12** sickle-
shaped

**hooligan**
**03** ned, yob **04** hoon, lout, thug
**05** droog, rough, rowdy, tough
**06** apache, mugger, skolly, tsotsi,
vandal **07** hoodlum, mobster, ruffian,
skollie **08** larrikin, tough guy **09** bovver
boy, roughneck **10** delinquent

**hoop**
**04** bail, band, gird, girr, loop, ring, tire
**05** round, wheel **06** basket, circle,
girdle **07** circlet, sleeper, stirrup,
trochus, trundle **08** encircle, hula-hoop
**10** laggen-gird

**hoot**
**03** boo, cry, jot, wit **04** beep, call, care,
hiss, hoop, howl, jeer, joke, mock,
riot, toot, yell **05** blare, comic, joker,
laugh, shout, sneer, taunt, whoop
**06** scream, shriek **07** screech, ululate,
whistle **08** howl down, ridicule
**09** character **12** tu-whit tu-whoo
**13** amusing person
• **not give a hoot 12** not care a toss,
not give a damn **13** not be bothered
**15** not give a monkey's

**hooter**
**03** owl **04** horn, nose **05** siren
• **little hooter 05** owlet

**hop**
**03** fly, nip, pop **04** jump, leap, limp,
skip, step, trip **05** bound, dance, disco,
frisk, jaunt, opium, party, vault
**06** bounce, flight, hobble, prance,
social, spring **07** journey, knees-up,
shindig **09** excursion **10** fly quickly
**11** quick flight
• **caught on the hop 07** unready
**11** ill-equipped **14** caught in the act,
caught unawares
• **stem of hop 04** bind, bine

**hope**
**03** aim **04** fear, long, pray, rely, wish
**05** await, combe, crave, dream, faith,
inlet, trust, yearn **06** aspire, assume,
belief, desire, expect **07** believe,
craving, foresee, longing, promise
**08** ambition, optimism, prospect,
reckon on, yearning **09** assurance, be
hopeful, enclosure, esperance, pipe
dream **10** anticipate, aspiration,
assumption, confidence, conviction,

expectance, expectancy **11** be
ambitious, contemplate, expectation,
hopefulness **12** anticipation **13** look
forward to **14** have confidence, pin
your hopes on **15** hope against hope

**hopeful**
**04** rosy **06** bright **07** assured, bullish,
buoyant **08** aspirant, aspiring, cheerful,
pleasant, positive, sanguine
**09** confident, expectant, promising
**10** auspicious, favourable, gladdening,
heartening, optimistic, propitious,
reassuring **11** encouraging

**hopefully**
**05** I hope **07** eagerly **08** probably, with
hope, with luck **09** bullishly
**10** expectedly, sanguinely
**11** conceivably, confidently,
expectantly **12** all being well **13** if all
goes well **14** optimistically

**hopefulness**
**04** wish **05** faith, trust **06** belief, desire
**07** craving, longing **08** ambition,
optimism, prospect, yearning
**09** assurance **10** aspiration,
assumption, confidence, conviction
**11** expectation **12** anticipation

**hopeless**
◊ *anagram indicator* **03** bad **04** lost,
poor, vain, weak **05** all up, awful,
bleak, grave, lousy **06** futile, gloomy,
no-hope **07** foolish, forlorn, useless
**08** dejected, downcast, helpless,
negative, pathetic, wretched **09** all up
with, defeatist, desperate, incurable,
pointless, worthless **10** despairing,
despondent, impossible
**11** demoralized, downhearted,
incompetent, irreparable, pessimistic
**12** beyond remedy, beyond repair,
irremediable, irreversible,
unachievable, unattainable
**13** impracticable **14** past praying for

**hopelessly**
◊ *anagram indicator* **05** badly **06** weakly
**07** awfully **08** gloomily **09** unhappily,
uselessly **10** dejectedly, negatively
**11** desperately **12** despairingly,
despondently, pathetically
**13** incompetently, inefficiently
**15** pessimistically

**hopelessness**
**05** blues, dumps, gloom **06** misery
**07** despair, wanhope **09** dejection,
pessimism **10** gloominess
**11** despondency, forlorn hope
**12** wretchedness **14** discouragement

**hophead**
*see* **addict**

**horde**
**03** mob **04** army, band, crew, gang,
herd, host, mass, pack **05** crowd,
drove, flock, swarm, troop **06** throng
**09** multitude

**horizon**
**05** range, scope, verge, vista
**07** compass, outlook, skyline
**08** prospect **10** experience, perception
**11** perspective **13** range of vision
• **on the horizon 04** near **05** close
**06** at hand, coming **07** brewing,

**horizontal**

looming 08 imminent, in the air, menacing, on the way 09 impending 11 approaching, forthcoming, in the offing, threatening 13 about to happen, almost upon you 15 fast approaching

**horizontal**

04 flat 05 level, plane 06 smooth, supine 08 levelled, straight 09 on its side

**hormone**

*Hormones include:*

05 kinin
06 orexin
07 gastrin, ghrelin, insulin, relaxin
08 abscisin, androgen, autacoid, estrogen, florigen, glucagon, oxytocin, secretin, thyroxin
09 adrenalin, cortisone, melatonin, oestrogen, pituitrin, prolactin, thyroxine
10 adrenaline, calcitonin, hypocretin
11 thyrotropin, vasopressin
12 androsterone, melanotropin, noradrenalin, progesterone, somatostatin, somatotropin, testosterone, thyrotrophin
14 erythropoietin, glucocorticoid

**horn**

04 butt, cusp, gore, push 05 bugle, corno, cornu 06 klaxon 07 keratin 08 cornicle, oliphant 09 telephone 10 corniculum 15 corno di bassetto
• **horn band** 04 frog
• **horn sound** 03 mot 04 beep, honk, hoot, parp 05 blast
• **part of horn** 03 bay, bez 04 tray, trey, trez 07 bay-tine, bez-tine 08 brow-tine, trey-tine 09 bay-antler, bez-antler 10 brow-antler, trey-antler

**hornless**

05 mooly, muley, poley 06 dodded, humble, hummel, mulley, polled

**horny**

04 hard, sexy 05 corny, randy 06 ardent 07 aroused, callous, lustful, ruttish 08 ceratoid, corneous 09 lecherous 10 keratinous, lascivious, libidinous 12 concupiscent

**horrendous**

08 dreadful, horrible, horrific, shocking, terrible 09 appalling, frightful 10 horrifying, terrifying 11 frightening

**horrible**

◇ *anagram indicator* 04 foul, grim, ugly 05 awful, black, grisy, nasty, scary 06 griesy, grisly, grysie, horrid, unkind 07 ghastly, hideous 08 dreadful, gruesome, horrific, shocking, terrible 09 appalling, frightful, harrowing, loathsome, monstrous, obnoxious, offensive, repulsive, revolting 10 abominable, detestable, disgusting, horrendous, horrifying, monstruous, terrifying, unpleasant 11 frightening, hair-raising 12 disagreeable 13 bloodcurdling

**horribly**

◇ *anagram indicator* 03 ill 06 grimly 07 awfully 08 terribly 09 hideously

10 dreadfully, gruesomely 11 appallingly, frightfully, repulsively 12 disagreeably, horrifically, unpleasantly

**horrid**

◇ *anagram indicator* 04 grim, mean 05 awful, cruel, nasty, rough 06 shaggy, unkind 07 beastly, ghastly, hateful, hideous 08 dreadful, gruesome, horrific, shocking, terrible 09 appalling, bristling, frightful, harrowing, obnoxious, repellent, repulsive, revolting 10 abominable, detestable, horrifying, terrifying 11 frightening, hair-raising 13 bloodcurdling

**horrific**

◇ *anagram indicator* 05 awful, scary 07 ghastly 08 dreadful, gruesome, shocking, terrible 09 appalling, frightful, harrowing 10 horrifying, terrifying 11 frightening 13 bloodcurdling

**horrifically**

07 awfully 08 terribly 10 dreadfully, shockingly 11 appallingly, frightfully, repulsively 12 disagreeably

**horrify**

05 abhor, alarm, appal, panic, repel, scare, shock, spook 06 agrise, agrize, agryze, dismay, offend, revolt, sicken 07 disgust, outrage, startle, terrify 08 frighten, nauseate 09 terrorize 10 intimidate, scandalize 12 put the wind up, scare to death

**horror**

04 fear, hate 05 alarm, dread, panic, shock 06 dismay, fright, terror 07 disgust, outrage 08 distaste, loathing 09 awfulness, revulsion 10 abhorrence, raggedness, repugnance, shagginess, shuddering 11 abomination, detestation, ghastliness, hideousness, trepidation 12 apprehension 13 consternation, frightfulness 14 unpleasantness
• **horror film** 07 chiller 10 hair raiser

**horror-struck**

06 aghast 07 shocked, stunned 08 appalled 09 horrified, petrified, terrified 10 frightened 11 scared stiff 14 horror-stricken

**hors d'oeuvre**

04 meze 05 mezze 06 hummus, matjes 07 ceviche, maatjes, zakuska 08 crudités 09 antipasto, carpaccio 11 smörgåsbord

**horse**

01 H 02 GG 03 pad 04 crib, hack, hoss, moke, pony, prad, yaud 05 filly, mount, neddy 06 dobbin, gee-gee, heroin, keffel, sorrel 07 broncho, cavalry, centaur, charger, pit pony, trotter 08 yarraman
*See also* **animal; heroin; pony**

*Horses and ponies include:*

03 Don
04 Arab, Barb, Fell
05 Dales, Iomud, Lokai, Pinto, Shire, Toric, Waler, Welsh

06 Auxois, Breton, Brumby, Exmoor, Morgan, Nonius, Tersky
07 Comtois, Criollo, Finnish, Furioso, Hackney, Hispano, Jutland, Masuren, Muraköz, Murgese, Mustang, Salerno
08 Budyonny, Danubian, Dartmoor, Friesian, Highland, Holstein, Kabardin, Karabair, Karabakh, Lusitano, Palomino, Paso Fino, Poitevin, Shetland, Welsh Cob
09 Akhal-Teké, Alter-Réal, Anglo-Arab, Appaloosa, Ardennias, Brabançon, Calabrese, Connemara, Falabella, Groningen, Kladruber, Knabstrup, Kustanair, Maremmana, New Forest, New Kirgiz, Oldenburg, Percheron, Sardinian, Tchenaran, Trakehner, Welsh Pony
10 Andalusian, Boulonnais, Clydesdale, Einsiedler, Freiberger, Gelderland, Hanoverian, Lipizzaner, Mangalarga, Shagya Arab
11 Anglo-Norman, Døle Trotter, Irish Hunter, Mecklenburg, Przewalski's, Trait du Nord, Württemberg
12 Cleveland Bay, Dutch Draught, East Friesian, French Saddle, Irish Draught, Metis Trotter, North Swedish, Orlov Trotter, Suffolk Punch, Thoroughbred
13 East Bulgarian, Frederiksborg, French Trotter, German Trotter, Welsh Mountain
14 American Saddle, Latvian Harness, Plateau Persian
15 American Quarter, American Trotter, Swedish Halfbred

*Parts of a horse include:*

03 ear, eye, hip
04 back, chin, dock, face, head, heel, hock, hoof, knee, lips, mane, neck, nose, poll, ribs, rump, shin, tail
05 atlas, belly, canon, cheek, chest, crest, croup, elbow, ergot, flank, girth, loins, mouth, thigh
06 breast, cannon, gaskin, haunch, muzzle, sheath, stifle, temple, throat
07 abdomen, brisket, buttock, coronet, crupper, fetlock, forearm, hind leg, pastern, quarter, shannon, tendons, withers
08 chestnut, forefoot, forehead, forelock, lower jaw, lower lip, nostrils, shoulder, under lip, upper lip, windpipe
09 hamstring, hock joint, nasal peak
10 chin groove, point of hip, wall of foot
11 back tendons, point of hock, stifle joint
12 fetlock joint, hindquarters, hollow of heel, point of elbow
13 dock of the tail, flexor tendons, jugular groove, root of the tail
14 Achilles tendon, crest of the neck
15 point of shoulder

*Horses' tack includes:*

**03** bit
**05** arson, cinch, girth, hames, reins
**06** bridle, cantle, collar, halter, numnah, pommel, saddle, traces
**07** alforja, crupper, housing, stirrup
**08** backband, blinders, blinkers, noseband, shabrack
**09** bellyband, breeching, hackamore, headstall, saddlebag, saddlebow, saddlepad, surcingle
**10** martingale, saddletree, shabracque, throatlash
**11** bearing rein, saddlecloth, saddle-girth, throatlatch
**13** saddle blanket

*See also* **bridle**

*Horse-related terms include:*

**03** bay, cob, dun, hie, hup, nag, shy
**04** bolt, buck, colt, foal, gait, grey, mare, roan, stud, trot, walk
**05** break, forge, gee up, groom, hands, lunge, mount, nappy, pinto, steed
**06** bronco, brumby, canter, equine, gallop, hippic, livery, manège, riding, stable
**07** astride, blanket, gelding, giddy-up, hacking, nosebag, paddock, passade, piebald
**08** chestnut, dismount, horse box, skewbald, stallion
**09** horseshoe, roughshod
**10** blood horse, draft horse, en cavalier, equestrian, heavy horse, side-saddle
**11** riding habit
**12** broken-winded, pony-trekking, thoroughbred
**13** champ at the bit, mounting block, put out to grass
**14** strawberry roan

*Racehorses include:*

**05** Arkle, Cigar, Pinza
**06** Nearco, Red Rum, Sir Ken
**07** Alleged, Dawn Run, Eclipse, Phar Lap, Sceptre, Shergar, Sir Ivor
**08** Aldaniti, Best Mate, Corbiere, Esha Ness, Hyperion, Istabraq, Mill Reef, Nijinsky
**09** John Henry, L'Escargot, Oh So Sharp
**10** Night Nurse, Persian War, Seabiscuit, See You Then, Sun Chariot
**11** Cottage Rake, Never Say Die, Pretty Polly
**12** Dancing Brave, Desert Orchid, Golden Miller, Hatton's Grace

*See also* **racecourse; racing**
• **call to horse** **03** hie, hup **04** high, proo, pruh
• **inferior horse** **03** nag, rip **04** moke
• **pair of horses** **04** span
• **shying horse** **03** jib **06** jibber
• **thin horse** **04** rake
• **working horse** **03** cut
• **worn-out horse** **03** tit **04** jade, plug **07** knacker

## horsefly
**04** cleg

## horseman, horsewoman
**05** rider **06** hussar, jockey, knight
**07** dragoon, hobbler, pricker
**08** stradiot, wrangler **09** caballero
**10** cavalryman, equestrian **12** horse soldier

*Horseriders, jockeys and trainers include:*

**04** **Anne** (Princess), **Hern** (Major Dick), **Leng** (Virginia), **Pipe** (Martin), **Tait** (Blyth), **Todd** (Mark)
**05** **Cecil** (Henry), **Green** (Lucinda), **Krone** (Julie), **Lukas** (D Wayne), **McCoy** (Tony), **Meade** (Richard), **Moore** (Ryan), **Smith** (Harvey), **Smith** (Robyn)
**06** **Arcaro** (Eddie), **Archer** (Fred), **Carson** (Willie), **Eddery** (Pat), **Fallon** (Kieren), **O'Brien** (Vincent), **O'Neill** (Jonjo), **Pitman** (Jenny)
**07** **Dettori** (Frankie), **Francis** (Dick), **Gifford** (Josh), **Piggott** (Lester), **Winkler** (Hans Günter)
**08** **Champion** (Bob), **Donoghue** (Steve), **Dunwoody** (Richard), **Phillips** (Captain Mark), **Richards** (Sir Gordon)
**09** **Scudamore** (Peter), **Shoemaker** (Willie)

*See also* **equestrian**

## horseplay
**03** rag **06** antics, capers, pranks
**07** foolery, fooling **08** clowning **09** high jinks **10** buffoonery, skylarking, tomfoolery **11** fun and games
**12** mucking about **13** fooling around, mucking around **14** monkey business, practical jokes, rough-and-tumble

## horsepower
**02** CV, hp, PS

## horseradish tree
**03** ben

## horsewoman
*see* **horseman, horsewoman**

## hortatory
**03** pep **08** didactic, edifying, inciting
**09** homiletic, hortative, practical
**10** heartening, preceptive
**11** encouraging, exhortative, exhortatory, inspiriting, instructive, stimulating

## horticulture
**09** gardening **11** agriculture, cultivation
**12** floriculture **13** arboriculture

## hosanna
**06** praise, save us **07** worship
**08** alleluia **09** laudation

## hose
**03** sox **04** duct, pipe, tube **05** socks
**06** piping, trunks, tubing **07** airline, channel, conduit **08** chausses
**09** stockings **12** galligaskins

## hosiery
**04** hose **05** socks **06** tights **07** hold-ups, stay-ups **08** leggings **09** knee-highs, panty hose, stockings **12** leg-coverings

## hospitable
**04** kind, warm **05** cadgy **06** genial, kidgie **07** cordial, helpful, liberal
**08** amicable, friendly, generous, gracious, sociable **09** bountiful, congenial, convivial, receptive, welcoming **10** open-handed **11** kind-hearted, neighbourly

## hospital
**01** H **03** CHE, san **04** GOSH, Guy's, home, lock, MASH **05** Bart's **06** clinic, spital **07** hospice, spittle **08** clinique, nuthouse, snake-pit **09** ambulance, funny farm, hôtel-Dieu, infirmary, institute, leprosery **10** booby hatch, leproserie, polyclinic, sanatorium
**11** nursing home **12** health centre
**13** lunatic asylum, medical centre
• **hospital department** **03** ENT
**04** gyny **05** A and E **08** casualty

## hospitality
**05** cheer **06** warmth **07** welcome
**08** kindness **09** open house
**10** generosity, liberality, philoxenia
**11** helpfulness, sociability
**12** congeniality, conviviality, friendliness, housekeeping
**13** accommodation, entertainment
**14** open-handedness, tea and sympathy **15** neighbourliness

## host
◇ *containment indicator* **02** MC **03** mob
**04** army, band, give, herd, mass, pack
**05** array, crowd, crush, emcee, horde, swarm, troop **06** anchor, myriad, throng **07** compère, linkman, present
**08** landlady, landlord, publican
**09** anchorman, announcer, harbinger, innkeeper, introduce, multitude, presenter **10** party-giver, proprietor
**11** anchorwoman, entertainer
**12** proprietress

## hostage
**04** pawn **06** pledge, surety **07** captive
**08** detainee, prisoner, security

## hostel
**01** Y **03** inn **04** hall, YMCA, YWCA
**05** entry, hotel, motel **07** hospice, pension **08** hospital **09** dormitory, dosshouse, flophouse, residence
**10** guesthouse **11** youth hostel
**13** boarding-house **15** bed-and-breakfast

## hostelry
**03** bar, inn, pub **05** hotel, motel
**06** tavern **07** canteen, pension
**09** public bar **10** guesthouse **11** public house **13** boarding-house

## hostile
**03** icy **05** enemy **06** averse, infest, wintry **07** adverse, glacial, opposed, warlike, wintery **08** contrary, inimical, opposite **09** bellicose, oppugnant
**10** aggressive, inveterate, malevolent, unfriendly **11** adversarial, belligerent, disinclined, ill-disposed
**12** antagonistic, antipathetic, disapproving, inauspicious, inhospitable, unfavourable
**13** unsympathetic **14** at daggers drawn
• **become hostile** **04** rise

## hostilities

**03** war **04** arms **06** action, battle, strife
**07** warfare **08** conflict, fighting
**09** bloodshed

## hostility

**03** war **04** envy, hate **05** anger
**06** animus, enmity, hatred, malice
**07** cruelty, dislike, ill-will **08** aversion,
disfavor **09** animosity, antipathy,
disfavour, militancy, prejudice
**10** abhorrence, aggression,
antagonism, bitterness, opposition,
resentment **11** bellicosity, malevolence
**12** belligerence, estrangement, hard
feelings **14** unfriendliness,
unpleasantness

## hot

**01** h **02** in **03** het, hip, new, red **04** chic,
cool, keen, warm **05** angry, balmy,
eager, fiery, fresh, funky, livid, quick,
ritzy, sharp, spicy **06** ardent, baking,
fervid, fierce, fuming, glitzy, heated,
latest, modern, piping, raging, recent,
red hot, snazzy, spiced, stolen, strong,
sultry, swanky, torrid, trendy, uncool,
with it **07** boiling, burning, candent,
current, devoted, earnest, enraged,
flushed, furious, illicit, intense, in
vogue, lustful, peppery, piquant,
popular, pungent, searing, stylish,
summery, violent, zealous
**08** animated, diligent, exciting,
feverish, incensed, inflamed, parching,
pilfered, powerful, roasting, scalding,
seething, sizzling, steaming, swinging,
toasting, tropical, up-to-date,
vehement **09** cut-throat, dangerous,
delirious, dog-eat-dog, ill-gotten,
indignant, scorching **10** all the rage,
blistering, candescent, contraband,
passionate, prevailing, sweltering
**11** fashionable **12** contemporary,
enthusiastic, incandescent **13** up-to-
the-minute
*See also* **warm**
• **be hot** **04** boil
• **blow hot and cold** **04** sway
**05** haver, waver **08** hesitate, hum and
ha **09** fluctuate, hum and haw,
oscillate, temporize, vacillate
**10** dilly-dally **12** shilly-shally
• **feel hot** **04** burn
• **hot air** **03** gas **04** bosh, bunk, foam
**05** bilge, froth **06** bunkum, piffle,
vapour **07** baloney, blather, blether,
bluster, bombast, eyewash, vapours
**08** blethers, claptrap, cobblers,
nonsense, verbiage **09** bullswool,
emptiness, empty talk, mere words
**10** balderdash, codswallop

## hotbed

**03** den **04** hive, nest **06** cradle, school
**07** nursery, seedbed **08** seed plot
**12** forcing-house **14** breeding-ground

## hot-blooded

**04** bold, rash, wild **05** eager, fiery, lusty
**06** ardent, heated **07** fervent, lustful,
sensual **08** spirited **09** excitable,
impetuous, impulsive, irritable,
perfervid **10** passionate **11** precipitate
**12** high-spirited, homothermous
**13** temperamental

## hotchpotch

◇ *anagram indicator* **03** mix, pie **04** mess
**06** jumble, medley **07** melange,
mixture **08** mishmash **09** confusion,
potpourri **10** collection, hodgepodge,
miscellany

## hotel

**01** H **03** inn, pub **04** Ritz **05** botel,
hydro, motel **06** boatel, hostel, tavern
**07** Gasthof, pension **08** Gasthaus,
hostelry **09** flophouse **10** aparthotel,
guesthouse, trust house
**11** hydropathic, public house
**13** boarding-house, sporting house
**15** bed and breakfast
• **hotel employee** **04** chef, page
**05** boots **06** porter **07** bell boy, bell hop
**11** chambermaid

## hotfoot

**07** flat out, hastily, in haste, quickly,
rapidly, swiftly **08** pell-mell, speedily
**09** hurriedly, posthaste **10** at top speed
**11** at the double **12** lickety-split,
without delay **13** helter-skelter **14** at a
rate of knots, hell for leather **15** like the
clappers
• **hotfoot it** **04** belt, dash, pelt, race,
rush, tear, zoom **05** hurry, speed
**06** career, gallop, hurtle, sprint
**07** quicken **08** step on it **09** bowl along
**10** accelerate **15** put your foot down

## hothead

**06** madcap, madman, terror **07** hotspur
**08** cacafogo, tearaway **09** cacafuego,
daredevil, desperado

## hotheaded

**04** rash, wild **05** fiery, hasty **08** reckless,
volatile, volcanic **09** excitable,
explosive, foolhardy, impetuous,
impulsive, irascible **10** headstrong
**11** hot-tempered **13** quick-tempered,
short-tempered

## hothouse

**05** stove **06** vinery **07** brothel
**08** orangery **10** glasshouse, greenhouse
**12** conservatory, forcing-house

## hotly

**04** near, nigh **06** keenly, nearly
**07** closely, tightly **08** ardently, fiercely,
narrowly, strongly **09** fervently,
intensely **10** forcefully, vehemently,
vigorously **12** at close range,
passionately **15** at close quarters

## hot-tempered

**05** fiery, hasty, ratty, testy **07** crabbit,
stroppy, violent **08** choleric, petulant,
volcanic **09** explosive, irascible,
irritable **10** splenative **13** quick-
tempered, short-tempered

## hound

**03** dog, nag **04** goad, hunt, lime, lyam,
lyme, prod, urge **05** brach, bully,
chase, drive, force, harry, stalk, track,
trail **06** badger, basset, beagle, chivvy,
follow, harass, jowler, pester, pursue,
talbot, tufter **07** coondog, disturb,
provoke **08** hunt down **09** persecute
• **pack of hounds** **03** cry **04** hunt
**06** kennel

## hour

**01** h **02** hr

*Hours include:*

**04** rush
**05** flexi, happy, lunch, small
**06** dinner, golden, office, waking
**07** trading, working
**08** business, eleventh, midnight,
unsocial, visiting, witching

*See also* **canonical**
• **early hours** **02** am
• **outside hours** **04** kerb

## house

◇ *containment indicator* **02** ho **03** Hse,
inn, ken, mas, pad **04** body, casa, clan,
crib, door, firm, gaff, hame, hold,
home, keep, line, race **05** bingo,
blood, board, cover, crowd, guard,
lodge, place, put up, store, tribe
**06** billet, family, ménage, reside, strain,
take in **07** chamber, company,
contain, convent, dynasty, harbour,
kindred, lineage, protect, quarter,
sheathe, shelter, turnout, viewers
**08** ancestry, assembly, audience,
building, business, congress,
domestic, domicile, dwelling
**09** gathering, household, listeners,
onlookers, residence **10** auditorium,
enterprise, habitation, parliament,
spectators **11** accommodate,
corporation, have room for, legislature
**12** family circle, have space for,
organization **13** establishment

*Houses include:*

**03** hut
**04** flat, hall, riad, semi, weem
**05** croft, igloo, lodge, manor, manse,
shack, villa, whare
**06** bedsit, chalet, datcha, duplex,
grange, mia-mia, pondok, prefab,
shanty, studio, wurley
**07** cottage, mansion, rectory
**08** bungalow, detached, hacienda,
log cabin, terraced, vicarage
**09** apartment, but and ben,
farmhouse, homestead,
parsonage, penthouse, single-
end, town house, treehouse, villa
home, villa unit
**10** granny flat, maisonette, pied-à-
terre, ranch house, state house
**11** condominium
**12** council house, semi-detached
**14** chalet bungalow
**15** thatched cottage

*See also* **accommodation; building;
zodiac**
• **House of Commons** **02** HC
• **House of Lords** **02** HL
• **on the house** **04** free **06** gratis
**08** at no cost **10** for nothing
**11** without cost **12** free of charge **13** at
no extra cost, without charge
**14** without payment

## household

**04** home **05** house, plain, set-up
**06** common, family, famous, ménage,
people **08** domestic, everyday,
familiar, ordinary **09** well-known
**11** established **12** family circle
**13** establishment

*Household items include:*

**03** bin, mop
**04** comb, hook, pram, vase
**05** broom, brush, diary, match, potty, range, towel
**06** basket, candle, duster, pet bed, sponge
**07** ashtray, coaster, dustpan, flannel, key rack, key ring, wash bag
**08** aquarium, bassinet, birdcage, calendar, coat hook, dish rack, fish tank, flatiron, hat stand, hip flask, ornament, place mat, shoe rack, soap dish, suitcase, tea towel, waste bin, wine rack
**09** cat basket, dishcloth, dog basket, door wedge, fireguard, hairbrush, hearth rug, highchair, memo board, phone book, pushchair, sponge bag, stair gate, stepstool, towel rail, washboard, washcloth
**10** baby bottle, baby walker, coathanger, laundry bag, letter rack, oven gloves, photo album, photo frame, stepladder, storage box, toothbrush
**11** address book, candlestick, changing mat, first aid kit, paperweight, toilet brush
**12** clothes airer, clothes-brush, clothes horse, ironing board, magazine rack, perambulator, picnic basket, thermos flask
**13** feather duster, laundry basket, satellite dish, soap dispenser, umbrella stand, washing-up bowl
**14** hot water bottle, phone directory
**15** draught excluder, photograph album, photograph frame

## householder
**05** owner **06** tenant **07** goodman, gudeman **08** landlady, landlord, occupant, occupier, resident **09** home-owner
**10** freeholder, proprietor
**11** leaseholder **13** owner-occupier

## housekeeping
**08** domestic **10** homemaking
**11** hospitality, housewifery
**12** domestic work, running a home
**13** home economics **15** domestic matters, domestic science

## houseman
**05** valet **06** butler, doctor, intern
**07** interne, servant **08** resident, retainer
**10** manservant **12** house-surgeon, junior doctor **14** house-physician

## house-trained
**04** tame **05** tamed **11** house-broken
**12** domesticated, well-mannered

## housing
◇ *containment indicator* **04** case
**05** cover, guard, homes **06** casing, holder, houses, jacket, sheath
**07** shelter **08** covering, shabrack
**09** container, dwellings **10** habitation, protection, shabracque
**13** accommodation

## hovel
**03** hut **04** dump, hole, shed, slum
**05** cabin, shack, whare **06** kennel, shanty **07** shelter

## hover
**03** fly **04** flap, hang, hove, wave
**05** drift, float, hoove, pause, poise, waver **06** linger, loiter, seesaw
**07** flutter **08** hesitate **09** alternate, fluctuate, hang about, oscillate, vacillate **10** helicopter **11** be suspended

## however
**03** but, yet **05** howbe, still **06** anyhow, even so, though **07** howbeit **08** actually
**09** as it comes, howsoever, in any case, leastways, leastwise
**10** howsomever, leastaways, regardless **11** howsomdever, just the same, nonetheless **12** nevertheless
**13** at the same time **15** notwithstanding

## howl
**03** bay, cry, wow **04** bawl, gowl, hoot, moan, roar, wail, yawl, yell, yelp, yowl **05** groan, laugh, shout **06** bellow, scream, shriek

## howler
**04** boob, flub, goof **05** boner, error, fluff, gaffe **07** bloomer, blunder, clanger, mistake, Mycetes **08** solecism
**11** malapropism

## HQ
*see* **headquarters**

## hub
**03** hob **04** axis, boss, core, nave
**05** focus, heart, pivot **06** centre, middle
**08** linchpin **10** focal point **11** nerve centre

## hubbub
**03** din, row **04** coil, riot **05** chaos, noise
**06** racket, rumpus, tumult, uproar
**07** clamour, whoobub **08** disorder, hubbuboo, rowdedow, rowdydow
**09** commotion, confusion, level-coil
**10** hullabaloo, hurly-burly
**11** disturbance, pandemonium

## hubris
**05** nerve, pride, scorn **06** vanity
**07** conceit, disdain, egotism, hauteur
**08** boasting, contempt **09** arrogance, contumely, insolence, lordiness, pomposity **11** haughtiness, overweening, presumption, superiority
**12** snobbishness **13** condescension, imperiousness **14** high-handedness, self-importance

## huckster
**04** hawk, tout **06** barker, dealer, hawker, kidder, peddle, pedlar, tinker, trader, vendor **07** haggler, kiddier, packman, pitcher **11** salesperson

## huddle
**04** cram, heap, herd, knot, mass, meet, pack, ruck **05** clump, crowd, flock, hunch, press **06** bundle, crouch, cuddle, curl up, fumble, gather, hustle, jumble, muddle, nestle, pester, powwow, throng **07** cluster, meeting, snuggle, squeeze **08** conclave, converge **09** confusion, gravitate
**10** conference, congregate, discussion
**12** consultation

## hue
**03** dye, hew **04** tint, tone **05** color,

light, shade, tinge **06** aspect, chroma, colour, nuance **07** clamour **08** shouting
**10** appearance, complexion

## hue and cry
**03** ado **04** fuss, to-do **05** chase, hoo-ha, tizzy **06** furore, outcry, rumpus, uproar
**07** carry-on, clamour, ruction
**08** ballyhoo, brouhaha **09** commotion, kerfuffle **10** hullabaloo **13** a song and dance

## huff
**03** pet **04** mood, rage, stew, tiff
**05** anger, bully, paddy, pique, snuff, sulks **06** hector, strunt **07** bad mood, bluster, passion **09** blusterer

## huffily
**07** angrily, crossly, in a huff **08** in a paddy, in a strop, morosely, snappily
**09** in a temper, irritably, peevishly
**11** resentfully

## huffy
**05** angry, cross, moody, short, sulky, surly, testy **06** crusty, grumpy, miffed, moping, morose, shirty, snappy, snuffy, touchy **07** crabbed, peevish, stroppy, waspish **08** offended, petulant
**09** crotchety, irritable, querulous, resentful **10** hoity-toity **11** disgruntled

## hug
◇ *containment indicator* **01** O **04** coll, grip, hold **05** clasp, press **06** clinch, clutch, cuddle, enfold **07** cherish, cling to, embrace, enclose, snuggle, squeeze **08** stay near **09** hold close
**11** keep close to, stay close to
**13** follow closely

## huge
**02** OS **03** big **04** mega, vast **05** bulky, enorm, giant, great, heavy, jumbo, large **06** immane **07** hideous, hugeous, immense, mammoth, massive, socking, titanic **08** colossal, enormous, gigantic, unwieldy **09** cavernous, extensive, frightful, gigantean, ginormous, Herculean, humongous, humungous, monstrous, swingeing
**10** Babylonian, gargantuan, monumental, prodigious, stupendous, superjumbo, tremendous
**11** mountainous, stupendious

## hugely
**04** very **06** highly, really, vastly
**07** awfully, greatly, largely **08** terribly, very much **09** extremely, immensely, massively **10** enormously, thoroughly
**11** frightfully **12** terrifically, tremendously **15** extraordinarily

## hugger-mugger
**03** sly **06** closet, covert, hidden, secret, sneaky, untidy **07** chaotic, furtive, jumbled, mixed-up, muddled, private, secrecy **08** backroom, confused, stealthy **09** concealed, confusion, underhand **10** behind-door, disordered, disorderly, fraudulent, out of order, undercover **11** clandestine, disarranged, underground
**12** disorganized **13** surreptitious
**14** cloak-and-dagger **15** under-the-counter

**Hughes**
03 Ted

**hulk**
03 oaf 04 clod, hull, lout, lump
05 frame, shell, wreck 06 lubber
07 remains 08 derelict 09 shipwreck
10 clodhopper

**hulking**
03 big 05 bulky, heavy, large 06 clumsy
07 awkward, massive, weighty
08 ungainly, unwieldy 09 lumbering
10 cumbersome

**hull**
03 pod 04 body, bulk, husk, pare, peel,
rind, skin, trim 05 frame, shell, shuck,
strip 06 casing, legume 07 capsule,
epicarp 08 covering, skeleton
09 framework, monocoque, structure

**hullabaloo**
03 din, hue 04 fuss, to-do 05 hoo-ha,
noise, tizzy 06 furore, hubbub, outcry,
racket, ruckus, rumpus, tumult, uproar
07 carry-on, palaver, ruction, turmoil
08 ballyhoo, brouhaha, razmataz
09 commotion, hue and cry, kerfuffle
10 razzmatazz 11 disturbance,
pandemonium, razzamatazz 13 a song
and dance

**hum**
03 bum 04 buzz, hoax, lilt, purr, sing
05 chirm, croon, drone, pulse, smell,
sough, throb, thrum, whirr 06 be busy,
mumble, murmur 07 applaud,
buzzing, purring, vibrate 08 whirring
09 bombilate, bombinate, pulsation,
throbbing, vibration 10 imposition
• **hum and haw** 04 sway 05 waver
06 dither 08 hesitate 09 fluctuate,
oscillate, vacillate 10 dilly-dally 12 be
indecisive, shilly-shally 14 blow hot
and cold

**human**
03 man 04 body, kind, soul, weak
05 child, woman 06 genial, humane,
mortal, person 07 fleshly 08 fallible,
physical, rational, tolerant
09 anthropic 10 anthropoid, human
being, individual, reasonable,
vulnerable 11 anthropical, considerate,
Homo sapiens, susceptible,
sympathetic 12 compassionate, flesh
and blood, understanding
• **human affairs** 04 life

**humane**
04 good, kind, mild 06 benign, gentle,
kindly, loving, polite, tender
07 elegant, lenient 08 generous,
merciful 09 classical, forgiving
10 benevolent, charitable, forbearing,
humanizing, thoughtful
11 considerate, good-natured, kind-
hearted, sympathetic 12 humanitarian
13 compassionate, understanding

**humanely**
06 gently, kindly, mildly 08 lovingly,
tenderly 10 generously, mercifully
12 thoughtfully 13 kind-heartedly
15 compassionately, sympathetically

**humanitarian**
04 kind 06 humane 07 welfare
08 altruist, do-gooder, generous

09 unselfish 10 altruistic, benefactor,
benevolent, charitable 11 considerate,
sympathetic 13 compassionate, good
Samaritan, philanthropic,
understanding 14 philanthropist,
public-spirited

**humanitarianism**
07 charity 08 goodwill, humanism
10 generosity 11 beneficence,
benevolence 12 philanthropy
14 charitableness, loving-kindness

**humanities**
04 arts 08 classics 10 literature,
philosophy 11 liberal arts

**humanity**
03 man 04 pity 05 mercy 06 mandom,
people, ubuntu 07 mankind, mortals
08 goodness, goodwill, kindness,
sympathy 09 humankind, human race,
mortality, tolerance, womankind
10 compassion, generosity, gentleness,
humaneness, tenderness
11 benevolence, Homo sapiens
13 brotherly love, fellow-feeling,
understanding 14 thoughtfulness
15 kind-heartedness

**humanize**
04 tame 05 edify 06 better, polish,
refine 07 educate, improve 08 civilize
09 cultivate, enlighten 11 domesticate

**humankind**
03 man 06 people 07 mankind, mortals
08 humanity 09 human race, mortality,
womankind 11 Homo sapiens

**humanness**
08 goodness, goodwill, humanity,
kindness, sympathy 09 tolerance
10 compassion, generosity, gentleness,
tenderness 11 benevolence, human
nature 13 understanding
14 thoughtfulness 15 kind-heartedness

**humble**
03 low 04 base, mean, meek, poor,
sink 05 abase, crush, lower, lowly,
plain, pluck, shame, silly, small
06 abased, common, demean, demiss,
hummel, modest, polite, simple,
subdue 07 afflict, awnless, chasten,
deflate, degrade, depress, mortify,
servile 08 belittle, bring low, disgrace,
hornless, inferior, ordinary, yeomanly
09 afflicted, bring down, demissive,
discredit, disparage, humiliate,
prideless, unrefined 10 low-ranking,
obsequious, put to shame, respectful,
submissive, unassuming
11 commonplace, deferential,
subservient, sycophantic, unassertive,
unimportant 12 self-effacing,
supplicatory 13 cut down to size,
insignificant, unpretentious
14 unostentatious 15 undistinguished

**humbleness**
07 modesty 08 humility, meekness
09 deference, lowliness, servility
10 diffidence 13 self-abasement 14 self-
effacement, submissiveness,
unassumingness 15 unassertiveness

**humbly**
03 low 06 meekly, simply 08 docilely,
modestly 09 cap in hand, servilely

10 sheepishly 11 diffidently
12 obsequiously, respectfully,
submissively, unassumingly
13 deferentially, subserviently
15 unpretentiously

**humbug**
03 con, gum, rot 04 bunk, cant, fake,
gaff, guff, hoax, sham 05 actor, balls,
bluff, cheat, fraud, fudge, poser, rogue,
trick 06 barney, berley, blague,
bunkum, burley, cajole, con man,
deceit, gammon, string 07 baloney,
bluffer, deceive, eyewash, rubbish,
swindle 08 buncombe, cheating,
claptrap, cobblers, flummery,
impostor, nonsense, pretence,
swindler, trickery 09 charlatan,
deception, gold brick, hypocrisy,
kidstakes, poppycock, trickster
10 balderdash, hollowness

**humdrum**
04 dull 05 banal, prosy 06 boring,
dreary 07 droning, mundane, routine,
tedious 08 everyday, monotony,
ordinary, tiresome, unvaried
09 bourgeois 10 monotonous,
uneventful 11 commonplace,
repetitious 12 run-of-the-mill
13 uninteresting

**humid**
03 wet 04 damp, dank 05 close, heavy,
mochy, moist, muggy 06 clammy,
mochie, steamy, sticky, sultry
10 oppressive

**humidity**
03 dew 04 damp, mist 07 wetness
08 dampness, dankness, moisture
09 closeness, heaviness, humidness,
moistness, mugginess, sogginess
10 clamminess, steaminess, stickiness,
sultriness, vaporosity 12 vaporousness

**humiliate**
05 abase, abash, break, crush, shame
06 demean, humble, wither
07 chasten, deflate, degrade, mortify,
put down 08 bring low, confound,
disgrace, take down 09 discomfit,
discredit, embarrass 11 make a fool of
12 bring shame on, take down a peg

**humiliating**
07 shaming 08 crushing, humbling,
snubbing 09 deflating, degrading,
humiliant, withering 10 chastening,
disgracing, inglorious, mortifying
11 disgraceful, humiliative,
humiliatory, ignominious
12 discomfiting, embarrassing

**humiliation**
04 snub 05 shame 06 ignomy, rebuff
07 affront, put-down 08 comedown,
crushing, disgrace, downfall,
humbling, ignominy, take-down
09 abasement, deflation, discredit,
dishonour, humble pie, indignity
10 chastening, loss of face
11 confounding, degradation
12 discomfiture 13 embarrassment,
mortification

**humility**
07 modesty 08 meekness 09 deference,
lowlihead, lowliness, servility

**10** diffidence, humbleness **13** self-abasement **14** self-effacement, submissiveness, unassumingness **15** unassertiveness

**humming**
see **smelly**

**hummingbird**
**05** sylph, topaz **06** hermit, hummer **07** colibri, jacobin, rainbow **08** coquette **09** sabrewing, swordbill, trochilus **10** racket-tail, rubythroat, sicklebill **11** whitethroat **12** sapphire-wing

**hummock**
**04** hump **05** knoll, mound **06** barrow **07** hillock **09** elevation **10** prominence

**humorist**
**03** wag, wit **05** clown, comic, joker **06** gagman, jester **08** comedian, satirist **10** cartoonist **12** caricaturist

**humorous**
**04** zany **05** comic, droll, funny, pawky, witty **06** absurd **07** amusing, comical, giocoso, jocular, playful, risible, waggish **08** farcical **09** facetious, funny ha-ha, hilarious, irregular, laughable, ludicrous, satirical, whimsical **10** capricious, Gilbertian, humoristic, ridiculous **11** Falstaffian, Rabelaisian **12** entertaining, knee-slapping **13** side-splitting

**humour**
**03** fun, wit **04** coax, gags, mood, vein **05** jokes, jolly, spoil **06** comedy, cosset, favour, kidney, pamper, pecker, permit, please, temper **07** flatter, gratify, indulge, jesting, mollify, observe, satisfy, spirits **08** badinage, drollery, hilarity, pander to, repartee, tolerate **09** absurdity, amusement, wittiness **10** comply with, jocularity, wisecracks **11** accommodate, acquiesce in, disposition, frame of mind, go along with, state of mind, temperament **13** facetiousness **14** ridiculousness

*The four bodily humours include:*

**05** blood
**06** choler, phlegm
**09** black bile
**10** melancholy, yellow bile

*Humour includes:*

**03** dry
**04** blue, sick
**05** black
**07** gallows, surreal
**08** farcical
**09** satirical, slapstick
**10** lavatorial
**11** barrack-room, Pythonesque
**12** Chaplinesque

**humourless**
**02** po **03** dry **04** dour, dull, glum, grim **05** grave **06** boring, morose, solemn, sombre **07** earnest, po-faced, serious, tedious **09** long-faced, unsmiling **10** unlaughing

**hump**
**03** hog, lug, pip, vex **04** arch, bend, bump, haul, knob, lift, lump, mass, ramp **05** annoy, bulge, bunch, carry, crook, curve, heave, hoist, humph, hunch, hurry, mound, ridge **08** shoulder, swelling **09** outgrowth, speed bump **10** projection, prominence, protrusion **11** excrescence **12** intumescence, protuberance
• **get the hump** **04** mope, sulk **09** be annoyed, get the pip **11** be irritated **13** be exasperated
• **give someone the hump** **03** bug, irk, nag, vex **04** gall, rile **05** anger, annoy, tease **06** bother, harass, hassle, madden, pester, plague, ruffle, wind up **07** disturb, hack off, provoke, tick off, trouble **08** brass off, irritate **09** aggravate, cheese off **10** exasperate **13** make sparks fly **14** drive up the wall **15** get someone's goat
• **over the hump** **12** over the worst **13** past the crisis

**hump-backed**
**06** humped **07** crooked, gibbose, gibbous, hunched, stooped **08** deformed, kyphotic **09** misshapen **11** bunch-backed, crookbacked, hunchbacked

**humped**
**04** bent **06** arched, curved **07** bunched, crooked, gibbose, gibbous, hunched

**humus**
**03** mor **04** mull **05** moder

**hunch**
**04** arch, bend, bump, hint, hump, idea, knob, lump, mass, ramp **05** bulge, curve, guess, mound, squat, stoop **06** crouch, curl up, draw in, huddle **07** feeling, inkling **08** swelling **09** intuition, outgrowth, suspicion **10** impression, projection, prominence, protrusion, sixth sense **11** premonition **12** presentiment, protuberance

**hundred**
**01** C **04** cent **05** centi- **06** centum **07** cantred, cantref **09** centenary

**hundredweight**
**03** cwt **07** quintal

**Hungary**
**01** H **03** HUN **04** Hung

**hunger**
**03** yen **04** ache, itch, long, need, pine, want, wish **05** crave, greed, raven, yearn **06** desire, famine, hanker, pining, starve, thirst **07** bulimia, craving, longing **08** appetite, voracity, yearning **09** emptiness, esurience, esuriency, hankering **10** famishment, greediness, hungriness, starvation **12** malnutrition, ravenousness **15** have a craving for, have a longing for

**hungrily**
**06** avidly **07** eagerly **08** greedily **09** longingly **10** covetously, insatiably, ravenously

**hungry**
**04** avid, lean, mean, poor, yaup **05** eager, empty, sharp **06** aching, greedy, hollow, pining, stingy **07** craving, itching, longing, needing, peckish, thirsty **08** covetous, desirous, esurient, famished, hungerly, ravenous, sharp-set, starving, underfed, yearning **09** ahungered, hankering, hungerful, voracious **10** insatiable **12** malnourished **14** could eat a horse, undernourished

**hunk**
**04** base, clod, dish, goal, lump, mass, safe, slab, stud **05** block, chunk, he-man, piece, wedge **06** dollop, gobbet, secure **08** beefcake, macho man **09** dreamboat, strong man **10** studmuffin

**hunt**
**03** cub, dog, rat, ren, rin, run **04** fish, hawk, meet, seal, seek, slug **05** chase, chevy, chivy, drive, hound, mouse, quest, scour, stalk, track, trail **06** battue, beagle, chivvy, course, ferret, follow, forage, halloo, prey on, pursue, rabbit, search, shadow, turtle **07** dismiss, look for, predate, pursuit, ransack, rummage, scare up **08** scouring, scrounge, stalking, tire down, tracking, venation **09** persecute, rummaging, still-hunt, try to find **11** investigate, run to ground **12** ride to hounds, spotlighting **13** investigation, kangaroo shoot **14** rabbit trapping

**hunter**
**05** hound, jäger **06** chaser, hawker, jaeger, Nimrod, ratter, shikar, wolfer **07** Actaeon, beagler, montero, shikari, turtler, venator, venerer, woodman **08** chasseur, free-shot, huntsman, rabbiter, shikaree, woodsman **10** lion-hunter, seal-fisher **11** still-hunter **13** rabbit trapper **15** kangaroo shooter

**hunting**
**05** chase **06** shikar, venery **07** birding, cubbing, ducking, lamping, ratting, wolfing, wolving **08** beagling, coursing, falconry, stalking, trapping, turtling, venation **11** field sports
• **expressions relating to hunting** **04** alew, so-ho **05** chevy, chivy **06** chivvy, halloa, halloo, hoicks, yoicks **07** tally-ho, tantivy
• **hunting-coat** **04** pink
• **hunting-cry** **04** alew **05** chevy, chivy **06** chivvy, halloa, halloo
• **hunting ground** **04** walk
• **hunting group** **04** meet

**huntsman**
**04** Peel **05** jäger, yager **06** jaeger **07** montero, skirter, venator, woodman **08** chasseur, woodsman

**hurdle**
**03** bar **04** doll, jump, snag, wall **05** fence, flake, hedge **06** raddle, wattle **07** barrier, problem, railing **08** handicap, obstacle **09** barricade, hindrance **10** difficulty, impediment **11** obstruction **12** complication **14** stumbling-block

**hurl**
◊ *anagram indicator* **03** bum, put **04** cast, dart, dash, fire, pelt, putt, send

## hurly-burly

toss **05** chuck, fling, heave, lanch, pitch, sling, swing, throw, wheel **06** hurtle, launch, let fly, propel **07** project **08** catapult **11** precipitate

## hurly-burly

**05** chaos **06** bedlam, bustle, frenzy, furore, hassle, hubbub, hustle, racket, tumult, unrest, uproar **07** trouble, turmoil **08** brouhaha, disorder, upheaval **09** agitation, commotion, confusion **10** disruption, turbulence **11** distraction, pandemonium

## hurricane

**04** gale, rout **05** storm **06** baguio, squall, tumult **07** cyclone, tempest, tornado, typhoon **09** commotion, whirlwind

## hurried

**03** ran **04** fast **05** brief, hasty, quick, rapid, short, swift **06** hectic, rushed, speedy **07** cursory, offhand, passing, rush job, shallow **08** careless, fleeting, slapdash **09** breakneck, festinate, transient **10** last minute, transitory **11** perfunctory, precipitate, superficial

## hurriedly

**07** flat out, hastily, hotfoot, in haste, quickly, rapidly, swiftly **08** pell-mell, speedily **09** posthaste **10** at top speed **11** at the double **12** lickety-split, without delay **13** helter-skelter **14** at a rate of knots, hell for leather **15** like the clappers

## hurry

**03** fly, hie, ren, rin, run **04** belt, dash, hare, hump, push, race, rush, tear **05** chase, drive, haste, mosey, press, speed **06** buck up, bustle, flurry, giddap, hasten, hubbub, hustle, pronto, scurry **07** press on, quicken, speed up, urgency, vamoose **08** celerity, chop-chop, despatch, dispatch, expedite, fastness, go all out, jump to it!, rapidity, step on it **09** beetle off, commotion, confusion, cut and run, festinate, hastiness, look alive, look sharp, look smart, make haste, quickness, swiftness **10** accelerate, expedition, hightail it, look slippy, look snappy **11** run like hell **12** get a wiggle on, make it snappy, step on the gas **13** precipitation **14** rattle your dags

## hurt

◇ *anagram indicator* **03** ake, cut, hit, mar, noy, sad **04** ache, burn, gall, harm, maim, pain, sore **05** abuse, annoy, grief, smart, spoil, sting, throb, upset, wound, wring **06** aching, be sore, blight, bruise, damage, grazed, grieve, impair, injure, injury, lesion, maimed, misery, offend, sadden, sorrow, tingle **07** afflict, annoyed, blemish, bruised, burning, disable, injured, painful, sadness, scarred, scratch, torture, wounded **08** distress, ill-treat, lacerate, maltreat, mischief, nuisance, offended, saddened, smarting, soreness, tingling **09** affronted, aggrieved, be painful, in anguish, lacerated, miserable, sorrowful, suffering, throbbing **10** affliction, debilitate, discomfort,

distressed **12** cause sadness **13** grief-stricken

## hurtful

**03** bad, ill **04** mean **05** catty, cruel, nasty **06** naught, nocent, shrewd, unkind **07** baleful, cutting, harmful, nocuous, noysome, ruinous, vicious **08** damaging, grievous, scathing, spiteful, wounding **09** injurious, malicious, obnoxious, offensive, pestilent, scatheful, upsetting **10** derogatory, maleficent, maleficial, pernicious **11** deleterious, destructive, detrimental, distressing, malefactory

## hurtle

**03** fly **04** belt, dash, dive, hurl, pelt, race, rush, spin, tear **05** clash, crash, shoot, speed **06** career, charge, plunge, rattle **08** brandish, step on it **12** step on the gas **14** step on the juice **15** put your foot down

## husband

**01** h **03** man **04** lord, mate, save **05** baron, groom, hoard, hubby, put by, store **06** budget, eke out, manage, master, old boy, old man, ration, save up, spouse **07** consort, goodman, manager, partner, reserve **08** conserve, preserve, put aside **09** cultivate, economize, other half **10** better half, hoddy-doddy, married man **12** gander-mooner, use carefully, use sparingly **15** mari complaisant

• **husband and wife 04** pair **06** couple

• **without husband or wife 04** sole

## husbandry

**06** saving, thrift **07** economy, farming, tillage **08** agronomy **09** frugality **10** agronomics, management **11** agriculture, cultivation, thriftiness **12** agribusiness, conservation **14** farm management, land management

## hush

**04** calm **05** peace, quiet, still **06** repose, settle, silent, soothe, subdue **07** be quiet, bestill, compose, mollify, quieten, silence **08** calmness, serenity **09** quietness, stillness **12** peacefulness, tranquillity

• **hush up 03** gag **04** smug **06** huddle, stifle **07** conceal, cover up, smother **08** keep dark, suppress **10** keep secret

## hush-hush

**06** secret **09** top-secret **10** classified, restricted, under wraps **12** confidential

## husk

**03** pod **04** bran, case, coir, hull, peel, pill, rind, skin **05** chaff, shale, sheal, sheel, shell, shiel, shill, shuck, strip **06** legume **07** capsule, epicarp **08** covering **09** corn shuck

## huskily

**06** deeply **07** gruffly, harshly **08** croakily, hoarsely **10** gutturally

## husky

**03** dry, low **04** deep **05** beefy, burly, gruff, harsh, hefty, Inuit, rough, thick **06** brawny, coarse, croaky, hoarse, strong **07** rasping, throaty **08** croaking,

gravelly, guttural, muscular **09** strapping, well-built

## hussy

**04** minx, slag, slut, tart, vamp **05** huzzy, tramp **06** hussif, limmer, wanton **07** floozie **08** scrubber **09** housewife, temptress **10** loose woman

## hustle

**03** fly, tew **04** dash, fuss, push, rush, sell, stir **05** crowd, elbow, force, fraud, hurry, nudge, shove **06** bounce, bundle, bustle, hasten, huddle, jostle, justle, rustle, thrust, tumult **07** swindle **08** activity **09** agitation, commotion, manhandle **10** hurly-burly, pressurize

## hut

**03** den **04** shed, skeo, skio, tilt **05** banda, booth, bothy, cabin, hogan, humpy, shack, sheal, shiel, whare **06** bothan, bothie, chalet, gunyah, lean-to, mia-mia, pondok, rancho, saeter, shanty, succah, sukkah, wiltja, wurley **07** caboose, shelter, wickiup **08** log cabin, rondavel, shealing, shieling **09** pondokkie, rancheria

## hybrid

◇ *anagram indicator* **05** cross, mixed **06** mosaic **07** amalgam, bigener, mixture, mongrel **08** combined, compound **09** composite, crossbred, half-blood, half-breed **10** crossbreed **11** combination, single-cross **13** heterogeneous **14** conglomeration

*Hybrids include:*

**02** zo
**03** dso, dzo, zho
**04** dzho, mule, OEIC, Ugli®
**05** oxlip, topaz
**06** oxslip
**07** beefalo, Bourbon, cattabu, cattalo, Jersian, lurcher, plumcot, tangelo, tea rose
**08** citrange, noisette, sunberry, tayberry
**09** perpetual, tiger tail, triticale
**10** clementine, loganberry, polyanthus
**11** boysenberry, bull-mastiff, Jacqueminot, marionberry, miracle rice
**13** polecat-ferret

## hybridize

**05** cross **10** bastardize, crossbreed, interbreed

## hydrant

**01** H **02** FP **08** fireplug

## hydrocarbon

*Hydrocarbons include:*

**03** wax
**05** halon
**06** aldrin, alkane, alkene, alkyne, butane, cetane, decane, ethane, hexane, indene, nonane, octane, olefin, picene, pyrene, retene
**07** benzene, heptane, methane, olefine, pentane, propane, styrene, terpene
**08** camphane, camphene, diphenyl,

isoprene, pristane, stilbene
**09** butadiene
**10** benzpyrene, mesitylene
**11** hatchettite, naphthalane
**12** cyclopropane

## hydrogen
**01** H

## hyena
**09** tiger wolf **10** strandwolf

## hygiene
**06** purity **09** sterility **10** sanitation
**11** cleanliness **12** disinfection,
sanitariness **13** wholesomeness

## hygienic
**04** pure **05** clean **07** aseptic, healthy,
sterile **08** germ-free, sanitary
**09** wholesome **10** salubrious, sterilized
**11** disinfected

## hymn
**03** air **04** song **05** carol, chant, dirge,
motet, paean, psalm **06** anthem,
choral, chorus, mantra, Te Deum
**07** cantata, chorale, introit, mantram,
Sanctus **08** canticle, cathisma, dies
irae, doxology, hymeneal, sequence
**09** dithyramb, offertory, spiritual,
sticheron, trisagion, troparion
**10** paraphrase, procession, Tantum
ergo **11** recessional, Stabat Mater
**12** Marseillaise, processional, song of
praise

## hype
**04** fuss, plug, puff **06** racket, talk up
**07** build up, build-up, promote, puffery
**08** ballyhoo, plugging **09** advertise,
deception, promotion, publicity,
publicize **10** razzmatazz **11** advertising
**13** advertisement

## hyped up
**04** fake, high, wild **05** eager, hyper,
moved **06** elated **07** anxious, excited,
fired up, frantic, stirred, uptight
**08** agitated, animated, frenzied,
restless, thrilled, worked up
**09** wrought-up **10** artificial, stimulated
**11** exhilarated, overwrought
**12** enthusiastic **13** in high spirits, on
tenterhooks **14** beside yourself, thrilled
to bits

## hyperbole
**06** excess **07** auxesis **08** overkill
**12** exaggeration, extravagance
**13** magnification, overstatement

## hypercritical
**05** fussy, picky **06** choosy, strict
**07** carping, finicky **08** captious,
niggling, pedantic **09** cavilling,
quibbling **10** censorious, nit-picking,
pernickety **11** persnickety **12** fault-
finding **13** hair-splitting **14** over-
particular

## Hypnos
**06** Somnus

## hypnotic
**07** numbing **08** magnetic, sedative
**09** soporific **10** compelling, magnetical
**11** fascinating, mesmerizing,
somniferous **12** irresistible,
spellbinding, stupefactive **13** sleep-
inducing

## hypnotism
**08** Braidism, hypnosis **09** mesmerism
**10** suggestion **12** neurypnology
**14** auto-suggestion, electrobiology,
neurohypnology **15** animal magnetism

## hypnotize
**06** dazzle **07** beguile, bewitch, enchant
**08** entrance **09** captivate, fascinate,
magnetize, mesmerize, spellbind
**10** put to sleep

## hypochondria
**03** hip, hyp **08** neurosis
**15** hypochondriasis

## hypochondriac
**08** neurotic **10** melancholy, phrenesiac
**11** atrabilious **14** hypochondriast,
valetudinarian **15** hypochondriacal

## hypocrisy
**04** cant **06** deceit **07** falsity **08** pretence
**09** deception, duplicity **10** dishonesty,
double-talk, lip service, pharisaism,
phoneyness **11** dissembling, insincerity
**12** two-facedness, wearing a mask
**13** deceitfulness, dissimulation,
double-dealing

## hypocrite
**05** fraud, Janus, pseud **06** canter,
mucker, phoney, pseudo **08** deceiver,
impostor, Pharisee, Tartuffe
**09** charlatan, Pecksniff, pretender
**10** dissembler, Holy Willie,
mountebank **15** whited sepulchre

## hypocritical
**05** false, lying **06** double, hollow,
phoney **08** specious, spurious, two-
faced **09** deceitful, deceptive,
dishonest, insincere, pharisaic, self-
pious, Tartufian, Tartufish **10** false-
faced, fraudulent, histrionic, Janus-
faced, perfidious, Tartuffian, Tartuffish
**11** dissembling, double-faced,
duplicitous, Janian-faced, pharisaical
**12** histrionical, Pecksniffian **13** double-
dealing, sanctimonious, self-righteous

## hypothesis
**03** hyp **05** axiom **06** notion, theory,
thesis **07** premise, theorem **09** postulate
**10** assumption, conjecture
**11** presumption, proposition,
speculation, supposition

## hypothetical
**03** hyp **07** assumed **08** imagined,
notional, presumed, proposed,
supposed **09** imaginary **11** conjectural,
speculative, theoretical
**13** suppositional

## hypothetically
**07** ideally **08** in theory **10** supposedly
**13** conjecturally, speculatively,
theoretically

## hysteria
**05** mania, panic **06** frenzy, mother
**07** habdabs, madness **08** delirium,
neurosis **09** agitation, hysterics **15** fits
of the mother

## hysterical
**03** mad **04** rich **06** crazed, raving
**07** berserk, frantic **08** demented,
farcical, frenzied, in a panic, neurotic
**09** delirious, hilarious, ludicrous,
priceless **10** ridiculous, uproarious
**11** overwrought **12** out of control
**13** side-splitting **14** beside yourself,
extremely funny, uncontrollable

## hysterically
**05** madly **08** absurdly, in a panic
**10** farcically **11** frantically, hilariously,
ludicrously, screamingly
**12** neurotically, out of control,
ridiculously, uproariously **13** out of
your mind **14** beside yourself,
uncontrollably

## hysterics
**05** mania, panic **06** frenzy **07** habdabs,
madness **08** delirium, hysteria,
neurosis **09** agitation **12** crise de nerfs

**I**

02 ch, me 03 aye, che, ego, ich, one, yes 05 India 06 indeed, iodine

**I am** 02 I'm 03 sum

**ice**
04 cool, kill 05 chill, frost, glaze 06 freeze, harden 07 diamond, iciness, reserve 08 coldness, coolness, diamonds, distance, enfreeze 09 formality 10 freeze over, frostiness 11 frozen water, refrigerate

*Ice types include:*
03 dry, pan, sea
04 floe, grew, grue, hail, pack, rime, slob, snow
05 black, brash, crust, drift, field, shelf, shell, sleet, virga
06 anchor, frazil, ground, icicle, stream
07 glacier, hummock, pancake, verglas
10 silver thaw
13 tickly-benders

**put on ice** 05 defer, delay 06 put off, shelve 07 suspend 08 postpone 14 hold in abeyance 15 leave in abeyance

**iceberg**
04 berg, calf 07 growler

**ice-cold**
03 icy, raw 04 hard, iced, numb 05 algid, fixed, gelid, polar, rigid, stiff 06 arctic, baltic, frigid, frosty, frozen 07 chilled, frosted, glacial 08 freezing, icebound, Siberian 10 solidified 11 frozen-stiff 12 bitterly cold

**ice cream**
*Types of ice cream include:*
04 cone
05 bombe, kulfi
06 bucket, cornet, gelato, ripple, slider, sorbet, sundae
07 cassata, choc-bar, granita, sherbet, spumone, spumoni, tortoni
08 hoky-poky, macallum
10 hokey-pokey, Neapolitan
11 tutti-frutti

**ice hockey**
*Ice hockey-related terms include:*
04 cage, goal, puck
05 bully, check, icing, stick, zones
06 assist, boards, period, sin-bin
07 face-off, forward, offside, penalty, red line, shut-out, Zamboni
08 blue line, boarding, defender, five-hole, linesman, one-timer, overtime, slap shot, slashing, spearing
09 blueliner, bodycheck, centreman, netminder, power play
10 centre line, cross-check, defenceman, goaltender, penalty box
11 penalty shot, short-handed, sudden-death
12 icing the puck, penalty bench
13 defending zone

**Iceland**
02 IS 03 ISL

**ice skating**
*Ice skaters include:*
04 **Dean** (Christopher), **Koss** (Johann Olav), **Kwan** (Michelle), **Witt** (Katarina), **Yang** (Yang 'A')
05 **Baiul** (Oksana), **Blair** (Bonnie), **Curry** (John), **Heiss** (Carol), **Henie** (Sonja), **Kania** (Karin), **Syers** (Madge)
06 **Button** (Dick), **Hamill** (Dorothy)
07 **Boitano** (Brian), **Cousins** (Robin), **Fleming** (Peggy), **Grinkov** (Sergei), **Harding** (Tonya), **Rodnina** (Irina), **Salchow** (Ulrich), **Torvill** (Jayne), **Yagudin** (Alexei)
08 **Browning** (Kurt), **Dijkstra** (Sjoukje), **Dmitriev** (Artur), **Eldredge** (Todd), **Gordeeva** (Ekaterina), **Hamilton** (Scott), **Kazakova** (Oksana), **Kerrigan** (Nancy), **Lipinski** (Tara), **Petrenko** (Viktor)
09 **Yamaguchi** (Kristi)
10 **Ballangrud** (Ivar)

*Ice skating-related terms include:*
04 Axel, edge, flip, loop, Lutz
05 blade, pairs, skate, waltz
06 figure, Mohawk, rocker, walley
07 bracket, Choctaw, Salchow, sit spin, toe jump, toe loop, toe pick
08 ice dance, Ina Bauer, stag leap
09 camel spin, crossover, free dance
10 inside edge
11 death spiral, flying camel, layback spin, outside edge, spread eagle, upright spin
12 headless spin, speed skating
13 Biellmann spin, figure skating, flying sit spin, free programme
14 short programme
15 compulsory dance, set pattern dance

**icily**
06 coldly, coolly, rudely 07 stiffly
08 formally, morosely 12 forbiddingly

**icon**
04 idol 05 image 06 figure, smiley, sprite, symbol 08 likeness, portrait
09 portrayal 14 representation

**iconoclast**
05 rebel 06 critic 07 heretic, radical, sceptic 08 opponent 09 denouncer, dissenter, dissident 10 questioner, unbeliever 11 denunciator 12 image-breaker

**iconoclastic**
07 impious, radical 08 critical

09 dissident, heretical, sceptical
10 innovative, irreverent, rebellious, subversive 11 dissentient, questioning
12 denunciatory

**icy**
03 raw 04 cold, cool, rimy, rude
05 aloof, chill, gelid, polar, stiff, stony
06 arctic, biting, bitter, chilly, formal, frigid, frosty, frozen, glassy, morose, slippy 07 distant, glacial, hostile, ice-cold 08 chilling, freezing, icebound, reserved, Siberian, slippery
10 forbidding, frostbound, restrained, unfriendly 11 indifferent

**id**
04 orfe

**Idaho**
02 ID

**idea**
03 aim, end 04 clou, clue, goal, idée, plan, view 05 fancy, guess, image, point, theme 06 belief, design, notion, object, reason, scheme, target, theory, vision 07 conceit, concept, feeling, inkling, opinion, purpose, thought, wrinkle 08 proposal 09 brainwave, intention, judgement, objective, obsession, suspicion, viewpoint
10 conception, conjecture, hypothesis, impression, perception, suggestion
11 abstraction, connotation, inspiration, proposition
13 understanding 14 interpretation, recommendation

**ideal**
04 acme, best, type 05 cause, dream, image, model 06 ethics, morals, unreal, Utopia 07 eidolon, epitome, example, highest, optimal, optimum, paragon, pattern, perfect, supreme, utopian 08 absolute, abstract, complete, exemplar, fanciful, notional, romantic, standard 09 archetype, benchmark, criterion, imaginary, nonpareil, principle, prototype, visionary, yardstick 10 archetypal, conceptual, consummate, idealistic, perfection 11 impractical, moral values, theoretical 12 hypothetical, unattainable 13 ethical values, philosophical 14 moral standards, quintessential
• **ideal state** 06 Utopia 07 nirvana

**idealism**
09 mentalism 10 utopianism
11 romanticism 13 perfectionism
14 impracticality

**idealist**
07 dreamer 08 optimist, romantic
09 visionary 11 romanticist
13 perfectionist

**idealistic**
07 utopian 08 quixotic, romantic
09 visionary 10 optimistic, starry-eyed
11 impractical, unrealistic
13 impracticable, perfectionist

**idealization**
07 worship 10 apotheosis, exaltation
11 ennoblement, idolization
13 glamorization, glorification, romanticizing 15 romanticization

## idealize

**05** exalt **07** glorify, idolize, worship
**09** glamorize **10** utopianize
**11** romanticize

## ideally

**06** at best **08** in theory, mentally
**09** perfectly **13** theoretically
**14** hypothetically, in an ideal world
**15** in a perfect world

## idée fixe

**06** hang-up **07** complex **08** fixation
**09** fixed idea, leitmotiv, monomania,
obsession

## identical

**04** like, same, self, twin **05** alike, equal,
right **06** cloned **07** identic, numeric,
precise, similar **08** matching, self-same
**09** analogous, congruent, duplicate,
syngeneic **10** coincident, consistent,
equivalent **11** a dead ringer
**12** doppelgänger **13** corresponding,
one and the same, spitting image
**15** interchangeable

## identically

**05** alike **07** equally **09** similarly
**11** analogously, congruently, just the
same **12** consistently, equivalently, in
the same way **15** correspondingly,
interchangeably

## identifiable

**05** known **10** detectable, noticeable
**11** discernible, perceptible
**12** recognizable, unmistakable
**13** ascertainable **15** distinguishable

## identification

**02** ID **03** PIN, tie **04** bond, link
**05** badge, label **06** naming, papers
**07** empathy, name tag, rapport,
surname **08** passbook, passport,
relation, spotting, sympathy
**09** biometric, detection, diagnosis,
documents, labelling **10** connection
**11** association, correlation, credentials,
involvement, pointing-out, recognition
**12** dactyloscopy, identity card,
relationship **13** fellow feeling,
interrelation **14** classification, driving
licence, fingerprinting

## identify

**03** tag **04** know, name, spot **05** label,
place **06** couple, detect, finger, notice,
relate **07** connect, discern, feel for, find
out, involve, make out, pick out, pin
down, specify **08** classify, diagnose,
discover, perceive, pinpoint, point out,
relate to **09** ascertain, associate,
catalogue, establish, recognize,
respond to, single out **11** distinguish
**13** associate with, empathize with
**14** put the finger on, sympathize with
**15** think of together

## identity

**02** ID **03** ego **04** face, name, self
**05** image, roots, seity, unity
**07** oneness, profile **08** equality,
likeness, property, sameness, selfhood
**09** character, closeness, existence
**10** appearance, background,
impression, personhood, public face,
similarity, uniqueness **11** equivalence,
personality, resemblance, singularity

**12** selfsameness **13** individuality,
particularity, public persona
**14** correspondence **15** distinctiveness

## ideologist

**07** teacher, thinker **08** theorist
**09** ideologue, visionary **11** doctrinaire,
philosopher

## ideology

**05** credo, creed, dogma, faith, ideas
**06** belief, tenets, theory, thesis
**07** beliefs, opinion **08** doctrine,
opinions, teaching **09** doctrines,
world-view **10** philosophy, principles
**11** convictions, metaphysics
*See also* **political**

## idiocy

**05** folly **06** lunacy **07** inanity
**08** daftness, insanity **09** absurdity,
craziness, silliness, stupidity
**10** imbecility **11** fatuousness
**13** foolhardiness, senselessness

## idiom

**04** talk **05** style, usage **06** jargon,
phrase, speech, Syrism **07** Arabism,
dialect, Grecism, Pahlavi, Pehlevi,
Persism, Slavism, Syriasm
**08** Aramaism, Graecism, Hebraism,
idiotism, Irishism, language, Latinism,
locution, parlance, polonism,
prosaism, Saxonism, Semitism,
Sinicism **09** anglicism, Celticism,
Chaldaism, Gallicism, Germanism,
Gothicism, Hellenism, Italicism,
Scoticism, Syriacism, Syrianism
**10** classicism, cockneyism, Englishism,
expression, feminimism, Italianism,
Johnsonese, Scotticism, vernacular,
Yiddishism **11** Americanism,
Hibernicism, phraseology
**12** classicalism, Hibernianism, turn of
phrase **13** Australianism,
colloquialism, vernacularism

## idiomatic

**06** native **07** correct, natural
**08** everyday **09** dialectal **10** colloquial,
idiolectal, vernacular **11** dialectical,
grammatical

## idiosyncrasy

**03** way **05** freak, habit, quirk, trait
**06** oddity **07** feature, quality
**09** mannerism **10** speciality
**11** peculiarity, singularity
**12** eccentricity **13** individuality
**14** characteristic

## idiosyncratic

**03** odd **06** quirky **08** peculiar, personal,
singular **09** eccentric **10** individual
**11** distinctive **14** characteristic

## idiot

**03** ass, mug, nit, nut, oaf **04** berk, clod,
clot, dill, dope, dork, fool, geek, jerk,
nana, nerd, nerk, nong, prat, putz, twit
**05** chump, clown, divvy, dumbo,
dunce, eejit, galah, klutz, moron,
nelly, ninny, schmo, twerp, wally
**06** bammer, bampot, cretin, dimwit,
doofus, drongo, dum-dum, muppet,
nidget, nitwit, numpty, schlub, sucker
**07** airhead, bampot, dumb-ass, fat-
head, halfwit, jughead, natural,
pillock, plonker, schmuck, wazzock

**08** bonehead, boofhead, dipstick,
flathead, imbecile, innocent,
numskull, pea-brain **09** birdbrain,
blockhead, cloth head, ignoramus,
lame brain, malt-horse, simpleton,
thickhead **10** bufflehead, nincompoop
**11** chowderhead, knuckle-head
*See also* **fool**

## idiotic

◇ *anagram indicator* **03** mad, twp
**04** daft, dozy, dumb **05** barmy, batty,
crazy, dorky, dotty, goofy, inane,
inept, nutty, potty, silly, wacky
**06** absurd, insane, oafish, simple,
stupid, unwise **07** asinine, dumb-ass,
fatuous, foolish, moronic, risible
**08** gormless, ignorant **09** dim-witted,
half-baked, ludicrous, pointless,
senseless **10** half-witted, ill-advised,
ridiculous **11** hare-brained,
injudicious, nonsensical, thick-headed
**12** crack-brained, short-sighted,
simple-minded, unreasonable **13** ill-
considered, knuckle-headed,
unintelligent

## idle

**03** lig **04** dead, doss, laze, lazy, loaf,
mike, move, vain **05** dally, empty,
light, petty, relax, shirk, skive, slack,
waste, while **06** bludge, casual, daidle,
dawdle, fester, fiddle, futile, loiter,
lollop, lounge, pootle, potter, putter,
unused, wanton **07** dormant, dronish,
foolish, fritter, goof off, jobless, loafish,
shallow, sit back, trivial, useless, work
shy **08** baseless, bone-idle, inactive,
indolent, kill time, lallygag, lollygag,
slothful, sluggish, sod about, tick over,
trifling **09** bum around, do nothing,
fruitless, gold-brick, lethargic, on the
dole, pointless, redundant, while
away, worthless **10** mothballed, not
working, take it easy, unedifying,
unemployed, unoccupied, whip the
cat **11** fiddle about, horse around,
ineffective, ineffectual, inoperative,
unimportant **12** be ready to run, fiddle
around, fiddle-faddle, unproductive,
unsuccessful **13** be operational, be
ready to work, insignificant,
lackadaisical

## idleness

**04** ease **05** sloth **06** lazing, torpor
**07** idlesse, inertia, leisure, loafing,
skiving, vacancy, vacuity **08** inaction,
laziness, otiosity **09** indolence,
pottering **10** inactivity, otioseness,
vegetating **12** slothfulness,
sluggishness, unemployment
**13** shiftlessness **14** dolce far niente

## idler

**04** slob, spiv **05** drone, sloth
**06** bumble, bummle, dodger, donnat,
donnot, dosser, loafer, skiver, truant,
waster **07** bludger, dawdler, goof-off,
laggard, Lollard, lounger, shirker,
slacker, wastrel **08** do-naught, fine
lady, layabout, sluggard **09** do-
nothing, gold brick, lazybones
**10** malingerer **11** couch potato
**12** carpet-knight, clock-watcher **13** fine
gentleman **14** good-for-nothing

## idol

**03** god, pet **04** hero, icon, joss, sham, star, wood **05** deity, image, pagod, pin-up, swami **06** effigy, fetish, figure, mammet, maumet, mawmet, mommet, pagoda **07** beloved, darling, fantasy, goddess, heroine, phantom **08** Baphomet, impostor, likeness **09** favourite, semblance, superstar **11** blue-eyed boy, graven image

## idolater

**06** adorer, votary **07** admirer, devotee, idolist **10** iconolater, idolatress, worshipper **14** idol-worshipper

## idolatrous

**05** pagan **07** adoring **09** adulatory, heretical, idolizing, lionizing **10** glorifying, uncritical **11** reverential, worshipping **15** idol-worshipping

## idolatry

**07** idolism **08** mammetry, maumetry, mawmetry, paganism, whoredom **09** adoration, adulation, fetishism, idolizing, reverence **10** admiration, exaltation, heathenism, iconolatry **11** deification, fornication, hero-worship, icon worship, worshipping **13** glorification

## idolize

**04** love **05** adore, deify, exalt **06** admire, dote on, revere **07** adulate, glorify, lionize, worship **08** venerate **09** reverence **11** hero-worship **14** put on a pedestal

## idyllic

**05** happy **06** rustic **07** perfect **08** blissful, charming, glorious, heavenly, pastoral, peaceful, romantic **09** idealized, unspoiled, wonderful **10** delightful **11** picturesque, Theocritean

## ie

**02** so

## if

**02** an **03** and, gin **06** though **07** suppose, whether **08** as long as, assuming, in case of, provided, so long as, whenever **09** condition, providing, supposing **11** supposition, uncertainty **12** assuming that, in the event of **13** supposing that **15** on condition that
• **even if 03** and, tho **04** albe **05** albee, all-be **06** albeit, though **07** suppose
• **if it 03** an't

## iffy

**04** suss **05** dodgy, risky **07** dubious **08** doubtful, low-grade **09** defective, imperfect, tentative, uncertain, undecided, unsettled **10** second-rate **11** substandard **13** disappointing **14** not up to scratch, unsatisfactory

## ignite

**04** burn, fire **05** light, torch **06** kindle **07** flare up, inflame **08** spark off, touch off **09** catch fire, set alight, set fire to, set on fire **11** conflagrate, put a match to **15** burst into flames

## ignoble

**03** low **04** base, mean, vile **05** petty, small **06** vulgar **07** heinous **08** infamous, shameful, unworthy, wretched **09** worthless **10** despicable **11** disgraceful **12** contemptible **13** dishonourable

## ignobly

**06** meanly, vilely **07** pettily **10** despicably, infamously, shamefully, wretchedly **12** contemptibly **13** disgracefully, dishonourably, without honour

## ignominious

**04** base **05** sorry **06** abject **08** infamous, shameful **09** degrading **10** despicable, mortifying, scandalous **11** disgraceful, humiliating, undignified **12** contemptible, disreputable, embarrassing **13** discreditable, dishonourable

## ignominiously

**10** despicably, shamefully **12** disreputably, scandalously **13** disgracefully, dishonourably

## ignominy

**05** odium, shame **06** infamy, stigma **07** obloquy, scandal **08** contempt, disgrace, reproach **09** discredit, dishonour, disrepute, indignity **10** opprobrium **11** degradation, humiliation **13** mortification

## ignoramus

**03** ass **04** dolt, fool **05** dunce **06** dimwit, duffer, ignaro **07** dullard, halfwit **08** bonehead, ignorant, imbecile, numskull **09** blockhead, simpleton **10** illiterate **11** know-nothing

## ignorance

**05** night **07** naivety **08** oblivion **09** greenness, innocence, nescience, stupidity, thickness **10** illiteracy **11** unawareness **12** inexperience **13** obliviousness, unfamiliarity **14** unintelligence **15** unconsciousness

## ignorant

**04** dumb, lewd, rude **05** blind, dense, naive, thick **06** ingram, ingrum, stupid, unread **07** ill-bred, redneck, unaware, unknown **08** backward, clueless, innocent, inscient, nescient, untaught **09** benighted, in the dark, lack-Latin, oblivious, unknowing, unlearned, untrained, unwitting **10** analphabet, illiterate, innumerate, uneducated, unfamiliar, uninformed, unschooled **11** analphabete, ill-educated, ill-informed, know-nothing, unconfirmed, unconscious, uninitiated **12** discourteous, having no idea, unacquainted **13** inexperienced, unenlightened

## ignore

◇ *deletion indicator* **03** cut **04** balk, omit, snub **05** baulk, blank, blink, spurn, waive **06** bypass, pass by, reject, slight **07** cut dead, high-hat, neglect, tune out **08** brush off, discount, overlook, pass over, set aside, shrug off **09** disregard **10** brush aside, scrub round, slight over **11** not listen to, run away from **12** cold-shoulder **13** be oblivious to, keep in the dark **14** shut your eyes to, take for granted, take no notice of, turn a deaf ear to, turn your back on **15** close your eyes to, look the other way, turn a blind eye to

## ilk

**04** each, kind, make, same, sort, type, ylke **05** brand, breed, class, stamp, style **07** variety **09** character **11** description

## ill

◇ *anagram indicator* **03** bad **04** down, evil, harm, hurt, pain, sick, weak **05** amiss, badly, cronk, crook, dicky, frail, harsh, rough, seedy, trial **06** ailing, barely, crummy, feeble, groggy, grotty, hardly, infirm, injury, laid up, naught, poorly, queasy, severe, sorrow, trials, unkind, unweal, unwell, wicked **07** adverse, ailment, cruelty, grieved, harmful, hostile, hurtful, ominous, peevish, problem, ruinous, run down, trouble, unlucky **08** critical, damaging, disaster, diseased, scantily, scarcely, sinister, unkindly **09** adversely, afflicted, bedridden, by no means, difficult, in a bad way, incorrect, injurious, off-colour, resentful, suffering, unhealthy, unluckily **10** affliction, broken-down, distressed, indisposed, misfortune, out of sorts, unfriendly, unpleasant, wickedness, wrongfully **11** belligerent, deleterious, destruction, destructive, detrimental, incompetent, peelie-wally, threatening, tribulation, unfortunate, unpromising **12** antagonistic, inadequately, inauspicious, infelicitous, unfavourable, unfavourably, unpropitious **13** reprehensible, unfortunately, inauspiciously, insufficiently, unpleasantness, unsuccessfully, valetudinarian **15** under the weather
• **ill at ease** ◇ *anagram indicator* **04** edgy **05** tense **06** on edge, uneasy, unsure **07** anxious, awkward, fidgety, nervous, strange, worried **08** farouche, hesitant, restless **09** disturbed, unrelaxed, unsettled **10** disquieted **11** embarrassed **13** on tenterhooks, self-conscious, uncomfortable
• **speak ill of 03** nag, pan **04** carp, slag, slam **05** blame, cut up, decry, knock, roast, score, slash, slate, trash **06** attack, hammer, impugn, niggle, peck at, tilt at **07** censure, condemn, nit-pick, rubbish, run down, scarify, slag off, snipe at **08** backbite, badmouth, denounce, wade into **09** castigate, criticize, denigrate, disparage, excoriate, have a go at, misreport, pull apart, take apart, tear apart **10** animadvert, come down on, go to town on, vituperate **11** pick holes in **12** disapprove of, pull to pieces, put the boot in, tear to shreds **13** find fault with, tear a strip off **15** do a hatchet job on, pass judgement on

## ill-advised

**04** rash **05** hasty **06** unwise **07** foolish **08** careless, overseen, reckless **09** ill-judged, imprudent, misguided **11** injudicious, thoughtless **12** short-sighted **13** ill-considered, inappropriate

**ill-assorted**
◊ *anagram indicator* **08** unsuited **09** misallied **10** discordant, mismatched **11** incongruous, uncongenial **12** incompatible, inharmonious

**ill-bred**
◊ *anagram indicator* **04** rude **05** crass, crude, ocker **06** coarse, vulgar **07** boorish, loutish, uncivil, uncouth **08** ignorant, impolite, unseemly **10** indelicate, misbehaved, unmannerly, unnurtured **11** bad-mannered, ill-mannered, uncivilized **12** discourteous

**ill-considered**
**04** rash **05** hasty **06** unwise **07** foolish **08** careless, heedless **09** ill-judged, imprudent, overhasty **10** ill-advised **11** improvident, injudicious, precipitate **12** misconceived

**ill-defined**
**03** dim **04** hazy **05** fuzzy, vague **06** blurry, woolly **07** blurred, mongrel, shadowy, unclear **08** nebulous **09** imprecise, shapeless **10** indefinite, indistinct

**ill-disposed**
**04** anti **06** averse **07** against, hostile, opposed **08** inimical **10** malevolent, unfriendly **11** disaffected, unwelcoming **12** antagonistic **13** uncooperative, unsympathetic

**illegal**
**05** wrong **06** banned, barred **07** bootleg, crooked, illicit **08** criminal, outlawed, unlawful, wrongful, wrongous **09** felonious, forbidden **10** adulterine, fraudulent, prohibited, proscribed **11** black-market, interdicted **12** criminalized, illegitimate, unauthorized **15** under-the-counter

**illegality**
**05** crime, wrong **06** felony **09** wrongness **11** criminality, illicitness, lawlessness, malfeasance **12** illegitimacy, unlawfulness, wrongfulness

**illegally**
**07** wrongly **08** guiltily **09** illicitly **10** criminally, unlawfully, wrongfully **13** against the law, disobediently **14** illegitimately

**illegible**
**05** faint **07** obscure **08** scrawled **10** hard to read, indistinct, unreadable **12** hieroglyphic **14** indecipherable, unintelligible

**illegitimacy**
**08** bastardy **10** bastardism **12** bend-sinister **13** baton-sinister **14** fatherlessness

**illegitimate**
**04** base, love **07** bastard, illegal, illicit, invalid, lawless, natural, unsound **08** base-born, improper, misbegot, nameless, spurious, unlawful

**09** illogical, incorrect **10** adulterine, fatherless, unfathered, unlicensed **11** misbegotten, unwarranted **12** inadmissible, unauthorized

**ill-equipped**
**07** exposed **10** unprovided, unsupplied **11** ill-supplied, underfunded, undermanned, unprotected **12** disappointed, understaffed **13** underfinanced, under strength, unprovided for **14** under-resourced

**ill-fated**
**06** doomed **07** hapless, unhappy, unlucky **08** blighted, luckless **09** ill-omened, star-crost **10** ill-starred **11** star-crossed, unfortunate

**ill-favoured**
**04** ugly **05** plain **06** homely **07** hideous **08** unlovely **09** repulsive, unsightly **12** unattractive **15** unprepossessing

**ill-feeling**
**05** anger, odium, pique, spite, wrath **06** animus, enmity, grudge, malice **07** dudgeon, ill-will, offence, rancour **08** bad blood, sourness **09** animosity, hostility **10** antagonism, bitterness, resentment, unkindness **11** frustration, indignation **12** hard feelings **14** disgruntlement **15** dissatisfaction

**ill-founded**
**07** unsound **08** baseless **10** groundless **11** unconfirmed, unjustified, unsupported **15** unsubstantiated

**ill-gotten**
**03** hot **04** bent **05** dodgy, taken **06** nicked, stolen, swiped **07** nobbled **08** pilfered **09** purloined, ripped off **10** knocked off

**ill-humour**
**03** dod **04** bile, dump **05** dumps, rheum **06** spleen **09** distemper

**ill-humoured**
**04** tart **05** cross, huffy, moody, ratty, sharp, sulky, testy **06** crabby, grumpy, morose, shirty, snappy, sullen **07** crabbed, grouchy, peevish, stroppy, waspish **08** petulant, snappish **09** crotchety, impatient, irascible, irritable **11** acrimonious, bad-tempered, distempered **12** cantankerous, disagreeable **13** quick-tempered

**illiberal**
**04** mean **05** petty, tight **06** stingy **07** bigoted, miserly **08** verkramp **09** hidebound, niggardly **10** intolerant, prejudiced, ungenerous **11** close-fisted, reactionary, small-minded, tight-fisted **12** narrow-minded, parsimonious, uncharitable **13** unenlightened

**illicit**
**03** sly **05** black, wrong **06** banned, barred, shonky **07** bootleg, furtive, illegal **08** criminal, improper, stealthy, unlawful **09** forbidden, ill-gotten, secretive **10** contraband, prohibited, unlicensed **11** black-market, clandestine **12** illegitimate,

unauthorized **13** surreptitious, under-the-table **15** under-the-counter

**illicitly**
**07** wrongly **08** guiltily **09** illegally **10** criminally, unlawfully, wrongfully **13** against the law, disobediently **14** illegitimately

**Illinois**
**02** IL **03** Ill

**illiteracy**
**09** ignorance **15** inability to read, lack of education, lack of schooling

**illiterate**
**08** ignorant, untaught **09** benighted, unlearned, untutored **10** letterless, uncultured, uneducated, unlettered, unschooled **12** analphabetic

**ill-judged**
**04** daft, rash **05** hasty **06** unwise **07** foolish **08** mistaken, reckless **09** foolhardy, impolitic, imprudent, misguided, overhasty, unadvised **10** ill-advised, incautious, indiscreet **11** injudicious, wrong-headed **12** short-sighted **13** ill-considered

**ill-mannered**
**04** rude **05** crude **06** coarse **07** boorish, cubbish, ill-bred, loutish, uncivil, uncouth **08** churlish, impolite, insolent **10** ill-behaved, unmannerly **11** bad-mannered, insensitive **12** badly behaved, discourteous

**ill-natured**
**03** wry **04** acid, mean, ugly **05** cross, nasty, sulky, surly **06** crabby, gnarly, shrewd, sullen, unkind **07** crabbed, vicious **08** churlish, perverse, petulant, shrewish, spiteful **09** malicious, malignant **10** malevolent, unfriendly, unpleasant, vindictive **11** bad-tempered **12** disagreeable

**illness**
**03** wog **04** bout, evil, tout, towt, weed, weid **05** touch **06** attack, malady **07** ailment, disease **08** disorder, sickness **09** complaint, condition, ill health, infirmity **10** affliction, disability, poor health **13** indisposition *See also* **disease**

**illogical**
**05** crazy, wrong **06** absurd, faulty **07** invalid, unsound **08** fallible, specious, spurious **09** casuistic, incorrect, senseless, untenable **10** fallacious, irrational **11** meaningless, sophistical **12** inconsequent, inconsistent, unreasonable, unscientific, woolly minded

**illogicality**
**07** fallacy **08** unreason **09** absurdity **10** invalidity **11** unsoundness **12** speciousness **13** inconsistency, irrationality, senselessness **14** fallaciousness

**ill-starred**
**06** doomed **07** hapless, unhappy, unlucky **08** blighted, ill-fated **09** star-crost **11** star-crossed, unfortunate **12** inauspicious

## ill-tempered
04 curt 05 cross, curst, ratty, sharp, testy 06 crabby, cranky, girnie, grumpy, morose, shirty, tetchy, touchy 07 crabbed, grouchy, stroppy, vicious 08 choleric, spiteful 09 crotchety, impatient, irascible, irritable 10 ill-natured 11 acrimonious, bad-tempered, ill-humoured 12 cantankerous

## ill-timed
05 crass, inept 07 awkward 08 mistimed, tactless, untimely 09 unwelcome 10 wrong-timed 11 inopportune, unfortunate 12 inconvenient, unseasonable 13 inappropriate

## ill-treat
◇ *anagram indicator* 04 harm 05 abuse, wrong 06 damage, demean, injure, misuse 07 neglect, oppress 08 maltreat, misguide, mistreat 09 mishandle

## ill-treatment
04 harm 05 abuse 06 damage, ill-use, injury, misuse 07 neglect 11 manhandling, mishandling 12 maltreatment, mistreatment

## illuminate
04 limn 05 adorn, edify, light 07 clarify, clear up, explain, lighten, light up, miniate, shine on 08 brighten, decorate, illumine, instruct, ornament, twilight 09 back-light, elucidate, embellish, enlighten, limelight, overshine 10 floodlight, illustrate 12 throw light on

## illuminating
07 helpful 08 edifying 09 revealing 10 revelatory 11 explanatory, informative, instructive 12 enlightening

## illumination
03 ray 04 beam 05 flash, light 06 lights 07 insight 08 learning, lighting, radiance 09 adornment, awareness, education, miniature, theosophy 10 brightness, decoration, perception, revelation 11 candlelight, elucidation, instruction, irradiation 12 illustration 13 clarification, embellishment, enlightenment, ornamentation, understanding, zodiacal light

## illusion
04 maya 05 error, fancy 06 déjà vu, mirage 07 chimera, fallacy, fantasy, mocking, phantom, spectre 08 delusion, phantasm, prestige 09 deception, phantosme 10 apparition 11 fata Morgana 12 misjudgement, will-o'-the-wisp 13 hallucination, misconception 15 false impression, misapprehension

## illusory
04 sham 05 false 06 unreal, untrue 07 fancied, phantom, seeming 08 apparent, deluding, delusive, delusory, illusive, imagined, mistaken, specious 09 deceptive, erroneous, imaginary 10 chimerical, fallacious, misleading 11 illusionary 13 unsubstantial

## illustrate
04 draw, show 05 adorn 06 depict, sketch 07 clarify, exhibit, explain, miniate, picture 08 decorate, instance, ornament, renowned 09 elucidate, embellish, enlighten, exemplify, interpret 10 illuminate 11 demonstrate

## illustrated
08 miniated 09 decorated, pictorial 11 embellished, illuminated 12 with drawings, with pictures

## illustration
04 case, note 05 bleed, chart, gloss, plate, quote 06 blow-up, design, figure, remark, sample, sketch 07 analogy, artwork, comment, diagram, drawing, example, graphic, picture 08 exemplar, exponent, half-tone, instance, specimen, vignette 09 adornment, hors texte, quotation, sidelight 10 decoration, photograph 11 case in point, elucidation, explanation, observation 12 frontispiece 13 clarification, demonstration, embellishment, ornamentation 14 interpretation, representation 15 exemplification

## illustrative
06 sample 07 graphic, typical 08 specimen 09 pictorial 10 expository 11 delineative, descriptive, explanatory, explicatory 12 diagrammatic, exemplifying, illustratory 14 illustrational, interpretative, representative

## illustrious
04 dull 05 famed, great, noble, noted 06 bright, famous 07 eminent, exalted, notable 08 esteemed, glorious, honoured, luminous, renowned, splendid 09 acclaimed, brilliant, excellent, prominent, well-known 10 celebrated, honourable, pre-eminent, remarkable 11 magnificent, outstanding 13 distinguished

## ill-will
04 envy, gall 05 anger, odium, spite, wrath 06 animus, enmity, grudge, hatred, malice, maugre 07 dislike, envying, maulgre, rancour 08 aversion, bad blood 09 animosity, antipathy, hostility, maltalent 10 antagonism, ill-feeling, resentment 11 indignation, malevolence 12 disaffection, hard feelings 14 unfriendliness

## image
03 pic 04 bust, copy, doll, face, icon, idea, idol, tiki, twin 05 clone, fancy, match 06 double, effigy, figure, idolon, idolum, mirror, notion, reflex, ringer, shadow, simile, statue, typify, vision 07 concept, eidolon, fantasy, imagery, imagine, persona, picture, portray, profile, replica, thought 08 figurine, identity, likeness, metaphor, phantasy, portrait 09 depiction, duplicate, facsimile, lookalike, portrayal, statuette 10 appearance, conception, dead ringer, impression, perception, photograph, projection, public face, reflection 11 graven image, resemblance 12 doppelgänger,

reproduction, turn of phrase 13 public persona, spitting image 14 figure of speech, representation

## imaginable
06 likely 08 credible, feasible, possible, probable 09 plausible, thinkable 10 believable, supposable 11 conceivable

## imaginary
06 dreamy, made-up, unreal 07 assumed, fancied, fictive, ghostly, phantom, pretend, shadowy 08 fabulous, fanciful, illusory, imagined, invented, mythical, notional, spectral, supposed 09 fantastic, fictional, legendary, visionary 10 chimerical, fictitious 11 fantastical, make-believe, non-existent 12 hypothetical, mythological 13 hallucinatory, insubstantial

## imagination
03 wit 05 dream, fancy 06 schema, vision 07 chimera, fantasy, imagery, insight, project 08 illusion, mind's eye, phantasy 09 dreamland, ingenuity 10 creativity, enterprise, mental view 11 inspiration, originality 12 fancifulness 13 contemplation, flight of fancy, ingeniousness, inventiveness 15 imaginativeness, resourcefulness

## imaginative
05 vivid 06 clever, poetic 07 lyrical 08 creative, fanciful, inspired, original, poetical 09 fantastic, ingenious, inventive, visionary, whimsical 10 innovative 11 full of ideas, resourceful 12 enterprising

## imagine
03 see 04 deem, plan, ween 05 dream, fancy, feign, guess, image, judge, think 06 assume, create, devise, figure, gather, ideate, invent, reckon, scheme, take it, vision 07 believe, conceit, dream up, picture, presume, pretend, project, propose, suppose, surmise, think up 08 conceive, contrive, daydream, envisage 09 conjure up, fantasize, visualize 10 conjecture 11 make believe 14 form a picture of

## imbalance
04 bias 08 inequity, variance 09 disparity 10 inequality, partiality, unevenness, unfairness 13 disproportion

## imbecile
◇ *anagram indicator* 03 ass, mug, nit 04 berk, clot, daft, dope, dork, dumb, fool, geek, jerk, nana, nerd, nerk, nong, prat, putz, twit 05 anile, barmy, batty, chump, crazy, dorky, dotty, dumbo, dunce, eejit, goofy, idiot, inane, klutz, moron, ninny, nutty, potty, silly, twerp, wacky, wally 06 absurd, bammer, bampot, cretin, dimwit, doofus, dum-dum, nitwit, numpty, stupid, sucker 07 asinine, bungler, fatuous, foolish, halfwit, idiotic, jughead, moronic, pillock, plonker, wazzock, witless 08 flathead, innocent, numskull 09 birdbrain, blockhead, cloth head, lame brain, ludicrous, simpleton, thickhead

**imbecility**

10 nincompoop 11 chowderhead, knuckle-head, thick-headed 12 crack-brained 13 knuckle-headed

**imbecility**

06 idiocy 07 amentia, fatuity, idiotcy, inanity 08 daftness 09 asininity, craziness, cretinism, stupidity 11 foolishness 12 childishness, incompetence

**imbibe**

◇ *containment indicator* 03 sip 04 gain, gulp, suck, swig 05 drink, lap up, quaff 06 absorb, gather, ingest, soak up, take in 07 acquire, consume, drink in, receive, swallow 09 knock back 10 assimilate

**imbroglio**

04 mess 06 muddle, scrape, tangle 07 dilemma 08 quandary 09 confusion 10 difficulty 11 embroilment, involvement 12 complication, entanglement

**imbue**

04 fill, tint 05 embay, steep, taint, tinct, tinge 06 charge, infuse, inject, instil, season 07 breathe, ingrain, inspire, moisten, pervade, possess, suffuse 08 permeate, saturate, tincture 09 inbreathe, inculcate, inoculate, transfuse 10 impregnate 12 indoctrinate

**imitate**

03 act, ape, hit 04 copy, echo, fake, mock 05 feign, forge, mimic, spoof 06 follow, hit off, mirror, parody, parrot, repeat, send up 07 copycat, emulate, take off 08 simulate 09 duplicate, replicate, reproduce 10 caricature, do likewise, follow suit 11 counterfeit, impersonate 12 take as a model

**imitation**

04 copy, echo, -ette, fake, faux, mock, sham 05 apery, aping, dummy, spoof 06 ersatz, parody, phoney, pseudo, send-up 07 forgery, man-made, mimesis, mimicry, mockery, mocking, replica, take-off 08 knock-off, likeness, parrotry, travesty 09 burlesque, duplicate, emulation, simulated, synthetic 10 artificial, caricature, impression, reflection, simulation 11 counterfeit, resemblance 12 reproduction 13 impersonation

**imitative**

04 mock 05 apish, me-too, mimic 07 copying, mimetic, servile 09 emulating, mimetical, mimicking, simulated 10 derivative, parrot-like, second-hand, unoriginal 11 plagiarized 12 onomatopoeic

**imitator**

03 ape 04 echo 05 mimic 06 copier, epigon, parrot 07 copycat, copyist, epigone 08 emulator, follower, parodist 10 plagiarist 12 impersonator 13 impressionist

**immaculate**

04 pure 05 clean 07 perfect, sinless 08 flawless, innocent, pristine, spotless, unsoiled 09 blameless, faultless, guiltless, incorrupt, stainless, undefiled, unstained, unsullied, untainted 10 impeccable 11 unblemished 12 spick and span, squeaky clean 15 whiter than white

**immaculately**

06 purely 09 perfectly, sinlessly 10 flawlessly, impeccably, innocently, spotlessly, without sin 11 blamelessly, faultlessly, guiltlessly, incorruptly 12 to perfection, without blame, without guilt

**immanent**

06 innate 08 inherent 09 ingrained, intrinsic, pervading 10 permeating, ubiquitous 11 omnipresent 12 all-pervading

**immaterial**

05 minor, petty 07 trivial 08 trifling 10 irrelevant 11 incorporeal, inessential, of no account, unessential, unimportant 13 insignificant 15 inconsequential

**immature**

◇ *tail deletion indicator* 03 raw 05 crude, green, naive, vealy, young 06 callow, jejune, unripe 07 babyish, budding, puerile, unbaked, unready 08 childish, juvenile, under-age, unformed, untimely 09 beardless, embryonic, fledgling, half-baked, infantile, ingenuous, unfledged, unsizable 10 adolescent, incomplete, unmellowed, unprepared, unsizeable 11 undeveloped 13 inexperienced

**immaturity**

05 youth 07 crudity, rawness 09 crudeness, greenness, puerility 10 callowness, juvenility, unripeness 11 adolescence, babyishness 12 childishness, immatureness, imperfection, inexperience 14 unpreparedness

**immeasurable**

04 vast 07 endless, immense 08 infinite 09 boundless, limitless, unbounded, unlimited 10 bottomless, fathomless 11 illimitable, inestimable, never ending 12 immensurable, incalculable, interminable, unfathomable 13 inexhaustible

**immeasurably**

06 vastly 09 endlessly, immensely 10 infinitely 11 boundlessly, illimitably, inestimably, limitlessly 12 incalculably, interminably 13 beyond measure, inexhaustibly

**immediacy**

07 urgency 08 instancy 09 freshness, imminence, swiftness 10 directness, importance, promptness 11 spontaneity 12 criticalness, simultaneity 13 instantaneity

**immediate**

04 main, near, next 05 basic, chief, close, swift, vital 06 direct, prompt, recent, speedy, sudden, urgent 07 closest, crucial, current, instant, nearest, present, primary, soonest 08 abutting, adjacent, critical, existing, next-door, pressing 09 adjoining, first-time, important, posthaste, principal, proximate 11 fundamental, top-priority 12 high-priority, without delay 13 instantaneous

**immediately**

03 now, pdq 04 anon, ASAP, next, stat, then, tite 06 at once, belive, pronto, statim, subito 07 bang off, quickly 08 as soon as, directly, promptly, right now, speedily, straight, urgently 09 at a glance, forthwith, instantly, like a shot, on the spot, out of hand, presently, right away, thereupon, yesterday 10 this minute 11 incessantly, incontinent, in the wake of, on the morrow, straightway, therewithal, this instant, tout de suite 12 lickety-split, no sooner than, on the instant, on the knocker, straight away, straightways, there and then, without delay 13 incontinently, straightforth 14 unhesitatingly, without more ado 15 before you know it, instantaneously, without question

**immemorial**

05 fixed, hoary 06 age-old, of yore 07 ancient, archaic 08 timeless 09 ancestral 11 traditional 12 long-standing, time-honoured

**immense**

04 fine, huge, mega, vast 05 enorm, giant, great, jumbo 06 bumper, cosmic, myriad 07 mammoth, massive, titanic 08 colossal, cyclopic, enormous, fabulous, gigantic, whopping 09 cyclopean, cyclopian, extensive, ginormous, herculean, humungous, limitless 10 gargantuan, monumental, tremendous 11 Brobdingnag, elephantine 14 Brobdingnagian, extremely large

**immensely**

04 very 05 jolly 06 highly, really, vastly 07 acutely, awfully, greatly, utterly 08 severely, terribly 09 decidedly, extremely, intensely, massively, unusually 10 dreadfully, enormously, remarkably, uncommonly 11 exceedingly, excessively, frightfully 12 immoderately, inordinately, terrifically, unreasonably 13 exceptionally 15 extraordinarily

**immensity**

04 bulk 07 expanse 08 hugeness, infinity, vastness 09 expansion, greatness, magnitude 11 massiveness 12 enormousness, giganticness 13 extensiveness, limitlessness

**immerse**

◇ *hidden indicator* 03 dip 04 bury, duck, dunk, sink, soak 05 bathe, douse, souse 06 absorb, blanch, drench, engage, engulf, occupy, plunge, wallow 07 baptize, demerge, demerse, embathe, engross, imbathe, immerge, involve 08 saturate, submerge, submerse, wrap up in 09 preoccupy

**immersed**

◇ *hidden indicator* 04 busy, deep, rapt, sunk 06 buried 07 taken up 08 absorbed, consumed, involved, occupied **09** engrossed, wrapped up **11** preoccupied

**immersion**
**03** dip **05** bathe **07** baptism, dipping, dousing, ducking, dunking, sinking, soaking **08** plunging **09** drenching **10** absorption, engagement, engrossing, saturation, submersion **11** involvement **13** concentration, preoccupation

**immigrant**
**03** pom **04** Balt **05** alien, issei, pommy **06** merino **07** greener, incomer, migrant, new chum, settler, wetback **08** newcomer, outsider **09** foreigner, Pakistani **10** Aussiedler, new arrival, overstayer **13** new Australian

**immigrate**
**06** come in, move in, remove, settle **07** migrate **08** resettle

**imminence**
**06** menace, threat **08** approach, instancy, nearness **09** closeness, immediacy **11** propinquity

**imminent**
**04** near **05** close **06** at hand, coming **07** brewing, in store, jutting, looming **08** in the air, menacing, on the way, upcoming **09** impending **11** approaching, forthcoming, in the offing, overhanging, threatening **12** on the horizon **13** about to happen, almost upon you **14** round the corner **15** fast approaching

**immobile**
**05** fixed, rigid, stiff, still **06** at rest, frozen, rooted, static **07** riveted **08** moveless, unmoving **09** immovable **10** motionless, stationary, stock-still **11** immobilized

**immobility**
**06** fixity **08** catatony, firmness **09** catatonia, fixedness, inertness, stability, stillness **10** disability, steadiness **12** immovability **14** motionlessness

**immobilize**
**04** halt, stop **05** Taser® **06** freeze **07** cripple, disable **08** paralyse, transfix **10** deactivate, inactivate **14** put out of action

**immoderate**
**03** OTT **05** steep, undue **06** lavish, wanton **07** extreme, fulsome **08** enormous, uncurbed **09** egregious, excessive, hubristic, unbridled, unlimited **10** exorbitant, inordinate, outrageous, over the top, profligate **11** exaggerated, extravagant, intemperate, overweening, uncalled-for, unjustified, unwarranted **12** distemperate, uncontrolled, unreasonable, unrestrained, unrestricted **13** self-indulgent **14** unconscionable

**immoderately**
**06** unduly **08** to excess, wantonly **09** extremely **11** excessively **12** exorbitantly, inordinately, out of all cess, unreasonably **13** exaggeratedly,

extravagantly, unjustifiably **14** unrestrainedly, without measure

**immoderation**
**06** excess **08** unreason **10** inordinacy, lavishness **11** dissipation, exorbitance, prodigality, unrestraint **12** extravagance, intemperance **13** excessiveness **14** immoderateness, overindulgence

**immodest**
**04** bold, lewd **05** cocky, fresh, saucy **06** brazen, cheeky, coarse, risqué **07** forward, immoral, obscene **08** boastful, improper, impudent, indecent **09** revealing, shameless **10** indecorous, indelicate

**immodesty**
**04** gall **05** brass **08** audacity, boldness, impurity, lewdness, temerity **09** bawdiness, impudence, indecorum, obscenity **10** coarseness, impudicity, indelicacy **11** forwardness **13** shamelessness **14** indecorousness

**immolate**
**04** burn, kill **05** offer **07** offer up **09** sacrifice

**immoral**
**03** bad **04** base, blue, evil, lewd, vile **05** juicy, loose, wrong **06** impure, naught, sinful, wanton, wicked **07** corrupt, godless, obscene, raunchy, vicious **08** depraved, indecent, unhonest **09** debauched, dishonest, dissolute, nefarious, reprobate, unethical **10** degenerate, iniquitous, licentious **11** promiscuous **12** pornographic, questionable, unprincipled, unscrupulous **13** against nature
• **immoral act 03** sin

**immorality**
**03** sin **04** evil, vice **05** wrong **07** badness **08** impurity, iniquity, lewdness, vileness **09** depravity, indecency, obscenity, turpitude **10** corruption, debauchery, dishonesty, profligacy, sinfulness, wickedness, wrongdoing **11** pornography **12** indiscretion **13** dissoluteness **14** licentiousness

**immortal**
**03** god **04** hero **05** deity, great **06** famous, genius **07** abiding, ageless, endless, eternal, goddess, lasting, undying **08** constant, divinity, enduring, fadeless, honoured, Olympian, timeless, unfading **09** amarantin, ambrosial, ceaseless, deathless, memorable, perennial, perpetual, well-known **10** celebrated, ever-living **11** divine being, everlasting, sempiternal **12** imperishable **13** distinguished, unforgettable **14** indestructible

**immortality**
**04** fame **05** glory **06** honour, renown **08** eternity **09** celebrity, greatness **10** amritattva, perpetuity **11** distinction, endlessness, eternal life **12** gloriousness, timelessness

**13** deathlessness, glorification **15** everlasting life, imperishability

**immortalize**
**04** laud **07** glorify **08** enshrine, eternize **09** celebrate **10** eternalize, perpetuate **11** commemorate, memorialize

**immovable**
**03** set **04** fast, firm, real **05** fixed, stuck **06** dogged, jammed, moored, rooted, secure, stable **07** adamant, riveted **08** anchored, constant, immobile, resolute, stubborn **09** impassive, obstinate, steadfast **10** determined, inflexible, motionless, unshakable, unswerving, unwavering, unyielding **11** unalterable, unshakeable **12** intransigent **14** marble-constant, uncompromising

**immune**
**04** free, safe **05** clear, proof **06** exempt, secure, spared **07** excused **08** absolved, released, relieved **09** protected, resistant **12** invulnerable **13** unsusceptible

**immunity**
**05** right **06** safety **07** freedom, liberty, licence, release **08** impunity **09** exception, exemption, franchise, indemnity, privilege **10** permission, protection, resistance **11** exoneration, inoculation, vaccination **12** immunization, mithridatism

**immunization**
**03** jab **09** injection **10** protection **11** inoculation, vaccination

**immunize**
**04** salt **06** inject, shield **07** protect **09** inoculate, safeguard, vaccinate

**immure**
**04** cage, jail **06** enwall, shut up, wall in **07** confine, enclose **08** cloister, imprison **11** incarcerate **13** put behind bars

**immutability**
**09** constancy, fixedness, stability **10** durability, permanence **13** immutableness, invariability **14** changelessness **15** unalterableness

**immutable**
**05** fixed **06** stable **07** abiding, lasting **08** constant, enduring **09** permanent, perpetual, steadfast **10** changeless, inflexible, invariable, sacrosanct **11** unalterable **12** unchangeable

**imp**
**03** elf **04** brat, limb, minx, puck, ympe **05** demon, devil, gamin, gnome, graft, Ralph, rogue, scamp, scion, shoot **06** goblin, rascal, sprite, urchin **09** hobgoblin, prankster, trickster **12** troublemaker **13** mischief-maker **15** flibbertigibbet

**impact**
**03** act, fix, hit **04** bang, belt, blow, bump, dush, jolt, work **05** brunt, clash, crash, crush, force, knock, poise, power, shock, smash, souse **06** affect, effect, glance, strike **07** apply to, collide, contact, impinge, meaning, results **09** collision, influence

**10** impression, percussion
**12** consequences, significance **13** press together, repercussions **14** have an effect on, reverberations

## impair

◇ *anagram indicator* **03** mar **04** harm, rust **05** alloy, blunt, craze, decay, spoil, wrong **06** damage, hinder, injure, lessen, reduce, weaken, worsen **07** cripple, disable, empeach, impeach, tarnish, vitiate, wear out **08** decrease, diminish, embezzle, emperish, enervate, enfeeble, wear away, wear down **09** undermine **10** debilitate **11** deteriorate

## impaired

◇ *anagram indicator* **04** poor, weak **05** rusty, stale **06** faulty, flawed, spoilt **07** damaged, unsound, vicious **08** disabled, vitiated, weakened **09** defective, imperfect **10** challenged **11** handicapped

## impairment

**04** flaw, harm, hurt, ruin, wear **05** allay, fault, spoil **06** damage, injury **07** empeach, impeach **08** handicap, weakness **09** paralogia, reduction, vitiation **10** disability **11** disablement, dysfunction **13** deterioration
*See also* **sight**

## impale

**04** spit, stab **05** ganch, lance, prick, spear, spike, stick **06** gaunch, pierce, skewer **08** puncture, transfix **09** perforate **10** disembowel, run through

## impalpable

**04** airy, fine, thin **06** subtle **07** elusive, shadowy, tenuous **08** delicate **10** indistinct, intangible **11** incorporeal, indefinable **13** imperceptible, insubstantial, unsubstantial **15** inapprehensible

## impart

**04** give, lend, shed, tell **05** break, grant, offer **06** accord, assign, bestow, confer, convey, pass on, relate, report, reveal **07** divulge **08** disclose, transmit **09** make known **10** contribute **11** communicate

## impartial

**04** fair, just **05** equal **06** candid **07** neutral **08** detached, judicial, unbiased **09** equitable, objective **10** crossbench, even-handed, fair-minded, open-minded **11** non-partisan, uncommitted, unconcerned **12** unprejudiced **13** disinterested, dispassionate

## impartiality

**06** candor, equity **07** candour, justice **08** equality, fairness **10** detachment, dispassion, neutrality **11** disinterest, objectivity **12** unbiasedness **14** even-handedness, open-mindedness **15** non-partisanship

## impassable

**06** closed **07** blocked, invious **08** pathless **09** trackless **10** invincible, obstructed, unpassable **11** insuperable, unnavigable **12** impenetrable, unassailable, unvoyageable **13** untraversable **14** insurmountable

## impasse

**04** halt **06** log jam **07** dead end **08** cul-de-sac, deadlock **09** checkmate, stalemate **10** blind alley, standstill **15** Mexican standoff

## impassioned

**05** eager, fiery **06** ardent, fervid, heated **07** blazing, earnest, excited, fervent, furious, glowing, intense, rousing, violent **08** animated, forceful, inflamed, inspired, spirited, stirring, vehement, vigorous **09** emotional, heartfelt **10** passionate **12** enthusiastic

## impassive

**04** calm, cool **05** bland **06** stolid **07** deadpan, stoical, unmoved **08** composed, laid-back **09** apathetic, immovable, unfeeling, unruffled **10** impassible, phlegmatic, stone-faced **11** emotionless, indifferent, unconcerned, unemotional, unemotioned, unexcitable, unflappable **13** dispassionate, imperturbable **14** expressionless

## impassively

**06** calmly, coolly **11** unfeelingly **13** apathetically, emotionlessly, imperturbably, unemotionally **14** phlegmatically **15** dispassionately

## impatience

**05** haste **07** anxiety **08** curtness, edginess, keenness, rashness **09** agitation, dysphoria, eagerness, shortness, tenseness **10** abruptness, indignance, uneasiness **11** brusqueness, impetuosity, intolerance, nervousness **12** excitability, irritability, restlessness
• **expression of impatience** **03** ach, dam, och, poh, tut **04** chut, damn, phew, push, toot, tush, tuts, when **05** damme, devil, pshaw, toots **06** dammit, tut-tut **07** crimine, crimini **10** tilly-fally, tilly-vally **12** Donnerwetter, tilley-valley

## impatient

**04** curt, edgy, keen **05** angry, eager, hasty, narky, ratty, short, tense, testy **06** abrupt, snappy **07** anxious, brusque, fidgety, fretful, jittery, nervous **08** restless **09** excitable, impetuous, irritable, querulous **10** intolerant **11** hot-tempered **13** on tenterhooks, quick-tempered

## impeach

**05** blame **06** accuse, attack, charge, damage, hinder, impair, impede, impugn, indict, revile **07** arraign, censure, prevent **08** denounce **09** criticize, detriment, disparage, hindrance **10** impairment, prevention

## impeachment

**06** appeal, charge **10** accusation, indictment **11** arraignment **13** disparagement

## impeccable

**04** pure **05** exact **06** just so **07** correct, perfect, precise, upright **08** flawless, innocent **09** blameless, exemplary,

faultless, stainless **10** immaculate **11** unblemished **12** squeaky clean **14** irreproachable

## impecunious

**04** poor **05** broke, needy, skint **07** boracic **08** dirt-poor, indigent, strapped **09** destitute, insolvent, penniless, penurious **10** cleaned out, stony-broke **12** impoverished, on your uppers **15** poverty-stricken

## impedance

**01** Z **09** hindrance
• **measure of impedance** **03** ohm

## impede

**03** bar, rub **04** clog, curb, slow, stop **05** block, check, delay **06** hamper, hinder, hogtie, hold up, retard, thwart **07** disrupt, empeach, impeach, trammel **08** encumber, handicap, hold back, incumber, obstruct, restrain, slow down, strangle

## impediment

**03** bar, bur, log, rub **04** burr, clog, curb, halt, snag **05** block, check **06** burden, defect, rubber **07** barrier, setback, stammer, stutter **08** handicap, obstacle **09** hindrance, restraint **10** difficulty **11** encumbrance, obstruction, restriction **14** stumbling-block

## impedimenta

**04** gear **05** stuff **06** things **07** baggage, effects, luggage **09** equipment **10** belongings **12** encumbrances **13** accoutrements, bits and pieces, paraphernalia

## impel

**03** put **04** goad, move, prod, push, spur, urge **05** drive, force, press **06** compel, excite, incite, oblige, prompt, propel, strike **07** inspire **08** get going, motivate, pressure **09** constrain, instigate, stimulate **10** pressurize

## impending

**04** near **05** close **06** at hand, coming, toward **07** brewing, looming **08** imminent, in the air, menacing, on the way, upcoming **11** approaching, forthcoming, in the offing, threatening **12** on the horizon **13** about to happen

## impenetrable

**04** dark **05** dense, solid, thick **07** cryptic, obscure **08** abstruse, airtight, baffling, puzzling **09** enigmatic, overgrown, recondite **10** adamantine, impassable, impervious, mysterious, soundproof **11** inscrutable **12** unfathomable **13** indiscernible **14** unintelligible

## impenitence

**08** defiance, obduracy **11** impenitency **12** stubbornness **15** hard-heartedness, incorrigibility

## impenitent

**07** defiant **08** hardened, obdurate **09** unabashed, unashamed **10** uncontrite, unreformed **11** remorseless, unrepentant **12** incorrigible, unregenerate, unremorseful **13** without regret **14** without remorse

## imperative

**05** vital **06** urgent **07** crucial **08** critical, pressing **09** essential, necessary **10** compulsory, obligatory, peremptory **13** authoritative, indispensable

## imperceptible

**04** fine, tiny **05** faint, small, vague **06** minute, slight, subtle **07** gradual, muffled, obscure, unclear **09** inaudible, minuscule **10** impalpable, indefinite, indistinct, negligible, unapparent **11** microscopic **12** undetectable, unnoticeable **13** inappreciable, indiscernible, infinitesimal

## imperceptibly

**06** slowly, subtly, unseen **08** bit by bit **09** gradually **10** insensibly **12** unnoticeably **13** inappreciably, indiscernibly, unobtrusively **14** little by little

## imperfect

◇ *anagram indicator* **04** lame **06** broken, faulty, flawed **07** chipped, damaged, sketchy **08** impaired **09** blemished, defective, deficient, embryonic, unperfect **10** inadequate, incomplete **12** insufficient

## imperfection

**03** cut **04** blot, dent, flaw, kink, spot, tear **05** break, crack, fault, stain, taint **06** blotch, defect, foible, hickey, mackle **07** blemish, failing, scratch **08** weakness **09** deformity **10** deficiency, impairment, inadequacy **11** shortcoming **13** insufficiency **15** malconformation

## imperial

**03** lmp **05** grand, great, lofty, noble, regal, royal **06** august, kingly **07** queenly, stately, supreme **08** absolute, glorious, majestic, splendid **09** sovereign **10** commanding **11** magnificent, monarchical

## imperialism

**10** flag-waving **11** adventurism, colonialism, flag-wagging **12** expansionism **14** empire-building **15** acquisitiveness

## imperil

**04** harm, risk **06** expose, hazard, injure **08** endanger, threaten **10** compromise, jeopardize **11** put in danger, take a chance **12** expose to risk **13** put in jeopardy

## imperious

**06** lordly **07** haughty **08** arrogant, despotic **09** assertive, masterful **10** autocratic, commanding, high-handed, peremptory, tyrannical **11** dictatorial, domineering, overbearing, overweening

## imperishable

**07** abiding, eternal, undying **08** enduring, immortal, unfading **09** deathless, perennial, permanent, perpetual **11** everlasting **13** immarcescible, incorruptible, unforgettable **14** indestructible

## impermanence

**09** briefness **10** transience, transiency **11** elusiveness, inconstancy **12** ephemerality **13** temporariness **14** transitoriness

## impermanent

**05** brief **06** flying, mortal **07** elusive, passing, unfixed **08** fleeting, fugitive, unstable **09** ephemeral, fugacious, momentary, temporary, transient, unsettled **10** evanescent, fly-by-night, inconstant, perishable, short-lived, transitory

## impermeable

**05** proof **06** sealed **08** airtight, hermetic **09** damp-proof, non-porous, resistant **10** impassable, impervious, waterproof, watertight **11** greaseproof **12** impenetrable **14** water-repellent, water-resistant

## impersonal

**04** cold, cool **05** aloof, stiff **06** formal, frigid, remote, stuffy **07** distant, neutral **08** clinical, detached, official, unbiased **09** objective, unfeeling **11** unemotional **12** businesslike, unprejudiced **13** dispassionate

## impersonally

**06** fairly, justly **09** equitably, neutrally **11** objectively, without bias **12** open-mindedly **14** with an open mind **15** dispassionately

## impersonate

**02** do **03** act, ape **04** mock **05** mimic **06** embody, parody, pose as, send up **07** imitate, portray, present, take off **09** incarnate, pass off as **10** caricature **12** masquerade as

## impersonation

**05** apery, aping, fraud, spoof **06** parody, send-up **07** mimicry, take-off **09** burlesque, imitation **10** caricature, impression

## impertinence

**03** lip **04** face, gall, sass **05** brass, cheek, crust, mouth, nerve, sauce, snash **08** attitude, audacity, backchat, boldness, chutzpah, rudeness **09** brass neck, flippancy, impudence, insolence, intrusion **10** brazenness, disrespect, effrontery **11** discourtesy, forwardness, presumption **12** flippantness, impoliteness **13** shamelessness

## impertinent

**04** bold, pert, rude **05** brash, fresh, sassy, saucy **06** brazen, cheeky **07** forward **08** impolite, impudent, insolent **09** audacious, intrusive, shameless **10** unmannerly **11** ill-mannered **12** discourteous, presumptuous **13** disrespectful

## imperturbability

**04** cool **08** calmness, coolness **09** composure, sangfroid **10** equanimity **11** complacency **12** tranquillity **14** self-possession

## imperturbable

**04** calm, cool **06** serene **07** unfazed, unmoved **08** composed, laid-back,

## impervious

tranquil **09** collected, impassive, supercool, unruffled **10** complacent, unruffable, untroubled **11** unexcitable, unflappable **12** even-tempered **13** self-possessed **15** cool as a cucumber

## impervious

**05** proof, tight **06** closed, immune, opaque, sealed **07** unmoved **08** gas-tight, hermetic **09** damp-proof, dustproof, non-porous, rainproof, resistant, star-proof, untouched **10** light-proof, smokeproof, smoketight, steamtight, unaffected, waterproof, watertight **11** adiathermic, impermeable, showerproof **12** impenetrable, invulnerable

## impetuosity

**04** birr, dash, élan, rush **05** haste **08** rashness **09** hastiness, vehemence **10** impatience **11** spontaneity **12** recklessness **13** foolhardiness, impetuousness, impulsiveness **15** precipitateness, thoughtlessness

## impetuous

**04** rash **05** brash, fiery, hasty **06** sturdy **07** violent **08** headlong, reckless, tearaway **09** foolhardy, hot-headed, impatient, impulsive, unplanned **10** bull-headed, unreasoned, unthinking **11** precipitate, spontaneous, thoughtless **12** ill-conceived, uncontrolled **14** unpremeditated **15** spur-of-the-moment

## impetuously

**06** rashly **10** recklessly, vehemently **11** impulsively **12** passionately, unthinkingly **13** precipitately, spontaneously

## impetus

**04** birr, goad, push, send, spur **05** boost, drive, force, power, sweep, swing **06** energy, travel, urging **07** impulse **08** momentum, stimulus **09** actuation, incentive, influence **10** motivation **11** inspiration **13** encouragement

## impiety

**06** hubris **08** iniquity **09** blasphemy, profanity, sacrilege **10** irreligion, sinfulness, unholiness, wickedness **11** godlessness, irreverence, profaneness, ungodliness **15** unrighteousness

## impinge

**03** hit **04** beat, fall **05** souse, touch **06** affect, invade, strike **07** intrude, touch on **08** encroach, infringe, trespass **09** influence

## impious

**06** sinful, unholy, wicked **07** godless, profane, ungodly **09** hubristic **10** iniquitous, irreverent **11** blasphemous, irreligious, unrighteous **12** sacrilegious

## impish

**05** elfin, gamin **07** naughty, puckish, roguish, tricksy, waggish **08** devilish, rascally, sportive **09** pranksome, tricksome **10** frolicsome **11** mischievous

### implacability
**12** pitilessness, ruthlessness, vengefulness **13** inexorability, inflexibility, intransigence, mercilessness, rancorousness **14** implacableness, intractability, relentlessness **15** remorselessness, unforgivingness

### implacable
**05** cruel **06** deadly, mortal **07** adamant **08** pitiless, ruthless, vengeful **09** heartless, impacable, merciless, rancorous **10** inexorable, inflexible, relentless, unyielding **11** intractable, remorseless, unforgiving, unrelenting **12** intransigent, unappeasable **14** irreconcilable, uncompromising

### implant
**03** fix, put, sow **04** root **05** embed, graft, inset, place, plant **06** enrace, enroot, insert, instil **07** embosom, engraft, imbosom **09** inculcate, introduce **10** inseminate, transplant

### implausible
**04** lame, thin, weak **06** flimsy **07** dubious, suspect **08** doubtful, unlikely **10** far-fetched, improbable, incredible **11** transparent **12** questionable, unbelievable, unconvincing **13** hard to believe, inconceivable

### implausibly
**10** doubtfully, improbably, incredibly **12** questionably, unbelievably **13** inconceivably

### implement
**02** do **04** celt, comb, loom, rake, tool **05** apply, brush, dolly, flail, raker, razor, steel, whisk **06** anchor, device, effect, eolith, fulfil, gadget, pusher, ricker, ripple, sickle, taster, tedder **07** enforce, execute, grubber, perform, realize, utensil **08** carry out, complete, fly whisk, scuffler, shoehorn, spreader, squeegee, squilgee, tint tool **09** apparatus, appliance, discharge, fire-stick, fish slice, microlith, poop scoop, requisite, scarifier **10** accomplish, bring about, cultivator, extirpator, fish-carver, fish-trowel, gold-washer, instrument, loggerhead, snowplough, sucket fork, wheel brace **11** contrivance, road scraper, sucket spoon, turfing iron **13** pooper-scooper, put into action, put into effect **14** rostrocarinate

### implementation
**06** action **09** discharge, effecting, execution, operation **10** completion, fulfilling, fulfilment, performing **11** application, carrying-out, enforcement, performance, realization **14** accomplishment

### implicate
◇ *anagram indicator* **05** imply **06** enfold **07** concern, connect, embroil, include, involve **08** entangle **09** associate, be a part of, be party to, inculpate **10** be a party to, compromise **11** incriminate

### implicated
◇ *anagram indicator* **07** party to

**08** included, involved **09** concerned, connected, embroiled, entangled, suspected **10** associated, inculpated **11** compromised, responsible **12** incriminated

### implication
**06** effect **07** meaning **08** overtone **09** deduction, inference, undertone **10** conclusion, connection, suggestion **11** association, consequence, embroilment, inculpation, insinuation, involvement **12** entanglement, ramification, repercussion, significance **13** incrimination **15** subintelligitur

### implicit
**04** full **05** sheer, tacit, total, utter **06** entire, hidden, hinted, latent, unsaid **07** implied, perfect **08** absolute, complete, indirect, inferred, inherent, positive, unspoken, unstated **09** deducible, entangled, steadfast, suggested **10** insinuated, understood, unreserved **11** intertwined, unexpressed, unqualified **12** unhesitating, wholehearted **13** unconditional, unquestioning

### implicitly
**06** firmly **07** totally, utterly **10** absolutely, completely **11** steadfastly **12** unreservedly **14** unhesitatingly, wholeheartedly **15** unconditionally, unquestioningly

### implied
**05** tacit **06** hinted **07** assumed **08** implicit, indirect, inherent, unspoken, unstated **09** suggested **10** insinuated, undeclared, understood **11** unexpressed

### implore
**03** ask, beg **04** pray **05** crave, plead, press **06** appeal, invoke **07** beseech, beseeke, conjure, entreat, request, solicit **09** importune, obsecrate **10** supplicate

### imply
**04** hint, mean **05** infer, state **06** denote, enfold, entail, signal **07** connote, involve, point to, require, signify, suggest, suppose **08** indicate, intimate **09** implicate, insinuate, predicate **10** presuppose, understand **13** say indirectly

### impolite
**04** rude **05** crude, rough **06** abrupt, cheeky, coarse, vulgar **07** boorish, ill-bred, loutish, uncivil **08** insolent **09** unrefined **10** indecorous, ungracious, unladylike, unmannerly **11** bad-mannered, ill-mannered, impertinent, uncivilized **12** discourteous **13** disrespectful, inconsiderate, ungentlemanly

### impolitely
**06** rudely **07** crudely **09** uncivilly **10** insolently **12** indecorously, ungraciously **13** impertinently **14** discourteously **15** disrespectfully, inconsiderately

### impoliteness
**08** rudeness **09** crassness, gaucherie,

indecorum, insolence, roughness **10** abruptness, bad manners, coarseness, disrespect, incivility, indelicacy **11** boorishness, discourtesy **12** churlishness, impertinence **14** indecorousness, unmannerliness

### impolitic
**04** daft, rash **06** unwise **07** foolish **09** ill-judged, imprudent, maladroit, misguided **10** ill-advised, indiscreet, unpolicied **11** inexpedient, injudicious **12** short-sighted, undiplomatic **13** ill-considered

### import
**03** nub **04** gist **05** buy in, drift, sense, state **06** amount, behove, convey, moment, ship in, thrust, weight **07** bring in, content, essence, meaning, message, portend, purport, signify **08** reimport, tendency **09** importing, intention, introduce, substance **10** importance **11** consequence, implication, seriousness **12** foreign goods, foreign trade, significance **13** buy from abroad, imported goods **14** foreign product **15** imported product

### importance
**04** mark, note, pith **05** power, state, value, worth **06** esteem, import, matter, status, weight **07** concern, urgency **08** eminence, gravitas, interest, prestige, standing **09** graveness, influence, magnitude, substance **10** prominence, usefulness **11** consequence, distinction **12** criticalness, significance **13** consideration, momentousness, signification **14** noteworthiness
• **anything of importance 04** much
• **anything of minor importance 02** by **03** bye
• **be of importance 04** mean **06** matter

### important
**03** big, key, top **04** main **05** chief, grave, heavy, major, noted, vital **06** mighty, of note, urgent, valued **07** big-time, capital, central, crucial, eminent, fateful, leading, notable, pivotal, pompous, primary, salient, seminal, serious, weighty **08** critical, esteemed, foremost, historic, material, powerful, priority, relevant, ultimate, valuable **09** essential, front-page, high-level, momentous, number one, of warrant, paramount, principal, prominent **10** meaningful, noteworthy, pre-eminent **11** epoch-making, far-reaching, fundamental, high-ranking, influential, outstanding, prestigious, significant, substantial **12** world-shaking **13** consequential, distinguished, of good warrant **15** world-shattering

### importunate
**06** dogged, urgent **08** annoying, pressing **09** impatient, insistent, tenacious **10** burdensome, persistent **11** inopportune, troublesome **12** pertinacious

**importune**
03 beg, dun, ply 04 prig, urge
05 annoy, beset, hound, press
06 appeal, badger, cajole, harass,
import, pester, plague, urgent
07 besiege, request, signify, solicit
08 untimely 09 flagitate, plead with
10 burdensome, lay siege to, resistless,
supplicate 11 inopportune

**importunity**
06 urging 07 urgency 08 cajolery,
hounding, pressing 09 harassing,
pestering 10 entreaties, harassment,
importance, insistence 11 persistence
12 solicitation

**impose**
03 fix, lay, put, set 04 levy, palm
05 abuse, apply, clamp, exact, foist,
force, lay on, place, put on 06 burden,
butt in, charge, decree, enjoin,
impone, saddle, thrust 07 break in,
command, enforce, exploit, inflict,
intrude, mislead, obtrude, place on,
presume, put over, put upon
08 encroach, encumber, trespass
09 establish, institute, introduce
13 force yourself, take liberties
14 thrust yourself 15 take advantage of

**imposing**
05 grand, lofty 06 august 07 stately
08 majestic, matronly, specious,
splendid, striking 09 deceptive,
dignified, grandiose, mausolean
10 commanding, impressive,
statuesque 12 high-sounding

**imposition**
03 hum, tax 04 bite, duty, levy, load,
task, toll 05 impot 06 burden, charge,
decree, fixing, hassle, pensum, tariff
07 levying, setting 08 exaction,
pressure, trickery 09 intrusion
10 constraint, infliction, punishment
11 application, encumbrance,
enforcement, institution, trespassing
12 encroachment, introduction
13 establishment
*See also* **tax**

**impossibility**
04 no-no 09 absurdity, inability 10 non-
starter 11 unviability 12 hopelessness,
untenability 13 ludicrousness
14 ridiculousness 15 unacceptability

**impossible**
03 out 06 absurd 08 hopeless
09 beyond you, insoluble, ludicrous
10 incredible, outlandish, ridiculous,
unbearable, unworkable
11 intolerable, prohibitive, unthinkable
12 pigs might fly, preposterous,
unacceptable, unachievable,
unattainable, unbelievable,
unimaginable, unobtainable,
unrealizable, unreasonable
13 anybody's guess, impracticable,
inconceivable 15 and pigs might fly

**impostor**
04 fake, idol, sham 05 cheat, fraud,
quack, rogue 06 bunyip, con man,
faitor, phoney, ringer 07 deluder,
faitour 08 deceiver, phantasm,
swindler 09 charlatan, defrauder,

pretender, trickster 10 hoodwinker,
mountebank 12 impersonator

**imposture**
03 con 04 hoax, sham 05 cheat, fraud,
trick 07 swindle 08 artifice, con trick,
pretence, quackery 09 deception
10 imposition 11 counterfeit
13 impersonation

**impotence**
07 frailty 08 ligature, weakness
09 inability, infirmity, paralysis
10 disability, enervation, feebleness,
inadequacy, incapacity, inefficacy
11 impuissance, uselessness
12 helplessness, incompetence
13 powerlessness 15 ineffectiveness

**impotent**
04 weak 05 frail 06 feeble, futile, infirm,
unable 07 useless, worn out
08 crippled, disabled, helpless
09 enervated, exhausted, incapable,
paralysed, powerless, worthless
10 impuissant, inadequate
11 debilitated, incompetent, ineffective
12 unrestrained 13 incapacitated

**impound**
04 cage 05 hem in, pen in, point, seize
06 coop up, immure, keep in, lock up,
remove, shut up 07 confine, pinfold
08 take away 10 commandeer,
confiscate 11 appropriate, expropriate,
incarcerate

**impoverish**
04 ruin 05 break, drain, waste
06 beggar, denude, reduce, weaken
07 deplete, exhaust 08 bankrupt,
diminish, distress, make poor
09 pauperize 11 depauperate

**impoverished**
04 bare, bust, dead, poor 05 broke,
empty, needy, skint, waste 06 barren,
ruined 07 boracic, decayed, drained,
reduced 08 bankrupt, desolate, dirt-
poor, indigent, weakened 09 destitute,
exhausted, penniless, penurious
10 cleaned out, distressed, down-and-
out, stony-broke 11 depauperate,
impecunious 12 on your uppers,
without a bean 14 on your beam ends
15 poverty-stricken

**impracticability**
08 futility 11 unviability, uselessness
12 hopelessness 13 impossibility,
infeasibility, unworkability
14 unsuitableness

**impracticable**
04 wild 07 useless 08 unviable, wild-
eyed 09 non-viable, visionary
10 impossible, inoperable, unfeasible,
unworkable 11 unrealistic
12 unachievable, unattainable,
unmanageable 13 unpracticable,
unserviceable

**impractical**
05 crazy 07 awkward 08 academic,
romantic 09 visionary 10 idealistic,
impossible, ivory-tower, starry-eyed,
unworkable 11 doctrinaire, unrealistic
12 inconvenient 13 impracticable,
unserviceable

**impracticality**
08 idealism 11 romanticism
12 hopelessness 13 impossibility,
infeasibility, unworkability
14 unworkableness

**imprecation**
04 oath, pize 05 abuse, curse
08 anathema, goodyear 09 blasphemy,
goodyears, profanity 10 execration
11 malediction 12 denunciation,
vilification, vituperation

**imprecise**
04 hazy 05 loose, rough, vague
06 sloppy, woolly 07 blurred, inexact
09 ambiguous, equivocal, estimated
10 ill-defined, inaccurate, indefinite,
inexplicit 11 approximate

**imprecision**
04 haze 08 estimate 09 ambiguity,
vagueness 10 inaccuracy, sloppiness
11 inexactness 12 inexactitude
13 approximation

**impregnable**
04 safe 05 solid 06 secure, strong
09 fortified 10 adamantine, invincible,
inviolable, unbeatable 11 irrefutable
12 impenetrable, inexpugnable,
invulnerable, unassailable
13 unconquerable 14 indestructible,
unquestionable

**impregnate**
03 pad 04 fill, melt, milt, soak
05 imbue, stain, steep 06 drench,
infuse 07 pervade, suffuse
08 permeate, saturate 09 fecundate,
fertilize, penetrate 10 inseminate
12 make pregnant

**impregnation**
07 imbuing 10 saturation
11 fecundation, fertilizing, fructifying
12 insemination 13 fertilization
14 fructification

**impresario**
07 manager, showman 08 director,
producer, promoter 09 exhibitor,
organizer

**impress**
03 gas, wow 04 drum, grab, mark,
move, slay, stir, sway 05 knock, press,
prest, print, rouse, stamp, touch
06 affect, deboss, emboss, excite,
incuse, indent, instil, stress, strike
07 enforce, engrave, impresa, imprint,
inspire, possess 08 astonish, bowl over,
knock out 09 beglamour, bring home,
emphasize, fix deeply, go over big,
highlight, inculcate, influence,
overwhelm, pressgang, underline,
watermark 10 bear in upon, hammer
home, prepossess 11 knock for six
13 go over big with

**impressed**
05 moved, taken, wowed 06 marked,
struck 07 excited, grabbed, stamped,
stirred, touched 08 affected, overawed
10 bowled over, influenced, knocked
out 13 knocked for six

**impression**
04 dent, feel, idea, mark, note, ring,
seal, sway 05 fancy, hunch, power,

print, sense, sound, spoof, stamp, vibes **06** belief, effect, impact, memory, notion, parody, repute, send-up **07** control, feeling, imprint, mimicry, opinion, outline, tableau, take-off, thought **08** illusion, pressure, printing **09** awareness, burlesque, imitation, influence, sensation, suspicion **10** caricature, conviction, gut feeling **11** indentation **12** funny feeling, recollection **13** consciousness, impersonation
• **confused impression**   **04** blur
• **give false impression**   **03** lie
• **make an impression**   **03** let
**08** register **10** come across

### impressionability
**07** naivety **09** greenness **11** gullibility, receptivity, sensitivity **13** ingenuousness, receptiveness, vulnerability **14** suggestibility, susceptibility

### impressionable
**04** open, waxy **05** naive **07** pliable **08** gullible **09** ingenuous, mouldable, receptive, sensitive **10** responsive, vulnerable **11** persuadable, susceptible

### impressive
**04** epic **05** grand, noble **06** awsome, killer, moving, rotund, solemn, superb, whizzo, whizzy **07** awesome, rousing, stately **08** dazzling, dramatic, emphatic, exciting, imposing, lapidary, powerful, stirring, stonking, striking, touching **09** affecting, effective, inspiring **10** commanding, emphatical, monumental, portentous **11** magnificent, spectacular **12** awe-inspiring, breathtaking **13** scintillating

### impressively
**07** grandly **09** awesomely **10** powerfully, strikingly **11** effectively **12** emphatically **13** magnificently, spectacularly

### imprint
**03** fix **04** etch, logo, mark, sign, tool **05** badge, brand, power, press, print, stamp **06** burn in, effect, emblem, emboss **07** engrave, impress, meaning, results **08** colophon, footmark **09** character, establish, footprint, influence **10** impression **11** indentation, rubber-stamp **12** consequences, significance **13** repercussions **14** reverberations
*See also* **publish**

### imprison
◊ *containment indicator* **03** jug, lag, pen **04** cage, gaol, jail, quad, quod, shop **06** bang up, cage in, detain, immure, intern, lock up, lumber, shut in, shut up **07** confine, put away **08** restrain, send down **11** incarcerate, put in prison **12** send to prison

### imprisoned
◊ *insertion indicator* **05** caged **06** inside, jailed **07** captive, immured, put away **08** banged up, confined, locked up, sent down **09** doing bird, doing time **10** behind bars **12** incarcerated

**13** doing porridge **15** under lock and key

### imprisonment
**04** bird, life **05** bonds **06** duress **07** custody, durance, duresse **08** porridge **09** captivity, committal, detention **10** commitment, internment **11** confinement **13** incarceration

### improbability
**05** doubt **07** dubiety **11** dubiousness, uncertainty **12** doubtfulness, unlikelihood, unlikeliness **14** far-fetchedness, implausibility, ridiculousness

### improbable
**06** farfet **07** dubious **08** doubtful, unlikely **09** uncertain **10** far-fetched, incredible, marvellous, ridiculous **11** implausible **12** preposterous, questionable, unbelievable, unconvincing

### impromptu
**05** ad-lib **07** offhand **09** ad libitum, extempore, makeshift **10** improvised, off the cuff, unprepared, unscripted **11** spontaneous, unrehearsed **13** spontaneously **14** extemporaneous

### improper
◊ *anagram indicator* **04** rude **05** false, unfit, wrong **06** risqué, vulgar **07** immoral **08** immodest, indecent, shocking, unlawful, unseemly **09** erroneous, incorrect, irregular, unfitting **10** inadequate, indecorous, indelicate, indiscreet, out of place, unbecoming, unsuitable **11** incongruous, inopportune **12** illegitimate **13** inappropriate

### improperly
◊ *anagram indicator* **05** amiss, wrong **06** rudely **07** falsely, wrongly **09** immorally **10** immodestly, indecently, unlawfully, unsuitably **11** erroneously, incorrectly, irregularly, unfittingly **12** indecorously, indiscreetly **13** incongruously **15** inappropriately

### impropriety
**04** slip **05** gaffe, lapse **07** blunder, faux pas, mistake **08** bad taste, solecism **09** gaucherie, immodesty, indecency, indecorum, vulgarity **11** incongruity **12** unseemliness **13** unsuitability **14** indecorousness

### improve
**04** beet, bete, do up, file, grow, help, mend, rise **05** amend, do for, emend, fix up, rally **06** better, buck up, enrich, look up, occupy, perk up, pick up, polish, reform, revamp, revise, uplift, work on **07** advance, correct, develop, enhance, perfect, recover, rectify, touch up, upgrade **08** increase, progress, put right, set right, work upon **09** get better, meliorate, modernize **10** ameliorate, convalesce, make better, recuperate, streamline **11** make headway **12** gain strength, mend your ways, rehabilitate **14** be on the up and up **15** give a facelift to

### improvement
**04** gain, rise **05** rally **06** growth, pick-up, profit, reform **07** advance, headway, upswing **08** increase, progress, recovery, revision **09** amendment, bettering, upgrading **10** betterment, correction, rectifying, refinement **11** development, enhancement, furtherance, modernizing, reformation **12** amelioration **13** rectification **14** rehabilitation

### improvident
**06** wastry **07** wastery **08** careless, heedless, prodigal, reckless, wasteful **09** imprudent, negligent, shiftless, unthrifty **10** profligate, thriftless, unprepared **11** extravagant, inattentive, Micawberish, spendthrift, thoughtless **12** uneconomical **13** underprepared

### improvisation
**04** vamp **05** ad-lib **06** improv, lash-up **08** ad hocery **09** ad-libbing, expedient, impromptu, invention, makeshift **11** spontaneity **13** autoschediasm, extemporizing **15** extemporization

### improvise
**03** jam **04** vamp, wing **05** ad-lib, rig up, run up **06** busk it, devise, invent, make do, noodle, wing it **07** concoct, knock up **08** contrive **09** play by ear **11** extemporize, play it by ear **13** throw together **14** cobble together, have a brainwave **15** speak off the cuff
• **improvise on**   **04** ride

### improvised
◊ *anagram indicator* **05** ad-lib, scrub **06** sudden **07** scratch **08** drumhead, on the fly **09** extempore, impromptu, makeshift **10** off-the-cuff, unprepared, unscripted **11** spontaneous, unrehearsed **12** extemporized **14** extemporaneous

### imprudence
**05** folly, haste **08** rashness **12** carelessness, heedlessness, recklessness **13** foolhardiness **15** thoughtlessness

### imprudent
**04** rash **05** hasty **06** unwise **07** foolish **08** careless, heedless, reckless **09** foolhardy, ill-judged, impolitic **10** ill-advised, incautious, indiscreet, unthinking **11** improvident, injudicious, thoughtless **12** short-sighted, ill-considered, inconsiderate, irresponsible

### impudence
**03** lip **04** face, gall, neck, sass **05** cheek, front, mouth, nerve, snash **06** bronze **07** hutzpah **08** attitude, boldness, chutzpah, pertness, rudeness **09** brass neck, insolence, sauciness **10** brazenness, effrontery **11** presumption **12** impertinence, impertinency

### impudent
**04** bold, calm, cool, pert, rude **05** bardy, cocky, fresh, hardy, nervy, sassy, saucy **06** brazen, cheeky, gallus **07** forward, gallows **08** immodest,

**impugn**

impolite, insolent, malapert, petulant
**09** audacious, barefaced, boldfaced,
out of line, shameless **10** brass-faced,
unblushing **11** impertinent
**12** presumptuous **13** disrespectful

**impugn**

**06** assail, attack, berate, oppose, resist,
revile, vilify **07** censure, dispute,
traduce **08** question, vilipend
**09** challenge, criticize **10** vituperate
**14** call in question

**impulse**

**04** push, send, urge, whim, wish
**05** drive, force, nisus, pulse, spike,
surge **06** desire, impact, motion,
motive, notion, signal, thrust
**07** caprice, conatus, feeling, impetus,
passion **08** instinct, momentum,
movement, pressure, stimulus
**09** brainwave, impulsion, incentive,
premotion **10** compulsion, incitement,
inducement, motivation, propulsion
**11** inclination, stimulation, thought-
wave
• **on impulse 06** rashly **07** hastily
**08** suddenly **10** recklessly
**11** impatiently, impetuously,
impulsively, intuitively
**13** automatically, instinctively,
irresponsibly, spontaneously,
thoughtlessly **15** without thinking

**impulsive**

**04** rash **05** hasty, quick **06** madcap,
sudden **08** reckless **09** automatic,
emotional, foolhardy, ill-judged,
impatient, impetuous, intuitive
**10** headstrong, passionate, unthinking
**11** instinctive, precipitate,
spontaneous, thoughtless **13** ill-
considered

**impulsively**

**06** rashly **07** hastily **08** suddenly **09** on
impulse **10** recklessly **11** impatiently,
impetuously, intuitively
**13** automatically, instinctively,
irresponsibly, spontaneously,
thoughtlessly **15** without thinking

**impulsiveness**

**05** haste **07** emotion, passion
**08** instinct, rashness **09** hastiness,
quickness **10** impatience, suddenness
**11** impetuosity, spontaneity
**12** recklessness **13** foolhardiness,
impetuousness, intuitiveness,
precipitation **15** precipitateness,
thoughtlessness

**impunity**

**07** amnesty, excusal, freedom, liberty,
licence **08** immunity, security
**09** exemption **10** permission
**12** dispensation
• **with impunity 06** freely, safely **08** in
safety **11** without risk

**impure**

**04** foul, lewd, sexy **05** bawdy, crude,
dirty, mixed **06** coarse, drossy, erotic,
filthy, ribald, risqué, smutty, vulgar
**07** alloyed, blended, corrupt, debased,
defiled, diluted, immoral, lustful,
obscene, sullied, tainted, unclean,
vicious **08** combined, depraved,
immodest, improper, indecent,

---

infected, polluted, unchaste
**09** lecherous, offensive, shameless,
unrefined **10** licentious, suggestive
**11** adulterated, promiscuous
**12** contaminated, pornographic

**impurity**

**04** dirt, mark, smut, spot **05** blend,
donor, dross, filth, grime, taint
**07** crudity, mixture **08** dilution,
foulness, lewdness **09** dirtiness,
eroticism, immodesty, indecency,
infection, looseness, obscenity,
pollutant, pollution, vulgarity
**10** coarseness, corruption,
debasement, immorality, unchastity
**11** contaminant, foreign body,
impropriety, lustfulness, pornography,
promiscuity **12** adulteration
**13** contamination, offensiveness,
shamelessness **14** licentiousness

**impute**

**03** lay, put **05** refer **06** assign, charge,
credit, object **07** ascribe **08** accredit
**09** attribute, put down to

**in**

◇ *containment indicator* ◇ *hidden
indicator* ◇ *insertion indicator* **01** i' **02** at,
by, of, on **03** hip, per **04** cool, each,
into, with **05** abode, among, every,
funky, smart **06** alight, during, inside,
modish, trendy, within **07** current,
enclose, in vogue, popular, stylish,
through **10** all the rage, enclosed by,
throughout **11** fashionable
**12** surrounded by **15** during the time of
• **in for 12** due to receive **13** going to
suffer
• **in itself 04** in se **05** per se
**13** intrinsically
• **in on 07** aware of **09** clued up on
**10** involved in **14** acquainted with
• **in with 07** liked by **12** friendly with
**15** on good terms with

**inability**

**08** handicap, weakness **09** impotence
**10** disability, inadequacy, incapacity,
ineptitude **11** uselessness
**12** incapability, incompetence
**13** powerlessness **15** ineffectiveness

**inaccessibility**

**08** distance **09** isolation **10** remoteness,
separation **15** unattainability

**inaccessible**

**06** remote **08** isolated **10** out of reach
**11** beyond reach, god-forsaken, out of
the way, unavailable, uncomatable,
unget-at-able, unreachable
**12** impenetrable, unattainable,
uncomeatable, unfrequented
**14** inapproachable, unapproachable

**inaccuracy**

**04** flub, goof, slip **05** error, fault, gaffe
**06** boo-boo, defect, howler, slip-up
**07** blunder, clanger, erratum, mistake
**11** corrigendum, imprecision,
inexactness **12** mistakenness
**13** erroneousness, unreliability
**14** fallaciousness, miscalculation

**inaccurate**

◇ *anagram indicator* **03** out **05** false,
loose, wrong **06** adrift, faulty, flawed,

---

untrue **07** inexact, unsound
**08** mistaken **09** defective, erroneous,
imperfect, imprecise, incorrect
**10** fallacious, unfaithful, unreliable
• **be inaccurate 03** err

**inaccurately**

**06** wildly **07** falsely, loosely, wrongly
**08** clumsily **09** inexactly **10** carelessly,
unreliably **11** defectively, erroneously,
imperfectly, imprecisely, incorrectly
**12** unfaithfully

**inaction**

**04** rest **06** torpor **07** inertia **08** idleness,
lethargy, slowness **09** passivity
**10** immobility, inactivity, stagnation
**12** lifelessness, sluggishness
**14** motionlessness

**inactivate**

**04** stop **07** cripple, disable, scupper
**08** mothball, paralyse **09** stabilize
**10** deactivate, immobilize

**inactive**

**04** dead, idle, lazy, slow **05** inert, still
**06** shadow, sleepy, torpid, unused
**07** dormant, languid, passive
**08** immobile, indolent, lifeless,
slothful, sluggish, stagnant, unactive
**09** dead-alive, lethargic, quiescent,
sedentary **10** motionless, stationary,
unemployed, vegetating
**11** hibernating, inoperative **12** dead-
and-alive

**inactivity**

**04** rest **05** sloth **06** stasis, torpor
**07** inertia, languor, vacancy
**08** abeyance, dormancy, dullness,
idleness, inaction, laziness, lethargy
**09** heaviness, indolence, inertness,
lassitude, passivity **10** immobility,
quiescence, quiescency, stagnation,
vegetation **11** hibernation
**12** dilatoriness, lifelessness,
sluggishness, unemployment

**inadequacy**

**04** flaw, lack, want **05** fault **06** dearth,
defect, foible **07** deficit, failing,
paucity, poverty **08** scarcity, shortage,
weakness **09** inability **10** deficiency,
inefficacy, inequality, meagreness,
scantiness **11** shortcoming
**12** imperfection, incapability,
incompetence **13** defectiveness,
insufficiency **15** ineffectiveness

**inadequate**

**03** bad **04** poor **05** scant, short, unfit
**06** faulty, meagre, scanty, scarce,
skimpy, sparse, too few **07** sketchy,
unequal, wanting **08** careless, derisory,
inexpert, pathetic **09** defective,
deficient, imperfect, incapable,
niggardly, too little **11** incompetent,
ineffective, ineffectual, substandard,
unqualified **12** insufficient,
unproficient **13** disappointing,
inefficacious, not good enough
**14** incommensurate, not up to scratch,
unsatisfactory **15** thin on the ground

**inadequately**

**05** badly **06** poorly, thinly **08** meagrely,
scantily, skimpily, sparsely **09** sketchily

**10** carelessly **11** imperfectly **14** insufficiently

**inadmissible**
**08** improper **09** precluded **10** disallowed, immaterial, inapposite, irrelevant, prohibited **11** unallowable **12** unacceptable **13** inappropriate

**inadvertent**
**06** chance **08** careless **09** negligent, unadvised, unguarded, unplanned, unwitting **10** accidental, unintended **11** inattentive, involuntary, thoughtless, unconscious **12** uncalculated **13** unintentional **14** unpremeditated

**inadvertently**
**08** by chance, remissly **09** by mistake **10** by accident, carelessly, heedlessly, mistakenly **11** negligently, unwittingly **12** accidentally, unthinkingly **13** involuntarily, thoughtlessly, unconsciously **15** unintentionally

**inadvisable**
**05** silly **06** unwise **07** foolish **09** ill-judged, imprudent, misguided **10** ill-advised, indiscreet **11** inexpedient, injudicious **13** ill-considered

**inalienable**
**08** absolute, inherent **09** permanent **10** inviolable, sacrosanct **11** unremovable **12** unassailable **13** non-negotiable **14** untransferable **15** imprescriptible, non-transferable

**inane**
**04** vain, void **05** empty, silly, vapid **06** absurd, drippy, futile, stupid, vacant **07** fatuous, foolish, idiotic, puerile, vacuous **08** mindless, trifling **09** frivolous, ludicrous, senseless, worthless **10** ridiculous **11** nonsensical **13** characterless, unintelligent

**inanely**
**08** absurdly, futilely, stupidly **09** fatuously, foolishly, vacuously **11** idiotically, ludicrously **12** ridiculously **13** nonsensically

**inanimate**
**04** dead, dull, lazy **05** inert **06** torpid, wooden **07** abiotic, defunct, dormant, extinct **08** immobile, inactive, lifeless, stagnant **09** apathetic, insensate, lethargic **10** insentient, spiritless **11** unconscious

**inanity**
**05** folly **06** waffle **07** fatuity, vacancy, vacuity **08** daftness, vapidity **09** absurdity, asininity, emptiness, frivolity, puerility, silliness, stupidity **10** imbecility **11** foolishness **13** ludicrousness, senselessness **14** ridiculousness

**inapplicable**
**05** inapt **08** unsuited **09** unrelated **10** immaterial, inapposite, irrelevant, unsuitable **11** unconnected **12** inconsequent **13** inappropriate

**inapposite**
**10** immaterial, irrelevant, out of place, unsuitable **13** inappropriate

**inappreciable**
**04** fine, tiny **05** faint, small, vague **06** minute, slight, subtle **07** gradual, muffled, obscure, unclear **09** inaudible, minuscule, priceless **10** impalpable, indefinite, indistinct, negligible, unapparent **11** microscopic **12** undetectable, unnoticeable **13** imperceptible, indiscernible, infinitesimal

**inappropriate**
**05** inapt, undue **08** ill-timed, improper, tactless, unseemly, untimely **09** facetious, ill-fitted, ill-suited, tasteless, unfitting **10** inapposite, indecorous, irrelevant, malapropos, out of place, unbecoming, unsuitable **11** incongruous, inopportune **12** infelicitous **13** unappropriate

**inappropriately**
**07** unfitly **08** off topic **10** malapropos, out of place, tactlessly, unsuitably **11** off the point, tastelessly **12** irrelevantly **13** incongruously, inopportunely **14** beside the point, infelicitously

**inapt**
**05** unfit **07** unhappy **08** ill-timed, unsuited **09** ill-fitted, ill-suited **10** inapposite, irrelevant, malapropos, out of place, unsuitable **11** inopportune, unfortunate, unqualified **12** infelicitous **13** inappropriate

**inarticulacy**
**08** mumbling **09** hesitancy, stumbling **10** stammering, stuttering **11** incoherence **14** indistinctness, speechlessness, tongue-tiedness

**inarticulate**
**04** dumb, mute **07** blurred, halting, muffled, mumbled, quavery, shaking, unclear **08** hesitant **09** faltering, gibbering, soundless, stumbling, trembling, voiceless **10** disjointed, hesitating, incoherent, indistinct, speechless, stammering, stuttering, tongue-tied **14** unintelligible

**inattention**
**07** absence **09** disregard, misregard **10** dreaminess, negligence **11** daydreaming, distraction **12** carelessness, heedlessness, unobservance **13** forgetfulness, preoccupation, unmindfulness **15** inattentiveness, thoughtlessness

**inattentive**
**04** deaf **05** loose, slack **06** absent, asleep, dreamy, remiss **08** careless, distrait, heedless **09** forgetful, incurious, miles away, negligent, unmindful **10** distracted, neglectful, regardless **11** daydreaming, inadvertent, preoccupied, thoughtless **12** absent-minded, disregarding, unrespective **13** somewhere else, wool-gathering

**inaudible**
**03** low **04** dull, soft **05** faint, muted **06** silent **07** muffled, mumbled, stifled **08** murmured, muttered **09** noiseless,

whispered **10** indistinct **13** imperceptible

**inaugural**
**05** first **06** maiden **07** initial, opening **08** exordial, original **09** launching **12** introductory

**inaugurate**
**04** open **05** begin, set up, start **06** hansel, induct, invest, launch, ordain **07** handsel, install, instate, swear in, usher in **08** commence, dedicate, enthrone, get going, initiate **09** auspicate, institute, introduce, originate **10** commission, consecrate **11** set in motion **13** admit to office **14** open officially

**inauguration**
**06** launch **07** opening **08** starting **09** induction, launching, setting up **10** initiation, installing, ordination, swearing-in **11** institution, investiture **12** commencement, consecration, enthronement, installation

**inauspicious**
**03** bad **05** black **07** ominous, unlucky **08** ill-fated, sinister, untimely **09** ill-boding, ill-omened **10** ill-starred, sinistrous **11** threatening, unfortunate, unpromising **12** discouraging, infelicitous, unfavourable, unpropitious

**inborn**
**06** inbred, innate, native **07** connate, natural **08** inherent, untaught **09** ingrained, inherited, intuitive **10** congenital, hereditary, ingenerate **11** in one's blood, instinctive, in the family

**inbred**
**03** sib **05** natal **06** innate, native **07** connate, natural **08** inherent **09** incrossed, ingrained **10** ingenerate **14** constitutional

**inbuilt**
**05** basic **07** built-in **08** inherent, integral **09** elemental, essential **11** constituent, fundamental

**incalculable**
**04** vast **06** untold **07** endless, immense, sumless **08** enormous, infinite **09** boundless, countless, limitless, unlimited **10** numberless **11** inestimable, innumerable, measureless **12** immeasurable **13** unpredictable, without number

**incandescence**
**04** fire, glow, leam **05** gleam, glory **07** glimmer, sunglow **08** outflush, radiance, richness **09** afterglow, splendour, vividness **10** brightness, brilliance, luminosity **15** phosphorescence

**incandescent**
**03** mad **05** aglow, angry, irate, livid **06** bright, fuming, raging **07** boiling, enraged, furious, glowing, shining **08** dazzling, frenzied, gleaming, incensed, inflamed, seething, sizzling, up in arms, white-hot **09** brilliant, in a

lather, indignant **10** hopping mad, infuriated **14** purple with rage

## incantation
**03** hex **04** rune **05** chant, charm, spell
**06** mantra **07** formula, karakia, mantram **10** invocation
**11** abracadabra, conjuration **12** magic formula

## incapable
◊ *anagram indicator* **04** weak **05** drunk, inept, unfit **06** feeble, unable **07** useless
**08** helpless, impotent, unfitted, unsuited **09** powerless **10** inadequate
**11** incompetent, ineffective, ineffectual, unqualified
**12** disqualified, not hacking it **14** not up to scratch **15** out of your league

## incapacitate
**05** lay up **07** cripple, disable, scupper
**08** paralyse **10** debilitate, disqualify, immobilize **14** put out of action

## incapacitated
**05** drunk, tipsy, unfit **06** laid up, unwell
**08** crippled, disabled **09** hamstrung, paralysed, prostrate, scuppered
**10** indisposed **11** immobilized, out of action **12** disqualified

## incapacity
**08** weakness **09** impotence, inability, unfitness **10** disability, feebleness, inadequacy, ineptitude, non-ability
**11** uselessness **12** incapability, incompetence, incompetency
**13** powerlessness **14** ineffectuality
**15** ineffectiveness

## incarcerate
**04** cage, gaol, jail **06** bang up, commit, coop up, detain, encage, immure, intern, lock up, wall in **07** confine, impound, put away **08** imprison, restrain, restrict, send down **09** put in jail, put inside **11** put in prison

## incarceration
**04** jail **07** bondage, custody
**09** captivity, detention, restraint
**10** internment **11** confinement, restriction **12** imprisonment

## incarnate
**04** heal **05** human **07** fleshly
**08** embodied, typified **09** corporeal, made flesh, personify **10** in the flesh
**11** impersonate, incardinate, in human form, personified

## incarnation
**06** avatar **09** human form
**10** embodiment **13** impersonation, manifestation **15** personification

*Incarnations include:*

**04** Rama
**07** Krishna
**09** Jugannath
**10** Juggernaut

## incautious
**04** rash **05** hasty **06** unwary **07** foolish
**08** careless, cavalier, reckless, wareless
**09** foolhardy, ill-judged, imprudent, impulsive, unguarded **10** ill-advised, unthinking, unwatchful **11** inattentive, injudicious, precipitate, thoughtless,

unobservant **13** ill-considered, inconsiderate, uncircumspect

## incendiary
**04** bomb, mine **06** charge **07** carcase, carcass, firebug, grenade **08** agitator, arsonist, fireball, firebomb, inciting, stirring **09** demagogue, explosive, firebrand, flammable, insurgent, pétroleur, seditious **10** fire-raiser, petrol bomb, pétroleuse, pyromaniac, rick-burner, subversive
**11** combustible, dissentious, fire-raising, provocative **12** inflammatory, rabble-rouser **13** rabble-rousing, revolutionary **14** proceleusmatic
**15** Molotov cocktail

## incense
**03** irk, vex **04** balm, rile, thus, urge
**05** anger, aroma, myrrh, scent
**06** enrage, excite, hassle, homage, incite, kindle, madden, nettle, stacte
**07** agitate, benzoin, bouquet, inflame, perfume, provoke **08** irritate, pastille
**09** adulation, aggravate, fragrance, infuriate, joss-stick **10** exasperate
**12** frankincense **14** drive up the wall

## incensed
**03** mad **04** waxy **05** angry, cross, irate, ratty, spewy **06** choked, fuming, ireful
**07** crooked, enraged, furious, ropable, stroppy, uptight **08** burned up, furibund, hairless, in a paddy, in a strop, maddened, up in arms, wrathful
**09** in a lather, indignant, raving mad, seeing red, steamed up, ticked off
**10** aggravated, hopping mad, infuriated **11** disgruntled, exasperated, fit to be tied **12** on the warpath

## incentive
**04** bait, goad, lure, spur **06** carrot, motive, reason, reward **07** impetus
**08** igniting, inciting, stimulus
**09** stimulant, sweetener **10** enticement, incitation, incitement, inducement, motivation **11** encouraging
**13** encouragement

## inception
**04** dawn, rise **05** birth, start **06** origin, outset **07** kick-off, opening
**09** beginning **10** initiation
**12** commencement, inauguration, installation **13** establishment

## incessant
**07** endless, eternal, non-stop
**08** constant, unbroken, unending
**09** ceaseless, continual, perpetual, recurrent, unceasing, weariless
**10** continuous, persistent
**11** everlasting, never-ending, unremitting **12** interminable
**13** uninterrupted

## incessantly
**07** for ever **09** endlessly, eternally
**10** constantly, unendingly **11** at every turn, ceaselessly, immediately, unceasingly **12** continuously, interminably **13** everlastingly, unremittingly **14** for ever and ever
**15** twenty-four seven, uninterruptedly

## incidence
**04** rate **05** range **06** amount, degree,

extent, to-fall **09** frequency
**10** commonness, occurrence, prevalence

## incident
**03** bar, row **04** baur, bawr, page
**05** brush, clash, event, fight, scene, upset **06** affair, comedy, fracas, matter, mishap, period **07** affaire, episode, falling, passage, subject **08** conflict, instance, occasion, skirmish
**09** adventure, commotion, happening
**10** consequent, experience, occurrence, proceeding
**11** disturbance **12** circumstance
**13** confrontation **14** unpleasantness

## incidental
**05** minor, petty, small **06** casual, chance, random **07** passing, related, trivial **08** by chance, striking
**09** ancillary, attendant, impinging, occurrent, secondary **10** accidental, background, fortuitous, occasional, peripheral, subsidiary **11** concomitant, contingency, facultative, subordinate
**12** accompanying, contributory, non-essential **13** supplementary

## incidentally
**07** apropos, by the by **08** by chance, by the way, casually **09** as an aside, en passant, in passing **10** by accident
**11** secondarily **12** accidentally, digressively, episodically, fortuitously, unexpectedly **13** as a digression
**14** coincidentally **15** parenthetically

## incinerate
**04** burn **07** cremate **09** carbonize
**13** reduce to ashes

## incineration
**07** burning **09** cremation
**13** carbonization **14** turning to ashes

## incipient
**07** nascent, newborn **08** inchoate, starting **09** beginning, embryonic, impending, inaugural, inceptive
**10** commencing, developing
**11** originating, rudimentary

## incise
**03** cut **04** etch, gash, nick, slit **05** carve, notch, slash **06** chisel, scribe, sculpt
**07** cut into, engrave **09** sculpture

## incision
**03** cut **04** gash, nick, slit **05** notch, slash, wound **07** coupure, cutting, opening **08** colotomy, incisure, lobotomy, oncotomy **09** cystotomy, insection, iridotomy **10** craniotomy, discission, enterotomy, episiotomy, nephrotomy, phlebotomy, pleurotomy, sclerotomy, trenchancy
**11** hysterotomy, myringotomy, thoracotomy, tracheotomy, venesection, venisection
**12** pharyngotomy, tonsillotomy

## incisive
**04** acid, keen **05** acute, sharp **06** astute, biting, shrewd **07** caustic, cutting, mordant, pungent **08** piercing, stinging, surgical **09** sarcastic, trenchant **10** perceptive **11** penetrating
**13** perspicacious

## incisively
**06** keenly, tartly **07** acutely, sharply
**08** astutely **09** mordantly, pungently
**10** piercingly **11** caustically,
trenchantly **13** penetratingly,
sarcastically

## incisiveness
**04** bite, edge **07** acidity, sarcasm
**08** astucity, keenness, pungency,
tartness **09** acuteness, sharpness
**10** astuteness, trenchancy
**11** penetration **12** perspicacity

## incite
**03** egg, hoi, hoy, put, set, sic, tar
**04** abet, fuel, goad, poke, prod, sick,
spur, urge, whet **05** drive, egg on,
impel, prick, put on, rouse, tarre
**06** arouse, excite, fillip, foment,
induce, kindle, prompt, stir up, whip
up, work up **07** actuate, agitate,
animate, incense, inflame, premove,
provoke, solicit **09** encourage,
instigate, stimulate **13** stir the possum

## incitement
**04** goad, prod, spur, whet **05** drive,
sting **06** motive, urging **07** impetus,
rousing **08** stimulus **09** agitation,
animation, incentive, onsetting,
prompting **10** inducement, motivation,
suggestion **11** instigation, provocation,
stimulation **13** encouragement

## inciting
**08** stirring **09** hortative, hortatory,
incentive, seditious **10** incendiary,
subversive **11** provocative
**12** inflammatory **13** rabble-rousing
**14** proceleusmatic

## incivility
**08** rudeness **09** indignity, roughness,
vulgarity **10** bad manners, coarseness,
disrespect, inurbanity **11** boorishness,
discourtesy, ill-breeding
**12** impoliteness **14** unmannerliness

## inclemency
**07** rawness **08** foulness, severity
**09** harshness, roughness **10** bitterness,
storminess **15** tempestuousness

## inclement
**03** raw, wet **04** cold, foul **05** harsh,
nasty, rough **06** bitter, severe, stormy
**07** squally **08** blustery **11** intemperate,
tempestuous

## inclination
**03** bow, maw, nod, set **04** bank, bend,
bent, bias, cant, kant, lift, list, mind,
rake, ramp, tilt **05** angle, pitch, slant,
slope, study, taste, trend **06** ascent,
liking, notion **07** incline, leaning
**08** affinity, fondness, gradient,
penchant, tendency **09** acclivity,
affection, declivity, deviation,
steepness **10** attraction, partiality,
preference, proclivity, propension,
propensity **11** disposition
**12** predilection, propenseness
**14** predisposition
• **with inclination towards** **02** on

## incline
**03** bow, dip, kip, nod, tip **04** bank,
bend, bias, hade, heel, hill, lean, list,
peck, rake, ramp, rise, slip, stay, sway,
tend, tilt, veer **05** curve, offer, slant,
slope, stoop, swell, swing, tempt,
verge **06** affect, ascent, direct, prefer,
shelve, steeve **07** descent, deviate,
dispose, diverge, propend, recline
**08** gradient, persuade **09** acclivity,
declivity, influence, prejudice

## inclined
**03** apt **04** bent, wont **05** given, ready
**06** liable, likely, minded **07** oblique, of
a mind, sloping, tending, willing
**08** disposed, proclive, propense
**10** well-minded **11** predisposed
• **be inclined** **04** care
• **inclined to** **01** -y

## include
◊ *containment indicator* ◊ *hidden
indicator* **03** add **04** hold, span **05** add
in, admit, carry, cover, enter, put in
**06** embody, insert, reckon, rope in,
take in **07** connote, contain, count in,
embrace, enclose, involve, let in on,
subsume, throw in **08** allow for,
classify, comprise, conclude
**09** encompass, introduce
**10** comprehend **11** incorporate **15** take
into account

## including
◊ *containment indicator* **03** inc **04** incl
with **08** as well as, counting, included
**11** inclusive of **12** together with

## inclusion
**08** addition **09** insertion
**10** embodiment **11** involvement,
subsumption **12** encompassing
**13** comprehension, incorporation

## inclusive
**03** inc **04** full, incl **05** all-in **07** blanket,
general, overall **08** catch-all, included,
sweeping **09** enclosing **12** all-
embracing, all-inclusive
**13** comprehensive **14** across-the-board

## incognito
**06** masked, veiled **07** unknown
**08** nameless, unmarked **09** disguised
**10** in disguise **11** camouflaged
**12** unidentified **14** unidentifiable,
unrecognizable **15** under a false name

## incognizant
**07** unaware **08** ignorant **09** unknowing
**10** uninformed **11** inattentive,
unconscious, unobservant
**12** unacquainted **13** unenlightened

## incoherence
**05** mix-up **06** jumble, muddle,
mumble, mutter **07** stammer, stutter
**08** wildness **09** confusion
**10** brokenness **11** garbledness
**12** illogicality **13** inconsistency
**14** disjointedness

## incoherent
**05** loose **06** broken **07** garbled,
jumbled, mixed-up, muddled,
mumbled, unclear **08** confused,
muttered, rambling, wandered
**09** illogical, rigmarole, scrambled,
unjointed, wandering **10** disjointed,
disordered, stammering, stuttering
**11** unconnected **12** disconnected,
inarticulate, inconsistent **14** skimble-
skamble, unintelligible

## incombustible
**09** fireproof **10** flameproof, unburnable
**12** non-flammable **13** fire-resistant
**14** flame-resistant, flame-retardant,
non-inflammable

## income
**03** pay **05** gains, means, rente, wages
**06** inflow, living, profit, salary
**07** arrival, profits, returns, revenue,
stipend, takings **08** benefice, earnings,
entrance, interest, proceeds, receipts,
rent roll **09** allowance, comings-in,
penny-rent **10** emoluments
**12** independency, remuneration

## incoming
**03** new **04** next **06** coming **07** ensuing,
revenue **08** accruing, arriving,
entering, homeward **09** returning
**10** succeeding **11** approaching

## incommensurate
**07** extreme, unequal **09** excessive
**10** inadequate, inordinate
**11** extravagant, inequitable
**12** insufficient **15** incommensurable

## incommunicable
**09** ineffable **11** unspeakable,
unutterable **12** unimpartable
**13** indescribable, inexpressible

## incomparable
**06** superb **07** supreme **08** peerless
**09** brilliant, matchless, nonpareil,
paramount, unmatched **10** inimitable,
unequalled, unrivalled **11** superlative,
unsurpassed **12** second to none,
unparalleled, without equal **13** beyond
compare **15** without parallel

## incomparably
**05** by far **06** easily **08** superbly
**09** eminently, supremely **10** far and
away, infinitely **11** brilliantly
**12** immeasurably **13** beyond compare,
superlatively

## incompatibility
**05** clash **08** conflict, mismatch,
variance **09** antipathy, disparity
**10** antagonism, difference
**11** discrepancy, incongruity
**12** disagreement **13** contradiction,
disparateness, inconsistency
**14** uncongeniality

## incompatible
**05** alien, wrong **06** at odds **08** clashing,
unsuited **09** disparate, dissonant,
exclusive, repugnant **10** at variance,
discordant, ill-matched, in conflict,
insociable, mismatched **11** conflicting,
disagreeing, ill-assorted, incongruous,
uncongenial **12** antagonistic,
inconsistent **13** contradictory
**14** irreconcilable

## incompetence
**08** bungling **09** inability, ineptness,
stupidity, unfitness **10** inadequacy,
ineptitude, inequality **11** uselessness
**12** incapability, inefficiency
**13** insufficiency, unsuitability
**14** ineffectuality **15** ineffectiveness,
ineffectualness

## incompetent
**03** ill **04** naff, poxy, ropy **05** awful,

flaky, lousy, pants, ropey, unfit
**06** clumsy, crummy, stupid, unable
**07** awkward, botched, no-hoper, the
pits, useless **08** bungling, fumbling,
handless, hopeless, inexpert, pathetic,
schleppy, terrible **09** deficient,
incapable, unskilful **10** amateurish,
inadequate, unsuitable **11** a load of
crap, ineffective, inefficient,
unqualified **12** insufficient **14** a load of
garbage, a load of rubbish

### incomplete
◊ *tail deletion indicator* **04** half, part
**05** short **06** broken, patchy **07** lacking,
partial, partial, pendent, scrappy,
sketchy, wanting **08** abridged
**09** defective, deficient, embryonic,
half-baked, imperfect, piecemeal,
shortened **10** catalectic, unfinished
**11** fragmentary, rudimentary,
undeveloped **14** unaccomplished

### incomprehensible
**04** deep **06** opaque **07** complex,
obscure, unaware **08** abstruse, baffling,
involved, profound, puzzling
**09** enigmatic, limitless, recondite
**10** mysterious, perplexing, unfamiliar,
unreadable **11** complicated, double
Dutch, inscrutable **12** impenetrable,
mind-boggling, over your head,
unfathomable **13** above your head, all
Greek to you, inconceivable
**14** unintelligible

### incomprehension
**09** ignorance, obscurity **10** complexity,
profundity **11** unawareness
**12** incognizance **13** unfamiliarity
**14** inscrutability, mysteriousness
**15** impenetrability

### inconceivable
**06** absurd **08** shocking **09** ludicrous,
unheard-of **10** impossible, incredible,
outrageous, ridiculous, staggering
**11** implausible, unthinkable **12** mind-
boggling, unbelievable, unimaginable

### inconclusive
**04** open, weak **05** vague
**09** ambiguous, uncertain, undecided,
unsettled **10** indecisive, indefinite, up
in the air **11** left hanging
**12** unconvincing, unsatisfying
**13** indeterminate **14** open to question

### incongruity
**05** clash **08** conflict **09** disparity,
inaptness **10** disharmony
**11** discrepancy **13** contradiction,
inconsistency, unsuitability
**14** dissociability **15** dissociableness,
incompatibility

### incongruous
**03** odd **06** absurd, at odds, patchy
**07** jarring, strange **08** clashing,
contrary, out of key **09** dissonant **10** out
of place, unsuitable **11** conflicting,
disharmonic, dissociable
**12** incompatible, inconsistent, out of
keeping **13** contradictory,
inappropriate **14** irreconcilable

### incongruously
**08** off topic **10** out of place, unsuitably
**11** off the point **12** irrelevantly

**13** inopportunely **14** beside the point,
infelicitously **15** inappropriately

### inconsequential
**05** minor, petty **07** trivial **08** trifling
**09** small beer **10** immaterial, negligible
**11** unimportant **13** inappreciable,
insignificant **14** of no importance

### inconsiderable
**04** mean, weak **05** minor, petty, small
**06** slight **07** nominal, trivial **08** trifling
**10** negligible **11** unimportant
**13** insignificant

### inconsiderate
**04** rash, rude **06** unkind **07** selfish
**08** careless, heedless, tactless,
uncaring **09** egotistic, imprudent
**10** dismissive, intolerant, regardless,
unthinking, unweighing **11** insensitive,
light-minded, self-centred,
thoughtless, unconcerned **12** light-
hearted, uncharitable, undiscerning

### inconsiderateness
**08** rudeness **09** unconcern
**10** unkindness **11** intolerance,
selfishness **12** carelessness,
tactlessness **13** insensitivity **15** self-
centredness, thoughtlessness

### inconsistency
**04** odds **07** paradox **08** conflict,
variance **09** disparity **10** divergence,
fickleness, repugnance **11** contrariety,
discrepancy, gallimaufry, incongruity,
inconstancy, instability
**12** disagreement, unsteadiness
**13** contradiction, unreliability
**14** changeableness **15** incompatibility

### inconsistent
**05** alien **06** at odds, fickle, spotty
**07** erratic, jarring, varying **08** contrary,
in and out, unstable, unsteady,
variable **09** differing, irregular,
mercurial, repugnant **10** at variance,
capricious, changeable, discordant,
dissimilar, inconstant, out of place
**11** conflicting, incongruent,
incongruous, unagreeable
**12** incompatible, in opposition, out of
keeping **13** contradictory, self-
repugnant, unpredictable
**14** disconformable, irreconcilable

### inconsolable
**08** desolate, wretched **09** miserable
**10** despairing, devastated
**11** heartbroken **12** disconsolate
**13** broken-hearted, grief-stricken

### inconspicuous
**05** plain, quiet **06** hidden, low-key,
modest **07** obscure **08** discreet,
ordinary, retiring **09** concealed
**10** indistinct, unassuming
**11** camouflaged, unobtrusive
**12** unremarkable **13** insignificant **15** in
the background, undistinguished

### inconspicuously
**07** faintly, quietly **08** modestly
**12** unassumingly **13** unobtrusively
**15** insignificantly, in the background

### inconstancy
**05** range, shift, swing **06** change
**08** wavering **09** variation **10** fickleness

**11** alternation, ambivalence,
fluctuation, instability, oscillation,
vacillation, variability **12** irresolution,
unsteadiness, variableness

### inconstant
**06** fickle, giglet, giglot **07** erratic,
moonish, mutable, Protean, vagrant,
varying, wayward **08** strumpet,
unstable, unsteady, variable, volatile,
wavering **09** changeful, faithless,
fluxional, mercurial, uncertain,
unsettled **10** capricious, changeable,
fluxionary, irresolute, unfaithful,
unreliable **11** fluctuating, vacillating
**12** inconsistent, undependable

### incontestable
**04** sure **05** clear **07** certain, evident,
obvious **08** cast-iron **10** undeniable
**11** indubitable, irrefutable, self-evident
**12** indisputable **14** unquestionable

### incontinent
**04** lewd **05** loose **06** wanton **07** lustful
**08** unchaste **09** debauched, dissolute,
lecherous, unbridled, unchecked
**10** dissipated, lascivious, licentious,
ungoverned, unstanched
**11** immediately, promiscuous,
unstaunched **12** uncontrolled,
ungovernable, unrestrained
**14** uncontrollable

### incontrovertible
**05** clear **07** certain **10** undeniable
**11** beyond doubt, indubitable,
irrefutable, self-evident **12** indisputable
**13** incontestable **14** beyond question,
unquestionable

### incontrovertibly
**07** clearly **09** certainly **10** undeniably
**11** beyond doubt, indubitably,
irrefutably **12** indisputably **14** beyond
question, unquestionably

### inconvenience
**03** irk **04** bind, bore, burr, drag, fuss,
pain **05** annoy, upset, worry **06** bother,
burden, hassle, put out **07** disrupt,
disturb, problem, trouble, turn-off
**08** drawback, flea-bite, headache,
nuisance, vexation **09** annoyance,
disoblige, hindrance, incommode
**10** difficulty, discommode, disruption,
disutility, impose upon
**11** awkwardness, disturbance,
incommodity **12** disadvantage,
discommodity

### inconvenient
**06** ungain **07** awkward **08** annoying,
ill-timed, untimely, untoward,
unwieldy **09** difficult **10** bothersome,
cumbersome, unhandsome,
unsuitable **11** inexpedient,
inopportune, troublesome
**12** embarrassing, incommodious,
unmanageable, unseasonable
**13** inappropriate

### incorporate
◊ *containment indicator* **03** mix **04** fuse
**05** blend, merge, unify, unite
**06** absorb, embody, imbody, take in
**07** build in, combine, contain,
embrace, include, piece up, subsume
**08** coalesce, incorpse **09** integrate,

**incorporated**

multiplex **10** amalgamate, assimilate **11** consolidate

**incorporated**
**03** inc

**incorporation**
**05** blend, union **06** fusion, merger **07** company, society **08** unifying **09** inclusion, subsuming **10** absorption, assumption, embodiment, federation **11** association, coalescence, combination, integration, unification **12** amalgamation, assimilation

**incorporeal**
**04** aery **05** aerie **06** unreal **07** ghostly **08** bodiless, ethereal, illusory, spectral, unfleshy **09** spiritual, unfleshly **10** immaterial, intangible, phantasmal, phantasmic

**incorrect**
◊ *anagram indicator* **03** bad, ill **05** false, wrong **06** faulty, untrue **07** inexact, off beam **08** improper, mistaken, not right **09** erroneous, imprecise **10** fallacious, inaccurate, unsuitable, way off beam **12** illegitimate **13** inappropriate, ungrammatical

**incorrectly**
**05** false, wrong **07** falsely, in error, wrongly **08** unfairly, unjustly **09** by mistake **10** mistakenly **11** erroneously, misguidedly **12** fallaciously, inaccurately **15** inappropriately

**incorrectness**
**05** error **07** fallacy **09** falseness, wrongness **10** faultiness, inaccuracy **11** imprecision, inexactness, unsoundness **12** inexactitude, mistakenness, speciousness **13** erroneousness, impreciseness, unsuitability

**incorrigible**
**08** hardened, hopeless **09** incurable **10** beyond hope, inveterate **12** irredeemable **13** dyed-in-the-wool, irreclaimable

**incorruptibility**
**06** honour, virtue **07** honesty, probity **08** justness, morality, nobility **09** integrity **11** uprightness **15** trustworthiness

**incorruptible**
**04** just **05** moral **06** honest **07** ethical, upright **08** straight, virtuous **10** honourable, unbribable **11** trustworthy **14** high-principled

**increase**
**02** up **03** add, ech, eik, eke, ich, wax **04** eche, eech, gain, go up, grow, hike, rise, soar, wave **05** add to, amp up, boost, breed, bulge, climb, mount, raise, surge, swell, widen **06** bump up, deepen, expand, extend, flow-on, gather, growth, hike up, mark-up, profit, pump up, rocket, spiral, spread, step up, step-up, uplift, uptick, upturn **07** advance, augment, broaden, build up, build-up, develop, enhance, enlarge, further, improve, inflate, magnify, produce, progeny, prolong, scale up, upsurge **08** addition,

escalate, heighten, interest, maximize, multiply, mushroom, progress, redouble, snowball **09** expansion, extension, increment, intensify, propagate, rocketing, skyrocket **10** accumulate, escalation, strengthen **11** development, enlargement, heightening, mushrooming, proliferate, snowballing **12** augmentation, bring to a head **13** become greater, proliferation **14** bring to the boil **15** be on the increase, intensification

**increasingly**
**06** more so **10** all the more **11** more and more **12** cumulatively **13** exponentially, on the increase, progressively

**incredible**
**04** tall **05** great, steep **06** absurd, unreal **07** amazing **08** smashing, terrific **09** fantastic, wonderful **10** astounding, cockamamie, far-fetched, formidable, impossible, improbable, marvellous, past belief, remarkable, surprising, tremendous **11** astonishing, cock-and-bull, exceptional, implausible, jaw-dropping, magnificent, unthinkable **12** beyond belief, mind-boggling, preposterous, unbelievable, unimaginable **13** extraordinary, inconceivable **14** out of this world

**incredibly**
**04** very **06** highly **07** greatly **09** amazingly, extremely **10** impossibly, remarkably **11** unspeakably, wonderfully **12** marvellously, surprisingly, terrifically, tremendously, unbelievably, unimaginably **13** exceptionally, fantastically, inconceivably, inexpressibly **15** extraordinarily

**incredulity**
**05** doubt **08** cynicism, distrust, mistrust, unbelief **09** amazement, disbelief, suspicion **10** scepticism

**incredulous**
**07** cynical, dubious **08** doubtful, doubting **09** sceptical, uncertain **10** suspicious **11** distrustful, distrusting, unbelieving, unconvinced **12** disbelieving, unbelievable

**increment**
**04** gain **06** growth, step-up **07** accrual **08** addendum, addition, increase **09** accretion, accrument, expansion, extension **10** growth ring, supplement **11** advancement, enlargement **12** augmentation

**incriminate**
**05** blame, set up **06** accuse, charge, indict **07** arraign, impeach, involve **08** stitch up **09** implicate, inculpate **13** put the blame on

**inculcate**
**03** fix **05** teach **06** infuse, instil, preach **07** din into, engrain, implant, impress, imprint **08** drum into **09** drill into **10** hammer into **12** indoctrinate

**inculpate**
**05** blame **06** accuse, charge, indict **07** arraign, censure, impeach, involve **09** implicate **11** incriminate, recriminate **13** put the blame on

**incumbent**
**04** up to **05** right **06** bearer, holder, member, parson **07** binding, officer **08** official **09** mandatory, necessary, overlying **10** compulsory, obligatory, prescribed **11** functionary, overhanging **12** office-bearer, office-holder **15** perpetual curate

**incur**
**03** ren, rin, run **04** earn, gain, risk **05** run up **06** arouse, suffer **07** provoke, sustain **08** contract, meet with **10** experience

**incurable**
**05** fatal **08** hardened, hopeless, terminal **10** beyond hope, inoperable, inveterate, remediless, unhealable, unrecuring **11** immedicable, untreatable **12** incorrigible **13** dyed-in-the-wool, unmedicinable

**incurably**
**07** fatally **10** beyond hope, hopelessly, inoperably, terminally **12** incorrigibly, inveterately

**incursion**
**04** raid, road, rode **05** foray, sally **06** attack, inroad, razzia, sortie **07** assault, inroads **08** invasion **09** intrusion, irruption, onslaught **11** penetration **12** infiltration

**indebted**
**05** owing **07** obliged **08** beholden, grateful, thankful **09** obligated **12** appreciative
• **be indebted** **03** owe

**indebtedness**
**09** gratitude **10** obligation **12** appreciation **15** debt of gratitude

**indecency**
**07** crudity **08** foulness, impurity, lewdness **09** grossness, immodesty, indecorum, obscenity, vulgarity **10** coarseness **11** pornography **13** offensiveness **14** licentiousness

**indecent**
◊ *anagram indicator* **04** blue, foul, free, lewd, ripe **05** bawdy, crude, dirty, gross, nasty **06** coarse, filthy, fruity, impure, ribald, risqué, sleazy, smutty, sultry, vulgar **07** corrupt, immoral, obscene, raunchy **08** depraved, immodest, improper, scabrous, shocking, uncomely, unhonest, unseemly **09** off colour, offensive, perverted **10** degenerate, indecorous, indelicate, licentious, outrageous, suggestive, unbecoming, unsuitable **11** near the bone, Rabelaisian **12** pornographic, unrepeatable **13** inappropriate **14** close to the bone, near the knuckle

**indecipherable**
**04** tiny **07** crabbed, cramped, unclear **09** illegible **10** indistinct, unreadable **14** unintelligible

**indecision**

05 doubt 06 dither 07 swither
08 suspense, wavering 09 hesitancy
10 hesitation 11 ambivalence,
fluctuation, uncertainty, vacillation
12 irresolution 13 tentativeness
14 indecisiveness 15 shilly-shallying

**indecisive**

04 open 06 unsure 07 dithery, unclear
08 doubtful, hesitant, wavering
09 faltering, tentative, uncertain,
undecided, unsettled 10 ambivalent,
hesitating, indefinite, in two minds,
irresolute, undecisive, up in the air,
weak-willed, wishy-washy
11 fluctuating, vacillating 12 feeble-
minded, inconclusive, pussyfooting,
undetermined 13 indeterminate
15 shilly-shallying

**indecorous**

04 rude 05 crude, rough 06 coarse,
vulgar 07 boorish, ill-bred, naughty,
uncivil, uncouth 08 churlish,
immodest, impolite, improper,
indecent, seemless, unseemly,
untoward 09 graceless, tasteless,
unfitting 10 high-kilted, in bad taste,
seemelesse, unladylike, unmannerly,
unsuitable 11 ill-mannered,
undignified 13 inappropriate,
ungentlemanly

**indecorum**

07 crudity 08 bad taste, rudeness
09 immodesty, indecency, roughness,
vulgarity 10 coarseness, uncivility
11 impropriety 12 impoliteness,
unseemliness 13 tastelessness

**indeed**

01 I 02 ay, la 03 aye, e'en, nay, yah,
yea, yes 04 deed, even, faix, just
05 faith, haith, marry, quite, sooth,
truly 06 atweel, in fact, quotha, rather,
really 07 for sure, insooth, in truth,
quite so, soothly 08 actually, forsooth,
to be sure 09 certainly, soothlich
10 absolutely, definitely, in good time,
positively, undeniably 11 doubtlessly,
undoubtedly 12 without doubt 13 for
that matter, in anyone's book, in point
of fact

**indefatigable**

06 dogged 07 patient, undying
08 diligent, tireless, untiring
09 unfailing, unresting, unwearied
10 relentless, unflagging, untireable,
unwearying 11 indomitable,
persevering, unremitting, unweariable
13 inexhaustible

**indefatigably**

08 doggedly 09 patiently 10 diligently,
tirelessly 11 indomitably, unfailingly,
unrestingly 12 relentlessly,
unflaggingly 13 unremittingly

**indefensible**

05 wrong 06 faulty, flawed 07 exposed,
unarmed 08 disarmed, specious
09 unguarded, untenable
10 unshielded, vulnerable
11 defenceless, ill-equipped,
inexcusable, unfortified, unprotected
12 undefendable, unforgivable,

unpardonable 13 insupportable,
unjustifiable

**indefinable**

03 dim 04 hazy 05 vague 06 subtle
07 obscure, unclear 08 nameless
10 impalpable, indistinct, unrealized
13 indescribable, inexpressible

**indefinite**

04 hazy 05 fuzzy, loose, vague
07 blurred, general, inexact, obscure,
unclear, unfixed, unknown
08 confused, doubtful, twilight
09 ambiguous, equivocal, imprecise,
uncertain, undecided, undefined,
unlimited, unsettled 10 ambivalent, ill-
defined, indistinct, unresolved
11 nondescript, unspecified
12 inconclusive, undetermined
13 indeterminate

**indefinitely**

06 always 07 for ever 09 endlessly,
eternally 11 ad infinitum, continually,
permanently 12 without limit

**indelible**

04 fast 07 lasting 08 enduring, unfading
09 ingrained, permanent
12 imperishable, ineffaceable,
ineradicable 14 indestructible

**indelibly**

10 enduringly 11 permanently
12 ineradicably 14 indestructibly

**indelicacy**

07 crudity 08 bad taste, rudeness
09 grossness, immodesty, indecency,
obscenity, vulgarity 10 coarseness,
smuttiness 11 impropriety
13 offensiveness, tastelessness
14 suggestiveness

**indelicate**

03 low 04 blue, rude, warm 05 crude,
gross 06 coarse, risqué, sultry, vulgar
07 obscene 08 immodest, improper,
indecent, tactless, unseemly,
untoward 09 off-colour, offensive,
tasteless 10 in bad taste, indecorous,
suggestive, unbecoming
12 embarrassing

**indemnify**

03 pay 04 free 05 repay 06 exempt,
insure, recoup, repair, secure
07 endorse, protect, requite, satisfy
09 guarantee, reimburse
10 compensate, remunerate,
underwrite

**indemnity**

07 amnesty, redress 08 immunity,
requital, security 09 assurance,
exemption, guarantee, insurance,
repayment, safeguard 10 protection,
reparation 11 restitution
12 compensation, remuneration
13 reimbursement

**indent**

03 cut 04 dent, dint, mark, nick, pink
05 notch, order 06 ask for, crenel,
demand, recess 07 bargain, impress,
request, scallop, serrate 08 apply for,
crenelle 09 penetrate 10 apprentice
11 requisition

**indentation**

03 cut, dip, pit 04 dent, nick 05 gouge,
notch, sinus 06 crenel, dimple, furrow,
groove, hollow, recess 08 crenelle
09 serration 10 depression
11 engrailment

**indenture**

04 bond, deal, deed 08 contract,
covenant 09 agreement
10 commitment, settlement
11 certificate

**independence**

01 I 05 uhuru 06 swaraj 07 autarky,
freedom, liberty 08 autonomy, home
rule, self-rule 10 competency,
separation 11 nationalism, sovereignty
12 independency, self-reliance
13 individualism 14 decolonization,
self-government 15 self-sufficiency

**independent**

01 I 03 Ind 04 fair, free, just 07 neutral,
private, unaided 08 absolute, autarkic,
discrete, distinct, separate, unbiased
09 autarchic, freelance, impartial,
liberated, objective, sovereign,
unrelated 10 autogenous, autonomous,
crossbench, individual, non-aligned,
self-ruling, unattacked 11 self-reliant,
unconnected 12 free-standing, free-
thinking, self-standing, unprejudiced,
unrestrained 13 autocephalous,
disinterested, dispassionate,
individualist, self-contained, self-
governing, unconstrained 14 self-
sufficient, self-supporting,
unconventional 15 going your own
way, individualistic, self-determining,
self-legislating

**independently**

04 solo 05 alone 07 unaided 09 on your
own, on your tod 10 by yourself,
separately 12 autonomously,
individually

**indescribable**

07 amazing 08 nameless 09 ineffable
10 incredible 11 exceptional,
indefinable, inenarrable, undefinable,
unspeakable, unutterable
13 extraordinary, inexpressible

**indescribably**

04 very 06 highly 07 greatly
09 amazingly, extremely 10 incredibly
11 unspeakably, unutterably
13 exceptionally, inexpressibly
15 extraordinarily

**indestructible**

05 tough 06 strong 07 abiding, durable,
endless, eternal, lasting 08 enduring,
immortal 09 permanent 10 undecaying
11 everlasting, infrangible,
unbreakable 12 imperishable 15 tough
as old boots

**indeterminate**

04 hazy 05 vague 07 inexact, unclear,
unfixed, unknown 08 unstated,
variable 09 ambiguous, equivocal,
imprecise, open-ended, uncertain,
undecided, undefined 10 ambivalent,
ill-defined, indefinite 11 unspecified
12 inconclusive, undetermined
13 unpredictable

## index

**03** BMI, key, RPI **04** clue, dial, hand, hint, list, mark, nose, rate, sign **05** guide, power, ratio, scale, style, table, token **06** alidad, gnomon, needle, number **07** average, formula, pointer, preface, symptom **08** card file, exponent, fraction, prologue **09** catalogue, directory, indicator **10** difference, forefinger, indication, percentage, proportion **11** concordance **12** introduction **13** card catalogue **14** correspondence

## India

**01** I **03** IND
*See also* **state**

## Indian

*see* **American; Asian**

## Indiana

**02** IN **03** Ind

## indicate

**03** put, say, tip **04** mark, mean, note, read, shew, show, sign, tell **05** argue, arrow, imply, point, spell, state, utter, voice **06** affirm, assert, denote, evince, record, report, reveal, set out **07** declare, display, divulge, express, point to, present, signify, specify, suggest **08** announce, disclose, evidence, manifest, point out, register **09** designate, formulate, make known, represent **10** articulate **11** communicate **15** be symptomatic of

## indicated

**06** marked, needed **08** required **09** advisable, called-for, desirable, necessary, suggested **11** recommended

## indication

**03** nod **04** clue, hint, lead, mark, note, omen, shew, show, sign **05** token, trace **06** augury, oracle, record, signal **07** glimpse, pointer, portent, symptom, warning **08** endeixis, evidence, monument, register, signpost **10** denotement, expression, intimation, suggestion **11** explanation **13** demonstration, manifestation

## indicative

**07** typical **08** indicant, symbolic, telltale **10** denotative, exhibitive, indicatory, suggestive **11** significant, symptomatic **13** demonstrative, significative **14** characteristic

## indicatively

**07** as a sign **09** as a symbol, typically **10** as evidence **12** symbolically **13** significantly **14** as an expression **15** symptomatically

## indicator

**04** dial, hand, mark, sign **05** bezel, gauge, guide, index, meter, token **06** gnomon, marker, needle, signal, symbol **07** display, flasher, pointer **08** signpost **09** barometer **10** litmus test, turn signal

## indict

**04** dite **06** accuse, charge, summon **07** arraign, article, impeach, summons, trounce **09** inculpate, prosecute **10** put on trial **11** incriminate

## indictment

**06** charge, dittay **07** summons **10** accusation, allegation **11** arraignment, impeachment, inculpation, prosecution **13** incrimination, recrimination

## indifference

**06** apathy, phlegm, slight **08** coldness, coolness **09** disregard, unconcern **10** negligence, neutrality **11** impassivity, inattention, nonchalance **12** heedlessness **13** lack of concern, lack of feeling **14** lack of interest

## indifferent

**02** OK **03** bad **04** cold, cool, easy, fair, so-so **05** aloof, blasé **06** medium **07** average, callous, distant, easy-osy, neutral, not good, unmoved **08** adequate, careless, detached, heedless, inferior, jack easy, mediocre, middling, moderate, ordinary, passable, uncaring **09** apathetic, impassive, incurious, unexcited, unfeeling **10** insouciant, nonchalant, uninvolved **11** cold-hearted, pococurante, unconcerned, unemotional **12** could be worse, run of the mill, uninterested, unresponsive **13** could be better, disinterested, dispassionate, uninteresting, unsympathetic **14** unenthusiastic **15** all the same to you, undistinguished

## indigence

**04** need, want **06** penury **07** poverty **08** distress **09** necessity, privation **11** deprivation, destitution

## indigenous

**05** local **06** native **08** original **09** home-grown **10** aboriginal, vernacular **13** autochthonous

## indigent

**04** bust, poor **05** broke, needy, skint **06** in need, in want **08** dirt-poor **09** destitute, penniless, penurious **10** cleaned out, down and out, stony-broke **11** impecunious, necessitous, up against it **12** impoverished, on your uppers **13** in dire straits **14** on your beam ends **15** poverty-stricken

## indigestion

**07** acidity, apepsia, pyrosis **08** dyspepsy **09** dyspepsia, heartburn **10** cardialgia, water-brash **13** grass staggers **15** stomach staggers

## indignant

**03** mad **05** angry, cross, irate, livid, riled **06** bitter, fuming, heated, miffed, narked, peeved **07** annoyed, enraged, furious, in a huff **08** in a strop, incensed, outraged, up in arms, wrathful **09** aggrieved, resentful, steamed up **10** got the hump, infuriated **11** acrimonious, disgruntled, exasperated

## indignantly

**07** angrily, crossly, in a huff, irately **08** bitterly, up in arms **09** furiously, steamed up **11** resentfully **13** acrimoniously, reproachfully

## indignation

**03** ire **04** fury, rage **05** anger, pique, scorn, wrath **06** furore **07** dudgeon, outrage **08** contempt **09** annoyance **10** resentment **12** exasperation **15** saeva indignatio

## indignity

**04** snub **05** abuse, shame **06** injury, insult, slight **07** affront, obloquy, offence, outrage, putdown **08** contempt, disgrace, reproach **09** contumely, dishonour **10** disrespect, incivility, opprobrium **11** humiliation **12** cold shoulder, mistreatment, unworthiness **13** slap in the face **14** kick in the teeth

## indigo

**04** anil

## indirect

**02** by **03** bye **06** remote, squint, ungain, zigzag **07** curving, devious, mediate, oblique, winding **08** allusive, rambling, tortuous **09** ancillary, divergent, secondary, wandering **10** back-handed, circuitous, discursive, incidental, meandering, roundabout, subsidiary, unintended **11** subordinate **12** periphrastic **14** circumlocutory

## indirectly

**05** round **09** deviously, hintingly, obliquely **10** allusively, second-hand **12** at second hand, incidentally, roundaboutly

## indiscernible

**04** tiny **06** hidden, minute **07** obscure, unclear **09** invisible, minuscule **10** impalpable, indistinct, unapparent **11** microscopic **12** undetectable, unnoticeable **13** imperceptible, undiscernible

## indiscreet

**04** rash **05** hasty **06** unwary, unwise **07** foolish **08** careless, heedless, immodest, reckless, tactless **09** foolhardy, ill-judged, impolitic, imprudent, shameless **10** ill-advised, indelicate, unthinking **11** injudicious, insensitive **12** undiplomatic **13** ill-considered

## indiscreetly

**06** rashly **08** unwisely **09** foolishly **10** carelessly, heedlessly, immodestly, recklessly, tactlessly **11** shamelessly **12** indelicately **13** insensitively

## indiscretion

**04** boob, flub, slip **05** error, folly, gaffe, lapse **06** slip-up **07** blunder, faux pas, mistake **08** rashness **09** immodesty **10** imprudence, indelicacy **11** foolishness **12** carelessness, recklessness, tactlessness **13** shamelessness

## indiscriminate

◊ *anagram indicator* **05** mixed **06** motley, random, varied **07** aimless, chaotic, diverse, general **08** careless, confused, pell-mell, sweeping **09** haphazard, hit or miss, wholesale **10** hit and miss **11** promiscuous, scattershot, unselective

**12** unmethodical, unrespective, unsystematic **13** miscellaneous

**indiscriminately**
**08** randomly **09** aimlessly, generally, in the mass, wholesale **10** carelessly **11** haphazardly **13** unselectively **14** unmethodically **15** indistinctively

**indispensable**
**03** key **05** basic, vital **06** needed **07** crucial, needful **08** required **09** essential, important, necessary, requisite **10** absolutely, imperative **11** fundamental

**indisposed**
**03** ill **04** sick **05** crook, loath **06** ailing, averse, groggy, laid up, poorly, unwell **09** reluctant, unwilling **10** not of a mind, not willing, out of sorts **11** disinclined **12** not of a mind to **13** confined to bed, incapacitated **15** under the weather

**indisposition**
**03** ail **06** malady **07** ailment, disease, dislike, illness **08** aversion, disorder, distaste, sickness **09** bad health, complaint, hesitancy, ill health **10** reluctance **13** unwillingness **14** disinclination, distemperature

**indisputable**
**04** sure **06** liquid **07** certain, dead set **08** absolute, definite, positive **10** inarguable, unarguable, undeniable, undisputed **11** indubitable, irrefutable **13** incontestable **14** beyond question, uncontrollable, unquestionable

**indissoluble**
**05** fixed, solid **07** abiding, binding, eternal, lasting **08** enduring **09** permanent **10** inviolable **11** inseparable, sempiternal, unbreakable **12** imperishable **13** incorruptible **14** indestructible

**indistinct**
**03** dim, low **04** hazy, pale **05** blear, faded, faint, fuzzy, misty, muted, vague **06** grainy, woolly **07** blurred, clouded, distant, muffled, obscure, shadowy, unclear **08** confused, muttered **09** ambiguous, undefined **10** ill-defined, indefinite, out of focus **14** indecipherable, unintelligible
• **indistinct appearance** **04** blur, loom

**indistinctly**
**05** dimly **06** hazily **07** fuzzily, vaguely **09** obscurely, unclearly **10** out of focus **14** unintelligibly

**indistinguishable**
**04** same, twin **05** alike **06** cloned **09** identical **10** tantamount **13** indiscernible **15** interchangeable

**indium**
**02** In

**individual**
**03** one, own **04** body, idio-, lone, poll, sole, sort, soul, type, unit **05** being, party **06** fellow, mortal, person, proper, single, unique, versal **07** private, several, special, typical **08** creature,

distinct, isolated, original, peculiar, personal, separate, singular, solitary, specific **09** character, exclusive **10** human being, particular, respective, subjective **11** distinctive, inseparable **12** personalized **13** idiosyncratic **14** characteristic

**individualism**
**06** egoism **09** anarchism **11** freethought, originality **12** eccentricity, freethinking, independence, self-interest, self-reliance **13** egocentricity, self-direction **14** libertarianism

**individualist**
**05** loner **06** egoist **08** bohemian, lone wolf, maverick, original **09** anarchist, eccentric **10** egocentric, free spirit **11** freethinker, independent, libertarian **13** nonconformist

**individualistic**
**06** unique **07** special, typical **08** bohemian, egoistic, original **09** eccentric **10** egocentric, individual, particular, unorthodox **11** anarchistic, independent, libertarian, self-reliant **13** idiosyncratic, nonconformist **14** unconventional

**individuality**
**07** oneness **08** identity, property **09** character, propriety **10** uniqueness **11** distinction, originality, peculiarity, personality, singularity **12** separateness **15** distinctiveness

**individually**
**06** singly **08** one by one **09** in several, severally **10** one at a time, personally, separately **12** in particular, particularly **13** independently

**indivisible**
**10** impartible **11** inseparable, intrenchant, undividable **12** indissoluble **14** indiscerptible

**indoctrinate**
**05** drill, teach, train **06** ground, instil, school **07** impress **08** instruct **09** brainwash, inculcate **12** propagandize

**indoctrination**
**08** drilling, teaching, training **09** grounding, schooling **10** catechesis, instilling **11** catechetics, inculcation, instruction **12** brainwashing

**Indo-European**
**02** IE
*See also* **European**

**indolence**
**05** sloth **06** apathy, torpor **07** inertia, languor **08** idleness, laziness, lethargy, shirking, slacking **09** heaviness, inertness, torpidity, torpitude **10** inactivity, torpidness **11** languidness **12** do-nothingism, listlessness, sluggishness

**indolent**
**04** idle, lazy, slow **05** inert, slack **06** otiose, supine, torpid **07** languid, lumpish **08** bone-idle, fainéant, inactive, listless, slothful, sluggard, sluggish **09** apathetic, do-nothing,

easy-going, lethargic, shiftless **13** lackadaisical

**indomitable**
**04** bold, firm **05** brave **07** staunch, valiant **08** fearless, intrepid, resolute, stalwart **09** steadfast, undaunted **10** courageous, determined, invincible, unbeatable, unyielding **11** impregnable, lion-hearted, unflinching **12** intransigent, unassailable, undefeatable **13** unconquerable

**Indonesia**
**02** RI **03** IDN

**indubitable**
**04** sure **07** certain, evident, obvious **08** absolute **09** undoubted **10** unarguable, undeniable **11** beyond doubt, irrefutable, undoubtable **12** indisputable, irrebuttable, irrefragable, unanswerable **13** beyond dispute, incontestable **14** unquestionable

**indubitably**
**05** truly **06** surely **07** clearly, no doubt **08** of course, probably **09** assuredly, certainly, doubtless, precisely **10** most likely, presumably **11** undoubtedly **12** indisputably, without doubt **14** unquestionably

**induce**
**03** get **04** coax, draw, lead, move, urge **05** cause, force, impel, press, tempt **06** effect, incite, lead to, prompt, seduce **07** actuate, bring on, entreat, inspire, intreat, procure, produce, provoke **08** generate, motivate, occasion, persuade, talk into **09** encourage, influence, instigate, originate **10** bring about, give rise to **11** prevail upon, set in motion

**inducement**
**04** bait, goad, lure, spur **05** bribe, cause, drink **06** carrot, motive, reason, reward **07** impetus **08** stimulus **09** incentive, influence, sweetener **10** attraction, back-hander, enticement, incitement, persuasion **11** seditionary **13** encouragement

**induct**
**05** admit, place, stall **06** enlist, invest, ordain **07** install, swear in **08** enthrone, initiate **09** conscript, introduce **10** consecrate, inaugurate

**inductance**
**01** L
• **measure of inductance** **01** H
**05** henry

**induction**
**07** epagoge, prelude **09** deduction, inference **10** conclusion, initiation, ordination **11** institution, investiture **12** consecration, enthronement, inauguration, installation, introduction **14** generalization

**indulge**
**03** pet **05** allow, spoil, treat **06** cocker, cosset, cuiter, favour, humour, pamper, pettle, regale **07** cater to, gratify, revel in, satisfy, yield to **08** give

in to, pander to, wallow in **09** give way to, make merry **11** go along with, luxuriate in, mollycoddle **14** give free rein to

**indulgence**
**03** law **04** luxe, riot **05** favor, swing, treat **06** excess, excuse, favour, luxury, pardon **08** lenience, spoiling **09** pampering, remission, tolerance **10** fulfilment, generosity, sensualism, sensuality **11** dissipation, forbearance **12** extravagance, immoderation, intemperance, satisfaction **13** dissoluteness, gratification, mollycoddling

**indulgent**
**04** fond, kind **06** humane, tender **07** lenient, liberal, patient **08** generous, merciful, spoiling, tolerant **09** compliant, cosseting, easy-going, forgiving, humouring, pampering **10** forbearing, permissive **11** sympathetic **13** compassionate, mollycoddling, understanding

**indulgently**
**06** fondly, kindly **08** humanely, tenderly **09** leniently, liberally, patiently, with mercy **10** generously, mercifully, tolerantly **12** with sympathy **14** with compassion **15** compassionately, sympathetically

**industrial**
**05** trade **08** business **09** technical **10** commercial **13** manufacturing

**industrialist**
**05** baron **06** tycoon **07** magnate **08** producer **09** financier **10** capitalist **12** manufacturer

**industrious**
**04** busy, hard **05** deedy **06** active, dogged, steady **07** notable, on the go, skilful, workful, zealous **08** diligent, sedulous, studious, tireless, vigorous, worksome **09** assiduous, dedicated, energetic, laborious **10** busy as a bee, determined, persistent, productive **11** hard-working, persevering **13** conscientious, indefatigable

**industriously**
**04** hard **08** doggedly, steadily **10** diligently, sedulously **11** assiduously **13** perseveringly **15** conscientiously

**industry**
**04** line, toil, zeal **05** field, trade **06** effort, energy, labour, vigour **07** service **08** activity, business, commerce, hard work, sedulity **09** assiduity, diligence **10** enterprise, intentness, production, steadiness **11** application, persistence **12** perseverance, sedulousness, stickability, tirelessness **13** assiduousness, concentration, determination, laboriousness, manufacturing **14** productiveness **15** industriousness

**inebriated**
◊ *anagram indicator* **04** full, high, inky, para **05** blind, drunk, happy, inked, lit up, merry, moppy, tight, tipsy, woozy **06** blotto, bombed, canned, corked,

jarred, juiced, loaded, mortal, ripped, rotten, soused, stewed, stinko, stoned, tanked, tiddly, wasted **07** bevvied, bonkers, bottled, crocked, drunken, half-cut, legless, maggoty, pickled, pie-eyed, sloshed, smashed, sozzled, squiffy, tiddled, toasted, trashed, wrecked **08** bibulous, footless, hammered, in liquor, juiced up, liquored, maggoted, moon-eyed, ossified, sow-drunk, steaming, stocious, tanked up, whiffled, whistled **09** bladdered, crapulent, paralytic, plastered, shickered, trolleyed, up the pole, well-oiled **10** blind drunk, in your cups, obfuscated **11** full as a boot, full as a goog, full as a tick, intoxicated, off your face **12** drunk as a lord, drunk as a newt, roaring drunk **13** drunk as a piper, drunk as a skunk, having had a few, under the table **14** Brahms and Liszt **15** one over the eight, the worse for wear, under the weather

**inedible**
**03** bad, off **05** stale **06** deadly, rancid, rotten **07** harmful, noxious **09** poisonous, uneatable **10** inesculent **11** not fit to eat, unpalatable **12** indigestible, unconsumable

**ineducable**
**08** indocile **11** unteachable **12** incorrigible

**ineffable**
**07** fearful **10** remarkable **11** beyond words, unspeakable, unutterable **12** unimpartible **13** indescribable, inexpressible **14** incommunicable

**ineffably**
**09** fearfully **10** absolutely, remarkably **11** beyond words, unspeakably, unutterably **13** indescribably, inexpressibly

**ineffective**
**03** dud **04** idle, lame, vain, weak **05** inept **06** feeble, futile **07** useless **08** abortive, impotent **09** burned out, fruitless, powerless, to no avail, toothless, worthless **10** inadequate, profitless, unavailing, unpregnant **11** incompetent, ineffectual **12** unproductive, unsuccessful

**ineffectiveness**
**08** futility, weakness **10** feebleness, inadequacy **11** uselessness **13** fruitlessness, worthlessness

**ineffectual**
**03** wet **04** lame, vain, void, weak **05** inept, resty, wimpy **06** feeble, futile, unable **07** useless **08** abortive, chinless, feckless, impotent **09** fruitless, frustrate, powerless, worthless **10** inadequate, unavailing **11** incompetent **12** unproductive **13** inefficacious, lackadaisical

**ineffectually**
**06** feebly, in vain, lamely, weakly **09** to no avail, uselessly **11** fruitlessly, to no purpose **14** unproductively, unsuccessfully

**inefficacy**
**08** futility **10** inadequacy **11** uselessness **14** ineffectuality **15** ineffectiveness, ineffectualness

**inefficiency**
**05** waste **06** laxity, muddle **09** slackness **10** ineptitude, negligence, sloppiness **12** carelessness, incompetence, wastefulness **15** disorganization

**inefficient**
**03** lax **05** inept, slack **06** flabby, sloppy **08** careless, inexpert, slipshod, wasteful **09** negligent, shiftless **10** uneconomic **11** incompetent, ineffective, time-wasting, unorganized **12** disorganized, money-wasting **13** unworkmanlike

**inelegant**
**04** ugly **05** crude, rough **06** clumsy, gauche, vulgar **07** awkward, ill-bred, uncouth **08** homespun, laboured, ungainly, unpolite **09** graceless, unrefined **10** uncultured, unfinished, ungraceful, unpolished **12** uncultivated **15** unsophisticated

**ineligible**
**05** unfit **08** ruled out, unfitted, unworthy **10** unequipped, unsuitable **11** incompetent, undesirable, unqualified **12** disqualified, unacceptable

**ineluctable**
**04** sure **05** fated **07** assured, certain **08** destined **10** ineludible, inevitable, inexorable **11** inescapable, irrevocable, unalterable, unavoidable

**inept**
◊ *anagram indicator* **04** void **05** flaky, lousy, silly **06** clumsy, stupid **07** awkward, foolish, useless **08** bungling, inexpert, pathetic **09** appalling, ham-fisted, incapable, maladroit, unskilful **10** cack-handed, inadequate, unsuitable **11** heavy-handed, incompetent **12** unsuccessful

**ineptitude**
**07** fatuity **08** bungling **09** crassness, gaucherie, ineptness, stupidity, unfitness **10** clumsiness, gaucheness, incapacity **11** awkwardness, glaikitness, unhandiness, uselessness **12** incapability, incompetence, inexpertness **13** unskilfulness

**inequality**
**03** rub **04** bias, odds, wave **05** whelk **08** contrast, imparity **09** disparity, diversity, imbalance, prejudice, roughness, variation **10** difference, inadequacy, unevenness **11** discrepancy, unequalness **12** incompetence, irregularity **13** disproportion, dissimilarity, nonconformity **14** discrimination

**inequitable**
**06** biased, unfair, unjust **07** bigoted, partial, unequal **08** one-sided, partisan, wrongful **10** intolerant, prejudiced **12** preferential **14** discriminatory

## inequity
**04** bias **05** abuse **09** injustice, prejudice **10** inequality, partiality, unfairness, unjustness **12** maltreatment, mistreatment, one-sidedness, wrongfulness **14** discrimination

## inert
**04** cold, dead, dull, idle, lazy **05** slack, still **06** leaden, sleepy, static, supine, torpid **07** dormant, languid, passive, restive **08** comatose, immobile, inactive, indolent, lifeless, listless, sluggish, stagnant, thowless, unmoving **09** apathetic, inanimate, lethargic, nerveless **10** motionless, stationary, stock-still **12** unresponsive

## inertia
**05** sloth **06** apathy, torpor **07** languor **08** idleness, inaction, laziness, lethargy **09** indolence, inertness, passivity, stillness **10** immobility, inactivity, Oblomovism, stagnation **12** listlessness, slothfulness **14** motionlessness

## inescapable
**04** sure **05** fated **07** assured, certain **08** destined **10** ineludible, inevitable, inexorable **11** ineluctable, irrevocable, unalterable, unavoidable

## inescapably
**06** surely **09** assuredly, certainly **10** definitely, inevitably, inexorably **11** irrevocably, necessarily, unavoidably **13** automatically

## inessential
**05** extra, spare **06** luxury **07** surplus **08** needless, optional, trimming **09** accessory, appendage, extrinsic, redundant, secondary **10** accidental, expendable, extraneous, immaterial, irrelevant, unasked-for **11** dispensable, superfluity, superfluous, uncalled-for, unessential, unimportant, unnecessary **12** extravagance, non-essential

## inestimable
**04** vast **06** untold **07** immense **08** infinite, precious **09** priceless, unlimited **10** invaluable, prodigious **11** measureless, uncountable **12** immeasurable, incalculable, incomputable, mind-boggling, unfathomable **13** worth a fortune

## inevitability
**04** fact **05** truth **07** reality, safe bet **08** dead cert, validity **09** certainty, sure thing **14** matter of course

## inevitable
**04** sure **05** fated, fixed **07** assured, certain, decreed, fateful, settled, unshun'd **08** definite, destined, ordained **09** automatic, necessary, unavoided, unshunned **10** inexorable, infallible **11** ineluctable, inescapable, irrevocable, predestined, unalterable, unavoidable **13** unpreventable

## inevitably
**06** surely **09** assuredly, certainly, fatefully, presently **10** definitely, inexorably, infallibly, willy-nilly **11** inescapably, irrevocably,

necessarily, unavoidably **13** automatically

## inexact
**03** lax **05** fuzzy, loose **06** untrue, woolly **07** muddled, of a sort, of sorts **09** erroneous, imprecise, incorrect **10** fallacious, inaccurate, indefinite, indistinct **11** approximate **13** indeterminate

## inexactitude
**05** error **07** blunder, mistake **09** looseness **10** inaccuracy, woolliness **11** imprecision, inexactness **13** approximation, impreciseness, incorrectness **14** indefiniteness, miscalculation

## inexcusable
**08** shameful **10** outrageous **11** blameworthy, intolerable **12** indefensible, unacceptable, unforgivable, unpardonable **13** reprehensible, unjustifiable

## inexcusably
**10** shamefully **12** indefensibly, outrageously, unacceptably **13** reprehensibly, unjustifiably

## inexhaustible
**07** endless **08** abundant, infinite, tireless, untiring **09** boundless, limitless, unbounded, unfailing, unlimited, unwearied, weariless **10** unflagging, unwearying **11** illimitable, measureless, never-ending **12** unrestricted **13** indefatigable

## inexorable
**04** sure **05** fated **07** certain **08** definite, destined, ordained **09** immovable, incessant, unceasing **10** implacable, inevitable, relentless, unyielding **11** ineluctable, inescapable, irrevocable, remorseless, unalterable, unavertable, unfaltering, unrelenting, unstoppable **12** intransigent, irresistible **13** unpreventable

## inexorably
**06** surely **09** certainly **10** definitely, implacably, inevitably, pitilessly **11** ineluctably, inescapably, irrevocably, mercilessly **12** irresistibly, relentlessly, resistlessly **13** remorselessly

## inexpedient
**05** wrong **06** unwise **07** foolish **09** ill-chosen, ill-judged, impolitic, imprudent, misguided, senseless **10** ill-advised, indiscreet, unsuitable **11** detrimental, impolitical, impractical, inadvisable, injudicious, unadvisable, undesirable **12** inconvenient, undiplomatic, unfavourable **13** inappropriate **15** disadvantageous

## inexpensive
**05** a snip, cheap **06** a steal, budget, modest **07** bargain, cut-rate, low-cost, reduced **08** dog-cheap, low-price, uncostly **09** dirt-cheap, low-priced, ten a penny **10** discounted, economical, reasonable **13** going for a song, on a shoestring

## inexperience
**07** newness, rawness **09** freshness, ignorance, innocence, naiveness **10** immaturity **11** strangeness **12** inexpertness **13** unfamiliarity

## inexperienced
**03** new, raw **04** puny **05** fresh, green, naive, young **06** callow, rookie, unseen **07** amateur **08** farouche, ignorant, immature, inexpert, innocent, unsifted, wide-eyed **09** fledgling, unfledged, unskilled, untrained, untutored **10** apprentice, fledgeling, unfamiliar, uninformed, unseasoned **11** new to the job, unexperient, unpractised, unqualified **12** probationary, unaccustomed, unacquainted **14** out of your depth, unsophisticate **15** unsophisticated
• **inexperienced person 03** cub **04** baby **09** fledgling **10** fledgeling

## inexpert
**03** ham **05** inept **06** clumsy **07** amateur, awkward, unhandy **08** bungling, untaught **09** ham-fisted, maladroit, unskilful, unskilled, untrained, untutored **10** amateurish, blundering, cack-handed **11** incompetent, unpractised, unqualified **13** unworkmanlike **14** unprofessional

## inexplicable
**05** weird **07** strange **08** abstruse, baffling, puzzling **09** enigmatic, insoluble **10** incredible, miraculous, mysterious, mystifying, perplexing **11** bewildering, inscrutable **12** inextricable, unbelievable, unfathomable **13** inexplainable, unaccountable, unexplainable **14** unintelligible

## inexplicably
**09** strangely **10** bafflingly, incredibly, puzzlingly **12** miraculously, mysteriously, mystifyingly **13** unaccountably, unexplainably

## inexpressible
**08** nameless, termless **09** ineffable, unsayable **10** untellable **11** indefinable, unspeakable, unutterable **12** inexpressive **13** indescribable, undescribable **14** incommunicable

## inexpressibly
**09** ineffably **11** beyond words, unspeakably, unutterably **13** indescribably

## inexpressive
**04** cold, dead **05** blank, empty **06** vacant **07** deadpan **08** lifeless **09** impassive **10** poker-faced **11** emotionless, inscrutable **12** unexpressive **14** expressionless

## inextinguishable
**07** eternal, lasting, undying **08** enduring, immortal **09** deathless **11** everlasting, unquellable **12** imperishable, unquenchable **13** irrepressible, unconquerable **14** indestructible, unsuppressible

## inextricable
**08** confused **09** intricate **11** indivisible, inescapable, inseparable

**inextricably**
12 indissoluble, inexplicable, irreversible 13 irretrievable

**inextricably**
11 indivisibly, inescapably, inseparably, intricately, irresolubly
12 indissolubly, irreversibly
13 irretrievably

**infallibility**
06 safety 08 accuracy, sureness
09 inerrancy, supremacy 10 perfection
11 omniscience, reliability
12 inerrability, unerringness
13 dependability, faultlessness, impeccability 14 irrefutability
15 trustworthiness

**infallible**
04 sure 05 sound 07 certain, perfect
08 accurate, fail-safe, flawless, reliable, sure-fire, unerring 09 faultless, foolproof, inerrable, unfailing
10 dependable, impeccable, inevitable
11 trustworthy

**infamous**
03 bad 04 base, evil, vile 06 wicked
07 hateful 08 ill-famed, shameful, shocking 09 dastardly, egregious, nefarious, notorious 10 abominable, detestable, iniquitous, outrageous, scandalous 11 disgraceful, ignominious, opprobrious
12 disreputable 13 discreditable, dishonourable

**infamy**
04 evil 05 shame 06 defame, ignomy
08 baseness, disgrace, ignominy, vileness, villainy 09 depravity, discredit, dishonour, disrepute, notoriety, turpitude 10 opprobrium, wickedness

**infancy**
04 dawn, rise 05 birth, roots, seeds, start, youth 06 cradle, nonage, origin, outset 07 genesis, origins, silence
08 babyhood 09 beginning, childhood, emergence, inception 11 early stages
12 commencement 14 speechlessness

**infant**
03 new, tot 04 babe, baby 05 bairn, child, early, sprog, young 07 dawning, growing, initial, nascent, newborn, toddler 08 emergent, immature, juvenile, nursling, youthful
09 beginning, fledgling, little one, nurseling 10 babe in arms, burgeoning, developing 11 rudimentary

**infantile**
05 young 07 babyish, puerile
08 childish, immature, juvenile, youthful 10 adolescent
11 undeveloped

**infantry**
02 LI 03 inf 06 pultan, pulton, pultun, tercio, tertia 07 phalanx, pultoon

**infantryman**
04 kern, naik, peon 05 grunt, kerne, Turco 06 ensign, evzone, Zouave
07 dragoon, footman, hoplite, pandoor, pandour 08 chasseur, doughboy 10 voetganger 11 foot soldier, landsknecht 13 beetle-crusher

**infatuated**
03 mad 06 assott, entêté, in love, sold on 07 entêtée, far gone, smitten, sweet on, wild for 08 assotted, besotted, mad about, obsessed, ravished
09 bewitched, daft about, enamoured, nuts about, wild about 10 bowled over, captivated, crazy about, enraptured, fascinated, lovestruck, mesmerized, potty about, spellbound
11 carried away 12 having a crush, having a thing, love-stricken

**infatuation**
04 love, mash, pash, rave 05 craze, crush, mania, shine, thing 07 passion
08 fixation, fondness 09 engoûment, obsession 10 engouement
11 fascination 12 besottedness

**infect**
03 mar, pox 04 clap, move, smit
05 spoil, taint, touch 06 affect, blight, canker, defile, excite, measle, pass on, poison 07 animate, corrupt, inspire, overrun, pervert, pollute, tainted
08 spread to, ulcerate 09 influence, stimulate, syphilize 10 parasitize
11 contaminate, tuberculize

**infection**
03 bug, wog 04 cold, germ, smit
05 taint, virus 06 blight, poison, sepsis
07 disease, fouling, illness 08 bacteria, epidemic, spoiling, tainting
09 complaint, condition, contagion, influence, pollution 10 corruption, defilement, pestilence
13 contamination
*See also* **disease**

**infectious**
05 toxic 06 deadly, septic, taking
07 noxious, smittle 08 catching, defiling, epidemic, virulent
09 infective, polluting, spreading
10 compelling, contagious, corrupting
12 communicable, irresistible
13 contaminating, transmissible, transmittable

**infelicitous**
03 sad 05 inapt 07 unhappy, unlucky
08 untimely, wretched 09 miserable, sorrowful, unfitting 10 despairing, unsuitable 11 incongruous, inopportune, unfortunate
13 inappropriate 15 disadvantageous

**infer**
05 educe, imply 06 allude, assume, deduce, derive, gather, induce, reason, render 07 conster, presume, surmise 08 conclude, construe
09 figure out 10 conjecture, generalize, understand 11 extrapolate

**inference**
07 reading, surmise 08 illation
09 corollary, deduction, reasoning
10 assumption, conclusion, conjecture
11 consequence, presumption
12 construction 13 extrapolation
14 contraposition, interpretation

**inferior**
03 bad, dog, inf, low 04 less, naff, poor, ropy, weak 05 awful, cheap, crook, grody, lousy, lower, lowly, minor,

ropey 06 bodgie, coarse, crummy, faulty, grotty, humble, impair, junior, lesser, menial, minion, ornery, second, shoddy, vassal 07 low-rent, of a sort, of sorts, provant, rubbish, shilpit, tinhorn, useless 08 hopeless, mediocre, paravail, pathetic, slipshod, underman
09 ancillary, cheap-jack, defective, deficient, imperfect, secondary, underling, underrate 10 fourth-rate, inadequate, low-quality, second-best, second-rate, subsidiary
11 incompetent, indifferent, not much chop, second-class, subordinate, subservient, substandard, under-sawyer 12 unacceptable
14 unsatisfactory

**inferiority**
08 meanness, ropiness 09 lowliness
10 bad quality, crumminess, faultiness, grottiness, humbleness, inadequacy, low quality, mediocrity, shoddiness
11 poor quality 12 imperfection, incompetence, slovenliness, subservience 13 defectiveness, subordination 14 insignificance

**infernal**
04 evil, vile 06 cursed, damned, darned, dashed, Hadean, wicked
07 blasted, demonic, fecking, flaming, hellish, satanic, Stygian 08 accursed, all-fired, blinking, blooming, devilish, fiendish, flipping, wretched
09 atrocious, execrable
10 confounded, diabolical, malevolent, outrageous, sulphurous

**infertile**
04 arid 06 barren, effete 07 dried-up, parched, sterile 08 infecund
09 childless 10 unfruitful
11 unfructuous 12 unproductive
13 non-productive

**infertility**
07 aridity 08 aridness 09 sterility
10 barrenness, effeteness
11 infecundity 14 unfruitfulness

**infest**
03 dog 04 teem 05 beset, crawl, flood, swarm 06 harass, invade, pester, plague, ravage, throng 07 bristle, disturb, overrun, pervade 08 permeate, take over 09 penetrate 10 infiltrate, overspread, parasitize, trichinize
13 spread through

**infestation**
04 pest 05 crabs 06 blight, plague
07 scourge 09 pervasion, taeniasis
10 affliction, ascariasis, giardiasis, pestilence, visitation 11 molestation, overrunning, parasitosis, phthiriasis, shigellosis 12 infiltration, strongylosis, uncinariasis 13 cysticercosis, helminthiasis, verminousness
14 trichinization

**infested**
04 mity 05 alive, batty, beset, buggy, lousy, midgy, mousy, ratty 06 chatty, grubby, mousey, ridden 07 haunted, overrun, plagued, rattish, ravaged, teeming, verminy, weevily
08 crawling, pervaded, swarming, thievish, vermined, weeviled, weevilly

**09** bristling, permeated, verminous, weevilled **10** overspread, stylopized **11** helminthous, infiltrated **12** pestilential

## infidel
**05** pagan **06** giaour **07** atheist, heathen, heretic, sceptic **09** miscreant, sceptical **10** unbeliever **11** disbeliever, freethinker, nullifidian, unbelieving **13** irreligionist

## infidelity
**05** amour **06** affair **07** liaison, perfidy, romance **08** adultery, betrayal, cheating, intrigue **09** duplicity, falseness, treachery **10** disloyalty **12** relationship **13** faithlessness, fooling around, playing around **14** unfaithfulness

## infiltrate
**04** seep, slip, soak **05** enter **06** filter, invade **07** intrude, pervade **08** permeate **09** creep into, insinuate, penetrate, percolate

## infiltration
**07** entrism **08** entryism, invasion **09** intrusion, pervasion **10** permeation **11** insinuation, penetration, percolation

## infiltrator
**03** spy **07** entrist **08** entryist, intruder **09** subverter **10** insinuator, penetrator, subversive **11** seditionary **14** fifth columnist

## infinite
**03** all **04** huge, vast **05** total **06** untold **07** endless, immense **08** absolute, enormous **09** boundless, countless, extensive, limitless, unbounded, unlimited **10** bottomless, fathomless, numberless **11** illimitable, inestimable, innumerable, never-ending, uncountable **12** immeasurable, incalculable, interminable, unfathomable **13** inexhaustible, unconditioned, without number **14** indeterminable

## infinitely
**03** all **09** endlessly, immensely **10** absolutely, enormously, without end **11** ad infinitum, boundlessly, inestimably, limitlessly **12** interminably, without limit **13** inexhaustibly

## infinitesimal
**03** wee **04** tiny **05** teeny **06** minute **08** trifling **09** minuscule **10** negligible **11** microscopic **13** imperceptible, inappreciable, insignificant **14** inconsiderable

## infinitesimally
**06** tinily **08** minutely **10** negligibly **13** imperceptibly, inappreciably **15** insignificantly, microscopically

## infinity
**07** allness **08** eternity, vastness **09** immensity **10** perpetuity **11** endlessness **12** enormousness **13** boundlessness, countlessness, extensiveness, limitlessness

## infirm
**03** ill, old **04** lame, weak **05** frail, shaky **06** ailing, feeble, poorly, sickly, unwell, wobbly **07** doddery, failing **08** decrepit, disabled, unstable, unsteady **09** faltering **11** debilitated

## infirmity
**06** malady **07** ailment, disease, failing, frailty, illness **08** debility, disorder, frailtee, senility, sickness, weakness **09** complaint, frailness, ill health **10** feebleness, sickliness **11** decrepitude, dodderiness, instability **13** vulnerability

## inflame
**03** fan **04** fire, fuel, heat, rile, stir **05** anger, rouse **06** arouse, enrage, excite, foment, ignite, incite, kindle, madden, stir up, whip up, work up, worsen **07** agitate, incense, provoke **08** enkindle, increase **09** aggravate, impassion, infuriate, intensify, make worse, stimulate **10** exacerbate, exasperate

## inflamed
**03** het, hot, raw, red **04** sore **05** angry, heady **06** heated, septic **07** fevered, flushed, glowing, swollen **08** festered, feverish, infected, poisoned, reddened **11** carbuncular

## inflammable
**06** ardent **07** piceous **08** burnable **09** flammable, ignitable **10** tinder-like **11** combustible, combustious

## inflammation
**04** fire, heat, rash **07** burning, hotness, redness **08** eruption, soreness, swelling **09** festering, infection **10** irritation, tenderness **11** painfulness

*Inflammations include:*

**03** RSI, sty
**04** acne, boil, bubo, sore, stye
**05** croup, felon, mange
**06** ancome, angina, bunion, canker, otitis, quinsy, sepsis, thrush, ulitis
**07** abscess, colitis, empyema, pink-eye, sycosis, tylosis, whitlow
**08** bursitis, carditis, cynanche, cystitis, erythema, mastitis, myelitis, neuritis, orchitis, prunella, rhinitis, windburn
**09** arthritis, carbuncle, enteritis, fasciitis, frostbite, gastritis, glossitis, hepatitis, keratitis, laminitis, nephritis, phlebitis, retinitis, septicity, sinusitis, vaginitis
**10** bronchitis, cellulitis, dermatitis, erysipelas, gingivitis, intertrigo, laryngitis, meningitis, sore throat, tendinitis, tonsilitis, tracheitis, vasculitis
**11** mad staggers, myocarditis, peritonitis, pharyngitis, pneumonitis, prickly heat, shin splints, spondylitis, tennis elbow, thyroiditis, tonsillitis
**12** appendicitis, encephalitis, endocarditis, pancreatitis, pericarditis, vestibulitis
**13** jogger's nipple, labyrinthitis

**14** conjunctivitis, diverticulitis, housemaid's knee, sleepy staggers
**15** gastroenteritis

## inflammatory
**04** sore **05** fiery, rabid **06** septic, tender **07** painful, riotous, swollen **08** allergic, anarchic, inciting, infected **09** demagogic, explosive, festering, inflaming, insurgent, seditious **10** incendiary, incitative, phlogistic **11** instigative, intemperate, provocative **13** rabble-rousing

## inflate
**05** blast, bloat, boost, elate, raise, swell **06** aerate, blow up, dilate, expand, extend, hike up, puff up, pump up, push up, step up **07** amplify, augment, balloon, bombast, distend, enlarge, magnify, puff out **08** escalate, increase, overrate, sufflate **09** intensify, overstate **10** aggrandize, daisy-chain, exaggerate **11** fill with air **12** overestimate

## inflated
**04** tall **05** tumid **06** puffed, raised, turgid **07** bloated, blown up, bombast, bullate, dilated, pompous, swollen, upblown **08** extended, puffed up, rhetoric, tumefied **09** ballooned, bombastic, distended, escalated, high-blown, increased, overblown, puffed out **10** euphuistic, rhetorical **11** exaggerated, intensified, overweening **12** magniloquent, ostentatious **13** grandiloquent

## inflation
**04** rise **08** afflatus, cost push, increase **09** expansion, turgidity **10** escalation **11** inspiration **14** hyperinflation
• **measure of inflation   03** RPI

## inflection
**04** tone **05** pitch **06** ending, rhythm, stress **07** bending, cadence **08** emphasis **09** deviation **10** comparison, modulation **11** conjugation **12** change of tone

## inflexibility
**06** fixity **08** hardness, obduracy, rigidity **09** obstinacy, stiffness **10** stringency **12** immovability, immutability, incompliance, inelasticity, stubbornness, unsuppleness **13** immutableness, intransigence **14** intractability

## inflexible
**03** set **04** fast, firm, hard, iron, taut **05** fixed, rigid, solid, stern, stiff **06** ramrod, steely, strict **07** adamant, uniform **08** obdurate, pitiless, resolute, rigorous, standard, stubborn, unsupple **09** calcified, immovable, immutable, merciless, obstinate, stringent, tramlined, unbending, unelastic, unvarying **10** entrenched, implacable, intolerant, relentless, unbendable, unyielding **11** hard and fast, intractable **12** intransigent, standardized, unchangeable **13** dyed-in-the-wool **14** uncompromising **15** unaccommodating

## inflict
**03** hit, lay **04** deal, levy **05** apply, exact,

lay on, wreak **06** burden, impose, strike, thrust **07** deal out, deliver, enforce, mete out **10** administer, perpetrate

**infliction**
**05** worry **06** burden **07** penalty, trouble **08** delivery, exaction, wreaking **10** affliction, imposition, punishment **11** application, castigation, enforcement, retribution **12** chastisement, perpetration **14** administration

**influence**
**03** say **04** bias, drag, hand, hold, mark, move, pull, rule, stir, sway, toll **05** alter, clout, force, guide, impel, mould, power, reign, rouse, shape **06** affect, arouse, change, colour, direct, effect, impact, incite, induce, inflow, modify, prompt, weight **07** control, dispose, holding, impress, incline, mastery **08** ambiance, ambience, dominate, guidance, impact on, interest, motivate, persuade, pressure, prestige, standing **09** authority, condition, determine, direction, dominance, have clout, instigate, manoeuvre, operation, prejudice, pull wires, restraint, supremacy, transform **10** domination, importance, manipulate **11** carry weight, pull strings **12** wheel and deal **14** have an effect on **15** hold over a barrel
• **easily influenced 09** malleable
• **unlucky influence 04** jinx

**influential**
**06** moving, potent, strong **07** guiding, leading, telling, weighty **08** dominant, powerful **09** effective, important, inspiring, momentous **10** compelling, convincing, meaningful, persuasive **11** charismatic, controlling, far-reaching, heavyweight, prestigious, significant, substantial **12** instrumental **13** authoritative

**influx**
**04** flow, rush, salt **05** flood **06** inflow, inrush, stream **07** arrival, ingress **08** invasion **09** accession, avalanche, incursion, influence, intrusion **10** inundation, visitation **11** instreaming

**inform**
◊ *homophone indicator* **03** dob, rat **04** blab, blow, fink, leak, mark, nark, shop, sing, tell **05** avail, brand, brief, cue in, dob in, dob on, grass, peach, split, stamp **06** advise, betray, clue in, clue up, direct, fill in, impart, notify, relate, report, rumble, snitch, squeak, squeal, tell on, tip off, typify, wise up **07** animate, apprise, certify, educate, inspire, let know, partake, possess, put wise, resolve, sing out, stool on **08** acquaint, announce, deformed, denounce, formless, identify, instruct, permeate, unformed **09** advertise, advertize, enlighten, misshapen, recommend **10** give notice, illuminate, keep posted **11** blow the gaff, communicate, distinguish, incriminate

**12** characterize **13** spill the beans **15** put in the picture, sing like a canary

**informal**
**03** inf **04** easy, free **06** candid, casual, simple **07** invalid, natural, relaxed **08** everyday, familiar, friendly, unsolemn **09** easy-going, officious **10** colloquial, unofficial, vernacular **12** off the record **13** go-as-you-please, unceremonious, unpretentious

**informality**
**04** ease **07** freedom **08** cosiness **10** casualness, homeliness, relaxation, simplicity **11** familiarity, naturalness **12** congeniality **15** approachability

**informally**
**06** easily, freely, simply **08** casually **09** privately **10** familiarly, on the quiet **12** colloquially, off the record, unofficially **13** sans cérémonie **14** confidentially **15** unceremoniously, without ceremony

**information**
**02** SP **03** gen, inf, wit **04** bumf, data, dope, file, info, news, poop, word **05** clues, facts, input, score **06** advice, notice, record, report **07** counsel, details, dossier, good oil, low-down, message, tidings, witting **08** briefing, bulletin, databank, database, evidence, izvestia **09** hard stuff, izvestiya, knowledge **10** communiqué, propaganda **11** instruction, particulars **12** intelligence **13** enlightenment
• **measure of information 03** bit, nit **05** field, nepit, qubit **08** location **11** binary digit

**informative**
**05** newsy **06** chatty, useful **07** gossipy, helpful **08** edifying **09** revealing **11** educational, forthcoming, instructive **12** constructive, enlightening, illuminating **13** communicative

**informed**
**02** up **03** hep, hip **05** aware **06** au fait, expert, posted, primed, sussed, versed **07** abreast, briefed, clued-up, erudite, knowing, learned **08** educated, familiar, up to date, well-read **09** au courant, in the know, in the loop, up to speed **10** acquainted, conversant, well-versed **11** enlightened, intelligent, well-briefed **12** well-informed **13** authoritative, knowledgeable **14** well-researched

**informer**
**03** dog, rat, spy **04** fink, mole, nark, nose, stag **05** grass, Judas, shelf, sneak, snout **06** canary, dobber, finger, fizgig, moiser, singer, snitch **07** fizzgig, grasser, peacher, pentito, stoolie, traitor **08** animator, approver, betrayer, inspirer, promoter, snitcher, squeaker, squealer, tell-tale **09** informant, sycophant, whisperer **10** discoverer, supergrass **11** stool pigeon **13** whistle-blower

**infraction**
**06** breach **08** breaking **09** violation

**12** encroachment, infringement **13** contravention, transgression

**infrared**
**02** ir

**infrequent**
**04** rare **06** scanty, seldom, sparse **07** unusual **08** sporadic, uncommon **09** spasmodic **10** occasional **11** exceptional **12** intermittent, like gold dust

**infringe**
**04** defy **05** break, flout **06** ignore, invade **07** disobey, impinge, infract, intrude, violate **08** encroach, overstep, trespass **10** contravene, transgress

**infringement**
**06** breach, piracy **07** evasion **08** breaking, defiance, invasion, trespass **09** intrusion, violation **10** infraction **12** disobedience, encroachment **13** contravention, non-compliance, non-observance, transgression

**infuriate**
**03** bug, vex **04** miff, nark, rile **05** anger, annoy, get at, rouse **06** enrage, madden, needle, nettle, wind up **07** incense, inflame, provoke **08** drive mad, irritate **09** aggravate **10** antagonize, drive crazy, exasperate **12** drive bananas **13** make sparks fly **14** drive up the wall

**infuriated**
**03** mad **04** wild **05** angry, cross, irate, radge, ratty, spewy, vexed **06** choked, heated, miffed, narked, peeved, roused **07** crooked, enraged, flaming, furious, ropable, stroppy, uptight, violent **08** agitated, burned up, hairless, in a paddy, incensed, maddened, provoked, up in arms **09** in a lather, irritated, raving mad, seeing red, ticked off **10** aggravated, apoplectic, hopping mad **11** disgruntled, exasperated, fit to be tied **12** on the warpath **14** beside yourself

**infuriating**
**05** pesky **07** galling **08** annoying **09** maddening, provoking, thwarting, vexatious **10** irritating, unbearable **11** aggravating, frustrating, intolerable **12** exasperating

**infuse**
◊ *insertion indicator* **04** brew, draw, fill, mash, mask, pour, shed, soak **05** imbue, immit, steep **06** inject, instil **07** implant, inspire, pervade **08** impart to, saturate **09** inculcate, introduce **11** breathe into

**infusion**
**03** tea **04** brew, mate **06** saloop, tisane **07** malt tea, sage tea, soaking, uva-ursi **08** infusing, senna tea, steeping, tar water **09** sassafras **10** capillaire **11** inculcation, inspiration **12** implantation, instillation

**ingenious**
**03** sly **04** neat, wily **05** adept, natty, nifty, sharp, slick, smart, witty

**ingeniously**

06 adroit, astute, bright, clever, crafty, gifted, patent, pretty, quaint, shrewd 07 cunning, skilful 08 creative, masterly, original, talented 09 brilliant, inventive 10 artificial, innovative 11 imaginative, resourceful

**ingeniously**

07 niftily 08 cleverly 09 cunningly, skilfully 10 originally 11 brilliantly 13 imaginatively

**ingenuity**

03 wit 04 gift 05 flair, knack, skill 06 engine, genius, ingine 07 cunning, faculty, slyness 08 deftness 09 invention, nattiness, niftiness, sharpness, slickness 10 adroitness, astuteness, cleverness, shrewdness 11 originality, skilfulness 12 creativeness 13 ingeniousness, ingenuousness, inventiveness 14 innovativeness 15 resourcefulness

**ingenuous**

04 open 05 frank, naive, plain 06 candid, direct, honest, simple 07 artless, genuine, sincere 08 freeborn, innocent, trustful, trusting 09 guileless 10 forthright, honourable 11 transparent 12 single-minded 13 undissembling 14 unsophisticate 15 unsophisticated

**ingenuously**

06 openly, simply 07 naively, plainly 08 directly, honestly 09 artlessly, genuinely, sincerely 10 innocently, trustingly 11 guilelessly 12 without guile

**ingenuousness**

07 candour, honesty, naiveté, naivety 08 openness 09 frankness, innocence, unreserve 10 directness 11 artlessness, genuineness 12 trustfulness 13 guilelessness 14 forthrightness

**inglorious**

06 unsung 07 ignoble, obscure, unknown 08 infamous, shameful, unheroic 10 irrenowned, mortifying, unhonoured 11 blameworthy, disgraceful, humiliating, ignominious 12 disreputable, unsuccessful 13 discreditable, dishonourable

**ingrain**

03 dye, fix 04 root 05 embed, imbue, infix 06 instil 07 build in, engrain, implant, impress, imprint 08 entrench 09 establish, ingrained

**ingrained**

05 fixed 06 inborn, inbred, rooted 07 built-in, inbuilt 08 embedded, inherent 09 immovable, implanted, permanent 10 deep-rooted, deep-seated, entrenched 11 established 12 ineradicable 13 thorough-going

**ingratiate**

04 fawn, sook 05 crawl, creep, toady 06 cozy up, grovel 07 flatter 08 play up to, soft-soap, suck up to 09 get in with 10 cozy up with 11 curry favour 12 bow and scrape 15 butter someone up

**ingratiating**

05 suave, sweet 06 greasy, silken 07 fawning, servile 08 crawling, toadying, unctuous 10 flattering, obsequious 11 bootlicking, sycophantic, time-serving 13 smooth-tongued

**ingratitude**

13 thanklessness 14 ungraciousness, ungratefulness, unthankfulness

**ingredient**

◇ *anagram indicator* 04 base, item, part, unit 05 basis 06 bottom, factor 07 amalgam, element, feature 09 component 11 constituent
*See also* **salad**
• **little boy ingredients** 05 frogs, snips 06 snails 14 puppy dogs' tails
• **little girl ingredients** 05 sugar, spice 13 all things nice 14 everything nice

**ingress**

05 entry 06 access 08 entrance 09 admission 10 admittance 12 means of entry, right of entry 15 means of approach

**inhabit**

05 dwell, haunt 06 live in, occupy, people, settle, stay in 07 denizen, dwell in, possess 08 colonize, populate, reside in 14 make your home in

**inhabitable**

09 habitable 11 fit to live in

**inhabitant**

03 son 05 child, towny 06 inmate, lodger, native, tenant 07 citizen, denizen, dweller, settler 08 habitant, occupant, occupier, resident 09 indweller 10 residenter 12 residentiary

**inhabited**

04 held 07 lived-in, peopled, settled 08 occupied, populate, populous, tenanted 09 colonized, developed, populated, possessed

**inhalation**

05 whiff 06 breath 07 suction 08 inhaling 09 breathing, spiration 11 inspiration, respiration

**inhale**

04 draw, take, toot, tout 05 whiff 06 draw in, suck in 07 inspire, respire 09 breathe in, inbreathe

**inharmonious**

03 out 04 sour 05 harsh 06 atonal, patchy 07 grating, jarring, raucous 08 clashing, jangling, perverse, strident, tuneless 09 dissonant, unmusical, untuneful 10 discordant, out of place, unfriendly 11 cacophonous, conflicting, disagreeing, inconsonant, quarrelsome, unmelodious 12 antipathetic, incompatible, unharmonious 13 contradictory, unsympathetic 14 irreconcilable

**inherent**

05 basic 06 inborn, inbred, innate, native, natura 07 built-in, inbuilt,

natural, radical 08 immanent, resident 09 essential, ingrained, inherited, intrinsic 10 hereditary, inexistant, inexistent, in the blood, subsistent 11 fundamental, intrinsical

**inherently**

08 inwardly 09 basically, centrally 10 integrally 11 essentially 13 constituently, fundamentally, intrinsically

**inherit**

04 heir 06 assume, be left 07 receive, succeed 08 accede to, be heir to, come into, take over 09 succeed to 10 fall heir to 12 be bequeathed

**inheritance**

03 fee 06 legacy 07 bequest, descent 08 heredity, heritage 09 accession, endowment, patrimony 10 birthright, proportion, succession 13 primogeniture 15 secundogeniture

**inheritor**

04 heir 05 scion 06 co-heir, tanist 07 devisee, heiress, heritor, legatee 08 heritrix, legatary 09 heritress, recipient, successor 10 fellow-heir, inheritrix, next in line, substitute 11 beneficiary, inheritress 12 reversionary

**inhibit**

04 balk, curb, stem, stop 05 baulk, check 06 bridle, hamper, hinder, hold in, impede, rein in, stanch, thwart 07 prevent, repress, staunch 08 hold back, obstruct, restrain, restrict, slow down, suppress 09 constrain, frustrate 10 discourage 12 put a damper on, straitjacket 13 interfere with

**inhibited**

03 shy 06 wooden 07 guarded, subdued, uptight 08 reserved, reticent 09 repressed, withdrawn 10 frustrated, restrained 11 constrained, embarrassed, introverted 13 self-conscious 14 self-restrained

**inhibition**

03 bar 04 curb 05 check 06 hang-up 07 coyness, reserve, shyness 09 hampering, hindrance, restraint, reticence, thwarting 10 impediment, repression 11 frustration, obstruction, restriction 12 interference 13 embarrassment

**inhospitable**

04 bare, cold, cool, wild 05 aloof, bleak, empty 06 barren, lonely, unkind 07 hostile, uncivil 08 desolate, inimical 09 hostlesse 10 antisocial, forbidding, unfriendly, ungenerous, uninviting, unsociable, xenophobic 11 uncongenial, unreceptive, unwelcoming 12 unfavourable 13 uninhabitable, unneighbourly

**inhuman**

03 odd 05 cruel, harsh 06 animal, brutal, savage 07 bestial, strange, vicious 08 barbaric, fiendish, non-human, ruthless, sadistic 09 barbarous, merciless 10 diabolical 11 cold-blooded

## inhumane

**05** cruel, harsh **06** brutal, unkind
**07** callous **08** pitiless, uncaring
**09** heartless, unfeeling **11** cold-hearted,
dehumanized, hard-hearted,
insensitive **13** inconsiderate,
unsympathetic

## inhumanity

**06** sadism **07** cruelty **08** atrocity
**09** barbarism, barbarity, brutality
**10** savageness, unkindness
**11** brutishness, callousness,
viciousness **12** pitilessness,
ruthlessness **13** heartlessness **15** cold-
bloodedness, cold-heartedness, hard-
heartedness

## inimical

**07** adverse, harmful, hostile, hurtful,
noxious, opposed **08** contrary
**09** injurious, repugnant **10** intolerant,
pernicious, unfriendly **11** destructive,
disaffected, ill-disposed, unwelcoming
**12** antagonistic, antipathetic,
inhospitable, unfavourable

## inimitable

**06** unique **07** sublime, supreme
**08** peerless **09** matchless, nonpareil,
unmatched **10** consummate,
unequalled, unexampled, unrivalled
**11** distinctive, exceptional, superlative,
unsurpassed **12** incomparable,
unparalleled **13** unsurpassable

## iniquitous

**04** base, evil **05** awful **06** sinful, unjust,
wicked **07** heinous, immoral, vicious
**08** accursed, criminal, dreadful,
infamous **09** atrocious, nefarious,
reprobate **10** abominable, facinorous,
flagitious, outrageous **11** unrighteous
**13** reprehensible

## iniquity

**03** sin **04** evil, vice **05** crime, wrong
**06** infamy **07** misdeed, offence
**08** baseness, enormity **09** evil-doing,
injustice **10** sinfulness, wickedness,
wrongdoing **11** abomination,
heinousness, lawlessness,
ungodliness, viciousness
**13** transgression **15** unrighteousness

## initial

◇ *head selection indicator* **04** sign
**05** basic, early, first, prime **07** bloomer,
endorse, opening, primary
**08** inchoate, original, starting
**09** autograph, beginning, formative,
inaugural, inceptive, incipient
**10** commencing, elementary
**11** countersign **12** foundational,
introductory

## initially

◇ *head selection indicator* **05** first **07** at
first, firstly **08** first off **10** at the start, first
of all, originally **11** at the outset, to
begin with, to start with **14** at the
beginning

## initiate

**04** open, tiro **05** admit, begin, blood,
cause, crash, drill, enrol, enter, lanch,
let in, set up, start, teach, train, tutor
**06** accept, induce, induct, instil, invest,
launch, novice, ordain, prompt,

rookie, sign up **07** convert, entrant,
install, kick off, learner, pioneer,
receive, recruit, start up, trigger,
welcome **08** activate, beginner,
bejesuit, commence, instruct,
neophyte, newcomer **09** auspicate,
establish, greenhorn, inculcate,
instigate, institute, introduce, new
member, novitiate, originate,
proselyte, stimulate **10** bring about,
catechumen, inaugurate, tenderfoot
**11** get under way, probationer, set in
motion **13** sow the seeds of **15** get off
the ground, get things moving

## initiation

**05** debut, entry, start **07** baptism,
opening **08** entrance **09** admission,
beginning, enrolment, inception,
induction, launching, reception,
setting-up **10** admittance, enlistment,
ordination **11** investiture, origination
**12** inauguration, installation,
introduction **13** rite of passage
• **initiation rite 04** bora

## initiative

**02** go **04** lead, plan, push **05** drive
**06** action, energy, scheme **07** lead-off
**08** ambition, démarche, dynamism,
gumption, proposal **09** first move, first
step **10** creativity, enterprise, get-up-
and-go, suggestion **11** opening move,
originality **12** introductory
**13** inventiveness **14** innovativeness,
recommendation **15** resourcefulness

## inject

**03** add, hit, jab **04** bang, hype **05** bring,
immit, shoot, spike **06** hype up, infuse,
insert, instil **07** bring in, crank up, hit it
up, inspire, shoot up, skin-pop, syringe
**08** immunize, mainline **09** inoculate,
introduce, vaccinate

## injection

**03** fix, jab, jag **04** bang, dose, shot
**06** needle **07** skin-pop **08** addition,
infusion **09** insertion **10** hypodermic,
instilling **11** inoculation, vaccination
**12** immunization, introduction **13** a
shot in the arm

## injudicious

**04** rash **05** hasty **06** stupid, unwise
**07** foolish **08** ill-timed **09** ill-judged,
impolitic, imprudent, misguided **10** ill-
advised, incautious, indiscreet,
unthinking **11** inadvisable,
inexpedient, wrong-headed
**13** inconsiderate

## injunction

**05** order **06** dictum, ruling
**07** command, dictate, mandate,
precept **09** direction, directive
**10** admonition **11** conjunction,
exhortation, instruction

## injure

◇ *anagram indicator* **03** cut, get, mar
**04** bomb, burn, dere, harm, hurt, kill,
lame, maim, maul, ruin, skin **05** abuse,
annoy, break, chill, choke, deare,
misdo, rifle, scald, scath, shend, spoil,
touch, upset, waste, wound, wring,
wrong **06** accloy, blight, damage,
deface, deform, impair, mangle,
nobble, offend, poison, put out, scaith,

scathe, skaith, strain, weaken
**07** blemish, carve up, cripple, disable,
outrage, shoot up **08** aggrieve, fracture,
ill-treat, maltreat, mutilate, override
**09** disfigure, disoblige, humiliate,
overshoot, prejudice, undermine
**10** vitriolize **11** hospitalize **13** stab in
the back

## injured

◇ *anagram indicator* **03** bad **04** hurt,
lame, sore **05** upset **06** abused,
harmed, pained, put out, tender
**07** bruised, damaged, defamed,
grieved, misused, unhappy, unsound,
wounded, wronged **08** crippled,
disabled, insulted, maligned,
offended, weakened **09** aggrieved
**10** displeased, ill-treated, maltreated,
vulnerable **11** disgruntled, wither-
wrung **13** cut to the quick
• **easily injured 04** nice

## injurious

**03** bad **06** malign, noyous, unjust
**07** adverse, baneful, harmful, hurtful,
noxious, ruinous **08** damaging,
wrongful **09** insulting, libellous,
unhealthy **10** calumnious, corrupting,
defamatory, derogatory, iniquitous,
offenceful, pernicious, slanderous
**11** deleterious, destructive,
detrimental, mischievous, prejudicial,
unconducive **15** disadvantageous

## injury

**03** cut, ill, RSI **04** bale, dere, gash,
harm, hurt, maim, ruin, scar, sore,
teen, tene, tort **05** abuse, deare, teene,
wound, wrong **06** bruise, damage,
insult, lesion, scathe, trauma
**07** offence, offense, outrage
**08** abrasion, fracture, mischief,
violence **09** annoyance, contusion,
grievance, injustice, prejudice
**10** affliction, contrecoup, disservice,
impairment, laceration, mutilation,
traumatism **12** endamagement, ill-
treatment **13** disfigurement
• **after injury** ◇ *anagram indicator*

## injustice

**04** bias **05** abuse, wrong **06** injury
**07** offence, unright **08** inequity,
iniquity, unreason **09** disparity,
prejudice **10** inequality, oppression,
partiality, unfairness, unjustness
**11** favouritism **12** ill-treatment, one-
sidedness, partisanship
**14** discrimination

## inkling

**04** clue, hint, idea, sign **06** notion
**07** glimmer, pointer, umbrage, whisper
**08** allusion, faintest, foggiest, innuendo
**09** suspicion **10** glimmering,
indication, intimation, suggestion
**11** insinuation

## inky

◇ *anagram indicator* **03** jet **05** black,
drunk, sooty **08** dark-blue, jet-black
**09** coal-black **10** pitch-black
• **inky blotch 04** monk

## inlaid

**03** set **05** inset, lined, tiled **06** mosaic
**07** studded **08** enchased **09** empaestic,

enamelled **10** damascened
**11** tessellated

### inland
**05** inner **06** upland **07** central, midland,
refined **08** domestic, interior, internal,
landward **09** up-country **10** within land
**13** sophisticated

### inlay
**05** embed, inset **06** enamel, insert,
lining, mosaic, tiling **07** emblema,
setting **08** damaskin, studding
**09** damascene, damaskeen,
damasquin **10** damasceene
**12** tessellation

### inlet
**03** arm, bay **04** cove, hope **05** bight,
creek, fiord, firth, fjord, haven, sound
**06** infall, ingate **07** opening, passage
**08** entrance

### inmate
**03** zek **04** case **06** client, intern
**07** convict, patient **08** detainee,
prisoner **09** collegian **10** collegiate

### inmost
**04** deep **05** basic **06** buried, hidden,
secret **07** central, closest, dearest,
deepest, private **08** esoteric, intimate,
personal **09** essential, innermost
**12** confidential

### inn
**03** bar, pub **04** khan **05** abode, hotel,
house, howff, local, lodge, put up
**06** boozer, hostel, imaret, posada,
public, ryokan, shanty, tavern
**07** albergo, auberge, canteen, potshop
**08** bona fide, groggery, hostelry **09** free
house, gin palace, lush-house,
posthouse, roadhouse **11** caravansary,
change-house, public house
**12** caravansarai, caravanserai, halfway
house **13** watering-house

### innards
◇ *middle selection indicator* **04** guts
**05** works **06** entera, organs, umbles,
vitals **07** giblets, insides, viscera
**08** entrails, interior **09** mechanism
**10** intestines **13** inner workings
**14** internal organs

### innate
**06** inborn, inbred, native **07** connate,
natural **08** inherent, original
**09** inherited, intrinsic, intuitive
**10** congenital, hereditary, indigenous,
ingenerate **11** in one's blood,
instinctive

### innately
**08** inwardly **09** basically, centrally
**10** inherently, integrally **11** essentially
**13** constituently, fundamentally,
intrinsically

### inner
**04** deep **06** entire, hidden, inside,
inward, mental, middle, secret
**07** central, obscure, private **08** esoteric,
interior, internal, intimate, personal,
profound **09** concealed, emotional,
innermost, spiritual **10** restricted
**13** psychological

### innermost
**04** deep **05** basic **06** buried, hidden,

inmost, secret **07** central, closest,
dearest, deepest, private **08** esoteric,
intimate, personal **09** essential
**12** confidential

### innkeeper
**04** host **07** hostess, manager, padrone
**08** boniface, hotelier, landlady,
landlord, mine host, publican
**09** barkeeper, innholder **10** aubergiste,
proprietor **11** hotel-keeper
**12** restaurateur

### innocence
**06** purity, safety, virtue **07** honesty,
naivety **08** chastity, openness
**09** credulity, frankness, ignorance,
integrity, naiveness, virginity
**10** simplicity **11** artlessness, gullibility,
naturalness, playfulness, sinlessness
**12** harmlessness, inexperience,
spotlessness, trustfulness
**13** blamelessness, childlikeness,
faultlessness, guilelessness,
guiltlessness, impeccability,
inculpability, ingenuousness,
innocuousness, righteousness,
stainlessness, unworldliness
**14** immaculateness **15** inoffensiveness

### innocent
**04** babe, lamb, naif, open, pure, safe
**05** bland, canny, child, clear, frank,
fresh, green, idiot, naive, seely, white
**06** benign, chaste, gentle, honest,
infant, novice, simple **07** angelic,
anodyne, artless, ingénue, natural,
playful, sinless, upright **08** Arcadian,
beginner, dewy-eyed, dovelike,
gullible, harmless, imbecile, lamblike,
neophyte, sackless, spotless, trustful,
trusting, virginal, virtuous
**09** blameless, childlike, credulous,
crimeless, faultless, greenhorn,
guileless, guiltless, incorrupt,
ingenuous, innocuous, righteous,
stainless, unsullied, untainted,
unworldly **10** babe in arms,
immaculate, impeccable, inculpable,
tenderfoot **11** inoffensive, offenceless,
unblemished, uncorrupted
**12** prelapsarian, simple-minded,
squeaky clean, unsuspecting,
unsuspicious **13** inexperienced,
unblameworthy, unimpeachable
**14** above suspicion, irreproachable,
uncontaminated **15** unsophisticated

### innocently
**06** simply **07** naively **09** artlessly
**10** harmlessly, trustfully, trustingly
**11** blamelessly, credulously,
ingenuously, innocuously
**13** inoffensively, unoffendingly
**14** unsuspiciously

### innocuous
**04** mild, safe **05** bland **07** anodyne,
playful **08** harmless, innocent
**11** inoffensive, unobtrusive
**15** unobjectionable

### innovation
**06** change, novity, reform **07** newness,
novelty **08** novation, novelism,
progress **09** departure, neologism, new
method, variation **10** alteration, new

product **12** introduction
**13** modernization

### innovative
**03** new **04** bold **05** fresh **06** daring
**07** go-ahead **08** creative, original
**09** inventive, reforming **10** avant-garde,
Promethean **11** adventurous,
imaginative, progressive, resourceful
**12** enterprising, trail-blazing
**14** groundbreaking

### innovator
**06** source **07** creator, deviser, pioneer
**08** novelist, reformer **09** developer
**10** modernizer, originator
**11** progressive, trailblazer **12** fresh
thinker

### innuendo
**04** hint, slur **07** whisper **08** allusion,
overtone **09** aspersion **10** intimation,
suggestion **11** implication, insinuation

### innumerable
**04** many, tons **05** heaps, loads, piles
**06** dozens, masses, oodles, stacks,
untold **07** umpteen **08** hundreds,
infinite, millions, numerous
**09** countless, thousands
**10** numberless, unnumbered
**11** uncountable **12** incalculable

### inoculate
**05** graft, imbue **06** inject **07** protect
**08** immunize **09** safeguard, syphilize,
vaccinate, variolate **10** give a jab to
**11** give a shot to

### inoculation
**03** jab, jag **04** shot **09** injection
**10** protection **11** vaccination,
variolation **12** immunization

### inoffensive
**04** mild, safe **05** bland, quiet
**07** anodyne **08** harmless, innocent,
pleasant, retiring **09** innocuous,
peaceable **11** unassertive, unobtrusive
**15** unexceptionable, unobjectionable

### inoperable
**05** fatal **06** deadly **08** hopeless, terminal
**09** incurable **10** unhealable
**11** intractable, irremovable,
unremovable, untreatable

### inoperative
**04** bust, duff, idle **05** kaput, resty
**06** broken, futile, kaputt, silent, unused
**07** invalid, useless **08** nugatory
**09** defective, worthless **10** broken-
down, inadequate, not working, on the
blink, on the fritz, out of order,
unworkable **11** ineffective, ineffectual,
inefficient, inofficious, out of action
**12** not operative, out of service
**13** inefficacious, unserviceable **14** non-
functioning **15** out of commission

### inopportune
**06** clumsy **08** ill-timed, mistimed,
tactless, untimely **09** ill-chosen,
importune **10** unsuitable, wrong-timed
**11** importunate, out of season,
unfortunate **12** inauspicious,
inconvenient, infelicitous,
intempestive, unpropitious,
unseasonable **13** inappropriate

## inordinate

◊ *anagram indicator* **03** OTT **05** great, undue **07** extreme **08** vaulting **09** excessive **10** exorbitant, immoderate, outrageous, over the top **11** God-almighty, unwarranted **12** preposterous, unmeasurable, unreasonable, unrestrained, unrestricted **14** unconscionable

## inorganic

**04** dead **07** mineral **08** lifeless **09** inanimate **10** artificial, non-natural

## input

**04** code, data, load **05** enter, facts, key in, put in, store **06** feed in, insert **07** capture, details, figures, process **08** material **09** resources **10** statistics **11** information, particulars **12** contribution

## inquest

**07** hearing, inquiry **10** inspection, post-mortem **11** examination **13** investigation

## inquietude

**05** worry **06** unease **07** anxiety **08** disquiet **09** agitation, jumpiness **10** solicitude, uneasiness **11** disquietude, disturbance, nervousness **12** apprehension, discomposure, perturbation, restlessness

## inquire, enquire

**03** ask, see **04** call, quiz, scan, seek **05** probe, query, snoop, speer, speir, study **06** quaere, search **07** examine, explore, inquere, inspect **08** look into, question, research **10** scrutinize **11** interrogate, investigate

## inquirer, enquirer

**06** seeker **07** querist, student **08** explorer, searcher **10** inquisitor, questioner, researcher **12** interrogator, investigator

## inquiring, enquiring

**04** nosy **05** eager, nosey **06** prying **07** curious, probing, zetetic **08** doubtful **09** sceptical, searching, wondering **10** analytical, interested **11** inquisitive, questioning **13** interrogatory, investigative, investigatory **14** outward-looking

## inquiringly, enquiringly

**06** keenly **07** eagerly **09** curiously **11** wonderingly **12** analytically **13** inquisitively, questioningly

## inquiry, enquiry

**04** poll **05** probe, query, quest, study **06** demand, quaere, search, survey **07** hearing, inquest, inquire **08** etiology, question, scrutiny, sounding **09** aetiology **10** inspection **11** examination, exploration, inquisition, star chamber **12** perquisition **13** interrogation, interrogatory, investigation **14** reconnaissance

## inquisition

**07** inquest, inquiry **08** grilling, quizzing **09** witch hunt **10** Holy Office **11** examination, questioning

**13** interrogation, investigation **14** the third degree

## inquisitive

**04** nosy **05** nosey **06** prying, snoopy, spying **07** curious, peeping, peering, probing **08** snooping **09** inquiring, intrusive, searching **10** meddlesome **11** interfering, questioning **12** scrutinizing

## inquisitively

**06** keenly **07** eagerly **09** curiously **11** inquiringly, searchingly **12** meddlesomely **13** interferingly, questioningly

## inquisitor

**04** Deza **07** Ximenes **10** Torquemada

## inroad

**04** raid **05** foray, sally **06** attack, charge, infall, sortie **07** advance, assault **08** invasion, progress, trespass **09** incursion, intrusion, irruption, offensive, onslaught, sea breach **11** impingement, trespassing **12** encroachment

## insane

◊ *anagram indicator* **03** ape, fey, mad **04** bats, daft, gyte, loco, nuts, wild, wood, yond **05** barmy, batty, buggy, crazy, daffy, dippy, dotty, flaky, gonzo, loony, loopy, manic, nutty, potty, queer, wacko, wacky, wiggy **06** absurd, crazed, cuckoo, dement, fruity, maniac, mental, raving, red-mad, screwy, stupid **07** bananas, barking, berserk, bonkers, cracked, foolish, frantic, horn-mad, idiotic, lunatic, meshuga **08** bughouse, crackers, crackpot, demented, deranged, dingbats, doolally, frenetic, frenzied, maniacal, unhinged, unstable **09** delirious, disturbed, half-baked, lymphatic, psychotic, senseless, up the wall **10** bestraught, distracted, distraught, frantic-mad, off the wall, off your nut, out to lunch, ridiculous, stone-crazy, unbalanced **11** hare-brained, impractical, nonsensical, not all there, off the rails, off your head **12** crackbrained, mad as a hatter, off your chump, round the bend **13** off your rocker, of unsound mind, out of your head, out of your mind, out of your tree, round the twist **14** off your trolley, wrong in the head **15** non compos mentis, out of your senses

## insanely

◊ *anagram indicator* **05** madly **08** absurdly **09** foolishly **11** ludicrously, senselessly **12** outrageously, ridiculously

## insanitary

**04** foul **05** dirty **06** filthy, impure **07** dirtied, noisome, noxious, unclean **08** feculent, infected, infested, polluted **09** unhealthy **10** unhygienic, unsanitary **11** unhealthful, unsanitized **12** contaminated, insalubrious **13** disease-ridden

## insanity

◊ *anagram indicator* **05** craze, folie,

folly, mania **06** frenzy, lunacy **07** madness **08** daftness, delirium, dementia, neurosis **09** absurdity, craziness, psychosis, stupidity **10** insaneness **11** derangement, foolishness, hebephrenia, psychopathy **13** mental illness, senselessness **14** ridiculousness *See also* **lunacy**

## insatiable

**04** avid **06** greedy, hungry **07** craving **08** ravenous, sateless **09** rapacious, voracious **10** gluttonous, immoderate, inordinate **12** unappeasable, unquenchable **13** unsatisfiable

## inscribe

**03** cut **04** etch, mark, sign **05** brand, carve, enrol, enter, print, stamp, write **06** endoss, enlist, incise, record, scrive **07** address, engrave, impress, imprint, scrieve **08** dedicate, register **09** autograph

## inscription

**04** ogam **05** ogham, title, words **06** legend **07** caption, epitaph, etching, message, trigram, wording, writing **08** colophon, epigraph, kakemono **09** autograph, engraving, lettering, signature, tetragram **10** chronogram, dedication **11** insculpture **15** circumscription

## inscrutable

**04** deep **06** arcane, hidden, invis'd **07** cryptic **08** baffling, puzzling **09** enigmatic **10** mysterious, unreadable **12** impenetrable, inexplicable, unfathomable, unsearchable **13** unexplainable **14** unintelligible

## insect

*Insects include:*

**03** ant, bee, bug, fly, ked, nit **04** cleg, flea, frit, gnat, kade, moth, tick, wasp **05** aphid, aphis, cimex, emmet, louse, midge, ox-bot, roach, sedge **06** bedbug, beetle, bembex, blowie, capsid, cicada, cootie, drongo, earwig, gadfly, gru-gru, hornet, jigger, locust, maggot, mantis, may bug, mayfly, muscid, red ant, sawfly, thrips, tipula, tsetse, tzetse, tzetze, weevil **07** antlion, blowfly, buzzard, chigger, cornfly, cricket, deer fly, fire ant, gallfly, gold-bug, hive bee, June bug, katydid, lace bug, ladybug, lamp fly, pill bug, rose bug, sand fly, soldier, termite, wood ant **08** berry bug, birch fly, blackfly, bookworm, cornworm, crane fly, fruit fly, gall wasp, glow-worm, greenfly, honey bee, horse-fly, house-fly, hoverfly, lacewing, ladybird, mealy bug, mosquito, onion fly, sand wasp, sedge fly, snake fly, stink bug, white ant, whitefly, woodworm **09** amazon ant, ant weaver, bumblebee, butterfly, caddis fly, carpet bug, cochineal, cockroach, coffee bug, damselfly, doodlebug, dragonfly, golden-eye, humble-bee, leaf miner, mason wasp, mining bee, mud dauber, paper wasp, shield bug, squash bug, stable fly, tsetse fly, tzetse fly, tzetze fly, velvet ant, wax insect, woodlouse

**10** blister fly, bluebottle, boll weevil, bulldog ant, cabbage-fly, cockchafer, dolphin-fly, drosophila, frog-hopper, grapelouse, kissing bug, leaf-cutter, leaf insect, Pharaoh ant, pond skater, puriri moth, silverfish, vinegar-fly, web spinner

**11** backswimmer, biting louse, biting midge, bristletail, bush cricket, caterpillar, froth-hopper, grasshopper, greenbottle, harvest mite, harvest tick, honeypot ant, stick insect, umbrella-ant, vine-fretter, walking leaf, walking twig

**12** house cricket, lightning bug, walking stick, water boatman

**13** daddy longlegs, diamond-beetle, leatherjacket, praying insect, praying mantis, water measurer, water scorpion

*See also* **animal; beetle; butterfly; invertebrate; moth**

*Insect parts include:*

**03** eye, jaw, leg
**04** head, vein, wing
**06** cercus, feeler, scutum, thorax
**07** abdomen, antenna, cuticle, maxilla, ocellus, pedicel, segment
**08** antennae, forewing, hindwing, mandible, peduncle, spiracle, tympanum
**09** mouthpart, proboscis
**10** epicuticle, integument, ovipositor
**11** compound eye

• **study of insects** **03** ent
**10** entomology

## insecticide

*Insecticides include:*

**02** Bt
**03** BHC, DDT
**05** timbó, zineb
**06** aldrin, derris
**07** cinerin, safrole
**08** camphene, carbaryl, chlordan, chromene, diazinon, dieldrin, flyspray, rotenone
**09** chlordane, Gammexane®, Malathion®, parathion, toxaphene
**10** carbofuran, dimethoate, Paris green, piperazine
**15** organophosphate

## insectivore

**04** mole, tody **05** shrew **06** agouta, desman, tanrec, tenrec, Tupaia
**08** hedgehog, serotine **09** solenodon, tree shrew **10** golden mole, otter shrew
**11** diamond bird, gnatcatcher
**13** elephant shrew

• **insectivorous plant** **06** sundew
**07** Dionaea, drosera **10** butterwort, sarracenia **11** gobe-mouches **12** pitcher plant, Venus flytrap **13** Venus's flytrap

## insecure

◇ *anagram indicator* **04** weak **05** frail, loose, shaky **06** afraid, flimsy, tickle, unsafe, unsure **07** anxious, exposed, fearful, nervous, worried **08** doubtful, hesitant, perilous, unstable, unsteady **09** dangerous, hazardous, unassured, uncertain, unguarded **10** precarious, vulnerable **11** defenceless, unprotected **12** apprehensive, open to attack

## insecurity

**04** fear **05** peril, worry **06** danger, hazard **07** anxiety **08** unsafety, weakness **09** frailness, shakiness
**10** flimsiness, uneasiness, unsafeness, unsureness **11** instability, nervousness, uncertainty **12** apprehension, unsteadiness **13** vulnerability
**14** precariousness **15** defencelessness

## insensate

**04** deaf, numb **05** blind **07** unaware **08** comatose, ignorant **09** inanimate, oblivious, senseless, unfeeling, unmindful **10** insensible, insentient **11** unconscious **12** unresponsive **13** anaesthetized

## insensible

**03** out **04** cold, deaf, dull, hard, numb **05** aloof, blind, faint **06** marble, slight, stupid, wooden, zonked **07** callous, distant, unaware, unmoved **08** comatose, detached, ignorant **09** oblivious, senseless, unfeeling, unmindful, untouched **10** insentient, iron-witted, knocked out, unaffected, unapparent **11** emotionless, hard-hearted, insensitive, unconscious **12** undetectable, unresponsive **13** anaesthetized, imperceptible, indiscernible **14** dead to the world, out for the count

## insensitive

**04** dead, hard, iron **05** crass, tough **06** immune, obtuse **07** callous, unmoved **08** hardened, tactless, uncaring **09** anomalous, heartless, impassive, oblivious, resistant, unfeeling, untouched **10** hypalgesic, impervious, unaffected **11** hard-hearted, indifferent, thoughtless, unconcerned **12** case-hardened, impenetrable, thick-skinned, unresponsive **13** unsusceptible, unsympathetic **14** pachydermatous

## insensitivity

**08** hardness, hypalgia, immunity **09** bluntness, crassness, toughness, unconcern **10** crassitude, hypalgesia, obtuseness, resistance **11** callousness **12** indifference, tactlessness **14** hard-headedness, imperviousness **15** hard-heartedness, impenetrability

## inseparable

**05** bosom, close **07** devoted **08** constant, intimate **10** individual **11** individuate, indivisible, undividable **12** indissoluble, inextricable

## inseparably

**05** as one **06** firmly **07** closely **08** arm in arm, together **10** hand in hand, intimately **11** indivisibly **12** indissolubly, inextricably

## insert

**03** cue, put, set **04** sink **05** embed, enter, immit, infix, inlay, inset, let in, place, plant, press, put in, stick **06** notice, push in, slip in **07** enchase, enclose, engraft, implant, ingraft, slide in, stick in **08** addition, circular, intromit, thrust in **09** enclosure, insertion, interject, interpose, introduce **10** interleave, supplement **11** intercalate, interpolate **13** advertisement

## insertion

**05** entry, inset, miter, mitre **06** insert **07** implant **08** addition **09** inclusion, intrusion **10** supplement **12** introduction, intromission **13** intercalation, interpolation

## inside

◇ *hidden indicator* ◇ *insertion indicator* **04** core, guts **05** belly, heart, inner **06** centre, indoor, inward, middle, secret, within **07** content, indoors, private **08** contents, hush-hush, implicit, inherent, interior, internal, intromit, inwardly, reserved, secretly **09** innermost, intrinsic, privately **10** classified, internally, restricted **12** confidential

## insider

**06** member **07** one of us **08** co-worker **11** participant, staff member **15** one of the in-crowd

## insides

**04** guts **05** belly, tummy **06** bowels, organs **07** abdomen, giblets, innards, stomach, viscera **09** entrails **10** intestines **14** internal organs

## insidious

**03** sly **04** wily **06** artful, crafty, sneaky, subtle, tricky **07** cunning, devious, furtive **08** sneaking, stealthy **09** cautelous, deceitful, deceptive, dishonest, insincere **10** perfidious **11** duplicitous, treacherous **13** Machiavellian, surreptitious

## insidiously

**05** slyly **06** subtly **09** cunningly

## insight

**05** grasp, sight **06** acumen, aperçu, vision, wisdom **08** epiphany **09** awareness, furniture, intuition, judgement, knowledge, sharpness **10** perception, shrewdness **11** discernment, observation, penetration, realization, sensitivity **12** apprehension, intelligence, perspicacity **13** comprehension, enlightenment, understanding

## insightful

**04** wise **05** acute, sharp **06** astute, seeing, shrewd **07** prudent **08** inscient **09** observant, sagacious **10** discerning, perceptive, percipient **11** intelligent, penetrating **13** knowledgeable, perspicacious, understanding

## insignia
**03** tab **04** arms, logo, mark, sign, type **05** armor, badge, brand, clasp, crest, eagle, order, signs **06** armour, emblem, ensign, ribbon, symbol **07** regalia **08** hallmark **09** hallmarks, medallion, trademark **10** coat of arms, decoration **11** cap and bells

## insignificance
**08** meanness, tininess **09** pettiness, smallness **10** paltriness, triviality **11** irrelevance, nothingness **12** nugatoriness, unimportance **13** immateriality, inconsequence, negligibility, worthlessness **15** meaninglessness

## insignificant
**04** tiny **05** C-list, dinky, minor, petit, petty, scrub, small **06** insect, meagre, paltry, puisne, puisny, scanty, slight **07** minimal, nebbich, scrubby, trivial **08** marginal, nugatory, piddling, trifling **09** jerkwater, no-account, small beer, small-time **10** fractional, immaterial, irrelevant, negligible, peripheral **11** meaningless, Mickey Mouse, unimportant **12** cutting no ice, non-essential **13** hole-in-the-wall, insubstantial, no great shakes **14** inconsiderable **15** inconsequential

## insincere
**04** jive **05** false, lying **06** double, forked, hollow, phoney, untrue **07** devious, feigned, lip-deep **08** disloyal, rhetoric, two-faced **09** deceitful, dishonest, faithless, mouth-made, pretended, underhand, unnatural **10** backhanded, mendacious, perfidious, rhetorical, unfaithful, untruthful **11** dissembling, duplicitous, pretentious, treacherous **12** disingenuous, hypocritical, meretricious **13** double-dealing

## insincerely
**07** falsely **09** deviously **10** disloyally **11** deceitfully, dishonestly **12** perfidiously, unfaithfully, untruthfully **13** duplicitously, pretentiously, treacherously **14** hypocritically

## insincerity
**04** cant **06** humbug **07** falsity, perfidy **08** bad faith, pretence **09** duplicity, falseness, hypocrisy, mendacity, phoniness **10** dishonesty, hollowness, lip service **11** deviousness, dissembling, evasiveness **13** artificiality, deceitfulness, dissimulation, faithlessness **14** untruthfulness **15** pretentiousness

## insinuate
**04** hint, wind **05** get at, imply **06** allude **07** mention, suggest, whisper **08** indicate, innuendo, intimate, work into **10** serpentine
• **insinuate yourself 04** work, worm **05** crawl, sidle **07** wriggle **09** brown-nose, get in with **10** ingratiate **11** curry favour

## insinuation
**04** hint, slur **05** slant **08** allusion, innuendo **09** aspersion, inference

**10** insinuendo, intimation, suggestion **11** implication **12** introduction

## insipid
**03** dry **04** blah, drab, dull, fade, flat, lash, tame, thin, weak **05** banal, bland, trite, vapid, wersh **06** boring, pallid, watery **07** anaemic, insulse, mawkish, missish, shilpit, tedious, wearish **08** lifeless, waterish **09** inanimate, sapidless, tasteless, unsavoury, wearisome **10** albuminous, colourless, monotonous, spiritless, wishy-washy **11** flavourless **12** milk-and-water, unappetizing **13** characterless, unimaginative, uninteresting

## insist
**03** vow **04** aver, hold, urge **05** claim, press, swear **06** assert, demand, harp on, repeat, strain, stress, threap **07** contend, declare, dwell on, entreat, persist, require, stand on **08** maintain **09** emphasize, reiterate, stand firm, stipulate **10** hang out for **11** state firmly, stick out for **12** ask for firmly **15** put your foot down, stand your ground, stick to your guns

## insistence
**05** claim **06** demand, stress, urging **08** emphasis, entreaty, firmness **09** assertion **10** contention, repetition, resolution **11** declaration, exhortation, maintenance, persistence, reiteration, requirement **13** assertiveness, determination

## insistent
**06** dogged, urgent **07** adamant, exigent **08** constant, emphatic, forceful, pressing, repeated, resolute **09** assertive, demanding, incessant, tenacious **10** determined, inexorable, persistent, relentless, unyielding **11** importunate, persevering, unrelenting, unremitting

## insobriety
**09** inebriety, tipsiness **10** crapulence **11** drunkenness, inebriation **12** hard drinking, intemperance, intoxication

## insolence
**03** gum, lip **04** gall, sass **05** abuse, cheek, mouth, nerve, sauce, snash **06** hubris, hybris **07** insults **08** attitude, audacity, boldness, chutzpah, defiance, pertness, rudeness **09** arrogance, contumely, impudence, sauciness **10** cheekiness, disrespect, effrontery, incivility **11** forwardness, presumption **12** impertinence **13** offensiveness **15** insubordination

## insolent
**04** bold, rude **05** bardy, brash, fresh, lairy, lippy, sassy, saucy **06** brazen, cheeky, mouthy, wanton **07** abusive, defiant, forward **08** arrogant, impudent **09** audacious, insulting **10** purse-proud **11** ill-mannered, impertinent **12** contemptuous, contumelious, presumptuous **13** disrespectful, insubordinate

## insoluble
**07** complex, obscure **08** baffling, involved, puzzling **09** enigmatic,

intricate **10** mysterious, mystifying, perplexing, unsolvable **11** inscrutable **12** impenetrable, inexplicable, unfathomable **13** unexplainable **14** indecipherable

## insolvency
**04** ruin **07** default, failure **10** bankruptcy **11** destitution, liquidation, queer street **12** indebtedness **13** impecuniosity, pennilessness **14** impoverishment

## insolvent
**04** bust **05** broke, skint **06** failed, in debt, ruined **07** boracic **08** bankrupt, in the red, strapped **09** destitute, gone under, penniless **10** liquidated, on the rocks **11** impecunious **12** impoverished **13** gone to the wall, in queer street **14** on your beam ends **15** strapped for cash

## insomnia
**11** wakefulness **12** insomnolence, restlessness **13** sleeplessness
• **insomnia drug 06** Ativan® **07** Mogadon® **08** Rohypnol® **09** lorazepam, Temazepam **10** nitrazepam

## insouciance
**04** ease **08** airiness **09** flippancy, unconcern **10** breeziness, jauntiness **11** nonchalance **12** carefreeness, heedlessness, indifference

## insouciant
**04** airy **06** breezy, casual, jaunty **07** buoyant **08** carefree, flippant, heedless **09** apathetic, easy-going, unworried **10** nonchalant, untroubled **11** free and easy, indifferent, unconcerned **12** happy-go-lucky, light-hearted

## inspect
**03** vet **04** case, scan, tour, view **05** audit, check, study, visit **06** assess, go over, review, search, survey **07** examine, oversee, see over **08** appraise, check out, look into, look over, pore over **09** supervise **10** scrutinize **11** investigate, perlustrate, reconnoitre, superintend

## inspection
**04** scan, tour, view **05** audit, check, dekko, recce, study, visit **06** alnage, muster, review, search, survey **07** autopsy, check-up, inspect, rag-fair, vetting, vidimus **08** analysis, autopsia, look-over, once-over, overview, scrutiny **09** appraisal, Cook's tour, look-round **10** assessment **11** examination, perspective, supervision **12** tracheoscopy **13** investigation

## inspector
**06** conner, critic, exarch, keeker, tester, viewer **07** alnager, auditor, checker, officer, scanner, visitor **08** assessor, examiner, overseer, provedor, providor, reviewer, searcher, surveyor **09** appraiser, provedore **10** controller, proveditor, scrutineer, supervisor **11** proveditore **12** investigator **14** superintendent

## inspiration
**04** goad, hoop, hwyl, idea, muse, spur
**05** estro, whoop **06** breath, duende,
fillip, genius **07** insight **08** afflatus,
Aganippe, arousing, inflatus, infusion,
stimulus, stirring, taghairm **09** afflation,
awakening, brainwave, inflation,
influence, theosophy **10** brainstorm,
bright idea, creativity, enthusiasm,
incitement, motivation, revelation
**11** imagination, originality,
stimulation, theopneusty
**12** illumination **13** encouragement,
enlightenment, inventiveness **14** stroke
of genius

## inspirational
**09** emotional, inspiring, spiritual
**10** devotional, heartening, motivating,
suggestive **11** encouraging, influential,
instinctive **13** psychological

## inspire
**04** fire, goad, spur, stir **05** guide,
imbue, rouse **06** arouse, enamor,
excite, inform, infuse, inject, kindle,
prompt, thrill **07** animate, breathe,
embrave, enamour, enliven, enthral,
enthuse, hearten, impress, inflame,
produce, provoke, quicken, trigger
**08** energize, instruct, motivate, spark
off, touch off **09** encourage, galvanize,
infatuate, influence, instigate,
stimulate **10** bring about, exhilarate

## inspired
**05** vatic **08** afflated, creative,
daemonic, daimonic, dazzling,
exciting, splendid, talented, visioned
**09** brilliant, memorable, thrilling,
wonderful **10** impressive, marvellous,
remarkable, theopneust **11** enthralling,
exceptional, imaginative, outstanding,
superlative **12** theopneustic

## inspiring
**06** moving **07** rousing **08** exciting,
stirring **09** affecting, memorable,
thrilling, uplifting **10** heartening,
impressive **11** encouraging,
enthralling, interesting, stimulating
**12** enthusiastic, exhilarating,
invigorating **13** inspirational

## inspirit
**04** fire, move **05** cheer, nerve, rouse
**06** incite **07** animate, enliven, gladden,
hearten, inspire, quicken, refresh
**08** embolden **09** encourage, galvanize,
stimulate **10** exhilarate, invigorate
**12** reinvigorate

## instability
**07** frailty **08** wavering **09** lubricity,
shakiness **10** fickleness, fitfulness,
flimsiness, insecurity, transience,
unsafeness, volatility **11** flightiness,
fluctuation, inconstancy, oscillation,
temperament, uncertainty,
unsoundness, vacillation, variability
**12** impermanence, irresolution,
unsteadiness **13** unreliability
**14** capriciousness, changeableness,
precariousness

## install
**03** fit, fix, lay, put **04** site **05** lodge,
place, plant, put in, set up, state
**06** induct, insert, invest, locate, nestle,

ordain, settle **07** instate, plumb in,
situate, station, swear in **08** ensconce,
enthrone, entrench, position
**09** establish, institute, introduce
**10** consecrate, inaugurate

## installation
**02** HQ **04** base, camp, post, site
**05** plant **06** centre, siting, system
**07** artwork, fitting, placing, station
**08** location **09** apparatus, equipment,
induction, insertion, machinery
**10** ordination, settlement, swearing-in
**11** instatement, investiture, positioning
**12** consecration, headquarters,
inauguration **13** establishment

## instalment
**02** HP **04** call, heft, part **06** lesson
**07** chapter, episode, payment, portion,
section, segment, tranche **08** division,
rhapsody **09** repayment **11** part
payment **12** continuation, hire
purchase **13** the never-never

## instance
**04** case, cite, give, name, suit **05** cause,
proof, quote **06** adduce, behest,
demand, motive, sample, urging
**07** example, mention, point to,
process, refer to, request, specify
**08** citation, entreaty, evidence,
occasion, pressure **09** exemplify,
prompting **10** incitement, initiative,
insistence, occurrence, particular
**11** case in point, exhortation,
importunity, instigation **12** illustration,
solicitation **15** exemplification
• **for instance** **02** as, eg, zB **10** for
example **13** exempli gratia

## instant
**02** mo **03** sec **04** fast, jiff, tick, time,
whip **05** flash, jiffy, quick, rapid, swift,
trice **06** direct, minute, moment,
prompt, second, urgent **07** current,
present **08** juncture, occasion
**09** immediate, on-the-spot, twinkling
**10** ready mixed **11** convenience, pre-
prepared, split second **12** unhesitating
**13** instantaneous **14** easily prepared
**15** quickly prepared

## instantaneous
**05** rapid **06** direct, prompt, snappy,
sudden **07** instant **09** immediate,
momentary, on-the-spot
**12** momentaneous, unhesitating

## instantaneously
**03** pdq **04** anon, ASAP **06** at once,
pronto **07** quickly, rapidly **08** directly,
in a jiffy, promptly, speedily
**09** forthwith, instantly, on the spot,
right away **11** immediately **12** straight
away, there and then, without delay
**14** unhesitatingly

## instantly
**03** now, pdq **04** ASAP **06** at once,
pronto **08** directly, in a jiffy, on the dot
**09** forthwith, like a shot, on the spot,
right away, zealously **11** immediately
**12** straight away, there and then,
without delay **13** importunately
**15** instantaneously

## instead
**04** else **06** rather **10** by contrast, in

contrast, preferably, substitute
**11** replacement **13** alternatively **15** as
an alternative
• **instead of** **04** vice **07** against **08** in
lieu of **09** in place of **10** in favour of, on
behalf of, rather than **11** as opposed to
**12** in contrast to **14** in preference to

## instigate
**04** goad, move, prod, spur, urge
**05** begin, cause, impel, press, rouse,
set on, spark, start **06** excite, foment,
incite, induce, kindle, prompt, stir up,
whip up **07** inspire, provoke
**08** generate, initiate, persuade
**09** encourage, influence, stimulate
**10** bring about

## instigation
**06** behest, motion, urging **07** bidding
**09** incentive, prompting, prompture
**10** incitement, inducement, initiation,
initiative, insistence **11** fomentation
**13** encouragement

## instigator
**04** goad, spur **06** leader **07** inciter
**08** agitator, fomenter, incensor,
provoker, putter-on **09** firebrand,
initiator, motivator **10** incendiary,
prime mover, ringleader
**12** troublemaker **13** mischief-maker

## instil
**05** drill, imbue, plant, teach **06** infuse,
inject **07** breathe, din into, implant,
impress, ingrain **09** inculcate,
insinuate, introduce, transfuse

## instinct
**04** bent, feel, gift, urge **05** drive, flair,
hunch, knack, moved **06** imbued,
nature, talent **07** ability, charged,
faculty, feeling, impulse, incited
**08** animated, aptitude, tendency
**09** intuition, principle **10** gut feeling,
instigated, sixth sense **11** gut reaction
**14** inbred response, predisposition
**15** natural response

## instinctive
**03** gut **06** inborn, innate, native, reflex
**07** natural **08** inherent, knee-jerk,
primeval, untaught, visceral
**09** automatic, immediate, impulsive,
intuitive, primaeval, unlearned
**10** mechanical, unthinking
**11** involuntary, spontaneous
**13** unintentional **14** seat-of-the-pants,
unpremeditated

## instinctively
**09** naturally **11** intuitively
**12** mechanically, unthinkingly
**13** automatically, involuntarily,
spontaneously **15** without thinking

## institute
**01** I **03** law **04** Inst, open, rule **05** begin,
enact, found, order, raise, set up, start
**06** create, custom, decree, induct,
invest, launch, ordain, school
**07** academy, appoint, college,
develop, educate, install, precept
**08** commence, initiate, organize,
seminary **09** establish, introduce,
originate, principle **10** foundation,
inaugurate, regulation **11** institution,

put in motion, set in motion
**12** conservatory, organization

*Institutes include:*

**02** IA, IM, WI
**03** BFI, CGI, CIB, CMI, EMI, ICA, MIT
**04** NICE, RIBA, RNIB, RNID, RTPI
**05** C and G, UMIST, UWIST
**07** Caltech

### institution
**03** law **04** club, home, rule **05** guild, usage **06** center, centre, custom, league, ritual, system **07** college, concern, society **08** creation, founding, hospital, practice, starting **09** enactment, formation, inception, institute, sacred cow, setting-up, tradition **10** convention, foundation, initiation **11** association, corporation **12** commencement, installation, introduction, organization **13** establishment

### institutional
**03** set **04** cold, drab, dull **06** dreary, formal **07** orderly, routine, uniform **08** accepted, clinical, orthodox **09** cheerless, customary, organized **10** forbidding, impersonal, methodical, monotonous, regimented, systematic **11** established, ritualistic, uninspiring, unwelcoming **12** bureaucratic, conventional **13** establishment

### instruct
**03** bid **04** shew, show, tell, warn **05** brief, coach, drill, guide, order, prime, study, teach, train, tutor **06** advise, charge, demand, direct, enjoin, gospel, ground, inform, lesson, notify, school, taught **07** call out, command, counsel, educate, inspire, lecture, mandate, prepare, require **09** catechize, enlighten, make known **10** discipline **12** indoctrinate

### instruction
**03** key **05** brief, order, rules **06** advice, charge, legend, lesson, manual, orders, ruling **07** classes, command, lecture, lessons, mandate, priming, telling, tuition **08** briefing, coaching, drilling, guidance, handbook, lectures, pedagogy, teaching, training, tutelage, tutoring **09** direction, directive, education, grounding, knowledge, schooling **10** directions, discipline, guidelines, injunction **11** book of words, edification, information, inspiration, preparation, requirement **13** enlightenment **14** indoctrination, recommendation **15** recommendations

### instructive
**06** useful **07** helpful **08** didactic, edifying, teaching **09** doctrinal, educative, improving, uplifting **10** didactical **11** educational, informative, informatory **12** enlightening, illuminating

### instructor
**04** guru **05** coach, guide, swami, tutor **06** master, mentor, sensei **07** adviser, teacher, trainer **08** educator, exponent, lecturer, mistress **09** maharishi,

pedagogue, preceptor **10** counsellor, instituter, institutor **11** preceptress **12** demonstrator

### instrument
**03** act, way **04** mean, rule, tool **05** agent, cause, gauge, gismo, means, meter, organ **06** agency, device, factor, gadget, medium **07** channel, measure, utensil, vehicle **09** apparatus, appliance, guideline, implement, indicator, mechanism, yardstick **11** contraption, contrivance

*See also* **measurement; optical; scientific; torture; writing**

*Musical instruments include:*

**02** gu
**03** gju, gue, lur, oud, sax, saz, uke, zel
**04** alto, bass, bell, dhol, drum, erhu, fife, gong, harp, horn, kora, koto, lure, lute, lyre, Moog®, oboe, pipe, rote, sang, tuba, vibe, vina, viol, zeze
**05** Amati, banjo, bells, bongo, bugle, cello, chime, conga, crwth, daiko, flute, gusla, gusle, gusli, hi-hat, kaval, kazoo, mbira, naker, organ, piano, pipes, rebec, shalm, shawm, sitar, strad, tabla, tabor, taiko, vibes, viola, zanze, zirna, zurna
**06** atabal, carnyx, cither, citole, cornet, cymbal, Fender, fiddle, guitar, rattle, spinet, tabret, tam-tam, timbal, tom-tom, tum-tum, tymbal, tympan, vielle, violin, zither
**07** alphorn, alto sax, bagpipe, bandore, bandura, baryton, bassoon, bazouki, bodhran, buccina, celeste, cembalo, cithara, cithern, cittern, clarion, clavier, cowbell, hautboy, lyricon, maracas, marimba, mridang, ocarina, pandora, Pianola®, piccolo, sackbut, sambuca, sarangi, saxhorn, serpent, sistrum, tambour, tambura, theorbo, timbrel, timpani, timpano, trumpet, tympani, tympano, ukulele, vihuela, whistle, zithern
**08** angklung, autoharp, bagpipes, barytone, bass drum, bass viol, bouzouki, calliope, carillon, charango, cimbalom, clappers, clarinet, clarsach, cornpipe, crumhorn, dulcimer, handbell, hornpipe, humstrum, jew's harp, keyboard, mandolin, manzello, melodeon, mridanga, Pan-pipes, polyphon, post horn, psaltery, recorder, side-drum, spinette, Steinway, surbahar, tamboura, tenor sax, theramin, theremin, timbales, triangle, trombone, tympanum, virginal, vocalion, zambomba
**09** accordion, alpenhorn, balalaika, banjolele, bugle-horn, castanets, chime bars, decachord, Dulcitone®, euphonium, flageolet, harmonica,

harmonium, Mellotron®, mridangam, nose flute, polyphone, saxophone, snare-drum, tenor-drum, vibraharp, wood block, Wurlitzer®, xylophone
**10** arpeggione, bass guitar, bird-scarer, bongo-drums, bullroarer, clavichord, concertina, cor anglais, didgeridoo, double bass, eolian harp, flugelhorn, French horn, grand piano, hurdy-gurdy, kettle-drum, mouth organ, oboe d'amore, pentachord, pianoforte, sousaphone, squeeze-box, tambourine, thumb piano, tin whistle, vibraphone
**11** aeolian harp, barrel organ, harpsichord, phonofiddle, player-piano, sleigh bells, synthesizer, viola d'amore, violoncello, wobble board
**12** glockenspiel, harmonichord, penny whistle, stock and horn, Stradivarius, tubular bells, viola da gamba
**13** contra-bassoon, Ondes Martenot, panharmonicon, slide trombone, Swanee whistle
**14** acoustic guitar, electric guitar, jingling Johnny
**15** Moog synthesizer®, wind synthesizer

### instrumental
**06** active, useful **07** helpful, organic **08** involved **09** auxiliary, conducive, important **10** subsidiary **11** implemental, influential, ministerial, significant, subservient **12** contributory

### insubordinate
**04** rude **06** unruly **07** defiant, riotous **08** impudent, mutinous **09** insurgent, seditious, turbulent **10** disorderly, rebellious, refractory **11** disobedient, impertinent **12** contumacious, recalcitrant, ungovernable **13** undisciplined

### insubordination
**06** mutiny, revolt **08** defiance, rudeness, sedition **09** impudence, rebellion **11** riotousness **12** disobedience, impertinence, indiscipline, insurrection, mutinousness **13** recalcitrance **15** ungovernability

### insubstantial
**04** idle, poor, thin, weak **05** false, frail, wispy **06** bubble, feeble, flimsy, frothy, meagre, slight, unreal, yeasty **07** tenuous **08** fanciful, illusory, tenuious, vaporous **09** airy-fairy, cardboard, ephemeral, imaginary, moonshine **10** chimerical, immaterial, intangible **11** incorporeal

### insufferable
**08** dreadful, shocking **09** loathsome, repugnant, revolting **10** detestable, impossible, outrageous, unbearable **11** intolerable, unendurable **13** insupportable, too much to bear

**insufferably**
**0** impossibly, shockingly, unbearably
**1** intolerably, repugnantly
**2** outrageously

**insufficiency**
**4** lack, need, want **06** dearth
**7** paucity, poverty **08** scarcity, shortage **10** deficiency, inadequacy
**1** short supply **14** inadequateness

**insufficient**
**5** scant, short **06** meagre, scanty, scarce, sparse **07** lacking, wanting
**9** defective, deficient, not enough
**0** inadequate **13** in short supply

**insular**
**5** aloof, petty **06** biased, closed, cut off, narrow, remote **07** bigoted, limited
**8** detached, isolated, separate, solitary **09** blinkered, insulated, parochial, withdrawn **10** prejudiced,·provincial, restricted, xenophobic
**2** narrow-minded, short-sighted
**3** inward-looking

**insularity**
**4** bias **07** bigotry **09** isolation, pettiness, prejudice **10** detachment, xenophobia **12** parochiality, solitariness **13** parochialness

**insulate**
**3** lag, pad **04** wrap **05** cover
**6** cocoon, cut off, detach, encase, shield **07** cushion, envelop, exclude, isolate, protect, shelter **08** separate
**9** segregate, sequester

**insulation**
**5** cover **06** shield **07** lagging, padding, shelter **08** asbestos, cladding, covering, sleeving, stuffing, wrapping
**9** cocooning, corkboard, exclusion, firebrefill, foam glass, isolation
**0** cushioning, detachment, fiberglass, fibreglass, protection, separation, Thermalite® **11** segregation **12** foam plastics **13** building paper, double-glazing, triple glazing **14** foamed plastics **15** contour feathers, vulcanized fibre

**insulator**

*insulators include:*

**3** lag
**4** mica
**7** bushing, tea cosy
**8** rock wool
**9** Pink Batts®
**0** dielectric
**1** vermiculite
**2** friction tape
**4** insulating tape, Willesden paper

**insult**
**4** bait, barb, gibe, hurt, slur, snub
**5** abuse, libel, taunt, wound
**6** damage, impugn, injure, injury, malign, mud pie, offend, rebuff, revile, slight, verbal **07** affront, mortify, offence, outrage, put-down, slander, traduce, trample, triumph **08** derogate, depriefe, ridicule, rudeness **09** call names, contumely, disparage, indignity, insolence **10** aspersions, calumniate, defamation, fling mud at,

insultment, revilement, sling mud at, throw mud at **11** triumph over
**13** disparagement, slap in the face
**14** fly in the face of, kick in the teeth

**insulting**
**04** rude **07** abusive, hurtful **08** insolent, reviling **09** degrading, injurious, libellous, offensive, slighting
**10** affronting, derogatory, outrageous, scurrilous, slanderous **11** disparaging, opprobrious **12** contemptuous, contumelious

**insuperable**
**10** formidable, impassable, invincible
**12** overwhelming, unassailable
**13** unconquerable **14** insurmountable

**insupportable**
**07** hateful **08** dreadful **09** loathsome, untenable **10** detestable, unbearable
**11** intolerable, unendurable
**12** indefensible, insufferable, irresistible, unacceptable
**13** unjustifiable

**insuppressible**
**06** lively, unruly **09** energetic, go-getting **11** unstoppable, unsubduable
**12** incorrigible, obstreperous, ungovernable **13** irrepressible
**14** uncontrollable

**insurance**
**02** NI **03** ins **05** cover **06** policy, surety
**07** premium **08** security, warranty
**09** assurance, guarantee, indemnity, provision, safeguard **10** protection
**15** indemnification

**insure**
**05** cover **06** assure, ensure **07** protect, warrant **08** reinsure **09** guarantee, indemnify **10** overinsure, underwrite

**insurer**
**07** assurer **09** abandonee, guarantor, protector, warrantor **11** indemnifier, underwriter

**insurgence**
**04** coup, riot **06** mutiny, putsch, revolt, rising **08** sedition, uprising **09** coup d'état, rebellion **10** revolution
**12** insurrection

**insurgent**
**05** pandy, rebel **06** rioter, rising
**07** riotous **08** Camisard, mutineer, mutinous, partisan, resister, revolted, revolter **09** revolting, seditious
**10** rebellious **11** disobedient, seditionist **13** insubordinate, revolutionary, revolutionist
**15** insurrectionary, insurrectionist

**insurmountable**
**08** hopeless **10** impossible, invincible
**11** insuperable **12** overwhelming, unassailable **13** unconquerable

**insurrection**
**04** coup, riot **06** mutiny, putsch, revolt, rising, uproar **08** sedition, uprising
**09** coup d'état, rebellion
**10** insurgence, insurgency, revolution

**intact**
**05** sound, whole **06** entire, unhurt
**07** perfect **08** complete, flawless,

integral, unbroken, unharmed
**09** faultless, undamaged, uninjured, unscathed, untouched **10** in one piece, unimpaired **12** undiminished **13** all in one piece

**intangible**
**04** airy **05** vague **06** subtle, unfelt, unreal **07** elusive, obscure, shadowy, unclear **08** abstract, fleeting
**09** invisible, touchless **10** impalpable, indefinite **11** incorporeal, indefinable, undefinable **12** immeasurable, imponderable **13** indescribable, insubstantial

**integer**
**04** unit **05** digit, whole **06** figure, number **07** numeral **11** whole number

**integral**
**04** full **05** basic, total, whole **06** entire, intact **07** built-in, inbuilt, unitary
**08** complete, inherent **09** component, elemental, essential, intrinsic, necessary, requisite, undivided
**10** integrated, unimpaired
**11** constituent, fundamental
**13** indispensable

**integrate**
**03** mix **04** fuse, join, knit, mesh
**05** blend, merge, unite, whole
**06** mingle **07** combine **08** coalesce, complete, intermix **09** harmonize
**10** amalgamate, assimilate, co-ordinate, homogenize, mainstream
**11** consolidate, desegregate, incorporate

**integrated**
**05** fused, mixed **06** hybrid, joined, merged, meshed, united **07** blended, mingled, mongrel, unified **08** cohesive, combined, joined-up **09** coalesced, connected, one-nation, tight-knit
**10** harmonious, harmonized
**11** amalgamated, assimilated, tightly knit, unseparated **12** consolidated, desegregated, incorporated, interrelated **13** part and parcel

**integration**
**03** mix **05** blend, unity **06** fusion, merger **07** harmony **11** combination, unification **12** amalgamation, assimilation **13** consolidation, desegregation, incorporation
**14** homogenization

**integrity**
**05** honor, unity **06** honour, purity, virtue **07** decency, honesty, justice, probity **08** cohesion, entirety, fairness, goodness, morality, totality
**09** coherence, principle, rectitude, sincerity, wholeness **10** entireness
**11** unification, uprightness
**12** completeness, impartiality, truthfulness **13** righteousness

**intellect**
**04** mind, nous **05** brain, sense
**06** brains, genius, noesis, reason, wisdom **07** egghead, noology, thinker, thought **08** academic, brainbox, highbrow **09** judgement
**10** brainpower, brilliance, mastermind

**12** intellectual, intelligence **13** comprehension, understanding

## intellectual
**04** blue **05** titan **06** boffin, brainy, far-out, genius, mental, noetic **07** bookish, egghead, erudite, learned, logical, thinker **08** academic, brainbox, cerebral, cultural, good mind, highbrow, studious, well-read **09** intellect, scholarly **10** mastermind, noematical, thoughtful **11** intelligent **12** bluestocking, pointy-headed, well-educated **15** rocket scientist

## intellectually
**08** mentally **10** cerebrally, culturally, studiously **12** academically, conceptually, noematically

## intelligence
**01** G **02** IQ **03** gen, wit **04** data, dope, news, nous, wits **05** brain, facts **06** acumen, advice, brains, notice, reason, report, rumour, spying, tip-off **07** account, low-down, thought, warning **08** aptitude, findings **09** alertness, espionage, intellect, knowledge, quickness, sharpness **10** brainpower, brightness, brilliance, cleverness, grey matter, perception **11** discernment, information, observation **12** notification, surveillance **13** comprehension, understanding **15** little grey cells
• **intelligence service** **02** MI **03** CIA, KGB, SIS **05** Stasi **06** Mossad

## intelligent
**05** acute, alert, quick, sharp, smart **06** brainy, bright, clever **07** knowing **08** all there, educated, informed, rational, sensible, thinking **09** brilliant, sagacious **10** discerning, perceptive **11** quick-witted **12** apprehensive, knowledgable, pointy-headed, well-informed **13** communicative, knowledgeable, perspicacious, understanding, using your loaf

## intelligently
**07** quickly **08** all there, cleverly, sensibly **09** knowingly **10** rationally **11** sagaciously **12** discerningly, perceptively **13** using your loaf **15** perspicaciously

## intelligentsia
**06** brains **08** eggheads, literati **09** academics, highbrows **10** illuminati **11** cognoscenti **13** intellectuals

## intelligibility
**07** clarity **08** lucidity **09** clearness, lucidness, plainness, precision **10** legibility, simplicity **11** exotericism **12** distinctness, explicitness

## intelligible
**04** open **05** clear, lucid, plain **07** legible **08** distinct, exoteric, explicit **10** exoterical, fathomable, penetrable **12** decipherable **14** comprehensible, understandable

## intemperance
**06** excess **07** licence **10** crapulence, debauchery, insobriety **11** drunkenness, inebriation, unrestraint **12** extravagance,

immoderation, intoxication **14** overindulgence, self-indulgence

## intemperate
**03** OTT **04** wild **06** severe, strong **07** drunken, extreme, violent **08** prodigal **09** dissolute, excessive, unbridled **10** immoderate, inebriated, inordinate, licentious, over the top, passionate, profligate **11** dissipation, distempered, extravagant, incontinent, intoxicated, tempestuous **12** uncontrolled, ungovernable, unreasonable, unrestrained **13** self-indulgent **14** irrestrainable, uncontrollable

## intend
**03** aim **04** mean, plan, plot, turn **05** ettle, hight, think **06** choose, design, devise, direct, expand, expect, extend, scheme, strain **07** be going, destine, earmark, express, mark out, project, propose, purport, purpose, resolve **08** foreman, meditate, set apart **09** be looking, calculate, destinate, determine, have a mind, intensify **10** have in mind **11** contemplate **12** be determined

## intended
**06** fiancé, future **07** fiancée, planned **08** destined, proposed, purposed, wife-to-be **09** betrothed, designate **10** deliberate, designated, future wife **11** husband-to-be, intentional, prospective **13** future husband
• **as intended** **15** according to plan

## intense
**04** deep, full, keen **05** acute, dense, eager, great, harsh, heavy, sharp, tense, vivid **06** ardent, fervid, fierce, opaque, potent, severe, strong **07** burning, earnest, excited, extreme, fervent, nervous, serious, violent, zealous **08** blinding, electric, forceful, powerful, profound, strained, vehement, vigorous **09** consuming, emotional, energetic, exquisite, intensive **10** heightened, passionate, thoughtful **11** impassioned **12** concentrated, enthusiastic

## intensely
**04** deep, very **06** deeply **07** greatly **08** ardently, fiercely, strongly **09** extremely, fervently, like stink **10** profoundly **12** passionately **14** with a vengeance

## intensification
**05** boost **07** build-up **08** emphasis, increase **09** deepening, intension, worsening **10** building-up, escalation, stepping-up **11** aggravation, enhancement, heightening **12** acceleration, augmentation, exacerbation **13** concentration, magnification, reinforcement, strengthening **14** exacerbescence

## intensify
**03** fan **04** fire, fuel, whet **05** add to, boost, hot up, raise, widen **06** bump up, deepen, fester, hike up, intend, step up, worsen **07** augment, broaden, build up, enhance, magnify, quicken, sharpen **08** compound, escalate,

heighten, increase, maximize **09** aggravate, emphasize, reinforce **10** exacerbate, exaggerate, strengthen **11** concentrate **12** bring to a head

## intensity
**04** fire, zeal **05** depth, force, power **06** accent, ardour, energy, strain, vigour **07** emotion, fervour, passion, potency, tension **08** fervency, fullness, keenness, severity, strength **09** acuteness, eagerness, extremity, greatness, intension, vehemence **10** enthusiasm, fanaticism, fierceness, profundity **11** earnestness, intenseness **13** concentration

## intensive
**04** full **05** total **06** all-out **07** in-depth, intense **08** detailed, rigorous, strained, thorough **10** exhaustive **11** unremitting **12** concentrated **13** comprehensive, thoroughgoing

## intensively
**05** fully **07** closely, totally **09** intensely **10** completely, rigorously, thoroughly **11** extensively **12** exhaustively **15** comprehensively

## intent
**03** aim, end, set **04** bent, firm, goal, hard, idea, keen, plan, rapt, view **05** alert, close, eager, ettle, fixed, point **06** design, enrapt, object, steady, target **07** earnest, focused, meaning, purpose, wistful **08** absorbed, hellbent, occupied, resolved, watchful **09** attentive, committed, engrossed, intention, objective, searching, wrapped up **10** determined **11** connotation, preoccupied **13** concentrating
• **to all intents and purposes**
**06** almost, nearly **07** morally **08** as good as, in effect **09** in essence, just about, virtually **10** more or less, pretty much, pretty well **11** effectively, practically

## intention
**03** aim, end **04** goal, hent, idea, plan, view, wish **05** point **06** animus, design, intent, object, target **07** concept, meaning, purpose, thought **08** ambition **09** objective **10** aspiration, attendment, designment **11** attendement

## intentional
**03** set **05** meant **06** wilful **07** planned, studied, willful, willing **08** designed, intended, prepense, purposed **09** conscious, on purpose, voluntary, weighed-up **10** calculated, considered, deliberate, purposeful, systematic **11** prearranged **12** preconceived, premeditated, systematical

## intentionally
**08** by design, wilfully **09** advisedly, knowingly, meaningly, on purpose, purposely, willingly **10** designedly, prepensely **11** in cold blood **12** deliberately

## intently
**04** hard **06** keenly **07** closely, fixedly **08** steadily **09** carefully, earnestly,

staringly **10** diligently, watchfully
**11** attentively, searchingly

**inter**
◇ *insertion indicator* **04** bury **05** earth,
inurn **06** entomb, inhume **07** inearth
**08** inhumate **09** lay to rest, sepulchre

**interbreed**
**03** mix **05** cross **09** hybridize
**10** crossbreed, mongrelize
**11** miscegenate **14** cross-fertilize

**interbreeding**
**07** syngamy **08** crossing **13** cross-
breeding, hybridization,
miscegenation

**intercede**
**05** plead, speak **07** beseech, entreat,
mediate **08** moderate, petition
**09** arbitrate, interpose, intervene,
negotiate

**intercept**
◇ *insertion indicator* **04** stop, take
**05** block, catch, check, cut in, delay,
seize **06** ambush, arrest, cut off,
impede, thwart, waylay **07** deflect,
head off **08** obstruct **09** frustrate,
interrupt **10** commandeer

**interception**
◇ *insertion indicator* **06** ambush
**07** seizure **08** blocking, checking,
stopping **10** cutting-off, deflection,
heading-off **11** obstruction

**intercession**
**04** plea **06** agency, prayer
**08** advocacy, entreaty, pleading
**09** mediation **10** beseeching
**11** arbitration, good offices,
negotiation **12** intervention,
solicitation, supplication
**13** interposition **14** interpellation

**intercessor**
**04** mean **05** agent **06** broker, prayer
**08** advocate, mediator **09** go-between,
middleman, moderator, paraclete
**10** arbitrator, negotiator
**12** intermediary

**interchange**
**04** swap **05** trade **06** barter, switch
**07** permute, replace, reverse, trading
**08** crossing, exchange, junction
**09** alternate, crossfire, crossroad,
interplay, permutate, transpose
**10** alternance, crossroads, substitute
**11** alternation, give-and-take,
reciprocate **12** intersection
**13** reciprocation

**interchangeability**
**04** swap **06** barter **08** exchange,
synonymy **10** congruence, similarity
**11** equivalence, interaction,
parallelism, reciprocity
**13** comparability, reciprocation
**14** correspondence
**15** exchangeability, transposability

**interchangeable**
**07** similar, the same **08** fungible,
standard **09** identical **10** comparable,
equivalent, permutable, reciprocal,
synonymous **11** commutative
**12** exchangeable, transposable
**13** corresponding

**interconnect**
**04** join, link **06** join up **07** network
**09** interlink, interlock **10** interweave
**11** communicate, interrelate

**intercourse**
**05** trade, trock, troke, truck **07** contact,
traffic **08** commerce, congress,
converse, dealings **10** connection
**11** association **12** conversation
**13** communication **14** correspondence

**interdependent**
**06** mutual, two-way **10** correlated,
reciprocal **11** interlinked
**12** interlocking, interrelated
**13** complementary **14** interconnected

**interdict**
**03** ban, bar **04** tabu, veto **05** debar,
taboo **06** forbid, outlaw **07** embargo,
prevent, rule out **08** disallow,
preclude, prohibit **09** proscribe
**10** injunction, preclusion
**11** prohibition **12** disallowance,
interdiction, proscription

**interest**
**03** fad, int **04** care, gain, good, grip,
heed, move, note, part, side **05** amuse,
bonus, charm, claim, hobby, rivet,
share, stake, stock, touch, value
**06** absorb, allure, appeal, divert,
engage, equity, moment, notice,
occupy, profit, regard, return, weight
**07** attract, benefit, concern, credits,
engross, gravity, involve, pastime,
portion, premium, pursuit, revenue,
urgency **08** activity, appeal to,
business, dividend, intrigue, priority,
proceeds, receipts **09** advantage,
amusement, attention, captivate,
curiosity, diversion, fascinate,
magnitude, relevance **10** attraction,
engagement, importance, investment,
percentage, prominence, recreation
**11** consequence, fascination,
involvement, seriousness
**12** partisanship, significance
**13** attentiveness, consideration,
participation **15** inquisitiveness
• **in the interests of 10** on behalf of
**12** for the sake of **15** for the benefit of
• **lack of interest 06** apathy
**07** boredom
• **object of interest 04** lion

**interested**
**04** into, keen **05** hot on **06** intent
**07** curious, devoted, engaged, gripped,
riveted **08** absorbed, affected, involved
**09** attentive, attracted, concerned,
engrossed, intrigued **10** captivated,
enthralled, fascinated, implicated
**12** enthusiastic, having the bug

**interesting**
**05** tasty **07** amusing, amusive, curious,
unusual **08** engaging, exciting,
gripping, readable, riveting, viewable
**09** absorbing, appealing **10** attractive,
compelling, compulsive, engrossing,
intriguing **11** captivating, fascinating,
stimulating **12** entertaining
**13** unputdownable

**interestingly**
**09** curiously **10** poignantly
**11** ingeniously **12** intriguingly

**interfere**
**03** jam, mar, pry **04** balk, rape
**05** abuse, block, check, choke, clash,
cramp, grope, upset **06** attack, butt in,
feel up, hamper, hinder, impede,
meddle, molest, tamper, thwart
**07** assault, barge in, inhibit, intrude,
touch up, trammel **08** conflict,
handicap, intromit, mess with,
obstruct, trespass **09** interpose,
interrupt, intervene, mess about
**10** mess around, muscle in on
**11** intermeddle **12** put your bib in, put
your oar in **13** get in the way of, poke
your bib in, touch sexually **14** poke
your nose in, stick your bib in, stick
your oar in **15** sexually assault, stick
your nose in

**interference**
**03** EMI **05** noise, shash **06** prying, static
**07** clutter, trammel **08** blocking,
checking, clashing, conflict, handicap,
meddling, trammels **09** cross-talk,
hampering, hindrance, intrusion,
thwarting **10** antagonism, impediment,
inhibiting, opposition **11** disturbance,
obstruction **12** interruption,
intervention, intromission
**13** interposition **14** meddlesomeness
**15** intermodulation

**interfering**
**04** nosy **05** nosey **06** prying
**08** meddling **09** intruding, intrusive
**10** meddlesome

**interim**
**06** acting, pro tem **07** stand-in, stopgap
**08** interval, meantime **09** caretaker,
makeshift, meanwhile, temporary
**10** improvised **11** interregnum,
provisional

**interior**
**03** int **04** core, home **05** heart, inner,
local **06** centre, depths, hidden, inland,
innate, inside, inward, mental, middle,
remote, secret **07** central, innards,
nucleus, private **08** domestic, internal,
intimate, personal **09** emotional,
impulsive, innermost, intrinsic,
intuitive, spiritual, up-country
**10** inside part **11** instinctive,
involuntary, spontaneous
**13** psychological

**interject**
**03** cry **04** call **05** shout, utter **06** insert,
pipe up **07** exclaim, throw in
**09** ejaculate, interpose, interrupt,
introduce **11** interpolate

**interjection**
**03** cry **04** call **05** shout **09** utterance
**11** ejaculation, exclamation
**12** interruption **13** interpolation,
interposition

**interlace**
**04** knit **05** braid, cross, plait, twine,
weave **06** enlace, inlace **07** entrail,
entwine, intwine **08** intermix
**09** interlock **10** intertwine, interweave,

reticulate **11** intersperse
**12** interwreathe

**interlink**
**04** knit, link, mesh **07** network
**09** intergrow, interlock **10** intertwine,
interweave **12** interconnect, link
together, lock together **13** clasp
together

**interlock**
**04** link, mesh **05** pitch, tooth **06** engage
**10** intertwine **12** interconnect, link
together, lock together **13** clasp
together, interdigitate

**interloper**
**07** invader **08** intruder **10** encroacher,
trespasser **11** gatecrasher **14** uninvited
guest

**interlude**
**03** jig **04** halt, rest, stop, wait **05** break,
delay, let-up, pause, spell **06** hiatus,
kyogen, recess, verset **07** respite
**08** antimask, breather, entr'acte,
interact, interval, stoppage **09** interrupt
**10** antimasque **11** parenthesis
**12** intermission **14** breathing space,
divertissement

**intermediary**
**05** agent **06** broker **08** linguist,
mediator **09** comprador, go-between,
in-between, middleman **10** arbitrator,
compradore, contact man, negotiator

**intermediate**
**03** mid **04** mean **05** mesne **06** medial,
median, medium, middle, midway
**07** halfway **09** in-between
**11** intervening **12** intermediary,
transitional

**interment**
**06** burial **07** burying, funeral, obsequy
**08** exequies **09** obsequies, sepulture
**10** inhumation

**interminable**
**04** dull, long **06** boring, prolix
**07** endless, eternal, tedious
**08** dragging, infinite **09** boundless,
ceaseless, limitless, perpetual,
unlimited, wearisome **10** long-winded,
loquacious, monotonous, without end
**11** everlasting, never-ending **12** long-
drawn-out

**intermingle**
**03** mix **04** fuse, lace **05** blend, merge,
mix up **06** commix **07** combine
**08** intermix **09** commingle, interlace
**10** amalgamate, interweave **11** mix
together

**intermission**
**04** halt, lull, rest, stop **05** break, let-up,
pause **06** recess **07** respite **08** apyrexia,
breather, interval, stoppage, suspense,
vacation **09** cessation, interlude,
remission **10** suspension
**12** interruption **14** breathing space

**intermittent**
**06** broken, cyclic, fitful **07** erratic **08** off
and on, on and off, periodic, sporadic
**09** irregular, spasmodic **10** now and
then, occasional **11** now and again,
spasmodical **13** discontinuous

**intermittently**
**08** off and on, on and off **09** sometimes
**11** erratically, irregularly
**12** occasionally, periodically,
sporadically **13** spasmodically **14** from
time to time **15** by fits and starts,
discontinuously, in fits and starts

**intern**
**04** hold, jail, tiro **05** cadet, pupil
**06** detain, inmate, novice **07** confine,
learner, recruit, starter, student, trainee
**08** beginner, graduate, imprison,
newcomer, prentice **10** apprentice
**11** probationer **13** hold in custody

**internal**
**03** int **04** home **05** civil, inner, local
**06** inside, inward, mental **07** in-house,
private **08** domestic, interior, intimate,
personal **09** emotional, intrinsic,
spiritual **10** subjective
**13** psychological

**internally**
**06** inside, within **07** at heart, locally
**08** deep down, inwardly, secretly
**09** privately **10** to yourself
**12** domestically, subjectively **13** deep
inside you

**international**
**01** I **03** cap, int **06** global, public
**07** general **09** test match, universal,
worldwide **12** cosmopolitan

**internecine**
**05** civil, fatal **06** bloody, deadly,
family, fierce, mortal **07** ruinous,
violent **08** internal **09** murderous
**11** destructive **13** exterminating

**Internet**
*see* **computer**

**interplay**
**08** exchange **11** alternation, give-and-
take, interaction, interchange
**13** reciprocation, transposition

**interpolate**
**03** add **05** put in **06** insert **09** interject,
interpose, intersert, introduce
**10** spatchcock **11** intercalate

**interpolation**
**03** gag **05** aside **06** insert **08** addition
**09** insertion **12** interjection,
introduction **13** intercalation

**interpose**
**03** add **05** cut in, put in **06** butt in, chip
in, horn in, insert, step in, strike
**07** barge in, intrude, mediate, stickle
**08** interlay, intermit, muscle in, strike
in, thrust in **09** arbitrate, intercede,
interfere, interject, interpone,
interrupt, intervene, introduce **10** put
between **11** come between, interpolate
**12** place between, put your oar in
**14** poke your nose in

**interpret**
**04** read, scan, take **05** aread, arede,
solve **06** decode, define, open up,
render, unfold **07** arreede, clarify,
conster, explain, expound **08** construe,
decipher **09** elucidate, explicate, make
clear, translate **10** paraphrase,
understand **11** make sense of,

rationalize, shed light on
**12** interpretate, throw light on

**interpretation**
**04** read, rede, spin, take **05** sense
**07** anagoge, anagogy, meaning,
opinion, reading, version **08** analysis,
construe, decoding, exegesis
**09** rendering **10** exposition,
expounding, paraphrase
**11** deciphering, elucidation,
explanation, explication,
performance, translation
**12** construction **13** clarification,
understanding

**interpretative**
**08** exegetic **10** expository
**11** explanatory, explicatory,
hermeneutic **12** interpretive
**13** clarificatory

**interpreter**
**06** lawyer, munshi **07** dobhash,
exegete, Latiner **08** dragoman,
exponent, lingster, linguist, linkster,
moonshee, truchman **09** annotator,
expositor, expounder **10** elucidator,
linguister, textualist, translator
**11** commentator, expositress
**12** hermeneutist, oneirocritic
**13** interpretress, oneiroscopist

**interrelate**
**04** link **09** interlink, interlock
**10** interweave **11** communicate
**12** interconnect

**interrogate**
**04** pump, quiz **05** grill **07** debrief,
examine **08** question **12** cross-examine
**13** cross-question, give a roasting
**14** give a going-over

**interrogation**
**04** quiz **07** inquest, inquiry, pumping
**08** grilling, question, quizzing
**09** going-over **11** examination,
inquisition, questioning, third degree
**14** the third degree

**interrogative**
**07** curious, probing **08** erotetic
**09** inquiring, quizzical **11** inquisitive,
questioning **12** catechetical
**13** inquisitional, inquisitorial,
interrogatory

**interrupt**
◊ *insertion indicator* **03** cut, end **04** halt,
stop **05** block, break, cut in, delay
**06** butt in, cancel, chip in, chop in, cut
off, heckle, hold up, snap up, take up
**07** barge in, barrack, break in,
chequer, disrupt, disturb, intrude,
suspend **08** cut short, obstruct,
postpone **09** intercept, interject,
interlude, interpose, intervene,
punctuate, take short **10** disconnect
**11** interpolate, take up short **12** put
your oar in **13** interfere with,
interjaculate

**interruption**
◊ *insertion indicator* **03** cut **04** halt, stop
**05** break, delay, hitch, let-up, pause
**06** cesure, hiatus, recess, remark
**07** wipeout **08** blocking, breather,
interval, obstacle, power cut, question
**09** abatement, barging-in, butting-in,

cessation, cutting-in, hindrance, interlude, intrusion **10** disruption, impediment, suspension **11** breaking-off, disturbance, obstruction **12** interference, interjection, intermission, solarization **13** disconnection, interpolation **14** discontinuance, interpellation

## intersect

**03** cut **04** meet **05** cross **06** bisect, divide **07** overlap **08** converge **09** cut across, decussate, intervein **10** criss-cross

## intersection

**04** edge, meet **06** carfax, carfox, chiasm, vertex **07** chiasma, meeting **08** crossing, junction **10** crossroads, roundabout **11** box junction, interchange **13** traffic circle **15** railway crossing

## intersperse

**03** dot **06** pepper, spread **07** scatter **08** dispense, intermix, sprinkle **09** diversify, interlard, interpose, punctuate **10** distribute

## interstice

**03** gap **04** gulf, hole, pore, rent, rift, void **05** blank, chink, cleft, crack, space **06** areola, breach, cavity, cranny, divide, lacuna **07** crevice, opening, orifice **08** aperture, fracture

## intertwine

**03** mix **04** coil, knit, lace **05** blend, braid, cross, plait, pleat, twine, twirl, twist, weave **06** pleach, writhe **07** connect, entwine **08** empleach, impleach **09** interlace, interlink, interwind **10** interweave **12** link together

## interval

**03** gap **04** leap, lull, rest, time, wait **05** break, comma, delay, pause, space, spell **06** period, recess, season **07** interim, opening **08** breather, distance, meantime, playtime **09** in-between, interlude, meanwhile **10** interspace **11** intervallum, parenthesis **12** intermission **14** breathing space

## intervene

**04** pass **05** arise, occur **06** befall, elapse, happen, step in **07** intrude, mediate **08** separate **09** arbitrate, intercede, interfere, interrupt, negotiate **10** come to pass
• **intervene boldly**   **02** up

## intervening

**06** middle **07** between, mediate **09** in-between **11** interjacent, interposing **12** intercurrent, intermediate, intervenient

## intervention

**06** agency **09** intrusion, mediation **10** stepping-in **11** arbitration, involvement, negotiation **12** intercession, interference, interruption **13** interposition

## interview

**03** vet **04** talk, viva **05** grill **06** assess, talk to **07** examine, meeting

**08** audience, dialogue, evaluate, one-to-one, question, sound out **09** appraisal, encounter, tête-à-tête **10** assessment, conference, discussion, evaluation **11** interrogate **12** consultation, cross-examine **13** cross-question **15** oral examination, press conference

## interviewer

**08** assessor, examiner, reporter **09** appraiser, evaluator **10** inquisitor, questioner **11** interrogant **12** interlocutor, interrogator, investigator **13** correspondent

## interweave

**03** mat, mix **04** coil, knit **05** blend, braid, cross, plash, twine, twist, weave **06** raddle, splice, tissue **07** connect, entwine, perplex **08** complect **09** interlace, interlink, interlock, interwind, interwork **10** criss-cross, intertwine, intertwist, reticulate **11** intermingle, intertangle **12** interconnect, interwreathe, link together

## intestinal

**05** ileac **07** coeliac, enteric, gastric **08** duodenal, internal, visceral **09** abdominal, stomachic **10** splanchnic

## intestines

**04** guts **05** colon, offal **06** bowels, casing, vitals **07** innards, insides, viscera **08** entrails **09** chidlings, chitlings **11** chitterling **12** chitterlings

## intimacy

**06** warmth **07** privacy **09** affection, closeness, connexion, knowledge **10** confidence, connection, friendship, inwardness **11** camaraderie, familiarity **13** understanding

## intimate

**03** pal **04** boon, chum, cosy, cozy, dear, deep, hint, mate, maty, near, pack, snug, tell, tosh, warm **05** bosom, buddy, chief, china, close, crony, imply, matey, pally, palsy, privy, state, thick, tight **06** allude, belamy, chummy, friend, impart, intime, inward, secret, signal, strict, throng **07** Achates, comrade, declare, gremial, in-depth, private, special, suggest **08** alter ego, announce, detailed, familiar, friendly, indicate, informal, internal, personal, profound, thorough **09** associate, cherished, confidant, gemütlich, innermost, insinuate, make known, welcoming **10** best friend, better half, confidante, deep-seated, exhaustive, give notice, palsy-walsy **11** bosom friend, cater-cousin, close friend, communicate, penetrating **12** affectionate, confidential, fidus Achates, heart-to-heart, let it be known **13** boon companion **14** well-acquainted
*See also* **friend**

## intimately

**04** well **05** fully **06** deeply, nearly, warmly **07** closely **08** commonly, in detail, tenderly **09** inside out, privately **10** familiarly, personally, thoroughly

**11** confidingly, hand in glove **12** exhaustively, hand and glove, particularly **14** affectionately, confidentially

## intimation

**04** hint, note **05** sniff **06** notice, signal **07** inkling, warning **08** allusion, innuendo, reminder **09** reference, statement **10** indication, suggestion **11** declaration, implication, insinuation **12** announcement **13** communication

## intimidate

**03** cow **05** alarm, appal, bully, daunt, get at, scare **06** coerce, compel, dismay, extort, lean on, menace, subdue **07** overawe, terrify, warn off **08** ballyrag, browbeat, bulldoze, bullyrag, domineer, frighten, pressure, psych out, threaten **09** blackmail, terrorize, tyrannize **10** pressurize **13** turn the heat on **14** put the screws on

## intimidation

**04** fear **06** screws, terror **07** menaces, threats **08** big stick, bullying, coercion, pressure **10** compulsion, terrifying **11** arm-twisting, browbeating, domineering, frighteners, frightening, terrorizing, threatening **12** scare tactics **13** sabre-rattling, terrorization, tyrannization

## intolerable

**05** awful **06** the end, too bad **08** dreadful, the limit **09** loathsome **10** detestable, impossible, unbearable **11** unendurable **12** insufferable, the last straw, unacceptable **13** beyond the pale, insupportable

## intolerably

**10** impossibly, shockingly, unbearably **11** repugnantly **12** insufferably, outrageously

## intolerance

**06** ageism, racism, sexism **07** bigotry **08** jingoism **09** dogmatism, extremism, prejudice, racialism **10** chauvinism, fanaticism, impatience, insularity, narrowness, xenophobia **12** anti-Semitism, illiberality **14** discrimination **15** small-mindedness

## intolerant

**06** ageist, biased, narrow, racist, sexist **07** bigoted, insular, redneck **08** dogmatic, one-sided, partisan **09** extremist, fanatical, illiberal, impatient, parochial, racialist **10** jingoistic, prejudiced, provincial, xenophobic **11** anti-Semitic, opinionated, persecuting, small-minded **12** chauvinistic, incompatible, narrow-minded, uncharitable **14** discriminating

## intonation

**02** Om **04** lilt, tone **05** pitch, twang **06** stress, timbre **07** cadence **08** emphasis **10** expression, inflection, modulation **12** accentuation

## intone

**03** say **04** sing **05** chant, croon, speak, utter, voice **06** chaunt, incant, recite

**07** declaim **08** intonate, monotone **09** enunciate, pronounce **10** cantillate

## intoxicate

◊ *anagram indicator* **04** corn **05** elate **06** excite, fuddle, poison, sozzle, thrill **07** animate, enthuse, inflame, inspire, stupefy **08** befuddle, disguise **09** inebriate, make drunk, stimulate **10** exhilarate

## intoxicated

◊ *anagram indicator* **04** full, high, inky, para, winy **05** blind, crunk, drunk, happy, inked, krunk, lit up, merry, moppy, moved, tight, tipsy, winey, woozy **06** blotto, bombed, canned, corked, elated, groggy, in wine, jarred, juiced, loaded, mortal, ripped, soused, stewed, stinko, stoned, tanked, tiddly, wasted, zonked **07** bevvied, blasted, blitzed, bonkers, bottled, coked-up, crocked, crunked, drunken, ebriate, ebriose, excited, half-cut, in drink, krunked, legless, maggoty, pickled, pie-eyed, sloshed, smashed, sozzled, squiffy, stirred, tiddled, toasted, trashed, wrecked **08** besotted, bibulous, ebriated, footless, hammered, in liquor, juiced up, liquored, maggoted, moon-eyed, sow-drunk, steaming, stocious, tanked up, thrilled, whiffled, whistled, worked up **09** crapulent, inebriate, paralytic, pixilated, plastered, shickered, trolleyed, up the pole, well-oiled, zonked out **10** blind drunk, inebriated, in your cups, obfuscated, pixillated, stimulated, whiskified **11** carried away, exhilarated, full as a boot, full as a goog, full as a tick, off your face, whiskeyfied **12** drunk as a lord, drunk as a newt, enthusiastic, roaring drunk **13** drunk as a piper, drunk as a skunk, having had a few, in high spirits, under the table **14** Brahms and Liszt **15** one over the eight, the worse for wear, under the weather

*See also* **drunk**

## intoxicating

**05** heady **06** moving, strong **07** rousing **08** dramatic, exciting, stirring **09** alcoholic, inebriant, inspiring, methystic, stimulant, thrilling **11** enthralling, stimulating **12** exhilarating **15** going to your head

## intoxication

**06** fuddle, thrill **07** elation, rapture **08** euphoria, methysis, pleasure **09** animation, inebriety, poisoning, temulence, temulency, tipsiness **10** alcoholism, crapulence, debauchery, dipsomania, enthusiasm, excitement, insobriety **11** drunkenness, inebriation, stimulation **12** bibulousness, exhilaration, hard drinking, intemperance **15** serious drinking

## intractability

**08** obduracy **09** obstinacy **10** perversity **11** awkwardness, waywardness **12** contrariness, indiscipline, perverseness, stubbornness **13** pig-

headedness, unamenability **15** incorrigibility, ungovernability

## intractable

**04** hard, wild **05** tough **06** kittle, unruly, wilful **07** awkward, frampal, haggard, problem, unwayed, wayward **08** contrary, frampold, obdurate, perverse, stubborn **09** difficult, fractious, obstinate, pig-headed, unbending **10** headstrong, monolithic, refractory, self-willed, unamenable, unyielding **11** disobedient, untreatable **12** cantankerous, cross-grained, intransigent, ungovernable, unmanageable **13** unco-operative, undisciplined **14** uncontrollable

## intransigence

**08** obduracy, tenacity **09** toughness **10** obstinacy **12** stubbornness **13** determination, implacability, inflexibility, pig-headedness **14** intractability, relentlessness

## intransigent

**05** rigid, tough **06** uppity **08** hardline, obdurate, stubborn **09** immovable, obstinate, pig-headed, tenacious, unbending **10** determined, implacable, inexorable, inflexible, relentless, unamenable, unyielding **11** intractable, unbudgeable, unrelenting **12** bloody-minded **13** unpersuadable **14** irreconcilable, uncompromising

## intrepid

**04** bold **05** brave, gutsy **06** daring, gritty, heroic, plucky, spunky **07** doughty, gallant, valiant **08** fearless, spirited, stalwart, unafraid, valorous **09** audacious, dauntless, undaunted **10** courageous, undismayed **11** lion-hearted, unflinching **12** stout-hearted

## intrepidness

**04** grit, guts **05** nerve, pluck **06** daring, spirit, valour **07** bravery, courage, heroism, prowess **08** audacity, boldness **09** fortitude, gallantry **11** doughtiness, intrepidity **12** fearlessness **13** dauntlessness, undauntedness **15** lion-heartedness

## intricacy

**06** enigma **09** obscurity **10** complexity, involution, knottiness, perplexity **11** complexness, convolution, involvement **12** complication, convolutions, entanglement **13** complexedness, elaborateness, intricateness **14** sophistication

## intricate

◊ *anagram indicator* **05** dedal, fancy **06** daedal, knotty, ornate, rococo, twisty **07** complex, finicky, Gordian, tangled **08** baffling, intrince, involved, puzzling, ravelled, tortuous **09** Byzantine, contrived, difficult, elaborate, enigmatic, entangled **10** convoluted, perplexing **11** complicated **12** intrinsicate, tirlie-wirlie **13** sophisticated

## intrigue

**03** web **04** draw, pack, plot, pull, ruse, wile **05** amour, cabal, charm, dodge,

junta, rivet **06** absorb, affair, brigue, puzzle, scheme **07** affaire, attract, connive, consult, liaison, romance, traffic **08** artifice, collogue, conspire, interest, intimacy, trickery **09** captivate, collusion, conniving, fascinate, gallantry, machinate, manoeuvre, stratagem, tantalize, undermine **10** conspiracy, courtcraft, dirty trick, love affair, manipulate **11** beguilement, machination **12** machinations **13** double-dealing, sharp practice, work the oracle **15** practise against

## intriguer

**06** Jesuit **07** plotter, schemer, wangler **08** conniver **09** intrigant, trinketer **10** intrigante, machinator, politician, wire-puller **11** conspirator **12** collaborator **13** Machiavellian, wheeler-dealer

## intriguing

**07** politic **08** charming, exciting, puzzling, riveting **09** absorbing, appealing, beguiling, diverting, stairwork **10** attractive, compelling **11** captivating, fascinating, interesting, tantalizing, titillating

## intrinsic

**05** basic **06** inborn, inbred, inward, native **07** built-in, central, genuine, in-built, natural, radical **08** inherent, integral, interior, internal **09** elemental, essential **10** congenital, indigenous, underlying **11** fundamental **14** constitutional

## intrinsically

**08** in itself, inwardly **09** basically, centrally **10** inherently, integrally **11** essentially **12** by definition **13** constituently, fundamentally

## introduce

◊ *containment indicator* **03** add **04** open **05** begin, float, found, immit, offer, plant, put in, start **06** induct, inject, insert, launch, lead in, prolog, submit **07** advance, bring in, develop, precede, preface, present, propose, suggest, usher in **08** acquaint, announce, commence, initiate, intromit, lead into, organize, prologue **09** establish, instigate, institute, originate **10** inaugurate, put forward **11** familiarize, put in motion, set in motion

• **be introduced to** **04** meet

## introduction

◊ *head selection indicator* **05** debut, intro, proem, start **06** basics, entrée, launch, lead-in **07** baptism, opening, preface, prelude **08** exordium, foreword, overture, preamble, prologue **09** beginning, knock-down, rudiments **10** essentials, initiation **11** acquainting, development, front matter, institution, origination, prolegomena **12** announcement, commencement, fundamentals, inauguration, intromission, organization, presentation, prolegomenon **13** establishment, preliminaries **15** familiarization, first principles

**introductory**
**05** basic, early, first **07** initial, opening **08** exordial, isagogic, starting **09** beginning, essential, inaugural, prefatory, prelusory **10** elementary, initiative, initiatory, precursory **11** fundamental, preliminary, preparatory, rudimentary

**introspection**
**08** brooding **11** navel-gazing, pensiveness **12** introversion, self-analysis **13** contemplation, soul-searching **14** heart-searching, thoughtfulness **15** self-centredness, self-examination, self-observation

**introspective**
**06** musing **07** pensive **08** brooding, reserved **09** withdrawn **10** meditative, subjective, thoughtful **11** introverted, self-centred **12** self-absorbed **13** contemplative, inward-looking, self-analysing, self-examining, self-observing

**introverted**
**03** shy **05** quiet **08** reserved **09** withdrawn **11** self-centred **12** self-absorbed **13** introspective, inward-looking, self-examining

**intrude**
**04** sorn **05** abate **06** butt in, chip in, invade, meddle, thrust **07** aggress, barge in, impinge, obtrude, violate **08** encroach, infringe, trespass **09** gatecrash, interfere, interject, interlope, interrupt

**intruder**
**05** thief **06** raider, robber **07** burglar, invader, prowler **08** Derby dog, pilferer **10** gooseberry, interloper, trespasser **11** gatecrasher, infiltrator **12** housebreaker **14** unwelcome guest

**intrusion**
**04** vein **08** invasion, lopolith, meddling, trespass **09** incursion, obtrusion, phacolith, violation **12** encroachment, gatecrashing, impertinence, impertinency, infringement, interference, interruption

**intrusive**
**04** nosy **05** nosey, pushy **06** prying **07** forward **08** annoying, intruded, invasive, snooping, unwanted **09** go-getting, obtrusive, officious, uninvited, unwelcome **10** disturbing, irritating, meddlesome **11** impertinent, importunate, interfering, trespassing, troublesome, uncalled-for **12** interrupting, presumptuous

**intuition**
**03** ESP **05** hunch **06** belief **07** feeling, insight **08** instinct **10** gut feeling, perception, sixth sense **11** discernment, premonition **12** anticipation, presentiment **13** light of nature

**intuitive**
**06** inborn, innate **08** untaught, visceral

**09** automatic, unlearned **11** instinctive, intuitional, involuntary, spontaneous

**intuitively**
**08** innately **10** by instinct **13** automatically, instinctively, spontaneously

**inundate**
**04** bury, soak **05** drown, flood, swamp **06** deluge, engulf **07** immerse, overrun **08** overflow, saturate, submerge **09** overwhelm **10** overburden

**inundation**
**04** glut **05** flood, spate, swamp **06** deluge, excess **07** surplus, torrent **08** diluvion, diluvium, overflow **09** land-flood, tidal wave **10** water flood

**inure**
**03** use **05** flesh, train **06** commit, harden, season, temper **07** toughen **08** accustom, practise **09** habituate **10** strengthen **11** acclimatize, desensitize, familiarize

**invade**
◇ *insertion indicator* **04** raid **05** enter, seize, storm **06** attack, infest, maraud, occupy **07** assault, burst in, conquer, intrude, obtrude, overrun, pervade, pillage, plunder, violate **08** encroach, infringe, take over, trespass **09** descend on, interrupt, march into, penetrate, swarm over **10** infiltrate **12** enter by force

**invader**
**04** Dane **06** raider **08** attacker, intruder, marauder, pillager **09** aggressor, assailant, infringer, plunderer **10** trespasser

**invalid**
◇ *anagram indicator* **03** ill **04** null, sick, void, weak **05** false, frail, wrong **06** ailing, feeble, infirm, poorly, sickly, unwell **07** chronic, expired, illegal, patient, quashed, revoked, unsound **08** baseless, disabled, informal, mistaken, sufferer **09** abolished, bedridden, cancelled, erroneous, illogical, incorrect, nullified, rescinded, unfounded, untenable, worthless **10** fallacious, groundless, ill-founded, irrational, overturned **11** debilitated, inoperative, null and void, unjustified, unwarranted **12** convalescent, unacceptable, unscientific **14** valetudinarian **15** unsubstantiated

**invalidate**
**04** undo, veto, void **05** annul, avoid, quash **06** cancel, negate, revoke, weaken **07** nullify, rescind, vitiate **08** abrogate, overrule **09** discredit, overthrow, terminate, undermine

**invalidity**
**07** fallacy, falsity, sophism **08** voidness **11** unsoundness **12** illogicality, speciousness **13** inconsistency, incorrectness, irrationality **14** fallaciousness

**invaluable**
**06** costly, useful **07** crucial **08** critical,

precious, valuable **09** priceless **11** inestimable **12** incalculable **13** indispensable

**invariable**
**03** set **05** fixed, rigid **06** stable, steady **07** regular, uniform **08** constant, habitual **09** immutable, invariant, permanent, unvarying **10** changeless, consistent, inflexible, unchanging, unwavering **11** unalterable **12** unchangeable

**invariably**
**06** always **09** regularly **10** constantly, habitually, inevitably, repeatedly **11** unfailingly, without fail **12** consistently

**invasion**
**04** raid **05** foray **06** attack, breach, sepsis **07** descent **08** Overlord, storming **09** incursion, intrusion, irruption, offensive, onslaught, violation **10** occupation **11** penetration **12** encroachment, infiltration, infringement, interference, interruption

**invective**
**05** abuse **06** rebuke, satire, tirade, verbal **07** censure, obloquy, sarcasm **08** berating, diatribe, reproach, scolding **09** contumely, philippic, reprimand **10** revilement **11** castigation, fulmination **12** denunciation, vilification, vituperation **13** recrimination, tongue-lashing

**inveigh**
**04** rail **05** blame, scold **06** berate, revile **07** censure, condemn, lambast, thunder, upbraid **08** denounce, reproach, sound off **09** castigate, criticize, fulminate **10** tongue-lash, vituperate **11** expostulate, recriminate

**inveigle**
**03** con **04** coax, lure, wile **05** decoy **06** allure, cajole, entice, entrap, lead on, seduce **07** beguile, ensnare, wheedle **08** persuade **09** bamboozle, manoeuvre, sweet-talk **10** manipulate

**invent**
**04** coin, fain, find, mint, plan **05** fable, faine, fayne, feign, frame **06** cook up, create, design, devise, father, make up **07** concoct, dream up, hit upon, imagine, pioneer, think up, trump up **08** conceive, contrive, discover, innovate **09** fabricate, formulate, improvise, originate **10** come up with **11** confabulate, manufacture **12** swing the lead

**invented**
**03** inv **06** made up **09** trumped-up **10** fictitious

**invention**
◇ *anagram indicator* **03** fib, lie, wit **04** baby, fake, gift, idea, myth **05** skill **06** deceit, design, device, gadget, genius, system, talent **07** coinage, coining, concept, fantasy, fiction, figment, forgery, machine, untruth **08** artistry, creation **09** discovery, falsehood, ingenuity, tall story

**10** brainchild, concoction, contriving, creativity, innovation **11** contrivance, development, fabrication, imagination, inspiration, originality, origination **12** construction, contrivement, excogitation **13** falsification, inventiveness **15** resourcefulness

**inventive**
**06** clever, gifted **07** fertile, skilful **08** artistic, creative, inspired, original, pregnant, talented **09** ingenious **10** innovative **11** imaginative, resourceful

**inventiveness**
**04** gift **05** power, skill **06** talent **10** creativity, enterprise, innovation **11** imagination, inspiration, originality **13** ingeniousness **14** innovativeness **15** imaginativeness, resourcefulness

**inventor**
**05** maker **06** author, coiner, father, framer, mother **07** creator, deviser **08** designer, engineer, producer **09** architect, developer, innovator, scientist, sloganeer **10** discoverer, mint master, originator **11** emblematist **12** palindromist

*Inventors include:*

**03** **Sax** (Antoine Joseph)
**04** **Abel** (Sir Frederick), **Bell** (Alexander Graham), **Benz** (Karl), **Biro** (Laszlo), **Colt** (Samuel), **Davy** (Sir Humphry), **Hood** (Thomas), **Jobs** (Steve), **Land** (Edwin Herbert), **Moon** (William), **Otis** (Elisha Graves), **Swan** (Sir Joseph Wilson), **Tull** (Jethro), **Watt** (James), **Yale** (Linus)
**05** **Baird** (John Logie), **Boehm** (Theobald), **Boyle** (Robert), **Cyril** (St), **Dyson** (James), **Hertz** (Heinrich), **Kilby** (Jack S), **Maxim** (Sir Hiram Stevens), **Monge** (Gaspard), **Morse** (Samuel), **Nobel** (Alfred), **Rubik** (Ernö), **Sousa** (John Philip), **Tesla** (Nikola), **Volta** (Alessandro, Count), **Zeiss** (Carl)
**06** **Ampère** (André Marie), **Brunel** (Isambard Kingdom), **Brunel** (Sir Marc Isambard), **Bunsen** (Robert Wilhelm), **Diesel** (Rudolf), **Dunlop** (John Boyd), **Eckert** (J Presper), **Edison** (Thomas Alva), **Frisch** (Otto), **Hansom** (Joseph Aloysius), **Hornby** (Frank), **Hubble** (Edwin Powell), **Lenoir** (Jean Joseph Étienne), **Lister** (Samuel, Lord), **McAdam** (John Loudon), **Napier** (John), **Newton** (Sir Isaac), **Pascal** (Blaise), **Pitman** (Sir Isaac), **Schick** (Jacob), **Singer** (Isaac Merritt), **Sperry** (Elmer Ambrose), **Talbot** (William Henry Fox), **Wallis** (Sir Barnes), **Wright** (Orville), **Wright** (Wilbur)
**07** **Babbage** (Charles), **Blériot** (Louis), **Carlson** (Chester Floyd), **Daimler** (Gottlieb), **Drebbel** (Cornelis), **Eastman** (George), **Faraday** (Michael), **Gaumont** (Léon), **Giffard** (Henri), **Goddard** (Robert Hutchings), **Huygens** (Christiaan),

**Jacuzzi** (Candido), **Janssen** (Zacharias), **Lumière** (Auguste), **Lumière** (Louis Jean), **Marconi** (Guglielmo), **Mauchly** (John W), **Maxwell** (James Clerk), **Pasteur** (Louis), **Pullman** (George Mortimer), **Thomson** (Elihu), **Whitney** (Eli), **Whittle** (Sir Frank)
**08** **Bessemer** (Sir Henry), **Birdseye** (Clarence), **Daguerre** (Louis Jacques Mandé), **De Forest** (Lee), **Ericsson** (John), **Ferranti** (Sebastian Ziani de), **Franklin** (Benjamin), **Gillette** (King Camp), **Goodyear** (Charles), **Huntsman** (Benjamin), **Newcomen** (Thomas), **Sandwich** (John Montagu, Earl), **Sinclair** (Sir Clive), **Zamenhof** (Lazarus Ludwig), **Zeppelin** (Ferdinand von, Count)
**09** **Arkwright** (Sir Richard), **Armstrong** (Edwin Howard), **Butterick** (Ebenezer), **Cockerell** (Sir Christopher Sydney), **Ctesibius**, **Fessenden** (Reginald Aubrey), **Gutenberg** (Johannes), **Hollerith** (Herman), **Macmillan** (Kirkpatrick), **McCormick** (Cyrus Hall), **Pinchbeck** (Christopher), **Remington** (Philo), **Whitworth** (Sir Joseph)
**10** **Archimedes**, **Berners-Lee** (Tim), **Cristofori** (Bartolommeo), **Fahrenheit** (Gabriel), **Lilienthal** (Otto), **Pilkington** (Sir Alastair), **Senefelder** (Aloys), **Stephenson** (George), **Torricelli** (Evangelista), **Trevithick** (Richard)
**11** **Montgolfier** (Jacques), **Montgolfier** (Joseph)
**12** **Friese-Greene** (William)

**inventory**
**04** file, list, roll **05** stock, sum up, tally **06** record, roster, scroll, supply **07** account, listing, terrier **08** register, schedule **09** catalogue, checklist, equipment **11** description, stocktaking

**inverse**
**05** other **07** counter, obverse, reverse **08** contrary, converse, inverted, opposite, reversed **10** reciprocal, retrograde, transposed, upside down **12** antistrophic

**inversion**
◇ *reversal indicator* **07** reverse **08** contrary, converse, opposite, reversal **09** entropion, entropium **10** anastrophe, antithesis, transposal **11** contrariety **13** transposition **14** antimetathesis, contraposition

**invert**
◇ *reversal indicator* **05** upset **06** turn up, upturn **07** capsize, reverse **08** overturn, turn down **09** transpose **10** homosexual, turn around, turn turtle **11** transsexual **13** turn inside out **14** turn upside down **15** turn back to front

**invertebrate**

*Invertebrates include:*

**05** coral, fluke, hydra, leech
**06** chiton, insect, spider, sponge

**07** bivalve, crinoid, mollusc, sea lily, sea wasp
**08** arachnid, flatworm, nematode, sea pansy, starfish, tapeworm
**09** arthropod, centipede, earthworm, gastropod, jellyfish, millipede, planarian, roundworm, sea spider, sea urchin, spoonworm, trilobite, water bear
**10** cephalopod, crustacean, echinoderm, sand dollar, sea anemone, tardigrade
**11** annelid worm, brittle star, chaetognath, feather star, sea cucumber
**12** box jellyfish, coelenterate, Venus's girdle
**13** crown-of-thorns, horseshoe crab, sea gooseberry
**15** dead-men's fingers

*See also* **animal; butterfly; crustacean; insect; mollusc; moth; spider; worm**

**invest**
◇ *hidden indicator* ◇ *insertion indicator* **03** put **04** belt, fund, give, gown, robe, sink, vest **05** admit, adorn, cover, crown, endow, endue, frock, grant, imbue, place, put in, spend, tie up **06** bestow, clothe, confer, create, devote, enrobe, induct, lay out, lock up, ordain, supply **07** besiege, dignify, empower, entrust, install, mandate, provide, swear in **08** dedicate, sanction, surround **09** authorize, beglamour, subsidize **10** contribute, inaugurate

**investigate**
**03** spy, sus **04** case, comb, feel, sift, suss **05** probe, study, trawl **06** go into, muzzle, nuzzle, pry out, search **07** analyse, check up, examine, explore, inspect, suss out **08** check out, consider, look into, research **09** delve into **10** scrutinize **11** inquire into **15** give the once-over

**investigation**
**05** probe, quest, study **06** review, search, survey **07** enquiry, hearing, inquest, inquiry, sifting, zetetic **08** analysis, research, scrutiny **10** inspection **11** examination, exploration, inquisition **13** consideration
• **bear investigation** **04** wash

**investigative**
**07** zetetic **08** research **09** heuristic **10** analytical, inspecting **11** exploratory, fact-finding, researching **13** investigating

**investigator**
**02** PI **04** dick **06** ferret, prober, sleuth **07** analyst **08** analyser, examiner, explorer, inquirer, quaestor, reviewer, searcher **09** detective, inspector, ombudsman **10** private eye, questioner, researcher, scrutineer **11** scrutinizer

**investiture**
**09** admission, induction, investing **10** coronation, investment, ordination, swearing-in **11** instatement

**12** enthronement, inauguration, installation

## investment
**04** cash, gilt, risk, spec **05** asset, funds, money, stake, stock **06** outlay, wealth **07** capital, finance, reserve, savings, venture **08** blockade, property **09** bonus bond, principal, resources **11** expenditure, investiture, speculation, transaction **12** contribution **14** venture capital

## inveterate
**05** sworn **06** inured **07** chronic, diehard **08** addicted, habitual, hard-core, hardened, stubborn **09** confirmed, incurable, obstinate **10** double-dyed, entrenched **11** established **12** incorrigible, irreformable, long-standing **13** dyed-in-the-wool

## invidious
**06** odious **07** awkward, hateful **08** enviable **09** difficult, obnoxious, offensive, repugnant, slighting **10** unpleasant **11** undesirable **13** objectionable **14** discriminating, discriminatory

## invigilate
**05** watch **06** direct **07** inspect, monitor, oversee **09** look after, supervise, watch over **11** keep an eye on, superintend **12** be in charge of **13** be in control of

## invigilation
**04** care **06** charge **07** control, running **08** guidance **09** direction, oversight **10** inspection **11** supervision **12** surveillance **15** superintendence

## invigilator
**07** monitor, proctor **08** director, examiner, overseer **09** inspector **10** supervisor **14** superintendent

## invigorate
**04** buck **05** brace, pep up, renew, rouse **06** buck up, excite, perk up, soup up **07** animate, enliven, fortify, freshen, inspire, liven up, quicken, refresh **08** energize, motivate, vitalize **09** stimulate **10** exhilarate, rejuvenate, revitalize, strengthen

## invigorating
**05** brisk, fresh, tonic, vital **07** bracing **08** generous **09** animating, healthful, uplifting, vivifying **10** energizing, fortifying, life-giving, quickening, refreshing, salubrious **11** inspiriting, restorative, stimulating **12** exhilarating, rejuvenating

## invincibility
**05** force, power **08** strength **13** inviolability **14** impregnability, insuperability **15** impenetrability, invulnerability, unassailability

## invincible
**08** almighty **10** unbeatable, unshakable, unyielding **11** all-powerful, impregnable, indomitable, insuperable, unshakeable **12** impenetrable, invulnerable, unassailable, undefeatable **13** unconquerable **14** indestructible, unsurmountable

## inviolability
**08** holiness, sanctity **09** inviolacy **10** sacredness **14** inalienability, inviolableness, sacrosanctness **15** invulnerability

## inviolable
**04** holy **06** sacred **08** hallowed **10** intemerate, sacrosanct **11** inalienable, unalterable, untouchable

## inviolate
**04** pure **05** whole **06** entire, intact, sacred, unhurt, virgin **08** complete, unbroken, unharmed **09** stainless, undamaged, undefiled, uninjured, unspoiled, unstained, unsullied, untouched **10** intemerate, unpolluted, unprofaned **11** undisturbed

## invisible
**05** blind **06** hidden, unseen **08** viewless **09** concealed, disguised, imaginary, occulting, sightless, unnoticed, unseeable **10** evaporated, out of sight, unobserved **11** microscopic, non-existent **12** undetectable **13** imperceivable, imperceptible, inconspicuous, indiscernible, infinitesimal, microscopical **14** dematerialized

## invitation
**04** bait, call, draw, lure **06** appeal, come-on, invite **07** bidding, request, summons, welcome **08** overture, petition **09** challenge **10** allurement, attraction, come-hither, enticement, incitement, inducement, temptation **11** proposition, provocation **12** solicitation **13** encouragement

## invite
**03** ask, bid, woo **04** call, draw, lead, seek, will **05** press, tempt **06** allure, appeal, ask for, entice, summon **07** attract, bring on, look for, provoke, request, solicit, welcome **08** have over, petition **09** encourage, entertain, have round **15** give the come-on to

## inviting
**07** winning **08** alluring, engaging, enticing, pleasant, pleasing, tempting **09** agreeable, appealing, beguiling, seductive, welcoming **10** attractive, bewitching, come-hither, delightful, enchanting, entrancing, intriguing **11** captivating, fascinating, tantalizing **12** irresistible

## invocation
**04** call **05** curse **06** appeal, prayer **07** request, summons **08** entreaty, petition **09** epiclesis **10** beseeching **11** benediction, conjuration, imploration **12** solicitation, supplication
• **expression of invocation** **02** io

## invoice
**03** inv **04** bill **07** account, charges **08** manifest, pro forma **09** reckoning

## invoke
**03** beg **04** cite, wish **05** curse, swear **06** call on, pray to, rabbit, turn to **07** beseech, conjure, entreat, implore, refer to, request, solicit, swear by

**08** appeal to, call down, call upon, petition, resort to **09** deprecate, imprecate, make use of **10** supplicate **14** have recourse to

## involuntary
**05** blind **06** forced, reflex **07** coerced **08** knee-jerk, unwilled **09** automatic, compelled, impulsive, mandatory, reluctant, unwilling **10** compulsory, mechanical, obligatory, unthinking **11** conditioned, instinctive, spontaneous, unconscious **12** uncontrolled **13** unintentional

## involve
◊ *anagram indicator* ◊ *insertion indicator* **03** mix **04** cost, grip, hold, mean, wind, wrap **05** cover, imply, infer, mix up, rivet **06** absorb, affect, assume, commit, denote, draw in, engage, entail, mess in, occupy, take in **07** concern, connect, connote, count in, dip into, embrace, embroil, engross, immerse, include, require **08** entangle, interest, mess with, walk into **09** associate, embarrass, encompass, implicate, inculpate, preoccupy **10** complicate, comprehend, compromise, presuppose **11** incorporate, incriminate, necessitate **15** cause to take part

## involved
◊ *anagram indicator* **04** deep, held, in on **06** implex, knotty **07** complex, engaged, gripped, jumbled, mixed up, riveted, tangled **08** absorbed, caught up, confused, immersed, intorted, involute, occupied, plighted, tortuous **09** complicit, concerned, confusing, difficult, elaborate, engrossed, intricate **10** associated, convoluted, implicated, inculpated, interested, taking part **11** anfractuous, complicated, preoccupied **12** incriminated, inextricable **13** participating
• **involved with** ◊ *insertion indicator* **02** in

## involvement
**04** part **05** share **06** action **07** concern **08** interest **09** immersion **10** attachment, connection **11** association, implication **12** contribution, entanglement **13** participation **14** responsibility

## invulnerability
**05** proof **06** safety **08** security, strength **13** invincibility, inviolability **14** impregnability **15** impenetrability, unassailability

## invulnerable
**04** safe **05** proof **06** secure **09** woundless **10** impervious, invincible **12** impenetrable, unassailable **14** indestructible

## inward
**02** in **05** inner **06** entire, hidden, infelt, inmost, inside, secret, toward **07** private **08** entering, homefelt, incoming, interior, internal, intimate, introrse, involute, personal, turned-in **09** heartfelt, incurrent, innermost, intrinsic **11** intrinsical **12** confidential

## inwardly
**04** inly **06** inside, within **07** at heart
**08** deep down, secretly **09** privately
**10** to yourself **13** deep inside you

## inwards
**06** inside, inward, within **07** indoors
**08** inwardly

## iodine
**01** I

## iota
**03** bit, jot, tad **04** atom, hint, mite, whit
**05** grain, scrap, speck, trace **06** morsel
**08** fraction, particle

## Iowa
**02** IA

## Iran
**02** IR **03** IRN

## Iraq
**03** IRQ

## irascibility
**06** choler **08** edginess **09** bad temper,
crossness, fieriness, ill-temper,
petulance, shortness, testiness
**10** crabbiness, impatience, irritation,
touchiness **12** irritability, snappishness

## irascible
**05** cross, hasty, narky, ratty, testy
**06** crabby, touchy **07** crabbed,
iracund, prickly, toustie **08** choleric,
petulant **09** irritable, querulous **10** ill-
natured **11** bad-tempered, hot-
tempered, ill-tempered
**12** cantankerous, iracundulous
**13** quick-tempered, short-tempered

## irate
**03** mad **04** waxy **05** angry, livid, vexed
**06** fuming, raging **07** annoyed,
enraged, furious, ranting **08** incensed,
up in arms, worked up **09** indignant,
irritated, steamed up **10** hopping mad,
infuriated **11** exasperated

## irately
**07** angrily, crossly, in a huff **08** bitterly
**09** furiously **11** indignantly,
resentfully **13** acrimoniously,
reproachfully

## ire
**04** fury, rage **05** anger, wrath **06** choler
**07** passion **09** annoyance
**11** displeasure, indignation
**12** exasperation

## Ireland
**03** IRL **04** Éire, Erin **08** Hibernia
**09** Green Isle **11** blarney-land, Emerald
Isle

*Irish cities and notable towns
include:*

**04** Cork
**05** Sligo
**06** Dublin, Galway
**07** Dundalk
**08** Drogheda, Limerick
**09** Waterford

*See also* **county; province**

## iridescent
**04** shot **06** flambé, pearly **07** rainbow
**08** dazzling **09** chatoyant, prismatic,
sparkling **10** glittering, opalescent,

shimmering, variegated **11** rainbow-
like **13** multicoloured, polychromatic
**15** rainbow-coloured

## iridium
**02** Ir

## iris
**03** lis, seg **04** flag, irid, ixia **05** orris,
sedge **07** gladdon **09** water flag
**10** fleur-de-lis, fleur-de-lys **12** flower-
delice, flower-deluce **13** flower-de-
leuce **14** roast-beef plant

## Irish
**02** Ir **04** Erse **08** Milesian **09** Hibernian
*See also* **Ireland**

*Irish first names include:*

**03** Ena, Kit, Pat, Una
**04** Aine, Cait, Colm, Edel, Elva, Eoin,
Erin, Euan, Ewan, Ewen, Finn,
Kath, Kyra, Liam, Maev, Maud,
Mona, Neal, Neil, Nola, Nora,
Owen, Rory, Ryan, Sean, Sine,
Tara
**05** Aidan, Aiden, Barry, Brona,
Cahal, Ciara, Colum, Conor,
Duane, Dwane, Elvis, Ethna,
Ethne, Fionn, Kelly, Kerry, Kevan,
Kevin, Kiera, Maeve, Maire,
Maude, Maura, Moira, Moyra,
Neale, Niall, Niamh, Norah,
Nuala, Oscar, Paddy, Ronan,
Rowan, Shane, Shaun, Shawn,
Ultan
**06** Aileen, Ailish, Arthur, Cathal,
Ciaran, Connor, Declan, Dervla,
Dympna, Eamonn, Eamunn,
Eileen, Eithna, Eithne, Finbar,
Fingal, Finola, Fintan, Garret,
Grania, Granya, Kieran, Kieron,
Kilian, Lorcan, Noreen, Roisin,
Seamas, Seamus, Shamus, Sheila,
Sinead, Sorcha, Tyrone
**07** Aisling, Brendan, Bronach,
Bronagh, Caitlin, Christy,
Clodagh, Colleen, Deirdre,
Desmond, Dymphna, Feargal,
Finbarr, Grainne, Killian,
Mairead, Maureen, Padraic,
Padraig, Patrick, Shannon,
Shelagh, Siobhan
**08** Kathleen, Ruaidhri
**09** Fionnuala

## irk
**03** bug, get, vex **04** gall, miff, rile
**05** anger, annoy, get at, get to, weary
**06** needle, nettle, put out, ruffle, wind
up **07** disgust, incense, provoke
**08** distress, drive mad, irritate
**09** aggravate, infuriate **10** drive crazy,
exasperate **12** drive bananas **13** make
sparks fly **14** drive up the wall

## irksome
**06** boring, trying, vexing **07** painful,
tedious **08** annoying, infernal, tiresome
**09** vexatious, wearisome
**10** bothersome, burdensome,
confounded, irritating, ungrateful
**11** aggravating, infuriating,
troublesome **12** disagreeable,
exasperating

## iron
**02** Fe **04** airn, firm, hard, Mars

**05** harsh, press, rigid, stern, tough
**06** fetter, pistol, robust, smooth, steely,
strong **07** adamant, flatten, grating,
stirrup **08** decrease, revolver, strength
**10** determined, inflexible **11** insensitive
**14** uncompromising
• **iron out 06** settle **07** clear up,
resolve, sort out **08** deal with, get rid
of, put right **09** eliminate, eradicate,
harmonize, reconcile **13** straighten out

## ironic, ironical
**03** wry **04** rich **05** bland **07** mocking
**08** derisive, sardonic, scoffing,
scornful, sneering **09** sarcastic, satirical
**10** ridiculing, ridiculous **11** paradoxical
**12** antiphrastic, contemptuous
**14** antiphrastical

## irons
**05** bonds **06** chains **07** fetters
**08** manacles, shackles, trammels

## irony
**04** hard **05** scorn **06** satire **07** asteism,
mockery, paradox, sarcasm **08** ridicule
**10** enantiosis **11** antiphrasis,
incongruity **12** contrariness **14** sting in
the tail

## irradiate
**06** expose, illume **07** lighten, light up,
radiate, shine on **08** brighten, illumine
**09** enlighten **10** illuminate

## irrational
**04** surd, wild **05** brute, crazy, silly
**06** absurd, phobic, unwise **07** brutish,
foolish, invalid, unsound **08** paranoid
**09** arbitrary, beastlike, illogical,
senseless **10** groundless, ridiculous
**11** implausible, nonsensical,
unreasoning **12** inconsistent,
unreasonable **14** beside yourself

## irrationality
**06** lunacy **07** madness **08** insanity,
unreason **09** absurdity **11** unsoundness
**12** illogicality **13** senselessness
**14** groundlessness, ridiculousness

## irreconcilable
**05** alien **06** at odds **07** opposed
**08** clashing, contrary, frondeur,
hardline, opposite **10** implacable, in
conflict, inexorable, inflexible,
unatonable **11** conflicting,
incongruous **12** incompatible,
inconsistent, intransigent
**13** contradictory, intransigeant
**14** uncompromising

## irrecoverable
**04** lost **09** unsavable **11** irreparable
**12** irredeemable, irremediable
**13** irreclaimable, irretrievable,
unrecoverable, unsalvageable

## irredeemable
**08** past hope **09** incurable **10** beyond
hope **11** irreparable, irrevocable
**12** incorrigible **13** irretrievable

## irrefutable
**04** sure **07** certain **08** decisive, definite,
positive **10** unarguable, undeniable
**11** beyond doubt, indubitable
**12** indisputable, unanswerable
**13** incontestable **14** beyond question,
unquestionable

## irregular

◇ *anagram indicator* **03** odd **04** bent, iffy **05** bumpy, false, fishy, freak, lumpy, rough, shady, shaky **06** fitful, haiduk, jagged, patchy, pitted, ragged, random, rugged, shifty, sniper, uneven **07** corrupt, crooked, devious, erratic, lawless, scraggy, snatchy, strange, unusual, wayward **08** aberrant, abnormal, cheating, improper, indecent, lopsided, partisan, peculiar, scraggly, sporadic, unsteady, variable, wavering **09** anomalous, deceitful, dishonest, guerrilla, haphazard, incondite, maquisard, spasmodic, terrorist **10** asymmetric, asyntactic, disorderly, fraudulent, immoderate, mendacious, occasional, out of order, perfidious, scraggling, unofficial, unorthodox **11** anomalistic, bushwhacker, duplicitous, exceptional, extravagant, fluctuating, fragmentary, franc-tireur, guerrillero, heteroclite **12** disorganized, disreputable, immethodical, inconsistent, intermittent, unmethodical, unprincipled, unscrupulous, unsystematic **13** against the law, anomalistical, dishonourable, extraordinary, unsymmetrical **14** freedom fighter, unconventional **15** against the rules

## irregularity

**05** fraud, freak, spasm **06** breach, deceit, oddity **07** anomaly, falsity, perfidy **08** cheating, trickery, wavering **09** arhythmia, asymmetry, bumpiness, chicanery, deviation, duplicity, falsehood, improbity, lumpiness, obliquity, roughness, shadiness, treachery **10** aberration, arrhythmia, corruption, dirty trick, dishonesty, fitfulness, jaggedness, misconduct, patchiness, raggedness, randomness, unevenness **11** abnormality, criminality, crookedness, fluctuation, fraudulence, impropriety, inconstancy, insincerity, lawlessness, malpractice, obliqueness, peculiarity, singularity, uncertainty, unorthodoxy, unusualness, variability **12** eccentricity, inordination, lopsidedness, perturbation, unsteadiness **13** double-dealing, haphazardness, inconsistency, intermittence, sharp practice, unpunctuality **14** disorderliness, occasionalness, untruthfulness **15** disorganization

## irregularly

**06** anyhow **07** jerkily **08** fitfully, off and on, unevenly **11** erratically, haphazardly, now and again **12** here and there, occasionally **13** eccentrically, interruptedly, spasmodically **14** disconnectedly, intermittently, unmethodically **15** by fits and starts, in fits and starts

## irrelevance

**07** tangent **09** inaptness **10** digression, red herring **11** irrelevancy **12** unimportance **13** inconsequence,

unrelatedness **14** extraneousness, inappositeness **15** inapplicability

## irrelevant

**05** inapt, inept **09** ungermane, unrelated **10** extraneous, immaterial, inapposite, irrelative, out of place, peripheral, tangential **11** off the point, unconnected, unimportant **12** inapplicable, inconsequent **13** beside the mark, inappropriate **14** beside the point **15** having no bearing, not coming into it

## irreligious

**05** pagan **06** sinful, unholy, wicked **07** godless, heathen, impious, profane, ungodly **08** agnostic, undevout **09** atheistic, heretical, sceptical **10** heathenish, irreverent **11** blasphemous, nullifidian, unbelieving, unreligious, unrighteous **12** free-thinking, iconoclastic, sacrilegious **13** rationalistic

## irremediable

**05** fatal, final **06** deadly, mortal **08** hopeless, terminal **09** incurable **10** inoperable, remediless **11** irreparable **12** incorrigible, irredeemable, irreversible **13** irrecoverable, irretrievable, unmedicinable

## irremovable

**03** set **04** fast **05** fixed, stuck **06** rooted **07** durable **08** obdurate **09** immovable, ingrained, obstinate, permanent **10** inoperable, persistent **12** ineradicable **14** indestructible

## irreparable

**09** incurable **12** irremediable, irreversible, unrepairable **13** irreclaimable, irrecoverable, irretrievable

## irreplaceable

**05** vital **06** unique **07** special **08** peerless, precious **09** essential, matchless, priceless, unmatched **13** indispensable

## irrepressible

**06** bubbly, lively **07** buoyant **08** animated **09** ebullient, energetic, resilient, vivacious **10** boisterous **11** uninhibited, unstoppable **12** effervescent, ungovernable **13** uncontainable **14** insuppressible, uncontrollable, unrestrainable

## irreproachable

**04** pure **07** perfect, sinless **08** flawless, innocent, spotless **09** blameless, faultless, guiltless, stainless **10** immaculate, impeccable, unblamable **11** unblemished **13** unimpeachable **14** beyond reproach **15** irreprehensible

## irresistible

**06** potent, urgent **07** killing **08** alluring, almighty, charming, enticing, forceful, pressing, tempting **09** ravishing, seductive **10** compelling, compulsive, enchanting, imperative, importable, inevitable, inexorable, opposeless, resistless **11** captivating, fascinating, inescapable, tantalizing, unavoidable

**12** overpowering, overwhelming **13** insupportable, irrepressible, overmastering, unpreventable **14** uncontrollable

## irresolute

**04** weak **06** fickle, unsure **07** dubious **08** doubtful, hesitant, shifting, unstable, unsteady, variable, wavering **09** dithering, tentative, uncertain, undecided, unsettled **10** ambivalent, hesitating, indecisive, in two minds, on the fence, unresolved, weak-willed, wishy-washy **11** fluctuating, half-hearted, vacillating **12** faint-hearted, invertebrate, pussyfooting, undetermined **15** shilly-shallying

## irrespective

• **irrespective of 07** however, whoever **08** ignoring, no matter, whatever **09** never mind, whichever **12** disregarding, not affecting, regardless of **15** notwithstanding

## irresponsible

**04** rash, wild **06** unwise **07** erratic, flighty **08** carefree, careless, heedless, immature, reckless **09** negligent **10** fly-by-night, unreliable **11** injudicious, thoughtless **12** light-hearted **13** ill-considered, untrustworthy **14** scatterbrained

## irretrievable

**04** lost **06** damned **08** hopeless **11** irreparable, irrevocable **12** irredeemable, irremediable, irreversible, unrecallable **13** irrecoverable, unrecoverable, unsalvageable

## irretrievably

**10** hopelessly **11** irreparably, irrevocably **12** irredeemably, irreversibly **13** irrecoverably

## irreverence

**05** cheek, sauce **06** heresy, levity **07** impiety, mockery **08** rudeness **09** blasphemy, flippancy, impudence, insolence, profanity, sacrilege **10** cheekiness, disrespect, irreligion **11** discourtesy, godlessness, ungodliness **12** impertinence, impoliteness

## irreverent

**04** rude **05** saucy **06** cheeky **07** godless, impious, mocking, profane, ungodly **08** flippant, impolite, impudent, insolent **09** heretical **10** unreverend **11** blasphemous, impertinent, irreligious **12** discourteous, sacrilegious **13** disrespectful

## irreversible

**05** final **07** lasting **08** hopeless **09** incurable, permanent **11** irreparable, irrevocable, unalterable **12** irremediable **13** irretrievable, unrectifiable

## irrevocable

**05** final, fixed **07** settled **09** immutable **10** changeless, invariable **11** unalterable **12** irreversible, unchangeable **13** irretrievable, predetermined

## irrevocably

**07** for good **10** hopelessly, inevitably
**11** inescapably, insuperably,
irreparably, unavoidably **13** for good
and all

## irrigate

**03** wet **04** soak **05** drink, flood, spray,
water **06** dampen, deluge **07** moisten
**08** inundate, sprinkle

## irritability

**04** bile, edge **08** edginess, erethism
**09** bad temper, crossness, hastiness, ill-
temper, petulance, rattiness, testiness
**10** crabbiness, grumpiness,
impatience, tetchiness, touchiness
**11** fretfulness, peevishness, prickliness,
stroppiness **12** irascibility
**13** fractiousness

## irritable

**04** edgy, sore **05** cross, fiery, gusty,
hasty, humpy, narky, ratty, riley, short,
spiky, techy, testy **06** chippy, crabby,
cranky, crusty, feisty, grumpy, livery,
on edge, shirty, snappy, snarky, tetchy,
touchy **07** bilious, crabbit, fretful,
gustful, peckish, peevish, peppery,
prickly, stroppy **08** liverish, scratchy,
snappish **09** crotchety, fractious,
impatient, irascible, splenetic
**10** capernoity, hot-blooded,
nettlesome **11** bad-tempered,
capernoitie, cappernoity, ill-tempered,
out of temper, thin-skinned
**12** cantankerous **13** quick-tempered,
short-tempered **14** hypersensitive

## irritant

**04** gall, goad, pain **05** CS gas, savin
**06** bother, menace, savine **07** trouble
**08** nuisance, urushiol, vexation
**09** annoyance **11** provocation **15** thorn
in the flesh

## irritate

**03** bug, eat, get, irk, jar, rub, try, vex
**04** fret, gall, goad, grig, hurt, itch, miff,
nark, rile **05** anger, annoy, chafe, get
at, grate, peeve, rouse, tease **06** bother,
emboil, enrage, excite, gravel, harass,
jangle, needle, nettle, niggle, put out,
rattle, ruffle, tickle, wind up
**07** enchafe, incense, inflame, provoke
**08** acerbate, drive mad **09** aggravate,
displease, drive nuts, infuriate,
stimulate **10** drive crazy, exasperate,
excruciate **12** drive bananas **13** get
your back up, make sparks fly **14** drive
up the wall, rub the wrong way **15** get
on your nerves, give the needle to

## irritated

◇ *anagram indicator* **03** mad **04** edgy,
sore **05** angry, cross, irked, raggy, ratty,
riled, spewy, vexed **06** choked, miffed,
narked, peeved, piqued, put out,
roused **07** annoyed, crooked, in a huff,
nettled, ropable, ruffled, stroppy,
uptight **08** bothered, harassed, in a
paddy, in a strop, up in arms
**09** flappable, flustered, impatient, in a
lather, irritable, raving mad, seeing
red, splenetic, ticked off
**10** aggravated, displeased, exasperate,
hopping mad **11** discomposed,

disgruntled, exacerbated, exasperated,
fit to be tied **12** on the warpath

## irritating

**04** sore **05** itchy, pesky **06** thorny,
trying, vexing **07** chafing, galling,
grating, irksome, nagging, rubbing
**08** abrasive, annoying, infernal,
ticklish, tiresome, urticant
**09** maddening, provoking, upsetting,
vexatious, worrisome **10** bothersome,
confounded, disturbing **11** aggravating,
displeasing, infuriating, troublesome
**12** excruciating

## irritation

**03** rub **04** bind, drag, fret, fury, pain,
pest **05** anger, pique **06** bother
**07** scunner, trouble **08** nuisance,
pinprick, vexation **09** annoyance,
crossness, testiness **10** impatience,
snappiness **11** aggravation,
displeasure, disturbance, indignation,
provocation, running sore, stimulation
**12** exasperation, excruciation, heeby-
jeebies, irritability **13** heebie-jeebies,
pain in the neck **15** dissatisfaction,
thorn in the flesh

*See also* **itch**

• **display of irritation** **04** tiff, tift

## is

**01** 's **03** est

## Islamic

*see* **month**

## island

**01** I **02** Is **03** ait, cay, île, Isl, key
**04** eyot, holm, inch, isle **05** atoll, islet
**06** skerry **07** isolate **11** archipelago

*Islands and island groups include:*

**03** Cos, Ely, Fyn, Hoy, IOM, Ios,
IOW, Man, Rab, Rum
**04** Bali, Coll, Cook, Corn, Cuba,
Eigg, Elba, Fiji, Gozo, Guam,
Holy, Iona, Java, Jura, Line, Long,
Mahe, Maui, Muck, Mull, Nias,
Niue, Oahu, Rhum, Rota, Sado,
Sark, Skye, Uist, Unst, Wake
**05** Arran, Barra, Bioko, Bonin, Capri,
Chios, Cocos, Coney, Corfu,
Crete, Delos, Éfaté, Ellis, Farne,
Faroe, Handa, Hondo, Hydra,
Ibiza, Islay, Kauai, Kuril, Lanai,
Lundy, Luzon, Malta, Melos,
Nauru, Naxos, North, Öland,
Orust, Palau, Paros, Pearl,
Pemba, Samoa, Samos, South,
Sunda, Timor, Tiree, Tonga,
Wight
**06** Aegean, Aegina, Andros, Azores,
Baffin, Bikini, Borneo, Caicos,
Canary, Chagos, Comino, Cyprus,
Devil's, Easter, Euboea, Flores,
Flotta, Hainan, Harris, Hawaii,
Honshu, Icaria, Ionian, Ischia,
Jersey, Kodiak, Komodo, Kosrae,
Kyushu, Lemnos, Lesbos,
Midway, Orkney, Patmos,
Penghu, Rhodes, Scilly, Sicily,
Skiros, Staffa, Staten, Tahiti,
Taiwan, Tinian, Tobago, Tubuai,
Tuvalu, Virgin
**07** Anjouan, Anthony, Antigua,
Bahamas, Bahrain, Bermuda,

Bonaire, Cabrera, Celebes,
Channel, Chatham, Comoros,
Corsica, Curaçao, Frisian, Gilbert,
Gotland, Grenada, Iceland,
Ireland, Iwo Jima, Jamaica, La
Digue, Leeward, Lofoten, Loyalty,
Madeira, Majorca, Mayotte,
Menorca, Mikonos, Mindoro,
Minorca, Molokai, Nicobar,
Norfolk, Oceania, Okinawa,
Palawan, Phoenix, Praslin,
Rathlin, Réunion, Siberut,
Society, Solomon, Stewart, St
Kilda, St Lucia, Sumatra, Surtsey,
Tokelau, Vanuatu, Visayan,
Westman, Wrangel, Zealand
**08** Aleutian, Anglesey, Anguilla,
Balearic, Bornholm, Colonsay,
Coral Sea, Cyclades, Dominica,
Falkland, Guernsey, Hawaiian,
Hebrides, Hokkaido, Hong Kong,
Jan Mayen, Johnston, Kiribati,
Lord Howe, Maldives, Marshall,
Mindanao, Moluccas, Pitcairn,
Sakhalin, Sandwich, São Tiago,
Sardinia, Shetland, Skiathos, Sri
Lanka, Sulawesi, Svalbard,
Tenerife, Trinidad, Victoria, Viti
Levu, Windward, Zanzibar
**09** Admiralty, Ascension, Australia,
Benbecula, Cape Verde,
Christmas, Ellesmere, Galápagos,
Greenland, Halmahera,
Indonesia, Irian Jaya, Isle of Man,
Kárpathos, Lanzarote, Las Palmas,
Macquarie, Manhattan,
Marquesas, Mascarene,
Mauritius, Melanesia, Nantucket,
New Guinea, North Uist,
Rodrigues, Santorini, Singapore,
South Seas, South Uist, Stromboli,
Vanua Levu, Zacynthus
**10** Ahvenanmaa, Basse-Terre, Cape
Breton, Cephalonia, Cook Strait,
Dodecanese, Formentera,
Heligoland, Hispaniola, Ile
d'Oléron, Kalimantan, Kiritimati,
Madagascar, Martinique,
Micronesia, Montserrat, New
Britain, New Ireland, Puerto Rico,
Samothrace, Seychelles,
Vesterålen, West Indies
**11** Gran Canaria, Grand Bahama,
Grand Cayman, Grande-Terre,
Guadalcanal, Iles d'Hyères, Iles
du Salut, Isla Cozumel, Isle of
Wight, North Island, Philippines,
Saint Helena, Scilly Isles, South
Island, South Orkney
**12** Bougainville, Grande Comore,
Great Britain, Isla de Pascua,
Newfoundland, Novaya Zemlya,
Prince Edward, Prince Rupert,
South Georgia
**13** American Samoa, British Virgin,
Inner Hebrides, Isla Contadora,
Isles of Scilly, New Providence,
Outer Hebrides, South Shetland
**14** Oki Archipelago, Papua New
Guinea, The Philippines, Tierra
del Fuego, Tristan da Cunha,
Turks and Caicos
**15** French Polynesia, Lewis with

Harris, Martha's Vineyard, Wallis and Futuna

See also **Channel Islands** under channel
• **reef island** 04 motu

**Isle of Man**
03 GBM, IMN 11 Ellan Vannin

**isn't**
03 nis, nys 04 ain't

**isolate**
06 cut off, detach, enisle, inisle, island, maroon, remove, strand 07 divorce, exclude, seclude, shut out 08 abstract, alienate, insulate, separate, set apart, shut away 09 keep apart, ostracize, segregate, sequester 10 disconnect, quarantine 11 marginalize 12 cold-shoulder 14 send to Coventry

**isolated**
04 lone 05 alone, apart, freak, stray 06 cut off, lonely, remote, single, unique 07 insular, special, unusual 08 abnormal, atypical, deserted, detached, outlying, secluded, solitary, uncommon 09 anomalous, separated, unrelated, untypical 10 segregated 11 exceptional, god-forsaken, in the sticks, out-of-the-way 12 unfrequented

**isolation**
05 exile 08 solitude 09 aloneness, seclusion 10 alienation, detachment, insulation, loneliness, quarantine, remoteness, retirement, separation, withdrawal 11 abstraction, segregation 12 dissociation, separateness, solitariness 13 disconnection, sequestration 15 marginalization

**Israel**
02 IL 03 ISR
See also **tribe**

**issue**
03 ish, jet, son 04 come, copy, emit, fall, fine, flow, flux, gush, mark, ooze, rise, rush, seed, seep, stem, turn 05 ensue, equip, exude, fit up, heirs, point, proof, spurt, topic, young 06 affair, debate, derive, effect, embryo, emerge, escape, family, finale, fit out, follow, kit out, matter, number, outlet, pay-off, put out, result, rig out, scions, spread, spring, stream, supply, upshot 07 concern, deal out, debouch, deliver, develop, dispute, edition, emanate, give out, handout, outcome, outflow, problem, proceed, produce, profits, progeny, provide, publish, release, send out, subject,

version 08 announce, argument, children, daughter, delivery, effusion, emission, printing, proclaim, question 09 broadcast, discharge, effluence, offspring, originate, supplying, terminate 10 break forth, burst forth, conclusion, dénouement, distribute, impression, instalment, promulgate, successors 11 circulation, consequence, controversy, descendants, disseminate, publication 12 announcement, distribution, promulgation 13 dissemination
• **at issue** 10 in question 12 being debated 14 being discussed 15 under discussion
• **final issue** 04 fate
• **side issue** 02 by 03 bye
• **take issue** 05 argue, fight 06 object 07 contest, dispute, protest, quarrel 08 be at odds, disagree 09 challenge 12 be at odds with 13 take exception
• **violent issue** 04 gush
• **without issue** 02 sp 03 dsp, osp 09 sine prole

**it**
01 a, 't 02 SA 05 oomph 08 vermouth 09 sex appeal
• **it is not** 05 'taint, 'tisn't 06 aikona
• **it's** 03 'tis
• **on it** 03 an't

**Italian**
◇ foreign word indicator 01 I 02 It 03 Sig 04 Ital, trat 05 Roman, tratt 08 Ausonian, Sicilian, Venetian 09 trattoria 10 Neapolitan

See also **day; month; number**
• **Italian family** 06 Medici

**Italy**
01 I 03 ITA 04 Ital

**itch**
03 die, euk, ewk 04 ache, burn, long, pine, yeuk, youk, yuck, yuke 05 crave, crawl, psora, yearn 06 desire, hanker, hunger, thirst, tickle, tingle 07 burning, craving, longing, passion, prickle, scabies 08 irritate, keenness, pruritus, tingling, yearning 09 cacoethes, eagerness, hankering, itchiness, prickling 10 irritation

**itching**
03 euk, ewk 04 avid, yeuk, youk, yuck, yuke 05 dying, eager 06 aching, greedy, raring 07 burning, longing 08 prurient, pruritus 09 hankering, impatient 11 inquisitive

**item**
03 job 04 also 05 entry, issue, piece, point, story, thing 06 aspect, detail, factor, matter, notice, number, object, report 07 account, article, element, feature 08 bulletin, likewise 09 component, paragraph 10 accidental, ingredient, particular 12 circumstance 13 consideration

**itemize**
04 list 05 count 06 detail, number, record 07 mention, specify 08 document, instance, overname, tabulate 09 catalogue, enumerate 13 particularize 15 make an inventory

**itinerant**
◇ anagram indicator 03 faw 04 hobo, Roma 05 caird, Gypsy, nomad, rover 06 gitano, hawker, pedlar, roamer, Romani, Romany, roving, tinker 07 chapman, didakai, didakei, didicoi, didicoy, nomadic, rambler, roadman, roaming, running, swagman, tzigany, vagrant, Zincalo, Zingaro 08 Bohemian, diddicoy, drifting, huckster, minstrel, preacher, rambling, rootless, stroller, vagabond, wanderer, Zigeuner 09 itinerary, migratory, muffin man, piepowder, strolling, sundowner, traveller, unsettled, wandering, wayfaring 10 evangelist, journeying, revivalist, travelling 11 gandy dancer, peripatetic, Scotch cuddy 12 on the wallaby, Scotch draper 15 New-Age Traveller, strolling player

**itinerary**
03 way 04 plan, tour 05 route 06 course 07 circuit, journey 08 schedule 09 itinerant, programme, timetable 10 travelling 12 arrangements

**itself**
• **of itself** 03 sui

**ivory**
07 dentine 08 eburnean 09 eburneous 10 whale's bone

**IVR code**
see **vehicle**

**ivy**
03 tod, udo 04 gill 06 aralia, fatsia, Hedera 07 ale-hoof 08 cat's-foot

**Ivy League**
see **university**

**izzard**
01 Z 03 zed

# J

**J**
03 jay 06 Juliet

**jab**
03 box, dig, tap 04 poke, prod, push, shot, stab 05 elbow, lunge, nudge, punch 06 thrust 09 injection

**jabber**
03 gab, jaw, yap 05 prate 06 babble, gabble, mumble, rabbit, ramble, rattle, tattle, witter, yabber, yatter 07 blather, blether, chatter, prattle, sputter

**jack**
01 J 02 AB 03 Dee, jak, nob, pam, pur, tar 04 Jock, John, mark 05 bower, fed up, kitty, knave, makar, money, noddy, tired, winch 06 hopper, runner, sailor 07 pantine, sticker 08 mistress, saw-horse, turnspit 09 detective, hand-screw
• **jack up** 04 hike, lift 05 hoist, put up, raise 06 hike up, push up, refuse, resist 07 elevate, inflate 08 increase

**jackal**
04 dieb 13 lion's provider

**jackass**
04 fool 09 blockhead 10 kookaburra

**jackdaw**
02 ka 03 daw, kae 04 jack 07 dawcock

**jacket**
02 DJ 03 tux 04 baju, beat, case, skin, wrap 05 acton, bania, cover, duvet, gilet, grego, jupon, polka, sayon, shell, tunic 06 anorak, banian, banyan, Basque, blazer, bolero, casing, dolman, folder, jerkin, railly, sheath, tuxedo, Zouave 07 Barbour®, Mae West, spencer, vareuse, wrapper 08 camisole, covering, envelope, water box, wrapping 09 night-rail, shortgown, slip cover 10 body-warmer, bumfreezer, duffel coat, sports coat, windjammer 11 Barbour® coat, windcheater

**jackpot**
03 pot 04 mess, pool 05 award, kitty, prize 06 reward, stakes 07 big time, bonanza 08 winnings 10 first prize
• **hit the jackpot** 05 score 06 arrive, make it 07 clean up, get rich, succeed 08 rake it in 09 make a pile 11 make a bundle, make a packet 13 hit the big time

**jade**
02 yu 03 nag 06 limmer 08 axe-stone, nephrite 11 spleenstone

**jaded**
04 done 05 all in, bored, fed up, spent, tired, weary 06 bushed, done in, dulled, fagged, pooped 07 wearied, whacked, worn out 08 fatigued, jiggered, tired out 09 disjaskit, exhausted, knackered, played-out, pooped out, shattered 10 cheesed off 11 ready to drop, tuckered out 14 unenthusiastic

**jag**
03 dag, fit 04 barb, bout, cart, load, snag, spur 05 cleft, notch, point, prick, slash, spell, spree, tooth 06 bundle, dentil, Jaguar, pierce 08 denticle, division, quantity 09 injection, saddlebag 10 projection, protrusion 11 inoculation

**jagged**
◇ *anagram indicator* 04 rag'd 05 drunk, ragde, rough 06 barbed, broken, craggy, hackly, nicked, ragged, ridged, snaggy, spiked, uneven 07 notched, pointed, snagged, toothed 08 indented, saw-edged, serrated 09 irregular 11 denticulate

**jaggedness**
09 roughness, serration, serrature 10 brokenness, raggedness, unevenness 12 irregularity

**jaguar**
03 Jag 05 ounce, tiger 07 leopard, tigress 10 leopardess 13 American tiger

**jail, gaol**
03 bin, can, jug, pen 04 nick, poky, quad, quod, stir 05 choky, clink, kitty, pokey 06 cooler, detain, immure, inside, intern, lock up, lock-up, prison 07 confine, custody, hoosgow, impound, put away, slammer 08 big house, hoosegow, imprison, porridge, send down 09 bridewell, jailhouse 10 guardhouse 11 incarcerate 12 penitentiary, send to prison 15 detention centre
*See also* **prison**

**jailbird**
*see* **prisoner**

**jailer, gaoler**
04 Adam 05 guard, screw 06 captor, keeper, warden, warder 07 alcaide, alcayde, turnkey 09 dungeoner 12 under-turnkey 13 prison officer

**jake**
02 OK 04 fine, okay 05 yokel 06 honest 07 correct 09 first-rate

**jam**
03 fix, mob, ram 04 bind, clog, cram, herd, hole, lock, pack, push, spot, stew 05 block, close, crowd, crush, force, horde, jeely, jelly, press, seize, stall, stick, stuff, swarm, wedge 06 hold-up, insert, jeelie, konfyt, pickle, plight, scrape, spread, squash, throng, thrust 07 confine, congest, seize up, squeeze, straits, the soup, trouble 08 close off, conserve, gridlock, obstruct, preserve, quandary 09 confiture, interfere, marmalade, multitude, tight spot 10 bottleneck, congestion 11 obstruction, predicament 12 damson cheese

**Jamaica**
02 JA 03 JAM

**jamb**
04 dern, durn, pole, post, prop 05 frame, shaft 06 greave, pillar 07 support, upright 08 doorpost, side post 09 stanchion 10 ingle-cheek

**jamboree**
04 fête 05 party, rally, spree 06 frolic, junket 07 carouse, jubilee, revelry, shindig 08 carnival, festival, field day 09 festivity, gathering, merriment 10 convention 11 celebration, get-together

**jammy**
05 lucky 06 timely 07 charmed 08 favoured 09 excellent, expedient, fortunate, opportune 10 auspicious, fortuitous, propitious, prosperous, successful 12 providential

**jangle**
◇ *anagram indicator* 03 din, jar 05 chime, clang, clank, clash, clink, upset 06 bother, jingle, racket, rattle 07 clatter, discord, disturb, jarring, quarrel, stridor, trouble, vibrate, wrangle 08 clangour, irritate 09 cacophony 10 contention, dissonance 11 make anxious 13 reverberation

**janitor**
06 porter 07 doorman, ostiary 08 servitor 09 attendant, caretaker, concierge, custodian 10 doorkeeper, servitress

**January**
03 Jan

**japan**
01 J 03 JPN 07 lacquer

**Japanese**
03 eta 07 Japonic 09 Nipponese
*See also* **Asian**

---

*Japanese art forms include:*

02 no
03 noh
04 raku
05 haiku, Hizen, Imari, kendo
06 gagaku, kabuki, nogaku, saikei, ukiyo-e
07 bunraku, chanoyu, ikebana, nihonga, origami
08 kakemono, kakiemon, tsutsumu
11 linked verse, tea ceremony

---

• **Japanese title** 03 san 04 sama

**jar**
◇ *anagram indicator* 03 irk, jug, mug, pot, urn 04 jerk, jolt, olla, pint, rasp, turn, vase 05 annoy, caddy, clash, crock, cruet, flask, grate, grind, shake, stave, upset 06 bicker, carafe, dolium, flagon, jampot, jangle, jostle, justle, kalpis, nettle, offend, pithos, rattle, tinaja, tureen, vessel 07 agitate, amphora, disturb, pitcher, quarrel, stamnos, terrine, trouble, vibrate 08 be at odds, canister, conflict, disagree, irritate 09 albarello, bell-glass, container, greybeard 10 receptacle

**11** water monkey **12** be at variance, be in conflict

**jargon**
**04** cant, jive **05** argot, Greek, idiom, lingo, slang, usage **06** patois, patter, pidgin **07** chatter, Kennick, twitter **08** legalese, nonsense, parlance, pig Latin **09** baragouin, buzz words, Eurospeak, gibberish **10** Eurobabble, greenspeak, journalese, mumbo-jumbo, twittering, vernacular **11** computerese, diplomatese, lingoa geral, officialese, sociologese, technospeak **12** gobbledegook, gobbledygook, lingua franca, psychobabble, technobabble, telegraphese **13** commercialese, computerspeak, pidgin English

**jarring**
**04** ajar **05** harsh, shock **06** off-key **07** grating, jolting, rasping **08** backlash, clashing, friction, jangling, strident **09** dissonant, troubling, upsetting **10** discordant, disturbing, irritating **11** cacophonous

**jasmine**
**07** jessamy **09** gelsemium, gessamine, jessamine **10** frangipani

**jaundiced**
**05** jaded **06** biased, bitter **07** bigoted, cynical, envious, hostile, jealous **09** distorted, resentful, sceptical **10** prejudiced, suspicious **11** distrustful, icteritious, pessimistic **12** disbelieving, misanthropic, preconceived **14** unenthusiastic

**jaunt**
**04** ride, spin, tour, trip **05** drive, sally **06** outing, ramble, stroll **07** holiday **09** excursion

**jauntily**
**06** airily **07** perkily, smartly **08** brightly, cheekily **10** cheerfully **13** energetically **15** self-confidently

**jaunty**
◇ anagram indicator **04** airy, pert, trim **05** perky, showy, smart **06** bouncy, breezy, cheeky, dapper, flashy, lively, rakish, spruce **07** buoyant, stylish **08** carefree, cheerful, debonair, sparkish **09** energetic, sprightly **11** gentlemanly, Micawberish **12** high-spirited **13** self-confident

**javelin**
**04** dart, pile **05** jerid, pilum, spear **06** jereed **07** harpoon **08** gavelock **09** handstaff

**jaw**
**03** gum, rap **04** chap, chat, chaw, chop, dash, jole, joll, jowl, talk, trap **05** chaft, chops, claws, grasp, mouth, power, scold, visit, wongi **06** babble, chafts, confab, gabble, gossip, jabber, muzzle, natter, rabbit **07** chatter, chinwag, control, lecture, maxilla **08** clutches, mandible, rabbit on, schmooze **09** threshold **10** discussion, masticator **12** conversation **13** talkativeness
• front of jaw **04** chin

**jay**
**01** J **10** whisky jack, whisky john

**jazz**
◇ anagram indicator

*Jazz types include:*

**03** bop, hot, rag
**04** acid, Afro, cool, jive, soul, trad
**05** bebop, blues, funky, kwela, modal, spiel, swing
**06** fusion, groove, modern
**07** classic, hard bop, New Wave, post-bop, ragtime
**08** free-form, high life
**09** Afro-Cuban, bossa nova, Dixieland, gutbucket, West Coast
**10** avant-garde, improvised, mainstream, neo-classic, New Orleans
**11** barrelhouse, third stream, traditional
**12** boogie-woogie

*See also* **singer**
• **jazz fan 03** cat
• **jazz up 07** enliven, liven up **08** ginger up **09** smarten up **10** brighten up

**jazzy**
**04** bold, wild **05** fancy, gaudy, smart **06** bright, flashy, lively, snazzy **07** stylish, zestful **08** spirited, swinging **09** vivacious

**jealous**
**04** wary **05** green **07** anxious, careful, envious, gealous, mindful **08** covetous, desirous, doubting, grudging, insecure, vigilant, watchful **09** defensive, green-eyed, jaundiced, resentful **10** begrudging, possessive, protective, solicitous, suspicious **11** distrustful

**jealously**
**08** with envy **09** enviously **10** covetously, desirously **11** resentfully **12** possessively **13** distrustfully

**jealousy**
**04** envy **05** doubt, spite **06** gelosy, grudge **07** envying, ill-will **08** distrust, gealousy, mistrust, wariness **09** emulation, suspicion, vigilance, zelotypia **10** bitterness, insecurity, resentment, yellowness **11** carefulness, mindfulness **12** covetousness, grudgingness, watchfulness **13** defensiveness **14** possessiveness, protectiveness

**jeans**
**05** Levis®

**jeer**
**03** boo, dig **04** gibe, gird, goof, hiss, hoot, jest, jibe, mock, razz, twit **05** abuse, chaff, fleer, flout, frump, geare, knock, scoff, scorn, sneer, taunt, tease **06** banter, chiack, deride, heckle **07** barrack, catcall, mockery, teasing **08** derision, ridicule **09** make fun of, shout down **10** cock a snook, sling off at **11** have a shot at, poke borak at **12** laugh to scorn

**jejune**
**03** dry **04** arid, dull **05** banal, empty,

naive, silly, trite, vapid **06** barren, boring, callow, meagre, simple **07** insipid, prosaic, puerile **08** childish, immature, juvenile **09** senseless **10** colourless, spiritless, unoriginal, wishy-washy **13** uninteresting **15** unsophisticated

**jell**
*see* **gel, jell**

**jelly**
**03** gel **04** agar, jeel **05** aspic, jeely, shape **06** jeelie, kanten, napalm, Sterno® **07** congeal **08** agar-agar, quiddany, Vaseline® **09** calf's-foot, gelignite **10** petrolatum **14** liquid paraffin

**jellyfish**
**05** jelly **06** medusa **07** blubber, sea wasp **08** sea jelly **09** sea nettle **10** nettle-fish, sea blubber

**jeopardize**
**04** risk **05** stake **06** chance, expose, gamble, hazard, menace **07** imperil, venture **08** endanger, threaten **09** put at risk **11** take a chance **13** put in jeopardy **14** expose to danger

**jeopardy**
**04** risk **05** peril **06** danger, hazard, menace, threat **07** venture **08** exposure **09** liability **10** insecurity **12** endangerment **13** vulnerability **14** precariousness

**jerk**
◇ anagram indicator **03** ass, bob, git, jar, jig, jog, mug, nit, sap, tug **04** berk, cant, clot, coot, dope, dork, fool, geek, goat, goof, goop, hoik, jolt, jump, kick, kook, nerd, nerk, peck, prat, pull, toss, twit, yank **05** braid, chump, dumbo, dweeb, flirt, hitch, hoick, idiot, lurch, neddy, ninny, pluck, quirk, shrug, surge, throw, twerp, wally **06** bounce, dum-dum, fillip, jiggle, josser, nitwit, sawney, sucker, switch, thrust, turkey, twitch, wrench **07** Charlie, charqui, gubbins, pillock, plonker, saphead, tosspot, wazzock **08** dipstick **09** birdbrain, cloth head, schlemiel **10** headbanger, nincompoop, silly-billy **11** kangaroo hop **13** proper Charlie

**jerkily**
**07** bumpily, jumpily, roughly **08** fitfully, unevenly **13** spasmodically

**jerky**
◇ anagram indicator **05** bumpy, jumpy, rough, shaky **06** bouncy, fitful, uneven **07** charqui, jolting, shaking, twitchy **08** lurching, saccadic **09** spasmodic **10** convulsive, incoherent **12** disconnected, uncontrolled **13** unco-ordinated

**jerry-built**
**04** Lego® **05** cheap **06** faulty, flimsy, shoddy **07** rickety **08** slipshod, unstable **09** cheapjack, defective, slop-built **10** ramshackle **12** quickly built **13** insubstantial, unsubstantial **14** thrown together **15** built on the cheap

## jersey
**03** GBJ, top **04** polo **05** frock **06** gansey, jumper, woolly, zephyr **07** maillot, sweater **08** guernsey, polo neck, pullover **09** sloppy joe **10** sweatshirt

## Jerusalem
**04** Zion

## jest
**03** cod, fun, gab, gag, jig, kid, toy **04** fool, game, hoax, jape, jeer, joke, mock, quip **05** bourd, crack, droll, gleek, prank, taunt, tease, trick **06** banter **07** fooling, kidding, leg-pull **08** drollery **09** Joe Miller, tell jokes, wisecrack, witticism **13** practical joke
• **in jest** **05** in fun **07** as a joke, to tease **08** jokingly **09** playfully **13** mischievously

## jester
**03** wag, wit **04** fool, scop, zany **05** clown, comic, droll, joker, patch **06** gagman, motley, mummer **07** bourder, buffoon, juggler **08** comedian, humorist, merryman, quipster **09** court-fool, harlequin, joculator, pantaloon, prankster **11** Jack-pudding, merry-andrew

## Jesuits
**02** SJ **09** Ignatians

## jet
**03** fly, jut **04** flow, gush, inky, jeat, rush, zoom **05** black, ebony, jumbo, raven, sable, shoot, sooty, spirt, spout, spray, spurt, strut **06** Airbus®, candle, career, douche, spring, squirt, stream **07** sprayer **08** encroach, fountain **09** delta wing, sprinkler **10** pitch-black, tankbuster
*See also* **aircraft**

## jettison
**04** drop, dump **05** chuck, ditch, eject, expel, heave, scrap **06** jetsam, unload **07** abandon, discard, offload **08** get rid of **09** throw away **14** throw overboard

## jetty
**04** dock, mole, pier, quay **05** jutty, wharf **06** groyne **07** harbour **10** breakwater **12** landing-place, landing-stage

## jewel
**03** gem **04** find, rock **05** bijou, pearl, prize **06** rarity **07** navette, paragon **08** gemstone, ornament, sparkler, treasure **09** jewellery, showpiece **10** ferronière **11** ferronnière, masterpiece, pride and joy **13** precious stone **14** crème de la crème

## jewellery
**03** tom **04** gems **05** bling, gauds **06** bijoux, finery, jewels **07** gemmery, regalia **08** treasure, trinkets **09** ornaments **10** bijouterie, tomfoolery **13** paraphernalia

---

*Jewellery types include:*

**04** prop, ring, stud
**05** beads, bindi, cameo, chain, tiara
**06** amulet, anklet, bangle, brooch, choker, corals, diadem, hatpin, locket, pearls, tiepin, torque
**07** armilla, coronet, ear cuff, earring,

necklet, pendant, rivière, sautoir, toe ring
**08** bracelet, cufflink, necklace, negligee, nose ring, wristlet
**09** medallion, navel ring
**10** signet ring
**11** mangalsutra
**12** eternity ring
**13** charm bracelet, solitaire ring
**15** belly-button ring

## Jewish calendar
*see* **month**

## Jezebel
**04** jade, tart, vamp **05** hussy, whore, witch **06** harlot, wanton **07** Delilah **08** man-eater, scrubber **09** temptress **10** loose woman, seductress **11** femme fatale **12** scarlet woman

## jib
**03** shy **04** balk, face, stop **05** baulk, genoa, stall, strip **06** boggle, fleece, recoil, refuse, shrink **07** back off, retreat **09** stop short **10** standstill

## jibe
*see* **gibe**

## jiffy
**02** mo **03** bit, sec **04** tick **05** flash, trice, whiff **06** minute, moment, no time, second **07** instant **08** two ticks **09** twinkling **11** split second

## jig
◇ *anagram indicator* **03** bob, hop **04** jerk, jest, jump, leap, skip **05** caper, prank, shake **06** bounce, jingle, prance, twitch, wiggle, wobble

## jigger
**04** damn, jerk, ruin **05** blast, break, shake, spoil, wreck **06** chigoe, chigre, jolley, kibosh **07** botch up, chigger, destroy, louse up, scupper, vitiate **08** sand flea **09** undermine **14** make a pig's ear of

## jiggery-pokery
**05** fraud **06** deceit **08** mischief, trickery **09** chicanery, deception **10** dishonesty, hanky-panky, subterfuge **13** funny business **14** monkey business

## jiggle
◇ *anagram indicator* **03** jig, jog **04** jerk, jump **05** shake, shift **06** bounce, fidget, joggle, twitch, waggle, wiggle, wobble **07** agitate

## jilt
**04** drop, dump **05** chuck, ditch, leave, spurn **06** begunk, betray, desert, pack in, reject **07** abandon, discard **08** brush off **09** cast aside, throw over, walk out on

## jingle
**03** jig **04** ding, poem, ring, song, tune **05** carol, chant, chime, chink, clang, clink, ditty, rhyme, verse **06** chorus, jangle, melody, rattle, slogan, tinkle **07** clatter, refrain, ringing **08** clangour, doggerel, limerick **14** tintinnabulate

## jingoism
**10** chauvinism, flag-waving, insularity, patriotism **11** imperialism, nationalism **13** sabre-rattling

## jinx
**03** hex, moz **04** doom, mozz **05** charm, curse, spell **06** hoodoo, plague, voodoo **07** bad luck, bedevil, bewitch, evil eye, gremlin **10** affliction, black magic, Indian sign **11** malediction **12** cast a spell on

## jitters
◇ *anagram indicator* **06** nerves **07** anxiety, fidgets, habdabs, jimjams **08** edginess **09** agitation, tenseness, the creeps, the shakes, trembling **10** the shivers, the willies, uneasiness **11** nervousness **12** collywobbles **13** heebie-jeebies

## jittery
◇ *anagram indicator* **04** edgy **05** het up, jumpy, nervy, shaky **06** on edge, uneasy **07** anxious, fidgety, in a stew, keyed up, nervous, panicky, quaking, shivery, twitchy, uptight, wound up **08** agitated, in a sweat, in a tizzy **09** flustered, perturbed, quivering, screwed-up, trembling

## job
**04** char, darg, duty, part, peck, post, prod, role, spot, task, work **05** berth, chore, place, punch, share, stint, trade **06** affair, career, charge, errand, métier, office, thrust **07** calling, concern, mission, project, pursuit, venture **08** activity, business, capacity, function, position, province, sinecure, vocation **09** situation, soft thing **10** assignment, commission, employment, enterprise, line of work, livelihood, occupation, proceeding, profession **11** appointment, consignment, piece of work, undertaking **12** contribution **14** line of business, responsibility
*See also* **burglary; occupation**
• **have a job doing something** **14** find it a problem
• **just the job** **12** just the thing **13** just the ticket

## jobless
**04** idle **07** laid off **08** inactive, workless **09** on the dole, out of work, redundant **10** unemployed **11** without work

## jock
**02** DJ **03** Mac **04** jack **06** deejay **08** Scotsman **10** disc jockey

## jockey
◇ *anagram indicator* **04** coax, ease, edge **05** rider **06** cajole, induce, manage **07** wheedle **08** engineer, horseman, inveigle, jockette **09** manoeuvre, negotiate **10** equestrian, horsewoman, jump-jockey, manipulate
*See also* **equestrian; horseman, horsewoman**

## jocose
**05** droll, funny, lepid, merry, witty **06** jovial, joyous **07** comical, jesting, playful, teasing, waggish **08** humorous, mirthful, pleasant, sportive **09** facetious **11** mischievous

## jocular
**05** comic, droll, funny, witty **06** jocose, joking, jovial **07** amusing, comical,

## jocularity

jesting, playful, roguish, scurril, teasing, waggish **08** humorous, scurrile **09** facetious, hilarious, whimsical **12** entertaining

## jocularity

**03** wit **05** sport **06** gaiety, humour **07** fooling, jesting, teasing **08** drollery, hilarity, jocosity, laughter **09** amusement, funniness, jolliness, joviality, merriment **10** comicality, desipience, jocoseness, pleasantry **11** playfulness, roguishness, waggishness **12** sportiveness, whimsicality **13** entertainment, facetiousness

## jog

◊ *anagram indicator* **03** hod, jar, run **04** bump, jerk, jolt, poke, prod, push, rock, shog, stir, trot, whig **05** dunch, dunsh, elbow, hotch, mosey, nudge, shake, shove **06** arouse, bounce, canter, jig-jog, joggle, jostle, prompt, remind **08** activate **09** stimulate

## john

**02** WC **03** bog, can, lat, lav, loo **04** jack, rear **08** lavatory
See also **toilet**

## joie de vivre

**03** joy **04** zest **05** gusto, mirth **06** bounce, esprit, gaiety, relish **08** buoyancy, pleasure **09** enjoyment, merriment **10** blitheness, ebullience, enthusiasm, exuberance, get-up-and-go, joyfulness **12** cheerfulness

## join

◊ *juxtaposition indicator* **03** add, mix, oop, oup, sew, tie, wed **04** abut, ally, bind, fuse, glue, knit, link, meet, weld, yoke **05** annex, enrol, enter, marry, merge, touch, unify, unite **06** adhere, adjoin, attach, border, cement, couple, enlist, fasten, sign up, solder, splice **07** combine, conjoin, connect, injoint, verge on **08** border on, coincide, converge, splinter **09** accompany, affiliate, associate, co-operate, interjoin, march with **10** amalgamate, team up with **11** collaborate, compaginate **15** become a member of
• **join in** **04** help **06** chip in, muck in **07** chime in, get in on, partake, pitch in **08** take part **09** co-operate, lend a hand **10** contribute, take part in **11** participate
• **join up** **04** link **05** enrol, enter **06** accede, enlist, sign up

## joint

**01** J **03** bar, fit, pub **04** club, dive, join, knot, lith, seam, weld **05** carve, cut up, haunt, hinge, nexus, place, roach, sever, stick, union, unite **06** common, couple, divide, fasten, joined, mutual, reefer, shared, spliff, united **07** connect, dissect, joining, segment **08** combined, communal, conjunct, coupling, dovetail, junction, juncture **09** cigarette, concerted, dismember, ginglymus, nightclub **10** articulate, collective, commissure, connection, cup-and-ball **11** amalgamated, co-operative, co-ordinated, enarthrosis

**12** articulation, consolidated, intersection
See also **bone; meat**

## jointly

**08** together, unitedly **09** in cahoots, in harmony **11** in agreement **13** co-operatively, in co-operation, in partnership **15** in collaboration

## joke

**03** bar, cod, fun, gag, guy, kid, one, pun, rot **04** baur, bawr, fool, hoax, hoot, jape, jest, josh, lark, mock, play, quip, yarn **05** chaff, clown, crack, farce, funny, kiddy, laugh, prank, spoof, sport, stunt, tease, trick **06** banter, frolic, gambol, parody, wheeze, whimsy **07** leg-pull, mockery, repartee, shambles, travesty **09** absurdity, booby trap, fool about, tell jokes, throwaway, wisecrack, witticism **10** break a jest, crack a joke, fool around, funny story, pleasantry, rib-tickler, running gag, whip the cat **11** apple-pie bed, old chestnut **12** take for a ride **13** have someone on, practical joke **14** pull a fast one on, ridiculousness

## joker

**03** wag, wit **04** card **05** clown, comic, droll, laugh, sport **06** gagman, hoaxer, jester, kidder **07** buffoon, farceur, funster **08** comedian, farceuse, humorist, jokester, quipster **09** character, prankster, trickster **11** wisecracker **14** practical joker

## jollity

**05** mirth **08** gladness **09** happiness, high jinks, merriment **11** high spirits, merrymaking **12** cheerfulness

## jolly

**02** RM **03** gay **04** coax, dead, glad, spur, trip, urge, very, well **05** buxom, egg on, gaucy, gawcy, gawsy, happy, merry, party, plump **06** bootee, cheery, ever so, gaucie, hearty, highly, jovial, joyful, lively, outing, prompt, titupy **07** awfully, festive, gleeful, greatly, healthy, playful, tittupy **08** cheerful, mirthful, persuade, splendid, terribly **09** certainly, convivial, encourage, enjoyable, extremely, exuberant, influence, intensely **10** delightful **11** celebration, pleasurable, royal marine **12** entertaining **13** exceptionally **15** extraordinarily

## jolt

◊ *anagram indicator* **03** hit, jar, jog **04** bang, blow, bump, jerk, push, stun **05** amaze, floor, knock, lurch, nudge, shake, shock, shove, start, upset **06** bounce, hotter, impact, jostle, jounce, jumble **07** astound, disturb, perturb, setback, shake up, startle **08** astonish, reversal, surprise **09** bombshell **10** discompose, disconcert **11** knock for six, thunderbolt **15** bolt from the blue

## Jordan

**03** HKJ, JOR

## jostle

◊ *anagram indicator* **03** jog, vie **04** bang, bump, jolt, push, tilt **05** crowd, elbow, fight, joust, shake, shove **06** battle, hustle, jockey, joggle, throng **07** collide, compete, contend, squeeze **08** shoulder, struggle **11** hog-shouther

## jot

**03** ace, bit, dot, fig **04** atom, hint, hoot, iota, mite, whit **05** aught, gleam, grain, scrap, speck, stime, styme, trace **06** detail, morsel, tittle, trifle **07** glimmer, smidgen **08** fraction, particle **09** scintilla
• **jot down** **04** list, note **05** enter **06** record **07** put down **08** note down, register, scribble, take down **09** write down

## jotting

**04** line, memo, note **05** lines, notes **07** comment, message **08** reminder, scribble **10** memorandum

## journal

**01** J **03** log **04** blog **05** diary, e-zine, paper **06** record, review, weekly **07** account, daybook, diurnal, fanzine, gazette, logbook, monthly, webzine **08** e-journal, magazine, register **09** chronicle, ephemeris, newspaper, waste book **10** periodical, trade paper **11** publication
See also **newspaper**

## journalism

**05** press **09** reportage, reporting **11** copy-writing, e-journalism, gutter press **12** broadcasting, fourth estate, news coverage **13** sportswriting, web journalism **14** correspondence, feature-writing, telejournalism

*Journalism-related terms include:*

**03** cub, cut, NPA, run, tip
**04** blat, bump, copy, deck, desk, kill, leak, news, op-ed
**05** angle, blatt, blurb, break, extra, local, media, pitch, quote, radio, scoop, squib, story, tie in
**06** anchor, Balaam, byline, column, editor, impact, kicker, leader, leg-man, rookie, source
**07** advance, article, caption, compact, editing, feature, journal, kill fee, spoiler, subhead, tabloid, topical, writing
**08** causerie, follow-up, headline, magazine, masthead, national, newshawk, news item, reporter, revision, stringer
**09** broadcast, columnist, editorial, exclusive, freelance, freesheet, front-page, interview, newshound, newspaper, paragraph, pull quote, reportage, scare-head, scare-line, soundbite, statement, stop-press, strapline
**10** broadsheet, centrefold, credit line, daily paper, journalist, leaderette, multimedia, newsreader, periodical, publishing, retraction, standfirst, television
**11** Fleet Street, Sunday paper
**12** breaking news, centre spread,

press council, press release, scare-heading

**13** correspondent, human interest, middle article

**14** banner headline, blind interview, current affairs, leading article

**15** photojournalism, press conference

## journalist

**02** Ed **03** man, sub **04** hack **06** editor, journo, scribe **07** diarist, wireman **08** hackette, pressman, reporter, reviewer, stringer **09** columnist, freelance, gazetteer, ink-jerker, newshound, paparazzo, sob sister, subeditor, thunderer **10** diarnalist, hatchet man, ink-slinger, news-writer, presswoman **11** broadcaster, commentator, contributor, e-journalist **12** gossip-writer, newspaperman, sportswriter **13** correspondent, feature-writer, web journalist **14** newspaperwoman, telejournalist

*Journalists and editors include:*

**03** Day (Sir Robin), Mee (Arthur)
**04** Adie (Kate), Bell (Martin), Birt (John, Lord), Ford (Anna), Gall (Sandy), Hogg (Sarah, Baroness), Jane (Frederick), Marr (Andrew), Neil (Andrew), Rook (Jean), Self (Will), Snow (Jon), Snow (Peter), Wade (Rebekah), Wark (Kirsty)
**05** Brown (Helen Gurley), Buerk (Michael), Cooke (Alistair), Dacre (Paul), Ensor (Sir Robert), Evans (Sir Harold), Frost (Sir David), Green (Charlotte), Hardy (Bert), James (Clive), Junor (Sir John), Laski (Marghanita), Levin (Bernard), Lewis (Martyn), Reith (John, Lord), Scott (C P), Waugh (Auberon), Wolfe (Tom), Young (Toby)
**06** Bailey (Trevor), Barron (Brian), Bierce (Ambrose), Burnet (Sir Alastair), Deedes (Bill, Lord), Fisher (Archie), Forman (Sir Denis), Gallup (George), Gordon (John), Greene (Sir Hugh), Hislop (Ian), Hulton (Sir Edward), Hutton (Will), Isaacs (Sir Jeremy), Martin (Kingsley), Morgan (Charles), Morgan (Piers), Murrow (Edward R), O'Brien (Conor Cruise), Paxman (Jeremy), Pilger (John), Proops (Marjorie), Reuter (Paul Julius von, Lord), Rippon (Angela), Stuart (Moira), Wilkes (John)
**07** Alagiah (George), Barclay (Sir David), Barclay (Sir Frederick), Boycott (Rosie), Bradlee (Ben), Brunson (Michael), Buckley (William F, Jnr), Cameron (James), Camrose (William Berry, Viscount), Cobbett (William), Dunnett (Sir Alastair), Edwards (Huw), Fairfax (John), Fleming (Peter), Gardner (Frank), Hellyer (Arthur George Lee), Ingrams (Richard), Jackson (Dame Barbara), Johnson (Boris), Kennedy (Helena, Baroness), Kennedy (Sir Ludovic), Leeming

(Jan), Malcolm (Derek), Mencken (H L), Perkins (Brian), Rowland (Tiny), Simpson (John), Sissons (Peter), Stanley (Sir Henry Morton), Thomson (Robert)
**08** Burchill (Julie), Cronkite (Walter), Dimbleby (David), Dimbleby (Jonathan), Dimbleby (Richard), Douglass (Frederick), Drawbell (James Wedgwood), Gellhorn (Martha), Hanrahan (Brian), Hobhouse (Leonard), Horrocks (Sir Brian), Humphrys (John), Lippmann (Walter), McCarthy (John), McDonald (Sir Trevor), Naughtie (James), Nevinson (Henry Wood), Rees-Mogg (William, Lord), Robinson (Henry Crabb), Thompson (Hunter S), Woodward (Bob)
**09** Bernstein (Carl), Bosanquet (Reginald), Hopkinson (Sir Tom), Macdonald (Gus, Lord), MacGregor (Sue), Mackenzie (Kelvin), Magnusson (Magnus), Plekhanov (Georgi), Streicher (Julius), Trethowan (Sir Ian)
**10** Greenslade (Roy), Guru-Murthy (Krishnan), Muggeridge (Malcolm), Rusbridger (Alan), Waterhouse (Keith), Worsthorne (Sir Peregrine)
**12** Street-Porter (Janet)

*See also* **newspaper**

## journey

**02** go, OE **03** fly, ren, rin, run, way **04** eyre, hike, mush, raik, rake, ride, roam, rove, sail, step, tour, trek, trip, went **05** drive, foray, jaunt, range, route, shlep, tramp **06** bummel, cruise, flight, outing, ramble, roving, safari, schlep, travel, voyage, wander **07** milk run, odyssey, passage, proceed, sailing, schlepp, stretch, travels **08** campaign, crossing, progress **09** excursion, gallivant, walkabout **10** expedition, pilgrimage, wanderings **11** peregrinate **13** globetrotting, peregrination

• **good journey, safe journey**
**08** godspeed **09** bon voyage
• **journey regularly** **03** ply
**07** commute

## journeyer

**07** pilgrim, rambler, tourist, trekker, tripper, voyager **08** wanderer, wayfarer **09** traveller **12** peregrinator

## joust

**03** vie **04** just, spar, tilt **05** fight, giust, trial **06** jostle, justle **07** compete, contest, quarrel, tourney, wrangle **08** skirmish **09** encounter, pas d'armes **10** engagement, tournament

## jovial

**03** gay **04** boon, glad **05** happy, jolly, merry **06** cheery, genial, joyous, lively, wanton **07** affable, Bacchic, buoyant, cordial, gleeful **08** animated, Bacchian, cheerful, mirthful, sociable **09** convivial **11** Falstaffian, full of beans **13** in good spirits

## joviality

**03** fun **04** glee **05** mirth **06** gaiety

**07** jollity **08** buoyancy, gladness, hilarity **09** happiness, merriment **10** affability, cheeriness, ebullience **12** cheerfulness

## joy

**03** gem **04** dear, glee, list, nuts **05** bliss, cheer, dream, exult, prize, treat **06** thrill **07** delight, ecstasy, elation, rapture, rejoice, success, victory **08** felicity, gladness, pleasure, treasure **09** cloud nine, enjoyment, happiness, rejoicing, transport **10** exultation, joyfulness, jubilation **11** achievement **12** entrancement, satisfaction **13** gratification, seventh heaven **14** accomplishment, positive result
• **expression of joy** **02** ah, ha, ho, io **03** aha, hah, hey, hoa, hoh, ooh, rah, say, wow, yay **04** I say!, whee **05** heigh, hurra, huzza, oh boy!, tra-la, wowee, yahoo, yummy, zowie **06** banzai, gotcha, heyday, hooray, hurrah, hurray, yippee, yum-yum **07** whoopee

## joyful

**04** fain, glad **05** happy, merry **06** elated **07** festive, gleeful, pleased **08** cheerful, ecstatic, euphoric, feastful, gleesome, jubilant, pleasing, thrilled **09** cock-a-hoop, delighted, gratified, overjoyed **10** exhilarant, triumphant **11** on cloud nine, over the moon, tickled pink **15** in seventh heaven, on top of the world

## joyfully

**06** gladly **07** happily **09** gleefully **10** cheerfully, jubilantly **12** ecstatically, euphorically, triumphantly

## joyless

**03** sad **04** dour, glum, grim **05** bleak, sober **06** dismal, dreary, gloomy, sombre **07** doleful, forlorn, serious, unhappy **08** dejected, downcast **09** cheerless, miserable **10** depressing, despondent, dispirited **12** discouraging

## joyous

**04** glad **05** happy, merry **06** festal, jovial, joyful **07** festive, gleeful **08** cheerful, ecstatic, frabjous, gladsome, jubilant **09** rapturous **10** blithesome, rollicking

## joyously

**06** gladly **07** happily, merrily **08** joyfully **10** cheerfully, jubilantly **11** rapturously **12** ecstatically

## jubilant

**06** elated, joyful **07** excited **08** ecstatic, euphoric, exultant, thrilled **09** delighted, exuberant, overjoyed, rejoicing, rhapsodic **10** triumphant **11** on cloud nine, over the moon, tickled pink **15** in seventh heaven, on top of the world

## jubilation

**03** joy **07** ecstasy, elation, jubilee, triumph **08** euphoria, jamboree **09** festivity, rejoicing **10** excitement, exultation **11** celebration **13** jollification

## jubilee

**04** fete, gala **07** holiday **08** carnival, feast day, festival **09** festivity

**11** anniversary, celebration
**13** commemoration
**14** semi-centennial

**Judas**
**07** traitor **08** betrayer, deceiver, quisling, renegade, turncoat
**11** backstabber **13** tergiversator

**judder**
◊ *anagram indicator* **05** quake, shake
**06** quiver **07** shudder, tremble, vibrate

**judge**
**01** J **03** lud, ref, see, try, ump, wig
**04** beak, damn, deem, doom, find, lord, rate, rule, scan **05** award, gauge, hakim, think, value, weigh **06** assess, critic, decern, decide, decree, expert, puisne, puisny, reckon, review, syndic, umpire **07** account, adjudge, arbiter, believe, censure, condemn, convict, coroner, discern, examine, her nibs, his nibs, justice, Law Lord, mediate, referee, set down, sheriff, weigh up **08** appraise, assessor, conclude, consider, deemster, doomsman, estimate, evaluate, mediator, recorder, reviewer, sentence
**09** arbitrate, ascertain, authority, criticize, determine, evaluator, judiciary, justiciar, moderator, ombudsman, seneschal, syndicate
**10** adjudicate, arbitrator, dijudicate, magistrate **11** adjudicator, connoisseur, distinguish **12** pass sentence **13** form an opinion, give a sentence **14** sit in judgement **15** deliver a verdict

*Judges include:*

**04** **Coke** (Sir Edward)
**05** **Allen** (Florence Ellinwood), **Burgh** (Hubert de), **Draco**, **Minos**, **Solon**
**06** **Aeacus**, **Burger** (Warren Earl), **Gideon**, **Holmes** (Oliver Wendell), **Irvine** (Alexander, Lord), **Mackay** (James, Lord), **Warren** (Earl)
**07** **Brennan** (William J), **Denning** (Alfred, Lord), **Erskine** (Thomas, Lord), **O'Connor** (Sandra Day), **Scarman** (Leslie, Lord)
**08** **Gardiner** (Gerald, Lord), **Ginsburg** (Ruth Bader), **Hailsham** (Quintin McGarel Hogg, Viscount), **Jeffreys** (George, Lord), **Marshall** (John), **Marshall** (Thurgood)
**09** **Rehnquist** (William), **Vyshinsky** (Andrei)
**10** **Elwyn-Jones** (Frederick, Lord)
**11** **Butler-Sloss** (Dame Elizabeth), **Montesquieu** (Charles-Louis de Secondat, Baron de)
**12** **Rhadamanthus**

**judgement**
**04** doom, fate, mind, view **05** award, order, sense, sight, taste **06** acumen, belief, decree, result, ruling, wisdom
**07** decreet, finding, opinion, verdict
**08** decision, estimate, prudence, sagacity, sapience, sentence, thinking
**09** appraisal, criticism, damnation, diagnosis, good sense, mediation, reckoning, sentiment **10** assessment, conclusion, conviction, evaluation, judication, misfortune, perception,

punishment, shrewdness
**11** arbitration, common sense, discernment, penetration, retribution **12** adjudication, condemnation, intelligence, perspicacity **13** enlightenment, judiciousness, understanding
**14** discrimination

**judgemental**
**07** carping **08** critical, scathing
**10** censorious, derogatory
**11** disparaging **12** condemnatory, disapproving, fault-finding
**13** hypercritical

**judicial**
**05** legal **08** critical, forensic, official
**09** decretory, impartial, judiciary, magistral **14** discriminating

**judicially**
**07** legally **10** officially **11** impartially
**12** forensically

**judiciary**
**06** judges, the law **07** justice **08** the bench **10** magistracy **11** court system, legal system

**judicious**
**04** wise **05** smart, sound **06** astute, clever, shrewd **07** careful, prudent
**08** cautious, discreet, informed, rational, sensible, wise-like
**09** sagacious, well-timed
**10** considered, discerning, reasonable, thoughtful, well-judged
**11** circumspect, common-sense, intelligent, well-advised
**14** discriminating

**judiciously**
**06** wisely **08** astutely, sensibly, shrewdly **09** carefully, prudently
**10** cautiously **11** sagaciously
**12** discerningly, thoughtfully
**13** circumspectly

**judo**
*see* **martial art**

**jug**
**03** jar, urn **04** ewer, olpe, Toby
**05** crock **06** carafe, flagon, pourie, prison, vessel **07** bombard, creamer, growler, pitcher, Toby jug **08** decanter, imprison **09** blackjack, container
**10** aquamanale, aquamanile, bellarmine, receptacle **11** Enghalskrug
*See also* **prison**

**juggle**
◊ *anagram indicator* **03** rig **04** cook, fake
**05** alter **06** adjust, change, doctor, fiddle, tamper **07** balance, conjure, falsify, massage **08** disguise, equalize
**09** rearrange **10** hocus-pocus, manipulate, tamper with
**12** misrepresent

**juice**
**03** jus, oil, sap **04** must **05** fluid, serum
**06** cremor, liquid, liquor, nectar, succus, walnut **07** enliven, essence, extract **08** piquancy, vitality
**09** secretion **10** pancreatin

**juicy**
**03** hot, wet **04** lush, racy **05** lurid, moist, sappy, spicy, vivid **06** risqué,

watery **07** flowing **08** exciting
**09** colourful, succulent, thrilling
**10** profitable, scandalous, suggestive
**11** interesting, sensational

**jujube**
**04** jube **05** lotus **08** zizyphus
**12** Christ's-thorn

**Juliet**
**01** J

**July**
**02** Jy **03** Jul

**jumble**
◊ *anagram indicator* **02** pi **03** mix, pie, pye **04** jolt, junk, mess **05** chaos, mix up, mix-up **06** garble, huddle, jabble, jumbal, medley, mingle, muddle, raffle, tangle, tumble, wuzzle
**07** clutter, confuse, jolting, mixture, rummage, shuffle **08** cast-offs, disarray, disorder, hotchpot, mishmash, mixy-maxy, oddments, pastiche, shambles
**09** bric-à-brac, confusion, pasticcio, potpourri, praiseach **10** disarrange, hodgepodge, hotchpotch, miscellany, mixty-maxty **11** disorganize, gallimaufry, printer's pie **12** mingle-mangle, mixter-maxter, mixtie-maxtie
**14** conglomeration

**jumbled**
◊ *anagram indicator* **06** untidy
**07** chaotic, garbled, huddled, mixed-up, muddled, tangled, tumbled **08** confused, shuffled, unsorted **10** disarrayed, disordered **11** farraginous
**12** disorganized, mingle-mangle
**13** miscellaneous

**jumbo**
**02** OS **04** huge, mega, vast **05** giant
**07** immense, mammoth, massive, outsize, Titanic **08** colossal, elephant, enormous, gigantic, whopping
**09** ginormous, walloping
**10** extra-large

**jump**
◊ *anagram indicator* **03** gap, hop, jar, lep, mug **04** axel, gain, gate, go up, hike, jerk, jolt, leap, lutz, miss, omit, rail, rise, risk, romp, skip **05** avoid, boost, bound, break, caper, clear, fence, frisk, halma, hedge, lapse, lurch, mount, ollie, quail, shake, shock, shoot, space, spasm, sport, start, surge, throb, vault, wince
**06** ascend, attack, beat up, bounce, breach, bypass, cavort, cut out, do over, flinch, frolic, gambol, go over, hazard, hiatus, hurdle, ignore, lacuna, leap up, pounce, prance, quiver, recoil, shiver, spiral, spring, switch, twitch, upturn **07** advance, assault, barrier, digress, exactly, flicker, salchow, set upon, shoot up, swoop on, toe loop, upsurge, venture
**08** batterie, bunny hop, escalate, go across, increase, interval, leave out, mounting, obstacle, omission, overlook, pass over, pounce on, spring on **09** barricade, disregard, elevation, entrechat, increment, stage-dive **10** appreciate, escalation, quersprung,

## jumper

trampoline **12** Becher's Brook, interruption
• **jump at**   **04** grab **05** seize **06** accept, leap at, snatch **07** agree to, fall for, seize on, swallow **08** pounce on **13** accept eagerly, accept quickly
• **jump on**   **05** blame, chide, fly at, scold **06** berate, rebuke, revile **07** censure, reprove, tick off, upbraid **08** reproach **09** castigate, criticize, reprimand
• **jump the gun**   **10** act hastily, act too soon, anticipate **13** start too early **14** act prematurely

## jumper

**03** roo **04** euro, flea **05** lammy **06** jersey, lammie, woolly **07** sweater **08** guernsey, kangaroo, pullover, wallaroo **09** sloppy joe **10** churn-drill, sweatshirt

## jumpy

**04** edgy **05** bumpy, het up, jerky, nappy, nervy, rough, shaky, tense **06** bouncy, fitful, on edge, uneasy **07** anxious, fidgety, in a stew, jittery, jolting, keyed up, nervous, panicky, restive, shaking, twitchy, uptight, wound up **08** agitated, in a sweat, in a tizzy, lurching **09** spasmodic, squirrely **10** convulsive, incoherent, squirrelly **12** apprehensive, disconnected, uncontrolled **13** unco-ordinated

## junction

**01** T **04** bond, cove, join, link, node, seam, toll **05** close, crown, graft, joint, raphe, union **06** circus, collar, infall, suture **07** cornice, joining, linking, meeting, welding **08** abutment, coupling, crossing, juncture, knitting **09** interface, symphysis, T-junction **10** confluence, connection, crossroads, match-joint **11** box junction, combination, interchange **12** intersection, meeting-point

## juncture

**04** crux, time **05** point, stage, union **06** crisis, minute, moment, period **07** article, joining **08** occasion **09** emergency, situation **11** predicament

## June

**03** Jun

## jungle

**03** web **04** bush, heap, mass, maze **05** chaos, shola, snarl **06** growth, medley, tangle **07** clutter **08** disarray, disorder, mishmash **09** confusion, labyrinth **10** hotchpotch, miscellany, rainforest **14** tropical forest

## junior

**02** Jr **03** Jnr, Jun, lad **04** fils, Junr **05** chota, lower, minor, young **06** lesser, minion, puisne, puisny, rating **07** servant, younger **08** dogsbody, inferior, under-boy **09** assistant, associate, secondary, underling **10** subsidiary **11** subordinate

## junk

◊ *anagram indicator* ◊ *deletion indicator*
**04** dump, spam **05** chuck, chunk,

ditch, dregs, scrap, trash, waste **06** debris, litter, refuse **07** clutter, discard, garbage, rubbish, rummage **08** cast-offs, get rid of, jettison, leavings, narcotic, nonsense, oddments, throw out, wreckage **09** bric-à-brac, dispose of, leftovers, throw away, worthless

## junket

**02** do **04** bash, trip **05** beano, feast, spree, visit **06** outing, picnic, regale **07** banquet, journey **09** entertain **11** celebration

## Juno

**04** Hera

## junta

**03** set **04** gang, ring **05** cabal, group, party **06** cartel, clique, league **07** coterie, council, faction, meeting **08** conclave **09** camarilla **11** confederacy

## Jupiter

**04** Zeus

## jurisdiction

**04** area, bail, rule, soke, sway, zone **05** field, orbit, power, range, reach, right, scope, soken, verge **06** bounds, region, sphere **07** command, control, mastery **08** capacity, district, dominion, province **09** authority, influence, territory **10** cognizance, competence, domination, judicature, leadership **11** prerogative, sovereignty **14** administration

## jury

**04** pais **05** panel, quest **06** assize, jurors **07** jurymen **09** grand jury, jurywomen, party-jury, petit jury, petty jury

## just

**03** all, apt, due **04** egal, even, fair, good, only, to a T **05** equal, exact, joust, legal, moral, quite, right, sound, valid **06** bang on, barely, earned, hardly, honest, indeed, lately, lawful, merely, normal, proper, purely, simply, spot-on **07** ethical, exactly, fitting, merited, neutral, sincere, upright **08** deserved, recently, rightful, scarcely, suitable, truthful, unbiased, virtuous **09** equitable, impartial, justified, objective, perfectly, precisely, righteous **10** absolutely, a moment ago, completely, even-handed, fair-minded, honourable, legitimate, nothing but, principled, reasonable, upstanding **11** appropriate, well-founded **12** unprejudiced, well-deserved, well-grounded **13** a short time ago, disinterested, incorruptible, true-disposing **14** irreproachable
• **just about**   **06** all but, almost, nearly **08** as good as, well-nigh **09** virtually **10** more or less **11** practically
• **just after**   **02** on

## justice

**01** J **02** CJ, JP, LJ **03** law **05** judge, right **06** amends, equity, ethics, honour,

morals **07** honesty, nemesis, penalty, redress, sheriff **08** fairness, fair play, justness, legality, validity **09** integrity, propriety, rectitude, rightness, soundness **10** lawfulness, legitimacy, magistrate, neutrality, punishment, recompense, reparation **11** objectivity, uprightness **12** compensation, impartiality, rightfulness, satisfaction **13** equitableness, righteousness **14** even-handedness, fair-mindedness, reasonableness **15** justifiableness

## justifiable

**03** fit **05** legal, right, sound, valid **06** lawful, proper **07** tenable **08** sensible **09** excusable, justified, plausible, warranted **10** acceptable, defensible, explicable, forgivable, legitimate, pardonable, reasonable **11** explainable, supportable, sustainable, warrantable, well-founded **12** within reason **14** understandable

## justifiably

**07** legally, rightly, validly **08** lawfully, properly **09** excusably, plausibly **10** acceptably, defensibly, reasonably **12** legitimately, within reason **14** understandably

## justification

**04** plea **05** basis **06** excuse, reason **07** apology, defence, defense, grounds, warrant **08** warranty **10** absolution, mitigation **11** explanation, vindication **12** confirmation, verification **15** rationalization

## justify

**04** aver, avow **05** clear, prove **06** acquit, defend, excuse, pardon, punish, uphold, verify **07** absolve, bear out, confirm, darrain, darrayn, deraign, deserve, explain, forgive, support, sustain, warrant **08** darraign, darraine, maintain, make good, validate **09** authorize, darraigne, establish, exculpate, exonerate, vindicate **10** stand up for **11** rationalize **12** substantiate **13** show to be right **14** give grounds for, give reasons for

## justly

**04** duly **05** right **06** fairly **07** equally, rightly **08** honestly, lawfully, properly **09** equitably **10** rightfully, with reason **11** deservingly, impartially, justifiably, objectively **12** even-handedly, legitimately

## jut, jut out

**03** jet **04** butt **05** jetty, jutty, stick **06** beetle, extend **07** extrude, project **08** overhang, protrude, stick out **10** projection

## jute

**03** tow **05** gunny, kenaf, urena **06** burlap **07** Hessian, hopsack **09** Corchorus **10** hop-sacking, Jews' mallow

**juvenile**
03 boy, juv, kid 04 girl 05 child, green, juvie, minor, young, youth 06 callow, infant, junior 07 babyish, puerile, teenage 08 childish, immature, teenager, youthful 09 infantile, youngster 10 adolescent 11 young person 13 inexperienced 15 unsophisticated

**Juventus**
04 Hebe

**juxtapose**
06 empale, impale 11 put together 13 place together, put side by side 15 place side by side

**juxtaposition**
07 contact 08 nearness, vicinity 09 closeness, immediacy, proximity 10 apposition, contiguity, impalement

# K

**K**
**03** Kay **04** kara, kesh, kilo **06** kaccha, kangha, kirpan

**kaleidoscopic**
**05** fluid **06** motley **08** manifold **10** changeable, poikilitic, polychrome, variegated **11** fluctuating **12** ever-changing, many-coloured, multifarious **13** multicoloured, parti-coloured, polychromatic **15** many-splendoured

**kame**
**02** ås **05** eskar, esker

**kangaroo**
**03** roo **04** euro, joey **06** boomer, old man **07** steamer, wallaby **08** forester, wallaroo

**Kansas**
**02** KS **04** Kans

**kaput**
**04** bust, phut **06** broken, ruined, undone **07** defunct, extinct, smashed, wrecked **08** finished **09** conked out, destroyed

**karate**
**08** Shotokan

*Shotokan belts include:*

**03** red
**05** black, brown, green, white
**06** orange, purple, yellow

*See also* **martial art**
• **karate costume** **02** gi **03** gie

**kay**
**01** K

**Kazakhstan**
**02** KZ **03** KAZ

**keel**
**04** back, base, cool, ship, skeg **05** barge, skegg **06** bottom, carina, ruddle **07** keelson **08** backbone **10** stabilizer **11** centreboard **12** cheesecutter
• **keel over** ◇ *reversal down indicator* **04** drop, fall **05** faint, swoon, upset **07** capsize, founder, pass out, stagger **08** black out, collapse, overturn **10** topple over, turn turtle **14** turn upside down

**keen**
**03** cry, mad, sob **04** acid, avid, cold, deep, fell, fine, gleg, howl, moan, nuts, wail, weep, wild, wise, yowl **05** acute, breem, breme, crazy, eager, groan, mourn, potty, quick, razor, sharp, smart, snell **06** argute, astute, biting, caring, clever, fierce, fond of, grieve, intent, lament, liking, loving, narrow, severe, shrewd, shrill, strong **07** anxious, devoted, earnest, fervent, hawking, hawkish, intense, mordant, nipping, pointed, pungent, sharpen, ululate **08** diligent, incisive, piercing, ruthless, stinging **09** assiduous, cut-throat, devoted to, dog-eat-dog, enamoured, impatient, quick-eyed, razor-like, sagacious, sensitive, trenchant, wide awake, wonderful **10** attached to, discerning, double-eyed, perceptive, razor-sharp **11** heavily into, industrious, lamentation, penetrating, quick-witted, sharp-witted **12** enthusiastic **13** conscientious, keen as mustard, perspicacious **14** discriminating

**keenly**
**06** deeply, shrewd **07** acutely, eagerly, quickly, sharply **08** astutely, cleverly, fiercely, shrewdly, strongly **09** earnestly, fervently, intensely **10** diligently, incisively **11** assiduously, sensitively **12** perceptively **13** penetratingly

**keenness**
**03** eye **04** edge **06** wisdom **08** industry, sagacity, sapience, sedulity **09** diligence, eagerness, sharpness **10** astuteness, cleverness, enthusiasm, shrewdness, trenchancy **11** discernment, earnestness, penetration, sensitivity **12** incisiveness **15** industriousness

**keep**
◇ *containment indicator* ◇ *hidden indicator* **03** own, run **04** curb, feed, food, fort, have, heap, hold, last, mark, mind, obey, pile, rear, save, stay, tend **05** amass, block, board, breed, carry, check, delay, deter, guard, hoard, limit, means, place, raise, stack, stock, store, tower, watch **06** arrest, castle, deal in, defend, detain, donjon, endure, foster, fulfil, hamper, hinder, hold up, honour, impede, keep at, keep on, keep up, living, manage, pile up, remain, retain, retard, shield, upkeep **07** abide by, care for, carry on, citadel, collect, conduct, confine, control, deposit, dungeon, furnish, inhibit, nurture, observe, perform, persist, possess, prevent, protect, refrain, reserve, respect, shelter, store up, support, sustain **08** adhere to, carry out, conserve, continue, fortress, hang on to, hold back, hold on to, keep back, maintain, obstruct, preserve, restrain, withhold **09** celebrate, constrain, look after, persevere, recognize, safeguard, solemnize, subsidize, watch over **10** accumulate, comply with, effectuate, livelihood, perpetuate, provide for, stronghold, sustenance, take care of **11** commemorate, keep waiting, maintenance, not part with, nourishment, subsistence, superintend **12** be in charge of, have charge of **13** have custody of, interfere with, keep faith with **15** keep in good order
• **for keeps** **06** always **07** for ever, for good **10** for all time

• **keep at** **03** nag **04** last, stay, toil **05** grind **06** badger, drudge, endure, finish, labour, remain, slog at **07** carry on, persist, stick at **08** complete, continue, fight off, maintain **09** persevere **10** plug away at **11** be steadfast **12** beaver away at
• **keep back** ◇ *reversal indicator* **04** curb, hide, save, stop **05** check, delay, hoard, limit, store **06** censor, hinder, hold up, hush up, impede, retain, retard, stifle **07** conceal, control, inhibit, repress, reserve **08** hold back, keep down, lay aside, prohibit, restrain, restrict, set aside, suppress, withhold **09** constrain, stockpile **10** accumulate, keep secret
• **keep from** **04** halt, help, stop **06** desist, resist **07** forbear, prevent, refrain **08** restrain
• **keep in** **04** hide **05** quell **06** coop up, detain, shut in, stifle, stop up **07** conceal, confine, control, inhibit, repress **08** bottle up, keep back, restrain, suppress
• **keep off** **05** avoid, expel, fence, parry **07** stay off **08** hands off, keep away **09** not go near **10** body-swerve **12** stay away from, steer clear of **14** avoid going near
• **keep on** **04** go on, last, stay **06** endure, hold on, remain, retain **07** carry on, persist **08** continue, keep at it, maintain **09** persevere, soldier on, stick at it **13** stay the course **14** continue to hire
• **keep on at** **03** nag **05** harry **06** badger, chivvy, go on at, harass, pester, plague, pursue **09** importune
• **keep secret** **04** hide **07** conceal **08** keep back, keep dark, suppress **09** dissemble **14** keep under wraps
• **keep to** **04** obey **06** fulfil **07** observe, respect, stick to **08** adhere to **10** comply with
• **keep up** **03** vie **05** equal, match, rival **06** retain **07** compete, contend, emulate, persist, support, sustain **08** continue, keep pace, maintain, preserve **09** entertain, persevere **10** keep tabs on **11** go along with **13** keep abreast of **15** keep in touch with

**keeper**
**03** nab **05** guard **06** custos, escort, gaoler, jailer, mahout, minder, parker, parkie, warden, warder **07** curator, granger, marshal, steward **08** defender, governor, guardian, overseer, surveyor, vesturer **09** archivist, attendant, bodyguard, caretaker, castellan, constable, custodian, guard ring, inspector **10** austringer, châtelaine, proprietor, supervisor **11** conservator, park-officer **13** administrator **14** superintendent

**keep fit**
**02** PE, PT

**keeping**
**04** care, cure, hand, ward **05** aegis, hands, store, trust **06** accord, charge **07** balance, custody, harmony, support

**08** auspices, tutelage **09** agreement, congruity, patronage, retention **10** compliance, conformity, observance, proportion, protection **11** consistency, maintenance, reservation, safe-keeping, supervision **12** guardianship, preservation, surveillance **14** correspondence

### keepsake
**05** relic, token **06** emblem, pledge **07** memento **08** reminder, souvenir **11** remembrance

### keg
**02** kg **03** tun, vat **04** butt, cask, drum **06** barrel, firkin **08** hogshead

### kelvin
**01** K

### ken
**04** know **05** field, grasp, range, reach, scope **06** notice **07** compass **09** awareness, knowledge **10** cognizance, perception **11** realization **12** acquaintance, appreciation **13** comprehension, understanding

### Kent
**02** SE

### Kentucky
**02** KY

### Kenya
**03** EAK, KEN

### kerfuffle
**03** ado **04** flap, fuss, to-do **05** hoo-ha, tizzy **06** bother, bustle, flurry, furore **07** agitate, carry-on, fluster, palaver **08** ballyhoo, brouhaha, disorder **09** agitation, commotion

### kernel
**03** nub, nut **04** core, corn, crux, germ, gist, seed **05** copra, gland, grain, heart, stone **06** almond, centre, marrow, nutmeg **07** essence, innards, nucleus **08** pichurim **09** pistachio, substance **11** nitty-gritty, quandong-nut **12** nuts and bolts, quintessence

### kestrel
**06** keelie **07** staniel, stannel, stanyel **08** stallion **09** windhover

### key
**01** A, B, C, D, E, F, G, H **03** cue **04** clue, code, crib, kaie, main, mood, note, sign, tone **05** basic, chief, gloss, guide, index, means, pitch, style, table, vital, wedge **06** answer, clavis, legend, secret, timbre, winder **07** central, crucial, leading, pointer, spanner **08** decisive, glossary, solution **09** character, essential, important, indicator, necessary, principal **11** explanation, explication, fundamental, translation **12** passe-partout **14** interpretation
*See also* **island**

*Keys on a computer keyboard include:*

**03** alt, del, end, esc, ins, tab **04** ctrl, home, pg dn, pg up **05** alt gr, enter **06** delete, insert, page up **07** control, num lock **08** caps lock, page down

• **key stem** **03** pin

### keynote
**01** C **04** core, gist, mese, pith **05** final, heart, point, theme, tonic **06** accent, centre, marrow, stress **07** essence **08** emphasis **09** substance

### keystone
**04** base, core, crux, root **05** basis, quoin **06** ground, motive, source, spring **07** sagitta **08** linchpin **09** principle **10** foundation, mainspring **11** cornerstone

### kick
◊ *anagram indicator* **03** fun, hit, pep, toe, zip **04** bite, blow, boot, buzz, chip, foot, hack, heel, high, hoof, jolt, knee, lark, lift, punt, quit, shin, spur, stop, tang, yerk, zing **05** break, fling, pause, power, punce, punch, react, shoot, spurn, wince **06** effect, falter, give up, jack in, let out, pack in, recoil, strike, thrill **07** abandon, dropout, fly-kick, grubber, lash out, misfire, penalty, potency, project, rebound, spurn at, tap-kick **08** back-heel, drop-kick, free kick, goal kick, grub kick, high kick, jump back, leave off, move back, pleasure, pungency, set piece, sixpence, spot kick, stimulus, strength, striking **09** boomerang, cross-kick, garryowen, place kick **10** desist from, excitement, pile-driver, point after, resilience, resistance, spring back **11** stimulation **12** recalcitrate, spurn against
• **kick against** **04** defy **05** rebel, spurn **06** oppose, resist **07** protest **09** withstand **14** hold out against
• **kick around** **03** use **05** abuse **07** discuss, exploit, toy with **08** ill-treat, maltreat, play with **09** mess about, push about, talk about, trample on **10** mess around, push around **15** take advantage of
• **kick off** **03** die **04** open **05** begin, start **08** commence, initiate **09** introduce **10** inaugurate **11** get under way
• **kick out** **04** oust, sack, spur **05** eject, evict, expel **06** reject, remove **07** boot out, dismiss, turf out **08** chuck out, get rid of, throw out **09** discharge **13** give the boot to, give the push to, give the sack to **14** give the elbow to

### kickback
**05** bribe **06** pay-off, recoil **07** rebound **08** backlash, reaction **09** incentive, sweetener **10** back-hander, inducement

### kick-off
**02** KO **05** start **06** outset, word go **07** opening **09** beginning, inception **12** commencement, introduction

### kid
**03** boy, con, imp, lad, rib, tot **04** brat, dupe, fool, girl, gull, hoax, jest, joke, wean **05** bairn, child, kiddy, sprog, tease, trick, youth **06** delude, have on, humbug, infant, nipper, rug rat, wind up **07** deceive, littlie, littlin, littl 'un, pretend, tiny tot, toddler, young 'un **08** cheverel, cheveril, hoodwink, juvenile, littling, teenager, yeanling, young one **09** bamboozle, deception, kiddywink, littleane, little boy, little one, youngster **10** adolescent, ankle-biter, little girl **11** young person

### kidnap
**05** seize, steal **06** abduct, hijack, snatch **07** capture **08** carry off **12** hold to ransom **13** hold as hostage, take as hostage

### kill
**03** axe, bag, end, ice, pip, sap, top, use, zap **04** ache, do in, dull, ease, fill, hang, hurt, pass, prey, ruin, slay **05** death, drain, mop-up, napoo, pound, quash, quell, shoot, smart, smite, spend, spoil, still, sting, throb, total, use up, waste, weary, whack **06** behead, be sore, climax, deaden, defeat, dilute, fag out, finish, lay low, muffle, murder, occupy, reject, rub out, settle, soothe, stifle, strain, suffer, twinge, weaken **07** abolish, bump off, butcher, cut down, destroy, discard, execute, exhaust, fatigue, kiss off, knacker, nullify, put down, relieve, scupper, smother, stonker, take out, tire out, wipe out **08** blow away, decimate, despatch, dispatch, knock off, massacre, moderate, ring-bark, shoot-out, snuff out, suppress **09** alleviate, be painful, cause pain, death-blow, devastate, dispose of, do to death, eliminate, eradicate, finish off, liquidate, overexert, polish off, shoot dead, slaughter, while away **10** annihilate, conclusion, decapitate, dénouement, do away with, extinguish, guillotine, neutralize, put an end to, put to death, put to sleep **11** assassinate, coup de grâce, electrocute, exterminate, stab to death, take it out of

### killer
**03** gun, orc **04** orca **06** gunman, hit-man, ice man, slayer **07** butcher, matador, shooter **08** assassin, hired gun, homicide, murderer **09** cut-throat, destroyer **10** hatchet man, liquidator, man-queller, stupendous **11** axe murderer, executioner, slaughterer **12** exterminator, mass murderer, serial killer, woman-queller
• **natural killer** **02** NK

### killing
**03** hit **04** coup, gain, hard **05** booty, death, funny **06** absurd, big hit, deadly, murder, profit, taxing, tiring **07** amusing, arduous, a scream, bonanza, carnage, clean-up, comical, fortune, slaying, success, wearing **08** butchery, draining, fatality, genocide, homicide, massacre, windfall **09** bloodshed, execution, fatiguing, gruelling, hilarious, ludicrous, mactation, matricide, patricide, predation, slaughter, uxoricide **10** enervating, exhausting, fratricide, hysterical, lucky break, sororicide, uproarious **11** destruction,

destructive, elimination, fascinating, infanticide, liquidation, rib-tickling **12** back-breaking, debilitating, irresistible, manslaughter, stroke of luck **13** assassination, extermination, side-splitting

**killjoy**
**05** cynic **06** damper, grouch, misery, moaner, whiner, wowser **07** sceptic **08** buzzkill, dampener **09** pessimist **10** complainer, spoilsport, wet blanket **11** Weary Willie **12** trouble-mirth **13** prophet of doom

**kiln**
**04** oast **05** stove **06** muffle

**kilo**
**01** K

**kilt**
**07** filabeg, filibeg **08** fillibeg, philabeg, philibeg **09** phillabeg, phillibeg **10** fustanella

**kilter**
• **out of kilter 04** awry **05** askew **08** confused, lopsided **09** skew-whiff **10** misaligned, unbalanced **12** out of balance

**kin**
**04** clan **05** blood, catty, stock, tribe **06** family, people **07** cousins, kindred, lineage, related **08** affinity **09** relations, relatives **10** extraction **12** relationship **13** consanguinity, flesh and blood

**kina**
**01** K

**kind**
**03** ilk, set **04** form, good, mild, nice, race, sort, type, warm **05** beget, brand, breed, class, genre, genus, stamp, style **06** benign, family, genial, gentle, giving, humane, kindly, loving, manner, nature, strain **07** amiable, clement, cordial, helpful, lenient, patient, pitying, species, tactful, variety **08** amicable, category, friendly, generous, gracious, merciful, obliging, selfless, tolerant **09** agreeable, bounteous, character, congenial, courteous, indulgent, unselfish **10** altruistic, benevolent, big-hearted, charitable, forbearing, persuasion, thoughtful **11** considerate, description, good-hearted, good-natured, kind-hearted, magnanimous, neighbourly, soft-hearted, sympathetic, temperament, warm-hearted **12** affectionate, humanitarian **13** compassionate, philanthropic, tender-hearted, understanding
• **in kind 08** in return, in specie **09** similarly, tit for tat **10** in exchange **12** in like manner
• **kind of** ◇ *anagram indicator* **04** a bit **05** kinda, quite **06** fairly, pretty, rather, sort of **07** a little **08** slightly, somewhat **10** moderately, relatively **12** to some degree, to some extent

**kind-hearted**
**04** kind, warm **06** benign, humane, kindly **07** helpful **08** amicable, generous, gracious, obliging **10** altruistic, big-hearted

**11** considerate, good-hearted, good-natured, sympathetic, warm-hearted **12** humanitarian **13** compassionate, philanthropic, tender-hearted

**kindle**
**03** fan **04** blow, fire, lunt, stir, tind, tine, tynd **05** brood, light, rouse, spark, teend, tynde **06** accend, arouse, awaken, excite, ignite, incite, induce, litter, thrill **07** enlight, incense, inflame, inspire, provoke **09** set alight, set fire to, set on fire, stimulate

**kindliness**
**06** nature, warmth **07** charity **08** kindness, sympathy **09** benignity **10** amiability, compassion, generosity **11** beneficence, benevolence **12** friendliness **14** loving-kindness

**kindly**
**04** fond, good, kind, mild, nice, warm **06** benign, couthy, genial, gentle, gently, giving, goodly, humane, native, please, polite, tender, warmly **07** benefic, cordial, couthie, helpful, natural, patient **08** amicable, benignly, friendly, generous, humanely, lovingly, pleasant **09** agreeable, avuncular, helpfully, indulgent, patiently, tactfully **10** benevolent, big-hearted, charitable, charitably, favourable, generously, mercifully, selflessly, thoughtful, tolerantly **11** considerate, courteously, good-natured, kind-hearted, magnanimous, neighbourly, sympathetic, unselfishly **12** benevolently, thoughtfully **13** compassionate, considerately, grandfatherly, kind-heartedly, magnanimously, understanding **14** affectionately, altruistically **15** compassionately, sympathetically

**kindness**
**03** aid **04** help, love **05** grace **06** favour, warmth **07** aggrace, benefit, candour, charity, service **08** altruism, courtesy, good deed, goodness, good turn, goodwill, humanity, leniency, mildness, niceness, patience, sympathy **09** affection, benignity, tolerance **10** assistance, benignancy, compassion, generosity, gentleness, humaneness, indulgence, kindliness **11** beneficence, benevolence, helpfulness, hospitality, magnanimity **12** friendliness, philanthropy, pleasantness **13** consideration, fellow feeling, Gemütlichkeit, understanding **14** loving-kindness, thoughtfulness **15** considerateness, humanitarianism, warm-heartedness

**kindred**
**03** kin, sib **04** akin, clan, folk, hapu, like **05** flesh, house, stock **06** allied, common, family, people **07** cognate, lineage, related, similar **08** affinity, kinsfolk, matching **09** congenial, connected, relations, relatives **10** affiliated, similarity **11** connections **12** relationship **13** consanguinity, corresponding, flesh and blood

**king**
**01** K, R **02** HM **03** Rex, Roi **04** Inca,

lord, shah, star **05** chief, ruler **06** bigwig, kaiser, leader, master, prince, top dog **07** big shot, emperor, kingpin, majesty, monarch, supremo **08** big noise **09** big cheese, chieftain, sovereign **11** head of state, the greatest **12** leading light

---

*Kings include:*

---

**03** Ban, Ida, Ine, Lot, Zog
**04** Ahab, Cnut, Cole, Edwy, Erik, Fahd, Ivan, Ivan (the Terrible), John, Karl, Knut, Lear, Offa, Olaf, Olav, Otto, Paul, Quin, Saud, Saul, Zeus
**05** Boris, Brian, Bruce (Robert), Capet (Hugo or Hugh), Carol, Creon, David, Edgar, Edred, Edwin (St), Henri, Henry, Herod (the Great), Hiero, Ixion, James, Louis, Midas, Murat (Joachim), Penda, Pepin (the Short), Priam, Svein, Sweyn
**06** Alaric, Albert, Alboin, Alfred, Alonso, Arthur, Attila, Baliol (Edward de), Canute, Cheops, Clovis, Darius, Donald, Duncan, Edmund, Edmund (Ironside), Edward, Egbert, Faisal, Farouk, George, Gustav, Haakon, Harald, Harold (Harefoot), Hassan, Khalid, Magnus, Oberon, Oswald (St), Philip, Ramses, Robert, Rudolf, Sargon, Xerxes
**07** Alfonso, Aragorn, Balliol (John de), Cepheus, Charles, Croesus, Emanuel, Francis, Fredrik, Humbert, Hussein, Ibn Saud, Kenneth, Leopold, Macbeth, Malcolm, Michael, Odoacer, Perseus, Ptolemy, Pyrrhus, Rameses, Richard, Romulus, Solomon, Stephen, Tarquin, Umberto, Wilhelm, William
**08** Baudouin, Birendra, Ethelred, Ethelred (the Unready), Frederik, Gaiseric, Gustavus, Jeroboam, Leonidas, Matthias, Ramesses, Sihanouk (Norodom), Thutmose
**09** Aethelred, Akhenaten, Alexander (the Great), Amenhotep, Antigonus, Antiochus, Athelstan, Christian, Cuchulain, Cymbeline, Ethelbert, Ethelwulf, Ferdinand, Frederick, Hammurabi, Hardaknut, Nadir Shah, Sigismund, Stanislaw, Taufa'ahau, Theodoric, Tuthmosis, Vortigern, Wenceslas, Wladyslaw, Zahir Shah (Mohammed)
**10** Aethelbert, Aethelstan, Aethelwulf, Artaxerxes, Carl Gustaf, Esarhaddon, Fisher King, Juan Carlos, Moshoeshoe, Ozymandias, Tarquinius, Wenceslaus
**11** Charlemagne, Constantine, Franz Joseph, Hardacanute, Hardicanute, Mithridates, Old King Cole, Sennacherib, Shalmaneser, Tut'ankhamun
**12** Assurbanipal, Boris Godunov, Herod Agrippa
**13** Chulalongkorn, Louis-Philippe
**14** Nebuchadnezzar, Philip Augustus, Victor Emmanuel
**15** Artaxerxes Ochus, Norodom Sihanouk

• **Three Kings** *see* **wise man** *under* **wise**
*See also* **Roman**

## kingdom
**04** land **05** realm, reign, state
**06** domain, empire, nation, sphere
**07** country, dynasty **08** division,
dominion, grouping, monarchy,
province **09** territory **11** sovereignty
**12** commonwealth, principality
*See also* **classification; empire**

## kingfisher
**07** halcyon **10** kookaburra

## kingly
**05** grand, noble, regal, royal **06** august,
lordly **07** stately, sublime, supreme
**08** glorious, imperial, imposing,
majestic, splendid **09** dignified,
grandiose, imperious, sovereign
**11** monarchical

## Kingsley
**03** Ben **04** Amis

## kink
◇ *anagram indicator* **03** bug **04** bend,
coil, curl, dent, flaw, gasp, knot, loop,
null, whim **05** chink, cough, crick,
crimp, curve, hitch, quirk, twirl, twist
**06** defect, fetish, foible, glitch, tangle
**07** blemish, caprice, crinkle, failing,
wrinkle **08** weakness **09** deviation,
weak point **10** deficiency, perversion
**11** indentation, peculiarity,
shortcoming **12** eccentricity,
entanglement, idiosyncrasy,
imperfection

## kinkajou
**05** potto **09** honey bear

## kinky
◇ *anagram indicator* **03** odd **04** wavy
**05** crazy, curly, funky, queer, weird
**06** coiled, curled, frizzy, quirky,
warped **07** bizarre, crimped, deviant,
strange, tangled, twisted, unusual
**08** abnormal, crumpled, depraved,
freakish, peculiar, wrinkled
**09** eccentric, perverted, unnatural,
whimsical **10** capricious, degenerate,
licentious, outlandish **13** idiosyncratic
**14** unconventional

## kinsfolk
**03** kin **04** clan, hapu **06** family
**07** cousins, kindred **09** relations,
relatives **11** connections

## kinship
**03** kin, sib, tie **04** ties **05** blood
**06** family **07** kindred, lineage
**08** affinity, alliance, ancestry, likeness,
relation **09** community **10** conformity,
connection, similarity **11** association,
equivalence **12** relationship
**13** consanguinity **14** correspondence

## kinsman
**03** sib **04** ally **06** cousin **07** brother

## kiosk
**03** box **05** booth, cabin, stall, stand
**07** counter **09** bandstand, bookstall,
news-stand

## Kiribati
**03** KIR

## Kirkpatrick
**01** K

## kismet
**03** lot **04** doom, fate **05** karma
**07** destiny, fortune, portion
**10** predestiny, providence

## kiss
**01** X **03** fan, lip, pax **04** buss, lick, neck,
pash, peck, snog **05** brush, cross,
graze, mouth, smack, touch **06** caress,
scrape, smooch, smouch **07** plonker,
smacker **08** canoodle, deep kiss,
osculate, suck face **09** baisemain,
glance off **10** bill and coo, contrecoup,
French kiss, osculation **11** touch gently
**12** touch lightly **13** butterfly kiss

## kit
**03** rig, set **04** gear, togs **05** get-up, strip,
stuff, tools **06** basket, kitten, outfit, rig-
out, tackle, things **07** baggage,
clobber, clothes, colours, effects,
luggage **08** clothing, supplies, utensils
**09** apparatus, equipment, trappings
**10** implements, provisions
**11** instruments **13** accoutrements,
appurtenances, paraphernalia
• **kit out** **03** arm **05** dress, equip, fix up
**06** fit out, outfit, rig out, supply **07** deck
out, furnish, garnish, prepare, provide

## kitchen
**03** but **06** galley **07** caboose, cookery,
cuisine **08** scullery **10** percussion
*See also* **utensil**

## kite
**04** gled **05** belly, glede **06** dragon,
elanet, Milvus, paunch **07** puttock,
rokkaku **08** aircraft

## kittenish
**04** cute **05** ludic **06** frisky **07** playful
**08** skittish, sportive **09** fun-loving
**10** coquettish, frolicsome **11** flirtatious

## kittiwake
**06** haglet **07** hacklet

## kitty
**04** fund **05** float

## knack
**03** art, toy **04** bent, feel, gift, hang, turn
**05** flair, forte, habit, quirk, skill, trick
**06** genius, talent **07** ability, faculty
**08** aptitude, capacity, facility,
ornament **09** dexterity, expertise,
handiness, quickness, technique
**10** adroitness, capability, competence,
propensity **11** proficiency, skilfulness

## knapsack
**03** bag **04** pack **06** kitbag **07** holdall,
musette **08** backpack, rucksack
**09** duffel bag, haversack

## knave
**01** J **03** boy, cad, nob, pam, pur **04** jack
**05** cheat, drôle, rogue, scamp, swine
**06** fripon, rascal, rotter, varlet
**07** bounder, custrel, dastard, villain
**08** blighter, coistrel, coistril, swindler
**09** reprobate, scallywag, scoundrel

## knavery
**05** fraud **06** deceit, ropery **07** devilry,
roguery **08** mischief, patchery, trickery,
villainy **09** chicanery, deception,

duplicity, imposture **10** corruption,
dishonesty, hanky-panky
**11** caddishness, friponnerie,
knavishness **13** double-dealing
**14** monkey business

## knavish
**06** rascal, wicked **07** caddish, corrupt,
roguish **08** devilish, fiendish, rascally
**09** dastardly, deceitful, deceptive,
dishonest, reprobate **10** fraudulent,
villainous **11** mischievous, scoundrelly
**12** contemptible, unprincipled,
unscrupulous **13** dishonourable

## knead
◇ *anagram indicator* **03** ply, rub **04** form,
mold, work **05** malax, mould, pound,
press, shape **06** conche, puddle,
pummel **07** knuckle, massage, squeeze
**08** malaxate **09** masticate
**10** manipulate

## kneel
**03** bow **04** bend **05** stoop **06** curtsy,
kowtow, revere **07** bow down, defer to
**09** genuflect **13** make obeisance **15** fall
to your knees

## knees
**03** lap

## knell
**03** end **04** peal, ring, toll **05** chime,
knoll, sound **07** ringing

## knickers
**05** pants, thong **06** briefs, smalls
**07** drawers, g-string, panties
**08** bloomers, frillies, lingerie, scanties
**09** underwear **10** underpants **12** bikini
briefs, camiknickers **14** knickerbockers

## knick-knack
**04** quip **05** knack **06** bauble, gewgaw,
jimjam, pretty, trifle **07** bibelot,
trangam, trinket **08** gimcrack,
jimcrack, nick-nack, ornament
**09** bagatelle, bric-à-brac, plaything
**11** whigmaleery **12** pretty-pretty,
whigmaleerie

## knife
**03** cut, rip **04** stab **05** blade, slash,
wound **06** cutter, pierce **08** lacerate

*Knives include:*

**02** da
**03** dah, hay, pen
**04** bolo, case, chiv, dirk, fish, jack,
moon, shiv, simi
**05** bowie, bread, clasp, craft, cutto,
flick, fruit, gully, kukri, panga,
paper, putty, skean, skene, spade,
steak, table
**06** barong, butter, carver, chakra,
cradle, cuttle, cuttoe, dagger,
gulley, oyster, parang, pocket,
sheath, trench
**07** bayonet, carving, catling,
drawing, dudgeon, hunting,
leather, machete, palette,
pruning, scalpel, Stanley®,
whittle
**08** bistoury, chopping, scalping,
skean-dhu, skene-dhu, tranchet
**09** box-cutter, butterfly, jockteleg,
Swiss army, toothpick
**10** skene-occle

**knight**

11 snickersnee, switchblade
13 Kitchen Devils®, pusser's dagger

*See also* **dagger; sword**
• **knife stand** 03 nef 05 block

**knight**

01 K, N 02 AK, Kt 03 dub, Sir 07 gallant, soldier, warrior, younker 08 champion, horseman 09 freelance, man-at-arms 10 cavalryman, equestrian 12 carpet-knight, knight-errant

*Knights include:*

04 grey
05 black, white
06 Bayard, carpet, errant, kemper, ritter
07 paladin
08 bachelor, banneret, cavalier, douzeper, vavasour
09 chevalier, doucepere, valvassor
10 kempery-man
14 knight-bachelor, preux chevalier

*Knights of the Round Table in Arthurian legend include:*

03 Kay
05 Lucan, Safer
06 Degore, Gareth
07 Alymere, Dagonet, Galahad, Gawaine, Lamorak, Lionell, Mordred, Pelleas, Tristan
08 Bedivere, Tristram
09 Bleoberis, Palomedes, Percivale
10 King Arthur
11 Bors de Ganis
12 Brunor le Noir, Ector de Maris
13 Lancelot Du Lac
15 La Cote Male Taile

**knightly**

04 bold 05 noble 06 heroic 07 courtly, gallant, valiant 08 gracious, intrepid, valorous 09 dauntless, soldierly 10 chivalrous, courageous, honourable

**knit**

03 set, tie 04 ally, bind, join, knot, link, loop, mend 05 unite, weave 06 crease, fasten, furrow, gather, secure 07 connect, tighten, wrinkle 08 contract, crotchet 09 interlace 10 intertwine 12 draw together

*Knitting-related terms include:*

03 rib, row
04 Aran, purl, wool
05 chart, pearl, plain
06 cast on, marker, needle, stitch
07 bind off, cast off, chevron, four-ply, tension, twin rib
08 ball band, Fair Isle, intarsia
09 box stitch, double rib, fingering, garter rib, single rib
10 double knit, French heel, moss stitch, rice stitch, row counter, seed stitch, tricoteuse
11 basketweave, cable needle, cable stitch, drop a stitch, plain stitch, thumb method
12 basket-stitch, garter-stitch, stitch holder
13 fisherman's rib, stocking frame
14 circular needle, double knitting, knitting needle, stocking stitch
15 knitting machine, knitting pattern

**knob**

03 bur, nub 04 ball, boll, boss, bump, burr, heel, knop, knot, knub, lump, node, noop, snub, stop, stud, umbo 05 berry, gnarl, knurl, mouse, offer, plook, plouk, rowel, swell, tuber, tuner 06 button, croche, handle, pommel, snubbe, switch, toorie, tourie, tumour 07 chesnut 08 chestnut, doorstop, eminence, pulvinar, register, swelling, tubercle 10 doorhandle, projection, protrusion, push-button 12 protuberance

**knock**

◇ *anagram indicator* 02 ca' 03 box, caa', con, dod, hit, pan, rap, tap 04 bang, bash, belt, blow, bump, chap, clip, cuff, dash, daud, dawd, daze, ding, jole, joll, jolt, jowl, pink, punt, slag, slam, slap, stun 05 clock, clour, clout, crash, joule, pound, punch, shock, slate, smack, stamp, swipe, thump, whack 06 attack, batter, defeat, nubble, rebuff, strike, wallop, whammy 07 bad luck, banging, censure, collide, condemn, failure, innings, knobble, knubble, rubbish, run down, setback, slag off 08 bump into, confound, pounding, reversal 09 criticism, criticize, deprecate, disparage, hammering, pull apart, rejection 10 misfortune 11 collide with, pick holes in 12 pull to pieces, tear to pieces 13 bad experience, find fault with

*See also* **beat**
• **knock about** 03 gad, hit 04 bash, hurt, roam, rove 05 abuse, punch, range, wound 06 bang up, batter, beat up, bruise, buffet, damage, injure, ramble, strike, travel, wander 07 consort, saunter, traipse 08 go around, maltreat, mistreat 09 associate, gallivant, hang about, manhandle 10 hang around
• **knock back** ◇ *reversal indicator* 04 cost, down, gulp, swig 05 drink, scoff, shock 06 devour, guzzle, rebuff, reject 07 swallow 08 gulp down 10 disconcert
• **knock down** 03 hit 04 fell, prop, raze 05 clout, floor, level, lower, pound, smash, wreck 06 batter, reduce, wallop 07 destroy, run down, run over, skittle 08 bowl over, decrease, demolish, pull down, take down 09 bring down, knock over
• **knocked down** 02 KD
• **knock off** 03 rob 04 do in, kill, lift, nick, slay, stop, whip 05 cease, filch, pinch, steal, swipe, waste 06 deduct, finish, murder, pack in, pilfer, pirate, rip off, snitch 07 bump off, snaffle 08 clock off, clock out, get rid of, pack it in, stop work, take away 09 polish off, terminate 10 do away with, finish work 11 assassinate, discontinue
• **knock out** 02 KO 04 beat, fell, kayo, rout, stun 05 amaze, crush, floor, level, shock 06 defeat, hammer, thrash 07 astound, destroy, disable, flatten, impress, startle 08 astonish, bowl over, demolish, overcome, surprise 09 eliminate, overwhelm, prostrate 10 strike down 11 knock for six 13 run rings round 14 get the better of 15 make unconscious
• **knock over** ◇ *anagram indicator* 04 fell 05 floor, level 07 run down, run over
• **knock up** 04 call, stir 05 awake, rouse, waken 06 awaken, wake up 07 wear out 09 improvise 10 impregnate, jerry-build 11 make quickly 12 build quickly, make pregnant, put in the club

**knockout**

02 KO 03 hit 04 coup, kayo 05 smash, socko 06 winner 07 king-hit, stunner, success, triumph 08 smash-hit 09 sensation 10 attraction

**knoll**

04 hill, rise 05 knell, knowe, mound 06 barrow, koppie 07 hillock, hummock 09 elevation

**knot**

◇ *anagram indicator* 02 kn, kt 03 bud, nur 04 band, bind, bond, boss, gnar, hill, knag, knar, knit, knob, knub, knur, lash, lump, node, nurr, ring, tags 05 bunch, clump, crowd, gnarl, group, joint, knurl, knurr, leash, mouse, ravel, snarl, twist, weave 06 circle, gaggle, nodule, secure, splice, tangle, tether 07 chignon, cluster, entwine 08 entangle, ligature, swelling 09 fastening, gathering 10 concretion, difficulty 14 marriage-favour

*Knots include:*

03 bow, tie
04 bend, flat, loop, love, reef, wale, wall
05 blood, chain, hitch, plait, thief, thumb, turle
06 Domhof, granny, lover's, prusik, square
07 bowline, Gordian, running, seizing, weaver's, Windsor
08 overhand, slipknot, spade-end, surgeon's, true-love
09 half hitch, lark's head, sheet bend, swab hitch, Turk's head
10 clove hitch, common bend, fisherman's, Flemish eye, sheepshank, true-lover's
11 carrick bend, donkey hitch, double blood, Englishman's, Hunter's bend, timber hitch
12 marling hitch, rolling hitch, simple sennit, weaver's hitch
13 drummer's chain, figure of eight, slippery hitch
14 Blackwall hitch, common whipping, double Cairnton, double-overhand, double-overhang, Englishman's tie, fisherman's bend, Matthew Walker's, running bowline

**knotty**

◇ *anagram indicator* 04 hard 05 bumpy,

## know

nirly, rough **06** knaggy, knobby, nirlie, nodose, nodous, rugged, thorny, tricky **07** complex, gnarled, gnarred, knarred, knobbly, knotted, nodular **08** baffling, puzzling **09** Byzantine, difficult, intricate **10** mystifying, perplexing **11** anfractuous, complicated, troublesome **13** problematical

## know

**03** con, ken, kon, see, wis, wit, wot **04** have, tell, weet, wish, wist **05** conne, savey, savvy, sense, weete **06** fathom, notice, savvey, weeten **07** approve, be aware, discern, make out, realize, undergo **08** identify, perceive **09** apprehend, be clued up, go through, have taped, recognize, tell apart **10** comprehend, experience, understand **11** distinguish, know by sight **12** be au fait with, discriminate **13** associate with, be cognizant of, be conscious of, be friends with, differentiate **14** be familiar with, be well-versed in
• **I don't know** **04** pass **08** search me

## know-all

**06** Jowett **07** wise guy **08** polymath, wiseacre **09** know-it-all, smart alec **10** clever dick **11** clever clogs, smartypants

## know-how

**04** bent **05** flair, knack, savey, savvy, skill **06** savvey, talent **07** ability, faculty **08** aptitude, cum-savvy, gumption **09** adeptness, dexterity, expertise, ingenuity, knowledge **10** adroitness, capability, competence, experience **11** proficiency, savoir-faire

## knowing

**03** fly, hep, hip **05** aware, canny, downy **06** astute, shrewd, sussed **07** cunning, gnostic, skilful

**08** informed **09** conscious, up to snuff **10** deliberate, discerning, expressive, meaningful, perceptive **11** intelligent, significant, worldly-wise

## knowingly

**08** by design, scienter, wilfully **09** on purpose, purposely, studiedly, willingly, wittingly **10** designedly **11** consciously **12** calculatedly, deliberately **13** intentionally

## knowledge

**03** art, gen, sus **04** data, suss **05** facts, grasp, jnana, light, skill, truth **06** gnosis, wisdom **07** ability, cunning, insight, knowhow, letters, tuition, witting **08** intimacy, learning, pansophy **09** awareness, cognition, education, erudition, expertise, judgement, schooling **10** cognizance **11** conversance, discernment, familiarity, information, instruction, proficiency, recognition, savoir-faire, scholarship **12** acquaintance, apprehension, intelligence **13** comprehension, consciousness, encyclopedism, enlightenment, understanding
• **full knowledge** **11** omniscience
• **range of knowledge** **03** ken

## knowledgeable

**02** up **05** aware, savey, savvy **06** au fait, expert, savvey **07** clued-up, erudite, learned **08** educated, familiar, genned up, informed, lettered, well-read, well up in **09** conscious, in the know, scholarly, up to speed **10** acquainted, conversant, well-versed **11** enlightened, experienced, intelligent **12** well-informed

## known

**04** kent **05** couth, noted, plain

**06** avowed, famous, patent **07** obvious **08** admitted, familiar, revealed **09** confessed, published, well-known **10** celebrated, proclaimed, recognized **11** commonplace **12** acknowledged
• **also known as** **03** aka **05** alias

## knuckle

• **knuckle down** **10** buckle down **12** begin to study **15** start to work hard
• **knuckle under** **05** defer, yield **06** accede, give in, submit **07** give way, succumb **09** acquiesce, surrender **10** capitulate **11** buckle under

## Koran

**05** Qoran, Quran **07** Alcoran
• **chapter of the Koran** **04** sura **05** surah

## Korea

**02** KP, KR **03** KOR, PRK, ROK

## kosher

• **not kosher** **04** tref **05** trefa, treif

## kowtow

**04** fawn **05** defer, kneel, toady **06** cringe, grovel, pander, suck up **07** flatter **08** pay court **11** curry favour **12** bow and scrape

## krypton

**02** Kr

## kudos

**04** fame, mana **05** glory **06** cachet, credit, esteem, honour, praise, regard, renown, repute **07** acclaim, laurels **08** applause, plaudits, prestige **09** laudation **10** reputation **11** distinction

## Kuwait

**03** KWT

## Kyrgyzstan

**02** KS **03** KGZ

# L

**L**
02 el 04 Lima

**label**
03 dub, tab, tag 04 call, logo, make, mark, name, seal, term 05 badge, brand, class, flash, stamp, tally, title 06 define, docket, marker, number, sticky, ticket 07 address, crowner, epithet, sticker 08 classify, describe, identify, nickname 09 bookplate, brand name, designate, dripstone, trademark 10 categorize, identifier, pigeonhole 11 description, designation 12 characterize 13 bumper sticker 14 attach a label to, categorization, classification, identification 15 proprietary name

**laboratory**

**laborious**
04 hard 05 heavy, tough 06 tiring, uphill 07 arduous, careful, onerous, operose, painful, slavish, tedious 08 diligent, tiresome, toilsome, wearying 09 assiduous, difficult, fatiguing, Sisyphean, strenuous, wearisome 10 laboursome, working-day 11 hard-working, industrious, painstaking 12 backbreaking 13 indefatigable

**laboriously**
09 arduously, operosely, slavishly 10 drudgingly, tiresomely, toilsomely 11 strenuously, wearisomely 14 with difficulty

**labour**
◊ *anagram indicator* 03 job, Lab 04 hard, moil, plod, roll, slog, task, toil, toss, turn, work 05 begar, birth, chore, grind, hands, pains, pangs, pitch, slave, sweat, yakka 06 drudge, duties, effort, overdo, strain, strive, suffer, throes 07 dwell on, katorga, travail, try hard, workers, workmen 08 belabour, be misled, delivery, drudgery, drudgism, exertion, go all out, hard work, struggle, work hard 09 be blinded, diligence, do to death, elaborate, employees, endeavour, hard yakka, labourers, reiterate, servitude, workforce 10 be deceived, childbirth, do your best, employment, overstress 11 flog to death, give your all, harp on about, labour pains, parturition 12 contractions, kill yourself 13 exert yourself, labor improbus, overemphasize 14 go on and on about 15 industriousness

**laboured**
◊ *anagram indicator* 05 heavy, stiff 06 forced, leaden, worked 07 awkward, stilted, studied 08 affected, overdone, strained 09 contrived, difficult, effortful, ponderous, unnatural 10 cultivated 11 complicated, overwrought

**labourer**
03 boy 04 hand, jack, peon 05 churl, grunt, navvy 06 bohunk, docker, drudge, hodman, Kanaka, menial, worker 07 Grecian, hobbler, pioneer, redneck, seagull, wharfie, workman 08 cottager, dataller, daytaler, farm hand, hireling 09 field hand, hired hand, operative 10 hod carrier, roustabout 11 gandy dancer 12 manual worker 15 unskilled worker

**labyrinth**
03 web 04 maze 06 enigma, jungle, puzzle, riddle, tangle, warren 07 mizmaze, network, winding 09 confusion, intricacy 10 complexity, perplexity 12 complication, entanglement

**labyrinthine**
◊ *anagram indicator* 04 mazy 06 knotty 07 complex, tangled, winding 08 confused, involved, mazelike, puzzling, tortuous 09 Byzantine, intricate 10 convoluted, perplexing 11 complicated

**lace**
◊ *anagram indicator* 03 net, tat, tie 04 bind, cord, do up 05 add to, blend, close, mix in, point, spike, thong, twine 06 attach, fasten, lacing, secure, string, tawdry, thrash, thread 07 crochet, flavour, fortify, latchet, netting 08 bobbinet, bootlace, filigree, mesh-work, open work, shoelace, stay tape 09 bobbin net 10 intertwine, interweave, strengthen 11 intermingle

**lacerate**
03 cut, rip 04 claw, gash, hurt, maim, rend, rent, tear, torn 05 ganch, slash, wound 06 gaunch, harrow, injure, mangle 07 afflict, cut open, scarify, torment, torture 08 distress, mutilate 09 lancinate

**laceration**
03 cut, rip 04 gash, maim, rent, tear 05 slash, wound 06 injury 10 mutilation

**lachrymose**
03 sad 05 teary, weepy 06 crying, woeful 07 maudlin, sobbing, tearful, weeping 08 dolorous, mournful 10 lugubrious, melancholy

**lack**
◊ *deletion indicator* 03 gap 04 miss, need, void, want 06 dearth, defect, penury 07 absence, not have, paucity, require, vacancy 08 scarcity, shortage 09 emptiness, privation 10 deficiency, have need of, scantiness 11 deprivation, destitution 12 be clean out of, be fresh out of 13 be deficient in, insufficiency 15 not have enough of

**lackadaisical**
04 dull, idle, lazy, limp 05 inert 06 dreamy 07 languid 08 careless, indolent, listless, lukewarm 09 apathetic, enervated, lethargic 10 abstracted, languorous, spiritless 11 half-hearted, indifferent

**lackey**
04 page, pawn, tool 05 gofer, guide, toady, valet 06 fawner, menial, minion, monkey, poodle, vassal, yes-man 07 doormat, equerry, footman, servant, steward 08 hanger-on, parasite, retainer 09 attendant, flatterer, sycophant 10 instrument, manservant, skip-kennel

**lacking**
◊ *deletion indicator* 03 shy 04 poor 05 minus 06 absent, flawed, to seek, wanted 07 missing, needing, short of, wanting, without 09 defective, deficient 10 inadequate

**lacklustre**
03 dim, dry 04 drab, dull, flat 05 vapid 06 boring, leaden 07 insipid, tedious 08 lifeless 10 spiritless, uninspired 11 commonplace 12 run-of-the-mill 13 unimaginative, uninteresting

**laconic**
04 curt 05 blunt, brief, crisp, pithy, short, terse 06 abrupt 07 concise, spartan 08 incisive, succinct, taciturn

**10** economical, to the point
**12** monosyllabic

**laconically**
**07** bluntly, briefly, in a word, in brief, pithily, tersely **08** abruptly **09** concisely **10** incisively, succinctly, to the point

**lacquer**
**05** japan **07** varnish **09** hairspray **12** vernis martin **14** Coromandel work

**lacuna**
**03** gap **04** void **05** blank, break, space **06** cavity, hiatus **08** omission

**lad**
**03** boy, guy, kid, son, tad **04** boyo, chap, sort, type **05** bloke, bucko, chiel, whelp, youth **06** callan, chield, fellow, nipper **07** callant, gossoon **08** juvenile, spalpeen **09** character, schoolboy, stripling, youngster **10** individual **13** gillie-wetfoot **14** whippersnapper **15** gillie-white-foot

**ladder**
**03** run, sty **04** rank, rung, trap **05** level, point, rungs, scala, scale, steps **06** étrier, series, stairs **07** fish-way, grading, potence, ranking **08** echelons **09** companion, hierarchy **10** set of steps **12** pecking order

**laden**
**04** full **05** heavy, taxed **06** jammed, loaded, packed **07** charged, fraught, gestant, stuffed **08** burdened, hampered, pregnant, weighted **09** chock-full, oppressed **10** encumbered **11** weighed down

**la-di-da**
**04** posh **05** pluty, put-on **06** snooty **07** foppish, stuck-up **08** affected, mannered, snobbish **09** conceited **11** highfalutin, over-refined, pretentious, toffee-nosed

**ladies**
see **toilet**

**ladle**
**03** dip **04** bail, bale, dish, lade **05** scoop, shank, spoon **06** dipper, shovel **07** divider
• **ladle out** **07** bail out, bale out, dish out, dole out, hand out **08** disburse **10** distribute

**lady**
**01** L **04** burd, dame, miss **05** begum, lakin, siren, woman **06** damsel, duenna, female, khanum, matron, Señora **07** hidalga, ladykin, old dear, sheikha, Signora **08** countess, Señorita **09** Signorina **10** demoiselle, grande dame, noblewoman, young woman **11** gentlewoman
See also **girl; woman**
• **lady's fingers** **04** okra **05** gumbo
• **lot of ladies** **04** bevy
• **organized ladies** **02** WI **15** Women's Institute

**ladylike**
**04** soft **06** modest, polite, proper **07** courtly, elegant, genteel, queenly, refined **08** cultured, decorous, delicate, matronly, polished, well-bred

**09** courteous **11** respectable **12** well-mannered

**lag**
**04** drag, idle, late **05** dally, delay, steal, tardy, tarry, trail **06** arrest, dawdle, linger, loiter, lounge, retard **07** convict, saunter, shuffle **08** hang back, hindmost, imprison, straggle **10** behindhand, fall behind, retardment **11** retardation **12** drag your feet, shilly-shally **13** kick your heels **14** bring up the rear
See also **prisoner**

**lager**
see **beer**

**laggard**
**05** idler, snail **06** loafer **07** dawdler, lounger **08** lingerer, loiterer, sluggard **09** saunterer, slowcoach, straggler

**lagoon**
**03** bog, fen **04** haff, lake, pond, pool **05** bayou, marsh, swamp **06** lagune, salina **08** shallows

**laid-back**
**04** calm, cool **06** at ease, casual **07** relaxed **09** easy-going, leisurely, unhurried, unworried **10** untroubled **11** free and easy, unflappable **13** imperturbable

**laid up**
**03** ill **04** sick **05** crook **07** injured **08** disabled **09** bedridden **10** housebound **11** immobilized, out of action **12** hors de combat **13** confined to bed, incapacitated, on the sick list

**lair**
**03** den, lie **04** mire **05** couch **07** retreat
See also **animal**

**laissez-faire**
**09** free-trade **10** free-market, permissive **14** free-enterprise, live and let live, non-interfering

**laity**
**03** lay **06** people **08** amateurs **09** lay people, outsiders **10** temporalty, unordained **12** parishioners **14** the non-ordained

**lake**
**01** L **03** dam, lac, sea **04** loch, meer, mere, pond, pool, tarn **05** basin, bayou, cowal, lough, playa, shott, water **06** lagoon, lagune, nyanza, salina **07** carmine **09** everglade, reservoir, saltchuck

*The Great Lakes:*

**04** Erie
**05** Huron
**07** Ontario
**08** Michigan, Superior

*Lakes, lochs and loughs include:*

**03** Awe, Van
**04** Abbé, Bala, Biwa, Bled, Chad, Como, Derg, Earn, Erie, Eyre, Kivu, Ness, Tana
**05** Foyle, Garda, Great, Huron, Leven, Morar, Neagh, Nyasa, Ohrid, Onega, Patos, Poopó, Tahoe, Taupo, Volta

**06** Albert, Baikal, Corrib, Crater, Finger, Geneva, Ladoga, Lomond, Louise, Malawi, Nasser, Saimaa, Taimyr, Taymyr, Vänern, Zurich
**07** Aral Sea, Balaton, Chapala, Dead Sea, Katrine, Lucerne, Ontario, Rannoch, Scutari, Torrens, Turkana
**08** Balkhash, Bodensee, Chiemsee, Issyk Kul, Lac Léman, Loch Earn, Loch Ness, Lough Awe, Maggiore, Michigan, Superior, Tiberias, Titicaca, Tonlé Sap, Victoria, Winnipeg
**09** Constance, Great Bear, Great Salt, Kammer See, Loch Leven, Loch Morar, Lough Derg, Maracaibo, Neuchâtel, Nicaragua, Ullswater, Willandra, Zeller See
**10** Caspian Sea, Great Slave, Loch Lomond, Lough Foyle, Lough Neagh, Okeechobee, Tanganyika, Windermere, Wörther See
**11** Great Bitter, Loch Katrine, Lough Corrib
**12** Derwent Water, Kielder Water
**13** Bassenthwaite, Coniston Water

**lam**
**03** hit **04** bash, beat, belt, pelt **05** clout, knock, pound, thump, whack **06** batter, escape, pummel, strike, thrash, wallop **07** leather

**lamb**
**04** cade, Elia, yean **08** yeanling

**lambast, lambaste**
**03** tan **04** beat, belt, drub, flay, flog, slag, whip **05** clout, roast, scold, thump, whack **06** batter, berate, rebuke, strike, thrash, wallop **07** censure, clobber, leather, reprove, rubbish, slag off, upbraid **08** badmouth **09** castigate, criticize, reprimand

**lambert**
**01** L

**lame**
**04** game, halt, hurt, maim, main, poor, tame, thin, weak **05** gammy **06** feeble, flimsy, maimed, mained, poorly **07** halting, injured, limping **08** disabled, hobbling, spavined **09** defective, hamstring, hamstrung **10** inadequate **11** handicapped **12** unconvincing **13** incapacitated **14** unsatisfactory
• **lame person** **04** gimp

**lamely**
**06** feebly, tamely, weakly **07** shakily **09** with a limp **10** hobblingly, unsteadily **12** inadequately **14** unconvincingly

**lament**
**03** cry, sob **04** howl, keen, mean, mein, mene, moan, wail, weep **05** dirge, dumka, elegy, groan, meane, mourn, plain, tears **06** bemoan, bewail, beweep, crying, grieve, regret, repine, sorrow, yammer **07** deplore, requiem, sobbing, ululate, wayment, weeping

**lamentable**

**08** complain, grieving, threnody **09** complaint **11** lamentation

**lamentable**

◊ *anagram indicator* **03** low, sad **04** mean, poor **05** lousy **06** crying, funest, grotty, meagre, measly, tragic, woeful **07** moanful, pitiful **08** grievous, mournful, terrible, wretched **09** miserable, niggardly, sorrowful, worthless **10** deplorable, inadequate **11** distressing, regrettable, unfortunate **12** insufficient **13** disappointing **14** unsatisfactory

**lamentably**

**08** woefully **09** miserably, pitifully **10** deplorably, tragically **11** regrettably **12** inadequately **14** insufficiently **15** disappointingly

**lamentation**

**03** cry **04** keen, moan **05** dirge, elegy, grief **06** lament, plaint, sorrow **07** keening, sobbing, wailing, wayment, weeping **08** grieving, jeremiad, mourning, threnody **09** ululation **11** deploration

**laminate**

**04** coat, face **05** cover, flake, layer, plate, split **06** veneer **07** foliate, overlay **08** separate, stratify **09** exfoliate

**lamp**

**03** eye **04** bulb, Davy **05** crusy, light, torch **06** argand, crusie, Leerie, sconce **07** cruisie, Geordie, lantern, lucigen, pendant, pendent, scamper **08** arc-light, fog light, torchier **09** light bulb, moderator, spotlight, torchière, veilleuse **10** Anglepoise®, Kleig light, Klieg light, night-light, photoflood **11** searchlight

**lampoon**

**04** mock, skit **05** spoof, squib **06** parody, satire, send up, send-up **07** Pasquil, Pasquin, take off, take-off **08** ridicule, satirize, travesty **09** burlesque, make fun of **10** caricature, pasquinade

**lampooner**

**07** Pasquil, Pasquin **08** parodist, satirist **09** pasquiler **10** pasquilant **11** pasquinader **12** caricaturist

**lance**

**03** cut **04** pike, slit **05** lanch, prick, rejón, shaft, spear **06** incise, lancet, launch, pierce **07** bayonet, cut open, harpoon, javelin **08** puncture, white arm

**land**

**03** bag, get, hit, nab, net, tax, win **04** area, deal, dock, drop, gain, give, loam, lord, moor, soil **05** acres, berth, catch, earth, end up, fetch, glebe, manor, reach, realm, state, tract **06** alight, anchor, arrive, burden, direct, domain, estate, fields, ground, lumber, nation, obtain, people, region, saddle, secure, settle, turn up, unload, whenua, wind up **07** achieve, acquire, acreage, capture, country, deliver, deplane, deposit, dry land, grounds, inflict, oppress, procure, terrain, trouble **08** dismount, district,

encumber, farmland, finish up, go ashore, property, province, take down **09** bring down, disembark, get hold of, open space, rural area, territory, touch down, weigh down **10** administer, come to rest, fatherland, motherland, real estate, terra firma **11** countryside, terrestrial **12** come in to land, find yourself **13** bring in to land, native country
*See also* **country; continent;**
• **amount of land 03** are, lot, rod, ure **04** acre, shot **07** hectare
• **arable land 03** lay, lea, ley

**landing**

**04** dock, pier, quay **05** jetty, wharf **07** arrival, greaser, harbour **08** coming in **09** alighting, belly flop, deplaning, touchdown **12** landing-place, landing-stage, three-pricker **13** putting ashore **14** coming in to land, coming to ground, disembarkation

**landing-stair**

**04** ghat **05** ghaut

**landlady, landlord**

**04** host **05** owner **06** lessor **07** hostess, Rachman **08** hotelier, mine host, publican, slumlord **09** innkeeper, landowner **10** freeholder, proprietor **11** hotel-keeper **12** proprietress, restaurateur

**landmark**

**05** cairn, meith **06** beacon, crisis **07** feature **08** boundary, milepost, monument, signpost **09** milestone, watershed **12** turning-point
*See also* **Africa; Asia; Australia; Canada; Europe; London; Middle East; New York; New Zealand; United Kingdom; United States of America**

**landscape**

**04** view **05** scene, vista **06** aspect, saikei **07** outlook, paysage, scenery **08** panorama, prospect **11** countryside, perspective

**landslide**

**04** slip **07** runaway **08** decisive, emphatic, landslip, rockfall **09** avalanche, earthfall **10** éboulement **12** overwhelming

**lane**

**02** La **03** gut, way **04** loan, loke, lone, path, wynd **05** alley, byway, entry, track **06** avenue, boreen, byroad, ruelle, vennel **07** bikeway, channel, footway, loaning, passage, pathway, sea road, towpath, twitten **08** alleyway, driveway, footpath, twitting **10** backstreet, passageway

**language**

**03** bat **04** cant, talk **05** argot, lingo, style **06** jargon, speech, tongue **07** diction, wording **08** converse, parlance, phrasing, rhetoric, speaking, swearing, uttering **09** discourse, utterance **10** expression, vocabulary, vocalizing **11** phraseology, terminology, verbalizing **12** conversation **13** communication

*Languages include:*

**02** Wu
**03** ASL, BSL, Edo, Gan, Giz, Ibo, Kru, Lao, Mam, Mon, Twi, Yue
**04** Chad, Cree, Crow, Dari, Erse, Fang, Gaul, Inca, Lapp, Manx, Maya, Moto, Nupe, Pali, Susu, Thai, Tshi, Urdu, Xosa, Zulu
**05** Attic, Aztec, Bantu, Cajun, Carib, Creek, Croat, Czech, Doric, Dutch, Farsi, Greek, Hindi, Inuit, Ionic, Iraqi, Irish, Karen, Kazak, Khmer, Latin, Malay, Maori, Masai, Norse, Osean, Punic, Saxon, Scots, Shona, Sioux, Tamil, Uzbek, Welsh, Xhosa, Yakut
**06** Arabic, Bangla, Basque, Berber, Bokmål, Celtic, Coptic, Creole, Dakota, Danish, French, Gaelic, German, Gothic, Hebrew, Lydian, Magyar, Micmac, Mohawk, Mongol, Polish, Romany, Sherpa, Slovak, Tartar
**07** Afghani, Amharic, Aramaic, Ayamará, Bengali, Bosnian, Catalan, Chinese, Chinook, Cornish, English, Euskera, Finnish, Flemish, Frisian, Guaraní, Italian, Kalmuck, Lappish, Latvian, Makaton, Maltese, Mohican, Nynorsk, Punjabi, Quechua, Russian, Semitic, Siamese, Slovene, Spanish, Swahili, Swedish, Tagálog, Turkish, Umbrian, Walloon, Yiddish, Zapotec
**08** Albanian, Armenian, Cherokee, Croatian, Demotiki, Estonian, Etruscan, Georgian, Japanese, Malagasy, Mandarin, Moldovan, Phrygian, Pilipino, Romanian, Romansch, Sanskrit, Setswana, Warlpiri
**09** Aborigine, Afrikaans, Algonquin, Bulgarian, Cantonese, Castilian, Dalmatian, Ethiopian, Gujarathi, Gujerathi, Hungarian, Icelandic, Kiswahili, Malayalam, Norwegian, Provençal, Sardinian, Ukrainian
**10** Anglo-Saxon, Babylonian, Belarusian, Hindustani, Lithuanian, Macedonian, Malayaalam, Phoenician, Portuguese, Serbo-Croat, Vietnamese
**12** ancient Greek, Katharevousa, Sign Language
**13** Middle English
**14** Lëtzebuergesch

*Invented languages include:*

**03** Ido, Neo
**06** Novial
**07** Volapük
**08** Newspeak
**09** Esperanto
**10** Occidental
**11** Interglossa, Interlingua
**12** Idiom Neutral

---

*Computer programming languages include:*

**01** C
**02** VB
**03** ADA, AWK, XML
**04** HTML, Java, Perl
**05** BASIC, COBOL
**06** Delphi, Pascal, Python
**07** FORTRAN
**10** Postscript
**11** Visual Basic

---

*Language terms include:*

**02** RP
**03** ASR, NLP
**04** cant
**05** argot, idiom, lingo, slang, usage
**06** accent, brogue, creole, jargon, patois, patter, pidgin, syntax, tongue
**07** dialect, grammar, lexicon, phoneme
**08** buzz word, localism, Mobspeak, morpheme, Newspeak, standard
**09** etymology, Franglais, phonetics, semantics
**10** cyberspeak, journalese, vernacular, vocabulary
**11** doublespeak, linguistics, non-standard, orthography, regionalism
**12** gobbledygook, lexicography, lingua franca, vulgar tongue
**13** colloquialism

• **bad language 04** cuss, oath **05** curse **07** cussing **08** swearing **09** expletive, swearword
• **language unit 04** word **07** phoneme

**languid**
**04** dull, lazy, limp, slow, weak **05** faint, heavy, inert, slack, weary **06** feeble, pining, sickly, torpid **07** relaxed **08** drooping, flagging, inactive, listless, sluggish **09** enervated, lethargic **10** languorous, spiritless **11** debilitated, indifferent **12** uninterested **13** lackadaisical **14** unenthusiastic

**languidly**
**05** dully **06** feebly, lazily, slowly, weakly **07** heavily, inertly **08** torpidly **10** inactively, listlessly **13** lethargically

**languish**
**03** die, rot **04** fade, fail, flag, long, mope, pine, sigh, sink, want, wilt **05** brood, droop, faint, quail, waste, yearn **06** desire, grieve, hanker, hunger, sicken, sorrow, weaken, wither **07** decline **08** fall away **09** waste away **11** deteriorate

**languor**
**04** calm, lull **05** ennui, sloth **06** pining, torpor **07** fatigue, frailty, inertia, silence **08** debility, laziness, lethargy, weakness **09** faintness, heaviness, indolence, lassitude, stillness, weariness **10** affliction, dreaminess, drowsiness, enervation, feebleness, relaxation, sleepiness **12** listlessness **14** oppressiveness

**languorous**
**04** lazy, weak **05** weary **06** dreamy, feeble, sleepy, torpid **07** relaxed **08** listless **09** lethargic

**lank**
**04** lean, limp, long, slim, tall, thin **05** gaunt, lanky **06** skinny **07** flaccid, scraggy, scrawny, slender **08** drooping, lifeless, rawboned **09** emaciated, slab-sided **10** lustreless, straggling

**lanky**
**04** lean, slim, tall, thin **05** gaunt, rangy, weedy **06** gangly **07** scraggy, scrawny, slender **08** gangling

**lantern**
**04** buat, glim, lamp **05** bowat, bowet, crown, darky **06** cupola, darkey, sconce **08** bull's-eye **09** Aldis lamp, belvedere **12** stereopticon

**lanthanum**
**02** La

**Laos**
**03** LAO

**lap**
**03** leg, lip, rag, sip, sup **04** beat, dash, flap, flow, fold, lick, loop, roll, rush, slop, tour, wash, wind, wrap **05** ambit, break, cover, drink, knees, orbit, round, slosh, stage, swish, twine **06** circle, course, encase, enfold, hollow, lappet, splash, swathe, thighs **07** circuit, compass, envelop, overlap, scoop up, section, stretch, swaddle **08** distance, surround
• **lap up 06** absorb, relish, savour **08** listen in **09** delight in **13** accept eagerly

**lapse**
**03** end, gap **04** drop, fail, fall, go by, go on, lull, pass, sink, slip, stop, trip **05** blank, break, cease, drift, error, fault, glide, pause, slide **06** course, elapse, expire, hiatus, run out, slip by, worsen **07** blunder, decline, descent, failing, go to pot, mistake, passage, relapse, resolve, stumble **08** downturn, interval, omission, slip away, slipping **09** backslide, oversight, prescribe, terminate, worsening **10** aberration, become void, degenerate, go downhill, negligence **11** backsliding, dereliction, deteriorate, go to the dogs **12** degeneration, indiscretion, intermission, interruption **13** become invalid, deterioration, fall from grace **14** go down the tubes **15** go to rack and ruin

**lapsed**
**04** once, void **05** ended **06** former, run out **07** expired, invalid **08** finished, obsolete, outdated **09** out of date, unrenewed **11** backslidden **12** discontinued **13** non-practising

**lapwing**
**05** pewit, tewit **06** peewit, tewhit **07** teuchat **08** teru-tero

**larceny**
**05** heist, theft **06** piracy **07** robbery **08** burglary, stealing **09** pilfering **10** purloining **13** expropriation

**lard**
**04** load, saim, seam **05** enarm, seame, smear, strew, stuff **06** fatten **07** garnish **14** interpenetrate

**larder**
**06** pantry, spence **08** scullery **09** storeroom **11** springhouse, storage room

**large**
**02** lg, OS **03** big, lge **04** full, high, huge, mega, tall, vast **05** ample, broad, bulky, giant, grand, great, heavy, jumbo, roomy **06** bumper **07** copious, diffuse, immense, liberal, mammoth, massive, monster, outsize, sizable **08** abundant, colossal, enormous, generous, gigantic, sizeable, spacious, spanking, sweeping, whopping **09** extensive, ginormous, good-sized, grandiose, humungous, king-sized, monstrous, plentiful **10** commodious, dirty great, exhaustive, monumental, prodigious, stupendous, voluminous **11** far-reaching, importantly, magnanimous, prominently, substantial, wide-ranging **12** considerable **13** comprehensive, wide-stretched **14** Brobdingnagian, ostentatiously
• **at large 03** out **04** free **06** abroad, mainly **07** chiefly **08** on the run **09** at liberty, generally, in general, in the main **10** by and large, on the loose, on the whole, unconfined **11** independent
• **by and large 06** mainly, mostly **07** as a rule **09** generally **10** on the whole **14** for the most part

**largely**
**06** mainly, mostly, widely **07** chiefly, greatly **09** generally, in the main, primarily **10** by and large, especially **11** extensively, principally **12** considerably **13** predominantly **14** for the most part, to a large extent

**largeness**
**04** bulk, size **08** vastness, wideness **09** ampleness, amplitude, broadness, grandness, greatness, heaviness, immensity **11** sizableness **12** enormousness, macrocephaly, sizeableness **13** expansiveness **14** stupendousness, voluminousness

**large-scale**
**04** epic, mega, vast, wide **05** broad **06** global **08** sweeping **09** expansive, extensive, universal, wholesale **10** nationwide **11** country-wide, far-reaching, wide-ranging **12** wide-reaching

**largesse**
**03** aid **04** alms, gift **05** grant **06** bounty **07** bequest, charity, handout, present **08** donation, kindness **09** allowance, endowment **10** generosity, liberality **11** benefaction, munificence **12** philanthropy **14** open-handedness

**lark**
◇ *anagram indicator* **03** guy, job **04** game, play, romp, task **05** antic, caper, chore, fling, prank, revel, sport, thing **06** cavort, frolic, gambol

**07** fooling, gammock, have fun, rollick, skylark **08** activity, business, escapade, mischief **09** cavorting, fool about, horseplay, mess about **10** fool around, play tricks

**larva**
**04** grub, moth, spat **05** ghost, naiad, ox-bot **06** caddis, chigoe, chigre, measle **07** budworm, chigger, hydatid, planula, pluteus, spectre, tadpole, veliger **08** army worm, bookworm, coenurus, cornworm, mealworm, wireworm, woodworm **09** auger-worm, bloodworm, doodlebug, glass-crab, joint-worm, screw-worm, sporocyst, strawworm, xylophage **10** bipinnaria, caddis-worm, cankerworm, miracidium, woolly bear **11** cabbage-worm, caterpillar, corn earworm, hellgramite **12** hellgrammite **13** leptocephalus, spruce budworm
• **larval stage 04** zoea **08** cercaria

**lascivious**
**04** blue, lewd **05** bawdy, crude, dirty, horny, randy, saucy **06** coarse, ribald, smutty, vulgar, wanton **07** lustful, obscene, Paphian, sensual, Sotadic **08** indecent, petulant, prurient, Sotadean, unchaste **09** lecherous, offensive, salacious **10** libidinous, licentious, scurrilous, suggestive **12** pornographic

**lash**
**03** cat, hit, tie, wag **04** beat, belt, bind, blow, dash, flog, join, rope, rush, slow, soft, stop, welt, whip, wire **05** affix, break, flail, flick, horse, pound, scold, seize, slack, slash, smash, strap, swipe, swish, thong, whack **06** attack, batter, berate, buffet, fasten, gammon, lavish, rebuke, secure, strike, stripe, stroke, swinge, switch, tether, thrash, wallop **07** bawl out, censure, insipid, lay into, reprove, scourge **08** bullwhip, make fast, squander **09** bullwhack, criticize, fulminate, horsewhip **12** tear to shreds **13** tear a strip off
• **lash out 04** yerk **06** thrash **07** lay into, run down **08** hit out at **09** have a go at **11** splash out on **12** tear to pieces, tear to shreds **13** tear a strip off, tear strips off **14** attack strongly **15** speak out against, spend a fortune on

**lashings**
**04** lots, tons **05** heaps, loads, piles **06** masses, oodles, stacks **11** large amount **13** great quantity

**lass**
**03** hen **04** bird, girl, miss **05** chick, filly, Jenny, popsy **06** damsel, lassie, maiden **10** schoolgirl, sweetheart, young woman **11** maid-servant
*See also* **girl**

**lassitude**
**06** apathy, torpor **07** fatigue, languor **08** dullness, lethargy, weakness **09** faintness, heaviness, tiredness, weariness **10** drowsiness, enervation, exhaustion **11** spring fever **12** listlessness, sluggishness

**lasso**
**04** lazo, rope **05** noose, reata, riata **06** lariat

**last**
◇ *tail selection indicator* **03** end, ult **04** back, dure, go on, hind, keep, live, load, stay, take, wear **05** abide, after, cargo, close, dying, exist, final **06** behind, ending, endure, finish, hold on, keep on, latest, live on, remain, utmost, yester **07** carry on, closing, dernier, endmost, extreme, finally, hold out, persist, stand up, subsist, survive, tail-end **08** at the end, continue, farthest, furthest, hindmost, previous, rearmost, remotest, terminal, ultimate **09** at the back, at the rear, finishing **10** completion, concluding, conclusion, get through, lattermost, most recent, stick it out, ultimately **11** least likely **12** most unlikely **13** least suitable **14** coming at the end, most improbable, most unsuitable
• **at last** ◇ *tail selection indicator* **07** finally **08** at length, in the end **10** eventually, ultimately **11** in due course **12** in conclusion
• **last word 04** amen, best, pick, rage **05** cream, vogue **06** latest **08** final say, ultimate **09** ultimatum **10** dernier cri, perfection **11** ne plus ultra **12** quintessence **13** final decision **14** crème de la crème, final statement **15** definite comment

**last-ditch**
**04** wild **05** final **06** all-out, heroic **07** frantic **08** frenzied, last-gasp **09** desperate, straining **10** last-chance, struggling **12** eleventh-hour

**lasting**
**05** fixed **07** abiding, durable, dureful, undying **08** enduring, external, lifelong, long-term, unending **09** ceaseless, endurable, long-lived, permanent, perpetual, surviving, unceasing **10** continuing, monumental, persisting, unchanging **11** everlasting, never-ending **12** interminable, long-standing

**lastly**
◇ *tail selection indicator* **07** finally, to sum up **08** in the end **10** ultimately **12** in conclusion

**last-minute**
**04** late **05** hasty **06** forced, rushed **07** overdue **11** superficial **12** eleventh-hour

**latch**
**03** bar **04** bolt, hasp, hook, lock, mire **05** catch, clink, sneck **06** fasten **07** clicket **09** fastening **10** make secure
• **latch on to 04** twig **05** grasp, learn **06** follow **07** realize **09** apprehend **10** comprehend, understand **14** not want to leave

**late**
**03** lag, new, old **04** dead, past, slow **05** fresh, tardy **06** behind, former, latest, recent, slowly, whilom **07** current, defunct, delayed, overdue, tardily **08** backward, deceased, departed, formerly, overtime, previous, recently, sometime, umquhile, up-to-date **09** belatedly, in arrears, preceding **10** after hours, behindhand, behind time, dilatorily, last-minute, unpunctual **12** unpunctually **13** up-to-the-minute **14** behind schedule
• **of late 05** newly **06** lately **08** latterly, recently **10** not long ago

**lately**
**05** alate, newly **06** of late **08** latterly, recently **09** now of late **10** not long ago

**lateness**
**05** delay **09** tardiness **11** belatedness, retardation **12** dilatoriness **13** unpunctuality

**latent**
**06** hidden, secret, unseen, veiled **07** dormant, lurking, passive **08** inactive, possible **09** concealed, invisible, potential, quiescent **10** underlying, unrealized, unrevealed **11** delitescent, undeveloped, unexpressed **12** undiscovered

**later**
**04** next, syne **05** after **06** latter **07** goodbye, later on **08** in a while **09** following, posterior **10** afterwards, eventually, subsequent, succeeding **11** in due course, in the future **12** at a later time, subsequently, successively **13** at a future date, at a future time, some other time **15** in the near future

**lateral**
**03** lat **04** side **05** fresh **06** clever **07** oblique **08** creative, edgeways, flanking, indirect, inspired, marginal, original, sideward, sideways, slanting **09** brilliant, illogical, ingenious **10** unorthodox **11** alternative, imaginative **13** outside the box **14** unconventional

**laterally**
**08** edgeways, sideways **09** obliquely **10** creatively, originally **11** illogically, ingeniously **13** imaginatively, outside the box

**latest**
**02** in **03** hip, now **04** last **05** funky **06** modern, newest, trendy, with it **07** current **08** ultimate, up-to-date **10** most recent **11** fashionable **13** up-to-the-minute

**lather**
**03** rub **04** flap, foam, fuss, soap, stew, suds **05** fever, froth, panic, state, sweat, tizzy **06** dither, whip up **07** anxiety, bubbles, fluster, flutter, shampoo **08** soapsuds **09** agitation

**Latin**
◇ *foreign word indicator* **01** L **03** Lat

*Latin words and expressions include:*

**03** sic
**04** idem, pace
**05** ad hoc, circa
**06** gratis, ibidem, passim
**07** alumnus, a priori, de facto, erratum, floruit, in vitro, sub rosa
**08** addendum, emeritus, ex gratia,

gravitas, infra dig, mea culpa, nota bene, subpoena **09** ad nauseam, alma mater, carpe diem, et tu, Brute, ex officio, inter alia, ipso facto, per capita, status quo, sub judice, vox populi **10** anno Domini, ante-bellum, ex cathedra, in absentia, in extremis, magnum opus, post mortem, prima facie, quid pro quo, sine qua non, tabula rasa **11** ad infinitum, memento mori, non sequitur, tempus fugit **12** ante meridiem, caveat emptor, compos mentis, habeas corpus, post meridiem **13** camera obscura, deus ex machina, modus operandi **14** annus mirabilis, in loco parentis, pro bono publico, terra incognita **15** annus horribilis, curriculum vitae, delirium tremens, persona non grata

*See also* **day; month; number**

## latitude
**01** l **03** lat **04** play, room, span **05** field, range, reach, scope, space, sweep, width **06** extent, laxity, leeway, spread **07** breadth, freedom, liberty, licence **09** allowance, clearance **10** indulgence **11** flexibility **12** carte blanche

## latter
**03** end **04** last **05** final, later **06** modern, recent, second **07** closing, ensuing **10** concluding, succeeding, successive **13** last-mentioned

## latter-day
**06** modern, recent **07** current **10** present-day **12** contemporary

## latterly
**06** lately, of late **08** hitherto, recently **12** most recently

## lattice
**03** web **04** grid, mesh **05** grate, grill **06** grille, jacket **07** grating, network, tracery, trellis **08** espalier, fretwork, openwork **10** portcullis **11** latticework **12** reticulation

## Latvia
**02** LV **03** LVA

## laud
**04** hail **05** extol **06** admire, honour, praise **07** acclaim, applaud, approve, glorify, magnify **09** celebrate

## laudable
**06** of note, worthy **08** sterling **09** admirable, estimable, excellent, exemplary **10** creditable **11** commendable, meritorious **12** praiseworthy

## laudation
**05** glory, kudos, paean **06** eulogy, homage, praise **07** acclaim, tribute **08** accolade, blessing, devotion, encomion, encomium **09** adulation, celebrity, extolment, panegyric, reverence **10** veneration **11** acclamation **12** commendation **13** glorification

## laudatory
**06** eulogy **09** adulatory, approving **10** eulogistic, glorifying **11** acclamatory, approbatory, celebratory, encomiastic, panegyrical **12** commendatory **13** complimentary, encomiastical **14** congratulatory

## laugh
**03** fun, wag, wit, yok **04** boff, card, ha-ha, he-he, hoax, hoot, howl, jest, joke, lark, peal, peel, play, roar, yock **05** clown, comic, joker, lauch, prank, risus, snirt, sport, te-hee, trick **06** cackle, giggle, guffaw, haw-haw, hoaxer, jester, nicher, nicker, scream, tee-hee, titter **07** break up, buffoon, chortle, chuckle, snicker, snigger, snirtle **08** comedian, crease up, humorist, irrision, quipster **09** character, fall about, prankster, trickster **10** belly-laugh, cachinnate, horse laugh **11** wisecracker **12** be in stitches, cachinnation **14** practical joker, shake your sides, split your sides **15** laugh like a drain
• **laugh at** **04** jeer, mock **05** scorn, taunt **06** deride **07** scoff at **08** ridicule **09** make fun of, poke fun at **11** make a fool of **14** make jokes about
• **laugh off** **06** ignore **07** dismiss **08** belittle, minimize, pooh-pooh, shrug off **09** disregard **10** brush aside **12** make little of

## laughable
**05** comic, droll, funny **06** absurd **07** amusing, comical **08** derisive, derisory, farcical, humorous **09** diverting, hilarious, ludicrous **10** ridiculous, uproarious **11** nonsensical **12** entertaining, preposterous **13** side-splitting

## laughably
**08** absurdly **10** farcically **11** ludicrously **12** ridiculously **14** preposterously

## laughing-stock
**04** butt, dupe **05** sport **06** stooge, target, victim **08** derision, fair game **09** Aunt Sally **10** outspeckle **11** figure of fun

## laughter
**03** haw **04** glee, ha-ha **05** mirth **06** cackle, haw-haw, tee-hee **07** fou rire, hooting **08** cackling, giggling, hilarity, irrision, laughing, paroxysm **09** amusement, chortling, chuckling, guffawing, happiness, hysterics, merriment, tittering **10** risibility, sniggering **11** convulsions **12** cachinnation, cheerfulness

## launch
**04** dart, fire, hurl, open, shot **05** begin, float, found, lance, set up, shoot, start, throw **06** attack, propel **07** lancing, project, roll out, send off, unstock **08** commence, dispatch, embark on, initiate, organize **09** discharge, establish, instigate, institute, introduce, set afloat **10** inaugurate **11** set in motion **12** presentation

## launder
◊ *anagram indicator* **04** wash **05** clean

**06** trough **07** cleanse **09** washerman **11** washerwoman

## laundry
**04** wash **07** bagwash, clothes, steamie, washing **08** lavatory **09** wash house **10** Laundromat® **11** dry cleaner's, launderette **12** dirty clothes, dirty washing

## laurel
**03** bay **04** Stan **06** aucuba, daphne, kalmia, Laurus **08** pichurim, sweet bay **09** sassafras, spicebush **10** greenheart, mock orange

## lava
**04** bomb, slag **05** lahar **06** cinder, coulée, pumice, scoria **07** clinker, lapilli **08** pahoehoe **09** toadstone **10** palagonite **12** volcanic bomb **13** volcanic glass

## lavatory
**02** WC **03** bog, can, lav, loo **04** dike, dyke, john, kazi, rear, toot **05** dunny, Elsan®, heads, karsy, karzy, khazi, lavvy, privy, rears **06** carsey, karsey, ladies', lavabo, lotion, office, throne, toilet, urinal **07** cludgie, cottage, crapper, latrine **08** bathroom, dunnakin, long drop, out-house, Portaloo®, rest room, superloo, washroom **09** cloakroom, necessary **10** facilities, little room, powder room, reredorter, thunderbox **11** convenience, earth-closet, water closet **12** smallest room **14** comfort station, little boys' room **15** little girls' room

## lavish
**04** free, heap, lash, lush, pour, rich, wild **05** grand, spend, waste **06** bestow, deluge, expend, lordly, shower, slap-up **07** copious, fulsome, liberal, profuse **08** abundant, generous, gorgeous, princely, prodigal, prolific, splendid, squander, wasteful **09** bountiful, dissipate, excessive, expensive, exuberant, luxuriant, plentiful, profusion, sumptuous, unlimited, unsparing **10** give freely, immoderate, open-handed, profligate, thriftless, unstinting **11** extravagant, intemperate, spendthrift **12** unrestrained **13** unwithdrawing

## lavishly
**06** freely, lushly, richly, wildly **07** grandly **09** liberally, profusely **10** abundantly, generously, splendidly **11** excessively, luxuriously, sumptuously, unsparingly **13** extravagantly, intemperately

## law
**03** act, lay, lex **04** code, cops, pigs, rule **05** axiom, canon, edict, maxim, order, tenet **06** decree **07** charter, command, coppers, formula, lawsuit, precept, rozzers, statute, the Bill, the fuzz **08** standard, the force **09** criterion, determine, direction, directive, enactment, guideline, ordinance, principle, the police **10** boys in blue, expediate, indulgence, litigation, regulation **11** commandment, instruction, legal action, legislation

**12** constitution **13** jurisprudence, pronouncement **14** police officers, the police force

*Laws and Acts include:*

**04** DORA
**07** Riot Act, Test Act
**08** Corn Laws, Poor Laws, Stamp Act, Sugar Act
**10** Act of Union, Magna Carta, Patriot Act, Reform Acts
**11** Abortion Act, Equal Pay Act
**12** Bill of Rights, Homestead Act
**13** Act of Congress, Enclosure Acts, Parliament Act
**14** Act of Supremacy, Cat and Mouse Act, Civil Rights Act, Corporation Act, Declaratory Act, Native Title Act, Taft-Hartley Act
**15** Act of Parliament, Act of Settlement, Act of Succession, Habeas Corpus Act

*Scientific and other laws include:*

**04** Ohm's, Oral, Sod's
**05** lemon, Roman, Salic
**06** Boyle's, Hooke's, Mosaic, Snell's, Stoke's
**07** Dalton's, Hubble's, Kepler's, Murphy's, natural
**08** Charles's
**09** Avogadro's
**10** Parkinson's
**13** inverse square

• **by law 04** iure, jure

**law-abiding**
**04** good **06** decent, honest, lawful **07** dutiful, orderly, upright **08** obedient, virtuous **09** complying, righteous **10** honourable, upstanding **15** whiter than white

**lawbreaker**
**05** crook, felon **06** outlaw, sinner **07** convict, culprit **08** criminal, offender **09** infractor, miscreant, wrongdoer **10** delinquent, trespasser **11** perpetrator **12** transgressor

**lawcourt**
**03** bar **05** bench, court, trial **07** assizes, session **08** tribunal **09** judiciary **10** court of law

**lawful**
**04** just **05** legal, legit, licit, valid **06** proper **08** rightful **09** allowable, legalized, warranted **10** authorized, legitimate, recognized, sanctioned **11** permissible **14** constitutional

**lawfully**
**05** by law **07** legally, validly **08** by rights, properly **10** rightfully **11** permissibly **12** legitimately

**lawless**
◊ *anagram indicator* **04** wild **05** rowdy **06** unruly **07** chaotic, illegal, riotous, rulesse **08** anarchic, criminal, mutinous, reckless, ruleless **09** insurgent, seditious, unsettled **10** anarchical, disorderly, rebellious, ungoverned, wrongdoing **11** lawbreaking **12** unrestrained

**13** revolutionary, wild and woolly **15** insurrectionary

**lawlessness**
**05** chaos **06** mob law, piracy **07** anarchy, mob rule **08** disorder, lynch-law, rent-a-mob, sedition **09** mobocracy, rebellion **10** insurgency, ochlocracy, revolution **12** insurrection, racketeering

**lawman**
**03** Ohm **05** Boyle, Hooke, Mufti **09** Parkinson

**Lawrence**
**02** DH, TE

**lawrencium**
**02** Lr, Lw

**lawsuit**
**04** case, plea, suit **05** cause, trial **06** action **07** contest, dispute, process **08** argument **10** indictment, litigation **11** legal action, proceedings, prosecution

**lawyer**
**02** Av, BL **03** Att **04** Atty, silk **05** brief **06** jurist **07** counsel, mukhtar, shyster, templar **08** advocate, attorney, greenbag, Man of Law **09** lawmonger **10** legal eagle **12** legal adviser
*See also* **barrister**

*Lawyer types include:*

**02** DA, KC, QC
**05** avoué, judge
**06** avocet
**07** bencher, coroner, counsel, justice, sheriff
**08** Recorder
**09** barrister, solicitor
**11** conveyancer, crown lawyer
**12** circuit judge, jurisconsult, Lord Advocate
**13** attorney at law, Crown attorney, district judge, Queen's Counsel, sheriff depute
**14** criminal lawyer, deputy recorder, High Court judge, Lord Chancellor, public defender, Vice-Chancellor
**15** ambulance-chaser, Attorney-General

*Lawyers include:*

**04** Hill (Anita), **John** (Otto), **Reno** (Janet)
**05** Booth (Cherie), **Finch** (Atticus), **Mason** (Perry), **Mills** (Dame Barbara Jean Lyon), **Nader** (Ralph), **Slovo** (Joe), **Vance** (Cyrus R)
**06** Bailey (F Lee), **Butler** (Benjamin Franklin), **Carton** (Sydney), **Darrow** (Clarence), **Devlin** (Patrick, Lord), **Holmes** (Oliver Wendell), **Martin** (Richard)
**07** Acheson (Dean), **Clinton** (Hillary Rodham), **Haldane** (Richard, Viscount), **Kennedy** (Helena, Baroness), **Mondale** (Walter), **O'Connor** (Sandra Day)
**08** Kunstler (William), **Marshall** (Thurgood), **Mortimer** (Sir John)
**09** La Guardia (Fiorello H), **Shawcross** (Hartley William, Baron)

**10** Birkenhead (Frederick Edwin Smith, Earl of), **Dershowitz** (Alan)
**11** Hore-Belisha (Leslie, Lord)
**12** Guicciardini (Francesco)
**14** Brillat-Savarin (Anthelme)

• **lawyers 03** bar

**lax**
◊ *anagram indicator* **04** wide **05** broad, loose, slack, vague **06** casual, remiss, salmon, sloppy **07** flaccid, general, inexact, lenient **08** careless, heedless, laid-back, slipshod, tolerant, wide-open **09** easy-going, imprecise, indulgent, negligent **10** inaccurate, indefinite, neglectful, permissive **11** inattentive **14** latitudinarian

**laxative**
**05** purge, salts, senna **06** ipecac, saline **07** cascara, Gregory **08** aperient, evacuant, lenitive, loosener, relaxant, solutive **09** aperitive, cathartic, purgative, taraxacum **10** eccoprotic, Epsom salts **11** health salts, ipecacuanha **14** cascara sagrada, Gregory's powder, liquid paraffin, Seidlitz powder **15** Gregory's mixture

**laxity**
**07** freedom, neglect **08** latitude, leniency, softness **09** looseness, slackness, tolerance **10** indulgence, negligence, sloppiness **11** imprecision, inexactness, nonchalance **12** carelessness, heedlessness, indifference, laissez-faire, slovenliness **14** indefiniteness, permissiveness

**lay**
**03** bet, ode, put, set **04** bear, bung, drop, laic, make, plan, poem, risk, song **05** allot, apply, beset, breed, civil cover, embed, imbed, leave, lodge, lyric, offer, place, plant, plonk, posit, stick, wager **06** arable, assign, ballad, burden, chance, charge, design, devise, gamble, hazard, impose, impute, locate, meadow, saddle, set out, settle, submit, thrust, waylay **07** amateur, arrange, ascribe, deposit, dispose, inflict, oppress, pasture, prepare, present, produce, secular, se down, station, work out **08** encumber, engender, exorcize, madrigal, oviposit, position **09** attribute, establish, weigh down **10** make it with put forward **11** give birth to **12** non-qualified **13** non-specialist **15** non-professional

• **lay aside 04** keep, save, void **05** defer, store **06** put off, reject, shelve **07** abandon, discard, dismiss **08** postpone, put aside, set aside **09** cast aside

• **lay bare 04** show **05** scale, strip, unrip **06** expose, reveal, uncase, unvei **07** divulge, exhibit, explain, uncover **08** disclose, manifest

• **lay down 04** drop, give **05** couch, plant, plonk, state, store, yield **06** affirm, assert, depone, give up, ordain, record, submit **07** deposit, discard **09** establish, formulate, postulate, prescribe, stipulate, surrender **10** relinquish

- **lay down the law** 07 dictate 09 crack down, dogmatize, emphasize 11 pontificate 12 rule the roost 14 read the riot act
- **lay hands on** 03 get 04 find, grab, grip 05 bless, catch, clasp, grasp, seize, set on 06 attack, beat up, clutch, locate, obtain, ordain 07 acquire, assault, confirm, lay into, unearth 08 discover 09 get hold of, lay hold of 10 consecrate 12 bring to light
- **lay in** 05 amass, glean, hoard, store 06 gather 07 build up, collect, stock up, store up 09 stockpile 10 accumulate
- **lay into** 06 assail, attack 08 hit out at, let fly at, set about, tear into 09 have a go at, lash out at, pitch into
- **lay it on** 07 flatter 08 butter up, overdo it, soft-soap 09 sweet-talk 10 exaggerate, overpraise
- **lay off** 04 doff, drop, quit, sack, stop 05 cease, hedge, let go, let up 06 desist, give up, pay off 07 dismiss, refrain 08 leave off 09 discharge 10 leave alone 11 discontinue 13 make redundant
- **lay on** 04 give 05 cater, pound, set up 06 impose, supply 07 furnish, inflict, provide 08 organize
- **lay out** 03 pay 04 fell, give, plan 05 floor, spend 06 design, expend, invest, put out, set out, streek 07 arrange, display, exhibit, flatten, fork out, stretch 08 demolish, disburse, knock out, shell out, straucht, straught 09 spread out 10 contribute
- **lay up** 04 hive, keep, save 05 amass, hoard, set by, store 07 deposit, put away, store up 08 mothball 10 accumulate
- **lay waste** 04 rape, raze, ruin, sack 05 havoc, spoil 06 locust, ravage 07 despoil, destroy, estrepe, pillage 08 demolish, desolate 09 depredate, devastate, vandalize

## layabout

05 idler 06 loafer, skiver, waster 07 goof-off, laggard, lounger, shirker, wastrel 09 corner-boy, corner-man, lazybones, sundowner 10 ne'er-do-well 14 good-for-nothing

## layer

01 E 03 bed, hen, lie, ply, row 04 band, coat, film, seam, skin, tier, vein 05 cover, flake, plate, sheet, table 06 course, lamina, mantle, scrape 07 blanket, coating, deposit, lamella, stratum 08 covering 09 mesoblast, thickness 10 integument, lamination 11 superficies

See also **atmosphere**
- **layers** 06 strata

## layman, layperson, laywoman

04 laic 07 amateur, secular 08 exhorter, outsider, tertiary 11 parabolanus, parishioner, terrestrial 12 impropriator 13 local preacher, unordained man 15 non-professional, unordained woman

## lay-off

05 cards 06 firing, papers 07 jotters, sacking, the boot, the push, the sack 08 the elbow 09 discharge, dismissal 10 redundancy 12 unemployment

## layout

◊ anagram indicator 03 map, set 04 plan, unit 05 draft 06 design, format, outfit, sketch 07 display, outline 09 blueprint, geography 11 arrangement 12 organization 13 comprehensive

## layperson

see **layman, layperson, laywoman**

## laze

03 veg 04 idle, loaf, loll, lusk 05 chill, relax 06 bludge, lounge, unwind, veg out 08 chill out 09 bum around, lie around, sit around

## lazily

◊ anagram indicator 04 idly 06 slowly 07 slackly 10 sluggishly 13 lethargically

## laziness

05 sloth 07 languor 08 idleness, lethargy, slowness 09 fainéance, indolence, slackness, tardiness 10 inactivity, Oblomovism 12 dilatoriness, slothfulness, sluggishness

## lazy

04 idle, lusk, slow 05 inert, slack, tardy 06 laesie, lither, torpid 07 dronish, languid, luskish, work-shy 08 bone-idle, fainéant, inactive, indolent, slothful, sluggish 09 lethargic 10 languorous, slow-moving 14 good-for-nothing

## lazybones

04 lusk, slob, slug 05 drone, idler 06 loafer, lubber, skiver, slouch 07 goof-off, laggard, lounger, lubbard, mollusc, shirker 08 do-nought, fainéant, layabout, slowback, slug-a-bed, sluggard 09 do-nothing, sluggabed, sundowner 10 bedpresser, ne'er-do-well, sleepyhead 14 good-for-nothing

## leach

04 seep 05 drain 06 filter, osmose, strain 07 extract 08 filtrate 09 lixiviate, percolate

## lead

◊ head selection indicator 02 Pb 03 gap, tip, top, van 04 clue, cord, edge, hand, have, head, hint, hold, line, live, main, move, pass, rein, rule, shot, show, slip, star, sway 05 balls, cause, chain, chief, excel, first, guide, leash, model, outdo, pilot, plumb, prime, slugs, spend, start, steer, usher 06 convey, direct, escort, exceed, govern, induce, manage, margin, minium, outrun, prompt, sinker, string, tether, tip-off, weight 07 bring on, bullets, command, conduct, dispose, eclipse, example, incline, leading, officer, pattern, pellets, plummet, pointer, precede, premier, primary, produce, provoke, running, surpass, undergo 08 foremost, guidance, interval, outstrip, persuade, priority, regulate, result in, star role,

vanguard 09 advantage, be in front, call forth, come first, direction, extension, forefront, indicator, influence, precedent, principal, supervise, supremacy, title role, transcend 10 ammunition, bring about, experience, first place, indication, initiative, leadership, leading man, precedence, suggestion 11 be in the lead, heavy weight, leading lady, leading role, outdistance, pre-eminence, preside over, tend towards 12 be in charge of, call the shots, contribute to, starring part 13 be at the head of, principal part 15 advance position, leading position
- **lead gradually** 04 drib
- **lead off** 04 open 05 begin, start 07 kick off 08 commence, get going, initiate, start off 10 inaugurate
- **lead on** 04 dupe, lure 05 tempt, trail, trick 06 draw on, entice, seduce 07 beguile, deceive, mislead 08 persuade 11 string along 12 put one over on, take for a ride 14 pull a fast one on
- **lead the way** 04 show 05 guide 07 go first, pioneer 09 go in front, set a trend 10 be a pioneer, pave the way, show the way 11 blaze a trail 14 break new ground
- **lead up to** 05 usher 07 prepare 08 approach 09 introduce 10 open the way, pave the way, prepare for 13 make overtures

## leaden

04 dull, grey, lead 05 ashen, dingy, heavy, inert, stiff 06 boring, cloudy, dismal, dreary, gloomy, sombre, wooden 07 greyish, humdrum, languid, onerous, stilted 08 laboured, lifeless, listless, overcast, plodding, sluggish 09 plumbeous 10 burdensome, cumbersome, depressing, lacklustre, oppressive, spiritless

## leader

◊ head selection indicator 02 PM 03 dux, gov, guv 04 boss, cock, head, imam 05 ariki, chief, guide, ruler, sheik, usher 06 bigwig, escort, expert, honcho, sachem, sheikh, top dog, zaddik 07 big shot, captain, coryphe, courier, founder, general, khalifa, kingpin, mahatma, manager, pioneer, skipper, tsaddik, tsaddiq, tzaddik, tzaddiq 08 big noise, caudillo, director, governor, inventor, khalifah, mocuddum, mokaddam, muqaddam, overseer, superior 09 architect, authority, big cheese, chieftain, commander, conductor, developer, editorial, innovator, liturgist, principal 10 coryphaeus, discoverer, figurehead, head honcho, pathfinder, ringleader, supervisor 11 front-runner, trailblazer 12 guiding light, leading light 13 groundbreaker 14 mover and shaker, superintendent

See also **governor; emperor; empress; king; leader; Maori; president; queen; Roman; ruler**

### leaderless

◇ *head deletion indicator* **08** headless
**10** acephalous

### leadership

◇ *head selection indicator* **04** lead, rule,
sway **07** command, control
**08** guidance, headship, hegemony
**09** authority, captaincy, direction
**10** apostolate, domination,
management **11** generalship, pre-
eminence, premiership, supervision
**12** directorship, governorship
**14** administration, rangatiratanga
**15** superintendency

### lead-in

**05** debut, intro, proem, start **06** launch
**07** opening, preface, prelude
**08** exordium, foreword, overture,
preamble, prologue **09** beginning
**11** front matter **12** inauguration,
introduction, presentation,
prolegomenon **13** preliminaries

### leading

◇ *head selection indicator* **03** top
**04** main, star **05** chief, first, front
**06** ruling, staple **07** guiding, highest,
premier, primary, supreme, top-rank
**08** dominant, foremost, greatest,
guidance, mistress, superior
**09** directing, governing, number one,
paramount, preceding, principal
**10** pre-eminent **11** outstanding

### leaf

**01** f, p **03** pad **04** flip, page, skim
**05** bract, calyx, folio, frond, sepal,
sheet, thumb **06** browse, folium,
glance, needle, troely **07** foliole,
leaflet, troelie, troolie **09** cataphyll,
clinquant, cotyledon, marijuana
**11** sclerophyll **12** thumb through

---

*Leaf parts include:*

**03** tip
**04** back, lobe, vein
**05** blade, lobus, stoma, thorn
**06** margin, midrib, sheath, stipel
**07** petiole, stipule, stomata
**08** leaf axil
**09** epidermis, leaf cells
**11** axillary bud, chloroplast

---

*Leaf shapes include:*

**04** oval
**05** acute, lobed, ovate
**06** cusped, entire, linear, lyrate
**07** acerose, ciliate, cordate, crenate,
dentate, falcate, hastate, obovate,
palmate, peltate, pinnate, ternate
**08** digitate, elliptic, reniform,
subulate
**09** orbicular, runcinate, sagittate
**10** lanceolate, pinnatifid, spathulate,
trifoliate
**13** doubly dentate
**15** abruptly pinnate

---

• **turn over a new leaf** **05** amend,
begin **06** change, reform **07** improve
**10** begin again, start again **11** start
afresh **12** mend your ways **14** better
yourself, change your ways
**15** improve yourself, make a fresh
start, pull your socks up

### leaflet

**04** bill **05** flier, flyer, pinna, tract
**06** dodger, mailer **07** booklet, foliole,
handout **08** brochure, circular,
handbill, pamphlet

### leafy

**05** bosky, green, shady, woody
**06** bowery, leafed, leaved, shaded,
wooded **07** foliose, verdant
**08** frondent, frondose **11** frondescent
**12** dasyphyllous

### league

**01** l **03** cup **04** ally, band, bond, Bund,
link **05** class, group, guild, Hansa,
Hanse, level, union, unite **06** cartel
**07** combine, compact, consort, contest
**08** alliance, category, conspire,
division **09** associate, coalition, co-
operate, syndicate **10** amalgamate,
consortium, federation, fellowship,
join forces, tournament **11** affiliation,
amphictyony, association, collaborate,
combination, competition,
confederacy, confederate, co-
operative, corporation, partnership
**12** band together, championship,
conglomerate, Holy Alliance
**13** confederation
*See also* **Australian football;
baseball; football; rugby**
• **in league** **06** allied, linked **08** in
tandem **09** in cahoots **10** conspiring,
in alliance **11** co-operating, hand in
glove, in collusion **13** collaborating,
in co-operation, in partnership

### leak

**03** cut, ren, rin, run **04** blab, drip, hole,
ooze, seep, tell, weep **05** break, chink,
crack, exude, let in, let on, spill
**06** escape, exposé, impart, let out,
oozing, pass on, relate, reveal, run out,
squeal **07** crevice, divulge, fissure,
leakage, leaking, let slip, opening,
seepage, seeping, trickle, urinate
**08** disclose, exposure, give away,
overflow, puncture, spillage
**09** discharge, make known, make
water, percolate **10** disclosure,
divulgence, make public, revelation,
uncovering **11** percolation **12** blow the
gaffe **13** spill the beans **15** bringing to
light

### leaky

**05** holey, split **06** gizzen, porous
**07** cracked, leaking **08** dripping
**09** permeable, punctured
**10** perforated, unstanched
**11** unstaunched

### lean

**03** lie **04** abut, arid, bank, bare, bend,
bony, hard, heel, lank, list, poor, prop,
rest, slim, tend, thin, tilt **05** gaunt,
lanky, slant, slink, slope, spare, tough
**06** barren, favour, hungry, meagre,
prefer, repose, scanty, skinny, slinky,
sparse **07** angular, austere, haggard,
incline, minceur, recline, scraggy,
scrawny, slender **09** difficult,
emaciated, fleshless, gravitate,
rigwiddie, rigwoodie **10** inadequate,
unfruitful, unpleasant **11** be at an angle
**12** insufficient, unproductive,

unprofitable, unsuccessful
**13** uncomfortable **15** all skin and bones
• **lean on** **04** rest **05** force **06** bank on,
coerce, rely on **07** trust in **08** depend
on, persuade **10** intimidate, pressurize
**13** put pressure on **14** put the screws on

### leaning

**04** bent, bias **06** liking **08** aptitude,
fondness, penchant, tendency
**10** attraction, partiality, preference,
proclivity, propensity **11** disposition,
inclination **12** predilection

### leanness

**08** boniness, lankness, slimness,
thinness **09** gauntness, lankiness
**11** scragginess, scrawniness,
slenderness

### lean-to

**03** hut **04** pent, shed **05** shack
**06** garage, lock-up **08** outhouse,
skilling, skillion **09** penthouse

### leap

◇ *anagram indicator* **03** hop, lep **04** jeté,
jump, lope, loup, over, rise, romp, skip,
skip, soar, volt **05** bound, caper, clear,
dance, fence, flier, flyer, frisk, mount,
pronk, salto, sault, spang, surge, vault,
volte **06** basket, bounce, breach,
cavort, curvet, frolic, gambol, rocket,
spring **07** échappé, falcade, soaring,
upsurge, upswing **08** assemblé,
cabriole, capriole, croupade, escalate,
fish-dive, increase, jump over,
overskip, somerset **09** elevation,
entrechat, pas de chat, skyrocket
**10** escalation, pigeon-wing, somersault
**11** summersault
• **by leaps and bounds, in leaps and
bounds** **07** quickly, rapidly, swiftly
**08** in no time **13** in no time at all
• **leap at** **04** grab **05** seize **06** jump at,
snatch **07** agree to, fall for, swallow
**08** pounce on **13** accept eagerly

### learn

**03** con, get, kon, see **04** cram, hear,
larn, lear, leir, lere, read **05** conne,
glean, grasp, leare, study, train
**06** absorb, detect, digest, gather, get
off, master, pick up, take in **07** acquire,
discern, find out, gen up on, prepare,
realize, receive, suss out **08** discover,
memorize, remember **09** ascertain,
determine, get wind of **10** assimilate,
comprehend, have off pat, understand
**12** get the hang of, learn by heart
**13** become aware of **14** acquire skill in,
commit to memory **15** gain knowledge
of

### learned

**04** cond, read, wise **06** savant, versed
**07** erudite, savante **08** academic,
cultured, educated, lettered, literary,
literate, pedantic, scienced, studious,
well-read **09** scholarly **10** widely read
**11** literatured **12** intellectual, well-
educated, well-informed
**13** knowledgeable

### learner

**01** L **04** tiro, tyro **05** pupil **06** conner,
intern, novice, rookie **07** scholar,
student, trainee **08** beginner, neophyte

**09** greenhorn **10** apprentice
**11** abecedarian
*See also* **beginner**

## learning
**04** lear, leir, lere, lore **05** leare, study
**06** wisdom **07** conning, culture, letters,
tuition **08** pedantry, research
**09** education, erudition, intellect,
knowledge, schooling **11** edification,
information, scholarship, schoolcraft
• **basic learning 03** RRR

## lease
**03** let, set **04** farm, hire, loan, rent, tack
**05** glean **06** let out, rental, sublet
**07** chapter, charter, hire out, pasture,
rent out, tenancy **08** contract
**09** agreement

## leash
**03** lym **04** bind, cord, curb, hold, lead,
lime, lyam, lyme, rein, slip **05** check,
trash **06** string, tether **07** control
**09** restraint **10** discipline
*See also* **three**
• **strain at the leash 07** be dying,
be eager **09** be anxious, be itching,
be longing **11** be impatient

## least
**06** fewest, lowest **07** minimum, poorest
**08** smallest **09** slightest
• **at least 06** anyhow **07** however **09** at
any rate, in any case **10** as a minimum,
at the least, for all that, in any event,
no less than **12** nevertheless, no matter
what **14** at the very least, nothing short
of **15** nothing less than, whatever
happens
• **to say the least 13** to put it mildly
**14** at the very least

## leather
**03** taw **04** beat, butt, hide, skin
**06** levant, spetch, thrash **08** studwork

*Leathers include:*

**03** kid
**04** buff, calf, napa, roan, shoe, wash,
yuft
**05** grain, Mocha, nappa, neat's,
plate, split, suede, waxed, white
**06** chrome, Nubuck®, patent,
Rexine®, Russia, shammy, skiver,
spruce
**07** chamois, cowhide, dogskin, hog-
skin, kidskin, kipskin, morocco,
pigskin, saffian
**08** buckskin, cabretta, calfskin,
capeskin, cheverel, cheveril,
cordovan, cordwain, deerskin,
goatskin, lambskin, maroquin,
shagreen
**09** crocodile, lacquered, sheepskin,
slinkskin, snakeskin
**10** artificial
**11** aqualeather, cuir-bouilli,
whitleather

## leathery
**04** hard **05** rough, tough **06** rugged
**07** corious, durable, wizened
**08** hardened, leathern, wrinkled
**10** coriaceous

## leave
◇ *deletion indicator* **02** go, OK **03** let,
vac **04** drop, dump, exit, jilt, levy, lose,
miss, move, park, part, quit, will
**05** allot, avoid, break, cause, cease,
chuck, congé, ditch, endow, go off,
raise, say-so, scoot, split **06** assign,
commit, congee, create, day off,
decamp, depart, desert, desist, devise,
forget, give up, go away, hook it, lead
to, mislay, resign, retire, set out, sickie,
vamose **07** abandon, consent, consign,
deliver, do a bunk, entrust, forsake,
freedom, holiday, liberty, licence,
license, produce, pull out, push off,
retreat, take off, time off, vamoose,
walk off, warrant **08** bequeath, choof
off, clear off, come away, emigrate,
evacuate, farewell, furlough, generate,
give over, hand down, hand over,
holidays, make over, misplace,
occasion, renounce, result in, run
along, run out on, sanction, shove off,
transmit, up sticks, vacation, withdraw
**09** allowance, disappear, push along,
sick leave, surrender **10** bring about,
concession, give rise to, green light, hit
the road, indulgence, make tracks,
permission, relinquish, sabbatical
**11** leave behind **12** dispensation, shoot
through **13** authorization, sling your
hook, take your leave **14** leave of
absence, turn your back on **15** leave
high and dry, take French leave
• **leave off 03** end **04** halt, omit, quit,
stop **05** cease **06** desist, lay off
**07** abstain, refrain **08** break off, give
over, knock off **09** terminate
**11** discontinue
• **leave out 03** bar, cut **04** miss, omit
**06** bypass, cut out, except, ignore,
reject **07** exclude, miss out, neglect
**08** count out, overlook, pass over,
suppress **09** cast aside, disregard,
eliminate
• **leave quickly 08** light out

## leaven
**04** barm, work, zyme **05** imbue, raise,
swell, yeast **06** expand, puff up
**07** enliven, ferment, inspire, lighten,
pervade, quicken, suffuse **08** permeate
**09** sourdough, stimulate **11** cause to
rise **12** raising agent

## leaves
**03** tea **04** atap **05** attap

## leavings
**04** bits **05** dregs, dross, spoil, waste
**06** debris, pieces, refuse, relics, scraps
**07** remains, residue, rubbish
**08** detritus, oddments, remnants
**09** alms-drink, fragments, leftovers,
remainder, sweepings **11** broken meats

## Lebanon
**02** RL **03** LBN

## lecher
**04** gate, goat, lech, perv, rake, roué,
wolf **05** Romeo, satyr **06** wanton
**07** Don Juan, flasher, seducer
**08** Casanova, Lothario, Lovelace
**09** adulterer, debauchee, libertine,
womanizer **10** fornicator, libidinist,
profligate, sensualist **11** dirty old man,
whoremonger

## lecherous
**04** lewd **05** horny, pervy, randy
**06** carnal, wanton **07** codding, leering,
lustful, rammish, raunchy **08** prurient,
unchaste **09** debauched, dissolute,
lickerish, liquorish, salacious
**10** degenerate, dissipated, lascivious,
libidinous, licentious, womanizing
**11** promiscuous **12** concupiscent

## lechery
**04** lust **08** lewdness, salacity
**09** carnality, prurience, randiness
**10** debauchery, rakishness, sensuality,
wantonness, womanizing
**11** libertinism, lustfulness, raunchiness
**13** concupiscence, lickerishness,
salaciousness **14** lasciviousness,
libidinousness, licentiousness

## lectern
**04** ambo, desk **05** eagle, stand, table
**07** lettern, oratory **11** reading-desk

## lecture
**03** act, jaw **04** read, talk **05** chide, class,
pi-jaw, scold, speak, teach **06** berate,
homily, lesson, preach, rebuke, rocket,
sermon, speech **07** address, censure,
chiding, expound, jawbone, prelect,
reproof, reprove, tell off **08** admonish,
berating, extender, harangue, instruct,
reproach, scolding, travelog **09** chalk
talk, discourse, give a talk, hold forth,
reprimand, talking-to **10** conférence,
prelection, rollicking, telling-off,
travelogue, upbraiding **11** instruction,
make a speech, pick holes in
**12** disquisition, dressing-down, pull to
pieces, tear to pieces **13** give lessons in
**14** curtain lecture

## lecturer
**01** L **03** don **04** lect **05** tutor **06** docent,
lector, orator, reader, talker **07** scholar,
speaker, teacher **08** academic,
preacher **09** declaimer, expounder,
haranguer, pedagogue, preceptor,
prelector, professor **10** instructor,
sermonizer, theologian **11** speechifier,
speechmaker **12** conférencier,
extensionist, instructress

## ledge
**04** berm, lode, sill, step, vein **05** altar,
bench, linch, ridge, shelf, stock
**06** gradin, mantel, offset, settle, shelve
**07** gradine, linchet, lynchet **08** fire-
step, overhang **10** buttery-bar, firing-
step, projection, scarcement
**11** mantelpiece, mantelshelf

## ledger
**05** books **07** journal **08** accounts,
register **09** inventory **10** record book
**11** account book

## lee
**05** cover, river **06** arable, meadow,
refuge **07** pasture, shelter **09** sanctuary
**10** protection

## leech
**05** drain, toady **06** usurer **07** clinger,
sponger **08** hanger-on, parasite
**09** physician, scrounger, sycophant
**10** freeloader **11** bloodsucker,
extortioner

## leer

**03** eye **04** grin, ogle, perv, wink
**05** gloat, smirk, sneer, stare, tweer,
twire **06** colour, goggle, squint **07** glad
eye **10** complexion **13** lecherous look

## leery

**04** wary **05** chary **06** unsure **07** careful,
dubious, guarded **08** cautious,
doubting **09** sceptical, uncertain
**10** suspicious **11** distrustful, on your
guard

## lees

**05** draff, dregs, grout **06** dunder, refuse
**07** deposit, grounds, residue
**08** sediment **09** settlings **11** precipitate

## leeway

**04** play, room **05** drift, scope, slack,
space **06** margin **07** freedom **08** latitude
**09** elbow-room **11** flexibility

## left

◊ *deletion indicator* **01** L **03** red **04** gone,
lorn, near, over, port, quit, went
**06** Maoist **07** liberal, Marxist, radical
**08** larboard, left-hand, left-wing,
Leninist **09** communist, sinistral,
socialist, Stalinist **10** Bolshevist,
Spartakist, Trotskyist, Trotskyite **11** left-
leaning, progressive, revisionist
**12** collectivist **13** revolutionary
• **turn left 03** hie **04** high

## left-handed

**06** clumsy, gauche **07** awkward,
dubious, unlucky **08** southpaw
**09** ambiguous, equivocal, insincere,
sinistral **10** backhanded, cack-handed,
kack-handed **11** cacky-handed
**12** corrie-fisted, hypocritical

## left-hander

**05** lefty **06** leftie **08** southpaw
**09** sinistral **11** cackyhander, molly-
dooker

## left-over

**04** orra **06** excess, unused **07** oddment,
settled, surplus, uneaten **09** remaining
**11** superfluous

## leftovers

**05** dregs **06** excess, refuse, scraps
**07** remains, residue, surplus
**08** leavings, remnants **09** remainder,
sweepings

## left-wing

**04** left **06** Maoist **07** liberal, Marxist,
radical **08** Leninist **09** communist,
socialist, Stalinist **10** Bolshevist,
Spartakist, Trotskyist, Trotskyite **11** left-
leaning, progressive, revisionist
**12** collectivist **13** revolutionary
• **left-winger 04** trot

## leg

**02** on **03** bit, gam, lap, peg, pin **04** crus,
gamb, limb, part, prop **05** brace,
shank, stage, stump **06** member, timber
**07** pleopod, portion, section, segment,
stretch, support, upright **08** swindler
**10** sheepshank **12** underpinning
• **leg it 03** run **04** walk **05** hurry **06** hoof
it **07** scarper **08** go by foot
• **not have a leg to stand on 10** be
unproved **11** lack support **12** lack an
excuse **13** be unjustified

• **on its last legs 04** weak **06** ailing
**07** failing **10** fading fast, near to ruin
**11** about to fail, near to death **12** at
death's door **15** about to collapse,
nearing collapse
• **pull someone's leg 03** kid, rib
**04** fool, joke **05** tease, trick **06** have on,
wind up **07** deceive **09** make fun of
**11** play a joke on **12** take for a ride
**14** pull a fast one on

## legacy

**04** gift **06** estate **07** bequest
**08** heirloom, heritage **09** endowment,
heritance, patrimony **10** bequeathal,
birthright **11** inheritance

## legal

**03** leg **05** legit, licit, right, sound, valid
**06** lawful, proper **07** allowed
**08** forensic, judicial, licensed, rightful
**09** allowable, judiciary, legalized,
permitted, statutory, warranted
**10** above-board, acceptable,
admissible, authorized, legitimate,
sanctioned **11** permissible **12** within
the law **14** constitutional
*See also* **court; crime**

---

*Legal terms include:*

---

**02** JP, QC
**03** bar, DPP, sue
**04** ASBO, bail, deed, dock, fine,
jury, oath, plea, will, writ
**05** alibi, asset, bench, brief, by-law,
claim, droit, felon, grant, judge,
juror, lease, party, proof, proxy,
title, trial
**06** appeal, arrest, bigamy, charge,
client, demand, equity, estate,
guilty, lawyer, legacy, pardon,
parole, patent, remand, repeal,
the bar, waiver
**07** accused, alimony, amnesty,
caution, charter, codicil, convict,
coroner, custody, damages,
defence, divorce, hearing,
inquest, inquiry, Law Lord,
lawsuit, mandate, penalty,
probate, sheriff, statute,
summons, tenancy, verdict,
warrant, witness
**08** act of God, adultery, advocate,
civil law, contract, covenant,
criminal, easement, eviction,
evidence, executor, freehold,
hung jury, innocent, judgment,
juvenile, legal aid, mortgage,
offender, prisoner, receiver,
reprieve, sanction, sentence,
subpoena, tribunal
**09** accessory, acquittal, affidavit,
agreement, annulment, barrister,
common law, copyright, court
case, defendant, endowment, fee
simple, indemnity, intestacy,
judgement, judiciary, leasehold,
liability, plaintiff, precedent,
probation, solicitor, testimony,
trademark
**10** accomplice, allegation, civil
union, conveyance, conveyance,
decree nisi, indictment,
injunction, liquidator, magistrate,
settlement

**11** adjournment, arbitration,
extradition, foreclosure,
inheritance, local search,
maintenance, plea bargain, plead
guilty, proceedings, ward of court
**12** age of consent, Bill of Rights,
constitution, court martial, cross-
examine, Lord Advocate,
misadventure, notary public
**13** King's evidence, public inquiry,
Queen's Counsel, young offender
**14** decree absolute, Lord Chancellor,
plead not guilty, Queen's
evidence
**15** Act of Parliament, Attorney-
General, clerk of the court,
contempt of court, power of
attorney

• **legal document 04** deed, writ

## legality

**08** validity **09** rightness, soundness
**10** lawfulness, legitimacy
**12** rightfulness **14** admissibleness,
permissibility

## legalize

**05** admit, allow **06** accept, permit,
ratify **07** approve, license, warrant
**08** sanction, validate **09** authorize,
make legal **10** legitimize
**13** decriminalize

## legally

**05** by law **07** validly **08** by rights,
lawfully, properly **10** rightfully
**11** permissibly **12** legitimately

## legate

**03** leg **05** agent, envoy **06** deputy,
exarch, nuncio **08** delegate, emissary
**09** messenger **10** ambassador
**12** commissioner **14** representative

## legatee

**04** heir **06** co-heir **07** devisee
**08** legatary, receiver **09** co-heiress,
inheritor, recipient **10** inheritrix
**11** beneficiary

## legation

**07** embassy, mission **08** ministry
**09** consulate **10** commission,
delegation, deputation
**14** representation

## legend

**03** key, VIP **04** myth, name, saga, star,
tale **05** celeb, fable, motto, story
**06** bigwig, cipher, legion, worthy
**07** big name, big shot, caption, fiction,
notable, romance **08** folk tale,
luminary **09** celebrity, dignitary,
narrative, personage, superstar,
underline **11** explanation, inscription,
personality **12** famous person, living
legend **13** household name
*See also* **mythology**

---

*Arthurian legend-related terms and
locations include:*

---

**03** Usk
**04** Bath, York
**06** Avalon, Camlan, Logres
**07** Camelot, Camlann, Carleon,
Chester
**08** Caerleon, Caliburn, Lyonesse,
Tintagel

**09** Badon Hill, Boscastle, Camelford, Excalibur, Holy Grail, Llyn Dinas, loadstone, Red Dragon, Roche Rock
**10** Cader Idris, Grail Table, Llyn Barfog, Round Table, Stonehenge, Tintagalon, Winchester
**11** Arthur's Seat, Cadbury Hill, Chalice Well, Craig y Dinas, Glastonbury, Merlin's Cave
**12** Alderley Edge, Arthur's Cross, Dozemary Pool, Isle of Avalon, Perilous Seat, Vale of Avalon
**13** Cadbury Castle, Questing Beast, Ship of Fairies, Siège Perilous, The Waste Lands
**14** Bamburgh Castle, Caerleon Castle, Carleon upon Usk, Dolorous Stroke, Glastonbury Tor, Island of Avalon, St Govan's Chapel, Tintagel Castle
**15** Slaughterbridge, St Michael's Mount, Sword in the Stone, The Tristan Stone, Valley of Delight

*Characters from Arthurian legend include:*

**03** Ban, Kay, Lot
**04** Bors
**05** Nimue, Uther
**06** Arthur, Elaine, Gareth (of Orkney), Gawain, Merlin, Modred
**07** Caradoc, Galahad, Gawayne, Igraine, Launfal, Mordred, Tristan
**08** Bedivere, Ironside, Lancelot, Palmerin, Parsifal, Perceval, Tristram
**09** Arondight, Guinevere
**10** Fisher King, King Arthur
**11** Morgan le Fay
**13** Lady of Shallot, Lady of the Lake
**14** Launcelot du Lac, Uther Pendragon

*See also* **knight**

*Characters from the Robin Hood legend include:*

**07** Sheriff (of Nottingham)
**08** Merry Men, Prioress (of Kirklees)
**09** Friar Tuck, Robin Hood
**10** Allan-A-Dale, Little John, Maid Marian, Prince John
**11** King Richard (the Lionheart), Will Scarlet
**13** Guy of Gisborne, Much the Miller

**legendary**
**06** fabled, famous **07** popular **08** fabulous, fanciful, glorious, honoured, immortal, mythical, renowned **09** acclaimed, fictional, storybook, well-known **10** celebrated, fictitious, remembered **11** illustrious, traditional

**legerdemain**
**05** feint **06** tricky **07** cunning **08** artifice, jugglery, juggling, trickery **09** chicanery, deception, sophistry **10** artfulness, craftiness, hocus-pocus, subterfuge **11** contrivance, logodaedaly, manoeuvring **12** manipulation **13** sleight of hand, thaumaturgics

**legibility**
**07** clarity **08** lucidity **09** clearness, lucidness, plainness, precision **10** simplicity **11** readability **12** distinctness, explicitness, readableness **15** intelligibility

**legible**
**04** neat **05** clear, lucid, plain **06** simple **07** precise **08** distinct, explicit, readable **10** easy to read **12** decipherable, intelligible **14** comprehensible

**legibly**
**06** simply **07** clearly, lucidly, plainly **08** readably **09** precisely **10** easily read, explicitly **12** intelligibly **14** comprehensibly

**legion**
**04** army, host, mass, unit **05** drove, force, horde, swarm, troop **06** cohort, legend, myriad, number, throng **07** brigade, company **08** division, numerous, regiment **09** battalion, countless, multitude **10** numberless **11** illimitable, innumerable **13** multitudinous
• **British Legion** 02 BL

**legislate**
**05** enact, order **06** codify, decree, ordain **08** make laws, pass laws **09** authorize, establish, formulate, prescribe

**legislation**
**03** act, law, leg **04** bill, code **05** legis, rules **06** ruling **07** charter, measure, statute **09** enactment, lawmaking, ordinance **10** regulation **11** formulation **12** codification, prescription **13** authorization

**legislative**
**03** leg **05** legis **08** judicial **09** lawgiving, lawmaking **10** senatorial **12** jurisdictive **13** congressional, parliamentary

**legislator**
**02** MP **06** deputy **07** senator **08** lawgiver, lawmaker **09** nomothete **10** nomothetes **11** congressman **13** congresswoman **15** parliamentarian

**legislature**
**03** leg **05** house, legis **06** senate, states **07** chamber **08** assembly, congress **10** parliament
*See also* **parliament**

**legitimacy**
**08** fairness, legality, validity **09** rightness, soundness **10** lawfulness **11** credibility, rationality **12** plausibility, rightfulness, sensibleness **13** acceptability, admissibility **14** admissibleness, justifiability, permissibility, reasonableness

**legitimate**
**04** fair, real, true **05** legal, legit, licit, loyal, sound, valid **06** kosher, lawful, proper **07** correct, genuine, logical, natural **08** credible, rational, rightful, sensible, true-born **09** competent, justified, plausible, statutory, warranted **10** acceptable, admissible,

authorized, reasonable, sanctioned **11** justifiable, well-founded **12** acknowledged

**legitimize**
**05** allow **06** permit **07** charter, entitle, license, warrant **08** legalize, sanction, validate **09** authorize **10** legitimate **13** decriminalize

**leisure**
**04** ease, rest, time **05** break, R and R, space **06** by-time **07** freedom, holiday, leisure, liberty, respite, time off, time out, vacancy **08** free time, off-hours, vacation **09** spare time **10** recreation, relaxation, retirement
• **at your leisure** 11 unhurriedly 13 in your own time, when you want to 14 when it suits you 15 in your spare time

**leisurely**
**04** easy, lazy, slow **05** loose **06** gentle **07** relaxed, restful, unhasty **08** carefree, laid-back, tranquil **09** easy-going, unhurried **10** leisurable **11** comfortable

**lemur**
**05** indri, loris **06** aye-aye, colugo, galago, indris, macaco, sifaka **07** half-ape, meercat, meerkat, nagapie **08** mongoose, mungoose **09** babacoote, mangouste **10** angwantibo **12** Cynocephalus **13** Galeopithecus

**lend**
**03** add, sub **04** give, loan, spot **05** grant, prest **06** bestow, confer, credit, donate, impart, on-lend, supply **07** advance, furnish, provide **08** overlend, put forth **10** allow to use, contribute **11** allow to have **13** let someone use
• **lend a hand** 03 aid 04 help 06 assist 07 help out, pitch in 09 do your bit 14 give assistance
• **lend an ear** 04 heed 06 listen 07 give ear, hearken 10 take notice 12 pay attention
• **lend itself to** 13 be suitable for 15 be easily used for

**length**
**01** l **04** span, term **05** piece, reach, space **06** extent, period **07** measure, portion, section, segment, stretch **08** distance, duration **09** prolixity
• **at length** 05 fully 06 at last, in full 07 finally 10 eventually, thoroughly 11 in due course 12 exhaustively, for a long time 13 in great detail 14 after a long time 15 comprehensively
• **go to any lengths** 10 do anything 11 try very hard 12 go to extremes

**lengthen**
**03** eik, eke **04** draw **06** eke out, expand, extend, pad out **07** draw out, prolong, spin out, stretch **08** continue, elongate, increase, protract **10** grow longer, prolongate

**lengthwise**
**05** along **07** endlong, endways, endwise **10** fore-and-aft, lengthways, vertically **12** horizontally

## lengthy
**04** long **05** wordy **06** prolix **07** diffuse, tedious, verbose **08** drawn-out, extended, overlong, rambling **09** prolonged **10** lengthened, long-winded, protracted **12** interminable, long-drawn-out

## leniency
**05** mercy **08** clemency, kindness, lenience, mildness, softness **09** tolerance **10** compassion, generosity, gentleness, humaneness, indulgence, moderation, tenderness **11** forbearance, forgiveness, magnanimity **14** permissiveness **15** soft-heartedness

## lenient
**04** kind, mild **06** gentle, humane, tender **07** liberal, sparing **08** generous, merciful, moderate, soothing, tolerant **09** emollient, forgiving, indulgent, softening **10** forbearing, permissive **11** magnanimous, soft-hearted **13** compassionate

## lenitive
**06** easing **07** calming **08** laxative, soothing **09** assuaging, relieving **10** mitigating, mollifying, palliative **11** alleviating

## lens
**03** eye **05** glass, optic, power **06** finder, lentil, pebble, peeper **07** aplanat, contact **08** achromat, bull's-eye, eyeglass, eyepiece, meniscus **09** amplifier, condenser, magnifier, telephoto **10** anastigmat, apochromat, pantoscope **11** object-glass **12** burning-glass

## Lent
**04** fast **06** carême, spring

## leopard
**04** pard **05** ounce, tiger **06** pardal **07** libbard, panther, pardale **08** pardalis **12** catamountain, cat o' mountain

## leper
**05** lazar, mesel **06** meazel, pariah **07** leprosy, outcast **11** undesirable, untouchable **13** social outcast

## leprechaun
**03** elf, imp **04** puck **05** bogey, demon, fiend, gnome, nixie, pooka, troll **06** goblin, kelpie, kobold, red-cap, spirit, sprite **07** brownie, gremlin **09** hobgoblin

## lesbian
**03** gay **07** Sapphic **08** sapphist **10** homosexual

## lesion
**03** cut **04** gash, hurt, sore **05** wound **06** bruise, injury, scrape, trauma **07** scratch **08** abrasion **09** contusion **10** impairment, laceration

## Lesotho
**02** LS **03** LSO

## less
**03** bar **04** meno, save **05** fewer, minor, minus **06** except **07** short of, smaller, wanting, without, younger **08** inferior **09** excepting, excluding, not as many, not as much, not so many, not so much **13** smaller amount **15** to a lesser degree, to a lesser extent

## lessen
**03** cut, dip, ebb **04** alay, bate, dull, ease, fail, flag, wane **05** abate, aleye, allay, erode, let up, lower, slack **06** absorb, deaden, go down, impair, narrow, plunge, reduce, shrink, weaken **07** abridge, curtail, decline, die down, dwindle, ease off, lighten, plummet, relieve, slacken, subside, tail off **08** belittle, come down, contract, decrease, derogate, diminish, minimize, mitigate, moderate, nosedive, peter out, slow down, tail away **09** disparage, extenuate **10** de-escalate

## lessening
**03** dip **05** allay, let-up **06** easing, ebbing, waning **07** cutting, decline, erosion, failure **08** batement, decrease, flagging **09** abatement, deadening, dwindling, reduction, shrinkage, weakening **10** derogation, diminution, imminution, mitigation, moderation, slackening **11** contraction, curtailment, extenuation, petering out **12** de-escalation, minimization

## lesser
**05** lower, minor **07** smaller **08** inferior, slighter **09** secondary **11** subordinate **13** less important

## lesson
**04** lear, leir, lere, task, text **05** class, drill, leare, model, moral, train **06** course, period, rebuke, sermon **07** example, lection, lecture, reading, seminar, warning **08** coaching, exercise, homework, instruct, liripipe, liripoop, practice, teaching, tutorial, workshop **09** deterrent, practical, scripture **10** assignment, recitation, schoolwork **11** application, instruction, master-class **12** Bible reading **13** demonstration

## lest
**06** in case, listen **07** for fear **11** for fear that **14** in order to avoid

## let
**02** OK **03** net **04** hire, make, rent **05** allow, cause, check, grant, lease **06** enable, hinder, let out, permit **07** agree to, hire out, prevent, rent out **08** assent to, obstacle, sanction, tolerate **09** authorize, consent to, give leave, give the OK, hindrance, restraint **10** constraint, give the nod, greenlight, impediment, obstructed **11** obstruction, prohibition, restriction **12** interference **14** give permission, give the go-ahead **15** say the magic word
• **let alone 04** also **08** as well as **09** apart from, never mind **12** not to mention **13** not forgetting
• **let down 04** fail, vail **05** lower **06** betray, desert **07** abandon, depress **09** fall short **10** disappoint, disenchant, dissatisfy **11** disillusion **14** disappointment **15** leave in the lurch

• **let fly 03** hit **05** fling, fly at, go for, shoot **06** attack, charge, strike **07** assault, lay into **08** fall upon **09** discharge, have a go at, lash out at
• **let go 04** drop, free, omit, quit, sack **06** give up, unhand **07** dismiss, hang off, manumit, release, set free, slacken, unleash **08** liberate, released **10** relinquish **11** stop holding **13** make redundant
• **let in 04** sink **05** admit, greet **06** accept, insert, take in **07** enchase, include, receive, welcome **11** incorporate **12** allow to enter
• **let in on 04** tell **06** inform **07** include, let know **11** allow to know **14** allow to share in
• **let off 04** emit, fire **05** spare **06** acquit, excuse, exempt, ignore, pardon **07** absolve, explode, forgive, give off, release **08** detonate, liberate, reprieve **09** discharge, exonerate
• **let on 04** blab, tell, impart, pass on, relate, reveal, squeal **07** divulge, let slip **08** disclose, give away **09** make known **10** make public **13** spill the beans **15** give the game away
• **let out 03** job **04** blab, emit, free, leak **05** let go, utter, widen **06** betray, reveal, squeal **07** enlarge, freight, let slip, release, slacken **08** disclose **09** discharge, make known **13** spill the beans
• **let up 03** end **04** ease, halt, stop **05** abate, cease **06** lessen **07** die down, ease off, slacken, subside **08** decrease, diminish, moderate

## let-down
**04** sell **07** setback, washout **08** betrayal **09** desertion **10** anticlimax **14** disappointment **15** disillusionment

## lethal
**05** fatal, toxic **06** deadly, mortal **07** deathly, noxious, ruinous, vicious **08** venomous **09** dangerous, murderous, poisonous **10** disastrous **11** destructive, devastating **12** death-dealing

## lethally
**07** fatally **08** mortally **09** noxiously, toxically **11** dangerously **12** disastrously **13** destructively, devastatingly

## lethargic
**04** dull, idle, lazy, logy, slow **05** heavy, inert, weary **06** drowsy, sleepy, torpid **07** dormant, languid, passive **08** hebetant, inactive, lifeless, listless, slothful, sluggish **09** apathetic, enervated, somnolent **11** debilitated

## lethargically
**04** idly **05** dully **06** lazily, slowly **07** heavily, inertly, wearily **08** drowsily, sleepily, torpidly **09** languidly **10** inactively, lifelessly, listlessly, slothfully, sluggishly **11** somnolently **13** apathetically

## lethargy
**05** sloth **06** apathy, stupor, torpor **07** inertia, languor **08** dullness, idleness, inaction, laziness, slowness

**09** lassitude, weariness **10** drowsiness, inactivity, sleepiness, somnolence **12** indifference, lifelessness, listlessness, sluggishness

## let-out

**04** cure **06** escape, excuse, get-out, remedy, way out **08** loophole **09** legal flaw **11** safety valve, way of escape **12** escape clause, technicality **13** error in the law, means of escape

## letter

**02** Ep **03** dak **04** chit, dawk, Epis, line, note, sign, sort, type **05** books, hirer, reply **06** device, figure, italic, lettre, scrawl, symbol, uncial **07** bloomer, capital, culture, epistle, message, missive, notelet, screeve, writing **08** academia, circular, dispatch, grapheme, learning, pastoral **09** character, education, epistolet, erudition, rune-stave **10** aerogramme, billet-doux, humanities, literature, round robin, semi-uncial **11** scholarship **13** belles-lettres, communication **14** correspondence **15** acknowledgement

*Letters include:*

**03** ash, edh, eth, wen, wyn
**04** aesc, ogam, wynn, yogh
**05** thorn

*See also* **alphabet; typeface**
• **to the letter 07** exactly **08** strictly **09** by the book, literally, precisely **10** accurately **11** religiously, word for word **13** in every detail, punctiliously

## lettered

**06** versed **07** erudite, learned, studied **08** academic, cultured, educated, highbrow, informed, literary, literate, well-read **09** scholarly **10** cultivated, widely read **12** accomplished, well-educated **13** knowledgeable

## letter-opener

**04** Dear

## letters

**04** mail, post

## lettuce

**07** Lactuca

*Lettuce varieties include:*

**03** cos
**04** flat
**05** lamb's, round
**06** frisée
**07** cabbage, Chinese, iceberg, romaine
**08** Batavian
**09** little gem
**10** butterhead, lollo rosso

## let-up

**03** end **04** lull **05** break, pause **06** recess, relief **07** ceasing, respite **08** breather, interval **09** abatement, cessation, lessening, remission **10** slackening

## level

**03** aim **04** avow, calm, even, flat, mark, rank, rase, raze, size, tell, tier, zone **05** admit, class, drawn, equal, flush,

focus, grade, guess, layer, plain, plane, plumb, point, range, stage, train **06** amount, degree, direct, even up, extent, height, on a par, open up, smooth, stable, status, steady, storey, volume **07** abreast, aligned, be frank, confess, destroy, divulge, echelon, even out, flatten, gallery, horizon, measure, regular, station, stratum, tell all, uniform **08** altitude, balanced, bulldoze, composed, constant, demolish, equalize, estimate, highness, lay waste, make flat, matching, position, pull down, quantity, standard, standing, tear down, zero in on **09** be upfront, champaign, come clean, devastate, elevation, knock down, magnitude, make level, stabilize **10** horizontal, unchanging **11** concentrate, neck and neck, unemotional, unflappable **12** level pegging, speak plainly, well-balanced **13** self-possessed **14** tell it like it is **15** keep nothing back, raze to the ground
• **on the level 04** fair, open **06** candid, honest **07** jannock, up-front **08** straight **10** above board, fair dinkum, straight-up **12** on the up and up **13** fair and square

## level-headed

**04** calm, cool, sane **06** steady **07** prudent **08** balanced, composed, rational, sensible **09** practical **10** cool-headed, dependable, reasonable **11** circumspect, unflappable **12** even-tempered **13** imperturbable, self-possessed

## lever

**03** bar, key, pry **04** lift, move, pull **05** brake, crank, force, heave, hoist, jemmy, peavy, pedal, pinch, prise, raise, shift **06** handle, peavey, switch, tiller **07** control, crowbar, treadle, treddle, trigger **08** backfall, crossbar, dislodge, joystick, knee-stop, throttle, tommy bar, water key **09** bell crank, handspike, knee-swell, rocker arm, whipstaff **10** pump-handle, tremolo arm **11** walking-beam

## leverage

**04** grip, hold, pull, rank **05** clout, force, grasp, power, prise, prize **06** weight **08** purchase, strength **09** advantage, authority, influence **10** ascendancy

## leviathan

**04** hulk **05** giant, Satan, Titan, whale **07** mammoth, monster **08** behemoth, colossus, gigantic **10** formidable, sea monster

## levitate

**03** fly **04** hang, waft **05** drift, float, glide, hover **07** suspend

## levitation

**06** flying **07** gliding, hanging, wafting **08** drifting, floating, hovering **10** suspension **11** yogic flying

## levity

**03** fun **08** hilarity **09** flippancy, frivolity, silliness, whifflery **10** fickleness, triviality **11** glaikitness, irreverence **12** carefreeness, flippantness

**13** facetiousness **15** light-mindedness, thoughtlessness

## levy

**03** due, fee, tax **04** duty, rate, toll **05** exact, leave, raise, stent, tithe, tythe **06** charge, demand, duties, excise, gather, impose, impost, tariff **07** collect, customs, estreat, militia, precept, tallage **10** assessment, collection **12** contribution, subscription

## lewd

**03** bad **04** bare, blue **05** bawdy, randy **06** carnal, harlot, impure, smutty, vulgar, wanton **07** Cyprian, lustful, obscene, raunchy, sensual, unclean **08** ignorant, indecent, unchaste **09** debauched, dissolute, lecherous, lubricous, salacious **10** degenerate, lascivious, libidinous, licentious, lubricious, suggestive **11** promiscuous **12** concupiscent, pornographic

## lewdly

**07** randily **08** impurely, smuttily, vulgarly **09** lustfully, obscenely, raunchily **10** indecently **11** dissolutely, lecherously **12** degenerately **13** promiscuously

## lewdness

**04** smut **07** crudity, lechery **08** impurity, priapism **09** bawdiness, carnality, depravity, indecency, lubricity, obscenity, randiness, vulgarity **10** debauchery, smuttiness, unchastity, wantonness **11** lustfulness, pornography **13** concupiscence, salaciousness **14** lasciviousness, licentiousness

## lexicographer

**10** vocabulist

*Lexicographers and philologists include:*

**04** **Bopp** (Franz)
**05** **Pliny** (Gaius 'the Elder'), **Sapir** (Edward), **Skeat** (Walter William)
**06** **Bierce** (Ambrose), **Brewer** (Ebenezer Cobham), **Fowler** (Henry Watson), **Freund** (Wilhelm), **Hornby** (A S), **Murray** (Sir James Augustus Henry), **Onions** (Charles Talbot), **Trench** (Richard Chenevix)
**07** **Chomsky** (Noam), **Craigie** (Sir William Alexander), **Diderot** (Denis), **Johnson** (Samuel, 'Dr'), **Mencken** (H L), **Tolkien** (J R R), **Ventris** (Michael George Francis), **Webster** (Noah)
**08** **Chambers** (Ephraim), **Chambers** (Robert), **Chambers** (William), **Larousse** (Pierre Athanase), **Saussure** (Ferdinand de)
**09** **Furnivall** (Frederick James), **Jespersen** (Otto Harry), **Partridge** (Eric)
**10** **Amarasimha**, **Burchfield** (Robert)

## lexicon

**03** lex, OED, TCD **08** glossary, wordbook, word-list **10** dictionary, phrase book, vocabulary **12** encyclopedia

## Leytonstone
03 E11

## liability
04 drag, dues, duty, onus 05 debit
06 burden, charge 07 arrears
08 drawback, nuisance 09 hindrance
10 impediment, obligation
11 culpability, encumbrance
12 disadvantage, indebtedness
13 answerability, inconvenience
14 accountability, responsibility
15 blameworthiness

## liable
03 apt 04 open 05 prone 06 likely 07 at
fault, exposed, fitting, subject, tending,
to blame 08 amenable, disposed,
inclined, suitable 10 answerable,
changeable, vulnerable
11 accountable, predisposed,
responsible, susceptible

## liaise
07 contact, network 08 relate to 09 co-
operate, interface 11 collaborate,
communicate 12 work together

## liaison
04 link 05 agent, amour, fling, union
06 affair, broker 07 affaire, carry-on,
contact, romance 08 intrigue, mediator
09 go-between, middleman, two-
timing 10 arbitrator, connection,
flirtation, love affair, negotiator 11 co-
operation, interchange 12 bit on the
side, entanglement, intermediary,
relationship 13 collaboration,
communication 15 working together

## liar
05 leear 06 falser, fibber 07 Ananias,
bouncer 08 deceiver, fabulist, perjurer
09 falsifier 11 pseudologue, storyteller
12 false witness, prevaricator

## libation
08 oblation 09 sacrifice 13 drink
offering

## libel
04 slur 05 abuse, smear 06 defame,
malign, revile, vilify 07 calumny,
slander, traduce 08 badmouth
09 aspersion, denigrate, disparage
10 calumniate, defamation, muck-
raking, throw mud at 11 denigration,
false report, mudslinging 12 vilification
13 disparagement 15 untrue statement

## libellous
05 false 06 untrue 07 abusive
09 injurious, maligning, traducing,
vilifying 10 defamatory, derogatory,
scurrilous, slanderous 11 denigratory,
disparaging 12 calumniatory

## liberal
◇ *anagram indicator* 01 L 03 Lib 04 free,
left, whig 05 ample, broad, frank
06 candid, giving, lavish, verlig
07 copious, leftish, lenient, profuse,
radical 08 abundant, advanced,
catholic, flexible, generous,
handsome, left-wing, moderate,
tolerant, unbiased 09 bountiful,
impartial, plentiful, reformist,
unsparing 10 altruistic, big-hearted,
broad-based, free-handed, munificent,
open-handed, open-minded 11 broad-

minded, enlightened, free-hearted,
libertarian, magnanimous, open-
hearted, progressive, wide-ranging
12 large-hearted, unprejudiced
13 philanthropic, unwithdrawing
14 forward-looking, latitudinarian

## liberalism
07 leftism 10 radicalism 12 free-
thinking 13 progressivism
14 libertarianism 15 humanitarianism

## liberality
06 bounty 07 breadth, candour, charity
08 altruism, kindness, largesse
09 tolerance 10 generosity, liberalism,
toleration 11 beneficence,
benevolence, catholicity, flexibility,
magnanimity, munificence, prodigality
12 generousness, impartiality,
magnificence, philanthropy
13 progressivism 14 free-handedness,
libertarianism, open-handedness,
open-mindedness, permissiveness
15 broad-mindedness, open-
heartedness

## liberalize
04 ease 05 relax 06 loosen, reduce,
soften 07 ease off, slacken 08 moderate
10 deregulate 14 lift controls on

## liberate
04 free 05 let go, steal 06 let out,
ransom, redeem, rescue, uncage
07 deliver, manumit, release, set free,
unchain 08 let loose, set loose, unfetter
09 discharge, disimmure, unshackle
10 emancipate 11 appropriate

## liberation
03 lib 07 freedom, freeing, liberty,
loosing, release 08 uncaging
09 discharge, ransoming, releasing,
unpenning 10 liberating, redemption,
unchaining 11 deliverance,
manumission, unfettering, unshackling
12 emancipation, resorgimento
13 franchisement 15 enfranchisement

## liberator
05 freer 07 rescuer, saviour
08 ransomer, redeemer 09 deliverer
10 manumitter 11 emancipator

## Liberia
02 LB 03 LBR

## Liber Pater
07 Bacchus

## libertine
04 rake, roué 05 Romeo 06 lecher
07 Don Juan, lustful, seducer
08 Casanova, freedman, Lothario,
Lovelace, palliard 09 debauched,
debauchee, dissolute, lecherous,
reprobate, salacious, womanizer
10 degenerate, licentious, profligate,
sensualist, voluptuary, womanizing
11 gay deceiver, promiscuous
*See also* **womanizer**

## liberty
03 ish 05 leave, right 07 freedom,
leisure, licence, release 08 autonomy,
boldness, disposal, sanction, self-rule
09 franchise, impudence, insolence,
privilege 10 discretion, disrespect,
indulgence, liberation, permission

11 deliverance, entitlement, familiarity,
impropriety, manumission,
prerogative, presumption, sovereignty
12 dispensation, emancipation,
impertinence, independence
13 authorization 14 self-government
15 overfamiliarity
• **at liberty** 04 free 05 loose
07 allowed, at large 08 entitled
09 available, permitted 10 disengaged,
unhindered, unoccupied 11 not
confined 12 unrestrained, unrestricted
13 unconstrained
• **take the liberty** 08 make bold 10 be
impudent 12 be so bold as to 13 be
impertinent 14 show disrespect

## libidinous
04 lewd 05 horny, loose, randy
06 carnal, impure, wanton, wicked
07 lustful, ruttish, sensual 08 prurient,
unchaste 09 debauched, lecherous,
salacious 10 cupidinous, lascivious
11 promiscuous 12 concupiscent
13 whoremasterly

## libido
04 lust 06 ardour 07 passion, the hots
08 sex drive 09 eroticism, randiness
10 sexual urge 12 erotic desire, sexual
desire 14 sexual appetite

## libra
01 l 02 lb

## librarian
03 ALA, lib

## library
02 BL, PL, RL 03 lib

## libretto
04 book, text 05 lines, words 06 lyrics,
script

*Librettists include:*

04 **Hart** (Lorenz), **Jouy** (Étienne), **Rice**
(Sir Tim), **Stow** (Randolph)
05 **Swann** (Donald)
06 **Berlin** (Irving), **Lerner** (Alan Jay),
**Malouf** (David), **Porter** (Cole)
07 **Gilbert** (Sir W S), **Harwood** (Gwen)
08 **Gershwin** (Ira), **Sondheim**
(Stephen)
11 **Hammerstein** (Oscar, II)

*See also* **composer**

## Libya
03 LAR, LBY

## licence
04 gale, pass 05 grant, leave, right,
slang 06 excess, indult, permit, ticket
07 abandon, anarchy, charter, consent,
faculty, freedom, liberty, warrant
08 approval, disorder, document,
sanction, warranty 09 authority,
decadence, deviation, exemption,
franchise, privilege 10 creativity,
debauchery, immorality, imprimatur,
indulgence, permission, unruliness
11 certificate, dissipation, entitlement,
impropriety, inspiration, lawlessness,
libertinage, miner's right, originality,
prerogative 12 carte blanche,
dispensation, exaggeration,
fancifulness, immoderation,
independence, intemperance
13 accreditation, authorization,

certification, dissoluteness, ticket of leave **14** letter-of-marque, licentiousness, self-indulgence **15** imaginativeness, letters-of-marque

**license**
**03** let **05** allow **06** permit **07** certify, consent, dismiss, empower, entitle, warrant **08** accredit, sanction **09** authorize, franchise, privilege **10** commission **14** give permission

**licentious**
**03** lax **04** lewd, wild **05** large, loose, randy **06** impure, ribald, ribaud, wanton **07** Cyprian, immoral, liberal, lustful, raunchy, rybauld **08** decadent, depraved, unchaste **09** abandoned, debauched, dissolute, lecherous, libertine **10** disorderly, dissipated, lascivious, profligate **11** promiscuous

**licentiousness**
**04** lust **07** abandon, lechery, licence, license **08** impurity, lewdness, priapism, salacity **09** prurience, randiness **10** debauchery, immorality, wantonness **11** dissipation, libertinism, lustfulness, promiscuity, raunchiness **13** dissoluteness, salaciousness **14** cupidinousness

**lichen**
**10** consortium
See also **alga, algae**

**licit**
**04** real **05** legal, legit **06** lawful, proper **07** correct, genuine **08** rightful **09** allowable, statutory, warranted **10** authorized, legitimate, sanctioned **12** acknowledged

**lick**
**03** bit, dab, lap, tad, wag, wet **04** beat, blow, dart, fawn, hint, spot, wash **05** brush, clean, flick, slake, smear, speck, taste, touch **06** defeat, hammer, little, ripple, sample, stroke, thrash, tongue **07** conquer, flicker, moisten, trounce **08** demolish, play over, smidgeon, vanquish **09** slaughter **13** run rings round **15** make mincemeat of
• **lick your lips** **05** enjoy **06** relish, savour **09** drool over **10** anticipate

**licking**
**06** defeat, hiding **07** beating, lambent, tanning **08** drubbing, flogging, smacking, spanking, whipping **09** thrashing

**lid**
**03** cap, hat, top **05** cover, slide **07** scuttle, stopper **08** covering, screw cap **09** operculum

**lie**
**02** be **04** cram, keep, lair, laze, lean, rest, stay **05** abide, couch, dwell, exist, lodge, press, reach, stand **06** belong, bounce, deceit, depend, extend, invent, lounge, remain, repose **07** be found, consist, falsify, perjure, perjury, recline, romance, stretch **08** be placed, continue, tell a lie, white lie **09** be located, dissemble, fabricate, sprawl out **10** equivocate, stretch out **11** dissimulate, prevaricate **12** be

positioned, make up a story, misrepresent

*Lies include:*

**03** bam, fib, gag
**04** cram, flam, oner, whid
**05** fable, one-er, porky, story
**06** deceit, unfact, wunner, yanker
**07** cretism, falsity, fiction, leasing, swinger, thumper, untruth, whacker, whopper
**08** porkypie, strapper, white lie
**09** fairy tale, falsehood, half-truth, invention, mendacity, tall story
**10** concoction, fairy story, taradiddle
**11** fabrication, made-up story, out-and-outer, pseudologia, tarradiddle
**13** dissimulation, falsification, prevarication

• **give the lie to** **05** rebut **08** disprove **10** contradict, invalidate, prove false
• **lie about** **03** lig
• **lie in sun** **04** bask
• **lie in wait for** **04** lurk, trap **06** ambush, attack, waylay **08** surprise **09** ambuscade **10** lie at lurch **11** lay a trap for
• **lie low** **04** hide, lurk **05** skulk **06** hole up **07** hide out, tappice **08** hide away, lie doggo **09** go to earth, take cover **12** go into hiding **15** conceal yourself, keep a low profile

**Liechtenstein**
**02** FL **03** LIE

**liege**
**04** king, lord **05** chief **06** master, vassal **07** subject **08** nobleman, overlord, superior **09** liege-lord **10** feudal lord

**lieutenant**
**02** DL, LL, Lt **04** loot **05** Lieut **06** deputy, guider, legate **09** assistant, number one, scavenger **11** subordinate **12** right-hand man **14** right-hand woman **15** second-in-command

**life**
**02** go **03** bio, man, pep, zip **04** élan, soul, span, time, vita, zest, zing **05** being, child, diary, fauna, flora, oomph, plant, verve, woman **06** breath, career, course, energy, entity, person, spirit, vigour **07** diaries, journal, memoirs, pizzazz, sparkle **08** activity, duration, lifespan, lifetime, vitality, vivacity **09** aliveness, animation, biography, existence, human life, life story, viability **10** animal life, enthusiasm, excitement, experience, exuberance, human being, individual, liveliness, travelling **11** continuance, high spirits **12** cheerfulness, living things **13** autobiography, effervescence, fauna and flora, meeting people **14** life expectancy, wide experience
• **come to life** **04** rise **06** wake up **09** come alive **12** become active, become lively **14** become exciting
• **enjoy life** **04** live
• **give your life** **06** die for **14** give up your life **15** offer up your life

• **in present life** **04** here
• **term of life** **04** date

**life-and-death**
**05** vital **07** crucial, serious **08** critical **09** important **12** all-important

**lifeblood**
**04** core, soul **05** heart **06** centre, lethee, spirit **09** life-force **11** inspiration **13** essential part **15** essential factor

**lifeless**
**04** arid, bare, cold, dead, dull, flat, gone, lank, slow **05** dusty, empty, stark, stiff **06** barren, wooden **07** defunct, insipid, key-cold, passive, sterile **08** clay-cold, deceased, desolate, listless, sluggish, soulless **09** apathetic, bloodless, cauldrife, exanimate, inanimate, lethargic, stone-dead **10** colourless, insensible, lacklustre, uninspired **11** unconscious, unemotional, uninhabited, uninspiring **12** unproductive

**lifelike**
**04** real, true **05** exact, vivid **06** lively **07** ad vivum, graphic, natural **08** faithful, speaking **09** authentic, breathing, realistic **10** true-to-life

**lifelong**
**07** abiding, lasting **08** constant, enduring, lifetime **09** permanent **10** persistent **11** long-lasting **12** long-standing **14** for all your life

**lifestyle**
**04** life **08** position **09** situation, way of life **11** way of living **14** manner of living

**lifetime**
**03** day **04** days, life, span, time **06** career, course, period **08** anthesis, duration, lifespan **09** existence **10** pilgrimage

**lift**
**02** up **03** air, end, fly, run, sky **04** copy, crib, jack, move, nick, pick, ride, rise, spur, stop **05** annul, arsis, boost, clear, dig up, drive, elate, exalt, hitch, hoist, mount, press, raise, relax, shift, spout, steal **06** arrest, borrow, buoy up, cancel, convey, fillip, hold up, pick up, pull up, remove, revoke, snatch, teagle, uplift, vanish **07** airlift, elevate, heavens, relieve, rescind, root out, scatter, support, thin out, unearth, upraise **08** disperse, dissolve, elevator, hold high, increase, pick-me-up, transfer, withdraw **09** disappear, encourage, escalator, terminate, transport **10** plagiarize **11** paternoster, reassurance **12** shot in the arm **13** encouragement
See also **steal**
• **lift off** **04** rear **05** climb **06** ascend, depart **07** take off **08** blast off

**lift-off**
**05** climb **06** ascent **07** take-off **08** blast-off **09** departure

**lift-shaft**
**04** well

**ligament**
**03** ACL, tie **04** bond **06** frenum **07** fraenum, urachus

**ligature**
**03** tie **04** aesc, band, bond, cord, link, rope, slur **05** strap, thong **06** string **07** bandage, binding, funicle **08** ligament **09** diphthong **10** connection, deligation, tourniquet

**light**
◊ *anagram indicator* **03** day, eye, gay, ray, way **04** airy, beam, bulb, clue, dawn, deft, easy, fair, fine, fire, flit, glow, hint, idle, lamp, lyte, mild, pale, rest, side, soft, thin, weak **05** agile, angle, blaze, blond, cheer, faded, faint, flash, funny, glare, gleam, glint, happy, loose, match, merry, petty, put on, quick, shaft, shine, slant, small, style, sunny, taper, torch, witty **06** active, aspect, beacon, blithe, blonde, bright, candle, cheery, facile, flimsy, floaty, gentle, ignite, kindle, lively, lustre, manner, modest, nimble, pastel, porous, scanty, settle, slight, turn on **07** amusing, animate, buoyant, cheer up, cresset, crumbly, daytime, friable, glowing, insight, lantern, lenient, lighten, lighter, light up, shining, sunrise, trivial, well-lit, whitish **08** approach, bleached, brighten, carefree, cheerful, cockcrow, daybreak, daylight, delicate, dismount, feathery, graceful, humorous, lambency, luminous, moderate, pleasing, portable, radiance, switch on, trifling, unchaste, untaxing **09** brilliant, dimension, diverting, easily dug, frivolous, irradiate, knowledge, set alight, set fire to, unheeding, worthless **10** brightness, brilliance, digestible, effortless, effulgence, first light, flashlight, floodlight, illuminate, luminosity, set burning, unexacting, weightless **11** crack of dawn, easily moved, elucidation, explanation, illuminated, lightweight, point of view, superficial, undemanding, unimportant **12** easy to digest, entertaining, illumination, light-hearted, luminescence, make cheerful **13** comprehension, enlightenment, incandescence, insubstantial, understanding **14** inconsiderable **15** inconsequential
• **bring to light** **04** rout **06** exhume, expose, notice, reveal **07** uncover, unearth **08** disclose, discover, disinter, exhumate **09** make known
• **come to light** **09** be exposed, be noticed, transpire **11** be made known, be uncovered **12** be discovered **13** become obvious
• **in the light of** **08** in view of **09** because of **11** considering, remembering **13** bearing in mind, keeping in mind **14** being mindful of
• **light on, light upon** **04** find, spot **05** hit on **06** notice **08** chance on, discover **09** encounter, stumble on **10** come across, happen upon
• **shed light on, throw light on, cast light on** **07** clarify, enlight, explain **09** elucidate, make clear, make plain **10** illuminate
• **speck of light** **04** peep

**lighten**
**04** calm, ease, glow, lift **05** allay, cheer, elate, shine **06** buoy up, lessen, perk up, reduce, revive, unload, uplift **07** assuage, cheer up, gladden, hearten, inspire, light up, relieve, restore **08** brighten, illumine, inspirit, levigate, mitigate **09** alleviate, encourage **10** illuminate **11** make lighter **12** make brighter
• **lighten up** **04** cool **05** chill, relax **06** unwind **08** calm down, chill out **09** hang loose **10** take it easy **13** let yourself go, put your feet up

**lighter**
**04** pram **05** barge, praam, Zippo **07** gondola, pontoon

**light-fingered**
**03** sly **06** crafty, shifty **07** crooked, furtive **08** filching, stealing, thieving, thievish **09** dishonest, pilfering **11** shoplifting

**light-footed**
**04** deft, spry **05** agile, lithe, swift **06** active, nimble **08** graceful **09** sprightly

**light-headed**
**04** airy **05** dizzy, faint, giddy, silly, woozy **07** flighty, foolish, shallow, vacuous **08** flippant, trifling, unsteady **09** airheaded, delirious, frivolous **11** empty-headed, superficial, thoughtless, vertiginous **14** feather-brained, scatter-brained

**light-hearted**
**03** gay **04** glad, high **05** happy, jolly, merry, sunny **06** blithe, bouncy, bright, chirpy, elated, jocund, jovial, joyful **07** amusing, playful **08** carefree, cheerful **10** frolicsome, untroubled **12** entertaining, happy-go-lucky **13** inconsiderate, in good spirits, in high spirits, irresponsible
• **light-heartedness** **06** levity

**lighthouse**
**05** fanal, phare, tower **06** beacon, pharos **12** danger signal **13** warning signal

**lightly**
**05** gaily **06** airily, easily, gently, mildly, softly, thinly **07** faintly, readily **08** breezily, casually, facilely, gingerly, slightly, sparsely **09** leniently, sparingly **10** carelessly, delicately, flippantly, heedlessly **11** frivolously, slightingly **12** effortlessly **13** thoughtlessly

**lightness**
**05** grace **06** gaiety, levity **07** agility **08** airiness, buoyancy, deftness, delicacy, mildness, porosity, thinness **09** animation, frivolity, litheness, sandiness **10** blitheness, cheeriness, fickleness, flimsiness, gentleness, liveliness, nimbleness, porousness, slightness, triviality **11** crumbliness **12** cheerfulness, delicateness, gracefulness **14** weightlessness

**lightning**
**04** fire **05** levin **08** fireball, wildfire **11** fulguration, thunderbolt, thunderclap, thunderdart

**12** thunderstorm **13** ball lightning, clap of thunder, electric storm **14** chain lightning, sheet lightning **15** forked lightning, lightning strike, summer lightning, zigzag lightning
• **like lightning** **07** a rocket, hastily, quickly, rapidly **08** speedily, wildfire **11** immediately

**lightweight**
**02** oz **04** thin **05** light, petty **06** flimsy, paltry, slight **07** trivial **08** delicate, feathery, nugatory, trifling **09** worthless **10** negligible, weightless **11** unimportant **13** insignificant, insubstantial **15** inconsequential

**likable, likeable**
**04** nice **06** genial **07** amiable, lovable, winning, winsome **08** charming, engaging, friendly, loveable, pleasant, pleasing **09** agreeable, appealing, congenial **10** attractive, personable **11** sympathetic

**like**
**02** as **03** à la, dig **04** akin, love, mate, peer, same, true, twin, want, wish **05** adore, alike, enjoy, equal, fancy, go for, match, prize, usual **06** admire, allied, choose, desire, esteem, fellow, normal, prefer, relish, select, such as, take to **07** approve, care for, cherish, of a kind, related, revel in, similar, suiting, typical, welcome **08** appeal to, be fond of, be keen on, decide on, hold dear, parallel, relating **09** analogous, befitting, delight in, identical, similar to **10** appreciate, comparable, equivalent, for example, resembling **11** counterpart, for instance, go a bundle on, much the same, would rather, would sooner **12** feel inclined, find pleasant, on the lines of, take a shine to, take kindly to **13** approximating, corresponding, find enjoyable **14** by way of example, characteristic, find attractive, in the same way as, opposite number, take pleasure in **15** along the lines of, find interesting

**likeable**
*see* **likable**

**likelihood**
**06** chance **08** prospect **09** liability **10** likeliness **11** possibility, probability

**likely**
**03** apt, fit **04** fair **05** prone, right **06** liable, odds-on, proper **07** fitting, hopeful, in order, no doubt, tending **08** credible, expected, feasible, inclined, pleasing, possible, probable, probably **09** in the wind, plausible, promising **10** acceptable, believable, calculated, on the cards, presumably, reasonable **11** anticipated, appropriate, doubtlessly, foreseeable, likely as not, predictable **12** to be expected **13** as likely as not

**like-minded**
**08** agreeing, in accord **09** in harmony, in rapport, of one mind, unanimous **10** compatible, harmonious **11** in agreement **13** of the same mind

## liken
**04** like, link **05** match **06** equate, relate
**07** compare **08** parallel, similize
**09** analogize, associate, correlate,
juxtapose, set beside

## likeness
**04** bust, copy, form, icon **05** guise,
image, shape, study **06** effigy, sketch,
statue **07** analogy, drawing, picture,
replica **08** affinity, painting, portrait
**09** depiction, facsimile, sculpture,
semblance **10** appearance, caricature,
comparison, expression, photograph,
similarity, similitude, simulacrum
**11** counterpart, parallelism,
personation, portraiture, resemblance
**12** reproduction **14** correspondence,
representation

## likewise
**02** do, so **03** als, eke, too **04** also, item
**05** ditto **06** as also, to boot **07** besides,
further **08** moreover, same here
**09** similarly **10** in addition
**11** furthermore **12** in like manner, in
the same way **14** by the same token
**15** in the same manner

## liking
**04** bent, bias, broo, brow, love
**05** fancy, taste, thing **06** desire, notion,
palate **07** leaning **08** affinity, fondness,
penchant, soft spot, tendency,
weakness **09** affection, proneness
**10** attraction, partiality, preference,
proclivity, propensity **11** inclination
**12** appreciation, predilection,
satisfaction

## lilac
**07** laylock, syringa **08** pipe-tree

## lilt
**03** air, hum **04** beat, lill, song, sway
**05** swing **06** rhythm **07** cadence,
measure **10** fingerhole **11** rise and fall

## lily

*Lilies include:*

**03** day, may
**04** aloe, arum, pond, sego
**05** calla, camas, lotus, regal, tiger,
torch, yucca
**06** camash, camass, Canada,
crinum, Easter, Nuphar, scilla,
smilax
**07** candock, day-lily, Madonna,
may-lily, quamash, Tritoma
**08** asphodel, galtonia, gloriosa,
hyacinth, martagon, nenuphar,
Phormium, trillium, Turk's cap,
victoria
**09** amaryllis, grass tree, herb-Paris,
kniphofia, Richardia
**10** agapanthus, aspidistra,
belladonna, fritillary
**11** cabbage-tree, Convallaria,
Madonna-lily, red-hot poker,
spatterdock
**12** Annunciation, Hemerocallis,
Solomon's seal, zantedeschia
**13** butcher's broom, lily of the Nile
**15** lily of the valley, star of
Bethlehem

• **lily leaf 03** pad

## lily-white
**04** pure **06** chaste, virgin **08** innocent,
spotless, virtuous **09** blameless,
faultless, incorrupt, milk-white,
uncorrupt, unsullied, untainted
**11** uncorrupted, untarnished
**14** irreproachable

## Lima
**01** L

## limb
**03** arm, leg **04** edge, fork, part, spur,
wing **05** bough, spald, spall, spaul
**06** border, branch, member, spalle,
spauld **07** flipper, quarter, section
**08** offshoot **09** appendage, extension,
extremity, pterygium **10** projection
• **out on a limb 07** exposed
**08** isolated **10** vulnerable **15** in a weak
position

## limber
**05** agile, lithe **06** lissom, pliant, supple
**07** elastic, plastic, pliable **08** flexible,
graceful **11** loose-limbed **12** loose-
jointed
• **limber up 06** warm up **07** prepare,
work out **08** exercise, loosen up

## limbo
• **in limbo 10** in abeyance, up in the
air **11** left hanging **12** left in the air
**14** awaiting action **15** on the back
burner

## lime
**04** bass, bast, lind, line, teil, trap
**05** leash, Tilia **06** linden, loiter, temper,
viscum **07** ensnare **08** basswood

## limelight
**04** fame **06** notice, renown **07** stardom
**08** eminence **09** attention, celebrity,
public eye, publicity, spotlight
**10** notability, prominence
**11** recognition

## limestone
**03** cam **04** calm, calp, caum **06** kunkar,
kunkur, oolite **07** coquina, scaglia
**08** Coral Rag, dolomite **09** caen-stone,
coral-rock, cornbrash, cornstone
**10** Kentish rag, stinkstone, travertine
**11** cement-stone, rottenstone,
sarcophagus **12** Forest Marble,
Purbeck stone **13** Purbeck marble
**15** coralline oolite, Kentish ragstone,
landscape-marble

## limit
◇ *containment indicator* ◇ *tail deletion
indicator* ◇ *ends selection indicator*
**03** cap, end, lid, rim, tie **04** brim, curb,
edge, goal, gole, line, mete, pale, rein,
roof, term **05** bound, brink, check, hem
in, stint, Thule, verge **06** border,
bounds, bridle, hinder, impede,
margin, ration, reduce, region, tropic,
utmost **07** appoint, ceiling, compass,
confine, contain, control, delimit,
extreme, margent, maximum, outside,
specify **08** boundary, confines,
deadline, division, frontier, outgoing,
restrain, restrict, terminus, ultimate
**09** condition, constrain, demarcate,
determine, extremity, perimeter,
prescribe, restraint, threshold
**10** constraint, limitation, parameters

**11** cut-off point, demarcation,
demarkation, hold in check, keep in
check, restriction, termination, ultima
Thule **12** circumscribe **14** greatest
amount, greatest extent **15** saturation
point
• **extend beyond limit 03** lap
• **the limit 06** enough, the end, utmost
**07** too much **08** the worst
**11** intolerable, the final bow **12** the
final blow, the last straw

## limitation
**04** curb, snag, tail **05** block, check
**06** burden, defect **07** control, reserve
**08** drawback, tail male, weakness
**09** condition, hindrance, inability,
restraint, weak point **10** constraint,
impediment, inadequacy
**11** demarcation, reservation,
restriction, shortcoming
**12** delimitation, disadvantage,
imperfection, incapability
**13** qualification **15** circumscription

## limited
◇ *ends deletion indicator* **03** Ltd **04** tail,
tyde **05** basic, borné, fixed, small
**06** finite, narrow, scanty **07** checked,
defined, minimal **08** confined
**09** blinkered, imperfect, qualified
**10** controlled, inadequate, incomplete,
restricted **11** constrained, determinate
**12** insufficient **13** circumscribed

## limitless
◇ *ends deletion indicator* ◇ *head deletion
indicator* ◇ *tail deletion indicator* **04** vast
**06** untold **07** endless, immense
**08** infinite, unending **09** boundless,
countless, illimited, unbounded,
undefined, unlimited **10** bottomless
**11** measureless, never-ending,
unspecified **12** immeasurable,
incalculable, interminable
**13** inexhaustible

## limp
**03** dot, hop, lax **04** flop, gimp, halt,
lank, soft, weak **05** frail, hilch, hitch,
loose, slack, spent, tired, weary
**06** falter, feeble, flabby, flaggy, floppy,
hamble, hobble, limber, totter
**07** flaccid, pliable, relaxed, shamble,
shuffle, stagger, stumble, worn out
**08** drooping, fatigued, flexible,
lameness **09** enervated, exhausted,
lethargic, out of curl **10** uneven walk
**11** debilitated, out of energy
**12** claudication, walk unevenly
**13** walk with a limp

## limpid
**04** pure **05** clear, lucid, plain, still
**06** bright, glassy **07** flowing
**08** coherent, pellucid **09** unruffled
**10** untroubled **11** translucent,
transparent **12** crystal-clear, intelligible
**14** comprehensible

## limply
**06** softly **07** loosely, slackly **08** flabbily,
flexibly **09** flaccidly

## limpness
**06** laxity **09** looseness, slackness
**10** flabbiness, flaccidity **11** flaccidness,
flexibility **12** claudication

## Lincoln
03 Abe

## line
01 l 03 bar, job, ley, pad, rew, rim, row, way 04 area, axis, back, band, bank, belt, book, card, ceil, ciel, cord, dash, draw, edge, face, file, fill, firm, flax, kind, lind, make, mark, memo, note, oche, part, path, race, rank, role, rope, rule, seam, side, sort, talk, text, tier, type, wire, word, work 05 bound, brand, breed, cable, canon, chain, cover, e-mail, field, forte, front, hatch, inlay, limit, panel, pitch, queue, route, score, shape, skirt, slash, spiel, stock, story, strip, stuff, style, track, trade, trail, twine, verge, words 06 avenue, belief, border, career, column, course, crease, encase, family, figure, fringe, furrow, groove, letter, margin, method, parade, patter, policy, report, scheme, script, series, strain, strand, streak, string, stripe, stroke, system, thread 07 calling, channel, company, contour, descent, lineage, message, outline, pattern, profile, pursuit, scratch, variety, wrinkle 08 activity, ancestry, approach, attitude, boundary, business, defences, filament, frontier, heritage, ideology, inscribe, interest, libretto, pedigree, position, postcard, practice, province, sequence, vocation 09 crow's feet, direction, formation, front line, parentage, perimeter, periphery, procedure, reinforce, sales talk, specialty, technique, underline 10 appearance, battle zone, borderline, department, employment, extraction, firing-line, line of work, memorandum, occupation, procession, profession, silhouette, specialism, speciality, strengthen, succession, trajectory, underscore 11 battlefield, corrugation, delineation, demarcation, information 12 battleground 13 configuration, modus operandi 14 course of action, line of business, specialization 15 draughtsmanship

See also **poetry; railway**
• **curved line** 03 tie
• **draw the line** 05 limit 06 refuse, reject 07 exclude, rule out, say no to 08 say not to 09 stand firm 11 stop short of 15 put your foot down
• **fishing line** 04 gimp, gymp 05 guimp
• **in line** 03 due 06 in a row, in step, likely 08 in accord, in a queue, in series 09 in a column, in harmony 10 on the cards 11 in agreement 12 in the running 15 being considered
• **lay on the line, put on the line** 04 risk 07 imperil 08 endanger 10 jeopardize 13 put in jeopardy
• **line up** 05 align, array, group, lay on, order, queue, range 06 fall in, obtain, secure 07 arrange, marshal, prepare, procure, produce, queue up 08 assemble, organize, regiment 09 form ranks 10 form a queue, straighten, wait in line 11 stand in line
• **new line** 03 zag

• **toe the line** 07 conform 12 keep the rules 14 be conventional, follow the rules

## lineage
04 line, race 05 birth, breed, house, stock 06 family, parage 07 descent, lignage, progeny 08 ancestry, heredity, pedigree 09 ancestors, forebears, genealogy, offspring, whakapapa 10 descending, extraction, succession 11 descendants

## lineaments
04 face 05 lines 06 aspect, traits, visage 07 outline, profile 08 features, outlines 10 appearance 11 countenance, physiognomy 13 configuration

## lined
04 worn 05 feint, ruled 07 creased, wizened 08 furrowed, wrinkled

## linen
04 duck, ecru, harn, lawn, line, lint, snow 05 crash, drill, toile 06 byssus, damask, dowlas, napery, sendal, sheets, sindon, whites 07 byssine, cambric, dornick, drabbet, holland, lockram, napkins, silesia 08 bed linen, drilling, gambroon, marcella, osnaburg 09 huckaback, Moygashel®, tea towels 10 seersucker, table linen, white goods 11 pillowcases, tablecloths
• **measure of linen** 03 lay, lea, ley
• **strip of linen** 04 amis 05 amice

## liner
04 boat, ship 07 steamer 10 cruise ship

## linesman
04 poet 06 author, writer

## line-up
03 row 04 bill, cast, line, list, team 05 array, queue 09 selection 11 arrangement

## linger
03 lag 04 hang, hove, idle, last, lurk, stay, stop, wait 05 dally, delay, hoove, hover, tarry 06 dawdle, endure, hang on, hanker, loiter, remain, taigle 07 hold out, persist, survive 08 continue, smoulder, straggle 10 dilly-dally, hang around 11 stick around 12 take your time 13 procrastinate
• **linger on scent** 03 tie

## lingerie
03 bra 04 slip 05 teddy 06 smalls, undies 07 panties 08 camisole, frillies, half-slip, knickers, scanties 09 brassiere, underwear 11 panty girdle 12 body stocking, camiknickers, underclothes 13 suspender belt, underclothing, undergarments 14 inexpressibles, unmentionables

## lingering
04 slow 08 dragging 09 prolonged, remaining, surviving 10 persistent, persisting, protracted 11 languishing 12 long-drawn-out

## lingo
03 bat 04 cant, talk 05 argot, idiom 06 jargon, patois, patter, speech, tongue 07 dialect 08 language,

parlance 10 mumbo-jumbo, vernacular, vocabulary 11 terminology

## liniment
04 balm, wash 05 cream, salve 06 balsam, lotion 07 unguent 08 ointment 09 carron oil, emollient, opodeldoc 11 embrocation 14 camphorated oil

## lining
◊ insertion indicator 03 lag 04 cush 05 inlay, stean, steen, stein 06 casing, facing, fettle 07 backing, cushion, furring, padding, sarking, tubbing 08 brattice, brattish, brettice, doublure, steaning, steening, steining, wainscot 09 alignment, panelling 10 encasement, incasement, stiffening 11 interfacing 13 reinforcement

## link
03 map, tie 04 ally, bind, bond, join, knot, loop, part, ring, yoke 05 cleek, joint, merge, piece, tie-up, torch, union, unite 06 attach, bridge, couple, fasten, hook up, liaise, member, relate, swivel, team up 07 bracket, connect, element, enchain, hot line, liaison, network, shackle 08 division, identify, osculate 09 air-bridge, associate, carabiner, component, interlink, karabiner 10 amalgamate, attachment, connection, join forces 11 association, concatenate, constituent, partnership 12 relationship 13 communication, concatenation
• **link up** 04 ally, dock, join 05 merge, unify 06 bridge, hook up, join up, meet up, team up 07 connect, network 10 amalgamate, join forces

## linkage
03 tie 04 bond, knot 05 joint, tie-in, tie-up, union 06 merger 07 liaison 08 alliance 09 valve gear 10 attachment, connection 11 association, partnership 12 amalgamation, relationship 13 communication

## link-up
05 tie-in, union 06 merger 08 alliance 10 connection 11 association, partnership 12 amalgamation, relationship

## lion
03 Leo 05 Aslan 12 king of beasts
• **lion's share** 04 bulk, mass, most 08 main part, majority 09 almost all, nearly all 11 largest part 12 greatest part 13 preponderance

## lion-hearted
04 bold 05 brave 06 daring, heroic 07 gallant, valiant 08 fearless, intrepid, resolute, stalwart, valorous 09 dauntless, dreadless 10 courageous 12 stout-hearted

## lionize
04 fête 05 exalt 06 honour, praise 07 acclaim, adulate, glorify, idolize, magnify 08 eulogize 09 celebrate 10 aggrandize 11 hero-worship 12 treat as a hero 14 put on a pedestal

## lip
03 jib, lap, rim 04 brim, edge, flew,

kiss, lave **05** brink, cheek, mouth, sauce, spout, verge **06** border, fipple, helmet, labium, labrum, ligula, margin, muffle **07** corolla, hare-lip **08** attitude, backchat, labellum, rudeness, underlip **09** impudence, insolence, submentum **10** effrontery **12** impertinence

**lippy**
**04** pert **05** fresh, sassy, saucy **06** brazen, cheeky, lippie, mouthy **07** forward **08** impudent, insolent **09** audacious **11** impertinent **12** overfamiliar **13** disrespectful

**liquefaction**
**06** fusion **07** melting, thawing **08** solation, syntexis **10** dissolving, karyolysis, liquefying **11** dissolution **13** deliquescence

**liquefy**
**03** run **04** flux, fuse, melt, thaw **05** smelt **08** dissolve, fluidize, liquesce **09** liquidize **10** deliquesce

**liqueur**

*Liqueurs include:*

**04** ouzo
**05** Aurum®, noyau
**06** Glayva®, Kahlúa®, kirsch, kümmel, Malibu®, Midori®, pastis, Pernod®
**07** Baileys®, curaçao, ratafia, sambuca
**08** absinthe, advocaat, amaretto, anisette, Drambuie®, Galliano®, Tia Maria®
**09** Cointreau®, mirabelle, Triple sec
**10** Chartreuse®, limoncello, maraschino
**11** Benedictine
**12** cherry brandy, crème de cacao, Grand Marnier®, kirschwasser, Parfait Amour
**13** crème de cassis, crème de menthe, Cuarenta y Tres
**15** Southern Comfort®

*See also* **cocktail; spirits**

**liquid**
**02** aq **03** sap, wet **04** even, pure, thin **05** clear, drink, fluid, juice, moist, runny **06** liquor, lotion, mellow, melted, molten, sloppy, smooth, steady, thawed, watery **07** aqueous, flowing, hydrous, regular, running, unfixed **08** solution, unbroken **09** liquefied, melodious **12** indisputable **13** uninterrupted
• **coloured liquid 03** dye, ink
• **liquid for washing 03** lye

**liquidate**
**03** pay **04** kill, sell **05** clear **06** cash in, murder, pay off, remove, rub out, wind up **07** abolish, break up, destroy, disband, sell off, wipe out **08** dispatch, dissolve, massacre **09** close down, discharge, eliminate, finish off, terminate **10** annihilate, do away with, put an end to **11** assassinate, exterminate **13** convert to cash

**liquidize**
**03** mix **05** blend, cream, crush, purée **07** process **10** synthesize

**liquor**
**03** liq **04** bree, broo, grog, malt, vino **05** boose, booze, bouse, broth, drink, gravy, hogan, hogen, hooch, juice, plonk, sauce, stock, tinct, turps **06** hootch, liquid, porter, rotgut, strunt, tiddly, tipple **07** alcohol, essence, extract, hokonui, shicker, spirits **08** infusion, potation **09** firewater, hard stuff, stiffener, stimulant, the bottle **10** intoxicant **11** aguardiente, jungle juice, strong drink, the creature, tickle-brain **12** Dutch courage
*See also* **drink**
• **liquor house** *see* **public house**

**liquorice**
**07** nail-rod, pomfret **09** jequirity, sugarally **10** sugarallie

**lissom**
**05** agile, light, lithe **06** limber, nimble, pliant, supple, svelte **07** pliable, willowy **08** flexible, graceful **09** lithesome **11** loose-limbed **12** loose-jointed

**list**
◇ *homophone indicator* **03** tip **04** bill, book, cant, file, heel, lean, leet, menu, note, roll, roon, rota, tilt **05** enrol, enter, index, slant, slate, slope, strip, table, tally **06** agenda, border, fillet, litany, recipe, record, roster, scroll, series, stripe **07** compile, incline, invoice, itemize, listing, scedule, selvage, set down **08** boundary, calendar, classify, contents, heel over, lean over, register, schedule, syllabus, tabulate **09** catalogue, checklist, directory, enumerate, inventory, programme, write down **10** tabulation **11** alphabetize, enumeration
*See also* **lean**

**listen**
◇ *homophone indicator* **04** hark, hear, heed, lest, list, mind **05** lithe **06** attend, intend **07** give ear, hearken, monitor **09** eavesdrop, lend an ear **10** auscultate, get a load of, take notice **12** pay attention **15** prick up your ears
• **listen in** ◇ *homophone indicator* **03** bug, tap **07** monitor, wiretap **08** overhear **09** eavesdrop **15** pin back your ears, prick up your ears

**listener**
**03** ear

**listless**
**04** dull, limp, waff **05** bored, heavy, inert **06** mopish, torpid, vacant **07** languid, passive **08** inactive, indolent, lifeless, sluggish, thowless, toneless **09** apathetic, depressed, enervated, impassive, lethargic, upsitting **10** spiritless **11** indifferent, languishing **12** uninterested **13** lackadaisical

**listlessly**
**05** dully **06** limply **07** inertly **09** passively **10** inactively, lifelessly, sluggishly **11** impassively **12** spiritlessly

**13** apathetically, lacking energy, lethargically

**listlessness**
**05** ennui, sloth **06** acedia, apathy, torpor **07** languor, vacuity **08** lethargy **09** indolence, torpidity, upsitting **10** enervation, supineness **11** inattention, languidness **12** indifference, lifelessness, sluggishness **14** spiritlessness

**lit**
◇ *anagram indicator* **02** in **05** drunk, light, merry, tight, tipsy **06** ablaze, blotto, rested, soused **07** drunken, legless, pickled, settled, sloshed, sozzled, squiffy **09** crapulent, paralytic, plastered **10** dismounted, inebriated **11** intoxicated

**litany**
**04** list **06** prayer **07** account, recital, synapte **08** devotion, irenicon, petition **09** catalogue, eirenicon **10** invocation, procession, recitation, repetition **11** enumeration **12** supplication

**literacy**
**07** culture **08** learning **09** education, erudition, knowledge **10** articulacy **11** cultivation, learnedness, proficiency, scholarship **12** intelligence **13** ability to read **14** ability to write, articulateness

**literal**
**03** lit **04** dull, true, typo **05** clear, close, error, exact, plain **06** actual, boring, strict, verbal **07** erratum, factual, genuine, humdrum, mistake, precise, prosaic, tedious **08** accurate, faithful, misprint, verbatim **10** colourless, uninspired **11** corrigendum, down-to-earth, undistorted, unvarnished, word-for-word **12** matter-of-fact **13** printing error, unembellished, unexaggerated, unimaginative

**literalism**
**06** letter **09** biblicism, verbalism **10** textualism **13** scripturalism **14** exact rendering, fundamentalism, letter of the law

**literally**
**03** lit **05** truly **06** really **07** closely, exactly, plainly **08** actually, strictly, verbatim **09** certainly, precisely **10** faithfully **11** to the letter, word for word

**literary**
**03** lit **06** formal, poetic **07** bookish, erudite, learned, refined, written **08** cultured, educated, lettered, literate, literose, well-read **09** scholarly **10** cultivated, epistolary, widely-read **12** old-fashioned

*Literary characters include:*

**02** Pi
**03** Eva (Little), **Fox** (Brer), **Jim** (Lord), **Kaa**, **Kim**, **Lee** (Lorelei), **Pan** (Peter), **Pip**, **Roo**, **Tom** (Uncle), **Una**
**04** Ahab (Captain), **Bede** (Adam), **Bond** (James), **Budd** (Billy), **Dent** (Arthur), **Eyre** (Jane), **Finn** (Huckleberry), **Finn** (Phineas), **Fogg**

(Phileas), **Gamp** (Sarah), **Gray** (Charlotte), **Gray** (Dorian), **Gunn** (Ben), **Haze** (Dolores), **Heep** (Uriah), **Hood** (Robin), **Hook** (Captain), **Hyde** (Mister), **Jack**, **Mole** (Adrian), **Pooh**, **Pope** (Giant), **Ridd** (John), **Slop** (Doctor), **Tigg** (Montague), **Toad** (Mister), **Trim** (Corporal), **Troy** (Sergeant Francis), **Tuck** (Friar), **Wilt** (Henry)

05 **Akela**, **Aslan**, **Athos**, **Avery** (Shug), **Baloo**, **Bates** (Miss), **Bloom** (Leopold), **Bloom** (Molly), **Boxer**, **Brown** (Father), **Celie**, **Chips** (Mister), **Clare** (Angel), **Darcy** (Fitzwilliam), **Darcy** (Mark), **Doone** (Lorna), **Drood** (Edwin), **Flint** (Captain), **Geste** (Beau), **Jones** (Bridget), **Jones** (Tom), **Kanga**, **Kipps** (Arthur), **Loman** (Willy), **Lucky**, **March** (Amy, Beth, Jo and Meg), **Maria** (Mad), **Mitty** (Walter), **Moore** (Mrs), **Mosca**, **Nancy**, **O'Hara** (Kimball), **O'Hara** (Scarlett), **Parry** (Will), **Piggy**, **Polly** (Alfred), **Porgy**, **Pozzo**, **Price** (Fanny), **Quilp** (Daniel), **Ralph**, **Ratty**, **Rebus** (Inspector John), **Remus** (Uncle), **Rudge** (Barnaby), **Satan**, **Sharp** (Becky), **Sikes** (Bill), **Slope** (Reverend Obadiah), **Sloth**, **Smike**, **Smith** (Winston), **Spade** (Sam), **Stubb**, **Tarka** (the Otter), **Titus**, **Topsy**, **Trent** (Little Nell), **Twist** (Oliver), **Wonka** (Willy), **Yahoo**

06 **Aramis**, **Archer** (Isabel), **Arthur** (King), **Badger**, **Barkis**, **Belial**, **Bennet** (Elizabeth), **Bourgh** (Lady Catherine de), **Bovary** (Emma), **Brodie** (Miss Jean), **Brooke** (Dorothea), **Bucket** (Charlie), **Bumble** (Mister), **Bumppo** (Natty), **Bunter** (Billy), **Butler** (Rhett), **Carton** (Sydney), **Crusoe** (Robinson), **Dombey** (Paul), **Dorrit** (Amy), **Dorrit** (William), **Du Bois** (Blanche), **Eeyore**, **Friday** (Man), **Gamgee** (Sam), **Gatsby** (Jay), **Gawain**, **Gollum**, **Grimes**, **Hagrid** (Rubeus), **Hannay** (Richard), **Holmes** (Sherlock), **Jeeves** (Reginald), **Jekyll** (Doctor Henry), **Legree** (Simon), **Little** (Vernon Gregory), **Lolita**, **Marley** (Jacob), **Marner** (Silas), **Marple** (Jane), **Morant** ('Breaker'), **Moreau** (Doctor), **Mowgli**, **Omnium** (Duke of), **Pickle** (Gamaliel), **Pickle** (Peregrine), **Piglet**, **Pinkie**, **Pliant** (Dame), **Poirot** (Hercule), **Potter** (Harry), **Rabbit**, **Random** (Roderick), **Rob Roy**, **Salmon** (Susie), **Sawyer** (Bob), **Sawyer** (Tom), **Shandy** (Tristram), **Silver** (Long John), **Subtle**, **Tarzan**, **Tigger**, **Tybalt**, **Tyrone** (James), **Varden** (Dolly), **Wadman** (Widow), **Watson** (Doctor John), **Weller** (Samuel), **Wimsey** (Lord Peter), **Wopsle** (Mister), **Yahoos**

07 **Andrews** (Pamela), **Ayeesha**, **Baggins** (Bilbo), **Baggins** (Frodo), **Beowulf**, **Biggles**, **Bramble** (Matthew), **Brer Fox**, **Bromden**

(Chief), **Clinker** (Humphry), **Corelli** (Captain Antonio), **Crackit** (Toby), **Danvers** (Mrs), **Dawkins** (Jack), **Dedalus** (Stephen), **Deronda** (Daniel), **Despair** (Giant), **Don Juan**, **Dorigen**, **Dorothy**, **Dracula** (Count), **Estella**, **Fairfax** (Jane), **Gandalf**, **Gargery** (Joe), **Granger** (Hermione), **Grendel**, **Harding** (Reverend Septimus), **Harlowe** (Clarissa), **Hawkins** (Jim), **Higgins** (Professor Henry), **Hopeful**, **Humbert** (Humbert), **Ishmael**, **Jaggers** (Mister), **Jellyby** (Mrs), **Le Fever** (Lieutenant), **Maigret** (Jules), **Marlowe** (Philip), **Mellors** (Oliver), **Newsome** (Chad), **Obadiah**, **Orlando**, **Peachum** (Thomas), **Pierrot**, **Porthos**, **Prefect** (Ford), **Proudie** (Doctor), **Raffles**, **Rebecca**, **Scarlet** (Will), **Scrooge** (Ebenezer), **Shalott** (Lady of), **Shipton** (Mother), **Slumkey** (Samuel), **Squeers** (Wackford), **Surface** (Charles), **Surface** (Joseph), **Tiny Tim**, **Weasley** (Ron), **Wemmick** (Mister), **Wickham** (George), **William**, **Witches** (The Three), **Wooster** (Bertie), **Would-be** (Sir Politic)

08 **Absolute** (Captain), **Anderson** (Pastor Anthony), **Backbite** (Sir Benjamin), **Bagheera**, **Bedivere** (Sir), **Belacqua** (Lyra), **Black Dog**, **Casaubon** (Reverend Edward), **Cratchit** (Bob), **Criseyde**, **Dalloway** (Mrs Clarissa), **Dashwood** (Elinor), **Dashwood** (Marianne), **de Winter** (Max), **de Winter** (Rebecca), **Everdene** (Bathsheba), **Faithful**, **Flanders** (Moll), **Flashman** (Harry), **Gloriana**, **Griselda** (Patient), **Gulliver** (Lemuel), **Havisham** (Miss), **Hrothgar**, **Jarndyce** (John), **Kowalski** (Stanley), **Kowalski** (Stella), **Ladislaw** (Will), **Lancelot** (Sir), **Lestrade** (Inspector), **MacHeath** (Captain), **Magwitch** (Abel), **Malaprop** (Mrs), **McMurphy** (Randle Patrick), **Micawber** (Wilkins), **Moriarty** (Dean), **Moriarty** (Professor James), **Napoleon**, **Nickleby** (Nicholas), **Paradise** (Sal), **Peggotty** (Clara), **Peterkin**, **Pickwick** (Samuel), **Queequeg**, **Ramotswe** (Precious), **Snowball**, **Starbuck**, **Svengali**, **Tashtego**, **Thatcher** (Becky), **The Clerk**, **The Friar**, **The Reeve**, **Trotwood** (Betsey), **Tulliver** (Maggie), **Twitcher** (Jemmy), **Vladimir**

09 **Archimago**, **Bounderby** (Josiah), **Britomart**, **Bulstrode** (Nicholas), **Caulfield** (Holden), **Cheeryble** (Charles), **Christian**, **Churchill** (Frank), **Constance**, **D'Artagnan**, **Doolittle** (Eliza), **Fezziwig** (Mister), **Golightly** (Holly), **Gradgrind** (Thomas), **Grandison** (Sir Charles), **Harlequin**, **Knightley** (George), **Lismahago** (Obadiah), **Lochinvar**, **Minnehaha**, **Pecksniff** (Seth), **Pendennis** (Arthur), **Pollyanna**, **Robin Hood**, **Rochester** (Edward

Fairfax), **Scudamour** (Sir), **Shere Khan**, **The Knight**, **The Miller**, **The Squire**, **The Walrus**, **Tiger Lily**, **Trelawney** (Squire), **Van Winkle** (Rip), **Voldemort** (Lord), **Woodhouse** (Emma), **Yossarian** (Captain John), **Zenocrate**

10 **Allan-a-Dale**, **Big Brother**, **Brer Rabbit**, **Challenger** (Professor), **Chatterley** (Lady Constance), **Chuzzlewit** (Martin), **Dumbledore** (Albus), **Evangelist**, **Fauntleroy** (Little Lord), **Great-heart** (Mister), **Heathcliff**, **Hornblower** (Horatio), **Houyhnhnms**, **Little John**, **Little Nell**, **Maid Marian**, **Quatermain** (Allan), **The Red King**, **The Tar Baby**, **Tinkerbell**, **Tweedledee**, **Tweedledum**

11 **Copperfield** (David), **D'Urberville** (Alec), **Durbeyfield** (Tess), **Mickey Mouse**, **Mutabilitie**, **Pumblechook** (Mister), **The Dormouse**, **The Franklin**, **The Man of Law**, **The Merchant**, **The Pardoner**, **The Prioress**, **The Red Queen**, **The Summoner**, **Tiggy-Winkle** (Mrs)

12 **Blatant Beast**, **Chaunticleer**, **Frankenstein** (Victor), **Humpty-Dumpty**, **Lilliputians**, **Osbaldistone** (Francis), **Rip Van Winkle**, **Silvertongue** (Lyra), **The Carpenter**, **The Mad Hatter**, **The March Hare**, **The Pied Piper** (of Hamelin), **The Red Knight**, **The Scarecrow**

13 **The Jabberwock**, **The Mock Turtle**, **The Tin Woodman**, **The Wife of Bath**, **Winnie-the-Pooh**

14 **Mephistopheles**, **Rikki-Tikki-Tavi**, **The White Rabbit**, **Worldly Wiseman** (Mister)

15 **The Artful Dodger**, **The Cowardly Lion**, **The Three Witches**, **Valiant-for-Truth**

*See also* **Shakespeare**

*Literary critics include:*

04 **Bell** (Clive), **Blum** (Léon), **Frye** (Northrop)
05 **Hicks** (Granville), **Lodge** (David), **Stead** (C K)
06 **Arnold** (Matthew), **Calder** (Angus), **Empson** (Sir William), **Leavis** (F R), **Leavis** (Q D), **Lukacs** (Georg), **Sontag** (Susan), **Wilson** (Edmund)
07 **Ackroyd** (Peter), **Alvarez** (A), **Barthes** (Roland), **Daiches** (David), **Derrida** (Jacques), **Hoggart** (Richard), **Kermode** (Frank)
08 **Bradbury** (Sir Malcolm), **Eagleton** (Terry), **Longinus**, **Nicolson** (Sir Harold), **Richards** (I A), **Trilling** (Lionel), **Williams** (Raymond)
10 **Saintsbury** (George Edward Bateman)
11 **Matthiessen** (F O), **Sainte-Beuve** (Charles Augustin)

• **literary work** 04 book, poem 05 essay 07 article

**literate**
07 learned 08 cultured, educated 09 scholarly 10 able to read, proficient

**11** able to write, intelligent
**12** intellectual, well-educated
**13** knowledgeable
• **Literate in Arts 02** LA **03** LLA

## literati

**06** brains **08** eggheads **09** academics, highbrows **10** illuminati, the erudite, the learned **11** cognoscenti, the studious **12** men of letters, the scholarly **13** intellectuals **14** intelligentsia, women of letters **15** the well-informed

## literature

**03** lit **04** bumf, data, page **05** facts, paper **06** papers **07** hand-out, leaflet, letters **08** brochure, circular, hand-outs, leaflets, pamphlet, writings **09** brochures, circulars, pamphlets **11** information **12** printed works **13** printed matter **14** published works

*Literature types include:*

**04** epic, play, saga
**05** drama, essay, novel, prose, verse
**06** comedy, parody, poetry, satire, thesis
**07** aga-saga, epistle, fantasy, fiction, lampoon, novella, polemic, tragedy, trilogy
**08** allegory, chick lit, libretto, pastiche, treatise
**09** anti-novel, biography, children's, novelette
**10** fan fiction, magnum opus, non-fiction, roman à clef, short story, travelogue
**11** black comedy, Gothic novel, pulp fiction
**12** bodice-ripper, crime fiction
**13** autobiography, belles-lettres, Bildungsroman, penny dreadful, travel writing
**14** science fiction
**15** epistolary novel, historical novel, picaresque novel

## lithe

**05** agile **06** limber, lissom, listen, pliant, supple, svelte **07** lissome, pliable **08** flexible **09** lithesome **11** loose-limbed **12** loose-jointed **13** double-jointed

## lithium

**02** Li

## Lithuania

**02** LT **03** LTU **04** Lith

## litigant

**05** party **08** claimant, opponent **09** contender, disputant, litigator, plaintiff **10** contestant **11** complainant

## litigate

**03** sue

## litigation

**03** law **04** case, suit **06** action **07** dispute, lawsuit, process **09** legal case **10** contention **11** legal action, prosecution

## litigious

**10** disputable **11** belligerent, contentious, quarrelsome **12** disputatious **13** argumentative

## litter

**03** bed, hay **04** grot, junk, mess, muck, team, teme **05** brood, chaff, issue, sedan, straw, strew, trash, wagon, waste, young **06** debris, doolie, family, farrow, jumble, kindle, mahmal, mess up, refuse, shreds **07** bedding, bracken, cacolet, clutter, garbage, progeny, rubbish, scatter **08** brancard, detritus, disarray, disorder, shambles **09** confusion, fragments, offspring, palankeen, palanquin, stretcher **10** light couch, make untidy, untidiness **11** make a mess of, odds and ends

## little

**03** bit, dab, sma, wee **04** baby, curn, cute, dash, drop, hint, leet, lite, lyte, mini, nice, poco, some, spot, tine, tiny, tyne, whit **05** brief, chota, dwarf, minor, petty, pinch, scant, short, small, speck, sweet, taste, teeny, touch, trace, young **06** barely, hardly, junior, meagre, midget, minute, paltry, petite, rarely, seldom, skimpy, slight, sparse, trifle **07** faintly, modicum, nominal, not much, passing, peanuts, shortly, slender, soupçon, trickle, trivial, younger **08** exiguous, fleeting, fragment, nugatory, particle, pint-size, pleasant, scarcely, skerrick, slightly, trifling **09** ephemeral, miniature, momentary, pint-sized, tiny weeny, transient **10** attractive, diminutive, negligible, short-lived, smattering, transitory **11** Lilliputian, microscopic, small amount, unimportant **12** infrequently, insufficient **13** infinitesimal, insignificant, next to nothing **14** inconsiderable **15** a drop in the ocean

*See also* **small**
• **a little 03** tad **04** some
• **little by little 04** Eric **06** slowly **08** bit by bit, inchmeal **09** by degrees, gradually, piecemeal, poco a poco **10** step by step **13** imperceptibly, progressively
• **take a little 04** drib

## liturgical

**06** formal, ritual, solemn **08** hieratic **10** ceremonial, sacerdotal **11** eucharistic, sacramental

## liturgy

**04** form, rite **05** usage **06** office, ritual **07** formula, service, worship **08** ceremony **09** ordinance, sacrament **10** observance **11** celebration

## livable, liveable

**08** adequate, bearable **09** endurable, habitable, tolerable **10** acceptable, worthwhile **11** comfortable, inhabitable, supportable **12** satisfactory
• **livable with, liveable with 08** bearable, passable, sociable **09** congenial, gemütlich, tolerable **10** compatible, harmonious **13** companionable

## live

**02** be **03** hot **04** hard, last, lead, pass, stay **05** abide, alert, alive, dwell, exist, lodge, spend, squat, vital, vivid **06** active, alight, behave, bodily, endure, lively, living, public, red hot, remain, reside, urgent **07** animate, be alive, blazing, breathe, burning, charged, comport, conduct, current, dynamic, flaming, glowing, have fun, ignited, inhabit, persist, see life, subsist, survive, topical, undergo **08** continue, existent, have life, in person, live it up, personal, pressing, real-time, relevant, stirring, unstable, vigorous, volatile **09** be settled, breathing, connected, energetic, enjoy life, explosive, important, pertinent, unwrought **10** applicable, draw breath, experience, having life, in the flesh, unexploded, unquarried **11** electrified, not recorded **12** have your home **13** controversial, enjoy yourself **14** earn your living, not prerecorded, with an audience **15** support yourself
• **live it up 05** revel **09** celebrate, have a ball, make merry **10** go on a spree **11** make whoopee **14** push the boat out **15** paint the town red
• **live on 04** feed, last **05** exist **06** rely on **07** live off, subsist **08** continue **09** subsist on
• **live wire 06** dynamo **08** go-getter, whizz kid **10** ball of fire **11** eager beaver, self-starter

## liveable

*see* **livable**

## livelihood

**03** job **04** keep, work **05** bread, crust, means, trade **06** income, living, upkeep **07** livelod, support **08** livelood **09** existence **10** daily bread, employment, livelihead, occupation, profession, sustenance **11** maintenance, subsistence **13** means of living **14** bread-and-butter, means of support, source of income

## liveliness

**04** brio, life, salt **05** oomph **06** energy, esprit, spirit, vigour **07** entrain, pizzazz **08** activity, dynamism, vitality, vivacity **09** animation, briskness, quickness, smartness **10** livelihead **11** refreshment **13** animal spirits, sprightliness, vivaciousness **14** boisterousness

## livelong

**04** full, long **05** whole **06** entire, orpine **08** complete, enduring **10** protracted

## lively

◊ *anagram indicator* **03** gay **04** busy, cant, go-go, keen, pacy, racy, spry, vive, vivo, warm, wick **05** agile, alert, alive, brisk, buxom, canty, cobby, kedge, kedgy, kidge, light, ludic, merry, pacey, peart, perky, piert, quick, rapid, vital, vivid, zappy, zippy **06** active, blithe, bouncy, breezy, bright, bubbly, chirpy, crouse, frisky, heated, hectic, jaunty, living, nimble, snappy, sporty, strong, titupy, vivace **07** buckish, buoyant, buzzing, crowded, dynamic, graphic, mettled, playful, slammin', teeming, tittupy, vibrant **08** animated, brushing, bustling, cheerful, eventful, exciting,

## liven

friskful, galliard, lifesome, rattling, skittish, slamming, spirited, stirring, striking, swarming, vigorous **09** colourful, energetic, lightsome, sparkling, sprightly, vivacious **10** frolicsome, mettlesome, mouvementé, refreshing **11** imaginative, interesting, stimulating **12** effervescent, enthusiastic, high-spirited, invigorating

## liven

**04** stir **05** cheer, hot up, pep up, rouse, spice **06** buck up, jazz up, perk up, stir up **07** animate, cheer up, enliven, spice up **08** brighten, energize, vitalize **10** invigorate **11** put life into

## liverish

**05** testy **06** crabby, crusty, grumpy, snappy, tetchy **07** crabbed, peevish **09** crotchety, irascible, irritable, splenetic **11** ill-humoured **12** disagreeable **13** quick-tempered

## livery

**04** garb, gear, suit, togs **05** dress, get-up, habit **06** attire **07** apparel, clobber, clothes, costume, regalia, uniform **08** clothing, garments **09** irritable, vestments **11** habiliments

## livid

**03** mad, wan **04** blae, blue, pale, waxy **05** angry, ashen, irate, pasty, white **06** fuming, leaden, pallid, purple, raging **07** bruised, enraged, furious, ghastly, greyish **08** blanched, incensed, outraged, purplish, seething **09** bloodless, indignant **10** infuriated **11** deathly pale, discoloured, exasperated, Hippocratic **12** black-and-blue

## living

**03** job **04** life, live, true, work **05** alive, being, bread, close, crust, exact, in use, trade, vital **06** active, extant, income, lively, strong **07** animate, current, genuine, precise, support **08** animated, benefice, existing, faithful, property, vigorous **09** animation, breathing, existence, identical, lifestyle, operative, surviving, way of life **10** continuing, daily bread, livelihood, occupation, profession, sustenance **11** going strong, maintenance, subsistence **13** means of living **14** bread-and-butter, means of support, source of income
• **mode of living** **04** diet

## living room

**06** lounge **07** day room, parlour **09** front room **11** drawing room, sitting room **13** reception room

## lizard

Lizards include:

**03** eft
**04** evet, gila, sand, seps, tegu, wall, worm
**05** blind, Draco, fence, gecko, skink
**06** agamid, dragon, flying, goanna, horned, iguana
**07** bearded, frilled, monitor, perenty
**08** basilisk, bungarra, perentie, slowworm, teguexin
**09** chameleon
**10** blue-tongue, chamaeleon
**11** gila monster
**12** Komodo dragon

See also **animal**

## llama

**06** alpaca **07** guanaco, huanaco

## load

**03** arm, jag, put, tax, tod **04** a lot, cram, duty, fill, haul, heap, lade, lard, lots, onus, pack, pile, plug, seam, slot, tons **05** cargo, enter, equip, goods, heaps, miles, piles, prime, put in, scads, slide, stack, stuff, todde, worry **06** burden, charge, dozens, fill up, hordes, insert, lading, masses, oodles, scores, stacks, strain, weight **07** fraught, freight, oppress, prepare, put into, trouble **08** a million, contents, encumber, hundreds, incumber, lashings, millions, pressure, shipment **09** abundance, albatross, great deal, millstone, overwhelm, thousands, weigh down **10** commitment, obligation, oppression, overburden, saddle with **11** consignment, encumbrance, large amount, tribulation **13** prepare to fire **14** responsibility

## loaded

◊ anagram indicator **03** fap, fou **04** full, high, inky, paid, rich **05** drunk, fixed, flush, foxed, happy, inked, laden, lit up, merry, moppy, piled, set up, tight, tipsy, woozy **06** biased, blotto, bombed, canned, corked, filled, heaped, jagged, juiced, mellow, mortal, packed, rigged, ripped, soused, stewed, stinko, stoned, tiddly, wasted **07** bevvied, bonkers, bottled, charged, crocked, drunken, ebriose, fairish, half-cut, legless, maggoty, pickled, pie-eyed, sloshed, smashed, sozzled, squiffy, stacked, tiddled, trashed, wealthy, well-off, wrecked **08** affluent, bibulous, burdened, footless, in liquor, juiced up, liquored, moon-eyed, overseen, overshot, pregnant, sow-drunk, stotious, tanked up, weighted, whiffled, whistled **09** blootered, crapulent, incapable, paralytic, plastered, shickered, trolleyed, up the pole, well-oiled **10** blind drunk, capernoity, inebriated, in the money, obfuscated, well-heeled **11** intoxicated, made of money, rolling in it, snowed under **12** drunk as a lord, drunk as a newt, on easy street, roaring drunk **13** drunk as a piper, having had a few, under the table **14** Brahms and Liszt **15** a sheet in the wind, one over the eight, the worse for wear, under the weather

## loaf

**03** bum, tin, veg **04** cake, cube, head, idle, laze, loll, lump, mass, mind, nous, pone, slab **05** block, brick, miche, mooch, relax, sense, slosh **06** bludge, brains, coburg, loiter, lounge, noddle, stotty, unwind, veg out **07** bloomer, brioche, challah, manchet, Panagia, stottie **08** baguette, corn pone, focaccia, gumption, Panhagia, scrapple **09** barmbrack, lie around, sit around **10** corn dodger, hang around, stand about, take it easy **11** common sense, French stick, spotted dick **12** lounge around
See also **bread; head**
• **loaf about** **04** laze **06** lounge

## loafer

**03** yob **04** slob **05** idler **06** bummer, skiver **07** goof-off, lounger, shirker, wastrel **08** layabout, sluggard **09** corner-boy, corner-man, lazybones, sundowner **10** ne'er-do-well **11** beachcomber
See also **footwear**

## loam

**04** clay, core, lome, malm, sand, soil **05** earth **09** brickclay, malmstone **10** brick-earth

## loan

**03** len', sub **04** lane, lend **05** allow, prest **06** credit, on-lend **07** advance, finance, imprest, lending **08** mortgage, overlend, put forth **09** allowance **12** floating debt, respondentia **13** accommodation

## loath

**04** ugly **05** laith **06** averse **07** against, hateful, opposed **08** grudging, hesitant **09** reluctant, repulsive, resisting, unwilling **10** indisposed **11** disinclined

## loathe

**02** ug **04** hate **05** abhor **06** detest **07** despise, dislike **08** execrate, nauseate, not stand **09** abominate **10** recoil from **15** feel revulsion at

## loathing

**04** hate **05** odium **06** hatred, horror, nausea **07** disgust, dislike, ill-will **08** aversion **09** antipathy, repulsion, revulsion **10** abhorrence, execration, repugnance **11** abomination, detestation

## loathsome

**04** foul, vile **05** nasty **06** odious **07** hateful, mawkish, obscene **08** horrible, nauseous **09** abhorrent, execrable, lothefull, obnoxious, offensive, repellent, repugnant, repulsive, revolting **10** abominable, despicable, detestable, disgusting, nauseating **12** contemptible, disagreeable

## lob

**03** shy **04** hurl, lift, loft, lout, lump, puck, toss **05** chuck, droop, fling, heave, pitch, throw **06** launch **07** lobworm, pollack

## lobby

**04** hall, urge **05** entry, foyer, porch **06** demand **07** call for, faction, hallway, passage, promote, push for, solicit **08** anteroom, box-lobby, campaign, corridor, entrance, persuade, press for, pressure **09** influence, lobbyists, vestibule **10** passageway **11** campaign for, ginger group, waiting room **12** entrance hall **13** pressure group

## lobster
**04** cock **08** crawfish, crayfish
**09** langouste **11** langoustine
• **lobster cage** **04** corf

## local
◇ *foreign word indicator* **02** PH **03** bar,
inn, pub **04** city, town **05** place, urban
**06** boozer, narrow, native, number,
parish, saloon, tavern **07** citizen,
limited, topical, vicinal, village
**08** district, hostelry, regional, resident
**09** community, municipal, parochial,
small-town **10** inhabitant, parish-
pump, provincial, restricted,
vernacular **11** anaesthetic,
examination, public house
**12** watering-hole **13** neighbourhood
*See also* **public house**
• **local worker** **06** barman
**09** bartender

## locale
**04** area, site, spot, zone **05** locus,
place, scene, venue **07** setting
**08** locality, location, position
**11** environment **13** neighbourhood

## locality
**04** area, site, spot **05** locus, place,
scene **06** locale, region **07** setting
**08** district, position, vicinity
**11** environment **12** neighborhood
**13** neighbourhood **15** surrounding area

## localize
**05** limit **06** assign **07** ascribe, confine,
contain, delimit, specify **08** identify,
pinpoint, restrain, restrict, zero in on
**10** delimitate, narrow down
**11** concentrate **12** circumscribe

## locate
**03** fix, lay, put, set **04** find, seat, site,
spot **05** build, place, plant **06** access,
detect, finger, settle **07** hit upon, pick
out, situate, station, uncover, unearth
**08** allocate, discover, identify,
pinpoint, position **09** establish, track
down **10** come across, run to earth
**14** lay your hands on
• **be located** **03** sit

## location
**04** farm, seat, site, spot **05** locus, place,
point, scene, venue **06** locale, ubiety
**07** setting **08** bearings, position
**09** situation **11** whereabouts

## loch
**01** L **03** dam, sea **04** lake, mere, pond,
pool, tarn **05** basin, lough, water
**09** reservoir
*See also* **lake**

## lock
**03** bar, hug, jam, tag **04** curl, join, link,
mesh, seal, shut, snap, snib, trap, tuft
**05** catch, clasp, grasp, latch, plait,
sasse, stick, tress, unite **06** clench,
clutch, engage, fasten, secure, strand
**07** embrace, enclose, entwine,
grapple, ringlet **08** encircle, entangle
**09** certainty, fastening, interlock
**12** scalping-tuft

*Locks include:*

**03** rim
**04** dead, Yale®

**05** child, Chubb®, wagon
**06** safety, spring
**07** mortice, mortise, padlock
**08** cylinder
**10** night latch
**11** combination

*Lock parts include:*

**03** bit, key, pin
**04** bolt, hasp, knob, post, rose, sash,
ward
**05** latch, talon
**06** barrel, keyway, spring, staple
**07** key card, keyhole, spindle,
tumbler
**08** cylinder, dead bolt, sash bolt
**09** face-plate, latch bolt
**10** escutcheon, latch lever, push-
button
**11** mortise bolt, spindle hole, strike
plate
**12** cylinder hole
**13** latch follower

• **lock out** **03** bar **05** debar
**07** exclude, keep out, shut out
• **lock up** ◇ *containment indicator*
◇ *hidden indicator* **03** pen **04** cage, jail
**06** detain, secure, shut in, shut up,
wall in **07** close up, confine, put
away **08** imprison **11** incarcerate
**13** put behind bars
• **open lock** **04** pick

## locker
**07** cabinet **08** cupboard **09** container
**11** compartment

## lock-up
**03** can, jug **04** cell, gaol, jail, quod
**05** choky, clink **06** chokey, cooler,
garage, prison **07** slammer
**08** storeroom, warehouse
**10** depository, roundhouse, watch
house **12** penitentiary, station house

## locomotion
**06** action, motion, moving, travel
**07** headway, walking **08** movement,
progress **10** ambulation, travelling
**11** progression **13** perambulation

## locus
**04** site **05** place, point, polar, venue
**06** locale, spiral **08** centroid,
conchoid, envelope, locality, location,
parabola, position, roulette
**09** directrix, situation, wavefront
**10** lemniscate **11** radical axis,
whereabouts **14** director circle

## locust
**08** devourer **10** devastator, voetganger

## locution
**04** term **05** idiom, style **06** accent,
cliché, phrase **07** diction, talking,
wording **08** phrasing, speaking
**10** expression, inflection, intonation
**11** collocation **12** articulation, turn of
phrase

## lode
**04** reef

## lodge
**03** box, cup, den, dig, fix, hut, inn, lay,
lie, put **04** bank, club, file, host, keep,
lair, live, make, nest, room, stay, stow,

tent **05** board, bower, cabin, dwell,
group, grove, haunt, house, imbed,
infix, layer, place, put in, put up
**06** billet, branch, chalet, grange, hand
in, harbor, loggia, record, reside, show
up, submit, teepee **07** barrack, chapter,
cottage, deposit, hang out, harbour,
implant, quarter, retreat, section,
shelter, society, sojourn **08** campfire,
get stuck, register **09** be settled,
gatehouse, get caught, longhouse
**10** habitation, put forward
**11** accommodate, association
**12** accumulation, have your home,
hunting-lodge, meeting-place

## lodger
**02** PG **05** guest **06** inmate, roomer,
tenant **07** boarder **08** resident **11** paying
guest

## lodgings
**03** pad **04** digs, ferm **05** abode, board,
place, rooms **06** bedsit, billet **07** flea-
bag **08** dwelling, quarters **09** bedsitter,
residence **13** accommodation,
boarding house **14** bedsitting-
room
*See also* **apartment**

## loftily
**07** proudly, stately **08** snootily
**09** haughtily **10** arrogantly
**12** disdainfully **14** superciliously

## lofty
**04** high, tall **05** brent, grand, noble,
proud, steep, wingy **06** aerial, lordly,
raised, skyish, snooty, winged
**07** exalted, haughty, sky-high, soaring,
stately, sublime **08** arrogant, elevated,
esteemed, imperial, imposing,
majestic, renowned, superior,
towering **09** dignified **10** disdainful
**11** illustrious, patronizing, toffee-nosed
**12** supercilious **13** condescending,
distinguished, high and mighty, high-
stomached

## log
**04** book, clog, file, note **05** block,
chart, chock, chunk, diary, piece,
stock, tally, trunk **06** billet, loggat,
record, timber **07** account, daybook,
journal, logbook, set down, write up
**08** register **09** logarithm

## logbook
**03** log **05** chart, diary, tally **06** record
**07** account, daybook, journal
**08** register

## loggerheads
• **at loggerheads** ◇ *anagram indicator*
**06** at odds **10** in conflict **11** disagreeing,
quarrelling **12** in opposition **13** like cat
and dog **14** at daggers drawn

## logic
**05** sense **06** reason **08** argument
**09** coherence, deduction, judgement,
rationale, reasoning, redecraft
**10** dialectics **13** argumentation,
ratiocination
*See also* **circuit**

## logical
**04** wise **05** clear, sound, valid
**06** cogent **07** Boolean **08** coherent,
rational, reasoned, relevant, sensible,

**logically**

thinking **09** deducible, deductive, dialectic, inductive, judicious **10** consistent, convergent, methodical, reasonable, sequacious **11** consecutive, dialectical, intelligent, syllogistic, well-founded **12** well-reasoned **13** well-organized **14** well-thought-out

**logically**

**07** clearly, validly **08** sensibly **10** coherently, rationally, relevantly **11** deductively, inductively **12** consistently, methodically **13** consecutively, dialectically, intelligently

**logistics**

**05** plans **07** tactics **08** planning, strategy **09** direction **10** management **11** arrangement, engineering **12** co-ordination, organization **13** masterminding, orchestration

**logo**

**04** mark, sign **05** badge, image **06** device, emblem, figure, symbol **08** insignia **09** trademark **14** representation

**loiter**

**03** lag **04** hove, idle, lime, loaf, lurk, mike **05** dally, delay, hoove, mooch, mouch, tarry **06** dawdle, linger, lounge, taigle **07** saunter **08** lallygag, lollygag **09** hang about, waste time **10** dilly-dally, hang around **12** take your time

• **loitering with intent**   **03** sus **04** suss

**loll**

**03** sag **04** drop, flap, flop, hang, lill, loaf **05** droop, relax, slump **06** dangle, lounge, slouch, sprawl **07** recline

**lollop**

**03** run **04** idle, lope **05** bound **06** canter, gallop, lounge, spring, stride

**lolly**

**05** money **06** sucker **07** lulibub **08** ice block, lollipop, Popsicle® 
*See also* **money**

**London**

**03** wen **08** great wen

*London boroughs:*

**05** Brent
**06** Barnet, Bexley, Camden, Ealing, Harrow, Merton, Newham, Sutton
**07** Bromley, Croydon, Enfield, Hackney, Lambeth
**08** Haringey, Havering, Hounslow, Lewisham
**09** Greenwich, Islington, Redbridge, Southwark
**10** Hillingdon, Wandsworth
**12** Tower Hamlets
**13** Waltham Forest
**17** City of Westminster
**18** Barking and Dagenham, Kingston upon Thames, Richmond upon Thames
**20** Hammersmith and Fulham, Kensington and Chelsea

*Other districts of London include:*

**02** EC
**03** Bow, Kew, Lee
**04** Bank, Oval, Soho
**05** Acton, Angel, Erith, Hayes, Penge
**06** Arkley, Balham, Barnes, Debden, Eltham, Epping, Euston, Fulham, Hendon, Heston, Hoxton, Ilford, Kenton, Leyton, Malden, Morden, Pinner, Poplar, Purley, Putney, Temple, Waddon
**07** Aldgate, Archway, Barking, Beckton, Belmont, Borough, Brixton, Catford, Chelsea, Clapham, Cranham, Dalston, Dulwich, East End, East Ham, Edgware, Elm Park, Feltham, Hampton, Hanwell, Holborn, Hornsey, Kilburn, Mayfair, Mile End, Mitcham, Neasden, Norwood, Old Ford, Olympia, Peckham, Pimlico, Selsdon, Stepney, The City, Tooting, Wapping, Welling, Wembley, West End, West Ham, Yeading
**08** Alperton, Bankside, Barbican, Brockley, Brompton, Chiswick, Coulsdon, Crayford, Dagenham, Deptford, Edmonton, Elmstead, Finchley, Finsbury, Grays Inn, Hanworth, Hatch End, Heathrow, Highbury, Highgate, Holloway, Homerton, Hyde Park, Ickenham, Kingston, Mill Hill, Mortlake, New Cross, Nine Elms, Northolt, Osterley, Perivale, Plaistow, Richmond, Shadwell, Southall, Stanmore, Surbiton, Sydenham, Tolworth, Uxbridge, Vauxhall, Victoria, Walworth, Wanstead, Waterloo, Woodford, Woolwich
**09** Abbey Wood, Addington, Barnsbury, Battersea, Bayswater, Beckenham, Becontree, Belgravia, Blackwall, Brentford, Brimsdown, Canonbury, Chalk Farm, Chingford, Colindale, Crouch End, Docklands, Fitzrovia, Foots Cray, Gant's Hill, Gidea Park, Gipsy Hill, Goodmayes, Gospel Oak, Greenford, Green Park, Hampstead, Harefield, Harlesden, Harringay, Herne Hill, Isleworth, Kidbrooke, Kingsbury, Kingsland, Limehouse, Maida Vale, Mark's Gate, Newington, Northwood, Orpington, Park Royal, Petts Wood, Plumstead, South Bank, Southgate, Stockwell, St Pancras, Stratford, Streatham, Tottenham, Tower Hill, Tulse Hill, Upminster, Whetstone, White City, Whitehall, Willesden, Wimbledon, Wood Green
**10** Addiscombe, Albany Park, Arnos Grove, Beddington, Bellingham, Bermondsey, Blackheath, Bloomsbury, Brent Cross, Camberwell, Chase Cross, Collier Row, Creekmouth, Dollis Hill, Earls Court, Earlsfield, Embankment, Farringdon, Forest

Gate, Forest Hill, Goddington, Green Lanes, Haggerston, Harlington, Harold Hill, Harold Wood, Horse Ferry, Isle of Dogs, Kennington, Kensington, King's Cross, Manor House, Marylebone, Mottingham, Paddington, Piccadilly, Queensbury, Raynes Park, Seven Dials, Seven Kings, Shad Thames, Shoreditch, Silvertown, Smithfield, Teddington, Thamesmead, Totteridge, Twickenham, Wallington, Wealdstone
**11** Bedford Park, Belsize Park, Bexleyheath, Blackfriars, Bounds Green, Brondesbury, Canada Water, Canary Wharf, Canning Town, Chessington, Clerkenwell, Cockfosters, Cricklewood, East Dulwich, Fortis Green, Gunnersbury, Hammersmith, Highams Park, Holland Park, Kensal Green, Kentish Town, Leytonstone, Lincoln's Inn, Little Italy, Ludgate Hill, Muswell Hill, Notting Hill, Pentonville, Regent's Park, Rotherhithe, Snaresbrook, St John's Wood, Surrey Quays, Tufnell Park, Walthamstow, Westminster, Whitechapel
**12** Bethnal Green, Billingsgate, Bromley-by-Bow, Charing Cross, City of London, Colliers Wood, Covent Garden, Crossharbour, Epping Forest, Finsbury Park, Golders Green, Hatton Garden, Havering Park, London Bridge, London Fields, Palmers Green, Parsons Green, Pool of London, Primrose Hill, Seven Sisters, Sloane Square, Stamford Hill, Swiss Cottage
**13** Ardleigh Green, Chadwell Heath, Crystal Palace, Harmondsworth, Knightsbridge, Ladbroke Grove, Lancaster Gate, North Woolwich, Petticoat Lane, Shepherd's Bush, Thornton Heath, Tottenham Hale, Wanstead Flats, Winchmore Hill
**14** Angel Islington, Becontree Heath, Hackney Marshes, Stoke Newington, Tottenham Green, Wormwood Scrubs
**15** Alexandra Palace, Leicester Square, Westbourne Green

*London streets include:*

**06** Strand
**07** Aldgate, Aldwych, The Mall, Westway
**08** Kingsway, Long Acre, Millbank, Minories, Pall Mall, Park Lane, York Road
**09** Bow Street, Cheapside, Drury Lane, Haymarket, King's Road, Maida Vale, Queensway, Tower Hill, Whitehall
**10** Bond Street, Dean Street, Eaton Place, Euston Road, Fetter Lane, Fulham Road, London Wall,

Onslow Road, Piccadilly, Queen's Gate, Soho Square, Vine Street

**11** Baker Street, Eaton Square, Edgware Road, Fleet Street, Goswell Road, Gower Street, High Holborn, Lambeth Road, Leather Lane, Ludgate Hill, Old Kent Road, Pimlico Road, Savoy Street, Warwick Road

**12** Albany Street, Belgrave Road, Birdcage Walk, Brompton Road, Cannon Street, Chancery Lane, Cromwell Road, Gray's Inn Road, Hatton Garden, Jermyn Street, Oxford Street, Regent Street, Sloane Square, Sloane Street, Tooley Street

**13** Bayswater Road, Bedford Square, Berwick Street, Carnaby Street, Downing Street, Garrick Street, Gerrard Street, Grosvenor Road, Knightsbridge, Lombard Street, Ludgate Circus, New Bond Street, New Fetter Lane, Newgate Street, Old Bond Street, Petticoat Lane, Portland Place, Portman Square, Russell Square, Wardour Street

**14** Belgrave Square, Berkeley Square, Coventry Street, Earl's Court Road, Earnshaw Street, Exhibition Road, Gloucester Road, Holborn Viaduct, Horseferry Road, Hyde Park Square, Kensington Road, Marylebone Road, Mayfair Gardens, Portobello Road, Stamford Street

**15** Albemarle Street, Blackfriars Road, Clerkenwell Road, Grosvenor Square, Horse Guards Road, Leicester Square, Liverpool Street, New Bridge Street, Pentonville Road, Southwark Street, St John's Wood Road, Trafalgar Square, Whitechapel Road

---

*London landmarks include:*

**03** ICA, Kew
**04** City, Eros, Oval, Soho
**05** Barts, Lord's, V and A
**06** Big Ben, Lloyds, Temple, Thames
**07** Harrods, Mayfair, St Paul's, The City, The Mall
**08** Bow bells, Cenotaph, Gray's Inn, Hyde Park, Liberty's, Monument, St Bride's
**09** Chinatown, Cutty Sark, George Inn, Green Park, Guildhall, London Eye, London Zoo, Old Bailey, Rotten Row, Royal Mews, South Bank, Staple Inn, The Temple, Trocadero
**10** Albert Hall, Camden Lock, Cock Tavern, Earl's Court, HMS Belfast, Jewel Tower, Kew Gardens, Marble Arch, Selfridge's, Serpentine, Tate Modern, the Gherkin
**11** Apsley House, Canary Wharf, Golden Hinde, Lincoln's Inn, OXO building, Queen's House, Regent's Park, River Thames, St

John's Gate, St Margaret's, St Mary-Le-Bow, Tate Britain, Tower Bridge

**12** Charterhouse, Covent Garden, Design Museum, Dickens House, Festival Hall, Globe Theatre, Guards Museum, Hatton Garden, Hay's Galleria, London Bridge, Mansion House, Spencer House, statue of Eros, St James's Park, Telecom Tower, Temple Church, Traitors' Gate

**13** Admiralty Arch, Bank of England, British Museum, Carnaby Street, Clarence House, Gabriel's Wharf, Geffrye Museum, Greenwich Park, Lambeth Palace, London Dungeon, Madam Tussaud's, Nelson's Column, Petticoat Lane, Queen's Gallery, Royal Exchange, Science Museum, Somerset House, Tower of London, Wesley's Chapel

**14** Albert Memorial, Barbican Centre, British Library, Hayward Gallery, Hermitage Rooms, Lancaster House, London Aquarium, Millennium Dome, Museum of London, Portobello Road, Speakers' Corner, St Clement Danes, St James's Palace, Waterloo Bridge, Wellington Arch

**15** Bankside Gallery, Banqueting House, Brompton Oratory, Burlington House, Cabinet War Rooms, Fortnum and Mason, National Gallery, Royal Albert Hall, Royal Opera House, Temple of Mithras, Trafalgar Square, Westminster Hall

---

*London Underground lines:*

**03** DLR
**06** Circle
**07** Central, Jubilee
**08** Bakerloo, District, Northern, Victoria
**10** East London, Piccadilly
**12** Metropolitan
**15** Waterloo and City
**18** Hammersmith and City
**21** Docklands Light Railway

---

*London Underground stations include:*

**04** Bank, Oval
**05** Angel
**06** Balham, Cyprus, Epping, Euston, Leyton, Morden, Pinner, Poplar, Temple
**07** Aldgate, Archway, Arsenal, Barking, Beckton, Borough, Bow Road, Brixton, Chesham, East Ham, Edgware, Holborn, Kilburn, Mile End, Neasden, Pimlico, Ruislip, St Paul's, Wapping, Watford, West Ham
**08** Amersham, Barbican, Chigwell, Hainault, Heathrow, Highgate, Lewisham, Monument, Moorgate, Mudchute, New Cross, Northolt, Perivale, Plaistow, Richmond, Royal Oak, Shadwell, Stanmore,

Uxbridge, Vauxhall, Victoria, Wanstead, Waterloo

**09** Acton Town, All Saints, Bayswater, Blackwall, Bow Church, Chalk Farm, Cutty Sark, East Acton, East India, Greenford, Green Park, Greenwich, Hampstead, Harlesden, Kingsbury, Limehouse, Maida Vale, Old Street, Park Royal, Queensway, South Quay, Southwark, Stockwell, Stratford, Tower Hill, Upton Park, West Acton, Westferry, White City, Wimbledon, Wood Green

**10** Bermondsey, Bond Street, Brent Cross, Camden Town, Canons Park, Devons Road, Dollis Hill, Earl's Court, East Putney, Embankment, Farringdon, Grange Hill, Hanger Lane, Heron Quays, Hillingdon, Hornchurch, Kennington, Kew Gardens, Manor House, Marble Arch, Marylebone, North Acton, Paddington, Queensbury, Queen's Park, Shoreditch, Tooting Bec

**11** Aldgate East, Baker Street, Barons Court, Beckton Park, Belsize Park, Blackfriars, Bounds Green, Canada Water, Canary Wharf, Canning Town, Chorleywood, Cockfosters, Custom House, Edgware Road, Gunnersbury, Hammersmith, Holland Park, Kensal Green, Kentish Town, Kilburn Park, Latimer Road, Leytonstone, North Ealing, Northfields, Regent's Park, Rotherhithe, Royal Albert, South Ealing, Southfields, St John's Wood, Surrey Quays, Tufnell Park, Wembley Park, Westminster, Whitechapel

**12** Bethnal Green, Bromley-by-Bow, Cannon Street, Chancery Lane, Charing Cross, Chiswick Park, Clapham North, Clapham South, Colliers Wood, Covent Garden, Dagenham East, Ealing Common, East Finchley, Elverson Road, Euston Square, Finchley Road, Finsbury Park, Golders Green, Goldhawk Road, Goodge Street, Holloway Road, Lambeth North, London Bridge, Mansion House, New Cross Gate, Oxford Circus, Parsons Green, Prince Regent, Putney Bridge, Seven Sisters, Sloane Square, Stepney Green, St James's Park, Swiss Cottage, Tower Gateway, Turnham Green, Turnpike Lane, Warren Street, West Brompton

**13** Clapham Common, Gallions Reach, Hendon Central, Island Gardens, Knightsbridge, Ladbroke Grove, Lancaster Gate, Rickmansworth, Royal Victoria, Russell Square, Shepherd's Bush, Stamford Brook, Tottenham Hale, Warwick Avenue, West Hampstead, West India Quay, Wimbledon Park

**lone**

14 Blackhorse Road, Caledonian Road, Deptford Bridge, Ealing Broadway, Fulham Broadway, Gloucester Road, Hyde Park Corner, North Greenwich, South Wimbledon, Westbourne Park, West Kensington, Willesden Green
15 Finchley Central, Harrow-on-the-Hill, Hounslow Central, Leicester Square, Liverpool Street, Notting Hill Gate, Pudding Mill Lane, Ravenscourt Park, South Kensington, Stonebridge Park, Tooting Broadway

**lone**
03 one 04 lane, only, sole 05 alone 06 barren, remote, single 07 widowed 08 deserted, desolate, divorced, forsaken, isolated, secluded, separate, solitary 09 abandoned, on your own, separated, unmarried 10 by yourself, unattached 11 out-of-the-way, uninhabited 12 unfrequented 15 without a partner

**loneliness**
08 solitude 09 aloneness, isolation, seclusion 10 desolation 12 lonesomeness, solitariness

**lonely**
03 sad 04 lone 05 alone, unked, unket, unkid 06 barren, remote 07 outcast, unhappy 08 deserted, desolate, forsaken, isolated, lonesome, rejected, secluded, solitary, wretched 09 abandoned, destitute, miserable, reclusive 11 god-forsaken, out-of-the-way, uninhabited 12 solitudinous, unfrequented 13 companionless, unaccompanied

**loner**
06 hermit 07 recluse 08 lone wolf, solitary 09 introvert 13 individualist 14 solitudinarian

**lonesome**
03 sad 04 lone 05 alone 06 barren, lonely, remote 07 outcast, unhappy 08 deserted, desolate, forsaken, isolated, rejected, secluded, solitary, wretched 09 abandoned, destitute, miserable, reclusive 10 friendless 11 out-of-the-way, uninhabited 12 unfrequented 13 companionless, unaccompanied

**long**
01 L 03 ake, die, far, yen 04 ache, hope, itch, lang, leng, lust, pant, pine, side, slow, tall, want, wish 05 covet, crave, dream, longa, tardy, yearn 06 desire, hanker, hunger, thirst 07 lengthy, spun out, tedious, verbose 08 expanded, extended, marathon, overlong 09 diuturnal, elongated, expansive, extensive, prolonged, spread out, stretched, sustained 10 protracted 11 far-reaching 12 interminable, long-drawn-out, stretched out
See also **want**
• **before long** 04 soon 07 by and by, shortly 09 in a moment, presently 12 in a short time 14 in a minute or two 15 in the near future
• **long ago** 03 eld 04 yore
• **Long Island** 02 LI
• **long live** 04 viva, vive 05 vivat 08 zindabad

**long-drawn-out**
06 prolix 07 lengthy, spun out, tedious 08 long-spun, marathon, overlong 09 long-drawn, prolonged 10 dragging on, long-winded, protracted 12 interminable, overextended

**longer**
04 more
• **no longer** 02 ex

**longing**
03 yen 04 avid, earn, erne, hope, itch, lust, urge, wish 05 brame, crave, dream, eager, greed, yearn 06 ardent, desire, hunger, hungry, pining, thirst 07 anxious, craving, wanting, wishful, wistful 08 ambition, appetent, coveting, desirous, yearning 09 breathing, cacoethes, hankering, hungering 10 aspiration, desiderium 11 languishing

**longingly**
06 avidly, wistly 07 eagerly 08 ardently 09 anxiously, wishfully, wistfully 10 yearningly

**long-lasting**
07 abiding, chronic 08 enduring, unfading 09 lingering, permanent, prolonged 10 continuing, protracted, unchanging 12 imperishable, long-standing

**long-lived**
07 durable, lasting 08 enduring 09 longevous, macrobian, vivacious 11 long-lasting, macrobiotic 12 long-standing

**long-standing**
07 abiding 08 enduring 09 long-lived 11 established, long-lasting, traditional 12 time-honoured 15 long-established, well-established

**long-suffering**
07 patient, stoical 08 resigned, tolerant 09 easy-going, forgiving, indulgent 10 forbearant, forbearing 13 uncomplaining

**long-winded**
05 wordy 06 prolix 07 diffuse, lengthy, tedious, verbose, voluble 08 overlong, rambling 09 garrulous, prolonged 10 discursive, protracted 11 repetitious 12 long-drawn-out

**long-windedness**
08 longueur 09 garrulity, macrology, prolixity, verbosity, wordiness 10 volubility 11 diffuseness, lengthiness, tediousness 14 discursiveness 15 repetitiousness

**loo**
02 WC 03 bog, lav 04 john, kazi, love, toot 05 dunny, Elsan®, gents', privy 06 ladies', throne, toilet, urinal 07 crapper, latrine 08 bathroom, lavatory, Portaloo®, rest room, superloo, washroom 09 cloakroom, lanterloo 10 facilities, powder room 11 convenience, water closet 12 smallest room 14 comfort station, little boys' room 15 little girls' room
See also **toilet**

**look**
02 hi, la, lo, oi 03 air, eye, ray, see, spy 04 deek, ecce, ecco, face, gape, gawp, gaze, geek, keek, leer, mien, peek, peep, peer, quiz, scan, seem, show, view, vise, vizy 05 check, decko, dekko, focus, front, frown, glout, guise, scowl, sight, squiz, stare, study, visie, watch 06 appear, aspect, behold, blench, effect, eyeful, façade, gander, give on, glance, gledge, manner, regard, review, shufti, shufty, squint, survey, take in, vision, vizzie 07 bearing, belgard, display, examine, exhibit, eyeball, front on, glimpse, inspect, observe 08 butcher's, consider, features, give on to, look onto, once-over, overlook, scrutiny 09 eye-glance, semblance, take a look 10 appearance, be opposite, complexion, expression, get a load of, impression, inspection, scrutinize 11 contemplate, countenance, examination, observation 12 butcher's hook, take a dekko at 13 contemplation, get an eyeful of, take a gander at, take a shufti at, take a squint at 14 give a going-over 15 give the once-over, run your eyes over
• **look after** 03 sit 04 heed, keep, mind, seek, tend 05 guard, nurse, see to, watch 06 expect 07 babysit, care for, protect 08 attend to, maintain 09 childmind, supervise, watch over 10 take care of 11 keep an eye on 12 take charge of
• **look back** 06 recall 08 remember 09 reminisce, think back 10 retrospect
• **look down on** 05 scorn, spurn 07 despise, disdain, sneer at 08 overpeer, pooh-pooh 09 disparage, patronize 10 talk down to 14 hold in contempt
• **look for** 04 seek 05 await, quest 06 expect 07 hunt for, hunt out 08 scavenge 09 forage for, search for, try to find 10 fossick out
• **look forward to** 05 await 06 expect 07 count on, hope for, long for, look for, wait for 08 envisage, envision 09 apprehend 10 anticipate
• **look into** 03 dig 05 delve, plumb, probe, study 06 fathom, go into 07 examine, explore, inspect 08 ask about, check out, look over, research 10 scrutinize, search into 11 investigate 12 inquire about
• **look like** 08 resemble 09 take after 11 be similar to, remind you of
• **look on, look upon** 03 eye 04 deem, hold, view 06 count, judge, think 06 regard 07 overeye 08 consider, spectate
• **look out** 04 mind 06 beware 07 Achtung, be alert 08 watch out 09 be careful 11 mind your eye 12 keep an eye out, pay attention 13 be on your guard, guard yourself 14 be on the qui vive

- **look over** 04 scan, view 05 check 07 examine, inspect, monitor, surview 08 check out 09 go through 11 look through, read through 13 cast an eye over, give a once-over 15 cast your eye over
- **look to** 05 await, besee, watch 06 expect, regard, rely on, turn to 07 count on, hope for, respect 08 consider, reckon on, resort to 10 anticipate, fall back on, think about 13 give thought to
- **look up** 04 find, seek 05 visit 06 call on, come on, drop by, perk up, pick up, stop by 07 advance, consult, develop, hunt for, improve 08 drop in on, look in on, progress, research 09 come along, get better, search for, track down 10 ameliorate 11 make headway, pay a visit to 12 make progress
- **look up to** 06 admire, esteem, honour, revere 07 respect 12 regard highly 13 think highly of

**lookalike**
04 spit, twin 05 clone, image 06 double, ringer 07 replica 10 dead ringer 11 living image 12 doppelgänger 13 exact likeness, spitting image

**lookout**
03 nit 04 huer, post, ward 05 guard, tower, watch, worry 06 affair, conder, conner, pigeon, sentry 07 concern, problem 08 business, cockatoo, prospect, sentinel, watchman, watch-out 09 nitkeeper 10 speculator, watch-tower 14 responsibility 15 observation post
- **keep a lookout** 05 watch 09 keep guard 10 be vigilant 11 remain alert 14 be on the qui vive

**loom**
04 loon, rise, soar, tool 05 frame, mount, tower 06 appear, emerge, impend, menace 07 overtop 08 dominate, hang over, jacquard, overhang, threaten 09 implement, take shape 10 be imminent, overshadow, receptacle 13 become visible

**loony**
◇ *anagram indicator* 03 mad, nut 04 daft, hook, wild 05 barmy, crank, crazy, loopy, nutty, potty, silly 06 crazed, insane, madman, maniac, nutter, psycho, stupid 07 berserk, bonkers, foolish, frantic, idiotic, lunatic, nutcase, oddball, strange 08 crackpot, demented, deranged, headcase, imbecile, madwoman, unhinged 09 disturbed, eccentric, fruitcake, psychotic, screwball 10 basket case, distracted, distraught, psychopath, unbalanced
*See also* **madman, madwoman**

**loop**
01 O 03 eye, lug, tab, tie, tug 04 bend, coil, curl, fold, hank, hoop, join, kink, knop, knot, oval, purl, ring, roll, turn, wind 05 braid, curve, noose, pearl, picot, sling, snare, twirl, twist, whorl 06 becket, cannon, circle, eyelet, fasten, lasket, runner, spiral, stitch 07 connect, latchet 08 carriage, écraseur, encircle, loophole, surround 09 billabong, eye splice 10 curve round, rubber band 11 convolution, elastic band, jubilee clip

**loophole**
04 plea 06 escape, excuse, eyelet, get-out, let-out, wicket 07 evasion, mistake, pretext 08 omission, pretence 09 ambiguity 12 escape clause

**loose**
◇ *anagram indicator* 03 lax, off 04 ease, fast, free, lose, open, undo 05 baggy, broad, let go, losen, lowse, relax, shaky, shoot, slack, solve, unpen, untie, vague 06 detach, flabby, lessen, loosen, reduce, solute, unbind, undone, unhook, unknit, unlock, unmoor, untied, wanton, weaken, wobbly 07 at large, corrupt, escaped, flowing, general, hanging, immoral, inexact, movable, relaxed, release, sagging, set free, slacken, unbound, unclasp, unleash 08 diffused, diminish, insecure, liberate, moderate, rambling, released, unchaste, uncouple, unfasten, unlocked, unpicked, unsteady 09 abandoned, debauched, desultory, discharge, disengage, dissolute, imprecise, shapeless, uncoupled 10 degenerate, disconnect, ill-defined, inaccurate, incoherent, indefinite, indistinct, licentious, unattached, unconfined, unfastened, untethered 11 inattentive, light-heeled, promiscuous 12 disreputable, loose-fitting, unrestrained
- **at a loose end** 04 idle 05 bored, fed up 07 aimless, off duty 09 désœuvré 11 out of action, purposeless 14 with time to kill 15 with nothing to do
- **on the loose** 04 free 07 at large, escaped 08 on the run 09 at liberty 10 unconfined

**loosely**
◇ *anagram indicator* 06 freely 07 baggily, broadly, movably, slackly, vaguely 09 generally, inexactly 10 insecurely, unsteadily 11 imprecisely, shapelessly 12 inaccurately

**loosen**
04 ease, free, undo 05 let go, loose, relax, untie 06 let out, unbind, unglue, weaken 07 deliver, release, set free, shake up, slacken, unscrew, work out 08 diminish, moderate, set loose, unfasten, unthread
- **loosen up** 05 let up, relax 06 cool it, ease up, go easy, lessen, unwind, warm up 07 prepare, work out 08 chill out, exercise, limber up, warm down 09 hang loose

**loot**
03 let, rob 04 haul, raid, sack, swag 05 booty, money, prize, rifle, steal 06 burgle, maraud, ravage, riches, spoils 07 despoil, pillage, plunder, ransack 08 pickings 09 steal from 10 lieutenant 11 stolen goods, stolen money

**lop**
03 cut 04 chop, clip, crop, dock, hack, sned, trim 05 prune, sever, shrub, trash 06 cut off, detach, reduce, remove, shroud 07 curtail, shorten, take off 08 truncate 10 detruncate

**lope**
03 run 05 bound 06 canter, gallop, lollop, spring, stride

**lopsided**
05 askew 06 squint, uneven 07 crooked, slanted, sloping, tilting, unequal 08 one-sided 09 skew-whiff 10 off balance, unbalanced 12 asymmetrical

**loquacious**
05 gabby, gassy, wordy 06 chatty 07 gossipy, voluble 08 babbling 09 garrulous, speechful, talkative 10 blathering, chattering 12 multiloquent, multiloquous

**loquacity**
09 garrulity, gassiness 10 chattiness, multiloquy, volubility 12 effusiveness 13 multiloquence, talkativeness

**lord**
01 D 02 Ld 03 Dom, God, lud 04 duke, earl, Herr, kami, king, land, losh, peer, sire, tuan 05 baron, chief, count, Maker, noble, omrah, ruler 06 bishop, Christ, Father, leader, master, prince, Yahweh 07 captain, Creator, emperor, Eternal, Holy One, Jehovah, Messiah, monarch, Saviour, the Word 08 Almighty, governor, nobleman, overlord, Redeemer, seigneur, seignior, Son of God, Son of Man, superior, suzerain, viscount 09 commander, patrician, sovereign 10 aristocrat 11 Jesus Christ, King of kings 13 grand seigneur
*See also* **nobility**
- **lord it over** 06 act big 07 oppress, repress, swagger 08 dominate, domineer, pull rank 09 put on airs, tyrannize 10 boss around, overoffice 11 order around, queen it over 13 be overbearing

**lordliness**
05 pride 07 disdain, majesty 09 arrogance, grandness, nobleness 11 haughtiness, imperiality 12 magnificence, splendidness 13 big-headedness, condescension, imperiousness 14 high-handedness, impressiveness, overconfidence

**lordly**
05 grand, lofty, noble, proud 06 lavish, uppity 07 haughty, stately, stuck-up 08 arrogant, imperial, majestic, splendid 09 big-headed, dignified, grandiose, hubristic, imperious 10 disdainful, high-handed, hoity-toity, impressive, peremptory, tyrannical 11 dictatorial, domineering, magnificent, overbearing, patronizing, toffee-nosed 12 aristocratic, supercilious 13 condescending, high and mighty, overconfident

**lore**
04 lair, lare, lear, leir, lere 05 leare,

**lorry**

myths, thong 06 cabala, kabala, wisdom 07 beliefs, cabbala, kabbala, legends, qabalah, sayings, stories 08 folklore, kabbalah, learning, teaching 09 erudition, knowledge, mythology 10 traditions 11 scholarship 13 superstitions

**lorry**

03 rig 04 drag 05 artic, float, truck, wagon 06 camion, pick-up, tipper 07 flatbed, trailer, vehicle 09 dump truck, Jugannath, semi-truck 10 juggernaut, removal van 11 dumper truck, semi-trailer 12 curtain-sider, double-bottom, flatbed truck, pantechnicon, trailer truck 13 drawbar outfit

**lose**

◊ deletion indicator 04 drop, fail, miss, tine, tyne 05 drain, elude, evade, leese, loose, losen, spend, use up, waste 06 expend, forget, go down, ignore, mislay, outrun 07 confuse, consume, deplete, exhaust, forfeit, fritter, get lost, neglect, not find 08 be beaten, bewilder, go astray, misplace, shake off, squander, throw off 09 disregard, dissipate, fall short, stray from 10 be defeated, depart from, escape from, stop having, wander from 11 be conquered, be taken away, come to grief, fail to grasp, leave behind 12 be bereaved of, be deprived of, be divested of, come a cropper, no longer have, suffer defeat 14 be unsuccessful 15 throw in the towel
• **lose out** 06 suffer 07 miss out 08 be beaten 14 be unsuccessful 15 be disadvantaged
• **lose yourself in something** 11 be riveted by 12 be absorbed in, be occupied in 13 be engrossed in, be taken up with 14 be captivated by, be enthralled by, be fascinated by 15 be preoccupied in

**loser**

04 flop 07 also-ran, failure, has-been, no-hoper, washout 08 dead loss, runner-up, write-off 10 non-starter 11 the defeated

**loss**

04 dead, debt, harm, hurt, miss 05 traik, waste 06 damage, defeat, tinsel 07 default, deficit, missing, undoing, wastage, wounded 08 casualty, decrease, deprival, dropping, fatality, write-off 09 death toll, detriment, disprofit, mislaying, privation 10 deficiency, diminution, forfeiture, forgetting, impairment 11 bereavement, deprivation, destruction 12 disadvantage, endamagement, misplacement 13 disappearance, dispossession
• **at a loss** 03 out 04 will, wull 07 at fault, baffled, puzzled 08 all at sea 09 mystified, perplexed 10 bewildered, nonplussed

**lost**

◊ anagram indicator 04 dead, gone, lore, lorn, past, tint 05 stray, tyned 06 astray, bushed, bygone, cursed, damned, doomed, dreamy, fallen, former, missed, ruined, wasted, way-out 07 at a loss, baffled, defunct, extinct, forlorn, mislaid, missing, puzzled, riveted, strayed, wrecked 08 absorbed, amissing, confused, occupied, vanished 09 condemned, destroyed, engrossed, misplaced, neglected, off course, perplexed 10 bewildered, captivated, demolished, enthralled, fascinated, nonplussed, spellbound, squandered, written off 11 disappeared, disoriented, out of the way, preoccupied, taken up with, untraceable 12 absent-minded, irredeemable 13 disorientated, frittered away, long-forgotten, unrecoverable 14 gone for a Burton
• **be lost** 04 tine, tyne
• **lost cause** 04 flop 07 also-ran, has-been, no-hoper, washout 08 dead loss, write-off 10 non-starter 12 hopeless case 14 hopeless person

**lot, lots**

03 cut, due, erf, set, tax 04 fall, fate, gobs, luck, many, part, plot, raft, scad, sort, tons 05 batch, bunch, cavel, crowd, group, heaps, loads, miles, piece, piles, quota, scads, share, weird 06 bundle, dozens, masses, oodles, parcel, ration, shower, stacks 07 destiny, fortune, portion, section 08 heritage, hundreds, jingbang, lashings, millions, quantity 09 a good deal, allotment, allowance, a quantity, gathering, shedloads, situation, sortilege, thousands 10 a great deal, assortment, collection, divination, percentage 11 bucketloads, consignment, great number, large amount, piece of land 13 circumstances, piece of ground
See also **fate; number**
• **a lot** 04 much, scad, slew, slue 05 loads, often 06 barrel 09 any amount 10 a great deal, frequently 12 for a long time 14 to a great degree, to a great extent
• **throw in your lot with** 06 muck in 07 pitch in 10 join forces, take part in, team up with 11 combine with 14 join forces with

**lotion**

04 balm, wash 05 cream, salve, scrub, toner 06 balsam, tanner 07 eyewash, washing 08 aftersun, cleanser, eye-water, lavatory, liniment, ointment 09 blackwash, collyrium, emollient, sunscreen 10 aftershave, astringent, witch-hazel, yellow wash 11 arquebusade, embrocation, fomentation 12 hairdressing, retinoic acid

**lottery**

04 draw, luck, risk 05 bingo, lotto, pools, sweep, Tatts 06 chance, gamble, hazard, raffle 07 tombola, venture 08 art union, Calcutta 09 crapshoot 10 Golden Kiwi, sweepstake 11 speculation, Tattersalls 12 gambling game

**loud**

01 f 02 ff 03 big 04 bold, high 05 brash, flash, forte, gaudy, lairy, noisy, rowdy, showy 06 brassy, brazen, flashy, garish, shrill, vulgar 07 blaring, booming, glaring, raucous, roaring 08 emphatic, gorblimy, piercing, plangent, resonant, strident, vehement 09 clamorous, deafening, gorblimey, insistent, obtrusive, tasteless 10 aggressive, flamboyant, fortissimo, resounding, stentorian, streperous, strepitant, thundering, thunderous, vociferous 11 ear-piercing, full-mouthed, loud-mouthed, penetrating 12 ear-splitting, ostentatious 13 reverberating
• **very loud** 02 ff 10 fortissimo

**loudly**

01 f 02 ff 03 out 05 aloud, forte 07 lustily, noisily, shrilly 08 strongly 10 fortissimo, stridently, vehemently, vigorously 11 clamorously, deafeningly 12 resoundingly, streperously, strepitantly, uproariously, vociferously
• **very loudly** 02 ff

**loudmouth**

04 brag 06 gasbag 07 boaster, windbag 08 big mouth, blowhard, braggart 09 blusterer, swaggerer 11 braggadocio

**loud-mouthed**

04 bold 05 noisy 06 brazen, coarse, vulgar 08 boasting, bragging 10 aggressive, blustering

**loudness**
• **unit of loudness** 04 phon, sone

**loudspeaker**

06 woofer 07 tweeter 09 subwoofer

**lough**

see **lake**

**Louisiana**

02 LA

**lounge**

04 hawm, idle, laze, loll 05 daker, relax, slump 06 dacker, daiker, lollop, repose, sprawl 07 day room, lie back, parlour, recline 08 kill time, lie about 09 front room, lie around, loll about, waste time 10 living room, take it easy 11 drawing room, sitting room 13 reception room
See also **laze**

**lour, lower**

04 loom 05 frown, glare, scowl 06 darken, glower, impend, menace 07 blacken 08 threaten 09 be brewing, cloud over 11 look daggers 14 give a dirty look

**louring, lowering**

04 dark, grey, grim 05 black, gurly, heavy 06 cloudy, gloomy 07 ominous 08 menacing, overcast 09 darkening, impending 10 forbidding, foreboding 11 threatening

**louse**

03 nit
See also **contemptible**

**lousy**

◊ anagram indicator 03 bad, ill, low 04 poor, ropy, sick 05 awful, mingy, ants, ropey, rough, seedy 06 chatty, nouldy, no good, poorly, queasy, ntten, unwell 07 rubbish 08 below ar, crawling, inferior, pathetic, rrible 09 miserable, off-colour, ediicular 10 inadequate, out of sorts, ediculous, second-rate 12 contemptible 14 unsatisfactory 15 under the weather

**out**
3 bow, hob, lob, oaf, oik, yob 4 boor, calf, clod, coof, cuif, dolt, awk, hick, hoon, jake, slob, swad 5 flout, loord, stoop, yahoo, yobbo 6 lubber 07 bumpkin, hallian, hallion, allyon, lumpkin 08 bull-calf, larrikin, oblolly 09 barbarian, roughneck 0 clodhopper 11 bushwhacker, huckle-head, hobbledehoy

**outish**
4 rude 05 crude, gawky, gruff, rough 6 coarse, oafish, rustic, vulgar 7 boorish, doltish, ill-bred, uncouth, obbish 08 churlish, clownish, norant, impolite 09 unrefined 0 uneducated, unmannerly 11 clodhopping, ill-mannered, ncivilized

**ovable, loveable**
4 cute, dear 05 sweet 06 lovely, taking 7 amiable, likable, winsome 8 adorable, charming, engaging, tching, likeable, pleasing 9 appealing, endearing 10 attractive, ewitching, delightful, enchanting 11 captivating

**ove**
4 O 03 lo'e, loo, luv, nil, pet 04 amor, are, dear, doat, dote, Eros, lust, zeal, ero 05 adore, agape, amour, angel, roha, Cupid, enjoy, fancy, honey, rize, sugar, taste 06 ardour, desire, ote on, liking, nought, poppet, gard, relish, savour, warmth 7 acushla, asthore, beloved, be mad n, care for, charity, cherish, concern, arling, dearest, dear one, delight, dolize, long for, machree, nothing, assion, rapture, sweetie, worship 8 amorance, be daft on, be fond of, e nuts on, be sold on, devotion, ndness, hold dear, intimacy, ndness, pleasure, precious, soft spot, mpathy, treasure, weakness 9 adoration, adulation, affection, be veet on, delight in, enjoyment, vourite, Platonics, tendresse 0 appreciate, attachment, ompassion, friendship, jeune amour, navourneen, partiality, sweetheart, nderness 11 amorousness, be evoted to, be partial to, brotherhood, nclination, infatuation, Platonicism 12 appreciation, belle passion, rauendienst, have a crush on, like ery much 13 amour courtois, be tracted to 14 have a liking for, have ne hots for, take pleasure in 15 think ne world of

**fall in love with** 05 fancy 06 take to 7 fall for 09 have it bad 12 be crazy bout, have a crush on, take a shine to 3 have a thing for 15 burn with

passion, lose your heart to
• **in love with** 06 doting, hooked, soft on 07 charmed, smitten, stuck on, sweet on 08 besotted, mad about, mashed on 09 enamoured, nuts about, wild about 10 crazy about, infatuated, potty about 11 attracted to, enamoured of
• **love affair** 05 amour, fling 06 affair 07 carry-on, liaison, passion, romance 08 amour fou, intrigue 12 relationship 13 grande passion
• **make love** 09 philander, sleep with 11 go to bed with, have sex with 13 sleep together

**loveable**
see **lovable**

**loveless**
03 icy 04 cold, hard 06 frigid 07 unloved 08 disliked, forsaken, unloving, unvalued 09 heartless, unfeeling 10 friendless, unfriendly 11 cold-hearted, insensitive, passionless, uncherished 12 unresponsive 13 unappreciated

**lovelorn**
06 pining 07 longing 08 desiring, lovesick, yearning 10 infatuated 11 languishing

**lovely**
04 fair 05 nasty, super, sweet 06 dreamy, pretty 07 amorous, winning 08 adorable, charming, handsome, pleasant, pleasing 09 agreeable, beautiful, enjoyable, exquisite, ravishing, wonderful 10 attractive, delightful, enchanting, marvellous 11 beautifully, good-looking 12 delightfully

**lover**
03 fan, lad 04 beau, bird, buff, date 05 fella, fiend, flame, freak, leman, swain 06 fiancé, friend, suitor, toy boy 07 admirer, amorist, amoroso, beloved, devotee, fanatic, fiancée, partner, servant 08 amoretto, follower, lady love, loved one, mistress, other man, paramour, Platonic 09 boyfriend, man friend, philander, supporter 10 enthusiast, girlfriend, lady friend, other woman, sweetheart 11 woman friend 12 bit on the side 13 live-in partner

*Lovers include:*

04 **Bess, Dido, Eros, Eyre** (Jane), **Hera, Hero, Ilsa, Joan, Lamb** (Lady Caroline), **Rick, Sand** (George), **Zeus**
05 **Byron** (Lord), **Cathy, Clyde, Dante, Darby, Darcy** (Mr), **Harry, Helen, Laura, O'Hara** (Scarlett), **Paris, Porgy, Pwyll, Romeo, Sally, Tracy** (Spencer)
06 **Aeneas, Antony, Bacall** (Lauren), **Bogart** (Humphrey), **Bonnie, Burton** (Richard), **Butler** (Rhett), **Caesar, Chopin, Isolde, Juliet, Marian** (Maid), **Nelson** (Lord), **Psyche, Samson, Taylor** (Elizabeth), **Thisbe**
07 **Abelard, Barrett** (Elizabeth),

**Bennett** (Elizabeth), **Delilah, Don Juan, Héloïse, Hepburn** (Katharine), **Leander, Louis XV, Mellors, Orlando, Orpheus, Pyramus, Rimbaud, Simpson** (Mrs), **Tristan, Troilus, Vronsky** (Count)
08 **Beatrice, Benedick, Browning** (Robert), **Casanova** (Giacomo Girolamo), **Cressida, Eurydice, Hamilton** (Lady Emma), **Karenina** (Anna), **Lancelot, Lothario, Napoleon, Nell Gwyn, Odysseus, Penelope, Petrarch, Rhiannon, Rosalind, Verlaine**
09 **Charles II, Cleopatra, Guinevere, Joséphine, Launcelot, Pompadour** (Madame de), **Robin Hood, Rochester** (Mr), **Valentino** (Rudolph)
10 **Chatterley** (Lady), **Edward VIII, Heathcliff**

**lovesick**
06 pining 07 longing 08 desiring, lovelorn, yearning 10 infatuated 11 languishing

**love story**
07 romance

**loving**
04 fond, kind, warm 06 ardent, caring, doting, lovely, tender 07 adoring, amorous, devoted 08 beloving, friendly 10 passionate 11 sympathetic, warmhearted 12 affectionate

**lovingly**
06 fondly, warmly 08 ardently, tenderly 12 passionately 14 affectionately 15 sympathetically

**low**
03 bad, law, moo, sad 04 base, bass, blue, deep, down, dull, evil, flat, glum, hill, late, mean, meek, mild, poor, rich, sale, slow, soft 05 a snip, blaze, cheap, early, fed up, flame, hedge, lowly, muted, nadir, nasty, plain, quiet, scant, short, small, squat 06 a steal, bellow, bottom, coarse, common, gentle, gloomy, humble, humbly, hushed, junior, little, meagre, modest, paltry, ribald, ribaud, scanty, scarce, shabby, simple, smutty, sparse, sunken, vulgar, wicked 07 adverse, debased, foolish, heinous, hostile, immoral, low-born, muffled, obscene, obscure, peasant, reduced, rybauld, shallow, slashed, stunted, subdued, tumulus, unhappy 08 degraded, dejected, depraved, dog-cheap, downcast, indecent, inferior, low-lying, low point, mediocre, moderate, negative, opposing, ordinary, plebeian, resonant, sea-level, sonorous, trifling 09 dastardly, deficient, depressed, dirt-cheap, knock-down, miserable, quietened, ten a penny, whispered 10 all-time low, cheesed off, despicable, despondent, inadequate, low-pitched, low-ranking, reasonable, rock-bottom, submissive 11 downhearted, ground-level, inexpensive, lowest point, low-spirited, subordinate, unimportant

**low-born**

12 antagonistic, contemptible, disconsolate, disheartened, insufficient, low-watermark, unfavourable 13 below standard, dishonourable, going for a song, insignificant, unintelligent 14 down in the dumps, unsatisfactory

**low-born**

04 poor 05 lowly 06 humble 07 obscure, peasant, plebean, villain 08 mean-born, plebeian 09 unexalted 10 low-ranking

**lowbrow**

04 rude 05 crude 07 tabloid 08 ignorant 09 unlearned, unrefined 10 downmarket, mass-market, uncultured, uneducated, unlettered 11 unscholarly 12 uncultivated

**lowdown**

03 gen 04 base, data, dope, info, mean, news, vile 05 facts 07 caitiff 08 shameful, wretched 09 dastardly, degrading, loathsome, reprobate, worthless 10 abominable, despicable, detestable, disgusting 11 disgraceful, information, inside story 12 contemptible, disreputable, intelligence 13 dishonourable, reprehensible

**lower**

03 cow, cut, dip 04 drop, hush, sink, vail 05 abase, abate, couch, demit, lowly, minor, slash, stoop, under 06 bottom, debase, demean, dilute, embace, embase, humble, imbase, junior, lessen, lesser, nether, reduce, settle, submit 07 beneath, cheapen, curtail, degrade, depress, descend, let down, let fall, quieten, set down 08 belittle, bring low, decrease, diminish, disgrace, inferior, look down, low-level, move down, take down 09 bring down, dishonour, disparage, secondary, undermost 10 nethermore, underneath 11 second-class, subordinate 12 speak quietly 13 move downwards
See also **lour, lower**
• **lower in estimation** 04 less

**lowering**

03 ebb 04 dark, drop, duck, grey, grim 05 black, gurly, heavy 06 cloudy, gloomy 07 ominous, sinking 08 menacing, overcast, reducing 09 darkening, degrading, demission, impending, reduction 10 depression, forbidding, foreboding 11 degradation, letting down, threatening
See also **louring, lowering**

**lowest**

03 net 04 nett

**low-grade**

03 bad 04 naff, poor, poxy, ropy 05 awful, lousy, pants, ropey 06 crummy 07 botched, the pits, useless 08 inferior, pathetic, terrible 09 cheap-jack, third-rate 10 second-rate 11 a load of crap, poor-quality, second-class, substandard 13 below standard 14 a load of garbage, a load of rubbish, not up to scratch

**low-key**

04 soft 05 muted, quiet 06 slight, subtle 07 relaxed, subdued 09 easy-going 10 restrained, undramatic 11 understated

**lowliness**

07 modesty, poverty 08 humility, meekness, mildness 09 obscurity 10 commonness, simplicity 11 inferiority 12 ordinariness, unimportance 14 submissiveness 15 subordinateness

**lowly**

04 base, mean, meek, mild, poor 05 plain 06 common, humble, junior, modest, simple 07 low-born, obscure, peasant 08 inferior, ordinary, plebeian 10 low-ranking, submissive 11 subordinate, unimportant

**low-pitched**

03 low 04 bass, deep, rich 08 resonant, sonorous

**low-spirited**

03 low, sad 04 down, glum 05 dowie, fed up, moody 06 gloomy 07 unhappy 08 dejected, downcast 09 depressed, miserable 10 cheesed off, despondent 11 discouraged, downhearted 12 heavy-hearted 14 down in the dumps

**loyal**

04 feal, firm, leal, true 06 stanch, trusty 07 devoted, sincere, staunch 08 constant, faithful, reliable 09 committed, dedicated, patriotic, steadfast 10 dependable, supportive, unchanging 11 true-hearted, trustworthy 12 well-affected

**loyalty**

06 fealty, lealty 08 devotion, fidelity 09 constancy, sincerity 10 allegiance, commitment, dedication, patriotism 11 reliability, staunchness 12 faithfulness 13 dependability, esprit de corps, steadfastness 15 trustworthiness

**lozenge**

05 rhomb 06 cachou, jujube, rustre, tablet, troche 07 gumdrop, rhombus 08 pastille, trochisk 09 cough drop 10 trochiscus

**LSD**

04 acid
• **LSD experience** 04 trip

**lubber**

03 oaf, yob 04 boor, clod, dolt, gawk, hick, lout, slob, swab 05 yahoo, yobbo 07 bumpkin 09 barbarian 10 clodhopper 11 hobbledehoy

**lubberly**

05 crude, dense, gawky 06 clumsy, coarse, oafish 07 awkward, doltish, loutish, lumpish, uncouth 08 bungling, churlish, clownish, ungainly 09 lumbering 10 blundering 11 clodhopping, heavy-handed

**lubricant**

03 fat, oil 04 lard, lube 06 ben-oil, grease 07 K-Y® jelly 08 oil of ben,

ointment, Vaseline® 11 lubrication 14 petroleum jelly

**lubricate**

03 oil, wax 04 ease, help, lard, lube 05 bribe, smear 06 assist, grease, polish, smooth 07 advance, forward, further, promote, speed up 08 expedit 09 encourage 10 accelerate, facilitate, make easier, make smooth 12 smooth the way

**luce**

03 ged

**lucid**

04 pure, sane 05 clear, plain, sober, sound 06 bright, glassy, limpid 07 beaming, evident, obvious, radian shining 08 distinct, explicit, gleaming luminous, pellucid, rational, sensible 09 brilliant, effulgent 10 diaphanous, reasonable 11 clear-headed, crystalline, of sound mind, perspicuous, resplendent, translucent transparent 12 compos mentis, intelligible 14 comprehensible

**lucidity**

06 sanity 07 clarity 09 plainness, soundness 11 rationality 12 compos mentis 14 reasonableness 15 clear-headedness, intelligibility

**lucidly**

07 clearly, plainly 09 evidently, obviously 10 explicitly 12 intelligibly 14 comprehensibly

**luck**

03 hap 04 fate, joss, seal, seel, seil, sel 05 break, fluke 06 chance, hazard 07 destiny, fortune, godsend, success 08 accident, fortuity, good luck, the stars 10 prosperity, providence 11 goo fortune, serendipity 14 predestination
• **bad luck** 06 hoodoo, mishap, mozzle 07 ambs-ace, ames-ace 08 deuce-ace 09 hard lines, mischanc 10 hard cheese, ill fortune 12 misadventure
• **bring bad luck** 03 hex 04 jinx
• **good luck** 05 sonce, sonse 06 pros 07 wassail 08 godspeed, waes hail 09 drink hail 11 bonne chance
• **in luck** 05 happy, jammy 06 timely 08 favoured 09 fortunate, opportune 10 advantaged, auspicious, successfu
• **out of luck** 07 hapless, unlucky 08 luckless 11 unfortunate 12 inauspicious, unsuccessful 13 disadvantaged 14 down on your luck

**luckily**

07 happily 08 by chance 10 by accident, by good luck, mercifully 11 fortunately 12 fortuitously, propitiously 14 providentially

**luckless**

06 cursed, doomed, jinxed 07 hapless unhappy, unlucky 08 hopeless, ill-fated 09 miserable 10 calamitous, disastrous, ill-starred 11 fortuneless, star-crossed, unfortunate 12 catastrophic, unpropitious, unsuccessful

**lucky**
05 canny, happy, jammy, tinny
06 chancy, in luck, spawny, timely
07 chancey, charmed 08 favoured
09 departure, expedient, fortunate,
opportune, promising 10 auspicious,
fortuitous, just as well, propitious,
prosperous, successful 12 providential
• **lucky chance** 03 hit

**lucrative**
07 gainful 08 well-paid 10 high-paying,
productive, profitable, worthwhile
11 moneymaking 12 advantageous,
profit-making, remunerative

**lucratively**
09 gainfully 10 profitably
12 productively 14 advantageously,
remuneratively

**lucre**
03 pay 04 cash, dosh, gain 05 brass,
bread, dough, dross, gains, lolly,
money, ready 06 income, mammon,
profit, riches, spoils, wealth 07 profits,
readies 08 greenies, proceeds,
winnings 11 spondulicks
12 remuneration

**ludicrous**
◊ anagram indicator 03 odd 04 zany
05 comic, crazy, droll, funny, silly
06 absurd 07 amusing, comical, risible
08 farcical, humorous, sportive
09 burlesque, eccentric, grotesque,
hilarious, laughable 10 outlandish,
ridiculous 11 nonsensical
12 preposterous
• **something ludicrous** 04 jest

**ludicrously**
08 absurdly 09 laughably
11 grotesquely, hilariously
12 outlandishly, ridiculously
13 nonsensically 14 preposterously

**lug**
03 ear, tow, tug 04 bear, drag, haul,
hump, lift, loop, pole, pull, tote
05 carry, heave, stick 06 handle

**luggage**
04 gear, swag 05 bluey, stuff, traps
06 things 07 baggage, clobber
10 belongings 11 impedimenta
13 paraphernalia

*Luggage includes:*

03 bag, box
04 case, grip
05 chest, trunk
06 basket, bergen, hamper, kitbag,
valise
07 holdall, satchel
08 backpack, knapsack, rucksack,
suitcase
09 briefcase, flight bag, haversack,
portfolio, travel bag
10 vanity case
11 attaché case, hand-luggage,
portmanteau
12 Gladstone bag, overnight bag

**lugubrious**
03 sad 04 glum 06 dismal, dreary,
gloomy, morose, sombre, woeful
07 baleful, doleful, serious 08 funereal,
mournful 09 sorrowful, woebegone

10 lachrymose, melancholy,
sepulchral

**lugworm**
03 lob 07 lobworm

**lukewarm**
03 lew 04 cool 05 tepid 07 coolish,
warmish 09 apathetic, impassive,
Laodicean 11 half-hearted, indifferent,
unconcerned 12 slightly warm,
uninterested, unresponsive
14 unenthusiastic

**lull**
04 calm, ease, hush 05 abate, allay, let-
up, pause, peace, quell, quiet, still
06 pacify, soothe, sopite, subdue
07 assuage, compose, silence, subside
08 calmness 09 stillness 11 quieten
down 12 tranquillity

**lullaby**
05 baloo 07 hushaby 08 berceuse
10 cradle song

**lumber**
04 junk, land, load, pawn, plod, wood
05 clump, stamp, stump, trash
06 burden, charge, hamper, impose,
jumble, prison, raffle, refuse, rumble,
saddle, timber, trudge 07 clutter,
rubbish, shamble, shuffle, stumble,
trundle 08 encumber, imprison,
pawnshop 10 flirtation 11 odds and
ends 13 bits and pieces

**lumbering**
05 heavy 06 bovine, clumsy
07 awkward, hulking, lumpish,
massive 08 bumbling, ungainly,
unwieldy 09 ponderous 10 blundering
11 elephantine, heavy-footed

**lumen**
02 lm, lu

**luminary**
03 VIP 04 star 05 celeb 06 bigwig,
candle, expert, leader, worthy 07 big
name, notable 09 authority, celebrity,
dignitary, personage, superstar
12 leading light

**luminence**
01 L
• **amount of luminence** 03 nit

**luminescent**
06 bright 07 glowing, radiant, shining
08 luminous 09 effulgent 10 luciferous
11 fluorescent 14 phosphorescent

**luminosity**
04 glow 05 light 06 lustre 08 radiance
10 brightness, brilliance
12 fluorescence, illumination

**luminous**
03 lit 05 clear, lucid 06 bright
07 glowing, lighted, radiant, shining
08 dazzling, lustrous 09 brilliant,
effulgent 11 fluorescent, illuminated,
illustrious, luminescent

**lump**
03 bur, cob, dab, dad, dod, gob, lob,
nub, nut, pat, wad 04 ball, bear, bees,
bump, burr, cake, clat, clod, core,
daud, dawd, fuse, hunk, knob, knot,
knub, loaf, mass, nirl, node, pool,
rock, slub, slug, take 05 blend, block,

bolus, brook, bulge, bunch, chuck,
chump, chunk, claut, clump, crowd,
gnarl, group, hunch, knarl, lunch,
piece, plook, plouk, slump, stand,
thole, tuber, unite, wedge, wodge
06 bruise, bunion, dallop, dollop,
endure, gather, gobbet, growth,
nodule, nubble, nugget, suffer, tumour
07 cluster, collect, combine, dislike,
knubble, pustule, stomach, swallow
08 bear with, coalesce, swelling,
tolerate 09 carbuncle, put up with
10 concretion, protrusion, tumescence
11 consolidate, mix together, put
together 12 conglomerate,
protuberance

**lumpish**
04 dull 05 gawky, gross, heavy
06 clumsy, oafish, obtuse, stolid,
stupid, sullen 07 awkward, boorish,
doltish, hulking 08 bungling, ungainly
09 lethargic, lumbering 10 dull-witted
11 elephantine

**lumpy**
04 slub 05 bumpy 06 cloggy, grainy,
nodose, nodous 07 bunched, clotted,
curdled, grumose, grumous, knobbly
08 granular 09 congealed
10 coagulated

**Luna**
06 Selene

**lunacy**
05 folly, mania 06 idiocy 07 inanity,
madness 08 dementia, insanity,
nonsense 09 absurdity, craziness,
silliness, stupidity 10 aberration,
imbecility 11 derangement,
foolishness, moon-madness
12 dementedness, illogicality
13 irrationality, senselessness
14 outrageousness, ridiculousness
• **fit of lunacy** 04 lune

**lunar**
*see* **moon**

**lunatic**
◊ anagram indicator 03 mad 04 daft,
nuts 05 barmy, crazy, inane, loony,
loopy, nutty, potty, silly 06 absurd,
insane, madman, maniac, nutter,
psycho, stupid 07 bonkers, foolish,
idiotic, nutcase, oddball 08 crackpot,
demented, deranged, headcase,
imbecile, madwoman, neurotic
09 disturbed, fruitcake, illogical,
psychotic, senseless 10 irrational,
moonstruck, psychopath, unbalanced
11 hare-brained, nonsensical 12 insane
person, moon-stricken, round the
bend 13 off your rocker, round the
twist

**lunch**
04 tiff, tift 05 piece, snack 06 brunch,
dinner, nacket, nocket, tiffin 07 tiffing
08 luncheon, nuncheon 10 light lunch,
midday meal 11 packed lunch, Sunday
lunch
• **out to lunch** ◊ anagram indicator
05 crazy

**lunge**
03 cut, hit, jab 04 dart, dash, dive,
grab, leap, pass, poke, stab 05 bound,

## lungs

hit at **06** charge, grab at, plunge, pounce, spring, strike, thrust **08** fall upon, strike at **09** pitch into

## lungs

• **goose lungs** **04** soul

## lurch

**04** list, reel, rock, roll, sway, swee, swey, veer, wait **05** filch, pitch, stoit **06** ambush, swerve, totter **07** defraud, stagger, stumble **09** forestall, overreach **11** weather roll **12** discomfiture
• **leave in the lurch** **04** fail **06** desert **07** abandon, let down **10** disappoint **13** leave stranded **15** leave high and dry

## lure

**03** jig **04** bait, draw, tole, toll **05** decoy, Devon, squid, stale, stool, tempt, train, troll **06** allure, carrot, entice, induce, lead on, seduce, trepan **07** attract, beguile, ensnare **08** inveigle **09** decoy-duck, honey-trap, seduction, spoonbait, spoonhook **10** allurement, attraction, enticement, inducement, temptation, trout-spoon **11** Devon minnow **12** trolling-bait **13** trolling-spoon **14** take a rise out of

## lurid

**04** gory, loud **05** showy, vivid **06** garish, Gothic, grisly, sultry **07** ghastly, glaring, graphic, intense, macabre **08** dazzling, explicit, gruesome, horrific, shocking **09** brilliant, brimstony, revolting, startling **11** exaggerated, sensational **12** melodramatic

## luridly

**07** vividly **08** garishly **09** intensely **10** explicitly, gruesomely, shockingly **11** brilliantly, graphically, revoltingly

## lurk

**04** dare, hide **05** dodge, prowl, skulk, slink, sneak, snoke, snook, snoop, snowk **06** crouch, lie low, loiter **07** swindle **09** lie in wait **15** conceal yourself

## luscious

**04** sexy **05** juicy, sweet, tasty, yummy **06** morish **07** cloying, fulsome, moreish, savoury **08** gorgeous, sensuous, smashing, stunning **09** beautiful, delicious, desirable, ravishing, succulent **10** appetizing, attractive, delectable, delightful, voluptuous **11** pleasurable, scrumptious **13** mouthwatering

## lush

**03** sot **04** posh, rich, soak, wino **05** alkie, dense, dipso, drink, drunk, grand, green, plush, ritzy, souse, toper **06** boozer, classy, glitzy, lavish, ornate, sponge, swanky **07** alcohol, bloater, drinker, fuddler, opulent, profuse, shicker, teeming, tippler, tosspot, verdant **08** abundant, drunkard, habitual, palatial, prolific **09** alcoholic, inebriate, luxuriant, luxurious, overgrown, sumptuous **10** wine-bibber **11** dipsomaniac, extravagant, flourishing, hard drinker **12** heavy drinker

## lust

**04** lech, will **05** greed **06** desire, hunger, libido, relish **07** avidity, craving, lechery, longing, passion, the hots **08** appetite, cupidity, lewdness, pleasure, yearning **09** horniness, prurience, randiness **10** greediness, sensuality **11** raunchiness, sexual drive **12** covetousness, sexual desire **13** concupiscence **14** lasciviousness, licentiousness
• **lust after** **04** need, want **05** covet, crave **06** desire, lecher, slaver **07** long for **08** yearn for **09** hunger for, thirst for

## lustful

**03** hot **04** lewd, rank **05** horny, radge, randy **06** carnal, randie, wanton **07** craving, goatish, rammish, raunchy, ruttish, sensual **08** prurient, unchaste **09** hankering, lecherous, lickerish, luxurious, salacious, venereous **10** cupidinous, lascivious, libidinous, licentious, passionate **12** concupiscent

## lustily

**04** hard **06** loudly **07** stoutly **08** heartily, robustly, strongly **10** forcefully, powerfully, vigorously

## lustiness

**05** power **06** energy, health, vigour **08** haleness, strength, virility **09** hardiness, stoutness, toughness **10** robustness, sturdiness **11** healthiness

## lustre

**04** fame, gaum, glow, gorm, silk **05** glare, gleam, glint, glory, gloss, merit, sheen, shine, water **06** credit, honour, renown **07** burnish, glitter, shimmer, sparkle, varnish **08** lambency, prestige, radiance, schiller **09** lovelight, splendour **10** brightness, brilliance, refulgence **11** distinction **12** resplendence **15** illustriousness

## lustreless

**03** mat **04** matt **05** matte

## lustrous

**05** glacé, shiny **06** bright, glossy, sheeny **07** glowing, lambent, radiant, shining **08** dazzling, gleaming, luminous **09** brilliant, burnished, sparkling, twinkling **10** glistening, glittering, shimmering

## lusty

**03** fit **04** hale, rank **05** beefy, bulky, frack, gutsy, stout, tough **06** hearty, lively, robust, rugged, strong, sturdy, virile **07** healthy, lustick **08** blooming, forceful, lustique, pleasant, pleasing, powerful, skelping, vigorous **09** energetic, strapping **13** hale and hearty

## lute

**03** oud **04** pipa **06** cither **07** bandura, cithern, cittern, dichord, pandora, pandore, theorbo **08** archlute, polyphon **09** orpharion, polyphone **10** chitarrone

## lutetium

**02** Lu

## Luxembourg

**01** L **03** LUX

## luxuriance

**06** excess **08** lushness, rankness, richness **09** abundance, denseness, fecundity, fertility, profusion **10** exuberance, exuberancy, lavishness, overgrowth **11** copiousnes **13** sumptuousness

## luxuriant

**04** lush, rank, rich **05** ample, dense, fancy **06** fecund, florid, lavish, ornate, rococo **07** baroque, copious, fertile, flowery, opulent, profuse, riotous, teeming **08** abundant, prolific, thriving, tropical **09** elaborate, excessive, exuberant, plenteous, plentiful, sumptuous **10** flamboyant, productive **11** extravagant, overflowing **12** overabundant **13** superabundant

## luxuriate

**04** bask, grow **05** bloom, enjoy, revel **06** abound, frowst, relish, savour, thrive, wallow **07** burgeon, delight, indulge, prosper, relax in **08** flourish **09** have a ball **12** live in clover

## luxurious

**04** high, lush, posh, rich **05** cushy, grand, plush, ritzy **06** costly, de luxe, glitzy, lavish, plushy, silken, swanky **07** Apician, elegant, lustful, opulent **08** affluent, delicate, feastful, pampered, splendid **09** expensive, sumptuous **10** Babylonian, mollitious **11** comfortable, magnificent **13** self-indulgent, well-appointed

## luxuriously

**04** high **06** poshly **07** plushly **08** glitzily, lavishly, swankily **09** opulently **10** affluently **11** comfortably, deliciously, sumptuously **13** magnificently

## luxury

**03** pie **04** luxe, Ritz **05** extra, treat **06** dainty **07** comfort **08** delicacy, delicate, grandeur, hedonism, opulence, pleasure, richness **09** affluence, grand luxe, grandness, splendour **10** costliness, indulgence, wantonness **11** lap of luxury **12** extravagance, magnificence, milk and honey, satisfaction **13** expensiveness, gratification, sumptuousness **14** self-indulgence

## lying

**05** false **06** deceit **07** crooked, falsity, fibbing, leasing, perjury **08** two-faced **09** deceitful, dishonest, duplicity, falsehood, invention, white lies **10** dishonesty, mendacious, untruthfu **11** crookedness, dissembling, fabrication, pseudologia **13** dissimulating, double-dealing, falsification **14** untruthfulness

## lynch

**04** hang, kill **06** dewitt **07** execute **08** string up **10** put to death **13** hang b the neck

## lyre string

**04** mese, nete **05** trite **06** hypate

## lyric

**03** lay, ode **04** lied, pean, song
**05** melic, paean **06** poetic **07** melodic,
musical **08** personal **09** emotional
**10** passionate, subjective

## lyrical

**04** odic **06** poetic **07** musical

**08** ecstatic, effusive, inspired, romantic
**09** emotional, rapturous, rhapsodic
**10** expressive, passionate **11** carried
away, impassioned **12** enthusiastic

## lyrically

**09** musically **10** effusively, poetically
**11** emotionally, rapturously

**12** ecstatically, expressively,
passionately, romantically

## lyricist

*see* **songwriter**

## lyrics

**04** book, text **05** words **08** libretto

# M

**M**
**02** em **04** Emma, Mike

**macabre**
◊ *anagram indicator* **04** gory, grim, sick
**05** eerie, sicko **06** Gothic, grisly,
morbid **07** ghastly, ghostly, hideous
**08** chilling, dreadful, gruesome,
horrible, horrific, shocking **09** frightful
**10** terrifying **11** frightening

**Macao**
**03** MAC

**macaroni**
**04** zite, ziti **05** dandy **06** medley
**10** rockhopper

**mace**
**03** rod **04** club, maul **05** poker, staff,
stick **06** cudgel

**mace-bearer**
**05** bedel **06** beadle

**Macedonia**
**02** MK **03** MKD

**macerate**
**04** mash, pulp, soak **05** blend, steep
**06** soften, squash **07** liquefy, mortify
**08** marinade

**Machiavellian**
**03** sly **04** foxy, wily **06** artful, astute,
crafty, shifty, shrewd **07** cunning,
devious **08** guileful, scheming
**09** deceitful, designing, underhand
**10** intriguing, perfidious **11** calculating,
opportunist **12** unscrupulous
**13** double-dealing

**machination**
**04** plot, ploy, ruse, wile **05** cabal,
dodge, trick **06** design, device,
scheme, tactic **08** artifice, intrigue
**09** manoeuvre, stratagem
**10** conspiracy **11** shenanigans

**machine**
**04** tool **05** motor, organ, robot
**06** agency, device, engine, gadget,
system, zombie **07** android, vehicle
**08** catalyst, hardware, workings
**09** apparatus, appliance, automaton,
influence, mechanism, structure
**10** instrument **11** contraption,
contrivance **12** organization

**machine-gun**
**02** MG **04** Bren **05** Maxim **07** Bren gun
**08** Lewis gun, Maxim-gun
**12** mitrailleuse

**machinery**
**04** gear **05** tools **06** agency, system,
tackle **07** channel **08** channels,
gadgetry, workings **09** apparatus,
equipment, mechanism, procedure,

structure **11** instruments
**12** organization

Machinery includes:
**03** Cat®, JCB®
**05** crane, dozer
**06** digger, dumper, grader, jigger
**07** dredger, grapple, gritter, skidder,
tractor
**08** dragline, dustcart, fork lift, jib
crane
**09** bulldozer, calfdozer, dump truck,
excavator
**10** angledozer, earthmover, pile-
driver, road roller, snowplough,
tower crane, tracklayer, truck
crane, water crane
**11** Caterpillar®, dumper truck,
gantry crane, road-sweeper,
wheel loader
**12** cherry picker, crawler crane,
luffing crane, pick-up loader
**13** concrete mixer, floating crane,
fork-lift truck, grabbing crane,
platform hoist
**14** container crane, crawler tractor,
tractor-scraper
**15** hydraulic shovel, luffing-jib
crane, walking dragline

**machinist**
**06** worker **08** mechanic, operator
**09** operative **11** factory hand

**machismo**
**08** maleness, strength, virility
**09** manliness, toughness **11** masculinity

**macrocosm**
**05** world **06** cosmos, entity, planet,
system **07** culture, society **08** creation,
humanity, totality, universe
**09** community, structure **11** solar
system **12** civilization, single entity

**mad**
◊ *anagram indicator* **03** ape, fay, fey, fie,
wud **04** avid, bats, daft, fond, gyte,
keen, loco, nuts, wild, wood, wowf,
yond **05** angry, barmy, batty, berko,
buggy, crazy, cross, daffy, dippy,
dotty, flaky, gonzo, hasty, irate, livid,
loony, loopy, manic, nutty, potty,
queer, rabid, rapid, ratty, silly, spewy,
wacko, wacky, wiggy **06** absurd,
ardent, choked, crazed, cuckoo, fruity,
fuming, insane, locoed, maniac,
mental, raging, raving, red-mad, red-
wud, screwy, stupid, troppo, whacko
**07** bananas, barking, berserk, blazing,
bonkers, cracked, crooked, devoted,
enraged, excited, flipped, foolish,
frantic, furious, hurried, idiotic,
intense, lunatic, meshuga, red-wood,
ropable, stroppy, uptight, violent,
zealous **08** burned up, choleric,
crackers, crackpot, demented,
deranged, dingbats, doolally, frenetic,
frenzied, hairless, in a paddy, in a
strop, incensed, maniacal, meshugga,
meshugge, reckless, unhinged,
unstable, up in arms **09** abandoned,
disturbed, energetic, fanatical,
foolhardy, illogical, in a lather,
infuriate, ludicrous, lymphatic,
psychotic, raving mad, seeing red,
ticked off, up the wall **10** aggravated,

bestraught, distracted, distraught,
frantic-mad, hopping mad, infatuated,
infuriated, irrational, off the wall, off
your nut, out to lunch, passionate,
stone-crazy, unbalanced
**11** disgruntled, fit to be tied, hare-
brained, nonsensical, not all there, off
the rails, off your head
**12** crackbrained, enthusiastic, mad as
a hatter, off your chump, on the
warpath, preposterous, round the
bend, uncontrolled, unreasonable,
unrestrained **13** off your rocker, of
unsound mind, out of your head, out
of your mind, out of your tree, round
the twist **14** off your trolley, wrong in
the head **15** non compos mentis, out of
your senses
• **go mad 04** flip **05** go ape **06** blow
up, wig out **07** go crazy **09** go bananas
**11** flip your lid, go ballistic **15** lose your
marbles
• **like mad 06** avidly, wildly
**07** quickly **09** furiously, hurriedly,
zealously **11** fanatically, frantically
**13** energetically

**Madagascar**
**02** RM **03** MDG

**madcap**
**04** cake, fury, rash, wild **05** crazy, silly
**06** lively **07** flighty, hothead
**08** crackpot, heedless, reckless,
tearaway **09** daredevil, desperado,
eccentric, firebrand, foolhardy,
hotheaded, imprudent, impulsive
**10** adventurer, ill-advised
**11** birdbrained, hare-brained,
thoughtless

**madden**
◊ *anagram indicator* **03** bug, irk, vex
**05** anger, annoy, bemad, upset
**06** enrage, hassle **07** agitate, incense,
inflame, provoke **08** distract, irritate
**09** aggravate, drive nuts, infuriate
**10** drive crazy, exasperate **13** get on
your wick, get up your nose, get your
back up **14** drive up the wall **15** get up
your nerves, get your dander up

**maddening**
◊ *anagram indicator* **07** galling
**08** annoying **09** upsetting, vexatious
**10** disturbing, irritating **11** aggravating,
infuriating, troublesome
**12** exasperating

**madder**
**04** chay **05** chaya, Rubia, shaya
**07** alizari **08** gardenia **10** buttonbush

**made**
• **made it 02** ff
• **recently made 03** new

**made-up**
◊ *anagram indicator* **05** false **06** done up
unreal, untrue **07** painted **08** invented,
mythical, powdered, specious
**09** fairytale, fictional, imaginary,
trumped-up **10** fabricated **11** make-
believe **13** wearing make-up

**madhouse**
**05** Babel, chaos **06** asylum, bedlam,
mayhem, uproar **07** turmoil
**08** disarray, disorder, loony bin,

nuthouse **09** funny farm
**11** pandemonium **13** lunatic asylum
**14** mental hospital

## madly
◇ *anagram indicator* **04** fast, very
**06** wildly **07** crazily, hastily, rapidly,
utterly **08** insanely **09** devotedly,
excitedly, extremely, fervently,
furiously, hurriedly, intensely,
violently **10** completely, dementedly,
frenziedly, recklessly **11** deliriously,
exceedingly, frantically
**12** distractedly, hysterically,
irrationally, unreasonably
**13** energetically, exceptionally

## madman, madwoman
**03** nut **04** gelt, kook **05** crank, loony
**06** bedlam, maniac, nutter, psycho
**07** cupcake, furioso, lunatic, nutcase,
oddball **08** crackpot, frenetic,
headcase, imbecile **09** bedlamite,
fruitcake, psychotic, screwball
**10** basket case, psychopath, Tom o'
Bedlam

## madness
◇ *anagram indicator* **03** ire **04** fury, rage,
riot, zeal **05** anger, craze, folie, folly,
mania, wrath **06** ardour, frenzy,
lunacy, raving, uproar **07** abandon,
inanity, passion **08** daftness, delusion,
dementia, hysteria, insanity, keenness,
nonsense, wildness **09** absurdity,
agitation, craziness, furiosity,
meshugaas, mishegaas, psychosis,
silliness, stupidity, theomania
**10** deliration, enthusiasm, excitement,
fanaticism, insaneness
**11** derangement, distraction,
foolishness, infatuation, lycanthropy,
unrestraint **12** exasperation,
intoxication **13** foolhardiness,
irrationality

## madrigal
**04** fa-la

## madwoman
*see* **madman, madwoman**

## Mae
**04** West

## maelstrom
**04** mess **05** chaos **06** bedlam, tumult,
uproar, vortex **07** turmoil **08** disorder
**09** Charybdis, confusion, whirlpool
**10** turbulence **11** pandemonium

## maestro
**03** ace **06** expert, genius, master,
wizard **07** prodigy **08** director, virtuoso
**09** conductor

## Mafia
**06** the Mob **10** Cosa Nostra
• **Mafia boss**   **03** don **04** capo
**09** godfather
• **Mafia code**   **06** omertà
• **Mafia member**   **07** made man,
pentito, soldier **09** goodfella

## magazine
**03** mag **04** pulp, zine **05** comic, depot,
e-zine, paper, slick **06** glossy, lad mag,
weekly **07** arsenal, fanzine, journal,
monthly, webzine **08** carousel,
ordnance **09** carrousel, quarterly

**10** periodical, powder room,
repository, storehouse, supplement
**11** fortnightly, publication
**12** contemporary **14** ammunition dump
*See also* **newspaper**

## maggot
**03** bot, fad **04** bott, mawk, whim, worm
**06** gentle **09** fleshworm

## Magi
*see* **wise man** *under* **wise**

## magic
**03** ace, art **04** cool, mega, mojo, pull
**05** brill, charm, curse, goety, great,
spell, wicca **06** allure, hoodoo, occult,
voodoo, wicked, wonder **07** conjury,
demonic, glamour, gramary, mystery,
sorcery **08** black art, charming,
diablery, gramarye, hermetic, illusion,
magnetic, prestige, romantic,
smashing, spellful, stardust, terrific,
trickery, wizardry **09** conjuring,
deception, diablerie, excellent,
magnetism, occultism, wonderful
**10** allurement, bewitching, black
magic, enchanting, enticement,
entrancing, marvellous, mysterious,
necromancy, tremendous, witchcraft
**11** captivating, enchantment,
fascinating, fascination, incantation,
legerdemain, thaumaturgy
**12** irresistible, metaphysical,
spellbinding, supernatural **13** magical
powers, sleight of hand, wonder-
working

## magical
**05** magic **06** occult **07** demonic
**08** charming, hermetic, spellful,
stardust **09** wonderful **10** enchanting,
hermetical, marvellous, mysterious
**11** captivating, fascinating
**12** spellbinding, supernatural

## magician
**03** ace **05** magus, pawaw, witch
**06** expert, genius, master, powwow,
wizard **07** juggler, maestro, warlock,
wise man **08** conjurer, conjuror,
sorcerer, virtuoso **09** archimage,
enchanter **11** enchantress, illusionist,
necromancer, spellbinder,
spellworker, thaumaturge, witch
doctor **12** wonder-worker **13** miracle-
worker

## magisterial
**05** bossy **06** lordly **08** arrogant,
despotic **09** assertive, imperious,
masterful **10** commanding, high-
handed, peremptory **11** dictatorial,
domineering, overbearing
**13** authoritarian, authoritative

## magistrate
**02** JP, RM **04** beak, cadi, doge, foud,
kadi, qadi **05** amman, edile, judge,
jurat, mayor, prior, reeve **06** aedile,
amtman, avoyer, bailie, bailli, censor,
cotwal, kotwal, pretor, sharif, sherif,
syndic **07** alcalde, bailiff, baillie,
burgess, justice, podestà, praetor,
prefect, provost, shereef, tribune
**08** dictator, landdros, mittimus,
praefect, quaestor **09** landamman,
landdrost, Lord Mayor, novus homo,
portreeve, proconsul **10** corregidor,

landammann, propraetor **11** baron
bailie, burgomaster, field cornet,
gonfalonier, stipendiary

## magnanimity
**05** mercy **07** charity **08** altruism,
kindness, largesse, nobility
**10** generosity, liberality
**11** beneficence, benevolence,
forgiveness, munificence
**12** generousness, philanthropy,
selflessness **13** bountifulness,
unselfishness **14** big-heartedness,
charitableness, high-mindedness,
open-handedness

## magnanimous
**03** big **04** kind **05** large, noble **06** kindly
**07** liberal **08** generous, merciful,
selfless **09** bountiful, forgiving,
unselfish **10** altruistic, beneficent,
benevolent, big-hearted, charitable,
munificent, open-handed, ungrudging
**11** large-minded **12** great-hearted
**13** philanthropic

## magnate
**05** baron, mogul, noble **06** bigwig, fat
cat, leader, tycoon **07** big shot, notable
**08** big noise, big timer **09** big cheese,
executive, financier, moneybags,
personage, plutocrat **12** entrepreneur
**13** industrialist
*See also* **newspaper**

## magnesium
**02** Mg

## magnet
**04** bait, draw, lure **05** charm, focus
**06** appeal, needle **08** solenoid
**09** loadstone, lodestone **10** allurement,
attraction, enticement, focal point

## magnetic
**03** mag **08** alluring, charming,
engaging, gripping, hypnotic, tempting
**09** absorbing, appealing, seductive
**10** attractive, bewitching, enchanting,
entrancing **11** captivating, charismatic,
enthralling, fascinating, mesmerizing,
tantalizing **12** irresistible

## magnetism
**02** it **03** mag **04** draw, grip, lure, pull
**05** charm, magic, oomph, power, spell
**06** allure, appeal, duende, glamor
**07** glamour **08** charisma **09** hypnotism,
mesmerism **10** attraction, temptation
**11** captivation, enchantment,
fascination **12** drawing power
**13** seductiveness

## magnification
**05** boost **07** build-up **08** dilation,
increase **09** deepening, expansion,
extolling, extolment, hyperbole,
inflation, overdoing **10** embroidery
**11** enhancement, enlargement,
heightening, lionization
**12** augmentation, exaggeration,
overemphasis **13** amplification,
dramatization, embellishment,
overstatement **14** aggrandizement
**15** intensification

## magnificence
**04** pomp **05** glory, pride **06** luxury
**07** majesty **08** grandeur, nobility,
opulence, splendor **09** splendour,

**magnificent**

sublimity 10 brilliance, excellence, lavishness 11 stateliness 12 gorgeousness, resplendence 13 luxuriousness, sumptuousness 14 impressiveness

**magnificent**

04 fine, rich 05 grand, noble, royal, state 06 august, lavish, lordly, superb 07 elegant, exalted, gallant, opulent, stately, sublime 08 dazzling, glorious, gorgeous, imposing, majestic, princely, splendid, striking 09 brilliant, excellent, grandiose, luxurious, splendent, sumptuous, wonderful 10 impressive, marvellous 11 resplendent

**magnify**

05 boost 06 blow up, deepen, dilate, expand, extend, overdo 07 amplify, broaden, build up, enhance, enlarge, greaten, signify 08 heighten, increase, multiply, overplay 09 dramatize, embellish, embroider, intensify, overstate 10 exaggerate 13 overemphasize

**magniloquence**

07 bombast, fustian 08 euphuism, rhetoric 09 loftiness, pomposity, turgidity 10 orotundity 14 grandiloquence 15 pretentiousness

**magniloquent**

05 lofty 06 turgid 07 exalted, fustian, orotund, pompous, stilted 08 elevated, sonorous 09 bombastic, high-flown, overblown 10 euphuistic, rhetorical 11 declamatory, pretentious 12 high-sounding 13 grandiloquent

**magnitude**

03 mag 04 bulk, fame, mass, note, size 05 space 06 amount, extent, import, moment, volume, weight 07 expanse, measure 08 capacity, eminence, muchness, quantity, strength 09 amplitude, greatness, intensity, largeness 10 dimensions, importance 11 consequence, distinction, proportions 12 significance 13 absolute value

**magnolia**

03 bay 05 yulan 07 champac, champak 08 sweet bay 09 star anise, tulip tree 10 beaver-tree, beaver-wood 12 cucumber tree, umbrella tree

**magnum opus**

10 masterwork 11 chef d'oeuvre, masterpiece

**magpie**

03 mag, pie 04 Pica, piet, pyat, pyet, pyot 05 madge 06 maggie 09 organ-bird 10 piping crow

**mahogany**

04 toon 05 carap, khaya 06 acajou 07 Cedrela 10 chinaberry 14 chittagong wood

**maid**

03 may 04 ayah, girl, lass 05 bonne, daily, wench 06 au pair, maiden, Mrs Mop, skivvy, slavey, tweeny, virgin 07 abigail, dresser, Mrs Mopp, pucelle, servant 08 bonibell, charlady, domestic, home help, spinster, suivante, tabby cat, waitress 09 bonnibell, charwoman, housemaid, lady's maid, soubrette, tire-woman 10 bowerwoman, Cinderella, handmaiden 11 chambermaid, kitchenmaid, maidservant, serving-maid 12 cleaning lady, kitchen-wench 13 maid-of-all-work 14 femme de chambre

**maiden**

01 M 03 new 04 burd, girl, kore, lass, miss, pure, wili 05 first, nymph, popsy, unwed 06 chaste, damsel, decent, demure, female, gentle, lassie, modest, proper, seemly, vestal, virgin 07 girlish, initial 08 celibate, decorous, reserved, virginal, virtuous 09 inaugural, undefiled, unmarried, unsullied, young girl, young lady 10 initiatory, unbroached, young woman 12 bachelorette, introductory

**maidenhood**

06 honour, purity, virtue 08 chastity 10 chasteness, maidenhead

**maidenly**

04 pure 05 unwed 06 chaste, decent, demure, female, gentle, modest, proper, seemly, vestal, virgin 07 girlish 08 becoming, decorous, reserved, virginal, virtuous 09 undefiled, unmarried, unsullied 10 immaculate, unbroached

**maidservant**

03 may 04 amah, girl, maid 05 daily 06 au pair, maiden, skivvy, slavey 07 abigail, dresser, Mrs Mopp, pucelle, servant 08 charlady, domestic, suivante, waitress 09 bonnibell, charwoman, housemaid, lady's maid, soubrette 10 bowerwoman, handmaiden 11 chambermaid, kitchenmaid, parlour-maid, serving-maid 13 maid-of-all-work

**mail**

03 dak 04 dawk, post, rent, send, spam, spot 05 armor, e-mail 06 armour 07 airmail, fan mail, forward, junk fax, letters, packets, panoply, parcels, payment 08 delivery, dispatch, hate mail, junk mail, packages 09 chain mail, habergeon, halfpenny, snail mail 10 cataphract, direct mail, Post Office 11 chain armour, general post, surface mail 12 all-up service, iron-cladding, postal system, recorded mail 13 postal service 14 communications, correspondence, electronic mail, first-class mail, registered mail 15 second-class mail, special delivery
• **Royal Mail** 02 RM

**mail-coach**

04 drag

**maim**

03 mar 04 hurt, lame, main 05 wound 06 impair, injure, injury, scotch 07 cripple, cut down, disable 08 crippled, mutilate, truncate 09 disfigure 10 disability 12 incapacitate 14 put out of action

**main**

03 key, sea 04 duct, head, lame, lead, line, maim, pipe 05 cable, chief, first, grand, great, major, prime, sheer, vital 06 staple, strong 07 capital, central, channel, conduit, crucial, general, leading, pivotal, premier, primary, purpose, supreme 08 cardinal, critical, dominant, foremost, strength 09 essential, extensive, important, necessary, paramount, principal 10 pre-eminent 11 exceedingly, fundamental, outstanding, predominant 13 most important
• **in the main** 06 mostly 07 as a rule, chiefly, largely, usually 08 commonly 09 generally, in general 10 by and large, especially, on the whole 14 for the most part

**Maine**

02 ME

**mainly**

04 much 06 mostly 07 as a rule, chiefly, largely, overall, usually 08 above all, commonly 09 generally, in general, in the main, primarily 10 by and large, especially, on the whole 11 principally 13 predominantly 14 for the most part

**mainspring**

05 cause 06 motive, origin, reason, source 07 impulse 09 generator, incentive 10 motivation, prime mover, wellspring 11 inspiration 12 driving force, fountainhead

**mainstay**

04 base, prop 05 basis 06 anchor, pillar 07 bulwark, support 08 backbone, buttress, linchpin 09 key player 10 foundation 11 cornerstone 12 right-hand man 14 right-hand woman 15 tower of strength

**mainstream**

06 normal 07 average, central, general, regular, typical 08 accepted, mainline, orthodox, received, standard 11 established 12 conventional

**maintain**

04 aver, avow, feed, hold, keep 05 carry, claim, escot, state 06 affirm, assert, avouch, defend, insist, keep up, retain, supply, uphaud, uphold 07 believe, care for, carry on, contend, declare, finance, nourish, nurture, observe, possess, profess, stand by, support, sustain 08 announce, conserve, continue, fight for, practise, preserve 09 keep going, look after 10 asseverate, perpetuate, provide for, take care of

**maintenance**

04 care, keep 05 title 06 living, upkeep 07 aliment, alimony, defence, feeding, keeping, nurture, repairs, running, support 08 altarage, appanage 09 allowance, financing 10 carrying-on, livelihood, protection, sustenance 11 continuance, nourishment, subsistence, traineeship 12 conservation, continuation, perpetuation, preservation

# maize

3 Zea 04 corn, maze, samp 05 maise, mealy, mease, stamp 06 hominy, mealie 07 mealies, popcorn 09 flint corn, sweetcorn 10 Indian corn, Indian meal, masa harina 12 corn on the cob
**maize dough** 04 masa
**maize loaf** 04 pone
**styles of maize** 04 silk

# majestic

5 grand, lofty, noble, regal, royal 6 august, kingly, lordly, superb 7 awesome, exalted, pompous, queenly, stately, sublime 08 elevated, glorious, imperial, imposing, princely, splendid 09 dignified 10 impressive, marvellous, monumental 1 magnificent, resplendent 3 distinguished

# majestically

5 nobly 07 grandly, regally, royally, stately 08 maestoso, superbly 9 pompously, sublimely 10 gloriously, imperially, splendidly 12 impressively, marvellously 13 magnificently, resplendently

# majesty

4 pomp 05 glory 06 beauty, Tuanku 7 dignity, royalty 08 grandeur, nobility, regality 09 grandness, loftiness, nobleness, splendour, sublimity 11 awesomeness, exaltedness, stateliness 2 magnificence, majesticness, resplendence 14 impressiveness, majesticalness
**Her Majesty** 02 ER, HM 06 Brenda
**His Majesty** 02 HM

# major

3 key, Maj 04 best, main 05 chief, great, older, prime, vital 06 bigger, higher, larger, senior 07 crucial, greater, highest, keynote, largest, leading, notable, serious, supreme, weighty 08 greatest, superior 9 important, paramount, uppermost 0 pre-eminent 11 outstanding, significant

# majority

4 bulk, many, mass, most 07 general, manhood, the many 08 legal age, maturity 09 adulthood, nearly all, plurality, womanhood 10 generality, larger part, lion's share 11 coming of age, greater part, pre-eminence 12 age of consent, larger number, more than half 13 greater number, preponderance 5 reaching full age

# make

◊ anagram indicator 02 do 03 fix, get, nag, net, win 04 cook, earn, flow, form, gain, give, kind, maik, mark, mate, name, sort, tell, tend, turn, type, urge, vote 05 act as, add up, brand, build, cause, clear, drive, elect, equal, erect, force, frame, gross, impel, model, mould, offer, press, put up, reach, score, shape, start, state, style, total, write 06 become, coerce, come to, commit, compel, convey, create, devise, draw up, effect, impart, marque, matter, oblige, obtain, ordain,

reckon, render, result, secure, select, settle, vote in, wrap up 07 achieve, acquire, add up to, appoint, arrange, attempt, bring in, chalk up, compose, compute, consort, convert, declare, deliver, dragoon, execute, fashion, install, notch up, perform, prepare, proceed, produce, promote, realize, require, serve as, shuffle, texture, think up, turn out, variety, work out 08 amount to, arrive at, assemble, bulldoze, carry out, comprise, conclude, contract, engender, estimate, generate, get ready, nominate, occasion, pressure, reckon up, set forth, take home 09 calculate, character, constrain, construct, designate, determine, discharge, establish, fabricate, formation, formulate, get down to, halfpenny, originate, pronounce, strongarm, structure, undertake 10 accomplish, bring about, constitute, contribute, function as, give rise to, perpetrate, pressurize 11 communicate, disposition, manufacture, mass-produce, prevail upon, put together 12 be to blame for 13 play the part of, play the role of 14 put the screws on 15 deliver the goods

*See also* **halfpenny**
• **make away with** 03 nab, rid 04 do in, kill, lift, nick 05 pinch, seize, steal, swipe 06 kidnap, murder, remove, snatch 07 bump off, destroy 08 carry off, fetch off, knock off 09 slaughter 10 do away with, run off with 11 assassinate, walk off with
• **make believe** 03 act 04 play 05 dream, enact, feign 07 imagine, play-act, pretend 09 fantasize
• **make do** 04 cope 05 get by 06 manage 07 make out, survive 08 get along, scrape by 09 improvise 13 muddle through
• **make for** 06 aim for, favour, lead to 07 forward, further, head for, produce, promote 09 go towards 10 facilitate 11 move towards 12 contribute to 13 be conducive to
• **make it** 05 get on, reach 06 arrive 07 prosper, succeed, survive 11 come through, pull through 12 be successful
• **make of** 04 rate 05 judge 06 assess, regard 07 think of, weigh up 08 consider, evaluate
• **make off** 03 fly 04 bolt 05 brush, leave, mosey, truss 06 beat it, decamp, depart, hook it, pop off, run off 07 run away, scarper 08 clear off, up sticks 09 cut and run, shemozzle, skedaddle 12 make a getaway 15 take to your heels
• **make off with** 03 nab 04 flog, nick, take 05 filch, pinch, steal, swipe 06 abduct, kidnap, pilfer 07 purloin 08 carry off, knock off 10 run off with 11 appropriate, walk off with
• **make out** 03 get, see, spy 04 aver, cope, espy, fare, read, scan 05 claim, get by, get on, grasp, imply, prove,

spell 06 affirm, assert, descry, detect, divine, draw up, fathom, fill in, follow, manage 07 achieve, declare, discern, fill out, succeed, work out 08 complete, decipher, describe, discover, get along, maintain, make love, perceive, progress, write out 09 establish, recognize 10 bear in hand, comprehend, understand 11 demonstrate, distinguish, manage to see 12 manage to hear 13 sleep together
• **make over** 05 leave 06 assign, convey 07 dispone, dispose 08 bequeath, sign over, transfer
• **make the rounds of** 02 do
• **make up** ◊ anagram indicator 04 fill, form, meet 05 feign, frame, hatch, paint, rouge 06 create, decide, devise, doll up, invent, parcel, powder, render, repair, repent, settle, supply, tart up 07 arrange, collect, compose, concoct, dream up, perfume, provide, think up 08 complete, compound, comprise, round off 09 construct, fabricate, formulate, make peace, originate 10 constitute, shake hands, supplement 11 call it quits, put make-up on 12 be reconciled 13 Birminghamize, put on your face 14 bury the hatchet
• **make up for** 06 offset 07 redress 08 atone for 13 compensate for, make amends for
• **make up to** 03 eik, eke 05 court 06 chat up, cozy up, fawn on 07 toady to 08 butter up, suck up to 10 compensate, cozy up with 15 curry favour with, make overtures to
• **make way** 06 gather 07 advance, gangway 11 allow to pass, clear the way, make room for 12 make space for, stand back for 14 allow to succeed

# make-believe

04 mock, sham 05 dream 06 made-up, unreal 07 charade, fantasy, feigned, pretend 08 dreaming, imagined, imitated, pretence, pretense, role-play 09 imaginary, pretended, simulated, unreality 10 fantasized, masquerade, play-acting 11 daydreaming, fabrication, imagination

# maker

06 author, wright 07 builder, creator, deviser 08 director, producer, repairer 09 architect 10 fabricator 11 constructor 12 manufacturer

# makeshift

06 cutcha, kludgy, make-do 07 Band-aid®, fig leaf, stand-by, stopgap 08 pis aller 09 expedient, impromptu, temporary, timenoguy 10 improvised, substitute 11 provisional, rudimentary 13 rough and ready 14 thrown together 15 cobbled together

# make-up

◊ anagram indicator 04 form, slap 05 get-up, paint, style 06 format,

nature, powder, temper **07** pancake
**08** assembly, panstick, war paint
**09** blackface, character, cosmetics,
formation, structure, whiteface
**10** foundation, maquillage
**11** arrangement, composition,
disposition, greasepaint, personality,
temperament **12** constitution,
construction, organization
**13** configuration

**making**
**04** form **06** income **07** forging, profits,
promise, returns, revenue, takings
**08** assembly, building, capacity,
creating, creation, earnings, moulding,
proceeds **09** materials, modelling,
potential, producing, qualities,
structure **10** beginnings, capability,
production **11** composition,
fabrication, ingredients, manufacture
**12** construction, potentiality
**13** possibilities
• **in the making** **06** coming
**07** budding, nascent **08** emergent
**09** incipient, potential, promising
**10** burgeoning, developing **11** up and
coming

**maladjusted**
◇ *anagram indicator* **04** gaga **05** dotty
**06** psycho, schizo **08** confused,
neurotic, unstable **09** alienated,
disturbed, estranged, screwed-up
**10** disordered **12** round the bend

**maladministration**
**07** misrule **08** bungling **09** stupidity
**10** blundering, corruption, dishonesty,
misconduct **11** malfeasance,
malpractice, misfeasance,
mishandling **12** incompetence,
inefficiency, malversation
**13** misgovernment, mismanagement

**maladroit**
**05** inept **06** clumsy, gauche
**07** awkward, unhandy **08** bungling, ill-
timed, inexpert, tactless, untoward
**09** graceless, ham-fisted, inelegant,
unskilful **10** cack-handed
**11** insensitive, thoughtless
**12** undiplomatic **13** inconsiderate

**maladroitness**
**10** clumsiness, inelegance, ineptitude
**11** awkwardness **12** tactlessness
**13** gracelessness, insensitivity,
unskilfulness **15** thoughtlessness

**malady**
**07** ailment, disease, illness, malaise
**08** disorder, sickness **09** breakdown,
complaint, infirmity **10** affliction
**13** indisposition
*See also* **disease**

**malaise**
**05** angst **06** unease **07** anguish, anxiety,
disease, illness **08** disquiet, doldrums,
sickness, weakness **09** lassitude,
weariness **10** depression, discomfort,
discontent, enervation, melancholy,
uneasiness **11** unhappiness
**12** restlessness **13** indisposition

**malapropism**
**06** misuse **08** slipslop, solecism
**09** wrong word **10** infelicity

**11** Dogberryism **14** misapplication
**15** slip of the tongue

**malapropos**
**05** inapt **07** inaptly **08** ill-timed,
tactless, unseemly, untimely
**10** inapposite, misapplied, tactlessly,
unsuitable, unsuitably **11** inopportune,
uncalled-for **12** inappositely,
unseasonably **13** inappropriate,
inopportunely **15** inappropriately

**malaria**
**04** ague

**Malawi**
**02** MW **03** MWI

**Malaysia**
**03** MAL, MYS

**malcontent**
**05** fed up, rebel **06** grouch, moaner,
morose **07** aginner, grouser, restive,
unhappy, whinger **08** agitator,
grumbler **09** nit-picker, resentful
**10** bellyacher, cheesed off,
complainer, rebellious **11** bellyaching,
disaffected, disgruntled, dissentious,
ill-disposed, unsatisfied
**12** discontented, dissatisfied, fault-
finding, troublemaker **13** mischief-
maker

**Maldives**
**03** MDV

**male**
**01** m **02** he **03** dog, man, tom **04** bull,
cock, mail, stag **05** macho, manly
**06** armour, boyish, virile **07** laddish,
manlike **09** masculine, staminate
*See also* **animal**

**malediction**
**04** oath, wish **05** curse **07** cursing,
damning, malison **08** anathema
**09** damnation **10** execration
**11** imprecation **12** denunciation

**malefactor**
**05** crook, felon **06** outlaw **07** convict,
culprit, villain **08** criminal, evildoer,
offender **09** miscreant, misfeasor,
wrongdoer **10** delinquent, lawbreaker
**12** transgressor

**malevolence**
**04** hate **05** spite, venom **06** hatred,
malice **07** cruelty, ill-will, rancour
**09** hostility, malignity **10** bitterness,
fierceness, malignancy **11** viciousness
**12** spitefulness, vengefulness
**13** maliciousness **14** unfriendliness,
vindictiveness

**malevolent**
**05** cruel **06** bitter, fierce, malign
**07** baleful, hostile, vicious **08** spiteful,
vengeful, venomous **09** malicious,
rancorous, resentful **10** evil-minded,
ill-natured, maleficent, pernicious,
unfriendly, vindictive
• **malevolent being** **04** peri

**malevolently**
**07** cruelly **08** bitterly, fiercely
**09** viciously **10** spitefully, vengefully,
venomously **11** maliciously, resentfully
**13** vindicatively

**malformation**
**04** warp **09** deformity **10** distortion
**12** irregularity **13** disfigurement,
misshapenness

**malformed**
◇ *anagram indicator* **04** bent **06** warped
**07** crooked, twisted **08** deformed
**09** distorted, irregular, misshapen
**10** disfigured

**malfunction**
◇ *anagram indicator* **04** fail, flaw
**05** crash, fault **06** defect, glitch, go
phut, hiccup, pack up **07** conk out,
failure, go kaput, go wrong
**08** disorder, hiccough **09** break down,
breakdown **11** stop working

**Mali**
**03** MLI, RMM

**malice**
**04** hate **05** spite, venom **06** animus,
enmity, hatred, spleen **07** despite, ill-
will, rancour **08** bad blood
**09** animosity, hostility **10** bitchiness,
bitterness, bone to pick, resentment
**11** malevolence **13** maliciousness
**14** vindictiveness

**malicious**
**04** evil, mean **05** snide **06** bitchy, bitte
malign **07** baleful, hostile, vicious
**08** narquois, spiteful, vengeful,
venomous **09** poisonous, rancorous,
resentful **10** dispiteous, evil-minded,
ill-natured, malevolent, pernicious
**11** mischievous

**maliciously**
**08** bitterly **09** unhappily, viciously
**10** spitefully, venomously
**11** resentfully **12** malevolently,
perniciously

**malign**
**03** bad **04** bait, evil, harm, slur
**05** abuse, libel, smear **06** defame,
injure, insult, vilify **07** baleful,
envenom, harmful, hostile, hurtful, ru
down, slander, traduce **08** badmouth
sinister **09** disparage, injurious,
malignant, misintend, poor-mouth
**10** calumniate, malevolent
**11** destructive **13** stab in the back
**14** kick in the teeth

**malignancy**
**08** fatality **09** lethality, mortality,
virulence **12** incurability

**malignant**
**04** evil **05** black, fatal, swart **06** deadl
lethal, malign, sullen, swarth
**07** baleful, harmful, hostile, hurtful,
vicious **08** cankered, Cavalier,
devilish, Royalist, spiteful, venomous
viperous, virulent **09** cancerous,
dangerous, incurable, injurious,
malicious, poisonous, rancorous
**10** malevolent, pernicious, rebellious
**11** destructive, disaffected
**14** uncontrollable **15** life-threatening

**malignity**
**04** gall, hate **05** spite, venom
**06** animus, hatred, malice, taking
**07** ill-will, rancour **08** bad blood
**09** animosity, hostility, virulence

**malinger**

**10** bitterness, deadliness, wickedness **11** balefulness, harmfulness, hurtfulness, malevolence, viciousness **12** vengefulness **13** maliciousness **14** perniciousness, vindictiveness **15** destructiveness

**malinger**

**04** loaf **05** dodge, shirk, skive, skulk, slack **07** pretend, put it on **09** gold-brick **12** swing the lead **14** pretend to be ill

**malingerer**

**06** dodger, loafer, skiver **07** shirker, slacker **11** lead-swinger

**mall**

**04** beat, maul, mell, walk **05** plaza **06** arcade **08** galleria, precinct **13** outlet village **14** shopping centre **15** shopping complex

**mallard**

**08** wild duck
• **mallard flock** **04** sord

**malleability**

**07** pliancy **08** softness **10** compliance, plasticity, pliability, suppleness **11** ductileness, flexibility **12** adaptability **13** manageability, receptiveness, tractableness **14** susceptibility

**malleable**

◊ *anagram indicator* **04** soft **06** pliant, supple **07** ductile, plastic, pliable **08** biddable, flexible, tractile, workable, yielding **09** adaptable, compliant, receptive, tractable **10** governable, manageable **11** persuadable, susceptible **14** impressionable

**mallow**

**04** sida

**malnourished**

**06** hungry **07** starved **08** anorexic, underfed **09** anorectic **14** undernourished

**malnutrition**

**06** hunger **08** anorexia **09** inanition **10** starvation **12** underfeeding **13** unhealthy diet **15** anorexia nervosa

**malodorous**

**04** rank **05** fetid, niffy **06** foetid, putrid, smelly **07** miasmal, miasmic, noisome, reeking **08** mephitic, miasmous, stinking **09** miasmatic, offensive **10** infragrant, miasmatous, nauseating **12** evil-smelling, foul-smelling

**malpractice**

**05** abuse **07** misdeed, offence **10** misconduct, negligence, wrongdoing **11** impropriety **12** carelessness **13** mismanagement

**malt**

**04** wort

**Malta**

**01** M **03** MLT

**maltreat**

◊ *anagram indicator* **04** harm, hurt, maul **05** abuse, bully, hound **06** damage, ill-use, injure, misuse **07** torture **08** ill-treat, mistreat **09** mishandle, victimize

**10** rough-house, treat badly **11** assassinate

**maltreatment**

**04** harm, hurt **05** abuse **06** damage, ill-use, injury, misuse **07** torture **08** bullying, ill-usage **12** ill-treatment, mistreatment **13** victimization

**mammal**

*Mammals include:*

**03** ape, ass, bat, cat, cow, dog, elk, fox, gnu, pig, rat, yak

**04** bear, boar, cavy, deer, goat, hare, ibex, kudu, lion, lynx, mink, mole, paca, puma, seal, soor, tahr, vole, wolf, zebu

**05** aguti, bison, camel, civet, coney, coypu, dingo, eland, genet, hippo, horse, human, hyena, hyrax, koala, lemur, llama, loris, moose, mouse, okapi, otter, ounce, panda, potto, rhino, sheep, shrew, skunk, sloth, stoat, takin, tapir, tiger, whale, zebra

**06** aye-aye, baboon, badger, beaver, beluga, bobcat, cattle, colugo, cougar, coyote, cuscus, dassie, dugong, duiker, ermine, ferret, galago, gerbil, gibbon, gopher, hacker, impala, jackal, jaguar, jerboa, langur, marmot, marten, monkey, numbat, ocelot, possum, rabbit, racoon, reebok, rhebok, sea cow, serval, tenrec, vicuna, walrus, wapiti, weasel, wombat

**07** ant-bear, bosvark, buffalo, caracal, caribou, chamois, cheetah, dolphin, echidna, fur seal, gazelle, gerenuk, giraffe, gorilla, grampus, grizzly, guanaco, guereza, gymnura, hamster, lemming, leopard, macaque, manatee, meercat, meerkat, mole rat, muntjac, muskrat, narwhal, opossum, pack rat, panther, peccary, polecat, potoroo, primate, raccoon, red deer, roe deer, sea lion, sun bear, tamarin, tarsier, wallaby, warthog, wild ass, wildcat

**08** aardvark, aardwolf, anteater, antelope, bushbaby, bushbuck, capybara, chipmunk, dormouse, duckbill, elephant, fruit bat, grey wolf, harp seal, hedgehog, house bat, kangaroo, mandrill, mangabey, marmoset, mongoose, musk deer, pacarana, pangolin, platypus, porpoise, red panda, reedbuck, reindeer, sea otter, sewer rat, squirrel, steenbok, steinbok, talapoin, wallaroo, warrigal, wild goat

**09** Arctic fox, armadillo, bamboo rat, bandicoot, black bear, blue sheep, blue whale, brown bear, dromedary, flying fox, grey whale, grindhval, guinea pig, jungle cat, mouse-deer, orang-utan, palm civet, phalanger, polar bear, porcupine, springbok, steinbuck, thylacine, waterbuck, wolverine

**10** Barbary ape, chevrotain,

chimpanzee, chinchilla, coatimundi, common seal, fallow deer, field mouse, giant panda, hartebeest, house mouse, human being, jack rabbit, kodiak bear, pilot whale, pine marten, prairie dog, rhinoceros, sperm whale, springbuck, springhare, vampire bat, white whale, wildebeest

**11** beaked whale, flying lemur, green monkey, grizzly bear, honey badger, killer whale, muntjac deer, pipistrelle, rat kangaroo, red squirrel, snow leopard

**12** Arabian camel, barbary sheep, elephant seal, grey squirrel, harvest mouse, hippopotamus, leaf-nosed bat, mountain goat, mountain lion, rhesus monkey, river dolphin, spider monkey, two-toed sloth, vervet monkey, water buffalo

**13** American bison, Bactrian camel, colobus monkey, dwarf antelope, elephant shrew, European bison, hanuman monkey, howling monkey, humpback whale, marsupial mole, mouse-eared bat, spiny anteater, Tasmanian wolf

**14** capuchin monkey, edible dormouse, flying squirrel, Indian elephant, marsupial mouse, mountain beaver, Patagonian hare, squirrel monkey, Tasmanian devil, three-toed sloth

**15** African elephant, black rhinoceros, brushtail possum, hamadryas baboon, humpbacked whale, proboscis monkey, ring-tailed lemur, Thomson's gazelle, white rhinoceros

*See also* **animal; ape; cat; cattle; deer; dog; horse; marsupial; monkey; pig; rodent; sheep; whale**

**mammoth**

**04** huge, vast **05** giant, jumbo **06** bumper, mighty **07** immense, massive **08** colossal, enormous, gigantic, whopping **09** ginormous, herculean, leviathan **10** gargantuan, monumental, prodigious, stupendous **14** Brobdingnagian

**man**

**01** b, k, m, n, p, q, r **02** bo, he, Mr, ou **03** boy, guy, IOM, lad, mun, pin **04** chap, cove, crew, gent, hand, homo, jack, king, male, page, pawn, rook, work **05** adult, bloke, cairn, human, joker, lover, piece, queen, staff, valet **06** bishop, castle, fellow, fiancé, geezer, helper, knight, Mister, mortal, occupy, people, person, spouse, toy boy, vassal, worker **07** chequer, draught, husband, mankind, mortals, operate, partner, servant, soldier, workman **08** employee, factotum, follower, houseboy, houseman, humanity, labourer **09** attendant, boyfriend, gentleman, humankind, human race, odd-jobman **10** human being, individual, manservant, sweetheart

**11** Homo sapiens, human beings **12** be in charge of, man-of-all-work, take charge of **15** jack-of-all-trades
*See also* **boy; chess**
• **first man 04** Adam
• **good man 01** S **02** St **04** sant **05** Saint
• **old man** *see* **old man**
• **to a man 05** as one **07** bar none **09** one and all **11** unanimously **12** with one voice
• **wise man 04** mage, sage **05** magus

**manacle**
**03** tie **04** bind, curb **05** chain, check **06** fetter, hamper, secure **07** inhibit, shackle **08** handcuff, restrain **11** put in chains

**manacles**
**05** bonds, cuffs, gyves, irons **06** chains **07** darbies, fetters, mittens, nippers **08** shackles **09** bracelets, handcuffs, snitchers, wristlets

**manage**
**03** ren, rin, run, use **04** boss, cope, fare, head, keep, lead, play, rule, work **05** cut it, get by, get on, guide, shift, wield **06** direct, effect, govern, handle, head up, honcho, make do, manure, master **07** achieve, carry on, command, conduct, control, make out, operate, oversee, solicit, succeed, survive **08** be head of, bring off, contrive, deal with, engineer, get along, maneuver, navigate, organize **09** influence, manoeuvre, negotiate, supervise **10** accomplish, administer, bring about, manipulate **11** preside over, superintend **12** be in charge of

**manageable**
**04** yare **05** handy **06** doable, docile, pliant, viable, wieldy **07** pliable **08** amenable, feasible, flexible, yielding **09** compliant, easy-to-use, tolerable, tractable **10** acceptable, attainable, functional, governable, reasonable, submissive **11** practicable **12** controllable **13** accommodating

**management**
**04** care **05** admin, board **06** bosses, charge, owners, ruling **07** command, conduct, control, dispose, running **08** disposal, handling, managers, ordering **09** direction, directors, employers, executive, governall, governors, husbandry, stewardry, treatment **10** executives, government, intendance, intendancy, leadership, overseeing **11** directorate, proprietors, stewardship, supervision, supervisors **12** organization **14** administration **15** superintendence

**manager**
**02** GM **03** guv, Mgr **04** boss, head, suit **05** agent, chair, chief **06** gaffer, honcho, serang **07** amildar, husband, planter, proctor **08** chairman, director, employer, governor, hotelier, landlady, landlord, motelier, overseer **09** conductor, contriver, directrix, executive, intendant, organizer, president, régisseur **10** chairwoman, controller, directress, head-bummer,

head serang, impresario, manageress, procurator, supervisor **11** businessman, chairperson, comptroller, head sherang, land-steward **12** commissioner, maître d'hôtel, manufacturer **13** administrator, businesswoman **14** chief executive, superintendent

**managerial**
**09** executive **10** industrial **11** legislative, supervisory **12** departmental, governmental **14** administrative, organizational, superintendent **15** entrepreneurial

**mandate**
**02** OK **03** law, let **04** okay **05** allow, edict, order **06** charge, decree, enable, permit, ratify, ruling **07** approve, bidding, command, confirm, dictate, empower, entitle, licence, precept, statute, warrant **08** legalize, sanction, validate **09** authority, authorize, consent to, direction, directive, make legal, ordinance **10** commission, injunction, king's brief **11** instruction **13** authorization **15** give authority to

**mandatory**
**07** binding **08** required **09** essential, necessary, requisite **10** compulsory, imperative, obligatory

**manful**
**04** bold **05** brave, hardy, manly, noble, stout **06** daring, heroic, strong **07** gallant, valiant **08** intrepid, powerful, resolute, stalwart, vigorous **09** steadfast **10** courageous, determined **11** indomitable, lion-hearted, noble-minded, unflinching **12** stout-hearted

**manfully**
**04** hard **05** nobly **06** boldly **07** bravely, man-like, stoutly **08** pluckily, strongly **09** gallantly, valiantly **10** heroically, intrepidly, powerfully, resolutely, stalwartly, vigorously **11** desperately, steadfastly **12** courageously, determinedly **13** unflinchingly

**manganese**
**02** Mn
• **manganese ore 03** wad **04** wadd, wadt

**manger**
**04** crib **06** cratch, feeder, trough **13** feeding trough

**mangle**
◇ *anagram indicator* **03** cut, mar **04** hack, maim, maul, rend, ruin, tear **05** botch, crush, mouth, spoil, twist, wreck **06** bungle, deform, garble, haggle, mess up **07** butcher, destroy, distort, mammock, screw up **08** calender, lacerate, mutilate **09** disfigure **11** make a hash of, make a mess of

**mangy**
**04** mean, worn **05** dirty, seedy, tatty **06** filthy, scabby, shabby, shoddy **07** roynish, scruffy **08** cowardly **09** moth-eaten

**manhandle**
**03** tug **04** haul, hump, maul, pull, push **05** abuse, heave, shove **06** jostle, misuse **07** rough up **08** maltreat, mistreat **10** knock about **13** handle roughly

**manhood**
**08** machismo, maleness, maturity, virility **09** adulthood, manliness **10** manfulness **11** masculinity

**mania**
**03** fad **04** rage, urge **05** craze, thing **06** desire, fetish, frenzy, lunacy, raving **07** craving, madness, passion **08** dementia, disorder, fixation, hysteria, insanity, wildness **09** craziness, gold-fever, obsession, psychosis, tarantism **10** aberration, compulsion, enthusiasm **11** derangement, fascination, infatuation **13** preoccupation

*Manias include:*

**08** egomania
**09** cynomania, demomania, ergomania, infomania, logomania, melomania, monomania, oenomania, opsomania, pyromania, theomania, tomomania, xenomania
**10** anthomania, dipsomania, erotomania, hippomania, hydromania, methomania, metromania, mythomania, narcomania, necromania, nostomania
**11** ablutomania, acronymania, ailuromania, bibliomania, cleptomania, demonomania, etheromania, graphomania, hedonomania, kleptomania, megalomania, nymphomania, technomania, toxicomania
**12** arithmomania, balletomania, pteridomania, thanatomania, theatromania
**13** flagellomania, morphinomania
**14** eleutheromania

**maniac**
**03** fan, nut **04** buff, kook **05** crank, fiend, freak, loony **06** madman, nutter, psycho **07** cupcake, fanatic, lunatic, nutcase, oddball **08** crackpot, headcase, madwoman **09** fruitcake, psychotic, screwball **10** enthusiast, psychopath **14** deranged person

**manic**
◇ *anagram indicator* **03** mad **04** amok, wild **05** barmy, batty, crazy, daffy, dippy, loopy **06** crazed, hectic, insane, raving **07** berserk, frantic, furious **08** demented, deranged, feverish, frenetic, frenzied **09** desperate, obsessive **10** distracted, distraught, hysterical **11** overwrought **12** uncontrolled **13** panic-stricken **14** beside yourself

**manically**
◇ *anagram indicator* **05** madly **06** wildly **09** excitedly, intensely **10** hectically **12** frenetically, hysterically

## manifest

◊ *anagram indicator* **04** open, shew, show **05** clear, plain, prove **06** appear, attest, evince, expose, patent, reveal **07** blatant, confess, declare, display, evident, exhibit, express, glaring, obvious, present, visible **08** apparent, distinct, indicate, set forth **09** establish, extrovert, make clear, make plain, show forth **10** illustrate, noticeable **11** conspicuous, demonstrate, perceptible, transparent, unconcealed **12** be evidence of, unmistakable **13** unmistakeable

## manifestation

◊ *anagram indicator* **04** mark, mode, show, sign **05** gleam, glory, token **06** avatar, reflex **07** display **08** Epiphany, evidence, exposure **09** theophany **10** appearance, disclosure, exhibition, exposition, expression, indication, revelation **11** angelophany, declaration, incarnation **12** illustration, presentation **13** demonstration **14** representation **15** exemplification

## manifesto

**08** platform, policies **09** programme, statement **11** declaration, publication **12** announcement, proclamation **14** pronunciamento

## manifold

**04** many **06** varied **07** copious, diverse, several, various **08** abundant, multiple, multiply, numerous **09** aggregate **12** multifarious **13** kaleidoscopic, multitudinous

## manipulate

◊ *anagram indicator* **03** cog, ply, rig, use **04** cook, hand, milk, tong, work **05** fit up, frame, guide, knead, nurse, steer, wield **06** direct, doctor, employ, fiddle, handle, juggle, manage, wangle **07** control, exploit, falsify, finesse, massage, operate, process, shuffle, utilize **08** cash in on, engineer **09** influence, manoeuvre, negotiate **10** juggle with, tamper with, thimblerig **11** gerrymander, pull strings **12** capitalize on, wheel and deal **15** have over a barrel

## manipulation

◊ *anagram indicator* **05** using **07** control, massage, milking, rigging, working **08** fiddling, guidance, handling, juggling, kneading, steering, wangling, wielding **09** directing, doctoring, influence, massaging, operation **11** manoeuvring, negotiation, utilization **12** exploitation, mobilization **13** falsification **14** pulling strings **15** cooking the books

## manipulative

**03** sly **04** foxy, wily **06** artful, crafty, tricky **07** cunning, devious **08** scheming, slippery **09** conniving, deceitful, designing, insidious, underhand **11** calculating, duplicitous **12** unscrupulous **13** Machiavellian

## manipulator

**04** user **05** slave **06** worker **07** handler, schemer, smoothy, wielder **08** director,

engineer, operator, smart guy **09** exploiter **10** controller, influencer, manoeuvrer, negotiator, wirepuller **13** wheeler-dealer

## Manitoba
**02** MB

## mankind

**03** man **05** flesh **06** Bimana, people, public **07** mortals **08** humanity **09** humankind, human race **11** Homo sapiens, human beings

## manliness

**06** mettle, valour, vigour **07** bravery, courage, heroism, manhood **08** boldness, firmness, machismo, maleness, strength, virility **09** fortitude, hardihood **10** manfulness, resolution **11** intrepidity, masculinity **12** fearlessness, independence, resoluteness, stalwartness

## manly

**04** bold, firm, male **05** brave, macho, noble, tough **06** heroic, manful, robust, rugged, strong, sturdy, virile **08** fearless, intrepid, powerful, vigorous **09** dignified, masculine **10** courageous, determined

## man-made

**04** faux, mock **06** ersatz **09** imitation, simulated, synthetic **10** artificial **12** manufactured

## manna

**07** trehala **08** honeydew

## manner

**03** air, how, way **04** form, look, mien, mode **05** means, style **06** aspect, custom, mainor, method, stance **07** bearing, conduct, decorum, fashion, posture, process, p's and q's, routine, variety **08** approach, attitude, courtesy, good form, practice, protocol **09** behaviour, character, demeanour, etiquette, procedure, propriety, technique **10** appearance, deportment, politeness **11** formalities **12** social graces, the done thing **13** way of behaving
• **in the manner of 02** as, of **03** à la, per
• **unconstrained manner 04** ease

## mannered

**05** posed, put-on **06** pseudo, thewed **07** stilted **08** affected, precious **10** artificial, euphuistic **11** pretentious
*See also* **bad-mannered**

## mannerism

**05** habit, quirk, trait, trick **06** foible **07** feature **10** foreignism **11** peculiarity, stiltedness **12** idiosyncrasy **14** characteristic

## mannerly

**05** civil **06** formal, polite **07** civilly, genteel, refined **08** decorous, gracious, ladylike, polished, well-bred **09** civilized, courteous **10** respectful **11** deferential, gentlemanly, well-behaved **12** well-mannered

## mannish

**05** butch **07** laddish, mankind **09** Amazonian, masculine, tomboyish,

unwomanly, viragoish **10** unfeminine, unladylike, viraginian, viraginous **11** virilescent

## mannishness

**08** virilism **09** butchness **11** masculinity **12** unfemininity, virilescence **13** unwomanliness **14** unladylikeness

## manoeuvre

◊ *anagram indicator* **04** dock, ease, loop, move, pick, plan, plot, ploy, roll, ruse, turn **05** berth, cut in, dodge, drive, guide, pilot, stall, steer, trick **06** action, device, devise, direct, gambit, handle, jockey, manage, pesade, scheme, tactic, wangle **07** wheelie **08** alley-oop, artifice, contrive, engineer, exercise, intrigue, movement, navigate, snap roll, wingover **09** chandelle, checkmate, decursion, half board, negotiate, operation, stratagem **10** deployment, manipulate, subterfuge **11** machination, pull strings, skilful plan, victory roll **12** countermarch, manipulation, renversement **13** Immelmann turn

## manor

**03** Hof **04** hall, seat, vill **05** house, villa **06** barony **07** château, Schloss **12** country house

## manpower

**05** staff **07** workers **09** employees, personnel, workforce **14** human resources, skilled workers

## manse

**07** deanery, rectory **08** vicarage **09** parsonage **10** glebe-house

## manservant

**05** valet **06** butler, Jeeves **08** retainer **09** attendant

## mansion

**04** casa, hall, home, seat **05** abode, house, manor, place, villa **06** castle **07** château, Schloss **08** dwelling **09** residence **10** habitation, manor-house

## manslaughter

**06** murder **07** carnage, killing, slaying **08** butchery, fatality, genocide, homicide, massacre **09** bloodshed, execution, matricide, patricide, slaughter, uxoricide **10** fratricide, sororicide **11** destruction, elimination, infanticide, liquidation **13** assassination, extermination

## mantle

**04** cape, hide, hood, mask, pall, veil, wrap **05** blush, cloak, cloud, cover, froth, layer, palla, shawl, vakas **06** bubble, capote, dolman, rochet, screen, shroud **07** blanket, conceal, envelop, obscure, pallium, pelisse, pluvial **08** covering, disguise, envelope **13** asthenosphere

## manual

**03** ABC **05** bible, guide, human **06** by hand **07** cambist, positif **08** handbook, physical **09** companion, guidebook, portolano, vade-mecum **10** directions, mechanical, prospectus **11** book of words, enchiridion **12** encheiridion, hand-operated, instructions **13** with your hands **15** instruction book

**manually**
**06** by hand **10** physically **13** with your hands

**manufacture**
◇ *anagram indicator* **04** form, make **05** build, forge, frame, model **06** create, devise, invent, make up, making **07** concoct, dream up, fashion, forming, process, produce, think up, turn out **08** assemble, assembly, building, creation **09** construct, fabricate, formation, modelling **10** fashioning, processing, production **11** fabrication, mass-produce, put together **12** construction **14** mass-production

**manufacturer**
**05** maker **07** builder, chemist, creator **08** producer **09** fabricant **10** paper-maker, soap boiler **11** chocolatier, constructor, tobacconist **12** factory-owner **13** industrialist
*See also* **car**

**manure**
**04** dung, hold, lime, muck, soil, tath **05** dress, guano, vraic **06** bedung, hen-pen, manage, occupy, ordure **07** compost **08** dressing **09** biosolids, cultivate, droppings, fish-guano **10** composture, fertilizer **11** top-dressing **12** animal faeces, police-manure **15** animal excrement

**manuscript**
**02** MS **04** text **05** codex, paper **06** scroll, uncial, vellum **07** papyrus **08** document **09** autograph, minuscule, parchment **10** Mabinogion, palimpsest, typescript **12** opisthograph

**Manx**
◇ *tail deletion indicator* **08** tailless

**many**
**01** C, D, K, L, M **04** a lot, lots, tons, wads **05** a mass, heaps, loads, piles, scads **06** a lot of, a wheen, hantle, lots of, masses, oodles, plenty, scores, stacks, sundry, untold, varied **07** copious, diverse, several, umpteen, various **08** billions, hundreds, manifold, millions, multiple, numerous, zillions **09** countless, hoi polloi, thousands **10** a multitude **11** any number of, innumerable **12** a large number **13** multitudinous **14** a large number of

**Maori**

*Maori leaders include:*

**05** **Ngata** (Sir Apirana Turupa)
**06** **Cooper** (Dame Whina), **Mahuta** (Sir Robert), **O'Regan** (Sir Tipene), **Pomare** (Sir Maui), **Ratana** (Tuhupotiki Wiremu), **Szászy** (Dame Miraka)
**07** **Rickard** (Eva), **Te Kooti** (Arikirangi Te Turuki)
**09** **Greensill** (Angeline Ngahina), **Heke Potai** (Hone Wiremu), **Hongi Hika**, **Rua Kenana** (Hepetipa)

**11** **Te Rauparaha**
**14** **Te Heuheu Tukino** (Sir Hepi)
*See also* **god, goddess; mythology**

**map**
**04** card, face, mark, plan, plot **05** atlas, chart, graph, inset **06** sketch **07** road-map **08** town plan **09** cartogram, delineate, gazetteer, horoscope, mappemond **10** projection, street plan **11** carte du pays, hypsography, planisphere, street guide **12** weather chart
• **map out** **04** draw **05** draft **06** draw up, sketch **07** outline, work out

**maple**
**04** acer **05** mazer, plane **08** box elder, sycamore

**mapmakers**
**02** OS

**mar**
◇ *anagram indicator* **04** harm, hurt, maim, ruin, scar **05** spoil, stain, sully, taint, wreck **06** damage, deface, deform, impair, injure, mangle, poison **07** blemish, tarnish **08** mutilate **09** disfigure, misguggle **10** mishguggle **11** contaminate, detract from

**maraud**
**04** loot, raid, sack **05** foray, harry **06** forage, ravage **07** despoil, pillage, plunder, raiding, ransack **08** spoliate **09** depredate **10** plundering

**marauder**
**05** rover **06** bandit, looter, mugger, outlaw, pirate, raider, robber **07** brigand, ravager, rustler **08** pillager, predator **09** buccaneer, plunderer **10** freebooter, highwayman

**marble**
**03** taw **04** ally, bool, bowl, dump, marl, onyx **05** agate, alley, bonce, touch **06** nicker, Parian **07** cipolin, knicker, paragon, plonker, plunker **08** commoney, onychite **09** cipollino, pavonazzo, scagliola **10** nero-antico **11** ophicalcite

**march**
**03** Mar **04** demo, file, gait, hike, Lide, pace, step, trek, walk, yomp **05** étape, hikoi, stalk, strut, tramp, tread, troop **06** border, defile, parade, stride **07** advance, debouch, en route, forward, headway, passage, swagger **08** boundary, footslog, progress **09** evolution, paso doble **10** procession, route-march, walk-around **11** development, make headway **12** countermarch **13** demonstration
• **March 15** **04** Ides
• **section of march** **04** trio

**marches**
**06** border **08** boundary, frontier, protests **10** borderland **14** border district

**mare**
**04** yaud

**margarine**
**04** oleo

**margin**
**03** rim **04** brim, curb, edge, kerb, marg, play, rand, room, side, tail **05** bound, brink, extra, limit, marge, scope, skirt, space, verge **06** border, leeway, limits, spread **07** confine, surplus, whisker **08** boundary, confines, frontier, latitude **09** allowance, perimeter, periphery **10** difference **12** differential **15** demarcation line

**marginal**
**03** low **04** marg, tiny **05** minor, small **06** minute, slight **07** minimal **08** doubtful **09** on the edge **10** borderline, negligible, peripheral **11** subordinate **13** insignificant
• **marginal note** **03** k'ri
• **of marginal value** **04** lean

**marginalization**
**05** exile **08** solitude **09** aloneness, isolation, seclusion **10** alienation, detachment, loneliness, remoteness, retirement, separation, withdrawal **11** abstraction, segregation **12** dissociation, separateness, solitariness **13** disconnection, sequestration

**marginalize**
**06** cut off, detach, maroon, remove, strand **07** divorce, exclude, isolate, seclude, shut out **08** abstract, alienate, separate, set apart, shut away **09** keep apart, ostracize, segregate, sequester **10** disconnect **12** cold-shoulder

**margosa**
**03** nim **04** neem, nimb **05** Melia, neemb

**marijuana**
*see* **cannabis**

**marina**
**04** dock, port **07** harbour, mooring **12** yacht station

**marinade**
**04** soak **05** imbue, souse, steep **06** infuse **07** immerse **08** marinate, permeate, saturate **09** chermoula, escabeche

**marine**
**02** RM **03** sea **05** jolly, naval **06** bootee **07** aquatic, oceanic, pelagic **08** maritime, nautical, seagoing, seascape, seawater **09** saltwater, seafaring, thalassic **10** ocean-going, thalassian **11** leatherneck

**mariner**
**02** AB **03** tar **04** salt **05** limey, matlo **06** matlow, sailor, sea dog, seaman **07** Jack Tar, matelot **08** deckhand, seafarer **09** navigator
*See also* **sailor**

**marital**
**06** wedded **07** married, nuptial, spousal, wedding **08** conjugal, marriage **09** connubial **11** matrimonial

**maritally**
**09** by wedlock, in wedlock, nuptially **10** by marriage, conjugally, in marriage **11** connubially **13** matrimonially

## maritime

**03** sea **05** naval **06** marine **07** coastal, oceanic, pelagic, seaside **08** littoral, nautical, sea-coast, seagoing, sea-trade **09** seafaring

## mark

**01** m **02** DM, mk, NB **03** aim, cut, dot, end, see, tag, tee, zit **04** blot, butt, chip, clue, dash, dent, dool, dule, flag, goal, heed, hint, keep, line, ling, logo, mind, name, nick, norm, note, scar, seal, sign, spot, stop, tatu, tick, tika, type **05** badge, brand, gauge, grade, issue, label, level, limit, model, motto, notch, patch, point, print, proof, scale, score, smear, speck, stage, stain, stamp, tally, token, trace, track **06** accent, assess, blotch, bruise, caract, denote, device, emblem, honour, listen, notice, object, picket, pimple, piquet, record, regard, smudge, smutch, stigma, symbol, target, tattoo, tattow, tittle, tracks, typify **07** blemish, correct, discern, feature, freckle, imprint, jot down, measure, observe, picquet, purpose, quality, scratch, signify, specify, symptom **08** appraise, boundary, bull's-eye, evaluate, evidence, identify, indicate, monogram, note down, remember, standard **09** attribute, birthmark, celebrate, character, criterion, designate, discolour, footprint, idiograph, intention, objective, recognize, represent, trademark, write down, yardstick **10** assessment, bear in mind, evaluation, impression, indication, percentage, take heed of, take note of **11** acknowledge, commemorate, distinguish, fingerprint, take to heart **12** characterize, fingerprints, pay tribute to **13** put your name on **14** characteristic, noteworthiness, pay attention to
• **encircling mark** **03** rim **04** ring
• **make your mark** **05** get on **06** make it **07** prosper, succeed **12** be successful, make the grade **13** hit the big time **14** make the big time
• **mark down** **03** cut **05** lower, slash **06** reduce **08** decrease
• **mark out** **03** fix **04** line **07** delimit, destine, measure **08** set apart **09** delineate, demarcate, designate, draw lines, single out, tell apart **11** distinguish **12** discriminate **13** differentiate
• **mark up** **05** put up, raise **06** hike up, jack up **08** increase
• **mark well** **02** nb **08** nota bene
• **miss mark** **03** err
• **up to the mark** **02** OK **10** acceptable, good enough **11** up to scratch **12** satisfactory
• **wide of the mark** **04** gone, wild **06** abroad, far out **09** imprecise, incorrect, off target **10** inaccurate, irrelevant **14** beside the point

## marked

**05** clear, noted, thick **06** doomed, pimply, signal, spotty, strong **07** blatant, blotchy, bruised, decided, evident, glaring, marcato, obvious, scarred, spotted, stained, watched **08** apparent, blotched, distinct, emphatic, freckled, striking **09** blemished, condemned, indicated, prominent, scratched, suspected **10** noticeable, pronounced, remarkable **11** conspicuous **12** considerable, unmistakable

## markedly

**07** clearly **08** signally **09** blatantly, decidedly, evidently, glaringly, obviously **10** distinctly, noticeably, remarkably, strikingly **11** prominently **12** considerably, emphatically, unmistakably **13** conspicuously

## marker

**03** dan, tag **04** buck, flag, goal **07** counter **08** bookmark, gybe mark, milepost, tidemark **09** milestone, stake boat

## market

**03** AIM, mkt, USM **04** call, fair, hawk, kerb, mall, mart, need, sale, sell, shop, souk, vent, want **05** agora, trade, value **06** bazaar, buying, demand, desire, outlet, peddle, retail **07** bargain, promote, selling, trading **08** business, dealings, exchange, industry, occasion, shambles **09** advertize **10** Smithfield **11** market-place, requirement **12** Billingsgate, Covent Garden, offer for sale **14** shopping centre
• **on the market** **06** on sale **07** for sale **09** available, up for sale

## marketable

**06** wanted **08** in demand, saleable, sellable, vendible **11** sought after **12** merchantable

## marketing

**04** hype **05** sales **07** pushing **08** plugging **09** promotion, publicity **11** advertising **12** distribution **13** merchandizing

## market-place

**03** suk **04** sook, souk, sukh, tron

## marksman, markswoman

**04** shot **06** sniper **07** deadeye **08** dead shot, free-shot, shootist, wing shot **09** crack shot **12** sharpshooter

## mark-up

**04** hike, leap, rise **07** upsurge **08** increase **10** escalation **13** price increase

## Marlowe

**03** Kit

## marmoset

**04** mico **07** jacchus, wistiti

## marmot

**05** bobac, bobak **08** whistler **09** woodchuck

## maroon

**05** leave **06** desert, strand **07** abandon, forsake, isolate **08** cast away **09** put ashore **11** leave behind **14** turn your back on **15** leave high and dry, leave in the lurch

## marriage

**04** link **05** match, noose, union **06** fusion, merger **07** spousal, wedding, wedlock **08** alliance, coupling, nuptials, shidduch, spousage, spousals **09** espousals, matrimony **10** connection **11** affiliation, association, combination, handfasting, partnership, unification **12** amalgamation, married state **13** confederation

*Marriage- and wedding-related terms include:*

**03** vow, wed
**04** ring, veil, wife
**05** aisle, altar, banns, bride, dowry, elope, groom, in-law, usher, vicar
**06** beenah, bigamy, digamy, favour, fiancé, garter, huppah, prenup, priest, speech, spouse
**07** best man, betroth, bouquet, chuppah, consort, divorce, espouse, exogamy, fiancée, husband, Ketubah, marital, merchet, Mr Right, nuptial, page boy, propose, punalua, trigamy, wedding
**08** bedright, best maid, confetti, conjugal, endogamy, hen night, jointure, levirate, maritage, minister, monogamy, monogyny, polygamy
**09** annulment, coemption, common-law, communion, connubial, honeymoon, hope chest, horseshoe, hypergamy, love match, matrimony, other half, reception, registrar, stag night, trousseau
**10** better half, bridesmaid, buttonhole, consortium, consummate, engagement, first dance, first night, flower girl, her indoors, him indoors, honeymonth, invitation, Lucy Stoner, maiden name, matrilocal, morganatic, patrilocal, separation, settlement, uxorilocal, wedding day
**11** deuterogamy, dissolution, Gretna Green, handfasting, misalliance, morning gift, mother in-law, outmarriage, wedding cake, wedding list
**12** bottom drawer, bridal shower, concubitancy, mariage blanc, open marriage, prothalamion, something new, something old, wedding dress, wedding march, wedding night
**13** church service, civil marriage, hedge-marriage, holy matrimony, marriage-lines, something blue
**14** matron of honour, pop the question, steal a marriage
**15** chief bridesmaid, going-away outfit, marriage-licence, plight one's troth

• **promise of marriage** **04** hand

## married

**01** m **03** wed **05** wived, yoked **06** joined, united, wedded, wifely **07** hitched, marital, nuptial, spliced,

## marrow

spousal **08** conjugal **09** connubial, husbandly **11** matrimonial

## marrow

**03** nub **04** core, gist, like, mate, pith, soul **05** equal, heart, match, quick, stuff **06** centre, couple, kernel, spirit **07** essence, medulla, nucleus **08** zucchini **09** companion, courgette, substance **11** nitty-gritty **12** nuts and bolts, quintessence

## marry

**03** wad, wed **04** ally, fuse, join, knit, link, mate, weld, wive **05** cleek, elope, match, merge, unite **06** couple, indeed!, spouse **07** combine, connect, hitch up **08** forsooth! **09** affiliate, associate **10** amalgamate, get hitched, get married, get spliced, intermarry, take to wife, tie the knot **12** go to the world, join together **13** take the plunge **14** become espoused, lead to the altar, lead up the aisle **15** join in matrimony

## Mars

**04** Ares

## marsh

**03** bog, fen **04** mire, salt, wash **05** bayou, swamp **06** marish, morass, muskeg, salina, slough **07** corcass **08** quagmire **09** everglade, marshland **10** Everglades

## marshal

◊ *anagram indicator* **04** lead, rank, take **05** align, array, group, guide, order, usher **06** deploy, draw up, escort, gather, line up, muster, parade **07** arrange, collect, conduct, dispose, farrier **08** assemble, organize, shepherd **09** mareschal, marischal **10** put in order **13** velt-mareschal **14** gather together

*Marshals include:*

**03** **Ney** (Michel)
**04** **Earp** (Wyatt), **Foch** (Ferdinand), **Saxe** (Maurice, Comte de), **Tito**
**06** **Hickok** (Wild Bill), **Pétain** (Philippe), **Tedder** (Arthur, Lord), **Zhukov** (Georgi)
**08** **MacMahon** (Patrice de)

*See also* **Field Marshal**

## Marshall Islands

**03** MHL

## marshy

**03** wet **04** miry **05** boggy, fenny, moory, muddy **06** quaggy, slumpy, spongy, swampy **07** fennish, moorish, paludal **08** paludine, paludose, paludous, squelchy **09** paludinal **10** paludinous **11** waterlogged

## marsupial

*Marsupials include:*

**03** roo
**04** euro, tuan
**05** koala, quoll
**06** boodie, cuscus, glider, numbat, possum, quokka, tammar, wombat
**07** bettong, dasyure, dibbler, dunnart, opossum, potoroo, wallaby
**08** kangaroo, macropod, tarsiped, wallaroo
**09** bandicoot, boodie-rat, koala bear, native cat, pademelon, petaurist, phalanger, thylacine, wambenger
**10** native bear, Notoryctes
**11** diprotodont, honey possum, rat kangaroo, rock wallaby
**12** marsupial rat, pouched mouse, tree kangaroo
**13** brush kangaroo, marsupial mole, Tasmanian wolf
**14** marsupial mouse, Tasmanian devil, vulpine opossum
**15** flying phalanger

*See also* **animal**

## mart

**04** fair, mall, souk **06** bazaar, market, outlet, staple **08** emporium, exchange **10** repository **11** market-place **14** shopping centre

## marten

**05** pekan, sable **06** fisher **07** Mustela **09** woodshock

## martial

**04** army **05** brave **06** heroic **07** hawkish, warlike **08** militant, military **09** bellicose, combative, soldierly **10** aggressive, pugnacious **11** belligerent

## martial art

*Martial arts and forms of self-defence include:*

**04** judo
**05** lai-do, sambo, wushu
**06** aikido, karate, kung fu, t'ai chi
**07** capuera, ju-jitsu
**08** capoeira, jiu-jitsu, ninjitsu, ninjutsu, Shotokan
**09** tae kwon do
**10** kick boxing
**11** self-defence, t'ai chi ch'uan

• **martial art expert 03** dan

## martinet

**06** martin, tyrant **08** stickler **09** formalist **10** taskmaster **11** slave-driver **12** taskmistress **14** disciplinarian

## Martinique

**03** MTQ

## martyr

**05** stone **06** victim **07** crucify, torment, torture **09** persecute **10** put to death **12** give the works, put on the rack **13** make a martyr of **14** burn at the stake **15** throw to the lions

## martyrdom

**05** agony, death, stake **06** ordeal **07** anguish, passion, torment, torture, witness **09** suffering **11** persecution **12** excruciation **13** baptism of fire **14** baptism of blood

## marvel

**04** gape, gawp, gaze, marl **05** marle, stare **06** genius, goggle, wonder **07** miracle, portent, prodigy **08** be amazed, surprise **09** eye-opener, fairy tale, not expect, sensation, spectacle **10** fairy story, phenomenon

**12** astonishment, be astonished **14** quite something **15** be flabbergasted

## marvellous

**03** ace, bad, def, fab, rad **04** cool, mean, mega, neat, phat **05** brill, great, magic, super **06** superb, wicked **07** amazing, awesome, crucial, épatant, mirific, radical, wondred **08** glorious, selcouth, splendid, terrific, wondered **09** bodacious, excellent, fantastic, mirifical, wonderful **10** astounding, improbable, incredible, miraculous, out of sight, remarkable, stupendous, super-duper, surprising **11** astonishing, fantabulous, magnificent, merveilleux, sensational, spectacular **12** merveilleuse, unbelievable **13** extraordinary

## marvellously

**04** very **06** highly, really **07** acutely, awfully, greatly, utterly **08** severely, terribly **09** decidedly, extremely, intensely, to a wonder, unusually **10** dreadfully, remarkably, thoroughly, uncommonly **11** exceedingly, excessively, frightfully **12** inordinately, terrifically **13** exceptionally **15** extraordinarily

## Maryland

**02** MD

## masculine

**01** m **02** he **03** mas **04** bold, male, masc **05** brave, butch, macho, manly **06** heroic, robust, rugged, strong, virile **07** gallant, manlike, mannish **08** fearless, muscular, powerful, resolute, vigorous **09** confident, strapping **10** determined, red-blooded **12** stout-hearted

## masculinity

**06** mettle, valour, vigour **07** bravery, courage, heroism, manhood **08** boldness, firmness, machismo, maleness, strength, virility **09** fortitude, hardihood, manliness **10** manfulness, resolution **11** intrepidity **12** fearlessness, independence, stalwartness

## mash

◊ *anagram indicator* **03** pap **04** beat, hash, mush, pulp **05** champ, crush, grind, paste, pound, purée, smash **06** bungle, infuse, muddle, pummel, squash **09** pulverize

## mask

**04** hide, show, veil **05** blind, cloak, cover, front, guise, matte, steep, visor, vizor **06** domino, façade, immask, infuse, masque, screen, shield, veneer, vizard **07** conceal, cover up, cover-up, goggles, inhaler, obscure, persona **08** disguise, joncanoe, junkanoo, pretence **09** dissemble, false face, gas helmet, John Canoe, John Kanoo, semblance **10** camouflage, gorgoneion, masquerade, respirator **11** concealment

## masquerade

◊ *anagram indicator* **03** mum **04** mask, mumm, play, pose **05** cloak, cover, front, guise **06** masque **07** cover-up, dress up, pretend, profess **08** disguise, pretence **09** deception **10** masked ball **11** costume ball, counterfeit, dissimulate, impersonate **14** fancy dress ball **15** fancy dress party, pass yourself off

## mass

**01** m **03** lot, mob, ped, sea, sum, wad **04** bags, ball, band, body, bulk, clod, hang, heap, herd, hunk, load, lots, lump, most, nest, pile, size, tons **05** amass, batch, block, bolus, bunch, chaos, chunk, crowd, group, heaps, horde, loads, piece, piles, plebs, rally, stack, swarm, total, troop, whole, wodge **06** dallop, dollop, gather, huddle, medley, muster, oodles, rabble, scores, tangle, throng, weight, welter **07** blanket, cluster, clutter, collect, general, popular **08** assemble, capacity, coagulum, entirety, indigest, majority, pandemic, quantity, riff-raff, sweeping, totality **09** abundance, aggregate, Communion, dimension, Eucharist, extensive, hoi polloi, immensity, magnitude, multitude, rotundity, universal, wholesale **10** accumulate, assemblage, collection, concretion, congregate, large-scale, Lord's Table, widespread **11** combination, greater part, large number, Lord's Supper, proletariat **12** accumulation, come together, common people, draw together, lower classes, working class **13** agglutination, bring together, comprehensive, Holy Communion, preponderance **14** across-the-board, conglomeration, indiscriminate, the rank and file, working classes

## Massachusetts

**02** MA **04** Mass

## massacre

**04** kill, slay **05** purge **06** murder, pogrom **07** butcher, carnage, killing, kill off, mow down, wipe out **08** butchery, decimate, genocide, homicide **09** bloodbath, holocaust, liquidate, slaughter **10** annihilate, blood purge, decimation **11** exterminate, liquidation **12** annihilation **13** extermination **15** ethnic cleansing

*Massacres include:*

**04** Hama, Lari
**05** Ambon, Katyn, My Lai, Paris, Sabra
**06** Bezier, Boston, Cataví, Herrin, Kanpur, Lidice, Rishon
**07** Amboyna, Babi Yar, Badajoz, Baghdad, Chatila, Glencoe, Halabja, Nanking, Tianjin
**08** Amritsar, Cawnpore, Drogheda, El Mozote, Kishinev, Novgorod, Peterloo, Tientsin
**09** Fetterman, Innocents, Jerusalem, Sand Creek, September, Trebizond
**10** Addis Ababa, Fort Pillow, Myall Creek, Paxton Boys, Sack of Rome, Srebrenica, Tlatelolco
**11** Janissaries, Sharpeville, Wounded Knee

**12** Bloody Sunday, Sabra/Chatila
**15** Oradour-sur-Glane, Sicilian Vespers, St Valentine's Day, Tiananmen Square

## massage

◇ *anagram indicator* **03** rub **04** an mo, cook, do-in **05** alter, knead, reiki, tui na **06** doctor, fiddle, pummel **07** falsify, Jacuzzi®, rubbing, rub down, rub-down, shampoo, shiatsu, shiatzu, tripsis **08** aerotone, kneading **10** manipulate, osteopathy, percussion, petrissage, pummelling, tamper with **11** acupressure, reflexology **12** aromatherapy, manipulation, misrepresent **13** interfere with, physiotherapy **15** Reichian therapy, thalassotherapy

## massive

**03** big **04** bull, gang, huge, vast **05** beamy, bulky, great, heavy, hefty, jumbo, large, solid **06** mighty **07** hulking, immense, mammoth, popular, weighty **08** colossal, enormous, gigantic, timbered, whopping **09** extensive, ginormous, ponderous **10** large-scale, monolithic, monumental, successful **11** substantial

## massively

**06** vastly **07** greatly, heavily **08** very much **09** immensely **10** enormously **11** extensively **12** monumentally **13** substantially

## mast

**03** bar, rod **04** boom, heel, nuts, pole, post, spar, yard **05** shaft, staff, stick **06** acorns, jigger **07** pannage, support, upright **10** topgallant

## master

**01** M **02** MA, PM, RM **03** ace, Dan, guv, Mas, Mes, pro **04** baas, beak, boss, buff, curb, guru, head, Herr, lord, main, Mass, Mess, rule, sire, tame, tuan **05** adept, bwana, check, chief, grand, grasp, great, guide, learn, maven, mavin, owner, prime, quell, ruler, tutor **06** bridle, defeat, expert, gaffer, genius, govern, honcho, leader, manage, mentor, pick up, pundit, season, subdue, temper **07** acquire, captain, conquer, control, dab hand, egghead, leading, maestro, manager, skilful, skilled, skipper, teacher, wise guy **08** director, employer, foremost, governor, masterly, overcome, overlord, overseer, suppress, vanquish, virtuoso **09** commander, dexterous, overpower, pedagogue, practised, preceptor, principal, Signorino, subjugate **10** controller, instructor, past master, proficient **11** controlling, experienced, grand master, predominate, symposiarch, triumph over **12** get the hang of, professional, schoolmaster **13** most important, schoolteacher **14** schoolmistress, superintendent

## masterful

**05** bossy, pithy **08** arrogant, despotic, powerful **09** imperious **10** autocratic, dominating, high-handed, peremptory, tyrannical **11** controlling, dictatorial,

domineering, overbearing **13** authoritative

## masterly

**03** ace **05** adept, crack **06** adroit, artful, expert, superb **07** skilful, skilled, supreme **08** polished, superior, top-notch **09** dexterous, excellent, first-rate, magistral **10** consummate **11** overbearing **12** accomplished, professional

## mastermind

**04** mind, plan **05** forge, frame, hatch **06** brains, design, devise, direct, genius, manage **07** control, creator, dream up, inspire, manager, planner, think up **08** be behind, conceive, contrive, director, engineer, organize, virtuoso **09** architect, authority, initiator, intellect, organizer, originate **10** originator, prime mover

## masterpiece

**05** jewel **08** creation **09** work of art **10** magnum opus, masterwork **11** chef d'oeuvre

## masterstroke

**04** coup, feat **07** success, triumph, victory **10** attainment **11** achievement **12** coup de maître **14** accomplishment

## mastery

**04** grip, rule **05** grasp, skill **07** ability, command, control, knowhow, prowess, triumph, victory **08** dominion **09** authority, dexterity, direction, expertise, knowledge, supremacy, upper hand **10** ascendancy, capability, domination, virtuosity **11** familiarity, proficiency, sovereignty, superiority **13** comprehension, understanding
• **strive for mastery  04** kemp

## masticate

**03** eat **04** chew **05** champ, chomp, knead, munch **06** crunch **08** ruminate **09** manduce **10** chew the cud

## mastication

**06** eating **07** chewing **08** champing, munching **10** rumination **11** manducation

## mat

**03** rug **04** dull, felt, knot, mass, matt, taut, tawt **05** frost, matte, tatty, twist **06** carpet, felter, paunch, tangle, tatami **07** cluster, coaster, doormat, drugget **08** place mat, table mat, underlay **09** underfelt **10** interweave, lustreless

## match

**03** fit, pit, tie, vie **04** ally, bout, copy, fuse, game, join, link, main, mate, meet, pair, peer, spar, suit, team, test, twin, yoke **05** adapt, agree, amate, blend, equal, event, fusee, fuzee, light, marry, rival, spill, tally, taper, trial, union, unite, vesta **06** accord, besort, couple, double, fellow, go with, marrow, merger, oppose, pair up, relate **07** combine, compact, compare, compete, connect, contend, contest, hitch up, Lucifer, pairing, paragon, pattern, replica **08** alliance, bonspiel, coupling, locofoco, marriage, parallel, tone with **09** accompany, companion, duplicate, encounter, harmonize, lookalike **10** competitor, complement, co-ordinate, correspond, dead ringer, equivalent, go together, keep up with, one of a pair, pit against, Promethean, tournament **11** affiliation, combination, competition, counterpart, measure up to, partnership, safety match **13** be in agreement

*See also* **game; sport**
• **match up to  04** meet **05** reach **08** approach, come up to, live up to **11** compare with, measure up to **12** make the grade
• **start of match, start the match 02** KO **05** break, bully **06** tee off **07** face-off, kick-off **13** break the balls

## matching
**04** like, same, twin **06** double, in sync, paired **07** coupled, in synch, similar **08** blending, parallel **09** analogous, duplicate, identical **10** comparable, equivalent **11** correlative, harmonizing **12** co-ordinating **13** complementary, complementing, corresponding

## matchless
**06** unique **07** perfect **08** makeless, peerless **09** nonpareil, unmatched **10** inimitable, unequalled, unexcelled, unrivalled **11** unsurpassed **12** incomparable, unparalleled, without equal **13** beyond compare

## mate
**03** fit, pal, wed, wus **04** chum, feer, fere, join, leap, line, maik, make, nick, oppo, pair, twin, wack, wife **05** breed, buddy, china, crony, cully, equal, feare, fiere, marry, match, rival **06** baffle, buffer, cobber, co-mate, couple, deputy, fellow, friend, gender, helper, hubbie, marrow, missis, missus, mucker, pheere, spouse, subdue **07** baffled, compeer, comrade, consort, daunted, husband, Mr Right, oldster, paragon, partner **08** confound, copulate, co-worker, sidekick, workmate **09** assistant, associate, boyfriend, checkmate, colleague, companion, exhausted, other half **10** accomplice, apprentice, better half, checkmated, china plate, confounded, equivalent, girlfriend **11** counterpart, subordinate **12** fellow worker **14** opposite number

## material
**03** gen, key **04** body, data, info, work **05** cloth, facts, gross, ideas, notes, stuff, vital **06** bodily, fabric, matter, medium **07** details, earthly, germane, low-down, numbers, serious, textile, weighty, worldly **08** apposite, concrete, evidence, palpable, physical, relevant, tangible **09** corporeal, essential, important, momentous, pertinent, substance **10** meaningful **11** information, particulars, significant, substantial **12** constituents **13** consequential, indispensable **15** facts and figures

*See also* **art; building; fabric**
• **set material in position 03** lay

## materialism
**05** greed **06** hylism **08** hylicism, somatism **11** consumerism, worldliness **12** corporealism **15** acquisitiveness

## materialistic
**07** worldly **08** banausic **09** bourgeois, mammonist, mercenary **11** acquisitive, consumerist, mammonistic **13** money-grabbing **14** bread-and-butter

## materialize
**05** arise, occur, reify **06** appear, happen, turn up **09** take place, take shape **12** show yourself **13** become visible, come into being **14** reveal yourself

## materially
**04** much **07** gravely, greatly **09** basically, seriously **11** essentially **12** considerably **13** fundamentally, significantly, substantially

## maternal
**04** fond, kind, warm **05** mumsy **06** caring, doting, gentle, loving, tender **08** motherly, vigilant **09** nurturing **10** comforting, motherlike, nourishing, protective **12** affectionate **13** understanding

## matey
*see* **maty, matey**

## mathematics

*Branches of mathematics include:*

**06** conics
**07** algebra, applied, fluxion
**08** calculus, geometry
**09** set theory
**10** arithmetic, game theory, statistics
**11** games theory, group theory
**12** number theory, trigonometry
**13** combinatorics
**14** biomathematics
**15** metamathematics, pure mathematics

*Mathematics terms include:*

**02** pi
**03** arc, set
**04** apex, area, axes, axis, base, cube, edge, face, line, mean, mode, plus, root, side, sine, skew, unit, zero
**05** angle, chaos, chord, curve, depth, equal, graph, group, helix, locus, minus, ogive, point, ratio, solid, speed, total, width
**06** binary, chance, convex, cosine, degree, factor, height, length, linear, matrix, median, number, origin, radian, radius, sample, secant, sector, spiral, square, subset, vector, vertex, volume
**07** algebra, average, bearing, bounded, breadth, chaotic, concave, decimal, divisor, formula, fractal, integer, mapping, maximum, measure, minimum, modulus, oblique, product, segment, tangent
**08** addition, analysis, antipode, argument, bar chart, bar graph, binomial, calculus, capacity, constant, converse, cube root,

diagonal, diameter, discrete, dividend, division, equation, exponent, fraction, function, geometry, gradient, identity, infinity, latitude, less than, multiple, parabola, pie chart, quadrant, quartile, quotient, rotation, symmetry, variable, variance, velocity, vertical
**09** algorithm, Cartesian, congruent, factorial, frequency, histogram, hyperbola, iteration, logarithm, longitude, numerator, odd number, operation, parameter, perimeter, remainder
**10** acute angle, arithmetic, complement, continuous, coordinate, covariance, derivative, even number, horizontal, hypotenuse, percentage, percentile, place value, proportion, protractor, Pythagoras, real number, reciprocal, reflection, regression, right-angle, square root, statistics, subtractor
**11** approximate, coefficient, combination, coordinates, correlation, denominator, determinant, enlargement, equidistant, exponential, greater than, integration, magic square, mirror image, Möbius strip, obtuse angle, permutation, plane figure, prime number, probability, Pythagorean, real numbers, reflex angle, translation, Venn diagram, whole number
**12** asymmetrical, Bayes' theorem, cross section, distribution, random sample, straight line, trigonometry, universal set
**13** circumference, complex number, Mandelbrot set, mixed fraction, natural number, ordinal number, parallel lines, perpendicular, quadrilateral, scalar segment, triangulation
**14** axis of symmetry, cardinal number, common fraction, directed number, mirror symmetry, multiplication, negative number, parallel planes, positive number, rational number, transformation, vulgar fraction
**15** conjugate angles, differentiation, imaginary number, scalene triangle

*Mathematicians include:*

**03** **Dee** (John), **Lie** (Sophus)
**04** **Abel** (Niels Henrik), **Hero** (of Alexandria), **Hopf** (Heinz), **Kerr** (Roy), **Pell** (John), **Tait** (Peter Guthrie), **Thom** (René), **Venn** (John), **Weil** (André), **Weyl** (Hermann)
**05** **Bayes** (Thomas), **Boole** (George), **Dirac** (Paul), **Euler** (Leonhard), **Gauss** (Carl Friedrich), **Gödel** (Kurt), **Green** (George), **Hardy** (Godfrey), **Hoyle** (Sir Fred), **Klein** (Felix), **Monge** (Gaspard), **Peano** (Giuseppe), **Serre** (Jean-Pierre),

**Snell** (Willebrod), **Vieta** (Franciscus)
**06** **Ampère** (André), **Argand** (Jean-Robert), **Bessel** (Friedrich), **Briggs** (Henry), **Cantor** (Georg), **Cauchy** (Augustin Louis, Baron), **Cayley** (Arthur), **Euclid**, **Fermat** (Pierre de), **Fields** (J C), **Fisher** (Sir Ronald), **Galois** (Évariste), **Halley** (Edmond), **Jacobi** (Carl), **Jordan** (Camille), **Kelvin** (William Thomson, Lord), **Lorenz** (Edward), **Markov** (Andrei), **Möbius** (August Ferdinand), **Moivre** (Abraham de), **Napier** (John), **Newton** (Sir Isaac), **Pappus** (of Alexandria), **Pascal** (Blaise), **Picard** (Émile), **Stokes** (Sir George), **Turing** (Alan), **Wallis** (John), **Wiener** (Norbert)
**07** **Alhazen**, **Babbage** (Charles), **Cardano** (Girolamo), **Carroll** (Lewis), **Eudoxus** (of Cnidus), **Fourier** (Joseph, Baron de), **Galileo**, **Germain** (Sophie), **Hilbert** (David), **Laplace** (Pierre, Marquis de), **Leibniz** (Gottfried), **Penrose** (Roger), **Poisson** (Siméon), **Riemann** (Bernhard), **Russell** (Bertrand, Earl), **Shannon** (Claude)
**08** **Alembert** (Jean le Rond d'), **Birkhoff** (George David), **Dedekind** (Julius), **De Morgan** (Augustus), **Guldberg** (Cato), **Hamilton** (Sir William Rowan), **Lagrange** (Joseph de, Comte), **Legendre** (Adrien-Marie), **Lovelace** (Ada, Countess of), **Mercator** (Nicolaus), **Playfair** (John), **Poincaré** (Jules)
**09** **Bernoulli** (Daniel), **Bernoulli** (Jacques), **Bronowski** (Jacob), **Descartes** (René), **Dirichlet** (Lejeune), **Fibonacci** (Leonardo), **Minkowski** (Hermann), **Whitehead** (Alfred)
**10** **Apollonius** (of Perga), **Archimedes**, **Diophantus**, **Hipparchus**, **Maupertuis** (Pierre Louis de), **Pythagoras**, **Sierpinski** (Wactaw), **Torricelli** (Evangelista), **Zeno of Elea**
**11** **al-Khwarizmi**
**12** **Eratosthenes**

## mating
**06** fusing **07** coition, joining, pairing, uniting **08** breeding, coupling, matching, twinning **10** copulating, copulation

## matriarch
**04** nana

## matrimonial
**06** wedded **07** marital, married, nuptial, spousal, wedding **08** conjugal, marriage
• **matrimonial duties** **03** bed

## matrimony
**05** union **07** wedlock **08** marriage, nuptials, spousage **09** espousals **12** married state

## matrix
**03** gel, mat **04** cast, form, mold, womb **05** array, frame, mould, plasm, table **06** stroma **07** context, matrice

**08** analysis, chondrin, Jacobian, template **09** composite, framework, transpose **11** arrangement

## matron
**04** dame

## matted
**05** taggy **06** tangly **07** knotted, tangled, tousled **08** uncombed **09** entangled **11** dishevelled **13** blood-boltered

## matter
**02** go **03** pus **04** body, case, hyle, note **05** count, event, issue, point, stuff, thing, topic, upset, value, worry **06** affair, bother, import, medium, weight **07** concern, content, episode, problem, subject, trouble **08** business, distress, incident, interest, material, nuisance, question, weakness **09** discharge, happening, make a stir, make waves, purulence, secretion, situation, substance **10** be relevant, difficulty, importance, occurrence, proceeding **11** be important, carry weight, consequence, shortcoming, suppuration **12** circumstance, cut a lot of ice, significance **13** have influence, inconvenience, mean something, momentousness **14** be of importance **15** make a difference
• **as a matter of fact** **05** truly **06** in fact, really **08** actually **11** as it happens **12** in actual fact
• **matter of no importance** **03** toy **10** triviality
• **no matter** **09** never mind **15** it does not matter, it is unimportant

## matter-of-fact
**03** dry **04** dull, flat **05** sober **06** thingy **07** deadpan, prosaic **08** lifeless, positive **09** practical, pragmatic, prosaical **10** pedestrian **11** down-to-earth, emotionless, pragmatical, unemotional **13** unimaginative, unsentimental **15** straightforward

## matting
**03** tat **04** bast

## mattress
**03** bed **04** Lilo® **05** futon **06** airbed, pallet **07** biscuit **08** crash-mat, water bed **09** paillasse, palliasse **10** feather bed

## maturation
**06** growth **08** fruition, ripening **09** seasoning **11** development

## mature
**03** age **04** bold, gray, grey, ripe, wise **05** adult, bloom, grown, of age, ready, ripen **06** evolve, grow up, mellow, nubile, season **07** concoct, develop, fall due, grown-up, perfect, prepare, ripened **08** balanced, complete, finished, joined-up, maturate, seasoned, sensible **09** come of age, finalized, full-grown, perfected **10** become ripe, precocious **11** become adult, draw to a head, experienced, responsible **12** become mellow, fully fledged **13** well-developed **14** become sensible, well-thought-out

## maturity
**03** age **06** summer, wisdom **07** manhood, puberty **08** majority, ripeness **09** adulthood, readiness, womanhood **10** experience, full growth, mellowness, perfection **11** coming of age **12** sensibleness **14** responsibility **15** age of discretion

## matweed
**04** nard

## maty, matey
**04** kind, warm **05** close, pally, thick, tight **06** blokey, chummy, folksy, genial **07** affable, cordial, helpful **08** amicable, blokeish, familiar, friendly, intimate, outgoing, sociable **09** agreeable, comradely, convivial, peaceable, receptive **10** favourable **11** good-natured, inseparable, neighbourly, sympathetic **12** affectionate, approachable, well-disposed **13** companionable

## maudlin
**05** drunk, gushy, mushy, soppy, tipsy, weepy **06** sickly, sloppy, slushy **07** fuddled, mawkish, tearful, weeping **09** emotional, half-drunk, schmaltzy **10** lachrymose **11** sentimental

## maul
◇ *anagram indicator* **03** mug, paw **04** beat, belt, claw, mall, mell **05** abuse **06** attack, batter, beat up, do over, mangle, molest, thrash, wallop **07** assault, rough up **08** ill-treat, lacerate, maltreat, mutilate **09** manhandle **10** knock about

## maunder
**04** ease, inch, laze, roam, rove **05** amble, mooch, mosey, stray **06** babble, beggar, drivel, gabble, jabber, mutter, natter, rabbit, ramble, stroll, waffle, wander, witter **07** blather, chatter, grumble, meander, prattle, shuffle **08** rabbit on

## Maureen
**02** Mo

## Mauritania
**03** MRT, RIM

## Mauritius
**02** MS **03** MUS

## mausoleum
**04** mole, tomb **05** crypt, vault **08** catacomb, Taj Mahal **09** sepulchre **10** undercroft **13** burial chamber

## maverick
**05** rebel **08** agitator, outsider **09** odd one out **13** individualist, nonconformist **14** fish out of water

## maw
**04** gulf, jaws **05** abyss, chasm, mouth **06** gullet, throat **07** seagull, stomach **08** appetite **11** inclination

## mawkish
**04** flat, foul **05** gushy, mawky, mushy, soppy **06** feeble, gloopy, sickly, slushy **07** insipid, maggoty, maudlin **08** nauseous **09** emotional, loathsome, offensive, schmaltzy, squeamish

**mawkishly**
10 disgusting, nauseating
11 sentimental

**mawkishly**
06 feebly 07 mushily, soppily
11 emotionally, loathsomely
12 nauseatingly 13 sentimentally

**maxim**
03 saw 04 rule 05 adage, axiom,
gnome, motto 06 byword, dictum,
saying 07 epigram, precept, proverb
08 aphorism, apothegm, moralism,
sentence 09 principle, sentiment,
watchword 10 apophthegm, prudential

**maximize**
05 add to, boost, breed, raise, widen
06 bump up, deepen, expand, extend,
hike up, spread, step up 07 advance,
augment, broaden, build up, develop,
enhance, enlarge, further, magnify,
prolong, scale up 08 heighten,
increase 09 intensify, propagate
10 accumulate, strengthen

**maximum**
03 max, top 04 acme, full, high, most,
peak 06 apogee, height, summit,
utmost, zenith 07 biggest, ceiling,
highest, largest, supreme, topmost
08 greatest, pinnacle, top point,
ultimate 09 extremity, uttermost
10 upper limit

**may**
04 mote 08 hawthorn
• **may it do** 04 dich

**maybe**
◊ anagram indicator 07 could be,
perhaps 08 possibly 09 perchance
11 conceivably, possibility
12 peradventure 13 for all you know

**mayfly**
06 day-fly 08 ephemera 09 caddis fly,
ephemerid 10 green-drake
11 Plectoptera, turkey brown

**mayhem**
◊ anagram indicator 04 mess, riot
05 chaos, havoc 06 bedlam, tumult,
uproar 07 anarchy, maiming
08 disorder, madhouse 09 confusion
10 disruption 11 lawlessness
15 disorganization

**mayor**
02 LM 05 maire 07 alcalde

**Mayotte**
03 MYT

**maze**
◊ anagram indicator 03 web 04 mesh
05 maise, maize, mease 06 jungle,
puzzle, tangle, warren 07 complex,
meander, network 09 confusion,
honeycomb, intricacy, labyrinth

**me**
02 mi, us 03 moi

**meadow**
03 ing, lay, lea, lee, ley 04 inch, mead
05 field, grass, green, haugh 06 leasow,
saeter 07 paddock, pasture, salting
09 grassland 11 pastureland

**meadow-grass**
03 poa

**meagre**
03 bar 04 arid, bony, lean, poor, puny,
thin, weak 05 gaunt, mingy, small,
spare 06 barren, frugal, jejune, Lenten,
maigre, measly, paltry, scanty, skimpy,
skinny, slight, sparse, stingy
07 scraggy, scrawny, slender
08 exiguous, roncador, scrannel
09 deficient, emaciated, niggardly
10 inadequate, negligible, threadbare
12 insufficient 13 insubstantial

**meagreness**
07 poverty 08 puniness 09 smallness
10 deficiency, inadequacy, measliness,
scantiness, slightness, sparseness,
stinginess 13 insufficiency

**meal**
03 kai 04 fare, feed, kail, kale, meat,
mess, mush 05 grout, scoff, skoff
06 farina, repast 07 meltith, surfeit
08 freeload, racahout 09 collation,
raccahout, refection, scambling
12 refreshments

*Meals include:*

| |
|---|
| 03 BBQ, kai, tea |
| 04 bite |
| 05 feast, lunch, snack |
| 06 barbie, brunch, buffet, dinner, nosh-up, picnic, repast, spread, supper, tiffin |
| 07 banquet, blow-out, high tea |
| 08 barbecue, cream tea, luncheon, takeaway, tea break, tea party, TV dinner |
| 09 breakfast, cold table, collation, elevenses |
| 10 fork supper, midday meal, slap-up meal |
| 11 dinner party, evening meal |
| 12 afternoon tea, safari supper |
| 13 harvest supper |

• **before a meal** 02 ap

**mealy-mouthed**
04 glib, prim 07 mincing 08 indirect,
reticent 09 equivocal, hestitant,
plausible 10 flattering 11 euphemistic
12 overdelicate 13 over-squeamish,
smooth-tongued

**mean**
03 ace, aim, low, rad 04 base, cool,
fate, fine, mega, mein, mene, mode,
neat, norm, plan, poor, rare, show,
vile, wish, wont 05 boffo, brill, cause,
crack, cross, cruel, dirty, footy, imply,
lowly, mangy, meane, mingy, nasty,
prime, scall, slink, snide, tight
06 abject, aspire, common, convey,
crabby, denote, design, dismal, divine,
effect, entail, humble, intend, lament,
lead to, mangey, matter, maungy,
median, medium, middle, normal,
ordain, ornery, paltry, ribald, ribaud,
shabby, simple, skimpy, snotty, sordid,
stingy, superb, unkind, way-out
07 appoint, average, beastly, betoken,
caitiff, chintzy, connote, crucial,
destine, express, grouchy, halfway,
involve, mesquin, miserly, niggard,
obscure, perfect, piggish, produce,
propose, purport, purpose, radical,
roynish, rybauld, selfish, signify,

skilful, spaniel, squalid, suggest, think
of 08 beggarly, complain, fabulous,
grasping, heavenly, indicate, intimate,
mesquine, middling, mid-point,
moderate, ordinary, result in,
smashing, sneaking, spiteful, splendid,
stand for, stunning, terrific, top-notch,
very good, whoreson, wretched
09 admirable, brilliant, crotchety,
cullionly, designate, earth-bred,
excellent, fantastic, first-rate,
malicious, matchless, middle way,
miserable, niggardly, represent,
symbolize, wonderful 10 base-minded,
bring about, compromise, contracted,
despicable, fast-handed, first-class,
give rise to, golden mean, have in
mind, ill-natured, marvellous, not half
bad, predestine, remarkable,
surpassing, threepenny, unequalled,
unfriendly, ungenerous, unpleasant
11 bad-tempered, be important, carry
weight, close-fisted, close-handed,
exceptional, happy medium, high-
quality, magnificent, near the bone,
necessitate, outstanding, sensational,
superlative, tight-fisted 12 cheeseparing, disagreeable, intermediate,
middle course, parsimonious, second
to none, unparalleled 13 have
influence, penny-pinching,
uncomfortable 14 inconsiderable, out
of this world 15 make a difference
• **mean time** 02 MT

**meander**
04 bend, ease, inch, laze, maze, roam,
rove, turn, wind 05 amble, curve,
mooch, mosey, snake, stray, twist
06 ramble, stroll, wander, wimple,
zigzag 07 shuffle, turning, whimple
09 sinuosity 10 perplexity

**meandering**
◊ anagram indicator 07 sinuous,
snaking, turning, winding 08 indirect,
rambling, tortuous, twisting
09 meandrous, wandering
10 circuitous, convoluted, roundabout,
serpentine

**meaning**
03 aim 04 feck, gist, goal, hang, idea,
plan, wish 05 drift, point, sense, trend,
value, worth 06 import, letter, object,
spirit, thrust 07 essence, message,
purport, purpose 08 sentence
09 intention, objective, substance
10 aspiration, definition, expression,
usefulness 11 connotation, elucidation,
explanation, explication, implication
12 construction, significance
13 signification 14 interpretation

**meaningful**
05 valid 06 useful 07 pointed, serious,
telling, warning 08 eloquent, material,
pregnant, relevant, speaking
09 effective, important 10 expressive,
purposeful, suggestive, worthwhile
11 significant

**meaningfully**
08 usefully 09 pointedly 10 eloquently,
relevantly 11 effectively, importantly
12 expressively, purposefully,
suggestively 13 significantly

## meaningless

**04** vain **05** empty **06** absurd, futile, hollow **07** aimless, trivial, useless, vacuous **08** trifling, unsensed **09** gibberish, pointless, senseless, worthless **10** irrational, motiveless **11** nonsensical, purposeless **13** insignificant, insubstantial **14** expressionless, unintelligible
• **meaningless word, meaningless refrain 05** nonny **07** ducdame, mirbane **08** falderal, fal de rol, folderol, rumbelow, rum-ti-tum **09** expletive **11** rumti-iddity **12** rumpti-iddity

## meaninglessly

**06** in vain, vainly **08** futilely **09** aimlessly, uselessly **11** pointlessly, senselessly **12** irrationally **13** purposelessly **14** unintelligibly

## meanly

**06** poorly, slight **07** cruelly, nastily **08** beggarly, commonly, scurvily, shabbily, unkindly **09** miserably, niggardly, selfishly **10** graspingly, spitefully **12** contemptibly, ungenerously, unpleasantly

## meanness

**09** parsimony **10** niggardise, niggardize, stinginess **11** mesquinerie, miserliness **12** illiberality **13** niggardliness, penuriousness **15** close-fistedness, close-handedness, tight-fistedness

## means

**03** way **04** mode **05** funds, money **06** agency, assets, avenue, course, income, manner, medium, method, riches, wealth **07** capital, channel, fortune, process, vehicle **08** property **09** affluence, resources, substance **10** instrument **11** wherewithal
• **by all means 06** surely **08** of course **09** certainly, naturally **10** of all loves **11** à toute force **12** with pleasure
• **by means of 03** per, via **04** with **05** using **07** through **08** by dint of **11** as a result of **12** with the aid of **13** with the help of
• **by no means 04** none **05** never, no way **07** in no way **08** not at all **11** anything but **12** certainly not
• **having enough means 04** able

## meantime, meanwhile

**05** among **06** for now **07** interim **12** concurrently, for the moment, in the interim **13** at the same time, in the interval, in the meantime **14** in the meanwhile, simultaneously **15** for the time being

## measly

**04** mean, poor, puny **05** mingy, petty **06** meagre, paltry, scanty, skimpy, spotty, stingy **07** miserly, pitiful, trivial **08** beggarly, pathetic, piddling **09** miserable, niggardly **10** ungenerous **12** contemptible

## measurable

**08** material, mensural, moderate **09** gaugeable **10** assessable, computable, fathomable, mensurable, noticeable **11** appreciable, perceptible,

significant **12** determinable, quantifiable, quantitative

## measure

**02** be **03** act, cut, lot, pit **04** area, bill, bulk, deed, gage, line, mass, mete, norm, pace, part, rate, read, rule, size, step, tape, test, time, unit **05** depth, gauge, judge, level, limit, means, meter, metre, piece, plumb, quota, range, ruler, scale, scope, share, sound, units, value, weigh, width **06** action, amount, assess, course, degree, extent, fathom, height, length, method, ration, record, rhythm, size up, strain, survey, system, volume, weight **07** compute, expanse, portion, rake-off, statute **08** acid test, appraise, capacity, division, estimate, evaluate, quantify, quantity, standard, traverse **09** allotment, barometer, benchmark, calculate, criterion, determine, dimension, enactment, expedient, magnitude, procedure, restraint, treatment, yardstick **10** allocation, dimensions, litmus test, measure off, measure out, moderation, proceeding, proportion, resolution, touchstone **11** proportions
*See also* **measurement**
• **beyond measure 08** out of cry **09** endlessly, immensely **10** extra modum, infinitely **11** excessively, inestimably, limitlessly **12** beyond belief, incalculably
• **for good measure 06** as well **07** besides **08** as a bonus **10** in addition **11** furthermore **12** over and above
• **get the measure of, take the measure of 04** rate **05** gauge, judge, value **06** assess, handle, reckon, size up **08** appraise, estimate, evaluate **09** calculate, determine **12** get a handle on
• **measure off 03** fix **05** limit **07** delimit, lay down, mark out, pace out **09** demarcate, determine **10** measure out **12** circumscribe
• **measure out 05** allot, issue **06** assign, divide **07** deal out, dole out, hand out, mete out, pour out **08** dispense, share out **09** apportion, parcel out **10** distribute, proportion
• **measure up 02** do **07** shape up, suffice **10** fit the bill, pass muster **11** fill the bill **12** make the grade **15** come up to scratch
• **measure up to 04** meet **05** equal, match, rival, touch **07** satisfy **08** come up to, live up to **09** match up to **11** compare with **12** make the grade

## measured

**04** slow **06** steady **07** careful, planned, precise, regular, studied **08** reasoned **09** unhurried **10** calculated, considered, deliberate, mensurable, restrained, rhythmical **12** premeditated **14** well-thought-out

## measureless

**04** vast **07** endless, immense **08** infinite **09** boundless, limitless, unbounded

**10** bottomless **11** inestimable, innumerable **12** immeasurable, incalculable

## measurement

**04** area, bulk, gage, mass, size, tare, unit **05** depth, range, width **06** amount, extent, height, length, sizing, survey, volume, weight **07** expanse, gauging, reading **08** capacity, quantity, weighing **09** amplitude, appraisal, dimension, judgement, magnitude **10** assessment, estimation, evaluation, proportion **11** calculation, calibration, computation, proportions **12** appreciation **14** quantification

*Measurement units include:*

**01** f, g, k, l, m, t, y

**02** as, cg, cm, ct, dg, em, en, ft, gm, gr, hg, kg, lb, li, mg, mm, oz, pt, st, yd

**03** amp, are, bar, bel, bit, cab, cor, cup, cwt, day, ell, erg, gal, grt, hin, kat, kin, kip, kos, lay, lea, ley, log, lux, mho, mil, mna, nit, ohm, oke, pin, rem, rod, tod, ton, tun, wey

**04** acre, aune, barn, bath, baud, boll, bolt, butt, cell, cord, coss, cran, demy, dyne, epha, foot, gill, gram, hand, hour, inch, kati, khat, knot, link, mile, mill, mina, mole, muid, nail, obol, omer, peck, pica, pint, pipe, pole, pood, ream, rood, rope, seer, sone, span, tael, thou, tola, torr, vara, volt, watt, week, yard, year

**05** cable, caneh, catty, chain, cubit, ephah, farad, henry, hertz, joule, kaneh, katti, litre, lumen, metre, month, ounce, perch, point, pound, quart, stere, stone, tesla, therm, tonne, weber

**06** ampere, barrel, bushel, decade, degree, denier, fathom, firkin, gallon, gramme, kelvin, league, minute, newton, noggin, parsec, pascal, radian, second

**07** calorie, candela, century, coulomb, decibel, fresnel, furlong, hectare, long ton, siemens, volt amp

**08** angstrom, cord foot, hogshead, kilogram, millibar, short ton

**09** becquerel, board foot, centigram, cubic foot, cubic inch, cubic yard, decimetre, foot-pound, kilolitre, kilometre, light year, metric ton, milligram, steradian

**10** atmosphere, barleycorn, centilitre, centimetre, cubic metre, fluid ounce, hectolitre, hoppus foot, horsepower, kilogramme, micrometre, millennium, millilitre, millimetre, millistere, square foot, square inch, square mile, square yard

**11** centigramme, milligramme, newton metre, square metre

**12** cable's length, nautical mile

**13** degree Celsius, hundredweight, volts per metre

**14** cubic decimetre, farads per metre, henrys per metre

**15** cubic centimetre, metres per second, newtons per metre, square decimetre, square kilometre

See also **measurement of pressure** under **pressure; timber; unit of weight** under **weight; wood**
• **Old Measurement 02** OM

## measuring instrument

Measuring instruments include:

**04** rule
**05** gauge, meter
**06** octant
**07** ammeter, balance, burette, pipette, sextant
**08** luxmeter, odometer, ohmmeter, quadrant
**09** altimeter, barometer, callipers, cryometer, dosimeter, flowmeter, focimeter, hodometer, hourglass, manometer, milometer, optometer, pedometer, plumb line, pyrometer, rheometer, steelyard, stopwatch, vinometer, voltmeter, volumeter, wattmeter, wavemeter
**10** anemometer, audiometer, bathometer, clinometer, cyclometer, gravimeter, hydrometer, hyetometer, hygrometer, hypsometer, micrometer, mileometer, multimeter, ombrometer, photometer, planimeter, protractor, pulsimeter, radiosonde, tachometer, tachymeter, theodolite, vibrograph, vibrometer, viscometer
**11** calorimeter, chronometer, colorimeter, dynamometer, pluviometer, pyranometer, salinometer, seismograph, seismometer, speedometer, spherometer, tape measure, tensiometer, thermometer, vaporimeter, velocimeter, weighbridge
**12** Breathalyser®, densitometer, evaporimeter, galvanometer, inclinometer, magnetometer, psychrometer, respirometer, spectrometer, sphygmometer, trundle wheel, viscosimeter
**13** accelerometer, decelerometer, Geiger counter, saccharometer
**14** geothermometer, interferometer

See also **gauge**

## meat

**03** nub **04** core, crux, eats, fare, food, gist, grub, nosh, pith, tuck **05** flesh, heart, point, scran **06** kernel, marrow, tucker, viands **07** essence, nucleus, rations **08** eatables, victuals **09** substance **10** provisions, sustenance **11** comestibles, nourishment, subsistence **12** fundamentals

Cold meats include:

**03** ham
**04** beef, game, pâté, pork, Spam®
**06** salami, tongue, turkey
**07** biltong, chicken, chorizo, kabanos, pork pie, sausage, terrine, venison
**08** bresaola, Cervelat, cold cuts, cured ham, meat loaf, ox tongue, parma ham, pastrami, salt beef
**09** Bierwurst, glazed ham, liver paté, Mettwurst, pepperoni, rillettes, saucisson, scotch egg
**10** breaded ham, corned beef, crumbed ham, liverwurst, mortadella, prosciutto, Serrano ham
**11** sausage roll
**12** Ardennes pâté, Brunswick ham, Brussels pâté, jamón serrano, liver sausage, luncheon meat, peppered beef, Wiltshire ham
**13** chicken breast, garlic sausage, honey roast ham, Schinkenwurst, smoked sausage
**15** luncheon sausage

Meat cuts include:

**03** leg, rib, sey
**04** chop, clod, hand, hock, loin, neck, rack, rump, shin
**05** baron, chine, chuck, flank, hough, round, scrag, shank
**06** breast, collar, cutlet, fillet, rib eye, saddle
**07** best end, brisket, buttock, knuckle, sirloin, topside
**08** escalope, forehock, noisette, popeseye, shoulder, spare rib
**09** aitchbone, médaillon
**10** silverside
**11** filet mignon, porterhouse

Meats and meat products include:

**03** emu, ham, MRM, red
**04** beef, bush, duck, hare, lamb, loaf, pâté, pork, Spam®, spek, veal
**05** bacon, brawn, goose, heart, liver, mince, offal, quail, speck, steak, tripe, vifda, vivda, white
**06** brains, burger, faggot, gammon, grouse, haggis, haslet, kidney, mutton, oxtail, pigeon, polony, rabbit, tongue, turkey
**07** biltong, chicken, fatback, griskin, harslet, long pig, pemican, poultry, rissole, sausage, variety, venison
**08** bushmeat, foie gras, fricadel, luncheon, meat loaf, pemmican, pheasant, scrapple, trotters
**09** forcemeat, frikkadel, hamburger, partridge, rillettes
**10** beefburger, horseflesh, minced beef, sweetbread
**11** pig's knuckle, sausage meat
**12** black pudding, luncheon meat
**13** shield of brawn, witchetty grub
**14** mousse de canard

## meaty

**04** rich **05** beefy, burly, heavy, hunky, pithy, solid **06** brawny, fleshy, hearty, sturdy **08** muscular, profound **09** strapping **10** meaningful **11** interesting, significant, substantial

## mechanic

**07** artisan **08** engineer, operator **09** artificer, grauncher, groundman, machinist, operative, repairman, tradesman **10** groundsman, millwright, technician **11** card-sharper, mechanician, tradeswoman **12** grease monkey

## mechanical

**04** cold, dead, dull **06** manual, reflex **07** organic, routine **08** electric, habitual, lifeless, soulless **09** automated, automatic, dynamical, technical, unfeeling **10** impersonal, mechanized, unthinking **11** emotionless, instinctive, involuntary, machine-like, mechanistic, perfunctory, power-driven, unconscious, unemotional **12** matter-of-fact **14** machine-powered

## mechanically

**09** routinely **10** as a machine, by a machine, habitually **11** intuitively, on autopilot **12** unthinkingly **13** automatically, instinctively, involuntarily, unconsciously **14** electronically

## mechanism

**04** guts, tool **05** gears, means, motor, works **06** action, agency, device, engine, gadget, medium, method, system **07** channel, machine, process **08** gimcrack, jimcrack, movement, workings **09** apparatus, appliance, interlock, machinery, operation, procedure, propeller, structure, technique **10** components, instrument, propelment **11** contraption, contrivance, functioning, performance

## mechanize

**07** program **08** automate **11** computerize

## medal

**04** gold, gong **05** award, cross, model, prize **06** bronze, honour, reward, ribbon, silver, trophy **08** contorno, vernicle **09** gold medal, medallion **10** decoration, touch-piece **11** bronze medal, contorniate, silver medal

See also **military**

## meddle

◇ anagram indicator **03** mix, pry **04** mell, mess **05** medle, snoop **06** butt in, fiddle, kibitz, tamper, temper, tinker **07** intrude **09** interfere, intervene **10** stickybeak **12** put your oar in **14** poke your nose in, stick your oar in **15** stick your nose in

## meddlesome

**04** nosy **05** nosey **06** prying **08** meddling, snooping **09** intruding, intrusive, pragmatic **11** interfering, mischievous, pragmatical

## mediaeval

see **medieval, mediaeval**

## mediate

**06** convey, middle, settle, step in, umpire **07** referee, resolve, stickle **08** indirect, moderate, transmit **09** arbitrate, intercede, interpose, intervene, negotiate, reconcile **10** conciliate **11** intervening

12 intermediate 13 act as mediator
15 act as peacemaker

## mediation
11 arbitration, good offices, negotiation, peacemaking
12 conciliation, intercession, intervention 13 interposition
14 reconciliation

## mediator
04 mean 05 judge 06 priest, umpire
07 arbiter, referee 08 stickler 09 go-between, middleman, moderator, Ombudsman, thirdsman 10 arbitrator, interceder, intervener, negotiator, peacemaker, reconciler 11 conciliator, intercessor, interventor 12 honest broker, intermediary

## medical
03 med
See also **disease**

*Medical and surgical equipment includes:*

03 ECG, MRI
05 clamp, swabs
06 canula, EpiPen®, scales
07 cannula, curette, dilator, forceps, inhaler, scalpel, scanner, syringe
08 catheter, iron lung, speculum, tweezers, X-ray unit
09 aspirator, auriscope, autoclave, CT scanner, dental dam, endoscope, incubator, inhalator, nebulizer, retractor
10 audiometer, CAT scanner, ear syringe, hypodermic, kidney dish, microscope, MRI scanner, oxygen mask, rectoscope, respirator, rhinoscope, sterilizer, ultrasound
11 body scanner, first aid kit, laparoscope, stethoscope, stomach pump, thermometer
12 bronchoscope, isolator tent, laryngoscope, resuscitator, surgical mask, urethroscope
13 aural speculum, defibrillator, specimen glass
14 oesophagoscope, operating table, ophthalmoscope, oxygen cylinder
15 instrument table

*Medical specialists include:*

07 dentist
08 optician
09 dietician, homeopath
10 homoeopath, oncologist, orthoptist, pharmacist
11 audiologist, chiropodist, neurologist, optometrist, pathologist, radiologist
12 anaesthetist, cardiologist, chiropractor, embryologist, geriatrician, immunologist, obstetrician, orthodontist, orthopaedist, psychiatrist, psychologist, toxicologist
13 dermatologist, gerontologist, gynaecologist, haematologist, paediatrician, vaccinologist
14 bacteriologist, microbiologist, pharmacologist, rheumatologist

15 endocrinologist, ophthalmologist, physiotherapist

See also **doctor; nurse**
• **medical man** see **doctor**
• **medical records** 04 case

## medicinal
06 physic 07 healing, medical
08 curative, physical, remedial
11 restorative, therapeutic 12 health-giving

## medicinally
09 medically 10 curatively, remedially
13 restoratively 15 therapeutically

## medicine
03 med 04 cure, drug 05 trade
06 remedy 07 nostrum, panacea
09 analeptic, physician
10 medicament, medication
12 prescription 14 pharmaceutical
See also **drug**

*Branches of medicine include:*

05 ob-gyn
07 otology, urology
08 nosology, obs/gynae, oncology, pharmacy
09 andrology, audiology, chiropody, dentistry, neurology, optometry, pathology, radiology
10 cardiology, embryology, geriatrics, immunology, obstetrics, osteopathy, pediatrics, psychiatry, psychology, toxicology
11 dermatology, diagnostics, gerontology, gynaecology, haematology, paediatrics, physiatrics
12 anaesthetics, bacteriology, kinesiatrics, microbiology, orthodontics, orthopaedics, perinatology, pharmacology, radiotherapy, rheumatology
13 brachytherapy, cytopathology, endocrinology, ophthalmology, physiotherapy, psychotherapy
14 electrotherapy, neuropathology, neuroradiology, sports medicine
15 neuropsychiatry

*Branches of complementary medicine include:*

04 yoga
05 reiki
07 massage, Pilates, Rolfing, shiatsu
08 Ayurveda
09 herbalism, iridology
10 art therapy, autogenics, homeopathy, meditation, osteopathy
11 acupressure, acupuncture, aura therapy, kinesiology, moxibustion, naturopathy, reflexology, ťai chi ch'uan
12 aromatherapy, Bach remedies, chiropractic, hydrotherapy, hypnotherapy, macrobiotics
14 autosuggestion, crystal healing, herbal medicine
15 Chinese medicine, thalassotherapy

*Medicine types include:*

04 pill
05 tonic
06 arnica, emetic, gargle, tablet
07 antacid, capsule, inhaler, linctus, lozenge, pessary, steroid
08 diuretic, ear drops, eye drops, hypnotic, laxative, narcotic, ointment, pastille, polypill, sedative
09 analgesic, paregoric, stimulant
10 antibiotic, antifungal, antiseptic, gripe-water, nasal spray, painkiller
11 anaesthetic, neuroleptic, suppository
13 antibacterial, anticoagulant, antihistamine, tranquillizer
14 anticonvulsant, antidepressant, bronchodilator, hallucinogenic

See also **antibiotic; drug**
• **medicine box** 04 inro

## medieval, mediaeval
03 med, old 07 antique, archaic
08 historic, obsolete, old-world, outmoded 09 primitive 10 antiquated
12 antediluvian, old-fashioned 13 of the Dark Ages, unenlightened 15 of the Middle Ages

## mediocre
04 hack, so-so 06 medium 07 average
08 adequate, inferior, middling, ordinary, passable 09 tolerable 10 not much cop, pedestrian, second-rate, uninspired 11 bog standard, commonplace, indifferent, not up to much, respectable 12 run-of-the-mill
13 insignificant, no great shakes, unexceptional 14 fair to middling
15 middle-of-the-road, undistinguished

## mediocrity
06 nobody 07 no-hoper, nothing
08 adequacy, dead loss, poorness
09 nonentity 10 non-starter
11 averageness, inferiority
12 indifference, ordinariness, passableness, unimportance
14 insignificance

## meditate
04 chew, muse, plan 05 brood, study, think 06 design, devise, intend, ponder, scheme 07 reflect 08 cogitate, consider, mull over, ruminate
09 speculate, think over 10 chew the cud, deliberate, have in mind
11 concentrate, contemplate

## meditation
02 TM 05 study, zazen 06 musing
07 reverie, thought 08 brooding
09 pondering 10 brown study, cogitation, reflection, ruminating, rumination 11 cerebration, mulling over, speculation 12 deliberation, excogitation 13 concentration, contemplation

## meditative
07 museful, pensive 08 ruminant, studious 09 prayerful 10 cogitative, reflective, ruminative, thoughtful
12 deliberative 13 contemplative

## Mediterranean
03 Med

## medium
01 m 03 med, way 04 fair, form, mean, mode, norm 05 ether, means, organ, stuff 06 agency, avenue, centre, medial, median, middle, midway, milieu 07 average, channel, element, habitat, midsize, psychic, setting, vehicle 08 ambience, material, middling, midpoint, moderate, standard 09 middle way, spiritist, substance 10 atmosphere, compromise, conditions, golden mean, influences, instrument 11 clairvoyant, environment, happy medium, necromancer 12 intermediate, middle ground, sound-carrier, spiritualist, surroundings 13 circumstances, fortune-teller 15 instrumentality, way of expressing
• by the medium of 02 in

## medley
◇ anagram indicator 03 mix 04 mess, olio, olla 05 fight, mêlée 06 jumble, mingle 07 farrago, melange, mixture, variety 08 macaroni, mishmash, mixed bag, pastiche 09 confusion, macédoine, patchwork, potpourri, quodlibet 10 assortment, collection, hodgepodge, hotchpotch, miscellany, salmagundi, salmagundy 11 gallimaufry, smorgasbord 13 helter-skelter 14 conglomeration, omnium-gatherum

## meek
04 mild, tame, weak 05 lowly, quiet, timid 06 docile, gentle, humble, modest 07 patient 08 peaceful, resigned, yielding 09 compliant, spineless 10 forbearing, spiritless, submissive, unassuming 11 deferential 13 long-suffering, unpretentious

## meekly
06 gently, humbly, mildly 07 quietly 08 modestly 09 patiently 12 submissively 13 deferentially

## meekness
07 modesty 08 docility, humility, mildness, patience, softness, tameness, timidity, weakness 09 deference, lowliness 10 compliance, gentleness, humbleness, submission 11 forbearance, resignation, wimpishness 12 acquiescence, peacefulness 13 long-suffering, self-abasement, spinelessness 14 self-effacement, spiritlessness, submissiveness

## meet
◇ juxtaposition indicator 03 get, pay, see 04 abut, bear, even, face, fill, game, give, hear, join, link, race, take 05 abide, cross, equal, event, greet, match, quits, rally, round, touch, unite 06 adjoin, answer, endure, fulfil, gather, handle, honour, hook up, link up, manage, muster, pay for, settle, suffer, tackle 07 balance, collect, connect, contest, convene, convoke, execute, fitting, fixture, meeting,

perform, react to, receive, run into, satisfy, undergo 08 assemble, bump into, chance on, come upon, come up to, converge, cope with, deal with, listen to 09 discharge, encounter, fittingly, forgather, go through, intersect, look after, qualified, respond to, run across 10 come across, comply with, congregate, engagement, experience, foregather, happen upon, join up with, rencounter, rendezvous, tournament 11 competition, get together, measure up to 12 come together, intersection 14 get to grips with 15 make contact with
• failure to meet 04 gape

## meeting
03 AGM, EGM, hui 04 date, meet, moot 05 rally, tryst, union, venue 06 caucus, roll-up 07 cabinet, contact, gorsedd, session 08 abutment, assembly, camporee, concours, congress, consulta, exercise, junction, wardmote 09 concourse, encounter, gathering, interface, interview 10 chautauqua, conference, confluence, convention, engagement, rencounter, rendezvous, watersmeet 11 appointment, assignation, conjunction, conventicle, convergence 12 intersection, introduction 13 confrontation 14 point of contact
See also greeting

## meeting-place
04 gild, moot, Pnyx 05 guild, house, joint, lodge, marae, venue 06 baraza, centre 07 cenacle 10 confluence, rendezvous, vestry-room 11 senate-house 12 chapterhouse

## megalomania
13 conceitedness 14 overestimation, self-importance 15 folie de grandeur

## meitnerium
02 Mt

## melancholy
03 low, sad 04 blue, down, glum 05 adust, blues, dumps, gloom, moody 06 dismal, gloomy, hipped, misery, rueful, somber, sombre, sorrow, spleen, woeful 07 doleful, pensive, sadness, unhappy 08 dejected, doldrums, downcast, mournful 09 allicholy, dejection, depressed, miserable, pessimism, sorrowful, splenetic, surliness, tristesse, woebegone 10 allycholly, deplorable, depression, despondent, dispirited, low spirits, lugubrious, pensieroso 11 atrabilious, despondency, downhearted, low-spirited, melancholia, melancholic, the black dog, unhappiness 12 disconsolate, heavy-hearted 13 hypochondriac, in the doldrums 14 down in the dumps
• make melancholy 03 hip, hyp

## melange
◇ anagram indicator 03 mix 06 jumble, medley 07 farrago, mixture, variety 08 mishmash, mixed bag, pastiche 09 confusion, patchwork, potpourri 10 assortment, collection,

hodgepodge, hotchpotch, miscellany, salmagundi 11 gallimaufry, smorgasbord 14 conglomeration, omnium-gatherum

## mêlée
◇ anagram indicator 04 fray, mess 05 brawl, broil, chaos, fight, mix-up, rally, scrum, set-to 06 affray, fracas, jumble, medley, mellay, muddle, ruckus, rumpus, tangle, tussle 07 clutter, ruction, scuffle 08 disorder, dogfight, stramash 09 confusion, scrimmage, scrummage 10 free-for-all 11 battle royal 15 disorganization

## Melia
03 nim 04 neem, nimb 05 neemb

## mellifluous
04 soft 05 sweet 06 dulcet, mellow, smooth 07 honeyed, silvery, tuneful 08 canorous, soothing 10 euphonious, harmonious 13 sweet-sounding

## mellow
04 full, kind, mild, rich, ripe, soft 05 happy, jolly, juicy, ripen, sweet 06 dulcet, fruity, genial, gentle, jovial, mature, placid, season, serene, smooth, soften, temper, tender 07 affable, amiable, cordial, improve, perfect, relaxed, rounded, sweeten, tuneful 08 amicable, cheerful, luscious, pleasant, resonant, tranquil 09 easy-going, melodious 10 euphonious, harmonious, pear-shaped 11 good-natured, kind-hearted 13 full-flavoured 15 make less extreme

## melodic
05 sweet 06 dulcet 07 musical, silvery, tuneful 09 melodious 10 euphonious, harmonious 13 sweet-sounding

## melodically
07 sweetly 09 musically, tunefully 11 melodiously 12 harmoniously

## melodious
05 sweet 06 dulcet, pretty 07 melodic, musical, Orphean, silvery, songful, tuneful 09 cantabile 10 euphonious, harmonious 13 sweet-sounding

## melodrama
07 tragedy 09 dramatics, high drama, staginess 10 overacting 11 histrionics, performance, tragicomedy 13 theatricality

## melodramatic
03 OTT 05 hammy, stagy 06 stagey 08 overdone, theatric 10 histrionic, over-the-top, theatrical 11 exaggerated, extravagant, sensational 12 histrionical, overdramatic, overstrained, transpontine 13 overemotional 15 blood-and-thunder

## melody
03 air 04 aria, ayre, part, song, tune 05 canto, chant, music, theme 06 cantus, rhythm, strain 07 euphony, harmony, melisma, musette, refrain 08 carillon, cavatina, part-song 09 cabaletta, cantilena, plainsong, sweetness 10 canto fermo, musicality 11 musicalness, tunefulness

**melon**

12 augmentation, counterpoint
13 ranz-des-vaches 14 harmoniousness

**melon**

04 pepo 06 casaba 07 cassaba
09 cantaloup, musk melon, Ogen
melon, rock melon 10 cantaloupe,
Charentais, Galia melon 11 winter
melon 13 honeydew melon

**melt**

◇ *anagram indicator* 03 ren, rin, run
04 blow, calm, flow, flux, fuse, move,
thaw 05 smelt, touch 06 affect, relent,
render, soften, spleen 07 defrost,
liquate, liquefy, resolve 08 discandy,
dissolve, moderate, unfreeze
09 discandie, uncongeal 10 colliquate,
deliquesce, impregnate, make tender
12 become tender
• **melt away** 04 fade 06 dispel, vanish
08 disperse, dissolve, evanesce, fade
away 09 disappear, evaporate

**meltdown**

06 defeat, fiasco 07 debacle, failure
08 abortion, calamity, collapse,
disaster, downfall 09 breakdown
11 frustration, miscarriage 15 coming
to nothing

**member**

01 M 02 MP 03 arm, leg, MBE, Mem
04 limb, part 05 organ 06 clause, fellow
07 comrade, dumaist, element
08 adherent 09 appendage, associate,
extremity, stretcher 10 subscriber
12 incorporator 14 representative

**membership**

04 body, seat 07 fellows, members
08 comrades 09 adherence, adherents,
enrolment 10 allegiance, associates,
fellowship 11 affiliation, subscribers
13 participation 15 representatives

**membrane**

03 haw, rim 04 fell, film, kell, skin, veil
05 hymen, layer, sheet, velum
06 mucosa, septum, tissue 08 patagium
09 arachnoid, diaphragm, partition
10 integument

**memento**

03 mem 04 Goss 05 relic, token
06 record, trophy 07 vestige
08 keepsake, memorial, reminder,
souvenir 11 remembrance

**memo**

03 fax 04 note 05 e-mail 06 letter
07 jotting, message 08 reminder
10 memorandum 11 aide-mémoire,
remembrance 12 memory-jogger

**memoir**

04 life 05 essay 06 record, report
07 account, journal 08 register
09 biography, chronicle, monograph,
narrative 13 autobiography

**memoirs**

05 diary 06 annals 07 diaries, records
08 journals, memories 09 life story
10 chronicles 11 confessions,
experiences 13 autobiography,
recollections, reminiscences

**memorable**

06 catchy, unique 07 notable, special
08 eventful, historic, striking

09 important, momentous
10 impressive, noteworthy, remarkable
11 distinctive, outstanding, significant
13 consequential, distinguished,
extraordinary, unforgettable

**memorandum**

03 fax, mem 04 memo, note, slip 05 e-
mail, jurat 06 letter 07 jotting, message
08 memorial, reminder 09 bordereau
11 aide-mémoire, remembrance
12 memory-jogger

**memorial**

03 mem 05 brass, relic, stone, stupa
06 dagaba, dagoba, marker, memory,
plaque, record, shrine, statue, trophy,
Yizkor 07 memento, relique
08 cenotaph, ebenezer, monument,
Pantheon, souvenir 09 altar-tomb,
headstone, mausoleum, tombstone
10 gravestone, memorandum,
monumental, remembered
11 celebratory, Norman cross,
remembrance, testimonial
13 commemorative
*See also* **monument**

**memorize**

05 learn 06 get off, record 08 remember
09 celebrate 11 learn by rote 12 learn
by heart 14 commit to memory

**memory**

03 RAM, ROM 04 mind, rote
06 honour, recall 07 tribute
09 retention, sovenance 10 observance
11 recognition, remembrance
12 recollection, reminiscence
13 commemoration 14 powers of recall
• **memory block** 04 page

**men**

02 OR
*See also* **man**
• **excluding men** 03 hen

**menace**

04 loom, lour, pain, pest, risk 05 alarm,
appal, bully, daunt, peril, press, scare,
shore 06 bother, coerce, danger,
dismay, hazard, screws, threat
07 terrify, warning 08 big stick,
browbeat, bullying, coercion, frighten,
jeopardy, nuisance, pressure, threaten
09 annoyance, terrorism, terrorize
10 intimidate, pressurize
11 browbeating, frighteners,
ominousness, public enemy,
terrorizing 12 intimidation,
troublemaker 13 tyrannization 15 thorn
in your side

**menacing**

04 grim 07 looming, louring, ominous,
warning 08 alarming, minatory, sinister
09 Damoclean, dangerous, impending,
minacious, threatful 10 portentous
11 frightening, threatening
12 intimidating, intimidatory

**mend**

03 fix, sew, toe 04 beet, bete, cure,
darn, heal 05 amend, clout, emend,
patch, plash, refit, renew, run up, stick
06 bushel, cobble, reform, remedy,
repair, revise, solder 07 correct,
improve, patch up, recover, rectify,
restore 08 put right, renovate, solution

09 get better, make whole
10 ameliorate, put in order, recuperate,
supplement 14 mend your fences
15 put back together
• **mend your ways** 06 reform
15 improve yourself, make a fresh start
• **on the mend** 07 healing 08 reviving
09 improving 10 recovering
12 convalescent, convalescing,
recuperating

**mendacious**

05 false, lying 06 untrue 08 perjured
09 deceitful, deceptive, dishonest,
insincere 10 fallacious, fictitious,
fraudulent, perfidious, untruthful
11 duplicitous

**mendacity**

03 lie 05 lying 06 deceit 07 perfidy,
perjury, untruth 09 duplicity, falsehood
10 dishonesty, distortion, inveracity
11 fraudulence, insincerity
13 deceitfulness, falsification
14 untruthfulness

**mendelevium**

02 Md

**mendicant**

03 bum 04 hobo 05 fakir, frate, friar,
sadhu, tramp 06 beggar, cadger,
canter, craver, pauper, saddhu, toerag
07 begging, bludger, cadging, jarkman,
moocher, sponger, vagrant
08 besognio, blighter, calender,
vagabond, whipjack 09 scrounger
10 down-and-out, freeloader,
panhandler, scrounging, supplicant
11 beachcomber, petitionary

**menial**

03 eta, low 04 base, dull 05 lowly,
slave 06 boring, drudge, humble,
minion, ribald, skivvy 07 humdrum,
routine, servant, servile, slavish,
waister 08 dogsbody, domestic,
labourer 09 attendant, degrading,
demeaning, underling, unskilled
10 after-guard 11 ignominious,
subservient

**menstruation**

04 flow 06 menses, period 07 courses
08 the curse, the usual 09 monthlies
10 menorrhoea 11 monthly flow
14 menstrual cycle, time of the month

**mensuration**

06 metage, survey 09 measuring,
surveying, valuation 10 assessment,
estimation, evaluation, planimetry
11 calculation, calibration,
computation, measurement

**mental**

◇ *anagram indicator* 03 ape, fey, mad
04 bats, gyte, loco, nuts, wild
05 barmy, batty, buggy, crazy, daffy,
dippy, dotty, flaky, gonzo, loony,
loopy, manic, nutty, potty, queer,
wacko, wacky, wiggy 06 crazed,
cuckoo, fruity, insane, maniac, raving,
red-mad, screwy, troppo 07 bananas,
barking, berserk, bonkers, cracked,
frantic, lunatic, meshuga 08 abstract,
cerebral, crackers, demented,
deranged, dingbats, doolally, frenetic,
frenzied, maniacal, rational,

unhinged, unstable **09** cognitive, disturbed, lymphatic, psychotic, up the wall **10** bestraught, conceptual, distracted, distraught, frantic-mad, off the wall, off your nut, out to lunch, ridiculous, stone-crazy, unbalanced **11** not all there, off the rails, off your head, theoretical, unconscious **12** intellectual, mad as a hatter, off your chump, round the bend **13** off your rocker, of unsound mind, out of your head, out of your mind, out of your tree, round the twist **14** off your trolley, wrong in the head **15** non compos mentis, out of your senses
• **mental health workers** **15** men in white coats

**mentality**
**04** mind **06** brains, make-up **07** faculty, mindset, outlook **08** attitude, ingenium **09** character, intellect **10** grey matter, psychology **11** disposition, frame of mind, personality, rationality **12** intelligence **13** comprehension, understanding, way of thinking **14** mental attitude **15** little grey cells

**mentally**
**07** ideally **08** inwardly **09** in the mind **10** rationally **11** emotionally **12** subjectively **14** intellectually **15** psychologically, temperamentally

**mention**
**03** say **04** cite, hint, mind, name, note, talk **05** hight, mensh, quote, speak, state **06** bename, broach, cast up, drag up, exhume, hint at, impart, notice, remark, report, reveal, speech **07** bring up, declare, divulge, let fall, refer to, speak of, specify, touch on, tribute **08** allude to, allusion, citation, disclose, instance, intimate, nominate, point out, remember **09** introduce, make known, namecheck, reference, statement **10** indication, particular **11** acknowledge, communicate, observation, recognition **12** announcement, notification **14** condescend upon **15** acknowledgement
• **don't mention it** **05** bitte **08** forget it, not at all **09** don't worry **12** it's a pleasure, it was nothing
• **not to mention** **05** let be **06** let-a-be **07** besides **08** as well as, let alone, much less **12** not including **13** not forgetting **14** to say nothing of

**mentioned**
**05** cited **06** quoted, stated **08** foresaid, reported **09** aforesaid, fore-cited, forenamed **10** fore-quoted **13** forementioned **14** above-mentioned, aforementioned

**mentor**
**03** rav **04** guru **05** coach, guide, swami, tutor **07** adviser, advisor, teacher, trainer **09** confidant, pedagogue, therapist **10** confidante, counsellor, instructor

**menu**
**04** card, list **06** tariff **10** bill of fare **11** carte du jour

**mercantile**
**05** trade **07** salable, trading **08** saleable **09** mercenary **10** commercial, marketable **12** merchantable

**mercenary**
**04** hack, merc, paid **05** hired, venal **06** greedy, rutter, sordid **07** Hessian, pindari, Switzer **08** covetous, grasping, hired gun, hireling, huckster, pindaree **09** freelance, on the make, warmonger **10** avaricious, galloglass, lansquenet, mercantile, prostitute **11** acquisitive, condottiere, landsknecht, mammonistic **12** hired soldier, professional **13** free companion, materialistic, money-grubbing **15** money-orientated

**merchandise**
**04** ware **05** cargo, goods, stock, trade, wares **07** dealing, freight, produce **08** products, shipment **09** vendibles **11** commodities

**merchandize**
**04** hype, plug, push, sell, vend **05** carry, trade **06** deal in, market, peddle, retail, supply **07** promote **09** advertise, publicize, traffic in **10** buy and sell, distribute

**merchant**
**05** agent, bunia, trade **06** broker, bunnia, dealer, factor, jobber, seller, trader, vendor **07** Antonio **08** hoastman, retailer, salesman **09** bourgeois, négociant **10** commercial, marcantant, saleswoman, shopkeeper, supercargo, trafficker, wholesaler **11** distributor, salesperson **14** sales executive

**merciful**
**04** kind, mild **06** humane **07** clement, lenient, liberal, pitying, sparing **08** generous, gracious, tolerant **09** forgiving, merciable **10** forbearing **11** soft-hearted, sympathetic **12** humanitarian **13** compassionate, tender-hearted

**mercifully**
**06** kindly **07** luckily **10** generously, graciously, thankfully, tolerantly **11** fortunately **15** compassionately, sympathetically, tender-heartedly

**merciless**
**04** hard **05** cruel, harsh, rigid, stern **06** severe, wanton **07** callous, inhuman **08** inhumane, pitiless, ruthless **09** barbarous, heartless, unfeeling, unpitying, unsparing **10** implacable, inexorable, intolerant, relentless, unmerciful **11** hard-hearted, remorseless, unforgiving **13** unsympathetic

**mercilessly**
**07** cruelly, harshly, sternly **08** severely **09** callously **10** implacably, inexorably, pitilessly, ruthlessly **11** heartlessly **12** relentlessly **13** hard-heartedly, remorselessly

**mercurial**
**06** active, fickle, lively, mobile **07** erratic, flighty **08** spirited, unstable, variable, volatile **09** impetuous,

impulsive, sprightly **10** capricious, changeable, inconstant **11** quicksilver **12** light-hearted **13** irrepressible, temperamental, unpredictable

**mercury**
**02** Hg **06** Hermes

**mercy**
**04** boon, pity **05** grace **06** favour, relief **07** godsend, quarter **08** blessing, clemency, good luck, kindness, leniency, mildness, sympathy **10** compassion, generosity, humaneness, misericord, tenderness **11** forbearance, forgiveness, misericorde **14** loving-kindness **15** humanitarianism
• **at the mercy of** **09** exposed to, prostrate **11** at the whim of **12** in the power of, vulnerable to **14** in the control of, unarmed against

**mere**
**04** bare, lake, meer, meri, pool, poor, pure, very **05** pound, petty, plain, sheer, stark, utter **06** common, paltry, simple **07** unmixed **08** absolute, boundary, complete **10** absolutely, no more than **13** pure and simple, unadulterated

**merely**
**03** but **04** just, only **06** barely, hardly, purely, simply **08** scarcely **10** nothing but

**meretricious**
**04** bold, loud **05** cheap, flash, gaudy, jazzy, showy, tacky **06** flashy, garish, glitzy, kitsch, made up, tawdry, vulgar **09** glamorous, insincere, tasteless **10** flamboyant **11** pretentious **12** ostentatious

**merganser**
**04** smew

**merge**
**03** die, dip, mix **04** fuse, join, meet, meld, sink **05** blend, unite, verge **06** mingle, plunge, team up **07** collate, combine, run into **08** coalesce, converge, intermix, liquesce, melt into **10** amalgamate, be engulfed, join forces **11** consolidate, incorporate **12** become lost in, come together **13** bring together **15** be assimilated in, be swallowed up in

**merger**
**05** blend, union **06** fusion **08** alliance **09** coalition **11** combination, convergence **12** amalgamation, assimilation **13** confederation, consolidation, incorporation

**merit**
**03** due **04** earn, good, plus **05** asset, claim, found, value, worth **06** credit, desert, praise, reward, talent, virtue **07** be worth, deserts, deserve, justify, quality, warrant **08** goodness **09** advantage **10** be worthy of, excellence, excellency, recompense, worthiness **11** distinction, high quality, strong point **12** be entitled to, have a right to **13** justification

## merited

**03** due **04** just **06** earned, worthy **07** condign, fitting **08** deserved, entitled, rightful **09** justified, warranted **11** appropriate **12** well-deserved

## meritorious

**04** good **05** right **06** worthy **08** laudable, virtuous, worthful **09** admirable, deserving, estimable, excellent, exemplary, righteous **10** creditable, honourable **11** commendable **12** praiseworthy

## mermaid

**05** siren **06** undine **07** seamaid **08** sea nymph, seawoman **11** water-spirit, water sprite

## merrily

**06** gladly **07** happily **08** blithely, chirpily, jovially **10** cheerfully, pleasantly

## merriment

**03** fun **04** glee **05** mirth **06** frolic, gaiety **07** jollity, revelry, waggery **08** buoyance, carnival, hilarity, laughter **09** amusement, festivity, jocundity, jolliment, joviality **10** blitheness, joyfulness, liveliness **11** high spirits **12** carefreeness, cheerfulness, conviviality, mirthfulness **13** jollification

## merry

◇ *anagram indicator* **03** gay **04** cant, daft, gean, glad **05** gaudy, happy, jolly, nitid, riant, tipsy, vogie **06** blithe, cheery, chirpy, frolic, jocose, jocund, jovial, joyful, lively, tiddly **07** amusing, festive, gleeful, squiffy **08** carefree, cheerful, gleesome, mirthful, pleasant, sportful, sportive **09** convivial, heartsome, hilarious **10** frolicsome **11** saturnalian **12** high-spirited, light-hearted **13** in good spirits, slightly drunk **15** one over the eight
• **make merry 04** gaud, rant, sing **05** dance, drink, revel **07** carouse, have fun, rejoice **09** celebrate **10** have a party **13** enjoy yourself

## merry-andrew

**05** clown **07** buffoon **11** Jack-pudding **13** pickle-herring

## merry-go-round

**08** carousel, galloper, joy-wheel **09** carrousel, gallopers, whirligig **10** roundabout

## merrymaking

**03** fun **05** party, revel **06** frolic, gaiety **07** revelry **08** carousal, merimake **09** carousing, festivity, galravage, gilravage, junketing, merriment **10** galravitch, gillravage, gilravitch, rejoicings **11** celebration, gillravitch **12** conviviality **13** jollification

## mesh

**03** net, web **04** trap **05** gauze, match, snare **06** engage, enmesh, inmesh, tangle **07** combine, connect, entwine, lattice, netting, network, tracery, trellis **08** dovetail, entangle **09** harmonize, interlock **10** co-ordinate, go together **11** fit together, latticework **12** come together, entanglement

## mesmerize

**04** grip **06** benumb **07** enthral, stupefy **08** entrance, transfix **09** captivate, fascinate, hypnotize, magnetize, spellbind **14** hold spellbound

## mess

◇ *anagram indicator* **03** fix, jam, mix, mux, tip **04** dine, dirt, dump, hash, hole, meal, muck, muss, soss, spot, stew **05** botch, chaos, farce, filth, mix-up, musse, slosh **06** bungle, cock-up, course, guddle, hiccup, jumble, lash-up, litter, medley, midden, mucker, muddle, pickle, plight **07** balls-up, clutter, dilemma, failure, jackpot, pig's ear, screw-up, squalor, trouble, turmoil **08** disarray, disorder, hot water, quandary, shambles, slaister, whoopsie **09** confusion, deep water, dirtiness, praiseach, shemozzle, shimozzle, tight spot **10** difficulty, dog's dinner, filthiness, pretty pass, schemozzle, shlemozzle, untidiness **11** predicament **13** dog's breakfast, embarrassment, pig's breakfast **15** disorganization
• **make a mess of 04** flub, goof
• **mess about, mess around 04** goof, play **05** upset **06** piddle, puddle, putter **09** faff about, goof about, muck about, play about **10** faff around, fool around, goof around, play around **11** potter about **12** fiddle around
• **mess about with, mess around with 05** upset **06** bother **07** trouble **08** play with **10** meddle with, tamper with, treat badly **13** fool about with, inconvenience, interfere with, play about with **14** fool around with, play around with
• **mess up 04** foul, muff, ruin **05** bitch, bodge, botch, dirty, fluff, spoil **06** bungle, cock up, foul up, jumble, muck up, muddle, tangle, untidy **07** confuse, disrupt, louse up, screw up **08** dishevel **09** clutter up **10** disarrange **11** make a hash of, make a mess of

## message

**03** fax **04** gist, idea, memo, news, note, task, wire, word **05** cable, drift, e-mail, moral, point, sense, telex, theme **06** errand, import, letter, notice, report, thrust **07** dépêche, epistle, essence, express, meaning, missive, purport, tidings **08** aerogram, bulletin, dispatch, irenicon, mailgram, telegram, Teletype® **09** autoreply, eirenicon, telegraph, telepheme **10** communiqué, intimation, memorandum **11** implication, marconigram, Telemessage® **12** significance **13** communication
• **end message 07** sign off
• **get the message 03** see **04** twig **05** get it, grasp **06** follow, take in **07** catch on, latch on **08** cotton on, tumble to **09** latch onto **10** comprehend, cotton on to, get the hang, get the idea, understand **11** get the point **13** catch the drift, get the picture

## messenger

**04** page, peon, post, send **05** agent, angel, caddy, cadee, cadie, envoy **06** beadle, bearer, caddie, herald, Hermes, nuncio, runner **07** carrier, courier, express, Mercury, missive **08** dispatch, emissary, footpost **09** chaprassi, chaprassy, chuprassy, errand-boy, go-between, harbinger, woman post **10** ambassador, errand-girl, forerunner, pursuivant, shellycoat **11** internuncio **12** ambassadress, valet de place **13** gillie-wetfoot, secretary-bird **14** commissionaire **15** corbie messenger, gillie-white-foot

## messy

◇ *anagram indicator* **05** dirty, gungy, yucky, yukky **06** filthy, grubby, grungy, sloppy, untidy **07** chaotic, muddled, unkempt **08** bungling, confused, littered, slobbish, slovenly **09** cluttered, shambolic **10** disordered, in disarray **11** dishevelled **12** disorganized

## metal

*Metals include:*

**01 K** (potassium), **U** (uranium), **V** (vanadium), **W** (tungsten), **Y** (yttrium)

**02 Ac** (actinium), **Ag** (silver), **Al** (aluminium), **Am** (americium), **Au** (gold), **Ba** (barium), **Be** (beryllium), **Bi** (bismuth), **Bk** (berkelium), **Ca** (calcium), **Cd** (cadmium), **Ce** (cerium), **Cf** (californium), **Cm** (curium), **Co** (cobalt), **Cr** (chromium), **Cs** (caesium), **Cu** (copper), **Dy** (dysprosium), **Er** (erbium), **Es** (einsteinium), **Eu** (europium), **Fe** (iron), **Fm** (fermium), **Fr** (francium), **Ga** (gallium), **Gd** (gadolinium), **Ge** (germanium), **Hf** (hafnium), **Hg** (mercury), **Ho** (holmium), **In** (indium), **Ir** (iridium), **La** (lanthanum), **Li** (lithium), **Lr** (lawrencium), **Lu** (lutetium), **Md** (mendelevium), **Mg** (magnesium), **Mn** (manganese), **Mo** (molybdenum), **Na** (sodium), **Nb** (niobium), **Nd** (neodymium), **Ni** (nickel), **No** (nobelium), **Np** (neptunium), **Os** (osmium), **Pa** (protactinium), **Pb** (lead), **Pd** (palladium), **Pm** (promethium), **Po** (polonium), **Pr** (praseodymium), **Pt** (platinum), **Pu** (plutonium), **Ra** (radium), **Rb** (rubidium), **Re** (rhenium), **Rh** (rhodium), **Ru** (ruthenium), **Sb** (antimony), **Sc** (scandium), **Sm** (samarium), **Sn** (tin), **Sr** (strontium), **Ta** (tantalum), **Tb** (terbium), **Tc** (technetium), **Th** (thorium), **Ti** (titanium), **Tl** (thallium), **Tm** (thulium), **Yb** (ytterbium), **Zn** (zinc), **Zr** (zirconium)

**03 tin** (Sn)

**04 gold** (Au), **iron** (Fe), **lead** (Pb), **zinc** (Zn)

**06 barium** (Ba), **cerium** (Ce), **cobalt** (Co), **copper** (Cu), **curium** (Cm), **erbium** (Er), **indium** (In), **nickel** (Ni),

## metallic

07 **bismuth** (Bi), **cadmium** (Cd), **caesium** (Cs), **calcium** (Ca), **fermium** (Fm), **gallium** (Ga), **hafnium** (Hf), **holmium** (Ho), **iridium** (Ir), **lithium** (Li), **mercury** (Hg), **niobium** (Nb), **rhenium** (Re), **rhodium** (Rh), **terbium** (Tb), **thorium** (Th), **thulium** (Tm), **uranium** (U), **yttrium** (Y)
08 **actinium** (Ac), **antimony** (Sb), **chromium** (Cr), **europium** (Eu), **francium** (Fr), **lutetium** (Lu), **nobelium** (No), **platinum** (Pt), **polonium** (Po), **rubidium** (Rb), **samarium** (Sm), **scandium** (Sc), **tantalum** (Ta), **thallium** (Tl), **titanium** (Ti), **tungsten** (W), **vanadium** (V)
09 **aluminium** (Al), **americium** (Am), **berkelium** (Bk), **beryllium** (Be), **germanium** (Ge), **lanthanum** (La), **magnesium** (Mg), **manganese** (Mn), **neodymium** (Nd), **neptunium** (Np), **palladium** (Pd), **plutonium** (Pu), **potassium** (K), **ruthenium** (Ru), **strontium** (Sr), **ytterbium** (Yb), **zirconium** (Zr)
10 **dysprosium** (Dy), **gadolinium** (Gd), **lawrencium** (Lr), **molybdenum** (Mo), **promethium** (Pm), **technetium** (Tc)
11 **californium** (Cf), **einsteinium** (Es), **mendelevium** (Md)
12 **praseodymium** (Pr), **protactinium** (Pa)

---

*Metal alloys include:*

03 pot
04 type
05 brass, Dutch, Invar®, Muntz, potin, steel, terne, white
06 Alnico®, billon, bronze, latten, occamy, ormolu, oroide, pewter, solder, tambac, tombac, tombak, Y-alloy
07 amalgam, Babbit's, chromel, Nitinol, prince's, shakudo, similor, tutania, tutenag
08 Babbitt's, cast iron, gunmetal, Manganin®, Nichrome®, orichalc, speculum, zircaloy, Zircoloy®
09 Britannia, Duralumin®, Dutch gold, Dutch leaf, magnalium, pinchbeck, shibuichi, white gold
10 constantan, ferro-alloy, iridosmine, iridosmium, mischmetal, Monel metal®, mosaic gold, osmiridium, white brass
11 chrome steel, cupro-nickel, nicrosilial, white copper
12 German silver, nickel silver
14 high-speed steel, phosphor-bronze, stainless steel

- **design on metal** 04 etch
- **join metal** 04 weld
- **metal after heating** 04 calx
- **metal bar** 03 zed 05 ingot
- **piece of metal** 03 gib
- **precious metal** 03 ore
- **thin metal** 04 foil

## metallic

03 tin 04 gold, iron, lead 05 harsh, rough, shiny, steel, tinny 06 copper, nickel, silver 07 grating, jarring 08 gleaming, jangling, polished 09 dissonant 10 unpleasant

## metamorphose

◊ *anagram indicator* 05 alter 06 change, modify, mutate, remake 07 convert, remodel, reshape 09 transform, translate, transmute 11 transfigure 12 transmogrify

## metamorphosis

◊ *anagram indicator* 06 change 07 rebirth 08 mutation 09 staminody 10 alteration, changeover, conversion, metabolism 12 modification, regeneration 13 transmutation 14 holometabolism, transformation 15 transfiguration

## metaphor

03 met 05 image, trope 06 emblem, metaph, symbol, visual 07 analogy, picture 08 allegory 10 emblematic 12 transumption 14 figure of speech, representation

## metaphorical

03 met 06 metaph, visual 08 symbolic 10 analogical, emblematic, figurative 11 allegorical

## metaphysical

04 deep 05 basic, ideal 06 unreal 07 eternal, general 08 abstract, abstruse, esoteric, fanciful, profound 09 essential, high-flown, recondite, spiritual, universal 10 immaterial, impalpable, intangible, subjective 11 fundamental, incorporeal, speculative, theoretical 12 intellectual, supernatural 13 insubstantial, philosophical, unsubstantial 14 transcendental

## mete

- **mete out** 05 allot 06 assign 07 deal out, dole out, hand out, portion 08 dispense, share out 09 apportion, divide out, ration out 10 administer, distribute, measure out

## meteor

05 comet, drake 06 bolide 08 aerolite, aerolith, fireball 09 meteorite, meteoroid 10 exhalation 11 falling star 12 shooting star

---

*Meteor showers include:*

06 Lyrids, Ursids
07 Leonids, Taurids
08 Geminids, Orionids, Perseids
11 Quadrantids
12 Eta Aquariids
14 Alpha-Scorpiids, Delta Aquariids

## meteoric

04 fast 05 brief, quick, rapid, swift 06 speedy, sudden 08 dazzling, flashing 09 brilliant, lightning, momentary, overnight, transient 11 spectacular 13 instantaneous

## meteorologist

06 met man 10 weatherman 11 weathergirl, weatherlady 13 climatologist 14 weather prophet

## meteorology

*Meteorology-related terms include:*

04 calm, eddy, flux, haar, haze, ITCZ, rime
05 flood, front, frost, Q-code, radar, ridge, SIGWX, solar, taiga, virga
06 arctic, el Niño, flurry, haboob, isobar, Kelvin, oxygen
07 Celsius, chinook, climate, cyclone, drizzle, drought, graupel, mistral, monsoon, rainbow, thunder, tornado, typhoon, weather
08 acid rain, blizzard, dewpoint, doldrums, forecast, humidity, isotherm, millibar, rainfall, udometer, windsock, wind vane
09 advection, aerograph, altimeter, barograph, barometer, cold front, hurricane, hyetology, jet stream, lightning, Met Office, nephology, radiation, rain gauge, satellite, sub-arctic, trade wind, warm front, wind chill, wind speed
10 aerography, air quality, anemometer, atmosphere, baroclinic, barotropic, cloud cover, conduction, convection, depression, Fahrenheit, Gulf stream, Hadley Cell, hemisphere, hyetograph, hyetometer, hygrometer, nephograph, nephoscope, nowcasting, ozone layer, rain shadow, rain shower, visibility, waterspout, wavelength
11 air pressure, anticyclone, climatology, evaporation, Fujita scale, ground frost, hyetography, pluviometer, pollen count, temperature, thermograph, thermometer, thermopause, troposphere, ultra violet, water vapour, wave cyclone
12 cloud seeding, condensation, cyclogenesis, meteorograph, microclimate, pilot balloon, thunderstorm, weather chart, weather watch
13 ball lightning, Beaufort scale, boundary layer, climate change, fork lightning, frontogenesis, magnetosphere, occluded front, onshore breeze, precipitation, scatterometer
14 air temperature, continentality, horse latitudes, offshore breeze, prevailing wind, sheet lightning, transmissivity, weather station
15 hyetometrograph, stationary front, weather forecast, wind-chill factor

## method

03 art, how, way 04 form, line, mode, plan, rule 05 means, order, route, style 06 course, design, manner, scheme, system 07 fashion, pattern, process, routine 08 approach, modality, planning, practice 09 procedure, programme, structure, technique 10 regularity 11 arrangement,

orderliness **12** organization **13** modus operandi **14** classification

**methodical**
**04** neat, tidy **06** formal **07** logical, ordered, orderly, planned, precise, regular **09** efficient, organized **10** deliberate, meticulous, scrupulous, structured, systematic **11** disciplined, painstaking, well-ordered **12** businesslike, systematical

**methodically**
**06** neatly, tidily **07** in place, orderly **08** formally **09** as planned, by the book, logically, precisely, regularly, to the rule, uniformly **11** efficiently **12** meticulously, scrupulously **13** painstakingly **14** systematically

**metical**
**02** Mt **03** MZM

**meticulous**
**05** exact, fussy, timid **06** strict **07** careful, precise **08** accurate, detailed, rigorous, thorough **10** fastidious, particular, scrupulous **11** overcareful, painstaking, punctilious **13** conscientious

**meticulously**
**07** exactly **08** strictly **09** carefully, precisely **10** accurately, rigorously, thoroughly **12** scrupulously **13** painstakingly, punctiliously **15** conscientiously

**métier**
**03** job **04** line **05** craft, field, forte, trade **06** sphere **07** calling, pursuit **08** business, vocation **09** specialty **10** occupation, profession, speciality **14** line of business

**metro**
*see* **underground**

**metropolis**
**04** city **07** capital **08** main city **09** large city **10** cosmopolis **11** capital city, megalopolis **12** municipality **14** cultural centre
*See also* **city**

**mettle**
**04** guts, pith **05** nerve, pluck, pride, spunk **06** daring, ginger, make-up, nature, spirit, valour, vigour **07** bravery, calibre, courage, resolve, smeddum **08** backbone, boldness **09** character, endurance, fortitude, gallantry **11** disposition, intrepidity, personality, temperament **12** fearlessness **13** determination, sprightliness **14** indomitability

**mettlesome**
**04** bold **05** brave **06** ardent, daring, lively, plucky, spunky **07** gallant, valiant **08** fearless, intrepid, resolute, spirited **10** courageous **11** lion-hearted, unflinching **12** high-spirited, stout-hearted

**mew**
**04** cast, coop, gull, meow, mewl, shed **05** miaow, miaul, moult, whine **07** confine, retreat **09** caterwaul

**mewl**
**03** cry **05** whine **06** snivel, whinge **07** blubber, grizzle, whimper

**Mexican**
**03** Mex

**Mexico**
**03** MEX

**miaow**
**03** mew **04** meow, mewl **05** miaul, whine **09** caterwaul

**miasma**
**04** reek **05** fetor, odour, smell, stink **06** stench **07** malaria **08** mephitis **09** effluvium, pollution

**miasmal**
**04** foul **05** fetid **06** foetid, putrid, smelly **07** miasmic, noisome, noxious, reeking **08** mephitic, miasmous, polluted, stinking **09** miasmatic **10** malodorous, miasmatous **11** unwholesome **12** foul-smelling

**mica**
**03** mic **04** daze **07** biotite

**Michigan**
**02** MI **04** Mich

**microbe**
**03** bug **04** germ **05** virus **08** bacillus, pathogen **09** bacterium **13** micro-organism

**Micronesia**
**03** FSM

**microphone**
**03** bug

**microscope**
**03** SEM, TEM

**microscopic**
**04** tiny **06** minute **09** minuscule **10** negligible **13** imperceptible, indiscernible, infinitesimal **14** extremely small

**microscopically**
**08** minutely **09** extremely **13** imperceptibly **15** infinitesimally

**midday**
**01** m, n **04** noon **06** twelve **07** noonday **08** meridian, noontide, noontime **09** lunchtime **10** meridional, twelve noon **12** twelve o'clock

**middle**
◇ *middle selection indicator* **03** med, mid **04** core, mean, noon **05** belly, heart, inner, midst, tummy, waist **06** centre, inside, medial, median, medium, mesial, midway, paunch **07** central, halfway, mediate, midriff, stomach **08** bull's eye, midpoint **11** bread basket, equidistant, intervening **12** halfway point, intermediate
• **in the middle of** **05** among, while **06** during **08** busy with **09** engaged in **12** in the midst of, occupied with, surrounded by **14** in the process of

**middle-class**
**08** suburban **09** bourgeois **10** gentrified **11** white-collar **12** conventional, professional

**Middle East**
*Middle Eastern landmarks include:*
**05** Kabaa
**06** Qumran, Red Sea, Tigris
**07** Dead Sea, Ephesus
**08** Bosporus
**09** Bosphorus, Gallipoli
**10** Persepolis
**11** Grand Mosque, Hagia Sophia, River Jordan, Via Dolorosa, Wailing Wall, Western Wall
**12** Sea of Galilee
**13** Dome of the Rock
**15** Elburz Mountains

**middleman**
**05** fixer **06** broker **08** bummaree, regrater, regrator, retailer **09** go-between **10** negotiator **11** distributer, distributor **12** entrepreneur, intermediary

**Middlesex**
**02** Mx

**middling**
**02** OK **04** fair, so-so **06** fairly, medium, modest **07** average **08** adequate, mediocre, moderate, ordinary, passable **09** tolerable **10** not much cop **11** indifferent, not up to much **12** intermediate, run-of-the-mill, unremarkable **13** no great shakes, unexceptional **14** fair to middling

**midget**
**03** toy **04** baby, tiny **05** dwarf, gnome, pygmy, small, teeny **06** little, minute, pocket **07** manikin **08** mannikin, Tom Thumb **09** itsy-bitsy, miniature **10** diminutive, homunculus, teeny-weeny **11** Lilliputian, pocket-sized, small person

**midpoint**
**11** middle point **12** central point, halfway point

**midshipman**
**03** mid **04** Easy **05** middy **06** reefer, snotty **07** oldster, snottie **11** midshipmate **12** brass-bounder

**midst**
**03** hub **04** core **05** bosom, heart, thick **06** centre, depths, middle **07** nucleus **08** interior, midpoint
• **in the midst** **04** amid **05** among **06** during **12** in the thick of, surrounded by **13** in the middle of

**midway**
**07** central, halfway **11** in the centre, in the middle **13** at the midpoint

**midwife**
**05** howdy **06** granny, howdie, Lucina **07** grannie **09** wise woman **10** accoucheur **11** accoucheuse

**mien**
**03** air **04** aura, look **06** allure, aspect, manner **07** bearing **08** carriage, presence **09** demeanour, semblance **10** appearance, complexion, deportment, expression **11** countenance

**miffed**
**04** hurt **05** irked, upset, vexed

**might**
**06** narked, peeved, piqued, put out
**07** annoyed, in a huff, nettled
**08** offended **09** aggrieved, chagrined, irritated, resentful **10** cheesed off, displeased **11** disgruntled

**might**
**04** sway **05** clout, force, power
**06** energy, muscle, valour, vigour
**07** ability, potency, prowess, stamina
**08** capacity, efficacy, strength
**09** heftiness, puissance **10** capability
**11** muscularity **12** forcefulness, powerfulness

**mightily**
**04** much, very **06** highly, hugely
**07** greatly, lustily **08** manfully, strongly, very much **09** decidedly, extremely, intensely **10** forcefully, powerfully, vigorously **11** exceedingly, strenuously
**13** energetically

**mighty**
**04** fell, huge, vast, very **05** bulky, felon, grand, great, hardy, hefty, large, lusty, stout, tough **06** highly, manful, potent, really, robust, strong **07** awfully, doughty, greatly, immense, massive, titanic, utterly, valiant **08** almighty, colossal, dominant, enormous, forceful, gigantic, mightful, muscular, powerful, puissant, stalwart, terribly, towering, vigorous **09** extremely, important, intensely, strapping, unusually, wonderful **10** dreadfully, monumental, prodigious, remarkably, stupendous, thoroughly, tremendous
**11** exceedingly, excessively, frightfully, indomitable, influential **12** terrifically, unreasonably **13** exceptionally
**15** extraordinarily

**mignonette**
**04** wald, weld **06** Reseda

**migrant**
**05** Gypsy, nomad, rover **06** roving, tinker **07** drifter, nomadic, swagger, swagman, vagrant **08** drifting, emigrant, shifting, wanderer
**09** immigrant, itinerant, migratory, transient, traveller, wandering
**10** travelling **11** peripatetic
**12** Gastarbeiter, globetrotter, transmigrant **13** globetrotting

**migrate**
**04** hike, move, roam, rove, trek **05** drift
**06** travel, voyage, wander **07** journey
**08** emigrate, relocate, resettle

**migration**
**03** ren, rin, run **04** trek **05** shift
**06** roving, travel, voyage **07** journey, passage **08** diaspora, movement
**09** walkabout, wandering
**10** emigration **11** immigration
**12** transhumance **15** Völkerwanderung

**migratory**
**05** Gypsy **06** roving **07** migrant, nomadic, vagrant **08** drifting, shifting
**09** immigrant, itinerant, transient, wandering **10** travelling **11** peripatetic
**13** globetrotting

**mike**
**01** M

**mild**
**04** calm, fair, kind, meek, soft, warm, weak **05** balmy, bland, faint, vague
**06** feeble, gentle, humane, mellow, modest, placid, slight, smooth, subtle, tender **07** amiable, clement, insipid, lenient, pacific **08** gall-less, mansuete, merciful, moderate, pleasant, soothing
**09** easy-going, peaceable, sensitive, tasteless, temperate **10** forbearing
**11** flavourless, good-natured, soft-hearted, sympathetic, warm-hearted
**13** compassionate, imperceptible, tender-hearted

**mildewy**
**05** fetid, fusty, mucid, musty **06** foetid, rotten **10** mucedinous

**mildly**
**06** calmly, gently, meekly, softly, subtly, warmly, weakly **07** faintly, vaguely **08** slightly, tenderly
**10** mercifully **11** sensitively
**13** imperceptibly **15** compassionately

**mildness**
**05** mercy **06** lenity, warmth
**08** calmness, clemency, docility, kindness, leniency, meekness, softness, sympathy **09** blandness, milkiness, passivity, placidity
**10** compassion, gentleness, indulgence, mellowness, moderation, smoothness, tenderness
**11** forbearance, insipidness
**12** tranquillity **13** tastelessness, temperateness

**mile**
**01** m **02** mi, ml, nm **05** n mile

**milieu**
**05** arena, scene **06** locale, medium, sphere **07** element, setting **08** location
**10** background **11** environment
**12** surroundings

**militancy**
**08** activism **09** extremism
**12** belligerence, vigorousness
**13** assertiveness **14** aggressiveness, British disease

**militant**
**07** fighter, soldier, warring, warrior
**08** activist, fighting, partisan, vigorous
**09** aggressor, assertive, combatant, combative, embattled, struggler
**10** aggressive, pugnacious
**11** belligerent, Black Muslim **12** Black Panther, militaristic

**militantly**
**10** vigorously **11** assertively
**12** aggressively **13** belligerently

**military**
**03** mil **04** army, navy **05** armed, milit
**06** forces **07** martial, militia, service, soldier, warlike **08** air force, services, soldiers, soldiery **09** soldierly **11** armed forces, disciplined

*Military decorations include:*
**02** GC, GM, MC, MM, VC
**03** AFC, AFM, BEM, CGM, CMH, DCM, DFC, DFM, DSC, DSM, DSO
**09** Iron Cross
**10** Bronze Star, Silver Star
**11** George Cross, George Medal, Purple Heart
**12** Pour le Mérite
**13** Air Force Cross, Air Force Medal, Croix de Guerre, Legion of Merit, Military Cross, Military Medal, Victoria Cross
**14** Oak-leaf Cluster

*Military units and groups include:*
**04** file, post, wing
**05** corps, flank, fleet, group, squad, troop
**06** cohort, convoy, flight, legion, patrol, picket
**07** battery, brigade, company, echelon, militia, phalanx, platoon, section
**08** division, flotilla, garrison, regiment, squadron
**09** battalion, commandos, effective, task force
**10** detachment, flying camp, rifle corps
**11** battle group, flying party
**12** flying column, Royal Marines
**13** guard of honour

• **military equipment 05** train
• **military life 04** camp
• **military men** *see* **soldiers** *under* **soldier**
• **military police 02** MP

**militate**
• **militate against 04** hurt **06** damage, oppose, resist **07** contend, counter
**09** go against, prejudice **10** act against, counteract, discourage **11** be harmful to, tell against, work against **12** count against, weigh against **15** be detrimental to
• **militate for 03** aid **04** back, help
**07** advance, further, promote **08** speak for

**militia**
**02** SA, TA **04** fyrd **06** Milice **07** reserve
**08** yeomanry **09** fencibles, home guard, minutemen, trainband
**10** reservists **13** National Guard
**15** Territorial Army

**milk**
**03** tap, use **04** draw, pump, skim, whig
**05** bleed, drain, press, screw, wring
**06** rip off, siphon, stroke **07** draw off, exploit, express, extract, oppress, squeeze **08** impose on, moo-juice
**10** manipulate **11** semi-skimmed
**15** take advantage of
• **milk producer 03** cow **04** teat
• **not yielding milk 04** eild, yeld, yell

**milk-can**
**04** kirn **05** churn

**milking**
• **place for milking 04** loan
**07** loaning

**milkman's cart**
**04** pram **05** float **09** milkfloat

**milksop**
**04** sook, wimp, wuss **05** cissy, molly
**06** coward, jessie **07** meacock

**milk-strainer**
08 weakling 09 mummy's boy
10 namby-pamby

**milk-strainer**
03 sye

**milky**
04 soft, weak 05 white 06 chalky, cloudy, gentle, opaque 07 clouded 08 lacteous 09 milk-white, snow-white, spineless

**mill**
◊ anagram indicator 03 box 04 nurl, roll, shop 05 crush, grate, grind, knurl, plant, pound, press, quern, works 06 crunch, powder, roller 07 crusher, factory, foundry, grinder 08 snuffbox, spinnery, workshop 09 comminute, pulverize 11 boxing match, molendinary 15 processing plant
• **mill around**   05 swarm 06 stream, throng 09 move about 11 crowd around, press around

**millet**
04 dari, dura, ragi 05 bajra, bajri, doura, durra, proso, ragee, raggy, whisk 06 bajree, dhurra, raggee 09 broom-corn 10 guinea corn

**million**
01 m

**millstone**
04 duty, load, onus 06 burden, ligger, runner, weight 07 trouble 09 buhrstone, burrstone 10 affliction, dead-weight, grindstone, obligation, quernstone 11 cross to bear, encumbrance
• **millstone support**   04 rind

**millstream**
04 lade

**Milne**
02 AA

**mime**
05 mimic 06 act out, signal 07 buffoon, charade, gesture, imitate, mimicry, mummery 08 dumb show, indicate, simulate 09 chironomy, pantomime, represent 11 impersonate

**mimic**
02 do 03 ape 04 copy, echo, mime, mina, mock, myna, play 05 mynah 06 mirror, monkey, parody, parrot, send up 07 copycat, copyist, emulate, imitate, mimetic, minnick, minnock, take off 08 imitator, look like, mimicker, resemble, simulate, starling 09 mimetical, personate 10 caricature 11 impersonate 12 caricaturist, impersonator 13 impressionist

**mimicry**
05 aping 06 parody 07 copying, mimesis, mockery, take-off 09 burlesque, imitating, imitation 10 caricature, impression, simulation 13 impersonation

**minatory**
04 grim 07 looming, ominous, warning 08 menacing, sinister 09 impending, minacious 10 cautionary, foreboding 11 threatening 12 inauspicious, intimidatory

**mince**
◊ anagram indicator 03 cut 04 chop, dice, hash, pose 05 grind, ponce 06 prance, simper 07 crumble, posture 11 strike a pose 12 attitudinize 14 walk affectedly
• **not mince your words**   11 talk plainly 13 speak directly

**mincing**
04 camp, nice 05 cissy, poncy 06 chi-chi, dainty, la-di-da 07 foppish, minikin 08 affected, chee-chee, precious 09 coxcombic 10 effeminate 11 coxcombical, pretentious 12 niminy-piminy

**mind**
03 wit 04 care, head, heed, mark, note, obey, soul, tend, urge, view, will, wish, wits 05 brain, fancy, guard, sense, watch 06 attend, belief, brains, desire, expert, follow, genius, memory, notion, object, psyche, reason, recall, record, resent, sanity, spirit 07 dislike, egghead, feeling, mention, observe, opinion, outlook, purpose, respect, scholar, thinker, thought 08 academic, attend to, attitude, brainbox, listen to, remember, take care, tendency, thinking, thoughts, watch out 09 attention, intellect, intention, judgement, look after, mentality, retention, sentiment, viewpoint 10 grey matter, mastermind 11 application, disposition, inclination, keep an eye on, personality, point of view, remembrance 12 intellectual, intelligence, pay attention, recollection, subconscious 13 commemoration, comprehension, concentration, consciousness, ratiocination, understanding, way of thinking 15 little grey cells
• **bear in mind, keep in mind**   04 note 06 retain 08 consider, remember 10 take note of 13 give thought to 15 take into account
• **be in two minds**   05 waver 06 dither 08 be unsure, hesitate 09 vacillate 10 be hesitant, dilly-dally 11 be uncertain, be undecided 12 shilly-shally 13 sit on the fence
• **cross your mind**   03 hit 06 come to, strike 07 occur to, think of 08 remember
• **have in mind**   03 aim 04 plan, talk, want 06 design, intend 07 think of 11 contemplate
• **make up your mind**   06 choose, decide, settle 07 resolve 09 determine 13 make a decision 14 reach a decision 15 come to a decision
• **mind out**   05 watch 06 beware 07 look out 08 take care, watch out 09 be careful 12 pay attention 13 be on your guard
• **mind's eye**   04 head 06 memory 11 imagination, remembrance 12 recollection 13 contemplation
• **never mind**   03 too 04 also 06 skip it! 08 as well as, forget it, let alone 09 apart from, don't worry 10 nix my dolly 12 not to mention 13 not forgetting 14 not bother about, take no notice of
• **out of your mind**   03 mad 04 nuts 05 barmy, batty, crazy, daffy, dippy,

loony, loopy, manic, nutty, potty 06 crazed, cuckoo, insane, maniac, mental, raving, screwy 07 bananas, bonkers, flipped, lunatic 08 crackers, demented, deranged, doolally, frenzied, maniacal, unhinged, unstable 09 psychotic, up the wall 10 barking mad, distracted, distraught, off the wall, unbalanced 11 not all there, off the rails, off your head 12 mad as a hatter, off your chump, round the bend 13 off your rocker, of unsound mind, round the twist 14 off your trolley, wrong in the head 15 non compos mentis, out of your senses
• **put you in mind of**   06 prompt, remind 10 call to mind 11 bring to mind 14 make you think of
• **put your mind to**   09 persevere, take pains 10 buckle down 13 concentrate on, exert yourself
• **sharpness of mind**   04 edge
• **speak your mind**   11 talk plainly 14 tell it like it is
• **to my mind**   04 heed, mark, note, obey 05 guard, watch 06 ensure, follow, I think, object, regard, resent 07 dislike, observe, respect 08 as I see it, attend to, I believe, in my view, listen to, make sure, object to, remember, take care, watch out 09 be careful, care about, look after, not forget, pay heed to, watch over 10 comply with, disapprove, personally, take care of 11 be annoyed by, in my opinion, keep an eye on, make certain, take offence 12 be bothered by, be offended by, be troubled by, have charge of, pay attention 13 concentrate on, take offence at

**mind-boggling**
07 amazing 10 astounding, formidable, impossible, incredible, surprising 11 astonishing, exceptional, unthinkable 12 unbelievable, unimaginable 13 extraordinary, inconceivable

**mindful**
04 wary 05 alert, alive, aware, chary 07 alive to, careful, heedful 08 inclined, sensible, watchful 09 attentive, cognizant, conscious, observant

**mindless**
04 dull, dumb 05 dopey, thick 06 stupid 07 foolish, robotic, routine, tedious, witless 08 knee-jerk 09 automatic, illogical, negligent, senseless 10 gratuitous, irrational, mechanical 11 birdbrained, instinctive, involuntary, thoughtless 13 unintelligent

**mindlessly**
08 stupidly 09 foolishly, routinely 11 illogically, senselessly 12 irrationally, mechanically 13 automatically, instinctively, involuntarily, thoughtlessly

**mine**
02 my 03 dig, egg, pit, win 04 bomb, fund, lode, seam, vein, well 05 delve,

dig up, hoard, shaft, stock, store, wheal **06** burrow, dig for, duffer, quarry, remove, search, source, supply, trench, tunnel, wealth **07** bonanza, coalpit, deposit, extract, reserve, unearth **08** claymore, colliery, excavate, landmine, treasury **09** coalfield, explosive, reservoir, undermine **10** excavation, repository, storehouse **11** depth charge
• **mine opening** **03** eye **04** adit
• **mine tunnel** **04** head
• **mining licence** **04** gale
• **surface over a mine** **03** day

## mine-passage
**04** road

## miner
**06** digger, hatter, pitman, tinner **07** collier, faceman **08** tributer **09** coalminer **10** faceworker, gold-digger, honeyeater, mineworker

## mineral
*Minerals include:*

**03** jet
**04** alum, mica, opal, ruby, salt, spar, talc
**05** beryl, borax, emery, flint, fluor, topaz, umber
**06** albite, blende, cerite, galena, gangue, garnet, glance, gypsum, halite, haüyne, humite, illite, jasper, kermes, lithia, maltha, natron, nosean, pyrite, quartz, rutile, silica, sphene, spinel, talcum, zircon
**07** anatase, apatite, axinite, azurite, barytes, biotite, bornite, brucite, calcite, cassite, crystal, cuprite, desmine, diamond, dysodil, epidote, jacinth, jadeite, jargoon, kandite, leucite, nacrite, olivine, pennine, peridot, pyrites, realgar, syenite, thorite, uralite, uranite, zeolite, zincite, zoisite
**08** allanite, ankerite, asbestos, autunite, blue john, boracite, brookite, calamine, calcspar, chlorite, chromite, cinnabar, corundum, crocoite, cryolite, diallage, diaspore, dolomite, dysodyle, epsomite, erionite, euxenite, feldspar, fluorite, goethite, graphite, gyrolite, hematite, hyacinth, idocrase, ilmenite, iodyrite, lazulite, lewisite, melilite, mimetite, nephrite, orpiment, plumbago, prehnite, pyroxene, rock salt, sanidine, sapphire, sardonyx, siderite, smaltite, sodalite, stannite, stibnite, stilbite, titanite, wurtzite
**09** alabaster, amphibole, anhydrite, aragonite, atacamite, bentonite, blacklead, cairngorm, celestite, cobaltite, elaterite, evaporite, fibrolite, fluorspar, fool's gold, goslarite, grossular, haematite, kaolinite, lodestone, magnesite, magnetite, malachite, marcasite, margarite, microlite, muscovite, nepholine, niccolite, olivenite,

pearl spar, quartzite, saltpetre, scheelite, soapstone, sylvanite, tantalite, turquoise, uraninite, vulpinite, wavellite
**10** antimonite, aquamarine, aventurine, bloodstone, chalcedony, chrysolite, glauconite, greenstone, hornblende, meerschaum, microcline, orthoclase, polyhalite, pyrolusite, samerskite, serpentine, sphalerite, tourmaline
**11** alexandrite, amphibolite, chrysoberyl, French chalk, lapis lazuli, pitchblende, sal ammoniac, smithsonite, vesuvianite
**12** chalcanthite, chalcopyrite, hemimorphite
**13** arsenopyrites
**14** hydroxyapatite, sodium chloride, yttro-columbite
**15** gooseberry-stone

## mineral water
*see* **water**

## Minerva
**06** Athene

## mingle
**03** mix **04** fuse, join, mell **05** alloy, blend, go out, merge, unite **06** hobnob, medley **07** combine, mixture **08** coalesce, compound, intermix **09** associate, circulate, commingle, interfuse, socialize **10** amalgamate **11** intermingle, run together **12** rub shoulders

## mingy
**04** mean, poor, puny **05** close **06** meagre, measly, paltry, scanty, skimpy, stingy **07** miserly, pitiful, sparing, trivial **08** grudging, pathetic, piddling, ungiving **09** miserable, niggardly **10** hard-fisted, ungenerous **11** close-fisted, close-handed, tight-fisted **12** cheese-paring, parsimonious

## miniature
**03** toy, wee **04** baby, mini, tiny **05** cameo, dwarf, small, teeny, young **06** little, midget, minute **07** diorama, reduced **08** pint-size **09** microcosm, pint-sized **10** diminutive, scaled-down, small-scale **11** microcosmic, pocket-sized, rubrication

## minimal
**05** least, token **06** minute **07** minimum, nominal **08** littlest, smallest **09** slightest **10** negligible

## minimize
**03** cut **05** decry, slash **06** lessen, reduce, shrink **07** curtail **08** belittle, decrease, diminish, discount, laugh off, play down **09** deprecate, disparage, soft-pedal, underrate **10** trivialize **11** make light of **12** make little of **13** underestimate

## minimum
◊ *head selection indicator* **03** min **05** least, nadir **06** bottom, lowest **07** minimal, tiniest **08** littlest, smallest **09** slightest **11** lowest point **12** lowest number

## minion
**05** leech **06** drudge, fawner, lackey, menial, stooge, yes-man **07** darling, flunkey, servant **08** follower, hanger-on, henchman, hireling, parasite **09** attendant, dependant, favourite, flatterer, sycophant, underling **10** bootlicker, henchwoman **11** henchperson

## minister
**02** PM **03** Min, Rev **04** aide, dean, tend **05** agent, dewan, diwan, elder, envoy, nurse, padre, serve, vezir, vicar, vizir **06** attend, cleric, consul, curate, deacon, divine, leader, legate, parson, pastor, priest, rector, supply, verger, visier, vizier, wait on, wizier **07** cater to, furnish, Mas-John, Mes-John, servant **08** chaplain, delegate, diplomat, emissary, Mass-John, Mess-John, official, preacher **09** churchman, clergyman, dignitary, executive, look after, presbyter **10** administer, ambassador, chancellor, politician, take care of **11** accommodate, clergywoman, Grand Vizier **12** ecclesiastic, office-holder, parish priest **13** administrator **14** representative **15** cabinet minister
*See also* **prime minister**

## ministration
**03** aid **04** care, help **06** favour, relief **07** backing, service, succour, support **09** patronage **10** assistance **11** disposition, supervision

## ministry
**03** Min, MOD, MOH **04** MAFF, METI **06** bureau, clergy, office **07** cabinet, service **08** the cloth **09** the church, the clergy **10** department, government, holy orders **13** the priesthood **14** administration

## Minnesota
**02** MN **04** Minn

## minnow
**04** pank, pink

## minor
**03** boy, kid, son, tot **04** baby, girl, less **05** child, light, lower, petty, small **06** infant, junior, lesser, nipper, slight **07** nominal, smaller, tiny tot, toddler, trivial, unknown, younger **08** daughter, inferior, juvenile, marginal, trifling, young one **09** little one, secondary, youngster **10** negligible, peripheral, subsidiary **11** little known, second-class, subordinate, unimportant, young person **12** unclassified **13** insignificant **14** inconsiderable
• **minor item** **02** by **03** bye

## minstrel
**04** bard, scop **05** rimer **06** rhymer, singer **07** gleeman **08** jongleur, musician **09** hamfatter, joculator **10** troubadour

## mint
◊ *anagram indicator* **03** aim, nep, new, nip **04** bomb, cast, coin, fake, heap, hint, make, pile **05** as new, forge, fresh, hatch, punch, stack, stamp **06** bundle, catnep, catnip, devise, invent, make

## minus

up, packet, riches, strike, unused, wealth **07** attempt, billion, concoct, falsify, fashion, fortune, million, mint-new, monarda, perfect, produce, purpose, trump up, venture **08** bergamot, billions, brand-new, millions **09** bugle-weed, construct, excellent, fabricate, megabucks, undamaged **10** first-class, immaculate, pennyroyal **11** king's ransom, loadsamoney, manufacture, unblemished

## minus

**03** bar **04** less, save **06** except **07** short of, without **08** negative **09** excepting, excluding **10** deficiency **11** subtraction

## minuscule

**04** fine, tiny **05** teeny **06** little, minute **09** itsy-bitsy, miniature, very small **10** diminutive, teeny-weeny **11** Lilliputian, microscopic **13** infinitesimal

## minute

**01** m **02** mo **03** min, sec **04** note, tick, tiny **05** close, exact, flash, jiffy, minim **06** moment, second, slight, strict **07** instant, precise, trivial **08** accurate, as soon as, critical, detailed, directly, no sooner, the point, trifling **09** miniature, minuscule, short time, the moment, very small **10** diminutive, exhaustive, meticulous, negligible, the instant **11** immediately, Lilliputian, microscopic, painstaking, punctilious **13** infinitesimal, insignificant, microscopical **14** circumstantial, inconsiderable
• **in a minute** **04** anon, soon **06** pronto **07** in a tick, shortly **08** in a flash, in a jiffy, very soon **09** in a moment **10** before long **15** in the near future
• **this minute** **03** now **04** next, then **06** at once, pronto **07** quickly **08** as soon as, directly, promptly, right now, speedily **09** forthwith, instantly, like a shot, right away, yesterday **11** immediately, this instant **12** no sooner than, straight away, there and then, without delay **14** unhesitatingly, without more ado **15** before you know it, instantaneously, without question
• **up to the minute** **02** in **03** now **06** latest, newest, with it **09** happening **10** all the rage, most modern, most recent **11** fashionable

## minutely

**07** closely, exactly **08** in detail **09** precisely **10** critically **12** exhaustively, meticulously, scrupulously **13** painstakingly **14** systematically

## minutes

**04** acta **05** notes, tapes **06** record **07** details, records **10** memorandum, transcript **11** proceedings **12** transactions

## minutiae

**07** details, trifles **08** niceties **10** small print, subtleties **11** fine details, finer points, intricacies, particulars **12** complexities, trivialities

## miracle

**04** sign **06** marvel, wonder **07** prodigy **10** phenomenon, wonderwork

## miraculous

**05** magic **07** amazing **09** monstrous, unnatural, wonderful **10** astounding, incredible, marvellous, monstruous, phenomenal, remarkable, superhuman, surprising, unexpected **11** astonishing **12** inexplicable, supernatural, unbelievable **13** extraordinary, unaccountable

## miraculously

**09** amazingly **10** incredibly, remarkably **11** wonderfully **12** inexplicably, superhumanly, surprisingly, unbelievably, unexpectedly **13** unaccountably **14** supernaturally **15** extraordinarily

## mirage

**04** loom **07** fantasy **08** illusion, phantasm **11** fata Morgana **13** hallucination **14** phantasmagoria **15** optical illusion

## mire

**03** bog, fen, fix, jam, mud **04** dirt, hole, lair, mess, muck, ooze, quag, sink, spot, stew **05** glaur, latch, letch, marsh, slime, swamp **06** deluge, morass, pickle, slough, sludge **07** bog down, trouble **08** loblolly, quagmire **09** marshland, overwhelm **12** difficulties

## mirror

**03** ape **04** copy, echo, show, twin **05** clone, glass, image, mimic, stone **06** depict, double, follow, parrot **07** emulate, imitate, reflect **08** busybody, likeness, speculum **09** coelostat, condenser, hand-glass, pier-glass, reflector, represent **10** dead ringer, reflection, siderostat, wing mirror **11** cheval-glass, pocket-glass, tiring-glass, toilet glass **12** keeking-glass, laryngoscope, looking-glass **13** driving-mirror, exact likeness, spitting image **14** rear-view mirror

## mirth

**03** fun **04** glee **05** dream, sport **06** gaiety, spleen **07** delight, frolics, jollity, revelry **08** buoyancy, hilarity, laughter, pleasure **09** amusement, enjoyment, merriment, merriness **10** blitheness, jocularity **11** high spirits **12** cheerfulness

## mirthful

**03** gay **04** glad **05** funny, happy, jolly, ludic, merry **06** amused, blithe, cheery, jocund, jovial **07** amusing, buoyant, festive, playful **08** cheerful, gladsome, laughful, laughing, sportive **09** hilarious, laughable, vivacious **10** frolicsome, uproarious **11** pleasurable **12** light-hearted **13** light-spirited

## mirthless

**03** sad **04** glum, sour **05** gruff, moody, sulky, surly **06** gloomy, grumpy, morose, sullen **07** doleful, unhappy **08** churlish, dejected, unamused **09** depressed, miserable

**10** despondent, humourless **11** crestfallen, ill-humoured, pessimistic

## miry

**04** oozy **05** boggy, dirty, fenny, mucky, muddy, slimy **06** glaury, marshy, sludgy, swampy

## misadventure

**06** mishap **07** bad luck, debacle, failure, ill luck, problem, reverse, setback, tragedy **08** accident, calamity, disaster, hard luck **09** cataclysm, misaunter, mischance **10** ill fortune, misfortune **11** catastrophe

## misanthrope

**05** cynic, loner, miser, Timon **06** hermit, meanie **07** recluse **08** solitary **14** unsocial person

## misanthropic

**05** surly **08** egoistic, inhumane **10** antisocial, malevolent, unfriendly, unsociable **13** unsympathetic

## misanthropy

**06** egoism **08** cynicism **10** inhumanity **11** malevolence **13** antisociality **14** unsociableness

## misapply

**05** abuse **06** misuse **07** exploit, pervert **09** misemploy **11** use unwisely **13** use unsuitably **14** misappropriate

## misapprehend

**07** misread, mistake **11** misconceive, misconstrue **12** misinterpret **13** miscomprehend, misunderstand **15** get the wrong idea

## misapprehension

**05** error, mix-up **07** fallacy, mistake **08** delusion **09** wrong idea **10** misreading **13** misconception **15** false impression

## misappropriate

**03** nab, rob **04** nick **05** abuse, filch, pinch, steal **06** misuse, pilfer, pocket, thieve **07** pervert, swindle **08** embezzle, misapply, misspend, peculate **09** defalcate, knock down

## misappropriation

**05** theft **06** misuse **07** robbing **08** stealing **09** pilfering, pocketing **10** peculation **11** defalcation **12** embezzlement **14** misapplication

## misbegotten

**05** shady **06** stolen **07** bastard, illicit, natural **08** abortive, unlawful **09** dishonest, ill-gotten, ill-judged, imprudent, monstrous, purloined, unadvised **10** ill-advised, monstruous **11** hare-brained **12** contemptible, disreputable, ill-conceived, illegitimate

## misbehave

◇ anagram indicator **05** act up, lapse **06** be rude, offend, play up **07** carry on, disobey **08** trespass **09** be naughty, fool about, mess about, misdemean, muck about **10** fool around, transgress **11** behave badly **15** be beyond the pale, get up to mischief

## misbehaviour

◇ *anagram indicator* **08** mischief, misguide **10** bad manners, carrying-on, misconduct **11** impropriety, naughtiness **12** bad behaviour, disobedience, misdemeanour, mucking about **15** insubordination

## misbelief

**05** error **06** heresy **07** fallacy, mistake **08** delusion, illusion **10** heterodoxy **11** unorthodoxy, wrong belief **13** misconception **15** misapprehension

## miscalculate

**03** err **04** boob **06** slip up **07** blunder, go wrong, miscast **08** get wrong, miscount, misjudge **09** misreckon **12** make a mistake, overestimate **13** underestimate

## miscalculation

**04** boob, slip **05** error, fault, gaffe, lapse **06** booboo, howler, slip-up **07** bloomer, blunder, clanger, mistake **08** miscount **09** oversight **10** aberration, inaccuracy **12** misjudgement, overestimate **13** underestimate **14** miscomputation **15** misapprehension

## miscarriage

**05** error **06** mishap **07** failure, misdeed **08** aborting, abortion **09** breakdown, ruination **10** misconduct, perversion **13** mismanagement **14** disappointment

## miscarry

**04** fail, flop, fold, warp **05** abort, slink **07** founder, go amiss, go wrong, misfire, miswend **10** not come off **11** bite the dust, come to grief, fall through, lose the baby **12** come a cropper **13** come to nothing

## miscellaneous

**04** chow **05** mixed **06** motley, sundry, varied **07** diverse, jumbled, mingled, various **08** assorted, eclectic **10** variegated **11** diversified, farraginous **12** multifarious **13** heterogeneous
• **miscellaneous lot 04** raft

## miscellany

**03** mix **04** olio, olla **06** jumble, medley **07** farrago, mixture, variety **08** mishmash, mixed bag, pastiche **09** anthology, bricolage, diversity, patchwork, potpourri **10** assortment, collection, hotchpotch, salmagundi, salmagundy **11** collectanea, gallimaufry, miscellanea, smorgasbord **14** conglomeration, omnium-gatherum

## mischance

**04** blow **06** mishap **07** ill luck, tragedy **08** accident, bad break, calamity, disaster **09** ill-chance **10** ill fortune, infelicity, misfortune **11** contretemps **12** misadventure

## mischief

**03** Ate, elf, hob, imp, wag **04** bale, bane, dido, evil, harm, hurt, lark, limb, pest, puck, tyke **05** cutty, devil, gamin, rogue, scamp **06** damage, gamine, injury, monkey, nickum, pranks, rascal, terror, tricks, urchin **07** carry-on, hellion, malicho, pliskie, stirrer, trouble, varmint, villain **08** diablery, escapade, makebate, nuisance, spalpeen **09** devilment, diablerie, scallywag, vengeance **10** cockatrice, disruption, disservice, hanky-panky, impishness, shenanigan, wrongdoing **11** limb of Satan, monkey shine, naughtiness, roguishness, shenanigans **12** bad behaviour, esprit follet, misbehaviour, monkey tricks **13** barnsbreaking, funny business, jiggery-pokery **14** monkey business **15** flibbertigibbet

## mischievous

◇ *anagram indicator* **03** bad **04** arch, evil **05** elfin, elvan, elven, rogue **06** elfish, elvish, impish, shrewd, wicked **07** gallows, harmful, hurtful, naughty, playful, roguish, teasing, tricksy, unhappy, vicious, waggish **08** litherly, rascally, spiteful **09** ill-deedly, injurious, malicious, malignant, pestilent **10** frolicsome, pernicious, up to no good **11** destructive, detrimental, disobedient, misbehaving, troublesome **12** badly behaved

## mischievously

◇ *anagram indicator* **08** impishly, wickedly **09** harmfully, naughtily, playfully, roguishly, teasingly, viciously, waggishly **10** spitefully **11** injuriously, maliciously **13** destructively, disobediently

## misconceive

**07** misread, mistake, suspect **08** misjudge **11** misconstrue **12** misapprehend, misinterpret **13** misunderstand

## misconception

**05** error **07** fallacy, mistake **08** delusion **09** wrong idea **10** misconceit, misreading **15** false impression, misapprehension

## misconduct

◇ *anagram indicator* **08** adultery, misusage **10** wrongdoing **11** impropriety, malpractice, miscarriage **12** bad behaviour, misbehaviour, misdemeanour **13** mismanagement

## misconstrue

◇ *anagram indicator* **07** misread, mistake, pervert **08** misjudge **09** misreckon **10** misconster **11** misconceive **12** misapprehend, misinterpret, mistranslate **13** misunderstand **15** take the wrong way

## miscreant

**05** knave, rogue, scamp **06** rascal, sinner, wicked, wretch **07** dastard, heretic, infidel, villain **08** criminal, evildoer, vagabond **09** reprobate, scallywag, scoundrel, wrongdoer **10** malefactor, profligate, villainous **11** misbeliever, scoundrelly, unbelieving **12** troublemaker **13** mischief-maker

## misdeed

**03** sin **05** amiss, crime, error, fault, wrong **06** felony **07** offence **08** trespass,

villainy **10** misconduct, peccadillo, wrongdoing **11** delinquency, miscarriage, misdemeanor, mistreading **12** misdemeanour **13** transgression

## misdemeanour

**05** error, fault, lapse, wrong **07** misdeed, offence **08** trespass **10** misconduct, peccadillo, wrongdoing **11** malfeasance **12** indiscretion, infringement, misbehaviour **13** transgression

## misdirect

◇ *anagram indicator* **05** avert **06** divert, misuse **07** mislead **08** misapply, misguide **09** misinform **10** misaddress **13** give a bum steer **14** misappropriate

## miser

**04** carl **05** hunks **06** meanie, wretch **07** niggard, save-all, Scrooge **08** muckworm, tightwad **09** skinflint **10** cheapskate, curmudgeon, scrapegood **11** cheeseparer, scrapepenny **12** money-grubber, penny-pincher

*Misers include:*

**05** **Burns** (Montgomery)
**06** **Mammon**, **Marner** (Silas)
**07** **Scrooge** (Ebenezer)
**08** **Nickleby** (Ralph), **Trabois**
**10** **Fardorough**, **Van Swieten** (Ghysbrecht)
**11** **Earlforward** (Henry)

## miserable

◇ *anagram indicator* **03** low, miz, sad **04** base, blue, down, glum, mean, mizz, poor, punk, vile **05** lousy, sorry, surly **06** dismal, dreary, gloomy, grumpy, meagre, measly, mouldy, paltry, rotten, scanty, shabby, sullen **07** crushed, forlorn, grouchy, joyless, pitiful, squalid, unhappy **08** dejected, desolate, downcast, pathetic, pitiable, shameful, wretched **09** cheerless, crotchety, depressed, irritable, niggardly, sorrowful, worthless **10** deplorable, depressing, despicable, despondent, detestable, distressed, unpleasant **11** bad-tempered, disgraceful, downhearted, god-forsaken, heartbroken, ignominious, ill-tempered, low-spirited, melancholic **12** contemptible, disagreeable, disconsolate, god-forgotten, impoverished **14** down in the dumps

## miserably

◇ *anagram indicator* **05** sadly **06** glumly, poorly **07** greatly **08** gloomily, markedly, paltrily, scantily, stingily, very much **09** niggardly, pitifully, unhappily **10** desolately **11** dangerously, desperately, sorrowfully **12** despondently, pathetically **14** disconsolately

## miserliness

**07** avarice **08** meanness **09** frugality, minginess, parsimony, tightness **10** stinginess **12** cheeseparing, covetousness **13** niggardliness, penny-pinching, penuriousness **15** close-fistedness, tight-fistedness

## miserly
**04** gare, mean **05** close, mingy, tight
**06** stingy **07** chintzy, sparing
**08** beggarly **09** niggardly, penurious
**11** close-fisted, close-handed, tight-fisted **12** candle-paring, cheeseparing, parsimonious **13** money-grubbing, penny-pinching

## misery
**02** wo **03** miz, woe **04** bale, hell, mizz, want **05** agony, gloom, grief **06** grouch, misère, moaner, penury, sorrow, whiner **07** anguish, avarice, despair, killjoy, poverty, sadness, whinger **08** buzzkill, distress, hardship, Jeremiah, sourpuss **09** adversity, indigence, perdition, pessimist, privation, suffering, the depths **10** affliction, complainer, depression, desolation, discomfort, melancholy, misfortune, oppression, spoilsport, wet blanket **11** deprivation, destitution, living death, melancholia, unhappiness **12** wretchedness **13** prophet of doom **14** dog in the manger

## misfire
**04** fail, flop **05** abort **06** go awry **07** founder, go amiss, go wrong **08** miscarry **09** fizzle out **10** not come off **11** bite the dust, come to grief, fall through **12** come a cropper

## misfit
◊ *anagram indicator* **04** geek **05** freak, loner **06** weirdo **07** dropout, oddball, sad sack **08** lone wolf, maverick **09** eccentric, odd one out **13** individualist, nonconformist **14** fish out of water

## misfortune
**02** wo **03** ill, woe **04** blow, evil, ruth, woes **05** trial **06** mishap, sorrow, wroath **07** bad luck, failure, ill luck, misfare, misluck, reverse, setback, tragedy, trouble **08** accident, calamity, casualty, disaster, distress, hard luck, hardship, judgment **09** adversity, judgement, mischance, mishanter **10** affliction, infelicity, mischanter **11** catastrophe, tribulation **12** misadventure

• **expression of misfortune 02** ah, ay, oh **03** out **04** alas, ay me, haro, waly **06** harrow **07** welaway **08** waesucks, welladay, wellaway **09** alack-a-day, wellanear **10** alas the day **12** alas the while

## misgiving
**04** fear **05** doubt, qualm, worry **06** niggle, unease **07** anxiety, scruple **08** distrust, misdoubt, mistrust **09** suspicion **10** hesitation **11** reservation, uncertainty **12** apprehension **14** second thoughts

## misguided
◊ *anagram indicator* **04** rash **05** wrong **06** erring, misled **07** deluded, foolish, off-beam **08** mistaken **09** erroneous, ill-judged, imprudent, misplaced **10** fallacious, ill-advised

**11** injudicious, misdirected, misinformed **12** misconceived **13** ill-considered

## mishandle
◊ *anagram indicator* **04** muff **05** botch, fluff **06** bungle, fumble, mess up **07** balls up, screw up **08** maltreat, misjudge **09** mismanage **11** make a hash of, make a mess of **12** make a balls of **14** make a balls-up of, make a pig's ear of

## mishap
◊ *anagram indicator* **04** blow **05** drere, shunt, trial **06** dreare, mucker **07** reverse, setback, trouble **08** accident, calamity, disaster, incident **09** adversity, misaunter, mischance **10** ill fortune, misfortune **11** catastrophe, disaventure, tribulation **12** disadventure, misadventure **15** stroke of bad luck

## mishit
**04** duff, thin **05** flier, flyer **06** sclaff

## mishmash
**04** hash, mess, olio, olla **05** salad **06** jumble, medley, muddle **07** farrago **08** pastiche **09** potpourri **10** hodgepodge, hotchpotch, salmagundi **11** gallimaufry **14** conglomeration

## misinform
**05** bluff **07** deceive, mislead **08** hoodwink, misguide **09** misdirect **12** take for a ride **13** give a bum steer

## misinformation
**04** dope, guff, hype, lies **05** bluff **07** baloney, eyewash **08** bum steer, nonsense **09** deception **10** misleading **12** misdirection **14** disinformation

## misinterpret
◊ *anagram indicator* **04** warp **05** wrest **06** garble **07** distort, misread, mistake **08** misjudge **11** misconceive, misconstrue **12** misapprehend **13** misunderstand **15** take the wrong way

## misinterpretation
**10** misreading **12** misjudgement **13** misconception **14** misacceptation **15** false impression, misapprehension, misconstruction

## misjudge
**07** mistake **08** miscount **11** misconstrue **12** miscalculate, misinterpret, overestimate **13** misunderstand, underestimate

## misjudgement
**07** mistake **09** wrong idea **10** misdeeming **12** wrong opinion **14** miscalculation **15** wrong conclusion

## mislay
**04** lose, miss **07** misfile **08** misplace **11** lose sight of, lose track of **14** be unable to find

## mislead
◊ *anagram indicator* **04** fool, snow **05** put on **06** delude **07** deceive **08** fool into, hoodwink, impose on, misguide **09** blindfold, misdirect, misinform

**10** impose upon, lead astray **12** misrepresent, take for a ride **13** give a bum steer, lead into error **14** pull a fast one on, put off the scent

## misleading
◊ *anagram indicator* **06** biased, loaded, tricky **07** evasive **08** delusive, illusive, illusory, sinister **09** ambiguous, confusing, deceiving, deceptive, equivocal **10** fallacious, unreliable

## mismanage
◊ *anagram indicator* **03** mar **04** muff **05** botch, waste **06** bungle, foul up, mess up **07** balls up, blunder, misrule, screw up **08** misjudge, misspend **09** mishandle **11** make a hash of, make a mess of **12** make a balls of **14** make a balls-up of, make a pig's ear of

## mismanagement
◊ *anagram indicator* **04** hash, mess **05** farce **06** bungle, cock-up, muddle **07** balls-up, failure, pig's ear **08** bungling, shambles **11** mishandling **12** misjudgement **13** pig's breakfast **14** misgovernaunce

## mismatched
**08** clashing, mismated, unsuited **09** disparate, irregular, misallied **10** discordant, unmatching **11** ill-assorted, incongruous **12** antipathetic, incompatible **14** unreconcilable

## misogynist
**03** MCP **06** sexist **10** woman-hater **12** anti-feminist **14** male chauvinist **15** male supremacist

## misogyny
**06** sexism **12** anti-feminism **13** male supremacy **14** male chauvinism

## misplace
◊ *anagram indicator* **04** lose, miss **06** mislay **07** misfile **08** misapply **09** misassign **11** lose sight of, lose track of **14** be unable to find

## misprint
◊ *anagram indicator* **04** typo **05** error **07** erratum, literal, mistake **11** corrigendum **12** literal error **13** printing error

## misquote
**05** twist **06** garble, muddle **07** distort, falsify, pervert **08** misstate **09** misreport **11** misremember **12** misrepresent

## misread
◊ *anagram indicator* **06** garble **07** distort, mistake **08** misjudge **11** misconceive, misconstrue **12** misapprehend, misinterpret **13** misunderstand **15** take the wrong way

## misrepresent
◊ *anagram indicator* **05** abuse, belie, color, slant, twist **06** colour, garble **07** distort, falsify, pervert **08** disguise, minimize, miscolor, misquote, misstate **09** miscolour, misreport **10** exaggerate, manipulate **11** misconstrue **12** misinterpret

## misrepresentation
◊ *anagram indicator* **08** twisting **10** distortion, perversion

**misrule** (continued)

**12** exaggeration, manipulation, misreporting **13** falsification **15** misconstruction

**misrule**
**04** riot **05** chaos **06** tumult **07** anarchy, turmoil **08** disorder, unreason **09** confusion **10** turbulence **11** lawlessness **12** indiscipline **13** misgovernment, mismanagement **15** disorganization

**miss**
**02** Ms **03** err **04** beat, blow, fail, flop, flub, girl, lack, lass, lose, maid, Mlle, muff, need, omit, skip, slip, trip, want, wish **05** avoid, dodge, error, evade, fault, forgo, let go, Mdlle, mourn **06** bypass, damsel, escape, fiasco, forego, kumari, lament, maiden, not see, pass up, regret **07** ache for, blunder, failure, let slip, long for, mistake, neglect, not go to, not spot, pine for **08** fräulein, leave out, miscarry, omission, overlook, pass over, Señorita, sidestep, teenager, yearn for **09** disregard, fail to get, fail to hit, grieve for, not notice, oversight, Signorina, sorrow for, young lady **10** be away from, circumvent, desiderate, not go to see, schoolgirl, young woman **11** fail to catch, fail to seize, not be part of **12** be absent from, be too late for, fail to attend, fail to notice, mademoiselle **13** feel the loss of, misunderstand, not take part in
*See also* **girl; woman**
• **miss out 04** jump, omit, skip **06** bypass, ignore **07** exclude **08** leave out, pass over **09** disregard **12** dispense with

**missal**
**08** breviary, mass-book, Triodion **09** formulary **10** office-book, prayerbook **11** euchologion, servicebook

**misshapen**
◊ *anagram indicator* **04** bent, ugly **06** inform, warped **07** crooked, dismayd, twisted **08** crippled, deformed **09** contorted, distorted, grotesque, malformed, monstrous **15** misproportioned

**missile**
**04** bomb, dart, shot **05** arrow, shaft, shell **06** rocket, weapon **07** grenade, torpedo **08** brickbat **10** flying bomb, projectile

*Missiles include:*

**02** MX, V-2
**03** AAM, ABM, AGM, ASM, ATM, SAM, SSM
**04** ALCM, ASBM, ICBM, IRBM, MIRV, MRBM, Scud, SLBM, TASM
**05** smart
**06** AMRAAM, cruise, Exocet®, guided
**07** javelin, Polaris, Trident
**08** Maverick
**09** ballistic, minuteman
**10** sidewinder, wire-guided

**11** heat-seeking
**12** surface-to-air

• **missile container 04** silo

**missing**
◊ *deletion indicator* **04** gone, lost **06** absent, astray **07** lacking, mislaid, strayed, wanting **08** awanting **09** misplaced **10** gone astray **11** disappeared **14** gone for a Burton, unaccounted-for

**mission**
**02** op **03** aim, job **04** duty, goal, raid, task, work **05** chore, quest **06** action, charge, errand, office, sortie **07** calling, crusade, embassy, purpose, pursuit **08** business, campaign, exercise, legation, ministry, vocation **09** manoeuvre, operation, task force **10** assignment, commission, delegation, deputation **11** raison d'être, undertaking

**missionary**
**05** envoy **07** apostle **08** champion, crusader, emissary, minister, preacher, promoter **09** converter **10** ambassador, campaigner, evangelist **12** propagandist, proselytizer

*Missionaries include:*

**03** **Fox** (George), **Huc** (Evariste Régis)
**04** **Luke** (St), **Mark** (St), **Paul** (St)
**05** **Carey** (William), **David** (Père Armand), **Eliot** (John), **Ellis** (William), **Moody** (Dwight L), **Ricci** (Matteo), **Smith** (Eli)
**06** **Damien** (Father Joseph), **Graham** (Billy), **Teresa** (Mother), **Wesley** (John)
**07** **Aylward** (Gladys), **Columba** (St), **Liddell** (Eric), **ten Boom** (Corrie)
**08** **Boniface** (St), **Crowther** (Samuel)
**09** **McPherson** (Aimee Semple), **Southwell** (Robert)
**10** **Huddleston** (Trevor), **Macpherson** (Annie), **Schweitzer** (Albert)
**11** **Livingstone** (David)
**13** **Francis Xavier** (St)

**Mississippi**
**02** MS **04** Miss

**missive**
**04** line, memo, note, sent **06** letter, report **07** epistle, message, missive **08** bulletin, dispatch **09** messenger **10** communiqué, memorandum **13** communication

**Missouri**
**02** MO

**misspell**
◊ *anagram indicator*

**misspent**
**04** idle **06** wasted **07** misused **08** prodigal **09** idled away **10** dissipated, misapplied, profitless, squandered, thrown away **12** unprofitable **13** frittered away

**misstate**
**05** twist **06** garble **07** distort, falsify, pervert **08** misquote **09** misrelate, misreport **11** misremember **12** misrepresent

**mist**
**03** dew, fog **04** drow, film, haar, haze, murk, rack, roke, smog, veil **05** cloud, spray, steam **06** mizzle, nimbus, vapour **07** dimness, drizzle **10** exhalation **12** condensation
• **mist over, mist up 03** dim, fog **04** blur, veil **05** fog up, glaze **07** obscure, steam up **09** cloud over **10** become hazy **12** become cloudy **13** become blurred

**mistake**
◊ *anagram indicator* **03** err **04** bish, blue, boob, boss, flaw, flub, goof, muff, slip, take, typo **05** error, fault, fluff, gaffe, lapse, mix up, mix-up **06** booboo, cock up, domino, duff it, foul up, foul-up, goof up, howler, mess up, miscue, muddle, ricket, slip up, slip-up, stumer **07** bad move, balls up, bloomer, blooper, blunder, botch-up, clanger, clinker, confuse, erratum, fallacy, faux pas, go wrong, louse up, misread, misstep, own goal, screw up, take for **08** confound, get wrong, mesprize, misfield, misjudge, misprint, misprise, misprize, muddle up, omission, solecism **09** make a slip, oversight **10** aberration, inaccuracy, misprision, misreading **11** corrigendum, make a booboo, misconceive, misconstrue, misspelling **12** come a cropper, drop a clanger, indiscretion, misapprehend, miscalculate, misjudgement **13** misunderstand **14** miscalculation **15** misapprehension, put your foot in it, slip of the tongue

**mistaken**
◊ *anagram indicator* **03** wet **05** false, wrong **06** faulty, misled, untrue **07** at fault, deluded, in error, inexact, off base, off-beam, vicious **08** deceived, overseen **09** erroneous, ill-judged, incorrect, misguided, misprised, unfounded **10** fallacious, inaccurate, up the booay **11** inauthentic, misinformed **13** inappropriate, wide of the mark **15** got the wrong idea

**mistakenly**
◊ *anagram indicator* **07** falsely, in error, wrongly **08** unfairly, unjustly **09** by mistake **11** erroneously, incorrectly, misguidedly **12** fallaciously, inaccurately **15** inappropriately

**Mister**
**02** Mr

**mistimed**
**08** ill-timed, tactless, untimely **10** malapropos **11** inopportune, unfortunate **12** inconvenient, infelicitous, unseasonable **14** unsynchronized

**mistiness**
*see* **mist**

**mistreat**
◊ *anagram indicator* **04** harm, hurt, maul **05** abuse, bully **06** batter, beat up, ill-use, injure, misuse, molest **08** ill-treat, maltreat, walk over **09** mishandle **10** knock about, treat badly **11** walk all over

## mistreatment
**04** harm, hurt **05** abuse **06** ill-use, injury, misuse **07** cruelty, mauling **08** bullying, ill-usage **09** battering **10** unkindness **11** manhandling, mishandling, molestation **12** ill-treatment, maltreatment **13** brutalization

## mistress
**04** amie, dame, doxy, lady, miss, wife **05** lover, tutor, wench, woman **06** ruling **07** Aspasia, herself, hetaera, leading, partner, stepney, teacher **08** goodwife, lady-love, paramour **09** belle amie, concubine, courtesan, courtezan, governess, housewife, inamorata, kept woman, principal **10** canary-bird, châtelaine, fancy woman, girlfriend, school dame **11** live-in lover **12** bit on the side **13** schoolteacher

## mistrust
**04** fear **05** doubt, qualm **06** beware **07** caution, suspect **08** be wary of, distrust, wariness **09** chariness, hesitancy, misgiving, suspicion **10** scepticism **11** uncertainty **12** apprehension, reservations **13** have no faith in **14** be suspicious of, have misgivings **15** have doubts about

## mistrustful
**03** shy **04** wary **05** chary, leery **07** cynical, dubious, fearful **08** cautious, doubtful, hesitant **09** sceptical, uncertain **10** suspicious **11** distrustful **12** apprehensive

## misty
**03** dim **04** hazy **05** foggy, fuzzy, murky, smoky, vague **06** cloudy, opaque, veiled **07** blurred, clouded, obscure, tearful, unclear **08** nebulous **10** indistinct

## misunderstand
**07** mishear, misknow, misread, mistake **08** get wrong, misjudge **11** misconstrue, misperceive **12** misapprehend, misinterpret, miss the point **13** miscomprehend **15** get the wrong idea

## misunderstanding
**03** row **04** rift, tiff **05** clash, error, mix-up **06** breach **07** discord, dispute, mistake, quarrel **08** argument, conflict, squabble **10** difference, falling-out, malentendu, misreading **12** crossed wires, disagreement, misjudgement **13** cross-purposes, misconception **15** false impression, misapprehension, misintelligence

## misunderstood
**07** misread **08** misheard, mistaken **09** ill-judged, misjudged **12** misconstrued, unrecognized **13** unappreciated **14** misappreciated, misinterpreted, misrepresented

## misuse
◇ *anagram indicator* **04** harm, hurt **05** abuse, waste, wrong **06** ill-use, injure, injury **07** abusion, corrupt, deceive, distort, exploit, pervert **08** ill-treat, misapply, mistreat, squander,

wrong use **09** dissipate, misemploy **10** corruption, perversion, treat badly **11** mishandling, squandering **12** exploitation, ill-treatment, maltreatment, mistreatment **13** misemployment **14** malappropriate, misapplication, misappropriate

## mite
**03** bit, jot, tad **04** atom, iota, whit, worm **05** grain, ounce, scrap, spark, touch, trace **06** acarus, lepton, morsel, varroa **07** modicum, smidgen **08** berry bug **09** red spider, Sarcoptes **11** trombiculid, tyroglyphid

## mitigate
**04** calm, dull, ease, help **05** abate, allay, blunt, check, mease, quiet, remit, slake, still **06** aslake, lenify, lessen, modify, pacify, reduce, soften, soothe, subdue, temper, weaken **07** appease, assuage, lighten, mollify, placate, qualify, relieve, sweeten **08** decrease, diminish, moderate, palliate, tone down **09** alleviate, extenuate

## mitigating
**08** lenitive, mitigant **09** assuasive, modifying, tempering **10** justifying, palliative, qualifying **11** extenuating, vindicating, vindicatory

## mitigation
**06** relief **07** remorse **08** allaying, decrease, easement, remission, lessening, reduction, remission, tempering **10** diminution, moderation, palliation **11** alleviation, appeasement, assuagement, extenuation **13** mollification, qualification

## mitre
**04** tiar **05** tiara

## mix
◇ *anagram indicator* **04** card, fuse, hash, join, mash, mell, meng, mess, ming, olio, stir, suit **05** agree, alloy, blend, cross, get on, menge, merge, union, unite, whisk **06** caudle, fold in, fusion, hobnob, jumble, meddle, medley, merger, mingle, muddle **07** amalgam, combine, consort, farrago, involve, mixture, shake up, swizzle **08** coalesce, compound, confound, emulsify, get along, intermix, mingling, mishmash, pastiche **09** associate, coalition, commingle, composite, harmonize, interfuse, introduce, potpourri, socialize, synthesis **10** amalgamate, assortment, complement, fraternize, go well with, hodgepodge, homogenize, hotchpotch, infiltrate, interbreed, meet others, salmagundi, synthesize **11** combination, gallimaufry, incorporate, intermingle, interpolate, olla-podrida, put together **12** amalgamation, be compatible, conglomerate
• **mix in** ◇ *anagram indicator* **05** add in, blend, merge **09** introduce **10** infiltrate **11** incorporate, interpolate
• **mix up** ◇ *anagram indicator* **05** upset **06** garble, jumble, muddle, puzzle **07** confuse, disturb, involve, mistake,

perplex, snarl up **08** bewilder, confound, muddle up **09** implicate **10** complicate **12** get jumbled up

## mixed
◇ *anagram indicator* **02** pi **03** pie, pye **04** chow, ment **05** fused, meint, meynt **06** hybrid, menged, minged, motley, united, unsure, varied **07** alloyed, blended, diverse, mingled, mongrel **08** assorted, combined, compound, confused **09** composite, crossbred, equivocal, half-caste, interbred, uncertain **10** ambivalent **11** amalgamated, conflicting, diversified, promiscuous **12** incorporated, through-other **13** contradicting, miscellaneous
• **mixed up** ◇ *anagram indicator* **04** in on **05** upset **06** hung up **07** chaotic, muddled, puzzled **08** caught up, confused, involved, messed up **09** disturbed, embroiled, entangled, perplexed, screwed up **10** bewildered, désorienté, disordered, distracted, distraught, implicated, inculpated **11** complicated, disoriented, maladjusted **12** incriminated

## mixer
**05** whisk **06** beater, joiner **07** blender, meddler, stirrer **08** busybody, makebate **09** disrupter, extrovert **10** interferer, liquidizer, socializer, subversive **12** troublemaker **13** food processor, mischief-maker

## mixing
**05** cross, union **06** fusion **08** blending, mingling **09** interflow, synthesis **10** commixtion, commixture, confection, minglement **11** association, coalescence, combination, socializing **12** amalgamation **13** hybridization, interbreeding, intermingling, miscegenation **14** fraternization

## mixture
◇ *anagram indicator* **03** mix **04** brew, mong, olio, olla, wash **05** alloy, blend, cross, union **06** fusion, hybrid, jumble, medley, mingle **07** amalgam, compost, farrago, melange, variety **08** compound, mishmash, mixed bag, pastiche **09** composite, organ stop, patchwork, potpourri, synthesis **10** assortment, composture, concoction, hodgepodge, hotchpotch, miscellany **11** coalescence, combination, olla-podrida, smorgasbord, temperature **12** amalgamation **14** conglomeration

## mix-up
◇ *anagram indicator* **04** mess **05** chaos, snafu **06** foul-up, jumble, muddle, tangle **07** balls-up, mistake, snarl-up **08** disorder, nonsense **09** confusion **12** complication

## moan
**03** sob **04** beef, carp, hone, howl, mean, mein, mene, sigh, wail, weep **05** bleat, gripe, groan, meane, mourn, whine **06** bemoan, charge, grieve, grouse, lament, whinge **07** beefing, carping, censure, grumble, whimper

**moaner**

**08** bleating, complain, grumbler **09** annoyance, bellyache, complaint, criticism, grievance, whingeing **10** accusation **11** bellyaching, kick up a fuss, lamentation **12** fault-finding **14** representation **15** dissatisfaction

**moaner**

**06** whiner **07** fusspot, grouser, niggler, whinger **08** grumbler **09** nit-picker **10** bellyacher, complainer, fussbudget **11** fault-finder

**mob**

**03** set **04** body, crew, fill, gang, herd, host, mass, pack **05** brood, crowd, drove, flock, group, horde, plebs, press, swarm, tribe, troop **06** attack, charge, jostle, masses, mobile, pester, proles, rabble, throng **07** besiege, company, king mob, overrun, set upon **08** canaille, fall upon, mobility, populace, riff-raff, surround **09** descend on, gathering, hoi polloi, multitude **10** assemblage, collection, common herd, crowd round, faex populi, rabble rout, swarm round **11** gather round, proletariat, rank and file **12** common people, ribble-rabble **13** great unwashed **15** many-headed beast

**mobile**

◇ *anagram indicator* **04** thin **05** agile, quick **06** active, lively, motile, moving, nimble, roving, supple **07** migrant, movable, roaming **08** changing, flexible, moveable, portable **09** adaptable, energetic, itinerant, revealing, wandering **10** able to move, adjustable, ambulatory, changeable, expressive, locomotive, suggesting, travelling **11** peripatetic **12** ever-changing **13** transportable

**mobility**

**06** motion **07** agility **08** motility, motivity, vivacity **09** animation **10** locomotion, movability, suppleness **11** flexibility, movableness, portability **12** locomobility, locomotivity **14** expressiveness

**mobilization**

**08** assembly **09** mustering, summoning **10** activation **11** marshalling, preparation **12** organization

**mobilize**

◇ *anagram indicator* **05** rally, ready **06** call up, enlist, muster, summon **07** animate, marshal, prepare **08** activate, assemble, get ready, organize **09** conscript, galvanize, make ready **14** call into action

**mob rule**

**06** mob law **08** lynch law **09** mobocracy **10** ochlocracy **13** kangaroo court, Reign of Terror

**mobster**

**04** thug **05** crook, heavy, rough, tough **06** bandit, robber **07** brigand, hoodlum, ruffian **08** criminal, gangster, hooligan, skinhead **09** bovver boy, desperado, racketeer, terrorist

**mock**

**03** ape, cod, dor, kid, rag, rib **04** fake, geck, gibe, goof, jape, jeer, rail, sham, slag **05** bogus, chaff, dummy, faked, false, fleer, flout, knock, mimic, scoff, scorn, scout, sneer, taunt, tease **06** bemock, deride, ersatz, forged, insult, parody, phoney, pseudo, send up **07** emulate, feigned, imitate, lampoon, laugh at, murgeon, pretend, slag off, take off **08** ridicule, satirize, simulate, spurious **09** burlesque, disparage, imitation, imitative, make fun of, poke fun at, pretended, simulated, synthetic **10** artificial, caricature, fraudulent, substitute **11** counterfeit, poke borak at **13** poke mullock at

*See also* **imitation**

**mocker**

**05** tease **06** critic, jeerer **07** clothes, derider, flouter, reviler, scoffer, scorner, sneerer **08** bellbird, satirist, vilifier **09** detractor, lampooner, ridiculer, tormentor **10** iconoclast, lampoonist **11** pasquinader

**mockery**

**03** dor, gab **04** jeer, quiz, sham **05** farce, fleer, scoff, scorn, serve, sneer, spoof, sport **06** banter, parody, satire, send-up **07** apology, disdain, horning, jeering, kidding, lampoon, mimicry, ragging, ribbing, sarcasm, take-off, teasing **08** contempt, derision, raillery, ridicule, scoffing, sneering, taunting, travesty **09** burlesque, charivari, contumely, emulation, imitation **10** caricature, disrespect **12** mickey-taking **13** disparagement

**mocking**

**03** wry **05** snide **07** cynical **08** derisive, derisory, illusion, impudent, irrisory, narquois, sardonic, scoffing, scornful, sneering, taunting **09** insulting, quizzical, sarcastic, satirical **10** disdainful, irreverent, wry-mouthed **12** contemptuous **13** disrespectful

**mock-up**

**04** copy **05** dummy, image, model **07** replica **09** facsimile, imitation **11** fabrication **14** representation

**mode**

**03** fad, way **04** form, kind, look, mood, plan, rage, rate **05** craze, modus, style, trend, vogue **06** custom, Dorian, Iastic, Ionian, Lydian, manner, method, system **07** Aeolian, fashion, Locrian, process **08** approach, modality, Phrygian, practice **09** condition, procedure, technique **10** convention, dernier cri **11** latest thing **13** manifestation **15** fashionableness

**model**

◇ *anagram indicator* **01** T **03** sit, toy **04** base, cast, copy, form, kind, make, mark, mode, mold, plan, pose, sort, type, wear, work **05** carve, dummy, ideal, image, medal, mould, poser, shape, sport, style **06** byword, create, design, lovely, mirror, mock-up, module, sample, sculpt, sitter **07** cutaway, display, epitome, example, exemple, fashion, paragon, pattern, perfect, reduced, replica, show off, subject, typical, variety, version **08** bozzetto, exemplar, maquette, original, paradigm, specimen, standard, template **09** archetype, dress form, exemplary, facsimile, imitation, mannequin, miniature, prototype, superwaif **10** archetypal, embodiment, small-scale, stereotype **11** guiding star **12** artist's model, fashion model, guiding light, prototypical, reproduction **14** perfect example, representation

**moderate**

**03** mod **04** calm, cool, curb, ease, fair, just, mean, mild, soft, so-so, tame **05** abate, allay, chair, check, slake, sober **06** decent, direct, gentle, lessen, medium, modest, modify, pacify, relent, soften, steady, subdue, temper **07** appease, assuage, average, chasten, control, die down, dwindle, fairish, liberal, qualify, repress, slacken, subside **08** adequate, attemper, centrist, chastise, decrease, diminish, don't know, mediocre, middling, mitigate, modulate, muscadin, ordinary, palliate, passable, play down, regulate, restrain, sensible, suppress, tone down **09** alleviate, attenuate, Menshevik, Octobrist, soft-pedal, soft-shell, supervise, temperate, tolerable, treatable **10** controlled, measurable, not much cop, reasonable, restrained **11** indifferent, keep in check, not up to much, preside over, soft-shelled **12** act as chair at, conservative, nonextremist **13** neutral person, no great shakes, well-regulated **14** fair to middling **15** act as chairman at, middle-of-the-road

**moderately**

**05** mezzo, quite **06** fairly, rather **08** passably, slightly, somewhat **10** reasonably **12** to some extent, within reason **13** within measure **14** conservatively

**moderation**

**02** ho **03** hoa, hoh **06** reason **07** caution, control, curbing, measure **08** chastity, decrease, sobriety **09** abatement, composure, lessening, reduction, restraint **10** golden mean, mitigation, regulation, relaxation, subsidence, temperance **11** alleviation, attenuation, self-control **13** self-restraint, temperateness **14** abstemiousness, reasonableness • **in moderation 10** moderately **12** within bounds, within limits, within reason **15** with self-control

**modern**

**02** AD, in **03** hip, mod, new, now **04** cool, late **05** fresh, novel **06** latest, latter, modish, recent, trendy, with it **07** current, faddish, go-ahead, in style, in vogue, present, stylish, voguish **08** advanced, everyday, existing, neoteric, space-age, up-to-date **09** in fashion, inventive, latter-day, newfangle, the latest **10** all the rage, avant-garde, futuristic, innovative, neoterical, newfangled, present-day

**11** commonplace, cutting edge, fashionable, modernistic, progressive, spanking new **12** contemporary **13** state-of-the-art, up-to-the-minute **14** forward-looking, hot off the press

## modernity

**07** newness, novelty **09** freshness **10** innovation, recentness **11** originality **14** innovativeness **15** contemporaneity, fashionableness

## modernization

**07** renewal **08** redesign, updating **09** revamping **10** renovation **11** improvement, remodelling **12** modification, regeneration **13** refurbishment **14** transformation

## modernize

**04** do up **05** fix up, renew **06** do over, modify, reform, remake, revamp, update **07** improve, refresh, remodel **08** progress, redesign, renovate **09** get with it, refurbish, transform **10** make modern, regenerate, rejuvenate, streamline **13** bring up-to-date

## modest

**03** coy, shy **04** fair, pure **05** lowly, plain, prude, pudic, quiet, small, timid **06** chaste, decent, demure, humble, proper, pudent, seemly, simple **07** bashful, limited, prudent **08** adequate, decorous, discreet, maidenly, moderate, ordinary, passable, reserved, retiring, verecund, virtuous **09** chastened, diffident, shamefast, tolerable **10** reasonable, shamefaced, unassuming **11** inexpensive, unobtrusive **12** satisfactory, self-effacing, unpretending **13** self-conscious, unexceptional, unpretentious **15** self-deprecating

## modestly

**05** coyly, shyly **06** humbly, purely **07** quietly, timidly **08** chastely, decently, demurely **09** bashfully **10** adequately, discreetly, moderately, reasonably, virtuously **11** diffidently **12** unassumingly **14** satisfactorily **15** self-consciously, unpretentiously

## modesty

**05** aidos, shame **07** coyness, decency, decorum, pudency, reserve, shyness **08** humility, pudicity, timidity **09** plainness, propriety, quietness, reticence **10** chasteness, demureness, humbleness, seemliness, simplicity **11** bashfulness **13** shamefastness **14** self-effacement, shamefacedness **15** inexpensiveness, self-deprecation

## modicum

**03** bit, tad **04** atom, dash, drop, hint, inch, iota, mite **05** crumb, grain, ounce, pinch, scrap, shred, speck, tinge, touch, trace, woman **06** degree, little **08** fragment, molecule, particle **09** little bit **10** suggestion **11** small amount

## modification

◊ anagram indicator **05** tweak **06** change **08** mutation, revision **09** recasting, reworking, tempering, variation

**10** adaptation, adjustment, alteration, limitation, moderation, modulation, refinement, remoulding **11** improvement, reformation, restriction **13** qualification **14** reorganization, transformation

## modify

◊ anagram indicator **04** dash, dull, vary **05** abate, adapt, alter, limit, touch, tweak, vowel **06** adjust, change, invert, lessen, recast, reduce, reform, revise, rework, sculpt, soften, temper, umlaut **07** convert, improve, qualify, remould, reshape **08** attemper, decrease, diminish, mitigate, moderate, overrule, redesign, retrofit, tone down, vowelize **09** diversify, transform **10** assimilate, reorganize **11** explain away **13** differentiate, trim your sails

## modish

**02** in **03** hip, mod, now **04** chic, cool **05** jazzy, smart, vogue **06** latest, modern, tonish, trendy, with it **07** à la mode, current, stylish, tonnish, voguish **10** all the rage, avant-garde **11** fashionable, modernistic **12** contemporary **13** up-to-the-minute **14** fashion-forward

## modulate

**04** tune, vary **05** alter, lower **06** adjust, change, modify, soften, temper **07** balance, inflect **08** moderate, regulate **09** harmonize

## modulation

**04** tone **05** shade, shift **06** accent, change, tuning **07** balance, cadence **08** lowering **09** inflexion, softening, variation **10** adjustment, alteration, inflection, intonation, moderation, regulation **12** modification **13** harmonization

## module

**02** LM **03** bug, LEM **04** item, part, SIMM, unit **05** image, model, piece **06** factor, plug-in **07** element, section **09** component

## modus operandi

**02** MO **03** way **04** plan, rule **06** manner, method, praxis, system **07** process **08** practice **09** operation, procedure, technique **11** rule of thumb

## mogul

**03** VIP **05** baron, Mr Big **06** big gun, big pot, bigwig, Mughal, top dog, tycoon **07** big shot, magnate, notable, supremo **08** big noise, big wheel, padishah **09** big cheese, personage, potentate

## moist

**03** wet **04** damp, dank, dewy **05** humid, juicy, muggy, rainy, soggy, washy **06** clammy, hydric, liquid, marshy, watery **07** drizzly, tearful, wettish **08** dripping **09** drizzling, humectant, hygrophil **12** hygrophilous

## moisten

**03** dew, dip, wet **04** damp, lick, soak, wash **05** bathe, bedew, bewet, imbue, latch, slake, water **06** dampen, embrue, humect, humefy, humify, imbrue, madefy, sloken, sparge

**07** embrewe, make wet, slocken, spairge **08** humidify, irrigate **09** humectate **10** moisturize

## moisture

**03** dew, wet **04** damp, rain **05** humor, spray, steam, sweat, water **06** humour, liquid, vapour **07** drizzle, soaking, wetness **08** dampness, dankness, humidity **09** mugginess **10** wateriness **11** humectation, precipitate **12** condensation, perspiration **13** precipitation

## molar

**04** wang **08** jaw-tooth **09** mill-tooth

## Moldova

**02** MD **03** MDA

## mole

**03** mol, spy **04** dyke, mark, pier, spot, want **05** agent, jetty, Talpa **06** blotch, groyne **07** barrier, blemish, freckle, speckle **08** causeway **09** mouldwarp, mowdiwort **10** breakwater, embankment, moudiewart, moudiewort, mowdiewart, Notoryctes **11** double agent, infiltrator, secret agent

## molest

**03** bug, nag, vex **04** harm, hurt, rape **05** abuse, annoy, harry, hound, tease, upset, worry **06** accost, assail, attack, badger, bother, chivvy, harass, hassle, injure, needle, pester, plague, ravish **07** agitate, assault, disturb, fluster, provoke, torment, trouble **08** ill-treat, irritate, maltreat, mistreat **09** aggravate, persecute **10** exasperate **13** interfere with **15** sexually assault

## molestation

**04** harm, rape **05** abuse **06** attack, injury **07** assault **11** disturbance, infestation **12** interference

## molester

**06** abuser, rapist **08** attacker, ravisher **09** assaulter

## mollify

**04** calm, ease, lull **05** abate, allay, blunt, quell, quiet, relax **06** lessen, mellow, modify, pacify, soften, soothe, temper **07** appease, assuage, compose, cushion, placate, quieten, relieve, sweeten **08** mitigate, moderate **10** conciliate, propitiate

## mollusc

Molluscs include:

**03** Mya
**04** clam, slug, Unio
**05** conch, cowry, ormer, snail, spoot, squid, whelk
**06** chiton, cockle, cowrie, cuttle, dodman, limpet, loligo, mussel, nerite, oyster, winkle
**07** abalone, octopus, piddock, scallop, sea slug
**08** escargot, nautilus, sea snail, shipworm, wallfish
**09** cone shell, hodmandod, land snail, pond snail, razorclam, razorfish, tusk shell, wing shell, wing snail
**10** cuttlefish, giant squid,

nudibranch, periwinkle, razor shell, Roman snail
**11** horse mussel, marine snail
**12** sea butterfly
**13** great grey slug, keyhole limpet, ramshorn snail, slipper limpet
**15** freshwater snail

*See also* **animal; crustacean**
• **mollusc's tongue  04** rasp

**mollycoddle**
**03** pet **04** baby, ruin **05** spoil **06** coddle, cosset, mother, pamper **07** indulge **08** pander to **09** spoon-feed **11** overprotect

**molten**
**05** fusil **06** fusile, melted **07** flowing **08** magmatic **09** liquefied **12** circumfusile

**molybdenum**
**02** Mo

**moment**
**02** mo **03** sec **04** hint, note, tick **05** flash, gliff, glift, jiffy, point, punto, trice, twink, value, worth **06** import, minute, puncto, second, stound, stownd, weight **07** concern, gravity, instant **08** as soon as, directly, glifing, interest, occasion, the point, two ticks **09** short time, substance, the minute, twinkling **10** importance, the instant **11** consequence, immediately, little while, point in time, seriousness, split second, weightiness **12** significance **13** very short time **14** less than no time
• **a moment ago  04** enow

**momentarily**
**07** briefly **10** fleetingly, for a moment, for a second **11** temporarily **12** for an instant **13** for a short time **15** instantaneously

**momentary**
**05** brief, hasty, quick, short **07** passing **08** fleeting **09** ephemeral, momentany, spasmodic, temporary, transient **10** evanescent, short-lived, transitory **12** momentaneous **13** instantaneous

**momentous**
**05** grave, major, vital **07** crucial, fateful, pivotal, serious, weighty **08** critical, decisive, eventful, historic, pregnant **09** important **11** epoch-making, significant **12** earth-shaking, of importance **13** consequential **14** of significance **15** earth-shattering, world-shattering

**momentum**
**04** push, urge **05** drive, force, poise, power, speed **06** energy, impact, thrust **07** impetus, impulse **08** stimulus, strength, velocity **09** incentive **10** propulsion **12** driving-power
• **angular momentum  01** L

**Monaco**
**02** MC **03** MCO

**monarch**
**01** K, Q, R **02** ER, GR, HM, VR **03** rex, roi **04** Cole, czar, Inca, king, ksar, tsar, tzar **05** queen, ruler **06** Caesar, prince, regina **07** czarina, emperor, empress, tsarina **08** autocrat, czarevna, czaritsa,

princess, the Crown, tsarevna, tsaritsa **09** cesarevna, czarevich, potentate, sovereign, tsarevich **10** cesarevich, cesarewich, czarevitch, tsarevitch, tsaresvna **11** cesarevitch, cesarewitch, crowned head, king of kings, tsesarevich, tsesarewich **12** tsesarevitch, tsesarewitch

*See also* **king; prince; princess; queen**

---

*Anglo-Saxon and English monarchs:*

**04** **Cnut** ('the Great'), **Edwy**, **Grey** (Lady Jane), **John** (Lackland), **Mary** (I, Tudor), **Offa**
**05** **Edgar**, **Edred**, **Henry** (I, II, III, IV, V, VI, VII, VIII), **Svein** (I Haraldsson, 'Fork-Beard')
**06** **Alfred** ('the Great'), **Canute**, **Edmund** (I, II 'Ironside'), **Edward** (I, II 'the Martyr', III 'the Confessor', IV, V, VI, 'the Elder'), **Egbert**, **Harold** (I Knutsson, 'Harefoot', II)
**07** **Richard** (I 'the Lion Heart', II, III), **Stephen**, **William** (I 'the Conqueror', II 'Rufus')
**08** **Ethelred** (I, II 'the Unready')
**09** **Athelstan**, **Elizabeth** (I), **Ethelbald**, **Ethelbert**, **Ethelwulf**
**11** **Hardicanute**
**13** **Edgar Atheling**, **Knut Sveinsson**

---

*Scottish monarchs:*

**03** **Aed**
**04** **Dubh**, **Duff**
**05** **Bruce** (Robert), **Culen**, **David** (I, II), **Edgar**, **Giric**, **James** (I, II, III, IV, V, VI)
**06** **Baliol** (Edward de), **Baliol** (John de), **Donald** (I, II, III 'Bane'), **Duncan** (I, II), **Indulf**, **Lulach**, **Robert** (I 'the Bruce', II, III)
**07** **Balliol** (Edward de), **Balliol** (John de), **Kenneth** (I, II, III), **Macbeth**, **Malcolm** (I, II, III 'Canmore', IV 'the Maiden'), **William** (I)
**08** **Margaret** ('Maid of Norway')
**09** **Alexander** (I, II, III)
**11** **Constantine** (I, II)
**16** **Mary** ('Queen of Scots')

---

*British monarchs:*

**04** **Anne**, **Mary** (II)
**05** **James** (VI and I), **James** (VII and II)
**06** **Edward** (VII, VIII), **George** (I, II, III, IV, V, VI)
**07** **Charles** (I, II), **William** (II and III of Orange, IV)
**08** **Victoria**
**09** **Elizabeth** (II)
**14** **William and Mary**

---

**monarchy**
**05** realm **06** domain, empire **07** kingdom, royalty, tyranny **08** dominion, kingship, royalism **09** autocracy, despotism, monocracy **10** absolutism **11** sovereignty **12** principality **14** sovereign state

**monastery**
**03** wat **04** cell **05** abbey, gompa **06** friary, priory, vihara **07** convent, minster, nunnery **08** cloister, lamasery

**09** coenobium, lamaserai
**12** Charterhouse

---

*Monasteries and convents include:*

**04** Iona
**05** Cluny
**07** Mt Athos, Shaolin
**08** Hilandar, Sénanque
**09** Melk Abbey, Tengboche
**10** Chartreuse, Douai Abbey, El Escorial, Ettal Abbey, San Lorenzo, Santa Croce, Worth Abbey
**11** Ealing Abbey, Glendalough, Lindisfarne, Parkminster, Simonopetra, Val-Duchesse, Whitby Abbey
**12** Belmont Abbey, Colwich Abbey, Monte Cassino, Mont St Michel, St John's Abbey
**13** Buckfast Abbey, Donglin Temple, Downside Abbey, Monasterboice, Rievaulx Abbey, Tyburn Convent
**14** Fountains Abbey, Stanbrook Abbey
**15** Ampleforth Abbey, Curzon Park Abbey, Portsmouth Abbey, St Cecilia's Abbey

---

*See also* **abbey; religious**

**monastic**
**07** ascetic, austere, monkish, recluse **08** celibate, eremitic, secluded, solitary **09** canonical, reclusive, withdrawn **10** anchoritic, cloistered, coenobitic, meditative **11** sequestered **13** contemplative

*See also* **religious**

**monasticism**
**07** monkery **08** monkhood **09** austerity, eremitism, monachism, reclusion, seclusion **10** asceticism **11** coenobitism, recluseness

**Monday**
**03** Mon

**monetary**
**04** cash **05** money **06** fiscal **07** capital **08** economic **09** budgetary, financial, pecuniary

**money**
**01** L, M, P **03** fat, LSD, oof, tin, utu **04** cash, cent, coin, dibs, dosh, dust, gelt, gilt, hoot, jack, kail, kale, loot, pelf **05** blunt, brass, bread, bucks, chink, dough, dumps, funds, gravy, lolly, means, Oscar, purse, ready, rhino, smash, sugar, wonga **06** argent, assets, greens, moolah, riches, stumpy, wealth **07** capital, dingbat, ooftish, readies, savings, scratch, shekels **08** currency, finances, greenies **09** affluence, banknotes, megabucks, resources **10** big bikkies, prosperity **11** legal tender, spondulicks **12** the necessary

*See also* **coin; currency**
• **get money from  03** tap
• **hand over money  03** pay
• **in the money  04** rich **05** flush **06** loaded **07** wealthy, well-off **08** affluent, well-to-do **10** prosperous,

well-heeled **11** rolling in it **12** stinking rich
• **large amount of money 03** wad **04** mint, pile, pots, scad
• **money collection 03** cap **04** whip **09** whip-round
• **provide with money 03** pay **04** fund
• **quantity of money 03** sum

**money-box**
**04** safe **05** chest **06** coffer **07** cash box, poor box **08** penny-pig **09** piggy-bank

**money-changing**
**04** agio

**moneyed**
**04** rich **05** flush, pluty **06** loaded **07** opulent, wealthy, well-off **08** affluent, well-to-do **10** prosperous, well-heeled **11** comfortable, rolling in it

**money-grubbing**
**07** miserly **08** grasping **09** mammonish, mercenary **10** quaestuary **11** acquisitive, mammonistic

**moneymaking**
**06** paying **09** lucrative **10** commercial, profitable, quaestuary, successful **12** profit-making, remunerative

**Mongolia**
**03** MGL, MNG

**mongoose**
**04** urva

**mongrel**
◊ *anagram indicator* **03** cur **04** kuri, mong, mutt **05** cross, mixed, pooch **06** bitser, hybrid **08** half-bred **09** crossbred, half-breed, yellow dog **10** crossbreed, ill-defined, mixed breed **12** of mixed breed

**monicker**
**04** name **05** alias **07** pen name **08** nickname **09** false name, pseudonym, sobriquet, stage name **10** soubriquet **11** assumed name

**monitor**
**03** VDU **04** CCTV, note, plot, scan **05** check, trace, track, varan, watch **06** detect, follow, goanna, iguana, leguan, marker, record, screen, survey, worral, worrel **07** adviser, advisor, display, head boy, leguaan, observe, oversee, perenty, prefect, scanner, Varanus **08** detector, head girl, observer, overseer, perentie, recorder, watchdog **09** supervise **10** supervisor **11** invigilator, keep an eye on, keep track of **12** dragon lizard, Komodo dragon, Komodo lizard **14** security camera

**monk**
**03** Dan, Dom **04** lama **05** abbot, friar, prior **06** beguin, frater, hermit **07** brother **08** cellarer, cenobite, monastic, talapoin **09** anchorite, bullfinch, coenobite, Dalai Lama, gyrovague, mendicant, religieux, religious **10** cloisterer, conventual, religioner **11** abbey-lubber, religionary **13** contemplative, possessionate

*Monks and nuns include:*
**02** Fa (Hsien), Fa (Xian)
**03** Orm
**04** Gall (St), Hume (Basil), Rule (St), Sava (St)
**05** Aidan (St), Barat (St Madeleine Sophie), Borde (Andrew), Jacob (Max), Ormin, Rancé (Armand Jean de), Sabas (St)
**06** Arnulf, Boorde (Andrew), Colman (St), Eadmer, Ernulf, Gildas (St), Gyatso (Geshe Kelsang), Gyatso (Tenzin), Merton (Thomas), Teresa (Mother), Tetzel (Johann), Turgot
**07** Adamnan (St), Adomnan (St), Arnauld (Angélique), Arnauld (Marie-Angélique), Beckett (Sister Wendy), Cabrini (St Francesca Xavier), Carpini (John of Plano), Cassian (St John), Gratian, Lydgate (John), Mortara (Edgar), Regulus (St), Schwarz (Berthold)
**08** Alacoque (St Marguerite Marie), Bonivard (François de), Duchesne (St Rose Philippine), Foucauld (Charles de), Houedard (Dom Sylvester), Pelagius, Rabelais (François), Rasputin (Grigori)
**09** Bonnivard (François de), MacKillop (Mary), Skobtsova (Maria)
**10** Bernadette (St), Fra Diavolo, Montfaucon (Bernard de), Torquemada (Tomás de), Walsingham (Thomas), Willibrord (St)
**11** Bodhidharma, Ponce de León (Luis), Scholastica (St)
**12** Guido d'Arezzo
**13** The Singing Nun
**14** Francis of Paola (St), Marianus Scotus, Peter the Hermit
**15** Bernard of Morval

*See also* **religious**

**monkey**
**03** imp, tup **04** brat, fool, mess, muck, play, tyke **05** anger, clown, mimic, rogue, scamp, sheep **06** fiddle, fidget, footle, lackey, meddle, potter, rascal, simian, tamper, tinker, trifle, urchin **07** primate **09** interfere, scallywag **10** jackanapes **13** mischief-maker

*Monkeys include:*
**03** ape, pug, sai
**04** douc, leaf, mico, mona, saki, titi, zati
**05** Diana, drill, green, magot, night, sajou, Satan, toque
**06** baboon, bandar, bonnet, coaita, grivet, guenon, howler, langur, malmag, rhesus, sagoin, saguin, spider, tee-tee, uakari, vervet, woolly
**07** cacajou, colobus, guereza, hanuman, jacchus, kipunji, macaque, sagouin, saimiri, sapajou, tamarin, tarsier, wistiti
**08** capuchin, durukuli, entellus, mandrill, mangabey, marmoset, squirrel, talapoin, wanderoo
**09** proboscis
**10** Barbary ape, moustached

**11** douroucouli, platyrrhine, white-eyelid
**13** platyrrhinian

*See also* **animal; ape**
• **monkey business 06** pranks **07** carry-on, foolery **08** clowning, mischief, trickery **09** chicanery **10** dishonesty, hanky-panky, tomfoolery **11** legerdemain, shenanigans, skulduggery **12** monkey tricks **13** funny business, jiggery-pokery, sleight-of-hand
• **monkey puzzle 09** araucaria, Chile pine **11** Chilean pine

**monochrome**
**05** sepia **08** monotone, unicolor **09** unicolour **10** monochroic, monotonous **11** unicolorate, unicolorous, unicoloured **13** black-and-white, monochromatic

**monocle**
**04** quiz **05** glass **08** eyeglass **13** quizzing-glass

**monogamous**
**09** monogamic **10** monandrous, monogynous

**monogamy**
**08** monandry, monogyny

**monolingual**
**08** monoglot **10** unilingual

**monolith**
**05** shaft **06** menhir, sarsen **08** megalith **13** standing stone

**monolithic**
**04** huge, vast **05** giant, rigid, solid **07** massive **08** colossal, faceless, gigantic, immobile, unmoving, unvaried **09** hidebound, immovable **10** fossilized, inflexible, monumental, unchanging **11** intractable

**monologue**
**03** rap **05** spiel **06** homily, sermon, speech **07** address, lecture, oration **09** soliloquy

**monomania**
**05** mania, thing **06** fetish **08** fixation, idée fixe, neurosis **09** fixed idea, obsession **10** fanaticism, hobby-horse **13** ruling passion **15** bee in your bonnet

**monopolize**
**03** hog **05** tie up **06** corner, occupy, take up **07** control, engross **08** dominate, take over **09** preoccupy **11** appropriate **14** have sole rights, have to yourself, keep to yourself

**monopoly**
**05** régie **06** corner **07** appalto, control **09** franchise, monopsony, privilege, sole right **10** ascendancy, domination, sole rights **14** exclusive right **15** exclusive rights

**monotonous**
**04** drab, dull, flat **05** ho-hum, samey **06** boring, deadly **07** humdrum, routine, tedious, uniform **08** plodding, tiresome, toneless, unvaried **09** unvarying, wearisome **10** all the same, colourless, mechanical,

monochrome, repetitive, unchanging, uneventful, unexciting **11** repetitious **12** run-of-the-mill **13** uninteresting **14** soul-destroying

## monotony
**06** tedium **07** boredom, humdrum, routine, taedium **08** ding-dong, dullness, flatness, sameness **10** repetition, uniformity **11** routineness **12** tiresomeness **13** wearisomeness **14** repetitiveness, uneventfulness

## monster
**04** huge, mega, vast **05** alien, beast, brute, devil, fiend, freak, giant, jumbo **06** mutant, savage **07** immense, mammoth, massive, villain **08** colossal, colossus, enormous, gigantic, teratism, whopping **09** barbarian, ginormous, monstrous **10** tremendous **11** miscreation, monstrosity **12** malformation **13** freak of nature **14** Brobdingnagian

*Monster types include:*

**03** orc, roc
**04** cete, gila, ogre
**05** alien, gulon, harpy, lamia, phoca, troll, yowie, zombi
**06** ajatar, bunyip, dragon, gorgon, kraken, nicker, ogress, sphinx, wivern, wyvern, zombie
**07** cyclops, griffin, griffon, gryphon, prodigy, satyral, taniwha, triffid, wendigo, windigo, ziffius
**08** basilisk, behemoth, bogeyman, dinosaur, lindworm, mooncalf, mushussu, seahorse
**09** leviathan, manticore, marakihau, rosmarine, sea satyre, wasserman, whirlpool
**10** chupacabra, cockatrice, criosphinx, salamander, sea monster
**11** amphisbaena, hippocampus

*Monsters include:*

**02** ET
**05** Hydra, Smaug, snark
**06** Balrog, Duessa, Empusa, Fafnir, Geryon, Medusa, Nazgul, Nessie, Python, Scylla, Shelob, Sphinx, Stheno, Typhon
**07** Bathies, Caliban, Cecrops, Chimera, Cyclops, Dracula, Echidna, Euryale, Grendel
**08** Cerberus, Chimaera, Godzilla, King Kong, Minotaur, Typhoeus
**09** Charybdis
**10** Black Annis, jabberwock, Jormangund, jubjub bird, Polyphemus
**12** bandersnatch, Blatant Beast, Count Dracula, Frankenstein
**13** Cookie Monster, Hecatonchires, Questing Beast
**14** Incredible Hulk, Midgard serpent
**15** Glatysaunt Beast, Loch Ness monster

*See also* **mythical; mythology**

## monstrosity
**04** evil **05** freak, teras **06** horror, mutant **07** eyesore, monster **08** atrocity, enormity, ugliness **09** carbuncle, obscenity **11** abnormality,

heinousness, hellishness, hideousness, miscreation **12** dreadfulness **13** frightfulness, loathsomeness

## monstrous
**04** evil, foul, huge, vast, vile **05** cruel, nasty **06** grisly, savage, wicked **07** heinous, hideous, immense, inhuman, mammoth, massive, vicious **08** abnormal, colossal, criminal, deformed, dreadful, enormous, freakish, gigantic, gruesome, horrible, misbegot, shocking, teratoid, terrible **09** abhorrent, atrocious, frightful, grotesque, malformed, misshapen, unnatural **10** abominable, horrifying, miraculous, outrageous, prodigious, scandalous, tremendous **11** disgraceful, misbegotten **12** preposterous

## monstrously
**06** hugely, vastly **08** terribly **09** immensely, massively **10** colossally, dreadfully, enormously, shockingly **11** atrociously, frightfully **12** gigantically, outrageously, scandalously, tremendously

## Montana
**02** MT **04** Mont

## month
**01** m **02** mo

*Months:*

**02** Jy
**03** Apr, Aug, Dec, Feb, Jan, Jul, Jun, Mar, May, Nov, Oct, Sep
**04** July, June, Sept
**05** April, March
**06** August
**07** January, October
**08** December, February, November
**09** September

*French month names:*

**02** Av
**03** mai
**04** août, juin, mars
**05** avril
**07** février, janvier, juillet, octobre
**08** décembre, novembre
**09** septembre

*French Revolutionary calendar month names:*

**06** Nivôse
**07** Floréal, Ventôse
**08** Brumaire, Frimaire, Germinal, Messidor, Pluviôse, Prairial
**09** Fructidor, Thermidor
**11** Vendémiaire

*German month names:*

**03** Mai
**04** Juli, Juni, März
**05** April
**06** August, Januar
**07** Februar, Oktober
**08** Dezember, November
**09** September

*Hindu calendar month names:*

**05** Magha, Pausa
**06** Asadha, Asvina

**07** Chaitra, Sravana
**08** Jyaistha, Karttika, Phalguna, Vaisakha
**10** Bhadrapada, Margasirsa
**13** Dvitiya Asadha
**14** Dvitiya Sravana

*Islamic calendar month names:*

**05** Rabi I, Rajab, Safar
**06** Rabi II, Shaban
**07** Jumada I, Ramadan, Shawwal
**08** Jumada II, Muharram
**10** Dhu al-Qadah
**11** Dhu al-Hijjah

*Italian month names:*

**05** marzo
**06** agosto, aprile, giugno, luglio, maggio
**07** gennaio, ottobre
**08** dicembre, febbraio, novembre
**09** settembre

*Jewish calendar month names:*

**02** Ab, Av
**04** Abib, Adar, Elul, Iyar
**05** Iyyar, Nisan, Sivan, Tebet, Tevet, Tisri
**06** Hesvan, Kisleu, Kislev, Shebat, Shevat, Tammuz, Tebeth, Tishri, Veadar
**07** Chislev, Heshvan
**09** Adar Sheni

*Latin month names:*

**05** Maius
**06** Julius, Junius
**07** Aprilis, Martius, October
**08** Augustus, December, November, Sextilis
**09** Januarius, Quintilis, September
**10** Februarius

*Spanish month names:*

**04** mayo
**05** abril, enero, julio, junio, marzo
**06** agosto
**07** febrero, octubre
**09** diciembre, noviembre
**10** septiembre

• **in the last month** **03** ult **04** ulto
**06** ultimo
• **the present month** **04** inst
**07** instant

## Montserrat
**03** MSR

## monument
**04** tomb **05** cairn, cross, folly, relic, token, trace **06** barrow, column, heroon, marker, pillar, record, shrine, statue **07** hogback, martyry, memento, obelisk, prodigy, pyramid, talayot, trilith, witness **08** cenotaph, evidence, memorial, reminder, sacellum **09** headstone, mausoleum, testament, tombstone, trilithon **10** gravestone, immortelle, indication **11** remembrance, war memorial
**13** commemoration

*Monuments and memorials include:*

04 Eros, Homo
05 Grant, Scott
06 Albert, Sphinx
07 Lincoln, Martyr's, Wallace
08 Boadicea, Cenotaph, Daibutsu, Lion Gate, Taj Mahal, Victoria
09 Charminar, Menin Gate, Qutb Minar, Tsar's Bell
10 Berlin Wall, Broken Ring, Ishtar Gate, Kutab Minar, London Wall, Marble Arch, Mt Rushmore, Navigators', Stonehenge, Washington
11 Civil Rights, Eiffel Tower, Grande Arche, Great Sphinx, Machu Picchu, Madara Rider, Silbury Hill, Voortrekker
12 Antonine Wall, Eleanor Cross, Glass Pyramid, Great Pyramid, Hadrian's Wall, Spanish Steps, Statue of Zeus, Tower of Babel
13 Admiralty Arch, Arc de Triomphe, Great Zimbabwe, Mount Rushmore, Nelson's Column, People's Heroes, Trajan's Column, Trevi Fountain
14 Albert Memorial, Eleanor Crosses, Gateway of India, Glastonbury Tor, Hands of Victory, Hiroshima Peace, Lenin Mausoleum, Spasskaya Tower, Stone of Destiny, Tomb of Mausolus, Wayland's Smithy, Wright Brothers
15 Angel of the North, Brandenburg Gate, Lincoln Memorial, Nubian monuments, Rollright Stones, Statue of Liberty, Thatta monuments

## monumental

04 huge, vast 05 great 07 abiding, amazing, awesome, classic, immense, lasting, massive, notable 08 colossal, enduring, enormous, historic, immortal, imposing, majestic, memorial, striking 09 important, memorable, permanent 10 impressive, remarkable, tremendous 11 celebratory, epoch-making, exceptional, magnificent, outstanding, significant 12 awe-inspiring, overwhelming 13 commemorative, extraordinary, unforgettable

## monumentally

06 hugely, vastly 09 immensely, massively 10 colossally, enormously 12 gigantically, tremendously

## mood

03 fit, tid 04 feel, mode, sulk, tone, vein, whim 05 anger, blues, dumps, pique, tenor 06 humour, plight, spirit, temper 07 bad mood, climate, feeling, spirits 08 ambience, doldrums, optative, the sulks 09 bad temper, potential 10 atmosphere, depression, imperative, indicative, infinitive, low spirits, melancholy 11 conjunctive, disposition, frame of mind, state of mind, subjunctive
• **in the mood for** 06 keen on, keen to 07 eager to 08 ready for 09 willing to

10 disposed to, inclined to 11 feeling like, wanting to do 13 wanting to have

## moody

04 glum, mopy 05 angry, faked, mopey, sulky, testy 06 broody, crabby, crusty, fickle, gloomy, morose, sullen, touchy 07 doleful, flighty, in a huff, in a mood 08 downcast, petulant, unstable, volatile 09 crotchety, impulsive, irascible, irritable, miserable, pretended 10 capricious, changeable, in a bad mood, melancholy 11 bad-tempered 12 cantankerous 13 short-tempered, temperamental, unpredictable

## moon

04 idle, loaf, mope, pine 05 brood, dream, month, mooch 06 Lucina, Phoebe 08 daydream, languish 09 fantasize, satellite 13 Paddy's lantern 15 MacFarlane's buat

*Lunar seas:*

08 Bay of Dew
09 Moscow Sea, Sea of Cold, Smyth's Sea
10 Bay of Heats, Central Bay, Eastern Sea, Foaming Sea, Mare Nubium, Sea of Waves, Sinus Medii, Sinus Roris
11 Lacus Mortis, Lake of Death, Mare Crisium, Mare Humorum, Mare Imbrium, Mare Ingenii, Mare Smythii, Mare Spumans, Mare Undarum, Mare Vaporum, Marginal Sea, Palus Somnii, Sea of Clouds, Sea of Crises, Sea of Nectar, Sinus Iridum, Southern Sea
12 Humboldt's Sea, Lake of Dreams, Mare Australe, Mare Frigoris, Mare Marginis, Mare Nectaris, Marsh of Decay, Marsh of Mists, Marsh of Sleep, Sea of Showers, Sea of Vapours, Sinus Aestuum
13 Bay of Rainbows, Mare Orientale, Ocean of Storms, Sea of Geniuses, Sea of Moisture, Sea of Serenity
14 Lacus Somniorum, Palus Nebularum, Sea of Fertility
15 Mare Moscoviense, Mare Serenitatis, Palus Putredinis
16 Mare Fecunditatis, Marsh of Epidemics, Palus Epidemiarum
17 Mare Humboldtianum, Sea of Tranquillity
18 Oceanus Procellarum
19 Mare Tranquillitatis

*Moons include:*

02 Io
04 Moon, Rhea
05 Ariel, Dione, Mimas, Titan
06 Charon, Deimos, Europa, Nereid, Oberon, Phobos, Tethys, Triton
07 Iapetus, Miranda, Proteus, Titania, Umbriel
08 Callisto, Cruithne, Ganymede, Hyperion
09 Enceladus

*Moon-related terms include:*

05 lunar, phase
06 waning, waxing
07 far side, gibbous, new moon
08 blue moon, crescent, dark side, full moon, half-moon, lunation, near side
09 blood moon, moonlight, moonscape, moonshine
11 harvest moon, hunter's moon, last quarter, quarter moon
12 first quarter, man in the moon, synodic month, third quarter

• **once in a blue moon** 06 seldom 08 not often 10 hardly ever, very rarely 11 almost never
• **over the moon** 06 elated, joyful 07 fervent 08 blissful, ecstatic, euphoric, frenzied, jubilant 09 delighted, delirious, overjoyed, rapturous, rhapsodic 10 enraptured 11 high as a kite, on cloud nine, tickled pink 13 jumping for joy 15 in seventh heaven, on top of the world

## moonlike

05 lunar, moony 06 lunate 07 lunular, selenic 08 crescent 09 meniscoid 10 crescentic, moon-shaped

## moonshine

03 rot 04 bosh, bunk, guff, tosh 05 hooch, month, stuff, tripe 06 bunkum, hootch, hot air, liquor, piffle, poteen 07 baloney, blather, blether, bootleg, eyewash, fantasy, hogwash, hokonui, potheen, rubbish, spirits, twaddle 08 blathers, blethers, bodiless, claptrap, nonsense, tommyrot 09 bull's wool

## moor

03 fix 04 bind, dock, fell, lash, muir 05 berth, heath, hitch, tie up 06 anchor, fasten, secure, upland 07 Moresco, Morisco, mudéjar, Saracen 08 make fast, moorland 09 fix firmly 10 drop anchor
• **tightly moored** 04 girt

## moot

04 open, pose, stir 05 argue, plead, raise, vexed 06 broach, debate, knotty, submit 07 advance, bring up, crucial, discuss, dispute, meeting, propose, suggest 08 academic, arguable, disputed, doubtful, propound 09 debatable, difficult, insoluble, introduce, undecided, unsettled 10 discussion, disputable, put forward, unresolved 11 contestable, problematic 12 open to debate, questionable, undetermined, unresolvable 13 controversial

## mop

03 mat 04 mane, mass, soak, swab, wash, wipe 05 clean, dwile, shock, wiper 06 absorb, malkin, mawkin, sponge, tangle, thatch 07 grimace, swabber 08 squeegee 10 head of hair
• **mop up** 04 swab, wash 06 absorb, secure, soak up, sponge, tidy up, wipe up 07 clean up, round up 08 deal with 09 dispose of, eliminate, finish off 10 account for, neutralize, take care of

## mope

**04** fret, mump, peak, pine, sulk **05** boody, brood, droop, grump, moper **06** grieve, grouch, misery, moaner **07** despair, killjoy **08** languish **09** introvert, pessimist **10** depressive **11** be miserable, melancholic **12** melancholiac

• **mope about**  **04** idle, loll, moon **05** mooch **06** lounge, wander **08** languish

## moral

**03** tag **04** good, just, pure **05** adage, maxim, noble, point, right **06** chaste, decent, dictum, honest, lesson, proper, saying, symbol **07** epigram, ethical, meaning, message, precept, proverb, upright **08** aphorism, straight, teaching, virtuous **09** blameless, certainty, emotional, righteous **10** high-minded, honourable, principled, upstanding **11** application, clean-living, encouraging **12** significance **13** incorruptible, psychological

## morale

**04** mood **05** heart **06** spirit **07** spirits **08** optimism **10** confidence, self-esteem **11** hopefulness, state of mind **13** esprit de corps **14** self-confidence

## moralistic

**04** smug **05** pious **08** priggish, superior **09** pietistic **10** complacent, goody-goody **11** pharisaical **12** hypocritical **13** sanctimonious, self-righteous **14** holier-than-thou

## morality

**04** good **06** ethics, ideals, morale, morals, purity, virtue **07** conduct, decency, honesty, justice, manners **08** chastity, goodness, moralism **09** integrity, principle, propriety, rectitude, standards **10** principles **11** moral values, uprightness **12** Sittlichkeit **13** righteousness

## moralize

**05** edify, pi-jaw **06** preach **07** lecture **08** ethicize **09** discourse, preachify, sermonize **11** pontificate

## morally

**05** nobly **06** justly **08** properly, socially **09** ethically **10** honourably **11** practically **13** behaviourally

## morals

**06** ethics, habits, ideals **07** conduct, manners **08** morality, scruples **09** behaviour, integrity, moral code, standards **10** principles **11** moral values **12** Sittlichkeit **13** right and wrong

• **lax in morals**  **04** wide

## morass

**03** bog, fen, jam **04** flow, mess, mire, moss, quag **05** chaos, marsh, mix-up, swamp **06** jumble, muddle, slough, tangle **07** clutter **08** quagmire **09** confusion, marshland, quicksand **10** can of worms

## moratorium

**03** ban **04** halt, stay **05** delay **06** freeze **07** embargo, respite **08** stoppage **10** standstill, suspension **12** postponement

## morbid

**04** down, grim, sick **06** ailing, gloomy, grisly, horrid, morose, sickly, sombre **07** ghastly, hideous, macabre, peccant, vicious **08** dejected, diseased, dreadful, ghoulish, gruesome, horrible **09** unhealthy **10** lugubrious, melancholy **11** pessimistic, unwholesome **12** insalubrious **14** down in the dumps

## morbidly

**06** grimly **08** horribly, horridly **09** hideously **10** dreadfully, ghoulishly, gruesomely

## mordant

**04** acid, base **05** edged, harsh, sharp **06** biting, bitter **07** acerbic, caustic, cutting, mixtion, pungent, vicious, waspish **08** critical, incisive, scathing, stinging, venomous, wounding **09** sarcastic, trenchant **10** astringent, iron-liquor **11** acrimonious

## more

**02** mo **03** mae, moe, new, più **04** root **05** added, again, extra, fresh, other, plant, spare, stump **06** better, longer, rather **07** another, further **08** moreover, repeated **09** increased **10** additional **11** alternative **13** greater number, supplementary **15** greater quantity

• **more or less**  **04** some **06** mainly, mostly **07** broadly **09** generally, in general, just about **10** by and large, on the whole, pretty much, pretty well **11** in most cases **13** predominantly **14** for the most part

• **more than**  **04** plus

• **yet more**  **03** nay

## moreover

**03** eft **04** also **06** as well, at that, either **07** besides, further **08** likewise **10** in addition, what is more **11** furthermore **12** additionally

## mores

**04** ways **06** custom, habits, usages **07** customs, manners **09** etiquette, practices **10** procedures, traditions, ways of life **11** conventions **14** ways of behaving

## morgue

**08** mortuary **09** arrogance, deadhouse **11** haughtiness **12** charnel house **14** funeral parlour

## moribund

**04** weak **05** dying **06** doomed, ebbing, fading, feeble, senile, waning **07** failing **08** comatose, expiring, lifeless, stagnant **09** crumbling, declining, dwindling **10** collapsing, in extremis, stagnating **11** obsolescent, on the way out, wasting away **14** on your last legs

## morning

**02** am **04** dawn, morn **05** matin **07** sunrise **08** cock-crow, daybreak, daylight, forenoon **10** before noon, break of day, first light **11** crack of dawn

• **morning star**  **05** Venus **07** daystar, Lucifer **08** Phosphor **09** precursor **10** Phosphorus **11** morgenstern

## Morocco

**02** MA **03** MAR, Mor

## moron

**03** ass, git, mug, nit **04** berk, butt, clot, dolt, dope, dork, dupe, fool, geek, goof, jerk, kook, nerd, nerk, nong, prat, twit **05** chump, clown, comic, dumbo, dunce, dweeb, idiot, neddy, ninny, twerp, wally **06** cretin, dimwit, drongo, jester, muppet, nitwit, stooge, sucker **07** buffoon, Charlie, fat-head, halfwit, pillock, plonker, tosspot **08** dipstick, imbecile **09** birdbrain, blockhead, cloth head, ignoramus, simpleton **10** nincompoop, silly-billy **13** laughing-stock, proper Charlie

## moronic

**03** mad **04** daft, dumb **05** barmy, batty, crazy, dotty, inane, inept, nutty, potty, silly, wacky **06** absurd, insane, simple, stupid, unwise **07** foolish, idiotic **08** gormless, ignorant **09** half-baked, ludicrous, pointless, senseless **10** half-witted, ill-advised, ridiculous **11** hare-brained, nonsensical **12** crack-brained, shortsighted, simple-minded, unreasonable **13** ill-considered, out of your mind, unintelligent **14** with a tile loose **15** with a screw loose

## morose

**04** acid, glum, grim, grum, sour **05** gruff, moody, sulky, surly **06** crabby, gloomy, severe, sombre, sullen **07** grouchy **08** mournful, taciturn **09** depressed, saturnine **10** lugubrious **11** bad-tempered, ill-tempered, melancholic, pessimistic

## morosely

**06** sourly **07** gruffly, moodily **08** gloomily, sullenly **10** mournfully **12** lugubriously

## morse

**06** walrus **09** Endeavour, iddy-umpty

## morsel

**03** bit **04** atom, bite, part **05** crumb, grain, piece, scrap, slice, taste **06** dainty, nibble, sippet, titbit **07** modicum, morceau, segment, soupçon **08** fraction, fragment, mouthful, particle **11** bonne bouche

## mortal

◇ *anagram indicator* **03** man **04** body, dire, Yama **05** awful, being, cruel, dying, fatal, grave, great, human, woman **06** bitter, bodily, deadly, lethal, person, severe **07** earthly, extreme, fleshly, intense, killing, worldly **08** creature, deathful, temporal, terrible, vengeful **09** corporeal, earthling, ephemeral, extremely, murderous, transient, worldling **10** human being, implacable, individual, perishable, relentless, thoroughly, unbearable **11** unrelenting **12** irremissible, unforgiving, unpardonable

• **first mortal**  **04** Adam, Yama

## mortality

**05** death **07** carnage, killing **08** casualty, fatality, humanity **09** death rate, slaughter **10** loss of life, transience

**11** earthliness, worldliness
**12** ephemerality, impermanence
**13** perishability

**mortally**
**07** awfully, fatally, finally, gravely, greatly **08** lethally, severely, terribly **09** extremely, intensely **12** disastrously

**mortgage**
**03** dip **04** bond, lien, loan **06** pledge, wadset **07** wadsett **08** home loan, security **09** debenture **11** hypothecate, impignorate

**mortification**
**05** shame **06** denial **07** chagrin, control **08** disgrace, ignominy, vexation **09** abasement, annoyance, dishonour, sphacelus **10** asceticism, chastening, conquering, discipline, loss of face, punishment, self-denial **11** confounding, humiliation, self-control, subjugation **12** discomfiture **13** embarrassment

**mortified**
**04** sick **06** shamed **07** ashamed, crushed, humbled **08** defeated **09** disgraced, horrified **10** confounded, gangrenous, humiliated **11** dishonoured, embarrassed

**mortify**
**03** die **04** deny, kill **05** abash, annoy, crush, shame **06** humble, offend, subdue, wither **07** affront, chagrin, chasten, conquer, control, crucify, deflate, horrify **08** bring low, chastise, confound, disgrace, gangrene, macerate, restrain, suppress **09** discomfit, dishonour, embarrass, humiliate **10** disappoint, discipline, put to shame

**mortifying**
**07** shaming **08** crushing, humbling, salutary **09** punishing, thwarting **10** chastening **11** humiliating, ignominious **12** discomfiting, embarrassing, overwhelming

**mortuary**
**06** morgue **09** deadhouse **12** charnel house **14** funeral parlour

**mosaic**
**06** musive, screen **08** terrazzo **10** pietra dura, pietre dure **11** opus musivum

**moss**
**03** hag **04** hagg **05** Musci

*Mosses include:*

**03** bog, bur, cup, fog
**04** burr, club, long, peat, tree
**05** fairy, usnea
**06** hypnum
**07** acrogen, foggage, lycopod
**08** sphagnum, staghorn
**09** wolf's claw, wolf's foot
**10** fontinalis, ground pine

• **stalk of moss capsule** **04** seta

**most**
◇ *tail deletion indicator* **04** bulk, mass **08** majority **09** almost all, nearly all **10** lion's share **11** largest part **12** greatest part **13** preponderance

**mostly**
◇ *deletion indicator* **06** feckly, mainly **07** as a rule, chiefly, largely, overall, usually **08** above all **09** generally, in general, in the main **10** especially, on the whole **11** principally **13** predominantly **14** for the most part

**moth**

*Moths include:*

**01** Y
**02** Io
**03** bag, pug, wax
**04** goat, hawk, luna, puss
**05** ghost, gypsy, tiger
**06** bogong, bugong, burnet, carpet, kitten, lackey, lappet, magpie, puriri, sphinx, turnip, winter
**07** buff-tip, clothes, codling, emerald, emperor, hook-tip, silver-Y, six-spot, tussock
**08** cinnabar, peppered, silkworm
**10** death's-head
**11** garden tiger, pale tussock, swallowtail
**12** Kentish glory, peach blossom, red underwing
**13** processionary

*See also* **animal; butterfly; insect**

**moth-eaten**
**03** old **04** worn **05** dated, mangy, musty, seedy, stale **06** mouldy, ragged, shabby **07** ancient, archaic, decayed, outworn, worn-out **08** decrepit, moribund, obsolete, outdated, tattered **10** antiquated, threadbare **11** dilapidated **12** old-fashioned

**mother**
**02** ma **03** dam, mam, mom, mum **04** baby, base, bear, mama, rear, scum, tend **05** cause, dregs, fount, mamma, mammy, mater, mommy, mummy, mumsy, nanny, nurse, raise, roots, spoil **06** foster, matron, minnie, origin, pamper, parent, source, spring, venter **07** care for, cherish, indulge, nurture, old lady, produce **08** ancestor, fuss over, hysteria, old woman **09** look after, matriarch **10** bring forth, derivation, foundation, procreator, take care of, wellspring **11** birth mother, give birth to, overprotect **12** progenitress **13** materfamilias
*See also* **dregs**

**motherly**
**04** fond, kind, warm **06** caring, gentle, loving, tender **08** maternal, matronal **09** nurturing **10** comforting, motherlike, protective **12** affectionate

**motif**
**04** form, idea, logo **05** shape, theme, topic **06** design, device, emblem, figure **07** concept, pattern **08** ornament **10** decoration

**motion**
**03** act, bid, nod **04** flow, plan, sign, wave **05** going, offer, usher **06** action, beckon, change, direct, moving, puppet, scheme, signal, travel **07** feeling, gesture, passage, passing, project, transit **08** activity, mobility, motility, movement, progress,

proposal **09** agitation, manifesto, prompting **10** indication, locomotion, suggestion, travelling **11** gesticulate, inclination, instigation, proposition **12** presentation **13** changing place, gesticulation **14** changing places, recommendation
• **in motion** ◇ *anagram indicator* **03** off **05** about, astir, going **06** agoing, moving **07** on the go, running **08** under way **09** on the move, on the wing **10** in progress, travelling **11** functioning, operational, upon the wing
• **set in motion** **04** move, open, stir **05** begin, found, start, steer, stire, styre **06** set off, winnow **07** actuate, kick off, promote, start up **08** activate, commence, embark on, get going, initiate, set about **09** instigate, institute, introduce **10** launch into **11** get cracking **13** begin to happen, take the plunge

**motionless**
**03** set **05** fixed, inert, rigid, still **06** at rest, frozen, halted, static **07** resting **08** becalmed, immobile, lifeless, moveless, sleeping, stagnant, standing, unmoving **09** immovable, inanimate, paralysed, unmovable **10** stationary, stock-still, transfixed **13** at a standstill

**motivate**
**04** draw, goad, lead, move, push, spur, stir, urge **05** bring, cause, drive, impel **06** arouse, excite, incite, induce, kindle, prompt, propel **07** actuate, inspire, provoke, trigger **08** activate, initiate, persuade **09** encourage, kick-start, stimulate

**motivation**
**04** push, spur, urge, wish **05** drive **06** desire, hunger, motive, reason **07** impulse **08** ambition, interest, momentum, stimulus **09** incentive, prompting **10** incitement, inducement, persuasion **11** inspiration, instigation, provocation

**motive**
**03** aim **04** goad, lure, spur, urge **05** basis, cause, motif **06** design, desire, ground, moment, object, reason **07** grounds, impulse, pretext, purpose **08** instance, occasion, sanction, stimulus, thinking **09** incentive, influence, intention, rationale **10** attraction, incitement, inducement, mainspring, motivation, persuasion, propellent **11** inspiration **13** consideration, encouragement

**motley**
**04** pied **05** mixed, tabby **06** jester, varied **07** dappled, diverse, mottled, piebald, pyebald, spotted, striped **08** assorted, brindled, many-hued, streaked **09** colourful, patchwork **10** variegated **11** diversified **12** multifarious **13** heterogeneous, miscellaneous, multicoloured, particoloured

**motor club**
*see* **motoring organization**

## motorcyclists
*see* **racing**

## motoring
*see* **car**

## motoring organization
**02** AA **03** AAA, BSM, FIA, RAC

## motor racing
*see* **racing**

## motor vehicle
*see* **car; vehicle**

## motorway
**01** M **02** AB, M1 **07** freeway, thruway **08** Autobahn, turnpike **09** autopista, autoroute **10** autostrada, expressway, throughway **12** superhighway

## mottled
**04** marl **05** chiné, jaspe, pinto, tabby **06** dapple **07** blotchy, brinded, brindle, dappled, flecked, marbled, piebald, spotted **08** blotched, brindled, freckled, speckled, splotchy, stippled, streaked **10** poikilitic, variegated

## motto
**03** cry, mot, saw **04** posy, rule **05** adage, axiom, gnome, maxim, poesy **06** byword, device, dictum, legend, saying, slogan, truism **07** epigram, formula, ich dien, ichthys, impresa, imprese, precept, proverb **08** aphorism, epigraph **09** catchword, watchword **10** golden rule **13** e pluribus unum **15** per ardua ad astra

## mould
◇ *anagram indicator* **03** cut, die, mix, rot **04** cast, form, fust, kind, line, make, must, sort, type, work **05** brand, build, carve, earth, forge, frame, knead, model, plasm, print, shape, stamp, style **06** affect, blight, create, design, direct, figure, format, fungus, matrix, mildew, nature, sculpt **07** calibre, casting, chessel, control, dariole, fashion, outline, pattern, quality, ramakin, ramekin **08** meringue, ramequin, template **09** character, construct, formation, framework, influence, mustiness, sculpture, structure **10** mouldiness **11** arrangement, blister pack **12** construction **13** configuration

## moulder
**03** rot **05** decay, waste **06** humify, perish **07** corrupt, crumble **09** decompose **10** turn to dust **12** disintegrate

## moulding
◇ *anagram indicator* **04** ogee, tore **05** torus

## mouldy
◇ *anagram indicator* **03** bad **04** fust, hoar **05** fusty, lousy, mochy, mucid, muggy, musty, stale **06** fousty, mochie, putrid, rotten **07** corrupt, foughty, spoiled, vinewed **08** blighted, decaying, mildewed **09** miserable **10** mucedinous

## moult
**03** mew **04** cast

## mound
**03** but, dun, hog, lot, orb, tel **04** bank, barp, butt, dike, dune, dyke, heap, hill, mote, pile, rise, tell, tump **05** agger, cairn, hoard, knoll, mogul, motte, mount, pingo, ridge, stack, store **06** barrow, bundle, kurgan, supply, tuffet **07** hillock, hummock, rampart, tumulus **08** mine dump, mountain **09** abundance, earthwork, elevation, monticule, stockpile, whaleback **10** collection, embankment **11** termitarium **12** accumulation
*See also* **hill**

## mound-bird
**05** lowan **08** megapode **09** mallee-hen **10** junglefowl, mallee-bird, mallee-fowl **11** brush turkey

## mount
◇ *reversal down indicator* **02** Mt **03** set, sty **04** back, base, go up, grow, lift, ride, rise, soar, stie, stye **05** build, climb, erect, frame, get on, get up, horse, put on, raise, scale, set up, stage, stand, swell, swell, tot up **06** accrue, ascend, jump on, launch, pile up, saddle, step up **07** arrange, backing, build up, climb on, climb up, display, exhibit, fixture, install, prepare, produce, support **08** escalade, escalate, increase, jump on to, mounting, multiply, organize, override, saddle up **09** clamber up, climb on to, inselberg, intensify, take horse **10** accumulate, get astride **12** passe-partout

## mountain
**03** alp, ben, lot, tor **04** berg, fell, heap, hill, mass, peak, pike, pile **05** guyot, jebel, mound, mount, stack **06** djebel, height, massif **07** backlog **08** pinnacle **09** abundance, elevation **12** accumulation

*Mountains and mountain ranges include:*

**02** K2
**03** Apo, Dom, Tai
**04** Alai, Alps, Blue, Cook, Etna, Fuji, Jura, Meru, Ossa, Rila, Sion, Ural
**05** Altai, Andes, Atlas, Coast, Downs, Eiger, Ghats, Halti, Huang, Kamet, Kékes, Kenya, Logan, Matra, Ozark, Qogir, Rocky, Sinai, Snowy, Table, Tatra
**06** Ararat, Cho Oyu, Deccan, Denali, Egmont, Elbert, Elbrus, Haltia, Hoggar, Lhotse, Makalu, Mourne, Musala, Pindus, Taurus, Vosges, Zagros
**07** Ahaggar, Belukha, Beskids, Everest, Fuji-san, Hua Shan, Lebanon, Manaslu, Nilgiri, Olympus, Rainier, Rhodope, Rockies, Roraima, Scafell, Skiddaw, Snowdon, Stanley, Tai Shan, Troödos
**08** Ben Nevis, Cameroon, Catskill, Caucasus, Cévennes, Damavand, Five Holy, Fujiyama, Heng Shan, Jungfrau, Kinabalu, Mauna Kea, Mauna Loa, McKinley, Pennines, Pyrenees, Rushmore, Song Shan,

St Helens, Taranaki
**09** Aconcagua, Allegheny, Altai Shan, Annapurna, Apennines, Blue Ridge, Broad Peak, Cotswolds, Dolomites, Grampians, Helvellyn, Himalayas, Hindu Kush, Inyangani, Karakoram, Kosciusko, Lenin Peak, Mont Blanc, Muz Tag Ata, Nanda Devi, Rakaposhi, Tirichmir, Tirol Alps, Zugspitze
**10** Adirondack, Cader Idris, Cairngorms, Cantabrian, Carpathian, Chimborazo, Dhaulagiri, Gasherbrum, Gosainthan, Great Smoky, Kosciuszko, MacDonnell, Matterhorn, Pobedy Peak, Puncak Jaya, Sagarmatha
**11** Appalachian, Arthur's Pass, Black Forest, Chomolungma, Drakensberg, Kilimanjaro, Mendip Hills, Mongo-Ma-Loba, Nanga Parbat, Pico Bolívar, Siula Grande
**12** Bavarian Alps, Cascade Range, Cheviot Hills, Darling Range, Dufourspitze, Kanchenjunga, Popocatepetl, Sierra Nevada, Southern Alps, Tibet Plateau, Ulugh Muztagh, Victoria Peak, Vinson Massif
**13** Carrantuohill, Chiltern Hills, Communism Peak, Great Dividing, Haltiatunturi, Kangchenjunga, Ojos del Salado, Stirling Range
**14** Australian Alps, Bavarian Forest, Bohemian Forest, Fichtelgebirge, Flinders Ranges, Grand St Bernard, Hamersley Range, Mackenzie Range, Musgrave Ranges, Qomolangma Feng, Thadentsonyane, Trans-Antarctic
**15** Guiana Highlands, Nevado de Illampu

*See also* **volcano**
• **mountain pass** **04** ghat

*Mountain passes include:*

**04** Ofen
**05** Haast, Lewis, South
**06** Khyber, Lindis, Shipka
**07** Arthur's, Brenner, Oberalp, Plöcken, Simplon, Wrynose
**08** Hongshan, Yangguan
**09** Khunjerab, St Bernard
**10** St Gotthard
**12** Roncesvalles
**13** Cilician Gates, San Bernardino
**14** Grand St Bernard
**15** Little St Bernard

• **mountain peak** **03** ben
• **mountain range** **04** tier

## mountaineering
*Mountaineers include:*

**04** **Hunt** (John, Lord)
**05** **Brown** (Joe), **Bruce** (C G), **Munro** (Sir Hugh), **Scott** (Doug), **Tabei** (Junko)
**06** **Haston** (Dougal), **Herzog**

(Maurice), **Irvine** (Andrew), **Smythe** (Frank), **Tilman** (Bill), **Uemura** (Naomi)
**07 Hillary** (Sir Edmund), **Mallory** (George), **Messner** (Reinhold), **Shipton** (Eric), **Simpson** (Myrtle), **Tazieff** (Haroun), **Tenzing** (Sherpa), **Whymper** (Edward)
**08 Coolidge** (W A B), **MacInnes** (Hamish), **Whillans** (Don)
**09 Bonington** (Sir Chris)
**10 Hargreaves** (Alison)
**13 Tenzing Norgay**

## mountainous
**04** high, huge, mega, vast **05** giant, hilly, jumbo, lofty, rocky, steep **06** alpine, craggy, upland **07** immense, mammoth, massive, soaring **08** colossal, enormous, gigantic, highland, towering **09** ginormous, humongous

## mountebank
**04** fake **05** antic, cheat, fraud, pseud, quack, rogue **06** antick, con man, phoney **07** anticke, antique, buffoon **08** impostor, jongleur, swindler **09** charlatan, pretender, trickster **11** saltimbanco

## mourn
**04** keen, miss, wail, weep **06** bemoan, bewail, grieve, lament, regret, sorrow **07** deplore

## mourner
**04** mute **06** keener, saulie, weeper **07** griever **08** bereaved, sorrower

## mournful
**03** sad **06** dismal, gloomy, rueful, sombre, tragic, woeful **07** dernful, doleful, elegiac, funèbre, unhappy **08** cast-down, dearnful, dejected, desolate, downcast, funereal **09** depressed, miserable, plaintive, sorrowful **10** lachrymose, lugubrious, melancholy **11** heartbroken, melancholic **12** disconsolate, heavy-hearted **13** broken-hearted, grief-stricken

## mournfully
**05** sadly **08** dismally, gloomily, ruefully, sombrely **09** con dolore, dolefully, miserably, unhappily **10** desolately **11** plaintively, sorrowfully **15** broken-heartedly

## mourning
**05** grief **06** sorrow **07** keening, sadness, wailing, weeping **08** grieving **09** sorrowing **10** desolation **11** bereavement, lamentation **13** sorry business

## mouse
**03** Mus **06** muscle, shiner **07** dunnart, Muridae, waltzer **08** black eye **09** Zapodidae

## mousey, mousy
**03** shy **04** drab, dull, meek **05** plain, quiet, timid **07** greyish **08** brownish, timorous **09** diffident, shrinking, withdrawn **10** colourless **11** unassertive **12** self-effacing **13** unforthcoming, uninteresting

## moustache
**04** tash **05** tache **06** walrus **07** Charley, Charlie **08** whiskers **09** excrement, mustachio **10** face fungus **15** zapata moustache

## mousy
*see* **mousey, mousy**

## mouth
◇ *head selection indicator* **03** cry, gab, gam, gas, gob, gub, mou, mug, say **04** door, form, gall, jaws, kiss, rant, trap, vent **05** bazoo, bocca, cheek, chops, delta, hatch, inlet, nerve, sauce, stoma, utter, voice **06** babble, cavity, hot air, kisser, oscule, outlet, portal **07** debouch, declaim, doorway, estuary, gateway, grimace, opening, orifice, speaker, whisper **08** aperture, backchat, boasting, bragging, cakehole, entrance, idle talk, rudeness, traphole **09** brass neck, empty talk, enunciate, impudence, insolence, pronounce, utterance **10** articulate, blustering, disrespect, effrontery, embouchure, potato trap, rattletrap **12** impertinence, laughing gear

*Mouth parts and features include:*

**03** gum, jaw, lip
**04** lips
**05** uvula
**06** tongue, tonsil
**07** hare lip
**08** lower lip, upper lip
**10** hard palate, soft palate
**11** cleft palate
**13** alveolar ridge
**15** isthmus of fauces

*See also* **teeth**
• **keep your mouth shut** **06** clam up, shut up **07** cover up, keep mum **08** pipe down **09** keep quiet **10** say nothing **14** hold your tongue **15** not breathe a word
• **sew up mouth** **04** cope

## mouthful
**03** bit, gag, gob, sip, sup **04** bite, drop, gulp, slug **05** taste **06** gobbet, morsel, nibble, sample, titbit **07** forkful, swallow **08** spoonful **11** bonne-bouche

## mouthpiece
**04** horn **05** agent, organ, voice **07** journal **08** delegate **09** spokesman **10** periodical **11** publication, spokeswoman **12** propagandist, spokesperson **14** representative

## movable
**06** mobile **08** flexible, portable **09** alterable, portative **10** adjustable, changeable **12** transferable **13** transportable

## movables
**04** gear **05** goods, stuff **06** things **07** clobber, effects **08** chattels, property **09** furniture **10** belongings **11** impedimenta, plenishings, possessions

## move
◇ *anagram indicator* **02** go **03** act, mix, wag **04** draw, lead, nose, pass, push, sell, step, stir, tack, take, urge, walk **05** bring, budge, carry, cause, drive, fetch, impel, leave, pal up, rouse, shift, shunt, swing, touch, upset **06** action, affect, arouse, change, decamp, depart, device, excite, gambit, gang up, go away, hobnob, incite, induce, mingle, motion, prompt, propel, remove, strike, submit, switch, travel **07** actuate, advance, agitate, consort, develop, disturb, gesture, hang out, impress, incline, inspire, measure, migrate, proceed, propose, provoke, quinche, removal, request, suggest **08** activity, advocate, go around, motivate, move away, movement, persuade, progress, relocate, transfer **09** associate, circulate, hang about, influence, instigate, manoeuvre, migration, move house, recommend, socialize, stimulate, stratagem, transport, transpose **10** fraternize, initiative, proceeding, put forward, relocation, take action **11** keep company, make strides, zwischenzug **12** rub shoulders **13** gesticulation, repositioning **15** change of address
• **get a move on** **07** hurry up, speed up **08** step on it **09** make haste, shake a leg **11** get cracking **12** step on the gas **15** put your foot down
• **make a move** **02** go **05** frame, leave, split **06** depart **07** push off **08** clear off, get going **10** make tracks **11** do something, get cracking **13** take the plunge, take your leave
• **move aimlessly** **04** mope
• **move around** **04** stir **05** steer, stire, styre
• **move gradually** **04** ease, edge
• **move in some direction** **04** tend
• **move lightly** **04** flit
• **move on** **03** gee, jee **06** avaunt
• **move quickly** **03** hop **04** tear, whid, whip, zoom **06** hurtle
• **move round** **04** eddy, turn
• **move sideways** **04** crab
• **move silently** **06** tiptoe
• **move slowly** **03** lag **04** inch
• **move unsteadily** **03** yaw
• **move up and down** **03** bob **04** yo-yo
• **move violently** **04** tear
• **on the move** **05** astir **06** active, around, moving **07** on the go **08** under way **09** advancing, on the hoof, walkabout **10** journeying, travelling **11** progressing **13** moving forward **14** making progress

## movement
◇ *anagram indicator* **03** act, bit **04** fall, flow, guts, move, pace, part, play, rise, stir, wing **05** drift, drive, group, party, piece, shift, swing, tempo, trend, works **06** action, change, moving, system **07** advance, crusade, current, emotion, faction, gesture, impulse, passage, portion, section **08** activity, campaign, division, progress, shifting, stirring, tendency, transfer, workings **09** agitation, coalition, evolution, machinery, mechanism, variation **10** relocation **11** development,

## movie

improvement, progression
**12** breakthrough, organization
**13** gesticulation, repositioning
**14** transportation
*See also* **art; poetry**
• **rapid eye movement** **03** REM
• **sudden movement** **04** dart, volt

## movie

**04** film **05** flick, video **06** cinema, talkie
**07** fleapit, picture **09** multiplex **10** silent
film **11** feature film, film theatre
**12** movie theatre, picture-house
**13** motion picture, picture-palace
*See also* **film**

## moving

◊ *anagram indicator* **05** astir **06** active,
mobile, motile, urging **07** driving,
dynamic, emotive, flowing, kinetic,
leading **08** arousing, exciting, in
motion, pathetic, poignant, stirring,
touching, worrying **09** affecting,
emotional, inspiring, thrilling,
upsetting **10** disturbing, impressive,
motivating, persuasive **11** influential,
stimulating **12** manoeuvrable
**13** inspirational

## movingly

**10** poignantly, touchingly **11** with
emotion, with feeling **12** expressively,
pathetically **15** inspirationally

## mow

**03** cut, moe **04** barb, clip, crop, tass,
trim **05** shear **06** scythe
• **mow down** **04** kill **07** butcher, cut
down, gun down **08** decimate,
massacre **09** shoot down, slaughter
**11** cut to pieces

## mowing

**04** math

## Mozambique

**03** MOC, MOZ

## much

**04** a lot, lots, many **05** ample, great,
heaps, loads, molto, often, piles, scads
**06** masses, mickle, muckle, oodles,
plenty, stacks **07** copious, greatly
**08** abundant, lashings **09** extensive,
plentiful **10** a great deal, frequently,
widespread **11** substantial
**12** considerable, considerably **14** a
great number of, to a great degree, to a
great extent
• **by so much** **03** the
• **how much** **03** the
• **not so much** **04** less
• **too much** **03** OTT **04** over **06** overly
**09** excessive
• **very much** **03** far **04** sore

## muck

**03** mud **04** crud, dirt, dung, gold, guck,
mess, mire, scum, yuck **05** filth, grime,
guano, gunge, slime **06** debris, faeces,
grunge, manure, ordure, rubble,
scunge, sewage, sludge **09** excrement
• **muck about, muck around**
**05** upset **06** bother, meddle, mess up,
potter, tamper, untidy **07** trouble
**08** dishevel, disorder **09** fool about,
goof about, interfere, lark about, mess
about, play about **10** disarrange, fool
around, goof around, lark around,

mess around, play around
**13** inconvenience **15** lead a merry
dance, make life hell for
• **muck up** **04** ruin **05** botch, spoil,
wreck **06** bungle, cock up, mess up
**07** louse up, screw up **11** make a mess
of

## mucky

**04** miry, oozy **05** dirty, grimy, gucky,
messy, muddy, nasty, slimy **06** filthy,
scungy, soiled, sticky **08** begrimed,
mud-caked **11** bespattered

## mucous

**05** gummy, slimy **06** snotty, viscid
**07** viscous **09** glutinous **10** gelatinous
**12** mucilaginous

## mud

**03** dub **04** clay, dirt, dubs, mire, moya,
ooze, silt, slab, soil **05** abuse, clart,
slake, slush **06** clarts, sleech, sludge
**07** clabber, slander **12** vilification
• **cover with mud** **04** lair

## muddle

◊ *anagram indicator* **03** mix **04** daze,
mash, mess, mull, muzz, stir **05** chaos,
mix up, mix-up **06** bemuse, bungle,
cock-up, fankle, guddle, jumble, mess
up, pickle, puddle, puzzle, tangle
**07** blunder, clutter, confuse, perplex
**08** befuddle, bewilder, confound,
disarray, disorder, jumble up,
scramble, shambles **09** confusion
**11** disorganize **12** bewilderment
**15** disorganization
• **muddle through** **04** cope **05** get by
**06** make do, manage **08** get along

## muddled

◊ *anagram indicator* **05** addle, at sea,
dazed, loose, messy, vague **06** tavert,
woolly **07** chaotic, jumbled, mixed-up,
taivert, tangled, unclear **08** confused
**09** befuddled, perplexed, scrambled,
stupefied **10** addle-pated, bewildered,
disarrayed, disordered, incoherent
**11** addle-headed, disoriented, muddy-
headed **12** addle-brained,
disorganized **13** disorientated

## muddy

◊ *anagram indicator* **04** dull, foul, hazy,
miry, oozy, soil **05** boggy, cloud,
dingy, dirty, fuzzy, grimy, mix up,
mucky, murky, slimy, smear, smoky
**06** bedash, bedaub, cloudy, dreggy,
drumly, filthy, grouty, grubby, jumble,
limous, marshy, muddle, opaque,
puddle, quaggy, slabby, sloppy,
sludgy, slushy, smirch, stupid,
swampy, tangle, turbid **07** begrime,
blurred, confuse, obscure, splashy,
trouble **08** confused, jumble up,
scramble **09** befuddled, bespatter,
make muddy **10** indistinct
**11** disorganize, make unclear,
waterlogged

## muff

◊ *anagram indicator* **04** miss, mitt
**05** botch, fluff, spoil **06** bungle, duffer,
mess up, mishit **07** bungler
**09** mishandle, mismanage

## muffle

**03** gag, mob **04** dull, hush, kill, mute,

wrap **05** cloak, cover, moble
**06** dampen, deaden, mobble, muzzle,
soften, stifle, swathe, wrap up **07** cover
up, envelop, quieten, silence, smother,
swaddle **08** suppress **09** blindfold

## mug

**03** can, cup, pot, rob, sap **04** bash,
bock, dupe, exam, face, fool, gull,
jump, mush, phiz, swot, Toby
**05** chump, clock, mouth, stein, tinny
**06** attack, batter, beaker, beat up, do
over, jump on, kisser, noggin, sconce,
sucker, tinnie, visage, waylay
**07** assault, muggins, rough up, set
upon, tankard **08** features
**09** simpleton, soft touch, steal from
**10** knock about **11** countenance,
physiognomy
*See also* **face; fool**
• **mug up** **03** con **04** cram, swot
**05** get up, study **06** bone up

## muggy

**04** damp **05** close, foggy, humid,
mochy, moist **06** clammy, mochie,
sticky, stuffy, sultry **07** airless
**10** oppressive, sweltering

## mulberry

**04** upas **05** Morus, mvule **06** murrey
**07** cowtree **08** cecropia, sycamine
**10** artocarpus **11** contrayerva, Osage
orange

## mule

**04** moyl, muil **05** moyle **06** hybrid
**07** slipper, sumpter **09** dziggetai

## mulish

**05** rigid **06** wilful **07** defiant
**08** perverse, stubborn **09** difficult,
obstinate, pig-headed **10** headstrong,
inflexible, refractory, self-willed
**11** intractable, stiff-necked, wrong-
headed **12** intransigent, recalcitrant,
unreasonable

## mull

• **mull over** **05** study **06** muse on,
ponder **07** examine, weigh up **08** chew
over, consider, meditate, ruminate
**09** reflect on, think over **10** deliberate,
think about **11** contemplate

## multicoloured

**04** pied **06** motley **07** dappled, piebald,
spotted, striped **08** brindled
**09** colourful **10** variegated
**11** psychedelic **13** kaleidoscopic,
particoloured

## multifarious

**04** many **06** legion, sundry, varied
**07** diverse **08** manifold, multiple,
numerous **09** different, multiform
**10** variegated **11** diversified
**13** miscellaneous, multitudinous

## multiple

**04** many **06** sundry **07** several, various
**08** compound, manifold, numerous,
repeated **10** collective, multiplied

## multiplicity

**03** lot **04** host, lots, mass, tons **05** array,
heaps, loads, piles **06** myriad, number,
oodles, scores, stacks **07** variety
**09** abundance, diversity, profusion
**12** manifoldness, numerousness

## multiplied with
**01** x **02** by

## multiply
**04** grow **05** boost, breed **06** double, expand, extend, spread **07** augment, build up, decuple, octuple **08** centuple, increase, manifold, septuple, sextuple **09** intensify, propagate, quadruple, quintuple, reproduce **10** accumulate **11** proliferate

## multipurpose
**05** handy **08** all-round, flexible, variable **09** adaptable, many-sided, versatile **10** adjustable, all-purpose, functional **11** resourceful **12** multifaceted **14** general-purpose

## multitude
**03** lot, mob **04** army, herd, hive, host, lots, mass, ruck **05** crowd, horde, plebs, shoal, swarm **06** hirsel, legion, number, people, public, rabble, throng **07** king mob **08** assembly, canaille, populace, riff-raff **09** hoi polloi **10** common herd, the million **11** rank and file **12** common people, congregation **13** great unwashed

## multitudinous
**04** many **05** great **06** legion, myriad **07** copious, profuse, teeming, umpteen **08** abundant, infinite, manifold, numerous, swarming **09** abounding, countless **11** innumerable **12** considerable

## mum
**02** ma **04** dumb, ma'am, mama, marm, mute **05** mummy, quiet **06** mother, silent **07** silence **08** reticent **09** secretive **10** masquerade **11** close-lipped, tight-lipped **12** close-mouthed **13** chrysanthemum, unforthcoming **15** uncommunicative

## mumble
**04** moop, moup, mump, slur **06** fumble, murmur, mutter, rumble **07** grumble, stutter **08** splutter **11** speak softly **14** speak unclearly, talk to yourself

## mumbo-jumbo
**04** cant, rite **05** chant, charm, magic, spell **06** humbug, jargon, ritual **07** mummery **08** claptrap, nonsense **09** gibberish, rigmarole **10** double talk, hocus-pocus **11** abracadabra, conjuration, incantation **12** gobbledygook, superstition

## mummer
**05** actor **06** guiser, guizer **07** guisard, scudler, skudler **09** scuddaler **11** masquerader

## munch
**03** eat **04** chew, moop, moup, mump **05** champ, chomp **06** crunch **09** masticate

## mundane
**04** dull **05** banal, stale, trite, usual **06** boring, common, cosmic, normal **07** earthly, fleshly, humdrum, prosaic, regular, routine, secular, terrene, typical, worldly **08** everyday, ordinary,

temporal, workaday **09** customary, hackneyed **11** commonplace, terrestrial

## municipal
**04** city, town **05** civic, civil, urban **06** public **07** borough **09** community **12** metropolitan

## municipality
**04** city, town **05** burgh **07** borough, council **08** district, precinct, township **10** department **11** département **15** local government

## munificence
**06** bounty **08** altruism, largesse **10** generosity, liberality **11** beneficence, benevolence, hospitality **12** generousness, philanthropy **13** bounteousness, bountifulness **14** charitableness, open-handedness **15** magnanimousness

## munificent
**04** rich **06** lavish **07** liberal **08** generous, princely **09** bounteous, bountiful **10** altruistic, beneficent, benevolent, big-hearted, charitable, free-handed, hospitable, open-handed, unstinting **11** magnanimous **15** philanthropical

## munitions
**03** kit **04** gear, guns **05** bombs, tools **06** shells, tackle **08** armament, materiel, ordnance, supplies **09** apparatus, equipment, materials **10** provisions

## murder
**03** hit, ice, rid **04** beat, do in, hell, kill, lick, rout, ruin, slay **05** agony, blood, botch, burke, spoil, stiff, waste, whack, wreck **06** fill in, hammer, mess up, misery, muller, ordeal, outwit, rub out, rubout, thrash **07** anguish, bump off, butcher, clobber, destroy, execute, killing, murther, outplay, removal, slaying, take out, torment, torture, trounce, wipe out **08** blow away, butchery, dispatch, femicide, filicide, foul play, homicide, knock off, massacre, outsmart **09** bloodshed, do to death, eliminate, execution, liquidate, matricide, nightmare, overwhelm, parricide, patricide, slaughter, suffering, uxoricide **10** annihilate, fratricide, put to death, sororicide **11** assassinate, infanticide, liquidation, make a mess of **12** defeat easily, manslaughter, petty treason, wretchedness **13** assassination, honour killing
*See also* **kill**

## murderer
**04** Cain **06** killer, slayer **07** butcher **08** assassin, filicide, homicide **09** bluebeard, cut-throat, matricide, murtherer, patricide **10** man-queller **11** slaughterer **12** serial killer

*Murderers, alleged murderers and assassins include:*

**03** **Ray** (James Earl)
**04** **Aram** (Eugene), **Cain**, **Edny** (Clithero), **Hare** (William), **Kray** (Reggie), **Kray** (Ronnie), **Retz** (Gilles de Laval, Baron), **Ruby**

(Jack), **Todd** (Sweeney), **West** (Fred), **West** (Rosemary)
**05** **Beane** (Sawney), **Booth** (John Wilkes), **Brady** (Ian), **Bundy** (Ted), **Burke** (William), **Craig** (Christopher), **Ellis** (Ruth), **Haigh** (John), **Havoc** (Jack), **Rudge**
**06** **Barrow** (Clyde), **Borden** (Lizzie), **Corday** (Charlotte), **Dahmer** (Jeffrey), **Lecter** (Dr Hannibal), **Manson** (Charles), **Misfit** (the), **Nilsen** (Dennis), **Oswald** (Lee Harvey), **Parker** (Bonnie), **Sirhan** (Sirhan)
**07** **Bathori** (Elizabeth), **Bentley** (Derek), **Bianchi** (Kenneth), **Chapman** (Mark), **Crippen** (Hawley Harvey), **Hindley** (Myra), **Macbeth**, **Manston** (Aeneas), **Neilson** (Donald), **Shipman** (Harold)
**08** **Barabbas**, **Christie** (John Reginald Halliday), **Claudius**, **Dominici** (Gaston), **Hanratty** (James), **Son of Sam**, **Thompson** (Edith)
**09** **Berkowitz** (David), **Bluebeard**, **Harmodius**, **McNaghten** (Daniel), **Sutcliffe** (Peter)
**10** **McNaughten** (Daniel), **McNaughton** (Daniel), **Nirdlinger** (Phyllis)
**11** **Anckarström** (Johan Jakob), **Quare Fellow** (the)
**13** **Jack the Ripper**
**14** **Moors Murderers**
**15** **Yorkshire Ripper**

## murderous
**05** cruel, fatal **06** bloody, brutal, carnal, deadly, lethal, mortal, savage **07** arduous, killing **09** barbarous, butcherly, cut-throat, dangerous, difficult, ferocious, gruelling, homicidal, punishing, strenuous **10** exhausting, unpleasant **11** internecine, internecive **12** bloodthirsty, slaughterous

## murderously
**06** grimly **07** fatally **09** ominously **10** alarmingly, menacingly, sinisterly **11** dangerously, homicidally **12** portentously, unpleasantly **13** threateningly **14** bloodthirstily

## murk
**04** dark, dusk, mirk **05** gloom, night, shade **06** gloomy **07** dimness, obscure, shadows **08** darkness, twilight **09** blackness, half-light, murkiness, shadiness, tenebrity **10** cloudiness, gloominess **11** sunlessness, tenebrosity

## murky
**03** dim, sus **04** dark, dull, grey **05** dingy, dirty, fishy, foggy, misty, muddy, rooky, shady **06** cloudy, dismal, dreary, gloomy, secret, turbid, veiled **07** obscure **08** overcast **09** cheerless, tenebrose, tenebrous **10** mysterious, suspicious, tenebrious **12** questionable

## murmur
◇ *homophone indicator* **03** bur, coo, hum **04** beef, burr, buzz, carp, fuss, moan, purl, purr **05** brawl, brool, bruit, drone, gripe, mourn, thrum, whine

**06** babble, burble, grouse, grudge, intone, mumble, mutter, object, repine, rumble, rumour, rustle, whinge **07** beefing, carping, censure, croodle, grumble, humming, protest, purring, whisper **08** complain, rumbling, syllable **09** annoyance, bellyache, complaint, criticism, criticize, find fault, grievance, muttering, objection, undertone, whingeing **11** bellyaching **12** fault-finding **15** dissatisfaction

## murmuring
**04** buzz, purl, purr **05** drone **06** babble, mumble, mutter, rumble **07** buzzing, droning, humming, purring, souffle, whisper **08** mumbling, rumbling, susurrus **09** murmurous, muttering **10** whispering **11** murmuration

## Murphy
**04** spud **05** praty, tater, tatie **06** potato, pratie, tattie

## muscle
**04** beef, thew **05** brawn, clout, force, might, power, sinew **06** mussel, tendon, weight **07** potency, stamina **08** ligament, strength **10** sturdiness **12** forcefulness

*Muscles include:*

**02** ab
**03** pec
**04** delt
**05** glute, psoas
**06** biceps, rectus, soleus
**07** cardiac, deltoid, gluteus, iliacus, omohyid, triceps
**08** detrusor, masseter, platysma, pronator, risorius, scalenus, splenius
**09** abdominal, complexus, eye-string, perforans, sartorius, stapedius, supinator, trapezius
**10** buccinator, quadriceps
**11** ciliary body, rhomboideus
**13** gastrocnemius
**14** xiphihumeralis
**15** latissimus dorsi, pectoralis major, pectoralis minor, peroneal muscles

**• muscle in   05** shove **06** butt in, jostle, push in **09** strongarm **13** interfere with **14** elbow your way in, force your way in, impose yourself

## muscular
**05** beefy, burly, hefty, husky, thewy **06** brawny, potent, robust, rugged, sinewy, strong, sturdy, thewed **07** fibrous **08** athletic, powerful, stalwart, vigorous **09** strapping **15** powerfully built

## muse
**04** mews **05** brood, dream, meuse, study, think, weigh **06** ponder, review **07** reflect **08** chew over, cogitate, consider, meditate, mull over, ruminate **09** speculate, think over **10** deliberate **11** contemplate **13** contemplation

*The Greek Muses:*

**04** Clio
**05** Erato
**06** Thalia, Urania
**07** Euterpe
**08** Calliope, Polymnia
**09** Melpomene
**10** Polyhymnia
**11** Terpsichore

**• the Muses   07** the nine

## museum
**03** mus **07** palazzo **10** art gallery, collection, repository **14** heritage centre

*Museums and galleries include:*

**02** BM, RA
**03** ICA
**04** MoMA, MOMI, Tate
**05** Prado, Terme, V and A
**06** Correr, London, Louvre, Uffizi
**07** British, Fogg Art, Hofburg, Mankind, Pushkin, Russian, Science, Vatican
**08** Bargello, Borghese, National, Pergamum
**09** Accademia, Albertina, Arnolfini, Ashmolean, Belvedere, Cloisters, Deutsches, Hermitage, Holocaust, Modern Art, Sans Souci, Tretyakov
**10** Guggenheim, Pinakothek, Pitt-Rivers, Serpentine, Tate Modern
**11** Fitzwilliam, Imperial War, Mauritshuis, Musée d'Orsay, Pitti Palace, Rijksmuseum, Tate Britain
**12** Royal Academy, Whitworth Art
**13** Jean Paul Getty, Peace Memorial, Royal Pavilion
**14** Barbican Centre, Natural History, State Hermitage
**15** Centre Beaubourg, Frick Collection, South Bank Centre

## mush
**03** pap **04** corn, glop, mash, pulp **05** cream, dough, gloop, notch, paste, purée, slush, swill **07** rubbish, scallop, shmaltz **08** schmaltz, umbrella **11** mawkishness **14** sentimentality

## mushroom
**04** boom, grow **06** expand, spread, sprout **07** burgeon, shoot up, upstart **08** flourish, increase, spring up, umbrella **09** luxuriate, pixy-stool **11** proliferate

*Mushrooms and toadstools include:*

**03** cep
**04** base, ugly, wood
**05** brain, field, gypsy, horse, magic, march, morel, naked
**06** agaric, blewit, button, elf cup, ink cap, meadow, mower's, oyster, satan's, winter
**07** amanita, blewits, blusher, boletus, Caesar's, griping, parasol, porcini, truffle
**08** death cap, deceiver, hedgehog, penny bun, shiitake, sickener
**09** cramp ball, earth ball, fairy ring, fly agaric, St George's, stinkhorn
**10** champignon, false morel,

lawyer's wig, liberty cap, panther cap, sweetbread, wood agaric
**11** chanterelle, clean mycena, common morel, dingy agaric, honey fungus, stout agaric, sulphur tuft, velvet shank
**12** common ink cap, dryad's saddle, false blusher, horn of plenty, larch boletus, lurid boletus, purple blewit, shaggy ink cap, slippery jack, white truffle, winter fungus, wood hedgehog
**13** buckler agaric, clouded agaric, copper trumpet, devil's boletus, emetic russula, firwood agaric, honey mushroom, Jew's ear fungus, purple boletus, satan's boletus, shaggy milk cap, shaggy parasol, summer truffle, trumpet agaric, woolly milk cap, yellow stainer
**14** common grisette, common laccaria, common puffball, fairies' bonnets, man on horseback, penny-bun fungus, saffron milk cap, yellow staining
**15** beefsteak fungus, chestnut boletus, common earthball, common stinkhorn, destroying angel, garlic marosmius, périgord truffle, stinking parasol, stinking russula, verdigris agaric

*See also* **fungus**

## mushy
◊ *anagram indicator* **03** wet **04** soft **05** pappy, pulpy, soppy, weepy **06** doughy, sloppy, slushy, sugary, syrupy **07** maudlin, mawkish, pulpous, squashy, squidgy **08** squelchy **09** schmaltzy **10** saccharine **11** sentimental

## music
**03** fun, mus **04** note, tune **05** dream **06** melody **07** harmony

*Music types include:*

**03** AOR, emo, MOR, pop, rai, rap, ska
**04** folk, funk, jazz, jive, mood, raga, rock, Romo, soca, soul, zouk
**05** bebop, blues, cajun, crunk, dance, disco, house, indie, krunk, muzak, R and B, salsa, samba, sokah, swing, world
**06** atonal, ballet, choral, doo-wop, fusion, garage, gospel, grunge, hip-hop, jungle, lounge, popera, reggae, sacred, skronk, techno, trance
**07** ambient, baroque, bhangra, Big Beat, calypso, chamber, gamelan, gangsta, karaoke, nu-metal, ragtime, skiffle, trip-hop
**08** acid jazz, ballroom, folk rock, glam rock, hardcore, hard rock, jazz-funk, jazz-rock, operatic, operetta, oratorio, punk rock, soft rock
**09** acid house, Americana, bluegrass, classical, dancehall, Dixieland, hard house, honky-tonk, reggaeton, technopop
**10** electronic, electropop, gangsta

rap, heavy metal, incidental, lovers' rock, orchestral, twelve-tone

**11** country rock, drum and bass, rock and roll, thrash metal

**12** boogie-woogie, electroclash, instrumental

**13** easy listening

**14** rhythm and blues

**15** middle-of-the-road

See also **jazz; opera**
• **compose music to** 03 set

**musical**
**03** mus **06** dulcet, mellow **07** lyrical, melodic, tuneful **09** melodious **10** euphonious, harmonious **11** mellifluous **13** sweet-sounding

See also **instrument; note**

Musicals include:

**04** Cats, Fame, Hair, Rent

**05** Annie, Blitz, Chess, Evita, Fosse, Zorba

**06** Grease, Joseph, Kismet, Oliver!, The Wiz

**07** Cabaret, Camelot, Chicago, Company, Follies

**08** Carnival, Carousel, Fiorello!, Godspell, Mamma Mia!, Oklahoma!, Peter Pan, Show Boat

**09** Brigadoon, Funny Girl, Girl Crazy, On the Town

**10** Hello Dolly!, Kiss Me Kate, Miss Saigon, My Fair Lady

**11** A Chorus Line, Babes in Arms, Billy Elliot, Bitter Sweet, Carmen Jones, Mary Poppins, Me and My Girl, Sweeney Todd, The King and I, The Lion King, The Music Man

**12** Anything Goes, Bombay Dreams, Bye Bye Birdie, Guys and Dolls, Martin Guerre, South Pacific, The Boy Friend, The Producers

**13** Aspects of Love, Blood Brothers, Les Miserables, Man of La Mancha, The Pajama Game, West Side Story

**14** Babes in Toyland, Victor/Victoria

**15** Annie Get Your Gun, La Cage aux Folles, Mister Wonderful, Sunset Boulevard, The Sound of Music, The Woman in White

Songs from musicals include:

**03** One
**04** Fame
**05** Maria
**06** Do-Re-Mi, Memory, People
**07** America, Bali Ha'i, Cabaret, Camelot, Tonight
**08** Aquarius, Day by Day, Oklahoma!, Time Warp, Tomorrow
**09** Edelweiss, Evergreen, Footloose, Somewhere, Superstar, Tradition
**10** 42nd Street, Be Our Guest, Big Spender, Friendship, Hello, Dolly, I Am What I Am, I Got Rhythm, Matchmaker, Night Fever, Ol' Man River, Too Darn Hot, Willkommen
**11** 76 Trombones, All That Jazz,

Luck Be a Lady, Night and Day, Old Man River, Summer Lovin', Where is Love?, You're The Top

**12** All I Ask of You, Broadway Baby, Circle of Life, Dancing Queen, Easter Parade, Hakuna Matata, Mack the Knife, Makin' Whoopee, Rich Man's Frug, Shall We Dance?, Sound of Music, Staying Alive, Summer Nights, There She Goes, We Go Together

**13** Skimbleshanks, Sunrise, Sunset

**14** Ain't Misbehavin', Any Dream Will Do, Chim Chim Cher-ee, Close Every Door, I Dreamed a Dream, I Know Him So Well, Lonely Goatherd, Mr Mistoffelees, New York, New York, So Long, Farewell, They All Laughed, We're in the Money

**15** A Bushel and a Peck, Bells Are Ringing, Greased Lightnin', Honeysuckle Rose, I Am the Starlight, If I Were a Rich Man, Music of the Night, Put On a Happy Face, Send in the Clowns, Singin' in the Rain, Sunset Boulevard, Tell Me on a Sunday, The Lady is a Tramp, Till There Was You

People associated with musicals include:

**04** Bart (Lionel), Hart (Lorenz), Kaye (Danny), Kern (Jerome), Nunn (Trevor), Rice (Tim)

**05** Black (Don), Donen (Stanley), Fosse (Bob), Kelly (Gene), Lenya (Lotte), Loewe (Frederick)

**06** Berlin (Irving), Coward (Sir Noel), Gaynor (Mitzi), Jolson (Al), Lerner (Alan Jay), Merman (Ethel), Porter (Cole), Prince (Hal), Rogers (Ginger), Steele (Tommy)

**07** Astaire (Fred), Burnett (Carol), Garland (Judy), Gilbert (Sir W S), Novello (Ivor), Rodgers (Richard)

**08** Berkeley (Busby), Gershwin (George), Gershwin (Ira), Minnelli (Liza), Robinson (Bill 'Bojangles'), Sondheim (Stephen), Ziegfeld (Florenz, Jnr)

**09** Bernstein (Leonard), Macintosh (Cameron), Offenbach (Jacques)

**10** D'Oyly Carte (Richard)

**11** Hammerstein (Oscar, II), Lloyd Webber (Andrew, Lord)

Musical composition types include:

**03** jig, lay, rag
**04** aria, duet, hymn, lied, opus, raga, song, trio, tune
**05** canon, carol, étude, fugue, gigue, march, opera, piece, polka, rondo, round, suite, tango, track, waltz
**06** aubade, ballad, bolero, lieder, masque, minuet, number, pavane, shanty, sonata
**07** ballade, bourrée, cantata, fanfare, gavotte, mazurka, partita, prelude, quartet, requiem, scherzo, toccata
**08** berceuse, cavatina, chaconne, concerto, fandango, fantasia, galliard, hornpipe, madrigal,

nocturne, operetta, overture, rhapsody, saraband, serenade, sonatina, symphony, zarzuela

**09** allemande, arabesque, bagatelle, cabaletta, capriccio, écossaise, farandole, impromptu, invention, pastorale, polonaise, sarabande, spiritual, voluntary

**10** barcarolle, bergamasca, concertino, humoresque, intermezzo, opera buffa, tarantella

**11** bacchanalia, ballad opera, composition, pastourelle, sinfonietta

**12** divertimento, extravaganza

**13** missa solemnis

**14** chorale fantasy, chorale prelude, concerto grosso

See also **song**

Musical compositions include:

**04** Saul
**05** Rodeo
**06** Boléro, Elijah, Études, Façade, Images
**07** Epitaph, Jephtha, Mazeppa, Messiah
**08** Ballades, Caprices, Creation, Drum Mass, Ode to Joy, Peer Gynt
**09** Capriccio, Fantaisie, Finlandia, Jerusalem, Nocturnes
**10** Arabesques, Bacchanale, Bagatelles, Concertino, Nelson Mass, The Planets, The Seasons, Water Music
**11** Curlew River, Gymnopédies, Harmony Mass, Minute Waltz, Requiem Mass, Stabat Mater, Winterreise
**12** A Sea Symphony, Danse Macabre, Golden Sonata, Karelia Suite, Kinderscenen, Linz Symphony, Piano Fantasy, Schéhérazade, Trout Quintet
**13** Alpensinfonie, Carmina Burana, Choral Fantasy, Ebony Concerto, Faust Symphony, Fêtes Galantes, German Requiem, Israel in Egypt, Metamorphoses, Missa Solemnis, On Wenlock Edge, The Art of Fugue
**14** Canticum Sacrum, Choral Symphony, Colour Symphony, Eroica Symphony, Glagolitic Mass, Prague Symphony, Rhapsody in Blue, Slavonic Dances, The Four Seasons
**15** A Child of our Time, Alexander's Feast, Children's Corner, Emperor Concerto, Haffner Symphony, Hungarian Dances, Italian Concerto, Judas Maccabaeus, Jupiter Symphony, Kossuth Overture, Manfred Symphony, Peter and the Wolf, Sicilian Vespers

See also **opera; oratorio; song**

Musical terms include:

**03** bar, bis, cue, key, tie
**04** a due, alto, arco, bass, beat, clef, coda, fine, flat, fret, hold, mode, mute, note, part, rest, root, slur, solo, tone, tune, turn

**05** ad lib, breve, buffo, chord, dolce, drone, forte, grave, largo, lento, lyric, major, metre, minim, minor, molto, outro, pause, piano, piece, pitch, scale, score, senza, shake, sharp, staff, stave, swell, tacet, tanto, tempo, tenor, theme, triad, trill, tutti
**06** adagio, al fine, a tempo, da capo, duplet, encore, finale, legato, manual, medley, melody, octave, phrase, presto, quaver, rhythm, sempre, subito, tenuto, timbre, treble, tuning, unison, upbeat, vivace
**07** agitato, allegro, al segno, amoroso, andante, animato, attacca, bar line, cadence, con brio, concert, con moto, descant, harmony, langsam, marcato, mediant, middle C, mordent, natural, recital, refrain, roulade, soprano, tremolo, triplet, vibrato
**08** acoustic, alto clef, arpeggio, baritone, bass clef, col canto, con fuoco, crotchet, diatonic, doloroso, dominant, downbeat, ensemble, interval, maestoso, moderato, movement, ostinato, perdendo, ritenuto, semitone, semplice, sequence, staccato, vigoroso, virtuoso
**09** alla breve, cantabile, cantilena, chromatic, contralto, crescendo, glissando, harmonics, imitation, larghetto, mezza voce, microtone, non troppo, obbligato, orchestra, pizzicato, semibreve, sextuplet, sforzando, smorzando, sostenuto, sotto voce, spiritoso, tablature, tenor clef
**10** accidental, affettuoso, allargando, allegretto, consonance, diminuendo, dissonance, dotted note, dotted rest, double flat, double stop, expression, fortissimo, intonation, ledger line, mezzo forte, modulation, pedal point, pentatonic, pianissimo, quadruplet, quintuplet, resolution, semiquaver, simple time, submediant, supertonic, tonic sol-fa, treble clef, two-two time
**11** accelerando, arrangement, decrescendo, double sharp, double trill, fingerboard, leading note, quarter tone, rallentando, rinforzando, subdominant, syncopation
**12** acciaccatura, alla cappella, appoggiatura, compound time, counterpoint, four-four time, key signature, six-eight time
**13** accompaniment, double bar line, fifth interval, improvisation, major interval, minor interval, orchestration, sixth interval, sul ponticello, third interval, three-four time, time signature, transposition
**14** cross-fingering, demisemiquaver, fourth interval, second interval

**15** perfect interval, seventh interval

## musician

*Musician types include:*

**03** duo
**04** band, bard, diva, duet, trio
**05** choir, griot, group, nonet, octet, piper, waits
**06** bugler, busker, folkie, jazzer, oboist, player, sextet, singer
**07** cellist, drummer, fiddler, harpist, maestro, Orphean, pianist, quartet, quintet, soloist, violist
**08** bluesman, clarsair, composer, ensemble, flautist, lutenist, minstrel, organist, virtuoso, vocalist
**09** balladeer, conductor, guitarist, itinerant, orchestra, performer, trumpeter, violinist
**10** bassoonist, one-man band, prima donna, trombonist
**11** accompanist, saxophonist
**12** backing group, clarinettist
**13** percussionist, session singer
**15** instrumentalist, session musician

*See also* **composer; conductor; libretto; pianist; singer; songwriter**

*Classical musicians include:*

**02** **Ax** (Emmanuel), **Ma** (Yo-Yo)
**03** **Mae** (Vanessa), **Pré** (Jacqueline du)
**04** **Bell** (Joshua), **Hahn** (Hilary), **Hess** (Dame Myra), **Lupu** (Radu), **Mork** (Truls), **Wild** (Earl)
**05** **Boehm** (Theobald), **Borge** (Victor), **Bream** (Julian), **Bülow** (Hans von), **Chung** (Kyung-Wha), **Dupré** (Marcel), **Elman** (Mischa), **Grove** (Sir George), **Isbin** (Sharon), **Ogdon** (John), **Sharp** (Cecil), **Stern** (Isaac)
**06** **Casals** (Pablo), **Czerny** (Karl), **Galway** (James), **Gitlis** (Ivry), **Kissin** (Evgeny), **Köchel** (Ludwig von), **Mutter** (Anne-Sophie), **Rizzio** (David), **Schiff** (András)
**07** **Blondel**, **Glennie** (Evelyn), **Heifetz** (Jascha), **Kennedy** (Nigel), **Menuhin** (Yehudi), **Perahia** (Murray), **Perlman** (Itzhak), **Pollini** (Maurizio), **Richter** (Sviatoslav), **Russell** (David), **Segovia** (Andrés), **Shankar** (Ravi), **Starker** (Janos)
**08** **Argerich** (Martha), **Bronfman** (Yefim), **Browning** (John), **Goossens** (Léon), **Helfgott** (David), **Holliger** (Heinz), **Horowitz** (Vladimir), **Kreisler** (Fritz), **Paganini** (Niccolò), **Sarasate** (Pablo), **Steinway** (Henry), **Vengerov** (Maxim), **Williams** (John)
**09** **Ashkenazy** (Vladimir), **Barenboim** (Daniel), **Benedetti** (Nicola), **Boulanger** (Nadia), **Broadwood** (John), **Dolmetsch** (Arnold), **Guarnieri**, **Tortelier** (Paul)
**10** **Cristofori** (Bartolomeo), **de Larrocha** (Alicia), **Paderewski** (Ignacy), **Rubinstein** (Anton), **Rubinstein** (Artur), **Stradivari** (Antonio), **Villa-Lobos** (Heitor), **Williamson** (Malcolm)

**11** **Theodorakis** (Mikis)
**12** **Guido d'Arezzo**, **Rostropovich** (Mstislav)
**14** **Jaques-Dalcroze** (Emile)

## musing
**05** study **07** reverie **08** dreaming, studying, thinking **10** brown study, cogitation, meditation, ponderment, reflection, rumination **11** abstraction, cerebration, daydreaming **13** contemplation, introspection, woolgathering

## musk
**04** must **05** civet, moust, muist, scent **07** mimulus

## musket
**05** fusee, fusil **06** gingal, jezail, jingal **07** caliver, dragoon, gingall **08** Biscayan **09** brown Bess, queen's-arm **10** musquetoon

## musketeer
**12** mousquetaire

*Musketeers include:*

**05** Athos
**06** Aramis
**07** Porthos
**09** D'Artagnan

## Muslim

*Muslims include:*

**04** Shia
**05** Shiah, Sunni
**06** Senusi, Shiite
**07** Alawite, dervish, Mevlevi, Senussi, Sonnite, Sunnite
**08** Senoussi
**10** Karmathian
**11** Black Muslim
**15** whirling dervish

## muslin
**04** leno, mull **05** sails **06** canvas, gurrah, mulmul **07** jamdani, mulmull, organdy **08** coteline, nainsook, organdie, tarlatan **09** persienne **10** mousseline

## muss
◇ *anagram indicator* **03** row **04** mess **06** ruffle, tousle **08** dishevel, disorder, scramble **09** confusion **10** disarrange, make untidy **11** disturbance, make a mess of

## mussel
**04** Unio **06** muscle, muskle **07** Modiola, Mytilus **08** deer horn, Modiolus **09** clabby-doo, clappy-doo, date-shell

## must
◇ *anagram indicator* **03** man, mun **04** amok, duty, maun, mote, musk, stum **05** amuck, basic, mould **06** frenzy, powder **09** essential, necessity, provision, requisite **10** imperative, obligation, sine qua non **11** fundamental, requirement, stipulation **12** fermentation, prerequisite

## mustard
**05** runch, senvy **08** charlock, flix-weed

**09** praiseach **10** sauce-alone **14** jack-by-the-hedge

## muster

**04** mass, meet **05** enrol, group, rally **06** call up, gather, number, parade, review, summon, throng **07** collect, convene, convoke, display, example, hosting, marshal, meeting, round up, round-up, turnout **08** assemble, assembly, mobilize, register, summon up **09** concourse, gathering, march past **10** assemblage, collection, congregate, convention, inspection **11** convocation **12** call together, come together, congregation, mobilization **13** bring together, demonstration **14** gather together
• **pass muster 07** shape up **09** measure up **10** be accepted, fit the bill **11** fill the bill **12** be acceptable, be good enough, make the grade **15** come up to scratch

## musty

◇ *anagram indicator* **04** amok, damp, dank **05** amuck, frowy, funky, fusty, mucid, stale **06** fousty, frowie, mochie, mouldy, smelly, stuffy **07** airless, decayed, foughty, froughy, mildewy, vinewed **08** decaying, mildewed

## mutability

**09** variation **11** variability **12** alterability **13** permutability **14** changeableness

## mutable

**06** fickle **08** changing, flexible, unstable, unsteady, variable, volatile, wavering **09** adaptable, alterable, uncertain, unsettled **10** changeable, inconstant, irresolute, permutable, unreliable **11** vacillating **12** inconsistent, undependable **15** interchangeable

## mutate

◇ *anagram indicator* **05** alter, morph **06** change, evolve, modify, remake **07** convert, remodel, reshape **09** transform, translate, transmute **11** transfigure **12** metamorphose, transmogrify

## mutation

◇ *anagram indicator* **06** change **07** anomaly **09** deviation, evolution, inversion, variation **10** adaptation, alteration, revolution **11** vicissitude **12** modification **13** metamorphosis **14** transformation

## mute

**03** mum **04** dull, dumb, stop **05** lower **06** dampen, damper, deaden, muffle, shtoom, silent, soften, stifle, subdue **07** aphasic, plosive, quieten, silence, smother, sordino **08** moderate, sourdine, suppress, taciturn, tone down, unspoken, wordless **09** noiseless, soft-pedal, voiceless **10** speechless **11** unexpressed **12** unpronounced **15** uncommunicative

## muted

**04** dull, soft **05** faint, quiet, sorda, sordo **06** low-key, subtle **07** muffled, stifled,

subdued **08** dampened, discreet, softened **10** restrained, suppressed

## mutely

**06** dumbly **08** silently **09** in silence **10** taciturnly **11** noiselessly, voicelessly **12** speechlessly

## mutilate

◇ *anagram indicator* **03** cut, mar **04** hack, lame, maim, ruin **05** cut up, spoil **06** censor, damage, garble, hack up, hamble, impair, injure, mangle **07** butcher, concise, cripple, disable, distort **08** lacerate **09** disfigure, dismember **10** bowdlerize, detruncate **11** cut to pieces

## mutilation

◇ *anagram indicator* **06** damage **07** maiming **10** amputation **12** detruncation, dismembering **13** disfigurement

## mutinous

◇ *anagram indicator* **06** unruly **07** bolshie, riotous **09** insurgent, seditious **10** disorderly, rebellious, refractory, subversive **11** anarchistic, disobedient **12** contumacious, ungovernable, unsubmissive **13** insubordinate, revolutionary **14** uncontrollable

## mutiny

**04** defy, riot **05** rebel **06** resist, revolt, rise up, rising, strife, strike, tumult **07** disobey, protest **08** defiance, uprising **09** rebellion **10** insurgence, resistance, revolution **12** disobedience, insurrection **15** insubordination

## mutt

**03** cur, dog **04** dolt, fool, kuri **05** bitch, hound, idiot, moron, pooch **07** mongrel **08** imbecile **09** blockhead, ignoramus, thickhead **10** dunderhead

## mutter

◇ *homophone indicator* **04** beef, carp, fuss, mump, roin **05** gripe, royne, whine **06** grouse, mumble, murmur, object, rumble, whinge, witter **07** chunder, chunner, chunter, grumble, maunder, protest, stutter, whitter **08** chounter, complain, splutter **09** bellyache, criticize, find fault, murmuring, mussitate **14** talk to yourself, whittie-whattie

## mutton

**02** em **05** gigot, macon, sheep, traik **07** haricot **09** Irish stew, Southdown **10** Fanny Adams **13** colonial goose

## mutual

**05** joint **06** common, shared **09** commutual, exchanged **10** collective, commonable, reciprocal **12** interchanged **13** complementary **15** interchangeable

## muzzle

**03** gag **04** mute **05** check, choke, snout **06** censor, fetter, stifle **07** inhibit, silence **08** gunpoint, restrain, suppress

## muzzy

**04** hazy **05** dazed, faint, fuzzy, mused, tipsy **06** addled, groggy **07** blurred, muddled, unclear **08** confused

**09** befuddled, unfocused **10** bewildered, indistinct

## my

**01** m' **02** ha **03** cor, gad, lor **04** gosh, well **08** 

## Myanmar

**03** BUR, MMR, MYA

## myopic

**06** narrow, unwise **08** purblind **09** half-blind, imprudent, localized, parochial, short-term **11** near-sighted, thoughtless **12** narrow-minded, short-sighted **13** ill-considered, unadventurous, uncircumspect, unimaginative

## myriad

**03** sea **04** army, host, raft **05** flood, horde, swarm, toman **06** scores, throng, untold **08** millions, mountain, zillions **09** boundless, countless, limitless, multitude, thousands **10** numberless **11** innumerable **12** immeasurable, incalculable **13** multitudinous

## mysterious

◇ *anagram indicator* **04** dark **05** shady, weird **06** arcane, creepy, hidden, mystic, occult, secret, veiled **07** cryptic, curious, furtive, obscure, shadowy, strange **08** abstruse, baffling, esoteric, mystical, puzzling, reticent, sinister **09** enigmatic, insoluble, recondite, secretive **10** mystifying, perplexing **11** as if by magic, inscrutable **12** inexplicable, unfathomable, unsearchable **13** surreptitious

## mysteriously

◇ *anagram indicator* **08** arcanely, in secret, secretly **09** curiously, magically, obscurely, strangely **10** abstrusely, mystically, puzzlingly **11** cryptically, inscrutably **12** esoterically, inexplicably **13** enigmatically **15** surreptitiously

## mystery

**06** enigma, puzzle, riddle, secret **07** arcanum, problem, secrecy **08** mystique, question **09** ambiguity, conundrum, curiosity, obscurity, reticence, sacrament, weirdness **10** closed book **11** concealment, furtiveness, miracle play, strangeness **12** question mark **14** inscrutability **15** inexplicability, unfathomability

## mystic

**04** Sofi, Sufi **05** swami **07** psychic **09** occultist, spiritist **11** allegorical, esotericist **12** spiritualist **13** metaphysicist **15** supernaturalist

## mystical

**05** weird **06** arcane, hidden, mystic, occult **07** obscure, strange **08** abstruse, baffling, esoteric **09** recondite, spiritual **10** mysterious, paranormal **12** inexplicable, metaphysical, other-worldly, supernatural, unfathomable **13** preternatural **14** transcendental

## mysticism

**05** deism **06** theism **07** mystery

**09** occultism, spiritism **10** arcaneness
**11** esotericism **12** spirituality
**14** mysteriousness **15** inexplicability,
supernaturalism

**mystification**
**03** awe, fog **04** daze **06** muddle
**08** surprise **09** confusion **10** perplexity,
puzzlement **11** uncertainty
**12** bewilderment, stupefaction
**13** disconcertion **14** disorientation

**mystify**
**04** hoax **06** baffle, puzzle **07** confuse,
flummox, perplex **08** bewilder,
confound **09** bamboozle **10** take to
town **13** metagrabolize, metagrobolize

**mystique**
**03** awe **05** charm, magic, spell
**06** appeal **07** glamour, mystery,
romance, secrecy **08** charisma
**09** adventure **11** fascination

**myth**
**03** fib, lie **04** saga, tale **05** fable, fancy,
story **06** legend **07** fallacy, fantasy,
fiction, parable, untruth **08** allegory,
bestiary, delusion, folk tale, pretence
**09** fairy tale, invention, tall story
**10** fairy story **11** fabrication
**13** misconception
• **book of myths** **04** Edda **09** Elder
Edda, Prose Edda **11** Younger Edda

**mythical**
**05** put-on **06** fabled, made-up, phoney,
unreal, untrue **07** fantasy, pretend
**08** fabulous, fanciful, invented
**09** fairytale, fantastic, imaginary,
legendary, pretended **10** chimerical,
fabricated, fictitious **11** make-believe,
non-existent **12** mythological

*Mythical creatures and spirits
include:*

**03** elf, hob, imp, orc, roc
**04** faun, fury, jinn, ogre, peri, pixy,
puck, yeti
**05** afrit, demon, devil, djinn, dobby,
dryad, dwarf, fairy, genie, ghost,
ghoul, giant, gnome, golem,
harpy, kelpy, lamia, naiad,
nymph, oread, pixie, satyr, shade,
Siren, sylph, troll, yowie
**06** afreet, bunyip, dobbie, dragon,
dybbuk, Fafnir, Furies, Geryon,
goblin, Gorgon, kelpie, kobald,
kraken, Lilith, Medusa, merman,
nereid, ogress, Scylla, selkie,
Sphinx, sprite, wivern,
yaksha
**07** banshee, Bigfoot, brownie,
Cecrops, centaur, Chimera,
Cyclops, Echidna, Erinyes,
gremlin, Grendel, griffin, Harpies,
incubus, Lorelei, mermaid,
Pegasus, phoenix, sandman,
taniwha, unicorn, vampire,
windigo
**08** basilisk, Cerberus, Gigantes,
lindworm, Minotaur,
seahorse, succubus,
werewolf
**09** Charybdis, hamadryad,
hobgoblin, mermaiden,
sasquatch

**10** cockatrice, hippogriff,
leprechaun, salamander, sea
serpent, tooth fairy
**11** hippocampus
**15** Loch Ness monster

*See also* **bird; monster**

*Mythical places include:*

**03** Dis, Hel
**04** Hell, Styx
**05** Argos, Babel, Hades, Lethe, Pluto,
Thule
**06** Albion, Anghar, Asgard, Avalon,
Heaven, Heorot, Nedyet, Utgard
**07** Acheron, Agartha, Alfheim,
Alpheus, Arcadia, Bifrost,
Boeotia, Elysium, Lemuria,
Nirvana, Pohjola, Tuonela
**08** Amazonia, Archeron, Atlantis, El
Dorado, Niflheim, Paradise, Tir-
na-nOg, Tlalocan, Valhalla,
Vanaheim
**09** Cockaigne, Fairyland, Purgatory,
River Styx, Yggdrasil
**10** River Lethe, Stymphalos
**11** Ultima Thule
**12** River Acheron, River Alpheus
**13** Jewel Mountain, River Archeron,
The Underworld
**14** Lake Stymphalos
**15** Cloudcuckooland, The Garden of
Eden, The Isle of Avalon, The
Tower of Babel

*See also* **mythology; river**

**mythological**
**06** fabled, mythic **08** fabulous,
mythical **09** fairytale, folkloric,
legendary **10** fictitious **11** traditional

**mythology**
**04** lore **05** myths, tales **06** legend
**07** stories **08** folklore, Pantheon **09** folk
tales, tradition **10** traditions

*Characters from Celtic mythology
include:*

**03** Anu, Lug
**04** Badb, Bran, Danu, Lugh, Medb,
Ogma
**05** Balor, Boann, Dagda, Macha,
Maeve, Neman, Nuada, Oisin,
Pwyll
**06** Brigit, Danaan, Deidre, Imbolc,
Isolde, Ogmios, Ossian
**07** banshee, Beltane, Branwen,
Brighid, Deirdre, Samhain, Tristan
**08** Manannan, Morrigan, Rhiannon,
The Dagda, Tir nan-Og
**09** Bean Sidhé, Cernunnos,
Conchobar
**10** Cú Chulainn, Lughnasadh
**11** Finn mac Cool
**13** Bendigeidfran, Finn mac
Cumhal
**14** Bran the Blessed, Finn mac
Cumhail, Tuatha dé Danaan

*Characters from Greek mythology
include:*

**02** Io
**04** Ajax, Dido, Echo, Eris, Hero,
Leda, Leto, Rhea
**05** Atlas, Chloe, Circe, Creon,
Danae, Helen, Horae, Hydra,

Irene, Ixion, Jason, Kreon, Laius,
Lamia, Medea, Midas, Minos,
Niobe, Orion, Paris, Priam,
Rheia
**06** Aeneas, Aeolus, Alecto, Amazon,
Atreus, Cadmus, Castor, Charon,
Chiron, Cronus, Danaoi, Daphne,
Dryads, Europa, Europe, Furies,
Graiae, Hecabe, Hector, Hecuba,
Hellen, Icarus, Iolaus, Kronos,
Latona, Medusa, Megara,
Memnon, Naiads, Nessus,
Nestor, Nymphs, Oreads, Peleus,
Pelops, Phoebe, Pollux, Python,
Satyrs, Scylla, Semele, Sileni,
Sirens, Stheno, Syrinx, Titans,
Triton, Typhon
**07** Actaeon, Alcyone, Arachne,
Ariadne, Calchas, Calypso,
Cecrops, Cepheus, Chimera,
Cyclops, Danaans, Daphnis,
Diomede, Echidna, Electra,
Epigoni, Erinyes, Euryale,
Galatea, Gorgons, Griffin,
Gryphon, Harpies, Iapetus,
Jocasta, Kekrops, Laocoon,
Lapiths, Leander, Maenads,
Marsyas, Nereids, Oceanus,
Oedipus, Orestes, Orpheus,
Pandora, Pegasus, Perseus,
Phaedra, Silenus,
Theseus, Titania, Troilus, Ulysses
**08** Achilles, Alcestis, Alcmaeon,
Anchises, Antigone, Arethusa,
Atalanta, Basilisk, Centaurs,
Cerberus, Chimaera, Cressida,
Cyclopes, Daedalus, Diomedes,
Endymion, Eteocles, Eurydice,
Ganymede, Gigantes, Halcyone,
Heracles, Hyperion, Iphicles,
Lycurgus, Meleager, Menelaus,
Minotaur, Nausicaa, Oceanids,
Odysseus, Pasiphae, Penelope,
Pentheus, Phaethon, Pleiades,
Sarpedon, Sisyphus,
Tantalus, Thyestes, Tiresias,
Typhoeus
**09** Aegisthus, Agamemnon,
Andromeda, Argonauts,
Autolycus, Cassandra, Charybdis,
Deucalion, Idomeneus,
Lotophagi, Mnemosyne,
Myrmidons, Narcissus, Patroclus,
Polynices, Pygmalion, Semiramis,
Tisiphone
**10** Amphitryon, Andromache,
Cassiopeia, Cockatrice,
Erechtheus, Hamadryads,
Hesperides, Hippolytus,
Iphigeneia, Polyneices,
Polyphemus, Procrustes,
Prometheus, Telemachus
**11** Bellerophon, Lotus-eaters,
Neoptolemus, Philoctetes
**12** Clytemnestra, Hyperboreans,
Rhadamanthus,
Rhadamanthys

*Characters from Maori mythology
include:*

**04** Kupe, Maui, Rona
**05** Pania
**07** Hinemoa, Mahuika
**09** Tutanekai

*Characters from Norse mythology include:*

03 Lif
06 Gudrun, Sigurd
09 Berserker
10 Lifthrasir

*Characters from Roman mythology include:*

05 Lamia, Lares, Manes, Remus, Sibyl
07 Danaans, Latinus, Lemures, Lucrece, Penates, Romulus, Sibylla, Tarpeia
08 Anchises, Callisto, Hercules, Lucretia, Verginia
09 Androcles
10 Coriolanus, Rhea Silvia, Rhea Sylvia

*Other mythological and legendary characters include:*

03 **Qat**
04 **Tell** (William)
05 **Adapa**, **El Cid**, **Faust**, **Frost** (Jack)
06 **Anansi**, **Arthur**, **Bunyan** (Paul), **Enkidu**, **George** (St), **Godiva** (Lady), **Kraken**, **Weland**
07 **Aladdin**, **Ali Baba**, **Beowulf**, **Grendel**, **Wayland**, **Weiland**, **Weyland**
08 **Baba Yaga**, **Brunhild**, **Hang Tuah**, **Hiawatha**, **Parsifal**
09 **Appleseed** (Johnny), **Bluebeard**, **Lohengrin**
10 **Yu the Great**
11 **Old King Cole**
12 **Lemminkainen**, **Rip Van Winkle**, **Scheherazade**, **Will-o'-the-Wisp**
14 **Flying Dutchman**
15 **Father Christmas**

*See also* **fate; fury; god, goddess; grace; monster; muse; sage**

# N

**N**
**02** en **08** November

**nab**
**03** hat **04** bone, grab, head, nail, nick
**05** catch, run in, seize **06** arrest, collar,
nobble, pull in, snatch **07** capture,
hilltop **09** apprehend **10** projection,
promontory

**nabob**
**03** VIP **05** celeb, nawab **06** bigwig,
tycoon **07** magnate **08** luminary
**09** celebrity, financier, personage
**11** billionaire, millionaire, zillionaire

**nadir**
**04** zero **06** bottom, depths **07** minimum
**08** low point **10** all-time low, rock
bottom **11** lowest point **12** low-
watermark

**nag**
**03** bug, rip, tit, vex **04** carp, hack, jade,
moan, moke, plug, yaff **05** annoy,
harry, horse, scold, tease, worry
**06** badger, berate, bother, grouse,
harass, hassle, keep at, keffel, niggle,
pester, pick on, plague, rouncy
**07** earbash, henpeck, torment, trouble,
upbraid **08** complain, ding-dong,
irritate, keep on at **09** aggravate,
Rosinante, Rozinante

**nagging**
**06** aching **07** moaning, painful
**08** critical, niggling, scolding,
shrewish, worrying **09** upsetting
**10** continuous, irritating, nit-picking,
persistent, tormenting **11** distressing

**nail**
**03** fix, nab, pin, toe **04** brad, brod,
claw, grab, join, nick, stub, stud, tack,
trap **05** catch, clout, rivet, screw, seize,
spick, spike, sprig, talon **06** arrest,
attach, collar, corner, detect, expose,
fasten, hammer, nipper, nobble,
pierce, pincer, reveal, secure, skewer,
snatch, tingle, unguis, unmask
**07** capture, clinker, pin down, toenail,
uncover, unearth **08** fastener, holdfast,
identify, panel pin, sparable
**09** apprehend **10** fingernail, tenterhook
• **hit the nail on the head 10** be
accurate **14** be exactly right, score a
bull's eye

**naïve**
**04** naif, open **05** frank, green
**06** candid, jejune, simple **07** artless,
natural **08** gullible, immature,
innocent, trusting, wide-eyed
**09** childlike, credulous, guileless,
ingenuous, primitive, simpliste, small-
town, unworldly **10** simplistic,

unaffected **11** unrealistic **12** having no
idea, pollyannaish, unsuspecting,
unsuspicious **13** born yesterday,
inexperienced, unpretentious
**14** bread-and-butter **15** unsophisticated

**naively**
**06** simply **08** gullibly **09** artlessly,
naturally **10** immaturely, innocently
**11** guilelessly, ingenuously
**14** simplistically, unsuspiciously

**naivety**
**08** openness **09** credulity, frankness,
innocence **10** candidness, immaturity,
simplicity **11** artlessness, gullibility,
naturalness **12** inexperience
**13** childlikeness, guilelessness,
ingenuousness

**naked**
**03** raw **04** bald, bare, nude, open,
weak **05** overt, plain, stark **06** Adamic,
barren, patent, simple **07** artless,
blatant, denuded, evident, exposed,
glaring, skyclad, unarmed
**08** Adamical, disrobed, flagrant,
helpless, in the raw, starkers, stripped,
treeless, undraped **09** au naturel,
grassless, in the buff, in the scud,
powerless, unadorned, unclothed,
uncovered, undressed, unguarded
**10** stark-naked, start-naked,
unprovided, vulnerable
**11** defenceless, mother-naked,
unconcealed, undisguised,
unprotected, unqualified, unvarnished
**12** not a stitch on **13** with nothing on
**15** in the altogether

**nakedness**
**06** nature, nudity **07** the buff, undress
**08** baldness, bareness, openness
**09** plainness, starkness **10** barrenness,
simplicity **13** the altogether

**namby-pamby**
**03** wet **04** prim, weak **05** cissy, soppy,
vapid, weedy, wussy **06** feeble, prissy
**07** anaemic, insipid, maudlin,
mawkish, wimpish **09** spineless, white-
shoe **10** colourless, wishy-washy
**11** sentimental **12** pretty-pretty

**name**
**01** n **03** dub, nom, tag, VIP **04** call, cite,
clan, fame, hero, nemn, note, noun,
pick, star, term **05** celeb, label, state,
style, title, utter **06** behalf, bigwig,
choose, esteem, expert, family,
famous, handle, honour, renown,
repute, select **07** appoint, baptize, big
name, entitle, epithet, mention,
specify **08** big noise, christen, classify,
cognomen, eminence, identify,
luminary, monicker, nominate,
prestige, somebody, standing
**09** authority, celebrity, character,
designate, dignitary, sobriquet, well-
known **10** commission, denominate,
give name to, popularity, prominence,
reputation, soubriquet **11** appellation,
designation, distinction
**12** denomination, leading light

*Names include:*

**03** pen, pet
**04** code, full, last

**05** alias, brand, false, first, given,
place, stage
**06** anonym, eponym, exonym,
family, maiden, middle, proper,
second
**07** agnomen, allonym, assumed,
autonym, surname, toponym
**08** nickname
**09** baptismal, Christian, cryptonym,
pseudonym, sobriquet, trademark
**10** diminutive, nom de plume,
soubriquet
**11** nom de guerre

*See also* **boy; cinema; French;
German; girl; Irish; public house;
Scottish; welsh**
• **in name only 07** titular
• **list of names 04** roll
• **name unknown 02** NU

**named**
**03** dit, hot **04** hote **05** cited, nempt
**06** called, chosen, dubbed, picked,
styled, termed, titled, yclept **07** known
as **08** baptized, entitled, labelled,
selected **09** appointed, mentioned,
nominated, specified **10** christened,
classified, designated, identified,
singled out **11** by the name of,
denominated **12** commissioned

**nameless**
**07** obscure, unknown, unnamed
**08** untitled **09** anonymous, titleless,
unheard-of **10** innominate, unlabelled
**11** unspeakable, unspecified,
unutterable **12** illegitimate,
undesignated, unidentified
**13** indescribable, inexpressible,
unmentionable **15** undistinguished

**namely**
**02** ie, sc **03** viz **04** scil, sciz **05** to wit
**06** famous, that is **08** scilicet
**09** videlicet **10** especially **11** that is to
say **12** in other words, specifically

**Namibia**
**03** NAM

**nanny**
**03** nan, pet **04** amah, ayah, baby, nana
**05** nanna, nurse, spoil **06** au pair,
coddle, cosset, mother, pamper
**07** indulge, she-goat **08** pander to, wet-
nurse **09** governess, nursemaid, spoon-
feed **11** childminder, grandmother,
mollycoddle, mother's help,
overprotect

**nanosecond**
**02** ns

**nap**
**03** kip, nod, ziz **04** down, doze, fuzz,
oose, ooze, pile, rest, shag, zizz
**05** fibre, grain, seize, sleep, steal,
weave **06** catnap, nod off, siesta,
snooze **07** bedding, bedroll, doze off,
drop off, lie down, lie-down, surface,
texture **08** meridian, napoleon
**09** downiness **10** forty winks, light
sleep **12** sleep lightly **14** get some shut-
eye, have forty winks

**napkin**
**05** doily, doyly, nappy **06** doyley
**09** muckender, serviette
**12** handkerchief

## nappy

**04** oosy, oozy **05** downy, heady, jumpy, terry, tipsy, towel **06** diaper, frothy, hippen, hippin, napkin, shaggy, strong **07** hipping, nervous **09** excitable, serviette **10** disposable

## narcissism

**06** vanity **07** conceit, egotism **08** egomania, self-love **10** self-regard **11** self-conceit **13** egocentricity, self-obsession **15** self-centredness

## narcissistic

**04** vain **09** conceited, egotistic **10** egocentric, self-loving **11** egomaniacal, self-centred **12** self-absorbed, self-obsessed

## narcotic

**03** hop **04** dopy, drug **05** dopey, upper **06** downer, opiate **07** anodyne, calming, dulling, numbing **08** hypnotic, sedative **09** analgesic, somnolent, soporific **10** painkiller, palliative, stupefying **11** anaesthetic, pain-dulling, painkilling **12** sleeping pill, stupefacient **13** sleep-inducing, tranquillizer **14** tranquillizing

*Narcotics include:*

**03** ava
**04** bang, benj, coca, dope, kava
**05** bhang, dagga
**06** charas, datura, pituri
**07** churrus, narceen
**08** narceine
**10** belladonna
**11** Indian berry, laurel-water
**15** cocculus indicus

*See also* **drug**
• **packet of narcotic 04** deck

## narked

**05** irked, riled, vexed **06** bugged, galled, miffed, peeved, piqued **07** annoyed, in a huff, nettled **08** bothered, in a paddy, provoked **09** irritated **10** brassed off, cheesed off, got the hump **11** exasperated

## narrate

◇ *homophone indicator* **04** read, tell **05** state **06** detail, recite, record, relate, report, set out, unfold **07** explain, portray, recount **08** describe, rehearse, set forth **09** chronicle

## narration

**04** tale **05** story **06** detail, report, sketch **07** account, history, reading, recital, telling **09** chronicle, portrayal, recountal, rehearsal, statement, voice-over **11** description, explanation **12** storytelling

## narrative

**04** saga, tale **05** fable, novel, prose, récit, story **06** detail, report, sketch **07** account, history, process, reading, romance **08** allegory, anecdote, periplus, relation **09** chronicle, portrayal, statement **10** short story **11** description

## narrator

**06** author, writer **07** relater, relator, sagaman **08** annalist, reporter **09** describer, raconteur, recounter **10** anecdotist, chronicler, tale-teller **11** commentator, storyteller **12** mythographer

## narrow

**03** set **04** fine, keen, slim, thin, true **05** close, cramp, exact, limit, petty, rigid, scant, small, spare, taper, tight **06** biased, meagre, reduce, strait, strict **07** bigoted, confine, cramped, insular, limited, literal, precise, slender, tighten **08** confined, contract, detailed, diminish, dogmatic, exiguous, original, restrict, simplify, squeezed, straiten, tapering, thorough **09** attenuate, coarctate, constrict, hidebound, illiberal **10** attenuated, contracted, intolerant, prejudiced, restricted **11** close-minded, constricted, incapacious, reactionary, small-minded, strait-laced **12** circumscribe, conservative, incommodious, narrow-minded, parsimonious **13** circumscribed, dyed-in-the-wool

## narrowing

**06** intake **08** stenosis, tapering, thinning **09** gathering, reduction, reductive **10** emaciation, rebatement **11** attenuation, compression, contraction, curtailment **12** constipation, constriction

## narrowly

**04** fine, just, near **06** barely, strait **07** closely, exactly **08** only just, scarcely, straitly, strictly **09** carefully, precisely **10** by a whisker **11** attentively **12** by a short head **13** painstakingly **14** scrutinizingly

## narrow-minded

**03** set **05** borné, petty, rigid **06** biased, warped **07** bigoted, diehard, insular, redneck, twisted **08** blimpish, verkramp **09** claustral, exclusive, hidebound, illiberal, jaundiced, parochial **10** entrenched, inflexible, intolerant, prejudiced, provincial **11** close-minded, opinionated, petty-minded, reactionary, small-minded, strait-laced **12** conservative, unreasonable **13** dyed in the wool

## narrow-mindedness

**04** bias **07** bigotry **08** rigidity **09** prejudice **12** parochialism **13** exclusiveness, inflexibility **15** close-mindedness, petty-mindedness, small-mindedness

## narrowness

**04** bias **07** bigotry **08** nearness, rigidity, thinness **09** closeness, pettiness, prejudice, tightness **10** insularity, limitation, meagreness **11** attenuation, intolerance, slenderness **12** conservatism, constriction, parochialism **13** exclusiveness, provincialism **14** restrictedness **15** small-mindedness

## narrows

**05** sound **07** channel, passage, straits **08** waterway

## nascent

**05** young **06** rising **07** budding, growing **08** evolving, naissant **09** advancing, beginning, embryonic, incipient **10** burgeoning, developing

## nastily

◇ *anagram indicator* **11** obnoxiously, offensively, repulsively **12** disagreeably, disgustingly, unpleasantly **13** objectionably

## nastiness

**04** porn **05** filth, spite **06** malice **07** squalor **08** foulness, impurity, meanness **09** dirtiness, indecency, obscenity, pollution **10** defilement, filthiness, smuttiness **11** malevolence, pornography, viciousness **12** horribleness, spitefulness **13** offensiveness, repulsiveness, uncleanliness, unsavouriness **14** unpleasantness

## nasty

◇ *anagram indicator* **03** wet **04** blue, foul, good, mean, rank, sore, vile, wild **05** awful, crook, cruel, dirty, dodgy, foggy, grave, mucky, rainy, ribby, rough, yucky **06** filthy, grotty, horrid, lovely, odious, ribald, smutty, stormy, tricky, unkind **07** awkward, hateful, noisome, obscene, serious, squalid, vicious **08** alarming, annoying, critical, delicate, horrible, indecent, nauseous, polluted, spiteful, ticklish, worrying **09** dangerous, difficult, loathsome, malicious, obnoxious, offensive, repellent, repugnant, repulsive, revolting, sickening **10** disgusting, ill-natured, malevolent, malodorous, unpleasant **11** bad-tempered, disquieting, distasteful, threatening **12** disagreeable, exasperating, pornographic **13** objectionable

## nation

**04** folk, land, race, volk **05** realm, state, tribe **06** people, public, vassal **07** country, kingdom, society **08** republic **09** community **10** population
*See also* **Africa; America; Asia; country; Europe**

## national

**01** N **03** Nat **05** civic, civil, state **06** native, public, social **07** citizen, federal, general, subject **08** domestic, internal, resident **10** inhabitant, nationwide, widespread **11** countrywide **12** governmental **13** comprehensive
*See also* **park**

## nationalism

**07** loyalty **08** jingoism **10** allegiance, chauvinism, patriotism, xenophobia

## nationalist

**01** N **03** Nat **07** patriot **08** jingoist, loyalist **09** flag-waver, xenophobe **10** chauvinist

## nationalistic

**05** loyal **09** patriotic **10** jingoistic, xenophobic **12** chauvinistic **13** ethnocentrist

## nationality

**04** clan, race **05** birth, tribe **06** nation **11** citizenship, ethnic group

*Nationalities include:*

**03** Lao
**04** Kiwi, Thai
**05** Bajan, Congo, Cuban, Czech, Dutch, Greek, Iraqi, Irish, Omani, Saudi, Swazi, Swiss, Tajik, Uzbek, Welsh
**06** Afghan, Danish, Fijian, French, German, Indian, Kenyan, Kyrgyz, Libyan, Malian, Polish, Qatari, Samoan, Somali, Syrian, Tongan, Yapese, Yemeni
**07** Angolan, Basotho, Belgian, Bosnian, British, Burmese, Chadian, Chilean, Chinese, Comoran, Cypriot, Emirati, English, Finnish, Gambian, Guinean, Haitian, Iranian, Israeli, Italian, Ivorian, Kosraen, Kuwaiti, Laotian, Latvian, Maltese, Mexican, Monacan, Mosotho, Nauruan, Palauan, Russian, Rwandan, Sahrawi, Serbian, Spanish, Swedish, Tadzhik, Turkish, Turkmen, Ugandan, Zambian
**08** Albanian, Algerian, American, Andorran, Antiguan, Armenian, Austrian, Bahamian, Bahraini, Barbudan, Batswana, Belizean, Beninese, Bolivian, Bruneian, Canadian, Chuukese, Croatian, Egyptian, Eritrean, Estonian, Filipina, Filipino, Gabonese, Georgian, Ghanaian, Grenadan, Guyanese, Honduran, Jamaican, Japanese, Lebanese, Liberian, Malagasy, Malawian, Moldovan, Moroccan, Motswana, Namibian, Nepalese, Nevisian, Nigerian, Nigerien, Peruvian, Romanian, Sahraoui, Scottish, St Lucian, Sudanese, Timorese, Togolese, Tunisian, Tuvaluan
**09** Argentine, Barbadian, Bhutanese, Brazilian, Bulgarian, Burkinabé, Burundian, Cambodian, Colombian, Congolese, Dominican, Ethiopian, Grenadian, Hungarian, Icelandic, I-Kiribati, Jordanian, Kittitian, Malaysian, Maldivian, Mauritian, Mongolian, Ni-Vanuatu, Norwegian, Pakistani, Pohnpeian, Sahrawian, Santoméan, São Toméan, Singapore, Slovakian, Slovenian, Sri Lankan, Taiwanese, Tanzanian, Ukrainian, Uruguayan
**10** Australian, Belarusian, Costa Rican, Djiboutian, Ecuadorean, Ecuadorian, Guatemalan, Indonesian, Lithuanian, Luxembourg, Macedonian, Monégasque, Mozambican, Myanmarese, New Zealand, Nicaraguan, Panamanian, Paraguayan, Philippine, Portuguese, Sahraouian, Salvadoran, Senegalese, Surinamese, Tobagonian, Venezuelan, Vietnamese, Vincentian, Zimbabwean

**11** Argentinian, Azerbaijani, Bangladeshi, Cameroonian, Cape Verdean, Kazakhstani, Marshallese, Mauritanian, Micronesian, Montenegrin, North Korean, Sammarinese, Seychellois, Singaporean, South Korean, Tajikistani, Trinidadian
**12** Luxembourger, Saudi Arabian, South African, St Vincentian
**13** Equatoguinean, Herzegovinian, Liechtenstein, Sierra Leonean
**14** Central African, Guinea-Bissauan
**15** Liechtensteiner, Papua New Guinean, Solomon Islander

**nationally**
**09** generally **10** nationwide
**11** countrywide **15** comprehensively

**National Trust**
**02** NT

**nationwide**
**05** state **07** general, overall **08** national
**09** extensive **10** widespread
**11** countrywide **12** coast-to-coast
**13** comprehensive

**native**
**03** nat, son **04** home **05** local, natal
**06** inborn, inbred, innate, mother, oyster **07** built-in, citizen, connate, dweller, genuine, natural **08** domestic, home-born, home-bred, indigene, inherent, national, original, resident
**09** aborigine, home-grown, ingrained, inherited, intrinsic, intuitive
**10** aboriginal, autochthon, congenital, hereditary, indigenous, inhabitant, vernacular **11** instinctive
**13** autochthonous, tangata whenua
**15** unsophisticated
*See also* **African; American; Asian; European**

**nativity**
**04** putz **05** birth **06** jataka **08** delivery
**09** horoscope **10** childbirth
**11** parturition

**NATO**

*NATO members:*

**02** UK
**03** USA
**05** Italy, Spain
**06** Canada, France, Greece, Latvia, Norway, Poland, Turkey
**07** Albania, Belgium, Croatia, Denmark, Estonia, Germany, Hungary, Iceland, Romania
**08** Bulgaria, Portugal, Slovakia, Slovenia
**09** Lithuania
**10** Luxembourg
**13** Czech Republic, United Kingdom
**14** The Netherlands
**21** United States of America

• **NATO phonetic alphabet** *see* **alphabet**

**natron**
**04** urao

**natter**
**03** gab, jaw **04** chat, talk **06** confab, gabble, gossip, jabber, rabbit, witter

**07** blather, blether, chatter, chinwag, prattle **08** chit-chat, rabbit on **10** chew the fat **11** confabulate **12** conversation
**14** shoot the breeze

**nattily**
**06** neatly **07** smartly **09** elegantly, stylishly **11** fashionably

**natty**
**04** chic, deft, neat, trim **05** ritzy, smart
**06** clever, dapper, snazzy, spruce, swanky **07** elegant, stylish, varment, varmint **09** ingenious **11** fashionable, well-dressed

**natural**
**03** nat, raw **04** open, pure, real
**05** frank, idiot, plain, usual, whole
**06** candid, common, inborn, inbred, innate, kindly, native, normal, physic, simple, virgin **07** artless, built-in, connate, genuine, organic, regular, relaxed, routine, sincere, typical, unmixed **08** everyday, inherent, lifelike, ordinary, standard, unforced
**09** authentic, certainty, guileless, ingenuous, ingrained, inherited, intuitive, unrefined, unstudied
**10** congenital, indigenous, unaffected, unlaboured, unstrained **11** instinctive, spontaneous, unprocessed **12** additive-free, chemical-free, illegitimate, run-of-the-mill, unregenerate
**13** unpretentious **15** unsophisticated
*See also* **fool**
• **natural order** **02** NO

**naturalist**
**08** botanist **09** biologist, Darwinist, ecologist, zoologist **11** creationist
**12** evolutionist **13** life scientist **14** plant scientist
*See also* **biology**

**naturalistic**
**07** factual, graphic, natural **08** lifelike, real-life **09** realistic **10** true-to-life
**12** photographic

**naturalize**
**05** adapt, adopt **06** accept **08** accustom
**09** acclimate, endenizen, habituate, introduce **10** assimilate **11** acclimatize, acculturate, domesticate, enfranchise, familiarize, incorporate, nationalize

**naturally**
**05** natch **06** simply **07** clearly, frankly
**08** candidly, normally, of course
**09** artlessly, certainly, genuinely, logically, obviously, sincerely, typically **10** absolutely **11** ingenuously, simpliciter **13** instinctively, spontaneously

**naturalness**
**04** ease **06** purity **07** realism
**08** openness, pureness **09** frankness, plainness, sincerity, wholeness
**10** candidness, simpleness, simplicity
**11** artlessness, genuineness, informality, spontaneity
**13** ingenuousness **14** unaffectedness
**15** spontaneousness

**nature**
**04** Gaia, kind, mood, sort, type
**05** being, class, earth, stamp, style,

world **06** cosmos, humour, make-up, temper **07** country, essence, outlook, quality, scenery, species, variety **08** category, creation, features, identity, universe **09** character, chemistry, landscape, nakedness **10** attributes, complexion, kindliness **11** countryside, description, disposition, environment, mother earth, personality, temperament **12** constitution, mother nature **14** characteristic, natural history **15** characteristics
• **according to nature 02** sn
• **of nature 04** akin

**naught**
**01** O **03** bad, ill, nil **04** evil, nowt, zero **05** zilch **06** cipher, cypher, foiled, nought, ruined **07** hurtful, immoral, nothing, sweet FA **09** worthless **10** wickedness **11** nothingness **15** sweet Fanny Adams

**naughtily**
**06** lewdly **07** bawdily **08** coarsely, vulgarly **09** defiantly, obscenely, playfully, waywardly **10** indecently, perversely **12** badly behaved **13** disobediently, mischievously

**naughtiness**
**08** defiance, lewdness, mischief **09** bawdiness, indecency, obscenity, vulgarity **10** coarseness, smuttiness **11** playfulness, waywardness **12** bad behaviour, disobedience, misbehaviour

**naughty**
◇ *anagram indicator* **03** bad **04** blue, bold, lewd **05** bawdy **06** coarse, ribald, risqué, smutty, unruly, vulgar, wicked **07** defiant, obscene, playful, roguish, wayward **08** indecent, perverse **09** off-colour, worthless **10** refractory **11** disobedient, misbehaving, mischievous, titillating **12** badly behaved, end of the pier, exasperating, incorrigible **13** undisciplined

**Nauru**
**03** NAU, NRU

**nausea**
**06** hatred, puking, wamble **07** disgust, gagging **08** aversion, distaste, loathing, retching, sickness, vomiting **09** revulsion **10** queasiness, repugnance, throwing up **11** airsickness, biliousness, carsickness, detestation, seasickness **12** sick headache **14** motion sickness, travel sickness **15** morning sickness

**nauseate**
**04** turn **05** repel **06** loathe, offend, revolt, sicken **07** disgust, scunner, turn off **08** gross out, make sick **14** turn the stomach **15** turn your stomach

**nauseating**
**06** odious **08** nauseous **09** abhorrent, loathsome, offensive, repellent, repugnant, repulsive, revolting, sickening **10** chunderous, detestable, disgusting **11** distasteful **14** stomach-turning **15** stomach-churning

**nauseous**
**03** ill **04** puky, sick **05** nasty, pukey **06** queasy **07** airsick, carsick, seasick **09** loathsome, nauseated **10** disgusting, travel sick **14** about to throw up **15** under the weather

**nautical**
**05** naval **07** boating, oceanic, sailing **08** maritime, seagoing, yachting **09** seafaring

**naval**
**03** nav, sea **06** marine **08** maritime, nautical, seagoing **09** seafaring

**navel**
**03** hub **06** centre, middle **07** nombril **08** omphalos **09** umbilicus **11** belly-button, tummy-button

**navigable**
**03** nav **04** open **05** clear **08** passable, sailable **09** crossable, dirigible, unblocked **10** negotiable, voyageable **11** traversable **12** surmountable, unobstructed

**navigate**
**04** helm, plan, plot, sail **05** cross, drive, guide, pilot, steer **06** cruise, direct, handle, voyage **07** journey, skipper **09** manoeuvre, negotiate **11** plan a course

**navigation**
**03** nav **05** canal **06** voyage **07** guiding, nautics, sailing **08** cruising, guidance, pilotage, piloting, seacraft, steering, voyaging **09** directing, direction **10** seamanship **11** manoeuvring **12** helmsmanship **13** contact flight

*Navigational aids and systems include:*

**03** gee, GPS, INS, log, map, Vor
**04** GNSS
**05** chart, loran, pilot, radar
**06** satnav
**07** compass, navarho, sextant
**08** bell buoy, dividers, VHF radio
**09** lightship, omnirange
**10** depth gauge, lighthouse, marker buoy
**11** chronometer, conical buoy, echo-sounder, gyrocompass
**13** nautical table, parallel ruler
**15** astronavigation, flux-gate compass, magnetic compass

**navigator**
**03** nav **05** navvy, pilot **06** master, sailor, seaman **07** mariner **08** helmsman **09** steersman

**navvy**
**06** digger, ganger, worker **07** workman **08** labourer **09** navigator **12** manual worker **14** common labourer

**navy**
**01** N **02** RN **03** RAN **05** fleet, ships **06** armada **08** flotilla, warships **10** naval fleet, naval force **12** merchant navy **15** merchant service
*See also* **rank**

**nay**
**02** no **03** nae **06** denial, indeed, in fact **07** in truth **08** actually, not at all, or

rather **09** not really **11** of course not **12** certainly not **13** absolutely not, in point of fact

**near**
**02** by, nr, ny, to **03** nie, nye **04** akin, come, dear, inby, left, like, nigh **05** alike, close, ewest, forby, handy, inbye, local **06** almost, at hand, beside, come by, coming, nearby, nearly, next to, stingy **07** cling to, close by, closely, close to, looming, related, similar **08** adjacent, approach, familiar, imminent, intimate, left-hand, narrowly **09** adjoining, alongside, bordering, close in on, immediate, impending, proximate, thriftily **10** accessible, adjacent to, close-range, come closer, come nearer, comparable, contiguous, convenient, draw near to, not far away **11** approaching, bordering on, come towards, forthcoming, get closer to, in the offing, move towards, surrounding, within cooee, within range, within reach **12** contiguous to, draw nearer to, neighbouring, parsimonious **13** corresponding, within reach of **14** advance towards, closely related, parsimoniously **15** at close quarters
• **draw near 04** come
• **near thing 08** near miss **09** close call **10** close shave **11** nasty moment **12** narrow escape, narrow squeak

**nearby**
**04** near **05** close, handy **06** beside **07** close by **08** adjacent **09** adjoining **10** accessible, convenient, not far away **11** close at hand, within cooee, within reach **12** neighbouring **13** in the vicinity **14** on your doorstep **15** at close quarters

**nearly**
◇ *deletion indicator* ◇ *tail deletion indicator* **02** ny **03** e'en, nie, nye **04** even, nigh **05** about, close **06** all but, almost, feckly, nigh on **07** closely, close on, close to, roughly **08** à peu près, as good as, nigh-hand, well-nigh **09** just about, verging on, virtually **10** intimately, more or less **11** practically **13** approximately **14** parsimoniously, scrutinizingly **15** close but no cigar

**nearness**
**06** degree **08** affinity, dearness, intimacy, vicinity **09** closeness, handiness, immediacy, imminence, proximity **10** chumminess, contiguity **11** familiarity, propinquity **12** availability, neighborhood **13** accessibility, appropinquity, neighbourhood

**near-sighted**
**06** myopic **08** purblind **09** half-blind **12** short-sighted

**neat**
**02** ox **03** apt, cow, net **04** bull, cool, deft, dink, feat, good, mega, nett, nice, oxen, pure, smug, snod, tidy, tosh, trig, trim **05** clean, clear, crisp, dinky, genty, great, handy, jemmy, jimpy, natty, nifty, short, slick, smart, super,

**neaten**

tight **06** adroit, cattle, clever, dainty, dapper, donsie, expert, nimble, pretty, simple, spruce, superb, wicked **07** band-box, cleanly, compact, elegant, featous, ordered, orderly, shining, skilful, unmixed **08** clean-cut, fabulous, feateous, featuous, finished, sensible, smashing, straight, terrific, well-made **09** admirable, dexterous, effective, efficient, excellent, fantastic, ingenious, organized, practised, shipshape, undiluted, wonderful **10** convenient, marvellous, tremendous **11** well-groomed, well-ordered **12** spick-and-span, undiminished, user-friendly, well-designed **13** unadulterated, well-organized **15** in apple-pie order

**neaten**

◊ *anagram indicator* **04** edge, prim, tidy, trim **05** clean, groom **06** tidy up **07** arrange, clean up, smarten **08** round off, spruce up **09** smarten up **10** square away, straighten **11** put to rights

**neatly**

**04** jimp **05** aptly **06** deftly, fairly, featly, jimply, nicely, nimbly, tidily **07** adeptly, agilely, handily, smartly **08** adroitly, cleverly, daintily, expertly, prettily, sprucely **09** elegantly, precisely, skilfully, stylishly **10** accurately, feateously, gracefully **11** dexterously, efficiently **12** conveniently, effortlessly, methodically **14** systematically

**neatness**

**05** grace, skill, style **06** nicety **07** agility, aptness **08** accuracy, deftness, elegance, niceness, tidiness, trimness **09** adeptness, dexterity, handiness, jemminess, precision, smartness **10** adroitness, cleverness, daintiness, efficiency, expertness, nimbleness, spruceness **11** orderliness, preciseness, skilfulness, stylishness **12** gracefulness, straightness **14** methodicalness

**Nebraska**

**02** NE **04** Nebr

**nebulous**

**03** dim **04** hazy **05** fuzzy, misty, vague **06** cloudy **07** obscure, shadowy, unclear **08** abstract, confused, formless, unformed **09** ambiguous, amorphous, imprecise, shapeless, uncertain **10** indefinite, indistinct **13** indeterminate

**necessarily**

**04** thus **06** needly **08** no remedy, obligate, of course, perforce **09** certainly, naturally, therefore **10** inevitably, inexorably, willy-nilly **11** accordingly, ineluctably, inescapably, of necessity, unavoidably **12** by definition, compulsorily, consequently, nolens volens **13** automatically, axiomatically, indispensably

**necessary**

**04** sure **05** money, needy, vital **06** needed, toilet **07** certain, crucial, needful **08** enforced, required **09** de rigueur, essential, mandatory, requisite

**10** compulsory, imperative, inevitable, inexorable, obligatory **11** ineluctable, inescapable, predestined, unavoidable **13** indispensable

**necessitate**

**04** mean, need, take **05** exact, force **06** compel, demand, entail, oblige **07** call for, involve, require **09** constrain **13** make necessary

**necessity**

**04** fate, must, need, want **06** ananke, demand, mister, need-be, penury **07** destiny, poverty **08** exigence, exigency, extremes, hardship **09** certainty, emergency, essential, indigence, privation, requisite **10** compulsion, obligation, sine qua non **11** deprivation, desideratum, destitution, fundamental, needfulness, requirement **12** prerequisite **13** indispensable, inevitability, inexorability **14** inescapability

• **of necessity** **05** needs **08** no remedy, perforce **09** certainly **10** inevitably, inexorably **11** inescapably, unavoidably **12** by definition, compulsorily **13** automatically, indispensably

**neck**

**03** col, pet **04** crag, kiss, nape, snog **05** drink, halse, hause, hawse, scrag **06** caress, cervix, scruff, smooch **08** audacity, canoodle **09** impudence • **neck and neck** **04** even **05** drawn, equal, level **06** on a par **07** aligned, uniform **08** balanced, matching **10** nip and tuck, side by side **12** level pegging

**necklace**

**04** band, torc **05** beads, chain **06** choker, corals, gorget, jewels, locket, pearls, string, torque **07** negligé, pendant, rivière, sautoir **08** carcanet, negligee **10** lavallière **11** mangalsutra

**necromancer**

**05** witch **06** wizard **07** diviner, warlock **08** conjurer, magician, sorcerer **09** sorceress, spiritist **11** thaumaturge **12** spiritualist **13** thaumaturgist

**necromancy**

**05** magic **06** hoodoo, voodoo **07** sorcery **08** black art, witchery, wizardry **09** spiritism **10** black magic, demonology, divination, nigromancy, witchcraft **11** conjuration, enchantment, thaumaturgy **12** spiritualism **13** magical powers, wonder-working

**necropolis**

**08** cemetery, God's acre **09** graveyard **10** burial site, churchyard **11** burial place **12** burial ground, charnel house

**need**

**04** call, lack, miss, must, want, wish **05** crave **06** besoin, demand, desire, egence, egency, have to, mister, rely on **07** call for, pine for, poverty, require **08** depend on, exigency, occasion, shortage, yearn for **09** cry out for, essential, necessity, neediness, requisite **10** have need of, inadequacy,

obligation **11** be obliged to, be reliant on, desideratum, necessitate, requirement **12** prerequisite **13** be compelled to, be dependent on, insufficiency, justification **14** be desperate for **15** have occasion for

• **in need** **04** poor **05** needy **06** hard up **08** deprived, dirt-poor, indigent **09** destitute, penniless, penurious **11** impecunious **12** impoverished **13** disadvantaged **14** on the breadline **15** poverty-stricken, underprivileged

**needed**

**06** wanted **07** desired, lacking **08** required **09** called for, essential, necessary, requisite **10** compulsory, obligatory

**needful**

**05** needy, vital **06** needed **08** required **09** essential, necessary, requisite **10** stipulated **13** indispensable

**needle**

**03** bug, irk, nag, nib, pin, sew **04** bait, barb, gall, goad, hand, hype, hypo, miff, nark, prod, rile, spud, spur **05** annoy, arrow, briar, get at, point, prick, quill, sharp, spike, spine, sting, taunt, thorn **06** bodkin, darner, enmity, harass, heckle, marker, nettle, niggle, pester, pierce, ruffle, stylus, thread, wind up **07** bramble, bristle, dislike, obelisk, pointer, prickle, provoke, spicule, syringe, torment **08** drive mad, dry-point, irritate, splinter **09** aggravate, indicator, penetrate **10** drive crazy **11** microneedle **12** drive bananas **13** darning-needle, make sparks fly, packing-needle **14** drive up the wall, knitting needle

**needless**

**06** luxury **07** useless **08** unwanted **09** pointless, redundant, undesired **10** expendable, gratuitous **11** dispensable, purposeless, superfluous, uncalled-for, unnecessary • **needless to say** **06** surely **07** no doubt **08** of course **09** certainly, naturally **10** by all means, definitely **11** doubtlessly, indubitably, undoubtedly **13** without a doubt

**needlessly**

**09** uselessly **11** dispensably, pointlessly, redundantly **13** superfluously, unnecessarily

**needlework**

**06** sewing **07** tatting **08** tapestry, woolwork **09** drawn work, fancywork, hemstitch, patchwork, piqué work, plainwork, stitching, white seam **10** crocheting, embroidery **11** cross-stitch, needlepoint, seamstressy, stitchcraft, worsted-work **12** saddle stitch

**needy**

**04** poor **06** hard up, in need, strait **07** needful, wanting **08** deprived, dirt-poor, indigent **09** destitute, necessary, penniless, penurious **11** impecunious **12** impoverished **13** disadvantaged **14** on the breadline **15** poverty-stricken, underprivileged

## ne'er-do-well
**04** spiv **05** idler **06** dodger, dosser, loafer, skelum, skiver, waster **07** bludger, goof-off, lounger, shirker, skellum, slacker, wastrel **08** layabout, schellum **09** do-nothing **10** black sheep **14** good-for-nothing

## nefarious
**04** base, evil, foul, vile **06** odious, sinful, unholy, wicked **07** heinous, satanic, vicious **08** criminal, depraved, dreadful, horrible, infamous, infernal, shameful, terrible **09** atrocious, execrable, loathsome, monstrous **10** abominable, detestable, horrendous, iniquitous, outrageous, villainous **11** opprobrious

## negate
**04** deny, undo, void **05** annul, quash **06** cancel, oppose, refute, reject, repeal, revoke, squash **07** explode, gainsay, nullify, rescind, retract, reverse, wipe out **08** abrogate, disprove, renounce **09** discredit, repudiate **10** contradict, invalidate, neutralize **11** countermand

## negation
**04** veto **06** denial, repeal **07** inverse, reverse **08** contrary, converse, opposite **09** disavowal, rejection **10** abrogation, antithesis, disclaimer **12** cancellation, renunciation **13** contradiction, nullification **14** countermanding, neutralization

## negative
**03** bad, neg **04** acid, deny, veto, weak **05** minus **06** denial, gloomy **07** adverse, counter, cynical, denying, harmful, hostile, hurtful, opposed, refusal, unlucky **08** contrary, critical, opposing, opposite, refusing, saying no **09** annulling, defeatist, injurious, rejection, spineless, unhelpful, unwilling **10** censorious, dissension, dissenting, gainsaying, neutralize, nullifying, unfriendly **11** conflicting, destructive, detrimental, obstructive, pessimistic, subtractive, uncongenial, unfortunate **12** antagonistic, inauspicious, invalidating, neutralizing, unfavourable, uninterested, unpropitious **13** contradiction, laevorotatory, unco-operative **14** unconstructive, unenthusiastic **15** disadvantageous

## negativity
**08** cynicism **09** defeatism, pessimism **10** gloominess **12** criticalness **13** unhelpfulness, unwillingness **14** lack of interest

## neglect
◇ *anagram indicator* **04** fail, omit **05** abuse, scorn, shirk, skimp, spurn **06** disuse, fail in, forget, ignore, laxity, pass by, pass up, pigeon, rebuff, slight **07** abandon, default, disdain, disobey, failure, forsake **08** ignoring, incivism, infringe, leave out, let slide, omission, overlook, spurning **09** desuetude, disregard, disrepair, mislippen, oversight, slackness **10** be lax about, culpa levis, disrespect, leave alone,

misprision, negligence, remissness **11** inattention, rack and ruin, shortcoming **12** carelessness, heedlessness, indifference **13** forgetfulness **14** non-performance

## neglected
◇ *anagram indicator* **04** waif **07** forlorn, run-down, squalid **08** derelict, deserted, forsaken, stranded, unheeded, untended, untilled, unweeded **09** abandoned, overgrown **10** uncared-for **11** dilapidated, disregarded, undervalued, unhusbanded **12** uncultivated, unmaintained **13** unappreciated

## neglectful
**03** lax **06** remiss, sloppy **08** careless, derelict, heedless, uncaring **09** forgetful, negligent, oblivious, slighting, unmindful **11** inattentive, indifferent, thoughtless **12** disregardful

## négligé dress
**03** mob

## negligence
◇ *anagram indicator* **06** laches, laxity, slight **07** default, failure, neglect **08** omission **09** culpa lata, disregard, oversight, slackness **10** remissness, sloppiness **11** inattention, shortcoming **12** carelessness, heedlessness, inadvertence, inadvertency, indifference **13** forgetfulness **15** inattentiveness, thoughtlessness

## negligent
◇ *anagram indicator* **03** lax **05** slack **06** casual, remiss, sloppy **07** cursory, offhand **08** careless, dilatory, heedless, uncaring **09** forgetful, unmindful **10** neglectful, neglecting, nonchalant **11** inattentive, indifferent, thoughtless

## negligible
**04** tiny **05** minor, petty, small **06** minute, paltry **07** minimal, trivial **08** trifling **09** off the map **11** neglectable, unimportant **13** imperceptible, inappreciable, insignificant

## negotiable
**03** neg **04** open **05** clear **08** arguable, passable **09** crossable, debatable, navigable, unblocked, undecided, unsettled **11** contestable, traversable **12** questionable, surmountable, unobstructed **14** open to question

## negotiate
◇ *anagram indicator* **04** deal, pass, talk **05** agree, broke, clear, cross, float, treat **06** broker, confer, debate, fulfil, haggle, manage, parley, settle **07** arrange, bargain, consult, discuss, execute, mediate, pull off, resolve, traffic, work out **08** complete, conclude, contract, get round, pass over, surmount, transact, traverse **09** arbitrate, hammer out, intercede, intervene, thrash out **11** pass through **12** wheel and deal

## negotiation
◇ *anagram indicator* **05** talks, treat **06** debate, parley, treaty **08** haggling, practice **09** diplomacy, mediation,

parleying **10** bargaining, conference, discussion, pulling-off **11** arbitration, transaction **12** hammering-out, thrashing-out

## negotiator
**06** broker **07** haggler **08** diplomat, mediator, parleyer **09** bargainer, go-between, moderator **10** ambassador, arbitrator **11** adjudicator, intercessor **12** intermediary **13** wheeler-dealer

## neigh
**04** bray **05** hinny **06** nicher, nicker, whinny **07** snicker, whicker

## neighbour
**03** bor **04** abut

## neighbourhood
**04** area, hood, part **06** locale, region **07** quarter **08** confines, district, environs, locality, precinct, presence, purlieus, vicinage, vicinity **09** community, proximity, voisinage **11** convicinity **12** surroundings
• **in the neighbourhood of** **04** near, up to **05** about, round **06** almost, around, nearby, next to **07** close to, roughly **13** approximately

## neighbouring
**04** near, next **05** local **06** nearby **07** nearest, vicinal **08** abutting, adjacent, next-door **09** adjoining, bordering, sistering **10** connecting, contiguous, near at hand **11** close at hand, surrounding

## neighbourly
**04** kind, warm **06** genial, social **07** affable, amiable, cordial, helpful **08** friendly, generous, obliging, sociable **10** hospitable **11** considerate **13** companionable

## nemesis
**04** fate, ruin **07** destiny **08** downfall **09** vengeance **10** punishment **11** destruction, retribution **14** just punishment

## neodymium
**02** Nd

## neologism
**07** coinage, new term, new word, novelty **09** new phrase, vogue word **10** innovation **13** new expression

## neon
**02** Ne

## neophyte
**01** L **04** tiro **06** newbie, novice, rookie **07** learner, recruit, trainee **08** beginner, newcomer **09** greenhorn, new member, noviciate, novitiate **10** apprentice, raw recruit **11** probationer

## Nepal
**03** NEP, NPL

## nephrite
**02** yu

## nepotism
**04** bias **10** partiality **11** favouritism **12** old school tie **13** Old Boy network **14** jobs for the boys

## Neptune
**08** Poseidon

## neptunium
**02** Np

## nerd
*see* **fool**

## nerk
*see* **fool**

## nerve
**03** lip **04** face, gall, grit, guts, neck, will **05** brace, cheek, force, mouth, pluck, sauce, sinew, spunk, steel **06** bottle, daring, mettle, spirit, valour, vigour **07** bolster, bravery, courage, fortify, hearten, prepare **08** audacity, boldness, chutzpah, embolden, firmness, strength, temerity **09** bowstring, brass neck, encourage, endurance, fortitude, hardihood, impudence, insolence **10** brazenness, effrontery, invigorate, resolution, strengthen **11** intrepidity, presumption **12** fearlessness, impertinence **13** determination, steadfastness **14** cool-headedness, self-confidence

*Nerves include:*

**05** optic, ulnar, vagus
**06** facial, lumbar, medial, median, radial, sacral, tibial
**07** femoral, phrenic, plantar, sciatic
**08** axillary, brachial, peroneal, thoracic
**09** cutaneous, laryngeal, occipital, olfactory
**10** splanchnic, trigeminal
**11** intercostal
**12** suboccipital
**15** lesser occipital, spinal accessory

## nerveless
**04** calm, weak **05** inert, slack, timid **06** afraid, feeble, flabby **07** nervous **08** cowardly, unnerved **09** enervated, spineless **11** debilitated

## nerve-racking
**05** tense **06** trying **07** anxious **08** worrying **09** difficult, harrowing, maddening, stressful **10** nail-biting **11** disquieting, distressing, frightening

## nerves
**05** shock, worry **06** strain, stress, wobbly **07** anxiety, jitters, tension, twitter, willies **11** butterflies, fretfulness, nervousness **12** collywobbles, crise de nerfs **13** heebie-jeebies **14** nervous tension
• **get on someone's nerves 03** bug, irk, nag, vex **04** fash, gall, rile **05** anger, annoy, tease **06** bother, harass, hassle, madden, molest, pester, plague, ruffle, wind up **07** disturb, hack off, provoke, tick off, trouble **08** brass off, irritate **09** aggravate, cheese off, displease, drive nuts **10** drive crazy, exasperate **12** drive bananas **13** make sparks fly **14** drive up the wall **15** get someone's goat, get your dander up

## nervous
◇ *anagram indicator* **03** shy **04** edgy, toey **05** het up, jumpy, nappy, nervy, shaky, tense, timid **06** on edge, sinewy, strong, uneasy **07** anxious, fearful, fidgety, fretful, in a stew, jittery, keyed up, quaking, twitchy, uptight, worried, wound up **08** agitated, in a sweat, in a tizzy, neurotic, skittish, strained, timorous, vigorous **09** excitable, flustered, perturbed, screwed-up, squirrely, tremulous **10** disquieted, squirrelly **11** overwrought **12** all of a dither, apprehensive, highly-strung **13** having kittens, on tenterhooks

## nervous breakdown
**06** crisis **08** neurosis **10** cracking-up, depression **11** melancholia **15** mental breakdown, nervous disorder

## nervously
◇ *anagram indicator* **06** edgily, on edge **07** in a stew, timidly **08** in a sweat, in a tizzy, uneasily **09** anxiously, fearfully, fretfully, twitchily **13** having kittens **14** apprehensively

## nervousness
**05** worry **06** strain, stress **07** anxiety, fluster, habdabs, tension, willies **08** disquiet, edginess, timidity **09** agitation **10** touchiness, uneasiness **11** stage fright **12** excitability, perturbation, restlessness, timorousness **13** heebie-jeebies, tremulousness

## nervy
**04** cool, edgy, high **05** het up, jumpy, shaky, tense **06** on edge, uneasy **07** anxious, fearful, fidgety, jittery, keyed up, twitchy, uptight, worried, wound up **08** agitated, impudent, neurotic, strained **09** audacious, excitable, flustered **12** apprehensive, highly-strung **13** having kittens

## nescient
**05** dense, thick **06** stupid, unread **07** unaware **08** backward, clueless, ignorant, untaught **09** unlearned, untrained, unwitting **10** illiterate, innumerate, uneducated, unfamiliar, uninformed, unschooled **11** ill-informed, uninitiated **12** unacquainted **13** inexperienced, unenlightened

## ness
**04** naze
*See also* **headland**

## nest
**03** den, mew, nid **04** aery, bike, bink, byke, cage, cote, dray, drey, eyry, lair, nide **05** aerie, ayrie, eyrie, haunt, lodge, nidus, perch, roost **06** refuge, settle, wurley **07** cabinet, hideout, retreat, shelter **08** hideaway, hive-nest, vespiary **09** bird-house, formicary, termitary **10** nesting-box **11** formicarium, hiding-place, termitarium **12** accumulation, nidification **14** breeding-ground
*See also* **animal**

## nest egg
**04** fund **05** cache, funds, store **07** deposit, reserve, savings **08** reserves **12** bottom drawer

## nestle
**06** cuddle, curl up, huddle, nuzzle **07** cherish, snuggle **08** cuddle up **09** snuggle up **14** huddle together

## nestling
**04** baby **05** chick **08** suckling, weanling **09** fledgling

## net
◇ *containment indicator* **03** bag, end, get, let, nab, web **04** caul, drag, earn, gain, lace, leap, make, mesh, neat, nett, nick, pure, sean, take, toil, trap, trim **05** broad, catch, clean, clear, drift, final, raise, seine, snare, toils, total, trawl **06** bright, cobweb, collar, enmesh, lowest, obtain, pocket, pull in, rake in, sagene, tunnel **07** bring in, capture, dragnet, drop-net, ensnare, fishnet, general, lattice, netting, network, overall, realize, receive, tracery, trammel, unmixed, webbing **08** after tax, drift-net, entangle, filigree, meshwork, open work, seine net, take home, take-home, ultimate **09** inclusive, reticulum **10** accumulate, after taxes, conclusive, difficulty **11** latticework, take captive **15** after deductions

## nether
**03** low **05** basal, below, lower, under **06** bottom **07** beneath, hellish, Stygian **08** inferior, infernal **09** Plutonian **10** lower-level, underworld **11** underground

## Netherlands
**02** NL **03** NLD **04** Neth

## Netherlands Antilles
**02** NA **03** ANT

## netherworld
**03** pit **04** fire, hell **05** abyss, below, Hades, Sheol **06** Erebus, Tophet **07** Abaddon, Acheron, Gehenna, inferno **08** Tartarus **09** down there, Malebolge, perdition **10** other place, underworld **12** lower regions **13** bottomless pit **15** abode of the devil, infernal regions

## nettle
**03** bug, vex **04** fret, goad, miff, nark, rami, rile **05** annoy, chafe, get at, pique, ramee, ramie, sting, tease, upset **06** harass, hassle, hen-bit, needle, ruffle, urtica, wind up **07** incense, provoke, torment **08** drive mad, irritate **09** aggravate, archangel, pellitory **10** drive crazy, exasperate **12** drive bananas **13** make sparks fly **14** artillery-plant, discountenance, drive up the wall **15** yellow archangel

## nettled
**05** angry, cross, got at, huffy, riled, stung, vexed **06** bugged, galled, goaded, miffed, narked, peeved, piqued **07** annoyed, needled, rattled, ruffled, wound up **08** harassed, incensed, offended, provoked **09** aggrieved, driven mad, irritable, irritated **10** aggravated **11** driven crazy, exasperated **13** driven bananas **15** driven up the wall

## network
**03** CNN, LAN, MAN, net, PCN, WAN, web **04** fret, grid, ISDN, lace, maze, mesh, PSTN, rete **05** grill, nexus **06** matrix, plexus, sagene, system,

**neurosis** (cont.)

tracks **07** complex, lattice, netting, tracery, webbing **08** channels, filigree, gridiron, meshwork, open work **09** circuitry, grapevine, labyrinth, reticulum, structure **10** Eurovision **11** arrangement, convolution, latticework **12** old school tie, organization, reticulation **13** bush telegraph, Old Boy network

**neurosis**

**05** mania **06** phobia **08** disorder, fixation **09** deviation, obsession **10** affliction **11** abnormality, derangement, disturbance, instability **13** maladjustment **14** mental disorder

**neurotic**

**05** manic **06** phobic **07** anxious, deviant, nervous **08** abnormal, deranged, paranoid, unstable **09** disturbed, obsessive, unhealthy **10** compulsive, hysterical, irrational **11** maladjusted, overanxious, overwrought **14** hypersensitive

**neuter**

**01** n **03** fix, gib **04** geld, neut, spay **05** dress **06** agamic, clonal, doctor, gib-cat **07** agamous, asexual, neutral, sexless **08** caponize, castrate, conidial **09** castrated, sterilize **10** emasculate **11** monogenetic **12** intransitive

**neutral**

**04** drab, dull, fawn, gray, grey, pale **05** beige, bland, white **06** neuter, pastel **07** anaemic, anodyne, insipid, mugwump **08** detached, ordinary, unbiased **09** anonymous, impartial, objective, undecided **10** colourless, even-handed, indefinite, indistinct, non-aligned, open-minded, uninvolved **11** indifferent, inoffensive, nondescript, non-partisan, unassertive, uncommitted **12** non-combatant, non-committal, unprejudiced, unremarkable **13** disinterested, dispassionate, uninteresting **14** expressionless **15** unexceptionable

**neutrality**

**10** detachment **11** disinterest **12** impartiality, non-alignment, unbiasedness **13** impartialness **14** non-involvement **15** non-intervention

**neutralize**

**04** kill, undo **05** annul **06** cancel, negate, offset **07** balance, nullify **08** negative **09** cancel out, frustrate, make up for **10** counteract, invalidate **12** incapacitate **13** compensate for **14** counterbalance

**Nevada**

**02** NV **03** Nev

**never**

**03** not **04** nary, ne'er **05** no way **07** not ever, Tib's Eve **08** at no time, not at all, Tibb's Eve **09** St Tib's Eve **10** St Tibb's Eve **11** on no account, when pigs fly **13** not for a moment, not on your life **15** not on your nellie

**never-ending**

◇ *tail deletion indicator* **07** endless, eternal, non-stop **08** constant, infinite, unbroken, unending **09** boundless,

incessant, limitless, permanent, perpetual, unceasing **10** continuous, persistent, relentless, unchanging, without end **11** everlasting, unremitting **12** interminable **13** uninterrupted

**nevertheless**

**03** but, tho, yet **05** still **06** algate, anyhow, anyway, at that, even so, howe'er, though, withal **07** algates, however **08** after all **09** in any case, quand même **10** all the same, by any means, for all that, in any event, malgré tout, not but what, regardless, still and on, tout de même **11** by some means, just the same, none but what, nonetheless, still and all **13** at the same time **15** notwithstanding

**new**

◇ *anagram indicator* **01** N **04** mint, more, span **05** added, alien, extra, fresh, green, novel, young **06** latest, maiden, modern, modish, recent, trendy, unused, virgin, way out **07** altered, another, changed, current, further, newborn, nouveau, renewed, resumed, strange, topical, unknown, unusual **08** advanced, brand-new, creative, ignorant, improved, nouvelle, original, reformed, restored, unversed, up-to-date **09** a stranger, born-again, different, fledgling, ingenious, refreshed **10** additional, avant-garde, fledgeling, futuristic, innovative, modernized, newfangled, pioneering, present-day, redesigned, remodelled, unfamiliar **11** imaginative, regenerated, resourceful, spanking-new, ultra-modern **12** contemporary, experimental, unaccustomed, unacquainted **13** inexperienced, reinvigorated, revolutionary, state-of-the-art, supplementary, up-to-the-minute **14** ground-breaking, unconventional **15** newly discovered

**New Brunswick**

**02** NB

**newcomer**

**04** tiro **05** alien, pupil **06** blow-in, gryfon, newbie, novice, rookie **07** arrival, griffin, griffon, gryphon, incomer, learner, new chum, pilgrim, recruit, settler, trainee **08** beginner, colonist, freshman, intruder, jackaroo, jackeroo, jillaroo, neophyte, outsider, stranger **09** foreigner, greenhorn, immigrant **10** apprentice, new arrival, tenderfoot **11** probationer

**newfangled**

**03** new **05** novel **06** modern, recent, trendy **08** gimmicky **10** futuristic **11** fashionable, modernistic, ultra-modern **12** contemporary **13** state-of-the-art

**Newfoundland and Labrador**

**02** NL

**New Hampshire**

**02** NH

**New Jersey**

**02** NJ

**newly**

◇ *anagram indicator* **04** anew, just

**05** fresh **06** afresh, lately, of late **07** freshly **08** latterly, recently

**New Mexico**

**02** NM **04** N Mex

**newness**

**06** novity, oddity **07** novelty, recency **09** freshness **10** innovation, uniqueness **11** originality, strangeness, unusualness **13** unfamiliarity

**news**

**03** gen, oil **04** data, dope, info, word **05** facts, story **06** advice, budget, exposé, gossip, latest, report, rumour **07** account, hearing, hearsay, lowdown, message, scandal, tidings **08** bulletin, dispatch, izvestia, newscast, news item **09** izvestia, newsflash, speerings, speirings, statement **10** communiqué, disclosure, revelation **11** information **12** announcement, developments, intelligence, press release **13** advertisement, communication

*News agencies include:*

**02** AP, PA
**03** AAP, AFP, UPI
**04** NZPA, Tass
**07** Reuters
**08** ITAR-Tass
**15** Associated Press

• **piece of news** **04** item, unco

**newspaper**

**03** rag **04** blat, post **05** blatt, daily, local, organ, paper, press, print, sheet **06** weekly **07** evening, gazette, journal, quality, tabloid, tribune **08** magazine, national, regional **09** telegraph **10** broadsheet, local paper, periodical, provincial **11** publication **12** evening paper, morning paper **13** national paper, regional paper **15** provincial paper

*Newspapers and magazines include:*

**02** FT, GQ, Ms, OK!
**03** FHM, NME, Red, She, Sun, TES, TLS, Viz
**04** Best, Chat, Chic, Elle, Heat, Judy, Life, Mail, Mind, Mizz, Mojo, More!, Real, THES, Time
**05** Bella, Bliss, Bunty, Hello!, Mandy, Maxim, Prima, Punch, Times, Vogue, Which?, Wired, Woman
**06** Forbes, Granta, Lancet, Loaded, Mirror, Nature, The Sun, War Cry
**07** Company, Esquire, Express, Fortune, Glamour, Hustler, Le Monde, Mayfair, Men Only, Newsday, Options, Playboy, Science, The Chap, The Face, The Lady, The Star, Time Out, Tribune, TV Times
**08** Campaign, Die Woche, Gay Times, Guardian, Le Figaro, Newsweek, New Woman, Scotsman, The Beano, The Dandy, The Eagle, The Field, The Month, The Oldie, The Times, USA Today
**09** Daily Mail, Daily Star, Ideal

Home, Penthouse, Q Magazine, Red Pepper, Smash Hits, Telegraph, The Friend, The Grocer, The Herald, The Mirror, The People, The Tablet, The Tatler, Woman's Own

10 Asian Times, Daily Sport, Irish Times, Private Eye, Racing Post, Radio Times, Sunday Post, Take a Break, Vanity Fair

11 Church Times, Country Life, Daily Record, Marie Claire, Melody Maker, Morning Star, Sunday Sport, The Big Issue, The European, The Guardian, The Observer, The Universe, Woman's Realm

12 Angling Times, Cosmopolitan, Daily Express, Family Circle, Fortean Times, History Today, Mail on Sunday, New Scientist, New Statesman, Poetry Review, Sunday Mirror, The Economist, The Pink Paper, The Spectator, Time Magazine, Woman's Weekly

13 Catholic Times, Daltons Weekly, Farmers Weekly, Homes and Ideas, Horse and Hound, Just Seventeen, Mother and Baby, People's Friend, Reader's Digest, Sunday Express, The Australian, The Bookseller, The Watchtower, Woman's Journal

14 Caribbean Times, Catholic Herald, Financial Times, House and Garden, Literary Review, News of the World, The Boston Globe, The Independent, The New York Post, The Sunday Times, The Times Higher, Washington Post

15 Evening Standard, Exchange and Mart, Harpers and Queen, Homes and Gardens, Sunday Telegraph, The Boston Herald, The Mail on Sunday, The New York Times

*Newspaper proprietors and magnates include:*

04 **King** (Cecil Harmsworth), **Ochs** (Adolph Simon), **Shah** (Eddy)
05 **Astor** (John Jacob, Lord), **Astor** (William Waldorf, Viscount), **Black** (Conrad, Lord)
06 **Aitken** (Sir Max), **Graham** (Katherine Meyer), **Hearst** (William Randolph), **Packer** (Sir Frank), **Ridder** (Bernard H, Jnr), **Walter** (John)
07 **Barclay** (Sir David), **Barclay** (Sir Frederick), **Camrose** (William Ewert Berry, Viscount), **Kemsley** (James Gomer Berry, Viscount), **Maxwell** (Robert), **Murdoch** (Rupert), **Pearson** (Sir Cyril Arthur), **Riddell** (George, Lord), **Scripps** (Edward Wyllis), **Thomson** (D C), **Thomson** (Roy, Lord)
08 **Pulitzer** (Joseph)
10 **Berlusconi** (Silvio), **Harmsworth** (Alfred, Viscount), **Harmsworth** (Harold, Viscount)
11 **Beaverbrook** (Max, Lord)

*See also* **journalist**

---

**newspaperman**
*see* **journalist**

**newsreader**
06 anchor 07 newsman 08 reporter 09 anchorman, announcer, newswoman, presenter 10 journalist, newscaster 11 anchorwoman, commentator 13 correspondent

**newsworthy**
07 notable, topical, unusual 09 arresting, important 10 noteworthy, remarkable, reportable 11 interesting, significant, stimulating

**newt**
03 ask, eft 05 asker

**New York**
◇ *dialect indicator* 02 NY

*New York boroughs:*

06 Queens
08 Brooklyn, The Bronx
09 Manhattan
12 Staten Island

*Other districts of New York include:*

04 Noho, Soho
06 Corona, Harlem, Hollis, Inwood, Nolita, Queens
07 Astoria, Chelsea, Clifton, Kips Bay, Midtown, Midwood, Tribeca
08 Brooklyn, Canarsie, East Side, El Barrio, Elmhurst, Flatbush, Flatiron, Flushing, Gramercy, Rego Park, Steinway, The Bronx, West Side
09 Briarwood, Chinatown, Flatlands, Manhattan, Ozone Park, Park Slope, Princeton, Ridgewood, The Bowery, Turtle Bay, Woodhaven, Yorkville
10 Cobble Hill, Douglaston, Greenpoint, Ground Zero, Kew Gardens, Marble Hill, Sunset Park
11 Borough Park, Central Park, Coney Island, East Village, Ellis Island, Forest Hills, Howard Beach, Little Italy, Little Korea, New Brighton, West Village
12 Alphabet City, Crown Heights, Cypress Hills, Hell's Kitchen, South Jamaica, Staten Island, Williamsburg
13 Brighton Beach, Lower East Side, Spanish Harlem, Upper East Side, Upper West Side
14 Jackson Heights, Long Island City, Lower Manhattan, Manhattan Beach, Stuyvesant Town
15 Brooklyn Heights, Garment District, Roosevelt Island

*New York streets include:*

06 Bowery
08 Broadway
10 14th Street, 34th Street, 42nd Street, Park Avenue, Wall Street
11 Canal Street, Fifth Avenue, Sixth Avenue, Union Square
13 Madison Square, Seventh Avenue
14 East 42nd Street, West 42nd Street

---

15 Central Park West, Lexington Avenue

*New York landmarks include:*

03 JFK, Met
04 CBGB, MoMA
05 Macy's
07 Barneys, Factory
08 Broadway, Bronx Zoo, Studio 54
09 East River, The Dakota
10 Bronx River, Cotton Club, FAO Schwarz, Ground Zero, Rose Center, Wall Street
11 Battery Park, Central Park, Coney Island, Ellis Island, Federal Hall, Harlem River, Hudson River, Penn Station, Shea Stadium, Times Square, Union Square
12 Carnegie Hall, Chelsea Hotel, Hotel Chelsea, Prospect Park, The Cloisters
13 Apollo Theater, Bloomingdale's, Lincoln Center, Lincoln Tunnel, Pan Am Building, St Paul's Church, Yankee Stadium
14 Brooklyn Bridge, Grand Army Plaza, Waldorf Astoria, Washington Arch
15 Flushing Meadows, Manhattan Bridge, Metlife Building, Saks Fifth Avenue, Seagram Building, Statue of Liberty, Trump World Tower

*New York districts, streets and landmarks include:*

03 JFK, Met
04 CBGB, MoMA, Soho
06 Bowery, Harlem, Queens
07 Tribeca
08 Broadway, Brooklyn, East Side, El Barrio, The Bronx, West Side
09 Chinatown, Manhattan, The Bowery
10 Ground Zero, Park Avenue, Wall Street
11 Battery Park, Central Park, Coney Island, East Village, Ellis Island, Harlem River, Hudson River, Little Italy, Penn Station, Shea Stadium, Times Square, Union Square, West Village
12 Carnegie Hall, Chelsea Hotel, Hell's Kitchen, Staten Island
13 Lincoln Center, Lower East Side, Madison Square, Seventh Avenue, Spanish Harlem, Upper East Side, Upper West Side, Yankee Stadium
14 Brooklyn Bridge, Waldorf Astoria
15 Statue of Liberty

**New Zealand**
02 NZ 03 NZL

*New Zealand cities and notable towns include:*

06 Napier, Nelson, Timaru
07 Dunedin, Manukau, Rotorua
08 Auckland, Gisborne, Hamilton, Hastings, Tauranga, Wanganui
09 Whangarei
10 Wellington
11 New Plymouth

**12** Christchurch, Invercargill
**15** Palmerston North

*New Zealand landmarks include:*

**05** Hawea
**06** Mt Cook, Te Anau, Wanaka
**07** Aorangi, Rotorua, Ruapehu, Waikato
**08** Mt Egmont, Wakatipu, Wanganui
**09** Fiordland, Lake Taupo
**10** Mt Victoria
**11** Rakaia Gorge
**12** Milford Sound, Southern Alps
**13** Stewart Island
**14** Otago Peninsula
**15** Mangere Mountain, Ninety Mile Beach, Whangaparaoa Bay

*See also* **electorate; governor; premier; prime minister; province; team**

**next**
**04** syne, then **05** along, later **06** beside
**07** closest, ensuing, nearest
**08** adjacent **09** adjoining, alongside, bordering, following, immediate, proximate **10** afterwards, contiguous, subsequent, succeeding, successive, tangential, thereafter **11** approximate **12** neighbouring, subsequently **13** after that time

**next-door**
**08** adjacent

**nibble**
**03** bit, eat **04** bite, gnaw, knap, moop, moup, nosh, peck, pick **05** crumb, munch, piece, snack, taste **06** morsel, pick at, titbit **07** knapple

**Nicaragua**
**03** NIC

**nice**
**03** bad, coy **04** cute, fine, good, kind **05** canny, civil, close, exact, sweet **06** dainty, decent, genial, kindly, lovely, minute, polite, strict, subtle, tickle, wanton **07** amiable, amusing, careful, likable, precise, refined, welcome **08** accurate, careless, charming, critical, delicate, friendly, likeable, pleasant, ticklish **09** agreeable, appealing, courteous, endearing, enjoyable, hazardous **10** acceptable, attractive, delectable, delightful, fastidious, meticulous, particular, satisfying, scrupulous **11** good-natured, pleasurable, respectable, sympathetic **12** entertaining, good-humoured, satisfactory, well-mannered **13** understanding **14** discriminating

**nicely**
**04** well **07** civilly **08** politely, properly **09** agreeably **10** pleasantly, pleasingly **11** courteously, pleasurably, respectably **12** attractively, delightfully **14** satisfactorily

**niceness**
**05** charm **08** kindness **10** amiability, politeness **11** likableness **12** friendliness, likeableness, pleasantness **13** agreeableness

**14** attractiveness, delightfulness, respectability

**nicety**
**06** nuance **07** coyness, finesse, quiddit **08** accuracy, delicacy, quiddity, subtlety **09** exactness, fine point, precision, punctilio **10** choiceness, minuteness, perjinkity, refinement **11** distinction **14** fastidiousness, meticulousness, scrupulousness

**niche**
**04** nook, slot **05** place **06** alcove, corner, cranny, exedra, hollow, métier, mihrab, recess, shrine **07** calling, exhedra, opening **08** position, vocation **09** cubbyhole **10** fenestella, pigeonhole, tabernacle **11** columbarium **14** specialist area **15** specialized area

**nick**
**02** do **03** can, cut, jug, lag, nab, rob **04** bust, chip, dent, deny, form, jail, mark, nail, quod, scar, snip, take **05** catch, choky, clink, Devil, notch, pinch, run in, score, shape, sneck, snick, state, steal, swipe **06** arrest, collar, cooler, damage, fettle, groove, health, indent, inside, pick up, pilfer, pocket, prison, pull in, snitch **07** capture, defraud, scratch, slammer **08** knock off, porridge **09** apprehend, condition, jailhouse **11** indentation **13** police station
*See also* **prison; steal**

**nickel**
**02** Ni

**nickname**
**06** byname, to-name **07** epithet, moniker, pet name **08** cognomen, monicker **09** sobriquet **10** diminutive, soubriquet **12** familiar name
*See also* **Australian football; football; state; team**

**nifty**
**03** apt **04** chic, deft, fine, neat **05** agile, nippy, quick, sharp, slick, smart **06** adroit, clever, spruce **07** skilful, stylish **08** pleasing **09** enjoyable, excellent

**Niger**
**02** RN **03** NER

**Nigeria**
**03** NGA, NGR, WAN

**Nigerian**
**03** Ibo, Tiv **04** Efik, Igbo, Nupe **05** Hausa

**niggardliness**
**08** meanness, scarcity **09** closeness, parsimony, smallness **10** inadequacy, meagreness, paltriness, scantiness, skimpiness, stinginess **11** miserliness **12** cheeseparing, grudgingness **13** insufficiency **14** ungenerousness **15** tight-fistedness

**niggardly**
**04** hard, mean **05** close, mingy, nippy, nirly, small **06** meagre, measly, niding, nirlie, paltry, scanty, skimpy, stingy **07** miserly, nithing, sparing **08** grudging, near-gaun, nidering,

ungiving **09** illiberal, miserable, niddering, niderling, penny-wise, penurious **10** hard-fisted, inadequate, near-begaun, nidderling, ungenerous **11** tight-fisted **12** cheeseparing, insufficient, parsimonious

**niggle**
**03** bug, nag **04** carp, gnaw, moan **05** annoy, cavil, query, upset, worry **06** bother, hassle, pick on, potter, trifle **07** henpeck, nit-pick, protest, quibble, trouble **08** complain, irritate, keep on at **09** complaint, criticism, criticize, objection **10** nit-picking **12** equivocation, pettifogging **13** prevarication

**night**
**04** dark, evil, nite **05** death **06** sorrow **07** evening **08** darkmans, darkness **09** ignorance, night-time, obscurity **10** affliction **11** dead of night **15** hours of darkness
• **pass the night 03** lie

**nightclub**
**04** club **05** disco **06** nitery **07** cabaret, hot spot, niterie **09** nightspot **11** boîte de nuit, discotheque

**nightfall**
**04** dark, dusk **06** sunset **07** evening, sundown **08** gloaming, twilight **10** crepuscule

**nightingale**
**04** Lind **06** bulbul, Progne **08** Philomel **09** Philomela, Philomene
• **sound of nightingale 03** jug

**nightly**
**07** at night **09** after dark, each night **10** every night **11** nocturnally **15** night after night

**nightmare**
**05** agony, trial **06** horror, ordeal **07** anguish, incubus, torment, torture **08** bad dream, calamity **09** cacodemon, cauchemar, ephialtes **10** cacodaemon **11** oneirodynia **13** hallucination **15** awful experience

**nightmarish**
**06** creepy, unreal **07** ghostly, scaring **08** alarming, dreadful, horrible, horrific **09** agonizing, harrowing **10** disturbing, terrifying **11** frightening

**night-time**
**04** dark **05** night **08** darkness **11** dead of night **15** hours of darkness

**nihilism**
**06** denial **07** anarchy, atheism, nullity **08** cynicism, disorder, negation, oblivion **09** disbelief, emptiness, pessimism, rejection, terrorism **10** abnegation, negativism, scepticism **11** agnosticism, lawlessness, nothingness, repudiation **12** non-existence, renunciation

**nihilist**
**05** cynic **07** atheist, sceptic **08** agitator, agnostic **09** anarchist, extremist, pessimist, terrorist **10** antinomian, negativist **11** disbeliever, negationist **13** revolutionary

**Nike**
08 Victoria

**nil**
01 O 04 duck, love, none, nowt, zero
05 zilch 06 cipher, cypher, naught,
nought 07 nothing

**nimble**
04 deft, spry, yald 05 agile, alert, brisk,
fleet, light, lithe, nippy, quick, ready,
smart, swack, swift, wanle, wight,
yauld 06 active, clever, lissom, lively,
prompt, quiver, volant, wandle,
wannel, wimble 07 deliver, lissome,
springe 08 flippant, graceful 09 fleet-
foot, sharp-eyed, sprightly 10 sure-
footed 11 light-footed, quick-moving,
quick-witted, sharp-witted 13 quick-
thinking

**nimbleness**
05 grace, skill 07 agility, finesse
08 alacrity, deftness, legerity, spryness
09 alertness, dexterity, lightness,
niftiness, nippiness, smartness
10 adroitness 13 sprightliness

**nimbly**
04 fast 06 deftly, easily, spryly
07 agilely, alertly, briskly, lightly,
quickly, readily, sharply, smartly,
swiftly 08 actively, promptly, snappily,
speedily 11 dexterously 12 proficiently
13 quick-wittedly

**nincompoop**
04 clot, dolt, fool, nerd, nong, poop,
twit 05 chump, dunce, idiot, twerp,
wally 06 dimwit, drongo, nitwit
07 plonker 08 numskull 09 blockhead,
ignoramus, simpleton

**nine**
02 IX 06 ennead 08 nonuplet,
novenary, Pierides

**nineteen**
03 XIX

**ninety**
02 XC

**ninny**
see **fool**

**niobium**
02 Nb

**nip**
02 go 03 fly, lop, nep, pop, ren, rin,
run, sip 04 bite, clip, dart, dash, dock,
dram, drop, grip, rush, shot, snip, tear
05 catch, chack, check, hurry, pinch,
smart, sneap, steal, taste, tweak
06 arrest, nibble, snatch 07 catmint,
draught, portion, squeeze, swallow
08 cutpurse, mouthful
• **nip in the bud** 04 curb, halt, stem,
stop 05 block, check 06 arrest, impede
08 obstruct 09 frustrate

**nipple**
03 dug, pap, tit 04 teat 05 diddy, udder
06 breast 07 mamilla, papilla
08 mammilla

**nippy**
03 icy, raw 04 cold, fast, spry 05 agile,
brisk, quick, sharp 06 active, biting,
chilly, frosty, nimble, speedy
07 nipping, pungent 08 piercing,

stinging, waitress 09 niggardly,
sprightly

**nirvana**
03 joy 05 bliss, peace 06 heaven
07 ecstasy 08 paradise, serenity
10 exaltation 12 tranquillity
13 enlightenment

**nit-picking**
05 fussy 07 carping, finicky
08 captious, pedantic 09 cavilling,
quibbling 12 pettifogging 13 hair-
splitting, hypercritical

**nitrogen**
01 N 02 az- 03 azo-

**nitty-gritty**
06 basics 09 key points 10 bottom line,
brass tacks, essentials, main points
12 fundamentals, nuts and bolts

**nitwit**
03 ass 04 clot, dope, fool, jerk, prat,
twit 05 chump, dumbo, idiot, neddy,
ninny, wally 06 dimwit, drongo
07 pillock, plonker 09 birdbrain,
blockhead, simpleton 10 nincompoop,
silly-billy

**Niue**
03 NIU

**no**
◊ *deletion indicator* 01 O 02 na 03 nae,
nay, non, not 04 none, nope, uh-uh,
zero 05 no way 06 aikona, denial,
never a 07 refusal 08 not at all, no
thanks 09 not really 11 of course not
12 certainly not, nothing doing
13 absolutely not, not on your life
14 not on your nelly, over my dead
body

**nob**
03 VIP 04 head, toff 06 bigwig, fat cat
07 big shot 09 personage 10 aristocrat

**nobble**
◊ *anagram indicator* 02 do 03 buy, nab
04 bust, dope, drug, foil, grab, nail,
nick, take 05 bribe, catch, check, get
at, pinch, run in, seize, steal, swipe
06 arrest, buy off, collar, defeat,
hinder, pick up, pilfer, pull in, snitch,
thwart 07 disable, swindle, warn off
08 knock off, threaten 09 frustrate,
hamstring, influence 10 intimidate
12 incapacitate 13 interfere with

**nobelium**
02 No

**Nobel Prize**

*Nobel Prize winners include:*

02 **Fo** (Dario), **Oë** (Kenzaburo)
03 **Kao** (Charles K), **Lee** (Tsung-Dao),
**Orr** (Lord Boyd), **Paz** (Octavio),
**Tum** (Rigoberta Menchú)
04 **Belo** (Carlos), **Bohr** (Aage), **Bohr**
(Niels), **Böll** (Heinrich), **Born** (Max),
**Buck** (Pearl S), **Cela** (Camilo José),
**Duve** (Christian de), **Ertl** (Gerhard),
**Fert** (Albert), **Fire** (Andrew Z), **Gide**
(André), **Gore** (Albert Arnold (Al)),
**Hume** (John), **Hunt** (Tim), **Katz** (Sir
Bernard), **King** (Martin Luther),
**Koch** (Robert), **Mann** (Thomas),
**Mott** (Sir Nevill F), **Nash** (John),

**Rabi** (Isidor Isaac), **Rous** (Peyton),
**Shaw** (George Bernard), **Tutu**
(Desmond), **Urey** (Harold C)
05 **Annan** (Kofi), **Bethe** (Hans), **Bloch**
(Felix), **Boyle** (Willard S), **Bragg** (Sir
Lawrence), **Bragg** (Sir William),
**Bunin** (Ivan), **Camus** (Albert),
**Chain** (Sir Ernst), **Crick** (Francis),
**Curie** (Marie), **Curie** (Pierre), **Debye**
(Peter), **Dirac** (Paul A M), **Ebadi**
(Shirin), **Eliot** (T S), **Euler** (Ulf von),
**Evans** (Sir Martin J), **Fermi** (Enrico),
**Golgi** (Camillo), **Grass** (Günter),
**Haber** (Fritz), **Hesse** (Hermann),
**Jerne** (Niels), **Klerk** (F W de), **Krebs**
(Sir Hans), **Kroto** (Sir Harold),
**Lewis** (Sinclair), **Libby** (Willard F),
**Lwoff** (André), **Mello** (Craig C),
**Monod** (Jacques), **Nambu**
(Yoichiro), **Nurse** (Sir Paul), **Obama**
(Barack), **Pamuk** (Orhan), **Pauli**
(Wolfgang), **Peres** (Shimon), **Rabin**
(Yitzhak), **Sachs** (Nelly), **Salam**
(Abdus), **Simon** (Claude), **Smith**
(George E), **Smoot** (George F),
**Soddy** (Frederick), **Stern** (Otto),
**Tsien** (Roger Y), **Yeats** (W B),
**Yunus** (Muhammad)
06 **Arafat** (Yasser), **Baeyer** (Adolf von),
**Bellow** (Saul), **Bordet** (Jules), **Calvin**
(Melvin), **Carrel** (Alexis), **Cronin**
(James Watson), **Debreu** (Gerard),
**Enders** (John F), **Florey** (Howard,
Lord), **France** (Anatole), **Frisch**
(Ragnar), **Glaser** (Donald A),
**Hamsun** (Knut), **Hausen** (Harald
zur), **Heaney** (Seamus), **Hevesy**
(George von), **Hewish** (Antony),
**Huxley** (Andrew F), **Lorenz**
(Konrad), **Maskin** (Eric S), **Mather**
(John C), **Müller** (Herta), **Myrdal**
(Gunnar), **Nernst** (Walther), **Neruda**
(Pablo), **O'Neill** (Eugene), **Ostrom**
(Elinor), **Pavlov** (Ivan), **Perutz** (Max
F), **Phelps** (Edmund S), **Pinter**
(Harold), **Planck** (Max), **Porter**
(George, Lord), **Sanger** (Frederick),
**Sartre** (Jean-Paul), **Singer** (Isaac
Bashevis), **Steitz** (Thomas A),
**Tagore** (Rabindranath), **Walesa**
(Lech), **Watson** (James), **Wiesel**
(Elie), **Wilson** (Robert), **Yonath** (Ada
E)
07 **Akerlof** (George A), **Alferov** (Zhores
I), **Alvarez** (Luis), **Axelrod** (Julius),
**Banting** (Sir Frederick G), **Beckett**
(Samuel), **Behring** (Emil von),
**Brenner** (Sydney), **Brodsky**
(Joseph), **Canetti** (Elias), **Chalfie**
(Martin), **Coetzee** (JM), **Dae-jung**
(Kim), **Ehrlich** (Paul), **Feynman**
(Richard P), **Fleming** (Sir Alexander),
**Glashow** (Sheldon), **Golding**
(William), **Greider** (Carol W),
**Hershey** (Alfred), **Hodgkin**
(Dorothy), **Hodgkin** (Sir Alan L),
**Hurwicz** (Leonid), **Jelinek** (Elfriede),
**Jiménez** (Juan Ramón), **Kendrew**
(John), **Kertész** (Imre), **Khorana** (H
Gobind), **Kipling** (Rudyard),
**Krugman** (Paul), **Laxness** (Halldór),
**Lessing** (Doris), **Maathai** (Wangari),
**Mahfouz** (Naguib), **Mandela**
(Nelson), **Marconi** (Guglielmo),

Márquez (Gabriel García), **Maskawa** (Toshihide), **Mauriac** (François), **Medawar** (Sir Peter), **Mistral** (Frédéric), **Mommsen** (Theodor), **Myerson** (Roger B), **Naipaul** (VS), **Pauling** (Linus), **Penzias** (Arno), **Röntgen** (Wilhelm Konrad), **Rotblat** (Joseph), **Russell** (Bertrand, Earl), **Seaborg** (Glen T), **Seifert** (Jaroslav), **Soyinka** (Wole), **Szostak** (Jack W), **Thomson** (J J), **Trimble** (David), **Waksman** (Selman A), **Walcott** (Derek), **Whipple** (George H), **Wilkins** (Maurice)

08 **Appleton** (Sir Edward V), **Asturias** (Miguel Angel), **Capecchi** (Mario R), **Chadwick** (Sir James), **Delbrück** (Max), **Einstein** (Albert), **Faulkner** (William), **Friedman** (Milton), **Gajdusek** (D Carleton), **Gell-Mann** (Murray), **Gordimer** (Nadine), **Grünberg** (Peter), **Hartwell** (Leland H), **Kornberg** (Roger D), **Langmuir** (Irving), **Le Clézio** (Jean-Marie Gustave), **Leontief** (Wassily), **Meyerhof** (Otto), **Millikan** (Robert A), **Milstein** (Cesar), **Morrison** (Toni), **Mulliken** (Robert S), **Northrop** (John H), **Sakharov** (Andrei), **Saramago** (José), **Shockley** (William B), **Smithies** (Oliver), **Tiselius** (Arne), **Tonegawa** (Susumu), **Weinberg** (Steven), **Xingjian** (Gao)

09 **Ahtisaari** (Martti), **Arrhenius** (Svante), **Becquerel** (Henri), **Blackburn** (Elizabeth H), **Cherenkov** (Pavel), **Churchill** (Sir Winston), **Dalai Lama**, **Gorbachev** (Mikhail), **Hemingway** (Ernest), **Kissinger** (Henry), **Kobayashi** (Makoto), **Markowitz** (Harry M), **Mechnikov** (Ilya), **Michelson** (Albert A), **Nirenberg** (Marshall W), **Pasternak** (Boris), **Prudhomme** (Sully), **Rainwater** (James), **Roosevelt** (Theodore), **Shimomura** (Osamu), **Sholokhov** (Mikhail), **Steinbeck** (John), **Tinbergen** (Jan), **Tinbergen** (Nikolaas)

10 **Galsworthy** (John), **Heisenberg** (Werner), **Hofstadter** (Robert), **Lagerkvist** (Pär), **McClintock** (Barbara), **Modigliani** (Franco), **Montagnier** (Luc), **Pirandello** (Luigi), **Ramos-Horta** (José), **Rutherford** (Ernest, Lord), **Szymborska** (Wislawa), **Williamson** (Oliver E)

11 **Joliot-Curie** (Frédéric), **Joliot-Curie** (Irène), **Kantorovich** (Leonid), **Landsteiner** (Karl), **Maeterlinck** (Maurice), **Ramón y Cajal** (Santiago), **Schrödinger** (Erwin), **van der Waals** (Johannes Diderik), **Zinkernagel** (Rolf M)

12 **Hammarskjöld** (Dag), **Mother Teresa**, **Ramakrishnan** (Venkatraman), **Solzhenitsyn** (Aleksandr), **Szent-Györgyi** (Albert)

13 **Aung San Suu Kyi**, **Barré-Sinoussi** (Françoise), **Chandrasekhar** (Subrahmanyan), **García Márquez** (Gabriel)

14 **Levi-Montalcini** (Rita)

## nobility

04 nobs, rank 05 élite, glory, lords, peers, toffs 06 family, gentry, honour, nobles, virtue 07 dignity, majesty, peerage 08 eminence, grandeur, noblesse 09 grandness, integrity, nobilesse, nobleness, splendour 10 excellence, generosity, worthiness 11 aristocracy, high society, magnanimity, stateliness, superiority, uprightness 12 generousness, magnificence 14 impressiveness 15 illustriousness

*The nobility includes:*

01 d, E, P
02 Bt, Kt, Pr
03 Dom, Don, Duc
04 Bart, dame, duke, earl, jarl, lady, lord, Marq, peer
05 baron, count, laird, liege, nawab, noble, ruler, thane
06 daimio, Junker, knight, squire, vidame
07 baronet, dowager, duchess, hidalgo, marquis, peeress, vicomte
08 baroness, countess, governor, life peer, margrave, marquess, nobleman, seigneur, starosta, toiseach, vavasour, viscount
09 grand duke, liege lord, magnifico, patrician
10 aristocrat, noblewoman
11 marchioness, viscountess
12 grand duchess
13 grand seigneur

## noble

04 fine, gent, high, lady, lord, peer 05 brave, grand, great, lofty, manly 06 gentle, landed, manful, titled, vidame, worthy 07 eminent, exalted, gallant, grandee, magnate, stately 08 atheling, douzeper, elevated, generous, glorious, handsome, high-born, honoured, imposing, majestic, nobleman, old money, splendid, virtuous 09 dignified, doucepere, excellent, patrician, unselfish, venerated 10 aristocrat, honourable, impressive, noblewoman 11 blue-blooded, high-ranking, illustrious, magnanimous, magnificent, noble-minded 12 aristocratic, great-hearted 13 distinguished 15 self-sacrificing
*See also* **nobility**

## nobly

07 bravely 08 manfully, worthily 09 gallantly 10 generously, honourably, virtuously 11 unselfishly

## nobody

04 Nemo 05 no one 06 cipher, menial, Pooter 07 naebody, nothing 09 nonentity 10 mediocrity 11 lightweight

## nocturnal

05 night 09 night-time 13 active at night

## nod

03 bow, dip, nap 04 beck, doze, sign 05 agree, sleep 06 accept, assent, beckon, drowse, nid-nod, noddle, nutate, salute, signal 07 approve, doze

off, drop off, gesture, incline, support 08 greeting, indicate, say yes to 10 fall asleep, indication 11 acknowledge 15 acknowledgement
• **give the nod to** 02 OK 03 buy 04 back, pass 05 adopt, allow, carry 06 accept, permit, ratify, second, uphold 07 agree to, approve, confirm, endorse, mandate, support 08 assent to, hold with, sanction, validate 09 authorize, consent to 10 greenlight 11 rubber-stamp
• **nod off** 03 nap 04 doze 05 sleep 06 drowse 07 doze off, drop off, slumber 10 fall asleep

## node

03 bud 04 bump, knob, knot, lump 05 joint, nodus 06 growth, nodule 08 junction, swelling 09 carbuncle 11 convergence 12 protuberance

## noise

◇ *homophone indicator* 03 cry, din, pop, row 04 bang, boom, chug, clap, coil, roar, talk, wham, zoom 05 blare, clash, clunk, sound, whang 06 babble, bicker, clamor, hubbub, jangle, outcry, racket, report, rumble, rumour, tumult, uproar 07 brattle, clamour, clangor, clatter, discord, thunder 08 announce, clangour 09 circulate, commotion, publicize 11 pandemonium
• **amount of noise** 02 dB 03 bel, dBA 04 phon, PNdB 07 decibel

## noiseless

04 mute, soft 05 mousy, quiet, still 06 hushed, mousey, silent 07 catlike 09 inaudible, soundless

## noiselessly

06 softly 07 quietly 08 silently 09 inaudibly 11 soundlessly

## noisily

06 loudly, wallop 07 rowdily 10 fortissimo 11 deafeningly 12 boisterously, resoundingly, tumultuously, vociferously

## noisome

03 bad 04 foul 05 fetid 06 foetid, putrid, smelly 07 harmful, hurtful, noxious, reeking 08 mephitic, stinking 09 injurious, obnoxious, offensive, poisonous, repulsive, unhealthy 10 disgusting, malodorous, nauseating, pernicious 11 deleterious, pestiferous, unwholesome 12 disagreeable, pestilential

## noisy

01 f 02 ff 04 loud 05 roary, rowdy, vocal 06 roarie 07 blaring, blatant, booming, rackety, roaring 08 blasting, blattant, boastful, piercing, plangent, strepent 09 clamorous, deafening, turbulent 10 blusterous, boisterous, hoity-toity, strepitant, strepitoso, thundering, tumultuous, vociferous 11 rumbustious 12 ear-splitting, obstreperous
• **not too noisy** 02 mf

## nomad

03 San 04 Bedu 05 rover 06 Beduin, roamer, Tuareg 07 Bedouin, Bushman, migrant, rambler, Saracen, swagger,

**nomadic**
swagman, vagrant **08** Khoikhoi, vagabond, wanderer **09** Hottentot, itinerant, transient, traveller

**nomadic**
**05** Gypsy **06** Beduin, roving, Tuareg **07** Bedouin, migrant, roaming, vagrant **08** drifting, Khoikhoi, Scythian **09** itinerant, migratory, unsettled, wandering **10** travelling **11** peripatetic **13** peregrinating

**nom-de-plume**
**05** alias **07** pen-name **09** pseudonym **11** assumed name

**nomenclature**
**06** naming **08** locution, taxonomy **10** vocabulary **11** phraseology, terminology **12** codification **14** classification

**nominal**
**03** nom **04** tiny **05** nomin, small, token **06** formal, puppet **07** minimal, titular, trivial **08** so-called, supposed, symbolic, trifling **09** professed, purported **10** figurehead, in name only, ostensible, peppercorn, self-styled **11** theoretical **13** insignificant

**nominally**
**08** formally **10** in name only, ostensibly **12** symbolically **13** theoretically

**nominate**
**04** name, term **05** elect, put up, voice **06** assign, choose, select, submit **07** appoint, elevate, present, propose, suggest **09** designate, postulate, recommend **10** commission, substitute

**nomination**
**06** choice, naming **08** election, proposal **09** selection **10** submission, suggestion **11** appointment, designation **14** recommendation

**nominative**
**01** n **03** nom

**nominee**
**06** runner **07** entrant **08** assignee **09** appointee, candidate **10** contestant

**nomogram**
**04** abac

**non-alcoholic drink**
see **drink**

**non-aligned**
**07** neutral **09** impartial, undecided **10** uninvolved **11** independent, non-partisan, uncommitted **13** disinterested

**nonchalance**
**04** calm, cool **06** aplomb **08** calmness, coolness **09** composure, sangfroid, unconcern **10** detachment, equanimity **11** insouciance **12** indifference **13** pococurantism **14** pococuranteism, self-possession

**nonchalant**
**04** calm, cool **05** blasé **06** casual **07** offhand **08** careless, detached, laid-back **09** apathetic, collected, easy-going **10** insouciant **11** indifferent, pococurante, unconcerned **13** dispassionate, imperturbable **15** cool as a cucumber

**non-combatant**
**06** dovish **07** conchie, neutral **08** civilian, pacifist **10** non-aligned, non-violent **11** non-fighting, peacemaking **12** conciliatory, unaggressive **14** non-belligerent **15** passive resister

**non-committal**
**04** wary **05** vague **07** careful, evasive, guarded, neutral, politic, prudent, tactful **08** cautious, discreet, reserved **09** ambiguous, equivocal, tentative **10** diplomatic, indefinite **11** circumspect, unrevealing

**non compos mentis**
**03** ape, fey, mad **04** bats, gyte, loco, nuts, wild **05** barmy, batty, buggy, crazy, daffy, dippy, dotty, flaky, gonzo, loony, loopy, manic, nutty, potty, queer, wacko, wacky, wiggy **06** crazed, cuckoo, fruity, insane, maniac, mental, raving, red-mad, screwy **07** bananas, barking, berserk, bonkers, cracked, frantic, lunatic, meshuga **08** crackers, demented, deranged, dingbats, doolally, frenetic, frenzied, maniacal, unhinged, unstable **09** disturbed, lymphatic, psychotic, up the wall **10** bestraught, distracted, distraught, frantic-mad, off the wall, off your nut, out to lunch, stone-crazy, unbalanced **11** not all there, off the rails, off your head **12** mad as a hatter, off your chump, round the bend **13** off your rocker, of unsound mind, out of your head, out of your mind, out of your tree, round the twist **14** off your trolley, wrong in the head **15** out of your senses

**nonconformist**
**05** rebel **06** chapel **07** heretic, oddball, radical, seceder **08** maverick **09** dissenter, dissident, eccentric, heretical, protester **10** iconoclast **11** dissentient **12** secessionist **13** individualist, unco-operative **14** fish out of water

**nonconformity**
**06** heresy **07** dissent **09** deviation, secession **10** heterodoxy **11** originality **12** eccentricity

**nondescript**
**04** dull **05** bland, plain, vague **07** anaemic, insipid, vanilla **08** ordinary **11** commonplace, featureless, uninspiring **12** cookie-cutter, run of the mill, unattractive, unclassified, unremarkable **13** indeterminate, no great shakes, undistinctive, unexceptional, uninteresting **14** common or garden **15** undistinguished

**non-drinking**
**02** TT **03** dry **10** on the wagon

**none**
**01** O **02** no **03** nil **04** zero **05** no one, zilch **06** nobody, not any, not one **07** nothing **08** not a soul **10** not even one **13** not a single one
• **none the ...** **02** no **07** not a bit **08** not at all **10** to no extent

**nonentity**
**06** cipher, cypher, menial, nobody **07** nothing **08** shlepper **09** non-person, schlepper **10** mediocrity **11** lightweight

**non-essential**
**08** unneeded **09** accessory, excessive, redundant **10** expendable, extraneous, peripheral **11** dispensable, inessential, superfluous, unimportant, unnecessary **13** supplementary

**nonetheless**
**03** but, yet **05** still **06** anyhow, anyway, even so, though **07** however **08** after all **09** in any case **10** all the same, by any means, for all that, in any event, regardless **11** by some means, just the same **12** nevertheless **13** at the same time **15** notwithstanding

**non-event**
**04** no-no **06** fiasco **07** let-down **08** comedown **09** damp squib **10** anticlimax **14** disappointment

**non-existence**
**05** fancy **07** absence, chimera, unbeing **08** illusion **09** unreality **11** nothingness **12** illusiveness

**non-existent**
**04** null **06** unborn, unreal **07** fancied, fantasy, missing, phantom, unbeing **08** fanciful, illusory, imagined, mythical **09** fictional, imaginary, legendary **10** chimerical, fictitious, immaterial **11** incorporeal **12** hypothetical **13** hallucinatory, insubstantial, suppositional

**non-fiction**
*Non-fiction works include:*

**06** Walden
**07** Capital, Who's Who
**08** Self-Help
**09** Kama Sutra, Leviathan, On Liberty, Table Talk, The Phaedo
**10** Das Kapital, The Annales, The Gorgias, The Poetics, The Timaeus
**11** Down the Mine, Mythologies, The Agricola, The Analects, The Germania, The Phaedrus, The Republic
**12** Novum Organum, Silent Spring, The City of God, The Second Sex, The Symposium
**13** The Story of Art
**14** A Room of One's Own, Birds of America, Eudemian Ethics, Inside the Whale, Modern Painters, Past and Present, Sartor Resartus, The Age of Reason, The Golden Bough, The Life of Jesus, The Rights of Man, The Selfish Gene
**15** Lives of the Poets, The Essays of Elia, The Female Eunuch, The Sleepwalkers

**non-flammable**
**09** fireproof **10** flameproof **12** not flammable **13** fire-resistant, incombustible, uninflammable **14** flame-resistant

**non-intervention**
**06** apathy **07** inertia **08** inaction

**09** passivity **12** laissez-faire, non-alignment **14** hands-off policy, non-involvement **15** non-interference

### non-Jew
**03** goy **07** gentile

### nonpareil
**06** unique **09** matchless **10** inimitable, unequalled, unrivalled **12** incomparable, unparalleled, without equal **13** beyond compare

### non-partisan
**07** neutral **08** detached, unbiased **09** impartial, objective **10** even-handed **11** independent **12** unprejudiced **13** dispassionate

### nonplus
**04** faze, stun **05** sew up, stick, stump **06** baffle, dismay, puzzle **07** astound, confuse, flummox, mystify, perplex, stagger **08** astonish, bewilder, confound **09** discomfit, dumbfound, embarrass, take aback **10** disconcert, perplexity **11** flabbergast **14** discountenance

### nonplussed
**05** blank, fazed **07** at a loss, baffled, floored, puzzled, stumped, stunned **08** dismayed **09** astounded, flummoxed, perplexed **10** astonished, bewildered, confounded, taken aback **11** dumbfounded, embarrassed **12** disconcerted **13** flabbergasted **14** out of your depth

### non-professional
**03** lay **04** laic **07** amateur

### nonsense
**03** gum, rot **04** blah, bosh, bull, bunk, gaff, guff, jazz, junk, kack, pulp, punk, tosh **05** balls, bilge, borak, borax, folly, fudge, haver, hooey, pants, squit, stuff, trash, tripe **06** blague, bunkum, drivel, faddle, footle, gammon, havers, hoop-la, humbug, kibosh, kybosh, piffle, waffle **07** baloney, blather, blether, boloney, doggrel, eyewash, flannel, garbage, hogwash, malarky, pisheog, rhubarb, rubbish, twaddle **08** all my eye, blah-blah, blathers, blethers, bumfluff, claptrap, cobblers, codology, doggerel, flimflam, malarkey, pishogue, tommyrot, trifling, unreason **09** absurdity, bull's wool, fandangle, gibberish, kidstakes, moonshine, mouthwash, poppycock, silliness, stupidity **10** balderdash, clamjamfry, codswallop, flapdoodle, galimatias, jabberwock, mumbo-jumbo, taradiddle, tomfoolery **11** clanjamfray, double Dutch, fiddle-de-dee, fiddlestick, foolishness, jabberwocky, tarradiddle **12** blah-blah-blah, clamjamphrie, fiddle-faddle, fiddlesticks, gobbledegook, gobbledygook **13** gas and gaiters, horsefeathers, senselessness **14** how's your father, ridiculousness
*See also* **rubbish**

### nonsensical
◇ *anagram indicator* **05** barmy, crazy, dotty, inane, nutty, potty, silly, wacky **06** absurd, stupid **07** fatuous, foolish

**08** crackpot **09** gibberish, ludicrous, senseless **10** irrational, ridiculous **11** hare-brained, meaningless **12** preposterous **14** unintelligible

### nonsmoker
**02** ns

### non-stop
**07** endless, ongoing **08** constant, steadily, unbroken, unending **09** ceaseless, endlessly, incessant, unceasing **10** constantly, continuous, persistent, relentless, unbrokenly, unendingly **11** ceaselessly, incessantly, never-ending, unceasingly, unfaltering **12** continuously, interminable, interminably, relentlessly **13** round-the-clock, unfalteringly, uninterrupted, unrelentingly, unremittingly **15** uninterruptedly

### non-violent
**06** dovish, irenic **07** pacific, passive **08** pacifist, peaceful **09** peaceable

### noodle
**04** head, udon **05** moony, Sammy **09** blockhead, improvise, simpleton
*See also* **head**

### nook
**03** den **04** neuk **05** angle, niche **06** alcove, cavity, corner, cranny, recess, refuge **07** hideout, opening, retreat, shelter **08** hideaway **09** cubbyhole

### noon
**01** m, n **06** midday, middle **08** twelve pm **09** lunchtime **10** meridional, twelve noon **12** twelve o'clock

### noose
**04** fank **05** snare **06** twitch **07** necktie **08** marriage, rope's end **12** hempen caudle

### norm
**03** par **04** mean, rule, type **05** gauge, model, scale **07** average, measure, pattern **08** standard **09** benchmark, criterion, principle, reference, usual rule, yardstick **10** touchstone

### normal
**05** stock, usual **06** common **07** average, general, natural, popular, regular, routine, typical **08** accepted, everyday, habitual, ordinary, rational, standard, straight **10** accustomed, mainstream, reasonable, regulation **11** bog standard, commonplace **12** conventional, run of the mill, twenty-twenty, well-adjusted **13** perpendicular

### normality
**06** reason **07** balance, routine **08** normalcy **09** usualness **10** adjustment, commonness, regularity, typicality **11** averageness, naturalness, rationality **12** ordinariness **14** reasonableness **15** conventionality

### normally
**07** as a rule, as usual, usually **08** commonly **09** generally, naturally, regularly, routinely, typically **10** ordinarily **14** conventionally

### Norse
**01** N
*See also* **god, goddess**

### north
**01** N

### North America
*see* **America; Canada; United States of America**

### North Atlantic Treaty Organization
*see* **NATO**

### North Carolina
**02** NC

### North Dakota
**02** ND **04** N Dak

### north-east, north-eastern
**02** NE

### northern
**01** N **05** north, polar **06** Arctic, boreal **09** northerly **11** hyperborean **13** septentrional

### Northern Ireland
*see* **district; town**

### north-west, north-western
**02** NW

### Northwest Territories
**02** NT

### Norway
**01** N **03** NOR

### nose
**03** neb, pry, pug **04** beak, bill, boko, conk, ease, edge, feel, inch, push, snub **05** aroma, flair, nudge, scent, sense, smell, snoot, snout **06** hooter, nozzle, nuzzle, schnoz, snitch **08** informer, instinct **09** proboscis, schnozzle **10** move slowly, perception, projection
• **get up your nose** **03** bug, irk, nag, vex **04** fash, gall, rile **05** anger, tease **06** bother, harass, hassle, madden, molest, pester, plague, ruffle, wind up **07** disturb, hack off, provoke, tick off, trouble **08** brass off, irritate **09** aggravate, cheese off, displease, drive nuts **10** drive crazy, exasperate **11** get your goat **12** drive bananas **13** get on your wick, get your back up, make sparks fly **14** drive up the wall, get your blood up, give you the hump **15** get on your nerves, get your dander up
• **nose around** **03** pry **05** snoop **06** search **10** poke around, rubberneck **14** poke your nose in
• **nose out** **06** detect, reveal **07** find out, inquire, uncover **08** discover, sniff out
• **poke your nose into** **03** pry **05** pry in, snoop **06** butt in, fiddle, tamper **07** intrude **08** meddle in **09** interfere, intervene **10** stickybeak, tamper with **11** interfere in **12** put your oar in **14** stick your oar in
• **under your nose** **07** clearly, plainly **09** obviously **10** plain to see **11** for all to see **12** in front of you

### nosedive
**04** dive, drop **05** swoop **06** go down,

header, plunge, purler **07** decline, plummet **08** get worse, submerge

## nosegay

**04** posy **05** bunch, spray **07** bouquet

## nosey, nosy

**06** prying **07** curious, probing
**08** fragrant, snooping **10** meddlesome
**11** inquisitive, interfering
**13** eavesdropping
• **Nosey Parker** **08** busybody

## nosh

**03** eat, kai **04** diet, dish, eats, fare, feed, food, grub, menu, tuck **05** board, meals, scran, table **06** fodder, nibble, stores, tucker, viands **07** cooking, cuisine, rations **08** delicacy, eatables, victuals **09** nutriment, nutrition **10** bush tucker, foodstuffs, provisions, speciality, sustenance **11** comestibles, nourishment, subsistence
**12** refreshments

## nosiness

**06** prying **08** snooping **11** curiousness
**12** interference **13** intrusiveness
**14** meddlesomeness **15** inquisitiveness

## nostalgia

**06** pining, regret **07** longing, regrets
**08** yearning **09** mal du pays
**11** remembrance, wistfulness
**12** homesickness, recollection, reminiscence **13** recollections, regretfulness, reminiscences

## nostalgic

**06** pining **07** longing, wistful
**08** homesick, yearning **09** emotional, regretful **11** reminiscent, sentimental

## nostril

**04** nare

## nostrum

**04** cure, drug, pill **06** elixir, potion, remedy, secret **07** cure-all, panacea
**08** medicine **13** universal cure **14** cure for all ills **15** universal remedy

## nosy

see **nosey, nosy**

## not

◇ *anagram indicator* ◇ *deletion indicator*
**02** na, ne, no, -n't **03** non **04** nary, ne'er
**05** never **06** polled
• **and not** **03** nor
• **has not** **03** nas **04** ain't, ha'n't
• **is not** **03** nis, nys **04** ain't
• **not out** **02** in, no

## notability

**03** VIP **04** fame, note **05** celeb
**06** bigwig, esteem, renown, worthy
**07** big shot, magnate, notable, someone **08** big noise, eminence, luminary, somebody, top brass **09** big cheese, celebrity, dignitary, personage
**10** importance **11** distinction, heavyweight **12** significance
**14** impressiveness, noteworthiness, observableness

## notable

**03** VIP **04** rare, star **05** celeb, great
**06** bigwig, clever, famous, marked, signal, worthy **07** big shot, capable, eminent, serious, someone, special,

unusual **08** big noise, luminary, renowned, somebody, striking, terrible, top brass, uncommon **09** big cheese, celebrity, dignitary, important, memorable, momentous, notorious, personage, well-known **10** celebrated, impressive, notability, noteworthy, noticeable, observable, particular, pre-eminent, remarkable **11** heavyweight, illustrious, outstanding, significant
**12** considerable **13** distinguished, extraordinary, unforgettable

## notably

**08** above all, markedly, signally
**09** eminently **10** distinctly, especially, noticeably, remarkably, strikingly, uncommonly **12** impressively, in particular, particularly
**13** conspicuously, outstandingly, significantly **15** extraordinarily

## notation

**04** code **05** Romic, signs **06** cipher, noting, record, script, system
**07** symbols **08** alphabet **09** shorthand, tablature **10** characters **11** Laban system **13** hieroglyphics, orchesography

## notch

**01** V **03** cut, gap, jag, lip **04** dent, gash, gimp, hack, kerf, mark, mush, nick, nock, snip, step **05** cleft, crena, gouge, grade, level, score, sinus, stage, tally
**06** degree, groove, indent, joggle, raffle
**07** achieve, scratch, serrate, vandyke
**08** incision, nail-hole, swan-mark, undercut **09** insection **11** indentation
• **notch up** **04** gain, make **05** score
**06** attain, record **07** achieve, chalk up
**08** register

## notched

**05** erose, jaggy **06** eroded, jagged, nicked, pinked **07** dentate, serrate
**08** dentated, serrated **09** serrulate
**10** crenellate, emarginate, serrulated
**11** crenellated, denticulate
**12** denticulated

## note

**01** A, B, C, D, E, F, G, n **02** NB **03** log, see **04** bill, care, chit, fame, heed, item, line, long, mark, memo, mese, nete, oner, show, tone, tune **05** breve, drone, e-mail, enter, entry, fiver, gloss, large, minim, music, one-er, token
**06** chitty, denote, detect, letter, minute, notice, postil, quaver, record, regard, remark, renown, signal, single, sticky, stigma, symbol, tenner, twenty, wunner **07** account, apostil, comment, element, epistle, jot down, jotting, mention, message, middle c, missive, observe, put down, receipt, refer to, touch on, voucher, witness **08** allude to, annotate, Bradbury, crotchet, eminence, footnote, indicate, perceive, prestige, register, reminder, sforzato **09** apostille, attention, greatness, non placet, semibreve, sforzando, write down **10** annotation, cognizance, commentary, fortepiano, importance, impression, indication, inflection, intimation, marginalia, memorandum, notability, reputation,

semiquaver, stigmatize
**11** consequence, distinction, explanation, explication, mindfulness, observation, pre-eminence
**12** acciaccatura, put in writing, significance **13** attentiveness, become aware of, communication, consideration **14** characteristic, demisemiquaver **15** illustriousness

*Musical notes of the sol-fa scale:*

**02 do** (first), **fa** (fourth), **la** (sixth), **me** (third), **mi** (third), **re** (second), **si** (seventh), **so** (fifth), **te** (seventh), **ti** (seventh), **ut** (first)
**03 doh** (first), **fah** (fourth), **lah** (sixth), **ray** (second), **soh** (fifth), **sol** (fifth)

*See also* **strings of a lyre** *under* **string**
• **highest note** **03** e-la
• **of note** **04** some
• **take note** **02** NB **03** dig

## notebook

**03** log **05** diary **06** cahier, jotter, record
**07** daybook, journal, logbook, notepad
**09** field book, table-book **10** index rerum, pocket-book **11** address book
**12** exercise book

## noted

**05** great **06** famous, marked, of note
**07** eminent, notable **08** renowned
**09** acclaimed, notorious, prominent, respected, well-known **10** celebrated, pre-eminent, recognized **11** illustrious
**13** distinguished

## notes

**05** draft **06** record, report, sketch
**07** minutes, outline **08** jottings, synopsis **10** adversaria, commentary, personalia, transcript **11** impressions

## noteworthy

**06** marked **07** notable, unusual
**08** striking **09** important, memorable
**10** impressive, particular, remarkable
**11** exceptional, outstanding, significant
**13** extraordinary

## nothing

**01** O **03** nil, nix, zip **04** love, nada, nowt, void, zero **05** nihil, squat, zilch, zippo **06** cipher, cypher, menial, naught, nix-nie, nobody, nought, sod all, trifle, vacuum **07** nullity, sweet FA
**08** naething, oblivion **09** emptiness, nonentity, not an iota, not a thing, worthless **10** mediocrity **11** diddly-squat, lightweight, nothingness
**12** non-existence **15** sweet Fanny Adams
• **doing nothing** **04** idle
• **for nothing** **04** free **06** gratis, in vain
**08** at no cost, futilely **09** to no avail
**10** as a freebie, needlessly, on the house **12** free of charge, with no result
**13** complimentary, without charge
**14** unsuccessfully
• **nothing but** **04** just, only **06** merely, simply, solely **11** exclusively
• **nothing more** **04** mere

## nothingness

**04** nada, void **06** vacuum **07** nullity, vacuity **08** nihilism, nihility, oblivion

**09** emptiness **12** non-existence
**13** worthlessness **14** insignificance

### notice
**02** ad **03** see **04** bill, crit, espy, gaum, gorm, heed, mark, mind, news, note, sign, spot, tent **05** order **06** advert, advice, behold, detect, poster, regard, remark, review, si quis **07** comment, discern, leaflet, make out, mention, observe, thought, warning, write-up **08** apprisal, bulletin, circular, civility, critique, handbill, interest, monition, pamphlet, perceive **09** attention, awareness, criticism **10** cognizance, get a load of, intimation, take heed of, take note of **11** declaration, distinguish, information, instruction, observation **12** announcement, intelligence, notification, watchfulness **13** advertisement, become aware of, communication, consideration **14** pay attention to
• **give in your notice** **04** quit **05** leave **06** resign **07** walk out **08** step down **09** stand down **13** pack in your job **14** chuck in your job
• **give someone notice** **03** axe **04** fire, sack, warn **05** eject **07** boot out, dismiss, kick out **08** get rid of **09** discharge

### noticeable
**04** bold **05** clear, plain **06** marked, patent **07** evident, notable, obvious, visible **08** distinct, manifest, powerful, striking **10** detectable, impressive, measurable, observable, pronounced **11** appreciable, conspicuous, discernible, distinction, perceptible, significant **12** unmistakable **15** distinguishable

### noticeably
**07** clearly, notably, plainly, visibly **08** markedly, patently **09** evidently, obviously **10** distinctly, strikingly **11** discernibly, perceptibly **12** unmistakably **13** conspicuously, significantly

### notification
**05** aviso **06** advice, notice **07** message, telling, warning **09** informing, statement **10** disclosure, divulgence **11** declaration, information, publication **12** announcement, intelligence **13** communication **14** acknowledgment **15** acknowledgement

### notify
**04** tell, warn **05** alert **06** advise, inform, reveal **07** apprise, caution, declare, divulge, placard, publish **08** acquaint, announce, disclose **09** broadcast, make known **11** communicate

### notion
**04** idea, mind, view, whim, wish **05** fancy, vapor **06** belief, desire, liking, notice, revery, theory, vapour **07** caprice, concept, impulse, inkling, opinion, project, reverie, thought, wrinkle **08** crotchet, supposal, whim-wham **10** assumption, conception, conviction, hypothesis, impression **11** abstraction, inclination

**12** anticipation, apprehension **13** understanding

### notional
**05** ideal **06** unreal **07** fancied **08** abstract, fanciful, illusory, thematic **09** imaginary, unfounded, visionary **10** conceptual, ideational **11** speculative, theoretical **12** hypothetical **14** classificatory

### notionally
**08** in theory **10** putatively **12** conceptually **13** conjecturally, theoretically **14** hypothetically

### notoriety
**06** infamy **07** obloquy, scandal **08** disgrace, ignominy **09** celebrity, dishonour, disrepute, esclandre, publicity **10** opprobrium

### notorious
**05** noted **06** arrant, notour **07** blatant, glaring **08** flagrant, ill-famed, infamous **09** egregious, well-known **10** proverbial, scandalous **11** disgraceful, ignominious, of ill repute, opprobrious **12** disreputable **13** dishonourable

### notoriously
**06** openly **07** notably, overtly **08** arrantly, patently **09** blatantly, glaringly, obviously **10** flagrantly, infamously **11** egregiously **12** disreputably, particularly, scandalously **13** disgracefully, dishonourably, ignominiously, opprobriously, spectacularly

### notwithstanding
**03** for, yet **05** howbe **06** even so, for all, maugre, though **07** despite, howbeit, however, maulgre **08** although, nathless, naythles **09** in spite of, natheless **10** for all that, nathelesse **11** nonetheless, non obstante **12** nevertheless, regardless of **13** at the same time

### nought
**01** O **03** nil, nix **04** nada, nowt, null, zero **05** zilch **06** cipher, cypher, naught **07** nothing **11** nothingness
*See also* **nothing**

### noun
**01** n **06** aptote, gerund **11** substantive

### nourish
**03** aid **04** feed, have, help, rear, tend **05** boost, nurse **06** assist, foster, suckle **07** advance, bring up, care for, cherish, educate, forward, further, nurture, promote, support, sustain **08** attend to, maintain **09** cultivate, encourage, stimulate **10** provide for, strengthen, take care of

### nourishing
**04** good **06** battle **08** nutrient **09** healthful, nutritive, wholesome **10** beneficial, nutritious **11** substantial **12** alimentative, health-giving, invigorating **13** strengthening

### nourishment
**04** diet, eats, food, grub, nosh, tuck **05** juice, scran **07** aliment, ingesta, pabulum **08** goodness **09** nouriture,

nutriment, nutrition **10** nourriture, sustenance **11** subsistence

### nouveaux riches
**08** parvenus, upstarts **10** arrivistes, the new rich

### Nova Scotia
**02** NS

### novel
◇ *anagram indicator* **03** new **04** book, epic, rare, tale **05** fresh, roman, story **06** modern, unique **07** Aga saga, fiction, romance, strange, unusual **08** creative, hardback, original, uncommon **09** different, ingenious, inventive, narrative, paperback **10** innovative, pioneering, unfamiliar, unorthodox, yellowback **11** imaginative, resourceful, three-decker **12** bodice-ripper, double-decker, nouveau roman **13** Bildungsroman, unprecedented **14** ground-breaking, unconventional

---

*Novels and fictional works include:*

**03** Kim, She, USA
**04** Emma, Jazz, Nana, Voss
**05** Kipps, Money, Porgy, Scoop, Sybil
**06** Ben Hur, Carrie, Herzog, Lolita, Nausea, Pamela, Rob Roy, The Sea, Trilby, Utopia
**07** Babbitt, Beloved, Candide, Catch-22, Cat's Eye, Dracula, Erewhon, Euphues, Ivanhoe, Justine, Lord Jim, Orlando, Rebecca, Shirley, The Bell, The Fall, Ulysses
**08** Adam Bede, Birdsong, Clarissa, Cranford, Disgrace, Germinal, Jane Eyre, Lavengro, Life of Pi, Lucky Jim, Moby Dick, Newcomes, Nostromo, Oroonoko, Peter Pan, Rasselas, The Idiot, The Trial, The Waves, The Years, Tom Jones, Tom Thumb, Villette, Waverley, Wolf Hall
**09** About a Boy, Amsterdam, Beau Geste, Billy Budd, Billy Liar, Dead Souls, Dubliners, Gargantua, Hard Times, Kidnapped, L'Étranger, On the Road, Rogue Male, The Devils, The Egoist, The Hobbit, The Warden, Tom Sawyer, White Fang
**10** A Man in Full, Animal Farm, Bleak House, Cancer Ward, Cannery Row, Clayhanger, Don Quixote, East of Eden, Edwin Drood, Fever Pitch, Goldfinger, Howards End, Kenilworth, Labyrinths, Lorna Doone, Persuasion, Rural Rides, The Leopard, The Rainbow, The Tin Drum, Titus Alone, Titus Groan, Uncle Remus, Vanity Fair, Westward Ho!, White Teeth
**11** A Tale of a Tub, Black Beauty, Burmese Days, Cakes and Ale, Daisy Miller, Gormenghast, Greenmantle, Little Women, Middlemarch, Mrs Dalloway,

Oliver Twist, Silas Marner, Steppenwolf, The Big Sleep, The Hireling, The Outsider, The Talisman, The Third Man, War and Peace, Women in Love

**12** Anna Karenina, A Severed Head, A Suitable Boy, Barnaby Rudge, Brighton Rock, Casino Royale, Dombey and Son, Fear of Flying, Frankenstein, Little Dorrit, Madame Bovary, Moll Flanders, Of Mice and Men, Old Mortality, Rip Van Winkle, Room at the Top, The Gathering, The Go-Between, The Golden Ass, The Lost World, The Moonstone, The Old Devils, Volsungasaga

**13** A Kind of Loving, Arabian Nights, Brave New World, Call of the Wild, Daniel Deronda, Doctor Zhivago, Finnegans Wake, Joseph Andrews, Just So Stories, Les Misérables, Mansfield Park, Metamorphosis, My Brother Jack, New Grub Street, North and South, Schindler's Ark, Sketches By Boz, Smiley's People, Sons and Lovers, Tarka the Otter, The Awkward Age, The Bostonians, The Golden Bowl, The Jungle Book, The Last Tycoon, The Mabinogion, The Naked Lunch, The Odessa File, Thérèse Raquin, The Thorn Birds, The Virginians, The White Tiger, Under Milk Wood, Winnie-the-Pooh, Zuleika Dobson

**14** A Handful of Dust, A Room with a View, A Town Like Alice, Cider with Rosie, Death on the Nile, Decline and Fall, Fathers and Sons, Humphry Clinker, Jude the Obscure, Le Morte d'Arthur, Lord of the Flies, Lord of the Rings, Robinson Crusoe, Roderick Random, The Ambassadors, The Coral Island, The Da Vinci Code, The First Circle, The Forsyte Saga, The Great Gatsby, The Human Comedy, The Kraken Wakes, The Long Goodbye, The Lovely Bones, The Secret Agent, The Time Machine, The Water-Babies, The Woodlanders, Treasure Island, Tristram Shandy, Tropic of Cancer, Uncle Tom's Cabin, What Maisie Knew

**15** A Christmas Carol, A Farewell to Arms, A Passage to India, Cold Comfort Farm, Daphnis and Chloe, Flaubert's Parrot, Gone with the Wind, Huckleberry Finn, Le Rouge et le Noir, Northanger Abbey, Oscar and Lucinda, Our Mutual Friend, Peregrine Pickle, Tarzan of the Apes, The African Queen, The Invisible Man, The Little Prince, The Old Wives' Tale, The Secret Garden, The Woman in White, Three Men in a Boat, To the Lighthouse, Under the Volcano, Vernon God Little, Where Eagles Dare

## novelist
**06** author, fabler, writer **09** innovator **10** newsmonger, news-writer **11** storyteller **12** man of letters **13** fiction writer **14** creative writer, woman of letters
*See also* **author**

## novelty
**06** bauble, gadget, trifle **07** gimmick, memento, newness, primeur, trinket **08** gimcrack, rareness, souvenir **09** curiosity, freshness **10** creativity, difference, innovation, knick-knack, uniqueness **11** originality, strangeness, unusualness **13** unfamiliarity **15** imaginativeness

## November
**01** N **03** Nov

## novice
**01** L **03** cub, kyu **04** noob, tiro, tyro **05** chela, pupil **06** gryfon, newbie, rookie **07** amateur, griffin, griffon, grommet, gryphon, learner, new chum, recruit, student, trainee **08** beginner, neophyte, newcomer **09** greenhorn, noviciate, novitiate **10** apprentice, raw recruit **11** probationer

## noviciate
**06** novice **08** training **09** novitiate, probation **10** initiation **11** trial period **13** trainee period **14** apprenticeship

## now
**02** AD **04** next, then **05** today **06** at once **07** just now, present **08** directly, nowadays, promptly, right now **09** at present, currently, instantly, presently, right away, these days **10** at this time **11** at the moment, immediately **12** straight away, without delay **15** for the time being
• **now and then** **07** at times **08** on and off **09** sometimes **10** on occasion **11** desultorily, now and again **12** infrequently, occasionally, once in a while, periodically, sporadically **13** spasmodically **14** from time to time, intermittently

## nowadays
**02** AD **03** now **05** today **09** at present, currently, presently, these days **10** at this time **11** at the moment **15** in this day and age

## noxious
**04** foul **05** toxic **06** deadly **07** harmful, nocuous, noisome, ruinous **08** damaging, menacing **09** injurious, malignant, obnoxious, poisonous, unhealthy **10** contagious, disgusting, pernicious **11** deleterious, destructive, detrimental, pestiferous, threatening, unwholesome

## nozzle
**03** jet **04** nose, rose **05** snout, spout, tweer, twier, twire, twyer **06** stroup, tuyère, twyere **07** ajutage, sparger, sprayer **08** adjutage **09** nosepiece, sprinkler **10** projection **13** sprinkler head

## nuance
**04** hint **05** shade, tinge, touch, trace

**06** degree, nicety **07** shading **08** overtone, subtlety **09** gradation, suspicion **10** refinement, suggestion **11** distinction **15** fine distinction

## nub
**04** core, crux, gist, hang, knob, lump, meat, pith **05** chunk, focus, heart, pivot, point **06** centre, kernel, marrow **07** essence, gallows, nucleus **12** central point, protuberance

## nubile
**04** sexy **05** adult **06** mature **09** desirable **10** attractive, voluptuous **12** marriageable

## nuclear
**01** N

## nucleus
◇ *middle selection indicator* **03** nub **04** core, crux, meat **05** basis, focus, heart, pivot **06** centre, kernel, marrow **08** eucaryon, eukaryon, heartlet, nucellus **09** karyosome

## nude
**03** raw **04** bare **05** naked **06** Adamic **07** denuded, exposed, skyclad **08** disrobed, in the raw, starkers, stripped, undraped **09** butt-naked, in the buff, in the scud, unclothed, uncovered, undressed **10** start-naked **11** mother-naked **12** not a stitch on **13** with nothing on **15** in the altogether
*See also* **bare**; **naked**

## nudge
**03** dig, jab, jog **04** bump, knee, poke, prod, push **05** dunch, dunsh, elbow, shove **06** prompt

## nudity
**04** scud **06** nudism **07** undress **08** bareness **09** nakedness **10** déshabillé, dishabille **14** state of undress **15** in the altogether

## nugatory
**04** vain **06** futile **07** invalid, trivial, useless **08** trifling **09** valueless, worthless **10** inadequate, negligible, unavailing **11** ineffectual, inoperative, null and void **13** insignificant **15** inconsequential

## nugget
**03** wad **04** hunk, lump, mass **05** chunk, clump, piece, wodge

## nuisance
**04** bore, chiz, drag, hoha, hoop, hurt, pain, pest **05** chizz, trial **06** bother, burden, hoop-la, injury, plague, weight **07** problem, scunner, trouble **08** drawback, irritant, vexation **09** annoyance **10** affliction, difficulty, irritation **11** tribulation **12** embuggerance **13** inconvenience **15** thorn in your side

## null
**04** kink, vain, void, zero **05** annul, empty, knurl **06** cipher, cypher, nought **07** invalid, nullify, revoked, useless **08** annulled **09** abrogated, cancelled, nullified, powerless, worthless **11** ineffectual, inoperative, invalidated

## nullify

**04** kill, null, void **05** abate, annul, quash **06** cancel, negate, offset, repeal, revoke **07** abolish, rescind, reverse **08** abrogate, evacuate, renounce, set aside **10** counteract, invalidate, neutralize **11** countermand, discontinue **12** bring to an end

## nullity

**08** voidness **10** invalidity **11** uselessness **12** non-existence **13** immateriality, powerlessness, worthlessness **14** incorporeality **15** ineffectualness

## numb

**04** daze, dead, drug, dull, stun **05** dazed **06** benumb, deaden, freeze, frozen, torpid **07** drugged, in shock, stunned, stupefy, torpefy **08** benumbed, deadened, paralyse, sleeping **09** insensate, paralysed, stupefied, unfeeling **10** immobilize, insensible **11** immobilized, insensitive **12** anaesthetize **13** anaesthetized **14** without feeling

## number

**01** C, D, K, L, M, n **02** no **03** act, add, num, sum **04** copy, data, item, many, song, tale, turn, unit **05** count, crowd, dance, digit, group, horde, issue, limit, local, score, tally, total, track **06** amount, cipher, figure, reckon, sketch, throng, volume **07** add up to, company, compute, decimal, delimit, edition, imprint, include, integer, numeral, ordinal, routine, several, specify **08** cardinal, estimate, fraction, printing, quantity, restrain, restrict **09** aggregate, apportion, calculate, character, enumerate, multitude **10** collection, impression, statistics **11** anaesthetic, performance **12** anaesthetist, piece of music

*Numbers include:*

**02** pi
**03** one, six, ten, two
**04** five, four, half, nine, zero
**05** eight, fifty, forty, seven, sixty, three
**06** eighty, eleven, googol, ninety, thirty, twelve, twenty
**07** billion, chiliad, fifteen, hundred, million, seventy, sixteen
**08** eighteen, fourteen, nineteen, thirteen, thousand, trillion
**09** decillion, nonillion, octillion, seventeen
**10** centillion, googolplex, one hundred, septillion, sextillion
**11** quadrillion, quintillion

*French numbers include:*

**02** un
**03** dix, six
**04** cent, cinq, deux, huit, neuf, onze, sept, zéro
**05** douze, mille, seize, trois, vingt
**06** quatre, quinze, treize, trente
**07** dix-huit, dix-neuf, dix-sept
**08** quarante, quatorze, soixante
**09** cinquante, deux mille, un million
**10** un milliard

**11** soixante-dix
**12** quatre-vingts

*German numbers include:*

**03** elf
**04** acht, drei, eins, fünf, neun, null, vier, zehn, zwei
**05** sechs, zwölf
**06** sieben
**07** achtzig, Billion, fünfzig, hundert, Million, neunzig, sechzig, siebzig, tausend, vierzig, zwanzig
**08** achtzehn, dreissig, dreizehn, fünfzehn, neunzehn, sechzehn, siebzehn, vierzehn
**09** Milliarde
**10** einhundert, eintausend

*Italian numbers include:*

**03** due, sei, tre, uno
**04** nove, otto
**05** cento, dieci, sette, venti
**06** cinque, dodici, sedici, trenta, undici
**07** novanta, ottanta, quattro, tredici
**08** diciotto, quaranta, quindici, sessanta, settanta
**09** cinquanta
**10** diciannove
**11** diciassette, quattordici

*Latin numbers include:*

**03** duo, nil, sex
**04** octo, tres, unus
**05** decem, mille, novem
**06** centum, septem
**07** quinque, sedecim, undecim, viginti
**08** duodecim, quattuor, tredecim, trigenta
**09** nonaginta, octoginta, sexaginta
**11** quadraginta, septendecim, septuaginta, undeviginti
**12** duodeviginti, quinquaginta, quinquedecim
**13** quattuordecim

*Spanish numbers include:*

**03** dos, mil, uno
**04** diez, doce, ocho, once, seis, tres
**05** cinco, nueve, siete, trece
**06** ciento, cuatro, quince, veinte
**07** catorce, noventa, ochenta, sesenta, setenta, treinta
**08** cuarenta, un millón
**09** cincuenta, dieciocho, dieciséis
**10** diecinueve, diecisiete, quinientos
**11** mil millones

• **any number 01** n
• **large number 01** n **03** lot, ten **04** army, host, raft, slew, slue **07** zillion **09** gazillion
*See also* **many**

## numberless

**04** many **06** myriad, untold **07** endless **08** infinite, unsummed **09** countless, uncounted **10** unnumbered **11** innumerable **12** immeasurable **13** multitudinous, without number

## numbness

**06** stupor, torpor **08** deadness, dullness **09** paralysis **10** night-palsy

**12** stupefaction **13** insensateness, insensibility, insensitivity, unfeelingness

## numeral

**03** num **04** unit **05** digit **06** cipher, figure, number **07** integer **09** character

*Roman numerals include:*

**01** C (hundred), D (five hundred), I (one), L (fifty), M (thousand), V (five), X (ten)
**02** II (two), IV (four), IX (nine), VI (six), XI (eleven), XV (fifteen), XX (twenty)
**03** III (three), VII (seven), XII (twelve), XIV (fourteen), XIX (nineteen), XVI (sixteen)
**04** VIII (eight), XIII (thirteen), XVII (seventeen)
**05** XVIII (eighteen)

## numerical

**05** whole **06** graded, ranked, scalar **07** digital, figural **08** integral **09** identical **11** statistical **12** hierarchical **13** computational

## numerically

**07** in order **09** digitally **10** measurably **12** quantifiably **13** algebraically, exponentially **14** arithmetically, mathematically

## numerous

**04** many **05** great **06** a lot of, legion, strong, sundry, untold **07** copious, endless, profuse, several, various **08** abundant, a good few, manifold, populous **09** countless, plentiful, quite a few **10** rhythmical **11** innumerable **13** great in number, multitudinous

## numerousness

**06** number **08** multeity **09** abundance, plurality, profusion **10** numerosity **11** copiousness **12** manifoldness, multiplicity **13** countlessness, plentifulness

## numinous

**04** holy **05** deity, numen **06** divine, sacred **08** divinity, mystical **09** religious, spiritual **10** mysterious **12** supernatural, transcendent

## numskull

**03** ass, git, mug, nit, sap **04** berk, clot, coot, dill, dope, dork, fool, geek, goat, goof, goop, jerk, kook, nana, nerd, nerk, nong, prat, putz, twit, yo-yo **05** chump, dumbo, dunce, dweeb, galah, neddy, ninny, schmo, twerp, wally **06** bampot, dimwit, doofus, dum-dum, josser, muppet, nitwit, sawney, sucker, turkey **07** Charlie, dingbat, gubbins, jughead, pillock, plonker, saphead, tosspot, wazzock **08** boofhead, dipstick, lunkhead **09** birdbrain, blockhead, cloth head, schlemiel, simpleton **10** headbanger, nincompoop, silly-billy **11** chowderhead **13** proper Charlie

## nun

**03** top **06** abbess, sister, vestal, vowess **07** ancress, blue tit, zelator **08** canoness, prioress, zelatrix **09** anchoress, deaconess, zelatrice

**Nunavut**

10 cloistress, conventual, religieuse
14 mother superior
*See also* **monk**

**Nunavut**

02 NU

**nuncio**

05 envoy 06 legate 09 messenger
10 ambassador 14 representative

**nunnery**

05 abbey 06 priory 07 convent,
nunship 08 cloister

**nuptial**

06 bridal, wedded 07 marital, spousal,
wedding 08 conjugal, hymeneal
09 connubial 11 epithalamic,
matrimonial 12 epithalamial

**nuptials**

06 bridal 07 wedding 08 espousal,
marriage, spousals 09 hymeneals,
matrimony

**nurse**

◇ *containment indicator* 03 aid 04 feed,
help, keep, tend 05 angel, boost, shark,
treat 06 assist, cradle, foster, suckle
07 advance, care for, cherish, dogfish,
further, harbour, nourice, nourish,
nurture, promote, support, sustain
08 attend to, preserve 09 encourage,
entertain, look after 10 breast-feed,
take care of

*Nurse types include:*

02 EN, RN
03 aia, CNN, dry, pro, RGN, SEN,
SRN, wet
04 amah, ayah, home, maid, sick
05 nanny, night, staff, tutor
06 charge, dental, matron, school,
sister
07 midwife, nursery
08 district
09 auxiliary, children's, community,
Macmillan
10 consultant, Iain Rennie, ward
sister
11 night sister, psychiatric
12 practitioner
13 health visitor, State Enrolled,
theatre sister
15 locality manager, State Registered

*Nurses include:*

05 **Kenny** (Elizabeth)
06 **Barton** (Clara), **Cavell** (Edith),
**Rayner** (Claire), **Sanger** (Margaret)
07 **Seacole** (Mary)
08 **Pattison** (Dorothy Wyndlow)
10 **Stephenson** (Elsie)
11 **Nightingale** (Florence)
14 **Queen Alexandra**

*See also* **medical**

**nurture**

03 aid 04 care, diet, eats, feed, food,
grub, help, nosh, rear, tend, tuck
05 boost, coach, nurse, scran, train,
tutor 06 assist, cradle, foster, school
07 advance, bring up, care for, cherish,
develop, educate, feeding, further,
nourish, promote, rearing, support,
sustain, tending 08 boosting, instruct,
training 09 cultivate, education,
fostering, nouriture, nutrition,
promotion, schooling, stimulate
10 assistance, discipline, nourriture,
sustenance, upbringing 11 cultivation,
development, environment,
furtherance, nourishment, stimulation,
subsistence 13 encouragement

**nut**

02 en 03 fan, pip 04 buff, butt, head,
seed 05 crank, fiend, freak, loony,
stone 06 kernel, madman, maniac,
nutter, psycho, zealot 07 admirer,
devotee, fanatic, lunatic, nutcase,
oddball 08 crackpot, follower,
headcase, madwoman 09 fruitcake,
screwball, supporter 10 aficionado,
basket-case, enthusiast, psychopath
12 insane person

*Nuts include:*

03 ben, oak, pig
04 cola, horn, kola, pará, pili, pine,
shea, wing
05 acorn, areca, arnut, beech, betel,
cedar, cream, earth, ivory, lichi,
pecan, tiger
06 almond, Brazil, cashew, castle,
cobnut, cohune, corozo, ginger,
hognut, illipe, lichee, litchi,
lychee, monkey, oilnut, peanut,
physic, poison, sleeve, souari,
walnut
07 babassu, bladder, buffalo,
chesnut, coconut, filberd, filbert,
gallnut, hickory, leechee,
locknut, marking, palmyra,
pilinut, saouari
08 chestnut, clearing, cocoanut,
cokernut, coquilla, hazelnut,
quandong, sapucaia, thumbnut
09 Barcelona, beech mast, butterfly,
butternut, groundnut,
macadamia, mockernut,
pistachio, sassafras, scaly-bark
10 locking-nut, Queensland, St
Anthony's
11 Molucca bean
13 earth-chestnut, horse chestnut

*See also* **head**

• **do your nut** 05 go mad 06 blow
up, lose it, see red 07 explode 08 boil
over, freak out 09 blow a fuse, go
berserk, raise hell 11 blow your top,
flip your lid, go ballistic, go up the
wall, have kittens, lose your rag
12 blow your cool, fly into a rage,
lose your cool, throw a wobbly 13 hit
the ceiling, throw a tantrum 14 foam
at the mouth 15 fly off the handle, go
off the deep end

**nutriment**

04 diet, eats, food, grub, nosh, tuck
05 scran 09 nutrition 10 sustenance
11 nourishment, subsistence

**nutrition**

04 diet, eats, food, grub, nosh, tuck
05 scran 08 eutrophy 09 nutriment
10 sustenance 11 nourishment,
subsistence

**nutritious**

04 good 09 healthful, nutritive,
wholesome 10 beneficial, nourishing,
sustaining 11 substantial 12 body-
building, health-giving, invigorating
13 strengthening

**nuts**

◇ *anagram indicator* 03 mad 04 avid,
bats, daft, fond, keen, loco, mast, wild
05 barmy, batty, crazy, daffy, dippy,
loony, loopy, nutty, potty 06 ardent,
crazed, insane 07 berserk, bonkers,
devoted, lunatic, smitten, zealous
08 demented, deranged, doolally,
unhinged 09 disturbed, enamoured,
fanatical 10 infatuated, out to lunch,
passionate, unbalanced
12 enthusiastic, round the bend 13 off
your rocker, out of your mind, round
the twist 14 off your trolley
*See also* **mad**

**nuts and bolts**

06 basics 07 details 10 components,
essentials 11 nitty-gritty
12 fundamentals 13 bits and pieces
14 practicalities

**nutty**

03 mad 04 nuts, wild 05 barmy, batty,
crazy, daffy, dippy, loony, loopy, potty
06 crazed, insane 07 berserk, bonkers,
lunatic 08 demented, deranged,
doolally, unhinged 09 disturbed 10 out
to lunch, unbalanced 12 round the
bend 13 off your rocker, out of your
mind, round the twist 14 off your
trolley

**nuzzle**

03 pet, rub 04 nose, poke, root
05 nudge, press, sniff, train 06 burrow,
caress, cuddle, fondle, foster, nestle
07 bring up, snoozle, snuggle, snuzzle

**nymph**

04 Echo, girl, lass, maid, pupa
05 dryad, houri, naiad, oread, sylph
06 damsel, maelid, maiden, nereid,
sprite, Tethys, undine 07 mermaid,
oceanid, rusalka 09 hamadryad

# O

**O**
05 Oscar 06 nought 07 nothing, spangle

**oaf**
03 auf, oik 04 boor, clod, dolt, gawk, hick, hoon, lout, ouph, slob 05 idiot, ocker, ouphe, yahoo, yobbo 06 lubber 07 bumpkin 09 barbarian, roughneck 10 changeling, clodhopper 11 hobbledehoy

**oafish**
05 gawky, gross, ocker, rough 06 clumsy, coarse, lumpen, stolid 07 boorish, doltish, idiotic, ill-bred, loutish, lumpish, swinish, uncouth, yobbish 08 bungling, churlish, lubberly 10 unmannerly 11 clodhopping, ill-mannered

**oak**
04 holm, ilex 05 roble 06 cerris, kermes 07 durmast, Quercus 08 corktree, flittern, wainscot 10 quercitron 13 partridge-wood 15 king of the forest
• **oak bark** 03 tan

**oar**
03 row 05 blade, scull, spoon, sweep 06 bow-oar, paddle, stroke 09 stroke oar
• **oar blade** 04 peel

**oasis**
05 haven 06 island, refuge, spring 07 hideout, retreat, sanctum 08 hideaway 09 sanctuary 12 watering-hole

**oath**
03 vow 04 bond, cuss, word 05 curse 06 avowal, pledge 07 promise 08 cussword 09 assurance, blasphemy, curse-word, expletive, obscenity, profanity, sacrament, swear-word 11 affirmation, attestation, bad language, imprecation, malediction 12 word of honour 14 four-letter word
• **oaths and euphemisms** 02 od 03 dod, dog, gad, gee, Gog, odd 04 drat, ecod, egad, gosh, heck, hell, igad, life, odso, oons, rats, 'slid, 'zbud 05 bedad, begad, gadso, nouns, 'sfoot, 'slife, zooks 06 cricky, crikey, 'sblood, 'sdeath, 'sheart, 'snails 07 begorra, by Jingo, crickey, jabbers, odzooks, strewth 08 begorrah, bejabers, gadzooks 09 bismillah, 'sbodikins 10 sapperment, 'sbuddikins

**obduracy**
08 firmness, tenacity 09 obstinacy 10 doggedness, mulishness, perversity, wilfulness 11 frowardness, persistence, pertinacity 12 perseverance, resoluteness, stubbornness 13 inflexibility, intransigence, pigheadedness 14 relentlessness 15 hard-heartedness, wrongheadedness

**obdurate**
04 firm, hard, iron 05 stony 06 dogged, flinty, wilful 07 adamant 08 hardened, stubborn 09 immovable, obstinate, pigheaded, steadfast, tenacious, unbending, unfeeling 10 determined, headstrong, implacable, inflexible, persistent, self-willed, unyielding 11 hard-hearted, intractable, stiff-necked, unrelenting 12 bloody-minded, intransigent, strong-minded

**obedience**
04 duty 07 respect 08 docility 09 agreement, deference, obeisance, passivity, reverence 10 accordance, allegiance, compliance, observance, submission 11 amenability, dutifulness 12 acquiescence, amenableness, malleability, subservience, tractability 14 conformability, submissiveness

**obedient**
04 bent, obdt 06 docile 07 duteous, dutiful, pliable 08 amenable, biddable, yielding 09 compliant, malleable, observant, tractable 10 bridle-wise, conforming, law-abiding, obsequious, respectful, submissive 11 acquiescent, deferential, disciplined, subservient, well-trained

**obeisance**
03 bow 06 cringe, curtsy, homage, kowtow, salaam, salute 07 curtsey, respect 09 deference, obedience, reverence 10 salutation, submission, veneration 12 genuflection

**obelisk**
06 column, dagger, needle, obelus, pillar 08 memorial, monument

**obese**
03 big, fat 05 beefy, bulky, gross, heavy, hefty, large, plump, podgy, porky, round, stout, tubby 06 chubby, flabby, fleshy, portly, rotund 07 outsize, paunchy 08 roly-poly 09 corpulent, ponderous 10 overweight 11 Falstaffian, well-endowed 15 well-upholstered

**obesity**
04 bulk 07 fatness 09 grossness, plumpness, podginess, stoutness, tubbiness 10 chubbiness, corpulence, flabbiness, overweight, portliness, rotundness

**obey**
04 heed, keep, mind 05 bow to, defer, yield 06 comply, follow, fulfil, keep to, submit 07 abide by, act upon, conform, defer to, execute, give way, observe, perform, respect, respond 08 adhere to, carry out 09 be ruled by, consent to, discharge, surrender 10 come to heel, toe the line 11 acquiesce in, go by the book 14 do as you are told, take orders from 15 stick to the rules

**obfuscate**
◇ *anagram indicator* 04 blur, hide, mask, veil 05 cloak, cloud, cover, shade 06 darken, muddle, shadow, shroud 07 conceal, confuse, obscure 08 bewilder, disguise 10 complicate, overshadow 14 muddy the waters

**obfuscation**
06 muddle 08 disguise 09 confusion, obscurity 11 concealment 12 complication

**obituary**
04 obit 06 eulogy 09 necrology 11 death notice

**object**
03 aim, end, jib 04 body, butt, goal, idea, item, sake 05 argue, cavil, demur, focus, point, rebut, thing 06 adduce, design, device, entity, gadget, impute, intent, motive, oddity, oppose, reason, recuse, refuse, resist, target, victim 07 article, exposed, opposed, present, protest, purpose 08 ambition, artefact, complain 09 challenge, intention, objective, recipient, repudiate, something, take issue, withstand 10 disapprove, interposed, phenomenon 11 beg to differ, expostulate, remonstrate 12 recalcitrate 13 interposition, take exception
• **provisional object** 02 it
• **with the object of** 02 to

**objection**
02 ob 03 but 05 cavil, demur 06 boggle 07 dislike, dissent, protest, quarrel, scruple 08 argument, demurrer, question 09 challenge, complaint, exception, grievance 10 difficulty, opposition, recusation 11 disapproval 13 expostulation, recalcitrance, remonstration, unwillingness 15 dissatisfaction

**objectionable**
04 pert 05 nasty 07 hateful 09 abhorrent, loathsome, obnoxious, offensive, repellent, repugnant, repulsive, revolting, sickening 10 deplorable, despicable, detestable, nauseating, unpleasant 11 distasteful, intolerable 12 contemptible, disagreeable, unacceptable 13 exceptionable, reprehensible

**objective**
03 aim, end, obj 04 fair, goal, idea, just, mark, real, true 05 point 06 actual, design, intent, object, target, thingy 07 factual, genuine, neutral, purpose 08 ambition, clinical, detached, unbiased 09 authentic, equitable, impartial, intention 10 even-handed, impersonal, open-minded, uninvolved 12 unprejudiced 13 disinterested, dispassionate

**objectively**
06 fairly, justly 09 equitably, neutrally 11 impartially 12 even-handedly 14 with an open mind 15 disinterestedly, dispassionately

**objectivity**
07 justice 08 fairness, justness, open

mind **10** detachment, thinginess
**11** disinterest, outwardness, thingliness
**12** impartiality **13** equitableness
**14** even-handedness, open-
mindedness

### objector
**05** rebel **07** opposer, striker **08** agitator,
opponent **09** dissenter, dissident,
protester **10** complainer
**12** demonstrator

### obligate
**04** bind, make **05** force, impel, press
**06** coerce, compel, oblige **07** require
**08** pressure **09** constrain **10** pressurize
**11** necessitate

### obligation
**03** job, tie **04** bond, cess, debt, deed,
duty, must, onus, task **05** trust
**06** burden, charge, demand, duress,
favour **07** astrict, burthen, command
**08** contract, covenant, function,
pressure **09** agreement, liability
**10** assignment, commitment,
compulsion, incumbency
**11** obstriction, requirement
**12** indebtedness **14** accountability,
responsibility

### obligatory
**03** set **05** usual **06** normal **07** binding,
bounden, regular, routine **08** accepted,
enforced, familiar, habitual, ordinary,
required **09** customary, essential,
incumbent, mandatory, necessary,
requisite, statutory **10** compulsory,
imperative **11** established, fashionable,
traditional, unavoidable
**12** conventional

### oblige
**03** put, tie **04** bind, help, make
**05** force, impel, press, serve **06** assist,
coerce, compel, please **07** gratify,
require **08** astringe, obligate, pressure
**09** constrain **10** pressurize
**11** accommodate, necessitate **15** be
given no option

### obliged
**05** bound **06** debted, forced, in debt
**08** beholden, grateful, having to,
indebted, in debt to, required, thankful
**09** compelled, duty-bound, gratified,
obligated **11** constrained, having got
to, honour-bound **12** appreciative
**15** under compulsion

### obliging
**04** kind **05** civil **06** polite **07** helpful,
willing **08** friendly, generous, pleasant
**09** agreeable, courteous, indulgent,
officious **11** complaisant, considerate,
co-operative, good-natured
**13** accommodating

### obligingly
**07** civilly **08** politely **09** agreeably,
helpfully, willingly **10** generously
**11** courteously **13** considerately

### oblique
◇ *anagram indicator* **03** obl **04** skew
**05** cross, slant, slash **06** angled, squint,
stroke, tilted, zigzag **07** awkward,
devious, sloping, solidus, virgule,
winding **08** bevelled, diagonal,
inclined, indirect, rambling, sidelong,

sideways, slanting, tortuous, traverse
**09** divergent, skew-whiff, underhand
**10** circuitous, discursive, meandering,
roundabout **12** forward slash,
periphrastic **14** circumlocutory,
slantendicular, slantindicular

### obliquely
**05** askew **06** askant, aslant, aslope,
squint **07** askance, asquint **08** sidelong
**09** at an angle, evasively, slantwise,
slopewise **10** diagonally, indirectly
**12** circuitously

### obliterate
**04** blot **05** erase **06** deface, delete,
efface, rub out **07** blot out, destroy,
expunge, wipe out **08** black out,
vaporize, wash away **09** eliminate,
eradicate, extirpate, overscore, strike
out **10** annihilate

### obliteration
**04** blot **06** rasure, razure **07** erasure
**08** deletion **10** effacement, expunction
**11** blotting out, destruction,
elimination, eradication, extirpation
**12** annihilation

### oblivion
**04** void **05** Lethe, limbo **06** disuse,
pardon, stupor **07** amnesty, silence
**08** darkness, deafness **09** blankness,
blindness, ignorance, obscurity
**11** forgiveness, nothingness
**12** carelessness, non-existence
**13** forgetfulness, insensibility,
unmindfulness **15** inattentiveness,
unconsciousness

### oblivious
**04** deaf **05** blind **07** unaware
**08** careless, heedless, ignorant
**09** forgetful, forgotten, negligent,
unheeding, unmindful **10** insensible
**11** inattentive, preoccupied,
unconcerned, unconscious **12** absent-
minded

### obliviousness
**07** naivety **09** greenness, ignorance,
innocence, stupidity, thickness
**10** illiteracy **11** unawareness
**12** inexperience **13** unfamiliarity
**14** unintelligence **15** unconsciousness

### obloquy
**05** abuse, blame, odium, shame
**06** attack, stigma **07** calumny, censure,
slander **08** bad press, disgrace,
ignominy, reproach **09** aspersion,
contumely, criticism, discredit,
disfavour, dishonour, invective
**10** defamation, detraction, opprobrium
**11** humiliation **12** vilification
**13** animadversion

### obnoxious
**04** vile **05** nasty **06** horrid, odious
**07** exposed, hateful, hurtful, noxious
**08** horrible **09** abhorrent, loathsome,
offensive, repellent, repugnant,
repulsive, revolting, sickening
**10** deplorable, detestable, disgusting,
nauseating, unpleasant **11** intolerable
**12** contemptible, disagreeable,
unacceptable **13** objectionable

### obscene
**03** paw **04** blue, foul, lewd, rude, sexy,

vile **05** bawdy, dirty, gross, nasty
**06** carnal, coarse, filthy, fruity, greasy,
impure, pawpaw, risqué, sleazy,
smutty, vulgar, X-rated **07** immoral,
raunchy **08** hard-core, immodest,
improper, indecent, prurient,
shocking, unchaste **09** loathsome, off-
colour, offensive, repellent, shameless
**10** disgusting, licentious, lubricious,
outrageous, scandalous, scurrilous,
suggestive **11** disgraceful, near the
bone **12** pornographic **14** near the
knuckle

### obscenity
**04** cuss, dirt, evil, smut **05** curse, filth
**06** sleaze **07** offence, outrage
**08** atrocity, cussword, foulness,
impurity, lewdness, ribaldry, ribaudry,
vileness **09** bawdiness, carnality,
dirtiness, eroticism, expletive,
grossness, immodesty, indecency,
lubricity, profanity, prurience,
rybaudrye, scatology, swear-word,
vulgarity **10** balderdash, coarseness,
filthiness, immorality, indelicacy,
wickedness **11** bad language,
heinousness, imprecation,
impropriety, malediction,
pornography, raunchiness
**12** unchasteness **13** salaciousness,
shamelessness **14** four-letter word,
lasciviousness, licentiousness,
scurrilousness, suggestiveness

### obscure
◇ *anagram indicator* **03** dim, fog **04** blur
dark, deep, hazy, hide, mask, mist,
veil, wrap **05** cloak, cloud, cover,
dusky, faint, fuzzy, lowly, minor,
misty, murky, shade, shady, vague
**06** arcane, cloudy, darken, fogged,
gloomy, hidden, humble, muddle,
occult, opaque, remote, screen,
shadow, shroud, unsung **07** blurred,
complex, conceal, confuse, cryptic,
eclipse, shadowy, unclear, unknown
**08** abstruse, block out, darkness,
disguise, doubtful, esoteric, involved,
nameless, oracular, puzzling, riddling
twilight **09** concealed, confusing,
enigmatic, obfuscate, oraculous,
recondite, uncertain, unheard-of
**10** complicate, indefinite, indistinct,
mysterious, overshadow, perplexing
**11** god-forsaken, little-known, out-of-
the-way, unexplained, unimportant
**12** impenetrable, inexplicable,
unfathomable, unrecognized
**13** inconspicuous, insignificant
**14** indistinctness **15** undistinguished

### obscurity
**03** fog **05** depth, night, shade
**07** mystery **09** ambiguity, confusion,
intricacy, lowliness, murkiness,
mysticism **10** complexity, lack of fame
**11** unclearness **12** abstruseness,
namelessness, unimportance
**13** reconditeness **14** insignificance
**15** impenetrability
• **bring out of obscurity** **04** fish

### obsequies
**04** wake **06** burial **07** funeral
**08** exequies **09** cremation, interment
**10** entombment, inhumation

## obsequious

**04** oily **06** abject, creepy, menial, smarmy **07** dutiful, fawning, fulsome, kiss-ass, servile, slavish **08** crawling, cringing, obedient, toadying, toadyish, unctuous **10** flattering, grovelling, submissive **11** bootlicking, deferential, subservient, sycophantic **12** ingratiating, knee-crooking

## observable

**04** open **05** clear **06** patent **07** evident, notable, obvious, visible **08** apparent **09** scrutable **10** detectable, measurable, noticeable **11** appreciable, discernible, perceptible, significant **12** recognizable

## observance

**04** Lent, puja, rite **06** custom, maying, notice, ritual **07** heeding, keeping, service, trinket, triumph **08** ceremony, festival, practice **09** adherence, attention, discharge, execution, following, formality, honouring, obedience, punctilio, reverence, sabbatism, tradition **10** compliance, fulfilment **11** celebration, performance **13** lectisternium

## observant

**05** alert, sharp **06** seeing **07** devoted, dutiful, heedful, mindful, on guard **08** hawk-eyed, obedient, orthodox, vigilant, watchful **09** attentive, beady-eyed, committed, eagle-eyed, sharp-eyed, wide-awake **10** perceptive, percipient, practising **11** observative **12** card-carrying, on the lookout, on the qui vive

## observation

**04** data, note **05** study **06** espial, notice, regard, remark, result, review, seeing **07** comment, finding, opinion, thought, viewing **08** eyesight, noticing, scrutiny, watching **09** attention, criticism, statement, utterance **10** annotation, cognizance, inspection, monitoring, perception, reflection **11** declaration, description, discernment, examination, information **13** consideration, pronouncement

## observatory

**06** orrery **09** viewpoint **11** planetarium, planisphere

*Observatories include:*

**04** Keck
**05** Royal, Tower
**06** Gemini
**07** Arecibo, Palomar, Paranal
**08** Kitt Peak, Mauna Kea
**09** Greenwich
**11** Jodrell Bank, Mount Wilson
**12** Herstmonceux
**13** Tower of London
**14** Royal Greenwich

## observe

**02** la, lo **03** eye, say, see, spy, use **04** espy, heed, hold, keep, mark, note, obey, spot, take, twig, view **05** clock, smoke, state, study, utter, watch **06** behold, detect, follow, fulfil,

honour, notice, regard, remark **07** abide by, comment, declare, discern, examine, execute, inspect, look you, mention, monitor, perform, respect **08** adhere to, maintain, perceive, remember, take note **09** celebrate, conform to, discharge, recognize, speculate, surveille **10** animadvert, comply with, keep tabs on, take notice **11** commemorate, contemplate, keep an eye on, keep watch on, miss nothing **12** catch sight of **14** watch like a hawk

## observer

**06** looker, viewer **07** watcher, witness **08** beholder, looker-on, onlooker, reporter **09** bystander, sightseer, spectator **10** eyewitness **11** commentator, speculation

## obsess

**04** grip, rule **05** beset, eat up, haunt, hound **06** plague, prey on **07** bedevil, besiege, consume, control, engross, possess, torment **08** dominate **09** preoccupy **10** monopolize **11** have a grip on, have a hold on

## obsessed

**05** beset **06** hipped **07** gripped, haunted, hounded, plagued **08** hung up on **09** dominated **10** bedevilled, immersed in, infatuated **11** in the grip of, preoccupied

## obsession

**03** bug **05** mania, siege, thing **06** fetish, hang-up, phobia **07** complex **08** fixation, idée fixe, neurosis **09** monomania **10** compulsion, enthusiasm, hobby-horse **11** fascination, infatuation **12** one-track mind **13** preoccupation, ruling passion **15** bee in your bonnet

## obsessive

**04** anal **05** fixed **08** gripping, haunting, neurotic **09** consuming, maddening **10** compulsive, tormenting **12** all-consuming, trainspotter

## obsolescence

**06** disuse **07** failure **09** rejection, scrapping **10** redundancy **12** obsoleteness **13** disappearance

## obsolescent

**05** aging, dated **06** ageing, fading, old hat, waning **08** dying out, moribund, outdated **09** declining, on the wane, out of date, redundant **10** on the shelf **11** on the way out, out of the ark **12** antediluvian, disappearing, old-fashioned, on the decline, past its prime

## obsolete

**03** obs, old **04** dead **05** dated, passé **06** bygone, old hat **07** ancient, antique, disused, expired, extinct, outworn **08** in disuse, outdated, outmoded **09** discarded, out of date **10** antiquated, on the shelf **11** on the way out, out of the ark **12** antediluvian, discontinued, old-fashioned, out of fashion, past its prime **13** superannuated **14** behind the times

## obstacle

**03** bar **04** boyg, curb, drag, gate, jump, oxer, rock, snag, stay, stop **05** catch, check, hitch, mogul, remora **07** barrier **08** blockade, blockage, drawback, handicap, stoppage, stubborn, tank trap **09** barricade, deterrent, hindrance **10** difficulty, hinderance, impediment **11** obstruction **12** Becher's Brook, entanglement, interference, interruption **14** stumbling-block

## obstinacy

**08** firmness, obduracy, self-will, tenacity **10** doggedness, mulishness, perversity, wilfulness **11** frowardness, persistence, persistency, pertinacity **12** perseverance, resoluteness, stubbornness **13** inflexibility, intransigence, pigheadedness **14** relentlessness **15** hard-heartedness, wrongheadedness

## obstinate

**04** dour, firm **05** rusty, stoor, stour, sture **06** cussed, dogged, kittle, mulish, stowre, sturdy, thrawn, wilful **07** adamant, bullish, diehard, hard-set, restive, willful **08** camelish, stubborn, thraward, thrawart **09** hidebound, immovable, pigheaded, steadfast, unbending **10** bull-headed, determined, headstrong, inflexible, persistent, refractary, refractory, self-willed, stomachful, unyielding **11** hard-hearted, intractable, persevering, stiff-necked, unrelenting, wrongheaded **12** bloody-minded, contumacious, intransigent, pertinacious, pervicarious, recalcitrant, stiff-hearted, strong-minded **13** high-stomached, intransigeant

*See also* **stubborn**

• **obstinate person 04** mule

## obstreperous

◇ *anagram indicator* **04** loud, wild **05** noisy, radge, rough, rowdy **06** unruly **07** bolshie, raucous, restive, riotous, stroppy **09** clamorous, out of hand, turbulent **10** boisterous, disorderly, disruptive, refractory, rip-roaring, tumultuous, uproarious, vociferous **11** intractable, tempestuous **12** bloody-minded, uncontrolled, unmanageable **13** undisciplined

## obstruct

◇ *containment indicator* **03** bar **04** clog, crab, curb, foul, halt, stap, stop **05** block, brake, check, choke, cross, delay, hedge, limit, stall, stimy, stuff **06** arrest, bridle, cut off, hamper, hinder, hold up, impede, retard, stimie, stymie, thwart, waylay **07** blanket, inhibit, obscure, prevent, sandbag, shut off **08** encumber, restrict, slow down **09** barricade, frustrate, hamstring, interfere, interrupt **10** portcullis **13** interfere with

## obstruction

**03** bar, let **04** clog, stop, veil **05** block, check, ileus, trump **07** barrier, embargo **08** blockade, blockage,

**obstructive**
obstacle, sanction, stoppage, traverse **09** barricade, body-check, deterrent, hindrance, roadblock **10** bottleneck, difficulty, filibuster, impediment, prevention **11** restriction **14** stumbling-block

**obstructive**
**07** awkward **08** blocking, delaying, negative, stalling **09** difficult, hindering, hindrance, unhelpful **10** inhibiting **11** restrictive **12** interrupting **13** unco-operative

**obtain**
**03** cop, get, pan **04** earn, gain, have, hold, make, rule, snag, take **05** exist, reach, reign, seize, stand **06** attain, come by, come to, derive, occupy, secure **07** achieve, acquire, be in use, compass, possess, prevail, procure, realize **08** hold sway **09** be in force, be the case, get hold of **11** be effective, be prevalent **14** get your hands on

**obtainable**
**05** on tap, ready **06** at hand, on call **07** to be had **09** available **10** accessible, achievable, attainable, procurable, realizable

**obtrude**
**04** sorn **05** abuse, foist **06** butt in, impose **07** break in, exploit, intrude, mislead, presume, put upon **08** encroach, protrude **13** force yourself **14** thrust yourself **15** take advantage of

**obtrusive**
**04** bold, loud, nosy **05** nosey, pushy **06** prying **07** blatant, forward, obvious **08** flagrant, meddling **09** intrusive, prominent **10** noticeable, projecting, protruding **11** conspicuous, interfering

**obtuse**
**03** dim **04** dozy, dull, dumb, slow **05** blunt, crass, dense, dopey, thick **06** stolid, stupid **09** dim-witted **10** dull-witted, slow-witted **11** insensitive **12** thick-skinned **13** unintelligent **15** slow on the uptake

**obverse**
**05** cross, heads **07** inverse, reverse **08** contrary, converse, opposite **10** antithesis **12** complemental

**obviate**
**04** save **05** avert **06** divert, remove **07** counter, prevent **08** preclude **09** forestall **10** anticipate, counteract

**obvious**
**04** bald, open, rank **05** broad, clear, plain **06** patent **07** blatant, evident, glaring, visible **08** apparent, clear-cut, distinct, manifest, palpable, pregnant **09** prominent, writ large **10** detectable, noticeable, pronounced, undeniable, well-marked **11** conspicuous, open-and-shut, perceptible, self-evident, transparent, unconcealed **12** crystal clear, recognizable, unmistakable **14** self-explaining **15** self-explanatory, straightforward

**obviously**
**03** duh **07** clearly, plainly **08** of course, patently **09** certainly, eminently, evidently **10** distinctly, manifestly, noticeably, undeniably **11** undoubtedly **12** unmistakably, without doubt

**occasion**
**02** do **04** bash, call, case, gala, hour, make, need, rise, room, time, turn **05** breed, cause, event, evoke, party, point, throw **06** affair, chance, create, effect, elicit, excuse, ground, induce, lead to, prompt, reason **07** bring on, episode, grounds, inspire, pretext, produce, provoke **08** accustom, engender, function, generate, incident, instance, juncture, persuade **09** encheason, happening, influence, originate, situation **10** bring about, experience, give rise to, occurrence **11** celebration, get-together, opportunity, requirement, social event **12** circumstance **13** justification
*See also* **event; party**

**occasional**
**03** odd **04** orra, rare **06** casual, daimen **08** fugitive, off and on, on and off, periodic, sometime, sporadic, uncommon **09** irregular **10** incidental, infrequent **12** intermittent

**occasionally**
**07** at times **08** casually, off and on, on and off **09** sometimes **10** now and then, once in a way, on occasion **11** at intervals, irregularly, now and again **12** every so often, infrequently, once in a while, periodically, sporadically **14** from time to time, intermittently

**occlude**
◇ *containment indicator* **03** bar **04** clog, fill, halt, plug, seal, shut, stop **05** block, check, choke, close, cover, dam up **06** absorb, arrest, bung up, clog up, hinder, impede, retain, stop up, thwart **08** obstruct

**occlusion**
**03** jam **04** clot **05** block **06** log jam **08** blockage, blocking, stoppage **09** hindrance **10** congestion, impediment **11** obstruction

**occult**
**03** art **04** arts **05** magic **06** arcane, hidden, secret, veiled **07** magical, obscure, unknown **08** abstruse, esoteric, mystical **09** black arts, concealed, mysticism, recondite **10** mysterious **12** metaphysical, supernatural **13** preternatural **14** transcendental **15** supernaturalism, the supernatural

*Occult- and supernatural-related terms include:*
**03** ESP, obi
**04** jinx, juju, omen, rune
**05** charm, coven, curse, relic, spell, totem, witch
**06** amulet, déjà vu, fetish, hoodoo, medium, séance, shaman, spirit, trance, vision, voodoo
**07** cabbala, diviner, evil eye, palmist, psychic, satanic, sorcery, warlock
**08** black cat, exorcism, exorcist, familiar, Satanism, Satanist, sorcerer, talisman
**09** astrology, black mass, ectoplasm, Hallowe'en, horoscope, influence, palmistry, pentagram, tarot card
**10** astrologer, black magic, broomstick, chiromancy, divination, evil spirit, hydromancy, necromancy, Ouija board®, paranormal, planchette, possession, sixth sense, white magic, witchcraft
**11** chiromancer, clairvoyant, crystal ball, divining-rod, hydromancer, incantation, necromancer, oneiromancy, poltergeist, premonition, psychometer, psychometry, second sight, witch doctor
**12** clairvoyance, oneiromancer, spiritualism, spiritualist, supernatural, superstition, tarot reading
**13** fortune-teller, witch's sabbath
**14** Walpurgis Night

**occupancy**
**03** use **04** term **06** tenure **07** holding, tenancy **09** ownership, residence **10** habitation, occupation, possession **11** inhabitancy **13** domiciliation **14** owner-occupancy

**occupant**
**04** user **05** owner **06** holder, inmate, lessee, renter, tenant **08** occupier, resident, squatter **09** homeowner, incumbent **10** inhabitant **11** householder, leaseholder **13** owner-occupier

**occupation**
**03** job, use **04** line, post, work **05** craft, field, trade **06** billet, career, employ, métier, tenure **07** calling, capture, control, holding, pursuit, seizure, tenancy **08** activity, business, conquest, interest, invasion, province, takeover, vocation **09** occupancy, overthrow, residence, residency **10** employment, habitation, possession, profession, walk of life **11** foreign rule, subjugation

*Occupations include:*
**02** AM, DJ, GP, MD, MP, PA
**03** MSP, nun, spy, vet
**04** aide, chef, cook, dean, dyer, hack, maid, monk, page, poet
**05** abbot, actor, agent, baker, boxer, buyer, caddy, clerk, coach, diver, envoy, friar, guide, judge, juror, mason, mayor, medic, miner, model, nanny, nurse, pilot, smith, tawer, tutor, usher, valet, vicar
**06** abbess, artist, au pair, author, banker, barber, barman, bishop, bookie, bowyer, brewer, broker, butler, cabbie, cleric, cooper, copper, coster, cowboy, critic, curate, dancer, dealer, doctor, draper, driver, editor, eggler, factor, farmer, fitter, forger, gaffer, glazer, grocer, herald, hermit, hosier, hunter, jailer, jester,

jockey, joiner, lawyer, mercer, miller, ostler, packer, parson, pastor, pig-man, pirate, player, porter, potter, priest, ragman, ranger, roofer, sailor, salter, server, singer, skater, sniper, sparks, spicer, tailor, tanner, teller, tinner, trader, tycoon, typist, vendor, verger, waiter, warden, warder, weaver, welder, writer

**07** acrobat, actress, actuary, admiral, adviser, almoner, analyst, artisan, artiste, athlete, attaché, auditor, aviator, bailiff, barista, barmaid, bellboy, bellhop, bottle-o, breeder, builder, butcher, cashier, chemist, cleaner, climber, coalman, cobbler, collier, coroner, courier, cowherd, crofter, curator, cyclist, dentist, doorman, dresser, drummer, equerry, farrier, fiddler, fighter, fireman, florist, footman, foreman, frogman, general, glazier, gymnast, hangman, haulier, hostess, janitor, junkman, lace-man, lineman, lorimer, luthier, magnate, manager, marshal, masseur, midwife, milkman, oculist, officer, orderly, painter, partner, pianist, planner, plumber, poacher, popstar, postman, prefect, printer, rancher, referee, saddler, scholar, senator, servant, shearer, sheriff, showman, soldier, spinner, stapler, steward, student, surgeon, teacher, trainee, trainer, trapper, vintner, warrior, woolman, workman

**08** advocate, animator, armourer, attorney, banksman, botanist, bottle-oh, brakeman, callgirl, cardinal, chairman, chandler, chaplain, comedian, compiler, composer, conjurer, conjuror, corporal, costumer, coxswain, croupier, dairyman, deckhand, designer, diplomat, director, druggist, educator, embalmer, engineer, engraver, essayist, executor, factotum, farmhand, ferryman, film star, fishwife, forester, gangster, gardener, goatherd, governor, gunsmith, handyman, henchman, herdsman, hireling, home help, hotelier, huntsman, inventor, jeweller, labourer, landlady, landlord, lecturer, linguist, lyricist, magician, maltster, mapmaker, masseuse, mechanic, merchant, milkmaid, milliner, minister, minstrel, muleteer, musician, novelist, operator, optician, organist, pardoner, perfumer, pig-woman, polisher, preacher, producer, promoter, publican, quarrier, recorder, reporter, retailer, reviewer, salesman, sales rep, satirist, scrap-man, sculptor, seedsman, sergeant, shepherd, showgirl,

smuggler, sorcerer, spaceman, spurrier, stockman, stripper, stuntman, supplier, surveyor, thatcher, upholder, waitress, watchman, wet nurse, wig-maker, woodsman, wrangler

**09** alchemist, anatomist, announcer, antiquary, architect, archivist, art critic, art dealer, assistant, associate, astronaut, attendant, barperson, barrister, biologist, bodyguard, bookmaker, brinjarry, buccaneer, bus driver, cab driver, caretaker, carpenter, charwoman, chauffeur, clergyman, coal miner, collector, columnist, commander, concierge, conductor, constable, cosmonaut, costumier, couturier, cricketer, decorator, detective, dietician, dramatist, ecologist, economist, executive, facialist, financier, fisherman, fruiterer, gas fitter, geologist, goldsmith, governess, guitarist, gutter-man, harvester, herbalist, historian, homeopath, horologer, housemaid, HR manager, hypnotist, innkeeper, inspector, ironsmith, jacksmith, landowner, launderer, laundress, librarian, life coach, lifeguard, locksmith, machinist, messenger, musketeer, navigator, newsagent, nursemaid, osteopath, outfitter, paralegal, paramedic, performer, physician, physicist, plasterer, ploughman, policeman, pop singer, poulterer, professor, publicist, publisher, puppeteer, registrar, robe maker, sailmaker, scientist, secretary, shoemaker, signaller, signalman, songsmith, spokesman, stagehand, stationer, staymaker, stevedore, subeditor, subtitler, swineherd, therapist, towncrier, tradesman, traveller, trumpeter, usherette, van driver, violinist, volunteer, whittawer, yachtsman, zookeeper, zoologist

**10** accountant, advertiser, air hostess, air steward, amanuensis, apothecary, apprentice, archbishop, astrologer, astronomer, auctioneer, baby sitter, bank teller, beautician, bellringer, bill-broker, biochemist, biographer, blacksmith, bookbinder, bookkeeper, bookseller, bricklayer, bureaucrat, campaigner, cartoonist, cartwright, chairmaker, clockmaker, coastguard, compositor, consultant, controller, copywriter, corn-dealer, corn-factor, councillor, counsellor, disc jockey, dishwasher, dramaturge, dressmaker, dry cleaner, equestrian, fellmonger, fishmonger, footballer, forecaster, frame-maker, fundraiser, gamekeeper, game warden, gangmaster, gatekeeper,

geneticist, geochemist, geographer, glassmaker, handmaiden, headhunter, headmaster, highwayman, horologist, instructor, ironmonger, journalist, junk-dealer, keyboarder, legislator, librettist, lumberjack, magistrate, manageress, manicurist, manservant, midshipman, millwright, missionary, naturalist, negotiator, newscaster, newsmonger, nurseryman, obituarist, pallbearer, park ranger, pawnbroker, peltmonger, perruquier, pharmacist, piano tuner, playwright, podiatrist, politician, postmaster, private eye, programmer, proprietor, prospector, railwayman, removal man, researcher, ringmaster, roadmender, sales clerk, saleswoman, sempstress, shipbroker, shipwright, shopfitter, shopkeeper, signwriter, songstress, stewardess, stock agent, stockinger, stonemason, supervisor, taxi driver, technician, translator, typesetter, undertaker, unguentary, wainwright, wharfinger, whitesmith, woodcarver, wholesaler, woodcutter

**11** accompanist, antiquarian, art director, astrologist, audio typist, bank manager, bingo caller, broadcaster, bullfighter, burn-the-wind, businessman, candlemaker, car salesman, chambermaid, cheerleader, chiropodist, clergywoman, commentator, coppersmith, delivery man, distributor, draughtsman, electrician, entertainer, estate agent, etymologist, executioner, firefighter, foot soldier, fund manager, glass blower, grave digger, greengrocer, haberdasher, hairdresser, hair stylist, head teacher, horse-dealer, illustrator, interpreter, interviewer, lifeboatman, linen-draper, lollipop man, lorry driver, metalworker, money broker, mountaineer, music-seller, neurologist, optometrist, panel beater, parlourmaid, pathologist, philatelist, philologist, philosopher, policewoman, proofreader, radiologist, relic-monger, secret agent, set designer, sharebroker, ship builder, silversmith, sociologist, steelworker, stockbroker, taxidermist, telephonist, ticket agent, tobacconist, travel agent, tree surgeon, truck driver, underwriter, upholsterer, vitraillist, wagonwright, wax-chandler, web designer, wheelwright, wool-stapler, youth worker

**12** anaesthetist, broker-dealer,

cabinet maker, calligrapher, cartographer, cheesemonger, chimney sweep, chiropractor, churchwarden, civil servant, coal merchant, corn-merchant, costermonger, demonstrator, dramaturgist, entomologist, entrepreneur, event manager, fent-merchant, film director, garret-master, hotel manager, immunologist, IT consultant, longshoreman, maitre d'hotel, make-up artist, media planner, metallurgist, mineralogist, nutritionist, obstetrician, orthodontist, photographer, physiologist, ploughwright, postal worker, practitioner, PR consultant, press officer, prison warder, psychologist, radiographer, receptionist, restaurateur, sales manager, schoolmaster, screenwriter, scriptwriter, ship chandler, slink butcher, social worker, spokesperson, stage manager, statistician, stenographer, toxicologist, urban planner, veterinarian, warehouseman, wine merchant, wood engraver

**13** administrator, antique dealer, archaeologist, charity worker, choreographer, civil engineer, crane operator, criminologist, dental surgeon, food scientist, groundskeeper, gynaecologist, harbour master, health visitor, home economist, industrialist, lab technician, lexicographer, lollipop woman, mathematician, meteorologist, nightwatchman, oceanographer, old-clothesman, police officer, prison officer, rag-and-bone-man, rent collector, retail manager, scrap merchant, security guard, ship's chandler, shop assistant, sound engineer, streetcleaner, streetsweeper, support worker, traffic warden, window cleaner

**14** anthropologist, camera operator, claims assessor, draughtsperson, market gardener, marriage-broker, merchant tailor, microbiologist, music therapist, naval architect, pharmacologist, pharmacopolist, store detective, superintendent, systems analyst, tallow chandler

**15** biotechnologist, business analyst, commission agent, computer analyst, conservationist, costume designer, dental hygienist, fashion designer, flight attendant, funeral director, graphic designer, marine biologist, military officer, ophthalmologist, personal trainer, physiotherapist, police constable, refuse collector, speech therapist, stock controller, ticket collector

**occupational**
**04** work **05** trade **06** career **08** business **10** employment, job-related, vocational **12** professional

**occupied**
**04** busy, full **05** in use, taken **06** tied up **07** engaged, taken up, working **08** absorbed, employed, hard at it, immersed, tenanted **09** engrossed **11** preoccupied, unavailable

**occupier**
**04** user **06** dealer, holder, inmate, lessee, renter, tenant **08** occupant, resident, squatter **09** homeowner, incumbent **10** inhabitant **11** householder, leaseholder **13** owner-occupier

**occupy**
◊ insertion indicator **03** own, use **04** busy, fill, have, hold, nest, rent, tire **05** amuse, beset, seize, trade, use up **06** absorb, divert, embusy, employ, engage, fill in, invade, live in, manure, move in, obsess, obtain, people, settle, stay in, take up, tenant **07** capture, cohabit, dwell in, engross, entreat, immerse, improve, inhabit, involve, overrun, possess **08** interest, occupate, overbusy, reside in, take over **09** entertain, preoccupy, stimulate **14** make your home in

**occur**
**03** hit **04** fall, meet **05** arise, exist **06** appear, befall, chance, crop up, dawn on, happen, obtain, result, sink in, strike, turn up **07** be found, develop, turn out **09** be present, come about, come to you, eventuate, take place, transpire **10** come to mind, come to pass **11** materialize **12** have its being, spring to mind **13** cross your mind, enter your head, present itself, suggest itself **14** manifest itself

**occurrence**
**04** case **05** event **06** action, affair **07** arising, episode **08** incident, instance **09** existence, happening, incidence **10** appearance **11** development, proceedings, springing-up **12** circumstance **13** manifestation
• **trying occurrence** **03** cow

**ocean**
**03** sea **04** main **05** briny **07** the deep **08** high seas, millpond, profound, the drink **11** herring pond

*Oceans:*

**06** Arctic, Indian
**07** Pacific
**08** Atlantic, Southern
**12** North Pacific, South Pacific
**13** North Atlantic, South Atlantic

*See also* **sea**

*Ocean trenches include:*

**03** Yap
**04** Java
**05** Japan, Kuril, Palau, Tonga
**06** Cayman, Ryukyu
**07** Atacama, Mariana
**08** Aleutian, Izu Bonin, Kermadec, Marianas, Mindanao, Romanche
**09** Peru-Chile
**10** Philippine, Puerto Rico
**11** Nansei Shoto

**12** Bougainville, West Caroline
**13** Middle America, South Sandwich

**ocean-going**
**05** naval **06** marine **07** sailing **08** maritime, nautical, seagoing **09** seafaring

**ochre**
**04** keel

**octave**
**04** utas

**October**
**03** Oct

**octopus**
**05** polyp, poulp **06** polype, poulpe **07** octopod **08** Octopoda **09** devilfish

**odd**
◊ anagram indicator ◊ hidden alternately indicator **03** god, rum **04** fent, orra, rare, wild, zany **05** barmy, drôle, droll, extra, funny, kinky, queer, spare, wacky, weird **06** casual, far-out, freaky, quaint, quirky, random, single, sundry, way-out, whimsy **07** bizarre, curious, deviant, oddball, odd-like, strange, surplus, uncanny, unusual, various, whimsey **08** abnormal, atypical, crackers, freakful, freakish, left-over, original, part-time, peculiar, periodic, seasonal, singular, uncommon, unpaired **09** different, eccentric, haphazard, irregular, remaining, temporary, unmatched, whimsical **10** additional, fortuitous, incidental, mismatched, occasional, off the wall, outlandish, remarkable **11** exceptional, superfluous **13** extraordinary, idiosyncratic, miscellaneous **14** unconventional
• **odd one out** **04** case, cure **05** freak **06** odd bod, weirdo **07** oddball, odd fish **09** eccentric, odd man out, queer fish, tall poppy **11** odd woman out **13** nonconformist **14** fish out of water

**oddball**
◊ anagram indicator **03** dag, nut, rum **04** card, case, geek, kook, loon, wack **05** crank, flake, freak **06** nutter, oddity, weirdo **07** cupcake, dingbat, odd fish, strange **08** crackpot, peculiar **09** character, eccentric, queer fish **13** nonconformist **14** fish out of water

**oddity**
**03** dag, nut, rum **04** card, case, geek, kook, loon, wack **05** flake, freak, quirk, twist **06** jimjam, misfit, nutter, object, rarity, weirdo **07** anomaly, cupcake, dingbat, oddball, odd fish **08** crackpot, queerity **09** character, curiosity, queer fish, queerness **10** phenomenon **11** abnormality, peculiarity, singularity, strangeness **12** eccentricity, idiosyncrasy **14** fish out of water

**odd-looking person**
**04** quiz

**oddly**
◊ anagram indicator ◊ hidden alternately indicator **07** weirdly **09** curiously, strangely, unusually **10** abnormally, remarkably **11** irregularly

## oddment
**03** bit, end **04** fent **05** patch, piece, scrap, shred **06** offcut **07** remnant, snippet **08** fragment, leftover

## odds
**02** SP **04** edge, lead, line **05** price **06** scraps **07** chances, dispute, the line **09** advantage, supremacy **10** ascendancy, inequality, likelihood **11** probability, superiority **13** starting price
• **at odds** **06** at outs **07** arguing **08** clashing **09** differing, out of step **10** at variance, in conflict **11** disagreeing, quarrelling **13** at loggerheads **14** in disagreement
• **ignore the odds** ◊ hidden alternately indicator
• **odds and ends** **03** tat **04** bits, junk, tatt **06** debris, job-lot, litter, scraps **07** rubbish **08** cuttings, leavings, oddments, remnants, snippets **09** bric-à-brac **11** bits and bobs, odds and sods, this and that **13** bits and pieces, odd-come-shorts

## ode
**04** awdl **06** monody, threne **07** epicede, threnos **08** Pindaric, stasimon, threnode, threnody **09** epicedium, epinicion, epinikion **12** genethliacon

## odious
**04** foul, vile **06** horrid **07** hateful, heinous **08** horrible **09** abhorrent, execrable, loathsome, obnoxious, offensive, repugnant, repulsive, revolting **10** abominable, despicable, detestable, disgusting, unpleasant **12** contemptible, disagreeable **13** objectionable

## odium
**05** blame, shame **06** hatred, infamy **07** censure, dislike, obloquy **08** contempt, disgrace **09** animosity, antipathy, discredit, disfavour, dishonour, disrepute **10** abhorrence, execration, opprobrium **11** detestation, disapproval, reprobation **12** condemnation **13** offensiveness **14** disapprobation

## odorous
**05** balmy **06** smelly **07** pungent, scented **08** aromatic, fragrant, perfumed, redolent **11** odoriferous **13** sweet-smelling

## odour
**02** bo **04** niff, pong, sent, waff **05** aroma, savor, scent, smell, stink, whiff **06** repute, savour, stench **07** bouquet, perfume **09** fragrance, redolence

## odourless
**09** inodorous, unscented **10** deodorized **12** without smell **13** having no smell

## odyssey
**04** trek **06** voyage **07** journey, travels **09** adventure, wandering **13** peregrination

## of
◊ hidden indicator **01** o' **02** de, du, on, to

## off
◊ anagram indicator **03** bad, far, ill, out **04** away, from, gone, high, kill, sick, sour **05** apart, aside, right, rough, seedy, slack, wrong **06** absent, depart!, mouldy, poorly, queasy, rancid, rotten, spoilt, turned, unwell **07** dropped, off form, shelved **08** below par, scrapped **09** abandoned, called off, cancelled, elsewhere, incorrect, off-colour, postponed **10** decomposed, indisposed, out of sorts **11** at a distance, substandard, unavailable **12** unobtainable **13** disappointing **14** unsatisfactory **15** under the weather

## offal
**03** fry **05** gurry, heart, liver **06** kidney, refuse, tongue **07** garbage **08** entrails, lamb's fry **11** variety meat

## offbeat
**05** kooky, wacky, weird **06** far-out, freaky, way-out **07** bizarre, oddball, strange, unusual **08** abnormal **09** eccentric **10** unorthodox **13** untraditional **14** unconventional

## off-colour
◊ anagram indicator **03** ill **04** blue, foul, lewd, rude, sexy, sick **05** crook, crude, dirty, gross, rough, seedy **06** coarse, crummy, filthy, impure, poorly, queasy, risqué, sleazy, smutty, unwell, vulgar **07** immoral, obscene, off form, run down **08** depraved, immodest, improper, indecent **09** offensive, perverted **10** degenerate, indelicate, indisposed, licentious, out of sorts, suggestive **11** peelie-wally **12** pornographic **15** under the weather

## offence
**03** ire, sin **04** hurt, snub **05** anger, crime, fault, pique, wrong **06** injury, insult, slight **07** affront, assault, misdeed, outrage, umbrage **08** atrocity, trespass **09** annoyance, antipathy, exception, indignity, stumbling, violation **10** illegal act, infraction, resentment, wrongdoing **11** disapproval, displeasure, indignation **12** exasperation, hard feelings, infringement, misdemeanour **13** transgression **14** breach of the law
See also **crime**
• **take offence** **04** huff, miff **06** be hurt, resent **07** be angry, be upset **08** be miffed, be put out, get huffy **09** be annoyed **10** be insulted, be offended, feel put out, get the hump **11** be indignant, go into a huff, take umbrage **13** be exasperated, take exception **14** take personally

## offend
**03** err, hip, hyp, sin **04** hurt, miff, snub **05** anger, annoy, repel, upset, wound, wrong **06** injure, insult, kittle, needle, put off, put out, revolt, sicken **07** affront, disgust, do wrong, incense, outrage, provoke, umbrage, violate **08** distaste, go astray, gross out, nauseate **09** disoblige, displease

**10** exasperate, transgress **11** break the law, displeasure

## offended
**04** hurt **05** huffy, stung, upset **06** hipped, miffed, pained, piqued, put out **07** angered, annoyed, in a huff, wounded **08** incensed, outraged, smarting **09** affronted, disgusted, resentful **10** displeased **11** disgruntled, exasperated

## offender
**07** culprit **08** criminal **09** defaulter, miscreant, wrongdoer **10** delinquent, lawbreaker, malefactor **11** guilty party, probationer **12** transgressor

## offensive
**03** bad **04** foul, push, raid, rude, vile **05** alien, drive, grody, nasty **06** attack, charge, frowsy, frowzy, odious, sortie, thrust, wicked **07** abusive, assault, hostile, hurtful **08** annoying, impolite, indecent, insolent, invading, invasion, stinking, wounding **09** abhorrent, attacking, incursion, insulting, loathsome, obnoxious, onslaught, repellent, repugnant, revolting, sickening, unsavoury, upsetting **10** abominable, affronting, aggressive, detestable, disgusting, nauseating, outrageous, unpleasant **11** belligerent, displeasing, impertinent **12** antagonistic, disagreeable, discourteous, disrelishing, exasperating **13** disrespectful, objectionable

## offensively
**10** detestably **12** disagreeably, disgustingly, nauseatingly, unpleasantly **13** objectionably

## offer
**03** bid, try **04** bode, give, make, sell, show **05** essay, shore **06** afford, extend, prefer, submit, supply, tender **07** advance, attempt, bidding, express, hold out, offer up, present, proffer, propine, propose, provide, suggest, worship **08** approach, dedicate, overture, proposal, propound **09** celebrate, put in a bid, recommend, sacrifice, volunteer **10** consecrate, put forward, submission, suggestion **11** come forward, proposition, show willing **12** presentation **13** make available **14** put on the market

## offering
**03** IPO **04** gift **05** tithe **06** ex voto, xenium **07** handout, present **08** donation, oblation **09** sacrifice **10** dedication **11** celebration **12** consecration, contribution, subscription **13** heave-shoulder

## offhand
**04** airy, curt, rude, snap **05** ad lib, blasé, terse **06** abrupt, at once, casual **07** brusque, cursory **08** careless, cavalier, informal, laid-back **09** brevi manu, extempore, impromptu **10** cavalierly, improvised, nonchalant, off the cuff **11** free-and-easy, immediately, indifferent, perfunctory, unconcerned **12** at first blush, discourteous, happy-go-lucky,

uninterested **13** unceremonious
**14** currente calamo **15** at the first blush,
take-it-or-leave-it, without checking

## office

**03** aid **04** base, dept, duty, help, hint,
part, post, role, wing, word, work
**05** aegis, place **06** agency, back-up,
branch, bureau, charge, favour, tenure
**07** backing, cockpit, section, service,
support **08** advocacy, auspices,
business, division, function, lavatory,
position, referral, workroom
**09** affiliate, mediation, patronage,
situation, workplace **10** assistance,
commission, department,
employment, obligation, occupation,
subsection, subsidiary **11** appointment,
local office, subdivision
**12** intercession, intervention
**14** recommendation, regional office,
responsibility **15** place of business
*See also* **toilet**

*Offices include:*

**02** CO, FO, PO, TO, WO
**03** box, COI, CRO, DLO, EPO, FCO,
GAO, GPO, IIP, IRO, Met, NAO,
OFT, OME, ONS, OPW, ORR,
OSS, OST, pay, PRO, RLO, SFO,
War
**04** back, BFPO, fire, HMSO, Holy,
Home, land, loan, Pipe, Post
**05** Assay, Crown, front, Ofcom,
Offer, Ofgas, Ofgem, Oflot, Oftel,
Ofwat, paper, press, stamp
**06** Ofsted, Patent, Pat Off, police,
Record, ticket
**07** booking, Foreign, sorting
**08** Chancery, Colonial, Eurostat,
incident, printing, register,
registry, Scottish
**09** personnel, receiving, telegraph
**10** dead-letter, employment, Quai
d'Orsay, registered, Stationery
**11** general post, left-luggage,
victualling
**12** Commonwealth, Serious Fraud
**13** Inland Revenue, National Audit
**14** European Patent, Meteorological,
returned letter
**15** Criminal Records

*Office furniture includes:*

**04** desk, safe
**07** lectern
**08** desk lamp, fire safe
**09** partition, plan chest, stepstool,
work table
**11** storage unit, swivel chair,
workstation
**12** computer desk, drawing-board,
fire cupboard, printer stand,
typist's chair
**13** executive desk, filing cabinet,
filing trolley
**14** boardroom table, display cabinet,
executive chair, filing cupboard,
reception chair
**15** conference table, secretarial desk

*Office equipment includes:*

**03** OHP, VDU
**05** mouse
**06** inkpad, screen, tacker

**07** cash box, monitor, planner,
printer, scanner, stapler, trimmer
**08** computer, intercom, keyboard,
mouse mat, plan file, shredder
**09** date-stamp, dust cover, laminator,
telephone, textphone, time clock,
wages book
**10** calculator, comb binder, copy
holder, Dictaphone®, duplicator,
fax machine, guillotine, letter
tray, monitor arm, paper punch,
printwheel, typewriter
**11** comb binding, hole puncher,
noticeboard, photocopier,
switchboard
**12** acoustic hood, letter opener,
letter scales, message board,
parcel scales, screen filter, telex
machine, visitors' book, wire
bindings
**13** data cartridge, desk organizer,
microcassette, planning board,
reference book, staple-remover,
thermal binder, waste-paper bin,
word processor
**14** adhesive binder, diskette mailer,
flip-chart easel, laptop computer,
slide projector, telephone index

*See also* **stationery**
- **branch office  02** bo
- **in office  02** in
- **office of bishop  03** see
- **office of cardinal  03** hat
- **out of office  04** late

## officer

**03** col, off **04** lead **05** agent, envoy,
polis **06** deputy, fantad, fantod, non-
com, pusser, schout, varlet
**07** command **08** dog's-body, official
**09** appointee, dignitary, executive,
inspector, messenger, subaltern
**10** bureaucrat **11** board member,
functionary **12** office-bearer, office-
holder **13** administrator, public servant
**14** representative **15** committee
member
*See also* **police officer; rank;
religious; ship**

## official

**03** off **05** legal **06** Bumble, formal,
kosher, lawful, proper, pusser, ritual,
solemn **07** officer, stately **08** accepted,
approved, bona fide, endorsed,
licensed **09** authentic, certified,
dignified, validated **10** accredited,
authorized, ceremonial, legitimate,
recognized, sanctioned **11** functionary
**12** Jack-in-office, office-bearer, office-
holder **13** authenticated, authoritative

*Officials include:*

**02** JP, MP
**05** agent, chief, clerk, druid, elder,
envoy, hakim, mayor, reeve,
usher
**06** atabeg, atabek, consul, Euro-MP,
notary, purser, pusser
**07** bailiff, captain, coroner, equerry,
manager, marshal, monitor,
prefect, proctor, senator, sheriff,
steward, vaivode, voivode
**08** chairman, delegate, diplomat,
director, Eurocrat, executor,

governor, mandarin, mayoress,
minister, mud-clerk, overseer,
provedor, providor
**09** commander, commissar,
executive, Gauleiter, inspector,
nipcheese, ombudsman,
president, principal, provedore,
registrar
**10** ambassador, bureaucrat,
chairwoman, chancellor,
councillor, magistrate, proprietor,
proveditor, railroader, supervisor
**11** chairperson, congressman,
proveditore
**12** baron-officer, borough-reeve,
civil servant, commissioner
**13** administrator, congresswoman,
fonctionnaire
**14** representative, superintendent

## officialdom

**04** them **08** ministry **09** mandarins,
officials, the system **10** government
**11** bureaucracy **12** civil service
**13** administrator, civil servants
**14** administration, the authorities
**15** local government

## officialese

**06** jargon **07** rubbish **08** nonsense
**09** buzz words, gibberish **10** journalese
**11** computerese **12** gobbledygook,
psychobabble

## officially

**08** formally, properly **09** correctly **11** on
the record **12** managerially,
procedurally **13** authentically
**15** authoritatively

## officiate

**03** run **05** chair **06** manage **07** conduct,
oversee, preside **10** be in charge, take
charge **11** superintend **12** take the chair

## officious

**05** bossy, pushy **06** prying, spoffy
**07** dutiful, forward **08** bustling,
informal, meddling, obliging,
overbusy, spoffish **09** diplomacy,
intrusive, obtrusive **10** meddlesome
**11** dictatorial, domineering,
importunate, inquisitive, interfering,
opinionated, over-zealous,
pragmatical **13** self-important

## officiously

**07** bossily, pushily **13** dictatorially,
over-zealously **15** self-importantly,
with importunity

## offing

- **in the offing  04** near **06** at hand
**07** in sight **08** coming up, imminent, on
the way **10** coming soon, on the cards
**11** close at hand **12** on the horizon
**13** happening soon

## offish

**04** cool **05** aloof **07** haughty, stuck-up
**10** unsociable **11** standoffish

## off-key

**07** jarring **09** dissonant, out of tune
**10** discordant, unsuitable **11** conflicting
**12** inharmonious, out of keeping
**13** inappropriate

## offload

**04** drop, dump, palm **05** chuck, shift

**off-putting**

**06** unload **07** deposit **08** get rid of, jettison, unburden **09** disburden, discharge

**off-putting**

**08** daunting **09** unnerving, upsetting **10** disturbing, formidable, unpleasant, unsettling **11** dispiriting, frightening, unappealing **12** demoralizing, discomfiting, discouraging, intimidating **13** disconcerting, disheartening

**offset**

**06** cancel **07** balance **09** cancel out, make up for **10** balance out, counteract, neutralize **11** countervail **12** counterpoise **13** compensate for **14** counterbalance

**offshoot**

**03** arm **04** limb, sien **05** bayou, plant, scion, swarm **06** branch, reform, result **07** outcome, product, spin-off **08** shoulder, sideslip **09** apophysis, appendage, billabong, by-product, outgrowth **11** consequence, development

**offspring**

**03** get, kid, son **04** baby, burd, kids, seed, sons **05** breed, brood, child, heirs, issue, spawn, young **06** babies, family, infant, litter, nipper, source **07** infants, nippers, product, progeny **08** ancestry, children, daughter, young one **09** daughters, little one, young ones, youngster **10** generation, little ones, successors, youngsters **11** descendants

**often**

**03** oft **04** much **08** commonly, frequent, ofttimes **09** generally, many a time, many times, regularly **10** frequently, repeatedly **11** day in day out **12** time and again **13** again and again, time after time, week in week out **15** month in month out

**ogle**

**03** eye **04** leer, look **05** eliad, eye up, stare **06** eyliad, illiad **07** eyeliad, glad eye **08** oeillade **10** make eyes at

**ogre**

**03** orc **04** boyg **05** beast, bogey, brute, demon, devil, fiend, giant, troll **06** savage **07** monster, villain **08** bogeyman **09** barbarian

**Ohio**

**02** OH

**oik**

*see* **cad**

**oil**

**03** fat **04** balm, news, oint **05** cream, salve, smear **06** anoint, grease, lotion **07** unguent **08** liniment, ointment **09** lubricant, lubricate **10** impregnate, make smooth **11** information

*Oils include:*

**03** ben, gas, nim, nut, til
**04** baby, cade, coal, corn, crab, derv, dika, fish, fuel, hair, neem, nimb, otto, palm, poon, rape, rock, rose, rusa, seed, tall,

tung, wood, wool, zest
**05** attar, carap, crude, grass, heavy, macaw, neemb, niger, olive, ottar, poppy, pulza, rosin, salad, savin, shale, shark, snake, sperm, spike, sweet, thyme, train, whale
**06** ajowan, almond, canola, castor, chrism, cloves, cohune, diesel, illipe, jojoba, macoya, neroli, peanut, savine, Seneca, sesame
**07** arachis, cajuput, camphor, coconut, gingili, jinjili, linseed, lumbang, mineral, mirbane, mustard, myrrhol, spindle, verbena, vitriol
**08** ambrosia, bergamot, camphine, cinnamon, cod-liver, creosote, gingelly, kerosene, kerosine, lavender, macahuba, macassar, North Sea, paraffin, pristane, rapeseed, rosewood
**09** black gold, candlenut, grapeseed, neat's-foot, patchouli, patchouly, safflower, sassafras, spikenard, sunflower, vanaspati, vegetable
**10** citronella, eucalyptus, peppermint, petit grain, turpentine, ylang-ylang
**11** camphorated, chaulmoogra, wintergreen
**12** brilliantine
**15** evening primrose

• **oil platform** **03** rig
• **oil receptacle** **04** sump

**oily**

**03** fat **04** glib **05** fatty, slimy, suave **06** greasy, smarmy, smooth, urbane **07** buttery, servile **08** slippery, unctuous **10** flattering, obsequious, oleaginous **11** subservient **12** ingratiating **13** smooth-talking

**ointment**

**03** gel **04** balm **05** cream, salve **06** balsam, cerate, lotion, pomade **07** pomatum, unction, unguent **08** eye-salve, liniment, lipsalve, Vaseline® **09** basilicon, cold cream, collyrium, emollient, inunction, lubricant, Tiger balm® **11** embrocation, preparation
• **ointment base** **07** lanolin

**OK**

**03** A-OK, oke, yes **04** fair, fine, good, jake, okay, pass, so-so, sure, well **05** right **06** agreed, not bad, righto **07** agree to, approve, consent, correct, go-ahead, in order, up to par **08** accurate, adequate, all right, approval, okey-doke, passable, passably, sanction, say yes to, thumbs-up, very good, very well **09** agreement, authorize, certainly, consent to, no worries, okey-dokey, permitted, tolerable, tolerably **10** acceptable, all correct, convenient, good as gold, green light, no problems, permission, reasonable, reasonably **11** approbation, endorsement, rubber-stamp, up to scratch **12** satisfactory, she'll be right **13** authorization, Bob's your uncle, she'll be apples **14** satisfactorily

**Oklahoma**

**02** OK **04** Okla

**okra**

**05** gumbo **06** bhindi **11** lady's finger **12** lady's fingers

**old**

◇ *archaic word indicator* **01** O **02** ex- **03** eld, set **04** aged, auld, folk, gaga, gray, grey, olde, oral, torn, wise, worn **05** aging, banal, corny, early, fixed, passé, stale, stock, tired, trite, usual **06** ageing, age-old, bygone, common, former, mature, past it, primal, senile, shabby **07** ancient, antique, archaic, cast-off, classic, cliché'd, decayed, earlier, elderly, lasting, one-time, quondam, routine, veteran, vintage, worn-out **08** clichéed, decaying, decrepit, earliest, enduring, habitual, historic, obsolete, original, outdated, overused, previous, primeval, pristine, sensible, sometime, time-worn **09** crumbling, customary, erstwhile, getting on, hackneyed, long-lived, out of date, primaeval, primitive, senescent, unwritten, worm-eaten **10** accustomed, antiquated, broken down, ceremonial, Dickensian, overworked, pedestrian, primordial, ramshackle, threadbare, tumbledown, uninspired, unoriginal, yawn-making **11** commonplace, established, on the way out, out of the ark, over the hill, prehistoric, stereotyped, traditional, wearing thin **12** antediluvian, cliché-ridden, conventional, long-standing, old-fashioned, run-of-the-mill, time-honoured **13** old as the hills, past your prime, platitudinous, unfashionable, unimaginative **14** behind the times, long in the tooth **15** advanced in years, long-established, no spring chicken

**old age**

**03** age, eld **04** hoar, hore **05** years **06** dotage **07** oldness **08** agedness, senility **09** antiquity **10** senescence **11** elderliness, vale of years **14** advancing years, declining years **15** second childhood

**old-fashioned**

◇ *archaic word indicator* **03** old **04** dead, past **05** corny, dated, dusty, fusty, mumsy, passé, steam **06** antick, bygone, old hat, past it, Podunk, quaint, rococo, square, uncool **07** ancient, antique, archaic, arriéré, old-time **08** medieval, obsolete, outdated, outmoded, shmaltzy, vieux jeu **09** mediaeval, moth-eaten, out of date, primitive, rinky-dink, schmaltzy **10** antiquated, auld-farand, fuddy-duddy, oldfangled, written off **11** auld-farrant, Neanderthal, obsolescent, on the way out, out of the ark **12** antediluvian, out of fashion **13** unfashionable **14** behind the times

**old maid**

**08** spinster

**old man**

**02** pa **03** OAP **04** boss, koro **05** elder, oldie **06** bodach, father, gaffer, geezer, Nestor **07** grandad, husband, oldster

## old-time

08 employer, granddad, kaumatua, old-timer, presbyte 09 greybeard, old codger, old geezer, old stager, patriarch, pensioner 10 fuddy-duddy, golden ager, white-beard 11 grandfather 13 senior citizen 14 elder statesman 15 old-age pensioner
*See also* **father; old woman**

## old-time

03 old 04 past 05 dated, passé 06 bygone 07 archaic 08 obsolete, outdated, outmoded 09 out of date 10 antiquated 12 old-fashioned, out of fashion 13 unfashionable 14 behind the times

## old woman

03 bag, hag, OAP 04 aunt, kuia, trot, wife 05 biddy, crone, oldie 06 beldam, gammer, granny, grouch, mother 07 beldame, carline, fusspot, grandma, grannie, old dear 08 caillach, grumbler 09 cailleach, cailliach, grandmama, pensioner 10 complainer, golden ager, grandmamma 11 grandmother 13 little old lady, senior citizen 15 old-age pensioner
*See also* **mother; old man**

## old-world

04 past 06 bygone, quaint 07 archaic 09 auld-warld 10 antiquated, olde-worlde 11 picturesque, traditional 12 old-fashioned

## olio

04 olla 06 medley 07 mixture 10 miscellany

## olive

04 Olea 05 wolly 08 oleaster

## Olympics

*Olympians include:*

03 **Coe** (Sebastian, Lord), **Hoy** (Sir Chris) 04 **Bolt** (Usain), **Clay** (Cassius), **Dean** (Christopher), **Ewry** (Ray), **Otto** (Kristin), **Papp** (Laszlo), **Todd** (Mark), **Witt** (Katarina) 05 **Blair** (Bonnie), **Bubka** (Sergei), **Chand** (Dhyan), **Cranz** (Christl), **Curry** (John), **Henie** (Sonja), **Killy** (Jean-Claude), **Lewis** (Carl), **Lewis** (Denise), **Longo** (Jeannie), **Meade** (Richard), **Nurmi** (Paavo), **Ottey** (Merlene), **Owens** (Jesse), **Popov** (Aleksandr), **Savon** (Felix), **Spitz** (Mark), **Tomba** (Alberto) 06 **Aamodt** (Kjetil), **Beamon** (Bob), **Bikila** (Abebe), **Biondi** (Matt), **Button** (Dick), **D'Inzeo** (Raimondo), **Fraser** (Dawn), **Heiden** (Eric), **Holmes** (Dame Kelly), **Korbut** (Olga), **Oerter** (Al), **Phelps** (Michael), **Ritola** (Ville), **Sailer** (Toni), **Thorpe** (Ian), **Thorpe** (Jim) 07 **Ainslie** (Ben), **Boitano** (Brian), **Cousins** (Robin), **Daehlie** (Bjorn), **Edwards** (Jonathan), **Fischer** (Birgit), **Johnson** (Michael), **Klammer** (Franz), **Mathias** (Bob), **Nykänen** (Matti), **Pinsent** (Sir Matthew), **Rodnina** (Irina), **Scherbo** (Vitaly), **Schmidt** (Birgit), **Torvill** (Jayne), **Voronin** (Mikhail), **Zatopek**

(Emil), **Zelezny** (Jan) 08 **Christie** (Linford), **Comaneci** (Nadia), **Cuthbert** (Betty), **De Bruijn** (Inge), **Dityatin** (Aleksandr), **Elvstrøm** (Paul), **Gerevich** (Aladár), **Jernberg** (Sixten), **Latynina** (Larissa), **Louganis** (Greg), **Ohuruogu** (Christine), **Redgrave** (Sir Steve), **Stenmark** (Ingemar), **Thompson** (Daley), **Zijlaard** (Leontien) 09 **Adlington** (Rebecca), **Andrianov** (Nikolay), **Babashoff** (Shirley), **Cáslavská** (Vera), **Egerszegi** (Krisztina), **Gräfström** (Gillis), **Pendleton** (Victoria), **Schneider** (Vreni), **Seizinger** (Katja), **Stevenson** (Teófilo) 10 **Linsenhoff** (Liselott), **Moser-Proll** (Annemarie), **van Moorsel** (Leontien) 11 **Mangiarotti** (Edoardo), **Weissmuller** (Johnny) 12 **Blankers-Koen** (Fanny), **Gebrselassie** (Haile), **Germeshausen** (Bernhard), **Joyner-Kersee** (Jackie), **Suleymanoglu** (Naim) 13 **Longo-Ciprelli** (Jeannie) 14 **Griffith-Joyner** (Florence)

## Oman

03 OMN

## omelette

08 frittata, tortilla

## omen

04 sign 05 freet, freit, purse, token 06 augury, boding 07 auspice, portent, presage, warning 08 bodement, dead-fire, forecast, prodrome, soothsay 09 abodement, harbinger, night-crow, prodromus, prognosis 10 foreboding, forerunner, indication, night-raven, prediction, prognostic 11 premonition, presagement 12 corpse candle, presentiment

## ominous

07 bodeful, fateful, unlucky 08 menacing, minatory, sinister 10 foreboding, portentous 11 threatening, unpromising 12 inauspicious, unfavourable, unpropitious

## ominously

06 grimly 10 alarmingly 11 dangerously 13 frighteningly

## omission

03 gap, out 04 balk, lack 05 baulk 06 lacuna 07 default, elision, erasure, failure, neglect 08 deletion 09 avoidance, disregard, exception, exclusion, haplology, oversight 10 expunction, leaving-out, lipography, negligence 11 dereliction

## omit

03 let 04 drop, fail, miss, pass, skip 05 erase 06 delete, except, forget, rub out 07 edit out, exclude, expunge, miss out, neglect 08 cross out, leave out, overlook, overskip, pass over, white out 09 disregard, eliminate, pretermit 11 leave undone 13 fail to mention

## omnibus

03 bus 09 anthology, inclusive 10 collection, compendium 11 compendious, compilation, wide-ranging 12 all-embracing, encyclopedia, encyclopedic 13 comprehensive

## omnipotence

07 mastery 09 supremacy 10 total power 11 divine right, sovereignty 12 almightiness, plenipotence 13 absolute power, invincibility 15 all-powerfulness

## omnipotent

07 supreme 08 almighty 10 invincible 11 all-powerful, plenipotent

## omnipresent

08 infinite 09 limitless, pervasive, universal 10 all-present, ubiquitary, ubiquitous 12 all-pervasive

## omniscient

07 all-wise 09 all-seeing, pansophic 10 all-knowing

## omnivorous

10 gluttonous 12 all-devouring, pantophagous 14 eating anything, indiscriminate

## on

◊ *anagram indicator* ◊ *juxtaposition down indicator* 01 o 02 an, by, in, of, re, to 03 leg, sur 04 atop, over, side, upon 05 abuse, tipsy 06 beside, tiddly 07 against, forward!, proceed!, stuck to, towards 08 feasible, touching 09 apropos of, as regards, regarding, resting on 10 acceptable, attached to, concerning, relating to 11 dealing with, practicable, referring to 12 with regard to 13 concerned with, connected with, in contact with, in the matter of, with respect to 14 on the subject of 15 with reference to
• **on and off** 08 fitfully, off and on, sporadic 09 sometimes 10 now and then, occasional, on occasion 11 at intervals, irregularly, now and again 12 every so often, intermittent, occasionally, periodically, sporadically 13 spasmodically 14 from time to time, intermittently 15 discontinuously
• **on and on** 03 e'er 04 ever 06 always 07 forever, non-stop 09 endlessly, eternally, regularly 10 all the time, constantly, frequently, habitually, repeatedly 11 ceaselessly, continually, incessantly, perpetually, recurrently 12 interminably, persistently 13 everlastingly

## once

◊ *archaic word indicator* 04 ance, onst, when 05 after 06 former 07 firstly, long ago, on a time, one time 08 as soon as, formerly 09 at one time, in the past, upon a time 10 at one point, previously 11 in times past 12 in the old days 13 in times gone by, once upon a time, on one occasion
• **at once** 03 now, tit 04 tite, tyte 05 alike, atone, ek dum, swith, tight 06 attone, presto, pronto, statim, titely

**07** at a word, attonce, attones, offhand **08** directly, promptly, right now, together **09** forthwith, hey presto, instantly, like a shot, on the spot, right away, yesterday **10** forthright **11** immediately, tout de suite **12** straightaway, without delay **13** at the same time **14** simultaneously **15** at the same moment, before you know it
• **more than once** **04** anew, over **05** again **10** repeatedly
• **once and for all** **07** finally, for good **10** decisively, positively **11** permanently **12** conclusively, definitively **14** for the last time
• **once in a while** **07** at times **08** off and on, on and off **09** sometimes **10** now and then, on occasion **11** now and again **12** infrequently, occasionally, periodically, sporadically **14** from time to time, intermittently **15** once in a blue moon

**once-over**
**04** gape, gaze, look, peek, peep, test **05** audit, check, dekko, probe, stare **06** eyeful, gander, glance, shufti, squint **07** checkup, glimpse, inquiry **08** analysis, butcher's, research, scrutiny **10** inspection, monitoring **11** examination **12** confirmation, verification **13** investigation

**oncoming**
**07** looming, nearing **08** approach, upcoming **09** advancing, gathering, onrushing **11** approaching

**one**
**01** a, I **02** ae, us **03** ace, ane, yin **04** lone, only, sole, tane, unit **05** alike, bound, equal, fused, monad, unity, whole **06** entire, joined, single, united, wedded **07** married **08** complete, solitary **09** identical, undivided **10** harmonious, individual, like-minded
• **French one** **02** un **03** une
• **German one** **03** ein **04** eine, eins
• **Italian one, Spanish one** **03** uno

**oneness**
**05** unity **07** unicity **08** identity, sameness **09** wholeness **10** singleness, uniqueness **11** consistency, homogeneity, singularity **12** completeness **13** identicalness, individuality

**onerous**
**04** hard **05** heavy **06** taxing, tiring **07** arduous, exigent, weighty **08** crushing, exacting, wearying **09** demanding, difficult, fatiguing, laborious, strenuous **10** burdensome, exhausting, oppressive **11** troublesome **12** back-breaking

**oneself**
• **by oneself** **04** solo **05** alone **06** lonely, singly **07** forlorn, unaided **08** deserted, desolate, forsaken, isolated, lonesome, solitary **09** abandoned, on your own, on your tod **10** by yourself, unassisted, unattended, unescorted **11** without help **12** single-handed

**13** independently, unaccompanied **15** on your Pat Malone

**one-sided**
**06** biased, one-way, uneven, unfair, unjust **07** bigoted, partial, unequal **08** lopsided, partisan, separate **09** separated **10** prejudiced, unbalanced, unilateral **11** independent, inequitable **12** disconnected, narrow-minded **14** discriminatory

**one-time**
**02** ex- **03** old **04** late, past **06** former **07** quondam **08** previous, sometime **09** erstwhile

**ongoing**
**05** event **07** current, growing, non-stop **08** constant, evolving, unbroken, unending **09** advancing, incessant, unfolding **10** continuing, continuous, developing, in progress, unfinished **11** progressing **13** uninterrupted

**onion**
**04** head, moly, ramp, sybo **05** cibol, ingan, syboe, sybow **06** chibol, shalot **07** shallot **08** scallion
See also **head**

**onlooker**
**06** gawper, viewer, voyeur **07** watcher, witness **08** beholder, looker-on, observer **09** bystander, sightseer, spectator **10** eyewitness, rubberneck

**only**
**03** but, one **04** just, lone, sole **05** alone **06** anerly, at most, barely, except, merely, nobbut, purely, simply, single, singly, solely, unique **07** onliest **08** solitary **09** allenarly, exclusive **10** individual, no more than, nothing but, one and only **11** exclusively, not more than

**onrush**
**04** flow, push, rush **05** flood, onset, surge, sweep **06** career, charge, stream **07** cascade **08** stampede **09** onslaught

**onset**
**04** dash, fall, push, raid, rush **05** break, start **06** access, affret, attack, charge, onding, onrush, outset **07** assault, kick-off **08** outbreak, storming **09** beginning, inception, onslaught **12** commencement

**onslaught**
**04** push, raid **05** blitz, drive, foray, onset, swoop **06** attack, charge, dismay, onfall, onrush, thrust **07** assault, dead-set **08** storming **09** offensive **11** bombardment

**Ontario**
**02** ON

**onus**
**04** duty, load, task **06** burden, charge, weight **09** albatross, liability, millstone **10** obligation **11** encumbrance **14** responsibility

**onward**
**04** away

**onwards**
**02** on **05** ahead, forth **06** beyond **07** forward, in front **08** forwards

**oodles**
**04** bags, lots, tons **05** heaps, loads **06** masses **08** lashings **09** abundance

**oomph**
**02** it, SA **03** pep **04** zing **06** bounce, energy, vigour **07** pizzazz, sparkle **08** sexiness, vitality, vivacity **09** animation, sex-appeal **10** enthusiasm, exuberance, get-up-and-go

**ooze**
**03** mud, nap, sap, sew **04** drip, drop, emit, flow, leak, mire, muck, seep, silt, sipe, slob, spew, spue, sype, weep **05** bleed, drain, exude, fluff, slime **06** escape, exhale, filter, sludge **07** deposit, dribble, excrete, secrete, seepage, trickle **08** alluvium, filtrate, sediment **09** discharge, percolate, pour forth **12** overflow with

**oozy**
**04** dewy, miry **05** moist, mucky, muddy, slimy, weepy **06** sloppy, sludgy, sweaty **07** weeping **08** dripping **09** uliginose, uliginous

**opacity**
**04** body, onyx **06** nebula **07** density, leucoma **08** dullness **09** filminess, milkiness, murkiness, obscurity **10** cloudiness, opaqueness **11** obfuscation, unclearness **14** impermeability **15** impenetrability

**opal**
**07** girasol, hyalite **08** girasole **09** cacholong **10** hydrophane

**opalescence**
**05** prism **07** glitter, rainbow **08** dazzling **09** sparkling **10** glittering, shimmering **11** iridescence, multicolour **14** rainbow colours

**opalescent**
**04** shot **06** pearly **07** rainbow **08** dazzling **09** prismatic, sparkling **10** glittering, iridescent, shimmering, variegated **11** cymophanous, rainbow-like **13** multicoloured, polychromatic **15** rainbow-coloured

**opaque**
**03** dim **04** dark, dull, hazy **05** dense, dingy, misty, muddy, murky, shady, thick **06** cloudy, turbid **07** blurred, clouded, cryptic, doltish, intense, muddied, obscure, unclear **08** abstruse, baffling, esoteric, puzzling **09** confusing, difficult, enigmatic, recondite **12** as clear as mud, impenetrable, unfathomable **14** unintelligible

**OPEC**

*OPEC members:*

**04** Iran, Iraq
**05** Libya, Qatar
**06** Angola, Kuwait
**07** Algeria, Ecuador, Nigeria
**09** Venezuela

11 Saudi Arabia
18 United Arab Emirates

## open
03 dup, pop 04 agee, airy, ajar, ajee, bare, fair, free, moot, undo, wide 05 apert, begin, blunt, broad, clear, crack, frank, holey, loose, overt, plain, split, start, unlid, unrip, untie 06 broach, candid, deploy, direct, expose, extend, flower, gaping, honest, launch, liable, ouvert, patent, porous, public, reveal, simple, spread, spring, unbolt, uncork, unfold, unfurl, unlock, unpack, unroll, unseal, unshut, vacant 07 blatant, divulge, evident, explain, exposed, general, kick off, lay bare, lidless, natural, obvious, ouverte, subject, topless, unblock, unclasp, unclose, uncover, unlatch, unscrew, upbreak, visible, yawning 08 apparent, arguable, cellular, commence, disclose, disposed, flagrant, initiate, manifest, openwork, passable, push open, separate, unbarred, unbolted, unclosed, unfasten, unfenced, unfolded, unfrozen, unhidden, unlocked, unripped, unsealed, wide open 09 available, break open, burst open, champaign, come apart, coverless, debatable, fenceless, force open, guileless, ingenuous, navigable, prise open, receptive, slide open, spread out, unblocked, uncovered, undecided, unlatched, unsettled, unstopped, well known 10 aboveboard, accessible, forthright, inaugurate, noticeable, obtainable, spongelike, unenclosed, unfastened, unoccupied, unreserved, unresolved, up in the air, vulnerable 11 conspicuous, get cracking, honeycombed, problematic, set in motion, susceptible, unconcealed, undisguised, unprotected, unsheltered, widely known 12 approachable, loosely woven, unobstructed, unrestricted 13 take the plunge 15 open to the risk of
• **opening words** 06 sesame
• **open onto** 04 face 06 lead to 08 give onto, overlook 14 command a view of
• **open up** 03 win

## open-air
06 afield 07 outdoor, outside 08 alfresco, plein-air 10 out-of-doors

## open-and-shut
05 clear 06 simple 07 obvious 12 easily solved 13 easily decided 15 straightforward

## opener
◊ head selection indicator

## open-handed
04 free 06 lavish 07 liberal 08 generous 09 bounteous, bountiful 10 munificent, unstinting 11 magnanimous 12 eleemosynary, large-hearted

## opening
◊ head selection indicator ◊ hidden indicator 02 os 03 gap, gat, job 04 adit, anus, bole, cave, dawn, gape, gate,

hole, pore, port, rent, scye, slit, slot, vent, yawn 05 birth, break, chasm, chink, cleft, crack, early, first, inlet, onset, place, space, split, start, stoma, thirl 06 breach, chance, hiatus, launch, outlet, outset, window 07 crevice, fissure, foramen, initial, kick-off, orifice, ostiole, portage, primary, rupture, undoing, vacancy 08 aperture, fenestra, occasion, position, starting 09 beginning, embrasure, embrazure, first base, inaugural, inception, mouse hole, square one, the word go 10 commencing, fenestella, interstice 11 opportunity, possibility 12 inauguration, introductory

## openly
06 barely 07 bluntly, frankly, overtly, plainly, up front 08 brazenly, candidly, directly, honestly, in public, patently, publicly 09 blatantly, glaringly 10 above board, flagrantly, immodestly, in full view 11 on the square, shamelessly, unashamedly 12 forthrightly, unreservedly

## open-minded
04 free 05 broad 07 liberal 08 catholic, tolerant, unbiased 09 impartial, objective, receptive 10 reasonable 11 broad-minded, enlightened 12 unprejudiced 13 dispassionate 14 latitudinarian

## open-mindedness
06 equity 07 justice 08 equality, fairness 10 detachment, dispassion, neutrality 11 disinterest, objectivity 12 impartiality, unbiasedness 14 even-handedness 15 non-partisanship

## open-mouthed
06 amazed, gaping, greedy 07 shocked 08 wide-eyed 09 astounded, clamorous, expectant, surprised 10 astonished, spellbound 11 dumbfounded, widechapped 13 flabbergasted, thunderstruck

## openwork
04 mode

## opera
03 ENO 05 works 08 burletta 09 pastorale 10 music drama 13 dramma giocoso 15 dramma per musica
See also **singer**

*Operas and operettas include:*

04 Aïda
05 Faust, Manon, Norma, Tosca
06 Carmen, Otello, Salome
07 Elektra, Fidelio, Macbeth, Nabucco, The Ring, Thespis, Werther, Wozzeck
08 Falstaff, Idomeneo, Iolanthe, La Bohème, Parsifal, Patience, Turandot
09 Billy Budd, Capriccio, Don Carlos, King Priam, Lohengrin, Rigoletto, Ruddigore, Siegfried, The Mikado, Véronique
10 Cinderella, Die Walküre, I Pagliacci, La Traviata, Oedipus Rex, Tannhäuser
11 Don Giovanni, Don Pasquale,

HMS Pinafore, Il Trovatore, La Périchole, Peter Grimes, Princess Ida, The Sorceror, Trial by Jury, William Tell
12 Boris Godunov, Cosí Fan Tutte, Das Rheingold, Eugene Onegin, Manon Lescaut, Nixon in China, Porgy and Bess, The Grand Duke, The Huguenots, The Rhinegold, The Valkyries
13 Albert Herring, Der Freischütz, Dido and Aeneas, Die Fledermaus, La Belle Hélène, Moses and Aaron, Powder Her Face, The Fairy Queen, The Gondoliers, The Knot Garden, The Magic Flute, Utopia Limited
14 Le Grand Macabre, Samson et Dalila
15 Ariadne auf Naxos, Götterdämmerung, Hansel and Gretel, Le Nozze di Figaro, Madama Butterfly, Madame Butterfly, Orfeo ed Euridice, Simon Boccanegra, The Beggar's Opera, The Pearl Fishers

*Opera houses include:*

03 Met, ROH
05 Cairo, Lyric, Royal, State
06 De Munt, Sydney, the Met, Zurich
07 La Scala
08 La Fenice, San Carlo
09 La Monnaie
10 Mussorgsky, Semper Oper
11 Oper Leipzig, Teatro Liceo, Verona Arena
12 Glyndebourne, Komische Oper, Metropolitan, Opéra-Comique
13 Kennedy Center, Muziektheater, Opera Bastille, Teatro Massimo
14 Bolshoi Theatre, Estates Theatre, Hungarian State, Kungliga Operan, London Coliseum, Unter den Linden
15 Gothenburg Opera, Teatro alla Scala, Zheng Yici Peking

*Opera characters include:*

03 **Eva**, **Liu**
04 **Aïda**, **Bess**, **Budd** (Billy), **Erda**, **Froh**, **Iago**, **Il Re**, **Loge**, **Luna** (Il Conte di), **Mime**, **Mimì**, **Pang**, **Pike** (Florence), **Ping**, **Pong**, **Tito**, **Vere** (Captain)
05 **Caius** (Dr), **Calaf**, **Falke** (Dr), **Faust**, **Freia**, **Gilda**, **Herod**, **Jeník**, **Kecal**, **Porgy**, **Rocco**, **Sachs** (Hans), **Titus**, **Tosca**, **Vasek**, **Wotan**
06 **Alcina**, **Alzira**, **Carmen**, **Donner**, **Emilia**, **Fafner**, **Fasolt**, **Figaro**, **Fricka**, **Gretel**, **Grimes** (Peter), **Hänsel**, **Isolde**, **Lockit** (Lucy), **Mantua** (Duke of), **Onegin** (Eugene), **Otello**, **Pamina**, **Pogner** (Veit), **Rosina**, **Salome**, **Tamino**, **Valery** (Violetta), **Wagner**
07 **Bartolo** (Dr), **Bastien**, **Billows**, **Despina**, **Don José**, **Douphol** (Baron), **Germont** (Alfredo), **Germont** (Giorgio), **Godunov** (Boris), **Gunther**, **Gutrune**, **Herring** (Albert), **Hunding**, **Jocasta**,

Leonora, Manrico, Marenka,
Micaëla, Musetta, Oedipus,
Peachum, Pelléas, Quickly
(Mistress), **Radamès**, Rodolfo,
Scarpia (Baron), **Susanna**, Tristan,
**Wozzeck**
08 Alberich, Almaviva (Count),
Almaviva (Countess), **Azeucena**,
Claggart (John), **Falstaff** (Sir John),
Ferrando, Herodias, Hoffmann,
Lucretia, Macheath, Marcello,
Mercédès, Orlofsky (Prince),
Papagena, Papageno, Parsifal,
Roderigo, Sarastro, Siegmund,
Turandot, Valentin, Woglinde,
Yamadori (Prince)
09 Angelotti (Cesare), Bastienne,
Butterfly (Madame), Cherubino,
Cio-Cio-San, Desdemona, Donna
Anna, Dorabella, Escamillo,
Esmerelda, Florestan, Guglielmo,
Leporello, Lohengrin, Maddalena,
Mélisande, Narraboth, Pinkerton
(Lieutenant), **Rigoletto**, Sharpless,
Siegfried, Sieglunde, Vogelsang
(Kunz), **Waltraute**
10 Beckmesser (Sixtus), Brünnhilde,
Don Alfonso, Don Basilio, Don
Ottavio, Eisenstein (Gabriele von),
Eisenstein (Rosalinde von),
Fiordiligi, Marcellina, Monostatos,
Prince Igor, Tannhäuser
11 Cavaradossi (Mario), **Don
Giovanni**, Donna Elvira,
Marschallin, Sparafucile, **The
Dutchman**
14 Henry the Fowler, John the
Baptist, Mephistopheles
15 Queen of the Night

## operate

◇ *anagram indicator* 02 go 03 act, fly,
ren, rin, run, set, use 04 play, trip, work
05 drive, pilot, serve 06 direct, employ,
handle, make go, manage 07 actuate,
conduct, control, perform, utilize
08 function, tick over 09 manoeuvre
12 be in charge of

## operation

02 op 03 job, ure, use 04 deal, game,
play, raid, task 05 using 06 action,
affair, agency, attack, charge, effect,
effort, motion 07 assault, control,
process, running, surgery, working
08 activity, business, campaign,
exercise, handling, movement
09 influence, manoeuvre, procedure
10 enterprise, management,
proceeding 11 functioning,
performance, transaction, undertaking,
utilization 12 manipulation
• **combined operations** 02 CO
• **in operation** 02 on 04 live 05 going,
valid 06 active, viable 07 in force,
working 08 in action, in effect,
prepared, workable 09 effective,
efficient, in service 10 functional
11 functioning, operational,
serviceable 12 taking effect

## operational

05 going, in use, ready 06 usable,
viable 07 running, working 08 in
action, prepared, workable 09 in

service 10 functional 11 functioning
12 up and running 14 in working order

## operative

03 key, spy 04 dick, hand, mole
05 agent, valid, vital 06 active, shamus,
sleuth, viable, worker 07 artisan,
crucial, gumshoe, in force, operant,
ouvrier, working, workman
08 employee, in action, in effect,
labourer, mechanic, operator,
ouvrière, relevant, workable
09 detective, effective, efficient,
important, machinist 10 functional,
private eye 11 double agent,
efficacious, functioning, in operation,
operational, secret agent, serviceable,
significant 12 investigator

## operator

02 op 05 mover 06 dealer, driver,
punter, trader, worker 07 functor,
handler, manager, operant, shyster
08 director, mechanic 09 machinist,
operative 10 contractor, machinator,
manoeuvrer, speculator, technician
11 manipulator 12 practitioner
13 administrator, wheeler-dealer

## operetta

*see* opera

## opiate

04 drug, dull 06 downer 07 anodyne,
bromide 08 narcotic, nepenthe,
pacifier, sedative 09 soporific
10 depressant 12 stupefacient
13 tranquillizer

## opine

03 say 05 guess, judge, think
07 believe, declare, presume, suggest,
suppose, surmise, suspect, venture
08 conceive, conclude 09 volunteer
10 conjecture

## opinion

03 bet 04 deem, doxy, idea, mind,
view, vote 05 sense, tenet 06 belief,
notion, stance, theory 07 feeling,
thought 08 attitude, feelings, suffrage,
thoughts 09 arrogance, judgement,
sentiment, viewpoint 10 assessment,
assumption, conception, conviction,
estimation, impression, perception,
persuasion, reputation, standpoint
11 point of view, supposition 13 way of
thinking 15 school of thought
• **in my opinion** 03 IMO 06 I think
08 à mon avis, as I see it, I believe, in
my book, in my view, me judice 10 for
my money, if you ask me, personally
• **opinion tester** 04 kite

## opinionated

06 biased, entêté 07 adamant, bigoted,
entêtée, pompous 08 arrogant,
cocksure, dogmatic, stubborn
09 obstinate, pigheaded, pragmatic
10 inflexible, pontifical, prejudiced
11 dictatorial, doctrinaire, pragmatical
12 single-minded 13 self-important
14 uncompromising

## opium

03 hop

## opossum

04 joey 05 yapok 06 yapock

07 marmose 09 phalanger
12 Didelphyidae

## opponent

03 foe 04 anti 05 enemy, rival
07 opposer 08 objector, opposite
09 adversary, contender, dissenter,
dissident, oppugnant 10 antagonist,
challenger, competitor, contestant,
opposition 11 dissentient
• **opponents** 02 NE, SW

## opportune

03 apt, fit 04 good 05 happy, lucky
06 proper, timely 07 fitting, in place
08 suitable 09 fortunate, pertinent,
well-timed 10 auspicious, convenient,
favourable, felicitous, propitious,
seasonable 11 appropriate
12 advantageous, providential

## opportunism

07 realism 10 expediency, pragmatism
12 exploitation 15 taking advantage

## opportunity

03 ren, rin, run 04 hour, pick, room,
roum, turn 05 break, power, scope,
space 06 chance, look-in, moment
07 fitness, opening, vantage
08 occasion, overture, prospect
09 privilege 11 possibility 14 crack of
the whip
• **alive to opportunity** 04 go-go

## oppose

03 bar, opp 04 defy, face 05 check,
fight, match 06 attack, breast, combat,
hinder, impugn, offset, oppugn,
repugn, resist, thwart 07 balance,
compare, contest, counter, dispute,
play off, prevent 08 confront, contrary,
contrast, disfavor, obstruct, traverse
09 be against, challenge, disfavour,
encounter, juxtapose, stand up to,
withstand 10 contradict, contravene,
controvert, set against 11 take against
12 argue against, disagree with,
disapprove of 13 take issue with
14 counterbalance, fly in the face of

## opposed

03 opp 04 anti 06 averse, object
07 adverse, against, hostile
08 clashing, contrary, inimical,
opposing, opposite 09 toto caelo
11 conflicting, disagreeing
12 antagonistic, incompatible, in
opposition
• **as opposed to** 01 v 02 vs 06 versus
09 as against, instead of 10 rather than
12 in contrast to

## opposing

05 enemy, rival 06 at odds 07 counter,
hostile, opposed, warring 08 clashing,
contrary, fighting, opponent, opposite
09 combatant, differing, oppugnant
10 at variance, contending
11 conflicting, contentious
12 antagonistic, antipathetic,
disputatious, incompatible
14 irreconcilable

## opposite

02 op 03 opp 06 at odds, en face,
facing, unlike 07 adverse, counter,
hostile, inverse, opposed, reverse
08 clashing, contrary, converse, flip

**opposition**

side, fronting, opponent, opposing
**09** different, differing, dissident
**10** antipathic, antithesis, at variance, contrasted, face to face, overthwart, poles apart **11** conflicting, over against **12** antagonistic, antithetical, inconsistent **13** contradiction, contradictory, corresponding
**14** irreconcilable

**opposition**

**03** foe **05** enemy, rival **06** syzygy
**07** dislike **08** clashing, contrast, distance, opponent **09** adversary, collision, hostility, other side
**10** antagonism, antagonist, antithesis, reluctance, resistance **11** competition, contrariety, counter-time, counter-view, disapproval **12** colluctation, counter-stand, opposing side
**13** confrontation **14** unfriendliness
**15** obstructiveness
• **set in opposition 04** play

**oppress**

**03** vex **04** ride **05** abuse, bully, crush, grind, gripe, press, quash, quell, tread
**06** burden, deject, hang on, harass, ravish, sadden, subdue, weight
**07** afflict, depress, enslave, overset, repress, smother, torment, trample
**08** desolate, dispirit, distress, hang over, maltreat, suppress **09** overpower, overpress, overwhelm, persecute, subjugate, suffocate, tyrannize, weigh down **10** discourage, dishearten, lie heavy on **11** walk all over **12** bear hard upon **13** treat like dirt, use as a doormat **15** bear heavily upon

**oppressed**

**06** abused **07** crushed, misused, subject **08** burdened, enslaved, harassed, troubled **09** repressed
**10** maltreated, persecuted, subjugated, tyrannized **11** downtrodden
**13** disadvantaged **15** underprivileged

**oppression**

**05** abuse **07** cruelty, tyranny
**08** hardship **09** brutality, despotism, harshness, injustice **10** repression, subjection **11** persecution, subjugation, suppression
**12** maltreatment, overpowering, overwhelming, ruthlessness

**oppressive**

**05** close, cruel, faint, harsh, heavy, muggy **06** brutal, leaden, stuffy, sultry, unjust **07** airless, inhuman, onerous, sweltry **08** crushing, despotic, pitiless, ruthless, stifling **09** burdenous, Draconian, merciless, troubling, tyrannous **10** broodiness, burdensome, iron-fisted, repressive, tyrannical
**11** domineering, heavy-handed, intolerable, overbearing, suffocating
**12** extortionate, overpowering, overwhelming

**oppressor**

**05** bully, tyran **06** despot, tyrant
**08** autocrat, dictator, torturer
**09** tormentor **10** persecutor, subjugator, taskmaster **11** intimidator, slave-driver **14** hard taskmaster

**opprobrious**

**07** abusive **08** damaging, infamous, insolent, venomous **09** insulting, invective, offensive, vitriolic
**10** calumnious, defamatory, derogatory, scandalous, scurrilous
**11** disgraceful, dyslogistic, reproachful
**12** calumniatory, contemptuous, contumelious, vituperative

**opprobrium**

**04** slur **05** odium, shame **06** infamy, stigma **07** calumny, censure, obloquy
**08** disgrace, ignominy, reproach
**09** contumely, discredit, disfavour, dishonour, disrepute **10** debasement, scurrility **11** degradation

**Ops**

**04** Rhea

**opt**

**04** pick **05** elect, go for **06** choose, decide, prefer, select **08** decide on, plump for, settle on **09** single out

**optical**

*Optical instruments and devices include:*

**05** laser
**06** camera
**07** sextant
**08** spyglass
**09** endoscope, periscope, telescope
**10** binoculars, microscope, opera-glass, theodolite
**12** field-glasses, stereocamera
**13** film projector
**14** slide projector
**15** magnifying glass, photomicroscope, telescopic sight, telestereoscope

**optimism**

**05** cheer **06** morale **08** buoyancy, idealism **10** brightness, confidence, expectancy **11** hopefulness
**12** cheerfulness, sanguineness
**13** Leibnizianism **14** feel-good factor, Leibnitzianism

**optimistic**

**06** bright, upbeat **07** assured, bullish, buoyant, hopeful **08** cheerful, positive, sanguine **09** confident, expectant
**10** idealistic, Panglossic
**11** Panglossian, pollyannish **12** happy-go-lucky, pollyannaish

**optimum**

**03** opt, top **04** best **05** ideal, model
**06** choice **07** highest, optimal, perfect, supreme, utopian **08** flawless
**11** superlative **14** most favourable

**option**

**03** put **04** call, wish **06** choice
**07** refusal **08** swaption **09** privilege, selection **10** preference **11** alternative, possibility

**optional**

**03** opt **04** free **08** elective, unforced
**09** voluntary **10** permissive
**11** facultative **13** discretionary

**options**

**04** menu

**opulence**

**06** luxury, plenty, riches, wealth
**07** fortune **08** fullness, richness
**09** abundance, affluence, profusion
**10** cornucopia, easy street, lavishness, luxuriance, prosperity **11** copiousness
**13** sumptuousness **14** superabundance

**opulent**

**04** posh, rich **05** plush, pluty **06** lavish
**07** copious, moneyed, profuse, wealthy, well-off **08** abundant, affluent, prolific, well-to-do
**09** luxuriant, luxurious, plentiful, sumptuous **10** prosperous, well-heeled **11** rolling in it
**13** superabundant

**opus**

**02** op **04** work **05** piece **06** oeuvre
**08** creation **10** brainchild, production
**11** composition

**or**

**04** gold **05** ossia **06** before, yellow
**10** conversely **13** alternatively **14** in preference to, on the other hand **15** as an alternative
*See also* **gold**

**oracle**

**04** guru, sage, seer, Urim **05** augur, sibyl **06** answer, augury, expert, mentor, pundit, vision, wizard
**07** adviser, prophet, Thummin
**08** forecast, prophecy **09** authority
**10** divination, forecaster, high priest, mastermind, prediction, prophetess, revelation, soothsayer, specialist
**13** fortune teller **14** Urim and Thummim **15** prognostication

**oracular**

**04** sage, wise **05** grave, vatic **06** arcane
**07** cryptic, Delphic, obscure, ominous
**08** abstruse, dogmatic, positive, two-edged **09** ambiguous, equivocal, prescient, prophetic, venerable
**10** auspicious, haruspical, mysterious, portentous, predictive **11** dictatorial, significant **13** authoritative

**oral**

◇ *homophone indicator* **04** quiz, said, viva **05** vocal **06** buccal, lively, spoken, verbal **07** uttered **08** viva voce **09** unwritten **11** nuncupative

**orally**

◇ *homophone indicator* **07** by mouth, vocally **08** verbally, viva voce

**orange**

**11** hesperidium

*Oranges include:*

**04** gold
**05** amber, chica, chico, coral, henna, tawny, tenné, tenny
**06** anatta, anatto, aurora, chicha, kamala, kamela, kamila, roucou, salmon, tawney
**07** annatta, annatto, apricot, arnotto, jacinth, nacarat, paprika, saffron
**08** croceate, croceous, mandarin
**09** bilirubin, tangerine
**13** cadmium yellow, canthaxanthin

## orate

*Orange varieties include:*

**04** mock, Ruta, sour
**05** blood, Jaffa, navel, sweet, topaz
**06** bitter
**07** cumquat, kumquat, naartje, nartjie, satsuma, Seville
**08** bergamot, bigarade, mandarin
**09** clockwork, mandarine, tangerine
**10** clementine

**• segment of orange 03** pig

## orate

**04** talk **05** speak **07** declaim, lecture
**08** harangue **09** discourse, hold forth, sermonize, speechify **11** pontificate

## oration

**05** éloge, elogy, spiel **06** eulogy, homily, korero, sermon, speech
**07** address, elogium, lecture
**08** eulogium, harangue **09** discourse, set speech **11** declamation

## orator

**06** Cicero, rhetor **07** speaker, spieler
**08** lecturer **09** Boanerges, declaimer, demagogue, spokesman, thunderer
**10** petitioner **11** Demosthenes, rhetorician, spellbinder
**12** phrasemonger, prevaricator
**13** public speaker

## oratorical

**08** eloquent, rhetoric, sonorous
**09** bombastic, high-flown
**10** Ciceronian, rhetorical
**11** declamatory, Demosthenic
**12** elocutionary, magniloquent
**13** grandiloquent, silver-tongued, smooth-tongued

## oratorio

*Oratorios include:*

**04** Saul
**06** Elijah, Esther, Joshua, Samson, Semele, St Paul
**07** Athalia, Deborah, Jephtha, Messiah, Solomon, Susanna
**08** Christus, Giuseppe, Hercules, Theodora
**09** Christmas
**10** Belshazzar, Oedipus Rex, The Seasons
**11** The Creation
**13** Israel in Egypt
**14** Alexander Balus, La Resurrezione
**15** Judas Maccabaeus

## oratory

**04** hwyl **06** chapel, speech **07** diction
**08** rhetoric **09** elocution, eloquence, proseucha, proseuche **11** chapel royal, declamation **12** speechifying, speechmaking **14** grandiloquence, public speaking

## orb

**03** eye **04** ball, pome, ring **05** globe, mound, orbit, round, world **06** circle, sphere **07** eyeball, globule
**08** bereaved, spherule

## orbit

**03** orb **04** path **05** ambit, cycle, range, reach, scope, sweep, track **06** circle, course, domain, sphere **07** circuit, compass, revolve **08** encircle, rotation

**09** eye socket, influence **10** revolution, trajectory **12** circumgyration, circumnavigate
**• point in orbit 04** apse **05** apsis
**06** apogee **07** apolune, perigee
**08** aphelion, perilune **10** perihelion
**12** pericynthion, periselenium

## orchestra

*Orchestras include:*

**03** LPO, NSO, OAE, OSM, RPO
**04** ASMF, CBSO, RLPO, RSNO
**05** Hallé
**06** Ulster
**09** Minnesota
**11** BBC Symphony, NBC Symphony
**12** Milan La Scala, Philadelphia, San Francisco
**13** Concertgebouw, Staatskapelle
**14** Boston Symphony, English Chamber, LA Philharmonic, London Symphony, Sydney Symphony, Vienna Symphony
**15** BBC Philharmonic, Chicago Symphony, Detroit Symphony, New York Symphony, Scottish Chamber, Seattle Symphony, The Philharmonia, Toronto Symphony

## orchestrate

**03** fix **05** score **07** arrange, compose, prepare, present **08** organize
**09** integrate **10** co-ordinate, mastermind **11** put together, stage-manage

## orchestration

**05** score **07** running, scoring, setting, version **08** planning **10** adaptation, management **11** arrangement, engineering, preparation **12** co-ordination, organization
**13** harmonization, masterminding, stage-managing **14** interpretation
**15** instrumentation

## orchid

*Orchids include:*

**03** bee, bog, bug, fen, fly, man, sun
**04** blue, disa, frog, king, kite, lady, moth, musk, wasp
**05** burnt, clown, comet, ghost, giant, pansy, queen, tiger, tulip
**06** lizard, monkey, spider
**07** leopard, slipper, vanilla
**08** calanthe, cattleya, crucifix, fragrant, military, oncidium
**09** bee-orchis, birds-nest, chocolate, Christmas, coralroot, cymbidium, false musk, fly orchis, pyramidal, twayblade
**10** early marsh, epidendrum, late spider, small white
**11** cockleshell, cypripedium, dancing lady, early purple, early spider, epidendrone, green-winged, helleborine
**12** black vanilla, heath spotted, ladys' tresses, Lapland marsh, narrow-leaved, one-leaved bog, western marsh
**13** Chinese ground, common spotted, dense-flowered, elder-flowered, ladies' tresses, loose-flowered, orange

blossom, southern marsh
**14** moccasin flower
**15** lesser butterfly, violet birds-nest

## ordain

**03** fix, set **04** call, fate, rule, will
**05** elect, frock, japan, order **06** anoint, assign, decree, invest, priest
**07** appoint, arrange, destine, dictate, dispose, foresay, lay down, require
**08** instruct, ordinate **09** destinate, establish, preordain, prescribe, pronounce **10** consecrate, foreordain, lay hands on, predestine
**12** predetermine

## ordeal

**04** pain, test **05** agony, trial **07** anguish, torment, torture, trouble **08** distress, troubles **09** bier right, gruelling, nightmare, suffering **10** affliction
**11** persecution, tribulation
**12** tribulations **13** baptism of fire

## order

◇ *anagram indicator* **02** OM **03** bid, law, OBE, ord **04** book, call, calm, chit, club, fiat, form, kind, line, nick, plan, rank, rota, rule, sect, sort, tell, type, writ **05** array, caste, class, cycle, edict, genus, grade, group, guild, level, lodge, peace, quiet, set-up, shape, state, union **06** codify, decree, degree, demand, direct, enjoin, family, fettle, kilter, lay out, layout, league, line-up, manage, method, ordain, system, tidy up **07** arrange, booking, call for, command, company, conduct, control, dictate, dispose, harmony, mandate, marshal, pattern, precept, request, require, reserve, society, sort out, species, station, summons, variety, warrant **08** apply for, classify, grouping, instruct, neatness, organize, position, practice, regulate, sequence, sorority, symmetry, tidiness
**09** authorize, catalogue, community, condition, direction, directive, hierarchy, legislate, ordinance, prescribe, structure **10** commission, discipline, fellowship, fraternity, injunction, lawfulness, regularity, regulation, sisterhood, uniformity
**11** application, arrangement, association, brotherhood, disposition, instruction, law and order, orderliness, requirement, requisition, reservation, send away for, stipulation, systematize, write off for
**12** codification, denomination, notification, organization, pecking order, tranquillity, working order
**13** secret society **14** categorization, classification
*See also* **command; honour; religious**
**• in order 02** OK **04** done, neat, tidy
**05** right **06** lawful, likely, mended, proper **07** allowed, correct, fitting, ordered, orderly, regular, working
**08** all right, arranged, suitable
**09** operative, organized, permitted, shipshape **10** acceptable, classified, good as gold, in sequence, methodical, systematic
**11** appropriate, categorized,

functioning **13** well-organized **15** secundum ordinem
• **in order that 02** so
• **in order to 02** to **05** for to **06** so that **11** intending to, with a view to **13** with the result **14** with the purpose
• **order around 05** bully **07** lay down **08** browbeat, bulldoze, dominate, domineer **09** push about, tyrannize **10** boss around, order about, push around **13** lay down the law
• **out of order** ◇ *anagram indicator* **04** bust **05** amiss, kaput, messy, wrong **06** broken, untidy **07** haywire, muddled **08** confused, gone phut, improper, unlawful, unseemly **09** conked out, incorrect, irregular, off kilter **10** broken down, disordered, not working, on the blink, on the fritz, out of sorts, out of whack, unsuitable **11** inoperative, out of course, out of kilter, uncalled-for **12** disorganized, unacceptable **13** inappropriate, out of sequence **14** not functioning **15** out of commission
• **set in order 02** do **03** red **04** redd, trim **05** dress, prank, right **06** betrim, fettle, pranck, snod up **07** dispone, prancke
• **special order, standing order 02** SO

## orderliness
**08** neatness, tidiness, trimness **09** smartness **10** regularity, spruceness **12** organization, straightness **14** methodicalness

## orderly
◇ *anagram indicator* **04** neat, ruly, tidy, trim **05** quiet **06** cosmic **07** in order, ordered, regular **09** chaprassi, chaprassy, chuprassy, efficient, regularly **10** controlled, law-abiding, methodical, restrained, systematic **11** disciplined, well-behaved **12** businesslike, methodically **13** well-organized, well-regulated **15** in apple-pie order

## ordinance
**03** law **04** fiat, rite, rule **05** canon, edict, order **06** bye-law, decree, dictum, ritual, ruling **07** command, statute **08** ceremony, planning, practice **09** directive, enactment, equipment, prescript, sacrament **10** dead-letter, injunction, observance, regulation **11** appointment, institution, preparation

## ordinarily
**07** as a rule, usually **08** commonly, normally **09** generally, in general **10** familiarly, habitually **11** customarily **14** conventionally

## ordinary
**01** O **03** ord **04** dull, fair **05** banal, bland, blunt, plain, usual **06** canton, common, cotise, modest, normal, simple **07** average, cottise, mundane, prosaic, quarter, regular, routine, typical, vanilla **08** everyday, familiar,

habitual, mediocre, standard, workaday **09** customary, plain-Jane, quotidian **10** mainstream, pedestrian, working-day **11** bog standard, commonplace, indifferent, nondescript, unmemorable **12** conventional, run-of-the-mill, unremarkable **13** garden-variety, penny-farthing, unexceptional, uninteresting, unpretentious **14** bread-and-butter, common-or-garden **15** undistinguished
• **out of the ordinary 04** rare **05** kinky **06** unique **07** unusual **09** different, left-field, memorable **10** noteworthy, remarkable, surprising, unexpected **11** exceptional, out of the way, outstanding **13** extraordinary

## ordnance
**03** ord **04** arms, guns **06** cannon **07** big guns, pelican, weapons **09** artillery, munitions **14** field artillery

## ordure
**03** poo **04** dirt, dung, poop **05** filth, frass, guano, scats, stool **06** egesta, faeces **09** droppings, excrement, excretion **11** waste matter

## ore
**03** o'er **04** over **06** tangle **07** mineral, seaweed **09** sea tangle

*Ores include:*

**03** wad
**04** wadd, wadt
**06** bog-ore, coltan, galena, rutile
**07** bauxite, bog-iron, bornite, cuprite, iron ore, oligist, schlich, uranite, wood tin
**08** beauxite, braunite, calamine, enargite, hematite, limonite, siderite, sinopite, stibnite, taconite, tenorite
**09** anglesite, blackband, coffinite, haematite, hedyphane, ironstone, kidney ore, lodestone, magnetite, malachite, manganite, minestone, morass ore, proustite, tantalite
**10** erubescite, melaconite, peacock-ore, pyrolusite, ruby silver, sphalerite, stephanite
**11** cassiterite, chloanthite, pyrargyrite, tetradymite
**12** babingtonite, chalcopyrite, pyromorphite, tetrahedrite
**13** copper pyrites, horseflesh ore
**15** stilpnosiderite

*See also* **seaweed**
• **vein of ore 04** rake

## Oregon
**02** OR **04** Oreg

## organ
**04** part, tool, unit **05** forum, paper, pedal, regal, voice **06** agency, device, medium, member **07** element, journal, process, vehicle **08** magazine, melodeon, melodion **09** component, harmonium, implement, newspaper, structure **10** instrument, mouthpiece, periodical **11** apollonicon, constituent, publication **13** kist o' whistles

*Organs include:*

**03** ear, eye
**04** lung, nose, skin
**05** bowel, brain, colon, liver, lungs, lymph, penis, vulva
**06** cervix, rectum, spleen, testes, throat, thymus, ureter, uterus, vagina
**07** bladder, kidneys, ovaries, oviduct, pharynx, scrotum, stomach, thyroid, tonsils, trachea, urethra
**08** adenoids, appendix, bronchus, clitoris, pancreas, prostate, windpipe
**09** diaphragm, pituitary, taste buds
**10** epididymis, intestines, lymph nodes, oesophagus, spinal cord
**11** gall bladder, parathyroid, vas deferens
**12** hypothalamus, thymus glands, thyroid gland
**13** adrenal glands, nervous system
**14** fallopian tubes, large intestine, small intestine
**15** ejaculatory duct, seminal vesicles

*Organ stops include:*

**04** echo, oboe, sext, tuba
**05** dolce, gamba, quint
**06** cornet, nasard, octave, tierce
**07** bombard, bourdon, clarino, clarion, fagotto, mixture, piccolo, salicet, trumpet
**08** carillon, crumhorn, diapason, diaphone, dulciana, gemshorn, krumhorn, register, waldhorn
**09** fifteenth, furniture, krummhorn, principal, pyramidon, vox humana, waldflute
**10** clarabella, fourniture, salicional
**11** superoctave, voix céleste
**12** sesquialtera
**15** corno di bassetto

## organic
**06** biotic, GM-free, living **07** animate, natural, ordered **08** coherent **09** organized **10** biological, harmonious, mechanical, structural, structured **11** non-chemical **12** additive-free, chemical-free, instrumental **13** not artificial, pesticide-free

## organism
**04** body, cell **05** being, biont, plant, set-up, unity, whole **06** animal, entity, system **08** creature **09** bacterium, structure **11** living thing **12** organization
*See also* **animal; cell; classification**

## organization
◇ *anagram indicator* **04** body, club, firm, plan **05** group, order, set-up, union, unity, whole **06** design, layout, league, method, outfit, system **07** company, concern, council, pattern, running, society **08** grouping, planning **09** authority, formation, institute, operation, structure, syndicate **10** consortium, federation, management, regulation **11** arrangement, association,

composition, corporation, development, institution, methodology **12** co-ordination **13** confederation, configuration, establishment **14** administration, classification, conglomeration

## Organization of Petroleum Exporting Countries
*see* OPEC

## organize
◇ *anagram indicator* **03** ren, rin, run **04** form **05** begin, found, frame, group, mould, order, see to, set up, shape, start **06** create, embody, imbody, manage, obtain **07** arrange, develop, dispose, marshal, prepare, sort out **08** assemble, classify, regiment, tabulate **09** catalogue, construct, establish, institute, lemmatize, originate, structure **10** administer, co-ordinate, put in order **11** orchestrate, put together, rationalize, standardize, systematize **12** be in charge of

## organized
◇ *anagram indicator* **04** neat, tidy **07** in order, ordered, orderly, organic, planned, regular **08** arranged **09** efficient **10** methodical, structured, systematic **11** well-ordered **12** businesslike **13** well-organized, well-regulated

## orgiastic
**04** wild **05** orgic **07** Bacchic **09** debauched, Dionysiac **12** bacchanalian

## orgy
**04** bout, riot **05** binge, party, revel, spree **06** excess, frenzy, revels **07** debauch, revelry, splurge **08** carousal, Dionysia **09** wild party **10** indulgence, Saturnalia **11** bacchanalia

## orient
**01** E **04** East **05** adapt, align **06** adjust, attune, rising **07** eastern, sunrise, the East **08** accustom **09** habituate, orientate **11** acclimatize, accommodate, familiarize **15** get your bearings

## oriental
**01** E **05** Asian **07** Asiatic, Eastern **10** Far Eastern
*See also* **Asian**

## orientation
**07** guiding, leading **08** attitude, bearings, location, position, training **09** alignment, direction, induction, placement, situation **10** adaptation, adjustment, initiation, settling-in **11** inclination, positioning **15** acclimatization, familiarization

## orifice
**03** gap **04** hole, pore, rent, rift, slit, slot, vent **05** break, cleft, crack, inlet, mouth, space, trema **06** breach, orifex **07** crevice, fissure, opening **08** aperture, spiracle **09** micropyle **10** blastopore **11** perforation

## origin
**04** base, dawn, germ, line, rise, root **05** basis, birth, cause, fount, roots, start, stock **06** family, launch, source, spring **07** dawning, descent, genesis, lineage **08** ancestry, creation, fountain, genetics, heritage, pedigree **09** beginning, emergence, etymology, inception, parentage, paternity, principle **10** conception, derivation, extraction, foundation, provenance, well-spring **12** commencement, fountainhead, inauguration **13** line of descent

## original
◇ *anagram indicator* **02** ur- **03** new **04** real, true, type **05** early, first, fresh, model, novel, prime **06** actual, innate, master, primal, unique **07** genuine, initial, opening, pattern, primary, radical, unusual **08** creative, earliest, paradigm, primeval, pristine, standard, starting **09** archetype, authentic, embryonic, first-hand, ingenious, inventive, primaeval, primitial, primitive, prototype **10** archetypal, commencing, indigenous, innovative, pioneering, primordial, protoplast, unborrowed, unorthodox **11** imaginative, primigenial, resourceful, rudimentary **13** autochthonous **14** ground-breaking, unconventional

## originality
**06** daring **07** newness, novelty **08** boldness **09** freshness, ingenuity **10** cleverness, creativity, innovation **11** imagination, singularity, unorthodoxy **12** creativeness, eccentricity **13** individuality, inventiveness **14** creative spirit, innovativeness **15** imaginativeness, resourcefulness
• **lacking originality** **07** clichéd **08** clichéed **09** hackneyed

## originally
◇ *head selection indicator* **05** first **07** at first, by birth **08** in origin **09** initially **10** at the start **11** at the outset, to begin with **12** by derivation **14** in the beginning **15** in the first place

## originate
**04** come, flow, form, head, rear, rise, seed, stem **05** arise, begin, found, hatch, issue, plant, set up, start **06** be born, create, derive, emerge, evolve, father, invent, launch, result, source, spring **07** develop, emanate, pioneer, proceed, produce **08** commence, conceive, discover, generate, take rise **09** establish, institute, introduce, set on foot **10** inaugurate, mastermind **11** give birth to, set in motion **13** be the father of, be the mother of

## origination
**07** forming **08** creation **09** invention, paternity **10** conception, generation, production **11** development

## originator
**06** author, father, mother **07** creator, founder, pioneer **08** designer, inventor **09** architect, developer, generator, initiator, innovator, the brains

**10** discoverer, prime mover **11** establisher

## ornament
**04** deck, fall, gaud, gild, knob, ouch, spar, tiki, trim **05** adorn, crown, décor, frill, gnome, jewel, mense, spray, sprig, wally **06** almond, bauble, bedeck, fallal, gewgaw, gorget, griffe, labret, relish, set-off **07** dress up, emblema, figgery, fleuron, frigger, frounce, garland, garnish, hei-tiki, lunette, netsuke, pattern, pendant, pendent, rellish, trinket, twiddle **08** barrette, bar slide, beautify, brighten, carcanet, decorate, furbelow, rocaille, sunburst, trimming **09** accessory, adornment, arabesque, dog collar, embellish, fandangle, medallion, multifoil, scalework **10** decoration, escutcheon, Japanesery, knick-knack **11** garden gnome, garnishment **12** curliewurlie, jingle-jangle **13** embellishment

## ornamental
**05** fancy, showy **06** florid **08** adorning **10** attractive, decorative **12** embellishing, embroidering

## ornamentation
**04** fret, seam **06** frills **07** barbola, die-work **09** adornment, fallalery, garniture, strap work **10** decoration, embroidery, enrichment, figuration, ornateness **11** barbola work, elaboration, whigmaleery **12** whigmaleerie **13** embellishment

## ornate
◇ *anagram indicator* **04** busy, fine **05** adorn, fancy, flash, fussy, showy **06** florid, rococo **07** baroque, elegant, flowery **08** barbaric, mandarin **09** barbarian, decorated, elaborate, grandiose, luxuriant, sumptuous **10** flamboyant, ornamented **11** embellished **12** ostentatious

## orotund
**04** deep, full, loud, rich **05** round **06** ornate, strong **07** booming, pompous **08** imposing, powerful, sonorous, strained **09** dignified **10** resonating **11** pretentious **12** magniloquent **13** grandiloquent

## orthodox
**04** true **05** sound, usual **06** devout, square, strict **07** canonic, correct, regular **08** accepted, catholic, faithful, official, received **09** canonical, customary, hardshell **10** conformist, recognized **11** bien pensant, established, traditional **12** conservative, conventional **13** authoritative **14** fundamentalist **15** well-established

## orthodoxy
**05** canon, credo, creed, dogma, tenet **06** belief **07** precept **08** devotion, doctrine, teaching, trueness **09** principle, soundness **10** conformism, conformity, conviction, devoutness, properness, strictness **11** correctness **12** conservatism, faithfulness **13** inflexibility **14** fundamentalism,

**oscar**

received wisdom, traditionalism
**15** conventionality

**oscar**
**01** O

**oscillate**
**03** wag **04** hunt, sway, vary, yo-yo
**05** pitch, squeg, swing, waver
**06** seesaw, wigwag **07** librate, vibrate
**09** fluctuate, vacillate **12** move to and
fro

**oscillation**
**05** surge, swing **07** flutter **08** sine wave,
swinging, wavering **09** seesawing,
squegging, variation, vibration
**10** swing-swang **11** fluctuation,
instability, vacillation **15** shilly-
shallying

**osmium**
**02** Os

**osprey**
**07** Pandion **08** fish-hawk **09** ossifrage

**ossify**
**06** harden **07** petrify **08** indurate, make
hard, rigidify, solidify **09** fossilize,
make fixed **10** become hard
**11** become fixed

**ostensible**
**07** alleged, claimed, feigned, outward,
seeming **08** apparent, presumed, so-
called, specious, supposed
**09** ostensive, pretended, professed,
purported **11** superficial

**ostensibly**
**09** allegedly, outwardly, reputedly,
seemingly **10** apparently, supposedly
**11** professedly, purportedly **12** on the
surface **13** superficially

**ostentation**
**03** dog **04** dash, fuss, pomp, puff, show
**05** flash, pride, swank **06** ostent,
parade, splash, tinsel, vanity **07** display
**08** boasting, flourish, pretence,
pretense, vaunting **09** flaunting,
pageantry, showiness, trappings
**10** flashiness, peacockery, phylactery,
pretension, showing-off **11** affectation,
fanfaronade, flamboyance
**13** exhibitionism **14** window-dressing
**15** pretentiousness

**ostentatious**
**03** OTT **04** loud **05** flash, gaudy, lairy,
showy **06** flashy, garish, glitzy, kitsch,
vulgar **07** splashy **08** affected, barbaric,
fastuous **09** barbarian, barbarous,
flaunting, obtrusive **10** flamboyant,
over the top **11** conspicuous,
extravagant, pretentious
**13** demonstrative

**ostentatiously**
**03** OTT **05** large **06** loudly **07** showily
**08** flashily, garishly **10** over the top
**11** obtrusively **12** flamboyantly
**13** conspicuously, extravagantly,
pretentiously **15** demonstratively

**ostracism**
**04** tabu **05** exile, taboo **07** barring,
boycott **09** avoidance, exclusion,
expulsion, isolation, rejection
**10** banishment **12** cold-shoulder,

proscription **13** disfellowship
**15** excommunication

**ostracize**
**03** bar, cut **04** shun, snub **05** avoid,
exile, expel **06** banish, outlaw, reject
**07** boycott, exclude, isolate
**09** blackball, proscribe, segregate
**12** cold-shoulder **13** excommunicate
**14** send to Coventry

**ostrich**
**04** rhea **05** nandu **06** nandoo, nhandu
**07** estrich **08** estridge, oystrige, Struthio

**OT**
*see* **Bible**

**other**
◊ *anagram indicator* **04** else, left, more
**05** extra, spare **06** second, unlike
**07** further, variant **08** distinct, separate
**09** alternate, different, disparate,
remaining **10** additional, dissimilar
**11** alternative, contrasting
**13** supplementary
• **all others** **04** rest

**otherwise**
◊ *anagram indicator* **02** or **03** aka **04** else
**05** alias, if not **06** or else, unless
**09** different **11** also known as,
differently, failing that **12** in another
way **15** in a different way, in other
respects

**otherworldly**
**03** fey **04** rapt **06** dreamy **07** bemused
**08** ethereal **11** preoccupied **12** absent-
minded

**otiose**
**05** extra, spare **06** excess, futile
**07** surplus, to spare **08** indolent,
needless, unneeded, unwanted
**09** excessive, redundant, remaining
**10** gratuitous, unoccupied
**11** superfluous, uncalled-for,
unnecessary, unwarranted
**12** functionless **13** supernumerary

**ottoman**
**04** pouf **05** squab

**ounce**
**02** oz **03** jot, tad **04** atom, drop, fl oz,
iota, lynx, spot, tael, unce, whit
**05** crumb, grain, liang, scrap, shred,
speck, touch, trace **06** jaguar, morsel
**07** cheetah, modicum **08** particle
**11** snow leopard

**oust**
**04** fire, sack **05** eject, evict, expel
**06** depose, put out, topple, unseat
**07** boot out, dismiss, kick out, replace,
turn out **08** dislodge, displace, drive
out, force out, get rid of, supplant,
throw out **09** overthrow, thrust out
**10** disinherit, dispossess **13** show the
door to

**out**
◊ *anagram indicator* ◊ *deletion indicator*
**02** to **03** KO'd, set **04** alas, away, bent,
dead, gone **05** dated, forth, known,
passé, ready **06** abroad, absent,
démodé, doused, intent, old hat,
public, remote, used up **07** evident,
expired, exposed, in bloom, in print,
out cold, outside, without

**08** blooming, comatose, divulged,
drawback, excluded, external,
finished, forcibly, in flower, manifest,
outlying, revealed, seawards
**09** available, disclosed, dismissed,
elsewhere, forbidden, insistent, in the
open, not at home, out-of-date,
published, unwelcome **10** antiquated,
blossoming, completely, determined,
disallowed, impossible, insensible,
knocked out, not burning, not shining,
obtainable, thoroughly, unsuitable
**11** in full bloom, unconscious,
undesirable **12** disadvantage,
extinguished, inadmissible, old-
fashioned, unacceptable, unreservedly
**13** inappropriate, unfashionable
• **not out** **02** no
• **out of** **04** frae, from, hors
• **out upon it** **04** haro **06** harrow

**out-and-out**
**04** fair, flat, rank **05** plumb, stark, total,
utter **06** arrant, full-on, proper
**07** perfect, regular **08** absolute,
complete, outright, positive, teetotal,
thorough, whole-hog **09** bald-faced,
downright, right-down, up and down
**10** consummate, definitely, heart-
whole, inveterate **11** honest-to-God,
straight-out, unmitigated, unqualified
**12** unreservedly **13** dyed-in-the-wool,
thoroughgoing **14** hundred-per-cent,
uncompromising

**outbreak**
**04** rash **05** burst, clash, flash, storm
**06** putsch **07** flare-up, upbreak,
upsurge **08** epidemic, eruption,
hysteria, outburst **09** explosion
**10** ebullition **11** disturbance,
excrescence, sudden start
**13** recrudescence

**outburst**
**03** fit, rag **04** flaw, gale, gush, gust,
song **05** blurt, burst, flaky, spasm,
storm, surge **06** attack, escape, outcry,
volley **07** boutade, flare-up, ovation,
passion, seizure **08** eruption, mouthful,
outbreak, paroxysm, sunburst
**09** explosion **10** exuberance,
exuberancy, outpouring, solar flare
**11** fit of temper

**outcast**
**05** cagot, exile, leper **06** abject, outlaw,
pariah, reject, wretch **07** evacuee,
quarrel, refugee **08** castaway, outsider,
rejected **11** untouchable **15** persona
non grata

**outclass**
**03** top **04** beat **05** outdo **07** eclipse,
outrank, surpass **08** outrival, outshine,
outstrip **09** excel over, transcend
**10** overshadow **11** outdistance **13** leave
standing, put in the shade

**outcome**
**05** issue, proof **06** answer, effect, pay-
off, result, sequel, upcome, upshot,
wash-up **07** proceed, product
**08** proceeds **09** end result, outspring
**10** conclusion, dénouement **11** after-
effect, consequence

### outcry

**03** cry, row **04** fuss **05** noise **06** clamor, racket, rumour, steven, tumult, uproar, yammer **07** clamour, dissent, exclaim, protest **08** outburst **09** commotion, complaint, hue and cry, objection **10** hullabaloo, humdudgeon **11** exclamation, indignation **12** protestation, vociferation

### outdated

**03** obs **05** dated, mumsy, passé, steam **06** démodé, old hat, past it, square, uncool **07** antique, archaic **08** obsolete, outmoded **09** out of date **10** antiquated, fuddy-duddy, oldfangled, superseded **11** obsolescent, old-fogeyish, on the way out, out of the ark **12** antediluvian, old-fashioned, out of fashion **13** unfashionable **14** behind the times

### outdistance

**04** pass **06** outrun **07** outpace, surpass **08** outstrip, overhaul, overtake, shake off **11** leave behind, pull ahead of **13** leave standing

### outdo

**03** cap **04** beat, best, whip **05** excel, lurch **06** defeat, exceed **07** eclipse, surpass **08** outclass, out-Herod, outshine, outstrip, overcome, superate **09** come first, transcend **10** outperform **11** outdistance **12** walk away from **13** knock spots off, put in the shade, run rings round **14** get the better of **15** go one better than, run circles round

### outdoors

**03** out **06** abroad **07** outside **08** alfresco **10** en plein air, out-of-doors **12** in the open air

### outer

**06** fringe, remote **07** distant, faraway, further, outside, outward, surface **08** exterior, external, outlying **09** outermost **10** peripheral **11** superficial

### outface

**04** defy **05** beard, brave **08** confront, outbrave, outstare **09** brazen out, stand up to, stare down

### outfit

**03** kit, rig, set **04** crew, firm, gang, garb, gear, suit, team, togs, unit, weed **05** dress, equip, fit up, get-up, group, samfu, set-up, squad, stock, tools **06** attire, clique, fit out, fit-out, kit out, layout, rig-out, samfoo, setout, supply **07** apparel, appoint, bloomer, clothes, company, costume, coterie, furnish, provide, sunsuit, turn out, turnout **08** accoutre, business, ensemble **09** apparatus, equipment, provision, separates, trappings **10** sailor suit **11** bag of tricks, corporation **12** organization **13** accoutrements, paraphernalia, shalwar-kameez

### outfitter

**06** sartor, tailor **07** modiste **08** clothier, costumer **09** costumier, couturier **10** couturière, dressmaker **11** haberdasher

### outflow

**03** ebb, jet **04** gush, rush **05** spout **06** efflux, spring **07** outfall, outrush **08** drainage, effluent, effusion **09** discharge, effluence, effluvium, effluxion, emanation, emergence **10** outpouring **11** debouchment **14** disemboguement

### outflowing

**07** emanant, gushing, leaking, rushing **08** effluent, spurting **10** debouching **11** discharging

### outfox

**03** con, kid **04** beat, best, dupe **05** trick **06** have on, outwit **07** deceive **08** outsmart, out-think **10** outperform **12** outmanoeuvre, take for a ride **14** get the better of, pull a fast one on

### outgoing

**02** ex- **04** last, open, past, warm **06** former, genial **07** affable, amiable, cordial, leaving **08** emissary, friendly, retiring, sociable **09** departing, easy-going, expansive, extrovert, talkative **10** gregarious, unreserved **11** expenditure, sympathetic, uninhibited **12** affectionate, approachable **13** communicative, demonstrative

### outgoings

**04** exes **05** costs **06** outlay **08** expenses, spending **09** disbursal, overheads **11** expenditure **12** disbursement

### outgrowth

**03** ala **04** aril, hair, horn **05** shoot **06** air-sac, effect, sprout, stolon **07** enation, product, spin-off, verruca **08** caruncle, offshoot, root hair, swelling, trichome **09** apophysis, appendage, by-product, emanation, emergence, flocculus, propagule, rostellum **10** osteophyte, pollen tube, propagulum **11** consequence, excrescence **12** appressorium, effiguration, protuberance

### outhouse

**04** shed

### outing

**03** out **04** hike, romp, spin, tour, trip **05** jaunt, jolly, sally **06** junket, picnic **08** ejection **09** coach tour, excursion **10** expedition **11** mystery tour **12** pleasure trip

### outlandish

◇ *anagram indicator* **03** odd **05** alien, wacky, weird **06** exotic, far-out, freaky, quaint, way-out **07** bizarre, curious, foreign, oddball, strange, unknown, unusual **08** peculiar **09** barbarous, eccentric, grotesque, peregrine, unheard-of, uplandish **10** ridiculous, unfamiliar **12** preposterous, unreasonable **13** extraordinary **14** unconventional

### outlandishness

**07** oddness **09** queerness, weirdness **10** exoticness, quaintness **11** bizarreness, peregrinity, strangeness, unusualness **12** eccentricity **13** grotesqueness

### outlast

**04** ride **07** outdure, outlive, outstay, survive, weather **11** come through

### outlaw

**03** ban, bar **04** horn, Tory **05** debar, exile **06** badman, bandit, banish, forbid, pirate, robber **07** brigand, condemn, embargo, exclude, outcast **08** criminal, disallow, fugitive, marauder, prohibit **09** broken man, desperado, interdict, proscribe, Robin Hood **10** bushranger, highwayman **12** put to the horn **13** excommunicate

### outlay

**04** cost, mise **05** price **06** charge, expend **07** expense, payment **08** expenses, spending **09** outgoings **11** expenditure **12** disbursement

### outlet

**04** duct, exit, port, shop, vent **05** issue, store, valve **06** egress, escape, let-off, market, nozzle, sluice, way out **07** channel, conduit, culvert, opening, outfall, release, sea gate **08** débouché, emissary, femerall, retailer, supplier **10** going forth **11** safety valve **12** retail outlet **14** means of release

### outline

**03** map **04** edge, form, plan, trim **05** braid, chart, draft, dress, shape, trace, trick **06** aperçu, design, figure, fringe, layout, précis, résumé, schema, sketch **07** balloon, contour, croquis, diagram, keyline, profile, skyline, summary, tracing **08** abstract, chalk out, contorno, esquisse, rough out, scenario, skeleton, synopsis **09** adumbrate, bare bones, bare facts, delineate, framework, lineament, programme, rough idea, sketch out, summarize, waterline **10** ground plan, main points, prospectus, silhouette **11** delineation **12** underdrawing **13** configuration **15** thumbnail sketch

### outlive

**07** outlast, outwear, survive, weather **08** overwear **11** come through, live through

### outlook

**04** view **05** angle, slant **06** aspect, future **07** mindset, opinion, picture **08** attitude, forecast, panorama, prospect **09** prognosis, prospects, viewpoint, world-view **10** standpoint **11** frame of mind, perspective, point of view **12** expectations **14** interpretation, Weltanschauung

### outlying

**03** out **05** outby, outer **06** far-off, forane, outbye, remote **07** distant, far-away, outland **08** detached, far-flung, isolated **10** provincial **11** out-of-the-way **12** inaccessible

### outmanoeuvre

**04** beat **05** outdo **06** outfox, outwit **07** sandbag **08** outflank, outsmart, outthink **10** circumvent, outgeneral **14** get the better of

### outmoded

**05** dated, passé, steam **06** démodé, old hat, past it, square, uncool **07** archaic

**out of date**
08 obsolete, outdated, shmaltzy 09 out of date, schmaltzy 10 antiquated, fuddy-duddy, oldfangled, superseded 11 obsolescent, old-fogeyish, on the way out, out of the ark 12 antediluvian, old-fashioned, out of fashion 13 unfashionable 14 behind the times

**out of date**
03 old 05 dated, passé, steam 06 démodé, old hat, passée, past it, square, uncool 07 archaic, belated, vintage 08 obsolete, outdated, outmoded, overworn 09 overdated 10 antiquated, behindhand, fuddy-duddy, oldfangled, superseded 11 obsolescent, old-fogeyish, on the way out, out of the ark, prehistoric 12 antediluvian, old-fashioned, out of fashion 13 horse-and-buggy, prehistorical, unfashionable 14 behind the times
*See also* **outdated**

**out-of-the-way**
03 odd 04 lost 05 outer 06 far-off, hidden, lonely, remote 07 distant, far-away, obscure, unusual 08 far-flung, isolated, outlying, secluded, singular, uncommon 10 outlandish, peripheral 11 god-forsaken, little-known 12 inaccessible, unfrequented

**out of work**
04 idle 07 jobless, laid off, resting 08 workless 09 on the dole, out of a job, redundant 10 unemployed 11 between jobs

**outpace**
04 beat, pass 05 outdo 06 outrun 07 surpass 08 outstrip, overhaul, overtake 11 outdistance

**outpouring**
04 flow, flux 05 blast, flood, spate, spurt 06 deluge, efflux, lavish, strain, stream 07 cascade, outflow, torrent, welling 08 effusion 09 effluence, emanation, word salad 11 debouchment 14 disemboguement

**output**
◇ *anagram indicator* 04 gain 05 yield 06 fruits, oeuvre, return 07 harvest, outturn, product, turnout 10 production, throughput 11 achievement, manufacture, performance 12 productivity 14 accomplishment

**outrage**
04 evil, fury, rage, rape 05 abuse, anger, appal, crime, shock, wrath 06 defile, enrage, horror, injure, injury, madden, offend, ravage, ravish 07 abusion, affront, assault, disgust, horrify, incense, offence, scandal, violate 08 atrocity, enormity, violence 09 barbarism, brutality, desecrate, infuriate, sacrilege, violation 10 scandalize 11 indignation

**outrageous**
◇ *anagram indicator* 04 foul, rich, vile, wild 05 enorm, gross 06 unholy 07 furious, ghastly, heinous, obscene, ungodly, violent 08 dreadful, enormous, flagrant, gruesome,

horrible, infernal, shocking, terrible 09 atrocious, egregious, excessive, monstrous, offensive, turbulent 10 abominable, diabolical, exorbitant, immoderate, inordinate, monstrous, scandalous, unbearable 11 disgraceful, extravagant, intolerable, unchristian, unspeakable 12 extortionate, insufferable, preposterous, unacceptable, unreasonable 14 unconscionable

**outrageously**
08 horribly, terribly 09 obscenely 10 dreadfully, unbearably 11 intolerably, unspeakably 12 scandalously, unacceptably 13 disgracefully

**outré**
◇ *anagram indicator* 03 odd 05 weird 06 far-out, freaky, way-out 07 bizarre, oddball, strange, unusual 08 shocking 09 eccentric, fantastic 10 outrageous 11 extravagant 13 extraordinary 14 unconventional

**outrider**
05 guard 06 escort, herald 08 vanguard 09 attendant, bodyguard, precursor 12 advance guard

**outright**
04 pure 05 clear, total, utter 06 at once, direct, openly, wholly 07 perfect, totally, utterly 08 absolute, complete, definite, directly, entirely, thorough 09 downright, instantly, out-and-out 10 absolutely, completely, explicitly, positively, thoroughly, undeniable 11 categorical, immediately, unequivocal, unmitigated, unqualified 12 straight away, there and then, unmistakable, unreservedly 13 categorically, thoroughgoing, unconditional, undisguisedly 15 instantaneously, straightforward

**outrun**
04 beat, lose, pass 05 excel, outdo 06 exceed 07 outpace, surpass 08 outstrip, overhaul, overtake, shake off 11 leave behind, outdistance, spread-eagle 13 run faster than

**outset**
05 onset, start 07 kick-off, opening 09 beginning, inception, threshold 12 commencement, inauguration

**outshine**
03 top 04 beat, best 05 dwarf, excel, outdo 07 eclipse, outrank, put down, surpass, upstage 08 outclass, outstrip 09 outlustre, transcend 10 overshadow, put to shame 13 put in the shade

**outside**
◇ *anagram indicator* ◇ *containment indicator* 03 exo- 04 ecto-, face, hors, rind, rine, slim 05 cover, extra, faint, front, outer, small, vague 06 casual, façade, remote, slight 07 distant, extreme, furth of, neutral, outdoor, outward, slender, surface, without 08 exterior, external, marginal, unbiased, unlikely, visiting 09 impartial, objective, outermost, temporary 10 appearance, consulting,

extramural, extraneous, improbable, negligible 11 independent, non-resident, peripatetic, superficial 12 outer surface, self-employed 13 subcontracted

**outsider**
05 alien 06 émigré, layman, misfit, ringer 07 outlier, roughie, visitor 08 emigrant, intruder, newcomer, stranger 09 foreigner, immigrant, non-member, odd one out, outlander 10 interloper 11 gatecrasher, non-resident

**outsize**
02 OS 04 huge, mega, vast 05 giant, great, jumbo 07 immense, mammoth, massive, titanic, very big 08 colossal, enormous, gigantic 09 extensive, frightful, ginormous, humongous, monstrous, very large 10 gargantuan, prodigious, stupendous, tremendous

**outskirts**
04 edge 05 edges, limit 06 margin 07 borders, fringes, suburbs 08 boundary, environs, frontier, purlieus, suburbia, vicinity 09 perimeter, periphery 13 neighbourhood

**outsmart**
03 con, kid 04 beat, best, dupe 05 trick 06 have on, outfox, outwit 07 deceive 08 out-think 10 outperform 12 outmanoeuvre, take for a ride 14 get the better of, pull a fast one on

**outsource**
07 farm out 08 delegate 11 contract out 12 give to others, pass to others

**outspoken**
04 free, rude 05 bluff, blunt, broad, frank, plain, vocal 06 candid, direct 07 brusque 08 explicit, straight 10 forthright, unreserved 11 plain-spoken, Rabelaisian, unequivocal 13 unceremonious 15 straightforward

**outspokenness**
07 freedom 08 rudeness 09 bluffness, bluntness, frankness, plainness 10 candidness, directness 11 brusqueness 14 forthrightness

**outspread**
04 open, wide 06 flared, opened 08 expanded, extended, unfolded, unfurled, wide-open 09 fanned out, spread out, stretched 12 outstretched

**outstanding**
03 ace, due 04 cool, some 05 brill, chief, famed, great, owing 06 famous, golden, superb, unpaid, wicked 07 eminent, notable, ongoing, payable, pending, radical, salient, special 08 left-over, renowned, smashing, striking, superior, to be done, top-notch 09 arresting, brilliant, excellent, important, memorable, prominent, remaining, unsettled, well-known 10 celebrated, impressive, noteworthy, pre-eminent, prosilient, remarkable, unfinished, unresolved 11 exceptional, superlative, uncollected 13 distinguished,

**outstandingly** (cont.)

extraordinary **14** extraordinaire, out of this world

**outstandingly**

**07** greatly, notably **09** amazingly, extremely **10** especially, remarkably, strikingly **12** impressively **13** exceptionally **15** extraordinarily

**outstrip**

**03** top **04** beat, cote, pass **05** outdo, outgo, strip **06** better, exceed, gain on, outrun **07** eclipse, outfoot, outpace, surpass **08** outshine, overtake **09** transcend **11** leave behind, outdistance **12** go faster than **13** leave standing

**outward**

**05** outer **06** carnal, extern, formal, public **07** evident, externe, obvious, outside, seeming, surface, visible, worldly **08** apparent, exterior, external, supposed **09** dissolute, outermost, posticous, professed **10** accidental, additional, noticeable, observable, ostensible **11** discernible, perceptible, superficial, without-door **13** superficially

**outwardly**

◇ *containment indicator* **07** visibly, without **09** seemingly **10** apparently, exteriorly, externally, supposedly **12** at first sight, on the outside, on the surface **13** on the face of it, superficially

**outweigh**

**06** exceed **07** surpass **08** overcome, override **09** cancel out, make up for, overpoise **10** be more than, outbalance **11** predominate, prevail over **12** be superior to, preponderate **13** be greater than, compensate for

**outwit**

**03** con, fox, kid **04** beat, best, dish, dupe **05** cheat, trick **06** better, euchre, have on, outfox **07** deceive, defraud, swindle **08** outsmart, outthink **09** crossbite, overreach **10** circumvent **12** outmanoeuvre, take for a ride **14** be cleverer than, get the better of, pull a fast one on

**outwork**

**04** moon

**outworn**

**05** stale **06** old hat, past it **07** ancient, archaic, defunct, disused **08** obsolete, outdated, outmoded, rejected **09** abandoned, exhausted, hackneyed, moth-eaten, out of date **10** antiquated **11** discredited, obsolescent **12** old-fashioned **14** behind the times

**oval**

**05** ovate, ovoid **07** navette, obovate, oviform **08** elliptic **09** egg-shaped, vulviform **10** elliptical **11** ellipsoidal

**ovation**

**06** bravos, cheers, praise **07** acclaim, bouquet, praises, tribute **08** accolade, applause, cheering, clapping, plaudits **09** laudation, rejoicing **11** acclamation **12** handclapping

**oven**

**03** Aga, oon, umu **04** kiln, lear, leer, lehr, oast **05** hangi, micro, stove **06** calcar, cooker **07** furnace, tandoor **09** microwave **11** copper Maori **13** microwave oven

**over**

◇ *containment indicator* ◇ *juxtaposition down indicator* ◇ *reversal down indicator* **02** of, on, re, up **03** o'er, ore **04** gone, left, ower, owre, past, upon **05** about, above, aloft, along, ended, extra, upper **06** across, beyond, closed, during, excess, no more, on high, unused **07** at an end, on top of, settled, surplus **08** done with, finished, in excess, left over, more than, overhead, superior, unwanted **09** apropos of, as regards, completed, concluded, exceeding, excessive, forgotten, in the past, regarding, remaining, unclaimed **10** concerning, higher than, in addition, in charge of, in excess of, relating to, superior to, terminated, throughout **11** dealing with, in command of, referring to, superfluous **12** accomplished, with regard to **13** concerned with, connected with, in the matter of, with respect to **14** ancient history, on the subject of **15** over and done with, with reference to

• **over and above** **04** plus **06** beside **07** added to, besides, on top of **08** as well as, let alone **09** along with **12** in addition to, not to mention, together with

• **over and over** **05** often **09** ad nauseam, endlessly **10** frequently, repeatedly **11** ad infinitum, continually **12** time and again **13** again and again

**overabundance**

**04** glut **06** excess **07** surfeit, surplus **08** plethora **09** profusion **10** oversupply **11** superfluity **14** superabundance **15** embarras de choix

**overact**

**03** ham **04** hoke **06** overdo **07** lay it on **08** overplay, pile it on **10** exaggerate **12** lay it on thick **13** pile it on thick

**overall**

**05** broad, pinny, total **06** global, pinnie **07** all-over, blanket, broadly, crawler, general, save-all, tablier **08** complete, dustcoat, out to out, pinafore, sweeping, umbrella **09** dungarees, inclusive, in general, siren suit, universal **10** altogether, boiler suit, by and large, everywhere, on the whole **12** all-embracing, all-inclusive **13** comprehensive **15** broadly speaking

**overalls**

**06** jumper, pinnie **07** crawler, save-all, tablier **08** coverall, dust-coat, fatigues, pinafore, workwear **09** dungarees **10** boiler suit

**overawe**

**03** awe, cow **05** abash, alarm, daunt, scare **06** dismay **07** buffalo, petrify, terrify, unnerve **08** browbeat, frighten **10** disconcert, intimidate

**overbalance**

**04** slip, trip **05** upset **06** topple, tumble **07** capsize, tip over **08** fall over, keel over, overturn **10** somersault, topple over, turn turtle **15** lose your balance, lose your footing

**overbearing**

**05** bossy, proud **06** la-di-da, lordly, snobby, snooty, snotty **07** haughty, stuck-up **08** arrogant, cavalier, despotic, dogmatic, masterly, smartass **09** imperious, officious, smartarse **10** autocratic, disdainful, dogmatical, high-handed, oppressive, tyrannical **11** dictatorial, domineering, toffee-nosed **12** contemptuous, presumptuous, supercilious

**overblown**

**03** OTT **07** exalted **08** inflated, overdone **09** amplified, bombastic, excessive **10** burlesqued, overstated, over the top **11** caricatured, embellished, extravagant, overcharged, pretentious **13** overestimated, self-important

**overcast**

**04** dark, dull, grey, hazy, whip **05** foggy, misty, shade **06** cloudy, dismal, dreary, gloomy, leaden, sombre **07** clouded, louring, recover, sunless **08** darkened **11** clouded over

**overcharge**

**02** do, o/c **04** clip, rook, rush, soak **05** cheat, sting **06** diddle, extort, fleece, rip off **07** swindle **09** surcharge **11** short-change

**overcoat**

*see* **coat**

**overcome**

**04** beat, best, lick, rout **05** break, cover, force, fordo, moved, outdo, worst **06** broken, byword, defeat, evince, excess, expugn, hammer, master, mither, moider, outwit, subdue, thrash **07** beat off, clobber, conquer, consume, moither, outplay, overget, prevail, refrain, surplus, trounce **08** affected, choked up, convince, dead-beat, knock out, outsmart, superate, surmount, vanquish, wear down **09** exhausted, hit for six, overmatch, overpower, overthrow, overwhelm, rise above, slaughter, subjugate, underfong **10** bowled over, speechless, surmounted **11** knock for six, overpowered, overwhelmed, triumph over **12** lost for words, put on the foil **13** have the edge on **14** get the better of

**over-confident**

**04** rash **05** brash, cocky **06** secure, uppish, uppity **08** arrogant, cocksure, sanguine **09** foolhardy, hubristic **10** blustering, incautious, swaggering **11** overweening, self-assured, temerarious **12** presumptuous **14** over-optimistic

**overcook**

**04** burn, char **05** singe **07** blacken

**overcritical**

**06** purist **07** carping, Zoilean

**overcrowded**

08 captious, over-nice, pedantic
09 cavilling 10 nit-picking, pernickety
11 persnickety 12 fault-finding, hard to
please 13 hair-splitting, hypercritical
14 overparticular

**overcrowded**

06 packed 07 chocker, overrun,
teeming 08 swarming 09 chock-full,
congested, jam-packed, packed out
10 overloaded 11 chock-a-block,
crammed full 13 overpopulated

**overdo**

05 excel 06 harass 07 fatigue, ham it
up, lay it on, overact 08 camp it up, go
too far, overplay, pile it on 09 overstate
10 exaggerate 11 cut it too fat, go
overboard, overindulge 12 lay it on
thick 13 carry to excess, pile it on
thick, stretch a point
• overdo it 07 crack up 08 overwork
09 do too much 10 sweat blood
11 work too hard 14 strain yourself
15 burn yourself out

**overdone**

03 OTT 05 burnt, hokey, undue
07 charred, dried up, fulsome, gushing,
percoct, spoiled 08 effusive, overshot
09 excessive, overbaked 10 histrionic,
immoderate, inordinate, overcooked,
overplayed, overstated, over the top
11 exaggerated, overwrought,
unnecessary 13 overelaborate 14 burnt
to a cinder 15 burnt to a frazzle

**overdose**

02 OD

**overdraft**

02 OD 04 debt 07 arrears, deficit
10 borrowings 11 liabilities 13 unpaid
amounts

**overdue**

03 due 04 late, slow 05 owing, tardy
06 unpaid 07 belated, delayed,
payable, pending 09 unsettled
10 behindhand, unpunctual 14 behind
schedule

**overeat**

05 binge, gorge 06 guzzle, pig out
10 eat too much, go on a binge,
gormandize 11 overindulge 13 stuff
yourself

**overeating**

07 bulimia 08 bingeing, gluttony,
guzzling 10 gormandise, gormandism
11 gourmandise, gourmandism
hyperphagia 14 overindulgence

**overemphasize**

06 labour 08 belabour 10 exaggerate,
overstress 13 make too much of,
overdramatize

**overexert**

• overexert yourself 07 fatigue
08 overdo it, overwork 11 work too
hard 14 strain yourself 15 overtax
yourself, wear yourself out

**overfeed**

04 cram, glut, sate

**overflow**

03 lip, ren, rin, run 04 ream, soak, teem
05 cover, flood, spill, surge, swamp,

water 06 back-up, deluge, shower
07 overrun, redound, run over, surplus
08 brim over, flow over, inundate,
outswell, pour over, spillage,
submerge, surround, well over
09 discharge, overspill, spill over
10 bubble over, inundation
13 overabundance

**overflowing**

04 full, rife 05 flush 06 filled 07 brimful,
copious, crowded, profuse, teeming
08 inundant, overfull, swarming,
thronged 09 abounding, bountiful,
exuberant, land-flood, plenteous,
plentiful, redundant 13 superabundant

**overgrown**

04 rank

**overgrowth**

05 naeve, nevus 06 naevus
09 gigantism 10 escalation, luxuriance,
luxuriancy, rhinophyma
11 gliomatosis, hyperplasia,
hypertrophy 13 overabundance
14 superabundance
15 overdevelopment

**overhang**

03 jut 04 loom, poke 05 bulge
06 beetle, extend, impend, jut out
07 poke out, project 08 bulge out,
protrude, stand out, stick out

**overhanging**

06 beetle, shelvy 07 bulging, jutting,
pendant, pendent, pensile 08 beetling,
imminent 09 incumbent, pendulous,
prominent 10 bulging out, jutting out,
projecting, protruding 11 standing out,
sticking out 14 superincumbent

**overhaul**

03 fix 04 mend, pass 05 check 06 gain
on, go over, repair, revamp, survey
07 check up, check-up, examine,
inspect, outpace, rummage, service
08 outstrip, overtake, renovate
09 check over, going-over, re-examine
10 get ahead of, inspection, renovation
11 examination, investigate,
outdistance, pull ahead of, recondition
14 reconditioning

**overhead**

03 air 05 above, aloft 06 aerial, on high,
raised, upward 07 average, general, up
above 08 all-round, elevated
11 overhanging

**overheads**

06 burden, oncost 07 oncosts
08 expenses 09 outgoings 10 fixed costs
11 expenditure 12 disbursement,
regular costs, running costs
14 operating costs

**overheated**

05 angry, fiery 06 roused 07 excited,
flaming 08 agitated, inflamed
10 passionate 11 impassioned,
overexcited, overwrought
• overheated state 04 stew

**overindulge**

03 pet 04 lush, sate 05 binge, booze,
gorge, spoil 06 cosset, guzzle, pamper,
pander, pig out 07 debauch, satiate
09 spoon-feed 10 eat too much,

gluttonize, gormandize
11 mollycoddle 12 drink too much

**overindulgence**

05 binge 06 excess 07 debauch, surfeit
10 overeating 12 immoderation,
intemperance

**overjoyed**

04 rapt 06 elated, joyful 08 ecstatic,
euphoric, jubilant, thrilled
09 delighted, rapturous 10 enraptured,
in raptures 11 high as a kite, on cloud
nine, over the moon, tickled pink
14 pleased as Punch 15 in seventh
heaven, on top of the world

**overlap**

03 lap 04 ride 05 cover 07 overlay,
overlie, shingle 08 coincide, flap over,
override 09 imbricate

**overlay**

04 ceil, face, line, span, whip, wrap
05 adorn, belay, cover, inlay, patch
06 spread, veneer 07 blanket, envelop,
surface, varnish 08 covering, decorate,
encumber, laminate, ornament

**overload**

03 tax 04 glut 06 burden, excess,
lumber, saddle, strain 07 oppress,
overtax, surfeit, surplus 08 encumber,
plethora 09 surcharge, weigh down
10 overburden, overcharge,
oversupply 11 hypercharge,
overfreight, superfluity
13 overabundance 14 superabundance

**overlook**

04 face, miss, omit 05 leave 06 excuse,
forget, ignore, pardon, pass by, slight,
wink at 07 condone, forgive, let pass,
let ride, neglect, oversee 08 look onto,
look over, open onto, overskip, pass
over 09 disregard, front onto,
mislippen 11 have a view of,
superintend 14 command a view of,
take no notice of 15 take no account
of, turn a blind eye to

**overlooked**

07 unnoted 08 unheeded, unprized,
unvalued 10 in the shade,
unhonoured, unregarded, unremarked
12 unconsidered

**overly**

03 too 04 over 06 casual, unduly
08 casually, superior 11 exceedingly,
excessively 12 immoderately,
inordinately, supercilious,
unreasonably 13 unnecessarily
14 superciliously

**overmuch**

06 unduly 07 too much 11 excessively
12 immoderately, inordinately,
unreasonably 13 unnecessarily

**overnice**

07 finical 08 kid glove 10 nit-picking,
oversubtle, pernickety 11 overprecise,
persnickety 13 oversensitive
14 overfastidious, over-meticulous,
overparticular, overscrupulous

**overplay**

06 colour, overdo, stress 07 amplify,
enhance, enlarge, lay it on, magnify
08 oversell, pile it on 09 dramatize,

embellish, embroider, emphasize, overstate **10** aggrandize, exaggerate, shoot a line **12** lay it on thick **13** make too much of, overdramatize, overemphasize, pile it on thick **15** stretch the truth

## overpopulated

**06** packed **07** overrun, teeming **08** swarming **09** chock-full, congested, jam-packed, packed out **10** overloaded **11** crammed full, overcrowded

## overpower

**04** beat, daze, move, rout **05** crush, floor, quash, quell, swelt, touch, whelm **06** dazzle, defeat, evince, master, overgo, subdew, subdue **07** confuse, conquer, perplex, stagger, swelter, trounce **08** bedazzle, bowl over, overbear, overcome, vanquish **09** dumbfound, hit for six, hypnotize, overthrow, overwhelm, subjugate, take aback **10** immobilize, overmaster **11** flabbergast, knock for six **12** affect deeply **14** affect strongly **15** gain mastery over, leave speechless

## overpowering

**06** strong **07** extreme **08** forceful, powerful, stifling **09** sickening, tyrannous **10** compelling, nauseating, oppressive, unbearable, undeniable **11** irrefutable, suffocating **12** irresistible, overwhelming **14** uncontrollable

## over-productive

**04** rank

## overrate

**06** blow up **07** magnify **09** overprize, overvalue **10** overpraise **12** overestimate **13** make too much of

## overreach

• **overreach yourself 08** go too far, overdo it **14** strain yourself, try to do too much **15** burn yourself out

## override

**05** annul, quash **06** cancel, exceed, ignore **07** nullify, overlap, rescind, reverse, surpass **08** abrogate, outweigh, overcome, overrule, overtake, set aside, vanquish **09** disregard, supersede **11** countermand, prevail over, trample over **12** be superior to **13** be greater than

## overriding

**05** final, first, major, prime, prior **06** ruling **07** pivotal, primary, supreme **08** cardinal, dominant, ultimate **09** essential, number one, paramount, principal **10** compelling, overruling, prevailing **11** determining, predominant **13** most important **15** most significant

## overrule

**05** annul **06** cancel, reject, revoke **07** nullify, outvote, prevail, rescind, reverse **08** abrogate, disallow, overbear, override, oversway, overturn, set aside, vote down **10** invalidate **11** countermand

## overrun

**03** lip **05** bleed, storm, swamp **06** attack, exceed, go over, infest, invade, occupy, ravage **07** besiege, run riot **08** inundate, overgrow, overstep, permeate **09** overreach, overshoot, overwhelm, penetrate, surge over, swarm over **10** depopulate, spread over

## overseas

**06** abroad, exotic, remote, widely **07** distant, faraway, foreign **08** external, outremer **10** far and wide **11** ultramarine **13** international **14** in foreign parts, to foreign parts **15** in foreign climes, out of the country, to foreign climes

## oversee

**03** ren, rin, run **05** guide, watch **06** direct, manage **07** conduct, control, inspect **09** disregard, look after, supervise, watch over **10** administer **11** keep an eye on, preside over, superintend **12** be in charge of **13** be in control of

## overseer

**03** guv **04** baas, boss **05** chief **06** bishop, critic, editor, gaffer, grieve, guv'nor, induna **07** captain, foreman, manager, overman, steward **08** banksman, decurion, oversman, surveyor **09** forewoman, woodreeve **10** foreperson, manageress, supervisor, workmaster **11** flock-master, mine-captain **12** workmistress **14** superintendent

## overshadow

◇ *containment indicator* **03** dim, mar **04** veil **05** cloud, dwarf, excel, shade, spoil **06** blight, darken **07** eclipse, obscure, protect, shelter, surpass **08** bescreen, dominate, hang over, outshine **09** adumbrate, obumbrate, rise above **10** tower above **12** be superior to, put a damper on **13** put in the shade **14** take the edge off

## oversight

**04** boob, care, flub **05** error, fault, lapse **06** charge, howler, slip-up **07** blunder, control, custody, keeping, mistake, neglect **08** handling, omission **09** direction **10** management, parablepsy **11** dereliction, parablepsis, supervision **12** carelessness, inadvertence, inadvertency, surveillance **14** administration, responsibility **15** superintendence

## oversize

**04** huge, mega, vast **05** giant, great, jumbo **07** immense, very big **08** colossal, enormous, gigantic **09** extensive, frightful, ginormous, humongous, monstrous, very large **10** gargantuan, monumental, prodigious, stupendous, tremendous

## overstate

**05** sex up **06** colour, overdo, stress **07** amplify, enhance, enlarge, lay it on, magnify **08** oversell, pile it on **09** dramatize, embellish, embroider, emphasize **10** aggrandize, exaggerate,

shoot a line **12** lay it on thick **13** make too much of, overdramatize, overemphasize, pile it on thick **15** stretch the truth

## overstatement

**06** excess, parody **08** emphasis **09** burlesque, hyperbole **10** caricature **11** enlargement **12** exaggeration, extravagance, overemphasis **13** amplification, embellishment, magnification **14** overestimation **15** pretentiousness

## overt

**04** open **05** plain **06** patent, public **07** evident, obvious, visible **08** apparent, manifest **09** professed **10** noticeable, observable **11** conspicuous, unconcealed, undisguised

## overtake

**03** lap **04** pass **05** catch **06** befall, engulf, gain on, go past, strike **07** forhent, run past **08** come upon, forehent, happen to, outstrip, overhaul, ride down **09** drive past, overcatch, overwhelm **10** come up with **11** catch up with, leave behind, outdistance, pull ahead of **13** catch unawares, draw level with **14** take by surprise

## over the top

*see* **over the top** *under* **top**

## overthrow

◇ *anagram indicator* **03** end **04** beat, best, down, fall, oust, rout, ruin **05** crush, quash, quell, smite, spill, upset, whelm, worst **06** defeat, depose, invert, lay low, master, subdue, topple, tumble, unseat, upturn **07** abolish, conquer, ousting, put down, run down, run over, stonker, subvert, tip over, trounce, undoing, whemmle, whomble, whommle, whummle **08** bear down, confound, dethrone, displace, downfall, keel over, overcast, overcome, overturn, ride down, supplant, turn over, vanquish **09** bring down, confusion, knock over, overpower, overwhelm, prostrate, unseating, upsetting **10** deposition, subversion **11** destruction, humiliation, labefaction, overbalance, suppression, vanquishing **12** dethronement **13** labefactation **14** bouleversement

## overtly

**06** openly **07** clearly, plainly **08** patently **09** obviously **10** in full view, manifestly, noticeably **11** for all to see **13** conspicuously

## overtone

**04** hint **05** sense **06** nuance **07** feeling, flavour **08** harmonic, innuendo **10** intimation, suggestion **11** association, connotation, implication, insinuation **12** undercurrent **13** hidden meaning

## overture

**04** move **05** moves, offer **06** feeler, gambit, motion, signal **07** advance, feelers, opening, prelude, toccata **08** advances, aperture, approach, proposal **09** beginning **10** invitation, suggestion **11** opening move, opportunity, proposition **12** introduction **13** opening gambit

*Overtures include:*

**05** Cuban, Herod, Wasps
**06** Adonis, Choral, Comedy, Esther, French, Heroic, Solemn, Spring, Thalia, Tragic
**07** Aladdin, Euterpe, Festive, Holiday, Idyllic, Jubilee, Leonora, Maytime, Othello
**08** Carnival, Columbus, Coriolan, Hebrides, Hyperion, In Autumn, King Lear, Romantic, Waverley
**09** Britannia, Children's, Fairy Land, In Bohemia, Pinocchio, The Naiads
**10** Amid Nature, In the South, Salutatory
**11** East and West, Fingal's Cave, Pickwickian, Shéhérazade, The Faithful, William Tell
**12** Fair Melusina, In London Town, Rip van Winkle, Street Corner, The Rehearsal
**13** In the Highland, Shadowy Waters, The Wood-Nymphs
**14** Eighteen Twelve, Eighteen-Twelve, In Nature's Realm, In the Mountains, Romeo and Juliet
**15** Comes Autumn Time, Portsmouth Point, The Fair Melusina

## overturn

◇ *anagram indicator* ◇ *reversal down indicator* **03** tip **04** beat, coup, cowp, oust, veto **05** annul, crush, quash, spill, upset, whelm **06** cancel, defeat, depose, invert, repeal, revoke, topple, unseat, upturn **07** abolish, capsize, conquer, destroy, nullify, rescind, reverse, skittle, subvert, tip over, whemmle, whomble, whommle, whumble **08** abrogate, confound, dethrone, displace, keel over, overcome, override, overrule, set aside, turn over, vanquish **09** bring down, knock over, overpower, overthrow, overwhelm **11** overbalance

## overused

**04** worn **05** stale, tired, trite **07** cliché'd **08** bromidic, clichéed **09** hackneyed, played out **10** overworked, threadbare, unoriginal **11** commonplace, stereotyped **13** platitudinous

## overview

**05** study **06** review, survey **08** panorama, scrutiny **09** appraisal, valuation **10** assessment, inspection **11** examination, measurement **13** consideration

## overweening

**04** vain **05** cocky, proud **06** hubris, hybris, lordly **07** haughty, pompous, swollen **08** arrogant, cavalier, cocksure, inflated, insolent, vaulting **09** conceited, excessive, hubristic,

overblown, upsetting **10** high-handed, immoderate **11** egotistical, extravagant, opinionated **12** presumptuous, supercilious, vainglorious **13** outrecuidance, over-confident, self-confident

## overweight

**03** fat **04** huge **05** ample, bulky, buxom, gross, heavy, hefty, obese, plump, podgy, stout, tubby **06** chubby, chunky, flabby, fleshy, portly **07** massive, outsize **09** corpulent **10** pot-bellied, voluptuous, well-padded **13** preponderance **15** well-upholstered

## overwhelm

**04** beat, best, bury, daze, kill, lick, move, rout **05** amaze, crush, floor, quash, quell, swamp, touch, worst **06** defeat, deluge, engulf, hammer, ingulf, outwit, subdue, thrash **07** clobber, confuse, destroy, engulph, ingulph, oppress, outplay, overrun, prevail, stagger, trounce **08** bowl over, inundate, knock out, outsmart, overbear, overcome, submerge, vanquish **09** devastate, hit for six, overpower, overthrow, slaughter, snow under, subjugate **10** overburden **11** knock for six **12** affect deeply **13** have the edge on, knock sideways **14** affect strongly, get the better of

## overwhelming

**04** huge, vast **05** great, large **06** strong **07** banging, extreme, immense, massive, runaway **08** crashing, enormous, forceful, powerful, stifling **09** sickening **10** compelling, formidable, foudroyant, nauseating, oppressive, unbearable, undeniable **11** irrefutable, suffocating **12** irresistible, overpowering **14** uncontrollable

## overwork

**05** weary **06** burden, strain **07** crack up, exhaust, exploit, oppress, overtax, overuse, wear out **08** overdo it, overload **09** do too much **10** overstrain, sweat blood **11** work too hard **14** strain yourself **15** burn yourself out

## overworked

**04** worn **05** stale, tired, trite **07** cliché'd, worn out **08** bromidic, clichéed, forswunk **09** exhausted, forswonck, hackneyed, overtaxed, played out **10** threadbare, unoriginal **11** commonplace, stereotyped, stressed out **12** overstrained **13** platitudinous

## overwrought

**04** edgy **05** nervy, tense **06** highly, on edge, strung **07** excited, frantic, keyed up, nervous, uptight, wound up **08** agitated, worked up **10** distraught **11** overcharged, overexcited **14** beside yourself

## owe

**10** be in debt to, be in the red, run up debts **11** be overdrawn, get into debt **12** be indebted to **13** be in arrears to

## owing

**03** dew, due **04** owed **06** unpaid **07** overdue, payable **09** imputable, in arrears, unsettled **11** outstanding
• **owing to** **02** of **05** due to **08** thanks to **09** because of **11** as a result of, on account of **15** in consequence of

## owl

**04** Bubo, ruru **05** madge **06** hooter, howlet, mopoke, strich **07** boobook, dullard, smuggle **08** longhorn, mopehawk, morepork, wiseacre **09** screecher **11** glimmer-gowk

## own

**03** ain, use **04** have, hold, keep, nain, nown **05** admit, enjoy **06** occupy, proper, retain **07** concede, confess, have got, possess, private **08** peculiar, personal **09** authentic, recognize **10** individual, monopolize, particular **11** acknowledge **12** be the owner of **13** idiosyncratic **14** have to yourself
• **on your own** **05** alone **06** singly **07** unaided **08** isolated **09** on your tod **10** by yourself, unassisted **13** independently, off your own bat, unaccompanied
• **own up** **05** admit **07** confess **09** come clean **11** acknowledge, plead guilty **12** tell the truth

## owner

**05** malik, melik **06** holder, keeper, master **08** landlady, landlord, mistress **09** homeowner, possessor **10** freeholder, proprietor **11** householder, proprietary **12** proprietress

## ownership

**04** uses **05** title **06** domain, rights **08** dominion, freehold, property **10** possession **11** proprietary **14** proprietorship

## owning

**02** of

## ox

**03** ure, yak **04** anoa, bull, gaur, gyal, mart, neat, urus, zebu **05** bison, bugle, gayal, steer, stirk **06** rother **07** aurochs, banteng, banting, buffalo, bullock **08** bull-beef, sapi-utan **09** sapi-outan
• **team of oxen** **04** span

## Oxford University

*see* **college**

## oxygen

**01** O

## oyster

**05** plant **06** native, Ostrea **07** spondyl **08** seedling
• **oyster bed** **04** stew

**P**

**p**
03 pee 04 papa

**pace**
04 gait, pass, rate, step, walk 05 amble, march, pound, speed, tempo, tramp, tread 06 flight, motion, patrol, stride 07 mark out, measure, passage, running 08 celerity, movement, progress, rapidity, velocity 09 quickness, swiftness 13 walk up and down 14 rate of progress

**pacific**
04 calm, mild 05 quiet, still 06 dovish, gentle, irenic, placid, serene, smooth 07 equable, halcyon 08 dovelike, friendly, irenical, pacifist, peaceful, tranquil 09 appeasing, peaceable, placatory, unruffled 10 diplomatic, non-violent 11 complaisant, peace-loving, peacemaking 12 conciliatory, pacificatory, propitiatory 14 nonbelligerent

**pacification**
07 calming 08 soothing 09 placating, silencing 10 moderating, moderation, quietening 11 appeasement, peacemaking 12 conciliation, propitiation 14 quietening down

**pacifism**
10 pacificism, satyagraha 11 non-violence, peacemaking

**pacifist**
02 CO 04 dove 06 conchy 08 peacenik 10 pacificist, peace-lover, peacemaker 11 peace-monger

**pacify**
04 calm, lull, tame 05 allay, crush, quell, quiet, still 06 defuse, soften, soothe, subdue 07 appease, assuage, compose, mollify, placate, put down, quieten, silence, sweeten 08 calm down, moderate 09 reconcile 10 conciliate, propitiate

**pack**
03 bag, box, jam, mob, ram, set, tin 04 bale, band, cram, crew, fill, gang, herd, load, plot, rout, stow, swag, wrap 05 bluey, bunch, cover, crate, crowd, drove, flock, group, press, put in, stock, store, stuff, tie up, troop, truss, wedge 06 bundle, burden, carton, charge, fardel, kitbag, packet, parcel, steeve, throng, wrap up 07 compact, company, dismiss, envelop, matilda, package, repack, squeeze 08 backpack, canister, compress, intrigue, knapsack, rucksack 09 container, haversack 10 collection 11 blister card, canisterize

• **pack in** 03 end, jam, mob, ram 04 fill, load, stop 05 chuck, crowd, leave, press, stuff, wedge 06 charge, cram in, give up, jack in, resign, throng 07 squeeze, throw in
• **pack off** 04 send 07 dismiss 08 dispatch 09 bundle off
• **pack round** 04 tamp
• **pack up** 03 end 04 fail, stop 05 crash, truss 06 bundle, finish, give up, go phut, jack in, tidy up, wrap up 07 clear up, conk out, go kaput, put away, seize up, throw in 08 empacket, tidy away 09 break camp, break down 10 call it a day 11 malfunction, stop working 12 go on the fritz 13 put things away

**package**
03 box, lot, set 04 bale, pack, roll, unit, wrap 05 batch, group, whole 06 bundle, carton, entity, packet, pack up, parcel, wrap up 08 gift-wrap, parcel up 09 container 10 collection, shrink-wrap 11 consignment, package deal

**packaging**
03 box 06 packet 07 packing, wrapper 08 wrappers, wrapping 09 container, wrappings 12 presentation
• **without packaging** 03 net 04 nett

**packed**
04 full 05 thick 06 filled, jammed 07 brimful, chocker, crammed, crowded, serried 08 thronged 09 chockfull, congested, jam-packed 10 overloaded 11 chock-a-block, overflowing

**packet**
03 bag, box 04 a lot, bomb, case, deck, lots, mint, pack, pile, post, pots 06 bundle, carton, parcel, sachet 07 fortune, package, packing, tidy sum, wrapper 08 envelope, Jiffy bag®, wrapping 09 a bob or two, container, megabucks, padded bag 11 king's ransom, loadsamoney, pretty penny 12 small fortune 14 padded envelope

**packhorse load**
04 seam

**packing-ring**
04 lute

**pact**
04 bond, deal 06 cartel, treaty 07 bargain, compact, concord, entente 08 alliance, contract, covenant 09 agreement, concordat 10 convention, settlement 11 arrangement 13 understanding

**pad**
03 paw, ren, rin, run, wad 04 fill, flat, foot, home, line, lope, move, mute, pack, path, roll, room, sole, step, sunk, walk, wase, wrap 05 block, guard, inker, place, print, quilt, rooms, squab, stuff, tramp, tread 06 bedsit, buffer, hamper, jotter, pillow, shield, tiptoe, trudge 07 blotter, bolster, bombast, bum roll, cushion, hang-out, memo pad, notepad, padding, pannier, pillion, protect, wadding 08 compress, dressing, leg-guard, notebook, quarters, stuffing 09 apartment, flip chart, footprint, penthouse 10 impregnate, protection, writing pad
• **pad out** 06 expand 07 amplify, augment, bolster, fill out, inflate, spin out, stretch 08 flesh out, increase, lengthen, protract 09 elaborate

**padding**
06 hot air, lining, waffle 07 bombast, filling, packing, wadding 08 crashpad, stuffing, verbiage 09 prolixity, verbosity, wordiness 10 cotton wool, cushioning, protection 11 verboseness

**paddle**
03 oar, row 04 pull, punt, slop, wade 05 canoe, scull, steer, sweep 06 dabble, finger, plunge, propel, splash, trifle 10 lumpsucker

**paddock**
03 pen 04 fold, frog, park, toad, yard 05 field, pound 06 corral 07 parrock 08 birdcage, compound, stockade 09 enclosure

**paddy**
03 pet 04 bate, fury, rage, tiff 05 sawah, strop 06 taking, temper 07 passion, tantrum 08 manrider 11 fit of temper 14 manriding train

**padlock**
03 bar 04 bolt, lock, seal, shut 05 catch, clasp, latch 06 fasten, secure 09 fastening 10 spring lock 11 mortise lock

**padre**
05 vicar 06 cleric, curate, deacon, father, parson, pastor, priest, rector 08 chaplain, minister, reverend 09 churchman, clergyman, deaconess

**paean**
04 hymn 05 psalm 06 anthem, eulogy 07 ovation 08 doxology, encomium, ode to joy 09 dithyramb, panegyric 10 exultation 12 song of praise

**pagan**
06 paynim 07 atheist, Gentile, godless, heathen, infidel, ungodly 08 idolater 09 atheistic 10 idolatrous, unbeliever 11 irreligious, nonbeliever, nullifidian, pantheistic

**page**
01 p 02 ro, vo 03 bid, era 04 call, leaf, side 05 epoch, event, folio, phase, recto, sheet, stage, title, verso 06 ask for, period, summon 07 bellboy, bellhop, chapter, episode, footman, pageboy, send for, servant 08 announce, henchman, incident, paginate 09 attendant, messenger, tearsheet 10 henchwoman 11 henchperson
• **pages** 02 pp
• **two pages** 04 leaf

**pageant**
04 play, show 05 antic, scene 06 antick, parade 07 anticke, antique, display, tableau, triumph 08 specious 09 cavalcade, spectacle 10 procession 12 extravaganza 14 representation

**pageantry**
04 pomp, show 05 drama 06 parade

**pageboy**

07 display, glamour, glitter
08 ceremony, flourish, grandeur
09 melodrama, showiness, spectacle, splendour 12 extravagance, magnificence 13 theatricality

**pageboy**
04 page 07 bellboy, bellhop, footman, servant 09 attendant, messenger

**paid-up**
05 loyal 06 active, red-hot 07 devoted, fervent, zealous 08 involved
09 committed, dedicated
11 evangelical 12 card-carrying, enthusiastic

**pail**
03 can, kit, tub 04 bail, dixy 05 churn, dixie 06 bucket, leglan, leglen, leglin, piggin, vessel 07 pitcher, scuttle
10 slop bucket

**pain**
02 wo 03 ake, gip, gyp, mal, woe
04 ache, bore, dole, dool, drag, hurt, pang, pest, rack, stab, sten, teen, tene
05 agony, cramp, dolor, doole, grief, gripe, shoot, smart, spasm, stend, sting, teene, thraw, throb, throe, throw, upset, worry 06 aching, be sore, bother, bummer, burden, cramps, dolour, grieve, misery, sadden, sorrow, stitch, throwe, twinge 07 afflict, agonize, ailment, anguish, anxiety, penalty, torment, torture, trouble 08 be tender, distress, headache, irritate, nuisance, smarting, soreness, vexation
09 annoyance, causalgia, heartache, suffering, throbbing 10 affliction, desolation, discomfort, heartbreak, irritation, tenderness 11 indigestion, lancination, make anxious, tribulation
12 collywobbles, wretchedness
13 make miserable, pain in the neck
• **expression of pain** 01 O 02 oh, ow
04 argh, ouch 05 aargh
• **freedom from pain** 04 ease

**pained**
03 sad 04 hurt 05 stung, upset, vexed
06 piqued 07 grieved, injured, unhappy, worried, wounded
08 offended, saddened 09 aggrieved
10 distressed 11 reproachful

**painful**
03 bad 04 achy, hard, sore 05 tough
06 aching, bitter, guilty, tender, touchy, trying 07 arduous, awkward, baleful, hurting, irksome, panging, pungent, shaming, tedious
08 exacting, grievous, inflamed, poignant, rigorous, shameful, smarting, stabbing, tortured, wretched
09 agonizing, difficult, harrowing, laborious, miserable, saddening, sensitive, strenuous, throbbing, traumatic, upsetting 10 disturbing, irritating, mortifying, unpleasant
11 disquieting, distressing, humiliating
12 disagreeable, discomfiting, embarrassing, excruciating
13 disconcerting, uncomfortable
• **be painful** 04 tine, tyne, work

**painfully**
◊ *anagram indicator* 04 sore 05 sadly
07 clearly 08 markedly, pitiably,

terribly, woefully 09 pitifully
10 alarmingly, deplorably, dreadfully, wretchedly 11 agonizingly, excessively
13 distressingly, unfortunately
14 excruciatingly

**painkiller**
04 bute, drug 06 remedy 07 anodyne, metopon, morphia, Nurofen®
08 lenitive, morphine, sedative
09 analgesia, analgesic 10 palliative
11 aminobutene, anaesthetic
*See also* **anaesthetic; analgesic**

**painless**
04 easy 05 cushy 06 simple 08 pain-free
10 child's play, effortless
11 comfortable, trouble-free, undemanding 12 a piece of cake, plain sailing

**painlessly**
06 easily, simply 11 comfortably
12 effortlessly 13 undemandingly

**pains**
04 care, fash, teen, tene 05 aches, labor, teene 06 bother, effort, labour, rheums 07 trouble 09 diligence
10 rheumatics 13 assiduousness
• **be at pains** 06 bother 07 try hard
08 take care 09 be anxious 11 be concerned 14 put yourself out 15 make every effort

**painstaking**
07 careful, devoted 08 diligent, sedulous, studious, thorough
09 assiduous, attentive, dedicated, searching 10 meticulous, scrupulous
11 hardworking, industrious, persevering, punctilious
13 conscientious

**paint**
03 dye 04 bice, coat, daub, draw, fard, gaud, limn, tell, tint, wash 05 adorn, apply, brush, color, cover, evoke, smear, stain 06 bister, bistre, colour, depict, finish, sketch, tipple 07 narrate, picture, pigment, plaster, portray, priming, recount, respray, stipple, topcoat 08 colorant, decorate, depeinct, describe 09 colouring, delineate, depicture, diversify, oil colour, represent, vinyl wash
10 redecorate 11 boot-topping

*Paints include:*

03 oil
04 matt, oils
05 glaze, gloss, satin, spray
06 enamel, fabric, pastel, poster, primer
07 acrylic, gouache, lacquer, masonry, scumble, shellac, stencil, tempera, varnish
08 eggshell, emulsion
09 anti-climb, distemper, undercoat, whitewash
10 colourwash, egg tempera
11 watercolour

• **paint the town red** 04 rave
05 binge, go out 07 have fun, rejoice
08 live it up 09 celebrate, have a ball, whoop it up 10 have a party 11 throw a party 13 enjoy yourself, go on the

razzle 14 go out on the town, push the boat out, put the flags out

**painted**
• **painted woman** 04 pict

**painter**
02 RA 06 artist, dauber, limner
07 Zeuxian 08 depicter 09 colourist, old master, paysagist, primitive, tactilist, vedutista 10 delineator, oil painter 11 landscapist, miniaturist, plein-airist 13 watercolorist
14 watercolourist

*Painters, printmakers and other artists include:*

03 **Arp** (Jean), **Dix** (Otto), **Ray** (Man)
04 **Bell** (Vanessa), **Boyd** (Arthur), **Dal** (Salvador), **Doré** (Gustave), **Dufy** (Raoul), **Eyck** (Jan van), **Goya** (Francisco de), **Gris** (Juan), **Hals** (Frans), **Hunt** (Holman), **John** (Augustus), **John** (Gwen), **Kent** (William), **Klee** (Paul), **Lely** (Sir Peter), **Long** (Richard), **Marc** (Franz), **Miró** (Joan), **Nash** (Paul)
05 **Bacon** (Francis), **Bakst** (Léon), **Blake** (Peter), **Blake** (William), **Bosch** (Hieronymus), **Brown** (Ford Madox), **Burra** (Edward), **Clark** (Kenneth, Lord), **Corot** (Camille), **David** (Jacques Louis), **Degas** (Edgar), **Dürer** (Albrecht), **Ernst** (Max), **Freud** (Lucian), **Gorky** (Arshile), **Greco** (El), **Grosz** (George), **Hirst** (Damien), **Homer** (Winslow), **Hooch** (Pieter de), **Johns** (Jasper), **Kahlo** (Frida), **Kitaj** (R B), **Klimt** (Gustav), **Kline** (Franz), **Léger** (Fernand), **Lewis** (Wyndham), **Lippi** (Filippino), **Lippi** (Fra Filippo), **Lowry** (L S), **Lucas** (Sarah), **Manet** (Edouard), **Monet** (Claude), **Mucha** (Alphonse), **Munch** (Edvard), **Nolan** (Sir Sidney), **Peake** (Mervyn), **Piper** (John), **Riley** (Bridget), **Sarto** (Andrea del)
06 **Braque** (Georges), **Bratby** (John), **Cassat** (Mary), **Claude**, **Derain** (André Louis), **Escher** (Maurits Cornelis), **Fuseli** (Henri), **Giotto**, **Gordon** (Douglas), **Ingres** (Jean), **Jarman** (Derek), **Knight** (Dame Laura), **Mabuse**, **Marini** (Marino), **Martin** (John), **Massys** (Quentin), **Millet** (Jean François), **Morley** (Malcolm), **Moroni** (Giovanni Battista), **Morris** (William), **Newman** (Barnett), **O'Keefe** (Georgia), **Orozco** (José), **Palmer** (Samuel), **Peploe** (Samuel John), **Pisano** (Nicola), **Ramsay** (Allan), **Renoir** (Pierre Auguste), **Rivera** (Diego), **Rothko** (Mark), **Rubens** (Sir Peter Paul), **Scarfe** (Gerald), **Searle** (Ronald), **Seurat** (Georges), **Sisley** (Alfred), **Strong** (Sir Roy), **Stubbs** (George), **Tanguy** (Yves), **Tissot** (James), **Titian**, **Turner** (J M W), **Warhol** (Andy), **Wilkie** (Sir David), **Wright** (Joseph)
07 **Attwell** (Mabel Lucie), **Bellini** (Giovanni), **Bonnard** (Pierre), **Boucher** (François), **Cézanne** (Paul), **Chagall** (Marc), **Chirico**

(Giorgio de), **Christo**, **Cimabué**, **Courbet** (Gustave), **Cranach** (Lucas, the Elder), **Daumier** (Honoré), **Delvaux** (Paul), **Duchamp** (Marcel), **El Greco**, **Gauguin** (Paul), **Hobbema** (Meindert), **Hockney** (David), **Hodgkin** (Sir Howard), **Hogarth** (William), **Hokusai** (Katsushika), **Holbein** (Hans), **Keating** (Tom), **Martini** (Simone), **Matisse** (Henri), **Millais** (Sir John Everett), **Morisot** (Berthe), **Pevsner** (Sir Nikolaus), **Picabia** (Francis), **Picasso** (Pablo), **Pollock** (Jackson), **Poussin** (Nicolas), **Rackham** (Arthur), **Raeburn** (Sir Henry), **Raphael**, **Sargent** (John Singer), **Schiele** (Egon), **Sickert** (Walter), **Spencer** (Sir Stanley), **Tenniel** (Sir John), **Thurber** (James), **Tiepolo** (Giovanni), **Uccello** (Paolo), **Utrillo** (Maurice), **Van Eyck** (Jan), **Van Gogh** (Vincent), **Vermeer** (Jan), **Watteau** (Antoine), **Wearing** (Gillian)

08 **Angelico** (Fra), **Annigoni** (Pietro), **Auerbach** (Frank), **Brueghel** (Pieter), **cummings** (e e), **Delaunay** (Robert), **Dubuffet** (Jean), **Goncourt** (Edmond de), **Gossaert** (Jan), **Hamilton** (Richard), **Hilliard** (Nicholas), **Landseer** (Sir Edwin), **Leonardo**, **Magritte** (René), **Malevich** (Kasimir), **Mantegna** (Andrea), **Masaccio**, **Mondrian** (Piet), **Munnings** (Sir Alfred), **Perugino**, **Piranesi** (Giambattista), **Pissarro** (Camille), **Reynolds** (Sir Joshua), **Rossetti** (Dante Gabriel), **Rousseau** (Henri, 'Le Douanier'), **Rousseau** (Théodore), **Ruisdael** (Jacob van), **Ruysdael** (Jacob van), **Topolski** (Feliks), **Vasarely** (Victor), **Veronese** (Paolo), **Vlaminck** (Maurice de), **Whistler** (James McNeill), **Whiteley** (Brett)

09 **Beardsley** (Aubrey), **Canaletto**, **Constable** (John), **Correggio**, **De Kooning** (Willem), **Delacroix** (Eugène), **Fergusson** (John Duncan), **Fragonard** (Jean), **Friedrich** (Caspar David), **Géricault** (Théodore), **Giorgione**, **Greenaway** (Kate), **Greenaway** (Peter), **Grünewald** (Matthias), **Kandinsky** (Wasily), **Kokoschka** (Oskar), **Lancaster** (Sir Osbert), **Nicholson** (Ben), **Nollekens** (Joseph), **Pisanello**, **Rembrandt**, **Rodchenko** (Alexander), **Velázquez** (Diego)

10 **Alma-Tadema** (Sir Lawrence), **Botticelli** (Sandro), **Burne-Jones** (Sir Edward), **Caravaggio** (Michelangelo), **Giacometti** (Alberto), **Modigliani** (Amedeo), **Motherwell** (Robert), **Parmigiano**, **Sutherland** (Graham), **Tintoretto**

12 **Bairnsfather** (Bruce), **Fantin-Latour** (Henri), **Gainsborough** (Thomas), **Lichtenstein** (Roy), **Michelangelo**

13 **Piero di Cosimo**

14 **Andrea del Sarto**, **Lucas van Leyden**

15 **Leonardo da Vinci**, **Toulouse-Lautrec** (Henri de)

---

**painting**
03 art, oil 04 daub, oils 08 likeness 09 cerograph, portrayal 11 delineation, scenography 13 belle peinture 14 representation
*See also* **art**

*Painting terms include:*

04 icon, tint, tone, wash
05 bloom, brush, easel, gesso, mural, paint, pieta, secco, tondo
06 canvas, fresco, frieze, primer, sketch
07 atelier, aureola, aureole, cartoon, collage, diptych, drawing, facture, gallery, gouache, impasto, limning, montage, palette, pastels, paysage, picture, pigment, scumble, sfumato, stipple, tempera
08 abstract, aquatint, bleeding, charcoal, esquisse, fixative, frottage, hard edge, hatching, paintbox, pastoral, portrait, seascape, skyscape, thinners, triptych, vignette
09 alla prima, aquarelle, brushwork, capriccio, encaustic, flat brush, grisaille, grotesque, landscape, mahlstick, maulstick, miniature, polyptych, scumbling, sgraffito, still life
10 art gallery, craquelure, dead colour, figurative, hair-pencil, monochrome, paintbrush, pentimento, pochade box, round brush, sable brush, silhouette, turpentine
11 canvas board, chiaroscuro, composition, fête galante, foreshorten, found object, illusionism, objet trouvé, oil painting, perspective, pointillism, trompe l'oeil, watercolour
12 anamorphosis, brush strokes, camera lucida, filbert brush, illustration, palette knife, pencil sketch
13 fête champêtre, genre painting, underpainting
14 foreshortening

---

*Paintings and other artworks include:*

04 Flag
05 Manga, Pietà, Trees
06 Spring
07 Bubbles, Erasmus, Gin Lane, Olympia, Targets, The Kiss
08 Guernica, L'Estaque, Maja Nude, Mona Lisa, The Dream
09 Bacchanal, Black Iris, Haystacks, Henry VIII, Jerusalem, L'Escargot, Night Café, Primavera, The Scream, The Tailor
10 Adam and Eve, Assumption, Beer Street, Blue Horses, Las Meninas, Sunflowers, The Angelus, The Hay Wain
11 100 Soup Cans, Arthur's Tomb, A Shrimp Girl, Crucifixion, Limp Watches, Maja Clothed, Starry Night, The Gleaners, View of Delft, Water Lilies
12 Autumn Rhythm, Beata Beatrix, Black on Black, Los Caprichos, Peasant Dance, The Nightmare, The Scapegoat, The Umbrellas
13 A Bigger Splash, Christ in Glory, Isenheim Altar, Man with a Glove, Sleeping Gypsy, The Last Supper, The Night Watch
14 A Rake's Progress, Disasters of War, Peasant Wedding, Random Sketches, Rouen Cathedral, Sistine Madonna, The Ambassadors, The Card Players, The Four Seasons, The Rokeby Venus, The Turkish Bath, View on the Stour
15 Absinthe Drinker, Commodore Keppel, Flight into Egypt, Madonna and Child, Madonna del Prato, Marriage à la Mode, The Annunciation, The Birth of Venus, The Charnel House, The Dance of Death, The Death of Marat, The Flagellation, The Potato Eaters, The Raft of Medusa, The Rape of Europa, Triumph of Caesar

---

**pair**
02 OO, pr 03 duo, set, twa, two, wed 04 duad, duet, join, link, mate, pack, team, twae, tway, twin, yoke 05 brace, marry, match, twain, twins, unite 06 couple, geminy, join up, link up, splice, team up 07 bracket, couplet, match up, partner, twosome 10 two of a kind 11 put together 14 arrange in pairs

**paired**
05 mated, yoked 06 double, in twos, joined, jugate, linked 07 coupled, matched, twinned 09 bracketed 10 associated

**Pakistan**
02 PK 03 PAK

**pal**
04 chum, mate 05 buddy, crony, cully 06 cobber, friend, winger 07 comrade, partner 08 intimate, sidekick, soul mate 09 companion, confidant 10 buddy-buddy, confidante
• **pal up**  06 chum up, gang up, join up 11 get together, make friends 13 become friends

**palace**
04 dome 05 court, hôtel 06 castle 07 alcázar, château, mansion, palazzo, schloss 08 basilica, seraglio 11 stately home

*Palaces include:*

05 Pitti, Royal, Savoy
06 Louvre, Mirror, Potala, Winter
07 Bishop's, Crystal, People's, Sultan's, Vatican
08 Alhambra, Blenheim, Borghese, Imperial, National, St James's, Valhalla, Walhalla
09 Episcopal, Maharaja's, Sans Souci, Tuileries, Whitehall
10 Buckingham, El Escorial,

Fishbourne, Generalife,
Kensington, Linlithgow,
President's, Qusayr Amra, Quseir
Amra, Schönbrunn, Versailles
**11** Archbishop's, Westminster
**13** Forbidden City, Holyrood House,
Royal Pavilion, Tower of London,
Windsor Castle
**14** Charlottenburg
**15** Palais de l'Elysée

**paladin**
**04** peer

**palaeontologist**

*Palaeontologists include:*

**04 Cope** (Edward Drinker), **Owen** (Sir
Richard)
**05 Gould** (Stephen Jay), **Marsh** (O C)
**06 Dubois** (Eugène), **Forbes** (Edward),
**Kurtén** (Björn), **Leakey** (Louis),
**Leakey** (Mary), **Leakey** (Richard),
**Osborn** (Henry Fairfield), **Zittel**
(Karl von)
**07 Colbert** (Ned), **Mantell** (Gideon),
**Simpson** (George Gaylord)
**08 Guettard** (Jean Étienne), **Johanson**
(Donald)

**palanquin**
**04** kago **05** palki, sedan **06** doolie,
litter, palkee **07** norimon

**palatable**
**04** nice **05** tasty, yummy **06** delish,
edible, morish **07** eatable, moreish,
savoury, scrummy **08** pleasant,
pleasing **09** agreeable, delicious,
enjoyable, flavorous, succulent,
toothsome **10** acceptable, appetizing,
attractive, delectable **11** done to a turn,
flavoursome, scrumptious
**12** satisfactory **13** mouthwatering

**palate**
**04** gout **05** heart, taste, velum **06** liking,
relish **07** stomach **08** appetite
**09** enjoyment, taste buds
**10** enthusiasm **12** appreciation, sense
of taste

**palatial**
**04** posh **05** grand, plush, regal, ritzy
**06** de luxe **07** opulent, stately
**08** imposing, majestic, spacious,
splendid **09** grandiose, luxurious,
sumptuous **11** magnificent

**Palau**
**03** PLW

**palaver**
**04** flap, fuss, talk, to-do **05** hoo-ha
**06** bother, bustle **07** carry-on, flatter,
fluster **08** activity, business
**09** commotion, kerfuffle, procedure,
rigmarole **10** conference, discussion
**12** song and dance

**pale**
**03** dim, wan **04** ashy, fade, gray, grey,
lily, melt, pall, pole, post, thin, waxy,
weak **05** appal, ashen, blank, crown,
faded, faint, fence, green, light, limit,
livid, lurid, mealy, muted, pasty,
peaky, shaft, stain, stake, vapid, verge,
waxen, white **06** blanch, bleach,
chalky, column, feeble, lessen, low-

key, mealie, pallid, pastel, sallow,
whiten **07** anaemic, drained, dwindle,
high-key, insipid, upright, whitely,
whitish **08** bleached, delicate,
diminish, encircle, etiolate, grow pale,
maid-pale **09** bloodless, enclosure,
etiolated, grow white, washed-out,
whey-faced **10** colourless, pallescent,
pasty-faced, restrained, wishy-washy
**11** peelie-wally **12** change colour
**14** complexionless
• **beyond the pale 08** improper,
unseemly **10** unsuitable **11** intolerable
**12** inadmissible, unacceptable,
unreasonable **13** inappropriate

**paleness**
**04** pale **06** pallor **07** anaemia, wanness
**09** pastiness, whiteness **10** sallowness
**11** pallescence **14** colourlessness

**palindromic**
**07** Sotadic **08** cancrine, Sotadean

**palisade**
**05** fence **06** fraise, paling **07** barrier,
bulwark, defence, stacket **08** stockade
**09** barricade, enclosure **13** fortification

**pall**
**04** cloy, jade, pale, sate, tire, veil
**05** cloak, cloud, daunt, gloom, weary
**06** damper, mantle, shadow, shroud,
sicken, weaken **07** curtain, frontal,
pallium, satiate, wear off **08** corporal,
covering **09** mortcloth **11** become
bored, become tired, hearse-cloth
• **cast a pall over 03** mar **04** harm,
ruin **05** spoil, upset, wreck **06** impair
**07** destroy

**palladium**
**02** Pd

**palliate**
**04** ease **05** abate, allay, cloak, cover
**06** excuse, lenify, lessen, soften,
soothe, temper **07** assuage, conceal,
lighten, mollify, relieve **08** diminish,
disguise, minimize, mitigate, moderate
**09** alleviate, extenuate

**palliative**
**07** anodyne, calming **08** lenitive,
sedative, soothing **09** analgesic,
assuasive, calmative, demulcent,
paregoric **10** mitigating, mitigative,
mitigatory, mollifying, painkiller
**11** alleviating, alleviative, extenuative,
extenuatory **13** tranquillizer

**pallid**
**03** wan **04** ashy, dull, pale, tame,
waxy, weak **05** ashen, bland, lurid,
pasty, tired, vapid, waxen, white
**06** boring, doughy, sallow, sickly
**07** anaemic, insipid, sterile, whitish
**08** lifeless **09** bloodless, etiolated,
whey-faced **10** colourless, pallescent,
pasty-faced, spiritless, unexciting,
uninspired **11** peelie-wally
**13** uninteresting **14** complexionless

**pallor**
**07** anaemia, wanness **08** paleness
**09** whiteness **10** chalkiness, etiolation,
pallidness, sallowness **11** pallescence
**13** bloodlessness

**pally**
**04** warm **05** close, thick, tight
**06** chummy, folksy **08** familiar,
friendly, intimate **12** affectionate

**palm**
**03** fob, paw **04** grab, hand, loof, mitt,
take, vola **05** bribe **06** snatch, thenar
**11** appropriate

*Palms include:*

**03** dum, ita, oil, wax
**04** atap, coco, date, doom, doum,
hemp, nipa, sago
**05** areca, assai, bussu, macaw,
nikau, peach, royal, Sabal, sugar,
toddy
**06** buriti, cohune, corozo, Elaeis,
gomuti, gru-gru, jupati, kentia,
kittul, miriti, raffia, Raphia, rattan,
troely
**07** babassu, cabbage, calamus,
coconut, coquito, Corypha,
Euterpe, moriche, palmyra,
paxiuba, pupunha, talipat, talipot,
troelie, troolie
**08** carnauba, coco-tree, date-tree,
groo-groo, palmetto
**10** Chamaerops
**12** chiquichiqui, Washingtonia
**15** cabbage-palmetto

• **have someone in the palm of
your hand 13** have power over
**15** have control over
• **palm off 05** foist **06** fob off,
impose, pass on, put off, thrust,
unload **07** offload, pass off, work off
**08** get rid of, pass upon

**palmist**
**10** palm reader **11** clairvoyant
**13** chirographist, fortune-teller

**palmistry**
**10** chirognomy, chiromancy **11** palm
reading **12** clairvoyancy **14** fortune-
telling

**palmy**
**05** happy **06** golden, joyous **07** halcyon
**08** carefree, glorious, thriving
**09** fortunate, luxurious **10** prosperous,
successful, triumphant **11** flourishing

**palpable**
**04** real **05** clear, gross, plain, solid
**06** patent **07** blatant, evident, glaring,
obvious, visible **08** apparent, concrete,
manifest, material, tangible
**09** touchable **11** conspicuous,
perceptible, substantial
**12** unmistakable **13** unmistakeable

**palpably**
**07** clearly, plainly, visibly **08** patently
**09** blatantly, evidently, glaringly,
obviously **10** apparently, manifestly
**12** unmistakably **13** conspicuously,
unmistakeably

**palpitate**
**04** beat, thud **05** pound, pulse, quake,
shake, throb, thump **06** pit-pat, quiver,
shiver **07** flutter, pitapat, pulsate,
tremble, twitter, vibrate **08** pitty-pat

**palpitation**
**05** shake, throb **06** quiver, shakes
**07** flutter, shaking **08** pounding

**09** quivering, throbbing, trembling, vibration **10** fluttering

## paltry
**03** low, tin **04** bald, bare, mean, poor, puny, vile, waff **05** cheap, minor, petty, scald, small, sorry, woful **06** jitney, meagre, measly, shabby, slight, tinpot, trashy, two-bit, vulgar, woeful **07** foolish, miserly, pelting, pimping, piteous, trivial **08** derisory, piddling, rubbishy, trifling, wretched **09** miserable, worthless **10** negligible, shoestring **11** unimportant **12** contemptible, pettifogging **13** insignificant **14** inconsiderable

## pamper
**03** pet **04** baby **05** spoil **06** cocker, coddle, cosher, cosset, cuiter, fondle, humour, pander, pompey **07** gratify, indulge **09** spoon-feed **10** featherbed **11** mollycoddle, overindulge

## pampered
**06** petted, spoilt **07** coddled, high-fed, overfed **08** cosseted, indulged, spoon-fed **10** lust-dieted **12** mollycoddled

## pamphlet
**03** pam **05** flyer, sheet, tract **06** dodger, folder, notice **07** booklet, handout, leaflet **08** brochure, chapbook, circular **10** mazarinade

## pan
**03** pit, pot, wok **04** bowl, cake, cave, face, flay, hole, lead, move, scan, slag, slam, turn, well **05** basin, betel, frier, fryer, knock, ladle, roast, scale, slate, sweep, swing, track, yield **06** cavern, cavity, circle, crater, Faunus, follow, hammer, hollow, obtain, spider, vessel **07** censure, channel, goat-god, rubbish, skillet, slag off **08** pancheon, panchion, pannikin, saucepan, traverse **09** bed-warmer, casserole, concavity, container, criticize, frying-pan, saltworks **10** corn popper, depression, excavation **11** calefactory **12** pull to pieces **13** find fault with
• **pan out**   **05** yield **06** happen, result **07** turn out, work out **09** culminate, eventuate **11** be exhausted, come to an end

## panacea
**06** elixir, tutsan **07** allheal, cure-all, nostrum **10** catholicon, parkleaves **12** panpharmacon **13** diacatholicon **15** universal remedy

## panache
**04** brio, dash, élan, zest **05** flair, plume, style, verve **06** energy, pazazz, pizazz, spirit, vigour **07** pazzazz, pizzazz, swagger **08** flourish **10** enthusiasm **11** flamboyance, ostentation

## Panama
**02** PA **03** PAN

## pancake
**04** flam, taco **05** blini, crêpe, flamm, flawn, latke, rösti, wafer **06** blintz, flaune, fraise, froise, roesti, waffle **07** bannock, blintze, crumpet, pikelet **08** flapjack, omelette, tortilla **09** drop scone **10** battercake, spring roll

**11** griddle-cake **12** crêpe suzette, dropped scone

## pandemic
**04** rife **06** common, global **07** general **09** extensive, pervasive, prevalent, universal **10** widespread **11** far-reaching

## pandemonium
**03** din **04** to-do **05** chaos **06** bedlam, hubbub, rumpus, tumult, uproar **07** turmoil **08** disorder **09** commotion, confusion, hue and cry, shemozzle **10** hullabaloo, turbulence

## pander
**04** bawd, pimp **06** broker **07** procure **08** procurer **11** whoremonger
• **pander to**   **06** fulfil, humour, pamper, please **07** cater to, gratify, indulge, provide, satisfy

## pane
**04** pean, peen, pein, pene **05** glass, panel **06** window **07** quarrel **10** windowpane

## panegyric
**05** éloge, elogy, paean **06** eulogy, homage, praise **07** elogium, glowing, tribute **08** accolade, citation, encomium, eulogium, praising **09** laudation, laudatory, praiseful **10** eulogistic, favourable, flattering **11** encomiastic, panegyrical **12** commendation, commendatory **13** complimentary **14** speech of praise

## panel
**03** orb **04** beam, jury, mola, pane, sign, slab, team, unit **05** array, board, dials, knobs, plank, plate, sheet, table **06** coffer, levers, screen, tablet, timber **07** buttons, console, council, inn sign, lacunar, valance, valence **08** controls, mandorla, switches, trustees **09** cartouche, committee, dashboard, faceplate, headboard, medallion **10** commission, focus group, patchboard **11** compartment, directorate, instruments **13** advisory group **15** instrument panel

## panelling
**04** dado **06** coffer **07** lacunar, reredos **08** wainscot **09** panelwork, reredorse, reredosse **11** wainscoting **12** wainscotting

## pang
**04** ache, cram, pain, stab **05** agony, gripe, prick, qualm, spasm, sting, stuff, thraw, throe, throw, tight **06** shower, stitch, stound, stownd, throwe, twinge **07** anguish, crammed, crowded, scruple, stuffed **08** distress **09** misgiving **10** discomfort, uneasiness

## pangolin
**05** Manis **08** anteater **13** scaly anteater

## panic
◇ *anagram indicator* **04** fear, flap, funk **05** alarm, amaze, scare **06** dismay, frenzy, fright, horror, panick, terror **07** pannick, unnerve **08** disquiet, flat spin, hysteria, tailspin **09** agitation, overreact, run scared **10** amazedness, go to pieces **11** have kittens,

trepidation **12** get the shakes, lose your cool, lose your head, perturbation, sauve qui peut **13** consternation, get the jitters, get the willies, lose your nerve **14** lose your bottle

## panic-stricken
**06** aghast, scared **07** alarmed, frantic, panicky **08** frenzied, in a tizzy **09** horrified, perturbed, petrified, terrified **10** frightened, hysterical **11** in a blue funk, in a flat spin, scared stiff **12** in a cold sweat **14** terror-stricken

## pannier
**03** pad, ped **06** dosser **07** cacolet, kajawah **09** ambulance

## panoply
**04** garb, gear, show **05** array, dress, get-up, range **06** armour, attire **07** raiment, regalia, turn-out **08** insignia **09** equipment, trappings

## panorama
**04** view **05** scene, vista **06** survey **07** scenery **08** overview, prospect, wide view **09** broad view, cyclorama, landscape, spectacle **11** perspective **12** bird's-eye view

## panoramic
**04** wide **05** broad **06** scenic **07** general, overall **08** sweeping **09** extensive, universal **10** widespread **11** far-reaching, wide-ranging **13** comprehensive

## pansy
**05** pance, viola **06** kiss-me, paunce, pawnce **10** effeminate, heart's-ease, homosexual **11** herb-trinity, kiss-me-quick **14** love-in-idleness

## pant
**03** yen **04** ache, blow, gasp, huff, long, pech, pegh, pine, puff, sigh, want **05** covet, crave, flaff, heave, throb, yearn **06** desire, hanker, thirst, wheeze **07** breathe **09** palpitate **11** huff and puff

## panting
**05** eager **06** puffed, winded **07** anxious, craving, gasping, longing, puffing **09** hankering, impatient, puffed out **10** breathless **11** out of breath, short-winded

## pantomime
**04** mime, show **05** farce, panto **06** masque **07** charade **08** dumbshow **12** harlequinade

*Pantomime characters include:*

**04** Jack, Jill
**05** Giant, Wendy
**06** Beauty, Gretel, Hansel
**07** Buttons, Dandini, Emperor, King Rat
**08** Abanazer, Idle Jack, Peter Pan, The Beast
**09** Alan-a-Dale, Columbine, Friar Tuck, Robin Hood
**10** Billy Goose, Cinderella, Goldilocks, Little John, Maid Marian, Maid Marion, Prince John, Tinkerbell
**11** Baron Hardup, Captain Hook, Daisy the Cow, Jack's Mother, King Richard, Mother Goose,

Simple Simon, Will Scarlet
12 Pantomime Cow, Principal Boy, Sarah the Cook, Widow Twankey, Will Scarlett, Wishee Washee
13 Principal Girl
14 Baroness Hardup, Fairy Godmother, Genie of the Lamp, Pantomime Horse, Prince Charming, Princess Aurora, Slave of the Ring, The Ugly Sisters
15 Alice Fitzwarren, Princess Jasmine, Rumpelstiltskin

*Pantomimes include:*

07 Aladdin, Ali Baba
08 Peter Pan, Rapunzel
09 Pinocchio, Robin Hood, Snow White
10 Cinderella, Goldilocks
11 Mother Goose, Old King Cole, Puss in Boots
12 The Pied Piper, The Snow Queen
13 Red Riding Hood
14 Babes in the Wood, Robinson Crusoe, Sleeping Beauty, Treasure Island
15 Dick Whittington, Hansel and Gretel, Rumpelstiltskin, Sinbad the Sailor, The Swan Princess

**pantry**
05 ambry, awmry 06 almery, aumbry, awmrie, larder, spence 07 butlery
08 scullery 09 stillroom, storeroom

**pants**
05 jeans, loons, teddy, thong 06 briefs, shorts, slacks, smalls, trunks, undies
07 drawers, joggers, panties, rubbish, Y-fronts 08 breeches, frillies, knickers, nonsense, trousers 09 long johns
10 underpants 11 boxer shorts, panty girdle 12 camiknickers

**pap**
03 goo, rot 04 mash, mush, pulp
05 purée, trash 06 breast, drivel, hot air, nipple 07 rubbish, twaddle
08 claptrap, nonsense, soft food
09 gibberish, poppycock 14 semi-liquid food

**papa**
01 P
*See also* **father**

**paper**
03 rag 04 ream, work 05 daily, essay, organ, study 06 report, thesis, weekly
07 article, journal, tabloid 08 analysis, magazine, treatise 09 monograph, newspaper 10 broadsheet, periodical
11 composition, examination
12 dissertation
*See also* **newspaper**

*Paper sizes and formats include:*

02 A0, A1, A2, A3, A4, A5
03 pot
04 demy, post, pott
05 atlas, crown, folio, jésus, legal, royal
06 letter, medium, quarto
07 emperor, tabloid
08 Berliner, elephant, foolscap, imperial

09 antiquary, music-demy
10 super-royal

*Paper types include:*

03 art, rag
04 bank, bond, card, note, rice, wall
05 crêpe, graph, sugar
06 carbon, manila, silver, tissue, toilet, vellum
07 papyrus, tracing, writing
08 acid-free, blotting, handmade, recycled, wrapping
09 cardboard, cartridge, parchment
10 pasteboard
11 greaseproof

• **on paper** 07 ideally 08 in theory, recorded 09 in writing, seemingly
10 officially, supposedly 11 on the record, written down 13 theoretically
14 hypothetically, in your mind's eye
15 in black and white
• **paper over** 04 hide 07 conceal, cover up, obscure 08 disguise
10 camouflage 13 put out of sight
• **paper size** 03 pot 04 demy, pott

**papers**
02 ID 04 bumf 05 bumph, deeds, sheaf
07 records 08 document, evidence, passbook, passport 10 despatches, dispatches 11 credentials
12 certificates, identity card
13 authorization, documentation
14 driving licence, identification, qualifications

**papery**
04 thin 05 frail, light 06 flimsy 07 fragile
08 delicate 09 paper-thin
10 glumaceous, membranous
11 chartaceous, lightweight, membraneous, papyraceous, translucent 13 insubstantial, membranaceous

**Papua New Guinea**
03 PNG

**par**
04 mean, norm, parr 05 level, usual
06 median, parity 07 average, balance
08 equality, standard 09 paragraph
10 accordance, similarity
11 equilibrium, equivalence 12 equal footing 14 correspondence
• **below par** 05 lousy, rough, tired
06 unwell 08 inferior, under par
10 inadequate, not up to par, out of sorts 11 at a discount 12 below average
14 not up to scratch, unsatisfactory
15 under the weather
• **deviation from par** 04 agio
• **on a par with** 07 equal to 08 as good as 12 equivalent to
• **par for the course** 05 usual
06 normal 07 typical 08 standard
11 predictable
• **up to par** 02 OK 04 fine 08 adequate
10 acceptable 11 up to scratch
12 satisfactory

**parable**
05 fable, story 06 lesson 07 proverb
08 allegory 09 discourse, moral tale
10 comparison, similitude 15 story with a moral

**parachute**
04 pack 05 chute 06 drogue, pappus
08 parafoil, patagium 09 aeroshell, parabrake

**parade**
03 row 04 file, pass, shew, show
05 array, march, parry, train, vaunt
06 column, flaunt, line-up, prance, review 07 display, exhibit, pageant, process, show off, stand-to
08 brandish, ceremony, file past
09 cavalcade, decursion, motorcade, spectacle 10 appearance, exhibition, procession 11 ostentation, progression
13 demonstration

**paradigm**
05 ideal, model 07 example, pattern
08 exemplar, original 09 archetype, framework, prototype

**paradise**
03 joy 04 Eden 05 bliss 06 heaven, parvis, Svarga, Swarga, utopia
07 delight, ecstasy, Elysium, rapture
08 felicity 09 afterlife, cloud nine, happiness, hereafter, home of God, next world, Shangri-La 10 life to come
12 Garden of Eden 13 Elysian Fields, seventh heaven

**paradox**
06 enigma, oddity, puzzle, riddle
07 anomaly, mystery 09 absurdity
11 incongruity 13 contradiction, inconsistency

**paradoxical**
06 absurd 08 baffling, puzzling
09 anomalous, enigmatic, illogical
10 impossible, improbable, mysterious
11 conflicting, incongruous
12 inconsistent 13 contradictory

**paraffin**
07 coal oil 08 earthwax, kerosene, kerosine, photogen 09 ozocerite, ozokerite, photogene 10 mineral wax
14 petroleum jelly

**paragon**
04 mate, rose 05 equal, ideal, match, model, pearl, rival 07 compare, epitome, paladin, pattern, phoenix, surpass 08 exemplar, standard
09 archetype, criterion, emulation, nonpareil, prototype 10 comparison
11 competition, masterpiece
12 quintessence, the bee's knees
14 crème de la crème, perfect example

**paragraph**
03 par 04 item, para, part 05 piece
06 clause 07 article, passage, portion, section, segment 08 causerie, te igitur
10 stand first, subsection 11 subdivision

**Paraguay**
02 PY 03 PRY

**parallel**
03 par 04 echo, like, twin 05 agree, equal, liken, match 06 be like
07 aligned, analogy, compare, conform, similar, uniform 08 analogue, likeness, matching, resemble
09 alongside, analogous, correlate, duplicate 10 co-existing, collateral, comparable, comparison, correspond,

**paralyse**

equivalent, homologous, resembling, side by side, similarity **11** be analogous, be similar to, coexist: correlation, counterpart, equidistant, equivalence, resemblance **12** be equivalent **13** corresponding **14** correspondence

**paralyse**

**04** dull, halt, lame, numb, stop **05** palsy, scram, shock **06** benumb, deaden, freeze **07** cripple, disable, terrify, torpefy **08** transfix **10** deactivate, debilitate, immobilize **12** anaesthetize, incapacitate

**paralysed**

**04** lame, numb **08** crippled, disabled **09** paralytic **10** paraplegic **11** immobilized **12** quadriplegic **13** incapacitated

**paralysis**

**04** halt **05** palsy, shock **07** paresis **08** deadness, diplegia, numbness, shutdown, stoppage **09** breakdown **10** Bell's palsy, hemiplegia, immobility, monoplegia, paraplegia, sideration, standstill **11** cycloplegia, paraparesis **12** debilitation, quadriplegia **13** cerebral palsy, powerlessness **15** ophthalmoplegia

**paralytic**

**04** lame, numb **05** drunk **06** blotto, canned, soused, stewed, stoned, wasted **07** legless, palsied, pie-eyed, sloshed, smashed, sozzled, wrecked **08** crippled, disabled, immobile **09** incapable, paralysed, plastered **10** hemiplegic, inebriated, monoplegic **11** immobilized, intoxicated **12** quadriplegic **13** incapacitated **15** a sheet in the wind

**parameter**

**05** limit **06** factor **08** boundary, variable **09** criterion, framework, guideline **10** indication, limitation **11** restriction **13** figure of merit, specification **14** limiting factor

**paramilitaries**

**04** sena

**paramount**

**04** main **05** chief, first, prime **07** highest, primary, supreme, topmost **08** cardinal, foremost, superior, suzerain **09** principal **10** pre-eminent **11** outstanding, predominant **13** most important

**paramour**

**04** beau **05** leman, lover, woman **07** beloved, franion, hetaera, hetaira **08** copemate, fancy man, mistress **09** concubine, copes-mate, courtesan, inamorata, inamorato, kept woman **10** bit of fluff, fancy woman **12** bit on the side

**paranoia**

**09** delusions, monomania, obsession, psychosis **11** megalomania

**paranoid**

**05** fazed **06** afraid **07** fearful **08** confused **10** bewildered, suspicious **11** distrustful

**paranormal**

◇ *anagram indicator* **05** eerie, magic, weird **06** hidden, mystic, occult **07** ghostly, magical, phantom, psychic **08** abnormal, mystical **09** spiritual, unnatural **10** miraculous, mysterious **12** metaphysical, otherworldly, supernatural **13** preternatural

**parapet**

**03** top **04** rail, wall **05** fence, guard **06** flèche, paling, parpen **07** barrier, bastion, bulwark, defence, parpane, parpend, parpent, perpend, perpent, railing, rampart **08** barbican, bartisan, bartizan, parpoint, traverse **09** barricade **10** balustrade, battlement, embankment **13** fortification

**paraphernalia**

**04** gear **05** stuff, tools **06** tackle, things **07** baggage, effects **09** apparatus, equipment, materials, trappings **10** belongings, implements **11** accessories, odds and ends, possessions **13** accoutrements, bits and pieces

**paraphrase**

**05** gloss **06** rehash, render, reword, Targum **07** restate, version **08** rephrase **09** interpret, rendering, rewording, translate **10** rephrasing **11** restatement, translation **14** interpretation **15** put in other words

**parasite**

**03** bum, fly **05** drone, leech **06** cadger, ligger, sponge, sucker **07** bludger, epizoan, epizoon, moocher, sponger, vampire **08** endozoon, entozoon, epiphyte, hanger-on, quandang, quandong, quantong **09** endophyte, passenger, scrounger, sycophant **10** freeloader **11** bloodsucker **12** lick-trencher **14** trencher-friend, trencher-knight

Parasites include:

**03** bot, ked, nit
**04** bott, chat, crab, flea, kade, mite, tick
**05** fluke, louse
**06** chigoe, chigre, cootie, jigger
**07** argulus, ascarid, ascaris, Babesia, bonamia, cestode, chalcid, chigger, Giardia, pinworm
**08** hookworm, itch-mite, lungworm, nematode, sheep ked, strongyl, tapeworm, toxocara, whipworm
**09** Bilharzia, bird louse, crab louse, fish louse, fluke-worm, head louse, pediculus, roundworm, sheep tick, sporozoan, strongyle, trematode
**10** Guinea worm, Plasmodium, threadworm
**11** biting louse, sarcocystis, scabies mite, trichomonad, trypanosome
**12** echinococcus, ectoparasite, endoparasite, semiparasite
**13** hyperparasite

**parasitic**

**07** cadging, epizoan, epizoic **08** sponging **09** biogenous, leechlike

**10** scrounging **11** freeloading, parasitical **12** bloodsucking

**parasol**

**04** veil **05** shade **06** shield **07** shelter **08** marquise, sunshade, umbrella **09** en tout cas **10** protection
*See also* **umbrella**

**parcel**

**03** box, dak, lot, mob, set **04** area, band, crew, dawk, deal, gang, herd, item, pack, plot, sort, wrap **05** bunch, crowd, flock, group, patch, piece, put up, tie up, tract, troop **06** bundle, carton, make up, packet, pack up, partly, wrap up **07** company, package, portion **08** bundle up, gift-wrap, quantity **09** allotment **10** collection **11** transaction
• **parcel out 05** allot, whack **06** divide **07** carve up, deal out, dole out, hand out, mete out **08** allocate, dispense, share out **09** apportion, divide out **10** distribute

**parch**

**03** dry **04** bake, burn, sear **05** dry up, toast **06** scorch, wither **07** blister, shrivel, torrefy **09** dehydrate, desiccate

**parched**

**03** dry **04** arid, sear, sere **05** baked **06** burned, seared **07** dried up, gasping, thirsty **08** scorched, withered **09** blistered, waterless **10** dehydrated, desiccated, dry as a bone, shrivelled

**parchment**

**04** pell, roll **05** forel, panel **06** mezuza, scroll, vellum **07** charter, diploma, mezuzah **08** document, membrane **09** sheepskin **10** palimpsest, phylactery **11** certificate

**pardon**

**02** eh? **04** free, what? **05** bitte, grace, mercy, remit, sorry **06** acquit, excuse, let off **07** absolve, amnesty, condone, forgive, release, you what? **08** clemency, excuse me, lenience, liberate, oblivion, overlook, reprieve, say again?, tolerate **09** acquittal, come again?, discharge, exculpate, exonerate, remission, vindicate **10** absolution, act of grace, indulgence **11** condonation, cry you mercy, exculpation, exoneration, forbearance, forgiveness **13** let off the hook, what did you say? **14** I beg your pardon

**pardonable**

**05** minor **06** slight, venial **09** allowable, excusable **10** condonable, forgivable **11** dispensable, justifiable, permissible, warrantable **14** understandable

**pare**

**03** cut, lop **04** chip, clip, crop, dock, peel, skin, trim **05** prune, shave, shear, skive **06** reduce **07** cut back, whittle **08** clip coin, decrease

**parent**

**02** ma, pa **03** dad, dam, mam, mom, mum, pop **04** papa, rear, root, sire **05** beget, cause, daddy, folks, mamma, mammy, mommy, mummy, mumsy, raise, teach, train **06** author, create,

**parentage**

father, foster, mother, old man, origin, source **07** bring up, creator, educate, genitor, nurture **08** begetter, generant, genetrix, genitrix, guardian, old woman, relative **09** architect, bioparent, look after, procreate, prototype **10** forerunner, originator, procreator, progenitor, solo parent, step-parent, take care of **11** birth mother, birth parent, empty-nester, progenitrix **12** foster parent, progenitress, single parent **13** be the father of, be the mother of **14** adoptive parent **15** custodial parent

**parentage**

**04** line, race **05** birth, brood, stock **06** family, origin, source, stirps **07** descent, lineage, origins **08** ancestry, pedigree **09** filiation, paternity, whakapapa **10** derivation, extraction **11** affiliation

**parenthetical**

**08** inserted **09** as an aside, bracketed **10** extraneous, incidental, interposed, qualifying **11** elucidative, explanatory, intervening **13** in parenthesis

**parenthetically**

**03** btw **08** by the way **09** as an aside **11** secondarily **12** incidentally **13** as a digression

**par excellence**

**02** A1 **03** ace **04** best, cool, fine, mean, neat, rare **05** brill, great, noted, prime **06** divine, select, superb, wicked **07** eminent, notable, perfect, shining **08** fabulous, flawless, heavenly, smashing, splendid, stunning, superior, terrific, top-notch, very good **09** brilliant, excellent, exemplary, fantastic, faultless, first-rate, matchless, wonderful **10** first-class, marvellous, noteworthy, pre-eminent, remarkable, surpassing, unequalled **11** commendable, exceptional, high-quality, magnificent, outstanding, sensational, superlative **12** praiseworthy, second to none, unparalleled **13** distinguished **14** out of this world

**pariah**

**05** exile, leper, pi-dog **06** outlaw, pie-dog, pye-dog **07** Ishmael, outcast **08** castaway, unperson **10** black sheep **11** undesirable, untouchable **15** persona non grata

**paring**

**04** peel, rind, skin **05** flake, shave, shred, slice **06** sliver **07** cutting, flaught, peeling, shaving, snippet **08** clipping, fragment, trimming **09** flaughter

**Paris**

*Paris districts include:*

**05** Bercy, Opéra
**06** Étoile, Louvre, Marais
**07** Pigalle
**08** Bastille, Chaillot, Left Bank, Sorbonne
**09** Chinatown, La Défense, Les Halles, Right Bank, Trocadero, Tuileries
**10** Belleville, La Villette, Montmartre, Rive Droite, Rive Gauche, Tour Eiffel
**11** Batignolles
**12** Latin Quarter, Les Invalides, Montparnasse, Place d'Italie
**13** Champs Élysées, Quartier Latin

*Paris streets include:*

**07** Pigalle
**09** Port Royal, Rue de Rome
**10** Avenue Foch, Quai d'Orsay, Rue d'Alésia
**11** Rue Dauphine, Rue de Clichy, Rue de Rennes, Rue de Rivoli, Rue de Sèvres, Rue Mazarine, Rue St-Honoré
**12** Périphérique, Place d'Italie, Place Vendôme, Quai du Louvre, Quai Voltaire, Rue St-Antoine
**13** Avenue George V, Place du Tertre, Rue des Rosiers, Rue Mouffetard
**14** Place des Vosges
**15** Avenue Montaigne, Quai d'Austerlitz

*Paris landmarks include:*

**05** Seine
**06** Bourse, Louvre
**07** Pyramid
**08** Bastille, Panthéon, Pont Neuf, Sorbonne
**09** Beaubourg, Bon Marché, Invalides, la Défense, Madeleine, Notre-Dame, Orangerie, St-Sulpice, Trocadero, Tuileries
**10** Gare du Nord, Île St-Louis, Montmartre, Musée Rodin, Sacré Coeur
**11** Champ de Mars, Eiffel Tower, Grande Arche, Grand Palais, Île de la Cité, Moulin Rouge, Musée d'Orsay, Palais Royal, Pont des Arts
**12** Hôtel de Ville, Montparnasse, Opéra Garnier, Père Lachaise
**13** Arc de Triomphe, Champs-Élysées, Les catacombes, Opéra Bastille
**14** Bois de Boulogne, École Militaire, Forum des Halles, Palais du Louvre, Place de l'Étoile, Pompidou Centre, Sainte Chapelle
**15** Bois de Vincennes, Cité des Sciences, Le stade de France, Palais de Justice

*Paris districts, streets and landmarks include:*

**05** Opéra, Seine
**06** Bourse, Louvre
**07** Pigalle
**08** Bastille, Left Bank, Pont Neuf, Sorbonne
**09** Invalides, la Défense, Les Halles, Madeleine, Notre-Dame, Orangerie, Right Bank, Trocadero, Tuileries
**10** Gare du Nord, Île St-Louis, Montmartre, Quai d'Orsay, Rive Droite, Rive Gauche, Sacré Coeur
**11** Eiffel Tower, Île de la Cité, Moulin Rouge, Musée d'Orsay
**12** Latin Quarter, Les Invalides, Montparnasse, Père Lachaise
**13** Arc de Triomphe, Champs-Élysées, Quartier Latin
**14** Pompidou Centre
**15** Le stade de France, Palais de Justice

**parish**

**03** par **04** fold, town **05** flock, title **06** church, county **07** village **08** district, parishen, parochin, peculiar, township **09** community, parischan, parochine **10** parischane **11** churchgoers **12** congregation, denomination, parishioners

**Parisian**

◊ *foreign word indicator*

**parity**

**03** par **05** unity **07** analogy **08** affinity, equality, likeness, sameness **09** agreement, congruity, semblance **10** conformity, congruence, consonance, similarity, similitude, uniformity **11** consistency, equivalence, parallelism, resemblance **14** correspondence

**park**

**01** P **02** Pk **03** put, set, sit, zoo **04** bung, stay, stop **05** field, leave, place, plonk, stand, walks **06** domain, draw up, garden, locate, pull up **07** deposit, gardens, grounds, reserve, situate **08** paradise, position, woodland **09** enclosure, grassland

*Parks include:*

**04** Hyde, West
**05** Green, Güell, Kings
**06** Albert, Domain
**07** Battery, Central, Phoenix, Regent's, Stanley
**08** Gramercy, Richmond, St James's, Victoria
**09** Battersea, Tuileries
**10** Tiergarten
**11** Champ de Mars, Vienna Woods
**13** Madison Square, Tivoli Gardens
**14** Bois de Boulogne
**15** Bois de Vincennes

*National parks in the UK:*

**06** Exmoor
**08** Dartmoor
**09** New Forest, Snowdonia, The Broads
**10** Cairngorms
**12** Lake District, Peak District
**13** Brecon Beacons
**14** Northumberland, North York Moors, Yorkshire Dales
**18** Pembrokeshire Coast
**25** Loch Lomond and the Trossachs

**parking**

**01** P

**parlance**

**04** cant, talk **05** argot, idiom, lingo **06** jargon, speech, tongue **07** diction **08** language, speaking **11** phraseology **12** conversation

## parley

**04** talk **05** parle, parly, speak, talks, treat **06** confab, confer, emparl, imparl, powwow **07** consult, council, discuss, meeting **08** colloquy, dialogue **09** negotiate, tête-à-tête **10** conference, deliberate, discussion, parliament **11** get together, get-together, negotiation **12** deliberation **14** parliament-cake

## parliament

**05** house, parly **06** parley **07** chamber **11** convocation, legislature

---

*Parliament types include:*

**04** diet, duma, moot
**05** boule, douma, gemot, jirga
**06** majlis, senate
**07** commons, council
**08** assembly, congress
**09** volksraad
**10** consistory, lower house, upper house
**12** lower chamber, upper chamber
**14** Council of State
**15** House of Assembly

---

*Parliaments and political assemblies include:*

**02** EP, HK, HP
**04** Dáil, Diet, Duma, Keys, Long, Pnyx, Rump, Sejm
**05** boule, Forum, gemot, Lords, Porte
**06** Cortes, kgotla, Majlis, Mejlis, Seanad, Senate, Senato, Senedd, Soviet
**07** Althing, comitia, Commons, Knesset, Lagting, Landtag, Rigsdag, Riksdag, Tynwald, zemstvo
**08** Assembly, Congress, ecclesia, European, folkmoot, Imperial, Lagthing, Lok Sabha, Scottish, Sobranje, Sobranye, Stannary, Storting
**09** Bundesrat, Bundestag, Directory, Eduskunta, Folketing, Landsting, Loya Jirga, Odelsting, Reichsrat, Reichstag, Skupstina, Ständerat, State Duma
**10** Bundesrath, Convention, Landsthing, lower house, Odelsthing, Oireachtas, Rajya Sabha, Reichsrath, Skupshtina, St Stephen's, upper house
**11** Dáil Eireann, Folketinget, House of Keys, Nationalrat, Star Chamber, Volkskammer, Westminster
**12** House of Lords
**13** House of States, Seanad Eireann, States General, Supreme Soviet, Welsh Assembly
**14** Council of State, Estates General, House of Commons, Long Parliament, Rump Parliament, Staten-Generaal
**15** Council of States, House of Assembly, People's Assembly, People's Congress

---

## parliamentary

**05** civil **07** elected, popular **08** decorous, official **09** lawgiving, lawmaking **10** democratic, republican, senatorial **11** legislative **12** governmental **13** congressional, legislatorial **14** representative

## parlour

**06** lounge, spence **09** front room **10** living room **11** drawing room, keeping-room, morning room, sitting room

## parlous

**04** dire **05** awful, grave **08** alarming, dreadful, horrible, perilous, shocking, terrible **09** appalling, atrocious, desperate, frightful **10** calamitous, disastrous **11** distressing **12** catastrophic

## parochial

**04** hick **05** petty **06** narrow **07** insular, limited **08** confined **09** blinkered, small-town **10** parish-pump, provincial, restricted **11** small-minded **12** narrow-minded **13** inward-looking **14** denominational

## parochialism

**09** pettiness **10** insularity, narrowness, parish pump **13** provincialism **15** small-mindedness

## parody

**03** ape **04** skit **05** mimic, spoof **06** satire, send up, send-up **07** imitate, lampoon, mimicry, take off, take-off **08** satirize, travesty **09** burlesque, imitation **10** caricature, corruption, distortion, pasquinade, perversion

## paroxysm

**03** fit **05** spasm, storm, thraw, throe, throw **06** attack, frenzy, throwe **07** flare-up, rapture, seizure **08** eruption, outbreak, outburst **09** explosion **10** convulsion

## parrot

**03** ape **04** copy, echo, Poll **05** mimic, Polly **06** repeat **07** copycat, imitate, phraser **08** imitator, popinjay, rehearse, repeater **09** reiterate

---

*Parrots include:*

**03** fig, kea
**04** grey, kaka, lory
**05** galah, macaw, pygmy
**06** Amazon, budgie, conure, kakapo, Nestor
**07** corella, hanging, rosella
**08** cockatoo, lorikeet, lovebird, parakeet, paroquet, Pesquet's, Strigops
**09** cockateel, cockatiel, green leek, owl-parrot, paraquito, parrakeet, parroquet, parrotlet, Psittacus, Stringops
**10** budgerigar, ring-necked
**11** African grey, night-parrot, shell-parrot
**13** Major Mitchell, zebra parakeet
**14** shell parrakeet

---

## parrot-fashion

**06** by rote **10** mindlessly **12** mechanically, unthinkingly **13** automatically

## parrot-wrasse

**04** scar

## parry

**04** duck, shun, ward **05** avert, avoid, block, dodge, evade, field, put by, repel, sixte **06** parade, rebuff **07** counter, deflect, fend off, keep off, repulse, ward off **08** sidestep, stave off, tac-au-tac **09** hold at bay, keep at bay, turn aside **10** bodyswerve, circumvent **12** steer clear of

## parsimonious

**04** mean, near **05** close, mingy, tight **06** frugal, narrow, saving, scanty, stingy **07** miserly, scrimpy, sparing **08** grasping, stinting **09** niggardly, penurious **10** Aberdonian **11** close-fisted, close-handed, tight-fisted **12** candle-paring, cheeseparing **13** penny-pinching

## parsimony

**08** meanness **09** frugality, minginess, tightness **10** stinginess **11** miserliness **12** cheeseparing **13** niggardliness, penny-pinching **15** tight-fistedness

## parson

**03** Rev **05** padre, vicar **06** cleric, curate, deacon, pastor, priest, rector **07** holy Joe **08** minister, preacher, reverend **09** churchman, clergyman, soul-curer **10** Jack-priest

## parson-bird

**03** tui

## part

◇ *hidden indicator* ◇ *hidden alternately indicator* ◇ *insertion indicator* **02** by, pt **03** bit, bye, job **04** area, book, duty, gift, half, hand, quit, role, shed, side, some, task, tear, twin, wing, work **05** break, chore, facet, leave, organ, party, piece, scene, scrap, sever, share, skill, slice, split, twine **06** aspect, branch, charge, cleave, depart, detach, divide, factor, genius, member, module, office, region, sector, talent, volume **07** ability, break up, calibre, chapter, concern, disband, disjoin, diverge, element, episode, excerpt, extract, faculty, limited, partial, passage, persona, portion, push off, quarter, scarper, scatter, section, segment, split up, take off **08** capacity, clear off, disperse, district, division, fraction, fragment, function, get going, interest, locality, particle, separate **09** attribute, character, come apart, component, dimension, direction, dismantle, endowment, expertise, imperfect, intellect, keep apart, portrayal, push along, take apart, territory **10** capability, depart from, department, disconnect, distribute, go away from, hit the road, ingredient, instalment, make tracks, percentage, proportion, restricted, say goodbye, unfinished **11** constituent, divorce from, fragmentary, hit the trail, involvement, not complete, split up from **12** intelligence, separate from, withdraw from **13** neighbourhood, participation, take your leave **14** accomplishment, representation,

responsibility **15** get divorced from, part company with
• **act the part of** **04** come
• **assign part** **04** cast
• **even parts** ◊ *hidden alternately indicator*
• **for the most part** **06** mainly, mostly **07** as a rule, chiefly, largely, overall, usually **08** above all, commonly **09** generally, in general, in the main **10** by and large, especially, on the whole **11** principally **13** predominantly
• **in part** ◊ *hidden indicator* **04** half **06** parcel, partim, partly **08** slightly, somewhat **10** up to a point **12** to some degree, to some extent
• **in the part of** **02** as
• **odd parts** ◊ *hidden alternately indicator*
• **on the part of** **02** by **08** caused by **10** on behalf of **12** carried out by **13** from the side of
• **part of** ◊ *hidden indicator*
• **part with** **04** drop **05** forgo, yield **06** forego, give up **07** abandon, discard, let go of **08** jettison, renounce **09** surrender **10** relinquish
• **principal part** **04** lead, main, mass
• **take part in** ◊ *hidden indicator* **05** opt in **06** join in **07** go in for, partake, share in **08** assist in, engage in, help with **11** play a part in, play a role in **12** be involved in, contribute to **13** participate in

**partake**
**05** enter, share **06** engage, inform **07** indulge **08** take part **10** be involved **11** participate
• **partake of** **03** eat **04** have, show, take **05** drink, evoke, share, taste **06** evince **07** consume, receive, suggest, undergo **08** manifest **11** demonstrate

**partial**
**04** half, part **06** biased, in part, unfair, unjust **07** ex parte, limited **08** affected, coloured, one-sided, partisan, twilight **09** component, imperfect **10** incomplete, prejudiced, restricted, unfinished **11** fragmentary, inequitable, predisposed, subordinate **12** preferential **14** discriminatory
• **partial to** **06** fond of, keen on, liking, loving **08** mad about **09** taken with **10** crazy about

**partiality**
**04** bias, love **05** favor **06** favour, liking **07** respect **08** fondness, inequity **09** injustice, prejudice **10** preference, proclivity, unfairness **11** inclination **12** partisanship, predilection **14** discrimination, predisposition **15** inequitableness

**partially**
**05** slack **06** in part, partly **08** halflins, not fully, somewhat **09** halflings **12** fractionally, incompletely

**participant**
**05** party **06** helper, member, sharer, worker **07** entrant, partner, sharing **09** associate **10** competitor, contestant,

co-operator **11** contributor, shareholder **12** participator

**participate**
◊ *insertion indicator* **04** be in, help **05** enter, opt in, share **06** assist, be in it, engage, join in, muck in **07** partake **08** take part **09** co-operate, play a part, play a role **10** be involved, contribute **12** be associated

**participation**
**04** part **07** sharing **09** mucking in, partaking **10** assistance **11** association, co-operation, involvement, partnership **12** contribution

**particle**
**03** bit, jot, tad **04** atom, corn, curn, drop, iota, mite, spot, whit **05** crumb, grain, piece, scrap, shred, spark, speck, stime, styme, touch, trace **06** morsel, prefix, sliver, suffix, tittle **07** globule, granule, smidgen **08** fragment, molecule, ribosome **09** inclusion **11** conjunction **12** interjection

*Particles include:*

**01** W, X, Z
**03** ion, psi
**04** kaon, muon, pion
**05** anion, boson, gluon, meson, omega, quark, sigma
**06** baryon, cation, hadron, kation, lambda, lepton, parton, photon, proton
**07** neutron, nucleon, upsilon
**08** electron, neutrino, positron, thermion
**09** carbanion, gravitron, tau lepton
**10** anti-proton, gauge boson, zwitterion
**11** anti-neutron
**12** anti-neutrino, nanoparticle

**parti-coloured**
**06** motley **07** piebald **10** variegated **11** polychromic **13** polychromatic, versicoloured

**particular**
**04** fact, item **05** exact, faddy, fussy, picky, point **06** choosy, detail, marked **07** certain, feature, finicky, minutia, notable, precise, respect, several, special, unusual **08** accurate, definite, detailed, distinct, especial, exacting, faithful, peculiar, specific, thorough, uncommon **09** favourite, selective **10** fastidious, individual, meticulous, noteworthy, pernickety, remarkable **11** exceptional, outstanding, painstaking, persnickety **12** circumstance **14** discriminating
• **in particular** **07** exactly **08** in detail **09** in special, precisely, severally **10** especially, in especial **12** individually, particularly, specifically, to be specific

**particularity**
**04** fact, item **05** point, quirk, trait **06** detail **07** feature **08** instance, property **10** uniqueness **11** peculiarity, singularity **12** circumstance, idiosyncrasy **13** individuality **14** characteristic **15** distinctiveness

**particularize**
**06** detail **07** itemize, specify **09** enumerate, stipulate **11** individuate **13** individualize

**particularly**
**07** notably **08** markedly **09** expressly, severally, unusually **10** distinctly, especially, explicitly, intimately, remarkably, uncommonly **12** individually, in particular, specifically, surprisingly **13** exceptionally **15** extraordinarily

**parting**
◊ *insertion indicator* **04** last, rift, shed **05** adieu, dying, final, going, leave, split **06** depart **07** closing, divorce, goodbye, leaving, rupture **08** breaking, division, farewell **09** departing, departure, partition, partitive **10** breaking-up, concluding, divergence, separation **11** leave-taking, valediction, valedictory **12** disseverance, disseverment **13** disseveration
*See also* **farewell**

**partisan**
**03** fan **06** backer, biased, unfair, unjust, votary **07** devotee, partial **08** adherent, champion, disciple, follower, henchman, loyalist, one-sided, party man, queenite, sidesman, stalwart, upholder **09** factional, guerrilla, irregular, sectarian, supporter **10** henchwoman, prejudiced **11** henchperson, imperialist, inequitable, out-and-outer, predisposed **14** discriminatory, freedom fighter

**partisanship**
**04** bias **08** interest, partyism **09** prejudice **10** partiality **12** factionalism, sectarianism

**partition**
**03** bar **04** wall, with **05** panel, score, sever, share, shoji, withe **06** divide, hallan, parpen, replum, screen, septum, tabula, travis, trevis **07** barrier, break up, break-up, cloison, divider, eardrum, grating, parpane, parpend, parpent, parting, perpend, perpent, split up, treviss, wall off **08** brattice, brattish, brettice, divide up, division, fence off, parpoint, separate, traverse **09** dashboard, diaphragm, parcel out, screen off, segregate, separator, severance, splitting, subdivide **10** rood screen, separation **11** dissepiment, false bottom, room-divider, segregation, separate off, subdivision **12** dividing wall **14** dividing screen

**partly**
**04** half, semi- **06** in part, parcel **07** little **08** slightly, somewhat, to a point **09** partially **10** moderately, relatively, up to a point **12** fractionally, incompletely, to some degree, to some extent **13** in some measure

**partner**
**03** man, pal, SOP **04** ally, lady, mate, oppo, pair, pard, wife **05** butty, catch, rival, woman **06** fiancé, friend, helper, lumber, sharer, spouse **07** comrade,

consort, fiancée, husband, kept man, pardner **08** cavalier, copemate, co-worker, sidekick, teammate, yoke-mate **09** associate, boyfriend, cohabitee, colleague, companion, copesmate, kept woman, other half **10** accomplice, better half, co-operator, girlfriend, yoke-fellow **11** confederate, live-in lover **12** bit on the side, collaborator **13** common-law wife **14** opposite number
• **former partner** **02** ex
• **partners** **02** EW, NS

## partnership
**04** firm **05** stand, union **06** cahoot **07** company, consort, sharing, society **08** alliance **09** symbiosis, syndicate **10** fellowship, fraternity **11** affiliation, association, brotherhood, combination, co-operation, co-operative, corporation **12** conglomerate **13** collaboration, confederation, participation

## partridge
**05** quail **06** chikor, chukar, chukor **07** chikhor, flapper, tinamou **08** paitrick, percolin

## part-song
**04** glee

## party
**03** jol **04** band, body, camp, crew, fest, gang, rage, rort, rout, sect, side, team, unit **05** binge, cabal, go out, group, posse, quest, squad **06** league, parted, person, thrash **07** carouse, company, divided, faction, have fun, large it **08** alliance, function, grouping, litigant, live it up **09** celebrate, defendant, festivity, gathering, have a ball, plaintiff, whoop it up **10** contingent, detachment, have a party, individual **11** affiliation, association, celebration, combination, get-together, have it large, throw a party **13** enjoy yourself, go on the razzle **14** go out on the town, push the boat out, put the flags out **15** paint the town red

*Parties include:*

**02** do
**03** hen, tea
**04** bash, drum, foam, luau, orgy, rave, stag, toga, wine, wrap
**05** beano, disco, hangi, house
**06** at-home, beer-up, bottle, dinner, drinks, garden, grog-on, grog-up, hooley, Kneipe, picnic, pyjama, rave-up, shivoo, social, soirée, supper
**07** blow-out, ceilidh, cookout, knees-up, leaving, new year, potluck, reunion, shindig, slumber
**08** barbecue, birthday, bunfight, clambake, cocktail, farewell, jamboree, tea fight, wingding
**09** acid-house, beanfeast, Christmas, Hallowe'en, hootnanny, reception, sleepover, welcoming
**10** after-party, baby shower, fancy dress, hootenanny, whist drive
**11** cookie-shine, discotheque, flat-warming, muffin-fight, muffin-worry
**12** bridal shower, house-warming
**13** cheese and wine, coffee klatsch, fête champêtre, small-and-early

*Political parties in the UK include:*

**01** L
**03** BNP, Con, DUP, Lab, Lib, PUP, SNP
**04** SDLP, Tory, UKIP, Whig
**05** Green
**06** Labour, Lib Dem
**07** Liberal, Respect
**08** Alliance, Sinn Féin
**09** Communist
**10** Democratic, Plaid Cymru, Republican, UK Unionist
**11** Co-operative
**12** Conservative
**13** National Front, Parliamentary
**14** UK Independence, Ulster Unionist
**15** British National, Liberal Democrat

*Political parties worldwide include:*

**02** AN, FN, PP
**03** ALP, CDU, FPD, NDP, NPD, UMP
**04** PSOE
**05** Green, Labor
**06** Labour
**07** Worker's
**08** Batasuna, Democrat, Fine Gael, National, Sinn Féin
**09** One Nation, Socialist
**10** Fianna Fáil, Republican
**12** Workers' Party
**13** Bloc Québécois, Front National, National Front
**14** Partido Popular
• **be a party to** **09** know about **12** be involved in
• **dancing party** **03** hop

## party-goer
**09** socialite

## parvenu
**07** climber, new rich, upstart **09** arriviste, pretender, vulgarian **12** nouveau riche **13** social climber

## pascal
**02** Pa

## pasha
**03** dey **06** bashaw

## pass
**02** go, OK **03** col, die, gap, hit, lap, nek, ren, rin, run, say, sit, tip, way **04** beat, chit, drag, emit, fill, flow, ghat, give, go by, hand, jark, kick, live, lose, make, move, okay, omit, pace, path, play, slap, turn, visa **05** adopt, allow, botte, cross, drive, enact, event, expel, ghaut, gorge, halse, hause, hawse, issue, lunge, notch, occur, outdo, poort, punto, reach, route, serve, sling, speak, spend, stand, state, swing, throw, use up, utter, voice **06** accept, assert, become, befall, be left, canyon, chalan, change, chitty, decree, defile, devote, elapse, employ, esteem, evolve, exceed, go over, go past, happen, let out, occupy, parade, permit, puncto, ratify, ravine, slip by, take up, thrust, ticket, travel **07** advance, agree to, approve, be given, challan, declare, deliver, develop, excrete, express, fade out, get over, licence, passage, proceed, qualify, release, run past, succeed, surpass, undergo, vote for, warrant **08** advances, announce, approach, be willed, currency, go across, go beyond, graduate, outstrip, overhaul, overtake, overture, passport, proclaim, progress, sanction, slip away, transfer, transmit, traverse, validate **09** authorize, be endowed, be granted, circulate, come about, condition, disappear, discharge, disregard, drive past, get across, go through, pronounce, take place, transpire, while away **10** adjudicate, be made over, experience, fulfilment, get through, permission, protection, reputation, suggestion **11** be consigned, be inherited, go unnoticed, leave behind, make your way, outdistance, predicament, proposition, pull ahead of, sail through **12** be bequeathed, be handed down, consummation **13** authorization, be transferred, breeze through, draw level with, laissez-passer, scrape through **14** successful in, identification, let someone have
*See also* **mountain pass** *under* **mountain**
• **pass as, pass for** **10** appear to be, be taken for **12** be regarded as **13** be mistaken for
• **pass away** **02** go **03** die **04** vade **05** forgo **06** elapse, expire, forego, pass on, peg out, pop off **07** decease **08** blow over **13** kick the bucket **14** depart this life, give up the ghost **15** breathe your last
• **pass degree** **04** poll
• **pass off** **04** fake **05** feign, go off, occur **06** happen, vanish **07** die down, palm off, put over, wear off **08** fade away, wear away **09** disappear, take place **11** counterfeit **12** misrepresent
• **pass out** **03** die **04** dole, drop **05** allot, faint, swoon **07** deal out, dole out, give out, hand out **08** allocate, black out, collapse, flake out, keel over, share out, spark out **10** distribute
• **pass over** **02** go **03** die **04** balk, miss, omit, skim **05** baulk, leave **06** forget, ignore, overgo, voyage **07** neglect **08** look over, overjump, overlook, overpass, override, overskip **09** disregard **14** take no notice of, turn a deaf ear to **15** turn a blind eye to
• **pass quickly** **03** fly, hie, ren, rin, run
• **pass the ball to** **04** feed
• **pass up** **04** miss **06** ignore, refuse, reject **07** let slip, neglect **08** renounce

## passable

**02** OK **04** fair, open, so-so **05** clear **06** decent **07** average **08** adequate, all right, mediocre, moderate, ordinary, pervious **09** allowable, navigable, tolerable, unblocked **10** acceptable, not much cop **11** practicable, presentable, respectable, traversable **12** run of the mill, satisfactory, unobstructed **13** no great shakes, unexceptional

## passably

**05** quite **06** fairly, rather **08** somewhat **09** tolerably **10** moderately, reasonably, relatively **13** after a fashion, indifferently

## passage

**03** cut, gap, gut, way **04** adit, coda, duct, exit, fare, flow, gate, hall, lane, lick, loan, main, neck, pace, pass, path, pend, pore, road, slap, text, tour, trek, trip **05** aisle, alley, alure, break, canal, chute, creep, cundy, entry, flume, fogou, gully, lapse, lento, lobby, locus, piano, piece, route, shaft, shoot, shute, sound, track, verse, vista **06** access, avenue, burrow, change, clause, condie, course, dromos, furrow, groove, gullet, gutter, legato, narrow, presto, screed, strait, street, throat, trance, transe, travel, trough, tunnel, voyage **07** advance, archway, cadenza, channel, conduit, doorway, episode, excerpt, extract, fistula, gallery, hallway, journey, offtake, opening, orifice, passing, prelude, running, sea lane, section, snicket, stretto, traffic, turning **08** adoption, alleyway, approval, citation, corridor, crossing, division, entrance, incident, longueur, movement, mutation, pericope, progress, ritenuto, sanction, southing, spiccato, staccato, straight, streight, thorough, transfer, waterway **09** admission, breezeway, enactment, migration, paragraph, quotation, ventiduct, vestibule **10** acceptance, occurrence, passageway, pianissimo, ritardando, scherzando, transition, tremolando, validation **11** development, safe conduct, watercourse **12** deambulatory, ratification, thoroughfare, transmission **13** authorization, metamorphosis

*Passages include:*

**04** Mona
**05** Drake, Gaspé, Umnak
**06** Akutan, Amukta, Burias, Caicos, Colvos, Mompog, Seguam, Unimak
**07** Oronsay, Palawan
**08** Amchitka, Dominica, Fenimore, Mouchoir, Saratoga, Windward
**09** Deception, Mayaguana, St Vincent
**10** Backstairs, Guadeloupe, Martinique, Mira Por Vos, Silver Bank
**11** Turks Island, Verde Island
**13** Crooked Island
**14** Jacques Cartier

## passageway

**03** way **04** exit, hall, lane, path, port **05** aisle, alley, lobby, track **06** arcade, runway **07** gangway, hallway, passage **08** corridor, entrance **11** back passage

## passé

**03** out **05** dated, faded **06** démodé, groovy, old hat, past it **07** outworn **08** obsolete, outdated, outmoded **09** out-of-date **10** antiquated **11** on the way out, past its best **12** old-fashioned **13** unfashionable

## passenger

**04** fare **05** drone, rider **07** outside, shirker, voyager **08** commuter, hanger-on **09** fare-payer, traveller **10** freeloader, hitchhiker **11** strap-hanger
• **turn away passenger** **04** bump

## passer-by

**06** gawper **07** witness **08** looker-on, observer, onlooker **09** bystander, spectator **10** eyewitness, rubberneck

## passing

**03** end **04** flow, loss, very **05** brief, death, hasty, march, quick, rapid, short **06** casual, course, demise, elapse, finish, slight **07** advance, cursory, decease, diadrom, passage, quietus, shallow **08** fleeting, movement **09** departure, ephemeral, momentary, perishing, temporary, transient **10** evanescent, expiration, incidental, short-lived **11** exceedingly, passing away, superficial, termination **12** transitional
• **in passing** **07** by the by **08** by the bye, by the way **09** en passant **12** incidentally **15** parenthetically

## passion

**03** fit, wax **04** fire, fury, heat, love, lust, pash, rage, zeal, zest **05** anger, brame, craze, mania, wrath **06** ardour, dander, desire, spirit, temper, warmth **07** avidity, craving, emotion, feeling, fervour, tantrum **08** fondness, keenness, outburst **09** adoration, affection, altitudes, eagerness, explosion, intensity, obsession, vehemence **10** enthusiasm, fanaticism **11** fascination, indignation, infatuation **12** sexual desire
• **burst of passion** **04** gust

## passionate

**03** hot, mad **04** avid, keen, nuts, sexy, warm, wild **05** crazy, eager, fiery, gutsy, horny, Latin, potty, randy **06** ardent, erotic, fervid, fierce, loving, stormy, strong, sultry, torrid, wilful **07** aroused, excited, fervent, intense, lustful, sensual, violent, zealous **08** choleric, frenzied, inflamed, turned on, vehement **09** emotional, excitable, fanatical, hotheaded, impetuous, impulsive, irritable, obstinate, perfervid **10** headstrong, hot-blooded, self-willed **11** impassioned, tempestuous, warm-blooded **12** affectionate, enthusiastic **13** quick-tempered, waspish-headed

## passionately

**05** hotly **06** keenly **08** ardently, fiercely, lovingly, strongly **09** con calore, fervently, intensely, lustfully, sensually, violently, zealously **10** erotically **11** fanatically **14** affectionately

## passionless

**03** icy **04** calm, cold **06** frigid, frosty **07** callous, neutral **08** detached, uncaring, unloving **09** apathetic, impartial, impassive, unfeeling, withdrawn **10** insensible, restrained, uninvolved **11** cold-blooded, cold-hearted, emotionless, indifferent, unemotional **12** unresponsive **13** dispassionate

## passive

**05** aloof, inert **06** docile, remote, supine **07** distant, patient, subdued, unmoved **08** detached, inactive, lifeless, resigned, yielding **09** apathetic, compliant, lethargic, receptive, suffering **10** effortless, non-violent, submissive, uninvolved **11** emotionless, indifferent, unassertive, unemotional, unresisting **13** dispassionate, long-suffering **14** unenterprising

## passively

**09** patiently **10** lifelessly **12** submissively **13** emotionlessly, unassertively

## passport

**02** ID **03** key, way **04** door, pass, path, visa **05** entry, route **06** avenue, papers, permit **07** doorway **09** admission **12** identity card **13** authorization, laissez-passer, means of access **15** travel documents

## password

**03** key **04** word **06** parole, signal **07** tessera **09** watchword **10** open sesame, shibboleth **11** countersign

## past

**02** by, pa, pt **03** ago, ygo **04** done, gone, last, late, life, near, over, ygoe, yore **05** after, agone, early, ended, forby, olden, round, since **06** behind, beside, beyond, bygone, by-past, former, gone by, latter, no more, recent, record **07** ancient, defunct, elapsed, extinct, history, long ago, one-time, worn-out **08** finished, foregone, overworn, preterit, previous, sometime **09** antiquity, completed, erstwhile, foregoing, forgotten, olden days, preceding, preterite, too old for, yesterday **10** background, bygone days, days gone by, days of yore, experience, olden times **11** bygone times, former times, good old days, track record **12** too mature for **15** over and done with

## pasta

*Pasta types include:*

**04** orza, ziti
**05** penne, ruoti
**06** anelli, ditali, noodle, trofie
**07** fusilli, gnocchi, lasagna, lasagne,

lumache, mafalde, maruzze,
mezzani, noodles, pennine,
ravioli
08 bucatini, farfalle, fedelini,
linguini, macaroni, rigatoni,
stelline
09 agnolotti, angel hair, casarecci,
crescioni, fiochetti, manicotti,
spaghetti
10 angel's hair, bombolotti,
cannelloni, conchiglie, farfalline,
fettuccine, strangozzi, tagliarini,
taglierini, tortellini, vermicelli
11 cappelletti, orecchiette,
pappardelle, tagliatelle
12 lasagne verde
13 elbow macaroni

## paste
03 fix, gum, pap 04 glue, miso, mush,
pack, pâté, pulp 05 blend, purée,
putty, stick 06 cement, cerate, fasten,
mastic, slurry, spread, thrash
07 mixture 08 adhesive

## pastel
04 pale, soft, woad 05 chalk, faint,
light, muted, quiet 06 crayon, low-key,
sketch, subtle 07 drawing, subdued
08 delicate, discreet, pastille, soft-
hued, vignette 11 sauce-crayon
13 light-coloured

## pastiche
◊ anagram indicator 03 mix 04 olio
06 jumble, medley 07 farrago,
melange, mixture, variety
08 mishmash, mixed bag 09 confusion,
pasticcio, patchwork, potpourri
10 assortment, collection,
hodgepodge, hotchpotch, miscellany,
salmagundi 11 gallimaufry, olla-
podrida, smorgasbord
14 conglomeration, omnium-gatherum

## pastille
05 sweet 06 jujube, pastel, tablet,
troche 07 lozenge 09 cough drop
10 confection, cough sweet

## pastime
03 fun 04 game, play 05 hobby, sport
08 activity, pastance 09 amusement,
avocation, diversion 10 abridgment,
recreation, relaxation, suppliance
11 abridgement, distraction
12 Zeitvertreib 13 entertainment
14 leisure pursuit 15 leisure activity
See also **hobby**

## past master
02 PM 03 ace 05 adept 06 artist, expert,
wizard 07 dab hand, old hand
08 virtuoso 10 proficient

## pastor
01 P 05 canon, vicar 06 cleric, deacon,
divine, parson, priest, rector
08 minister, shepherd 09 churchman,
clergyman 10 prebendary
12 ecclesiastic

## pastoral
03 oat 04 idyl 05 idyll, rural 06 rustic,
simple 07 bucolic, country, crosier,
crozier, eclogue, idyllic 08 agrarian,
Arcadian, clerical, priestly, serenata
09 bucolical, siciliano 11 ministerial,

Theocritean 12 agricultural
14 ecclesiastical

## pastry
*Pastry types include:*

04 filo, flan, puff
05 choux, flaky, plain, short, sweet
06 cheese, Danish
07 pork-pie
08 one-stage, piecrust
09 rough-puff, suetcrust
10 pâte brisée, pâte frolle, pâte
sablée, pâte sucrée, shortcrust,
wholewheat
12 biscuit-crumb, pâte à savarin
13 American crust, hot-water crust
14 rich shortcrust

See also **cake**

## pasture
03 alp, lay, lea, lee, ley, tie, tye 04 feed,
fell, food, gang, mead, raik, rake,
soum, sowm, walk 05 downs, field,
grass, graze, lease, leaze, range
06 leasow, meadow, saeter 07 feeding,
grazing, leasowe, paddock
08 mountain, shealing, shieling
09 grassland, pasturage, sheepwalk
11 grazing land
• **pasture grass** 04 bent 05 grama
06 fescue 07 timothy 08 paspalum, rye
grass 09 bent grass 10 grama grass
12 meadow fescue, sheep's fescue,
timothy grass 13 dog's-tail grass,
Flinders grass

## pasty
03 wan 04 pale, waxy 06 doughy,
pallid, sallow, sickly 07 anaemic
08 empanada 09 unhealthy 10 pasty-
faced 11 oyster-patty

## pat
03 dab, pet, pot, tap 04 ball, burp, clap,
easy, glib, lump, mass, slap, tick
05 bepat, chunk, print, ready, slick,
touch 06 caress, facile, fluent, fondle,
patter, simple, smooth, stroke
07 exactly 08 coquille, fluently
09 perfectly, precisely 10 flawlessly,
simplistic 11 faultlessly, word-for-word
• **pat someone on the back**
06 praise 10 compliment
12 congratulate 13 say well done to

## patch
03 bed, fix, lot, sew 04 area, mend,
plot, snip, spot, term, time, zona
05 botch, cloth, clout, cover, phase,
piece, scrap, spell, tract 06 parcel,
period, plaque, pocket, repair, shield,
stitch 07 stretch 08 covering, dressing,
fragment, material 09 reinforce
10 protection

## patchwork
04 hash 06 jumble, medley, motley
07 farrago, mixture 08 mishmash,
pastiche 10 assortment, hotchpotch
11 gallimaufry

## patchy
◊ anagram indicator 05 bitty 06 fitful,
random, spotty, uneven 07 blotchy,
erratic, macular, sketchy, varying
08 variable 09 centonate, irregular

10 incomplete 11 incongruous
12 inconsistent, inharmonious

## patent
03 pat 04 open 05 clear, overt, plain,
right 07 blatant, charter, evident,
glaring, licence, obvious, visible
08 apparent, flagrant, manifest,
palpable 09 copyright, expanding,
ingenious, invention, privilege,
spreading 10 undeniable 11 certificate,
conspicuous, self-evident, transparent,
unequivocal 12 crystal clear,
unmistakable 13 unmistakeable
15 clear as daylight

## patently
06 openly 07 clearly, plainly, visibly
08 palpably 09 blatantly, glaringly,
obviously 10 manifestly
12 unmistakably 13 conspicuously,
unequivocally, unmistakeably

## paternal
08 fatherly, vigilant 09 concerned
10 benevolent, fatherlike, protective

## path
02 go 03 pad, sty, way 04 berm, gate,
lane, road, trod, walk, went 05 allée,
orbit, route, track, trail, troad, trode
06 avenue, course, troade 07 circuit,
highway, passage, pathway, slidder,
towpath, walkway 08 approach,
cycleway, footpath 09 bridleway,
direction, footsteps 10 bridle-road,
forthright

## pathetic
◊ anagram indicator 03 sad 04 poor
05 sorry 06 dismal, feeble, meagre,
moving, tender, woeful 07 pitiful,
useless 08 derisory, pitiable, poignant,
touching, wretched 09 affecting,
miserable, plaintive, worthless
10 deplorable, inadequate, lamentable
11 distressing 12 contemptible, heart-
rending 13 heartbreaking
14 unsatisfactory

## pathetically
05 sadly 08 dismally, pitiably, woefully
09 miserably, pitifully 10 deplorably,
lamentably, wretchedly
12 contemptibly, inadequately

## pathological
07 chronic 08 addicted, habitual,
hardened 09 confirmed, dependent,
obsessive 10 compulsive, inveterate,
persistent

## pathos
06 misery 07 sadness, tragedy 08 sob
stuff 09 poignancy 10 inadequacy
11 pitifulness 12 pitiableness
13 plaintiveness

## patience
04 cool 07 bistort 08 calmness,
Klondike, Klondyke, serenity, stoicism,
tenacity 09 composure, diligence,
endurance, fortitude, restraint,
solitaire, tolerance 10 doggedness,
equanimity, submission, sufferance
11 forbearance, persistence,
resignation, self-control 12 monk's
rhubarb, perseverance, stickability,

## patient

tranquillity **13** long-suffering **14** inexcitability, unflappability

## patient

**04** calm, case, cool, kind, mild **06** client, extern, serene, tender **07** externe, invalid, lenient, stoical, subject **08** ambulant, composed, enduring, laid-back, resigned, resolute, sufferer, tolerant **09** easy-going, forgiving, indulgent, leisurely, unhurried **10** forbearant, forbearing, out-patient, persistent, restrained, submissive **11** persevering, susceptible, unflappable **12** even-tempered, patient as Job **13** accommodating, imperturbable, long-suffering, philosophical, self-possessed, uncomplaining, understanding **14** hanging in there, self-controlled
• **be patient 04** bear
• **hospital patients 04** ward

## patiently

**06** calmly, kindly, mildly **08** tenderly **09** leisurely **10** enduringly, resolutely, tolerantly **11** unflappably, unhurriedly **12** persistently **13** considerately, perseveringly

## patois

**04** cant, argot, Gumbo, lingo, slang **06** Creole, jargon, patter **07** dialect **08** Guernsey **10** vernacular **11** local speech **12** lingua franca **13** local parlance

## patriarch

**04** pope, sire **05** abuna, elder **06** father **07** founder **09** greybeard **10** Catholicos **11** grandfather, grand old man **13** paterfamilias

*Patriarchs include:*

**04** Levi, Noah
**05** Aaron, Abram, Enoch, Isaac, Jacob
**06** Joseph
**07** Abraham, Ishmael
**10** Methuselah, Theophilus

## patrician

**03** nob **04** peer **05** noble **06** gentle, lordly, patron **07** grandee **08** high-born, nobleman, well-born **09** gentleman, high-class **10** aristocrat, upper-crust **11** blue-blooded **12** aristocratic, thoroughbred

## patrimony

**05** share **06** estate, legacy **07** bequest, portion, revenue **08** heritage, property **10** birthright **11** inheritance, possessions

## patriot

**05** jingo **06** jingoist, loyalist **09** flag-waver **10** chauvinist **11** nationalist

## patriotic

**05** loyal **08** loyalist **10** flag-waving, jingoistic **11** nationalist **12** chauvinistic **13** nationalistic

## patriotism

**07** loyalty **08** jingoism **10** chauvinism, flag-waving **11** nationalism

## patrol

**04** beat, tour **05** guard, round, vigil, watch **06** defend, picket, piquet, police, sentry **07** defence, inspect, monitor, picquet, protect **08** defender, policing, sentinel, sentry-go, watchman **09** milk train, patrolman **10** patrolling, protection **11** be on the beat, do the rounds, go the rounds, keep guard on, keep watch on, patrolwoman, perambulate **12** surveillance **13** keep watch over, make the rounds, night-watchman, perambulation, police officer, security guard **14** make your rounds

## patron

**05** angel, buyer, stoop, stoup, Venus **06** Apollo, backer, client, fautor, friend, helper, Hermes **07** pattern, regular, shopper, sponsor **08** advocate, champion, customer, defender, guardian, Maecenas, promoter, upholder **09** protector, purchaser, supporter **10** benefactor, frequenter, subscriber **11** sympathizer **12** benefactress **13** guardian angel **14** fairy godmother, philanthropist

## patronage

**05** aegis, trade **06** buying, custom **07** backing, funding, support **08** auspices, business, commerce, shopping **09** promotion **10** protection, purchasing **11** countenance, sponsorship **12** financial aid, subscription **13** encouragement, financial help

## patronize

**03** aid **04** back, fund, help **05** scorn **06** assist, foster, shop at **07** buy from, despise, finance, promote, protect, sponsor, support **08** champion, deal with, empatron, frequent, maintain **09** disparage, encourage **10** look down on, talk down to **12** be a regular at

## patronizing

**05** lofty **06** snooty **07** haughty, stuck up **08** scornful, snobbish, stooping, superior **10** disdainful, high-handed **11** overbearing, toffee-nosed **12** contemptuous, supercilious **13** condescending, high-and-mighty **14** holier-than-thou **15** on your high horse

## patter

**03** pat, rap, tap, yak **04** beat, drum, line, pelt, trip **05** lingo, pitch, pound, spiel **06** bicker, gabble, gammon, jabber, jargon, pit-pat, scurry, verbal **07** beating, chatter, pitapat, scuttle, tapping, verbals **08** pitty-pat **09** monologue, pattering **12** pitter-patter

## pattern

**03** key **04** copy, form, mold, norm, plan, trim, type **05** guide, ideal, match, model, motif, mould, order, shape, style, whirl **06** design, device, dicing, figure, follow, method, sample, stripe, swatch, system **07** emulate, example, fashion, Gestalt, grecque, imitate, stencil, tracery **08** decorate, Greek key, markings, original, ornament, parallel, standard, template **09** blueprint, criterion, influence, prototype,

scantling **10** craquelure, decoration **11** arrangement, instruction **13** ornamentation

## patterned

**05** moiré **07** figured, printed, watered **09** decorated **10** ornamented

## paucity

**04** lack, want **06** dearth, rarity **07** fewness, poverty **08** scarcity, shortage, sparsity **09** smallness **10** deficiency, meagreness, paltriness, scantiness, slightness, sparseness **11** slenderness **12** exiguousness **13** insufficiency

## paunch

**03** gut, pod **04** kite, kyte **05** belly, rumen, tripe **07** abdomen, beer gut **08** pot-belly **09** beer belly **10** eviscerate, fat stomach **11** corporation

## paunchy

**03** fat **05** podgy, pudgy, tubby **06** portly, rotund **07** adipose **08** stomachy **09** corpulent **10** pot-bellied

## pauper

**06** beggar **07** have-not **08** bankrupt, indigent **09** insolvent, mendicant **10** down-and-out **11** church mouse

## pause

**03** gap **04** halt, hold, kick, lull, rest, stay, stop, wait **05** break, cease, close, delay, demur, dwell, let up, let-up, limma **06** cesura, desist **07** adjourn, breathe, caesura, fermata, respite, sit down, time out **08** break off, breather, dieresis, hesitate, hold back, interval, stoppage, take five **09** cessation, diaeresis, interlude, interrupt, take a rest **10** hesitation, take a break **11** discontinue, freeze-frame **12** intermission, interruption **13** take a breather **14** breathing space

## pave

**03** tar **04** flag, tile **05** cover, floor, pitch **06** cobble, tarmac **07** asphalt, surface **08** concrete **10** macadamize, tessellate **11** cobblestone
• **pave the way for 08** lead up to **09** introduce, take steps **10** prepare for **11** get ready for **12** make ready for, take measures **14** clear the ground

## pavement

**03** bed, way **04** path **05** floor **07** footway, walkway **08** causeway, flagging, footpath, platform, sidewalk, trottoir **11** plainstanes, plainstones

## pavilion

**04** flag, tent **05** kiosk **06** canopy, ensign, houdah, howdah **09** belvedere **14** jingling Johnny

## paving-block

**03** set **04** sett

## paw

**03** pad, pah, pud **04** foot, foul, hand, maul, poke **05** mouse, puddy, touch **06** molest, stroke **07** obscene, touch up **08** forefoot **09** manhandle, mishandle

## pawn

**01** P **03** dip, pan, pop, toy **04** dupe, fine, hock, paan, pown, tool **05** betel, powin, spout, stake **06** impawn, lumber, pledge, puppet, stooge, wadset **07** cat's paw, deposit, gallery, peacock, wadsett **08** mortgage **09** pignerate, pignorate, plaything **10** instrument **11** impignorate, oppignerate, oppignorate **13** lay in lavender

## pawnbroker

**05** uncle **06** lender, sheeny, usurer **07** pop-shop **08** lumberer, pawnshop **10** gombeen-man **11** money-lender, mont-de-piété **12** monte di pietà

## pay

**02** do **03** fee **04** ante, bung, foot, give, make, pony, sold **05** atone, grant, offer, remit, repay, solde, spend, wages, yield **06** afford, answer, ante up, bestow, defray, expend, extend, income, invest, lay out, net pay, outlay, pay off, pay out, profit, rake in, refund, return, reward, salary, settle, square, suffer, supply **07** benefit, bring in, cough up, fork out, imburse, pay back, payment, produce, proffer, stipend, stump up **08** disburse, earnings, gross pay, hand over, settle up, shell out **09** discharge, indemnify, reimburse **10** be punished, commission, compensate, emoluments, honorarium, make amends, recompense, remunerate **11** foot the bill, take-home pay **12** compensation, pick up the tab, remuneration, satisfaction **13** meet the cost of, reimbursement **14** be beneficial to, be worthwhile to, let someone have
• **pay back** **05** repay **06** pay off, punish, refund, return, settle, square **08** give back **09** reimburse, retaliate **10** recompense **11** get even with, reciprocate, take revenge **13** counter-attack **14** get your own back
• **pay for** **04** take **05** atone, escot, prize, pryse **06** suffer **09** answer for **10** compensate, cost dearly, make amends **12** count the cost, face the music **13** be punished for **14** count the cost of, get your deserts, pay a penalty for, pay the price for
• **pay off** **03** fix **04** fire, meet, sack, work **05** bribe, clear, repay **06** buy off, grease, honour, lay off, settle, square, suborn **07** dismiss, requite, succeed **08** amortize **09** discharge, pay in full **10** extinguish, get results, take care of **12** be successful **13** make redundant
• **pay out** **04** veer **05** remit, spend **06** ante up, expend, lay out **07** cough up, dispend, fork out **08** disburse, hand over, part with, shell out

## payable

**03** due **04** owed **05** owing **06** mature, unpaid **08** to be paid **09** in arrears **10** profitable **11** outstanding **13** contributable

## payload

**04** haul, load **05** cargo, goods **06** lading

**07** baggage, freight, tonnage **08** contents, shipment **11** consignment, merchandise

## payment

**03** fee, pay, sub **04** ante, dole, fare, farm, hire, mail, rent, scot, shot, toll, wage **05** arles, modus **06** amount, hansel, outlay, payola, reward **07** advance, annuity, deposit, expense, handsel, pension, premium, primage **08** danegeld, danegelt, donation, soul-scat, soul-scot, soul-shot **09** allowance, clearance, discharge **10** instalment, prestation, punishment, quarterage, recompense, remittance, settlement **12** compensation, contribution, remuneration, satisfaction **13** consideration
• **demand payment** **03** dun

## pay-off

**03** fee, pay **05** bribe, wages **06** crunch, income, net pay, result, reward, salary, upshot **07** benefit, outcome, payment, stipend **08** earnings, gross pay **09** advantage, hush money, punchline, slush fund, sweetener **10** allurement, back-hander, commission, dénouement, emoluments, enticement, honorarium, inducement, recompense, settlement **11** consequence, take-home pay **12** compensation, remuneration **13** moment of truth, reimbursement **15** protection money

## PC

*see* **police officer**

## pea

**03** dal **04** daal, dahl, dhal **05** dholl, pease **06** legume **08** kaka beak, kaka bill **09** chickling, mangetout, marrowfat, parrot-jaw, rounceval **10** parrot-beak, parrot-bill **14** chickling vetch

## peace

**03** pax **04** calm, ease, hush, pact, rest **05** amity, frith, olive, quiet, still, truce **06** accord, repose, shalom, treaty **07** concord, harmony, silence **08** calmness, goodwill, serenity **09** agreement, armistice, ceasefire, composure, placidity, quietness, stillness **10** friendship, relaxation **11** contentment, law and order, non-violence, peace treaty, restfulness **12** amicableness, conciliation, peacefulness, tranquillity **13** non-aggression

## peaceable

**04** mild **05** douce **06** dovish, gentle, irenic, placid **07** cordial, pacific **08** amicable, friendly **09** easy-going, unwarlike **10** harmonious, non-violent **11** good-natured, inoffensive, peace-loving **12** conciliatory, even-tempered **13** non-aggressive

## peaceably

**06** gently, mildly **08** amicably, placidly **09** cordially **11** pacifically **12** harmoniously **13** inoffensively

## peaceful

**04** calm **05** quiet, still **06** gentle, irenic,

placid, serene, sleepy **07** halcyon, pacific, restful **08** amicable, friendly, in repose, relaxing, tranquil **09** peaceable, reposeful, unruffled **10** harmonious, untroubled **11** undisturbed

## peacefully

**06** calmly, gently **07** quietly **08** amicably, placidly, serenely, sleepily **09** restfully **12** harmoniously

## peacemaker

**04** dove **06** broker **08** appeaser, mediator, pacifier, pacifist, revolver **09** make-peace **10** arbitrator **11** conciliator, intercessor, pacificator, peace-monger

## peacemaking

**06** irenic **07** pacific **09** appeasing, mediating, mediative, mediatory **11** mediatorial **12** conciliatory, pacification

## peach

**03** dob **06** accuse, betray, inform **07** sing out, whittle **08** quandang, quandong, quantong **09** melocoton, nectarine, victorine **10** melicotton, melocotoon **11** malakatoone

## peacock

**03** pea **04** Pavo, pawn, pown **05** powin **06** paiock, pajock, pavone **07** paiocke, pajocke

## peak

**02** pk **03** ben, nib, pin, tip, top **04** apex, hill, mope, peag, rise **05** crest, crise, crown, droop, mount, pique, point, prick, spike, spire, visor, vizor **06** apogee, climax, height, summer, summit, zenith **07** maximum **08** aiguille, high noon, mountain, pinnacle **09** culminate, elevation, high point **11** come to a head, culmination

## peaky

**03** ill, wan **04** pale, sick **05** dicky, seedy **06** crummy, pallid, poorly, queasy, sickly, unwell **09** off-colour, washed-out **10** out of sorts **15** under the weather

## peal

**04** boom, clap, howl, ring, roar, roll, toll **05** chime, clang, crash, knell **06** firing, grilse, rumble, triple **07** resound, ringing, ring out **08** carillon, resonate **10** resounding **11** reverberate **13** reverberation

## peanut

**05** arnut **06** goober **07** arachis **08** earth-nut, earth-pea **09** goober pea, groundnut, monkey nut

## pear

**04** tuna **05** nashi, nelis, nopal **06** Colmar, comice, nelies, pepino, seckel, seckle, warden **07** avocado, poperin **08** aguacate, bergamot, blanquet, muscadel, muscatel **09** Indian fig, poppering **10** Conference, jargonelle **11** bon chrétien, queez-maddam **12** cuisse-madame

## pearl

**04** purl, Unio **05** nacre, union

## peasant

**06** barock, orient **07** barocco, baroque, granule, paragon **10** granulated
• **string of pearls** **04** rope

## peasant

**03** oaf **04** boor, hick, kern, lout, rude, ryot **05** churl, kerne, kisan, kulak, mujik, rural, swain, yokel **06** carlot, cottar, cotter, fellah, jungli, moujik, muzhik, raiyat, rustic **07** bumpkin, Cossack, cottier **09** campesino, contadina, contadino **10** blue-bonnet, clodhopper, provincial **13** country person **14** country bumpkin

## pebble

**04** chip, pelt, pumy, rock **05** agate, chuck, pumie, stone **06** gallet **07** chuckie **09** pumy stone **10** dreikanter, pumie stone **12** chuckie-stane, chuckie-stone

## peccadillo

**04** boob, slip **05** error, fault, lapse **06** slip-up **07** misdeed **10** infraction **11** delinquency **12** indiscretion, minor offence, misdemeanour

## peck

**02** pk **03** dab, hit, jab, job, nip, rap, tap **04** bite, food, jerk, kiss, pick **05** pitch, prick **06** pickle, strike

## peculiar

◇ *anagram indicator* **03** ill, odd, own **04** sick **05** dizzy, droll, ferly, funny, queer, weird **06** exotic, poorly, proper, quaint, queasy, unique, unwell, way-out **07** bizarre, curious, oddball, offbeat, special, strange, unusual **08** abnormal, distinct, freakish, personal, singular, specific **09** eccentric, grotesque, preserved **10** individual, outlandish, out of sorts, particular, remarkable **11** distinctive, exceptional **12** appropriated **13** extraordinary, idiosyncratic **14** characteristic, distinguishing, unconventional **15** individualistic, under the weather
• **peculiar to** **04** like **08** unique to **09** typical of **11** belonging to **12** indicative of **13** in keeping with

## peculiarity

**04** mark **05** quirk, trait **06** foible, jimjam, oddity **07** feature, quality **08** hallmark, property **09** attribute, exception, mannerism, weirdness **10** shibboleth **11** abnormality, bizarreness, singularity **12** eccentricity, idiosyncrasy **13** individuality, particularity **14** characteristic **15** distinctiveness

## peculiarly

◇ *anagram indicator* **05** oddly **08** quaintly, uniquely **09** bizarrely, curiously, strangely, unusually **10** distinctly, remarkably, singularly **12** particularly **13** distinctively, exceptionally **15** extraordinarily

## pecuniary

**06** fiscal **07** nummary **08** monetary **09** financial, nummulary **10** commercial

## pedagogic

**08** academic, didactic, teaching

**09** tuitional **10** scholastic **11** educational **13** instructional

## pedagogue

**03** don **05** teach **06** master, pedant **07** dominie, teacher **08** educator, mistress **09** dogmatist, preceptor **10** instructor **12** educationist, schoolmaster **13** schoolteacher **14** educationalist, schoolmistress

## pedagogy

**07** tuition **08** teaching, training, tutelage **09** didactics **10** pedagogics **11** instruction

## pedal

**01** P **07** treadle

## pedant

**06** purist **07** academe, casuist, egghead **08** academic, highbrow, quibbler **09** dogmatist, Dryasdust, formalist, nit-picker, pedagogue, precisian **10** literalist, scholastic, schoolmarm **11** doctrinaire, pettifogger **12** hair-splitter, intellectual, precisionist, schoolmaster **13** perfectionist

## pedantic

**04** blue **05** exact, fussy, heavy **06** purist, stuffy **07** bookish, erudite, finical, inkhorn, pompous, precise, stilted **08** academic **09** formalist, quibbling **10** literalist, meticulous, nit-picking, particular, scholastic, scrupulous **11** pretentious, punctilious, sesquipedal **12** intellectual **13** hair-splitting, perfectionist, schoolmarmish **14** schoolmasterly, sesquipedalian

## pedantry

**09** cavilling, dogmatism, exactness, pedantism, pomposity, quibbling **10** finicality, nit-picking, pedagogism, stuffiness **11** bookishness, donnishness **12** academicness **13** hair-splitting **14** meticulousness **15** intellectualism, pedagoguishness, pretentiousness, punctiliousness

## peddle

◇ *anagram indicator* **04** flog, hawk, push, sell, tout, vend **05** trade **06** market, smouch, trifle **07** traffic **08** huckster **12** offer for sale **14** present for sale

## pedestal

**04** base, dado, foot **05** basis, stand, trunk **06** column, pillar, plinth, podium **07** acroter, support **08** mounting, platform **09** axle-guard, stylobate **10** acroterion, acroterium, foundation **11** pillow-block
• **put on a pedestal** **05** exalt **06** admire, revere **07** adulate, idolize **08** look up to **11** hero-worship

## pedestrian

**03** ped **04** dull, flat **05** banal, hiker **06** boring, hicker, stodgy, turgid, walker **07** humdrum, mundane, prosaic **08** mediocre, ordinary, plodding **09** jaywalker **10** unexciting, uninspired, voetganger **11** commonplace, indifferent, not up to much, peripatetic **12** matter-of-fact, run-of-the-mill **13** foot-traveller, no great shakes, unimaginative

## pedigree

**03** set **04** line, race, tree **05** blood, breed, stirp, stock **06** family, series, stemma, stirps, strain **07** descent, lineage **08** ancestry, breeding, pure-bred **09** genealogy, parentage, phylogeny **10** derivation, extraction, family tree, succession **11** full-blooded **12** aristocratic, phylogenesis, thoroughbred **13** line of descent

## pediment

**07** frontal, fronton **08** frontoon **09** fastigium **12** frontispiece

## pedlar

**06** bodger, cadger, coster, hawker, jagger, pedder, pether, seller, smouch, smouse, vendor, walker, yagger **07** camelot, chapman, packman, smouser **08** huckster **09** boxwallah, cheap-jack, gutter-man, itinerant **10** colporteur **12** costermonger, street-trader **14** gutter-merchant

## pee

**01** P
*See also* **urinate**

## peek

**03** spy **04** look, peep, peer **05** blink, dekko, squiz **06** gander, glance, shufti, squint **07** glimpse, look-see **11** have a gander **12** have a look-see

## peel

◇ *ends deletion indicator* **04** bark, pale, pare, peal, pill, rind, skin, zest **05** flake, scale, shell, shuck, stake, strip **06** grilse, remove, shovel **07** epicarp, exocarp, peeling, pillage, plunder, take off, undress **08** flake off **10** desquamate, integument **11** decorticate
• **keep your eyes peeled** **07** be alert, monitor, observe **12** watch closely **15** keep a lookout for

## peep

**03** cry, eye, pip, pry, spy **04** cook, keek, kook, look, peek, peer, pink, pipe, slit, toot, word **05** blink, cheep, chirp, dekko, issue, noise, sound, speck, tweet **06** appear, emerge, gander, glance, shufti, squeak, squint, warble **07** chatter, chirrup, glimpse, look-see, twitter **09** quick look, utterance

## peephole

**04** hole, slit **05** chink, cleft, crack, slink **07** crevice, eyehole, fissure, keyhole, opening, pinhole, spyhole **08** aperture **09** Judas hole **10** interstice **11** Judas window

## peer

**03** pry, spy **04** dick, duke, earl, gaze, lady, like, look, lord, peep, pink, scan, toot **05** baron, count, equal, match, noble, snoop, stime, styme, trier, tweer, twire **06** appear, fellow, squint, squiny **07** compeer, examine, inspect, Law Lord, marquis, peeress, squinny **08** confrère, marquess, nobleman, protrude, viscount **09** patrician **10** antagonist, aristocrat, equivalent, scrutinize **11** counterpart **12** backwoodsman
*See also* **nobility**

## peerage
**07** Debrett, red book **08** nobility **09** top drawer **10** upper crust **11** aristocracy **14** lords and ladies

## peeress
**04** dame, lady **05** noble **07** duchess **08** baroness, countess **10** aristocrat, noblewoman **11** marchioness, viscountess

## peerless
**06** unique **07** supreme **09** excellent, matchless, nonpareil, paramount, unmatched **10** incompared, unbeatable, unequalled, unexcelled, unrivalled **11** outstanding, superlative, unsurpassed **12** incomparable, second to none, unparalleled, without equal **13** beyond compare

## peeve
**03** bug, irk, vex **04** gall, nark, rile **05** annoy **06** grouse, hassle, wind up **07** hack off, tick off **08** brass off, irritate **09** aggravate, cheese off, drive nuts, grievance **10** drive crazy, exasperate **12** drive bananas **13** make sparks fly **14** drive up the wall

## peeved
**04** sore **05** irked, riled, upset, vexed **06** bugged, galled, miffed, narked, piqued, put out, shirty **07** annoyed, hassled, in a huff, nettled, stroppy **08** in a paddy **09** irritated, ticked off **10** brassed off, cheesed off, driven nuts, got the hump **11** driven crazy, exasperated

## peevish
**03** ill **04** sour **05** cross, moody, ratty, sulky, surly, testy **06** crusty, franzy, girnie, grumpy, hipped, snappy, sullen, tetchy, touchy **07** crabbed, foolish, frabbit, frampal, fretful, grouchy, nattery, pettish, wayward **08** captious, churlish, frampold, nattered, perverse, petulant **09** crotchety, fractious, irritable, querulous, splenetic, vexatious **10** capernoity, in a bad mood **11** capernoitie, cappernoity, complaining, ill-tempered, out of temper **12** cantankerous **13** short-tempered

## peevishly
**07** crossly **08** grumpily, sullenly **09** fretfully, irritably **10** churlishly, in a bad mood, petulantly **11** fractiously

## peevishness
**03** dod, pet **05** pique **08** acrimony, fretting **09** curstness, ill-temper, petulance, testiness **10** perversity, protervity **12** captiousness, irritability **13** querulousness

## peg
**03** fix, key, leg, nog, pin, set, tap **04** brad, hook, join, knag, knob, mark, nail, plug, poke, post, step **05** dowel, limit, perch, piton, score, screw, spike, stake, theme, thole, throw **06** attach, degree, fasten, freeze, hatpeg, marker, picket, piquet, secure, spigot, target, thrust **07** control, picquet, tent pin

**08** cheville, hold down, thole pin **09** soft spile, stabilize, tuning pin
• **peg away** **06** hang in **07** persist **08** keep at it, plug away, work away, work hard **09** persevere, plod along, stick at it **10** beaver away **13** apply yourself
• **take down a peg or two, bring down a peg or two** **06** humble **09** humiliate **13** cut down to size **15** bring down to size

## pejorative
**03** bad **08** negative **09** slighting **10** belittling, derogatory, unpleasant **11** deprecatory, disparaging **12** depreciating, unflattering **15** uncomplimentary

## pellet
**04** ball, drop, pill, shot, slug **05** prill **06** bullet **07** capsule, granule, lozenge **08** pithball **09** coprolite, paintball

## pell-mell
◇ *anagram indicator* **06** rashly **07** hastily **08** disorder, headlong **09** hurriedly, posthaste **10** at full tilt, confusedly, feverishly, heedlessly, recklessly, vehemently **11** hurry-scurry, impetuously **13** helter-skelter, precipitously **14** indiscriminate

## pellucid
**04** pure **05** clear **06** bright, glassy, limpid **10** diaphanous **11** translucent, transparent

## pelt
**03** fur, hit, ren, rin, run, zip **04** beat, belt, blow, clod, coat, dash, fell, hide, hurl, pour, race, rush, skin, tear, teem **05** hurry, scoot, speed, stone, throw **06** assail, attack, batter, bucket, career, charge, fleece, pebble, pellet, pelter, pepper, shower, sprint, squail, strike **07** bombard **08** bearskin, bepepper, coonskin, downpour, lapidate, squirrel, wolfskin **10** bucket down **15** rain cats and dogs

## pen
◇ *containment indicator* **03** Bic®, cub, dam, mew, nib, sty **04** Biro®, cage, coop, fold, J-pen, note, reed, shut, stie, stye, weir **05** crawl, cruve, draft, fence, hedge, hem in, hutch, kraal, penne, pound, quill, stall, write **06** author, corral, croove, cruive, estate, shut up **07** compose, confine, dash off, enclose, felt pen, felt-tip, gladius, jot down, rastrum, writing **08** compound, note down, scribble, take down **09** ballpoint, enclosure, marker pen, sheepfold, write down **10** felt-tip pen, plantation, Rollerball®, self-filler, stylograph **11** fountain pen, highlighter, Magic Marker® **12** ballpoint pen, penitentiary
*See also* **author**

## penal
**08** punitive **10** corrective, vindictive **11** retaliatory, retributive **12** disciplinary, penitentiary

## penalize
**04** fine **06** punish **07** correct, forfeit **08** chastise, handicap, sanction

**09** castigate **10** discipline **12** disadvantage

## penal servitude
**03** lag **04** bird, time **07** katorga, stretch **08** porridge **10** hard labour

## penalty
**04** fine, pain, snag **05** minus, mulct **06** amende **07** forfeit **08** downside, drawback, handicap, sentence **09** weak point **10** punishment **11** castigation, retribution **12** chastisement, demerit point, disadvantage
• **pay penalty** **03** aby **04** abye

## penance
**06** shrift **07** penalty **08** hardship **09** atonement, expiation, penitence **10** punishment, reparation, repentance **13** mortification, self-abasement **14** self-punishment

## penchant
**04** bent, bias **05** taste **06** foible, liking **07** leaning **08** affinity, fondness, soft spot, tendency, weakness **09** proneness **10** partiality, preference, proclivity, propensity **11** disposition, inclination **12** predilection **14** predisposition

## pencil
**03** cam **04** calm, caum **05** stump **06** crayon **09** keelivine, keelyvine, tortillon **10** Chinagraph®

## pendant
**03** bob **04** drop, tika, tiki **05** cross **06** locket, luster, lustre **07** eardrop, earring, heitiki, necklet, pennant, sautoir **08** appendix, necklace, pear drop **09** girandola, girandole, lavaliere, medallion **10** lavallière, Rouen cross, stalactite

## pendent
**06** nutant **07** hanging, pensile **08** dangling, drooping, swinging **09** pendulous, suspended **11** overhanging

## pending
**02** to **04** near, till **05** until, while **06** before, coming, during, whilst **07** hanging, nearing **08** awaiting, imminent, so long as **09** impending, uncertain, undecided, unsettled **10** throughout, unresolved, up in the air **11** approaching, forthcoming, in the offing **12** in the balance

## pendulous
**06** droopy **07** hanging, pendent, sagging, swaying **08** dangling, drooping, swinging **09** suspended **11** overhanging

## penetrable
**04** open **05** clear **06** porous **08** passable, pervious **09** permeable **10** accessible, explicable, fathomable **12** intelligible **14** comprehensible, understandable

## penetrate
◇ *insertion indicator* **03** cut, see **04** bite, bore, fill, seep, sink, stab, twig **05** crack, enter, grasp, imbue, prick, probe, sease, shear, spike **06** fathom,

**penetrating**

indent, invade, needle, pierce, rain in, sink in, strike **07** get into, make out, pervade, suffuse, suss out, work out **08** cotton on, permeate, perviate, puncture, register, saturate **09** perforate **10** comprehend, infiltrate, understand **11** make your way

**penetrating**

◇ *insertion indicator* **04** deep, hard, keen, loud, wise **05** acute, clear, sharp **06** biting, shrewd, shrill **07** cutting, in-depth, ingoing, intrant, probing **08** carrying, incisive, invasive, piercing, poignant, profound, stinging, strident **09** observant, searching **10** discerning, insightful, perceptive **14** discriminating

**penetration**

◇ *insertion indicator* **03** wit **05** entry **06** acumen, fathom, inroad **07** insight **08** entrance, incision, invasion, keenness, piercing, pricking, stabbing **09** acuteness, pervasion, sharpness **10** astuteness, perception, permeation, puncturing, shrewdness **11** discernment, perforation **12** infiltration, perspicacity

**penguin**

**05** diver **06** gentoo, korora **07** pinguin **08** macaroni **10** rockhopper, Spheniscus **11** king penguin **12** fairy penguin **13** little penguin **14** emperor penguin

**peninsula**

**03** Pen **04** cape, doab, mull **05** point **06** tongue **10** chersonese

*Peninsulas include:*

**04** Ards, Cape, Eyre, Gyda, Huon, Kola
**05** Gaspé, Gower, Italy, Lleyn, Malay, Otago, Qatar, Sinai
**06** Alaska, Avalon, Azuero, Balkan, Carnac, Crimea, Iberia, Istria, Jaffna, Korean, Recife, Seward, Taymyr, Wirral
**07** Alaskan, Arabian, Cape Cod, Chukchi, Florida, Furness, Iberian, Jiulong, Jutland, Kintyre, Kowloon, Olympic, Yucatán
**08** Apsheron, Cape York, Cotentin, Musandam, Pinellas, Sorrento, Yorktown
**09** Cape Verde, Gallipoli, Kamchatka, Paraguana, Peary Land
**10** Arnhem Land, Graham Land, Isle of Dogs, Nova Scotia
**11** Peloponnese
**12** Scandinavian
**14** Baja California, Isle of Portland
**15** Rinns of Galloway

*See also* **cape**

**penitence**

**05** shame **06** regret, sorrow **07** remorse **10** contrition, repentance, ruefulness **11** compunction **12** self-reproach

**penitent**

**05** sorry **06** humble, rueful **07** ashamed, mourner **08** contrite **09** regretful, repentant, sorrowful **10** apologetic, remorseful, shamefaced

**pen-name**

**06** anonym **07** allonym **09** false name, pseudonym, stage-name **10** nom de plume **11** assumed name, nom de guerre

**pennant**

**04** flag, jack **06** banner, burgee, ensign, guidon, pennon **07** colours, pendant, pendent **08** banderol, gonfalon, standard, streamer

**penniless**

**04** bust, poor **05** broke, skint, stony **06** ruined **07** boracic **08** bankrupt, dirt-poor, indigent **09** destitute **10** cleaned out, down and out, on the rocks, stone-broke, stony-broke **11** impecunious **12** impoverished, on your uppers **14** on the breadline, on your beam-ends **15** poverty-stricken, strapped for cash

**Pennsylvania**

**02** PA **04** Penn

**penny**

**01** d, p **03** win **04** cent, wing, winn **08** denarius, sterling

**penny-pincher**

**05** miser **06** meanie **07** niggard, Scrooge **09** skinflint **10** cheapskate **11** cheeseparer **12** money-grubber

**penny-pinching**

**04** mean **05** close, mingy, tight **06** frugal, stingy **07** miserly **09** niggardly, scrimping **10** ungenerous **11** tight-fisted **12** cheeseparing, parsimonious

**pension**

**04** SIPP **05** board **06** corody, income **07** annuity, benefit, corrody, support, welfare **09** allowance **11** deferred pay **12** state pension **13** old-age pension **14** company pension, superannuation **15** personal pension

**pensioner**

**03** OAP **07** boarder **09** dependant **12** out-pensioner **13** retired person, senior citizen **15** gentleman-at-arms, old-age pensioner

**pensive**

**05** sober **06** dreamy, musing, solemn **07** serious, wistful **08** absorbed, thinking **09** pondering **10** cogitative, meditative, melancholy, reflective, ruminative, thoughtful **11** preoccupied **12** absent-minded **13** contemplative, lackadaisical

**pensively**

**08** dreamily **09** seriously, wistfully **12** meditatively, thoughtfully **14** absent-mindedly **15** contemplatively

**Pentateuch**

**05** Torah

**penthouse**

**03** cat **04** pent

**pent-up**

**06** curbed, held in **07** bridled, stifled **09** bottled-up, inhibited, repressed **10** restrained, suppressed

**penurious**

**04** bust, mean, poor **05** close, mingy, tight **06** hard up, scanty, stingy **07** lacking, miserly **08** beggarly, grudging, indigent **09** destitute, flat broke, niggardly, penniless **10** inadequate, ungenerous **11** close-fisted, close-handed, impecunious, tight-fisted **12** cheeseparing, impoverished, on your uppers, parsimonious **14** on your beam-ends **15** poverty-stricken

**penury**

**04** lack, need, want **06** dearth **07** beggary, poverty, straits **09** indigence, mendicity, pauperism **10** deficiency, insolvency **11** destitution **14** impoverishment

**people**

**03** men, mob **04** clan, folk, gens, land, race **05** folks, laity, ngati, plebs, tribe, tuath **06** family, hordes, humans, masses, nation, occupy, proles, public, rabble, settle, voters **07** inhabit, mankind, mortals, parents, persons, punters, society **08** citizens, colonize, humanity, populace, populate, riff-raff, servants, subjects **09** community, employees, followers, hoi polloi, humankind, relations, relatives, retainers **10** attendants, electorate, kith and kin, population **11** ethnic group, human beings, individuals, inhabitants, rank and file **12** congregation, the human race **13** general public, great unwashed

*Peoples include:*

**03** Han, Ibo, Jat, Kru, Mam, Mon, San, Tiv, Twi
**04** Ainu, Cham, Efik, Goth, Hutu, Igbo, Jute, Kroo, Lett, Moor, Motu, Nair, Nupe, Roma, Saba, Shan, Sulu, Susu, Tshi, Zulu
**05** Bajau, Bantu, Hausa, Iceni, Inuit, Karen, Khmer, Maori, Masai, Nayar, Nguni, Oriya, Saxon, Swazi, Taino, Tamil, Temne, Tonga, Tutsi, Vedda, Wolof, Yakut, Yupik
**06** Angles, Aymara, Griqua, Gurkha, Herero, Innuit, Kabyle, Kalmyk, Kikuyu, Manchu, Nyanja, Ostiak, Ostyak, Sherpa, Tswana, Tungus, Yoruba, Zyrian
**07** Barotse, Basotho, Calmuck, Cossack, Goorkha, Hittite, Kalmuck, Manchoo, Maratha, Pashtun, Punjabi, Quechua, Quichua, Samoyed, Swahili, Tagálog, Walloon
**08** Khoikhoi, Mahratta, Polabian, Yanomami
**09** Himyarite, Ostrogoth, Ruthenian, Sinhalese, Tocharian, Tokharian

**pep**

**02** go **03** zip **04** life, zing **05** oomph, verve **06** energy, ginger, spirit, vigour **07** pizzazz, sparkle **08** dynamism, vitality **10** ebullience, exuberance, get-up-and-go, liveliness **11** high spirits **13** effervescence

• **pep up** **06** excite **07** animate,

## pepper

improve, inspire, liven up, quicken
**08** energize, vitalize **09** stimulate
**10** exhilarate, invigorate

## pepper

**03** dot **04** bomb, pelt, stud **05** blitz,
Piper, strew **06** assail, attack, shower
**07** bombard, scatter, spatter **08** sprinkle
**09** bespatter

*Pepper and peppercorns include:*

**03** ava, red
**04** bird, kava, pink
**05** black, chile, chili, green, sweet, white
**06** cherry, chilli, yellow
**07** cayenne, Jamaica, paprika, pimento
**08** allspice, capsicum, habañero, jalapeño, pimiento, piquillo
**12** Scotch bonnet

## peppermint

**06** humbug **07** pan drop **08** bull's-eye

## peppery

**03** hot **05** fiery, sharp, spicy, testy
**06** biting, grumpy, touchy **07** caustic,
piquant, pungent, waspish **08** choleric,
incisive, seasoned, snappish, stinging
**09** irascible, irritable, sarcastic,
trenchant **10** astringent **11** hot-
tempered **13** quick-tempered

## peppy

**04** spry **05** agile, alert, alive, brisk,
quick **06** active, lively, nimble
**07** dynamic **08** animated, spirited,
vigorous **09** energetic, sprightly,
vivacious **12** enthusiastic, high-spirited

## per

**01** a **02** by, pr **07** through

## perceive

**03** see **04** espy, feel, hear, know, note,
spot, twig, view, wind **05** grasp, learn,
sense, smell, taste **06** behold, deduce,
detect, gather, notice, remark, survey
**07** believe, discern, glimpse, make out,
observe, realize, suppose **08** conclude,
discover, subitize **09** apprehend, be
aware of, get wind of, recognize,
undertake **10** appreciate, comprehend,
understand **11** distinguish **12** catch
sight of **13** be cognizant of

## perceptible

**05** clear, plain **06** patent **07** evident,
obvious, tactile, visible **08** apparent,
distinct, manifest, palpable, sensible,
tangible **10** detectable, noticeable,
observable **11** appreciable,
conspicuous, discernible, perceivable
**15** distinguishable

## perception

**04** idea, view **05** grasp, sense, taste
**06** vision **07** feeling, insight, percept
**09** awareness, cognition, knowledge
**10** cognizance, conception,
experience, impression
**11** discernment, observation,
recognition, sensitivity
**12** appreciation, apprehension
**13** consciousness, light of nature,
understanding **14** discrimination,
interpretation, responsiveness
• **fine perception** **04** tact

## perceptive

**04** deep, keen **05** acute, alert, aware,
quick, sharp **06** astute, shrewd
**08** delicate **09** observant, sensitive,
sharp-eyed **10** discerning, insightful,
percipient, responsive **11** penetrating,
quick-witted **12** perspicacious
understanding **14** discriminating

## perceptively

**06** keenly **07** sharply **08** astutely
**11** observantly, sensitively
**12** insightfully **15** perspicaciously

## perch

**03** bar, lug, rod, sit **04** bass, land, perk,
pole, rest, rood, ruff **05** basse, gaper,
Perca, roost, ruffe **06** alight, anabas,
comber, darter, fogash, sander, sauger,
settle, zander, zingel **07** balance,
kahawai, walleye **09** blackfish,
overperch, stone bass, wreckfish
**12** walleyed pike

## perchance

**05** maybe **07** percase, perhaps
**08** feasibly, possibly **11** conceivably

## percipience

**07** insight **08** sagacity **09** acuteness,
alertness, awareness, intuition,
judgement **10** astuteness, perception
**11** discernment, penetration, sensitivity
**12** perspicacity **13** understanding

## percipient

**05** alert, alive, aware, sharp **06** astute
**07** knowing **09** judicious, observant,
wide-awake **10** discerning, perceptive
**11** intelligent, penetrating, quick-
witted **13** perspicacious
**14** discriminating

## percolate

**03** sop **04** drip, leak, ooze, perk, seep,
sift **05** drain, leach, sieve **06** filter, strain
**07** pervade **08** filtrate, permeate
**09** penetrate **11** pass through **13** spread
through **14** trickle through

## perdition

**04** doom, hell, loss, ruin **08** downfall,
hellfire **09** confusion, damnation,
ruination **11** destruction
**12** annihilation, condemnation

## peregrination

**04** tour, trek, trip **06** roving, travel,
voyage **07** journey, odyssey, roaming
**08** trekking **09** excursion, wandering,
wayfaring **10** expedition, pilgrimage,
travelling **11** exploration
**13** globetrotting

## peremptory

**04** curt **05** bossy, final, utter **06** abrupt,
lordly **07** summary **08** absolute,
dogmatic **09** arbitrary, assertive,
imperious **10** autocratic, commanding,
high-handed, imperative, tyrannical
**11** dictatorial, domineering, irrefutable,
overbearing **13** authoritative

## perennial

**07** abiding, endless, eternal, lasting,
undying **08** constant, enduring,
immortal, unending **09** ceaseless,
continual, incessant, permanent,
perpetual, unceasing, unfailing
**10** persistent, unchanging

**11** everlasting, never-ending
**12** imperishable **13** uninterrupted

## perfect

**04** full, mint, perf, pure, true **05** exact,
ideal, model, prize, right, sheer, total,
utter **06** better, entire, expert, finish,
fulfil, mature, polish, refine, spot on,
superb, triple **07** certain, correct,
improve, precise, sinless, skilful
**08** absolute, accurate, complete,
copybook, faithful, finished, flawless,
peerless, spotless, textbook, thorough,
ultimate, unmarred **09** blameless,
completed, convinced, downright,
elaborate, excellent, exemplary,
faultless, matchless, out-and-out,
wonderful **10** consummate,
immaculate, impeccable, just the job,
to the nines **11** experienced,
superlative, unblemished
**12** accomplished, incomparable

## perfection

**04** acme, best **05** bloom, crown, ideal,
model, prime **06** flower **07** paragon
**08** maturity, pinnacle, ripeness,
ultimate **09** polishing **10** betterment,
completion, excellence, refinement
**11** improvement, ne plus ultra, point-
device, point-devise, realization,
roundedness, superiority
**12** consummation, flawlessness
**13** faultlessness, impeccability, one in
a million **14** immaculateness, the cat's
pyjamas **15** the cat's whiskers

## perfectionism

**06** purism **08** idealism, pedantry
**09** formalism **10** Utopianism

## perfectionist

**06** pedant, purist **08** idealist, stickler
**09** formalist, Free-lover **12** precisionist

## perfectly

**04** very **05** fully, quite **06** à point,
wholly **07** down pat, exactly, ideally,
totally, utterly **08** entirely, superbly
**09** correctly **10** absolutely, altogether,
completely, flawlessly, impeccably,
like a charm, thoroughly **11** faultlessly,
wonderfully **12** consummately,
immaculately, to perfection **14** without
blemish

## perfidious

**05** false, Punic **07** corrupt **08** disloyal,
two-faced **09** deceitful, dishonest,
faithless **10** traitorous, treasonous,
unfaithful **11** double-faced,
duplicitous, treacherous **13** double-
dealing, Machiavellian, untrustworthy

## perfidy

**06** deceit **07** falsity, treason **08** betrayal
**09** duplicity, treachery **10** disloyalty,
infidelity **13** double-dealing,
faithlessness **14** perfidiousness,
traitorousness

## perforate

**04** bore, gore, hole, stab, tear **05** burst,
drill, prick, punch, spike, split
**06** pierce **07** rupture **08** puncture,
trephine **09** penetrate **11** make holes in

## perforated

**05** bored, holed **06** porous **07** drilled,
ethmoid, pierced, punched

**perforation**

09 fenestral, punctured 10 cribriform, fenestrate, fenestrial, foraminous 11 fenestrated

**perforation**
04 bore, hole 05 prick 06 pierce 07 foramen 08 fenestra, puncture 10 dotted line 12 fenestration

**perforce**
10 inevitably, willy-nilly 11 necessarily, of necessity, unavoidably

**perform**
◇ anagram indicator 02 do, go 03 act, cut, run 04 make, play, sing, take, work 05 dance, enact, put on, stage, throw 06 behave, effect, fulfil, recite, render 07 achieve, conduct, execute, operate, portray, present, produce, pull off, satisfy 08 appear as, atchieve, bring off, carry out, complete, despatch, dispatch, function, make good, transact 09 discharge, implement, represent 10 accomplish, bring about 12 give effect to

**performance**
03 act 04 deed, duet, play, show, solo, spot, trio 05 doing, going, house 06 acting, action, acture, ballet, try-out 07 account, benefit, concert, conduct, recital, running, showing, working 08 hierurgy, première, set piece 09 behaviour, discharge, effecting, execution, happening, operation, portrayal, prolusion, rendering, rendition 10 appearance, completion, conducting, fulfilling, fulfilment, last hurrah, peroration, production 11 achievement, carrying-out, functioning, presentment, tour de force 12 presentation 14 accomplishment, implementation, interpretation, representation

**performer**
04 doer, hand, moke, star, turn 05 actor, clown, comic 06 artist, author, dancer, mummer, player, singer 07 actress, artiste, old hand, ripieno, trouper 08 achiever, comedian, executor, Fancy Dan, film star, musician, operator, star turn, Thespian, topliner 09 ecdysiast, executant 10 rope-walker 11 entertainer 12 improvisator, vaudevillean, vaudevillian 15 jerry-come-tumble

**performers**
04 cast

**perfume**
04 balm, musk, otto, sent 05 aroma, attar, odour, ottar, scent, smell 06 chypre 07 bouquet, cologne, essence, incense 08 fumigate, opoponax 09 aromatize, fragrance, redolence, sweetness 10 frangipane, frangipani, heliotrope, Jockey Club 11 millefleurs, toilet water 12 eau-de-cologne 13 eau-de-toilette, lavender water

**perfunctorily**
07 quickly 09 cursorily, hurriedly

10 carelessly 13 inattentively, superficially

**perfunctory**
05 brief, quick 06 wooden 07 cursory, hurried, offhand, routine 08 careless, heedless, slipshod, slovenly 09 automatic, desultory, negligent 10 mechanical 11 inattentive, indifferent, superficial

**perhaps**
◇ anagram indicator 03 say 05 haply, maybe 06 ablins, belike, happen, mayhap 07 aiblins, could be, happily, percase, yibbles 08 feasibly, possibly 09 perchance 11 conceivably 12 peradventure, you never know

**peril**
04 risk 06 danger, hazard, menace, threat 07 apperil 08 apperill, distress, jeopardy 10 insecurity 11 uncertainty 12 endangerment

**perilous**
04 dire 05 dicey, dodgy, hairy, risky 06 chancy, unsafe, unsure 07 exposed, parlous, perlous 08 high-risk, insecure, menacing 09 dangerous, hazardous 10 precarious, vulnerable 11 threatening

**perimeter**
04 edge 05 limit 06 border, bounds, fringe, limits, margin 07 circuit 08 boundary, confines, frontier 09 periphery 11 outer limits 13 circumference

**period**
03 age, end, eon, era, per 04 aeon, date, span, spin, stop, term, time, turn 05 class, cycle, epoch, phase, point, shift, space, spell, stage, stint, while, years 06 finish, lesson, menses, season 07 lecture, seminar, session, stretch 08 duration, full stop, interval, semester, the curse, tutorial 09 full point, monthlies 10 conclusion, end of story, generation 11 instruction 12 menstruation 13 menstrual flow 14 menstrual cycle, time of the month *See also* **geology; historical; time**

**periodic**
05 round 06 cyclic 07 regular 08 cyclical, repeated, seasonal, sporadic 09 recurrent, recurring 10 infrequent, occasional, periodical 12 intermittent, once in a while

**periodical**
03 mag 05 organ 06 review, weekly 07 etesian, journal, monthly, regular 08 bi-weekly, bulletin, magazine 09 pictorial, quarterly, thunderer, tri-weekly 11 illustrated, publication, semi-monthly 12 trade journal *See also* **newspaper**

**periodically**
07 at times 08 off and on, on and off 09 sometimes 10 now and then, on occasion 11 at intervals, irregularly, now and again 12 every so often, infrequently, occasionally, once in a while, sporadically 14 from time to time, intermittently 15 every now and then

**peripatetic**
06 mobile, roving 07 migrant, nomadic, roaming, vagrant 08 ambulant, vagabond 09 itinerant, migratory, traveling, wandering 10 ambulatory, journeying, pedestrian, travelling 12 Aristotelian

**peripheral**
05 add-on, input, minor, outer 06 lesser, output 07 storage, surface 08 computer, marginal, outlying 09 ancillary, auxiliary, disk drive, outermost, secondary, sidelined 10 additional, borderline, incidental, irrelevant, subsidiary, tangential 11 superficial, surrounding, unimportant, unnecessary 14 beside the point, graphics tablet

**periphery**
03 hem, rim 04 brim, edge 05 ambit, brink, skirt, verge 06 border, fringe, margin 07 circuit 08 boundary 09 outskirts, perimeter 12 outer regions 13 circumference

**periphrastic**
07 oblique 08 indirect, rambling, tortuous 09 wandering 10 circuitous, discursive, roundabout 12 long-drawn-out 14 circumlocutory

**perish**
02 go 03 die, rot 04 cark, exit, fail, fall, pass, ruin, tine, tyne, vade 05 choke, croak, decay, drown, go off, quell, swelt 06 depart, expire, famish, go bung, go west, pass on, peg out, pip out, pop off, starve, sterve, vanish 07 crumble, decease, destroy, die away, fall off, forfair, kick off, kiss off, snuff it, succumb 08 collapse, flatline, pass away, spark out 09 decompose, disappear, go belly up, have had it 10 hop the twig 11 bite the dust, come to an end 12 disintegrate, lose your life, pop your clogs, slip the cable 13 close your eyes, kick the bucket, meet your maker, push up daisies 14 depart this life, give up the ghost, turn up your toes 15 breathe your last, cash in your chips

**perishable**
10 short-lived 12 decomposable, destructible 13 biodegradable

**periwinkle**
05 vinca 06 winkle 08 Apocynum, dog-whelk 11 pennywinkle 12 strophanthus

**perjure**
• **perjure yourself** 03 lie 12 lie under oath 13 commit perjury

**perjury**
09 false oath, mendacity 11 crimen falsi, forswearing 12 false witness, hard swearing, oath-breaking 13 false evidence, false swearing, falsification 14 false statement, false testimony, lying under oath

**perk**
03 tip 04 plus 05 bonus, brisk, extra, perch 07 benefit, freebie 08 dividend, gratuity 09 advantage, baksheesh, percolate 10 percolator, perquisite 13 fringe benefit 15 golden handshake

**perky**

• **perk up** 05 pep up, rally 06 buck up, cock up, look up, revive 07 cheer up, improve, liven up, recover 08 brighten 09 take heart 10 brighten up, make lively, revitalize 12 become lively

**perky**
03 gay 04 pert 05 cocky, peppy, sunny 06 bouncy, bright, bubbly, cheery, gallus, jaunty, lively 07 buoyant, gallows 08 animated, cheerful, spirited 09 ebullient, sprightly, vivacious 12 effervescent

**permanence**
09 constancy, endurance, fixedness, stability 10 durability, perpetuity 11 persistence 13 steadfastness 15 imperishability

**permanent**
04 firm 05 fixed, pakka, pucka, pukka, solid 06 stable 07 abiding, durable, eternal, lasting, regular, stative 08 constant, enduring, lifelong, standing, unfading 09 immutable, indelible, perennial, perpetual, steadfast 10 invariable, unchanging 11 established, everlasting, long-lasting 12 imperishable, unchangeable 14 indestructible

**permanently**
06 always 07 for ever, for good 08 ever more, for keeps 09 endlessly, eternally, indelibly 10 constantly, for all time, unendingly 11 ceaselessly, continually, incessantly, perpetually, unceasingly 12 in perpetuity, till doomsday 13 everlastingly, for good and all, once and for all, unremittingly 14 for ever and ever 15 till kingdom come

**permeable**
06 porous, spongy 08 passable, pervious 09 absorbent, poromeric 10 absorptive, penetrable

**permeate**
04 fill 05 imbue 06 leaven 07 diffuse, pervade, suffuse 08 saturate 09 penetrate, percolate 10 impregnate, infiltrate 11 impenetrate, pass through, seep through, soak through, transpierce 13 filter through, spread through

**permissible**
02 OK 05 legal, legit 06 kosher, lawful, proper, venial 07 allowed 08 all right 09 allowable, permitted, tolerable 10 acceptable, admissible, authorized, legitimate, sanctioned

**permission**
03 out 04 loan, pass 05 congé, exeat, leave, power 06 access, assent, congee, permit, placet, square 07 consent, freedom, go-ahead, liberty, licence, license, mandate, warrant 08 approval, pratique, sanction, thumbs-up, wayleave 09 admission, agreement, allowance, authority, clearance 10 green light, imprimatur 11 approbation, bill of sight, congé d'élire, permittance

12 dispensation 13 authorization 14 leave of absence, permis de séjour

**permissive**
03 lax 04 free 07 lenient, liberal 08 optional, tolerant 09 easy-going, indulgent, permitted 10 forbearing 11 broad-minded 13 overindulgent 14 latitudinarian

**permit**
03 let 04 give, pass, visa 05 admit, agree, allow, grant, smoke 06 carnet, docket, enable, suffer, ticket 07 consent, docquet, empower, indulge, licence, license, placard, warrant 08 intromit, passport, sanction, tolerate 09 authorize, green card 10 greenlight, permission 11 safe-conduct 12 give the nod to 13 authorization, laissez-passer 14 permis de séjour

• **it is not permitted** 02 nl

**permutation**
04 perm 05 shift 06 barter, change 09 obversion, variation 10 alteration 11 commutation 13 configuration, transmutation, transposition 14 transformation

**pernicious**
03 bad 04 evil 05 fatal, ready, swift, toxic 06 deadly, prompt, wicked 07 baneful, harmful, hurtful, noisome, noxious, ruinous 08 damaging, damnable, venomous 09 dangerous, injurious, malicious, malignant, offensive, pestilent, poisonous, unhealthy 10 maleficent, malevolent 11 deleterious, destructive, detrimental, unwholesome

**pernickety**
04 fine, nice 05 fussy, picky 06 choosy, fiddly, tricky 07 careful, carping, finical, finicky 08 detailed, exacting 10 fastidious, nit-picking, particular 11 over-precise, painstaking, persnickety, punctilious 13 hair-splitting 14 over-particular

**peroration**
04 talk 06 korero, speech 07 address, lecture, oration, summary 08 diatribe, pirlicue, purlicue 09 recapping, summing-up 10 conclusion 11 declamation, reiteration 14 closing remarks, recapitulation

**perpendicular**
04 sine 05 atrip, erect, plumb, right, sheer, steep 06 abrupt, normal, offset 07 apothem, upright 08 cathetus, straight, vertical 09 downright, erectness 10 anticlinal 11 precipitous, verticality 13 at right angles

**perpetrate**
02 do 05 wreak 06 commit, effect 07 execute, inflict, perform 08 carry out 10 accomplish, effectuate 12 be to blame for

**perpetration**
05 doing 09 committal, execution 10 commitment 11 achievement, carrying-out, performance 14 accomplishment, implementation

**perpetrator**
04 doer, perp 05 agent 08 executor, offender 09 committer, executant

**perpetual**
07 abiding, endless, eternal, lasting, undying 08 constant, enduring, infinite, repeated, unbroken, unending 09 ceaseless, continual, incessant, perennial, permanent, recurrent, unceasing, unfailing, unvarying 10 continuous, persistent, persisting, unchanging 11 everlasting, never-ending, unremitting 12 interminable, intermittent 13 uninterrupted

**perpetually**
09 endlessly, eternally 10 constantly 11 ceaselessly, continually, incessantly, permanently, unceasingly 12 interminably, persistently 13 unremittingly

**perpetuate**
06 keep up 07 sustain 08 continue, maintain, preserve 09 keep alive, keep going 10 eternalize 11 commemorate, immortalize, memorialize

**perpetuation**
09 extension 10 sustaining 11 lengthening, maintenance, protraction 12 continuation, keeping alive, preservation, prolongation 13 commemoration

**perpetuity**
• **in perpetuity** 06 always 07 for ever 08 ever more 09 endlessly, eternally 10 for all time 11 perpetually 14 for ever and ever

**perplex**
◇ anagram indicator 04 pose 05 beset, stump, throw 06 baffle, bother, feague, fickle, gravel, hobble, muddle, pother, pudder, puzzle, tangle, tickle 07 bumbaze, confuse, flummox, mystify, nonplus 08 bewilder, confound, entangle, throw off 09 bamboozle, dumbfound, embarrass, embrangle, imbrangle 10 complicate, difficulty, distrouble, interweave

**perplexed**
05 spiny 07 at a loss, baffled, fuddled, muddled, puzzled, stumped, worried 08 confused 09 flummoxed, mystified, quizzical 10 bamboozled, bewildered, confounded, distraught, nonplussed, tosticated 11 embarrassed 12 disconcerted

**perplexing**
04 hard 05 weird 06 knotty, taxing, thorny 07 amazing, complex, strange 08 baffling, involved, puzzling 09 confusing, difficult, enigmatic, intricate 10 mysterious, mystifying 11 bewildering, complicated, paradoxical 12 inexplicable, labyrinthine

**perplexity**
05 doubt, tweak, worry 06 bother, enigma, puzzle, taking, tangle 07 dilemma, meander, mystery, nonplus, paradox 09 confusion, intricacy, labyrinth, obscurity

**10** bafflement, complexity, difficulty, fickleness, puzzlement **11** distraction, disturbance, involvement, obfuscation, tostication **12** bewilderment, complication, entanglement **13** embarrassment, mystification **15** incomprehension

**perquisite**
**03** tip **04** lock, perk, plus, vail **05** bonus, extra, vales **07** apanage, benefit, freebie **08** appanage, dividend, gratuity **09** advantage, baksheesh, royal fish **10** emoluments, kitchen-fee **13** fringe benefit

**persecute**
**04** bait, hunt **05** abuse, annoy, hound, worry **06** badger, bother, harass, hassle, martyr, molest, pester, pursue **07** afflict, crucify, oppress, torment, torture **08** distress, hunt down, ill-treat, maltreat, mistreat **09** tyrannize, victimize

**persecution**
**05** abuse **07** torture, tyranny **09** martyrdom **10** dragonnade, harassment, oppression, punishment **11** crucifixion, molestation, subjugation, suppression **12** ill-treatment, maltreatment, mistreatment **13** victimization **14** discrimination

**Persephone**
**10** Proserpina

**perseverance**
**07** purpose, resolve, stamina **08** tenacity **09** assiduity, constancy, diligence, endurance **10** commitment, dedication, doggedness, resolution **11** application, persistence, persistency, pertinacity **12** stickability **13** determination, intransigence, steadfastness **14** purposefulness

**persevere**
**04** go on **05** truck **06** bash on, hang on, hold on, remain **07** carry on, persist, stick in **08** continue, plug away **09** keep going, prosecute, soldier on, stand fast, stand firm, stick at it **10** be resolute, hammer away, struggle on **11** hang in there **12** be determined, be persistent, mean business **15** stick to your guns

**Persian**
**04** Babi, Mede **05** Babee, Farsi

**persist**
**04** go on, hold, last **05** abide **06** endure, hang in, hang on, hold on, insist, keep on, linger, remain **07** carry on **08** continue, keep at it, plug away **09** hang about, keep going, persevere, soldier on, stand fast, stand firm, stick at it **10** be resolute, hang around **11** hang in there **12** be determined, be persistent

**persistence**
**04** grit **07** stamina **08** sedulity, tenacity **09** assiduity, constancy, diligence, endurance, obstinacy **10** doggedness, resolution **11** pertinacity **12** continuation, perseverance, stickability, tirelessness

**13** assiduousness, determination, steadfastness

**persistent**
**05** fixed **06** dogged, steady, urgent **07** endless, lasting, zealous **08** constant, diligent, enduring, obdurate, repeated, resolute, stubborn, tireless, unabated **09** assiduous, ceaseless, continual, incessant, obstinate, perpetual, steadfast, tenacious, unceasing **10** continuous, determined, persisting, purposeful, relentless, unflagging **11** importunate, intractable, never-ending, persevering, unrelenting, unremitting **12** interminable, pertinacious, stick-to-it-ive **13** indefatigable

**persistently**
**10** constantly, diligently, resolutely, stubbornly, tirelessly **11** assiduously, ceaselessly, continually, incessantly, obstinately, tenaciously, unceasingly **12** continuously, interminably, relentlessly

**person**
**03** bod, chi, man, per **04** body, chai, chal, cove, fish, pers, soul, type **05** being, human, woman **06** geezer, mortal **07** someone **08** somebody **09** character **10** human being, individual
• **good person** **01** S **02** St **04** sant **05** Saint
• **individual person** **03** one
• **in person** **06** bodily, myself **08** actually **10** face to face, in the flesh, personally **13** as large as life

**persona**
**04** face, mask, part, role **05** front, image **06** façade **09** character **10** public face **11** personality

**personable**
**04** nice, warm **07** affable, amiable, winning **08** charming, handsome, likeable, outgoing, pleasant, pleasing **09** agreeable **10** attractive **11** good-looking, presentable

**personage**
**03** VIP **04** name **05** celeb **06** bigwig, figure, worthy **07** big shot, notable **08** big noise, identity, luminary, somebody **09** big cheese, celebrity, dignitary, headliner **11** personality **12** public figure

**personal**
**03** gut, own **04** live, pers, rude **05** privy **06** bodily, secret, unique **07** abusive, hurtful, private, special **08** critical, in person, intimate, peculiar, wounding **09** exclusive, insulting, offensive, upsetting **10** derogatory, individual, in the flesh, particular, subjective **11** distinctive **12** confidential **13** disrespectful, idiosyncratic **14** characteristic

**personality**
**03** VIP **04** mind, self, star **05** charm **06** figure, make-up, nature, person, psyche, temper, traits, worthy **07** notable **08** charisma, identity, selfhood, selfness **09** celebrity,

character, dignitary, magnetism, personage **10** the real you **11** beastlyhead, disposition, temperament **12** public figure **13** individuality

**personalize**
**03** fit **04** suit **05** adapt, alter **06** adjust, modify, tailor **07** convert **09** customize, personify, transform

**personally**
**05** alone **06** I think, solely **08** as I see it, I believe, in my book, in my view, in person, uniquely **09** as a slight, ourselves, privately, specially **10** for my money, if you ask me **11** exclusively, in my opinion, insultingly, offensively **12** individually, particularly, subjectively, the way I see it **13** distinctively, independently **14** confidentially

**personification**
**05** image **07** epitome, essence **08** likeness **09** portrayal, semblance **10** embodiment, recreation **11** delineation, incarnation **12** quintessence **13** manifestation **14** representation

**personify**
**06** embody, imbody, mirror, typify **09** epitomize, exemplify, incarnate, personize, represent, symbolize **11** hypostatize, impersonate, personalize

**personnel**
**04** crew **05** staff **06** people **07** members, service, workers **08** liveware, manpower **09** employees, workforce **11** labour force **14** human resources

**perspective**
**04** take, view **05** angle, scene, slant, vista **06** aspect, optics **07** balance, optical, outlook **08** attitude, peepshow, prospect, relation **09** viewpoint **10** inspection, proportion, standpoint **11** equilibrium, frame of mind, point of view **12** vantage point

**perspicacious**
**04** keen **05** alert, aware, quick, sharp **06** astute, shrewd **09** judicious, observant, sagacious, sensitive, sharp-eyed **10** discerning, perceptive, percipient, responsive **11** penetrating, quick-witted **13** understanding **14** discriminating

**perspicacity**
**03** wit **06** acumen, brains **07** insight **08** keenness, sagacity **09** acuteness, sharpness **10** astuteness, cleverness, shrewdness **11** discernment, penetration, percipience, perspicuity **13** sagaciousness **14** discrimination, perceptiveness

**perspicuity**
**07** clarity **08** lucidity **09** clearness, limpidity, plainness, precision **10** limpidness **12** distinctness, explicitness, transparency **13** penetrability **15** intelligibility

**perspicuous**
**05** clear, lucid, plain **06** limpid **07** obvious **08** apparent, distinct,

explicit, manifest **11** self-evident, transparent, unambiguous **12** crystal-clear, intelligible **14** comprehensible, understandable **15** straightforward

## perspiration
**04** foam **05** sudor, suint, sweat **07** wetness **08** hidrosis, moisture **09** exudation, secretion **11** diaphoresis

## perspire
**04** drip **05** exude, sweat **06** exhale, sudate **07** secrete, swelter

## persuadable
**07** pliable **08** amenable, flexible **09** agreeable, compliant, malleable, receptive **10** susceptive **11** acquiescent, persuasible **14** impressionable

## persuade
**03** con, win **04** coax, lure, move, snow, sway, urge **05** argue, lobby, moody, plead, tempt **06** cajole, coerce, incite, induce, lead on, lean on, nobble, prompt **07** convert, prevail, satisfy, swing it, wheedle, win over **08** convince, fast-talk, get round, inveigle, lamb down, perswade, soft-soap, talk into, talk over **09** argue into, influence, sweet-talk **10** bring round **11** prevail upon, pull strings **13** bring yourself **14** put the screws on

## persuasion
**04** camp, kind, pull, sect, side, sway, view **05** clout, creed, faith, party, power **06** belief, come-on, school, urging **07** coaxing, faction, opinion, suasion **08** cajolery, coercion, pressure, soft sell **09** influence, prompting, sweet talk, viewpoint, wheedling **10** conversion, conviction, enticement, incitement, inducement, philosophy, prevailing **11** affiliation, arm-twisting, point of view, talking into, winning over **12** denomination, sweet-talking **15** school of thought

## persuasive
**05** pushy, slick, sound, valid **06** cogent, moving, potent **07** telling, weighty, winning **08** eloquent, forceful, touching **09** effective, effectual, plausible **10** compelling, convincing **11** influential **12** high-pressure, honey-tongued, smooth-spoken **13** smooth-talking, smooth-tongued

## persuasively
**08** cogently **09** plausibly **10** forcefully, powerfully **11** effectively, effectually **12** compellingly, convincingly **13** influentially

## pert
**03** gay **04** bold, coxy, flip, open **05** brash, brisk, cocky, fresh, perky, sassy, saucy, smart, tossy **06** adroit, cheeky, cocksy, daring, jaunty, lively **07** forward **08** flippant, impudent, insolent, spirited **09** sprightly **11** flourishing, impertinent, unconcealed **12** presumptuous **13** objectionable

## pertain
**04** long **05** apply, befit, refer **06** bear on, belong, regard, relate **07** concern

**08** be part of **09** appertain, come under **10** be relevant **13** be appropriate **14** have a bearing on

## pertinacious
**05** stiff **06** dogged, mulish, wilful **08** obdurate, perverse, resolute, stubborn **09** obstinate, tenacious **10** determined, headstrong, inflexible, persistent, purposeful, relentless, self-willed, unyielding **11** intractable, persevering **12** strong-willed **13** inquisitorial **14** uncompromising

## pertinent
**03** apt **05** ad rem **07** apropos, fitting, germane, related **08** apposite, material, relating, relevant, suitable **10** applicable, to the point **11** appropriate

## pertness
**04** face, sass **05** brass, cheek **08** audacity, boldness, chutzpah, rudeness **09** brashness, cockiness, freshness, impudence, insolence, sassiness, sauciness **10** brazenness, cheekiness, effrontery **11** forwardness, presumption **12** impertinence

## perturb
◇ *anagram indicator* **03** vex **04** faze **05** alarm, feese, feeze, phase, phese, upset, worry **06** aerate, bother, didder, dither, pheese, pheeze, rattle, ruffle **07** agitate, confuse, disturb, fluster, trouble **08** disquiet, unsettle **10** discompose, disconcert **11** make anxious **12** put the wind up

## perturbation
**04** faze, fear, flap **05** alarm, panic, scare, shock, worry **06** didder, dismay, dither, fright, horror, terror **07** anxiety **08** disquiet, distress **10** uneasiness **11** nervousness, trepidation **12** apprehension, irregularity **13** consternation

## perturbed
◇ *anagram indicator* **05** upset **06** shaken, uneasy **07** alarmed, anxious, fearful, nervous, worried **08** agitated, flurried, harassed, restless, troubled **09** disturbed, flustered, unsettled **11** discomposed **12** disconcerted **13** uncomfortable

## Peru
**02** PE **03** PER

## perusal
**04** look, read, skim **05** check, sight, study **06** browse, glance **07** reading **08** scrutiny **10** inspection, run-through **11** examination

## peruse
**04** read, scan, skim **05** check, study **06** browse, revise **07** examine, inspect **08** pore over **10** run through, scrutinize **11** leaf through, look through **13** glance through

## pervade
**04** fill **05** imbue **06** affect, charge, infuse **07** diffuse, suffuse **08** permeate, saturate **09** penetrate, percolate **10** impregnate, infiltrate **11** pass

through **13** spread through **14** interpenetrate

## pervasive
**04** rife **06** common **07** diffuse, general **08** immanent **09** extensive, prevalent, universal **10** ubiquitous, widespread **11** inescapable, omnipresent

## perverse
◇ *anagram indicator* **03** wry **05** balky **06** cussed, donsie, thrawn, thwart, unruly, wilful **07** adverse, awkward, bolshie, crabbed, deviant, froward, peevish, stroppy, wayward **08** alarming, contrary, improper, obdurate, stubborn, worrying **09** camstairy, camsteary, difficult, incorrect, obstinate, pig-headed, senseless, unhelpful **10** camsteerie, headstrong, overthwart, rebellious, refractary, refractory, unyielding **11** disobedient, ill-tempered, intractable, obstructive, troublesome, wrong-headed **12** bloody-minded, cantankerous, cross-grained, intransigent, unmanageable, unreasonable **13** unco-operative **14** uncontrollable

## perversely
◇ *anagram indicator* **04** awry **09** waywardly **10** alarmingly, stubbornly, worryingly **11** obstinately, thwartingly, unhelpfully **12** cross-grained **13** obstructively **15** unco-operatively

## perversion
◇ *anagram indicator* **04** vice **06** misuse **08** deviance, travesty, twisting **09** depravity, deviation, kinkiness **10** aberration, corruption, debauchery, distortion, immorality, paraphilia, subversion, wickedness **11** abnormality **12** irregularity **13** exhibitionism, falsification **14** misapplication

## perversity
◇ *anagram indicator* **03** gee **08** obduracy **09** adversity, contumacy, obstinacy **10** cussedness, gallusness, protervity, unruliness, wilfulness **11** awkwardness, frowardness, gallowsness, waywardness **12** contrariness, disobedience, stubbornness **13** intransigence, senselessness **14** rebelliousness, refractoriness **15** troublesomeness, wrong-headedness

## pervert
◇ *anagram indicator* **03** wry **04** perv, turn, vert, warp **05** abuse, avert, sicko, twist, wrest **06** debase, divert, garble, misuse, weirdo **07** corrupt, debauch, deflect, degrade, deprave, deviant, deviate, distort, falsify, oddball, subvert, vitiate **08** misapply **09** debauchee, misdirect, turn aside **10** degenerate, lead astray **11** misconstrue, prevaricate **12** misinterpret, misrepresent

## perverted
◇ *anagram indicator* **04** evil **05** kinky, pervy, sicko **06** warped, wicked **07** corrupt, debased, deviant, immoral,

twisted **08** abnormal, depraved, vitiated **09** corrupted, debauched, distorted, unhealthy, unnatural

**pesky**
**06** thorny, trying, vexing **07** galling, grating, irksome, nagging **08** annoying, infernal, tiresome **09** maddening, provoking, upsetting, vexatious, worrisome **10** bothersome, confounded, disturbing, irritating **11** aggravating, displeasing, infuriating, troublesome

**pessimism**
**05** gloom **07** despair **08** cynicism, distrust, fatalism, glumness **09** defeatism, dejection, doomwatch **10** depression, gloominess, melancholy **11** despondency, Weltschmerz **12** hopelessness

**pessimist**
**05** cynic **07** doubter, killjoy, no-hoper, worrier **08** alarmist, doomsman, doomster, fatalist **09** defeatist, saturnist **10** wet blanket **11** crapehanger, crepehanger, dismal Jimmy, doomwatcher, gloom-monger, melancholic **12** doom merchant **13** prophet of doom **14** doubting Thomas

**pessimistic**
**04** glum **05** bleak, doomy **06** dismal, gloomy, morose, negate **07** cynical **08** alarmist, dejected, doubting, hopeless, negative, resigned **09** defeatist, depressed **10** depressing, despairing, despondent, fatalistic, melancholy, off-putting, suspicious **11** distrustful, downhearted **12** discouraging

**pest**
**03** bug, fly, nun **04** bane, frit, pain, pize **05** brize, curse, trial **06** blight, bother, breese, breeze, capsid, May bug, plague **07** blister, cane rat, fritfly, scourge **08** irritant, meal moth, mealy bug, nuisance, onion fly, vexation, viticide **09** annoyance, capsid bug, carrot fly, chinch bug, cornborer, May beetle, squash bug, stable fly **10** cicadellid, cockchafer, codlin moth, fowl-plague, house mouse, irritation, spider mite **11** codling moth, spermophile **13** jointed cactus, pain in the neck, red spider mite **14** American blight, Colorado beetle, Japanese beetle **15** thorn in the flesh

**pester**
**03** bug, dun, irk, nag **04** clog, fret **05** annoy, chevy, chivy, devil, get at, hound, worry **06** badger, bother, chivvy, earwig, harass, hassle, huddle, infest, mither, moider, pick on, plague **07** besiege, disturb, moither, provoke, torment **08** doorstep, irritate **09** annoyance, beleaguer **12** rhyme to death **14** drive up the wall

**pestilence**
**04** lues **06** plague **07** cholera, disease, murrain **08** epidemic, pandemic, sickness **09** contagion, infection **11** infestation

**pestilent**
**06** deadly, vexing **07** harmful, irksome, ruinous **08** annoying, catching, diseased, infected, tiresome **09** poisonous, vexatious **10** bothersome, contagious, corrupting, infectious, irritating, pernicious **11** deleterious, destructive, detrimental, infuriating, mischievous, troublesome **12** communicable, contaminated, plague-ridden **13** disease-ridden

**pestilential**
**06** vexing **07** baneful, harmful, irksome, ruinous **08** annoying, diseased, infected, tiresome **09** pestering, poisonous **10** bothersome, contagious, detestable, infectious, irritating, pernicious **11** destructive, infuriating, troublesome **12** contaminated, plague-ridden **13** disease-ridden

**pet**
**04** cade, chou, coax, daut, dawt, dear, huff, hump, idol, kiss, neck, snog, stew, sulk, tame, tiff, tift, tout, towt **05** jewel, paddy, strop, sulks **06** caress, chosen, cosset, cuddle, dautie, dawtie, fondle, grumps, pamper, pettle, prized, smooch, stroke, temper **07** bad mood, darling, dearest, embrace, indulge, special, subdued, tantrum, the pits, trained **08** canoodle, favoured, fondling, indulged, personal, treasure **09** bad temper, cherished, favourite, preferred **10** manageable, particular **11** blue-eyed boy, teacher's pet **12** blue-eyed girl, domesticated, house-trained **14** apple of your eye

*Pets include:*

**03** cat, cow, dog, pig, rat
**04** bird, fish, goat, newt, pony
**05** goose, horse, llama, mouse, sheep
**06** alpaca, canary, donkey, ferret, gerbil, jerboa, lizard, parrot, rabbit, turtle
**07** chicken, hamster
**08** chipmunk, cyberpet, goldfish, parakeet, terrapin, tortoise
**09** guinea pig, tarantula
**10** budgerigar, chinchilla, salamander, virtual pet
**11** stick insect

*See also* **cat; dog; fish; horse; rabbit**

**peter**
**03** jar, jug **05** half-g **06** flagon
• **peter out  03** ebb **04** fade, fail, stop, wane **05** cease **06** go cold **07** die away, dwindle **08** diminish, taper off **09** evaporate, fizzle out **11** come to an end **13** come to nothing

**petite**
**05** bijou, dinky, small **06** dainty, little, slight **08** delicate

**petition**
**03** ask, beg, bid, sue **04** boon, plea, pray, suit, urge **05** axiom, crave, plead, press **06** adjure, appeal, prayer **07** beseech, entreat, implore, protest, request, solicit **08** call upon, entreaty

**09** postulate, supplicat **10** invocation, round robin, supplicate **11** application, deprecation, memorialize **12** solicitation, supplication **14** representation

**pet name**
**03** mog, nan **04** nana **05** bunny, moggy, nanna, nanny **06** moggie **08** nickname **10** diminutive, endearment, hypocorism **11** hypocorisma

**petrel**
**05** ariel, nelly, prion **06** fulmar **07** pintado, stinker **09** stormbird **10** Cape pigeon, sea swallow **11** Procellaria

**petrified**
**04** numb **05** dazed **06** aghast, frozen **07** shocked, stunned **08** appalled, benumbed **09** horrified, stupefied, terrified **10** speechless, transfixed **11** dumbfounded, in a blue funk, scared stiff **13** having kittens, scared to death **14** horror-stricken, terror-stricken

**petrify**
**04** numb, stun **05** alarm, appal, panic, spook **06** boggle, ossify, rattle **07** horrify, stupefy, terrify **08** frighten, paralyse **09** dumbfound, fossilize **11** turn to stone **12** put the wind up

**petrol**
**03** gas, LRP **05** ethyl, juice, super **08** gasolene, gasoline
*See also* **fuel**

**petticoat**
**04** coat, slip **05** jupon, woman **06** female, kirtle **07** placket **08** balmoral, basquine, feminine **09** crinoline, wyliecoat **10** underskirt

**pettifogging**
**04** mean **05** petty **06** paltry, subtle **07** trivial **08** captious, niggling **09** casuistic, cavilling, quibbling **10** nit-picking **11** over-refined, sophistical **12** equivocating **13** hair-splitting

**pettiness**
**08** meanness **09** quibbling **10** nit-picking **12** spitefulness **15** small-mindedness

**pettish**
**05** cross, dorty, huffy, sulky **06** grumpy, tetchy, touchy **07** fretful, peevish, waspish **08** petulant, snappish **09** fractious, irritable, querulous, splenetic **11** bad-tempered, ill-humoured, thin-skinned

**petty**
**04** mean **05** minor, petit, potty, small **06** grotty, lesser, little, measly, paltry, poking, puisne, puisny, slight **07** pimping, scantle, trivial **08** grudging, niggling, picayune, piddling, piffling, spiteful, trifling **09** parochial, quibbling, scantling, secondary, small-town **10** negligible, nit-picking, parish-pump, shoestring, ungenerous **11** in a small way, inessential, small-minded, unimportant **12** contemptible, narrow-

minded **13** insignificant
**14** inconsiderable **15** inconsequential

**petulance**
**05** pique **06** spleen **09** bad temper, ill-humour, ill-temper, procacity, sulkiness **10** crabbiness, sullenness **11** crabbedness, peevishness, waspishness **12** irritability **13** querulousness

**petulant**
**04** sour **05** cross, mardy, moody, ratty, sulky **06** crabby, sullen, touchy, toutie, wanton **07** crabbed, forward, fretful, in a stew, peevish **08** in a paddy, snappish **09** crotchety, impatient, irritable, querulous **10** browned off, humoursome, lascivious, ungracious **11** bad-tempered, complaining, ill-humoured

**pew**
**03** box **04** seat **05** stall **08** horse box

**phalanger**
**04** tait **06** cuscus, glider, possum **07** opossum **08** Tarsipes **09** petaurist **10** honey-mouse **11** honey possum **14** flying squirrel, vulpine opossum

**phantasmagorical**
**06** unreal **07** surreal **08** ethereal, illusory **09** dreamlike, fantastic, visionary **10** chimerical, trance-like **13** hallucinatory, insubstantial, unsubstantial **14** phantasmagoric

**phantom**
**04** idol **05** ghost, spook **06** fantom, spirit, unreal, vision, wraith **07** eidolon, feature, figment, specter, spectre **08** illusion, illusory, revenant, spectral **09** imaginary **10** apparition, Scotch mist **12** Pepper's ghost **13** hallucination

**pharaoh**
**04** faro **11** river-dragon

*Pharaohs include:*
**07** Rameses
**08** Thutmose
**09** Akhenaten
**10** Hatshepsut
**11** Tut'ankhamun

**pharisaical**
**06** formal **07** preachy **09** insincere, pietistic **10** goody-goody, moralizing **12** hypocritical **13** sanctimonious, self-righteous **14** holier-than-thou

**Pharisee**
**05** fraud **06** humbug, phoney **07** pietist **09** formalist, hypocrite **10** dissembler **12** dissimulator **15** whited sepulchre

**phase**
**04** beat, faze, form, part, step, time **05** drive, morph, point, shape, spell, stage, state, worry **06** aspect, period, season **07** chapter, perturb **08** juncture, position, unsettle **09** condition **11** development
• **phase in** **05** start **06** ease in **07** bring in **08** initiate **09** introduce **10** start using
• **phase out** **04** stop **05** close **06** remove, wind up **07** ease off, run down **08** get rid of, taper off, wind

down, withdraw **09** dispose of, eliminate, stop using, terminate

**pheasant**
**05** argus, monal **06** coucal, monaul **08** fireback, lyrebird, tragopan **09** francolin
• **brood of pheasants** **03** eye, nid, nye **04** nide

**phenomenal**
**06** unique **07** amazing, unusual **08** singular **09** fantastic, unheard of, wonderful **10** astounding, incredible, marvellous, remarkable, stupendous **11** astonishing, exceptional, mind-blowing, sensational **12** breathtaking, mind-boggling, unbelievable, unparalleled **13** extraordinary, unprecedented **15** too good to be true

**phenomenally**
**09** amazingly **10** incredibly, remarkably **11** wonderfully **12** astoundingly, marvellously, unbelievably **13** astonishingly, exceptionally, sensationally **15** extraordinarily

**phenomenon**
**04** fact **05** event, sight **06** marvel, phenom, rarity, wonder **07** episode, miracle, prodigy **08** incident **09** curiosity, happening, sensation, spectacle **10** appearance, experience, occurrence **12** circumstance

**philander**
**05** dally, flirt, lover **08** womanize **10** fool around, play around **11** sleep around **12** have an affair, philandering, play the field

**philanderer**
**04** rake, roué, stud, wolf **05** flirt **07** dallier, Don Juan, playboy **08** Casanova **09** ladies' man, libertine, womanizer **10** lady-killer

**philanthropic**
**04** kind **06** humane **07** liberal **08** generous, selfless **09** bounteous, bountiful, unselfish **10** alms-giving, altruistic, benevolent, charitable, munificent, open-handed **11** kind-hearted **12** humanitarian **14** public-spirited

**philanthropist**
**05** donor, giver **06** backer, helper, patron **07** sponsor **08** altruist **09** alms-giver **10** benefactor **11** contributor **12** humanitarian

**philanthropy**
**04** help **06** giving **07** backing, charity **08** altruism, kindness **09** patronage **10** alms-giving, generosity, liberality **11** beneficence, benevolence, munificence, sponsorship **12** selflessness **13** bounteousness, bountifulness, social concern, unselfishness **14** open-handedness **15** humanitarianism, kind-heartedness, social awareness

**Philip**
**04** Phil

**philippic**
**05** abuse **06** attack, insult, rebuke,

tirade **07** reproof **08** diatribe, harangue, reviling **09** criticism, invective, onslaught, reprimand **10** upbraiding **12** denunciation, vituperation

**Philippines**
**02** RP **03** PHL

**philistine**
**04** boor, lout **05** crass, enemy, yahoo **06** gigman, unread **07** bailiff, boorish, lowbrow **08** ignorant **09** barbarian, bourgeois, ignoramus, tasteless, unrefined, vulgarian **10** uncultured, uneducated, unlettered **12** uncultivated

**Phillip**
**04** Phil

**philologer**
*see* **lexicographer**

**philosopher**
**04** guru, sage **06** expert **07** scholar, thinker **08** academic, analyser, logician, theorist **09** theorizer **12** dialectician **13** deipnosophist, metaphysicist, philosophizer **14** epistemologist

*Philosophers include:*
**04 Ayer** (Sir A J), **Hume** (David), **Joad** (C E M), **Kant** (Immanuel), **Mach** (Ernst), **Marx** (Karl), **Mill** (James), **Mill** (John Stuart), **More** (Henry), **Otto** (Rudolf), **Ryle** (Gilbert), **Vico** (Giambattista), **Weil** (Simone)
**05 Bacon** (Francis), **Bacon** (Roger), **Bayle** (Pierre), **Benda** (Julien), **Bodin** (Jean), **Broad** (Charlie Dunbar), **Bruno** (Giordano), **Buber** (Martin), **Burke** (Edmund), **Comte** (Auguste), **Croce** (Benedetto), **Dewey** (John), **Dunne** (John William), **Frege** (Gottlob), **Gödel** (Kurt), **Hegel** (Georg Wilhelm Friedrich), **Hulme** (T E), **James** (William), **Locke** (John), **Moore** (George Edward), **Occam** (William of), **Plato**, **Smith** (Adam), **Vivés** (Juan Luis)
**06 Adorno** (Theodor), **Anselm** (St), **Berlin** (Sir Isaiah), **Bonnet** (Charles), **Carnap** (Rudolf), **Celsus**, **Engels** (Friedrich), **Fichte** (Johann Gottlieb), **Goedel** (Kurt), **Herder** (Johann Gottfried von), **Hobbes** (Thomas), **Langer** (Suzanne Knauth), **Lukács** (Georg), **Ockham** (William of), **Palach** (Jan), **Popper** (Sir Karl), **Pyrrho**, **Sartre** (Jean-Paul), **Singer** (Peter), **Strato**, **Thales**
**07 Aquinas** (St Thomas), **Bentham** (Jeremy), **Buridan** (Jean), **Derrida** (Jacques), **Diderot** (Denis), **Dilthey** (Wilhelm), **Edwards** (Jonathan), **Erasmus** (Desiderius), **Gentile** (Giovanni), **Gorgias**, **Haldane** (Richard, Viscount), **Husserl** (Edmund), **Hypatia**, **Jaspers** (Karl), **Leibniz** (Gottfried Wilhelm), **Marcuse** (Herbert), **Mencius**, **Proclus**, **Russell** (Bertrand, Earl), **Sankara**, **Schlick** (Moritz), **Spencer** (Herbert), **Spinoza** (Baruch),

Steiner (Rudolf), **Thoreau** (Henry David), **Tillich** (Paul)
08 **Alcmaeon**, **Alembert** (Jean le Rond d'), **Averroës**, **Avicenna**, **Beauvoir** (Simone de), **Berkeley** (Bishop George), **Boethius** (Anicius Manlius Severinus), **Buchanan** (George), **Cassirer** (Ernst), **Cudworth** (Ralph), **Epicurus**, **Foucault** (Michel), **Habermas** (Jürgen), **Hamilton** (Sir William), **Hobhouse** (Leonard), **Longinus** (Dionysius), **Plotinus**, **Porphyry**, **Ram Singh**, **Rousseau** (Jean Jacques), **Sidgwick** (Henry), **Socrates**, **Spengler** (Oswald)
09 **Althusser** (Louis), **Aristotle**, **Avicebrón**, **Bronowski** (Jacob), **Condorcet** (Marie-Jean-Antoine-Nicolas de Caritat, Marquis de), **Confucius**, **Descartes** (René), **Feuerbach** (Ludwig), **Heidegger** (Martin), **Nietzsche** (Friedrich), **Plekhanov** (Giorgiy), **Santayana** (George), **Schelling** (Friedrich), **Whitehead** (Alfred North)
10 **Anaxagoras**, **Aristippus**, **Democritus**, **Duns Scotus** (John), **Empedocles**, **Heraclitus**, **Horkheimer** (Max), **Maimonides** (Moses), **Parmenides**, **Posidonius**, **Protagoras**, **Pythagoras**, **Schweitzer** (Albert), **Xenocrates**, **Xenophanes**, **Zeno of Elea**
11 **Anaximander**, **Kierkegaard** (Sören), **Montesquieu** (Charles-Louis, Baron de), **Reichenbach** (Hans), **Shaftesbury** (Anthony Ashley Cooper, Earl of), **Vivekananda**
12 **Merleau-Ponty** (Maurice), **Philo Judaeus**, **Schopenhauer** (Arthur), **Theophrastus**, **Wittgenstein** (Ludwig), **Zeno of Citium**
14 **Albertus Magnus** (St), **Schleiermacher** (Friedrich)
15 **William of Ockham**

## philosophical
04 calm, cool, wise 05 stoic 06 placid, serene 07 erudite, learned, logical, patient, pensive, stoical 08 abstract, composed, rational, resigned 09 collected, impassive, realistic, unruffled 10 analytical, meditative, phlegmatic, reflective, thoughtful 11 theoretical, unemotional, unflappable 12 metaphysical 13 contemplative, dispassionate, imperturbable, self-possessed
See also **philosophy**

## philosophically
06 calmly 08 placidly 09 logically, patiently, stoically 10 abstractly, resignedly 11 impassively, unflappably 12 analytically 13 theoretically, unemotionally 14 metaphysically

## philosophy
04 view 06 reason, tenets, values, wisdom 07 beliefs, thought 08 attitude, doctrine, ideology, stoicism, thinking 09 knowledge, reasoning, viewpoint, world-view 10 principles 11 convictions, point of view

*Branches of philosophy include:*

03 est, law
04 mind, yoga
05 logic, moral
06 ethics
07 biology, eastern, history, Sankhya, science, Vedanta
08 axiology, language, medicine, ontology, politics, religion
09 bioethics, economics, education, semiotics
10 aesthetics, literature, psychology
11 informatics, mathematics, metaphysics
12 epistemology
13 applied ethics, jurisprudence, phenomenology

*Philosophical schools, doctrines and theories include:*

05 deism
06 egoism, monism, Taoism, theism
07 atheism, atomism, dualism, fideism, Marxism, realism, Thomism
08 altruism, ascetism, cynicism, fatalism, feminism, hedonism, humanism, idealism, nihilism, Stoicism
09 dogmatism, pantheism, Platonism, pluralism, solipsism
10 absolutism, Eleaticism, empiricism, gnosticism, Kantianism, naturalism, nominalism, positivism, pragmatism, Pyrrhonism, relativism, scepticism
11 agnosticism, determinism, Hegelianism, historicism, materialism, objectivism, rationalism, Sankhya-Yoga
12 behaviourism, Cartesianism, Confucianism, Epicureanism, essentialism, Neoplatonism, reductionism, subjectivism
13 antinomianism, conceptualism, descriptivism, immaterialism, Neo-Kantianism, occasionalism, phenomenalism, scholasticism, structuralism
14 existentialism, interactionism, intuitionalism, libertarianism, Nyaya-Vaisesika, prescriptivism, Pythagoreanism, sensationalism, utilitarianism, Vedanta-Mimamsa
15 Aristotelianism, experimentalism, Frankfurt School, instrumentalism

*Philosophy terms include:*

05 deism, logic, moral
06 egoism, ethics, monism, theism
07 a priori, atheism, atomism, dualism, falsafa, Marxism, realism
08 altruism, ascetism, axiology, cynicism, fatalism, feminism, hedonism, humanism, idealism, identity, nihilism, ontology, stoicism
09 deduction, dogmatism, induction, intuition, pantheism, Platonism, pluralism, sense data, solipsism, substance, syllogism, teleology
10 absolutism, aesthetics, deontology, empiricism, entailment, gnosticism,

Kantianism, naturalism, nominalism, positivism, pragmatism, relativism, scepticism
11 agnosticism, a posteriori, determinism, historicism, materialism, metaphysics, objectivism, rationalism
12 behaviourism, Confucianism, Epicureanism, epistemology, Neoplatonism, reductionism, subjectivism
13 antinomianism, conceptualism, immaterialism, jurisprudence, neo-Kantianism, phenomenalism, phenomenology, scholasticism, structuralism
14 existentialism, interactionism, intuitionalism, libertarianism, prescriptivism, sensationalism, utilitarianism
15 Aristotelianism, experimentalism, instrumentalism

## phlegmatic
04 calm, cool 06 placid, stolid 07 stoical 08 tranquil 09 impassive, saturnine 11 indifferent, unconcerned, unemotional, unflappable 12 matter-of-fact 13 dispassionate, imperturbable 14 self-controlled

## phobia
04 fear 05 dread, thing 06 hang-up, hatred, horror, terror 07 anxiety, dislike 08 aversion, loathing, neurosis 09 antipathy, obsession, repulsion, revulsion 11 detestation 14 irrational fear

*Phobias include:*

09 apiphobia, neophobia, panphobia, zoophobia
10 acrophobia, algophobia, aquaphobia, autophobia, canophobia, cynophobia, demophobia, hodophobia, musophobia, nosophobia, pyrophobia, toxiphobia, xenophobia
11 agoraphobia, astraphobia, cnidophobia, cyberphobia, gymnophobia, hippophobia, hydrophobia, hypnophobia, necrophobia, nyctophobia, ophiophobia, photophobia, scotophobia, tachophobia, taphephobia
12 achluophobia, ailurophobia, belonephobia, brontophobia, coulrophobia, entomophobia, phasmophobia, technophobia
13 arachnophobia, arithmophobia, bacillophobia, herpetophobia
14 anthropophobia, bacteriophobia, claustrophobia, ereuthrophobia, thalassophobia

## Phoebus
03 Sol, sun 05 Titan 06 Apollo, Helios

## phoenix
03 fum 04 fung, huma 07 paragon 12 bird of wonder

## phone
04 bell, buzz, call, cell, dial, ring

**06** blower, call up, mobile, ring up, tinkle **07** contact, handset **08** car phone, receiver **09** cell phone, give a bell, give a buzz, make a call, phone call, telephone **10** dog and bone, get in touch **11** give a tinkle, mobile phone **13** cordless phone

## phonetic alphabet
*see* **alphabet**

## phoney
◇ *anagram indicator* **04** fake, mock, sham **05** bogus, faker, false, fraud, hokey, pseud, put-on, quack, trick **06** ersatz, forged, humbug, pseudo, unreal **07** assumed, feigned, forgery **08** affected, impostor, spurious **09** contrived, imitation, pretender, simulated **10** fraudulent, mountebank **11** counterfeit, pretentious

## phosphorescent
**06** bright **07** glowing, radiant **08** luminous **09** refulgent **11** luminescent, noctilucent, noctilucous

## phosphorus
**01** P

## photocopy
**04** copy **05** print, Xerox® **06** run off **09** duplicate, facsimile, Photostat®

## photograph
**03** pap, pic, pin **04** film, shot, snap, take, X-ray **05** image, Kodak®, panel, photo, piccy, print, sepia, shoot, slide, still, video **06** blow up, blow-up, record, retake **07** close-up, enlarge, montage, mug shot, picture **08** abstract, exposure, headshot, hologram, likeness, microdot, portrait, seascape, skiagram, snapshot, sun print **09** angiogram, ferrotype, karyotype, landscape, mammogram, microgram, nephogram, photogene, photogram, radiogram, rotograph, skiagraph, visual aid, wirephoto **10** centrefold, chromatype, ferro-print, micrograph, radiograph, sun picture **11** composition, enlargement, heliochrome, platinotype, spectrogram **12** cathodograph, röntgenogram, transparency **13** capture on film, chlorobromide, daguerreotype, encephalogram **14** pyrophotograph, take a picture of **15** microphotograph, take a snapshot of

## photographer
**07** snapper **09** cameraman, paparazzo **11** camerawoman **14** camera operator

*Photographers include:*

**03** **Ray** (Man)
**04** **Capa** (Robert), **Hill** (David Octavius), **Penn** (Irving)
**05** **Adams** (Ansel), **Arbus** (Diane), **Hardy** (Bert), **Karsh** (Yousuf), **Lange** (Dorothea), **Ritts** (Herb), **Smith** (W Eugene)
**06** **Arnold** (Eve), **Avedon** (Richard), **Bailey** (David), **Beaton** (Sir Cecil), **Brandt** (Bill), **Godwin** (Fay), **McBean** (Angus), **Miller** (Lee), **Newton** (Helmut), **Niepce** (Joseph Nicéphore), **Rankin**, **Talbot**

(William Henry Fox), **Warhol** (Andy)
**07** **Brassaï**, **Cameron** (Julia Margaret), **Carroll** (Lewis), **Dodgson** (Charles Lutwidge), **Eastman** (George), **Lumière** (Auguste), **McCurry** (Steve), **Salgado** (Sebastião), **Siskind** (Aaron), **Snowdon** (Antony Armstrong-Jones, Earl of), **Waddell** (Rankin)
**08** **Daguerre** (Louis), **McCullin** (Don), **Sielmann** (Heinz), **Steichen** (Edward)
**09** **Leibovitz** (Annie), **Lichfield** (Patrick, Earl of), **Muybridge** (Eadweard James), **Rodchenko** (Alexander), **Rosenblum** (Walter), **Stieglitz** (Alfred), **Winogrand** (Garry)
**10** **Moholy-Nagy** (László)
**11** **Bourke-White** (Margaret), **Wakabayashi** (Yasuhiro)
**12** **Friese-Greene** (William)
**13** **Ducos du Hauron** (Louis)
**14** **Armstrong-Jones** (Antony), **Cartier-Bresson** (Henri)

## photographic
**05** exact, vivid **06** filmic, minute, visual **07** graphic, natural, precise **08** accurate, detailed, faithful, lifelike **09** cinematic, pictorial, realistic, retentive **12** naturalistic

*Photographic equipment includes:*

**06** camera, tripod, viewer
**08** enlarger, light-box, stop bath
**09** camcorder, safelight
**10** fixing bath, paper drier, Vertoscope®
**11** print washer, slide viewer
**13** developer bath, enlarger timer, film projector, flash umbrella
**14** contact printer, developing tank, focus magnifier, slide projector
**15** negative carrier, print-drying rack

*Photographic accessories include:*

**04** film, lens
**06** eye-cup, filter
**07** battery, hot shoe, lens cap
**08** diffuser, disc film, flashgun, lens hood, long lens, zoom lens
**09** camera bag, flashbulb, flash card, flashcube, flash unit, macro lens, polarizer, spot meter
**10** afocal lens, lens shield, light meter, memory card, slide mount, video light, video mixer, viewfinder
**11** close-up lens, fish-eye lens, sepia filter, video editor
**12** cable release, colour filter, memory reader
**13** auxiliary lens, cartridge film, exposure meter, remote control, teleconverter, telephoto lens, wide-angle lens

## Photostat®
**04** copy **05** print, Xerox® **06** run off **09** duplicate, facsimile, photocopy

## phrase
**03** phr, put, say **04** cant, hook, riff, word **05** couch, frame, idiom, style,

usage, utter **06** clause, cliché, mantra, remark, saying **07** comment, express, flatter, formula, mantram, present, wheedle **08** laconism, language, locution **09** catchword, formulate, pronounce, utterance **10** expression, laconicism, mondegreen **11** phraseology **12** construction, group of words, put into words **13** way of speaking **15** style of speaking

## phraseology
**04** cant **05** argot, idiom, style **06** patois, phrase, speech, syntax **07** diction, wording, writing **08** language, parlance, phrasing **10** expression **11** terminology

## phrasing
**05** idiom, style, words **07** diction, wordage, wording **08** language, verbiage **10** expression **11** phraseology, terminology **13** choice of words

## physical
**04** real **05** brute, solid **06** actual, bodily, carnal, fleshy, mortal **07** earthly, fleshly, medical, somatic, spatial, visible **08** concrete, material, palpable, tangible **09** corporeal, incarnate, medicinal, wholesome **11** substantial, unspiritual **13** materialistic

## physically
**06** bodily, really **07** visibly **08** actually, animally, tangibly **10** concretely, in your body, materially **13** substantially **15** physiologically

## physician
**02** GP **03** doc **05** hakim, leech, medic, Paean, quack **06** doctor, healer, intern, medico **08** external, houseman, medicine **09** internist, mediciner, registrar **10** consultant, medicaster, specialist **11** physicianer **12** school doctor
*See also* **doctor**

## physics
*Physics terms include:*

**03** gas, GUT, ion, law, QCD, QED, TOE
**04** area, atom, barn, flux, gate, heat, lens, mass, node, rule, spin, wave, WIMP, work, X-ray
**05** chaos, fermi, field, focus, force, laser, lever, light, phase, power, quark, ratio, sound, speed, SQUID, state
**06** atomic, charge, couple, energy, engine, liquid, mirror, moment, motion, optics, phonon, photon, proton, scalar, SI unit, string, theory, volume, weight
**07** circuit, density, digital, entropy, formula, gravity, inertia, neutron, nuclear, nucleus, orbital, process, statics, tension
**08** alpha ray, dynamics, electron, equation, friction, gamma ray, half-life, harmonic, infrared, molecule, momentum, neutrino, particle, polarity, pressure, rest mass, spectrum, velocity
**09** acoustics, amplitude, black body, cosmology, dimension,

frequency, induction, magnetism, mechanics, Mohs scale, potential, principle, radiation, radio wave, resonance, sound wave, sparticle, subatomic, substance, vibration, viscosity, white heat

**10** efficiency, elasticity, flash point, focal plane, gauge boson, heavy water, Higgs boson, hydraulics, latent heat, Mach number, microwaves, reflection, refraction, relativity, resistance, separation, shear force, ultrasound, wavelength

**11** diffraction, electricity, equilibrium, evaporation, light source, oscillation, periodic law, sensitivity, temperature, ultraviolet

**12** absolute zero, acceleration, boiling point, centre of mass, critical mass, hydrostatics, interference, Kelvin effect, laws of motion, luminescence, nanoparticle, radioisotope, spectroscopy, speed of light, standing wave, string theory, time dilation, wave property

**13** Appleton layer, beta particles, Big Bang theory, bubble-chamber, chain reaction, freezing point, hydrodynamics, incandescence, kinetic energy, kinetic theory, light emission, magnetic field, nuclear fusion, optical centre, quantum theory, radioactivity, semiconductor, supersymmetry, Thomson effect

**14** alpha particles, analogue signal, applied physics, circuit-breaker, Coriolis effect, light intensity, nuclear fission, nuclear physics, parallel motion, states of matter, superconductor, surface tension, thermodynamics, transverse wave

**15** angular momentum, capillary action, centre of gravity, charged particle, electric current, electrodynamics, Fourier analysis, moment of inertia, perpetual motion, potential energy, specific gravity, visible spectrum

_Physicists include:_

**02 Wu** (Chien-Shiung)
**03 Lee** (Tsung-Dao), **Ohm** (Georg Simon)
**04 Abbe** (Ernst), **Biot** (Jean-Baptiste), **Bohr** (Niels), **Born** (Max), **Bose** (Satyendra Nath), **Dick** (Robert Henry), **Gray** (Stephen), **Haüy** (René Just), **Hess** (Victor Francis), **Katz** (Sir Bernard), **Kerr** (John), **Land** (Edwin Herbert), **Laue** (Max Theodor Felix von), **Lenz** (Heinrich Friedrich Emil), **Mach** (Ernst), **Mott** (Sir Nevill Francis), **Néel** (Louis Eugène Félix), **Rabi** (Isidor Isaac), **Saha** (Meghnad), **Ting** (Samuel Chao Chung), **Wien** (Wilhelm), **Yang** (Chen Ning)
**05 Aston** (Francis William), **Auger** (Pierre Victor), **Bethe** (Hans Albrecht), **Bloch** (Felix), **Bondi** (Sir

Hermann), **Boyle** (Robert), **Bragg** (Sir Lawrence), **Bragg** (Sir William Henry), **Braun** (Ferdinand), **Curie** (Marie), **Curie** (Pierre), **Debye** (Peter), **Dewar** (Sir James), **Dirac** (P A M), **Dyson** (Freeman), **Esaki** (Leo), **Fermi** (Enrico), **Fuchs** (Klaus), **Gabor** (Dennis), **Gamow** (George), **Gauss** (Carl Friedrich), **Gibbs** (Josiah Willard), **Grove** (Sir William Robert), **Henry** (Joseph), **Hertz** (Heinrich Rudolf), **Higgs** (Peter), **Hooke** (Robert), **Jeans** (Sir James Hopwood), **Joule** (James Prescott), **Milne** (Edward Arthur), **Pauli** (Wolfgang), **Raman** (Sir Chandrasekhara Venkata), **Rossi** (Bruno), **Salam** (Abdus), **Segrè** (Emilio), **Stern** (Otto), **Tesla** (Nikola), **Vleck** (John Hasbrouck van), **Volta** (Alessandro Giuseppe Anastasio, Count), **Waals** (Johannes van der), **Young** (Thomas)
**06 Ampère** (André Marie), **Bunsen** (Robert Wilhelm), **Carnot** (Sadi), **Dalton** (John), **Edison** (Thomas Alva), **Frisch** (Otto Robert), **Geiger** (Hans Wilhelm), **Glaser** (Donald Arthur), **Huxley** (Hugh Esmor), **Kelvin** (William Thomson, Lord), **Lorenz** (Ludwig Valentin), **Newton** (Sir Isaac), **Pascal** (Blaise), **Planck** (Max), **Rohrer** (Heinrich), **Stokes** (Sir George Gabriel), **Taylor** (Sir Geoffrey Ingram), **Teller** (Edward), **Wigner** (Eugene Paul), **Wilson** (Robert), **Zwicky** (Fritz)
**07 Alferov** (Zhores I), **Alvarez** (Luis Walter), **Bednorz** (Georg), **Broglie** (Louis-Victor Pierre Raymond de), **Charles** (Jacques), **Compton** (Arthur Holly), **Coulomb** (Charles Augustin de), **Doppler** (Christian Johann), **Eastman** (George), **Faraday** (Michael), **Feynman** (Richard Phillips), **Fresnel** (Augustin Jean), **Galilei** (Galileo), **Galileo**, **Glashow** (Sheldon Lee), **Goddard** (Robert Hutchings), **Hawking** (Stephen), **Huygens** (Christiaan), **Langley** (Samuel Pierpont), **Lorentz** (Hendrik Antoon), **Marconi** (Guglielmo, Marchese), **Maxwell** (James Clerk), **Meitner** (Lise), **Oersted** (Hans Christian), **Peierls** (Sir Rudolf Ernst), **Penzias** (Arno Allan), **Poisson** (Siméon Denis), **Réaumur** (René Antoine Ferchault de), **Richter** (Burton), **Röntgen** (Wilhelm Konrad von), **Rotblat** (Sir Joseph), **Seaborg** (Glen Theodore), **Szilard** (Leo), **Thomson** (Sir George Paget), **Thomson** (Sir J J), **Vernier** (Pierre)
**08 Ångström** (Anders Jonas), **Appleton** (Sir Edward Victor), **Avogadro** (Amedeo), **Beaufort** (Sir Francis), **Chadwick** (Sir James), **Clausius** (Rudolf), **De Forest** (Lee), **Delbrück** (Max), **Einstein** (Albert), **Foucault** (Jean Bernard Léon), **Gell-Mann** (Murray), **Langevin** (Paul), **Lemaître** (Georges Henri), **Millikan** (Robert Andrews), **Mulliken** (Robert Sanderson), **Oliphant** (Sir Mark),

**Regnault** (Henri Victor), **Sakharov** (Andrei), **Shockley** (William Bradford), **Tomonaga** (Sin-Itiro), **Van Allen** (James Alfred), **Weinberg** (Steven)
**09 Aristotle**, **Bartholin** (Erasmus), **Becquerel** (Antoine Henri), **Birkeland** (Kristian Olaf Bernhard), **Boltzmann** (Ludwig), **Cavendish** (Henry), **Cherenkov** (Pavel), **Cockcroft** (Sir John Douglas), **Gay-Lussac** (Joseph Louis), **Heaviside** (Oliver), **Helmholtz** (Hermann von), **Michelson** (Albert Abraham)
**10 Anaximenes**, **Fahrenheit** (Daniel), **Heisenberg** (Werner Karl), **Rutherford** (Ernest, Lord), **Torricelli** (Evangelista), **Weizsäcker** (Carl Friedrich, Baron von), **Wheatstone** (Sir Charles), **Xenocrates**
**11 Chamberlain** (Owen), **Joliot-Curie** (Frédéric), **Joliot-Curie** (Irène), **Leeuwenhoek** (Antoni van), **Oppenheimer** (Robert), **Schrödinger** (Erwin), **Tsiolkovsky** (Konstantin), **Van de Graaff** (Robert Jemison)
**13 Chandrasekhar** (Subrahmanyan)

## physiognomy

**03** mug **04** dial, face, look, phiz **05** clock **06** aspect, kisser, phizog, visage **07** visnomy **08** features, fisnomie, phisnomy, visnomie **09** character **11** countenance, craniognomy

## physiology

_Physiologists include:_

**04 Best** (Charles Herbert), **Dale** (Sir Henry Hallett), **Hess** (Walter Rudolf)
**05 Hubel** (David Hunter), **Kühne** (Wilhelm), **Lower** (Richard), **Marey** (Etienne-Jules), **Mayow** (John), **Prout** (William), **Yalow** (Rosalyn)
**06 Adrian** (Edgar Douglas, Lord), **Bordet** (Jules), **Cannon** (Walter Bradford), **Haller** (Albrecht von), **Huxley** (Sir Andrew), **Ludwig** (Karl), **Müller** (Johannes Peter), **Pavlov** (Ivan), **Pincus** (Gregory Goodwin)
**07 Banting** (Sir Frederick Grant), **Bayliss** (Sir William), **Beddoes** (Thomas Lovell), **Bernard** (Claude), **Borelli** (Giovanni Alfonso), **Diamond** (Jared Mason), **Galvani** (Luigi), **Haldane** (John Scott), **Helmont** (Johannes Baptista van), **Hodgkin** (Sir Alan Lloyd), **Schwann** (Theodor)
**08 Flourens** (Pierre Jean Marie), **Magendie** (François), **Mariotte** (Edmé), **Meyerhof** (Otto Fritz), **Purkinje** (Jan Evangelista), **Starling** (Ernest Henry)
**09 Blakemore** (Colin), **Dutrochet** (Henri), **Einthoven** (Willem), **Helmholtz** (Hermann von)
**11 Sherrington** (Sir Charles Scott)

## physique

**04** body, form **05** build, frame, set-up, shape **06** figure, make-up **09** structure **12** constitution

## pi

03 pie, pye 05 pious 09 confusion, religious 13 sanctimonious

## pianist

*Pianists include:*

02 **Ax** (Emmanuel)
04 **Bush** (Alan), **Cole** (Nat 'King'), **Hess** (Dame Myra), **John** (Sir Elton), **Lupu** (Radu), **Monk** (Thelonious Sphere), **Wild** (Earl)
05 **Alkan**, **Arrau** (Claudio), **Basie** (Count), **Beach** (Mrs H H A), **Blake** (Eubie), **Bolet** (Jorge), **Borge** (Victor), **Bülow** (Hans), **Corea** (Chick), **Evans** (Bill), **Evans** (Gil), **Field** (John), **Friml** (Rudolf), **Gould** (Glenn), **Hallé** (Sir Charles), **Harty** (Sir Hamilton), **Henri** (Florence), **Hines** (Earl 'Fatha'), **Joyce** (Eileen), **Lewis** (Jerry Lee), **Liszt** (Franz), **Nyman** (Michael), **Ogdon** (John Andrew Howard), **Szell** (George), **Tatum** (Art), **Tovey** (Sir Donald), **Weber** (Carl Maria von)
06 **Arnaud** (Yvonne), **Atwell** (Winifred), **Busoni** (Ferruccio), **Chopin** (Frédéric), **Cortot** (Alfred), **Cramer** (Johann), **Curzon** (Sir Clifford), **Czerny** (Karl), **Domino** (Fats), **Dussek** (Jan), **Garner** (Errol), **Hummel** (Johann), **Joplin** (Scott), **Kenton** (Stan), **Kissin** (Evgeny), **Koppel** (Herman D), **Lamond** (Frederic), **Levine** (James), **Martin** (Frank), **Morton** (Jelly Roll), **Powell** (Bud), **Schiff** (András), **Serkin** (Rudolf), **Sitsky** (Larry), **Stoker** (Richard), **Taylor** (Cecil), **Tracey** (Stan), **Turina** (Joaquín), **Waller** (Fats), **Wilson** (Teddy)
07 **Albéniz** (Isaac), **Bennett** (Sir William), **Bentzon** (Niels), **Brendel** (Alfred), **Brubeck** (Dave), **Charles** (Ray), **d'Albert** (Eugen), **Goodman** (Isador), **Hancock** (Herbie), **Ibrahim** (Abdullah), **Johnson** (James P), **Kentner** (Louis), **Lipatti** (Dinu), **Malcolm** (George), **Mathias** (William), **Matthay** (Tobias), **Medtner** (Nikolai), **Perahia** (Murray), **Richter** (Svyatoslav), **Solomon**, **Sorabji** (Kaikhosru), **Taneyev** (Sergei), **Vaughan** (Sarah)
08 **Argerich** (Martha), **Bronfman** (Yefim), **Browning** (John), **Clementi** (Muzio), **Dohnanyi** (Ernst), **Fou Ts'ong**, **Franklin** (Aretha), **Godowsky** (Leopold), **Grainger** (Percy), **Henschel** (Sir George), **Horowitz** (Vladimir), **Leighton** (Kenneth), **Lhévinne** (Josef), **Pachmann** (Vladimir de), **Peterson** (Oscar), **Richards** (Henry), **Schnabel** (Artur), **Schumann** (Clara), **Scriabin** (Aleksandr), **Skriabin** (Aleksandr), **Thalberg** (Sigismond), **Williams** (Mary Lou)
09 **Ashkenazy** (Vladimir), **Barenboim** (Daniel), **Bernstein** (Leonard), **Butterley** (Nigel), **Ellington** (Duke), **Gieseking** (Walter), **Henderson** (Fletcher), **Landowska** (Wanda), **MacDowell** (Edward), **Moscheles**

(Ignaz), **Stevenson** (Ronald), **Westbrook** (Mike)
10 **de Larrocha** (Alicia), **Gottschalk** (Louis), **Moszkowski** (Moritz), **Paderewski** (Ignacy), **Rubinstein** (Anton), **Rubinstein** (Artur), **Scharwenka** (Xaver)
11 **Farren-Price** (Ronald), **Mitropoulos** (Dimitri), **Reizenstein** (Franz)
12 **Michelangeli** (Arturo), **Moiseiwitsch** (Benno), **Shostakovich** (Maxim)
13 **Little Richard**

## piano

01 p 05 grand 06 flügel, joanna 07 upright 08 music box 09 baby grand, semi-grand 12 boudoir grand, concert grand

## pick

04 best, bite, cull, hack, open, peck, pull, wale 05 begin, cause, crack, cream, elect, élite, fix on, go for, pique, pluck, prize, start 06 choice, choose, favour, flower, gather, lead to, nibble, opt for, option, pickle, pilfer, prefer, prompt, select, take in 07 collect, harvest, mandrel, mandril, produce, provoke 08 choicest, decide on, decision, plectrum, plump for, settle on 09 break open, force open, prise open, selection, single out 10 give rise to, preference 14 crème de la crème, make up your mind
• **pick at**    04 peck 06 nibble 07 toy with 08 play with
• **pick off**    03 hit 04 kill 05 shoot, snipe 06 detach, fire at, remove, strike 07 gun down, pull off, take out 08 take away
• **pick on**    03 nag 04 bait 05 blame, bully, get at 06 needle 07 torment 09 criticize, have a go at, persecute, victimize 13 find fault with
• **pick out**    04 cull, sort, spot 05 fix on, go for 06 choose, favour, notice, opt for, prefer, select, single 07 discern, make out 08 decide on, hand-pick, perceive, separate, settle on 09 recognize, single out, tell apart 11 distinguish 12 discriminate 14 make up your mind
• **pick up**   ◊ *reversal down indicator* 03 buy, get, nab 04 bust, find, gain, go on, hear, lift, nick, peck, pull, tong 05 catch, fetch, glean, grasp, hoist, learn, pinch, raise, rally, run in 06 arrest, collar, detect, gather, master, obtain, perk up, resume, take in, take up 07 acquire, call for, carry on, collect, improve, receive, recover 08 continue, contract, discover, purchase 09 apprehend, get better, get to know, give a lift, give a ride 10 begin again, chance upon, come across, cop off with, get off with, go down with, start again 11 make headway 12 make progress 13 become ill with 15 take into custody

## picket

03 peg 04 pale, pike, post 05 guard, rebel, spike, stake, watch 06 paling, patrol, piquet, sentry 07 boycott, enclose, lookout, outpost, picquet, protest, striker, upright 08 blockade,

objector, picketer, surround 09 dissident, protester, stanchion 11 demonstrate 12 demonstrator 15 go on a picket line

## pickings

04 loot, take 05 booty, gravy, yield 06 spoils 07 plunder, profits, returns, rewards 08 earnings, proceeds

## pickle

◊ *anagram indicator* 03 fix, jam 04 bind, cure, mess, peck, pick, salt, spot 05 achar, pinch, sauce, souse, steep 06 crisis, muddle, pilfer, plight, relish, scrape 07 chutney, dilemma, put down, straits, vinegar 08 conserve, cucumber, exigency, hot water, marinade, preserve, quandary 09 condiment, seasoning, tight spot 10 difficulty, flavouring, piccalilli 11 predicament

## pick-me-up

05 boost, tonic 06 fillip 07 cordial 08 roborant, stimulus 09 stimulant 11 refreshment, restorative 12 shot in the arm

## pickpocket

03 dip 04 bung, file, wire 05 diver, thief 06 dipper, nipper 07 whizzer 08 cly-faker, cutpurse, snatcher 09 pick-purse 11 bagsnatcher

## pick-up

02 PU 03 ute, van 04 gain, rise 05 float, lorry, rally, truck, wagon 06 bakkie, growth, reform 07 advance, headway, upswing, utility 08 increase, progress, recovery, revision 09 amendment, humbucker, reception, upgrading 10 betterment, correction, rectifying 11 development, enhancement, furtherance, improvement, modernizing, reformation 12 amelioration, utility truck 13 rectification 14 rehabilitation, utility vehicle

## picky

05 faddy, fussy 06 choosy 07 finicky 08 exacting 09 selective 10 fastidious, particular, pernickety 11 persnickety 14 discriminating

## picnic

05 cinch, gipsy, gypsy 06 doddle, junket, outing 08 clambake, pushover, tailgate, walkover, waygoose 09 excursion, wasegoose, wayzgoose 10 child's play 11 outdoor meal, piece of cake 13 a kettle of fish, fête champêtre

## pictorial

05 vivid 06 scenic 07 graphic 08 striking 09 schematic 10 expressive, in pictures 11 illustrated, picturesque 12 diagrammatic 13 in photographs

## picture

03 pic, see 04 draw, film, show, tale 05 flick, movie, paint, story 06 appear, cinema, depict, flicks, movies, report 07 account, epitome, essence, imagine, outlook, portray 08 conceive, describe, envisage, envision, exemplar 09 archetype, delineate, depiction,

multiplex, narrative, portrayal, represent, reproduce, semblance, situation, visualize **10** call to mind, embodiment, illustrate, impression, similitude **11** delineation, description, film theatre **12** picture-house, quintessence **13** motion picture, picture-palace **15** personification

*Pictures include:*

**04** E-fit®, icon, ikon, snap
**05** cameo, image, mural, pin-up, plate, print, slide, still, study
**06** bitmap, canvas, design, doodle, effigy, fresco, kit-cat, mosaic, sketch, veduta
**07** cartoon, collage, diptych, drawing, etching, modello, montage, mugshot, tableau, tracing, vanitas
**08** abstract, anaglyph, graffiti, graphics, kakemono, likeness, monotype, negative, painting, panorama, Photofit®, portrait, snapshot, tapestry, transfer, triptych, vignette
**09** bricolage, engraving, identikit, landscape, miniature, old master, oleograph, still life
**10** altarpiece, caricature, photograph, silhouette
**11** oil painting, trompe l'oeil, watercolour
**12** illustration, photogravure, reproduction, self-portrait, transparency
**13** passport photo
**14** action painting, cabinet picture, representation

• **get the picture** **03** see **05** get it, grasp **06** follow, take in **07** catch on, latch on **08** cotton on, tumble to **10** comprehend, get the idea, understand **11** get the point **13** get the message

• **put someone in the picture** **04** clue up, fill in, inform, notify, update **07** explain **10** keep posted **11** communicate

## pictures
**03** pix

## picturesque
**05** vivid **06** lovely, pretty, quaint, scenic, vulgar **07** graphic, idyllic **08** charming, pleasant, pleasing, romantic, striking **09** beautiful, colourful, depictive **10** attractive, delightful, impressive **11** descriptive, picture-book

## piddling
**03** low **04** mean, poor, puny **05** minor, petty, small, sorry **06** meagre, measly, paltry, slight **07** trivial **08** derisory, piffling, trifling, wretched **09** miserable, worthless **10** negligible **11** unimportant **12** contemptible **13** inconsiderate, insignificant

## pie
◊ *anagram indicator* **02** pi **03** mag, pye **04** flan, pâté, Pica, piet, pyat, pyet, pyot, tart **05** madge, pasty, patty, pirog **06** chewet, maggie, magpie, pastry

**07** cobbler, floater **08** pandowdy **09** chatterer, confusion, coulibiac, croquante, vol-au-vent **10** Florentine, koulibiaca, tarte tatin **11** Banbury cake, oyster-patty

• **pie in the sky** **05** dream **06** hot air, mirage, notion **07** fantasy, reverie, romance **08** daydream, delusion **11** jam tomorrow **13** castle in Spain **14** castle in the air

## piebald
**04** pied **05** pinto **06** motley **07** dappled, flecked, mottled, spotted **08** brindled, skewbald, speckled **10** variegated **13** black and white, heterogeneous

## piece
◊ *anagram indicator* ◊ *hidden indicator* **01** b, k, n, p, q, r **03** bar, bit, cut, die, dod, écu, end, gun, man, nip, pce **04** bite, chip, daud, dawd, dice, hunk, item, king, lump, opus, part, pawn, peso, rook, slab, snip, solo, unit, work, zack **05** block, cameo, chunk, crown, crumb, dumka, flake, fleck, patch, queen, quota, scrap, shard, share, sherd, shred, slice, small, speck, stick, story, strip, study, wedge **06** bishop, bittie, castle, dollop, jitney, knight, length, lesson, morsel, offcut, report, review, sample, scliff, skliff, sliver, tidbit, titbit **07** allegro, article, combine, element, example, intrada, mammock, mummock, peeling, portion, quarter, scaling, section, segment, snippet **08** creation, division, fraction, fragment, instance, louis-d'or, mouthful, nocturne, particle, picayune, quantity, specimen, splinter **09** allotment, component, dandiprat, dandyprat, interlude, truncheon **10** allegretto, allocation, comedietta, embodiment, percentage, production, smithereen **11** composition, constituent **12** illustration **14** morceau de salon **15** exemplification

• **all in one piece** **05** whole **06** entire, intact, unhurt **08** complete, integral, unbroken, unharmed **09** undamaged, uninjured

• **go to pieces** **05** break **06** blow up **07** break up, crack up, go to pot **08** collapse **09** break down, fall apart **10** be overcome **11** lose control **14** have a breakdown

• **in pieces** ◊ *anagram indicator* **05** kaput **06** broken, in bits, ruined **07** damaged, smashed **09** shattered **13** disintegrated, in smithereens

• **piece together** **03** fit, fix **04** join, mend **05** patch, unite **06** attach, repair **07** compose, restore **08** assemble **10** rhapsodize **11** put together

• **pull to pieces, tear to pieces** **03** nag, pan **04** slag, slam **05** blame, knock, slate, snipe **06** attack, tear up **07** censure, condemn, mammock, rubbish, run down, slag off **08** badmouth, denounce **09** criticize, dismember **10** come down on, go to town on **11** pick holes in **12** disapprove of, put the boot in, tear to shreds **13** find fault with, tear a strip off **15** do a hatchet job on

## pièce de résistance
**05** jewel, joint, prize **09** showpiece **10** magnum opus, masterwork **11** chef-d'oeuvre, masterpiece

## piecemeal
**06** patchy, slowly **07** partial **08** bit by bit, discrete, fitfully, in detail, sporadic **09** by degrees, dismember, partially, scattered **10** parcel-wise **11** at intervals, fragmentary, interrupted **12** intermittent, unsystematic **14** intermittently, little by little **15** in dribs and drabs

## pied
**04** piet, pyat, pyet, pyot **06** motley **07** brindle, dappled, flecked, mottled, piebald, spotted **08** brindled, skewbald, streaked **09** irregular **10** variegated **12** varicoloured **13** multicoloured, parti-coloured

## pier
**04** dock, mole, pile, post, quay **05** jetty, jutty, wharf **06** column, pillar **07** slipway, support, upright **08** buttress **09** Swiss roll **10** breakwater **12** landing-stage **15** clustered column

## pierce
◊ *insertion indicator* **03** jag, peg, ren, rin, run, tap **04** barb, bore, fill, gore, hurt, move, nail, pain, pike, pink, pith, prog, rive, slap, stab **05** drift, drill, enter, gride, gryde, lance, perce, perse, prick, probe, punch, spear, spike, spile, stake, steek, stick, sting, thirl, touch **06** broach, cleave, engore, gimlet, impale, launce, launch, needle, pearce, percen, skewer, thrill, thrust **07** bayonet, emperce, light up **08** empierce, puncture, transfix **09** lancinate, penetrate, perforate, stick into **10** run through **11** pass through, perforation, transpierce **12** burst through **13** cut to the quick, thrill through

## pierced
**05** grypt, stung **06** pearst, pierst, pinked **07** impaled, pertuse **08** pertused **09** perforate, pertusate, punctured **10** fenestrate, foraminous, penetrated, perforated **11** fenestrated, foraminated

## piercing
◊ *insertion indicator* **03** raw **04** cold, keen, loud **05** acute, alert, sharp **06** Arctic, astute, biting, bitter, fierce, frosty, severe, shrewd, shrill, wintry **07** extreme, intense, numbing, painful, probing **08** freezing, perceant, shooting, stabbing **09** agonizing, searching, thrillant **10** discerning, lacerating, perceptive **11** ear-piercing, high-pitched, penetrating, penetrative, sharp-witted **12** ear-splitting, excruciating

## piercingly
**06** keenly, loudly **07** alertly, sharply, shrilly **08** astutely, bitterly, fiercely, severely **09** extremely, intensely, numbingly, painfully **11** agonizingly **12** discerningly **13** penetratingly **14** excruciatingly

**piety**
04 fear, pity 05 faith 07 respect
08 devotion, holiness, religion, sanctity
09 deference, fear of God, godliness,
piousness, reverence 10 devoutness
11 dutifulness, saintliness 12 spirituality
13 religiousness

**piffle**
03 rot 04 blah, bosh, bull, bunk, guff,
tosh 05 balls, hooey, trash, tripe
06 bunkum, drivel, trifle 07 baloney,
eyewash, hogwash, rhubarb, rubbish,
twaddle 08 malarkey, nonsense,
tommyrot 09 bull's wool, moonshine,
poppycock 10 balderdash, codswallop
11 tarradiddle

**piffling**
04 idle 05 empty, minor, petty, silly,
small 06 paltry, slight 07 foolish,
shallow, trivial 08 trifling 09 frivolous,
worthless 10 inadequate, negligible
11 superficial, unimportant
12 insufficient 13 insignificant
14 inconsiderable 15 inconsequential

**pig**
03 elt, hog, sow 04 boar, boor, cram,
gilt, runt, slip, wolf, yelt 05 beast,
brute, feast, gorge, piggy, scoff, shoat,
shote, snarf, stuff, swine 06 animal,
gobble, guffie, guzzle, piggie, piglet,
porker, sucker, weaner 07 Anthony,
glutton, grunter, guzzler, monster,
pigling, roaster, tantony 08 gourmand,
grumphie, porkling, potsherd, wild
boar 09 policeman 10 greedy guts
11 earthenware, gormandizer
13 Captain Cooker

*Pigs include:*

05 Duroc
07 Old Spot
08 landrace, Pietrain, Tamworth,
wild boar
09 Berkshire, Hampshire, Yorkshire
10 Large White, potbellied,
saddleback
11 Middle White
15 Chinese Meishian

**pigeon**
03 nun, owl 04 barb, clay, dove, girl,
gull, hoax, kuku, rock, ront, ruff, runt,
spot 05 goura, homer, piper, quest,
quist, ronte, squab, wonga 06 affair,
culver, cushat, pouter, queest, quoist,
roller, turbit, zoozoo 07 carrier,
concern, cropper, fantail, jacinth,
jacobin, laugher, manumea, pintado,
tumbler 08 business, capuchin,
horseman, ringdove, rock dove,
squealer 09 archangel, solitaire,
trumpeter 10 bronze-wing,
Didunculus, wonga-wonga
12 mourning dove

**pigeonhole**
03 box, tag 04 file, slot, sort 05 class,
defer, label, niche, place 06 locker, put
off, shelve 07 cubicle, section
08 category, classify, postpone
09 catalogue, cubby-hole
10 categorize 11 alphabetize,
compartment 14 classification

**pigeon pea**
03 dal 04 daal, dahl, dhal 05 dholl

**pig-headed**
06 mulish, stupid, wilful 07 froward
08 contrary, perverse, stubborn
09 obstinate 10 bull-headed,
headstrong, inflexible, self-willed,
unyielding 11 intractable, stiff-necked,
wrong-headed 12 intransigent

**piglet**
*see* **pig**

**pigment**
03 dye, hue 04 tint 05 paint, stain
06 colour, piment 08 tincture
09 colouring

*Pigments include:*

03 hem
04 haem, heme
05 henna, ochre, sepia, smalt, umber
06 bister, bistre, cobalt, cyanin,
lutein, madder, sienna, zaffer,
zaffre
07 carmine, etiolin, gamboge,
melanin, sinopia, turacin
08 cinnabar, luteolin, orpiment,
rose-pink, verditer, viridian
09 anthocyan, bilirubin, colcothar,
Indian red, lamp-black,
lithopone, phycocyan, quercetin,
vermilion, zinc white
10 Berlin blue, biliverdin, Chinese
red, chlorophyl, green earth,
lipochrome, madder-lake, Paris-
green, pearl white, rhodophane,
terre verte
11 anthochlore, anthocyanin,
chlorophyll, King's-yellow,
phycocyanin, phycophaein,
phytochrome, ultramarine,
Venetian red
12 anthoxanthin, Cappagh-brown,
Chinese white, chrome yellow,
Naples-yellow, phaeomelanin,
phycoxanthin, Prussian blue,
turacoverdin, Tyrian purple,
xanthopterin
13 cadmium yellow, phycoerythrin,
Scheele's green, titanium white,
xanthopterine
15 purple of Cassuis

*See also* **colour; dye**

**pike**
03 gar, ged 04 jack, luce, pick, toll
05 speed 06 renege 07 garfish, walleye
08 jackfish, pickerel, turnpike
11 Lepidosteus

*Pikes include:*

03 Esk, Red
04 Cold, High
05 Heron, Rispa
06 Causey, Kidsty, Ullock
07 Rossett, Scafell
08 Kentmere, Langdale
09 Angletarn, Grisedale, Sheffield
10 Dollywagon, Nethermost

**pilaster**
04 anta

**pile**
03 bar, fur, jam, nap 04 a lot, beam,

bing, bomb, cock, down, fuzz, hair,
heap, load, lots, mass, mint, pack,
post, rush, shag, tons, wool 05 amass,
crowd, crush, flock, flood, fluff, heaps,
hoard, loads, mound, plush, stack,
store 06 bundle, charge, column,
fibres, gather, heap up, masses,
oodles, packet, piling, riches, stacks,
stream, wealth 07 build up, collect,
edifice, fortune, mansion, rouleau,
squeeze, stack up, support, surface,
texture, threads, upright 08 assemble,
big bucks, hundreds, lashings,
millions, mountain 09 arrowhead,
megabucks, stockpile, thousands
10 accumulate, a great deal,
assemblage, assortment, collection,
foundation, quantities
11 loadsamoney, soft surface
12 accumulation 13 large building,
large quantity
• **pile it on** 06 overdo, stress 07 lay it
on, magnify 08 overplay 09 dramatize,
emphasize, overstate 10 exaggerate
12 lay it on thick 13 make too much of,
overdramatize, overemphasize, pile it
on thick
• **pile up** 03 big 04 deck, grow, soar
07 mount up 08 escalate, increase,
multiply 10 accumulate

**pile-up**
04 bump 05 crash, prang, smash,
wreck 07 smash-up 08 accident
09 collision

**pilfer**
03 bag, lag, mag, nim, rob 04 blag, lift,
mill, nick, pick, pull, smug, whip
05 boost, filch, heist, hoist, miche,
mooch, mouch, pinch, sneak, steal,
swipe 06 finger, nobble, pickle, snitch,
thieve 07 purloin, snaffle 08 knock off,
peculate, shoplift 10 run off with
12 make away with

**pilfering**
*see* **theft**

**pilgrim**
05 hadji 06 palmer 07 devotee
08 crusader, newcomer, wanderer,
wayfarer 09 peregrine, traveller
10 worshipper

**pilgrimage**
03 haj 04 hadj, hajj, tour, trip
06 wander 07 crusade, journey,
mission 08 lifetime 10 expedition
13 peregrination

**pill**
03 dex, tab 04 ball, husk, peel 05 bolus,
upper 06 bomber, cachou, caplet,
doctor, pellet, pilula, pilule, tablet
07 capsule, globule, lozenge, plunder
08 goofball, microdot, spansule
09 blackball 10 integument, number
nine 12 multivitamin 13 pain in the
neck

**pillage**
03 rob 04 loot, peel, raid, raze, sack
05 booty, rifle, spoil, strip 06 maraud,
rapine, ravage, spoils 07 despoil,
plunder, ransack, robbery, seizure
08 freeboot, harrying, spoliate
09 depredate, marauding, vandalize

**10** spoliation **11** depredation, devastation

### pillar
**03** lat, man **04** goal, mast, pier, pile, pole, post, prop, rock **05** newel, shaft, stack, stoop, stoup **06** cippus, column **07** bastion, obelisk, respond, support, telamon, trumeau, upright **08** baluster, caryatid, gendarme, lamppost, mainstay, monolith, pilaster, stalwart, standard **09** pillarbox, sandspout, stanchion **12** lamp-standard **15** tower of strength

### pillory
**04** cang, lash, mock **05** brand **06** attack, cangue, show up **07** laugh at, tumbrel, tumbril **08** denounce, ridicule **09** criticize **10** little-ease, stigmatize **11** cast a slur on, pour scorn on **13** hold up to shame

### pillow
**03** bed, cod **04** rest **07** bolster, cushion **08** headrest, pulvinar

### pillowcase
**04** bear, beer, bere, slip

### pilot
**03** fly, run **04** crew, lead, test **05** drive, flier, flyer, guide, model, prune, steer, trial **06** airman, direct, George, handle, leader, manage, sample **07** aircrew, aviator, captain, conduct, control, hobbler, operate, shipman **08** airwoman, aviatrix, coxswain, director, governor, helmsman, lodesman, navigate **09** aviatress, commander, manoeuvre, navigator, rocketeer, steersman **10** cowcatcher, cropduster **12** experimental, first officer **14** flight engineer

### pimp
**04** bawd, hoon, mack **05** ponce **06** broker, pandar, pander **07** hustler, procure **08** fancy man, mackerel, panderer, procurer **09** solicitor **11** fleshmonger, whoremonger

### pimpernel
**06** burnet **09** brookweed, wincopipe, wink-a-peep **12** weather glass **14** shepherd's glass

### pimple
**03** zit **04** boil, quat, spot **05** botch, plook, plouk, whelk **06** button, milium, papula, papule, rum-bud **07** bubukle, pustule **08** swelling **09** blackhead, carbuncle, whitehead **10** rum-blossom

### pin
**03** fix, lay, leg, nog, peg, put **04** axle, bolt, clip, hold, join, nail, peak, stud, tack **05** affix, dowel, drift, pitch, pivot, place, preen, press, rivet, screw, spike, stage, stick, wrist **06** attach, brooch, cotter, degree, fasten, impute, pintle, secure, skewer, staple **07** ascribe, enclose, gudgeon, skittle, trenail **08** chessman, fastener, hold down, hold fast, restrain, treenail **09** attribute, constrain, thumbtack **10** immobilize
• **pin down** **03** peg **04** make, nail **05** force, press **06** compel, define **07** specify **08** hold down, hold fast, identify, nail down, pinpoint, restrain

**09** constrain, determine **10** pressurize **15** put your finger on

### pinafore
**04** brat, tire **05** apron, pinny **06** jumper, pinner, pinnie **07** gym slip, overall, save-all **08** gym tunic

### pincers
**06** forfex **07** forceps, nippers **08** pinchers, tweezers **10** Jaws of Life®

### pinch
◇ *containment indicator* **03** bag, bit, jot, nab, nip, tad **04** bite, book, bust, carp, dash, grip, hurt, lace, lift, mite, nail, nick, nirl, pook, pouk, save, shut, spot, tait, tate, whip **05** catch, chack, check, cramp, crush, filch, grasp, gripe, pleat, press, pugil, run in, seize, sneap, snuff, speck, steal, stint, swipe, taste, touch, trace, tweak, wring **06** arrest, budget, collar, crisis, detain, eke out, hamper, harass, narrow, pick up, pilfer, pincer, pull in, snatch, sneesh, stress, twinge, twitch **07** capture, confine, cut back, purloin, smidgen, snaffle, soupçon, squeeze **08** compress, encroach, half-inch, hardship, knock off, peculate, pressure, restrict, sneeshan, sneeshin, souvenir **09** economize, emergency, sneeshing **10** difficulty **11** appropriate, predicament, walk off with **13** keep costs down, scrape a living, scrimp and save **14** live on the cheap **15** tighten your belt
*See also* **steal**
• **at a pinch** **11** if necessary **13** in an emergency
• **feel the pinch** **06** be poor **12** hit a bad patch **13** have a hard time **14** be short of money, scratch a living **15** strike a bad patch, tighten your belt

### pinched
**04** pale, thin, worn **05** drawn, gaunt, peaky **07** haggard, starved **08** careworn, narrowed, strained **12** straightened

### pine
**04** ache, fade, fret, hone, long, sigh, wish **05** crave, dwine, mourn, yearn **06** desire, grieve, hanker, hunger, repine, thirst, weaken **08** languish **09** waste away

*Pine trees include:*

**03** nut, red
**04** blue, Huon, jack
**05** Chile, kauri, pinon, Scots, stone, sugar, white
**06** arolla, celery, cembra, Jersey, Korean, limber, Paraná, Scotch, spruce
**07** Amboina, Chilean, cluster, Mexican, radiata
**08** Japanese, Jeffrey's, knobcone, laceback, loblolly, longleaf, mountain, Pandanus, pinaster, Scots fir, umbrella
**09** lodgepole, Scotch fir
**11** bristlecone
**12** monkey puzzle
**13** Norfolk Island

### pineapple
**04** bomb, piña, pine **05** anana **06** ananas **07** grenade **10** tillandsia

### pining
**04** sick

### pinion
**03** cog, tie **04** bind, wing **05** chain, penne, truss **06** fasten, fetter, hobble, pennon **07** confine, manacle, pin down, shackle **10** immobilize

### pink
**03** cut, top **04** acme, best, peak, peep, peer, penk, rosy, stab, wink **05** blink, knock, notch, pinky, prick, prime, punch, score, small **06** eyelet, flower, height, incise, minnow, pierce, pinkie, samlet, summit, tiptop **07** extreme, flushed, reddish, roseate, scallop, serrate **08** blinking, detonate **09** chaffinch, exquisite, perforate **10** crenellate, perfection, rose colour **12** rose-coloured

*Pinks include:*

**04** puce, rose
**05** coral, peach
**06** oyster, salmon, shrimp
**07** old rose
**08** cyclamen
**09** carnation, pompadour, shell pink
**12** mushroom pink, shocking pink

• **in the pink** **03** fit **04** trim, well **07** healthy **08** very well **10** in good nick, in good trim, on good form **11** in good shape, right as rain **12** in fine fettle, in good health **15** in perfect health

### pinnacle
**03** cap, top **04** acme, apex, cone, peak **05** crest, crown, spire **06** apogee, height, hoodoo, needle, pinnet, summit, turret, vertex, zenith **07** minaret, obelisk, pyramid, steeple, sublime **08** eminence **11** culmination

### pinpoint
**04** spot **05** exact, place, right **06** define, locate **07** pin down, precise, specify **08** accurate, discover, home in on, identify, nail down, rigorous, zero in on **09** determine **10** meticulous, scrupulous **11** distinguish, punctilious **15** put your finger on

### pint
**02** pt
• **nearly a pint** **03** log

### pint-size
**03** wee **04** mini, tiny **05** dinky, dwarf, pygmy, small, teeny **06** little, midget, pocket **09** miniature, pint-sized **10** diminutive, teeny-weeny **11** pocket-sized

### pioneer
**05** begin, chips, found, set up, start **06** create, invent, launch, leader, open up **07** develop, founder, planter, settler **08** colonist, discover, explorer, initiate, inventor, labourer, way-maker **09** developer, establish, excavator, harbinger, innovator, instigate, institute, introduce, originate, spearhead **10** discoverer, lead the way,

## pious

pathfinder, pave the way, sandgroper **11** bandeirante, blaze a trail, trailblazer, voortrekker **12** First Fleeter, frontiersman **13** groundbreaker **14** break new ground, founding father, frontierswoman
See also **explorer**

## pious

**02** pi **03** pia **04** good, holy, wise **05** godly, moral **06** devout **07** devoted, dutiful, saintly **08** faithful, priggish, reverent, unctuous, virtuous **09** dedicated, insincere, religious, righteous, spiritual **10** goody-goody, sanctified **12** hypocritical **13** sanctimonious, self-righteous **14** holier-than-thou

## piously

**07** morally **08** devoutly **10** faithfully, priggishly, reverently, virtuously **11** insincerely, religiously, righteously, spiritually **14** hypocritically **15** sanctimoniously, self-righteous

## pip

**03** die **04** hump, kill, peep, roup, seed, spot, star **05** chirp, peepe, speck, wound **06** acinus, pippin, spleen **07** ailment, disgust, offence **08** fruitlet, syphilis **09** blackball, distemper **10** grapestone

## pipe

**03** ait, jet, oat, tap **04** clay, duct, fife, flue, hose, line, main, peep, play, pule, reed, sing, take, tube, vent, weep, worm **05** aulos, brier, bring, carry, cheep, chirp, crane, cutty, drone, flute, kelly, quill, riser, sound, tibia, trill, tweet **06** convey, dudeen, faucet, funnel, hookah, kalian, piping, shrike, shrill, siphon, supply, tubing, uptake, warble **07** calumet, channel, chanter, chibouk, chirrup, cob-pipe, conduct, conduit, dead-end, deliver, dip-pipe, nargile, nargily, passage, tweedle, twitter, whistle **08** aqueduct, bagpipes, blow pipe, claypipe, conveyor, cornpipe, cylinder, dry riser, feed-pipe, manifold, mirliton, narghile, narghily, nargileh, nargilly, overflow, pipeline, recorder, soil pipe, stopcock, tailpipe, transmit **09** blast-pipe, chibouque, drainpipe, goose-neck, narghilly, peace-pipe, pitch-pipe, standpipe, stovepipe, ventiduct, wastepipe, water pipe **10** chimney pot, gas-bracket, kill string, meerschaum **11** clyster-pipe, exhaust pipe, service pipe, tobacco-pipe **12** churchwarden, hubble-bubble, penny whistle, throttle-pipe **13** woodcock's-head **15** injection string
See also **tobacco**
• **pipe down** **06** shut up **07** be quiet **11** stop talking

## pipeclay

**03** cam **04** calm, caum

## pipe dream

**05** dream **06** mirage, notion, vagary **07** chimera, fantasy, reverie, romance **08** daydream, delusion **09** false hope **11** pie in the sky **13** castle in Spain **14** castle in the air

## pipeline

**04** duct, line, pipe, tube **07** channel, conduit, passage **08** conveyor
• **in the pipeline** **07** planned **08** on the way, under way **13** in preparation **14** already started

## pipsqueak

**05** creep, twerp **06** nobody, squirt **07** nothing, upstart **09** nonentity **11** hobbledehoy **14** whippersnapper

## piquancy

**03** pep, zip **04** bite, edge, kick, race, salt, tang, zest **05** juice, oomph, punch, spice **06** colour, ginger, relish, spirit, vigour **07** flavour, pizzazz **08** interest, pungency, raciness, vitality **09** sharpness, spiciness **10** excitement, liveliness **11** pepperiness **13** strong flavour

## piquant

**04** racy, tart **05** juicy, salty, sharp, spicy, tangy, zesty **06** biting, lively **07** peppery, pungent, savoury **08** poignant, seasoned, spirited, stinging **09** colourful, sparkling **10** appetizing, intriguing **11** fascinating, interesting, provocative, stimulating **14** highly seasoned

## pique

**03** bug, get, irk, vex **04** gall, goad, huff, miff, nark, peak, rile, spur, stir, whet **05** anger, annoy, get at, peeve, point, rouse, sting, wound **06** arouse, excite, grudge, kindle, needle, nettle, offend, put out, wind up **07** affront, dudgeon, incense, mortify, offence, provoke, umbrage **08** drive mad, irritate, vexation **09** aggravate, animosity, annoyance, displease, galvanize, punctilio, stimulate **10** drive crazy, ill-feeling, irritation, resentment **11** displeasure **12** drive bananas **13** make sparks fly **14** drive up the wall

## piqued

**03** mad **05** angry, cross, ratty, riled, vexed **06** choked, miffed, narked, peeved, put out **07** annoyed, stroppy, uptight **08** in a paddy, offended, up in arms **09** in a lather, irritated, raving mad, resentful, seeing red **10** aggravated, displeased, hopping mad **11** disgruntled, fit to be tied **12** on the warpath

## piracy

**05** theft **06** rapine **07** robbery **08** stealing **09** hijacking, sea-roving **10** plagiarism **11** bootlegging, freebooting **12** buccaneering, infringement
• **practise piracy** **04** rove

## piranha

**05** perai, pirai **06** caribe, piraña, piraya **08** characid, characin

## pirate

**04** copy, crib, lift, nick **05** pinch, poach, rover, steal **06** borrow, marque, raider, sea dog, sea rat, viking **07** brigand, corsair, sea wolf **08** algerine, knock off, marauder, picaroon, sea rover, water rat **09** buccaneer, infringer, sallee-man,

sea robber **10** arch-pirate, filibuster, freebooter, plagiarist, plagiarize, water-thief **11** appropriate, plagiarizer
Pirates include:
**03** Tew (Thomas)
**04** Bart (Jean), Gunn (Ben), Hook (Captain), Kidd (William), Otto, Read (Mary), Smee
**05** Barth (Jean), Bones (Billy), Bonny (Anne), Bunce (Jack), Drake (Sir Francis), Every (Henry), Ewart (Nanty), Flint (Captain), Tache (Edward), Teach (Edward)
**06** Aubery (Jean-Benoit), Conrad, Jonsen (Captain), Morgan (Sir Henry), Silver (Long John), Thatch (Edward), Walker (William)
**07** Dampier (William), Lafitte (Jean), O'Malley (Grace), Pugwash (Captain), Rackham (John), Roberts (Bartholomew), Sparrow (Captain Jack), Trumpet (Solomon)
**08** Altamont (Frederick), Black Dog, Blackett (Nancy), Blackett (Peggy), Blind Pew, Redbeard, Ringrose (Basil)
**09** Black Bart, Cleveland (Clement)
**10** Barbarossa (Khair-ed-din), Blackbeard, Calico Jack
**14** Long John Silver

## pirouette

**04** spin, turn **05** pivot, twirl, whirl **06** gyrate **08** gyration **15** turn on a sixpence

## pistol

**03** dag, gat, gun, pop, rod **04** Colt®, iron **05** Luger®, piece **06** barker, heater, puffer, zip gun **07** handgun, pistole, sidearm **08** revolver, water gun **09** derringer, squirt gun **10** six-shooter **11** barking iron
See also **gun**

## piston

**03** ram

## pit

**03** bed, den, put **04** dent, gulf, hole, khud, mark, mine, play, scar, silo, sump **05** abyss, chasm, ditch, fossa, fovea, notch, stone **06** cavity, crater, dimple, hollow, indent, quarry, trench **07** blemish, depress, measure, moss hag, pothole **08** alveolus, coalmine, diggings, moss hagg, pockmark, punctule, workings **10** depression, scrobicule **11** excavations, indentation
• **pit against** **05** match **06** oppose **07** compete **10** set against
• **the pits** **04** naff **05** awful, lousy, pants, spewy **06** cruddy, crummy **07** abysmal **08** dreadful, inferior, pathetic, terrible, very poor **09** third-rate **10** inadequate, second-rate **14** a load of rubbish, unsatisfactory

## Pitcairn Island

**03** PCN

## pitch

**03** aim, fix, lob, pin, pop, set, tar, yak **04** bowl, cant, cast, dive, drop, face, fall, fire, hurl, keel, line, list, mark, nets, park, peck, reel, roll, stud, sway, talk, tilt, tone, toss **05** angle, arena,

**pitch-black**

chuck, cover, erect, field, fling, grade, heave, level, lurch, place, plant, point, put up, set up, slant, sling, slope, sound, spiel, throw **06** alight, bounce, degree, direct, encamp, extent, gabble, ground, height, jargon, launch, maltha, patter, plunge, settle, timbre, topple, tumble, wallow, wicket **07** asphalt, bitumen, chatter, descent, incline, plummet, set down, stadium, station **08** flounder, gradient, position, tonality **09** determine, establish, frequency, intensity, interlock, steepness **10** modulation **11** inclination, sports field **12** fall headlong, playing-field **13** move up and down
• **make a pitch for 05** offer, put up **06** bid for, submit, tender **07** advance, proffer, propose **08** put in for, try to get **09** try to sell **10** put forward **11** try to obtain
• **pitch in 04** help **06** join in, muck in **07** help out **09** co-operate, do your bit, lend a hand **10** be involved **11** participate
• **too low in pitch, too high in pitch 04** flat **05** sharp

**pitch-black**

**04** dark, inky **05** black, unlit **08** jet-black **09** coal-black, pitch-dark **13** unilluminated

**pitcher**

**03** can, jar, jug, urn **04** ewer, jack, sett **05** crock **06** bottle, closer, vessel **07** growler **09** container **11** screwballer **13** knuckleballer
• **pitcher plant 08** nepenthe **09** Nepenthes **10** Sarracenia **12** Darlingtonia

**piteous**

**03** sad **06** moving, paltry, rueful, woeful **07** pitiful, ruthful **08** mournful, pathetic, pitiable, poignant, touching, wretched **09** plaintive, sorrowful **10** lamentable **11** distressing **12** heart-rending **13** compassionate, heartbreaking

**pitfall**

**04** risk, snag, trap **05** catch, peril, snare **06** danger, hazard **08** drawback, trapfall **10** difficulty **14** stumbling-block

**pith**

**03** nub **04** core, crux, gist, meat **05** heart, point, value **06** import, kernel, marrow, matter, mettle, moment, vigour, weight **07** essence, medulla, papyrus **09** substance **10** importance **11** consequence **12** forcefulness, quintessence, salient point, significance **13** essential part

**pithead**

**04** brow

**pithily**

**07** in a word, in brief, tersely **09** compactly, concisely **10** succinctly, to the point **11** in a few words, in a nutshell **12** meaningfully

**pithy**

**05** brief, meaty, short, terse **06** cogent, strong **07** compact, concise, marrowy,

pointed, summary, telling **08** forceful, forcible, incisive, lapidary, material, pregnant, succinct **09** condensed, energetic, matterful, trenchant **10** expressive, meaningful

**pitiable**

**03** sad **04** poor **05** silly, sorry **06** woeful **07** doleful, piteous, woesome **08** grievous, mournful, pathetic, wretched **09** miserable **10** distressed, lamentable **11** distressful, distressing **12** commiserable, contemptible **14** compassionable

**pitiful**

**03** low, sad **04** base, mean, poor, vile **05** lousy, seely, sorry, waefu' **06** crummy, meagre, moving, paltry, shabby, waeful, woeful **07** doleful, piteous, ruthful, the pits, waesome **08** hopeless, mournful, pathetic, pitiable, terrible, wretched **09** affecting, miserable, worthless **10** deplorable, despicable, inadequate, lamentable **11** distressing **12** contemptible, heart-rending **13** compassionate, heartbreaking, insignificant

**pitifully**

**05** sadly **08** terribly, woefully **09** miserably, piteously **10** deplorably, despicably, hopelessly, lamentably **12** contemptibly, pathetically **13** distressingly

**pitiless**

**05** cruel, harsh, stony **06** brutal, severe **07** callous, inhuman **08** inhumane, ruthless, uncaring **09** heartless, merciless, unfeeling **10** dispiteous, hard-headed, inexorable, relentless **11** cold-blooded, cold-hearted, hard-hearted, unremitting **13** unsympathetic

**pitilessly**

**07** cruelly, harshly **08** brutally **09** callously **10** ruthlessly **11** mercilessly **13** cold-bloodedly, cold-heartedly, hard-heartedly

**pittance**

**04** dole, drop **05** crumb **06** trifle **07** modicum, peanuts **11** chickenfeed **14** drop in the ocean

**pitted**

**05** holey, rough **06** dented, marked **07** foveate, notched, scarred **08** alveolar, indented, lacunose, potholed, punctate **09** alveolate, blemished, depressed, punctated **10** pockmarked

**pity**

**03** rew, rue, sin **04** ruth **05** bleed, grace, mercy, piety, shame **06** bemoan, bepity, bowels, regret, sorrow **07** bad luck, emotion, feel for, feeling, mercify, remorse, sadness, weep for **08** distress, kindness, sympathy **09** grieve for **10** compassion, condolence, have a heart, misericord, misfortune, tenderness **11** crying shame, forbearance, forgiveness, misericorde **12** feel sorry for **13** commiseration, empathize with, fellow-feeling, understanding

**14** disappointment, sympathize with **15** commiserate with
• **take pity on 03** rue **05** spare **06** pardon **07** feel for **09** show mercy **11** have mercy on **12** feel sorry for **13** empathize with **14** emphathize with, sympathize with **15** commiserate with

**pivot**

**03** hub, lie **04** axis, axle, hang, rely, spin, turn **05** focus, heart, hinge, swing **06** centre, depend, rotate, swivel **07** fulcrum, kingpin, revolve, spindle **08** cardinal, linchpin **10** focal point **12** be contingent, central point

**pivotal**

**05** axial, focal, vital **07** central, crucial **08** critical, decisive **09** climactic, important **11** determining

**pixie**

**03** elf, imp **04** pixy **05** fairy, pisky **06** goblin, sprite **07** brownie **10** leprechaun

**pizzazz**

**04** brio, life **05** oomph **06** energy, esprit, spirit, vigour **07** entrain **08** activity, dynamism, vitality, vivacity **09** animation, briskness, quickness, smartness **10** liveliness **11** refreshment **13** sprightliness, vivaciousness **14** boisterousness

**placard**

**02** ad **04** bill, sign **05** title **06** advert, notice, poster **07** affiche, placcat, placket, sticker **13** advertisement

**placate**

**04** calm, lull **05** quiet **06** disarm, pacify, soothe **07** appease, assuage, mollify, win over **08** calm down **10** conciliate, propitiate

**placatory**

**07** calming **08** soothing **09** appeasing **10** mollifying **11** peace-making **12** conciliatory, pacificatory, propitiative, propitiatory

**place**

**01** P **02** do, Pl **03** fix, job, lay, pad, put, set **04** area, city, digs, duty, flat, home, know, lieu, park, part, pose, post, rank, rest, role, room, seat, site, sort, spot, sted, task, town **05** abode, class, grade, group, hotel, house, leave, locus, lodge, niche, order, plant, point, right, scene, space, stand, state, stead, stedd, stede, steed, topic, venue **06** assign, hamlet, induct, invest, locale, locate, region, settle, square, status, stedde **07** appoint, arrange, concern, country, deposit, footing, install, lay down, put down, set down, setting, situate, station, village **08** allocate, building, business, classify, district, domicile, dwelling, fortress, function, identify, locality, location, pinpoint, position, property, remember, standing **09** apartment, establish, recognize, residence, situation **10** categorize, restaurant **11** appointment, battlefield, find a job for, institution, whereabouts **13** accommodation, establishment, neighbourhood **14** responsibility

## placement

*See also* **Bible; entertainment; fictional; mythical**
• **all over the place** ◇ *anagram indicator* **04** awry **05** messy **07** muddled **08** confused **09** dispersed, scattered **12** disorganized
• **at that place 05** there
• **at the right place 03** pat
• **at this place 04** here
• **in place 05** set up **07** in order, working **08** arranged **10** in position
• **in place of 04** lieu, vice **08** in lieu of **09** instead of **13** in exchange for
• **in the same place 02** ib **04** ibid **06** ibidem
• **no place 02** np
• **out of place** ◇ *anagram indicator* **04** away **08** improper, out of key, tactless, unseemly **09** unfitting **10** inapposite, malapropos, unbecoming, unsuitable **12** unseasonable **13** inappropriate
• **put someone in their place 05** crush, shame **06** humble **07** deflate **08** bring low **09** humiliate
• **take place 02** be **04** fall **05** occur **06** befall, be held, betide, happen **07** come off **09** come about, transpire **10** come to pass
• **take the place of 06** act for **07** replace, serve as, succeed **09** supersede **10** stand in for **12** take over from **13** substitute for

## placement

**03** job **07** placing, ranking, setting **08** locating, location, ordering **10** assignment, deployment, employment, engagement, internship, stationing **11** appointment, arrangement, disposition, emplacement, positioning **12** distribution, installation **14** classification

## placid

**04** calm, cool, mild **05** quiet, still **06** gentle, serene **07** equable, pacific, restful, unmoved **08** composed, peaceful, tranquil **09** easy-going, peaceable, unruffled **10** untroubled **11** level-headed, undisturbed, unemotional, unexcitable, unflappable **12** even-tempered **13** imperturbable, self-possessed

## placidly

**06** calmly, gently, mildly **08** serenely **09** restfully **10** peacefully **11** unflappably **13** imperturbably

## plagiarism

**04** crib **05** theft **06** piracy **07** copying, lifting **08** cribbing **09** borrowing **12** infringement, reproduction **13** appropriation **14** counterfeiting

## plagiarist

**05** thief **06** copier, pirate, robber **08** imitator **09** Autolycus

## plagiarize

**04** copy, crib, lift, nick **05** poach, steal **06** borrow, pirate **07** imitate **09** reproduce **11** appropriate, counterfeit

## plague

**03** bug, dog, dun, pox, vex **04** bane, blow, pest **05** annoy, curse, death, haunt, hound, swarm, tease, trial, upset, worry, wound **06** bother, hamper, harass, hassle, hinder, influx, pester **07** afflict, bedevil, cholera, disease, disturb, murrain, scourge, torment, torture, trouble **08** calamity, distress, epidemic, goodyear, invasion, irritate, nuisance, pandemic, sickness, vexation **09** aggravate, annoyance, contagion, goodyears, infection, persecute **10** affliction, Black Death, huge number, pestilence **11** infestation **13** bubonic plague, pain in the neck **15** pneumonic plague, thorn in the flesh

*The ten Biblical plagues:*

**04** lice
**05** boils, flies, frogs
**07** locusts
**08** darkness
**09** hailstorm
**18** disease of livestock
**19** death of the firstborn
**21** Nile waters turn to blood

## plain

**04** even, flat, open, ugly **05** basic, blunt, clear, frank, level, lucid, muted, overt, prose, quite, secco, stark, utter **06** candid, direct, homely, honest, lament, modest, patent, rustic, simple, simply **07** austere, clearly, evident, obvious, plateau, sincere, spartan, totally, unruled, utterly, visible **08** apparent, clinical, complain, flatland, home-bred, home-made, homespun, manifest, ordinary, truthful, uncurled, unlovely **09** downright, grassland, outspoken, plain-Jane, practical, tableland, unadorned **10** accessible, completely, distinctly, forthright, noticeable, restrained, thoroughly, unaffected, unassuming, uncoloured, undeniably **11** discernible, perceptible, plain-spoken, transparent, unambiguous, undecorated, unelaborate, unpatterned **12** intelligible, self-coloured, unattractive, unmistakable, unobstructed, unvariegated **13** uncomplicated, unembellished, unpretentious **14** understandable **15** clear as daylight, not much to look at, straightforward, undistinguished, unprepossessing, unsophisticated

*Plains include:*

**04** vega
**05** carse, lande, llano
**06** maidan, pampas, sabkha, steppe, tundra
**07** lowland, prairie, sabkhah, sabkhat
**08** savannah

## plain-spoken

**04** open **05** blunt, frank, round **06** candid, direct, honest **08** explicit, outright, truthful **09** downright, outspoken **10** forthright **11** unequivocal **15** straightforward

## plaintive

**03** sad **06** woeful **07** doleful, piteous, pitiful, unhappy, wistful **08** mournful, wretched **09** lacrimoso, lagrimoso, querulous, sorrowful **10** melancholy **11** heartbroken, high-pitched **12** disconsolate, heart-rending **13** grief-stricken

## plaintively

**05** sadly **08** woefully **09** dolefully, lacrimoso, lagrimoso, pitifully, unhappily, wistfully **10** mournfully, wretchedly **14** disconsolately

## plait

**04** plat **05** braid, pedal, pleat, tress **06** plight **07** frounce, leghorn **08** doubling **09** Dunstable

## plan

◇ *anagram indicator* **03** aim, lay, map, way **04** case, dart, hang, idea, mean, plat, plot, ploy, seek, want, wish **05** block, chart, draft, frame, means, model, shape, trace **06** design, device, devise, intend, invent, layout, map out, method, policy, schema, scheme, sketch, system **07** arrange, complot, concoct, develop, diagram, drawing, foresee, formula, outline, prepare, project, propose, purpose, resolve, road map, think of, work out **08** conspire, contrive, envisage, organize, platform, proposal, scenario, schedule, strategy **09** architect, blueprint, formulate, intention, itinerary, procedure, programme, timetable **10** conception, mastermind, suggestion **11** arrangement, contemplate, contrivance, delineation, ichnography, premeditate, projectment, proposition **12** illustration, scale drawing **14** representation

## plane

**03** bus, fly, jet **04** even, flat, rank, rung, sail, skim, soar, VTOL, wing **05** class, flush, glide, jumbo, level, plain, skate, stage **06** bomber, degree, glider, planar, smooth, thrust **07** echelon, fighter, footing, jointer, regular, stratum, uniform **08** aircraft, airplane, jumbo jet, position, seaplane, sycamore, volplane **09** aeroplane, condition, fillister, swing-wing **10** buttonball, buttonwood, homaloidal, horizontal **11** flat surface **12** level surface
*See also* **aircraft**

## planet

**05** world

*Planets:*

**04** Mars
**05** Earth, Pluto, Venus
**06** Saturn, Uranus
**07** Jupiter, Mercury, Neptune

## plank

**04** beam, slab, slat **05** board, panel, sheet **06** planch, timber **08** stringer **09** washboard **12** weatherboard

## planner

**05** maker **06** author **07** creator, deviser,

**planning**

stylist **08** arranger, designer, inventor, producer **09** architect, contriver, developer, fashioner, organizer **10** mastermind, originator

**planning**

**06** design **07** control, running **09** ordinance **10** management, projection, regulation **11** arrangement, development, preparation **12** co-ordination, organization **13** establishment **14** administration

**plant**

**03** fix, put, set, sow **04** bury, gear, hide, land, mill, post, root, salt, seed, shop, slip, yard **05** found, imbed, inter, lodge, place, scion, stock, works **06** cudgel, insert, instil, locate, settle **07** conceal, cutting, factory, foundry, implant, scatter, secrete, situate, station **08** colonize, disguise, offshoot, position, workshop **09** apparatus, equipment, establish, introduce, machinery **10** transplant **11** put secretly **13** put out of sight
See also **flower; leaf**

Plant types include:

**03** air, pot
**04** bean, beet, bulb, bush, cane, corm, fern, herb, moss, tree, vine, weed
**05** algae, grass, house, sedge, shrub, water
**06** annual, cactus, cereal, flower, fungus, hybrid, lichen
**07** bedding, climber, foliage, sapling
**08** biennial, cultivar, epiphyte, seedling
**09** aerophyte, evergreen, perennial, succulent, vegetable
**10** herbaceous, wild flower
**11** carnivorous
**13** insectivorous

See also **alga, algae; bean; bulb; cactus; cereal; crop; disease; grass; herb; lily; orchid; palm; poison; seaweed; sedge; shrub; tree; vegetable; weed**

**plantation**

**03** pen **04** tope **06** bosket **07** bosquet, fazenda, pinetum **08** vineyard **09** cornbrake, salicetum, shrubbery, tea garden, viticetum

**plaque**

**04** sign, slab **05** badge, brass, medal, panel, plate **06** brooch, shield, tablet **07** plateau **09** cartouche, medallion, plaquette

**plaster**

**03** mud **04** coat, daub, leep, teer **05** cover, gesso, grout, parge, patch, smarm, smear **06** bedaub, clatch, gypsum, laying, mortar, parget, peloid, render, screed, spread, stucco **07** bandage, Band-aid®, overlay, pugging **08** dressing, plaister, sinapism **09** beplaster, cataplasm, emplaster, Polyfilla®, rendering, roughcast **10** emplastron, emplastrum **11** Elastoplast®, plasterwork, scratchcoat **12** cover thickly,

plasterboard **13** butterfly clip **14** plaster of Paris **15** sticking-plaster

**plastered**

◊ anagram indicator
See **drunk**

**plastic**

◊ anagram indicator **04** soft **05** false **06** phoney, pliant, supple **07** ductile, man-made, pliable, shaping **08** flexible, modeller, sculptor **09** compliant, formative, malleable, mouldable, receptive, shapeable, synthetic, tractable, unnatural **10** artificial, manageable, modifiable **14** impressionable

Plastics include:

**03** PVC
**04** PTFE, uPVC
**05** vinyl
**06** Biopol®, Teflon®
**07** Perspex®
**08** Bakelite®, laminate, silicone
**09** Celluloid®, Plexiglas®, polyester, polythene, Styrofoam®
**10** epoxy resin, plexiglass
**11** polystyrene
**12** polyethylene, polyurethane
**13** phenolic resin, polypropylene
**14** polynorbornene

**plasticity**

**07** pliancy **08** softness **10** pliability, suppleness **11** flexibility, pliableness **12** malleability, tractability

**plate**

**01** L, T **03** seg, tin, web **04** bowl, coat, dish, foil, gild, pane, rove, sign, slab **05** ashet, cover, layer, ortho, panel, paten, print, sheet **06** baffle, lamina, latten, muffin, plaque, remark, salver, silver, tablet, veneer **07** anodize, gravure, helping, lamella, ossicle, overlay, picture, plateau, platter, portion, serving **08** laminate, mazarine, pattress, trencher **09** galvanize, osteoderm, platinize **10** lithograph, photograph, zincograph **11** photo-relief **12** electroplate, illustration, mazarine dish
See also **platter**

**plateau**

**04** mesa, roof **05** grade, level, plane, stage, table **06** meseta, upland **08** highland, platform **09** Altiplano, stability, tableland

**platform**

**03** pad, rig, top **04** aims, bema, dais, deck, kang, plan, site **05** basis, bench, crane, dolly, floor, ideas, stage, stand, stoep, stoop, stump **06** bridge, cradle, device, flotel, gantry, machan, oil rig, pallet, perron, podium, policy, pulpit, scheme, sketch, tenets **07** balcony, decking, estrade, floatel, foretop, maintop, plateau, rostrum, soapbox, sponson, terrace, tribune **08** barbette, flooring, labellum, predella, round top, scaffold, strategy **09** crow's-nest, drillship, footplate, gangboard, manifesto, party line, programme, traverser, turntable **10** dumb waiter, intentions, objectives, principles,

roundabout **11** emplacement, entablement, monkey board, paint-bridge **12** landing stage, launching-pad

**platinum**

**02** Pt

**platitude**

**06** cliché, truism **07** bromide, inanity **08** banality, chestnut, flatness **10** generality, stereotype **11** commonplace **15** trite expression

**platitudinous**

**03** set **04** dull, flat **05** banal, corny, inane, stale, stock, tired, trite, vapid **07** cliché'd **08** clichéed, truistic, well-worn **09** hackneyed **10** overworked **11** commonplace, stereotyped

**platonic**

**05** ideal **09** non-sexual, spiritual **10** idealistic **11** incorporeal, non-physical, non-romantic **12** intellectual, transcendent

**platoon**

**04** team, unit **05** group, squad, troop **06** outfit, patrol, volley **07** battery, company **08** squadron

**platter**

**04** dish, lanx, tray **05** graal, grail, plate **06** grayle, salver **07** charger **08** trencher
See also **plate**

**plaudits**

**04** hand **06** praise **07** acclaim, bouquet, hurrahs, ovation **08** accolade, applause, approval, clapping **09** good press **10** rave review **11** acclamation, approbation **12** commendation, pat on the back **15** congratulations, standing ovation

**plausible**

**04** fair, glib **06** cogent, likely **07** logical, proball **08** credible, possible, probable, specious **10** acceptable, believable, colourable, convincing, imaginable, persuasive, reasonable, soft-spoken **11** conceivable, smooth-faced **12** smooth-spoken **13** silver-tongued, smooth-talking, smooth-tongued

**plausibly**

**08** possibly, probably **09** logically **10** imaginably, pleasantly, reasonably **11** commendably, conceivably **12** convincingly, persuasively

**play**

◊ anagram indicator **02** do, no **03** act, fun, noh, pit, ply, toy **04** game, give, jest, laik, lake, plot, romp, room, show, work **05** caper, dance, drama, farce, flash, frisk, gleam, hobby, kicks, laugh, range, revel, rival, scope, slack, space, sport, wield **06** action, cavort, comedy, frolic, gamble, gambol, glance, join in, joking, leeway, margin, nogaku, oppose, take on, trifle **07** compete, flicker, flutter, freedom, have fun, holiday, leisure, liberty, licence, operate, pastime, perform, portray, shimmer, teasing, tragedy, twinkle, vie with **08** activity, exercise, free rein, gambling, latitude, movement **09** amusement, challenge, dalliance, diversion, enjoyment, interplay, looseness, melodrama, operation, play games, represent **10** recreation, take part in **11** flexibility, impersonate, interaction, merrymaking, move lightly, performance, transaction **12** be involved in **13** amuse yourself, enjoy yourself, entertainment, participate in, play the part of **14** compete against, divert yourself, occupy yourself

*Plays include:*

**03** RUR
**04** Loot
**05** Equus, Faust, Le Cid, Medea, Médée, Roots, Yerma
**06** Becket, Phèdre, St Joan
**07** Amadeus, Candida, Electra, Endgame, Galileo, La Ronde, Oedipus, Oleanna, Orestes, Volpone, Woyzeck
**08** Antigone, Betrayal, Everyman, Hay Fever, Huis Clos, Oresteia, Peer Gynt, Tartuffe, The Birds, The Flies, The Frogs, The Miser, The Price, The Wasps
**09** All My Sons, Happy Days, Miss Julie, Party Time, Pygmalion, Saint Joan, The Chairs, The Clouds, The Father, The Rivals, The Vortex
**10** A Dream Play, All for Love, Andromache, Andromaque, Lysistrata, Misery Guts, No Man's Land, The Bacchae, The Robbers, The Seagull, Uncle Vanya
**11** A Doll's House, Blood and Ice, Hedda Gabler, The Blue Bird, The Crucible, The Wild Duck, Trojan Women
**12** Anna Christie, Blithe Spirit, Blood Wedding, Major Barbara, Private Lives, Punch and Judy, The Alchemist, The Caretaker, The Mousetrap
**13** Arms and the Man, A Taste of Honey, Doctor Faustus, Educating Rita, Le Misanthrope, The Homecoming, The Jew of Malta, The White Devil, The Winslow Boy
**14** Can't Pay? Won't Pay!, Krapp's Last Tape, Man and Superman, Orlando Furioso, Riders to the Sea, Separate Tables, The Country Wife, The Entertainer, The Silent Woman
**15** Bartholomew Fair, Look Back in Anger, Prometheus Bound, The Beggar's Opera, The Iceman Cometh, The Three Sisters, Waiting for Godot

*See also* **Shakespeare**
• **out of play** **04** dead
• **part of play** **03** act
• **play around with** ◊ *anagram indicator* **07** toy with **08** fool with **09** dally with, flirt with **10** fiddle with, fidget with, meddle with, tamper with, trifle with **12** womanize with **13** interfere with, philander with **14** mess around with
• **play at** **06** affect **07** make out,

pretend **10** put on an act **11** pretend to be
• **play down** **08** downplay, minimize **09** gloss over, underplay **10** understate, undervalue **11** make light of **13** underestimate
• **play harshly** **03** saw
• **play on** **07** exploit, trade on **08** profit by **12** capitalize on **13** turn to account **15** take advantage of
• **play out** **03** act **04** go on **05** enact **06** act out, unfold **07** carry on, exhaust, wear out **08** continue **10** be revealed
• **play the fool** **03** fon **04** daff, fool **07** act dido, tomfool
• **play up** **04** fool, hurt **05** annoy, boost **06** bother, stress **07** go wrong, not work, point up, trouble **09** be naughty, emphasize, highlight, misbehave, spotlight, underline **10** accentuate, exaggerate **11** give trouble, malfunction **12** be on the blink, go on the blink **13** be mischievous **15** call attention to
• **play up to** **04** fawn **05** toady **06** cozy up **07** flatter **08** blandish, bootlick, butter up, soft-soap, suck up to **15** curry favour with
• **play with** ◊ *anagram indicator*

## play-act
**03** act **04** fake, mime, sham **05** bluff, feign, put on **06** affect, assume **07** pretend **08** simulate **09** dissemble, fabricate **10** put on an act **11** counterfeit, impersonate **15** pass yourself off

## playboy
**04** rake, roué **09** debauchee, ladies' man, libertine, socialite, womanizer **10** lady-killer **11** philanderer **12** man about town

## player
**01** E, N, S, W **03** ace, ham, man **04** east, pone, star, west **05** actor, north, south **06** artist **07** actress, artiste, trifler, trouper **08** comedian, musician **09** performer, sportsman **10** all-rounder, competitor, contestant **11** accompanist, entertainer, participant, sportswoman **15** instrumentalist

*See also* **Australian football; baseball; basketball; chess; footballer; instrument; rugby; tennis**
• **bit player** **05** extra
• **opposing player** **02** it

## players
**04** band, cast, wind **05** brass **07** strings

*See also* **football; orchestra**

## playful
**03** gay, mad **05** funny, ludic **06** frisky, impish, joking, lively, toyish **07** jesting, kitteny, puckish, roguish, teasing, toysome, waggish **08** espiègle, flippant, friendly, gamesome, humorous, skittish, spirited, sportive **09** facetious, fun-loving, kittenish, piacevole **10** frolicsome, rollicking

**11** mischievous **12** high-spirited, light-hearted **13** tongue-in-cheek

## playfully
**06** in jest **08** jokingly **09** piacevole **10** humorously **11** facetiously **14** light-heartedly

## playground
**04** park **08** play area **12** playing-field **13** amusement park **14** pleasure ground

## playmate
**03** pal **04** chum, mate **05** buddy **06** friend **07** comrade **09** companion, neighbour **10** playfellow

## plaything
**03** toy **04** game **05** sport **06** bauble, gewgaw, puppet, trifle **07** pastime, trinket **08** gimcrack **09** amusement

## playwright
**06** writer **09** dramatist, tragedian **10** dramaturge **12** dramaturgist, screen writer, scriptwriter

*Playwrights and screenwriters include:*

**02** Fo (Dario)
**03** Fry (Christopher), Gay (John), Hay (Ian), Kyd (Thomas), May (Elaine)
**04** Bolt (Robert), Bond (Edward), Coen (Ethan), Coen (Joel), Dane (Clemence), Ford (John), Hare (David), Rowe (Nicholas), Shaw (George Bernard), Vega (Lope de)
**05** Albee (Edward), Allen (Woody), Arden (John), Bates (Herbert Ernest), Behan (Brendan), Dumas (Alexandre), Eliot (T S), Frayn (Michael), Friel (Brian), Genet (Jean), Gogol (Nikolai), Havel (Vaclav), Ibsen (Henrik), Lodge (Thomas), Lorca (Federico García), Mamet (David), Nashe (Thomas), Odets (Clifford), Orton (Joe), Otway (Thomas), Sachs (Hans), Sachs (Nelly), Smith (Dodie), Stone (Oliver), Synge (J M), Udall (Nicholas), Wilde (Oscar), Yeats (W B)
**06** Barrie (Sir J M), Brecht (Bertolt), Bridie (James), Colman (George), Coward (Sir Noël), Dekker (Thomas), Dryden (John), Galdós (Benito Pérez), Goethe (Johann Wolfgang von), Greene (Robert), Herzog (Werner), Hilton (James), Huston (John), Jerome (Jerome K), Jonson (Ben), Kaiser (Georg), Lerner (Alan Jay), Mercer (David), Miller (Arthur), Miller (Henry), Musset (Alfred de), O'Casey (Sean), O'Neill (Eugene), Pinero (Sir Arthur Wing), Pinter (Harold), Powell (Michael), Racine (Jean), Sardou (Victorien), Sartre (Jean-Paul), Steele (Sir Richard), Storey (David), Tagore (Rabindranath), Wesker (Arnold), Wilder (Thornton)
**07** Anouilh (Jean), Arrabal (Fernando), Beckett (Samuel), Bennett (Alan), Büchner (Georg), Chapman (George), Chekhov (Anton), Cocteau (Jean), Coppola (Francis

Ford), **Diderot** (Denis), **Garrick** (David), **Gregory** (Lady Isabella Augusta), **Holberg** (Ludvig, Baron), **Ionesco** (Eugène), **Klinger** (Friedrich Maximilian von), **Kubrick** (Stanley), **Labiche** (Eugène), **Lardner** (Ring), **Marlowe** (Christopher), **Marston** (John), **McGough** (Roger), **Mishima** (Yukio), **Molière**, **Novello** (Ivor), **Osborne** (John), **Plautus** (Titus Maccius), **Richler** (Mordecai), **Rostand** (Edmond), **Russell** (Willy), **Shaffer** (Peter), **Shepard** (Sam), **Terence**, **Ustinov** (Sir Peter), **Vicente** (Gil), **Walcott** (Derek), **Webster** (John)

08 **Andersen** (Hans Christian), **Banville** (Théodore de), **Beaumont** (Francis), **Björnson** (Björnstjerne), **Brentano** (Clemens), **Burgoyne** (John), **Congreve** (William), **Davenant** (Sir William), **Fielding** (Henry), **Fletcher** (John), **Hochhuth** (Rolf), **Lochhead** (Liz), **Menander**, **Mortimer** (Sir John), **Polanski** (Roman), **Rattigan** (Sir Terence), **Schiller** (Friedrich), **Shadwell** (Thomas), **Sheridan** (Richard Brinsley), **Stoppard** (Sir Tom), **Suckling** (Sir John), **Tourneur** (Cyril), **Vanbrugh** (Sir John), **Wedekind** (Frank), **Williams** (Emlyn), **Williams** (Tennessee)

09 **Aeschylus**, **Ayckbourn** (Sir Alan), **Corneille** (Pierre), **D'Annunzio** (Gabriele), **Euripides**, **Goldsmith** (Oliver), **Hauptmann** (Gerhart), **Isherwood** (Christopher), **Mankowitz** (Wolf), **Marinetti** (Filippo Tommaso), **Middleton** (Thomas), **Poliakoff** (Stephen), **Priestley** (J B), **Rosenthal** (Jack), **Sophocles**, **Wycherley** (William)

10 **Galsworthy** (John), **Pirandello** (Luigi), **Strindberg** (August)

11 **Maeterlinck** (Maurice), **Shakespeare** (William)

12 **Aristophanes**, **Beaumarchais** (Pierre-Augustin Caron de)

---

**plea**
05 alibi, claim, fains 06 appeal, excuse, fains I, placet, placit, prayer 07 defence, defense, lawsuit, pretext, request 08 demurrer, entreaty, fainites, petition, placitum, pleading 10 invocation 11 declinature, explanation, imploration, vindication 12 supplication 13 justification 14 nolo contendere

**plead**
03 ask, beg 04 moot, urge 05 argue, claim, state 06 adduce, allege, appeal, assert 07 beseech, entreat, implore, request, solicit 08 maintain, persuade, perswade, petition 09 intercede 10 put forward 12 intercede for
• **refusing to plead** 04 mute

**pleasant**
04 cute, fine, nice 05 amene, lepid, merry, tipsy 06 genial, groovy, jocund, lekker, lovely 07 affable, amiable, amusing, likable, welcome, winsome

08 all roses, charming, cheerful, friendly, gorgeous, likeable, pleasing, savorous, sunshiny 09 agreeable, congenial, enjoyable, piacevole, toothsome 10 acceptable, delightful, gratifying, refreshing, salubrious, satisfying 11 inoffensive 12 entertaining, good-humoured 14 roses all the way

**pleasantly**
07 nice and 09 enjoyably, piacevole, plausibly 10 pleasingly 12 delightfully, refreshingly 14 entertainingly

**pleasantry**
04 jest, joke, quip 05 sally 06 banter, bon mot 08 badinage 09 enjoyment, witticism 10 jocularity 12 casual remark, pleasantness 13 polite comment 14 friendly remark

**please**
04 like, list, suit, want, will, wish 05 agree, amuse, bitte, charm, cheer, queme 06 arride, choose, desire, divert, fulfil, humour, kindly, prefer, see fit, tickle 07 aggrate, attract, cheer up, content, delight, flatter, gladden, gratify, indulge, prithee, prythee, satisfy 08 appeal to, think fit 09 captivate, entertain, make happy 11 if you please 12 je vous en prie 14 give pleasure to
• **hard to please** 04 nice 09 difficult

**pleased**
04 glad, rapt 05 happy 06 elated 07 chuffed 08 cheerful, euphoric, grateful, gruntled, thrilled 09 contented, delighted, delirious, gratified, satisfied 10 complacent 11 on cloud nine, over the moon, tickled pink

**pleasing**
04 cute, fair, fine, good, nice 05 lusty 06 comely, liking, taking 07 amusing, likable, savoury, winning 08 charming, engaging, likeable, pleasant 09 agreeable, desirable, enjoyable 10 acceptable, attractive, delectable, delightful, gratifying, satisfying 11 pleasurable 12 entertaining, heartwarming, honey-tongued 13 prepossessing

**pleasurable**
03 fun 04 good, nice 06 groovy, lovely 07 amusing, welcome 08 luscious, pleasant 09 agreeable, congenial, diverting, enjoyable 10 delightful, gratifying 12 entertaining

**pleasure**
03 fun, gem, joy 04 will, wish 05 glory, mirth, prize 06 choice, desire, heaven, solace, thrill 07 command, delight, elation, leisure, purpose 08 gladness, treasure 09 amusement, enjoyment, happiness, hog heaven, pleasance 10 preference, recreation, sensuality 11 complacence, complacency, contentment, dissipation, inclination 12 satisfaction 13 entertainment, gratification
• **expression of pleasure** 03 aha, boy, oho, ooh, wow 05 good-o, oh boy, tra-la, whack, wowee, zowie

06 good-oh, gotcha, whacko 07 way to go!, whoopee 10 hubba hubba
• **it's a pleasure** 07 any time 08 forget it, not at all 09 no problem 10 my pleasure 11 it's all right 12 it's no trouble, it was nothing, you're welcome 13 don't mention it, that's all right
• **with pleasure** 04 fain 06 gladly 07 happily, readily 08 of course 09 willingly 11 avec plaisir

**pleasure-flight**
04 flip

**pleat**
04 fold, kilt, purl, tuck 05 braid, crimp, flute, pinch, plait, prank 06 crease, gather, goffer, pranck, pucker 07 folding, gauffer, plicate, prancke 09 plication 10 intertwine

**plebeian**
03 low 04 base, boor, mean, non-U, pleb 05 prole 06 coarse, common, vulgar, worker 07 ignoble, low-born, peasant, popular 08 commoner, roturier 09 unrefined, vulgarian 10 lower-class, uncultured 11 proletarian 12 common person, uncultivated, working-class 15 undistinguished

**plebiscite**
04 poll, vote 06 ballot 09 straw poll 10 referendum

**pledge**
03 vow, wad, wed 04 bail, band, bond, fine, gage, hand, oath, pass, pawn, wage, word 05 swear, vouch, wager 06 borrow, commit, engage, impawn, plight, secure, surety 07 betroth, deposit, earnest, hostage, promise, propine, warrant 08 contract, covenant, impledge, mortgage, security 09 assurance, committal, guarantee, pignorate, sacrament, undertake 10 collateral, commitment, take an oath 11 impignorate, undertaking 12 give your word, word of honour

**plenary**
04 full, open 05 whole 06 entire 07 general 08 absolute, complete, integral, sweeping, thorough 09 unlimited 11 unqualified 12 unrestricted 13 unconditional

**plenipotentiary**
05 envoy 06 legate, nuncio 08 absolute, diplomat, emissary, minister 09 dignitary 10 ambassador

**plenitude**
06 bounty, excess, plenty, wealth 08 fullness, plethora 09 abundance, amplitude, profusion, repletion 10 cornucopia, entireness 11 copiousness 12 completeness 13 plenteousness, plentifulness

**plenteous**
04 rich 05 ample 06 bumper, lavish 07 copious, fertile, liberal, profuse 08 abundant, fruitful, generous, infinite, prolific 09 abounding, bounteous, bountiful, luxuriant,

**plentiful**
**10** productive **11** overflowing **13** inexhaustible

**plentiful**
**04** easy **05** ample, routh, rowth **06** bumper, lavish **07** copious, liberal, profuse, teeming **08** abundant, fruitful, generous, infinite **09** bounteous, bountiful **10** productive **11** overflowing **13** inexhaustible

**plentifully**
**05** amply **08** lavishly **09** copiously, liberally, profusely **10** abundantly, fruitfully, generously **11** bountifully

**plenty**
**04** bags, fund, mass, mine **05** ample, store **06** enough, foison, riches, scouth, scowth, volume, wealth **07** fortune, fulness **08** fullness, plethora, quantity **09** abundance, affluence, plenitude, profusion, substance **10** abundantly, cornucopia, plentitude, prosperity **11** copiousness, sufficiency, wealthiness **12** milk and honey **13** plenteousness **14** stouth and routh
• **plenty of** **04** bags, lots, many **05** heaps, loads, piles **06** enough, masses, stacks **09** shedloads **11** large amount, large number **14** more than enough

**plethora**
**04** glut **06** excess **07** surfeit, surplus **09** abundance, profusion, repletion **11** repleteness, superfluity **12** overfullness **13** overabundance **14** superabundance

**pliability**
**08** docility **09** ductility **10** compliance, elasticity, plasticity **11** amenability, bendability, flexibility **12** adaptability, malleability **13** tractableness **14** suggestibility, susceptibility

**pliable**
**05** bendy, lithe **06** docile, pliant, supple **07** elastic, plastic **08** bendable, biddable, cheveril, cheveril, flexible, yielding **09** adaptable, compliant, malleable, receptive, tractable **10** manageable, responsive **11** persuadable, susceptible **12** superplastic **13** accommodating **14** impressionable

**pliant**
**05** bendy, lithe, swack, swank, wanle **06** docile, limber, supple, wandle, wannel, whippy **07** elastic, plastic, pliable **08** bendable, biddable, flexible, yielding **09** adaptable, compliant, malleable, receptive, tractable **10** manageable, responsive, sequacious **11** persuadable, susceptible **13** accommodating **14** impressionable

**plight**
**03** fix, jam, vow **04** case, fold, hole, mood, risk, trim **05** array, plait, point, state, swear, vouch, weave **06** enfold, engage, liking, pickle, pledge, scrape, secure, taking **07** dilemma, pliskie, promise, propose, straits, trouble **08** affiance, contract, covenant, quandary **09** condition, extremity,

guarantee, situation, tight spot **10** difficulty, engagement **11** dire straits, predicament **13** circumstances

**plimsoll**
**03** dap **05** tacky **07** gym shoe **08** sandshoe

**plod**
**04** plot, slog, thud, toil **05** clump, grind, stomp, stump, tramp **06** drudge, labour, lumber, stodge, trudge **07** peg away **08** plug away **09** persevere, policeman, soldier on **11** police force, walk heavily **13** plough through

**plodder**
**03** mug, sap **06** drudge, toiler **07** dullard, slogger

**plot**
**03** bed, erf, lay, lot, map, web **04** area, brew, burn, draw, mark, pack, plan, plod, ruse **05** block, cabal, chart, draft, frame, hatch, patch, piece, ploat, scald, story, theme, tract **06** action, cook up, design, devise, fleece, garden, locate, map out, parcel, scheme, scorch, sketch, thread **07** collude, concoct, connive, dispose, outline, project, section, subject **08** conspire, contrive, intrigue, scenario **09** allotment, calculate, machinate, narrative, storyline, stratagem **10** conspiracy **11** machination

**plotter**
**06** dabble, potter **07** planner, schemer **08** dabbling, designer, paddling **09** intriguer **10** machinator **11** conspirator

**plough**
◇ *anagram indicator* **03** ard, dig, ear, ere, pip, rib **04** beam, fail, list, plow, rive, sill, till, work **05** break, ridge, spade **06** Dipper, fallow, furrow, lister, pleuch, pleugh, rafter, ridger, thwart, turn up **07** break up, scooter, tractor, triones, wrinkle **08** the Wagon **09** Big Dipper, cultivate, Great Bear, subsoiler, Ursa Major **10** Seven Stars **11** agriculture, drill-plough, swing-plough, wheel plough **12** Charles's Wain, septentrions **13** septentriones
• **plough into** **03** hit **06** go into **07** collide, run into **08** bump into **09** crash into, drive into, smash into
• **plough through** **11** plod through, wade through **13** trudge through

**ploughshare**
**04** sock **05** share

**plover**
**04** dupe **06** godwit **07** dottrel, killdee, lapwing **08** dotterel, killdeer, wire bird **09** thick knee **10** Charadrius, prostitute, stone snipe
• **flock of plovers** **04** wing

**ploy**
**04** game, move, ruse, wile **05** dodge, trick **06** device, scheme, tactic **08** artifice **09** manoeuvre, stratagem **10** subterfuge **11** contrivance

**pluck**
**03** pip, rob, tug **04** draw, fail, grit, guts, pick, plot, pook, pouk, pull, race, rase,

yank **05** heart, nerve, ploat, plunk, spunk, strip, strum, thrum, twang **06** avulse, daring, evulse, finger, fleece, gather, humble, mettle, remove, rescue, snatch, spirit, take in, tweeze, twitch, valour **07** bravery, collect, courage, despoil, extract, harvest, pull off, swindle **08** audacity, backbone, boldness **09** fortitude **10** resolution **11** divellicate, intrepidity **12** fearlessness **13** determination

**pluckily**
**06** boldly **07** bravely **08** daringly **09** valiantly **10** fearlessly, heroically, intrepidly **11** audaciously, confidently **12** courageously **13** adventurously

**plucky**
**04** bold, game, gamy **05** brave, gamey, gutsy, gutty **06** daring, feisty, gallus, gritty, heroic, spunky **07** gallows, valiant **08** fearless, intrepid, spirited **09** audacious **10** courageous, determined

**plug**
**02** ad **03** DIN, wad **04** blow, bung, cake, chew, cork, dook, fill, hype, neck, pack, puff, push, seal, stem, stop, tent, tout **05** block, blurb, choke, close, promo, punch, SCART, shoot, spile, stuff, twist **06** dossil, dottle, fipple, market, spigot, stop up, tampon **07** go-devil, mention, pessary, promote, stopper, stopple, tampion, tompion **08** good word **09** access eye, advertise, promotion, publicity, publicize **10** commercial **11** suppository **13** advertisement **14** recommendation
• **plug away** **04** toil **06** plod on **07** peg away **08** preserve, slog away, toil away **09** persevere, soldier on **10** keep trying

**plum**
**04** best, kaki **05** cushy, prize, prune **06** choice, damson, mussel **07** bullace, quetsch **08** damaskin, prunello, victoria **09** damascene, damaskeen, damasquin, excellent, greengage, mirabelle, myrobalan, naseberry, persimmon, sapodilla **10** damasceene, first-class

**plumb**
**04** bang, dead, slap, true **05** gauge, level, probe, right, sheer, sound **06** bullet, fathom, search, spot-on **07** exactly, examine, explore, measure, plummet, utterly **08** sound out, vertical **09** delve into, out-and-out, penetrate, precisely, search out, up and down **10** straight up, vertically **11** investigate, verticality **12** straight down **13** thorough-going **15** perpendicularly
• **plumb in** **03** fit, fix, put **05** place, put in, set up **07** install **08** position
• **plumb the depths of** **13** reach the nadir **15** experience fully, reach rock bottom

**plumbing**

*Plumbing fittings and equipment include:*

**02** WC
**03** pan, tap, tee

**plume**

**04** bath, bend, bowl, flux, hose, pipe, plug, pump, sink, tank, trap
**05** auger, basin, bidet, float, joint, P-trap, U-bend, union, valve
**06** boiler, faucet, gasket, geyser, hopper, nipple, shower, solder, toilet, urinal, washer
**07** cistern, coupler, plunger, reducer, stop end, Y-branch
**08** ballcock, cylinder, drain rod, lavatory, lever tap, mixer tap, pedestal, pipe clip, radiator, soil vent, stopcock, sump pump, valve key
**09** ball valve, blowtorch, draincock, gate valve, mains pipe, nipple key, waste pipe
**10** back boiler, bottle trap, check valve, copper pipe, copper tube, elbow joint, flare joint, header tank, pipe bender, pipe cutter, pipe wrench, programmer, septic tank, shower head, Teflon® tape, thermostat, tube cutter
**11** water closet
**12** basin spanner, ceiling joint, monkey wrench, overflow bend, pipe coupling, siphon washer
**13** deburring tool, expansion tank, lavatory chain
**14** gas water heater, Stillson® wrench
**15** immersion heater

**plume**

**04** tuft **05** crest, preen, quill **06** osprey, pappus, pinion **07** feather, marabou, panache, plumule **08** aigrette, marabout, streamer
• **plume yourself on** **07** exult in **10** boast about **13** preen yourself, pride yourself

**plummet**

**04** dive, drop, fall, lead **05** plumb, sound **06** fathom, hurtle, plunge, tumble **07** descend **08** nose-dive **09** plumb line **11** drop rapidly, fall rapidly **15** decrease quickly

**plummy**

**01** U **04** posh **07** refined **08** affected **09** desirable, high-class **10** profitable, upper-class **12** aristocratic

**plump**

**03** fat **04** blow, bold, drop, dump, fall, flop, full, plop, sink, soss, swap, swop, tidy **05** ample, beefy, blurt, bonny, buxom, clump, dumpy, gross, jolly, large, obese, plunk, podgy, round, shoot, slump, sonsy, souse, squab, stout, swell, tubby **06** bonnie, chubby, cuddly, flabby, fleshy, plunge, portly, rotund, sonsie, strike **07** cluster, deposit, descend, put down, set down, well-fed **08** chopping, collapse, generous, matronly **09** corpulent, downright **10** cuddlesome, embonpoint, roundabout, well-liking, well-padded **11** well-covered, well-rounded **15** well-upholstered
• **plump for** **04** back **06** choose, favour, opt for, prefer, select **07** support **08** side with

**plumpness**

**03** fat **07** fatness, obesity **09** podginess, pudginess, rotundity, stoutness, tubbiness **10** chubbiness, corpulence, fleshiness, portliness

**plunder**

**03** rob **04** loot, peel, pill, prey, raid, rape, reif, sack, swag **05** berob, booty, harry, prize, reave, reive, rifle, scoff, shave, skoff, spoil, steal, strip **06** fleece, forage, maraud, ravage, spoils, spulye **07** despoil, escheat, hership, pillage, ransack, spulyie, spulzie, stick up **08** lay waste, pickings, spoliate, spuilzie **09** depredate, devastate, herriment, herryment, sprechery **10** spreaghery **14** ill-gotten gains

**plunge**

**03** dip, jab, ram **04** bull, dash, dive, drop, duck, enew, fall, jump, mire, push, rush, sink, stab, tank, tear **05** crash, douse, dowse, drive, lunge, merge, pitch, plump, raker, shove, souse, stick, swoop, throw, whelm **06** beduck, career, charge, go down, hurtle, launch, thrust, tumble **07** demerge, demerse, descend, descent, immerge, immerse, plummet **08** bull into, dive-bomb, emplonge, implunge, nose-dive, submerge **09** immersion **10** submersion **11** drop rapidly, fall rapidly **12** enew yourself **15** decrease quickly
• **take the plunge** **07** go for it **13** bite the bullet **14** commit yourself

**plurality**

**04** bulk, mass, most **06** galaxy, number **07** variety **08** majority **09** diversity, profusion **12** multiplicity, numerousness **13** preponderance

**plus**

**03** and **04** gain, perk, with **05** asset, bonus, extra **06** credit **07** added to, benefit, surplus **08** addition, as well as, increase, positive **09** advantage, good point **10** additional **12** advantageous, in addition to, not to mention, over and above, together with

**plush**

**04** posh, rich **05** ritzy **06** costly, de luxe, glitzy, lavish, luxury, swanky **07** opulent, stylish **08** affluent, palatial **09** luxurious, sumptuous

**Pluto**

**03** Dis **05** Hades

**plutocrat**

**05** Dives **06** fat cat, tycoon **07** Croesus, gold-bug, magnate, rich man **09** moneybags **10** capitalist **11** billionaire, millionaire, zillionaire

**plutonium**

**02** Pu

**ply**

◇ *anagram indicator* **02** go **03** ren, rin, run, set, use **04** bend, birl, feed, fold, leaf, lush, play **05** apply, beset, birle, ferry, layer, sheet, trade, wield **06** assail, employ, follow, handle, harass, lavish, pursue, strand, supply, travel, work at **07** bombard, carry on, furnish, provide, utilize **08** engage in,

exercise, practise **09** condition, importune, thickness **10** manipulate **13** keep supplying

**PM**

*see* **prime minister**

**poach**

**04** copy, lift, nick, poke, take **05** potch, steal **06** borrow, pilfer, potche, thrust **07** intrude, trample **08** encroach, infringe, trespass **11** appropriate **13** hunt illegally **14** catch illegally

**pocket**

◇ *containment indicator* **03** bag, bin, fob, pot **04** gain, lift, mini, nick, poke, take, whip **05** filch, funds, means, money, patch, pinch, pouch, purse, small, steal, touch **06** assets, budget, cavity, hollow, little, pilfer, potted **07** capital, compact, concise, placket, purloin, trouser **08** abridged, envelope, finances, fob-watch, pint-size, portable, souvenir **09** miniature, plaid-neuk, resources, small area **10** receptacle, small group **11** appropriate, compartment, wherewithal, win unfairly **12** isolated area **14** help yourself to
*See also* **steal**

**pockmark**

**03** pit **04** pock, scar **07** blemish, pockpit

**pod**

**03** cod **04** case, hull, husk, pipi **05** chile, chili, shell, shuck **06** chilli, legume, loment, paunch, peacod, school **07** musk-bag, peascod, silicle, siliqua, silique **08** lomentum, peasecod, silicula, silicule, strombus, sugar pea, tamarind **09** green bean, mangetout **10** cotton boll **11** pudding-pipe **12** mangetout pea

**podgy**

**03** fat **05** dumpy, plump, squat, stout, tubby **06** chubby, chunky, fleshy, rotund, spuddy, stubby, stumpy **07** paunchy **08** roly-poly **09** corpulent, roll-about

**podium**

**04** dais, foot, hand **05** stage, stand **07** rostrum **08** platform **09** stylobate

**poem**

*Poem types include:*

**03** dit, lay, ode
**04** awdl, ditt, epic, epos, idyl, song, waka
**05** ditty, elegy, epode, haiku, idyll, lyric, rhyme, tanka, verse
**06** ballad, epopee, monody, sonnet
**07** bucolic, couplet, eclogue, epigram, georgic, pantoum, rondeau, sestina, triolet, virelay
**08** cinquain, clerihew, limerick, lipogram, madrigal, palinode, pastoral, thin poem, verselet, versicle
**09** roundelay, shape poem
**10** villanelle
**12** concrete poem, epithalamium, nursery rhyme, prothalamion

*Poems and poetry collections include:*

**02** If
**04** A Red, Crow, Days, Edda, Hope, Howl, Maud, Odes
**05** Comus, Lamia
**06** Façade, Heaven, Hellas, Marina, The Fly, Villon
**07** A Vision, Beowulf, Don Juan, Lycidas, Mariana, Marmion, Red Rose, Requiem, Rondeau, The Quip, Ulysses
**08** Bermudas, Endymion, Georgics, Gunga Din, Hiawatha, Hudibras, Hysteria, Insomnia, Kalevala, Lupercal, Queen Mab, Ramayana, The Iliad, The Night, The Pearl, The Tyger, Tithonus, To Autumn
**09** Decameron, Human Life, Jerusalem, Kubla Khan, The Aeneid, The Cantos
**10** Cherry Ripe, Christabel, Dream Songs, In Memoriam, Lalla Rookh, On an Island, The Dunciad, The Odyssey, The Poetics, The Prelude, The Village, Up in the Air, Very Old Man, View of a Pig
**11** Ars Amatoria, Empty Vessel, High Windows, Holy Sonnets, Humming-Bird, Jabberwocky, Mahabharata, Memorabilia, Remembrance, Song of My Cid, Sudden Light, Tall Nettles, Tam O'Shanter, The Eclogues, The Extasie, The Peasants, The Retreate, The Sick Rose, The Sluggard, The Woodlark
**12** A Glass of Beer, Ash Wednesday, A Song to Celia, A Song to David, Auld Lang Syne, Bhagavad Gita, Eugene Onegin, Faith Healing, Four Quartets, Goblin Market, Hawk Roosting, Homage to Clio, Jubilate Agno, Mercian Hymns, Morte d'Arthur, Ode to Evening, Paradise Lost, Piers Plowman, The Hill-Shade, The Lucy Poems, The Troop Ship, The Visionary, The Waste Land, The Windhover
**13** Arms and the Boy, Behind the Line, Gilgamesh Epic, Leaves of Grass, Metamorphoses, Missing the Sea, Naming of Parts, Roman de la Rose, September Song, Song by Isbrand, The Book of Thel
**14** A Shropshire Lad, Divina Commedia, Leda and the Swan, Les Fleurs du Mal, Love Songs in Age, Lyrical Ballads, Orlando Furioso, Song of Hiawatha, Strange Meeting, The Divine Image, The Feel of Hands, The Garden Party, The Lotus-Eaters, The Ship of Death, Venus and Adonis
**15** Canterbury Tales, Cautionary Tales, Love without Hope, Magna est Veritas, Ode on Melancholy, Summoned by Bells, The Age of Anxiety, The Divine Comedy, The Eve of St Agnes, The Faerie Queene, The Garden of Love,

The Grauballe Man, The Second Coming, The Sorrow of Love

*See also* **poetry; song**

**poet**
**04** bard, scop **06** rhymer **07** elegist, rhymist **08** beat poet, idyllist, lyricist, minstrel **09** balladeer, poetaster, poeticule, rhymester, sonneteer, versifier **10** verse-maker
**15** performance poet

*Poets include:*

**03** Gay (John), Lee (Laurie), Paz (Octavio), Poe (Edgar Allan)
**04** Amis (Kingsley), Blok (Alexander), Cope (Wendy), Dunn (Douglas), Dyer (Sir Edward), Gray (Thomas), Gunn (Thom), Hill (Geoffrey), Hogg (James), Hood (Thomas), Hunt (Leigh), Lear (Edward), Maro (Publius Vergilius), Muir (Edwin), Nash (Ogden), Ovid, Owen (Wilfred), Pope (Alexander), Rich (Adrienne), Seth (Vikram), Vega (Lope de)
**05** Auden (W H), Basho (Matsuo), Benét (Stephen Vincent), Blake (William), Burns (Robert), Byron (George, Lord), Clare (John), Crane (Hart), Dante, Donne (John), Duffy (Carol Ann), Eliot (T S), Frost (Robert), Hardy (Thomas), Harte (Brett), Heine (Heinrich), Henri (Adrian), Hesse (Hermann), Homer, Ibsen (Henrik), Iqbal (Sir Muhammad), Keats (John), Keble (John), Lodge (Thomas), Lorca (Federico García), Marot (Clément), Meung (Jean de), Moore (Thomas), Myers (Frederic William Henry), O'Hara (Frank), Opitz (Martin), Plath (Sylvia), Pound (Ezra), Prior (Matthew), Pulci (Luigi), Raine (Craig), Rilke (Rainer Maria), Sachs (Hans), Sachs (Nelly), Scott (Sir Walter), Smart (Christopher), Smith (Stevie), Spark (Dame Muriel), Tasso (Torquato), Wyatt (Sir Thomas), Yeats (W B)
**06** Adcock (Fleur), Aragon (Louis), Arnold (Matthew), Artaud (Antonin), Atwood (Margaret), Barnes (William), Bellay (Joachim du), Belloc (Hilaire), Benoît, Binyon (Laurence), Bishop (Elizabeth), Brecht (Bertolt), Brontë (Anne), Brontë (Emily), Brooke (Rupert), Camäes (Luís de), Carver (Raymond), Cowper (William), Crabbe (George), Dunbar (William), Eluard (Paul), Empson (Sir William), Ennius (Quintus), Fuller (Roy), Goethe (Johann Wolfgang von), Graves (Robert), Gurney (Ivor), Haller (Albrecht von), Heaney (Seamus), Herder (Johann Gottfried von), Hesiod, Horace, Hughes (Langston), Jensen (Johannes Vilhelm), Larkin (Philip), Lorris (Guillaume de), Lowell (Amy), Lowell (Robert), Millay (Edna St Vincent), Milosz (Czeslaw), Milton (John), Morris (William), Musset (Alfred de),

Neruda (Pablo), Ossian, Patten (Brian), Pindar, Porter (Peter), Racine (Jean), Ramsay (Allan), Riding (Laura), Sappho, Sidney (Sir Philip), Surrey (Henry Howard, Earl of), Tagore (Rabindranath), Thomas (Dylan), Thomas (Edward), Thomas (R S), Valéry (Paul), Villon (François), Virgil, Waller (Edmund)
**07** Addison (Joseph), Akahito (Yamabe no), Alberti (Leon Battista), Aneurin, Angelou (Maya), Aretino (Pietro), Ariosto (Ludovico), Ashbery (John), Barbour (John), Beckett (Samuel), Beddoes (Thomas Lovell), Blunden (Edmund Charles), Boiardo (Matteo Maria), Brodsky (Joseph), Büchner (Georg), Caedmon, Campion (Thomas), Causley (Charles), Chapman (George), Chaucer (Geoffrey), Cocteau (Jean), Da Ponte (Lorenzo), Douglas (Gawain), Durrell (Lawrence), Emerson (Ralph Waldo), Flecker (James Elroy), Fröding (Gustaf), Gautier (Théophile), Herbert (George), Herrick (Robert), Holberg (Ludvig, Baron), Hopkins (Gerard Manley), Housman (A E), Jiménez (Juan Ramón), Johnson (Samuel), Kipling (Rudyard), Layamon, Lydgate (John), Macbeth (George), MacCaig (Norman), MacLean (Sorley), Manzoni (Alessandro), Martial, Marvell (Andrew), McGough (Roger), Mishima (Yukio), Mistral (Frédéric), Mistral (Gabriela), Montale (Eugenio), Newbolt (Sir Henry), Novalis, Orléans (Charles Duc d'), Patmore (Coventry), Pushkin (Alexander), Quarles (Francis), Rimbaud (Arthur), Roethke (Theodore), Ronsard (Pierre de), Rostand (Edmond), Sassoon (Siegfried), Seferis, Seifert (Jaroslav), Shelley (Percy Bysshe), Sitwell (Dame Edith), Sitwell (Sir Sacheverell), Skelton (John), Spender (Sir Stephen), Spenser (Edmund), Stevens (Wallace), Terence, Thomson (James), Thoreau (Henry David), Vaughan (Henry), Vicente (Gil), Walcott (Derek), Whitman (Walt), Wieland (Christoph Martin)
**08** Anacreon, Andersen (Hans Christian), Ausonius (Decimus Magnus), Banville (Théodore de), Berryman (John), Brentano (Clemens), Brittain (Vera), Browning (Elizabeth Barrett), Browning (Robert), Campbell (Roy), Carducci (Giosuè), Catullus (Gaius Valerius), Claudian, Congreve (William), cummings (e e), Cynewulf, Davenant (Sir William), De La Mare (Walter), Drummond (William, of Hawthornden), Firdausi, Ginsberg (Allen), Henryson (Robert), Laforgue (Jules), Langland (William), Lawrence (D H), Leopardi

(Giacomo), **Lovelace** (Richard),
**Macaulay** (Dame Rose), **Macaulay**
(Thomas), **MacLeish** (Archibald),
**MacNeice** (Louis), **Malherbe**
(François de), **Mallarmé** (Stéphane),
**Menander**, **Milligan** (Spike),
**Palgrave** (Francis Turner), **Paterson**
(Andrew Barton), **Petrarch**,
**Robinson** (Edwin Arlington),
**Rossetti** (Christina), **Rossetti**
(Dante Gabriel), **Sandburg** (Carl),
**Schiller** (Friedrich), **Schlegel**
(August Wilhelm von), **Suckling**
(Sir John), **Taliesin**, **Tibullus**,
**Traherne** (Thomas), **Verlaine** (Paul),
**Whittier** (John Greenleaf)

09 **Aeschylus**, **Akhmatova** (Anna),
**Bronowski** (Jacob), **Coleridge**
(Samuel Taylor), **D'Annunzio**
(Gabriele), **Dickinson** (Emily),
**Froissart** (Jean), **Goldsmith**
(Oliver), **Hölderlin** (Friedrich),
**Lamartine** (Alphonse de),
**Lucretius**, **Marinetti** (Filippo
Tommaso), **Pasternak** (Boris),
**Rochester** (John Wilmot, Earl of),
**Rosenberg** (Isaac), **Santayana**
(George), **Southwell** (Robert),
**Swinburne** (Algernon Charles),
**Ungaretti** (Giuseppe), **Zephaniah**
(Benjamin)

10 **Baudelaire** (Charles), **Bradstreet**
(Anne), **Chatterton** (Thomas),
**Chesterton** (G K), **Empedocles**,
**FitzGerald** (Edward), **La Fontaine**
(Jean de), **Lagerkvist** (Pär),
**Longfellow** (Henry Wadsworth),
**MacDiarmid** (Hugh), **Mayakovsky**
(Vladimir), **McGonagall** (William),
**Propertius** (Sextus), **Theocritus**

11 **Apollinaire** (Guillaume),
**Callimachus**, **Omar Khayyám**,
**Shakespeare** (William),
**Yevtushenko** (Yevegeny)

12 **Ferlinghetti** (Lawrence)
13 **Sackville-West** (Vita)
14 **Dante Alighieri**, **Saint-John Perse**
15 **Thomas the Rhymer**

• **poet laureate** 02 PL

*Poets laureate:*

03 **Pye** (Henry)
04 **Rowe** (Nicholas), **Tate** (Nahum)
05 **Duffy** (Carol Ann)
06 **Austin** (Alfred), **Cibber** (Colley),
**Dryden** (John), **Eusden** (Laurence),
**Hughes** (Ted), **Jonson** (Ben),
**Motion** (Andrew), **Warton** (Thomas)
07 **Bridges** (Robert), **Southey** (Robert)
08 **Betjeman** (Sir John), **Davenant** (Sir
William), **Day-Lewis** (Cecil),
**Shadwell** (Thomas), **Tennyson**
(Alfred, Lord)
09 **Masefield** (John), **Whitehead**
(William)
10 **Wordsworth** (William)

## poetic
06 moving 07 flowing, lyrical, rhyming
08 artistic, creative, graceful, metrical,
poetical, symbolic 09 beautiful,
sensitive 10 expressive, figurative,
rhythmical 11 imaginative

## poetry
04 muse 05 poems, poesy, rhyme,
verse 06 epopee, lyrics 07 doggrel,
iambics, pennill, rhyming, versing
08 doggerel, epopoeia 09 free verse,
macaronic, Parnassus, vers libre
10 macaronics 13 versification

*Poetry movements include:*

04 Beat
05 found, sound
07 Acmeism, digital, epitaph,
erasure, imagism
08 concrete, medieval, pastoral,
Trouvère
09 automatic, modernism,
symbolism, Troubador, Victorian
10 Parnassian
11 Minnesinger, objectivist,
performance, Romanticism, The
Movement, traditional
12 metaphysical
13 Black Mountain, New York
School, non-conformism, post-
modernism
14 chanson de geste

*See also* **poem**

## pogrom
06 murder 07 carnage, killing
08 butchery, genocide, homicide,
massacre 09 bloodbath, holocaust,
slaughter 10 decimation 11 liquidation
12 annihilation 13 extermination
15 ethnic cleansing

## poignancy
04 pain 06 misery, pathos 07 emotion,
feeling, sadness, tragedy 08 distress,
keenness, piquancy, pungency
09 intensity, sentiment, sharpness
10 bitterness, tenderness
11 painfulness, piteousness
12 wretchedness 13 evocativeness

## poignant
03 sad 05 sharp 06 moving, tender,
tragic 07 painful, piquant, piteous,
poynant, pungent, tearful 08 haunting,
pathetic, pricking, stinging, touching,
wretched 09 affecting, agonizing,
emotional, heartfelt, miserable,
sorrowful, upsetting 11 distressing,
penetrating 12 heart-rending
13 heartbreaking

## poignantly
05 sadly 08 movingly, tenderly
09 miserably, painfully, tearfully
10 tragically, wretchedly
11 emotionally, sorrowfully
12 pathetically

## point
01 E, N, S, W 02 pt 03 ace, aim, dot,
end, hit, neb, nib, nub, ord, tip, top,
use 04 apex, area, cape, case, core,
crag, crux, cusp, fang, feat, gist, goal,
head, hint, item, lace, mark, meat,
ness, node, peak, pike, pith, show,
site, spot, stop, time, tine, vein, whit
05 drift, facet, heart, issue, level, place,
score, sense, speck, spike, stage, state,
sting, taper, tenor, theme, topic, total,
train, trait, value, verge 06 aspect,
burden, clause, denote, detail, direct,

marrow, matter, moment, motive,
object, period, plight, reason, signal,
thrust 07 essence, feature, heading,
instant, keynote, meaning, purpose,
quality, sharpen, signify, subject,
suggest 08 evidence, foreland, full
stop, headland, indicate, juncture,
locality, location, position, property,
pungency, question, sharp end
09 attribute, condition, designate,
extremity, full point, gesture at,
intention, main point, north pole,
objective, situation, south pole
10 conclusion, importance, particular,
promontory, resolution 11 culmination
12 central point, decimal point,
significance 14 characteristic, gesture
towards

*See also* **compass; horse**

• **beside the point** 09 unrelated
10 immaterial, irrelevant, out of
place, red herring 11 unconnected
• **chief points** 03 sum
• **in point of fact** 03 nay 06 indeed,
in fact, really 08 actually 09 in reality
15 as a matter of fact
• **lowest point** 04 zero
• **main point** 04 clou, gist
• **on the point of** 07 about to, going
to, ready to 10 in danger of 11 just
about to, preparing to 12 on the brink
of, on the verge of
• **point of view** 03 POV 04 view
05 angle, slant 06 aspect, belief,
stance 07 feeling, opinion, outlook
08 approach, attitude, position
09 judgement, sentiment, viewpoint
10 Anschauung, standpoint
11 perspective
• **point out** 04 shew, show 05 judge
06 remind, reveal 07 bring up,
mention, point to, presage, specify
08 allude to, identify, indicate
09 highlight 15 call attention to, draw
attention to
• **point up** 06 stress 09 emphasize,
highlight, underline 15 call attention
to
• **to the point** 05 ad rem
07 germane, related 08 apposite,
pregnant, relevant 09 connected,
pertinent 10 applicable
11 appropriate
• **up to a point** 06 partly 08 slightly,
somewhat 12 to some degree, to
some extent

## point-blank
04 flat, near, open 05 blunt, frank,
level, plain, reach 06 candid, direct,
openly, rudely 07 bluntly, closely,
close to, frankly, plainly 08 abruptly,
candidly, directly, explicit, outright,
straight, touching 10 explicitly,
forthright, unreserved 12 at close
range, forthrightly 13 unequivocally
15 straightforward

## pointed
04 keen, urdé, urdy 05 clear, edged,
sharp, spicy, urdée 06 barbed, biting,
Gothic, lancet 07 cutting, mordant,
obvious, precise, telling 08 acicular,
aculeate, explicit, forceful, incisive,

## pointedly

striking, tapering **09** aculeated, cuspidate, mucronate, trenchant **10** cuspidated, fastigiate, lanceolate, mucronated **11** lanceolated, near the bone, penetrating **12** epigrammatic **14** epigrammatical

## pointedly

**07** bluntly, plainly **09** defiantly, on purpose **10** explicitly **13** intentionally, provocatively

## pointer

**03** rod, tip **04** cane, clue, hand, hint, pole, sign **05** arrow, guide, index, stick, style **06** advice, fescue, needle, tongue **07** caution, warning **09** guideline, hyperlink, indicator **10** indication, suggestion **11** trafficator **13** piece of advice **14** recommendation

## pointless

◇ *tail deletion indicator* **04** vain **05** blunt, inane **06** absurd, futile **07** aimless, foolish, useless **08** muticous **09** a mug's game, fruitless, senseless, to no avail, valueless, worthless **10** ridiculous, unavailing **11** meaningless, nonsensical **12** a waste of time, unproductive, unprofitable **13** insignificant **14** a waste of effort

## pointlessly

**06** in vain **09** aimlessly **11** senselessly **12** unprofitably **13** meaninglessly **14** unproductively

## poise

**04** bias, cool, hang **05** grace, hover, pease, peaze, peise, peize, peyse, weigh **06** aplomb, impact, ponder, steady, weight **07** balance, dignity, librate, support, suspend **08** calmness, coolness, elegance, momentum, position, serenity, suspense **09** assurance, composure **10** equanimity **11** equilibrium, self-control **13** self-assurance **14** presence of mind, self-confidence, self-possession

## poised

**03** set **04** calm, cool **05** paysd, ready, suave **06** all set, serene, urbane **07** assured, waiting **08** balanced, composed, graceful, prepared **09** collected, dignified, expectant, unruffled **11** unflappable **13** self-confident, self-possessed **14** self-controlled

## poison

**03** mar **04** warp **05** spoil, taint **06** blight, cancer, canker, defile, infect, rankle **07** corrupt, deprave, envenom, pervert, pollute **08** embitter **09** contagion, pollution **10** adulterate, corruption, envenomate, malignancy **11** contaminate **13** contamination

*Poisonous creatures include:*

**03** asp
**04** fugu, gila, seps, weta
**05** adder, cobra, viper
**06** dugite, katipo, taipan
**07** redback, sea wasp
**08** blowfish, cerastes, jararaca, jararaka, mocassin, moccasin,

ringhals, rinkhals, scorpion, sea snake
**09** berg-adder, boomslang, funnel-web, globe fish, hamadryad, king cobra, puff adder, stonefish, tarantula
**10** bandy-bandy, black snake, black widow, bushmaster, copperhead, coral snake, death adder, puffer fish
**11** cottonmouth, gaboon viper, gila monster, rattlesnake
**12** box jellyfish, scorpion fish, sea porcupine, violin spider
**13** water moccasin
**15** funnel-web spider

*Poisonous plants include:*

**04** upas
**05** dwale
**06** antiar, gidgee, karaka
**07** aconite, amanita, anemone, cowbane, hemlock, lantana
**08** banewort, foxglove, laburnum, mandrake, oleander, poroporo, wild arum
**09** digitalis, monkshood, naked boys, naked lady, poison ivy, stinkweed, wake-robin, wolfsbane
**10** belladonna, cuckoo pint, jimson weed, stramonium, thorn apple, windflower
**12** giant hogweed, helmet flower
**13** meadow saffron
**14** castor oil plant, lords-and-ladies
**15** black nightshade

*Poisons and toxic substances include:*

**03** BHC
**04** bane, lead
**05** abrin, conin, lysol, ozone, ricin, sarin, toxin, venin, venom, VX gas
**06** arsine, curare, dioxin, G-agent, iodine, ketene, V-agent, wabain, war gas
**07** arsenic, bromine, cacodyl, coniine, cyanide, digoxin, dioxane, mercury, mineral, neurine, ouabain, stibine, tanghin
**08** antimony, atropine, chlordan, chlorine, cyanogen, cytisine, fluorine, gossypol, lobeline, melittin, nerve gas, Paraquat®, phosgene, ptomaine, ratsbane, rotenone, thebaine, urushiol
**09** aflatoxin, amygdalin, chaconine, chlordane, muscarine, mycotoxin, nux vomica, saxitoxin, white damp
**10** acrylamide, aqua Tofana, bufotenine, ciguatoxin, domoic acid, heptachlor, mustard gas, neurotoxin, oxalic acid, phosphorus, phytotoxin, picrotoxin, strychnine, tetrotoxin
**11** enterotoxin, hyoscyamine, nitric oxide, prussic acid, sugar of lead
**12** strophanthin, tetrodotoxin
**13** Scheele's green, silver nitrate
**14** carbon monoxide
**15** hydrogen cyanide, nitrogen dioxide

## poisoning

**03** obi **04** obia **05** obeah

*Poisoning types include:*

**04** food, lead
**05** algae, blood
**06** iodism
**07** bromism, gassing, pyaemia, sausage, toxemia
**08** botulism, ergotism, plumbism, ptomaine, toxaemia
**09** brominism, crotalism, fluorosis, lead colic, mephitism, sapraemia, saturnism, zinc colic
**10** alcoholism, molybdosis, salicylism, salmonella, stibialism, strychnism
**11** phosphorism, septicaemia
**12** hydrargyrism, intoxication, strychninism
**13** mycotoxicosis

## poisonous

**05** fatal, toxic, venom **06** deadly, lethal, mortal, virose **07** baneful, harmful, noxious, vicious **08** mephitic, spiteful, toxicant, venomous, virulent **09** cancerous, cankerous, malicious, malignant, offensive **10** corrupting, pernicious **11** deleterious **13** contaminating
*See also* **poison**

## poke

**03** bag, dig, hit, jab, peg **04** butt, pick, pock, pote, prod, prog, push, root, rout, stab **05** elbow, goose, grope, nudge, poach, prick, proke, punch, shove, stick, stoop, wroot **06** incite, nuzzle, pocket, potter, powter, stir up, thrust **07** scuffle, snuzzle **08** itchweed, protrude **10** stickybeak
• **poke around 04** root, rout **07** look for **09** search for **11** grope around, rake through **13** rummage around **14** look all over for
• **poke fun at 03** cod, rag, rib **04** jeer, joke, mock, quiz **05** get at, spoof, taunt, tease **06** parody, send up **08** ridicule **09** make fun of **11** poke borak at **13** poke mullock at, take the mickey
• **poke out 06** beetle, extend, jut out **07** extrude, project **08** overhang, protrude, stick out

## poker

*Poker-related terms include:*

**03** pat, shy
**04** ante, call, flop, pair, stay, stud
**05** blind, bluff, check, flush
**06** kicker, suited
**08** hole card, showdown, stand pat, straight
**09** four-flush, full house
**10** royal flush
**11** busted flush, pass the buck
**13** community card, straight flush

## poker-faced

**05** blank, empty **06** glazed, vacant **07** deadpan, vacuous **08** lifeless **09** apathetic, impassive **10** stone-faced **11** emotionless, indifferent, inscrutable

**poky**

**12** uninterested **14** expressionless, without feeling **15** uncomprehending

**poky**

**04** slow, tiny **05** small, tight **06** narrow, poking **07** cramped, crowded **08** confined, powerful **10** restricted **12** incommodious
*See also* **prison**

**Poland**

**02** PL **03** POL

**polar**

**03** icy **04** cold **05** axial **06** arctic, frozen **07** glacial **08** freezing, opposite, Siberian **09** Antarctic **10** ambivalent **11** conflicting, dichotomous **12** antithetical **13** contradictory

**polarity**

**07** duality, paradox **09** dichotomy **10** antithesis, difference, opposition, separation **11** ambivalence, contrariety **12** oppositeness **13** contradiction

**polarize**

**05** split **06** divide **07** break up, split up **08** alienate, disunite, estrange, separate **09** segregate **10** drive apart **11** come between

**pole**

**01** N, S **02** po **03** bar, lug, nib, oar, rod **04** bail, boom, kent, mast, post, rood, spar **05** caber, limit, perch, quant, shaft, staff, stake, stang, stick, sting **06** janker, pillar, Polack, ripeck, rypeck **07** extreme, heavens, ryepeck, support, upright **08** Polander **09** cowl-staff, extremity, stanchion **10** river horse **11** clothes-prop **12** Venetian mast
• **poles apart** **11** worlds apart **12** incompatible **14** irreconcilable

**polecat**

**05** fitch, skunk **06** ferret **07** fitchet, fitchew, foumart **08** foulmart **10** prostitute

**polemic**

**06** debate **07** dispute, eristic **08** argument, diatribe **09** eristical, invective, polemical **11** contentious, controversy **12** disputatious **13** argumentative, controversial

**polemicist**

**06** arguer **07** debater **08** disputer, polemist **09** contender, disputant **11** logomachist

**polemics**

**06** debate **07** dispute **08** argument **09** logomachy **10** contention **11** controversy, disputation **13** argumentation

**police**

◇ *anagram indicator* **04** cops, fuzz, heat, pigs, plod **05** check, filth, guard, polis, watch **06** defend, patrol, the law **07** bizzies, control, coppers, monitor, observe, Old Bill, oversee, peelers, protect, rozzers, the Bill, the fuzz **08** Mounties, regulate, the force **09** gendarmes, keep watch, supervise **10** boys in blue, the Old Bill **11** police force **12** constabulary, keep the peace **13** the boys in blue **14** police officers

*Police forces and branches include:*

**02** AP, KP, MP, PD, SS
**03** CIB, CID, KGB, Met, MGB, RMP
**04** Ogpu, PSNI, RCMP, SWAT
**05** cheka, Garda, Stasi
**07** Europol, Gestapo, sweeney, the Yard
**08** Interpol
**09** Air Police, bomb squad, drug squad, porn squad, riot squad, task force, vice squad
**10** riot police, Securitate, water guard
**11** flying squad, gendarmerie, strike force, sweeney todd, Yardie squad
**12** mobile police, Scotland Yard, secret police, Texas Rangers
**13** Garda Siochana, mounted police, Schutzstaffel, Special Branch, traffic police
**14** military police
**15** New Scotland Yard

*Police-related terms include:*

**04** ACPO, beat, book, bust, cell, nick, raid, rank, shop, tana, tank
**05** ACPOS, baton, cuffs, fit-up, force, frame, go off, grass, manor, plant, pound, set-up, snout, sting, tanna, thana, tunic
**06** arrest, batoon, charge, cordon, curfew, fisgig, fizgig, helmet, line-up, rumble, search, tannah, thanah, thanna, wanted
**07** caution, copshop, custody, dragnet, epaulet, jemadar, manhunt, mugshot, pentito, round-up, station, stinger, stoolie, thannah, uniform, warrant
**08** evidence, mouchard, panda car, precinct, prowl car, speed gun, squad car
**09** blue light, centenier, handcuffs, identikit, meat wagon, on the beat, police dog, radar trap, shakedown, speed trap, truncheon
**10** body armour, police cell, police trap, supergrass, tenderloin, tracker dog, watch house
**11** fingerprint, flying squad, jam sandwich, Judges' Rules, stool pigeon, utility belt, warrant card
**12** bertillonage, incident room, police escort, police-manure, surveillance, walkie-talkie
**13** police station, rogues' gallery, search warrant, stop-and-search
**14** catch red-handed, criminal record, identity parade
**15** bullet-proof vest, long arm of the law, scene of the crime

**police officer**

**02** DI, PC, PS, PW, SC **03** cop, pig, 'tec, WPC **04** bogy, bull, flic, gill, nark, peon, plod, slop, SOCO, trap **05** beast, bizzy, bobby, bogey, Dixon, garda, jawan, polis, sepoy, sowar, traps, wolly **06** askari, copper, escort, lawman, Mounty, peeler, redcap, rozzer, sbirro, the law **07** captain, crusher, gumshoe, John Hop, marshal, Mountie, officer, trooper, zabtieh, zaptiah, zaptieh **08** flat-foot, gendarme, sergeant, serjeant, speed-cop, walloper **09** centenier, commander, constable, detective, inspector, patrolman, policeman, woodentop **10** bluebottle, carabinero, gangbuster, lieutenant, traffic cop **11** Black and Tan, carabiniere, patrolwoman, policewoman **12** master-at-arms, peace officer, state trooper **13** beetle-crusher, branch officer **14** police sergeant, superintendent, warrant officer

*Police ranks in the UK:*

**03** DCI
**08** Sergeant
**09** Commander, Constable, Inspector
**12** Commissioner
**14** Chief Constable, Chief Inspector, Superintendent
**18** Deputy Commissioner
**19** Chief Superintendent
**20** Deputy Chief Constable
**21** Assistant Commissioner
**23** Assistant Chief Constable
**27** Deputy Assistant Commissioner
• **police search** **04** heat **07** dragnet, manhunt **09** shakedown

**police station**

**04** nick, tana **05** tanna, thana **06** tannah, thanah, thanna **07** copshop, thannah **08** precinct **10** watch house **11** gendarmerie

**policy**

**04** line, plan **05** rules **06** course, custom, method, scheme, stance, system **07** cunning **08** approach, position, practice, protocol, prudence, schedule, strategy **09** guideline, insurance, procedure, programme **10** guidelines, statecraft **12** constitution **14** code of practice, course of action
• **the best policy** **07** honesty

**polish**

**03** lap, rub, wax **04** buff, bull, file, posh, sand **05** class, clean, glass, glaze, gloss, grace, poise, rub up, scour, sheen, shine, slick, style **06** finish, lustre, Polack, Poland, posh up, refine, smooth, veneer **07** beeswax, brush up, burnish, enhance, finesse, furbish, improve, perfect, planish, slicken, sparkle, touch up, varnish **08** breeding, brighten, elegance, glaciate **09** brilliant, cultivate **10** brightness, brilliance, refinement, smoothness **11** cultivation, rottenstone, satin finish **13** supercalender **14** sophistication
• **polish off** **03** zap **04** bolt, do in, down, kill, wolf **05** eat up, stuff, waste **06** devour, finish, gobble, murder, rub out **07** bump off, consume, destroy, put away, take out, wipe out **08** blow away, complete, dispatch, knock off **09** dispose of, eliminate, liquidate

**polished**

**05** adept, filed, shiny, suave, waxed **06** expert, glassy, glossy, polite, sanded, smooth, snappy, urbane

**07** elegant, genteel, perfect, refined, shining, skilful **08** cultured, flawless, gleaming, graceful, lapidary, lustrous, masterly, slippery, well-bred **09** burnished, civilized, excellent, faultless, perfected **10** consummate, cultivated, impeccable, proficient, remarkable **11** outstanding, superlative **12** accomplished, professional, well-mannered **13** sophisticated

**polite**
**05** bland, civil, suave **06** glossy, humane, urbane **07** elegant, gallant, genteel, refined, tactful **08** cultured, delicate, gracious, ladylike, obliging, polished, well-bred **09** civilized, courteous, courtlike **10** chivalrous, cultivated, diplomatic, respectful, thoughtful **11** considerate, deferential, gentlemanly, well-behaved **12** Grandisonian, well-mannered **13** sophisticated

**politely**
**09** gallantly, tactfully **10** graciously, obligingly **11** courteously **12** chivalrously, respectfully, thoughtfully **13** considerately **14** diplomatically

**politeness**
**04** tact **05** grace **06** polish **07** culture, manners, respect **08** civility, courtesy, elegance **09** attention, deference, diplomacy, gentility, politesse **10** cordiality, discretion, refinement **11** courtliness, cultivation, good manners, savoir-vivre **12** complaisance, good breeding, graciousness, mannerliness **14** respectfulness, thoughtfulness **15** considerateness, gentlemanliness

**politic**
**04** sage, wise **06** shrewd **07** prudent, tactful **08** discreet, sensible **09** advisable, expedient, judicious, opportune, political, sagacious **10** diplomatic **12** advantageous **14** constitutional

**political**
**05** civil **06** public **08** judicial **09** executive **11** ministerial **12** bureaucratic, governmental **13** parliamentary **14** administrative, constitutional, party political
See also **parliament; party**

Political ideologies include:

**06** holism, Maoism, Nazism
**07** fascism, Marxism
**08** third way, Whiggism
**09** anarchism, communism, democracy, neo-Nazism, pluralism, socialism, theocracy
**10** absolutism, Bolshevism, federalism, liberalism, neo-fascism, Trotskyism
**11** imperialism, nationalism, syndicalism, Thatcherism
**12** collectivism, conservatism
**13** individualism, republicanism, unilateralism
**14** egalitarianism, neocolonialism

**15** neoconservatism, social democracy, totalitarianism

**politician**
**02** MP **07** senator **08** minister **09** president **13** vice president
See also **president; prime minister**

Politicians include:

**03** Coe (Sebastian, Lord), Fox (Charles James), Fox (Liam), Fox (Sir Marcus), Jay (Margaret, Lady), Lee (Jennie, Lady), Lie (Trygve), May (Theresa), Pym (John), Wet (Christian de), Yeo (Timothy)
**04** Amos (Valerie, Baroness), Aziz (Tariq), Bell (Martin), Benn (Anthony Wedgwood 'Tony'), Benn (Hilary), Bush (George), Bush (George W), Cato (Marcus Porcius), Cook (Robin), Debs (Eugene Victor), Dole (Robert), Foot (Michael), Gore (Albert), Haig (Alexander), Hain (Peter), Hess (Rudolf), Hoon (Geoff), Howe (Geoffrey, Lord), Hume (John), Hurd (Douglas, Lord), Koch (Ed), Kohl (Helmut), More (Sir Thomas), Nagy (Imre), Opik (Lembit), Owen (David, Lord), Pitt (William, the elder), Reid (John), Reno (Janet), Rice (Condoleezza), Röhm (Ernst), Rusk (Dean), Vane (Sir Henry)
**05** Adams (Gerry), Agnew (Spiro), Astor (Nancy, Viscountess), Bacon (Francis), Baker (James Addison), Baker (Kenneth, Lord), Balls (Ed), Bevan (Aneurin), Bevin (Ernest), Biden (Joe), Blair (Tony), Brown (Gordon), Burke (Edmund), Cecil (Robert), Cecil (William), Cimon, Clark (Alan), Clegg (Nick), Cleon, Cowen (Brian), Davis (David), Dayan (Moshe), Dewar (Donald), Field (Frank), Freud (Sir Clement), Hague (William), Huhne (Chris), Kelly (Ruth), Kirov (Sergey), Krenz (Egon), Lenin (Vladimir Ilyich), Marat (Jean Paul), Maude (Francis), Nkomo (Joshua), Obama (Barack), Perón (Eva), Perón (Isabelita), Perón (Juan), Scott (Sir Nicholas), Scott (Sir Richard), Short (Clare), Smith (Chris), Smith (Jacqui), Smith (John), Solon, Steel (David, Lord), Straw (Jack), Sulla (Lucius Cornelius), Sully (Maximilien de Béthune, Duc de), Tambo (Oliver), Timms (Stephen), Vance (Cyrus Roberts)
**06** Abacha (Sani), Abbott (Diane), Antony (Mark), Archer (Jeffrey, Lord), Benton (Thomas Hart), Blears (Hazel), Bonner (Neville), Boyson (Sir Rhodes), Brandt (Willy), Bright (John), Browne (Des), Butler (Richard, Lord), Caesar (Julius), Castle (Barbara, Baroness), Cicero (Marcus Tullius), Clarke (Charles), Clarke (Kenneth), Cobden (Richard), Cripps (Sir Stafford), Curzon (George, Marquis), Danton (Georges), Davies (Denzil), Djilas (Milovan),

**Dobson** (Frank), **Dubček** (Alexander), **Dulles** (John Foster), **Erhard** (Ludwig), **Fowler** (Sir Norman), **Gummer** (John), **Hardie** (Keir), **Harman** (Harriet), **Healey** (Denis, Lord), **Hewitt** (Patricia), **Hitler** (Adolf), **Horthy** (Miklós), **Howard** (Michael), **Hughes** (Simon), **Hutton** (John), **Irvine** (Alexander, Lord), **Jinnah** (Muhammad Ali), **Joseph** (Keith, Lord), **Jowell** (Tessa), **Kaunda** (Kenneth), **Lamont** (Norman), **Lawson** (Nigel, Lord), **Letwin** (Oliver), **Lilley** (Peter), **Mallon** (Seamus), **Marius** (Gaius), **Mellon** (Andrew William), **Mellor** (David), **Merkel** (Angela), **Morgan** (Rhodri), **Mornay** (Philippe de), **Morton** (John), **Mosley** (Sir Oswald), **Mowlam** (Doctor Marjorie 'Mo'), **Nansen** (Fridtjof), **Necker** (Jacques), **Norris** (Steven), **Pandit** (Vijaya Lakshmi), **Pompey**, **Powell** (Enoch), **Prasad** (Rajendra), **Quayle** (Dan), **Roland** (Jean Mari), **Sidney** (Algernon), **Somers** (John, Lord), **Steele** (Sir Richard), **Suslov** (Mikhail), **Tebbit** (Norman, Lord), **Thorpe** (Jeremy), **Waller** (Edmund), **Walter** (Hubert), **Warren** (Earl), **Wilkes** (John), **Wolsey** (Thomas)
**07** Acheson (Dean), Allende (Salvador), Arundel (Thomas), Ashdown (Paddy), Beckett (Margaret), Bedford (John of Lancaster, Duke of), Boateng (Paul), Bormann (Martin), Brittan (Sir Leon), Cameron (David), Canning (George), Cassius, Clinton (Bill), Clinton (Hillary), Colbert (Jean Baptiste), Collins (Michael), Comines (Philippe de), Crassus (Marcus Licinius), Dalyell (Tam), Dandolo (Enrico), Darling (Alistair), De Klerk (Frederik William), Dorrell (Stephen), Fischer (Joschka), Fouquet (Nicolas), Gemayel (Amin), Gemayel (Bashir), Gemayel (Sheikh Pierre), Grattan (Henry), Grimond (Jo, Lord), Haldane (Richard, Viscount), Halifax (Edward Frederick Lindley Wood, Earl of), Halifax (George Savile, Marquis of), Harlech (William David Ormsby Gore, Lord), Hunyady (János Corvinus), Hussein (Saddam), Jackson (Andrew), Jackson (Glenda), Jackson (Jesse), Jameson (Sir Leander Starr), Jenkins (Roy, Lord), Johnson (Alan), Johnson (Lyndon B), Kalinin (Mikhail), Kaufman (Gerald), Kaunitz (Wenzel Anton, Fürst von), Kennedy (Charles), Kennedy (Edward M), Kennedy (John F), Kennedy (Robert F), Kinnock (Neil), Kossuth (Lajos), Lepidus (Marcus Aemilius), MacLeod (Iain), Malraux (André), Maxwell (Robert), Mazarin (Jules, Cardinal), Meacher (Michael), Mikoyan (Anastas), Milburn (Alan), Mondale (Walter Frederick),

Osborne (George), **Paisley**
(Reverend Ian), **Profumo** (John),
**Redmond** (John), **Redwood** (John),
**Rifkind** (Sir Malcolm), **Russell**
(William, Lord), **Salmond** (Alec),
**Sarkozy** (Nicolas), **Schmidt**
(Helmut), **Sithole** (Reverend
Ndabaningi), **Skinner** (Dennis),
**Tallien** (Jean Lambert), **Trimble**
(David), **Warwick** (Richard Neville,
Earl of), **William** (of Wykeham)

08 **Adenauer** (Konrad), **Albright**
(Madeleine), **Antonius** (Marcus),
**Blunkett** (David), **Campbell** (Kim),
**Campbell** (Sir Menzies), **Catiline**,
**Constant** (Benjamin), **Cromwell**
(Oliver), **Cromwell** (Thomas),
**Crossman** (Richard), **Daladier**
(Edouard), **Dimitrov** (Georgi),
**Dollfuss** (Engelbert), **Falconer**
(Charles, Lord), **Franklin**
(Benjamin), **Genscher** (Hans-
Dietrich), **Giuliani** (Rudolph
'Rudy'), **Goebbels** (Joseph),
**Hailsham** (Quintin McGarel Hogg,
Viscount), **Hamilton** (Alexander),
**Harriman** (William Averell),
**Honecker** (Erich), **Humphrey**
(Hubert Horatio), **Ibárruri** (Dolores),
**Jumblatt** (Kemal), **Karadžić**
(Radovan), **Khomeini** (Ayatollah
Ruhollah), **Lansbury** (George),
**Lucullus** (Lucius Licinius),
**Malenkov** (Giorgiy), **Marshall**
(George Catlett), **Maudling**
(Reginald), **McCarthy** (Eugene
Joseph), **McCarthy** (Joseph
Raymond), **McGovern** (George
Stanley), **McNamara** (Robert
Strange), **Medvedev** (Dmitry),
**Miliband** (David), **Miliband** (Ed),
**Mirabeau** (Honoré Gabriel Riqueti,
Comte de), **Montfort** (Simon de),
**Morrison** (Herbert, Lord), **Pericles**,
**Polignac** (Auguste Jules Armand
Marie, Prince de), **Portillo**
(Michael), **Prescott** (John),
**Rathenau** (Walther), **Sandwich**
(John Montagu, Earl of), **Schröder**
(Gerhard), **Schüssel** (Wolfgang),
**Shephard** (Gillian), **Shinwell**
(Manny, Lord), **Stanhope** (James,
Earl), **Thatcher** (Margaret,
Baroness), **Ulbricht** (Walter),
**Whitelaw** (William 'Willie',
Viscount), **Williams** (Shirley, Lady),
**Zinoviev** (Grigoriy)

09 **Alexander** (Douglas), **Armstrong**
(Hilary), **Boothroyd** (Betty,
Baroness), **Bottomley** (Virginia),
**Buthelezi** (Chief Mangosuthu),
**Ceauşescu** (Nicolae), **Churchill**
(Randolph, Lord), **Churchill** (Sir
Winston), **Gaitskell** (Hugh),
**Godolphin** (Sidney, Earl of),
**Goldwater** (Barry Morris), **Heseltine**
(Michael, Lord), **Kissinger** (Henry),
**Kitchener** (Herbert, Earl), **Lafayette**
(Marie Joseph, Marquis de), **La
Guardia** (Fiorello Henry),
**Luxemburg** (Rosa), **Mandelson**
(Peter, Lord), **Milošević** (Slobodan),
**Miltiades**, **Parkinson** (Cecil, Lord),
**Podgorniy** (Nikolay), **Ramaphosa**

(Cyril), **Richelieu** (Armand Jean du
Plessis, Cardinal and Duc de),
**Robertson** (George, Lord),
**Stevenson** (Adlai), **Strafford**
(Thomas Wentworth, Earl of),
**Streicher** (Julius), **Vyshinsky**
(Andrei)

10 **Alcibiades**, **Carrington** (Peter,
Lord), **Cunningham** (Doctor Jack),
**Enver Pasha**, **Hattersley** (Roy,
Lord), **McGuinness** (Martin),
**Metternich** (Klemens, Fürst von),
**Ribbentrop** (Joachim von),
**Stresemann** (Gustav), **Talleyrand**
(Charles Maurice de), **Waldegrave**
(William), **Walsingham** (Sir
Francis), **Weinberger** (Caspar),
**Widdecombe** (Ann)

11 **Beaverbrook** (Max Aitken, Lord),
**Bolingbroke** (Henry St John,
Viscount), **Castlereagh** (Robert
Stewart, Viscount), **Chamberlain**
(Sir Joseph Austen), **Chamberlain**
(Neville), **Cincinnatus** (Lucius
Quinctius), **Demosthenes**, **George-
Brown** (Lord), **Hore-Belisha** (Leslie,
Lord), **Livingstone** (Ken),
**Machiavelli** (Niccolò), **Mountbatten**
(Louis, Earl), **Shaftesbury** (Anthony
Ashley Cooper, Earl of),
**Wilberforce** (William)

12 **Boutros-Ghali** (Boutros),
**Hammarskjöld** (Dag),
**Themistocles**

13 **Chateaubriand** (François Auguste
René, Viscount of), **Fabius
Maximus** (Quintus)

14 **Heathcoat-Amory** (David)

15 **Giscard d'Estaing** (Valéry),
**Macapagal-Arroyo** (Gloria)

## politics

05 state 06 civics 09 diplomacy, power
game 10 government, statecraft
11 machination, manoeuvring,
Weltpolitik 12 machinations,
Machtpolitik, manipulation 13 party
politics, power politics, power
struggle, public affairs, statesmanship
14 affairs of state, haute politique,
political views, wheeler-dealing
15 local government

## poll

03 cut, dod, get, net, pow, win 04 clip,
gain, head, trim, vote 05 count, shear,
tally 06 ballot, census, obtain, parrot,
return, sample, survey, voting
07 canvass, dishorn, pollard, receive,
returns, solicit, sondage 08 campaign,
question, register, sampling 09 ballot-
box, head count, interview, straw poll,
straw vote 10 Gallup poll, individual,
plebiscite, referendum 11 electioneer,
opinion poll, show of hands 14 market
research

## pollack

03 lob 05 coley, lythe 06 saithe
08 coalfish 09 sea salmon

## polled

03 not 04 nott

## pollen

06 farina 08 bee-bread 09 witchmeal

## pollute

◇ anagram indicator 03 mar 04 file, foul,
soil, warp 05 blend, dirty, spoil, stain,
sully, taint 06 befoul, canker, debase,
defile, infect, poison 07 besmear,
blacken, corrupt, defiled, deprave,
profane, tarnish, vitiate 09 make dirty
10 adulterate 11 contaminate

## pollution

◇ anagram indicator 03 fug 04 smog
05 stain, taint 07 fouling, soilure
08 foulness, impurity, staining, sullying
09 depravity, dirtiness, infection,
muckiness 10 blackening, corruption,
debasement, defilement, filthiness,
tarnishing 12 adulteration
13 contamination

## polonium

02 Po

## polychromatic

06 motley 07 mottled, rainbow
08 many-hued 10 polychrome,
variegated 12 many-coloured,
varicoloured 13 kaleidoscopic,
multicoloured, parti-coloured

## polyglot

08 linguist 11 multiracial, polyglottal,
polyglottic 12 cosmopolitan,
multilingual 13 international,
multilinguist

## polymath

06 oracle 07 know-all 10 all-rounder,
pansophist, polyhistor

## pomp

04 show 05 glory, state 06 parade,
ritual, vanity 07 display, glitter,
majesty, triumph 08 ceremony,
flourish, grandeur 09 formality,
pageantry, solemnity, spectacle,
splendour 10 brilliance, ceremonial,
procession 11 ostentation
12 magnificence 14 self-importance
15 ceremoniousness

## pomposity

04 airs 05 pride 06 vanity 07 bombast,
fustian 08 euphuism, rhetoric
09 arrogance, loftiness, turgidity
10 pretension, stuffiness 11 affectation,
haughtiness, preachiness, presumption
13 condescension, imperiousness,
magniloquence 14 grandiloquence,
self-importance 15 pretentiousness

## pompous

03 big 04 vain 05 budge, grant, heavy,
lofty, proud, state, windy 06 la-di-da,
snooty, solemn, stuffy, turgid
07 flowery, fustian, haughty, orotund,
preachy, stately, stilted 08 affected,
arrogant, inflated, magnific
09 bombastic, conceited, elaborate,
grandiose, high-flown, imperious,
important, ororotund, overblown
10 aldermanly, euphuistic, magnifical,
portentous 11 highfalutin, magisterial,
magnificent, overbearing, patronizing,
pretentious 12 aldermanlike,
highfaluting, high-sounding,
magniloquent, ostentatious,
presumptuous, supercilious
13 condescending, self-important

## pond

**03** dam **04** lake, mere, pool, rink, stew, tank, tarn **05** flash, pound, viver **06** puddle **07** piscary, piscina, piscine **08** Atlantic, fish-stew, turlough **09** waterhole **10** oceanarium, seaquarium **12** watering-hole

## ponder

**04** mull, muse, pore **05** brood, poise, study, think, volve, weigh **06** muse on, reason **07** analyse, examine, reflect, revolve **08** cogitate, consider, incubate, meditate, mull over, pore over, turn over **09** cerebrate, ponderate **10** deliberate, excogitate, puzzle over **11** contemplate, ratiocinate **12** ruminate over **13** give thought to

## ponderous

**04** dull, huge **05** bulky, heavy, hefty **06** clumsy, dreary, prolix, stodgy, stolid **07** awkward, massive, serious, stilted, tedious, verbose, weighty **08** laboured, lifeless, pedantic, plodding, unwieldy **09** graceless, laborious, lumbering **10** cumbersome, flat-footed, humourless, long-winded, pedestrian, slow-moving **11** elephantine, heavy-footed, heavy-handed

## ponderously

**06** slowly **07** heavily **08** clumsily, stodgily **09** awkwardly, seriously, tediously, verbosely **11** gracelessly, laboriously **12** cumbersomely, pedantically

## ponderousness

**06** tedium **08** gravitas **09** heaviness, stolidity **10** stodginess **11** seriousness, weightiness **13** laboriousness **14** humourlessness

## pong

*see* **smell**

## pontifical

**05** papal **06** snooty **07** Aaronic, pompous, preachy **08** didactic, dogmatic, prelatic, splendid **09** Aaronical, apostolic, imperious **10** portentous **11** magisterial, overbearing, pretentious, sermonizing **13** condescending, self-important **14** ecclesiastical

## pontificate

**05** spiel **06** preach **07** declaim, expound, lecture **08** harangue, moralize, perorate, sound off **09** dogmatize, hold forth, pronounce, sermonize **13** lay down the law

## pontoon

**05** float **07** caisson, vingt-un **09** blackjack, twenty-one, vingt-et-un

## pony

*see* **horse**

## pooh-pooh

**04** pish **05** scoff, scorn, sneer, spurn **06** deride, reject, slight **07** disdain, dismiss, sniff at **08** belittle, minimize, play down, ridicule **09** disparage, disregard **10** brush aside **12** make little of **15** laugh out of court

## pool

**03** dub, hag, lin, pot, spa **04** ante, bank, bath, dump, flow, fund, hagg, lake, lido, linn, meer, mere, pond, ring, sump, tank, tarn, team **05** flash, group, kitty, merge, plash, plesh, purse, share, stank **06** cartel, chip in, lasher, muck in, puddle, supply **07** combine, jackpot, Jacuzzi®, piscina, piscine, reserve **08** Bethesda **09** backwater, composite, syndicate, waterhole **10** accumulate, amalgamate, collective, consortium, contribute, natatorium **11** put together **12** accumulation, paddling-pool, swimming-bath, swimming-pool, watering-hole **13** swimming-baths

## poor

◊ *anagram indicator* **03** bad, low, sad **04** bare, duff, mean, mere, naff, puir, ropy, thin, weak **05** broke, cronk, crook, jerry, lowly, needy, pants, ropey, skint, sober, sorry, stony **06** barren, cruddy, crummy, faulty, feeble, hard-up, humble, hungry, ill off, in need, meagre, measly, ornery, paltry, rotten, scanty, shoddy, skimpy, sparse **07** hapless, lacking, low-rent, obolary, pitiful, reduced, rubbish, unhappy, unlucky, useless, wanting **08** badly off, bankrupt, beggared, beggarly, below par, depleted, deprived, dirt-poor, exiguous, ill-fated, indigent, inferior, low-grade, luckless, mediocre, one-horse, pathetic, pitiable, shameful, strapped, waterish, wretched **09** defective, deficient, destitute, exhausted, flat broke, fruitless, imperfect, miserable, penniless, penurious, third-rate, worthless **10** cleaned-out, distressed, ill-starred, inadequate, low-quality, second-rate, spiritless, stony-broke, straitened, threadbare **11** impecunious, near the bone, necessitous, substandard, unfortunate **12** impoverished, insufficient, on your uppers, unproductive, without means **13** below standard, disadvantaged, in Queer Street **14** on the breadline, on your beam ends, unsatisfactory **15** poverty-stricken, strapped for cash, underprivileged

## poorly

◊ *anagram indicator* **03** ill **04** sick **05** badly, crook, seedy **06** ailing, feebly, groggy, meanly, rotten, sickly, unwell **08** below par, faultily, rottenly, shabbily, shoddily **09** off colour **10** indisposed, inexpertly, inferiorly, out of sorts **12** inadequately **13** incompetently **14** insufficiently, unsuccessfully **15** under the weather

## pop

◊ *anagram indicator* **03** nip, put **04** bang, boom, cola, dash, drop, papa, pawn, push, rush, shot, slip, snap, soda **05** burst, crack, go off, hurry, poppa, shoot, shove, slide **06** insert, pistol, poppet, report, thrust **07** darling, explode, popular, propose **08** protrude, suddenly **09** explosion, go quickly **10** fizzy drink **12** leave quickly **13** fizzy lemonade **15** go for a short time

*See also* **father; pawn; singer; song**
• **pop off** **03** die **06** pass on, peg out **07** snuff it **08** flatline, pass away **09** have had it **13** kick the bucket
• **pop up** **05** occur **06** appear, crop up, show up, turn up **09** come along **11** materialize

## pope

**03** SSD **04** ruff **05** ruffe **06** Il Papa **07** pontiff **10** Holy Father **11** His Holiness **12** Bishop of Rome **13** Vicar of Christ

*Popes:*

**03** Leo
**04** Cono, Joan, John, Mark, Paul, Pius
**05** Caius, Donus, Felix, Lando, Linus, Peter, Soter, Urban
**06** Adrian, Agatho, Albert, Fabian, Julius, Lucius, Martin, Philip, Sixtus, Victor
**07** Anterus, Clement, Damasus, Gregory, Hadrian, Hilarus, Hyginus, Marinus, Paschal, Pontian, Romanus, Sergius, Stephen, Ursinus, Zosimus
**08** Agapetus, Anicetus, Benedict, Boniface, Calixtus, Eugenius, Eulalius, Eusebius, Formosus, Gelasius, Honorius, Innocent, John Paul, Liberius, Nicholas, Novatian, Pelagius, Siricius, Theodore, Vigilius, Vitalian
**09** Adeodatus, Alexander, Anacletus, Callistus, Celestine, Cornelius, Deusdedit, Dionysius, Dioscorus, Evaristus, Hormisdas, Marcellus, Miltiades, Severinus, Silverius, Sisinnius, Sylvester, Symmachus, Theodoric, Valentine, Zacharias
**10** Anastasius, Hippolytus, Laurentius, Sabinianus, Simplicius, Zephyrinus
**11** Christopher, Constantine, Eleutherius, Eutychianus, Marcellinus, Telesphorus

## popinjay

**03** fop **04** beau, dude, toff **05** dandy, swell **06** parrot **07** coxcomb, peacock

## poplar

**03** asp **05** abele, aspen **06** aspine **09** tacamahac, tacmahack, tulip tree **10** cottonwood

## poppy

**07** Papaver, ponceau **08** argemone **09** bloodroot **10** coquelicot **12** eschscholzia **13** eschscholtzia

## poppycock

**03** rot **04** blah, bosh, bull, bunk, guff, tosh **05** balls, bilge, folly, hooey, trash, tripe **06** drivel, humbug, piffle, waffle **07** baloney, blether, flannel, hogwash, rhubarb, rubbish, twaddle **08** blathers, claptrap, cobblers, nonsense, tommyrot **09** gibberish, silliness, stupidity **10** balderdash, codswallop **11** foolishness **12** gobbledygook

## populace

**03** mob **04** folk, herd **05** crowd, plebs

## popular

**06** masses, people, proles, public, rabble **07** natives, punters, society **08** canaille, citizens, riff-raff **09** community, hoi polloi, multitude, occupants, residents **10** common herd, multitudes **11** inhabitants, proletariat, rank and file, third estate **12** common people **13** general public, great unwashed

## popular

**02** in **03** big, hip, lay, now, pop **04** cool, laic **05** famed, liked, noted, stock, usual **06** common, famous, modish, simple, trendy, vulgar, wanted **07** admired, amateur, current, demotic, desired, general, massive **08** accepted, approved, exoteric, favoured, idolized, in demand, in favour, ordinary, plebeian, renowned, standard **09** acclaimed, customary, favourite, household, prevalent, universal, well-known, well-liked **10** accessible, all the rage, celebrated, democratic, mass-market, prevailing, simplified, well-graced, widespread **11** fashionable, sought-after **12** conventional, non-technical **13** non-specialist **14** understandable

## popularity

**04** fame **05** glory, kudos, vogue **06** esteem, favour, regard, renown, repute **07** acclaim, worship **08** approval, currency **09** adoration, adulation **10** acceptance, mass appeal, reputation **11** approbation, idolization, lionization, recognition

## popularize

**06** spread **08** simplify **09** propagate, vulgarize **10** generalize **11** democratize, familiarize **12** universalize **14** give currency to, make accessible

## popularly

**03** pop **05** vulgo **06** widely **07** usually **08** commonly **09** generally, regularly **10** ordinarily **11** customarily, universally **13** traditionally **14** conventionally, non-technically

## populate

**05** dwell **06** live in, occupy, people, settle **07** inhabit, overrun, peopled **08** colonize **09** devastate, inhabited

## population

**03** pop **04** folk **06** people **07** natives, society **08** citizens, populace **09** community, occupants, residents, stabilate **11** inhabitants

## populous

**06** packed **07** crowded, teeming **08** crawling, numerous, swarming **11** overpeopled **13** overpopulated

## porcelain

*Porcelain makes include:*

**03** Bow
**04** Ming, Noke, Wade
**05** Arita, Delft, Derby, Spode
**06** Minton, Sèvres, Vienna
**07** Belleek, Bristol, Chelsea, Dresden, Limoges, Meissen, Nanking, Satsuma

**08** Caughley, Coalport, Copeland, Wedgwood
**09** Chantilly, Davenport, Worcester
**10** Cookworthy, Crown Derby, Rockingham
**12** Royal Doulton
**14** Royal Worcester

*Porcelain types include:*

**04** bisk, frit
**05** Hizen, Imari, ivory, Kraak
**06** bamboo, bisque, Canton, jasper, Parian, tender
**07** biscuit, crackle, faience, nankeen
**08** eggshell, kakiemon, Yingqing
**09** bone china, copper red, hard-paste, soft-paste
**10** jasperware, salt-glazed
**11** Capodimonte, chinoiserie, clair de lune, famille rose
**12** blanc-de-Chine, blue and white, famille jaune, famille verte
**14** soapstone paste

*See also* **pottery**

## porch

**04** hall, stoa **05** foyer, lobby, stoep, stoop **07** galilee, hallway, portico, veranda **09** colonnade, vestibule **12** entrance-hall

## porcupine

**05** urson **10** porpentine

## pore

**04** hole, vent **05** stoma **06** outlet, stigma **07** foramen, opening, orifice **08** aperture, lenticel, nanopore **09** micropore **11** perforation
• **pore over** **03** con, kon **04** read, scan **05** brood, conne, study **06** go over, peruse, ponder **07** dwell on, examine **10** scrutinize **11** contemplate **14** examine closely, study intensely

## porgy

**04** scup **06** braise, braize **08** scuppaug

## porker

*see* **pig**

## pornographic

**04** blue, lewd, pink, porn **05** adult, bawdy, dirty, gross, nasty, porno **06** coarse, erotic, filthy, risqué, X-rated **07** obscene **08** indecent, prurient **09** off-colour, salacious **11** titillating

## pornography

**04** dirt, porn, smut **05** filth, nasty, porno **07** curiosa, erotica **08** facetiae, peep-show **09** bawdiness, grossness, indecency, obscenity, skinflick, snuff film **10** snuff movie, snuff video, video nasty **13** sexploitation **15** girlie magazines

## porous

**04** airy, open **05** holey **06** spongy **07** foveate **08** cellular, pervious **09** absorbent, permeable **10** cancellate, cancellous, foraminous, penetrable, spongelike **11** cancellated, cavernulous, foraminated, honeycombed

## porpoise

**06** seahog, sea-pig **07** dolphin, pellach, pellack, pellock, porpess **08** Phocaena,

porpesse, sea swine **09** mere swine, porcpisce

## porridge

**04** gaol, jail, samp, stir **05** kasha, sadza **06** hominy, supawn **07** brochan, polenta, pottage, suppawn **08** parritch, sentence **09** mealie pap, praiseach, stirabout **12** hasty pudding

## port

**01** L **02** pt **03** bag **04** dock, gate, left, ruby **05** carry, haven, hithe, jetty, roads **06** convey **07** bearing, borough, harbour, retinue, seaport **08** dockland, larboard, porthole, suitcase **09** anchorage, demeanour, docklands, roadstead **10** deportment, harbourage

*Ports include:*

**03** Gao, Lae, Rio, Vac
**04** Aden, Apia, Baku, Bari, Caen, Cebu, Ciba, Cork, Deal, Doha, Elat, Faro, Hull, Kiel, Kobe, Linz, Lomé, Lüda, Nice, Oban, Omsk, Oran, Oslo, Oulu, Pula, Riga, Safi, Sfax, Suez, Suva, Tyre, Vigo, Wick
**05** Accra, Agana, Aqaba, Arica, Basle, Basra, Beira, Belém, Blyth, Brest, Busan, Colón, Dakar, Davao, Dover, Dubai, Emden, Galle, Gavle, Genoa, Ghent, Gijon, Haifa, Ibiza, Izmir, Kayes, Kazan, Koper, Lagos, Larne, Leith, Liège, Macao, Malmo, Masan, Miami, Nampo, Natal, Omaha, Osaka, Ostia, Palma, Paris, Poole, Praia, Pusan, Rouen, Sakai, Salem, Ségou, Sitra, Skien, Split, Surat, Tampa, Tanga, Tokyo, Tomsk, Torun, Tulsa, Tunis, Turku, Ulsan, Vaasa, Varna, Worms, Wuhan
**06** Aarhus, Abadan, Agadir, Albany, Ancona, Annaba, Ashdod, Avarua, Aveira, Aviles, Balboa, Bamako, Banjul, Bastia, Batumi, Beirut, Bergen, Bissau, Bombay, Boston, Bremen, Bruges, Calais, Callao, Camden, Cannes, Cochin, Dalian, Dammam, Darwin, Denver, Dieppe, Douala, Dublin, Duluth, Dundee, Durban, Durres, El Paso, Galway, Gdansk, Gdynia, Grodno, Hamina, Havana, Hobart, Huelva, Inchon, Jarrow, Jeddah, Juneau, Kalgar, Kandla, Kaunas, Khulna, Lisbon, Lobito, London, Luanda, Lübeck, Madras, Malabo, Malaga, Manama, Manaus, Manila, Maputo, Matrah, Mersin, Mobile, Muscat, Nacala, Nagoya, Nantes, Napier, Naples, Narvik, Nassau, Nelson, Newark, Niamey, Ningbo, Nouméa, Nyborg, Odense, Odessa, Oporto, Ostend, Penang, Phuket, Quebec, Recife, Rijeka, Rimini, Samara, Samsun, Santos, Sasebo, Sittwe, Sousse, St John, St-Malo, St Paul, Sydney, Szeged, Tacoma, Thurso, Timaru, Toledo, Toulon, Toyama, Treves, Vannes, Velsen, Venice, Warsaw,

Whitby, Xiamen, Yangon
**07** Aalborg, Abidjan, Ajaccio,
Alcudia, Algiers, Almeria,
Antibes, Antwerp, Augusta,
Bangkok, Belfast, Berbera,
Bizerta, Bourgas, Bristol, Buffalo,
Cabinda, Calabar, Caldera,
Calicut, Cardiff, Catania,
Cayenne, Chicago, Cologne,
Colombo, Conakry, Corinth,
Corinto, Cotonou, Dampier,
Detroit, Douglas, Dunedin,
Dunkirk, Esbjerg, Fukuoka,
Funchal, Geelong, Glasgow,
Grimsby, Halifax, Hamburg,
Harstad, Harwich, Hodeida,
Honiara, Honiari, Houston,
Ipswich, Iquique, Jakarta,
Karachi, Kowloon, Kuching,
Kushiro, La Plata, Larnaca, La
Union, Le Havre, Livorno,
Marsala, Melilla, Memphis,
Messina, Mindelo, Mombasa,
Newport, New Ross, Niigata,
Niterói, Oakland, Okayama,
Palermo, Papeete, Paradip,
Pasajes, Piraeus, Portree,
Rangoon, Ravenna, Rosaria,
Rosario, Rostock, Salerno, San
José, San Juan, San Remo, Santa
Fe, São Tomé, Saratov, Seattle,
Seville, Shimizu, Stanley, St
John's, St Louis, Swansea, Tallinn,
Tampico, Tangier, Taranto, Tel
Aviv, Tianjin, Tilbury, Toronto,
Trieste, Tripoli, Vitebsk, Vitoria,
Wroclaw, Xingang, Zhdanov
**08** Aberdeen, Abu Dhabi, Acajutla,
Acapulco, Adelaide, Alicante,
Arbroath, Asunción, Auckland,
Benghazi, Bordeaux, Boulogne,
Brindisi, Brisbane, Cagliari,
Calcutta, Cape Town, Castries,
Changsha, Chimbote, Djibouti,
Dortmund, Duisburg, Dunleary,
Falmouth, Flushing, Freeport,
Freetown, Gisborne, Godthaab,
Greenock, Guyaquil, Hakodate,
Halmstad, Hamilton, Hay Point,
Helsinki, Holyhead, Honolulu,
Istanbul, Kawasaki, Keflavik,
Kingston, Kinshasa, Kirkaldy,
Kirkwall, Kismaayo, Klaipeda, La
Coruna, La Guaira, La Spezia,
Lattakia, Limassol, Limerick,
Mandalay, Mannheim, Marbella,
Matanzas, Mazatlan, Monrovia,
Montreal, Montrose, Mormugao,
Moulmein, Mulhouse,
Murmansk, Nagasaki, New
Haven, Pago Pago, Plymouth,
Portland, Port Said, Port-Vila,
Ramsgate, Richmond, Roskilde,
Rosslare, Salonica, Salvador, San
Diego, San Pedro, Santarém,
Savannah, Semarang, Shanghai,
Simbirsk, Smolensk, St Helier,
Stockton, St-Tropez, Surabaya,
Syracuse, Szczecin, Takoradi,
Tauranga, Torshavn, Ullapool,
Valencia, Valletta, Veracruz,
Voronezh, Weymouth,
Yokohama, Zanzibar
**09** Algeciras, Amsterdam,

Anchorage, Archangel,
Astrakhan, Baltimore, Barcelona,
Botany Bay, Bujumbura,
Cartagena, Cherbourg,
Cleveland, Constance, Constanta,
Dordrecht, Dubrovnik,
Esztergom, Europoort, Famagusta,
Fleetwood, Flensburg, Fortaleza,
Frankfurt, Fremantle, Galveston,
Gateshead, Gibraltar, Gravesend,
Heraklion, Hiroshima,
Immingham, Kagoshima,
Kaohsiung, Karlsrühe, King's
Lynn, Kingstown, Kozhikode,
Langesund, Las Palmas,
Launceton, Liverpool, Long
Beach, Lowestoft, Magdeburg,
Mahajanga, Maracaibo,
Mariehamn, Melbourne,
Milwaukee, Mizushima,
Mogadishu, Nashville,
Newcastle, Nuku'alofa,
Palembang, Palm Beach,
Paranagua, Peterhead, Phnom
Penh, Port Blair, Port Limon, Port
Louis, Port Natal, Port Sudan,
Reykjavík, Rio Grande,
Rochester, Rotterdam, Santander,
Sassandra, Sheerness, Singapore,
Stavanger, St-Nazaire,
Stockholm, Stornoway, Stralsund,
Stranraer, Sundsvall, Takamatsu,
Tarragona, Toamasina,
Trebizond, Trondheim, Tuticorin,
Vancouver, Vicksburg, Vientiane,
Volgograd, Walvis Bay, Yaroslavl,
Zeebrugge, Zhenjiang, Zrenjanin
**10** Alexandria, Basseterre, Baton
Rouge, Belize City, Bratislava,
Bridgeport, Bridgetown, Cap
Haitian, Casablanca, Charleston,
Chittagong, Cienfuegos,
Copenhagen, East London,
Felixstowe, Folkestone, Fray
Bentos, Fredericia, Georgetown,
Gothenburg, Hartlepool,
Hildesheim, Iskenderun, Kansas
City, Kitakyushu, Kompong Som,
Kuwait City, Leeuwarden,
Libreville, Little Rock, Los
Angeles, Louisville, Manchester,
Manzanillo, Marseilles, Mina
Qaboos, Mina Sulman, Montego
Bay, Montevideo, Mostaganem,
New Orleans, Nouadhibou,
Nouakchott, Oranjestad,
Paramaribo, Pittsburgh, Port
Gentil, Portishead, Portsmouth,
Port Talbot, Providence,
Sacramento, Salina Cruz, San
Lorenzo, Santa Marta,
Sebastopol, Sevastopol,
Strasbourg, Sunderland,
Talcahuano, Thunder Bay,
Townsville, Valparaiso,
Wellington, Willemstad,
Wilmington, Workington,
Zaporozhye
**11** Antofagasta, Bahia Blanca,
Bandar Abbas, Brazzaville,
Bremerhaven, Bridlington,
Brownsville, Buenos Aires,
Charlestown, Chattanooga, Dar
es Salaam, Fraserburgh,

Grangemouth, Helsingborg,
Krasnoyarsk, Livingstone,
Lossiemouth, Mar del Plata,
Minneapolis, Narayanganj, New
Plymouth, New York City,
Novosibirsk, Panama Canal, Pasir
Gudang, Pointe-Noire,
Pondicherry, Port Cartier, Port
Moresby, Porto Alegre, Port of
Spain, Punta Arenas,
Qinhuangdao, Richards Bay,
Rostov-on-Don, Southampton,
Three Rivers, Vladivostok
**12** Barranquilla, Buenaventura, Fort
de France, Frederikstad,
Jacksonville, Kota Kinabalu,
Kristiansand, Ludwigshafen, New
Amsterdam, New Mangalore,
Novorossiysk, Philadelphia,
Point-à-Pitre, Ponta Delgada, Port
Adelaide, Port-au-Prince, Port
Harcourt, Port Victoria, Puerto
Cortes, Rio de Janeiro, Saint
George's, San Francisco, San
Sebastian, Santo Domingo, St
Petersburg, Tel Aviv-Jaffa, Ujung
Pandang, Villahermosa
**13** Ellesmere Port, Frederikshavn,
Great Yarmouth, Ho Chi Minh
City, Hook of Holland,
Middlesbrough, Port Elizabeth,
Semipalatinsk, Sihanoukville
**14** Dnepropetrovsk, Port
Georgetown, Santiago de Cuba
**15** Barrow-in-Furness, Charlotte
Amalie, Frankfurt am Main,
Nizhniy Novgorod

• **port authority** **03** PLA

## portability
**09** handiness **10** movability
**11** compactness, convenience
**13** manageability

## portable
**05** handy **07** compact, movable
**08** luggable **09** endurable, portatile
**10** convenient, conveyable,
manageable **11** lightweight
**13** transportable

## portal
**04** door, gate **05** way in **06** access
**07** doorway, gateway, opening
**08** entrance

## portend
**04** bode, omen **05** augur **06** herald,
import, warn of **07** bespeak, betoken,
point to, predict, presage, promise,
purport, signify **08** announce,
forebode, forecast, foreshow, foretell,
forewarn, indicate, threaten
**09** adumbrate, be a sign of, foretoken,
harbinger **10** foreshadow
**13** prognosticate

## portent
**04** omen, sign **05** augur, token
**06** augury, boding, marvel, ostent,
threat **07** presage, prodigy, warning
**08** forecast, prodrome **09** harbinger,
precursor **10** foreboding, forerunner,
indication, prognostic **11** forewarning,
ominousness, premonition
**12** presentiment **13** foreshadowing,

prefiguration, signification
**15** prognostication

**portentous**
**04** dire, vain **05** proud **06** snooty,
solemn **07** amazing, crucial, fateful,
haughty, ominous, pompous
**08** affected, arrogant, menacing,
sinister **09** conceited, grandiose,
imperious, important, momentous
**10** astounding, foreboding, impressive,
miraculous, prodigious, remarkable
**11** epoch-making, magisterial,
overbearing, patronizing, pretentious,
significant, threatening **12** awe-
inspiring, earth-shaking, ostentatious,
presumptuous, supercilious
**13** condescending, extraordinary, self-
important

**portentously**
**08** snootily **09** haughtily, pompously
**10** arrogantly **11** conceitedly
**13** patronizingly **14** superciliously
**15** condescendingly, self-importantly

**porter**
**04** page **05** caddy, cadee, cadie, hamal
**06** bearer, caddie, entire, hammal,
humper, redcap **07** bell-boy, bellhop,
carrier, doorman, dvornik, janitor
**08** bummaree, doorsman **09** caretaker,
concierge, out-porter **10** door-keeper,
gatekeeper **11** double-stout, night-
porter **12** ticket-porter **13** door
attendant **14** baggage-carrier, baggage-
handler, commissionaire

**portico**
**04** stoa **05** porch **06** exedra, parvis,
xystus **07** distyle, exhedra, narthex,
parvise, veranda **08** prostyle, verandah
**09** colonnade, decastyle, hexastyle,
octastyle, octostyle **10** pentastyle,
tetrastyle **11** dodecastyle

**portion**
◊ *hidden indicator* **02** go **03** bit, cut, dot,
lot, rag **04** deal, dole, dose, fate, luck,
meed, mite, part, tait, tate, what
**05** allot, dowry, grist, order, piece,
quota, ratio, share, slice, small, space,
taste, wedge, whack, wodge **06** assign,
chance, divide, kismet, morsel, parcel,
ration, region **07** carve up, destiny,
dole out, fortune, helping, kenning,
measure, rake-off, scantle, section,
segment, serving, slice up, tranche
**08** allocate, division, fraction,
fragment, particle, pittance, quantity,
share out **09** allotment, allowance,
apportion, partition, scantling,
something **10** allocation, distribute,
percentage, proportion

**portliness**
**07** fatness, obesity **08** fullness
**09** ampleness, beefiness, dumpiness,
heaviness, plumpness, rotundity,
roundness, stoutness, tubbiness
**10** chubbiness, corpulence, fleshiness
**11** paunchiness

**portly**
**03** fat **05** ample, gaucy, gawcy, gawsy,
heavy, large, obese, plump, round,
stout **06** gaucie, rotund, stocky
**08** matronly **09** corpulent

**10** aldermanly, overweight
**12** aldermanlike

**portrait**
**04** icon **05** image, pin-up, story, study
**06** Kit-Cat, sketch **07** account, drawing,
picture, profile, retrate **08** likeness,
painting, pourtray, retraitt, vignette
**09** composite, depiction, miniature,
portrayal **10** caricature, full-length,
half-length, photograph, pourtraict
**11** description, whole-length **12** carte-
de-viste, self-portrait **14** representation
**15** thumbnail sketch

**portray**
**03** act **04** draw, play, take **05** evoke,
image, paint **06** depict, sketch
**07** perform, picture, present
**08** describe, portrait, pourtray
**09** pantomime, personify, represent
**10** illustrate **11** impersonate **12** act the
part of, characterize **13** play the part of

**portrayal**
**05** study **06** acting, sketch **07** drawing,
picture **08** painting **09** depiction,
evocation, rendering **11** delineation,
description, performance
**12** presentation **14** interpretation,
representation

**Portugal**
**01** P **02** Pg **03** PRT

**Portuguese**
**02** Pg

**pose**
**03** act, air, ask, put, set, sit **04** airs, role,
sham **05** cause, claim, feign, front,
model, posit **06** affect, assert, create,
façade, lead to, puzzle, stance, submit
**07** advance, arrange, bearing, posture,
present, pretend, produce, propose,
suggest **08** attitude, carriage, position,
pretence, propound, result in
**09** postulate, put on airs **10** constitute,
deportment, give rise to, masquerade,
put forward, put on an act
**11** affectation, impersonate
**12** attitudinize, contrapposto **15** pass
yourself off

**Poseidon**
**07** Neptune

**poser**
**04** sham **05** pseud **06** enigma, phoney,
poseur, puzzle, riddle, sitter
**07** dilemma, mystery, poseuse,
problem, show-off, sticker **08** impostor,
posturer **09** charlatan, conundrum,
play-actor **10** mind-bender
**11** brainteaser **12** brain-twister
**13** attitudinizer, exhibitionist, vexed
question

**poseur**
**04** sham **05** poser, pseud **06** phoney
**07** poseuse, show-off **08** impostor,
posturer **09** charlatan, play-actor
**13** attitudinizer, exhibitionist

**posh**
**01** U **04** rich, swag **05** dandy, fancy,
grand, money, plush, pluty, smart,
swish **06** classy, de-luxe, la-di-da,
lavish, luxury, select, snazzy, superb,
swanky **07** elegant, opulent, stylish

**08** top-class, up-market **09** exclusive,
expensive, halfpenny, high-class,
luxurious, sumptuous **10** upper-class
**11** fashionable

**posit**
**03** set **04** pose **05** state **06** assert,
assume, submit **07** advance, dispose,
presume **08** propound **09** postulate,
predicate **10** put forward

**position**
**03** fix, job, lie, pos, put, set **04** area,
case, duty, pose, post, rank, role, site,
spot, view **05** array, grade, level, place,
point, pozzy, scene, stand, state
**06** belief, deploy, factor, lay out,
locate, office, orient, plight, possie
settle, stance, status **07** arrange,
bearing, dispose, factors, install,
opinion, outlook, posture, ranking,
setting, situate, station **08** attitude,
capacity, function, locality, location,
prestige, standing **09** condition,
establish, influence, postulate,
situation, viewpoint **10** background,
employment, occupation, standpoint
**11** appointment, arrangement,
disposition, point of view,
predicament, whereabouts
**13** circumstances **14** state of affairs
• **in fixed position 02** to

**positive**
**01** p **03** pos **04** firm, good, plus, rank,
real, sure **05** basic, clear, sheer, utter
**06** actual, direct, upbeat, useful
**07** assured, certain, express, helpful,
hopeful, perfect, positif, precise, reality
**08** absolute, cheerful, clear-cut,
complete, concrete, decisive, definite,
emphatic, explicit, material, outright,
thorough **09** assertive, categoric,
confident, convinced, downright, out-
and-out, practical, promising, veritable
**10** conclusive, consummate,
convincing, definitive, encouraged,
favourable, optimistic, productive,
undeniable **11** affirmative, categorical,
encouraging, irrefutable, unequivocal,
unmitigated **12** constructive,
indisputable, matter-of-fact,
unmistakable **13** incontestable
**14** dextrorotatory

**positively**
**06** firmly, surely **07** finally **09** assuredly,
certainly, expressly **10** absolutely,
decisively, definitely, undeniably
**12** conclusively, emphatically,
indisputably, unmistakably
**13** categorically, incontestably,
unequivocally **14** unquestionably

**possess**
◊ *containment indicator* **03** get, own
**04** gain, have, hold, take **05** enjoy,
enjoy, haunt, imbue, seize, wield
**06** attain, inform, obsess, obtain,
occupy **07** acquire, bedevil, bewitch,
control, enchant, inhabit, inherit,
overget **08** acquaint, demonize,
dominate, maintain, take over
**09** infatuate, influence **12** be gifted
with **13** be blessed with, be endowed
with, take control of

## possessed

**03** mad **06** crazed, cursed, raving **07** berserk, haunted **08** besotted, consumed, demonized, dominated, maddened, obsessed, spirited **09** bewitched, demonized, dominated, enchanted, hag-ridden **10** bedevilled, controlled, infatuated, mesmerized

## possession

**03** fee **04** grip, hand, hold **05** craze, thing, title **06** having, tenure **07** control, custody, holding, tenancy **08** haunting **09** obsession, occupance, occupancy, ownership **10** domination, occupation **11** infatuation **14** proprietorship
• **in possession** ◇ *containment indicator*

## possessions

**03** all, ana **04** aver, gear, good, swag **05** goods, stuff, worth **06** assets, estate, riches, things, wealth **07** baggage, clobber, effects, luggage **08** chattels, movables, outsight, property **09** sprechery, territory **10** belongings, spreaghery **12** temporalties **13** accoutrements, paraphernalia, temporalities, worldly wealth **15** personal effects

## possessive

**06** greedy **07** jealous, selfish **08** clinging, covetous, genitive, grasping **10** dominating **11** acquisitive, controlling, domineering **14** overprotective

## possessiveness

**05** greed **08** jealousy **11** selfishness **12** covetousness **13** exclusiveness **15** acquisitiveness

## possibility

**04** fear, hope, odds, risk **05** maybe, posse **06** chance, choice, danger, hazard, option, talent **07** promise **08** prospect, recourse **09** off-chance, potential, prospects **10** advantages, likelihood, preference **11** alternative, contingency, feasibility, probability, proposition **12** capabilities, expectations, potentiality **13** attainability **14** conceivability, practicability

## possible

◇ *anagram indicator* **06** doable, likely, odds-on, viable **07** tenable **08** credible, feasible, probable, workable **09** potential, promising **10** achievable, attainable, imaginable, on the cards, realizable **11** conceivable, practicable **13** that can be done **14** accomplishable

## possibly

◇ *anagram indicator* **03** e'er **04** ever, well **05** at all, maybe **07** in posse, perhaps **09** hopefully **10** by any means **11** by any chance, conceivably **12** peradventure

## possum

**04** tait **07** opossum **08** Tarsipes **09** phalanger **10** honey-mouse **11** sugar glider

## post

**03** dak, job, leg, pin, put **04** beat, bitt,

jamb, mail, move, pale, pole, prop, send **05** affix, e-mail, haste, newel, pin up, place, put up, shaft, stake, strut **06** assign, attach, column, locate, office, picket, pillar, report, second **07** airmail, appoint, display, forward, letters, packets, parcels, publish, situate, station, stick up, support, upright, vacancy **08** announce, baluster, banister, delivery, dispatch, junk mail, packages, palisade, position, standard, transfer, transmit **09** advertise, broadcast, circulate, mail-coach, make known, publicize, put on duty, situation, snail mail, stanchion **10** assignment, direct mail, employment, packet-boat, Post Office **11** appointment, surface mail **12** all-up service, postal system, recorded mail **13** postal service **14** communications, correspondence, electronic mail, first-class mail, registered mail **15** second-class mail, special delivery
• **keep someone posted** **06** fill in, inform **12** keep informed, keep up to date **13** keep in the loop

## postal order

**02** PO

## postcard

**02** pc

## poster

**02** ad **04** bill, sign **05** solus **06** advert, notice **07** placard, sticker **08** bulletin, play bill, show bill **12** announcement **13** advertisement

## posterior

**03** ass, bum **04** back, butt, hind, rear, rump, seat, tail **05** after, later **06** behind, bottom, dorsal, hinder, jacksy, latter **07** ensuing, jacksie **08** backside, buttocks, haunches, rearward **09** following, hinder end, posterity, posticous **10** subsequent, succeeding **12** hindquarters

## posterity

**04** seed **05** heirs, issue **07** progeny **08** children, mokopuna **09** offspring, posterior **10** succession, successors **11** descendants

## posthaste

**06** at once, pronto, speedy **07** hastily, quickly, swiftly **08** directly, full tilt, promptly, speedily **09** immediate **11** double-quick, immediately **12** straightaway, with all speed

## postman, postwoman

**04** post **06** postie **07** courier, mailman **11** mail-carrier, mail handler **12** postal worker **13** letter-carrier **15** delivery officer

## post-mortem

**02** PM **06** review **07** autopsy **08** analysis, autopsia, necropsy **10** dissection, necroscopy **11** examination

## Post Office

**01** P **02** PO **03** GPO **04** BFPO

## postpone

**04** stay, wait **05** defer, delay, frist, refer, table, waive **06** freeze, put off, retard,

shelve **07** adjourn, do later, prolong, put back, rejourn, sleep on, suspend **08** hold over, mothball, postpose, prorogue, protract, put on ice, roll back, withhold **09** carry over, sleep on it, stand over **10** pigeonhole, reschedule **11** subordinate **13** procrastinate

## postponed

**05** on ice **06** frozen, put off **07** shelved **08** deferred, held over **09** adjourned, suspended **10** in abeyance, protracted **11** carried over, pigeonholed **15** on the back burner

## postponement

**04** stay **05** delay **06** freeze, put-off **07** respite **08** deferral **09** deferment **10** moratorium, suspension **11** adjournment, prorogation **13** backwardation

## postscript

**02** PS **03** PPS **07** codicil **08** addendum, addition, appendix, epilogue **09** afterword **10** supplement **12** afterthought

## postulate

**05** axiom, claim, posit **06** assume **07** advance, lay down, presume, propose, suppose **08** nominate, petition, theorize **09** stipulate **10** assumption, postulatum, presuppose, put forward **11** hypothesize, stipulation

## posture

**03** set **04** pike, pose, site, view **05** guard, mudra, stand, strut **06** affect, belief, motion, sprawl, stance **07** bearing, gesture, opinion, outlook, show off **08** attitude, carriage, position **09** arabesque, decubitus, defensive, offensive, put on airs, viewpoint **10** decumbence, decumbency, deportment, standpoint **11** counter-view, disposition, point of view **12** attitudinize **15** strike attitudes

## postwoman

*see* **postman, postwoman**

## posy

**05** motto, poesy, spray **07** bouquet, corsage, nosegay **08** affected **09** sentiment **10** buttonhole **12** tussie mussie

## pot

**02** po **03** box, can, cup, jar, pan, pat, tea, urn **04** bank, bowl, fund, lota, olla, pool, stew, test, vase **05** basin, crewe, crock, cruse, kitty, lotah, purse **06** aludel, bowpot, caster, chatti, chatty, pipkin, pocket, pottle, tajine, teapot, tipple, trivet, trophy, vessel **07** marmite, pitcher, planter, pothole, reserve **08** boughpot, cauldron, crucible, gallipot, plantpot, pot-au-feu **09** casserole, coffee pot, flowerpot **10** chamberpot, receptacle **11** earthenware, manufacture **13** potentiometer
*See also* **cannabis**

## potable

**04** safe **05** clean **08** beverage **09** drinkable **10** fit to drink

**potassium**
01 K

**potato**
03 alu, yam 04 aloo, chat, spud
05 boxty, early, tater, tatie 06 batata,
camote, murphy, pratie, tattie
07 scallop, scollop

---

*Potatoes include:*

---

04 Cara, chat, seed, ware
05 praty, Sante, Saxon, sweet
06 camote, Estima, kidney, kumara
07 Desiree
09 Charlotte, Kerr's Pink, Maris Peer
10 Duke of York, King Edward, Maris
   Piper
12 Golden Wonder
15 Pentland Javelin

---

**pot-bellied**
03 fat 05 kedge, kedgy, kidge, obese,
tubby 06 portly 07 bloated, paunchy
09 corpulent, distended
10 abdominous, gor-bellied,
overweight

**pot-belly**
03 gut, pot 05 belly 06 paunch
08 tunbelly 09 beer belly, bow
window, spare tyre 11 corporation

**potency**
04 kick, sway 05 force, might, power,
punch 06 energy, muscle, vigour
07 cogency, control 08 capacity,
efficacy, strength 09 authority,
headiness, influence, potentate,
potential, puissance 12 potentiality,
powerfulness 13 effectiveness
14 persuasiveness 15 efficaciousness

**potent**
06 active, cogent, mighty, prince,
strong, virile 07 dynamic, pungent
08 dominant, eloquent, forceful,
powerful, puissant, vigorous
09 effective, energetic, potentate
10 commanding, compelling,
convincing, impressive, persuasive
11 efficacious, influential
12 intoxicating, overpowering
13 authoritative

**potentate**
04 czar, king, tsar, tzar 05 chief, mogul,
queen, ruler 06 despot, dynast, huzoor,
leader, prince, tyrant 07 emperor,
empress, monarch 08 autocrat,
dictator, overlord 09 chieftain,
sovereign 10 panjandrum 11 head of
state

**potential**
◊ *anagram indicator* 04 gift 05 flair
06 future, hidden, latent, likely,
powers, talent 07 ability, budding,
dormant, promise, virtual, would-be
08 aptitude, aspiring, capacity,
implicit, inherent, possible, powerful,
probable 09 concealed, embryonic,
promising, resources 10 capability,
developing, unrealized 11 efficacious,
possibility, prospective, undeveloped

**potentiality**
05 power 07 ability, potence, potency,
promise 08 aptitude, capacity,

prospect 09 potential 10 capability,
likelihood, virtuality 13 possibilities

**potentially**
◊ *anagram indicator* 07 in posse
08 latently, possibly, probably
09 dormantly, virtually 10 implicitly,
inherently, in potentia 15 in all
likelihood

**potion**
04 brew, dose 05 drink, tonic 06 elixir
07 draught, mixture, philtre
08 beverage, medicine, potation
10 concoction

**potpourri**
04 olio 06 jumble, medley 07 melange,
mixture 08 mishmash, pastiche
09 confusion, patchwork, selection
10 assortment, collection,
hodgepodge, hotchpotch, miscellany
11 gallimaufry, olla-podrida,
smorgasbord

**potter**
04 muck, poke 05 amble, daker
06 dacker, daidle, daiker, dawdle,
dodder, fettle, footle, loiter, niggle,
pootle, putter, tiddle, tinker, toddle
07 plotter, plouter, plowter 09 mess
about 10 dilly-dally
• **potter about** 05 truck 06 humbug,
muddle 09 fart about, fool about, mess
about, muck about, play about 10 fart
around, fool around, mess around,
muck around, play around 11 fiddle
about, tinker about 12 fiddle around,
tinker around 13 do nothing much

**pottery**
04 bank

---

*Pottery includes:*

---

04 Ming, Tang, Wade
05 Bizen, china, Crown, delft, Poole
06 basalt, bisque, Dunoon, flambé,
   Hummel, jasper, Parian, Sèvres
07 biscuit, ceramic, Dresden,
   faience, Meissen, redware
08 ceramics, Coalport, crockery,
   maiolica, majolica, rakuware,
   Rookwood, slipware
09 agateware, bone china,
   creamware, Davenport,
   delftware, hard-paste, ironstone,
   Jackfield, pearlware, porcelain,
   red figure, saltglaze, soft-paste,
   stoneware, tin-glazed, Worcester
10 jasperware, lead-glazed,
   lustreware, Parian ware, Queen's
   ware, terracotta, Wemyss ware
11 black figure, earthenware, Florian
   ware, pâte-sur-pâte, Portmeirion,
   soufflé ware, spatter ware
12 Royal Doulton, transfer ware,
   Wedgwood ware
13 Claremont ware, Hazledene
   ware, Staffordshire, tortoiseshell,
   willow pattern
14 ironstone china
15 cauliflower ware, Royal Crown
   Derby, Wedgwood pottery

---

*Pottery makers include:*

---

03 **Fry** (Laura), **Rie** (Dame Lucie)
04 **Boyd** (Arthur), **Boyd** (Merric), **Vyse**

(Charles), **Wood** (Aaron), **Wood**
(Enoch), **Wood** (John), **Wood**
(Ralph), **Wood** (Ralph, Jnr), **Wyse**
(Henry Taylor)
05 **Adams** (Truda), **Adams** (William),
**Amour** (Elizabeth), **Carter** (Clarice),
**Coper** (Hans), **Finch** (Alfred
William), **Korin** (Ogata), **Leach**
(Bernard), **Mason** (Miles), **Moore**
(Bernard), **Perry** (Grayson)
06 **Cardew** (Michael), **Carter** (Truda),
**Dwight** (John), **Hamada** (Shoji),
**Kenzan** (Ogata), **Murray** (William
Staite), **Taylor** (William Howson)
07 **Astbury** (John), **Britton** (Alison),
**Doulton** (Sir Henry), **Execias**,
**Exekias**, **Forsyth** (Gordon), **Fritsch**
(Elizabeth), **Gardner** (Peter), **Grotell**
(Maija), **Palissy** (Bernard), **Twyford**
(Joshua)
08 **Fujiwara** (Kei), **Robineau**
(Adelaide), **Wedgwood** (Josiah),
**Whieldon** (Thomas), **Yamamoto**
(Toshu)
09 **Kaneshige** (Toyo), **Moorcroft**
(William)
10 **Euphronios**

---

*Pottery terms include:*

---

04 kiln, raku, slip
05 delft, glaze, model
06 basalt, enamel, figure, firing,
   flambé, ground, jasper, lustre,
   sagger
07 celadon, ceramic, crazing,
   faience, fairing
08 armorial, bronzing, flatback,
   maiolica, majolica, monogram,
   slip-cast
09 china clay, cloisonné,
   creamware, grotesque, ironstone,
   overglaze, porcelain, sgraffito,
   stoneware
10 art pottery, maker's mark,
   spongeware, terracotta,
   underglaze
11 crackleware, earthenware,
   scratch blue
12 blanc-de-chine
13 Staffordshire, willow pattern
15 mandarin palette

*See also* **porcelain**

**potty**
◊ *anagram indicator* 03 ape, fey, mad
04 avid, bats, daft, fond, gyte, keen,
loco, nuts, wild 05 barmy, batty,
buggy, crazy, daffy, dippy, dotty, flaky,
gonzo, loony, loopy, manic, nutty,
petty, queer, silly, wacko, wacky,
wiggy 06 ardent, crazed, cuckoo,
fruity, insane, maniac, mental, raving,
red-mad, screwy 07 bananas, barking,
berserk, bonkers, cracked, devoted,
frantic, lunatic, meshuga, zealous
08 crackers, demented, deranged,
dingbats, doolally, frenetic, frenzied,
gazunder, maniacal, trifling,
unhinged, unstable 09 disturbed,
fanatical, lymphatic, psychotic, up the
wall 10 bestraught, chamberpot,
distracted, distraught, frantic-mad,
infatuated, off the wall, off your nut,
out to lunch, passionate, stone-crazy,

unbalanced **11** not all there, off the rails, off your head **12** enthusiastic, mad as a hatter, off your chump, round the bend **13** off your rocker, of unsound mind, out of your head, out of your mind, out of your tree, round the twist **14** off your trolley, wrong in the head **15** non compos mentis, out of your senses

## pouch
**03** bag, sac, tip **04** poke, sack, spur **05** bursa, cecum, purse, scrip **06** caecum, ovisac, pocket, wallet **07** papoose, sporran **08** codpiece, pappoose, reticule **09** container, marsupium, spleuchan **10** receptacle **11** gaberlunzie **12** diverticulum

## poultry

*Poultry and game birds include:*

**03** hen
**04** duck, teal
**05** goose, quail, snipe
**06** grouse, pigeon, turkey, wigeon
**07** chicken, ostrich, pochard
**08** pheasant, woodcock
**09** partridge, ptarmigan
**10** guinea fowl, woodpigeon

*See also* **chicken; duck; game**

## pounce
**04** dart, dive, drop, fall, grab, jump, leap, pink **05** bound, lunge, punch, swoop **06** ambush, attack, dive on, fall on, jump on, powder, snatch, spring, strike, thrust **07** assault, descend, swoop on **08** puncture, sandarac, sprinkle **09** descend on, sandarach **10** cuttle-bone **12** take unawares **13** catch off guard, catch unawares **14** take by surprise

## pound
**01** L **02** as, lb **03** bar, pen, pun, sov **04** bang, bash, beat, bray, drum, fold, mash, pace, pelt, plod, pond, punt, quid, thud, walk, yard **05** crush, grind, lay on, libra, nevel, oncer, pownd, smash, squid, stamp, stomp, throb, thump, tramp, tread **06** batter, bruise, corral, hammer, nicker, pestle, powder, pummel, shower, strike, trudge **07** balance, confine, contund, contuse, enclose, iron man, penfold, pinfold, pulsate, smacker **08** compound, levigate **09** comminute, enclosure, granulate, palpitate, pound coin, pulverize, smackeroo, sovereign, triturate **12** jimmy-o'goblin **13** pound sterling

## pour
**03** jet, ren, rin, run, tip **04** emit, flow, gush, hush, leak, ooze, rain, rush, spew, teem **05** crowd, drain, flood, issue, serve, spill, spout, spurt, swarm **06** course, decant, stream, throng **07** cascade, come out, let flow, pour out **08** disgorge, make flow, pelt down, sprinkle, teem down **09** discharge **10** bucket down, disembogue **15** rain cats and dogs
• **pour forth** **04** gush, vent, well
• **pour out** **04** lave

## pout
**03** bib **04** lour, mope, moue, poot, sulk, tout, towt **05** blain, boody, poult, scowl **06** brassy, glower **07** grimace **08** long face, make a lip **09** make a moue, pull a face

## poverty
**04** lack, need, want **06** dearth, penury **07** beggary, paucity **08** distress, hardship, poorness, poortith, scarcity, shortage **09** depletion, indigence, necessity, privation **10** bankruptcy, deficiency, inadequacy, insolvency, meagreness, shabbiness **11** deprivation, destitution, locust-years **13** impecuniosity, insufficiency, pennilessness **14** impoverishment

## poverty-stricken
**04** poor **05** broke, needy, skint, stony **07** obolary, squalid **08** bankrupt, beggared, dirt-poor, indigent, strapped **09** destitute, flat broke, penniless, penurious **10** cleaned-out, distressed, stony-broke **11** impecunious **12** impoverished, on your uppers **13** in Queer Street **14** on your beam-ends

## powder
**04** beat, blue, bran, bray, dust, kohl, mash, must, pulv, salt, seed, talc **05** cover, crush, grind, moust, muist, smalt, smash, strew **06** farina, grains, pestle, pounce, pulvil, saline **07** alcohol, araroba, scatter, smeddum **08** amberite, coal dust, levigate, magnesia, pemoline, pulvilio, pulville, sprinkle, woodmeal **09** comminute, granulate, pulverize, pulvillio, triturate, wood flour **10** icing sugar, ivory-black, thimerosal **11** mould-facing, washing-blue **13** efflorescence, platinum black

## powdered
**04** semé **05** semée **06** seméed

## powdery
**03** dry **04** ashy, fine **05** dusty, loose, mealy, sandy **06** chalky, floury, grainy, ground, mealie **07** crumbly, friable **08** granular, levigate, powdered **09** pulverous **10** granulated, pulverized **11** pulverulent **12** efflorescent

## power
**01** P **03** arm, eon, say, vis **04** aeon, mana, pull, rule, sway, watt **05** clout, force, index, juice, might, oomph, right, state, teeth **06** energy, muscle, nation, people, vigour **07** ability, command, control, country, faculty, licence, mastery, potency, warrant **08** capacity, clutches, dominion, exponent, strength **09** authority, influence, intensity, potential, privilege, supremacy **10** ascendancy, capability, competence, domination, superpower **11** prerogative, sovereignty **12** forcefulness, potentiality, powerfulness **13** authorization, effectiveness

*Power stations include:*

**06** Huntly
**07** Benmore, Heysham, Torness

**08** Bankside, Dounreay, Sizewell, Yallourn
**09** Battersea, Chernobyl, Dungeness, Manapouri, Windscale
**10** Eggborough, Hunterston, Sellafield
**11** Wallerawang
**12** Hinkley Point, Marsden Point
**14** Snowy Mountains
**15** Three Mile Island

• **have sufficient power** **03** can
• **having enough power** **04** able
• **the powers that be** **04** them
**09** the system **14** the authorities

## powerful
**03** hot **04** high **05** burly, gutty, hardy, tough **06** brawny, cogent, mighty, potent, punchy, robust, strong, studly **07** intense, leading, telling, winning **08** dominant, forceful, forcible, mightful, muscular, puissant **09** effective, energetic, knock-down, prevalent, strapping **10** commanding, compelling, convincing, impressive, noticeable, persuasive, prevailing **11** all-powerful, efficacious, exceedingly, high-powered, influential **12** overwhelming **13** authoritative

## powerfully
**04** hard, high **06** highly, strong **08** cogently, forcibly, mightily, potently, strongly **09** tellingly **10** forcefully, vigorously **12** convincingly, impressively, persuasively

## powerless
**04** numb, weak **05** frail, unfit **06** feeble, infirm, unable **07** unarmed **08** benumbed, disabled, helpless, impotent **09** castrated, hamstrung, incapable, paralysed, toothless **10** impuissant, vulnerable, weak-handed **11** debilitated, defenceless, ineffective, ineffectual **13** incapacitated

## practicability
**03** use **05** value **07** utility **09** handiness, viability **10** usefulness **11** feasibility, operability, possibility, workability **12** practicality, workableness

## practicable
**02** on **06** doable, viable **08** feasible, operable, passable, possible, workable **09** practical, realistic **10** achievable, attainable **11** functioning, performable

## practical
**04** real **05** handy **06** active, actual, strong, useful **07** applied, hands on, skilled, trained, virtual, working **08** everyday, feasible, in effect, ordinary, sensible, suitable, workable, workaday **09** effective, efficient, essential, hard-nosed, pragmatic, qualified, realistic **10** functional, hard-boiled, hard-headed, proficient **11** applicative, commonsense, down-to-earth, experienced, practicable, pragmatical, serviceable, utilitarian **12** accomplished, businesslike, matter-of-fact **14** bread-and-butter
• **practical joke** **03** gag **04** feat, hoax,

**practicality**

jape, joke, scam **05** antic, caper, prank, stunt, trick **06** frolic **07** fast one, frame-up, leg-pull **09** booby trap **11** apple-pie bed

**practicality**

**05** sense **06** basics **07** realism, utility **08** practice **09** soundness **10** experience, pragmatism, usefulness **11** common sense, feasibility, nitty-gritty, workability **12** nuts and bolts **13** practicalness **14** practicability, serviceability

**practically**

**06** all but, almost, nearly **07** morally **08** in effect, sensibly, well-nigh **09** just about, virtually **10** pretty much, pretty well, rationally, reasonably **11** essentially, in principle **13** fundamentally, pragmatically, realistically **14** matter-of-factly

**practice**

**03** ism, job, net, ure, use, way **04** firm, wont, work **05** drill, habit, study, trade, usage **06** action, career, custom, dry run, effect, method, policy, system, try-out, warm-up **07** company, pursuit, reality, routine, work-out **08** business, dummy run, exercise, plotting, scheming, training, trickery **09** actuality, following, operation, procedure, rehearsal, tradition **10** convention, employment, experience, occupation, profession, run-through **11** application, partnership, performance, preparation **13** establishment
• **out of practice** **05** rusty **07** disused **10** out of habit **11** unpractised **13** disaccustomed, out of the habit
• **put into practice** **03** use **05** apply **07** perform **08** exercise, put to use **09** make use of **13** put into action, put into effect

**practise**

**02** do **03** use **04** plot **05** apply, drill, study, train **06** effect, follow, go over, polish, pursue, refine, repeat, tamper, work at, work on **07** execute, observe, perfect, perform, prepare **08** carry out, engage in, exercise, frequent, maintain, rehearse **09** go through, implement, prosecute, undertake **10** run through **15** put into practice

**practised**

**03** old **04** able **05** adept **06** expert, traded, versed **07** knowing, skilful, skilled, trained, veteran **08** finished, masterly, seasoned **09** prevalent, qualified **10** consummate, proficient **11** experienced **12** accomplished, experimented **13** knowledgeable

**practitioner**

**03** ace, pro **04** buff, doer **05** crack **06** expert, master, pundit **07** dab hand, maestro, old hand **08** virtuoso **09** authority **10** practician, proficient, specialist **12** professional

**pragmatic**

**05** edict **08** busybody, sensible **09** efficient, hard-nosed, practical, realistic **10** hard-headed, meddlesome

**11** opinionated, utilitarian **12** businesslike, matter-of-fact **13** unsentimental

**pragmatism**

**07** realism **08** ad hocery, humanism **10** unidealism **11** opportunism **12** practicalism, practicality **14** hard-headedness, utilitarianism **15** instrumentalism

**pragmatist**

**07** realist **08** humanist **11** opportunist, utilitarian **12** practicalist

**praise**

**03** los, rap **04** hail, hery, laud, loos, puff, rave, sell, tout, wrap **05** adore, bless, blurb, carol, cheer, cry up, exalt, extol, glory, herry, herye, kudos, roose **06** admire, eulogy, homage, honour, talk up, thanks, wrap-up **07** acclaim, applaud, bouquet, build up, commend, crack up, flatter, glorify, hosanna, magnify, ovation, promote, tribute, worship **08** accolade, applause, appraise, approval, bouquets, cheering, devotion, emblazon, encomium, eulogium, eulogize, flattery, plaudits, rave over, set forth **09** adoration, adulation, laudation, panegyric, recognize **10** admiration, compliment, hallelujah, wax lyrical **11** acknowledge, approbation, recognition, speak well of, testimonial **12** commendation, congratulate, pay tribute to, thanksgiving **13** glorification, speak highly of **14** congratulation
• **expression of praise** **07** hosanna **08** alleluia **10** halleluiah, hallelujah

**praiseworthy**

**04** fine **06** worthy **08** laudable, sterling **09** admirable, deserving, estimable, excellent, exemplary, reputable **10** creditable, honourable **11** commendable

**praising**

**09** adulatory, approving, laudative, laudatory, panegyric **10** eulogistic, favourable, flattering, plauditory, worshipful **11** approbatory, encomiastic, promotional **12** commendatory **13** complimentary **14** congratulatory, recommendatory

**pram**

**05** buggy, praam **08** bassinet, stroller **09** Baby Buggy®, pushchair **12** baby carriage, perambulator

**prance**

◇ *anagram indicator* **04** jump, leap, romp, skip **05** bound, brank, caper, dance, frisk, prank, stalk, strut, swank, titup, vault **06** canary, cavort, curvet, frolic, gambol, jaunce, jaunse, parade, spring, tittup **07** caracol, prankle, show off, swagger, trounce **08** caracole

**prank**

**03** jig, rig **04** fold, gaud, joke, lark, reak, reik **05** antic, caper, pleat, stunt, trick **06** escape, frolic, prance, pranck, vagary, wedgie **07** prancke **08** capering, escapade, fredaine,

prancing **11** monkey shine **13** practical joke

**prankster**

**05** joker, rogue **06** hoaxer, jester **07** funster **08** jokester, quipster **09** trickster **14** practical joker

**praseodymium**

**02** Pr

**prat**

**03** ass, mug, nit, oaf **04** berk, clot, dope, dork, fool, geek, jerk, nerd, twit **05** chump, clown, dumbo, dunce, idiot, ninny, pratt, twerp, wally **06** cretin, dimwit, dum-dum, muppet, nitwit, sucker **07** fat-head, halfwit, pillock, plonker **08** buttocks, imbecile, innocent, numskull **09** birdbrain, ignoramus, lamebrain, simpleton, thickhead **10** nincompoop **11** knuckle-head
*See also* **bottom**

**prattle**

**03** gab, gup, jaw, yap **04** chat, talk **06** babble, drivel, gabble, gossip, hot air, jabber, patter, rattle, tattle, witter **07** blabber, blather, blether, chatter, gabnash, nashgab, prating, twaddle, twattle, twitter **08** chitchat, nonsense **09** bavardage, gibberish **11** foolishness

**prattler**

**06** gossip, magpie, rattle, talker, tatler **07** babbler, blether, gabbler, tattler, windbag **09** chatterer, loudmouth **10** chatterbox **12** blabbermouth

**pray**

**03** ask, beg, bid, say **05** adore, crave, daven, plead, thank **06** call on, invoke, praise, talk to **07** beseech, beseeke, confess, entreat, implore, prithee, prythee, request, solicit, speak to, worship **08** petition **09** imprecate **10** be at prayer, say a prayer, supplicate **11** commune with **14** say your prayers, wrestle with God

**prayer**

**03** act, ave, cry **04** bead, bede, bene, plea **06** appeal, litany, mantra, novena, orison, praise **07** collect, karakia, request, worship **08** devotion, doxology, entreaty, petition, suffrage **09** adoration, communion **10** confession, fellowship, invocation **11** imprecation **12** intercession, supplication, thanksgiving

*Prayers include:*

**02** Om
**03** act
**05** adhan, Ardas, grace, salat, Shema
**06** Amidah, Gloria, rosary, Yizkor
**07** angelus, khotbah, khutbah
**08** Agnus Dei, Ave Maria, Habdalah, Hail Mary, Havdalah, Kaddhish, Kol Nidre, shahadah
**09** Confiteor, Our Father
**10** Benedictus, Lychnapsia, Magnificat, requiescat
**11** Lord's Prayer, Paternoster, Sursum Corda

**12** Divine Office, Kyrie eleison, Nunc Dimittis
**15** act of contrition

• **call to prayer  04** azan

**prayer-book**
**06** mahzor, missal, primer, siddur
**07** liturgy, machzor, ordinal, primmer
**08** breviary, Triodion **09** euchology, formulary **11** euchologion, service-book

**preach**
**04** urge **05** teach **06** advise, exhort, sermon **07** address, deliver, lecture
**08** admonish, advocate, harangue, moralize, proclaim, prophesy
**09** inculcate, preachify, predicate, recommend, sermonize **10** apostolize, evangelize **11** give a sermon, pontificate **15** spread the gospel

**preacher**
**05** molla **06** mollah, moolah, mullah, parson, ranter **07** apostle, holy Joe, martext, prophet **08** homilist, minister, pulpiter, sermoner, spintext
**09** Boanerges, clergyman, gospeller, itinerant, moralizer, predicant, predikant, pulpiteer, sermoneer
**10** ecclesiast, evangelist, Holy Roller, licentiate, missionary, revivalist, sermonizer, tub-thumper **11** Bible-basher, devil-dodger, lay preacher, probationer **12** Bible-pounder, Bible-thumper, circuit rider, pontificater, tent preacher **13** field preacher, local preacher, televangelist **15** open-air preacher

**preaching**
**05** dogma **06** gospel, pulpit **07** evangel, kerygma, message, sermons
**08** doctrine, homilies, precepts, prophecy, teaching **09** predicant
**10** evangelism, homiletics
**11** exhortation, instruction, sermonizing, tub-thumping **12** Bible-bashing **13** pontificating, tent preaching

**preachy**
**02** pi **05** pious **08** didactic, dogmatic, edifying **09** homiletic, hortatory, pharisaic, pietistic, religiose
**10** moralistic, moralizing, pontifical
**11** exhortatory, sermonizing
**13** pontificating, sanctimonious, self-righteous **14** holier-than-thou

**preamble**
**05** proem **06** lead-in **07** preface, prelude **08** exordium, foreword, overture, prologue **11** preparation
**12** introduction, prolegomenon
**13** preliminaries

**prearrange**
**07** diarize, prepare, pre-plan
**08** organize, schedule **09** plan ahead
**12** predetermine

**prearranged**
**03** set

**precarious**
◇ *anagram indicator* **04** iffy **05** dicey, dicky, dodgy, hairy, risky, shaky
**06** chancy, unsafe, unsure, wobbly
**07** dubious, trickle **08** doubtful,

insecure, ticklish, unstable, unsteady
**09** dangerous, hazardous, uncertain, unsettled **10** touch and go, unreliable, vulnerable **11** treacherous
**12** supplicating, undependable
**13** unpredictable

**precariously**
◇ *anagram indicator* **07** riskily, shakily
**08** unsafely, unstably **10** insecurely, unreliably, unsteadily **11** dangerously, hazardously **13** unpredictably

**precaution**
**04** care **07** caution **08** forewarn, prudence, security **09** foresight, insurance, provision, safeguard
**10** protection, providence, safety belt
**11** forethought, preparation
**12** anticipation **13** attentiveness
**14** circumspection, farsightedness

**precautionary**
**06** safety **07** prudent **08** cautious
**09** judicious, provident **10** far-sighted, preventive, protective **11** preliminary, preparatory **12** preventative

**precede**
**04** head, lead **06** forego, herald
**07** forerun, preface, prelude, prevene, prevent, usher in **08** antecede, antedate, go before **09** come first, go ahead of, harbinger, introduce
**10** anticipate, come before **14** take precedence

**precedence**
**03** pas **04** lead, rank **05** place
**08** eminence, priority **09** seniority, supremacy **10** ascendancy, first place, preference, right of way
**11** preaudience, pre-eminence, superiority **12** pride of place
• **take precedence over  09** take place **10** come before, take rank of

**precedent**
**04** case, lead **05** model, token
**07** example, pattern **08** exemplar, instance, paradigm, parallel, standard
**09** criterion, yardstick

**preceding**
**04** past **05** above, prior, supra
**06** former **07** earlier, leading
**08** anterior, previous **09** aforesaid, foregoing, precedent **10** antecedent, precursive, prevenient **11** preliminary
**14** aforementioned

**precept**
**03** law **04** rule **05** axiom, canon, maxim, motto, order **06** charge, decree, dictum, rubric, saying
**07** command, mandate, statute
**08** doctrine, sentence **09** direction, directive, guideline, institute, ordinance, principle **10** convention, injunction, regulation
**11** commandment, instruction

**precinct**
**04** area, land, mall, zone **05** bound, close, court, lands, limit, verge
**06** milieu, sector, vihara **07** confine, quarter, section, temenos, village
**08** boundary, building, district, division, environs, galleria, locality, purlieus, vicinity **09** buildings,

enclosure, food court, peribolos, peribolus, surrounds
**13** neighbourhood **14** shopping centre

**preciosity**
**06** chichi **08** tweeness **11** affectation, floweriness, marivaudage
**13** artificiality **14** over-refinement
**15** pretentiousness

**precious**
**04** dear, fine, nice, rare, twee **05** ditsy, ditzy, grand, loved, tatty **06** adored, chichi, choice, costly, dainty, prized, valued **07** beloved, darling, dearest, flowery, revered **08** affected, idolized, mannered, valuable **09** cherished, contrived, egregious, expensive, extremely, favourite, priceless, simulated, treasured **10** artificial, dearbought, fastidious, high-priced
**11** inestimable, overrefined, pretentious **12** confoundedly
• **precious stone**  *see* **gem**

**precipice**
**04** crag, drop **05** bluff, brink, cliff, krans, kranz, scarp, steep **06** escarp, height, krantz **08** precepit **09** cliff face, sheer drop **10** escarpment

**precipitate**
**04** hurl, rash **05** brief, cause, fling, flock, hasty, heave, hurry, quick, rapid, shoot, speed, swift, throw
**06** abrupt, flocks, hasten, induce, plunge, sludge, speedy, sudden, thrust
**07** advance, bring on, frantic, further, hurried, quicken, speed up, trigger, violent **08** expedite, headlong, heedless, occasion, reckless
**09** breakneck, hot-headed, impatient, impetuous, impulsive, magistery
**10** accelerate, bring about, indiscreet, unexpected **11** precipitant, precipitous

**precipitately**
**06** rashly **07** hastily, quickly, rapidly
**08** abruptly, headlong, suddenly
**09** violently **10** recklessly **11** frantically, impetuously, impulsively
**12** unexpectedly

**precipitation**

*Precipitation includes:*

**03** dew, fog
**04** hail, mist, rain, snow
**05** sleet
**06** shower
**07** drizzle
**08** downpour, rainfall, snowfall
**09** rainstorm, snowflake

*See also* **ice; snow; weather**

**precipitous**
**04** high **05** sharp, sheer, steep
**06** abrupt, sudden **07** steepup
**08** headlong, steepeup, vertical
**10** steepdowne **11** steepedowne
**13** perpendicular

**précis**
**05** sum up, table **06** aperçu, digest, résumé, sketch **07** abridge, epitome, outline, run-down, shorten, summary
**08** abstract, compress, condense, contract, synopsis **09** epitomize, summarize, synopsize **10** abbreviate,

**precise**

compendium, conspectus
**11** abridgement, contraction,
encapsulate **12** abbreviation,
condensation **13** encapsulation

**precise**

**03** dry **04** nice, prim, very **05** exact,
fixed, razor, right, rigid, tight **06** actual,
formal, minute, narrow, strict
**07** buckram, careful, correct, express,
factual, finical, literal, pointed, starchy
**08** accurate, clear-cut, definite,
detailed, distinct, explicit, faithful,
preceese, priggish, punctual, rigorous,
specific, succinct, surgical
**09** authentic, identical **10** blow-by-
blow, fastidious, meticulous,
particular, scrupulous **11** ceremonious,
punctilious, puritanical, unambiguous,
unequivocal, word-for-word
**13** conscientious

**precisely**

**03** yes **04** just, slap, to a T, true
**05** plumb, quite, right, sharp, smack
**06** agreed, bang on, dead on, indeed,
just so, spot-on **07** clearly, exactly
**08** minutely, of course, on the dot,
strictly, verbatim, you got it
**09** certainly, correctly, literally
**10** absolutely, accurately, distinctly,
that's right **11** to the squire, on the
button, word for word

**precision**

**04** care **06** detail, rigour **08** accuracy,
neatness **09** exactness **10** exactitude
**11** correctness, preciseness, reliability
**12** distinctness, explicitness,
faithfulness **13** particularity
**14** fastidiousness, meticulousness,
scrupulousness **15** punctiliousness

**preclude**

**03** bar **04** stop **05** avoid, check, debar,
estop **06** hinder **07** exclude, inhibit,
obviate, prevent, rule out **08** prohibit,
restrain **09** eliminate, foreclose,
forestall

**precocious**

**04** fast **05** ahead, early, quick, smart
**06** bright, clever, farand, gifted, mature
**07** farrand, farrant, forward
**08** advanced, far ahead, talented
**09** brilliant, developed, premature
**11** auld-farrant **13** old for your age

**preconceive**

**06** assume, expect, ideate **07** imagine,
picture, presume, project **08** conceive,
envisage **09** visualize **10** anticipate,
presuppose **12** predetermine

**preconception**

**04** bias, idea **06** notion **09** prejudice,
prenotion **10** assumption, conjecture
**11** expectation, presumption
**12** anticipation, prejudgement
**14** predisposition, presupposition

**precondition**

**04** must **09** condition, essential,
necessity **10** sine qua non
**11** requirement, stipulation
**12** prerequisite

**precursor**

**04** sign **05** usher **06** herald **07** pioneer,
prelude **08** ancestor, forebear, way-

maker **09** harbinger, messenger
**10** antecedent, forerunner, indication,
progenitor **11** morning star,
predecessor, trailblazer **13** curtain-
raiser

**precursory**

**05** prior **07** warning **08** anterior,
previous **09** preceding, prefatory,
preludial, prelusive, prodromal
**10** antecedent, precursive, prevenient
**11** preliminary, preparatory
**12** introductory **13** preambulatory

**predator**

*see* bird; cat; spider

**predatory**

**06** greedy, lupine **07** hunting, preying,
wolfish **08** covetous, ravaging, thieving
**09** marauding, pillaging, predative,
rapacious, raptorial, voracious,
vulturine, vulturous **10** avaricious,
despoiling, plundering, predaceous,
predacious **11** acquisitive, carnivorous,
deleterious, destructive, raptatorial

**predecessor**

**08** ancestor, forebear **09** precursor
**10** antecedent, antecessor, forefather,
forerunner, progenitor

**predestination**

**03** lot **04** doom, fate **07** destiny
**11** reprobation **14** foreordination

**predestine**

**04** doom, fate, mean **06** intend
**07** destine **08** foredoom, pre-elect
**09** preordain **10** foreordain
**12** predestinate, predetermine

**predetermined**

**03** set **05** fated, fixed **06** agreed,
doomed **07** settled **08** arranged,
destined, ordained **11** prearranged,
predestined **12** foreordained

**predicament**

**03** box, fix, jam **04** cart, hole, mess,
pass, spot, stew **06** crisis, hiccup,
pickle, plight, scrape, taking
**07** dilemma, impasse, trouble
**08** chancery, hot water, how-d'ye-do,
quandary **09** deep water, emergency,
situation, tight spot **10** praemunire
**12** kettle of fish

**predicate**

**04** aver, avow, base, rest **05** build,
found, imply, posit, state **06** affirm,
assert, avouch, ground, preach
**07** contend, declare, premise
**08** maintain, proclaim **09** establish,
postulate **11** be dependent

**predict**

**03** bet **04** cast **05** augur **06** divine
**07** foresay, foresee, portend, presage,
project, warrant **08** forecast, foreshew,
foreshow, foretell, prophesy
**09** auspicate, forespeak **10** vaticinate
**11** second-guess **13** prognosticate

**predictable**

**04** sure **05** trite, usual **06** likely, odds-
on **07** certain **08** expected, foregone,
foreseen, knee-jerk, probable, reliable
**09** customary **10** dependable,
imaginable, on the cards, unoriginal

**11** anticipated, foreseeable
**12** unsurprising

**prediction**

**03** bet **06** augury **07** fortune **08** forecast,
prophecy, soothsay **09** horoscope,
prognosis **10** divination, prognostic
**11** auspication, soothsaying **14** fortune-
telling **15** prognostication

**predictive**

**07** augural **09** prophetic **10** diagnostic,
divinatory, prognostic **11** foretelling
**12** anticipating

**predilection**

**04** bent, bias, love **05** fancy, taste
**06** liking **07** leaning **08** affinity,
fondness, penchant, soft spot,
tendency, weakness **09** affection
**10** enthusiasm, partiality, preference,
proclivity, propensity **11** inclination
**14** predisposition

**predispose**

**04** bias, make, move, sway **06** affect,
induce, prompt **07** dispose, incline
**08** persuade **09** influence, prejudice
**10** make liable

**predisposed**

**05** prone, ready **06** biased, liable,
minded **07** subject, willing
**08** amenable, disposed, inclined,
prepared **09** agreeable **10** favourable,
prejudiced **11** susceptible **12** not
unwilling, well-disposed

**predisposition**

**04** bent, bias **07** leaning **08** penchant,
tendency **09** liability, prejudice,
proneness **10** likelihood, preference,
proclivity, propensity **11** disposition,
inclination, willingness **12** potentiality,
predilection **13** vulnerability
**14** susceptibility

**predominance**

**04** edge, hold, rain, sway **05** power,
raine, reign **06** weight **07** control,
mastery, numbers **08** dominion,
hegemony **09** dominance, influence,
supremacy, upper hand
**10** ascendancy, leadership,
prepotence, prepotency, prevalence
**11** paramountcy, prepollence,
prepollency, superiority
**13** preponderance

**predominant**

**04** main **05** chief, prime **06** master,
potent, ruling, strong **07** capital,
leading, primary, supreme
**08** dominant, forceful, powerful
**09** ascendant, ascendent, important, in
control, paramount, principal,
sovereign **10** prevailing **11** controlling,
influential, most obvious
**12** preponderant **13** most important
**14** most noticeable, preponderating
**15** in the ascendancy

**predominantly**

**06** mainly, mostly **07** as a rule, chiefly,
largely, overall, usually **08** above all,
commonly **09** generally, in general, in
the main, primarily **10** by and large,
especially, on the whole **11** principally
**14** for the most part

**predominate**
04 rule, tell 05 reign 06 obtain
07 prevail 08 dominate, outweigh,
override, overrule 09 outnumber,
transcend 10 overshadow
12 preponderate, rule the roast 15 be in
the majority

**pre-eminence**
04 fame, palm 06 renown, repute
08 majority, prestige 09 supremacy
10 excellence, prominence
11 distinction, paramountcy,
sovereignty, superiority
12 peerlessness, predominance
13 matchlessness, transcendence
15 incomparability

**pre-eminent**
03 gun 04 arch, star 05 chief, first,
grand, great 06 famous, unique
07 eminent, extreme, leading,
palmary, supreme, topping
08 foremost, renowned, singular,
superior 09 excellent, first-rate,
matchless, palmarian, prominent,
unmatched 10 inimitable, unequalled,
unrivalled 11 exceptional, outstanding,
superlative, unsurpassed
12 incomparable, transcendent
13 distinguished, most important

**pre-eminently**
04 only 06 notably 08 paravant,
signally 09 eminently, paravaunt,
primarily, supremely 10 especially,
inimitably, peerlessly, singularly,
strikingly 11 exclusively, matchlessly,
principally 12 emphatically,
incomparably, particularly,
surpassingly 13 conspicuously,
exceptionally, par excellence,
superlatively

**pre-empt**
05 seize, usurp 06 assume, secure,
thwart 07 acquire, prevent, replace
08 arrogate, supplant 09 forestall
10 anticipate 11 appropriate

**preen**
03 pin 04 bask, deck, do up, trim, whet
05 adorn, array, clean, exult, gloat,
groom, pique, plume, pride, primp,
prink, proin, proyn, prune, slick 06 doll
up, proign, proine, proyne, smooth,
tart up 07 dress up, trick up 08 beautify,
prettify, spruce up, trick out
12 congratulate

**preface**
04 open 05 begin, index, proem, start
06 launch, prefix, prolog 07 epistle,
precede, prelims, prelude
08 exordium, foreword, lead up to,
preamble, prologue 09 introduce
11 avant-propos, frontmatter
12 introduction, prolegomenon
13 preliminaries

**prefatory**
07 opening 08 exordial, proemial
09 preludial, prelusive, prelusory
10 antecedent, precursory
11 explanatory, prefatorial,
preliminary, preparatory
12 introductory, prolegomenal
13 preambulatory

**prefect**
05 grave 07 monitor 08 praefect
09 commander, prepostor
10 magistrate, praepostor, prepositor,
supervisor 13 administrator

**prefer**
03 opt 04 back, file, pick, want, wish
05 adopt, bring, elect, exalt, fancy, go
for, lodge, place, press, raise
06 choose, desire, favour, honour,
move up, opt for, select 07 advance,
elevate, pick out, present, promote,
support 08 advocate, plump for
09 recommend, single out
10 aggrandize, like better 11 be partial
to, would rather, would sooner

**preferable**
05 nicer 06 better, chosen 08 favoured,
superior 09 advisable, desirable,
preferred 11 more desired,
recommended 12 advantageous

**preferably**
05 first 06 rather, sooner 07 ideally
09 for choice 10 from choice, if
possible, much rather, much sooner
12 by preference 13 for preference

**preference**
03 fad 04 bent, bias, kink, mark, pick,
will, wish 05 fancy 06 choice, desire,
liking, option 07 leaning 08 cup of tea,
druthers, forehand, priority
09 favourite, selection 10 partiality,
precedence 11 favouritism, first
choice, inclination, pre-election
12 predilection 14 discrimination
• in preference to 06 before 08 by
choice 09 for choice, in place of,
instead of 10 from choice, rather than

**preferential**
06 better, biased 07 partial, special
08 favoured, partisan, superior
10 favourable, privileged
12 advantageous

**preferment**
04 rise 06 step up 07 dignity
09 elevation, prelation, promotion,
upgrading 10 betterment, exaltation
11 advancement, furtherance,
improvement 14 aggrandizement

**preferred**
03 pet 06 choice, chosen 07 desired
08 approved, favorite, favoured
selected 09 favourite, predilect
10 authorized, sanctioned
11 recommended

**prefigure**
04 bode, mean, type 05 augur 06 signal
07 portend, predict, presage, promise,
signify, suggest 08 indicate, prophesy
10 foreshadow 13 prognosticate

**pregnancy**
06 cyesis 09 family way, gestation,
gravidity 10 conception 11 parturition
12 child-bearing, impregnation
13 fertilization 14 being with child

**pregnant**
04 full, gone, rich 05 clear, great,
heavy, in pig, in pup, pithy, quick,
witty 06 cogent, filled, gravid, in calf,
in foal, loaded 07 charged, fertile,

fraught, obvious, pointed, replete,
teeming, telling, weighty 08 eloquent,
enceinte, fruitful, preggers, swelling,
with calf, with foal 09 expectant,
expecting, in the club, in trouble,
inventive, momentous, up the duff, up
the pole, with child, with young
10 big-bellied, convincing, expressive,
fertilized, meaningful, parturient,
productive, suggestive, up the spout,
up the stick 11 impregnated, significant
12 great-bellied 14 in the family way

**prehistoric**
03 old 05 early 06 Minoan 07 ancient,
archaic, Ogygian 08 earliest, obsolete,
outmoded, Pelasgic, primeval 09 out-
of-date, primaeval, primitive
10 antiquated, primordial 11 out of the
ark 12 antediluvian 14 before the flood

**prejudge**
06 assume 07 presume 09 forejudge,
prejudice 10 anticipate, presuppose
11 prejudicate 12 predetermine

**prejudice**
03 mar 04 bias, harm, hurt, load, loss,
ruin, sway 05 slant, spoil, wreck
06 ageism, colour, damage, hinder,
impair, injure, injury, racism, sexism,
weight 07 bigotry, distort, incline
08 classism, endanger, jaundice,
misogyny 09 condition, detriment,
influence, injustice, preoccupy,
undermine 10 chauvinism,
impairment, partiality, predispose,
preference, prepossess, unfairness,
xenophobia 11 intolerance,
misanthropy, prejudicate
12 anticipation, anti-Semitism,
disadvantage, one-sidedness,
partisanship, prejudgement
13 preoccupation 14 discrimination
15 be detrimental to

**prejudiced**
06 ageist, biased, loaded, racist, sexist,
unfair, unjust, warped 07 bigoted, ex
parte, insular, partial, slanted 08 one-
sided, partisan, weighted 09 blinkered,
distorted, illiberal, jaundiced,
parochial 10 chauvinist, influenced,
intolerant, subjective, xenophobic
11 anti-Semitic, conditioned,
predisposed, prejudicial
12 chauvinistic, narrow-minded,
prepossessed 14 discriminatory

**prejudicial**
07 harmful, hurtful, noxious
08 damaging, inimical 09 injurious
11 deleterious, detrimental
12 unfavourable 15 disadvantageous

**preliminary**
04 test 05 early, first, pilot, prior,
proem, start, trial 06 basics
07 advance, initial, opening, preface,
prelude, primary 08 earliest, exordial,
exordium, foreword, preamble,
prodrome 09 beginning, inaugural,
prefatory, rudiments 10 groundwork,
precursory, qualifying 11 exploratory,
formalities, foundations, preparation,
preparative, preparatory
12 experimental, introduction,
introductory, prolegomenon

## prelude

**05** proem, start **06** entrée, herald, opener, verset **07** intrada, opening, preface **08** exordium, foreword, overture, preamble, prodrome, prologue **09** beginning, harbinger, induction, praeamble, precursor **10** forerunner, praeludium **11** preliminary, preparation **12** commencement, introduction, prolegomenon **13** curtain-raiser

## premature

**04** prem, rash, soon **05** early, hasty **07** preemie, too soon **08** ill-timed, previous, timeless, too early, untimely **09** impetuous, impulsive, precocial **10** praecocial **11** inopportune, precipitate **13** ill-considered, jumping the gun

## prematurely

**05** early **06** rashly **07** hastily, too soon **08** too soon, untimely **11** impetuously, impulsively **12** incompletely

## premeditated

**06** wilful **07** planned **08** intended, prepense, propense **09** conscious, contrived **10** calculated, considered, deliberate, preplanned **11** cold-blooded, intentional, prearranged **12** aforethought **13** predetermined

## premeditation

**06** design **07** purpose **08** planning, plotting, scheming **09** intention **11** forethought **12** aforethought, deliberation **13** determination **14** deliberateness, prearrangement

## premier

**03** top **04** head, main **05** chief, first, prime **07** highest, initial, leading, primary, supreme **08** cardinal, earliest, foremost, original **09** paramount, principal **10** chancellor, pre-eminent **13** chief minister, first minister, prime minister

*Premiers of New Zealand:*

**03** **Fox** (William)
**04** **Grey** (Sir George), **Hall** (John), **Weld** (Frederick Aloysius)
**05** **Stout** (Sir Robert), **Vogel** (Sir Julius)
**06** **Domett** (Alfred), **Pollen** (Daniel), **Seddon** (Richard John), **Sewell** (Henry)
**08** **Atkinson** (Sir Harry Albert), **Ballance** (John), **Stafford** (Edward William), **Whitaker** (Frederick)
**10** **Waterhouse** (George Marsden)

*See also* **prime minister**

## première

**05** debut **07** opening **10** first night **12** first showing, opening night

## premise

**05** basis, lemma, posit, state **06** assert, assume, prefix, reason, thesis **07** lay down **08** argument **09** assertion, postulate, predicate, statement, stipulate **10** assumption, hypothesis, presuppose, take as true **11** hypothesize, proposition, supposition **14** presupposition

## premises

**04** site **05** place **06** estate, office **07** grounds, section **08** building, property **13** establishment

## premium

**02** ap, pm **05** bonus, prize **06** bounty, reward **07** grassum **08** extra sum, interest, key money **09** insurance, surcharge **10** instalment **11** extra charge **12** an arm and a leg, overcharging **14** regular payment **15** daylight robbery
• **at a premium** **04** rare **06** scarce **08** above par **12** hard to come by, like gold dust **13** in great demand, in short supply
• **put a premium on** **06** favour **08** hold dear, treasure **10** appreciate **12** regard highly, value greatly **15** set great store by

## premonition

**04** fear, idea, omen, sign **05** hunch, worry **07** anxiety, feeling, portent, presage, specter, spectre, warning **09** intuition, misgiving, suspicion **10** foreboding, gut feeling, prevention, sixth sense **11** forewarning **12** apprehension, funny feeling, presentiment

## preoccupation

**05** thing **06** hang-up **07** concern, reverie **08** fixation, interest, oblivion **09** obsession, prejudice **10** absorption, enthusiasm, hobby-horse **11** abstraction, daydreaming, distraction, engrossment, pensiveness **12** heedlessness, one-track mind **13** obliviousness, prepossession, wool-gathering **15** bee in your bonnet, inattentiveness

## preoccupied

**06** intent **07** engaged, faraway, fixated, pensive, taken up **08** absorbed, distrait, heedless, immersed, involved, obsessed **09** engrossed, oblivious, wrapped up **10** abstracted, distracted **11** daydreaming **12** absent-minded **13** deep in thought

## preoccupy

**03** eat **04** bias **05** eat up **06** absorb, engage, fixate, obsess, occupy, take up **07** involve **09** prejudice **10** prepossess

## preordain

**04** doom, fate **07** destine **10** foreordain, prearrange, predestine **12** predestinate, predetermine

## preparation

◇ *anagram indicator* **04** plan, prep **05** study **06** basics, lotion, potion, supply **07** address, mixture **08** assembly, coaching, compound, cosmetic, homework, medicine, planning, practice, revision, training **09** equipping, provision, readiness, rudiments, spadework **10** concoction, foundation, groundwork, production **11** application, arrangement, composition, development, mise en place **12** construction, organization **13** preliminaries

## preparatory

**05** basic **07** initial, opening, primary **09** prefatory **10** antecedent, elementary, precursory **11** fundamental, preliminary, rudimentary **12** introductory
• **preparatory to** **06** before **07** prior to **10** previous to **11** in advance of **15** in expectation of

## prepare

◇ *anagram indicator* **02** do **03** fix, mix **04** boun, busk, cock, edit, make, plan **05** bowne, coach, draft, dress, equip, prime, set up, study, teach, tee up, train **06** adjust, attire, cooper, devise, digest, draw up, fit out, gear up, rig out, supply, warm up **07** arrange, compose, concoct, fashion, produce, provide, psych up **08** assemble, contrive, exercise, get ready, instruct, organize, practise **09** construct, make ready **10** pave the way **11** put together **12** get into shape **13** throw together **14** set the scene for
• **prepare yourself** **12** gird yourself **13** brace yourself, steel yourself **15** fortify yourself, gird up your loins

## prepared

◇ *anagram indicator* **03** fit, set **04** yare **05** fixed, ready **07** in order, planned, waiting, willing **08** arranged, disposed, inclined **09** organized **11** predisposed
• **prepared with** **03** à la

## preparedness

**05** order **07** fitness **08** procinct **09** alertness, readiness **10** expectancy **11** preparation **12** anticipation

## preponderance

**04** bulk, mass, sway **05** force, power **06** weight **08** dominion, majority **09** dominance, supremacy **10** ascendancy, domination, lion's share, overweight, prevalence **11** superiority **12** predominance **13** extensiveness, greater number

## preponderant

**06** larger **07** greater **08** dominant, foremost, superior **09** important **10** overriding, overruling, prevailing **11** controlling, predominant, significant

## preponderate

**04** rule, tell **07** prevail **08** dominate, outweigh, override, overrule **09** outnumber, weigh with **11** predominate **13** turn the scales **14** turn the balance **15** be in the majority

## prepossessing

**04** fair **06** taking **07** amiable, lovable, winning, winsome **08** alluring, charming, engaging, fetching, handsome, inviting, likeable, loveable, magnetic, pleasing, striking **09** appealing, beautiful **10** attractive, bewitching, delightful, enchanting **11** captivating, fascinating, good-looking

## preposterous

◇ *anagram indicator* ◇ *reversal indicator* **05** crazy **06** absurd **07** asinine, foolish

## preposterously

**08** farcical, shocking **09** ludicrous, monstrous, senseless **10** impossible, incredible, irrational, monstruous, outrageous, ridiculous **11** intolerable, nonsensical, unthinkable **12** unbelievable, unreasonable

## preposterously

**08** absurdly **10** incredibly, shockingly **11** intolerably, ludicrously **12** outrageously, ridiculously, unbelievably, unreasonably

## prerequisite

**04** must **05** basic, vital **06** needed **07** needful, proviso **08** required **09** condition, essential, mandatory, necessary, necessity, requisite **10** imperative, obligatory, sine qua non **11** fundamental, requirement **12** precondition **13** indispensable, qualification

## prerogative

**03** due **05** claim, droit, right **06** choice, purvey **07** liberty, licence, royalty **08** immunity, sanction **09** advantage, authority, exemption, privilege **10** birthright **11** entitlement **12** carte blanche

## presage

**04** bode, omen, sign **05** abode, augur **06** augury, herald, reveal, threat, warn of **07** bespeak, betoken, point to, portend, portent, predict, promise, signify, warning, warrant **08** announce, forebode, forecast, foretell, forewarn, indicate, threaten **09** adumbrate, be a sign of, foretoken, harbinger, precursor **10** foreboding, forerunner, foreshadow, indication, prognostic **11** forewarning, premonition **12** presentiment **13** foreshadowing, prefiguration, prognosticate, signification **15** prognostication

## Presbyterian

**04** Whig

## prescience

**08** prophecy **09** foresight, prevision **11** second sight **12** clairvoyance, precognition **13** foreknowledge, propheticness **14** far-sightedness

## prescient

**06** divine **07** psychic **08** divining **09** far-seeing, prescious, prophetic **10** discerning, divinatory, far-sighted, perceptive **11** clairvoyant, foreknowing, foresighted, previsional

## prescribe

**03** act, fix, set **04** rule **05** lapse, limit, order **06** advise, decree, define, direct, enjoin, impose, ordain **07** appoint, command, confine, dictate, lay down, require, specify **09** stipulate

## prescribed

**03** set **07** decreed **08** assigned, laid down, ordained **09** formulary, prescript, specified, statutory **10** regulation, statutable, stipulated

## prescription

**04** drug **05** scrip **06** advice, recipe, remedy, script **07** formula, mixture **08** leechdom, medicine **09** direction,

guideline, optometry, treatment **10** concoction, guidelines **11** instruction, preparation **14** recommendation

## prescriptive

**05** rigid **08** didactic, dogmatic **09** customary, normative **10** preceptive **11** dictatorial, legislating, prescribing **13** authoritarian

## presence

**03** air **04** aura, face **05** being, ghost, poise **06** appeal, person, shadow, spirit **07** bearing, company, dignity, phantom, spectre **08** assembly, carriage, charisma, nearness, Shekinah, vicinity, visitant **09** closeness, demeanour, existence, magnetism, occupancy, proximity, residence, Shechinah **10** apparition, appearance, attendance, attraction **11** personality, propinquity **13** companionship, neighbourhood, self-assurance **14** self-confidence
• **in the presence of** **02** by
• **presence of mind** **04** cool **05** poise **06** aplomb **08** calmness, coolness **09** alertness, composure, sangfroid **10** equanimity **11** self-command **13** self-assurance **14** self-possession, unflappability **15** level-headedness

## present

**02** pr **03** box, gie, now, tip **04** gift, give, here, host, near, perk, pres, show **05** apply, award, being, endow, grant, mount, offer, put on, ready, stage, there **06** at hand, bestow, bounty, cadeau, confer, convey, depict, donate, extend, favour, moment, nearby, prefer, submit, tender, to hand **07** compère, current, deliver, display, douceur, entrust, exhibit, fairing, freebie, handout, hold out, instant, perform, picture, porrect, portray, pressie, prezzie, proffer, propine **08** announce, describe, donation, existent, existing, gratuity, hand over, largesse, offering, organize **09** attending, available, delineate, endowment, immediate, introduce, make known, represent, sweetener **10** present-day, put forward **11** benefaction, close at hand, demonstrate **12** bring forward, characterize, contemporary, contribution, in attendance, put on display
• **at present** **03** now **05** today **06** the now **07** just now **09** currently **10** at this time **11** at the moment
• **for the present** **03** now **06** for now, pro tem **12** for the moment **13** in the meantime **15** for the time being
• **present yourself** **05** arise, occur, pop up **06** appear, arrive, attend, crop up, emerge, happen, show up, turn up **11** come to light, materialize
• **the present day** **03** now **05** today **08** nowadays **09** currently **10** at this time, here and now

## presentable

**04** neat, tidy **05** clean, smart **06** decent, spruce **08** passable **09** quite good,

tolerable **10** acceptable **11** respectable **12** satisfactory **14** smartly dressed

## presentation

**04** form, show, talk **05** award **06** format, launch, layout, object, speech, system **07** address, display, lecture, program, recital, seminar, showing, staging **08** awarding, bestowal, donating, exterior, granting, mounting **09** collation, conferral, packaging, programme, rendition, structure, unveiling **10** appearance, exhibition, presenting, production **11** arrangement, investiture, making known, performance **12** disquisition, introduction, organization **13** demonstration, poster session **14** representation

## present-day

**02** AD **06** latest, living, modern **07** current, present **08** existing, up-to-date **11** fashionable **12** contemporary

## presenter

**02** MC **04** host **05** emcee **06** anchor **07** compère **08** frontman **09** anchorman, announcer **10** postulator **11** anchorwoman, sportcaster **12** sportscaster
*See also* **radio; television**

## presentiment

**04** fear **05** hunch **07** feeling, presage **08** bad vibes, bodement, forecast **09** intuition, misgiving **10** foreboding, presension **11** expectation, forethought, premonition **12** anticipation, apprehension, forebodement

## presently

**03** now **04** enow, soon **05** in a mo **06** pronto, the now **07** by and by, in a tick, shortly **08** directly, in a jiffy **09** at present, currently, in a minute, in a moment, in a second, ipso facto, these days **10** before long, inevitably **11** at the moment, immediately, necessarily **12** in a short time **13** in a short while

## preservation

**06** repair, safety, upkeep **07** defence, keeping, storage, support **08** guarding, security **09** retention, upholding **10** protection **11** cold storage, maintenance, reservation, safekeeping **12** conservation, continuation, freeze-drying, perpetuation, safeguarding **13** refrigeration

## preserve

**03** can, dry, jam, tin **04** area, corn, cure, hain, keep, salt, save **05** candy, chase, chill, field, guard, jelly, lay up, realm, salve, smoke, store **06** bottle, cocoon, defend, domain, embalm, forest, freeze, keep up, kipper, konfyt, pickle, retain, season, secure, shield, sphere, uphold **07** care for, confect, kyanize, mummify, protect, put down, reserve, shelter, sustain **08** chow-chow, conserve, continue, creosote, maintain **09** desiccate, freeze-dry, look after, marmalade, powellize, safeguard, sanctuary **10** perpetuate, safari park, speciality, take care of **11** commemorate, game reserve,

quick-freeze, reservation **13** nature
reserve

**preside**
**03** run **04** head, lead, rule **05** chair
**06** direct, govern, head up, manage
**07** conduct, control **08** moderate
**09** hold court, officiate **10** administer
**12** be in charge of, be in the chair, be
the chair of, call the shots, take the
chair **15** be the chairman of

**president**
**01** P **04** boss, dean, head, Pres, prex,
prez **05** chief, prexy, ruler **06** leader,
preses **07** manager, praeses, speaker
**08** director, governor **09** commodore,
moderator, principal **10** chancellor,
chief-baron, controller **11** chief barker,
Earl Marshal, head of state **13** Dean of
Faculty, Earl Marischal **15** Grand
Pensionary

*Presidents include:*

**03** **Moi** (Daniel arap), **Rau** (Johannes),
**Zia** (Muhammad)
**04** **Amin** (Idi), **Díaz** (Porfirio), **Khan**
(Ayub), **Ozal** (Turgut), **René**
(France-Albert), **Rhee** (Syngman),
**Tito** (Josip Broz)
**05** **Ahmed** (Shehabuddin), **Assad**
(Hafez al-), **Banda** (Hastings),
**Botha** (P W), **Havel** (Vaclav), **Heuss**
(Theodor), **Klerk** (F W de), **Mbeki**
(Thabo), **Menem** (Carlos), **Obote**
(Milton), **Perón** (Juan), **Perón**
(Martínez de), **Putin** (Vladimir),
**Ramos** (Fidel), **Sadat** (Anwar el-)
**06** **Aideed** (Mohammed), **Aquino**
(Corazon), **Banana** (Canaan), **Bao**
**Dai**, **Bhutto** (Zulfikar Ali), **Biswas**
(Abdur Rahman), **Calles** (Plutarco
Elías), **Castro** (Fidel), **Chirac**
(Jacques), **Ciampi** (Carlo Azeglio),
**Gaulle** (Charles de), **Geisel**
(Ernesto), **Herzog** (Chaim), **Juárez**
(Benito), **Kruger** (Paul), **Kuchma**
(Leonid), **Lahoud** (Émile), **Marcos**
(Ferdinand), **Mobutu**, **Mugabe**
(Robert), **Nasser** (Gamal Abdel),
**Nathan** (Sellapan Ramanathan),
**Ortega** (Daniel), **Pierce** (Franklin),
**Préval** (René), **Rahman** (Ziaur),
**Renner** (Karl), **Santos** (José
Eduardo dos), **Somoza** (Anastasio),
**Somoza** (Luis), **Valera** (Éamon de),
**Vargas** (Getúlio), **Walesa** (Lech)
**07** **Atatürk** (Mustapha Kemal), **Batista**
(Fulgencio), **Bolívar** (Simón),
**Cardoso** (Fernando Henrique),
**Demirel** (Süleyman), **Estrada**
(Joseph Ejercito), **Gaddafi**
(Muammar), **Gemayel** (Amin),
**Gromyko** (Andrei), **Habibie** (Jusuf),
**Hussein** (Saddam), **Iliescu** (Ion),
**Khatami** (Sayed Ayatollah
Mohammad), **Mancham** (James),
**Mandela** (Nelson), **Masaryk**
(Tomás), **Mubarak** (Hosni),
**Nkrumah** (Kwame), **Parnell**
(Charles Stewart), **Sampaio** (Jorge),
**Sarkozy** (Nicolas), **Suharto** (Thojib
N J), **Sukarno** (Ahmed), **Tudjman**
(Franjo), **Weizman** (Ezer), **Yanayev**
(Gennady), **Yeltsin** (Boris), **Zhivkov**
(Todor)

**08** **Andropov** (Yuri), **Aristide** (Jean-
Bertrand), **Bani-Sadr** (Abolhassan),
**Brezhnev** (Leonid), **Chamorro**
(Violeta), **Childers** (Erskine),
**Cosgrave** (William Thomas),
**Duvalier** (François 'Papa Doc'),
**Duvalier** (Jean-Claude 'Baby Doc'),
**Fujimori** (Alberto), **Galtieri**
(Leopoldo), **Griffith** (Arthur),
**Karadzic** (Radovan), **Kenyatta**
(Jomo), **Khamenei** (Sayed Ali),
**Kravchuk** (Leonid), **MacMahon**
(Patrice de), **Makarios**, **McAleese**
(Mary), **Medvedev** (Dmitry
Anatolyevich), **Mengistu** (Haile
Mariam), **Museveni** (Yoweri),
**Napoleon**, **Pinochet** (Augusto),
**Poincaré** (Raymond), **Pompidou**
(Georges), **Rawlings** (Jerry),
**Robinson** (Mary), **Waldheim** (Kurt),
**Weizmann** (Chaim), **Zia Ul-Haq**
(Muhammad)
**09** **Ceauşescu** (Nicolae), **Chernenko**
(Konstantin), **Gorbachev** (Mikhail),
**Ho Chi Minh**, **Kim Il-sung**, **Kim**
**Jong Il**, **Mao Zedong**, **Milosevic**
(Slobodan), **Narayanan** (Kocheril
Raman), **Pilsudski** (Józef), **Sun Yat-**
**Sen**
**10** **Alessandri** (Arturo), **Betancourt**
(Rómulo), **Hindenburg** (Paul von),
**Jaruzelski** (Wojciech), **Jiang**
**Zemin**, **Khrushchev** (Nikita),
**Kubitschek** (Juscelino),
**Mannerheim** (Carl Gustav, Baron
von), **Mitterrand** (François),
**Najibullah** (Mohammad),
**Rafsanjani** (Ali Akbar Hashemi),
**Stroessner** (Alfredo), **Voroshilov**
(Kliment)
**13** **Paz Estenssoro** (Víctor)
**14** **Mobutu Seze Seko**
**15** **Giscard d'Estaing** (Valéry)

*Presidents of the United States of
America:*

**03** **Abe**, **Ike**, **Ron**
**04** **Bill**, **Bush** (George), **Bush** (George
W), **Ford** (Gerald R), **Polk** (James
K), **Taft** (William H)
**05** **Adams** (John), **Adams** (John
Quincy), **Buren** (Martin van), **Grant**
(Ulysses S), **Hayes** (Rutherford B),
**Nixon** (Richard M), **Obama**
(Barack), **Tyler** (John)
**06** **Arthur** (Chester A), **Carter** (Jimmy),
**Hoover** (Herbert), **Monroe** (James),
**Pierce** (Franklin), **Reagan** (Ronald),
**Taylor** (Zachary), **Truman** (Harry S),
**Wilson** (Woodrow)
**07** **Clinton** (Bill), **Harding** (Warren G),
**Jackson** (Andrew), **Johnson**
(Andrew), **Johnson** (Lyndon B),
**Kennedy** (John F), **Lincoln**
(Abraham), **Madison** (James)
**08** **Buchanan** (James), **Coolidge**
(Calvin), **Fillmore** (Millard),
**Garfield** (James A), **Harrison**
(Benjamin), **Harrison** (William
Henry), **McKinley** (William)
**09** **Cleveland** (Grover), **Jefferson**
(Thomas), **Roosevelt** (Franklin D),
**Roosevelt** (Theodore)
**10** **Eisenhower** (Dwight D),
**Washington** (George)

**press**
**02** AP, UP **03** AAP, CUP, hug, jam, lie,
mob, OUP, sit, vex **04** airn, bear, cram,
iron, mash, pack, push, roll, urge
**05** beset, clasp, crowd, crush, flock,
force, grasp, hacks, horde, hurry,
knead, pinch, plead, print, stamp,
stuff, surge, swarm, troop, worry,
wring **06** caress, closet, coerce,
compel, cuddle, demand, enfold,
exhort, harass, lean on, nuzzle,
papers, praise, smooth, squash, strain,
stress, strive, throng, thrust **07** afflict,
besiege, call for, depress, embrace,
entreat, express, flatten, implore,
imprint, oppress, push for, reports,
reviews, squeeze, swing it, thrutch,
trample, trouble, urgency **08** articles,
bookcase, campaign, compress,
coverage, expedite, fast-talk, insist on,
petition, pressmen, pressure, push
down, soft-soap, the media
**09** constrain, criticism, hold close,
importune, multitude, news media,
paparazzi, reporters, smooth out,
sweet-talk, treatment **10** journalism,
newspapers, pressurize, presswomen,
supplicate **11** Fleet Street, journalists,
pull strings, push forward, rotary press
**12** fourth estate, newspapermen
**13** photographers, printing press, put
pressure on **14** correspondents,
newspaperwomen, put the screws on
**15** printing-machine, the fourth estate,
turn the screws on
*See also* **news**
• **member of the press** *see*
**journalist**
• **press close** **04** serr **05** serre
• **press forward** **04** push, spur,
urge **05** drive
• **press on** **04** go on, toil **05** crowd
**06** plod on **07** carry on, go ahead,
peg away, proceed **08** continue, plug
away, slog away, toil away **09** keep
going, persevere, soldier on, stick at
it **10** keep trying, press ahead

**pressed**
**04** laid, lain **06** forced, pushed, rushed
**07** bullied, coerced, hard-run, hurried,
lacking, short of **08** harassed
**09** pressured **10** bludgeoned,
browbeaten, railroaded
**11** constrained, deficient in,
pressurized **15** having too little, not
having enough

**pressing**
**03** key **05** acute, vital **06** urgent
**07** burning, crucial, exigent, serious
**08** critical, crowding **09** demanding,
essential, important **10** imperative
**11** importunate **12** high-priority

**pressman**
*see* **journalist**

**pressure**
**01** P **04** heat, load, push **05** aggro,
bully, drive, force, power, press, stamp
**06** burden, coerce, compel, demand,
duress, hassle, lean on, oblige, strain,
stress, weight **07** dragoon, problem,
swing it, tension, trouble, urgency
**08** bludgeon, browbeat, bulldoze,
bullying, coercion, crushing, fast-talk,

railroad, soft-soap **09** adversity,
constrain, heaviness, squeezing,
sweet-talk **10** compulsion, constraint,
difficulty, harassment, impression,
obligation, pressurize **11** compression,
constraints, pull strings **13** put pressure
on **14** put the screws on
• **blood pressure 02** BP **03** ABP
• **extreme/high/low pressure 02** EP,
HP, LP
• **measurement of pressure 02** mb,
Pa **03** atm, bar, psi **04** torr **05** barye
**06** pascal **07** megabar **08** microbar,
millibar **10** atmosphere

### pressurize
**05** bully, drive, force, press **06** coerce,
compel, lean on, oblige **07** dragoon,
swing it **08** bludgeon, browbeat,
bulldoze, fast-talk, pressure, railroad,
soft-soap **09** constrain, sweet-talk
**11** pull strings **12** put the acid on **13** put
pressure on **14** put the screws on

### prestige
**04** fame, mana **05** charm, izzat, kudos,
magic **06** credit, esteem, honour,
regard, renown, status **07** glamour,
stature **08** eminence, standing
**09** authority, influence **10** ascendancy,
importance, reputation **11** distinction

### prestigious
**05** great **06** famous **07** eminent, exalted
**08** blue-chip, esteemed, imposing,
juggling, renowned, up-market
**09** deceitful, important, prominent,
reputable, respected, well-known
**10** celebrated, impressive **11** high-
ranking, illustrious, influential
**13** distinguished

### presumably
**06** I guess **07** no doubt **08** I presume,
probably **09** doubtless, seemingly
**10** apparently, most likely, very likely
**11** doubtlessly **15** in all likelihood

### presume
**04** dare **05** infer, think **06** assume,
deduce, take it **07** believe, go so far,
imagine, suppose, surmise, venture
**09** undertake **10** make so bold,
presuppose, take as read
**11** hypothesize **14** take for granted,
take the liberty **15** have the audacity
• **presume on 05** trust **06** bank on,
rely on **07** count on, exploit **08** depend
on **15** take advantage of

### presumption
**03** lip **04** gall, neck **05** cheek, guess,
mouth, nerve, sauce **06** belief
**07** opinion, surmise **08** assuming,
audacity, boldness, chutzpah, temerity
**09** arrogance, assurance, brass neck,
deduction, impudence, inference,
insolence, upsetting **10** assumption,
conjecture, effrontery, hypothesis,
likelihood **11** forwardness, probability,
supposition **12** impertinence
**13** outrecuidance **14** presupposition

### presumptive
**06** likely **07** assumed **08** believed,
credible, expected, inferred, possible,
probable, supposed **09** designate,
plausible **10** believable, reasonable,

understood **11** conceivable,
conjectural, prospective
**12** hypothetical

### presumptuous
**04** bold **05** cocky, fresh, lippy, pushy,
saucy **06** cheeky, mouthy **07** forward
**08** arrogant, cocksure, impudent,
insolent, malapert **09** audacious,
bigheaded, conceited **11** impertinent
**12** over-familiar **13** over-confident

### presuppose
**05** imply, posit **06** accept, assume
**07** premise, presume, suppose
**08** consider **09** postulate **11** necessitate
**14** take for granted

### presupposition
**06** belief, theory **07** premise, premiss
**10** assumption, hypothesis
**11** presumption, supposition
**13** preconception

### pretence
**03** act, lie **04** cant, mask, ruse, sham,
show, veil, wile **05** bluff, cloak, cover,
feint, front, guise **06** acting, deceit,
excuse, façade, faking, humbug,
posing, veneer **07** charade, daubery,
display, pretext **08** feigning, trickery
**09** deception, falsehood, false show,
hypocrisy, invention, posturing,
semblance, showiness **10** appearance,
masquerade, play-acting, pretension,
profession, simulation **11** affectation,
dissembling, fabrication, make-
believe, ostentation **12** false colours
**13** dissimulation **15** pretentiousness

### pretend
**03** act, kid **04** fake, mime, play, sham
**05** bluff, claim, feign, frame, kiddy, let
on, offer, put on **06** affect, allege,
assume, semble **07** imagine, play-act,
profess, purport, purpose, put it on,
suppose **08** indicate, simulate
**09** dissemble, fabricate, imaginary
**10** put on an act **11** counterfeit,
impersonate, make believe **15** pass
yourself off

### pretended
**04** fake, sham **05** bogus, false, moody,
put on **06** avowed, phoney, pseudo
**07** alleged, assumed, feigned, pretend
**08** affected, so-called, specious,
spurious, supposed, vizarded
**09** imaginary, professed, purported,
soi-disant **10** artificial, fictitious,
ostensible, self-styled **11** counterfect,
counterfeit **14** supposititious

### pretender
**06** suitor **07** claimer, would-be
**08** aspirant, claimant **09** candidate

### pretension
**04** airs, show **05** claim **06** demand,
vanity **07** conceit, pretext **08** ambition,
pretence **09** hypocrisy, pomposity,
showiness **10** aspiration, profession,
purporting **11** affectation, floweriness,
ostentation **12** snobbishness
**13** dissimulation, magniloquence
**14** self-importance **15** pretentiousness

### pretentious
**03** big, OTT **04** fine, twee **05** false,
large, pseud, showy **06** chichi,

phoney, pseudo, shoddy, uppish
**07** kitschy, pompous, tinhorn
**08** affected, fantoosh, immodest,
inflated, mannered, pseudish,
snobbish **09** ambitious, bombastic,
conceited, elaborate, flaunting,
grandiose **10** artificial, flamboyant,
over-the-top **11** exaggerated,
extravagant **12** high-sounding,
magniloquent, ostentatious,
vainglorious **13** overambitious, self-
important

### pretentiously
**07** showily **08** uppishly **09** pompously
**10** snobbishly **12** artificially,
flamboyantly **14** ostentatiously **15** self-
importantly

### pretentiousness
**04** show, side **05** swank **06** chichi,
kitsch, posing **08** flummery, grandeur,
paraffle, pretence, pretense, pseudery
**09** posturing **10** flatulence, flatulency,
floridness, pretension, uppishness
**11** flamboyance, floweriness,
ostentation **13** ambitiousness,
theatricality **14** attitudinizing

### preternatural
**07** no' canny, unusual **08** abnormal
**11** exceptional **12** supernatural
**13** extraordinary

### pretext
**04** hook, mask, plea, ploy, ruse, sham,
show, veil **05** cloak, cloke, color,
cover, guise, salvo, stale **06** colour,
excuse **07** off-come, umbrage
**08** occasion, pretence, pretense
**09** semblance **10** appearance,
pretension, red herring **13** alleged
reason

### prettify
**04** deck, do up, gild, trim **05** adorn
**06** bedeck, doll up, tart up **07** deck out,
garnish, trick up **08** beautify, decorate,
ornament, trick out **09** embellish,
smarten up

### prettily
**06** neatly, nicely **08** daintily
**09** elegantly, winsomely
**10** charmingly, engagingly, gracefully,
pleasantly, pleasingly **11** beautifully
**12** attractively, delightfully

### pretty
**04** cute, fair, fine, neat, nice, twee,
very **05** bonny, grand, purty, quite
**06** bonnie, clever, comely, dainty,
fairly, incony, lovely, rather, tricky
**07** elegant, fairway, inconie, not half,
winsome **08** charming, delicate,
engaging, graceful, handsome,
keepsake, keepsaky, pleasant,
pleasing, somewhat, stalwart
**09** appealing, beautiful, extremely,
ingenious, tolerably **10** attractive,
decorative, delightful, knick-knack,
moderately, personable, reasonably
**11** commendable, good-looking,
substantial **12** chocolate-box,
considerable **13** prepossessing

### prevail
**03** win **04** ring, rule **05** avail, occur,
reign **06** abound, have it, obtain, win

## prevailing

out **07** conquer, succeed, triumph **08** be common, be normal, hold sway, overcome, override, overrule, persuade, perswade **09** be current, be present **10** be accepted, win through **11** be customary, carry the day, gain mastery, predominate **12** be victorious, preponderate **14** gain ascendancy
• **prevail upon 03** win **04** rule, sway, urge **06** induce, lean on, prompt **07** incline, win over **08** convince, persuade, pressure, soft-soap, talk into **09** influence, sweet-talk **10** bring round, pressurize **11** pull strings

## prevailing

**03** set **04** main **05** chief, usual **06** common, ruling **07** average, current, general, in style, in vogue, popular, supreme **08** accepted, dominant, powerful, reigning **09** ascendant, customary, effective, in fashion, most usual, prepotent, prevalent, principal **10** compelling, mainstream, most common, widespread **11** controlling, established, fashionable, influential, predominant **12** preponderant

## prevalence

**03** ren, rin, run **04** hold, rule, sway **07** mastery, primacy **08** currency, ubiquity **09** frequency, profusion **10** acceptance, ascendancy, commonness, popularity, regularity **11** commonality **12** omnipresence, predominance, universality **13** order of the day, pervasiveness, preponderance

## prevalent

**03** set **04** rife **05** usual **06** common, vulgar **07** current, endemic, general, popular, rampant, regnant **08** accepted, dominant, enzootic, epidemic, everyday, frequent, powerful **09** customary, extensive, pervasive, universal **10** prevailing, ubiquitous, victorious, widespread **11** established

## prevaricate

**03** lie **05** cavil, dodge, evade, hedge, mudge, shift **06** waffle **07** deceive, deviate, pervert, quibble, shuffle, whiffle **09** be evasive, pussyfoot, stonewall **10** equivocate, transgress **12** shilly-shally, tergiversate **13** sit on the fence

## prevarication

**03** fib, lie **04** fibs **06** deceit **07** evasion, fibbing, untruth **08** pretence **09** cavilling, deception, falsehood, half-truth, quibbling **12** equivocation, pussyfooting **13** falsification **14** tergiversation **15** shilly-shallying

## prevaricator

**04** liar **06** dodger, evader, fibber, Jesuit **07** casuist, sophist **08** caviller, deceiver, quibbler **09** hypocrite **10** dissembler **11** equivocator, pettifogger

## prevent

**02** sa' **03** bar, let **04** balk, foil, halt, help, keep, save, stop **05** avert, avoid, block, check, debar, deter, stimy **06** arrest, hamper, hinder, impede, stimie,

stymie, thwart **07** fend off, head off, inhibit, obviate, precede, ward off **08** hold back, keep from, obstruct, preclude, prohibit, restrain, stave off **09** foreclose, forestall, frustrate, intercept **10** anticipate **11** hold in check

## prevention

**03** bar **05** check **07** balking, empeach, foiling, halting, impeach **08** obstacle **09** arresting, avoidance, exclusion, hampering, hindrance, obviation, safeguard **10** deterrence, fending off, heading off, hinderance, impediment, precaution, preclusion, staving off, warding off **11** elimination, frustration, obstruction, premonition, prophylaxis **12** anticipation **13** contraception

## preventive

**05** block **06** remedy, shield **08** obstacle **09** deterrent, hindrance, safeguard **10** impediment, inhibitory, pre-emptive, prevenient, prevention, protection, protective **11** neutralizer, obstruction, obstructive **12** anticipatory, preventative, prophylactic **13** counteractive, precautionary

## previous

**02** ex- **04** past **05** prior **06** before, former **07** earlier, one-time, quondam **08** sometime **09** erstwhile, foregoing, preceding, premature **10** antecedent

## previously

**04** erst, fore, once **05** afore **06** before **07** already, earlier **08** formerly, hitherto, until now **09** at one time, earlier on, erstwhile, in the past **10** beforehand, heretofore

## prey

**03** mug **04** game, kill **05** booty, ravin, soyle **06** quarry, rapine, target, victim **07** afflict, fall guy, plunder, spreagh **08** distress **11** depredation
• **prey on 03** con, eat **04** hunt, kill **05** bleed, catch, haunt, prowl, seize, worry **06** burden, devour, feed on, fleece, plague **07** exploit, live off, moth-eat, oppress, predate, raven on, torment, trouble, vampire **08** distress, hang over, pounce on **09** depredate, weigh down **15** take advantage of

## price

**02** pr **03** fee, sum **04** bill, cost, fare, levy, rate, toll **05** prise, prize, value, worth **06** amount, assess, charge, figure, outlay, result, reward **07** expense, forfeit, payment, penalty **08** appraise, estimate, evaluate, expenses, valorize **09** quotation, sacrifice, valuation **10** assessment **11** consequence, expenditure **12** consequences, preciousness **13** fix the price at, set the price at
• **at any price 09** at any cost, à tout prix **15** whatever it takes, whatever the cost
• **at a price 04** dear **09** expensive **11** at a high cost **12** at a high price
• **fix price 03** peg

## priceless

**04** dear, rare, rich **05** comic, funny **06** costly, prized **07** amusing, a scream, killing, riotous **08** precious, unvalued, valuable **09** cherished, expensive, hilarious, treasured **10** invaluable **11** inestimable **12** incalculable, incomparable **13** inappreciable, irreplaceable, side-splitting

## pricey

**04** dear **05** steep **06** costly **07** sky-high **09** excessive, expensive **10** exorbitant, high-priced **11** over the odds **12** costing a bomb, extortionate **15** costing the earth, daylight robbery

## prick

**03** dot, jab, jag, pin **04** acme, bite, bore, brod, brog, cloy, gash, hole, itch, mark, nick, pain, pang, peak, prod, prog, slit, stab **05** harry, point, punch, rowel, smart, spike, sting, thorn, worry, wound **06** accloy, gnaw at, harass, incite, pierce, plague, prey on, target, tingle, twinge **07** pinhole, prickle, torment, trouble **08** distress, puncture, smarting **09** perforate **11** perforation
• **prick up your ears 06** attend **09** lend an ear **10** take note of **12** pay attention, take notice of **13** listen eagerly **15** listen carefully, pin back your ears

## prickle

**03** nip **04** barb, itch, pang, spur, tine **05** point, prick, prong, smart, spike, spine, sting, thorn **06** needle, tingle, twinge **07** acantha, aculeus, itching, spicula **08** smarting, stinging **09** sensation **11** formication **12** paraesthesia **14** pins and needles

## prickly

**04** edgy, hard **05** armed, jaggy, ratty, rough, spiky, spiny, tough **06** barbed, crabby, grumpy, on edge, shirty, spiked, thorny, touchy, tricky **07** bearded, brambly, bristly, grouchy, pronged, stroppy **08** aculeate, delicate, echinate, scratchy **09** aculeated, crotchety, difficult, echinated, irritable, sensitive **10** acanaceous **11** bad-tempered, complicated, problematic, thin-skinned, troublesome **12** acanthaceous **13** problematical, short-tempered

## prickly pear

**04** tuna **05** nopal **07** opuntia **09** Indian fig

## pride

**03** ego, joy **05** prime **06** flower, honour, mettle, vanity **07** conceit, delight, dignity, disdain, egotism, elation, stomach **08** pleasure, smugness, snobbery **09** arrogance, proudness, self-image, self-worth, splendour **10** exuberance, self-esteem **11** haughtiness, ostentation, presumption, self-conceit, self-respect **12** boastfulness, magnificence, satisfaction, triumphalism **13** bigheadedness, gratification **14** self-importance **15** pretentiousness
• **pride and joy 03** joy **04** best, pick **05** élite, glory **06** finest, flower

## priest

**07** darling, delight **10** choice part, select part **14** apple of your eye, crème de la crème, pick of the bunch
• **pride yourself on 05** vaunt **07** exult in, glory in, revel in **09** brag about, crow about **10** boast about **11** take pride in **13** plume yourself, preen yourself **15** flatter yourself

## priest

**01** P **02** Pr **03** Eli **05** Aaron, clerk, Zadok **06** cleric, Elijah, Elisha, father, orator **07** prelate, secular **08** man of God **09** churchman, clergyman **10** hierophant, woman of God **11** churchwoman, clergywoman **12** ecclesiastic **13** man of the cloth **15** woman of the cloth

*Priests include:*

**02** HP, PP
**04** abbé, arch, curé, high, lama, papa, pope
**05** bonze, druid, magus, mambo, padre, rabbi, vicar
**06** deacon, flamen, Levite, lucumo, parish, parson, pastor, pujari, rector, shaman, zymite
**07** Brahman, patrico, pontiff, Pythian, tohunga
**08** bacchant, corybant, hierarch, minister, neophyte, seminary, Syriarch
**09** bacchanal, confessor, deaconess, lack-Latin, oratorian, patercove, presbyter
**10** arch-flamen, masspriest, seminarian, seminarist
**11** hedge-parson, hedge-priest
**12** concelebrant, Redemptorist

## priestess

**03** nun **05** mambo **06** abbess, Pythia, sister, vestal **07** beguine, Pythian **08** canoness, prioress **09** bacchante, deaconess, Pythoness, religious **11** clergywoman

## priesthood

**08** the cloth **09** the church **10** full orders, hierocracy, holy orders, priestship **11** the ministry **12** the pastorate **13** sacerdotalism

## priestly

**07** Aaronic **08** clerical, hieratic, pastoral **09** Aaronical, canonical **10** priestlike, sacerdotal **14** ecclesiastical

## prig

**05** filch, prude, thief **06** haggle, tinker **07** coxcomb, entreat, holy Joe, killjoy, old maid, puritan **09** importune, Mrs Grundy, precisian **10** goody-goody, holy Willie

## priggish

**04** prim, smug **05** prude **06** stuffy **07** prudish, starchy **10** goody-goody **11** puritanical, strait-laced **12** narrow-minded **13** sanctimonious, self-righteous **14** holier-than-thou

## prim

**03** mim **04** smug **05** fussy, mimsy **06** demure, formal, mimsey, neaten, prissy, proper, quaint, stuffy **07** perjink,
precise, primsie, prudish, starchy **08** priggish **10** fastidious, fuddy-duddy, governessy, old-maidish, particular **11** puritanical, strait-laced **12** primigravida **13** schoolmarmish

## primacy

**07** command **08** dominion **09** dominance, seniority, supremacy **10** ascendancy, leadership, paramouncy **11** pre-eminence, sovereignty, superiority

## prima donna

**04** diva **10** female lead **11** leading lady, moody person **14** leading soprano

## primaeval

*see* **primeval, primaeval**

## primal

**04** main **05** basic, chief, first, major, prime **07** central, highest, initial, primary **08** earliest, greatest, original, primeval **09** paramount, primaeval, primitive, principal **10** primordial **11** fundamental, primigenial, primogenial

## primarily

◊ *head selection indicator* **05** first **06** mainly, mostly **07** chiefly, firstly **09** basically, in essence, in the main **10** especially **11** essentially, principally **12** nothing if not, particularly **13** fundamentally, predominantly **15** in the first place

## primary

**04** main **05** basic, chief, first, prime **06** direct, simple **07** capital, highest, initial, leading, opening, radical, supreme **08** cardinal, dominant, earliest, foremost, greatest, original, primeval, ultimate **09** beginning, elemental, essential, first-hand, paramount, primaeval, primitive, principal **10** elementary, idiopathic, primordial **11** fundamental, predominant, rudimentary **12** introductory

## primate

**06** bishop **07** Bigfoot **10** archbishop

*Primates include:*

**03** ape
**04** mico
**05** chimp, drill, human, indri, jocko, lemur, loris, orang, pigmy, pongo, pygmy, satyr
**06** aye-aye, baboon, bonobo, chacma, colugo, dog-ape, galago, gelada, gibbon, indris, macaco, malmag, monkey, sifaka, wou-wou, wow-wow
**07** gorilla, hoolock, jacchus, macaque, meercat, meerkat, nagapie, siamang, tarsier, wistiti
**08** bushbaby, great ape, hylobate, mandrill, marmoset, mongoose, night-ape
**09** babacoote, catarhine, hamadryad, orang-utan, prosimian
**10** angwantibo, catarrhine, chimpanzee, protohuman, silverback
**11** Homo sapiens, orang-outang
**12** Cynocephalus, ourang-outang, paranthropus
**13** Galeopithecus, Kenyapithecus
**15** pygmy chimpanzee

*See also* **ape; monkey**

## prime

**03** top **04** acme, best, fang, fill, main, peak **05** bloom, brief, chief, coach, equip, gen up, phang, pride, train **06** charge, choice, clue up, fill in, flower, gear up, height, heyday, inform, notify, select, zenith **07** blossom, classic, highest, leading, premier, prepare, primary, quality, supreme, typical **08** best part, foremost, get ready, maturity, original, pinnacle, standard, top-grade **09** excellent, first-rate, make ready, principal **10** first-class, perfection, pre-eminent **11** culmination, predominant **12** paradigmatic, prototypical **14** characteristic, quintessential

## prime minister

**02** PM **05** dewan, diwan **07** premier **08** quisling **09** Taoiseach **10** chancellor **11** Grand Vizier **13** chief minister, first minister

*Prime Ministers of Australia:*

**04** **Cook** (Joseph), **Holt** (Harold), **Page** (Earle), **Reid** (George), **Rudd** (Kevin)
**05** **Bruce** (Stanley), **Forde** (Francis Michael), **Hawke** (Bob), **Lyons** (Joseph)
**06** **Barton** (Edmund), **Curtin** (John), **Deakin** (Alfred), **Fadden** (Arthur), **Fisher** (Andrew), **Fraser** (Malcolm), **Gorton** (John), **Howard** (John), **Hughes** (Billy), **McEwen** (John), **Watson** (Chris)
**07** **Chifley** (Ben), **Gillard** (Julia), **Keating** (Paul), **McMahon** (William), **Menzies** (Robert), **Scullin** (James), **Whitlam** (Gough)

*Prime Ministers of Canada:*

**04** **King** (William Lyon Mackenzie)
**05** **Abbot** (John J C), **Clark** (Joseph)
**06** **Borden** (Robert), **Bowell** (Mackenzie), **Harper** (Stephen), **Martin** (Paul), **Tupper** (Charles), **Turner** (John)
**07** **Bennett** (R B), **Laurier** (Wilfrid), **Meighen** (Arthur), **Pearson** (Lester B), **Trudeau** (Pierre)
**08** **Campbell** (Kim), **Chrétien** (Jean), **Mulroney** (Brian), **Thompson** (John S D)
**09** **Macdonald** (John A), **Mackenzie** (Alexander), **St Laurent** (Louis)
**11** **Diefenbaker** (John G)

*Prime Ministers of New Zealand:*

**03** **Key** (John)
**04** **Bell** (Francis), **Kirk** (Norman Eric), **Nash** (Walter), **Ward** (Joseph)
**05** **Clark** (Helen), **Lange** (David), **Moore** (Mike)
**06** **Bolger** (James), **Coates** (Gordon), **Forbes** (George William), **Fraser** (Peter), **Massey** (William), **Palmer** (Geoffrey), **Savage** (Michael Joseph), **Seddon** (Richard)

**07** Holland (Sidney), **Muldoon** (Sir Robert), **Rowling** (Wallace), **Shipley** (Jenny)

**08** Holyoake (Sir Keith), **Marshall** (John Ross)

**09** Hall-Jones (William), **Mackenzie** (Thomas)

*See also* **premier**

*Prime Ministers of the United Kingdom:*

**04** Bute (John Stuart, Earl), **Eden** (Sir Anthony), **Grey** (Charles Grey, Earl), **Home** (Alec Douglas, Earl), **Peel** (Robert), **Pitt** (William)

**05** Blair (Tony), **Brown** (Gordon), **Cecil** (Robert), **Derby** (Edward Stanley, Earl), **Heath** (Sir Edward), **Major** (Sir John), **North** (Frederick North, Lord)

**06** Attlee (Clement), **Pelham** (Henry), **Wilson** (Harold, Lord)

**07** Asquith (Herbert), **Baldwin** (Stanley), **Balfour** (Arthur), **Cameron** (David), **Canning** (George), **Grafton** (Augustus Henry Fitzroy, Duke), **Russell** (John, Lord), **Walpole** (Robert)

**08** Aberdeen (George Hamilton-Gordon, Lord), **Bonar Law** (Andrew), **Disraeli** (Benjamin), **Goderich** (Frederick John Robinson, Viscount), **Perceval** (Spencer), **Portland** (William Henry Cavendish Bentinck, Duke), **Rosebery** (Archibald Philip Primrose, Earl), **Thatcher** (Margaret, Lady)

**09** Addington (Henry), **Callaghan** (James, Lord), **Churchill** (Sir Winston), **Gladstone** (William), **Grenville** (George), **Grenville** (William Wyndham, Lord), **Liverpool** (Robert Jenkinson, Earl), **MacDonald** (Ramsay), **Macmillan** (Harold, Earl of Stockton), **Melbourne** (William Lamb, Viscount), **Newcastle** (Thomas Pelham-Holles, Duke), **Salisbury** (Robert Gascoyne-Cecil, Marquess), **Shelburne** (William Petty-Fitzmaurice, Earl)

**10** Devonshire (William Cavendish, Duke), **Palmerston** (Henry John Temple, Viscount), **Rockingham** (Charles Watson Wentworth, Marquess), **Wellington** (Arthur Wellesley, Duke), **Wilmington** (Spencer Compton, Earl)

**11** Chamberlain (Neville), **Douglas-Home** (Alec), **Lloyd George** (David)

**17** Campbell-Bannerman (Henry)

*Prime Ministers of other countries include:*

**02** Nu (U)

**03** Ito (Hirobumi)

**04** Meir (Golda), **Moro** (Aldo), **Tojo** (Hideki)

**05** Ahern (Bertie), **Assad** (Hafez al-), **Azaña** (Manuel), **Aznar** (José María), **Banda** (Hastings Kamuzu), **Barak** (Ehud), **Barre** (Raymond), **Begin** (Menachem), **Botha** (Louis), **Botha** (P W), **Craxi** (Bettino), **Desai**

(Morarji), **Faure** (Edgar), **Hoxha** (Enver), **Juppé** (Alain), **Khama** (Sir Seretse), **Laval** (Pierre), **Lynch** (Jack), **Malan** (Daniel), **Nehru** (Jawaharlal), **Obote** (Milton), **Pasic** (Nikola), **Peres** (Shimon), **Prodi** (Romano), **Putin** (Vladimir), **Rabin** (Yitzhak), **Sadat** (Anwar el-), **Singh** (Manmohan), **Smith** (Ian), **Smuts** (Jan), **Spaak** (Paul Henri)

**06** Bhutto (Benazir), **Bhutto** (Zulfikar Ali), **Briand** (Aristide), **Bruton** (John), **Castro** (Fidel), **Chirac** (Jacques), **Fabius** (Laurent), **Gandhi** (Indira), **Gandhi** (Rajiv), **Hun Sen**, **Jospin** (Lionel), **Li Peng**, **Manley** (Michael), **Mugabe** (Robert), **Neguib** (Mohammed), **O'Neill** (Terence, Lord), **Pétain** (Philippe), **Pol Pot**, **Pombal** (Sebastião de Carvalho, Marquês de), **Rahman** (Sheikh Mujibur), **Rhodes** (Cecil), **Shamir** (Yitzhak), **Sharif** (Nawaz), **Sharon** (Ariel), **Thiers** (Adolphe)

**07** Berisha (Sali), **Cresson** (Édith), **Halifax** (Charles Montagu, Earl of), **Haughey** (Charles), **Hertzog** (J B M), **Kosygin** (Alexei), **Lubbers** (Ruud), **Molotov** (Vyacheslav), **Nkrumah** (Kwame), **Nyerere** (Julius), **Vorster** (John), **Yeltsin** (Boris)

**08** Ben Bella (Ahmed), **Bismarck** (Otto, Fürst von), **Bulganin** (Nikolai), **Daladier** (Édouard), **de Gaulle** (Charles), **de Valera** (Éamon), **González** (Felipe), **Kenyatta** (Jomo), **Mahathir** (bin Mohamad), **Nakasone** (Yasuhiro), **Poincaré** (Raymond), **Pompidou** (Georges), **Quisling** (Vidkun), **Reynolds** (Albert), **Vajpayee** (Atal Bihari), **Verwoerd** (Hendrik), **Zapatero** (José Luis Rodríguez)

**09** Andreotti (Giulio), **Ben-Gurion** (David), **de Gasperi** (Alcide), **Hashimoto** (Ryutaro), **Kim Il-sung**, **Kim Jong Il**, **Mussolini** (Benito), **Netanyahu** (Binyamin), **Stanishev** (Sergei), **Wen Jiabao**

**10** Balkenende (Jan Peter), **Berlusconi** (Silvio), **Clemenceau** (Georges), **FitzGerald** (Garret), **Jaruzelski** (Wojciech), **Lee Kuan Yew**

**11** Verhofstadt (Guy)

**12** Bandaranaike (S W R D), **Chernomyrdin** (Viktor)

**13** Brookeborough (Basil Brooke, Viscount)

**primer**
**05** Donat, Donet **06** manual **08** prodrome, textbook **09** absey-book, detonator, prodromus **12** introduction

**primeval, primaeval**
**03** old **05** basic, early, first **06** inborn, innate, primal **07** ancient, natural, Ogygian **08** earliest, inherent, original **09** intuitive, primitial, primitive **10** primordial **11** instinctive, prehistoric **12** autochthonal

**primitive**
**02** ur- **03** pro- **04** wild **05** crude, early, first, naive, rough **06** primal, savage, simple **07** ancient, natural, primary,

radical **08** backveld, earliest, original, primeval **09** barbarian, primaeval **10** aboriginal, antiquated, elementary, primordial, uncultured **11** fundamental, rudimentary, uncivilized, undeveloped **12** antediluvian, old-fashioned, protomorphic **15** unsophisticated

**primly**
**07** fussily **08** prissily, stuffily **09** prudishly

**primordial**
**03** old **05** early, first **07** ancient **08** earliest, original, primeval **09** primaeval, primitive **11** instinctive, prehistoric, rudimentary **12** autochthonal, protomorphic

**primp**
**04** tidy **05** groom, preen **06** doll up, tart up **07** brush up, dress up, smarten **08** beautify, spruce up, titivate

**prince**
**01** P **02** Pr **03** mir, ras **04** amir, duke, khan, king, lord, raja, rana **05** ameer, chief, Mirza, nawab, nizam, queen, rajah, ruler, Tunku **06** leader, lucumo, potent, sharif, sherif, Tengku **07** infante, monarch, shereef **08** archduke, atheling, gospodar, hospodar, maharaja, tetrarch **09** Beelzebub, maharajah, potentate, princekin, princelet, royal duke, sovereign **10** princeling, Upper Roger **13** prince consort **14** porphyrogenite

*Princes include:*

**03** Hal

**04** Igor, Ivan, **John** (of Gaunt)

**05** Edgar (the Atheling), **Harry**, **Henry** (the Navigator), **James**

**06** Albert, Andrew, **Arthur**, **Edward**, **Edward** (the Black Prince), **Philip**

**07** Charles, Michael (of Kent), **Rainier**, **Richard**, **William**

**08** Llywelyn, Vladimir

**09** Ferdinand

**11** James Stuart

**15** Alexander Nevski, **Bernhard**, **Leopold**

**Prince Edward Island**
**02** PE

**princely**
**04** huge, vast **05** grand, noble, regal, royal **06** lavish, superb **07** immense, liberal, mammoth, massive, prenzie, stately **08** colossal, enormous, en prince, generous, glorious, handsome, imperial, imposing, majestic, splendid **09** bounteous, sovereign, sumptuous **10** impressive, large-scale, stupendous, tremendous **11** magnanimous, magnificent **12** considerable

**princess**
**04** lady, rani **05** begum, ruler **07** infanta, monarch **09** potentate, sovereign **11** archduchess **13** crown princess

*Princesses include:*

**02** Di

**03** Ida

**04** Anne
**05** Alice, Diana, Fiona, Grace, Regan
**06** Salome
**07** Eudocia, Eugenie, Goneril, Jezebel, Matilda
**08** Beatrice, Caroline, Cordelia, Margaret
**09** Alexandra, Charlotte, Elizabeth, Stephanie
**10** Pocahontas
**11** Anna Comnena

## principal

**03** key **04** arch, boss, head, main **05** chief, first, major, money, prime, ruler **06** assets, leader, rector **07** capital, central, decuman, highest, leading, manager, primary, supreme, truncal **08** cardinal, director, dominant, especial, foremost, in charge, mistress **09** essential, paramount **10** capital sum, controller, headmaster, pre-eminent **11** controlling, head teacher **12** capital funds, headmistress **13** most important **14** superintendent

## principality

**05** duchy, realm, Wales **06** empire, Monaco, Orange **07** Andorra, dukedom, earldom, kingdom, Muscovy **08** dominion, Walachia **09** archduchy, princedom, sultanate, Wallachia **10** dependency, federation, grand duchy, palatinate, principate **11** archdukedom **12** protectorate **13** confederation, Liechtenstein

## principally

**06** mainly, mostly **07** chiefly **08** above all **09** capitally, in the main, primarily **10** especially **12** particularly **13** predominantly **14** for the most part

## principle

**03** key, law **04** code, germ, idea, root, rule, seed, soul **05** axiom, basis, canon, creed, dogma, geist, maxim, Sakti, tenet, truth **06** dictum, ethics, honour, morals, origin, reason, Shakti, source, spirit, theory, virtue **07** brocard, decency, element, formula, precept, probity, theorem **08** doctrine, morality, rudiment, scruples, standard **09** beginning, component, criterion, essential, headstone, institute, integrity, postulate, rationale, rectitude, standards **10** classicism, conscience, golden rule, groundwork, primordial, principium, seminality **11** fundamental, proposition, uprightness **12** classicalism
• **in principle** **07** ideally **08** in theory **09** in essence **10** en principe **13** theoretically

## principled

**04** just **05** moral **06** decent **07** ethical, upright **08** virtuous **09** righteous **10** high-minded, honourable, scrupulous **11** respectable, right-minded **13** conscientious

## print

**04** copy, etch, font, lith, mark, oleo, snap, type **05** fount, issue, mould, photo, stamp **06** design, record, run off, strike **07** bromide, edition, engrave, impress, imprint, letters, picture, publish, replica **08** aquatint, put to bed, register, snapshot, typeface **09** aquatinta, engraving, facsimile, footprint, lettering, newspaper, oleograph, reproduce, strike off **10** characters, exactitude, impression, lithograph, photograph, typescript **11** fingerprint **12** reproduction
*See also* **painter**
• **in print** **07** in stock **09** available, published **10** obtainable **13** in circulation
• **out of print** **02** op **07** sold out **10** out of stock **11** unavailable **12** off the market, unobtainable

## printer

• **instruction to printer** **04** dele, hash, stet **05** caret

## printing

*Printing methods include:*

**03** CTP
**05** laser, litho
**06** ink-jet, offset, screen
**07** etching, gravure
**08** intaglio
**09** bubble-jet, collotype, engraving
**10** silk-screen, xerography
**11** die-stamping, duplicating, flexography, letterpress, lithography, rotary press, stencilling, twin-etching
**12** lino blocking, thermography
**13** colour-process, electrostatic
**14** photoengraving
**15** computer-to-plate, copper engraving

*Printing and publishing terms include:*

**02** em, en
**03** CTP, TLS, TPS
**04** bulk, case, CMYK, copy, demi, font, kern, laid, logo, sewn, stet, text, tint, trim, type, typo
**05** bleed, caret, chase, cloth, cover, flong, forme, litho, moiré, press, proof, quoin, roman, widow, zinco
**06** galley, gutter, indent, italic, jacket, mackle, margin, matrix, octavo, orphan, Ozalid®, quarto, take in, unsewn, web-fed
**07** bromide, carding, cast-off, compact, compose, dot gain, end even, foiling, leaders, leading, literal, opacity, Pantone®, reprint, strip in, woodcut
**08** bad break, bold face, Linotype®, logotype, misprint, Monotype®, mottling, offprint, spoilage, strike-on, take over, typeface, type spec
**09** backing-up, catchword, condensed, duodecimo, finishing, Intertype®, letterset, lower-case, makeready, newsprint, overprint, run-around, sans serif, signature, trim marks, type scale, upper-case, web offset
**10** back margin, collograph, column inch, compositor, dot-etching,

dustjacket, feathering, first proof, hard hyphen, imposition, impression, large print, manuscript, perfecting, ragged left, see-through, soft hyphen, stereotype, typescript
**11** drum printer, electrotype, initial caps, line printer, ragged right, running head, running text, typesetting, typographer
**12** author's proof, character set, expanded type, flat-bed press, inking roller, machine proof, registration, specimen page
**13** composing room, cylinder press, image printing, justification, printing press, small capitals, wood engraving
**14** relief printing, thermal printer
**15** camera-ready copy

*See also* **typeface**

## printmaker

*see* **painter**

## prior

**05** elder **06** former **07** earlier **08** previous **09** foregoing, preceding **10** antecedent, magistrate
• **prior to** **03** pre **04** till, up to **05** until **06** before **09** preceding **11** earlier than, in advance of

## priority

**04** rank **07** the lead **09** essential, main thing, seniority, supremacy **10** first place, paramouncy, precedence, preference, right of way **11** pre-eminence, requirement, superiority **12** first concern, highest place, pole position, primary issue, top of the tree **13** supreme matter

## priory

**05** abbey **06** friary **07** convent, nunnery **08** cloister, priorate **09** béguinage, monastery **14** religious house

## prise

**03** pry **04** lift, move **05** force, hoist, jemmy, lever, raise, shift **06** winkle **08** dislodge, leverage, purchase

## prison

**03** bin, can, HMP, jug, pen, pit **04** bird, brig, cage, cell, coop, gaol, jail, nick, quad, quod, stir, tank **05** choky, clink, gulag, kitty, limbo **06** bagnio, chokey, cooler, inside, lock-up, lumber **07** bull pen, confine, custody, dungeon, enclose, hoosgow, slammer **08** bastille, big house, hoosegow, porridge, restrain, the hulks, the joint **09** bridewell, calaboose, detention, jailhouse, Lob's pound, massymore **10** guardhouse **11** confinement **12** imprisonment, penitentiary **15** detention centre

*Prisons include:*

**04** Maze
**05** Fleet, Pozzi
**06** Albany, Attica, Folsom
**07** Brixton, Feltham, Newgate
**08** Alcatraz, Bastille, Belmarsh, Dartmoor, Holloway, Long Kesh, Lubyanka, Sing Sing
**09** Fremantle, Parkhurst, the Scrubs

10 San Quentin, Wandsworth
11 Hanoi Hilton, Pentonville, Strangeways
12 Devil's Island, Rikers Island, Robben Island
13 Tower of London
14 Wormwood Scrubs

## prisoner
03 con, lag, POW 05 lifer, trust
06 détenu, inmate, old lag, trusty
07 captive, convict, culprit, détenue, hostage, passman 08 detainee, internee, jailbird, yardbird 10 recidivist
13 prisoner of war, state prisoner

## prissily
06 primly 07 fussily 08 stuffily
09 prudishly

## prissy
04 prim 05 fussy 06 demure, formal, proper, stuffy 07 finicky, po-faced, precise, prudish, starchy 08 priggish
09 squeamish 10 effeminate, fastidious, old-maidish, particular 11 puritanical, strait-laced 13 schoolmarmish

## pristine
04 pure 05 clean, first, fresh 06 former, primal, unused, virgin 07 initial, primary 08 earliest, original, primeval, unspoilt 09 primaeval, primitive, unchanged, undefiled, unspoiled, unsullied, untouched 10 immaculate, primordial 11 primigenial, uncorrupted

## privacy
07 private, privity, retreat, secrecy
08 solitude 09 isolation, quietness, seclusion 10 retirement
11 concealment, privateness
12 independence 13 sequestration
15 confidentiality

## private
03 own, Pte, Pvt 04 swad 05 alone, aside, close, privy, quiet, Tommy
06 closed, closet, gunner, hidden, remote, secret, swaddy 07 postern, privacy, soldier, special, squaddy
08 domestic, familiar, homefelt, hush-hush, intimate, isolated, personal, reserved, retiring, secluded, separate, singular, solitary, squaddie
09 concealed, exclusive, innermost, top secret, withdrawn 10 classified, commercial, free-market, individual, particular, privatized, privileged, unofficial 11 clandestine, enlisted man, independent, introverted, out-of-the-way, sequestered, Tommy Atkins, undisturbed 12 confidential, off the record 13 intraparietal, self-contained, self-governing, single soldier
14 denationalized, free-enterprise, private soldier 15 non-governmental, self-determining
• **in private** 07 sub rosa 08 in camera, in secret, secretly 09 privately 12 in confidence 14 confidentially 15 behind the scenes
• **private detective** see detective

## privateer
06 marque, pirate 07 brigand, corsair, cruiser, sea wolf 09 buccaneer, sea robber 10 filibuster, freebooter

## private eye
see **detective**

## privately
05 aside 06 inside, within 07 at heart, privily, sub rosa 08 deep down, in camera, in secret, inwardly, secretly
09 in private 10 personally, to yourself
12 in confidence, under the rose
13 deep inside you 14 confidentially

## privation
04 lack, loss, need, want 06 misery, penury 07 poverty 08 distress, hardship
09 austerity, indigence, neediness, suffering 10 affliction 11 deprivation, destitution

## privilege
03 due 05 honor, prise, right, title
06 honour, octroi, patent 07 benefit, faculty, freedom, liberty, licence
08 immunity, priority, sanction
09 advantage, authority, commodity, exemption, franchise 10 birthright, concession, seignorage 11 entitlement, prerogative, seigniorage
12 dispensation, status symbol

## privileged
04 rich 05 élite 06 exempt, immune, ruling, secret 07 private, special, wealthy 08 excepted, favoured, honoured, hush-hush, powerful
09 chartered, indulgent, top secret
10 advantaged, authorized, classified, sanctioned, unofficial 12 confidential, off the record

## privy
02 WC 03 bog, can, lav, loo 04 Ajax, kazi 05 dunny, gents', heads, jakes, siege 06 cloaca, closet, ladies', secret, toilet, urinal 07 cottage, crapper, draught, latrine, private 08 familiar, intimate, lavatory, rest room, washroom 09 cloakroom, garderobe
10 powder room, thunderbox 11 water closet 12 draught-house, smallest room
14 comfort station
• **privy to** 04 in on 06 wise to 07 aware of 09 clued up on 10 apprised of, genned up on 11 cognizant of
13 informed about 14 in the know about

## prize
03 aim, cup, lot, pie, top 04 best, gain, goal, gree, hope, loot, love, palm, plum, tern 05 award, booty, great, honor, match, medal, plate, price, purse, stake, value 06 desire, esteem, honour, revere, reward, spoils, stakes, trophy 07 capture, cherish, jackpot, laurels, pennant, perfect, pillage, plunder, premium, seizure, winning
08 accolade, champion, hold dear, leverage, pickings, purchase, smashing, terrific, top-notch, treasure, winnings 09 excellent, first-rate, treasured 10 appreciate 11 outstanding, wooden spoon 12 award-winning, prize-winning 13 think highly of 14 out of this world 15 set great store by
See also **award**

## prize-winner
03 dux 05 champ 06 winner

08 champion, prizeman 09 cup-winner, medallist 10 prizewoman
See also **Nobel Prize**

## pro
03 ace, aye, for 06 expert, master, wizard 07 backing, dab hand, old hand 08 virtuoso 09 authority
10 consultant, in favour of, past master, prostitute, specialist, supporting
12 practitioner, probationary, professional
See also **prostitute**

## probability
04 odds 06 chance 07 chances
08 prospect 10 likelihood, likeliness
11 expectation, possibility

## probable
06 likely, odds-on 07 seeming 08 a fair bet, apparent, credible, expected, feasible, possible 09 plausible
10 believable, forseeable, on the cards
11 anticipated, predictable 12 to be expected

## probably
04 like 05 maybe 06 belike, likely
07 perhaps 08 a fair bet, arguably, possibly 09 doubtless, like as not
10 most likely, presumably 11 as like as not, it looks like 13 as likely as not, the chances are 15 in all likelihood

## probation
04 test 05 proof, trial 07 testing
09 noviciate 10 test period
11 supervision, trial period
14 apprenticeship

## probationer
04 tiro 05 pupil 06 novice, rookie
07 amateur, learner, recruit, student, trainee 08 beginner, neophyte, newcomer, stibbler 09 greenhorn, noviciate 10 apprentice, raw recruit

## probe
04 bore, feel, poke, prod, sift, tent, test
05 check, drill, plumb, sound, study, style 06 device, go into, pierce, search, stilet, stylet, tracer 07 analyse, examine, explore, inquest, inquire, inquiry 08 analysis, look into, research, scrutiny, searcher 09 penetrate
10 instrument, scrutinize
11 examination, exploration, investigate 13 investigation
14 scrutinization

*Space probes include:*

04 Luna
06 Viking
07 Galileo, Mariner, Pioneer, Voyager
09 Messenger
10 Deep Impact
14 Cassini-Huygens

## probity
05 worth 06 equity, honour, virtue
07 honesty, justice 08 fairness, fidelity, goodness, morality 09 integrity, rectitude, sincerity 11 uprightness
12 truthfulness 13 righteousness
14 honourableness 15 trustworthiness

## problem

◊ *anagram indicator* **02** BO **03** fix, sum **04** bore, boyg, drag, hole, knot, mess, pain, pest, prob, snag **05** facer, issue, poser, thing, worry **06** bother, enigma, hassle, indaba, matter, pickle, plight, puzzle, riddle, unruly **07** dilemma, toughie, trouble, wrinkle **08** irritant, nuisance, quandary, question, vexation **09** annoyance, conundrum, dichotomy, difficult, tight spot **10** conclusion, delinquent, difficulty, irritation, mind-bender **11** brainteaser, dire straits, disobedient, predicament, troublesome **12** brain-twister, complication, intransigent, recalcitrant, unmanageable **13** Chinese puzzle, inconvenience, pain in the neck **14** no-win situation, uncontrollable **15** thorn in your side

*See also* **economics; environment**

## problematic

◊ *anagram indicator* **04** hard, moot **06** thorny, tricky **07** awkward, dubious **08** doubtful, involved, puzzling **09** debatable, difficult, enigmatic, intricate, uncertain **10** a minefield, perplexing **11** a can of worms, troublesome **12** questionable **13** problematical

## procedure

**02** op **03** way **04** move, play, step **05** drill, means **06** action, course, custom, fetich, fetish, method, policy, scheme, system **07** conduct, fetiche, formula, measure, process, routine, tactics **08** practice, strategy, technics **09** mechanics, operation, technique **11** advisedness, methodology, performance **12** plan of action **13** modus operandi **14** course of action

## proceed

**02** go, on **03** put **04** come, fand, flow, fond, go on, make, pass, rake, stem, sway, yead, yede, yeed **05** arise, begin, ensue, get on, issue, start, trace **06** come on, derive, follow, happen, move on, pass on, result, spring **07** advance, carry on, emanate, go ahead, press on, prosper **08** continue, progress **09** go forward, originate, prosecute, take steps **10** make a start **11** get under way, make your way, set in motion

• **proceed with difficulty** **04** limp

## proceedings

**04** acta, case, diet **05** deeds, moves, steps, trial **06** action, annals, doings, events, report **07** account, affairs, lawsuit, matters, minutes, process, records, reports **08** archives, business, dealings, measures, ongoings **10** activities, happenings, litigation, manoeuvres, operations, procedures **12** transactions **14** course of action

## proceeds

**04** gain, gout **05** motza, yield **06** avails, income, motser, profit, return **07** produce, profits, returns, revenue, takings **08** earnings, receipts **12** intromission

## process

◊ *anagram indicator* **03** way **04** mode, sort, step **05** alter, edict, means, stage, train, treat **06** action, change, course, growth, handle, manner, method, refine, system **07** advance, changes, convert, prepare **08** attend to, deal with, movement, practice, progress **09** evolution, formation, narrative, operation, procedure, technique, transform **10** proceeding **11** development, progression

• **in the process of** **05** being **11** in the making **13** in preparation, in the course of, in the middle of

## procession

**03** run **04** demo, file, pomp, walk **05** corso, march, train **06** column, course, exequy, parade, series, stream **07** cortège, funeral, pageant, triumph **08** Moharram, Muharram, Muharrem, progress, sequence **09** cavalcade, motorcade **10** succession **11** hunger march **13** demonstration, manifestation

## proclaim

**03** ask, bid, cry **04** ring, show, sing **05** knell, sound **06** affirm, blazon, herald, notify, out-ask, preach, summon **07** declare, enounce, give out, profess, protest, publish, testify, trumpet **08** announce, denounce, indicate **09** advertise, broadcast, circulate, make known, preconize, pronounce, show forth **10** annunciate, annuntiate, apostolize, promulgate **11** blaze abroad

## proclamation

**03** ban **04** oyes, oyez, rule **05** banns, edict, order **06** decree, notice **07** command, kerygma, placard **08** proclaim **09** broadcast, hue and cry, indiction, manifesto, preaching **11** affirmation, circulation, declaration, publication **12** announcement, annunciation, notification, promulgation, proscription **13** advertisement, order of the day, pronouncement **14** pronunciamento

## proclivity

**04** bent, bias **07** leaning **08** penchant, tendency, weakness **09** liability, proneness **10** liableness, propensity **11** disposition, inclination **12** predilection **14** predisposition

## procrastinate

**05** dally, defer, delay, stall **06** put off, retard **07** prolong **08** postpone, protract **09** temporize **10** dilly-dally **11** play for time **12** drag your feet

## procrastination

**08** deferral, delaying, stalling **10** cunctation **11** temporizing **12** dilatoriness **13** dilly-dallying **15** delaying tactics

## procreate

**04** sire **05** beget, breed, spawn **06** father, mother **07** produce **08** conceive, engender, generate, multiply **09** propagate, reproduce

## proctor

**04** prog **08** proggins

## procure

**03** buy, get, win **04** earn, find, gain, hire, hook, pimp, sort **05** ponce **06** come by, hustle, induce, obtain, pander, pick up, secure **07** acquire, provide, solicit **08** purchase **09** get hold of, importune **10** lay hands on **11** appropriate, requisition

## procurer

**04** bawd, hoon, mack, pimp **05** madam, ponce **06** broker, pander **07** hustler **08** fancy man, mackerel, panderer **09** procuress, solicitor **11** fleshmonger, whoremonger

## prod

**03** awl, dig, jab, job **04** brod, butt, goad, move, poke, push, spur, stir, urge **05** egg on, elbow, goose, nudge, prick, probe, punch, shove **06** incite, needle, prompt, skewer, thrust **08** motivate, reminder, stimulus **09** encourage, prompting, stimulate **10** motivation **13** encouragement

## prodigal

**06** lavish, wanton, waster **07** copious, profuse, wastrel **08** profuser, reckless, spendall, unthrift, wasteful **09** bounteous, bountiful, excessive, exuberant, luxuriant, sumptuous, unsparing, unthrifty **10** big spender, immoderate, profligate, squanderer **11** extravagant, improvident, intemperate, spendthrift, squandering

## prodigality

**05** waste **06** excess, plenty, wastry **07** abandon, wastery **08** richness **09** abundance, amplitude, profusion **10** exuberance, lavishness, luxuriance, profligacy, wantonness **11** copiousness, dissipation, squandering **12** extravagance, immoderation, intemperance, recklessness, wastefulness **13** bounteousness, plenteousness, sumptuousness, unthriftiness

## prodigious

**04** huge, vast **05** giant **07** amazing, immense, mammoth, massive, unusual **08** abnormal, colossal, enormous, fabulous, gigantic, striking, terrific **09** fantastic, monstrous, startling, wonderful **10** astounding, gargantuan, impressive, inordinate, marvellous, miraculous, monumental, phenomenal, portentous, remarkable, staggering, stupendous, tremendous **11** exceptional, spectacular **12** immeasurable **13** extraordinary **14** flabbergasting

## prodigiously

**06** vastly **09** amazingly, immensely, massively, unusually **10** remarkably **11** wonderfully **12** astoundingly, impressively, phenomenally, staggeringly **13** exceptionally, fantastically, spectacularly

## prodigy

**05** freak **06** genius, marvel, phenom, rarity, wonder **07** miracle, monster,

## produce

portent **08** moniment, monument, virtuoso, whizz kid **09** curiosity, sensation **10** mastermind, phenomenon, wonderwork, wunderkind **11** child genius, gifted child, phaenomenon, wonder child

## produce

◊ *anagram indicator* **04** bear, crop, eggs, food, give, grow, kind, make, show **05** beget, breed, build, cause, crops, dig up, evoke, fruit, issue, mount, offer, put on, raise, stage, stuff, throw, wheel, yield **06** create, direct, effect, extend, get out, invent, manage, output, put out, supply, upcome **07** advance, arrange, compose, deliver, develop, execute, exhibit, fashion, furnish, harvest, perform, prepare, present, product, proffer, provide, provoke **08** assemble, bring out, engender, generate, increase, knock out, occasion, organize, proceeds, products, put forth, result in **09** construct, fabricate, originate **10** bring about, bring forth, come up with, foodstuffs, give rise to, put forward, vegetables **11** commodities, demonstrate, give birth to, manufacture, put together **12** bring forward **13** dairy products

## producer

**04** hand **05** maker **06** farmer, grower **07** manager **08** director, generant **09** generator, presenter, régisseur **10** impresario, undertaker **12** manufacturer
*See also* **director**

## product

◊ *anagram indicator* **04** item, work **05** fruit, goods, issue, wares, yield **06** effect, legacy, output, result, return, upshot **07** article, outcome, produce, spin-off **08** artefact, creation, offshoot **09** by-product, commodity, invention, offspring, outgrowth **10** end-product, production **11** consequence, merchandise, producement

## production

◊ *anagram indicator* **04** film, play, show, work **05** drama, fruit, opera, revue, yield **06** fruits, making, output, return **07** concert, harvest, musical, returns, staging **08** assembly, building, creation, mounting **09** direction, extension, formation, producing **10** management **11** achievement, composition, development, fabrication, manufacture, origination, performance, preparation **12** construction, organization, presentation, productivity **13** manufacturing

## productive

**04** busy, rich **06** fecund, useful **07** fertile, gainful, teeming **08** creative, fructive, fruitful, pregnant, prolific, valuable, vigorous **09** effective, efficient, energetic, inventive, rewarding **10** beneficial, generative, profitable, worthwhile **11** increaseful, procreative **12** constructive, fructiferous, high-yielding

## productivity

**05** yield **06** output **08** capacity, work rate **10** efficiency, production **12** fruitfulness **14** productiveness

## profanation

**05** abuse **06** misuse **08** violence **09** blasphemy, sacrilege, violation **10** debasement, defilement, perversion **11** desecration **12** dishonouring

## profane

**03** lay **04** foul **05** abuse, crude **06** coarse, debase, defile, filthy, misuse, unholy, vulgar **07** abusive, godless, impious, pervert, pollute, secular, unclean, ungodly, violate, worldly **08** temporal **09** desecrate, misemploy **10** foul-spoken, idolatrous, irreverent, unhallowed **11** blasphemous, contaminate, foul-mouthed, irreligious **12** sacrilegious, unsanctified **13** disrespectful, unconsecrated

## profanity

**04** oath **05** abuse, curse **07** cursing, impiety **08** swearing **09** blasphemy, expletive, obscenity, sacrilege, swear-word **10** execration **11** imprecation, irreverence, malediction, profaneness **14** four-letter word

## profess

**03** own **04** aver, avow **05** admit, claim, state **06** affirm, allege, assert **07** certify, confess, confirm, declare, make out, pretend, purport **08** announce, maintain, proclaim **09** dissemble **10** lay claim to **11** acknowledge

## professed

**06** avowed **07** alleged, would-be **08** apparent, declared, so-called, supposed **09** certified, confirmed, pretended, purported, soi-disant **10** ostensible, proclaimed, self-styled **12** acknowledged **13** self-confessed

## profession

**03** job **04** line, post **05** claim, craft, trade **06** avowal, career, métier, office **07** calling **08** averment, business, position, pretence, vocation **09** admission, assertion, situation, statement, testimony **10** confession, employment, line of work, occupation, walk of life **11** affirmation, appointment, declaration **12** announcement **15** acknowledgement

## professional

**03** ace, pro **04** able **05** adept, buppy, maven, mavin, whizz, yuppy **06** expert, master, wizard, yuppie **07** dab hand, maestro, old hand, regular, skilful, skilled, trained **08** educated, licensed, masterly, virtuoso **09** authority, competent, dexterous, efficient, practised, qualified **10** consultant, past master, proficient, specialist **11** experienced **12** accomplished, businesslike, practitioner **13** knowledgeable

## professor

**02** RP **03** don, STP **04** dean, prof **05** chair, hodja, khoja **06** fellow,

khodja, reader, regent **07** adjoint, provost **08** academic, emeritus, lecturer **09** principal **12** intellectual **13** head of faculty **14** vice chancellor

## proffer

**04** hand **05** offer **06** extend, submit, tender **07** advance, hold out, present, propose, suggest **09** volunteer

## proficiency

**05** knack, skill **06** talent **07** ability, aptness, finesse, mastery **08** aptitude **09** adeptness, dexterity, expertise, technique **10** capability, competence, experience **11** skilfulness **14** accomplishment
• **level of proficiency** **03** dan **05** grade

## proficient

**03** apt **04** able, wise **05** adept **06** clever, expert, gifted, useful **07** capable, skilful, skilled, trained **08** masterly, talented **09** competent, effective, efficient, qualified **10** past master **11** experienced **12** accomplished, passed master

## profile

**02** CV **04** biog, form, line, vita **05** cameo, chart, graph, lines, shape, study **06** figure, purfle, résumé, review, sketch, survey, talweg **07** contour, diagram, drawing, outline, thalweg **08** analysis, half-face, portrait, side view, template, vignette **09** biography, half-cheek **10** silhouette **11** description, examination **15** curriculum vitae, thumbnail sketch
• **high profile** **08** exposure **10** prominence, visibility **12** the limelight, the spotlight **15** public attention
• **keep a low profile** **06** lie low **12** escape notice, hide yourself **14** avoid publicity

## profit

**03** pay, use **04** boot, gain, gelt, perk, vail **05** avail, bonus, bunce, gravy, gross, serve, value, worth, yield **06** excess, income, margin, return **07** benefit, bestead, improve, killing, rake-off, revenue, surplus, takings, vantage **08** dividend, earnings, fast buck, increase, interest, proceeds, receipts, winnings **09** advantage, commodity, make money **10** bottom line, percentage, perquisite, usefulness **11** improvement **13** make megabucks **15** line your pockets, make loadsamoney
• **profit by, profit from** **03** use **04** milk **07** exploit, utilize **08** cash in on **12** capitalize on, put to good use **15** take advantage of, turn to advantage
• **share of profit** **03** lay

## profitable

**03** fat **05** juicy, utile **06** paying, plummy, useful **07** gainful, helpful, payable **08** behovely, economic, fruitful, valuable **09** available, expedient, lucrative, rewarding **10** beneficial, commercial, in the black, productive, successful,

worthwhile **11** moneymaking
**12** advantageous, remunerative
**13** advantageable, cost-effective

**profitably**
**08** usefully, valuably **10** fruitfully
**12** beneficially, commercially,
economically, productively,
successfully

**profiteer**
**06** extort, fleece **07** exploit **09** exploiter,
racketeer **10** overcharge **11** extortioner
**12** extortionist **13** make a fast buck
**14** make a quick buck

**profiteering**
**09** extortion **10** Rachmanism
**12** exploitation, racketeering

**profitless**
**04** idle, vain **06** futile **07** useless
**08** gainless, wasteful **09** fruitless,
pointless, thankless, to no avail,
worthless **10** unavailing **11** ineffective,
ineffectual, to no purpose
**12** unproductive, unprofitable
**14** unremunerative

**profligacy**
**05** waste **06** excess **09** abundance,
depravity, profusion **10** corruption,
debauchery, degeneracy, immorality,
lavishness, wantonness **11** dissipation,
libertinism, prodigality, promiscuity,
squandering, unrestraint
**12** extravagance, improvidence,
recklessness, wastefulness
**13** dissoluteness, unthriftiness
**14** licentiousness

**profligate**
**04** rake, roué **05** loose **06** wanton,
waster, wicked **07** corrupt, Don Juan,
immoral, wastrel **08** defeated,
depraved, prodigal, reckless, wasteful
**09** abandoned, debauched,
debauchee, dissolute, excessive,
libertine, reprobate **10** Corinthian,
degenerate, dissipated, immoderate,
iniquitous, licentious, overthrown,
squanderer **11** extravagant,
improvident, promiscuous, spendthrift,
squandering **12** unprincipled

**profound**
**03** sea **04** deep, wise **05** abyss, great,
ocean **06** marked **07** erudite, extreme,
intense, learned, radical, serious,
sincere, weighty **08** absolute, abstruse,
complete, esoteric, thorough
**09** extensive, heartfelt, recondite,
sagacious **10** deep-seated, discerning,
exhaustive, thoughtful **11** far-reaching,
penetrating **12** impenetrable
**13** philosophical, thoroughgoing

**profoundly**
**04** deep **06** deeply, keenly **07** acutely,
greatly **08** heartily **09** extremely,
intensely, seriously, sincerely
**10** thoroughly

**profundity**
**05** depth **06** acumen, wisdom
**07** insight **08** learning, sagacity,
severity, strength **09** erudition,
extremity, intensity **11** penetration,
perspicuity, seriousness
**12** abstruseness, intelligence,

perspicacity, profoundness
**14** perceptiveness

**profuse**
**04** rich **05** ample **06** lavish **07** copious,
fulsome, liberal **08** abundant, generous
**09** excessive, luxuriant, plentiful,
unsparing **10** immoderate, inordinate,
over the top, unstinting **11** extravagant,
large-handed, overflowing
**12** colliquative, overabundant
**13** superabundant

**profusely**
**08** lavishly **09** copiously, liberally
**10** abundantly **11** unsparingly
**12** immoderately, unstintingly
**13** extravagantly

**profusion**
**04** glut, lots, riot, tons **05** heaps, loads,
waste **06** excess, lavish, plenty, wealth
**07** surplus **08** plethora **09** abundance,
multitude, plenitude **10** profligacy
**11** copiousness, prodigality, superfluity
**12** extravagance **13** unsparingness
**14** superabundance

**progenitor**
**05** stock **06** father, mother, parent,
source, tupuna **07** founder **08** ancestor,
begetter, forebear **09** precursor
**10** antecedent, forefather, forerunner,
instigator, originator, procreator
**11** predecessor **12** primogenitor

**progeny**
**04** burd, race, seed **05** breed, issue,
stock, young **06** family, scions
**07** lineage **08** children, increase,
mokopuna **09** offspring, posterity,
quiverful **10** generation **11** descendants

**prognosis**
**07** outlook, surmise **08** forecast,
prospect **09** diagnosis **10** assessment,
evaluation, prediction, projection
**11** expectation, forecasting,
speculation **15** prognostication

**prognosticate**
**05** augur **06** divine, herald **07** betoken,
portend, predict, presage **08** forebode,
forecast, foretell, indicate, prophesy,
soothsay **09** harbinger **10** foreshadow

**prognostication**
**04** omen **07** surmise **08** forecast,
precurse, prophecy **09** horoscope,
prejudice, prejudize, prognosis
**10** prediction, projection
**11** expectation, speculation

**programme**
**04** book, list, plan, prog, show **05** lay
on **06** agenda, course, design, line up,
line-up, map out, scheme **07** arrange,
episode, itemize, listing, project, work
out **08** calendar, schedule, syllabus
**09** broadcast, formulate, simulcast,
timetable **10** curriculum, prearrange,
production, prospectus
**11** performance **12** plan of action,
presentation, transmission **13** order of
events
*See also* **radio; television**

**programming**
*see* **language**

**progress**
**02** go **03** ren, rin, run, way **04** gain, go
on, grow, sail **05** bloom, going
**06** better, career, come on, course,
growth, mature, thrive **07** advance,
blossom, circuit, develop, headway,
improve, journey, onwards, passage,
proceed, prosper, recover, shape up,
success **08** continue, distance, flourish,
increase, movement, traverse **09** come
along, evolution, go forward,
promotion, upgrading **10** betterment,
forge ahead, periegesis, proceeding,
procession **11** advancement,
development, improvement, make
headway, make strides, make your
way, move forward, progression, step
forward **12** breakthrough,
continuation, make progress, steps
forward **14** be getting there **15** forward
movement
• **in progress** **02** on **06** on foot **07** en
train, going on, in train, on-going
**08** on the way, under way
**09** happening, occurring
**10** continuing, proceeding **11** not
finished, on the stocks **12** not
completed **13** in preparation, in the
pipeline
• **make progress** **04** roll

**progression**
**05** chain, cycle, order, train **06** course,
motion, series, stream, string
**07** advance, headway, passage,
process **08** movement, progress, pub-
crawl, sequence **10** paraphonia,
precession, resolution, succession
**11** advancement, development
**12** direct motion **15** forward movement

**progressive**
**04** left, prog **06** modern **07** creator,
deviser, dynamic, go-ahead, gradual,
growing, liberal, pioneer, radical
**08** advanced, left-wing, reformer
**09** advancing, developer, innovator,
reformist **10** avant-garde, continuing,
developing, escalating, increasing,
innovative, modernizer, originator
**11** enlightened, trailblazer, up-and-
coming **12** accelerating, enterprising,
fresh thinker, intensifying
**13** revolutionary **14** forward-looking
**15** forward-thinking

**progressively**
**07** forward **08** bit by bit, by stages,
forwards, in stages **09** by degrees,
gradually, piecemeal **10** step by step
**12** hand over hand, increasingly
**14** little by little

**prohibit**
**03** ban, bar **04** stop, veto **06** defend,
enjoin, forbid, hamper, hinder,
impede, outlaw **07** exclude, injunct,
prevent, rule out **08** obstruct, preclude,
restrict **09** interdict, proscribe

**prohibited**
**05** taboo **06** banned, barred, vetoed
**07** illegal **08** verboten **09** embargoed,
forbidden, off-limits **10** contraband,
disallowed, proscribed **11** interdicted

**prohibition**
**03** ban, bar **04** tabu, veto **07** embargo,

forbode **08** negation **09** exclusion, forbiddal, interdict **10** constraint, forbidding, injunction, prevention **11** forbiddance, obstruction, restriction **12** disallowance, interdiction, proscription

**prohibitionist**
**03** dry **09** pussyfoot **11** teetotaller **12** abolitionist

**prohibitive**
**05** steep **07** sky-high **09** excessive **10** exorbitant, forbidding, impossible, repressive **11** prohibiting, prohibitory, restraining, restrictive, suppressive **12** extortionate, preposterous, proscriptive

**project**
**03** job, jut **04** cast, hurl, idea, kick, plan, sail, task, work **05** bulge, chuck, fling, gauge, jetty, throw **06** beetle, design, devise, expect, extend, intend, jut out, launch, map out, notion, propel, reckon, reflex, scheme, screen **07** obtrude, predict, propose, venture **08** activity, campaign, contract, estimate, exercise, forecast, outstand, overhang, proposal, protrude, stand out, stick out, workshop **09** calculate, discharge, programme **10** assignment, conception, enterprise, occupation **11** externalize, extrapolate, undertaking **12** predetermine

**projectile**
**04** ball, bomb, shot **05** shell **06** bullet, mortar, rocket, tracer **07** grenade, missile **08** case-shot, fireball **09** ballistic, impelling **13** guided missile

**projecting**
**05** proud **08** beetling, exserted **09** exsertile, extrusive, extrusory, obtrusive, prominent **10** protrudent, protruding, protrusive **11** overhanging, sticking out
• **projecting part 03** arm, ear, fin **04** nose, tang

**projection**
**03** cam, cog, jut, lug, nab, out, rag **04** beak, nose, peak, plan, sail, sill, spur, tusk **05** bulge, ledge, prong, ridge, sally, scrag, shelf, snout, spike, strap, tooth **06** calcar, corner, design, nozzle, outjet, outjut, relief, tongue **07** jutting, process **08** estimate, forecast, overhang, oversail, planning **09** dentation, reckoning **10** estimation, prediction, prominence, promontory **11** calculation, computation, excrescence, expectation, orthography **12** protuberance **13** extrapolation

**proletarian**
**06** common **08** ordinary, plebeian **12** working-class

**proletariat**
**03** mob **04** herd **05** plebs **06** lumpen, masses, proles, rabble **08** canaille, riff-raff **09** commoners, hoi polloi **10** commonalty **11** rank and file, third estate **12** common people, lower classes, working class **13** great unwashed

**proliferate**
**05** breed **06** expand, extend, rocket, spread, thrive **07** build up, burgeon **08** escalate, flourish, increase, multiply, mushroom, snowball **09** intensify, reproduce **11** grow quickly **15** increase rapidly

**proliferation**
**06** spread **07** build-up **08** increase **09** expansion, extension, rocketing **10** escalation **11** duplication, ecblastesis, mushrooming, snowballing **13** concentration, rapid increase **14** multiplication **15** intensification

**prolific**
**04** rank **06** broody, fecund **07** copious, fertile, profuse **08** abundant, fruitful **09** luxuriant, plentiful **10** productive **11** fertilizing **12** reproductive

**prolix**
**04** long **05** prosy, wordy **07** diffuse, lengthy, tedious, verbose **08** rambling, tiresome **09** prolonged, rigmarole **10** digressive, discursive, long-winded, pleonastic, protracted

**prolixity**
**06** length **08** longueur, pleonasm, rambling, verbiage **09** prosiness, verbosity, wandering, wordiness **10** boringness **11** diffuseness, tediousness, verboseness **13** copia verborum **14** discursiveness, long-windedness

**prologue**
**05** index, proem **07** preface, prelude **08** exordium, foreword, preamble **09** introduce, prooemion, prooemium **11** preliminary, prolegomena **12** introduction

**prolong**
**05** delay **06** extend, linger **07** drag out, draw out, respite, spin out, stretch, sustain **08** continue, elongate, lengthen, postpone, prorogue, protract **10** perpetuate, stretch out

**prolongation**
**04** tail **08** appendix, urostyle **09** extension, gonophore **10** androphore, carpophore, stretching, trichogyne **11** lengthening, protraction **12** continuation, perpetuation

**promenade**
**04** pier, prom, turn, walk **05** front, mosey, paseo, strut **06** airing, parade, stroll **07** saunter, swagger, terrace, walkway **08** breather, seafront **09** boulevard, esplanade, polonaise, walkabout **10** sally forth **11** perambulate **14** constitutional

**promethium**
**02** Pm

**prominence**
**03** rib **04** boss, bump, crag, cusp, fame, hump, lump, name, note, rank, rise **05** bulge, cliff, crest, mound, torus **06** height, renown, rising, tragus, weight **07** jutting, mastoid, process, stature **08** eminence, emphasis,

headland, pinnacle, prestige, standing, swelling **09** celebrity, elevation, greatness **10** antitragus, colliculus, embossment, importance, projection, prominency, promontory, protruding, reputation, top billing **11** distinction, pre-eminence **12** pride of place, protuberance **15** conspicuousness, illustriousness
• **into prominence 02** up

**prominent**
**03** top **04** main **05** A-list, chief, noted **06** famous, goggle, marked **07** bulging, eminent, jutting, leading, notable, obvious, popular, salient **08** beetling, foremost, renowned, striking **09** acclaimed, egregious, important, obtrusive, respected, to the fore, well-known **10** celebrated, jutting out, noticeable, pre-eminent, projecting, protrudent, protruding, protrusive **11** conspicuous, eye-catching, high-profile, illustrious, outstanding, protuberant, standing out, sticking out **12** unmistakable **13** distinguished, unmistakeable

**promiscuity**
**06** laxity **09** depravity, looseness **10** debauchery, immorality, profligacy, protervity, wantonness **11** dissipation **13** dissoluteness **14** licentiousness, permissiveness, sleeping around

**promiscuous**
◇ *anagram indicator* **04** fast **05** loose, mixed, slack **06** casual, random, wanton **07** immoral **08** sluttish, swinging **09** abandoned, debauched, dissolute, haphazard **10** accidental, dissipated, licentious, profligate **12** of easy virtue **14** indiscriminate, sleeping around

**promise**
**03** vow **04** avow, bond, hand, hete, hint, oath, sign, word **05** augur, flair, hecht, hight, swear, vouch **06** assure, behote, commit, denote, engage, hint at, pledge, plight, talent **07** ability, behight, betoken, betroth, compact, presage, signify, suggest, warrant **08** aptitude, contract, covenant, evidence, indicate, look like **09** assurance, be a sign of, committal, guarantee, potential, undertake **10** capability, commitment, engagement, indication, suggestion, take an oath **11** expectation, undertaking **12** give your word, word of honour **13** pollicitation **15** give an assurance
• **promised land 04** Zion **06** Canaan, heaven, Utopia **07** Elysium **08** El Dorado, paradise **09** Shangri-la **13** Elysian fields
*See also* **heaven**

**promising**
**04** able, rosy **06** bright, gifted, likely **07** budding, hopeful **08** talented, towardly **09** favorable **10** auspicious, favourable, optimistic, propitious **11** encouraging, up-and-coming

**promissory note**
**02** pn **03** IOU

## promontory

**03** hoe, nab **04** bill, cape, head, mull, naze, ness, spur **05** bluff, cliff, point, ridge **08** eminence, foreland, headland **09** peninsula, precipice **10** projection, prominence

## promote

**03** aid, ren, rin, run **04** back, help, hype, make, plug, push, sell, urge **05** boost, exalt, raise **06** assist, foster, honour, market, move up, peddle, prefer, puff up **07** advance, elevate, endorse, espouse, forward, further, nurture, sponsor, support, upgrade **08** advocate, champion **09** advertise, encourage, publicize, recommend, stimulate **10** aggrandize, popularize **11** merchandize **12** contribute to, kick upstairs

## promoter

**07** pleader, speaker, sponsor **08** advocate, champion, exponent, upholder **09** furtherer, projector, proponent, spokesman, supporter **10** campaigner, evangelist, vindicator **11** spokeswoman **12** spokesperson

## promotion

**02** ad **04** hype, puff, rise **05** promo **06** advert, move-up, payola, remove, urging **07** backing, puffery, pushing, support, venture **08** advocacy, boosting, campaign, espousal, plugging, speeding **09** elevation, fostering, marketing, prelation, publicity, upgrading **10** exaltation, preferment, propaganda **11** advancement, advertising, development, furtherance **12** contribution **13** advertisement, encouragement **14** aggrandizement, recommendation

## prompt

**02** OP **03** cue **04** help, hint, jolt, lead, make, move, prod, spur, urge **05** alert, cause, eager, early, frack, impel, quick, rapid, ready, sharp, swift **06** bang on, dead on, direct, elicit, incite, induce, on time, remind, speedy, spot-on, sudden, timely **07** exactly, inspire, instant, premove, produce, provoke, willing **08** expedite, motivate, occasion, on the dot, promptly, punctual, reminder, result in, stimulus **09** call forth, encourage, immediate, instigate, refresher, stimulate **10** give rise to, pernicious, punctually, responsive **11** expeditious, to the minute **12** unhesitating **13** encouragement, instantaneous

## prompting

**04** hint, urge **06** advice, motion, urging **07** jogging, pushing **08** pressing, pressure, prodding, reminder **09** influence, reminding **10** admonition, assistance, incitement, persuasion, protreptic, suggestion **13** encouragement

## promptly

**03** pdq, tit **04** asap, tite, tyte **05** sharp, tight **06** bang on, dead on, on time, pronto, spot-on, titely, yarely **07** exactly, lightly, quickly, smartly,

swiftly **08** chop-chop, directly, on target, on the dot, speedily **09** forthwith, instantly, like a shot, posthaste, yesterday **10** punctually **11** immediately, to the minute **12** in short order, on the knocker **14** unhesitatingly, without more ado **15** before you know it, pretty damn quick

## promptness

**05** haste, speed **08** alacrity, dispatch **09** alertness, briskness, eagerness, quickness, readiness, swiftness **10** expedition **11** promptitude, punctuality, willingness

## promulgate

**05** issue **06** decree, notify, spread **07** declare, promote, publish **08** announce, proclaim **09** advertise, broadcast, circulate, make known, publicize **10** make public **11** communicate, disseminate

## promulgation

**08** issuance **11** declaration, publication, publicizing **12** announcement, proclamation, promulgating **13** communication, dissemination

## prone

**03** apt **04** bent, flat **05** eager, given, ready **06** homily, liable, likely **07** subject, tending, willing **08** disposed, face down, inclined, proclive **09** prostrate, recumbent, stretched **10** full-length, horizontal, procumbent, vulnerable **11** predisposed, susceptible

## proneness

**04** bent, bias **07** aptness, leaning **08** penchant, tendency, weakness **09** liability **10** proclivity, propensity **11** disposition, inclination **14** susceptibility

## prong

**03** tip **04** fang, fork, spur, tang, tine **05** grain, point, spike, tooth **10** projection

## pronounce

◇ *homophone indicator* **03** say **04** give, pass, vote **05** judge, mouth, sound, speak, utter, voice **06** affirm, assert, decree, stress, tongue **07** bring in, declare, deliver, express **08** announce, proclaim, vocalize **09** enunciate **10** adjudicate, articulate

## pronounceable

**07** sayable, vocable **09** speakable, utterable **10** enunciable **11** articulable, expressible

## pronounced

◇ *homophone indicator* **05** broad, clear, thick **06** marked, strong **07** decided, evident, obvious **08** definite, distinct, positive, striking, terrible **10** noticeable **11** conspicuous **12** unmistakable **13** unmistakeable

## pronouncement

**05** edict **06** decree, dictum **09** assertion, ipse dixit, judgement, manifesto, statement **11** declaration

**12** announcement, notification, proclamation, promulgation **14** pronunciamento

## pronunciation

**06** accent, saying, speech, stress **07** diction, voicing **08** delivery, orthoepy, uttering **09** elocution, phonetics **10** inflection, intonation, modulation **11** enunciation **12** articulation, vocalization

## proof

**02** ap **04** pull, slip, test **05** assay, issue, prief, repro, tight **06** galley, priefe, strong, upshot **07** outcome, proofed, testing, treated, warrant, witness **08** argument, evidence **09** bombproof, fireproof, foolproof, leakproof, probation, rainproof, repellent, resistant, testimony, windproof **10** argumentum, childproof, experience, impervious, smoking gun, soundproof, validation, waterproof **11** attestation, bulletproof, tamperproof **12** confirmation, impenetrable, invulnerable, verification, weatherproof **13** certification, corroboration, demonstration, documentation **14** authentication, substantiation **15** impenetrability, invulnerability
• **adduce as proof** **04** cite

## prop

**03** leg, set **04** lean, post, rest, stay **05** brace, punch, rance, shaft, shore, sprag, staff, stand, stick, stilt, stoop, stoup, strut, stull, truss **06** anchor, brooch, column, crutch, hold up, pillar, steady, tiepin, uphold **07** balance, bolster, bunting, fulcrum, shore up, studdle, support, sustain, upright **08** buttress, mainstay, maintain, property, underpin, underset, upholder **09** bolster up, crippling, propeller, stanchion, supporter **10** underwrite **11** clothespole, point d'appui, proposition **14** flying buttress

## propaganda

**04** hype **08** Agitprop, ballyhoo **09** promotion, publicity **11** advertising, information **12** brainwashing **14** disinformation, indoctrination

## propagandist

**07** plugger **08** advocate, promoter **09** canvasser, proponent, publicist **10** evangelist **11** pamphleteer **12** hot gospeller, proselytizer **13** indoctrinator

## propagandize

**06** preach, uphold **07** promote, win over **08** advocate, argue for, champion, persuade, press for, talk into **09** brainwash, re-educate **10** pressurize **11** campaign for **12** indoctrinate

## propagate

**04** grow, pipe **05** beget, breed, layer, spawn **06** spread **07** diffuse, produce, promote, propage, provine, publish, traduce **08** generate, increase, multiply, proclaim, seminate, transmit **09** broadcast, circulate, procreate, publicize, reproduce **10** distribute,

## propagation

promulgate **11** communicate, disseminate, proliferate

## propagation

**06** spread **08** breeding, increase, spawning **09** diffusion, promotion, spreading **10** generation **11** circulation, procreation **12** distribution, promulgation, reproduction, transmission **13** communication, dissemination, proliferation **14** multiplication

## propel

**02** ca' **03** caa', leg, oar, row **04** loft, move, pole, pump, punt, push, sail, send, swim, waft **05** drive, force, impel, power, scull, shoot, shove, shunt, wheel **06** launch, paddle, thrust **07** project **09** frogmarch **11** push forward

## propeller

**03** fan **04** prop, vane **05** helix, rotor, screw **06** pusher **07** tractor **08** airscrew, thruster **09** tail rotor, tilt-rotor

## propensity

**04** bent, bias **06** foible **07** aptness, leaning **08** penchant, tendency, weakness **09** liability, proneness, readiness **10** proclivity **11** disposition, inclination **14** predisposition, susceptibility

## proper

**01** U **03** ain, due, own **04** prim, real, true, very **05** exact, moral, right **06** actual, comely, decent, dueful, formal, goodly, kosher, polite, seemly, strict **07** correct, dewfull, fitting, genteel, genuine, gradely, precise, prudish, refined **08** accepted, accurate, decorous, graithly, ladylike, orthodox, peculiar, singular, suitable, thorough **09** befitting, out-and-out, shipshape **10** acceptable **11** appropriate, comme il faut, established, exceedingly, gentlemanly, respectable **12** conventional, well-becoming

## properly

**04** duly **05** right **07** exactly, gradely, rightly **08** actually, entirely, graithly, strictly, suitably **09** correctly, extremely, fittingly, precisely **10** acceptably, accurately, flawlessly, unerringly **11** faultlessly, respectably **13** appropriately **14** conventionally
• **properly so called 04** true

## property

**03** fee **04** gear, land, mark, prop **05** acres, fonds, goods, house, means, quirk, trait **06** assets, estate, houses, living, riches, things, wealth **07** capital, clobber, effects, feature, fitness, holding, quality **08** chattels, holdings, premises **09** affection, attribute, buildings, ownership, propriety, resources, substance **10** belongings, real estate **11** appropriate, peculiarity, possessions **12** idiosyncrasy **13** individuality, paraphernalia **14** characteristic

## prophecy

**06** augury **07** message **08** forecast **09** preaching, prognosis **10** divination,

prediction **11** second sight, soothsaying **12** vaticination **14** fortune-telling **15** prognostication

## prophesy

**05** augur **06** preach **07** foresee, predict **08** forecast, foretell, forewarn **10** vaticinate **13** prognosticate

## prophet, prophetess

**04** seer **05** sibyl **06** oracle **07** tipster, völuspa **10** forecaster, foreteller, soothsayer **11** clairvoyant, vaticinator **13** fortune-teller, prophet of doom **14** prognosticator

---

*Prophets and prophetesses include:*

**02** Is
**03** Dan, Hag, Hos, Isa, Jer, Jon, Mic, Nah, Sam
**04** Amos, Ezek, Joel, Obad, Zeph
**05** Hosea, Jonah, Micah, Moses, Nahum
**06** Barton (Elizabeth), Daniel, Elijah, Elisha, Haggai, Isaiah, Nathan, Samuel, St John
**07** Ezekiel, Malachi, Obadiah
**08** Jeremiah, Mohammed, Muhammad, Nehemiah
**09** al-Mokanna, Zephaniah, Zoroaster
**11** Zarathustra
**12** the Nun of Kent
**13** the Maid of Kent
**14** John the Baptist

---

• **prophet of doom 08** doomster, Jeremiah **09** Cassandra, doomsayer, pessimist **11** doomwatcher **12** doom merchant

## prophetic

**03** fey **05** vatic **06** mantic **07** augural, fateful **08** oracular **09** fatidical, oraculous, presaging, prescient, sibylline, vaticidal **10** divinatory, predictive, prognostic **11** apocalyptic, forecasting **13** foreshadowing

## prophylactic

**04** safe **06** condom, rubber, sheath **07** Femidom®, johnnie, scumbag, treacle **09** deterrent **10** inhibitory, precaution, pre-emptive, preventive, protective **11** obstructive **12** anticipatory, female condom, French letter, immunization, preservative, preventative **13** contraceptive, counteractive, precautionary, viper's bugloss

## propinquity

**03** tie **05** blood **07** kinship **08** affinity, nearness, relation, vicinity **09** adjacency, closeness, proximity **10** connection, contiguity **11** affiliation, kindredness, kindredship **12** relationship **13** consanguinity, neighbourhood

## propitiate

**06** pacify, soothe **07** appease, mollify, placate, satisfy **09** reconcile **10** conciliate

## propitiation

**09** atonement, pacifying, placation **11** appeasement, peacemaking **12** conciliation, pacification **13** mollification **14** reconciliation

## propitiatory

**08** soothing **09** appeasing, assuaging, expiatory, pacifying, placative, placatory **10** mollifying **11** peacemaking **12** conciliatory, pacificatory, propitiative **14** reconciliatory

## propitious

**04** rosy **05** happy, lucky **06** benign, bright, kindly, timely **08** friendly, gracious **09** favorable, fortunate, opportune, promising, wholesome **10** auspicious, beneficial, benevolent, favourable, prosperous, reassuring **11** encouraging **12** advantageous, well-disposed

## proponent

**06** backer, friend, patron **08** advocate, champion, defender, exponent, favourer, partisan, proposer, upholder **09** apologist, proposing, supporter **10** enthusiast, propounder, subscriber, vindicator

## proportion

**03** cut **04** bulk, mass, part, size **05** depth, quota, ratio, scale, share, split, whack, width **06** amount, extent, height, length, volume **07** analogy, balance, breadth, measure, portion, segment **08** capacity, division, fraction, graduate, quotient, symmetry **09** magnitude **10** dimensions, percentage **11** temperature **12** distribution, measurements, relationship **14** correspondence, slice of the cake

## proportional

**04** even **08** logistic, relative, relevant **09** analogous, equitable **10** comparable, consistent, equivalent, logistical **12** commensurate **13** corresponding, proportionate

## proportionally

**06** evenly **07** pro rata **10** comparably, relatively **14** commensurately **15** correspondingly, proportionately

## proposal

**03** bid **04** plan **05** offer, terms **06** design, motion, scheme, tender **07** project **08** overture, supposal **09** manifesto, programme **10** resolution, suggestion **11** proposition **12** presentation **14** recommendation

## propose

**03** aim, bid, pop **04** face, mean, moot, move, name, plan, talk, vote **05** offer, place, put up, slate, table **06** design, intend, motion, submit, tender **07** advance, bethink, bring up, imagine, present, proffer, propone, purpose, suggest, suppose **08** advocate, converse, nominate, propound, put forth **09** discourse, enunciate, introduce, recommend **10** ask to marry, have in mind, put forward **14** pop the question **15** plight your troth

## proposition

**03** job **04** pass, plan, prop, task **05** offer **06** accost, come-on, motion, scheme, tender, theory **07** advance, premise,

project, solicit, theorem, venture
**08** activity, approach, disjunct,
overture, proposal **09** alternant,
manifesto, programme, universal
**10** hypothesis, suggestion **11** make a
pass at, subcontrary, undertaking
**14** recommendation

**propound**
**03** put, set **04** move, pose **06** submit
**07** advance, contend, lay down,
present, propone, propose, purpose,
suggest **08** advocate, set forth
**09** postulate **10** put forward

**proprietary**
**03** pty

**proprietor, proprietress**
**04** lord **05** owner **06** patron **07** esquire
**08** landlady, landlord, zemindar
**09** landowner, possessor, publisher
**10** deed holder, freeholder, landholder
**11** leaseholder, proprietrix, title-holder
**12** entrepreneur
*See also* **newspaper**

**propriety**
**05** mense **07** aptness, decency,
decorum, fitness, manners, modesty,
p's and q's, quality **08** breeding,
civility, courtesy, delicacy, elegance,
elegancy, property, protocol, standard
**09** character, etiquette, ownership,
punctilio, rectitude, rightness
**10** bienséance, convention, politeness,
refinement, seemliness **11** correctness,
good manners **12** becomingness,
ladylikeness, social graces,
suitableness, the done thing
**14** respectability, social niceties
**15** appropriateness, gentlemanliness

**propulsion**
**04** push **05** drive, power **06** thrust
**07** impetus, impulse **08** momentum,
pressure, traction **09** impulsion
**10** propelment **11** motive force
**12** driving force

**pro rata**
**06** evenly **10** comparably, relatively
**14** commensurately, proportionally
**15** correspondingly, proportionately

**prosaic**
**03** dry **04** dull, flat, tame **05** banal,
bland, stale, trite, vapid **06** boring
**07** humdrum, mundane, routine,
vacuous **08** everyday, ordinary,
workaday **09** hackneyed
**10** monotonous, pedestrian,
uninspired, unpoetical
**11** commonplace, uninspiring
**12** matter-of-fact **13** unimaginative

**prosaically**
**05** dully **07** blandly **09** mundanely
**10** ordinarily **12** monotonously
**13** uninspiringly **15** unimaginatively

**proscribe**
**03** ban, bar **04** damn, doom **05** black,
exile, expel **06** banish, deport, forbid,
outlaw, reject **07** boycott, censure,
condemn, embargo, exclude
**08** denounce, disallow, prohibit
**09** blackball, interdict, ostracize
**10** expatriate **13** excommunicate

**proscription**
**03** ban, bar **05** exile **07** barring,
boycott, censure, damning, embargo
**08** ejection, eviction, outlawry
**09** exclusion, expulsion, interdict,
ostracism, rejection **10** banishment
**11** deportation, prohibition
**12** condemnation, denunciation,
expatriation, proclamation
**15** excommunication

**prosecute**
**02** do **03** sue, try **05** chase **06** accuse,
charge, indict, pursue, summon
**07** arraign, proceed, process **08** litigate
**10** put on trial **11** take to court **12** bring
charges **13** prefer charges

**prosecution**
**05** trial **08** charging **10** accusation,
indictment, litigation **11** impeachment
**13** taking to court **15** bringing charges

**prosecutor**
**02** DA, PF **06** fiscal **08** quaestor
**10** avvogadore **11** prosecutrix **12** Lord
Advocate **13** judge advocate
**14** advocate-depute

**proselyte**
**07** convert, recruit **08** neophyte **09** new
person **10** catechumen **11** new believer
**13** changed person

**proselytize**
**07** convert, win over **08** persuade
**10** bring to God, evangelize **12** make
converts, propagandize **15** spread the
gospel

**Proserpina**
**10** Persephone

**prosody**

*Prosody terms include:*

**04** foot, iamb
**05** canto, envoy, epode, ictus, Ionic,
metre, paeon
**06** choree, dactyl, dipody, dizain,
laisse, miurus, rondel, sonnet
**07** ballade, caesura, couplet, distich,
elision, pantoum, pyrrhic,
rondeau, Sapphic, spondee,
strophe, triolet, tripody, triseme,
trochee, virelay
**08** anapaest, choriamb, cinquain,
eye rhyme, Pindaric, quatrain,
tribrach, trimeter
**09** anacrusis, assonance, catalexis,
dispondee, ditrochee, free verse,
half-rhyme, hexameter,
macaronic, monometer,
monorhyme, rime riche,
tetrapody
**10** amphibrach, amphimacer, blank
verse, consonance, enjambment,
galliambic, heptameter,
pentameter, rhyme royal,
tetrameter, villanelle
**11** Alcaic verse, alexandrine, broken
rhyme, linked verse, long-
measure, septenarius
**12** alliteration, antibacchius,
Leonine rhyme, Pythian verse,
sprung rhythm
**13** abstract verse, feminine rhyme,
heroic couplet, hypermetrical,
internal rhyme

**14** feminine ending, masculine
rhyme, rime suffisante
**15** feminine caesura, masculine
ending, poulters' measure

**prospect**
**04** face, hope, nose, odds, seek, view
**05** quest, scene, sight, vista, visto
**06** aspect, chance, future, search,
survey **07** chances, examine, explore,
fossick, inspect, look for, lookout,
opening, outlook, promise **08** belle
vue, likeness, panorama **09** landscape,
spectacle, viewpoint **10** likelihood
**11** expectation, opportunity,
perspective, possibility, probability
**12** anticipation

**prospective**
**04** -to-be **06** coming, future, likely
**07** awaited, would-be **08** aspiring,
destined, expected, hoped-for,
imminent, intended, possible,
probable **09** designate, potential
**11** anticipated, approaching,
forthcoming

**prospectus**
**04** list, plan **06** scheme **07** leaflet,
outline **08** brochure, pamphlet,
syllabus, synopsis **09** catalogue,
manifesto, programme **10** conspectus,
literature **11** description
**12** announcement

**prosper**
**04** boom, thee **05** bloom, get on **06** do
well, flower, thrive **07** advance,
blossom, burgeon, proceed, succeed
**08** flourish, get ahead, grow rich,
progress **09** get on well **11** turn out well
**12** be successful, make progress, make
your pile **13** hit the big time, hit the
jackpot **14** go up in the world **15** get on
in the world

**prosperity**
**04** boom, good **06** clover, luxury,
plenty, riches, thrift, wealth **07** fortune,
success, welfare **08** sunshine
**09** affluence, wellbeing **10** bed of
roses, easy street **11** good fortune, lap
of luxury, the good life **14** the life of
Riley
• **spell of prosperity** **02** up **04** boom

**prosperous**
**04** fair, rich **05** blest, lucky, sleek
**06** well in **07** blessed, bonanza,
booming, opulent, thrifty, wealthy,
well-off **08** affluent, blooming, thriving,
well-to-do **09** fortunate **10** burgeoning,
felicitous, successful, well-heeled,
well-to-live **11** flourishing, rolling in it

**prostitute**
**02** ho **03** pro, pug, tom **04** bawd, dell,
drab, moll, punk, road, stew, tart
**05** brass, broad, poule, quail, quiff,
stale, tramp, trull, wench, whore
**06** betray, bulker, callet, debase,
demean, floosy, floozy, geisha, harlot,
hooker, misuse, mutton, plover
**07** cheapen, cocotte, degrade,
devalue, floosie, floozie, hetaera,
hetaira, hostess, hustler, lorette,
pervert, polecat, profane, rent-boy,
trollop, venture **08** bona-roba, call-girl,

dolly-mop, magdalen, misapply, strumpet **09** courtesan, courtezan, hackneyed, hierodule, loose fish, mercenary, sacrifice, sex worker **10** cockatrice, convertite, fancy woman, loose woman, rough trade, vizard-mask **11** fallen woman, fille de joie, laced mutton, night-walker, poule de luxe, public woman, working girl **12** fille des rues, scarlet woman, street-walker **13** grande cocotte **14** lady of the night, woman of the town

**prostitution**
**04** vice **07** the game, whoring **08** harlotry, whoredom **10** social evil **13** street-walking

**prostrate**
**03** sap **04** fell, flat, laid, ruin, tire **05** all-in, crush, drain, level, prone **06** bushed, fallen, lay low, pooped **07** crushed, exhaust, fatigue, flatten, laid low, wear out, whacked, worn out **08** dead beat, flatling, flatlong, helpless, overcome, tired out, trailing **09** exhausted, flatlings, knock down, lying down, lying flat, overthrow, overwhelm, paralysed, pooped out, powerless **10** devastated, horizontal, procumbent **11** defenceless, overwhelmed, tuckered out
• **prostrate yourself 05** kneel **06** cringe, grovel, kowtow, submit **07** bow down **13** abase yourself

**prostration**
**03** bow **05** grief **06** kowtow **07** despair **08** collapse, kneeling, weakness **09** abasement, dejection, obeisance, paralysis, weariness **10** depression, desolation, exhaustion, submission **11** despondency **12** genuflection, helplessness **15** slough of despond

**protactinium**
**02** Pa

**protagonist**
**04** hero, lead **06** banker, leader **07** heroine **08** adherent, advocate, champion, exponent, mainstay **09** principal, proponent, supporter, title role **10** prime mover **12** moving spirit **13** leading figure, leading player, main character **14** chief character, standard-bearer

**protean**
◇ *anagram indicator* **07** amoebic, mutable **08** variable, volatile **09** many-sided, mercurial, multiform, versatile **10** changeable, inconstant **11** polymorphic **12** ever-changing, polymorphous

**protect**
◇ *containment indicator* **04** keep, save **05** cover, guard **06** defend, escort, screen, secure, shield **07** buckler, care for, harbour, shelter, support, warrant **08** bestride, conserve, enshield, keep safe, preserve, savegard **09** look after, ring-fence, safeguard, watch over **10** overshadow, strengthen, take care of

**protected**
**06** immune

**protection**
**03** lee **04** care, egis, ward, wing **05** aegis, bield, cover, guard **06** armour, asylum, buffer, charge, refuge, safety, screen, shield **07** barrier, buckler, bulwark, custody, defence, defense, shelter **08** security, umbrella, wardship **09** insurance, patronage, safeguard **11** concubinage, defensative, maintenance, safekeeping **12** conservation, entrenchment, guardianship, intrenchment, preservation
• **in protection from 04** agin **07** against

**protective**
**04** wary **06** condom **07** careful **08** armoured, covering, fatherly, maternal, motherly, paternal, vigilant, watchful **09** defensive, fireproof, shielding, windproof **10** insulating, possessive, sheltering, waterproof **14** over-protective

**protector**
**03** pad **04** faun **05** guard **06** buffer, father, keeper, minder, patron, regent, screen, shield **07** bolster, buckler, counsel, cushion, gardant **08** advocate, champion, Cromwell, defender, guardant, guardian, pectoral **09** bodyguard, safeguard **10** benefactor, protectrix **11** patron saint, protectress **12** father-figure

**protégé, protégée**
**04** ward **05** pupil **06** charge **07** student **08** disciple, follower **09** dependant, discovery **11** blue-eyed boy **12** blue-eyed girl **14** white-headed boy **15** white-headed girl

**protein**
*Proteins include:*

**03** TSP, TVP
**04** zein
**05** abrin, actin, opsin, prion, renin
**06** avidin, casein, cyclin, enzyme, fibrin, globin, gluten, kinase, lectin, leptin, myosin, papain, pepsin, rennin
**07** albumen, albumin, elastin, gliadin, histone, hordein, insulin, plasmin, sericin, trypsin, tubulin
**08** aleurone, amandine, collagen, cytokine, ferritin, gliadine, globulin, glutelin, integrin, lysozyme, protease, thrombin
**09** apoenzyme, fibrillin, invertase, isomerase, luciferin, myoglobin, myostatin, phaseolin, prolamine, protamine, sclerotin
**10** calmodulin, complement, conchiolin, dystrophin, factor VIII, fibronogen, interferon
**11** angiostatin, angiotensin, haemoglobin, interleukin, lipoprotein, plasminogen, transferrin, tropomyosin
**12** immunoglobin, neurotrophin, proteoglycan
**13** ceruloplasmin, lactoglobulin

**protest**
**03** vow **04** avow, demo, fuss, riot

**05** abhor, argue, demur, gripe, hikoi, march, sit in, sit-in **06** affirm, appeal, assert, attest, avowal, insist, object, obtest, oppose, outcry, picket, reject, squawk, strike, whinge, work-in **07** boycott, contend, declare, dissent, profess, reclaim, scruple, testify **08** announce, complain, demurral, disagree, insist on, maintain, proclaim, speak out **09** assertion, complaint, deprecate, down tools, exception, objection, take issue **10** contention, disapprove, go on strike, opposition, work to rule, work-to-rule **11** affirmation, attestation, declaration, demonstrate, disapproval, kick up a fuss, mass meeting, remonstrate **12** announcement, disagreement, hunger strike, proclamation, protestation, remonstrance **13** demonstration, remonstration, take exception
• **expression of protest 01** O **02** oh **03** say, why **04** come, I say!, what **07** come now **08** come come

**protestation**
**03** vow **04** oath **06** avowal, outcry, pledge **07** dissent, protest **09** assurance, complaint, objection, statement, testimony **10** profession **11** affirmation, declaration **12** asseveration, disagreement, remonstrance **13** expostulation, remonstration

**protester**
**05** rebel **06** picket **07** opposer, striker **08** agitator, mutineer, objector, opponent **09** dissenter, dissident **10** complainer **11** Remonstrant **12** demonstrator

**protocol**
**02** IP **03** FTP, TCP, WAP **04** HTTP, IMAP, kawa, MIDI **05** TCP/IP **06** custom **07** decorum, manners, p's and q's **08** good form **09** etiquette, procedure, propriety **10** civilities, convention **11** formalities **15** code of behaviour

**prototype**
**04** type **05** model **06** mock-up **07** example, pattern **08** exemplar, original, paradigm, standard **09** archetype, precedent

**protract**
**06** extend, linger **07** drag out, draw out, prolong, spin out, sustain **08** continue, lengthen, postpone, protrude **09** keep going **10** make longer, stretch out

**protracted**
**04** long **07** endless, lengthy, spun out **08** drawn-out, extended, livelong, overlong **09** postponed, prolonged **12** interminable, long-drawn-out, stretched out

**protrude**
**03** jut, pop **04** peer, poke, pout **05** bulge, stick, strut **06** beetle, exsert, extend, goggle, jut out, strout **07** extrude, obtrude, poke out, project **08** protract, stand out, stick out **11** come through

## protruding
**05** goofy, proud **06** astrut **07** jutting
**09** exsertive, extrusive, extrusory,
obtrusive, prominent, underhung
**10** jutting out, protrudent, protrusive
**11** protuberant, sticking out

## protrusion
**03** jag, jut **04** bump, knob, lump
**05** bulge **06** hernia **07** pedicle, process
**08** shoulder, swelling **09** obtrusion,
outgrowth **10** projection, staphyloma
**11** cephalocele, eventration,
meningocele **12** exophthalmia,
exophthalmos, exophthalmus,
protuberance **13** encephalocele

## protuberance
**03** bud, nub **04** ball, boss, bulb, bump,
hump, knap, knob, lump, nurl, teat,
wame, wart, welt **05** bulge, caput,
ergot, gemma, inion, knurl, mount,
nodus, tuber, whelk **06** casque, nipple,
paunch, pimple, tumour, venter,
wallet **07** condyle, crankle, mamelon,
mamilla, papilla, process
**08** mammilla, pot-belly, swelling,
tubercle **09** apophysis, beer belly,
outgrowth **10** bulging-out, projection,
prominence, protrusion
**11** excrescence

## protuberant
**04** full **05** proud **06** astrut, rotund
**07** bottled, bulbous, bulging, bunched,
gibbous, jutting, popping, swollen
**08** beetling, swelling **09** exsertive,
extrusive, extrusory, prominent
**10** protrudent, protruding, protrusive

## proud
**04** brag, glad, smug, vain **05** cocky,
dicty, grand, happy, noble, stout
**06** dickty, lordly, snooty, superb,
worthy **07** content, haughty, jutting,
notable, pleased, pompous, stately,
stuck-up, sublime **08** arrogant,
boastful, fearless, glorious, honoured,
imposing, jumped-up, misproud,
pleasing, proudful, puffed up, scornful,
snobbish, splendid, swelling, thrilled,
top-proud **09** bigheaded, cockhorse,
conceited, contented, delighted,
dignified, gratified, hubristic,
imperious, memorable, prominent,
red-letter, satisfied, untamable,
wonderful **10** complacent, gratifying,
high-handed, honourable, jutting out,
marvellous, projecting, satisfying
**11** egotistical, magnificent,
outstanding, overbearing,
overweening, protuberant, sticking
out, toffee-nosed, walking tall **12** high-
spirited, presumptuous, supercilious
**13** high and mighty, self-important,
self-satisfied **14** full of yourself, self-
respecting

## proudly
**04** brag **06** smugly, vainly **08** snootily
**09** haughtily **10** arrogantly, boastfully
**11** bigheadedly, conceitedly,
contentedly, delightedly, with delight
**14** appreciatively

## provable
**08** testable **09** evincible **10** attestable,
verifiable **11** confirmable

**12** corroborable, demonstrable
**13** establishable

## prove
**03** try **04** shew, show, test, trie
**05** argue, check **06** attest, pan out,
prieve, suffer, try out, verify **07** analyse,
bear out, certify, confirm, darrain,
darrayn, deraign, examine, justify,
make out, qualify, stand up, turn out
**08** darraign, darraine, document,
evidence, validate **09** ascertain, be the
case, bring home, come about,
darraigne, determine, establish,
eventuate, transpire **10** experience
**11** corroborate, demonstrate
**12** authenticate, substantiate **13** bear
witness to

## proven
**05** tried, valid **06** proved, tested
**07** checked **08** accepted, attested,
definite, reliable, verified **09** authentic,
certified, confirmed, undoubted
**10** dependable **11** established,
trustworthy **12** corroborated

## provenance
**06** origin, source, spring **10** birthplace,
derivation **11** provenience

## provender
**03** kai **04** chow, eats, fare, feed, food,
grub, nosh, tuck **05** scoff **06** fodder,
forage, stores, tucker, viands
**07** aliment, edibles, pabulum, pasture,
provand, provend, rations **08** eatables,
proviant, supplies, victuals
**09** groceries, repasture **10** foodstuffs,
provisions, sustenance **11** comestibles

## proverb
**03** saw **05** adage, axiom, gnome,
maxim, motto **06** byword, dictum,
saying **07** parable, precept
**08** aphorism, paroemia
**10** apophthegm, whakatauki

## proverbial
**05** famed **06** famous **07** typical
**08** accepted, infamous, renowned
**09** axiomatic, customary, legendary,
notorious, well-known **10** archetypal
**11** traditional **12** acknowledged,
conventional, time-honoured

## provide
◇ *anagram indicator* **02** do **03** add
**04** give, lend, suit **05** allow, besee,
bring, cater, equip, lay on, offer, put
on, serve, state, stock, yield **06** afford,
fit out, impart, kit out, outfit, purvey,
supply **07** compare, furnish, lay down,
plan for, prepare, present, require,
specify **09** stipulate, take steps
**10** anticipate, arrange for, contribute,
prepare for **11** accommodate **12** make
plans for, take measures **13** make
provision **15** take precautions
• **provide for** **04** fend, keep **05** besee,
cover, do for, endow **07** support,
sustain **08** maintain **09** look after
**10** take care of

## provided
**02** so **05** given **06** sobeit **08** as long as,
assuming, so long as **09** presuming
**10** in the event **11** on condition **14** with
the proviso

## providence
**04** care, fate, luck **06** thrift, wisdom
**07** caution, destiny, economy, fortune
**08** disaster, God's will, prudence,
sagacity **09** foresight, judgement
**11** forethought **13** judiciousness
**14** circumspection, far-sightedness

## provident
**06** frugal **07** careful, prudent, thrifty
**08** cautious **09** judicious, sagacious
**10** economical, far-sighted
**11** circumspect

## providential
**05** happy, lucky **06** timely **07** welcome
**09** fortunate, opportune **10** convenient,
fortuitous, heaven-sent

## providentially
**07** happily, luckily **11** fortunately,
opportunely **12** conveniently,
fortuitously

## provider
**05** angel, donor, giver **06** earner,
funder, patron, source **07** sponsor
**08** mainstay, supplier **09** supporter
**10** benefactor, wage-earner
**11** breadwinner

## providing
**02** if **05** given **08** as long as, assuming,
provided **09** presuming **10** in the event
**11** on condition **14** with the proviso

## province
**04** area, dorp, duty, line, nome, role,
zone **05** field, realm, reame, shire, state
**06** charge, circar, colony, county,
domain, office, pigeon, region, sircar,
sirkar, sphere **07** concern, eparchy,
mudiria, rectory, satrapy, vilayet
**08** business, district, function,
mudirieh **09** backwater, backwoods,
eparchate, territory, the sticks
**10** department, dependency, the
boonies **12** patriarchate, the
boondocks **14** responsibility **15** middle
of nowhere

*Canadian provinces and territories:*

**05** Yukon
**06** Quebec
**07** Alberta, Nunavut, Ontario
**08** Labrador, Manitoba
**10** Nova Scotia
**12** New Brunswick, Newfoundland,
Saskatchewan
**14** Yukon Territory
**15** British Columbia
**18** Prince Edward Island
**20** Northwest Territories
**23** Newfoundland and Labrador

*Ireland's ancient provinces:*

**06** Ulster
**07** Munster
**08** Connacht, Leinster

*New Zealand provinces:*

**05** Otago
**06** Nelson
**08** Auckland, Taranaki, Westland
**09** Fiordland, Hawke's Bay,
Northland, Southland
**10** Canterbury, Wellington
**11** Marlborough

*South African provinces:*

07 Gauteng, Limpopo
09 Free State, North West
10 Mpumalanga
11 Eastern Cape, Western Cape
12 KwaZulu-Natal, Northern Cape

**provincial**
04 hick 05 local, naive, rural, yokel
06 narrow, rustic 07 country, hayseed,
insular, limited, peasant 08 mofussil,
outlying, regional, suburban
09 hillbilly, home-grown, parochial,
presidial, small-town 10 intolerant,
parish-pump, unpolished 11 small-
minded 12 narrow-minded 13 inward-
looking 14 country bumpkin
15 unsophisticated

**provincialism**
08 localism 10 insularity, Patavinity
11 regionalism 12 parochialism,
sectionalism 13 provinciality

**provision**
04 food, plan, step, term 05 rider,
stock, store, stuff 06 clause, giving,
stocks, stores, supply, viands
07 measure, proviso, rations, service
08 eatables, services, supplies, victuals
09 allowance, amenities, condition,
equipping, foodstuff, groceries,
resources, stouthrie 10 concession,
facilities, furnishing, outfitting,
precaution, stoutherie, sustenance
11 arrangement, contingency,
preparation, requirement, stipulation
12 contribution 13 qualification,
specification

**provisional**
05 Provo 06 pro tem 07 interim,
stopgap 09 makeshift, temporary,
tentative 11 conditional, pencilled in
12 transitional

**provisionally**
06 pro tem 07 interim 09 meanwhile
11 temporarily, tentatively 15 for the
time being

**proviso**
04 term 05 rider 06 clause 07 strings
09 condition, provision 10 limitation
11 requirement, reservation,
restriction, stipulation 13 qualification

**provocation**
04 dare 05 cause, taunt 06 injury,
insult, motive, reason, red rag
07 affront, grounds, offence
08 angering, enraging, stimulus,
vexation 09 annoyance, challenge,
eliciting, grievance 10 generation,
incitement, inducement, irritation,
motivation, production 11 aggravation,
inspiration, instigation, stimulation
12 exasperation 13 justification

**provocative**
04 sexy 05 tarty 06 erotic 07 abusive,
galling, piquant, teasing 08 alluring,
annoying, arousing, exciting, inviting,
tempting 09 insulting, in-yer-face,
offensive, seductive 10 in-your-face,
irritating, outrageous, suggestive
11 aggravating, challenging,

infuriating, stimulating, tantalizing,
titillating 12 exasperating

**provocatively**
06 sexily 08 sexually 10 alluringly,
annoyingly, erotically, invitingly,
temptingly 11 offensively, seductively
12 outrageously, suggestively
13 infuriatingly 14 exasperatingly

**provoke**
03 bug, vex 04 goad, miff, move, nark,
prod, rile, spur, stir 05 anger, annoy,
cause, egg on, evoke, get at, pique,
rouse, sound, taunt, tease 06 appeal,
elicit, enrage, entice, excite, harass,
hassle, incite, induce, insult, kindle,
madden, needle, nettle, offend,
prompt, summon, wind up 07 incense,
inflame, inspire, produce, promote
08 drive mad, engender, generate,
irritate, motivate, occasion
09 aggravate, call forth, challenge,
infuriate, instigate, stimulate, tantalize
10 drive crazy, exacerbate, exasperate,
give rise to 12 drive bananas 13 make
sparks fly 14 drive up the wall

**provoking**
06 irking, vexing 07 agaçant, galling,
irksome 08 agaçante, annoying,
tiresome 09 maddening, offensive,
vexatious 10 irritating 11 aggravating,
infuriating, obstructive, stimulating
12 exasperating

**prow**
03 bow 04 bows, fore, head, nose,
ship, stem 05 front, prore 07 valiant
08 cut-water, forepart

**prowess**
04 grit, guts 05 nerve, pluck, skill,
spunk 06 bottle, daring, genius, talent,
valour 07 ability, bravery, command,
courage, heroism, mastery 08 aptitude,
audacity, facility 09 adeptness,
dexterity, expertise, gallantry,
vassalage 10 adroitness, attainment,
capability 11 intrepidity, proficiency,
skilfulness 12 fearlessness
13 dauntlessness 14 accomplishment

**prowl**
04 hunt, lurk, nose, roam, rove
05 creep, lurch, mouse, prole, proll,
proul, range, ratch, skulk, sneak,
snoke, snook, snoop, snowk, stalk,
steal 06 cruise, patrol, search
08 scavenge 14 move stealthily

**prowler**
06 patrol, proler, roamer 07 proller,
prouler, stalker 08 tenebrio
09 nighthawk, scavenger

**proximity**
08 nearness, vicinity 09 adjacency,
closeness 10 contiguity 11 propinquity
13 juxtaposition, neighbourhood

**proxy**
05 agent 06 deputy, factor 07 stand-in
08 attorney, delegate 09 surrogate
10 substitute 14 representative
• **by proxy** 02 pp

**prude**
04 prig 06 wowser 07 old maid, puritan

09 Mrs Grundy 10 goody-goody,
schoolmarm

**prudence**
04 care 05 Metis 06 policy, saving,
thrift, wisdom 07 caution, economy
08 planning, sagacity, wariness
09 canniness, foresight, frugality, good
sense, husbandry, judgement,
vigilance 10 discretion, precaution,
providence 11 advisedness, common
sense, forethought, happy medium,
heedfulness, penny-wisdom
12 cautiousness, preparedness
13 judiciousness 14 circumspection,
far-sightedness 15 circumspectness

**prudent**
04 ware, wary, wise 06 frugal, shrewd
07 careful, politic, thrifty 08 cautious,
discreet, sensible, vigilant
09 judicious, provident, sagacious
10 discerning, economical, far-sighted
11 circumspect, ware and wise, well-
advised, wise-hearted 13 considerative

**prudently**
06 warily, wisely 08 sensibly, shrewdly
09 advisedly, carefully 10 discreetly,
vigilantly 11 providently
12 economically, far-sightedly

**prudery**
08 primness 09 Grundyism
10 prissiness, puritanism, strictness,
stuffiness 11 overmodesty, starchiness
12 priggishness 13 squeamishness
14 old-maidishness

**prudish**
04 prim 05 mimsy 06 demure, mimsey,
prissy, proper, stuffy 07 po-faced,
starchy 08 overnice, priggish,
pudibund 09 squeamish, Victorian,
wowserish 10 goody-goody, old-
maidish, overmodest 11 puritanical,
strait-laced 12 narrow-minded
13 schoolmarmish, ultra-virtuous

**prune**
03 cut, lop 04 clip, dock, pare, plum,
sned, snip, spur, trim 05 preen, proin,
proyn, shape, shred 06 cut off, dehorn,
prewyn, proign, proine, proyne,
pruine, reduce, reform, switch 07 cut
back, shorten 08 prunello 10 French
plum

**prurient**
04 blue, lewd 05 dirty 06 erotic, smutty
07 itching, lustful, obscene 08 desirous,
indecent 09 lecherous, salacious
10 cupidinous, lascivious, libidinous
11 voyeuristic 12 concupiscent,
pornographic

**pry**
03 dig 04 nose, peep, peer, poke, toot
05 delve, prise, snoop 06 ferret, meddle
07 gumshoe, intrude 08 prodnose
09 interfere 10 stickybeak 12 put your
oar in 14 poke your nose in 15 stick
your nose in

**prying**
04 nosy 05 nosey, peery 06 snoopy,
spying 07 curious, peering
08 meddling, snooping 09 intrusive
10 meddlesome 11 inquisitive,
interfering

## psalm

02 Ps 03 Psa 04 hymn, poem, song
05 chant, paean, tract 06 choral,
prayer, proper, venite 07 cantate,
chorale, introit, tractus 08 canticle,
Jubilate, Miserere 09 neckverse
10 paraphrase

## psalm tune

04 tone

## pseud

04 sham 05 false, fraud, poser
06 humbug, phoney, poseur, trendy
11 pretentious

## pseudo

04 fake, mock, sham 05 bogus, false,
pseud, quasi- 06 ersatz, phoney
08 spurious 09 imitation, pretended,
ungenuine 10 artificial 11 counterfeit,
pretentious

## pseudonym

05 alias 06 anonym 07 allonym, pen-
name 09 false name, incognito, stage
name 10 nom de plume 11 assumed
name, nom de guerre

*Pseudonyms include:*

03 Day (Doris), Pop (Iggy), Tey
(Josephine)
04 Alda (Alan), Bell (Acton), Bell
(Currer), Bell (Ellis), Cage (Nicolas),
Dors (Diana), Ford (Ford Madox),
Gish (Lillian), Hite (Shere), Holm
(Sir Ian), John (Sir Elton), Lulu,
Lynn (Dame Vera), Piaf (Edith),
Reed (Lou), Rhys (Jean), Ross
(Diana), Saki, Sand (George), West
(Nathanael), West (Dame
Rebecca), Wood (Natalie), York
(Susannah)
05 Allen (Woody), Bizet (Georges),
Black (Cilla), Bowie (David), Caine
(Sir Michael), Clark (Petula), Cline
(Patsy), Dylan (Bob), Eliot (George),
Flynn (Errol), Garbo (Greta), Gorky
(Maxim), Grant (Cary), Grant
(Richard E), Hardy (Oliver), Henry
(O), Holly (Buddy), Jason (David),
Keith (Penelope), Lanza (Mario),
Leigh (Vivien), Loren (Sophia),
Moore (Demi), Moore (Julianne),
Niven (David), Queen (Ellery),
Ryder (Winona), Scott (Ronnie),
Seuss (Dr), Smith (Stevie), Solti (Sir
Georg), Stern (Daniel), Sting,
Stone (Sly), Twain (Mark), Wayne
(John), Welch (Raquel)
06 Bacall (Lauren), Bardot (Brigitte),
Berlin (Irving), Brooks (Mel),
Burton (Richard), Conrad (Joseph),
Crosby (Bing), Curtis (Tony), Fields
(Dame Gracie), Foster (Jodie),
France (Anatole), Gibbon (Lewis
Grassic), Harlow (Jean), Heston
(Charlton), Irving (Sir Henry),
Jolson (Al), Keaton (Diane), Laurel
(Stan), London (Jack), Lugosi
(Bela), McBain (Ed), Mirren (Dame
Helen), Monroe (Marilyn), Morton
(Jelly Roll), Neeson (Liam), Orwell
(George), Peters (Ellis), Rogers
(Ginger), Salten (Felix), Sapper,
Scales (Prunella), Simone (Nina),
Spacey (Kevin), Steele (Tommy),

Turner (Lana), Turner (Tina),
Waters (Muddy), Weldon (Fay),
Wesley (Mary), Wonder (Stevie)
07 Andrews (Dame Julie), Bachman
(Richard), Bennett (Tony), Bogarde
(Sir Dirk), Bronson (Charles),
Carroll (Lewis), Deneuve
(Catherine), Diddley (Bo), Dinesen
(Isak), Douglas (Kirk), Gardner
(Ava), Garland (Judy), Hepburn
(Audrey), Higgins (Jack), Holiday
(Billie), Jacques (Hattie), Karloff
(Boris), Kincaid (Jamaica), Le Carré
(John), Lindsay (Robert), Lombard
(Carole), Matthau (Walter), Mercury
(Freddie), Michael (George),
Miranda (Carmen), Molière,
Montand (Yves), Novello (Ivor),
Richard (Sir Cliff), Robbins
(Harold), Russell (Lillian), Shepard
(Sam), Swanson (Gloria),
Wyndham (John), Wynette (Tammy)
08 Bancroft (Anne), Coltrane (Robbie),
Coolidge (Susan), Costello (Elvis),
Crawford (Joan), Dietrich
(Marlene), Gershwin (George),
Gershwin (Ira), Goldberg (Whoopi),
Hayworth (Rita), Kingsley (Sir Ben),
MacLaine (Shirley), Ma Rainey,
Pickford (Mary), Robinson (Edward
G), Stanwyck (Barbara), Stoppard
(Tom), Voltaire, Williams
(Tennessee)
09 Bernhardt (Sarah), Charteris
(Leslie), Fairbanks (Douglas),
Lancaster (Burt), Leadbelly,
Offenbach (Jacques), Streisand
(Barbra), Valentino (Rudolph)
10 Howlin' Wolf, Washington (Dinah),
Westmacott (Mary)
11 Springfield (Dusty)

## pshaw

03 och

## psych

• **psych out** 03 cow 05 alarm, appal,
bully, daunt, get to, scare, throw, upset
06 coerce, compel, dismay, lean on,
menace, rattle 07 overawe, terrify,
warn off 08 browbeat, bulldoze,
domineer, frighten, pressure, unsettle
09 terrorize, tyrannize 10 intimidate,
pressurize 13 put off balance, turn the
heat on 14 put the screws on
• **psych yourself up** 13 brace
yourself, nerve yourself, steel yourself
14 gear yourself up, pluck up courage,
work yourself up

## psyche

03 ego 04 mind, self, soul 05 anima
06 pneuma, spirit 08 superego
09 awareness, inner self, intellect
10 inmost self 11 personality
12 intelligence, subconscious
13 consciousness, heart of hearts,
individuality, innermost self,
understanding 15 deepest feelings

## psychiatrist

06 shrink 07 analyst 08 alienist
09 therapist 10 head doctor, psychiater
12 headshrinker, psychologist, trick
cyclist 13 psychoanalyst

14 psychoanalyser 15 man in a white
coat, psychotherapist

*Psychiatrists and psychoanalysts
include:*

04 Beck (Aaron), Jung (Carl), Rank
(Otto)
05 Adler (Alfred), Clare (Anthony),
Freud (Anna), Freud (Sigmund),
Fromm (Erich), Jones (Ernest),
Klein (Melanie), Lacan (Jacques),
Laing (Ronald David), Meyer
(Adolf), Reich (Wilhelm), Szasz
(Thomas)
06 Berger (Hans), Bowlby (John),
Hitzig (Julius), Snyder (Solomon)
07 Bleuler (Eugen), Erikson (Erik),
Persaud (Raj)
08 Maudsley (Henry), Sullivan (Harry
Stack), Wernicke (Carl)
09 Alexander (Franz), Alzheimer
(Alois), Kraepelin (Emil), Menninger
(Karl), Rorschach (Hermann)
11 Krafft-Ebing (Richard, von)
13 Wagner-Jauregg (Julius)

*See also* **psychology**

## psychic

04 seer 05 augur 06 medium, mental,
mystic, occult, oracle 07 diviner,
prophet 08 mystical, telepath
09 cognitive, emotional, spiritual,
visionary 10 mind-reader, prophetess,
soothsayer, telepathic 11 clairvoyant,
telekinetic 12 extrasensory,
intellectual, supernatural 13 fortune-
teller, psychological 14 spiritualistic

## psychoanalyst

*see* **psychiatrist**

## psychological

06 mental, unreal 08 cerebral
09 cognitive, emotional, imaginary
10 conceptual, irrational, subjective
11 theoretical, unconscious 12 all in
the mind, intellectual, subconscious
13 psychosomatic

## psychologically

08 mentally 11 cognitively,
emotionally 12 conceptually,
subjectively 13 theoretically,
unconsciously 14 intellectually

## psychology

04 mind 06 habits, make-up
07 mindset, motives 08 conation,
hedonics, psychics 09 attitudes
10 child-study, gestaltism
12 pneumatology 14 metapsychology,
study of the mind 15 mental chemistry

*Branches of psychology include:*

03 bio
04 para
05 child, depth, neuro, sport
06 health, social
08 abnormal, clinical, criminal,
forensic, hedonics
09 cognitive, narrative
10 industrial, structural
11 educational
12 evolutionary, experimental,
occupational
13 developmental, environmental,
psychobiology,

psychometrics, transpersonal
**14** organizational, psychoanalysis
**15** psychopathology

*Psychology theories include:*

**07** atomism, Gestalt, Jungian
**08** Adlerian, Freudian, Jamesian, Lacanian
**09** cognitive, Pavlovian
**10** functional, humanistic, Skinnerian, structural
**11** behavioural, personality
**13** connectionism, functionalism, structuralism
**14** associationism, psychoanalytic

*Psychological conditions and disorders include:*

**06** autism, manias
**07** agnosia, bulimia, phobias
**08** dementia, neurosis, paranoia
**09** addiction, anhedonia, Asperger's, psychosis, Tourette's
**10** abreaction, Alzheimer's, blindsight, depression, dysmorphia, Munchausen, sociopathy
**11** kleptomania, psychopathy
**12** hypochondria
**13** acatamathesia, battle fatigue, schizophrenia
**15** anorexia nervosa, bipolar disorder

*Psychological therapies include:*

**03** art
**05** drama, group, hypno
**06** colour, psycho
**07** Gestalt
**08** aversion
**09** cognitive
**10** regression
**11** behavioural, counselling
**12** electroshock
**13** interpersonal, person-centred, psychodynamic

*Psychologists include:*

**04 Bain** (Alexander)
**05 Binet** (Alfred), **James** (William), **Pratt** (Joseph Gaither), **Rhine** (Joseph Banks)
**06 De Bono** (Edward), **Kinsey** (Alfred Charles), **Morris** (Robert Lyle), **Murphy** (Gardner), **Piaget** (Jean), **Pinker** (Steven), **Terman** (Lewis Madison)
**07 Cattell** (Raymond Bernard), **Eysenck** (Hans Jürgen), **Skinner** (Burrhus Frederic)
**09 Thorndike** (Edward Lee)
**10 Wertheimer** (Max)

*See also* **psychiatrist**

## psychopath
**06** madman, maniac, psycho
**07** lunatic **08** madwoman **09** mad person, psychotic, sociopath

## psychopathic
**03** mad **06** insane, psycho **07** lunatic
**08** demented, deranged, maniacal
**09** psychotic **10** unbalanced

## psychosomatic
**06** unreal **09** imaginary **10** irrational, subjective **12** all in the mind
**13** psychological

## psychotic
**03** fey **04** bats, gyte, loco, nuts, wild
**05** barmy, batty, buggy, crazy, daffy, dippy, dotty, flaky, gonzo, loony, loopy, manic, nutty, potty, queer, wacko, wacky, wiggy **06** crazed, cuckoo, fruity, insane, maniac, mental, raving, red-mad, screwy
**07** bananas, barking, berserk, bonkers, cracked, frantic, lunatic, meshuga
**08** crackers, demented, deranged, dingbats, doolally, frenetic, frenzied, maniacal, unhinged, unstable
**09** disturbed, lymphatic, up the wall
**10** bestraught, distracted, distraught, frantic-mad, off the wall, off your nut, out to lunch, stone-crazy, unbalanced
**11** not all there, off the rails, off your head **12** mad as a hatter, off your chump, round the bend **13** off your rocker, of unsound mind, out of your head, out of your mind, out of your tree, round the twist **14** off your trolley, wrong in the head **15** non compos mentis, out of your senses

## ptarmigan
**04** rype

## pub
*see* **public house**

## puberty
**05** teens, youth **08** maturity **09** growing up **10** pubescence **11** adolescence
**12** teenage years **14** young adulthood

## public
**03** out **04** fans, open **05** civic, civil, crowd, known, overt, plain, state
**06** buyers, common, famous, masses, nation, people, social, tavern, voters
**07** country, eminent, exposed, federal, general, obvious, patrons, popular, society **08** audience, citizens, communal, everyone, national, official, populace **09** available, clientèle, community, consumers, customers, followers, important, multitude, prominent, published, respected, universal, well-known
**10** accessible, celebrated, collective, electorate, government, population, recognized, spectators, supporters, widespread **11** illustrious, influential, unconcealed **12** acknowledged, nationalized, unrestricted
**13** international
• **in public 06** openly **08** publicly **09** in the open **10** in full view **11** for all to see

## publican
**04** host **06** barman **07** barmaid, tapster
**08** hotelier, landlady, landlord, mine host, taverner **09** barperson, bartender, innkeeper, tax farmer **11** hotel-keeper
**12** saloon-keeper, tax collector

## publication
**04** blog, book, buik, buke **05** daily, forum, issue, title **06** serial, volume, weekly **07** booklet, fanzine, journal, leaflet, monthly, podcast, release
**08** brochure, handbill, hardback,

magazine, pamphlet, printing
**09** newspaper, paperback, quarterly, reporting **10** disclosure, half-yearly, newsletter, periodical, production, publishing **11** circulation, declaration, festschrift **12** announcement, broadcasting, distribution, notification, proclamation
• **prepare for publication 04** edit

## public house
**02** PH **03** bar, inn, pub **04** houf, howf
**05** grill, hotel, houff, house, howff, local, table **06** boozer, lounge, saloon, shanty, tavern **07** brewpub, canteen, counter, potshop, shebeen, taproom, wine bar **08** ale house, bona fide, groggery, hostelry **09** brasserie, free house, gin palace, jerry-shop, lounge bar, lush-house **12** watering-hole

*Public house names include:*

**04** Bell, Bull, Ship, Swan
**05** Crown, Globe
**06** Anchor, Castle, George, New Inn, Plough
**07** Railway, Red Lion
**08** Green Man, Nags Head, Royal Oak, Victoria
**09** Black Bull, Cross Keys, King's Arms, King's Head, White Hart, White Lion, White Swan
**10** Black Horse, Golden Lion, Queen's Head, Wheatsheaf, White Horse
**12** Fox and Hounds, Rose and Crown
**13** Hare and Hounds, Prince of Wales
**14** Coach and Horses
**15** George and Dragon

## publicity
**03** air **04** hype, plug, puff **05** boost
**06** splash **07** acclaim, build-up, réclame **08** ballyhoo **09** attention, limelight, marketing, notoriety, promotion **10** propaganda
**11** advertising
• **publicity agent 02** PA

## publicize
**04** hype, plug, push **05** blaze **06** market
**07** promote **08** announce, headline
**09** advertise, broadcast, make known, spotlight **10** make public, promulgate
**11** disseminate

## public-spirited
**08** generous **09** unselfish **10** altruistic, charitable **12** humanitarian
**13** conscientious, philanthropic
**15** community-minded

## public transport
*see* **transport**

## publish
**03** run **04** vent **05** carry, issue, print, sound **06** delate, import, notice, notify, pirate, poster, put out, report, reveal, spread **07** declare, diffuse, divulge, gazette, placard, produce, release
**08** announce, bring out, disclose, evulgate, proclaim, put about, put forth, set forth **09** advertise, broadcast, celebrate, circulate, divulgate, fulminate, give forth, make known,

paperback, paragraph, publicize, serialize, syndicate **10** distribute, make public, promulgate **11** communicate, disseminate

*See also* **printing**

*Publishers and imprints include:*

**02** DK
**03** CUP, OUP, Pan
**04** Reed
**05** Corgi, Letts, Orion
**06** Europa, Puffin, Viking, Virago
**07** Berlitz, Cassell, Collins, Longman, Merriam, Methuen, Pearson, Penguin, Picador, Pimlico, Usborne
**08** BBC Books, Chambers, Everyman, Flamingo, Gollancz, Ladybird, Larousse, Michelin, Palgrave
**09** Allen Lane, Black Swan, Blackwell, Doubleday, Harlequin, Heinemann, Macmillan, Routledge
**10** A and C Black, Bloomsbury, Bodley Head, Hutchinson, McGraw-Hill, Paul Hamlyn, Scholastic, Times Books, Transworld
**11** Bantam Press, Bertelsmann, Fodor Guides, Rand McNally, Random House, Rough Guides
**12** André Deutsch, Butterworths, Edward Arnold, Fourth Estate, Jonathan Cape, Lonely Planet, Mills and Boon, Penguin Books, Reed Elsevier
**13** Allen and Unwin, AOL/Time Warner, Atlantic Books, Faber and Faber, Hachette Livre, HarperCollins, Reader's Digest
**14** Canongate Books, Chambers Harrap, Chrysalis Books, Hodder Headline, Springer-Verlag
**15** Chatto and Windus, Houghton Mifflin, Mitchell Beazley, Sweet and Maxwell, Thames and Hudson

**pucker**
**04** fold, ruck, shir **05** pleat, purse, shirr **06** cockle, crease, furrow, gather, ruckle, ruffle **07** crinkle, crumple, screw up, shrivel, wrinkle **08** compress, contract **09** agitation, confusion **11** corrugation

**puckered**
**05** pursy **06** plissé, rucked **07** bullate, creased, ruckled **08** gathered, wrinkled

**puckering**
**04** shir **05** shirr

**puckish**
**03** sly **06** impish **07** naughty, playful, roguish, teasing, waggish **08** sportive **09** whimsical **10** frolicsome **11** mischievous

**pudding**
**03** pie, pud **04** tart **05** sweet **06** afters, pastry **07** dessert
*See also* **cake; dessert**

**puddle**
**03** dub, sop **04** pant, pool, slop, soss,

sump **05** flush, plash, plesh **06** muddle **07** muddler, plashet

**puddock**
**04** frog, toad

**puerile**
**05** inane, silly **07** babyish, foolish, trivial **08** childish, immature, juvenile, trifling **09** infantile **10** adolescent **13** irresponsible

**Puerto Rico**
**03** PRI

**puff**
**02** ad **04** blow, drag, draw, fuff, gasp, gulp, gust, huff, pant, plug, pull, push, suck, toke, waff, waft, waif **05** blast, extol, flaff, pluff, skiff, smoke, swell, whiff, whift **06** breath, expand, flatus, flurry, market, praise, wheeze **07** breathe, commend, draught, inflate, promote **09** advertise, marketing, promotion, publicity, publicize **10** homosexual **11** ostentation **12** commendation **13** advertisement
• **puff out   03** bag, sag **04** bulb, hump **05** belly, bloat, bulge, heave, swell **06** bepuff, billow, blouse, dilate, expand **07** balloon, distend, enlarge, project **08** protrude

**puffed**
**06** done in, winded **07** gasping, panting **08** inflated **09** distended, exhausted **10** breathless **11** out of breath
• **puffed up   05** bloat, elate, proud **06** pluffy **07** swollen, ventose **08** arrogant, prideful **09** bigheaded **13** high and mighty, self-important, swollen-headed **14** full of yourself

**puffin**
**08** rock-bird, Tom-noddy **09** sea parrot **10** Fratercula **11** Tammie Norie

**puffy**
**05** pursy **07** bloated, dilated, swollen **08** engorged, enlarged, inflated, puffed up **09** bombastic, distended **10** oedematous

**pugilism**
**04** ring **06** boxing **07** the ring **08** fighting, fistiana, the fancy **11** the noble art **12** the prize-ring **13** prize-fighting **15** the noble science

**pugilist**
**03** ham, pug **05** boxer **07** bruiser, fighter **12** prize-fighter

**pugnacious**
**07** hostile **09** bellicose, combative **10** aggressive **11** bad-tempered, belligerent, contentious, hot-tempered, quarrelsome **12** antagonistic, disputatious **13** argumentative

**puke**
**03** cat **04** barf, boke, honk, sick, spew **05** heave, retch, vomit **06** emesis, emetic, sick up **07** bring up, chuck up, chunder, fetch up, throw up, upchuck **08** disgorge, parbreak, retching **10** egurgitate **11** regurgitate

**pull**
**03** lug, rip, row, tow, tug **04** drag, draw, fire, haul, jerk, lure, raid, sole, sowl, suck, sway, tear, turn, yank **05** charm, clout, heave, pluck, power, proof, soole, sowle, steal, tempt, trail, tweak **06** allure, arrest, damage, entice, muscle, pull in, pull up, remove, snatch, sprain, strain, twitch, uproot, weight, wrench **07** attract, bring in, draught, draw out, extract, pull out, root out, stretch, take out **08** exertion, withdraw **09** advantage, dislocate, influence, magnetism, magnetize **10** allurement, attraction, resistance **12** drawing power, forcefulness
• **pull apart   03** pan **04** part, pick, slam **05** slate **06** attack **07** run down **08** demolish, distrain, separate **09** criticize, dismantle, dismember, take apart, tear apart **11** pick holes in **12** pick to pieces, pull to pieces, take to pieces, tear to shreds **15** do a hatchet job on
• **pull back   04** draw **06** retire **07** back out, retreat **08** draw back, fall back, withdraw **09** disengage
• **pull down   07** destroy, unbuild **08** bulldoze, demolish, take down **09** dismantle, knock down **10** dilapidate **15** raze to the ground
• **pull in   03** nab **04** book, bust, draw, earn, halt, lure, make, nick, park, stop **05** clear, run in, seize **06** allure, arrest, arrive, be paid, collar, detain, draw in, entice, pull up, rake in **07** attract, bring in, capture, collect, receive **08** take home **09** apprehend **15** take into custody
• **pull off   05** pluck **06** detach, fulfil, manage, remove, rip off **07** achieve, succeed, take off, tear off **08** bring off, carry off, carry out, separate **10** accomplish
• **pull out   04** quit **05** leave **06** depart, desert **07** abandon, back out, draw out, move out, pluck up, retreat **08** evacuate, withdraw
• **pull through   05** rally **07** improve, recover, survive, weather **09** get better **10** recuperate **11** come through **12** get well again
• **pull together   04** draw **05** rally **06** team up **09** co-operate **11** collaborate **12** work together
• **pull up   04** balk, halt, park, stop **05** baulk, blame, brake, chide, scold **06** arrest, berate, carpet, draw up, pull in, rebuke, uproot, uptear **07** censure, lecture, reprove, tell off, tick off **08** admonish, draw rein, pull over **09** castigate, criticize, eradicate, reprimand **10** take to task **11** come to a halt **14** read the riot act
• **pull yourself together   11** snap out of it **15** buck up your ideas, control yourself

**pulled up**
**02** pu

**pulley**
**04** swig

## pullover
03 top 06 jersey, jumper, woolly
07 sweater, tank top 10 sweatshirt
11 windcheater

## pulp
03 pap 04 beat, gush, mash, mush,
must, pith 05 chyme, cream, crush,
flesh, gloop, paste, pound, purée,
shred, slush 06 bathos, marrow,
pomace, squash 07 furnish
08 nonsense, schmaltz 09 corniness,
liquidize, nostalgia, pulverize, triturate
10 sloppiness, tenderness
11 mawkishness, romanticism
12 chemical wood, emotionalism
14 sentimentalism, sentimentality

## pulpit
03 tub 04 ambo, dais, desk, tent, wood
05 stand 06 mimbar, minbar, podium
07 lectern, rostrum, soapbox
08 platform 11 three-decker

## pulpy
04 soft 05 mushy, pappy 06 fleshy,
sloppy 07 baccate, crushed, squashy
09 succulent

## pulsate
04 beat, drum, thud 05 pound, pulse,
throb, thump 06 hammer, quiver
07 vibrate 09 oscillate, palpitate

## pulsating
07 pulsing 09 pulsatile, pulsative,
pulsatory, vibratile, vibrating, vibrative
11 oscillating, palpitating

## pulsation
04 beat 05 ictus, throb 07 beating
09 heartbeat, throbbing, vibration
11 oscillation, palpitation
12 vibratiuncle

## pulse
03 dal, pea 04 bean, beat, daal, dahl,
dhal, drum, gram, thud, tick 05 pound,
throb, thump 06 legume, rhythm,
stroke, thrill 07 beating, flutter, pulsate,
vibrate 08 drumming, pounding,
sphygmus, thudding, thumping
09 calavance, caravance, pulsation,
throbbing, vibration 11 oscillation
*See also* **bean**

## pulverize
◇ *anagram indicator* 04 mill, pulp
05 crush, grind, pound, smash
06 bruise, defeat, hammer, powder,
squash, thrash 07 crumble, destroy
08 demolish, vanquish 09 comminute,
triturate 10 annihilate 12 contriturate

## puma
05 tiger 06 cougar 07 couguar, panther
09 catamount 12 mountain lion

## pummel
◇ *anagram indicator* 03 fib, hit 04 bang,
beat, soak 05 knock, pound, punch,
thump 06 batter, hammer, pommel,
strike

## pump
03 jet 04 draw, gush, push, quiz, send,
shoe 05 drain, drive, force, grill, spout,
spurt, surge 06 bowser, inject, siphon
08 inflater, inflator 09 grease gun,
hydropult 11 interrogate 12 cross-

examine 13 cross-question 14 put the
screws on
*See also* **footwear**
• **pump out**    05 drain, empty
06 siphon 07 bail out, draw off
08 force out
• **pump up**    04 fill 06 blow up, puff
up 07 inflate 08 increase

## pumpkin
06 cashaw, cushaw 07 pompion,
pumpion 12 Jack-o'-lantern
14 Queensland blue 15 vegetable
marrow

## pun
03 ram 04 quip 05 pound 06 clinch
07 quibble 08 equivoke 09 calembour,
equivoque, jeu de mots, witticism
10 pundigrion 11 paronomasia, play on
words 13 double meaning, play upon
words 14 double entendre

## punch
03 bop, box, cut, die, fib, hit, jab, job,
mat, zap 04 bash, biff, bite, blow, boff,
bore, bust, clip, cuff, dong, hole, kick,
lamp, plug, poke, prod, slug, sock,
wind 05 black, check, clout, drill,
drive, force, knock, power, prick,
rumbo, stamp, thump, verve
06 energy, impact, pierce, pounce,
pummel, stingo, strike, thwack, vigour,
wallop, whammy 07 king hit, panache,
pizzazz 08 keypunch, puncture,
strength 09 bolo punch, perforate
10 roundhouse 11 coup de poing,
make a hole in, sucker-punch
12 bunch of fives, counter-punch,
forcefulness, fourpenny one
13 effectiveness 15 knuckle sandwich

## punch-drunk
05 dazed, dizzy, woozy 06 groggy
07 reeling 08 confused, unsteady
09 befuddled, slap-happy, stupefied
10 staggering

## punch-up
03 row 05 brawl, fight, scrap, set-to
06 dust-up, fracas, ruckus, shindy,
stoush 07 scuffle 08 argument, ding-
dong 10 free-for-all 12 stand-up fight

## punchy
05 dazed, zappy 06 lively, strong
07 dynamic 08 forceful, incisive,
powerful, spirited, vigorous
09 effective 10 aggressive

## punctilio
05 pique, punto 06 detail, nicety,
puncto 08 ceremony, delicacy
09 exactness, fine point, formality,
precision 10 convention, exactitude,
particular, refinement, strictness
11 distinction, finickiness, preciseness
13 particularity 14 meticulousness,
scrupulousness 15 punctiliousness

## punctilious
04 prim 05 exact, fussy, picky
06 choosy, formal, picked, proper,
strict 07 careful, finicky, precise
08 punctual 10 meticulous, nit-picking,
particular, pernickety, scrupulous
11 ceremonious, persnickety
13 conscientious

## punctiliously
07 exactly 09 carefully, precisely
12 meticulously, scrupulously
15 conscientiously

## punctual
05 early, exact, on cue 06 on time,
prompt 07 precise 08 on the dot, up to
time 09 well-timed 10 bang on time,
dead on time, in good time
11 punctilious

## punctuality
09 readiness 10 promptness, regularity,
strictness 11 promptitude

## punctually
05 sharp 06 bang on, dead on, on time,
prompt, spot-on 07 exactly 08 on the
dot, promptly, up to time 09 precisely
11 on the button, on the stroke, to the
minute 13 on the stroke of

## punctuate
04 stop 05 break, point 06 pepper
07 break up 08 sprinkle 09 emphasize,
interject, interrupt 10 accentuate
11 intersperse

## punctuation

*Punctuation marks include:*

04 dash, star
05 colon, comma
06 hyphen, period, quotes
07 solidus
08 asterisk, brackets, ellipsis, full
stop
09 backslash, semicolon
10 apostrophe
11 parentheses, speech marks
12 question mark
13 oblique stroke
14 inverted commas, quotation
marks, square brackets
15 exclamation mark

## puncture
◇ *insertion indicator* 03 cut 04 bite, bore,
flat, hole, leak, nick, slit 05 burst, prick,
spike 06 holing, pierce, pounce
07 blow-out, deflate, flatten, let down,
put down, rupture 08 centesis, flat tyre,
piercing 09 humiliate, penetrate,
perforate, spinal tap 11 make a hole in,
perforation

## pundit
04 buff, guru, sage 05 maven, mavin
06 expert, gooroo, master, savant
07 adviser, maestro, teacher
09 authority

## pungency
03 nip 04 bite, kick, tang 05 oomph,
point, power, sting 07 pizzazz,
sarcasm 08 mordancy, strength
09 sharpness, spiciness 10 causticity,
trenchancy 11 pepperiness
12 incisiveness 13 strong flavour

## pungent
03 hot 04 acid, fell, keen, racy, salt,
sour, tart 05 acrid, acute, fiery, nippy,
sharp, spicy, tangy 06 biting, bitter,
strong 07 burning, caustic, cutting,
mordant, painful, peppery, piquant,
pointed 08 aromatic, incisive, piercing,

poignant, powerful, scathing, stinging **09** sarcastic, trenchant **11** penetrating

## punish
◊ *anagram indicator* **03** log **04** beat, cane, fine, flog, gate, hang, harm, lash, slap, sort, whip **05** abuse, scold, scour, shend, smack, spank, visit, wreak **06** amerce, batter, damage, defeat, ground, hammer, misuse, pay out, strafe, straff, thrash **07** chasten, correct, crucify, justify, knee-cap, rough up, scourge, sort out, trounce **08** chastise, decimate, imprison, keelhaul, maltreat, masthead, penalize, serve out **09** castigate, strappado **10** come down on, discipline **11** bring to book **12** come down upon, give it laldie **14** bring to justice, make someone pay, throw the book at **15** give someone hell, make an example of
• **be punished** **03** pay

## punishable
**07** illegal **08** criminal, culpable, unlawful **10** chargeable, indictable **11** blameworthy, convictable

## punishing
**04** hard **05** cruel, harsh **06** severe, taxing, tiring **07** arduous, testing **08** crushing, grinding, grueling, wearying **09** crippling, demanding, fatiguing, gruelling, strenuous **10** burdensome, exhausting **12** backbreaking

## punishment
**04** harm, pine, toco, toko **05** force, impot **06** damage, ill-use, injury **07** deserts, penalty, revenge **08** ferocity, sentence **10** correction, discipline, imposition, storminess, turbulence **11** retribution **12** chastisement, maltreatment **13** rough handling **15** short sharp shock

*Punishments include:*
**04** cane, fine, gaol, jail, rope
**05** exile, lines, strap
**06** gating, hiding, prison
**07** beating, belting, borstal, capital, flaying, hanging, hitting, jankers, lashing, the cane, the rack, the rope
**08** corporal, demotion, flogging, slapping, smacking, solitary, spanking, the birch, whipping
**09** chain gang, detention, exclusion, execution, expulsion, grounding, larruping, pack-drill, probation, scourging, strappado, the stocks, thrashing, torturing
**10** banishment, cashiering, decimation, defrocking, internment, leathering, suspension, the slipper, unfrocking
**11** confinement, deportation, house arrest, keelhauling, knee-capping, mastheading, penal colony
**12** confiscation, dressing-down, imprisonment
**13** electric chair, horsewhipping, incarceration, sequestration, tar and feather
**14** transportation

**15** excommunication, walking the plank

---

• **place of punishment** **04** cang, gaol, Hell, jail, tron **05** Hades, trone **06** cangue, prison, sin bin **07** borstal, dungeon, gallows, pillory, tumbrel, tumbril **08** scaffold, solitary, Tartarus **09** black hole, cart's-tail, the stocks **10** little-ease **11** penal colony **12** cucking stool, whipping-post
*See also* **prison**

## punitive
**04** hard **05** cruel, harsh, penal, stiff **06** severe **08** crushing **09** crippling, demanding, gruelling, punishing **10** burdensome, chastising, corrective, vindictive **11** castigatory, retaliatory, retributive, vindicatory **12** disciplinary

## punter
**03** guy **04** chap **05** bloke, joker **06** backer, better, bettor, client, fellow, person **07** gambler, wagerer **08** consumer, customer **10** individual **11** handicapper

## puny
**04** tiny, weak **05** frail, minor, petty, scram, small, weary **06** feeble, little, measly, puisne, puisny, sickly **07** pimping, shilpit, stunted, trivial **08** piddling, reckling, trifling **10** diminutive, undersized **11** undeveloped **13** inexperienced, insignificant **14** underdeveloped **15** inconsequential

## pupil
**01** L **04** coed, prep, ward **05** cadet **06** alumna, bursar, day-boy, grader, junior, novice, old boy, preppy, senior **07** alumnus, ashrama, boarder, day-girl, learner, monitor, old girl, prefect, protégé, scholar, student **08** beginner, bluecoat, disciple, grey-coat, praefect, protégée, schoolie **09** classmate, schoolboy, St Trinian **10** abiturient, academical, apprentice, charity-boy, day-boarder, day-scholar, gymnasiast, schoolgirl, Wykehamist **11** charity-girl, class-fellow, Westminster **12** pupil teacher **13** apple of the eye, kindergärtner **14** kindergartener, parlour-boarder
• **former pupil** **02** OB **06** alumna, old boy **07** alumnus, old girl

## puppet
**04** doll, dupe, gull, Judy, pawn, tool **05** Punch, puppy **06** mammet, maumet, mawmet, mommet, motion, poppet, stooge **07** cat's-paw, Guignol **08** creature, quisling **09** dependant, fantoccio, rod puppet **10** fantoccino, figurehead, hand puppet, instrument, Jack of Lent, marionette, mouthpiece **11** glove puppet, Punchinello **12** finger puppet

## puppy
**03** pup **05** whelp **06** lapdog **08** young dog

## purchase
**03** buy, get, win **04** deal, earn, gain, grip, hold **05** asset, booty, goods, grasp, lay-by, price, prise, prize

**06** assets, obtain, pay for, pick up, secure, snap up, strive **07** acquire, bargain, emption, procure, seizure, shop for **08** foothold, holdings, invest in, leverage, property **09** advantage **10** go shopping, investment, possession **11** acquisition, possessions, splash out on

## purchaser
**05** buyer, hirer **06** client, emptor, patron, vendee **07** shopper **08** consumer, customer **11** perquisitor

## pure
**03** net, pur **04** fair, fine, free, good, holy, meer, mere, neat, nett, puer, real, true **05** clean, clear, fresh, moral, noble, sheer, snowy, solid, total, utter, white **06** chaste, decent, honest, kosher, modest, purity, refine, simple, virgin, worthy **07** aseptic, cleanly, cleanse, genuine, natural, perfect, sincere, sterile, unmixed, upright, utterly **08** absolute, abstract, academic, complete, flawless, germ-free, heavenly, hygienic, innocent, pristine, sanitary, spotless, straight, thorough, undrossy, unsoiled, virginal, virginly, virtuous **09** authentic, blameless, downright, essential, excellent, incorrupt, righteous, Saturnian, snow-white, spiritous, stainless, unalloyed, undefiled, undiluted, unsullied **10** antiseptic, completely, homozygous, honourable, immaculate, intemerate, sterilized, uninfected, unpolluted **11** conjectural, disinfected, speculative, theoretical, unblemished, unmitigated, unqualified **12** unadulterate **13** unadulterated **14** heavenly-minded, uncontaminated **15** whiter than white

## pure-bred
**07** blooded **08** pedigree, true-born, true-bred **09** pedigreed, pure-blood **11** full-blooded, pure-blooded **12** thoroughbred

## purée
**03** dal **04** fool **06** coulis, hummus, humous, kissel **07** houmous **08** hoummous **10** baba ganouj **11** baba ganoush **12** baba ghanouzh

## purely
**04** just, only **06** merely, simply, solely, wholly **07** totally, utterly **08** chastely, entirely **09** unmixedly **10** absolutely, completely, thoroughly **11** exclusively, wonderfully **15** unconditionally

## purgative
**05** aloes, enema, jalap, purge, salts, yapon, yupon **06** cacoon, emetic, ipecac, yaupon **07** calomel, drastic, jalapin, purging, rhubarb **08** aperient, elaterin, evacuant, laxative, lenitive **09** cathartic, cleansing, colocynth, croton oil, physic nut **10** abstersive, cholagogue, depurative, eccoprotic, Epsom salts, hiera-picra, higry-pigry, number nine **11** bitter aloes, cathartical, chrysarobin, ipecacuanha **12** black draught **13** diacatholicon **14** hickery-pickery

### purgatory
**04** hell **05** agony, swamp **06** misery, ordeal, ravine **07** anguish, purging, torment, torture **09** cleansing, expiatory **12** hopelessness, wretchedness

### purge
**03** rid **04** kill, oust, soil, work **05** clear, eject, expel, scour **06** depose, purify, remove **07** absolve, clarify, cleanse, dismiss, expiate, ousting, removal, root out, wipe out **08** absterge, clean out, clear out, disposal, ejection, get rid of **09** catharize, cleansing, eradicate, expulsion, expurgate, purgative, witch hunt **10** rooting-out **11** eradication, exterminate **13** extermination

### purification
**05** purge **06** lustre **07** elution, lustrum **08** cleaning **09** catharsis, cleansing, epuration, purgation **10** absolution, depuration, filtration, fumigation, lustration, redemption, refinement **11** sublimation **12** desalination, disinfection, sanitization, zone refining **13** deodorization **14** reverse osmosis, sanctification **15** decontamination

### purify
**03** try **04** clay, fine **05** clean, purge, scrub **06** distil, filter, redeem, refine, retort, shrive **07** absolve, chasten, clarify, cleanse, epurate, expurge, freshen, furbish, mundify, rectify, sublime **08** chastise, defecate, depurate, filtrate, fumigate, lustrate, sanctify, sanitize **09** catharize, deodorize, disinfect, expurgate, sterilize, sublimate, sublimize **10** circumcise **13** decontaminate

### purifying
**06** fining **07** lustral, purging **08** refining **09** cathartic, cleansing, purgative **10** depurative, lustration **11** cathartical, expurgation **12** purificatory **13** mundificative

### purism
**08** Atticism, pedantry **09** austerity, formalism, fussiness, orthodoxy, restraint **10** classicism, strictness **13** over-precision **14** fastidiousness

### purist
**05** fussy **06** pedant, strict **07** finicky **08** captious, pedantic, puristic, quibbler, stickler **09** dogmatist, formalist, nit-picker, over-exact, quibbling **10** fastidious, literalist, nit-picking **11** over-precise **12** precisionist **13** hypercritical **14** over-fastidious, over-meticulous, over-particular, uncompromising

### puritan
**04** prig **05** prude **06** wowser, zealot **07** fanatic, killjoy, pietist **08** Cromwell, Ironside, moralist, rigorist **09** Ironsides, precisian, Roundhead **10** goody-goody, spoilsport **14** disciplinarian

### puritanical
**04** prim **05** rigid, stern, stiff **06** proper, severe, strict, stuffy **07** ascetic, austere, bigoted, precise, prudish, puritan, zealous **09** fanatical **10** abstemious,

goody-goody, moralistic **11** round-headed, strait-laced **12** disapproving, narrow-minded **14** disciplinarian

### puritanism
**07** bigotry **08** primness, rigidity, severity, zealotry **09** austerity, propriety, sternness, stiffness **10** abstinence, asceticism, fanaticism, narrowness, self-denial, strictness **11** prudishness **12** priggishness, rigorousness **14** abstemiousness, self-discipline

### purity
**04** pure **05** truth **06** candor, honour, orient, virtue **07** candour, clarity, decency, honesty **08** chastity, goodness, morality, nobility, pureness, sanctity **09** chiarezza, cleanness, clearness, freshness, innocence, integrity, rectitude, sincerity, virginity **10** perfection, simplicity, worthiness **11** cleanliness, genuineness, uprightness **12** authenticity, flawlessness, virtuousness **13** blamelessness, untaintedness, wholesomeness
• **person of purity 04** lily

### purlieus
**06** bounds, limits **07** borders, fringes, suburbs **08** confines, environs, vicinity **09** outskirts, perimeter, periphery, precincts **12** surroundings **13** neighbourhood

### purloin
**03** bag, rob **04** lift, nick, take, whip **05** annex, filch, pinch, steal, swipe **06** finger, nobble, pilfer, pocket, remove, rip off, snitch, thieve **07** cabbage, snaffle **08** abstract, scrounge, souvenir **10** run off with **11** appropriate **12** make away with

### purple
*Purples include:*

**04** anil, plum, puce, puke
**05** lilac, mauve, pansy, prune
**06** cerise, damson, indigo, maroon, violet
**07** fuchsia, fuschia, heather, magenta, purpure
**08** amethyst, burgundy, hyacinth, lavender, mulberry
**09** aubergine
**11** royal purple

### purport
**04** bear, gist, idea, mean, seem, show **05** claim, drift, imply, point, sense, tenor, theme **06** allege, assert, convey, denote, import, intend, pose as, spirit, thrust **07** bearing, betoken, declare, express, meaning, portend, pretend, profess, purpose, signify, suggest **08** indicate, maintain, proclaim, tendency **09** direction, substance **11** implication **12** significance

### purportedly
**09** allegedly, dubiously **10** apparently, doubtfully, ostensibly, putatively, reportedly, supposedly **13** by all accounts

### purpose
**03** aim, end, use **04** gain, goal, good, hope, idea, mean, plan, talk, wish, zeal **05** basis, drive, point, teleo-, telos, value **06** aspire, decide, design, desire, effect, intend, motive, object, reason, result, settle, target, vision **07** benefit, outcome, propose, purport, resolve **08** ambition, backbone, converse, devotion, firmness, function, meditate, tenacity **09** advantage, constancy, determine, intention, objective, principle, rationale **10** aspiration, dedication, doggedness, motivation, resolution, usefulness **11** application, contemplate, persistence **12** conversation, perseverance **13** determination, justification, steadfastness
• **on purpose 08** à dessein, by design, wilfully **09** knowingly, purposely, wittingly **11** consciously **12** deliberately **13** intentionally **14** premeditatedly

### purposeful
**04** firm **06** dogged **07** decided **08** constant, positive, purposed, resolute, resolved **09** steadfast, tenacious **10** deliberate, determined, persistent, unwavering **11** persevering, unfaltering **12** single-minded, strong-willed

### purposefully
**10** resolutely **11** steadfastly, tenaciously **12** persistently, unwaveringly **13** perseveringly, unfalteringly **14** single-mindedly

### purposeless
**04** vain **05** empty **06** wanton **07** aimless, useless, vacuous **08** goalless, needless **09** pointless, senseless, shapeless, unmeaning **10** gratuitous, motiveless, objectless, unasked-for **11** nonsensical, thoughtless, uncalled-for, unnecessary

### purposely
**08** by design, wilfully **09** expressly, knowingly, on purpose **10** designedly **11** consciously **12** calculatedly, deliberately, specifically **13** intentionally **14** premeditatedly

### purse
◇ *containment indicator* **04** bung, fisc, fisk, gift, prim **05** award, burse, close, funds, means, money, pouch, prize **06** pocket, pucker, reward, wallet **07** coffers, present, tighten, wrinkle **08** compress, contract, crumenal, finances, money-bag, treasury **09** exchequer, resources, spleuchan **10** pocketbook **12** draw together, porte-monnaie **13** press together

### pursuance
**07** pursuit **08** pursuing **09** discharge, effecting, execution, following **10** completion, fulfilment **11** achievement, performance, prosecution **12** effectuation **14** accomplishment

### pursue
**03** dog, sew, sue **04** hunt, seek, tail

## pursuit

**05** chace, chase, harry, hound, stalk, track, trail **06** aim for, follow, harass, hold to, keep on, keep up, persue, pursew, shadow, try for **07** carry on, conduct, go after, perform, poursew, poursue, run down **08** aspire to, continue, engage in, follow up, hunt down, maintain, practise, run after **09** give chase, make after, persecute, persist in, prosecute, search for, strive for **10** whore after **11** inquire into, investigate, persevere in, work towards **12** have your goal **15** apply yourself to

## pursuit

**03** aim **04** goal, hunt, line, suit **05** caper, chase, chevy, chivy, craft, hobby, quest, trade, trail **06** attain, chivvy, search **07** hot trod, hunting, pastime, pursual, tailing **08** activity, interest, poursuit, pursuing, stalking, tracking, vocation **09** endeavour, following, hue and cry, poursuitt, pursuance, shadowing, specialty **10** aspiration, employment, occupation, speciality **11** continuance, persistence, wildfowling **12** perseverance **13** investigation

## purvey

**04** sell **05** cater, stock **06** deal in, pass on, retail, spread, supply **07** furnish, provide, publish, trade in, victual **08** put about, transmit **09** propagate, provision, publicize **11** communicate, disseminate

## purveyor

**06** dealer, seller, trader, vendor **08** manciple, provedor, provider, providor, provisor, retailer, stockist, supplier **09** provedore **10** propagator, proveditor, victualler **11** proveditore, transmitter **12** communicator, disseminator

## pus

**06** matter **07** quitter, quittor, seropus **09** diapyesis, discharge **11** suppuration

## push

**02** go **03** jog, put, ram **04** birr, bunt, butt, cram, goad, horn, hype, jolt, plug, poke, pole, prod, raid, spur, urge **05** boost, bully, drive, dunch, dunsh, egg on, elbow, foray, force, impel, knock, nudge, onset, press, shove **06** charge, coerce, effort, energy, firing, hustle, incite, jostle, market, notice, papers, peddle, plunge, propel, ramrod, squash, the axe, thrust, vigour **07** advance, assault, company, depress, impulse, promote, sacking, squeeze, the boot, the chop **08** ambition, dynamism, invasion, persuade, press for, pressure, the elbow, vitality **09** advertise, constrain, discharge, dismissal, encourage, incursion, influence, manhandle, offensive, onslaught, publicize, your cards **10** enterprise, get-up-and-go, initiative, pressurize **12** forcefulness **13** determination **14** marching orders, put the screws on

• **push around** **05** bully **06** pick on **07** torment **09** terrorize, victimize **10** intimidate

• **push off** **04** move, scat **05** leave, scram **06** beat it, depart, go away **07** buzz off, scarper **08** clear off, clear out, run along, shove off **09** make a move, push along **10** make tracks

• **push on** **04** go on, toil, urge **06** plod on **07** advance, carry on, go ahead, peg away, press on, proceed **08** continue, plug away, slog away, toil away **09** keep going, persevere, soldier on, stick at it **10** keep trying

## pushed

**06** hard-up, rushed **07** harried, hurried, pinched, pressed, short of **08** harassed, strapped **09** stretched **11** hard-pressed **13** under pressure **14** in difficulties

## pushover

**03** mug **04** dupe, gull **05** cinch **06** doddle, picnic, stooge, sucker **07** fall guy **08** duck soup, walkover, weakling **09** easy touch, soft touch **10** child's play **11** piece of cake, sitting duck **13** sitting target

## pushy

**04** bold **05** bossy, brash **07** forward **08** arrogant, assuming, forceful **09** ambitious, assertive **10** aggressive **11** impertinent **12** presumptuous **13** over-confident, self-assertive

## pusillanimity

**08** timidity, weakness **10** cravenness, feebleness **11** fearfulness, gutlessness, poltroonery **12** cowardliness, timorousness **13** spinelessness

## pusillanimous

**04** weak **05** timid **06** craven, feeble, scared, yellow **07** chicken, fearful, gutless, wimpish **08** cowardly, timorous **09** spineless, weak-kneed **11** lily-livered **12** faint-hearted, mean-spirited **14** chicken-hearted

## pussyfoot

**03** pad **05** creep, hedge, prowl, slink, steal **06** tiptoe **09** mess about **10** equivocate **11** prevaricate **12** tergiversate **14** prohibitionist

## pustule

**04** boil, pock **05** ulcer **06** blotch, fester, papule, pimple **07** abscess, blister, whitlow **08** eruption **09** carbuncle, whitehead **10** uredosorus

## put

**02** do **03** add, bet, fix, lay, pin, pit, say, set **04** cast, dump, flow, give, have, hurl, levy, park, post, push, rank, rest, risk, sink, sort, turn, word **05** affix, apply, class, couch, drive, exact, force, frame, gauge, grade, group, guess, impel, offer, place, plonk, speak, spend, stake, stand, state, throw, utter, voice **06** append, assert, assign, attach, call on, chance, charge, commit, convey, demand, devote, gamble, impose, impute, incite, invest, locate, oblige, phrase, reckon, reduce, render, repose, set out, settle, submit, tender, thrust **07** arrange, ascribe, bumpkin, connect, convert, deposit, dispose, express, inflict, lay down, present, proceed, proffer, propose, require, set down, situate, station, subject, suggest,

venture, work out **08** classify, dedicate, estimate, position, propound, set forth **09** attribute, constrain, establish, formulate, greenhorn, lay before, pronounce, set before, translate, transport **10** categorize, contribute, transcribe **11** guesstimate **12** bring forward

• **put about** **04** tell **06** spread **07** publish **08** announce, distress **09** circulate, make known **11** disseminate

• **put across** **06** convey **07** clarify, explain, express, get over, put over **08** bring off, spell out **09** get across, make clear **11** bring home to, communicate **12** get through to **14** make understood

• **put aside** **04** keep, save, stow **05** hoard, lay by, put by, set by, stash, store **06** retain, shelve **07** reserve **08** lay aside, salt away, set apart, set aside **09** stockpile **12** put to one side **13** keep in reserve

• **put away** **03** eat **04** down, jail, keep, kill, save, stow, wolf **05** drink, eat up, lay by, put by, scoff, snarf, store, waive **06** bang up, commit, devour, guzzle, lock up, pack up, retain, tuck in **07** cashier, certify, confine, consume, divorce, reserve, swallow **08** imprison, lay aside, put aside, renounce, send down, set aside **09** polish off, stockpile **11** incarcerate **13** keep in reserve

• **put back** **05** defer, delay, remit **06** freeze, return, shelve, tidy up **07** adjourn, clear up, replace, repulse, restore, suspend **08** postpone, put on ice, tidy away **09** clear away, reinstate **10** reschedule **13** procrastinate **14** take a raincheck

• **put down** **03** fix, lay, log **04** alay, drop, kill, laid, list, snub, stop **05** abase, aleye, allay, blame, crush, enter, lower, plonk, quash, quell, shame, sneap **06** attach, charge, defeat, humble, reckon, record, slight, squash **07** ascribe, confute, deflate, degrade, destroy, jot down, mortify, repress, set down, silence, squelch, surpass **08** belittle, note down, outshine, register, stamp out, suppress, underlay **09** attribute, deprecate, disparage, humiliate, write down **10** put to sleep, transcribe **12** take down a peg

• **put forward** **03** lay, run **04** move, pose, urge **05** offer, table **06** assign, obtend, prefer, submit, tender **07** advance, present, proffer, propone, propose, suggest **08** nominate **09** hold forth, introduce, recommend

• **put in** ◇ *insertion indicator* **03** fit **05** enter, input **06** insert, submit **07** install, present **09** introduce

• **put in for** **05** order **06** ask for **07** request **08** apply for **11** requisition, write off for **14** fill in a form for

• **put off** **03** fob, fub **04** daff, doff **05** daunt, defer, delay, deter, lay by, shift **06** dismay, divert, shelve, sicken **07** adjourn, confuse, deflect, dismiss,

## putative

respite, suspend **08** dissuade, distract, nauseate, postpone, put on ice, turn away **09** sidetrack, talk out of, turn aside **10** demoralize, disconcert, discourage, dishearten, intimidate, reschedule **13** procrastinate **14** take a raincheck
• **put on** ◇ **02** do **03** add, don **04** fake, give, robe, sham, wear **05** affix, apply, feign, lay on, mount, place, stage, try on **06** affect, assume, attach, impose, plug in, supply, turn on **07** connect, dress in, get into, perform, present, pretend, produce, provide, start up, throw on **08** activate, organize, simulate, slip into, switch on **10** change into **11** make believe **12** get dressed in **13** get dolled up in
• **put out** ◇ *anagram indicator* **03** irk **04** dout, faze, hurt **05** anger, annoy, douse, dowse, issue, snuff, upset, utter **06** bother, offend, quench **07** dismiss, disturb, extinct, perturb, provoke, publish, smother, trouble **08** announce, bring out, disclose, impose on, irritate, stamp out, unsettle **09** broadcast, circulate, infuriate, make known **10** discommode, disconcert, exasperate, extinguish, mistrysted **13** inconvenience
• **put through** **06** manage **07** achieve, execute, process **08** bring off, complete, conclude, finalize **10** accomplish
• **put together** **04** join **05** build, frame, marry **06** cobble, made up, make up **07** compile, concoct **08** assemble **09** carpenter, construct **11** fit together **13** piece together
• **put up** ◇ *reversal down indicator* **03** inn, pay **04** give **05** build, erect, float, house, lodge, offer, raise, sling, stake **06** bump up, choose, hike up, invest, jack up, pledge, supply **07** advance, propose, provide, sheathe, shelter, suggest **08** assemble, compound, escalate, increase, nominate **09** construct, recommend **10** put forward **11** accommodate, give a room to
• **put upon** **07** exploit **08** impose on **13** inconvenience, take liberties **14** take for granted **15** take advantage of
• **put up to** **04** goad, urge **05** egg on **06** incite, prompt **08** persuade **09** encourage
• **put up with** **04** bear, lump, take, wear **05** abide, allow, brook, stand **06** accept, endure, suffer **07** stomach, swallow **08** stand for, tolerate **13** take lying down

## putative
**07** alleged, assumed, reputed

**08** presumed, reported, supposed **10** reputative **11** conjectural, theoretical **12** hypothetical, suppositious **13** suppositional

## put-down
**03** dig **04** gibe, snub **05** sneer **06** insult, rebuff, slight **07** affront, sarcasm **11** humiliation **13** disparagement, slap in the face

## put-off
**04** curb **05** damper, excuse **07** evasion **08** obstacle **09** deterrent, hindrance, restraint **10** constraint **12** disincentive, postponement **14** discouragement

## putrefaction
**03** rot **05** decay, mould **06** fungus, mildew, sepsis **07** rotting **08** going bad **09** perishing, putridity **11** putrescence **13** decomposition

## putrefy
**03** rot **05** addle, decay, go bad, mould, spoil, stink, taint **06** fester, perish **07** corrupt **08** gangrene **09** decompose **11** deteriorate

## putrescent
**07** rotting **08** decaying, mephitic, stinking **09** festering, perishing **10** putrefying **11** decomposing

## putrid
**03** bad, off **04** foul, rank **05** addle, fetid **06** addled, foetid, mouldy, rancid, rotten, turned **07** corrupt, decayed, tainted **08** decaying, polluted, stinking **10** decomposed, disgusting **11** decomposing **12** contaminated

## put-upon
**04** used **06** abused **09** exploited, imposed on **10** maltreated, persecuted **14** inconvenienced

## puzzle
◇ *anagram indicator* **04** beat, crux, pose **05** brood, floor, poser, stump, think **06** baffle, bemuse, enigma, fickle, figure, gravel, kittle, ponder **07** bumbaze, confuse, dilemma, flummox, mystery, mystify, nonplus, paradox, perplex, problem, stagger, tickler **08** bewilder, confound, consider, entangle, intrigue, meditate, mull over, muse over, question **09** bamboozle, fascinate **10** complicate, deliberate, mind-bender, perplexity **11** brainteaser **12** bewilderment, brain-twister **13** metagrabolize, metagrobolize **14** beat your brains, rack your brains, think hard about

Puzzles include:

**06** hanjie, jigsaw, kakuro, riddle, sudoku
**07** anagram, hangman, sorites, tangram
**08** acrostic, wordgame
**09** conundrum, crossword
**10** alphametic, cryptogram, Rubik's Cube®, wordsearch
**12** magic pyramid

• **puzzle out** **03** get **04** suss **05** crack, solve **06** decode **07** clear up, resolve, sort out, suss out, unravel, work out **08** decipher, think out, untangle **09** figure out **13** metagrabolize, metagrobolize, piece together **15** find the answer to

## puzzled
**04** lost **05** at sea **06** beaten **07** at a loss, baffled, floored, in a haze, stumped **08** confused **09** flummoxed, mystified, perplexed **10** bamboozled, bewildered, confounded, nonplussed

## puzzlement
**05** doubt **06** wonder **08** surprise **09** confusion **10** bafflement, bemusement, perplexity **11** incertitude, uncertainty **12** astonishment, bewilderment, doubtfulness **13** bamboozlement, mystification **14** disorientation
• **expression of puzzlement** **02** ha **03** hah, hey, huh **04** anan, anon **05** heigh **06** indeed

## puzzling
**05** queer, trick **06** arcane, knotty, posing **07** bizarre, cryptic, curious, strange, unclear **08** abstruse, baffling, involved, mystical, peculiar, riddling, tortuous **09** ambiguous, confusing, damnedest, enigmatic, equivocal, intricate **10** misleading, mysterious, mystifying, perplexing, Sphynx-like **11** bewildering, enigmatical, mind-bending **12** impenetrable, inexplicable, labyrinthine, mind-boggling, unfathomable **13** unaccountable

## pygmy
**03** elf, toy, wee **04** baby, tiny **05** atomy, dwarf, elfin, small **06** midget, minute, pocket **07** manikin, Negrito, stunted **08** dwarfish, half-pint, Tom Thumb **09** miniature, minuscule, pint-sized, thumbling **10** diminutive, fingerling, homunculus, undersized **11** hop-o'-my-thumb, Lilliputian

## pyramid
**05** stack **08** teocalli, ziggurat, zikkurat

## pyromaniac
**04** pyro **07** firebug **08** arsonist **10** fire-raiser, incendiary

# Q

**Q**
03 cue 06 Quebec 13 trichosanthin

**Qatar**
01 Q 02 QA 03 QAT

**quack**
04 fake, sham 05 bogus, false, fraud,
pseud 06 cowboy, crocus, doctor,
humbug, phoney 07 empiric
08 impostor, so-called, spurious,
supposed, swindler 09 charlatan,
pretended, pretender, trickster
10 fraudulent, medicaster,
mountebank 11 counterfeit,
masquerader, quacksalver,
saltimbanco, unqualified

**quackery**
04 sham 05 fraud 06 humbug
09 imposture, phoniness 10 empiricism
11 fraudulence 12 charlatanism
13 mountebankery, mountebankism

**quadrangle**
04 quad 05 court, plaza 06 piazza,
square 08 cloister 09 courtyard,
enclosure, esplanade

**quaff**
04 down, gulp, swig 05 booze, drain,
drink, swill 06 guzzle, imbibe, quaich,
tipple 07 carouse, draught, swallow,
toss off 08 drink off 09 crush a cup,
knock back

**quagmire**
03 bog, fen, fix 04 hole, mess, mire,
quag 05 marsh, swamp 06 morass,
pickle, slough 07 dilemma, problem
08 entangle, hot water, quandary,
wagmoire 09 deep water, quicksand,
tight spot 10 perplexity

**quail**
05 colin, cower, daunt, quake, shake,
whore 06 blench, caille, cringe, falter,
flinch, recoil, shiver, shrink, subdue
07 decline, shudder, shy away,
slacken, tremble 08 back away,
bobwhite, draw back, hemipode,
languish, percolin, pull back
09 partridge

**quaint**
◇ *anagram indicator* 03 odd 04 fine,
twee 05 droll, funky, queer, sweet
06 queint, whimsy 07 bizarre, cunning,
curious, skilful, strange, unusual,
whimsey 08 charming, fanciful, old-
world 09 ingenious, whimsical
10 antiquated, attractive, auld-farand,
olde-worlde 11 picturesque 12 old-
fashioned

**quaintly**
05 oddly 09 curiously, strangely,

unusually 10 charmingly
11 whimsically 12 attractively
13 picturesquely

**quaintness**
05 charm 11 unusualness
13 whimsicalness 14 attractiveness
15 picturesqueness

**quake**
◇ *anagram indicator* 04 move, rock,
sway 05 heave, quail, shake, throb
06 didder, dither, quiver, shiver,
tremor, wamble, wobble 07 pulsate,
shudder, tremble, vibrate 08 convulse
09 the big one 10 earthquake

**qualification**
05 rider, skill 06 caveat, degree
07 ability, diploma, fitness, proviso
08 aptitude, capacity, training
09 allowance, condition, exception,
exemption, provision 10 adaptation,
adjustment, capability, competence,
limitation 11 certificate, eligibility,
proficiency, reservation, restriction,
stipulation, suitability 12 modification
13 certification 14 accomplishment

*Qualifications include:*

02 AB, AM, AS, BA, BD, BE, BL, BM,
   BS, DC, DD, DS, IB, MA, MB,
   MD, MS
03 BAI, BAS, BCh, BCL, BDS, BEd,
   BRE, BSc, ChB, ChM, CSE, DCh,
   DCL, DDS, DEd, DPh, DSc, DTh,
   EdB, EdD, FPC, LHD, LLB, LLD,
   LLM, MBA, MCh, MDS, MEd,
   MSc, NVQ, ONC, OND, PhD,
   ScB, ScD, SCE, SVQ, ThD, VMD
04 BAgr, BCom, BEng, B ès L, B ès S,
   BLit, BMus, BTEC, DEng, DIng,
   DLit, DMus, GCSE, GNVQ, LitB,
   LitD, MBSc, MCom, MDSc,
   MMus, MusB, MusD
05 BArch, BComm, BLitt, BPhil,
   DLitt, DPhil, LittB, LittD, Lower,
   MEcon, MLitt, MPhil, MTech
06 A level, BAgric, BPharm, degree,
   DTheol, Higher, MPharm, O
   grade, O level
07 AS level
10 eleven-plus, Lower grade, School
   Cert
11 Higher grade, Legum doctor
12 Doctor of Laws, Master of Arts,
   Master of Laws
13 Advanced level, Bachelor of Law,
   Doctor of Music, Legum magister,
   Master of Music, Ordinary grade,
   Ordinary level, Standard grade
14 Advanced Higher, Artium
   Magister, Bachelor of Arts,
   Bachelor of Laws, Magister
   Artium
15 Bachelor of Music, Doctor of
   Letters, Doctor of Science, Doctor
   of Surgery, Master of Letters,
   Master of Science, Master of
   Surgery, Medicinae Doctor

**qualified**
03 fit 04 able, meet 05 adept 06 expert,
fitted 07 bounded, capable, guarded,
limited, skilful, skilled, trained
08 cautious, eligible, equipped,
licensed, modified, prepared,

reserved, talented 09 certified,
chartered, competent, efficient,
equivocal, practised 10 contingent,
proficient, restricted 11 conditional,
experienced, provisional
12 accomplished, professional
13 circumscribed, knowledgeable

**qualify**
03 fit 04 ease, pass, vary 05 abate,
allow, alloy, coach, equip, limit,
prove, teach, train 06 adjust, define,
ground, lessen, modify, permit,
reduce, soften, temper, weaken
07 appease, certify, confirm, delimit,
empower, entitle, license, prepare,
warrant 08 classify, diminish, graduate,
instruct, mitigate, moderate, restrain,
restrict, sanction 09 alleviate,
authorize, be allowed, contemper,
make ready 10 be eligible, capacitate,
habilitate 12 characterize 15 make
conditional

**quality**
01 Q 02 it 04 cast, kind, make, mark,
rank, sort, type 05 class, grade, level,
merit, skill, trait, value, worth
06 aspect, make-up, manner, nature,
status, timbre 07 calibre, feature,
variety 08 eminence, property,
standard 09 attribute, character,
condition 10 excellence, profession,
refinement 11 distinction, peculiarity,
pre-eminence, superiority
14 accomplishment, characteristic
• **quality assurance** 02 QA

**qualm**
04 fear 05 doubt, worry 07 anxiety,
concern, scruple 08 disquiet
09 hesitancy, misgiving 10 hesitation,
reluctance, uneasiness
11 compunction, uncertainty
12 apprehension 14 disinclination

**quandary**
03 fix, jam 04 hole, mess 06 muddle,
pickle 07 dilemma, impasse, problem
09 confusion, tight spot 10 difficulty,
perplexity 11 predicament
12 bewilderment

**quantify**
05 count, weigh 06 number
07 measure, specify 08 evaluate
09 calculate, calibrate, determine,
enumerate

**quantity**
02 qt 03 lot, qty, sum 04 area, bulk,
deal, dose, lots, many, mass, much,
part, size, tons 05 heaps, loads, quota,
reams, scrap, share, total 06 amount,
extent, length, masses, number,
oodles, stacks, volume, weight
07 breadth, content, expanse,
measure, portion 08 capacity, fragment
09 aggregate, allotment, extension,
magnitude 10 proportion
*See also* **measurement**
• **in equal quantities** 01 ā 02 āā
03 ana
• **small quantity** 04 curn, drib, lock
• **unknown quantity** 01 X, Y, Z

**quarantine**
09 detention, isolation, lazaretto,

**quarrel**

quarenden, quarender **10** quarrender **11** quarrington, segregation

**quarrel**
**03** jar, row, wap **04** beef, feud, miff, slam, spat, tiff, tift, whid **05** argue, brawl, broil, cavil, chide, clash, fault, fight, flite, flyte, knock, run-in, scrap, set-to, slate **06** barney, bicker, breach, breeze, bust-up, charge, differ, dust-up, fracas, fratch, jangle, quar'le, quarry, ruffle, rumble, schism, square, strife **07** brattle, cast out, censure, contend, dispute, dissent, fall out, outcast, outfall, punch-up, wrangle **08** argument, conflict, disagree, squabble, vendetta **09** caterwaul, complaint, criticize, have words, objection **10** contention, difference, differency, difficulty, dissension, falling-out **11** altercation, controversy, disputation, pick holes in **12** be at variance, disagreement, pull to pieces **13** exchange blows, exchange words, find fault with, part brass rags, shouting match, slanging match **15** be at loggerheads

**quarrelling**
**06** at odds, rowing, strife **07** discord, feuding, warring **08** fighting, variance **09** bickering, scrapping, wrangling **10** at variance, contending, contention, discordant, disharmony, dissension, squabbling **11** altercation, disputation, dissentient **12** argy-bargying **13** argumentation, at loggerheads **14** vitilitigation

**quarrelsome**
**06** chippy **07** scrappy, stroppy **09** bellicose, camstairy, camsteary, debateful, irascible, irritable **10** camsteerie, pugnacious **11** belligerent, contentious, hot-tempered, ill-tempered **12** cantankerous, disputatious **13** argumentative **14** ready for a fight

**quarry**
**04** game, goal, kill, mark, prey **05** chase, curry, prize, spoil **06** currie, object, target, victim **07** quarrel **08** stone pit **09** glory hole, slaughter

**quarter**
**01** E, N, q, S, W **02** qr, qu **03** pad **04** airt, area, digs, east, hand, part, pity, post, side, spot, west, zone **05** board, grace, house, lodge, mercy, north, place, point, put up, quart, rooms, south **06** billet, favour, fourth, ghetto, medina, pardon, region, sector **07** Moorery, section, shelter, station, two bits **08** barracks, clemency, district, division, domicile, dwelling, leniency, locality, lodgings, province, quartern, vicinity **09** direction, residence, territory **10** compassion, habitation, indulgence **11** accommodate, forgiveness **13** accommodation, neighbourhood
See also **compass**

**quarterly**
**02** qu **04** quar **12** three-monthly

**quarters**
**04** camp **05** house **06** ghetto **07** lodging

See also **accommodation**

**quartz**
**04** jasp **05** flint, prase **06** jasper, morion **07** crystal **08** amethyst, tiger eye **09** buhrstone, burrstone, cacholong, cairngorm, carnelian, cornelian, goldstone, tiger's eye **10** avanturine, aventurine, chalcedony **11** rock crystal **12** Bohemian ruby, Spanish topaz **14** Bristol-diamond, cairngorm-stone **15** occidental topaz

**quash**
**04** void **05** annul, crush, quell **06** cancel, defeat, repeal, revoke, scotch, squash, subdue **07** nullify, rescind, reverse **08** abrogate, override, overrule, overturn, set aside, suppress **09** overthrow **10** invalidate, put an end to **11** countermand

**quaver**
**03** sob **05** break, quake, shake, throb, trill, waver **06** quiver, tremor, warble, wobble **07** flicker, flutter, pulsate, shudder, tremble, tremolo, vibrate, vibrato **09** oscillate, trembling, vibration **10** eighth note **11** quaveriness

**quay**
**03** kay, key **04** dock, pier **05** jetty, levee, wharf **07** harbour

**queasiness**
**06** nausea **07** gagging **08** retching, sickness, vomiting **11** airsickness, biliousness, carsickness, seasickness **12** sick headache **14** motion sickness, travel sickness **15** morning sickness

**queasy**
**03** ill **04** sick **05** dizzy, faint, giddy, green, queer, rough **06** groggy, uneasy, unwell **07** bilious **08** nauseous, sickened **09** hazardous, nauseated, squeamish, unsettled **10** fastidious, out of sorts, scrupulous **15** under the weather

**Quebec**
**01** Q **02** QC

**queen**
**01** Q, R **02** ER, FD, HM, Qu, VR **03** VIR **04** idol, rani **05** belle, charm, ranee, ruler, Venus **06** beauty, regina **07** consort, empress, majesty, monarch **08** princess **09** sovereign **11** head of state

*Queens include:*

**03** Mab
**04** Anne, Anne (of Cleves), Emma, Grey (Jane, Lady), Joan (of Navarre), Mary, Mary (of Teck), Mary (Queen of Scots), Parr (Catherine)
**05** Maeve, Maria, Marie (de Médici), Sheba
**06** Boleyn (Anne), Esther, Hearts, Himiko, Howard (Catherine), Louisa, Nzinga, Salote, Silvia, Soraya
**07** Beatrix, Eleanor (of Aquitaine), Eleanor (of Castile), Juliana, Macbeth (Lady), Seymour (Jane), Titania, Zenobia
**08** Adelaide, Berenice, Boadicea,

Boudicca, Caroline (of Ansbach), Caroline (of Brunswick), Clotilda (St), Gloriana, Isabella (of Castile), Kristina, Margaret, Margaret (of Anjou), Margaret (St), Philippa (of Hainault), Victoria
**09** Alexandra, Artemisia, Brunhilde, Catherine (de Médici), Catherine (of Aragon), Catherine (of Braganza), Christina, Cleopatra, Elizabeth, Fredegond, Margrethe, Mary Tudor, Nefertiti, Semiramis, Woodville (Elizabeth)
**10** Hatshepsut, Lakshmi Bai, Wilhelmina
**13** Margaret Tudor
**14** Henrietta Maria
**15** Charlotte Sophia, Marie Antoinette

**queenly**
**05** grand, noble, regal, royal **06** august **07** reginal, stately, sublime **08** gracious, imperial, majestic, splendid **09** dignified, imperious, sovereign **11** monarchical

**queer**
◇ *anagram indicator* **03** ill, mar, odd, rum **04** foil, harm, iffy, ruin, sick **05** botch, cheat, dizzy, faint, fishy, funny, giddy, quare, rough, shady, spoil, upset, weird, wreck **06** Fifish, impair, quaint, queasy, shifty, stymie, thwart, unwell **07** bizarre, curious, deviant, dubious, strange, suspect, unusual **08** abnormal, doubtful, endanger, peculiar, puzzling, ridicule, singular, uncommon **09** eccentric, frustrate, irregular, unnatural **10** jeopardize, mysterious, outlandish, out of sorts, remarkable, suspicious, unorthodox **11** counterfeit, light-headed **13** extraordinary, funny peculiar **14** unconventional **15** under the weather

**queerness**
**06** oddity **11** abnormality, bizarreness, curiousness, peculiarity, singularity, strangeness, unorthodoxy, unusualness **12** eccentricity, irregularity, uncommonness **13** anomalousness, unnaturalness

**quell**
**03** die **04** alay, calm, hush, kill, rout, stay **05** abash, abate, aleye, allay, crush, quash, quiet **06** defeat, pacify, perish, soothe, squash, stifle, subdue **07** appease, conquer, put down, silence, slaying, subside **08** mitigate, moderate, overcome, suppress, vanquish **09** alleviate, overpower **10** disconcert, extinguish, put an end to, spifflicate **11** spifflicate

**quench**
**04** cool, sate, stop **05** douse, slake **06** put out, sloken, stanch, stifle **07** destroy, satiate, satisfy, slocken, smother, staunch **08** snuff out, stamp out **10** extinguish

**querulous**
**04** sour **05** cross, fussy, ratty, testy **06** shirty **07** carping, fretful, grouchy, peevish **08** captious, critical, petulant **09** fractious, grumbling, irascible,

irritable, plaintive **11** complaining
**12** cantankerous, discontented,
dissatisfied, fault-finding

## query

**01** Q **02** qy **03** ask **05** doubt, qualm
**06** quaere, qualms **07** dispute, inquire,
inquiry, problem, quibble, suspect
**08** distrust, mistrust, question
**09** challenge, suspicion **10** disbelieve,
hesitation, scepticism, uneasiness
**11** quarrel with, reservation,
uncertainty **12** question mark **13** be
sceptical of, throw doubts on

## quest

**03** aim **04** bark, goal, hunt, yelp
**06** search, voyage **07** crusade, inquiry,
journey, mission, purpose, pursuit,
seeking, venture **08** ringdove
**09** adventure **10** enterprise, expedition,
pilgrimage, wood pigeon
**11** exploration, undertaking
**13** investigation
• **in quest of** **03** for, out **06** out for
**08** questing **09** hunting for **11** in pursuit
of **12** harking after, searching for,
seeking after, trying to find **14** trying to
obtain

## question

**01** Q **02** Qu **03** ask **04** chin, poll, pose,
pump, quiz **05** demur, doubt, grill,
issue, point, poser, probe, query,
theme, topic **06** debate, matter,
motion, quaere, riddle, teaser
**07** debrief, discuss, dispute, enquiry,
eroteme, eroteme, examine, inquire,
inquiry, problem, scruple, subject
**08** argument, converse, erotesis,
proposal **09** backspeer, backspeir,
catechize, challenge, conundrum,
interview, objection **10** difficulty,
disbelieve, discussion **11** controversy,
interrogate, investigate, proposition,
uncertainty **12** conversation, cross-
examine, peradventure, point at issue
**13** cross-question, interrogation,
interrogatory **15** have doubts about,
have qualms about
• **in question** **07** at issue
**09** concerned **14** being discussed
**15** under discussion
• **out of the question** **06** absurd
**10** impossible, ridiculous
**11** unthinkable **12** unacceptable,
unbelievable
• **without question** **07** on trust
**11** immediately **14** unhesitatingly,
unquestionably, without arguing

## questionable

◇ *anagram indicator* **04** iffy **05** fishy,
shady, vexed **07** dubious, immoral,
suspect **08** arguable, doubtful,
improper, unproven **09** debatable,
equivocal, uncertain, unsettled **10** at
question, disputable, suspicious
**11** problematic **12** undetermined
**13** controversial, problematical

## questioner

**07** counsel, doubter, sceptic
**08** agnostic, examiner, inquirer
**09** catechist **10** catechizer, inquisitor,
quizmaster **11** disbeliever, interrogant,
interviewer **12** interlocutor,

interrogator, investigator **14** question-
master

## questionnaire

**04** form, quiz, test **06** survey **11** opinion
poll **14** market research

## queue

**03** row **04** file, line, tail **05** chain, order,
train **06** back up, column, fall in, in
line, line up, series, string **07** pigtail
**08** sequence, tailback **09** breadline,
crocodile, form a line **10** form a queue,
procession, succession, wait in line
**11** stand in line **13** concatenation

## quibble

**03** pun **04** carp, quip **05** cavil, dodge,
query, quirk **06** haggle, niggle, peck at,
snatch **07** brabble, nit-pick, protest,
quiblin, quiddit, quillet **08** equivoke,
pettifog, quiddity **09** complaint,
criticism, equivoque, objection
**10** equivocate, nit-picking, split hairs
**11** prevaricate **12** carriwitchet,
equivocation, pettifogging **13** avoid
the issue, find fault with, prevarication

## quibbler

**07** casuist, niggler, sophist **08** caviller,
chicaner **09** nit-picker **11** equivocator,
pettifogger **12** hair-splitter

## quibbling

**07** carping, evasive **08** captious,
critical, niggling, overnice
**09** ambiguous, casuistic, cavilling,
chicanery, chicaning **10** nit-picking
**12** equivocating, pettifogging **13** hair-
splitting, logic-chopping, word-
splitting

## quick

**03** hot, pdq **04** fast, keen, rath, soon,
yare **05** agile, alive, brief, brisk, flash,
hasty, nifty, nippy, rapid, rathe, ready,
sharp, smart, swift, zippy **06** astute,
clever, dapper, living, mobile, nimble,
presto, prompt, shrewd, snappy,
speedy, sudden **07** cursory, express,
flutter, hurried, instant, rapidly, schnell
**08** expedite, fleeting, pregnant, shifting
**09** immediate, receptive, sensitive,
sprightly **10** discerning, perceptive,
responsive **11** expeditious, intelligent,
perfunctory, quick-witted, sharp-
witted **12** without delay
**13** instantaneous **15** pretty damn quick,
quick off the mark

## quicken

**04** stir, whet **05** couch, hurry, rouse,
speed **06** arouse, excite, hasten, incite,
kindle, revive, stir up **07** advance,
animate, enliven, hurry up, inspire,
refresh, speed up **08** activate, dispatch,
energize, expedite, revivify
**09** galvanize, instigate, stimulate
**10** accelerate, couch grass, invigorate,
reactivate, revitalize, strengthen
**11** precipitate **12** reinvigorate

## quickly

**04** cito, fast, soon, vite **05** apace, quick,
slick, swith **06** presto, pronto
**07** briskly, express, hastily, rapidly,
readily, smartly, swiftly **08** abruptly,
promptly, smartish, speedily
**09** cursorily, hurriedly, instantly, like a

shot, like smoke, overnight, posthaste
**11** at the double, immediately,
prestissimo **12** a mile a minute, lickety-
split, with dispatch **13** expeditiously,
perfunctorily **14** at a rate of knots, hell
for leather, unhesitatingly
**15** instantaneously, like the clappers

## quickness

**05** speed **06** acumen **07** agility
**08** celerity, keenness, rapidity
**09** acuteness, alertness, briskness,
hastiness, immediacy, nimblesse,
readiness, sharpness, swiftness
**10** astuteness, expedition, nimbleness,
promptness, shrewdness, speediness,
suddenness **11** penetration,
promptitude **12** intelligence
**13** precipitation **15** quick-wittedness

## quick-tempered

**05** fiery, testy **06** snappy, touchy
**07** waspish **08** choleric, petulant,
shrewish, volcanic **09** excitable,
explosive, impatient, impulsive,
irascible, irritable, splenetic **11** hot-
tempered, quarrelsome
**13** temperamental

## quick-witted

**04** keen **05** acute, alert, sharp, smart,
witty **06** astute, bright, clever, crafty,
shrewd **09** ingenious, wide-awake
**10** perceptive **11** intelligent,
penetrating, ready-witted, resourceful
**12** nimble-witted **15** quick off the mark

## quid

**01** L **03** sov **04** chew, oner **05** libra,
pound, squid **06** guinea, nicker
**07** smacker **09** sovereign, substance
**12** jimmy-o'goblin **13** pound sterling
*See also* **pound**

## quid pro quo

**04** swap **07** damages **08** exchange,
trade-off **09** mutuality, tit for tat
**10** equivalent **11** co-operation,
equivalence, give-and-take,
reciprocity **12** compensation,
remuneration **13** reciprocation

## quiescent

**04** calm **05** inert, quiet, still **06** asleep,
at rest, latent, placid, serene, silent
**07** dormant, passive, resting
**08** inactive, peaceful, sleeping,
tranquil **09** reposeful **10** in abeyance,
motionless, untroubled **11** undisturbed

## quiet

**01** p **02** QT, sh **03** dry, low, shy
**04** calm, ease, hush, loun, lown, lull,
meek, mild, pale, rest, soft **05** doggo,
faint, lound, lownd, muted, peace,
shtum, sober, still, stoic, stumm
**06** gentle, hushed, lonely, low-key,
pastel, placid, repose, secret, serene,
settle, shtoom, shtumm, silent, sleepy,
stilly, subtle **07** appease, easeful,
muffled, orderly, private, schtoom,
silence, subdued **08** composed,
discreet, isolated, man-to-man,
peaceful, personal, reserved, reticent,
retiring, secluded, serenity, taciturn,
tranquil **09** inaudible, introvert,
noiseless, quietness, soundless,
stillness, withdrawn **10** indistinct,
phlegmatic, restrained, thoughtful,

untroubled **11** inoffensive, sequestered, undisturbed, unexcitable, unflappable **12** confidential, off-the-record, peacefulness, tranquillity, unfrequented, woman-to-woman **13** imperturbable, noiselessness, soundlessness, unforthcoming, without a sound **15** uncommunicative, undemonstrative
*See also* **silence**

**quieten**
**04** calm, dull, hush, mute **05** lower, quell, quiet, shush, sober, still **06** deaden, muffle, pacify, reduce, shut up, smooth, soften, soothe, stifle, subdew, subdue **07** compose, silence **08** calm down, diminish **12** tranquillize

**quietly**
**01** p **04** loun, lown, soft **05** lound, lownd, still **06** calmly, gently, meekly, mildly, mutely, softly **08** modestly, placidly, secretly, silently **09** inaudibly, privately **10** peacefully, tranquilly **11** noiselessly, soundlessly **12** deliberately **13** unobtrusively **15** surreptitiously

**quietness**
**04** calm, hush, lull **05** peace, quiet, still **06** repose **07** inertia, silence **08** calmness, dullness, quietude, serenity **09** composure, placidity, stillness **10** inactivity, quiescence **12** peacefulness, tranquillity **14** uneventfulness

**quietude**
**04** calm, hush, rest **05** peace, quiet **06** repose **07** ataraxy, silence **08** ataraxia, calmness, coolness, serenity **09** composure, placidity, quietness, stillness **10** equanimity, sedateness **11** restfulness **12** peacefulness, tranquillity

**quietus**
**03** end **05** death **06** demise **07** decease, release **08** dispatch, quashing **09** death-blow, discharge, silencing **10** extinction **11** acquittance, coup de grâce, death-stroke, elimination **15** finishing stroke

**quilt**
**05** doona, duvet, twilt **06** downie, kantha, thrash **07** comfort **08** bedcover, coverlet **09** bedspread, comforter, eiderdown **11** counterpane **12** counterpoint **14** patchwork quilt

**quince**
**03** bel **04** bael, bhel **06** feijoa **08** japonica **11** chaenomeles, queene-apple

**quinine**
**04** kina **05** china, quina **08** cinchona, kinakina **09** quinquina **10** chinachina, quinaquina

**quinsy**
**06** angina **08** cynanche, prunella **09** squinancy **11** tonsillitis

**quintessence**
**04** core, gist, pith, soul **05** heart **06** elixir, kernel, marrow, spirit **07** essence, extract, pattern

**08** exemplar, quiddity **10** embodiment **12** distillation **15** personification, sum and substance

**quintessential**
**05** ideal **06** entire **07** perfect, typical **08** complete, ultimate **09** essential **10** archetypal, consummate, definitive **12** archetypical, prototypical

**quip**
**03** gag **04** gibe, jest, joke **05** crack, quirk **06** retort, zinger **07** epigram, quibble, riposte **08** one-liner **09** wisecrack, witticism **10** knick-knack, pleasantry **12** carriwitchet

**quirk**
**03** way **04** kink, quip, turn, whim **05** fluke, freak, habit, knack, thing, trait, trick, twist **06** foible, hang-up, oddity, vagary **07** caprice, feature, quibble **09** curiosity, mannerism, obsession **11** peculiarity **12** eccentricity, idiosyncrasy **14** characteristic

**quirkiness**
**06** oddity **07** anomaly **08** zaniness **09** wackiness, weirdness **10** aberration, freakiness **11** abnormality, bizarreness, peculiarity, singularity, strangeness, unorthodoxy **12** eccentricity, freakishness, idiosyncrasy **13** nonconformity **14** capriciousness

**quirky**
◊ *anagram indicator* **03** odd **04** wild, zany **05** barmy, drôle, droll, funky, funny, kinky, queer, wacky, weird **06** far-out, freaky, way-out, whimsy **07** bizarre, curious, deviant, oddball, strange, uncanny, unusual **08** aberrant, abnormal, atypical, crackers, freakish, original, peculiar, singular, uncommon **09** different, eccentric, irregular, whimsical **10** capricious, off the wall, outlandish, remarkable **11** exceptional **13** extraordinary, idiosyncratic **14** unconventional

**quisling**
**05** Judas **06** puppet **07** traitor **08** betrayer, renegade, turncoat **12** collaborator **14** fifth columnist

**quit**
**02** go **03** end, rid **04** drop, exit, free, part, stop, void **05** avoid, cease, clear, leave, quite, quyte, repay, shift, stash **06** acquit, decamp, depart, desert, desist, give up, go away, pack in, quight, resign, retire, vacate **07** abandon, abstain, forsake, requite **08** leave off, renounce, withdraw **09** surrender **10** chicken out, relinquish **11** discontinue

**quite**
**03** all, yes **04** full, just, real, tout, very **05** clean, clear, fully, right, sheer **06** depart, enough, fairly, indeed, quight, rather, really, resign, wholly **07** absolve, exactly, totally, utterly **08** actually, entirely, every bit, somewhat **09** every whit, perfectly, precisely **10** absolutely, completely, moderately, reasonably, relatively **12** to some degree, to some extent

**13** comparatively
• **not quite** ◊ *tail deletion indicator* **06** almost, nearly

**quits**
**04** even, meet **05** equal, evens, level **06** square
• **call it quits 04** stop **05** cease **08** break off **09** make peace **10** call it a day **11** discontinue **12** stop fighting **14** bury the hatchet **15** lay down your arms

**quitter**
**03** pus, rat **06** skiver **07** shirker **08** apostate, defector, deserter, recreant, renegade **10** delinquent

**quiver**
◊ *anagram indicator* **05** quake, shake, throb **06** active, bicker, nimble, quaver, shiver, thrill, tingle, tremor, wobble **07** feather, flicker, flutter, pulsate, shudder, tremble, twinkle, vibrate **08** flichter **09** oscillate, palpitate, pulsation, vibration **11** oscillation, palpitation

**quixotic**
**06** errant **07** Utopian **08** fanciful, romantic **09** impetuous, impulsive, unworldly, visionary **10** chivalrous, idealistic, starry-eyed **11** extravagant, fantastical, unrealistic **13** impracticable

**quiz**
**03** eye **04** hoax, pump, test, yo-yo **05** grill, smoke, trail **07** examine, monocle **08** question **09** bandalore **11** competition, examination, interrogate, questioning **12** cross-examine **13** cross-question, interrogation, questionnaire

*Radio and television quiz shows include:*

**02** QI
**05** 15 to 1
**08** Bullseye, Eggheads
**09** Countdown, Odd One Out, Small Talk
**10** Mastermind, Masterteam, Screen Test
**11** Call My Bluff, Catchphrase, Give Us a Clue, Just a Minute, Spot the Tune, The Food Quiz, The News Quiz, What's My Line?
**12** Ask the Family, Blockbusters, Bognor or Bust, Deal or No Deal, Face the Music, Fifteen to One, Going for Gold, Lucky Numbers, Name That Tune, Strike It Rich, Take Your Pick, Telly Addicts, Winning Lines
**13** Blankety Blank, Bob's Full House, Going for a Song, Strike It Lucky
**14** Brain of Britain, Family Fortunes, The Weakest Link, Wheel of Fortune, Winner Takes All
**15** Double Your Money, The Price Is Right

**quizzical**
**06** amused **07** amusing, baffled, comical, curious, mocking, puzzled, teasing **08** humorous, sardonic

**quizzically**
**09** inquiring, mystified, perplexed, satirical, sceptical **11** questioning

**quizzically**
**06** askant **07** askance **09** curiously, mockingly **11** inquiringly, sceptically **13** questioningly

**quoit**
**04** coit, disc, disk, ring
*See also* **buttocks**
• **target in quoits**   **03** hub, pin, tee

**quota**
**03** cut **04** part **05** share, slice, whack **06** quotum, ration **07** portion **09** allowance **10** allocation,

assignment, contingent, percentage, proportion **11** slice of cake **14** numerus clausus

**quotation**
**03** bid, tag **04** cost, line, rate **05** piece, price, quote **06** charge, figure, tender **07** cutting, excerpt, extract, listing, passage, remnant **08** allusion, citation, estimate **09** reference, selection **14** locus classicus

**quote**
**04** cite, coat, cote, echo, name **05** coate **06** adduce, allege, drag up, recall, recite, repeat **07** examine,

mention, refer to **08** allude to **09** recollect, reproduce **10** scrutinize

**quoted**
**05** cited **06** stated **08** reported **09** instanced **10** referred to, reproduced **13** forementioned **14** above-mentioned

**quotidian**
**05** daily **06** common, normal **07** diurnal, regular, routine **08** day-to-day, everyday, habitual, ordinary, repeated, workaday **09** customary, recurrent **11** bog-standard, commonplace **12** run-of-the-mill

**R**
02 ar 05 Romeo

## rabbi

## rabbit

03 bun, doe 04 buck, cony, go on, talk
05 bunny, coney, daman, drone, hyrax
06 dassie, dodder, wander, wibble
07 go-devil, maunder 08 confound
09 give forth 11 bunny rabbit

• **rabbit on** 03 gab, yap 04 go on
06 babble, natter, waffle, witter
07 blather, blether, chatter, maunder
08 witter on 09 go on and on,
maunder on

## rabble

03 mob, tag 04 herd, rout 05 crowd,
horde, meiny, plebs 06 gabble,
masses, meiney, meinie, menyie,
proles, raffle, ragtag, rascal, tagrag,
throng 07 doggery 08 canaille,
populace, riff-raff, varletry
09 colluvies, hoi polloi, rascaille,
rascality 10 clamjamfry 11 clanjamfray,
proletariat, rank and file
12 clamjamphrie, common people,
raggle-taggle 13 great unwashed

## rabble-rouser

08 agitator 09 demagogue, firebrand
10 incendiary, ringleader, tub-thumper
12 troublemaker

## rabble-rousing

10 stirring up 11 tub-thumping
13 troublemaking

## Rabelaisian

04 lewd, racy 05 bawdy, gross
06 coarse, earthy, ribald, risqué, vulgar
08 indecent 09 exuberant, satirical
11 extravagant, uninhibited
12 unrestrained

## rabid

03 mad 04 wild 06 ardent, crazed,
raging 07 berserk, bigoted, burning,
extreme, fervent, frantic, furious,
violent, zealous 08 frenzied, maniacal
09 fanatical, ferocious, obsessive
10 hysterical, intolerant, irrational
11 hydrophobic, overzealous,
unreasoning 12 narrow-minded

## rabies

05 lyssa 08 rabidity 09 rabidness
11 hydrophobia

## race

03 cut, fly, ren, rin, run, sex, zap, zip
04 bolt, clan, dart, kind, line, rach,
rase, raze, rush, seed, slit, tear, zoom
05 blood, breed, chase, erase, genus,
house, hurry, pluck, quest, ratch,
scoot, slash, speed, stock, trial, tribe
06 career, colour, family, gallop,
ginger, hasten, nation, people, snatch,
stirps, strain 07 contest, dynasty,
kindred, lineage, rivalry, scratch,
species 08 ancestry, go all out,
piquancy 09 parentage 10 accelerate,
contention, extraction, get a move on
11 competition, ethnic group, get
cracking, racial group, run like hell
15 take part in a race

## racecourse

03 lap 04 turf 05 track 06 course,
dromos 07 circuit 08 speedway
09 racetrack 10 hippodrome

## racehorse

05 neddy, stiff 06 mudder, novice
07 no-hoper 08 cocktail, outsider,
yearling 12 morning glory,
thoroughbred
*See also* **horse**

## racial

04 folk 06 ethnic, tribal 07 genetic
08 national 09 ancestral, inherited
12 ethnological, genealogical

## raciness

03 pep 04 zest 06 energy 07 pizzazz
08 dynamism, lewdness, ribaldry
09 animation, bawdiness, crudeness,
freshness, indecency, vulgarity
10 coarseness, ebullience, indelicacy,
liveliness, smuttiness 11 naughtiness,
zestfulness 12 exhilaration
14 suggestiveness

## racing

12 handicap race, National Hunt, starting gate, steeplechase, thoroughbred, weighing room
14 conditions race
15 stewards' enquiry

*Formula One Grand Prix circuits include:*

05 Imola, Monza
06 Sakhir, Sepang, Suzuka
07 Bahrain
08 Istanbul, Shanghai
10 Albert Park, Hockenheim, Interlagos, Magny-Cours, Monte Carlo
11 Hungaroring, Nurburgring, Silverstone
12 Indianapolis
13 Francorchamps

*Formula One motor racing teams include:*

05 Honda
06 Toyota
07 Ferrari, McLaren, Midland, Red Bull, Renault
08 Williams
09 BMW Sauber, Toro Rosso
10 Super Aguri
13 Red Bull Racing

*Motor racing drivers, motorcyclists and associated figures include:*

04 Foyt (A J), Hill (Damon), Hill (Graham), Hunt (James), Ickx (Jacky), Moss (Sir Stirling)
05 Alesi (Jean), Clark (Jim), Clark (Roger), Hulme (Denny), Lauda (Niki), McRae (Colin), Olsen (Ole), Petty (Richard), Prost (Alain), Rossi (Valentino), Sainz (Carlos), Senna (Ayrton), Unser (Al), Unser (Bobby)
06 Ascari (Alberto), Berger (Gerhard), Briggs (Barry), Button (Jensen), Doohan (Michael), Dunlop (Joey), Fangio (Juan), Irvine (Eddie), Lawson (Eddie), Mauger (Ivan), Piquet (Nelson), Sheene (Barry), Walker (Murray)
07 Brabham (Sir Jack), Brundle (Martin), Ferrari (Enzo), Fogarty (Carl), Guthrie (Janet), Mäkinen (Tommi), Mansell (Nigel), McLaren (Bruce), Mikkola (Hannu), Roberts (Kenny), Rosberg (Keke), Rosberg (Nico), Segrave (Sir Henry), Stewart (Sir Jackie), Surtees (John)
08 Agostini (Giacomo), Andretti (Mario), Campbell (Donald), Campbell (Sir Malcolm), Hailwood (Mike), Häkkinen (Mika), Hawthorn (Mike), Oldfield (Barney), Williams (Sir Frank)
09 Blomqvist (Stig), Chevrolet (Louis), Coulthard (David), Earnhardt (Dale), Kankkunen (Juha)
10 Fittipaldi (Emerson), Schumacher (Michael), Schumacher (Ralf), Villeneuve (Jacques)
12 Rickenbacker (Eddie)

*Motor-racing-related terms include:*

03 lap, pit
04 apex, grid, oval, pits, pole, T-car
05 apron, shunt
06 out lap, slicks
07 chicane, cockpit, hairpin, marshal, pace car, paddock, pit lane, pit stop, stagger, steward
08 dirty air, drafting, fishtail, lollipop, outbrake, pit board, straight
09 Brickyard, parade lap, parc fermé, safety car, telemetry
10 back marker, gravel trap, qualifying, racing line, run-off area, slipstream, team orders
11 braking zone, pit straight, victory lane
12 formation lap, pole position
13 launch control, scrutineering, start straight, stop-go penalty, superspeedway
14 finish straight

## racism

04 bias 08 jingoism 09 apartheid, prejudice, racialism 10 chauvinism, xenophobia 14 discrimination 15 racial prejudice

## racist

04 Nazi 05 bigot 07 bigoted 09 racialist 10 chauvinist, intolerant 13 discriminator 14 discriminatory

## rack

04 bink, hack, haik, hake, heck, pain, tear 05 agony, crash, creel, drift, drive, flake, frame, pangs, shake, shelf, stand, touse, touze, towse, towze, track, wrack, wrest, wring 06 extort, harass, harrow, holder, misery, strain, stress, wrench 07 afflict, agonize, anguish, crucify, distort, oppress, remnant, stretch, support, torment, torture, trestle 08 convulse, distress, lacerate, vertebra 09 framework, structure, suffering, vengeance 10 affliction, canterbury, excruciate, overstrain, punishment 11 destruction, devastation, persecution, portmanteau 13 umbrella stand
• **on the rack** 06 in pain 07 in agony 09 in trouble, suffering 10 in distress 11 under stress 13 under pressure 14 in difficulties
• **rack your brains** 05 study 09 think hard 11 concentrate, think deeply 13 put your mind to

## racket

03 bat, con, din, job, row 04 fuss, game, rort, scam 05 dodge, fraud, noise, trick 06 fiddle, hubbub, outcry, rattle, scheme, tumult, uproar 07 clamour, swindle, yelling 08 ballyhoo, business, shouting, snowshoe 09 commotion, deception, gold brick 10 hullabaloo, hurly-burly, occupation 11 dissipation, disturbance, pandemonium 14 responsibility

## racketeering

05 fraud 08 cheating, fiddling, fleecing, stealing, stinging 09 extortion, swindling 10 chiselling, defrauding,

ripping off 12 overcharging 14 taking for a ride 15 cooking the books

## raconteur

07 relater 08 narrator, reporter 09 describer 10 anecdotist, chronicler 11 commentator, storyteller

## racquet

*see* **racket**

## racy

04 blue, rude 05 bawdy, crude, dirty, peppy, salty, spicy, witty, zippy 06 coarse, lively, ribald, risqué, smutty, vulgar 07 buoyant, dynamic, naughty, piquant, pungent, zestful 08 animated, indecent, spirited, vigorous 09 ebullient, energetic, off-colour, sparkling, vivacious 10 boisterous, fast-moving, indelicate, suggestive 12 enthusiastic

## radar

• **radar image** 04 blip
• **radar signal** 04 echo 05 angel

## raddled

◇ *anagram indicator* 05 drawn, gaunt 06 wasted 07 haggard, in a mess, unkempt, worn out 11 dishevelled 15 the worse for wear

## radiance

03 joy 04 glow 05 bliss, gleam, light, sheen, shine 06 lustre 07 delight, ecstasy, elation, glitter, rapture 08 pleasure 09 beaminess, happiness, radiation, splendour 10 brightness, brilliance, effulgence, luminosity, refulgence 12 resplendence 13 incandescence

## radiant

05 beamy, happy, lit up 06 bright, elated, joyful 07 beaming, beamish, glowing, lambent, pleased, shining 08 blissful, ecstatic, gleaming, glorious, luminous, splendid 09 brilliant, delighted, effulgent, refulgent, sparkling 10 glittering, in raptures, profulgent 11 illuminated, magnificent, on cloud nine, over the moon, resplendent 12 incandescent 15 in seventh heaven, on top of the world

## radiate

03 ray 04 beam, emit, glow, pour, shed 05 gleam, issue, shine 06 branch, spread 07 diffuse, diverge, emanate, give off, scatter, send out 08 disperse 09 oscillate, send forth, spread out 10 divaricate 11 disseminate

## radiation

04 rays 05 waves 08 emission 09 emanation 12 transmission

*Radiation includes:*

02 ir, UV
03 UVA, UVB, UVC, UVR
04 beta, hard, heat, soft
05 alpha, gamma, light, X-rays
06 cosmic
07 Hawking, visible
08 Cerenkov, gamma ray, infrared, ionizing
09 black body
10 background, black light,

insolation, microwaves, radio
waves, synchroton
**11** ultraviolet
**12** beta particle
**13** alpha particle
**14** bremsstrahlung
**15** electromagnetic

• **radiation unit** **03** rad, rem, rep

**radical**
**03** rad, red **04** amyl, aryl, dyad, root
**05** allyl, basic, butyl, cetyl, group,
hexad, hexyl, monad, rebel, total,
triad, utter, vinyl, yippy **06** acetyl,
benzal, benzil, benzyl, entire, heptad,
innate, ligand, methyl, native, pentad,
phenyl, propyl, tetrad, yippie
**07** benzoyl, carbene, drastic, extreme,
fanatic, Jacobin, natural, oxonium,
primary, radicle **08** absolute,
ammonium, carbonyl, carboxyl,
complete, glyceryl, glycosyl, hydroxyl,
inherent, left-wing, militant, original,
profound, reformer, sweeping,
thorough **09** elemental, essential,
extremist, fanatical, intrinsic,
isopropyl, primitive, reformist **10** deep-
seated, elementary, exhaustive, nitro-
group, rebellious, vinylidene
**11** benzylidine, far-reaching,
fundamental, methyl group,
phosphonium, rudimentary
**13** comprehensive, ferricyanogen,
ferrocyanogen, revolutionary,
thoroughgoing **14** fundamentalist

**radio**
**08** wireless

*Radio stations include:*

**03** LBC, XFM
**04** Kiss
**06** Jazz FM, Kiss FM, Radio 1, Radio
2, Radio 3, Radio 4
**08** Five Live
**09** BBC London, Capital FM, Classic
FM, Radio Five, Talksport
**11** Virgin Radio
**12** World Service
**13** Radio Caroline, Radio Scotland
**15** Radio Luxembourg

*Radio programmes include:*

**02** PM
**04** ITMA
**05** Today
**10** Home Truths, The Archers,
Woman's Hour
**11** Just a Minute, You and Yours
**12** Any Questions?, Poetry Please,
Start the Week
**13** Book at Bedtime, Pick of the
Week, Round the Horne, The
World at One
**14** Brain of Britain
**15** It's That Man Again

*See also* **quiz**
• **on the radio** ◇ *homophone
indicator* **02** DJ **10** disc jockey
• **radio presenter** **02** DJ **10** disc
jockey

*Radio presenters include:*

**04** **Mayo** (Simon), **Peel** (John), **Ross**
(Jonathan), **Tong** (Pete)

**05** **Cooke** (Alistair), **Evans** (Chris),
**Stern** (Howard), **Vance** (Tommy),
**Wogan** (Sir Terry), **Young** (Kirsty),
**Young** (Sir Jimmy)
**06** **Harris** (Bob), **Jensen** (Kid), **Lamacq**
(Steve), **Lamarr** (Mark), **Lawley**
(Sue), **Moyles** (Chris), **Murray**
(Jenni), **Savile** (Sir Jimmy), **Travis**
(Dave Lee), **Walker** (Johnnie),
**Whiley** (Jo), **Wright** (Steve)
**07** **Edmonds** (Noel), **Everett** (Kenny),
**Freeman** (Alan 'Fluff'), **Keillor**
(Garrison), **Kershaw** (Andy),
**Pickles** (Wilfred), **Plomley** (Roy),
**Redhead** (Brian), **Tarrant** (Chris)
**08** **Anderson** (Marjorie), **Campbell**
(Nicky), **Humphrys** (John), **Metcalfe**
(Jean), **Westwood** (Tim)
**09** **Blackburn** (Tony), **MacGregor**
(Sue), **Radcliffe** (Mark)
**10** **Gambaccini** (Paul), **Hardcastle**
(William)
**11** **Nightingale** (Annie)

**radioactive**
**03** hot

**radish**
**05** mooli, runch **06** daikon
**08** Raphanus

**radium**
**02** Ra

**radon**
**02** Rn

**raffish**
**04** loud **05** cheap, gaudy, gross, showy
**06** casual, coarse, flashy, garish,
jaunty, rakish, sporty, tawdry, trashy,
vulgar **07** dashing, uncouth
**08** bohemian, careless, improper
**09** dissolute, tasteless **10** dissipated,
flamboyant **12** devil-may-care,
disreputable, meretricious

**raffle**
**04** draw **05** notch, sweep **06** jumble,
lumber, rabble, tangle **07** crumple,
lottery, rubbish, tombola **08** Calcutta,
riff-raff **10** sweepstake

**raft**
**04** heap **05** balsa, crowd, float
**09** catamaran **11** Carley float

**rag**
◇ *anagram indicator* **03** kid, lap, rib,
row, tat **04** bait, duds, flag, fray, goof,
haze, jeer, mock, sail, slut, tatt
**05** argue, cloth, clout, lapje, scold,
scrap, shred, taunt, tease, towel
**06** badger, banter, duster, lappie,
tagrag, tatter, wallop **07** duddery,
flannel, garment, remnant, torment,
wrangle **08** farthing, ridicule
**09** newspaper, schmutter **10** floorcloth,
paper money, raggedness
**12** handkerchief
*See also* **newspaper**
• **bunch of rags** **03** mop

**ragamuffin**
**04** waif **05** gamin, ragga **06** urchin
**09** street kid **11** guttersnipe
**14** tatterdemalion **15** tatterdemallion

**ragbag**
**03** mix **04** olio **05** salad **06** jumble,

medley **07** mixture **08** mishmash,
pastiche, slattern **09** confusion,
potpourri **10** assemblage, assortment,
hodgepodge, hotchpotch, miscellany
**11** olla-podrida **14** omnium-gatherum

**rage**
◇ *anagram indicator* **03** ire **04** bait, bate,
bayt, fume, fury, ramp, rant, rave, tear
**05** anger, craze, flame, flood, go mad,
mania, paddy, party, radge, storm,
vogue, wrath **06** ardour, choler, frenzy,
raving, see red, seethe, temper, tumult
**07** bluster, explode, madness, passion,
rampage, tantrum, thunder, violent
**08** boil over, paroxysm, violence
**09** blow a fuse, do your nut, raise hell,
spit blood **10** hit the roof, paddy-
whack **11** blow a gasket, blow your
top, flip your lid, go up the wall, lose
your rag **12** blow your cool, lose your
cool, spit feathers **14** foam at the
mouth **15** fly off the handle, go off the
deep end
• **all the rage** **02** in **03** now **04** cool
**06** trendy **07** in vogue, popular, stylish
**08** the craze **10** the in thing
**11** fashionable

**ragged**
◇ *anagram indicator* **04** poor, rag'd,
rent, torn **05** duddy, holey, ragde,
rough, tatty **06** duddie, frayed, jagged,
raguly, ripped, rugged, shabby,
shaggy, tagrag, uneven, untidy
**07** erratic, in holes, notched, scruffy,
tattery, unkempt, worn-out
**08** indented, indigent, serrated,
tattered **09** destitute, in tatters, irregular
**10** down and out, down-at-heel,
fragmented, straggling, threadbare
**12** disorganized **14** tatterdemalion
**15** falling to pieces, tatterdemallion

**raging**
**03** mad **04** amok, wild **05** amuck,
angry, irate, rabid **06** fuming, ireful,
raving, stormy **07** enraged, furious,
violent **08** flagrant, frenzied, furibund,
incensed, seething, wrathful
**09** turbulent **10** infuriated, tumultuous
**11** fulminating

**raid**
**02** do **04** bust, loot, pull, road, rode,
rush, sack **05** blitz, foray, onset, rifle,
sally, storm, swoop **06** assail, attack,
bodrag, charge, forage, hold-up,
inroad, invade, maraud, sortie, strike
**07** air raid, assault, break-in, descent,
pillage, plunder, ram-raid, ransack,
robbery, set upon, spreagh **08** dawn
raid, invasion **09** break into, descend
on, excursion, incursion, onslaught,
sneak-raid **12** Baedeker raid

**raider**
**05** crook, shark, thief **06** looter, pirate,
robber, viking **07** brigand, invader,
villain **08** attacker, criminal, marauder,
pillager **09** plunderer, ransacker

**rail**
**03** bar **04** flow, gush, jeer, mock, rung,
sora, spar **05** abuse, cloak, decry, raile,
rayle, scoff **06** attack, banter, Rallus,
revile **07** arraign, censure, garment,
inveigh, protest, upbraid **08** denounce,

reviling, ridicule **09** castigate, criticize, fulminate **10** slang-whang, vituperate, vociferate **11** neckerchief

## railing

**04** rail **05** fence, rails **06** paling, pulpit **07** barrier, fencing, manrope, parapet, pushpit **08** banister, parclose, raillery **09** bannister, fireguard **10** balustrade

## raillery

**04** joke **05** chaff, irony, sport **06** banter, joking, satire **07** jeering, jesting, kidding, mockery, ragging, railing, ribbing, teasing **08** badinage, diatribe, dicacity, repartee, ridicule **09** chiacking, invective **10** persiflage, pleasantry

## railway

**02** Ry **03** rly, Rwy **04** line, rail **05** rails, track **08** railroad

*Railways include:*

**01** L
**02** el
**03** cog, ell
**04** rack, ship, tube
**05** cable, light, metro, model
**06** garden, scenic, siding, subway
**07** cutting, express, freight, tramway
**08** cable-car, electric, elevated, main line, monorail, mountain
**09** funicular, goods line, InterCity®, trunk line
**10** branch line, broad gauge, feeder line
**11** crémaillère, narrow gauge, underground
**12** rapid transit
**13** high-speed line, passenger line, rack-and-pinion, standard gauge

*Railway-related terms include:*

**02** CN
**03** ABC, ATC, ATP, bay, cab, car, CPR, EWS, GWR, lie, LMS, LNE, lye, RMT, rod, RPC, SRA, Sta, tie, TOC, van
**04** APEX, bank, crew, dock, dome, frog, halt, LNER, RUCC, slot, SPAD, spur, stay, TPWS
**05** aisle, berth, bogey, bogie, brake, brute, coach, coupé, crank, depot, diner, grate, guard, local, Mogul, shunt, T-rail, train, wagon
**06** balise, banker, boiler, branch, buffer, buffet, coaler, diesel, gricer, hopper, piston, points, porter, reefer, saloon, siding, stoker, target, tender, tunnel, up-line, waggon, Y-track
**07** ballast, banking, bay-line, buckeye, bulgine, butcher, caboose, cocopan, cutting, drag-bar, drawbar, entrain, fettler, firebox, fireman, hostler, lineman, locoman, network, off-peak, Pullman, railage, railbed, railbus, railcar, railman, roadbed, signals, sleeper, station, tank car, turnout, viaduct, whistle, yardman
**08** box-wagon, Bradshaw, brakeman, brake van, bullgine, cant-rail, carriage, catenary, choo-choo, corridor, coupling,

crosstie, down-line, draw-gear, firehole, fire-tube, fly-under, horse box, junction, live-rail, loop-line, main line, manrider, motorail, motorman, overpass, pilotman, platform, puff-puff, rack rail, railcard, railhead, roomette, side-line, smokebox, subgrade, terminus, trackage, trackbed, wagon-lit
**09** brakesman, buffet car, checkrail, concourse, conductor, couchette, crossover, cross-sill, day return, dining-car, drag-chain, fishplate, footboard, footplate, funicular, goods line, goods yard, guardrail, guard's van, interrail, iron horse, jerkwater, lengthman, overshoot, palace-car, parlor car, plate rail, pointsman, rail-borne, rail-motor, railwoman, second man, sidetrack, signal box, signalman, slip-coach, steam pipe, tank wagon, third rail, train mile, trunk line, turntable, vestibule, wheelbase
**10** baggage-car, brake block, branch line, broad-gauge, centre-rail, draught-bar, embankment, Eurotunnel, feeder line, griddle car, home-signal, lengthsman, locomotive, luggage-van, parlour car, platelayer, Pullman car, railroader, railwayman, smokestack, steam brake, supersaver, surfaceman, switchback, tank engine, zone-ticket
**11** compartment, gandy dancer, goods engine, left-luggage, people mover, pilot engine, rack railway, railroad car, ship railway, side cutting, sleeping car, strap-hanger, throatplate, track-walker, underbridge, underground, vacuum brake, whistle stop
**12** double-header, driving wheel, engine-driver, euroterminal, footplateman, loading gauge, rolling stock, running board, shunting yard, station house, trainspotter
**13** conductor rail, dead man's pedal, level crossing, sleeping coach, standard gauge, stationmaster, through-ticket
**14** dead man's handle, shuttle service, superelevation
**15** marshalling yard

*See also* **train**
• **railway station**

*Railway stations include:*

**05** Crewe
**06** Euston
**08** Victoria, Waterloo, Waverley
**09** St Pancras
**10** Gare de Lyon, Gare du Nord, Kings Cross, Marylebone, Paddington, Piccadilly
**11** Penn Station
**12** Charing Cross, Gare St Lazare, Grand Central,

Hauptbahnhof, Montparnasse
**15** Clapham Junction, Gare d'Austerlitz, Liverpool Street

*See also* **London**

## rain

**03** wet **04** pelt, pour, roke, sile, smir, smur, spet, spit, teem, weep **05** blash, brash, raine, reign, smirr, storm, water **06** bucket, deluge, mizzle, shower, squall, volley **07** drizzle, skiffle, torrent **08** down-come, downfall, downpour, pour down, rainfall, sprinkle **09** raindrops, rainstorm, sunshower **10** bucket down, cloudburst, Scotch mist, tipple down **12** thunderstorm **13** precipitation, the clouds open **15** rain cats and dogs

## rainbow

**03** arc, bow **04** arch, iris **05** prism **06** bruise, dew-bow, fog-bow, irised, sunbow **07** moon-bow **08** irisated, spectral, spectrum **09** arc-en-ciel, prismatic, steelhead, water gall **10** iridescent, opalescent, variegated, weather gaw **11** rainbow-like, weather gall **13** kaleidoscopic

*Colours of the rainbow:*

**03** red
**04** blue
**05** green
**06** indigo, orange, violet, yellow

## raincoat

**03** mac **04** mack, mino **08** Burberry® **09** macintosh **10** mackintosh

## rainy

**03** wet **04** damp, soft **05** moist **06** hyetal, watery **07** drizzly, pluvial, showery **08** pluviose, pluvious **09** inclement

## raise

◊ *reversal indicator* **02** up **03** get **04** buoy, grow, jack, levy, lift, moot, rear, rise, stir **05** amass, boost, breed, build, cairn, cause, elate, erect, evoke, exalt, extol, hoist, leave, mount, put up, rally, rouse, set up, utter, weigh **06** araise, arayse, arouse, broach, bump up, create, excite, gather, hike up, hold up, jack up, lift up, muster, obtain, push up, step up, stir up, take up, uplift **07** advance, amplify, augment, bring up, collect, develop, educate, elevate, enhance, heave up, magnify, nurture, present, produce, provoke, recruit, suggest, upgrade **08** activate, assemble, escalate, heighten, increase, purchase **09** construct, cultivate, establish, institute, intensify, introduce, propagate **10** accumulate, give rise to, put forward, strengthen **11** get together

## raised

◊ *reversal down indicator* **05** cameo **06** relief **07** applied, relievo **08** appliqué, elevated, embossed

## rake

**03** hoe **04** comb, hunt, roam, roué **05** amass, graze, level, rifle, scour, slope, track **06** gather, gay dog, harrow, lecher, scrape, search,

smooth, strafe, straff, string, wanton
**07** collect, incline, journey, pasture,
playboy, ransack, rummage, scratch,
swinger **08** buckrake, hedonist,
Lothario, muck-rake, prodigal,
rakehell **09** debauchee, dissolute,
horse rake, libertine **10** accumulate,
degenerate, profligate, sensualist
**11** spendthrift, stubble rake
**14** pleasure-seeker
• **rake in** **03** net **04** earn, make, reap
**05** fetch, gross **06** haul in, pull in
**07** bring in, get paid, receive
• **rake up** **05** dig up, raise **06** drag up,
remind, revive **07** bring up, mention
**08** dredge up **09** introduce

**rake-off**
**03** cut **04** part **05** share, slice **07** portion
**10** percentage, proportion

**rakish**
**05** loose, natty, sharp, smart **06** breezy,
casual, dapper, flashy, jaunty, sinful,
snazzy, sporty **07** dashing, immoral,
raffish, stylish **08** debonair, depraved,
prodigal **09** abandoned, debauched,
dissolute, lecherous, libertine
**10** degenerate, dissipated, flamboyant,
licentious, nonchalant, profligate
**11** adventurous **12** devil-may-care

**rally**
**04** demo, rely **05** group, march, unite
**06** banter, gather, morcha, muster,
perk up, pick up, really, reform, revive,
summon **07** collect, convene, get well,
improve, marshal, meeting, recover,
regroup, renewal, reunion, revival,
round up **08** assemble, assembly,
comeback, jamboree, mobilize,
organize, recovery **09** gathering, get
better, re-enforce **10** assemblage,
bounce back, conference, congregate,
convention, reassemble, recuperate,
reorganize, resurgence **11** be on the
mend, convocation, get together,
improvement, mass meeting, pull
through **12** band together, come
together, gain strength, recuperation
**13** bring together, demonstration

**ram**
**03** hit, jam, pun, tup **04** beat, bump,
butt, cram, dash, drum, pack, slam,
stem, tamp **05** Aries, crash, crowd,
drive, force, pound, smash, stuff,
wedge **06** corvus, hammer, punner,
strike, thrust, wether **07** block up,
squeeze **08** compress

**ramble**
◇ *anagram indicator* **03** gas, jaw **04** hike,
roam, rove, tour, trek, trip, walk, wind
**05** amble, drift, jaunt, range, stray,
tramp, troll **06** babble, dodder, natter,
rabbit, stroll, waffle, wander, wanton,
witter, zigzag **07** blather, blether,
chatter, digress, diverge, meander,
saunter, traipse **08** bushwalk, rabbit
on, straggle, witter on **09** excursion,
expatiate **15** go off at a tangent

**rambler**
**05** hiker, rover **06** roamer, walker
**07** drifter **08** stroller, wanderer,
wayfarer **09** saunterer, traveller
**10** bushwalker

**rambling**
◇ *anagram indicator* **05** wordy **06** errant,
vagary **07** verbose **08** errantry, trailing
**09** desultory, excursive, sprawling,
spreading, wandering **10** circuitous,
digressive, disjointed, incoherent,
long-winded, roundabout, straggling
**12** disconnected, long-drawn-out,
periphrastic **14** skimble-skamble

**rami**
**04** rhea **10** China grass, grass cloth

**ramification**
**04** limb **06** branch, effect, result,
sequel, upshot **07** outcome **08** offshoot
**09** branching, outgrowth
**11** consequence, development,
implication **12** complication,
divarication

**ramp**
**03** rob **04** rage, rise, romp **05** climb,
grade, slope **06** ramson, snatch,
tomboy **07** incline, swindle **08** gradient
**09** acclivity, declivity **10** cattle-grid

**rampage**
◇ *anagram indicator* **04** fury, rage, rant,
rave, rush, tear **05** storm **06** charge,
frenzy, furore, mayhem, uproar **07** run
amok, run riot, run wild, turmoil
**08** violence **09** go berserk **10** rush
wildly **11** destruction **13** rush violently
• **on the rampage** ◇ *anagram indicator*
**04** amok, wild **06** wildly **07** berserk,
violent **08** frenzied **09** in a frenzy,
violently **12** out of control

**rampant**
◇ *anagram indicator* ◇ *reversal indicator*
**04** rank, rife, wild **06** fierce, raging,
wanton **07** profuse, rearing, riotous,
violent **08** epidemic, pandemic
**09** excessive, out of hand, prevalent,
unbridled, unchecked **10** widespread
**12** high-spirited, out of control,
uncontrolled, unrestrained

**rampart**
**04** bank, fort, ring, wall **05** fence, guard
**06** abatis, vallum **07** abattis, bastion,
bulwark, defence, parapet, rampire
**08** security **09** barricade, earthwork
**10** breastwork, embankment,
stronghold **13** fortification

**ramshackle**
◇ *anagram indicator* **05** shaky **06** flimsy,
ruined, unsafe **07** rickety, run-down
**08** decrepit, derelict, unsteady
**09** crumbling, neglected, tottering
**10** broken-down, jerry-built,
tumbledown **11** dilapidated

**ranch**
**04** farm, tear **05** range **06** estate, spread
**07** fazenda, station **08** estancia,
hacienda, property **09** dude ranch
**10** plantation **12** sheep station **13** cattle
station

**rancid**
**03** bad, off **04** foul, high, rank, sour
**05** fetid, frowy, musty, stale **06** foetid,
frowie, putrid, rotten, turned
**07** froughy, noisome, noxious
**08** overripe **10** malodorous, unpleasant

**rancorous**
**06** bitter **07** acerbic, hostile **08** spiteful,
vengeful, venomous, virulent
**09** malignant, resentful, splenetic
**10** implacable, malevolent, vindictive
**11** acrimonious

**rancour**
**04** hate **05** spite, venom **06** animus,
enmity, grudge, hatred, malice, spleen
**07** ill-will **08** acrimony, sourness
**09** animosity, antipathy, hostility,
malignity, virulence **10** bitterness, ill-
feeling, resentment **11** malevolence
**13** resentfulness **14** vindictiveness

**rand**
**01** R

**random**
◇ *anagram indicator* **04** spot, wild
**05** stray **06** casual, chance **07** aimless,
freedom **08** sporadic **09** arbitrary,
desultory, haphazard, hit-or-miss,
irregular, unplanned **10** accidental, at
a venture, fortuitous, hit-and-miss,
hitty-missy, incidental, stochastic,
unarranged **11** purposeless, scattershot
**12** uncontrolled, unmethodical,
unsystematic **13** serendipitous
**14** indiscriminate
• **at random** ◇ *anagram indicator*
**06** hobnob **07** at large **08** at rovers,
randomly **09** aimlessly, haphazard
**11** arbitrarily, haphazardly, irregularly
**12** fortuitously, incidentally,
sporadically **13** purposelessly
**14** unmethodically **15** à tort et à travers

**randomly**
◇ *anagram indicator* **08** at random
**09** aimlessly **11** arbitrarily,
haphazardly, irregularly
**12** incidentally, sporadically
**13** purposelessly **14** unmethodically

**randy**
**03** hot **04** sexy **05** horny, rudas
**06** virago **07** amorous, aroused,
goatish, lustful, raunchy, satyric
**08** turned-on **09** lecherous
**10** boisterous, lascivious
**12** concupiscent

**range**
**02** go **03** ren, rin, row, run **04** area, file,
kind, line, oven, raik, rank, roam, rove,
sort, span, type, vary **05** align, ambit,
amble, array, carry, chain, class,
cover, drift, field, gamut, genus, grade,
grass, group, level, orbit, order, reach,
ridge, scale, scope, stove, stray, sweep
**06** bounds, cooker, domain, draw up,
extend, extent, limits, line up,
meadow, radius, ramble, series, sierra,
sphere, spread, string, stroll, wander
**07** arrange, compass, dispose, earshot,
grazing, paddock, pasture, purview,
species, stretch, variety **08** classify,
confines, distance, latitude, province,
spectrum **09** amplitude, catalogue,
diversity, fluctuate, grassland,
pasturage, selection **10** assortment,
categorize, cordillera, parameters,
pigeonhole, straighten **11** grazing land
**12** distribution

## rangy

See also **mountain**
• **range over** 04 scur, sker 05 skirr
06 squirr

## rangy

05 lanky, leggy, roomy, weedy
06 skinny 08 gangling, rawboned
10 long-legged, long-limbed
11 mountainous

## rank

03 row 04 état, file, foul, gree, line,
lush, mark, nobs, rate, sort, tier, type,
vile 05 acrid, align, caste, class, dense,
élite, fetid, grade, gross, group, level,
lords, lusty, order, peers, place, range,
sheer, stale, toffs, total, utter 06 arrant,
coarse, column, degree, draw up,
estate, family, foetid, gentry, line up,
nobles, putrid, rancid, series, status,
string, strong 07 arrange, blatant,
dispose, echelon, glaring, peerage,
profuse, pungent, station, stratum,
swollen, utterly, violent 08 absolute,
abundant, classify, complete, division,
flagrant, mephitic, nobility, organize,
position, shocking, standing, stinking,
thorough, vigorous 09 condition,
downright, formation, luxuriant,
offensive, out-and-out, overgrown,
repulsive, revolting, violently
10 categorize, disgusting, graveolent,
malodorous, outrageous, unpleasant
11 aristocracy, high society,
unmitigated, unqualified
12 disagreeable, evil-smelling
14 classification

Air force ranks:

05 major
07 captain, colonel, general
08 corporal, sergeant
10 air marshal
11 aircraftman
12 air commodore, aircraftsman,
group captain, major general,
pilot officer
13 aircraftwoman, flying officer,
wing commander
14 aircraftswoman, air vice-marshal,
flight sergeant, squadron leader,
warrant officer
15 air chief marshal, first lieutenant
16 brigadier general, flight
lieutenant, second lieutenant
17 lieutenant colonel, lieutenant
general
19 leading aircraftsman
20 general of the air force
21 leading aircraftswoman
25 marshal of the Royal Air Force

Army ranks:

05 major
07 captain, colonel, general,
marshal, private
08 corporal, sergeant
09 brigadier
10 bombardier, lieutenant
12 field marshal, major general
13 lance-corporal, staff sergeant
14 warrant officer
15 first-lieutenant, lance-bombardier
16 brigadier-general, general of the
army, second-lieutenant

17 lieutenant colonel, lieutenant-
general

Naval ranks:

06 ensign, rating, seaman
07 admiral, captain
09 captain RN, commander,
commodore
10 able seaman, lieutenant,
midshipman
11 rear admiral, vice-admiral
12 fleet admiral, petty officer
13 leading seaman, sublieutenant
14 warrant officer
16 commodore admiral
17 admiral of the fleet, chief petty
officer
19 lieutenant-commander
21 lieutenant junior grade

See also **nobility; police**
• **other ranks** 02 OR
• **rank and file** 03 mob 04 herd
05 crowd, plebs 06 masses, proles,
rabble 08 populace, riff-raff, soldiers
09 hoi polloi 10 grass-roots
11 ordinary men, proletariat
12 common people 15 private
soldiers

## rankle

03 bug, irk, vex 04 gall, rile 05 anger,
annoy, peeve 06 fester, nettle, poison
08 embitter, irritate 11 get your goat
13 get on your wick, get up your nose,
get your back up 14 get your blood up
15 get on your nerves

## rank-smelling

04 olid

## ransack

04 comb, fish, hunt, loot, raid, rake,
ripe, sack 05 harry, rifle, scour, strip
06 maraud, ravage, search 07 despoil,
pillage, plunder, rummage
09 depredate, devastate, go through,
ranshakle 10 ranshackle 13 turn inside
out 14 rummage through, turn upside
down

## ransom

04 free 05 atone, money, price 06 buy
off, pay-off, redeem, rescue 07 deliver,
freedom, payment, release, set free
08 liberate 09 atonement 10 liberation,
redemption 11 deliverance,
restoration, setting free 15 buy the
freedom of

## rant

03 cry 04 rand, rave, roar, yell
05 mouth, shout, storm 06 bellow,
crying, tirade 07 bluster, bombast,
declaim, oration, roaring, yelling
08 diatribe, harangue, rhetoric,
shouting, tear a cat, tub-thump 09 hold
forth, philippic 10 slang-whang, tear
the cat, vociferate 11 declamation, rant
and rave 12 vociferation

## rap

03 hit, pan, tap 04 bang, blow, clip,
cuff, flak, grab, knap, rail, slam, whit,
wrap 05 blame, boost, clout, crime,
flick, flirt, knock, ragga, scold, slate,
stick, swear, thump, whack 06 batter,
hammer, hip-hop, patter, punish,

rattle, rebuke, snatch, strike, yanker
07 censure, commend, gangsta,
reprove, run down, slating, testify
08 knocking, slamming 09 castigate,
criticize, reprimand 10 come down on,
punishment 11 acclamation,
castigation, pick holes in 12 pull to
pieces, tear to pieces, tear to shreds
• **take the rap** 08 pay for it 10 be
punished 12 face the music, take the
blame 14 get it in the neck

## rapacious

06 greedy 07 preying, wolfish, wolvish
08 esurient, grasping, ravening,
ravenous, uncaring, usurious
09 marauding, predatory, voracious,
vulturine, vulturish, vulturous
10 avaricious, insatiable, plundering
12 extortionate
• **rapacious person** 04 kite

## rapacity

05 greed, usury 07 avarice, avidity
08 voracity 09 esurience, esuriency,
vulturism 10 greediness 11 wolfishness
12 graspingness, ravenousness
13 predatoriness, rapaciousness,
shark's manners, voraciousness
14 insatiableness

## rape

03 rob 04 loot, raid, sack 05 abuse,
navew, strip 06 defile, rapine, ravage,
ravish 07 assault, despoil, looting,
outrage, pillage, plunder, ransack,
sacking, seizure, violate, vitiate
08 coleseed, date rape, deflower, gang
rape, gang-rape, maltreat, ravaging,
spoliate, violence 09 depredate,
devastate, stripping, transport,
violation 10 defilement, plundering,
ransacking, ravishment, spoliation
11 depredation, devastation
12 despoliation, maltreatment
13 sexual assault, statutory rape
15 assault sexually, sexual violation

## rapid

03 pdq 04 fast 05 brisk, chute, hasty,
nifty, quick, shoot, shute, swift, zippy
06 lively, prompt, speedy 07 express,
hurried, stickle 08 headlong 09 splitting
11 expeditious, precipitate 13 like
lightning 15 pretty damn quick

## rapidity

04 rush 05 haste, hurry, speed
08 alacrity, celerity, dispatch, velocity
09 briskness, fleetness, quickness,
swiftness 10 expedition, promptness,
speediness 11 promptitude
15 expeditiousness, precipitateness

## rapidly

04 fast 05 quick 06 pronto 07 briskly,
hastily, like fun, quickly, swiftly
08 promptly, speedily 09 hurriedly
11 at the double, like winking 12 a mile
a minute, lickety-split
13 expeditiously, precipitately 14 at a
rate of knots, hell for leather 15 like the
clappers

## rapine

04 prey, rage, raid, rape 05 raven, ravin
06 ravine 07 looting, sacking, seizure
08 ravaging 09 stripping, transport,
violation 10 defilement, plundering,

ransacking, ravishment, spoliation
**11** depredation, devastation
**12** despoliation

## rapport
**04** bond, link **07** empathy, harmony
**08** affinity, relation, sympathy
**10** connection **12** relationship
**13** understanding

## rapprochement
**07** détente, reunion **09** agreement,
softening **13** harmonization,
reconcilement **14** reconciliation

## rapt
**06** intent, way-out **07** charmed,
gripped **08** abducted, absorbed,
ecstatic, ravished, snatched, thrilled
**09** bewitched, delighted, enchanted,
engrossed, entranced **10** captivated,
enraptured, enthralled, fascinated,
spellbound **11** preoccupied,
rhapsodical, transported
**12** concentrated

## rapture
**03** joy **05** bliss **07** delight, ecstasy,
elation **08** euphoria, felicity, paroxysm
**09** cloud nine, happiness, transport
**10** enragement, exaltation
**11** delectation, enchantment
**12** exhilaration **13** seventh heaven, top
of the world
• **go into raptures 04** fire, gush, rave
**05** drool **06** excite, praise **07** enthuse,
inspire **08** motivate **10** bubble over,
effervesce, wax lyrical

## rapturous
**05** happy **06** joyful, joyous **07** exalted
**08** blissful, ecstatic, euphoric, ravished
**09** delighted, entranced, overjoyed,
rhapsodic **11** dithyrambic, on cloud
nine, over the moon, tickled pink,
transported **12** enthusiastic **15** in
seventh heaven, on top of the world

## rare
◇ *anagram indicator* **04** seld, thin
**05** early **06** choice, geason, scarce,
sparse, superb **07** curious, unusual
**08** precious, sporadic, superior,
uncommon **09** excellent, exquisite,
matchless, recherché, underdone
**10** far between, infrequent, remarkable
**11** exceptional, outstanding,
superlative **12** incomparable, like gold
dust, unparalleled **13** extraordinary,
one in a million **15** thin on the ground

## rarefied
**04** high, thin **05** noble **06** select, subtle
**07** private, refined, special, sublime,
tenuous **08** esoteric, tenuious
**09** exclusive **10** attenuated

## rarely
**04** seld **06** hardly, little, seldom
**08** choicely, scarcely **10** hardly ever,
once in a way **12** infrequently,
occasionally, once in a while, scarcely
ever, sporadically **13** spasmodically
**14** intermittently **15** once in a blue
moon

## raring
**04** keen **05** eager, ready **07** itching,
longing, willing **09** desperate,
impatient **12** enthusiastic

## rarity
**03** gem **04** find **05** curio, pearl
**06** marvel, wonder **08** scarcity,
shortage, thinness, treasure
**09** curiosity, nonpareil **10** sparseness
**11** infrequency, strangeness,
unusualness **12** uncommonness
**14** collector's item

## rascal
**03** imp **04** loon, lown **05** devil, knave,
lorel, losel, lowne, rogue, scamp,
skelm, smaik **06** lozell, rabble, ratbag,
schelm, skelum, tinker, toerag, varlet
**07** a bad hat, bounder, cullion, hallian,
hallion, hallyon, knavish, lorrell,
skellum, villain, wastrel **08** scalawag,
schellum, spalpeen, vagabond,
wretched **09** rascaille, scallawag,
scallywag, scoundrel, skeesicks, son of
a gun **10** ne'er-do-well, rascallion,
scapegrace **11** rapscallion **13** mischief-
maker **14** good-for-nothing, two-for-
his-heels

## rascally
**03** bad, low **04** base, evil, mean
**06** arrant, wicked **07** crooked,
hangman, knavish, roguish, vicious
**09** dishonest, reprobate **10** villainous
**11** furciferous, mischievous,
scoundrelly **12** disreputable,
unscrupulous **14** good-for-nothing

## rash
◇ *anagram indicator* **03** run **04** dash,
drag, fast, itch, rush, tear, wave
**05** flood, hasty, heady, hives, slash,
spate, stick **06** deluge, madcap,
plague, series, unwary **07** rosacea,
roseola, torrent **08** careless, epidemic,
eruption, headlong, heat rash,
heedless, madbrain, outbreak,
reckless, temerous **09** audacious, daredevil, foolhardy, hot-headed,
impetuous, imprudent, impulsive,
over-hasty, pompholyx, premature,
unadvised, unguarded, urticaria
**10** headstrong, ill-advised, indiscreet,
irritation, madbrained, nettlerash,
unthinking **11** adventurous,
furthersome, hare-brained, harum-
scarum, hasty-witted, precipitate,
temerarious **13** ill-considered,
inconsiderate

## rashly
**07** hastily **08** headlong, unwarily **09** on
impulse **10** carelessly, heedlessly,
recklessly **11** audaciously,
impetuously, imprudently,
impulsively, over-hastily
**12** indiscreetly **15** without thinking

## rashness
**08** audacity, hazardry, temerity
**09** brashness, hastiness, incaution
**10** imprudence **12** carelessness,
heedlessness, indiscretion,
precipitance, precipitancy,
recklessness **13** foolhardiness,
impulsiveness, precipitation
**14** incautiousness **15** adventurousness,
thoughtlessness

## rasp
**03** bug, jar, rub **04** file, risp, sand
**05** croak, grate, grind, peeve, scour

**06** abrade, cackle, scrape, squawk
**07** grating, scratch, screech
**08** grinding, irritate **09** excoriate,
harshness, raspberry **10** hoarseness
**15** get on your nerves

## rasping
**05** gruff, harsh, husky, raspy, rough
**06** croaky, filing, hoarse **07** grating,
jarring, raucous **08** creaking, croaking,
gravelly, scratchy **10** stridulant

## rat
**03** rot, spy **04** blab, blow, fink, mole,
nark, nose, shop, sing, stag, vole
**05** dob on, grass, hutia, Judas, peach,
puppy, sneak, snout, split **06** agouta,
betray, canary, finger, fizgig, gopher,
inform, ratton, rumble, snitch, squeal,
tell on **07** peacher, stoolie, traitor
**08** approver, Arvicola, betrayer,
denounce, informer, musk-cavy,
promoter, renegade, sand mole,
snitcher, squeaker, squealer, tell-tale,
turncoat **09** bandicoot, informant,
sycophant, water vole, whisperer
**10** discoverer, supergrass
**11** incriminate, stool pigeon **12** cutting
grass **13** strike-breaker, whistle-blower

## rate
**03** fee, MPH, pay, ret, sum, tax **04** cess,
cost, deem, duty, hire, mode, pace,
rank, time, toll **05** allot, basis, chide,
class, count, grade, judge, merit, price,
prize, ratio, scale, scold, speed, sum
up, tempo, value, weigh, worth
**06** admire, amount, assess, charge,
degree, esteem, extent, figure, manner,
rating, reckon, regard, tariff
**07** adjudge, deserve, justify, measure,
payment, reprove, respect, tallage,
warrant, weigh up **08** appraise,
classify, consider, estimate, evaluate,
relation, standard, velocity
**09** calculate **10** be worthy of,
categorize, estimation, percentage,
proportion **12** be entitled to, have a
right to
*See also* **scold**
• **at any rate 05** at all **06** anyhow,
anyway **07** at least **09** in any case
**10** at the least, in any event,
regardless **12** nevertheless

## rather
**03** gay, gey, yes **04** a bit, more, some,
very **05** quite **06** a bit of, fairly, indeed,
pretty, sooner, sort of **07** a little, instead
**08** by choice, slightly, somewhat **09** for
choice **10** from choice, moderately,
much rather, much sooner, noticeably,
preferably, relatively **12** by preference,
to some degree, to some extent **13** for
preference, significantly

## ratification
**08** approval **10** validation
**11** affirmation, endorsement
**12** confirmation **13** authorization,
certification, corroboration
**14** authentication, seal of approval
**15** stamp of approval

## ratify
**02** OK **04** amen, seal, sign **06** affirm,
strike, uphold **07** agree to, approve,
certify, confirm, endorse, warrant

**rating**

**08** legalize, sanction, validate
**09** authorize, establish, preconize
**10** homologate **11** corroborate, countersign **12** authenticate

**rating**

**02** AB **04** mark, rank **05** class, grade, order, score **06** degree, status
**07** grading, placing, ranking, set-down
**08** category, position, standing
**09** adjudging, appraisal **10** assessment, evaluation **14** classification

**ratio**

**04** rate **05** index **07** balance, portion
**08** fraction, quotient, relation, symmetry **09** allowance **10** percentage, proportion **11** correlation
**12** relationship **14** correspondence

**ration**

**03** lot **04** food, part, save **05** allot, issue, limit, point, quota, share **06** amount, budget, stores, supply, viands
**07** control, deal out, dole out, hand out, helping, measure, mete out, portion **08** allocate, conserve, dispense, restrict, supplies, victuals
**09** allotment, allowance, apportion, divide out **10** allocation, distribute, foodstuffs, iron ration, measure out, percentage, proportion, provisions
**11** compo ration

**rational**

**04** sane, wice, wise **05** lucid, sober, sound **06** normal **07** logical, prudent
**08** balanced, cerebral, grounded, sensible, thinking **09** cognitive, judicious, realistic, reasoning, sagacious **10** Apollonian, discursive, reasonable **11** circumspect, clear-headed, enlightened, intelligent, well-founded **12** intellectual
**13** philosophical, ratiocinative **15** in your right mind

**rationale**

**05** basis, logic **06** motive, reason, theory, thesis **07** grounds, purpose, reasons **09** principle, reasoning
**10** hypothesis, motivation, philosophy
**11** explanation, raison d'être

**rationalization**

**06** excuse **08** excusing, updating
**11** explanation, vindication
**12** streamlining **13** justification, modernization **14** reorganization

**rationalize**

**04** trim **06** excuse, update **07** explain, justify **09** cut back on, modernize, vindicate **10** account for, pragmatize, reorganize, streamline **11** cut out waste, explain away

**rationally**

**06** sanely **07** lucidly **08** sensibly
**09** logically, prudently **10** reasonably, thinkingly **11** judiciously, sagaciously, without bias **13** intelligently
**15** philosophically

**rattle**

◇ *anagram indicator* **03** jar, rap **04** bang, bump, faze, jolt, reel, tirl **05** alarm, clang, clank, clink, knock, shake, upset **06** bounce, hurtle, jangle, jingle, put off, put out, racket, ruckle

**07** clapper, clatter, confuse, disturb, fluster, jarring, jolting, shaking, sistrum, unnerve, vibrate **08** clanking, clinking, irritate, unsettle **09** crepitate, vibration **10** disconcert
**13** tintinnabulum **15** throw off balance
• **rattle off** **04** list **06** recite, repeat
**07** reel off **10** run through **11** list quickly
• **rattle on** **03** gab **04** yack **05** prate
**06** cackle, gabble, jabber, natter, witter
**07** blether, chatter, chunter, prattle
**08** rabbit on

**ratty**

**05** angry, cross, short, testy **06** peeved, snappy, touchy, untidy **07** annoyed, crabbed, grouchy, unkempt
**08** wretched **09** impatient, irritable
**13** short-tempered

**raucous**

**04** loud **05** harsh, husky, noisy, rough, rusty, sharp **06** hoarse, raucid, shrill
**07** grating, jarring, rasping **08** piercing, strident **10** discordant, scratching, screeching **11** ear-piercing

**raunchy**

**04** lewd, sexy **05** bawdy **06** earthy, erotic, nubile, shabby, slinky
**07** sensual **08** alluring, arousing, inviting **09** desirable, provoking, salacious, seductive **10** attractive, suggestive, voluptuous **11** flirtatious, provocative, stimulating, titillating
**12** pornographic

**ravage**

◇ `anagram indicator` **04** loot, raze, ruin, sack **05** harry, havoc, level, spoil, wreck **06** damage, maraud **07** despoil, destroy, looting, pillage, plunder
**08** demolish, lay waste, wreckage
**09** depredate, devastate, ruination
**10** desolation, ransacking, spoliation
**11** depredation, destruction, devastation **12** despoliation, leave in ruins

**ravaged**

◇ *anagram indicator* **06** spoilt **07** war-torn, war-worn, wrecked **08** desolate
**09** destroyed, ransacked, shattered, war-wasted **10** battle-torn, devastated

**rave**

◇ *anagram indicator* **02** do **03** cry
**04** bash, fume, hail, orgy, rage, rant, roar, yell **05** crazy, disco, extol, go ape, go mad, party, shout, storm, taver
**06** babble, bellow, blow up, jabber, ramble, rave-up, see red, seethe, sizzle, taiver **07** acclaim, blow-out, enthuse, explode, knees-up, thunder
**08** boil over, carousal, ecstatic, freak out, praising **09** blow a fuse, do your nut, excellent, go bananas, go berserk, laudatory, raise hell, rapturous, wonderful **10** be mad about, favourable, hit the roof, talk wildly, wax lyrical **11** blow a gasket, blow your top, celebration, flip your lid, go up the wall, have kittens, infatuation, lose your rag, rant and rave **12** blow your cool, enthusiastic, fly into a rage, lose your cool, throw a wobbly
**13** throw a tantrum **14** acid-house party, foam at the mouth, go into

raptures, lose your temper **15** fly off the handle, get all steamed up, go off the deep end

**raven**

**03** jet **04** Grip, inky, prey **05** black, crake, dusky, ebony, ravin, sable
**06** corbie, rapine **07** preying **08** jet-black **09** coal-black

**ravenous**

**06** greedy, hungry **07** starved, wolfish, wolvish **08** famished, starving
**09** rapacious, voracious **10** insatiable, plundering, very hungry

**rave-up**

**02** do **04** bash, orgy **05** party **06** thrash
**07** blow-out, debauch, shindig
**08** carousal **11** celebration

**ravine**

**03** gap, lin **04** gill, khor, khud, linn, nala, pass, prey **05** abyss, cañon, chine, flume, ghyll, gorge, goyle, grike, gryke, gulch, gully, heuch, heugh, kloof, nalla, nulla **06** arroyo, canyon, clough, coulée, gullet, gulley, nallah, nullah, rapine **07** preying
**09** purgatory
*See also* **gorge**

**raving**

◇ *anagram indicator* **03** mad **04** wild
**05** barmy, batty, crazy, loony, loopy
**06** insane, maniac, mental **07** berserk, furious **08** demented, deranged, frenzied **09** delirious **10** barking mad, frantic-mad, hysterical, irrational, unbalanced **12** round the bend **13** out of your mind, round the twist

**ravings**

**06** drivel, yammer **07** prattle, rubbish, twaddle **08** nonsense **09** gibberish
**10** balderdash, mumbo-jumbo
**12** gobbledygook

**ravish**

**04** rape **05** abuse, charm, force
**06** abduct, defile **07** assault, bewitch, delight, enchant, enthral, oppress, outrage, overjoy, violate **08** entrance, maltreat, stuprate, suppress
**09** captivate, enrapture, fascinate, spellbind **11** constuprate **15** assault sexually, force yourself on

**ravishing**

**06** lovely, raping **07** radiant **08** alluring, charming, dazzling, gorgeous, stunning **09** beautiful, seductive
**10** bewitching, delightful, enchanting
**11** enthralling **12** transporting

**raw**

**03** new, red, wet **04** bare, cold, damp, hard, open, sore **05** basic, bleak, blunt, chill, crude, crudy, cruel, frank, fresh, green, harsh, naive, naked, nippy, plain, rough, wersh **06** biting, bitter, bloody, brutal, callow, candid, chafed, chilly, grazed, strong, tender
**07** abraded, exposed, intense, natural, scraped, tartare **08** freezing, ignorant, immature, piercing, uncooked, ungenial **09** outspoken, realistic, scratched, sensitive, unrefined, unskilled, untrained, untreated, untutored, unwrought **10** excoriated,

**ray**

forthright, true-to-life, unfinished, unprepared **11** unpractised, unprocessed **13** inexperienced

**ray**

**02** re **04** beam, hint, look **05** array, dirty, dress, flash, gleam, glint, manta, roker, shaft, skate, spark, trace **06** defile, glance, streak, stream **07** flicker, glimmer, homelyn, radiate, torpedo, twinkle **09** cramp-fish, thornback **10** indication, sea vampire, suggestion

**raze**

**04** fell, race, rase, ruin **05** erase, graze, level, wreck **06** scrape, slight **07** destroy, flatten **08** bulldoze, demolish, pull down, tear down **09** dismantle, knock down

**razor**

**04** keen **05** sharp **06** shaver **07** precise **09** cut-throat **11** cutting edge

**re**

**03** are, ray **05** about **09** regarding **10** concerning **12** with regard to **14** on the subject of **15** with reference to

**reach**

**03** arm, bay, fax, hit, rax, win **04** call, come, deal, gain, hand, hent, hold, make, pass, ring, shot, span, take **05** ambit, get at, get to, grasp, phone, power, range, retch, scope, seize, touch **06** amount, arrive, attain, come at, come to, extend, extent, go up to, snatch, spread, strike **07** achieve, command, compass, contact, control, get onto, project, speak to, stretch, write to **08** amount to, arrive at, artifice, come up to, continue, distance, go down to, latitude, make it to **09** authority, extension, get hold of, go as far as, influence, telephone **10** come down to, stretch out **12** get through to, jurisdiction **14** get in touch with **15** communicate with
*See also* **retch**
• **reach down**   **03** dip
• **reach out**   **04** push

**react**

◊ *anagram indicator* **03** act **04** defy **05** rebel, reply **06** answer, behave, oppose, resist, rise up **07** dissent, respond **08** freak out, kick back, retroact **09** retaliate **11** acknowledge, reciprocate

**reaction**

**05** reply, stink **06** answer, recoil, reflex **08** backlash, backwash, feedback, kickback, response, reversal **09** reversion, swing-back **11** retaliation **12** repercussion **13** counteraction, reciprocation **14** antiperistasis, counterbalance **15** acknowledgement

**reactionary**

◊ *anagram indicator* ◊ *reversal indicator* **06** Junker **07** Bourbon, diehard, redneck **08** mandarin, rightist, Sadducee **09** right-wing, young fogy **10** Neandertal, young fogey **11** Neanderthal, right-winger, traditional **12** conservative, Neandertaler **13** Neanderthaler

**14** Neanderthal man, traditionalist **15** backward-looking

**read**

**03** maw, rad **04** look, name, scan, show, skim **05** solve, speak, study, teach, utter **06** advise, browse, decode, glance, look at, peruse, recite, record, saying **07** counsel, declaim, declare, deliver, dip into, display, examine, expound, learned, measure, perusal **08** abomasum, browsing, construe, decipher, indicate, pore over, register, scanning, scrutiny, skimming **09** interpret, speed-read **10** comprehend, scrutinize, understand **11** leaf through **12** flick through, thumb through **13** browse through **14** interpretation
• **read aloud**   ◊ *homophone indicator*
• **read into**   **05** infer **06** deduce, reason **08** construe **09** interpret **12** misinterpret

**readable**

**05** clear **07** legible **08** gripping **09** enjoyable **10** easy to read **11** captivating, enthralling, interesting, stimulating **12** decipherable, entertaining, intelligible, worth reading **13** unputdownable **14** comprehensible, understandable

**reader**

**06** hearer, lector, taster **08** audience, bookworm, epistler, lectress, lecturer, listener **09** addressee, epistoler, prelector **10** pocketbook **13** bibliophagist

**readership**

**08** audience, regulars **09** following **11** subscribers

**readily**

**04** soon **06** easily, freely, gladly **07** eagerly, happily, lightly, quickly, rapidly, swiftly **08** promptly, smoothly, speedily, with ease **09** willingly **12** effortlessly **14** unhesitatingly

**readiness**

**04** ease **05** alert, skill **07** fitness **08** alacrity, aptitude, facility, gameness, keenness, rapidity **09** eagerness, handiness, quickness **10** promptness **11** inclination, preparation, promptitude, willingness **12** availability, preparedness
• **in readiness**   **05** ready **06** on call **07** at point **08** at a point, at points, prepared **09** available, on standby **10** standing by **11** at all points, on full alert **13** in preparation

**reading**

**04** scan, text **05** piece, study **06** figure, lesson, record **07** display, edition, lection, passage, perusal, recital, section, version **08** browsing, decoding, register, scrutiny **09** rendering, rendition **10** indication, inspection, recitation **11** deciphering, examination, measurement **13** understanding **14** interpretation
• **variant reading**   **02** vl

**reading-desk**

**04** ambo **07** lectern

**ready**

**02** go **03** apt, fit, set **04** boun, cash, easy, free, game, keen, near, ripe, yare **05** alert, bound, bowne, close, eager, equip, handy, happy, order, prest, prime, prone, quick, rapid, sharp, swift **06** all set, astute, at hand, clever, direct, on hand, prompt, speedy, to hand **07** about to, addrest, ad manum, arrange, attired, dressed, forward, pleased, prepare, present, scratch, waiting, willing **08** arranged, disposed, equipped, finished, geared up, hard cash, inclined, liable to, likely to, organize, pregnant, prepared **09** addressed, available, completed, dexterous, fitted out, immediate, organized, psyched up, rigged out **10** accessible, convenient, discerning, perceptive, pernicious, ready money, the needful **11** predisposed, resourceful, within reach **12** enthusiastic, on the point of, on the verge of, unhesitating **14** argent comptant
• **at the ready**   **03** set **06** all set, poised **08** prepared **09** mobilized

**real**

**04** rial, ryal, sure, trew, true **05** quite, right, royal, truly, utter, valid **06** actual, dinkum, honest, proper, really, thingy **07** certain, dinki-di, dinky-di, factual, fervent, genuine, sincere **08** absolute, bona fide, complete, concrete, dinky-die, existing, material, official, physical, positive, rightful, tangible, thorough, truthful, unfabled **09** authentic, heartfelt, immovable, occurring, simon-pure, unfeigned, veritable **10** fair dinkum, legitimate, sure-enough, unaffected **11** substantial, substantive **12** from the heart

**realign**

◊ *anagram indicator* **09** reshuffle **10** straighten

**realism**

**06** sanity **08** saneness **09** actuality **10** naturalism, pragmatism, televérité **11** genuineness, naturalness, rationality **12** authenticity, cinéma vérité, faithfulness, lifelikeness, practicality, sensibleness, truthfulness

**realistic**

**04** real, true **05** close, vivid **07** genuine, graphic, logical, natural **08** detached, faithful, lifelike, rational, real-life, sensible, truthful **09** authentic, hard-nosed, objective, practical, pragmatic **10** figurative, hard-boiled, hard-headed, true-to-life, unromantic **11** commonsense, down-to-earth, level-headed **12** businesslike, clear-sighted, matter-of-fact **13** unsentimental

**realistically**

**05** truly **07** vividly **08** sensibly **09** genuinely, logically **10** faithfully, rationally, truthfully **11** graphically, objectively, practically **12** figuratively **13** authentically, pragmatically **14** unromantically **15** unsentimentally

## reality

**04** fact **05** truth **06** effect, verity **07** realism **08** positive, real life, validity **09** actuality, certainty, existence, real world, thingness **10** thinginess **11** genuineness, materiality, tangibility, thingliness **12** authenticity, corporeality **14** substantiality
• **in reality** **05** truly **06** indeed, in fact, really **07** for real, in truth **08** actually **09** in earnest **10** in practice **12** in actual fact, in all but name **13** in point of fact **15** as a matter of fact

## realization

**04** gain **05** grasp **06** making **07** earning, selling **08** clearing, fetching **09** awareness **10** acceptance, cognizance, completion, fulfilment, perception **11** achievement, discernment, performance, recognition **12** appreciation, apprehension, consummation **13** actualization, comprehension, consciousness, understanding **14** accomplishment, implementation
• **expression of realization** **03** why

## realize

**03** get, net, see **04** earn, gain, make, twig **05** clear, fetch, glean, grasp, learn **06** accept, effect, encash, fulfil, obtain, take in **07** achieve, bring in, catch on, discern, perform, produce, sell for **08** complete, cotton on, discover, perceive, register, tumble to **09** actualize, apprehend, ascertain, implement, recognize **10** accomplish, appreciate, articulate, bring about, comprehend, concretize, consummate, effectuate, understand **11** see the light **13** become aware of

## really

**03** way **04** very **05** quite, rally, truly **06** highly, indeed, in fact, quight, simply, surely, verily **08** actually, honestly, in effect, severely **09** certainly, extremely, genuinely, intensely, sincerely **10** absolutely, positively, remarkably, straight up, thoroughly **11** undoubtedly **13** as large as life, categorically, exceptionally

## realm

**04** area, land **05** field, orbit, reame, reign, state, world **06** domain, empire, region, sphere **07** country, kingdom, royalty **08** monarchy, province, queendom **09** territory **10** department **12** principality

## reap

**03** cut, get, mow, win **04** crop, gain, swap, swop **05** shear **06** derive, garner, gather, obtain, secure **07** acquire, collect, harvest, realize, receive

## rear

◇ *reversal indicator* ◇ *tail selection indicator* **03** end **04** back, grow, hind, last, lift, loom, rise, rump, soar, tail **05** breed, erect, hoist, nurse, raise, rouse, set up, stern, tower, train **06** behind, bottom, foster, hinder, hold up, lift up, parent, rise up, stir up, take up **07** bring up, build up, care for, educate, elevate, nurture, tail-end

**08** backside, buttocks, hindmost, instruct, lavatory, rearmost **09** cultivate, look after, originate, posterior
*See also* **toilet**

## rearrange

◇ *anagram indicator* **04** vary **05** alter, rejig, shift **06** adjust, change **07** reorder **08** rejigger **09** reshuffle **10** reposition, reschedule **11** consolidate

## reason

**03** aim, end, wit **04** case, goal, mind, nous **05** argue, basis, brain, cause, color, infer, logic, sense, solve, think **06** colour, debate, deduce, excuse, ground, induce, motive, object, reckon, remark, sanity, wisdom **07** defence, discuss, examine, grounds, impetus, premise, pretext, purpose, resolve, thought, warrant, work out **08** argument, cogitate, conclude, converse, gumption, occasion, think out **09** cerebrate, discourse, encheason, incentive, intellect, intention, judgement, rationale, reasoning, syllogize **10** inducement, moderation, motivation, proportion **11** common sense, explanation, raison d'être, ratiocinate, rationality **12** intelligence, use your brain **13** comprehension, consideration, justification, ratiocination, understanding **15** intellectuality
• **reason with** **04** coax, move, urge **08** persuade **09** argue with, plead with **10** debate with **11** discuss with, expostulate **15** remonstrate with
• **within reason** **10** moderately **12** in moderation, within bounds, within limits **15** with self-control

## reasonable

**02** OK **03** low **04** fair, just, okay, sane, wise **05** sound **06** modest, viable **07** average, logical **08** credible, moderate, possible, rational, reasoned, sensible **09** judicious, plausible, practical, sagacious, tolerable, wholesome **10** acceptable **11** competitive, inexpensive, intelligent, justifiable, well-advised **12** satisfactory **13** no great shakes **14** understandable, well-thought-out

## reasonably

**02** OK **04** okay **05** quite **06** fairly, rather, wisely **08** passably, sensibly, somewhat **09** plausibly, tolerably **10** adequately, moderately, rationally **13** intelligently

## reasoned

**05** clear, sound **07** logical **08** rational, sensible **09** judicious, organized **10** methodical, systematic **14** well-thought-out

## reasoning

**04** case **05** logic, proof **07** ijtihad, thought **08** analysis, argument, thinking **09** casuistry, deduction, induction, rationale, syllogism, synthesis **10** hypothesis, philosophy **11** cerebration, supposition **13** argumentation, ratiocination **14** interpretation **15** rationalization

## reassemble

◇ *anagram indicator* **05** rally **07** rebuild **09** re-enforce **11** reconstruct

## reassurance

**05** cheer **06** urging **07** coaxing, comfort, succour **08** cheering **10** heartening, incitement, motivation, persuasion **11** consolation, exhortation, inspiration, stimulation **13** encouragement
*See also* **encouragement**

## reassure

**05** brace, cheer, nerve, rally **06** buoy up, stroke **07** bolster, cheer up, comfort, confirm, hearten, inspire **08** inspirit, reinsure **09** cosy along, encourage

## rebate

**04** dull **05** abate, blunt **06** rabbet, reduce, refund **08** decrease, discount **09** allowance, deduction, reduction, repayment

## rebel

◇ *anagram indicator* **04** defy, riot **06** flinch, mutine, mutiny, oppose, recoil, resist, revolt, rise up, shrink **07** aginner, beatnik, defiant, disobey, dissent, heretic, run riot, shy away **08** agitator, apostate, mutineer, mutinous, pull back, recusant, revolter **09** dissenter, guerrilla, insurgent **10** malcontent, rebellious, schismatic **11** disobedient, turn against **12** malcontented, paramilitary **13** insubordinate, nonconformist, revolutionary **14** freedom fighter **15** insurrectionary

*Rebels include:*

**04** Aske (Robert), Ball (John), Cade (Jack), Kett (Robert)
**05** Lalor (Peter)
**06** Fawkes (Guy)
**09** Glendower (Owen)
**10** Engelbrekt

*See also* **revolutionary**

## rebellion

**04** coup, riot **06** heresy, mutine, mutiny, revolt, rising **07** dissent, treason **08** defiance, uprising **09** coup d'état **10** insurgence, insurgency, opposition, resistance, revolution **12** disobedience, insurrection **15** insubordination

*Rebellions include:*

**03** Rum
**07** Fifteen, Whiskey
**08** Jacobite
**09** Forty-Five
**10** The Fifteen
**12** Easter Rising, The Forty-Five
**14** Eureka Stockade

## rebellious

◇ *anagram indicator* ◇ *reversal indicator* **06** unruly **07** defiant, rioting **08** mutinous **09** insurgent, malignant, obstinate, rebelling, resistant, seditious **10** disorderly, refractory **11** disobedient, intractable **12** contumacious, recalcitrant,

**rebirth**
ungovernable, unmanageable
**13** insubordinate, revolutionary
**15** insurrectionary

**rebirth**
**07** renewal, revival **11** reawakening,
renaissance, restoration
**12** regeneration, rejuvenation,
resurrection, risorgimento
**13** reincarnation **14** revitalization

**rebound**
**04** fail **05** carom **06** bounce, double,
recoil, re-echo, resile, result, return,
spring **07** bricole, redound **08** backfire,
ricochet **09** boomerang, carambole,
reflexion, throw back **10** backfiring,
bounce back, reflection, spring back
**11** reverberate **12** defeat itself,
repercussion **13** reverberation **14** score
an own goal **15** be self-defeating,
come home to roost

**rebuff**
**03** cut **04** snub **05** check, noser, spurn
**06** refuse, reject, rubber, slight
**07** decline, put down, put-down,
refusal, repulse, set-down, squelch
**08** brush-off, spurning, turn down
**09** knock back, rejection, repudiate
**10** discourage **11** counterbuff, one in
the eye, repudiation **12** cold shoulder,
cold-shoulder **13** slap in the face **14** a
flea in your ear, discouragement, kick
in the teeth

**rebuild**
◇ *anagram indicator* **06** reform, remake
**07** re-edify, remodel, restore
**08** renovate **09** reaedifye, refashion
**10** reassemble **11** reconstruct
**12** haussmannize, rehabilitate

**rebuke**
**04** rate, slap, snub, trim **05** blame,
check, chide, sauce, scold, score, stick
**06** carpet, earful, lesson, talk to,
threap, threep **07** censure, lecture,
reproof, reprove, rollick, speak to, tell
off, tick off, trounce, upbraid, wigging
**08** admonish, call down, keelhaul,
reproach, restrain, scolding, trimming
**09** carpeting, castigate, dress down, go
crook at, go crook on, objurgate, pitch
into, raspberry, reprimand
**10** admonition, go to town on,
rollicking, telling-off, ticking-off
**11** castigation, comeuppance,
remonstrate **12** countercheck,
dressing-down, give an earful
**13** remonstration, tear off a strip
**14** throw the book at **15** give someone
hell

**rebut**
**05** elide, quash, repel **06** defeat,
negate, recoil, refute **07** confute,
explode **08** disprove, overturn
**09** discredit **10** invalidate **12** give the lie
to

**rebuttal**
**06** defeat **08** disproof, negation
**09** overthrow **10** refutation
**11** confutation **12** invalidation

**recalcitrance**
**08** defiance **09** obstinacy **10** wilfulness
**11** waywardness **12** disobedience,

stubbornness **13** unwillingness
**14** refractoriness **15** insubordination

**recalcitrant**
**06** unruly, wilful **07** defiant, wayward
**08** contrary, renitent, stubborn
**09** obstinate, unwilling **10** refractory
**11** disobedient, intractable
**12** contumacious, ungovernable,
unmanageable, unsubmissive
**13** insubordinate, unco-operative
**14** uncontrollable

**recall**
◇ *reversal indicator* **05** annul, evoke
**06** call up, cancel, go over, memory,
repeal, revoke, summon **07** nullify,
reclaim, rescind, retract, retreat, think
of, unswear **08** abrogate, call back,
dredge up, recision, remember,
summon up, withdraw **09** annulment,
bring back, order back, recollect,
reminisce **10** abrogation, call to mind,
retraction, revocation, summon back,
withdrawal **11** countermand,
remembrance, think back to
**12** cancellation, recollection
**13** nullification, order to return
**14** countermanding

**recant**
**04** deny **05** unsay **06** abjure, disown,
recall, revoke **07** disavow, rescind,
retract **08** abrogate, disclaim, forswear,
renounce, unpreach, withdraw
**09** repudiate **10** apostatize

**recantation**
**06** denial, revoke **08** apostasy,
palinode, palinody **09** disavowal
**10** abjuration, disclaimer, disownment,
revocation, withdrawal **11** repudiation
**12** renunciation, retractation

**recapitulate**
**05** recap, sum up **06** go over, repeat,
review **07** recount, restate, run over
**09** reiterate, summarize

**recapitulation**
**06** review **07** summary **08** epanodos
**09** summing-up **10** repetition
**11** reiteration, restatement,
summarizing

**recast**
◇ *anagram indicator* **05** alter **06** modify,
revamp, revise, rework **07** rewrite
**08** rephrase, revision

**recce**
**04** case, scan **05** probe **06** patrol,
search, spy out, survey **07** examine,
explore, inspect, observe **08** check out,
scouting, scrutiny **10** expedition,
inspection, scrutinize **11** examination,
exploration, investigate, observation,
reconnoitre **13** investigation,
reconnoitring **14** reconnaissance

**recede**
◇ *reversal indicator* **03** ebb **04** drop,
fade, sink, wane **05** abate **06** go back,
lessen, retire, return, shrink **07** decline,
dwindle, fall off, regress, retreat,
slacken, subside **08** decrease,
diminish, move away, withdraw
**10** retrograde

**receipt**
**03** pay, rec **04** chit, note, rept, slip, stub
**05** gains, paper, recpt, tally **06** chitty,
docket, income, recipe, return, ticket
**07** gaining, getting, profits, returns,
takings, voucher, warrant **08** capacity,
delivery, deriving, earnings, proceeds,
turnover **09** obtaining, quittance,
receiving, reception **10** acceptance
**11** acquittance, counterfoil, dock-
warrant **13** money received **14** deposit-
receipt **15** acknowledgement, proof of
purchase

**receive**
◇ *containment indicator* **03** get **04** bear,
draw, gain, hear, hold, take **05** admit,
fence, greet, latch, let in **06** accept,
come by, derive, gather, obtain, pick
up, suffer, take up **07** acquire, be
given, collect, contain, embrace,
harbour, inherit, react to, sustain,
undergo, welcome **08** meet with,
perceive **09** apprehend, encounter,
entertain, entertake, go through,
respond to **10** experience, learn about
**11** accommodate, take on board **12** be
informed of, find out about

**receiver**
**03** tap **05** donee, fence, radio, tuner
**07** catcher, grantee, handset, legatee
**08** assignee, receptor, wireless
**09** apparatus, recipient, televisor
**10** radiopager **11** beneficiary
**13** satellite dish **14** stamp collector
**15** direction-finder, superheterodyne

**recent**
**03** low, new **04** late **05** fresh, novel,
young **06** latest, latter, modern
**07** current **08** ci devant, neoteric, up-
to-date **09** latter-day **10** neoterical,
present-day **11** Post-Glacial
**12** contemporary **13** up-to-the-minute

**recently**
**04** late **05** newly **06** lately, of late
**07** freshly **09** yesterday **10** not long ago
**13** a short time ago

**receptacle**
**04** bath, sink, tank **05** bosom, purse
**06** holder, vessel **07** hanaper
**08** canister **09** container, reliquary,
reservoir **10** monstrance, reliquaire,
repository **11** conceptacle, reservatory
**12** receptaculum
*See also* **bag; basket; bin; can;
container**

**reception**
**02** do **04** bash **05** beano, levee, party
**06** accoil, at-home, durbar, pick-up,
rave-up, ruelle, social **07** ovation,
receipt, reunion, shindig, welcome
**08** assembly, function, greeting,
occasion, reaction, response
**09** admission, gathering, treatment
**10** acceptance, assumption, bel-
accoyle, bon accueil, recipience,
recipiency **11** get-together, recognition
**12** entertaining **13** entertainment
**15** acknowledgement

**receptive**
**04** open **05** quick **07** willing
**08** amenable, flexible, friendly,
pregnant **09** recipient, sensitive,

welcoming **10** accessible, favourable, hospitable, interested, open-minded, responsive **11** suggestible, susceptible, sympathetic **12** approachable, open to reason **13** accommodating

**recess**
◇ *reversal indicator* **03** bay, cwm **04** apse, bole, bunk, cove, ingo, nook, rest **05** ambry, awmry, bower, break, heart, hitch, niche, oriel, press, sinus **06** alcove, almery, aumbry, awmrie, bowels, bunker, cavity, cirque, closet, corner, corrie, depths, exedra, hollow, indent, locule **07** adjourn, exhedra, holiday, innards, loculus, mortice, mortise, outshot, reaches, respite, time off, time out **08** cupboard, interior, interval, playtime, vacation **09** blank door, breaktime, embrasure, embrazure, seclusion, sepulcher, sepulchre **10** depression, penetralia, retirement **11** blank window, columbarium, indentation **12** confessional, intermission

**recession**
**05** crash, slide, slump **06** trough **07** decline, failure **08** collapse, downturn, shake-out **10** depression, withdrawal **15** economic decline

**recherché**
**04** rare **06** arcane, choice, exotic, select **07** obscure, refined, tenuous **08** abstruse, esoteric **10** far-fetched

**recipe**
**01** r **03** rec, way **04** dish, take **05** guide, means **06** method, system **07** formula, process, receipt **09** procedure, technique **10** directions **11** ingredients **12** instructions, prescription

**recipient**
**05** donee **06** vessel **07** grantee, legatee **08** assignee, donatory, receiver **09** receiving, receptive **10** suscipient **11** beneficiary

**reciprocal**
**05** joint **06** mutual, reflex, shared **07** inverse **08** requited, returned **09** commutual, exchanged, reflexive **10** equivalent, quid pro quo **11** alternating, correlative, give-and-take **13** complementary, corresponding **14** interdependent **15** interchangeable

**reciprocate**
**04** swap **05** equal, match, repay, reply, trade **06** return **07** requite, respond **08** exchange **09** alternate, do the same **10** correspond **11** interchange **12** give in return

**reciprocity**
**08** exchange **09** isopoly, mutuality **11** alternation, equivalence, give-and-take **14** correspondence **15** interdependence

**recital**
**04** show **06** report **07** account, concert, reading, telling **08** relation **09** narration, rendering, rendition **10** recitation, repetition **11** commination, declamation, description, enumeration,

performance, solmization **14** interpretation

**recitation**
**03** ave **04** poem, tale **05** piece, story, verse **07** passage, reading, recital, telling **09** monologue, narration, rendering **10** party piece **11** incantation, performance

**recite**
**04** scan, tell **05** chant, chime, daven, speak **06** chaunt, relate, repeat **07** declaim, deliver, itemize, narrate, perform, recount, reel off **08** say aloud **09** enumerate, improvise, rattle off **10** articulate, rhapsodize **11** improvisate

**reckless**
◇ *anagram indicator* **04** rash, wild **05** brash, hasty, perdu, ton-up **06** madcap, perdue **07** wildcat **08** careless, heedless, kamikaze, mindless, tearaway **09** blindfold, daredevil, desperate, foolhardy, imprudent, negligent, rantipole, rechlesse, retchless **10** ill-advised, incautious, indiscreet **11** harum-scarum, inattentive, precipitate, temerarious, thoughtless **12** devil-may-care **13** irresponsible

**recklessly**
◇ *anagram indicator* **06** rashly **07** hastily **09** full fling, like water **10** carelessly, mindlessly **11** desperately, negligently **13** irresponsibly, thoughtlessly

**recklessness**
**06** Bayard **07** madness **08** rashness **09** incaution **10** gallusness, imprudence, negligence **11** desperation, gallowsness, inattention **12** carelessness, heedlessness, mindlessness **13** foolhardiness **15** thoughtlessness

**reckon**
**03** sum **04** call, deem, make, rate **05** add up, class, count, fancy, gauge, guess, judge, place, sum up, tally, think, total, value, vogue **06** assess, assume, esteem, expect, figure, impute, number, regard **07** account, believe, compute, imagine, put down, suppose, surmise, think of, work out **08** appraise, consider, estimate, evaluate, look upon **09** calculate, designate, enumerate, figure out **10** conjecture
• **reckon on** **04** face **06** bank on, expect, rely on **07** count on, foresee, hope for, plan for, trade on, trust in **08** depend on, figure on **10** anticipate, bargain for **14** take for granted **15** take into account
• **reckon with** **04** cope, deal, face **05** treat **06** expect, handle **07** foresee, plan for **08** consider **10** anticipate, bargain for **15** take into account
• **reckon without** **06** ignore **08** overlook **09** disregard, not expect, not notice **13** fail to think of
• **to be reckoned with** **05** great **06** mighty, strong **07** weighty **08** forceful, powerful **09** important

**10** formidable **11** influential, significant **12** considerable

**reckoning**
**03** due, tab **04** bill, doom, tale, time **05** count, datal, lawin, score, tally, total **06** charge, lawing, number, paying **07** account, daytale, opinion, payment **08** addition, counting, estimate **09** appraisal, damnation, judgement **10** assessment, estimation, evaluation, fellowship, imputation, punishment, settlement, working-out **11** calculation, computation, enumeration, retribution

**reclaim**
**04** tame **05** waste **06** appeal, assart, polder, recall, redeem, regain, rescue **07** get back, recover, restore, salvage **08** civilize, retrieve, take back, wildness **09** claim back, recapture, reinstate **10** regenerate, submersion

**reclamation**
**06** rescue **07** salvage **08** recovery **09** regaining, retrieval **11** restoration **12** regeneration **13** reinstatement

**recline**
**03** lie **04** bend, loll, rest **06** lounge, repose, sprawl **07** incline, lie down **08** lean back **09** recumbent **10** stretch out

**recluse**
**04** monk **05** loner **06** anchor, hermit **07** ascetic, eremite, stylite **08** anchoret, enclosed, monastic, retiring, secluded, solitary **09** anchoress, anchorite, solitaire **10** monastical, solitarian **11** monasterial

**reclusive**
**07** ascetic, recluse **08** eremitic, isolated, monastic, retiring, secluded, solitary **09** withdrawn **10** anchoritic, cloistered, hermitical **11** sequestered

**recognition**
**06** honour, recall, reward, salute, thanks **07** grating, knowing, placing, respect **08** allowing, approval, sanction, spotting **09** admission, awareness, detection, discovery, gratitude, knowledge **10** acceptance, admittance, cognizance, confession, perception, validation **11** endorsement, realization, remembrance **12** appreciation, recognizance, recollection, thankfulness **13** consciousness, understanding **14** identification **15** acknowledgement

**recognize**
**03** ken, own, see, wit **04** know, nose, spot, tell **05** admit, adopt, allow, grant, place **06** accept, acknow, honour, notice, recall, reward, salute **07** approve, concede, confess, discern, endorse, not miss, pick out, realize, respect **08** identify, perceive, remember, sanction, validate **09** apprehend, be aware of, recollect **10** appreciate, call to mind, legitimate, not mistake, understand **11** acknowledge, know by sight **13** be conscious of, be thankful for

## recoil

◊ *reversal indicator* **03** shy **04** kick
**05** quail, react, rebut **06** falter, flinch, recule, resile, revert, shrink, spring **07** misfire, rebound, recoyle, recuile, redound, retreat, shy away **08** backfire, backlash, draw back, jump back, kickback, move back, reaction, requoyle, undertow, withdraw **09** boomerang **10** degenerate, resilience, resiliency, spring back **11** reverberate **12** repercussion **15** come home to roost

## recollect

◊ *anagram indicator* ◊ *reversal indicator*
**05** think **06** recall **07** bethink **08** récollet, remember, summon up **09** reminisce **10** call to mind

## recollection

◊ *anagram indicator* **06** memory, recall **08** souvenir **09** anamnesis **10** impression **11** remembrance **12** reminiscence

## recommend

**04** move, plug, tout, urge, wish **05** guide **06** advise, commit, exhort, inform, praise, preach **07** advance, approve, commend, consign, counsel, endorse, propose, suggest **08** advocate, set forth, vouch for **10** put forward

## recommendation

**03** tip **04** plug **06** advice, coupon, praise, urging **07** counsel **08** advocacy, approval, blessing, good word, guidance, proposal, sanction **09** reference **10** suggestion **11** endorsement, testimonial **12** commendation, exhortations **14** special mention

## recompense

**03** fee, pay **05** repay, wages **06** amends, answer, return, reward **07** damages, guerdon, payment, redress, requite, satisfy **08** requital **09** indemnify, make up for, reimburse, repayment **10** compensate, remunerate, reparation **11** restitution **12** compensation, remuneration, remuneratory, satisfaction **13** consideration, gratification **15** indemnification

## reconcile

**04** mend, wean **05** agree, atone **06** accept, accord, adjust, attone, make up, pacify, regain, remedy, settle, square, submit, upknit **07** appease, compose, mollify, patch up, placate, rectify, resolve, reunite **08** face up to, put right **09** harmonize, make peace **10** conciliate, propitiate, shake hands **11** accommodate **12** come to accept, reconsecrate **13** bring together, make your peace **14** bury the hatchet

## reconciliation

**05** peace **06** accord **07** détente, harmony, reunion **08** squaring **09** agreement, atonement **10** adjustment, compromise, resolution, settlement, syncretism **11** appeasement, explanation, harmonizing **12** conciliation,

pacification, propitiation **13** accommodation, mollification, rapprochement

## recondite

**04** dark, deep **06** arcane, hidden, secret **07** obscure, retired **08** abstruse, esoteric, involved, mystical, profound **09** concealed, difficult, intricate **10** mysterious **11** complicated

## recondition

◊ *anagram indicator* **03** fix **05** refit, renew **06** repair, revamp **07** remodel, restore **08** overhaul, renovate **09** refurbish

## reconfigure

◊ *anagram indicator*

## reconnaissance

**04** scan **05** probe, recce, recco, reccy, recon **06** patrol, search, survey **08** scouting, scrutiny **09** discovery **10** expedition, inspection **11** examination, exploration, observation **13** investigation, reconnoitring

## reconnoitre

**04** case, scan **05** probe, recce, scout **06** patrol, spy out, survey **07** examine, explore, inspect, observe **08** check out, remember **10** scrutinize **11** investigate

## reconsider

**06** modify, review, revise **07** rethink **08** reassess **09** re-examine, think over **10** think twice **13** think better of

## reconsideration

**06** review **07** rethink **09** fresh look **12** reassessment **13** re-examination **14** second thoughts

## reconstitute

◊ *anagram indicator*

## reconstruct

◊ *anagram indicator* **04** redo **06** recast, reform, remake, revamp **07** rebuild, remodel, restore **08** make over, recreate, renovate **09** refashion, reproduce **10** reassemble, regenerate, reorganize **11** recondition, re-establish

## record

**02** CD, EP, LP **03** can, cut, log, rec **04** best, burn, case, data, disc, disk, edit, file, -gram, keep, list, make, mark, mono, note, read, show, tape **05** album, chart, diary, elpee, enrol, enter, entry, notes, score, trace, video, vinyl **06** annals, career, enroll, manage, memoir, memory, minute, obtain, report, single **07** account, achieve, archive, chalk up, display, dossier, express, fastest, history, journal, lay down, logbook, minutes, myogram, narrate, notch up, produce, put down, release, set down, supreme, swinger, tracing, witness **08** aerogram, annalize, archives, best ever, calendar, cassette, complete, document, evidence, indicate, inscribe, kymogram, memorial, MiniDisc®, preserve, protocol, rap sheet, register, reminder, take down **09** anemogram, catalogue, celebrate, chronicle, documents, recording, testimony,

videotape, write down **10** accomplish, background, enregister, instrument, memorandum, seismogram, tape-record, top-ranking, transcribe, unequalled **11** compact disc, fastest time, meteorogram, photography, put on record, remembrance, sphygmogram, superlative, track record, unsurpassed, world record **12** personal best, unparalleled, without equal, world-beating **13** documentation **14** autoradiograph, record-breaking **15** best performance, curriculum vitae
*See also* **recording**
• **off the record** **07** private, sub rosa **09** privately **10** unofficial **12** confidential, unofficially **14** confidentially
• **on record** **04** ever **05** noted **06** on file **10** documented **11** written down **13** publicly known

## recorder

**03** VCR, VTR **05** clerk, video **06** marker, scorer, scribe **07** diarist, Walkman® **08** annalist, black box, CD burner **09** archivist, DVD burner, flûte-à-bec, historian, registrar, secretary **10** chronicler, Dictaphone® **11** chronologer, fipple flute, score-keeper, tape machine **12** English flute, remembrancer, stenographer, tape recorder **13** video recorder **14** cassette-player

## recording

*Recordings include:*

**02** 45, 78, CD, EP, LP
**03** DAT, DVD, MP3, vid
**04** disc, mono, tape, tele
**05** album, video, vinyl
**06** record, single, stereo
**08** cassette, MiniDisc®
**09** audiotape, phonogram, video disc, videotape
**11** compact disc, compact disk, long-playing
**12** extended play, magnetic tape
**13** microcassette, video cassette

## recount

**04** tell **05** refer **06** depict, detail, impart, recite, relate, repeat, report, run off, unfold **07** account, narrate, portray **08** describe, rehearse **09** reminisce **11** communicate

## recoup

**05** repay **06** refund, regain **07** get back, recover, recruit, win back **08** claw back, make good, retrieve **09** indemnify, reimburse, repossess **10** compensate, recompense

## recourse

**04** flow **06** access, appeal, choice, option, refuge, remedy, resort, return, way out **09** turning to **10** recurrence, withdrawal **11** alternative, possibility
• **have recourse to** **03** use **04** take **06** betake, employ, turn to **07** utilize **08** exercise, resort to **09** make use of **10** fall back on **15** avail yourself of

## recover

◊ *anagram indicator* **04** cure, heal, menc

**05** amend, rally **06** attain, pick up, recoup, recure, redeem, regain, rescue, retake, revive **07** fetch up, get back, get over, get well, improve, reclaim, recoure, recower, recruit, recycle, replevy, restore, salvage, win back **08** overcast, replevin, retrieve **09** come round, get better, recapture, repossess **10** ameliorate, bounce back, convalesce, feel better, recuperate **11** be on the mend, get stronger, pull through, revendicate **12** gain strength **13** turn the corner

**recovered**
**04** over **06** better

**recovery**
**05** rally **06** pick-up, recure, regain, rescue, upturn **07** healing, mending, recover, revival, salvage, upswing **08** comeback, rallying **09** recapture, recouping, recycling, regaining, retrieval **10** second wind **11** improvement, reclamation, restoration **12** amelioration, recuperation, regeneration, repossession **13** convalescence, convalescency, dead-cat bounce **14** electrowinning, rehabilitation **15** reconvalescence

**recreate**
◇ *anagram indicator* **05** amuse, renew **07** refresh **09** replicate, reproduce **11** reconstruct **12** reinvigorate

**recreation**
**03** fun, rec **04** game, play **05** hobby, sport **07** leisure, pastime **08** pleasure **09** amusement, diversion, enjoyment **10** relaxation **11** distraction, refreshment **12** intermission **13** entertainment **14** leisure pursuit **15** leisure activity

**recrimination**
**06** retort **07** quarrel **08** comeback, reprisal **09** bickering **10** accusation **11** retaliation **13** counter-attack, countercharge

**recruit**
**02** AR **03** yob **04** levy, tiro **05** draft, enrol, raise, rooky, sprog **06** engage, enlist, gather, muster, novice, nozzer, obtain, rookie, sign up, swabby, take on **07** acquire, convert, draftee, learner, procure, renewal, restore, trainee **08** assemble, beginner, headhunt, initiate, mobilize, newcomer, unionize, yardbird **09** conscript, greenhorn, reinforce, replenish **10** apprentice, new entrant, talent-spot **11** put together, restoration **12** reinvigorate **13** reinforcement

**recruitment**
**05** press **08** drafting, engaging **09** enlisting, enrolment, signing-up **10** engagement **12** conscription, mobilization

**rectification**
**09** amendment **10** adjustment, correction, making good **11** improvement, reformation **12** putting right, setting right

**rectify**
**03** fix **04** cure, mend **05** amend, emend, right **06** adjust, better, reform, remedy, repair **07** correct, improve, redress **08** make good, put right, set right **10** ameliorate **11** dephlegmate

**rectitude**
**06** honour, virtue **07** decency, honesty, justice, probity **08** goodness, morality **09** exactness, integrity, rightness **11** correctness, uprightness **12** straightness **13** righteousness **14** scrupulousness

**recto**
**02** ro

**rector**
**01** R **04** Rect **06** parson

**recumbent**
**04** flat **05** lying, prone **06** supine **07** leaning, recline, resting **08** lounging, reclined **09** lying down, prostrate, reclining, sprawling **10** horizontal

**recuperate**
**04** mend **05** rally **06** pick up, revive **07** get well, improve, recover **09** get better **10** bounce back, convalesce **11** be on the mend, get stronger, pull through **13** turn the corner

**recuperation**
**05** rally **06** recure, upturn **07** healing, mending, revival **08** rallying, recovery **11** improvement, restoration **12** amelioration **13** convalescence, convalescency **14** rehabilitation **15** reconvalescence

**recur**
**03** ren, rin, run **05** prime **06** repeat, return, revert **07** persist **08** reappear **09** come round **11** happen again, perseverate **12** repeat itself **14** come round again

**recurrence**
**06** return, rhythm **08** paroxysm, recourse **09** flashback, reversion **10** appearance, regularity, repetition, restenosis, revolution **11** persistence **12** alliteration, continuation, reminiscence **14** redintegration

**recurrent**
◇ *reversal indicator* **07** chronic, regular **08** cyclical, frequent, habitual, periodic, repeated **09** continual, recurring **10** persistent, repetitive **12** intermittent

**recycle**
◇ *anagram indicator* **04** save **05** re-use **07** reclaim, recover, salvage **09** reprocess

**red**
◇ *anagram indicator* **01** c **04** cent, comb, redd, rede, rosy **06** florid, refuse, rubric **07** clear up, flaming, flushed, glowing, leftist, reddish, rubbish, vacated **08** blushing, inflamed, rubicund **09** bloodshot, Bolshevik, communist, rubescent, rufescent, socialist **10** erubescent, shamefaced, testaceous **11** carbuncular, disentangle, embarrassed, incarnadine, lateritious,

sanguineous **12** Cain-coloured **13** revolutionary

*Reds include:*

**04** guly, pink, rose, ruby, rust, wine **05** brick, gules, henna, ruddy **06** auburn, cerise, cherry, claret, damask, ginger, maroon, minium, modena, murrey, rufous, russet, Titian, tomato, Tyrian **07** carmine, carroty, cramesy, crimson, fuchsia, lobster, nacarat, scarlet, stammel, vermeil **08** beetroot, blood-red, brick-red, burgundy, cardinal, chestnut, cinnabar, cramoisy, sanguine **09** carnation, solferino, vermilion **10** Chinese red, coccineous, coquelicot, terracotta **11** burnt sienna, incarnadine, sang-de-boeuf

• **in the red** **04** bust **05** broke **06** in debt **08** bankrupt **09** in arrears, insolvent, overdrawn, penniless **10** on the rocks, owing money **12** impoverished, on your uppers **13** gone to the wall **14** on your beam ends
• **red and inflamed** **03** raw
• **see red** **05** go mad **07** explode **08** boil over **09** do your nut **10** hit the roof **11** become angry, blow your top, lose your rag **12** blow your cool, fly into a rage, lose your cool **14** lose your temper **15** fly off the handle

**red-blooded**
**05** lusty, manly **06** hearty, lively, robust, strong, virile **08** vigorous **09** masculine

**redcap**
**02** MP

**redden**
**03** rud **04** gild, rosy, ruby **05** blush, flush, go red **06** colour, rubefy **07** crimson, scarlet, suffuse

**reddish**
**03** red **04** pink, rosy **05** ruddy, sandy **06** flushy, ginger, rufous, russet **08** pyrrhous, rubicund **09** bloodshot, gingerous, rufescent
• **reddish brown** **03** bay **04** rust, sore **06** russet

**redecorate**
**04** do up, redo **09** refurbish

**redeem**
**03** buy **04** cash, free, save **05** lowse, trade **06** acquit, cash in, change, offset, ransom, recoup, regain, rescue **07** absolve, buy back, convert, deliver, expiate, get back, reclaim, recover, release, reprive, repryve, salvage, set free, trade in **08** atone for, exchange, liberate, outweigh, repreeve, reprieve, retrieve **09** discharge, make up for, repossess **10** emancipate, recuperate, repurchase **13** compensate for **14** give in exchange **15** remove guilt from

**redemption**
**06** ransom, rescue **07** freedom, release, trade-in **08** exchange, recovery **09** atonement, expiation, retrieval,

salvation **10** fulfilment, liberation, reparation, repurchase **11** deliverance, reclamation **12** compensation, emancipation, repossession **13** reinstatement

**redeploy**
◇ *anagram indicator*

**redevelop**
◇ *anagram indicator*

**redevelopment**
◇ *anagram indicator*

**red-handed**
**07** napping **08** in the act, off-guard, on the hop, unawares **10** by surprise **12** in the very act

**redistribute**
◇ *anagram indicator*

**redistribution**
◇ *anagram indicator*

**redness**
**03** rud **04** glow, heat **05** flush

**redolent**
**07** odorous, scented **08** aromatic, fragrant, perfumed **09** evocative, remindful **10** suggestive **11** reminiscent **13** sweet-smelling

**redoubtable**
**05** awful **06** mighty, strong **07** fearful, valiant **08** dreadful, fearsome, powerful, resolute, terrible **10** formidable

**redound**
**04** cast, tend **05** ensue, surge **06** effect, result, return **07** conduce, rebound, reflect **08** overflow **10** contribute

**redraft**
◇ *anagram indicator* **06** revise, rework **07** rewrite

**redress**
**03** aid **04** help **05** amend, right **06** adjust, avenge, reform, relief, remead, remede, remedy, remeid **07** balance, correct, justice, payment, rectify, requite, restore **08** put right, readjust, regulate, requital **09** atonement **10** assistance, compensate, correction, recompense, reparation **11** restitution **12** compensation, satisfaction **15** indemnification

**reduce**
◇ *tail deletion indicator* **02** ax **03** axe, cut, put **04** alay, clip, diet, dock, ruin, slim, trim **05** abate, adapt, aleye, allay, annul, drive, force, halve, lower, scant, slake, slash **06** absorb, adjust, deduct, demote, dilute, draw in, humble, impair, lessen, master, rebate, shrink, subdue, weaken **07** conquer, curtail, cut back, cut down, deflate, degrade, deplete, devalue, disband, shorten, thicken **08** beat down, come down, condense, contract, decrease, diminish, discount, downsize, make less, minimize, mitigate, moderate, overcome, restrict, separate, step down, take down, vanquish, wear down, wind down **09** bring down, comminute, deoxidate, deoxidize,

downgrade, go on a diet, humiliate, knock down, overpower, translate, water down **10** abbreviate, de-escalate, impoverish, lose weight **11** make smaller, weight-watch **12** disintegrate **13** whittle away at **14** take the edge off

**reduction**
◇ *tail deletion indicator* **03** cut **04** drop, fall, loss, wear **06** rebate **07** cutback, decline **08** batement, clipping, decrease, discount, drawdown **09** allowance, deduction, lessening, narrowing, shrinkage, weakening **10** concession, correction, diminution, downsizing, hatchet job, limitation, moderation, rebatement, shortening **11** compression, contraction, curtailment, devaluation, discounting, restriction, subjugation, subtraction **12** abbreviation, condensation, depreciation, minimization

**redundancy**
**04** boot, push, sack **05** cards, elbow **06** excess, firing, notice, papers **07** jotters, removal, sacking, surplus **08** cheville, pleonasm **09** discharge, dismissal, expulsion, laying-off, prolixity, tautology, verbosity, wordiness **10** downsizing, exuberance, exuberancy, repetition **11** superfluity, uselessness **12** outplacement **14** marching-orders

**redundant**
**05** extra, fired, wordy **06** excess, otiose, padded, sacked **07** copious, jobless, laid off, surging, surplus, verbose **08** unneeded, unwanted **09** dismissed, excessive, out of work **10** pleonastic, unemployed **11** inessential, overflowing, repetitious, superfluous, unnecessary **12** periphrastic, tautological **13** supernumerary

**redwood**
**07** big tree, sequoia

**re-edit**
◇ *anagram indicator*

**reef**
**03** cay, key **04** bank, motu, scar **05** ridge, scaur, shoal **06** skerry **07** bombora, sandbar **08** sandbank **10** square knot
• **reefer** **05** coral
*See also* **cannabis**

**reek**
**03** hum **04** fume, honk, ming, niff, pong **05** fetor, fumes, odour, reech, smell, smoke, stink, whiff **06** exhale, stench, vapour **08** malodour, mephitis **09** effluvium **10** exhalation

**reel**
◇ *anagram indicator* **03** din **04** pirn, rock, roll, spin, sway, swim **05** fling, lurch, pitch, spool, swift, swirl, twirl, waver, wheel, whirl, wince, winch **06** bobbin, falter, gyrate, rattle, totter, wobble **07** revolve, stagger, stumble **08** hoolican **09** eightsome, hoolachan **10** multiplier
• **reel off** **04** list **06** recite, repeat

**09** rattle off **10** run through **11** list quickly

**refashion**
◇ *anagram indicator* **06** adjust, reform, rehash **07** convert, rebuild **11** reconstruct

**refer**
**04** cite, mean, send **05** apply, guide, point, quote, remit **06** advert, allude, appeal, assign, belong, commit, direct, hand on, hint at, look at, look up, pass on, permit, relate, turn to **07** bring up, concern, consult, deliver, mention, pertain, put over, speak of, touch on **08** describe, indicate, relegate, resort to, transfer **09** recommend, represent, reproduce **10** be relevant
• **refer to** **03** see

**referee**
**03** ref, ump **05** judge, zebra **06** umpire **07** arbiter, mediate **08** linesman, mediator **09** arbitrate, intercede **10** adjudicate, arbitrator **11** adjudicator, commissaire, referendary

**reference**
**03** ref **04** hint, note **05** mensh **06** regard, remark, source, squint **07** bearing, mention, respect **08** allusion, citation, footnote, innuendo, instance, relation **09** authority, character, quotation **10** connection, pertinence, retrospect **11** credentials, endorsement, testimonial **12** illustration **13** applicability **14** recommendation
• **with reference to** **02** re **05** about **07** apropos **09** as regards, regarding **10** concerning, relating to, relevant to, respecting **11** referring to **12** with regard to **13** in the matter of, with respect to **14** on the subject of

**referendum**
**04** poll, vote **06** survey, voting **10** plebiscite

**referral**
**07** sending **08** handover, pointing, transfer **09** direction, handing on, passing on

**refine**
◇ *anagram indicator* **03** try **04** fine, hone, pure, sift, test **05** clear, exalt, treat **06** distil, filter, polish, purify, rarefy, repure, strain **07** chasten, clarify, cleanse, elevate, improve, perfect, process **08** chastise, civilize, freebase, repurify **09** cultivate, elaborate, sublimize, subtilize **11** cut and carve **12** spiritualize

*Products and byproducts of refining include:*

**03** tar
**05** sugar
**07** asphalt, bitumen, treacle
**08** molasses
**11** golden syrup

*See also* **fuel; hydrocarbon; sugar**

**refined**
**04** fine, pure **05** Attic, civil, clear, couth, exact, horsy **06** gentle, horsey, inland, picked, polite, subtle, urbane

**07** classic, courtly, elegant, foppish, genteel, precise, stylish, treated **08** Augustan, cultured, cutglass, delicate, educated, filtered, gracious, ladylike, polished, precious, purified, rarefied, well-bred **09** civilized, distilled, processed, sensitive, spiritual **10** cultivated **11** gentlemanly **12** well-mannered **13** gentlewomanly, sophisticated **14** discriminating

**refinement**
**05** grace, style, taste **06** nicety, polish **07** culture, exility, finesse **08** addition, breeding, chastity, civility, delicacy, elegance, elegancy, subtlety, urbanity **09** amendment, gentility, technique **10** alteration, subtleness **11** cultivation, elaboration, good manners, improvement **12** amelioration, modification **14** discrimination, sophistication

**refit**
◊ *anagram indicator* **04** mend **05** renew **06** repair, revamp **07** furbish **08** facelift, renovate **09** refurbish **10** renovation

**reflect**
◊ *reversal indicator* **04** cast, chew, echo, mull, muse, shed, show **05** brood, dwell, glass, glint, image, shine, study, think **06** advise, depict, mirror, ponder, reveal **07** bespeak, display, exhibit, express, imitate, portray, redound, scatter, tarnish **08** cogitate, consider, disgrace, indicate, manifest, meditate, mull over, ruminate, send back **09** bounce off, cerebrate, discredit, repercuss, reproduce, speculate, throw back **10** chew the cud, deliberate **11** communicate, contemplate, demonstrate, reverberate **14** give a bad name to, put in a bad light

**reflection**
◊ *reversal indicator* **04** baby, echo, idea, life, slur, view **05** blame, image, shame, study **06** belief, musing, reflex **07** censure, display, eidolon, feeling, opinion, rebound, thought **08** disgrace, feelings, likeness, reproach, thinking **09** aspersion, criticism, discredit, disrepute, portrayal, snowblink, viewpoint **10** cogitation, epiphonema, expression, impression, indication, meditation, rumination **11** cerebration, mirror image, observation **12** deliberation, repercussion **13** consideration, contemplation, demonstration, manifestation

**reflective**
**06** dreamy **07** pensive **08** absorbed **09** pondering, reasoning **10** cogitating, meditative, ruminative, thoughtful **12** deliberative **13** contemplative

**reflex**
**06** direct **07** natural, project **08** autonomy, knee-jerk, unwilled **09** automatic, re-entrant **10** expression, mechanical, reciprocal, re-entering **11** instinctive, involuntary, spontaneous **13** manifestation **14** Babinski effect, uncontrollable **15** without thinking

**reform**
◊ *anagram indicator* **04** mend **05** amend, prune, purge **06** anneal, better, change, repair, revamp, revise **07** correct, disband, dismiss, improve, rebuild, rectify, redress, remodel, restore, shake up, shake-up **08** chastise, renovate, revision **09** amendment, refashion, transform **10** ameliorate, betterment, correction, rebuilding, regenerate, renovation, reorganize **11** improvement, reconstruct, remodelling, restoration **12** reconstitute, rehabilitate **13** rectification, revolutionize **14** reconstruction, rehabilitation, reorganization

**reformat**
◊ *anagram indicator*

**reformation**
◊ *anagram indicator* **08** progress, revision **09** amendment **10** renovation **11** improvement, restoration **12** amelioration, palingenesis, regeneration **13** rectification **14** rehabilitation

**reformer**
**03** rad **06** mucker **07** Hussite, liberal, Lollard, Owenite, radical **08** do-gooder, Lutheran **09** Calvinist, reformado, Wyclifite, Zwinglian **10** Wycliffite **11** progressive **12** Pestalozzian **13** bleeding heart, revolutionary, whistle-blower

---

*Reformers include:*

**03** Hus (Jan)
**04** Huss (John), **Knox** (John), **Mill** (John Stuart), **Owen** (Robert)
**05** Perón (Eva)
**06** Calvin (John), **Luther** (Martin), **Wiclif** (John), **Wyclif** (John)
**07** Stanton (Elizabeth Cady), **Wycliff** (John), **Zwingli** (Huldreich), **Zwingli** (Ulrich)
**08** Wicliffe (John), **Wycliffe** (John)
**10** Pestalozzi (Johann)
**11** Wilberforce (William)

---

**refractory**
**05** balky, surly, tough **06** mulish, sturdy, unruly, wilful **07** defiant, naughty, restive **08** perverse, stubborn **09** difficult, obstinate, resistant **10** headstrong, rebellious **11** contentious, disobedient, intractable **12** cantankerous, contumacious, disputatious, recalcitrant, unmanageable **13** fire-resistant, unco-operative **14** uncontrollable

**refrain**
**03** bob, tag **04** curb, fa la, juba, keep, quit, song, stop, tune **05** avoid, cease, forgo, spare, wheel **06** burden, chorus, desist, eschew, fading, fa la la, forego, give up, melody, strain **07** abstain, burthen, ducdame, forbear, hold off **08** faburden, falderal, leave off, overcome, overture, renounce, repetend, response, restrain, rum-ti-tum, surcease, withhold **09** do without, hemistich, supersede, tirra-lyra,

turnagain, undersong **10** epistrophe, ritornello, tirra-lirra **11** rumti-iddity **12** rumpti-iddity

**refresh**
**03** jog **04** cool, prod, stir **05** brace, renew, slake **06** arouse, prompt, refect, remind, repair, repose, revive **07** enliven, fortify, freshen, restore **08** activate, energize, recreate, revivify **09** reanimate, recomfort, stimulate **10** exhilarate, invigorate, rejuvenate, revitalize **11** refocillate **12** reinvigorate

**refreshing**
**03** new **04** cool **05** fresh, novel **06** caller **07** bracing, welcome **08** original, reviving **09** different, inspiring **10** energizing, freshening, not another, unexpected **11** inspiriting, refrigerant, stimulating **12** exhilarating, invigorating **15** thirst-quenching

**refreshment**
**03** tea **04** bait, food **05** drink, snack **06** drinks, repast **07** elevens, renewal, revival **09** elevenses, four-hours, refection, twalhours **10** freshening, recreation, sustenance **11** reanimation, restoration, stimulation, water of life **12** food and drink, invigoration **14** reinvigoration, revitalization

**refreshments**
**04** eats, food, grub, nosh **06** drinks, snacks, tucker **07** aliment, titbits **08** eatables **09** elevenses **10** provisions, sustenance **12** food and drink

**refrigerate**
**03** ice **04** cool **05** chill **06** freeze **08** keep cold

**refuge**
**04** dive, hole, holt, home **05** haven **06** asylum, burrow, harbor, island, resort **07** harbour, hideout, hospice, retreat, shelter **08** bolthole, funkhole, hideaway, security **09** sanctuary **10** protection, stronghold, subterfuge **11** sheet anchor **13** place of safety

**refugee**
**05** exile **06** asylee, émigré **07** escapee, runaway **08** fugitive **10** contraband **12** asylum seeker **15** displaced person, stateless person

**refulgent**
**06** bright **07** beaming, lambent, radiant, shining **08** gleaming, lustrous **09** brilliant, irradiant **10** glistening, glittering **11** resplendent

**refund**
**05** repay **06** rebate, return **07** imburse, pay back, restore **08** give back **09** reimburse, repayment **10** redisburse **13** reimbursement

**refurbish**
◊ *anagram indicator* **04** do up, mend **05** refit **06** repair, revamp **07** re-equip, remodel, restore **08** overhaul, renovate **10** redecorate **11** recondition

**refurbishment**
◊ *anagram indicator* **07** doing-up **09** refitting, repairing, revamping **10** renovation **11** recondition, restoration **12** redecoration

## refusal

**02** no **04** veto **06** denial, nay-say, rebuff **07** repulse **08** negation, spurning **09** knock-back, raspberry, rejection **11** repudiation, turning-down, withholding **12** incompliance, non-admission, nothing doing **13** non-acceptance **14** nolo episcopari
• **first refusal 06** choice, option **11** opportunity **13** consideration **15** right of purchase

## refuse

◊ *anagram indicator* **03** ban, jib, red **04** bran, deny, junk, marc, nill, rape, redd, scum **05** draff, dregs, dross, flock, husks, offal, repel, say no, spurn, trash, waste **06** debris, litter, naysay, pass up, rebuff, reject, resist, scoria, sewage **07** decline, garbage, offscum, rubbish, sullage **08** leavings, renounce, tailings, turn down, withhold **09** knock back, repudiate, riddlings, throw back **11** offscouring **12** kitchen-stuff, offscourings, rejectamenta **13** draw the line at, shake your head **14** dig your heels in

## refutation

**08** disproof, elenchus, negation, rebuttal **09** overthrow **11** confutation

## refute

**04** deny, meet **05** rebut, refel **06** negate **07** confute, counter, reprove, silence **08** disprove, redargue **09** discredit, overthrow **12** deny strongly, give the lie to

## regain

**04** find **06** recoup, retake **07** get back, reclaim, recover, win back **08** recovery, retrieve, return to, take back **09** recapture, reconcile, repossess

## regal

**05** noble, royal **06** kingly, lordly **07** queenly, stately **08** imperial, majestic, princely, sceptred **09** sceptered, sovereign **11** magnificent

## regale

**03** ply **05** amuse, feast, serve **06** divert, junket **07** delight, gratify, kitchen, refresh **09** captivate, entertain, fascinate

## regard

**03** eye, see **04** care, deem, gaum, gorm, heed, look, love, mark, note, rate, view **05** gauge, judge, point, think, value, watch **06** aspect, behold, detail, esteem, follow, gaze at, hold of, honour, look at, look on, matter, notice, repute, tender **07** believe, concern, imagine, observe, respect, set down, subject, suppose, weigh up **08** appraise, approval, consider, estimate, listen to, look upon, relation, respects, sympathy **09** affection, attention, deference, greetings, intention, reference **10** admiration, advertence, advertency, bear in mind, best wishes, estimation, good wishes, particular, retrospect, scrutinize **11** approbation, compliments, contemplate, observation, salutations **12** take notice of **13** consideration

**14** loving kindness, pay attention to **15** give the once-over, take into account
• **with regard to, in regard to 02** re **04** as to **05** about, anent **07** apropos, vis-à-vis **09** as regards, in terms of **10** as concerns, concerning **12** in relation to **13** with respect to **14** on the subject of **15** with reference to

## regardful

**05** aware **07** careful, dutiful, heedful, mindful **08** noticing, watchful **09** attentive, observant **10** respectful, respective, thoughtful **11** circumspect, considerate

## regarding

**02** re **04** as to **05** about **07** apropos, vis-à-vis **09** as regards **10** concerning, in regard to **12** in relation to, with regard to **13** when it comes to, with respect to **14** on the subject of **15** with reference to

## regardless

◊ *deletion indicator* **06** anyhow, anyway **08** careless, heedless **09** at any cost, negligent, unmindful **10** at any price, neglectful **11** come what may, inattentive, indifferent, nonetheless, respectless, unconcerned **12** disregarding, irregardless, nevertheless, no matter what **13** inconsiderate

## regenerate

◊ *anagram indicator* **05** renew **06** change, revive, uplift **07** refresh, renewed, restore **08** inspirit, reawaken, rekindle, renovate, revivify **09** reproduce, twice-born **10** invigorate, rejuvenate, revitalize **11** reconstruct, re-establish **12** reconstitute, reinvigorate

## regenerated

◊ *anagram indicator* **03** new

## regeneration

**07** renewal **10** neogenesis, renovation **11** reformation, restoration **12** morphallaxis, palingenesis, rejuvenation, reproduction **13** homomorphosis **14** reconstitution, reconstruction, reinvigoration **15** re-establishment

## regime

**03** way **04** diet, fast, rule **05** order, reign **06** method, system **07** command, control, formula, pattern, regimen, routine **08** practice, schedule, tyrannis **09** direction, procedure, programme **10** abstinence, government, leadership, management **11** kleptocracy **13** establishment **14** administration **15** short sharp shock

## regiment

**04** army, band, body, crew, gang **05** group **06** cohort, pultun, tercio **07** battery, brigade, company, platoon **08** squadron

*Army regiments include:*

**02** RA, RE, TA
**03** SAS
**04** REME

**05** Kings, Paras
**06** London
**07** Gurkhas, Lowland
**08** Cheshire
**09** Fusiliers, Parachute, Royal Tank
**10** Black Watch, Life Guards, Royal Irish, Royal Scots, Royal Welsh
**11** Highlanders, Horse Guards, Irish Guards, Scots Guards, Welsh Guards
**12** Army Air Corps, Close Support, Green Howards, Green Jackets, Gurkha Rifles, Rifle Brigade, Royal Anglian, Royal Hussars, Royal Lancers, Royal of Wales
**13** Artists' Rifles, Light Dragoons, Light Infantry, Staffordshire
**14** General Support, Royal Artillery, Royal Engineers
**15** Grenadier Guards, Rifle Volunteers, Territorial Army

## regimented

**06** strict **07** ordered **09** organized, regulated **10** controlled, methodical, systematic **11** disciplined **12** standardized, systematized

## region

**01** E **03** end **04** area, belt, high, land, part, wild, zona, zone **05** ambit, bundu, burgh, duchy, field, manor, orbit, place, range, realm, reame, scope, shire, state, tract, waste, wilds, world **06** county, domain, empire, estate, garden, ghetto, parish, riding, sector, sphere **07** borough, climate, country, diocese, emirate, expanse, granary, heavens, hundred, kingdom, mission, quarter, section, suburbs, terrain **08** autonomy, badlands, district, division, dominion, foreland, interior, province, time zone **09** backwoods, bailiwick, climature, continent, goldfield, heartland, inner city, outskirts, periphery, territory **10** borderland, hemisphere, playground, wilderness **11** breadbasket, God's country, reservation, terra ignota **12** municipality, principality, subcontinent **13** catchment area, neighbourhood **14** God's own country, postal district, terra incognita

*Regions include:*

**03** Zug
**04** Jura, León, Midi, Ruhr, Vaud
**05** Angus, Dixie, Gower, Lazio, Liège, Loire, Marne, Namur, Norte, Otago, Rhine, Rhône, Rioja, Somme, Taupo, Tyrol, Urals
**06** Acadia, Alsace, Apulia, Aragón, Argyll, Azores, Bayern, Beiras, Burgos, Centro, Crimea, Hessen, Iberia, Latium, Lisboa, Molise, Mt Cook, Murcia, Nelson, Ozarks, Puglia, Savoie, Saxony, Sicily, Top End, Umbria, Valais, Veneto, Vosges, Wanaka
**07** Abruzzo, Algarve, Almería, Ardenne, Bavaria, Bohemia, Borders, Brabant, Castile, Corsica, Drenthe, Galicia, Hainaut,

Jutland, La Loire, La Rioja, Liguria, Limburg, Lucerne, Madeira, Marches, Midwest, Moselle, Navarra, Navarre, Picardy, Riviera, Rotorua, Ruapehu, Shannon, Siberia, Silesia, Thurgau, Tuscany, Utrecht, Venetia, Waikato, Zeeland

08 Alentejo, Alicante, Ardennes, Asturias, Auvergne, Bretagne, Brittany, Burgundy, Calabria, Calvados, Campania, Canaries, Cataluña, Caucasus, Charente, Chechnya, Dalmatia, Dordogne, Eastland, Flanders, Grampian, Hebrides, Holstein, Lappland, Limousin, Lombardy, Lorraine, Manawatu, Normandy, Picardie, Piedmont, Provence, Pyrenees, Rust Belt, Saarland, Sardinia, Taranaki, Trentino, Val d'Oise, Valencia, Wallonia, Wanganui

09 Andalucía, Andalusia, Aquitaine, Bible Belt, Bourgogne, Cantabria, Carinthia, Castellón, Catalonia, Champagne, Charentes, Côte d'Azur, Deep South, Fiordland, Flevoland, Friesland, Groningen, Gulf Coast, Hawkes Bay, Highlands, Languedoc, Maritimes, Neuchâtel, Northland, Pomerania, Red Centre, Rhineland, Schleswig, Snowdonia, Southland, Southwest, The Burren, Thuringia, Trossachs, Wairarapa, West Coast

10 Appalachia, Basilicata, Canterbury, Coromandel, Costa Brava, Gelderland, Graubünden, Great Lakes, Horowhenua, New England, Overijssel, Palatinate, Westphalia

11 Bay of Plenty, Black Forest, Brandenburg, Central Belt, Costa Blanca, Costa del Sol, Costa Dorada, Extremadura, Great Plains, Île-de-France, Marlborough, Mid-Atlantic, Zuid-Holland

12 American West, Bay of Islands, Noord-Brabant, Noord-Holland, The Kimberley

13 Barossa Valley, Basque Country, Brecon Beacons, Canary Islands, Emilia-Romagna, Middle America, Pays-de-la-Loire

14 Castile and Leon, Channel Islands, Snowy Mountains

15 Balearic Islands, Bernese Oberland, Eastern Seaboard

*See also* **council; county; department; district; electorate; geography; province; state**
• **in the region of** 03 odd 04 near, some 05 about, circa 06 around, nearly 07 close to, loosely, roughly 09 just about, not far off, rounded up 10 give or take, more or less, round about 11 approaching, rounded down 13 approximately, or thereabouts, something like 14 in round numbers 15 in the vicinity of

## regional
05 local, zonal 08 district 09 localized, parochial, sectional 10 provincial

## register
03 log, say, tax 04 cast, file, list, mark, note, poll, read, roll, show, tone 05 album, clock, diary, enrol, enter, files, index, notes, range, voice 06 annals, betray, book in, docket, enlist, enroll, ledger, lidger, muster, record, regest, reveal, roster, sign on, turn in 07 almanac, check in, diptych, display, exhibit, express, journal, listing, notitia, put down, set down, terrier 08 archives, cadastre, indicate, inscribe, manifest, menology, obituary, schedule, take down 09 cartulary, catalogue, chronicle, directory, enrolment, matricula, registrar 10 enregister, enrollment 11 demonstrate, matriculate, patent-rolls 12 put in writing, transfer book

## registrar
05 clerk 07 actuary 08 annalist, greffier, official, recorder, register 09 archivist, secretary 10 cataloguer, chronicler 11 protocolist, protonotary 12 prothonotary, sheriff clerk 13 administrator

## registration
04 list, rego 05 reggo 06 noting, record 07 logging 08 entering, register 09 enrolment, recording, signing-on 10 checking-in 11 inscription

## regress
◇ *reversal indicator* 03 ebb 04 wane 05 lapse 06 recede, return, revert 07 re-entry, relapse, retreat 09 backslide, retrocede, reversion 10 degenerate, retrogress 11 deteriorate

## regret
03 rew, rue 04 weep 05 grief, mourn, shame 06 bemoan, desire, grieve, lament, relent, repent, sorrow 07 be sorry, deplore, remorse 08 had-I-wist 09 deprecate, feel sorry, penitence 10 bitterness, contrition, repentance 11 compunction 12 be distressed, feel bad about, self-reproach 14 be disappointed, disappointment
• **expression of regret** 02 ay 03 ach, och 04 alas 05 alack, ewhow 06 if only 07 out upon 09 alack-a-day

## regretful
03 sad 05 sorry 06 rueful 07 ashamed 08 contrite, penitent 09 repentant, sorrowful 10 apologetic, remorseful 12 disappointed

## regrettable
03 sad 05 sorry, wrong 06 too bad 07 unhappy, unlucky 08 shameful 09 upsetting 10 deplorable, ill-advised, lamentable 11 disgraceful, distressing, unfortunate 13 disappointing, reprehensible

## regrettably
04 alas 05 sadly 08 sad to say 09 unhappily, unluckily, worse luck 11 sad to relate 13 unfortunately

## regular
01 M 03 set 04 even, flat 05 daily, fixed, level, loyal, swell, usual 06 common, giusto, hourly, normal, proper, smooth, stated, steady, strict, weekly, yearly 07 average, canonic, certain, classic, correct, monthly, orderly, private, routine, typical, uniform 08 approved, balanced, constant, everyday, frequent, habitual, official, ordinary, orthodox, periodic, rhythmic, standard, standing, thorough 09 canonical, customary, out-and-out, permanent, recurring, unvarying, veritable 10 consistent, methodical, periodical, systematic, unchanging 11 commonplace, established, symmetrical 12 conventional, evenly spread, professional, time-honoured 13 well-organized

## regularly
◇ *hidden alternately indicator* 05 often 10 frequently 13 like clockwork

## regulate
◇ *anagram indicator* 03 run, set 04 rule, tune 05 align, aline, guide, order 06 adjust, baffle, direct, govern, handle, manage, settle, square 07 arrange, balance, conduct, control, monitor, oversee 08 moderate, modulate, organize 09 supervise 10 administer 11 superintend, synchronize

## regulation
02 AR 03 act, law, set 04 code, rule 05 by-law, edict, fixed, order, usual 06 bye-law, curfew, decree, dictum, dosage, normal, pusser, ruling 07 command, control, dictate, precept, statute 08 accepted, guidance, official, orthodox, required, standard 09 customary, direction, directive, mandatory, ordinance, principle, procedure, statutory 10 management, obligatory 11 commandment, requirement, supervision 12 dispensation 13 pronouncement 14 administration 15 superintendence

## regurgitate
04 puke, spew 05 heave, retch, vomit 06 posset, repeat, sick up, spit up 07 bring up, fetch up, regorge, restate, throw up 08 disgorge, ruminate, say again 09 reiterate, tell again 12 recapitulate

## rehabilitate
04 mend, save 05 clear, rehab, renew 06 adjust, redeem, reform 07 convert, rebuild, restore 08 renovate 09 normalize, reinstate 11 recondition, reconstruct, re-establish, reintegrate 12 reconstitute, reinvigorate

## rehash
◇ *anagram indicator* 05 alter, rejig 06 change, rework 07 restate, rewrite 08 rejigger 09 rearrange, refashion, rejigging, reshuffle, reworking 11 restatement 13 rearrangement

## rehearsal
05 drill 06 dry run 07 hersall, reading,

**rehearse**
recital **08** band-call, dummy run, exercise, practice, trial run, woodshed **09** narration **10** repetition, run-through **11** enumeration, preparation, read-through, walk-through

**rehearse**
**05** block, drill, train **06** go over, recite, relate, repeat, try out **07** narrate, pour out, prepare, recount **08** block out, practise **09** enumerate, pour forth **10** run through

**reign**
**04** rain, ring, rule, sway **05** exist, occur, power, raine, rayne, realm **06** be king, domain, empire, govern, obtain **07** be queen, command, control, kingdom, prevail **08** dominion, hold sway, monarchy **09** be in power, be present, influence, Silver Age, supremacy **10** ascendancy, be in charge, government **11** be in command, be in control, pontificate, predominate, sovereignty **12** predominance **14** be in government, sit on the throne

**reigning**
**05** world **06** ruling **07** current, in power, present, regnant **09** governing, in command, in control, incumbent, presiding **10** victorious

**reimburse**
**05** repay **06** refund, return **07** pay back, restore **08** give back **09** indemnify **10** compensate, recompense, remunerate

**reimbursement**
**06** refund **09** indemnity, repayment **10** recompense **12** compensation

**rein**
**04** curb, halt, hold, stop **05** brake, check, limit **06** answer, arrest, bridle **07** control, harness **08** hold back, reindeer, restrain, restrict **09** overcheck, restraint **11** restriction
• **free rein** **07** freedom, liberty **08** free hand **10** free-for-all **11** blank cheque, open slather **12** carte blanche, laissez-faire

**reincarnation**
**07** rebirth, samsara **12** palingenesis **14** metempsychosis

**reindeer**
**04** deer, rein **06** tarand **07** caribou

*Father Christmas's reindeer:*

**05** Comet, Cupid, Vixen
**06** Dancer, Dasher, Donner
**07** Blitzen, Prancer, Rudolph

**reinforce**
◇ *containment indicator* **04** line, prop, stay **05** brace, shore, steel **06** beef up, harden, stress, supply **07** augment, enforce, fortify, recruit, stiffen, support, toughen **08** buttress, increase, renforce **09** emphasize, re-enforce, underline **10** strengthen, supplement **11** consolidate

**reinforcement**
**04** help, prop, stay **05** brace, shore **06** back-up **07** recruit, support **08** addition, buttress, emphasis,

increase, reserves **09** hardening **10** supplement **11** auxiliaries, enlargement **12** augmentation **13** amplification, fortification, re-enforcement, strengthening **15** supplementaries

**reinstate**
**06** recall, return **07** replace, reseize, restore **08** give back **09** reappoint, reinstall **11** re-establish **12** rehabilitate

**reinstatement**
**06** recall, return **10** giving-back, reposition **11** replacement, restoration **15** re-establishment

**reiterate**
**04** ding **05** recap, resay **06** repeat, retell, stress **07** iterate, restate **08** rehearse **09** emphasize **10** ingeminate **12** recapitulate

**reject**
◇ *anagram indicator* ◇ *reversal indicator*
**03** bin, nix, pip **04** cast, deny, dice, jilt, kill, spin, veto **05** repel, scrap, spurn, trash **06** rebuff, recuse, refuse, second **07** cast off, cast-off, condemn, decline, despise, discard, dismiss, exclude, failure, forsake, outcast, repulse, say no to **08** athetize, brush off, disallow, disclaim, jettison, renounce, set aside, throw out, turn away, turn down **09** eliminate, knock back, reprobate, repudiate, throw away **10** disapprove **11** give the push **13** kick into touch **14** throw overboard, turn your back on **15** wash your hands of

**rejection**
**04** push, veto **05** spurn **06** denial, rebuff **07** heave-ho, refusal **08** brush-off, turn-down **09** athetesis, declining, dismissal, exclusion, knock-back **10** discarding **11** elimination, jettisoning, reprobation, repudiation, turning-down **12** cold shoulder, renunciation **14** Dear John letter

**rejig**
◇ *anagram indicator* **07** re-equip, shake up **09** modernize, rearrange **10** reorganize, streamline **11** rationalize, restructure

**rejoice**
**03** joy **05** exult, glory, revel **07** be happy, delight, gladden **08** be joyful, jubilate **09** be pleased, celebrate, make merry, whoop it up **10** jump for joy **11** be delighted **12** take pleasure

**rejoicing**
**03** joy **05** glory **07** delight, elation, ovation, revelry, triumph **08** euphoria, gladness, jubilant, pleasure **09** festivity, happiness **10** exaltation, exultation, jubilation **11** celebration, merrymaking

**rejoin**
◇ *anagram indicator* **04** quip **05** reply **06** answer, retort **07** respond, riposte **08** repartee

**rejoinder**
**04** quip **05** reply **06** answer, retort **07** riposte **08** comeback, repartee, response

**rejuvenate**
**05** renew **06** revive **07** refresh, restore **08** recharge, rekindle, revivify **09** freshen up, reanimate **10** regenerate, revitalize **12** reinvigorate

**rejuvenation**
**07** renewal, revival **11** restoration, shunamitism **12** regeneration **14** reinvigoration, revitalization

**relapse**
**04** fail, sink, weed, weid **05** lapse **06** revert, weaken, worsen **07** decline, regress, setback **08** fall away **09** backslide, reversion, weakening, worsening **10** degenerate, recurrence, regression, retrogress **11** backsliding, deteriorate, hypostrophe **13** deterioration, retrogression

**relate**
**04** ally, join, link, rede, tell **05** apply, fable, refer, story **06** couple, detail, empart, impart, recite, report **07** compare, concern, connect, feel for, narrate, pertain, present, recount, respect **08** describe, hit it off, identify **09** appertain, associate, bring back, correlate, delineate, discourse, empathize, get on with, make known **10** be relevant, sympathize, understand **11** communicate **12** have a rapport **13** get on well with **14** have a bearing on

**related**
**03** kin, rel **04** akin **05** joint, of kin **06** affine, agnate, allied, kinred, linked, mutual **07** affined, cognate, kindred **08** narrated, referred, relevant **09** connected, pertinent **10** affiliated, associated, correlated **11** concomitant **12** accompanying, interrelated **14** consanguineous, interconnected **15** of the same family

**relation**
**03** kin, rel, sib **04** bond, link, term **05** ratio **06** affine, family, regard, rellie **07** bearing, kindred, kinsman, linking, rapport, recital, respect **08** alliance, kinsfolk, relative **09** connexion, kinswoman, narrative, reference, relevance, statement **10** collateral, comparison, connection, pertinence, similarity **11** affiliation, application, correlation, information **12** relationship **13** interrelation **14** correspondence, correspondency **15** interconnection, interdependence
*See also* **narrative; relative**

**relations**
**03** kin, sex **05** folks, terms, union **06** coitus, family **07** affairs, coition, contact, kindred, kinsman, liaison, quarter, rapport, rellies **08** contacts, dealings, intimacy, kinsfolk **09** kinswoman, relatives **10** copulation, love-making **11** connections, interaction, intercourse **12** associations, consummation, relationship **14** communications **15** carnal knowledge

**relationship**
**03** kin, tie **04** bond, link, ties **05** blood,

fling, ratio, thing, tie-up **06** affair
**07** account, kinship, liaison, rapport,
romance, sibship **08** affinity, alliance,
intimacy, parallel **09** chemistry,
closeness **10** connection, flirtation,
friendship, love affair, proportion,
similarity **11** association, correlation
• **end relationship 04** dump, jilt
**07** break up, divorce, split up

**relative**
**03** kin, rel **05** in-law **06** family, rellie
**07** germane, kindred, kinsman, related
**08** apposite, kinsfolk, moderate,
parallel, relation, relevant
**09** connected, connexion, dependant,
dependent, kinswoman, pertinent
**10** applicable, comparable,
connection, reciprocal, respective
**11** appropriate, comparative,
correlative **12** commensurate,
interrelated, proportional
**13** corresponding, proportionate

*Relatives include:*

**02** ex
**03** bro, dad, mom, mum, sis, son
**04** aunt, gran, heir, nana, twin, wife
**05** aunty, daddy, mummy, nanna,
nanny, niece, uncle
**06** auntie, cousin, ex-wife, father,
german, godson, grampa, granny,
mother, nephew, parent, sister,
spouse
**07** brother, grandad, husband,
partner, sibling, stepdad,
stepmum, stepson
**08** daughter, godchild, grandson,
son-in-law
**09** ex-husband, godfather,
godmother, stepchild
**10** grandchild, half-sister, stepfather,
stepmother, step-parent,
stepsister, twin-sister
**11** father-in-law, first cousin, foster-
child, goddaughter, grandfather,
grandmother, grandparent, half-
brother, mother-in-law, sister-in-
law, stepbrother, twin-brother
**12** brother-in-law, foster-parent,
second cousin, stepdaughter
**13** daughter-in-law, granddaughter

**relatively**
**05** quite **06** fairly, rather **08** somewhat
**12** by comparison, in comparison
**13** comparatively

**relax**
◇ *anagram indicator* **03** veg **04** calm,
ease, fall, rest **05** abate, chill, loose,
lower, remit, slump **06** cool it, lessen,
loosen, reduce, relent, sedate, soften,
unbend, unknit, unrein, unwind, veg
out, weaken **07** ease off, mollify,
resolve, slacken, unbrace, unclasp,
unpurse **08** calm down, chill out, de-
stress, diminish, kick back, loosen up,
moderate, unbend **09** hang loose,
lighten up **10** liberalize, take it easy
**12** tranquillize **13** let yourself go, put
your feet up **14** take a chill pill, take
things easy **15** let it all hang out, let
your hair down

**relaxation**
**03** fun **04** rest **05** let-up **06** easing,

repose **07** détente, leisure, relâche
**08** chill-out, pleasure **09** abatement,
amusement, enjoyment, lessening,
loosening, reduction, softening,
unwinding, weakening **10** autogenics,
meditation, misericord, moderation,
recreation, slackening **11** délassement,
distraction, loosening up, misericorde,
refreshment **13** entertainment

**relaxed**
◇ *anagram indicator* **04** calm, cool, easy
**05** loose **06** at ease, atonic, casual,
comodo, unbent **07** commodo,
languid, restful **08** carefree, composed,
downbeat, informal, laid-back,
toneless, unbraced, unstrung
**09** collected, easy-going, graspless,
leisurely, unhurried **10** chilled-out
**11** comfortable, uninhibited **12** happy-
go-lucky

**relay**
◇ *anagram indicator* **04** send, time, turn
**05** carry, shift, spell, stint **06** hand on,
pass on, period, spread, supply
**07** message **08** dispatch, transmit
**09** broadcast, circulate, programme
**11** communicate **12** transmission
**13** communication

**release**
**04** free, undo **05** exeem, exeme, issue,
let go, loose, remit, untie **06** acquit,
convey, excuse, exempt, launch, let
off, let-off, loosen, reveal, unbind,
unlock, unveil **07** absolve, acquite,
deliver, divulge, freedom, liberty,
present, publish, relieve, set free,
slacken, unchain, unclasp, unleash,
unloose **08** acquight, announce,
bulletin, disclose, liberate, uncouple,
unfasten **09** acquittal, circulate,
discharge, disengage, exemption,
exonerate, make known, quitclaim,
quittance, remission, surrender,
unshackle **10** absolution, disclosure,
distribute, emancipate, liberation,
make public, publishing, relinquish,
revelation **11** acquittance, declaration,
deliverance, enlargement,
exoneration, manumission,
publication **12** announcement,
emancipation, proclamation **13** make
available

**relegate**
**05** eject, exile, expel, refer **06** assign,
banish, demote, deport, reduce
**07** consign, degrade, entrust
**08** delegate, dispatch, sideline, transfer
**09** downgrade **10** expatriate
**12** Stellenbosch

**relent**
**04** ease, melt **05** abate, allow, let up,
relax, yield **06** give in, regret, repent,
soften, unbend, weaken **07** die down,
ease off, give way, melting, slacken,
slowing **08** moderate **09** come round
**10** capitulate **14** change your mind

**relentless**
**04** grim, hard **05** cruel, harsh, stern
**06** fierce **08** pitiless, ruthless **09** cut-
throat, incessant, merciless, punishing,
unceasing **10** implacable, inexorable,
inflexible, persistent, unflagging,

unyielding **11** cold-hearted, hard-
hearted, remorseless, unforgiving,
unrelenting, unremitting
**14** uncompromising

**relevance**
**07** aptness, bearing **10** pertinence
**11** suitability **12** appositeness,
significance **13** applicability
**15** appropriateness

**relevant**
**03** apt **04** live **06** german, proper
**07** apropos, fitting, germane, related
**08** apposite, material, relative, suitable
**09** congruous, pertinent **10** admissible,
applicable, to the point **11** appropriate,
significant **12** proportional, to the
purpose

**reliability**
**07** honesty **09** certainty, constancy,
integrity, precision **10** steadiness
**12** faithfulness **13** dependability
**14** responsibility **15** trustworthiness

**reliable**
**04** safe, sure, true **05** solid, sound,
white **06** honest, stable, tested, trusty
**07** certain, devoted, dutiful, regular,
staunch **08** bankable, constant,
credible, faithful **09** unfailing
**10** dependable **11** predictable,
responsible, trustworthy, well-founded
**12** well-grounded **13** authoritative,
conscientious **14** copper-bottomed

**reliance**
**05** faith, trust **06** belief, credit
**09** assurance **10** confidence,
conviction, dependance, dependence

**relic**
**05** scrap, shell, token, trace **06** corpse,
fossil, relict **07** antique, memento,
relique, remains, remanié, remnant,
vestige **08** artefact, fragment, heirloom,
holdover, keepsake, moniment,
monument, reminder, souvenir,
survival **09** antiquity **11** remembrance

**relief**
**03** aid **04** alms, cure, help, rest
**05** break, let-up, locum, proxy
**06** back-up, easing, remedy, repose,
rescue, saving, succor, supply
**07** comfort, redress, release, relievo,
reserve, respite, rilievo, stand-by,
stand-in, succour, support **08** allaying,
breather, calmness, easement,
soothing **09** abatement, assuaging,
diversion, happiness, lessening,
reduction, remission, surrogate
**10** assistance, mitigation, palliation,
relaxation, substitute, sustenance,
understudy **11** alleviation, consolation,
deliverance, reassurance, refreshment,
replacement **12** interruption
• **expression of relief 04** phew,
whew **06** wheugh **08** thank God
**12** thank heavens **13** thank goodness

**relieve**
**03** aid **04** beet, bete, cure, ease, feed,
free, heal, help, save, stop **05** abate,
allay, break, expel, pause, spare, spell
**06** assist, excuse, exempt, lessen,
reduce, remove, rescue, soften,
soothe, succor **07** assuage, bestead,

break up, comfort, console, deliver, dismiss, release, replace, set free, slacken, succour, support, sustain **08** liberate, mitigate, palliate, reassure, unburden **09** alleviate, discharge, interrupt, punctuate **10** stand in for, substitute **11** discontinue **12** bring to an end, take over from **14** take the place of

## relieved
**04** glad **05** eased, happy **07** cheered, pleased **08** thankful **09** refreshed **10** encouraged

## religion
**04** code **05** creed, dogma, faith **07** beliefs **08** doctrine **12** belief system

*Religions include:*

**03** Bon, Zen
**04** Shi'a
**05** Amish, Baha'i, Druze, Islam, Sunni
**06** Sufism, Taoism, voodoo
**07** animism, Baha'ism, Essenes, Jainism, Jesuits, Judaism, Lamaism, Moonies, Opus Dei, Orphism, Quakers, Saivism, Saktism, Sikhism
**08** Baptists, Buddhism, Druidism, Hasidism, Hinduism, paganism, Tantrism, Wahhabis
**09** Ahmadiyya, Cabbalism, Calvinism, Methodism, Mithraism, Mormonism, occultism, Parseeism, shamanism, Shintoism, Vedantism, Waldenses
**10** Adventists, Brahmanism, Evangelism, Gnosticism, iconoclasm, Puritanism, Soka Gakkai
**11** Anabaptists, Anglicanism, Catholicism, Creationism, Freemasonry, Hare Krishna, Lutheranism, Manichaeism, Scientology, Zen Buddhism
**12** Albigensians, Christianity, Confucianism, Nestorianism, Unitarianism
**13** Church in Wales, Protestantism, Reform Judaism, Salvation Army
**14** Fundamentalism, Oxford Movement, Pentecostalism, Rastafarianism, Rosicrucianism, Society of Jesus, Ultramontanism, Zoroastrianism
**15** ancestor-worship, Church of England, Presbyterianism

## religious
**02** pi **03** pia **04** holy **05** godly, pious **06** devout, divine, sacred, strict **07** serious **08** reverent, rigorous **09** believing, committed, doctrinal, righteous, spiritual **10** devotional, God-fearing, meticulous, practising, scriptural, scrupulous **11** church-going, theological **13** conscientious
*See also* **Bible; festival; scripture; service; symbol**

*Religious buildings include:*

**04** Kaba
**05** Ka'aba

**06** Kasbah
**07** Abu Mena, al-Azhar
**08** Pantheon
**09** Abu Simbel, Acropolis, Borobudur, Eye Temple, Kinkakuji, Parthenon, Propylaea, Sacred Way, Sun Temple, Temple Bar
**10** Blue Mosque, Erechtheum, Harimandir, Sacré Coeur
**11** Ajanta caves, Ellora caves, Erechtheion, Great Sphinx, Hagia Sophia, Temple Mount, Wailing Wall, Western Wall, York Minster
**12** Boyana Church, Ely Cathedral, Golden Temple, Great Pyramid, Monte Cassino, Norton Priory, Pagan temples, Temple of Hera, Temple of Isis, Watton Priory
**13** Cordoba Mosque, Dome of the Rock, Horyuji Temple, Kailasa Temple, Muhammad's Tomb, Rila Monastery, Vézelay Church
**14** Belém Monastery, Dilwara temples, Golden Pavilion, Kazan Cathedral, Mahamuni Pagoda, My Son Sanctuary, Reims Cathedral, Ripon Cathedral, Sagrada Familia, Suleiman Mosque, Temple of Amon-Ra, Temple of Apollo, Temple of Athena, Temple of Heaven, Ummayad Mosque, Wells Cathedral
**15** Aachen Cathedral, Amiens Cathedral, Chavín de Huantar, Durham Cathedral, Exeter Cathedral, Ggantija temples, Pyramid of Cheops, Pyramid of the Sun, Shwe Dagon Pagoda, Shwezigon Pagoda, Speyer Cathedral, Temple of Artemis, Temple of Hathoor, Temple of Solomon, Temple of Somnath

*See also* **abbey; cathedral; worship**

*Religious figures include:*

**03 Fry** (Elizabeth), **Hus** (Jan), **Roy** (Ram Mohan)
**04 Bede** (St, 'the Venerable'), **Eddy** (Mary), **Huss** (John), **John** (of Leyden), **King** (Martin Luther), **Knox** (John), **Penn** (William), **Pire** (Dominique), **Shaw** (Anna Howard), **Tutu** (Desmond), **Weil** (Simone)
**05 Amman** (Jacob), **Booth** (William), **Condé** (Louis Prince de), **Farel** (Guillaume), **Grove** (Sir George), **Jesus**, **Keble** (John), **Lao Zi**, **Lewis** (Clive Staples), **Mahdi** (El), **Paley** (William), **Paris** (Matthew), **Smith** (Joseph), **Soper** (Donald, Lord), **Waite** (Terry), **Young** (Brigham)
**06 Arnold** (of Brescia), **Baxter** (Richard), **Becket** (St Thomas à), **Besant** (Annie), **Boehme** (Jakob), **Borgia**, **Browne** (Robert), **Browne** (Sir Thomas), **Buddha**, **Bunyan** (John), **Calvin** (John), **Christ**, **Gandhi** (Mohandas), **Garvey** (Marcus), **Graham** (Billy), **Hillel**, **Hutter** (Leonhard), **Jowett** (Benjamin), **Julian** (of Norwich),

**Kempis** (Thomas à), **Lao-tzu**, **Luther** (Martin), **Mather** (Cotton), **Mesmer** (Franz Anton), **Olcott** (Colonel Henry Steel), **Pilate** (Pontius), **Raikes** (Robert), **Ridley** (Nicholas), **Rogers** (John), **Sieyès** (Emmanuel Joseph Comte), **Tetzel** (Johann), **Wesley** (John)
**07 Aga Khan**, **al-Banna** (Hassan), **Ayeshah**, **Buchman** (Frank), **Coligny** (Gaspard de), **Cranmer** (Thomas), **Crowley** (Aleister), **Erasmus** (Desiderius), **Falwell** (Jerry), **Fénelon** (François), **Hubbard** (L Ron), **Jackson** (Jesse), **Latimer** (Hugh), **Mahatma**, **Müntzer** (Thomas), **Paisley** (Reverend Ian), **Photius**, **Russell** (Charles Taze), **Russell** (Jack), **Sithole** (Reverend Ndabaningi), **Spooner** (William Archibald), **Steiner** (Rudolf), **Tyndale** (William), **William** (of Malmesbury), **William** (of Ockham), **William** (of Tyre), **Wishart** (George), **Zwingli** (Huldreich)
**08 Agricola** (Johann), **Andrewes** (Lancelot), **Barabbas**, **Buchanan** (George), **Caiaphas**, **Khomeini** (Ayatollah Ruhollah), **Mahavira** (Vardhamana), **Mohammed**, **Muhammad**, **Pelagius**, **Rasputin** (Grigoriy), **Selassie** (Emperor Haile), **Williams** (Roger), **Wycliffe** (John)
**09 Akhenaten**, **Bar Kokhba** (Simon), **Blavatsky** (Madame Helena), **Confucius**, **Dalai Lama**, **Guru Nanak**, **Joan of Arc** (St), **McPherson** (Aimee Semple), **Niemöller** (Martin), **Zoroaster**
**10 Belshazzar**, **Fateh Singh** (Sant), **Huntingdon** (Selina Hastings, Countess of), **Manichaeus**, **Savonarola** (Girolamo), **Swedenborg** (Emmanuel), **Torquemada** (Tomás de), **Whitefield** (George)
**11 Bodhidharma**, **Jesus Christ**, **Prester John**, **Ramakrishna**, **Wilberforce** (William)
**12 Krishnamurti** (Jiddu)
**13 Judas Iscariot**
**15 Francis of Assisi** (St)

*Religious officers include:*

**03** nun
**04** dean, guru, imam, monk, pope
**05** abbot, canon, elder, friar, imaum, kohen, padre, prior, rabbi, rebbe, swami, vicar
**06** abbess, bishop, clergy, curate, deacon, father, mullah, parson, pastor, priest, rector
**07** muezzin, prelate, proctor
**08** cardinal, chaplain, minister, preacher
**09** ayatollah, clergyman, Dalai Lama, deaconess, Monsignor, Tashi Lama
**10** archbishop, archdeacon, arch-priest, chancellor
**11** clergywoman, Panchen Lama
**14** mother superior

See also **archbishop; cardinal; missionary; pope; theologian**

*Religious orders include:*

**04** IBVM, Sufi
**05** Taizé
**06** Culdee, Essene, Jesuit, Loreto, Marist
**07** Jesuits, Marists, Rifaite
**08** Buddhist, Capuchin, Grey nuns, Minorite, Trappist, Ursuline
**09** Barnabite, Capuchins, Carmelite, Dominican, Marianist, Mawlawite, mendicant, Salesians, Trappists, Ursulines
**10** Bernardine, Carmelites, Carthusian, Celestines, Cistercian, Conventual, Dominicans, Franciscan, Gilbertine, Grey friars, Norbertine, Oratorians, Poor Clares
**11** Augustinian, Benedictine, Black friars, Camaldolite, Carthusians, Cistercians, Franciscans, Ignorantine, Sylvestrine, White friars
**12** Augustinians, Austin friars, Benedictines
**13** Society of Mary
**14** Knights Templar, Sisters of Mercy, Society of Jesus

See also **monastery; sect**
• **religious education 02** RE, RI

**religiously**
**08** strictly **10** rigorously **11** doctrinally, spiritually **12** meticulously, scrupulously **13** theologically **15** conscientiously

**relinquish**
**04** cede, drop, part, quit **05** cease, demit, forgo, let go, waive, yield **06** desert, desist, forego, give up, resign **07** abandon, abstain, discard, forsake, give out, release, retreat **08** abdicate, hand over, part with, renounce **09** repudiate, surrender **11** discontinue

**reliquary**
**04** chef, tope **09** encolpion **10** tabernacle

**relish**
**03** sar **04** gout, gust, like, love, lust, tang, zest **05** adore, charm, enjoy, gusto, sauce, savor, smack, spice, taste, tooth **06** bumalo, degust, flavor, palate, pickle, savour, vigour **07** botargo, bummalo, chutney, delight, flavour, garnish, kitchen, rellish, revel in, stomach **08** appetite, bumaloti, caponata, opsonium, piquancy, pleasure, vivacity **09** appetizer, bummaloti, condiment, delight in, enjoyment, seasoning **10** appreciate, Bombay duck, experience, flavouring, liveliness **12** appreciation, satisfaction
• **lose relish 04** pall

**relocate**
**02** go **04** move **05** leave **06** go away, remove **08** move away, transfer, up sticks **09** move house **13** change address

**reluctance**
**07** dislike **08** aversion, distaste, loathing **09** hesitancy, renitency **10** hesitation, opposition, repugnance, resistance **12** backwardness **13** indisposition, recalcitrance, unwillingness **14** disinclination

**reluctant**
**03** shy **04** loth, slow **05** loath **06** averse **08** backward, grudging, hesitant, loathful, renitent **09** resisting, squeamish, unwilling **10** indisposed, struggling **11** disinclined **14** unenthusiastic

**rely**
**04** bank, lean, rest **05** count, trust **06** be sure, depend, reckon **07** swear by

**remain**
**02** be **03** lie **04** bide, keep, last, rest, stay, wait **05** abide, abode, await, dwell, leave, stand, stick, tarry **06** endure, linger, stay on **07** climate, persist, prevail, subsist, survive **08** continue, outstand **09** hang about, stand good **10** be left over, hang around, stay behind **11** stick around

**remainder**
**04** lave, rest **06** excess **07** balance, remains, remanet, remnant, residue, surplus **08** remanent, residuum, vestiges **09** carry-over, leftovers **11** superfluity

**remaining**
**03** odd **04** last, left, over **05** other, spare **06** unused **07** abiding, lasting, remnant, unspent **08** left over, remanent, residual **09** lingering, surviving **10** persisting, unfinished **11** outstanding

**remains**
**03** ash **04** body, dust, rest, ruin **05** ashes, bones, dregs, ruins **06** corpse, crumbs, debris, relics, scraps, traces **07** cadaver, carcase, residue **08** dead body, detritus, leavings, oddments, remnants, vestiges **09** fragments, leftovers, reliquiae, remainder, reversion **11** odds and ends

**remake**
◊ *anagram indicator* **06** mutate **07** rebuild **09** modernize, reproduce, transmute **11** reconstruct **12** metamorphose

**remark**
**03** hit, say **04** barb, jeer, note, quip, shot **05** ad-lib, sally, state **06** assert, insult, notice, reason **07** clanger, comment, declare, mention, observe, opinion **08** brickbat, cynicism, intimacy, one-liner, remarque **09** assertion, gallantry, pronounce, reference, statement, stricture, utterance, witticism **10** commentary, reflection, trivialism **11** commonplace, declaration, discourtesy, non sequitur, observation **12** obiter dictum **13** pronouncement **14** noteworthiness **15** acknowledgement

**remarkable**
◊ *anagram indicator* **03** odd **04** fine, rare, some, tall, unco **06** signal **07** amazing, notable, strange, unusual **08** singular, striking, uncommon **09** damnedest, important, memorable, momentous, prominent **10** hellacious, impressive, inimitable, miraculous, noteworthy, phenomenal, pre-eminent, surpassing, surprising **11** conspicuous, exceptional, outstanding, significant **12** considerable, unbelievable **13** distinguished, extraordinary
• **remarkable thing 04** lulu

**remarkably**
**04** unco **08** signally, uncommon **09** unusually **10** uncommonly **12** considerably, surprisingly **13** exceptionally, outstandingly, significantly **15** extraordinarily

**remedy**
◊ *anagram indicator* **03** fix **04** cure, ease, heal, help, mend, sort **05** azoth, dinic, salve, solve, tonga, treat **06** answer, bicarb, nosode, physic, posset, recure, relief, remead, remede, remeid, repair, soothe **07** arcanum, control, correct, nostrum, panacea, plaster, rectify, redress, relieve, restore, sort out, therapy **08** antidote, cephalic, corn-cure, leechdom, lungwort, medicine, mitigate, pilewort, put right, solution, specific **09** echinacea, eyebright, Galenical, hoarhound, horehound, magistery, prescript, salvarsan, treatment **10** catholicon, corrective, counteract, medicament, medication, reparation, simillimum, tarantella **11** oil of cloves, restorative **12** panpharmacon **13** antiscorbutic, antispasmodic, viper's bugloss **14** countermeasure, white horehound

**remember**
**03** mem **04** keep, mark, mind **05** evoke, learn, place, think **06** honour, recall, record, remind, retain **07** mention, think of **08** hark back, look back, memorize, summon up **09** celebrate, recognize, recollect, reminisce, think back **10** bear in mind, call to mind **11** commemorate, hold against, reconnoitre **12** learn by heart, pay tribute to **13** send greetings **14** commit to memory, send best wishes, send good wishes **15** send your regards

**remembrance**
**04** mind **05** relic, token **06** memory, recall, record **07** memento, thought **08** keepsake, memorial, monument, reminder, souvenir **09** nostalgia, sovenance **10** memorandum, retrospect **11** recognition, recordation, testimonial **12** recollection, reminiscence **13** commemoration

**remind**
**04** hint **05** evoke, nudge **06** call up, prompt **08** remember, take back **10** call to mind **11** bring to mind **13** jog your memory **14** make you think of, put you in mind of

**reminder**
**04** hint, memo, note, prod **05** nudge, token **06** prompt **07** memento **08** keepsake, souvenir **09** red letter **10** memorandum, phylactery, prompt-

note, suggestion, verbal note **11** aide-mémoire, remembrance **12** reality check

## reminisce
**06** recall, review **08** hark back, look back, remember **09** recollect, think back **10** retrospect

## reminiscence
**06** memoir, memory, recall, review **08** anecdote **10** reflection **11** remembrance **12** recollection **13** retrospection
• **collection of reminiscences**
**03** ana

## reminiscent
**08** redolent **09** evocative, nostalgic, remindful **10** suggestive

## remiss
**03** lax **04** slow **05** slack, tardy **06** casual, sloppy **07** wayward **08** careless, culpable, dilatory, heedless, slipshod **09** forgetful, negligent, unmindful **10** neglectful **11** inattentive, indifferent, slack-handed, thoughtless **13** lackadaisical

## remission
**03** ebb **04** lull **05** let-up **06** excuse, pardon, repeal **07** amnesty, release, respite **08** decrease, remittal, reprieve **09** abatement, acquittal, annulment, discharge, exemption, lessening, reduction, remitment, weakening **10** abrogation, absolution, diminution, indulgence, indulgency, moderation, relaxation, rescinding, revocation, slackening, suspension **11** alleviation, exoneration, forgiveness **12** cancellation **13** acceptilation

## remit
**03** pay **04** mail, post, send **05** abate, brief, refer, relax, scope, untax **06** cancel, desist, direct, give up, orders, pardon, pass on, repeal, revoke, settle **07** forward, release, rescind, suspend **08** abrogate, dispatch, hold over, set aside, transfer, transmit **10** guidelines, overslaugh **12** instructions **13** authorization **14** responsibility

## remittance
**03** fee **07** payment, sending **08** dispatch **09** allowance, remitment **13** consideration

## remnant
**03** bit, end, tag **04** butt, fent, rump **05** piece, scrap, shred, trace, wrack **06** offcut **07** balance, oddment, outlier, remains, residue, vestige, witness **08** fragment, leftover, remanent **09** quotation, remainder, remaining **12** odd-come-short

## remodel
◇ *anagram indicator* **04** turn **05** adapt, alter, renew, shape **06** adjust, change, mutate, reform **07** convert, furbish, rebuild **08** renovate **09** modernize, refurbish, transform **11** recondition, reconstruct **12** metamorphose

## remonstrance
**07** protest, reproof **08** petition

**09** complaint, exception, grievance, objection, reprimand **10** opposition **12** protestation **13** expostulation **14** representation

## remonstrate
**05** argue, gripe **06** object, oppose **07** dispute, dissent, protest **08** complain **09** challenge **11** demonstrate, expostulate **13** take issue with **15** take exception to

## remorse
**03** rew, rue **04** bite, pity, ruth, worm **05** grief, guilt, shame **06** regret, sorrow **08** ayenbite, had-I-wist **09** penitence **10** contrition, mitigation, repentance, ruefulness **11** compunction **12** contriteness, self-reproach **13** bad conscience

## remorseful
**03** sad **05** sorry **06** guilty, rueful **07** ashamed **08** contrite, penitent **09** chastened, regretful, repentant, sorrowful **10** apologetic **11** guilt-ridden **12** compunctious, on a guilt trip **13** compassionate

## remorseless
**04** hard **05** cruel, harsh, stern **06** savage **07** callous **08** inhumane, pitiless, ruthless **09** merciless **10** implacable, inexorable, relentless, unmerciful **11** hard-hearted, undeviating, unforgiving, unrelenting, unremitting, unstoppable **12** unremorseful

## remorselessly
**07** cruelly, harshly **08** savagely **09** callously **10** implacably, inexorably, ruthlessly **11** mercilessly **12** relentlessly **13** unremittingly

## remote
**03** far, out **04** back, long, poor, slim **05** aloof, faint, inapt, small **06** far-off, lonely, meagre, slight, upland **07** devious, distant, dubious, faraway, outback, outside, removed, slender **08** backveld, detached, doubtful, isolated, outlying, reserved, secluded, unlikely **09** ungermane, unrelated, up the bush, withdrawn **10** extraneous, immaterial, improbable, inapposite, in the mulga, irrelative, irrelevant, negligible, never-never, out of place, peripheral, tangential, uninvolved, up the mulga **11** back-country, god-forsaken, in the sticks, off the point, out-of-the-way, standoffish, unconcerned, unconnected, unimportant, up the Boohai **12** back of beyond, back of Bourke, inaccessible, inapplicable, inconsequent, in the wop-wops, long-distance **13** beside the mark, inappropriate, insignificant **14** beside the point, inconsiderable, unapproachable **15** having no bearing, in the back blocks, in the never-never, not coming into it, uncommunicative

## removable
**07** movable **09** separable **10** detachable, eradicable **12** transferable

## removal
**04** boot, move, push, sack **05** elbow,

shift **06** firing, murder **07** ousting, purging, sacking **08** ablation, deletion, disposal, ejection, eviction, riddance, shifting **09** abolition, clearance, departure, discharge, dismissal, expulsion, taking-off, uprooting **10** conveyance, deposition, detachment, displacing, evacuation, extraction, relegation, relocation, taking away, withdrawal **11** subtraction, transferral **12** dislodgement, obliteration, transference, transporting **14** transportation

## remove
**03** nip, rid **04** dele, doff, fire, flit, lift, move, oust, pick, sack, shed, take, void, weed **05** amove, carry, eject, eloin, erase, evict, expel, purge, raise, shift, strip **06** ablate, convey, cut off, cut out, delete, depose, detach, efface, eloign, excise, extort, get out, go away, lop off, remble, rub out, unseat **07** abolish, absence, boot out, cart off, cashier, cast out, collect, destroy, dismiss, edge out, expurge, extract, pull off, pull out, put away, removal, take off, take out, tear off **08** amputate, cross out, dislodge, disloign, displace, elbow out, estrange, get rid of, relegate, relocate, separate, subtract, take away, throw out, transfer, withdraw **09** discharge, eliminate, enucleate, go off with, strike out, translate, transport **10** blue-pencil, obliterate **11** deaccession

## remunerate
**03** pay **05** repay **06** reward **07** redress **09** indemnify, reimburse **10** compensate, recompense

## remuneration
**03** fee, pay **04** sold **05** solde, wages **06** income, profit, reward, salary **07** payment, stipend **08** earnings, retainer **09** emolument, indemnity, repayment **10** honorarium, recompense, remittance **12** compensation **13** reimbursement

## remunerative
**04** rich **06** paying **07** gainful **08** fruitful **09** lucrative, rewarding **10** profitable, worthwhile **11** moneymaking

## renaissance
**07** new dawn, rebirth, renewal, revival **08** new birth **09** awakening **10** renascence, resurgence **11** reawakening, re-emergence, restoration **12** reappearance, regeneration, rejuvenation, resurrection, Risorgimento **13** recrudescence

## renascent
**06** reborn **07** renewed, revived **09** born again, redivivus, resurgent **10** reanimated, reawakened, re-emergent **11** resurrected

## rend
**03** rip **04** rent, rive, stab, tear **05** break, burst, sever, smash, split, wring **06** cleave, divide, pierce, to-rend **07** rupture, shatter **08** fracture, lacerate,

separate, splinter **09** tear apart
**10** dilacerate

## render

◇ *anagram indicator* **02** do **03** gie, pay,
put, try **04** give, make, melt, play,
show, sing, turn **05** leave, yield
**06** change, depict, give up, make up,
return, submit, supply, tender
**07** clarify, deliver, display, exhibit,
explain, furnish, perform, present,
proffer, provide **08** describe, give back,
hand over, manifest **09** cause to be,
interpret, represent, reproduce,
surrender, translate **10** contribute,
transcribe

## rendering

**04** crib, show **05** gloss **06** acting
**07** reading, version **09** portrayal,
rendition, rewording **10** appearance,
paraphrase, production, rephrasing
**11** explanation, metaphrasis,
performance, translation
**12** presentation **13** transcription
**14** interpretation, representation,
simplification **15** transliteration

## rendezvous

**02** RV **04** date, meet **05** haunt, rally,
tryst, venue **06** gather, muster, resort
**07** collect, convene, meeting
**08** assemble, converge **10** engagement
**11** appointment, assignation **12** come
together, meeting-place **13** trysting-
place

## rendition

**05** gloss **07** reading, version **08** delivery
**09** depiction, execution, portrayal,
rendering, rewording, surrender
**10** paraphrase, rephrasing
**11** arrangement, explanation,
performance, translation
**12** construction, presentation
**13** transcription **14** interpretation,
simplification **15** transliteration

## renegade

◇ *anagram indicator* **03** rat **05** rebel
**06** outlaw **07** runaway, traitor
**08** apostate, betrayer, defector,
deserter, disloyal, mutineer, mutinous,
recreant, runagate, turncoat
**09** dissident **10** backslider, perfidious,
rebellious, traitorous, unfaithful
**11** backsliding, treacherous
**13** tergiversator

## renege

**04** deny, pike **05** renig, welsh **06** refuse
**07** default, renague, renegue
**08** renounce **09** backslide, repudiate
**10** apostatize **13** cross the floor

## renegotiate

◇ *anagram indicator*

## renew

◇ *anagram indicator* **03** new **04** mend,
stum **05** boost, refit **06** extend, reform,
reline, repair, repeat, reseat, resume,
revive **07** brush up, prolong, refresh,
remodel, replace, reprise, reprize,
restart, restate, restock, restore, retrace
**08** continue, innovate, overhaul,
reaffirm, recreate, renforce, renovate
**09** modernize, refurbish, reiterate,
replenish, transform **10** invigorate,

recommence, regenerate, rejuvenate,
revitalize **11** recondition, re-establish,
resuscitate **12** reconstitute, reinvigorate

## renewal

**05** flush **06** repair **07** rebirth, recruit,
revival **08** new birth, nidation
**09** recruital **10** kiss of life, re-creation,
renovation, repetition, resumption
**11** continuance, reiteration,
restatement **12** instauration,
regeneration, rejuvenation,
resurrection **13** reaffirmation,
refurbishment, replenishment,
resuscitation **14** recommencement,
reconditioning, reconstitution,
reconstruction, reinvigoration,
revitalization, revivification

## renounce

**03** cut **04** deny, reny, shun **05** forgo,
renay, reney, renig, spurn, waive
**06** abjure, desist, disown, eschew,
forego, forsay, give up, pass up, recant,
recede, refuse, reject, renege, resign,
revolt **07** abandon, abstain, discard,
disgown, foresay, forsake, put away,
renague, renegue **08** abdicate,
abnegate, disclaim, forswear, sign
away, swear off **09** repudiate,
surrender **10** declare off, disinherit,
disprofess, relinquish **14** forisfamiliate
**15** wash your hands of

## renovate

◇ *anagram indicator* **04** do up **05** refit,
renew **06** reform, repair, revamp
**07** furbish, improve, remodel, restore
**08** overhaul **09** modernize, refurbish,
translate **10** redecorate, regenerate
**11** recondition **12** rehabilitate **13** give a
facelift

## renovation

**05** refit **06** repair **07** renewal **08** facelift
**11** improvement, restoration
**13** modernization, refurbishment
**14** reconditioning

## renown

**04** bays, fame, mana, mark, note
**05** glory, kudos, rumor **06** esteem,
honour, luster, lustre, repute, rumour
**07** acclaim, stardom **08** eminence,
prestige **09** celebrate, celebrity
**10** prominence, reputation
**11** distinction, pre-eminence
**15** illustriousness

## renowned

**05** famed, noted **06** fabled, famous
**07** eminent, notable **08** of repute
**09** acclaimed, prominent, splendent,
well-known **10** celebrated, illustrate,
pre-eminent **11** illustrious, prestigious
**13** distinguished

## rent

◇ *anagram indicator* **03** fee, let, rip
**04** cost, farm, gale, hire, mail, rate, ript,
take, tare, tear, tore, torn **05** cuddy,
gavel, lease, riven, split **06** let out,
rental, ripped, screed, sublet
**07** charter, divided, fissure, hire out,
payment, rent out, revenue, severed
**08** lacerate, purchase, ruptured
**09** lacerated, torn apart **11** ripped apart

## renunciation

**06** denial **07** kenosis, waiving **08** giving
up, shunning, spurning **09** disowning,
forsaking, rejection, surrender
**10** abdication, abnegation, abstinence,
desistance, discarding, disclaimer
**11** abandonment, disclaiming,
recantation, repudiation
**13** disinheriting **14** relinquishment,
self-abnegation

## reorder

◇ *anagram indicator* **04** edit
**09** rearrange, transpose

## reorganize

◇ *anagram indicator* **05** rejig **07** shake up
**09** modernize, rearrange **10** streamline
**11** rationalize, restructure
**12** reconstitute

## repackage

◇ *anagram indicator*

## repair

◇ *anagram indicator* **02** go **03** fix, sew
**04** darn, form, heal, mend, move, nick,
turn **05** order, patch, refit, renew,
shape, state **06** adjust, doctor, fettle,
kilter, make up, remead, remede,
remedy, remeid, remove, resort, retire,
return, tinker **07** mending, patch up,
rectify, redress, refresh, restore, service
**08** maintain, make good, overhaul, put
right, renovate, revivify, stitch up,
withdraw **09** concourse, condition
**10** adjustment, reparation
**11** improvement, maintenance,
restoration, wend your way
**12** preservation, working order

## reparable

**07** curable, savable **10** corrigible,
remediable, restorable **11** recoverable,
rectifiable, retrievable, salvageable

## reparation

**04** boot **06** amends, remead, remede,
remedy, remeid, repair **07** damages,
redress, renewal **08** requital, solatium
**09** atonement, indemnity
**10** assythment, recompense
**11** restitution **12** compensation,
propitiation, satisfaction

## repartee

**03** wit **06** banter, retort **07** jesting,
riposte **08** backchat, badinage,
wordplay **09** bantering, cross-talk,
witticism **11** give and take

## repast

**04** feed, food, meal **05** board, lunch,
snack, table **06** spread **08** victuals
**09** collation, refection **11** nourishment
*See also* **meal**

## repatriate

**04** oust **05** exile, expel **06** banish,
deport **09** extradite, ostracize, transport

## repay

**03** pay **04** apay, quit **05** appay, quite,
quyte, yield **06** avenge, quight, rebate,
refund, return, reward, settle, square
**07** pay back, requite, revenge **09** get
back at, quittance, reimburse, retaliate
**10** compensate, recompense,
remunerate **11** get even with,

reciprocate **12** settle up with **14** settle the score

## repayment
**06** amends, rebate, refund, reward **07** payment, redress, revenge **08** requital **09** tit for tat, vengeance **10** recompense, reparation **11** eye for an eye, restitution, retaliation, retribution **12** compensation, remuneration **13** reciprocation, reimbursement

## repeal
**04** lift, void **05** annul, quash, unlaw **06** abjure, cancel, recall, recant, revoke **07** abolish, nullify, repress, rescind, retract, reverse **08** abrogate, quashing, reversal, set aside, withdraw **09** abolition, annulment **10** abrogation, invalidate, rescinding, rescission, revocation, withdrawal **11** countermand, rescindment **12** cancellation, invalidation **13** nullification

## repeat
◇ *repetition indicator* **03** rep, rpt **04** copy, echo, redo **05** ditto, labor, quote, recap, recur, renew, rerun, thrum **06** do over, go over, labour, parrot, patter, recite, record, re-echo, relate, replay, reshow, retail, retell, reword, run off, screed **07** confirm, divulge, iterate, persist, recount, replica, reprise, reprize, restate **08** redouble, rehearse, remurmur, say again **09** celebrate, circulate, do to death, duplicate, reiterate, replicate, reproduce, reshowing **10** repetition **11** duplication, perseverate, rebroadcast, reduplicate, restatement **12** recapitulate, reproduction **14** recapitulation

## repeated
◇ *repetition indicator* **07** regular **08** constant, frequent, multiple, periodic **09** continual, recurrent, recurring **10** persistent, reiterated, rhythmical **12** repercussive

## repeatedly
◇ *repetition indicator* **05** often **10** frequently **11** over and over **12** time and again **13** again and again, time after time

## repel
◇ *reversal indicator* **05** check, fight, parry, rebut, spurn **06** offend, oppose, rebuff, refuse, reject, resist, revolt, sicken **07** beat off, decline, disgust, hold off, repulse, turn off, ward off **08** beat back, drive off, fight off, nauseate, push back **09** drive back, force back, keep at bay, repudiate **11** make you sick **13** be repugnant to **15** turn your stomach

## repellent
**04** foul, grim, vile **05** nasty **06** horrid **07** hateful, obscene **08** shocking **09** abhorrent, loathsome, obnoxious, offensive, repugnant, repulsive, revolting, sickening **10** abominable, despicable, disgusting, nauseating, off-putting, unpleasant **11** distasteful, rebarbative **12** contemptible,

disagreeable **13** objectionable
• **insect repellent** **04** deet **07** camphor

## repent
**03** rue **04** turn **06** lament, recant, regret, relent, sorrow **07** be sorry, confess, deplore, reptant **08** do a U-turn **09** be ashamed **10** be contrite **11** be converted, feel remorse, see the light **14** beat your breast

## repentance
**03** rue **05** grief, guilt, ruing, shame, U-turn **06** regret, rueing, sorrow **07** penance, remorse **08** metanoia **09** penitence **10** confession, contrition, conversion **11** compunction, recantation

## repentant
**05** sorry **06** guilty, rueful **07** ashamed, attrite **08** contrite, penitent **09** chastened, regretful, sorrowful **10** apologetic, remorseful

## repercussion
**04** echo **06** effect, recoil, result, ripple **07** rebound, spin-off **08** backlash, backwash, blowback **09** shock wave **10** reflection, side-effect **11** consequence **13** reverberation

## repertoire
**04** list **05** range, stock, store **06** supply **07** reserve **09** repertory, reservoir **10** collection, repository

## repetition
◇ *repetition indicator* **04** echo, rote **05** troll **06** answer, repeat, return **07** copying, echoing, quoting, reprise **08** iterance **09** echolalia, iteration, rehearsal, replicate, tautology **10** recurrence, redundancy **11** duplication, epanalepsis, reiteration, restatement, superfluity **12** reappearance **14** recapitulation

## repetitious
**04** dull **05** windy, wordy **06** boring, prolix **07** tedious, verbose **08** unvaried **09** redundant **10** long-winded, monotonous, pleonastic, unchanging **12** pleonastical, tautological

## repetitive
**04** dull **05** samey **06** boring **07** tedious **08** unvaried **09** automatic, iterative, recurrent **10** mechanical, monotonous, unchanging **14** soul-destroying

## rephrase
**06** recast, reword **07** rewrite **10** paraphrase **13** put another way **14** ask differently, say differently **15** put in other words

## repine
**04** beef, fret, moan, mope, pine, sulk **05** brood **06** grieve, grouch, grouse, grudge, lament, murmur **07** grumble **08** complain, languish

## replace
◇ *anagram indicator* **04** oust **06** act for, change, follow, hang up, refund, return **07** pre-empt, put back, relieve, replant, restore, succeed **08** deputize, displace, exchange, make good, supplant **09** come after, fill in for,

reinstate, supersede **10** stand in for, substitute **11** re-establish **14** take the place of

## replaceable
**09** throwaway **10** disposable, expendable **12** exchangeable **13** biodegradable, non-returnable, substitutable **15** interchangeable

## replacement
**05** proxy **06** fill-in, supply **07** bionics, reserve, stand-in **09** spare part, successor, surrogate **10** jury-rudder, substitute, understudy **12** arthroplasty, substitution

## replenish
**04** fill **05** renew, stock, top up **06** fill up, make up, people, refill, reload, supply **07** furnish, provide, recruit, refresh, replace, restock, restore **08** recharge

## replenishment
**06** supply **07** filling, renewal **09** provision, refilling **10** recharging, restocking, supplyment **11** replacement, restoration

## replete
**04** full **05** sated **06** filled, full up, gorged, jammed **07** brimful, charged, chocker, crammed, glutted, implete, stuffed, teeming, well-fed **08** brimming, satiated **09** abounding, chock-full, jam-packed **11** chock-a-block, well-stocked **12** well-provided

## repletion
**04** glut **07** satiety **08** fullness, plethora **09** plenitude, satiation **11** superfluity **12** completeness, overfullness **14** superabundance

## replica
**04** copy, spit **05** clone, dummy, model **06** repeat **08** gold disc, gold disk **09** duplicate, facsimile, imitation **10** immortelle **12** reproduction

## replicate
**03** ape **04** copy **05** clone, mimic, reply **06** follow, repeat **08** recreate **09** duplicate, reproduce **10** repetition **11** reduplicate

## reply
**04** echo **05** duply, react **06** answer, come in, rejoin, retort, return, triply **07** counter, respond, riposte **08** come back, comeback, reaction, rebutter, repartee, response, surrebut, talk back **09** drink-hail, quadruply, rejoinder, replicate, retaliate, surrejoin, write back **11** acknowledge, reciprocate, replication, retaliation, surrebutter **12** surrejoinder, triplication **13** counter-signal **15** acknowledgement

## report
◇ *homophone indicator* **03** air, cry, rat, rpt **04** bang, boom, buzz, fame, file, item, name, news, note, rept, shop, shot, tale, talk, tell, word **05** blast, brief, bruit, cover, crack, crash, grass, noise, piece, relay, split, state, story, voice **06** cahier, convey, credit, detail, esteem, furphy, gossip, honour, notify, pass on, record, relate, renown, repute, return, rumour, squeal, tell on,

**reportedly**

update **07** account, article, declare, divulge, dossier, give out, hearsay, message, minutes, narrate, opinion, publish, recount, stature, stool on, whisper, write-up **08** announce, blue book, bulletin, complain, describe, disclose, document, inform on, proclaim, register, relation, set forth, standing **09** appraisal, broadcast, celebrity, character, chronicle, circulate, delineate, explosion, judgement, narrative, statement, testimony **10** assessment, communiqué, evaluation, inspection, reputation, stenograph **11** communicate, compte rendu, declaration, delineation, description, distinction, examination, information **12** announcement, press release, procès-verbal **13** communication, reverberation

**reportedly**

◇ *homophone indicator* **09** allegedly **10** apparently, ostensibly, putatively, supposedly **13** by all accounts

**reporter**

**03** cub **04** hack **05** press **06** leg-man **07** fireman, Jenkins **08** leg-woman, newshawk, pressman **09** announcer, columnist, newshound, roundsman **10** journalist, newscaster, news-writer, presswoman, tripehound **11** commentator **12** newspaperman **13** correspondent **14** newspaperwoman

**repose**

**03** kef, kif, lay, lie, put, set **04** affy, calm, ease, kaif, laze, lean, rest **05** lodge, peace, place, poise, quiet, relax, sleep, store **06** aplomb, invest **07** confide, deposit, dignity, entrust, recline, respite, slumber **08** calmness, quietude, serenity **09** composure, night-rest, quietness, stillness **10** equanimity, inactivity, relaxation **11** restfulness **12** tranquillity **14** self-possession

**reposition**

◇ *anagram indicator* **05** shift **09** rearrange

**repository**

**03** urn **04** bank, mart, safe, tomb **05** depot, store, vault **06** museum **07** archive, dustbin, spicery **08** magazine, treasury **09** confidant, container, repertory, salvatory, sepulchre, warehouse **10** collection, depository, promptuary, receptacle, storehouse

**reprehensible**

**03** bad, ill **04** base **06** errant, erring, remiss **07** ignoble **08** blamable, culpable, shameful, unworthy **10** censurable, delinquent, deplorable **11** blameworthy, condemnable, disgraceful, opprobrious **13** discreditable, objectionable

**represent**

◇ *anagram indicator* **02** be **03** act, set **04** draw, mark, mean, show **05** act as, enact, evoke, refer **06** act for, allege, denote, depict, embody, figure,

render, sketch, typify **07** display, exhibit, express, perform, picture, portray, present **08** amount to, appear as, describe, speak for, stand for **09** appear for, character, depicture, designate, epitomize, exemplify, personify, sculpture, symbolize **10** constitute, illustrate **11** deputize for **12** characterize, correspond to **13** act on behalf of **14** act in the name of, be equivalent to **15** speak on behalf of

**representation**

◇ *anagram indicator* **02** MP **04** bust, icon, ikon, play, show **05** envoy, image, model, proxy, stage **06** deputy, reflex, report, shadow, sketch, statue **07** account, drawing, picture, protest, request, showing, stand-in **08** delegate, likeness, petition, portrait, prospect **09** complaint, depiction, depicture, pictogram, portrayal, spectacle, spokesman, statement, tablature **10** allegation, ambassador, councillor, delegation, deputation, mouthpiece, production, thermoform **11** Congressman, delineation, description, explanation, performance, presentment, restoration, spokeswoman **12** cross-section, illustration, presentation, remonstrance, reproduction, spokesperson **13** Congresswoman, expostulation, tableau vivant **14** reconstruction, representative

**representative**

**02** MP **03** rep **05** agent, envoy, proxy, rider, usual, vakil **06** bagman, chosen, deputy, exarch, legate, normal, nuncio, sample, vakeel **07** drummer, elected, stand-in, typical **08** delegate, devolved, elective, salesman, specimen, symbolic **09** appointed, delegated, exemplary, nominated, spokesman, traveller **10** ambassador, archetypal, authorized, councillor, delegation, deputation, emblematic, exhibitive, indicative, mouthpiece, saleswoman **11** congressman, salesperson, spokeswoman **12** ambassadress, commissioned, commissioner, illustrative, representant, spokesperson **13** decentralized, heir-portioner **14** characteristic **15** governor-general, knight of the road

**repress**

◇ *containment indicator* **04** cork, curb **05** check, crush, quash, quell, sit on, sneap **06** cork up, master, muffle, repeal, stifle, subdue **07** control, inhibit, oppress, put down, reprime, silence, sit upon, smother, swallow **08** bottle up, dominate, domineer, hold back, keep back, keep down, overcome, restrain, suppress, vanquish **09** overpower, subjugate **11** bite your lip

**repressed**

**06** hung-up, pent-up **07** uptight **09** inhibited, withdrawn **10** frustrated **11** introverted **14** self-restrained

**repression**

**07** control, gagging, tyranny **08** coercion, crushing, muffling, quashing, quelling, stifling **09** despotism, restraint **10** censorship, constraint, domination, inhibition, oppression, smothering **11** holding-back, subjugation, suffocation, suppression **12** dictatorship

**repressive**

**05** cruel, harsh, tough **06** severe, strict **08** absolute, coercive, despotic **10** autocratic, dominating, oppressive, tyrannical **11** dictatorial **12** totalitarian **13** authoritarian

**reprieve**

**05** let-up, spare **06** acquit, let off, pardon, redeem, relief, rescue **07** amnesty, forgive, relieve, reprive, reprove, respite **08** abeyance, repreeve, show pity **09** abatement, deferment, remission, show mercy **10** suspension **12** postponement **13** let off the hook **15** stay of execution

**reprimand**

**04** jobe, lace **05** blame, check, chide, scold, slate, targe **06** berate, bounce, carpet, earful, rebuke, rocket, see off **07** bawl out, censure, chew out, go off at, lambast, lecture, reproof, reprove, rouse on, tell off, tick off, wigging **08** admonish, lace into, lambaste, reproach **09** carpeting, castigate, criticize, dress down, pull apart, schooling, take apart, talking-to **10** admonition, telling-off, ticking-off, upbraiding **11** castigation **12** dressing-down **13** call to account, tongue-lashing **14** bring to account, slap on the wrist **15** smack on the wrist

**reprisal**

**05** prize **06** ultion **07** redress, reprise, reprize, revenge **08** requital **09** recaption, recapture, tit for tat, vengeance **11** eye for an eye, retaliation, retribution **12** compensation **13** counter-attack, recrimination

**reprise**

**03** act **04** play, sing **05** prize, put on, renew **06** relate, repeat **07** copying, echoing, narrate, perform, quoting, reissue **08** iterance, reprisal **09** iteration, recapture, rehearsal **10** repetition **11** reiteration, restatement **12** compensation **14** recapitulation

**reproach**

**04** blot, slur, twit, wite, wyte **05** blame, braid, chide, scold, scorn, shame, shend, slate, smear, stain, taunt, touch, wight **06** bounce, carpet, defame, earful, rebuke, rocket, see off, stigma, upcast **07** bawl out, blemish, catch it, censure, chew out, condemn, nayword, obloquy, reproof, reprove, tell off, tick off, upbraid, wigging **08** admonish, contempt, disgrace, dishonor, ignominy, repriefe, scolding **09** carpeting, criticism, criticize, discredit, dishonour, disparage, dispraise, disrepute, dress down, mispraise, pull apart, reprehend,

## reproachful

reprimand, take apart, talking-to
**10** admonition, cri de coeur,
disrespect, imputation, opprobrium,
reflection, telling-off, ticking-off
**11** degradation, disapproval
**12** condemnation, dressing-down
**13** find fault with **14** slap on the wrist
**15** smack on the wrist
• **term of reproach 03** gib **04** runt
**05** besom, bisom, madam **06** ronyon,
truant **07** Cataian, Catayan, runnion
**09** rigwiddie, rigwoodie

## reproachful

**08** critical, scolding, scornful
**09** reproving **10** censorious, upbraiding
**11** castigating, disgraceful,
disparaging, opprobrious
**12** disappointed, disapproving, fault-
finding

## reprobate

**03** bad, rep **04** base, rake, roué, vile
**05** knave, rogue, scamp **06** damned,
disown, rascal, reject, sinful, sinner,
wicked, wretch **07** censure, corrupt,
dastard, immoral, villain **08** criminal,
depraved, evildoer, hardened,
vagabond **09** abandoned, dissolute,
miscreant, scallywag, scoundrel,
shameless, wrongdoer **10** degenerate,
ne'er-do-well, profligate
**11** reprobative, reprobatory
**12** condemnatory, incorrigible,
troublemaker, unprincipled
**13** mischief-maker

## reprocess

◇ *anagram indicator* **07** recycle

## reproduce

◇ *anagram indicator* **03** ape **04** copy,
echo, redo **05** breed, cline, clone,
match, mimic, print, refer, spawn,
Xerox® **06** follow, mirror, pirate,
remake, render, repeat **07** emulate,
enlarge, express, gemmate, imitate,
reflect **08** autotype, generate, multiply,
recreate, refigure, simulate **09** bear
young, duplicate, facsimile, give birth,
photocopy, Photostat®, phototype,
procreate, propagate, replicate
**10** hectograph, regenerate, transcribe
**11** proliferate, reconstruct

## reproduction

**04** copy, hi-fi, mono **05** clone, print,
repro, Xerox® **06** ectype, piracy
**07** edition, picture, replica
**08** breeding, monogeny, monogony
**09** duplicate, facsimile, imitation,
photocopy, Photostat® **10** amphimixis,
generation, viviparism
**11** gamogenesis, monogenesis,
procreation, propagation, replication
**12** regeneration **14** multiplication,
representation

## reproductive

**03** sex **06** sexual **07** genital **08** prolific
**10** generative **11** procreative,
progenitive, propagative

## reproof

**04** rate **05** shame, sloan **06** earful,
lesson, rebuke, rocket, sermon
**07** censure, jarring, lecture, upbraid,
wigging **08** berating, disgrace,

disproof, repriefe, reproach, reproval,
scolding **09** carpeting, criticism,
reprimand, reproving, schooling,
talking-to **10** admonition, correction,
telling-off, ticking-off, upbraiding
**11** castigation **12** condemnation,
dressing-down, reprehension
**14** curtain lecture, disapprobation, slap
on the wrist **15** smack on the wrist
• **expression of reproof 03** now, tut
**04** come, toot, tuts **05** toots **06** tut-tut
**07** come now, now then **08** come
come

## reprove

**03** rap **04** rate **05** chide, scold, slate
**06** berate, bounce, carpet, rebuke,
refute, see off, take up **07** bawl out,
censure, chew out, condemn, lecture,
rouse on, tell off, tick off, upbraid
**08** admonish, call down, disprove,
reprieve, reproach **09** castigate,
criticize, dress down, pull apart,
reprehend, reprimand, take apart
**10** take to task

## reptile

*Reptiles include:*

**04** croc, tegu
**05** gator
**06** caiman, cayman, garial, gavial,
mugger, turtle
**07** gharial, hicatee, snapper, tuatara
**08** aligarta, galapago, hiccatee,
matamata, stinkpot, synapsid,
teguexin, terrapin, tortoise
**09** alligarta, alligator, crocodile,
hawksbill, mud turtle, sea turtle
**10** loggerhead, musk turtle
**11** green turtle, leatherback
**13** giant tortoise, water tortoise
**14** leathery turtle, snapping turtle
**15** hawksbill turtle

*See also* **animal; dinosaur; lizard; snake**

## republic

*Republics include:*

**03** USA
**04** Chad, Cuba, Fiji, Iran, Iraq, Laos,
Mali, Peru, Togo
**05** Benin, Burma, Chile, China,
Congo, Egypt, Gabon, Ghana,
Haiti, India, Italy, Kenya, Malta,
Nauru, Niger, Palau, Sudan,
Syria, Yemen
**06** Angola, Brazil, Cyprus, France,
Greece, Guinea, Guyana, Israel,
Latvia, Malawi, Mexico, Panama,
Poland, Russia, Rwanda, Serbia,
Taiwan, Turkey, Uganda, Zambia
**07** Albania, Algeria, Armenia,
Austria, Belarus, Bolivia, Burundi,
Croatia, Ecuador, Estonia,
Finland, Georgia, Germany,
Hungary, Iceland, Ireland,
Lebanon, Liberia, Moldova,
Myanmar, Namibia, Nigeria,
Romania, Senegal, Somalia,
Tunisia, Ukraine, Uruguay,
Vanuatu, Vietnam
**08** Botswana, Bulgaria, Cameroon,
Colombia, Djibouti, Ethiopia,

Honduras, Kiribati, Maldives,
Mongolia, Pakistan, Paraguay,
Portugal, Slovakia, Slovenia, Sri
Lanka, Suriname, Tanzania,
Zimbabwe
**09** Argentina, Cape Verde, Costa
Rica, East Timor, Guatemala,
Indonesia, Lithuania, Macedonia,
Mauritius, Nicaragua, San
Marino, Singapore, The Gambia,
Venezuela
**10** Azerbaijan, Bangladesh, El
Salvador, Kazakhstan,
Kyrgyzstan, Madagascar,
Mauritania, Montenegro,
Mozambique, North Korea,
Seychelles, South Korea,
Tajikistan, Uzbekistan
**11** Burkina Faso, Côte d'Ivoire,
Philippines, Sierra Leone, South
Africa, Switzerland
**12** Guinea-Bissau, Turkmenistan
**13** Czech Republic, Western Sahara
**15** Marshall Islands

*See also* **country**

## repudiate

**04** deny **05** repel **06** abjure, desert,
disown, nochel, reject, revoke
**07** abandon, cast off, disavow, discard,
divorce, forsake, notchel, rescind,
retract, reverse **08** denounce, disclaim,
renounce **09** disaffirm **10** disprofess
**14** turn your back on

## repudiation

**06** denial **09** disavowal, disowning,
rejection **10** abjuration, disclaimer,
retraction **11** recantation
**12** renunciation **13** disaffirmance
**14** disaffirmation

## repugnance

**05** odium **06** hatred, horror, nausea,
revolt **07** allergy, disgust, dislike
**08** aversion, distaste, loathing
**09** abhorring, antipathy, repulsion,
revulsion **10** abhorrence, reluctance,
repugnancy **11** reluctation
**13** inconsistency

*See also* **disgust; distaste**

## repugnant

**04** foul, vile **05** alien **06** averse, horrid,
odious **07** adverse, hateful, hostile,
noisome, opposed **08** inimical
**09** abhorrent, loathsome, obnoxious,
offensive, repellent, resisting,
revolting, sickening, unwilling
**10** abominable, disgusting, nauseating
**11** distasteful **12** antagonistic,
antipathetic, incompatible,
inconsistent, unacceptable
**13** contradictory, objectionable

## repulse

**04** foil, snub **05** check, refel, repel,
spurn **06** defeat, rebuff, refuse, reject
**07** beat off, disdain, failure, put back,
refusal, reverse **08** spurning
**09** disregard, drive back, rejection
**11** repudiation **14** disappointment

## repulsion

**06** action, effect, hatred **07** disgust
**08** aversion, distaste, loathing
**09** disrelish, revulsion **10** abhorrence,

repellence, repellency, repugnance **11** detestation, raison d'être

## repulsive
**04** cold, foul, icky, loth, ugly, vile **05** gross, loath, nasty **06** horrid, odious **07** hateful, heinous, hideous, squalid **08** reserved, shocking **09** abhorrent, loathsome, obnoxious, offensive, repellent, repelling, repugnant, revolting, sickening **10** abominable, despicable, disgusting, forbidding, nauseating, off-putting, unpleasant **11** distasteful **12** contemptible, disagreeable, evil-favoured, unattractive **13** objectionable, reprehensible

## repulsively
**10** abominably, despicably, shockingly **11** obnoxiously **12** disagreeably, disgustingly, nauseatingly, unpleasantly **13** objectionably

## reputable
**04** good, gude, guid **06** honest, worthy **07** upright **08** esteemed, reliable, virtuous **09** admirable, estimable, excellent, respected **10** creditable, dependable, honourable **11** respectable, trustworthy **12** of good repute, of high repute **13** well-thought-of **14** irreproachable

## reputation
**03** los, rep **04** fame, loos, name, note, pass, rank **05** image, izzat, voice **06** credit, esteem, honour, infamy, renown, repute, status **07** opinion, respect, stature **08** estimate, good name, position, prestige, standing **09** celebrity, character, notoriety **10** estimation **11** distinction **12** good standing **14** respectability

## repute
**04** fame, name, odor **05** odour, rumor, savor, stock **06** esteem, regard, renown, report, rumour, savour **07** stature **08** good name, standing **09** celebrity **10** estimation, reputation **11** distinction
• **of doubtful repute** **03** shy

## reputed
**03** dit **04** held, said **06** judged **07** alleged, assumed, seeming, thought **08** apparent, believed, presumed, putative, reckoned, regarded, rumoured, supposed **09** estimated **10** considered, ostensible, reputative

## reputedly
**09** allegedly, seemingly **10** apparently, ostensibly, supposedly **12** reputatively **13** by all accounts

## request
**03** ask, beg, hit **04** boon, call, plea, seek, suit, wish **05** apply, order **06** adjure, appeal, ask for, behest, demand, desire, invite, prayer **07** beseech, bespeak, call for, call out, entreat, require, send for, solicit **08** apply for, entreaty, petition, pleading, put in for **09** impetrate **10** invitation, supplicate, write in for **11** application, imploration,

petitioning, requisition, write off for **12** solicitation, supplication

## require
**03** ask **04** draw, lack, make, miss, need, take, want, will, wish **05** crave, exact, force, order **06** call on, compel, demand, desire, direct, enjoin, entail, govern, oblige **07** call for, command, involve, requere, request, solicit **08** insist on, instruct **09** be short of, constrain, stipulate **11** necessitate **13** be deficient in

## required
**03** set **05** vital **06** needed **07** advised **08** demanded **09** de rigueur, essential, mandatory, necessary, requisite **10** compulsory, obligatory, prescribed, stipulated **11** recommended, unavoidable

## requirement
**04** fike, lack, must, need, term, want **06** demand **07** proviso **08** occasion **09** condition, essential, necessity, provision, requisite **10** obligation, sine qua non **11** desideratum, stipulation **12** precondition, prerequisite **13** qualification, specification

## requisite
**03** due, set **04** must, need **05** vital **06** needed **07** needful **08** required **09** condition, essential, implement, mandatory, necessary, necessity **10** compulsory, obligatory, prescribed, sine qua non **11** desideratum, requirement, stipulation **12** desiderative, precondition, prerequisite **13** indispensable, qualification, specification

## requisition
**03** use **04** call, take **05** order, press, seize **06** demand, indent, occupy **07** request, seizure, summons **08** put in for, take over, takeover **10** commandeer, confiscate, occupation **11** application, appropriate **12** confiscation **13** appropriation, commandeering

## requital
**06** amends, pay-off, return **07** payment, quittal, redress **09** indemnity, quittance, repayment **10** recompence, recompense, reparation **11** restitution, retribution **12** compensation, satisfaction **15** indemnification

## requite
**03** pay **04** apay, quit **05** repay **06** avenge, pay off, return, reward **07** redress, respond, satisfy **08** even up on, requight **09** reimburse, retaliate **10** compensate, recompense, remunerate **11** reciprocate **14** counterbalance

## rescind
**04** void **05** annul, quash **06** cancel, negate, recall, repeal, revoke **07** cut away, nullify, retract, reverse **08** abrogate, overturn, set aside, withdraw **10** invalidate **11** countermand

## rescission
**06** recall, repeal **08** negation, reversal,

voidance **09** annulment **10** abrogation, retraction, revocation **11** rescindment **12** cancellation, invalidation **13** nullification

## rescue
**04** free, save **05** pluck **06** ransom, redeem, relief, reskew, reskue, saving **07** deliver, freeing, recover, release, relieve, reprive, repryve, salvage, set free **08** bring off, liberate, recovery, repreeve, reprieve, retrieve **09** extricate, salvation **10** emancipate, liberation, redemption **11** deliverance **12** emancipation

## research
**03** res **04** test **05** probe, study, tests **06** assess, review, search **07** analyse, examine, explore, inquiry, inspect, postdoc, testing **08** analysis, look into, scrutiny **10** assessment, experiment, groundwork, inspection, scrutinize **11** examination, exploration, fact-finding, investigate **13** investigation **15** experimentation

## researcher
**06** boffin **07** analyst, student **08** inquirer **09** inspector **11** field worker **12** investigator

## resemblance
**04** like **05** image, match **06** parity **07** analogy **08** affinity, likeness, nearness, parallel, sameness **09** agreement, assonance, closeness, congruity, facsimile, homophyly **10** appearance, comparison, conformity, likelihood, similarity, similitude, uniformity **11** parallelism **13** comparability **14** correspondence

## resemble
**04** echo **05** favor, mimic **06** be like, depict, favour, mirror **07** compare **08** approach, look like, parallel **09** duplicate, take after **11** be similar to

## resent
**04** envy **06** grudge **07** dislike, stomach **08** begrudge, object to **09** be angry at, grumble at, take amiss **12** have a derry on **13** take offence at, take umbrage at **15** feel aggrieved at, feel bitter about, take exception to

## resentful
**04** hurt **05** angry, irked **06** bitter, ireful, miffed, peeved, piqued, put out **07** envious, jealous, wounded **08** grudging, incensed, offended, spiteful **09** aggrieved, indignant, irritated, malicious **10** embittered, stomachful, stomachous, vindictive **13** in high dudgeon

## resentment
**03** ire **04** envy, hurt, miff **05** anger, derry, pique, snuff, spite **06** grudge, malice **07** dudgeon, ill-will, offence, umbrage **08** bad blood, ill blood, jealousy, vexation **09** animosity, annoyance, hostility **10** bad feeling, bitterness, ill-feeling, irritation **11** displeasure, high dudgeon, indignation **12** hard feelings **14** vindictiveness

## reservation

**03** res, rez **04** park **05** demur, doubt, order, qualm, salvo, tract **06** doubts, qualms, safety, saving, upkeep **07** booking, defence, enclave, keeping, proviso, reserve, scruple, storage, support **08** guarding, homeland, preserve, scruples, security **09** condition, hesitancy, misgiving, retention, sanctuary, upholding **10** engagement, hesitation, limitation, misgivings, protection, scepticism **11** appointment, arrangement, maintenance, safekeeping, stipulation **12** conservation, continuation, perpetuation, preservation, safeguarding **13** arrière-pensée, qualification **14** advance booking, prearrangement, second thoughts
• **without reservation 07** utterly **08** entirely, outright **09** gloves-off **10** completely **11** boots and all **12** unreservedly **14** unhesitatingly, wholeheartedly

## reserve

**02** TA **03** AVR, ice, MNR, res, RNR, sub **04** area, bank, book, fund, help, hold, keep, park, pool, RNVR, save **05** cache, defer, delay, extra, hoard, order, proxy, spare, stock, store, tract **06** backup, engage, fill-in, put off, retain, secure, shelve, supply **07** adjourn, backlog, earmark, enclave, modesty, savings, shyness, stand-in, support, suspend **08** coldness, coolness, distance, hold back, hold over, keep back, Landwehr, lay aside, postpone, preserve, set apart, set aside, Wavy Navy **09** aloofness, auxiliary, reservoir, restraint, reticence, ring-fence, sanctuary, secondary, stockpile, successor, surrogate **10** accumulate, additional, arrange for, arrière-ban, detachment, limitation, prearrange, remoteness, substitute, understudy **11** alternative, auxiliaries, replacement, reservation, restriction **12** accumulation, put on one side, put to one side **13** secretiveness, self-restraint **14** reinforcements **15** supplementaries
• **in reserve 02** by **05** spare **06** in hand, stored, to hand, unused **07** in petto, in store **08** set aside **09** available, in pectore

## reserved

**03** shy **04** cold, cool, held, kept **05** aloof, close, meant, saved, taken **06** booked, modest, remote, silent **07** distant, engaged, on appro, ordered, private, retired, strange **08** arranged, backward, cautious, destined, intended, retained, reticent, retiring, set aside, taciturn **09** diffident, earmarked, repulsive, secretive, spoken for, withdrawn **10** designated, restrained, unsociable **11** introverted, prearranged, standoffish **12** unresponsive **13** self-contained, unforthcoming **14** unapproachable **15** uncommunicative

## reservoir

**03** vat **04** bank, fund, lake, loch, pond, pool, sump, tank, well **05** basin, stock, store **06** gilgai, header, holder, source, supply **07** cistern, gas tank, ghilgai, hot well, urinary **08** fountain, reserves **09** container, inkholder, stockpile, wind chest **10** header tank, receptacle, repository, steam chest **11** reservatory **12** accumulation

## resettle

◇ *anagram indicator* **07** migrate **08** emigrate **09** immigrate **10** transplant

## reshape

◇ *anagram indicator* **05** alter **06** adjust, modify, mutate **07** convert **12** metamorphose

## reshuffle

◇ *anagram indicator* **05** shift **06** change, revise **07** realign, regroup, shake up, shake-up, shuffle **08** revision, upheaval **09** rearrange **10** regrouping, reorganize **11** interchange, realignment, restructure **12** redistribute **13** rearrangement, restructuring **14** redistribution, reorganization

## reside

**03** lie, sit **04** hive, keep, live, rest, stay **05** abide, board, dwell, exist, house, lodge **06** inhere, occupy, remain, settle **07** hang out, inhabit, sojourn **09** be present **10** be inherent **11** be contained

## residence

**03** pad, res **04** digs, flat, hall, home, nest, seat, stay **05** abode, house, lodge, manor, place, villa **06** des res, palace **07** cottage, domicil, lodging, mansion, sojourn **08** domicile, dwelling, lodgings, mansonry, quarters **09** apartment, residency **10** habitation, mansionary, praetorium, presidency, second home **11** country seat, inhabitance, inhabitancy, squarsonage, summerhouse **12** country house **13** dwelling-place **14** winter quarters

## resident

**05** guest, local **06** client, inmate, ledger, leiger, lieger, live-in, lodger, tenant **07** citizen, dweller, en poste, gremial, leidger, patient, resiant, resider, settled **08** dwelling, inherent, living-in, occupant, occupier **09** commorant, permanent, sojourner, transient **10** inhabitant, inhabiting, stationary **11** householder **13** neighbourhood

## residential

**07** exurban **08** commuter, suburban **09** dormitory

## residual

**03** net **06** excess, unused **07** surplus **08** left-over **09** reliquary, remaining **10** unconsumed

## residue

**04** coke, gunk, lees, rest **05** dregs, extra, mazut, pitch, scrap, snuff **06** excess, mazout, pomace, slurry **07** asphalt, astatki, balance, clinker, remains, remnant, surplus, tankage, vinasse **08** charcoal, mine dump, overflow, residuum **09** asphaltum, carry-over, leftovers, remainder

**10** difference, racemation, terra rossa **11** apiezon oils **12** caput mortuum

## resign

**04** quit **05** demit, forgo, leave, waive, yield **06** forego, give up, retire, submit, vacate **07** abandon, entrust, forsake, throw up **08** abdicate, forelend, renounce, step down **09** stand down, surrender **10** relinquish
• **resign yourself 03** bow **05** yield **06** accept, comply, submit **09** acquiesce **11** come to terms

## resignation

**06** notice **07** waiving **08** giving-up, patience, stoicism, yielding **09** defeatism, demission, departure, passivity, surrender **10** abdication, acceptance, compliance, retirement, submission **12** acquiescence, renunciation, standing-down, stepping-down **13** non-resistance **14** reconciliation, relinquishment
• **expression of resignation 04** well **05** ho-hum **07** heigh-ho

## resigned

**07** passive, patient, stoical **08** yielding **09** defeatist **10** reconciled, submissive **11** acquiescent, unresisting **12** unprotesting **13** long-suffering, philosophical, uncomplaining

## resignedly

**09** patiently, stoically **12** submissively **15** philosophically, uncomplainingly

## resilience

**04** give, kick **06** bounce, recoil, spring **07** granite **08** buoyance, buoyancy, strength **09** hardiness, toughness **10** bounciness, elasticity, plasticity, pliability, suppleness **11** flexibility, springiness **12** adaptability **14** unshockability

## resilient

**05** hardy, tough **06** bouncy, strong, supple **07** buoyant, elastic, plastic, pliable, rubbery, springy **08** flexible **09** adaptable, recoiling, springing **10** rebounding **11** unshockable **13** irrepressible

## resin

**03** lac **04** aloe, hing, kino **05** alkyd, aloes, amber, animé, copal, damar, elemi, epoxy, pitch, rosin, Saran®, vinyl **06** balsam, conima, dammar, dammer, guaiac, mastic, storax **07** acrylic, caranna, carauna, copaiba, copaiva, gamboge, hashish, jalapin, ladanum, mastich, Perspex®, shellac, xylenol **08** Araldite®, Bakelite®, cannabin, galbanum, guaiacum, hasheesh, kauri gum, olibanum, opopanax, propolis, retinite, sandarac, scammony, sweet gum **09** asafetida, courbaril, elaterite, sagapenum, sandarach, tacamahac, tacamahack **10** asafoetida, assafetida, euphorbium, turpentine **11** assafoetida, gum ammoniac, podophyllin **12** Canada balsam, frankincense, gum sandarach **13** Burgundy pitch, spirit varnish, thermoplastic

## resist
**04** buck, curb, defy, face, fend, halt, stem, stop, wear **05** avoid, check, fight, repel **06** battle, combat, defend, hinder, impede, jack up, oppose, refuse, thwart **07** contend, counter, deforce, prevent, weather **08** confront, fight off, obstruct, restrain, stick out, struggle **09** stand up to, withstand **10** counteract, gainstrive **12** stand against **14** hold out against

## resistance
**01** R **04** drag, kick, pull **05** fight, stand **06** battle, combat **07** refusal **08** defiance, fighting, struggle **09** avoidance, contumacy, hindrance, impedance, repulsion, restraint, thwarting **10** contention, impediment, opposition, prevention **11** contumacity, counter-time, obstruction **12** counter-stand, withstanding **13** confrontation, counteraction, intransigence **14** antiperistasis
• **passive resistance** **09** passivism **10** satyagraha **11** vis inertiae

## resistant
**04** anti- **05** proof, stiff, tough **06** immune, strong **07** defiant, opposed, viscous **08** renitent **09** unwilling, windproof **10** impervious, shellproof, shockproof, unaffected, unyielding, waterproof **12** antagonistic, intransigent, invulnerable **13** unsusceptible

## resolute
**03** set **04** bold, firm **05** fixed, hardy, stout, tough **06** dogged, intent, steady, strong, sturdy **07** adamant, decided, diehard, earnest, granite, serious, staunch **08** constant, obdurate, resolved, stalwart, stubborn **09** dauntless, dedicated, obstinate, steadfast, tenacious, unbending, undaunted **10** determined, flat-footed, inflexible, relentless, unswerving, unwavering, unyielding **11** persevering, unflinching **12** bloody-minded, single-minded, strong-willed

## resolutely
**06** firmly **08** steadily, strongly **09** adamantly, earnestly, seriously, staunchly **10** inflexibly, resolvedly, stubbornly **11** dauntlessly, obstinately, steadfastly **12** relentlessly, unswervingly, unwaveringly **13** unflinchingly **14** single-mindedly

## resolution
◇ *anagram indicator* **03** res **04** rede, zeal **05** point **06** answer, decree, motion, result **07** courage, finding, granite, melting, resolve, solving, thought, verdict **08** analysis, boldness, decision, devotion, firmness, solution, tenacity **09** constancy, judgement, willpower **10** abreaction, commitment, dedication, doggedness, intentness, sorting out, working out **11** declaration, earnestness, persistence, proposition, seriousness, unravelling **12** perseverance

**13** determination, disentangling, inflexibility, steadfastness

## resolve
◇ *anagram indicator* **03** fix, vow **04** melt, zeal **05** lapse, patch, relax, solve, untie **06** answer, assure, bottle, decide, detail, divide, inform, pecker, reduce, settle **07** analyse, analyze, break up, convert, courage, itemize, sort out, sublate, talk out, unravel, work out **08** boldness, conclude, devotion, dissolve, firmness, separate, settle on, tenacity **09** anatomize, break down, constancy, decompose, determine, dissipate, factorize, transform, willpower **10** commitment, dedication, doggedness, intentness **11** disentangle, earnestness, persistence, seriousness **12** disintegrate, perseverance **13** determination, inflexibility, steadfastness, straighten out **14** make up your mind, sense of purpose

## resonance
**05** depth **08** fullness, richness, sonority, strength, vibrancy **09** plangency **10** mesomerism, resounding **12** canorousness **13** reverberation

## resonant
**04** deep, full, rich **06** fruity, plummy, strong **07** booming, echoing, ringing, vibrant **08** canorous, plangent, sonorous **10** pear-shaped, resounding **11** reverberant **13** reverberating

## resonate
**04** boom, echo, ring **05** sound **06** re-echo **07** resound, thunder **11** reverberate

## resort
◇ *anagram indicator* **02** go **03** spa, use **04** dive, draw, seek, spot, step **05** apply, frame, haunt, trade, visit **06** appeal, center, centre, chance, course, lounge, museum, option, refuge, repair, revert **07** doggery, measure **08** frequent, recourse **09** concourse, dude ranch, frequency, patronize, thronging **10** rendezvous, sanatorium, sanitarium **11** alternative, night-cellar, possibility **12** health resort **13** holiday centre **14** course of action, stamping-ground

*Resorts include:*

**04** Nice, Rhyl
**05** Aspen, Davos
**06** Cairns, Cannes, St Ives, St-Malo, Whitby
**07** Funchal, Margate, Newquay, Torquay, Ventnor, Zermatt
**08** Alicante, Aviemore, Benidorm, Biarritz, Chamonix, Honolulu, Klosters, Marbella, Montreux, Penzance, Skegness, St Helier, St Moritz, St-Tropez, Weymouth
**09** Albufeira, Blackpool, Galveston, Gold Coast, Kitzbühel, Lanzarote, Morecambe, Nantucket
**10** Baden Baden, Bondi Beach, Costa Brava, Eastbourne, Lake Placid, Long Island, Miami Beach, Monte Carlo, Windermere
**11** Bognor Regis, Bournemouth,

Bridlington, Cleethorpes, Coney Island, Costa Blanca, Costa del Sol, Costa Dorada, Gran Canaria, Grand Bahama, Palm Springs, Scarborough
**12** San Sebastian, Santa Barbara, Waikiki Beach
**13** Great Yarmouth, Southend-on-Sea
**15** Martha's Vineyard, Weston-super-Mare

*See also* **spa**
• **in the last resort** **06** at last **07** finally **08** after all, in the end **10** eventually, ultimately **13** fundamentally, sooner or later
• **resort to** **03** use **04** seek **06** employ, invoke, turn to **07** utilize **08** exercise, frequent **09** make use of **10** fall back on **14** have recourse to **15** avail yourself of

## resound
**04** boom, echo, ring **05** sound **06** re-echo **07** thunder, vibrate **08** resonate **11** reverberate

## resounding
**04** full, loud, rich **05** great, vocal **07** booming, echoing, notable, reboant, ringing, roaring, vibrant **08** decisive, emphatic, plangent, resonant, rumorous, sonorous, striking, thorough **09** memorable, resonance **10** conclusive, impressive, remarkable, resonating, thunderous **11** outstanding **13** reverberating

## resource
**03** wit **04** fund, pool **05** funds, means, money, power, store **06** assets, course, device, fodder, resort, riches, source, supply, talent, wealth **07** ability, capital, reserve **08** artifice, holdings, property, reserves, supplies **09** expedient, ingenuity, materials, stockpile **10** capability, chevisance, enterprise, initiative **11** contrivance, imagination, wherewithal **12** accumulation **13** inventiveness **15** resourcefulness

## resourceful
**04** able **05** fendy, sharp, witty **06** adroit, bright, clever **07** capable **08** creative, original, talented **09** ingenious, inventive, versatile **10** innovative **11** imaginative, quick-witted **12** enterprising

## resourceless
**06** feeble **07** useless **08** feckless, helpless, hopeless **09** shiftless **10** inadequate

## respect
**03** way **04** duty, face, heed, obey **05** facet, honor, point, sense, value **06** admire, aspect, detail, esteem, follow, fulfil, homage, honour, matter, notice, praise, regard, revere **07** bearing, devoirs, feature, observe, regards, worship **08** adhere to, consider, courtesy, relation, venerate **09** approve of, attention, deference, greetings, obeisance, reference, reverence **10** admiration, appreciate,

best wishes, cognizance, comply with, connection, good wishes, high regard, particular, politeness, veneration **11** approbation, compliments, high opinion, recognition, salutations **12** appreciation **13** attentiveness, consideration, show regard for, think highly of **14** characteristic, pay attention to, thoughtfulness **15** set great store by, take into account
• **title of respect, word of respect**
**01** U **03** Esq, oom, sir **04** Esqr, tuan **05** hodja, honor, khoja, molla **06** father, gaffer, honour, khodja, kumari, mollah, moolah, mullah **07** Bahadur, effendi, esquire **08** holiness, talapoin **10** burra sahib, worshipful
• **with respect to** **02** of, on, re **03** for, wrt **04** as to **05** about **07** apropos **09** as regards **10** concerning, in regard to **12** in relation to, with regard to **14** on the subject of **15** with reference to

## respectability
**07** decency, honesty **09** gentility, integrity **10** worthiness **11** uprightness **15** trustworthiness

## respectable
**02** OK **04** fair, good, neat, nice, tidy **05** clean **06** decent, honest, not bad, seemly, worthy **07** savoury, upright **08** adequate, all right, clean-cut, decorous, mediocre, menseful, passable, superior **09** dignified, reputable, respected, sponsible, tolerable **10** above-board, acceptable, fairly good, honourable, reasonable, salubrious **11** appreciable, clean-living, presentable, trustworthy **12** considerable

## respected
**06** valued **07** admired **08** esteemed **12** highly valued **14** highly esteemed, highly regarded **15** thought highly of

## respectful
**05** civil **06** humble, polite **07** courtly, dutiful **08** reverent **09** courteous, regardful **11** deferential, reverential, subservient **12** well-mannered

## respectfully
**07** civilly **08** mannerly, politely **10** reverently **11** courteously **13** deferentially, reverentially

## respecting
**05** about **07** vis-à-vis **09** regarding **10** concerning **11** considering, in respect of **12** with regard to **13** with respect to

## respective
**03** own **07** heedful, several, special, various **08** personal, relative, relevant, separate, specific **09** regardful **10** individual, particular **11** considerate **13** corresponding **14** discriminating

## respectively
**06** in turn **08** one by one **09** severally, specially **12** individually, particularly, specifically **15** correspondingly, in the order given

## respite
**03** gap **04** halt, lull, rest, stay **05** break,

delay, frist, let-up, pause, truce **06** give up, hiatus, put off, recess, relief **07** leisure, prolong **08** breather, interval, reprieve **09** abatement, breathing, cessation, deferment, remission **10** moratorium, relaxation, suspension **11** adjournment **12** intermission, interruption, postponement **14** breathing space

## resplendent
**06** bright, snazzy **07** beaming, fulgent, radiant, shining **08** dazzling, gleaming, glorious, luminous, lustrous, splendid **09** brilliant, effulgent, irradiant, refulgent **10** glittering **11** magnificent **13** splendiferous

## respond
**04** rise **05** react, reply **06** answer, behave, rejoin, retort, return **07** counter **10** answer back **11** acknowledge, reciprocate

## response
**03** tic **04** echo, rise **05** reply, touch **06** answer, retort, return **07** riposte **08** comeback, feedback, reaction **09** rejoinder **10** phototaxis **11** respondence **15** acknowledgement

## responsibility
**04** baby, care, duty, onus, role, task **05** blame, fault, guilt, power, trust **06** affair, burden, charge, pidgin, racket **07** concern, honesty **08** business, maturity **09** adulthood, authority, soundness, stability **10** obligation **11** culpability, reliability **13** answerability, dependability **14** accountability **15** trustworthiness

## responsible
**04** sane **05** adult, sober, sound **06** guilty, honest, liable, mature, stable, steady **07** at fault, leading, to blame **08** culpable, managing, powerful, rational, reliable, sensible, solidary **09** executive, high-level, important **10** answerable, dependable, in charge of, reasonable **11** accountable, blameworthy, controlling, in control of, level-headed, trustworthy **13** authoritative, conscientious, correspondent **14** decision-making

## responsibly
**08** honestly, reliably, sensibly, steadily **10** dependably, rationally, reasonably **15** conscientiously

## responsive
**04** open **05** alert, alive, awake, aware, quick, sharp **06** with it **08** amenable, reactive, sentient, swinging **09** answering, excitable, on the ball, receptive, sensitive, teachable **10** perceptive, respondent, stimulable, switched on **11** forthcoming, susceptible, sympathetic **12** responsorial **13** correspondent **14** impressionable

## responsiveness
**05** mouth **08** openness **09** alertness, awareness **11** sensitivity **13** receptiveness **14** susceptibility

## rest
**03** alt, lie, nap, sit, veg **04** base, calm, doze, ease, halt, hang, last, laze, lean, lull, noon, prop, rely, stay, stop **05** break, cease, hinge, light, pause, quiet, relax, sleep, smoko, spell, stand **06** alight, anchor, bottom, cradle, depend, endure, excess, feutre, fewter, holder, lounge, others, recess, remain, repose, settle, siesta, snooze, steady, veg out **07** balance, be based, breathe, holiday, leisure, lie down, lie-down, persist, recline, relâche, remains, remnant, residue, respite, sit down, slumber, support, surplus, time off **08** breather, continue, idleness, interval, quietude, remnants, residuum, vacation **09** anchorage, cessation, interlude, leftovers, remainder, sabbatism, stillness **10** inactivity, quiescence, quiescency, relaxation, standstill, take a break, take breath, take it easy **12** intermission, tranquillity **13** put your feet up **14** breathing space, motionlessness
• **and the rest** **07** and so on **08** et cetera, et ceteri **10** and so forth
• **lay to rest** **04** bury **05** inter
• **rest upon** **04** ride

## restaurant

*Restaurant types include:*

**04** café, caff
**05** diner, grill, NAAFI
**06** bistro, buffet, chippy, eatery, pull-in
**07** canteen, carvery, chipper, eaterie, milk bar, taverna, tea room, tea shop
**08** creperie, mess room, pizzeria, snack-bar, sushi bar, taqueria, teahouse
**09** brasserie, burger bar, cafeteria, coffee bar, dining-car, grill room, refectory, trattoria
**10** dining room, health food, rotisserie, steakhouse
**11** eating-house, greasy spoon, sandwich bar, self-service
**12** drivethrough, Internet café, luncheonette, motorway café
**13** transport café
**15** fish-and-chip shop, ice-cream parlour

*Restaurants include:*

**06** The Ivy
**07** El Bulli
**09** L'Escargot
**10** Paul Bocuse, Savoy Grill, The Fat Duck
**11** The Wolseley
**12** Gordon Ramsay, Heinz Winkler, The River Café, Waterside Inn
**15** Les Pres d'Eugenie, Patrick Guilbaud

*Fast food restaurant chains include:*

**03** KFC
**06** Wendy's
**08** Pizza Hut, Taco Bell
**09** Harvester, McDonald's
**10** Burger King, Dairy Queen, Little Chef

**12** Domino's Pizza, Dunkin' Donuts,
Hard Rock Café, Pizza Express
**13** Baskin-Robbins, Harry Ramsden's
**14** Subway Sandwich

**restaurateur**
*see* **chef**

**restful**
**04** calm **05** quiet, still **06** placid, serene
**07** calming, languid, relaxed
**08** peaceful, relaxing, soothing,
tranquil **09** leisurely, unhurried
**11** comfortable, undisturbed

**restitution**
**06** amends, refund, return **07** damages,
redress, restore **08** requital
**09** indemnity, repayment, restoring
**10** recompense, reparation
**11** restoration **12** compensation,
remuneration, satisfaction
**13** reimbursement **15** indemnification

**restive**
**04** edgy, toey **05** inert, jumpy, resty,
tense **06** on edge, uneasy, unruly,
wilful **07** anxious, fidgety, fretful,
nervous, restiff, stroppy, uptight,
wayward **08** agitated, restless
**09** fidgeting, fractious, impatient,
obstinate, turbulent, unsettled **10** hot-
mouthed, refractory **12** recalcitrant,
unmanageable **13** undisciplined
**14** uncontrollable

**restiveness**
**10** turbulence, unruliness, wilfulness
**11** waywardness **12** restlessness

**restless**
◊ *anagram indicator* **04** edgy, toey
**05** jumpy **06** broken, on edge, uneasy,
unruly **07** agitato, anxious, fidgety,
fretful, jittery, nervous, restive,
unquiet, uptight, worried **08** agitated,
disquiet, troubled **09** disturbed,
fidgeting, impatient, sleepless,
turbulent, unsettled **10** changeable,
wanrestful **13** uncomfortable

**restlessly**
**09** anxiously, fretfully, nervously
**11** impatiently, turbulently

**restlessness**
**04** fike **05** hurry **06** bustle, fidget, unrest
**07** anxiety, jitters, turmoil **08** activity,
disquiet, dynamism, edginess,
insomnia, movement **09** agitation,
dysphoria, gate fever, jumpiness
**10** fitfulness, inquietude, transience,
turbulence, uneasiness **11** disturbance,
fretfulness, inconstancy, instability,
jactitation, nervousness, restiveness,
spring fever, worriedness
**12** fermentation **13** heebie-jeebies,
unsettledness

**restoration**
◊ *anagram indicator* **06** repair, return
**07** recruit, renewal, revival **08** recovery
**09** recruital **10** kiss of life, rebuilding,
renovation **11** refreshment,
replacement, restitution
**12** instauration, refurbishing,
rejuvenation **13** reinstatement
**14** reconstitution, reconstruction,

rehabilitation, reinstallation,
revitalization **15** re-establishment

**restore**
◊ *anagram indicator* **03** fix **04** do up,
heal, mend, stet **05** renew **06** reform,
repair, return, revamp, revive **07** build
up, rebuild, recover, recruit, redress,
refresh, replace, retouch **08** give back,
hand back, refigure, re-impose,
renovate, retrieve, revivify, undelete
**09** reanimate, redeliver, re-enforce,
refurbish, reinstate, restitute **10** bring
round, redecorate, rejuvenate,
revitalize, strengthen **11** recondition,
reconstruct, re-establish, reintegrate,
reintroduce, restitution **12** reconstitute,
redintegrate, rehabilitate, reinvigorate

**restrain**
◊ *containment indicator* **03** bit, dam, tie
**04** bank, bind, curb, heft, hold, jail,
keep, rein, stay, stop **05** bound, chain,
check, still, stint, trash **06** arrest,
behold, bridle, coerce, detain, fetter,
forbid, govern, hinder, hold in,
hopple, impede, keep in, prison,
rebuke, strain, subdue, tether
**07** abstain, chasten, cohibit, confine,
contain, control, impound, inhibit,
injunct, manacle, prevent, refrain,
repress, tighten **08** bottle up, chastise,
compesce, conclude, hold back, hold
down, imprison, keep back, keep
down, obstruct, regulate, restrict,
suppress, withhold **09** immanacle,
temperate **10** hamshackle **11** hold
captive, hold in check, keep in check

**restrained**
**03** dry **04** calm, cold, cool, mild, soft
**05** aloof, muted, quiet, sober **06** chaste,
formal, low-key, modest, severe,
steady, subtle **07** captive, classic,
ordered, refined, relaxed, subdued
**08** discreet, measured, moderate,
reserved, ritenuto, tasteful
**09** forbidden, temperate
**10** abstemious, controlled
**11** unemotional, unobtrusive **14** self-
controlled, self-restrained
**15** uncommunicative

**restraint**
**03** dam, lid, tie **04** curb, grip, hold,
rein, stay **05** block, bonds, check,
cramp, limit, stint, trash **06** bridle,
chains, duress, limits **07** barrier,
bondage, control, fetters, measure,
reserve **08** coercion, prudence
**09** captivity, hindrance **10** constraint,
inhibition, limitation, moderation,
prevention **11** confinement, restriction,
self-control, suppression
**12** countercheck, imprisonment,
restrictions, straitjacket
**13** judiciousness **14** self-discipline

**restrict**
◊ *containment indicator* **03** tie **04** bind,
curb, fast, hold **05** bound, cramp, hem
in, limit, pinch, scant, stint, thirl **06** go
slow, hamper, hinder, impede, ration
**07** astrict, combine, confine, contain,
control, curtail, inhibit, peg down,
tighten **08** handicap, localize, regulate,
restrain, straiten, strangle **09** condition,

constrain, constrict, demarcate
**15** draw in your horns, pull in your
horns

**restricted**
**05** close, small, tight **06** closed,
narrow, secret, strict **07** bounded,
cramped, limited, private **08** confined
**09** exclusive, parochial, regulated
**10** controlled **11** constricted

**restriction**
**03** ban **04** curb, rule **05** bound, check,
limit, stint **06** burden, chains, ration
**07** confine, control, embargo, proviso,
reserve **08** handicap **09** condition,
restraint, stricture **10** constraint,
limitation, regulation **11** stipulation
**13** qualification

**restructure**
**05** rejig **07** shake up **09** modernize,
rearrange **10** reorganize, streamline
**11** rationalize

**result**
**03** end, sum, win **04** flow, make, mark,
stem, turn **05** arise, ensue, event, fruit,
grade, issue, occur, score **06** answer,
derive, effect, emerge, evolve, finish,
follow, fruits, happen, pan out, pay-
off, revert, sequel, spring, upshot
**07** develop, emanate, outcome,
proceed, product, rebound, spin-off,
verdict **08** decision, reaction **09** by-
product, come out of, corollary,
culminate, eventuate, judgement,
terminate **10** conclusion, end-product,
resolution, side effect **11** consequence,
implication, termination
**12** repercussion

**resultant**
**07** ensuing **09** following, resulting
**10** consequent, subsequent

**resume**
**04** go on **06** reopen, take up **07** carry
on, proceed, restart **08** continue, re-
occupy, take back **09** reconvene,
summarize **10** begin again,
recommence, start again
**11** rejuvenesce, take up again

**résumé**
**02** CV **05** recap **06** digest, précis,
review, sketch, wrap-up **07** epitome,
outline, run-down, summary
**08** abstract, overview, pirlicue,
purlicue, synopsis **09** breakdown
**14** recapitulation **15** curriculum vitae

**resumption**
**06** sequel **07** re-entry, renewal, reprise,
restart **09** reopening **10** proceeding,
resurgence **11** epanalepsis
**12** continuation **14** recommencement
**15** re-establishment

**resurgence**
**06** return **07** rebirth, revival
**10** renascence, resumption **11** re-
emergence, renaissance **12** reappearance, resurrection, risorgimento
**13** recrudescence **14** revivification

**resurrect**
**05** renew **06** revive **07** restore
**08** disinter **09** bring back, re-install
**10** reactivate, revitalize **11** re-establish,

**resurrection**
reintroduce, resuscitate **13** restore to life **15** bring back to life

**resurrection**
**06** return **07** rebirth, renewal, revival **08** comeback **09** anastasis **10** resurgence **11** renaissance, restoration **12** reappearance **13** resuscitation **14** revitalization **15** re-establishment

**resuscitate**
**04** save **05** renew **06** rescue, revive **07** quicken, restore **08** revivify **09** reanimate, resurrect **10** bring round, revitalize **12** reinvigorate

**resuscitated**
**07** revived **08** restored **09** redivivus **11** resurrected **12** redintegrate **13** redintegrated

**resuscitation**
**03** CPR **07** renewal, revival **10** quickening **11** restoration **12** resurrection, revitalizing **14** reinvigoration, revivification

**retain**
◇ *containment indicator* **03** pay, ret **04** grip, heft, hire, hold, keep, save **05** brief, grasp **06** employ, engage, keep on, keep up, recall **07** contain, occlude, reserve **08** conserve, continue, contract, hang on to, hold back, maintain, memorize, preserve, remember **09** recollect **10** bear in mind, call to mind, commission, hold fast to, keep hold of, keep in mind

**retainer**
**03** fee **05** valet **06** lackey, menial, vassal **07** advance, deposit, footman, jackman, samurai, servant **08** domestic, follower **09** attendant, dependant, supporter **10** galloglass **11** gallowglass **12** retaining fee

**retaliate**
**06** avenge, pay out **07** hit back, pay home **09** fight back, get back at **10** strike back **11** get even with, reciprocate, take revenge **13** counter-attack **14** get your own back, pay someone back

**retaliation**
**06** retort, talion, ultion **07** revenge **08** reprisal **09** retorsion, retortion, tit for tat, vengeance **10** quid pro quo **11** eye for an eye, lex talionis, like for like, retribution **13** an eye for an eye, counter-attack, reciprocation

**retard**
**03** lag **04** curb, slow **05** brake, check, delay, tardy **06** belate, hinder, hold up, impede **07** slacken **08** handicap, obstruct, postpone, restrict, slow down **10** decelerate **11** put a brake on **12** incapacitate **13** put the brake on

**retardation**
**03** lag **05** delay **07** slowing **08** dullness, impeding, slowness **09** hindering, hindrance **10** deficiency, hysteresis, incapacity, inhibition, retardment **11** obstruction **12** incapability **14** mental handicap

**retch**
**03** gag **04** barf, boak, bock, boke, keck, puke, reck, spew **05** heave, reach, vomit **06** sick up, strain **07** chuck up, fetch up, throw up **08** disgorge **11** regurgitate **13** heave the gorge

**retching**
**04** heft, keck **06** nausea, puking **07** gagging, spewing **08** reaching, vomiting **12** vomiturition

**retention**
**05** gripe **06** saving **07** custody, holding, keeping **09** hanging-on, holding on **11** continuance, keeping hold, maintenance **12** preservation

**rethink**
**06** modify, review, revise **08** forthink, reassess **09** re-examine, think over **10** reconsider, think twice **13** think better of

**reticence**
**07** reserve, silence **08** muteness **09** quietness, restraint **10** diffidence **11** taciturnity **13** secretiveness

**reticent**
**03** shy **05** quiet **06** silent **08** boutonné, reserved, taciturn **09** boutonnée, diffident, inhibited, secretive **10** restrained **11** close-lipped, tight-lipped **12** close-mouthed, close-tongued **13** unforthcoming **15** uncommunicative

**reticule**
*see* **bag**

**retinue**
**04** many, port, tail **05** aides, meiny, staff, suite, train **06** escort, meiney, meinie, menyie **07** cortège, sowarry **08** equipage, servants, sowarree **09** comitatus, entourage, followers, following, personnel **10** attendancy, attendants

**retire**
◇ *reversal indicator* **02** go **03** den **04** move, step **05** leave **06** bow out, decamp, depart, go away, recede, resign, return **07** go aside, retreat, scratch **08** draw back, step down, stop work, withdraw **09** leave work **10** give up work, retirement **11** stop working **14** lick your wounds

**retired**
◇ *reversal indicator* **02** ex- **03** ret, rtd **04** past, retd **06** former **07** private **08** emeritus, secluded, solitary **09** recondite, withdrawn **11** sequestered

**retirement**
**04** exit **06** recess **07** bedtime, privacy, retreat **08** solitude **09** departure, obscurity, seclusion **10** loneliness, withdrawal **11** recluseness, resignation

**retiring**
◇ *reversal indicator* **03** coy, shy **05** quiet, timid **06** humble, modest **07** bashful, recluse **08** reserved, reticent **09** diffident, shrinking **10** retreating, unassuming **11** unassertive, unobtrusive **12** self-effacing

**retort**
**04** quip **05** reply, sally **06** answer, clinch, rejoin, return, zinger **07** counter, floorer, respond, riposte, squelch **08** backword, comeback, outfling, repartee, response, turn upon **09** rejoinder, retaliate, squelcher, throw back, wisecrack **10** answer back, backanswer **11** retaliation

**retract**
◇ *reversal indicator* **04** deny **05** unsay **06** abjure, cancel, disown, draw in, move in, recant, renege, repeal, revoke **07** disavow, rescind, reverse, unspeak, unswear **08** abrogate, disclaim, draw back, move back, pull back, renounce, take back, withdraw **09** repudiate

**retreat**
◇ *reversal indicator* **03** den, mew **04** flee, lair, nest, neuk, nook, quit, rout **05** arbor, haven, leave, lodge, tower **06** alcove, arbour, ashram, asylum, bug out, decamp, depart, flight, recede, recoil, recule, reduit, refuge, retire, shrink **07** back off, give way, harbour, hideout, privacy, recoyle, recuile, redoubt, retrait, retrate, shelter **08** crawfish, draw back, fall back, funkhole, growlery, hideaway, pull back, pull-back, retraict, retraite, solitude, turn back, turn tail, withdraw **09** back-pedal, climb down, climb-down, departure, hermitage, katabasis, sanctuary, seclusion **10** disadvance, evacuation, give ground, ivory tower, retirement, withdrawal **11** drawing-back, falling-back, pulling-back **12** beat a retreat, hibernaculum, interglacial, interstadial

**retrench**
**03** cut **04** pare, sack, save, trim **05** limit, prune **06** lessen, reduce **07** curtail, cut back, husband **08** decrease, diminish, downsize, slim down **09** economize **15** tighten your belt

**retrenchment**
**03** cut **07** cutback, economy, pruning, run-down, the sack **09** reduction, shrinkage **11** contraction, cost-cutting, curtailment, cutting back

**retribution**
**03** utu **05** karma **06** reward, talion **07** justice, Nemesis, payment, redress, revenge **08** reprisal, requital **09** reckoning, repayment, vengeance, vengement **10** punishment, recompense **11** just deserts, retaliation **12** compensation, satisfaction

**retrieve**
**04** mend, read, save **05** fetch **06** access, recoup, redeem, regain, remedy, repair, rescue, return **07** get back, read out, reclaim, recover, restore, salvage **08** make good **09** bring back, recapture, repossess **11** put to rights

**retro**
**03** old **04** past **05** passé **06** bygone, former, period **07** antique, old-time **10** olde-worlde **12** old-fashioned **13** in period style

## retrograde
◇ *reversal indicator* **06** recede
**07** inverse, regrede, reverse
**08** backward, contrary, downward,
negative **09** declining, reverting,
worsening **10** retrogress **11** deteriorate
**12** degenerating **13** deteriorating,
retrogressive

## retrogress
◇ *reversal indicator* **03** ebb **04** drop, fall,
sink, wane **06** recede, retire, return,
revert, worsen **07** decline, regress,
relapse, retreat **08** withdraw
**09** backslide **10** degenerate, retrograde
**11** deteriorate **12** degeneration

## retrogression
**03** ebb **04** drop, fall **06** return
**07** decline, regress, relapse
**09** worsening **10** recidivism, regression
**13** deterioration **14** retrogradation

## retrospect
**06** regard, review, survey **08** look back
**09** hindsight **10** reflection
**11** remembrance **12** afterthought,
recollection, thinking back **13** re-
examination
• **in retrospect** ◇ *reversal indicator*
**11** looking back **12** on reflection,
thinking back **13** retroactively, with
hindsight **15** retrospectively

## retrospective
◇ *reversal indicator* **11** ex post facto,
retro-active **14** retro-operative
**15** backward-looking

## retrospectively
**11** ex post facto, looking back **12** in
retrospect, on reflection, thinking back
**13** retroactively, with hindsight

## return
◇ *reversal indicator* **03** ret **04** data, form,
gain, turn **05** equal, match, recur,
remit, repay, reply, yield **06** answer, go
back, income, profit, record, refund,
rejoin, render, report, retort, retour,
revert, reward **07** account, benefit,
bring in, counter, declare, deliver, get
back, pay back, put back, redound,
regress, replace, requite, respond,
restore, revenue, riposte, takings
**08** announce, come back, comeback,
come home, delivery, document,
exchange, give back, hand back, hand
down, interest, proceeds, reappear,
recourse, requital, send back, take
back, turn away, turn back
**09** advantage, backtrack, come again,
do the same, pronounce, recursion,
reimburse, reinstate, repayment,
reversion, round-trip, statement
**10** correspond, giving-back, homecoming, recompense, recurrence,
taking-back **11** handing-back, happen
again, reciprocate, replacement,
restoration **12** reappearance
**13** reciprocation, reinstatement
• **in return** ◇ *reversal indicator*
**08** mutually **10** in exchange, in
response **12** equivalently, reciprocally
• **point of no return** **07** Rubicon

## Réunion
**03** REU

## re-use
◇ *anagram indicator* **07** recycle
**12** reconstitute

## revamp
◇ *anagram indicator* **04** do up **05** refit
**06** recast, repair, revise **07** rebuild,
restore **08** overhaul, renovate
**09** modernize, refurbish
**11** recondition, reconstruct
**12** rehabilitate

## reveal
◇ *anagram indicator* **04** ingo, leak,
show, tell **05** let on **06** betray, bewray,
descry, expose, impart, let out, unfold,
unmask, unveil **07** confess, display,
divulge, exhibit, express, ingoing, lay
bare, lay open, let slip, presage,
publish, throw up, unbosom, uncover,
unearth, unshale **08** announce,
decipher, disbosom, disclose,
discover, give away, manifest,
proclaim, unshadow **09** broadcast,
make aware, make known, publicize,
undeceive **10** make public
**11** communicate **12** blow the lid on,
bring to light, expose to view, lift the
lid on **15** take the wraps off

## revealing
**05** sheer **06** daring, low-cut
**08** giveaway, telltale **09** décolleté
**10** diaphanous, indicative, revelatory,
see-through **11** significant

## revel
◇ *anagram indicator* **02** do **03** fug, joy
**04** bask, crow, gala, orgy, rave, riot,
wake **05** comus, enjoy, gloat, glory,
lap up, party, roist, spree **06** rave-up,
relish, savour, shivoo, thrive, wallow
**07** carouse, debauch, delight, indulge,
knees-up, large it, rejoice, roister,
royster **08** carousal, live it up
**09** bacchanal, celebrate, festivity,
luxuriate, make merry, night-rule,
whoop it up **10** have a party, saturnalia
**11** celebration, have it large,
merrymaking, take delight **12** raise the
roof, take pleasure **13** jollification
**14** push the boat out **15** kick up your
heels, paint the town red

## revelation
**04** fact, leak, news, show **06** detail,
vision **07** display **08** betrayal,
epiphany, exposure, giveaway
**09** admission, eye-opener, unmasking,
unveiling **10** apocalypse, confession,
disclosure, divulgence, exhibition,
expression, revealment, uncovering,
unearthing **11** information, publication
**12** announcement, broadcasting,
proclamation **13** communication,
manifestation

## reveller
**05** raver **07** roister, royster **08** bacchant,
carouser, corybant **09** bacchanal,
party-goer, roisterer, wassailer
**10** celebrator, goodfellow,
merrymaker, roaring boy
**12** bacchanalian **14** pleasure-seeker

## revelry
**03** fun **04** riot **05** party, reels **07** booze-
up, jollity, wassail **08** carousal
**09** festivity **10** debauchery

**11** celebration, festivities, merrymaking
**12** celebrations **13** jollification

## revenge
**03** get, utu **05** repay **06** avenge, pay off,
ultion **07** hit back, payback, redress,
wreak of **08** avenging, reprisal,
requital, revanche, serve out, vendetta
**09** fight back, get back at, retaliate, tit
for tat, vengeance **10** avengement,
punishment **11** eye for an eye, get even
with, retaliation, retribution
**12** satisfaction, settle a score **14** get
your own back, pay someone back
**15** take vengeance on

## revengeful
**06** bitter **08** pitiless, spiteful, vengeful,
wreakful **09** malicious, malignant,
merciless, resentful, vengeable
**10** implacable, malevolent,
unmerciful, vindictive **11** unforgiving,
vindicative

## revenue
**04** fisc, fisk, gain, rent **05** yield
**06** income, profit, return **07** profits,
rewards, takings **08** incoming, interest,
proceeds, receipts **09** patrimony,
primitiae

## reverberate
**04** boom, echo, ring **06** recoil, re-echo
**07** rebound, reflect, resound, vibrate
**08** resonate **09** repercuss

## reverberation
**04** echo, wave **06** effect, recoil, result,
ripple **07** rebound, ringing **09** re-
echoing, resonance, shock wave,
vibration **10** reflection, resounding
**11** consequence, replication
**12** repercussion

## revere
**04** fear **05** adore, exalt **06** admire,
esteem, honour **07** idolize, respect,
worship **08** look up to, venerate
**09** reverence **11** pay homage to
**13** think highly of

## reverence
**03** awe **04** fear **05** adore, dread
**06** admire, esteem, hallow, homage,
honour, revere **07** idolism, overawe,
respect, worship **08** devotion, venerate
**09** adoration, deference, obeisance
**10** admiration, exaltation, high esteem,
necrolatry, veneration
**11** acknowledge, bibliolatry
**13** ecclesiolatry

## reverent
**04** awed **05** pious **06** devout, humble,
loving, solemn **07** adoring, devoted,
dutiful **08** admiring, obeisant
**10** respectful **11** deferential,
reverential, worshipping

## reverie
**05** study **06** musing, trance
**08** daydream **10** brown study
**11** abstraction, daydreaming,
inattention **13** preoccupation,
woolgathering

## reversal
◇ *reversal indicator* **02** un- **04** blow,
swap **05** check, delay, knock, trial,
upset, U-turn **06** defeat, mishap, repeal

**reverse**
07 failure, problem, reverse, setback, turning, undoing 08 exchange, hardship, negation 09 about face, adversity, annulment, inversion, revulsion, turnabout, turnround, volte-face 10 affliction, difficulty, misfortune, rescinding, revocation, turnaround 12 cancellation, misadventure 13 nullification 14 countermanding, disappointment

**reverse**
◇ reversal indicator 04 back, blow, pile, rear, swap, turn, undo 05 alter, annul, check, delay, quash, tails, trial, up-end, upset, U-turn, verso, woman 06 back up, cancel, change, defeat, invert, mishap, negate, repeal, return, revert, revoke, stroke 07 backset, counter, failure, inverse, problem, regress, rescind, retract, retreat, setback, transit 08 backward, contrary, converse, exchange, flip-flop, flipside, hardship, inverted, opposite, overrule, overturn, renverse, reversal, set aside, withdraw 09 adversity, back-pedal, backtrack, disaffirm, other side, overthrow, transpose, turn round, underside 10 affliction, antithesis, backhanded, difficulty, invalidate, misfortune, transverse, turn around 11 change round, countermand, vicissitude 12 misadventure 13 move backwards 14 disappointment, drive backwards, put back to front, turn upside-down

**reversion**
◇ reversal indicator 06 return 07 atavism, escheat, regress 09 puerilism, throwback 10 giving-back, regression, taking-back 11 handing-back, hypostrophe, restoration 13 reinstatement, retrogression

**revert**
◇ reversal indicator 04 fall 05 lapse, recur 06 a tempo, fall in, go back, recoil, resort, result, resume, return 07 cut back, regress, relapse, reverse, run wild, try back 08 fail safe 09 throw back, turn again 10 retrogress

**review**
◇ anagram indicator ◇ reversal indicator 03 pan 04 crit, view 05 judge, slate, study, weigh 06 appeal, assess, go over, notice, rating, report, revise, size up, survey 07 analyse, discuss, examine, inspect, journal, rethink, weigh up, write up, write-up 08 analysis, appraise, critique, evaluate, magazine, reassess, reviewal, revision, scrutiny 09 appraisal, comment on, criticism, criticize, judgement, recension, re-examine, summing-up 10 assessment, commentary, evaluation, periodical, reconsider, re-evaluate, retrospect, scrutinize 11 examination, take stock of 12 reassessment, recapitulate, re-evaluation, tour d'horizon 13 re-examination 14 recapitulation 15 reconsideration

**reviewer**
05 judge 06 critic 07 arbiter 08 essayist, observer 11 commentator, connoisseur

**revile**
04 hate, rail 05 abuse, libel, scorn, smear 06 defame, malign, missay, vilify 07 despise, inveigh, miscall, slander, traduce 08 reproach 09 denigrate 10 blackguard, calumniate, vituperate

**revise**
◇ anagram indicator 03 Rev 04 cram, edit, swot 05 alter, amend, emend, learn, mug up, study 06 change, go over, modify, peruse, recast, revamp, review, reword, rework, swot up, update 07 correct, recense, redraft, rewrite 08 bone up on, memorize, optimize 09 expurgate, re-examine 10 reconsider 13 think better of

**revision**
03 Rev 06 change, recast, review 07 editing 08 homework, learning, studying, swotting, updating 09 amendment, recasting, recension, rereading, reworking, rewriting 10 alteration, correction, diorthosis, emendation, memorizing 12 modification 13 re-examination 14 reconstruction

**revitalize**
05 renew 06 revive 07 refresh, restore 08 revivify 09 reanimate, resurrect 10 reactivate, rejuvenate 12 reinvigorate

**revival**
04 Romo 06 upturn 07 Odinism, rebirth, renewal, upsurge 08 comeback, wakening 09 awakening, lightning 10 quickening, resurgence 11 neopaganism, reawakening, renaissance, restoration 12 resurrection, risorgimento 13 resuscitation, the kiss of life 14 reintroduction, revitalization 15 re-establishment

**revive**
04 wake 05 rally, renew, rouse 06 awaken, rake up, relive 07 animate, cheer up, comfort, quicken, recover, refresh, restore 08 reawaken, rekindle, revivify 09 reanimate, resurrect 10 bring round, invigorate, reactivate, revitalize 11 re-establish, reintroduce, resuscitate 12 reinvigorate
• revivers 10 Epsom salts

**revivify**
05 renew 06 repair, revive 07 refresh, restore 08 inspirit 09 reanimate 10 invigorate, reactivate, revitalize 11 resuscitate

**reviving**
05 tonic 07 bracing, cordial 11 reanimating, revivescent, revivifying, reviviscent, stimulating 12 enheartening, exhilarating, invigorating, refreshening, regenerating 13 resuscitative 14 reinvigorating

**revocation**
06 repeal, revoke 08 negation, quashing, reversal, revoking 09 abolition, annulment, repealing 10 rescinding, rescission, retraction, revokement, withdrawal 11 countermand, repudiation 12 cancellation, invalidation, retractation 13 nullification 14 countermanding

**revoke**
04 lift 05 annul, check, quash, recal, renig 06 cancel, negate, recall, recant, renege, repeal, unpray 07 abolish, nullify, renague, renegue, rescind, retract, reverse, unshoot, unshout 08 abrogate, withdraw 09 unpredict 10 invalidate, revocation 11 countermand

**revolt**
◇ anagram indicator 04 coup, riot, rise 05 rebel, repel, shock 06 defect, mutiny, offend, putsch, resist, rise up, rising, sicken 07 disgust, dissent, fall off, outrage 08 apostasy, fall away, futurism, nauseate, uprising 09 breakaway, coup d'état, defection, Jacquerie, rebellion, revulsion, secession 10 revolution, scandalize, take up arms 12 insurrection 13 expressionism 15 Romantic Revival, the Paris Commune, turn your stomach

**revolting**
◇ anagram indicator 02 up 04 foul, vile 05 grody, nasty 07 hateful, heinous 08 horrible, shocking 09 abhorrent, appalling, insurgent, loathsome, obnoxious, offensive, repellent, repugnant, repulsive, sickening 10 abominable, disgusting, nauseating, off-putting 11 distasteful 13 reprehensible

**revolution**
◇ anagram indicator ◇ reversal indicator 04 coup, roll, spin, turn 05 cycle, orbit, round, wheel, whirl 06 change, circle, mutiny, putsch, revolt, rising 07 circuit, inqilab, revolve 08 gyration, mutation, rotation, upheaval, uprising 09 cataclysm, coup d'état, rebellion, sex change 10 innovation, insurgence, revolvency 11 reformation 12 insurrection 13 metamorphosis 14 transformation

*Revolutions include:*

04 July
06 French
07 October, Russian
08 American, Cultural, February, Glorious
10 Industrial
12 Agricultural

**revolutionary**
◇ anagram indicator ◇ reversal indicator 03 new, red 04 trot 05 novel, rebel 07 drastic, radical 08 complete, Leninist, mutineer, mutinous 09 anarchist, Bolshevik, different, extremist, insurgent, Menshevik, seditious 10 avant-garde, filibuster,

## revolutionize

innovative, rebellious, Sandinista, subversive, Trotskyist, Trotskyite **11** anarchistic, progressive, sansculotte **12** experimental **13** revolutionist, thoroughgoing **14** ground-breaking **15** insurrectionary, insurrectionist

*Revolutionaries include:*

**03 Che**
**04 Biko** (Steve), **Cade** (Jack), **Kett** (Robert), **Marx** (Karl)
**05 Allen** (Ethan), **Fanon** (Frantz), **Gorky** (Maxim), **Henry** (Patrick), **Kirov** (Sergey), **Lenin** (Vladimir Ilyich), **Marat** (Jean Paul), **Paine** (Tom), **Radek** (Karl), **Rykov** (Alexey), **Sands** (Bobby), **Sucre** (Antonio José de), **Tyler** (Wat), **Villa** (Pancho)
**06 Arafat** (Yasser), **Baader** (Andreas), **Barras** (Paul François Jean Nicolas, Comte de), **Castro** (Fidel), **Corday** (Charlotte), **Danton** (Georges), **Fawkes** (Guy), **Fuller** (Margaret), **Hébert** (Jacques René), **Kassem** (Abdul Karim), **Madero** (Francisco), **Moreno** (Mariano), **Qassim** (Abd al-Krim), **Stalin** (Joseph), **Zapata** (Emiliano)
**07 Bakunin** (Mikhail), **Barnave** (Antoine), **Blanqui** (Auguste), **Bolívar** (Simón), **Catesby** (Robert), **Goldman** (Emma), **Guevara** (Che), **Mandela** (Nelson), **Meinhof** (Ulrike Marie), **Princip** (Gavrilo), **Sandino** (Augusto César), **Savimbi** (Jonas), **Tallien** (Jean Lambert), **Trotsky** (Leon), **Wallace** (William)
**08 Abu Nidal**, **Bin Laden** (Osama), **Bukharin** (Nikolay), **Hereward** (the Wake), **Kerensky** (Alexander), **Lilburne** (John), **Mirabeau** (Honoré Gabriel Riqueti, Comte de), **Proudhon** (Pierre Joseph), **Santerre** (Antoine Joseph), **Zinoviev** (Grigoriy)
**09 Christian** (Fletcher), **Garibaldi** (Giuseppe), **Guillotin** (Joseph), **Kropotkin** (Knyaz Peter), **Luxemburg** (Rosa), **Mao Zedong**, **Nana Sahib**, **Plekhanov** (Georgi), **Saint-Just** (Louis de), **Spartacus**, **Sun Yat-Sen**
**10 Delescluze** (Charles), **Desmoulins** (Camille)
**11 Jiang Jieshi**, **Robespierre** (Maximilien de)
**13 Chiang Kai-Shek**, **Paz Estenssoro** (Víctor)

## revolutionize

**06** reform **09** transform **10** reorganize **11** restructure, transfigure **14** turn upside-down

## revolve

**02** go **03** ren, rev, rin, run **04** move, spin, turn **05** orbit, pivot, swirl, think, twist, wheel, whirl **06** circle, gyrate, hang on, ponder, return, rotate, swivel, turn on **07** focus on, hinge on, turning **08** centre on, roll back **10** circumduct, revolution **11** circumvolve **13** concentrate on

## revolver

**03** gat, gun, rod **04** Colt®, iron **05** rifle **06** airgun, pistol **07** bulldog, firearm, handgun, shooter, shotgun **10** peacemaker, six-shooter **12** shooting iron

## revolving

**07** turning **08** gyrating, gyratory, rotating, spinning, whirling **12** peristrephic

## revulsion

**04** hate **06** hatred, nausea, recoil, revolt **07** disgust, dislike **08** aversion, distaste, loathing **09** repulsion **10** abhorrence, repugnance, withdrawal **11** abomination, detestation
*See also* **disgust; distaste**

## reward

**03** pay **04** gain, meed, wage **05** bonus, medal, merit, prise, prize, repay, wages, yield **06** bounty, desert, honour, pay-off, profit, quarry, return **07** benefit, guerdon, payment, premium, present, requite, salvage, testern, warison **08** consider, decorate, requital, sanction, warrison **09** head money, recognize, reguerdon, repayment **10** compensate, decoration, punishment, recompense, remunerate **11** just deserts, retribution **12** compensation, remuneration

## rewarding

**08** edifying, fruitful, pleasing, valuable **09** enriching, lucrative **10** beneficial, fulfilling, gratifying, productive, profitable, satisfying, worthwhile **11** retributive **12** advantageous, remunerative

## rewording

**04** edit **08** revision **09** rewriting **10** metaphrase, paraphrase, rephrasing **11** metaphrasis

## rework

◊ *anagram indicator* **04** edit **05** alter, amend, emend **06** change, go over, modify, peruse, recast, revamp, review, revise, reword, update **07** correct, recense, redraft, rewrite **09** expurgate, re-examine, refashion **10** reconsider **13** think better of

## rewrite

◊ *anagram indicator* **04** edit **05** emend, tweak **06** recast, revise, reword, rework **07** correct, redraft, rescore **08** inscribe, rescript

## Rex

**01** R

## rhea

**03** Ops **04** rami **05** nandu, ramee, ramie **06** nandoo, nhandu

## rhenium

**02** Re

## rhesus

**02** Rh

## rhetoric

**07** bombast, fustian, oratory, periods **09** eloquence, hyperbole, pomposity, prolixity, verbosity, wordiness **10** oratorical **11** speechcraft
**13** magniloquence **14** grandiloquence, long-windedness

## rhetorical

**05** grand, showy, wordy **06** florid, prolix **07** aureate, flowery, pompous, verbose **09** bombastic, high-flown, insincere, stylistic **10** artificial, flamboyant, long-winded, oratorical **11** declamatory, pretentious **12** Churchillian, high-sounding, magniloquent **13** grandiloquent

*Rhetorical devices include:*

**03** pun
**05** irony, trope
**06** aporia, bathos, climax, simile, zeugma
**07** auxesis, epigram, erotema, litotes, meiosis, paradox
**08** anaphora, chiasmus, diallage, diegesis, ellipsis, epanodos, erotetic, innuendo, metaphor, metonymy, oxymoron, parabole, symploce
**09** asyndeton, cataphora, dissimile, epizeuxis, euphemism, hendiadys, hypallage, hyperbole, increment, prolepsis, syllepsis, tautology
**10** abscission, anastrophe, anticlimax, antithesis, apostrophe, dysphemism, enantiosis, epanaphora, epiphonema, epistrophe, metalepsis, synchrysis, synecdoche
**11** anacoluthon, anadiplosis, antiphrasis, antonomasia, catachresis, enumeration, epanalepsis, hypostrophe, hypotyposis, paraleipsis, parenthesis
**12** alliteration, antimetabole, epanorthosis, onomatopoeia
**13** amplification, dramatic irony, epanadiplosis, mixed metaphor, vicious circle
**14** antimetathesis, double entendre, figure of speech
**15** pathetic fallacy, personification

## rheumatoid arthritis

**02** RA

## rhino

*see* **money**

## Rhode Island

**02** RI

## rhodium

**02** Rh

## rhubarb

**03** rot, row **05** Rheum **06** rumpus **08** nonsense, pie-plant, squabble **09** rhapontic

## rhyme

**03** ode **04** poem, rime, song, tink **05** chime, ditty, rhime, verse **06** crambo, jingle, poetry, rhythm, verses **07** couplet **08** clerihew, limerick **09** harmonize **13** versification

*Rhymes include:*

**03** end, eye
**04** half, head, male, near, rich, tail

**05** slant, vowel
**06** female, riding, tailed
**08** feminine, internal
**09** assonance, identical, masculine, pararhyme, rime riche
**10** apocopated, cynghanedd, rhyme royal
**13** rime suffissant

## rhythm
**04** beat, flow, lilt, stot, time **05** metre, pulse, rhyme, swing, tempo, throb
**06** accent **07** cadence, cadency, harmony, measure, numbers, pattern
**08** movement **09** voltinism

## rhythmic
**04** go-go **06** metric, steady **07** flowing, lilting, pulsing, regular **08** metrical, periodic, repeated **09** pulsating, throbbing **10** rhythmical
• **rhythmic pattern** **04** raga, tala
**05** talea

## rib
**03** bar **04** band, bone, cord, gill, vein, wale, welt, wife **05** costa, groin, nerve, ogive, ridge, shaft, tease **06** cutlet, lierne, purlin **07** feather, futtock, nervure, ribbing, support **08** moulding, pork-chop, ridicule **09** tierceron
**10** mutton chop **13** cross-springer
**14** pleurapophysis

## ribald
**03** low **04** base, blue, lewd, mean, racy, rude **05** bawdy, gross **06** coarse, earthy, filthy, ribaud, risqué, smutty, vulgar **07** jeering, mocking, naughty, obscene, rybauld **08** derisive, indecent
**09** off-colour, satirical **10** irreverent, licentious, scurrilous **11** foul-mouthed, Rabelaisian **13** disrespectful

## ribaldry
**04** smut **05** filth **07** jeering, lowness, mockery **08** baseness, derision, raciness, ribaudry, rudeness
**09** bawdiness, grossness, indecency, obscenity, rybaudrye, vulgarity
**10** coarseness, earthiness, scurrility, smuttiness **11** naughtiness
**14** licentiousness

## ribbing
**06** banter **07** baiting, goading, kidding, mocking, ragging, teasing
**08** annoying, ridicule, taunting
**09** badgering **11** provocation

## ribbon
**03** jag, pad, tie **04** band, cord, line, pads, sash, tape **05** braid, cloth, flash, shred, strip, tenia **06** caddis, cordon, ferret, fillet, radula, riband, streak, stripe, taenia, tassel, tatter **07** caddice, caddyss, elastic, hatband, ribband, tieback **08** hair-band, headband, quilling, streamer **09** petersham, sword knot **10** cordon bleu, ticker tape
**11** multistrike, watchspring

## rice
**04** reis, twig **05** paddy **07** arborio, zizania **09** brushwood

## rich
**03** fat **04** busy, deep, fine, full, high, lush, oily, oofy, warm **05** ample, fatty,

flush, grand, heavy, juicy, ritzy, spicy, sweet, tasty, vivid **06** absurd, active, bright, costly, creamy, fecund, fruity, ironic, lavish, lively, loaded, mellow, monied, ornate, packed, strong
**07** copious, fertile, intense, moneyed, opulent, profuse, replete, rolling, savoury, steeped, vibrant, wealthy, well-off **08** abundant, affluent, eventful, exciting, fruitful, gorgeous, luscious, palatial, precious, prolific, resonant, sonorous, splendid, valuable, well-to-do **09** abounding, brilliant, delicious, elaborate, expensive, laughable, luxurious, pecunious, plenteous, plentiful, priceless, sumptuous **10** filthy rich, full-bodied, in the money, outrageous, productive, prosperous, ridiculous, well-heeled **11** made of money, magnificent, mellifluous, overflowing, rolling in it **12** preposterous, rhinocerical, stinking rich, unreasonable, well-provided, well-supplied **13** full-flavoured **15** with money to burn

## riches
**04** dosh, gold, loot, pelf **05** brass, bread, dough, gravy, lolly, lucre, means, money, ready, smash **06** assets, greens, mammon, moolah, stumpy, wealth **07** fortune, readies, scratch, shekels **08** greenies, opulence, property, treasure **09** affluence, megabucks, resources, substance
**10** prosperity **11** filthy lucre, spondulicks **12** the necessary

## richly
**04** well **05** fully **08** floridly, lavishly, properly, strongly, suitably
**09** elegantly, opulently **10** completely, gorgeously, palatially, splendidly, thoroughly **11** elaborately, expensively, exquisitely, luxuriously, sumptuously **13** appropriately

## richness
**05** depth, taste **07** fatness **08** business, elegance, fullness, loudness, oiliness
**09** abundance, fattiness, fertility, heaviness, intensity, juiciness, provision, resonance, splendour
**10** creaminess, excitement, lavishness, liveliness, luxuriance, mellowness
**12** eventfulness, magnificence
**13** exquisiteness, luxuriousness, plentifulness, sumptuousness

## rickety
◊ *anagram indicator* **05** crazy, shaky
**06** feeble, flimsy, wobbly **07** tottery
**08** decrepit, derelict, insecure, unstable, unsteady **10** broken-down, jerry-built, ramshackle, tumbledown
**11** dilapidated

## ricochet
**03** bob, dap **04** jump, leap, stot
**05** bound, carom, stoit, throw
**06** bounce, recoil, spring **07** rebound
**10** bounce back, spring back

## rid
**04** free, quit **05** clear, expel, purge, shift
**06** purify, remove **07** cleanse, deliver, relieve **08** unburden **11** disencumber

• **get rid of** **04** cast, dump, junk
**05** chuck, ditch, eject, expel, scrap, shake, shunt **06** remove, see off, unload **07** abolish, deep-six, discard
**08** choke off, chuck out, clear off, clear out, elbow out, jettison, railroad, shake off, shrug off, throw out
**09** dispose of, eliminate, eradicate, get shot of, throw away **10** do away with, put an end to **12** dispense with, make away with

## riddance
**06** relief **07** freedom, release, removal
**08** disposal, ejection **09** clearance, expulsion, purgation **11** deliverance, elimination **13** extermination

## riddle
**03** mar **04** fill, koan, sift **05** guess, poser, sieve, solve **06** enigma, filter, infest, pepper, pierce, puzzle, strain, teaser, winnow **07** charade, cribble, mystery, pervade, problem
**08** permeate, puncture **09** conundrum, logograph, perforate **10** conclusion, mind-bender **11** brainteaser **12** brain-twister

## ride
**02** go **03** sit **04** burn, hack, lift, move, road, rode, spin, surf, trip, trot
**05** cycle, drive, jaunt, pedal, steer
**06** gallop, handle, manage, outing, saddle, travel **07** bobsled, control, journey, overlap **08** bestride, dominate, progress **09** bobsleigh, promenade **12** steeplechase

## rider
**02** PS **05** biker, bikie **06** hussar, jockey, knight **07** dragoon, eventer
**08** horseman, reinsman **09** corollary
**10** cavalryman, equestrian, horsewoman, showjumper
**11** mosstrooper **12** equestrienne, horse soldier

## ridge
**02** ås **03** bur, hoe, rib, rig **04** balk, band, bank, burr, drum, edge, hill, kame, keel, list, lump, nurl, rand, reef, wale, welt **05** arête, baulk, costa, crest, esker, halse, hause, hawse, knurl, ledge, linch, raphe, torus **06** crista, ripple, saddle **07** corn rig, crinkle, drumlin, hogback, hummock, linchet, lynchet, wrinkle, yardang **08** eminence, hog's back, sastruga **09** knife-edge, razorback **10** escarpment, promontory
**12** superciliary, thank-you-ma'am

## ridicule
**03** guy, kid, rag, rib **04** gibe, goof, jeer, jest, josh, mock **05** chaff, irony, mimic, queer, scoff, scorn, smoke, sneer, taunt, tease **06** banter, deride, parody, poo-poo, satire, send up **07** crucify, jeering, lampoon, laugh at, mockery, pillory, reticle, sarcasm, teasing
**08** badinage, derision, laughter, pooh-pooh, reticule, satirize, taunting
**09** absurdity, burlesque, humiliate, make fun of, poke fun at **10** caricature, make game of, sling off at **11** make a game of **12** depreciation **13** have a game with, poke mullock at

## ridiculous

◇ *anagram indicator* **04** rich **05** crazy, droll, funny, silly **06** absurd, mental, stupid **07** comical, damfool, foolish, risible **08** derisory, farcical, humorous, shocking **09** facetious, hilarious, laughable, ludicrous **10** cockamamie, incredible, outrageous **11** nonsensical **12** contemptible, preposterous, unbelievable

## ridiculously

◇ *anagram indicator* **08** absurdly **09** laughably **10** incredibly, shockingly **11** ludicrously **12** outrageously, surprisingly, unbelievably, unreasonably **14** preposterously

## rife

**06** common, raging **07** current, general, rampant, teeming **08** abundant, epidemic, frequent, swarming **09** abounding, extensive, plenteous, prevalent **10** ubiquitous, widespread **11** overflowing, predominant

## riff-raff

**03** mob **04** raff, scum **05** dregs, scaff **06** rabble, raffle **07** rubbish **08** canaille, rent-a-mob **09** hoi polloi, scaff-raff **12** undesirables

## rifle

◇ *anagram indicator* **02** M1 **03** gun, gut, rob, SLR **04** loot, pick, sack **05** fusil, strip **06** burgle, injure, maraud, Mauser, musket, search, weapon **07** bandook, bundook, carabin, carbine, despoil, express, firearm, Martini, pillage, plunder, ransack, rummage, shotgun **08** Armalite®, carabine, disarray, firelock, petronel **09** chassepot, flintlock **10** Lee Enfield, Winchester® **11** elephant gun **12** Martini-Henry

## rift

**03** gap, row **04** feud, hole, slit **05** belch, break, chink, cleft, crack, fault, fight, space, split **06** breach, cavity, cleave, cranny, schism **07** crevice, fissure, opening **08** argument, conflict, division, fracture **10** alienation, difference, separation **11** altercation **12** disagreement, estrangement

## rig

◇ *anagram indicator* **03** kit **04** cook, fake, garb, gear **05** dress, equip, fit up, forge, prank, ridge, set up, trick, twist **06** clothe, doctor, fiddle, fit out, frolic, gunter, jack-up, outfit, tackle **07** distort, falsify, massage, pervert, swindle **08** fittings, fixtures **09** apparatus, equipment, machinery, structure **10** manipulate, tamper with **12** misrepresent **13** accoutrements
• **rig out 03** fit **04** garb, robe, trim, wear **05** array, dress, equip, get up, put on **06** attire, clothe, fit out, kit out, outfit, supply **07** dress up, furnish, get into, provide, trick up, turn out **08** accoutre, trick out **10** make ready
• **rig up 05** build, dress, equip, erect, fit up, fix up **07** arrange, knock up **08** assemble **09** construct, improvise

**11** put together **13** throw together **14** cobble together

## right

**01** r **02** OK, rt **03** due, fit, fix, oke **04** fair, good, just, lien, okay, real, Tory, true, user, well **05** claim, droit, exact, legal, moral, power, quite, sound, title, truth, utter, valid **06** actual, avenge, bang-on, direct, equity, ethics, fairly, honest, honour, justly, lawful, pronto, proper, repair, seemly, settle, spot on, virtue, wholly **07** charter, correct, ethical, exactly, factual, fitting, freedom, genuine, honesty, justice, licence, precise, rectify, redress, stand up, totally, upright, utterly, warrant **08** absolute, accepted, accurate, approved, becoming, business, complete, directly, entirely, fairness, goodness, legality, morality, properly, put right, sanction, slap bang, straight, suitable, thorough, true-blue, virtuous **09** all the way, authentic, authority, by the book, correctly, desirable, equitable, factually, impartial, integrity, like a shot, opportune, precisely, privilege, propriety, rectitude, righteous, rightness, right-wing, territory, title deed, veritable, vindicate, yesterday **10** absolutely, acceptable, accurately, admissible, auspicious, birthright, completely, convenient, favourable, favourably, honourable, lawfulness, permission, preferable, principled, propitious, put in order, reasonable, straighten **11** appropriate, entitlement, immediately, opportunity, prerogative, reactionary, straightway, uprightness **12** advantageous, conservative, impartiality, satisfactory, the done thing, truthfulness, without delay **13** perpendicular, righteousness, straighten out **14** as the crow flies, characteristic, satisfactorily **15** before you know it, in a straight line
• **by rights 06** de jure, justly **07** legally, rightly **08** lawfully, properly **09** correctly **10** in fairness, rightfully **11** justifiably **12** legitimately
• **in the right 09** justified, warranted **10** vindicated
• **put to rights, set to rights 03** fix **04** sort **05** fix up **06** remedy, settle **07** correct, rectify **10** put in order, straighten **13** straighten out
• **right away 03** now **04** ASAP **06** at once, pronto **08** directly, in a jiffy, promptly **09** forthwith, instantly, like a shot, yesterday **11** immediately **12** straight away, without delay **13** from the word go **15** before you know it
• **right-hand man, right-hand woman 02** PA **04** aide **06** deputy, helper **08** henchman **09** assistant, man Friday, number two, secretary **10** girl Friday, henchwoman, lieutenant, understudy **11** backroom boy, helping hand, henchperson, subordinate **12** backroom girl **15** second-in-command
• **right of way 04** lead, rank **08** eminence, priority **09** seniority, supremacy **10** first place, precedence,

preference **11** pre-eminence, superiority
• **within your rights 07** allowed **08** entitled **09** justified, permitted **10** reasonable

## righteous

**04** fair, good, just, pure **05** legal, moral, valid **06** honest, lawful, proper, worthy **07** ethical, saintly, sinless, upright **08** virtuous **09** blameless, equitable, excellent, excusable, guiltless, incorrupt, justified, warranted **10** acceptable, defensible, God-fearing, honourable, law-abiding, legitimate, reasonable **11** explainable, justifiable, supportable, well-founded **14** irreproachable

## righteousness

**06** dharma, equity, honour, purity, virtue **07** honesty, justice, probity **08** goodness, holiness, morality **09** integrity, rectitude **11** ethicalness, uprightness **12** faithfulness **13** blamelessness **14** sanctification

## rightful

**03** due **04** just, real, true **05** legal, valid **06** de jure, lawful, proper **07** correct, genuine **08** bona fide, suitable **10** authorized, legitimate

## rightfully

**06** de jure, justly **07** legally, rightly **08** by rights, lawfully, properly **09** correctly **11** justifiably **12** legitimately

## rightly

**04** well **06** fairly, justly **07** legally, morally **08** by rights, lawfully, properly **09** correctly, equitably, fittingly **10** reasonably **11** justifiably **12** legitimately **13** appropriately

## rigid

**03** set **04** firm, hard **05** fixed, harsh, stern, stiff, stony, tense **06** ramrod, severe, starch, strict **07** austere, hard-set, spartan **08** cast-iron, rigorous, stubborn **09** inelastic, stringent, tramlined, unbending **10** inflexible, invariable, unyielding **11** unalterable, unrelenting **12** intransigent **14** uncompromising

## rigidity

**06** fixity **08** hardness, obduracy **09** obstinacy, stiffness **10** stringency **12** immovability, immutability, inelasticity, stubbornness, unsuppleness **13** immutableness, inflexibility, intransigence **14** intractability

## rigmarole

**04** fuss, to-do **06** bother, hassle, jargon, ragman **07** carry-on, palaver, process, ragment, twaddle **08** nonsense **09** gibberish **11** performance, riddle-me-ree

## rigorous

**04** firm, hard **05** close, exact, harsh, rigid, stern, tough **06** severe, strait, strict **07** ascetic, austere, precise, spartan, violent **08** accurate, exacting, straight, streight, thorough **09** laborious, stringent, unsparing

**rigorously**

10 meticulous, scrupulous
11 painstaking, punctilious
12 intransigent 13 barrack square,
conscientious 14 uncompromising

**rigorously**

06 strait 07 exactly 08 straight, streight
09 precisely 10 accurately, thoroughly
12 meticulously, scrupulously
13 painstakingly, punctiliously

**rigour**

05 trial 06 ordeal 08 accuracy,
firmness, hardness, hardship, rigidity,
severity 09 austerity, exactness,
harshness, precision, privation,
sternness, stiffness, suffering,
toughness 10 strictness, stringency
11 preciseness 12 thoroughness
13 inflexibility, intransigence
14 meticulousness 15 punctiliousness

**rig-out**

03 kit 04 garb, gear, togs 05 dress, get-
up, habit 06 livery, outfit, things
07 apparel, clobber, clothes, costume,
raiment, uniform 08 clothing,
garments, glad rags

**rile**

◇ *anagram indicator* 03 bug, irk, vex
04 roil 05 anger, annoy, peeve, pique,
upset 06 hassle, nettle, put out, wind
up 07 agitate, hack off, tick off 08 brass
off, irritate 09 aggravate, cheese off,
drive nuts 10 drive crazy, exasperate
11 get your goat 12 drive bananas
13 get on your wick, get up your nose,
get your back up, make sparks fly
14 drive up the wall, get your blood
up, give you the hump 15 get on your
nerves, get your dander up

**rill**

*see* **brook**

**rim**

03 lip 04 brim, edge, ring, shoe, wood
05 apron, bezel, brink, chimb, chime,
chine, felly, helix, rymme, skirt,
velum, verge 06 border, felloe, fiddle,
girdle, margin, strake 08 membrane
10 peritoneum 13 circumference

**rind**

04 bark, husk, peel, rine, rynd, skin,
zest 06 crust, gourd, shell 06 citron
07 epicarp, outside 09 crackling
10 integument, orange peel

**ring**

01 O 03 mob, rim 04 area, band, bell,
belt, buzz, call, cell, club, crew, dial,
ding, disc, disk, echo, gang, gird, halo,
hoop, link, loop, peal, sing, tang, ting,
toll, tore 05 arena, atoll, chime, clang,
clink, group, hem in, knell, phone,
reach, reign, round, sound, torus
06 cage in, call up, cartel, circle,
clique, collar, girdle, jingle, keeper,
league, re-echo, ring up, signet, terret,
territ, tingle, tinkle, torret, turret
07 annulet, annulus, circlet, circuit,
combine, coterie, enclose, resound,
society, vibrate 08 alliance, ding-dong,
encircle, proclaim, pugilism, resonate,
sorority, surround 09 enclosure,
encompass, gathering, give a bell, give
a buzz, phone call, syndicate,
telephone 10 fraternity 11 association,
give a tinkle, reverberate, wedding
band 12 circumscribe, organization
14 tintinnabulate
• **prize ring** 02 PR
• **ring of wagons** 04 laer 06 corral,
laager

**ringleader**

05 chief 06 brains, leader 08 fugleman
09 spokesman 10 bell-wether,
mouthpiece 11 spokeswoman
12 spokesperson

**ringlet**

04 curl, lock

**rinse**

03 dip, wet 04 sind, synd, wash
05 bathe, clean, flush, swill 06 sloosh
07 cleanse, wash out 09 flush away,
wash clean

**riot**

◇ *anagram indicator* 03 row 04 fray,
hoot, orgy, rage, rant, rave, rout, show,
tear 05 brawl, fight, laugh, mêlée,
rebel, revel, storm 06 affray, charge,
fracas, hubbub, mutiny, rave-up,
revolt, rise up, rising, scream, strife,
tumult, uproar 07 anarchy, display,
quarrel, rampage, revelry, run amok,
run riot, run wild, turmoil, whoobub
08 disorder, feasting, flourish,
hubbuboo, partying, race riot, uprising
09 commotion, confusion, go berserk,
rebellion 10 debauchery, exhibition,
indulgence, insurgence, rush wildly,
turbulence 11 disturbance,
lawlessness, merrymaking
12 extravaganza, insurrection 14 go on
the rampage
• **run riot** ◇ *anagram indicator* 04 rage,
rant, rave, tear 05 storm 06 charge
07 rampage, run amok, run wild 09 go
berserk 10 rush wildly 14 go on the
rampage

**riotous**

◇ *anagram indicator* 04 loud, wild
05 noisy, rowdy 06 unruly, wanton
07 lawless, roaring, violent
08 mutinous 10 boisterous, disorderly,
ragmatical, rebellious, tumultuous,
uproarious 12 ungovernable,
unrestrained 13 insubordinate
14 uncontrollable 15 insurrectionary

**riotously**

◇ *anagram indicator* 05 ariot 06 loudly,
wildly 07 noisily 12 tumultuously
14 uncontrollably

**rip**

◇ *anagram indicator* 03 cut 04 coop,
gash, hack, hole, rend, rent, ripp, slit,
tear 05 burst, shred, slash, split
06 ladder 07 handful, rupture
08 cleavage, lacerate, separate
• **rip off** 02 do 03 con, rob 04 dupe
05 cheat, steal, sting, trick 06 diddle,
fleece 07 defraud, exploit, swindle
09 gold-brick 10 overcharge

**ripe**

03 fit 05 grope, grown, ready, right
06 mature, mellow, search, timely
07 forward, perfect, ransack, ripened
08 complete, drop-ripe, finished, in
season, rare-ripe, seasoned, spoiling,
suitable, thorough 09 developed,
excellent, excessive, opportune,
premature, ratheripe, under-ripe
10 auspicious, favourable, fully grown,
propitious 11 spoiling for
12 advantageous 14 fully developed

**ripen**

03 age 06 mature, mellow, season
07 develop 13 gather to a head
14 come to maturity 15 bring to
maturity

**rip-off**

03 con 04 scam, swiz 05 cheat, fraud,
sting, theft 06 diddle 07 robbery,
swindle 08 cheating, con trick, stealing
09 gold brick 12 exploitation
15 daylight robbery

**riposte**

04 quip 05 reply, sally 06 answer,
rejoin, retort, return 07 respond
08 comeback, repartee, response
09 rejoinder 11 reciprocate

**ripple**

◇ *anagram indicator* 04 curl, eddy, flow,
fret, pirl, purl, ring, wave 06 babble,
burble, crease, effect, gurgle, jabble,
pucker, result, riffle, ruffle, wimple
07 crumple, lapping, ripplet, wavelet,
whimple, wrinkle 08 undulate
09 shock wave 10 crispation,
undulation 11 consequence,
disturbance 12 repercussion
13 reverberation

**rise**

◇ *reversal down indicator* 02 up 03 sty,
try 04 buoy, flow, go up, grow, head,
hill, leap, lift, loom, riot, soar, stie, stye
05 arise, begin, climb, get up, issue,
mount, pluff, prove, raise, rebel, slope,
start, swell, tower 06 appear, ascend,
ascent, come in, defect, emerge,
growth, harden, jump up, leap up,
mutiny, origin, resist, revolt, rising,
rocket, source, spring, upturn, volume
07 advance, attempt, climb up, dissent,
emanate, improve, incline, prosper,
react to, respond, slope up, soaring,
stand up, upsurge 08 approach,
commence, escalate, increase,
occasion, overgrow, progress,
response, spring up, surmount,
towering 09 acclivity, ascendant,
ascendent, elevation, get higher,
increment, intensify, originate,
promotion 10 be promoted, do your
best, escalation, take up arms
11 advancement, get out of bed,
improvement, move upwards, upward
slope 12 amelioration, make progress
13 exert yourself, get to your feet
14 aggrandizement
• **give rise to** ◇ *reversal down indicator*
04 make 05 cause, evoke, raise, spawn
06 create, effect, elicit, induce, lead to,
prompt 07 bring on, inspire, produce,
provoke 08 engender, generate,
persuade 09 influence, originate
10 bring about

**risible**

05 comic, droll, funny 06 absurd
07 amusing, comical 08 farcical,

humorous **09** hilarious, laughable,
ludicrous **10** ridiculous **11** rib-tickling
**13** side-splitting

**rising**

◊ *reversal down indicator* **04** bull, hill,
riot, rise **06** émeute, origin, revolt,
uprest, uprise, uprist **07** growing,
soaring **08** emerging, mounting,
naissant, swelling, uprising
**09** advancing, ascendant, ascendent,
ascending, assurgent, insurgent
**10** increasing, prominence, revolution
**11** approaching **12** insurrection,
intensifying

**risk**

**04** dare, dice, fear **05** flier, peril, stake,
throw **06** chance, danger, gamble,
hazard, impawn, threat **07** imperil,
venture **08** chance it, endanger,
jeopardy **09** adventure **10** go for broke,
jeopardize, self-danger **11** possibility,
speculation, take a chance,
uncertainty **12** lay on the line, play
with fire, put on the line **13** put in
jeopardy
• **against all risks** **03** aar
• **at the risk of** **02** on

**risky**

**04** iffy **05** dicey, dodgy, hairy
**06** chancy, risqué, touchy, tricky,
unsafe **07** chancey **08** high-risk,
perilous **09** dangerous, hazardous,
uncertain **10** precarious, touch-and-go
**11** venturesome

**risqué**

**04** blue, racy, rude **05** adult, bawdy,
crude, dirty, risky, saucy, spicy
**06** coarse, earthy, fruity, ribald, smutty
**07** naughty **08** immodest, improper,
indecent **09** off-colour **10** indelicate,
suggestive **14** near the knuckle

**rite**

**03** act **04** bora, form, orgy **05** pawaw,
right, usage **06** custom, office,
powwow, ritual, symbol **07** dry Mass,
liturgy, service, worship **08** ceremony,
practice **09** formality, ordinance,
procedure, sacrament **10** ceremonial,
commixtion, commixture, dry service,
initiatory, observance **11** subincision
**12** confirmation, superstition

**ritual**

**03** act, set **04** form, rite, wont **05** habit,
usage **06** Agadah, cultus, custom,
fetich, fetish, formal, lavabo **07** fetiche,
Haggada, liturgy, routine, sacring,
service **08** ceremony, habitual,
Haggadah, lavatory, practice,
trumpery **09** customary, custumary,
formality, formulary, ordinance,
procedure, sacrament, solemnity,
tradition **10** ceremonial, consuetude,
convention, mumbo-jumbo,
observance, prescribed, procedural
**11** apotropaism, celebration,
traditional **12** conventional,
prescription **14** consuetudinary

**ritualistic**

**06** formal, ritual, solemn **07** festive,
stately **08** official **09** customary,
dignified, formulaic, formulary
**10** ceremonial **11** traditional

**ritzy**

**04** posh, rich **05** cushy, grand, plush
**06** costly, de luxe, glitzy, lavish,
swanky **07** elegant, opulent, stylish
**08** affluent, pampered, splendid
**09** expensive, luxurious, sumptuous
**11** comfortable, magnificent **13** self-
indulgent, well-appointed

**rival**

**03** vie **04** mate, peer, vier **05** equal,
match, touch **06** fellow, oppose
**07** emulate, nemesis, opposed,
paragon, partner, vie with **08** corrival,
opponent, opposing, parallel
**09** adversary, competing, contender
**10** antagonist, challenger, collateral,
competitor, contestant, in conflict,
opposition **11** compare with, compete
with, competitive, conflicting, contend
with, measure up to **12** in opposition
**13** in competition

**rivalry**

**05** vying **06** strife **07** contest **08** conflict,
rivality, struggle **09** emulation
**10** antagonism, contention, corrivalry,
in-fighting, opposition **11** competition
**12** corrivalship **15** competitiveness

**riven**

**04** rent **05** split **07** divided, severed
**08** ruptured **09** torn apart **11** ripped
apart

**river**

**01** R **03** lee, rio **05** flood **11** watercourse

*River and watercourse types include:*

**02** ea
**03** cut, pow, sny
**04** beck, burn, flow, khor, kill, lake,
lane, nala, rill, snye, wadi, wady
**05** bourn, brook, canal, creek, delta,
ditch, drain, firth, flume, fresh,
frith, inlet, mouth, nalla, nulla,
rhine, shott, whelm
**06** arroyo, broads, influx, nallah,
nullah, rapids, rillet, runnel,
source, spruit, stream
**07** channel, estuary, freshet, riveret,
rivulet, torrent
**08** affluent, brooklet, effluent,
influent, waterway
**09** anabranch, backwater, billabong,
confluent, headwater, streamlet,
tributary
**10** confluence, head-stream,
millstream, streamling
**11** trout stream, water splash
**12** distributary, embranchment,
water-channel
**14** mountain stream

*Rivers include:*

**02** Ob, Po
**03** Ain, Axe, Bug, Cam, Dee, Don,
Ems, Esk, Exe, Fal, Fly, Han, Ill,
Inn, Lea, Lee, Lim, Lot, Mun, Nid,
Our, Red, San, Tay, Taz, Ure,
Usk, Váh, Wye
**04** Aare, Adur, Aire, Amur, Arno,
Avon, Bann, Cher, Coco, Dart,
East, Ebro, Eden, Elbe, Gail,
Hong, Huon, Isis, Kemi, Lena,
Nene, Neva, Nile, Oder, Ohio,
Ouse, Oxus, Ping, Ravi, Ruhr,

Saar, Spey, Swan, Taff, Tees, Test,
Towy, Tyne, Ural, Vaal, Wear,
Yalu, Yare
**05** Adige, Argun, Benue, Boyne,
Cauca, Chari, Clyde, Congo,
Donau, Douro, Fleet, Forth,
Glåma, Indus, Jumna, Loire,
Marne, Meuse, Mosel, Neath,
Negro, Neman, Niger, Peace,
Pearl, Pecos, Plata, Plate, Rhine,
Rhône, Saône, Seine, Snake,
Somme, Tagus, Tamar, Teifi,
Tiber, Tisza, Trent, Tweed, Volga,
Volta, Weser, Yarra, Yukon, Zaire
**06** Amazon, Angara, Brazos,
Chenab, Clutha, Danube, Dnestr,
Escaut, Fraser, Gambia, Ganges,
Grande, Hudson, Humber,
Hunter, Irtysh, Jhelum, Jordan,
Kagera, Kistna, Kolyma, Liffey,
Mekong, Mersey, Murray,
Orange, Ottawa, Pahang, Paraná,
Rakaia, Ribble, Salado, Severn,
Seyhan, Sutlej, Thames, Tigris,
Tornio, Ubangi, Vltava, Wabash,
Yamuna, Yellow
**07** Alpheus, Darling, Derwent,
Dnieper, Garonne, Glommen,
Helmand, Huang He, Huang Ho,
Lachlan, Limpopo, Lualaba,
Madeira, Marañón, Maritsa,
Narmada, Orinoco, Pechora,
Potomac, Salween, Schelde,
Selenga, Sénégal, Shannon, Tarim
He, Ucayali, Uruguay, Vistula,
Waikato, Waitaki, Yangtze,
Yenisei, Zambezi
**08** Arkansas, Blue Nile, Canadian,
Cherwell, Colorado, Columbia,
Delaware, Dniester, Dordogne,
Margaret, Missouri, Okavango,
Paraguay, Tunguska, Wanganui,
Zhu Jiang
**09** Churchill, Crocodile, Euphrates,
Great Ouse, Irrawaddy,
Mackenzie, Rio Grande,
Tennessee, White Nile
**10** Albert Nile, Bass Strait, Des
Plaines, Parramatta, Sacramento,
San Joaquin, Shenandoah, St
Lawrence, Walla Walla
**11** Mississippi, Shatt al-Arab
**12** Murrumbidgee, Saskatchewan,
Victoria Nile

*Mythical rivers include:*

**04** Alph, Styx
**05** Lethe
**07** Acheron, Alpheus, Cocytus,
Oceanus
**08** Achelous, Eridanos
**10** Phlegethon

• **river valley** **04** wadi, wady
**05** water **07** wind gap

**rivet**

**04** grip **05** clink **06** absorb, arrest,
clinch, excite **07** engross, enthral
**08** intrigue **09** captivate, fascinate
• **fix rivet** **04** pane, pean, peen, pein,
pene

**riveting**

**08** exciting, gripping, hypnotic,
magnetic **09** absorbing, arresting

**10** engrossing **11** captivating, enthralling, fascinating, interesting **12** spellbinding

### road
**03** via **04** raid, ride, rode, tour **06** course **07** railway, roadway **09** dismissal, incursion **10** journeying, prostitute, travelling

*Road types include:*

**01** A, B, C, E
**02** Rd, St
**03** Ave, way
**04** drag, high, lane, mews, pass, ring, side, slip, toll
**05** alley, byway, close, gated, Roman, route, strip, track, trunk
**06** avenue, bypass, parade, rat run, relief, strand, street, subway
**07** beltway, dead end, flyover, freeway, highway, off ramp, parkway, private, through
**08** alleyway, autobahn, causeway, clearway, crescent, cul-de-sac, metalled, motorway, overpass, red route, short cut, speedway, trackway, turnpike
**09** autoroute, boulevard, bridleway, cart track, dirt track, esplanade, green lane, promenade, underpass
**10** autostrada, bridlepath, cloverleaf, expressway, interstate, unmetalled
**11** gravel track, scenic route, single track
**12** mountain pass, superhighway, thoroughfare, unclassified
**14** gyratory system
**15** dual carriageway

*Roads include:*

**02** A1, M1, M2, M3, M4, M5, M6, M8, M9
**03** M25, M40, M62
**07** Route 66, Westway
**08** Fosse Way, Highway 1, Silk Road
**09** Appian Way, Burma Road, Highway 61
**10** Cassian Way, Dere Street, Khyber Pass
**12** El Camino Real, King's Highway, Périphérique, Sturt Highway
**13** North Circular, South Circular, Stuart Highway, Watling Street
**14** Great Ocean Road, Great River Road, Le Périphérique, Pacific Highway

### roadhouse
*see* **public house**

### roam
**04** rake, rove, trek, walk **05** amble, drift, prowl, range, raven, stray, tramp, wheel **06** ramble, stroam, stroll, travel, wander **07** meander **08** ambulate, squander, traverse **09** wandering **11** perambulate, peregrinate

### roar
**03** cry **04** bawl, bell, boom, hoot, howl, roin, rore, rote, rout, yell **05** blare, crash, laugh, royne, shout **06** bellow, guffaw, holler, rumble, scream, shriek

**07** break up, thunder **08** crease up **09** fall about **14** split your sides **15** laugh like a drain

### roaring
**04** full, loud, rich **05** great **07** bluster, booming, echoing, notable, ringing, riotous, vibrant **08** decisive, emphatic, resonant, sonorous, striking, thorough **09** memorable **10** conclusive, impressive, remarkable, resonating, resounding, thunderous **11** outstanding **13** reverberating

### roast
**04** bake, rost **05** brown, parch, swale, swayl, sweal, sweel **06** banter **07** torrefy **08** barbecue **11** decrepitate

### rob
**02** do **03** mug, pad, rub **04** blag, fake, loot, mill, nick, raid, ramp, roll, sack **05** berob, bunco, bunko, cheat, flimp, heist, pluck, reave, reive, rifle, screw, stiff, sting **u6** burgle, do over, hijack, hold up, pirate, rip off **07** bereave, defraud, deprive, despoil, pillage, plunder, ransack, stick up, swindle **08** highjack, knock off, turn over **09** depredate, steal from

### robber
**04** Tory **05** cheat, fraud, rover, thief **06** bandit, con man, dacoit, dakoit, latron, looter, mugger, pirate, raider **07** brigand, burglar, cateran, ladrone, pandour, pandour, stealer **08** hijacker, swindler **09** embezzler, plunderer **10** highjacker, highwayman, land-pirate, roberdsman, robertsman **11** motor-bandit

*See also* **thief**

### robbery
**04** blag, raid, toby **05** fraud, heist, theft **06** hold-up, piracy, rip-off, snatch **07** break-in, dacoity, dakoiti, larceny, low toby, mugging, pillage, plunder, stick-up, swindle **08** burglary, high toby, stealing **09** dacoitage, latrociny, pilferage **10** plundering **11** latrocinium **12** embezzlement, smash-and-grab **13** housebreaking

### robe
**04** garb, gown, vest, wrap **05** camis, camus, drape, dress, habit, talar **06** attire, chimer, clothe, dolman, khalat, khilat, killut, kimono, peplos, peplus, purple **07** apparel, cassock, chimere, chrisom, costume, kellaut, wrapper **08** bathrobe, christom, parament, peignoir, vestment, wardrobe **09** housecoat, nightgown **10** palliament **12** chrisom-cloth, dressing-gown

### Robert
**03** Bob, Rob **05** Bobby **06** Bobbie, Rabbie, Robbie

### Robin Hood
*see* **legend**

### robot
**05** golem **06** cyborg, zombie **07** android, chatbot, machine, nanobot **08** telechir **09** automaton

### robust
**03** fit, raw **04** hale, iron, rude, well **05** crude, hardy, sonsy, stout, tough **06** brawny, coarse, direct, earthy, hearty, ribald, risqué, rugged, sonsie, strong, sturdy **07** healthy, sthenic **08** athletic, forceful, muscular, powerful, stalwart, thickset, vigorous **09** energetic, strapping, well-built **10** able-bodied, no-nonsense **11** down-to-earth **15** straightforward, tough as old boots

### rock
◊ *anagram indicator* **03** AOR, jow, tip **04** cill, coin, crag, daze, reef, reel, roll, sill, stun, sway, tilt, toss, trap, tuff, whin **05** crack, lurch, pitch, shake, shock, stone, swing **06** danger, pebble, totter, wobble **07** astound, boulder, diamond, distaff, outcrop, shoggle, stagger, startle **08** astonish, bewilder, hard core, obstacle, surprise, take back, undulate **09** dumbfound, oscillate **12** move to and fro
*See also* **singer**

*Rocks include:*

**02** aa
**03** ore
**04** coal, lava, marl
**05** chalk, chert, flint, shale, slate
**06** basalt, gabbro, gneiss, gravel, marble, schist
**07** breccia, granite
**08** dolerite, hornfels, obsidian, porphyry
**09** argillite, greywacke, limestone, sandstone, soapstone
**10** greenstone, serpentine
**11** pumice stone
**12** conglomerate

• **on the rocks 06** doomed, failed, in a fix, in a jam **07** failing, in a hole, in a mess **08** hopeless, in pieces, in shreds, slipping, unstable **09** in a bad way, in a scrape, penniless **11** at an impasse **12** in difficulty **14** in difficulties

### rocket
**02** V-1, V-2 **04** soar, wald, weld **05** onion, retro, tower **06** rucola **07** arugula, missile, shoot up **08** Congreve, escalate, roquette, thruster **09** reprimand **10** flying bomb, projectile **13** guided missile, launch vehicle **15** increase quickly, St Barbara's cress

### rocky
◊ *anagram indicator* **04** hard, weak **05** rough, shaky, stony, tipsy **06** craggy, flinty, pebbly, rugged, wobbly **08** unstable, unsteady, wobbling **09** difficult, tottering, uncertain **10** staggering, unpleasant, unreliable **14** unsatisfactory

### rococo
**04** bold **05** showy **06** florid, ornate **07** baroque, flowery **08** fanciful, rocaille, vigorous **09** decorated, elaborate, exuberant, fantastic, grotesque, whimsical **10** convoluted, flamboyant **11** embellished,

extravagant, overwrought
**13** overdecorated, overelaborate
**15** churrigueresque

**rod**
**03** bar, cue, lug **04** calm, came, cane,
mace, pole, reed, rood, spit, twig,
vare, wand **05** baton, perch, shaft, staff,
stave, stick, strut, swits **06** pistol,
switch **07** ellwand, probang, sceptre,
scollop, tringle **08** caduceus,
metewand, meteyard, revolver,
stanchel, stancher **09** metestick,
stanchion
*See also* **gun**

**rodent**
*Rodents include:*

**03** rat
**04** cavy, cony, degu, hare, paca,
pika, vole
**05** aguti, coypu, mouse
**06** agouti, beaver, ferret, gerbil,
gopher, hog-rat, jerboa, marmot,
rabbit
**07** bush rat, cane rat, hamster,
lemming, meerkat, muskrat,
ondatra, potoroo
**08** black rat, brown rat, capybara,
chipmunk, dormouse, hampster,
hedgehog, musquash, sewer rat,
squirrel, tucutuco, viscacha,
water rat
**09** bandicoot, groundhog, guinea
pig, porcupine, water vole,
woodchuck
**10** chinchilla, fieldmouse, prairie
dog, springhaas, springhase
**11** kangaroo rat, red squirrel,
spermophile
**12** grey squirrel, harvest mouse

**roe**
**04** melt, milt, raun, rawn **06** caviar,
cavier **07** caviare **08** caviarie

**roentgenium**
**02** Rg

**rogue**
◇ *anagram indicator* **05** cheat, crook,
drôle, fraud, Greek, hempy, knave,
scamp **06** con man, donder, limmer,
rascal, scally, terror, varlet **07** skellum,
vagrant, villain, wastrel, wrong 'un
**08** deceiver, dummerer, palliard,
swindler **09** fraudster, miscreant,
prankster, reprobate, scallywag,
scoundrel, son of a gun **10** disruptive,
ne'er-do-well, rascallion, slip-string
**11** mischievous, rapscallion **12** hedge-
creeper **14** good-for-nothing

**roguish**
**04** arch **05** hempy, shady **06** cheeky,
impish, wicked **07** crooked, knavish,
playful, waggish **08** criminal, espiègle,
rascally **09** deceitful, deceiving,
dishonest, swindling **10** confounded,
coquettish, fraudulent, frolicsome,
rascal-like, slip-string, villainous
**11** mischievous **12** unprincipled,
unscrupulous

**roister**
**04** brag, romp **05** boast, revel, strut
**06** frolic **07** bluster, carouse, large it,

rollick, swagger **09** blusterer,
celebrate, make merry, whoop it up
**11** have it large **15** paint the town red

**roisterer**
**06** buster, ranter **07** boaster, roister
**08** braggart, carouser, reveller
**09** blusterer, swaggerer

**roisterous**
**04** loud, wild **05** noisy, rowdy
**09** clamorous, exuberant **10** boisterous,
disorderly, uproarious **12** obstreperous

**role**
**03** bit, fat, job **04** duty, lead, part, post,
task **05** cameo, place, stead
**08** capacity, function, name part,
position **09** cameo-part, character,
portrayal, situation **11** comprimario
**12** principal boy, spear carrier
**13** character part, impersonation
**14** representation

**roll**
◇ *anagram indicator* **02** go **03** bap, bun,
ren, rin, rob, run, wad **04** bind, boom,
bowl, coil, curl, drum, echo, file, flow,
fold, furl, list, move, pass, peal, reel,
roar, rock, spin, sway, toss, turn, waul,
wawl, wind, wrap **05** crush, cycle,
dandy, index, level, lurch, pitch, press,
spool, start, swell, swing, trill, twirl,
twist, wheel, whirl **06** annals, billow,
bobbin, census, elapse, enfold,
enwrap, gyrate, rafale, record, rental,
roller, roster, rotate, rumble, scroll,
smooth, tumble, volley, volume,
volute, wallow, wander, welter
**07** envelop, flatten, go round, grumble,
notitia, reeling, resound, revolve,
rocking, rouleau, stagger, swagger,
terrier, thunder, tossing, trindle,
trundle **08** crescent, cylinder, gyration,
pitching, register, rotation, schedule,
undulate **09** billowing, catalogue,
chronicle, directory, inventory, press
down, resonance, turn round
**10** muster-file, revolution, undulation
**11** reverberate **13** reverberation
*See also* **bread**
**• roll in** **04** come **06** appear, arrive,
blow in, come in, flow in, pour in,
rush in, show up, turn up **07** flood in
**09** be present **10** be received
**• rolling in it** **04** rich **05** flush
**06** loaded **07** moneyed, wealthy,
well-off **08** affluent, well-to-do
**10** filthy rich, in the money,
prosperous, well-heeled **11** made of
money **12** stinking rich **15** with
money to burn
**• roll up** **04** furl **06** arrive, gather
**07** convene **08** assemble
**10** congregate, intervolve

**roller**
**02** RR **07** trundle **10** Rolls-Royce®

**rollicking**
◇ *anagram indicator* **05** merry, noisy
**06** banzai, frisky, hearty, jaunty, jovial,
joyous, lively, rebuke, rocket
**07** censure, chiding, lecture, playful,
reproof, romping **08** berating, carefree,
harangue, reproach, roisting, scolding,
spirited, sportive **09** cavorting,

exuberant, reprimand, sprightly,
talking-to **10** boisterous, frolicsome,
rip-roaring, roisterous, telling-off,
upbraiding **12** devil-may-care,
dressing-down, light-hearted
**13** swashbuckling

**rolling**
◇ *anagram indicator* **06** goggle, waving
**07** heaving, surging **08** rippling,
undulant **10** undulating, volutation

**roll-on roll-off**
**04** ro-ro

**roly-poly**
**03** fat **05** buxom, plump, podgy,
pudgy, round, tubby **06** barrel,
chubby, rotund **07** rounded
**10** butterball, overweight

**Roman**
*Roman emperors:*

**03** Leo
**04** Geta, Nero, Otho, Zeno
**05** Carus, Gaius, Galba, Nerva, Titus
**06** Avitus, Decius, Gallus, Julian,
Philip, Probus, Trajan, Valens
**07** Carinus, Florian, Gordian, Gratian,
Hadrian, Marcian, Maximin,
Maximus, Severus, Tacitus
**08** Aemilian, Arcadius, Augustus,
Aurelian, Balbinus, Caligula,
Claudius, Commodus, Constans,
Domitian, Galerius, Honorius,
Licinius, Macrinus, Majorian,
Maximian, Numerian, Olybrius,
Pertinax, Tiberius, Valerian
**09** Anthemius, Caracalla, Gallienus,
Hostilian, Maxentius, Procopius,
Vespasian, Vitellius
**10** Diocletian, Elagabalus,
Magnentius, Quintillus,
Theodosius
**11** Constantine, Constantius, Julius
Nepos, Lucius Verus, Valentinian
**13** Antoninus Pius, Libius Severus
**14** Didius Julianus, Marcus Aurelius
**15** Romulus Augustus
**16** Alexander Severus, Petronius
Maximus, Septemius Severus

*Roman kings:*

**07** Romulus
**12** Ancus Marcius
**13** Numa Pompilius
**14** Servius Tullius
**15** Tullus Hostilius
**17** Tarquinius Priscus
**18** Tarquinius Superbus

*Romans include:*

**04** Cato, Livy, Ovid
**05** Lucan, Pliny
**06** Antony (Mark), Brutus, Cicero
(Marcus Tullius), Horace, Pilate
(Pontius), Pompey, Seneca, Vergil,
Virgil
**07** Atticus (Titus Pomponius),
Cassius, Juvenal, Martial, Plautus
(Titus Maccius), Roscius, Tacitus,
Terence
**08** Agricola (Gnaeus Julius), Catilina
(Lucius Sergius), Catiline, Catullus
(Gaius Valerius), Claudian,

Gracchus (Tiberius Sempronius),
Lucretia
09 **Agrippina**, **Lucretius**, **Spartacus**,
**Suetonius**
10 **Coriolanus** (Gaius), **Quintilian**
14 **Marcus Antonius**

*See also* **god, goddess; mythology;
numeral**

## romance
03 lie, see, woo 04 date, gest, tale
05 amour, charm, chase, court, fling,
geste, idyll, novel, story, thing 06 affair,
colour, legend, whimsy 07 crusade,
fantasy, fiction, glamour, liaison,
mystery, passion, Romanic, romaunt
08 intrigue 09 adventure, fairytale,
fantasize, go out with, love story,
melodrama, overstate, sentiment
10 attachment, exaggerate,
excitement, fairy story, love affair
11 fascination 12 bodice-ripper, go
steady with, relationship 15 romantic
fiction

## Romania
02 RO 03 ROU

## romantic
04 fond, wild 05 soppy 06 dreamy,
Gothic, loving, sloppy, tender
07 amorous, dreamer, idyllic, utopian
08 exciting, fanciful, idealist, quixotic,
stardust, unlikely 09 fairytale, fantastic,
imaginary, legendary, visionary
10 fictitious, idealistic, improbable,
lovey-dovey, mysterious, optimistic,
passionate, starry-eyed 11 extravagant,
fascinating, impractical, sentimental,
unrealistic 14 sentimentalist

## romantically
06 fondly 08 lovingly, tenderly
09 amorously 10 excitingly, fancifully
12 mysteriously, passionately
13 extravagantly, impractically,
sentimentally 14 idealistically,
optimistically 15 unrealistically

## Rome
*see* **hill**

## Romeo
01 R 05 lover 06 gigolo 07 Don Juan
08 Casanova, Lothario 09 ladies' man
10 lady-killer

## romp
03 rig 04 lark, play, ramp, skip
05 caper, frisk, hempy, revel, sport,
spree 06 cavort, frolic, gambol,
hoiden, hoyden, tomboy 07 roister,
rollick

## rondo
04 rota

## roof
05 vault 06 canopy 07 ceiling, rigging,
shelter 08 covering, dwelling
11 culmination

*Roof types include:*

03 hip
04 bell, dome, flat, helm, ogee, span
05 gable
06 cupola, French, lean-to, saddle
07 gambrel, mansard, monitor,
pitched

08 flat roof, imperial, pavilion,
sawtooth, thatched
09 onion dome
10 imbricated, saucer dome
12 geodesic dome, sloped turret
13 conical broach
14 gable-and-valley, pendentive
dome

• **hit the roof** 05 go mad 06 blow up,
see red 07 explode 08 boil over, freak
out 09 do your nut 11 blow your top,
flip your lid, go up the wall, lose
your rag 12 blow your cool, lose
your cool 15 fly off the handle, go off
the deep end

## roof-gutter
04 roan, rone 05 rhone 08 roanpipe,
ronepipe

## rook
01 R 02 do 03 con 04 bilk, crow
05 cheat, squab, sting 06 castle, diddle,
fleece, rip off 07 defraud, swindle
09 card-sharp, gold-brick, simpleton
10 overcharge 12 take for a ride

## room
02 rm 03 ben, but, end, oda 04 area,
seat 05 range, scope, space, stead
06 chance, extent, leeway, margin,
volume 07 expanse, legroom
08 capacity, headroom, latitude,
occasion 09 allowance, elbow-room
10 Lebensraum 11 appointment,
compartment, opportunity

*Rooms include:*

02 WC
03 bed, box, day, den, loo
04 ante, bath, cell, dark, hall, loft,
play, rest, sick, tack, wash, work
05 attic, board, cabin, class, cloak,
court, foyer, front, games, green,
guard, guest, lobby, music, porch,
salon, spare, staff, state, stock,
store, study
06 cellar, common, dining, engine,
family, larder, living, locker,
lounge, lumber, office, pantry,
rumpus, saddle, strong, studio,
toilet
07 boudoir, buttery, chamber,
control, cubicle, drawing, fitting,
kitchen, landing, laundry, lecture,
library, meeting, morning,
nursery, parlour, reading,
seminar, sitting, smoking, utility,
waiting
08 assembly, basement, chambers,
changing, dressing, lavatory,
scullery, workshop
09 breakfast, dormitory, mezzanine,
reception, sun lounge
10 consulting, laboratory, recreation
11 kitchenette, lounge-diner
12 conservatory, kitchen-diner
15 en suite bathroom

• **have room for** 04 stow

## roomy
04 wide 05 ample, broad, large, rangy
07 sizable 08 generous, sizeable,
spacious 09 capacious, extensive
10 commodious, voluminous

## root
03 fix, nub, rad, set, tap, yam 04 axis,
base, core, germ, grub, hail, home,
moor, more, pull, seat, seed, spur,
stem 05 basis, cause, cheer, embed,
fount, heart, radix, shout, stick, tuber
06 anchor, bottom, etymon, family,
fasten, ground, kernel, nuzzle, origin,
radish, reason, sinker, source
07 applaud, calamus, cheer on,
essence, ginseng, implant, nucleus,
origins, parsnep, parsnip, radical,
radicle, rhizome, rummage, snuzzle,
support, turbith, turpeth, vetiver
08 entrench, heritage, radicate,
scammony 09 beginning, encourage,
establish, principle 10 background,
beginnings, birthplace, derivation,
foundation 11 fundamental
12 fountainhead, sarsaparilla
13 starting point
• **put down roots** 09 set up home
10 settle down 12 make your home
• **root and branch** 06 wholly
07 finally, totally, utterly 08 complete,
entirely, thorough 10 radically
10 completely, thoroughly
• **root around** 03 dig, pry 04 hunt,
nose, poke 05 delve 06 burrow, ferret,
forage 07 rummage
• **root out** 06 dig out, remove, uproot
07 abolish, destroy, outweed, uncover
unearth 08 discover, get rid of 09 clear
away, eliminate, eradicate, extirpate
10 put an end to 11 exterminate
• **take root** 08 take hold 11 become
fixed 15 establish itself

## rooted
04 deep, felt, firm 05 fixed, rigid
06 deeply 07 radical 08 radicate
09 confirmed, ingrained, radicated
10 deep-seated, entrenched
11 established

## rootless
04 free 06 moving 07 nomadic
08 carefree, drifting, floating, homeless
09 itinerant, transient, unsettled,
wandering 14 of no fixed abode

## rootstock
04 race 05 orris

## rope
03 tie 04 bind, jeff, lash, moor, stay
05 hitch, lasso 06 fasten

*Rope types include:*

03 guy, tow
04 cord, drag, fall, head, line, seal,
stay, tack, vang, warp
05 brace, cable, lasso, noose, widdy
06 bridle, halter, hawser, hobble,
lariat, runner, strand, string,
tackle, tether
07 bobstay, bowline, cordage,
cringle, halyard, lanyard, lashing,
marline, mooring, outhaul,
painter, ratline
08 buntline, clew-line, dockline,
downhaul, dragline, gantline
09 hackamore

• **know the ropes** 05 learn
06 master 12 know the drill, know the
score 13 know what's what

### rope in
**06** engage, enlist
**07** involve **08** inveigle, persuade, talk into

### ropy, ropey
**04** duff, poor **05** rough **06** unwell
**07** stringy **08** below par, inferior
**09** deficient, glutinous, off colour
**10** inadequate **11** substandard **14** not up to scratch, unsatisfactory

### rose
**03** riz **04** geum, Jack, moss **05** avens, brere, briar, brier **07** Bourbon, monthly, paragon, rambler, rosette
**08** noisette, primrose **09** crampbark, eglantine, perpetual, remontant
**10** erysipelas, floribunda, water elder
**12** snowball tree **13** cranberry bush, cranberry tree
• **rose fruit**   **03** hep, hip

### rosette
**04** chou, rose **06** rosace, rosula
**07** cockade **13** wedding favour
**14** provincial rose

### rosin
**05** resin, roset, rosit, rozet, rozit
**09** colophony

### roster
**04** list, roll, rota **05** index **07** listing
**08** register, schedule **09** directory

### rostrum
**04** beak, bema, dais **05** stage
**06** podium **08** platform

### rosy
**03** red **04** pink, rose **05** fresh, ruddy, sunny **06** bright, florid **07** auroral, flushed, glowing, hopeful, reddish, roseate, rose-red **08** aurorean, blooming, blushing, cheerful, inflamed, rose-hued, roselike, rose-pink, rubicund **09** bloodshot, promising **10** auspicious, favourable, optimistic, reassuring **11** encouraging, rose-scented **12** rose-coloured
**14** healthy-looking

### rot
◇ *anagram indicator* **03** rat, ret **04** blah, bosh, bunk, halt, joke, rait, rate, rust, tosh **05** decay, go bad, go off, hooey, mould, spoil, taint, tease **06** bluing, bunkum, drivel, fester, go sour, humbug, kibosh, kybosh, perish, piffle
**07** baloney, blueing, corrode, corrupt, crumble, garbage, hogwash, putrefy, rhubarb, rubbish **08** claptrap, cobblers, collapse, malarkey, Merulius, nonsense **09** corrosion, decompose, moonshine, poppycock
**10** codswallop, corruption, degenerate
**11** deteriorate **12** disintegrate, putrefaction **13** decomposition, deterioration **14** disintegration

### rota
**04** list, roll **05** canon, index, rondo, round **06** course, roster **07** listing, routine **08** register, schedule
**09** directory

### rotary
**07** turning **08** gyrating, gyratory, rotating, spinning, whirling
**09** revolving **10** roundabout

### rotate
◇ *reversal indicator* **04** reel, roll, spin, turn **05** pivot, rabat, whirl **06** gyrate, swivel **07** go round, rabatte, revolve, twiddle **09** alternate, move round, spin round, turn about, turn round
**10** change face **11** interchange, reciprocate, take in turns **13** take it in turns

### rotation
**04** spin, turn **05** cycle, orbit, round, whirl **06** swivel **07** turning **08** gyration, sequence, spinning, whirling
**10** revolution, succession, swivelling
**11** alternation

### rote
• **learn by rote**   **08** memorize **11** learn off pat **14** commit to memory **15** learn from memory, learn off by heart

### rotten
◇ *anagram indicator* **03** bad, ill, off, rat
**04** evil, foul, mean, poor, poxy, punk, rank, ropy, sick, sour **05** awful, dirty, fetid, lousy, manky, nasty, putid, ropey, rough **06** addled, bloody, crummy, damned, darned, dashed, foetid, grotty, guilty, mouldy, poorly, putrid, spoilt, unwell, wicked
**07** beastly, blasted, corrupt, decayed, flaming, gone off, immoral, rotting, tainted, unsound **08** blinking, blooming, decaying, dratting, dreadful, flipping, horrible, inferior, infernal, low-grade, stinking, terrible, wretched **09** dishonest, off colour, putrefied **10** confounded, decomposed, despicable, inadequate, mouldering, putrescent, unpleasant **12** contemptible, unprincipled **13** dishonourable
**14** disintegrating

### rotter
**03** cad, cur, pig, rat **04** fink, heel
**05** beast, louse, rogue, swine
**07** bounder, dastard, stinker **08** blighter
**09** scoundrel **10** blackguard

### rotund
**03** fat **04** full, rich **05** heavy, obese, plump, podgy, round, stout, tubby
**06** chubby, fleshy, portly **07** bulbous, orotund, rounded, spheral, spheric
**08** globular, resonant, roly-poly, sonorous **09** corpulent, orbicular, rotundate, spherical, spherular
**10** impressive **12** magniloquent
**13** grandiloquent

### roué
**04** rake **06** lecher, wanton **08** rakehell
**09** debauchee, libertine **10** profligate, sensualist

### rough
◇ *anagram indicator* **03** ill, ned, row, yob **04** curt, hard, hazy, rude, sick, thug, wild **05** asper, basic, blunt, bully, bumpy, crude, cruel, dirty, draft, gruff, gurly, hairy, harsh, hasty, husky, lousy, lumpy, model, nasty, noisy, plain, quick, raggy, raspy, rocky, rowdy, ruggy, rusty, scaly, sharp, stern, stony, tough, tousy, touzy, towsy, towzy, vague, yobbo **06** brutal, choppy, coarse, craggy, grotty, hoarse, jagged,

### roughneck
lively, mock-up, poorly, raucle, rotten, ruffle, rugged, severe, shaggy, sketch, stormy, uneven, unkind, unwell, vulgar **07** bristly, bruiser, brusque, brutish, cursory, drastic, extreme, general, gnarled, grained, hirsute, inexact, of a sort, of sorts, outline, prickly, rasping, raucous, ruffian, sketchy, throaty, unkempt, unshorn, violent **08** agitated, aspirate, below par, croaking, forceful, gravelly, guttural, hooligan, impolite, muricate, scabrous, scratchy, strident, unbroken, ungentle, unshaven **09** difficult, energetic, estimated, harrowing, imprecise, iron-sided, irregular, merciless, muricated, off colour, primitive, roughneck, turbulent, unfeeling, unhealthy, unrefined
**10** aggressive, astringent, boisterous, broadbrush, discordant, disorderly, hard-handed, incomplete, unfinished, unpleasant, unpolished
**11** approximate, belligerent, insensitive, ramgunshoch, rudimentary, tempestuous, uncivilized
**12** tiger country, unelaborated
**15** under the weather
• **rough out**   **05** draft **06** mock up, sketch **07** outline **11** draw in rough
**14** give a summary of
• **rough up**   **03** mug **04** bash, do in
**06** beat up **08** maltreat, mistreat
**09** manhandle **10** knock about

### rough-and-ready
**05** basic, crude, plain **06** bodgie, make-do, simple **07** hurried, sketchy, stop-gap **09** makeshift, unrefined
**10** unpolished **11** approximate, provisional

### rough-and-tumble
**04** blue **05** brawl, fight, mêlée, scrap
**06** affray, dust-up, fracas, rumpus
**07** punch-up, scuffle **08** struggle

### roughen
◇ *anagram indicator* **04** chap, hack, rasp, stab **05** chafe, graze, rough, scuff, spray **06** abrade, ruffle **07** coarsen, harshen, spreaze, spreeze **08** asperate, spreathe, spreethe, unsmooth
**09** granulate

### roughly
◇ *anagram indicator* **01** c **02** ca **03** cir
**04** circ **05** about, circa **06** around, nearly, wildly **07** close to, cruelly, harshly, loosely, noisily, rowdily, toughly **08** brutally, unkindly **09** just about, not far off, rounded up, violently **10** forcefully, give or take, more or less, round about
**11** approaching, mercilessly, rounded down **12** boisterously
**13** approximately, energetically, insensitively, in the region of, or thereabouts, something like **14** in round figures, in round numbers **15** in the vicinity of

### roughneck
**04** lout, thug **05** rough, rowdy, tough, yobbo **06** keelie **07** bruiser, ruffian
**08** bully boy, hooligan, larrikin

## roulade
03 run 05 trill

## round
◇ *anagram indicator* ◇ *containment indicator* ◇ *reversal indicator* **01** ◯ **03** fat, lap, orb **04** ball, band, beat, bend, bout, coil, disc, disk, full, game, heat, hoop, past, path, ring, rota, tour, walk **05** about, ample, cycle, flank, globe, globy, level, plump, rough, route, scope, skirt, stage, stout **06** around, beyond, bypass, candid, chubby, circle, course, curved, honest, patrol, period, portly, rotund, series, sphere, sphery **07** all over, circlet, circuit, discoid, globate, go round, rounded, routine, session, whisper **08** circular, cylinder, disclike, framed by, globular, hooplike, milk-walk, move past, sequence, sonorous, spheroid, to and fro, vigorous **09** corpulent, discoidal, enclosing, estimated, finish off, full-orbed, globelike, imprecise, orbicular, spherical, unsparing **10** ball-shaped, disc-shaped, encircling, enveloping, everywhere, indirectly, on all sides, ring-shaped, succession, throughout, to all parts **11** approximate, cylindrical, on every side, plain-spoken, surrounding, travel round, unqualified **12** circuitously, encompassing, everywhere in, here and there, on all sides of, to all parts of **13** on every side of **15** in all directions
• **round about 01** c **02** ca **03** cir **04** circ **05** about, circa **06** around, nearly **07** close to, loosely, roughly **09** just about, not far off, rounded up **10** give or take, more or less **11** approaching, rounded down **13** approximately, in the region of, or thereabouts, something like **14** in round numbers **15** in the vicinity of
• **round off 03** cap, end **04** turn **05** close, crown **06** finish, parcel, top off **08** complete, conclude **09** finish off
• **round on 05** abuse **06** attack, turn on **07** lay into, set upon
• **round up 04** herd **05** group, rally **06** gather, muster **07** collect, marshal **08** assemble **13** bring together

## roundabout
**05** plump **06** rotary **07** devious, evasive, oblique, waltzer, winding **08** carousel, indirect, tortuous, twisting **09** whirligig **10** circuitous, meandering **12** merry-go-round, periphrastic **13** traffic circle **14** circumlocutory **15** circumambagious

## roundly
**06** openly **07** bluntly, frankly, sharply **08** fiercely, severely **09** intensely, violently **10** completely, forcefully, rigorously, thoroughly, vehemently **11** outspokenly

## round-up
**05** rally, rodeo **06** muster, précis, survey **07** herding, summary **08** assembly, overview **09** collation, gathering **10** collection **11** marshalling **14** bang-tail muster

## rouse
◇ *anagram indicator* **04** call, fire, firk, move, rear, send, stir, wake, yerk **05** abray, amove, anger, awake, evoke, flush, get up, impel, raise, roust, scold, set up, shake, start, steer, stire, styre, unbed, waken **06** abrade, abraid, arouse, awaken, bumper, call up, excite, incite, induce, kindle, ruffle, stir up, summon, turn on, wake up, whip up, work up **07** agitate, disturb, inflame, knock up, provoke, shake up **08** carousal, enkindle, irritate, reveille **09** galvanize, instigate, look alive, reprimand, stimulate, suscitate

## rousing
**05** brisk, great **06** lively, moving **07** beating, violent, wakeful **08** exciting, spirited, stirring, vigorous **09** awakening, inspiring **10** incitation **11** stimulating **12** electrifying, exhilarating **13** heart-stirring **14** spirit-stirring

## rout
**04** beat, fuss, grub, herd, lick, pack, riot, roar, rowt **05** brawl, chase, crush, flock, snore **06** bellow, defeat, dispel, flight, grub up, hammer, rabble, thrash, turn up **07** beating, clamour, clobber, conquer, retreat, scatter, trounce, turn out **08** conquest, drubbing, stampede, vanquish **09** discomfit, hurricane, overthrow, shoot down, slaughter, subjugate, thrashing, trouncing **11** disturbance, put to flight, subjugation, walk all over

## route
**03** run, way **04** beat, line, path, road, send, tail, walk **05** round, trail **06** avenue, bypass, convey, course, direct **07** airline, circuit, forward, journey, passage, transit **08** delivery, despatch, dispatch, main line, sideline **09** direction, itinerary, milk round **10** flight path, navigation **11** long paddock **12** wallaby track

## routine
**03** act, run, rut, way, yak **04** dull, rota, wont **05** banal, chain, chore, drill, habit, heigh, ho-hum, lines, order, piece, round, spiel, usage, usual **06** boring, common, custom, groove, method, normal, patter, regime, schtik, shtick, system, wonted **07** formula, heigh-ho, humdrum, jogtrot, milk run, mundane, pattern, schtick, tedious, typical **08** day-to-day, everyday, familiar, habitual, heich-how, ordinary, practice, schedule, standard, tiresome, workaday **09** customary, hackneyed, mechanics, procedure, programme, treadmill, unvarying **10** monotonous, unoriginal **11** journey-work, performance, perfunctory, predictable **12** conventional, run-of-the-mill **13** institutional **14** bread-and-butter

## routinely
**07** usually **08** commonly, normally **09** regularly, typically **10** habitually **11** customarily **14** conventionally

## rove
◇ *anagram indicator* **04** roam **05** drift, range, stray **06** cruise, ramble, stroll, wander **07** meander, traipse **08** stravaig **09** gallivant, wandering **11** go walkabout

## rover
**05** Gypsy, nomad **06** nomade, pirate, ranger, robber **07** drifter, rambler, seacock, vagrant **08** gadabout, wanderer **09** itinerant, transient, traveller **10** stravaiger

## row
**03** din, oar, rag **04** bank, deen, file, line, pull, rank, roll, tier, tiff **05** argue, brawl, chain, fight, noise, queue, rammy, range, rough, scold, scrap, set to **06** assail, bicker, column, dust-up, fracas, hubbub, racket, rumpus, series shindy, splore, string, stroke, tumult, uproar **07** bobbery, clamour, dispute, quarrel, ruction, shindig, wrangle **08** argument, conflict, rebuking, remigate, scolding, sequence, squabble **09** commotion **10** falling-out **11** altercation, arrangement, controversy, disturbance **12** disagreement **13** slanging match
• **in a row 04** arew, arow **06** in turn, serial **09** on the trot **10** back to back **12** continuously, sequentially, successively **13** consecutively **15** uninterruptedly

## rowan
**04** sorb

## rowdy
**03** yob **04** loud, lout, wild **05** money, noisy, rorty, rough, tough, yahoo, yobbo **06** apache, blowsy, blowzy, keelie, unruly **07** brawler, hoodlum, lawless, riotous, ruffian, stroppy **08** hooligan, larrikin, tearaway **09** bovver boy **10** boisterous, brat packer, disorderly **12** obstreperous, unrestrained

## rower
**03** oar **06** stroke **07** oarsman, sculler **09** oarswoman, stroke oar

## rowing
*Rowing-related terms include:*

**03** bow, cox, rig
**04** crew, easy, four, gate, keel, loom, pair, quad, rate, skeg, span, wash
**05** blade, catch, coxed, drive, eight, pitch, scull, shell, stern
**06** boatie, button, collar, gunnel, length, puddle, rating, rigger, skying, stroke
**07** bowside, coxless, gunwale, regatta, row over, sculler
**08** coxswain, paddling, rowlocks
**09** ergometer, head races, outrigger, slide seat, stretcher
**10** catch a crab, feathering, pivot point, strokeside
**11** double scull, single scull, the Boat Race
**13** getting spoons
**15** jumping the slide
• **rowing boat 04** four, pair **05** eight

## royal

**04** king, real, rial, ryal **05** grand, queen, regal **06** august, kingly, prince, regius, superb **07** queenly, stately **08** imperial, imposing, kinglike, majestic, princely, princess, splendid **09** basilical, queenlike, sovereign **10** impressive **11** magnificent, monarchical

## royally

**07** grandly, greatly **08** superbly **10** splendidly **11** wonderfully **12** impressively, tremendously **13** magnificently

## royalty

**08** residual

## rub

◇ *anagram indicator* **03** dub, pat, rob, wax **04** buff, faze, fret, snag, soap, wipe **05** apply, catch, chafe, clean, curry, emery, grate, grind, hitch, knead, pinch, put on, rosin, scour, scrub, shine, smear, stone, towel **06** abrade, buff up, caress, fondle, fridge, impede, liquor, nuzzle, polish, rubber, scrape, smooth, spread, stroke, work in **07** burnish, flannel, furbish, massage, problem, rub-down, scratch, snuzzle, trouble **08** drawback, irritate, kneading, obstacle, soft-soap **09** embrocate, hindrance, triturate **10** difficulty, impediment
• **rub along 04** cope **05** get by, get on **06** manage **08** get along
• **rub down 03** dry **04** wash, wisp **05** clean, curry **06** smooth, sponge **07** massage **08** wash down
• **rub in 06** harp on, stress **08** insist on **09** emphasize, highlight, underline **10** make much of
• **rub off on 05** alter **06** affect, change **09** influence, transform **14** have an effect on
• **rub out 04** do in, kill **05** erase **06** cancel, delete, efface, murder **07** bump off **09** eliminate, finish off, liquidate **10** do away with, obliterate, put to death **11** assassinate
• **rub up the wrong way 03** bug, get, irk, vex **05** anger, annoy, get to, peeve **06** needle, niggle, wind up **08** irritate **11** get your goat **13** get up your nose

## rubber

*Rubber types and trees include:*

**03** ule
**04** buna, cold, foam, hard, hule, pará, root
**05** butyl, crêpe, hevea, India, Lagos, sorbo
**06** sponge
**07** ebonite, guayule, seringa
**08** Funtumia, neoprene, Silastic®
**09** camelback, vulcanite
**10** caoutchouc, gum elastic, mangabeira
**14** high-hysteresis

## rubberneck

**04** gape, gawk, gawp, view **05** stare, watch **06** goggle, look at **07** tourist

## rubbish

◇ *anagram indicator* **03** red, rot, tat **04** blah, bosh, bull, bunk, dirt, gash, grot, guff, junk, kack, mush, redd, tosh **05** balls, bilge, brock, chaff, culch, dreck, dross, garbo, hokum, hooey, pants, scrap, stuff, trade, trash, tripe, truck, waste **06** bunkum, cultch, debris, drivel, litter, piffle, raffle, refuse, rubble **07** baloney, eyewash, garbage, gubbins, hogwash, mullock, rhubarb, twaddle **08** bulldust, claptrap, cobblers, detritus, malarkey, nonsense, riff-raff, tommyrot, trashery, trumpery **09** bull's wool, criticize, gibberish, moonshine, mouthwash, poppycock, sweepings **10** balderdash, clamjamfry, codswallop, excrementa, tomfoolery **11** clanjamfray **12** clamjamphrie, gobbledegook, gobbledygook
*See also* **nonsense**

## rubbish heap

**03** tip **04** coup, cowp, dump, toom **06** midden **08** laystall **09** scrapheap **13** kitchen midden

## rubbishy

**05** cheap, junky, petty, tatty, tripy **06** cruddy, crummy, grotty, paltry, shoddy, tawdry, tinpot, trashy, tripey **08** gimcrack, inferior, riff-raff **09** third-rate, throw-away, valueless, worthless **10** low-quality, second-rate **14** unsatisfactory

## rubble

**04** muck **05** ruins, waste, wreck **06** debris **07** moellon, remains, rubbish **08** hard core, wreckage **09** fragments

## rubidium

**02** Rb

## ruby

**05** agate, balas, blood **06** redden **09** starstone **12** pigeon's-blood

## ruction

**03** din, row **04** fuss, rout, to-do **05** brawl, noise, scrap, storm **06** fracas, racket, ruckus, ruffle, rumpus, uproar **07** carry-on, dispute, protest, quarrel, rookery, trouble **09** commotion, hue and cry, kerfuffle **11** altercation, disturbance

## ruddy

**03** red **04** rosy **05** fresh **06** bloody, blowsy, blowzy, bright, cherry, darned, dashed, florid, rubric **07** blasted, crimson, flushed, glowing, healthy, reddish, rubious, scarlet **08** annoying, blooming, blushing, flipping, infernal, rubicund, sanguine, sunburnt **10** confounded **11** carnationed, flammulated **12** apple-cheeked, high-coloured

## rude

◇ *anagram indicator* **04** blue, curt, lewd **05** basic, bawdy, crude, dirty, gross, harsh, nasty, rough, sharp, short **06** abrupt, cheeky, coarse, filthy, ribald, risqué, robust, rugged, simple, smutty, sudden, vulgar **07** abusive, bestial, boorish, brusque, ill-bred, naughty, obscene, peasant, uncivil, uncouth, violent **08** barbaric, churlish, ignorant, impolite, improper, impudent, indecent, insolent **09** barbarian, giant rude, goustrous, insulting, makeshift, offensive, primitive, salacious, startling, unrefined, unskilled, untutored, unwrought **10** heathenish, illiterate, indelicate, uncultured, uneducated, unexpected, unpleasant, unpolished **11** bad-mannered, bad-tempered, ill-mannered, impertinent, near the bone, rudimentary, uncivilized, undeveloped **12** disagreeable, discourteous **13** disrespectful, rough-and-ready **14** near the knuckle

## rudely

**06** curtly **07** harshly **08** abruptly, suddenly **09** abusively, brusquely **10** impolitely, impudently, insolently **12** disagreeably, unexpectedly, unpleasantly **14** discourteously **15** disrespectfully

## rudeness

**05** abuse **09** barbarism, Gothicism, impudence, insolence, rusticity **10** bad manners, disrespect, ill manners, incivility **11** discourtesy, grossièreté, uncouthness **12** impertinence, impoliteness **14** unpleasantness

## rudimentary

**03** pro- **05** basic, crude, rough **06** simple **07** initial, primary, reduced, seminal **08** inchoate **09** embryonic, embryotic, essential, imperfect, makeshift, primitive, remaining, surviving, vestigial **10** elementary, incomplete, primordial **11** abecedarian, fundamental, undeveloped **12** functionless, introductory **13** rough-and-ready **15** unsophisticated

## rudiments

**03** ABC **05** abcee, absey **06** basics **08** elements **10** beginnings, essentials, principles **11** foundations **12** fundamentals **15** first principles

## rue

**03** rew **04** pity, Ruta **05** mourn **06** bemoan, bewail, grieve, lament, regret, repent, sorrow **07** be sorry, deplore, harmala **09** herb-grace **10** repentance, thalictrum **11** be regretful, herb-of-grace **14** feel remorse for

## rueful

**03** sad **05** sorry **06** dismal, woeful **07** doleful, piteous, pitiful **08** contrite, grievous, mournful, penitent, pitiable **09** plaintive, regretful, repentant, sorrowful, woebegone **10** apologetic, deplorable, lugubrious, melancholy, remorseful **15** self-reproachful

## ruff

**03** ree **04** band, pope, slam **05** frill, reeve, rough, trump **06** fraise, ruffle, tippet **07** applaud, elation, partlet **08** applause **09** blackfish **10** excitement

## ruffian

**03** ned, yob **04** hoon, lout, thug **05** brute, bully, rogue, rough, rowdy, tough, yobbo **06** Apache, booner, brutal, rascal, thuggo, toerag

**07** bruiser, hoodlum, sweater, villain, violent **08** bully-boy, hooligan, larrikin, plug-ugly **09** bovver boy, bully-rook, cut-throat, desperado, lager lout, miscreant, roughneck, ruffianly, scoundrel **10** highbinder **11** trailbaston

**ruffle**

◇ *anagram indicator* **03** bug, irk, vex **04** fold, line, rile, ruff, tuck **05** anger, annoy, frill, pleat, rough, rouse, upset **06** bustle, crease, fringe, furrow, gather, hassle, nettle, pucker, put out, rattle, ripple, rumple, snatch, tangle, tousle, tumult, wind up **07** agitate, bluster, confuse, crinkle, crumple, falbala, flounce, fluster, flutter, perturb, quarrel, swagger, trouble, valance, wrinkle **08** brass off, dishevel, disorder, irritate, struggle, trimming **09** aggravate, agitation, annoyance, cheese off, drive nuts, encounter, pantalets **10** disarrange, discompose, drive crazy, exasperate **11** pantalettes **12** drive bananas **13** make sparks fly **14** drive up the wall

**rug**

**03** mat, rya, tug, wig **04** felt, haul, kali, snug **05** kelim, kilim, pilch, share, throw **06** carpet, khilim, Kirman, numdah, secure, toupee, toupet **07** bergama, doormat, flokati, matting **08** bergamot, covering, underlay **09** hairpiece, prayer mat, underfelt **11** buffalo robe **13** floor-covering, Persian carpet

*See also* **carpet**

**rugby**

**02** RL, RU **05** Union **06** footie, League **08** football **10** Rugby Union **11** Rugby League

*Rugby League teams and nicknames include:*

**04** Eels, Reds
**05** Bears, Bulls, Kiwis, Lions, Storm
**06** Eagles, Giants, Hull FC, Kumuls, Rhinos, Sharks, Tigers, Wolves
**07** Blue Sox, Broncos, Cowboys, Dragons, Knights, Raiders
**08** Bulldogs, Panthers, Roosters, Warriors, Wildcats
**09** Kangaroos, Rabbitohs, Tomahawks
**10** Lionhearts
**11** Bravehearts, Leeds Rhinos, St Helens RFC
**13** Bradford Bulls, London Broncos, Widnes Vikings, Wigan Warriors
**15** Irish Wolfhounds, Leigh Centurions, Les Chanticleers, Salford City Reds

*Rugby League-related terms include:*

**02** RL
**03** try
**04** back, feed, lock, pack, prop, punt
**05** dummy, put-in, scrum
**06** centre, hooker, in-goal, tackle, winger
**07** dropout, forward, hand-off, knock on, offload, offside, penalty, try line

**08** blood bin, drop goal, free-kick, front row, full back, gain line, goal line, halfback, handover, open side, scissors, sidestep, stand-off, turnover
**09** blind side, dummy half, field goal, place kick, scrum half
**10** charge down, conversion, five-eighth, penalty try, up and under, zero tackle
**11** forward pass, grubber kick, play-the-ball, sixth tackle, touch-in-goal
**12** dead-ball line, loose forward, three-quarter
**13** loose-head prop
**14** acting halfback
**15** twenty-metre line

*Rugby players include:*

**03** Fox (Neil)
**04** Hare (William Henry 'Dusty'), Hill (Richard), John (Barry), Lomu (Jonah), Sole (David), Tait (Alan), Wood (Keith)
**05** Batty (Grant), Bevan (Brian), Botha (Naas), Ellis (William Webb), Lydon (Joe), Meads (Colin), Price (Graham), Rives (Jean-Pierre), Sella (Philippe)
**06** Andrew (Rob), Blanco (Serge), Boston (Billy), Brooke (Zinzan), Calder (Finlay), Cotton (Fran), Craven (Danie), Davies (Jonathan), Gibson (Mike), Irvine (Andy), Kirwan (John)
**07** Bennett (Phil), Campese (David), Carling (Will), Duckham (David), Edwards (Gareth Owen), Edwards (Shaun), Farrell (Andy), Gregory (Andy), Guscott (Jeremy), Jenkins (Neil), Laidlaw (Roy), McBride (Willie John), Meninga (Mal), O'Reilly (Tony)
**08** Beaumont (Bill), Hastings (Gavin), Millward (Roger), Scotland (Ken), Slattery (Fergus), Sullivan (Jim), Williams (John Peter Rhys 'JPR'), Williams (John 'JJ'), Woodward (Sir Clive)
**09** Dallaglio (Lawrence), Farr-Jones (Nick), McGeechan (Ian), Patterson (Chris), Underwood (Rory), Wilkinson (Jonny)
**10** Rutherford (John)
**11** Fitzpatrick (Sean)
**12** Starmer-Smith (Nigel)

*Rugby Union teams and nicknames include:*

**04** Oaks, Reds
**05** Lelos, Lions, Pumas, Wasps
**06** Eagles
**07** Canucks, Dragons
**08** Brumbies, Les Bleus, Los Teros, Saracens, Waratahs
**09** All Blacks, Bath Rugby, Wallabies
**10** Gli Azzurri, Gloucester, Harlequins, Leeds Tykes, Sale Sharks, Springboks
**11** London Irish
**13** Brave Blossoms
**14** Cherry Blossoms
**15** Leicester Tigers

*Rugby Union-related terms include:*

**02** RU
**03** gas, tee, try
**04** back, cite, feed, hack, lock, mark, maul, pack, ping, prop, ruck
**05** clear, drive, dummy, phase, put-in, scrum, touch, wheel
**06** centre, hooker, in-goal, jumper, sevens, tackle, uglies, winger
**07** back row, binding, box kick, dropout, flanker, fly hack, fly-half, forward, hand-off, knock on, lifting, line-out, offload, offside, recycle, restart, try line
**08** blood bin, crossing, drop goal, free-kick, front row, full back, gain line, goal line, halfback, miss move, open side, scissors, scrum cap, set piece, sidestep, stand-off, turnover
**09** back three, blind side, breakdown, crash ball, front five, grand slam, place kick, scrum half, second row, tap tackle, third half, tight five, touchline, twenty-two
**10** charge down, conversion, pack leader, penalty try, tap penalty, touch judge, up and under
**11** cover tackle, forward pass, grubber kick, number eight, outside half, pushover try, ten-man rugby, triple crown, up the jumper, wing forward
**12** dead-ball line, inside centre, loose forward, three-quarter
**13** dummy scissors, loose-head prop, outside centre, tight-head prop
**14** against the head
**15** truck and trailer

*Rugby-related terms include:*

**03** try
**04** back, feed, hack, lock, mark, maul, pack, prop, punt, ruck
**05** clear, drive, dummy, put-in, scrum, touch, wheel
**06** centre, hooker, in-goal, jumper, sevens, tackle, winger
**07** back row, binding, dropout, flanker, fly-half, forward, hand-off, knock on, lifting, line-out, offload, offside, penalty, restart, try line
**08** crossing, drop goal, free-kick, front row, full back, goal line, half-back, open side, scissors, scrum cap, set piece, sidestep, standoff, turnover
**09** blind side, dummy half, field goal, grand slam, place kick, scrum-half, second row, tap tackle, touchline
**10** charge down, conversion, penalty try, tap penalty, touch judge, up and under
**11** cover tackle, forward pass, number eight, outside half, pushover try, spear tackle, triple crown, wing forward
**12** dead-ball line, inside centre, loose forward, three-quarter
**13** dummy scissors, loose-head prop,

outside centre, tight-head prop
**14** acting half-back

## rugged
**04** firm, rude, wild **05** bumpy, burly,
hardy, rocky, rough, stark, stony,
tough **06** craggy, jagged, knaggy,
knotty, robust, shaggy, sinewy, stormy,
strong, sturdy, uneven **07** gnarled,
uncouth **08** furrowed, muscular,
resolute, stalwart, vigorous **09** iron-
bound, irregular, tenacious, well-built
**10** determined, unwavering
**11** unflinching **13** weather-beaten

## ruggedly
**07** rockily, roughly, starkly, toughly
**08** strongly, unevenly **10** muscularly,
vigorously **11** irregularly

## ruin
◊ *anagram indicator* **03** mar **04** cook,
dish, do in, doom, fall, harm, heap,
Hell, loss, raze, sink **05** botch, break,
chaos, crash, crush, decay, do for,
folly, fordo, havoc, smash, spoil,
whelm, wreck **06** banjax, damage,
debris, defeat, injure, jigger, mess up,
penury, perish, ravage, relics, rubble,
traces, unmake **07** carcase, carcass,
cripple, destroy, failure, remains,
screw up, scupper, scuttle, shatter,
stuff up, subvert, undoing **08** bankrupt,
collapse, demolish, detritus, disaster,
down-come, downfall, lay waste,
remnants, shambles, vestiges,
wreckage **09** breakdown, devastate,
disrepair, fragments, indigence,
overthrow, overwhelm, perdition,
ruination, seduction, shipwreck
**10** bankruptcy, demolition,
impoverish, insolvency, subversion,
wreak havoc **11** destruction,
devastation **12** do violence to, make
bankrupt **13** make insolvent
**14** bouleversement, disintegration
• **in ruins** **04** sunk **06** ruined
**07** damaged, ruinate, wrecked
**08** decrepit **09** destroyed **10** broken-
down, devastated, ramshackle,
tumbledown **11** dilapidated **12** falling
apart

## ruination
**04** fall **05** decay, havoc **06** damage,
defeat **07** failure, undoing **08** collapse,
downfall, wreckage **09** breakdown,
disrepair, overthrow **11** destruction,
devastation **14** disintegration

## ruined
◊ *anagram indicator*
See **bankrupt**

## ruinous
**05** waste **06** ruined **07** damaged,
decayed, in ruins, wrecked
**08** decrepit, tottered **09** crippling,
destroyed, excessive, shattered
**10** broken-down, calamitous,
devastated, disastrous, exorbitant,
immoderate, ramshackle
**11** cataclysmic, devastating,
dilapidated **12** catastrophic,
extortionate, unreasonable

## ruinously
**11** excessively **12** exorbitantly,

immoderately, unreasonably
**14** extortionately

## rule
**01** r **03** law, raj **04** dash, find, form,
lead, line, norm, rain, ring, sway, wont
**05** axiom, canon, guide, habit, judge,
maxim, norma, order, power, raine,
reign, sutra, tenet, truth **06** custom,
decide, decree, direct, govern,
manage, method, regime, rubric,
ruling, settle, squier, squire, truism
**07** command, conduct, control,
dictate, formula, lay down, mastery,
ordinar, plummet, precept, prevail,
resolve, routine, royalty, statute
**08** dominate, dominion, kingship,
ordinary, practice, protocol, regulate,
standard, thearchy **09** authority,
criterion, determine, direction,
establish, guideline, gynocracy,
hagiarchy, influence, mobocracy,
officiate, ordinance, prescript,
principle, procedure, pronounce,
queenship, supremacy **10** adjudicate,
administer, convention, corrective,
government, leadership, mastership,
ochlocracy, prevalence, regulation
**11** be in control, commandment,
gubernation, instruction, preside over,
restriction, sovereignty, stratocracy,
tridominium **12** call the shots,
jurisdiction **14** administration
• **as a rule** **06** mainly **07** usually
**08** normally **09** generally, in general, in
the main **10** by and large, on the
whole, ordinarily **14** for the most part
• **collection of rules** **03** pie, pye
**04** code
• **rule out** **03** ban **06** forbid, reject
**07** dismiss, exclude, prevent
**08** disallow, preclude, prohibit
**09** eliminate

## ruler
*Rulers include:*

**03** aga, mir, oba
**04** amir, czar, duce, emir, head, jarl,
kaid, khan, king, ksar, lord, meer,
naik, raja, rana, rani, ratu, shah,
tsar, tzar
**05** begum, mpret, nawab, nizam,
queen, rajah, ratoo
**06** atabeg, atabek, Caesar, caliph,
consul, Führer, gerent, kaiser,
leader, mikado, prince, regent,
satrap, sheikh, shogun, sultan
**07** czarina, emperor, empress,
monarch, pharaoh, sultana,
toparch, tsarina, viceroy
**08** dictator, governor, maharani,
overlord, padishah, princess,
suzerain
**09** commander, maharajah,
potentate, president, sovereign
**10** controller
**11** gouvernante, head of state
**15** governor-general

*See also* **emperor; empress; king;
monarch; president; prime
minister; queen**

## ruling
**04** main **05** chief **06** decree **07** finding,
leading, supreme, verdict **08** decision,

dominant, in charge, judgment,
reigning **09** governing, in control,
judgement, principal, sovereign
**10** commanding, resolution
**11** controlling, on the throne,
predominant **12** adjudication
**13** pronouncement **15** most influential

## rum
◊ *anagram indicator* **03** odd **04** good
**05** droll, funny, queer, tafia, weird
**06** taffia **07** Bacardi®, bizarre,
cachaça, curious, strange, suspect,
unusual **08** abnormal, demerara,
freakish, peculiar, singular
**10** suspicious **13** funny-peculiar

## rumble
**04** boom, roar, roll **05** grasp, groan
**06** lumber, mutter **07** grumble, quarrel,
thunder **11** disturbance, reverberate
**13** reverberation

## rumbustious
**04** loud, wild **05** noisy, rough, rowdy
**06** robust, unruly, wilful **07** wayward
**08** roisting **09** clamorous, exuberant
**10** boisterous, disorderly, refractory,
roisterous, uproarious **12** obstreperous,
unmanageable

## ruminant
**10** meditative

*Ruminants include:*

**02** ox
**03** cow
**04** goat
**05** camel, sheep
**06** musk ox
**07** giraffe
**08** antelope, cavicorn
**09** pronghorn

*See also* **cattle; antelope**

*Stomachs of ruminants include:*

**05** bible, rumen
**06** bonnet, fardel, paunch
**09** king's-hood, manyplies, rennet-
bag, reticulum

## ruminate
**04** muse **05** brood, think **06** ponder
**07** reflect **08** chew over, cogitate,
consider, meditate, mull over **10** chew
the cud, deliberate **11** contemplate

## rummage
**03** tat **04** fish, hunt, junk, root, stir
**05** delve, rifle, touse, touze, towse,
towze, wroot **06** ferret, forage, jumble,
powter, search **07** examine, explore,
fossick, ransack **08** overhaul, turn over,
upheaval **09** bric-à-brac, commotion
**10** poke around, root around **11** odds
and ends **13** search through

## rumour
**03** cry, say **04** buzz, fame, goss, hint,
kite, news, talk, tell, word **05** bruit,
noise, on-dit, say-so, sough, story,
voice **06** breeze, canard, furphy,
gossip, murmur, outcry, renown,
report, repute, speech **07** clamour,
hearsay, publish, scandal, tidings,
whisper **08** put about **09** circulate,
grapevine **10** bruit about **11** bruit
abroad, fama clamosa, information,

noise abroad, scuttlebutt, speculation, underbreath **12** tittle-tattle **13** bush telegraph

## rump

**03** ass, bum, can **04** butt, coit, dock, duff, prat, rear, seat, tail, tush **05** booty, croup, fanny, nache, natch, podex, quoit, stern, trace **06** behind, bottom, breech, croupe, haunch, heinie **07** keister, remains, remnant, residue, vestige **08** backside, buttocks, derrière, haunches **09** fundament, leftovers, posterior, remainder, uropygium **12** hindquarters

## rumple

**04** fold **05** crush, touse, touze, towse, towze **06** crease, pucker, ruffle, tousle, tumble **07** crinkle, crumple, derange, scrunch, wrinkle **08** dishevel, disorder

## rumpus

**03** row **04** fuss, rout **05** brawl, noise **06** fracas, furore, ruckus, shindy, tumult, uproar **07** bagarre, rhubarb, ruction **08** brouhaha **09** commotion, confusion, kerfuffle, shemozzle, shimozzle **10** disruption, schemozzle, shlemozzle **11** disturbance

## run

◇ *anagram indicator* **01** r **02** do, go **03** cut, hit, jet, jog, own, pen, ply, ren, rin, rip, set, sty, use, way **04** bolt, call, coop, dart, dash, drip, emit, flee, flow, fold, fuse, gash, goal, go on, gush, hare, have, head, hole, hunt, keep, kind, last, lauf, lead, leak, line, lope, mark, melt, move, need, pass, pour, race, ride, road, roll, romp, rush, show, slip, slit, snag, sort, spew, spin, take, tear, tend, trip, trot, type, work, yard **05** bleed, brush, carry, chain, chase, class, corso, cross, cycle, drive, enter, glide, hurry, incur, issue, jaunt, point, pound, print, range, reach, round, route, scoot, score, shoal, slash, slide, speed, spell, split, spurt, stand, track, tract, trill **06** become, career, chance, charge, convey, course, curdle, demand, direct, elapse, extend, follow, fulfil, gallop, hasten, ladder, manage, outing, period, pierce, schuss, scurry, series, spread, sprint, stream, string, thrust, travel **07** average, be valid, carry on, cascade, clamour, compete, conduct, contend, control, execute, feature, include, journey, operate, oversee, paddock, passage, perform, possess, proceed, promote, publish, revolve, roulade, run away, scamper, scarper, scutter, scuttle, shuttle, smuggle, stretch, trickle, variety **08** be played, be staged, carry out, category, continue, distance, function, maintain, organize, overflow, pressure, progress, regulate, sequence, step on it, traverse **09** be mounted, broadcast, challenge, coagulate, discharge, enclosure, excursion, free use of, give a lift, give a ride, implement, supervise, transport, undertake **10** administer, be in effect, be produced, co-ordinate, flight path, prevalence, succession, take part in **11** be performed, be presented,

communicate, opportunity, superintend **12** be in charge of **13** be in control of, be in operation **15** travel regularly
• **in the long run** **06** at last **08** in the end **10** eventually, ultimately
• **on the run** **04** free **07** at large, escaped, pursued **08** on the lam **09** at liberty **10** on the loose, unconfined **11** running away **14** trying to escape
• **run across** **04** meet **07** run into **08** bump into **09** encounter **10** chance upon, come across **12** meet by chance
• **run after** **04** tail **05** chase **06** follow, pursue
• **run along** **04** scat **05** be off, leave **06** go away **07** buzz off, scarper **08** clear off, off you go **09** on your way **10** off with you **11** away with you
• **run along the ground** **04** taxi
• **run away** **03** cut **04** bolt, bunk, flee, lift, nick **05** avoid, dodge, elope, evade, filch, leave, pinch, scapa, steal **06** beat it, decamp, desert, escape, ignore, pocket, run off, scarpa **07** abscond, make off, neglect, nick off, purloin, scarper, vamoose **08** cheese it, clear off, overlook **09** coast home, disregard, do a runner, skedaddle, win easily **10** brush aside **11** appropriate, make off with, walk off with **12** win hands down **13** make a run for it **14** shut your eyes to, take no notice of, turn your back on
• **run down** **03** cut, hit, pan **04** bust, drop, slag, slam, tire, trim **05** knock, slate, weary **06** attack, defame, pooped, reduce, strike, weaken **07** curtail, exhaust, rubbish, run over, slag off, whacked **08** belittle, decrease, denounce, lose time **09** criticize, cut back on, denigrate, disparage, knock down, knock over **12** pull to pieces, tear to pieces
• **run for it** **03** fly **04** bolt, flee **05** scram **06** escape **07** do a bunk, make off, retreat, scarper, vamoose **09** skedaddle **11** give leg bail
• **run in** **03** nab **04** bust, jail, lift, nail, nick **05** pinch **06** arrest, collar, pick up **09** apprehend
• **run into** **03** hit, ram **04** face, meet **05** crash, equal **06** come to, strike **07** add up to **08** amount to, bump into **09** encounter, run across **10** chance upon, come across, experience **11** collide with **12** meet by chance **13** come up against
• **run off** **04** bolt, copy **05** elope, print, Xerox® **06** decamp, escape, repeat **07** abscond, make off, produce, recount, run away, scarper **09** duplicate, photocopy, Photostat®, skedaddle
• **run off with** **04** lift, nick **05** filch, pinch, steal **06** pocket **07** purloin **08** take away **09** elope with **11** appropriate, make off with, run away with, walk off with **12** make away with
• **run on** **04** go on, last **05** reach **06** extend **07** carry on **08** continue
• **run out** **02** ro **03** end **04** fail, leak

**05** cease, close, dry up **06** elapse, expire, finish **07** exhaust, give out **08** be used up **09** terminate **10** be finished **11** be exhausted
• **run out on** **04** dump, jilt **05** chuck, ditch, leave **06** desert, maroon, strand **07** abandon, forsake **09** walk out on **15** leave in the lurch
• **run over** **03** hit **04** flow, heat **05** recap **06** go over, repeat, review, strike, survey **07** run down **08** overflow, practise, rehearse **09** knock down, overthrow, reiterate **10** run through **12** recapitulate
• **run through** **04** read **05** spend, waste **06** review, survey **07** examine, exhaust, run over **08** practise, rehearse, squander **09** dissipate, go through **11** fritter away, read through
• **run to** **05** equal, total **06** afford, come to **07** add up to **08** amount to **12** have enough of
• **run together** **03** mix **04** fuse, join **05** blend, merge, unite **06** concur, mingle **07** combine **08** coalesce **09** commingle **10** amalgamate

## runaway

**04** wild **05** fugie, loose **06** flight, truant **07** escaped, escapee, escaper, refugee **08** deserter, fugitive **09** absconder **11** loup-the-dyke **12** out of control, uncontrolled

## run-down

**03** cut, ill **04** drop, weak **05** dingy, peaky, recap, seedy, tired, weary **06** grotty, résumé, review, shabby, sketch, unwell **07** cutback, decline, drained, outline, summary, worn-out **08** analysis, briefing, decrease, decrepit, fatigued, synopsis **09** enervated, exhausted, knackered, neglected, reduction, unhealthy **10** broken-down, ramshackle, run-through, tumble-down, uncared-for **11** curtailment, debilitated, dilapidated

## rune

**03** ash, wen, wyn **04** aesc, wynn

## run-in

**05** brush, fight, set-to **06** dust-up, stoush, tussle **07** dispute, quarrel, wrangle **08** approach, argument, skirmish **11** altercation, contretemps **13** confrontation

## runnel
*see* **brook**

## runner

**03** ski **04** scud, skid, slip, stem, tout **05** agent, blade, miler, racer, shoot, slide, slipe, sprig **06** bearer, jogger, sprout, stolon **07** athlete, courier, courser, harrier, slipper, tendril **08** fugitive, offshoot, smuggler, sprinter **09** flagellum, lampadist, messenger, racehorse, sarmentum **10** competitor **11** participant **13** dispatch rider
• **do a runner** **02** go **04** exit, quit **05** scoot **06** decamp, depart, go away, hook it, set out **07** do a bunk, pull out, push off, take off, vamoose **08** clear off, shove off, up sticks **09** disappear, push along **10** make tracks **13** sling your

**running**

hook, take your leave **15** take French leave
• **runners 05** field

**running**
◊ *anagram indicator* **04** easy **05** hasty **06** charge, in a row, moving, racing **07** conduct, contest, control, current, cursive, flowing, jogging, ongoing, rushing, working **08** constant, stampede, unbroken **09** candidacy, ceaseless, direction, incessant, itinerant, on the trot, operation, perpetual, shortlist, sprinting, unceasing **10** contention, continuous, leadership, management, regulation, successive **11** competition, consecutive, controlling, discharging, functioning, performance, supervision **12** co-ordination, in succession, organization **13** uninterrupted **14** administration **15** superintendency

**runny**
◊ *anagram indicator* **05** fluid **06** liquid, melted, molten, watery **07** diluted, flowing **09** liquefied

**run-of-the-mill**
**02** OK **04** fair, so-so **06** common, normal **07** average **08** everyday, mediocre, middling, ordinary **09** tolerable **11** bog standard, not up to much **12** unimpressive, unremarkable **13** no great shakes, unexceptional **14** common-or-garden **15** undistinguished

**rupture**
◊ *anagram indicator* **04** rend, rent, rift, tear **05** break, burst, crack, sever, split **06** breach, bust-up, cut off, divide, hernia, rhexis, schism **07** quarrel **08** breaking, bursting, division, fracture, puncture, scissure, separate **09** amniotomy **10** falling-out, separation **12** disagreement, estrangement

**rural**
**04** hick **06** forane, rustic, sylvan, upland **07** bucolic, country, peasant, predial **08** agrarian, agrestic, mofussil, pastoral, praedial **09** bucolical, uplandish **11** countryside **12** agricultural **13** cracker-barrel

**ruse**
**04** hoax, plan, plot, ploy, sham, wile **05** blind, dodge, stall, trick **06** device, scheme, tactic **08** artifice **09** deception, imposture, manoeuvre, stratagem **10** subterfuge

**rush**
**03** fly, ren, rin, rip, run **04** belt, bolt, bomb, call, dart, dash, fall, flaw, flow, gush, lash, leap, need, pelt, push, race, raid, rash, star, stir, tear **05** fling, flood, haste, hurry, onset, press, run at, scour, shoot, spate, speat, speed, starr, storm, surge **06** attack, bustle, career, charge, demand, flurry, gallop, hasten, random, sprint, streak, stream, strike **07** assault, cariere, clamour, defraud, quicken, speed up, tantivy, urgency,

viretot **08** activity, despatch, dispatch, pressure, rapidity, scramble, stampede **09** commotion, make haste, onslaught, star grass, swiftness **10** accelerate, excitement, get a move on, hurly-burly, overcharge, shave-grass, spring tide, starr grass **11** run like hell **13** precipitation **14** hive of activity **15** hustle and bustle

**rushed**
**04** busy, fast **05** brisk, hasty, quick, rapid, swift **06** hectic, prompt, urgent **07** cursory, hurried **08** careless **09** emergency **11** expeditious, superficial

**Russia**
**03** RUS

*Russian cities and notable towns include:*

**04** Omsk
**05** Kazan
**06** Moscow, Moskva, Samara
**07** Irkutsk
**08** Novgorod
**09** Archangel, Volgograd
**11** Archangelsk, Chelyabinsk, Novosibirsk, Rostov-on-Don, Vladivostok
**12** Ekaterinburg, St Petersburg
**13** Yekaterinburg
**15** Nizhniy Novgorod

**Russian**
**04** czar, tsar, tzar **05** Lenin, Putin, Raisa **07** czarina, Trotsky, tsarina, Yeltsin **08** czaritsa, Rasputin, tsaritsa **09** Gorbachev

*Russians include:*

**05** Khant
**06** Buryat, Ostyak
**07** Bashkir, Cossack
**08** Siberian
**09** Muscovite
**10** Volga Tatar

**rust**
**03** rot **05** decay, dross, stain, uredo **07** corrode, decline, ferrugo, oxidize, tarnish **09** corrosion, oxidation, verdigris **11** deteriorate

**rust-coloured**
**03** red **05** brown, rusty, sandy, tawny **06** auburn, copper, ginger, russet, titian **07** coppery, gingery, reddish **08** chestnut **10** rubiginose, rubiginous **11** ferruginous **12** ferrugineous, reddish-brown

**rustic**
◊ *anagram indicator* **03** hob, oaf **04** boor, carl, clod, hick, hind, rude **05** bacon, borel, churl, clown, crude, Hodge, plain, rough, rural, swain, yokel **06** borrel, clumsy, coarse, forest, hodden, oafish, russet, simple, sylvan **07** artless, awkward, boorish, borrell, bucolic, bumpkin, Corydon, country, culchie, hayseed, peasant, uncouth, woollen **08** backveld, clownish, homespun, pastoral, Strephon

**09** bucolical, chawbacon, graceless, hillbilly, Hobbinoll, ingenuous, maladroit, unrefined, uplandish **10** bogtrotter, clodhopper, countryman, indelicate, provincial, uncultured **11** clodhopping, countrified, countryside **12** countrywoman **13** country cousin, cracker-barrel **15** unsophisticated

**rustle**
◊ *anagram indicator* **04** raid, sigh **05** steal, swish **06** bustle, fissle, hustle, whoosh **07** crackle, whisper **08** crepitus, rustling, susurrus **09** crinkling, susurrate **10** whispering **11** crepitation, susurration
• **rustle up 04** make **07** scare up **10** get quickly **11** get together, put together **14** prepare quickly, provide quickly

**rusty**
**03** red **04** dull, poor, weak **05** brown, dated, rough, sandy, stale, stiff, tawny **06** auburn, copper, ginger, russet, rusted, titian **07** coppery, gingery, raucous, reddish **08** chestnut, corroded, creaking, impaired, outmoded, oxidized, time-worn **09** deficient, obstinate, tarnished **10** aeruginous, antiquated, rubiginose, rubiginous **11** discoloured, ferruginous, rust-covered, unpractised **12** ferrugineous, old-fashioned, reddish-brown, rust-coloured **13** out of practice

**rut**
**05** ditch, gouge, grind, habit, track **06** furrow, groove, gutter, system, trough **07** channel, humdrum, pattern, pothole, routine **09** treadmill, wheelmark **10** daily grind, wheel track **11** indentation **12** same old place, same old round

**ruthenium**
**02** Ru

**rutherfordium**
**02** Rf

**ruthless**
**04** fell, grim, hard **05** cruel, harsh, stern **06** brutal, fierce, savage, severe **07** callous, inhuman, vicious **08** felonous, pitiless **09** barbarous, cut-throat, dog-eat-dog, Draconian, ferocious, heartless, merciless, unfeeling, unsparing **10** hard-bitten, implacable, inexorable, relentless, unmerciful **11** hard-hearted, remorseless, third-degree, unforgiving, unrelenting

**ruthlessly**
**06** grimly **07** cruelly, harshly **08** brutally, fiercely, savagely, severely **09** callously **10** inexorably, pitilessly **11** mercilessly, unfeelingly **12** unmercifully **13** hard-heartedly, remorselessly

**Rwanda**
**03** RWA

# S

**S**
02 es 03 ess 06 sierra
• **S-shape** 04 ogee 08 swan neck

**Sabbath**
01 S 03 Sat, Sun 06 Sunday 07 Shabbat
08 Saturday

**sable**
03 jet 04 dark, inky 05 black, dusky,
ebony, raven 06 darken, pitchy,
sombre 08 midnight, zibeline 09 coal-
black, pitch-dark, zibelline 10 pitch-
black

**sabotage**
◇ *anagram indicator* 03 mar 04 ruin
05 spoil, wreck 06 damage, impair,
ratten, thwart, weaken 07 cripple,
destroy, disable, disrupt, scupper
08 spoiling, wrecking 09 crippling,
disabling, rattening, undermine,
vandalism, vandalize, weakening
10 disruption, impairment
11 destruction 12 incapacitate

**sac**
03 bag, pod 04 cyst 05 bursa, pouch,
theca 06 ink-bag, pocket, vesica
07 bladder, capsule, saccule, vesicle
08 aerostat, cisterna, follicle,
tympanum, vesicula 09 lithocyst, spore
case 10 air-bladder, nematocyst,
sporangium, vitellicle 11 gall bladder,
pericardium 12 diverticulum

**saccharine**
05 gushy, mushy, soppy, sweet
06 sickly, sloppy, sugary, syrupy
07 cloying, dulcite, dulcose, honeyed,
maudlin, mawkish 08 dulcitol
09 oversweet, schmaltzy 10 nauseating
11 sentimental, sickly-sweet

**sachet**
03 bag 04 pack 06 packet 07 musk-bag,
package 08 envelope, musk-ball, scent
bag, wrapping 09 container
12 bouquet garni

**sack**
◇ *anagram indicator* ◇ *deletion indicator*
03 axe, bag, bed, can, mat, rob 04 fire,
loot, muid, pack, raid, rape, raze, ruin
05 cards, gunny, level, pouch, rifle,
spoil, strip, waste 06 budget, firing, lay
off, maraud, notice, papers, pocket,
rapine, ravage, razing, remove, the
axe 07 boot out, despoil, destroy,
dismiss, dust bag, jotters, looting,
pillage, plunder, sacking, satchel, the
boot, the chop, the push 08 demolish,
earth-bag, lay waste, the elbow
09 depredate, desecrate, devastate,
discharge, dismissal, hop-pocket,
levelling, marauding, select out

10 give notice, plundering, the heave-
ho 11 depredation, desecration,
destruction, devastation, send packing
12 despoliation 13 make redundant
14 marching orders

**sacrament**
04 rite 05 order 06 ritual 07 mystery,
nagmaal, penance 08 ceremony,
practice 09 communion, Eucharist,
ordinance 10 holy orders, observance
11 institution 13 Holy Communion
14 extreme unction

**sacred**
04 holy 05 godly 06 divine, secure
07 blessed, devoted, revered, sainted,
saintly 08 accursed, defended,
hallowed, heavenly, priestly
09 dedicated, protected, religious,
respected, spiritual, venerable
10 devotional, inviolable, sacrosanct,
sanctified 11 consecrated,
impregnable, untouchable
14 ecclesiastical

**sacredness**
08 divinity, holiness, sanctity
09 godliness, solemnity 11 saintliness
13 inviolability, sacrosanctity
15 invulnerability

**sacrifice**
◇ *deletion indicator* 04 loss 05 forgo, let
go, offer 06 forego, gambit, give up,
victim 07 abandon, forfeit, offer up,
sacrify 08 giving-up, hecatomb,
immolate, lustrate, oblation, offering,
renounce 09 holocaust, martyrize,
molochize, sacrifide, slaughter,
surrender 10 immolation, juggernaut,
lustration, relinquish 11 abandonment,
destruction, sin-offering, taurobolium
12 propitiation, renunciation
13 acceptilation, burnt-offering, heave-
offering, heave-shoulder, suovetaurilia
14 blood-sacrifice

**sacrificial**
06 votive 07 atoning 08 oblatory,
piacular 09 expiatory 10 reparative
12 propitiatory

**sacrilege**
06 heresy 07 impiety, mockery,
outrage 09 blasphemy, profanity,
violation 10 disrespect, irreligion
11 desecration, irreverence,
profanation

**sacrilegious**
06 unholy 07 godless, impious,
profane, ungodly 09 heretical
10 irreverent 11 blasphemous,
desecrating, irreligious, profanatory
13 disrespectful

**sacrosanct**
06 sacred, secure 08 hallowed
09 protected, respected 10 inviolable
11 impregnable, untouchable

**sad**
◇ *anagram indicator* 02 wo 03 low, woe
04 blue, down, dull, glum 05 dowie,
dusky, fed up, grave, heavy, mesto,
sated, sober, sorry, staid, stiff, upset
06 dismal, doughy, gloomy, sedate,
tragic 07 doleful, earnest, joyless,
painful, pitiful, serious, tearful,

unhappy, wistful 08 constant,
dejected, downcast, grievous,
lovesick, mournful, pathetic, pitiable,
poignant, shameful, subtrist, touching,
tragical, wretched 09 depressed, heart-
sore, long-faced, miserable, sorrowful,
sportless, steadfast, upsetting,
woebegone 10 calamitous, deplorable,
depressing, despondent, disastrous,
distressed, lamentable, melancholy,
rock bottom 11 crestfallen, disgraceful,
distressing, downhearted, low-spirited,
regrettable, unfortunate 12 at rock
bottom, disconsolate, heart-rending,
heavy-hearted, in low spirits 13 grief-
stricken, heartbreaking 14 down in the
dumps

**Sadat**
05 Anwar

**sadden**
05 upset 06 deject, dismay, grieve
07 attrist, depress 08 cast down,
contrist, dispirit, distress 09 bring down
10 discourage, dishearten 14 break
your heart, drive to despair, get
someone down

**saddle**
03 col, pad, tax 04 land, load, seat, sell
05 panel, pilch, selle 06 burden,
charge, impose, lumber 07 kajawah,
pigskin, pillion 08 encumber

**sadism**
05 spite 07 cruelty 08 savagery
09 barbarity, brutality 10 bestiality,
inhumanity 11 callousness,
malevolence, viciousness
12 ruthlessness 13 heartlessness, sado-
masochism, schadenfreude,
unnaturalness

**sadist**
05 brute 06 abuser, savage, terror
07 monster 08 molester, torturer
09 barbarian

**sadistic**
05 cruel 06 brutal, savage 07 bestial,
inhuman, vicious 08 pitiless
09 barbarous, merciless, perverted,
unnatural

**sadly**
◇ *anagram indicator* 04 alas 08 dismally,
gloomily, sad to say 09 miserably,
tearfully, unhappily, unluckily,
weepingly, worse luck 10 dejectedly
11 regrettably, sad to relate,
sorrowfully 12 despondently
13 unfortunately 14 heavy heartedly

**sadness**
03 woe 04 pain 05 grief 06 dismay,
misery, pathos, regret, sorrow
07 tragedy, waeness 08 distress,
glumness 09 bleakness, dejection,
heartache, poignancy 10 depression,
desolation, dismalness, gloominess,
low spirits, melancholy, misfortune,
sombreness 11 despondency,
dolefulness, joylessness, tearfulness,
unhappiness, Weltschmerz
12 mournfulness, wretchedness
13 cheerlessness, contristation,
sorrowfulness 14 lugubriousness

## safe

**04** fine, good, hunk, sure **05** ambry, awmry, chest, peter, sound, timid, tried, vault **06** almery, aumbry, awmrie, coffer, condom, honest, immune, intact, proven, secure, tested, unhurt **07** cash box, certain, guarded, keister, prudent, upright **08** all right, cautious, defended, harmless, nontoxic, reliable, unharmed **09** innocuous, protected, sheltered, strongbox, undamaged, uninjured, unscathed **10** dependable, deposit box, depository, home and dry, honourable, repository **11** circumspect, impregnable, in good hands, out of danger, responsible, trustworthy **12** conservative, invulnerable, non-poisonous, safe and sound, safe as houses, unassailable **13** out of harm's way, unadventurous, with whole skin **14** copper-bottomed, uncontaminated, unenterprising

## safe-conduct

**04** jark, pass **06** convoy, permit **07** licence, warrant **08** passport **09** safeguard **13** authorization, laissez-passer

## safeguard

**05** cover, guard **06** defend, screen, secure, shield, surety **07** defence, protect, shelter **08** preserve, security **09** assurance, guarantee, insurance, look after, palladium **10** precaution, preventive, protection, take care of **11** safe-conduct **12** preservative, preventative

## safekeeping

**04** care, ward **05** trust **06** charge **07** custody, keeping **08** wardship **10** protection **11** supervision **12** guardianship, surveillance

## safely

**06** surely **08** securely **11** impregnably, out of danger, without harm, without risk **13** out of harm's way, without injury

## safety

**05** cover **06** refuge **07** shelter, welfare **08** fail-safe, immunity, safeness, security **09** safeguard, sanctuary, soundness **10** preventive, protection, protective **11** reliability **12** harmlessness, preventative **13** dependability, precautionary **14** impregnability **15** trustworthiness

## sag

**03** bag, dip, low **04** bend, drop, fail, fall, flag, flop, give, hang, sink, slip, swag, wilt **05** droop, slide, slump **06** falter, weaken **07** decline, spinach, subside **08** downturn, low point **09** dwindling, reduction **10** depression **11** hang loosely

## saga

**04** Edda, epic, epos, tale, yarn **05** story **06** epopee **07** history, romance **08** epopoeia **09** adventure, chronicle, narrative, soap opera **11** roman fleuve

## sagacious

**03** fly **04** able, sage, wary, wily, wise

**05** acute, canny, quick, sharp, smart **06** astute, shrewd **07** knowing, prudent, sapient **09** judicious, wide-awake **10** discerning, far-sighted, insightful, long-headed, perceptive, percipient **11** intelligent, long-sighted, penetrating **13** perspicacious

## sagacity

**05** sense **06** acumen, wisdom **07** insight **08** judgment, prudence, sapience, wariness, wiliness **09** acuteness, canniness, foresight, judgement, sharpness **10** astuteness, shrewdness **11** discernment, knowingness, penetration, percipience **12** perspicacity **13** judiciousness, understanding

## sage

**04** guru, wise **05** canny, clary, elder, hakam, orval, rishi **06** astute, expert, master, Nestor, oracle, pundit, salvia, saulge, savant **07** knowing, learned, mahatma, politic, prudent, sapient, Solomon, teacher, tohunga, wise man **08** sensible, wiseacre **09** authority, judicious, maharishi, sagacious, wise woman **10** discerning, wise person **11** intelligent, philosopher **13** knowledgeable, perspicacious

*The Seven Sages:*

**04 Bias** (of Priene in Caria)
**05 Solon** (of Athens)
**06 Chilon** (of Sparta), **Thales** (of Miletus)
**08 Pittacus** (of Mitylene)
**09 Cleobulus** (tyrant of Lindus in Rhodes), **Periander** (tyrant of Corinth)

## sagely

**04** ably **06** wisely **07** acutely, quickly, sharply **08** astutely, shrewdly **09** knowingly, prudently **11** judiciously **12** discerningly, perceptively **13** intelligently **15** perspicaciously

## saggy

**03** lax **04** limp, weak **05** loose, slack **06** droopy, feeble, floppy **07** falling, sagging **08** drooping, dropping

## said

◇ *homophone indicator* **03** quo', sed **04** quod **05** quoth

## sail

**03** fan, fly, ply, rag, van **04** boat, scud, ship, skim, soar, Vela, waft, wing **05** coast, float, glide, pilot, plane, steer, sweep, yacht **06** cruise, embark, put off, voyage **07** captain, go by sea, sea wing, set sail, skipper **08** navigate, put to sea **09** leave port **11** travel by sea, weigh anchor

*Sails include:*

**03** jib, lug, rig, sky, top, try
**04** fore, gaff, head, kite, main, moon, stay, stun
**05** drift, genoa, royal, smoke, sprit, storm
**06** bonnet, canvas, course, jigger, lateen, mizzen, square, stuns'l
**07** foretop, gaff-top, jury rig,

maintop, spanker, spencer
**08** forestay, gennaker, storm try, studding
**09** crossjack, foreroyal, moonraker, spinnaker, stargazer
**10** Bermuda rig, fore-and-aft, main course, skyscraper, topgallant
**13** fore-and-aft rig
**14** fore-topgallant

• **part of a sail 04** bunt, luff, nock, reef **05** belly **06** bonnet
• **sail into 05** shoal **06** attack, let fly, turn on **07** assault, lay into **08** set about, tear into
• **sail through 10** pass easily
**11** romp through **15** succeed in easily

## sailing

**07** boating **08** yachting

*Sailing-related terms include:*

**04** beat, gybe, helm, jibe, port
**05** abaft, fetch, lay up
**06** astern, course, leeway, upwind, yawing
**07** backing, bearing, beating, heeling, lee helm, running, tacking, yardarm
**08** downwind, gennaker, port tack, reaching, under way, windward
**09** alongside, laying off, letting go, starboard
**10** broad reach, casting off, close reach, going about, ready about!
**11** close-hauled, coming about, goose-winged, steerage way
**12** sail trimming, spilling wind
**13** across the wind, hard on the wind, starboard tack
**15** fixing a position, stepping the mast, taking soundings

## sailor

*Sailor types include:*

**02** AB, OS, PO
**03** cox, gob, mid, tar
**04** hand, jack, mate, salt, tarp, Wren
**05** bosun, janty, limey, matlo, middy, pilot, rower
**06** bargee, hearty, jaunty, lascar, marine, master, matlow, pirate, purser, rating, sea boy, seadog, seaman, swabby, topman, Triton
**07** boatman, captain, crewman, Jack tar, jauntie, mariner, matelot, oarsman, old salt, sculler, shipman, skipper, waister
**08** Argonaut, cabin boy, coxswain, deck hand, helmsman, leadsman, seafarer, shipmate, water dog, water rat
**09** boatswain, buccaneer, fisherman, galiongee, greenhand, navigator, sailor-man, sea lawyer, shellback, steersman, tarpaulin, yachtsman
**10** able rating, able seaman, bluejacket, liberty-man, midshipman, tarpauling
**11** foremastman, leatherneck, tarry-breeks, yachtswoman
**12** able seawoman
**13** canvas-climber

## saint

*Sailors include:*

**04 Ahab** (Captain), **Byng** (George), **Byng** (John), **Cook** (James), **Diaz** (Bartolomeu), **Gama** (Vasco da), **Hood** (Samuel, Viscount), **Howe** (Richard, Earl), **Kidd** (William), **Ross** (Sir James Clark), **Ross** (Sir John), **Ross** (Horatio), **Spee** (Count Maximilian von)
**05 Adams** (Will), **Blake** (Robert), **Bligh** (William), **Cabot** (John), **Cabot** (Sebastian), **Doria** (Andrea), **Drake** (Sir Francis), **Hawke** (Edward, Lord), **Henry** (the Navigator), **James** (Dame Naomi), **Jones** (Paul), **Peary** (Robert Edwin), **Tromp** (Maarten)
**06 Baffin** (William), **Beatty** (David, Earl), **Benbow** (John), **Bering** (Vitus), **Dönitz** (Karl), **Fisher** (John, Lord), **Hudson** (Henry), **Nelson** (Horatio, Viscount), **Nimitz** (Chester), **Ruyter** (Michiel Adriaanzoon de), **Tasman** (Abel Janszoon), **Vernon** (Edward)
**07 Barentz** (William), **Decatur** (Stephen), **Fitzroy** (Robert), **Hawkins** (Sir John), **Hawkyns** (Sir John), **Kolchak** (Alexander), **Lord Jim**, **Marryat** (Captain Frederick), **Pytheas**, **Raleigh** (Sir Walter), **Selkirk** (Alexander), **Tirpitz** (Alfred von), **Weddell** (James)
**08 Beaufort** (Sir Francis), **Columbus** (Christopher), **Cousteau** (Jacques Yves), **Elvström** (Paul), **Jellicoe** (John Rushworth, Earl), **Magellan** (Ferdinand), **Pitcairn** (Robert), **Sandwich** (Edward Montagu, Earl of), **Vespucci** (Amerigo)
**09 Christian** (Fletcher), **Frobisher** (Sir Martin), **Grenville** (Sir Richard), **MacArthur** (Dame Ellen), **St Vincent** (John Jervis, Earl of), **Vancouver** (George)
**10 Chichester** (Sir Francis), **Erik the Red**, **Villeneuve** (Pierre de)
**11 Collingwood** (Cuthbert, Lord), **Elphinstone** (George Keith, Viscount Keith), **Mountbatten** (Louis, Earl)
**12 Bougainville** (Louis Antoine, Comte de), **Knox-Johnston** (Sir Robin), **Themistocles**

*See also* **admiral; pirate; ship**
• **sailors** **02** MN, RM, RN **03** RAN, RFA, RYA, RYS **04** navy

## saint

**01** S **02** St **03** Ste **04** hagi-, holy, sant **05** angel, hagio-, saunt **06** hallow, patron, santon **07** tutelar **08** tutelary **11** patron saint **13** guardian saint

*Saints include:*

**03 Ivo, Leo**
**04 Adam, Anne, Bede, Gall, Joan** (of Arc), **John, John** (Chrysostom), **John** (of the Cross), **John** (the Baptist), **Jude, Lucy, Luke, Mark, Mary, Mary** (Magdalene), **Paul, Zita**
**05 Agnes, Aidan, Alban, Amand, Basil** (the Great), **Bruno** (of Cologne), **Clare, Cyril, Cyril** (of Alexandria), **David, Denis, Edwin,**

**Giles, James, Louis, Paula, Peter, Titus, Vitus**
**06 Albert** (the Great), **Andrew, Anselm, Antony, Antony** (of Padua), **Aquila, Cosmas, Damian, Dismas, Edmund, Edmund** (Campion), **Edward** (the Martyr), **Fiacre, George, Helena, Hilary** (of Poitiers), **Jerome, Joseph, Joseph** (of Arimathea), **Justin, Martha, Martin, Monica, Oliver, Oliver** (Plunket), **Oswald, Philip, Prisca, Robert, Simeon, Teresa** (of Avila), **Thomas, Thomas** (Aquinas), **Thomas** (Becket), **Thomas** (More), **Thomas** (à Becket), **Ursula**
**07 Adamnan, Ambrose, Anthony, Anthony** (of Padua), **Barbara, Bernard** (of Clairvaux), **Bernard** (of Menthon), **Bridget, Cecilia, Clement, Columba, Crispin, Cyprian, Dominic, Dorothy, Dunstan, Erasmus, Francis** (Romulus), **Francis** (Xavier), **Francis** (of Assisi), **Francis** (of Sales), **Gabriel, Gregory** (of Nazianzus), **Gregory** (of Tours), **Gregory** (the Great), **Isidore** (of Seville), **Leonard, Matthew, Michael, Pancras, Patrick, Stephen, Swithin, Theresa** (of Lisieux), **Timothy, Vincent** (de Paul), **Wilfrid**
**08 Albertus** (Magnus), **Angelico, Barnabas, Benedict** (of Nursia), **Boniface, Cuthbert, Genesius, Ignatius** (of Loyola), **Irenaeus, Lawrence, Margaret, Matthias, Nicholas, Polycarp, Veronica, Vladimir, Walpurga**
**09 Alexander, Alexander** (Nevsky), **Augustine** (of Canterbury), **Augustine** (of Hippo), **Catherine, Genevieve, Homobonus, Honoratus, John Bosco, John of God, Kentigern, Ladislaus, Methodius, Sebastian, Valentine, Wenceslas**
**10 Appollonia, Athanasius, Bernadette, Crispinian, John Fisher, Stanislaus, Thomas More, Wenceslaus**
**11 Bonaventure, Christopher**
**12 Justin Martyr**
**13 Martin of Tours, Thomas Apostle, Thomas Aquinas**
**14 Albert the Great, Francis de Sales, Francis of Paola**
**15 Aquila and Prisca, Cosmas and Damian, Francis of Assisi, Gregory the Great, Our Lady of Loreto, Raymond Nonnatus**

## saintliness

**05** faith, piety **06** purity, virtue **08** chastity, goodness, holiness, morality, sanctity **09** godliness, innocence **10** asceticism, devoutness, sanctitude, self-denial **11** blessedness, sinlessness, uprightness **12** selflessness, spirituality, spotlessness **13** blamelessness, righteousness, self-sacrifice, unselfishness

## saintly

**04** good, holy, pure **05** godly, moral,

pious **06** devout, worthy **07** angelic, blessed, ethical, sinless, upright **08** innocent, spotless, virtuous **09** believing, blameless, religious, righteous, saintlike, spiritual **10** God-fearing

## sake

**03** aim **04** gain, goal, good, saki **05** cause **06** behalf, object, profit, reason, regard **07** account, benefit, purpose, respect, welfare **08** interest **09** advantage, objective, wellbeing **13** consideration

## salacious

**04** blue, lewd, salt **05** bawdy, horny, randy **06** carnal, coarse, erotic, fruity, ribald, smutty, steamy, wanton **07** lustful, obscene, raunchy, ruttish **08** improper, indecent, prurient **09** lecherous **10** lascivious, libidinous, lubricious, scurrilous **12** concupiscent, pornographic

## salaciousness

**08** lewdness **09** bawdiness, indecency, obscenity, prurience **10** smuttiness, steaminess **11** lustfulness, pornography **13** concupiscence, lecherousness **14** lasciviousness

## salad

◊ *anagram indicator*

*Salads include:*

**04** herb, rice, slaw
**05** fruit, Greek, green, pasta
**06** Caesar, potato, tomato
**07** mesclum, mesclun, Niçoise, Russian, seafood, tabouli, Waldorf
**08** coleslaw, couscous
**09** mixed leaf, tabbouleh, three bean
**11** bulgar wheat
**15** mustard and cress

*Salad ingredients include:*

**03** egg, ham, nut
**04** meat, tuna
**05** bacon, chard, cress, olive
**06** borage, carrot, celery, endive, lovage, potato, rocket, tomato
**07** anchovy, arugula, chicken, chicory, crouton
**08** bacon bit, beetroot, cold meat, coleslaw, cucumber
**09** boiled egg, corn-salad, green bean, new potato, radicchio, sweetcorn
**10** cos lettuce, lollo rosso, mayonnaise, salad cream, watercress
**11** salad burnet, spring onion
**12** cherry tomato, lamb's lettuce, round lettuce
**13** hard-boiled egg, roasted pepper, salad dressing
**14** iceberg lettuce, sundried tomato

*See also* **lettuce**

*Salad dressings include:*

**06** Caesar, French
**07** Italian, Russian
**10** blue cheese, mayonnaise, salad cream

11 vinaigrette
14 Thousand Island

## salamander
03 olm 07 axolotl 08 mudpuppy
10 hellbender 12 springkeeper

## salaried
04 paid 05 waged 11 emolumental,
remunerated, stipendiary
12 emolumentary

## salary
03 fee, pay 05 screw, wages 06 income
07 stipend 08 earnings 09 allowance,
emolument 10 honorarium
12 remuneration

## sale
04 deal, seal, vend, vent 05 trade
06 wicker, willow 07 for sale, selling,
traffic, vending 08 disposal
09 marketing 10 bargaining
11 transaction

*Sales include:*

04 boot, fair, work
06 autumn, bazaar, forced, garage,
jumble, market, online, public,
spring, summer, winter
07 auction, car-boot, charity,
January, private, rummage,
warrant
08 bazumble, clearing, cold call, e-
auction, tabletop
09 clearance, end-of-line, mail
order, mid-season, pre-season,
remainder, telesales, trade show
10 exhibition, exposition,
fleamarket, open market, second-
hand
11 bring-and-buy, closing-down,
end-of-season, on-promotion,
stocktaking
12 bargain offer, church bazaar,
grand opening, of the century,
special offer
13 online auction
14 pyramid selling
15 of bankrupt stock

• **for sale** 06 on sale, to sell 07 in
stock 09 available, up for sale 10 in
the shops, obtainable, up for grabs
11 for purchase, on the market
12 wanted to sell
• **sale or return** 03 SOR

## saleable
08 vendible 09 desirable 10 marketable
11 sought-after 12 merchantable

## salesperson
03 rep 05 clerk 07 shop-boy
08 salesman, shop-girl 09 salesgirl,
saleslady 10 salesclerk, saleswoman,
shopkeeper 13 sales engineer, shop
assistant 14 representative, sales
assistant

## salient
04 main 05 bulge, chief 06 signal
07 leaping, obvious, saltant 08 striking
09 arresting, important, principal,
prominent, springing 10 noticeable,
pronounced, remarkable
11 conspicuous, outstanding,
significant

## saliva
04 foam, spit 05 drool, spawl, water
06 phlegm, slaver, sputum 07 dribble,
spittle 13 expectoration

## sallow
03 wan 04 pale, sale, seal 05 adust,
ashen, pasty, sally, sauch, saugh,
waxen 06 pallid, sickly, willow, yellow
07 anaemic 09 jaundiced, unhealthy,
yellowish 10 colourless, goat-willow

## sally
04 dash, jest, joke, quip, raid, rock,
rush, sway, trip 05 amble, bound,
crack, drive, erupt, foray, issue, jaunt,
mosey, surge 06 attack, bon mot,
breeze, charge, escape, frolic, outing,
retort, sallee, sallow, sortie, stroll,
thrust, wander 07 assault, outrush,
riposte, saunter, venture 08 escapade
09 excursion, incursion, offensive,
promenade, wisecrack, witticism
10 jeu d'esprit, projection 11 snatch
squad

## salmon
03 fry, lax, lox 04 chum, cock, coho,
kelt, keta, masu, mort, parr 05 cohoe,
nerka, smolt, sprod 06 baggit, dorado,
grilse, kipper, ligger, samlet
07 bluecap, gravlax, kokanee, quinnat,
redfish, salamon, shedder, skegger,
sockeye 08 blueback, humpback,
rockfish, springer 09 blackfish,
brandling, bull trout, gravadlax
10 fingerling, ouananiche
12 Oncorhynchus

## salt
02 AB 03 sal, tar, wit, zip 04 corn, cure,
dear, leap, saut, zest 05 briny, punch,
rapid, salty, sault, smack, taste
06 marine, rating, relish, sailor, saline,
salted, savour, seaman, vigour
07 flavour, mariner, pungent, saltish,
sea-salt 08 brackish, interest, merum
sal, mordancy, piquancy, pungency,
seafarer 09 expensive, salacious,
seasoning, waterfall 10 liveliness,
trenchancy 11 acclimatize 14 sodium
chloride

*Salts include:*

05 azide
06 aurate, borate, folate, halite,
iodate, iodide, malate, oleate
07 bay salt, caprate, citrate, cyanate,
ferrate, formate, lactate, maleate,
nitrate, nitrite, oxalate, sorbate,
tannate, toluate, viscose
08 arsenite, benzoate, butyrate,
caproate, chlorate, chloride,
chromate, plumbate, pyruvate,
rock salt, silicate, stearate,
sulphate, sulphide, sulphite,
tartrate, vanadate, xanthate
09 ascorbate, bath salts, carbamate,
carbonate, glutamate,
manganate, molybdate,
periodate, phosphate, phthalate,
solar salt, succinate, table salt
10 antimonite, bichromate,
dichromate, Epsom salts, liver
salts, salicylate
11 bicarbonate, health salts,
persulphate, sal volatile

12 borosilicate, permanganate,
Rochelle-salt
13 smelling salts

• **salt away** 04 bank, hide, save
05 amass, cache, hoard, stash
07 collect, put away, store up 08 put
aside, set aside 09 stockpile
10 accumulate
• **take with a pinch of salt, take
with a grain of salt** 08 hesitate,
question 10 disbelieve 14 have
misgivings 15 have hesitations, not
fully believe

## salty
04 racy, salt 05 briny, spicy, tangy,
witty 06 lively, saline, salted
07 mordant, piquant, savoury
08 animated, brackish, exciting,
vigorous 09 trenchant 11 salsuginous,
stimulating

## salubrious
06 benign, decent 07 healthy
08 hygienic, pleasant, salutary,
sanitary 09 healthful, wholesome
10 beneficial, refreshing 11 respectable
12 health-giving, invigorating

## salutary
04 good 06 timely, useful 07 healthy,
helpful 08 hygienic, sanitary, valuable
09 practical, wholesome 10 beneficial,
profitable, refreshing 12 advantageous,
health-giving, invigorating

## salutation
03 ave, hat 04 g'day, hail, skol
05 jambo, skoal 06 homage, prosit,
salaam, salute 07 address, all-hail, ave
Mary, good-day, good-den, good-e'en,
wassail, welcome 08 ave Maria, good-
even, greeting, Hail Mary, regreets,
respects 09 goodnight, obeisance,
reverence, time of day 10 excitement,
good-morrow 11 good-evening, good-
morning 13 good afternoon
*See also* **greeting**

## salute
03 bow, cap, nod 04 hail, mark, move,
wave 05 coupé, greet, halse, salue,
salvo 06 banzai, coupee, homage,
honour 07 address, gesture, half-cap,
present, tribute, welcome 08 greeting,
Sieg Heil 09 celebrate, handshake,
recognize, reverence 11 acknowledge,
celebration, present arms, recognition
12 pay tribute to 15 acknowledgement,
make your manners

## salvage
04 save 05 salve 06 redeem, repair,
rescue, retain, savage, saving 07 get
back, raising, reclaim, recover, restore
08 conserve, preserve, recovery,
retrieve 09 regaining, retrieval
10 recuperate 11 reclamation,
restoration 12 regeneration
13 reinstatement

## salvation
06 rescue, saving 08 lifeline
10 liberation, redemption
11 deliverance, reclamation,
soteriology 12 preservation

## salve
03 saw 04 balm, calm, ease, hail, heal

**05** cream, smear **06** anoint, lotion, remedy, soothe **07** clear up, comfort, explain, lighten, relieve, salvage **08** greeting, liniment, ointment **09** harmonize, vindicate **10** medication **11** application, embrocation, preparation

**salver**
**04** dish, tray **05** plate **06** server, waiter **07** charger, platter **08** trencher

**samarium**
**02** Sm

**same**
**02** ae, do, id **03** ilk, one **04** idem, like, self, twin, very, ylke **05** alike, ditto, equal, samey, thick, thilk **06** all one, as much, mutual, thicky **07** similar, uniform **08** matching, selfsame, unvaried **09** duplicate, identical, unchanged, unvarying **10** carbon copy, changeless, comparable, consistent, equiparate, equivalent, reciprocal, synonymous, unchanging, unvariable **11** the very same **12** the aforesaid **13** corresponding, one and the same, substitutable, the above-named **15** interchangeable
• **all the same**   **03** but, yet **05** still **06** anyhow, anyway, even so **07** however **09** in any case **10** by any means, for all that, in any event, not but what, regardless, tout de même **11** by some means, nonetheless **12** nevertheless **15** birds of a feather, notwithstanding
• **the same as**   **02** iq **08** idem quod

**sameness**
**06** déjà vu, tedium **07** oneness **08** ding-dong, equality, identity, likeness, monotone, monotony **09** dead-level, mannerism **10** repetition, similarity, uniformity **11** consistency, duplication, resemblance **13** identicalness, indistinction, invariability **14** changelessness, predictability **15** standardization

**samey**
**04** same **05** alike **07** similar, tedious, uniform **09** identical **10** monotonous, unchanging **11** predictable **12** cookie-cutter

**Samoa**
**02** WS **03** WSM

**sample**
◇ *hidden indicator* **03** sip, try **04** blad, cast, core, sign, test, type **05** dummy, match, model, piece, pilot, taste, toile, trial **06** muster, swatch, taster, try out **07** examine, example, inspect, pattern, typical **08** instance, prospect, sampling, specimen, transect **09** breakbeat, foretaste, scantling **10** assay-piece, experience, indication **12** cross-section, illustration, illustrative **13** demonstration, demonstrative **14** representative **15** depleted uranium

**sanatorium**
**03** san **06** clinic **07** sick bay **08** hospital **09** infirmary **10** health farm, sanitarium

**12** health centre, health resort **13** medical centre

**sanctification**
**05** piety **06** purity **08** devotion, holiness **09** godliness **10** sacredness **11** blessedness **12** spirituality **13** righteousness

**sanctify**
**04** back, wash **05** allow, bless, exalt **06** anoint, hallow, permit, purify, ratify **07** absolve, approve, cleanse, confirm, endorse, license, support, warrant **08** accredit, canonize, dedicate, make holy, sanction, set apart **09** authorize **10** consecrate, legitimize, make sacred, underwrite

**sanctimonious**
**02** pi **04** holy, smug **05** pious **08** priggish, superior, unctuous **09** pietistic **10** goody-goody, moralizing **11** pharisaical **12** hypocritical **13** self-righteous **14** holier-than-thou

**sanctimoniousness**
**04** cant **06** humbug **07** pietism **08** saintism, smugness **09** hypocrisy **10** moralizing, pharisaism **11** complacency, preachiness **12** priggishness, unctuousness **13** righteousness

**sanction**
**02** OK **03** ban, oke **04** back, fiat, okay **05** allow **06** permit, ratify **07** approof, approve, backing, boycott, confirm, embargo, endorse, go-ahead, licence, license, penalty, support, sustain, warrant **08** accredit, approval, royalize, sanctify, sentence, suffrage, thumbs-up **09** agreement, authority, authorize, deterrent **10** green light, legitimize, permission, punishment, underwrite **11** approbation, countenance, endorsement, prohibition, restriction **12** confirmation, ratification, subscription **13** accreditation, authorization

**sanctity**
**05** grace, piety **06** purity, virtue **08** devotion, goodness, holiness **09** godliness, saintship **10** sacredness **11** blessedness, saintliness **12** spirituality **13** inviolability, religiousness, righteousness, sacrosanctity **14** sanctification

**sanctuary**
**04** area, park **05** altar, frith, girth, grith, haven, tract **06** asylum, church, oracle, refuge, safety, shrine, temple **07** Alsatia, chancel, enclave, hideout, reserve, retreat, sanctum, shelter **08** delubrum, hideaway, immunity, preserve, security **09** holy place, nymphaeum, privilege, sacrarium, safeguard **10** frithsoken, protection, tabernacle **11** reservation **12** holy of holies **14** place of worship

**sanctum**
**03** den **05** study **06** refuge, shrine **07** hideout, retreat **08** hideaway

**09** cubbyhole, holy place, sanctuary **12** holy of holies

**sand**
**04** grit, rock **05** beach, sands, shore **06** desert, strand **08** ironsand, seashore **10** wilderness
• **sand dune, sand dunes**   **03** erg **04** areg, dene, down, seif **06** barkan **07** barchan, barkhan **08** barchane

**sandal**
**04** geta, zori **05** jelly, thong **06** galosh, golosh, Jandal® **07** chappal, galoche, talaria **08** flip-flap, flip-flop, huarache, slipslop **09** alpargata **12** calceamentum

**sandalwood**
**05** algum, almug **06** santal **07** sanders **08** quandang, quandong, quantong **10** buffalo-nut **11** sanderswood **13** Barbados pride

**sandarac**
**04** arar

**sandbank**
**02** ås **03** bar, key **04** dune, kaim, kame, reef **05** esker, hurst, shelf, shoal **07** sand bar, yardang **08** sandhill **10** harbour-bar
• **opening between sandbanks**   **03** gat

**sand-eel**
**04** grig, lant **05** lance **06** launce

**Sandhurst**
**03** RMA **04** RMAS

**sandpiper**
**03** ree **04** knot, ruff **05** reeve, terek **06** dunlin, ox-bird, willet **07** sea lark **08** peetweet, redshank, sand-lark, sand-peep, sea snipe **10** greenshank, sanderling, yellowlegs

**sandstone**
**04** grit **05** fakes **06** arkose, dogger, faikes, Flysch, kingle **07** hassock **08** sand-flag **09** bluestone, firestone, greensand, gritstone, holystone, quartzite, tile stone **10** brownstone **13** millstone grit

**sandwich**
◇ *containment indicator* **03** bap, BLT, wad **04** roti, wrap **05** butty, piece, round **06** burger, hoagie, sarney, sarnie **07** toastie **09** submarine **10** jeely piece **11** intercalate, three-decker **12** double-decker **14** croque-monsieur

**sandy**
◇ *dialect indicator* **03** red **04** Scot **05** light, rusty, tawny **06** auburn, ginger, gritty, Titian, yellow **07** coppery, gingery, reddish, yellowy **08** sabulose, sabulous **09** gingerous, psammitic, yellowish **10** arenaceous **13** reddish-yellow

**sane**
**04** wice, wise **05** lucid, sober, sound **06** formal, normal, stable **07** herself, himself **08** all there, balanced, moderate, rational, sensible, yourself **09** judicious **10** reasonable **11** level-headed, of sound mind, responsible, right-minded **12** compos mentis, well-balanced **15** in your right mind

## sangfroid
**04** cool **05** nerve, poise **06** aplomb, phlegm **08** calmness, coolness **09** assurance, composure **10** dispassion, equanimity **11** nonchalance, self-control **12** indifference **14** cool-headedness, self-possession, unflappability

## sanguinary
**04** gory, grim **05** cruel **06** bloody, brutal, savage **08** bloodied, pitiless, ruthless **09** merciless, murderous **12** bloodthirsty

## sanguine
**03** red **04** gory, pink, rosy **05** fresh, ruddy **06** ardent, bloody, florid, lively **07** assured, buoyant, flushed, hopeful, roseate, unbowed **08** animated, blood-red, cheerful, rubicund, spirited **09** confident, expectant, unabashed **10** optimistic **13** over-confident **14** over-optimistic

## sanitary
**04** pure **05** clean **07** aseptic, healthy, sterile **08** germ-free, hygienic **09** wholesome **10** antiseptic, salubrious, unpolluted **11** disinfected **14** uncontaminated

## sanitize
**05** clean **06** filter, purify, refine **07** cleanse, clean up, freshen **08** fumigate **09** deodorize, disinfect, expurgate, sterilize **13** decontaminate, make palatable **14** make acceptable **15** make presentable

## sanity
**04** mind **05** sense **06** health, reason, wisdom **08** lucidity, prudence **09** good sense, normality, soundness, stability **11** common sense, rationality **13** balance of mind, judiciousness **14** responsibility **15** level-headedness, right-mindedness, soundness of mind

## San Marino
**03** RSM, SMR

## Santa Claus
**06** St Nick **10** St Nicholas **11** Kris Kringle **12** Kriss Kringle **15** Father Christmas

## São Tomé and Príncipe
**02** ST **03** STP

## sap
**03** box, git, mug, nit **04** clot, fink, fool, jerk, nong, ooze, prat, sura, twit **05** bleed, drain, erode, idiot, juice, moron, toddy **06** energy, impair, nitwit, reduce, trench, vigour, weaken **07** deplete, essence, exhaust **08** diminish, enervate, enfeeble, imbecile, palm wine, vitality, wear away, wear down **09** lifeblood, palm-honey, undermine **10** debilitate, karyolymph, plant fluid, vital fluid

## sapi-utan
**04** anoa

## sapling
**05** plant **06** tellar, teller, tiller **08** ash-plant, flittern **09** ground-ash, ground oak

## sapper
**02** RE

## sarcasm
**04** jibe, wipe **05** irony, scorn **06** gibing, satire **07** acidity, mockery **08** acrimony, contempt, cynicism, derision, mordancy, ridicule, scoffing, sneering **09** invective **10** bitterness, resentment, trenchancy **12** spitefulness
• **expression of sarcasm 03** gee

## sarcastic
**04** acid **05** sarky, sharp, snide, witty **06** biting, snarky **07** acerbic, caustic, cutting, cynical, jeering, mocking, mordant, pungent, satiric **08** derisive, derisory, incisive, ironical, sardonic, scathing, scoffing, scornful, sneering, taunting **09** invective, satirical **10** backhanded, Juvenalian, Voltairian **11** disparaging **12** sharp-tongued

## sarcastically
**09** cynically, jeeringly **10** ironically, scathingly, scornfully, tauntingly **11** satirically

## sardonic
**03** dry, wry **05** cruel **06** biting, bitter **07** acerbic, cynical, jeering, mocking, mordant **08** derisive, scornful, sneering **09** heartless, malicious, sarcastic **11** acrimonious **12** contemptuous

## sash
**03** obi **04** belt **05** lungi, scarf, shash **06** girdle **07** baldric, burdash, chassis **08** baldrick, cincture **09** waistband **10** cummerbund

## Saskatchewan
**02** SK

## sassy
**04** pert **05** fresh, lippy, saucy **06** brazen, cheeky, mouthy **07** forward **08** impudent, insolent **09** audacious **11** impertinent **12** overfamiliar **13** disrespectful

## Satan
**05** devil **06** Belial **07** Abaddon, arch-foe, Lucifer, Old Nick, Shaitan **08** Apollyon, the Devil, the Enemy **09** arch-enemy, arch-felon, arch-fiend, Beelzebub, leviathan **10** the Evil One, the serpent, the Tempter **12** the Adversary **13** the old serpent **14** Mephistopheles

## satanic
**04** dark, evil **05** black **06** damned, sinful, wicked **07** demonic, hellish, inhuman **08** accursed, devilish, diabolic, fiendish, infernal **09** satanical **10** abominable, diabolical, iniquitous, malevolent, sulphurous

## sate
**04** cloy, fill, glut **05** gorge, satay, slake **06** accloy, sicken, stodge **07** gratify, satiate, satisfy, surfeit **08** overfill, saturate

## sated
**03** sad

## satellite
**03** sat **04** aide, moon **06** colony, lackey, minion, planet, puppet, vassal **07** moonlet **08** adherent, disciple, dominion, follower, hanger-on, parasite, province, retainer, sidekick, smallsat **09** attendant, dependant, spaceship, sycophant **10** dependency, spacecraft **11** subordinate **12** orbiting body, protectorate, space station

*Satellites include:*

**03** CAT
**04** ECHO
**05** Astra, TIROS
**06** Oshumi, Rohini
**07** Asterix, Horizon, Sputnik, Transit
**08** Explorer, INMARSAT, Intelsat, Prospero
**09** Early Bird, Long March
**11** Black Knight

*See also* **moon**

## satiate
**04** cloy, fill, glut, jade, sate **05** gorge, slake, stuff **07** engorge, glutted, satisfy, surfeit **08** nauseate, overfeed, overfill

## satiety
**07** surfeit **08** cloyment, fullness **09** repletion, satiation **10** saturation **11** repleteness **12** over-fullness, satisfaction **13** gratification **14** overindulgence

## satire
**03** wit **04** jeer, skit **05** irony, satyr, spoof, squib **06** glance, parody, send-up, taxing **07** lampoon, Pasquil, Pasquin, sarcasm, Sotadic, take-off **08** raillery, ridicule, Sotadean, travesty **09** burlesque, invective **10** caricature, mazarinade **12** mickey-taking **15** comedy of manners

## satirical
**06** biting, bitter **07** abusive, acerbic, caustic, cutting, cynical, mocking, mordant **08** derisive, incisive, ironical, sardonic, Swiftian, taunting **09** invective, sarcastic, trenchant **10** irreverent, ridiculing **12** Archilochian

## satirist
**05** satyr **06** mocker, satire **07** Pasquil, Pasquin **08** parodist **09** lampooner, pasquiler, ridiculer **10** cartoonist, lampoonist, pasquilant **11** pasquinader **12** caricaturist

*Satirists include:*

**03** Loy (Myrna)
**04** Cech (Svatopluk), Isla (José Francisco de), Pope (Alexander)
**05** Börne (Ludwig), Brown (Thomas), Cooke (Ebenezer), Ellis (George), Larra (Mariano José de), Meung (Jean de), Nashe (Thomas), Nesin (Aziz), Swift (Jonathan)
**06** Butler (Samuel), Giusti (Giuseppe), Horace, Lucian, Murner (Thomas), Pindar (Peter), Wolcot (John)
**07** Barclay (John), Juvenal, Marston (John), Mencken (Henry Louis), Persius, Régnier (Mathurin), Thurber (James)
**08** Apuleius (Lucius), Beerbohm (Max), Fischart (Johann), Lucilius (Gaius), Rabelais (François)

**09** Churchill (Charles), **Delavigne** (Casimir), **Junqueiro** (Ablio Manuel Guerra), **Petronius** (Arbiter), **Whitehead** (Paul)
**10** **Mandeville** (Bernard)
**12** **Konstantinov** (Aleko)

*See also* **comedian**

**satirize**
**04** mock **06** deride, parody, send up **07** lampoon, Pasquil, Pasquin, take off **08** ridicule **09** burlesque, criticize, make fun of, poke fun at **10** caricature

**satisfaction**
**03** pay **04** ease **05** pride **06** amends, change, liking **07** comfort, content, damages, delight, payment, redress **08** pleasure, requital **09** atonement, enjoyment, happiness, indemnity, quittance, wellbeing **10** conviction, fulfilment, recompense, reparation, settlement, suffisance **11** complacence, complacency, contentment, restitution, vindication
**12** compensation **13** gratification, reimbursement **15** indemnification

**satisfactorily**
**06** nicely **08** passably **10** acceptably, adequately, favourably **11** competently **12** sufficiently

**satisfactory**
**02** OK **03** A-OK, oke **04** fair, fine, nice, okay, well **05** sweet **06** cushty, proper **07** atoning, average **08** adequate, all right, passable, suitable **09** competent, copacetic, copasetic, favorable, kopasetic **10** acceptable, convincing, favourable, sufficient, tickety-boo **11** tickettyboo, up to scratch, up to the mark

**satisfied**
**04** full, paid, smug, sure **05** happy, sated **07** certain, content, pleased, replete **08** pacified, positive, satiated **09** contented, convinced, persuaded, reassured **13** self-satisfied

**satisfy**
**03** pay **04** apay, fill, meet, sate, stay **05** agree, appay, serve, slake **06** answer, assure, defray, fulfil, please, quench, settle, supply **07** appease, assuage, content, delight, gratify, indulge, placate, qualify, requite, satiate, suffice, surfeit **08** convince, live up to, persuade, reassure **09** discharge, indemnify **10** comply with **13** be adequate for, compensate for **15** be sufficient for

**satisfying**
**04** cool **06** enough, far-out, square, way-out **07** filling **08** cheering, pleasing **10** convincing, fulfilling, gratifying, harmonious, persuasive, refreshing **11** pleasurable
**12** satisfactory

**saturate**
**03** wet **04** fill, glut, sate, soak **05** flood, imbue, souse, steep **06** drench **07** pervade, suffuse, surfeit **08** overfill, permeate, waterlog **09** surcharge **10** impregnate **14** make wet through

**saturated**
**05** drunk **06** imbued, soaked, sodden, soused **07** flooded, soaking, sopping, steeped **08** drenched, dripping, suffused, wringing **09** permeated **11** impregnated, waterlogged

**saturation**
**06** sating **07** filling, soaking **08** flooding, glutting **09** pervading, satiation, suffusion **10** permeation

**Saturday**
**03** Sat

**Saturn**
**06** Cronus

**saturnine**
**04** dour, dull, glum **05** grave, heavy, moody, stern **06** dismal, gloomy, morose, severe, sombre **07** austere **08** taciturn **09** withdrawn
**10** melancholy, phlegmatic, unfriendly **15** uncommunicative

**satyr**
**05** silen **06** satire **07** silenus **08** satirist, woodwose **09** orang-utan, woodhouse

**sauce**
**03** dip, lip **04** sass **05** brass, cheek, mouth, nerve **06** rebuke, relish **08** audacity, backchat, belabour, dressing, pertness, rudeness **09** condiment, flippancy, freshness, impudence, insolence, sauciness **10** brazenness, cheekiness, disrespect, flavouring **11** irreverence, presumption **12** impertinence, malapertness

*Sauces include:*

**02** HP®
**03** jus, red, soy
**04** fish, hard, mint, mole, ragu, soja, soya, wine
**05** apple, bread, brown, caper, cream, curry, fudge, garum, gravy, melba, pesto, salsa, satay, shoyu, white
**06** catsup, cheese, chilli, coulis, fondue, fu yung, hoisin, mornay, nam pla, oxymel, oyster, panada, reform, tamari, tartar, tomato, tommy K
**07** catchup, custard, Daddies®, harissa, ketchup, nuoc mam, passata, rouille, sabayon, soubise, supreme, Tabasco®, tartare, velouté
**08** barbecue, béchamel, bigarade, chasseur, marinara, piri-piri, salpicon, yakitori
**09** béarnaise, black bean, bolognese, carbonara, chocolate, cranberry, demi-glace, espagnole, Marie Rose, remoulade, Worcester
**10** avgolemono, chaudfroid, Cumberland, mayonnaise, mousseline, napoletana, puttanesca, salad cream, salsa verde, stroganoff
**11** bourguignon, beurre blanc, hollandaise, horseradish, vinaigrette
**12** brandy butter, sweet-and-sour
**13** crème anglaise, salad dressing
**14** Worcestershire

**saucepan**
**03** pan, pot, wok **05** fryer **06** chafer, goblet, vessel **07** milk pan, skillet **08** pancheon **09** casserole, container, frying-pan **12** double boiler

**saucy**
**04** pert, rude **05** fresh, lippy, peart, piert, sassy **06** brazen, cheeky, fruity, gallus **07** forward, gallows **08** flippant, impudent, insolent, malapert **10** disdainful, irreverent, lascivious **11** impertinent **12** presumptuous **13** disrespectful

**Saudi Arabia**
**02** SA **03** SAU

**saunter**
**04** walk **05** amble, daker, mooch, mosey, shool, shule **06** dacker, daiker, dander, dauner, dawdle, dawner, ramble, shoole, stroll, toddle, wander **07** daunder, meander **09** promenade **10** knock about **11** knock around **14** constitutional

**sausage**

*Sausages include:*

**04** beef, lamb, lola, pork
**05** blood, liver, Lorne, Lyons, snags, weeny, wurst
**06** banger, bumbar, garlic, German, hot dog, kishke, lolita, mumbar, polony, salami, square, summer, weenie, Wiener, wienie
**07** Abruzzo, baloney, Bologna, boloney, cabanos, chorizo, corn dog, kabanos, klobasa, merguez, saveloy, snarler, zampone
**08** cervelat, chaurice, chourico, cocktail, drisheen, kielbasa, linguica, peperoni, Toulouse
**09** andouille, bierwurst, blutwurst, boerewors, bratwurst, chipolata, cotechino, frankfurt, lap cheong, loukanika, pepperoni, saucisson
**10** bauerwurst, boudin noir, cervellata, Cumberland, knackwurst, knockwurst, liverwurst, mortadella
**11** boudin blanc, boudin rouge, frankfurter, Wienerwurst
**12** andouillette, black pudding, Lincolnshire

**savage**
**04** bite, boor, claw, fell, grim, maul, slam, tear, wild **05** beast, brute, churl, cruel, feral, harsh, slate **06** attack, bloody, brutal, fierce, immane, mangle **07** beastly, furious, inhuman, monster, rubbish, run down, salvage, untamed, vicious, wild man **08** barbaric, denounce, lacerate, pitiless, ruthless, sadistic, terrible, warrigal **09** barbarian, barbarous, cut-throat, dog-eat-dog, ferocious, merciless, murderous, primitive, wild woman **10** go to town on, wild person **11** pick holes in, uncivilized **12** bloodthirsty, catamountain, cat o' mountain, pull to pieces, pull to shreds, tear to pieces, tear to shreds **14** undomesticated **15** do a hatchet job on

## savagely

**07** cruelly, harshly **08** brutally, fiercely **09** viciously **10** pitilessly, ruthlessly **11** barbarously, ferociously, mercilessly **12** barbarically

## savagery

**06** ferity, sadism **07** cruelty **08** ferocity, wildness **09** barbarism, barbarity, brutality, roughness **10** bestiality, fierceness, inhumanity **11** brutishness, viciousness **12** pitilessness, ruthlessness **13** mercilessness, murderousness, primitiveness

## savant

**04** guru, sage **06** master, pundit **07** learned, scholar **09** authority **10** mastermind **11** philosopher **12** accomplished, intellectual, man of letters **14** woman of letters

## save

**02** sa' **04** free, hain, hold, keep, safe **05** guard, hoard, lay up, put by, spare, stash, store **06** budget, but for, except, export, gather, hinder, redeem, rescue, retain, screen, shield, snudge, unless **07** bail out, collect, cut back, deliver, obviate, prevent, protect, reclaim, recover, release, reserve, salvage, set free, use less **08** conserve, cut costs, excepted, keep safe, liberate, preserve, put aside, retrieve, set aside, sock away **09** apart from, aside from, be thrifty, economize, except for, excluding, safeguard, stockpile **10** buy cheaply **11** not counting **13** scrimp and save **14** live on the cheap **15** get someone out of, tighten your belt

## saving

**03** cut **04** fund **05** store **06** frugal, thrift **07** bargain, capital, careful, economy, nest egg, sparing, thrifty **08** discount, reserves **09** excepting, redeeming, reduction, resources, salvatory **10** economical, mitigating, preserving, protecting, qualifying **11** extenuating, investments, reservation **12** compensating, compensatory, conservation, preservation

## saviour

**04** Jesu **05** Jesus **06** Christ **07** Messiah, rescuer **08** champion, defender, Emmanuel, guardian, Mediator, redeemer **09** deliverer, Lamb of God, liberator, protector **11** emancipator

## savoir-faire

**04** tact **05** poise **07** ability, finesse, knowhow **08** urbanity **09** assurance, diplomacy, expertise **10** capability, confidence, discretion **11** social grace **12** social graces **14** accomplishment

## savour

**03** sar **04** hint, like, odor, sair, salt, tang, zest **05** aroma, enjoy, odour, scent, smack, smell, speak, spice, taste, touch, trace **06** relish, repute, resent, season **07** bouquet, flavour, perfume, revel in, suggest **08** piquancy, seem like **09** delight in, fragrance **10** appreciate, smattering, suggestion **14** enjoy to the full, take pleasure in, taste to the full

## savoury

**04** tapa **05** gusty, salty, sapid, snack, spicy, tangy, tapas, tasty, umami, yummy **06** canapé, gustie, nibble, samosa, spiced **07** gustful, piquant, scrummy **08** aigrette, aromatic, fragrant, luscious **09** appetizer, delicious, palatable **10** appetizing **11** amuse-bouche, amuse-gueule, bonne-bouche, flavoursome, hors d'oeuvre, respectable, scrumptious **13** mouthwatering

## savvy

**03** sly **04** keen, know, wily **05** acute, alert, canny, sharp, skill, smart **06** artful, astute, callid, clever, crafty, shrewd **07** cunning, know-how, knowing **09** judicious, observant, sagacious **10** calculated, discerning, far-sighted, perceptive, understand **11** calculating, intelligent, well-advised **13** knowledgeable, perspicacious **14** discriminating

## saw

**03** mot, say, sow **05** adage, axiom, gnome, maxim, salve **06** byword, decree, dictum, saying **07** epigram, proverb **08** aphorism **10** apophthegm **11** commonplace

*Saws include:*

**03** jig, rip
**04** band, fret, hack, hand
**05** bench, chain, panel, tenon
**06** coping, rabbet, scroll
**07** compass, pruning
**08** circular, crosscut
**09** radial-arm
**11** power-driven

## say

◇ *homophone indicator* **02** eg **03** add, put, saw **04** read, sway, tell, vote, word **05** assay, claim, clout, drawl, grunt, guess, imply, judge, orate, order, power, reply, speak, state, utter, voice **06** affirm, allege, answer, assert, assume, convey, mutter, phrase, recite, reckon, rejoin, remark, render, repeat, report, retort, reveal, rumour, speech, weight **07** comment, declare, deliver, divulge, exclaim, express, imagine, mention, observe, opinion, perform, presume, respond, signify, suggest, suppose, surmise **08** announce, disclose, estimate, indicate, instruct, intimate, maintain, rehearse **09** authority, ejaculate, enunciate, influence, pronounce **10** articulate, for example **11** come out with, communicate, turn to speak **12** put into words **13** approximately, chance to speak

• **that is to say** **02** ie, sc **03** viz **05** id est, to wit **06** namely, that is **09** c'est-à-dire, videlicet **12** in other words

## saying

◇ *homophone indicator* **03** mot, saw **04** cant, dict, read, rede, reed, word **05** adage, axiom, gnome, maxim, motto, reede **06** bon mot, byword, cliché, dictum, phrase, remark, slogan, wisdom **07** diction, epigram, fadaise, precept, proverb **08** aphorism,

apothegm, overword **09** platitude, quotation, rusticism, statement **10** apophthegm, expression **11** catch phrase **12** word of wisdom **13** household word, pearl of wisdom

## say-so

**02** OK **04** word **06** dictum, rumour **07** backing, consent, go-ahead, hearsay **08** approval, sanction, thumbs-up **09** agreement, assertion, assurance, authority, guarantee **10** green light, permission **11** affirmation **12** asseveration, ratification **13** authorization

## scab

**03** rat **08** blackleg **13** strike-breaker

## scabies

**04** itch **05** psora

## scaffold

**05** stage, tower **06** gantry, gibbet **07** catasta, gallows, hanging, sustain, the rope **08** platform **09** framework **11** scaffolding

## scald

**04** burn, leep, plot, poet, sear **05** brand, ploat, scaud, skald **06** paltry, scabby, scorch, scurfy **07** blister **09** cauterize

## scalding

**07** boiling, burning **08** steaming **09** piping hot **10** blistering **12** extremely hot

## scale

**04** coat, film, go up, leaf, scan **05** climb, crust, flake, gamme, gamut, layer, level, Libra, mount, order, palea, plate, range, ratio, reach, scope, scurf, shell, skail, weigh **06** ascend, degree, extent, furfur, gunter, ladder, lamina, plaque, series, shin up, spread, squama, tartar **07** clamber, coating, compass, conquer, deposit, measure, ranking **08** escalade, register, scramble, sequence, spectrum, surmount **09** hierarchy, limescale **10** graduation, proportion **11** calibration, progression **12** encrustation, pecking order, relative size **15** measuring system

• **scale down** **04** drop **06** lessen, reduce, shrink **07** cut back, cut down **08** contract, decrease, make less

• **scale up** **05** boost, raise **06** bump up, expand, hike up, step up **07** augment, build up, develop, enhance, further, improve **08** increase **09** intensify **10** accumulate, strengthen

## scaliness

**06** furfur **08** dandruff **09** flakiness, leprosity **10** scurfiness, squamation, squamosity **12** scabrousness

## scallop

**03** dag **04** clam, gimp, mush **05** grill **06** pecten **07** queenie **08** coquille

## scaly

**05** flaky, rough **06** branny, scabby, scurfy, shabby **07** leprose, leprous **08** lepidote, scabrous, scarious, squamate, squamose, squamous **09** furfurous **10** squamulose

**12** desquamative, desquamatory, furfuraceous

**scam**
**03** con **04** game **05** dodge, fraud, trick **06** fiddle, racket, rip-off, scheme **07** swindle **08** business **09** deception, gold brick

**scamp**
**03** imp **05** devil, losel, rogue **06** fripon, monkey, rascal, skelum, wretch **07** skellum **08** blighter, scalawag, schellum, spalpeen, vagabond **09** reprobate, scallawag, scallywag **10** highwayman **12** troublemaker **13** mischief-maker **14** good-for-nothing, whippersnapper

**scamper**
**03** fly, ren, rin, run **04** dart, dash, lamp, race, romp, rush **05** hurry, scoot, scoup, scowp **06** decamp, frolic, gambol, hasten, scurry, sprint **07** scuttle, skitter **08** scramble

**scan**
**03** con, kon **04** read, skim, test **05** check, climb, conne, judge, probe, scale, spell, study, sweep **06** go over, review, search, survey **07** CAT scan, examine, inspect, run over **08** glance at, scrutiny **09** interpret, screening **10** inspection, run through, scrutinize, sector scan **11** examination, flip through, investigate, leaf through **12** flick through, thumb through **13** browse through, investigation, scintilliscan **14** run your eye over

**scandal**
**04** blot, dirt, -gate, pity, slur **05** libel, shame, shock, smear, stain **06** defame, furore, gossip, outcry, uproar **07** calumny, obloquy, offence, outrage, rumours, slander **08** disgrace, ignominy, reproach **09** black mark, discredit, dishonour **10** defamation, dirty linen, opprobrium **11** crying shame **12** dirty laundry, dirty washing **13** embarrassment

**scandalize**
**05** appal, repel, shock **06** dismay, insult, offend, revolt **07** affront, disgust, horrify, outrage, slander **08** disgrace

**scandalmonger**
**06** gossip, tattle **07** defamer, tattler **08** busybody, quidnunc, traducer **09** muck-raker **10** talebearer **11** calumniator, Nosey Parker, sweetie-wife **12** gossip-monger

**scandalous**
**05** gamey, juicy **06** untrue **07** blatant **08** flagrant, improper, infamous, shameful, shocking, unseemly **09** appalling, atrocious, libellous, malicious, monstrous **10** abominable, defamatory, outrageous, scurrilous, slanderous **11** disgraceful, opprobrious, sensational, unspeakable **12** disreputable **13** dishonourable

**Scandinavian**
**05** Norse

*Scandinavians include:*

**04** Dane, Finn
**05** Swede
**06** Norman, viking
**08** Norseman
**09** Icelander, Norwegian, Varangian

**scandium**
**02** Sc

**scanner**

*Scanners include:*

**02** CT
**03** CAT, PET
**04** body, SPET
**07** barcode, flatbed
**10** Emi-Scanner®

**scant**
**04** bare, jimp **05** short, stint **06** barely, jimply, little, measly, reduce, slight, sparse **07** limited, minimal, sparing **08** exiguous, restrict, scantily, scarcity **09** deficient, hardly any **10** inadequate, little or no **12** insufficient

**scantily**
**06** barely, poorly **08** meagrely, scarcely, skimpily, sparsely **11** deficiently **12** inadequately **14** insufficiently

**scanty**
**03** low, shy **04** bare, hard, poor, thin **05** brief, light, scant, short, skimp, spare **06** little, meagre, narrow, scrimp, skimpy, sparse **07** limited, scrimpy **08** exiguous **09** deficient, penurious **10** inadequate, restricted **12** insufficient **13** insubstantial

**scapegoat**
**05** bunny, patsy **06** stooge, sucker, victim **07** fall guy **11** whipping-boy

**scar**
**04** mark, wipe **05** brand, cliff, hilum, scare, scaur, shock, spoil, wound **06** blotch, damage, deface, injure, injury, keloid, lesion, stigma, trauma, ulosis **07** blemish, desmoid, pockpit **08** cicatrix, pockmark, sword-cut **09** cicatrice, cicatrize, discolour, disfigure **10** cicatricle, defacement, stigmatize, traumatize **11** cicatricula, leaf-cushion **12** cicatrichule, parrot-wrasse **13** disfigurement **14** discolouration

**scarce**
**03** few **04** dear, rare **05** scant, tight **06** meagre, scanty, sparse **07** lacking, sparing, unusual **08** uncommon **09** deficient, not enough, too little **10** inadequate, infrequent **12** insufficient, like gold dust **13** in short supply
• **make yourself scarce** **05** scoot **06** go fast **07** dash off **08** run for it, rush away **10** make tracks **12** leave quickly **15** take to your heels

**scarcely**
**03** not **05** uneth **06** barely, hardly, uneath **08** no sooner, not at all, only just, scantily, scrimply, uneathes, unnethes **12** certainly not **13** definitely not

**scarcity**
**04** lack, want **05** scant **06** dearth, famine, rarity **07** paucity **08** exiguity, rareness, shortage **09** scantness **10** deficiency, scantiness, sparseness **11** infrequency **12** uncommonness **13** insufficiency, niggardliness

**scare**
**04** scar, scat, shoo **05** alarm, appal, daunt, gally, gliff, glift, panic, scaur, shock, skear, skeer, start **06** affray, dismay, fright, horror, menace, rattle, scarre, terror **07** perturb, petrify, startle, terrify, unnerve **08** frighten, hysteria, threaten **09** terrorize **10** intimidate, make afraid, scare silly **11** fearfulness **12** put the wind up **14** make frightened

**scarecrow**
**04** bogy **05** bogle, sewel **06** boggle, malkin, mawkin, shewel **07** boggard, boggart **09** galli-crow, gally-crow **10** crow-keeper **11** galli-bagger, galli-beggar, gally-bagger, gally-beggar, potato bogle, tattiebogle

**scared**
**03** rad **05** cowed **06** afraid, shaken **07** alarmed, anxious, chicken, fearful, jittery, nervous, panicky, quivery, worried **08** startled, unnerved **09** petrified, terrified **10** frightened, terrorized **11** in a blue funk **13** having kittens, panic-stricken, scared to death **14** terror-stricken

**scaremonger**
**08** alarmist **09** Cassandra, jitterbug, pessimist **11** doomwatcher **13** prophet of doom

**scarf**
**10** chaplaincy

*Scarfs, veils and other head cloths include:*

**04** caul, doek, haik, hyke, rail, sash, veil
**05** curch, fichu, haick, hejab, hijab, nikab, niqab, pagri, patka, shawl, stole, volet, whisk
**06** chadar, chador, cravat, haique, khimar, kiss-me, madras, rebozo, screen, tippet, turban, weeper, wimple
**07** belcher, chaddar, chaddor, chuddah, chuddar, dopatta, dupatta, foulard, kufiyah, modesty, muffler, necktie, orarium, puggery, puggree, whimple, yashmak
**08** babushka, chrismal, kaffiyeh, kalyptra, keffiyeh, kerchief, mantilla, neckatee, puggaree, vexillum
**09** comforter, headcloth, headscarf, muffettee
**10** fascinator, headsquare, lambrequin
**11** kiss-me-quick, neckerchief, nightingale

**scarlet**
**03** red **06** redden, vermil **07** vermeil, vermell, vermily **08** cardinal **09** vermeille, vermilion

## scarper
**02** go **04** bolt, flee, flit **05** leave, scram **06** beat it, decamp, depart, escape, vanish **07** abscond, bunk off, do a bunk, run away, vamoose **08** clear off, run for it **09** disappear, skedaddle **10** hightail it **13** make a run for it

## scary
**05** eerie, hairy **06** creepy, skeary, skeery, spooky **08** alarming, chilling, daunting, fearsome, shocking, timorous **10** disturbing, forbidding, formidable, horrifying, petrifying, terrifying **11** frightening, hair-raising **12** intimidating, white-knuckle **13** bloodcurdling, spine-chilling

## scathing
**04** acid **05** harsh **06** biting, bitter, brutal, fierce, savage, severe **07** caustic, cutting, mordant **08** critical, scornful, stinging **09** ferocious, sarcastic, trenchant, unsparing, vitriolic, withering **11** detrimental, devastating

## scatter
◇ *anagram indicator* **03** dot, sow **05** blind, fling, flurr, scail, scale, shake, skail, strew **06** berley, burley, dispel, divide, litter, shower, spread **07** break up, diffuse, disband, disject, scamble, shatter, spatter **08** disperse, disunite, separate, splutter, sprinkle, squander **09** bescatter, broadcast, dissipate **10** dispersion, scattering, sprinkling **11** backscatter, disseminate, intersperse **12** disintegrate **14** cast to the winds **15** fling to the winds, throw to the winds

## scatterbrained
**05** ditsy, ditzy, dizzy **06** scatty **08** carefree, careless **09** airheaded, forgetful, frivolous, impulsive, slaphappy **10** unreliable **11** empty-headed, hare-brained, inattentive, thoughtless **12** absent-minded **13** irresponsible, wool-gathering **14** feather-brained

## scattering
**03** few **07** break-up, handful, poor-oot, pour-out **10** dispersion, smattering, sprinkling **12** disgregation

## scatty
◇ *anagram indicator* **10** abstracted **11** empty-headed, hare-brained, harum-scarum **12** absent-minded **14** scatterbrained

## scavenge
**04** hunt, rake **06** forage, search **07** cleanse, look for, rummage **08** scrounge

## scavenger
**04** dieb, hyen **05** hyena, raker **06** hyaena, jackal **07** forager, gorcrow, scaffie, vulture **08** caracara, night-man, rummager, scavager **09** scrounger **13** lion's provider

## scenario
**04** plan, plot **05** scene, state **06** résumé, scheme, script **07** outline, summary **08** sequence, synopsis **09** programme, situation, storyline **10** continuity, projection, screenplay **13** circumstances **14** state of affairs

## scene
**03** act, set **04** area, clip, fuss, part, show, site, spot, to-do, veil, view **05** arena, drama, field, place, scena, sight, stage, vista **06** circus, furore, locale, milieu, screen **07** context, curtain, display, episode, outlook, pageant, picture, scenery, setting, tableau, tantrum **08** backdrop, division, incident, locality, location, outburst, panorama, position, prospect **09** commotion, induction, kerfuffle, landscape, situation, spectacle **10** background, exhibition, proceeding, speciality **11** environment, performance, streetscape, whereabouts **13** tableau vivant **14** area of activity, area of interest **15** three-ring circus
• **behind the scenes** **06** within **08** secretly **09** backstage, in private, privately **10** on the quiet, out of sight **11** not in public **15** surreptitiously
• **scenes** **04** play

## scenery
**03** set **04** view **05** décor, scene, vista **07** film set, outlook, scenary, setting, terrain **08** backdrop, panorama, prospect **09** landscape **10** background **11** mise-en-scène **12** surroundings

## scenic
**05** grand **06** pretty **08** striking **09** beautiful, panoramic **10** attractive, impressive **11** picturesque, spectacular **12** awe-inspiring, breathtaking

## scent
**04** nose, odor, sent, vent, waft **05** aroma, fumet, odour, sense, smell, sniff, spoor, trace, track, trail **06** detect **07** bouquet, cologne, discern, essence, fumette, nose out, perfume **08** perceive, sniff out **09** fragrance, recognize, redolence **11** toilet water **12** eau-de-cologne **13** become aware of, eau-de-toilette

## scented
**04** rank **07** roseate **08** aromatic, fragrant, perfumed **13** sweet-smelling

## sceptic
**05** cynic **07** atheist, doubter, scoffer **08** agnostic **10** questioner, unbeliever **11** disbeliever, rationalist **14** doubting Thomas

## sceptical
**07** cynical, dubious, infidel **08** academic, doubtful, doubting, hesitant, scoffing **10** hesitating, suspicious, Voltairian **11** distrustful, incredulous, mistrustful, pessimistic, questioning, unbelieving **12** disbelieving

## scepticism
**05** doubt **07** atheism, dubiety **08** cynicism, distrust, nihilism, unbelief **09** disbelief, hesitancy, pessimism, Sadducism, suspicion **10** Pyrrhonism **11** agnosticism, incredulity, rationalism, Sadduceeism **12** doubtfulness
• **expression of scepticism** **02** ha **04** umph **09** away you go! **11** away with you! **12** pigs might fly

## sceptre
**03** rod **05** baton, staff **06** bauble

## schedule
**04** book, form, list, plan, time **05** diary, slate, table **06** agenda, assign, scheme **07** appoint, arrange **08** calendar, organize, syllabus **09** catalogue, inventory, itinerary, programme, timetable **10** enschedule
• **behind schedule** **04** late **07** overdue **10** behindhand, behind time **11** running late
• **on schedule** **05** on tap **06** on time **07** on track **08** on course, on target **15** according to plan
• **place in schedule** **04** slot **06** window

## schema
**03** map **04** form, plan **05** chart, shape **06** design, figure, layout, scheme, sketch **07** diagram, outline, profile, tracing **09** lineament **11** delineation **13** configuration

## schematic
**07** graphic **08** symbolic **10** simplified **12** diagrammatic, illustrative

## scheme
◇ *anagram indicator* **03** gin, key, map **04** dart, game, idea, lurk, plan, plat, plot, ploy, ruse **05** angle, chart, draft, frame, shape, shift, table **06** bubble, design, device, devise, layout, method, schema, sketch, system, tactic **07** collude, connive, diagram, nostrum, outline, pattern, project, tactics, work out **08** conspire, contrive, escapade, intrigue, pedigree, platform, practice, practise, proposal, scenario, schedule, strategy **09** blueprint, machinate, manoeuvre, procedure, programme, stratagem, underplot **10** conspiracy, manipulate, mastermind, suggestion **11** arrangement, delineation, disposition, proposition, pull strings **12** machinations **13** configuration **14** course of action

## schemer
**03** fox **07** plotter, wangler **08** conniver, deceiver **09** contriver, intrigant, intriguer **10** intrigante, machinator, mastermind, politician, wire-puller **11** intriguante, Machiavelli **13** éminence grise, Machiavellian, wheeler-dealer

## scheming
**03** sly **04** foxy, wily **06** artful, crafty, tricky **07** cunning, devious **08** practice, slippery **09** conniving, deceitful, designing, insidious, underhand **11** calculating, duplicitous **12** manipulative, unscrupulous **13** Machiavellian

## schism
**04** rift, sect **05** break, group, split **06** breach **07** discord, faction, rupture **08** disunion, division, scission, splinter

**schismatic**
09 severance 10 detachment, separation 12 estrangement

**schismatic**
05 rebel 08 apostate, renegade, seceding 09 breakaway, heretical 10 dissenting, separatist 12 secessionist

**schmaltz**
04 glop, gush, mush, pulp 05 slush 09 soppiness 10 sloppiness 11 mawkishness, romanticism 12 emotionalism 14 sentimentality

**scholar**
01 L 02 BA, MA 05 clerk, pupil 06 day-boy, expert, pundit, savant 07 artsman, bookman, Dantist, day-girl, egghead, Grecian, learner, Maulana, Pauline, savante, student 08 academic, bookworm, boursier, disciple, polymath, Saxonist, schoolie, Semitist, taberdar 09 authority, Gothicist, schoolboy, schoolman, Talmudist 10 Carthusian, day-scholar, mastermind, postmaster, scholastic, schoolgirl 11 philosopher, schoolchild 12 intellectual, man of letters 14 woman of letters 15 person of letters

**scholarly**
06 school 07 bookish, clerkly, erudite, learned 08 academic, highbrow, lettered, literate, studious, well-read 09 clerklike 10 analytical, scholastic, scientific 12 intellectual 13 conscientious, knowledgeable

**scholarship**
05 award, burse, grant 06 wisdom 07 bursary 08 learning 09 education, endowment, erudition, knowledge, schooling 10 exhibition, fellowship 11 learnedness, Orientalism

**scholastic**
06 subtle 07 bookish, learned, precise, teacher 08 academic, lettered, literary, pedantic 09 pedagogic, scholarly, schoolman 10 analytical 11 educational

**school**
02 GS 03 gam, pod, Sch, set 04 club, coed, high, prep, scul, sect 05 class, coach, drill, flock, group, guild, lycée, prime, scull, shoal, teach, train, troop, tutor, verse 06 circle, clique, infant, junior, league, pupils, sculle 07 academy, college, company, coterie, educate, faction, faculty, madrasa, prepare, primary, society, yeshiva 08 admonish, division, instruct, madrasah, madrassa, seminary, students, yeshivah 09 institute, madrassah, medresseh, palaestra, pre-school, secondary 10 assemblage, department, discipline, foundation, kohanga reo, playcentre, university 11 association, institution, pedagoguery 12 indoctrinate, kindergarten

Schools include:

03 LSE
04 Eton
05 Rugby, Slade
06 Ascham, Fettes, Harrow, Te Aute
07 Loretto, Roedean, St Paul's

08 Bluecoat, Hogwarts
09 Cranbrook
10 Ampleforth, Grange Hill, Greyfriars, Shrewsbury, Stonyhurst, St Trinian's, The Friends, Winchester
11 Abbotsleigh, Giggleswick, Gordonstoun, Marlborough, Perth Modern, Westminster
12 Chalet School, Charterhouse, Linbury Court, Malory Towers, Marcia Blaine
13 Dotheboys Hall, James Ruse High, Queen Victoria
14 Fort Street High, Geelong Grammar, The Kings School
15 Merchant Taylors'

See also **art; educational**

**schoolboy, schoolgirl**
see **pupil**

**schooling**
05 drill 07 reproof, tuition 08 coaching, guidance, learning, teaching, training 09 education, grounding, reprimand 10 discipline 11 instruction, preparation 12 book-learning 14 indoctrination

**schoolteacher**
03 sir 04 miss 06 master 07 dominie, teacher 08 educator, mistress, schoolie 09 pedagogue 10 instructor, schoolmarm 12 schoolmaster 14 schoolmistress

**schooner**
04 tern 12 fore-and-after

**science**
03 art, sci 05 skill 09 dexterity, expertise, knowledge, technique 10 discipline, technology 11 proficiency 14 specialization

Sciences include:

04 agri, food, life
05 earth
06 botany
07 anatomy, biology, ecology, geology, medical, natural, physics, zoology
08 chemurgy, computer, domestic, dynamics, genetics, robotics
09 acoustics, astronomy, chemistry, dietetics, economics, materials, mechanics, pathology, political, sociology
10 biophysics, entomology, geophysics, graphology, hydraulics, metallurgy, mineralogy, morphology, physiology, psychology, toxicology, veterinary
11 aeronautics, archaeology, behavioural, climatology, cybernetics, diagnostics, electronics, engineering, linguistics, mathematics, meteorology, ornithology, ultrasonics
12 aerodynamics, agricultural, anthropology, astrophysics, biochemistry, geochemistry, geographical, macrobiotics, microbiology, pharmacology

13 environmental
14 geoarchaeology, nuclear physics, radiochemistry, thermodynamics
15 electrodynamics, space technology

See also **science fiction** under **fiction**

**scientific**
05 exact 07 orderly, precise 08 accurate, thorough 09 regulated, scholarly 10 analytical, controlled, methodical, systematic 12 mathematical 13 demonstrative

See also **law**

Scientific concepts include:

04 area, heat, mass, time, work
05 force, power
06 energy, length, stress, torque, volume
07 density
08 enthalpy, momentum, pressure, velocity
09 frequency, impedance, reactance, viscosity
10 admittance, plane angle, solid angle
11 capacitance, conductance, power factor, susceptance, temperature
12 acceleration, electric flux, illumination, luminous flux, magnetic flux, permeability, permittivity
13 electric force, kinetic energy, moment of force
14 electric charge, mass rate of flow, self inductance, surface tension
15 angular momentum, electric current, moment of inertia, potential energy, velocity of light

Scientific instruments include:

06 strobe
07 coherer, vernier
08 barostat, cryostat, rheocord, rheostat
09 decoherer, heliostat, hodoscope, hydrostat, hygrostat, image tube, microtome, slide rule, telemeter, tesla coil, thyratron, zymoscope
10 centrifuge, collimator, eudiometer, heliograph, humidistat, hydrophone, hydroscope, hygrograph, iconoscope, microscope, nephograph, pantograph, radarscope, radiosonde, tachograph, teinoscope, thermostat
11 chronograph, fluoroscope, stactometer, stauroscope, stroboscope, transformer, transponder, tunnel diode
12 dephlegmator, electrosonde, oscillograph, oscilloscope, spectroscope
13 Geiger counter, phonendoscope, tachistoscope
14 absorptiometer, image converter, interferometer, torsion balance
15 electromyograph, telethermoscope

## scientist

05 brain 06 boffin, doctor, expert, genius 07 analyst, ologist, planner, thinker 08 designer, engineer, inventor 09 alchemist, intellect, magnetist 10 mastermind, researcher 11 backroom-boy 12 entomologist, experimenter, intellectual, investigator, technologist 14 explorationist, research worker
*See also* **anatomy; anthropology; archaeology; astronomer; bacteriology; biochemistry; biology; botany; chemist; computer; economist; engineer; genetics; geography; inventor; mathematics; palaeontologist; physics; physiology; psychology; zoology**

## scintilla

03 bit, jot 04 atom, hint, iota, mite, spot, whit 05 grain, piece, scrap, shred, spark, speck, trace 07 modicum, remnant, snippet 08 fragment, particle, skerrick

## scintillate

04 wink 05 blaze, flash, gleam, glint, shine, spark 07 glisten, glitter, sparkle, twinkle 09 coruscate

## scintillating

05 witty 06 bright, lively 07 shining 08 animated, dazzling, exciting, flashing 09 brilliant, ebullient, sparkling, twinkling, vivacious 10 glittering 11 stimulating 12 exhilarating, invigorating

## scion

03 imp 04 cion, heir, sien, syen, twig 05 child, graft, plant, seyen, shoot, sient, sprig 06 branch, sprout 08 offshoot 09 offspring, successor 10 descendant 11 engraftment

## scissors

06 cizers, forfex, shears 13 pinking shears

## scoff

03 dor, eat, rib 04 bolt, chow, eats, food, gall, geck, gibe, grub, gulp, jeer, jibe, meal, mock, nosh, rail, tuck, wolf 05 binge, knock, scaff, scorn, scran, snarf, sneer, taunt, tease 06 deride, devour, gall at, geck at, gobble, guzzle, nosh-up, revile 07 consume, despise, laugh at, mockery, plunder, poke fun, put away 08 belittle, chow down, eatables, pooh-pooh, ridicule 09 disparage, finish off, nutriment, nutrition 10 foodstuffs, provisions, sustenance 11 comestibles, nourishment, subsistence 12 refreshments

## scoffing

07 cynical, mocking 08 derisive, derisory, fiendish, scathing, sneering, taunting 09 sarcastic 11 disparaging 14 Mephistophelic 15 Mephistophelean, Mephistophelian

## scold

03 jaw, nag, rag, row, wig, yap 04 Fury, rage, rant, rate, yaff 05 blame, brawl, chide, flite, flyte, go off, shrew, slang,

vixen 06 berate, blow up, callet, dragon, rattle, rebuke, virago, yankie 07 censure, earbash, go off at, jawbone, lambast, lecture, reprove, rouse on, speak to, start on, tell off, tick off, trimmer, upbraid 08 admonish, harridan, reproach, spitfire, tear into, Xantippe 09 brimstone, castigate, go crook at, henpecker, objurgate, reprimand, start in on, take apart, termagant 10 take to task 11 clapperclaw 15 give it to someone

## scolding

03 row 05 doing 06 dirdam, dirdum, earful, rating, rebuke 07 chiding, hearing, lecture, reproof, rollick, wigging 08 jobation, sasarara, siserary, slanging 09 carpeting, jawbation, reprimand, sassarara, sisserary, talking-to, termagant 10 earbashing, earwigging, telling-off, ticking-off, upbraiding 11 castigation, throughgaun 12 dressing-down, through-going

## scombroid fish

04 seer, seir

## scoop

03 dig, dip, lap 04 bail, coup, grab, lade, pale 05 empty, gouge, ladle, spoon 06 bailer, bucket, dipper, exposé, hollow, latest, remove, scrape, shovel 07 helping, portion 08 excavate, ladleful, spoonful 09 exclusive, sensation 10 revelation 11 inside story

## scoot

03 run, zip 04 belt, bolt, dart, dash, rush, scud, tear 05 hurry, scout, shoot 06 beat it, career, scurry, sprint, squirt, tootle 07 scarper, scuttle, vamoose 09 skedaddle

## scope

03 aim, VDU, way 04 area, play, room, span, wale 05 ambit, field, orbit, range, reach, realm, remit, round, space, sweep, swing, verge 06 cinema, domain, extent, leeway, limits, scouth, scowth, sphere 07 breadth, compass, display, freedom, liberty, monitor, purpose, purview 08 capacity, confines, coverage, latitude 09 dimension, elbow-room 11 opportunity 12 spaciousness

## scorch

03 fry 04 burn, char, plot, sear 05 adust, blast, dry up, parch, ploat, roast, scald, scath, singe, slash, swale, swayl, sweal, sweel 06 birsle, scaith, scathe, sizzle, skaith, wither 07 blacken, frizzle, scowder, shrivel, torrefy 08 scouther, scowther 09 discolour

## scorching

05 blast 06 baking, red-hot, torrid 07 boiling, burning, searing 08 roasting, sizzling, tropical 09 withering 10 blistering, scowdering, sweltering 11 scouthering 12 extremely hot

## score

02 XX 03 cut, get, law, net, rit, run, set, sum, win 04 case, earn, gain, gash, hail, hits, line, lots, make, mark, nick,

ritt, runs, slit 05 adapt, basis, count, facts, goals, gouge, graze, hosts, issue, marks, notch, put on, slash, tally, total, truth, write 06 aspect, attain, crowds, droves, groove, grudge, incise, indent, masses, matter, points, reason, record, result, scotch, scrape, shoals, swarms, target, the gen, twenty 07 account, achieve, arrange, be one up, chalk up, concern, dispute, engrave, grounds, legions, motives, myriads, notch up, outcome, quarrel, scratch, subject 08 argument, hundreds, incision, millions, question, register 09 complaint, enumerate, grievance, reckoning, situation, thousands, what's what 10 instrument, keep a tally, multitudes, the picture 11 explanation, have the edge, orchestrate 12 be successful 13 hit the jackpot 14 state of affairs 15 the whole picture
• **even the score** 06 avenge 07 get back 09 retaliate 14 settle the score
• **score off** 09 humiliate 11 have the edge 12 get one over on
• **score out** 05 erase 06 cancel, delete, efface, remove 07 expunge 08 cross out 09 strike out 10 obliterate

## scorn

04 geck, mock, shun, spit, zing 05 blurt, spurn 06 deride, rebuff, refuse, reject, scorch, slight 07 crucify, despise, disdain, disgust, dismiss, laugh at, mockery, sarcasm, scoff at, sneer at, sniff at 08 contempt, derision, mesprise, mesprize, misprise, misprize, ridicule, sneering 09 contumely, disparage 10 look down on 11 haughtiness 12 scornfulness 13 disparagement

## scornful

07 haughty, jeering, mocking 08 arrogant, derisive, sardonic, scathing, scoffing, sneering 09 insulting, sarcastic, slighting 10 disdainful, dismissive 11 disparaging 12 contemptuous, supercilious

## scornfully

09 haughtily 10 arrogantly, derisively, scathingly, sneeringly 11 slightingly, witheringly 12 disdainfully, dismissively 13 disparagingly 14 contemptuously, superciliously

## scorpion

07 Scorpio 08 ballista, pedipalp 11 Eurypterida

## Scot

◊ *dialect indicator* 03 Mac 04 Gael
*See also* **Scottish**

## scotch

04 gash, halt, maim, ruin, stop 05 block, quash, score, strut, wedge, wreck 07 scupper, scuttle 09 frustrate 10 put an end to, put a stop to 11 put the lid on 12 bring to an end 13 pull the plug on

## scot-free

04 safe 05 clear 06 unhurt 07 untaxed 08 shot-free, unharmed 09 undamaged, uninjured, unrebuked, unscathed

**10** unpunished **12** unreproached **13** unreprimanded **15** without a scratch

## Scotland
*see* **council; town**

## Scotsman
*see* **Scot; Scottish**

## Scottish
◇ *dialect word indicator*
*See also* **monarch**

*Scottish first names include:*

**03** Ian, Rab, Rae
**04** Doug, Euan, Ewan, Ewen, Greg, Iain, Iona, Isla, Jess, Jock
**05** Ailsa, Angus, Arran, Blair, Calum, Clyde, Colin, Craig, Isbel, Logan, Lorna, Lorne, Sandy
**06** Aileen, Callum, Dougie, Elspet, Gordon, Gregor, Hamish, Kelvin, Lilias, Mhàiri, Rabbie, Ranald, Vanora
**07** Cameron, Douglas, Elspeth, Malcolm
**08** Campbell, Catriona

*Scottish clans include:*

**04** Ross
**05** Baird, Bruce, Grant, Innes, Munro, Scott
**06** Brodie, Buchan, Dunbar, Duncan, Dundas, Eliott, Elliot, Forbes, Fraser, Gordon, Graeme, Graham, Irvine, Irving, Lennox, Mackay, Macnab, Macrae, Moffat, Monroe, Murray, Napier, Ogilvy, Ramsay, Stuart
**07** Balfour, Cameron, Douglas, Macduff, Maclean, Macleod, Macneil, Malcolm, Ogilvie, Stewart, Wallace
**08** Anderson, Campbell, Drummond, Ferguson, Hamilton, Macaulay, MacInnes, Macneill, Oliphant, Sinclair, Stirling, Urquhart
**09** Armstrong, Colquhoun, Fergusson, Henderson, Johnstone, MacAlpine, MacAndrew, MacArthur, MacCallum, Macdonald, Macgregor, Macintosh, Macintyre, Mackenzie, Mackinnon, Macmillan, Nicholson, Robertson
**10** Macdonnell, Macdougall, Mackintosh, Macpherson, Sutherland
**11** MacAllister, MacLauchlan, MacLaughlan, Macnaughton

## scoundrel
**03** cur, dog, rat **04** scab **05** cheat, hound, louse, rogue, scamp, swine **06** donder, louser, rascal, rotter, scally **07** bounder, dastard, ruffian, stinker, villain **08** blighter, spalpeen, vagabond **09** miscreant, reprobate, scallywag **10** blackguard, hounds-foot, ne'er-do-well **14** good-for-nothing

## scour
◇ *anagram indicator* **03** rub **04** comb, drag, full, hunt, rake, scur, sker, wash, wipe **05** clean, flush, purge, scout,

scrub, skirr, skirt **06** abrade, forage, polish, punish, scrape, search, squirr **07** burnish, cleanse, ransack, rummage **08** clear out **14** turn upside-down

## scourge
**04** bane, beat, cane, evil, flog, lash, whip **05** birch, curse, flail, strap, trial **06** burden, menace, plague, punish, switch, terror, thrash **07** afflict, penalty, torment, torture **08** chastise, nuisance, scorpion **09** devastate, flagellum **10** affliction, discipline, misfortune, punishment **13** cat-o'-nine-tails **14** disciplinarium **15** thorn in your side

## scout
**03** cub, spy **04** case, hunt, look, mock, seek **05** flout, probe, recce, rover, scoot, sixer, snoop, spial, watch **06** beaver, escort, person, search, spying, spy out, survey **07** explore, inspect, look for, lookout, observe, pickeer, scourer, spotter, wolf cub **08** check out, outrider, scurrier, vanguard **09** recruiter, scurriour **10** discoverer, tenderfoot **11** investigate, reconnoitre, voortrekker **12** advance guard **13** talent spotter

## scowl
**04** lour, pout **05** frown, glare, gloom, lower **06** glower **07** grimace **09** black look, dirty look, overgloom **13** look daggers at

## scrabble
◇ *anagram indicator* **03** dig, paw **04** claw, grub, root **05** grope **06** scrape, scrawl **07** clamber, scratch **08** scramble

## scraggy
◇ *anagram indicator* **04** bony, lean, thin **05** gaunt, lanky **06** skinny, wasted **07** angular, scrawny, unkempt **08** raw-boned **09** emaciated, irregular **10** straggling **14** undernourished

## scram
**04** bolt, flee, puny, quit, scat **05** leave, scoot **06** beat it, depart, get out, go away **07** buzz off, do a bunk, scarper, vamoose **08** clear off, clear out, shove off, withered **09** disappear, skedaddle **15** take to your heels

## scramble
◇ *anagram indicator* **03** mix, ren, rin, run, vie **04** dash, muss, push, race, rush **05** climb, crawl, grope, hurry, mêlée, mix up, musse, scale, vying **06** battle, bustle, hasten, hustle, infuse, jockey, jostle, jumble, muddle, scurry, strive, swerve, tussle **07** clamber, compete, contend, disturb, grabble, rat race, scaling, scamble, shuffle **08** scrabble, sprattle, stampede, struggle **09** commotion, confusion **10** free-for-all **11** competition, disorganize

## scrap
**03** axe, bit, ort, rag, row **04** atom, bite, bits, drop, dump, glim, iota, junk, mite, part, shed, snap, tiff **05** argue, brawl, crumb, crust, ditch, fight, grain, patch, piece, scrip, set-to, shard, sherd, shred, trace, waste **06** battle, bicker, bundle,

cancel, dust-up, fracas, morsel, sliver, splore, stitch, tatter, verset **07** abandon, break up, discard, dispute, fall out, punch-up, quarrel, remains, remnant, residue, scissel, scissil, scuffle, snippet, vestige, wrangle **08** argument, chuck out, demolish, disagree, fraction, fragment, get rid of, jettison, leavings, leftover, mouthful, particle, quantity, skerrick, squabble, write off **09** leftovers, scrapings, throw away **11** bits and bobs, odds and ends, odds and sods **12** disagreement **13** bits and pieces
• **on the scrap heap** **06** dumped **07** ditched **08** rejected **09** discarded, forgotten, redundant **10** jettisoned, written off

## scrape
**03** cut, fix, hoe, paw, rub **04** bark, clat, claw, file, hole, mess, rake, rase, rasp, raze, skin **05** claut, clean, curet, erase, flesh, grate, graze, grind, scalp, scart, scour, scrab, scuff, shave, shred **06** abrade, hobble, pickle, plight, remove, splore **07** curette, descale, dilemma, scratch, snapper, trouble **08** abrasion, distress, scrabble, wrong box **09** curettage, shemozzle, shimozzle, tight spot **10** difficulty, praemunire, schemozzle, shlemozzle **11** predicament
• **scrape by** **05** get by, skimp **06** eke out, scrimp **13** muddle through
• **scrape through** **08** just pass **09** barely win **11** only just win **13** just succeed in
• **scrape together** **07** round up, scuffle **11** get together **12** pool together **15** just manage to get

## scrappy
◇ *anagram indicator* **05** bitty **06** untidy **07** sketchy **08** slapdash, slipshod **09** piecemeal **10** disjointed, incomplete **11** belligerent, fragmentary, quarrelsome, superficial **12** disconnected, disorganized

## scraps
**04** odds **05** brock, trash **08** dog's-meat

## scratch
◇ *anagram indicator* ◇ *deletion indicator* **03** cut, rit, rub **04** cash, clat, claw, etch, gash, line, mark, nick, race, rase, ritt, skin, tear **05** claut, curry, Devil, fluke, gouge, graze, rough, scart, score, scrab, scram, scrat, scuff, tease, wound **06** abrade, casual, incise, scramb, scrape, scrawm, streak **07** engrave **08** abrasion, lacerate, scrabble **09** haphazard, impromptu **10** improvised, laceration, ready money **11** clapperclaw, unrehearsed **13** rough-and-ready
• **up to scratch** **02** OK **08** adequate **09** competent, tolerable, up to snuff **10** acceptable, good enough, reasonable **11** up to the mark **12** satisfactory

## scrawl
**03** jot, pen **06** doodle **07** dash off, jot down, scratch, writing **08** scrabble, scribble, squiggle **10** cacography

11 handwriting 12 write quickly 14 bad handwriting

## scrawny

04 bony, lean, thin 05 lanky 06 meagre, skinny, sparse 07 angular, scraggy, scranny 08 raw-boned, underfed 09 emaciated 14 undernourished

## scream

03 cry, eek, wit 04 bawl, hoot, howl, riot, roar, wail, yawp, yell, yelp 05 comic, joker, laugh, shout 06 holler, shriek, squawk, squeal 07 screech 08 comedian 09 character 13 cry blue murder 15 shout blue murder

## screech

03 cry 04 howl, yell, yelp 06 screak, scream, shriek, squawk, squeal 07 scraich, scraigh, screich, screigh, scriech, scritch, shriech, shritch, skreigh, skriech, skriegh, ululate

## screen

03 net, VDU, vet 04 grid, hide, mask, mesh, scan, show, sift, sort, test, veil 05 blind, check, chick, cloak, cover, front, gauge, grade, grill, guard, scope, shade, sieve 06 awning, canopy, defend, façade, filter, grille, purdah, riddle, sconce, shield, shroud 07 conceal, cribble, curtain, divider, examine, monitor, netting, picture, present, process, protect, reredos, shelter 08 abat-jour, disguise, evaluate, parclose, traverse 09 broadcast, dashboard, faceplate, partition, reredorse, reredosse, safeguard 10 camouflage, protection 11 concealment, investigate, room-divider 12 clothes-horse
• **screen off**   04 hide 06 divide 07 conceal, protect 08 fence off, separate 09 divide off, partition 11 separate off 12 partition off

## screenwriter
see **playwright**

## screw

◊ *anagram indicator* 03 fix, pay, pin, rob 04 bolt, brad, milk, nail, spin, tack, turn, wind 05 bleed, cheat, clamp, force, rivet, twist, wages, wrest, wring 06 adjust, burgle, extort, fasten, pucker, salary, warder 07 defraud, distort, extract, squeeze, tighten, wrinkle 08 compress, contract, fastener, pressure 09 constrain, skinflint 10 pressurize 12 extortionist
• **put the screws on**   05 force 06 coerce, compel, lean on 07 dragoon 09 constrain, strongarm 10 pressurize
• **screwed up**   05 upset 06 hung up 07 mixed up, muddled, puzzled 08 confused, messed up 09 disturbed, perplexed 10 bewildered, disordered, distracted, distraught 11 disoriented, maladjusted
• **screw up**   04 knot, ruin 05 botch, spoil, twist 06 bungle, cock up, mess up, pucker 07 contort, crumple, disrupt, distort, louse up, squinch, stuff up, tighten, wrinkle 08 contract, summon up 09 mishandle, mismanage 11 make a hash of

## screwy

◊ *anagram indicator* 03 mad, odd 04 daft 05 batty, crazy, dotty, nutty, queer, tipsy, weird 07 bonkers 08 crackers 09 eccentric 12 round the bend 13 round the twist

## scribble

03 jot, pen 05 write 06 doodle, scrawl 07 dash off, jot down, scratch, writing 08 bescrawl, scrabble, squiggle 10 bescribble, cacography 11 handwriting 14 bad handwriting

## scribbler

04 hack 06 jotter, writer 07 note-pad 09 ink-jerker, pen-pusher, pot-boiler 10 ink-slinger 11 inkhorn-mate, verse-monger 12 paper-stainer

## scribe

04 hack 05 clerk, write 06 author, incise, mallam, penman, writer 07 copyist 08 recorder, reporter 09 pen-pusher, scrivener, secretary 10 amanuensis 11 transcriber 12 calligrapher, hierographer

## scrimmage

03 row 04 fray, riot 05 brawl, bully, fight, mêlée, rouge, scrap, scrum, set-to 06 affray, bovver, dust-up, shindy 07 scuffle 08 skirmish, squabble, struggle 10 free-for-all 11 disturbance

## scrimp

04 save 05 limit, pinch, skimp, stint 06 barely, reduce, scanty, scrape 07 curtail, shorten, stinted 08 restrict 09 cut back on, economize 15 tighten your belt

## script

02 MS 04 book, copy, hand, Jawi, text 05 Cufic, Kufic, lines, ronde, words 06 Arabic, nagari 07 letters, linear A, linear B, writing 08 dialogue, Gurmukhi, libretto, longhand, nastalik, nasta'liq, Sumerian 09 minuscule 10 devanagari, manuscript, screenplay 11 calligraphy, Cypro-Minoan, handwriting, running-hand 14 rustic capitals, shooting script
• **insert into script**   03 cue

## scripture
02 RE, RI

---

*Religious writings include:*

---

02 NT, OT
05 Bayan, Bible, Koran, Qur'an, sutra, Torah, Vedas, Zohar
06 Gemara, gospel, Granth, Hadith, I Ching, Kojiki, Mishna, Talmud, Tantra
07 epistle, Li Ching, Puranas, Shari'ah
08 Haft Wadi, Halakhah, Ramayana, Shu Ching
09 Adi Granth, Apocrypha, Chuang-tzu, Chu'un Ch'iu, Decalogue, Digambara, Hexateuch, scripture, Shih Ching, Tripitaka
10 Heptateuch, Lotus Sutra, Nohon Shoki, Pentateuch, Svetambara, Tao-te-ching, Upanishads, Zend-Avesta
11 Bardo Thodol, Mahabharata
12 Bhagavad Gita, Kitab al-Aqdas,

Milindapanha, New Testament, Old Testament
14 Dead Sea Scrolls, Mahayana Sutras, Revised Version
15 Ten Commandments

*See also* **Bible**

## scroll

04 curl, list, roll 05 draft, paper, scrow, Sefer, Torah 06 mezuza, scrowl, stemma, Thorah, volume, volute 07 mezuzah, scrowle 08 cartouch, makimono, megillah, rocaille, schedule 09 cartouche, inventory, parchment 10 monkey tail, phylactery, Sefer Torah

## Scrooge

05 crowd, miser 06 meanie 07 niggard, squeeze 08 tightwad 09 skinflint 10 cheapskate 12 money-grubber, penny-pincher

## scrounge

03 beg, bot, bum 04 blag 05 cadge 06 bludge, borrow, scunge, sponge 07 purloin

## scrounger

03 bum 05 mooch, mouch 06 beggar, cadger, scunge 07 bludger, moocher, sponger 08 borrower, parasite 10 freeloader

## scrub

◊ *deletion indicator* 03 axe, rub 04 bush, drop, wash, wipe 05 brush, clean, scour, shrub 06 cancel, delete, drudge, forget, give up, purify 07 abandon, abolish, cleanse, garigue, thicket 08 garrigue 09 backwoods, brushwood, exfoliate, holystone, scrubland 10 improvised, undersized 11 discontinue, undergrowth 13 insignificant

## scruff

04 nape 05 scuff, scuft

## scruffy

◊ *anagram indicator* 05 daggy, dirty, messy, seedy 06 grotty, ragged, scurvy, shabby, sloppy, untidy 07 run-down, squalid, unkempt, worn-out 08 dog-eared, slovenly, sluttish, tattered 09 ungroomed 10 bedraggled, down-at-heel, slatternly 11 dishevelled 12 disreputable
• **scruffy person**   03 dag 04 slob 06 scruff

## scrum
04 ruck

## scrumptious

05 tasty, yummy 06 morish 07 moreish, scrummy 08 gorgeous, luscious 09 delicious, exquisite, succulent 10 appetizing, delectable, delightful 11 magnificent 13 mouthwatering

## scrunch

04 chew, mash 05 champ, crush, grate, grind, screw, twist 06 crunch, squash 07 crumple, screw up 09 crumple up

## scruple

03 scr 04 balk 05 demur, doubt, qualm, stick 06 boggle, ethics, morals, shrink 07 protest, stickle 08 hesitate, hold

## scrupulous

back, question **09** disbelief, misgiving, objection, standards, vacillate **10** difficulty, hesitation, perplexity, principles, reluctance, think twice, uneasiness **11** be reluctant, compunction, reservation, vacillation **13** point of honour **14** second thoughts

## scrupulous

**04** nice **05** exact, moral **06** honest, minute, queasy, queazy, spiced, strict, tender **07** careful, ethical, precise, upright **08** captious, rigorous, thorough **09** religious **10** fastidious, honourable, meticulous, principled **11** painstaking, punctilious **13** conscientious **14** high-principled

## scrutinize

**03** vet **04** coat, cote, scan, sift **05** coate, probe, quote, study **06** go over, peruse, search **07** analyse, canvass, examine, explore, inspect, run over **08** look over **09** go through **10** run through, take a squiz **11** investigate, look through

## scrutiny

**05** probe, study **06** search **07** canvass, check-up, close-up, inquiry, perusal **08** analysis, docimasy **10** inspection **11** examination, exploration **13** investigation

## scud

**03** fly **04** blow, dart, East, gust, race, sail, skim, slap **05** shoot, speed, spoom, spoon

## scuff

**03** rub **04** cuff, drag **05** brush, graze, scuft **06** abrade, scrape, scruff **07** scratch

## scuffle

◇ anagram indicator **03** hoe, row **04** fray **05** brawl, clash, fight, scrap, set-to **06** affray, cuffle, dust-up, rumpus, tussle **07** bagarre, contend, grapple, punch-up, quarrel, scarify, shuffle **08** pull caps, struggle **09** commotion **11** come to blows, disturbance **14** rough-and-tumble

## sculpt

◇ anagram indicator **03** cut, hew **04** cast, form **05** carve, model, mould, shape **06** chisel **07** fashion **09** represent, sculpture
• he/she sculpted **02** sc **08** sculpsit

## sculptor

**05** hewer, mason **06** artist, carver, caster **07** moulder, plastic **08** figurist, modeller **09** chiseller, craftsman **10** sculptress **11** craftswoman, stone-carver

Sculptors include:

**03** Arp (Hans), Ray (Man)
**04** Bell (John), Bone (Phyllis), Caro (Sir Anthony), Gabo (Naum), Gill (Eric), King (Philip), Mach (David), Rude (François)
**05** Andre (Carl), Bacon (John), Beuys (Joseph), Cragg (Tony), Davey (Grenville), Frink (Dame Elisabeth), Johns (Jasper), Koons (Jeff), Manzú (Giacomo), Moore (Henry), Myron, Rodin (Auguste), Smith (David

Roland), Story (William)
**06** Calder (Alexander), Canova (Antonio), Cousin (Jean), Deacon (Richard), Hatoum (Mona), Kapoor (Anish), Marini (Marino), Pisano (Andrea), Pisano (Giovanni), Robbia (Luca della), Scopas, Walker (Dame Ethel)
**07** Bernini (Gianlorenzo), Cellini (Benvenuto), Christo, Duchamp (Marcel), Epstein (Sir Jacob), Gormley (Antony), Klinger (Max), Longman (Evelyn), Millett (Kate), Phidias, Samaras (Lucas)
**08** Boccioni (Umberto), Brancusi (Constantin), Chadwick (Lynn), Ghiberti (Lorenzo), Hepworth (Dame Barbara), Landseer (Sir Edwin), Paolozzi (Eduardo Luigi), Pheidias, Tinguely (Jean)
**09** Borromini (Francesco), Bourgeois (Louise), Donatello, Oldenburg (Claes), Roubiliac (Louis François), Whiteread (Rachel)
**10** Giacometti (Alberto), Polyclitus, Praxiteles, Schwitters (Kurt), Verrocchio (Andrea del)
**11** Della Robbia (Luca), Goldsworthy (Andy)
**12** Jeanne-Claude, Michelangelo
**14** Gaudier-Brzeska (Henri)
**15** Leonardo da Vinci

## sculpture

◇ anagram indicator

Sculpture types include:

**04** bust, cast, head, herm, kore
**05** group
**06** bronze, effigy, figure, kouros, marble, relief, statue
**07** carving, kinetic, telamon, waxwork
**08** caryatid, Daibutsu, figurine, maquette, moulding
**09** bas-relief, statuette
**10** high-relief
**11** plaster cast

Sculptures and statues include:

**04** Adam, Kore, Zeus
**05** Angel, Cupid, David, House, Medea, Moses, Pietà, Torso
**06** Balzac
**07** Bacchus, Genesis, Liberty, Lincoln, Mercury, Merzbau, Spiders, The Kiss, The Wall
**08** Cantoria, Ecce Homo, Eggboard, Have Pity!, Mahamuni, Piscator
**09** A Universe, Seated Man, Slate Cone
**10** Discobolus, Doryphorus, Double Talk, Ledge Piece, Orange Bath, Running Man, Single Form, The Thinker
**11** Gomateswara, Kiss and Tell, Pierced Form, Spear Bearer, Venus de Milo
**12** Cactus People, Elgin Marbles, Feast of Herod
**13** Discus Thrower, Fallen Warrior, People in a Wind, Veduggio Sound
**14** Cosimo de' Medici, Fontana Magiore, Horse Lying Down,

Japanese War God, Sailing Tonight, The Age of Bronze, The Gates of Hell, The Three Graces
**15** Angel of the North, Athena Promachos, Buddhas of Bamian, Christ in Majesty, Figure and Clouds, Giant Clothespin, Madonna and Child, Recumbent Figure

## scum

**04** dirt, film, foam, slag **05** dregs, dross, froth, layer, plebs, spume, trash **06** mantle, mother, rabble **07** rubbish, sullage **08** covering, pellicle, riff-raff, sandiver **09** epistasis, glass-gall **10** impurities **12** undesirables **13** great unwashed **14** dregs of society, lowest of the low

## scupper

**03** axe **04** foil, kill, ruin, sink **05** do for, wreck **06** cock up, defeat, mess up **07** destroy, disable, louse up, screw up, scuttle, torpedo **08** demolish, submerge **09** overthrow, overwhelm

## scurf

**05** scald, scale **06** furfur, scruff **07** furfair **08** dandriff, dandruff **09** flakiness, scaliness **12** scabrousness

## scurfy

**05** flaky, lepra, scald, scaly **06** scabby, scurvy **07** leprose, leprous, scabrid **08** lepidote, scabrous, scarious **09** furfurous **11** scaberulous **12** furfuraceous

## scurrility

**05** abuse **07** obloquy **08** foulness, rudeness **09** grossness, indecency, invective, nastiness, obscenity, vulgarity **10** coarseness **11** abusiveness **12** vituperation **13** offensiveness **14** scurrilousness

## scurrilous

**04** foul, rude **06** coarse, vulgar **07** abusive, obscene, Sotadic **08** indecent, Sotadean **09** insulting, libellous, offensive, salacious **10** defamatory, Fescennine, scandalous, slanderous **11** disparaging **12** vituperative

## scurry

**03** fly, ren, rin, run **04** dart, dash, race, rush, scud, scur, sker, skim, trot **05** hurry, scoot, scour, skirr, whirl **06** beetle, bustle, flurry, hasten, skurry, sprint, squirr **07** scamper, scutter, scuttle, skelter **08** bustling, scramble **09** beetle off **10** scampering **15** hustle and bustle

## scurvy

**03** bad, low **04** base, mean, vile, yaws **05** dirty, scall, sorry **06** abject, rotten, scurfy, shabby **07** ignoble, low-down, pitiful, roynish, scruffy **08** whoreson **09** worthless **10** despicable **12** contemptible **13** dishonourable

## scuttle

◇ anagram indicator **03** hod, ren, rin, run **04** rush, scud, sink **05** hurry **06** bustle, hasten, scurry **07** scamper, scuddle,

**scythe**
scutter, skuttle **08** scramble, scrattle **09** purdonium

**scythe**
**03** mow **07** cut down **11** bushwhacker
• **part of scythe** **04** sned **05** snath, snead **06** snathe, sneath

**sea**
**03** mer **04** deep, host, main, mass, salt, tide **05** briny, ocean, swell, waves **06** afloat, marine **07** aquatic, expanse, oceanic **08** maritime **09** abundance, multitude, profusion, roughness, saltwater, seafaring **11** large number

*Seas include:*

**03** Med, Red
**04** Aral, Azov, Dead, East, Java, Kara, Ross, Sulu
**05** Banda, Black, Coral, Crete, Irish, Japan, North, Timor, White
**06** Aegean, Baltic, Bering, Celtic, Flores, Inland, Ionian, Laptev, Nan Hai, Scotia, Tasman, Yellow
**07** Andaman, Arabian, Arafura, Barents, Caspian, Celebes, Dong Hai, Galilee, Marmara, Okhotsk, Solomon, Weddell
**08** Adriatic, Amundsen, Beaufort, Bismarck, Hebrides, Huang Hai, Labrador, Ligurian, McKinley, Sargasso
**09** Caribbean, East China, Greenland, Norwegian
**10** Philippine, Setonaikai, South China, Tyrrhenian
**11** Yam Kinneret
**12** East Siberian
**13** Mediterranean
**14** Bellingshausen

*See also* **moon; ocean**
• **at sea** ◇ *anagram indicator* **04** lost **06** adrift, afloat **07** baffled, puzzled **08** confused **09** mystified, perplexed **10** bewildered **11** disoriented **12** disorganized **13** disorientated

**seabird**
*see* **bird**

**seaborgium**
**02** Sg

**sea bream**
**03** sar, tai **05** porgy, sargo **06** braise, braize, porgie, sargos, sargus **07** old wife **08** tarwhine

**seafaring**
**05** naval **06** marine **07** oceanic, sailing **08** maritime, nautical, sea-going **10** ocean-going

**seafood**
*Seafood and seafood dishes include:*

**04** bisk, clam, crab
**05** prawn, squid, sushi, whelk
**06** bisque, cockle, mussel, oyster, paella, scampi, shrimp, winkle
**07** abalone, lobster, octopus, risotto, scallop, tempura, toheroa
**08** calamari, coquille, crawfish, crevette, marinara, zarzuela
**09** jambalaya, king prawn, surf'n'turf
**10** tiger prawn
**11** clam-chowder, Dublin prawn,

fritto misto, fruits de mer, langoustine, tiger shrimp
**13** bouillabaisse, Norway lobster, prawn cocktail
**14** Dublin Bay prawn

*See also* **crustacean; fish; mollusc**

**seahorse**
**06** tangie, walrus **08** pipefish **09** hippodame, sea dragon **11** hippocampus, lophobranch

**seal**
**04** chop, cork, jark, lute, plug, seel, shut, stop **05** bulla, close, O-ring, plumb, puppy, sigil, stamp, tie up **06** cachet, clinch, enseal, fasten, obsign, ratify, secure, settle, signet, stop up, wicker, willow **07** close up, confirm, consign, enclose, stopper, tar-seal, tighten, ziplock **08** bachelor, conclude, finalize, insignia, set apart **09** assurance, footprint, obsignate **10** impression, imprimatur, shake hands, waterproof **11** attestation, counterseal **12** confirmation, make airtight, ratification **14** authentication, make watertight

*Seals include:*

**03** fur
**04** grey, hair, harp, monk
**05** otary, phoca, silky
**06** common, hooded, ribbon, sea dog, sealch, sealgh, selkie, silkie
**07** harbour, sea bear, sea calf, sea lion, Weddell
**08** Atlantic, elephant, seecatch
**09** crab-eater, Greenland, whitecoat
**10** saddleback, sea leopard
**11** sea elephant

• **in the place of the seal** **02** LS **11** loco sigilli
• **seal off** **03** cap **06** cut off, fasten **07** block up, isolate, shut off **08** close off, fence off **09** cordon off, segregate **10** quarantine

**sealed**
**04** shut **06** closed, corked **07** plugged **08** hermetic **09** sigillate **10** hermetical, watertight **12** draught-proof

**seam**
**04** fell, join, line, lode, saim, vein, weld **05** joint, layer, quilt, raphe, seame **06** grease, suture, thread **07** closure, joining, stratum, wrinkle **08** cartload, edge coal, junction, wayboard **09** stitching **10** weighboard **12** dorsal suture **15** middle-stitching

**seaman**
**02** AB **03** Kru, tar **04** Kroo **06** merman, sailor **07** killick, killock
*See also* **sailor**

**sea-mist**
**04** haar

**sea-monster**
**03** orc **04** cete **05** Phoca **06** kraken **07** ziffius **08** seahorse **09** leviathan, rosmarine, sea satyre, wasserman, whirlpool **11** hippocampus
*See also* **monster**

**seamy**
**03** low **04** dark **05** nasty, rough **06** sleazy, sordid **07** squalid **09** unsavoury **10** unpleasant **12** disreputable

**sear**
**03** dry, fry **04** burn, char, seal, sere, wilt **05** brand, brown, dry up, parch, seare, singe **06** scorch, sizzle, wither **07** burning, shrivel **08** withered **09** cauterize

**search**
**03** pry **04** comb, fish, hunt, rake, ripe, scur, seek, sift, sker **05** check, frisk, grope, probe, quest, rifle, scour, sieve, skirr, sweep **06** ferret, forage, squirr, survey **07** enquire, enquiry, examine, explore, fossick, inquire, inquiry, inspect, look for, pursuit, ransack, rifling, rummage **08** prospect, research, scrutiny **09** cast about, go through, ranshakle **10** inspection, ransacking, ranshackle, scrutinize **11** examination, exploration, investigate, look through **12** perquisition **13** investigation, perscrutation, turn inside-out **14** turn upside-down
• **in search of** **07** seeking **09** in quest of **10** looking for **11** in pursuit of **12** searching for **15** on the lookout for
• **search me** **05** dunno **09** I don't know, it beats me, I've no idea **12** ask me another **15** I haven't got a clue, you've got me there
• **search out** **04** scan **06** ferret **07** explore **08** indigate **10** run to earth **11** run to ground

**searching**
**04** home, keen **05** alert, close, quest, sharp **06** intent, minute, trying **07** probing **08** piercing, thorough **09** observant **10** discerning **11** penetrating, prospecting **13** inquisitional **14** strand-scouring

**searing**
**05** cruel **06** brutal, fierce, savage, severe **07** blazing, burning, extreme, intense, mordant **08** scathing **09** ferocious, scorching, trenchant, vitriolic **10** unbearable **11** devastating **12** insufferable

**seaside**
**05** beach, coast, sands, shore **06** strand **08** seashore

**season**
**03** age **04** fall, salt, seal, seel, seil, sele, span, term, tide, time **05** inure, pep up, phase, prime, ripen, savor, spell, spice, train, treat **06** harden, haysel, master, mature, mellow, period, savour, temper **07** flavour, prepare, toughen **08** festival, interval, moderate, tone down **09** condiment, condition **10** add herbs to, add sauce to, fence month, summertide, summertime **11** add pepper to, add relish to **13** add flavouring

*Seasons include:*

**03** dry, wet
**04** high, open
**05** close, rainy, silly

## seasonable

**06** autumn, closed, spring, summer, winter
**07** festive, holiday, monsoon
**08** breeding, shooting
**12** Indian summer

• **in season** **02** in **07** growing
**09** available **10** obtainable **11** on the market

## seasonable

**04** tidy **06** timely, timous **07** fitting, timeous, welcome **08** suitable
**09** opportune, well-timed
**10** convenient, forehanded, tempestive
**11** appropriate **12** providential

## seasoned

**03** old **04** salt **06** mature, spiced
**07** veteran **08** cayenned, hardened
**09** practised, toughened, weathered
**10** habituated, well-versed
**11** conditioned, established, experienced, long-serving
**12** acclimatized **13** battle-scarred, weather-beaten

## seasoning

**04** salt **05** herbs, salad, sauce, spice
**06** pepper, relish, spices **07** salting
**08** dressing, duxelles **09** condiment
**10** celery salt, flavouring, weathering
**11** fines herbes
*See also* **herb**

## seat

**03** fit, fix, hub, pew, put, see, set, sit
**04** axis, base, form, hold, home, pouf, sell, site, sofa, sunk, take **05** abode, bench, cause, chair, heart, house, perch, place, sedes, selle, siege, slide, stall, stool, swing, villa **06** bottom, centre, dukery, ground, humpty, locate, origin, pouffe, reason, saddle, sedile, settle, source, throne **07** capital, contain, deposit, footing, install, mansion, pillion, sitting, station
**08** location, position, sociable, tribunal
**09** faldstool, residence, situation
**10** foundation, metropolis, strapontin
**11** accommodate, have room for, reservation, stately home
**12** confessional, headquarters, rumble-tumble
*See also* **chair**

## seating

**04** room **05** seats **06** chairs, places
**07** sedilia **13** accommodation

## sea trout

**04** peal, peel **05** sewen, sewin
**06** finnac **07** finnack, finnock, herling, hirling

## seaweed

*Seaweeds include:*

**03** ore, red
**04** agar, alga, kelp, kilp, nori, tang, ulva, ware
**05** arame, domoi, dulse, fucus, kombu, laver, varec, vraic, wrack
**06** fucoid, tangle, varech, wakame
**07** oarweed, oreweed, redware, sea lace, sea moss, seaware
**08** agar-agar, bull kelp, gulfweed, porphyra, rockweed, sargasso,

sea wrack, whipcord
**09** carrageen, coralline, coral weed, drift-weed, Irish moss, Laminaria, nullipore, sargassum, seabottle, sea girdle, sea tangle, thongweed
**10** badderlock, carragheen, Ceylon moss, green laver, sea lettuce, sea whistle, tangleweed
**11** purple laver, sea furbelow
**12** bladderwrack, peacock's tail, Phaeophyceae, Rhodophyceae

*See also* **alga, algae**

## secede

**04** quit **05** break, leave **06** resign, retire
**08** separate, split off, withdraw
**09** break away **10** apostatize
**12** disaffiliate **14** turn your back on

## seceders

**04** cave

## secession

**05** break, split **06** revolt, schism
**08** apostasy, seceding **09** breakaway, defection **10** withdrawal
**14** disaffiliation

## secluded

**03** shy **05** close **06** cut off, hidden, lonely, remote, secret **07** private, recluse, retired, shadowy **08** in purdah, isolated, purdahed, shut away, solitary, umbratic **09** claustral, cloistral, concealed, sheltered, withdrawn **10** cloistered **11** out-of-the-way, sequestered, umbratilous
**12** unfrequented

## seclusion

**04** nook **06** bypath, hiding, purdah, recess **07** byplace, privacy, retreat, secrecy, shelter **08** bolt hole, retiracy, solitude **09** hermitage, isolation, reclusion, sequester **10** remoteness, retirement, withdrawal
**11** concealment, recluseness
**13** sequestration

## second

**01** s **02** mo **03** aid, sec **04** back, beta, help, jiff, move, next, send, tick, twin
**05** extra, flash, jiffy, lower, other, shift, spare, trice, vouch **06** assign, assist, backer, back up, back-up, change, deputy, double, helper, lesser, minute, moment **07** advance, another, approve, endorse, forward, further, helpful, instant, promote, support
**08** inferior, relocate, repeated, transfer
**09** agree with, alternate, assistant, attendant, duplicate, encourage, favouring, following, secondary, supporter, twinkling **10** additional, subsequent, succeeding, supporting
**11** alternative, split second, subordinate **12** right-hand man
**13** supplementary **14** right-hand woman **15** second-in-command

• **second to none** **04** best **06** superb
**07** supreme **08** peerless **09** brilliant, matchless, nonpareil, paramount
**10** inimitable, unrivalled
**11** superlative, unsurpassed
**12** incomparable, without equal
**13** beyond compare, nulli secundus
**15** without parallel

## secondary

**05** extra, lower, minor, spare **06** back-up, deputy, feeder, lesser, relief, second **07** derived, reserve
**08** delegate, indirect, inferior, Mesozoic **09** ancillary, auxiliary, resulting **10** derivative, subsidiary, supporting **11** alternative, subordinate, unimportant **12** non-essential

## second-class

**01** B **08** inferior, mediocre **10** second-best, second-rate, uninspired
**11** indifferent, unimportant, uninspiring **15** undistinguished

## second-hand

**03** old **04** used, worn **08** borrowed, indirect, pre-owned **09** nearly-new, obliquely, secondary, vicarious
**10** derivative, hand-me-down, indirectly **11** reach-me-down
**12** incidentally, tralaticious, tralatitious
**13** formerly owned **14** on the grapevine

## second-in-command

**06** backer, deputy, helper **09** assistant, attendant, number two, supporter
**12** right-hand man **14** right-hand woman

## secondly

**03** too **04** also, next **06** as well
**07** besides, further **08** moreover
**09** what's more **10** in addition
**11** furthermore **12** additionally **14** into the bargain

## second-rate

**04** poor, ropy **05** cheap, crook, lousy, ropey, tacky **06** grotty, lesser, shoddy, tawdry, tinpot **08** inferior, low-grade, mediocre **10** second-best, uninspired
**11** second-class, substandard, unimportant, uninspiring
**15** undistinguished

## secrecy

**04** dern **05** dearn, wraps **07** hidling, hidlins, mystery, privacy, privity, silence, stealth **08** disguise, hidlings
**09** seclusion **10** camouflage, confidence, covertness
**11** concealment, furtiveness **12** hugger-mugger, stealthiness **15** confidentiality

## secret

**03** key, sly **04** code, dark, deep, dern, rune **05** close, dearn, hushy, privy
**06** answer, arcane, closet, covert, cut off, enigma, hidden, inward, lonely, mystic, occult, recipe, remote, unseen
**07** arcanum, covered, cryptic, formula, furtive, hidling, hidlins, mystery, nostrum, private, retired, unknown
**08** abstruse, back-door, discreet, esoteric, hidlings, hush-hush, isolated, secluded, shrouded, shut away, sneaking, solitary, solution, stealthy
**09** concealed, disguised, recondite, sensitive, sheltered, tête-à-tête, top secret, underhand **10** backstairs, classified, cloistered, confidence, mysterious, restricted, undercover, unrevealed **11** camouflaged, clandestine, inside story, know-nothing, out-of-the-way, sequestered, underground, undisclosed,

unpublished **12** confidential, hugger-mugger, Naples yellow, unfrequented, unidentified **13** hole-and-corner, private matter, surreptitious **14** cloak-and-dagger **15** between you and me, under-the-counter
• **in secret 07** in petto, on the qt, privily, quietly **08** covertly, in camera, on the sly, secretly **09** furtively, in pectore, in private, privately **10** on the quiet, stealthily, under cover, unobserved **12** hugger-mugger, in confidence, subterranean **13** clandestinely **14** confidentially **15** surreptitiously
• **secret agent 03** spy **04** Bond, mole **05** scout **07** snooper **10** enemy agent **11** double agent **12** foreign agent **14** fifth columnist **15** undercover agent

### secretary
**02** PA **03** Sec **04** Secy, temp **05** clerk **06** munshi, scribe, typist **07** famulus **08** moonshee **09** assistant, man Friday, town clerk **10** amanuensis, chancellor, girl Friday, secretaire **11** protonotary **12** person Friday, prothonotary, stenographer

### secrete
**04** bury, emit, hide, leak, ooze, take, veil **05** cache, cover, exude, leach, plant, water **06** screen, secern, shroud **07** conceal, cover up, emanate, excrete, give off, lactate, produce, release, send out **08** disguise, salivate **09** discharge, sequester, stash away **11** appropriate

### secretion
**04** lerp **05** sebum, slime **06** liquor, oozing, pruina, smegma, succus **07** cerumen, hormone, leakage, osmosis, release **08** autacoid, emission, honeydew **09** discharge, emanation, exudation, incretion, lactation, recrement **10** osmidrosis, production, royal jelly, secernment **12** lachrymation

### secretive
**03** sly **04** cagy, deep **05** cagey, close, quiet **06** intent **07** cryptic **08** reserved, reticent, taciturn **09** enigmatic, withdrawn **11** tight-lipped **13** unforthcoming **15** uncommunicative

### secretively
**07** quietly **08** silently **10** reticently, taciturnly **13** enigmatically

### secretly
**05** close **06** dernly **07** dearnly, on the qt, privily, quietly **08** covertly, in camera, in secret, on the sly **09** furtively, in private, privately **10** on the quiet, stealthily, under-board, under cover, unobserved **11** underground **12** in confidence **13** clandestinely **14** confidentially **15** surreptitiously

### sect
**03** sex **04** camp, clan, cult, wing **05** group, order, party **06** church, school **07** cutting, faction **08** division

**09** tradition **11** subdivision **12** denomination **13** splinter group

*Religious sects include:*
**05** Amish
**07** Ahmadis, Cathars, Moonies, Shakers, Zealots
**09** Ahmadiyya, Lubavitch
**10** Mennonites
**11** Hare Krishna, Therapeutae

*See also* **sectarian**

### sectarian
**04** Babi **05** Amish, Babee, bigot, Cynic, hodja, khoja, rigid, Saiva, Yezdi **06** Berean, Cathar, Dunker, khodja, Marist, Moonie, Mormon, Mucker, narrow, Ophite, ranter, Sabian, Seeker, Senusi, Shaiva, Shiite, Tunker, Wahabi, Yezidi, Zabian, zealot **07** Adamite, Alawite, Baptist, bigoted, Cainite, Dunkard, extreme, fanatic, hillmen, insular, Ismaili, Karaite, limited, Senussi, Tsabian, Wahabee, Wahhabi, Yezidee, Zezidee **08** Calixtin, cliquish, Darbyite, dogmatic, Donatist, Dukhobor, Familist, hillfolk, Mandaean, Maronite, Mendaite, partisan, Pharisee, Senoussi, Stundist **09** Calixtine, dogmatist, Doukhobor, Encratite, exclusive, extremist, factional, fanatical, Harmonist, Harmonite, Hesychast, hidebound, Israelite, Mennonite, Nasoraean, parochial, Paulician **10** anabaptist, Holy Roller, Karmathian, prejudiced, separatist **11** abecedarian, Albigensian, Black Muslim, Campbellite, doctrinaire, Hare Krishna, Lubavitcher, Plymouthist, Plymouthite, Sandemanian **12** denomination, Muggletonian, narrow-minded **13** convulsionary, fractionalist, Hemerobaptist, Perfectionist, Philadelphian, Schwenkfelder **14** denominational, Schwenkfeldian **15** Christadelphian, Plymouth Brother

### section
**01** s **03** bit **04** area, part, plot, sect, unit, wing, zone **05** block, conic, piece, share, slice **06** branch, region, sector **07** article, chapter, passage, portion, segment **08** campfire, district, division, fraction, fragment **09** Caesarean, Caesarian, component, induction, paragraph **10** department, instalment **11** subdivision
• **all sections 02** AS

### sectional
**05** class, local **06** racial **07** divided, partial **08** regional, separate **09** exclusive, factional, localized, sectarian **10** individual, separatist

### sector
**04** area, gore, part, zone **05** field **06** branch, octant, region **07** quarter, section, sextant **08** category, district, division, precinct, quadrant **11** subdivision

### secular
**03** lay **05** civil, state **06** age-old, layman **07** agelong, earthly, profane, worldly

**08** temporal **12** non-religious, non-spiritual

### secure
◊ *containment indicator* **03** bag, bar, fix, get, pin, pot, rug, tie, win **04** bolt, bond, fast, firm, gain, hunk, land, lash, lock, moor, nail, safe, shut, sure, take, vest **05** chain, close, cover, fixed, guard, happy, quoin, rivet, solid, tie up, tight **06** anchor, assure, attach, closed, come by, defend, ensure, fasten, immune, line up, locked, lock up, obtain, screen, sealed, shield, stable, steady, sturdy, take up **07** acquire, assured, certain, confirm, endorse, padlock, procure, protect, relaxed, settled, sponsor, warrant **08** anchored, careless, definite, fastened, make fast, make safe, reliable, shielded, unharmed **09** confident, contented, establish, fortified, get hold of, guarantee, immovable, protected, reassured, safeguard, sheltered, steadfast, undamaged **10** batten down, conclusive, dependable, home and dry, strengthen, underwrite **11** comfortable, established, impregnable, make certain, self-assured, well-founded **13** make certain of, out of harm's way, self-confident

### securely
**06** firmly, safely, stably **07** tightly **08** robustly, steadily, strongly, sturdily **09** immovably **11** impregnably, out of danger, steadfastly

### security
**03** wad, wed **04** care, ease, gage, gilt, lock **05** cover **06** anchor, asylum, pledge, refuge, safety, surety **07** caution, custody, defence **08** guaranty, immunity, warranty **09** assurance, certainty, guarantee, insurance, safeguard, sanctuary **10** collateral, confidence, conviction, precaution, protection, safeguards **11** peace of mind, precautions, safe-keeping **12** carelessness, positiveness, preservation, surveillance **14** over-confidence **15** invulnerability

### sedan
**05** chair **06** jampan, litter **09** palanquin

### sedate
**03** sad **04** calm, cool, dull **05** douce, grave, noble, quiet, relax, sober, staid, stiff **06** demure, pacify, proper, seemly, serene, solemn, soothe, worthy **07** earnest, serious **08** calm down, composed, decorous, tranquil **09** collected, dignified, unruffled **10** deliberate, slow-moving, unexciting **11** quieten down, unflappable **12** tranquillize **13** imperturbable

### sedately
**05** nobly **06** calmly **07** quietly, soberly **08** demurely, serenely, worthily **09** earnestly, seriously **10** decorously **11** with dignity **12** deliberately **13** imperturbably

### sedative
**06** downer, opiate **07** anodyne, calming **08** lenitive, narcotic, quietive,

**sedentary**

relaxing, soothing **09** calmative, composing, soporific **10** depressant **11** barbiturate **12** sleeping-pill **13** tranquillizer **14** tranquillizing

*Sedatives and tranquillizers include:*

**06** Amytal®, Ativan®, Valium®
**07** codeine, Librium®, lupulin
**08** diazepam, Nembutal®, Rohypnol®, tetronal, thridace
**09** barbitone, clozapine, lorazepam, Temazepam
**10** clonazepam
**11** amobarbital, deserpidine, laurel-water, scopalamine, thalidomide
**12** meprobramate, methaqualone, promethazine
**14** chloral hydrate, cyclobarbitone, pentobarbitone, phenobarbitone

**sedentary**

**05** still **06** seated **07** sessile, sitting **08** immobile, inactive, unmoving **09** desk-bound **10** stationary

**sedge**

*Sedges include:*

**04** star
**05** Carex, chufa, starr
**07** bulrush, papyrus
**08** clubrush, sawgrass, tiger nut
**09** deergrass
**13** umbrella plant, water chestnut

**sediment**

**03** lee **04** lees, silt, warp **05** crust, dregs, feces, grout, varve **06** bottom, faeces, fecula **07** bottoms, deposit, grounds, residue **08** residuum **09** turbidite **10** deposition, hypostasis **11** precipitate **13** coffee grounds

**sedition**

**06** mutiny, revolt **07** treason **09** agitation, rebellion, treachery **10** disloyalty, subversion **11** fomentation **12** insurrection **13** rabble-rousing **15** insubordination

**seditious**

**08** disloyal, factious, inciting, mutinous **09** agitating, dissident, fomenting **10** rebellious, refractory, subversive, traitorous **13** insubordinate, rabble-rousing, revolutionary **15** insurrectionist

**seduce**

◇ *insertion indicator* **04** jape, lure, pull, ruin, undo, vamp **05** charm, tempt, wrong **06** allure, betray, chat up, entice **07** attract, beguile, corrupt, debauch, deceive, deprave, ensnare, mislead **08** bejesuit, dishonor, inveigle **09** dishonour **10** get into bed, lead astray **12** make a play for **15** take advantage of

**seducer**

**04** goat, rake, wolf **05** flirt, Romeo **06** undoer **07** charmer, Don Juan **08** betrayer, Casanova, deceiver, lady's man, Lothario **09** ladies' man, libertine, womanizer **11** philanderer

**seduction**

**04** lure, ruin **05** charm **06** allure, appeal, come-on **09** deception

**10** allurement, attraction, corruption, enticement, misleading, temptation **11** beguilement

**seductive**

**04** sexy **06** honied, luring, sultry **07** honeyed **08** alluring, arousing, charming, enticing, inviting, tempting **09** appealing, beguiling, deceiving **10** attractive, bewitching, come-hither, misleading **11** captivating, flirtatious, provocative, tantalizing, temptatious **12** honey-tongued, irresistible

**seductress**

**04** vamp **05** Circe, siren **07** Delilah, Lorelei **09** temptress **11** femme fatale

**sedulous**

**04** busy **08** constant, diligent, resolved, tireless, untiring **09** assiduous, laborious **10** determined, persistent, unflagging **11** industrious, painstaking, persevering, unremitting **13** conscientious

**see**

**01** C, v **02** la, lo **03** ask, Ely, get **04** date, deek, deem, ecce, espy, know, lead, look, mark, meet, note, seat, show, spot, take, vide, view **05** court, get it, grasp, judge, learn, sight, think, usher, visit, voilà, watch **06** behold, decide, escort, fathom, follow, go with, look at, notice, regard, take in **07** consult, diocese, discern, find out, foresee, glimpse, imagine, inquire, make out, observe, picture, predict, realize, reflect, run into, speak to, take out, witness **08** bump into, consider, discover, envisage, forecast, identify, perceive **09** accompany, apprehend, ascertain, determine, encounter, go out with, interview, latch onto, lay eyes on, recognize, set eyes on, visualize **10** anticipate, appreciate, chance upon, clap eyes on, come across, comprehend, confer with, cotton onto, experience, get a look at, understand **11** distinguish, investigate **12** catch sight of **15** keep company with

*See also* **diocese**

• **see about** **02** do **03** fix **06** manage, repair **07** arrange, sort out **08** attend to, consider, deal with, organize **09** look after **10** take care of
• **see around** ◇ *containment indicator*
• **see through** **06** fathom, hang in, rumble **07** persist, realize, support, sustain **08** continue, stick out **09** encourage, get wise to, keep going, not give up, penetrate, persevere **10** get through, understand **14** not be taken in by **15** not be deceived by
• **see to** **02** do **03** fix **04** mind **06** ensure, manage, repair **07** arrange, sort out **08** attend to, deal with, make sure, organize **09** look after **10** take care of **11** make certain

**seed**

**03** egg, nut, pea, pip, pit, sow, urd **04** bean, corn, dust, germ, moit, mote, ovum, race, root **05** argan, carvy,

cause, child, grain, heirs, lupin, ovule, piñon, semen, spawn, sperm, start, stone, young **06** bonduc, embryo, family, kernel, lentil, lupine, origin, powder, reason, source **07** genesis, nucleus, reasons **08** chickpea, children, peaberry, sprinkle, young one **09** beginning, fruit body, jequirity, offspring, sword-bean, young ones **10** successors **11** descendants **12** fruiting body, spermatozoon **13** jequirity bean, water chestnut
• **go to seed, run to seed** **04** bolt **05** decay **07** decline, go to pot **08** get worse, go to hell **10** degenerate, go downhill **11** deteriorate, go to the dogs **14** go down the tubes
• **seed covering** **03** bur, ear **04** aril, burr, husk

**seediness**

**05** decay, scuzz **09** dirtiness **10** shabbiness, untidiness **11** squalidness **12** dilapidation

**seedy**

◇ *anagram indicator* **03** ill **04** sick **05** crook, dirty, mangy, ribby, rough, tatty **06** ailing, chippy, crummy, groggy, grotty, mangey, maungy, poorly, shabby, sleazy, untidy, unwell **07** run-down, scruffy, squalid **08** decaying **09** off-colour **10** out of sorts **11** dilapidated **15** under the weather

**seek**

**03** aim, ask, beg, try **04** cast, hunt, want **05** chase, court **06** aspire, desire, follow, gun for, invite, lay out, pursue, resort, search, strive **07** attempt, enquire, entreat, examine, hunt for, inquire, look for, mole out, request, solicit **08** petition, prospect **09** endeavour, look after, search for, try to find

**seeker**

**05** chela, hound **06** novice **07** student, zetetic **08** disciple, enquirer, inquirer, searcher

**seem**

**04** feel, look **05** befit, sound **06** appear, semble **08** look like **11** pretend to be, show signs of, strike you as **12** come across as **13** have the look of

**seeming**

**05** quasi- **06** pseudo **07** assumed, outward, surface **08** apparent, external, semblant, specious, supposed **09** pretended **10** ostensible, semblative **11** superficial

**seemingly**

**09** allegedly, outwardly **10** apparently, ostensibly **12** on the surface **13** on the face of it, superficially

**seemly**

**03** fit **04** meet, nice **06** comely, decent, honest, proper, suited **07** fitting **08** becoming, decorous, handsome, maidenly, suitable **09** befitting **10** attractive **11** appropriate, comme il faut, respectable

**seep**

**04** drip, leak, oose, ooze, sipe, soak,

**seepage**

sype, well 05 drain, exude 07 dribble, trickle 08 permeate 09 percolate

**seepage**

04 leak 06 oozing 07 leakage, osmosis 08 dripping 09 exudation 11 percolation

**seer**

04 seir 05 augur, sibyl 07 prophet, seeress, spaeman, wise man 08 spaewife 10 prophetess, soothsayer

**seesaw**

04 yo-yo 05 pitch, swing 06 teeter 08 wild mare 09 alternate, fluctuate, oscillate

**seethe**

◇ *anagram indicator* 04 boil, fizz, foam, fume, rage, rise, teem 05 froth, go ape, storm, surge, swarm, swell 06 blow up, bubble, buller, see red, simmer 07 be angry, be livid, explode, ferment 08 boil over, smoulder 09 be furious, blow a fuse 10 be incensed, be outraged, effervesce 11 blow a gasket, go ballistic 12 blow your cool, lose your cool 14 foam at the mouth 15 fly off the handle, go off the deep end

**see-through**

05 filmy, gauzy, sheer 06 flimsy 08 gossamer 09 gossamery 11 translucent, transparent

**segment**

03 bit, pig 04 exon, link, lith, part, ring 05 cut up, femur, halve, joint, piece, slice, split, urite, wedge 06 divide, scliff, skliff, somite, telson 07 article, isomere, overlay, portion, section, uromere 08 division, metamere, separate 09 anatomize, propodeon, prothorax, sternebra 10 arthromere, metathorax, proglottid, proglottis, trochanter 11 compartment 12 articulation

**segregate**

06 cut off 07 exclude, isolate, seclude 08 separate, set apart 09 keep apart, ostracize, sequester 10 dissociate, quarantine

**segregation**

09 apartheid, isolation 10 quarantine, separation 12 dissociation, setting apart 13 sequestration 14 discrimination

**seize**

◇ *containment indicator* 03 bag, cly, nab, nap 04 bone, grab, grip, hend, hold, nail, snap, take 05 annex, catch, ceaze, cleek, grasp, latch, reach, sease, seaze, seise, usurp 06 abduct, areach, arrest, attach, attain, clutch, collar, graple, hijack, kidnap, nobble, ravish, snatch, tackle 07 capture, forhent, grapple, impound, possess, prehend 08 forehent 09 apprehend, deprehend, get hold of, lay hold of, lay hold on, penetrate 10 commandeer, confiscate, grab hold of, lay hands on, take hold of 11 appropriate, catch hold of, requisition, sequestrate
• **seize on** 04 grab 07 exploit 08 fasten on 12 grasp eagerly
• **seize up** 03 jam 04 stop 06 go phut,

pack up 07 conk out 09 break down 11 malfunction, stop working

**seizure**

03 fit 04 grab, rape 05 catch, prise, prize, spasm 06 arrest, attack, extent, hijack, rapine, taking 07 capture, seysure 08 paroxysm, purchase, reprisal, wingding 09 abduction, distraint, snatching 10 annexation, attachment, convulsion, pre-emption 12 apprehension, confiscation 13 appropriation, commandeering, sequestration

**seldom**

04 rare 06 rarely 07 unoften 10 hardly ever, infrequent, once in a way 12 infrequently, occasionally, once in a while, scarcely ever 15 once in a blue moon

**select**

03 top 04 best, cull, pick, posh, sort 05 elect, élite, prime 06 choice, choose, favour, finest, invite, opt for, prefer 07 appoint, extract, limited, special, supreme 08 decide on, selected, settle on, superior 09 excellent, exclusive, first-rate, single out 10 cherry-pick, first-class, hand-picked, privileged 11 high-quality 12 make choice of

**selection**

04 blad, farm, pick 05 blaud, range 06 choice, dim sum, line-up, medley, option 07 Auslese, palette, variety 08 property 09 anthology, cold table, potpourri 10 assortment, collection, miscellany, preference 11 block of land, smörgåsbord

**selective**

05 fussy, picky 06 choosy 07 careful, finicky 10 discerning, fastidious, particular, pernickety 11 persnickety 14 discriminating

**selectively**

08 by choice 09 carefully 12 discerningly, particularly 14 differentially, preferentially

**Selene**

04 Luna

**selenium**

02 Se

**self**

01 I 03 ego, own, sel 04 same, sell, soul, very 05 atman, seity 06 person 08 identity 09 identical, number one, the real me 10 inner being, yours truly 11 body and soul, personality 13 heart of hearts

**self-assembly**

03 DIY 07 kit-form 08 flat-pack 13 prefabricated

**self-assertive**

05 bossy, perky, pushy 07 pushing 08 forceful, immodest 10 aggressive, commanding, high-handed, peremptory 11 dictatorial, domineering, heavy-handed, overbearing, overweening 13 authoritarian

**self-assurance**

06 aplomb 09 assurance, cockiness 10 confidence 11 assuredness 12 cocksureness, positiveness 14 overconfidence, self-confidence, self-possession

**self-assured**

05 cocky 07 assured 08 cocksure 09 confident, hubristic 13 overconfident, self-collected, self-confident, self-possessed 14 sure of yourself

**self-centred**

07 selfish 09 egotistic 10 egocentric 11 egotistical, self-seeking, self-serving 12 narcissistic, self-absorbed 14 self-interested

**self-confidence**

03 ego 05 poise 06 aplomb 07 opinion 09 assurance, composure 10 confidence 12 positiveness, self-reliance 13 self-assurance

**self-confident**

04 bold, cool 07 assured 08 cocksure, composed, fearless, positive 09 confident, unabashed 11 self-assured, self-reliant 13 self-possessed

**self-conscious**

03 coy, shy 05 timid 07 awkward, bashful, nervous 08 blushing, insecure, retiring, sheepish, timorous 09 diffident, ill at ease, shrinking 10 shamefaced 11 embarrassed 12 self-effacing 13 uncomfortable

**self-contained**

02 s/c 05 quiet 07 private 08 discrete, reserved, separate 09 secretive 11 independent, self-reliant 12 free-standing 14 self-sufficient

**self-control**

04 cool 06 temper 07 dignity, encraty 08 calmness, patience 09 composure, restraint, willpower 10 self-denial, temperance 11 self-mastery 13 self-restraint 14 self-discipline
• **lose self-control** 04 flip, snap 05 break

**self-defence**

*see* **martial art**

**self-denial**

10 asceticism, moderation, temperance 12 selflessness 13 self-sacrifice, unselfishness 14 abstemiousness, self-abnegation

**self-discipline**

07 resolve 09 willpower 11 persistence, self-control, self-mastery 13 determination

**self-employed**

06 casual 08 part-time 09 freelance, temporary 10 consultant, out-of-house 11 independent

**self-esteem**

03 ego 05 pride 07 conceit, dignity 09 self-image, self-pride 10 self-regard 11 amour-propre, self-respect 13 self-assurance 14 self-confidence

**self-evident**

05 clear, plain 07 obvious 08 manifest

**self-explanatory**
09 axiomatic 10 undeniable
11 inescapable 14 unquestionable

**self-explanatory**
05 clear, plain 07 obvious
10 accessible, easy-to-read 11 self-evident 12 approachable, easy-to-follow, intelligible 14 comprehensible, understandable

**self-glorification**
07 egotism 09 egotheism 14 self-admiration, self-exaltation

**self-governing**
04 free 09 autonomic, sovereign
10 autonomous 11 independent 15 self-determining

**self-government**
06 swaraj 08 autarchy, autonomy, home rule 09 democracy
11 sovereignty 12 independence
15 self-sovereignty

**self-importance**
04 pomp 06 vanity 07 conceit, donnism
09 arrogance, cockiness, pomposity, pushiness 10 pretension
11 pompousness, self-opinion
13 bigheadedness, bumptiousness, conceitedness 15 self-consequence

**self-important**
04 coxy, vain 05 cocky, proud, pushy
06 chesty, cocksy 07 pompous
08 arrogant, egoistic 09 bigheaded, bumptious, conceited, egotistic, strutting 10 portentous, swaggering
11 egotistical, overbearing, pragmatical, pretentious, swell-headed
13 consequential, swollen-headed
14 self-consequent

**self-indulgence**
06 excess 08 hedonism 10 high living, profligacy, sensualism 11 dissipation
12 extravagance, intemperance
13 dissoluteness

**self-indulgent**
06 wanton 09 dissolute 10 dissipated, hedonistic, immoderate, profligate
11 extravagant, intemperate
15 pleasure-seeking

**self-interest**
04 self 08 self-love 10 expediency, self-regard 11 selfishness, self-serving

**selfish**
04 mean 06 greedy 07 miserly
08 covetous 09 egotistic, mercenary
10 egocentric 11 calculating, egotistical, self-centred, self-seeking, self-serving 13 inconsiderate 14 self-interested

**selfishly**
08 greedily 12 ungenerously
13 egotistically 14 egocentrically
15 inconsiderately, only for yourself

**selfishness**
05 greed 06 egoism 07 egotism
08 meanness, self-love 10 self-regard
11 self-seeking, self-serving 12 self-interest 15 self-centredness

**selfless**
08 generous 09 unselfish 10 altruistic

11 magnanimous, self-denying
13 philanthropic 15 self-sacrificing

**selflessness**
08 altruism 10 generosity, self-denial
11 magnanimity 12 philanthropy
13 self-sacrifice, unselfishness

**self-possessed**
04 calm, cool 06 poised 07 assured
08 composed, together 09 collected, confident, unruffled 11 self-assured, unflappable 13 self-collected

**self-possession**
04 cool, head 05 nerve, poise
06 aplomb 08 calmness, coolness
09 assurance, composure, sangfroid
10 confidence 11 self-command
13 collectedness, self-assurance
14 self-confidence, unflappability

**self-reliance**
07 autarky 11 self-support
12 independence 14 self-sustenance
15 self-sufficiency, self-sustainment

**self-reliant**
08 autarkic 10 autarkical
11 independent 14 self-sufficient, self-supporting, self-sustaining

**self-respect**
05 pride 07 dignity 10 self-esteem, self-regard 11 amour-propre 13 self-assurance 14 self-confidence

**self-restraint**
07 encraty 08 patience 09 willpower
10 continence, continency, moderation, self-denial, temperance
11 forbearance, self-command, self-control 14 abstemiousness, self-discipline, self-government

**self-righteous**
02 pi 04 smug 05 pious 08 priggish, superior 09 pietistic 10 complacent, goody-goody, moralistic 11 pharisaical
12 hypocritical 13 sanctimonious
14 holier-than-thou

**self-righteousness**
09 goodiness, piousness 10 pharisaism
12 priggishness 14 goody-goodiness
15 pharisaicalness

**self-sacrifice**
08 altruism 10 generosity, self-denial
12 selflessness 13 unselfishness 14 self-abnegation

**self-satisfaction**
05 pride 08 smugness 11 complacency, contentment 12 self-approval 15 self-approbation

**self-satisfied**
04 smug 05 proud 08 puffed up
10 complacent 13 self-righteous

**self-seeking**
07 selfish 09 careerist, mercenary, on the make 10 self-loving 11 acquisitive, calculating, gold-digging, self-serving
12 self-endeared 13 opportunistic
14 fortune-hunting, self-interested

**self-styled**
07 would-be 08 so-called
09 pretended, professed, soi-disant
10 self-titled 13 self-appointed

**self-sufficient**
11 independent, self-reliant 13 self-contained 14 self-supporting, self-sustaining

**self-supporting**
11 independent, self-reliant 13 self-financing 14 self-sufficient, self-sustaining

**self-willed**
05 elvan, elven 06 cussed, elfish, elvish, wilful 07 froward, willful
08 perverse, stubborn 09 obstinate, pig-headed 10 headstrong, refractory
11 intractable, opinionated, stiff-necked 12 bloody-minded, ungovernable 15 self-opinionated

**sell**
04 flog, hawk, hype, mart, push, seat, self, tout, vend, vent 05 carry, cry up, go for, selle, shift, stock, trade, trick
06 barter, betray, deal in, export, handle, import, market, peddle, praise, retail, saddle, smouch 07 auction, chaffer, let-down, promote, trade in, win over 08 exchange, persuade, retail at 09 advertise, deception, dispose of, traffic in 10 be priced at, bring round
11 merchandize 13 get support for
14 disappointment, get approval for
• **sell out** 04 fail 05 rat on 06 betray, fink on 07 stool on 08 run out of 11 be exhausted, double-cross 12 be out of stock, have none left 13 stab in the back

**seller**
06 trader, vendor 08 huckster, merchant, stockist, supplier
• **seller's opinion** 02 so

**selling**
07 dealing, trading, traffic, vending
09 marketing, promotion, vendition
11 trafficking 12 salesmanship, transactions 13 merchandizing

**selvage**
04 list, roon, rund 05 royne

**semblance**
03 air 04 copy, garb, idol, life, look, mask, show, sign 05 front, ghost, guise, image 06 aspect, façade, veneer
07 seeming 08 likeness, pretence, pretense 10 apparition, appearance, likelihood, similarity, similitude, simulacrum 11 resemblance

**semen**
03 cum 04 seed 05 sperm, spoof
09 ejaculate 12 seminal fluid

**semi-liquid**
04 slab 05 slimy 06 blashy, globby

**seminal**
05 major 08 creative, germinal, original, seminary 09 formative, important 10 generative, innovative, productive 11 imaginative, influential, rudimentary

**seminar**
05 class, forum 07 lecture, meeting, session, webinar 08 colloquy, tutorial, workshop 09 symposium
10 colloquium, conference, convention, discussion, study group

**seminary**
**03** Sem **06** school **07** academy, college, nursery, yeshiva **08** yeshivah **09** institute **10** theologate **11** institution **15** training college

**send**
**04** beam, cast, emit, fire, hurl, mail, make, move, post, turn **05** drive, fling, grant, radio, relay, remit, shoot, swash, throw **06** arouse, commit, convey, direct, excite, get off, launch, propel, thrill, turn on **07** address, consign, deliver, forward, project **08** despatch, dispatch, redirect, televise, transmit **09** broadcast, cause to be, discharge, give a buzz, give a kick, messenger, stimulate **11** communicate **12** put in the mail, put in the post **14** give pleasure to
• **send away** **04** hunt, pack, void **05** drive **07** dismiss, pack off **08** despatch, dispatch
• **send for** **05** get in, order **06** summon **07** call for, command, request
• **send forth** **04** beam, pour **05** fling, shoot, speed **08** expedite **09** discharge
• **send off** **04** ship **06** let fly, set off **08** despatch, dispatch, order off **12** order to leave
• **send up** ◊ reversal down indicator **04** mock **05** mimic **06** parody **07** imitate, take off **08** ridicule, satirize

**send-off**
**05** start **07** goodbye, push-off **08** farewell **09** departure **11** leave-taking

**send-up**
**04** skit **05** spoof **06** parody, satire **07** mockery, take-off **09** burlesque, imitation **10** mickey-take

**Senegal**
**02** SN **03** SEN

**senile**
**03** old **04** aged, gaga **06** doited, doitit **07** failing **08** confused, decrepit **09** doddering, senescent

**senility**
**03** eld **04** eild **06** dotage, old age **07** anility, paracme **08** caducity **09** infirmity **10** senescence **11** decrepitude **14** senile dementia **15** second childhood

**senior**
**02** Sr **03** Sen, Snr **04** âiné, sire **05** âinée, chief, doyen, elder, first, major, older **06** higher **07** ancient, doyenne **08** superior **11** high-ranking
• **senior citizen** **03** OAP **09** pensioner **10** golden ager **12** coffin-dodger **13** retired person **15** old-age pensioner

**seniority**
**03** age **04** rank **06** status **08** priority, standing **09** anciority, antiquity, signeurie **10** importance, precedence **11** superiority

**sensation**
**03** hit, wow **04** aura, itch, stir **05** sense, vibes **06** furore, pit-pat, splash, thrill, tingle, winner **07** emotion, feeling,

outrage, pitapat, prickle, scandal, success, symptom, triumph **08** goneness, pitty-pat **09** agitation, awareness, commotion **10** Empfindung, excitement, impression, perception **13** consciousness

**sensational**
**04** gamy, pulp **05** gamey, juicy, lurid, shock **06** superb, yellow **07** amazing **08** dramatic, drop-dead, exciting, fabulous, galvanic, gorgeous, shocking, smashing, stirring, terrific **09** excellent, fantastic, revealing, startling, thrilling, wonderful **10** astounding, eye-popping, horrifying, impressive, incredible, marvellous, scandalous, staggering **11** exceptional, spectacular **12** breathtaking, electrifying, melodramatic **15** blood-and-thunder

**sense**
**03** wit **04** feel, gist, mind, nous, wits **05** brain, drift, grasp, logic, point, savvy, tenor **06** brains, detect, divine, import, intuit, notice, nuance, pick up, reason, wisdom **07** ability, discern, faculty, feeling, meaning, observe, opinion, purport, purpose, realize, suspect **08** gumption, judgment, perceive, prudence **09** awareness, be aware of, direction, intuition, judgement, recognize, sensation, substance **10** appreciate, cleverness, comprehend, definition, denotation, experience, impression, perception, understand **11** common sense, discernment, implication, sensibility **12** appreciation, apprehension, intelligence, significance **13** be conscious of, comprehension, consciousness, judiciousness, understanding **14** interpretation, reasonableness
• **in this sense** **02** hs **08** hoc sensu
• **make sense of** **05** grasp **06** fathom **07** make out **09** figure out **10** comprehend, make much of, understand

**senseless**
**03** mad, out **04** daft, numb, surd **05** batty, crazy, dotty, inane, silly **06** absurd, futile, insane, stupid, unwise **07** fatuous, foolish, idiotic, moronic, out cold, stunned **08** deadened, mindless **09** illogical, insensate, ludicrous, pointless, unfeeling **10** insensible, irrational, ridiculous **11** meaningless, nonsensical, purposeless, unconscious **12** unreasonable **13** anaesthetized, load of rubbish **14** load of nonsense

**sense-organ**
**03** ear, eye **04** nose, palp **06** tongue **09** sensillum **15** mechanoreceptor

**sensibility**
**05** taste **07** feeling, insight **08** delicacy, emotions, feelings **09** awareness, intuition, sentiment **10** sentiments **11** discernment, sensitivity **12** appreciation **13** sensitiveness, sensitivities **14** perceptiveness,

responsiveness, sentimentality, susceptibility

**sensible**
**04** sane, wise **05** aware, sharp, sober, solid, sound, tough, witty **06** clever, mature, shrewd, strong **07** evident, logical, prudent, working **08** everyday, ordinary, rational, wise-like **09** judicious, practical, realistic, sagacious, sensitive, wholesome **10** discerning, far-sighted, functional, no-nonsense, perceptive, reasonable, responsive, vulnerable **11** appreciable, clear-headed, commonsense, down-to-earth, hard-wearing, intelligent, level-headed, perceptible, serviceable, susceptible, well-advised **12** compos mentis **14** commonsensical
• **sensible of** **07** alive to, aware of **09** mindful of **11** cognizant of, conscious of, convinced of, observant of, sensitive to **13** understanding **14** acquainted with

**sensibly**
**06** wisely **07** handily **08** cleverly, shrewdly, strongly, suitably, usefully **09** logically, prudently **10** rationally, reasonably **11** judiciously, practically, sagaciously, serviceably **12** functionally **13** realistically

**sensitive**
**04** fine, soft **05** aware, exact, quick **06** kittly, tender, touchy, tricky **07** awkward, brittle, careful, fragile, precise, tactful **08** delicate, discreet, reactive, sentient **09** cold-short, difficult, emotional, irritable **10** diplomatic, discerning, perceptive, responsive, sensitized, vulnerable **11** considerate, problematic, susceptible, sympathetic, thin-skinned **12** appreciative, highly strung **13** controversial, hyperesthetic, temperamental **14** hyperaesthesic, hyperaesthetic, impressionable, well-thought-out

**sensitivity**
**07** algesia **08** delicacy, esthesia, fineness, softness, sympathy **09** aesthesia, aesthesis, awareness, fragility **11** discernment **12** appreciation, radiesthesia, reactiveness **13** receptiveness, vulnerability **14** perceptiveness, responsiveness, susceptibility

**sensual**
**04** lewd, sexy **05** brute, gross, horny, randy **06** animal, bodily, brutal, carnal, erotic, sexual, sultry **07** fleshly, lustful, swinish, worldly **08** embodied, physical **09** lecherous, pandemian **10** licentious, voluptuary, voluptuous **11** animalistic **12** encarnalized **13** self-indulgent

**sensuality**
**08** lewdness, pleasure, sexiness **09** animalism, carnality, eroticism, prurience **10** debauchery, profligacy **11** gourmandise, libertinism, lustfulness **13** lecherousness, salaciousness **14** lasciviousness, licentiousness, voluptuousness

## sensuous
04 lush, rich 08 pleasant, pleasing
09 aesthetic, luxurious, sumptuous
10 gratifying, voluptuous
11 pleasurable

## sensuously
06 lushly, richly 11 luxuriously,
pleasurably, sumptuously
12 gratifyingly, voluptuously

## sentence
03 swy 04 bird, doom, time 05 curse,
judge, lifer, maxim, order 06 decree,
period, punish, ruling 07 condemn,
opinion, verdict 08 aphorism,
decision, judgment, penalize, porridge
09 judgement 10 adjudgment,
punishment 11 adjudgement
12 condemnation 13 pronouncement
15 pass judgement on

## sententious
05 brief, pithy, short, terse 06 gnomic
07 canting, compact, concise, laconic,
pointed, pompous, preachy
08 succinct 09 axiomatic 10 aphoristic,
moralistic, moralizing 11 judgemental
12 epigrammatic 13 sanctimonious

## sentient
04 live 05 aware 06 living 07 feeling,
sensile 08 reactive 09 conscious,
sensitive 10 responsive

## sentiment
04 idea, posy, view 05 maxim, slops
06 belief, hobnob, pledge 07 emotion,
feeling, opinion, romance, thought
08 attitude, judgment, softness
09 judgement 10 persuasion,
tenderness 11 mawkishness, point of
view, romanticism, sensibility
14 sentimentality 15 soft-heartedness

## sentimental
05 corny, gooey, gucky, gushy, hokey,
mushy, soppy, weepy, yucky, yukky
06 gloopy, loving, sickly, sloppy,
slushy, sugary, tender, too-too 07 boy-
girl, gushing, maudlin, mawkish,
missish, treacly 08 cornball, pathetic,
romantic, rose-pink, shmaltzy,
touching 09 emotional, nostalgic,
rosewater, schmaltzy 10 lovey-dovey,
Wertherian 11 soft-hearted, tear-
jerking 12 affectionate, chocolate-box
13 lackadaisical

## sentimentality
03 goo, yuk 04 gush, mush, pulp, yuck
05 gloop, slush 06 bathos 07 feeling,
shmaltz, treacle 08 schmaltz
09 corniness, nostalgia, sentiment
10 sloppiness, tenderness
11 mawkishness, romanticism,
sensibility 12 emotionalism
14 sentimentalism

## sentry
03 nit 05 guard, watch 06 centry, picket
07 lookout, vedette 08 cockatoo,
sentinel, watchman 09 out-sentry

## separable
08 distinct, dividant, dividual, partible
09 different, divisible, removable
10 detachable, particular
11 independent 15 distinguishable

## separate
03 red, sep, try 04 comb, part, redd,
shed, sort, twin 05 alone, apart, break,
sever, shear, split, twine 06 cut off,
demark, depart, detach, divide,
reduce, remove, secede, single,
sunder, sundry, winnow 07 break up,
discerp, disjoin, dislink, dispart,
diverge, divided, divorce, isolate,
seclude, several, sort out, split up
08 abstract, break off, detached,
discreet, discrete, disperse, dissever,
distinct, distract, disunite, divorced,
isolated, offprint, prescind, set apart,
solitary, uncouple, withdraw 09 come
apart, demarcate, different, disengage,
dismantle, disparate, disunited,
intervene, keep apart, partition,
segregate, single out, take apart,
uncombine, unrelated 10 autonomous,
disconnect, disjointed, dissociate,
individual, particular, segregated,
unattached 11 disentangle,
independent, part company,
unconnected 12 disaffiliate,
disconnected 15 become estranged

## separated
05 apart 06 parted, remote 07 divided,
split up 08 isolated, separate, sundered
09 disunited 10 dissociate, poles apart,
segregated 12 disconnected, poles
asunder 13 disassociated,
discontinuous

## separately
05 alone, apart 06 singly 07 asunder,
divisim 08 one by one 09 in several,
severally 10 absolutely, discretely,
personally 12 individually
13 independently 14 discriminately

## separating
07 parting, sifting 08 abducent,
dividing, divisive 09 isolating,
precisive 10 discretive 11 intervening,
segregating 12 partitioning
13 disengagement

## separation
03 gap 04 gulf, rift 05 split 06 schism,
wrench 07 break-up, divorce, freedom,
parting, split-up 08 avulsion, dialysis,
disunion, dividing, division, farewell,
interval, solution 09 apartheid,
isolation, severance 10 detachment,
divergence, uncoupling
11 demarcation, demarkation,
disjunction, distinction, leave-taking,
segregation 12 disgregation,
disseverment, dissociation,
estrangement 13 disconnection,
disengagement 14 centrifugation

## separatist
05 rebel 08 apostate, renegade,
seceding 09 breakaway, dissenter,
heretical 10 dissenting, schismatic
11 Independent 12 secessionist

## separatists
03 ETA

## September
03 Sep 04 Sept

## septic
06 putrid 08 infected, poisoned

09 festering 10 putrefying
11 suppurating 12 putrefactive

## sepulchral
03 sad 04 deep 05 grave 06 dismal,
gloomy, hollow, morbid, solemn,
sombre, woeful 07 charnel 08 funereal,
mournful 09 cheerless 10 lugubrious,
melancholy 11 sepulchrous

## sepulchre
04 tomb 05 grave, vault 06 burial,
entomb 09 mausoleum 10 repository
11 burial place

## sequel
03 end 05 issue, suite 06 pay-off, result,
upshot 07 outcome 08 follow-up,
sequence 09 after-clap, followers
10 conclusion, successors
11 consequence, development
12 consequences, continuation

## sequence
03 run, set 04 line, suit 05 chain, cycle,
order, track, train 06 course, series,
string 10 procession, succession
11 arrangement, consequence,
progression

## sequester
04 take 05 seize 06 detach, remove
07 impound, isolate, seclude, shut off
08 alienate, insulate, set apart, set
aside, shut away 09 seclusion
10 commandeer, confiscate
11 appropriate, sequestrate

## sequestered
05 quiet 06 lonely, remote 07 outback,
private, retired 08 isolated, secluded
10 cloistered 11 out-of-the-way
12 unfrequented

## sequestrate
04 take 05 seize 07 impound
09 sequester 10 commandeer,
confiscate 11 appropriate

## seraphic
04 holy, pure 06 divine, serene
07 angelic, saintly, sublime 08 beatific,
blissful, heavenly, innocent
09 celestial 10 seraphical

## Serbia and Montenegro
03 SCG, YUG

## serenade
04 wake 07 horning 08 chivaree,
shivaree 09 charivari

## serendipitous
05 happy, lucky 06 chance 09 fortunate
10 accidental, fortuitous, unexpected

## serendipity
04 luck 06 chance 07 fortune
08 accident, fortuity 11 coincidence,
good fortune

## serene
04 calm, cool 05 clear, quiet, still
06 placid, serein 07 halcyon
08 composed, peaceful, seraphic,
tranquil 09 unclouded, unruffled
10 seraphical, untroubled
11 undisturbed, unflappable
12 tranquillize 13 imperturbable

## serenely
06 calmly 07 quietly 08 placidly

**10** peacefully, tranquilly
**13** imperturbably

**serenity**
**04** calm, cool **05** peace **06** repose
**08** calmness, quietude **09** composure,
placidity, quietness, stillness
**12** peacefulness, tranquillity
**14** unflappability

**serf**
**05** helot, slave, thete, thirl **06** thrall
**07** bondman, servant, villein
**08** adscript, bondmaid, bondsman
**09** bond-slave, bondwoman
**10** bondswoman **11** bondservant

**sergeant**
**02** PS **03** NCO, Sgt **04** Cuff, Serg, Troy
**05** Bilko, chips, sarge, Sergt **06** Buzfuz
**08** havildar

**series**
**03** row, run, ser, set **04** line **05** chain,
cycle, early, order, train **06** catena,
course, stream, string **07** library
**08** bead-roll, pedigree, sequence
**10** succession **11** arrangement,
progression **13** concatenation
• **new series** **02** NS

**serious**
**03** bad, big, sad **04** deep, dour, grim,
tidy **05** acute, ample, grave, great,
heavy, large, quiet, sober, staid, stern
**06** honest, lavish, no joke, severe,
solemn, somber, sombre, urgent
**07** crucial, earnest, genuine, pensive,
sincere, sizable, weighty **08** abundant,
critical, generous, grievous, perilous,
pressing, sizeable, worrying
**09** dangerous, difficult, important,
long-faced, momentous, plentiful,
unsmiling **10** humourless, precarious,
thoughtful, unlaughing **11** far-reaching,
preoccupied, significant, substantial
**12** considerable, life-and-death
**13** consequential, of consequence

**seriously**
**04** very **05** badly, jolly **06** highly, really,
sorely **07** acutely, awfully, for real,
gravely, greatly, utterly **08** severely,
solemnly, terribly **09** au sérieux,
decidedly, earnestly, extremely,
intensely, sincerely, unusually
**10** critically, dreadfully, grievously,
remarkably, thoroughly, uncommonly
**11** dangerously, exceedingly,
excessively, frightfully, joking apart,
joking aside **12** immoderately,
inordinately, terrifically, thoughtfully,
unreasonably **13** distressingly,
exceptionally **15** extraordinarily

**seriousness**
**06** moment, weight **07** gravity, urgency
**08** gravitas, sobriety **09** solemnity,
staidness, sternness **10** importance,
sedateness **11** earnestness
**12** significance **14** humourlessness

**sermon**
**03** ser **04** talk **06** homily, preach
**07** address, karakia, khotbah, khotbeh,
khutbah, lecture, message, oration,
reproof **08** harangue **09** discourse,
talking-to **10** preachment
**11** declamation, exhortation

**serow**
**04** thar

**serpent**
**05** lamia, snake **06** ellops **08** basilisk,
sea snake **09** ouroboros **10** cockatrice
*See also* **snake**

**serpentine**
**05** snaky **06** ophite **07** coiling, crooked,
sinuous, snaking, winding **08** asbestos,
tortuous, twisting **09** ophiolite,
snakelike **10** chrysotile, meandering,
retinalite **12** serpentiform

**serrated**
**06** jagged, pinked **07** notched, sawlike,
toothed **08** indented, saw-edged
**09** crenulate **10** crenulated, saw-
toothed, serrulated **11** serratulate
**12** diprionidian **14** monoprionidian

**serried**
**05** close, dense **06** massed **07** compact,
crowded **08** close-set **13** close together

**servant**
**03** boy, man **04** drug, help, jack
**06** drudge, helper **07** subject
**08** hireling **09** ancillary, assistant,
attendant **10** ministrant

*Servants include:*

**03** fag, gip, gyp
**04** char, chef, cook, hind, maid,
page
**05** boots, carer, daily, groom, nanny,
slave, valet, wench
**06** au pair, barman, batman, butler,
chokra, garçon, haiduk, lackey,
menial, ostler, skivvy, tweeny,
waiter
**07** barmaid, bellboy, bellhop,
cleaner, equerry, flunkey,
footman, gossoon, pageboy,
steward, tapsman
**08** charlady, coachman, dogsbody,
domestic, factotum, handmaid,
henchman, home help, house
boy, retainer, scullion, servitor,
turnspit, waitress, wet nurse
**09** chauffeur, errand boy, governess,
housemaid, lady's maid,
seneschal
**10** chauffeuse, handmaiden,
henchwoman, manservant,
stewardess
**11** body servant, boot-catcher,
chambermaid, henchperson,
housekeeper, kitchen-maid,
parlour-maid
**12** domestic help, scullery maid
**13** care assistant, lady-in-waiting,
livery-servant
**14** commissionaire

**serve**
◊ *anagram indicator* **02** do, ka **03** ace,
act, aid, kae, let **04** deal, help, sair,
wait **05** avail, valet **06** answer, assist,
attend, dish up, fulfil, lackey, supply,
wait on **07** benefit, deliver, dish out,
dole out, further, give out, lacquey,
perform, present, provide, satisfy,
succour, suffice, support, undergo,
work for, work out, worship **08** carry
out, complete, function, wait upon
**09** be of use to, discharge, go through

**10** distribute, minister to, take care of
**11** do the work of **12** be employed by
**13** be of benefit to, be of service to, do
a good turn to
• **serve up** ◊ *reversal down indicator*

**service**
**02** RN **03** ace, fee, job, let, RAF, use
**04** army, duty, help, navy, rite, sorb,
tune, turn, work **05** check, usage
**06** course, duties, forces, go over,
labour, repair, ritual **07** amenity,
benefit, repairs, utility, worship
**08** activity, air force, business,
ceremony, disposal, facility, function,
maintain, military, overhaul, resource
**09** advantage, ordinance, sacrament,
servicing **10** assistance, employment,
expediting, observance, usefulness
**11** maintenance, performance,
recondition **12** availability

*Religious services include:*

**04** Mass
**06** matins
**07** baptism, evening, funeral,
morning, wedding
**08** compline, evensong, High Mass,
marriage, memorial
**09** communion, Eucharist
**10** bar mitzvah, bat mitzvah,
dedication
**11** christening, Christingle, Lord's
Supper, nuptial Mass,
remembrance, Requiem Mass
**12** confirmation, Midnight Mass,
thanksgiving
**13** Holy Communion, Holy
Matrimony
**14** First Communion, morning
prayers
**15** harvest festival

• **in service** **05** in use **07** working
**09** operative **10** functional **11** in
operation **12** in regular use **14** in
working order
• **of service** **06** useful **07** helpful
**09** of benefit **10** beneficial, profitable
**12** advantageous
• **on active service** **03** oas
• **out of service** **04** phut **05** kaput
**06** broken, faulty, kaputt **08** out of
use, packed up **09** conked out,
defective **10** not working, on the
blink, on the fritz, out of order

**serviceable**
**04** good **05** plain, tough **06** simple,
strong, usable, useful **07** durable,
helpful **08** availful, sensible
**09** effective, efficient, practical,
unadorned **10** beneficial,
commodious, convenient,
dependable, functional, profitable
**11** hard-wearing, utilitarian
**12** advantageous

**serviceman**
*see* **aircraftman; sailor; soldier**

**servicemen**
*see* **air force; army; navy**

**servile**
**03** low **04** base, mean **05** lowly, slimy
**06** abject, humble, menial, vassal
**07** fawning, slavish, subject

**08** cringing, toadying, unctuous
**09** groveling **10** controlled, grovelling, obsequious, submissive **11** bootlicking, subservient, sycophantic

### servility

**05** slime **07** fawning **08** baseness, meanness, toadyism **09** abjection
**10** abjectness, grovelling, sycophancy
**11** bootlicking, slavishness
**12** subservience, unctuousness **13** self-abasement **14** obsequiousness, submissiveness

### serving

**05** share **06** amount, ration **07** bowlful, helping, portion **08** plateful, spoonful
**11** ministering

### servitude

**05** bonds **06** chains, thrall **07** bondage, peonage, peonism, serfdom, slavery
**08** thirlage, thraldom **09** obedience, vassalage **10** stillicide, subjection, villeinage **11** enslavement, subjugation

### sesame

**03** til **04** beni, teel **05** benne, benni
**06** semsem **07** gingili, jinjili **08** gingelly

### session

**04** bevy, sesh, Sess, term, time, year
**05** bevvy, drill, shoot, spell **06** clinic, grog-on, grog-up, period, séance
**07** hearing, meeting, sitting, stretch
**08** assembly, semester **09** scrimmage, talkathon **10** conference, discussion
**11** church court, down-sitting
*See also* **term**
• **be in session** **03** set, sit
• **close a session** **04** rise

### set

◊ *anagram indicator* **02** TV **03** dip, dot, fix, gel, kit, lay, lot, pit, ply, put
**04** band, bulb, cake, club, dump, firm, gang, give, jell, knit, look, name, park, plan, rate, rest, sink, stud, turn
**05** adapt, apply, array, batch, befit, begin, cause, class, crowd, embed, fixed, frame, grant, group, jelly, lodge, mount, pitch, place, plant, plonk, posit, radio, ready, rigid, scene, score, set up, stage, stake, start, stick, stock, telly, usual, value, wings, write
**06** adjust, agreed, all set, assign, become, choose, circle, clique, create, decide, devise, direct, formal, go down, harden, impose, incite, insert, lead to, locate, ordain, outfit, prompt, select, series, set off, set out, settle, strict, vanish **07** agree on, appoint, arrange, bearing, compose, confirm, congeal, consign, coterie, decided, decline, deposit, dispose, faction, install, lay down, posture, prepare, produce, provide, regular, resolve, routine, scenery, setting, settled, sharpen, situate, specify, station, stiffen, subside, thicken, trigger
**08** allocate, arranged, backdrop, category, conclude, delegate, equipped, everyday, finished, get ready, habitual, occasion, ordained, organize, position, prepared, propound, put right, regulate, result in, schedule, sequence, solidify, sprinkle, standard **09** appointed, coagulate,

completed, customary, designate, determine, direction, disappear, establish, harmonize, ingrained, make ready, organized, prescribe, scheduled, specified, stipulate, variegate **10** assemblage, assortment, background, become firm, become hard, bring about, collection, compendium, complement, co-ordinate, deliberate, determined, entrenched, expression, give rise to, inaugurate, inflexible, prescribed, television, trigger off **11** crystallize, established, inclination, intentional, mise-en-scène, orchestrate, prearranged, stereotyped, synchronize, traditional
**12** conventional **13** predetermined
**14** bring into being
• **set about** **05** begin, frame, start
**06** attack, tackle **08** commence, embark on **09** get down to, undertake
• **set against** **05** weigh **06** assail, divide, oppose **07** balance, compare
**08** alienate, contrast, disunite, estrange
**09** juxtapose
• **set apart** **04** seal **06** divide, ordain
**07** mark off, reserve **08** put aside, separate **09** segregate, sequester
**11** distinguish, peculiarize **12** put on one side, put to one side
**13** differentiate, make different
• **set aside** **04** keep, save **05** allot, annul, break, lay by, put by **06** cancel, ignore, reject, repeal, revoke, select
**07** discard, earmark, put away, reserve, reverse **08** abrogate, discount, keep back, lay aside, mothball, overrule, overturn, put aside, separate, set apart
**09** sequester, slight off, stash away, supersede **10** give over to **13** keep in reserve
• **set back** ◊ *reversal indicator* **04** cost, slow **05** check, delay **06** hinder, hold up, impede, retard, thwart **07** reverse
**08** surprise
• **set down** **03** lay **04** drop, land, note, snub, take **05** judge, pitch, state
**06** affirm, assert, depose, encamp, esteem, record, regard **07** ascribe, deposit, lay down **08** note down
**09** attribute, discharge, establish, formulate, prescribe, stipulate, subscribe, write down **12** put in writing
• **set forth** **03** say **04** shew, show
**05** leave, state **06** depart, praise, record, set off, set out **07** clarify, declare, display, exhibit, explain, expound, present, publish **08** describe, start out **09** delineate, elucidate, explicate, recommend
• **set in** ◊ *insertion indicator* **04** come
**05** begin, inset, start **06** arrive
**08** commence
• **set off** **05** begin, leave, light, start
**06** blow up, depart, ignite, prompt, set out **07** commend, display, enhance, explode, show off, trigger **08** activate, contrast, detonate, heighten, initiate, set forth, start out, touch off
**09** encourage, intensify **10** trigger off
**11** set in motion, take the road
**14** counterbalance **15** throw into relief

• **set on** **03** mug, out, sic, tar **04** bent, firm, sick, sool **05** fixed, go for, tarre
**06** attack, beat up, dogged, intent, strong, turn on **07** assault, dead set, decided, lay into, set upon **08** fall upon, hell-bent, resolute, resolved, stubborn **09** insistent, steadfast, tenacious **10** determined, persistent, purposeful, unwavering
**11** persevering, unflinching **12** single-minded, strong-minded, strong-willed
**14** uncompromising
• **set out** ◊ *anagram indicator* **03** put
**04** boun, laid **05** adorn, begin, bowne, leave, start **06** depart, lay out, set off, strike **07** arrange, display, exhibit, explain, expound, present, take off
**08** describe, start out
• **set up** ◊ *reversal down indicator* **02** up
**03** rig **04** form, rear, trap **05** array, begin, build, erect, fit up, found, frame, pitch, raise, sport, start
**06** create, settle **07** arrange, compose, dispose, elevate, mounted, prepare
**08** assemble, initiate, organize
**09** construct, establish, institute, introduce **10** constitute, inaugurate
**11** incriminate **13** accuse falsely
**14** bring into being

### setback

◊ *reversal indicator* **04** blip, blow, snag
**05** check, delay, hitch, knock, upset
**06** blight, defeat, hiccup, hold-up, rebuff, whammy **07** problem, relapse, reverse **08** body blow, hiccough, reversal **09** hindrance, throwback
**10** difficulty, impediment, misfortune
**11** obstruction **14** disappointment, stumbling-block

### settee

**04** sofa **05** couch, futon, squab
**06** canapé, day-bed, lounge
**07** bergère, dos-à-dos, sofa bed **09** bed-settee, davenport, tête-à-tête
**12** chesterfield

### setter

**01** I **02** me **03** spy **07** dropper
• **setter's** **04** mine
*See also* **crossword**

### setting

**04** site, vail **05** frame, scene **06** chaton, locale, milieu, period **07** context, framing, monture, scenery **08** fixation, location, mounting, position
**09** placement **10** background
**11** environment, mise-en-scène, perspective **12** surroundings

### setting-up

**05** start **08** creation, founding
**09** inception **10** foundation, initiation
**11** institution **12** inauguration, introduction **13** establishment

### settle

**03** fix, pay **04** drop, fall, foot, kill, land, lite, live, nest, perk, rest, sink, stun
**05** agree, bench, clear, fix up, ledge, light, lodge, lower, order, perch, pitch, plant, quiet, solve, squat, state
**06** accept, adjust, alight, ante up, choose, clinch, decide, defray, go down, occupy, people, repose, reside,

**settlement**

square **07** agree on, appoint, arrange, compact, compose, confirm, cough up, descend, discuss, dispose, fork out, inhabit, install, patch up, resolve, subside **08** colonize, come down, complete, conclude, decide on, organize, populate, regulate, settle up, square up **09** determine, discharge, establish, light upon, reconcile **10** compromise, put in order **12** make your home, put down roots **13** do the business
• **settle down**  **05** still **06** shut in, soothe **07** compose, quieten **08** calm down **09** buy a house, get down to, gravitate **10** get married **12** buckle down to, put down roots, start a family **13** concentrate on, knuckle down to **15** apply yourself to, make comfortable

**settlement**
◇ *anagram indicator* **02** pa **03** pah, utu **04** camp, fine, post **05** truce **06** bustee, colony, hamlet **07** kibbutz, manyata, outpost, payment, sinking, village **08** clearing, contract, decision, defrayal, manyatta, ordering, presidio **09** agreement, Ausgleich, bandobast, Botany Bay, bundobust, clearance, community, discharge, rancherie **10** completion, conclusion, encampment, occupation, patching up, plantation, population, resolution, subsidence **11** arrangement, down-sitting, liquidation, penal colony, termination **12** colonization, lake dwelling, organization, satisfaction **13** accommodation, convict colony, establishment **14** reconciliation

**settler**
**07** bushman, incomer, new chum, pilgrim, pioneer, planter **08** colonist, newcomer, shagroon, squatter **09** colonizer, immigrant, inhabiter, Varangian **10** pure Merino **11** beachcomber, Cromwellian **12** frontiersman **14** frontierswoman

**set-to**
**03** row **04** bout, spat **05** brush, fight, scrap **06** barney, bust-up, dust-up, fracas **07** contest, quarrel, wrangle **08** argument, conflict, exchange, squabble **09** argy-bargy **11** altercation **12** disagreement **13** slanging-match

**set-up**
◇ *reversal down indicator* **06** format, system **08** business **09** framework, structure **10** conditions **11** arrangement, composition, disposition **12** organization **13** circumstances

**seven**
**01** S **03** VII **06** heptad, Pleiad **08** hebdomad **09** septenary

## Seven Against Thebes

*The Seven Greek champions who attacked Thebes:*

**06** Tydeus
**08** Adrastus, Capaneus
**09** Polynices
**10** Amphiaraus, Hippomedon
**13** Parthenopaeus

## Seven Deadly Sins
*see* **sin**

## seven hills of Rome
*see* **hill**

## Seven Sisters colleges
*see* **university**

**seventeen**
**04** XVII

**seventy**
**03** LXX

## Seven Wonders of the World
*see* **wonder**

**sever**
**03** cut, end, hew, nip **04** chop, hack, part, pith, rend **05** break, cease, split **06** cleave, cut off, detach, divide, lop off, nip off **07** chop off, disjoin, divorce, tear off **08** alienate, amputate, break off, dissever, dissolve, disunite, estrange, separate **09** disbranch, terminate **10** disconnect, dissociate **13** cut the painter

**several**
**04** a few, many, some **06** divers, sundry **07** diverse, various **08** assorted, distinct, separate **09** a number of, different, disparate, quite a few **10** individual, particular

**severally**
**06** apiece, singly **08** seriatim **10** discretely, separately **12** individually, in particular, particularly, respectively, specifically

**severe**
**03** bad, ill **04** cold, dour, grim, hard **05** acute, cruel, eager, grave, harsh, penal, plain, rigid, sharp, snell, sober, stark, stern, tough **06** fierce, modest, morose, shrewd, simple, strict, strong, taxing, trying **07** arduous, ascetic, austere, caustic, drastic, extreme, intense, serious, spartan, violent **08** Catonian, critical, Draconic, exacting, forceful, grievous, grinding, perilous, pitiless, powerful, rigorous, ruthless **09** agonizing, dangerous, demanding, difficult, Draconian, Dracontic, inclement, merciless, punishing, splitting, stringent, swingeing, unadorned, unbending, unsmiling, unsparing **10** astringent, burdensome, forbidding, functional, hard-handed, inexorable, iron-fisted, iron-handed, relentless, tyrannical, unbearable **11** strait-laced, undecorated **12** businesslike, disapproving, excruciating **13** Rhadamanthine, unembellished, unsympathetic

**severely**
**04** hard, sore **05** badly **06** coldly, dourly, grimly, hardly, sorely **07** acutely, gravely, harshly, sharply, sternly **08** bitterly, strictly **09** extremely, intensely **10** critically, rigorously **11** dangerously **14** disapprovingly

**severity**
**05** wrath **06** rigour **07** gravity **08** bareness, coldness, grimness, hardness, strength **09** acuteness,

austerity, extremity, harshness, intensity, plainness, sharpness, sternness, toughness **10** asceticism, fierceness, severeness, simplicity, spartanism, strictness, stringency **11** seriousness **12** forcefulness, pitilessness, ruthlessness, ungentleness **13** mercilessness

**sew**
**03** hem, run, sue **04** bind, darn, mend, ooze, seam, tack, whip, work **05** baste, drain **06** needle, stitch **08** overcast, overhand **09** embroider **10** buttonhole, whipstitch **12** saddle-stitch

**sewage**
**04** soil **07** sullage

**sewer**
**04** sure **05** drain, shore, sough **06** cloaca, needle, tailor

**sex**
**01** f, m **04** male **05** union **06** allure, coitus, female, gender, libido **07** coition, glamour **08** congress, embraces, intimacy, sexiness **09** magnetism, sex appeal, sexuality **10** commixtion, copulation, lovemaking, sensuality **11** fornication, intercourse **12** consummation, desirability, reproduction **13** seductiveness **14** voluptuousness **15** carnal knowledge, sexual relations

**sex appeal**
**02** it, SA **05** oomph

**sexless**
**01** n **06** neuter **07** asexual, unsexed **08** unsexual **10** undersexed, unfeminine **11** unmasculine **15** parthenogenetic

**sexton**
**06** fossor, verger **09** caretaker, sacristan **10** grave-maker **11** grave-digger

**sexual**
**03** sex **05** gamic **06** carnal, coital, erotic **07** genital, raunchy, sensual **08** venereal **11** procreative **12** reproductive

**sexuality**
**04** lust **06** desire **08** sexiness, virility **09** carnality, eroticism **10** sensuality, sexual urge **12** sexual desire **14** voluptuousness **15** sexual instincts

**sexy**
**04** phat **06** erotic, nubile, slinky, steamy **07** raunchy, sensual **08** alluring, arousing, beddable, exciting, inviting, tempting **09** desirable, provoking, salacious, seductive **10** attractive, suggestive, voluptuous **11** fascinating, flirtatious, provocative, stimulating, titillating **12** pornographic

**Seychelles**
**02** SY **03** SYC

**shabbily**
**08** rottenly, unfairly **09** scruffily **10** despicably, shamefully **11** inelegantly **12** contemptibly, disreputably, unacceptably **13** dishonourably, unfashionably

## shabby

**03** low **04** mean, poky, worn **05** cheap, dingy, dirty, dowdy, faded, mangy, oorie, ourie, owrie, pokey, scaly, seedy, tacky, tatty **06** frayed, mangey, maungy, paltry, poking, ragged, rotten, scurvy, shoddy, unfair **07** raunchy, run-down, scruffy, squalid, worn-out **08** dog-eared, low-lived, shameful, tattered, unworthy **09** moth-eaten, out at heel **10** broken-down, despicable, down-at-heel, flea-bitten, ramshackle, threadbare, tumbledown **11** dilapidated, in disrepair **12** contemptible, disreputable, unacceptable **13** discreditable, dishonourable

## shack

**03** hut **04** dump, hole, shed **05** cabin, hovel, hutch **06** lean-to, shanty

## shackle

**03** tie **04** bind, bond, gyve, iron, rope **05** chain, limit **06** couple, fetter, hamper, hobble, impede, secure, tether, thwart **07** darbies, inhibit, manacle, trammel **08** encumber, handcuff, handicap, obstruct, restrain, restrict **09** bracelets, constrain, hamstring, hindrance, restraint **10** constraint, fetterlock, hamshackle **11** encumbrance, obstruction, restriction

## shad

**05** allis **06** allice, twaite

## shade

**03** dim, hue, tad **04** cast, dash, dusk, hide, hint, part, tint, tone, ugly, veil **05** blind, cloud, color, cover, ghost, gloom, swale, tinge, touch, trace, umbra, visor, vizor **06** amount, awning, canopy, colour, darken, degree, memory, nuance, screen, shadow, shield, shroud, spirit **07** conceal, curtain, dimness, obscure, parasol, phantom, protect, shadows, shelter, spectre, umbrage, variety **08** bongrace, covering, darkness, gloaming, overcast, reminder, sunblind, sunshade, tincture, twilight, umbrella **09** gradation, inumbrate, murkiness, obscurity, represent, semblance, shadiness, suspicion **10** apparition, difference, gloominess, overshadow, protection, suggestion **12** semi-darkness **14** block light from See also **black; blue; colour; dye; green; grey; orange; pigment; pink; purple; rainbow; red; white; yellow**
• **a shade** **04** a bit **06** a touch, a trace, rather **07** a little, a trifle **08** slightly
• **put in the shade** **03** top **04** beat **05** dwarf, excel **07** eclipse, outrank, surpass **08** outclass, outshine
• **shade off** **04** melt, pass **05** blend **07** gradate **10** intergrade

## shadow

**03** dog, pal **04** dusk, hide, hint, pall, scog, scug, skug, stag, tail **05** cloud, cover, ghost, gloom, image, scoog, scoug, shade, shape, stalk, trace, trail, umbra, watch **06** blight, darken, follow, screen, shield, sleuth, spirit, typify, unreal **07** dimness, feigned, obscure, outline, remnant, sadness, shelter, trouble, umbrage, vestige **08** darkness, follower, gloaming, overhang, penumbra, sidekick, twilight **09** companion, detective, obscurity, remainder, suspicion **10** foreboding, overshadow, protection, silhouette, suggestion **11** tenebrosity **12** semi-darkness **14** Brocken spectre, representation
• **a shadow of your former self** **07** apology, remnant, vestige **13** poor imitation, weaker version
• **without a shadow of a doubt** **05** truly **06** surely **07** clearly, no doubt **08** of course **09** assuredly, certainly, doubtless **10** most likely **11** indubitably, undoubtedly **12** indisputably, without doubt **14** unquestionably

## shadowy

**03** dim **04** dark, hazy **05** faint, murky, shady, vague **06** gloomy, unreal **07** ghostly, obscure, phantom, unclear **08** ethereal, illusory, nebulous, secluded, spectral, symbolic **09** dreamlike, imaginary, tenebrose, tenebrous **10** ill-defined, indistinct, intangible, mysterious, tenebrious **11** crepuscular, umbratilous **13** indeterminate, unsubstantial

## shady

**03** dim **04** cool, dark, iffy **05** bosky, fishy, leafy **06** bowery, louche, opaque, shaded, shifty, veiled **07** clouded, covered, crooked, dubious, obscure, shadowy, suspect, umbrose, umbrous **08** screened, shielded, shrouded, sinister, slippery **09** dishonest, protected, tenebrose, tenebrous, umbratile, underhand, unethical **10** caliginous, mysterious, suspicious, tenebrious, umbrageous, unreliable **11** umbratilous, umbriferous **12** disreputable, questionable, unscrupulous **13** untrustworthy

## shaft

**03** ash, bar, fil, pit, ray, rod **04** beam, butt, dart, duct, dupe, fill, flue, fust, hilt, pole, sink, stem, tige, well **05** arbor, arrow, scape, shank, stale, stalk, stave, steal, steel, steil, stele, stick, stock, stulm, winze **06** handle, pencil, pillar, rachis, scapus, steale, tunnel **07** missile, passage, swindle, upright, winning **08** hoistway **09** truncheon

## shaggy

**04** rag'd **05** bushy, hairy, nappy, ragde, tousy, touzy, towsy, towzy **06** horrid, ragged, woolly **07** crinose, hirsute, unkempt, unshorn **09** mop-headed **10** long-haired **11** dishevelled

## shake

◊ anagram indicator **03** jog, wag, wap **04** bump, faze, jerk, jolt, pump, rock, roll, shog, stir, sway, wave **05** alarm, alert, crack, heave, lower, quake, rouse, shock, split, swing, throb, trill, upset, waver, wield, wring **06** bounce, didder, dindle, dinnle, dismay, dodder, happen, hustle, jigger, jiggle, joggle, jostle, judder, justle, lessen, moment, quiver, rattle, reduce, shiver, summon, totter, trillo, twitch, weaken, wobble **07** agitate, concuss, disturb, fissure, perturb, quaking, rocking, shake up, shoggle, shoogle, shudder, tremble, unnerve, vibrate **08** brandish, convulse, diminish, distress, flourish, frighten, unsettle **09** oscillate, shivering, throbbing, trembling, undermine, vibration **10** convulsion, discompose, intimidate, shuddering, unsettling **11** disturbance, oscillation
• **shake a leg** **05** hurry **07** hurry up **08** step on it **10** get a move on, look lively **11** get cracking **15** get your skates on
• **shake off** **04** heal, lose, mend **05** elude, rally **06** escape, pick up, revive **07** get away, get over, get well, improve **08** dislodge, get rid of, outstrip, shrug off **09** get better **10** bounce back, convalesce, feel better, recuperate **11** be on the mend, get away from, give the slip, leave behind, outdistance, pull through, recover from **12** gain strength **13** turn the corner
• **shake up** **03** mix **05** alarm, rouse, shock, upset **06** jumble, rattle **07** disturb, succuss, unnerve, upbraid **08** distress, unsettle **09** rearrange, reshuffle **10** reorganize **11** restructure

## Shakespeare

**02** WS **07** the Bard **13** The Swan of Avon

*Shakespeare's characters include:*

**03** Hal (Prince), **Nym**, **Sly** (Christopher)
**04** **Ajax**, **Anne** (Lady), **Dull**, **Fool** (The), **Ford** (Mistress), **Hero**, **Iago**, **John** (Don), **John** (King), **Kate**, **Kent** (Earl of), **Lear** (King), **Moth**, **Page** (Mistress), **Puck**, **Snug**
**05** **Ariel**, **Bagot**, **Belch** (Sir Toby), **Bushy**, **Celia**, **Diana**, **Edgar**, **Feste**, **Flute**, **Gobbo** (Launcelot), **Green**, **Julia**, **Maria**, **Nurse**, **Paris** (Count), **Pedro** (Don), **Regan**, **Romeo**, **Snout**, **Speed**, **Timon**, **Titus**, **Viola**
**06** **Alonso**, **Angelo**, **Antony** (Mark), **Armado** (Don Adriano de), **Audrey**, **Banquo**, **Bianca**, **Bottom** (Nick), **Brutus**, **Cassio**, **Cloten**, **Cobweb**, **Dromio**, **Duncan** (King), **Edmund**, **Emilia**, **Fabian**, **Hamlet**, **Hecate**, **Hector**, **Helena**, **Henry V** (King), **Hermia**, **Imogen**, **Jaques**, **Juliet**, **Launce**, **Marina**, **Oberon**, **Oliver** (de Bois), **Olivia**, **Orsino**, **Oswald**, **Pistol**, **Pompey**, **Porter**, **Portia**, **Quince**, **Silvia**, **Thisbe**, **Ursula**, **Verges**, **Yorick**
**07** **Adriana**, **Antonio**, **Berowne**, **Bertram** (Count of Rousillon), **Caliban**, **Capulet**, **Cesario**, **Claudio**, **Costard**, **Fleance**, **Goneril**, **Gonzalo**, **Henry IV** (King), **Henry VI** (King), **Horatio**, **Hotspur**, **Iachimo**, **Jessica**, **Laertes**, **Lavinia**, **Leontes**, **Lepidus**, **Lorenzo**, **Luciana**, **Macbeth**, **Macbeth** (Lady), **Macduff**,

Malcolm, Mariana, Martext (Sir Oliver), Miranda, Nerissa, Octavia, Ophelia, Orlando, Othello, Paulina, Perdita, Proteus, Pyramus, Quickly (Mistress), Shallow, Shylock, Sycorax, Theseus, Titania, Troilus

**08** Bardolph, Bassanio, Beatrice, Benedick, Benvolio, Charmian, Claudius, Cordelia, Cressida, Dogberry, Falstaff (Sir John), Florizel, Fluellen, Ganymede, Gertrude, Hermione, Isabella, Laurence (Friar), Lucretia, Lysander, Malvolio, Mercutio, Montague, Pandarus, Parolles, Pericles, Polonius, Prospero, Rosalind, Rosaline, Stephano, Trinculo

**09** Aguecheek (Sir Andrew), Antigonus, Cleopatra, Collatine, Cornelius, Cymbeline, Demetrius, Desdemona, Enobarbus, Ferdinand, Ferdinand (King of Navarre), Frederick (Duke), Henry VIII (King), Hippolyta, Hortensio, Katharina, Katharine (Princess of France), Nathaniel (Sir), Petruchio, Polixenes, Richard II, Sebastian, Valentine, Vincentio (Duke)

**10** Antipholus (of Ephesus), Antipholus (of Syracuse), Collatinus, Coriolanus, Fortinbras, Gloucester (Earl of), Holofernes, Jaquenetta, Richard III, Starveling, Tarquinius, Touchstone

**11** Mustard-seed, Peasblossom, Rosencrantz

**12** Guildenstern, Julius Caesar, Three Witches

**15** Robin Goodfellow, Titus Andronicus

*Shakespeare's plays:*

**06** Hamlet, Henry V
**07** Macbeth, Othello
**08** King John, King Lear, Pericles
**09** Cymbeline, Henry VIII, Richard II
**10** Coriolanus, Richard III, The Tempest
**11** As You Like It
**12** Julius Caesar, Twelfth Night
**13** Timon of Athens
**14** Henry IV Part One, Henry IV Part Two, Henry VI Part One, Henry VI Part Two, Romeo and Juliet, The Winter's Tale
**15** Titus Andronicus
**16** Henry VI Part Three, Love's Labours Lost
**17** Measure for Measure, The Comedy of Errors
**18** Antony and Cleopatra, Troilus and Cressida
**19** Much Ado About Nothing, The Merchant of Venice, The Taming of the Shrew
**20** All's Well That Ends Well
**21** A Midsummer Night's Dream, Hamlet, Prince of Denmark
**22** The Merry Wives of Windsor
**23** The Two Gentlemen of Verona

**shake-up**
**08** upheaval **09** reshuffle

**11** disturbance **13** rearrangement, restructuring **14** reorganization

**shaky**
◊ *anagram indicator* **04** weak **05** dicky, loose, quaky, rocky, wonky **06** coggly, cranky, dickey, flimsy, wobbly **07** dubious, quavery, rickety, suspect, tottery, unsound **08** insecure, unstable, unsteady, wavering **09** doddering, faltering, quivering, tentative, tottering, trembling, tremulous, uncertain, unfounded **10** precarious, staggering, ungrounded, unreliable **11** unsupported **12** questionable **13** untrustworthy

**shale**
**04** husk, till **05** blaes, fakes, shell **06** blaise, blaize, faikes **09** torbanite **12** porcellanite **14** Kupferschiefer

**shall**
**02** 'll

**shallow**
**03** ebb **04** bank, flat, flew, flue, idle **05** empty, fleet, petty, shoal **06** flimsy, shoaly, simple, slight, spread **07** foolish, surface, trivial **08** ignorant, skin-deep, trifling **09** frivolous, insincere **11** meaningless, superficial, unscholarly **13** rattle-brained **14** one-dimensional

**sham**
◊ *anagram indicator* **03** cod **04** copy, fake, hoax, idol, mock **05** bogus, cheat, dummy, false, feign, fraud, mimic, pseud, put on, put-on, snide **06** affect, con man, humbug, phoney, pseudo, shoddy, stumer **07** feigned, forgery, imitate, pretend **08** deceiver, fakement, feigning, imposter, impostor, pretence, pretense, simulate, spurious, swindler **09** brummagem, charlatan, dissemble, gold brick, imitation, imposture, pinchbeck, pretended, pretender, simulated, synthetic **10** artificial, pasteboard, simulation **11** counterfeit, make believe, make-believe, mock-modesty, synthetical **12** impersonator

**shaman**
**05** pawaw **06** healer, powwow **07** angekok, tohunga **08** angekkok, magician, sorcerer **11** medicine man, witch doctor **13** medicine woman

**shamble**
**04** drag, limp **06** doddle, falter, hobble, scrape, toddle **07** bauchle, scamble, shuffle

**shambles**
**04** mess **05** chaos, havoc, wreck **06** bedlam, muddle, pigsty **07** anarchy **08** abattoir, butchery, disarray, disorder, madhouse **09** confusion **10** slaughtery **14** slaughterhouse **15** disorganization

**shambling**
**05** loose **06** clumsy **07** awkward **08** lurching, ungainly, unsteady **09** lumbering, shuffling **10** disjointed **13** unco-ordinated

**shambolic**
**05** messy **07** chaotic, muddled **08** confused **10** in disarray **12** disorganized **14** all over the shop

**shame**
**03** fie, fye, out, sin **04** alas, pity **05** abash, aidos, guilt, pudor, shend, stain, sully, taint **06** ashame, debase, humble, infamy, rebuke, show up, stigma, too bad **07** bad luck, beshame, degrade, modesty, mortify, remorse, reproof, scandal **08** confound, disgrace, dishonor, ignominy, repriefe, reproach, ridicule **09** confusion, discredit, dishonour, disrepute, embarrass, humiliate **10** misfortune, opprobrium, put to shame **11** bashfulness, compunction, degradation, humiliation **13** embarrassment, mortification **14** disappointment, shamefacedness
• **put to shame 05** shend **06** humble, rebuke, show up **07** eclipse, mortify, surpass, upstage **08** disgrace, outclass, outshine, outstrip **09** embarrass, humiliate

**shamefaced**
**05** sorry **06** guilty **07** abashed, ashamed **08** blushing, contrite, penitent, pudibund, red-faced, sheepish **09** mortified, regretful **10** apologetic, humiliated, remorseful **11** embarrassed **13** uncomfortable

**shameful**
**03** low **04** base, foul, mean, poor, vile **06** wicked **07** heinous, ignoble, shaming **08** indecent, shocking, unworthy **09** atrocious, pudendous **10** abominable, inglorious, mortifying, outrageous, scandalous **11** disgraceful, humiliating, ignominious **12** contemptible, embarrassing **13** discreditable, dishonourable, reprehensible

**shamefully**
**10** shockingly **11** atrociously **12** confoundedly, outrageously, scandalously **13** disgracefully, ignominiously, reprehensibly **14** embarrassingly

**shameless**
**05** brash **06** brazen, wanton **07** blatant, corrupt, defiant **08** blattant, browless, depraved, flagrant, hardened, immodest, improper, impudent, indecent, insolent, unseemly, unshamed **09** abashless, audacious, bald-faced, barefaced, dissolute, frontless, unabashed, unashamed, unbashful **10** brass-faced, impenitent, indecorous, unbecoming, unblushing **11** ithyphallic, unregretful, unrepentant **12** incorrigible, unprincipled

**shamelessly**
**09** blatantly, defiantly **10** immodestly, improperly, indecently **11** unashamedly **12** incorrigibly

**shanty**
**03** hut **04** shed **05** bothy, cabin, hovel, hutch, shack **06** chanty, lean-to **07** chantey, chantie, shantey
• **shanty town 06** favela **10** bidonville

## shape

◇ *anagram indicator* **03** air, cut, hew **04** cast, form, look, make, plan, trim, turn **05** adapt, alter, block, build, carve, forge, frame, guide, guise, image, lines, model, mould, state **06** adjust, aspect, create, define, design, devise, direct, embody, fettle, figure, format, health, kilter, modify, sculpt **07** conduce, develop, fashion, outline, pattern, prepare, produce, profile, purpose, remodel, whittle **08** contours, likeness, organize, physique, regulate **09** character, condition, construct, determine, influence, sculpture, semblance, structure **10** apparition, appearance, silhouette **11** accommodate **13** configuration
*See also* **circle; figure; triangle**
• **shape up  06** come on **07** develop, improve **08** flourish, progress **09** take shape **11** make headway, move forward **12** make progress
• **take shape  03** gel **04** form **06** inform **11** become clear, materialize **12** come together **14** become definite

## shapeless

◇ *anagram indicator* **05** dumpy **07** chaotic **08** deformed, formless, indigest, nebulous, unformed, unframed **09** amorphous, irregular, misshapen **11** purposeless, undeveloped, unfashioned **12** unstructured **13** unfashionable **15** ill-proportioned

## shapely

**04** neat, tidy, trig, trim **06** comely, gainly, pretty **07** elegant, featous **08** feateous, featuous, graceful **09** well-set-up **10** attractive, curvaceous, forehanded, voluptuous, well-formed, well-turned **11** clean-limbed

## shard

**03** bit, gap **04** chip, part **05** piece, scrap, sherd **06** shiver, sliver **08** fragment, particle, splinter

## share

**03** cut, due, lot, rug **04** divi, dole, part, snap, snip, sock **05** allot, divvy, halve, quota, snack, split, whack **06** assign, common, divide, finger, ration **07** carve up, deal out, dole out, give out, go Dutch, hand out, partake, portion, rake-off, section **08** allocate, dividend, division, go halves, interest, ordinary, share out **09** allotment, allottery, allowance, apportion, bank-stock, co-portion **10** allocation, contingent, distribute, percentage, plough-iron, proportion **11** go halvesies, participate **12** compare notes, contribution, go fifty-fifty, have a share in **14** slice of the cake
• **shareholder  09** ploughman
• **share out  05** allot, split **06** assign **07** divvy up, give out, hand out, mete out **08** divide up **09** apportion, parcel out **10** distribute

## shark

**05** crook **07** fleecer, sharper, slicker,

sponger **08** man-eater, operator, parasite, swindler **11** extortioner **12** extortionist **13** wheeler-dealer

*Sharks include:*

**03** cat, fox, saw
**04** blue, bull, mako
**05** blind, dusky, ghost, gummy, lemon, night, nurse, sagre, swell, tiger, whale, zebra
**06** beagle, carpet, goblin, salmon, school, sea cat
**07** basking, bramble, dogfish, leopard, requiem, sleeper, soupfin
**08** blacktip, grey reef, mackerel, thresher, whitetip
**09** angelfish, epaulette, Greenland, man-eating, porbeagle, sand tiger, sevengill, sharpnose, wobbegong
**10** Colclough's, great white, hammerhead, Portuguese, shovelhead
**11** ragged-tooth, smooth-hound

## sharp

**03** fit, sly **04** able, acid, cold, curt, edgy, fine, gleg, keen, neat, sour, tart, tidy, wily **05** acidy, acrid, acute, alert, brisk, clear, crisp, cruel, eager, edged, harsh, natty, nifty, quick, rapid, razor, smart, snell, spiky, stark, tangy, tight **06** abrupt, acidic, artful, astute, barbed, biting, bitter, bright, clever, crafty, fierce, hungry, jagged, marked, severe, shrewd, snappy, strong, sudden **07** acerbic, brusque, burning, caustic, cunning, cutting, elegant, exactly, extreme, hairpin, hurtful, intense, nipping, piquant, pointed, pungent, stylish, varment, varmint, violent **08** abruptly, all there, clear-cut, definite, distinct, freezing, incisive, on the dot, peracute, piercing, poignant, promptly, sardonic, scathing, serrated, shooting, stabbing, stinging, suddenly, venomous, vinegary **09** deceptive, dishonest, malicious, observant, on the ball, precisely, sarcastic, trenchant, vitriolic, voiceless **10** astringent, discerning, knife-edged, needle-like, perceptive, punctually, razor-edged, razor-sharp, unexpected **11** acrimonious, fashionable, intelligent, penetrating, quick-witted, well-defined **12** twenty-twenty, unexpectedly

## sharpen

**03** set **04** edge, file, hone, keen, whet **05** frost, grind, point, stone, strop **09** acuminate

## sharp-eyed

**08** hawk-eyed, noticing **09** eagle-eyed, observant **10** perceptive **11** keen-sighted **12** eagle-sighted

## sharply

**05** smack **06** curtly **07** acutely, clearly, harshly, quickly, rapidly, starkly, tightly **08** abruptly, bitterly, fiercely, markedly, suddenly **09** brusquely **10** definitely, distinctly, venomously **12** unexpectedly **13** acrimoniously, sarcastically, vitriolically

## sharpness

**04** edge, whet **05** venom **06** acuity, acumen **07** clarity, cruelty, sarcasm, vitriol **08** keenness, severity **09** acuteness, crispness, eagerness, harshness, intensity, precision **10** astuteness, definition, fierceness, shrewdness **11** brusqueness, discernment, observation, penetration **12** incisiveness **14** perceptiveness

## shatter

◇ *anagram indicator* **04** bust, dash, ruin, star **05** blast, break, burst, crack, craze, crush, smash, split, upset, wreck **06** shiver **07** destroy, explode, scatter **08** demolish, fragment, overturn, splinter **09** devastate, overwhelm, pulverize **10** disappoint, smithereen **14** break your heart

## shattered

◇ *anagram indicator* **05** all in, weary **06** broken, done in, pooped, zonked **07** crushed, worn out **08** dead beat, dog-tired, tired out **09** exhausted, fagged out, knackered, plastered, pooped out **10** devastated **11** overwhelmed, ready to drop, tuckered out

## shattering

**06** severe **08** crushing, damaging, smashing **10** paralysing **11** devastating **12** overwhelming

## shave

**03** cut **04** barb, crop, pare, trim **05** brush, graze, plane, shear, touch **06** barber, fleece, paring, scrape **07** plunder
• **close shave  09** close call, near touch **10** close thing, narrow miss **11** lucky escape **12** narrow escape

## Shaw

**03** GBS

## shawl

**04** wrap **05** scarf, stole, tozie **06** afghan, tonnag, zephyr **07** blanket, dopatta, dupatta, tallith, whittle **08** pashmina, shatoosh, turnover **09** shahtoosh **10** India shawl **11** prayer shawl **12** Kashmir shawl, Paisley shawl

## she

**01** a **03** her **04** elle
*See also* **girl**

## sheaf

**04** gait, garb **05** bunch, garbe, gerbe, truss **06** armful, bundle **07** dorlach

## shear

**03** cut **04** clip, crop, trim **05** shave, strip **06** barber, fleece **07** scissor, tonsure **08** clipping, separate **09** penetrate

## sheath

**04** case **05** ocrea, shard, shell, theca, volva **06** casing, cocoon, condom, ochrea, rubber, sleeve, vagina **07** johnnie, root cap, velamen **08** covering, envelope, scabbard, urceolus, vaginula, vaginule, wrapping **09** epidermis **10** caddis-case, coleoptile, endodermis, neurilemma, neurolemma, rhinotheca, thumbstall, zoothecium **11** perineurium **12** French letter, perichaetium, prophylactic, rhamphotheca

## shed

◊ *deletion indicator* **03** hut, mew, sow **04** cast, drop, emit, give, molt, part, pour, skeo, skio **05** hovel, linny, moult, shack, shine, spend, spill, spilt, throw **06** impart, lean-to, linhay, linney, remove, shower, slough **07** cast off, diffuse, discard, emitted, fall off, let fall, parting, radiate, scatter, send out, shippen, shippon **08** building, disperse, get rid of, give away, outhouse, separate, skillion **10** besprinkle

• **shed tears 03** sob **04** bawl, howl, wail, weep **05** whine **06** snivel **07** blubber, whimper **09** be in tears **14** burst into tears, cry your eyes out

## sheen

**05** gleam, gloss, shine, water **06** bright, luster, lustre, patina, polish **07** burnish, shimmer, shining, sparkle, varnish **08** radiance **09** beautiful, shininess **10** brightness, brilliance

## sheep

**03** ewe, hog, joe, keb, mug, ram, teg, tup, yeo, yow **04** fold, hogg, lamb, tegg, yowe **05** crone, flock, yowie **06** bident, gimmer, hidder, hirsel, hogget, lamber, theave, wether, woolly **07** jumbuck, twinter **08** hoggerel **09** shearling **10** bell-wether, woollyback

*Sheep include:*

**03** Rya
**04** Dala, Gute, Soay
**05** ammon, ancon, aodad, Jacob, Lleyn, Lonck, Masai, Rygja, Texel, Tunis, urial
**06** aoudad, Arcott, argali, Awassi, Balwen, Beltex, bharal, burhel, burrel, Dorper, Galway, Masham, merino, muflon, Romney
**07** Barbary, bighorn, burrell, burrhel, caracul, Cheviot, Colbred, Gotland, karakul, Karaman, Lincoln, Loghtan, Loghtyn, mouflon, Romanov, Roussin, Ryeland, St Croix, Steigar, Suffolk, Tibetan, Vendeen
**08** Columbia, Cotswold, herdwick, Katahdin, Loaghtan, Meatlinc, moufflon, Ouessant, Peliquey, Portland, Shetland, thinhorn, troender
**09** blackface, Costentin, Leicester, Marco Polo, Southdown, Teeswater
**10** Charollais
**11** Wensleydale
**15** Border Leicester

• **flock of sheep 04** fold, trip

## sheepish

**05** silly **07** abashed, ashamed, foolish **09** chastened, mortified **10** shamefaced **11** embarrassed **13** self-conscious, uncomfortable

## sheepskin

**04** napa, roan **05** basan, Mocha, nappa **06** mouton, shammy, skiver **07** chamois, morocco **11** wash leather **13** shammy leather

• **sheepskin coat 07** posteen, zamarra, zamarro **08** poshteen **10** Afghan coat

## sheer

**04** bend, fine, flat, full, main, mere, pure, rank, thin, turn, veer **05** blank, clear, drift, gauzy, light, plumb, quite, sharp, shift, stark, steep, swing, total, utter **06** abrupt, bright, flimsy, simple, swerve **07** deflect, deviate, diverge, perfect **08** absolute, complete, delicate, gossamer, thorough, unbroken, vertical **09** deviation, downright, out-and-out, unmingled, veritable **10** diaphanous, see-through, vertically **11** precipitous, translucent, transparent, unmitigated, unqualified **12** unadulterate **13** perpendicular, thoroughgoing, unadulterated, unconditional

## sheet

**03** cel, sht, web **04** cell, coat, film, leaf, page, pane, sail, sill, skin, slab **05** cover, folio, layer, panel, piece, plate, reach, sweep **06** lamina, shroud, veneer **07** blanket, blotter, coating, expanse, overlay, stratum, stretch, surface **08** bed linen, covering, membrane, pamphlet **09** Celluloid®, newspaper **10** broadsheet

## shelf

**03** bar **04** bank, bink, rack, reef, sill, step **05** bench, ledge, shoal, stage **06** shelve, shrine **07** bracket, counter, retable, sand bar, terrace **08** credence, credenza, informer, sandbank, shelving **11** mantelpiece, mantelshelf **12** chimney piece

• **on the shelf 06** single **09** on your own, unmarried **10** spouseless, unattached **15** without a partner

## shell

◊ *anagram indicator* ◊ *ends deletion indicator* **03** pod **04** body, bomb, case, clam, hull, husk, mail, rind, shot **05** blitz, chank, conch, cowry, crust, frame, ormer, shale, shard, sheal, sheel, shiel, shill, shuck, testa **06** attack, bullet, casing, cockle, cowrie, fire on, mussel, pellet, sea pen **07** admiral, barrage, bombard, carcase, carcass, chassis, cochlea, grenade, limacel, missile, scallop, scollop **08** carapace, covering, sea acorn, skeleton, univalve **09** explosive, framework, Midas's ear, structure, turbinate **10** integument, projectile **11** globigerina **12** pelican's-foot

• **shell money 04** peag, peak **06** wakiki, wampum **10** wampumpeag

• **shell out 04** ante, give **05** pay up, spend **06** ante up, donate, expend, lay out, pay out **07** cough up, fork out **08** disburse **10** contribute

## shellfish

• **young shellfish 04** spat
*See also* **fish; mollusc; seafood**

## shelter

◊ *containment indicator* **03** cot, lee **04** cote, hide, loun, lown, roof, scog, scug, skug, tent **05** bield, bivvy, bothy, cover, guard, haven, house, hovel, lound, lownd, put up, scoog, scoug, shade **06** asylum, bunker, covert, defend, dugout, harbor, hole up, maimai, refuge, safety, sconce, screen, shadow, shield, shroud, wiltja **07** conceal, defence, embower, harbour, imbower, lodging, protect, retreat, roofing **08** bolthole, funkhole, security, snow-hole **09** coverture, safeguard, sanctuary, screening **10** overshadow, protection **11** accommodate, cold harbour, weather-fend **13** accommodation

## sheltered

**03** lee **04** cosy, loun, lown, snug, warm **05** lound, lownd, quiet, shady **06** shaded **07** covered, retired, sharded **08** isolated, screened, secluded, shielded **09** protected, reclusive, unworldly, withdrawn **10** cloistered, in the shade

## shelve

**04** halt **05** defer, ledge, shelf, shunt, slope **06** put off **07** incline, suspend **08** lay aside, mothball, postpone, put aside, put on ice **09** sidetrack **10** pigeonhole

## shepherd

**04** Acis, herd, lead **05** guide, steer, swain, usher **06** convoy, escort, feeder, pastor, tar-box **07** conduct, herdboy, herdess, marshal **08** guardian, herdsman **09** herd-groom, protector **11** flockmaster, shepherd boy, shepherdess **12** shepherdling

## sheriff

**06** grieve, lawman, shirra **07** bailiff **08** landdros, shireman, viscount **09** landdrost **10** shire-reeve

## sherry

**04** fino **05** Xeres **06** doctor **07** amoroso, oloroso, sherris **08** Montilla **10** manzanilla **11** amontillado, Bristol-milk

• **sherry glass 06** copita **08** schooner

## shield

**05** cover, fence, guard, pelta, shade, targe **06** buckle, defend, screen, shadow **07** buckler, bulwark, defence, forfend, mantlet, protect, rampart, shelter, support, ward off **08** keep safe, mantelet, plastron **09** protector, safeguard **10** escutcheon, protection

## shift

◊ *anagram indicator* **03** rid **04** core, move, post, quit, sell, slip, span, tack, time, tour, turn, vary, veer, warp, work **05** alter, budge, carry, cimar, cymar, evade, relay, smock, spell, stint, swing, U-turn **06** adjust, change, fidget, go away, hirsle, manage, modify, period, put off, remove, swerve, switch, wrench **07** chemise, consume, removal, stretch, swallow **08** artifice, dislodge, displace, get rid of, movement, pis aller, relocate, transfer **09** cutty-sark, expedient, fluctuate, rearrange, transpose, variation **10** alteration, relocation, reposition **11** contrivance, fluctuation, lodging turn, prevaricate **12** displacement, modification, tergiversate **13** rearrangement, transposition

### shiftless
**04** idle, lazy **05** inept **07** aimless **08** feckless, goalless, indolent, slothful **11** incompetent, ineffectual, inefficient, unambitious **12** resourceless **13** directionless, irresponsible, lackadaisical **14** good-for-nothing, unenterprising

### shifty
◊ *anagram indicator* **04** iffy, wily **05** shady **06** crafty, louche, tricky **07** cunning, devious, dubious, evasive, furtive **08** scheming, slippery **09** deceitful, dishonest, underhand **10** contriving **11** duplicitous **13** untrustworthy

### shilling
**01** s **03** bob, hog **06** deaner, teston **09** twalpenny **11** shovelboard, twalpennies, twelve-penny **12** shuffleboard

### shilly-shally
**05** waver **06** dither, falter, seesaw, teeter **08** hesitate, hum and ha **09** fluctuate, hem and haw, mess about, vacillate **10** dilly-dally **11** prevaricate, vacillation **12** be indecisive, indecisively **13** sit on the fence **14** whittie-whattie

### shimmer
◊ *anagram indicator* **04** glow, haze, play **05** gleam, glint **06** lustre **07** flicker, glimmer, glisten, glitter, sparkle, twinkle **10** glistening **11** iridescence, scintillate

### shimmering
◊ *anagram indicator* **05** shiny **07** glowing, shining **08** gleaming, luminous, lustrous **09** chatoyant **10** avanturine, aventurine, glistening, glittering, iridescent **12** incandescent

### shin
**03** sin **04** soar **05** climb, mount, scale, shoot, skink, swarm **06** ascend, shinny **07** clamber **08** scrabble, scramble

### shine
**03** rub, wax **04** beam, buff, dash, emit, glow, lamp, leam, leme, star **05** brush, excel, flash, glare, glaze, gleam, glint, gloss, light, party, rub up, sheen, skyre **06** beacon, come up, dazzle, lustre, patina, polish, shindy **07** burnish, effulge, flicker, give off, glimmer, glisten, glitter, radiate, shimmer, sparkle, twinkle **08** lambency, radiance, resplend, stand out **09** irradiate **10** brightness, effulgence, incandesce **11** be brilliant, be excellent **12** be pre-eminent, luminescence, phosphoresce **13** be outstanding, incandescence

### shingle
**06** chesel, chisel

### shingles
**04** zona **06** zoster **12** herpes zoster

### shininess
**05** gleam, sheen, shine **06** lustre, polish

**07** burnish, glitter **10** brightness, effulgence, glossiness

### shining
**04** glow, neat **05** beamy, glary, light, lucid, moony, nitid, sheen **06** bright, candid, glossy, golden, lucent, marble, starry **07** aeneous, beaming, eminent, fulgent, glowing, lamping, leading, perfect, radiant **08** flashing, gleaming, glinting, glooming, glorious, luculent, luminous, lustrous, relucent, rutilant, splendid **09** brilliant, effulgent, excellent, sparkling, splendent, twinkling **10** celebrated, flickering, glistening, glittering, pre-eminent, profulgent, shimmering **11** conspicuous, illustrious, magnificent, outstanding, resplendent **12** incandescent **13** distinguished **14** phosphorescent

### shiny
**05** raven, silky, sleek **06** bright, glossy, sheeny **07** shining **08** gleaming, lustrous, polished **09** burnished **10** glistening, shimmering

### ship
**04** boat, post, send **05** craft **06** embark, vessel **07** send off **08** aircraft

---

*Ship and boat types include:*

**01** E, Q, U
**02** el, mv, NS, SS, TB
**03** air, ark, bum, cat, cog, cot, day, dow, fly, gig, gun, HMS, hoy, ice, jet, kit, man, MTB, mud, pig, RMS, row, sub, tow, tub, tug, USS, war
**04** bark, brig, buss, cock, cott, dhow, dory, falt, fire, flag, flat, fold, four, grab, HMAS, HMCS, hulk, hush, junk, keel, koff, life, long, mail, maxi, pair, pink, pont, post, pram, prau, proa, prow, punt, ro-ro, saic, scow, show, snow, surf, tall, tern, tilt, trow, Turk, waka, well, wind, yawl, zulu
**05** aviso, barca, barge, botel, butty, cabin, canal, canoe, casco, coble, coper, crare, dandy, dingy, drake, ferry, funny, guard, gulet, hatch, horse, house, jolly, kayak, ketch, laker, light, liner, motor, oiler, peter, pilot, plate, power, praam, prahu, prore, razee, river, rotor, saick, scout, scull, seine, shell, shore, skiff, slave, sloop, smack, speed, stake, steam, store, swamp, tanka, track, tramp, troop, umiak, wager, waist, whale, whiff, xebec, yacht, zabra
**06** advice, argosy, banker, barque, bateau, battle, bethel, bireme, caique, carvel, castle, coaler, cobble, cockle, codder, coffin, convoy, cooper, crayer, cutter, dingey, dinghy, dogger, dragon, droger, dromon, drover, dugout, flying, galiot, galley, gay-you, hooker, hopper, jigger, lateen, launch, lorcha, lugger, masula, monkey, mother, narrow, nuggar, oomiac, oomiak, packet, paddle, pedalo, pirate, prison, puffer,

pulwar, puteli, randan, reefer, rowing, runner, sailer, saique, sampan, sandal, sanpan, school, schuit, schuyt, settee, slaver, tanker, tartan, torpid, trader, turret, wangan, wangun, wherry
**07** assault, Berthon, birlinn, budgero, capital, caravel, clipper, coaster, collier, consort, coracle, corsair, cruiser, currach, curragh, dredger, drifter, drogher, dromond, factory, felucca, four-oar, frigate, gabbard, gabbart, galleon, galliot, Geordie, gondola, landing, liberty, lighter, lymphad, man-o'-war, mistico, mudscow, mystery, nacelle, oomiack, pair-oar, passage, patamar, pearler, pinnace, piragua, pirogue, polacca, pontoon, sailing, scooter, shallop, sharpie, sponger, steamer, tartane, torpedo, trawler, trireme, vedette, victory, wanigan, warship, weather, Yngling
**08** bilander, billyboy, budgerow, car ferry, corocore, corocoro, corvette, dahabieh, dispatch, eight-oar, galleass, galliass, gallivat, hospital, hoveller, Indiaman, ironclad, johnboat, log-canoe, longship, mackinaw, man-of-war, masoolah, massoola, merchant, monohull, montaria, periagua, pleasure, repeater, row barge, runabout, sally-man, schooner, skipjack, smuggler, Spaniard, training, trimaran, water bus, woodskin
**09** bomb-ketch, Bucentaur, catamaran, commodore, container, dahabeeah, dahabiyah, dahabiyeh, daysailer, daysailor, destroyer, firefloat, flying jib, freighter, herringer, Hollander, hydrofoil, klondiker, klondyker, lapstrake, lapstreak, leviathan, long-liner, minelayer, monoxylon, motoscafo, multihull, Norwegian, oil-burner, oil tanker, outrigger, privateer, randan gig, receiving, sallee-man, speedster, steamship, store ship, submarine, surf canoe, transport, two-decker, two-master, vaporetto, well smack
**10** armour-clad, bomb-vessel, brigantine, free-trader, hovercraft, icebreaker, minehunter, quadrireme, seal-fisher, tea clipper, trekschuit, triaconter, victualler, windjammer
**11** bulk carrier, cockleshell, dreadnought, galley-foist, merchantman, minesweeper, motor launch, penteconter, purse-seiner, quinquereme, sallee-rover, salmon coble, side-wheeler, steam launch, steam packet, steam vessel, submersible, three-decker, three-master, victualling, wooden horse
**12** cabin cruiser, deepwaterman, double-decker, East-Indiaman,

line-of-battle, screw steamer, single-decker, square-rigger, stern-wheeler, tangle-netter, tramp steamer, troop carrier
13 Canadian canoe, paddle steamer, revenue cutter, roll-on roll-off
14 ocean-greyhound, turbine steamer
15 aircraft-carrier, floating battery, logistics vessel

*Ships include:*

03 QE2
04 Ajax, Argo, Hood, Nina
05 Argus, Maine, Pinta
06 Beagle, Bounty, Cathay, Oriana, Pequod, Renown
07 Alabama, Amistad, Belfast, Blücher, Olympic, Pelican, Potomac, Repulse, Tirpitz, Titanic, Victory
08 Ark Royal, Bismarck, Canberra, Fearless, Graf Spee, Intrepid, Iron Duke, Mary Rose, Royal Oak
09 Adventure, Aquitania, Britannia, Britannic, Carinthia, Cutty Sark, Discovery, Endeavour, Gipsy Moth, Gneisenau, Lexington, Lusitania, Mayflower, Normandie, Queen Mary, Sheffield, Téméraire, Terranova
10 Golden Hind, Hispaniola, Invincible, Mauretania, Prinz Eugen, Resolution, Santa Maria, Washington
11 Dawn Treader, Dreadnought, Illustrious, Scharnhorst
12 African Queen, Great Britain, Great Eastern, Great Western, Marie Celeste
13 Prince of Wales
14 Flying Dutchman, Queen Elizabeth
15 Admiral Graf Spee, General Belgrano, Queen Elizabeth 2

*Ship parts include:*

03 bow, box, oar, rig
04 beam, brig, brow, bunk, cant, deck, head, hold, hull, keel, mast, poop, port, prow, sail
05 berth, bilge, cabin, cable, cleat, davit, hatch, hawse, stern, wheel, winch
06 anchor, bridge, fender, fo'c'sle, funnel, galley, gunnel, hawser, rigger, rudder, tiller
07 bollard, bulwark, caboose, capstan, counter, gangway, gun deck, gunwale, hammock, landing, quarter, rowlock, top deck, transom
08 binnacle, boat deck, bulkhead, hatchway, main deck, poop deck, porthole, wardroom
09 afterdeck, chart room, crosstree, crow's nest, forecabin, gangplank, lower deck, radio room, stanchion, starboard, stateroom, waterline
10 boiler room, engine room, figurehead, flight deck, forecastle, pilot house, stabilizer

11 chain locker, paddle wheel, quarter deck
12 companion way, Plimsoll line
13 promenade deck
14 superstructure
15 companion ladder

*Ships' crewmen and officers include:*

02 AB
04 mate
06 master, purser
07 captain, steward
08 cabin-boy, ship's boy
09 first mate
10 able rating, able seaman

*See also* **sailor**

### shipping

*Shipping forecast areas:*

04 Sole, Tyne
05 Dover, Forth, Lundy, Malin, Wight
06 Bailey, Biscay, Dogger, Faroes, Fisher, Humber, Thames, Viking
07 Fastnet, FitzRoy, Forties, Rockall, Shannon
08 Cromarty, Fair Isle, Hebrides, Irish Sea, Plymouth, Portland
09 Trafalgar
10 Finisterre
11 German Bight, North Utsire, South Utsire
16 South-East Iceland

• **shipping order** 02 so

### shipshape

04 neat, tidy, trig, trim 06 proper, spruce 07 orderly 11 well-planned
12 businesslike, spick and span
13 well-organized, well-regulated
14 Bristol fashion

### shirk

04 balk, duck, funk, shun 05 avoid, baulk, dodge, evade, skive, slack
06 bludge 07 goof off, soldier 08 get out of 09 duck out of, duckshove, goldbrick 10 play truant, shrink from
12 wriggle out of

### shirker

05 idler, piker, poler, shirk 06 dodger, loafer, skiver, truant 07 bludger, goof-off, quitter, slacker, sneak-up, soldier
08 absentee, embusqué, layabout
09 gold brick 10 duckshover, malingerer 12 carpet-knight

### shirt

01 T 04 sark, serk 05 kurta, parka
06 caftan, camese, camise, kaftan, khurta 07 dasheki, dashiki, partlet
08 guernsey, subucula

### shiver

◊ *anagram indicator* 03 bit 04 chip, grew, grue 05 break, crack, flake, piece, quake, shake, shard, shred, shrug, smash, split, start 06 didder, dither, quiver, sliver, tremor, twitch
07 chitter, flutter, frisson, shatter, shaving, shudder, tremble, vibrate
08 cold sore, fragment, splinter
09 disshiver, palpitate, vibration
10 smithereen 11 smithereens

### shivery

04 cold 05 ourie 06 chilly 07 brittle, chilled, nervous, quaking, quivery, shaking, trembly 08 fluttery, shuddery
09 trembling

### shoal

03 bar, mob, ren, rin, run 04 bank, mass, reef 05 flock, group, horde, shelf, swarm 06 school, throng 07 schoole, shallow 08 sandbank 09 multitude
10 assemblage

### shock

◊ *anagram indicator* 03 jar, mat, mop
04 blow, daze, head, jerk, jolt, mane, mass, numb, shog, stun, turn
05 amaze, appal, crash, knock, repel, shake, shook, sixty, start, stook, upset
06 dismay, fright, horror, impact, offend, poodle, revolt, sicken, stound, stownd, tangle, thatch, trauma, whammy 07 agitate, astound, disgust, horrify, jarring, outrage, perturb, scandal, stagger, startle, stupefy, unnerve 08 astonish, bewilder, bowl over, confound, disquiet, distress, gross out, nauseate, paralyse, surprise, unsettle 09 bombshell, collision, dumbfound, knock back, take aback
10 scandalize, traumatize
11 thunderbolt 12 perturbation
13 consternation, rude awakening
15 bolt from the blue
• **shock absorber** 04 oleo 07 oleo leg, snubber
• **shocked** 06 aghast
• **shock treatment** 03 ECT, EST

### shocking

04 foul, vile 05 awful 06 daring
07 épatant, ghastly, hideous
08 dreadful, horrible, horrific, terrible
09 abhorrent, appalling, atrocious, execrable, frightful, loathsome, monstrous, offensive, repugnant, repulsive, revolting, sickening
10 abominable, deplorable, detestable, diabolical, disgusting, horrifying, nauseating, outrageous, perturbing, scandalous, unbearable, unsettling
11 disgraceful, disquieting, distressing, intolerable, unspeakable

### shockingly

08 terribly 10 abominably, deplorably, dreadfully, unbearably 11 appallingly, atrociously, frightfully, repulsively, revoltingly, sickeningly
12 disgustingly, outrageously, scandalously 13 disgracefully

### shoddy

◊ *anagram indicator* 04 poor, ropy, sham 05 cheap, crook, ropey, tacky, tatty 06 tawdry, trashy 07 rag-wool, rubbish 08 careless, gimcrack, inferior, jimcrack, rubbishy, slapdash, slipshod
09 cheapjack, third-rate 10 devil's dust, second-rate 11 poor-quality

### shoe
*see* **footwear**

### shoemaker

04 snab, snob 05 sutor 06 cosier, cozier, soutar, souter, sowter

## shoemaking

07 cobbler, crispin 08 cordiner
09 bootmaker 10 cordwainer

## shoemaking

08 cobblery, cobbling 10 bootmaking
14 the gentle craft

## shoot

03 aim, bud, fly, gun, hit, imp, lob, pop, pot, rod, tip, zap, zip 04 belt, bolt, cast, chit, cyme, dart, dash, dump, film, fire, germ, grow, hurl, kick, kill, plug, poot, pout, race, rush, slip, snap, tear, twig, wand, whip, whiz 05 blast, chute, fling, graft, hurry, loose, pluff, rapid, scion, scoot, shell, slide, spear, speed, spire, spray, sprig, start, throw, tower, video, whisk, wound 06 branch, charge, direct, hurtle, injure, launch, let fly, let off, propel, sprint, sprout, streak, strike, sucker 07 bombard, burgeon, cutting, gun down, mow down, pick off, project, shoot up, snipe at, stretch, tendron 08 detonate, go all out, offshoot, open fire 09 bring down, discharge, germinate, spindling 10 get a move on, photograph 11 crystallize, precipitate

## shooter

*see* **gun; gunman**

## shop

03 buy, get, rat 05 grass, split, store 06 betray, pick up, prison, squeal, tell on 07 stool on 08 emporium, imprison, inform on, purchase 09 buy things, stock up on 10 go shopping 11 tell tales on 12 retail outlet 13 do the shopping

*Shop types include:*

01 e
02 op, PX
03 toy
04 book, chip, deli, farm, grog, shoe, tuck
05 baker, dairy, dress, offie, phone, stall, sweet, video
06 barber, bazaar, bookie, bottle, chippy, corner, draper, grocer, market, online, record, tailor
07 betting, butcher, charity, chemist, chipper, clothes, florist, saddler
08 boutique, hardware, jeweller, milliner, pharmacy, takeaway
09 bookmaker, drugstore, newsagent, outfitter, stationer, superette
10 candy store, chain store, electrical, fishmonger, health-food, ironmonger, mini-market, off-licence, pawnbroker, post office, radio and TV, second-hand, superstore
11 bottle store, fish and chip, five-and-dime, greengrocer, haberdasher, hairdresser, hypermarket, launderette, online store, opportunity, supermarket, tobacconist
12 cash-and-carry, confectioner, delicatessen, general store, indoor market
13 computer store, farmers' market
15 department store

*French shops include:*

05 tabac
08 boutique, épicerie
09 boucherie, librairie
10 bijouterie, confiserie, fromagerie, parfumerie, pâtisserie, rôtisserie
11 boulangerie, charcuterie
12 chocolaterie, grand magasin, poissonnerie

*Shops include:*

03 BHV
04 Tati
05 Macy's
07 Hamleys, Harrods, Jenners, Liberty
08 Tiffany's
09 Century 21, Printemps
10 FAO Schwarz, Selfridge's
11 Le Bon Marché
12 Tiffany and Co
13 Bloomingdale's, Harvey Nichols, La Samaritaine, Lord and Taylor
15 Bergdorf Goodman, Fortnum and Mason, Saks Fifth Avenue

## shopkeeper

05 owner 06 dealer, trader 07 manager 08 merchant, retailer, salesman, stockist 09 bourgeois, boxwallah, tradesman 10 proprietor, saleswoman 11 storekeeper, tradeswoman 13 counter-jumper 14 counter-skipper

## shopper

05 buyer 06 client 08 consumer, customer 09 purchaser

## shore

04 bank, hold, prop, sand, stay, warn 05 beach, brace, coast, drain, front, offer, rance, sands, sewer 06 hold up, menace, prop up, rivage, strand 07 seaside, shingle, support 08 buttress, lakeside, littoral, seaboard, seashore, threaten, underpin 09 foreshore, promenade, reinforce, waterside 10 strengthen, waterfront 11 threatening

## shorebird

04 knot 06 dunlin, ox-bird 07 sea lark 08 sand-lark, surfbird
*See also* **bird**

## shorn

03 cut 04 bald 06 polled, shaved, shaven 07 crew-cut, cropped 08 deprived, stripped 09 beardless

## short

◊ *tail deletion indicator* 03 low, shy, wee 04 curt, neat, poor, rude 05 blunt, brief, crisp, dumpy, gruff, hasty, pithy, quick, scant, sharp, small, squat, swift, teeny, terse, tight 06 abrupt, curtly, direct, little, meagre, petite, scanty, scarce, slight, snappy, sparse, stubby, teensy 07 briefly, brittle, brusque, compact, concise, cursory, lacking, limited, passing, summary, uncivil, wanting 08 abridged, abruptly, fleeting, impolite, pint-size, snappish, succinct, suddenly 09 condensed, curtailed, deficient, ephemeral, fugacious, minuscule, momentary, pint-sized, shortened, temporary, transient, truncated 10 aphoristic, compressed, diminutive, evanescent, inadequate, short-lived, summarized, to the point, transitory 11 abbreviated, Lilliputian 12 abbreviation, discourteous, insufficient, unexpectedly
• **fall short** 05 fault, under 09 be lacking 12 be inadequate 14 be insufficient
• **in short** 04 once 05 in sum 06 in fine 07 at a word, briefly, in a word, in brief, to sum up 09 concisely, in one word 11 in a few words, in a nutshell, summarizing 12 in conclusion
• **little short of** 02 on 07 towards
• **short of** 03 bar, but 04 save 05 low on, under 06 but for 07 barring, besides, lacking, missing, short on, wanting 08 less than, omitting 09 apart from, aside from, except for, excepting, excluding, other than, pushed for 10 leaving out, this side of 11 deficient in, not counting

## shortage

04 lack, need, shtg, want 06 dearth, drouth 07 absence, deficit, drought, paucity, poverty, wantage 08 scarcity 09 shortfall, skills gap 10 deficience, deficiency, inadequacy 13 insufficiency

## shortcoming

03 sin 04 flaw 05 fault 06 defect, foible 07 failing, frailty 08 drawback, weakness 09 weak point 12 imperfection

## shorten

◊ *tail deletion indicator* 03 cut 04 clip, crop, dock, pare, trim 05 check, prune, sum up 06 lessen, reduce, take up 07 abridge, curtail, cut down, scantle 08 compress, condense, contract, decrease, diminish, pare down, truncate 09 epitomize, telescope 10 abbreviate 11 make shorter 13 become shorter

## shortened

◊ *tail deletion indicator* 03 cut 06 curtal 07 curtate 08 abridged 09 condensed 10 abbreviate, abstracted, contracted, summarized 11 abbreviated 12 abbreviatory

## shortfall

04 lack, loss 07 arrears, default, deficit 08 shortage 10 deficiency

## shorthand

02 s/h 11 phonography, stenography, tachygraphy 12 Speedwriting®

## short-lived

05 brief, short 07 passing 08 caducous, fleeting, volatile 09 ephemeral, fugacious, momentary, temporary, transient 10 evanescent, transitory 11 impermanent

## shortly

◊ *tail deletion indicator* 04 soon 06 curtly, rudely 07 bluntly, briefly, by and by, gruffly, sharply, tersely 08 abruptly, directly, in a while 09 brusquely, presently, uncivilly 10 before long, impolitely 14 discourteously, in a little while

## shorts
07 baggies, cut-offs 08 Bermudas, hot pants

## short-sighted
04 rash 05 hasty 06 myopic, unwise 08 careless, heedless 09 impolitic, imprudent 10 ill-advised, unthinking 11 improvident, injudicious, near-sighted, thoughtless 13 ill-considered, uncircumspect

## short-staffed
11 shorthanded 12 understaffed 13 below strength

## short-tempered
05 fiery, ratty, testy 06 crusty, touchy 07 grouchy, stroppy 08 choleric 09 crotchety, impatient, irascible, irritable 10 crotcheted 11 bad-tempered, hot-tempered 13 quick-tempered

## short-winded
05 puffy, pursy 07 gasping, panting, puffing, purfled 10 breathless

## shot
◇ *anagram indicator* 02 go 03 ace, aim, fix, get, hit, jab, lob, peg, pop, pot, shy, try 04 ball, bang, bash, burl, dink, dose, dram, kick, putt, scot, slug, snap, stab, turn 05 blast, crack, fling, guess, image, moiré, photo, pluff, print, range, reach, set-up, shoat, shote, slide, snipe, spell, throw, whack 06 bullet, corner, effort, gunner, header, hunter, jumper, pellet, ruined, shotte, sitter, sniper, strike, stroke 07 attempt, gunfire, missile, mottled, payment, pelican, penalty, picture, shooter, watered 08 advanced, marksman, moon-ball, snapshot 09 discharge, endeavour, explosion, injection, mitraille 10 ammunition, cannonball, iridescent, markswoman, photograph, point-blank, projectile, variegated 11 inoculation, vaccination 12 contribution, immunization, transparency
• **call the shots** 04 head, lead 06 direct, head up, manage 07 command 09 give a lead, supervise 10 be in charge 15 wear the trousers
• **good shot** 07 deadeye
• **like a shot** 06 at once 07 eagerly, quickly 09 instantly, willingly 11 immediately 12 without delay 14 unhesitatingly
• **not by a long shot** 04 ne'er 05 never, no way 07 in no way 08 not at all 09 by no means 12 certainly not 13 not in the least
• **shot in the arm** 04 lift 05 boost 06 fillip, uplift 07 impetus 08 stimulus 11 fresh talent 13 encouragement
• **shot in the dark** 05 guess 09 guesswork, wild guess 10 blind guess, conjecture 11 speculation

## shoulder
04 bear, hump, push 05 carry, elbow, force, press, shove, spald, spall, spaul 06 accept, assume, jostle, spalle, spauld, take on, thrust 07 support, sustain 09 undertake 10 coathanger 13 heave-offering

• **give someone the cold shoulder** 03 cut 04 shun, snub 05 blank, shame, spurn 06 humble, ignore, insult, rebuff, rebuke, slight, squash 07 mortify, put down 08 brush off 09 disregard, humiliate 13 slap in the face 14 kick in the teeth
• **rub shoulders with** 07 mix with 08 meet with 10 hobnob with 13 associate with, hang about with, socialize with 14 fraternize with, hang around with, knock about with 15 knock around with
• **shoulder to shoulder** 06 united 07 closely 08 together 10 hand in hand, in alliance, side by side 13 co-operatively 15 working together

## shout
03 bay, cry 04 bawl, call, howl, roar, rort, yawp, yell 05 cheer, claim, clame, jodel, round, stand, treat, yodel, yodle 06 bellow, cry out, heckle, holler, scream, shriek, squawk 07 barrack, call out, exclaim, glory be, sing out 11 acclamation, rant and rave, stand a round 12 buy drinks for, conclamation 14 raise your voice

*Shouts and cries include:*

02 io
03 hup, nix
04 euoi, evoe, fall, fore, haro, I-spy, rivo, shoo, sola
05 chevy, chivy, evhoe, evohe, havoc, heigh, holla, hollo, hooch, huzza
06 banzai, chivvy, eureka, halloa, halloo, harrow, hoicks, yoicks
07 glory be, heureka, kamerad, tally-ho, tantivy
08 alleluia, gardyloo, Geronimo, harambee
09 scaldings, stop thief!
10 halleluiah, hallelujah, view-halloo, westward ho!

*See also* **war cry** *under* **war**

## shouting
03 hue

## shove
04 bump, bung, jolt, push 05 barge, crowd, drive, elbow, force, press 06 jostle, propel, thrust 07 thrutch 08 shoulder
• **shove off** 04 scat 05 hop it, leave, scoot, scram 06 beat it, depart, go away 07 buzz off, do a bunk, get lost, push off, rack off, scarper, vamoose 08 choof off, clear off, clear out, run for it 09 skedaddle

## shovel
03 dig, van 04 heap, main, move, peel 05 clear, scoop, shift, shool, spade 06 bucket, dredge 07 backhoe, dust-pan 08 excavate 09 excavator 13 backhoe loader

## show
◇ *hidden indicator* 03 air, con 04 come, expo, fair, give, lead, mean, pose, shew, sign, take, wear 05 array, front, guide, guise, offer, prove, sight, steer, teach, usher 06 affair, appear, arrive, attend, chance, depict, direct, escort,

expose, façade, parade, record, reveal, set out, turn up 07 clarify, conduct, display, divulge, exhibit, explain, expound, express, panache, pizzazz, portray, present, produce, showing, signify, staging, suggest, uncover 08 disclose, evidence, illusion, indicate, instruct, manifest, point out, pretence, register 09 accompany, elucidate, exemplify, make clear, make known, make plain, operation, programme, semblance, showiness, spectacle 10 appearance, be evidence, exhibition, exposition, illustrate, impression, indication, play-acting, production, profession 11 affectation, arrangement, demonstrate, flamboyance, make it clear, make visible, materialize, opportunity, ostentation, performance, proceedings, undertaking 12 extravaganza, organization, plausibility, presentation 13 bear witness to, demonstration, entertainment, exhibitionism, manifestation 14 representation, window dressing
*See also* **musical; pantomime**
• **show off** ◇ *anagram indicator* 04 brag 05 boast, pronk, strut, swank, vapor 06 flaunt, hot-dog, parade, set off, vapour 07 display, enhance, exhibit, swagger 08 brandish, flourish 09 advertise 10 grandstand, put on an act 11 demonstrate 15 show to advantage
• **show up** 04 come 05 lodge, shame 06 appear, arrive, bewray, expose, hand in, reveal, turn up, unmask 07 lay bare, let down, mortify, uncloak 08 disgrace, pinpoint 09 embarrass, highlight, humiliate 10 put to shame 11 make visible, materialize

## showdown
05 clash 06 climax, crisis 07 face-off 10 dénouement 11 culmination 13 confrontation, moment of truth

## shower
◇ *anagram indicator* 04 fall, hail, heap, load, pang, pelt, play, pour, rain, scat, scud, skit 05 drift, pound, skatt, spray, water 06 attack, deluge, lavish, pelter, pepper, stream, volley 07 barrage, scowder, torrent 08 inundate, rainfall, scouther, scowther, sprinkle 09 aspersion, avalanche, drizzling, overwhelm 10 kitchen tea, sprinkling 13 thunder-shower
*See also* **meteor**

## showiness
05 glitz, swank 07 glitter, pizzazz, varnish 09 ritziness 10 flashiness, razzmatazz 11 flamboyance, ostentation 12 razzle-dazzle 15 pretentiousness

## showing
04 expo, show 06 record 07 account, display, staging 08 evidence, symbolic 09 endeictic, ostensive, statement 10 appearance, exhibition, impression, indicative, revelatory 11 descriptive, elucidative, explanatory, explicatory,

## showing-off

performance, significant, track record
**12** illustrative, presentation
**13** demonstrative **14** representation,
representative **15** past performance

## showing-off

**05** swank **07** egotism, swagger
**08** boasting, bragging **09** vainglory
**10** peacockery **11** braggadocio
**13** exhibitionism

## showjumper

*see* **equestrian**

## showman

**07** show-off **09** performer, publicist
**10** impresario, ring-master
**11** entertainer **14** self-advertiser

## show-off

**05** poser, skite **06** poseur **07** boaster,
egotist, know-all, peacock, swanker
**08** braggart **09** swaggerer
**13** exhibitionist

## showy

**03** gay **04** fine, loud **05** brave, fancy,
flash, flory, gaudy, lairy, ritzy, spicy,
viewy **06** blingy, branky, brassy,
dressy, flashy, flossy, garish, glitzy,
ornate, swanky, tawdry **07** buckeye,
dashing, pompous, splashy, stylish
**08** fantoosh, gorgeous, sparkish,
specious, tinselly **10** bling-bling,
flamboyant, glittering **11** conspicuous,
pretentious **12** ostentatious

## shred

**03** bit, cut, jot, rag, rip, tag **04** atom,
chop, iota, mite, snip, spot, tear, whit,
wisp **05** cut up, grain, grate, piece,
prune, rip up, scrap, slice, speck,
taver, trace **06** agnail, cut off, paring,
ribbon, screed, sliver, taiver, tatter, tear
up **07** frazzle, mammock, modicum,
mummock, peeling, remnant, snippet,
vestige **08** clipping, fragment,
hangnail, julienne, particle

## shrew

**03** nag **04** Fury, Kate, tana **05** bitch,
curse, scold, shrow, sorex, vixen
**06** dragon, Tupaia, virago **07** muskrat,
sondeli **08** banxring, harridan, spitfire
**09** bangsring, henpecker, Katharina,
termagant, Xanthippe **10** petrodrome

## shrewd

**03** sly **04** arch, evil, hard, keen, wily,
wise **05** acute, alert, canny, savey,
savvy, sharp, smart **06** argute, artful,
astute, biting, callid, clever, crafty,
keenly, savvey, severe, shrowd
**07** cunning, gnostic, hurtful, knowing,
prudent **08** piercing, shrewish, spiteful,
vixenish **09** judicious, observant,
sagacious **10** calculated, discerning,
far-sighted, formidable, hard-headed,
ill-natured, long-headed, perceptive
**11** calculating, intelligent,
mischievous, well-advised **12** sharp-
sighted **13** perspicacious
**14** discriminating, ill-conditioned

## shrewdly

**05** slyly **06** wisely **07** cannily
**08** argutely, artfully, astutely, cleverly,
craftily **09** knowingly, unhappily
**11** judiciously, sagaciously

**12** far-sightedly, perceptively
**15** perspicaciously

## shrewdness

**05** grasp **06** acumen, wisdom
**08** astucity, gumption, prudence,
sagacity **09** acuteness, callidity,
canniness, judgement, sharpness,
smartness **10** astuteness
**11** discernment, knowingness,
penetration **12** intelligence,
perspicacity **14** perceptiveness

## shrewish

**06** shrewd **07** nagging, peevish
**08** captious, petulant, scolding,
vixenish **09** querulous, termagant
**10** henpecking, ill-natured, wasp-
tongu'd **11** bad-tempered,
complaining, ill-humoured, ill-
tempered, quarrelsome
**12** discontented, fault-finding, sharp-
tongued

## shriek

**03** cry **04** howl, wail, yell, yelp
**05** pling, shout, skirl **06** cry out,
scream, scrike, shreek, shreik, shrike,
squawk, squeal **07** screech, screich,
screigh, sreich, shright, shritch,
skreigh, skriech, skriegh **08** screamer
**09** caterwaul **11** exclamation
**15** exclamation mark

## shrill

**04** high, keen **05** acute, sharp
**06** argute, treble **08** piercing, screechy,
strident **09** screaming **10** screeching
**11** ear-piercing, high-pitched,
penetrating **12** ear-splitting

## shrimp

**05** krill, prawn **06** squill **07** squilla
**08** crevette **09** Euphausia, schizopod
**10** stomatopod

## shrine

**04** dome, fane, tope **05** chest, darga,
image, stupa **06** chapel, church,
dagaba, dagoba, pagoda, scrine,
scryne, temple, vimana **07** cabinet,
martyry **08** delubrum, feretory,
marabout **09** holy place, sanctuary
**10** tabernacle **11** sacred place

## shrink

**04** balk, dare, nirl, shun **05** cling,
cower, crine, quail, shrug, wince
**06** blench, cringe, flinch, gizzen,
lessen, narrow, recoil, reduce, retire,
shy off, swerve, wither **07** atrophy,
drop off, dwindle, fall off, give way,
retreat, shorten, shrivel, shy away,
wrinkle **08** back away, contract,
decrease, diminish, draw back,
withdraw **09** cower away, start back
**10** constringe, withdrawal
**11** contraction, grow smaller
**12** psychiatrist **13** become smaller
**15** have qualms about

## shrivel

**03** dry **04** burn, nirl, sear, welk, wilt
**05** cling, crine, dry up, parch **06** blight,
gizzen, pucker, scorch, shrink, wither
**07** dwindle, frizzle, wrinkle **08** pucker
up **09** dehydrate, desiccate

## shrivelled

**03** dry **04** sere **06** gizzen, shrunk

**07** dried up, wizened **08** puckered,
shrunken, withered, wrinkled, writhled
**09** emaciated **10** desiccated

## shroud

**03** fog, lop **04** hide, pall, veil, wrap
**05** cloak, cloth, cloud, cover, shade
**06** branch, mantle, screen, sindon,
swathe **07** blanket, clothes, conceal,
envelop, garment, shelter **08** cerement,
covering, enshroud, loppings
**09** cerecloth **12** graveclothes, winding-
sheet

## shrouded

**06** hidden, veiled **07** cloaked, clouded,
covered, swathed, wrapped
**09** blanketed, concealed, enveloped
**10** enshrouded

## shrub

**04** bush **07** arboret

*Shrubs include:*

**03** box, ivy, til
**04** coca, hebe, nabk, Rosa, rose
**05** brere, briar, brier, broom, buaze,
buchu, bucku, bwazi, hakea,
holly, lilac, nebek, peony, yucca
**06** azalea, daphne, laurel, mallow,
mimosa, myrtle, nebbuk,
nebeck, privet, protea,
sesame
**07** arbutus, Banksia, boronia,
bramble, dogwood, fuchsia,
heather, jasmine, phlomis,
rhatany, spiraea, waratah,
weigela
**08** barberry, berberis, bilberry,
buddleia, camellia, clematis,
euonymus, gardenia, japonica,
krameria, laburnum, lavender,
magnolia, musk rose, viburnum,
wistaria, wisteria
**09** beach plum, bean caper,
eucryphia, firethorn, forsythia,
hydrangea
**10** bitter-king, buffalo-nut,
buttonbush, mock orange, witch
hazel
**11** bottlebrush, calycanthus,
cotoneaster, honeysuckle
**12** blackcurrant, buffalo-berry,
rhododendron
**13** Barbados pride, butcher's broom,
mountain avens
**15** Siberian ginseng

*See also* **plant**

## shrug

• **shrug off** **06** ignore **07** dismiss,
neglect **08** brush off **09** disregard
**14** take no notice of

## shrunken

**05** gaunt **06** shrunk, wasted **07** reduced
**09** emaciated **10** cadaverous,
contracted, shrivelled, sphacelate
**11** sphacelated

## shudder

**04** grew, grue, grue **05** creep, grise, heave,
quake, shake, shrug, spasm **06** judder,
quiver, shiver, tremor **07** frisson,
tremble, vibrate **08** convulse
**10** convulsion

## shuffle

◇ *anagram indicator* 03 mix 04 drag, limp, make, pack 05 dodge, hedge, mix up, scuff, stack 06 doddle, falter, hobble, jumble, riffle, scrape, switch, toddle 07 confuse, evasion, patch up, scuffle, shamble 08 artifice, disorder, intermix, jumble up, scramble, shauchle 09 rearrange, reshuffle 10 move around, reorganize 11 shift around 12 tergiversate

## shun

◇ *deletion indicator* 03 shy 04 snub 05 avoid, elude, evade, evite, spurn 06 eschew, ignore 09 attention, ostracize 11 shy away from 12 cold-shoulder, keep away from, steer clear of 14 send to Coventry

## shunt

04 move, take 05 bring, budge, carry, crash, fetch, shift, swing 06 bypass, mishap, shelve, switch 08 relocate, transfer 09 sidetrack, transport, transpose

## shut

02 to 03 bar 04 bolt, jail, lock, seal, slam, spar, tine 05 close, latch, put to, shoot, steek 06 cage in, closed, coop up, fasten, immure, intern, lock up, secure 07 confine 08 imprison 11 incarcerate, put the lid on
• **shut down** 04 halt, stop 05 cease, close, scram 07 suspend 09 close down, switch off, terminate 10 inactivate 11 discontinue
• **shut in** 04 cage 05 box in, embar, hem in, imbar 06 cage in, empale, immure, impale, intern, keep in 07 confine, enclose, fence in, inclose, occlude 08 imprison, restrain 10 encloister
• **shut off** 06 cut off 07 exclude, isolate, occlude, seclude 08 obstruct, separate 09 segregate, switch off
• **shut out** 03 bar 04 fend, hide, mask, veil 05 cover, debar, exile 06 banish, outlaw, screen 07 conceal, cover up, exclude, lock out 08 block out 09 ostracize
• **shut up** 03 gag, pen 04 hush, jail, lock, pent 05 cabin, close, frank, quiet 06 bang up, cage in, clam up, closet, coop up, encage, hush up, immure, incage, intern, lock up 07 confine, keep mum, quieten, silence 08 button up, imprison, pipe down 09 endungeon 11 incarcerate 13 button your lip 14 hold your tongue

## shutter

05 blind, shade 06 douser, louver, louvre, screen 07 scuttle 08 abat-jour, jalousie

## shuttle

03 ply, run 05 flute, shunt 06 seesaw, travel 07 commute, shottle 09 alternate 10 go to and fro 11 shuttlecock 13 netting-needle

## shy

03 coy, jib 04 cagy, gibe, shot, shun, toss, wild 05 cagey, chary, fling, mousy, squab, throw, timid 06 demure, modest, mousey, scanty, skeigh 07 attempt, bashful, indrawn, nervous, startle, strange 08 backward, cautious, farouche, hesitant, reserved, reticent, retiring, secluded, timorous, willyard, willyart 09 diffident, inhibited, shrinking, withdrawn 10 suspicious 11 embarrassed, introverted 12 self-effacing, unproductive 13 self-conscious
• **fight shy of** 04 shun 05 avoid, spurn 06 eschew 12 steer clear of
• **shy away** 03 jib 04 balk, buck, rear 05 avoid, quail, spook, start, wince 06 flinch, recoil, shrink, swerve 07 startle 08 back away

## shyly

05 coyly 06 cagily 07 charily, timidly 09 bashfully 10 cautiously, hesitantly, reticently 11 diffidently 15 self-consciously

## shyness

07 coyness, modesty 08 caginess, timidity 09 chariness, hesitancy, mousiness, reticence, timidness 10 constraint, diffidence, inhibition 11 bashfulness, nervousness 12 timorousness 13 embarrassment

## SI

*SI prefixes include:*

03 exa
04 atto, deca, deci, giga, kilo, mega, nano, peta, pico, tera
05 centi, femto, hecto, micro, milli, yocto, yotta, zepto, zetta

## sibling

03 sis 04 twin 06 german, sister 07 brother

## sibyl

04 seer 06 oracle, Pythia 07 seeress, völuspa 09 pythoness, sorceress, wise woman 10 prophetess

## sick

◇ *anagram indicator* 03 ill 04 weak 05 angry, black, bored, chase, crook, cruel, fed up, gross, rough, seedy, tired, weary 06 ailing, feeble, groggy, laid up, pining, poorly, puking, queasy, sickly, unwell, vulgar 07 airsick, annoyed, bilious, carsick, enraged, heaving, macabre, seasick, set upon 08 diseased, gruesome, nauseous, retching, vomiting 09 disgusted, hacked off, mortified, nauseated, off colour, spewing up, tasteless, uncle Dick 10 browned off, cheesed off, in bad taste, indisposed, out of sorts, throwing up, travel-sick 11 disgruntled 12 disappointed, sick and tired 15 under the weather
• **be sick** 03 ail, gag 04 barf, puke, spew, spue 05 heave, retch, vomit 07 fetch up, throw up 10 feel queasy 12 feel nauseous

## sicken

03 ail, get 05 appal, catch, repel 06 pick up, put off, revolt 07 develop, disgust, turn off 08 contract, nauseate 09 become ill, succumb to 10 go down with 12 come down with 13 become ill with 15 turn your stomach

## sickening

04 foul, vile 08 nauseous, shocking 09 appalling, loathsome, offensive, repellent, repulsive, revolting 10 chunderous, disgusting, nauseating, off-putting 11 distasteful 12 cringe-making, cringeworthy 14 stomach-turning

## sickly

03 wan 04 pale, puly, sick, weak 05 faint, frail, gushy, mushy, soppy, sweet, wersh 06 ailing, donsie, feeble, infirm, morbid, pallid, slushy, sugary, syrupy, weakly 07 anaemic, bilious, cloying, insipid, languid, mawkish, pimping, queachy, queechy 08 delicate 09 revolting, schmaltzy, unhealthy, washed out 10 indisposed, nauseating 14 valetudinarian

## sickness

03 bug, mal 04 dwam, puna 05 dwalm, dwaum, qualm, virus 06 malady, nausea, puking 07 ailment, disease, heaving, illness, soroche, surfeit 08 disorder, retching, vomiting 09 complaint, ill-health, infirmity, spewing up 10 affliction, queasiness, throwing up 11 airsickness, biliousness, carsickness, seasickness 13 indisposition 14 motion sickness, travel sickness 15 morning sickness

## side

◇ *ends selection indicator* 01 L, R 02 11, XI, XV 03 end, rim 04 area, bank, camp, edge, face, hand, jamb, left, long, page, sect, team, teme, view, wing, zone 05 angle, brink, cause, facet, flank, limit, minor, party, right, shore, slant, verge 06 aspect, border, eleven, fringe, lesser, margin, region, sector 07 faction, fifteen, lateral, oblique, profile, quarter, section, surface 08 boundary, district, division, flanking, interest, marginal, sidelong, sideward, sideways 09 arrogance, direction, periphery, secondary, viewpoint 10 department, incidental, standpoint, subsidiary 11 point of view, subordinate 13 neighbourhood, splinter group
*See also* **football**
• **at the side of** 02 by
• **both sides** ◇ *ends selection indicator*
• **change sides** 06 defect 08 come over
• **from side to side** 04 over 06 across
• **side by side** 06 jugate 07 abreast 10 collateral 11 cheek by jowl, neck and neck 14 heads and thraws 15 next to each other
• **side-effect** 04 echo 06 effect, recoil, result, ripple 07 outcome, rebound, spin-off 08 backwash 09 aftermath, by-product 11 consequence 12 repercussion 13 reverberation
• **side with** 04 back 06 favour, prefer 07 support, vote for 08 join

with **09** agree with **10** team up with **13** be on the side of **15** give your backing, give your support
• **take someone's side** **04** back, help **06** favour, prefer **07** support, vote for **08** join with, motivate **09** encourage **13** be on the side of **14** sympathize with

**sideline**
**04** game, omit **05** eject, exile, expel, hobby, sport **06** banish, demote, deport **07** degrade, exclude, pastime, pursuit **08** interest, relegate, transfer **09** amusement, diversion, downgrade, second job **10** expatriate, recreation, relaxation **13** entertainment **14** divertissement, leisure pursuit **15** leisure activity

**sidelong**
**06** covert, secret, tilted **07** oblique, sloping **08** indirect, sideward, sideways **13** surreptitious

**side-splitting**
**05** funny **07** amusing, a scream, comical, killing, riotous **08** farcical, humorous **09** hilarious, laughable **10** hysterical, uproarious

**sidestep**
**04** duck **05** avoid, dodge, elude, evade, shirk, skirt **06** bypass **09** give a miss **10** circumvent **14** find a way around

**sidetrack**
**05** shunt **06** divert **07** deflect, head off **08** distract **12** lead away from

**sideways**
**04** side **07** askance, athwart, lateral, oblique, slanted **08** crabwise, edgeways, edgewise, indirect, sidelong, sideward **09** laterally, obliquely, sidewards, to the side **14** from side to side

**siding**
**03** lie, lye **04** spur **07** turnout **09** sidetrack

**sidle**
**04** edge, inch **05** creep, slink, sneak

**siege**
**04** dung, rank, seat **05** class, privy, sedge **06** throne **07** leaguer **08** blockade **09** obsession, offensive **11** besiegement, distinction **12** encirclement **13** beleaguerment

*Sieges include:*

**04** Acre, Metz, Troy, Waco
**05** Alamo, Derry, Kuito, Paris, Rouen
**06** Janina, London, Quebec, Toulon, Vienna
**07** Antioch, Bristol, Granada, Lucknow, Orléans
**08** Damascus, Drogheda, Limerick, Mafeking, Roxburgh, Sarajevo, Syracuse, The Alamo
**09** Barcelona, Jerusalem, Kimberley, Ladysmith, Leningrad, Silistria, Singapore, Vicksburg
**10** Charleston, Kut al-amara, Montevideo, Sevastopol
**12** Tenochtitlán
**14** Balcombe Street, Constantinople, Entebbe Airport, Iranian Embassy, Munich Olympics, Spaghetti House

**sierra**
**01** S

**Sierra Leone**
**03** SLE, WAL

**siesta**
**03** nap **04** doze, rest **05** sleep **06** catnap, repose, snooze **10** forty winks, relaxation **12** afternoon nap

**sieve**
**03** sye **04** sift, sort, tems **05** temse **06** bolter, filter, girdle, remove, riddle, screen, searce, search, sifter, strain, winnow **07** boulter, cribble, griddle, trommel **08** colander, separate, strainer

**sift**
**03** try **04** bolt, sort, tems **05** boult, probe, sieve, study, temse **06** filter, garble, review, riddle, screen, searce, search, strain, winnow **07** analyse, cribble, discuss, examine **08** pore over, separate **10** scrutinize **11** investigate

**sigh**
**04** moan **05** heave, sithe, sough, swish **06** besigh, exhale, grieve, lament, rustle **07** breathe, crackle, suspire, whisper **08** complain **09** susurrate
• **sigh for** **03** cry **04** long, pine, weep **05** mourn, yearn **06** grieve, lament **08** languish **13** cry for the moon

**sight**
**03** eye, see **04** bead, espy, look, show, spot, vane, view **05** range, scene, skill, visor **06** beauty, behold, fright, glance, marvel, seeing, vision, wonder **07** amenity, discern, display, eyesore, feature, glimpse, insight, make out, observe, perusal **08** eyesight, judgment, landmark, perceive, prospect **09** beholding, curiosity, judgement, spectacle, splendour **10** appearance, estimation, exhibition, perception, visibility **11** distinguish, monstrosity, observation **12** ability to see, conspectuity, sense of sight **13** field of vision, range of vision **14** faculty of sight **15** place of interest

*Ways of describing sight impairment include:*

**06** myopic
**08** purblind
**09** amaurotic, cataracts, half-blind, sand-blind, snow-blind
**10** astigmatic, far-sighted, night-blind, nyctalopic, presbyopic, stone-blind
**11** blind as a bat, colour-blind, hemeralopic, long-sighted, near-sighted
**12** glaucomatous, short-sighted, trachomatous
**13** hypermetropic

• **catch sight of** **03** see, spy **04** espy, mark, note, spot, view **05** watch **06** look at, notice **07** discern, glimpse, make out **08** identify, perceive **09** recognize, set eyes on **10** clap eyes on
• **lose sight of** **04** omit **06** forget, ignore **07** neglect **08** overlook, put aside **09** disregard **12** slip your mind **14** fail to remember
• **set your sights on** **05** aim at **06** seek to **07** plan for **08** intend to **09** strive for **11** work towards **13** aspire towards

**sightless**
**05** blind **07** eyeless **08** unseeing **09** invisible, unsighted, unsightly **10** visionless

**sightseer**
**07** tourist, tripper, visitor **10** rubberneck **12** excursionist, holidaymaker

**sign**
**01** V **03** act, nod, tag **04** bode, clue, code, hint, levy, logo, mark, omen, shew, show, wave, wink, word **05** badge, board, draft, enrol, frank, proof, raise, sigil, stamp, token, trace, write **06** action, attest, augury, banner, beckon, caract, cipher, effigy, emblem, engage, enlist, ensign, figure, gather, marker, motion, muster, notice, obelus, obtain, poster, ratify, signal, sign up, symbol, take on **07** acquire, ale-bush, ale-pole, betoken, bus stop, earnest, endorse, express, gesture, glimmer, initial, insigne, placard, pointer, portent, presage, promise, recruit, symptom, witness **08** ale-stake, assemble, evidence, headhunt, ideogram, indicate, inscribe, insignia, mobilize, movement, signpost **09** autograph, character, conscript, harbinger, ideograph, indicator, sacrament, subscribe **10** death-token, denotement, foreboding, indication, suggestion, talent-spot, three balls **11** barber's pole, communicate, countersign, forewarning, gesticulate, phraseogram, put together, recognition, significant **12** shilling mark **13** gesticulation, manifestation **14** representation **15** prognostication

*See also* **zodiac**
• **from the sign** **02** DS **08** dal segno
• **sign over** **06** convey **07** consign, deliver, entrust **08** make over, transfer, turn over **09** surrender
• **sign up** **04** hire, join **05** enrol **06** employ, engage, enlist, join up, sign on, take on **07** recruit **08** register **09** volunteer **15** join the services

**signal**
◊ *anagram indicator* **04** clue, hint, mark, show, sign, toll, waff, waft **05** alert, recal, token **06** beckon, convey, famous, gryfon, maroon, motion, recall, target, tip-off **07** eminent, express, gesture, griffin, griffon, gryphon, message, notable, pointer, signify, symptom, warning **08** evidence, glorious, indicate, intimate, striking **09** important, memorable, momentous, telegraph **10** impressive, indication, intimation, noteworthy, remarkable **11** communicate, conspicuous, exceptional, gesticulate, outstanding,

## signature

significant **13** distinguished, extraordinary

---

*Signals and warnings include:*

**03** cue, gun, nod, pip, SOS
**04** bell, buoy, fire, flag, gong, home, honk, horn, pips, taps, toot, wave, wink
**05** alarm, bugle, flare, knell, larum, light, pager, robot, shout, siren, vigia
**06** beacon, buzzer, hooter, klaxon, mayday, rocket, tattoo, tocsin, war cry, winker
**07** bleeper, car horn, foghorn, go-ahead, red card, red flag, torpedo, whistle
**08** car alarm, diaphone, drumbeat, high sign, password, red alert, red light, reveille
**09** alarm-bell, detonator, fire alarm, indicator, larum-bell, Morse code, signal box, storm cone, Very light, watch fire, watchword, white flag
**10** alarm clock, amber light, Bengal fire, curfew bell, green light, hand signal, heliograph, lighthouse, Lutine bell, smoke alarm, time signal, yellow card, yellow flag
**11** Bengal light, bicycle bell, gale warning, smoke signal, starter's gun, storm signal, trafficator, trumpet call, warning shot
**12** burglar alarm, final warning, storm warning, warning light
**13** Belisha beacon, flashing light, personal alarm, police whistle, security alarm, signal letters, traffic lights
**14** distress signal
**15** semaphore signal

---

## signature

**01** X **03** sig, tag **04** hand, mark, name **05** cross, frank, sheet **08** initials **09** autograph, theme song, theme tune **10** criss-cross, sign-manual **11** endorsement, inscription, John Hancock **12** subscription

## significance

**04** gist, pith **05** ethos, force, point, sense **06** import, matter, slight, weight **07** essence, meaning, message, purport **08** interest **09** magnitude, relevance, solemnity **10** importance, inwardness **11** consequence, implication, seriousness **12** implications **13** consideration

## significant

**03** big, key **04** sign **05** vital **06** cosmic, marked, of note **07** crucial, fateful, meaning, ominous, serious, telling, weighty **08** critical, eloquent, material, pregnant, relevant, senseful, symbolic **09** important, memorable, momentous **10** expressive, indicative, meaningful, noteworthy, suggestive **11** appreciable, symptomatic **12** considerable **13** consequential

## significantly

**07** notably, vitally **09** crucially, knowingly, meaningly **10** critically, eloquently, materially, noticeably, remarkably **11** appreciably, perceptibly **12** considerably, expressively, meaningfully, suggestively

## signify

**04** mark, mean, show **05** count, imply, skill, spell **06** bemean, convey, denote, import, matter, signal **07** betoken, connote, declare, exhibit, express, magnify, portend, suggest **08** indicate, intimate, proclaim, stand for, transmit **09** be a sign of, importune, make waves, represent, symbolize **10** be relevant **11** be important, carry weight, communicate **13** have influence **14** be of importance **15** be of consequence

## signpost

**04** clue, sign **06** marker **07** placard, pointer, waypost **08** handpost **09** guidepost, indicator **10** fingerpost, indication

## silence

**03** gag **04** calm, hush, lull, mute **05** abate, burke, peace, quell, quiet, still **06** deaden, muffle, muzzle, stifle, subdue **07** clamour, infancy, put down, quieten, reserve, secrecy **08** calmness, cut short, dumbness, muteness, oblivion, suppress **09** cough down, dumbfound, quietness, reticence, stillness **10** quiescence, strike dumb **11** taciturnity **12** peacefulness, tranquillity, wordlessness **13** noiselessness, secretiveness, soundlessness, voicelessness **14** altum silentium, speechlessness

### • expressions invoking silence

**02** sh, st **03** mum, shh **04** hist, hush, tace **05** dry up, peace, quiet, shush, whish, whist **06** belt up, shut up, wheesh, whisht, wrap up **07** wheesht **08** button it, give over, pack it in, pipe down **09** say no more **10** enough said, keep shtoom, stay shtoom **11** give it a rest **12** cut the cackle, put a sock in it, shut your face **13** hold your peace, shut your mouth **14** hold your tongue, not another word

*See also* **quiet**

## silent

**03** mum **04** calm, dumb, hush, mute **05** dummy, muted, quiet, shtum, still, stumm, tacit, whist **06** hushed, schtum, shtoom, shtumm, sullen, whisht **07** implied, schtoom, sulking, wheesht **08** implicit, peaceful, reserved, reticent, taciturn, tuneless, unspoken, unvoiced, wordless **09** conticent, inaudible, mumchance, noiseless, quiescent, secretive, soundless, voiceless **10** creepmouse, dumbstruck, speechless, tongue-tied, understood **11** inoperative, obmutescent, tight-lipped, unexpressed **12** languageless

## silently

**06** calmly, dumbly, mutely, stilly **07** quietly, tacitly, unheard **08** ex tacito **09** inaudibly **10** wordlessly **11** noiselessly, quiescently, soundlessly **12** speechlessly, without a word

## silhouette

**04** form **05** shape **06** shadow **07** contour, outline, profile, skyline **08** stand out **09** configure, delineate **11** configurate, delineation **12** shadow figure **13** configuration

## silicon

**02** Si

## silk

**02** KC, QC **03** bur **04** burr **05** crape, moire, satin, surah, tulle **06** crepon, faille, pongee, sendal **07** alamode, challie, challis, marabou, organza, ottoman, taffeta **08** boulting, marabout, prunella, prunelle, prunello, taffetas **09** barrister, filoselle, grenadine **10** peau de soie **11** Canton crepe **12** bolting cloth, King's Counsel, moire antique **13** Queen's Counsel

### • silk yarn **04** tram **08** chenille **09** organzine

## silky

**04** fine, seal, soft **05** sleek **06** glossy, satiny, selkie, silken, silkie, smooth **07** velvety **08** lustrous **09** sericeous **10** diaphanous

## silliness

◊ *anagram indicator* **05** folly **06** idiocy **08** daftness, rashness **09** absurdity, barminess, frivolity, inaneness, looniness, loopiness, pottiness, stupidity **10** immaturity **11** fatuousness, foolishness **12** childishness, recklessness **13** foolhardiness, frivolousness, irrationality, ludicrousness, pointlessness, senselessness **14** ridiculousness **15** meaninglessness

## silly

◊ *anagram indicator* **03** nit **04** berk, clot, daft, dope, dumb, fool, rash, soft, twit **05** apish, barmy, bunny, dazed, dilly, dizzy, dotty, dumbo, goose, idiot, inane, inept, loopy, ninny, nutty, potty, seely, wally **06** absurd, cuckoo, dotish, drippy, duffer, feeble, humble, nitwit, simple, spoony, stupid, unwise **07** fatuous, foolish, halfwit, idiotic, missish, puerile, spooney, strange, stunned **08** childish, harmless, immature, pitiable, reckless **09** airheaded, brainless, foolhardy, frivolous, hen-witted, ignoramus, illogical, imprudent, ludicrous, pointless, senseless, simpleton **10** irrational, nincompoop, ridiculous, silly-billy **11** defenceless, hair-brained, hare-brained, injudicious, meaningless, nonsensical, thoughtless **12** feeble-minded, preposterous, unreasonable **13** irresponsible, unintelligent **14** feather-brained, scatterbrained

*See also* **muddled**

## silt

**03** mud **04** ooze **06** sludge **07** deposit, residue, sullage **08** alluvium, illuvium, sediment **10** brick-earth

### • silt up **03** dam **04** clog **05** block, choke **06** clog up **07** block up, congest

## silvan

**04** bush **05** leafy **06** forest, wooded

**silver**

08 arcadian, forestal, forested, woodland 09 arboreous, forestine 11 tree-covered

**silver**

02 Ag 05 plate, snowy 06 albata, argent, pirate, siller 07 bonanza, cutlery 08 pale grey 11 whitish-grey 12 British plate, greyish-white

**similar**

04 akin, like, same 05 alike, close, samey 07 related, uniform 08 such like 09 analogous, semblable 10 coincident, comparable, equivalent, homologous, resembling 11 homogeneous, much the same 13 corresponding

**similarity**

06 kinred 07 analogy, kindred, kinship 08 affinity, homogeny, likeness, relation, sameness 09 agreement, closeness 10 conformity, congruence, similitude, uniformity 11 concordance, equivalence, homogeneity, isomorphism, parallelism, resemblance 13 comparability, compatibility 14 correspondence

**similarly**

08 likewise 09 by analogy, uniformly 12 in the same way 14 by the same token 15 correspondingly

**similitude**

07 analogy, parable 08 affinity, likeness, relation, sameness 09 agreement, closeness, semblance 10 comparison, congruence, likelihood, similarity, uniformity 11 equivalence, parallelism, resemblance 13 comparability, compatibility 14 correspondence

**simmer**

04 boil, burn, fume, rage, stew 06 bubble, seethe 08 smoulder 10 boil gently, cook gently
• **simmer down** 06 lessen 07 subside 08 calm down, cool down 15 become less angry, collect yourself, control yourself

**simpering**

03 coy 05 silly 06 smirky 07 missish 08 affected, giggling 13 schoolgirlish, self-conscious

**simple**

04 bald, easy, mean, mere, open, slow 05 afald, basic, blunt, clear, crude, cushy, green, lucid, naive, naked, plain, seely, sheer, silly, sorry, stark 06 a cinch, aefald, afawld, candid, direct, honest, semple, soigné, stupid 07 a doddle, aefauld, artless, austere, classic, foolish, gullish, idiotic, low-tech, natural, onefold, sincere, soignée, spartan, unfussy 08 Arcadian, backward, homespun, innocent, inornate, no-frills, ordinary, retarded, semplice 09 a cakewalk, a pushover, a walkover, boastless, credulous, easy as pie, easy-peasy, Galenical, guileless, ingenuous, primitive, Saturnian, unadorned, unlearned, unskilled 10 effortless, elementary, half-witted, unaffected, uninvolved 11 incomposite, inelaborate, Mickey Mouse, open-and-shut, rudimentary, unambiguous, undecorated 12 a piece of cake, feeble-minded, inartificial, simple-minded, unsuspecting 13 low technology, rough and ready, uncomplicated, unembellished, unpretentious 14 comprehensible, understandable, unsophisticate 15 straightforward, unsophisticated

**simple-minded**

03 twp 05 dopey, goofy, idiot 06 simple, stupid 07 artless, foolish, idiotic, moronic, natural 08 backward, clueless, imbecile, innocent, retarded 09 brainless, cretinous, dim-witted 12 addle-brained, feeble-minded 14 not the full quid 15 unsophisticated

**simpleton**

03 daw, mug 04 clot, dolt, dope, dupe, flat, fool, gaby, loon, nong, poop, rook, simp, tony, twit, zany 05 booby, bunny, cokes, dunce, goose, idiot, moron, ninny, noddy, patsy, spoon, sumph, twerp 06 drongo, gander, Johnny, nincom, nincum, nitwit, noodle, simple, stupid 07 dawcock, dullard, gomeral, gomeril, jackass, Johnnie, juggins, mafflin 08 Abderite, flathead, imbecile, maffling, numskull, shot-clog, softhead, wiseacre, woodcock 09 blockhead, Gothamist, Gothamite, greenhorn, nicompoop 10 green goose, hoddy-doddy, nickumpoop, nincompoop 11 ninny-hammer
*See also* **fool**

**simplicity**

04 ease 06 purity 07 candour, clarity, honesty, naiveté, naivety 08 easiness, facility, lucidity, openness, simplism 09 frankness, gracility, innocence, niaiserie, plainness, restraint, rusticity, simplesse, sincerity, starkness 10 clean lines, directness, simpleness 11 artlessness, naturalness 13 guilelessness 14 elementariness 15 intelligibility

**simplification**

09 reduction 10 paraphrase 11 abridgement, explanation 13 clarification 14 interpretation, popularization

**simplify**

06 reduce 07 abridge, clarify, explain, sort out, unravel 08 decipher, make easy, untangle 09 interpret 10 make easier, paraphrase, popularize, streamline 11 disentangle 14 make accessible

**simplistic**

03 pat 04 naif 05 naive 06 facile, simple 07 shallow 08 sweeping 10 oversimple 11 superficial 14 oversimplified

**simplistically**

06 simply 07 naively 08 facilely 09 shallowly 13 superficially

**simply**

04 just, only 05 quite, truly 06 easily, merely, purely, really, solely, wholly 07 clearly, lucidly, plainly, totally, utterly 08 directly, semplice 09 naturally, obviously, shallowly, tout court 10 absolutely, altogether, completely, positively, undeniably 11 simpliciter 12 intelligibly, unreservedly, without doubt 14 unquestionably 15 unconditionally

**Simpson**

02 OJ 04 Bart, Lisa 05 Homer, Marge 06 Maggie, Wallis

**simulate**

03 act 04 copy, echo, fain, fake, mock, sham 05 faine, fayne, feign, mimic, put on 06 affect, assume, parrot 07 feigned, imitate, pretend, reflect 08 parallel 09 duplicate, reproduce 11 counterfeit, make believe

**simulated**

04 fake, faux, mock, sham 05 bogus, put-on 06 phoney, pseudo 07 assumed, feigned, man-made 08 spurious 09 imitation, insincere, pretended, synthetic 10 artificial, substitute 11 inauthentic, make-believe

**simultaneous**

05 simul 08 parallel 10 coexistent, coinciding, concurrent, synchronic 11 concomitant, synchronous 15 coinstantaneous, contemporaneous

**simultaneously**

06 at once 07 at one go 08 in unison, together 09 all at once, at one time 10 in parallel 11 all together 13 at the same time, synchronously 14 synchronically

**sin**

03 err 04 debt, evil, fall, pity, shin, sine 05 crime, error, fault, folly, guilt, lapse, shame, since, stray, wrong 06 offend 07 badness, do wrong, go wrong, impiety, misdeed, offence, offense 08 go astray, iniquity, trespass 09 misbehave 10 commit a sin, immorality, peccadillo, sinfulness, transgress, wickedness, wrongdoing 11 ungodliness 12 misdemeanour 13 fall from grace, transgression 15 irreligiousness, unrighteousness

*The Seven Deadly Sins:*

04 envy, lust 05 anger, greed, pride, sloth, wrath 06 acedia 07 accidie, avarice 08 gluttony 12 covetousness

**since**

02 as 03 ago, sin 04 past, sens, sine, sith, syne, ygoe 05 after, agone, being, until 06 seeing, sithen 07 because, owing to, sithens, through 08 sithence, until now 09 following 10 inasmuch as, seeing that 11 as a result of, on account of 12 from that time, subsequent to 13 from the time of 15 considering that, from the time that

**sincere**

04 open, pure, real, true 05 afald, frank 06 aefald, afawld, candid, dinkum, direct, hearty, honest, simple, single

**07** aefauld, artless, cordial, dinki-di, earnest, fervent, genuine, natural, serious, unmixed, up front **08** bona fide, truthful **09** guileless, heartfelt, ingenuous, unfeigned **10** above board, fair dinkum, heart-whole, no-nonsense, unaffected **11** plain-spoken, true-hearted, trustworthy, undesigning **12** plain-hearted, wholehearted **13** simple-hearted, single-hearted, unadulterated **15** straightforward

### sincerely

**05** truly **06** entire, really, simply **08** honestly **09** earnestly, genuinely, in earnest, seriously **10** truthfully **11** unfeignedly **12** unaffectedly **14** wholeheartedly

### sincerity

**05** truth **06** candor, honour, purity **07** candour, honesty, probity, realtie **08** openness **09** frankness, integrity **10** directness **11** artlessness, earnestness, genuineness, seriousness, uprightness **12** truthfulness **13** guilelessness, ingenuousness **15** trustworthiness

### sinecure

**05** cinch **06** doddle, picnic **07** plum job **08** cushy job **10** gravy train, soft option **11** money for jam **15** money for old rope

### sinewy

**04** wiry **05** burly **06** brawny, robust, strong, sturdy **07** nervous, stringy **08** athletic, muscular, stalwart, vigorous **09** strapping

### sinful

**03** bad **04** evil **05** wrong **06** erring, fallen, guilty, unholy, wicked **07** corrupt, immoral, impious, ungodly **08** criminal, depraved, wrongful **10** iniquitous **11** irreligious, unrighteous

### sinfulness

**03** sin **05** guilt **07** impiety **08** iniquity, peccancy **09** depravity **10** corruption, immorality, wickedness **11** peccability, ungodliness **13** transgression **15** unrighteousness

### sing

**03** hum **04** lilt, pipe, rant, ring, scat, slur **05** carol, chant, chirp, croon, grass, jodel, trill, yodel, yodle **06** chaunt, chorus, intone, quaver, record, second, squall, squeal, strain, warble **07** confess, measure, perform, whistle **08** serenade, vocalize **09** celebrate **13** burst into song
• **sing out** **03** cry **04** bawl, call, yell **05** cooee, peach, shout **06** bellow, cry out, holler, inform

### Singapore

**03** SGP

### singe

**04** burn, char, sear **05** swale, swayl, sweal, sweel **06** scorch, swinge **07** blacken, scowder **08** scouther, scowther

## singer

*Singer types include:*

**03** pop
**04** alto, bard, bass, diva, folk, wait
**05** carol, mezzo, opera, tenor
**06** cantor, chorus, treble
**07** crooner, pop star, soloist, soprano, warbler
**08** baritone, barytone, castrato, choirboy, falsetto, minstrel, songster, vocalist
**09** balladeer, chanteuse, choirgirl, chorister, contralto, precentor, sopranist
**10** prima donna, songstress, troubadour
**11** Heldentenor
**12** counter-tenor, mezzo-soprano
**13** basso profondo, basso profondo

*See also* **bird**

*Singers include:*

**03** **Day** (Doris)
**04** **Cole** (Nat 'King'), **Lynn** (Dame Vera), **Piaf** (Edith)
**05** **Lloyd** (Marie), **Paige** (Elaine)
**06** **Atwell** (Winifred), **Bassey** (Dame Shirley), **Church** (Charlotte), **Crosby** (Bing), **Fields** (Dame Gracie), **Jolson** (Al), **Lauder** (Sir Harry), **Lillie** (Beatrice), **Steele** (Tommy)
**07** **Andrews** (Dame Julie), **Garland** (Judy), **Miranda** (Carmen), **Robeson** (Paul), **Secombe** (Sir Harry), **Sinatra** (Frank)
**08** **Bygraves** (Max), **Liberace**
**09** **Belafonte** (Harry), **Chevalier** (Albert)

*Classical singers include:*

**04** **Butt** (Dame Clara), **Lind** (Jenny), **Popp** (Lucia), **Tear** (Robert)
**05** **Baker** (Dame Janet), **Craig** (Charles), **Evans** (Sir Geraint), **Ewing** (Maria), **Field** (Helen), **Gigli** (Beniamino), **Lanza** (Mario), **Lenya** (Lotte), **Melba** (Dame Nellie), **Patti** (Adelina), **Pears** (Sir Peter)
**06** **Bowman** (James), **Callas** (Maria), **Caruso** (Enrico), **Davies** (Ryland), **Deller** (Alfred), **Kirkby** (Emma), **Norman** (Jessye), **Terfel** (Bryn), **Turner** (Dame Eva), **Van Dam** (José)
**07** **Baillie** (Dame Isobel), **Bartoli** (Cecilia), **Caballé** (Montserrat), **Domingo** (Plácido), **Ferrier** (Kathleen), **Garrett** (Lesley), **Hammond** (Dame Joan), **Lehmann** (Lotte), **Nilsson** (Birgit), **Vickers** (Jon)
**08** **Carreras** (José), **Flagstad** (Kirsten), **Te Kanawa** (Dame Kiri)
**09** **Chaliapin** (Fyodor), **Forrester** (Maureen), **McCormack** (John), **Pavarotti** (Luciano)
**10** **Söderström** (Elisabeth), **Sutherland** (Dame Joan)
**11** **Schwarzkopf** (Dame Elisabeth)
**12** **De Los Angeles** (Victoria)

*Folk singers, musicians and bands include:*

**03** **Gow** (Niel)
**04** **Baez** (Joan), **Bain** (Aly), **Reid** (Robert)
**05** **Sharp** (Cecil James), **Simon** (Paul)
**06** **Browne** (Ronnie), **Fisher** (Archie), **Foster** (Stephen Collins), **Fraser** (Marjory Kennedy), **Mackay** (Charles), **Martyn** (John), **Nairne** (Carolina), **Pogues**, **Runrig**, **Seeger** (Pete)
**07** **Burgess** (John Davey), **Cassidy** (Eva), **Clannad**, **Donegan** (Lonnie), **Donovan**, **Gaughan** (Dick), **Guthrie** (Woody), **MacColl** (Ewan), **Robeson** (Paul), **Skinner** (James Scott), **Thomson** (George)
**08** **Marshall** (William), **Morrison** (Van), **O'Donnell** (Daniel), **Rafferty** (Gerry)
**09** **Dubliners**, **Henderson** (Hamish), **Leadbelly**, **Robertson** (Jeannie), **The Pogues**
**10** **Williamson** (Roy)

*Jazz singers and musicians include:*

**04** **Cole** (Nat 'King'), **Getz** (Stan), **Kidd** (Carole), **King** (B B), **Monk** (Thelonius), **Pine** (Courtney), **Shaw** (Artie)
**05** **Baker** (Chet), **Basie** (Count), **Corea** (Chick), **Davis** (Miles), **Evans** (Gil), **Hines** (Earl), **Jones** (Quincy), **Krupa** (Gene), **Laine** (Dame Cleo), **Roach** (Max), **Scott** (Ronnie), **Smith** (Bessie), **Smith** (Tommy), **Sun Ra**, **Tatum** (Art), **Young** (Lester)
**06** **Barber** (Chris), **Bechet** (Sidney), **Blakey** (Art), **Domino** (Fats), **Dorsey** (Tommy), **Garner** (Errol), **Gordon** (Dexter), **Herman** (Woody), **Hodges** (Johnny), **Hooker** (John Lee), **Joplin** (Scott), **Kenton** (Stan), **Miller** (Glenn), **Mingus** (Charles), **Morton** (Jelly Roll), **Oliver** (King), **Parker** (Charlie), **Powell** (Bud), **Simone** (Nina), **Tracey** (Stan), **Walker** (T-Bone), **Waller** (Thomas 'Fats'), **Waters** (Muddy)
**07** **Bennett** (Tony), **Broonzy** (Big Bill), **Brubeck** (Dave), **Charles** (Ray), **Coleman** (Ornette), **Goodman** (Benny), **Hampton** (Lionel 'Hamp'), **Hancock** (Herbie), **Hawkins** (Coleman), **Holiday** (Billie 'Lady Day'), **Hot Five**, **Ibrahim** (Abdullah), **Jackson** (Milt), **Jarrett** (Keith), **Johnson** (James Price), **Metheny** (Pat), **Mezzrow** (Mezz), **Rollins** (Sonny), **Shorter** (Wayne), **Vaughan** (Sarah)
**08** **Adderley** (Cannonball), **All Stars**, **Calloway** (Cab), **Coltrane** (John), **Eldridge** (Roy), **Franklin** (Aretha), **Gershwin** (George), **Hot Seven**, **Marsalis** (Wynton), **Mulligan** (Gerry), **Peterson** (Oscar)
**09** **Armstrong** (Louis 'Satchmo'), **Christian** (Charlie), **Dankworth** (Sir John), **Ellington** (Duke), **Gillespie** (Dizzy), **Grappelli** (Stephane), **Henderson** (Fletcher), **Leadbelly**, **Lunceford** (Jimmie), **Lyttelton** (Humphrey), **Reinhardt** (Django),

Teagarden (Jack)
10 Fitzgerald (Ella), McLaughlin (John), Thielemans (Toots), Washington (Dinah)
11 Beiderbecke (Bix), Howling Wolf
12 Jazz Warriors

---

*Opera singers include:*

03 Mei (Lanfang)
04 Lind (Jenny), Pons (Lily), Popp (Lucia), Tear (Robert), Ward (David)
05 Allen (Sir Thomas), Baker (Dame Janet), Evans (Sir Geraint), Ewing (Maria), Freni (Mirella), Gedda (Nicolai), Gigli (Beniamino), Gobbi (Tito), Horne (Marilyn), Jones (Dame Gwyneth), Kollo (René), Kraus (Alfredo), Lanza (Mario), Luxon (Benjamin), Melba (Dame Nellie), Patti (Adelina), Pears (Sir Peter), Pinza (Ezio), Price (Leontyne), Siepi (Cesare), Sills (Beverly), Teyte (Dame Maggie)
06 Bowman (James), Callas (Maria), Caruso (Enrico), Davies (Ryland), Dawson (Peter), Deller (Alfred), de Luca (Giuseppe), Farrar (Geraldine), García (Manuel), Garden (Mary), Harper (Heather), Hotter (Hans), Ludwig (Christa), Minton (Yvonne), Norman (Jessye), Reszke (Jean de), Scotto (Renata), Studer (Cheryl), Tauber (Richard), Terfel (Bryn), Turner (Dame Eva), Van Dam (José)
07 Barstow (Dame Josephine), Bartoli (Cecilia), Caballé (Montserrat), Domingo (Placido), Farrell (Eileen), Ferrier (Kathleen), Garrett (Lesley), Jurinac (Sena), Lehmann (Lilli), Lehmann (Lotte), Migenes (Julia), Milanov (Zinka), Nilsson (Birgit), Stratas (Teresa), Tebaldi (Renata), Tibbett (Lawrence), Traubel (Helen), Vickers (Jon)
08 Anderson (Marian), Berganza (Teresa), Bergonzi (Carlo), Björling (Jussi), Carreras (José), Dernesch (Helga), Flagstad (Kirsten), Lawrence (Marjorie), Melchior (Lauritz), Piccaver (Alfred), Ponselle (Rosa), Schumann (Elisabeth), Seefried (Irmgard), Te Kanawa (Dame Kiri)
09 Berberian (Cathy), Brannigan (Owen), Chaliapin (Feodor), Christoff (Boris), Della Casa (Lisa), Del Monaco (Mario), Forrester (Maureen), Hendricks (Barbara), McCormack (John), McCracken (James), Pavarotti (Luciano)
10 Galli-Curci (Amelita), Los Angeles (Victoria de), Martinelli (Giovanni), Söderström (Elisabeth), Sutherland (Dame Joan), Tetrazzini (Luisa)
11 Schwarzkopf (Dame Elisabeth)
12 de los Angeles (Victoria), Shirley-Quirk (John)
14 Fischer-Dieskau (Dietrich)

---

*Pop and rock singers, musicians and bands include:*

02 U2
03 ELO, Eno (Brian), Jam, Lee

(Peggy), Pop (Iggy), REM, Yes
04 Abba, AC/DC, B52s, Baez (Joan), Blur, Bush (Kate), Cash (Johnny), Cher, Cray (Robert), Crow (Sheryl), Cure, Devo, Dion (Celine), Dury (Ian), Gaye (Marvin), Joel (Billy), John (Sir Elton), King (Carole), Kiss, Lulu, Piaf (Edith), Pulp, Reed (Lou), Ross (Diana), Rush, Sade, Shaw (Sandie), UB40, Vega (Suzanne), Wham!
05 Adams (Bryan), Berry (Chuck), Black (Cilla), Bolan (Marc), Bowie (David), Brown (James), Byrds, Byrne (David), Carey (Mariah), Clash, Cohen (Leonard), Davis (Sammy, Junior), Doors, Dylan (Bob), Ferry (Bryan), Flack (Roberta), Haley (Bill, and the Comets), Jarre (Jean-Michel), Jones (Grace), Jones (Tom), Kinks, Lewis (Jerry Lee), Melua (Katie), Moyet (Alison), Oasis, Queen, Simon (Carly), Simon (Paul), Smith (Patti), Starr (Ringo), Twain (Shaniah), Verve, Waits (Tom), White (Barry), Wings, Young (Neil), Zappa (Frank), ZZ Top
06 Atwell (Winifred), Bassey (Shirley), Cocker (Joe), Cooper (Alice), Crosby (Bing), Damned, Denver (John), Domino (Fats), Eagles, Easton (Sheena), Fields (Dame Gracie), Jolson (Al), Joplin (Janis), Knight (Gladys, and the Pips), Lauper (Cyndi), Lennon (John), Lennox (Annie), Marley (Bob), Midler (Bette), Newman (Randy), Palmer (Robert), Pitney (Gene), Pogues, Police, Prince, Richie (Lionel), Sedaka (Neil), Simone (Nina), Smiths, Summer (Donna), Taylor (James), The Who, Turner (Tina), Wonder (Stevie)
07 Animals, Beatles, Bee Gees, Blondie, Bon Jovi, Charles (Ray), Clapton (Eric), Cochran (Eddie), Collins (Phil), Diamond (Neil), Diddley (Bo), Donovan, Gabriel (Peter), Garland (Judy), Genesis, Hendrix (Jimi), Hollies, Houston (Whitney), Jackson (Janet), Jackson (Michael), Madonna, Mercury (Freddie), Michael (George), Minogue (Kylie), Monkees, Orbison (Roy), Osmonds, Pickett (Wilson), Presley (Elvis), Redding (Otis), Richard (Sir Cliff), Santana (Carlos), Shadows, Sinatra (Frank), Squeeze, Stevens (Cat), Stewart (Rod), Vincent (Gene), Warwick (Dionne)
08 Coldplay, Costello (Elvis), Franklin (Aretha), Green Day, Harrison (George), Liberace, Mitchell (Joni), Morrison (Van), New Order, Oldfield (Mike), Robinson (Smokey), Vandross (Luther), Van Halen, Williams (Robbie)
09 Aerosmith, Beach Boys, Chevalier (Albert), Garfunkel (Art), Kraftwerk, McCartney (Paul), Motorhead, Pink

Floyd, Radiohead, Roxy Music, Simply Red, Status Quo, Steely Dan, Streisand (Barbra), Thin Lizzy
10 Carpenters, Deep Purple, Def Leppard, Duran Duran, Eurythmics, Guns 'n' Roses, Iron Maiden, Moody Blues, Portishead, Pretenders, Sex Pistols, Shangri-las, Spice Girls, Stranglers
11 Armatrading (Joan), Culture Club, Cypress Hill, Dire Straits, Human League, Joy Division, Judas Priest, Led Zeppelin, Public Enemy, Simple Minds, Springfield (Dusty), Springsteen (Bruce), Temptations
12 Black Sabbath, Dead Kennedys, Fleetwood Mac, Grateful Dead, Talking Heads
13 Little Richard, Rolling Stones, Spandau Ballet
14 Everly Brothers, Pointer Sisters, Public Image Ltd
15 Neville Brothers

---

## single

01 I 03 ane, one 04 free, lone, only, poor, sole, solo, thin, unit, weak 05 afald, alone, small, unwed 06 aefald, afawld, honest, one run, simple, slight, unique, versal 07 aefauld, one-fold, simplex, sincere 08 by itself, celibate, distinct, isolated, man-to-man, one-to-one, separate, singular, solitary, unbroken, unshared 09 available, exclusive, on your own, undivided, unmarried 10 by yourself, determined, individual, one and only, particular, unattached, uncombined 12 woman-to-woman 14 person-to-person
• single out 04 pick 05 hit on 06 choose, pick on, select 07 hit upon, isolate 08 decide on, hand-pick, identify, pinpoint, separate, set apart 09 highlight, victimize 11 distinguish, separate out

## single-handed

04 solo 05 alone 07 unaided 09 on your own 10 by yourself, unassisted 11 independent, without help 13 independently, unaccompanied

## single-minded

03 set 05 afald, fixed 06 aefald, afawld, dogged 07 aefauld, devoted, onefold 08 resolute, tireless 09 committed, dedicated, ingenuous, obsessive, steadfast 10 determined, unswerving, unwavering 11 persevering, undeviating 12 monomaniacal

## singly

04 only 05 alone 06 solely 08 one by one 10 distinctly, one at a time, on their own, separately, singularly 12 individually 13 independently

## singular

01 s 03 odd 04 sing 05 queer 06 proper, single, unique 07 curious, eminent, private, strange, unusual 08 atypical, peculiar, uncommon 09 eccentric 10 noteworthy, pre-eminent, remarkable 11 conspicuous, exceptional, out-of-the-way,

outstanding **12** unparalleled
**13** extraordinary

**singularity**
**05** quirk, twist **06** oddity **07** oddness, oneness **09** queerness **10** uniqueness **11** abnormality, curiousness, peculiarity, strangeness **12** eccentricity, idiosyncrasy, irregularity **13** individuality, particularity

**singularly**
**06** singly **07** notably **08** signally **09** bizarrely, strangely, unusually **10** especially, peculiarly, remarkably, uncommonly **12** particularly, pre-eminently, prodigiously, surprisingly **13** conspicuously, exceptionally, outstandingly **15** extraordinarily

**sinister**
**01** L **02** lh **04** dark, evil, left **05** cruel, shady **06** Gothic, louche, malign, wicked **07** harmful, ominous, unlucky, vicious **08** menacing **09** underhand **10** disturbing, forbidding, malevolent, misleading, portentous, terrifying **11** disquieting, frightening, threatening **12** inauspicious

**sink**
◇ *anagram indicator* **03** bog, dig, dip, ebb, lay, pay, pot, sag, set **04** bore, damn, dive, drop, fade, fail, fall, flag, foil, fund, mire, risk, ruin, slip **05** abate, basin, bason, decay, drill, drive, droop, drown, embed, lapse, let in, lower, merge, put in, shaft, slump, stoop, wreck **06** cloaca, devall, engulf, fall in, go down, insert, invest, jawbox, lay out, lessen, plough, plunge, settle, vanish, weaken, worsen **07** abandon, abolish, capsize, conceal, decline, degrade, descend, destroy, dwindle, founder, go lower, go to pot, go under, immerse, plummet, put down, scupper, scuttle, subside, succumb, venture **08** cesspool, collapse, decrease, demolish, diminish, excavate, submerge, suppress **09** devastate, disappear, gravitate, penetrate **10** degenerate, go downhill **12** draught-house

**sinless**
**04** pure **08** innocent, virtuous **09** faultless, guiltless, undefiled, unspotted, unsullied **10** immaculate, impeccable **11** unblemished, uncorrupted

**sinner**
**08** criminal, evil-doer, offender **09** miscreant, reprobate, wrongdoer **10** backslider, impenitent, malefactor, trespasser **12** transgressor

**sinuous**
**04** ogee, wavy **05** lithe **06** curved, slinky **07** bending, coiling, curling, curving, sinuate, turning, weaving, winding, wriggly **08** tortuous, twisting **10** meandering, serpentine, undulating

**sip**
**03** sup **04** drop, sowp, tiff, tift **05** drink, taste **06** sample, sipple **08** delibate, mouthful, spoonful **11** drink slowly

**sir**
**02** Sr **03** Dan, Don **04** baas, Herr, stir, tuan **05** bwana, sahib, Señor **06** Mister, Signor, sirrah, stirra **07** lording, mynheer, Signior, Signore, stirrah **08** Monsieur

**siren**
**04** vamp **05** alarm, Circe, syren **06** hooter, tocsin **07** charmer, Delilah, foghorn, Lorelei, mermaid **08** car alarm **09** fire alarm, temptress **10** seductress **11** femme fatale **12** burglar alarm **13** moaning minnie, personal alarm, security alarm

**sissy**
*see* **cissy**

**sister**
**02** Sr **03** nun, sib, sis **04** siss **05** nurse, titty **06** abbess, fellow, friend, german, vowess **07** comrade, partner, sibling **08** prioress, relation, relative **09** associate, colleague, companion **10** full sister, half-sister, twin-sister **11** blood-sister

**sit**
**02** do **03** fit, lie, put **04** bear, hang, hold, meet, pass, pose, rest, seat, take **05** befit, brood, clock, model, perch, place, press, roost, serve, squat, stand, weigh **06** gather, locate, reside, settle **07** consult, contain, convene, deposit, sit down, situate **08** assemble, be seated, position, study for, take part **09** be a member, squat down **10** deliberate, take part in **11** accommodate, be a member of, be in session, have room for **12** have space for, take your seat
• **sit back** **05** relax **09** do nothing **15** not be involved in
• **sit in on** **04** join **05** watch **06** attend **07** observe **11** be present at
• **sit on** **04** ride **05** brood, cover
• **sit upright** **04** perk

**site**
**03** lot, put, set **04** area, plot, seat, spot **05** place, scene, venue **06** ground, locate **07** install, posture, setting, situate, station, website **08** locality, location, platform, position **09** situation

**sitting**
**04** seat **05** spell **06** assize, clutch, period, seated, sejant **07** hearing, meeting, sejeant, session **08** assembly, brooding, sederunt **12** consultation

**sitting room**
**06** lounge, parlor, sitter **07** day room, parlour **08** anteroom **09** front room **10** living room **11** drawing room **13** reception room

**situate**
**03** put, set **04** site **05** place **06** locate **07** install, station **08** position **12** circumstance

**situation**
**03** job, lie **04** case, post, rank, seat, site, spot **05** place, score, set-up, state **06** locale, milieu, office, status **07** affairs, climate, picture, setting, station **08** juncture, locality, location,

position, scenario **09** condition **10** conditions, employment **11** appointment, environment, predicament, state of play **12** lie of the land, what's going on **13** circumstances **14** state of affairs

**six**
**02** VI **04** sice, size **05** hexad **06** senary, sestet **07** sestett **08** sestette **09** half-dozen **10** half-a-dozen

**six-footer**
*see* **insect**

**sixpence**
**04** kick, zack **05** tizzy **06** bender, tanner, tester, teston **07** testern, testril **08** testrill

**sixteen**
**03** XVI

**sixty**
**02** LX

**sizable, sizeable**
**05** hefty **06** decent, goodly **07** biggish, largish **08** generous **11** fairly large, respectable, substantial **12** considerable

**size**
**04** area, bulk, mass **05** range, scale **06** amount, assize, extent, height, length, volume **07** bigness, expanse, measure **08** quantity, vastness **09** allowance, dimension, greatness, immensity, largeness, magnitude **10** dimensions **11** measurement, proportions **12** measurements
• **size up** **04** rate **05** gauge, judge **06** assess **07** measure, suss out, weigh up **08** appraise, estimate, evaluate

**sizeable**
*see* **sizable, sizeable**

**sizzle**
**03** fry **04** hiss, sear, spit **06** scorch **07** crackle, frizzle, sputter

**skate**
**03** ray **04** rink **06** rocker
*See also* **ice skating**

**skeletal**
**05** drawn, gaunt **06** wasted **07** haggard **08** shrunken **09** emaciated, fleshless, unfleshed **10** cadaverous **11** skin-and-bone **13** hollow-cheeked

**skeleton**
**04** plan **05** atomy, basic, bones, draft, frame **06** lowest, sketch **07** anatomy, minimum, outline, reduced, support **08** corallum, smallest **09** bare bones, blueprint, framework, polyzoary, structure, tentorium **10** coenosteum **11** polyzoarium **12** endoskeleton

**sketch**
**03** act **04** draw, line, plan, skit, turn **05** draft, paint, rough, scene, skiff, spoof, trick **06** aperçu, depict, design, memoir, parody, pencil, précis, résumé, satire, send-up, visual **07** cartoon, croquis, diagram, draught, drawing, ébauche, modello, outline, portray, profile, summary, take-off **08** abstract, block out, bozzetto, esquisse, platform, rough out,

scenario, skeleton, synopsis, vignette **09** bare bones, bare facts, burlesque, delineate, framework, programme, represent, rough idea, thumbnail **10** caricature, designment, main points, pencilling, prospectus **11** delineation, description **12** mickeytaking **13** prosopography **14** representation **15** thumbnail sketch

### sketchily
**07** hastily, roughly, vaguely **08** patchily **09** cursorily **11** imperfectly **12** inadequately, incompletely **13** perfunctorily

### sketchy
◇ *anagram indicator* **05** bitty, crude, hasty, rough, vague **06** meagre, patchy, slight **07** cursory, scrappy **09** defective, deficient, imperfect **10** inadequate, incomplete, unfinished, unpolished **11** perfunctory, provisional, superficial **12** insufficient

### skew
**04** awry, bias **05** slant, twist, weigh **06** biased, colour **07** distort, falsify, oblique **09** obliquity **12** asymmetrical, misrepresent

### skewer
**04** prod **05** kebab **06** skiver **09** brochette

### skier
*Skiers include:*

**04** Hess (Erika)
**05** Cranz (Christl), Killy (Jean Claude), Maier (Hermann), Tomba (Alberto)
**06** Dahlie (Björn), Figini (Michela), Sailer (Toni), Wenzel (Hanni)
**07** Edwards (Eddie 'The Eagle'), Klammer (Franz), Nykänen (Matti), Simpson (Myrtle)
**08** Kostelic (Janica), Nykaenen (Matti), Stenmark (Ingemar), Walliser (Maria)
**09** Schneider (Vreni), Smetanina (Raisa)
**10** Girardelli (Marc), Moser-Pröll (Annemarie), Zurbriggen (Pirmin)

### skiing
*Skiing events include:*

**05** grass, mogul, relay, speed
**06** aerial, alpine, nordic, slalom, sprint, super-g
**07** jumping, pursuit
**08** combined, downhill, halfpipe
**09** classical, dual mogul, freestyle, snowboard
**11** giant slalom
**12** cross-country

*Skiing-related terms include:*

**04** gate
**05** daffy, glide, inrun, piste, split
**06** basket, big air, edging, kicker, k point, outrun, p point, schuss
**07** grip wax, hairpin, harries, kick wax, takeoff
**08** freeride, glide wax, table top, Telemark
**09** aerialist, freestyle, large hill, mass start, Steilhang, V-position

**10** Hahnenkamm, helicopter, normal hill
**11** carving skis, egg position, scramble leg, spread eagle
**12** starting gate, tuck position, vertical gate
**13** backscratcher, critical point, herringboning

### skilful
**03** hot, sly **04** able, deft, good, hend, mean, wise **05** adept, canny, handy, smart **06** adroit, artful, clever, expert, gifted, quaint, skeely, versed **07** capable, cunning, knowing, learned, skilled, trained **08** dextrous, masterly, tactical, talented, well-seen **09** competent, dexterous, efficient, ingenious, practised **10** diplomatic, proficient, well-versed **11** experienced, industrious, workmanlike **12** accomplished, diplomatical, professional **14** nimble-fingered

### skilfully
**04** ably, well **06** deftly, yarely **07** capably, handily **08** cleverly, expertly **11** competently **12** proficiently

### skill
**03** art **04** chic, feat, hand **05** craft, knack, power, savey, savvy, sight, touch **06** matter, reason, savvey, talent **07** ability, cunning, finesse, knowhow, mastery, quality, science, signify **08** aptitude, artifice, deftness, facility, training **09** adeptness, expertise, handiness, knowledge, smartness, technique **10** adroitness, cleverness, competence, efficiency, experience, expertness **11** proficiency, skilfulness **12** intelligence **14** accomplishment, discrimination **15** professionalism

### skilled
**04** able, good **05** adept **06** expert, gifted **07** capable, skilful, trained **08** complete, masterly, schooled, talented **09** competent, efficient, practised, qualified **10** consummate, proficient **11** experienced **12** accomplished, professional

### skim
**03** fly **04** ream, sail, scan, skip **05** brush, cream, float, glide, graze, plane, skate, skiff, touch **06** bounce **07** run over, skitter, take off **08** glance at, separate **09** despumate **10** hydroplane, run through **11** flip through, leaf through, look through, read quickly **12** flick through, thumb through **13** browse through

### skimp
**05** pinch, spare, stint **06** scanty, scrimp **08** withhold **09** cut back on, economize **10** be mean with, cut corners **12** be economical **15** tighten your belt

### skimpy
**04** mean, thin **05** brief, short, small, tight **06** meagre, measly, scanty, sparse, stingy **07** miserly, sketchy **08** beggarly, exiguous **09** niggardly **10** inadequate **12** insufficient **13** insubstantial

### skin
**03** pod **04** drum, fell, film, flay, hide, hull, husk, peel, pelt, rind, rine **05** cover, crust, graze, layer, strip **06** casing, fleece, scrape **07** coating, outside, surface, swindle **08** covering, membrane, tegument **10** complexion, integument

*Skin parts include:*

**04** derm, hair, hide, pore
**05** cutis, derma
**06** corium, dermis
**07** cuticle, papilla
**09** epidermis
**10** sweat gland
**11** lower dermis
**12** hair follicle
**14** sebaceous gland

*Skin diseases and conditions include:*

**02** EB, XP
**04** acne, boba, buba, rash, yaws
**05** favus, tinea, warts
**06** eczema, herpes, ulcers
**07** anthrax, gum rash, leprosy, scabies, serpigo
**08** dandruff, melanoma, ringworm
**09** keratosis, psoriasis
**10** dermatitis, dermatosis, framboesia
**11** acne rosacea, prickly heat
**12** athlete's foot, button scurvy

### • by the skin of your teeth
**06** barely **08** narrowly, only just **10** a near thing, by a whisker **11** a close thing

### skin-deep
**05** empty **07** outward, shallow, surface **08** external **10** artificial **11** meaningless, superficial **13** superficially

### skinflint
**05** miser, screw **06** meanie **07** niggard, Scrooge **08** tightwad **09** flay-flint **11** cheeseparer **12** penny-pincher

### skinny
**04** lean, thin **07** scraggy, scrawny **08** skeletal, underfed **09** emaciated **11** skin-and-bone **12** tight-fitting **14** undernourished

### skip
◇ *anagram indicator* ◇ *deletion indicator* **03** bob, cut, hop **04** dart, jump, leap, miss, omit, pass, race, rush, tear **05** bound, caper, dance, dodge, flisk, frisk, slipe **06** bounce, cavort, gambol, prance, spring, tittup **07** captain, miss out, scamper, skipper, trounce **08** dumpster, leave out, overleap, overskip, ricochet **10** bottle bank **11** move quickly

### skirmish
**05** argue, brawl, brush, clash, fight, mêlée, scrap, set-to **06** affray, battle, combat, dust-up, fracas, tussle **07** contend, dispute, fall out, pickeer, punch-up, quarrel, scuffle, wrangle **08** argument, conflict, scarmoge **09** encounter **10** engagement, velitation **11** altercation, escarmouche **13** confrontation, running battle

## skirt

**03** hug, rim **04** coat, edge, gore, kilt, maxi, mini, tutu **05** avoid, evade, flank, woman, women **06** border, bypass, circle, margin, piupiu **07** go round, midriff **08** lava-lava, wrapover **09** move round, petticoat **10** circumvent, wraparound **13** find a way round **14** circumnavigate

## skit

**03** act **04** hoax, turn **05** scene, spoof **06** parody, satire, send-up, sketch **07** take-off **09** burlesque **10** caricature **12** mickey-taking

## skittish

**03** coy **05** jumpy **06** fickle, frisky, lively, skeigh, wanton **07** fidgety, kitteny, nervous, playful, restive **08** startish, unsteady, volatile **09** excitable, frivolous, kittenish **10** changeable **11** light-headed **12** highly-strung

## skittles

**04** pins **05** bowls, kails **07** tenpins **08** ninepins **10** kettle-pins, kittle-pins **11** skittle-pins **13** tenpin bowling

## skive

**04** idle, laze **05** dodge, evade, shirk, skulk, slack **07** bunk off, goof off **08** malinger **09** avoid work **12** swing the lead

## skiver

**05** idler **06** dodger, loafer, skewer **07** goof-off, shirker, slacker **09** do-nothing **10** malingerer

## skivvy

*see* **servant**

## skulduggery

**08** trickery **09** chicanery, duplicity, swindling **10** hanky-panky **11** fraudulence, shenanigans **12** machinations **13** double-dealing, jiggery-pokery **15** underhandedness

## skulk

**03** pad **04** hide, lurk, lusk **05** creep, miche, mooch, mouch, prowl, shool, shule, slide, slink, sneak, steal **06** loiter, shoole **08** malinger **09** lie in wait, pussyfoot

## skunk

**04** atoc, atok **05** zoril **06** zorino **07** polecat, zorilla, zorille, zorillo

## sky

**03** air **04** blue, lift **05** azure, carry, space **06** welkin **07** ambient, heavens, the blue, weather **08** empyrean **09** firmament **10** atmosphere **12** upper regions **13** vault of heaven

## skyscraper

**10** tower block **14** sliver building

## slab

**03** mud, tab **04** blad, hawk, hunk, lump, pane, slat, tile, turf **05** blaud, block, board, brick, chunk, dalle, piece, plate, slate, slice, stela, stele, table, wedge, wodge **06** bunker, ice pan, ledger, lidger, marble, marver, metope, mihrab, peever, planch, plaque, quarry, sheave, tablet **07** briquet, portion, viscous

## slack

◇ *anagram indicator* **03** lax **04** ease, give, idle, lash, lazy, limp, play, room, slow, veer **05** baggy, dodge, loose, quiet, shirk, skive, surge, tardy **06** excess, flabby, leeway, lessen, reduce, remiss, sloppy, softly **07** flaccid, get less, hanging, languid, neglect, relaxed, sagging, slacken **08** careless, decrease, diminish, flapping, flexible, inactive, malinger, moderate, slapdash, slow down, sluggish **09** easy-going, looseness, negligent, nerveless, partially **10** neglectful, permissive **11** inattentive, promiscuous **12** become slower **13** spare capacity **14** insufficiently

## slacken

• **slacken off** **04** ease, slow **05** abate, relax **06** lessen, loosen, reduce **07** ease off, get less, release **08** decrease, diminish, forslack, moderate, slow down **10** take it easy **12** become slower

## slacker

**05** idler **06** loafer, skiver **07** dawdler, shirker **08** embusqué, layabout **10** malingerer **12** clock-watcher **14** good-for-nothing

## slag

• **slag off** **04** mock, slam **05** abuse, knock, slate **06** berate, deride, insult, malign **07** lambast, run down **08** lambaste **09** criticize

## slake

**03** mud **04** daub, lick, sate **05** abate, allay, slime, smear **06** deaden, quench, reduce, sloken **07** assuage, gratify, hydrate, moisten, mudflat, satiate, satisfy, slacken, slocken, subside **08** mitigate, moderate **10** extinguish

## slam

**03** pan **04** bang, clap, dash, hurl, ruff, slag, slap, swap, swop **05** clash, crash, fling, slate, smash, throw, thump, trump **06** attack **07** censure, rubbish, run down, slag off **08** denounce **09** criticize **12** pull to pieces, tear to pieces, tear to shreds **13** find fault with **15** do a hatchet job on

## slander

**03** mud **04** slur **05** libel, smear **06** defame, malign, missay, vilify **07** asperse, calumny, obloquy, scandal, traduce **08** backbite, badmouth, vilipend **09** aspersion, denigrate, disparage, sclaunder **10** backbiting, calumniate, defamation, detraction, fling mud at, muck-raking, scandalize, sling mud at, throw mud at **11** denigration, mudslinging, speak evil of, traducement **12** evil-speaking, vilification **13** disparagement, smear campaign **14** cast aspersions

## slanderous

**05** false **06** untrue **07** abusive

## slang

**04** cant **05** argot, chain, lingo, scold **06** jargon, patois, patter **07** cockney **09** vulgarism **10** mumbo-jumbo, vituperate, watch chain **11** criminalese, doublespeak **12** gobbledygook **13** colloquialism

## slanging match

**03** row **04** spat **05** set-to **06** barney **07** dispute, quarrel **08** argument **09** argy-bargy **11** altercation **13** shouting match

## slant

**03** dip **04** bend, bias, jibe, lean, list, ramp, skew, spin, tilt, view, warp **05** angle, bevel, pitch, slash, slope, splay, twist **06** camber, chance, colour, glance, shelve, sklent, weight **07** be askew, distort, incline, leaning, oblique, opinion, sloping **08** attitude, diagonal, emphasis, gradient **09** embrasure, embrazure, obliquity, prejudice, viewpoint **10** distortion **11** inclination, point of view **12** forward slash, one-sidedness

## slanting

**05** askew, bevel, slope **06** aslant, tilted **07** asklent, dipping, leaning, listing, oblique, sloping, tilting **08** at a slant, diagonal **09** inclining **11** on an incline

## slap

**03** hit, set **04** bang, biff, blow, clap, cuff, daub, dead, scud, slam, snub, sock, spat, swap, yank **05** apply, clout, pandy, plonk, plumb, plump, punch, right, skelp, smack, spank, stick, thump, twank, whack **06** breach, buffet, clatch, make-up, pierce, rebuke, sclaff, spread, strike, wallop **07** clobber, exactly, plaster, put down, set down **08** directly, slap-bang, straight, suddenly **09** precisely, violently **10** paddy-whack **11** strike hands

• **slap in the face** **04** blow, snub **06** insult, rebuff, rebuke **07** affront, put-down, repulse **09** indignity, rejection **11** humiliation

• **slap on the wrist** **04** flak **05** blame, stick **06** earful, rebuke **07** censure, slating **08** knocking, slamming **09** carpeting, reprimand **10** punishment, rollicking, telling-off, ticking-off **11** castigation, comeuppance **12** dressing-down

## slapdash

◇ *anagram indicator* **04** rash **05** hasty, messy **06** clumsy, sloppy, untidy **07** hurried, offhand **08** careless, slipshod, slovenly **09** haphazard, negligent, roughcast **10** disorderly, last-minute **11** perfunctory, thoughtless **14** thrown-together

## slap-happy

**05** dazed, giddy, woozy **06** casual **07** reeling **08** reckless, slapdash **09** haphazard, hit-or-miss

**slapstick**
10 boisterous, nonchalant, punch-drunk 12 happy-go-lucky
13 irresponsible

**slapstick**
05 farce 06 comedy 09 horseplay, low comedy 10 buffoonery, custard pie, knockabout, tomfoolery

**slap-up**
06 lavish, superb 08 princely, splendid 09 elaborate, excellent, first-rate, luxurious, sumptuous 10 first-class
11 magnificent, superlative

**slash**
03 axe, cut, jag, rip 04 curb, gash, hack, race, rase, rash, raze, rend, rent, slit, snip, tear 05 knife, prune, score, slant, slice 06 reduce, scorch, stroke
07 curtail, oblique, solidus, urinate, virgule 08 decrease, diagonal, incision, lacerate 09 carbonado 10 laceration, separatrix 12 forward slash
*See also* **urinate**

**slate**
03 cam, pan, rag 04 calm, caum, ragg, slag, slam, slat 05 abuse, blame, knock, scold, set on 06 berate, killas, rebuke, sklate 07 censure, propose, rubbish, run down, slag off
08 schedule, tomahawk 09 alum-shale, criticize, pull apart, reprimand, spilosite 10 black chalk, tabula rasa
11 sclate-stane 12 pull to pieces, tear to pieces, tear to shreds
14 Knotenschiefer 15 do a hatchet job on
• **size of roofing slate** 04 lady
05 peggy, queen, small 06 double
07 duchess 08 countess, princess
09 small lady 11 marchioness, viscountess

**slatternly**
05 dirty, dowdy 06 blowsy, blowzy, frowzy, frumpy, sleazy, sloppy, untidy
07 unclean, unkempt 08 frumpish, slipshod, slovenly, sluttish
10 bedraggled

**slaughter**
04 beat, best, drub, kill, lick, rout, slay
05 halal, worst 06 battue, defeat, hallal, hammer, murder, outwit, subdue, thrash 07 butcher, carnage, clobber, conquer, killing, murther, outplay, trounce 08 butchery, massacre, outsmart, overcome, vanquish
09 bloodbath, bloodshed, holocaust, liquidate, mactation, overpower, overwhelm, sacrifice, subjugate
10 annihilate, put to death
11 exterminate, liquidation, meat packing 12 annihilation
13 extermination, have the edge on
14 get the better of, putting to death

**slaughtered**
◊ *anagram indicator*
*See also* **drunk**

**slaughterhouse**
08 abattoir, butchery, shambles

**Slav**
04 Serb, Sorb, Wend 05 Sclav
06 bohunk
*See also* **European**

**slave**
03 boy 04 esne, gimp, serf, slog, toil
05 grind, sweat, theow 06 abject, addict, drudge, labour, lackey, maroon, menial, sclave, skivvy, thrall, vassal 07 bondman, captive, odalisk, predial, servant, villein 08 bondmaid, bondsman, Mameluke, odalique, praedial, servant, villein 08 bondmaid, Gibeonite, odalisque 10 bondswoman, contraband 11 bondservant, galley slave 15 work your guts out

**slave-driver**
05 bully 06 despot, tyrant 08 autocrat, dictator, martinet 09 oppressor
10 taskmaster

**slaver**
05 drool, spawl 06 drivel 07 dribble, slobber, spittle 08 salivate 09 beslobber

**slavery**
04 yoke 06 thrall 07 bondage, serfdom
08 drudgery, nativity, slabbery, thraldom 09 captivity, servitude, thralldom, vassalage 11 bond-service, enslavement, enthralment, subjugation 12 enthrallment

**slavish**
03 low 04 mean, meek 06 abject, menial, strict 07 fawning, literal, servile 08 cringing 09 imitative, laborious 10 grovelling, obsequious, submissive, uninspired, unoriginal
11 deferential, subservient, sycophantic 13 unimaginative

**slavishly**
06 meekly 08 strictly 12 submissively, unoriginally 13 unresistingly
15 unimaginatively

**slay**
04 kill 06 murder, rub out 07 butcher, destroy, execute 08 despatch, dispatch, massacre 09 eliminate, slaughter 10 annihilate 11 assassinate, exterminate

**slaying**
05 quell 06 murder 07 killing
08 butchery, despatch, dispatch, massacre 09 mactation, slaughter
11 destruction, elimination
12 annihilation 13 assassination, extermination

**sleazy**
03 low 05 grody, seedy, tacky
06 crummy, sleezy, sordid 07 corrupt, squalid 10 slatternly 12 disreputable

**sledge**
03 bob 04 dray, luge, pulk, sled
05 pulka, slide, slipe, train 06 hurdle, pulkha, Ski-doo®, sleigh 07 bobsled, dogsled, kibitka, travois 08 toboggan
09 bobsleigh 10 fore-hammer 11 hurly-hacket, skeleton bob 12 sledgehammer

**sleek**
04 calm, smug, soft 05 glide, shiny, silky, slick, smalm, smarm 06 glossy, oilily, silken, smooth, soothe 07 stylish
08 lustrous, smoothly, thriving
10 prosperous 11 insinuating, well-groomed

**sleep**
03 kip, nap, ziz 04 bunk, doss, doze, rest, zizz 05 death, dover, go off
06 catnap, drowse, nod off, repose, siesta, snooze 07 bye-byes, drop off, shut-eye, slumber 08 be asleep, crash out, dormancy, doss down, drift off, flake out, REM sleep 09 hibernate
10 fall asleep, forty winks 11 have a snooze, hibernation 12 get some sleep
13 sleep like a log 14 have forty winks
15 go out like a light
• **go to sleep** 03 kip 04 dove, doze
05 go off 06 catnap, nod off, snooze
07 doze off, drop off 08 crash out, drift off, fall over 10 fall asleep 14 have forty winks
• **put to sleep** 06 sopite 07 destroy, put down

**sleepily**
06 slowly 07 heavily, quietly, wearily
08 drowsily, torpidly 09 languidly
10 inactively, sluggishly
13 lethargically

**sleepiness**
06 torpor 07 languor 08 doziness, lethargy 09 drowsihed, heaviness, oscitancy 10 drowsihead, drowsiness, oscitation, somnolence, somnolency

**sleeping**
04 idle 06 asleep 07 dormant, passive, unaware 08 abeyance, becalmed, dormient, inactive, off guard
10 slumbering 11 daydreaming, hibernating, inattentive 12 spine-bashing

**sleepless**
05 alert, awake 07 wakeful 08 restless, vigilant, watchful 09 disturbed, insomniac, wide-awake 10 unsleeping

**sleeplessness**
08 insomnia 11 wakefulness
12 insomnolence

**sleepwalker**
10 somnambule 11 night-walker
12 noctambulist, somnambulist

**sleepwalking**
12 noctambulism, somnambulism
13 somnambulance
14 noctambulation, somnambulation

**sleepy**
04 dull, slow 05 heavy, quiet, still, tired, weary 06 drowsy, lonely, torpid
07 languid, slumbry 08 comatose, hypnotic, inactive, isolated, peaceful, sleepery, sluggish, slumbery, soporose, soporous, tranquil
09 lethargic, slumbrous, somnolent, soporific 10 languorous, slumberous
11 lethargical, sequestered, undisturbed 12 unfrequented

**sleeve**
03 arm 04 bush 05 brass, gigot, gland, liner 06 drogue, manche 08 wind cone

**sleigh**
04 dray, luge 05 pulka, slide, slipe, train 06 Ski-doo®, sledge 07 bobsled, dogsled, kibitka, travois 08 toboggan
09 bobsleigh 10 snowmobile 11 hurly-hacket, skeleton bob

### sleight of hand
05 magic, skill 08 artifice, trickery
09 deception, dexterity 10 adroitness
11 legerdemain 12 manipulation

### slender
04 fine, jimp, lean, slim, thin, trim
05 faint, scant, small, swank 06 feeble,
flimsy, little, meagre, narrow, remote,
scanty, slight, svelte 07 gracile,
tenuous, thready, willowy
08 exiguous, graceful, tenuious
09 deficient, sylphlike, willowish
10 inadequate 12 insufficient
14 inconsiderable

### sleuth
04 dick, tail 05 track, trail 06 shadow
07 gumshoe, tracker 09 detective,
Pinkerton 10 bloodhound, private eye
*See also* **detective**

### slice
◇ *hidden indicator* 03 cut 04 chip, chop,
fade, hunk, part, slab 05 carve, chunk,
crisp, cut up, lunch, piece, round,
sever, share, shive, slash, swipe, wafer,
wedge, whack, whang 06 cantle,
collop, croûte, divide, rasher, runner,
sheave, sliver 07 frustum, helping,
portion, scallop, scollop, section,
segment, shaving, tranche 08 doorstep,
separate 09 allotment 10 allocation
14 slice of the cake

### slick
04 deft, easy, glib, trim 05 quick, sharp,
sheen, shiny, sleek, smart, suave
06 adroit, deftly, glibly, glossy, polish,
smarmy, smooth, tidy up, urbane
07 quickly, skilful 08 masterly,
polished, smoothly, unctuous
09 dexterous, efficient, insincere,
plausible, well-oiled 10 altogether,
persuasive, simplistic 11 streamlined
12 professional 13 smooth-talking,
smooth-tongued, sophisticated, well-
organized 14 smooth-speaking

### slide
◇ *anagram indicator* 03 ski 04 drop, fall,
skid, skim, slip 05 chute, coast, glide,
lapse, mount, plane, shoot, skate
06 decamp, hirsle, ice run, lessen,
plunge, runner, sledge, worsen
07 decline, descend, descent, falling,
plummet, relapse, slidder, slither
08 decrease, get worse, glissade,
landslip, toboggan 10 depreciate, go
smoothly 11 deteriorate, diapositive
12 depreciation, move smoothly,
transparency 13 helter-skelter

### slight
03 cut, pet 04 raze, slim, slur, snub,
thin 05 elfin, frail, light, minor, petty,
scant, scorn, small, spurn, wispy
06 dainty, flimsy, ignore, insult, little,
meanly, minute, modest, offend,
paltry, petite, rebuff, single, smooth,
subtle 07 affront, despise, disdain,
fragile, neglect, sketchy, sleight,
slender, tenuous, trivial 08 brush-off,
contempt, delicate, misprise, misprize,
overlook, rudeness, tenuious, trifling
09 disparage, disregard 10 diminutive,
disrespect, negligence, negligible
11 discourtesy, unimportant 12 cold

shoulder, cold-shoulder, indifference
13 imperceptible, inappreciable,
insignificant, insubstantial, slap in the
face 14 inconsiderable, kick in the
teeth 15 inconsequential

### slighting
07 abusive 08 mesprise, mesprize,
misprise, misprize, scornful
09 insulting, offensive 10 belittling,
defamatory, derogatory, disdainful,
neglectful, slanderous 11 disparaging
12 supercilious 13 disrespectful
15 uncomplimentary

### slightly
04 a bit 05 quite 06 rather 07 a little, a
trifle, halfway, lightly 08 somewhat
12 to some degree, to some extent

### slim
03 axe 04 diet, lean, poor, thin, trim
05 faint, leggy, lower, scant, small
06 crafty, flimsy, lessen, little, meagre,
reduce, remote, scanty, shrink, slight,
svelte, weaken 07 curtail, cut back, cut
down, slender, tenuous, willowy
08 contract, decrease, downsize,
graceful, make less, minimize,
moderate, restrict, sylphine, sylphish,
wind down 09 bring down, go on a
diet, sylphlike, willowish
10 inadequate, lose weight 11 make
smaller 12 insufficient
14 inconsiderable

### slime
03 goo, mud 04 gunk, mess, muck,
ooze, yuck 05 slake 06 matter, sludge
07 bitumen

### slimy
04 miry, oily, oozy 05 gucky, muddy
06 glairy, greasy, limous, mucous,
sludgy, smarmy, sticky 07 servile,
viscous 08 creeping, glareous,
slippery, toadying, unctuous
09 glaireous, uliginose, uliginous
10 disgusting, grovelling, obsequious
11 sycophantic 12 ingratiating

### sling
03 lob, shy 04 band, give, hang, hurl,
loop, pass, toss 05 bribe, chuck, fling,
heave, pitch, put up, scarf, strap,
sweep, swing, throw 06 dangle, prusik
07 bandage, support, suspend
08 ballista, catapult, selvagee
09 parbuckle

### slink
04 lean, lurk, mean, slip 05 creep,
droop, miche, prowl, sidle, skulk,
sneak, steal 07 starved

### slinky
04 lean 05 sleek, tight 07 sinuous
08 clinging 09 skin-tight 12 close-
fitting, tight-fitting 13 figure-hugging

### slip
◇ *anagram indicator* 03 don, err, ren, rin,
run 04 boob, cast, chit, drop, fall, flub,
goof, note, shim, sink, skid, skip, trip,
wear 05 creep, error, fault, glide,
jupon, lapse, leash, paper, piece,
plant, put on, scape, scrap, skate,
slide, slink, slive, slump, sneak, steal,
strip 06 booboo, cave in, cock-up,
coupon, escape, howler, kirtle, lapsus,

piping, plunge, pull on, runner, sledge,
slip-up, worsen 07 bloomer, blunder,
clanger, cutting, decline, failure, get
into, go to pot, incline, mistake,
plummet, scedule, slidder, slither,
stumble, take off, voucher 08 decrease,
get worse, omission, quickset,
schedule 09 disengage, landslide,
oversight, petticoat 10 change into,
descendant, underskirt 11 certificate,
change out of, deteriorate, galley
proof, go to the dogs 12 get dressed in,
indiscretion, lapsus calami 13 lapsus
linguae 14 go down the tubes, lapsus
memoriae 15 lose your balance, lose
your footing
• **a slip of a** 04 slim, thin 05 small,
young 06 slight 07 fragile, slender
08 delicate
• **give someone the slip** 04 duck
05 dodge 08 flee from, shake off
10 escape from 11 get away from, run
away from 14 break loose from
• **let slip** 04 balk, blab, leak, miss, tell
05 baulk 06 betray, let out, reveal,
squeal 07 divulge 08 disclose, give
away, overslip 13 spill the beans
15 give the game away
• **slip away** 05 evade 06 elapse
• **slip up** 03 err 04 boob, fail, goof
05 botch, fluff 06 bungle, cock up, goof
up 07 blunder, deceive, go wrong,
screw up, stumble 08 get wrong
10 disappoint 12 make a mistake,
miscalculate

### slipper
04 muil, mule, pump 06 loafer, panton,
sandal 07 baboosh, babuche
08 babouche, flip-flop, mocassin,
moccasin, pabouche, pantable,
pantofle, slip-shoe 09 houseshoe,
pantoffle, pantoufle 13 carpet-slipper

### slippery
◇ *anagram indicator* 03 icy, wet 04 foxy,
glib, glid, oily 05 false, slime, slimy
06 clever, crafty, glassy, greasy, shifty,
skiddy, slippy, smarmy, smooth
07 cunning, devious, elusive, evasive,
glidder, slither 08 glibbery, gliddery,
perilous, sliddery, slithery, two-faced,
unstable 09 dangerous, deceitful,
dishonest, lubricous, uncertain
10 lubricious, perfidious, unreliable
11 duplicitous, treacherous
13 unpredictable, untrustworthy

### slipshod
◇ *anagram indicator* 03 lax 06 casual,
sloppy, untidy 08 careless, slapdash,
slovenly 09 negligent 12 disorganized

### slip-up
04 boob, flub, gaff, goof, slip 05 error,
fault, gaffe 06 booboo, cock-up,
howler 07 bloomer, blunder, clanger,
failure, mistake 08 omission
09 oversight 12 indiscretion

### slit
03 cut, rip, rit 04 fent, gash, loop, loup,
peep, race, rend, rent, ritt, sipe, slot,
snip, tear, vent 05 knife, lance, slash,
slice, spare, speld, split 06 pierce
07 fissure, opening, pertuse, placket
08 aperture, incision, loophole,

pertused **09** pertusate, pertusion
**10** buttonhole **11** placket-hole

**slither**
**04** skid, slip, worm **05** creep, glide,
slide, slink, snake **08** slippery

**sliver**
**03** bit **04** chip, rove **05** flake, piece,
scrap, shard, shred, slice, wafer
**06** paring, shiver **07** shaving
**08** fragment, splinter

**slob**
**03** mud, oaf, yob **04** boor, lout, ooze
**05** churl, yobbo **06** sloven, sludge
**07** mud-flat **08** layabout **10** philistine
**14** good-for-nothing

**slobber**
**04** slop **05** drool **06** drivel, slaver
**07** dribble **08** salivate **14** foam at the
mouth

**slog**
**03** hit **04** bash, belt, hike, plod, slug,
sock, toil, trek, work **05** clout, graft,
grind, slave, slosh, smite, sweat,
thump, tramp **06** effort, labour, strike,
trudge, wallop **08** exertion, struggle,
work hard **09** peg away at, persevere
**10** plug away at, sweat blood
**13** plough through **15** work till you
drop

**slogan**
**03** cry **04** logo **05** chant, motto
**06** jingle, splash, war cry **07** tag line
**08** slughorn **09** battle-cry, catchword,
slughorne, watchword **10** shibboleth
**11** catch phrase, rallying cry **12** back to
basics

**sloop**
**03** hoy **05** dandy, smack **06** cutter

**slop**
**05** slosh, slush, spill **06** puddle, splash
**07** slather, slobber, spatter **08** overflow,
slattern, splatter, wash away
**09** policeman

**slope**
**03** bow, dip, lie, tip **04** bank, brae,
cant, drop, fall, heel, kant, lean, rake,
ramp, rise, tilt **05** pitch, slant, splay,
verge **06** ascent, aslant, breast,
decamp, escarp, glacis, shelve
**07** decline, descent, incline, upgrade
**08** fall away, shelving, slanting
**09** acclivity, disappear, downgrade,
watershed **11** inclination
• **slope off** **06** decamp, go away
**08** slip away, sneak off **09** steal away
**12** leave quietly

**sloping**
**03** dip **05** askew, slant **06** angled,
canted, supine **07** canting, leaning,
oblique, tilting **08** at a slant, bevelled,
inclined, shelving, sidelong, slanting
**09** acclivous, declivous, inclining
**11** acclivitous, declivitous

**sloppily**
**07** hastily, messily **08** untidily
**09** hurriedly **10** carelessly
**11** haphazardly **15** lackadaisically

**sloppy**
◇ *anagram indicator* **03** wet **05** baggy,

corny, gooey, gucky, gushy, hasty,
messy, muddy, mushy, runny, slack,
soggy, soppy **06** clumsy, liquid, sickly,
slushy, sozzly, untidy, watery
**07** gushing, hurried, maudlin,
mawkish, splashy **08** careless,
romantic, slapdash, slattery, slipshod,
slovenly **09** haphazard, hit-or-miss,
schmaltzy **10** amateurish, wishy-washy
**11** sentimental **12** disorganized
**13** lackadaisical

**slosh**
◇ *anagram indicator* **03** hit **04** bash, beat,
biff, pour, slap, slog, slop, slug, sock,
wade **05** clout, punch, spray, swash,
swipe, thump **06** shower, splash, strike,
thwack, wallop **08** flounder

**slot**
**03** bar, fit, gap, put **04** bolt, hole, slit,
spot, time, vent **05** crack, niche, notch,
place, space, track **06** assign, groove,
insert, tracks, window **07** channel,
install, opening, vacancy **08** aperture,
position **10** pigeonhole

**sloth**
**02** ai **04** unau **06** acedia, torpor
**07** accidie, inertia, mylodon
**08** idleness, laziness, mylodont
**09** fainéance, indolence, slackness
**10** inactivity **12** listlessness,
slothfulness, sluggishness

**slothful**
**04** idle, lazy **05** inert, slack, sweer,
sweir **06** sweert, sweirt, torpid
**07** skiving, sweered, workshy
**08** fainéant, inactive, indolent, listless,
sluggish **09** do-nothing

**slouch**
**04** bend, loll **05** droop, hunch, mooch,
slump, stoop **06** lounge **07** shamble,
shuffle **08** drooping

**Slovakia**
**02** SK **03** SVK

**Slovenia**
**03** SLO, SVN

**slovenly**
◇ *anagram indicator* **05** dirty, messy
**06** sloppy, untidy **07** scruffy, unclean,
unkempt **08** careless, slattery, slipshod,
sluttish **09** slammakin **10** slammerkin,
slatternly **12** disorganized

**slow**
**03** dim, twp **04** daft, dead, dull, dumb,
lash, late, lazy, poky **05** delay, dense,
dopey, gross, largo, lento, loath,
pokey, quiet, slack, tardy, thick, unapt
**06** adagio, averse, boring, obtuse,
retard, sleepy, stupid **07** andante,
delayed, glacial, gradual, lagging,
slacken, slack up, tedious
**08** backward, creeping, dawdling,
dilatory, hesitant, measured, plodding,
retarded, sluggish, stagnant, tiresome
**09** larghetto, leisurely, lingering,
loitering, ponderous, prolonged,
reluctant, slacken up, unhurried,
unwilling, wearisome **10** deliberate,
dull-witted, indisposed, lentissimo,
protracted, slow-motion, slow-
moving, slow-witted, uneventful
**11** disinclined **12** long-drawn-out **13** at

a snail's pace, time-consuming,
unintelligent, uninteresting **14** slow off
the mark **15** slow on the uptake
• **slow down** **04** curb, stem **05** brake,
check, delay, relax **06** detain, do less,
ease up, hold up, relent, retard, wait
up **08** calm down, chill out, handicap,
hold back, keep back, restrict **09** hang
loose **10** decelerate, take it easy
**11** reduce speed **12** throttle back,
throttle down **14** put the brakes on
• **slowing down** **03** rit **04** rall
**08** ritenuto **10** ritardando
**11** rallentando
• **slow up** **04** rein

**slowly**
**05** largo, lento **06** adagio, lazily
**08** steadily **09** by degrees, gradually,
larghetto, leisurely **10** lentissimo,
ploddingly, sluggishly **11** ponderously,
unhurriedly **13** at a snail's pace **14** little
by little **15** slowly but surely

**sludge**
**03** mud **04** gunk, mire, muck, ooze,
silt, slag, slob, slop **05** dregs, gunge,
mudge, slime, slush, swill **07** residue
**08** sediment

**slug**
**04** bash, boff, gulp, oner, swat
**05** douse, dowse, limax, one-er, slosh,
souse, swash **06** bullet, lander, wallop,
wunner **07** lounder, swallow
**08** Linotype®, sea lemon **10** bêche-de-
mer

**sluggish**
**04** dull, idle, lazy, slow **05** heavy, inert,
resty, tardy **06** jacent, torpid **07** languid
**08** inactive, indolent, lifeless, listless,
slothful **09** apathetic, lethargic,
somnolent **10** languorous, phlegmatic,
slow-moving **12** unresponsive

**sluggishness**
**05** sloth **06** apathy, lentor, phlegm,
torpor **07** inertia, languor **08** dullness,
lethargy, slowness **09** fainéance,
heaviness, indolence, lassitude
**10** drowsiness, somnolence, stagnation
**12** listlessness, slothfulness

**sluice**
**04** wash **05** drain, flush, inlet, koker,
sasse, slosh, sluse, slush, swill
**06** drench, outlet **07** channel, cleanse,
conduit, passage **08** irrigate, lock gate,
penstock **09** floodgate, water gate

**slum**
**05** hovel **06** favela, ghetto **07** rookery
**10** shanty town **11** cabbagetown
**15** across the tracks

**slumber**
**03** kip, nap **04** doze, rest **05** sleep,
sloom **06** drowse, repose, snooze
**07** shut-eye **08** lethargy **10** forty winks

**slummy**
**05** dirty, seedy **06** sleazy, sordid
**07** decayed, run-down, squalid
**08** wretched **10** ramshackle
**11** overcrowded

**slump**
**03** low, sag **04** bend, drop, fail, fall,
flop, loll, sink **05** crash, droop, flump,

plump, slide, stoop **06** go down, lounge, plunge, slouch, trough, worsen **07** decline, failure, plummet, subside **08** collapse, decrease, downturn, lowering, nosedive **09** downswing, recession, worsening **10** depression, go downhill, stagnation **11** deteriorate, devaluation **13** deterioration

**slur**
**04** blot, blur **05** cheat, libel, smear, stain **06** insult, mumble, slight, stigma **07** affront, calumny, slander, stumble **08** besmirch, disgrace, innuendo, ligature, reproach, splutter **09** aspersion, discredit, disparage **11** insinuation **13** disparagement **14** speak unclearly

**slush**
**04** gush, mush, pulp, slop, snow **05** slosh, sposh, swash **06** lapper, lopper **07** wet snow **08** schmaltz **09** soppiness **10** sloppiness **11** mawkishness, melting snow, romanticism **12** emotionalism **14** sentimentality

**slut**
**04** drab, slag, tart **05** bitch, hussy **06** clatch, drazel, hooker, pussel, puzzle, sloven **07** floozie, pucelle, trollop **08** dolly-mop, scrubber, slattern, slummock **09** dratchell **10** loose woman, prostitute **11** draggle-tail
*See also* **prostitute**

**sly**
**03** fly **04** foxy, leer, slee, wily **05** canny, carny, peery, smart **06** artful, astute, carney, clever, covert, crafty, expert, impish, secret, shifty, shrewd, sleeky, sneaky, subtle, tricky **07** cunning, devious, furtive, illicit, knowing, roguish, sleekit **08** guileful, scheming, stealthy, weaselly **09** conniving, insidious, secretive, underhand **11** clandestine, mischievous **13** surreptitious
• **on the sly** **07** on the qt **08** covertly, in secret, secretly **09** furtively, in private, privately **10** stealthily, under cover **13** clandestinely, underhandedly **15** surreptitiously
• **sly person** **03** tod **06** weasel

**slyly**
◊ *anagram indicator* **07** cannily **08** artfully, covertly, shrewdly **09** cunningly, deviously, furtively **10** stealthily **13** underhandedly **15** surreptitiously

**smack**
**03** box, hit, pat, tap **04** bang, belt, biff, blow, clap, cuff, dash, hint, kiss, like, slap, sock, tack, tang, thud, zest **05** clout, crack, crash, enjoy, evoke, plumb, punch, right, smell, spank, speck, spice, taste, thump, tinge, touch, trace, twang, whack, whiff **06** bawley, flavor, heroin, hint at, hooker, nuance, relish, savour, smatch, smouch, strike, thwack, wallop **07** clobber, coaster, exactly, flavour, revel in, sharply, smacker,

suggest **08** directly, intimate, piquancy, savour of, slap-bang, straight **09** delight in, precisely **10** absolutely, appreciate, impression, intimation, paddy-whack, suggestion **11** bring to mind, remind you of **13** give a hiding to **14** take pleasure in **15** put over your knee
*See also* **hit; kiss**
• **smack your lips** **05** enjoy **06** relish, savour **09** delight in, drool over **10** anticipate

**smacker**
*see* **kiss**

**small**
◊ *deletion indicator* **01** S **03** low, sma, wee **04** mean, mini, pink, poky, puny, tiny **05** bitsy, diddy, dwarf, minor, petty, pinky, short, teeny, tiddy, totty, young **06** broken, dilute, humble, little, meagre, minute, narrow, paltry, peerie, peewee, petite, pinkie, pocket, scanty, single, slight, stupid, teensy, tottie **07** ashamed, compact, cramped, crushed, foolish, ignoble, limited, slender, trivial **08** confined, deflated, degraded, delicate, dwarfish, pint-size, trifling **09** disgraced, miniature, minuscule, pint-sized **10** diminutive, humiliated, inadequate, negligible, ungenerous, unimposing **11** embarrassed, microscopic, pocket-sized, unimportant **12** insufficient, teensy-weensy **13** inappreciable, infinitesimal, insignificant **14** inconsiderable

**small-minded**
**04** mean **05** petty, rigid **06** biased, little **07** bigoted, insular **09** cat-witted, hidebound, illiberal, parochial **10** intolerant, prejudiced, ungenerous **12** narrow-minded

**smallness**
**07** exility, fewness, paucity **08** tininess **09** small size **10** littleness, minuteness, slightness **11** compactness, parvanimity **12** microcephaly **14** diminutiveness

**small-time**
**05** minor, petty **08** piddling **09** no-account **10** small-scale **11** unimportant **13** insignificant **15** inconsequential

**smarminess**
**07** suavity **08** oiliness, toadying **09** servility **10** sycophancy, unctuosity **12** unctuousness **14** obsequiousness

**smarmy**
**04** oily **05** suave **06** smooth **07** fawning, servile **08** crawling, toadying, unctuous **10** obsequious **11** bootlicking, sycophantic **12** ingratiating

**smart**
**01** U **03** nip **04** ache, bite, burn, chic, cool, fine, flip, hurt, neat, pacy, pert, posh, smug, tidy, trim **05** acute, brisk, dandy, gemmy, janty, jemmy, kooky, natty, nifty, nobby, pacey, prick, ritzy, saucy, sharp, slick, smoke, spiff, sting, swank, sweat, swish, throb, tippy, witty **06** astute, brainy, bright, clever, dapper, glitzy, jaunty, kookie, larney,

modish, pusser, shrewd, snappy, snazzy, spiffy, spruce, swanky, tiddly, tingle, trendy, twinge **07** crabbit, elegant, stylish, swagger, tiddley **08** all there, rattling, sprauncy **09** expensive, on the ball, vivacious **11** fashionable, intelligent, presentable, well-dressed, well-groomed **13** well-turned-out
• **smart alec** **07** know-all, wise guy **08** wiseacre **09** smartarse **10** clever dick **11** clever clogs, smartyboots, smartypants

**smarten**
**04** tidy **05** clean, groom, primp, prink **06** neaten, polish, spruce, tidy up **08** beautify, make neat, make tidy, spruce up

**smartly**
**06** neatly, tidily **07** briskly, hastily, nattily, quickly, rapidly, readily, swiftly **08** abruptly, directly, promptly, snazzily, speedily **09** elegantly, hurriedly, instantly, stylishly **11** fashionably, immediately, presentably **14** unhesitatingly **15** instantaneously

**smash**
◊ *anagram indicator* **02** go **03** hit, run, wow **04** bang, bash, bump, cash, dash, ruin **05** break, crack, crash, crush, drive, knock, prang, thump, wreck **06** bingle, defeat, pile-up, plough, shiver, strike, winner **07** collide, destroy, shatter, smash-up, success, triumph **08** accident, demolish, knockout, smash hit, splinter, squabash, stramash **09** collision, pulverize, sensation **12** disintegrate

**smashing**
**05** great, super **06** superb **07** dashing **08** crushing, fabulous, terrific **09** excellent, fantastic, first-rate, wonderful **10** first-class, marvellous, shattering, stupendous, tremendous **11** magnificent, sensational, superlative **12** exhilarating

**smattering**
**03** bit **04** dash **06** basics, smatch **07** modicum **08** elements **09** rudiments **10** sprinkling

**smear**
**03** dab, gum, oil, pay, rub, tar, wax **04** blot, blur, coat, daub, gaum, gild, gorm, lard, lick, mark, slap, slur, soot, spot **05** blood, cover, libel, patch, pitch, salve, slake, slime, smalm, smarm, stain, sully, taint **06** anoint, bedaub, blotch, defame, grease, malign, slairg, smudge, spread, streak, vilify **07** blacken, obloquy, plaster, slander, slather, slubber, splodge, splotch, tarnish, treacle **08** badmouth **09** aspersion **10** calumniate, defamation, muck-raking, turpentine **11** false report, mudslinging **12** vilification

**smell**
**03** fug, hum **04** funk, fust, gale, guff, ming, must, niff, nose, odor, pong, ponk, reek **05** aroma, fetor, odour, scent, sniff, snuff, stink, trace, whiff **06** miasma, savour, stench **07** bouquet

**08** malodour, mephitis, pungency
**09** effluvium, fragrance, redolence

---

*Particular smells include:*

---

**02** BO
**04** feet, musk, rose
**05** basil, booze, ozone, smoke, spice
**06** cheese, coffee, garlic, nutmeg, pepper
**07** alcohol, camphor, incense, menthol, perfume, vanilla
**08** bergamot, lavender
**09** body odour, patchouli, pot pourri, woodsmoke
**10** eucalyptus, peppermint
**11** wintergreen

## smelly
**03** bad, off **04** foul, high, nosy, olid, rank, ripe **05** fetid, nosey, olent, pongy **06** foetid, mingin', putrid **07** honking, humming, minging, noisome, reeking **08** mephitic, stinking **09** on the nose **10** malodorous **12** foul-smelling **14** strong-smelling

## smile
**04** beam, grin, leer **05** drink, laugh, smirk, sneer, treat **06** favour, giggle, simper, smoile, smoyle, titter **07** chuckle, snigger **11** be all smiles

## smirk
**04** grin, leer, trim **05** sneer **06** simper, spruce **07** grimace, snigger

## smitten
**05** beset, épris **06** éprise, in love, struck **07** charmed, hard-hit, plagued **08** beguiled, burdened, obsessed, troubled **09** afflicted, attracted, bewitched, enamoured **10** bowled over, captivated, infatuated **12** enthusiastic

## smock
**04** slop **05** frock, shift **07** chemise, smicket
• **lady's smock** **05** spink **09** cardamine **12** cuckoo flower

## smog
**03** fog **04** haze, mist **05** fumes, smoke **06** vapour **07** exhaust **09** pea-souper, pollution

## smoke
**03** dry, fog, gas **04** cure, draw, fume, lunt, mist, puff, quiz, reek, roke, smog **05** fumes, reast, reest, reist, smart, smoor **06** draw on, puff on, smudge, suffer, thrash, vapour **07** exhaust, light up, smother, tear gas **08** preserve, ridicule, smoulder **09** London ivy
*See also* **cigarette; tobacco**

## smoky
**04** dark, grey, hazy **05** black, foggy, fuggy, grimy, murky, peaty, reeky, sooty **06** cloudy, rechie, reechy, reekie, smoggy, smudgy **07** reechie **10** suspicious

## smooch
**03** hug, pet **04** hold, kiss, neck, snog **05** clasp, nurse **06** caress, cuddle, enfold, fondle, nestle **07** embrace, snuggle **08** canoodle

## smooth
**03** aid, dub **04** calm, ease, easy, even, file, flat, glib, help, iron, mild, rich, roll, sand, smug, snod, soft, trim **05** allay, bland, brent, dress, filed, float, flush, grind, level, plane, press, shiny, silky, sleek, slick, sooth, still, suave, sweet, terse, thick **06** assist, classy, creamy, fluent, glassy, glossy, legato, mature, mellow, pacify, polish, serene, silken, simple, sleeky, smarmy, soothe, steady, urbane **07** appease, assuage, elegant, equable, even out, fawning, flatten, flatter, flowing, mollify, plaster, regular, rub down, sleekit, slicken, uniform, velvety, worsted **08** blandish, calm down, charming, crawling, glabrate, glabrous, hairless, levigate, mitigate, palliate, peaceful, polished, rhythmic, slippery, tranquil, unbroken, unctuous **09** agreeable, alleviate, burnished, encourage, plausible, press down, unruffled **10** continuous, effortless, facilitate, horizontal, make easier, persuasive, unwrinkled **11** legatissimo, like a mirror, mellifluent, mellifluous, plaster down, problem-free, trouble-free, undisturbed **12** ingratiating, plain sailing **13** full-flavoured, over-confident, smooth-talking, sophisticated, uninterrupted **14** clear the way for **15** straightforward

## smoothly
**06** calmly, easily, evenly, legato, mildly **07** cleanly, equably, sleekly, slickly, volubly **08** fluently, serenely, steadily **10** peacefully, pleasantly, soothingly, swimmingly, tranquilly **11** legatissimo **12** effortlessly

## smoothness
**04** ease, flow **05** shine **06** finish, polish, rhythm **07** fluency **08** calmness, evenness, facility, flatness, serenity, softness **09** levelness, lubricity, silkiness, sleekness, stillness **10** efficiency, glassiness, regularity, steadiness **11** velvetiness **12** unbrokenness **14** effortlessness

## smooth-talking
**04** glib **05** bland, slick, suave **06** facile, smooth **09** plausible **10** flattering, persuasive **12** conciliatory **13** silver-tongued

## smother
**04** damp, hide, wrap **05** choke, cover, smoke, smoor, smore, snuff **06** cocoon, dampen, muffle, put out, shroud, stifle, welter **07** conceal, envelop, oppress, overlie, repress **08** damp down, inundate, keep back, smoulder, strangle, suppress, surround, throttle **09** overwhelm, suffocate **10** asphyxiate, extinguish **11** suffocation

## smoulder
**04** boil, burn, foam, fume, rage **05** smoke **06** fester, seethe, simmer **07** smother

## smudge
**04** blot, blur, daub, mark, soil, spot **05** dirty, smear, stain **06** blotch, offset,

smouch, smutch, streak **07** blacken, blemish **08** besmirch **09** dirty mark, make dirty

## smug
**04** neat, prim **05** sleek, steal **06** hush up, smooth, spruce **08** priggish, smirking, superior, unctuous **09** conceited **10** complacent **13** self-righteous, self-satisfied **14** holier-than-thou

## smuggle
**03** owl, ren, rin, run **05** steal **07** bootleg

## smuggler
**04** mule **05** owler **06** runner **07** courier **10** bootlegger, drug-runner, free-trader, moonshiner **13** contrabandist

## smutty
**04** blue, lewd, racy, rude **05** bawdy, crude, dirty, gross **06** coarse, filthy, fruity, ribald, risqué, sleazy, vulgar **07** obscene, raunchy **08** improper, indecent, prurient **09** off colour, salacious **10** indelicate, suggestive **12** pornographic

## snack
**04** bite, gorp, meze, snap, tapa, wrap **05** bever, butty, chack, fours, lunch, share, tapas, taste **06** buffet, canapé, crisps, nacket, nibble, nocket, snatch, supper, tidbit, titbit **07** bar meal, elevens, fourses, nibbles, zakuska **08** bar lunch, pick-me-up, sandwich, scroggin, trail mix **09** appetizer, bite to eat, Bombay mix, elevenses, light meal **11** amuse-bouche, hors d'oeuvre, refreshment **12** potato crisps, refreshments **15** pork scratchings

## snaffle
**03** bag, nab, win **04** gain, grab, grip, nail, pull, take **05** grasp, pluck, seize, steal, swipe, wrest **06** arrest, clutch, collar, secure, wrench **07** bridoon, capture, purloin, snabble **08** pounce on **09** get hold of **10** take hold of **11** make off with

## snag
**03** bug, jag, nog, rip **04** hole, sneb, snub, tear **05** catch, hitch, stump **06** banger, ladder, obtain, secure, snubbe **07** problem, sausage, setback **08** drawback, obstacle **10** difficulty **12** complication, disadvantage **13** inconvenience **14** stumbling-block

## snail
**05** crawl, helix **06** dodman, nerite **08** escargot, wallfish **09** hodmandod, wing shell

## snake
**04** bend, drag, loop, naga, wind, worm **05** creep, curve, twine **06** drudge, ramble, spiral, wretch, zigzag **07** deviate, meander, serpent **08** Joe Blake, ophidian

---

*Snakes include:*

---

**03** asp, boa, rat, sea
**04** boma, bull, corn, file, hoop, king, milk, naga, Naia, Naja, pine, pipe, ring, rock, sand, seps, tree, whip, worm
**05** adder, black, blind, brown,

cobra, coral, Elaps, grass, green, krait, mamba, racer, tiger, viper, water
**06** carpet, dipsas, dugite, elapid, ellops, flying, gaboon, garter, gopher, indigo, karait, python, ribbon, smooth, taipan
**08** anaconda, cerastes, colubrid, cylinder, jararaca, jararaka, mocassin, moccasin, pit viper, ringhals, rinkhals, sucurujú
**09** berg-adder, boomslang, coachwhip, hamadryad, hamadryas, king cobra, puff adder, river-jack
**10** bandy-bandy, bushmaster, copperhead, death adder, dendrophis, fer-de-lance, Gabon viper, massasauga, rock python, sidewinder
**11** constrictor, cottonmouth, diamondback, gaboon viper, horned viper, massasauger, rattlesnake
**12** carpet python
**13** diamond python, water moccasin
**14** boa constrictor, river-jack viper

## snap
**03** nip, pic **04** bark, bite, chop, film, grip, knap, shot, snip, span, take, tick, time, whit **05** break, catch, cheat, click, clink, crack, flick, gnash, grasp, growl, hanch, photo, print, scrap, seize, share, shoot, snack, snarl, snick, spell, split, still, stint **06** abrupt, bark at, fillip, period, record, retort, snatch, sudden **07** crackle, earring, give way, growl at, instant, offhand, picture, sharper, snarl at, stretch **08** collapse, fracture, separate, snapshot, splinter **09** crepitate, immediate, lash out at, on-the-spot **10** photograph, unexpected **14** speak angrily to, speak sharply to
• **snap up 03** nab **04** grab **05** grasp, pluck, seize **06** pick up, snatch **08** pounce on **10** buy quickly

## snappy
**04** chic, edgy **05** brisk, cross, hasty, natty, quick, ratty, smart, testy **06** crabby, crusty, lively, modish, snazzy, touchy, trendy **07** brusque, crabbed, elegant, grouchy, stroppy, stylish **08** polished, up-to-date **09** crotchety, energetic, irascible, irritable **10** ill-natured **11** bad-tempered, fashionable, ill-tempered **13** instantaneous, quick-tempered, short-tempered, up-to-the-minute
• **make it snappy 05** hurry **06** buck up **07** hurry up **08** go all out, jump to it, step on it **09** come along, look sharp, shake a leg **10** look lively **11** get cracking **15** get your skates on

## snare
◇ *containment indicator* **03** gin, net, web **04** grin, hook, toil, trap, weel, wire **05** catch, fraud, noose, seize, toils **06** cobweb, engine, entrap, spring, trepan **07** capture, ensnare, pitfall, springe **08** lime-twig **09** spider web **10** allurement, temptation **12** entanglement

## snarl
◇ *anagram indicator* **04** bark, girn, gnar, gurn, howl, knar, knot, snap, snar, yelp **05** gnarl, gnarr, growl, ravel, twist **06** enmesh, jumble, muddle, tangle **07** confuse, embroil, ensnare, entwine, grumble **08** complain, entangle **09** lash out at **10** complicate **13** show your teeth

## snarl-up
**04** mess **05** mix-up **06** jumble, muddle, tangle **08** gridlock **09** confusion **10** traffic jam **12** entanglement

## snatch
**03** bag, bit, nab, nip, rap, win **04** gain, glom, grab, grip, nail, part, pull, race, ramp, rase, snap, snip, take **05** catch, grasp, piece, pluck, reach, seize, snack, spell, steal, swipe, whiff, wrest **06** abduct, clutch, collar, gobble, kidnap, ruffle, secure, twitch, wrench **07** clauht, claught, quibble, robbery, section, segment, snippet **08** fraction, fragment, pounce on **09** get hold of **10** kidnapping, smattering, take hold of **11** make off with **13** take as hostage

## snazzy
**05** jazzy, ritzy, showy, smart **06** flashy, snappy, sporty, with it **07** dashing, raffish, stylish **08** swinging **10** attractive, flamboyant **11** fashionable **13** sophisticated

## sneak
**03** pad, rat **04** lurk, mole, peak, shop, slip **05** creep, grass, prowl, quick, sidle, skulk, slide, slink, snoke, snook, snowk, split, steal **06** covert, cringe, secret, snitch, spirit, squeal, suck-up **07** furtive, grass on, smuggle, stoolie, stool on **08** informer, inform on, squealer, stealthy, surprise, tell-tale **09** tell tales **11** clandestine, stool pigeon **13** surreptitious, whistle-blower

## sneaking
**04** mean **06** hidden, secret **07** furtive, lurking, nagging, private, sleekit **08** grudging, niggling, unvoiced, worrying **09** crouching, intuitive, underhand **10** persistent, suppressed **11** sheep-biting, unexpressed **13** surreptitious, uncomfortable

## sneaky
**03** low, sly **04** base, mean **05** nasty, shady, snide **06** shifty **07** cunning, devious, furtive, low-down **08** cowardly, guileful, slippery **09** deceitful, dishonest, malicious, unethical **10** unreliable **12** contemptible, disingenuous, unscrupulous **13** double-dealing, untrustworthy

## sneer
**04** gibe, grin, jeer, mock **05** laugh, scoff, scorn, smirk, taunt **06** deride, insult, slight, twitch **07** disdain, mockery, snicker, snigger **08** derision, ridicule **10** look down on **12** curl your lips

## sneeze
**05** neese, neeze **07** atishoo

## sneezing
**12** sternutation

## snicker
**05** laugh, neigh, sneer **06** giggle, nicker, titter **07** chortle, chuckle, snigger, snirtle

## snide
**04** base, mean, sham **05** false, nasty **06** biting, snarky, unkind **07** caustic, cynical, hurtful, jeering, mocking **08** derisive, scathing, scoffing, scornful, sneering, spiteful, taunting **09** dishonest, malicious, sarcastic **10** derogatory, ill-natured **11** counterfeit, disparaging

## sniff
**04** hint, nose, sent, vent **05** aroma, scent, shmek, smell, snift, snuff, trace, whiff **06** inhale, nuzzle, snivel **07** breathe, schmeck, sniffle, snifter, snuffle **10** impression, intimation, suggestion **11** get a whiff of
• **sniff at 04** mock, shun, vent **05** scorn, spurn **06** deride, refuse, reject, slight **07** disdain, dismiss, laugh at, scoff at, smell at, sneer at **08** overlook **09** disparage, disregard **10** look down on

## sniffy
**06** snobby **07** haughty **08** scoffing, scornful, sneering, snobbish, superior **10** disdainful **12** contemptuous, supercilious **13** condescending

## snifter
*see* **dram**

## snigger
**05** laugh, smirk, sneer **06** giggle, nicher, nicker, titter **07** chortle, chuckle, snicker, whicker

## snip
**03** bit, cut **04** clip, crop, dock, nick, slit, snap, trim **05** notch, piece, prune, scrap, share, shred, slash, sneck, snick, steal **06** incise, snatch, tailor **07** bargain, good buy, snippet **08** clipping, discount, fragment, giveaway **09** certainty, reduction **12** special offer **13** value for money

## snipe
**04** fool, walk, wisp **05** scape **06** attack **09** criticism, criticize **12** heather-bleat **14** heather-bleater, heather-bluiter, heather-blutter

## sniper
**06** haiduk **08** partisan **09** guerrilla, irregular, terrorist **11** bushwhacker, franc-tireur, guerrillero **14** freedom fighter

## snippet
**03** bit **04** part, snip **05** piece, scrap, shred **06** snatch **07** cutting, portion, section, segment **08** clipping, fragment, particle

## snivel
**03** cry, sob **04** bawl, blub, cant, moan, weep **05** sniff, snift, whine **06** whinge **07** blubber, grizzle, sniffle, snuffle, whimper

### snivelling

**06** crying **07** moaning, weeping, whining **09** grizzling, sniffling, snuffling, whingeing **10** blubbering, whimpering

### snob

**04** scab **05** swank **07** bighead, cobbler, élitist, high-hat, parvenu **08** blackleg, townsman **09** shoemaker **13** social climber

### snobbery

**04** airs, side **05** pride **07** disdain **09** arrogance, loftiness **10** pretension, snootiness, uppishness **11** haughtiness, superiority **12** snobbishness **13** airs and graces, condescension **15** pretentiousness

### snobbish

**05** dicty, lofty, proud **06** dickty, snobby, snooty, uppish, uppity **07** haughty, stuck-up **08** affected, arrogant, jumped-up, superior **10** disdainful, hoity-toity, toffee-nose **11** patronizing, pretentious, toffee-nosed **12** supercilious **13** condescending, high and mighty

### snog

**03** hug, pet **04** hold, kiss, neck **05** clasp, nurse **06** caress, cuddle, enfold, fondle, nestle, smooch **07** embrace, snuggle **08** canoodle

### snoop

**03** pry, spy **04** nose **05** sneak **06** meddle **07** gumshoe, meddler, Paul Pry, snooper **08** busybody, meddling **09** interfere **10** stickybeak **11** Nosey Parker **12** interference, put your oar in **14** poke your nose in, stick your oar in **15** stick your nose in

### snooper

**03** pry, spy **05** snoop **07** meddler, Paul Pry **08** busybody **10** stickybeak **11** Nosey Parker **12** eavesdropper

### snooty

**05** lofty, proud **06** snobby, uppity **07** haughty, stuck-up **08** affected, arrogant, jumped-up, snobbish, superior **10** disdainful, hoity-toity **11** patronizing, pretentious, toffee-nosed **12** supercilious **13** condescending, high and mighty

### snooze

**03** kip, nap **04** calk, doze **05** caulk, dover, sleep **06** catnap, nod off, repose, siesta **07** drop off, shut-eye, slumber **10** forty winks **14** have forty winks

### snout

**03** neb **04** beak, nose **05** sword, trunk **06** muzzle, nozzle, snitch **07** gruntle, tobacco **08** informer **09** cigarette, proboscis, schnozzle
See also **nose**

### snow

**03** ice **05** linen **06** heroin, whiten, winter **07** cocaine **08** blizzard, morphine, snowfall **09** snowdrift, snowstorm **10** snowflakes **12** snow flurries

*Snow types and formations include:*

**03** red
**04** corn, crud, firn, névé
**05** drift, flake, sleet, slush
**06** powder, sludge, yellow
**07** cornice, flaught
**08** sastruga
**09** avalanche, spindrift

*See also* **ice**

### snowman

**04** yeti **06** frosty

### snub

**03** cut **04** knob, shun, slap, snag, sneb, snib, stop, stub **05** blank, check, frump, shame, sloan, sneap, snool, spurn **06** humble, ignore, insult, rebuff, rebuke, slight, squash **07** affront, heave-ho, mortify, put down, put-down, set-down, squelch **08** brush off, brush-off **09** disregard, humiliate **11** down-setting, humiliation **12** cold shoulder, cold-shoulder **13** slap in the face **14** give the heave-ho, kick in the teeth

### snuff

**04** stop, vent **06** pulvil, rappee, sneesh
• **snuff out** **03** end **04** kill **05** choke, crush, douse, erase **06** put out, quench, remove, stifle **07** abolish, blow out, destroy, smother **08** suppress **09** eliminate, eradicate **10** dampen down

### snug

**03** rug **04** cosh, cosy, cozy, snod, warm **05** comfy, tight **06** couthy, homely, secure **07** compact, couthie **08** friendly, intimate **09** sheltered, skintight **11** comfortable **12** close-fitting **13** figure-hugging

### snuggle

**03** hug **04** cose **06** cozy up, cuddle, curl up, nestle, nuzzle **07** croodle, embrace

### snugly

**06** cosily, warmly **07** tightly **08** securely **11** comfortably

### so

**02** as **03** sae, sic, soh, sol **04** ergo, thus, well **05** hence **06** soever **08** insomuch, likewise, provided **09** therefore, thereupon **10** thereafter **11** accordingly

### soak

**03** mop, ret, sog, sop, wet **04** beat, buck, rait, rate, sipe, sype **05** bathe, imbue, souse, steep **06** drench, embrue, guzzle, imbrue, infuse, pummel, seethe, sodden, sponge **07** embrewe, immerse **08** macerate, marinate, permeate, saturate, submerge **09** drenching, penetrate **10** overcharge
See also **drunkard**

### soaking

**03** sop **04** ret **05** steep **06** sluicy, soaked, sodden **07** sopping **08** drenched, dripping, wringing **09** saturated, streaming **10** sopping wet, wet through **11** waterlogged **15** soaked to the skin

### soap

**04** ball, cake, curd **05** money **06** sudser, tablet **07** flannel, flatter **08** flattery, washball **09** soap opera **12** shaving-stick

*Soaps include:*

**03** Lux®
**04** Dove®, hard, soft
**05** glass, Pears®, sugar
**06** liquid, marine, saddle, toilet, yellow
**07** Castile, coal-tar, shaving, Spanish, Windsor
**08** carbolic, mountain, olive-oil
**09** Palmolive®
**10** coconut-oil

*Soap operas include:*

**06** Dallas
**07** Dynasty, The Bill
**08** Casualty
**09** Brookside, Emmerdale, Holby City, Hollyoaks, River City
**10** EastEnders, Neighbours, The Archers
**11** Home and Away

### soar

**03** fly **04** rise, sore, wing, zoom **05** climb, fly up, glide, mount, plane, soare, tower **06** ascend, rocket, sorrel, spiral **07** take off **08** escalate **09** skyrocket **15** increase quickly

### sob

**03** cry, sab **04** bawl, blub, howl, weep, yoop **06** boohoo, snivel **07** blubber, singult, snotter **09** shed tears

### sober

**02** TT **03** dry, sad **04** calm, cool, dark, drab, dull, poor, sane **05** douce, grave, plain, quiet, staid **06** demure, feeble, sedate, serene, severe, solemn, sombre, steady **07** austere, earnest, serious, subdued **08** composed, moderate, rational, teetotal **09** abstinent, dignified, drying out, practical, realistic, temperate, unexcited, unruffled **10** abstemious, on the wagon, reasonable, restrained, thoughtful, unliquored **11** clear-headed, level-headed, unconcerned **12** off the bottle **13** dispassionate, sober as a judge **14** self-controlled, stone-cold sober
• **sober up** **06** dry out **10** sleep it off **13** clear your head

### sobriety

**07** gravity **08** calmness, coolness **09** composure, restraint, soberness, solemnity, staidness **10** abstinence, moderation, sedateness, steadiness, temperance **11** seriousness, teetotalism **13** self-restraint **14** abstemiousness **15** level-headedness

### sobriquet, soubriquet

**03** tag **04** name, term **05** label, style, title **06** handle **07** epithet **08** cognomen, monicker, nickname **11** appellation, designation **12** denomination

### so-called

**07** alleged, nominal, would-be

**soccer**

**08** supposed **09** pretended, professed, purported, soi-disant **10** ostensible, self-styled

**soccer**
*see* **football**

**sociability**
**10** affability, chumminess, cordiality **12** congeniality, conviviality, friendliness **14** gregariousness **15** neighbourliness

**sociable**
**04** maty, warm **05** matey **06** chummy, clubby, folksy, genial, social **07** affable, cordial **08** clubable, familiar, friendly, outgoing **09** clubbable, convivial, extrovert **10** accessible, gregarious, hospitable **11** companiable, conversable, neighbourly **12** approachable **13** companionable

**social**
**02** do **04** bash **05** civic, dance, group, party **06** at-home, common, public, rave-up, thrash **07** blow-out, general, knees-up, leisure **08** communal, function, sociable, societal **09** amusement, community, convivial, gathering, organized **10** collective, gregarious, neighborly, sociologic **11** get-together, neighbourly, sympathetic **12** recreational, sociological **13** entertainment
• **social insect** **03** ant **05** queen
• **social standing** **04** rank **05** class **11** consequence

**socialism**
**07** leftism, Marxism **08** Leninism **09** communism, Stalinism, welfarism **10** Trotskyism **12** collectivism

**socialist**
**03** red, Soc **04** pink, Trot **05** pinko **06** commie, leftie **07** leftist **08** hard-left, left-wing **09** Bolshevik, communist, Menshevik, welfarist **10** left-winger, Trotskyist, Trotskyite **11** parlour pink

**socialize**
**03** mix **05** go out **06** hobnob, mingle **08** converse **09** entertain **10** be sociable, fraternize, meet people **11** get together **12** meet socially

**society**
**01** S **03** Soc **04** band, body, club, nobs, tong **05** élite, group, guild, toffs, union **06** circle, gentry, league, nation, people, public, swells **07** company, culture, mankind **08** alliance, humanity, nobility, sorority **09** community, humankind, human race, top drawer **10** federation, fellowship, fraternity, friendship, population, sisterhood **11** aristocracy, association, brotherhood, camaraderie, corporation, high society, the smart set **12** civilization, organization, upper classes **13** companionship, polite society, Sloane Rangers, the upper crust

*Societies include:*

**03** BCS, BPS, CSP, ENS
**04** BNES, BRCS

**05** ASLEF, Royal
**06** burial, choral, Dorcas, masons
**07** benefit, Camorra
**08** affluent, building, friendly, Red Cross
**10** freemasons

**sock**
**04** drub, hose, tabi **06** argyle, Argyll, thrash **07** bedsock **08** half-hose, knee-high, stocking **11** ploughshare

**socket**
**03** pod **04** hose, jack, ouch, port **05** hosel, point **06** budget, eye-pit, keeper **07** eyehole, hot shoe, torulus **08** alveolus **10** lampholder, power point, tabernacle

**sod**
**04** delf, fail, turf **05** delph, divot, scraw, sward **06** ground

**sodden**
**03** wet **04** miry **05** boggy, soggy **06** boiled, doughy, marshy, poachy, soaked **07** drookit, soaking, sopping **08** drenched **09** saturated **11** waterlogged

**sodium**
**02** Na

**sofa**

*Sofas include:*

**05** couch, divan, futon, squab
**06** canapé, day bed, litter, lounge, settee, sunbed
**07** bergère, casting, dos-à-dos, lounger, sofa bed
**09** banquette, bed-settee, davenport, tête-à-tête, twoseater
**10** sun lounger
**11** studio couch
**12** chaise-longue, chesterfield

**soft**
**01** B, p **02** mp, pp **03** dim, lax, low **04** easy, fool, hold, kind, lash, mild, pale, waxy, weak **05** bland, cushy, downy, faint, fuffy, furry, light, milky, mulch, mulsh, mushy, muted, piano, pulpy, quiet, rainy, silky, sweet **06** crumby, doughy, dulcet, fleecy, gentle, gently, hushed, low-key, mellow, pastel, pliant, shaded, silken, smooth, sonant, spongy, supple, tender, voiced **07** cottony, diffuse, ductile, elastic, flaccid, flowing, fungous, lenient, liberal, pillowy, plastic, pliable, quietly, springy, squashy, squishy, subdued, unsized, velvety **08** cushiony, delicate, diffused, flexible, generous, merciful, pleasant, soothing, squelchy, tolerant, yielding **09** easy-going, forgiving, indulgent, luxurious, malleable, melodious, sensitive, spineless, whispered **10** bituminous, effeminate, forbearing, mezzo-piano, permissive, pianissimo, prosperous, restrained, successful, unarmoured **11** a bed of roses, comfortable, mellifluous, soft-hearted, sympathetic, unprotected **12** affectionate, dough-kneaded
• **soft in the head** **04** daft **05** barmy, dotty, loopy, nutty, potty **06** stupid,

unwise **07** foolish, puerile **08** childish, immature **09** senseless **13** irresponsible, unintelligent
• **soft spot** **06** liking **08** fondness, penchant, weakness **10** fontanelle, partiality, proclivity

**soften**
**03** pad, ret **04** blet, calm, cree, ease, melt, rait, rate, soak **05** abate, lower, malax, quell, relax, still, water **06** digest, lessen, mellow, muffle, reduce, relent, soothe, subdue, temper **07** appease, assuage, cushion, lighten, liquefy, mollify, quicken, unsteel **08** calm down, diminish, dissolve, humanize, macerate, malaxate, mitigate, moderate, modulate, palliate, tone down **09** alleviate, emolliate **10** intenerate
• **soften up** **04** melt **06** disarm, weaken **07** win over **08** butter up, persuade, soft-soap **10** conciliate

**soft-hearted**
**04** kind **06** gentle, tender **08** generous **10** benevolent, charitable **11** sentimental, sympathetic, warm-hearted **12** affectionate **13** compassionate, tender-hearted

**softly-softly**
**06** low-key **07** careful, patient **08** cautious, delicate, indirect **09** tentative **10** diplomatic, restrained **11** circumspect

**soft-pedal**
**06** go easy, subdue **08** minimize, moderate, play down, tone down

**soggy**
**03** wet **04** damp **05** boggy, heavy, moist, pulpy, soppy **06** marshy, soaked, sodden, spongy, sultry, swampy **07** soaking, sopping **08** drenched, dripping **09** saturated **10** sopping wet, spiritless **11** waterlogged

**soil**
**04** clay, dirt, dung, dust, foul, lair, land, loam, mire, smut, spot, tash **05** black, dirty, earth, filth, humus, mould, muddy, smear, solum, stain, sully, tilth **06** befoul, damage, defile, fatten, ground, region, sewage, smudge **07** begrime, country, pollute, slubber, tarnish **08** besmirch **09** territory **10** terra firma

**soiled**
**05** dingy, dirty, grimy, manky, tarry **06** grubby **07** spotted, stained, sullied **08** maculate, polluted **09** tarnished

**sojourn**
**04** rest, stay, stop **05** abide, dwell, lodge, tarry, visit **06** reside **08** stopover **09** tarriance **10** tabernacle **13** peregrination

**Sol**
**06** Helios

**solace**
**05** allay, cheer **06** relief, soften, soothe **07** comfort, console, succour, support **08** mitigate, pleasure **09** alleviate,

amusement **10** condolence
**11** alleviation, consolation

## soldier

**03** ant, Joe, man, vet **04** swad **05** shirk
**06** swaddy **07** shirker, veteran **10** red
herring
*See also* **rank**

*Soldier types include:*

**02** GI
**03** NCO
**04** merc, para, peon
**05** Anzac, cadet, poilu, tommy
**06** digger, ensign, gunner, hussar,
lancer, marine, sapper, sentry,
sniper, troops
**07** dragoon, fighter, officer, orderly,
private, recruit, regular, terrier,
trooper, warrior
**08** commando, fusilier, partisan,
rifleman
**09** centurion, conscript, guardsman,
guerrilla, irregular, mercenary,
minuteman
**10** cavalryman, serviceman
**11** infantryman, legionnaire,
paratrooper, Territorial
**12** sharpshooter

*Soldiers include:*

**02** Li (Hongzhang)
**03** Cid (El), Lee (Robert E), Ney
(Michel), Wet (Christian de), Zia
(Muhammad)
**04** Alba (Ferdinand Alvarez de Toledo,
Duke of), Alva (Ferdinand Alvarez
de Toledo, Duke of), Cade (Jack),
Foch (Ferdinand), Haig
(Alexander), Haig (Douglas, Earl),
Jodl (Alfred), John (Don), Khan
(Ayub), Röhm (Ernst), Tojo (Hideki)
**05** Allen (Ethan), Bader (Sir Douglas),
Barak (Ehud), Botha (Louis), Bowie
(James), Bruce (Robert), Cimon
(Clive (Robert, Lord), Dayan
(Moshe), Essex (Robert Devereux,
Earl of), Gates (Horatio), Grant
(Ulysses S), Inönü (Ismet), Monck
(George), Murat (Joachim), Perón
(Juan), Pride (Sir Thomas), Rabin
(Yitzhak), Smuts (Jan), Sucre
(Antonio José de), Sully
(Maximilien de Béthune, Duc de),
Timur, Zhu De
**06** Anders (Wladyslaw), Antony
(Mark), Arnold (Benedict), Blamey
(Sir Thomas Albert), Brutus
(Marcus Junius), Butler (Benjamin
Franklin), Caesar (Julius), Cortés
(Hernán), Custer (George
Armstrong), Dundee (John Graham,
Viscount of), Dunois (Jean
d'Orléans Comte), Edward (the
Black Prince), Egmont (Graaf van
Gavre), Ershad (Hossain
Muhammad), Eugene (of Savoy),
Franco (Francisco), Gaulle (Charles
de), Gordon (Charles George),
Granby (John Manners, Marquis
of), Greene (Nathanael), Ireton
(Henry), Keitel (Wilhelm), Marius
(Gaius), Moltke (Helmuth, Graf
von), Napier (Robert, Lord), Nasser
(Gamal Abd al-), Neguib

(Mohammed), Patton (George),
Pétain (Philippe), Pompey, Prokop
(the Bald), Raglan (Fitzroy James
Henry Somerset, Lord), Rahman
(Ziaur), Revere (Paul), Rommel
(Erwin), Rupert (Prince), Scipio
(Publius Cornelius), Vauban
(Sébastien le Prestre de), Wavell
(Archibald, Earl), Zhukov (Giorgiy)
**07** Agrippa (Marcus Vipsanius),
Allenby (Edmund, Viscount),
Almagro (Diego de), Artigas (José
Gervasio), Atatürk (Mustapha
Kemal), Baldwin, Bazaine (Achille),
Bedford (John of Lancaster, Duke
of), Blücher (Gebhard Leberecht
von Fürst von), Bourbon (Charles),
Boycott (Charles Cunningham),
Bradley (Omar Nelson), Cadogan
(William, Earl), Cassius, Coligny
(Gaspard de), Dreyfus (Alfred),
Fairfax (Thomas, Lord), Farnese
(Alessandro), Gaddafi (Muammar),
Gemayel (Bashir), Hunyady (János
Corvinus), Jackson (Thomas
Jonathan), Kolchak (Alexander),
Kutuzov (Mikhail, Knyaz), Lambert
(John), Masséna (André), Maurice
(Prince), Metaxas (Ioannis), Mortier
(Edouard Adolphe Casimir Joseph),
Pizarro (Francisco), Ptolemy,
Roberts (Frederick, Earl), Sherman
(William Tecumseh), St Leger
(Barry), Tancred, Turenne (Henri de
la Tour d'Auvergne, Vicomte de),
Vendôme (Louis Joseph Duc de),
Warwick (Richard Neville, Earl of),
William (Prince of Orange),
Wrangel (Pyotr, Lord)
**08** Agricola (Gnaeus Julius), Alvarado
(Pedro de), Anglesey (Henry
William Paget, Marquis of),
Antonius (Marcus), Arminius,
Badoglio (Pietro), Bentinck
(William, Lord), Boadicea
(Burgoyne (John), Burnside
(Ambrose Everett), Campbell (Sir
Colin), Cardigan (James Thomas
Brudenell, Earl of), Cromwell
(Oliver), Eichmann (Adolf),
Ginckell (Godert de), Guiscard
(Robert), Hamilton (James, Duke
of), Hannibal, Harrison (William
Henry), Hereward (the Wake),
Horrocks (Sir Brian), Ironside
(William, Lord), Itúrbide (Agustín
de), Lawrence (Thomas Edward),
Lucullus (Lucius Licinius),
MacMahon (Marie Edme Patrice
Maurice de), Marshall (George
Catlett), Mengistu (Haile Mariam),
Montfort (Simon de), Montrose
(James Graham, Marquis of),
Napoleon, Nobunaga (Oda),
Pershing (John Joseph), Potemkin
(Grigoriy), Pugachev (Emelyan),
Seleucus, Sheridan (Philip Henry),
Sikorski (Wladyslaw), Skorzeny
(Otto), Stanhope (James, Earl),
Tokugawa (Ieyasu), Valdivia (Pedro
de), Wolseley (Garnet, Viscount),
Xenophon, Yamagata (Prince
Aritomo), Zia Ul-Haq (Muhammad)
**09** Alexander (Harold, Earl),

Antonescu (Ion), Bonaparte
(Jérôme), Carausius (Marcus
Aurelius Mausaeus), Cavendish
(William), Garibaldi (Giuseppe),
Gneisenau (August, Graf Neithardt
von), Hasdrubal, Hideyoshi
(Toyotomi), Kim Il-sung, Kitchener
(Horatio, Earl), Lafayette (Marie
Joseph, Marquis de), MacArthur
(Douglas), Miltiades, Spartacus
**10** Abercromby (Sir Ralph),
Alanbrooke (Alan Francis Brooke,
Viscount), Alcibiades, Auchinleck
(Sir Claude), Belisarius, Clausewitz
(Karl von), Cornwallis (Charles,
Marquis), Cumberland (William,
Duke of), Eisenhower (Dwight D),
Germanicus, Hindenburg (Paul
von), Karageorge, Montgomery
(Bernard, Viscount), Schlieffen
(Alfred, Graf von), Stroessner
(Alfredo), Voroshilov (Kliment),
Washington (George), Wellington
(Arthur Wellesley, Duke of)
**11** Baden-Powell (Robert, Lord), Black
Prince, Genghis Khan,
Marlborough (John Churchill, Duke
of), Mohammed Ali, Münchhausen
(Baron von)
**12** Ptolemy Soter, Stauffenburg
(Claus, Graf von)
**13** Fabius Maximus (Quintus), Rouget
de Lisle (Claude Joseph)
**14** Pinochet Ugarte (Augusto)
**15** Scipio Africanus (Publius
Cornelius), Seleucus Nicator

• **soldier on** **06** hang on, hold on,
keep on, remain **08** continue, keep at
it, plug away **09** keep going,
persevere, stick at it **11** hang in there
• **soldiers** **02** OR, RE, TA **03** GIs
**04** army **06** legion **08** garrison

## sole

**03** one **04** lone, only, palm, pull, sill,
slip, sowl **05** alone, capon, clump,
mered, soole, sowle **06** meered, single,
thenar, unique **07** uniform **08** singular,
solitary **09** exclusive, scaldfish
**10** individual

## solecism

**04** boob **05** error, gaffe, lapse
**06** booboo, howler **07** blunder, faux
pas, mistake **08** cacology **09** absurdity,
gaucherie, indecorum **11** anacoluthon,
impropriety, incongruity

## solely

**04** just, only **05** alone **06** merely,
simply, singly **08** entirely, uniquely
**09** allenarly **10** completely
**11** exclusively **14** single-handedly

## solemn

**02** po **04** awed, glum **05** grand, grave,
pious, sober, state **06** august, devout,
formal, honest, owlish, ritual, sedate,
sombre **07** earnest, genuine, po-faced,
pompous, serious, sincere, stately
**08** imposing, majestic **09** committed,
dignified, momentous, venerable
**10** ceremonial, impressive, portentous,
thoughtful **11** ceremonious, reverential
**12** awe-inspiring, wholehearted

### solemnity
04 rite 06 ritual 07 dignity, gravity
08 ceremony, grandeur, sanctity
09 formality 10 ceremonial,
observance, sacredness 11 celebration,
earnestness, proceedings, seriousness,
stateliness 13 momentousness
14 impressiveness, portentousness

### solemnize
04 keep 06 honour 07 dignify, observe,
perform 09 celebrate 11 commemorate

### solemnly
07 gravely, soberly 08 formally
09 earnestly, seriously 10 faithfully

### sol-fa
*see* note

### solicit
03 ask, beg, sue, woo 04 bash, drum,
pray, seek, tout 05 apply, court, crave,
plead 06 accost, ask for, hustle, incite,
manage 07 accoast, beseech, canvass,
conduct, entreat, implore, request,
require 08 apply for, petition
09 importune 10 supplicate
11 proposition

### solicitor
02 QC, SL, WS 03 Att, Sol, SSC 04 Atty,
Solr, tout 06 lawyer 08 advocate,
attorney, law agent, recorder
09 barrister, canvasser 10 crown agent

### solicitous
05 eager 06 caring, uneasy 07 anxious,
careful, earnest, jealous, worried,
zealous 08 troubled 09 attentive,
concerned 11 considerate
12 apprehensive

### solicitude
04 care, cark, fear 05 worry 06 regard
07 anxiety, concern, trouble
08 disquiet 10 uneasiness
13 attentiveness, consideration
15 considerateness

### solid
04 firm, hard, pure, real 05 cubic,
dense, gross, sober, sound, thick, valid
06 cogent, decent, square, stable,
strong, sturdy, trusty, worthy
07 compact, cubical, durable,
genuine, serious, unmixed, upright,
wealthy, weighty 08 concrete, reliable,
sensible, tangible, unbroken, unvaried
09 steadfast, unalloyed, unanimous,
undivided, well-built 10 compressed,
continuous, dependable, holosteric,
unshakable, upstanding 11 level-
headed, long-lasting, respectable,
substantial, trustworthy, unshakeable,
well-founded 12 well-grounded
13 authoritative, unadulterated,
uninterrupted

### solidarity
05 unity 06 accord 07 concord,
harmony 08 cohesion 09 agreement,
consensus, soundness, stability,
unanimity 10 team spirit
11 camaraderie 13 esprit de corps
14 like-mindedness

### solidify
03 gel, set 04 cake, clot, jell 06 go hard,
harden 07 congeal 09 coagulate,

corporify 10 become hard
11 crystallize

### soliloquy
06 homily, sermon, speech 07 address,
lecture, monolog, oration
09 monologue

### solitary
03 one 04 lone, monk, sole 05 alone,
loner 06 hermit, lonely, remote, single
07 ancress, ascetic, dernful, eremite,
recluse, retired, stylite 08 dearnful,
desolate, isolated, lonesome, lone
wolf, monastic, secluded, separate
09 anchoress, anchorite, reclusive,
untrodden, unvisited, withdrawn 10 by
yourself, cloistered, friendless,
hermitical, monastical, unsociable
11 introverted, monasterial, out-of-the-
way, sequestered 12 inaccessible,
Jimmy Woodser, unfrequented
13 companionless, individualist

### solitude
07 privacy 09 aloneness, isolation,
seclusion 10 desolation, loneliness,
remoteness, retirement, singleness
12 introversion, lonesomeness
13 reclusiveness, unsociability
14 friendlessness

### solo
04 aria, ayre, lone 05 alone, break,
récit 06 single 07 cadenza 09 on your
own 10 by yourself, unattended,
unescorted 12 single-handed
13 unaccompanied

### Solomon Islands
03 SLB

### solution
◇ *anagram indicator* 02 aq 03 fix, gel,
key, lye, mix, sol 05 blend, brine
06 answer, liquid, liquor, remedy,
result, saline, way out 07 cure-all,
formula, mixture, panacea, solvent
08 compound, emulsion, quick fix
09 rationale, unfolding 10 resolution,
suspension 11 elucidation,
explanation, unravelling
12 decipherment 13 clarification
15 disentanglement

### solve
◇ *anagram indicator* 04 read, undo,
work 05 crack, guess, loose, untie
06 answer, assoil, fathom, puzzle,
remedy, riddle, settle, unbind, unfold
07 clarify, clear up, explain, expound,
rectify, resolve, unravel, work out
08 decipher, put right, solution, think
out, unriddle 09 figure out, interpret,
puzzle out 11 disentangle 12 think
through

### solvent
04 DMSO 05 ether, sound 06 dioxan,
toluol 07 benzine, dioxane, toluene
08 alcahest, alkahest, methanol,
terebene 09 able to pay, banana oil,
detergent, financial, menstruum, out of
debt 10 chloroform, extractant, in the
black, in the clear, unindebted
11 cyclohexane 12 banana liquid,
creditworthy, ethyl acetate,
nitromethane, salt of sorrel 14 banana

solution, petroleum ether 15 propylene
glycol, trichloroethane

### solver
11 solutionist
• **solvers** 02 ye 03 you

### Somalia
02 SO 03 SOM

### sombre
03 dim, sad 04 dark, drab, dull
05 dingy, grave, morne, shady, sober
06 dismal, gloomy, morose, solemn
07 doleful, joyless, obscure, serious,
shadowy, subfusc, subfusk 08 funereal,
mournful 09 depressed 10 lugubrious,
melancholy

### some
◇ *hidden indicator* 03 any, few, one
04 they 07 certain, several
10 remarkable 11 outstanding, such-
and-such 12 considerable

### somebody
03 one, VIP 04 name, star 05 mogul,
nabob 06 bigwig, quidam 07 big shot,
magnate, notable, someone 08 big
noise, big wheel, luminary
09 celebrity, dignitary, personage,
superstar 10 panjandrum
11 heavyweight 13 household name

### someday
05 later 06 one day 07 by and by, later
on 08 sometime 10 eventually,
ultimately 11 in due course 13 sooner
or later 14 one of these days

### somehow
◇ *anagram indicator* 06 in a way 10 in a
fashion 11 by some means, come what
may 13 after a fashion 15 by hook or by
crook, one way or another

### someone
*see* **somebody**

### somersault
◇ *anagram indicator*

### sometime
02 ex 04 late, then 06 former, one day
07 earlier, one-time, quondam, retired,
someday 08 emeritus, formerly,
previous 09 erstwhile, in the past
10 occasional, previously 11 another
time

### sometimes
07 at times 08 off and on, on and off
09 somewhile 10 now and then, on
occasion, otherwise, somewhiles
11 now and again, on occasions,
otherwhiles 12 every so often,
occasionally, once in a while 14 from
time to time

### somewhat
04 a bit 05 kinda, quite 06 a bit of,
fairly, kind of, pretty, rather, sort of
07 a little 08 slightly 10 moderately,
relatively 12 to some degree, to some
extent

### somnolent
04 dozy 06 drowsy, sleepy, torpid
08 comatose, oscitant 09 half-awake,
heavy-eyed, soporific

### Somnus
06 Hypnos

## son

**01** s **03** boy, lad **04** fils **05** child, lewis **06** epigon, filius, laddie, native **07** epigone **08** disciple **09** offspring **10** descendant, inhabitant

*Sons include:*

**04 Abel**, **Amis** (Martin), **Bush** (George W), **Cain**, **Esau**, **Pitt** (William)
**05 Dumas** (Alexandre), **Groan** (Titus), **Harry** (Prince), **Isaac**, **Jacob**, **Milne** (Christopher Robin), **Morel** (Paul), **Waugh** (Auberon)
**06 Andrew** (Prince), **Edward** (Prince), **Gandhi** (Rajiv), **Hamlet**, **Joseph**
**07 Absalom**, **Charles** (Prince), **Douglas** (Michael), **Hotspur**, **Laertes**, **Oedipus**, **Simpson** (Bart), **William** (Prince)
**08 Benjamin**, **Dimbleby** (David), **Dimbleby** (Jonathan), **Florizel**, **Pontifex** (Ernest)
**09 Dumas fils**
**10 Duke of York**
**11 Jesus Christ**
**13 Prince of Wales**
**14 Pitt the Younger** (William)

• **son of 01** M', O' **02** Mc **03** Mac

## song

*Songs include:*

**03** air, art, fit, lay, oat, ode, pop, pub, war
**04** aria, bird, duet, folk, glee, hymn, lied, lilt, love, pean, rock, rune, tune
**05** blues, carol, catch, chant, dirge, ditty, elegy, lyric, paean, plain, psalm, torch, yodel
**06** amoret, anthem, ballad, chorus, gospel, jingle, lieder, lyrics, melody, number, shanty
**07** calypso, cantata, canzone, chanson, descant, lullaby, refrain, requiem, wassail
**08** birdcall, canticle, canzonet, madrigal, serenade, threnody
**09** barcarole, cantilena, dithyramb, epinikion, roundelay, spiritual
**10** plainchant, recitative
**11** bothy ballad, chansonette, rock and roll
**12** epithalamium, nursery rhyme

*See also* **poem**

*Pop songs include:*

**03** Bad
**04** 1999, Gold, Help!, True
**05** Clair, Diana, Faith, Layla, My Way, Relax, Shout
**06** Atomic, The End, Vienna, Volare
**07** Delilah, D.I.V.O.R.C.E., Hey Jude, Holiday, Imagine, Jamming, Let It Be, Rat Trap, Respect, Sailing, Starman
**08** Answer Me, Antmusic, At the Hop, Baby Love, Downtown, Love Me Do, Mamma Mia, Our House, Parklife, Peggy Sue, The Boxer, The Model, Thriller, Wannabee, Waterloo
**09** Dance Away, I Feel Love, Maggie

May, Metal Guru, Penny Lane, Praise You, Release Me, Something, Stand By Me, Wild Thing, Yesterday
**10** All Shook Up, Annie's Song, Band of Gold, Billie Jean, Blue Monday, Bye Bye Baby, House of Fun, King Creole, Lazy Sunday, Living Doll, Millennium, Moving On Up, Night Fever, Perfect Day, Purple Haze, Reet Petite, Ring of Fire, Wonderwall
**11** All Right Now, American Pie, Back for Good, Baker Street, Cathy's Clown, Firestarter, From Me to You, Glad All Over, Golden Brown, I Got You Babe, I'm Not in Love, Light My Fire, Like a Virgin, Lily the Pink, Mrs Robinson, Oliver's Army, Space Oddity, Tainted Love, Voodoo Chile
**12** All or Nothing, Bat Out of Hell, Born in the USA, Born to be Wild, Come on Eileen, Common People, Dancing Queen, Eleanor Rigby, God Only Knows, Material Girl, No Woman No Cry, The Birdy Song, West End Girls
**13** Blueberry Hill, Brass in Pocket, Design for Life, Don't You Want Me, Into the Groove, It's Not Unusual, It's Now or Never, Jailhouse Rock, Last Christmas, Long Tall Sally, Mary's Boy Child, Mull of Kintyre, Oh, Pretty Woman, Only the Lonely, Pinball Wizard, Summer Holiday, Tears in Heaven
**14** 20th Century Boy, A Hard Day's Night, Blue Suede Shoes, Good Vibrations, Karma Chameleon, Stand By Your Man, Sunny Afternoon, That'll Be the Day, The Power of Love, Waterloo Sunset, White Christmas, Wonderful World
**15** Baby One More Time, Begin the Beguine, Blowin' in the Wind, Candle in the Wind, Careless Whisper, Congratulations, God Save the Queen, Heartbreak Hotel, Hotel California, I Shot the Sheriff, Jumpin' Jack Flash, Killing me Softly, Love is all Around, Paperback Writer, Puppet on a String, Rivers of Babylon, Unchained Melody, When I Fall In Love, Yellow Submarine

*See also* **musical**
• **song and dance 03** ado **04** flap, fuss, stir, to-do **05** hoo-ha, tizzy **06** bother, furore, pother, tumult **09** commotion, kerfuffle **11** performance

## songster

**06** singer **07** crooner, soloist, warbler **08** minstrel, vocalist **09** balladeer, chanteuse, chorister **10** troubadour

## songwriter

*Songwriters and lyricists include:*

**03 Pop** (Iggy)
**04 Bart** (Lionel), **Cahn** (Sammy), **Cash**

(Johnny), **Hart** (Lorenz), **John** (Sir Elton), **Kern** (Jerome), **Reed** (Lou), **Rice** (Sir Tim)
**05 Berry** (Chuck), **Brown** (James), **Cohan** (George Michael), **Davis** (Miles), **Dylan** (Bob), **Holly** (Buddy), **Loewe** (Frederick), **Simon** (Paul), **Smith** (Tommy), **Sousa** (John Philip), **Swann** (Donald), **Weill** (Kurt)
**06 Berlin** (Irving), **Coward** (Sir Noël), **Fields** (Dorothy), **Joplin** (Scott), **Lennon** (John), **Lerner** (Alan Jay), **Marley** (Bob), **Mercer** (Johnny H), **Morton** (Jelly Roll), **Oliver** (King), **Parker** (Charlie), **Porter** (Cole), **Seeger** (Pete), **Waller** (Thomas 'Fats'), **Warren** (Harry)
**07 Collins** (Phil), **Dickson** (Barbara), **Donovan**, **Gilbert** (Sir Wiliam), **Guthrie** (Woody), **Hendrix** (Jimi), **Loesser** (Frank), **MacColl** (Ewan), **Mancini** (Henry), **Novello** (Ivor), **Orbison** (Roy), **Rodgers** (Richard), **Romberg** (Sigmund)
**08 Coltrane** (John), **Costello** (Elvis), **Gershwin** (George), **Mitchell** (Joni), **Morrison** (Van), **Sondheim** (Stephen)
**09 Bernstein** (Leonard), **Ellington** (Duke), **Faithfull** (Marianne), **Gillespie** (Dizzy), **McCartney** (Sir Paul)
**10 Carmichael** (Hoagy)
**11 Armatrading** (Joan), **Hammerstein** (Oscar), **Lloyd Webber** (Andrew, Lord), **Springsteen** (Bruce)

## sonorous

**04** full, loud, rich **05** round **07** orotund, ringing, rounded **08** plangent, resonant, sounding **09** high-flown, ororotund **10** full-voiced, resounding **11** full-mouthed **12** full-throated, high-sounding **13** grandiloquent

## soon

**04** anon **05** early, quick **06** pronto, timely **07** betimes, ere long, in a tick, just now, readily, shortly **08** in a hurry, in a jiffy, in no time **09** any minute, in a minute, in a moment, presently, willingly **10** before long **12** any minute now, in a short time, without delay **13** in no time at all **14** in a little while, in a moment or two, round the corner **15** in the near future
• **as soon as 04** once, when **07** whene'er **08** directly, eftsoons, whenever **10** right after **11** immediately, in the wake of **13** directly after

## sooner

**06** before, rather **07** earlier, instead **08** by choice **09** for choice, in advance **10** beforehand, from choice, much rather, preferably **12** by preference **13** for preference
• **no sooner than 06** barely, hardly **08** only just, scarcely
• **sooner or later 06** at last **07** finally **08** after all, at length, in the end **10** eventually, ultimately **11** in due

course **12** in the long run, subsequently

## soot
**04** coom, smut **05** colly **06** smutch **08** gas black **09** lampblack

## soothe
**04** balm, calm, coax, ease, hush, lull **05** accoy, allay, quiet, salve, sleek, still **06** augury, back up, cajole, pacify, settle, smooth, soften, temper **07** appease, assuage, comfort, compose, confirm, flatter, mollify, quieten, relieve, support **08** blandish, calm down, mitigate, palliate **09** alleviate **10** settle down **11** quieten down **12** foretokening, tranquillize

## soothing
**04** soft **05** balmy **06** anetic, gentle **07** anodyne, calming, easeful, lenient, pacific, restful **08** balsamic, lenitive, relaxing **09** assuasive, demulcent, emollient, paregoric **10** palliative

## soothsayer
**04** seer **05** augur, sibyl **06** oracle **07** Chaldee, diviner, prophet **08** Chaldaic, haruspex **10** foreteller, prophetess **14** prognosticator

## sophisticated
**04** cool, gold **05** couth, slick, suave **06** hi-tech, inland, subtle, urbane **07** complex, elegant, refined, stylish, worldly **08** advanced, cultured, delicate, high-tech, joined-up, polished, seasoned, space-age **09** civilized, elaborate, executive, expensive, falsified, intricate **10** cultivated **11** adulterated, complicated, experienced, worldly-wise **12** cosmopolitan **13** state-of-the-art **15** highly developed

## sophistication
**05** poise **07** culture, finesse **08** elegance, urbanity **10** experience **11** savoir-faire, savoir-vivre, worldliness

## sophistry
**07** fallacy, quibble, sophism **08** elenchus **09** casuistry, choplogic **10** paralogism **14** false reasoning

## soporific
**06** hypnic, opiate, sleepy **07** poppied, Seconal® **08** hypnotic, narcotic, sedative **09** dormitive, somnolent **10** poppy water **11** anaesthetic **12** sleeping pill **13** sleep-inducing, tranquillizer **14** benzodiazepine, sleeping tablet, tranquillizing

## soppy
**03** wet **04** daft, soft, wild **05** corny, crazy, gooey, mushy, silly, soggy, weepy **06** cheesy, gloopy, sloppy, slushy **07** cloying, maudlin, mawkish, wimpish **08** drenched **09** schmaltzy **10** lovey-dovey **11** sentimental **13** overemotional

## soprano
**01** S **03** sop **05** mezzo **06** treble **08** castrato

## sorcerer
**04** mage **05** magus, witch **06** magian, voodoo, wizard **07** angekok, warlock **08** angekkok, magician **09** enchanter, sorceress **10** reim-kennar **11** enchantress, necromancer **13** thaumaturgist

## sorcery
**05** charm, magic, spell, wicca **06** voodoo **07** pisheog **08** diablery, malefice, pishogue, witching, wizardry **09** diablerie, warlockry **10** black magic, necromancy, witchcraft **11** enchantment, incantation, thaumaturgy

## sordid
**03** low **04** base, foul, mean, vile **05** dirty, grimy, mucky, seamy, seedy **06** filthy, scungy, shabby, sleazy, soiled, tawdry **07** corrupt, debased, immoral, miserly, squalid, stained, unclean **08** degraded, grasping, shameful, wretched **09** abhorrent, debauched, dishonest, mercenary, niggardly **10** degenerate, despicable **11** ignominious, self-seeking **12** disreputable **13** dishonourable

## sore
**03** cut, raw, red **04** bite, boil, gall, hard, hurt, sair **05** angry, blain, botch, chafe, felon, graze, grief, nasty, nerve, ulcer, upset, vexed, wound **06** aching, bitter, chafed, fester, lesion, miffed, peeved, scrape, shiver, sorrel, tender, the raw, touchy **07** abscess, annoyed, anthrax, bruised, burning, eagerly, hurting, injured, painful, quittor, wounded **08** abrasion, grievous, inflamed, offended, reddened, severely, smarting, stinging, swelling **09** afflicted, aggrieved, irritable, irritated, painfully, resentful, sensitive **10** affliction, cheesed off, distressed, grievously, laceration **12** inflammation **13** distressingly

## sorely
**04** much **06** highly **07** greatly, notably **08** markedly, very much **09** extremely **10** noticeably, powerfully, remarkably **11** exceedingly **13** significantly, substantially

## sorrel
**03** oca **04** soar, sore **05** soare, sorel **06** oxalis, sorell **07** bilimbi, sourock **08** shamrock, sourwood **09** carambola, sour-gourd

## sorrow
**03** rew, rue, woe **04** moan, pain, pine, pity, ruth, weep **05** be sad, grief, mourn, night, sorra, trial, worry **06** bemoan, bewail, dolour, grieve, lament, misery, regret, repent **07** agonize, anguish, feel sad, remorse, sadness, trouble **08** distress, hardship, mourning **09** dejection, heartache, suffering, tristesse **10** affliction, compassion, contrition, heartbreak, misfortune **11** be miserable, lamentation, tribulation, unhappiness, Weltschmerz **12** wretchedness **13** feel miserable
*See also* **grief**

## sorrowful
**02** wo **03** sad, wae, woe **05** sorry, trist, woful **06** dismal, rueful, triste, woeful **07** baleful, careful, doleful, painful, piteous, ruthful, tearful, unhappy, wailful **08** dejected, grievous, mournful, wretched **09** afflicted, depressed, miserable, woebegone **10** lamentable, lugubrious, melancholy **11** distressing, heartbroken **12** disconsolate, heart-rending, heavy-hearted

## sorry
◇ *anagram indicator* **02** wo **03** bad, sad, woe **04** mean, poor **05** moved, upset **06** dismal, rueful, simple **07** ashamed, pitiful, pitying, unhappy **08** contrite, grievous, pathetic, penitent, shameful, wretched **09** concerned, miserable, regretful, repentant, worthless **10** apologetic, distressed, remorseful, shamefaced **11** distressing, guilt-ridden, sympathetic, unfortunate **12** contemptible, heart-rending **13** compassionate, understanding
• **be sorry for** **03** rew, rue **06** repent **08** forthink

## sort
◇ *anagram indicator* **03** fit, ilk, lot, set **04** beat, geld, kind, make, race, rank, sift, type **05** agree, allot, befit, brand, breed, class, genre, genus, grade, group, order, stamp, style, woman **06** accord, adjust, assign, codify, divide, family, kidney, manner, nature, parcel, person, punish, screen, select **07** arrange, company, consort, dispose, fashion, procure, provide, quality, species, variety **08** category, classify, organize, separate **09** catalogue, character, segregate **10** categorize, collection, distribute, put in order **11** description, systematize **12** denomination
• **out of sorts** ◇ *anagram indicator* **03** ill **04** mean, sick, weak **05** crook, cross, dicky, frail, narky, nohow, ratty, rough, seedy **06** ailing, crabby, crummy, feeble, groggy, grumpy, infirm, laid up, poorly, queasy, rotten, shirty, snappy, unwell **07** crabbed, grouchy, in a huff, in a mood, in a sulk, run down, run-down, stroppy **08** below par, choleric, diseased, nohowish **09** bedridden, crotchety, fractious, impatient, in a bad way, irritable, off-colour, unhealthy **10** in a bad mood **11** bad-tempered **13** mops and brooms, quick-tempered **14** down in the dumps, down in the mouth **15** under the weather
• **sort of** ◇ *anagram indicator* **04** a bit **05** kinda, quite **06** fairly, kind of, pretty, rather **07** a little **08** slightly, somewhat **10** moderately, relatively **12** to some degree, to some extent
• **sort out** **04** rank **05** class, grade, group, order, solve **06** choose, divide, select **07** arrange, clear up, resolve, work out **08** classify, organize, put right, separate **09** segregate **10** categorize, put in order

## sortie
**04** raid, rush **05** foray, sally, swoop

**so-so**

06 attack, charge 07 assault, outfall 08 invasion 09 offensive

**so-so**

02 OK 04 fair 06 not bad 07 average, neutral 08 adequate, mediocre, middling, moderate, ordinary, passable 09 tolerable 11 indifferent, respectable 12 run-of-the-mill 13 no great shakes, unexceptional 14 comme ci comme ça, fair to middling 15 undistinguished

**soubriquet**

see **sobriquet, soubriquet**

**sought-after**

02 in 03 big, hip, hot, now 04 cool 05 liked 06 modish, trendy, wanted 07 admired, desired, popular 08 approved, favoured, in demand, in favour 09 favourite, well-liked 10 all the rage 11 fashionable 13 in great demand

**soul**

02 ba, ka 03 âme, ego, man 04 alma, life, mind 05 anima, model, shade, woman 06 person, pneuma, psyche, reason, spirit 07 element, epitome, essence, example, feeling, passion 08 creature, humanity, inner man, sympathy 09 character, inner self, intellect 10 compassion, embodiment, human being, individual, inner being, inner woman, tenderness, vital force 11 inspiration, sensitivity 12 appreciation 13 heart of hearts, understanding 15 personification

**soulful**

06 moving 08 eloquent, mournful, profound 09 emotional, heartfelt, sensitive 10 expressive, meaningful

**soulless**

04 cold, dead, mean 05 bleak, cruel, empty 06 unkind 07 callous, ignoble, inhuman 08 lifeless 09 unfeeling 10 mechanical, spiritless 11 dehumanized 12 mean-spirited 13 characterless, uninteresting, unsympathetic 14 soul-destroying

**sound**

◇ *homophone indicator* 03 din, fit, say, voe 04 deep, firm, goad, good, hale, look, mean, safe, sane, seem, tend, test, toll, tone, trig, true, vibe, well 05 fiord, firth, fjord, gauge, go off, inlet, noise, plumb, probe, radio, right, sense, solid, swoon, tease, tenor, utter, valid, voice, whole 06 appear, cogent, deeply, fathom, intact, notion, proven, robust, secure, severe, strait, strong, sturdy, timbre, unhurt 07 channel, declare, earshot, estuary, examine, express, extreme, feeling, greatly, healthy, inspect, intense, logical, measure, passage, perfect, provoke, publish, resound, serious, weighty 08 announce, complete, orthodox, proclaim, profound, rational, reliable, resonate, severely, thorough, unbroken, very much, vigorous 09 enunciate, excellent, extremely, intensely, judicious, pronounce, resonance, seriously, undamaged, uninjured, very great, wholesome

10 articulate, completely, dependable, impression, profoundly, reasonable, thoroughly, unimpaired, vigorously 11 disease-free, implication, in good shape, investigate, reverberate, substantial, trustworthy, well-founded 12 in fine fettle, in good health, sound as a bell, well-grounded 13 authoritative, reverberation 15 in good condition

*Sounds include:*

03 cry, hum, pip, pop, sob, tap 04 bang, beep, boom, buzz, chug, clap, echo, fizz, hiss, honk, hoot, moan, peal, ping, plop, ring, roar, sigh, slam, snap, thud, tick, ting, toot, wail, whiz, yell, yoop 05 blare, blast, bleep, chime, chink, chirm, clack, clang, clank, clash, click, clink, clunk, crack, crash, creak, drone, grate, groan, knock, plonk, skirl, slurp, smack, sniff, snore, snort, swish, throb, thump, twang, vroom, whine, whirr, whish, whizz, whoop 06 bubble, crunch, gabble, gollar, goller, gurgle, hiccup, jangle, jingle, murmur, patter, rattle, report, rumble, rustle, scrape, scream, sizzle, splash, squeak, squeal, tinkle, whoosh 07 brattle, chatter, clatter, crackle, explode, graunch, grizzle, pitapat, screech, squelch, thunder, whimper, whistle 08 splutter 11 taratantara

*Animal sounds include:*

03 baa, bay, caw, coo, kaw, low, mew, moo, wee, yap 04 bark, bell, blat, bray, bump, crow, hiss, honk, hoot, howl, purr, roar, woof, yawp, yelp, yowl 05 bleat, cheep, chirp, cluck, crake, croak, groin, growl, grunt, miaow, neigh, pewit, quack, scape, snarl, tweet 06 bellow, cackle, gobble, peewit, squawk, squeak, warble, whinny 07 chirrup, gruntle, looning, screech, trumpet, twitter, whicker 09 caterwaul

*Geographical sounds include:*

03 Hoy, Rum 04 Bute, Calf, Crow, Deer, Eigg, Holm, Iona, Jura, King, Mull, Papa, Rock, Yell 05 Barra, Canna, Cross, Exuma, Gigha, Inner, Islay, Luing, Puget, Sanda, Shuna, Sleat 06 Breton, Harris, Norton, Pabbay, Raasay, Ramsey, Sanday, Shiant, Turner 07 Arisaig, Bardsey, Caswell, Cuillin, Gairsay, McMurdo, Milford, Pamlico, St Mary's 08 Auskerry, Bluemull, Breaksea, Colgrave, Doubtful, Kotzebue, Taransay 09 Albemarle, Casiguran, Currituck, Eynhallow, Lancaster, Shapinsay

10 Chandeleur, Cumberland, Kilbrannan, King George, Long Island, New Georgia, Possession 11 Mississippi, Roes Welcome 12 Prince Albert 13 Prince William

• **by the sound of it** ◇ *homophone indicator*
• **sound measure/unit** 02 dB 03 bel 04 phon, sone 07 decibel, phoneme, segment 09 kilohertz
• **sound out** 03 ask 04 pump 05 probe 06 survey 07 canvass, examine, suss out 08 question, research 11 investigate

**soundly**

04 fast 05 fully, quite, tight 06 deeply 07 greatly, solidly, totally, utterly, validly 08 entirely, securely, severely, very much 09 downright, extremely, intensely, logically, perfectly, seriously 10 absolutely, completely, dependably, profoundly, reasonably, thoroughly, vigorously 15 authoritatively

**soundtrack**

10 theme music

**soup**

◇ *anagram indicator*

*Soups include:*

03 dal, pea, pho 04 cawl, crab, dhal, game, miso 05 adrak, blaff, broth, egusi, gumbo, locro, misua, rasam, snert, stock 06 ajiaco, asapao, barley, birria, bisque, borsch, cocido, congee, fennel, guacho, harira, lentil, noodle, oxtail, pazole, posole, potage, potato, reuben, sambar, tomato, turtle, won ton 07 borscht, chicken, chowder, tarator, turbana 08 borschch, broccoli, callaloo, chirmole, consommé, ful nabed, gazpacho, halászlé, julienne, mondongo, mushroom, okroshka, sancocho, solianka, split pea 09 asparagus, bird's nest, cacciucco, Clanallen, escabeche, fasolatha, pea and ham, pepperpot, picadillo, quimbombo, royal game, rozsolnyk, shark's fin, tom kha gai, white foam 10 avgolemono, caldo verde, minestrone, mock turtle, mole de olla, sauerkraut, superkanja, watercress 11 clam chowder, cock-a-leekie, cullen skink, French onion, gaeng som kai, gaeng som pla, Scotch broth, tom yam goong, vichyssoise 12 bouneschlupp, brown Windsor, cockieleekie, guriltai shul, mulligatawny 13 bouillabaisse, chicken noodle, cream of tomato, potato and leek, stracciatella 14 lentil and bacon 15 Queen Anne's broth

## sour

**03** bad, off **04** acid, rank, tart, tiff, tift, turn **05** acerb, acidy, aygre, eager, heavy, nasty, ratty, sharp, spoil, surly, tangy, wersh **06** acetic, bitter, canker, crusty, morose, rancid, shirty, strong, turned **07** acerbic, acetous, austere, crabbed, curdled, envenom, grouchy, peevish, pungent, subacid **08** alienate, churlish, embitter, verjuice, vinegary **09** acidulent, acidulous, resentful **10** disenchant, embittered, exacerbate, exasperate, make bitter, unpleasant **11** acrimonious, bad-tempered, ill-tempered **12** disagreeable, inharmonious, unsuccessful

## source

◊ *head selection indicator* **03** urn **04** font, head, mine, rise, root, well, ylem **05** cause, fount, radix, start, stock **06** author, origin, sourse, spring, supply, whence **07** surging **08** wellhead **09** authority, beginning, generator, good hands, informant, principle, rootstock, water head **10** derivation, originator, primordium, provenance, springhead, wellspring **11** fons et origo **12** commencement, fountainhead

## sourpuss

**04** crab **05** grump, shrew **06** grouse, kvetch, misery, whiner **07** killjoy, whinger **08** buzzkill, grumbler **10** crosspatch **14** dog in the manger

## souse

**03** dip, ear, sou **04** dash, duck, dunk, sink, soak, wash **05** douse, plump, smite, souce, sowce, sowse, steep, thump **06** drench, impact, pickle, plunge, sowsse, strike **07** ducking, immerse, impinge **08** drunkard, marinade, marinate, saturate, submerge, suddenly **09** drenching

## south

◊ *tail selection down indicator* **01** S **02** So **03** Sth **04** Midi

## South Africa

**02** SA, ZA **03** RSA, ZAF **04** S Afr

## South African

**02** SA **04** S Afr

## South America

*see* **America; god, goddess**

## South Carolina

**02** SC

## South Dakota

**02** SD **04** S Dak

## south-east, south-eastern

**02** SE

## southern

**01** S **05** south **07** austral **09** southerly **10** meridional

## south-west, south-western

**02** SW

## souvenir

**05** relic, steal, token **06** trophy **07** memento, purloin, relique **08** keepsake, reminder **11** remembrance

## sovereign

**01** K, L, Q **02** ER, HM **03** bar, sov **04** king, quid, tsar **05** chief, crown, pound, queen, royal, ruler, squid **06** canary, couter, kingly, nicker, prince, ruling, shiner, sovran, utmost **07** emperor, empress, extreme, monarch, queenly, smacker, supreme, thick'un **08** absolute, autocrat, dominant, imperial, majestic, princely **09** paramount, potentate, principal, unlimited **10** autonomous, self-ruling, unequalled, unrivalled **11** independent, outstanding, predominant **12** jimmy-o'goblin **13** pound sterling, self-governing

*See also* **king; queen**

## sovereignty

**03** raj **04** sway **07** primacy, royalty **08** autonomy, chiefdom, dominion, imperium, kingship, regality, synarchy **09** chiefship, princedom, queenship, supremacy **10** ascendancy, domination, suzerainty **11** condominium, pre-eminence **12** independence **13** thalassocracy, thalattocracy **14** rangatiratanga, self-government

## sow

**03** elt, saw **04** gilt, seed, yelt **05** drill, lodge, plant, strew **06** spread **07** bestrew, implant, scatter **08** disperse, seminate **09** broadcast **10** distribute, inseminate **11** disseminate

*See also* **pig**

## sozzled

◊ *anagram indicator* **05** happy, merry, tight, tipsy **06** blotto, tiddly **07** drunken, pickled, squiffy, tiddley **09** crapulent, plastered **10** inebriated **11** intoxicated

## spa

**06** spring **07** Kurhaus

*Spas include:*

**03** Dax

**04** Bath

**05** Baden, Baños, Epsom, Sochi, Vichy

**06** Aachen, Boston, Buxton, Ilkley, Trebon

**07** Lourdes, Malvern, Matlock

**08** Carlsbad, Shearsby, Woodhall

**09** Bad Elster, Droitwich, Harrogate, Marienbad, Velingrad

**10** Baden Baden, Cheltenham, Leamington

**11** Bad Dürrheim, Scarborough

**12** Strathpeffer

**13** Aix-la-Chapelle, Knaresborough

**14** Tunbridge Wells

## space

**02** em, en **03** gap **04** area, lung, play, room, seat, span, time, void **05** array, blank, break, chasm, order, place, range, scope, shift, spell, stint, sweep **06** cosmos, extent, galaxy, lacuna, leeway, margin, period, volume **07** arrange, be apart, dispose, expanse, opening, stretch **08** capacity, interval, latitude, omission, set apart, space out, universe **09** amplitude, clearance, deep space, elbow-room, expansion, string out **10** empty space, interstice, Lebensraum, outer space, put in order, stretch out **11** the Milky Way **12** intermission **13** accommodation

*Space travel-related terms include:*

**03** bus, ELV, ESA, ISS, LOX, LRV, MCC

**04** NASA

**05** abort, flyby, orbit

**06** CAPCOM, drogue, G force, hydyne, launch, module, rocket

**07** booster, coolant, docking, lift-off, mission, payload, re-entry, shuttle, vidicon

**08** attitude, blast-off, free-fall, fuel cell, fuel tank, impactor, lunanaut, moonwalk, nose cone, sloshing

**09** astronaut, cosmonaut, hydrazine, launch pad, light year, lunarnaut, spaceship, space suit, taikonaut

**10** heat shield, pogo effect, propellant, rendezvous, spacecraft, space probe, trajectory

**11** lunar module, solar system, zero gravity

**12** ascent module, launch window, lunar landing, man on the moon, microgravity, space station

**13** command module, descent module, jet propulsion, launch vehicle, space sickness

**14** escape velocity, mission control, weightlessness

**15** re-entry corridor

*Spacecraft include:*

**02** LM

**03** ISS, LEM, Mir

**06** Skylab, Tardis

**07** Gemini 4, Vostok 1, Vostok 5, Vostok 6

**08** Apollo 11, Apollo 13, Apollo 17, Columbia, Freedom 7, Nostromo, Red Dwarf, Sputnik 1, Sputnik 2, Voskhod 1, Voskhod 2

**09** Discovery, Endeavour, Liberator, Pioneer 10, Shenzhou V

**10** Challenger, USS Voyager

**11** Fireball XL5, Heart of Gold

**12** SS Discovery 1, Thunderbird 3, Thunderbird 5

**13** Moonbase Alpha, USS Enterprise

*See also* **probe**

## spaceman, spacewoman

*see* **astronaut**

## spacious

**03** big **04** huge, open, vast, wide **05** ample, broad, large, roomy **07** immense, sizable **08** palatial, sizeable **09** capacious, expansive, extensive, uncrowded **10** commodious

## spade

**01** S **03** loy **04** pick, spay, spit **05** graft, slane, spado, spayd **06** paddle, pattle, pettle, spayad, tuskar, tusker **07** cas crom, tushkar, tushker, twiscar **08** caschrom **09** flaughter **11** paddle-staff **12** breastplough

• **spades** **01** S

**spadework**
**06** labour **08** drudgery, homework
**10** donkey-work, foundation,
groundwork **11** preparation
**15** preliminary work

**Spain**
**01** E **03** ESP **06** España
• **in Spain** ◇ *foreign word indicator*

**span**
**04** arch, last, link, term, time, yoke
**05** cover, cross, fresh, piece, range,
reach, scope, spell, vault **06** bridge,
extend, extent, length, period, spread,
wind up **07** compass, include,
measure, overlay, stretch **08** bestride,
distance, duration, interval, traverse
**09** encompass **10** overbridge

**spangle**
**01** O **06** sequin **07** glitter **09** paillette

**Spaniard**
**03** don

**spaniel**
**04** mean **07** fawning

*Spaniels include:*

**03** toy
**04** land
**05** field, water
**06** cocker, Sussex
**07** clumber
**08** Blenheim, papillon, springer
**10** Irish water, Maltese dog
**11** King Charles

**Spanish**
*see* **day; month; number**

**spank**
**03** tan **04** cane, slap **05** smack, whack
**06** paddle, strike, thrash, thwack,
wallop **07** slipper **15** put over your
knee

**spanking**
**04** fast, fine, very **05** brand, brisk,
quick, scuds, smart, swift **06** lively,
snappy, speedy **07** exactly, totally,
utterly **08** gleaming, spirited, striking,
vigorous **09** energetic **10** absolutely,
completely, paddy-whack, positively,
strikingly **12** invigorating

**spanner**
**03** key **06** wrench **12** monkey wrench

**spar**
**03** bar, box **04** gaff, pole, rail, shut,
spat, tiff **05** argue, scrap, sprit **06** barite,
bicker, fasten, rafter, ricker, steeve
**07** barytes, contend, contest, dispute,
fall out, quarrel, wrangle, wrestle
**08** bowsprit, cryolite, mainboom,
skirmish, squabble **09** outrigger
**10** martingale **11** torpedo boom
**12** swinging-boom, wollastonite
**13** rhodochrosite

**spare**
**04** bony, free, gash, give, hain, lank,
lean, over, save, slim, thin **05** allow,
avoid, extra, gaunt, grant, guard,
hoard, scant, skimp, stint **06** afford,
defend, frugal, let off, meagre, modest,
pardon, scanty, secure, skimpy,
skinny, unused **07** forbear, forgive,
leisure, not harm, protect, provide,

refrain, release, reserve, scraggy,
scrawny, slender, sparing, surplus
**08** buckshee, leftover, part with,
reprieve, unwanted, withhold
**09** auxiliary, do without, emergency,
remaining, safeguard, subsecive
**10** additional, subsidiary, take care of,
unoccupied **11** show mercy to,
superfluous **12** dispense with
**13** manage without, supernumerary,
supplementary **15** all skin and bones
• **to spare** **05** extra **06** unused
**07** surplus **08** left over **09** in reserve,
remaining
• **with little to spare** **04** fine
**06** narrow

**sparing**
**05** canny, mingy, scant **06** frugal,
meagre, scarce, stingy, strait
**07** careful, miserly, prudent, thrifty
**09** penurious **10** economical **11** close-
fisted, tight-fisted

**sparingly**
**06** nighly **08** frugally, meagrely,
scrimply, stingily **09** carefully,
prudently **12** economically

**spark**
**03** bit, jot **04** atom, beau, funk, hint,
iota **05** flake, flame, flare, flash, gleam,
glint, lover, scrap, spunk, touch, trace
**06** kindle **07** animate, bluette, flaught,
flicker, glimmer, sparkle, vestige
**08** skerrick **09** scintilla **10** suggestion
**11** electrician
• **spark off** **04** stir **05** cause, start
**06** excite, incite, kindle, prompt, set off
**07** inspire, provoke, trigger
**08** occasion, start off, touch off
**09** stimulate **10** give rise to, trigger off
**11** precipitate

**sparkle**
**03** vim **04** beam, brio, dash, fire, fizz,
glow, life, zest **05** flash, gleam, glint,
shine, spark **06** bubble, dazzle, energy,
spirit **07** be witty, emicate, flicker,
glimmer, glisten, glister, glitter,
pizzazz, shimmer, twinkle **08** be
bubbly, be lively, radiance, vitality,
vivacity **09** animation, coruscate,
emication **10** be animated, be spirited,
brilliance, ebullience, effervesce,
enthusiasm, get-up-and-go, liveliness
**11** be ebullient, be vivacious,
coruscation, scintillate **13** scintillation
**14** be effervescent, be enthusiastic

**sparkling**
**05** fizzy, witty **06** bubbly, lively
**07** emicant **08** aglitter, animated,
flashing, gleaming, spritzig **09** brilliant,
frizzante, pétillant, twinkling
**10** carbonated, glistening, glittering
**11** coruscating, scintillant
**12** effervescent **13** scintillating
• **make sparkling** **09** carbonate

**sparrow**
**04** tody **05** sprug **06** mossie
**07** dunnock, pinnock, spadger, titling
**08** accentor, prunella, ricebird
**09** paddy-bird **11** whitethroat **13** hedge-
accentor

**sparse**
**04** rare, thin **06** meagre, scanty, scarce,
slight **07** light on, scrawny **08** scattery,
sporadic **09** scattered **10** infrequent

**sparsely**
**08** meagrely, scantily, scarcely, slightly
**12** sporadically

**spartan**
**05** bleak, hardy, harsh, plain **06** frugal,
severe, simple, strict **07** ascetic,
austere, harmost, joyless, laconic
**08** rigorous **09** stringent, temperate
**10** abstemious **11** disciplined, self-
denying **12** militaristic

**spasm**
**03** fit, tic **04** bout, grip, jerk **05** burst,
cramp, crick, gripe, spell, start, thraw,
throe, throw, tonus **06** access, attack,
clonus, frenzy, hippus, throwe, twitch
**07** seizure, trismus **08** eruption,
outburst, paroxysm **10** blepharism,
convulsion, tonic spasm **11** clonic
spasm, contraction, laryngismus
**12** childcrowing

**spasmodic**
◇ *anagram indicator* **05** jerky **06** fitful
**07** erratic, spastic **08** periodic, sporadic
**09** irregular **10** convulsive, occasional
**12** intermittent

**spasmodically**
**08** off and on, on and off **11** now and
again **12** occasionally, periodically,
sporadically **14** intermittently

**spate**
**04** flow, rush **05** flood, speat **06** deluge,
series **07** torrent **10** outpouring

**spatter**
◇ *anagram indicator* **03** jap **04** daub,
jaup, soil **05** dirty, spray **06** bedaub,
dabble, shower, splash **07** bestrew,
scatter, speckle, splodge **08** splatter,
sprinkle **09** bespatter **10** besprinkle

**spawn**
**03** fry, roe **04** blot, make, redd, seed,
spat, spit, teem **05** brood, cause, culch,
sperm **06** create, cultch, lead to
**07** bring on, produce **08** engender,
generate **09** offspring, originate
**10** bring about, give rise to

**spay**
**03** fix **04** geld **05** spade, spayd
**06** doctor, neuter, spayad **08** castrate
**09** sterilize **10** emasculate

**speak**
◇ *homophone indicator* **03** gab, say, yak
**04** chat, mang, pipe, talk, tell, word
**05** argue, sound, state, utter, voice
**06** witter **07** address, chatter, comment,
declaim, declare, discuss, expound,
express, lecture, mention **08** converse,
describe, harangue, platform
**09** enunciate, hold forth, pronounce
**10** articulate **11** communicate **13** have
a word with
• **speak angrily** **04** pelt
• **speak for** **06** act for **08** stand for
**09** represent **15** speak on behalf of
• **speak of** **05** voice **07** discuss,
mention, refer to **13** make mention of
**15** make reference to

**speak out** 03 ope 04 open
06 defend 07 protest, support 11 say publicly, speak openly
**speak tediously** 05 prose
**speak to** 04 warn 05 scold
06 accost, attest, bounce, carpet, rebuke 07 address, bawl out, discuss, lecture, rouse on, tell off, tick off, upbraid 08 admonish 09 dress down, go crook at, pull apart, reprimand, take apart 10 go to town on 11 bring to book 13 have a word with 14 throw the book at 15 give someone hell
**speak up** 06 defend 07 protest, support 10 talk loudly 11 say publicly, speak openly 14 raise your voice, talk more loudly

**speaker**
05 mouth 06 orator, talker, woofer 07 tweeter 08 lecturer, top tweet 09 spokesman, subwoofer
10 mouthpiece, prolocutor 11 first person, spokeswoman
12 spokesperson

**spear**
03 ash, gad, gig 04 dart, gade, gaid, pike, pile, reed 05 lance, pilum, spire, stick 06 glaive, gleave, waster
07 assagai, assegai, harpoon, javelin, leister, trident 08 assegaai, gavelock, lancegay 09 boar-spear, demi-lance, fish-spear, handstaff, truncheon
12 burn the water

**spearhead**
03 van 04 head, lead 05 front, guide 06 launch, leader 07 pioneer
08 initiate, overseer, vanguard 09 front line 11 cutting edge, trailblazer
15 leading position

**special**
◇ anagram indicator 01 S 02 sp 05 exact, major 06 choice, select, unique
07 notable, precise, unusual
08 detailed, intimate, peculiar, singular, specific 09 different, dividuous, exclusive, important, memorable, momentous, red-letter
10 individual, noteworthy, particular, remarkable 11 distinctive, exceptional, outstanding, significant
13 distinguished, extraordinary
14 characteristic

**specialist**
06 brains, expert, master 07 attaché 08 boutique 09 authority 10 consultant 11 connoisseur 12 professional
See also **medical**

**speciality**
03 bag 04 gift 05 field, forte 06 talent 07 feature 08 strength 09 specialty 11 area of study 12 field of study

**specialization**
05 focus 12 special study
13 concentration 14 special subject 15 special interest

**specialize**
05 major, study 06 follow 07 focus on, major in, specify 13 concentrate on, differentiate

**specially**
◇ anagram indicator 07 express 08 uniquely 09 expressly 10 distinctly, explicitly 11 exclusively 12 in particular, particularly, specifically

**species**
02 sp 03 spp 04 kind, sort, type 05 breed, class, genus, group 07 variety 08 category 10 collection
11 description

**specific**
03 set 05 exact, fixed 07 express, limited, precise, special, trivial
08 clear-cut, concrete, definite, detailed, explicit 09 determined, particular 11 unambiguous, unequivocal, well-defined

**specifically**
07 clearly, exactly, plainly
09 expressly, specially 10 definitely, distinctly 11 exclusively 12 in particular, particularly
13 unambiguously

**specification**
04 item, spec 06 detail, naming 07 listing 09 condition, statement
10 particular 11 delineation, description, designation, instruction, requirement, stipulation
13 qualification

**specify**
04 cite, list, name 05 limit, state 06 assign, define, detail, set out
07 frutify, itemize, mention
08 describe, indicate, spell out
09 delineate, designate, enumerate, stipulate 10 condescend, specialize 13 particularize 14 condescend upon

**specimen**
04 copy, sort, swab, type 05 assay, model, piece 06 person, sample
07 example, exhibit, pattern
08 exemplar, instance, paradigm
12 illustration 14 representative

**specious**
04 fair 05 false, showy 06 untrue 07 pageant, unsound 08 imposing
09 beautiful, casuistic, deceptive, fair-faced, plausible, sophistic
10 fallacious, misleading 11 sophistical

**speck**
03 bit, dot, fat, jot, pip 04 atom, blot, flaw, iota, mark, mite, mote, peep, spek, spot, whit 05 bacon, fault, fleck, grain, peepe, shred, stain, trace
06 defect, sheave, tittle 07 blemish, floater, spangle, speckle 08 particle

**speckled**
03 gay 05 mealy 06 dotted, mealie, spotty, ticked 07 brinded, brindle, dappled, flecked, mottled, spotted
08 brindled, freckled, stippled
09 fleckered, sprinkled 11 lentiginous 13 trout-coloured

**spectacle**
04 shew, show 05 scene, sight
06 marvel, object, parade, wonder
07 display, pageant, picture
09 bullfight, curiosity, pageantry, raree-show 10 exhibition, outspeckle,

phenomenon 11 performance
12 extravaganza, son et lumière

**spectacles**
02 OO 05 specs 06 specks 07 eyewear, glasses, goggles, lorgnon, sunnies
08 bifocals, cheaters, gig-lamps, horn-rims 09 barnacles, glass eyes, lorgnette, preserves, trifocals
10 eyeglasses, sunglasses, varifocals
13 granny glasses, pebble-glasses
14 National Health, pinhole glasses

**spectacular**
04 show 05 grand 06 daring
07 amazing, display, opulent, pageant
08 dazzling, dramatic, glorious, splendid, striking, stunning
09 colourful, spectacle 10 exhibition, flamboyant, impressive, remarkable, staggering 11 astonishing, eye-catching, magnificent, outstanding, resplendent, sensational
12 breathtaking, extravaganza, ostentatious 13 extraordinary

**spectacularly**
09 amazingly 10 gloriously, remarkably, strikingly, stunningly
12 impressively, staggeringly
13 astonishingly, magnificently, outstandingly, sensationally
15 extraordinarily

**spectator**
06 viewer 07 watcher, witness
08 beholder, looker-on, observer, onlooker, passer-by 09 bystander, ringsider 10 eyewitness, groundling, rubberneck, supervisor, wallflower

**spectral**
05 eerie, weird 06 spooky 07 ghostly, phantom, shadowy, uncanny
08 eldritch 09 phantosme, unearthly
11 disembodied, incorporeal
12 supernatural 13 insubstantial

**spectre**
04 fear 05 bogle, dread, ghost, larva, shade, spook 06 bodach, Empusa, menace, shadow, spirit, threat, vision, wraith 07 phantom 08 phantasm, presence, revenant, visitant
09 phantosme 10 apparition

**spectrum**
05 gamme, prism, range 07 rainbow 10 after-image

**speculate**
04 muse, risk, view 05 guess
06 gamble, hazard, wonder
07 examine, imagine, observe, reflect, suppose, surmise, venture 08 cogitate, consider, meditate, theorize
10 conjecture, deliberate
11 contemplate, hypothesize

**speculation**
04 risk, spec 05 flier, flyer, guess
06 gamble, hazard, theory, vision, wisdom 07 flutter, surmise, theoric, venture, viewing 08 gambling, ideology, observer 09 adventure, guesswork, theorique 10 conjecture, hypothesis, theorizing 11 imagination, supposition 12 deliberation
13 consideration, contemplation, flight of fancy 14 a shot in the dark

## speculative

**04** iffy **05** dicey, risky, vague **06** chancy
**08** abstract, academic, notional,
unproven **09** hazardous, tentative,
theoretic, uncertain **10** indefinite
**11** conjectural, theoretical
**12** hypothetical, transcendent
**13** suppositional, unpredictable

## speculator

**04** bear, bull **05** piker **07** gambler,
lookout **08** boursier, watchman
**09** pinhooker **10** adventurer, land-
jobber **11** adventuress, speculatist,
speculatrix, stockjobber **12** money-
spinner

## speech

◇ *anagram indicator* ◇ *homophone*
*indicator* **03** say **04** rant, talk **05** lingo,
spiel, voice **06** accent, homily, jargon,
korero, parole, patter, rumour, saying,
sermon, tirade, tongue **07** address,
dialect, diction, lecture, mention,
message, oration **08** colloquy,
delivery, dialogue, diatribe, harangue,
language, parlance **09** discourse,
elocution, monologue, philippic,
soliloquy, utterance **11** enunciation
**12** articulation, conversation
**13** communication, pronunciation

---

*Parts of speech include:*

**01** a, n, v
**02** vb, vi, vt
**03** adj, adv, art
**04** noun, prep, verb
**06** adnoun, adverb, gerund, plural,
prefix, suffix
**07** article, pronoun
**08** singular
**09** adjective, gerundive
**10** common noun, connective,
copulative, participle, proper
noun
**11** conjunction, phrasal verb,
preposition
**12** abbreviation, interjection
**13** auxiliary verb
**14** transitive verb
**15** definite article, relative pronoun

---

• **speech defect** **04** lisp **07** stammer,
stutter **10** impediment

## speechless

**03** mum **04** dumb, mute **06** aghast,
amazed, silent **07** shocked
**08** unworded **09** astounded, voiceless
**10** dumbstruck, struck dumb, tongue-
tied **11** dumbfounded, obmutescent
**12** inarticulate, languageless, lost for
words **13** thunderstruck

## speed

**01** v **02** AS **03** bat, mph **04** belt, clip,
dash, fare, knot, pace, pelt, race, rate,
rush, tear, zoom **05** haste, hurry,
tempo, whisk **06** career, cruise, gallop,
hasten, hurtle, sprint **07** quicken,
succeed, success **08** alacrity, celerity,
despatch, dispatch, momentum,
rapidity, step on it, velocity **09** bowl
along, quickness, swiftness
**10** accelerate, promptness
**11** amphetamine **12** acceleration, step
on the gas **14** step on the juice

**15** expeditiousness, put your foot
down
• **increase speed** **03** gun
**10** accelerate, give the gun
• **speed up** **05** hurry **06** hasten, open
up, spur on, step up **07** advance,
forward, further, promote, quicken
**08** expedite, go faster, step on it
**09** stimulate **10** accelerate, facilitate
**11** drive faster, gather speed, pick up
speed, precipitate, put on a spurt
**12** gain momentum, step on the gas
**14** step on the juice **15** put your foot
down

## speedily

**04** fast, post **06** pronto **07** betimes,
hastily, on wings, quickly, rapidly,
swiftly **08** in a hurry, promptly
**09** hurriedly, posthaste **11** at the double
**12** a mile a minute, lickety-split
**13** expeditiously **14** at a rate of knots,
hell for leather **15** like the clappers

## speedwell

**06** hen-bit **08** bird's-eye, fluellin,
neckweed, veronica **09** brooklime

## speedy

**03** pdq **04** fast **05** hasty, nippy, quick,
rapid, swift, zappy, zippy **06** nimble,
prompt **07** cursory, express, hurried,
summary **09** immediate, posthaste
**11** expeditious, precipitate **15** pretty
damn quick

## spell

**02** go **03** fit, hex, jag, ren, rin, run
**04** bout, mean, mojo, pull, rest, rune,
rung, scan, scat, span, tack, term, time,
turn **05** augur, charm, imply, magic,
patch, shift, skatt, spurt, stint, trick,
weird **06** allure, course, extent, grigri,
herald, lead to, lesson, period, season,
signal, snatch, trance, whammy
**07** cantrip, enchant, glamour, innings,
portend, presage, promise, relieve,
session, signify, sorcery, stretch,
suggest **08** amount to, greegree,
grisgris, indicate, interval, splinter,
witchery **09** discourse, influence,
magnetism **10** attraction, Indian sign,
open sesame **11** abracadabra,
bewitchment, conjuration,
contemplate, enchantment,
fascination, incantation, paternoster
**12** drawing power, entrancement,
supplication
• **cast a spell on** **05** charm **07** attract,
bewitch, enchant, encharm, enthral
**09** captivate, fascinate, mesmerize
• **spell out** **06** detail **07** clarify,
explain, specify **09** elucidate,
emphasize, make clear, stipulate

## spellbinding

**08** gripping, riveting **10** bewitching,
enchanting, entrancing **11** captivating,
enthralling, fascinating, mesmerizing

## spellbound

**04** rapt **07** charmed, gripped, riveted
**09** bewitched, enchanted, entranced
**10** captivated, enraptured, enthralled,
fascinated, hypnotized, mesmerized,
transfixed **11** transported

## spelling

**02** sp **11** orthography

## spend

**02** do **03** use **04** blow, fill, kill, live,
pass, shed, ware **05** apply, put in, use
up, waste **06** devote, employ, expend,
finish, invest, lay out, occupy, pay out,
take up **07** consume, cough up,
exhaust, fork out, fritter, outwear,
stump up **08** contrive, disburse, shell
out, squander **09** splash out, while
away **14** spend like water

## spendthrift

**06** waster **07** wastrel **08** prodigal,
profuser, unthrift, wasteful **10** high-
roller, profligate, squanderer
**11** extravagant, improvident,
scattergood, squandering

## spent

**04** gone, used **05** all in, weary
**06** bushed, done in, effete, fagged,
pooped, used up, zonked **07** drained,
wearied, whacked, worn out **08** burnt
out, consumed, dead beat, dog-tired,
expended, finished, jiggered,
overworn, tired out, weakened
**09** exhausted, fagged out, knackered,
pooped out, shattered **11** debilitated,
tuckered out

## sperm

**04** eggs **05** brood, semen, spawn
**06** gamete **07** sex cell **08** germ cell
**09** offspring **10** spermaceti
**11** spermatozoa **12** seminal fluid,
spermatozoon

## spew

**04** barf, emit, gush, puke **05** belch,
issue, retch, spurt, vomit **06** sick up
**07** bring up, chuck up, chunder, fetch
up, spit out, throw up **08** disgorge
**11** regurgitate

## sphere

**03** orb, set **04** area, ball, band, rank
**05** class, crowd, field, globe, group,
orbit, range, realm, round, scope,
world **06** circle, clique, domain,
extent, planet **07** compass, globule
**08** capacity, function, province,
universe **09** territory **10** department,
discipline, speciality

## spherical

**05** round **06** global, rotund **07** globate,
globoid, globose **08** globular
**09** orbicular **10** ball-shaped **11** globe-
shaped

## spice

**03** pep, zap, zip **04** kick, life, mull, stir,
tang, vary, zest **05** gusto, hot up, liven,
pep up, rouse, touch **06** buck up,
colour, jazz up, perk up, relish,
savour, stacte, stir up **07** animate,
enliven, liven up **08** brighten,
energize, ginger up, piquancy,
tincture, vitalize **09** diversify,
seasoning **10** excitement, flavouring,
invigorate, sweetmeats **11** put life into
*See also* **herb**

## spick and span

**04** neat, tidy, trim **05** clean **06** spruce
**08** polished, scrubbed, spotless, well-

**spicy**

kept **09** shipshape **10** immaculate **11** uncluttered

**spicy**
**03** hot **04** blue, racy, tart **05** adult, juicy, sharp, showy, tangy **06** ribald, risqué **07** peppery, picante, piquant, pointed, pungent, raunchy **08** aromatic, fragrant, improper, indecent, seasoned, unseemly **09** flavoured **10** indecorous, indelicate, scandalous, suggestive **11** flavoursome, near the bone, sensational **12** well-seasoned **14** near the knuckle

**spider**
**07** beastie, spinner

*Spiders and arachnids include:*
**03** red
**04** bird, mite, tick, wolf
**05** bolas, money, water, zebra
**06** diadem, epeira, katipo, mygale, violin
**07** araneid, harvest, hunting, jumping, limulus, redback
**08** huntsman, scorpion, trapdoor
**09** funnel-web, harvester, phalangid, tarantula
**10** black widow, cheesemite, harvestman, saltigrade
**11** harvest mite, harvest tick
**12** book-scorpion, whip scorpion
**13** horseshoe crab

**spiel**
**04** line **05** pitch **06** patter, speech **07** oration, recital **11** sales patter

**spies**
*see* **spy**

**spignel**
**03** meu **09** baldmoney

**spike**
**03** add, ear, gad, nib **04** barb, brod, cloy, drug, lace, nail, spit, tang, tine **05** beard, chape, mix in, point, prick, prong, rowel, spear, spick, spine, spire, stake, stick **06** catkin, impale, reject, skewer, spadix **07** bayonet, pricket **09** dosshouse, frustrate, strobilus **10** filopodium, projection **11** contaminate **13** Anglo-Catholic

**spill**
**03** ren, rin, run, tip **04** drip, fall, flow, kill, leak, pour, shed, slop, well **05** scail, scale, skail, spile, taper, throw, upset, waste **06** escape, oozing, run out, tumble **07** cropper, destroy, fidibus, leakage, leaking, run over, scatter, seepage, seeping, slatter, swatter **08** accident, disgorge, overflow, overturn, spillage, spilling **09** discharge, pipe-light **11** lamplighter, percolation, pipe-lighter **13** candle-lighter
• **spill the beans** **03** rat **04** blab, tell **05** grass, split **06** inform, squeal, tell on **07** tell all **11** blow the gaff **15** give the game away

**spin**
◊ *anagram indicator* **03** cut, run **04** flap, play, reel, ride, tell, tizz, trip, turn **05** drive, jaunt, panic, spirt, state, swirl, tizzy, twirl, twist, wheel, whirl, whirr **06** circle, dither, gyrate, hurtle, invent, make up, outing, relate, rotate, swivel **07** draw out, dream up, fluster, go round, journey, narrate, revolve, twizzle **08** gyration, rotation **09** agitation, commotion, fabricate, pirouette, turn about, turn round **10** revolution
• **spin doctor** **03** pro **07** spinner
• **spin out** **06** extend, pad out **07** amplify, prolong **08** lengthen, protract, wiredraw **09** keep going
• **spin round** **04** gyre, purl

**spindle**
**03** pin, rod **04** axis, axle, spit **05** arbor, fusee, fuzee, pivot, staff, verge

**spindly**
**04** long, thin **05** lanky, weedy **06** gangly, skinny **07** spidery **08** fusiform, gangling, skeletal **09** attenuate **10** attenuated **14** spindle-shanked

**spine**
**04** barb, grit, guts **05** chine, pluck, quill, spike, spunk, thorn **06** bottle, dorsum, mettle, needle, rachis, spirit **07** bravery, bristle, courage, prickle, rhachis, spinule **08** backbone, spiculum, strength **09** fortitude, Jew's-stone, ridge bone, vertebrae **10** resolution **12** spinal column **13** determination **15** ichthyodorulite, ichthyodorylite, vertebral column

**spine-chilling**
**05** eerie, scary **06** spooky **10** horrifying, terrifying **11** frightening, hair-raising **13** bloodcurdling

**spineless**
**03** wet **04** soft, weak **05** cissy, milky, timid, wussy **06** feeble, yellow **07** chicken, wimpish **08** boneless, cowardly, muticous, timorous **09** weak-kneed **10** indecisive, irresolute, spiritless, submissive **11** ineffective, lily-livered, vacillating **12** faint-hearted, invertebrate

**spin-off**
**06** effect, result **10** side effect **11** consequence **12** repercussion **13** reverberation

**spinster**
**07** old maid **12** bachelorette

**spiny**
**05** spiky **06** briery, thorny **07** prickly, spinose, spinous, thistly **08** spicular **09** acanthoid, acanthous, perplexed, spiculate **11** spiniferous, spinigerous, troublesome **12** acanthaceous

**spiral**
**04** coil, dive, go up, gyre, rise, soar, wind **05** climb, helix, screw, spire, twist, whorl **06** circle, coiled, gyrate, plunge, rocket, volute, wreath **07** cochlea, helical, plummet, voluted, whorled, winding, wreathe **08** circular, cochlear, curlicue, dive-bomb, escalate, gyroidal, increase, nosedive, scrolled, tailspin, twisting, volution **09** cochleate, corkscrew, skyrocket **10** cochleated **11** convolution, drop rapidly, fall rapidly **15** decrease quickly

**spire**
**03** tip, top **04** coil, cone, peak, reed **05** crest, crown, point, shoot, spear, spike, spyre, stalk, tower **06** belfry, broach, flèche, spiral, sprout, summit, turret **07** shoot up, steeple **08** pinnacle

**spirit**
**02** ka **03** air, div, fay, imp, nix, pep, zip **04** atua, brio, deev, deva, fire, gist, grit, guts, jinn, kick, life, mind, mood, nixy, soul, zeal, zest **05** angel, anima, cheer, demon, devil, drift, fairy, fiend, force, genie, ghost, jinni, monad, nixie, pluck, sense, shade, spook, spunk, tenor, verve **06** ardour, bottle, breath, djinni, energy, humour, jinnee, kidnap, make-up, mettle, morale, psyche, shadow, sprite, temper, vigour, wraith **07** bravery, courage, essence, feeling, meaning, mindset, outlook, phantom, pizzazz, purport, quality, sparkle, spectre **08** attitude, backbone, feelings, presence, revenant, tendency, visitant, vivacity **09** animation, breathing, character, élan vital, elemental, encourage, inner self, kidnapper, principle, substance, willpower **10** apparition, atmosphere, complexion, enterprise, enthusiasm, inner being, liveliness, motivation, resolution, vital force **11** disposition, frame of mind, implication, state of mind, temperament **13** dauntlessness, determination **14** characteristic
*See also* **mythical**
• **spirit away** **05** carry, seize, steal, whisk **06** abduct, convey, kidnap, remove **07** capture, purloin, snaffle **08** abstract

**spirited**
**04** bold, gamy, racy **05** fiery, gamey, gutty **06** active, ardent, feisty, gallus, lively, plucky, spunky **07** dashing, gallows, valiant, zealous **08** animated, resolute, spanking, stomachy, valorous, vigorous **09** confident, energetic, sparkling, vivacious **10** courageous, determined, mettlesome, passionate, sprightful, stomachful, stomachous **12** high-spirited

**spiritless**
**03** low **04** cold, dead, dowf, dull, poor, tame, weak **05** amort, soggy **06** craven, droopy, jejune, mopish, torpid **07** anaemic, hilding, languid, unmoved **08** dejected, enervate, lifeless, listless **09** apathetic, bloodless, depressed, exanimate, inanimate **10** despondent, dispirited, lacklustre, melancholy, wishy-washy **11** sprightless **12** faint-hearted, muddy-mettled **14** unenthusiastic

**spirit-level**
**04** vial

**spirits**
**04** ginn, jinn, mood **05** djinn, hooch **06** humour, liquor, temper **07** alcohol **08** attitude, emotions, feelings **09** firewater, moonshine **11** strong

drink, temperament **12** strong liquor, the hard stuff

*Spirits include:*

**03** gin, kir, rum, rye
**04** feni, grog, ouzo, raki, sake
**05** fenny, Pimm's®, pisco, vodka
**06** brandy, cognac, eggnog, geneva, grappa, kirsch, mescal, mezcal, pastis, Pernod®, poteen, Scotch, whisky
**07** aquavit, Bacardi®, bitters, bourbon, Campari, dark rum, genever, pink gin, sloe gin, tequila, whiskey
**08** Armagnac, Calvados, eau de vie, Hollands, hot toddy, sambucca, schnapps, vermouth, white rum, witblits
**09** apple-jack, aqua vitae, framboise, golden rum, mirabelle, slivovitz, spiced rum
**10** malt whisky, usquebaugh
**11** gold tequila, Hollands gin, peach brandy
**12** añejo tequila
**13** peach schnapps, silver tequila
**15** reposado tequila

*See also* **cocktail; liqueur**

**spiritual**
**04** aery, holy **05** aerie, witty **06** clever, divine, sacred **07** psychic **08** ethereal, heavenly **09** pneumatic, psychical, religious, unfleshly, unworldly **10** devotional, immaterial, intangible **11** incorporeal **12** metaphysical, otherworldly, supernatural, transcendent **14** ecclesiastical

**spit**
**03** dig, gob, yex **04** fuff, hawk, hiss, hook, jack, rasp, slag, spet, yesk **05** drool, eject, issue, spade, spawl, spawn, spume, sword **06** bespit, broach, phlegm, saliva, skewer, slaver, sputum **07** dribble, replica, spittle, sputter **08** broacher, emptysis, spadeful, splutter, turnspit **09** brochette, discharge, smoke-jack **10** rotisserie **11** expectorate **13** expectoration
• **spitting image 04** twin **05** clone **06** double, ringer **07** picture, replica **08** dead spit, likeness **09** lookalike **10** dead ringer **13** exact likeness

**spite**
**03** irk, vex **04** evil, gall, hate, hurt **05** annoy, upset, venom, wound **06** grudge, hatred, injure, malice, maugre, offend, put out, rancor, spight, thwart **07** ill-will, maulgre, provoke, rancour **08** irritate **09** animosity, hostility, ill nature, malignity, vengeance **10** bitterness, ill-feeling, resentment **11** malevolence **12** hard feelings, spitefulness **13** maliciousness **14** vindictiveness
• **in spite of 03** for **04** with **06** malgré, maugre **07** against, defying, despite, maulgre **08** after all, malgrado **11** in the face of **12** nevertheless, regardless of, undeterred by **13** be that as it may **15** notwithstanding

**spiteful**
**05** catty, cruel, nasty, petty, snide **06** barbed, bitchy, bitter, shrewd, wicked **07** cattish, hostile, vicious, waspish **08** vengeful, venomous, viperish **09** cat-witted, malicious, malignant, rancorous, resentful, splenetic **10** ill-natured, malevolent, vindictive **11** ill-disposed **12** evil-tempered

**spitefully**
**07** cruelly **08** bitchily, bitterly **10** venomously **11** maliciously, resentfully **12** malevolently, vindictively

**spitting image**
*see* **spit**

**splash**
◇ *anagram indicator* **03** jap, lap, wet **04** beat, dash, daub, jaup, plop, show, slop, soss, spat, spot, stir, wade, wash **05** bathe, blash, blaze, break, burst, patch, plash, slosh, slush, smack, spray, stain, surge, swash, touch **06** batter, bedash, blazon, buffet, dabble, effect, flaunt, flouse, floush, impact, jabble, paddle, plunge, shower, sozzle, splish, splosh, spread, squirt, streak, strike, wallow **07** beating, display, exhibit, plaster, scatter, slatter, spatter, splatch, splodge, splotch, splurge, swatter, trumpet **08** splatter, sprinkle, squatter **09** publicity, publicize, sensation **10** excitement, impression **11** ostentation
• **splash out 05** spend **07** lash out, splurge **08** invest in **13** be extravagant **14** push the boat out

**spleen**
**03** pip **04** bile, gall, lien, melt, milt **05** anger, miltz, mirth, pique, spite, venom, wrath **06** animus, hatred, malice **07** boredom, caprice, ill-will, impulse, rancour, stomach **08** acrimony **09** animosity, bad temper, hostility, ill-humour, malignity **10** bitterness, melancholy, resentment **11** biliousness, malevolence, peevishness **12** spitefulness **14** vindictiveness

**splendid**
**04** braw, fine, rich **05** bonny, grand, great, jolly, super **06** bonnie, bright, divine, lavish, superb **07** gallant, glowing, opulent, radiant, stately, sublime, supreme **08** dazzling, fabulous, glorious, gorgeous, imposing, lustrous, pontific, renowned, terrific **09** admirable, brilliant, effulgent, excellent, luxurious, refulgent, sumptuous, wonderful **10** celebrated, first-class, glittering, impressive, marvellous, pontifical, remarkable **11** exceptional, illustrious, magnificent, outstanding, resplendent **13** distinguished

**splendidly**
**07** grandly **08** superbly **09** admirably **10** remarkably **11** brilliantly, wonderfully **12** impressively,

marvellously **13** exceptionally, magnificently, outstandingly

**splendour**
**04** glow, pomp, show **05** éclat, gleam, glory, pride **06** dazzle, finery, fulgor, luster, lustre, luxury **07** display, fulgour, majesty, panache **08** ceremony, flourish, grandeur, opulence, radiance, richness **09** solemnity, spectacle **10** brightness, brilliance **12** magnificence, resplendence **13** sumptuousness **15** illustriousness

**splenetic**
**04** acid, sour **05** angry, cross, ratty, testy **06** bitchy, crabby, morose, sullen, touchy **07** bilious, crabbed, fretful, peevish **08** choleric, churlish, petulant, spiteful **09** envenomed, irascible, irritable, irritated, rancorous **10** melancholy **11** atrabilious, bad-tempered

**splice**
◇ *anagram indicator* **03** tie **04** bind, join, knit, mesh **05** braid, graft, marry, plait, unite **06** fasten **07** connect, entwine **09** interlace **10** intertwine, interweave
• **get spliced 03** wed **10** get hitched, get married, tie the knot **13** take the plunge **15** plight your troth

**splinter**
**03** bit **04** chip, flaw **05** break, flake, piece, shard, shred, skelf, smash, spale, spall, spalt, speel, spelk, spell, split **06** cleave, paring, shiver, sliver, splint **07** crumble, flinder, shatter, shaving, spicula, spicule **08** flinders, fracture, fragment **11** smithereens **12** disintegrate **15** break into pieces

**split**
◇ *insertion indicator* **03** cut, gap, rat, rip **04** chop, dual, open, part, rend, rent, rift, rive, shop, slit, tear **05** allot, break, burst, cleft, crack, grass, halve, leave, peach, sever, shake, share, slash, spall, spalt, wreck **06** betray, bisect, breach, broken, cleave, cloven, divide, rumble, schism, shiver, sliver, spring, sprung, squeal, stitch, tell on **07** break up, break-up, carve up, cracked, crevice, disband, discord, disrupt, divided, divorce, divulge, dole out, fissure, hand out, rupture, spalted, stool on, twofold **08** allocate, bisected, cleavage, crevasse, disunion, disunite, division, inform on, ruptured, separate, set apart, share-out, splinter **09** apportion, fractured, parcel out, partition **10** alienation, difference, dissension, distribute, divergence, separation **11** incriminate, part company **12** estrangement **14** dissociate from **15** become alienated, become estranged
• **split up 04** part **06** divide **07** break up, disband, divorce **08** separate **11** get divorced, part company

**split-up**
**07** break-up, divorce, parting **10** alienation, separation **12** estrangement

## spoil

◊ *anagram indicator* **03** end, gum, mar, mux, pie, ret, rot **04** baby, cook, foul, game, harm, hurt, kill, rait, rate, ruin, sour, turn **05** bitch, blunk, bodge, booty, botch, bribe, decay, go bad, go off, gum up, louse, queer, strip, taint, upset, wreck, wrong **06** boodle, coddle, cosset, curdle, damage, deface, deform, foul up, go sour, impair, injure, mangle, mess up, murder, pamper, poison, prizes, quarry, wash up **07** bauchle, bitch up, blemish, butcher, corrupt, deprive, despoil, destroy, distort, indulge, louse up, pillage, plunder, pollute, screw up, tarnish, viciate, vitiate **08** distaste, go rotten, mutilate **09** decompose, disfigure, spoon-feed, vulgarize **10** impairment, obliterate, spoliation **11** contaminate, deteriorate, mollycoddle, overindulge, prejudicate **12** acquisitions, become rotten, put a damper on **15** cast a shadow over, pour cold water on
• **spoil for 07** long for **08** be keen on, yearn for **10** be eager for, be intent on

## spoils

**04** gain, haul, loot, swag **05** booty, bribe **06** boodle, damage, prizes, profit, trophy **07** benefit, pillage, plunder, spulzie, the game **08** pickings, winnings **10** impairment, spoliation **11** spolia opima **12** acquisitions, despoliation

## spoilsport

**04** nark **06** damper, misery, wowser **07** killjoy, meddler **08** buzzkill **10** wet blanket **11** party-pooper **14** dog in the manger

## spoke

**04** rung **06** radius

## spoken

◊ *homophone indicator* **03** sed **04** oral, said, told **06** stated, verbal, voiced **07** uttered **08** declared, phonetic, viva voce **09** expressed, unwritten

## spokesman, spokeswoman

**05** agent, mouth, voice **06** broker, orator **07** foreman **08** delegate, mediator **09** forewoman, go-between **10** arbitrator, foreperson, mouthpiece, negotiator, prolocutor **12** intermediary, propagandist, spokesperson **14** representative

## sponge

**03** beg, bum, mop **04** mump, swab, wash, wipe **05** cadge, clean, mooch, mouch, shool, shule **06** bludge, borrow, loofah, shoole, spunge, sucker **07** monaxon, zimocca **08** bedeguar, drunkard, freeload, hanger-on, parasite, quandang, quandong, quantong, scrounge, victoria **09** glass-rope, hyalonema, sea orange **13** mermaid's glove, sulphur sponge
*See also* **drunkard**
• **sponge cake 06** coburg, trifle **09** lamington, madeleine, Swiss roll **11** lady's finger **12** lady's fingers **14** charlotte russe
• **sponge spicule 06** hexact, sclere,

tylote **07** monaxon, pentact, rhabdus, tetract, triaxon **08** polyaxon, tetraxon, triaxial **09** polyaxial, spiraster

## sponger

**03** bum **06** beggar, bummer, cadger **07** bludger, moocher **08** borrower, hanger-on, parasite, scambler **09** scrounger **10** freeloader, smell-feast

## spongy

◊ *anagram indicator* **04** fozy, soft **05** light **06** poachy, porous **07** drunken, elastic, fungous, springy, squashy **08** cushiony, yielding **09** absorbent, cushioned, resilient **10** absorptive, cancellate, cancellous **11** cancelled

## sponsor

**04** back, fund **05** angel, vouch **06** backer, friend, gossip, patron, surety **07** finance, promise, promote, support **08** bankroll, promoter, stand for **09** godfather, godmother, guarantee, guarantor, patronize, subsidize, supporter, susceptor **10** subsidizer, undertaker, underwrite **11** be a patron of, underwriter

## sponsorship

**03** aid **05** funds, grant **07** backing, finance, subsidy, support **09** patronage, promotion **10** assistance **11** endorsement **12** financial aid

## spontaneity

**07** impulse **08** instinct **11** naturalness **13** improvisation **15** extemporization, instinctiveness

## spontaneous

**04** free **06** reflex **07** natural, willing **08** free-will, knee-jerk, unbidden, unforced, untaught **09** automatic, autonomic, extempore, impromptu, impulsive, unplanned, unstudied, voluntary **10** ultroneous, unprompted **11** instinctive, uncompelled, unrehearsed **12** unhesitating **14** unpremeditated **15** spur of the moment

## spontaneously

**05** ad-lib **06** freely **09** extempore, impromptu, on impulse, unplanned, willingly **10** off the cuff, unprompted **11** impulsively, voluntarily **13** instinctively **15** of your own accord

## spoof

**03** con **04** fake, game, hoax, joke **05** bluff, prank, trick **06** parody, satire, send-up **07** lampoon, leg-pull, mockery, take-off **08** travesty **09** burlesque, deception **10** caricature

## spooky

**05** eerie, scary, weird **06** creepy **07** ghostly, macabre, uncanny **08** chilling **09** unearthly **10** mysterious **11** frightening, hair-raising **12** supernatural **13** spine-chilling

## spool

**04** pirn, reel **06** bobbin **07** trundle

## spoon

**05** court, labis, ladle, scoop **07** spatula **08** cochlear **09** cochleare, courtship, simpleton

## spoon-feed

**04** baby **05** spoil **06** cosset, pamper **07** indulge **10** featherbed **11** mollycoddle, overindulge

## sporadic

**06** random, uneven **07** erratic **08** episodic, isolated **09** irregular, scattered, spasmodic **10** episodical, infrequent, now and then, occasional **11** now and again **12** intermittent

## sporadically

**08** off and on, on and off **10** now and then **11** now and again **12** occasionally, periodically **13** spasmodically **14** intermittently

## sport

◊ *anagram indicator* **03** fun, gig **04** game, jest, joke, laik, lake, play, wear **05** amuse, mirth, wager **06** banter, frolic, humour, joking, trifle **07** display, exhibit, jesting, kidding, mockery, pastime, show off, teasing **08** activity, exercise, pleasure, ridicule, sneering, squander **09** amusement, dalliance, diversion, plaything **10** recreation **13** entertainment
*See also* **American football; athletics; Australian football; baseball; boxing; competition; cricket; football; golf; gymnastics; ice hockey; race; rugby; stadium; tennis**

*Sports include:*

**04** golf, judo, polo, pool
**05** bowls, darts, fives, rugby
**06** boules, boxing, discus, diving, futsal, hockey, karate, kung fu, luging, Nascar®, pelota, quoits, rowing, shinty, skiing, slalom, soccer, squash, tennis
**07** angling, aquafit, archery, camogie, cricket, croquet, curling, fencing, fishing, gliding, hunting, hurling, jogging, jujitsu, keep-fit, netball, Parkour, putting, running, sailing, shot put, snooker, surfing, walking
**08** aerobics, baseball, biathlon, canoeing, climbing, football, handball, high-jump, hurdling, lacrosse, long-jump, pétanque, ping-pong, ringette, rounders, shooting, swimming, trotting, yachting
**09** athletics, badminton, billiards, bobsleigh, decathlon, go-karting, ice-hockey, pole vault, pot-holing, sky-diving, tae kwon do, triathlon, water polo, wrestling
**10** basketball, drag-racing, gymnastics, ice-skating, motorsport, pentathlon, real tennis, skin-diving, triple-jump, volleyball
**11** cycle racing, free running, horse-racing, kitesurfing, motor racing, show-jumping, table-tennis, tobogganing, water-skiing, windsurfing
**12** aqua aerobics, cross-country, kiteboarding, landboarding, orienteering, pitch and putt, rock-

climbing, snowboarding, speed skating, trampolining
**13** bungee jumping, coarse fishing, Nordic walking, roller-skating, tenpin bowling, weightlifting
**14** downhill skiing, Gaelic football, mountaineering, speedway racing, stock-car racing
**15** greyhound-racing

*Sports equipment includes:*

**03** bow, cue, fly, jig, mat, net, oar, ski, tee
**04** bail, bait, beam, bolt, bowl, épée, foil, gaff, hook, jack, lure, mask, mitt, nets, pins, puck, rack, reel, rest, rope, shot, wood
**05** arrow, boule, brush, caman, chalk, float, rings, sabre, stump, table, trace
**06** bridge, discus, fly rod, hammer, hurley, priest, spider, wicket
**07** cue ball, fly reel, javelin, keep-net, netball, snorkel
**08** aqualung, baseball, crossbow, football, gang-hook, golf ball, golf club, ice-skate, punch-bag, ski stick, toboggan, water-ski
**09** disgorger, face-guard, grind rail, gum shield, kiteboard, longboard, punch-ball, rugby ball, sailboard, snow board, surfboard
**10** basketball, cricket bat, fishing-rod, hockey ball, roller boot, skateboard, speed skate, tennis ball, trampoline, volleyball
**11** balance beam, baseball bat, bowling ball, boxing glove, cricket ball, fishing-line, hockey skate, hockey stick, in-line skate, paternoster, pommel horse, racket press, rollerblade, roller-skate, shuttlecock, snooker ball, spinning rod, springboard
**12** billiard ball, curling stone, golfing glove, grinding rail, isometric bar, parallel-bars, tennis racket
**13** catcher's glove, horizontal bar, mountainboard, vaulting horse
**14** ice-hockey stick
**15** badminton racket

*Sports positions include:*

**04** lock, slip, wing
**05** cover, gully, mid-on, point, rover
**06** batter, centre, goalie, hooker, libero, long on, mid-off, setter, winger
**07** batsman, catcher, fine leg, flanker, fly-half, fly slip, forward, leg slip, long leg, long off, number 8, pitcher, ruckman, sweeper, torpedo
**08** attacker, backstop, defender, fullback, halfback, left back, left wing, long stop, short leg, split end, third man, tight end, wing back
**09** deep cover, deep point, first base, first slip, left field, left guard, leg gulley, mid-wicket, right back, right wing, ruck rover, scrum-half, short stop, square leg, third base, third slip

**10** back pocket, cover point, defenceman, extra cover, goal attack, goalkeeper, goaltender, inside left, left tackle, midfielder, point guard, right field, right guard, second base, second slip, silly mid-on, silly point, wing attack
**11** centre field, deep fine leg, full-forward, goal defence, goal shooter, inside right, left forward, prop forward, quarterback, right tackle, silly mid-off, wing defence
**12** left half-back, power forward, right forward, short fine leg, small forward, stand-off half, wicketkeeper
**13** backward point, centre-forward, deep mid-wicket, deep square leg, forward pocket, half-back flank, loosehead prop, right half-back, shooting guard, tighthead prop
**14** centre half-back, deep extra cover, left corner-back, short mid-wicket
**15** left half-forward, right corner-back, short extra cover

## sporting

◇ *anagram indicator* **04** fair, just
**06** decent, modest **08** ladylike
**10** honourable, reasonable
**11** considerate, gentlemanly, respectable **13** sportsmanlike

## sportive

**03** gay **05** ludic, merry **06** frisky, jaunty, lively, wanton **07** amorous, coltish, playful, toysome **08** gamesome, prankish, skittish **09** kittenish, ludicrous, sprightly, vivacious
**10** frolicsome, rollicking

## sportsperson

**04** blue, jock

*Sportspeople include:*

**04** **Bird** (Larry), **Dean** (Christopher), **Khan** (Jahangir), **Lowe** (John), **Nudd** (Bob), **Witt** (Katerina)
**05** **Curry** (John), **Davis** (Fred), **Davis** (Joe), **Davis** (Steve), **Ender** (Kornelia), **Kelly** (Sean), **O'Neal** (Shaquille), **Spitz** (Mark), **White** (Jimmy)
**06** **Briggs** (Karen), **Bryant** (David), **Davies** (Sharron), **Fraser** (Dawn), **Hendry** (Stephen), **Jordan** (Michael), **LeMond** (Greg), **Malone** (Karl), **Merckx** (Eddy), **Pulman** (John), **Wilkie** (David), **Wilson** (Jocky)
**07** **Allcock** (Tony), **Bristow** (Eric), **Cousins** (Robin), **Gretzky** (Wayne), **Harding** (Tonya), **Higgins** (Alex 'Hurricane'), **Hinault** (Bernard), **Johnson** (Earvin 'Magic'), **O'Reilly** (Wilfred), **Reardon** (Ray), **Rodnina** (Irina), **Torvill** (Jayne), **Zaitsev** (Aleksandr)
**08** **Boardman** (Chris), **Indurain** (Miguel), **Kerrigan** (Nancy), **Redgrave** (Sir Steve), **Williams** (Rex)
**09** **Cipollini** (Mario), **Hazelwood** (Mike)

**10** **Barrington** (Jonah)
**11** **Abdul-Jabbar** (Kareem), **Chamberlain** (Wilt 'the Stilt'), **Weissmuller** (Johnny)

*See also* **athlete; Australian football; baseball; boxer; chess; cricket; footballer; golfer; gymnastics; horseman, horsewoman; mountaineering; rugby; skier; tennis**

## sporty

**03** fit **04** loud **05** natty, showy
**06** casual, flashy, jaunty, lively, snazzy, trendy **07** outdoor, stylish
**08** athletic, informal **09** energetic

## spot

**03** bit, dot, eye, fix, jam, pin, pip, see, zit **04** area, bite, blob, blot, blur, boil, daub, drop, espy, flaw, fret, give, hole, lend, mail, mark, meal, mess, moil, mold, mole, peep, plot, pock, show, site, slot, smut, soil, some, sore, time, turn **05** cloud, fleck, freak, hilum, naeve, nerve, nevus, niche, patch, peepe, place, plook, plouk, point, pupil, scene, speck, stain, sully, swale, taint **06** blotch, descry, detect, garden, little, locale, locate, macula, morsel, naevus, notice, papula, papule, pickle, pimple, plight, recess, scrape, smudge, splash, stigma **07** airtime, blemish, discern, flecker, freckle, lentigo, make out, observe, ocellus, opening, pick out, pustule, setting, spangle, speckle, splodge, splotch, tarnish, trouble
**08** fenestra, identify, locality, location, maculate, position, quandary
**09** birthmark, blackhead, freckling, programme, recognize, reprehend, situation **10** cicatricle, death-token, difficulty, maculation **11** cicatricula, performance, predicament, small amount **12** catch sight of, cicatrichule **13** discoloration
• **on the spot** **02** in **04** down, next **05** alert **06** at once, pronto **07** quickly **08** directly, in a jiffy, promptly, right now, speedily, sur place **09** forthwith, instantly, like a shot, right away **10** this minute **11** immediately, this instant
**12** straight away, there and then, without delay **13** straightforth, with a siserary **14** unhesitatingly, without more ado **15** before you know it, instantaneously, without question
• **spot-on** **04** true **05** close, exact, right
**06** bang on, dead-on, strict **07** correct, factual, precise **08** accurate, definite, detailed, explicit, flawless, specific, unerring **09** excellent, faultless, on the nail **10** on the money **11** on the button

## spotless

**04** pure **05** clean, white **06** chaste, virgin **07** shining **08** gleaming, innocent, unmarked, virginal
**09** blameless, faultless, snow-white, unstained, unsullied, untainted, untouched **10** immaculate
**11** unblemished **12** spick and span, squeaky clean **14** irreproachable

## spotlight

**04** baby, fame, spot **05** brute **06** stress

**07** feature, focus on, point up **08** emphasis, interest **09** attention, emphasize, highlight, limelight, notoriety, public eye, underline **10** accentuate, foreground, illuminate **15** draw attention to, public attention, throw into relief

**spotted**
**03** gay **04** pied **06** dotted, macled, parded, spotty **07** brindle, dappled, flecked, guttate, macular, mottled, piebald **08** brindled, freckled, guttated, maculose, polka-dot, speckled

**spotty**
**04** pied, poxy **05** acned, bitty **06** dotted, measly, patchy, pimply, uneven **07** blotchy, dappled, erratic, flecked, mottled, piebald, pimpled, spotted, varying **08** speckled **12** inconsistent

**spouse**
**04** feer, fere, mate, wife **05** feare, fiere, hubby **06** missus, pheere **07** consort, husband, partner **09** companion, other half **10** better half

**spout**
**03** jet **04** blow, emit, flow, go on, gush, pawn, pour, rant, rose, spew **05** chute, erupt, mouth, orate, shoot, spiel, spray, spurt, surge **06** geyser, nozzle, outlet, squirt, stream, stroup, waffle, witter **07** bespout, declaim **08** disgorge, fountain, gargoyle, pawnshop, rabbit on, spout off, witter on **09** discharge, expatiate, hold forth, sermonize **10** spout forth, waterspout **11** pontificate

**sprain**
**03** hip **04** pull, rick, turn **05** crick, stave, twist, wrest, wrick **06** injure, wrench **09** dislocate **12** shoulder slip

**sprat**
**04** brit, Jack **06** garvie **07** garvock **08** brisling

**sprawl**
**04** flop, loll **05** slump, trail **06** lounge, ramble, repose, slouch, spread **07** recline, scamble, stretch **08** sprangle, straggle

**spray**
◇ *anagram indicator* **03** jet, wet **04** Alar®, foam, gush, Mace®, mist, posy, scud, twig **05** froth, shoot, spout, sprig, spume, swish **06** branch, drench, mister, shower, spritz, squirt, wreath **07** aerosol, bouquet, corsage, diffuse, drizzle, garland, nosegay, scatter, spatter, sprayer **08** aigrette, atomizer, disperse, moisture, mothball, nebulize, spray gun, sprinkle, vaporize **09** aspersion, nebulizer, spindrift, sprinkler, squirt gun, vaporizer **10** golden rose, propellant, spoondrift, waterspout **11** disseminate **13** water-sprinkle

**spread**
◇ *anagram indicator* **03** air, lay, ren, rin, run, set, sow, ted **04** coat, grow, laid, open, span, teer, walk **05** apply, cover, feast, flare, layer, order, party, put on, ranch, reach, scale, smear, spray, strew, sweep, swell, treat, widen

**06** dilate, dinner, effuse, expand, extend, extent, fan out, lay out, mantle, repast, slairg, smooth, sprawl, unfold, unfurl, unroll **07** advance, arrange, banquet, blow-out, broaden, compass, develop, diffuse, enlarge, expanse, go round, open out, overlay, publish, radiate, scatter, stretch **08** disperse, escalate, extended, get round, increase, mushroom, swelling, transmit **09** advertise, broadcast, circulate, diffusion, displayed, expansion, large meal, make known, percolate, propagate, publicize, spill over **10** dispersion, distribute, escalation, gain ground, grow bigger, make public, promulgate **11** communicate, development, dinner party, disseminate, mushrooming, proliferate, propagation **12** become bigger, broadcasting, distribution, transmission **13** communication, dissemination, proliferation

*Spreads include:*

**03** jam
**04** marg, oleo, pâté
**05** honey, marge
**06** butter
**07** Marmite®, Nutella®
**08** dripping, Vegemite®
**09** butterine, lemon curd, margarine, marmalade
**11** lemon cheese
**12** peanut butter
**13** oleomargarine

**spree**
**03** bat, bum, jag **04** bout, bust, orgy, tear **05** binge, blind, fling, revel, skite, skyte **06** bender, junket, randan, razzle, splore **07** blinder, carouse, debauch, splurge **08** jamboree **12** razzle-dazzle

**sprig**
**04** brad, stem, twig **05** bough, scion, shoot, spray **06** branch

**sprightly**
**04** airy, spry **05** agile, brisk, perky **06** active, blithe, gallus, hearty, jaunty, lively, nimble, sprack **07** gallows, ghostly, playful **08** animated, cheerful, spirited **09** energetic, mercurial, vivacious **10** frolicsome, spirituous **12** light-hearted

**spring**
◇ *anagram indicator* **03** eye, gin, hop, lep, spa **04** bend, bolt, come, dawn, give, grow, hair, jump, leap, Lent, open, rise, root, skip, stem, stot, voar, ware, warp, well **05** arise, basis, bound, burst, cause, copse, crack, dance, issue, prime, shoot, spang, split, start, vault, youth **06** appear, bounce, derive, emerge, energy, geyser, origin, pounce, recoil, salina, source, spirit, sprout, strain **07** descend, develop, emanate, explode, proceed, rebound **08** balneary, brine-pan, brine-pit, buoyancy, wellhead **09** animation, beginning, briskness, originate **10** bounciness, elasticity, liveliness, resilience, wellspring **11** black smoker,

flexibility, springiness, undergrowth **12** cheerfulness, fountainhead **14** reveal suddenly
• **spring up 04** grow, rise **05** start **06** upblow **07** develop, shoot up **08** fountain, mushroom, sprout up **11** proliferate **13** come into being **14** appear suddenly

**springtime**
*see* **spring**

**springy**
**05** crisp, lofty **06** bouncy, spongy **07** buoyant, elastic, rubbery, squidgy, tensile **08** flexible, stretchy, tensible **09** resilient

**sprinkle**
◇ *anagram indicator* **03** dot, set **04** drop, dust, salt, sand, seed, sift **05** bedew, flake, flour, spang, spray, strew, sugar **06** dredge, pepper, pounce, powder, shower, sparge, splash **07** asperge, sawdust, scatter, spairge, spatter, trickle **08** beflower, disponge, dispunge, lavender, strinkle **09** bespatter, diversify **10** scowdering **11** aspersorium, scouthering

**sprinkling**
**03** few **04** dash **05** touch, trace **07** baptism, dusting, handful, scatter, sifting, trickle **08** sprinkle **09** admixture, aspersion **10** scattering, smattering

**sprint**
**03** fly, run, zip **04** belt, dart, dash, race, tear **05** scoot, shoot **06** career, scurry

**sprite**
**03** elf, imp, pug **04** bogy, puck **05** bogle, dryad, fairy, gnome, kelpy, naiad, nymph, pixie, pouke, sylph **06** goblin, kelpie, spirit **07** apsaras, brownie, spright **10** apparition, leprechaun **11** water spirit

**sprout**
**03** bud **04** chit, germ, grow **05** scion, shoot, spire, spirt **06** come up, spring **07** develop, tendron **08** put forth, spring up **09** germinate, pullulate, turnip top **10** descendant

**spruce**
**04** chic, cool, neat, smug, trim **05** brisk, natty, nifty, Picea, sleek, smart, smirk, spiff, Tsuga **06** dapper, snazzy, spiffy, sprush **07** band-box, elegant, finical, hemlock, smarten **11** well-dressed, well-groomed **13** well-turned-out
• **spruce up 04** tidy **05** groom, preen, primp **06** neaten, tart up, tidy up **08** titivate **09** smarten up

**spry**
**05** agile, alert, brisk, nippy, peppy, quick, ready **06** active, nimble, supple **09** energetic, sprightly

**spud**
*see* **potato**

**spume**
**04** fizz, foam, head, scum, spit, suds **05** froth, yeast **06** lather **07** bubbles **13** effervescence

**spunk**
**04** grit, guts **05** heart, match, nerve,

pluck, spark **06** bottle, fire up, mettle, spirit, tinder **07** courage **08** backbone, chutzpah, gameness **09** touchwood, toughness **10** resolution

## spur

**04** goad, heel, limb, poke, prod, stud, urge **05** drive, ergot, impel, prick, prong, rowel, spica, spike, strut **06** branch, calcar, fillip, hasten, incite, induce, motive, offset, prompt, propel, Rippon, siding, spurne **07** impetus **08** motivate, stimulus **09** encourage, incentive, star wheel, stimulant, stimulate **10** incitement, inducement, motivation, projection, protrusion **12** embranchment, protuberance **13** encouragement

• **on the spur of the moment**
**08** suddenly **09** extempore, impromptu, on impulse, on the spot **10** upon the gad **11** impetuously, impulsively **12** unexpectedly **13** spontaneously, thoughtlessly **15** without planning

## spurious

◇ *anagram indicator* **03** bad, dog **04** fake, mock, sham **05** bogus, cronk, false **06** forged, phoney, pseudo **07** feigned **08** pseudish **09** contrived, deceitful, imitation, pretended, simulated, trumped-up **10** adulterate, adulterine, apocryphal, artificial, fraudulent **11** counterfeit, make-believe **12** illegitimate **14** supposititious

## spurn

**04** kick, snub, trip **05** scorn, tread **06** ignore, rebuff, reject, slight **07** condemn, despise, disdain, repulse, say no to **08** turn away, turn down **09** disregard, repudiate **10** look down on **12** cold-shoulder

## spurt

**03** fit, jet **04** boak, bock, boke, gush, kick, pour, pump, rush, spin, well **05** burst, erupt, issue, shoot, spate, spray, start, surge **06** access, skoosh, squirt, stream **07** welling **08** eruption, increase **10** outpouring

## spy

**03** eye, see **04** espy, look, mole, nark, spie, spot, tout, wait **05** agent, plant, scout, spial, spook, spyal **06** beagle, descry, notice, setter, shadow, survey **07** discern, glimpse, make out, observe, sleeper, snooper **08** discover, emissary, mouchard **10** enemy agent **11** double agent, secret agent, under-espial **12** catch sight of, foreign agent **13** intelligencer **14** fifth columnist **15** undercover agent

*Spies include:*

**03** **Pym** (Magnus)
**04** **Bond** (James), **Hale** (Nathan), **Hiss** (Alger)
**05** **André** (John), **Blake** (George), **Blunt** (Anthony Frederick), **Fuchs** (Klaus Emil Julius), **Karla**, **Szabo** (Violette), **Wynne** (Greville)
**06** **Howell** (James), **Philby** (Kim), **Smiley** (George), **Tubman** (Harriet),

**Vidocq** (Eugène François), **Werner** (Ruth)
**07** **Burgess** (Guy Francis de Moncy), **Maclean** (Donald)
**08** **Lonsdale** (Gordon Arnold), **Mata Hari**
**09** **Carstares** (William), **Rosenberg** (Ethel), **Rosenberg** (Julius)
**10** **Cairncross** (John)

• **spies** **02** MI **03** CIA, KGB, MI5, MI6 **05** Stasi **06** Mossad
• **spy on** **04** tout **05** watch **07** observe **10** keep tabs on **11** keep an eye on **14** observe closely

## spymaster
**01** M

## squabble

**03** row **04** spat, tiff, tift **05** argue, brawl, clash, fight, scrap, set to, set-to **06** barney, bicker **07** dispute, quarrel, rhubarb, wrangle **08** argument **09** have words **12** disagreement

## squad

**03** set **04** band, crew, gang, team, unit **05** force, group, troop **06** outfit **07** brigade, company, platoon

## squadron

**03** red, RYS, sqn **04** blue **10** escadrille

## squalid

**03** low **04** foul, mean, vile **05** dingy, dirty, grimy, mucky, nasty, ribby, seedy **06** filthy, grotty, grubby, sleazy, slummy, sordid, untidy **07** obscene, run-down, unclean, unkempt **08** improper, shameful, slovenly, wretched **09** neglected, offensive, repulsive **10** broken-down, Dickensian, disgusting, ramshackle, uncared-for, unpleasant **11** dilapidated, disgraceful

## squall

**03** cry **04** blow, drow, gale, gust, howl, moan, wail, wind, yell, yowl **05** groan, storm **06** flurry **07** sumatra, tempest **08** williwaw **09** hurricane, windstorm

## squally

**04** wild **05** blowy, gusty, rough, windy **06** stormy **07** gustful **08** blustery **09** turbulent **10** blustering **11** tempestuous

## squalor

**04** dirt, slum **05** decay, filth, grime **07** neglect, skid row **08** dung-heap, dung-hill, foulness, meanness, skid road **09** dinginess, dirtiness, griminess, muckiness **10** filthiness, grubbiness, sleaziness **11** squalidness, uncleanness **12** wretchedness

## squander

**04** blow, blue, lash, muck, roam **05** spend, sport, waste **06** bezzle, expend, gamble, lavish, misuse, mucker, plunge, wander **07** consume, fritter, scamble, scatter, slather, splurge **08** disperse, fool away, misspend, straggle **09** dissipate, sport away, throw away **10** muddle away **11** fritter away, splash out on

## square

**01** S, T **02** sq **03** fit, pay **04** even, fair,

full, just, quad, rule, suit, true **05** adapt, agree, align, bribe, canon, exact, fogey, level, match, order, plaza, scarf, solid, tally **06** accord, adjust, dinkum, equity, evenly, fairly, honest, settle, tailor **07** balance, conform, diehard, ethical, fitting, genuine, honesty, quarrel, resolve, solidly, swagger, upright **08** complete, directly, fairness, honestly, old fogey, put right, regulate, set right, settle up, standard, straight, suitable, thick-set **09** conformer, criterion, equitable, harmonize, headscarf, make equal, reconcile **10** above-board, conformist, correspond, dissension, fuddy-duddy, honourable, on the level, quadrangle, satisfying, straighten, town square **11** marketplace, rectangular, right-angled, strait-laced, unequivocal **12** buttoned-down, conservative, market square, old-fashioned **13** perpendicular, quadrilateral, stick-in-the-mud **14** traditionalist **15** be congruous with, conventionalist

*Squares include:*

**03** Red
**05** Times
**06** Sloane
**07** Central, Madison, People's
**08** Berkeley, Victoria
**09** Leicester, Tiananmen, Trafalgar
**10** Bloomsbury, Washington
**12** Covent Garden

## squarely

**04** bang, dead, just **05** plumb, right, smack **07** exactly **08** directly, straight **09** precisely **12** unswervingly

## squash

**03** jam **04** mash, pack, pulp, snub **05** crowd, crush, grind, pound, press, quash, quell, smash, stamp **07** distort, flatten, put down, silence, squeeze, squelch, squidge, trample **08** compress, macerate, suppress **09** dilutable, humiliate, pulverize, squeezing **10** annihilate

## squashy

**04** soft **05** mushy, pappy, pulpy **06** spongy **07** sopping, springy, squidgy, squishy **08** squelchy, yielding **10** squelching

## squat

**03** sit **04** bend, ruck **05** croup, dumpy, fubby, fubsy, hunch, kneel, podgy, pudgy, short, stoop **06** chunky, crouch, croupe, hunker, pyknic, stocky, stubby **07** squabby **08** thickset **09** crouching **10** hunker down **12** absquatulate, Humpty-dumpty

## squawk

**03** cry, nag **04** beef, carp, crow, fuss, hoot, moan, yelp **05** bitch, bleat, croak, gripe, groan, growl, grump, whine **06** cackle, grouch, grouse, object, scream, shriek, squeal, whinge **07** carry on, grumble, protest, scrauch, scraugh, screech **08** complain **09** bellyache, criticize, find fault **11** kick up a fuss, raise a stink **15** have a bone to pick

## squeak
**squeak**
03 eek 04 peep, pipe 05 cheep, chirk, creak, whine 06 inform, squeal 07 confess

**squeal**
03 cry, rat, wee 04 howl, shop, sing, tell, wail, yell, yelp 05 grass, shout, sneak, split, stool 06 betray, inform, scream, shriek, snitch, squawk 07 screech, sell out 08 complain 09 tell tales

**squeamish**
03 coy 04 sick 06 queasy, queazy 07 finicky, mawkish, missish, prudish 08 delicate, nauseous 09 nauseated 10 fastidious, particular, scrupulous 11 punctilious, strait-laced 12 mealy mouthed

**squeeze**
◇ containment indicator 03 hug, jam, nip, ram 04 cram, grip, hold, mash, milk, pack, pulp, push, shoe, suck 05 bleed, chirt, clasp, crowd, crush, force, grasp, gripe, juice, pinch, press, shove, stuff, sweat, twist, wedge, wrest, wring 06 clutch, cuddle, enfold, extort, fleece, jostle, lean on, mangle, scruze, squash, strain, thrust 07 embrace, extract, rubbing, scrooge, scrouge, squidge, thrutch, tighten 08 compress, pressure, sandwich, scrowdge, shoehorn, wring out 09 boyfriend, hold tight 10 congestion, girlfriend, pressurize 14 put the screws on

**squid**
01 L 04 quid 05 pound 06 loligo, nicker 07 ink-fish, smacker 08 calamari, calamary 10 sleeve fish

**squiffy**
◇ anagram indicator 05 happy, merry, tight, tipsy 06 blotto, tiddly 07 drunken, pickled, sozzled, tiddley 09 crapulent, plastered 10 inebriated 11 intoxicated

**squint**
03 aim 04 awry, cast, gaze, glee, gley, hint, peep, peer, pink, scan 05 askew, blink, twire 06 aslant, glance, gledge, gleyed, skelly, squiny 07 crooked, glimpse, oblique, skellie, squinny 08 cockeyed, cross-eye, indirect, strabism, tendency, walleyed 09 obliquely, off-centre, skew-whiff 10 hagioscope, side-glance, strabismic, strabismus 11 look askance 12 sideways look

**squire**
04 rule 05 canon 06 attend, donzel, escort, Junker, squier 08 scutiger, squarson 12 armour-bearer

**squirm**
◇ anagram indicator 04 move, worm 05 shift, twist 06 fidget, wiggle, writhe 07 agonize, wriggle 08 flounder, squiggle

**squirrel**
03 bun 04 skug, vair 05 hoard 06 gopher, suslik, taguan 07 meercat, meerkat 08 chipmuck, chipmunk 09 chickaree 10 prairie dog 11 flickertail, spermophile

• **squirrel away** 04 hide, save 05 hoard, lay in, lay up, put by, store 06 save up 07 conceal, put away, stock up 08 salt away, set aside 09 stash away, stockpile
• **squirrel's nest** 04 cage, dray, drey

**squirt**
03 jet 04 emit, gush, pour, spew, well 05 chirt, eject, expel, issue, scoot, shoot, spirt, spout, spray, spurt, surge 06 scoosh, skoosh, stream 07 spew out 09 discharge, ejaculate
• **sea squirt** 08 ascidian, cunjevoi

## Sri Lanka
**Sri Lanka**
02 CL 03 LKA

**stab**
02 go 03 cut, jab, try 04 ache, bash, dirk, fork, gash, gore, kris, pain, pang, pink, push, shot 05 crack, essay, knife, prick, prong, slash, spasm, spear, stick, throb, whirl, wound 06 injure, injury, pierce, skewer, thrust, twinge 07 attempt, bayonet, poniard, venture 08 incision, puncture, stiletto, transfix 09 endeavour
• **stab in the back** 06 betray 07 deceive, let down, sell out, slander 08 inform on 11 double-cross

**stabbing**
05 acute, sharp 07 knifing, painful 08 piercing, shooting, stinging 09 throbbing

**stability**
06 fixity, fixure 07 balance 08 firmness, solidity 09 constancy, soundness 10 durability, regularity, secureness, steadiness, sturdiness, uniformity 11 reliability 15 unchangeability

**stabilize**
03 fix, peg 06 firm up, freeze, secure, steady 07 balance, support 08 equalize, valorize 09 establish 10 keep steady, make stable 11 make uniform

**stable**
04 barn, fast, firm, sure 05 fixed, solid, sound, stall 06 secure, static, steady, strong, sturdy 07 abiding, durable, lasting, regular, uniform 08 balanced, constant, enduring, reliable, together 09 permanent 10 deep-rooted, dependable, invariable, unchanging, unswerving, unwavering 11 established, long-lasting, substantial, well-founded 12 unchangeable 13 self-balancing
• **stablehand** 06 ostler

**stack**
03 lot 04 fill, flue, heap, load, many, mass, pile, rick, ruck, save, tons, vent 05 amass, clamp, heaps, hoard, loads, mound, piles, shaft, stash, stock, store 06 funnel, gather, granum, masses, oodles 07 chimney 08 assemble 09 a good deal, stockpile 10 accumulate, a great deal, collection 12 accumulation, a large amount, great numbers

**stadium**
04 bowl, park, ring 05 arena, field, pitch, track, venue 06 ground 08 coliseum 09 colosseum, velodrome 11 sports field 12 amphitheatre, sports ground

*Sports stadia and venues include:*
04 Oval
05 Ascot, Epsom, Ibrox, Imola, Lords, Monza, Troon
06 Henley, Le Mans
07 Aintree, Anfield, Daytona, Olympia, San Siro, The Oval
08 Highbury, Sandwich
09 Cresta Run, Edgbaston, Longchamp, Muirfield, Newmarket, St Andrews, The Belfry, Turnberry, Villa Park, Wimbledon
10 Brooklands, Carnoustie, Celtic Park, Cheltenham, Elland Road, Fairyhouse, Headingley, Hockenheim, Interlagos, Meadowbank, Millennium, Monte Carlo, Twickenham
11 Belmont Park, Brands Hatch, Hampden Park, Murrayfield, Old Trafford, Royal Lytham, Sandown Park, Silverstone, The Crucible, The Rose Bowl, Trent Bridge, Windsor Park
12 Goodison Park, Texas Stadium, Wembley Arena
13 Azteca Stadium, Caesar's Palace, Crystal Palace, Heysel Stadium, Royal Birkdale, The Albert Hall, White Hart Lane
14 Anaheim Stadium, Churchill Downs, Stamford Bridge, Wembley Stadium
15 Bernabeu Stadium, Cardiff Arms Park, Flushing Meadows, Maracana Stadium

**staff**
03 man, rod 04 cane, crew, mace, pike, pole, prop, team, wand, work 05 baton, crook, cross, equip, stave, stick 06 burden, crutch, cudgel, occupy, stanza, supply, taiaha, warder 07 bourdon, crosier, crozier, operate, provide, scepter, sceptre, support, workers 08 arbalest, ash-plant, manpower, officers, pastoral, teachers 09 employees, entourage, personnel, truncheon, workforce 10 alpenstock 11 secretariat, walking-cane 12 secretariate, walking-stick 13 establishment 14 human resources

**stag**
03 dog 04 colt, male 05 royal, staig 06 follow, humble, hummel, shadow 07 brocket, knobber 08 imperial, informer, stallion 10 ten-pointer

## stage
**stage**
02 do 03 lap, leg, pin 04 dais, give, step, tier, time, trek 05 apron, arena, field, floor, lay on, level, mount, phase, point, put on, realm, scene, shelf, stand 06 direct, length, period, podium, sphere, storey 07 arrange, perform, present, produce, rostrum, setting, soapbox 08 backdrop, division, engineer, juncture, organize, platform, scaffold 10 background 11 orchestrate, put together, stage-manage
• **the stage** 03 rep 05 drama

07 theatre, the play 09 dramatics, theatrics, the boards 11 Thespian art 12 show business 13 the footlights

## stagecoach
03 fly 05 dilly 09 diligence

## stagger
◇ *anagram indicator* 04 reel, rock, roll, step, stot, stun, sway 05 amaze, lurch, pitch, shake, shock, stoit, waver 06 bumble, daidle, falter, recoil, recule, teeter, totter, wintle, wobble 07 astound, blunder, nonplus, recoyle, recuile, stoiter, stotter, stupefy 08 astonish, bowl over, confound, hesitate, keel over, surprise, titubate, wavering 09 dumbfound, overwhelm 11 flabbergast

## staggered
◇ *anagram indicator* 05 dazed 06 amazed 07 shocked, stunned 08 open-eyed, startled 09 astounded, surprised 10 astonished, bewildered, bowled over, confounded, gobsmacked, taken aback 11 dumbfounded 12 lost for words 13 flabbergasted, knocked for six

## staggering
◇ *anagram indicator* 06 groggy 07 amazing, rolling 08 dramatic, shocking, stunning 09 titubancy 10 astounding, stupefying, surprising, titubation, unexpected, unforeseen 11 astonishing 12 mind-boggling

## stagnant
04 dull, foul, slow 05 dirty, dying, inert, quiet, stale, still 06 filthy, smelly, torpid 08 brackish, inactive, moribund, sluggish, standing 09 lethargic, unflowing, unhealthy 10 motionless

## stagnate
03 rot 04 idle, rust 05 decay 06 fester 07 decline, putrefy 08 languish, vegetate 09 do nothing 10 degenerate 11 deteriorate 14 become stagnant

## staid
03 sad 04 calm, prim 05 grave, quiet, sober, stiff 06 demure, formal, proper, sedate, solemn, sombre, steady 07 serious, starchy 08 composed, decorous 09 permanent 12 buttoned-down 13 serious-minded

## stain
03 dye 04 blot, mail, mark, meal, mote, slur, smit, soil, spot, tint 05 bedye, black, chica, chico, cloud, color, dirty, henna, paint, shame, smear, sully, taint, tinge 06 blotch, chicha, colour, damage, embrue, imbrue, injure, injury, marble, smirch, smudge, smutch 07 attaint, blacken, blemish, corrupt, embrewe, inkspot, soilure, splodge, splotch, tarnish, varnish 08 besmirch, Congo red, discolor, disgrace, maculate, sanguine 09 discolour, dishonour, osmic acid, pollution, soiliness 10 ensanguine, trypan blue 11 contaminate 12 methyl violet, picrocarmine 13 Coomassie Blue®, discoloration 14 discolouration

## stair, stairs
04 ghat, pair, trap, vice 05 ghaut,

grece, scale, sweep 06 perron, stayre 07 caracol 08 caracole, escalier, turnpike 09 escalator, forestair 10 backstairs, scale stair 11 common stair 12 companionway, winding stair 13 scale and platt, turnpike stair 14 apples and pears, escalier dérobé, scale staircase 15 companion ladder, moving staircase, spiral staircase

## stake
02 go 03 bet, peg, pot, put, rod, set, tie, vie 04 ante, gage, hold, mise, pale, pawn, pile, play, pole, post, prop, race, rest, risk, stob 05 brace, claim, prize, put in, put on, put up, share, spike, spile, stang, state, stick, tie up, wager 06 assert, chance, demand, fasten, gamble, hazard, hold up, loggat, paling, picket, pierce, piquet, pledge, prop up, secure, tether 07 concern, contest, declare, picquet, support, venture 08 interest, standard, winnings 09 establish 10 investment, lay claim to 11 competition, involvement, requisition
• **stake out** 05 watch 06 define, survey 07 delimit, mark off, mark out, outline, reserve 08 stake off 09 demarcate 11 keep an eye on

## stakes
03 bet 04 pool
• **row of stakes** 04 wear, weir 05 orgue 06 paling, zareba, zariba, zereba, zeriba 07 zareeba 08 estacade, palisade, stockade 09 worm fence

## stale
03 dry, off, old 04 flat, hard, lure, sour 05 banal, blown, corny, fusty, jaded, musty, shaft, stalk, stock, tired, trite, urine 06 handle, mouldy 07 gone off, insipid, pretext, tainted, urinate, worn-out 08 clichéed, hardened, overused 09 hackneyed, tasteless, worthless 10 uninspired, unoriginal 11 commonplace, stereotyped 12 cliché-ridden, overfamiliar, run-of-the-mill 13 platitudinous

## stalemate
03 tie 04 draw, halt 07 impasse 08 blockade, deadlock, stand-off, zugzwang 10 standstill 15 Mexican standoff

## stalk
03 bun, kex 04 haft, hunt, keck, pace, rush, seta, stem, step, tail, twig, walk 05 chase, haunt, kecks, march, quill, shaft, shoot, spire, stale, stipe, strig, track, trail, trunk 06 bennet, branch, follow, kecksy, keksye, pursue, shadow, stride 07 pedicel, pedicle, petiole 08 peduncle 09 creep up on, give chase, track down 10 sporophore *See also* **stem**

## stall
03 bay, pen, pew 04 bulk, coop, crib, ruse, slow, staw, trap 05 booth, decoy, defer, delay, dwell, hedge, kiosk, place, stand, table, trick 06 corral, hold up, induct, put off, stable, travis, trevis 07 counter, cowshed, cubicle, install, shamble, surface, surfeit, sutlery, treviss, tribune 08 fauteuil, flypitch,

horse box, obstruct, platform, postpone, put on ice, slow down 09 enclosure, news-stand, stasidion, stonewall, temporize 10 equivocate, standstill 11 compartment, play for time 12 drag your feet

## stallion
04 stag 05 staig 06 cooser, cusser, entire 07 cuisser, kestrel, staniel, stannel, stanyel 09 courtesan, stud horse 10 stonehorse

## stalwart
05 burly, hardy, loyal, stout 06 brawny, daring, pretty, robust, rugged, steady, strong, sturdy, trusty 07 buirdly, devoted, staunch, valiant 08 athletic, faithful, intrepid, muscular, reliable, resolute, vigorous 09 committed, stalworth, steadfast, strapping 10 dependable, determined 11 indomitable

## stamina
04 grit, guts 05 fiber, fibre, force, power 06 bottom, energy, vigour 07 stamens 08 strength 09 endurance, fortitude 10 resilience, resistance 12 staying power

## stammer
03 hum 04 lisp 06 babble, falter, gibber, mumble 07 stumble, stutter 08 hesitate, splutter 12 speech defect

## stamp
03 cut, die, fix, tag 04 beat, cast, coin, form, kind, mark, mash, mint, pulp, seal, sort, type 05 brand, breed, crush, frank, grind, label, mould, pound, press, print, punch, tread 06 cachet, emboss, enface, incuse, preace, prease, signet, squash, stramp, strike 07 engrave, fashion, impress, imprint, mintage, preasse, quality, trample, variety 08 hallmark, identify, inscribe 09 character, designate, signature 10 categorize, definitive, impression, tripudiate 11 attestation, description 12 characterize 13 authorization

---

*Famous and rare stamps include:*

08 Bull's eye, Penny Red
09 Basel dove, Penny Blue
10 Mount Athos, Penny Black, Red Mercury, Scinde Dawk, VR official
11 Jenny invert, St Louis bear
12 Inverted swan
13 Black Honduras, Inverted Jenny, Uganda Cowries

---

• **stamp out** 03 end 04 curb, kill 05 crush, quash, quell 06 quench, scotch 07 destroy, put down 08 suppress 09 eliminate, eradicate, extirpate 10 extinguish, put an end to

## stampede
03 fly, ren, rin, run 04 dash, flee, race, rout, rush, tear 05 shoot 06 charge, flight, gallop, onrush, sprint 07 debacle, scatter 09 breakaway 10 scattering 12 sauve qui peut

## stance
04 line 05 angle, slant, stand 06 policy, stanza 07 bearing, opinion, posture,

stretch **08** attitude, carriage, position **09** viewpoint **10** deportment, standpoint **11** point of view

## stanch
**03** dam **04** halt, plug, stay, stem, stop **05** allay, block, check, loyal **06** arrest, hearty, quench, trusty **07** styptic, zealous **08** constant **09** floodgate, seaworthy **10** watertight

## stand
**02** be **03** bin, nef, put, set **04** base, bear, bier, case, dais, desk, hold, line, park, post, rack, rise, wait **05** abide, allow, angle, bipod, booth, brook, erect, exist, frame, get up, place, plant, shelf, slant, stage, stall, stool, table, up-end **06** cradle, endure, locate, obtain, policy, remain, stance, suffer, tripod **07** be erect, be valid, counter, dumpbin, monopod, opinion, prevail, stand up, station, stomach, support, sustain, swallow, tribune, undergo, weather **08** attitude, cope with, guéridon, live with, monopode, pedestal, platform, position, stillage, stilling, stillion, stoppage, tolerate **09** be in force, be upright, put up with, viewpoint, withstand **10** be in effect, experience, resistance, standpoint **11** point of view **12** be on your feet, straighten up **13** get on your feet, get to your feet **14** rise to your feet
• **stand by   04** back **06** affirm, defend, hold to, uphold **07** stick by, support **08** adhere to, champion, side with **10** stand up for, stick up for
• **stand down   04** quit **06** give up, resign, retire **08** abdicate, step down, withdraw
• **stand for   04** bear, mean **05** allow, brook **06** denote, endure **07** betoken, signify, stomach **08** indicate, tolerate **09** put up with, represent, symbolize
• **stand in for   07** replace **08** cover for **10** understudy **11** deputize for **13** substitute for **14** hold the fort for, take the place of
• **stand out   04** show **06** extend, jut out, strout **07** jump out, poke out, project **08** stick out **09** be obvious **11** catch the eye **12** be noticeable **13** be conspicuous, stick out a mile
• **stand up   04** jilt, rise, wash **05** get up **06** cohere, hold up **07** let down, upstare **09** hold water **10** fail to meet **11** remain valid **12** straighten up **13** get to your feet **14** rise to your feet
• **stand up for   06** adhere, defend, uphold **07** protect, stand by, support **08** champion, fight for, side with **10** stick up for **13** remain loyal to
• **stand up to   04** defy, face **05** brave **06** endure, oppose, resist **08** confront, face up to **09** challenge, withstand

## standard
**03** par, set, std **04** base, code, flag, mark, norm, rate, rule, type **05** basic, color, ethic, fixed, gauge, grade, guide, ideal, level, model, moral, norma, stock, usual **06** banner, colors, colour, ensign, normal, pennon, sample, square, staple **07** average,

classic, colours, example, labarum, measure, pattern, pennant, popular, quality, regular, routine, scruple, typical **08** accepted, approved, exemplar, gonfalon, habitual, official, ordinary, orthodox, paradigm, streamer, vexillum **09** archetype, benchmark, criterion, customary, guideline, horsetail, principle, yardstick **10** definitive, prevailing, recognized, touchstone **11** established, Lesbian rule, requirement **12** conventional **13** authoritative, specification

## standard-bearer
**06** cornet, ensign **07** alférez, ancient **08** standard **09** vexillary **11** gonfalonier

## standardize
**08** equalize, regiment **09** normalize **10** homogenize, regularize, stereotype **11** mass-produce, systematize

## stand-in
**03** sub **04** temp **05** locum, proxy **06** deputy, second **08** delegate, stuntman **09** surrogate **10** stuntwoman, substitute, understudy **11** pinch-hitter **14** representative **15** second-in-command

## standing
**04** foul, rank **05** dirty, erect, fixed, stale, still **06** filthy, repute, smelly, status **07** footing, lasting, rampant, regular, settled, station, up-ended, upright **08** brackish, duration, eminence, position, repeated, stagnant, vertical **09** existence, permanent, perpetual, seniority, unflowing, unhealthy **10** experience, motionless, on your feet, reputation **11** continuance, established **13** perpendicular

## stand-off
**03** tie **04** draw, halt **07** impasse **08** blockade, deadlock **10** five-eighth, standstill

## standoffish
**04** cold, cool **05** aloof **06** remote **07** distant **08** detached, reserved **09** withdrawn **10** unfriendly, unsociable **14** unapproachable **15** uncommunicative

## standpoint
**05** angle, slant **06** stance **07** station **08** position **09** viewpoint **11** perspective, point of view **12** vantage point

## standstill
**03** jam, jib **04** halt, lull, rest, stop **05** pause, stall, stand, tie-up **06** hold-up, log jam **07** dead-set, impasse **08** deadlock, dead stop, gridlock, stoppage, unmoving **09** cessation, stalemate **10** dead-finish, stationary, still-stand
• **to a standstill   02** up **04** down

## staple
**03** key **04** main **05** basic, chief, major, sadza, vital **06** matoke **07** leading, matooke, primary, stapple, stopple **08** foremost, plantain, standard **09** essential, fastening, important,

necessary, principal **11** fundamental, ship biscuit **13** indispensable

## star
**03** orb, sun **04** idol, lead, moon, nova **05** celeb, major, shine **06** bigwig, famous, planet, shiner, sphere **07** big name, big shot, leading **08** asterisk, asteroid, luminary, megastar, talented **09** bespangle, brilliant, celebrity, paramount, personage, principal, prominent, satellite, superstar, well-known **10** celebrated, leading man, pre-eminent **11** illustrious, leading lady **12** heavenly body, leading light **13** celestial body, household name

*Stars include:*

**03** Dog, sun
**04** Mira, nova, Pole, Vega
**05** Deneb, Dubhe, Merak, North, Rigel, Spica
**06** Castor, meteor, Pollux, pulsar, quasar, Sirius
**07** Alphard, Antares, Canopus, Capella, falling, neutron, Polaris, Procyon
**08** Achernar, Arcturus, Barnard's, red dwarf, red giant, shooting
**09** Aldebaran, Alderamin, Fomalhaut, supernova
**10** Beta Crucis, Betelgeuse, brown dwarf, supergiant, white dwarf
**11** Alpha Boötis, Alpha Crucis, Delta Cephei
**12** Alpha Doradus
**13** Alpha Centauri
**15** Proxima Centauri

*See also* **constellation**

## starboard
**01** R **05** right

## starchy
**04** prim **05** staid, stiff **06** formal, stuffy **07** precise **11** ceremonious, punctilious, strait-laced **12** conventional

## stare
**04** dare, gape, gawk, gawp, gaze, gorp, look, ogle **05** glare, watch **06** glower, goggle **07** fisheye, outface **08** starling **10** rubberneck
• **be staring you in the face   09** be blatant **13** be conspicuous, be very obvious, stick out a mile

## starfish
**07** asterid **08** asteroid **09** stellerid **10** asteridian, bipinnaria, fivefinger **11** fivefingers, stelleridan **13** crown of thorns

## stark
**04** bald, bare, grim, pure **05** bleak, blunt, clean, clear, empty, harsh, plain, quite, sharp, sheer, stern, stiff, total, utter **06** arrant, barren, dreary, gloomy, severe, simple, wholly **07** austere, obvious, totally, utterly **08** absolute, clear-cut, complete, desolate, distinct, entirely, flagrant, forsaken, starkers, thorough **09** downright, out-and-out, unadorned **10** absolutely, altogether, completely, consummate, depressing, stark-naked, start-naked **11** undecorated,

**stark-naked**

unmitigated, unqualified
**13** unembellished

**stark-naked**

**04** nude **05** naked, stark **06** unclad
**08** en cuerpo, in the raw, starkers,
stripped **09** in the buff, in the nude,
undressed **15** in the altogether

**start**

◇ *head selection indicator* **03** bug, fit,
gin, law, off, set **04** dart, dawn, fire,
jerk, jump, leap, make, open, roll
**05** abray, arise, begin, birth, braid,
break, burst, debut, found, get-go, go-
off, issue, leave, onset, rouse, set up,
shoot, spasm, spurt, wince **06** abrade,
abraid, appear, boggle, create, depart,
flinch, kick in, launch, origin, outset,
recoil, set off, set out, shrink, spring,
turn on, twitch **07** combust, getaway,
jump-off, kick off, kick-off, opening,
pioneer, trigger **08** activate,
commence, conceive, embark on, fire
away, get going, initiate, outburst
**09** beginning, emergence, establish,
inception, instigate, institute,
introduce, originate, set on foot
**10** convulsion, embark upon,
foundation, inaugurate, initiation,
trigger off **11** get cracking, get under
way, institution, origination
**12** commencement, inauguration,
introduction **13** come into being
**14** bring into being **15** get things
moving
• **did not start, fail to start** ◇ *head
deletion indicator*

**starter**

◇ *head selection indicator* **04** meze, whet
**05** tapas **06** bhajee, canapé, entrée,
relish **08** antepast, apéritif, cocktail
**09** appetizer **11** first course, hors
d'oeuvre **13** prawn cocktail

**starting point**

**03** tee **04** base **06** origin **07** scratch
**08** terminus **11** springboard

**startle**

**03** shy **04** rock **05** alarm, amaze, scare,
shock, spook, start, upset **06** affray
**07** agitate, astound, disturb, perturb
**08** astonish, frighten, surprise, unsettle
**11** make you jump

**startling**

**06** sudden **07** épatant **08** alarming,
dramatic, galvanic, shocking
**10** astounding, eye-popping,
staggering, surprising, unexpected,
unforeseen **11** astonishing
**12** electrifying **13** extraordinary

**starvation**

**04** pine **05** death **06** famine, hunger
**07** fasting **10** famishment
**12** malnutrition **13** extreme hunger

**starve**

**03** die **04** clem, deny, diet, fast, pine
**05** faint **06** famish, hunger, perish,
sterve **07** atrophy, deprive
**11** deteriorate

**starving**

**05** dying, faint **06** hungry **08** famished,
ravenous, underfed **10** very hungry
**14** undernourished

**stash**

**04** fund, heap, hide, mass, pile, quit,
stop, stow **05** cache, hoard, lay up,
store **06** closet, desist, save up
**07** conceal, reserve, secrete **08** salt
away **09** reservoir, stockpile
**10** collection **12** accumulation, squirrel
away

**state**

◇ *homophone indicator* **03** put, say
**04** aver, case, état, flap, land, name,
pomp, tell **05** endow, glory, panic,
phase, realm, shape, stage, tizzy, utter,
voice **06** affirm, assert, bother, canopy,
dither, estate, formal, nation, plight,
public, report, reveal, set out, settle,
status, tizwas **07** council, country,
declare, dignity, display, divulge,
express, fluster, install, kingdom,
majesty, pompous, present, specify,
stately **08** announce, ceremony,
disclose, grandeur, national, official,
position, proclaim, property, republic
**09** condition, establish, formulate,
make known, situation, splendour,
statement, territory **10** articulate,
ceremonial, federation,
government, parliament, promulgate
**11** authorities, communicate,
magnificent, predicament
**12** governmental **13** circumstances,
Establishment, parliamentary
**14** administration
*See also* **province**

*Australian states and territories:*

**02** NT, SA, WA
**03** ACT, NSW, QLD, TAS, VIC
**08** Tasmania (TAS), Victoria (VIC)
**10** Queensland (QLD)
**13** New South Wales (NSW)
**14** South Australia (SA)
**16** Western Australia (WA)
**17** Northern Territory (NT)
**26** Australian Capital Territory (ACT)

*Australian state residents'
nicknames:*

**08** Top Ender
**09** cornstalk, Croweater, gumsucker,
Taswegian
**10** sandgroper
**11** Territorian, Vandemonian
**12** bananabender
**13** Apple Islander
**14** Cabbage Patcher
**15** Cabbage Gardener

*Indian states and union territories:*

**03** Goa
**05** Assam, Bihar, Delhi
**06** Kerala, Orissa, Punjab, Sikkim
**07** Gujarat, Haryana, Manipur,
Mizoram, Tripura
**08** Nagaland
**09** Jharkhand, Karnataka,
Meghalaya, Rajasthan, Tamil
Nadu
**10** Chandigarh, West Bengal
**11** Daman and Diu, Lakshadweep,
Maharashtra, Pondicherry,
Uttaranchal
**12** Chhattisgarh, Uttar Pradesh
**13** Andhra Pradesh, Madhya Pradesh

**15** Himachal Pradesh, Jammu and
Kashmir
**16** Arunachal Pradesh
**17** Andaman and Nicobar
**19** Dadra and Nagar Haveli

*US states:*

**04** Iowa, Ohio, Utah
**05** Idaho, Maine, Texas
**06** Alaska, Hawaii, Kansas, Nevada,
Oregon
**07** Alabama, Arizona, Florida,
Georgia, Indiana, Montana, New
York, Vermont, Wyoming
**08** Arkansas, Colorado, Delaware,
Illinois, Kentucky, Maryland,
Michigan, Missouri, Nebraska,
Oklahoma, Virginia
**09** Louisiana, Minnesota, New
Jersey, New Mexico, Tennessee,
Wisconsin
**10** California, Washington
**11** Connecticut, Mississippi, North
Dakota, Rhode Island, South
Dakota
**12** New Hampshire, Pennsylvania,
West Virginia
**13** Massachusetts, North Carolina,
South Carolina
**18** District of Columbia

*US state abbreviations and zip
codes:*

**02** AK (Alaska), AL (Alabama), AR
(Arkansas), AZ (Arizona), CA
(California), CO (Colorado), CT
(Connecticut), DC (District of
Columbia), DE (Delaware), FL
(Florida), GA (Georgia), HI
(Hawaii), IA (Iowa), ID (Idaho), IL
(Illinois), IN (Indiana), KS (Kansas),
KY (Kentucky), LA (Louisiana), MA
(Massachusetts), MD (Maryland),
ME (Maine), MI (Michigan), MN
(Minnesota), MO (Missouri), MS
(Mississippi), MT (Montana), NC
(North Carolina), ND (North
Dakota), NE (Nebraska), NH (New
Hampshire), NJ (New Jersey), NM
(New Mexico), NV (Nevada), NY
(New York), OH (Ohio), OK
(Oklahoma), OR (Oregon), PA
(Pennsylvania), RI (Rhode Island),
SC (South Carolina), SD (South
Dakota), TN (Tennessee), TX
(Texas), UT (Utah), VA (Virginia),
VT (Vermont), WA (Washington),
WI (Wisconsin), WV (West
Virginia), WY (Wyoming)
**03** Ala (Alabama), Ark (Arkansas), Del
(Delaware), Fla (Florida), Ill
(Illinois), Ind (Indiana), Nev
(Nevada), Tex (Texas), Wis
(Wisconsin), W Va (West Virginia),
Wyo (Wyoming)
**04** Ariz (Arizona), Colo (Colorado),
Conn (Connecticut), Kans (Kansas),
Mass (Massachusetts), Mich
(Michigan), Minn (Minnesota), Miss
(Mississippi), Mont (Montana), N
Dak (North Dakota), Nebr
(Nebraska), N Mex (New Mexico),
Okla (Oklahoma), Oreg (Oregon), S
Dak (South Dakota), Tenn

(Tennessee), **Wash** (Washington)
05 **Calif** (California)

---

*US state nicknames:*

08 **Bay State** (Massachusetts), **Gem State** (Idaho)
09 **Beef State** (Nebraska), **Corn State** (Iowa), **Free State** (Maryland), **Old Colony** (Massachusetts)
10 **Aloha State** (Hawaii), **First State** (Delaware), **Peach State** (Georgia), **Sioux State** (North Dakota)
11 **Beaver State** (Oregon), **Coyote State** (South Dakota), **Creole State** (Louisiana), **Empire State** (New York), **Garden State** (New Jersey), **Golden State** (California), **Gopher State** (Minnesota), **Little Rhody** (Rhode Island), **Nutmeg State** (Connecticut), **Show Me State** (Missouri), **Silver State** (Nevada), **Sooner State** (Oklahoma), **Sunset State** (Oklahoma)
12 **Beehive State** (Utah), **Buckeye State** (Ohio), **Bullion State** (Missouri), **Chinook State** (Washington), **Diamond State** (Delaware), **Granite State** (New Hampshire), **Hawkeye State** (Indiana), **Heart of Dixie** (Alabama), **Hoosier State** (Indiana), **Old Line State** (Maryland), **Prairie State** (Illinois), **Tar Heel State** (North Carolina)
13 **Big Sky Country** (Montana), **Camellia State** (Alabama), **Equality State** (Wyoming), **Keystone State** (Pennsylvania), **Land of Lincoln** (Illinois), **Lone Star State** (Texas), **Magnolia State** (Mississippi), **Mainland State** (Alaska), **Mountain State** (West Virginia), **Old North State** (North Carolina), **Palmetto State** (South Carolina), **Pine Tree State** (Maine), **Sunshine State** (Florida, New Mexico, South Carolina), **Treasure State** (Montana)
14 **Bluegrass State** (Kentucky), **Evergreen State** (Washington), **Great Lake State** (Michigan), **Jayhawker State** (Kansas), **North Star State** (Minnesota), **Panhandle State** (West Virginia), **Sagebrush State** (Nevada), **Volunteer State** (Tennessee), **Wolverine State** (Michigan)
15 **Centennial State** (Colorado), **Plantation State** (Rhode Island), **The Last Frontier** (Alaska)
16 **Flickertail State** (North Dakota), **Grand Canyon State** (Arizona), **Peace Garden State** (North Dakota)
17 **America's Dairyland** (Wisconsin), **Constitution State** (Connecticut), **Land of Enchantment** (New Mexico), **Land of Opportunity** (Arkansas)
18 **Green Mountain State** (Vermont), **Mother of Presidents** (Virginia)

• **in a state** 05 het up, upset
07 anxious, hassled, in a stew, ruffled, worried 08 agitated, in a tizzy, troubled, worked up

---

09 flustered 10 distressed 13 panic-stricken
• **state of affairs** 03 job 04 case
05 scene 06 crisis, plight, status
07 posture 08 juncture, position
09 condition, situation
11 predicament 12 kettle of fish, lie of the land 13 circumstances

---

*US states and zip codes:*

04 **Iowa** (IA), **Ohio** (OH), **Utah** (UT)
05 **Idaho** (ID), **Maine** (ME), **Texas** (TX)
06 **Alaska** (AK), **Hawaii** (HI), **Kansas** (KS), **Nevada** (NV), **Oregon** (OR)
07 **Alabama** (AL), **Arizona** (AZ), **Florida** (FL), **Georgia** (GA), **Indiana** (IN), **Montana** (MT), **New York** (NY), **Vermont** (VT), **Wyoming** (WY)
08 **Arkansas** (AR), **Colorado** (CO), **Delaware** (DE), **Illinois** (IL), **Kentucky** (KY), **Maryland** (MD), **Michigan** (MI), **Missouri** (MO), **Nebraska** (NE), **Oklahoma** (OK), **Virginia** (VA)
09 **Louisiana** (LA), **Minnesota** (MN), **New Jersey** (NJ), **New Mexico** (NM), **Tennessee** (TN), **Wisconsin** (WI)
10 **California** (CA), **Washington** (WA)
11 **Connecticut** (CT), **Mississippi** (MS), **North Dakota** (ND), **Rhode Island** (RI), **South Dakota** (SD)
12 **New Hampshire** (NH), **Pennsylvania** (PA), **West Virginia** (WV)
13 **Massachusetts** (MA), **North Carolina** (NC), **South Carolina** (SC)
18 **District of Columbia** (DC)

---

**stately**
05 grand, lofty, noble, proud, regal, royal 06 august, solemn 07 courtly, elegant, pompous 08 glorious, graceful, imperial, imposing, majestic, measured, splendid 09 dignified, mausolean 10 ceremonial, deliberate, impressive, majestical
11 ceremonious, magnificent

**statement**
04 note 05 state, story, table 06 exposé, report, verbal 07 account, preface
08 averment, bulletin, manifest, relation 09 assertion, testimony, utterance 10 communiqué, disclosure, divulgence, revelation, white paper
11 affirmation, declaration, enunciation, presentment
12 announcement, constatation, presentation, press release, procès-verbal, proclamation, promulgation
13 communication 14 representation

**state-of-the-art**
02 in 03 hip, new 04 cool 05 fresh, novel 06 hi-tech, latest, modern, modish, recent, trendy, with it
07 complex, go-ahead, in vogue, present 08 advanced, high-tech, space-age, up-to-date 09 inventive, the latest 10 futuristic, innovative, newfangled, present-day
11 complicated, cutting edge, modernistic, progressive
12 contemporary 13 up-to-the-minute

---

14 forward-looking 15 highly developed

**statesman, stateswoman**
03 GOM 06 leader 08 diplomat, wealsman 10 homme d'état, politician
11 grand old man 14 elder statesman
*See also* **politician**

**static**
05 fixed, inert, still 06 stable, steady
07 resting 08 constant, immobile, unmoving 09 unvarying 10 changeless, motionless, stationary, unchanging
11 undeviating 13 at a standstill, Maginot-minded

**station**
03 lay, set, Sta 04 base, camp, farm, halt, post, rank, seat, send, site, stop
05 class, depot, grade, level, place, plant, point, rowme, stand 06 assign, centre, locate, office, status 07 appoint, channel, habitat, install, quarter
08 exchange, garrison, location, position, standing, terminus
09 establish, fare-stage 10 wavelength
11 park-and-ride, place of duty, whistle stop 12 headquarters 13 establishment, stopping-place
*See also* **London; police station; power; radio; railway station** *under* **railway**

**stationary**
05 fixed, inert, still 06 at rest, ledger, lidger, moored, parked, static
07 resting, sessile, settled 08 constant, immobile, standing, unmoving
09 sedentary 10 motionless, standstill
13 at a standstill

**stationery**

*Stationery items include:*

03 ink, pen, pin
04 file
05 diary, label, ruler, toner
06 eraser, folder, marker, pencil, rubber, staple, Tipp-Ex®
07 blotter, Blu-Tack®, divider, file tab, Filofax®, memo pad
08 calendar, cash book, envelope, Jiffy bag®, notebook, scissors, stamp pad
09 card index, clipboard, desk diary, flip chart, index card, notepaper, paper clip, Sellotape®, wall chart
10 calculator, drawing pin, filing tray, floppy disk, graph paper, paper knife, Post-it note®, ring binder, rubber band
11 account book, address book, bulldog clip, carbon paper, elastic band, rubber stamp, treasury tag
12 adhesive tape, computer disk, copying paper, pocket folder, printer label, printer paper, writing paper
13 expanding file, lever arch file, paper fastener, printer ribbon, tape dispenser
14 document folder, document wallet, manila envelope, spiral notebook, suspension file, window envelope

**15** cartridge ribbon, correcting paper, correction fluid, headed notepaper, pencil-sharpener

**statue**
**02** ka **04** bust, head, idol, kore, tiki **05** gnome, image, torso **06** bronze, effigy, figure, kouros, xoanon **07** carving, stookie **08** acrolith, colossus, figurine, monument **09** sculpture, statuette **10** polychrome **11** garden gnome, whole-length **14** representation
*See also* **sculpture**

**statuesque**
**04** tall **05** regal **07** stately **08** handsome, imposing, majestic **09** dignified, junoesque **10** impressive

**stature**
**04** fame, rank, size **06** height, inches, renown, weight **08** attitude, eminence, prestige, standing, tallness **09** elevation, loftiness **10** importance, prominence, reputation **11** consequence

**status**
**04** rank **05** class, grade, level, state **06** degree, weight **07** quality, station **08** eminence, position, prestige, standing **09** character, condition **10** importance, reputation **11** consequence, distinction **14** territoriality

**statute**
**03** act, law **04** rule **05** edict, ukase **06** assize, decree **07** Riot Act **09** capitular, enactment, ordinance **10** lex scripta, regulation, written law **13** interlocution, Septennial Act **15** act of parliament

**staunch**
**04** firm, halt, plug, stay, stem, stop, sure, true **05** allay, block, check, loyal, sound, stout **06** arrest, hearty, quench, stanch, strong, trusty **07** devoted, styptic, zealous **08** constant, faithful, reliable, resolute, yeomanly **09** committed, floodgate, seaworthy, steadfast **10** dependable, watertight **11** trustworthy

**staunchly**
**06** firmly **08** yeomanly **10** implacably, resolutely **11** steadfastly **12** unswervingly **13** unfalteringly, unflinchingly

**stave**
**03** bar, lag, rod **05** break, shaft, staff **06** sprain, stanza **07** break up
• **stave off** **04** foil **05** avert, avoid, parry, repel **07** deflect, fend off, prevent, repulse, ward off **08** keep back **09** keep at bay, turn aside

**stay**
**04** curb, halt, hold, keep, last, live, prop, rest, sist, stop, wait, wire **05** abide, abode, allay, await, block, board, brace, cease, check, defer, delay, dwell, lodge, pause, put up, quell, strut, tarry, visit **06** arrest, desist, detain, endure, hinder, linger, put off, remain, reside, settle **07** adjourn,

appease, control, holiday, persist, prevent, satisfy, shoring, sojourn, stay put, support, suspend **08** buttress, continue, obstacle, obstruct, postpone, prorogue, put on ice, reprieve, restrain, stopover, suppress, vacation **09** deferment, endurance, hang about, remission, restraint, stanchion **10** hang around, suspension **11** continuance, discontinue, take a room at **12** postponement **13** reinforcement

**staying power**
**04** grit, guts **05** fibre, force, power, steel **06** bottom, energy, vigour **07** stamina **08** strength **09** endurance, fortitude **10** resilience, resistance

**steadfast**
**03** sad **04** fast, firm **05** fixed, loyal **06** intent, manful, stable, steady, strong, sturdy **07** adamant, staunch **08** constant, faithful, reliable, resolute **09** dedicated, immovable **10** dependable, implacable, unswerving, unwavering **11** established, perseverant, persevering, unfaltering, unflinching **12** single-minded, stout-hearted

**steadily**
**06** calmly, evenly **07** soberly **08** sensibly **09** regularly, seriously **10** constantly, rationally **12** all year round, on an even keel **13** round the clock **15** uninterruptedly

**steady**
**03** fix **04** calm, even, firm, rest **05** brace, check, fixed, relax, sober, staid, still, usual **06** poised, secure, soothe, stable, subdue **07** balance, compose, control, regular, serious, settled, support, uniform **08** balanced, constant, habitual, reliable, resolute, restrain, sensible, unbroken, unmoving **09** boyfriend, ceaseless, customary, immovable, incessant, perpetual, rock-solid, stabilize, steadfast, unexcited, unvarying **10** consistent, controlled, dependable, girlfriend, motionless, persistent, unchanging, unvariable, unwavering **11** consistence, consistency, established, industrious, unexcitable, unfaltering, unflappable, unremitting **12** on an even keel, tranquillize, well-balanced **13** imperturbable, uninterrupted **14** self-controlled

**steak**
**05** T-bone **08** pope's eye **09** entrecôte **11** porterhouse **13** Chateaubriand

**steal**
**03** bag, cly, dip, lag, mag, nap, nim, nip, rob **04** blag, bone, crib, duff, glom, knap, lift, magg, mill, nick, pick, pull, slip, smug, snip, take, whip **05** annex, boost, bribe, creep, filch, heist, hoist, miche, mooch, mouch, pinch, poach, purse, shaft, shank, slide, slink, sneak, steel, steil, stele, swipe, theft **06** abduct, burgle, convey, finger, handle, hijack, kidnap, nobble, pickle, pilfer, pocket, rip off, rustle, scrump, skrimp, skrump, snatch, snitch, steale, thieve, tiptoe, twitch **07** bargain, break

in, cabbage, good buy, knock up, purloin, slither, smuggle, snaffle **08** abstract, discount, embezzle, giveaway, half-inch, high-jack, knock off, liberate, peculate, scrounge, shoplift, souvenir **09** condiddle, duckshove, go off with, reduction, relieve of **10** burglarize, plagiarize, run off with **11** appropriate, make off with, pick a pocket, walk off with **12** make away with, special offer **13** value for money **14** help yourself to, misappropriate

**stealing**
**05** swipe, theft **06** piracy, snatch **07** break-in, larceny, mugging, nicking, robbery, stick-up **08** burglary, filching, pinching, poaching, thievery, thieving **09** pilferage, pilfering, sprechery **10** peculation, plagiarism, purloining, spreaghery **11** shoplifting **12** embezzlement, smash-and-grab **13** appropriation

**stealth**
**05** theft **07** secrecy, slyness **10** covertness, sneakiness **11** furtiveness **12** stealthiness **15** unobtrusiveness
• **by stealth** **08** stowlins **09** stownlins **10** à la dérobée, stolenwise

**stealthily**
**05** slyly **08** covertly, secretly **09** by stealth, cunningly, furtively, stownlins **10** à la dérobée, stolenwise **15** surreptitiously

**stealthy**
**03** sly **05** mousy, quiet **06** covert, mousey, secret, sneaky **07** catlike, cunning, furtive **09** secretive, underhand **11** clandestine, unobtrusive **13** surreptitious

**steam**
**04** haze, mist, roke **05** force **06** energy, exhale, spirit, vapour, vigour **07** stamina **08** activity, dampness, moisture, momentum, outdated **09** eagerness **10** enthusiasm, exhalation, liveliness **11** water vapour **12** condensation, old-fashioned
• **get steamed up** **07** explode **08** boil over, get angry, get het up **09** blow a fuse, do your nut **10** get annoyed, get excited, hit the roof **11** have kittens, lose your rag **12** blow your cool, fly into a rage, get flustered, lose your cool **15** fly off the handle
• **let off steam** **08** sound off **13** let yourself go **15** air your feelings
• **steam up** **05** fog up **06** mist up
• **under your own steam** **05** alone **07** unaided **10** by yourself **11** without help **13** independently

**steamer**
**02** SS **03** str, USS **06** packet, puffer **09** propeller, steamboat, steamship, vaporetto, whaleback **10** packet-boat, packet-ship, paddle-boat **11** side-wheeler, steam-packet, steam vessel **12** screw steamer **13** paddle steamer **14** ocean-greyhound

## steaming

◇ *anagram indicator see* **drunk**

## steamy

**03** hot **04** blue, damp, hazy, sexy
**05** close, humid, misty, muggy, stewy
**06** erotic, sticky, sultry, sweaty
**07** amorous, gaseous, lustful, raunchy,
sensual, vapoury **08** steaming,
vaporous **09** seductive, vapourish
**10** lubricious, passionate, sweltering,
vaporiform

## steed

**03** nag **04** hack, jade, sted
**05** horse, mount, stedd, stede
**06** stedde **07** charger
**09** Rosinante

## steel

**05** brace, nerve, psych, shaft, shank,
steal, steil, stele, sword **06** handle,
harden, steale **07** fortify, prepare,
toughen **15** trustworthiness

## steely

**04** firm, grey, hard **05** harsh **06** strong
**08** blue-grey, pitiless, resolute
**09** merciless, steel-blue **10** determined,
inflexible, unyielding **13** steel-
coloured

## steep

**03** sop **04** bold, buck, damp, dear, fill,
high, mask, plot, soak, stey **05** bathe,
bluff, brent, brine, embay, imbue,
lofty, sharp, sheer, souse, stiff
**06** abrupt, costly, drench, imbrue,
infuse, pickle, rennet, seethe, steepy,
sudden **07** arduous, cragged, ensteep,
extreme, immerse, moisten, pervade,
stickle, suffuse **08** headlong, macerate,
marinate, permeate, saturate,
submerge, vertical **09** difficult,
excessive, expensive **10** exorbitant,
incredible, inordinate, overpriced,
over the top, precipiced **11** acclivitous,
declivitous, exaggerated, exponential,
high-pitched, precipitous, uncalled-for
**12** extortionate, unreasonable
**13** perpendicular

## steeple

**05** spire, tower **06** belfry, turret **11** rood-
steeple **12** spire-steeple

## steeply

**07** rapidly, sharply **08** abruptly,
suddenly

## steer

**03** con, cox **04** beef, cann, conn, helm,
lead, stir, stot, tack **05** drive, guide,
pilot, usher **06** direct, govern, steare
**07** conduct, control **08** navigate
• **steer clear of** **04** shun **05** avoid,
dodge, evade, skirt **06** bypass, escape,
eschew **10** circumvent **12** keep away
from

## stem

**03** dam, pin, ram **04** axis, beam, bine,
cane, come, corm, culm, curb, flow,
halm, halt, plug, race, runt, stop, tail,
tamp **05** arise, block, check, haulm,
issue, shaft, shank, shoot, stalk, stock,
trunk **06** arrest, bamboo, branch,
breast, derive, family, oppose, resist,
spring, stanch **07** contain, develop,
emanate, hop-vine, staunch **08** kail-
runt, peduncle, restrain **09** originate
**11** pipe-stapple, pipe-stopple **14** have
its origins

## stench

**04** niff, pong, reek **05** odour, smell,
stink, whiff **06** miasma **08** mephitis

## stentorian

**04** full, loud **06** strong **07** booming,
ringing, vibrant **08** carrying, powerful,
resonant, sonorous, strident
**10** thundering, thunderous
**13** reverberating

## step

**03** act, fix, pas, peg **04** deed, gait, gree,
gris, move, pace, rank, rung, trip, walk
**05** glide, grade, grece, grees, grese,
grice, grise, grize, level, notch, phase,
point, print, stage, stair, stamp, stile,
titup, trace, track, tramp, tread
**06** action, degree, effort, gradin,
greece, greese, griece, pit-pat, remove,
stride, tittup **07** advance, gradine,
grecian, measure, pitapat, process,
shuffle, stempel, stemple, twinkle
**08** démarche, footfall, footstep,
greesing, gressing, halfpace,
movement, pitty-pat, progress
**09** expedient, footprint, gradation,
manoeuvre, procedure **10** impression,
proceeding **11** development, pas de
basque, progression **14** course of
action
*See also* **dance**
• **in step** **08** in accord, in unison,
together **09** in harmony **11** in
agreement
• **out of step** **06** at odds **09** not in
step **13** at loggerheads **14** in
disagreement
• **step by step** **06** slowly **08** bit by
bit, gradatim **09** gradually
**13** progressively **14** little by little, one
step at a time
• **step down** **04** quit **05** leave
**06** resign, retire **08** abdicate,
withdraw **09** stand down **14** give up
your post
• **step in** **07** intrude, mediate
**09** arbitrate, intercede, interfere,
interrupt, intervene
• **step up** **05** boost, raise
**07** augment, build up, speed up
**08** escalate, increase **09** intensify
**10** accelerate
• **watch your step** **07** look out
**08** take care, watch out **09** be careful
**11** be attentive **12** mind how you go

## stereotype

**03** tag **04** cast **05** label, model, mould
**06** cliché, stereo **07** formula, pattern
**08** typecast **09** formalize **10** categorize,
convention, pigeonhole **11** mass-
produce, standardize
**15** conventionalize, fixed set of ideas

## stereotyped

**05** banal, corny, fixed, stale, stock,
tired, trite **07** cliché'd **08** clichéed,
overused, standard **09** hackneyed
**10** threadbare, unoriginal **12** cliché-
ridden, conventional, mass-produced,
standardized, unchangeable
**13** platitudinous, stereotypical

## sterile

**03** dry **04** arid, bare, pure, vain
**05** clean, moory, stale **06** barren, futile
**07** aseptic, moorish, useless
**08** abortive, acarpous, germ-free,
germless, infecund, lifeless **09** fruitless,
infertile, pointless **10** antiseptic,
sterilized, unfruitful, uninfected,
uninspired, unyielding **11** disinfected,
ineffectual **12** unproductive,
unprofitable **13** unimaginative
**14** uncontaminated

## sterility

**06** atocia, purity **07** asepsis **08** futility
**09** cleanness, impotence
**10** barrenness, inefficacy **11** infertility,
unfecundity, uselessness
**12** disinfection **13** fruitlessness,
pointlessness **14** unfruitfulness
**15** ineffectiveness

## sterilize

**04** geld, spay **05** clean **06** doctor,
neuter, purify, retort **07** cleanse
**08** castrate, fumigate **09** autoclave,
disinfect **13** make infertile

## sterling

**03** ace, stg **04** mean, neat, pure, real,
ster, true **05** brill, great, sound
**06** worthy **07** genuine **08** smashing,
standard, starling, terrific, top-notch
**09** authentic, excellent **10** first-class
**11** superlative **12** second to none
**14** out of this world

## stern

**04** back, grim, hard, helm, iron, poop,
rear, rump, star, tail **05** cruel, harsh,
rigid, stark, starn, tough **06** ramrod,
severe, sombre, strict **07** austere, tail
end **08** exacting, rigorous
**09** demanding, Draconian, stringent,
unsmiling, unsparing **10** forbidding,
inflexible, relentless, tyrannical,
unyielding **11** unrelenting
**13** authoritarian

## sternly

**06** grimly **07** cruelly, harshly
**08** severely, sombrely, strictly
**10** inflexibly **12** forbiddingly,
relentlessly

## Stevenson

**03** RLS

## stew

◇ *anagram indicator* **03** fix, jug **04** boil,
cook, fret, fuss, hash, hole **05** daube,
salmi, stove, sweat, tizzy, worry
**06** bother, braise, burgoo, hotpot,
paella, pother, ragout, salmis, scouse,
simmer, tajine, tizwas **07** agonize,
bouilli, cholent, chowder, fluster,
goulash, haricot, navarin, stovies,
swelter, tzimmes **08** matelote,
mulligan, pot-au-feu, zarzuela
**09** agitation, carbonade, carbonado,
casserole, cassoulet, Irish stew,
lobscouse, potpourri, succotash
**10** carbonnade, lob's course,
maconochie, prostitute **11** olla-
podrida, ratatouille, slumgullion
**13** bouillabaisse

## steward

**05** dewan, diwan, reeve **06** bailie,

butler, commis, factor, waiter
**07** bailiff, baillie, foreman, maître d', marshal, mormaor **08** khansama, manciple, official, overseer, waitress **09** attendant, caretaker, custodian, khansamah, major-domo, seneschal, sommelier **10** air hostess, stewardess, supervisor **11** chamberlain **12** maître d'hôtel, trolley dolly **14** homme d'affaires **15** flight attendant

## St Helena
**03** SHN

## stick
**03** fix, gad, gum, jab, jam, jut, lay, pin, put, set **04** bear, bind, bond, clog, drop, flak, fuse, glue, grip, hang, hold, join, last, poke, push, rest, site, stab, stay, stop, tack, tape, trap, twig, weld, yard **05** abide, abuse, affix, blame, cling, dwell, paste, place, prick, spear, stand, tally **06** adhere, attach, branch, cement, clog up, endure, fasten, impale, insert, linger, locate, pierce, remain, rocket, secure, solder, switch, thrust **07** carry on, confine, deposit, install, persist, reproof, scruple, set down, stomach, swallow **08** continue, position, protrude, puncture, tolerate, transfix **09** criticism, hostility, penetrate, put up with **10** punishment **11** come to a halt **12** dressing-down **13** get bogged down

*Sticks include:*

**02** ko
**03** bat, lug, rod
**04** cane, club, cosh, pike, pole, post, wand, whip
**05** baton, billy, birch, crook, lathi, staff, stake, waddy
**06** alpeen, crutch, cudgel, hockey, kierie, tripod
**07** sceptre, walking, woomera
**08** bludgeon, cocktail
**09** truncheon
**10** alpenstock, knobkerrie, shillelagh

• **stick at 04** balk **05** demur, doubt, pause **06** keep at, recoil, stop at **07** persist, scruple **08** continue, hesitate, plug away **09** persevere **10** shrink from **13** draw the line at
• **stick by 04** back **06** defend, hold to, uphold **07** stand by, support **08** adhere to, champion, side with **10** stand up for, stick up for
• **stick it out 07** persist **08** continue, keep at it, plug away **09** persevere **11** hang in there **13** grin and bear it
• **stick out 04** perk **05** bulge **06** extend, jut out, tongue **07** poke out, project **08** protrude **09** be obvious **12** be noticeable **13** be conspicuous
• **stick to 04** obey **06** accept, follow, fulfil, hold to, keep to, uphold **07** abide by, agree to, observe, respect, stand by **08** adhere to, carry out, submit to **09** conform to, discharge **10** comply with, toe the line **11** go along with, go by the book
• **stick up for 06** defend, uphold **07** protect, stand by, support **08** champion, fight for **10** speak up

for, stand up for **13** take the part of, take the side of
• **the sticks 04** bush, wops **05** scrub **07** boonies, hickdom, outback, wop-wops **08** backveld, yokeldom **09** backwoods, boondocks **10** backblocks **11** remote areas, up the Boohai **13** end of the earth **15** middle of nowhere

## sticker
**03** bur **04** tine

## stickiness
**03** goo **04** gaum, gorm, tack **09** glueyness, gooeyness, gumminess, tackiness, viscidity **10** syrupiness **12** adhesiveness **13** glutinousness

## stick-in-the-mud
**05** fogey **06** fossil, square **08** fogeyish, old fogey, outmoded **09** Victorian **10** antiquated, back number, fossilized, fuddy-duddy **12** antediluvian, buttoned-down, conservative **13** unadventurous

## stickler
**03** nut **06** backer, maniac, pedant, purist, second, umpire **07** fanatic, fusspot **08** mediator **09** regulator **10** fussbudget **12** precisianist **13** perfectionist, quarterdecker

## sticky
**04** limy **05** chewy, close, dauby, gluey, gooey, goopy, gummy, humid, jammy, muggy, tacky, tough **06** claggy, clammy, clarty, clingy, cloggy, gummed, smeary, stodgy, sultry, sweaty, thorny, tricky, viscid **07** awkward, viscous **08** adhesive, delicate, ticklish **09** difficult, glutinous, sensitive, tenacious **10** oppressive, sweltering, unpleasant **12** embarrassing
• **sticky substance 03** goo, gum **04** glit, goop, gunk, lime **05** gunge **06** viscin **08** mucilage, propolis

## stiff
**03** rob **04** cold, dead, firm, hard, prim, taut, very **05** brisk, cheat, dense, fresh, harsh, large, rigid, solid, stark, stoor, stour, sture, tense, thick, tight, tough, windy **06** aching, chilly, corpse, formal, murder, potent, severe, stowre, strict, strong, tiring **07** arduous, austere, awkward, certain, drastic, extreme, pompous, stilted, unlucky, viscous **08** decorous, exacting, forceful, hardened, priggish, reserved, rigorous, stubborn, vigorous **09** alcoholic, arthritic, demanding, difficult, Draconian, excessive, extremely, inelastic, laborious, resistant, rheumatic, stringent, unbending **10** ceremonial, formidable, inflexible, solidified, unyielding **11** ceremonious, challenging, constrained, rheumaticky, standoffish **12** intoxicating, pertinacious

## stiffen
**03** gel, set **04** jell **05** brace, stark, steel, tense **06** harden, starch **07** congeal, fortify, tense up, thicken, tighten **08** ankylose, solidify **09** anchylose,

bandoline, coagulate, reinforce, Trubenise, Trubenize® **10** strengthen

## stiff-necked
**05** proud **06** formal **07** haughty **08** arrogant, stubborn **09** obstinate, pig-headed, unnatural **11** opinionated **12** contumacious **14** uncompromising

## stifle
**04** curb, funk, hush **05** check, choke, crush, quash, quell, stive **06** dampen, deaden, hush up, keep in, muffle, subdue **07** repress, silence, smother, swallow **08** gulp back, gulp down, hold back, restrain, scomfish, strangle, suppress, throttle **09** constrain, suffocate **10** asphyxiate, extinguish

## stigma
**04** blot, mark, note, pore, scar, slur, spot **05** brand, shame, stain, taint **07** blemish **08** disgrace, spiracle **09** dishonour

## stigmatize
**04** mark, note **05** brand, label, shame, stain **06** vilify **07** blemish, condemn **08** demonize, denounce, disgrace, vilipend **09** discredit

## still
**03** but, e'en, ene, yet **04** calm, deep, even, hush, kill, mild **05** abate, accoy, allay, inert, peace, quiet **06** always, distil, even so, hushed, pacify, serene, settle, silent, smooth, soothe, static, subdue, though **07** appease, assuage, however, quieten, quietly, restful, silence **08** although, constant, immobile, inactive, lifeless, moderate, peaceful, restrain, serenity, stagnant, tranquil, unmoving, until now **09** continual, noiseless, quiescent, quietness, sedentary, stillness, unruffled **10** constantly, for all that, inactively, motionless, stationary, stock-still, unstirring **11** nonetheless, undisturbed **12** nevertheless, peacefulness, tranquillity, tranquillize, up to this time **13** in spite of that, in spite of this, noiselessness **15** notwithstanding
• **be still 03** lie **04** hush, rest **06** remain, repose

## stillness
**04** calm, hush, rest **05** peace, quiet **06** repose **07** silence **08** calmness, coolness, quietude, serenity **09** composure, placidity, quietness **10** equanimity, sedateness **11** restfulness **12** peacefulness, tranquillity

## stilted
**05** stiff **06** forced, wooden **08** laboured, mannered **09** unnatural **10** artificial **11** constrained

## stimulant
**01** E **03** kat, qat **04** khat **05** betel, chile, chili, tonic, upper **06** chilli, cinder **07** caffein, cardiac, digoxin, ecstasy, guaraná, pep pill, reviver **08** caffeine, coramine, doxapram, excitant, incitant, lobeline, pemoline, pick-me-up **09** analeptic, cantharis, dance drug, digitalin, nux vomica, sassafras,

**stimulate**

whetstone **11** nikethamide, purple heart, restorative, winter's bark **13** dexamfetamine, smelling salts **14** dexamphetamine **15** methamphetamine

**stimulate**

**03** fan, jog **04** fire, goad, hype, spur, urge **05** gee up, hop up, impel, rouse **06** arouse, buck up, excite, fillip, hype up, incite, induce, kindle, prompt, whip up **07** animate, hearten, inflame, inspire, provoke, quicken, trigger **08** activate, irritate, motivate **09** challenge, encourage, instigate **10** potentiate, trigger off

**stimulating**

**07** bracing, piquant, rousing **08** excitant, exciting, galvanic, stirring **09** inspiring, provoking, stimulant **10** intriguing, suggestive **11** interesting, provocative **12** exhilarating

**stimulation**

**06** ginger **07** arousal **08** kindling **09** animation, prompting **10** excitement, incitement, irritation, motivation, quickening **11** inspiration, instigation, provocation **13** encouragement

**stimulus**

**03** jog **04** goad, jolt, kick, prod, push, spur, whet **05** drive, sting **06** fillip **07** impetus **09** incentive **10** incitement, inducement **11** provocation **12** shot in the arm **13** encouragement

**sting**

**02** do **03** con, nip, rob **04** barb, bite, burn, edge, goad, hurt, lurk, pain, pole, scam, tang **05** annoy, cheat, fraud, point, prick, smart, spite, stang, trick, upset, wound **06** diddle, fiddle, fleece, grieve, injure, injury, malice, needle, nettle, offend, racket, rip off, rip-off, tingle **07** aculeus, deceive, defraud, incense, piercer, provoke, sarcasm, swindle, torment **08** distress, irritate, pungency, stimulus, trickery, urticate **09** deception, gold brick, gold-brick, heartache, sharpness **10** causticity, exasperate, incitement, irritation **11** causticness, viciousness **12** incisiveness, take for a ride **13** double-dealing, sharp practice

**stinging**

**05** smart, urent **07** burning, hurtful, piquant **08** aculeate, poignant, smarting, tingling, urticant, wounding **09** aculeated, injurious, offensive **10** irritating **11** distressing

**stingy**

**04** hard, mean, near **05** close, mingy, tight **06** hungry, skimpy, snippy **07** costive, miserly, niggard, save-all **09** niggardly, penurious **11** bad-tempered, tight-fisted **12** candle-paring, cheeseparing, parsimonious **13** penny-pinching

**stink**

**03** hum, row **04** flap, fuss, guff, honk, ming, niff, pong, reek, stir, suck **05** be bad, hoo-ha, odour, smell **06** bother, furore, hassle, stench **07** be awful, be

nasty, fluster, trouble **08** bad smell, malodour, mephitis **09** commotion, foul smell **12** be despicable, be unpleasant, song and dance

**stinker**

**03** cur, dog, rat **04** scab **05** cheat, hound, louse, rogue, scamp, swine **06** fulmar, horror, louser, petrel, plight, rascal, rotter **07** bounder, dastard, problem, ruffian, shocker, villain **08** blighter, stinkard, vagabond **09** miscreant, reprobate, scallywag, scoundrel **10** blackguard, difficulty, impediment, ne'er-do-well **11** predicament **14** good-for-nothing

**stinking**

**03** bad **04** foul, vile **05** awful, fetid, nasty, niffy, pongy **06** foetid, mingin', rotten, smelly **07** honking, humming, minging **08** mephitic, terrible **10** disgusting, unpleasant **11** odoriferous **12** contemptible

**stint**

**03** bit **04** bout, save, stop, time, turn **05** allot, cease, check, limit, pinch, quota, scant, share, shift, skimp, spare, spell, stent **06** period, scrimp **07** scantle, skimp on, stretch **08** begrudge, restrain, restrict, withhold **09** allowance, apportion, economize, restraint **11** restriction

**stipend**

**03** ann **05** annat, grant **06** income, salary **07** alimony, annuity, benefit, payment, pension **08** expenses **09** allowance **10** assistance **11** maintenance **12** contribution

**stipulate**

**06** demand **07** article, lay down, provide, require, set down, specify **08** covenant, insist on **09** guarantee

**stipulation**

**05** point, rider **06** clause, demand **07** proviso **08** contract **09** condition, postulate, provision **11** requirement **12** precondition, prerequisite **13** specification

**stir**

◇ anagram indicator **03** ado, jee, jog, mix, wag **04** beat, flap, fuss, moot, move, to-do, turn, whip **05** blend, budge, churn, hoo-ha, pique, quich, raise, rouse, shake, shift, steer, stire, tizzy, touch **06** affect, bustle, excite, flurry, muddle, prison, puddle, quatch, quetch, quitch, quiver, racket, riffle, rustle, thrill, tumult, twitch, uproar **07** agitate, clutter, disturb, ferment, flutter, inspire, provoke, quinche, rummage, tempest, torment, tremble **08** activity, disorder, movement **09** agitation, commotion, kerfuffle, sensation **10** excitement **11** disturbance **12** song and dance

See also **prison**

• **stir up** **03** jog **04** fire, poke, rear, spur, wake **05** amove, awake, drive, impel, poach, raise, rouse, roust, waken **06** arouse, awaken, excite, incite, kindle, prompt, racket, rustle **07** agitate, animate, disturb, inflame, inspire, provoke, quicken, rummage

**08** motivate **09** electrify, encourage, galvanize, instigate, stimulate

**stirring**

◇ anagram indicator **04** live **05** afoot, heady **06** lively, moving **07** emotive, rousing, working **08** dramatic, exciting, spirited **09** animating, inspiring, thrilling **11** impassioned, stimulating **12** exhilarating, intoxicating

**stitch**

**03** hem, sew **04** darn, mend, seam, tack **06** repair **09** embroider

See also **embroidery**
• **stitch up** **03** con **04** shop, trap **05** fit up, grass, plant, set up **06** rumble, suture **07** swindle **11** double-cross, incriminate **13** stab in the back

**St Kitts and Nevis**

**03** KNA, SCN

**St Lucia**

**02** WL **03** LCA

**stock**

**03** box, log, set **04** cows, fund, heap, keep, line, name, pack, pigs, pile, post, race, sell, team **05** banal, basic, block, blood, bonds, breed, cache, carry, equip, fumet, funds, goods, herds, hoard, money, plant, range, sheep, store, stump, talon, tired, trite, trunk, usual, wares **06** assets, cattle, common, credit, deal in, family, flocks, handle, horses, kit out, market, repute, shares, source, strain, supply, trough **07** animals, average, capital, descent, fumette, furnish, holding, kindred, lineage, opinion, plenish, provide, regular, reserve, routine, species, stretch, trade in, variety, worn-out **08** accoutre, ancestry, clichéed, equities, good name, ordinary, overused, pedigree, pressure, quantity, standard, standing, stoccado **09** amassment, customary, equipment, essential, genealogy, hackneyed, inventory, livestock, parentage, portfolio, provision, relatives, reservoir, selection, stockpile, traffic in **10** assortment, background, collection, estimation, extraction, investment, repertoire, reputation, securities **11** commodities, farm animals, merchandise, merchandize, stereotyped, traditional **12** accumulation, conventional, run-of-the-mill
• **in stock** **06** on sale **07** for sale **09** available **11** on the market **12** on the shelves
• **stock up** **03** buy **04** fill, heap, load, save **05** amass, buy up, hoard, lay in, store **06** fill up, gather, heap up, pile up **07** put away, stack up, store up **08** put aside, salt away **09** provision, replenish, stash away, stockpile **10** accumulate
• **take stock** **06** assess, review, size up, survey **07** weigh up **08** appraise, estimate, evaluate, reassess **09** re-examine **10** re-evaluate

## stockade
**06** zareba, zariba, zereba, zeriba
**07** zareeba

## stocking
**05** nylon, stock **06** hogger, moggan
**07** popsock, spattee **08** boothose,
knee-high **10** understock
**11** netherstock
*See also* **sock**

## stockings
**04** hose **07** hold-ups, legwear
**11** netherlings

## stockpile
**04** fund, heap, keep, pile, save
**05** amass, cache, hoard, stock, store
**06** gather, heap up, pile up **07** put
away, reserve, store up **08** put aside
**09** amassment, reservoir
**10** accumulate **12** accumulation

## stock-still
**05** inert, still **06** static **08** immobile,
inactive, unmoving **10** motionless,
stationary, unstirring

## stocky
**05** broad, dumpy, short, solid, squat
**06** blocky, chunky, stubby, stumpy,
sturdy **07** nuggety **08** thickset
**11** mesomorphic

## stodgy
**04** dull **05** heavy, solid, staid **06** boring,
formal, leaden, solemn, stuffy, turgid
**07** filling, starchy, tedious **08** laboured
**10** fuddy-duddy, spiritless, unexciting,
uninspired **11** substantial
**12** indigestible **13** unimaginative
**14** unenterprising

## stoical
**04** calm, cool **07** patient **08** resigned
**09** accepting, impassive **10** forbearing,
phlegmatic **11** indifferent,
unemotional, unexcitable
**13** dispassionate, imperturbable, long-
suffering, philosophical,
uncomplaining **14** self-controlled
**15** self-disciplined

## stoicism
**07** ataraxy **08** ataraxia, calmness,
fatalism, patience **09** fortitude, stolidity
**10** acceptance, dispassion, philosophy
**11** forbearance, impassivity,
resignation **12** indifference **13** long-
suffering **14** unexcitability

## stoke
**04** tend **09** add coal to, add fuel to, add
wood to **11** keep burning **12** feed with
fuel

## stokes
**01** S

## stolen
**03** hot **04** bent **05** taken **06** nicked,
swiped **07** nobbled, punched
**08** pilfered **09** ill-gotten, purloined,
ripped off **10** knocked off
• **stolen goods** **03** tom **04** crib, loot,
soup, waif **05** cheat, theft **07** stealth
**08** tweedler **09** stouthrie **10** stoutherie,
tomfoolery

## stolid
**02** po **04** dull, slow **05** beefy, heavy

**06** bovine, solemn, wooden
**07** lumpish, po-faced **08** blockish
**09** apathetic, impassive **10** phlegmatic
**11** indifferent, unemotional,
uninspiring **13** unimaginative

## stomach
**03** gut, maw, tum **04** bear, craw, guts,
puku, read, take, vell, zest **05** abide,
belly, bible, bingy, brook, gorge,
pride, rumen, stand, taste, tummy
**06** bonnet, desire, digest, endure,
fardel, hunger, inside, liking, omasum,
paunch, relish, rennet, resent, spirit,
spleen, suffer, tum-tum, venter
**07** abdomen, courage, gizzard,
insides, passion **08** abomasum,
appetite, pot-belly, submit to, tolerate
**09** approve of, king's-hood, manyplies,
put up with, rennet-bag, reticulum
**10** little Mary, psalterium **11** bread
basket, corporation, disposition,
inclination **13** determination
*See also* **ruminant**
• **without stomach** ◇ *middle
deletion indicator*

## stomach ache
**05** colic **06** gripes, gut rot **09** bellyache,
dyspepsia, tummy ache
**12** hypochondria **13** grass staggers
**15** stomach staggers

## stone
**02** st **03** gem, pip, pit, rag, set **04** flag,
hone, plum, rock, seed, sett, slab
**05** jewel, lapis **06** cobble, gibber,
gonnie, goolie, kernel, mirror, pebble,
yonnie **07** boondie, boulder, brinnie
**08** endocarp, gemstone, sardonyx,
testicle **09** flagstone, headstone,
tombstone **10** concretion, gravestone
*See also* **birth; gem; rock**

## stoned
*see* **drunk**

## stonewall
**03** lie **05** dodge, evade, hedge, shift
**06** waffle **07** deceive, quibble, shuffle
**09** be evasive, pussy-foot
**10** equivocate **11** prevaricate **12** shilly-
shally **13** sit on the fence

## stony
**03** icy **04** cold, hard **05** blank, rigid,
rocky, stern **06** chilly, frigid, frosty,
gritty, pebbly, severe, steely
**07** adamant, callous, deadpan, hostile,
petrous, shingly **08** gravelly, obdurate,
pitiless **09** heartless, lapideous,
merciless, unfeeling **10** inexorable,
petrifying, poker-faced, unfriendly
**11** indifferent, unforgiving
**12** unresponsive **14** expressionless

## stooge
**04** butt, dupe, feed, foil, pawn
**06** drudge, lackey, puppet **07** cat's
paw, fall guy **08** henchman
**09** scapegoat **11** subordinate

## stool
**05** coppy, stand **06** buffet, sunkie,
tripod **07** creepie, cricket, taboret,
tumbrel, tumbril **08** stillage, tabouret

## stoop
**03** bow, sag **04** bend, curb, duck, lean,
lout, lowt, poke, post, prop, sink

**05** courb, deign, droop, hunch, kneel,
lower, porch, slump, squat, steep,
stoep, stope, stoup, swoop **06** bucket,
cringe, crouch, patron, resort, slouch,
stoope, submit **07** bending, decline,
descend, descent, ducking, incline
**08** hunching, lowering, verandah **09** go
so far as, go so low as, supporter,
vouchsafe **10** condescend
**11** inclination **13** condescension, lower
yourself

## stop
**03** bar, can, dit, end **04** bung, cork,
halt, hold, kick, kill, live, plug, poop,
quit, rein, rest, seal, sist, snub, stap,
stay, stem **05** block, board, break,
cease, check, choke, close, cover,
dwell, embar, imbar, lodge, media,
pause, put up, snuff, sprag, stage, stall,
stash, stimy, tarry, visit **06** anchor,
arrest, cut off, desist, detain, devall,
draw up, finish, hinder, impede, keep
up, pack in, pack up, rein in, reside,
scotch, settle, stanch, stimie, stop up,
stymie, thwart, wind up **07** abandon,
bus stop, chuck it, close up, occlude,
prevent, refrain, sojourn, station,
staunch, suspend **08** conclude, draw
rein, give over, hold hard, knock off,
leave off, obstacle, obstruct, pack it in,
pack it up, restrain, stopover,
stoppage, suppress, terminus, withhold
**09** cessation, diaphragm, fare stage,
foreclose, frustrate, hindrance,
intercept, interrupt, obstruent,
punctuate, terminate **10** conclusion,
standstill **11** come to an end, come to a
rest, destination, discontinue,
termination **12** bring to an end, bring
to a rest, interruption **13** stopping-
place **14** discontinuance
**15** discontinuation
*See also* **organ**
• **expressions ordering a stop**
**02** ha, ho, wo **03** hoa, hoh **04** easy,
proo, pruh, toho, whoa **05** avast

## stopgap
**05** shift **06** resort **09** emergency,
expedient, impromptu, makeshift,
temporary **10** improvised, substitute
**11** provisional **12** expediential
**13** improvisation, rough-and-ready

## stopover
**04** rest, stop **05** break, visit **07** layover,
sojourn, stop-off **13** overnight stay

## stoppage
**03** cut, jam **04** blin, halt, stop **05** check,
choke, hitch, sit-in, stand, stick
**06** arrest, freeze, hartal, hold-up,
outage, pull-up, strike **07** closure,
embargo, removal, shut-off, walk-out
**08** asphyxia, blackout, blockage,
decrease, discount, obstacle,
shutdown, stayaway **09** allowance,
breakdown, cessation, deduction,
hindrance, occlusion, reduction,
taking off **10** inhibition, standstill,
taking away, withdrawal
**11** haemostasis, obstruction,
subtraction, suppression, termination
**12** heart failure, interruption
**14** discontinuance **15** discontinuation

## stopper
**03** tap **04** bung, cork, plug, seal
**06** spigot **07** stopple **08** screwtop

## storage
• **computer storage** **03** RAM, ROM

## store
**03** lot **04** bank, barn, fund, heap, keep, load, mine, pack, save, shop, stow **05** cache, hoard, house, lay by, lay in, lay up, stash, stock, stuff, value **06** coffer, esteem, garner, gather, larder, panary, plenty, supply, vintry **07** buttery, collect, deposit, furnish, keeping, lay down, put down, reserve **08** cupboard, minimart, multiple, put aside, quantity, salt away, treasury **09** abundance, amassment, livestock, provision, reservoir, stockpile, storeroom, warehouse **10** accumulate, chain store, corner shop, depository, groceteria, repository, storehouse **11** hypermarket, stock up with, sufficiency, supermarket **12** accumulation, retail outlet, squirrel away **15** department store
• **set store by, lay store by** **05** value **06** admire, esteem **13** think highly of **14** consider highly

## storehouse
**04** barn, fund, hold, silo **05** depot, étape, vault **06** cellar, garner, larder, pantry, pataka, wealth **07** armoury, arsenal, buttery, granary **08** dene-hole, elevator, entrepot, magazine, treasury **09** repertory, thesaurus, warehouse **10** depository, repository **12** conservatory

## storey
**04** deck, flat, tier **05** attic, étage, floor, level, stage **06** flight **07** stratum **08** basement, bel étage, entresol **09** triforium **10** clearstory, clerestory, downstairs, first floor **11** ground floor

## stork
**06** argala, jabiru **08** adjutant, shoebill **09** whale-head **10** saddlebill

## storm
◇ *anagram indicator* **03** row **04** fume, rage, rand, rant, rave, roar, rush, stir, tear, to-do **05** shout, stamp **06** assail, attack, charge, furore, outcry, rumpus, seethe, tumult, uproar **07** assault, clamour, explode, flounce, turmoil **08** brouhaha, outbreak, outburst, paroxysm **09** agitation, commotion, kerfuffle, offensive, onslaught **10** hit the roof **11** disturbance **12** lose your cool **14** foam at the mouth

*Storms include:*

**03** ice, sea, sun
**04** dust, gale, hail, line, rain, sand, snow
**05** buran, devil
**06** baguio, calima, haboob, meteor, pelter, squall
**07** cyclone, monsoon, Shaitan, tempest, thunder, tornado, twister, typhoon, violent
**08** blizzard, downpour, magnetic
**09** bourasque, dust devil, hurricane, whirlwind
**10** cloudburst, electrical

## stormy
◇ *anagram indicator* **04** foul, wild **05** dirty, gusty, rainy, rough, windy, wroth **06** choppy, raging, rugged, unruly, wintry **07** gustful, squally, wintery **08** blustery, oragious, stormful **09** inclement, turbulent **10** boisterous, passionate **11** tempestuous

## story
**03** bar, fib, gag, lie, rib **04** baur, bawr, epic, idyl, item, joke, myth, plot, saga, tale, tier, yarn **05** fable, floor, idyll, novel, rumor, theme **06** legend, record, relate, report, rumour, serial, storey **07** account, article, episode, fantasy, feature, fiction, history, recital, romance, shocker, untruth **08** anecdote, jeremiad, nouvelle, oratorio, phantasy, relation, thriller **09** chronicle, falsehood, narrative, statement, storyline **10** allegation, Munchausen, rib-tickler **11** fabrication, historiette, Munchausen **12** old wives' tale, spine-chiller
*See also* **novel; tale**

## storyteller
**04** bard, liar **06** author, writer **08** narrator, novelist, romancer, tell-tale **09** raconteur **10** anecdotist, chronicler, raconteuse

## stout
**03** big, fat **04** bold, tall **05** beefy, brave, bulky, burly, cobby, gutsy, hardy, heavy, lusty, obese, plump, proud, solid, thick, tough, tubby **06** brawny, entire, fierce, fleshy, gritty, heroic, manful, plucky, portly, robust, spunky, stanch, stocky, strong, stuffy, stuggy, sturdy **07** durable, gallant, hulking, staunch, valiant **08** arrogant, athletic, chopping, enduring, fearless, forceful, intrepid, muscular, resolute, stalwart, stubborn, thickset, valorous, vigorous **09** corpulent, dauntless **10** courageous, determined, embonpoint, overweight, unyielding **11** substantial

## stoutly
**06** boldly **07** toughly **08** fiercely, strongly **09** staunchly **10** fearlessly, resolutely

## stove
**03** Aga **04** kiln, oven, stew **05** grill, range **06** cockle, cooker, heater, Primus® **07** caboose, chaufer, furnace **08** chauffer, hothouse, pot-belly **09** gas cooker, kitchener **10** base-burner, calefactor, salamander **12** cooking-range

## stow
◇ *containment indicator* **04** cram, crop, load, pack **05** place, stash, store, stuff **06** bundle **07** deposit, put away **11** flemish down
• **stow away** **04** hide, snug, tuck **05** put up **07** put away **14** travel secretly **15** conceal yourself

## straggle
**03** gad, lag **04** roam, rove, tail **05** amble, drift, range, stray, trail **06** loiter, ramble, sprawl, spread, wander **07** scatter, vagrant **08** sprangle, squander **09** string out **10** dilly-dally

## straggly
**05** loose **06** random, untidy **07** aimless **08** drifting, rambling, straying **09** irregular, spreading, strung out **10** straggling **12** disorganized

## straight
**03** het, str **04** even, fair, flat, gain, just, neat, pure, slap, tidy, true **05** blunt, frank, level, right, smack, spang **06** at once, candid, decent, direct, honest, normal, pronto, square, unbent **07** aligned, bluntly, clearly, frankly, in order, orderly, plainly, settled, sincere, unmixed, upright **08** accurate, arranged, balanced, candidly, directly, faithful, honestly, promptly, reliable, slap-bang, unbroken, uncurved, vertical **09** downright, instantly, on the trot, organized, outspoken, right away, shipshape, tramlined, unbending, uncurving, undiluted **10** consistent, continuous, forthright, honourable, horizontal, law-abiding, point-blank, successive, unswerving, upstanding **11** consecutive, immediately, outspokenly, rectilineal, rectilinear, respectable, trustworthy, undeviating **12** continuously, conventional, forthrightly, heterosexual, orthotropous, successively, without delay **13** consecutively, unadulterated, uninterrupted **14** as the crow flies **15** straightforward, uninterruptedly
• **off the straight** **04** agee, ajee **08** cockeyed
• **straight away** **03** now **06** at once, pronto **08** directly, like that **09** instantly, right away **11** immediately, incontinent **12** just like that, there and then, without delay **13** incontinently

## straighten
◇ *anagram indicator* **04** tidy, yelm **05** align, dress, order, range, yealm **06** adjust, neaten, tidy up, unbend **07** arrange, stretch **08** put right **10** put in order **12** make straight **14** become straight
• **straighten out** **06** extend, settle, tidy up **07** clear up, correct, realign, rectify, resolve, sort out, untwist **08** put right **10** put in order, regularize **11** disentangle
• **straighten up** **05** stand **07** stand up **10** stand erect **12** stand upright

## straightforward
**04** easy, even, open **05** clear, frank, pakka, plain, pucka, pukka **06** candid, direct, honest, simple **07** genuine, jannock, sincere, up-front **08** no frills, truthful **09** outspoken **10** child's play, elementary, forthright, on the level, penny-plain, point-blank, unexacting **11** undemanding, undesigning **12** a piece of cake **13** plain-speaking, uncomplicated, without frills

## strain
**03** air, fit, rax, sye, tax, try, tug, way **04** aria, fitt, hurt, kind, play, pull, race,

rack, rick, seil, sift, sile, sing, song, sort, tear, tire, tune, type, vein, work **05** blood, breed, drain, drive, exert, fitte, force, fytte, heave, labor, music, point, press, retch, shear, sieve, sound, stock, theme, trace, trait, twist, worry, wrick, wring **06** burden, demand, duress, effort, extend, family, filter, goggle, injure, injury, labour, melody, purify, riddle, screen, sprain, spring, streak, stress, stripe, strive, tauten, weaken, wrench **07** anxiety, descent, distend, element, embrace, express, fatigue, lineage, measure, overtax, quality, squeeze, stretch, tension, tighten, variety **08** ancestry, compress, elongate, exertion, go all out, overwork, pedigree, pressure, restrain, separate, struggle, tendency **09** endeavour, offspring, percolate, suspicion, tiredness, weariness **10** exhaustion, extraction, proclivity, suggestion **11** disposition **12** do your utmost **14** beyond the limit, characteristic, push to the limit **15** make every effort

**strained**
**05** drawn, false, heavy, stiff, tense **06** forced, sprung, uneasy, wooden **07** awkward, intense **08** laboured **09** intensive, unnatural, unrelaxed **10** artificial, non-natural **11** constrained, embarrassed **13** self-conscious, uncomfortable

**strainer**
**03** sye **04** seil, sile, tems **05** sieve, siler, tammy, temse **06** filter, milsey, riddle, screen, sifter **08** colander **09** cullender

**strait**
**02** St **03** fix, gat, gut, jam **04** belt, hole, kyle, mess **05** close, inlet, needy, sound, tight **06** crisis, narrow, pickle, plight, strict **07** channel, closely, dilemma, narrows, poverty, tighten, tightly **08** distress, hardship, narrowly, rigorous, straight, streight, strictly **09** emergency, extremity **10** difficulty, perplexity, rigorously **11** hard-pressed, predicament **13** embarrassment

*Straits include:*

**03** Rae
**04** Adak, Bass, Cook, Haro, Irbe, Kara, Palk, Pitt, Soya
**05** Banks, Bohai, Cabot, Canso, Davis, Dease, Dover, Kerch, Korea, Luzon, Menai, Osumi, Sunda, Tatar
**06** Bering, Dundas, Etolin, Fisher, Hecate, Hormuz, Hudson, Lombok, Solent, Sunday, Tablas, Taiwan, Tokara, Torres, Vitiaz
**07** Balabac, Chatham, Dampier, Denmark, Florida, Formosa, Foveaux, Georgia, Le Maire, Makasar, Malacca, McClure, Messina, Mindoro, Otranto, Polillo, Rosario, Tsugaru
**08** Bosporus, Clarence, Karimata, Kattegat, Mackinac, Magellan, Makassar, Shelikof, Tsushima, Victoria
**09** Belle Isle, Bonifacio, Bosphorus,

Gibraltar, Great Belt, La Pérouse, Linapacan, Van Diemen
**10** Juan de Fuca, Little Belt
**11** Dardanelles
**12** Bougainville, Investigator
**13** San Bernardino
**14** Northumberland, Queen Charlotte
**15** Dolphin and Union

**straitened**
**04** poor **07** limited, reduced **09** difficult **10** distressed, restricted **11** embarrassed **12** impoverished

**strait-laced**
**04** prim **06** narrow, proper, strict, stuffy **07** prudish, starchy, uptight **08** priggish, unstuffy **09** tight-lace **10** moralistic, tight-laced **11** puritanical **12** narrow-minded **13** prim and proper

**strand**
**03** ply **04** kemp, lock, sand, wire, wisp **05** beach, fibre, front, piece, sands, shore, tress, twist **06** bundle, factor, gutter, length, maroon, sliver, string, strond, thread **07** element, feature, monofil, rivulet **08** filament, multifil, seashore **09** component, foreshore **10** ingredient, waterfront **11** homopolymer **12** optical fibre **13** multifilament **14** vascular bundle

**stranded**
**07** aground, beached, wrecked **08** forsaken, grounded, helpless, marooned **09** abandoned, penniless **10** high and dry, in the lurch **11** shipwrecked **14** left in the lurch

**strange**
◇ *anagram indicator* **03** new, odd, rum, shy **04** unco **05** alien, crazy, fraim, fremd, funny, kinky, novel, queer, silly, unked, unket, unkid, wacky, weird **06** exotic, freaky, fremit, stupid, unreal **07** bizarre, curious, foreign, oddball, offbeat, surreal, uncanny, uncouth, unknown, untried, unusual **08** abnormal, peculiar, selcouth, singular, straunge, uncommon, unversed, wondrous **09** eccentric, estranged, fantastic, irregular, unheard-of, wonderful, wonderous **10** mysterious, mystifying, off the wall, outlandish, perplexing, remarkable, surprising, unexpected, unfamiliar **11** exceptional, unexplained **12** inexplicable, unaccustomed, unacquainted **13** extraordinary

**strangely**
◇ *anagram indicator* **05** oddly **07** weirdly **08** wondrous **09** bizarrely, curiously, unusually, wonderous **10** abnormally, peculiarly, remarkably, singularly, uncommonly **12** inexplicably, unexpectedly **13** exceptionally

**strangeness**
**01** S **06** oddity **07** oddness **08** eeriness **09** queerness **10** exoticness **11** abnormality, bizarreness, peculiarity, singularity, uncanniness **12** eccentricity, irregularity

**stranger**
**04** unco **05** alien, fraim, fremd, guest

**06** fremit, frenne **07** incomer, pilgrim, visitor **08** newcomer, outsider **09** foreigner, non-member **10** new arrival
• **a stranger to 10** unversed in **14** unaccustomed to, unfamiliar with **15** inexperienced in

**strangle**
**03** gag **04** kill **05** check, choke **06** impede, keep in, stifle **07** garotte, garrote, inhibit, repress, smother **08** garrotte, hold back, restrain, suppress, thrapple, thropple, throttle **09** bowstring, constrict, suffocate **10** asphyxiate **11** strangulate

**strap**
**03** tab, tie **04** band, beat, belt, bind, cord, flog, hang, jess, lash, rein, taws, whip **05** leash, sling, strop, tawse, thong, truss **06** barber, credit, fasten, muzzle, secure **07** bandage, leather, scourge **08** backband, selvagee **10** watchguard

**strapping**
**03** big **05** beefy, burly, hefty, hunky, husky **06** brawny, robust, strong, sturdy **07** hulking **08** chopping, swanking **09** thrashing, two-handed, well-built

**stratagem**
**04** coup, plan, plot, ploy, ruse, wile **05** dodge, fetch, guile, guyle, trick **06** device, feeler, scheme, tactic **08** artifice, intrigue, maneuver, trickery **09** deception, malengine, manoeuvre **10** subterfuge **11** counter-plot, machination **12** ruse de guerre

**strategic**
**03** key **05** vital **07** crucial, planned, politic **08** critical, decisive, tactical **09** essential, important **10** calculated, commanding, deliberate, diplomatic **11** strategical

**strategy**
**03** ESS **04** plan **06** design, policy, scheme **07** maximin, minimax, tactics **08** approach, game plan, planning, schedule **09** blueprint, procedure, programme **11** generalship, geostrategy **12** plan of action **14** shark repellent

**stratification**
**07** bedding, ranking, sorting **08** division, layering **09** gradation, hierarchy **10** graduation **14** categorization, classification

**stratum**
**03** bed **04** lode, post, rank, seam, tier, vein **05** caste, class, grade, group, layer, level, table **06** region **07** bracket, cap rock, coal-bed, day-coal, station **08** category, wayboard **09** Corallian **10** weighboard **14** stratification

**straw**
**04** halm, wase **05** chaff, haulm, strae **06** buntal, litter, thatch **07** stubble **08** strammel, strummel
• **bundle of straw, bundles of straw**
**04** wisp, yelm **05** truss, yealm **06** kemple
• **straw hat 04** hive **06** basher, boater

**stray**
07 leghorn 09 coolie hat, Dunstable
10 balibuntal

**stray**
◊ *anagram indicator* 03 err, odd, tag
04 lost, roam, rove, waff, waif
05 amble, drift, freak, range, traik
06 casual, chance, common, estray,
ramble, random, wander, wilder
07 deviate, digress, diverge, erratic, get
lost, go wrong, meander, roaming,
saunter 08 alleycat, drifting, go astray,
homeless, isolated, maverick, straggle,
stravaig, stray cat, stray dog
09 abandoned, forwander, scattered,
straggler, wandering, wander off
10 accidental, exorbitate, occasional
15 go off at a tangent, go off the subject

**streak**
03 fly 04 band, belt, dart, dash, daub,
lace, line, mark, race, rach, roll, rush,
tear, time, vein, waif, wake, wale,
wave, weal, zoom 05 flash, fleck,
freak, layer, ratch, smear, speed, spell,
stint, stria, strip, sweep, touch, trace,
vibex, whizz 06 beat it, gallop, hurtle,
period, ribbon, scurry, smudge, sprint,
strain, strake, stripe, stroke 07 element,
scarper, scratch, stretch, striate,
vamoose, whistle 09 skedaddle

**streaked**
05 lined 06 banded, barred, hawked,
hawkit, veined 07 brinded, brindle,
flecked, streaky, striate, striped
08 brindled 09 fleckered 11 tear-stained

**stream**
03 fly, jet, pow, ren, rin, run 04 beck,
burn, flap, flow, gush, kill, lake, lane,
nala, pour, rill, rush, shed, tide, well
05 brook, burst, creek, crowd, drift,
float, flood, issue, nalla, nulla, river,
spill, spout, surge, trail 06 course,
deluge, efflux, gutter, nallah, nullah,
rillet, runnel, streel, volley 07 cascade,
current, flutter, rivulet, torrent
08 affluent, influent, tendency
09 tributary 10 outpouring, succession
11 watercourse

**streamer**
04 flag, vane 05 plume 06 banner,
ensign, fallal, pennon, pinnet, ribbon
07 bandrol, pennant 08 banderol,
bannerol, gonfalon, standard, vexillum
09 banderole, bannerall

**streamlined**
05 sleek, slick 06 smooth 07 well-run
08 graceful 09 efficient, organized
10 modernized, time-saving
11 aerodynamic 12 rationalized
13 smooth-running, up-to-the-minute

**street**
02 St 03 rue, way 04 gate, lane, road
06 avenue 12 thoroughfare
*See also* **London; New York; Paris;
road**
• **man in the street, woman in the
street** 07 Joe Blow 09 Joe Bloggs,
Joe Public, Mr Average 10 Joe
Sixpack, Mrs Average 11 John
Citizen 13 average person, average
punter, ordinary bloke 14 ordinary
person 15 ordinary citizen

**streetwalker**
*see* **prostitute**

**strength**
04 bant, bent, gift, grit, guts, iron,
main, thew 05 asset, brawn, clout,
depth, force, forte, might, nerve, point,
power, sinew, thing, truth, vigor
06 ardour, energy, fizzen, foison,
fusion, health, métier, muscle, spirit,
talent, vigour, weight 07 ability,
bravery, cogency, courage, fitness,
fushion, passion, potence, potency,
stamina, urgency 08 aptitude,
fervency, firmness, keenness,
pungency, solidity, validity
09 advantage, fortitude, hardiness,
influence, intensity, sharpness,
solidness, soundness, specialty,
stoutness, toughness, vehemence,
vividness 10 brute force, complement,
durability, resilience, resistance,
resolution, robustness, speciality,
sturdiness 11 athleticism, graphicness,
persistence, strong point
12 forcefulness, might and main
13 assertiveness, determination,
effectiveness 14 impregnability,
persuasiveness
• **lose strength** 04 fade, pall 05 faint,
waste 08 wind down
• **on the strength of** 07 based on
09 because of 10 by virtue of 11 on
account of 12 on the basis of

**strengthen**
03 arm, man 04 fish, line, stay 05 brace,
cleat, edify, force, rally, serve, sinew,
steel, wharf 06 anneal, back up, beef
up, harden, munite, picket, piquet,
prop up, turn up 07 afforce, bolster,
build up, confirm, fortify, hearten,
nourish, picquet, protect, refresh,
restore, shore up, stiffen, support,
toughen 08 buttress, heighten, increase
09 encourage, intensify, reinforce
10 invigorate, work-harden
11 consolidate, corroborate
12 substantiate

**strenuous**
04 bold, hard, keen, warm 05 eager,
heavy, tough 06 active, taxing, tiring,
uphill, urgent 07 arduous, earnest,
weighty, zealous 08 forceful, resolute,
spirited, tireless, vigorous
09 demanding, difficult, energetic,
gruelling, laborious, tenacious
10 blistering, determined, exhausting
13 indefatigable

**strenuously**
06 boldly 08 actively 10 forcefully,
resolutely, tirelessly, vigorously
11 tenaciously

**stress**
◊ *anagram indicator* 04 beat, birr, rack
05 brunt, force, ictus, shear, value,
worry 06 accent, burden, hassle,
repeat, strain, trauma, weight
07 anxiety, point up, straits, tension,
trouble 08 distress, emphasis,
hardship, pressure, priority 09 distraint,
emphasize, highlight, spotlight,
underline 10 accentuate, difficulty,
exaggerate, importance, underscore,

uneasiness 12 accentuation,
apprehension, significance, thermal
shock

**stressed**
04 edgy 05 jumpy, tense 06 on edge,
strong, uneasy 07 anxious, fidgety,
jittery, keyed up, nervous, uptight,
worried 08 emphatic, restless, strained
09 screwed up 10 distraught,
emphatical 11 overwrought, stressed
out 12 apprehensive 13 under pressure

**stressful**
05 tense 06 uneasy 07 charged, fraught
08 strained, worrying 10 nail-biting
12 high-pressure, nerve-racking

**stretch**
03 rax, ren, rin, run, tax, try 04 area,
last, line, pull, push, rack, span, term,
test, time 05 offer, perch, range, reach,
space, spell, stint, sweep, tract, widen
06 bouncy, expand, extend, extent, go
up to, lay out, length, period, pliant,
return, spread, strain, streek, supple,
tauten, unfold, unroll 07 broaden,
buoyant, draw out, elastic, expanse,
hold out, plastic, pliable, present,
proffer, project, prolong, rubbery,
springy, tighten 08 come up to,
continue, distance, elongate, flexible,
go down to, lengthen, protract, reach
out, straucht, straught, stretchy,
yielding 09 challenge, extension, go as
far as, make wider, resilient, spread
out, stimulate 10 come down to,
exaggerate, make longer, straighten
11 become wider, elasticated,
stretchable 12 become longer,
exaggeration, put demands on
13 extensibility
• **stretch out** 05 crane, reach, relax
06 extend, intend, put out, sprawl,
string 07 hold out, lie down, recline
• **stretch your legs** 06 stroll
08 exercise 09 move about,
promenade, take a walk 10 go for a
walk, take the air 13 take a breather

**stretcher**
04 rack 06 gurney, litter

**strew**
03 sow 04 lard, rush, snow, toss
05 level, straw, strow 06 litter, spread
07 bestrew, scatter 08 bespread,
disperse, sprinkle 10 besprinkle

**stricken**
03 hit 06 struck 07 injured, smitten,
wounded 08 affected 09 afflicted

**strict**
04 firm, hard, true 05 clear, close,
exact, harsh, rigid, stern, tight, total,
tough, utter 06 giusto, narrow, proper,
severe, strait 07 austere, literal, precise,
regular 08 absolute, accurate, clear-
cut, complete, faithful, intimate,
orthodox, rigorous, straight, streight
09 Draconian, religious, stringent
10 inflexible, iron-fisted, iron-handed,
meticulous, no-nonsense, particular,
restricted, scrupulous 11 hard and fast
13 authoritarian, barrack square,
conscientious, thoroughgoing
14 disciplinarian, uncompromising

### strictly

**04** only **06** firmly, purely, strait, wholly **07** sternly, totally **08** narrowly, properly, severely, straight, straitly, streight, uniquely **10** absolutely, completely, definitely, in every way, inflexibly, positively, rigorously **11** exclusively **13** categorically, unambiguously, unequivocally **14** in every respect, unquestionably
• **strictly speaking** **07** exactly **09** literally, precisely **11** to the letter

### strictness

**06** rigour **08** accuracy, firmness, rigidity, rigorism, severity **09** austerity, exactness, harshness, precision, rigidness, sternness **10** stringency **12** rigorousness **13** barrack square, stringentness **14** meticulousness, scrupulousness

### stricture

**04** flak **05** blame, bound, limit **06** rebuke **07** binding, censure, closure, confine, control, reproof **09** criticism, restraint, tightness **10** constraint, strictness **11** restriction **13** animadversion

### stride

**04** lamp, lope, pace, sten, step, walk **05** stalk, stend, tread **06** stroam **07** advance, galumph **08** bestride, gallumph, movement, progress, straddle **10** overstride **11** progression
• **take something in your stride** **11** do blindfold, make light of **14** cope with easily, deal with easily, think nothing of

### strident

**04** loud **05** harsh, rough **06** shrill, urgent **07** booming, grating, jarring, rasping, raucous, roaring **08** clashing, jangling **09** clamorous, unmusical **10** discordant, screeching, stentorian, stridulant, thundering, vociferous

### strife

**03** row **04** bate, feud **05** sturt **06** barrat, battle, brigue, combat, debate, hassle, mutiny **07** bargain, conteck, contest, discord, dispute, ill-will, quarrel, rivalry, trouble, warfare **08** argument, conflict, fighting, friction, striving, struggle, variance **09** animosity, bickering, hostility, wrangling **10** contention, dissension, ill-feeling **11** controversy, quarrelling **12** colluctation, contestation, disagreement

### strike

**03** bop, box, cob, fix, hit, lam, pat, ram, rap, tip, wap, zap **04** bang, beat, belt, biff, blad, blow, buff, chap, chip, clap, coin, cuff, dart, deal, draw, feel, find, fist, flog, gowf, hook, knee, look, neck, pane, pash, pean, peck, peen, pein, pene, pole, raid, rush, seem, slam, slap, slat, sock, swap, swop, take, toll, tonk, trap, yerk **05** adopt, bandh, blast, blaud, catch, chime, clout, crash, douse, dowse, fight, impel, knock, lower, plump, pound, prang, print, punch, reach, shoot, sit-in, slant, smack, smite, sound, souse,

spank, stamp, storm, swipe, thump, touch, whack **06** affect, affrap, alight, ambush, appear, assail, assume, attack, batter, blight, broach, buffet, cancel, charge, clinch, come to, dawn on, delete, go-slow, hammer, hit out, mutiny, paddle, poleax, ratify, revolt, sclaff, set out, settle, smooth, stroke, take on, thrash, thwack, wallop **07** achieve, afflict, agree on, assault, bewitch, clobber, come out, compute, deliver, embrace, impinge, impress, inflict, occur to, percuss, poleaxe, protest, torpedo, uncover, unearth, walk out, walk-out **08** arrive at, come upon, describe, discover, estimate, look like, pounce on, register, set about, settle on, siderate, stayaway, stoppage, stop work, storming, strickle **09** dismantle, down tools, encounter, événement, interpose, penetrate, surrender **10** bird impact, chance upon, come to mind, constitute, happen upon, work to rule, work-to-rule **11** collide with **13** have the look of
• **on strike** **03** out
• **strike back** **07** hit back **09** fight back, get back at, retaliate **11** get even with, reciprocate **14** get your own back, pay someone back
• **strike down** **04** fell, kill, ruin, slay **06** smite **07** afflict, destroy **11** assassinate
• **strike out** **03** paw **05** erase **06** cancel, delete, efface, remove, rub out **08** cross out **09** strike off **10** obliterate **13** strike through
• **strike up** **05** begin, start **07** kick off **08** commence, initiate **09** establish, instigate, introduce

### strike-breaker
see **scab**

### striking

**04** bold, dash, fine **06** pretty, strike **07** beating, evident, obvious, salient, visible **08** dazzling, distinct, frappant, gorgeous, sizzling, spanking, stunning **09** arresting, beautiful, distingué, glamorous, memorable **10** attractive, distinguée, impressive, incidental, noticeable, percussion, percutient, photogenic, remarkable **11** astonishing, conspicuous, eye-catching, good-looking, outstanding **13** extraordinary

### string

**01** G **03** row, tie **04** cord, file, hang, hoax, lace, line, link, loop, nete, rake, rope, yarn **05** cable, chain, chord, drove, fibre, leash, queue, quint, sling, strap, tie up, train, twine **06** column, fasten, humbug, number, series, strand, stream, thairm, thread **07** connect, elastic, festoon, suspend **08** lichanos, nicky-tam, paramese, paranete, sequence, shoelace **10** procession, succession
• **string along** **04** dupe, fool, hoax **05** bluff **06** humbug **07** deceive, mislead **09** co-operate, play false **12** put one over on, take for a ride
• **string out** **06** extend, fan out, wander **08** disperse, lengthen, protract,

space out, straggle **09** spread out **10** stretch out
• **strings of a lyre** **04** mese, nete **05** trite **06** hypate **08** lichanos, paramese, paranete **09** parhypate
• **string up** **03** top **04** hang, kill, kilt **05** lynch, run up, truss **15** send to the gibbet
• **with no strings attached** **13** unconditional

### stringency

**06** rigour **07** demands **08** firmness **09** exactness, toughness **10** strictness **12** rigorousness **13** inflexibility

### stringent

**04** firm, hard **05** harsh, rigid, tight, tough **06** severe, strict **07** binding, extreme **08** exacting, rigorous **09** demanding **10** inflexible **14** uncompromising

### stringy

**04** ropy, wiry **05** chewy, ropey, tough **06** sinewy **07** fibrous, gristly **08** leathery

### strip

**03** bar, bit, gut, jib, rig **04** area, band, bare, bark, belt, bend, doff, flay, gear, husk, lath, list, loot, peel, pull, rand, roon, rund, sash, skin, slat, slip, tack, tirl, tirr, togs, welt, zona, zone **05** clear, empty, get-up, ledge, linch, piece, pluck, press, royne, ruler, shear, shred, shuck, spoil, strap, thong, tract, unrip **06** denude, devest, divest, expose, extent, lardon, outfit, peeler, ribbon, rig-out, screed, splent, spline, splint, straik, strake, stripe, stroke, swathe, things, uncase, unload **07** clobber, clothes, colours, deprive, despoil, disrobe, expanse, feather, flaught, flitter, fumetto, lardoon, lay bare, parking, peeling, pillage, plunder, ransack, stretch, tear off, uncover, undress **08** airstrip, clean out, clothing, degrease, flake off, separate, unclothe **09** dismantle, excoriate, pull apart, take apart **10** disfurnish, dispossess, striptease **11** disassemble **12** straightedge, take to pieces **13** swaddling-band

### stripe

**03** bar **04** band, belt, blow, lash, line, list, pale, snip, zone **05** flash, fleck, guard, slash, strip, vitta, whelk **06** ribbon, straik, strain, strake, streak **07** chevron, endorse **09** laticlave, pin-stripe

### striped

**06** banded, barred, pirnie, pirnit, stripy **07** bausond, guarded, streaky, vittate **08** endorsed, streaked, striated **10** variegated **11** finch-backed

### stripling

**03** boy, lad **05** youth **07** young 'un **08** teenager **09** fledgling, youngster **10** adolescent **11** hobbledehoy

### strive

**03** try, tug, vie **04** toil, work **05** bandy, fight, force, heave, press **06** aspire, battle, combat, engage, follow, labour, pingle, preace, prease, resist, strain **07** attempt, bargain, compete,

**stroke**

contend, contest, enforce, preasse, try hard, wrestle **08** campaign, do battle, endeavor, purchase, struggle **09** endeavour, persevere **10** do your best **11** give your all **12** do your utmost **13** exert yourself

**stroke**

**03** cut, hit, pat, pet, rub **04** beat, bell, belt, biff, blow, coup, dash, dint, hand, jole, joll, jowl, line, milk, move, push, shot, slap, touk, tuck, whet **05** boast, chuck, cross, ictus, joule, knock, pulse, scoop, shock, smack, spasm, strip, sweep, swipe, thump, touch, trait, whack **06** action, attack, buffet, caress, fondle, glance, motion, stound, stownd, strike, struck, thwack, tittle, wallop **07** clobber, flatter, massage, nobbler, outlash, reverse, reverso, seizure, solidus, strooke, upright, whample **08** collapse, flourish, movement **09** encourage, grand coup **10** back-hander, coup d'éclat, piledriver, sideration, thrombosis **11** achievement **12** punto reverso, punto riverso, repercussion **14** accomplishment
*See also* **swimming**

**stroll**

**04** turn, walk **05** amble, troll **06** bummel, dander, dauner, dawdle, dawner, lounge, ramble, toddle, wander **07** daunder, meander, saunter **08** ambulate **10** go for a walk **14** constitutional **15** stretch your legs

**stroller**

**06** walker **07** dawdler, flâneur, rambler, vagrant **08** wanderer **09** itinerant, pushchair, saunterer

**strong**

**01** f **03** fit, hot, str **04** able, bull, deep, firm, full, hale, keen, rank, sour, very, well, yald **05** beefy, brave, burly, clear, eager, great, gross, gutsy, hardy, heady, heavy, lusty, nappy, pithy, sharp, solid, sound, spicy, stiff, stout, thewy, tough, valid, vivid, wight, yauld **06** active, ardent, biting, brawny, cogent, fierce, marked, mighty, potent, robust, rugged, secure, severe, sinewy, sturdy, trusty, urgent **07** devoted, doughty, durable, evident, fervent, graphic, healthy, intense, marrowy, obvious, piquant, pollent, pungent, telling, violent, weighty **08** athletic, cast-iron, clear-cut, decisive, definite, forceful, forcible, grievous, muscular, numerous, positive, powerful, profound, resolute, stalwart, stressed, vehement, vigorous **09** assertive, committed, competent, confident, effective, efficient, excelling, heavy-duty, plausible, resilient, resistant, steadfast, strapping, undiluted, well-built **10** aggressive, compelling, convincing, courageous, determined, emphasized, fast-moving, formidable, hogen-mogen, passionate, persistent, persuasive, pronounced, reinforced, remarkable **11** efficacious, hard-wearing, long-lasting, substantial **12** concentrated, enthusiastic, single-minded, strong-minded, strong-willed

**13** well-protected **14** highly seasoned **15** highly flavoured
• **strong point 04** bent, gift **05** asset, forte, thing **06** métier, talent **08** aptitude, strength **09** advantage, specialty **10** speciality

**strongarm**

**06** terror **07** violent **08** bully-boy, bullying, coercive, forceful, physical, thuggish **10** aggressive, oppressive **11** threatening **12** intimidatory

**strongbox**

**04** safe **05** chest, vault **06** coffer **07** cash box **10** deposit box, depository, repository

**stronghold**

**04** aery, eyry, fort, hold, holt, keep **05** aerie, ayrie, eyrie, tower **06** castle, center, centre, refuge **07** bastion, citadel, outpost **08** fastness, fortress, hill-fort

**strongly**

**06** deeply, firmly **07** durably, solidly, toughly **08** markedly **09** intensely **10** definitely, forcefully, muscularly, positively, powerfully, resolutely **11** resiliently **12** athletically **13** substantially

**strong-minded**

**04** firm **08** resolute **09** steadfast, tenacious, unbending **10** determined, iron-willed, unwavering **11** independent **12** strong-willed **14** uncompromising

**strong-willed**

**06** wilful **07** wayward **08** obdurate, stubborn **09** obstinate **10** inflexible, refractory, self-willed **11** intractable **12** intransigent, recalcitrant

**strontium**

**02** Sr

**stroppy**

**05** ratty, rowdy **06** shirty **07** awkward, bolshie **08** perverse **09** difficult, unhelpful **10** refractory **11** bad-tempered, quarrelsome **12** bloody minded, cantankerous, obstreperous **13** unco-operative

**structural**

**06** design **07** organic **08** tectonic **09** edificial **11** formational **14** constructional, organizational **15** configurational

**structure**

◇ *anagram indicator* **04** form, make **05** build, frame, set-up, shape **06** design, fabric, make-up, system **07** arrange, build up, chassis, edifice **08** assemble, building, erection, organize **09** construct, formation, framework **10** contexture **11** arrangement, composition **12** architecture, conformation, constitution, construction, organization **13** configuration

**struggle**

◇ *anagram indicator* **03** tug, vie, war **04** agon, camp, toil, work **05** agony, brawl, clash, fight, pains, scrum **06** battle, combat, effort, engage,

hassle, labour, ruffle, strain, strife, strift, strive, tussle **07** agonize, compete, contend, contest, grapple, problem, scuffle, trouble, try hard, tuilyie, tuilzie, warfare, wrestle **08** conflict, exertion, flounder, skirmish, slugfest, sprangle **09** encounter, handgrips, luctation, scrimmage, scrummage **10** difficulty, do your best **11** competition, give your all, hostilities **12** do your utmost **13** exert yourself, passage of arms

**strumpet**
*see* **prostitute**

**strut**

**03** jet **04** cock, prop, spur **05** brank, bulge, dwang, glory, major, pronk, raker, stalk, swank **06** flaunt, parade, prance, scotch, strout, strunt **07** nervure, peacock, swagger **08** protrude, stanchel, stancher, tail boom **09** stanchion

**stub**

**03** end **04** butt, grub, snub, stob **05** stump **06** dog-end, fag end, snubbe **07** remnant **11** counterfoil

**stubborn**

**05** rigid, stiff, stoor, stour, stout, sture **06** dogged, mulish, ornery, stowre, thrawn, wilful **07** adamant **08** obdurate, obstacle, perverse **09** difficult, hidebound, obstinate, opinioned, pig-headed, rigwiddie, rigwoodie, tenacious, unbending **10** headstrong, inflexible, inveterate, persistent, refractory, self-willed, unyielding **11** intractable, opinionated, stiff-necked **12** cantankerous, contumacious, intransigent, opinionative, pertinacious, recalcitrant, stiff-hearted, strong-willed, unmanageable **14** overdetermined, uncompromising **15** not open to reason, stubborn as a mule
*See also* **obstinate**

**stubbornly**

**08** doggedly, wilfully **10** inflexibly, perversely **11** obstinately, pig-headedly, tenaciously **12** persistently **14** intransigently

**stubby**

**05** dumpy, short, squat **06** chunky, stumpy **08** thickset

**stuck**

**04** fast, firm **05** fixed, glued **06** beaten, jammed, joined, rooted **07** at a loss, baffled, stalled, stumped **08** cemented, embedded, fastened, immobile **09** perplexed, unmovable **10** bogged down, nonplussed **13** at your wits' end
• **get stuck into 05** begin, start **06** tackle **08** embark on, set about **09** get down to
• **stuck on 05** mad on **06** fond of, keen on, nuts on **07** sweet on **09** wild about **10** crazy about, dotty about **12** obsessed with **14** infatuated with

**stuck-up**

**05** proud **06** snooty, uppish **07** haughty **08** arrogant, snobbish, toplofty

**stud**
09 bigheaded, conceited 10 hoity-toity
11 patronizing, toffee-nosed,
toploftical 12 supercilious
13 condescending, high and
mighty

**stud**
03 seg, set 04 boss, knob, nail, race,
spur, stop, tack 05 pitch, prick, rivet,
stump 06 popper 07 clinker 08 doornail
11 pop-fastener 12 clip-fastener, snap-
fastener 13 press fastener

**studded**
03 set 06 dotted 07 flecked, spotted,
starred 08 mamillar, spangled,
speckled 09 mamillary, scattered,
sprinkled 10 bejewelled, bespangled,
icy-pearled, ornamented 12 star-
spangled

**student**
01 L 04 semi, soph 05 bejan, pupil,
semie, softa, welly 06 bejant, bursar,
medico, premed, tosher, wellie
07 alumnus, bookman, fresher,
grinder, learner, scarfie, scholar,
Templar, trainee 08 disciple, freshman,
premedic 09 collegian, schoolboy,
semi-bajan, sophomore 10 apprentice,
green welly, schoolgirl 11 collegianer,
probationer 12 extensionist,
postgraduate 13 undergraduate
• **student group** 03 NUS

**studied**
05 voulu 06 forced, versed, wilful
07 planned 08 affected, designed, well-
read 09 conscious, contrived,
unnatural 10 artificial, calculated,
deliberate, purposeful 11 intentional
12 premeditated 13 over-elaborate

**studio**
06 school 07 atelier, bottega, gallery
08 workroom, workshop

**studious**
05 eager 07 bookish, careful, earnest,
serious 08 academic, diligent,
sedulous, thorough 09 assiduous,
attentive, scholarly 10 deliberate,
meticulous, reflective, thoughtful
11 hard-working, industrious
12 intellectual

**study**
03 con, den, dig, kon 04 cram, muse,
plod, read, scan, swot, work, zeal
05 conne, essay, learn, mug up, paper,
train 06 bone up, devise, digest, office,
peruse, ponder, read up, report,
review, revise, studio, survey, thesis
07 analyse, article, examine, inquiry,
library, major in, perusal, reading,
reflect, reverie, subject, thought
08 analysis, bone up on, consider,
cramming, critique, homework,
instruct, interest, learning, meditate,
pore over, research, revision, scrutiny,
swotting, workroom 09 attention,
monograph, workplace 10 deliberate,
inspection, scrutinize 11 contemplate,
examination, inclination, investigate,
lucubration, preparation,
prolegomena, scholarship
12 propaedeutic 13 consideration,
contemplation, investigation

*Subjects of study include:*

02 IT
03 art, ICT, law, PSE
04 PHSE
05 craft, dance, D and T, drama,
music, sport
06 botany, design
07 anatomy, biology, driving,
ecology, fashion, fitness, geology,
history, physics, pottery, science,
zoology
08 commerce, eugenics, genetics,
heraldry, medicine, penology,
politics, theology
09 astrology, astronomy, chemistry,
cosmology, economics,
education, erotology, ethnology,
forensics, geography, languages,
logistics, marketing, mechanics,
mythology, pathology, shorthand,
sociology, surveying, web design
10 humanities, journalism, literature,
metallurgy, philosophy,
physiology, psychology,
publishing, statistics, technology,
visual arts
11 accountancy, agriculture,
archaeology, calligraphy,
citizenship, dressmaking,
electronics, engineering,
linguistics, mathematics,
metaphysics, meteorology,
ornithology, photography, the
Classics, typewriting
12 anthropology, architecture,
astrobiology, horticulture,
lexicography, media studies,
oceanography, pharmacology
13 gender studies, home economics,
librarianship, marine studies,
nutrigenomics, women's studies
14 food technology, leisure studies,
natural history, quantum physics,
social sciences, toxicogenomics,
word processing
15 building studies, business studies,
computer studies, creative
writing, hotel management

**stuff**
03 jam, kit, pad, ram, wad 04 clog,
cram, fill, gear, hoax, lard, line, load,
pack, pang, push, sate, stap, stow, trig,
tuck 05 binge, blash, block, cloth,
crowd, farce, force, fudge, goods,
gorge, items, money, press, shove,
squab, store, wedge 06 bung up,
fabric, gobble, guzzle, liquor, matter,
pig out, steeve, stodge, tackle, things,
thrust 07 bombast, clobber, essence,
filling, furnish, luggage, objects,
rubbish, satiate, squeeze, woollen
08 articles, compress, garrison, gross
out, material, nonsense, obstruct,
stuffing 09 equipment, furniture,
materials, provision, substance
10 belongings, gormandize
11 overindulge, possessions
13 paraphernalia

**stuffing**
◇ *containment indicator* ◇ *hidden
indicator* 05 farce, kapok 07 bombast,
farcing, filling, packing, padding,
pudding, wadding 08 dressing,

quilting, stopping 09 deafening,
forcemeat, taxidermy

**stuffy**
04 dull, prim 05 close, fuggy, fusty,
heavy, muggy, musty, staid, stale, stiff,
stivy, stout, sulky 06 dreary, frowsy,
frowzy, poking, stodgy, sturdy, sultry
07 airless, pompous, starchy 08 stifling
10 fuddy-duddy, oppressive 11 strait-
laced, suffocating 12 buttoned-down,
conventional, old-fashioned,
unventilated 13 uninteresting

**stultify**
04 dull, numb 05 blunt 06 negate, stifle,
thwart 07 nullify, smother, stupefy
08 hebetate, suppress 10 invalidate

**stumble**
◇ *anagram indicator* 03 err 04 fall, peck,
reel, slip, trip 05 lapse, lurch, stoit
06 falter, hamble 07 blunder, founder,
snapper, stagger, stammer, stotter,
stutter 08 flounder, hesitate, titubate
09 false step 10 disconcert 15 lose your
balance
• **stumble across, stumble on**
04 find 08 discover 09 encounter
10 chance upon, come across, happen
upon

**stumbling-block**
03 bar 04 snag 06 hurdle 07 barrier,
scandal 08 obstacle 09 hindrance
10 difficulty, impediment
11 obstruction 12 Becher's Brook

**stump**
03 end, leg, nog, peg 04 butt, dare, foil,
more, runt, snag, stob, stub, stud
05 floor, scrag, stock, stool, trunk
06 baffle, defeat, dog-end, fag end,
outwit, puzzle, wicket 07 confuse,
flummox, mystify, nonplus, perplex,
remains, remnant, staddle, stubble
08 bewilder, confound 09 bamboozle,
challenge, dumbfound, tortillon
• **stump up** 03 pay 05 pay up 06 ante
up, chip in, donate, pay out 07 cough
up, fork out 08 hand over, shell out
10 contribute

**stumped**
02 st 05 stuck 07 baffled, floored,
stymied 09 flummoxed, perplexed,
stonkered 10 bamboozled, nonplussed

**stumpy**
04 cash 05 dumpy, heavy, nirly, short,
squat, thick 06 chunky, nirlie, stocky,
stubby 07 stubbed 08 thickset

**stun**
02 KO 04 daze, kayo 05 amaze, devel,
dover, knock, shock, stonn, stoun,
Taser® 06 abrade, bruise, deafen,
devvel, settle, stonne, stound
07 astound, confuse, stagger, stupefy
08 astonish, bedeafen, bewilder, bowl
over, confound, knock out, overcome
09 dumbfound, overpower
11 flabbergast, knock for six

**stunned**
04 numb 05 dazed, silly 06 aghast,
amazed, stupid 07 floored, in a daze,
shocked 09 astounded, staggered,
stupefied 10 astonished, devastated,

gobsmacked **11** dumbfounded **13** flabbergasted

**stunner**
**02** KO **03** wow **05** peach, siren **06** beauty, looker, lovely **07** charmer, cracker, dazzler, smasher **08** knockout **09** sensation **10** eye-catcher, good-looker, heart-throb **11** femme fatale

**stunning**
**05** great **06** dazing, lovely **07** amazing **08** dazzling, drop-dead, fabulous, gorgeous, smashing, striking **09** beautiful, brilliant, ravishing, wonderful **10** impressive, incredible, marvellous, remarkable, staggering, stupefying **11** sensational, spectacular **12** stupefaction **13** extraordinary

**stunningly**
**09** amazingly **10** fabulously, gorgeously, remarkably, strikingly **11** beautifully, brilliantly, wonderfully **12** impressively, marvellously, staggeringly **13** spectacularly **15** extraordinarily

**stunt**
**03** act **04** curb, deed, feat, hype, nirl, ramp, slow, stop, turn **05** check, dwarf, stock, trick **06** action, arrest, hamper, hinder, impede, retard, wheeze **07** exploit, inhibit **08** restrict **10** enterprise **11** performance

**stunted**
**04** puny, tiny **05** nirly, small **06** little, nirlie **07** dwarfed, scroggy, scrubby **08** dwarfish, scroggie, scrubbed, withered **10** diminutive, undersized, wanthriven

**stupefaction**
**04** daze **06** wonder **08** blackout, numbness, stunning **09** amazement **10** amazedness, bafflement **12** astonishment, bewilderment, state of shock **13** senselessness

**stupefy**
**04** daze, drug, dull, mull, numb, stun **05** amaze, dozen, hocus, shock **06** bemuse, benumb, drowse, fuddle, mither, moider **07** astound, moither, stagger **08** bowl over, etherize, knock out, somniate **09** devastate, dumbfound **11** knock for six

**stupendous**
**04** huge, vast **06** killer, superb **07** amazing, immense **08** colossal, enormous, fabulous, gigantic, stunning **09** fantastic, wonderful **10** astounding, marvellous, phenomenal, prodigious, staggering, tremendous **12** breathtaking, overwhelming **13** extraordinary

**stupid**
◇ *anagram indicator* **03** dim, jay, mad, twp **04** dopy, dull, dumb, rash, slow **05** barmy, brute, crass, crazy, dazed, dense, divvy, dopey, doted, dovie, dunny, flaky, foggy, goofy, gross, inane, looby, loony, loopy, muddy, potty, silly, stupe, thick **06** absurd, boring, bovine, donsie, facile, futile, groggy, lumpen, obtuse, owlish, tavert, wooden **07** damfool, doltish, donnard,

donnart, donnerd, donnert, fatuous, foolish, glaiket, glaikit, idiotic, insulse, lunatic, moronic, puerile, stunned, taivert, witless **08** anserine, backward, besotted, blockish, Boeotian, boobyish, clueless, donnered, gaumless, gormless, mindless, purblind, sluggish **09** brainless, dim-witted, fat-witted, foolhardy, half-assed, imbecilic, laughable, ludicrous, pointless, senseless, stupefied **10** beef-witted, dull-witted, fatbrained, half-witted, ill-advised, indiscreet, insensible **11** beef-brained, blunt-witted, clay-brained, conceitless, hair-brained, hare-brained, heavy-headed, injudicious, meaningless, nonsensical, not all there, thickheaded, unconscious **12** feeble-minded, hammer-headed, muttonheaded, simple-minded, sodden-witted, thick-skulled, woodenheaded **13** chuckle-headed, irresponsible, pudding-headed, semiconscious, thick as a plank **15** slow on the uptake

**stupidity**
**05** folly **06** bêtise, idiocy, lunacy, torpor **07** dimness, duncery, fatuity, goosery, inanity, madness, naivety **08** dopiness, doziness, dullness, dumbness, futility, insanity, rashness, slowness **09** absurdity, asininity, bruteness, crassness, denseness, insulsity, oscitancy, puerility, silliness, thickness **10** crassitude, imbecility, ineptitude, obtuseness **11** fatuousness, foolishness, glaikitness **12** cluelessness, indiscretion **13** brainlessness, foolhardiness, ludicrousness, pointlessness, senselessness **14** impracticality
• **expression of stupidity 03** doh, duh

**stupidly**
◇ *anagram indicator* **07** inanely, sillily **08** absurdly **09** fatuously, foolishly **10** mindlessly **12** unthinkingly **13** irresponsibly

**stupor**
**04** coma, daze **06** torpor, trance **07** inertia **08** blackout, lethargy, numbness, oblivion **12** state of shock, stupefaction **13** insensibility **15** unconsciousness

**sturdy**
**03** gid **04** dunt, firm **05** burly, giddy, hardy, husky, rough, solid, stout **06** hearty, mighty, robust, rugged, steeve, stieve, stocky, strong, stuffy **07** durable, staunch, violent **08** athletic, lubberly, muscular, powerful, resolute, stalwart, turnsick, vigorous, well-made **09** impetuous, obstinate, steadfast, tenacious, well-built **10** determined, refractory **11** flourishing, substantial

**sturgeon**
**04** huso **05** elops **06** beluga, ellops **07** osseter, sevruga, sterlet **10** shovelnose

**stutter**
**04** lisp **06** falter, mumble **07** sputter,

stammer, stumble **08** hesitate, splutter **12** speech defect

**St Vincent and the Grenadines**
**02** WV **03** VCT

**style**
◇ *anagram indicator* **03** cut, dub, pen, tag, way **04** call, chic, dash, form, hand, kind, make, mode, name, sort, term, tone, type, vein **05** adapt, flair, genre, index, label, shape, taste, tenor, title, trend, vogue **06** custom, design, format, gnomon, luxury, manner, method, phrase, polish, tailor, wealth **07** address, comfort, diction, entitle, fashion, panache, pattern, pointel, pointer, produce, variety, wording **08** approach, category, elegance, grandeur, language, phrasing, urbanity **09** affluence, designate, smartness, suaveness, technique **10** appearance, denominate, dressiness, expression, refinement **11** flamboyance, methodology, stylishness **14** sophistication
• **in the style of 03** à la **05** after, -esque

**stylish**
**03** fly **04** chic, posh **05** janty, natty, nifty, ritzy, sharp, showy, smart, swish **06** chichi, classy, dressy, jaunty, modish, snappy, snazzy, sporty, trendy, urbane **07** à la mode, dashing, elegant, in vogue, refined, voguish **08** polished **11** fashionable **13** sophisticated

**stylus**
**03** gad, pen **04** hand **05** index, probe, style **06** needle **07** pointer **08** graphium

**stymie**
**04** balk, foil **05** block, stump **06** baffle, defeat, hamper, hinder, hogtie, impede, puzzle, thwart **07** flummox, mystify, nonplus, snooker **08** confound **09** bamboozle, frustrate, interfere

**styptic**
**06** amadou, matico, stanch **07** staunch **10** astringent **11** haemostatic

**suave**
**04** glib **05** bland, civil **06** polite, smooth, urbane **07** affable, refined, worldly **08** charming, debonair, polished, unctuous **09** agreeable, civilized, courteous **10** soft-spoken **13** sophisticated

**suavity**
**05** charm **08** civility, courtesy, urbanity **09** blandness **10** politeness, refinement, smoothness **11** worldliness **12** agreeability, unctuousness **14** sophistication

**sub**
**04** dues, gift, lend, temp **05** agent, locum, proxy, U-boat **06** deputy, fill-in, relief, supply **07** advance, payment, reserve, stand-by, stand-in, stopgap **08** donation, offering **09** makeshift, surrogate **10** substitute, understudy **11** locum tenens, pinch-hitter, replacement **12** contribution, subscription **13** membership fee

## subaquatic
07 subaqua 08 demersal, undersea
09 submarine, submersed
10 subaqueous, underwater

## subatomic particle
*see* **particle**

## subconscious
02 id 03 ego 04 deep, mind 05 inner
06 hidden, latent, psyche 08 super-ego
09 innermost, inner self, intuitive,
repressed 10 inner being, subliminal,
suppressed, underlying 11 instinctive,
unconscious 15 unconscious self

## subcontract
07 farm out 08 delegate 09 outsource
11 contract out 12 give to others, pass
to others

## subdue
03 cow 04 adaw, damp, mate, tame
05 accoy, allay, break, charm, check,
crush, daunt, quail, quash, quell
06 defeat, do down, humble, master,
mellow, pacify, reduce, soften, starve,
step on, stifle, subact, subdew, take in
07 achieve, chasten, conquer, control,
crucify, daunton, mortify, overrun,
quieten, repress, subject 08 chastise,
moderate, overcome, restrain,
suppress, vanquish 09 overpower, soft-
pedal, subjugate 10 bring under,
discipline 12 put a damper on 14 get
the better of 15 gain mastery over

## subdued
03 dim, sad 04 soft 05 grave, muted,
quiet, sober, still 06 abated, hushed,
low-key, pastel, shaded, silent,
solemn, sombre, subtle 07 captive,
passive, serious, submiss 08 dejected,
delicate, downcast, lifeless, softened
09 depressed, noiseless, toned-down,
unexcited 10 restrained 11 crestfallen,
unobtrusive 13 irrepressible 14 down
in the dumps

## subject
03 apt, put, sub 04 case, open, subj
05 bound, field, issue, liege, motif,
point, prone, theme, thirl, topic
06 affair, aspect, client, expose,
ground, liable, likely, matter, native,
subdew, subdue, submit, vassal,
victim 07 caitive, captive, citizen,
exposed, hanging, lay open, patient,
resting, servant, servile 08 amenable,
business, disposed, inferior, liegeman,
national, obedient, question, resident
09 dependant, dependent, depending,
guinea pig, subjugate, substance,
underling 10 answerable, cognizable,
contingent, discipline, inhabitant,
subjugated, submissive, underlying,
vulnerable 11 accountable, area of
study, conditional, constrained,
participant, subordinate, subservient,
susceptible 12 field of study
*See also* **study**

## subjection
06 chains, defeat 07 bondage, mastery,
slavery 08 exposure, question,
shackles 09 captivity, servitude,
vassalage 10 discipline, domination,
oppression 11 enslavement,
subjugation

## subjective
06 biased 07 bigoted 08 personal
09 emotional, intuitive 10 individual,
nominative, prejudiced 11 instinctive
13 idiosyncratic, introspective

## subjugate
04 tame 05 crush, quell 06 defeat,
master, reduce, subdue, thrall
07 conquer, enslave, oppress
08 overcome, suppress, vanquish
09 overpower, overthrow 14 get the
better of 15 gain mastery over

## sublimate
04 turn 05 exalt 06 divert, purify, refine
07 alcohol, channel, elevate, flowers
08 heighten, redirect, transfer
09 transmute

## sublime
04 high 05 exalt, grand, great, lofty,
noble, utter 06 august, winged
07 Dantean, exalted, extreme, intense,
supreme 08 complete, elevated,
empyreal, glorious, heavenly,
imposing, majestic 09 celestial,
Dantesque, spiritual 10 majestical
11 magnificent 12 transcendent 14 out
of this world

## subliminal
06 hidden 09 concealed
11 unconscious 12 subconscious,
subthreshold

## submarine
03 sub 05 U-boat 06 hoagie, X-craft
07 pigboat

## submerge
03 dip 04 bury, dive, duck, dunk, sink,
take 05 drown, flood, swamp, whelm
06 deluge, engulf, go down, plunge
07 conceal, immerse, plummet
08 implunge, indrench, inundate,
overflow, submerse, suppress
09 overwhelm 12 go under water
13 put under water

## submerged
04 sunk 06 hidden, sunken, unseen,
veiled 07 cloaked, drowned, swamped
08 immersed, obscured 09 concealed,
inundated, submersed 10 underwater

## submission
05 entry 06 assent, tender 07 tabling
08 averment, giving in, meekness,
offering, proposal 09 agreement,
assertion, deference, obedience,
passivity, statement, surrender,
tendering 10 compliance, confession,
suggestion 11 proposition, resignation
12 acquiescence, capitulation,
contribution, introduction,
presentation, resignedness,
subscription 13 subordination
14 submissiveness

## submissive
04 meek, weak 06 docile, humble,
supine 07 passive, patient, servile,
subdued 08 biddable, obedient,
resigned, yielding 09 compliant,
malleable 10 weak-willed
11 acquiescent, deferential,
downtrodden, reverential,
subordinate, subservient, unresisting

12 ingratiating, self-effacing
13 accommodating, uncomplaining

## submissively
06 humbly, meekly, weakly 09 cap in
hand, passively, patiently
10 obediently 13 deferentially,
subserviently 15 uncomplainingly

## submit
03 bow, put 04 aver, bend, move
05 agree, argue, claim, defer, lower,
offer, posit, refer, state, stoop, table,
yield 06 accede, assert, comply,
expose, give in, permit, prefer, render,
resign, send in, tender 07 consent, give
way, lay down, passage, present,
proffer, propose, subject, succumb,
suggest, violate 08 propound
09 acquiesce, introduce, lay before,
subscribe, surrender 10 bow the knee,
capitulate, come to heel, kiss the rod,
put forward 11 bend the knee, come to
terms, subordinate 12 knuckle under
13 bite the bullet 15 lay down your
arms

## subnormal
03 low 04 slow 08 backward, inferior,
retarded 11 below normal 12 below
average, feeble-minded

## subordinate
◇ *juxtaposition down indicator* 04 aide
05 lower, lowly, minor, under
06 deputy, junior, lesser, menial,
second, skivvy, stooge, submit, vassal
07 subject 08 dogsbody, inferior,
marginal, offsider, servient, sidekick
09 ancillary, assistant, attendant,
auxiliary, dependant, dependent,
secondary, subaltern, underling
10 submissive, subsidiary, underlying
11 lower in rank, subservient 12 lower-
ranking, second fiddle
14 understrapping

## subordination
09 servitude 10 dependence
subjection, submission 11 inferiority
12 subservience

## subscribe
04 back, give, sign, take 05 agree
06 answer, assent, chip in, donate,
pledge, submit 07 approve, endorse,
fork out, support 08 advocate, shell
out, sign up to 10 contribute,
underwrite 12 buy regularly 13 take
regularly 15 pay for regularly

## subscriber
06 member 08 customer 13 regular
reader

## subscription
04 dues, gift 06 assent 07 payment
08 donation, offering, sanction
09 signature 10 abonnement,
submission 11 endorsement
12 contribution 13 membership fee

## subsequent
04 next 05 later 06 future 07 ensuing
09 following, resulting 10 consequent,
succeeding 12 postliminary

## subsequently
05 after, later 09 afterward
10 afterwards 12 consequently

### subservience
**08** humility **09** deference, obedience, servility, servitude **10** subjection **11** dutifulness **12** acquiescence **13** subordination **14** submissiveness

### subservient
**05** lower, minor **06** junior, lesser **07** fawning, servile, slavish, subject **08** inferior, toadying, unctuous **09** ancillary, auxiliary, dependent, secondary **10** obsequious, submissive, subserving, subsidiary **11** bootlicking, deferential, subordinate, sycophantic **12** ingratiating, instrumental, subalternate **13** less important

### subside
**03** ebb **04** adaw, drop, ease, fall, lull, sink, wane **05** abate, let up, lower, quell, slake, sound, swoon, swoun **06** cave in, lessen, quench, recede, settle, swound **07** assuage, decline, descend, die down, dwindle, founder, quieten, slacken **08** collapse, decrease, diminish, dissolve, get lower, moderate, peter out, pipe down

### subsidence
**03** ebb, sag **04** swag **07** decline, descent, sinking **08** collapse, decrease, settling **09** abatement, lessening **10** diminution, settlement, slackening **12** de-escalation, detumescence

### subsidiary
**02** by **03** bye **04** part, side, wing **05** minor **06** aiding, branch, feeder, lesser **07** section **08** division, offshoot **09** accessory, adjective, affiliate, ancillary, assistant, auxiliary, secondary, succursal **10** additional, collateral, supporting **11** subordinate, subservient **12** contributory **13** supplementary

### subsidize
**03** aid **04** back, fund **07** endorse, finance, promote, sponsor, support **08** invest in **10** underwrite **12** contribute to **14** give a subsidy to

### subsidy
**03** aid **04** help **05** grant **07** backing, finance, funding, headage, support **09** allowance **10** assistance, investment, subvention **11** endorsement, sponsorship **12** contribution, underwriting

### subsist
**04** last, live **05** exist **06** endure, remain **07** consist, hold out, survive **08** continue

### subsistence
**04** food, keep **06** living **07** aliment, rations, support **08** survival **09** existence **10** livelihood, provisions, sustenance **11** continuance, maintenance, nourishment

### substance
**03** sum **04** body, gist, mass, meat, pith, quid, text **05** basis, being, force, means, money, power, stuff, theme, topic, truth **06** amount, assets, burden, entity, fabric, ground, import, matter, medium, riches, wealth, weight **07** essence, fortune, meaning, reality,

subject **08** material, property, solidity, validity **09** actuality, affluence, influence, marijuana, resources **10** foundation, prosperity **11** consistence, consistency, materiality, tangibility **12** concreteness, corporeality, significance **13** subject matter **14** meaningfulness

### substandard
**04** poor **05** crook **06** shoddy **07** damaged **08** below par, inferior **09** imperfect **10** inadequate, second-rate **12** unacceptable **14** not up to scratch

### substantial
**03** big **04** firm, hard, main, real, rich, tidy, true **05** ample, basic, bulky, great, large, solid, sound, stout, tough **06** actual, hearty, pretty, stable, strong, sturdy **07** central, durable, filling, notable, primary, sizable, wealthy, weighty **08** affluent, cast-iron, concrete, enduring, existing, generous, inherent, material, powerful, sizable, tangible, valuable, well-to-do **09** corporeal, essential, heavy-duty, important, intrinsic, principal, well-built **10** meaningful, measurable, prosperous, remarkable, successful, worthwhile **11** fundamental, influential, significant **12** considerable

### substantially
**06** mainly **07** at heart, largely **08** in effect **09** in the main **10** materially **11** essentially **12** considerably **13** fundamentally, significantly **14** to a great extent

### substantiate
**05** prove **06** back up, embody, uphold, verify **07** bear out, confirm, support **08** validate **11** corroborate **12** authenticate

### substantive
**02** sb **04** noun, real **05** solid, subst, valid **07** factual **08** concrete, material **09** intrinsic **11** fundamental, substantial

### substitute
**03** sub **04** -ette, heir, lieu, swap, temp **05** agent, cover, locum, proxy, vicar **06** acting, change, deputy, double, ersatz, fill in, fill-in, relief, ring-in, supply, switch **07** commute, fig leaf, relieve, replace, reserve, stand-by, stand in, stand-in, stopgap **08** deputize, exchange, replacer, take over **09** alternate, makeshift, prorector, subrogate, surrogate, temporary **10** changeling, proproctor, understudy, use instead **11** alternative, interchange, locum tenens, pinch-hitter, replacement **12** act instead of **14** take the place of

### substitution
**04** swap **06** change, switch **08** exchange, novation, swapping **09** switching **10** delegation, innovation, resolution **11** interchange, replacement

### subsume
**03** add **04** hold **05** add in, admit, cover,

enter, put in **06** embody, insert, take in **07** contain, count in, embrace, enclose, include, swallow **08** comprise, take over **09** encompass, introduce **10** comprehend **11** incorporate

### subterfuge
**04** hole, ploy, ruse, wile **05** blind, dodge, trick **06** excuse, refuge, scheme **07** evasion, off-come, pretext **08** artifice, intrigue, pretence **09** creep-hole, deception, duplicity, expedient, manoeuvre, stratagem **11** deviousness, machination

### subtle
◊ *anagram indicator* **03** sly **04** deep, fine, mild, nice, wily **05** faint **06** artful, astute, clever, crafty, low-key, minute, shrewd, slight, subtil, suttle, tricky **07** complex, cunning, devious, elusive, implied, refined, tactful, tenuous **08** abstruse, delicate, dextrous, discreet, indirect, profound, rarefied, ticklish **09** dexterous, insidious, intricate, sophistic, strategic, toned-down **10** impalpable, indefinite, indistinct, scholastic **11** overrefined, sophistical, understated **13** sophisticated **14** discriminating

### subtlety
**05** guile, skill **06** acumen, nicety, nuance **07** cunning, finesse, quillet, slyness **08** delicacy, sagacity, wiliness **09** acuteness, faintness, intricacy, mutedness, suttletie **10** artfulness, astuteness, cleverness, craftiness, refinement **11** deviousness, discernment **14** discrimination, indefiniteness, indistinctness, sophistication

### subtly
◊ *anagram indicator* **05** slyly **06** mildly, suttly **07** faintly **08** artfully, astutely, cleverly **09** cunningly, deviously, tenuously **10** indirectly **11** deceitfully **12** indefinitely, indistinctly

### subtract
**04** dock, take **05** debit **06** deduct, remove **07** detract **08** diminish, take away, withdraw, withhold

### suburb
**04** burb **08** banlieue, faubourg, purlieus, suburbia **09** dormitory, outskirts **12** commuter belt **13** bedroom suburb, dormitory town **15** dormitory suburb, residential area

### suburban
**04** dull **06** narrow **07** insular **08** commuter **09** bourgeois, parochial **10** provincial **11** middle-class, residential **12** conventional, narrow-minded **13** unimaginative **14** common-or-garden

### subversive
**07** riotous, traitor **08** quisling **09** dissident, seditious, terrorist, weakening **10** disruptive, incendiary, traitorous, treasonous **11** destructive, seditionist, treacherous, undermining **12** discrediting, inflammatory, troublemaker **13** revolutionary,

troublemaking **14** fifth columnist, freedom fighter

## subvert
**04** raze, ruin **05** upset, wreck **06** debase, poison **07** corrupt, deprave, destroy, disrupt, pervert, vitiate **08** confound, demolish, overturn, sabotage **09** overthrow, undermine **10** demoralize, invalidate **11** contaminate

## subway
**04** dive, tube **05** metro **06** tunnel **09** underpass **11** underground

## succeed
**04** fare, work **05** cut it, ensue, fadge, get on, reach, speed **06** answer, attain, come on, do well, follow, fulfil, make it, manage, result, thrive, walk it, win out **07** achieve, crack it, devolve, inherit, make out, prevail, prosper, pull off, realize, replace, triumph, turn out, work out **08** approach, bring off, carry out, complete, flourish, get there, go places, make good, take over **09** come after, win the day **10** accomplish, get results, strike gold, take effect, win through **11** come through, squeeze home **12** be successful, make the grade, steal the show, turn up trumps **13** hit the jackpot **14** fall on your feet, land on your feet, take the place of
• **succeed to** **06** accede, assume **07** inherit, replace **08** come into, take over **09** enter upon, supersede

## succeeding
**04** next **05** later **06** coming, to come **07** ensuing **09** following **10** hereditary, subsequent, successive

## success
**02** go, up **03** hit, VIP, win, wow **04** fame, luck, riot, star **05** celeb, fluke, smash **06** bigwig, upshot, winner **07** big name, big shot, fortune, sell-out, triumph, victory **08** eminence, sequence, smash hit, somebody, speeding **09** celebrity, happiness, sensation **10** attainment, bestseller, completion, fulfilment, prosperity, succession **11** achievement, realization **12** box-office hit **13** coup de théâtre, flash in the pan, flying colours **14** accomplishment, positive result
• **expression of success** **03** Jai **05** bingo **06** eureka, hurrah **07** heureka, hey pass **09** hey presto

## successful
**03** top **05** boffo, lucky, socko **06** famous **07** booming, leading, popular, thriven, wealthy, winning **08** affluent, fruitful, thriving, unbeaten **09** fortunate, lucrative, rewarding, well-known **10** home and dry, productive, profitable, prosperous, riding high, satisfying, triumphant, victorious **11** bestselling, flourishing, moneymaking **12** chart-busting

## successfully
**04** fine, well **05** great **08** famously **09** feliciter **10** swimmingly **11** beautifully **12** victoriously

## succession
**03** run **04** flow, line **05** chain, cycle, order, train **06** course, series, string **08** pedigree, sequence **09** accession, attaining, elevation, posterity **10** assumption, procession, survivance **11** continuance, inheritance, progression **12** continuation
• **in succession** **06** in a row, in turn **07** by-and-by, en suite, running **08** seriatim, straight **09** on the trot **12** sequentially, successively **13** consecutively **15** uninterruptedly

## successive
**06** serial **07** running, sequent **09** following **10** hereditary, sequential, succeeding **11** consecutive

## successively
**07** running **09** on the trot **12** in succession, sequentially **13** consecutively **15** uninterruptedly

## successor
**04** heir **05** ⊂uarb **06** co-heir, comarb, epigon, relief **07** epigone, khalifa **08** khalifah **09** inheritor, succeeder **10** descendant, next in line, substitute **11** beneficiary, replacement

## succinct
**05** brief, crisp, pithy, short, terse **07** compact, concise, in a word, summary **08** Laconian **09** condensed **10** to the point **12** close-fitting

## succinctly
**07** briefly, crisply, in a word, in brief, pithily, tersely **09** compactly, concisely **10** to the point

## succour
**03** aid **04** help **05** nurse **06** assist, foster, relief **07** comfort, help out, relieve, support **08** befriend **09** encourage **10** assistance, minister to **11** helping hand **13** ministrations

## succulent
**04** lush, rich **05** juicy, moist, sappy, tasty **06** cactus, fleshy, mellow **08** ice plant, luscious, spekboom, stapelia **09** echeveria, kalanchoe **11** sempervivum **13** mouthwatering

## succumb
**03** die **04** fall **05** catch, die of, yield **06** give in, pick up, submit **07** die from, give way **08** collapse, contract **09** surrender **10** capitulate, go down with **12** knuckle under

## suck
**04** draw, pull **05** drain **06** absorb, blot up, draw in, hoover, imbibe, soak up, sponge, suckle **07** exhaust, extract, suction
• **suck up to** **04** fawn **05** creep, toady **06** grovel **07** flatter, truckle **10** ingratiate **11** curry favour

## sucker
**03** mug, sap **04** butt, dupe, fool **05** graft, leech, patsy, sweet, toady **06** sponge, stooge, tellar, teller, tiller, victim **07** cat's-paw, muggins, osculum **08** lollipop, parasite, pushover, surculus **10** acetabulum

## suckle
**04** feed **05** nurse **07** nourish **08** wet-nurse **10** breastfeed

## suction
**07** sucking **08** draining **09** absorbing, drawing-in **10** extraction

## Sudan
**03** SDN, SUD

## sudden
**04** fast, rash, snap **05** ferly, flash, hasty, quick, rapid, sharp, swift **06** abrupt, prompt, speedy **07** hurried, quantum **08** dramatic, meteoric **09** extempore, immediate, impetuous, impulsive, overnight, startling **10** improvised, surprising, unexpected, unforeseen **11** subitaneous **13** instantaneous, unanticipated **15** spur-of-the-moment

## suddenly
**03** pop **04** slap, swap, swop **05** souse **06** astart, subito **07** asudden, at a blow, quickly, sharply **08** abruptly, unwarely **09** all at once, extempore **11** immediately **12** à l'improviste, all of a sudden, out of the blue, unexpectedly **13** with a siserary **14** at one fell swoop, in one fell swoop, without warning **15** instantaneously

## suddenness
**05** haste **09** hastiness **10** abruptness **11** hurriedness **13** impulsiveness **14** unexpectedness

## suds
**04** beer, foam **05** froth **06** lather **07** bubbles **09** soapiness

## sue
**03** beg **05** court, plead **06** appeal, charge, follow, indict, pursue, summon **07** beseech, entreat, implead, process, solicit **08** petition **09** prosecute **11** beg for a fool, take to court **12** bring to trial

## suffer
◊ *anagram indicator* **03** die, let, pay **04** ache, bear, feel, have, hurt **05** abide, allow, gripe, incur, prove, stand, thole **06** endure, grieve, permit, sorrow **07** agonize, support, sustain, undergo **08** be in pain, meet with, tolerate **09** go through, put up with **10** experience **11** be afflicted

## suffering
◊ *anagram indicator* **04** hurt, pain, pine **05** agony, trial **06** misery, ordeal, plight **07** anguish, hurting, passion, torment, torture **08** distress, hardship **09** adversity, afflicted, endurance **10** affliction, discomfort **12** wretchedness

## suffice
**02** do **05** serve **06** answer **07** content, satisfy **08** be enough **09** measure up **10** be adequate, fit the bill **11** fill the bill **12** be sufficient

## sufficiency
**05** store **06** enough, plenty **07** satiety **08** adequacy, bellyful **09** abundance **10** competence, competency **11** sufficience **12** adequateness

## sufficient
**04** enow, good **05** ample **06** decent, enough, plenty **08** adequate **09** competent, effective **12** satisfactory
• **a sufficient quantity** **02** qs **15** quantum sufficit

## suffocate
**05** choke, smoke, smoor, smore, stive **06** stifle **07** oppress, smother **08** strangle, throttle **10** asphyxiate **12** be breathless **14** make breathless

## suffrage
**04** vote **06** prayer **08** sanction **09** franchise **11** right to vote **15** enfranchisement

## suffuse
**03** dip **04** gild **05** bathe, cover, flood, imbue, steep, tinge **06** colour, infuse, mantle, redden, spread **07** pervade **08** permeate **09** transfuse

## sugar
**03** LSD **05** money, sweet **06** heroin **08** flattery

*Sugars include:*

**03** gur
**04** beet, cane, date, goor, loaf, lump, milk, palm, spun, wood
**05** brown, fruit, grape, icing, maple, syrup, white
**06** aldose, barley, caster, castor, golden, hexose, invert, ketose, xylose
**07** glucose, glycose, jaggery, lactose, maltose, mannose, pentose, refined, sucrose, treacle
**08** demerara, dextrose, fructose, levulose, molasses, powdered
**09** arabinose, galactose, laevulose, raffinose, sucralose, trehalose, unrefined
**10** granulated, saccharose
**11** glucosamine
**12** crystallized
**13** confectioner's

## sugary
**05** corny, gushy, mushy, soppy, sweet **06** sickly, sloppy, slushy, syrupy **07** gushing, maudlin, mawkish, sugared **08** touching **09** emotional, schmaltzy, sweetened **10** lovey-dovey, saccharine **11** sentimental

## suggest
**04** hint, move, vote **05** evoke, float, imply, smack, smell, table, tempt **06** advise, allude, hint at, prompt, savour, submit **07** connote, counsel, present, propose, smack of, smell of **08** advocate, envisage, indicate, intimate, nominate **09** insinuate, recommend **10** come up with, put forward **11** bring to mind **12** bring forward

## suggestion
**04** hint, idea, kite, note, plan, ring, wind **05** smack, touch, trace, twang, whiff **06** motion **07** pointer, wrinkle **08** allusion, innuendo, proposal **09** prompting, prompture, suspicion **10** incitement, indication, intimation, submission, temptation **11** implication,

insinuation, proposition **12** aesthesiogen **13** piece of advice **14** recommendation

## suggestive
**04** blue, lewd **05** bawdy, dirty **06** ribald, risqué, sexual, smutty **07** meaning **08** immodest, improper, indecent, redolent **09** evocative, off-colour **10** expressive, indelicate, indicative **11** provocative, reminiscent, stimulating, titillating

## suicide
**06** suttee **07** seppuku **08** felo de se, hara-kiri, hari-kari **10** self-murder **11** ending it all, parasuicide **12** self-violence **13** happy dispatch, self-slaughter **14** self-immolation **15** killing yourself, self-destruction, topping yourself
• **commit suicide** **08** end it all **11** top yourself **12** do yourself in, kill yourself, take your life **14** commit hari-kiri **15** take your own life

## suit
**03** fit, gee, hit, set **04** case, meet **05** agree, apply, befit, besit, cause, clubs, do for, match, queme, suite, trial **06** action, answer, attire, become, drapes, effeir, effere, hearts, outfit, please, series, spades, square **07** contest, costume, crawler, dispute, fashion, flatter, furnish, gratify, lawsuit, overall, process, provide, pursuit, satisfy, suffice **08** argument, clothing, diamonds, ensemble, petition, sequence, tailleur **09** agree with, courtship, plus fours, tally with **10** complement, fit the bill, go well with, litigation, look good on, qualify for **11** fill the bill, proceedings, prosecution **12** set of clothes **13** be suitable for, harmonize with **14** be acceptable to, be applicable to **15** be convenient for

*Suits include:*

**01** g
**03** cat, dry, Mao, NBC, sun, wet
**04** body, Eton, jump, play, swim, zoot
**05** drape, dress, noddy, pants, shell, siren, sleep, space, sweat, track, union
**06** boiler, diving, flying, lounge, monkey, riding, safari, sailor, tsotsi
**07** bathing, leisure, penguin, trouser
**08** birthday, business, pressure, skeleton, sleeping

## suitability
**07** aptness, fitness **09** congruity, rightness **10** competence, competency, congruence, congruency, timeliness **11** convenience, fittingness **12** appositeness **13** opportuneness **14** correspondence, correspondency **15** appropriateness

## suitable
**03** apt, due, fit **04** able, good **05** right **06** giusto, liable, proper, seemly, suited **07** fitting **08** adequate, agreeing, all right, apposite, becoming, decorous,

relevant **09** agreeable, befitting, competent, congruent, consonant, in keeping, opportune, pertinent **10** acceptable, applicable, compatible, convenient, well-suited **11** appropriate, well-matched **12** satisfactory

## suitably
**05** fitly, quite **06** as well **08** properly **09** fittingly **10** acceptably **11** accordingly **13** appropriately

## suitcase
**03** bag **04** case, port **05** trunk **06** valise **07** holdall, suitbag **09** flight bag, portfolio, travel bag **10** vanity-case **11** attaché case, hand-luggage, portmanteau **12** overnight-bag

## suite
**03** set **04** flat, tail **05** court, rooms, train **06** ballet, escort, sequel, series **07** partita, retinue **08** chambers, sequence, servants **09** apartment, cassation, entourage, followers, furniture, household, retainers **10** attendants, collection, set of rooms **11** hospitality **12** divertimento

## suitor
**04** beau **05** lover, swain, wooer **07** admirer **08** follower, young man **09** boyfriend, pretender **10** petitioner, pretendant, pretendent **11** detrimental

## sulk
**03** dod, pet **04** dort, huff, miff, mood, mope, mump, pout **05** boody, brood, grump, pique **06** grouse, temper **07** bad mood **08** be miffed **09** bad temper, be in a huff **13** pull a long face
• **the sulks** **03** pet **04** dods, hump, tout, towt **05** glout, grump **06** glumps, strunt **07** strunts

## sulkily
**07** crossly, moodily **08** morosely, sullenly **10** grudgingly **11** resentfully

## sulky
**05** aloof, cross, huffy, humpy, moody, pouty, ratty **06** glumpy, grouty, grumpy, jinker, miffed, moping, morose, put out, stuffy, sullen **07** pettish **08** brooding, grudging, stunkard **09** resentful **10** out of sorts, unsociable **11** bad-tempered, disgruntled **13** gumple-foisted

## sullen
**04** dark, dour, dull, glum, grim, sour **05** black, cross, heavy, moody, sulky, surly **06** broody, dismal, dogged, gloomy, leaden, morose, silent, solein, sombre **07** lumpish, mumpish **08** churlish, farouche, perverse, stubborn, stunkard **09** cheerless, obstinate, resentful, simpleton **11** black-browed **15** uncommunicative

## sullenly
**06** glumly, sourly **07** crossly, moodily, sulkily **08** gloomily, morosely **10** churlishly, stubbornly **11** obstinately, resentfully

## sullenness
**05** gloom **08** brooding, glumness, sourness **09** glowering, heaviness,

**sully**
moodiness, sulkiness, surliness
**10** moroseness

**sully**
**03** mar **04** soil, spot **05** dirty, spoil,
stain, taint **06** assoil, befoul, damage,
darken, defile, smirch, smutch
**07** blemish, distain, pollute, tarnish
**08** besmirch, disgrace **09** dishonour
**11** contaminate

**sulphur**
**01** S **09** brimstone

**sultan, sultana**
**06** despot, fiddle, raisin, sharif, sherif,
soldan **07** shereef **08** padishah
**09** Grand Turk **12** Grand Signior
**13** Grand Seignior

**sultanate**
**04** Oman **06** Brunei

**sultry**
**03** hot **04** sexy **05** close, humid, lurid,
muggy, soggy **06** sticky, stuffy
**07** airless, sensual, sweltry **08** alluring,
stifling, tempting **09** seductive
**10** attractive, indelicate, oppressive,
passionate, sweltering, voluptuous
**11** provocative, suffocating

**sum**
**03** add **05** penny, score, tally, total,
whole **06** amount, answer, height,
number, result **07** summary **08** entirety,
quantity, sum total **09** abatement,
aggregate, carry-over, exemplify,
reckoning, summarize, summation
**10** completion, remittance
**11** culmination
• **large sum  04** pots **11** golden hello
**12** a king's ransom, a pretty penny
**15** golden handshake
• **small sum  04** dime **05** groat, penny
**08** pittance
• **sum up  03** add **04** foot, wind
**05** close, compt, count, gauge, recap
**06** assess, embody, review, size up,
upknit **08** conclude, consider, evaluate
**09** epitomize, exemplify, inventory,
summarize **11** encapsulate
**12** recapitulate **14** put in a nutshell

**summarily**
**07** hastily, swiftly **08** abruptly,
promptly, speedily **09** forthwith
**11** arbitrarily, immediately
**12** peremptorily, without delay
**13** expeditiously

**summarize**
**03** pot, sum **05** recap, sum up
**06** docket, minute, précis, resume,
review, sketch **07** abridge, outline,
shorten **08** abstract, condense,
pirlicue, purlicue **09** epitomize,
synopsize **10** abbreviate
**11** encapsulate

**summary**
**02** CV **04** curt, plan **05** brief, creed,
hasty, recap, short, summa, swift
**06** aperçu, digest, direct, docket,
précis, prompt, résumé, review,
speedy, summar, wrap-up **07** cursory,
docquet, epitome, instant, minutes,
offhand, outline, rundown, sylloge,
tabloid **08** abstract, argument,

overview, succinct, synopsis
**09** arbitrary, condensed, immediate,
summation, summing-up
**10** compendium, conspectus,
Hitopadesa, main points,
memorandum, peremptory
**11** abridgement, aide-mémoire,
compendious **12** balance-sheet,
condensation, without delay **13** bank
statement, instantaneous,
unceremonious **14** recapitulation
**15** abstract of title, curriculum vitae

**summerhouse**
**06** gazebo **08** pavilion **09** belvedere,
root house **11** garden-house

**summit**
◇ *head selection indicator* **03** top
**04** acme, acro-, apex, head, peak, pike
**05** crest, crown, glory, point, spire,
talks **06** apogee, climax, height, vertex,
zenith **07** hilltop, meeting **08** pinnacle
**09** sublimity **10** conference, discussion
**11** culmination, negotiation
**12** altaltissimo, consultation

**summon**
**03** bid **04** buzz, call, cite, gong, hail,
hist, hoop, page, ring, sist, toll, warn
**05** knell, order, rally, rouse, shake,
whoop **06** accite, arouse, beckon, call
up, demand, drum up, gather, invite,
muster, ring up, work up **07** call out,
conjure, convene, convent, convoke,
history, pluck up, provoke, screw up,
send for, trumpet, whistle **08** assemble,
mobilize, muster up **09** challenge,
preconize, recollect
• **summon up  05** evoke, rally, rouse
**06** arouse, gather, muster, revive, work
up **07** convene, pluck up, screw up
**08** assemble, mobilize **09** recollect
**10** call to mind

**summons**
**04** call, writ **05** bluey, cital, order,
rouse **06** gather, what ho, wo ha ho
**07** warning, war note, whistle
**08** citation, monition, reveille,
subpoena **09** challenge **10** arrière-ban,
injunction, invocation **11** clarion call,
curtain call **12** gathering-cry **13** parking
ticket **14** interpellation

**sumptuous**
**04** dear, rich **05** grand, plush **06** costly,
de luxe, lavish, slap-up, superb
**07** opulent **08** gorgeous, palatial,
princely, splendid **09** expensive,
luxurious **11** extravagant, magnificent

**sun**
**01** S **03** day, tan **04** bake, bask, star,
year **05** brown, light **07** daystar
**08** daylight, eye of day, insolate,
sunbathe, sunlight, sunshine
• **sun god  02** Ra, Re **03** Sol **05** Horus,
Surya **06** Apollo, Helios, Tammuz
**07** Phoebus

**sunbathe**
**03** sun, tan **04** bake, bask **05** brown
**07** sunbake **08** insolate

**sunburnt**
**03** red **05** brown, burnt **07** peeling
**08** inflamed **09** blistered **10** blistering
**13** weather-beaten

**Sunday**
**01** S **03** Sun

**sunder**
**03** cut **04** chop, part **05** sever, split
**06** cleave, divide, sundra, sundri
**07** disally, sundari **08** dissever,
disunite, separate **09** dissunder

**sundry**
**04** a few, some **06** divers, varied
**07** diverse, several, various **08** assorted,
separate **09** different **13** miscellaneous

**sunk**
◇ *anagram indicator* **03** pad **04** bank,
deep, lost **06** doomed, failed, in a fix,
in a jam, ruined **07** done for
**08** finished, knee-deep **09** submerged
**10** up the creek, up the spout

**sunken**
**05** drawn, laigh, lower **06** buried,
hollow **07** concave, drowned,
haggard, lowered **08** hollowed,
recessed **09** cellarous, depressed,
submerged

**sunless**
**04** dark, grey, hazy **05** bleak **06** cloudy,
dismal, dreary, gloomy, sombre
**08** overcast **09** cheerless **10** depressing

**sunlight**
**03** sun **05** light **08** daylight, sun's rays
**12** natural light

**sunny**
**04** fine, glad **05** clear, happy, merry
**06** blithe, bouncy, bright, bubbly,
cheery, genial, joyful, sunlit
**07** beaming, buoyant, hopeful, radiant,
smiling, summery **08** cheerful,
pleasant, sunshiny **09** brilliant,
cloudless, unclouded **10** optimistic
**12** light-hearted

**sunrise**
**04** dawn **05** sun-up **06** aurora, orient
**07** morning **08** cock-crow, daybreak,
daylight **10** break of day, first light
**11** crack of dawn

**sunset**
**04** dusk **07** evening, sundown
**08** gloaming, twilight **09** nightfall
**10** close of day

**sup**
*see* **eat; dine**

**super**
**03** ace **04** cool, good!, mega, neat
**05** brill, great **06** lovely!, superb,
wicked **08** glorious, peerless,
smashing, terrific, top-notch
**09** excellent, matchless, wonderful
**10** delightful, marvellous
**11** magnificent, outstanding,
sensational **12** incomparable

**superannuated**
**03** old **04** aged **06** past it, senile
**07** elderly, retired **08** decrepit,
moribund, obsolete **10** antiquated
**12** pensioned off **13** put out to grass

**superb**
**03** ace **04** fine, neat, posh **05** brill,
grand, great, proud **06** choice, lavish,
tiptop **07** haughty **08** clipping,
dazzling, fabulous, gorgeous, jim-

dandy, smashing, splendid, superior, terrific **09** admirable, brilliant, excellent, exquisite, first-rate, wonderful **10** first-class, impressive, marvellous, remarkable, unrivalled **11** fantabulous, magnificent, outstanding, superlative, unsurpassed **12** breathtaking **14** out of this world

## supercilious
**05** lofty, proud **06** lordly, overly, snooty, snotty, snouty, uppish, uppity **07** haughty, stuck-up **08** arrogant, cavalier, insolent, jumped-up, scornful, superior **09** imperious **10** disdainful, hoity-toity, toffee-nose **11** high-sighted, overbearing, patronizing, toffee-nosed **12** contemptuous, vainglorious **13** condescending

## superficial
◊ *containment indicator* **05** hasty, outer **06** casual, facile, slight **07** alleged, cursory, hurried, outside, outward, passing, seeming, shallow, sketchy, surface, trivial **08** apparent, careless, cosmetic, exterior, external, skin-deep, slapdash **09** frivolous, surficial **10** ostensible, peripheral **11** lightweight, perfunctory **13** insignificant **14** one-dimensional

## superficiality
**09** lightness **10** simplicity, slightness, triviality **11** externality, shallowness **13** frivolousness, worthlessness

## superficially
**07** outward **08** casually, skin-deep **09** hurriedly, outwardly, seemingly **10** apparently, carelessly, externally, ostensibly **12** on the surface

## superfine
**03** sup **04** supe **05** super **09** rosewater

## superfluity
**04** glut **05** extra **06** excess **07** surfeit, surplus **08** pleonasm, plethora **09** overflush, superflux **10** exuberance, overgrowth, redundancy, surplusage **13** excessiveness **14** superabundance

## superfluous
**05** extra, spare, waste **06** de trop, excess, frilly, otiose **07** surplus, to spare **08** needless, unneeded, unwanted **09** excessive, redundant, remaining **10** excrescent, fifth-wheel, gratuitous, prolixious **11** at a discount, uncalled-for, unnecessary, unwarranted **13** supernumerary

## superhuman
**03** god **04** hero **05** great **06** bionic, divine, heroic **07** goddess, immense **09** herculean **10** paranormal, phenomenal, prodigious, stupendous **12** supernatural **13** extraordinary, preternatural

## superimpose
**03** add **05** lay on, put on **07** lay over, overlay **08** transfer **10** overstrike

## superintend
**03** run **05** steer **06** direct, handle, manage **07** control, inspect, oversee **08** overlook **09** supervise **10** administer **12** be in charge of **13** be in control of

## superintendence
**04** care **06** charge, survey **07** control, running **08** episcopy, guidance **09** direction, oversight **10** government, inspection, management **11** supervision **12** surveillance **14** administration

## superintendent
**04** boss, Supt **05** chief, super **06** gaffer, viewer, warden **07** curator, manager **08** curatrix, director, governor, overseer **09** conductor, inspector, intendant **10** controller, provincial, supervisor **13** administrator

## superior
**03** sup **04** boss, fine, over **05** chief, elder, fancy, lofty, prime, prize, upper **06** better, choice, de luxe, higher, la-di-da, lordly, select, senior, snooty, uppish, uppity **07** foreman, generic, greater, haughty, manager, premium, quality, stuck-up, upstage **08** director, jumped-up, lah-di-dah, overlord, snobbish, top-notch **09** admirable, excellent, exclusive, first-rate, high-class, high-grade, high-toned, paramount, preferred, principal, top-drawer, top-flight, top-sawyer **10** disdainful, first-class, supervisor, unrivalled **11** exceptional, good-quality, high-quality, outstanding, patronizing, pretentious, toffee-nosed **12** higher in rank, supercilious, transcendent **13** condescending, distinguished, par excellence
• **without superior** **04** odal, udal **07** alodial, topless **08** allodial

## superiority
**04** edge, gree, lead **07** numbers **08** eminence **09** advantage, dominance, supremacy **10** ascendancy, mastership **11** pre-eminence **12** predominance

## superlative
**03** ace, -est, sup **04** best **05** brill **06** superl **07** highest, supreme **08** greatest, peerless, unbeaten **09** brilliant, excellent, first-rate, matchless **10** consummate, first-class, unbeatable, unrivalled **11** magnificent, outstanding, unsurpassed **12** transcendent, unparalleled

## supermarket
**08** minimart **09** superette **10** superstore **11** hypermarket **12** cash-and-carry

## supernatural
**03** fay, fey, fie **05** eerie, magic, weird **06** hidden, mystic, occult **07** ghostly, magical, phantom, psychic, uncanny **08** abnormal, daemonic, daimonic, eldritch, mystical **09** spiritual, unnatural, witchlike **10** miraculous, mysterious, paranormal **12** metaphysical, otherworldly **13** hyperphysical, preternatural **14** transcendental
*See also* **occult**

## supernumerary
**04** orra **05** extra, spare **06** excess

**07** surplus **09** excessive, redundant **11** superfluous **13** extraordinary

## supersede
**04** oust **05** usurp **06** desist, remove **07** discard, refrain, replace, succeed **08** displace, override, set aside, supplant **12** Stellenbosch, take over from **14** take the place of

## supersonic transport
**03** AST, SST

## superstition
**04** myth **05** magic **07** fallacy **08** delusion, illusion **10** Aberglaube **11** apotropaism **12** old wives' tale

## superstitious
**05** false **06** freety, freity **08** delusive, illusory, mythical **10** fallacious, groundless, irrational

## supervise
**03** run **04** edit **05** guide, nanny, targe, watch **06** direct, handle, manage, umpire **07** conduct, control, inspect, monitor, oversee **08** bear-lead **09** look after, watch over **10** administer, invigilate **11** keep an eye on, preside over, superintend **12** be in charge of **13** be in control of

## supervision
**04** care, duty **06** charge **07** control, running **08** guidance **09** direction, oversight **10** inspection, management **11** instruction **12** surveillance **14** administration **15** superintendence

## supervisor
**04** boss **05** chief **06** umpire, warden **07** foreman, manager, monitor, proctor, steward **08** director, governor, overseer **09** forewoman, inspector, roundsman, spectator **10** brewmaster, foreperson, sheep-biter, toolpusher **11** floorwalker, invigilator **12** floor manager **13** administrator **14** superintendent

## supervisory
**09** executive **10** managerial, overseeing **11** directorial **14** administrative, superintendent

## supine
**03** sup **04** flat, idle, lazy, weak **05** bored, inert **06** torpid **07** languid, passive, sloping, upright **08** careless, heedless, inactive, inclined, indolent, listless, resigned, slothful, sluggish **09** apathetic, lethargic, negligent, prostrate, recumbent, spineless **10** horizontal, spiritless **11** indifferent, unresisting **12** uninterested

## supper
**03** tea **04** mass **05** snack **06** dinner, hawkey, hockey, horkey **07** nagmaal **10** rere-supper **11** aftersupper, evening meal

## supplant
**04** oust **05** usurp **06** cut out, remove, topple, unseat, uproot **07** pre-empt, replace **08** displace **09** overthrow, supersede **12** take over from **14** take the place of

## supple
**05** agile, leish, lithe, lofty, wanle **06** limber, pliant, souple, wannel, whippy **07** bending, elastic, fawning, plastic, pliable, sinuous **08** flexible, graceful, yielding **09** willowish **10** stretching **11** loose-limbed **12** loose-jointed **13** double-jointed

## supplement
**02** PS **03** eik, eke, SCP, sup, TES, TLS **04** mend, supp **05** add-on, add to, annex, boost, extra, relay, rider, suppl, top up **06** eke out, extend, fill up, insert, make up, sequel, supply **07** augment, codicil, help out, pull-out **08** addendum, addition, additive, appendix, increase, salt lick, schedule **09** Beta fibre, reinforce, sooterkin **10** Beres drops, complement, Incaparina, postscript, suppletion

## supplementary
**05** added, extra **06** bolt-on, second **07** ripieno **08** attached **09** ancillary, auxiliary, corollary, expletory, secondary, suppliant **10** additional **12** accompanying **13** complementary

## suppliant
**07** begging, craving **09** imploring **10** beseeching, entreating **11** importunate, reinforcing **12** supplicating **13** supplementary

## supplicant
**06** suitor **07** pleader **09** applicant, postulant, suppliant **10** petitioner

## supplicate
**04** pray **05** plead **06** appeal, invoke **07** beseech, entreat, request, solicit **08** petition

## supplication
**04** plea, suit **06** appeal, orison, prayer **07** request **08** entreaty, petition, pleading, rogation **10** invocation **11** conjuration, imploration, obsecration **12** solicitation

## supplicatory
**06** humble **07** begging **09** imploring, precative, precatory **10** beseeching **11** imprecatory, petitioning, postulatory **12** supplicating

## supplier
**05** donor **06** dealer, seller, vendor **08** provider, retailer **09** connexion, outfitter **10** connection, wholesaler **11** contributor

## supply
◊ *anagram indicator* **03** due, fit, gas **04** bank, crop, feed, fill, find, food, fund, give, heap, help, lend, load, mass, pile, sell, temp, wood **05** cache, cater, endew, endow, endue, equip, grant, grist, hoard, indew, indue, labor, plumb, serve, stake, stock, store, yield **06** amount, donate, fit out, labour, occupy, outfit, output, plenty, purvey, source, stores **07** furnish, plenish, produce, proffer, provide, rations, reserve, satisfy, service, victual **08** minister, quantity **09** equipment, materials, reinforce, replenish, reservoir, stockpile **10** contribute,

cornucopia, provisions, substitute, supplement **11** necessities **15** cut and come again

## support
◊ *juxtaposition down indicator* **03** aid, arm, bra, cup, leg, tee **04** abet, axle, back, base, bear, care, feed, food, fund, help, keep, pier, pole, post, prop, raft, rest, root, skid, stay **05** brace, carry, grant, truss **06** assist, back up, be with, corset, crutch, defend, endure, foster, hold up, pillar, prop up, ratify, relief, second, uphold, verify **07** backing, barrack, bear out, bolster, capital, care for, comfort, confirm, defence, endorse, espouse, finance, funding, further, loyalty, nourish, promote, run with, shore up, sponsor, subsidy, sustain, trestle **08** advocate, approval, be behind, befriend, be kind to, buttress, champion, document, donation, espousal, evidence, maintain, motivate, skeleton, strength, sympathy, underpin, validate **09** bolster up, encourage, look after, patronage, provision, reinforce, subsidize **10** allegiance, assistance, barrack for, foundation, friendship, motivation, protection, provide for, rally round, strengthen, sustenance, take care of, underwrite, validation **11** corroborate, foundations, maintenance, sponsorship, subsistence **12** authenticate, be in favour of, confirmation, contribute to, contribution, moral support, ratification, substantiate, substructure, underpinning, verification **13** encouragement **14** authentication, be supportive to, give strength to, substantiation, sympathize with **15** give a donation to, take the weight of, tower of strength
• **be supported** **04** live, rest **05** float
• **expression of support** **03** olé

## supporter
◊ *juxtaposition down indicator* **03** bra, fan, leg **04** ally, beam, belt, foot, prop **05** angel, donor, stoop, voter **06** braces, friend, helper, patron, pillar, second **07** apostle, booster, partner, sponsor **08** adherent, advocate, champion, co-worker, defender, follower, henchman, janizary, militant, promoter, seconder, upholder **09** apologist, crossbeam **10** ideologist, well-wisher **11** contributor, sympathizer **12** bottle-holder, understander

## supporting
**03** pro- **06** behind

## supportive
**06** caring **07** helpful **08** positive **09** attentive, sensitive **10** comforting, reassuring **11** affirmative, encouraging, sympathetic **13** understanding **14** on someone's side

## suppose
**02** if **03** say **04** take **05** fancy, guess, imply, infer, judge, opine, posit, sepad, think **06** assume, devise, expect, reckon, uphold **07** believe,

dare say, imagine, presume, propose, put case, require, surmise, warrant **08** conceive, conclude, consider, perceive **09** calculate, postulate **10** conjecture, presuppose, put the case **11** expectation, hypothesize **14** take for granted

## supposed
**07** alleged, assumed, feigned, reputed, thought **08** believed, imagined, presumed, putative, reported, rumoured, so-called **11** conjectured **12** hypothetical **14** supposititious
• **supposed to** **07** meant to **09** obliged to **10** expected to, intended to, required to

## supposedly
**09** allegedly **10** apparently, ostensibly, putatively, reportedly **13** by all accounts

## supposing that
**02** if

## supposition
**02** if **04** idea **05** guess **06** notion, theory **07** fiction, opinion, surmise **10** assumption, conjecture, hypothesis **11** postulation, presumption, speculation **14** presupposition

## suppress
**04** kill, sink, stay, stop **05** burke, check, choke, crush, elide, mince, quash, quell, sit on **06** cancel, censor, hold in, hush up, ravish, squash, stifle, subdue **07** conceal, contain, control, cushion, inhibit, put down, repress, silence, sit upon, smother, squelch **08** black out, blank out, block out, gulp back, gulp down, hold back, moderate, restrain, stamp out, strangle, submerge, throttle, vanquish, vote down, withhold **09** choke back, choke down **10** put an end to **11** clamp down on, crack down on, keep in check, strangulate **14** knock on the head, put the tin hat on, put the tin lid on

## suppression
**05** check **07** cover-up, elision **08** blackout, crushing, ischuria, quashing, quelling, stoppage **09** clampdown, crackdown, epistasis **10** censorship, ecthlipsis, extinction, inhibition, smothering **11** comstockery, concealment, dissolution, elimination, prohibition, termination

## suppurate
**04** ooze, weep **06** fester, gather **08** maturate **09** discharge

## suppuration
**03** pus **09** diapyesis, festering, mattering, pyorrhoea

## supremacy
**04** rule, sway **05** power **07** control, mastery, primacy **08** dominion, hegemony, lordship, regalism **09** dominance **10** ascendancy, domination **11** paramountcy, pre-eminence, sovereignty **12** predominance

## supreme
**03** sup, top **04** best, head, last, Supr

**05** chief, final, first, grand, prime
**06** sudden, utmost **07** extreme, highest, leading, sublime **08** crowning, foremost, greatest, imperial, peerless, ultimate **09** excellent, first-rate, matchless, paramount, principal, sovereign **10** consummate, first-class, pre-eminent, prevailing **11** culminating, predominant, superlative, unsurpassed **12** incomparable, second-to-none, transcendent, world-beating

**supremely**
**04** very **06** highly, really **07** acutely, greatly, utterly **08** severely
**09** decidedly, extremely, intensely, unusually **10** remarkably, thoroughly, uncommonly **11** exceedingly, excessively, sovereignly
**12** inordinately, terrifically
**13** exceptionally **15** extraordinarily

**sure**
**02** OK **03** yes **04** fast, fine, firm, okay, safe **05** bound, clear, loyal, pakka, pucka, pukka, right, sewer, solid
**06** agreed, indeed, secure, siccar, sicker, stable, steady, tested
**07** assured, certain, decided, precise
**08** accurate, all right, definite, faithful, of course, positive, reliable, sure-fire, unerring, very well **09** certainly, confident, convinced, effective, foolproof, steadfast, undoubted, unfailing **10** dependable, guaranteed, home and dry, inevitable, infallible, sure-footed, undeniable, unwavering
**11** efficacious, irrevocable, trustworthy, undoubtedly, unfaltering
**12** indisputable, never-failing, safe as houses, unmistakable
**14** unquestionable
• **for sure 06** indeed **07** clearly, plainly **09** certainly, obviously
**10** absolutely, definitely, for certain, positively, undeniably **11** indubitably, undoubtedly **12** unmistakably, without doubt **13** categorically
**14** unquestionably **15** without question
• **make sure 04** look **05** check
**06** assure, ensure, insure, secure, verify
**07** betroth, confirm **09** ascertain, guarantee **11** make certain
• **make sure of having 03** see

**surely**
**05** syker **06** firmly, safely, siccar, sicker
**07** no doubt **09** assuredly, certainly
**10** definitely, inevitably, inexorably
**11** confidently, doubtlessly, indubitably, undoubtedly **12** without doubt **14** unquestionably

**surety**
**04** bail, bond **06** borrow, pledge, safety
**07** caution, deposit, hostage, sponsor, warrant **08** bondsman, security, warranty **09** assurance, cautioner, certainty, frithborh, guarantee, guarantor, indemnity, insurance, mortgagor, safeguard **10** undertaker

**surface**
**03** top **04** area, face, pile, rise, side, skin **05** arise, outer, plane **06** appear, come up, emerge, façade, patina,

veneer **07** outside, outward **08** aerofoil, apparent, covering, exterior, external, reappear **11** come to light, materialize, superficial
• **on the surface 04** upon
**09** seemingly **10** apparently, externally, ostensibly **13** at first glance, superficially

**surfeit**
**04** cram, fill, glut, staw **05** gorge, stall, stuff **06** excess, gutful **07** gorging, satiate, satiety, surplus **08** bellyful, cloyment, gluttony, overcloy, overfeed, overfill, plethora
**09** repletion, satiation **11** overfulness, repleteness, superfluity
**14** overindulgence, superabundance

**surge**
**03** jaw **04** eddy, flow, gush, jerk, pour, rise, roll, rush, wave **05** break, heave, spike, sweep, swell, swirl, waves, whelm **06** billow, efflux, roller, seethe, stream, upgush, uprush, wallow, welter **07** breaker, pouring, redound, upsurge, upswell, upswing **08** escalate, increase **09** transient **10** escalation
**15** intensification

**surgeon**
**02** BS, ch, CM, DS, MS **03** BCh, ChB, ChM, DCh, LCh, MCh, vet **04** surg
**05** LChir **06** doctor, extern, intern
**07** externe, interne **08** orthopod, sawbones **09** trephiner **10** chirurgeon
**11** lithotomist **12** lithotritist
**13** lithotriptist **14** lithontriptist

*Surgeons include:*

**04 Bell** (Sir Charles), **Mayo** (Charles Horace), **Reed** (Walter)
**05 Broca** (Paul Pierre), **Paget** (Sir James)
**06 Carrel** (Alexis), **Cooper** (Sir Astley), **Hunter** (John), **Lister** (Joseph, Lord), **Treves** (Sir Frederick), **Yacoub** (Sir Magdi)
**07 Barnard** (Christiaan), **Burkitt** (Denis Parsons), **Cushing** (Harvey Williams), **MacEwen** (Sir William), **McIndoe** (Sir Archibald)
**08 Beaumont** (William), **Billroth** (Theodor), **Charnley** (Sir John)

*See also* **doctor; medical**
• **sea surgeon 04** tang **06** doctor
**10** doctor-fish

**surgery**
**03** ops **09** operation

*Surgery types include:*

**06** biopsy
**07** keyhole, nose job, plastic
**08** cosmetic, elective, facelift, lobotomy
**09** Caesarean, colostomy, open-heart, sex change, skin graft, spare-part, tummy tuck
**10** autoplasty, cordectomy, discectomy, iridectomy, laparotomy, lumpectomy, mastectomy, nip and tuck, phlebotomy, thymectomy, transplant, varicotomy
**11** angioplasty, cryosurgery,

enterostomy, gastrectomy, laparoscopy, mammoplasty, rhinoplasty, splenectomy, tracheotomy, trepanation
**12** appendectomy, circumcision, corneal graft, hysterectomy, laryngectomy, microsurgery, neurosurgery, tonsilectomy, tracheostomy, trephination
**13** adenoidectomy, prostatectomy, psychosurgery, stomatoplasty, thyroidectomy, tonsillectomy
**14** abdominoplasty, appendicectomy, coronary bypass, fundoplication, pancreatectomy, reconstructive
**15** cholecystectomy, thoracocentesis

*Surgery-related terms include:*

**02** op
**04** CABG, seam
**05** couch, curet, donor, graft, stoma, taxis, truss
**06** canula, domino, dossil, garrot, hobday, lancet, post-op, reduce, stitch, trepan, trocar
**07** cannula, catling, curette, forceps, garotte, myotome, operate, scalpel, section, theatre, torsion
**08** ablation, adhesion, bistoury, cannular, capeline, centesis, clinical, compress, cosmesis, crow-bill, curarine, écraseur, garrotte, incision, incisure, invasive, trephine
**09** abduction, autograft, cannulate, capelline, collodion, crow's-bill, curettage, depressor, dermatome, diastasis, enucleate, operation, osteotome, piggyback, resection, retractor, tamponade, tamponage, tenaculum
**10** deligation, diorthosis, discussion, guillotine, lithotrite, lithotrity, osteoclast
**11** anaesthetic, arthrodesis, autoplastic, cannulation, curettement, decapsulate, exteriorize, incarnation, laparoscope, lithotripsy, lithotritor, prosthetics
**12** fenestration, lithotripter, lithotriptor, lunar caustic, paracentesis, scarificator, short circuit, tissue-typing
**13** cyclodialysis, decompression, herniorrhaphy, operating room, post-operative, premedication, under the knife
**14** embryo transfer, operating table

**surgical**
*see* **medical**

**Suriname**
**03** SME, SUR

**surly**
**04** grum **05** bluff, cross, cynic, gruff, gurly, stoor, stour, sture, sulky, testy
**06** crabby, crusty, grumpy, morose, stowre, sullen **07** brusque, crabbed, cynical, grouchy, haughty, uncivil
**08** churlish **09** crotchety, irascible
**10** ill-natured, refractory, ungracious
**11** bad-tempered **12** cantankerous

## surmise

**04** idea **05** fancy, guess, infer, opine **06** assume, deduce, notion **07** imagine, opinion, presume, suppose, suspect, thought **08** conclude, consider **09** deduction, inference, speculate, suspicion **10** allegation, assumption, conclusion, conjecture, hypothesis **11** possibility, presumption, speculation, supposition

## surmount

**03** top **04** rise, rush **05** crest **06** breast, exceed, master **07** conquer, get over, surpass **08** overcome, superate, vanquish **09** transcend **11** prevail over, triumph over

## surpass

**03** cap, top **04** bang, beat, ding, pass, whap, whop **05** excel, outdo, outgo **06** better, exceed, overgo **07** eclipse, outbrag, outpeer, overtop, paragon, put down **08** go beyond, outclass, outrival, outshine, outstrip, surmount, underlay **09** transcend **10** overshadow, tower above **12** beat to sticks, leave for dead **13** knock spots off

## surpassing

**04** rare **07** corking, supreme, topping **08** frabjous **09** bettering, exceeding, matchless **10** inimitable, phenomenal, unrivalled **11** exceptional, outstanding, unsurpassed **12** incomparable, transcendent **13** extraordinary

## surplice

**04** sark **05** cotta, ephod, stole **06** rochet

## surplus

**04** glut, over, plus **05** extra, spare **06** excess, unused **07** balance, o'ercrome, overage, residue, surfeit **08** left over, overcome, overplus, owrecome, wine lake **09** carry-over, leftovers, redundant, remainder, remaining **11** superfluity, superfluous

## surprise

**03** wow **04** drop, find, stun **05** alert, amaze, seize, shock, start **06** dismay, expose, unmask, wonder **07** astound, confuse, find out, nonplus, stagger, startle **08** astonish, bewilder, blow away, bowl over **09** amazement, bombshell, burst in on, curveball, surprisal, take aback **10** disconcert, revelation, wonderment **11** flabbergast, incredulity, knock for six, thunderbolt **12** astonishment, bewilderment **13** catch in the act, catch unawares **14** catch red-handed **15** bolt from the blue

• **expression of surprise 01** O **02** ah, eh, ha, ho, my, oh **03** aha, coo, cor, gee, god, hah, hoa, hoh, law, lor, man, oho, ooh, ook, say, wow **04** dear, egad, gosh, hech, igad, I say, Jeez, lawk, lord, losh, odso, phew, well, what, whew, yike **05** arrah, blimy, fancy, gadso, glory, godso, golly, hallo, hello, hullo, Jeeze, Jesus, lawks, lordy, lumme, lummy, ma foi, mercy, musha, my God, my hat, never, wowee, yikes, zowie **06** blimey, by Jove, Christ, cricky, crikey, cripes, crumbs, dear me, gemini, geminy,

gemony, heaven, indeed, jiminy, my word, oh dear, wheugh, whoops, zounds **07** bless me, brother, caramba, cravens, crickey, crimine, crimini, crivens, deary me, gee whiz, glory be, good-now, heavens, jeepers, stone me, too much **08** crivvens, dearie me, good-lack, goodness, gorblimy, gracious, I declare, man alive, stroll on, well well **09** blood oath, cor blimey, fancy that, good grief, gorblimey, I never did, Jesus wept, mercy on us, son of a gun **10** conscience, gracious me, Great Scott, hell's bells, hell's teeth, hoity-toity, upon my soul, upon my word, well I never **11** bless my soul, good heavens, to think of it **12** good gracious, heavens above, my conscience, strike a light, well I declare **13** Gordon Bennett, just think of it, stone the crows **14** it's a small world **15** jeepers creepers

## surprised

**05** agape **06** amazed **07** shocked, stunned **08** jiggered, startled **09** astounded, staggered **10** astonished, gobsmacked, nonplussed, speechless **11** dumbfounded, open-mouthed **12** lost for words **13** flabbergasted, thunderstruck

## surprising

◊ *anagram indicator* **05** funny **07** amazing, strange **08** shocking, stunning **09** obreption, startling, wonderful **10** astounding, eye-popping, incredible, remarkable, staggering, unexpected, unforeseen **11** astonishing, jaw-dropping, unlooked-for **13** extraordinary **14** eyebrow-raising

## surprisingly

◊ *anagram indicator* **07** funnily **09** amazingly, strangely **10** incredibly, remarkably, stunningly **11** wonderfully **12** staggeringly, unexpectedly **13** astonishingly **15** extraordinarily

## surrender

**04** cede, quit **05** forgo, waive, yield **06** bail up, forego, give in, give up, remise, render, resign, strike, submit, turn in **07** abandon, cession, concede, enfeoff, kamerad, let go of, release, succumb, waiving **08** abdicate, renounce, yielding **09** rendition, sacrifice, surrendry **10** abdication, capitulate, relinquish, submission **11** abandonment, leave behind, resignation **12** capitulation, lower the flag, renunciation **13** cessio bonorum, strike the flag **14** relinquishment **15** lay down your arms, throw in the towel, throw in your hand

## surreptitious

**03** fly, sly **06** covert, hidden, secret, sneaky, veiled **07** furtive **08** stealthy **09** underhand **10** behind-door, subreptive **11** clandestine **12** unauthorized

## surrogate

**05** locum, proxy **06** deputy **07** stand-in **10** substitute **11** locum tenens,

replacement **12** locum tenency **14** representative

## surround

◊ *containment indicator* **03** lap, orb, rim **04** brim, edge, gird, halo, moat, pack, ring, zone **05** beset, bound, brink, hedge, hem in, limit, round, verge, water **06** begird, border, bounds, edging, empale, encase, enhalo, fringe, garter, girdle, impale, incase, invest, margin, picket, piquet **07** besiege, compass, confine, embosom, enclave, enclose, enround, envelop, environ, fence in, go round, imbosom, inclose, picquet, rampart, setting **08** cincture, confines, encircle, overflow, palisade, stockade **09** encompass, perimeter, periphery **10** circumvent, water about **11** close in upon **13** circumference, circumvallate

## surrounding

◊ *containment indicator* **06** gherao, nearby **07** ambient **08** adjacent **09** adjoining, bordering **10** encircling **12** encompassing, neighbouring

## surroundings

**05** scene **06** milieu **07** context, element, habitat, setting **08** ambience, environs, locality, vicinity **10** background **11** environment, mise en scène **12** circumstance **13** neighbourhood

## surveillance

**04** care **05** check, watch **06** charge, spying **07** control **08** scrutiny **09** direction, vigilance **10** inspection, monitoring, regulation **11** observation, stewardship, supervision **12** guardianship, suicide watch **15** superintendence

## survey

**03** map, spy **04** form, plan, plot, poll, quiz, scan, test, view **05** chart, level, probe, recce, study, sweep, watch **06** assess, look at, review, size up **07** examine, inspect, measure, observe, overeye, surview **08** appraise, consider, episcopy, estimate, evaluate, look over, once-over, overview, perceive, prospect, research, scrutiny, traverse **09** appraisal, summing-up, supervise, valuation **10** assessment, conspectus, inspection, plane-table, scrutinize **11** contemplate, examination, measurement, opinion poll, reconnoitre, triangulate **12** Domesday book, Doomsday book, tour d'horizon **13** consideration, perambulation, questionnaire, triangulation **14** market research, reconnaissance **15** superintendence

## surveyor

**02** CS **08** assessor, examiner, overseer **09** geodesist, inspector

## survival

**06** coping **08** hangover, leftover, managing **09** endurance, existence **10** will to live **11** continuance, persistence, withholding **12** perseverance, staying power

## survive

**04** cope, last, live, stay **05** exist, rally **06** endure, live on, make it, manage, remain **07** die hard, hold out, live out, outlast, outlive, persist, recover, weather **08** be extant, continue **09** withstand **10** get through **11** come through, live through, pull through

## susceptibility

**07** feeling **08** openness, tendency, weakness **09** liability, proneness **10** proclivity, propensity **11** gullibility, sensitivity **13** sensibilities, vulnerability **14** predisposition, responsiveness, suggestibility **15** defencelessness

## susceptible

**04** open, weak **05** given, prone **06** at risk, liable, tender **07** capable, patient, subject **08** disposed, gullible, inclined **09** credulous, easily led, receptive, sensitive **10** responsive, vulnerable **11** defenceless, impressible, predisposed, suggestible **14** impressionable

## suspect

◇ *anagram indicator* **03** sus **04** fear, feel, iffy, suss **05** dodgy, doubt, fancy, fishy, guess, infer, smoke, sniff, snuff **07** believe, dubious, jalouse, misdeem, suppose, surmise **08** be wary of, conclude, consider, distrust, doubtful, jealouse, misdoubt, mistrust **09** debatable, mislippen, smell a rat, speculate, suspicion **10** conjecture, have a hunch, inadequate, suspicious, unreliable **11** misconceive **12** insufficient, questionable **13** be uneasy about **15** have doubts about, have qualms about

## suspend

**04** hang, hold, side, stay **05** cease, debar, defer, delay, expel, swing **06** arrest, dangle, ground, hang up, put off, recess, remove, shelve **07** adjourn, dismiss, entrain, exclude, keep out, shut out, unfrock **08** disperse, postpone, prorogue, put on ice, sideline, stand off **09** interrupt **10** pigeonhole **11** discontinue **13** put in abeyance

## suspended

**06** put off **07** delayed, hanging, pendent, pending, pensile, shelved **08** dangling, deferred, put on ice **09** postponed **10** underslung

## suspense

**05** doubt, poise **07** anxiety, tension **09** cessation, deferring **10** excitement, expectancy, indecision, insecurity **11** expectation, nervousness, uncertainty **12** anticipation, apprehension, doubtfulness, intermission
• **in suspense 06** on edge **07** eagerly, keyed up **09** anxiously **11** expectantly **13** on tenterhooks **15** with bated breath

## suspension

**03** sol **04** foam, mist, stay **05** break, delay **07** removal, respite **08** abeyance, abeyancy, deferral **09** cessation, debarment, deferment, dismissal, exclusion, expulsion, grounding,

remission **10** inhibition, moratorium, unfrocking **11** adjournment, standing-off **12** intermission, interruption, postponement **14** pseudosolution

## suspicion

**03** sus **04** dash, hint, idea, suss **05** doubt, hunch, qualm, shade, sniff, tinge, touch, trace, whiff **06** belief, breath, notion, qualms, shadow **07** caution, feeling, glimmer, inkling, opinion, soupçon, surmise, suspect, umbrage **08** distrust, misdoubt, mistrust, paranoea, paranoia, wariness **09** chariness, intuition, misgiving, scintilla **10** conjecture, intimation, misdeeming, misgivings, scepticism, sixth sense, suggestion **12** apprehension, funny feeling

## suspicious

◇ *anagram indicator* **03** odd **04** iffy, suss, wary **05** chary, dodgy, fishy, funny, queer, shady, smoky **06** guilty, shifty, uneasy, unsure **07** dubious, strange, suspect **08** doubtful, peculiar **09** dishonest, equivocal, irregular, sceptical **10** misdeeming, suspectful, suspecting **11** distrustful, mistrustful, unbelieving **12** apprehensive, disbelieving, questionable

## suspiciously

**05** oddly **06** warily **07** shadily **09** dubiously, strangely **10** doubtfully **11** dishonestly, sceptically **12** questionably **13** distrustfully, mistrustfully, unbelievingly **14** apprehensively, disbelievingly

## Sussex

• **division of Sussex 04** rape

## sustain

**03** aid **04** bear, buoy, face, feed, help, hold, prop, ride **05** abide, carry, stand **06** assist, buoy up, endure, foster, hold up, keep up, prop up, suffer, upbear, uphold, upstay **07** aliment, carry on, comfort, endorse, nourish, nurture, prolong, receive, relieve, ride out, support, suspend, undergo **08** continue, happen to, maintain, protract, sanction, scaffold **09** encourage, go through, keep going, underbear **10** experience, provide for, sustentate **14** give strength to

## sustained

**06** steady, tenuto **07** ongoing **08** constant **09** perpetual, prolonged, sostenuto **10** continuing, continuous, protracted **11** unremitting **12** long-drawn-out

## sustenance

**04** fare, food, grub, nosh **05** scoff **06** viands **07** aliment, support **08** victuals **09** autophagy, provender, refection **10** autophagia, livelihood, provisions **11** comestibles, maintenance, nourishment, subsistence, sufficience

## svelte

**04** slim **05** lithe **06** lissom, urbane **07** elegant, shapely, slender, willowy **08** graceful, polished **09** sylphlike **13** sophisticated

## swag

**03** sag **04** drum, sway **05** bluey **07** bed roll, festoon, matilda, plunder **10** depression, subsidence

## swagger

**04** brag, cock, crow, roll, show **05** boast, brank, pronk, smart, strut, swank, vapor **06** parade, prance, ruffle, square, vapour **07** bluster, panache, roister, royster, show off **08** parading, prancing, tigerism **09** arrogance **11** ostentation **12** go over the top

## swallow

◇ *containment indicator* **03** buy, eat, pop **04** bear, bolt, down, gulp, slug, swig, take **05** abide, abyss, ariel, drink, gorge, gulch, quaff, scoff, shift, stand, thole, trust **06** accept, devour, endure, englut, gobble, guzzle, ingest, martin, Progne, stifle, take in, throat, up with **07** believe, consume, contain, fall for, martlet, repress, smother, stomach, subsume, take off **08** down with, gobble up, gulp down, hold back, martinet, suppress, tolerate **09** knock back, polish off, put up with, worry down **11** be certain of, house martin
• **swallow hole 04** sink **06** dolina, doline **07** swallet **08** sinkhole
• **swallow up 06** absorb, enfold, engulf **07** engulph, envelop, ingulph, overrun **08** take over **09** overwhelm **10** assimilate **11** ingurgitate

## swamp

**03** bog, fen, mud, vly **04** mire, quag, sink, vlei **05** beset, cowal, flood, Lerna, Lerne, marsh **06** deluge, Dismal, drench, engulf, morass, muskeg, slough **07** besiege, bog down, Dismals, wash out **08** inundate, loblolly, overload, quagmire, saturate, submerge, waterlog **09** overwhelm, purgatory, quicksand, swampland, weigh down

## swampy

**03** wet **04** miry **05** boggy, fenny, soggy **06** marshy, quaggy **07** paludal **08** squelchy **09** uliginose, uliginous **11** waterlogged

## swan

**03** cob, pen **04** Leda **06** cygnet, Cygnus

*Swans include:*

| |
|---|
| **04** mute |
| **05** black |
| **07** Bewick's, whooper |
| **08** whooping |
| **09** trumpeter, whistling |

## swank

**04** brag, show, swot **05** agile, boast, pronk, smart, strut **06** parade, pliant **07** conceit, display, posture, show off, slender, swagger **08** bragging **09** vainglory **10** showing-off **11** ostentation **12** attitudinize, boastfulness **13** conceitedness, preen yourself **15** pretentiousness

## swanky

**04** posh, rich **05** fancy, flash, grand, plush, ritzy, showy, smart, swish **06** de luxe, flashy, lavish, plushy **07** stylish

**09** exclusive, expensive, glamorous, luxurious, sumptuous **11** fashionable, pretentious **12** ostentatious

## swap, swop

◊ *anagram indicator* **03** hit **04** blow, flop, slam **05** bandy, plump, smite, trade **06** barter, strike, stroke, switch **07** traffic **08** exchange, suddenly, trade-off **09** transpose **10** substitute **11** interchange **12** substitution **13** transposition

## sward

**03** sod **04** turf

## swarm

**03** fry, mob **04** army, bike, body, byke, cast, herd, host, mass, nest, pack, shin, teem **05** crowd, drove, flock, flood, horde, shoal, surge, troop **06** abound, colony, hotter, myriad, stream, swerve, throng **08** offshoot **09** multitude **10** congregate
• **be swarming with** **08** abound in **13** be crowded with, be overrun with, be teeming with **14** be crawling with, be hotching with, be thronged with **15** be bristling with

## swarthy

**04** dark **05** black, brown, dusky **06** tanned **08** blackish **11** black-a-vised, dark-skinned

## swashbuckling

**04** bold **06** daring, robust **07** dashing, gallant **08** exciting, spirited **09** daredevil **10** courageous, flamboyant, swaggering **11** adventurous

## swat

**03** hit **04** biff **05** lunge, swipe, whack **06** strike, wallop **07** fly-flap, lash out

## swathe

**03** lap **04** bind, fold, furl, wind, wrap **05** cloak, drape **06** enwrap, shroud **07** bandage, envelop, sheathe, swaddle **08** enshroud, wrapping

## sway

**04** bend, lean, reel, rock, roll, rule, shog, swag, swee, swey, veer, wave **05** clout, hoist, lurch, power, sally, shake, swale, swing, thraw, wield **06** affect, direct, divert, govern, induce, swerve, swinge, teeter, titter, totter, waddle, wobble **07** command, control, convert, incline, proceed, reeling, rocking, shoogie, shoogle, stagger, win over **08** convince, dominate, dominion, hegemony, overrule, persuade, rotation **09** authority, dominance, fluctuate, influence, oscillate, supremacy, vacillate **10** ascendancy, bring round, government, leadership **11** fluctuation, oscillation, prevail upon, sovereignty **12** jurisdiction, predominance **13** preponderance
• **hold sway** **04** rule **05** reign **07** prevail **09** have power **10** wield power **13** exercise power, have authority, have influence, lay down the law

## Swaziland

**02** SD **03** SWZ

## swear

**03** eff, rap, vow **04** aver, avow, cuss, damn, oath **05** abuse, blind, curse **06** abjure, adjure, affirm, assert, attest, depose, insist, invoke, objure, pledge **07** declare, promise, testify **08** be on oath, forswear, maledict **09** blaspheme, imprecate, overswear **10** asseverate, take an oath **11** be under oath, eff and blind, take the oath **12** damn and blast **14** abjure the realm, pledge yourself, turn the air blue, use bad language **15** promise solemnly
• **swear by** **06** rely on **07** trust in **08** depend on **09** believe in **11** have faith in **14** put your faith in

## swearing

**07** cursing, cussing **08** language **09** blasphemy, profanity **10** coprolalia, expletives **11** bad language **12** foul language, imprecations, maledictions **14** strong language

## swear-word

**04** cuss, oath **05** curse **08** cussword, swearing **09** blasphemy, expletive, obscenity, profanity **11** bad language, imprecation **12** foul language **14** four-letter word

## sweat

**04** drip, flap, fuss, toil **05** chore, exude, panic, smart, sudor, tizzy, worry **06** dither, effort, labour, lather, sudate, tizwas **07** anxiety, fluster, secrete, soldier, swelter **08** drudgery, hidrosis, moisture, perspire, sudation **09** agitation, cold sweat, death-damp, mucksweat **10** osmidrosis, perspirate, stickiness **11** bloody-sweat, diaphoresis **12** perspiration, sweat buckets **13** sweat like a pig

## sweaty

**04** damp **05** moist **06** clammy, sticky **08** forswatt, sudorous, sweating **10** perspiring

## Sweden

**01** S **03** SWE

## sweep

**03** arc, fly **04** bend, drag, dust, lash, move, pass, poke, push, race, roll, sail, scud, skim, soop, span, sway, tear, wash, whip, wipe **05** besom, broom, brush, clean, clear, curve, drive, elbow, force, glide, range, scoop, scope, shove, sling, surge, swath, swing, swipe, swoop, vista, whisk **06** action, extent, glance, hurtle, jostle, onrush, remove, search, stroke, swathe, thrust, vacuum **07** clean up, clear up, compass, ensweep, expanse, gesture, impetus, stretch **08** besom out, movement, overrake, snowball, vastness **09** besom away, clearance, curvature, immensity, sooterkin **10** blackguard, pump-handle **11** move quickly **13** spread quickly
• **sweep under the carpet** **04** hide **06** hush up **07** conceal, cover up **08** suppress **09** gloss over, paper over

## sweeper

**05** broom **06** libero

## sweeping

**04** sway, wide **05** broad, swing **06** global **07** blanket, general, radical, rubbish **08** thorough **09** extensive, universal, wholesale **10** simplistic **11** far-reaching, wide-ranging **12** all-embracing, all-inclusive **13** comprehensive, thoroughgoing **14** across-the-board, indiscriminate, oversimplified

## sweepstake

**04** draw **05** sweep, Tatts **07** lottery **08** gambling **11** sweepstakes, Tattersall's

## sweet

**03** pud **04** cute, dear, easy, icky, kind, mild, pure, ripe, soft, soot, twee **05** balmy, candy, clean, clear, dolce, fresh, glacé **06** afters, benign, dulcet, gentle, kindly, lovely, mellow, pretty, sickly, sugary, syrupy, tender **07** amiable, beloved, candied, darling, dessert, honeyed, lovable, musical, odorous, pudding, sweetie, tuneful, winning, winsome **08** adorable, all right, aromatic, charming, engaging, fragrant, gracious, likeable, loveable, luscious, perfumed, pleasant, pleasing, precious, redolent **09** agreeable, ambrosial, appealing, beautiful, cherished, delicious, melodious, sweetened, sweetmeat, treasured, wholesome **10** attractive, confection, delightful, euphonious, harmonious, saccharine **11** mellifluous, odoriferous, sickly sweet **12** affectionate, ingratiating, satisfactory, sweet-scented **13** confectionery, sweet-sounding

*Sweets include:*

**03** gum, ice
**04** jube, Mars®, mint, rock
**05** fudge, halva, jelly
**06** bonbon, confit, humbug, jujube, nougat, tablet, toffee
**07** alcorza, caramel, fondant, gumdrop, lozenge, Mars Bar®, pomfret, praline, truffle, wine gum
**08** acid drop, bull's eye, confetti, lollipop, marzipan, noisette, pastille, pear drop
**09** chocolate, jelly baby, jelly bean, lemon drop, liquorice, nougatine
**10** candyfloss, chewing-gum, gobstopper, peppermint
**11** aniseed ball, barley sugar, marshmallow, toffee apple
**12** butterscotch, dolly mixture
**13** Edinburgh rock, fruit pastille
**14** pineapple chunk, Turkish delight

*See also* **cake; dessert**
• **sweet on** **06** fond of, keen on, liking **08** mad about **09** far gone on **10** crazy about **12** ravished with **14** infatuated with

## sweetbread

**03** bur **04** burr

## sweeten

**04** ease **05** honey, sugar **06** mellow, pacify, soften, soothe, temper

**07** appease, cushion, mollify, relieve
**08** mitigate **09** alleviate **10** add sugar to, edulcorate

**sweetheart**
**02** jo **03** joe **04** beau, dear, dona, duck, girl, lass, love **05** bonny, donah, flame, honey, leman, lover, Romeo, swain, toots **06** amoret, bonnie, steady, suitor, sweety, tootsy **07** admirer, beloved, darling, sweetie **08** Dulcinea, follower, lady-love, truelove, young man **09** betrothed, boyfriend, inamorata, inamorato, valentine, young lady **10** girlfriend

**sweetly**
**04** soot **05** dolce, soote **06** easily, evenly, in tune, kindly, softly **08** lovingly, mellowly, smoothly, steadily, tenderly **09** tunefully, winsomely **10** charmingly, dolcemente, pleasantly **11** melodiously **12** delightfully, effortlessly, euphoniously, harmoniously **14** affectionately

**sweetness**
**04** love **05** aroma, charm, sirup, syrup **07** douceur, euphony, harmony **08** kindness **09** balminess, dulcitude, fragrance, freshness, saccharin **10** amiability, loveliness, mellowness, saccharine, succulence, sugariness, tenderness **11** sweet temper, winsomeness **12** lusciousness, mellifluence, pleasantness

**sweet-smelling**
**05** balmy **07** odorous **08** aromatic, fragrant, perfumed, redolent **09** ambrosial **11** odoriferous **12** sweet-scented

**swell**
**03** bag, don, fop, sea **04** beau, blab, boll, bulb, bulk, dude, grow, hove, huff, lord, plim, posh, puff, rise, toff, wave **05** adept, belly, berry, blast, bloat, bulge, bunch, dandy, elate, farce, grand, great, heave, mount, plump, raise, ritzy, smart, surge **06** bigwig, billow, blow up, de luxe, dilate, expand, extend, fatten, flashy, louden, puff up, step up, strout, swanky, tumefy, volume, wallow **07** augment, balloon, distend, enlarge, ferment, heaving, incline, inflate, stylish, tumesce **08** belly out, escalate, heighten, increase, mushroom, outswell, snowball **09** backwater, cockscomb, excellent, exclusive, intensify, intumesce, loudening, roughness, skyrocket, wonderful **10** accelerate, distension, grow larger, undulation **11** enlargement, fashionable, proliferate

**swelling**
**03** sty **04** boil, boll, bulb, bump, gall, knob, knot, lump, node, stye **05** bulge, heave, mouse, nodus, proud, tuber, tumor **06** bruise, nodule, pimple, rising, torose, torous, tumour, venter **07** blister, chancre, pillowy, tympany, vesicle **08** nodosity, pulvinus, scirrhus, tubercle **09** chilblain, gathering, puffiness **10** distension, tumescence,

turgescent **11** enlargement, tumefaction **12** inflammation, intumescence, protuberance

**sweltering**
**03** hot **05** humid, muggy, stewy **06** baking, clammy, steamy, sticky, sultry, torrid **07** airless, boiling **08** roasting, sizzling, stifling, tropical **09** scorching **10** oppressive **11** suffocating

**swerve**
**03** wry **04** bend, lean, skew, sway, swee, swey, turn, veer, warp **05** faint, sheer, shift, stray, swarm, swing, twist **06** shrink, wander **07** deflect, deviate, diverge, incline, inswing **08** outswing, scramble **09** deviation **10** deflection

**swift**
**04** fast **05** agile, brief, brisk, fleet, hasty, nippy, quick, rapid, ready, short, wight **06** abrupt, flying, lively, nimble, prompt, speedy, sudden, winged **07** express, flighty, hurried **09** feathered, immediate, screecher **10** pernicious **11** dispatchful, expeditious, tiger-footed **13** screech-martin

**swiftly**
**04** fast **05** apace **07** express, hotfoot, quickly, rapidly **08** promptly, speedily **09** hurriedly, instantly, posthaste **10** at full tilt **11** double-quick **13** expeditiously

**swiftness**
**05** speed **08** alacrity, celerity, despatch, dispatch, rapidity, velocity **09** fleetness, immediacy, quickness, readiness **10** expedition, promptness, speediness, suddenness **13** immediateness, instantaneity

**swill**
◊ anagram indicator **04** gulp, swig, wash **05** drain, drink, quaff, rinse, slops, waste **06** gargle, guzzle, imbibe, refuse, sluice **07** consume, hogwash, pigwash, swallow, toss off **08** pig's-wash, pigswill **09** knock back, scourings
• swill out **05** clean, flush, rinse **06** drench, sluice **07** cleanse, wash out **08** wash down

**swim**
◊ anagram indicator **03** bob, dip, fin, ren, rin, run **04** soom, swan, whim **05** bathe, crawl, float **06** paddle **07** snorkel **08** take a dip **09** strike out **10** tread water

**swimmer**
see **fish**

**swimming**
◊ anagram indicator

*Swimming strokes include:*

**03** fly
**05** crawl
**07** trudgen
**09** back-crawl, butterfly, dog-paddle, freestyle
**10** backstroke, front crawl, sidestroke
**11** doggy-paddle

**12** breaststroke
**15** Australian crawl

*Swimming- and diving-related terms include:*

**02** IM
**03** fly, rip
**04** pike, tuck
**05** block, boost, entry, scull, split
**06** inward, layout, length, medley
**07** forward, reverse
**08** armstand, backward, flamingo
**09** ballet leg, eggbeater, elevation
**10** tumble turn
**11** dolphin kick, flutter kick, rocket split
**12** combined spin
**13** negative split
**14** continuous spin
**15** backstroke flags

*Swimmers and divers include:*

**04** **Klim** (Michael), **Otto** (Kristin), **Rose** (Murray), **Webb** (Matthew)
**05** **Crapp** (Lorraine), **Curry** (Lisa), **Ender** (Kornelia), **Evans** (Janet), **Gould** (Shane), **Gross** (Michael), **Lewis** (Hayley), **Riley** (Samantha), **Spitz** (Mark)
**06** **Biondi** (Matt), **Davies** (Sharron), **Durack** (Fanny), **Ederle** (Gertrude), **Fraser** (Dawn), **Loader** (Danyon), **O'Neill** (Susie), **Phelps** (Michael), **Thorpe** (Ian), **Wilkie** (David)
**07** **Goodhew** (Duncan), **Hackett** (Grant), **Perkins** (Kieren), **Wickham** (Tracey)
**08** **Champion** (Malcolm), **Charlton** (Boy), **De Bruijn** (Inge), **Louganis** (Greg), **Streeter** (Alison), **Van Wisse** (Tammy), **Williams** (Esther)
**09** **Adlington** (Rebecca), **Armstrong** (Duncan), **Kellerman** (Annette)
**11** **Beaurepaire** (Sir Frank), **Weissmuller** (Johnny)

• **swimming organ** **03** oar **05** ctene
**swimming costume**
see **swimsuit**
**swimmingly**
**06** easily **08** smoothly, very well **12** successfully **13** like clockwork, without a hitch

**swimming-pool**
**04** lido **05** baths **10** natatorium **11** leisure pool **12** swimming-bath, swimming-pond **13** swimming-baths

**swimsuit**
**03** tog **04** togs **05** tanga, thong **06** bikini, cossie, trunks **07** bathers, maillot, tankini **08** monokini, one-piece **11** bathing suit **12** bathing dress **14** bathing costume **15** swimming costume

**swindle**
**02** do **03** con, gyp, rig **04** beat, chiz, dupe, fake, have, lurk, ramp, rook, scam, skin, take **05** bunco, bunko, cheat, chizz, fraud, gouge, grift, let in, mulct, pluck, shaft, sting, trick, twist **06** bucket, chouse, diddle, fiddle, fleece, hustle, nobble, racket, rip off, rip-off **07** con game, deceive, defraud,

**swindler**

exploit, skelder, tweedle **08** clean-out, con trick, fakement, sell a pup, stitch up, trickery **09** bamboozle, deception, financier, gold brick, gold-brick, sell smoke **10** overcharge **12** put one over on, take for a ride **13** double-dealing, sharp practice

**swindler**

**03** con, leg **04** hood, rook **05** cheat, crook, fraud, rogue, shark **06** chouse, con man, escroc, rascal **07** fiddler, grifter, hoodlum, hustler, magsman, shyster, slicker, spieler **08** blackleg, con woman, impostor **09** charlatan, chiseller, con artist, fraudster, trickster **10** mountebank **12** bunko-steerer

**swine**

**03** hog, pig **04** boar, boor **05** beast, brute, rogue **06** rascal **09** scoundrel **14** good-for-nothing
• **bit of a swine** **03** ham **05** bacon

**swing**

◇ anagram indicator **03** fix, get **04** bend, hang, hurl, jive, lean, make, move, rock, shog, spin, sway, swee, swey, turn, vary, veer, wave, wind **05** curve, fix up, pivot, scope, set up, shift, sling, sweep, twist, wheel, whirl **06** change, dangle, excite, motion, rhythm, rotate, stroke, swerve, waving **07** achieve, arrange, attract, control, impetus, incline, shoogie, vibrate **08** brandish, fishtail, movement, organize, sweeping **09** fluctuate, oscillate, pendulate, variation, vibration **11** fluctuation, oscillating, oscillation

**swingeing**

**04** huge **05** great, harsh, heavy **06** severe **07** drastic, extreme, serious **08** thumping **09** Draconian, excessive, punishing, stringent **10** exorbitant, oppressive **11** devastating **12** extortionate

**swinging**

◇ anagram indicator **03** hip **06** lively, modern, trendy, with it **07** dynamic, hanging, stylish, swaying, turning **08** exciting, up-to-date **10** jet-setting **11** fashionable, oscillatory **12** contemporary **13** up-to-the-minute

**swipe**

**03** hit **04** biff, blow, gulp, lift, nick, slap, sock, swat, whip, wipe **05** clout, filch, lunge, pinch, slice, smack, steal, swath, whack **06** pilfer, strike, stroke, wallop **07** lash out, purloin

**swirl**

◇ anagram indicator **04** curl, eddy, purl, spin, wind **05** churn, twirl, twist, wheel, whirl **07** agitate, revolve, swizzle **09** circulate **10** tourbillon **11** tourbillion

**swish**

**04** cane, flog, lash, posh, wave, whip **05** birch, flash, grand, plush, ritzy, smart, swell, swing, swirl, twirl, whirl, whisk, whizz **06** de luxe, rustle, swanky, swoosh, thrash, whoosh **07** elegant, stylish, whistle **08** brandish, flourish **09** exclusive, sumptuous **11** fashionable

**switch**

◇ anagram indicator ◇ reversal indicator **03** put, rod **04** beat, cane, jerk, lash, swap, turn, twig, veer, whip **05** birch, lever, prune, relay, shift, shoot, shunt, thong, trade, tress, whisk **06** barter, beat up, branch, button, change, divert, gain-up, scutch, toggle, twitch **07** control, convert, deflect, deviate, replace **08** cryotron, exchange, reversal **09** about-turn, rearrange, transpose **10** alteration, changeover, substitute **11** interchange, on-off device, replacement **12** substitution **13** chop and change **14** circuit-breaker
• **switch off** **03** cut **07** shut off, turn off, turn out **08** flick off **09** close down **11** stop working
• **switch on** **05** put on **06** set off, turn on **07** flick on, operate **08** activate **10** trigger off

**Switzerland**

**02** CH **03** CHE

**swivel**

**04** spin, turn **05** pivot, twirl, wheel **06** gyrate, rotate **07** revolve **09** pirouette

**swollen**

**04** rank **05** bloat, puffy, tumid **06** bolled, bollen, gourdy, turgid **07** blabber, bloated, bulbous, bulging, dilated, distent, gibbose, gibbous **08** blubbery, engorged, enlarged, expanded, hydropic, inflamed, inflated, puffed up **09** blubbered, distended, tumescent **11** incrassated

**swoop**

**04** dive, drop, fall, rush **05** lunge, souse, stoop **06** attack, plunge, pounce **07** descend, descent **09** onslaught
• **at one fell swoop** **07** in one go **08** suddenly **09** all at once, at one time, by one blow **13** on one occasion **15** by a single action

**swop**

see **swap, swop**

**sword**

**03** war **04** spit

_Swords include:_

**03** fox
**04** back, épée, foil, simi
**05** bilbo, blade, brand, broad, court, estoc, kukri, saber, sabre, short, skean, skene, small, steel
**06** espada, glaive, hanger, katana, kirpan, rapier, sweard, Toledo, waster
**07** curtana, curtaxe, cutlass, gladius, hunting, Morglay, shabble, spurtle, whinger, yatagan
**08** claymore, curtalax, damaskin, falchion, schläger, scimitar, spadroon, whiniard, whinyard, white arm, yataghan
**09** curtalaxe, damascene, damaskeen, damasquin, Excalibur
**10** damasceene

**12** spurtle-blade, toasting fork, toasting iron

_See also_ **dagger; knife**
• **cross swords** **05** argue, fight **06** bicker **07** contend, contest, dispute, quarrel, wrangle **08** be at odds, disagree **15** be at loggerheads

**sworn**

**07** devoted, eternal **08** attested **09** confirmed **10** implacable, inveterate, relentless

**swot**

**03** mug **04** cram, work **05** learn, mug up, study, swank **06** bone up, revise **08** memorize

**sybarite**

**07** epicure, playboy **08** hedonist, parasite **09** bon vivant, epicurean, pleasurer **10** sensualist, voluptuary **14** pleasure-seeker

**sybaritic**

**04** easy **07** sensual **09** epicurean, luxurious, parasitic **10** hedonistic, voluptuous **13** self-indulgent **14** pleasure-loving **15** pleasure-seeking

**sycophancy**

**07** fawning **08** cringing, flattery, toadyism **09** adulation, kowtowing, servility, truckling **10** grovelling, toad-eating **11** bootlicking, slavishness **14** backscratching, obsequiousness, oleaginousness

**sycophant**

**05** slave, toady **06** fawner, yes-man **07** crawler, cringer, placebo, sponger **08** claqueur, hanger-on, parasite, truckler **09** flatterer, groveller, toad-eater **10** bootlicker **12** cookie-pusher **13** apple polisher, backscratcher

**sycophantic**

**05** slimy **06** smarmy **07** fawning, servile, slavish **08** cringing, toadying, unctuous **09** truckling **10** flattering, grovelling, obsequious, oleaginous, toad-eating **11** bootlicking, parasitical, time-serving **12** ingratiating **13** sycophantical **14** backscratching

**syllabus**

**03** syl **04** plan **05** table **06** course **07** outline **08** schedule **09** programme **10** curriculum

**syllogism**

**08** argument **09** abduction, deduction, enthymeme **11** epicheirema, proposition

**sylph-like**

**04** slim **05** lithe **06** slight, svelte **07** elegant, slender, willowy **08** graceful **11** streamlined

**sylvan**

see **silvan**

**symbiotic**

**07** epizoan, epizoic **09** commensal, epizootic **10** endophytic, synergetic

11 co-operative, interactive
14 interdependent

**symbol**
04 mark, rune, sign, type 05 creed, image 06 figure 09 character, ideograph 14 representation

*Symbols include:*

01 A, B, C, D, E, F, G, H, I, J, K, L, M, N, O, P, Q, R, S, T, U, V, W, X, Y, Z
02 Ac, Ag, Al, Am, Ar, As, At, Au, Ba, BB, Be, Bh, Bi, Bk, Bq, Br, Ca, Cd, Ce, Cf, Cl, Cm, Co, CQ, Cr, Cs, Cu, Db, Ds, Dy, Er, Es, Eu, Fe, ff, Fm, Fr, Ga, Gd, Ge, Gy, Ha, He, Hf, Hg, HH, Ho, Hs, Hz, In, Ir, kg, Kr, La, Li, Im, Lr, Lu, Lw, Ix, Md, Mg, Mn, Mo, Mt, MV, Na, Nb, Nd, Ne, Ni, No, Np, Oe, Os, Pa, Pb, Pd, Pm, Po, Pr, Pt, Pu, Ra, Rb, Re, Rf, Rg, Rh, Rn, Ru, Sb, Sc, Se, Sg, Si, Sm, Sn, Sr, Sv, Ta, Tb, Tc, Te, Th, Ti, Tl, Tm, Wb, Xe, Yb, Zn, Zr
03 BBB, dBA, kat, LXX, mol, rad
04 icon, ikon, logo
05 badge, brand, crest, motif, token, totem
06 cipher, emblem, smiley, uraeus
08 caduceus, ideogram, insignia, logogram, monogram, swastika
09 pentagram, trademark, watermark
10 coat of arms, hieroglyph, pictograph
12 yellow ribbon

*Religious symbols include:*

02 Om
03 IHC, IHS
04 ankh, fish, yoni
05 cross, linga
06 chakra, filfot, fylfot, lingam
07 Ik Onkar, mandala, menorah, yin-yang
08 crescent, swastika
11 Christingle, star of David

*See also* **element**

**symbolic**
05 token 07 shadowy, typical
10 emblematic, figurative, meaningful, symbolical 11 allegorical, significant
12 illustrative, metaphorical
14 representative

**symbolically**
07 as a sign 09 as a symbol 10 as an emblem 11 by this token 12 figuratively
14 emblematically

**symbolize**
04 mean, type 05 agree 06 denote, emblem, figure, symbol, typify
07 betoken, combine, express, present, signify 08 stand for 09 epitomize, exemplify, personate, personify, represent

**symmetrical**
03 sym 04 even 07 dimeric, regular, uniform 08 balanced, parallel
10 consistent, harmonious 11 well-rounded, zygopleural 12 isobilateral,

proportional, right-and-left
13 actinomorphic, corresponding

**symmetry**
07 balance, harmony 08 evenness
09 agreement, congruity 10 proportion, regularity, uniformity 11 consistency, parallelism, proportions
14 correspondence

**sympathetic**
04 kind, soft, warm 06 caring, genial, kindly, social, tender 07 feeling, pitying 08 friendly, likeable, pleasant, sociable, tolerant 09 agreeable, concerned, congenial, consoling, simpatico 10 comforting, compatible, favourable, interested, like-minded, solicitous, supportive 11 considerate, encouraging, kind-hearted, neighbourly, warm-hearted
12 affectionate, appreciative, well-disposed 13 commiserating, commiserative, companionable, compassionate, sympathetical, understanding

**sympathetically**
06 kindly, warmly 09 feelingly, pityingly 11 consolingly, sensitively
12 comfortingly, responsively, supportively 13 warm-heartedly
14 appreciatively 15 compassionately, understandingly

**sympathize**
03 rap 04 pity 07 care for, comfort, condole, console, feel for
09 empathize, encourage, respond to
10 appreciate, correspond, understand
11 commiserate, show concern 12 be supportive, feel sorry for, identify with, show interest

**sympathizer**
03 fan 06 backer 07 admirer
08 adherent, condoler, partisan
09 supporter 10 copperhead, well-wisher 15 fellow-traveller

**sympathy**
04 pity 05 aroha 06 accord, solace, warmth 07 comfort, empathy, harmony, rapport, support 08 affinity, approval, kindness 09 agreement, closeness 10 compassion, tenderness
11 approbation, condolences, consolation, correlation, Weltschmerz
12 appreciation 13 commiseration, consideration, encouragement, fellow-feeling, understanding
14 correspondence, thoughtfulness
15 warm-heartedness
• **expression of sympathy** 02 ah, aw
04 dear 05 shame, sorry, there 06 dear me, oh dear, too bad 07 deary me
08 dearie me, good-lack
09 hard lines, tough luck 10 hard cheese

**symptom**
03 sym 04 mark, note, sign 05 fever, hives, rigor, token 06 signal 07 anxiety, display, feature, hard pad, warning
08 evidence, merycism, necrosis, prodrome 09 ketonuria, prodromus, rosetting 10 diagnostic, expression, indication, nettle rash, prognostic

11 hydrophobia, proteinuria
13 demonstration, epiphenomenon, malabsorption, manifestation
14 characteristic
*See also* **disease**

**symptomatic**
07 typical 10 associated, indicative, suggesting, suggestive 14 characteristic

**synagogue**
04 shul 06 temple

**synchronize**
04 sync, tune 05 synch

**syndicate**
04 bloc, ring 05 group, judge 06 cartel
07 censure, combine, council
08 alliance 11 association, combination

**synonymous**
07 similar, the same 09 identical
10 comparable, equivalent, tantamount 13 corresponding, substitutable 15 interchangeable

**synopsis**
05 recap 06 digest, précis, résumé, review, schema, sketch 07 outline, run-down, summary 08 abstract
09 summation 10 abridgment, compendium, conspectus, tabulation
11 abridgement 12 condensation
14 recapitulation

**synthesis**
05 alloy, blend, union 06 fusion
07 amalgam, welding 08 compound, pastiche 09 anabolism, composite
11 coalescence, combination, integration, pantheology, unification
12 amalgamation, glycogenesis
13 individuation

**synthesize**
04 fuse, weld 05 alloy, blend, merge, unify, unite 07 combine 08 coalesce, compound 09 integrate
10 amalgamate

**synthetic**
◇ *anagram indicator* 03 syn 04 fake, faux, mock, sham 05 bogus 06 ersatz, pseudo 07 man-made, plastic
09 imitation, simulated 10 artificial
12 manufactured

**Syria**
03 SYR

**syrup**
03 rob 05 sirup 06 orgeat 07 glucose, linctus, treacle 08 quiddany 09 cocky's joy, diacodion, diacodium, grenadine, moskonfyt 10 capillaire, maple syrup

**syrupy**
05 corny, gushy, mushy, soppy, sweet, weepy 06 loving, sickly, sloppy, slushy, sugary 07 gushing, honeyed, maudlin, mawkish 08 pathetic, romantic 09 emotional, oversweet, schmaltzy, sweetened 10 lovey-dovey, saccharine 11 sentimental, sickly sweet, tear-jerking
12 affectionate

## system

**03** way **04** mode, plan, rule, them **05** logic, means, order, set-up, usage **06** method, scheme **07** network, process, routine **08** approach, practice **09** apparatus, framework, mechanism, procedure, structure, technique **11** arrangement, methodology, orderliness **12** co-ordination, organization **13** modus operandi, the government **14** classification, the authorities **15** systematization, the powers that be

## systematic

**07** logical, ordered, orderly, planned **08** habitual, methodic **09** efficient, organized **10** methodical, scientific, structured **11** intentional, well-ordered, well-planned **12** businesslike, standardized, systematized **13** well-organized

## systematize

**04** plan **05** order **06** codify **07** arrange, dispose **08** classify, organize, regiment, regulate, tabulate **09** methodize, structure **10** schematize **11** make uniform, rationalize, standardize

**T**
03 tee, toc 04 tock 05 tango

**TA**
10 volunteers 15 Territorial Army

**tab**
03 fob, tag 04 bill, cost, drug, flap, pill 05 check, label, strap, tally 06 marker, tablet, ticket 07 Ecstasy, sticker, trimmer 08 ring pull, tabulate 09 cigarette, tabulator
• **keep tabs on** 07 observe 11 keep an eye on 12 watch closely

**tabby**
04 girl, wavy 05 woman 06 banded, stripy 07 brindle, mottled, striped 08 brindled, streaked 10 variegated

**table**
03 bar 04 chow, diet, dish, fare, food, grub, list, menu, move, nosh, plan, slab, tuck 05 bench, chart, graph, index, layer, panel, stand 06 figure, record, submit 07 diagram, picture, propose, suggest, worktop 08 register, schedule, syllabus, tabulate 09 catalogue, committee, inventory, programme, timetable 10 put forward, speciality, tabulation 12 string-course 13 entertainment

*Tables include:*

03 bed, loo, tea, top
04 bird, card, desk, draw, drum, high, pier, pool, sand, side, sofa, work
05 altar, board, lunch, night
06 bureau, coffee, dining, dinner, dolmen, gaming, inking, lowboy, picnic, teapoy, toilet, vanity
07 capstan, console, counter, cricket, drawing, draw-top, dresser, gateleg, snooker, trestle, writing
08 billiard, credence, credenza, draw-leaf, dressing, drop-leaf, guéridon, mahogany, pembroke, piecrust
09 breakfast, communion, operating, refectory
10 dissecting, gate-legged, greencloth, occasional
12 council-board
13 bonheur-du-jour

*Tableware includes:*

03 cup, jug, mug
04 bowl
05 ashet, cruet, plate
06 goblet, saucer, teacup, teapot, tureen
07 creamer, milk jug, platter, tumbler

08 cream jug, flatware, mazarine, rice bowl, salt mill
09 coffee cup, coffee pot, gravy boat, pasta bowl, pasta dish, pepper pot, salad bowl, sauceboat, side plate, soup plate, sugar bowl, toast rack, wineglass
10 bread plate, butter dish, cereal bowl, cruet-stand, pepper mill, salt shaker, soup tureen
11 butter plate, cheese plate, dessert bowl, dessert dish, espresso cup, serving bowl, serving dish
12 dessert plate, mazarine dish, pudding-plate
13 mazarine plate
14 serving platter

• **inner table** 04 home

**tableau**
05 scene 07 diorama, picture 08 vignette 09 portrayal, spectacle 13 tableau vivant 14 representation

**tableland**
04 mesa, puna 05 Karoo 06 Karroo 07 plateau

**tablet**
01 E 03 pad, tab 04 ball, dove, pill, slab 05 album, benny, bolus, panel, plate, stela, stele 06 abacus, caplet, marker, pellet, plaque, Roofie, tabula, troche 07 capsule, diptych, lozenge, sleeper, surface 08 monument, triglyph 09 medallion, tablature, wobbly egg 10 osculatory, tabula rasa 11 purple heart 12 disco biscuit, Rosetta stone

**tabletalk**
03 ana

**tabloid**
*see* **newspaper**

**taboo**
03 ban 04 tabu, tapu, veto 05 curse 06 banned, vetoed 08 anathema, ruled out 09 exclusion, forbidden, interdict, ostracism, restraint 10 prohibited, proscribed, sacrosanct 11 prohibition, restriction, unthinkable 12 interdiction, proscription, unacceptable 13 unmentionable

**tabulate**
03 tab 04 list, sort 05 chart, index, order, range, table 06 codify 07 arrange 08 classify 09 catalogue 10 categorize, tabularize 11 systematize

**tabulation**
07 listing, sorting, tabling 08 indexing, ordering 11 arrangement, cataloguing 14 categorization, classification

**tacit**
06 silent 07 implied 08 implicit, inferred, unspoken, unstated, unvoiced, wordless 10 understood 11 unexpressed

**taciturn**
04 cold, dumb, mute 05 aloof, quiet 06 silent 07 distant 08 detached, reserved, reticent 09 withdrawn 10 of few words 11 tight-lipped, untalkative 12 close-mouthed 13 unforthcoming 15 uncommunicative

**tack**
03 add, fix, pin, sew, tag, way 04 line, nail, path, plan, take, turn, veer 05 affix, annex, baste, catch, lease, smack, spell 06 append, attach, attack, course, fasten, method, policy, sleaze, staple, stitch, swerve, tactic, tenure, tingle, zigzag 07 bearing, go about, heading, process, tintack 08 approach, club-haul, strategy 09 come about, direction, procedure, technique, thumbtack 10 drawing-pin, stickiness 12 change course, line of action 14 course of action 15 change direction
*See also* **horse**

**tackle**
◊ *containment indicator* 03 cat, rig, try 04 chin, foul, gear, grab, halt, sack, stop, take, whip 05 begin, block, catch, grasp, hoist, seize, stuff, tools 06 attack, burton, garnet, handle, jigger, outfit, pulley, take on, things 07 address, attempt, clobber, deflect, go about, harness, have a go, rigging, weapons 08 attend to, confront, deal with, embark on, face up to, obstruct, set about, wade into 09 apparatus, challenge, encounter, equipment, get down to, intercept, trappings, undertake 10 clew-garnet, get to grips, ground-hold, implements, take hold of 11 come to grips, grapple with, topping lift 12 interception, intervention 13 accoutrements, paraphernalia 14 get to grips with 15 apply yourself to, come to grips with

**tacky**
03 wet 04 naff 05 dingy, gaudy, gluey, gooey, gummy, messy, tatty 06 flashy, grotty, ragged, shabby, shoddy, sleazy, sloppy, sticky, tawdry, untidy, vulgar 07 kitschy, scruffy 08 adhesive, plimsoll, tattered 09 tasteless 10 threadbare

**tact**
05 skill 07 finesse 08 delicacy, judgment, prudence, subtlety 09 dexterity, diplomacy, judgement 10 adroitness, discretion, perception 11 discernment, savoir-faire, sensitivity, tactfulness 13 consideration, judiciousness, understanding 14 thoughtfulness

**tactful**
06 adroit, polite, subtle, tender 07 careful, politic, prudent, skilful 08 delicate, discreet, kid-glove 09 judicious, sensitive 10 diplomatic, discerning, perceptive, thoughtful 11 considerate 12 diplomatical 13 understanding

**tactfully**
08 politely, tenderly 09 carefully, prudently, skilfully 10 delicately, discreetly 11 judiciously, sensitively 12 thoughtfully 14 diplomatically

**tactic**
03 way 04 move, plan, ploy, ruse 05 means, moves, shift, trick 06 course, device, method, policy, scheme 07 audible 08 approach, campaign,

**game plan**, hardball, soft sell, strategy **09** expedient, manoeuvre, procedure, stratagem **10** manoeuvres, subterfuge **12** line of attack **14** course of action, full-court press

**tactical**
**05** smart **06** adroit, artful, clever, shrewd **07** cunning, planned, politic, prudent, skilful **09** judicious, strategic **10** calculated

**tactician**
**05** brain **07** planner **08** diplomat, director **10** campaigner, mastermind, politician, strategist **11** co-ordinator **12** orchestrator

**tactless**
**04** rude **05** crass, rough **06** clumsy, gauche, unkind **07** awkward, hurtful **08** careless, impolite, unsubtle **09** impolitic, imprudent, maladroit, unfeeling **10** blundering, indelicate, indiscreet **11** injudicious, insensitive, thoughtless **12** discourteous, undiplomatic **13** inappropriate, inconsiderate

**tactlessness**
**08** rudeness **09** bad timing, gaucherie **10** clumsiness, crassitude, indelicacy, ineptitude, maladdress **11** boorishness, discourtesy **12** impoliteness, indiscretion **13** insensitivity, maladroitness **15** thoughtlessness

**tadpole**
**08** polliwig, polliwog, pollywig, pollywog **09** porwiggle

**tag**
**03** add, dag, dub, tab, tig **04** call, flap, mark, name, note, slip, tack, term **05** affix, aglet, annex, badge, label, maxim, moral, motto, quote, shred, strap, style, tally, title **06** adjoin, aiglet, anklet, append, attach, cliché, dictum, docket, fasten, phrase, rabble, saying, ticket **07** entitle, epithet, kabaddi, proverb, refrain, remnant, sticker **08** allusion, bracelet, christen, identify, nickname **09** designate, quotation **10** aglet babie, expression, Kimball tag **11** aiguillette, description, stock phrase, treasury tag **12** identity disc **14** identification
• **tag along** **04** tail **05** trail **06** follow, shadow **09** accompany

**tail**
◊ *tail selection indicator* **03** dog, end, fan, fud, uro- **04** back, flag, herd, rear, rump, scut **05** brush, queue, stalk, stern, suite, track, trail, train **06** behind, bottom, follow, pursue, shadow, shamus, sleuth **07** gumshoe, limited, rear end, retinue **08** backside, buttocks, cynosure, straggle **09** appendage, detective, extremity, posterior **10** conclusion, private eye **11** termination **12** investigator
• **part of tail** **03** fin **04** dock
• **tail back** **03** jam **04** line **05** queue **06** back up
• **tail off** **03** die **04** drop, fade, wane **06** die out **07** decline, drop off, dwindle **08** decrease, fall away,

peter out, taper off
• **turn tail** **04** bolt, flee **06** beat it, decamp, escape **07** abscond, run away, scarper **09** skedaddle

**tailback**
**03** row **04** file, line, tail **05** queue, train **06** backup, column **09** crocodile **10** procession

**tailor**
◊ *anagram indicator* **03** cut, fit **04** dung, snip, suit, trim **05** adapt, alter, darzi, flint, mould, shape, style **06** adjust, cutter, modify, sartor, teller **07** convert, fashion, modiste, whipcat **08** clothier, costumer, seamster **09** costumier, couturier, customize, outfitter **10** dressmaker, prick-louse, seamstress, whipstitch **11** accommodate, personalize **13** prick-the-louse

**tailor-made**
**05** ideal, right **06** fitted, suited **07** bespoke, perfect **08** tailored **11** custom-built **13** made-to-measure

**taint**
◊ *anagram indicator* **04** blot, flaw, harm, ruin, soil, spot, wilt **05** dirty, fault, muddy, shame, smear, smoke, spoil, stain, sully, tinge **06** befoul, blight, damage, defect, defile, infect, injure, mildew, poison, stigma, weaken, wither **07** blacken, blemish, corrupt, deprave, envenom, pollute, tarnish **08** disgrace **09** attainder, contagion, dishonour, infection, pollution **10** adulterate, corruption **11** contaminate **12** adulteration **13** contamination

**Taiwan**
**02** RC **03** TWN

**Tajikistan**
**02** TJ **03** TJK

**take**
◊ *containment indicator* **01** r **02** do **03** bag, buy, eat, fet, get, nim, rec, use, win **04** bear, bite, book, deem, draw, fall, fett, gain, gate, give, grab, grip, haul, have, help, hent, hire, hold, last, lead, lift, need, nick, note, pick, read, rent, seat, show, twig, view, work **05** abide, admit, adopt, angle, begin, bring, carry, catch, charm, cheat, drink, drive, ferry, fetch, filch, grasp, guide, learn, lease, pinch, scoff, seize, slant, stand, steal, study, teach, think, use up, usher, visit, whisk, yield **06** abduct, accept, aspect, assume, attain, become, betake, blight, choose, clutch, come by, convey, decide, deduct, demand, derive, detect, devour, endure, engage, escort, fathom, follow, freeze, gather, guzzle, handle, imbibe, income, ingest, inhale, kidnap, obtain, occupy, pay for, profit, pursue, recipe, reckon, regard, remove, return, secure, select, snatch, strike, suffer, tuck in **07** achieve, acquire, be given, believe, bewitch, call for, capture, conduct, conquer, consume, contain, deceive, deliver, detract, examine, execute, extract, find out, go along, major in,

measure, mistake, observe, perform, portray, presume, procure, profits, purloin, react to, receive, require, returns, revenue, set down, stomach, succeed, suppose, swallow, swindle, takings, undergo **08** attitude, be taught, carry off, consider, cope with, cotton on, deal with, discover, look upon, proceeds, purchase, receipts, remember, research, settle on, shepherd, submerge, subtract, surprise, take away, tolerate, vanquish **09** accompany, apprehend, ascertain, captivate, determine, eliminate, establish, fathom out, gate-money, get hold of, lay hold of, put up with, respond to, transport, undertake, viewpoint, withstand **10** bear in mind, comprehend, confiscate, drive along, experience, photograph, standpoint, take effect, understand **11** accommodate, acknowledge, appropriate, be effective, frame of mind, have room for, necessitate, perspective, point of view, subscribe to, travel along **12** have space for, vantage point **13** be efficacious **14** interpretation, produce results **15** have a capacity of
• **let him/her take** **03** cap
• **take after** **04** echo **06** be like, favour, mirror **08** look like, resemble, surprise **11** be similar to
• **take against** **06** oppose **07** despise, dislike **08** object to **12** disapprove of
• **take apart** **03** nag, pan **04** carp, slag, slam **05** blame, knock, slate, snipe **06** attack **07** analyse, censure, condemn, nit-pick, rubbish, run down, slag off **08** badmouth, denounce, separate **09** criticize, dismantle, disparage **10** come down on, go to town on **11** disassemble, pick holes in **12** disapprove of, pull to pieces, put the boot in, take to pieces, tear to shreds **13** find fault with, tear a strip off **15** do a hatchet job on, pass judgement on
• **take back** **04** deny **05** evoke **06** call up, recant, regain, remind, resume, retake, return **07** get back, reclaim, replace, restore, retract **08** disclaim, give back, hand back, renounce, send back, withdraw **09** repossess, repudiate **12** eat your words **14** make you think of, put you in mind of
• **take down** **04** note, raze **05** level, lower **06** record, reduce, remove **07** demount, get down, put down, set down **08** demolish, pull down **09** dismantle, write down **10** put on paper, transcribe **11** disassemble, make a note of
• **take in** ◊ *containment indicator* **03** con, lap **04** dupe, fool **05** admit, cheat, cover, grasp, trick **06** absorb, digest **07** contain, deceive, embrace, include, mislead, realize, receive, shelter, swindle, welcome **08** comprise, hoodwink **09** bamboozle, encompass **10** appreciate, assimilate, comprehend, understand **11** accommodate, incorporate

• **take off** ◇ *deletion indicator* **02** go **03** ape, fly **04** bolt, doff, drop, flee, mock, rise, shed, soar, work **05** climb, leave, mimic, mount, strip **06** ascend, decamp, deduct, depart, detach, divest, do well, make it, parody, remove, send up **07** abscond, bunk off, catch on, discard, imitate, lift off, prosper, pull off, run away, scarper, succeed, tear off, undress **08** discount, flourish, go places, satirize, subtract, take away, throw off **09** disappear, do a runner, skedaddle **10** caricature, strike gold **11** impersonate **12** get undressed **13** become popular, hit the jackpot **14** become airborne

• **take on** ◇ *containment indicator* ◇ *juxtaposition indicator* **04** copy, face, hire, kill **05** enrol, fight **06** accept, assume, defeat, employ, engage, enlist, escort, oppose, retain, tackle **07** acquire, destroy, extract, recruit, vie with **08** get angry, get upset **09** entertain, make a fuss, undertake **11** compete with, contend with

• **take out** **03** fix, see, zap **04** dele, do in, draw, kill **05** set up, shoot, waste **06** be lent, borrow, cut out, defeat, delete, detach, escort, except, excise, get out, go with, murder, remove, rub out **07** arrange, bump off, butcher, destroy, execute, extract, pull out, wipe out, work out **08** blow away, despatch, dispatch, knock off, massacre, organize, settle on **09** accompany, eliminate, finish off, go out with, have a loan, liquidate, polish off **10** do away with, put to death **11** assassinate, exterminate **14** use temporarily

• **take over** **05** adopt **06** buy out **07** subsume **10** run the show **12** take charge of **13** gain control of

• **take to** **04** like **05** begin, start **08** commence, set about **09** undertake **10** appreciate, launch into **12** become keen on, find pleasant **14** find attractive

• **take up** ◇ *insertion indicator* ◇ *reversal down indicator* **03** use **04** fill, lift, rear **05** adopt, begin, raise, start, use up **06** absorb, accept, assume, engage, occupy, pick up, pursue, resume **07** agree to, carry on, consume, engross **08** commence, continue, embark on **10** monopolize **13** hang about with **14** knock about with **15** get involved with

## take-off
**05** spoof **06** ascent, flight, flying, parody, send-up **07** lift-off, mimicry **08** climbing, drawback, scramble, travesty **09** departure, imitation **10** caricature **13** impersonation

## takeover
**04** coup **06** buyout, merger **09** coalition **11** combination **12** amalgamation **13** incorporation

## taking
◇ *juxtaposition indicator* **04** gain, gate **05** yield **06** income, plight **07** profits, returns, revenue, winning, winsome **08** alluring, catching, charming, earnings, engaging, fetching, pickings, pleasing, proceeds, receipts, winnings **09** agitation, appealing, beguiling, gate-money **10** attractive, compelling, delightful, enchanting, infectious, intriguing, perplexity **11** bewitchment, captivating, fascinating **13** prepossessing

## tale
**03** bam, fib, lie, toy **04** epic, gest, hoax, myth, rede, reed, saga, talk, yarn **05** blood, fable, geste, novel, porky, reede, roman, spiel, story, total, weird **06** legend, number, report, rumour **07** account, fabliau, Märchen, mystery, novella, odyssey, parable, romance, untruth, whopper **08** allegory, anecdote, jeremiad, sob story **09** discourse, fairytale, falsehood, folk story, narrative, reckoning, storiette, storyette, tall story, tradition **10** fairy story, hair-raiser **11** fabrication **13** old wives' tale, superstition **14** traveller's tale

## talent
**04** bent, feel, gift, nous **05** flair, forte, knack, power, skill, talon **06** genius **07** ability, aptness, faculty **08** aptitude, capacity, facility, ingenium, long suit, new blood, strength **09** endowment **11** disposition, showmanship, strong point **12** shot in the arm

## talented
**04** able, deft **05** adept **06** adroit, clever, gifted **07** capable, skilful **08** artistic **09** brilliant, versatile **10** proficient **11** well-endowed **12** accomplished

## talisman
**04** idol, ju-ju **05** charm, totem **06** amulet, fetish, mascot, symbol, telesm **07** abraxas, periapt **10** phylactery

## talk
**03** gab, gas, jaw, mag, rap, say, yak **04** blab, bull, cant, chat, tell, yack **05** grass, haver, lingo, moody, mouth, noise, noyes, orate, parle, slang, speak, spiel, utter, voice, words **06** babble, confab, confer, debate, devise, gasbag, gossip, haggle, havers, jabber, jargon, jaw-jaw, korero, natter, parley, patter, rabbit, report, rumour, sermon, speech, squeal, yabber **07** address, baloney, bargain, blether, boloney, chatter, chinwag, clatter, confess, dialect, discuss, earbash, express, hearsay, lecture, malarky, meeting, oration, palaver, prattle, seminar, twaddle **08** badinage, chitchat, conclave, converse, dialogue, flimflam, haggling, idiolect, inform on, language, malarkey **09** discourse, gibberish, interview, negotiate, symposium, tell tales, tête-à-tête, utterance **10** articulate, balderdash, bargaining, chew the fat, chew the rag, conference, discursion, discussion, namby-pamby **11** communicate, negotiation **12** consultation, conversation, disquisition, tittle-tattle **13** rabbit and pork, spill the beans, spread rumours **15** give the game away

• **foolish talk** **04** bosh **05** haver **06** havers

• **impudent talk** **03** lip **08** slack jaw

• **talk back** **06** retort **07** riposte **09** retaliate **10** answer back, be cheeky to **12** answer rudely

• **talk big** **04** brag, crow **05** boast, swank, vaunt **07** bluster, show off **10** exaggerate

• **talk down to** **07** despise **09** patronize **10** look down on

• **talk into** **04** coax, sway **07** win over **08** convince, persuade **09** encourage **10** bring round

• **talk nonsense** **03** gum, rot **04** jive **05** bleat, haver **06** havers

• **talk out of** **04** stop **05** deter **06** put off **07** prevent **08** dissuade **10** discourage

## talkative
**04** gash **05** gabby, gassy, gobby, talky, vocal, wordy **06** chatty, mouthy **07** gossipy, verbose, voluble **09** expansive, garrulous **10** long-winded, loquacious, unreserved **11** forthcoming, long-tongued **13** communicative

## talker
**05** prose **06** orator, tatler **07** speaker, tattler, twaddle **08** lecturer **09** chatterer **10** chatterbox, motormouth **11** speechmaker **12** blatherskite, bletherskate, communicator **14** bletheranskate

## talking-to
**06** rebuke, rocket **07** lecture, reproof, wigging **08** reproach, scolding **09** carpeting, criticism, reprimand **10** telling-off, ticking-off **12** dressing-down

## tall
**03** big **04** hard, high, long **05** giant, great, lanky, lofty, stout, taunt **06** absurd, taxing, towery, trying **07** doughty, dubious, sky-high, soaring **08** elevated, exacting, gigantic, towering, unlikely **09** bombastic, demanding, difficult, overblown **10** far-fetched, improbable, incredible, remarkable **11** challenging, exaggerated, implausible **12** preposterous, unbelievable

## tallness
**06** height **07** stature **08** altitude **09** loftiness, procerity

## tally
**03** add, fit, sum, tab, tag **04** list, nick, roll, stub, suit, tick **05** adapt, add up, agree, count, label, match, score, stick, stock, tie in, total **06** accord, concur, credit, figure, reckon, record, square, ticket **07** account, conform **08** coincide, register **09** calculate, duplicate, harmonize, nickstick, reckoning **10** correspond **11** counterfoil, counterpart, enumeration

## tame
**03** pet **04** calm, curb, dull, flat, lame,

**tamper**

mail, meek, weak **05** bland, break, quell, train, vapid **06** boring, bridle, docile, entame, feeble, gentle, humble, master, mellow, pacify, soften, subdue, temper, wonted **07** amenage, break in, conquer, humdrum, insipid, reclaim, repress, subdued, tedious, trained **08** amenable, biddable, broken in, domestic, lifeless, mansuete, obedient, overcome, suppress **09** kids' stuff, subjugate, tractable, wearisome **10** accustomed, cultivated, discipline, house-train, manageable, spiritless, submissive, unexciting, uninspired **11** bring to heel, disciplined, domesticate, uninspiring, unresisting **12** domesticated **13** unadventurous, uninteresting **14** unenterprising

**tamper**

**03** fix, rig **04** work **05** alter **06** bishop, damage, doctor, fiddle, juggle, meddle, monkey, temper, tinker **07** falsify **08** contrive, medicate, practise **09** interfere, mess about, muck about, undermine **10** manipulate **11** interpolate **12** put your oar in **14** poke your nose in, stick your oar in **15** stick your nose in

**tan**

**04** bark, beat, belt, cane, flay, flog, lash, whip **05** beige, birch, brown, clout, spank, strap, tawny, whack **06** bronze, thrash, wallop **07** go brown, tangent **09** turn brown **10** light brown, make darker **12** become darker **14** yellowish brown

**tang**

**03** pep **04** barb, bite, edge, hint, kick, ring **05** aroma, point, prong, punch, scent, smack, smell, spice, spike, sting, taste, tinge, touch, trace, whiff **06** savour **07** flavour **08** overtone, piquancy, pungency **09** sharpness **10** sea-surgeon, suggestion

**tangible**

**04** hard, real **05** solid **06** actual **07** evident, tactile, visible **08** concrete, definite, manifest, material, palpable, physical, positive **09** corporeal, touchable **11** discernible, perceptible, substantial, well-defined **12** unmistakable

**tangle**

◊ *anagram indicator* **03** mat, ore, web **04** coil, fank, knot, maze, mesh, mess, nest, taut, tawt, trap **05** catch, mix-up, ravel, skein, snarl, twist **06** burble, enmesh, entrap, fankle, hamper, icicle, jumble, muddle, raffle **07** confuse, embroil, ensnare, involve, perplex, snarl-up **08** argument, conflict, convolve, entangle, mess with **09** confusion, drift-weed, embroglio, imbroglio, implicate, interlace, labyrinth, Laminaria **10** intertwine, intertwist, interweave, perplexity, wilderness **11** convolution, embroilment, intertangle **12** complication, entanglement

**tangled**

◊ *anagram indicator* **05** messy **06** knotty,

matted **07** complex, haywire, jumbled, knotted, mixed up, muddled, snarled, tousled, twisted **08** confused, involved, tortuous **09** entangled, intricate **10** convoluted **11** complicated, dishevelled

**tango**

**01** T

**tangy**

**04** acid, tart **05** fresh, sharp, spicy **06** biting, strong **07** piquant, pungent

**tank**

**03** vat **04** pond, pool, stew **05** basin **06** defeat, header, panzer, refuel, thrash **07** cistern, sponson, whippet **08** aquarium, flush-box, sponsing **09** baptistry, container, gasholder, gasometer, reservoir, Valentine **10** baptistery, receptacle, septic tank, shield pond **11** armoured car **12** precipitator **13** shielding pond **15** armoured vehicle

**tanning material**

**04** puer, pure **07** valonea, valonia **08** vallonia

**tantalize**

**04** bait, balk, mock **05** taunt, tease, tempt **06** allure, entice, lead on, thwart **07** beguile, provoke, torment, torture **09** frustrate, titillate **10** disappoint

**tantalum**

**02** Ta

**tantamount**

**05** equal **08** as good as **09** the same as **10** equivalent, synonymous **12** commensurate

**tantrum**

**03** fit, pet **04** fury, rage **05** paddy, scene, storm **06** blow-up, temper, wobbly **07** flare-up **08** hissy fit, outburst, paroxysm, tirrivee, tirrivie **10** conniption **11** fit of temper

**Tanzania**

**03** EAT, TZA

**tap**

**03** bob, bug, hit, pat, rap, tat, tip, tit, top, use **04** beat, blip, bung, cock, drum, milk, mine, plug, tack, tick, toby, touk, tuck **05** bleed, chuck, drain, knock, spout, touch, valve **06** broach, draw on, faucet, pierce, pirate, pit-pat, quarry, siphon, spigot, strike, stroup **07** bibcock, draw off, exploit, monitor, percuss, petcock, pitapat, stopper, utilize, wiretap **08** draw upon, listen to, pitty-pat, receiver, stopcock **09** light blow, make use of **10** listen in on **11** eavesdrop on **15** listening device, take advantage of • **on tap** **05** handy, ready **06** at hand, on hand **09** available **10** accessible

**tape**

**03** tie **04** band, bind, seal **05** stick, strip, video **06** fasten, record, ribbon, secure, string **07** binding **08** cassette **09** audiotape, recording, Sellotape®, videotape **10** gaffer tape, Scotch tape®, sticky tape, tape-record **11** masking tape, video-record **12** adhesive tape, magnetic tape,

passe-partout **13** audio cassette, tape-recording, video cassette **14** video recording

**taper**

**04** fade, nose, slim, thin, wane, wick **05** spill **06** acumen, candle, die off, lessen, narrow, reduce **07** die away, dwindle, tail off, thin out **08** decrease, diminish, make thin, peter out, wax light **09** attenuate **10** become thin, make narrow **12** become narrow

**tapir**

**04** anta **07** sladang **08** seladang

**tar**

**05** set on **06** maltha, sailor **11** pissasphalt
*See also* **sailor**
• **smear with tar** **03** pay
• **tar derivative** **05** furan, indol, pitch **06** cresol, furane, indene, indole, phenol, picene, retene, xylene **07** acridin, aniline, benzene, indulin, naphtha, picamar, skatole, styrene **08** acridine, cerulein, creasote, creosote, heavy oil, induline, nigrosin, pyridine, safranin **09** carbazole, coumarone, nigrosine, primuline, safranine **10** anthracene, benzpyrene **11** creosote oil, naphthalene, phenanthene

**tardily**

**04** late **06** slowly **09** belatedly **10** sluggishly **12** late in the day, unpunctually **13** not before time **15** at the last minute

**tardiness**

**05** delay **08** dawdling, lateness, slowness **11** belatedness **12** dilatoriness, sluggishness **13** unpunctuality **15** procrastination

**tardy**

**03** lag **04** late, slow **05** slack **06** retard **07** belated, delayed, overdue **08** backward, dawdling, dilatory, retarded, sluggish **09** loitering **10** behindhand, last-minute, unpunctual **12** eleventh-hour **15** procrastinating

**tare**

**01** t **04** tine, weed **05** vetch **06** darnel

**target**

**03** aim, end **04** butt, game, goal, mark, prey, seek **05** aim at **06** aim for, object, quarry, try for, victim **07** purpose **08** ambition, bull's eye **09** intention, objective **11** destination **14** have as your goal
• **centre of target** **03** pin **04** bull **06** carton **08** bull's-eye
• **on target** **05** exact **06** bang on, on time, spot-on **07** precise **08** accurate, on course **10** on schedule **15** according to plan

**tariff**

**03** tax **04** duty, levy, menu, rate, toll **06** excise, zabeta **07** charges, customs **08** schedule **09** price list **10** bill of fare **13** list of charges

**tarnish**

**03** dim, mar **04** blot, dull, film, rust,

**taro**
soil, spot **05** spoil, stain, sully, taint
**06** befoul, darken, impair, patina
**07** blacken, blemish, corrode
**08** besmirch **09** discolour
**10** blackening **13** discoloration

**taro**
**04** coco, eddo **05** cocco **07** dasheen

**tarry**
**03** lag **04** bide, leng, rest, stay, stop,
wait **05** abide, await, dally, delay,
pause **06** dawdle, linger, loiter, remain,
stay on **07** sojourn

**tart**
**03** pie, pro, tom **04** acid, bawd, drab,
flan, moll, slut, sour **05** brass, broad,
patty, quiff, sharp, tangy, tramp,
wench, whore **06** biting, bitter, geisha,
harlot, hooker, pastry, quiche
**07** acerbic, caustic, cocotte, cutting,
floozie, hetaera, hostess, hustler,
lorette, piquant, pungent, rent-boy,
strudel, tartlet, trollop **08** call girl,
incisive, magdalen, mirliton, sardonic,
scathing, scrubber, strumpet, vinegary
**09** acidulous, charlotte, courtesan,
croquante, hierodule, loose fish,
sarcastic, trenchant **10** astringent,
fancy woman, loose woman,
prostitute, rough trade, vizard-mask
**11** fallen woman, fille de joie, night-
walker, poule de luxe, working girl
**12** fille des rues, scarlet woman, street-
walker **13** grande cocotte **14** lady of
the night, woman of the town
• **tart up** **06** doll up **07** dress up,
smarten **08** decorate, renovate
**09** embellish, smarten up **10** redecorate

**tartar**
**05** scale, Tatar **08** beeswing, calculus

**task**
**03** job, tax **04** darg, duty, pain, snap,
toil, work **05** chore, grind, stint
**06** burden, charge, errand, killer,
labour, pensum **07** mission, stretch
**08** activity, business, exercise, hard
time, trauchle **09** challenge, job of
work, soft thing **10** assignment,
commission, employment,
engagement, enterprise, imposition,
occupation **11** piece of work,
undertaking
• **take to task** **04** slam **05** blame,
knock, scold, slate **06** attask, pull up,
rebuke **07** censure, chapter, lecture,
reprove, tell off, tick off, upbraid
**08** reproach **09** criticize, reprimand

**Tasmania**
**03** Tas **06** Tassie

**taste**
**03** bit, eat, sar, sip, try **04** bent, bite,
dash, drop, feel, gout, know, meet,
pree, tang, test **05** enjoy, fancy, grace,
piece, smack, style **06** choice, desire,
hunger, liking, morsel, nibble, polish,
relish, sample, savour, thirst, titbit
**07** culture, decorum, discern, finesse,
flavour, leaning, make out, soupçon,
undergo **08** appetite, breeding,
elegance, fondness, judgment,
mouthful, penchant, perceive
**09** encounter, etiquette, hankering,
judgement, propriety **10** experience,

partiality, perception, preference,
refinement **11** cultivation,
discernment, distinguish, inclination,
sensitivity, stylishness **12** appreciation,
predilection, tastefulness
**13** differentiate **14** discrimination

*Tastes include:*

**03** hot
**04** acid, sour, tart
**05** acrid, bland, fishy, meaty, nutty,
salty, sapid, sharp, spicy, sweet,
tangy, umami
**06** acidic, bitter, citrus, creamy,
fruity, sugary
**07** insipid, peppery, piquant,
pungent, savoury
**08** vinegary
**11** bittersweet

**tasteful**
**05** smart, tasty **06** dainty, pretty
**07** correct, elegant, refined, stylish
**08** artistic, charming, cultured,
delicate, graceful, gracious, pleasing,
polished **09** aesthetic, beautiful,
exquisite, judicious **10** cultivated,
fastidious, harmonious, restrained,
well-judged **14** discriminating

**tastefully**
**07** smartly **09** elegantly, stylishly
**10** charmingly, delicately, graciously
**11** beautifully, exquisitely, judiciously
**12** artistically, harmoniously

**tasteless**
**04** dull, flat, loud, mild, naff, rude, thin,
weak **05** bland, cheap, crass, crude,
gaudy, plain, showy, stale, tacky,
vapid, wersh **06** boring, flashy, garish,
kitsch, tawdry, vulgar, watery
**07** insipid, insulse, uncouth, wearish
**08** improper, tactless, unseemly
**09** graceless, inelegant, unfitting,
unsavoury **10** indiscreet **11** flavourless,
watered-down **13** uninteresting

**tasting**
**05** assay, smack, trial **07** testing
**08** sampling **09** gustation **10** assessment

**tasty**
**04** nice **05** spicy, sweet, tangy, umami,
yummy **06** morish **07** gustful, moreish,
piquant, savoury **08** luscious, tasteful
**09** delicious, flavorous, palatable,
succulent, toothsome **10** appetizing,
attractive, delectable **11** flavoursome,
interesting, scrumptious
**13** mouthwatering

**tatter**
• **in tatters** **03** rag **06** broken, in bits,
in rags, ragged, ruined **07** in ruins,
wrecked **08** in pieces, in shreds
**09** destroyed, in ribbons, shattered
**10** devastated

**tattered**
◊ *anagram indicator* **04** torn **05** tatty
**06** frayed, ragged, ripped, shabby
**07** scruffy **10** threadbare
**14** tatterdemalion **15** tatterdemallion

**tattie**
*see* **potato**

**tattler**
**04** blab **06** gossip **08** busybody, tell-tale
**09** chatterer **10** newsmonger,
talebearer, tale-teller **12** rumour-
monger **13** scandalmonger

**tattoo**
**03** tat **04** moko, tatu **06** tattow
**08** drumming

**taunt**
**03** dig, rib **04** bait, barb, gibe, gird,
goad, jeer, jest, jibe, jive, mock, twit
**05** fling, sneer, tease **06** deride, insult,
revile **07** catcall, censure, mockery,
provoke, sarcasm, teasing, torment
**08** brickbat, derision, reproach,
ridicule, taunting **09** make fun of, poke
fun at **11** provocation

**taut**
**03** mat **05** rigid, stiff, tense, tight
**06** tangle, tensed **07** anxious, fraught,
worried **08** strained **09** stretched,
tightened, unrelaxed **10** contracted

**tautological**
**05** wordy **07** verbose **09** redundant
**10** pleonastic, repetitive **11** superfluous

**tautology**
**08** pleonasm **09** iteration, verbosity
**10** redundancy, repetition
**11** duplication, perissology, superfluity
**14** repetitiveness

**tavern**
**03** bar, inn, pub **04** bush, dive
**05** fonda, joint, local **06** boozer,
Kneipe, public **08** alehouse, hostelry,
tap-house **09** roadhouse **10** night-
house, trust-house **11** night-cellar,
public house

**taw**
**03** tew **04** ally, flog, whip **05** alley,
thong

**tawdry**
**05** cheap, fancy, gaudy, showy, tacky,
tatty **06** cheapo, flashy, garish, vulgar
**07** chintzy **08** tinselly, trumpery
**09** tasteless **10** glittering **11** gingerbread

**tawny**
**03** tan **04** fawn **05** khaki, sandy
**06** fulvid, golden, yellow **07** fulvous
**08** xanthous **11** golden brown

**tax**
**03** aid, lot, sap, try **04** cess, duty, levy,
load, rate, scot, sess, soak, test, tire
**05** drain, exact, stent, weary, weigh
**06** assess, burden, charge, demand,
impose, impost, strain, stress, tariff,
weaken, weight **07** exhaust, stretch,
wear out **08** encumber, enervate,
overload, pressure **09** agistment, weigh
down **10** accusation, assessment,
imposition **12** contribution **13** make
demands on

*Taxes include:*

**02** PT
**03** GST, sur, VAT
**04** geld, gelt, PAYE, poll, scat, skat,
toll
**05** green, rates, scatt, tithe, Tobin
**06** carbon, excise, income
**07** airport, council, customs, gabelle

**08** property, Rome-scot, windfall
**09** death duty, head money, insurance
**10** capitation, estate duty, value added
**11** corporation, inheritance, Peter's pence
**12** capital gains, pay as you earn
**15** capital transfer, community charge

• **tax collectors** **02** IR **03** IRS

**taxi**
**03** cab **06** fiacre, samlor **07** hire-car, Joe Baxi, minicab, taxicab **09** hansom-cab **10** hackney cab **12** hackney coach **15** hackney carriage

**taxing**
**04** hard **05** heavy, tough **06** satire, tiring, trying **07** censure, onerous, testing, wearing **08** draining, exacting, wearying **09** demanding, punishing, stressful, wearisome **10** burdensome, enervating, exhausting

**taxman**
**02** IR **03** IRS

**tea**
**03** cha, tay **04** char **05** cuppa **06** tisane **07** Rosy Lee **08** infusion, Rosie Lee, stroupan **09** stroupach
*See also* **cannabis**

*Teas and herbal teas include:*

**03** ice, kat, qat
**04** beef, bush, chai, herb, iced, khat, mate, mint, sage
**05** Assam, black, bohea, brick, caper, China, congo, fruit, green, hyson, lemon, pekoe, senna, white, yerba
**06** Ceylon, congou, herbal, oolong, oulong
**07** cambric, instant, jasmine, lapsang, redbush, rooibos, rosehip, Russian, twankay
**08** camomile, Earl Grey, Lady Grey, souchong, switchel
**09** breakfast, chamomile, gunpowder
**10** Darjeeling
**11** orange pekoe
**13** decaffeinated
**15** lapsang souchong

**teach**
**03** con, kon **04** cram, larn, lear, leir, lere, read, show, take **05** coach, conne, din in, drill, edify, guide, leare, learn, train, tutor, verse **06** advise, direct, ground, impart, inform, parrot, preach, school **07** counsel, din into, educate, lecture, perfect **08** accustom, disciple, hammer in, instruct **09** brainwash, condition, enlighten, foreteach, inculcate, pedagogue **10** discipline, hammer into, potty-train **11** demonstrate, give lessons **12** indoctrinate

**teacher**
**03** rav **04** Miss **05** guide **07** chalkie, dominie, prophet, tohunga **08** educator, reliever, schoolie **09** pedagogue, schoolman

**10** instructor, scholastic
**12** demonstrator, instructress
**13** gerund-grinder

*Teacher types include:*

**03** AST, don, NQT
**04** dean, form, guru, head
**05** barbe, coach, molla, rabbi, rebbe, tutor, usher
**06** docent, doctor, duenna, fellow, gooroo, mallam, master, mentor, mollah, moolah, mullah, munshi, pedant, pundit, reader, school, supply
**07** acharya, adviser, crammer, starets, staretz, student, trainer
**08** lecturer, mistress, moonshee, sol-faist
**09** governess, maharishi, mnemonist, pedagogue, preceptor, principal, professor, rebbetzin, reception
**10** counsellor, deputy head, headmaster, head of year, instructor, paedotribe, schoolmarm
**11** housemaster, preceptress, upper school
**12** demonstrator, headmistress, mademoiselle, middle school, pastoral head, posture-maker, private tutor, schoolmaster
**13** housemistress, nursery school, posture-master, primary school
**14** schoolmistress, senior lecturer
**15** college lecturer, secondary school

*Teachers include:*

**04** Beck (Madame), Eyre (Jane), Hart (Sheba), King (Anna), Lamb (Michael), Nunn (Sir Percy), Wilt (Henry)
**05** Brill (Miss), Chips (Mr), Crane (Edwina), Crick (Tom), Dixon (Jim), Doyle (Patrick), Handy (Charles Brian), Henri (Frances), Levin (Sam), Odili, Snape (Severus)
**06** Alcott (Bronson), Angelo (Albert), Arnold (Thomas), Brodie (Miss Jean), Coppin (Fanny Marion Jackson), Cotton (George Edward Lynch), Covett (Barbara), Graham (Martha), Grimes (Captain), Gyatso (Geshe Kelsang), Hagrid (Rubeus), Harris (Crocker), Hillel, Hornby (A S), Ramsay (Dunstan), Solent (Wolf)
**07** Darling (Sir James Ralph), Eckhart (Miss), Enketei (Mira), Fischer (Marcus), Keating (John), Krishna, Lowther (Gordon), Matthay (Tobias), Mr Chips, Mulcahy (Henry), Peecher (Emma), Porpora (Nicola), Saville (Colin), Squeers (Wackford), Vaughan (Barbara), Wackles (Sophy)
**08** Bridgman (Laura Dewey), Caldwell (George), Chipping (Mr), Doubloon (Maggie), Lewisham (George), Prodicus, Sullivan (Anne)
**09** Batchelor (Barbie), Bellgrove (Professor), Braidwood (Thomas), Hartright (Walter), Headstone (Bradley), Strasberg (Lee)

**10** Dumbledore (Albus), Leadbetter (David), Madame Beck, Madam Hooch, McGonagall (Minerva), Protagoras
**12** Pennyfeather (Paul), Stanislavsky
**13** M'Choakumchild (Mr)

• **teachers** **03** ATL, NUT
**06** NASUWT

**teaching**
**04** lair, lare, lore, TEFL, TESL
**05** dogma, tenet, TESOL **06** loring, wisdom **07** precept, tuition **08** doctrine, pedagogy **09** didactics, education, principle, tradition **10** pedagogism **11** instruction, instructive, pedagoguism

**team**
**02** 11, XI, XV **03** set **04** band, crew, gang, pair, side, yoke **05** brood, bunch, chain, group, shift, squad **06** équipe, line-up, litter, outfit, pick-up, stable, troupe **07** company, offence, offense, turn-out **08** equipage

*National team nicknames in Australia and New Zealand include:*

**05** Opals
**07** Boomers, Olyroos
**08** Matildas
**09** All Blacks, All Whites, Kangaroos, Socceroos, Wallabies
**10** Hockeyroos
**11** Kookaburras, Silver Ferns

*See also* **Australian football; baseball; basketball; cricket; football; racing; rugby**
• **team up** **04** join, yoke **05** match, unite **06** couple **07** combine **09** co-operate **10** join forces **11** collaborate **12** band together, come together, work together

**teamwork**
**10** fellowship, team spirit **11** co-operation, joint effort **12** co-ordination **13** collaboration, esprit de corps

**tear**
**03** fly, nip, rag, ren, rin, rip, run, zap, zip **04** bead, belt, blob, bolt, bomb, claw, dart, dash, gash, grab, hole, plow, pull, race, rage, rash, rend, rent, rive, rush, slip, slit, snag, tire, yank, zing, zoom **05** hurry, pluck, ranch, scoot, seize, sever, shoot, shred, slash, speed, split, spree, vroom, whizz, wound, wrest **06** career, charge, divide, gallop, injure, injury, ladder, mangle, plough, screed, snatch, sprint, sunder, tatter, unroot **07** eye-drop, mammock, rupture, scratch **08** lacerate, mutilate, step on it **09** pull apart, water drop **10** break apart, laceration, mutilation
• **in tears** **03** sad **05** upset, weepy **06** crying **07** sobbing, tearful, wailing, weeping **09** emotional, sorrowful **10** blubbering, distressed, whimpering
• **tear down** **07** destroy **08** demolish, pull down **09** dismantle, knock down

**tearaway**
**04** hoon **05** rough, rowdy, tough **06** madcap, rascal **07** hoodlum, hothead, ruffian **08** hooligan, reckless

**09** daredevil, impetuous, roughneck
**10** delinquent **14** good-for-nothing

**tearful**
**03** sad, wet **05** misty, moist, upset,
weepy **06** crying **07** doleful, in tears,
sobbing, weeping **08** mournful
**09** emotional, sorrowful, upsetting
**10** blubbering, distressed, lachrymose,
whimpering **11** distressing

**tease**
◊ *anagram indicator* **03** kid, mag, rag,
rib, rot, vex **04** bait, chip, gibe, goad,
goof, grig, josh, mock, nark, tose, toze
**05** annoy, chaff, kiddy, sound, taunt,
teaze, toaze, touse, touze, towse,
towze, worry **06** badger, banter,
bother, chiack, chyack, needle, pester,
plague, wind up **07** mamaguy,
perplex, provoke, torment **08** back-
comb, irritate, ridicule **09** aggravate,
give heaps, have a go at, make fun of,
poke fun at, tantalize **11** have a lend of
**12** poke the borax

**technetium**
**02** Tc

**technical**
**06** expert **07** applied **09** practical
**10** artificial, electronic, industrial,
mechanical, scientific, specialist
**11** specialized **12** computerized,
professional **13** technological

**technically**
**11** practically **12** mechanically
**14** electronically, professionally,
scientifically **15** technologically

**technician**
**06** fitter **08** engineer, mechanic,
operator **09** machinist, operative,
rocketeer **11** mechanician, vision
mixer **12** phlebotomist, radiographer

**technique**
**03** art, way **04** mode **05** craft, ELISA,
knack, means, skill, style, touch, trick
**06** course, manner, method, system
**07** ability, fashion, knowhow, mastery,
technic **08** approach, artistry, delivery,
facility, technics **09** animation,
dexterity, execution, expertise,
procedure, serialism **10** capability,
holography, millefiori, rag-rolling
**11** performance, proficiency,
skilfulness **12** oil immersion
**13** craftsmanship, modus operandi

**technology**
• **appropriate technology,
alternative technology 02** AT
• **information technology 02** IT
**08** infotech **11** informatics

**tedious**
**04** drab, dull, flat, long **05** a drag,
banal, prosy, samey, weary **06** boring,
draggy, dreary, dreich, tiring
**07** humdrum, irksome, operose,
prosaic, routine **08** lifeless, long-spun,
tiresome, unvaried, wearying
**09** laborious, wearisome **10** dragsville,
long-winded, monotonous,
unexciting, uninspired **11** balls-aching
**12** long-drawn-out, run-of-the-mill
**13** uninteresting
• **tedious person 04** bore **06** foozle

**tedium**
**03** rut **05** ennui **07** boredom, routine
**08** banality, drabness, dullness,
monotony, sameness, vapidity
**09** prosiness **10** dreariness
**11** irksomeness, tediousness
**12** lifelessness **14** monotonousness

**tee**
**01** T

**teem**
**04** bear, brim, pour, rain **05** burst,
crawl, empty, spawn, swarm
**06** abound, be full **07** bristle, produce
**08** increase, multiply, overflow, pelt
down **09** pullulate **10** bucket down
**11** chuck it down, proliferate **15** rain
cats and dogs

**teeming**
**04** full **05** alive, great, thick **06** packed
**07** copious, crowded, replete
**08** abundant, brimming, bursting,
childing, crawling, fruitful, numerous,
pregnant, seething, swarming
**09** bristling, chock-full, plentiful
**11** chock-a-block, overflowing,
pullulating

**teenage**
**05** young **08** immature, juvenile,
teenaged, youthful **10** adolescent

**teenager**
**03** boy, Mod, yob **04** girl, teen
**05** minor, youth **06** rocker **07** sharpie
**08** juvenile **09** rangatahi **10** adolescent,
bobbysoxer, junior miss, young adult
**11** teeny-bopper, young person
**13** emerging adult

**teeny**
**03** wee **04** tiny **06** minute, teensy,
teenty, titchy **07** teentsy **09** miniature,
minuscule **10** diminutive, teeny-weeny
**11** microscopic **12** teensy-weensy

**teeter**
◊ *anagram indicator* **04** reel, rock, roll,
sway **05** lurch, pitch, pivot, shake,
waver **06** seesaw, totter, wobble
**07** balance, stagger, tremble
**08** hesitate **09** vacillate

**teeth**
---
*Teeth include:*
---
**03** cap, dog, egg, eye, gag, gam, jaw
**04** baby, back, buck, fang, fore,
gold, milk, mill, tush, tusk, wang,
wolf
**05** cheek, colt's, crown, false, first,
molar, plate, store, sweet, upper
**06** bridge, canine, chisel, corner,
cuspid, wisdom
**07** denture, grinder, incisor, scissor,
snaggle
**08** bicuspid, dentures, impacted,
premolar
**09** milk-molar, permanent, sectorial,
serration
**10** carnassial, first molar, masticator,
molendinar, third molar
**11** multicuspid, second molar
**12** snaggletooth
**13** first premolar
**14** central incisor, lateral incisor,
second premolar

**teetotal**
**02** TT **05** sober **06** tee-tee **08** complete
**09** abstinent, out-and-out, temperate
**10** abstemious, on the wagon

**teetotaller**
**02** TT **06** tee-tee, wowser **09** abstainer,
nephalist, Rechabite **10** non-drinker
**12** water-drinker

**telegram**
**03** fax **04** wire **05** cable, telex
**09** cablegram, radiogram, telegraph
**11** night letter, Telemessage®

**telegraph**
**04** send, wire **05** cable, telex **06** signal
**08** telegram, transmit **10** radiograph
**11** teleprinter **12** Telautograph®
**14** radiotelegraph
• **telegraph office 02** TO

**telepathy**
**03** ESP **10** sixth sense **11** mind-reading,
second sight **12** clairvoyance

**telephone**
**03** tel **04** buzz, call, dial, ring, tele-
**05** phone **06** blower, call up, ring in,
ring up **07** contact, handset, hot line
**08** receiver **09** give a bell, give a buzz,
make a call **10** get in touch **11** give a
tinkle
• **on the telephone** ◊ *homophone
indicator*

**telescope**
**03** cut **04** trim, tube **05** crush, optic,
scope **06** reduce, shrink, squash
**07** abridge, compact, curtail, shorten,
squeeze **08** compress, condense,
contract, spyglass, truncate
**09** binocular, optic tube, reflector,
refractor **10** abbreviate, binoculars,
concertina, equatorial **11** perspective
**13** prospect-glass

**televise**
**03** air **04** beam, show **05** cable, put on,
relay **06** screen **08** transmit
**09** broadcast

**television**
**02** TV **03** box, set **04** tele, tube **05** cable,
telly **06** the box **07** the tube **08** boob
tube, idiot box, receiver **09** goggle-box
**11** cablevision, small screen
**13** narrowcasting
---
*Television programme types include:*
---
**04** news, soap
**05** anime, drama
**06** repeat, sitcom
**07** cartoon, phone-in, reality
**08** bulletin, chat show, docusoap,
game show, quiz show
**09** panel game, soap opera
**11** documentary
**12** makeover show, mockumentary
---
*Television channels include:*
---
**02** E4
**03** ABC, CNN, Fox, HBO, MTV,
NBC, QVC, S4C, VH1
**04** BBC1, BBC2, BBC3, BBC4,
CBBC, CNBC, Dave, Five, ITV1,
ITV2, ITV3, ITV4
**05** More4
**06** Sky One

**07** BBC News, Fox News, History, Sky News
**08** BBC World, Cbeebies, Channel 4, FilmFour, Living TV
**09** al-Jazeera, Bloomberg, Discovery, Eurosport, Sky Movies, Sky Sports
**11** Nickelodeon
**13** BBC Parliament

---

*Television programmes include:*

**02** ER, QI
**03** CSI, QED
**04** Glee, GMTV, Lost, M*A*S*H
**05** Arena, Bread, Kojak, LA Law, Shaft
**06** Batman, Bottom, Cheers, Dallas, Hi-De-Hi, Lassie, Mad Men, Minder, Mr Bean, Quincy, Sharpe, Tiswas
**07** Bagpuss, Blake's 7, Columbo, Dynasty, Frasier, Friends, Holiday, Horizon, Lovejoy, Maigret, Mr Magoo, Omnibus, Poldark, Pop Idol, Rainbow, Rawhide, Spender, Taggart, The Bill, The Wire, The Word, Tonight, Top Gear
**08** 'Allo 'Allo, Baywatch, Bergerac, Casualty, Dad's Army, Eldorado, Faking It, NYPD Blue, Panorama, Porridge, Red Dwarf, Roseanne, Seinfeld, Sgt Bilko, Star Trek, Stingray, The Saint, Time Team, Trumpton, Watchdog, Wife Swap
**09** Andy Pandy, Blind Date, Blue Peter, Brookside, Countdown, Doctor Who, Dr Kildare, Emmerdale, Father Ted, Happy Days, Heartbeat, Holby City, Hollyoaks, I Love Lucy, Jackanory, Miami Vice, News at Ten, Newsnight, Newsround, Parkinson, South Park, That's Life, The X Files, Twin Peaks, Up Pompeii!, Wallander
**10** Ally McBeal, Big Brother, Blackadder, Crossroads, Deputy Dawg, EastEnders, Gladiators, Grandstand, Grange Hill, Howards' Way, Jim'll Fix It, Kavanagh QC, Masterchef, Mastermind, Miss Marple, Neighbours, On the Buses, Pebble Mill, Perry Mason, Play School, Postman Pat, Quatermass, Rising Damp, The Goodies, The Monkees, The Sweeney, The Waltons, The Wombles, The X-Factor, Wacky Races
**11** Animal Magic, Call My Bluff, Catchphrase, Come Dancing, Crackerjack, Fame Academy, Give Us a Clue, Ground Force, Hawaii Five-O, Home and Away, Juke Box Jury, Life on Earth, Teletubbies, The Avengers, The Fast Show, The Fugitive, The Good Life, The Prisoner, The Simpsons, The Sopranos, Tom and Jerry, What's My Line?, Yes, Minister
**12** As Time Goes By, Blockbusters,

Candid Camera, Citizen Smith, Fawlty Towers, Fifteen to One, It's a Knockout, Knots Landing, Melrose Place, Moonlighting, Mork and Mindy, Open All Hours, Peak Practice, Points of View, Question Time, Sesame Street, Terry and June, The Thick of It, The Young Ones, Thunderbirds, Top of the Pops
**13** A Touch of Frost, Blankety Blank, Bob the Builder, Breakfast Time, Emmerdale Farm, Hamish Macbeth, Ivor the Engine, Little Britain, Match of the Day, May to December, Muffin the Mule, Pinky and Perky, Ready, Steady, Go!, Sex and the City, Songs of Praise, Spitting Image, Steptoe and Son, The Likely Lads, The Liver Birds, The Lone Ranger, The Muppet Show, The Sky at Night, The Two Ronnies, The World at War, Whicker's World
**14** Animal Hospital, Ballykissangel, Cagney and Lacey, Captain Pugwash, Charlie's Angels, Family Fortunes, Gardener's World, Inspector Morse, Murder, She Wrote, My Friend Flicka, Record Breakers, The Flintstones, The Frost Report, The Weakest Link, This Is Your Life, Tomorrow's World, To the Manor Born, Wheel of Fortune, Worzel Gummidge
**15** Birds of a Feather, Camberwick Green, Hill Street Blues, Midsomer Murders, One Man and His Dog, Ready Steady Cook, Remington Steele, Starsky and Hutch, The Addams Family, The Big Breakfast, The Man from UNCLE, The New Statesman, The Price is Right, The Twilight Zone, Watch with Mother, You've Been Framed

*See also* **quiz**

---

*Television presenters include:*

**03** **Ant** (Anthony McPartlin), **Dec** (Declan Donnelly)
**04** **Muir** (Frank), **Ross** (Jonathan)
**05** **Aspel** (Michael), **Black** (Cilla), **Bragg** (Melvyn, Lord), **Evans** (Chris), **Frost** (Sir David), **James** (Clive), **Moore** (Sir Patrick), **Negus** (Arthur), **Wogan** (Sir Terry)
**06** **Carson** (Johnny), **Norden** (Denis), **Norman** (Barry), **Paxman** (Jeremy), **Rayner** (Claire), **Savile** (Sir Jimmy)
**07** **Andrews** (Eamonn), **Bellamy** (David), **Edmonds** (Noel), **Forsyth** (Bruce), **Kennedy** (Sir Ludovic), **Madeley** (Richard), **Rantzen** (Esther), **Starkey** (David), **Tarrant** (Chris), **Wheldon** (Sir Huw), **Whicker** (Alan), **Winfrey** (Oprah)
**08** **Bakewell** (Joan), **Campbell** (Nicky), **Finnigan** (Judy), **Stoppard** (Miriam), **Sullivan** (Ed)
**09** **Ant and Dec** (Anthony McPartlin/ Declan Donnelly), **Magnusson** (Magnus), **Parkinson** (Sir Michael)

**10** **Titchmarsh** (Alan)
**12** **Attenborough** (Sir David)
**14** **Richard and Judy** (Richard Madeley/Judy Finnigan)

---

• **television system 03** PAL **10** flat-screen **13** closed circuit

**tell**

**03** bid, rat, say, see **04** blab, shop, show, talk **05** alter, brief, count, drain, grass, order, speak, state, story, utter **06** advise, affect, assure, betray, change, charge, decree, direct, gossip, impart, inform, notify, recite, relate, report, reveal, sketch, squeal, tattle, unfold **07** apprise, command, confess, declare, dictate, discern, divulge, exhaust, explain, let know, make out, mention, narrate, portray, recount, require, versify **08** acquaint, announce, count out, denounce, describe, disclose, discover, identify, inform on, instruct, perceive, proclaim **09** authorize, broadcast, delineate, elucidate, make known, recognize, tell apart, tell tales, transform **10** comprehend, understand **11** blow the gaff, communicate, distinguish **12** discriminate **13** differentiate, spill the beans, take its toll of **14** give the low-down, have an effect on **15** give the game away

• **tell off 04** slam **05** chide, knock, scold, slate **06** berate, bounce, carpet, rebuke, see off **07** bawl out, catch it, censure, chew out, lecture, reprove, tick off, upbraid **08** reproach **09** dress down, pull apart, reprimand, take apart **14** give a talking-to

**teller**

**05** clerk, griot **06** banker, tailor, tellar, tiller **07** cashier, sapling **09** bank clerk, raconteur, treasurer **10** Munchausen, raconteuse **11** Munchhausen

**telling**

**06** cogent, marked **07** pointed **08** powerful **09** effective, narration, narrative, numbering, revealing **10** convincing, impressive, meaningful, persuasive **11** instruction, significant

**telling-off**

**03** row **06** earful, rebuke, rocket **07** chiding, lecture, reproof, wigging **08** reproach, scolding **09** carpeting, reprimand, talking-to **10** bawling-out, ticking-off, upbraiding **11** castigation **12** dressing-down **14** kick in the pants, slap on the wrist **15** smack on thewrist

**tell-tale**

**03** spy **05** clype, grass, sneak **06** buzzer, snitch **07** stoolie, tattler **08** blabbing, give-away, informer, snitcher, squealer **09** betraying, revealing **10** indicating, meaningful, noticeable, revelatory, suggestive, tale-teller, tattle-tale **11** perceptible, secret agent **12** unmistakable **15** snake in the grass

**tellurium**

**02** Te

## telly
*see* television

## temerity
**04** gall **05** cheek, nerve **06** daring
**08** audacity, boldness, rashness
**09** impudence **10** effrontery
**11** presumption **12** impertinence,
recklessness **13** impulsiveness

## temper
**03** wax **04** alay, calm, cool, fury,
mood, rage, tone, trim, tune **05** aleye,
allay, alloy, anger, assay, blood, delay,
paddy, radge, scene, storm **06** adjust,
anneal, attune, harden, humour,
lessen, master, meddle, modify,
nature, reduce, season, soften, soothe,
tamper, weaken **07** assuage, bad
mood, chasten, flare-up, fortify,
passion, roughen, tantrum, toughen
**08** attitude, calmness, comeddle,
mitigate, moderate, palliate, tone
down **09** alleviate, annoyance,
character, composure, condition,
fireworks, ill-humour, petulance
**10** resentment, strengthen
**11** disposition, fit of temper, frame of
mind, self-control, state of mind,
temperament **12** constitution,
irritability, pyrotechnics, tranquillity

*See also* **bad-tempered**
• **lose your temper 05** go mad
**06** lose it, see red **07** explode **08** boil
over, freak out, get angry **09** blow a
fuse, do your nut, go bananas, go up
a wall, raise hell **10** hit the roof
**11** blow a gasket, blow your top, flip
your lid, get up in arms, go up the
wall, lose your rag **12** blow your
cool, fly into a rage, lose your cool,
throw a wobbly **13** get aggravated,
have a hissy fit, hit the ceiling, throw
a tantrum **14** foam at the mouth **15** fly
off the handle, get all steamed up, go
off the deep end

## temperament
**04** bent, mood, soul **05** blood, humor
**06** humour, kidney, make-up, mettle,
nature, phlegm, spirit, temper
**07** climate, outlook **08** attitude,
tendency **09** character, composure,
fieriness, moodiness, tempering
**10** complexion, compromise,
impatience, touchiness, volatility
**11** disposition, frame of mind,
personality, sensitivity, state of mind
**12** constitution, excitability,
idiosyncrasy, irritability
**13** explosiveness, hot-headedness, red-
headedness

## temperamental
**05** fiery, moody **06** inborn, innate,
touchy **07** natural **08** artistic, inherent,
neurotic, petulant, volatile
**09** emotional, excitable, explosive,
hot-headed, impatient, ingrained,
irritable, mercurial, sensitive
**10** capricious, congenital, hot-
blooded, passionate, unreliable
**12** highly strung **13** over-emotional,
over-sensitive, unpredictable
**14** constitutional, hypersensitive

## temperamentally
**08** innately **09** basically, naturally
**10** inherently **13** fundamentally

## temperance
**08** sobriety **09** austerity, restraint
**10** abstinence, continence,
moderation, self-denial **11** prohibition,
self-control, teetotalism **13** self-
restraint **14** abstemiousness, self-
discipline

## temperate
**04** calm, fair, mild **05** balmy, sober
**06** gentle, stable **07** clement, equable
**08** balanced, composed, moderate,
pleasant, sensible, teetotal
**09** abstinent, agreeable, continent
**10** abstemious, controlled, reasonable,
restrained **11** self-denying **12** even-
tempered **14** self-controlled, self-
restrained

## temperature
**01** t **04** temp **05** fever **07** mixture
**10** proportion **12** constitution

## tempest
**04** gale **05** storm **06** furore, squall,
tumult, uproar **07** cyclone, ferment,
tornado, turmoil, typhoon **08** upheaval
**09** bourasque, commotion, hurricane
**11** disturbance
*See also* **wind**

## tempestuous
**04** high, wild **05** gusty, rough, windy
**06** fierce, heated, raging, stormy,
wrathy **07** furious, intense, squally,
violent **08** blustery, feverish
**09** turbulent **10** boisterous, passionate,
tumultuous **11** impassioned
**12** uncontrolled

## template
**03** jig **04** form, mold **05** frame, model,
mould **06** master, matrix **07** pattern,
profile **08** strickle **09** blueprint,
prototype **10** master page, stylesheet
**12** cookie-cutter

## temple
**03** wat **04** fane, naos **06** church, haffet,
haffit, mandir, mosque, pagoda, shrine
**07** mandira **08** teocalli **09** joss house,
sanctuary, synagogue **10** tabernacle
**14** place of worship
*See also* **religious; worship**

## tempo
**04** beat, pace, rate, time **05** agoge,
metre, pulse, speed, throb **06** rhythm
**07** cadence, measure **08** movement,
velocity

## temporal
**04** good **05** civil **06** carnal, mortal,
timely **07** earthly, fleshly, profane,
secular, worldly **08** material
**11** terrestrial **12** temporaneous

## temporarily
**06** for now, pro tem **07** briefly **08** for a
time **10** fleetingly **11** momentarily,
transiently **12** in the interim, transitorily
**15** for the time being

## temporary
**05** brief **06** fill-in, pro tem **07** Band-
aid®, interim, passing, stopgap
**08** fleeting, temporal **09** ephemeral,

fugacious, makeshift, momentary,
provisory, short-term, transient
**10** evanescent, short-lived, transitory
**11** impermanent, provisional
**12** temporaneous **14** extemporaneous

## temporize
**05** delay, pause, stall **08** hang back
**09** hum and haw **10** equivocate **11** play
for time **12** tergiversate **13** procrastinate

## tempt
**03** woo **04** bait, bayt, coax, draw, lure,
tice **05** assay, educe, egg on **06** allure,
cajole, entice, incite, induce, invite
**07** attempt, attract, dispose, incline,
provoke, suggest **08** inveigle, persuade
**09** tantalize

## temptation
**04** bait, draw, lure, pull **05** snare, trial
**06** allure, appeal, urging **07** attempt,
coaxing **08** cajolery **09** influence,
seduction, tentation **10** allurement,
attraction, cloven hoof, enticement,
incitement, inducement, invitation,
invitement, persuasion, suggestion

## tempting
**04** sexy **08** alluring, enticing, inviting
**09** lickerish, liquorish, seductive
**10** appetizing, attractive **11** tantalizing
**13** mouthwatering

## temptress
**04** vamp **05** Circe, flirt, siren **06** Dalila
**07** Dalilah, Delilah, Lorelei
**08** coquette **09** sorceress **10** seductress
**11** enchantress, femme fatale

## ten
**01** X **02** 10 **05** decad **06** decade, dectet,
denary

## tenable
**05** sound **06** viable **08** arguable,
credible, feasible, rational **09** plausible
**10** believable, defendable, defensible,
reasonable **11** justifiable, supportable
**12** maintainable

## tenacious
**04** fast, firm **05** tight, tough **06** claggy,
dogged, grippy, secure, sticky
**07** adamant **08** adhesive, clinging,
cohesive, obdurate, resolute, stubborn
**09** obstinate, retentive, steadfast
**10** determined, persistent, purposeful,
relentless, unshakable, unswerving,
unyielding **11** persevering,
unshakeable **12** intransigent, single-
minded

## tenacity
**04** guts, hold **05** force, power
**07** resolve **08** fastness, firmness,
obduracy, solidity, strength
**09** diligence, obstinacy, solidness,
toughness **10** doggedness, resolution
**11** application, persistence,
pertinacity, staunchness
**12** forcefulness, perseverance,
resoluteness, stubbornness
**13** determination, inflexibility,
intransigence, steadfastness
**14** indomitability

## tenancy
**05** lease **06** tenure **07** holding, renting
**09** leasehold, occupancy, residence

**10** incumbency, occupation, possession

## tenant
**04** ryot **05** baron, dwell, gebur, thane **06** farmer, lessee, mailer, occupy, raiyat, renter, socman **07** cottier, métayer, socager, sokeman **08** gavelman, occupant, occupier, resident, suckener **09** incumbent, pendicler **10** inhabitant, landholder **11** householder, leaseholder
• **be a tenant  03** sit

## tend
**02** go **03** aim, ren, rin, run **04** bear, bend, grow, head, herd, keep, lamb, lead, lean, make, mind, move, wait **05** dress, groom, guard, nurse, offer, point, see to, serve, sound, verge, watch **06** affect, attend, escort, handle, invite, manage, wait on **07** care for, conduce, hearken, incline, nurture, protect **08** attend to, be liable, maintain, wait upon **09** cultivate, gravitate, look after, watch over **10** be inclined, minister to, take care of **11** keep an eye on **13** show a tendency

## tendency
**03** set **04** bent, bias, turn **05** drift, trend **06** course, genius, levity **07** aptness, bearing, conatus, heading, leaning **08** movement **09** direction, liability, proneness, readiness **10** partiality, proclivity, propensity **11** disposition, inclination **14** predisposition, susceptibility

## tendentious
**06** biased **07** at issue **08** disputed, doubtful **09** debatable, polemical **10** disputable **11** contentious **12** questionable **13** controversial

## tender
**03** bid, new, raw, red **04** care, fond, give, kind, nesh, plan, pram, sair, soft, sore, warm, weak **05** chary, coins, early, frail, green, juicy, money, offer, praam, price, value, young **06** aching, callow, caring, dainty, extend, feeble, fleshy, gentle, humane, kindly, loving, regard, render, submit **07** advance, amoroso, amorous, beloved, bruised, cherish, concern, fragile, painful, pinnace, present, proffer, propose, suggest **08** currency, delicate, estimate, fondness, footsore, generous, immature, inflamed, merciful, pathetic, proposal, romantic, smarting, youthful **09** banknotes, easy to cut, emotional, evocative, quotation, sensitive, soft-paste, succulent, throbbing, volunteer **10** affettuoso, benevolent, easy to chew, scrupulous, submission, suggestion, vulnerable **11** considerate, proposition, sentimental, soft-hearted, sympathetic **12** affectionate **13** compassionate, inexperienced, tender-hearted **14** impressionable

## tender-hearted
**04** fond, kind, mild, warm **06** benign, caring, gentle, humane, kindly, loving **07** feeling, pitying **08** merciful **09** sensitive **10** benevolent, responsive

**11** considerate, kind-hearted, sentimental, soft-hearted, sympathetic, warm-hearted **12** affectionate **13** compassionate

## tenderly
**06** fondly, gently, warmly **08** lovingly **10** affettuoso, generously **11** emotionally, sensitively **12** benevolently, romantically **13** considerately, sentimentally **14** affectionately **15** compassionately, sympathetically

## tenderness
**04** ache, care, love, pain, pity **05** mercy, youth **06** aching, liking, warmth **07** feeling, rawness **08** bruising, delicacy, devotion, fondness, humanity, kindness, softness, soreness, sympathy, weakness **09** affection, fragility, frailness, greenness, juiciness, sweetness **10** attachment, callowness, compassion, feebleness, gentleness, humaneness, immaturity, irritation, succulence **11** amorousness, benevolence, painfulness, sensitivity **12** delicateness, inexperience, inflammation, youthfulness **13** consideration, sensitiveness, vulnerability **14** loving-kindness, sentimentality **15** soft-heartedness, warm-heartedness

## tendon
**05** sinew **06** leader, paxwax **09** hamstring **11** aponeurosis, heart-string

## tenet
**04** rule, view **05** canon, credo, creed, dogma, maxim **06** belief, thesis **07** opinion, precept **08** doctrine, teaching **09** principle **10** adiaphoron, conviction **11** presumption **14** article of faith

## Tennessee
**02** TN **04** Tenn

## tennis
**10** jeu de paume **12** sphairistike

*Tennis players include:*

**04 Ashe** (Arthur), **Borg** (Björn), **Cash** (Pat), **Graf** (Steffi), **Hoad** (Lew), **King** (Billie Jean), **Ryan** (Elizabeth), **Wade** (Virginia)
**05 Budge** (Don), **Bueno** (Maria), **Court** (Margaret), **Evert** (Chris), **Henin** (Justine), **Jones** (Ann), **Laver** (Rod), **Lendl** (Ivan), **Lloyd** (Chris), **Nadal** (Rafael), **Perry** (Fred), **Roche** (Tony), **Seles** (Monica), **Stich** (Michael), **Vilas** (Guillermo), **Wills** (Helen)
**06 Agassi** (Andre), **Austin** (Tracy), **Barker** (Sue), **Becker** (Boris), **Cawley** (Evonne), **Drobny** (Jaroslav), **DuPont** (Margaret), **Edberg** (Stefan), **Gibson** (Althea), **Henman** (Tim), **Hewitt** (Lleyton), **Hingis** (Martina), **Hopman** (Harry), **Kramer** (Jack), **Murray** (Andy), **Rafter** (Pat), **Tilden** (Bill)
**07 Borotra** (Jean), **Brookes** (Sir Norman Everard), **Connors**

(Jimmy), **Emerson** (Roy), **Federer** (Roger), **Godfree** (Kitty), **Lacoste** (Rene), **Lenglen** (Suzanne), **Maskell** (Dan), **McEnroe** (John), **Nastase** (Ilie), **Novotna** (Jana), **Renshaw** (Willie), **Sampras** (Pete), **Sedgman** (Frank), **Shriver** (Pam)
**08 Capriati** (Jennifer), **Connolly** (Maureen 'Little Mo'), **del Potro** (Juan Martin), **Gonzales** (Pancho), **Krajicek** (Richard), **Newcombe** (John), **Rosewall** (Ken), **Rusedski** (Greg), **Sabatini** (Gabriela), **Williams** (Serena), **Williams** (Venus)
**09 Clijsters** (Kim), **Davenport** (Lindsay), **Goolagong** (Evonne), **Sharapova** (Maria), **Woodforde** (Mark), **Wozniacki** (Caroline)
**10 Ivanisevic** (Goran), **Kafelnikov** (Yevgeny), **Kournikova** (Anna), **Wills Moody** (Helen), **Woodbridge** (Todd)
**11 Navratilova** (Martina)
**15 Goolagong Cawley** (Evonne)

*Tennis-related terms include:*

**03** ace, ATP, let, lob, LTA, set, WTA **04** love, pass **05** AELTC, break, deuce, drive, fault, rally, serve, slice, smash **06** return, umpire, volley, winner **07** ballboy, net cord, runback **08** backhand, ballgirl, baseline, drop shot, forehand, line call, love game, midcourt, net judge, overhead, overrule, set point, tie-break, wood shot **09** advantage, backcourt, baseliner, break back, foot fault, forecourt, hold serve, line judge, mini-break, sweet spot, tramlines, two-handed **10** break point, cross court, deuce court, match point **11** block volley, double fault, service game, service line **12** approach shot, ground stroke, mixed doubles, service court **13** second service **14** advantage court, serve and volley

## tenor
**01** T **03** aim, way **04** feck, gist, path **05** drift, point, sense, theme, trend, Trial **06** burden, course, intent, spirit **07** essence, meaning, purport, purpose, texture **08** tendency **09** direction, substance

## tense
**01** t **04** edgy, taut, work **05** brace, drawn, heavy, jumpy, rigid, stiff, tight **06** narrow, on edge, strain, taught, uneasy **07** anxious, charged, fidgety, fraught, jittery, keyed up, nervous, stiffen, stretch, tighten, uptight, worried **08** contract, exciting, restless, strained, worrying **09** inflexion, screwed up, stressful, stretched **10** distraught, inflection, nail-biting **11** overwrought, stressed out **12** apprehensive, nerve-racking **13** under pressure

*Grammatical tenses include:*

**02** pt
**03** pat
**04** past
**06** aorist, future
**07** perfect, present
**08** preterit
**09** imperfect, preterite
**10** pluperfect
**11** conditional, past perfect
**12** gnomic aorist, past historic
**13** future perfect
**14** present perfect
**15** paragogic future

**tensely**
**08** in a state, uneasily **09** anxiously,
nervously, worriedly **10** restlessly
**11** stressed out **14** apprehensively

**tension**
**04** feud **05** clash, worry **06** nerves,
strain, stress, strife, unrest, wobbly
**07** anxiety, discord, dispute, ill-will,
jitters, quarrel, willies **08** conflict,
disquiet, distress, edginess, friction,
pressure, rigidity, suspense, tautness,
variance **09** agitation, antipathy,
hostility, stiffness, straining, tightness
**10** antagonism, contention, dissension,
opposition, stretching, uneasiness
**11** butterflies, nervousness
**12** apprehension, collywobbles,
disagreement, hypertension,
restlessness **13** confrontation, heebie-
jeebies
• **equal tension 08** isotonic
• **high tension 02** HT
• **low tension 02** LT
• **premenstrual tension 03** PMT
• **surface tension 01** T

**tent**
**04** camp, heed **05** probe

*Tents include:*

**03** box, ger, gur, mat
**04** bell, dome, kata, tilt, tipi, yurt
**05** bivvy, black, frame, lodge, ridge,
tepee, tupik, yourt
**06** big top, canopy, canvas, teepee,
tunnel, wigwam
**07** conical, marquee, touring, trailer,
yaranga
**10** single hoop, tabernacle
**11** hooped bivvy
**12** sloping ridge, sloping wedge
**13** barrel-vaulted, crossover pole
• **tent village 04** duar **05** douar,
dowar

**tentacle**
**03** arm **04** horn **06** feeler
**12** hectocotylus

**tentative**
**04** test **05** pilot, timid, trial **06** unsure
**08** cautious, doubtful, hesitant,
unproven, wavering **09** diffident,
faltering, peirastic, uncertain,
undecided **10** indefinite **11** conjectural,
exploratory, provisional, speculative,
unconfirmed **12** experimental **13** to be
confirmed

**tentatively**
**06** on spec **07** timidly **08** gingerly

**10** cautiously, doubtfully, hesitantly
**12** indefinitely **13** peirastically,
provisionally, speculatively
**14** experimentally

**tenterhooks**
• **on tenterhooks 05** eager
**07** anxious, excited, keyed up,
nervous, waiting **08** watchful
**09** expectant, impatient **10** in suspense
**15** with bated breath

**tenuous**
**04** fine, hazy, slim, thin, weak
**05** shaky, vague **06** flimsy, slight, subtle
**07** dubious, fragile, slender **08** delicate,
doubtful, rarefied **09** recherché
**10** indefinite **12** questionable
**13** insubstantial

**tenure**
**03** fee, feu **04** tack, term, time **05** lease,
tenor **06** papacy, socage **07** burgage,
fee-farm, holding, popedom, soccage,
tenancy **08** frank-fee, steelbow,
vavasory, venville **09** commendam,
gavelkind, leasehold, occupancy,
pastorate, priorship, rabbinate,
residence, sokemanry, villenage
**10** archontate, cottierism, government,
habitation, incumbency, occupation,
possession, villeinage **12** frankalmoign
**13** knight service **14** proprietorship,
subinfeudation

**tepee**
**04** tent, tipi

**tepid**
**03** lew **04** cool **07** warmish
**08** lukewarm **09** apathetic **11** half-
hearted, indifferent **14** unenthusiastic

**terbium**
**02** Tb

**term**
**03** dub, end, tag **04** call, fees, name,
span, time, word **05** bound, close,
costs, label, limit, point, rates, space,
spell, style, title **06** clause, course,
detail, finish, period, phrase, prices,
season, tariff **07** charges, entitle,
epithet, footing, proviso, session,
stretch **08** boundary, duration, fruition,
interval, locution, position, semester,
standing, terminus **09** condition,
designate, provision, relations,
trimester **10** conclusion, denominate,
expression, particular **11** appellation,
culmination, designation, restriction,
stipulation **12** denomination,
relationship **13** qualification,
specification

*Terms and sessions include:*

**04** Lent
**06** Easter, Hilary
**07** Trinity
**10** Michaelmas
• **come to terms 06** accept, submit
**08** compound **10** articulate
**11** accommodate **12** come to accept
**14** resign yourself
• **in terms of 09** as regards **10** in
regard to **12** in relation to, with
regard to **13** with respect to
• **on good terms 02** in

**terminal**
◊ *tail selection indicator* **03** end, VDU
**04** last, pole, POST, RJET **05** acute,
depot, dying, fatal, final, limit
**06** deadly, ending, garage, lethal,
mortal, utmost **07** console, extreme,
killing, monitor, station **08** boundary,
desinent, keyboard, last stop, limiting,
railhead, terminus, ultimate
**09** confining, extremity, incurable
**10** concluding **11** desinential,
termination, untreatable, workstation
**12** end of the line
• **terminal part 03** cap **06** cloaca,
rectum **12** sigmoid colon **14** sigmoid
flexure

**terminally**
**07** fatally **08** lethally, mortally
**09** incurably **11** malignantly

**terminate**
**03** end **04** fall, stop **05** abort, cease,
close, issue, lapse **06** cut off, expire,
finish, result, run out, wind up
**07** dismiss **08** complete, conclude,
dissolve, leave off **10** put an end to
**11** come to an end, discontinue
**12** bring to an end **14** close the book
on
*See also* **kill**

**termination**
**03** end **05** close, finis, issue **06** demise,
effect, ending, expiry, finale, finish,
result **07** success **08** abortion,
boundary, naricorn **09** cessation
**10** completion, conclusion,
dénouement **11** consequence
**15** discontinuation

**terminology**
**05** terms, words **06** jargon **08** language
**10** glossology, vocabulary
**11** expressions, phraseology
**12** nomenclature

**terminus**
◊ *tail selection indicator* **03** end **04** goal
**05** close, depot, limit **06** garage, target
**07** station **08** boundary, terminal
**09** extremity **11** air terminal,
destination, termination **12** end of the
line **13** starting-point

**termite**
**03** ant **07** duck-ant, royalty, wood ant
**08** white ant **09** woodlouse

**Terra**
**04** Gaia

**terrace**
**03** Ter **04** Terr **05** beach, bench, linch,
shelf **06** offset, perron, tarras
**07** balcony, sun deck, veranda
**08** barbette, crescent, platform,
verandah **09** promenade **10** undercliff

**terrain**
**04** land **06** ground **07** country, terrane,
terrene **09** landscape, territory
**10** topography **11** countryside

**terrapin**
**04** emys **06** slider **08** redbelly
**11** diamondback **13** water tortoise

**terrestrial**
**04** land **06** global, layman **07** earthly,

mundane, terrene, worldly
**09** subastral, tellurian

**terrible**
◊ *anagram indicator* **03** bad, big, ill
**04** foul, grim, naff, poor, poxy, ropy,
sick, vile, weak **05** awful, great, large,
lousy, nasty, pants, ropey, sorry
**06** aching, crappy, crummy, faulty,
gloomy, guilty, horrid, in pain, poorly,
severe, unwell **07** ashamed, extreme,
fearful, hateful, hideous, intense,
notable, painful, serious, tearing, the
pits, unhappy, useless **08** contrite,
diseased, dreadful, gruesome,
hopeless, horrible, horrific, inferior,
mediocre, pathetic, pokerish, shocking
**09** abhorrent, appalling, defective,
deficient, frightful, harrowing,
imperfect, monstrous, obnoxious,
offensive, repulsive, revolting, third-
rate **10** abortional, apologetic,
despondent, disgusting, hellacious,
inadequate, indisposed, outrageous,
pronounced, remorseful, second-rate,
shamefaced, unpleasant **11** a load of
crap, distressing, exceptional,
incompetent, ineffective, substandard,
unspeakable **12** unacceptable **14** a
load of garbage, a load of rubbish,
unsatisfactory **15** under the weather

**terribly**
◊ *anagram indicator* **04** evil, much, very
**06** evilly **07** awfully, greatly
**09** decidedly, extremely, seriously
**10** thoroughly **11** desperately,
exceedingly, frightfully

**terrier**
**04** roll **08** register, rent-roll **09** inventory
**11** territorial

*Terriers include:*

**03** fox
**04** bull, Skye
**05** cairn, foxie, Irish, Welsh
**06** Border, Boston, Scotch, Scotty,
   Westie, Yorkie
**07** pit bull, Scottie, Tibetan
**08** Aberdeen, Airedale, Doberman,
   Scottish, Sealyham, wire-hair
**09** Kerry blue, schnauzer, Yorkshire
**10** Australian, Bedlington,
   Manchester, wire-haired
**11** Jack Russell
**12** West Highland
**13** Dandie Dinmont
**15** American pit bull

**terriers**
**02** TA

**terrific**
**03** ace **04** cool, huge, mega, neat, wild
**05** brill, crack, great, large, super, triff
**06** superb, wicked **07** amazing,
awesome, crucial, extreme, hell of a,
intense **08** dreadful, enormous,
fabulous, gigantic, smashing
**09** brilliant, excellent, excessive,
fantastic, wonderful **10** marvellous,
prodigious, remarkable, stupendous,
terrifying, tremendous **11** frightening,
magnificent, outstanding, sensational
**12** breathtaking **13** extraordinary **14** out
of this world

**terrifically**
**04** very **05** jolly **06** highly, really
**07** acutely, awfully, greatly, utterly
**08** severely, terribly **09** decidedly,
extremely, intensely, unusually
**10** dreadfully, remarkably, thoroughly,
uncommonly **11** exceedingly,
excessively, frightfully
**12** immoderately, inordinately,
unreasonably **13** exceptionally
**15** extraordinarily

**terrified**
**04** awed **06** aghast, scared **07** alarmed
**08** appalled, dismayed **09** horrified,
petrified **10** frightened **11** in a blue
funk, intimidated, scared stiff
**12** horror-struck **13** having kittens,
panic-stricken, scared to death

**terrify**
**04** fear, gast, numb **05** alarm, appal,
ghast, grise, panic, scare, shock
**06** agrise, agrize, agryze, dismay, rattle
**07** horrify, petrify **08** affright, frighten,
paralyse **09** terrorize **10** intimidate,
scare stiff **12** put the wind up

**territorial**
**04** area **05** zonal **08** district, domainal,
regional **09** localized, sectional
**11** topographic **12** geographical

**territorials**
**02** TA

**territory**
**03** Ter **04** area, land, mark, Terr, turf,
zone **05** field, state, tract **06** county,
domain, region, sector **07** abthane,
apanage, country, outland, terrain
**08** appanage, backyard, district,
outlands, preserve, province,
sheikdom, toparchy, township
**09** khedivate, sheikhdom
**10** dependency, home ground,
khedivate, possession, Reichsland
**11** trusteeship **12** jurisdiction
*See also* **province; state**

**terror**
**03** bug **04** bogy, fear **05** alarm, bogle,
demon, devil, dread, fiend, panic,
poker, rogue, shock **06** dismay, fright,
horror, rascal **07** bugbear, monster
**08** affright, blue funk, tearaway **09** cold
sweat, scarecrow, terrorism
**10** amazedness **11** trepidation
**12** intimidation **13** consternation

**terrorist**
**06** bomber, gunman, player **07** butcher
**08** agitator, assassin, attacker, militant
**09** aggressor, anarchist, assailant,
guerrilla **11** seditionist **13** revolutionary
**14** freedom fighter, fundamentalist,
urban guerrilla
• **terrorist militia** **02** SA

**terrorize**
**04** prey **05** alarm, bully, scare, shock
**06** coerce, menace **07** horrify, oppress,
petrify, terrify **08** browbeat, frighten,
threaten **09** strongarm **10** intimidate
**12** put the wind up

**terse**
**04** curt **05** blunt, brief, crisp, pithy,
short **06** abrupt, gnomic, smooth,
snappy **07** brusque, compact, concise,

laconic **08** clean-cut, incisive, succinct
**09** condensed **10** elliptical, to the point
**12** epigrammatic, monosyllabic

**test**
**03** MOT, pix, pyx, sap, SAT, try, van
**04** Esda, exam, load, pass, quiz, tire
**05** assay, check, drain, exact, probe,
proof, prove, study, testa, touch, trial,
trier, weary **06** assess, burden, dry run,
impose, ordeal, prieve, sample,
screen, strain, try out, try-out, verify,
weaken **07** analyse, check-up,
examine, exhaust, inspect, reagent,
scratch, stretch, wear out **08** analysis,
appraise, audition, check out,
crucible, encumber, enervate,
evaluate, overload, prospect,
sounding, trial run **09** challenge,
criterion, probation, questions,
testimony, time trial **10** assessment,
evaluation, experience, experiment,
inspection, pilot study, scrutinize,
shibboleth **11** examination,
exploration, investigate
**13** investigation, make demands on,
questionnaire **14** scrutinization
*See also* **examination**
• **stand the test** **04** wash

**testament**
**02** NT, OT **04** Test, will **05** proof
**07** earnest, tribute, witness
**08** covenant, evidence **09** testimony
**11** attestation **13** demonstration
**15** exemplification

**testicles**
**04** nads, nuts **05** balls, groin
**07** cojones, doucets, dowsets, gooleys,
goolies **08** cobblers, knackers, lamb's
fry **12** family jewels

**testify**
**03** rap **04** avow, show **05** state, swear,
vouch **06** affirm, assert, attest, back up,
depone, verify **07** certify, confirm,
declare, endorse, speak to, support
**08** proclaim **09** establish **11** bear
witness, corroborate, demonstrate
**12** give evidence, substantiate

**testimonial**
**04** chit **06** chitty **07** tribute **09** character,
reference **10** credential **11** certificate,
endorsement **12** commendation
**14** recommendation

**testimony**
**05** proof **06** attest, report **07** support,
tribute, witness **08** evidence
**09** affidavit, assertion, statement
**10** deposition, indication, profession,
submission **11** affirmation, attestation,
declaration **12** confirmation,
verification **13** corroboration,
demonstration, manifestation

**testy**
**05** cross, ratty **06** crusty, grumpy,
shirty, snappy, sullen, tetchy, touchy
**07** crabbed, fretful, peevish, stroppy,
waspish **08** captious, petulant,
snappish **09** crotchety, impatient,
irascible, irritable, splenetic **11** bad-
tempered, quarrelsome
**12** cantankerous **13** quick-tempered,
short-tempered

## tetchy

**05** ratty **06** crusty, grumpy, shirty, touchy **07** grouchy, peevish, teachie **08** scratchy, snappish **09** crotchety, irascible, irritable **11** bad-tempered **13** short-tempered

## tête-à-tête

**03** jaw **04** chat, talk **06** confab, natter, secret **07** twasome, twosome **08** chitchat, dialogue **10** face to face **12** a quattr'occhi, confidential, conversation, heart-to-heart

## tether

**03** tie **04** bind, bond, cord, lash, lead, line, rope **05** chain, hitch, leash, tie up **06** fasten, fetter, picket, piquet, secure **07** manacle, picquet, shackle **08** restrain **09** fastening, restraint

## Teutonic

**03** Ger **04** Teut **05** Dutch **06** German **08** Germanic

## Texas

**02** TX **03** Tex

## text

**04** body, book **05** Bible, issue, point, theme, topic, verse, words **06** matter, source **07** chapter, content, passage, reading, set book, subject, wording **08** libretto, sentence, textbook **09** paragraph **10** main matter **11** boilerplate **13** subject matter

## texture

**03** web **04** feel, wale, woof **05** grain, touch, weave **06** fabric, finish, tissue **07** quality, surface, weftage **09** character, structure, texturize **10** appearance **11** composition, consistency **12** constitution

## Thailand

**01** T **03** THA

## thallium

**02** Tl

## thank

**03** owe **06** credit **07** aggrate, remercy **09** recognize **10** appreciate, be grateful **11** acknowledge **13** say thank you to

## thankful

**07** obliged, pleased **08** beholden, grateful, indebted, relieved **09** contented **12** appreciative

## thankfulness

**09** gratitude **10** obligation **12** appreciation, indebtedness

## thankless

**07** useless **09** fruitless **10** ungrateful, unrequited, unrewarded **11** unrewarding **12** unprofitable, unrecognized **13** unappreciated **14** unacknowledged

## thanks, thank you

**02** ta **05** mercy **06** cheers, credit **08** bless you, gramercy, thank you **09** gratitude **10** many thanks **11** much obliged, recognition **12** appreciation, gratefulness, thanksgiving **13** thank-offering **14** acknowledgment **15** acknowledgement
• **thanks to 05** due to **07** owing to,

through **09** because of **11** as a result of, on account of

## that

**02** as, so, yt **03** how, yon **04** such **05** which **07** because
• **that French 03** que, qui
• **that is, that's 02** dh, ie **05** id est **09** das heisst

## thatching

**04** atap, reed **05** attap

## thaw

**04** melt, warm **05** de-ice, fresh, relax **06** heat up, soften **07** defrost, liquefy **08** defreeze, dissolve, loosen up, unfreeze **09** uncongeal

## the

**01** t' **02** ye
• **the French 02** la, le **03** les
• **the German 03** das, der, die
• **the Italian 01** i **02** il, la, le
• **the Spanish 02** el, la **03** las, los

## theatre

**04** hall, shop **05** drama **06** cinema **08** the stage **09** dramatics, playhouse, theatrics, the boards **10** hippodrome, opera house **11** Thespian art **12** amphitheatre, show business **13** the footlights
*See also* **cinema**

*Theatres include:*

**03** Pit
**04** Rose, Swan
**05** Abbey, Globe, Lyric, Savoy
**06** Albery, Apollo, Donmar, Lyceum, Old Vic, Palace, Queen's
**07** Adelphi, Aldwych, Almeida, Garrick, Gielgud, Mermaid, Olivier, Phoenix
**08** Barbican, Broadway, Coliseum, Crucible, Dominion, Festival, National, Young Vic, Ziegfeld
**09** Cottesloe, Criterion, Drury Lane, Haymarket, Lyttelton, Palladium, Playhouse
**10** Royal Court
**11** Comedy Store, Duke of York's, Her Majesty's, Moulin Rouge, Royal Lyceum, Shaftesbury
**12** Covent Garden, Sadler's Wells, Theatre Royal, Winter Garden
**13** Folies Bergère, Prince of Wales, The Other Place, The Roundhouse
**14** Barbican Centre
**15** Donmar Warehouse, London Palladium

*Theatre parts include:*

**03** box, pit, set
**04** area, drop, flat, grid, loge
**05** apron, decor, flies, house, logum, spots, stage, wings
**06** border, bridge, circle, floats, floods, lights, loggia, scruto, stalls
**07** balcony, catwalk, curtain, cut drop, gallery, leg drop, rostrum, the gods, upstage
**08** backdrop, coulisse, trapdoor
**09** backstage, cyclorama, downstage, forestage, green room, mezzanine,

open stage, tormentor
**10** auditorium, footlights, fourth wall, ghost light, prompt side, proscenium
**11** drop-curtain, house lights, upper circle
**12** orchestra pit
**13** safety curtain
**14** opposite prompt, proscenium arch, revolving stage
**15** proscenium doors

*Theatre-related terms include:*

**02** BS, LX, OB, OP, PS
**03** act, cue, fée, fly, gel, rep, run, vis, yok
**04** call, cast, flat, grid, juve, loge, plot, pong, rake, tabs, wash, yock
**05** actor, ad lib, angel, aside, derig, dry up, fit-up, genre, get-in, lines, lodge, props, re-rig, scene, spike, usher
**06** baffle, chorus, corpse, critic, double, dry ice, Equity, flyman, fringe, get-out, make-up, miscue, places, prompt, review, script, walk-on
**07** actress, costume, curtain, dresser, matinee, pittite, preview, project, rhubarb, rigging, scenery, tableau, upstage, West End
**08** audience, audition, blackout, block out, Broadway, business, coulisse, dialogue, director, duologue, entr'acte, interval, libretto, overture, pass door, play-goer, producer, ring down, thespian, wardrobe, white out
**09** backlight, backstage, beginners, box office, break a leg, chaperone, curtain up, cyclorama, double act, downstage, footlight, full house, limelight, monologue, periaktos, programme, rehearsal, repertory, soliloquy, soubrette, spotlight, stage crew, stage door, stage hand, stage left, usherette, visual cue
**10** book-holder, dénouement, first night, followspot, fourth wall, get the bird, in the wings, prompt book, prompt copy, prompt desk, prompt side, stagecraft, stage right, understudy, walk-around
**11** bastard side, centre stage, curtain call, curtain time, die the death, greasepaint, house lights, iron curtain, leading lady, off-Broadway, quick change, read-through, stage fright, top one's part, wind machine
**12** breeches part, breeches role, first-nighter, front of house, intermission, jeune premier, juvenile lead, monstre sacré, principal boy, prompt corner, prompt script, stage manager, travesty role
**13** bastard prompt, curtain-raiser, curtain speech, grande vedette, jeune première, safety curtain
**14** dress rehearsal, opposite prompt, special effects
**15** genteel business, opposite bastard

See also **director**
• **theatre award** 04 Tony

**theatrical**

◇ *anagram indicator* 03 OTT 04 camp
05 showy, stagy 06 forced, scenic,
unreal 07 actorly, pompous
08 actorish, actressy, affected,
dramatic, mannered, overdone,
thespian 09 emotional 10 artificial,
histrionic, over the top 11 exaggerated,
extravagant 12 histrionical,
melodramatic, ostentatious

*Theatrical forms include:*

03 Noh
04 mime, play
05 farce, opera, revue
06 Absurd, ballet, circus, comedy,
fringe, kabuki, masque, puppet,
street
07 cabaret, Cruelty, mummery,
musical, pageant, tableau,
tragedy
08 duologue, operetta
09 burlesque, melodrama,
monologue, music hall,
pantomime
10 in-the-round
11 black comedy, kitchen-sink,
miracle play, mystery play
12 Grand Guignol, morality play,
Punch and Judy
13 fringe theatre, musical comedy,
puppet theatre, street theatre
14 comedy of menace
15 comedy of humours, comedy of
manners, legitimate drama

**Thebes**
*see* **Seven Against Thebes**

**theft**

03 job 04 blag, crib 05 fraud, heist,
steal, sting, swipe, touch 06 mainor,
rip-off, stouth, walk-in 07 larceny,
lifting, mugging, nicking, pilfery,
robbery, stealth, stick-up, swiping
08 burglary, filching, nobbling,
pinching, plagiary, rustling, stealing,
thieving 09 autocrime, pilferage,
pilfering, stouthrie, swindling
10 conversion, purloining, stoutherie,
stouthrief 11 kleptomania, shoplifting
12 embezzlement, smash-and-grab

**them**
02 'em 03 hem 04 some

**thematic**
08 notional 09 taxonomic
10 conceptual 14 classificatory

**theme**
03 peg 04 gist, idea, song, talk, text,
tune 05 essay, lemma, motif, paper,
story, topic, topos 06 burden, matter,
melody, mythos, mythus, thesis,
thread 07 burthen, essence, keynote,
o'ercome, subject, subtext
08 argument, overcome, owrecome
09 leitmotif, leitmotiv 11 composition
12 dissertation 13 subject matter

**then**
03 now, tho, too 04 also, next, soon,
syne, thus 05 after, and so 06 as well
07 besides, further 08 moreover 09 as a

result, therefore, whereupon
10 afterwards, at that time, by that
time, in addition 11 accordingly, at
that point, furthermore, in those days
12 additionally, at a later date, at that
moment, consequently, subsequently

**theocracy**
04 Zion 08 thearchy

**theologian**
02 DD 03 ThD 06 divine 09 schoolman

*Theologians include:*

03 **Eck** (Johann), **Ela** (Jean-Marc)
04 **Baur** (Ferdinand Christian), **Bede**
('the Venerable', St), **John** (of
Damascus, St), **More** (Henry), **Otto**
(Rudolf), **Paul** (St)
05 **Arius**, **Barth** (Karl), **Buber** (Martin),
**Colet** (John), **Cyril** (of Alexandria,
St), **Llull** (Ramón), **Mbiti** (John S),
**Paley** (William), **Pusey** (Edward
Bouverie), **Young** (Thomas)
06 **Alcuin**, **Anselm** (St), **Butler**
(Joseph), **Calvin** (John), **Hooker**
(Richard), **Jansen** (Cornelius),
**Jerome** (St), **Luther** (Martin),
**Mather** (Increase), **Newman** (John
Henry, Cardinal), **Ockham** (William
of), **Origen**, **Pascal** (Blaise), **Rahner**
(Karl)
07 **Abelard** (Peter), **Aquinas** (St
Thomas), **Arnauld** (Antoine),
**Bernard** (of Clairvaux, St), **Clement**
(of Alexandria), **Cyprian** (St),
**Eckhart** (Johannes), **Edwards**
(Jonathan), **Gregory** (of Nazianzus,
St), **Gregory** (of Nyssa), **Grotius**
(Hugo), **Lombard** (Peter), **Sankara**,
**Spinoza** (Baruch), **Tillich** (Paul
Johannes), **William** (of Ockham)
08 **Arminius** (Jacobus), **Berengar** (of
Tours), **Bultmann** (Rudolf Karl),
**Chalmers** (Thomas), **Cudworth**
(Ralph), **Eusebius**, **Ignatius** (of
Loyola, St), **Irenaeus** (St), **Sprenger**
(Jacob)
09 **Augustine** (St), **Bessarion** (John),
**Nagarjuna**, **Söderblom** (Nathan)
10 **Athanasius** (St), **Bellarmine** (St
Robert), **Bonhoeffer** (Dietrich),
**Duns Scotus** (John), **Macquarrie**
(John), **Rosenzweig** (Franz),
**Schweitzer** (Albert), **Swedenborg**
(Emanuel), **Tertullian**, **Weizsäcker**
(Karl Heinrich)
11 **Bonaventure** (St), **Kierkegaard**
(Sören Aabye)
12 **Justin Martyr** (St)
14 **Schleiermacher** (Friedrich)

**theological**
06 divine 09 doctrinal, religious
10 scriptural 12 hierological
14 ecclesiastical

**theology**
08 divinity 09 dogmatics 14 school-
divinity

**theorem**
04 rule 06 dictum 07 formula
09 deduction, postulate, principle,
statement 10 hypothesis 11 proposition

**theoretical**
04 pure 05 ideal 07 a priori, on paper

08 abstract, academic, armchair,
notional 10 conceptual 11 conjectural,
doctrinaire, speculative
12 hypothetical 13 suppositional

**theoretically**
07 a priori, ideally, on paper 08 in
theory 09 nominally, seemingly
10 notionally 11 in principle
12 conceptually 14 hypothetically

**theorize**
05 guess 07 suppose 08 propound
09 formulate, postulate, speculate
10 conjecture 11 hypothesize

**theory**
03 ism, law 04 idea, plan, view
05 guess 06 notion, scheme, system,
thesis 07 opinion, surmise 08 proposal
09 principle, rationale 10 assumption,
conjecture, hypothesis, philosophy
11 abstraction, postulation,
presumption, speculation, supposition

*Theories include:*

01 M
03 GUT, TOE
04 game
05 chaos
06 atomic, number, string
07 Big Bang, quantum
09 collision, Darwinism, evolution
10 panspermia, relativity
11 catastrophe
12 Grand Unified, Milankovitch
14 plate tectonics
15 butterfly effect

• **in theory** 07 a priori, ideally, on
paper 09 seemingly 10 notionally
11 in principle 12 conceptually 13 in
the abstract, theoretically
14 hypothetically

**therapeutic**
04 good 05 tonic 06 curing 07 healing
08 curative, remedial, salutary,
sanative 09 medicinal 10 beneficial,
corrective 11 restorative
12 advantageous, ameliorative, health-
giving

**therapy**
04 cure 05 tonic 06 remedy 07 healing
09 treatment 12 therapeutics

*Therapies include:*

02 OT
03 art, CST, HRT, LDT, ORT, sex
04 drug, play, zone
05 aroma, chemo, drama, group,
hydro, hypno, music, photo,
radio, reiki
06 beauty, family, Gerson, physio,
primal, psycho, retail, speech
07 electro, Gestalt, Rolfing, shiatsu
08 aversion
09 behaviour, cognitive, herbalism
10 homeopathy, osteopathy,
regression, ultrasound
11 acupressure, acupuncture,
biofeedback, homoeopathy,
irradiation, mesotherapy,
moxibustion, naturopathy,
reflexology
12 chiropractic, craniosacral,
electroshock, faith healing,

horticulture, occupational, reminiscence **13** confrontation, dream analysis, heat treatment

*See also* **psychological**

## there
**04** ecco **06** yonder

## thereabouts
**05** about **07** roughly **12** near that date **13** approximately **14** near that number

## thereafter
**02** so **04** next, upon **09** after that **10** afterwards **11** accordingly **12** subsequently **13** after that time

## therefore
**02** so **04** ergo, then, thus **05** and so, argal **06** forthy, so then **09** as a result **11** accordingly **12** consequently **13** for that reason

## thereupon
**02** so **06** withal **08** with that, with this **11** immediately

## thesaurus
**05** Roget **07** lexicon **08** synonymy, treasury, wordbook **10** dictionary, repository, storehouse, vocabulary, wordfinder **12** encyclopedia

## these
**04** thir

## thesis
**04** idea, view **05** essay, paper, theme, topic **06** theory **07** opinion, premise, subject **08** argument, position, proposal, treatise **09** monograph, statement **10** contention, hypothesis **11** composition, proposition **12** disquisition, dissertation

## thick
**03** big, fat, hub **04** daft, deep, dull, dumb, fast, full, slow, this, warm, wide **05** broad, bulky, close, dense, dippy, dopey, focus, foggy, gross, gruff, heart, heavy, husky, lumpy, midst, murky, rough, solid, soupy, stiff, stout **06** centre, chunky, creamy, croaky, filled, grouty, hoarse, marked, middle, opaque, packed, simple, smoggy, strong, stupid, turbid, unfair **07** chocker, closely, clotted, compact, crowded, foolish, muffled, obvious, rasping, teeming, thicket, thickly, throaty, unclear, viscous, woollen **08** abundant, brimming, bursting, close-set, crawling, croaking, definite, frequent, gormless, gravelly, guttural, intimate, numerous, striking, swarming **09** abounding, brainless, bristling, condensed, dim-witted, excessive, semi-solid, squabbish **10** coagulated, frequently, indistinct, noticeable, pronounced **11** chock-a-block, overflowing, substantial **12** concentrated, impenetrable **13** thick as a plank, unintelligent

## thicken
**03** gel, set **04** cake, clot, curd, jell, meal **05** upset **06** curdle, reduce **07** congeal, stiffen **08** condense, solidify **09** coagulate **10** incrassate,

inspissate **13** make more solid **15** become more solid

## thickening
**04** roux **08** clubbing **09** callosity **14** hyperkeratosis **15** atherosclerosis, middle-age spread, primitive streak

## thicket
**04** bosk, wood **05** brake, brush, copse, cover, grove, shola **06** bosket, greave, maquis, queach **07** bosquet, coppice, spinney **08** chamisal, fernshaw, reed-rand, reed-rond **09** canebrake, chaparral, salicetum **10** dead-finish **11** bramble-bush

## thickhead
**03** git, oaf **04** berk, clot, dope, dork, fool, geek, prat, twit **05** chump, dummy, dunce, idiot, moron, ninny, twerp **06** dimwit, nitwit **07** buffoon, fathead, halfwit, pinhead **08** imbecile, numskull **09** blockhead **10** nincompoop

## thick-headed
**04** dumb, slow **05** barmy, dense, dopey, loony, loopy, potty, thick **06** obtuse, stupid **07** asinine, doltish, foolish, idiotic, moronic **08** gormless **09** brainless, dim-witted, imbecilic **10** dull-witted, slow-witted **11** blockheaded, not all there **13** thick as a plank **15** slow on the uptake

## thickness
**03** bed, ply **04** band, body, bulk, coat, film, loft, seam, vein **05** layer, sheet, width **06** extent, lamina **07** breadth, density, deposit, stratum **08** diameter **09** bulkiness, closeness, solidness, viscosity **11** consistency, pachydermia **14** third dimension

## thickset
**05** beefy, bulky, burly, dense, heavy, solid, squat **06** brawny, robust, stocky, strong, sturdy **07** nuggety, squabby **08** muscular, powerful **09** well-built **12** heavily built

## thick-skinned
**05** tough **06** inured **07** callous **08** hardened **09** hard-nosed, unfeeling **10** hard-boiled, impervious **11** insensitive **12** case-hardened, invulnerable **14** pachydermatous **15** tough as old boots

## thief
**05** crook **06** magpie, nicker **07** filcher, stealer, tea leaf **08** larcener, pilferer **09** Autolycus, larcenist, plunderer **12** kleptomaniac

*Thieves and robbers include:*

**03** dip, pad
**04** bung, file, prig, Tory, wire, yegg
**05** diver, fraud, heist, kiddy, rover, sneak
**06** bandit, bulker, chummy, con man, dacoit, dakoit, dipper, hotter, ice man, latron, lifter, limmer, looter, mugger, nipper, pirate, raider, robber
**07** abactor, blagger, booster, brigand, burglar, cateran, cosh boy, footpad, hoister, ladrone,

land-rat, nobbler, nut-hook, pandoor, pandour, poacher, prigger, rustler, twoccer, whizzer, yeggman
**08** cly-faker, cutpurse, hijacker, huaquero, rapparee, river-rat, swindler
**09** area-sneak, cracksman, embezzler, fraudster, pick-purse, ram-raider, sea robber
**10** cat-burglar, gully-raker, highjacker, highwayman, horse-thief, land-pirate, man-stealer, pickpocket, roberdsman, robertsman, shoplifter, sneak thief, water thief
**11** motor-bandit, poddy-dodger, safe-breaker, safe-cracker, snatch-purse, snow-dropper, stair-dancer
**12** appropriator, baby-snatcher, cattle duffer, cattle-lifter, housebreaker, sheep-stealer, snow-gatherer
**13** highway robber
**15** resurrectionist, resurrection man

## thieve
**03** bag, lag, rob **04** blag, flog, lift, nick, pull, whip **05** cheat, filch, heist, hoist, pinch, poach, steal, swipe **06** burgle, nobble, pilfer, rip off **07** plunder, purloin, snaffle, swindle **08** abstract, embezzle, knock off, peculate **10** run off with **11** make off with **14** misappropriate

## thieving
**05** theft **06** piracy **07** crooked, larceny, lifting, mugging, nicking, pugging, robbery **08** banditry, burglary, filching, stealing, thievery **09** dishonest, furacious, larcenous, pilferage, pilfering, predatory, rapacious **10** conversion, fraudulent, peculation, plundering, ripping off **11** crookedness, knocking off, sheep-biting, shoplifting **12** embezzlement **13** light-fingered **14** sticky-fingered

## thievish
**07** crooked, furtive **08** thieving **09** dishonest, furacious, larcenous, predatory, rapacious, theftuous **10** fraudulent **13** light-fingered, tarry-fingered **14** nimble-fingered, sticky-fingered

## thin
**04** bony, fine, lame, lank, lean, poor, rare, slim, soft, trim, weak **05** faint, filmy, gaunt, gauzy, lanky, light, quiet, runny, scant, sheer, spare, wispy **06** dilute, feeble, flimsy, lessen, meagre, narrow, paltry, rarefy, reduce, refine, scanty, scarce, single, skimpy, skinny, slight, sparse, svelte, wasted, watery, weaken **07** diluted, dwindle, scraggy, scrawny, slender, spindly, tenuous, weed out **08** anorexic, decrease, delicate, diminish, gossamer, rarefied, scrannel, shrunken, skeletal, straggly, tenuious, tinkling **09** attenuate, defective, deficient, emaciated, paper-thin, scattered, untenable, wafer-thin, water down **10** attenuated, diaphanous,

## thing

inadequate, see-through, wishy-washy
**11** high-pitched, implausible,
lightweight, thin as a rake, translucent,
transparent, underweight
**12** inconclusive, unconvincing
**13** insubstantial **14** make more watery,
undernourished
• **on thin ice  06** at risk, unsafe
**08** insecure **10** in jeopardy, precarious,
vulnerable **12** open to attack

## thing

**02** it **03** act, aim, bag, job **04** baby,
bent, bias, body, deed, fact, fear, feat,
gear, idea, item, love, task, togs, tool
**05** chore, court, event, fancy, gismo,
goods, mania, point, stuff, taste, tools,
trait, waldo **06** action, affair, aspect,
attire, desire, detail, device, dinges,
doodah, entity, factor, fetish, gadget,
hang-up, horror, liking, matter, notion,
object, phobia, tackle, thingy
**07** apparel, article, baggage, clobber,
clothes, concept, council, dislike,
effects, element, episode, exploit,
feature, leaning, luggage, machine,
problem, quality, thought, whatsit
**08** activity, affinity, assembly,
aversion, clothing, creature, cup of
tea, fixation, fondness, garments, idée
fixe, incident, oddments, penchant,
property, soft spot, tendency,
thingamy, weakness **09** affection,
apparatus, attribute, condition,
doodackie, equipment, happening,
implement, mechanism, obsession,
proneness, situation, substance,
thingummy **10** attraction, belongings,
instrument, occurrence, parliament,
partiality, particular, phenomenon,
possession, preference, proceeding,
proclivity, propensity, speciality
**11** arrangement, bits and bobs,
contrivance, eventuality, inclination,
odds and ends, possessions,
undertaking, what you like
**12** appreciation, circumstance, one-
track mind, predilection,
thingummybob, thingummyjig, what's-
its-name **13** bits and pieces,
paraphernalia, preoccupation
**14** characteristic, responsibility, what-
d'you-call-it, what turns you on
• **the thing  03** hip **04** cool **06** latest,
modish, trendy **07** current, in vogue,
popular **09** in fashion, the latest **10** all
the rage **11** fashionable

## think

**04** deem, feel, hold, muse, seem
**05** brood, cense, guess, judge, opine
**06** design, esteem, expect, figure,
intend, look on, ponder, reason, recall,
reckon, regard, review **07** believe,
conceit, foresee, imagine, presume,
purpose, reflect, suppose, surmise,
thought, weigh up **08** chew over,
cogitate, conceive, conclude,
consider, envisage, estimate, meditate,
mull over, remember, ruminate
**09** calculate, cerebrate, determine,
recollect, sleep on it, take stock,
visualize **10** anticipate, assessment,
cogitation, conjecture, deliberate,
evaluation, meditation, reflection
**11** concentrate, contemplate

**12** deliberation **13** consideration,
contemplation
• **think better of  06** revise **07** rethink
**10** reconsider, think again, think twice
**11** get cold feet **13** decide not to do
• **think much of  04** rate **05** prize,
value **06** admire, esteem, reckon
**07** respect **10** set store by **13** think
highly of
• **think nothing of  13** consider usual
**14** consider normal
• **think over  06** digest, ponder
**07** weigh up **08** chew over, consider,
meditate, mull over, ruminate
**11** contemplate, reflect upon
• **think up  06** create, design, devise,
invent **07** concoct, dream up, imagine
**08** conceive, contrive **09** visualize

## thinkable

**06** likely **08** feasible, possible
**09** cogitable **10** imaginable,
reasonable, supposable
**11** conceivable

## thinker

**04** sage **05** brain **07** scholar **08** theorist
**09** intellect **10** ideologist, mastermind,
philosophe **11** philosopher
**12** theoretician

## thinking

**04** idea, view **06** theory **07** logical,
opinion, outlook, thought **08** cultured,
judgment, position, rational, sensible,
thoughts **09** appraisal, judgement,
reasoning **10** analytical, assessment,
conclusion, evaluation, meditative,
philosophy, reflective, thoughtful
**11** conclusions, intelligent
**12** excogitation, intellectual
**13** contemplative, philosophical,
sophisticated

## thin-skinned

**04** soft **06** tender, touchy **07** prickly
**08** snappish **09** irritable, sensitive
**10** vulnerable **11** easily upset,
susceptible **14** hypersensitive

## third-rate

**03** bad **04** naff, poor, poxy, ropy
**05** awful, lousy, pants, ropey
**06** crappy, crummy, shoddy
**07** botched, the pits, useless **08** inferior,
low-grade, mediocre, pathetic,
slipshod, terrible **10** low-quality **11** a
load of crap, indifferent, poor-quality,
substandard **13** cheap and nasty **14** a
load of garbage, a load of rubbish, not
up to scratch, unsatisfactory

## thirst

**03** yen **04** long, lust, want **05** crave,
yearn **06** desire, drouth, hanker,
hunger, thirst, thrust **07** aridity,
craving, drought, dryness, longing,
passion **08** appetite, keenness,
yearning **09** eagerness, hankering
**11** drouthiness, have a yen for,
parchedness, thirstiness

## thirsty

**03** dry **04** adry, arid, avid, keen
**05** dying, eager **06** greedy, hungry
**07** athirst, burning, craving, drouthy,
gasping, itching, longing, parched,
thristy **08** desirous, droughty, hydropic,

yearning **09** hankering, thirsting
**10** dehydrated

## thirteen

**04** XIII

## thirty

**03** XXX

## this

**03** hic, hoc

## Thomas

**03** Tom

## thong

**03** taw **04** band, belt, cord, lash, lore,
riem **05** strap, strip, tawse, whang
**06** Jandal® **07** latchet **08** flip-flop
**11** shoe latchet

## thorium

**02** Th

## thorn

**04** barb **05** doorn, point, prick, spike,
spine **06** needle **07** acantha, aculeus,
bristle, prickle

## thorny

**05** armed, dicey, sharp, spiky, spiny,
tough, vexed **06** barbed, briery, knotty,
sticky, tricky, trying **07** awkward,
bristly, complex, irksome, pointed,
prickly, spinose, spinous **08** delicate,
ticklish, worrying **09** acanthous,
difficult, harassing, intricate, upsetting
**10** convoluted **11** problematic,
troublesome

## thorough

**04** deep, full, good, pure **05** close,
pakka, pucka, pukka, sheer, sound,
total, utter **06** damned, entire, narrow,
proper **07** careful, in-depth, ingoing,
perfect, radical, regular, through
**08** absolute, complete, rigorous,
sweeping **09** downright, efficient,
extensive, intensive, out-and-out,
searching **10** exhaustive, methodical,
meticulous, resounding, scrupulous,
widespread **11** down-the-line,
painstaking, unmitigated, unqualified
**12** all-embracing, all-inclusive
**13** comprehensive, conscientious,
thoroughgoing

## thoroughbred

**07** blooded, pur sang **08** pedigree,
pure-bred **09** pedigreed, pure-blood
**11** full-blooded, pure-blooded **12** high-
spirited

## thoroughfare

**03** way **04** road **05** corso **06** access,
avenue, street **07** highway, passage,
roadway **08** broadway, motorway,
turnpike **09** boulevard, concourse
**10** passageway **12** king's highway

## thoroughgoing

**04** deep, full, pure **05** sheer, total, utter
**06** entire, strict **07** careful, in-depth,
perfect **08** absolute, complete, deep-
dyed, outright, rigorous, sweeping
**09** downright, extensive, intensive,
out-and-out **10** exhaustive,
methodical, meticulous, scrupulous,
widespread **11** painstaking,
unmitigated, unqualified **12** all-

**thoroughly**
embracing, all-inclusive
**13** comprehensive **14** uncompromising

**thoroughly**
**02** up **03** out **04** well **05** à fond, fully, good-o, quite **06** good-oh, mortal **07** soundly, totally, utterly **08** entirely, even-down **09** carefully, downright, every inch, inside out, perfectly, throughly **10** absolutely, completely, sweepingly **11** assiduously, back to front, efficiently, intensively **12** exhaustively, meticulously, scrupulously, well and truly **13** painstakingly, root and branch **15** comprehensively, conscientiously

**those**
**03** tho **04** thae, them, they

**though**
**02** if **03** but, yet **05** still, while **06** even if, even so **07** granted, however **08** allowing, although **09** admitting **10** all the same, for all that **11** nonetheless **12** nevertheless **15** notwithstanding

**thought**
**03** aim **04** care, heed, hint, hope, idea, idée, mind, muse, plan, view **05** dream, fancy, grief, study, think, touch, trace **06** belief, design, musing, notion, pensée, reason, regard, theory **07** anxiety, conceit, concept, concern, feeling, gesture, opinion, purpose **08** judgment, kindness, prospect, scrutiny, sympathy, thinking **09** appraisal, attention, intention, judgement, pondering, reasoning **10** aspiration, assessment, cogitation, compassion, conception, conclusion, conviction, estimation, meditation, reflection, resolution, rumination, solicitude, tenderness **11** cerebration, expectation, point of view **12** anticipation, deliberation **13** consciousness, consideration, contemplation, introspection **14** thoughtfulness **15** considerateness

**thoughtful**
**04** deep, kind, wary **05** quiet **06** caring, dreamy, solemn, tender **07** careful, heedful, helpful, mindful, pensive, prudent, serious, wistful **08** absorbed, cautious, profound, sobering, studious, thinking **09** attentive, unselfish **10** abstracted, cogitative, conceitful, methodical, pensieroso, reflective, solicitous **11** considerate, sympathetic **13** compassionate, considerative, contemplative, in a brown study, introspective, lost in thought

**thoughtfully**
**06** deeply **07** quietly **08** dreamily **09** carefully, helpfully, mindfully, pensively, seriously, wistfully **10** cautiously, profoundly **11** unselfishly **12** methodically, reflectively **13** considerately **15** compassionately, contemplatively, introspectively, sympathetically

**thoughtless**
**04** rash, rude, vain **05** hasty, silly **06** remiss, stupid, unkind, unwise **07** étourdi, foolish, selfish **08** carefree,

careless, étourdie, heedless, impolite, mindless, reckless, tactless, uncaring **09** blindfold, frivolous, imprudent, negligent, unfeeling **10** ill-advised, incogitant, indiscreet, unthinking, unweighing **11** giddy-headed, improvident, inattentive, insensitive, light-headed, precipitate **12** absent-minded, undiplomatic **13** ill-considered, inconsiderate

**thoughtlessly**
**06** rashly, rudely **08** stupidly **09** foolishly **10** carelessly, impolitely, recklessly, tactlessly **11** unfeelingly **12** indiscreetly **13** inattentively, insensitively **15** inconsiderately

**thousand**
**01** G, K, M **04** thou **05** grand, mille **07** chiliad **09** millenary

**thrall**
**04** grip, serf **05** hands, power, slave **07** bondage, control, enslave, serfdom, slavery **08** clutches, enslaved, thraldom **09** servitude, vassalage **10** subjection **11** enslavement, subjugation

**thrash**
**02** do **03** hit, lam, pay, tan **04** beat, belt, cane, drub, flog, jerk, lace, lash, lick, rout, rush, sock, tank, toss, trim, whap, whip, whop **05** bless, cream, crush, dress, flail, party, paste, pound, quilt, smoke, spank, swish, targe, towel, whack, whale **06** beat up, defeat, donder, hammer, larrup, lather, punish, raddle, thresh, wallop, writhe **07** clobber, lambast, lay into, leather, scourge, swaddle, trounce **08** beat up on, demolish, lambaste, vanquish, work over **09** dress down, horsewhip, marmelize, overwhelm, pulverize, slaughter, surcingle **11** walk all over **13** have the edge on
• **thrash out** **06** debate, settle **07** discuss, hash out, resolve **09** hammer out, negotiate **11** clear the air

**thrashing**
**04** rout **05** doing, laldy **06** caning, defeat, hiding, laldie, wiping **07** beating, belting, lamming, lashing, licking, pasting, tanking, tanning, whaling **08** crushing, dressing, drubbing, flogging, quilting, strap-oil, whacking, whipping, whopping **09** hammering, strapping, towelling, trouncing, walloping **10** clobbering, leathering, punishment **12** chastisement, dressing-down

**thread**
**03** end **04** ease, inch, line, move, pass, plot, push, silk, wind, yarn **05** braid, drift, fibre, Lurex®, motif, seton, shoot, strip, tenor, theme, thrid, thrum, twine, twist, weave **06** course, lingel, lingle, needle, strand, streak, string, suture **07** meander, subject, worsted **08** filament **09** direction, storyline **14** train of thought

**threadbare**
**03** old **04** bare, poor, worn **05** corny, stale, stock, tatty, tired, trite **06** frayed,

meagre, ragged, shabby **07** napless, scruffy, worn-out **08** overused, overworn, tattered, well-worn **09** hackneyed, moth-eaten **11** commonplace, stereotyped **12** cliché-ridden

**threat**
**04** omen, risk **05** peril, stick **06** danger, hazard, menace **07** portent, presage, war drum, warning **08** big stick **09** blackmail, ultimatum **10** foreboding **11** commination **12** brutum fulmen, denunciation **14** enemy at the door

**threaten**
**03** cow, vow **04** burn, loom, lour, mint, warn **05** augur, bully, flank, shore **06** extort, impend, lean on, loom up, menace, scorch **07** imperil, portend, presage, scowder, warn off **08** approach, browbeat, endanger, forebode, hang over, look like, scouther, scowther **09** blackmail, comminate, terrorize **10** be imminent, foreshadow, intimidate, jeopardize, pressurize, push around **11** lift a hand to **13** be in the offing **14** lift your hand to, put the screws on

**threatening**
**04** grim, ugly **05** lurid, nasty, shore **07** bravado, looming, ominous, warning **08** frowning, imminent, menacing, minatory, sinister **09** impending, minacious **10** broodiness, cautionary, forbidding, foreboding **11** commination, comminative **12** denunciatory, inauspicious, intimidatory
• **threatening character** **04** omen

**three**
**03** III, ter-, tri- **04** tern, tray, trey, trio **05** leash, prial, triad **06** parial **07** pairial, triplet **09** pair-royal
• **Three Wise Men** see **wise man** under **wise**

**threesome**
**04** trio **05** triad **06** triple, triune, troika **07** trilogy, trinity, triplet **08** triptych **11** triumvirate

**thresh**
**03** hit **04** flog, jerk, rush, toss **05** flail, swish **06** thrash, writhe

**threshold**
**04** cill, dawn, door, sill **05** brink, entry, limen, start, verge **06** outset **07** doorway, opening **08** door-sill, doorstep, entrance **09** beginning, inception **12** commencement **13** starting-point

**thrice**
see **three**

**thrift**
**04** gain **06** saving **07** economy, savings, sea pink **08** prudence, sea grass **09** frugality, husbandry, parsimony **10** prosperity, providence **11** carefulness **12** conservation **14** sea gillyflower

**thriftless**
**06** lavish **08** prodigal, wasteful **09** imprudent, unthrifty **10** profligate

**11** dissipative, extravagant, improvident, spendthrift

**thrifty**
**04** wary **05** fendy **06** frugal, saving
**07** careful, prudent, sparing
**09** husbandly, provident
**10** conserving, economical, prosperous **12** parsimonious

**thrill**
**03** gas, joy **04** bang, buzz, dirl, glow, kick, move, stir **05** flush, pulse, rouse, shake, thirl, throb **06** arouse, charge, dindle, dinnle, excite, pierce, quiver, shiver, tingle, tremor **07** delight, feeling, flutter, frisson, pulsate, shudder, tremble, vibrate **08** pleasure **09** adventure, electrify, galvanize, sensation, stimulate, vibration **10** excitement, exhilarate, the shivers **11** give a buzz to, give a kick to, stimulation

**thrilling**
**07** quaking, rousing, shaking, vibrant **08** electric, exciting, gripping, riveting, stirring, tinglish **09** shivering, trembling, vibrating **10** rip-roaring, shuddering **11** hair-raising, sensational, stimulating **12** action-packed, electrifying, exhilarating, soul-stirring **13** heart-stirring

**thrive**
**02** do **04** boom, gain, grow, thee **05** bloom **06** come on, do well, profit **07** advance, blossom, burgeon, develop, prosper, succeed **08** flourish, increase **11** make headway **12** make progress

**thriving**
**04** well **07** booming, growing, healthy, wealthy **08** affluent, blooming **10** blossoming, burgeoning, developing, prosperous, successful **11** comfortable, flourishing

**throat**
**04** crag, craw **05** gorge, halse, hause, hawse **06** fauces, gullet **07** pharynx, swallow, trachea, weasand **08** prunella, thrapple, thropple, throttle, windpipe **10** oesophagus, the Red Lane
• **part of throat** **04** gula

**throaty**
**03** low **04** deep **05** gruff, husky, thick **06** hoarse **07** rasping, raucous **08** croaking, guttural **12** full-throated

**throb**
◊ *anagram indicator* **04** beat, drum, jump, pant, quop **05** pound, pulse, thump **06** stound, stownd, tingle **07** pulsate, vibrate **08** drumming, pounding, thumping **09** heartbeat, palpitate, pulsation, vibration **11** palpitation

**throe**
**03** fit **04** pain, pang, stab **05** agony, spasm, thraw **07** anguish, seizure, torture, travail **08** distress, paroxysm **09** deid-thraw, suffering **10** convulsion
• **in the throes of** **08** busy with **12** in the midst of **13** in the middle of,

wrestling with **14** in the process of, struggling with **15** preoccupied with

**thrombosis**
**03** DVT **08** apoplexy, coronary **09** blood clot **11** heart attack

**throne**
**03** see **04** gadi, seat **05** exalt, siege, stool **07** tribune **08** cathedra, enthrone, kingship, lavatory **09** mercy-seat **12** bed of justice
*See also* **toilet**

**throng**
**03** jam, mob **04** bevy, busy, cram, fill, herd, host, mass, pack **05** bunch, crowd, crush, flock, horde, press, swarm **06** jostle, preace, prease, thrang **07** besiege, crowded, preasse **08** converge, crowding, intimate **09** multitude **10** assemblage, congregate, mill around **12** congregation, grex venalium

**throttle**
**03** gag, gun **05** check, choke, scrag **06** keep in, stifle **07** inhibit, silence, smother **08** hold back, restrain, strangle, suppress, thrapple, thropple, wiredraw **09** suffocate **10** asphyxiate **11** accelerator, strangulate

**through**
**02** by, in **03** per, tra-, via **04** done, yond, yont **05** among, clear, due to, ended, fully, using **06** across, direct, during **07** between, by way of, clear of, express, non-stop, owing to, totally **08** entirely, finished, thanks to **09** because of, by means of, completed, connected, throughly **10** by virtue of, completely, terminated, thoroughly, throughout, to the end of **11** as a result of, on account of **12** continuously **13** until the end of, with the help of **15** all the way across, uninterruptedly, without a break in
• **through and through** **05** fully **06** wholly **07** totally, utterly **08** entirely, to pieces **09** to the core **10** altogether, completely, thoroughly **11** all to pieces **12** unreservedly **13** to the backbone **14** in every respect **15** from top to bottom

**throughout**
**04** over **05** along **06** during, widely **07** all over **08** all round **09** up and down **10** all through, completely, everywhere, in all parts **11** extensively, in every part **12** in the whole of, ubiquitously **13** in every part of, in the course of

**throughput**
**05** yield **06** fruits, output, return **07** harvest, outturn, product, turnout **10** production **11** manufacture **12** productivity

**throw**
◊ *anagram indicator* **02** go **03** hip, lob, peg, put, shy, wap **04** blow, bung, cast, dash, emit, faze, fell, flip, give, host, hurl, lose, puck, putt, scat, send, shed, shot, toss, turn, whap, whop, work, yerk **05** chuck, ditch, fling, floor, force, heave, lay on, pitch, put on, skatt,

sling, spang, spasm, spill, upset, whang, while **06** baffle, bemuse, direct, launch, propel, purler, put out, rattle, unseat, upcast, wheech, wuther **07** arrange, confuse, disturb, execute, give off, operate, perform, perplex, produce, project, radiate, unhorse, whither **08** astonish, catapult, confound, dislodge, jaculate, occasion, organize, overturn, paroxysm, surprise, switch on, unsaddle **09** bring down, discomfit, dumbfound, prostrate **10** disconcert **11** cause to fall, move quickly
*See also* **wrestling**
• **throw away** **04** blow, dump, lose **05** ditch, scrap, waste **06** reject **07** discard **08** chuck out, get rid of, jettison, squander, throw out **09** chuck away, dispose of **11** fritter away **12** dispense with
• **throw headlong** **04** purl
• **throw off** **04** cast, drop, shed **05** elude **06** divest **07** abandon, cast off, discard, discuss **08** get rid of, jettison, shake off **10** escape from
• **throw out** **04** cast, dump, emit **05** ditch, eject, evict, expel, exude, fling, scrap **06** reject, unseat **07** bring up, diffuse, discard, dismiss, emanate, give off, mention, produce, project, radiate, refer to, send out, turf out, turn out **08** distance, distract, jettison, point out, turn down **09** introduce, throw away **10** disconcert, speak about **12** dispense with
• **throw over** **04** drop, jilt, quit **05** chuck, leave **06** desert, reject **07** abandon, discard, forsake **10** finish with
• **throw up** **03** gag **04** barf, jack, puke, quit, spew, toss **05** heave, leave, retch, vomit **06** cast up, give up, jack in, pack in, resign, reveal, sick up **07** abandon, bring up, chuck in, chuck up, chunder, fetch up, upchuck **08** disgorge, renounce **10** relinquish **11** regurgitate

**throwaway**
**05** cheap **06** casual **07** offhand, passing **08** careless **10** disposable, expendable, undramatic, unemphatic **13** biodegradable, non-returnable

**throwback**
**06** return **07** setback **09** reversion **10** taking back **11** restoration **13** reinstatement, retrogression

**thrush**
**04** chat **05** mavis, sprue, veery **06** missel, sylvia, Turdus **07** antbird, redwing, wagtail **08** throstle **09** fieldfare, olive-back, ring ouzel, solitaire, stormcock **10** bush-shrike, missel-bird **12** throstle-cock

**thrust**
**03** dig, jab, jam, pop, put, ram, ren, rin, run **04** bear, butt, chop, dash, foin, gist, poke, pote, prod, prog, push, rash, side, sock, stab, stap, stop, tilt, urge **05** crowd, drift, drive, foist, force, impel, lunge, pitch, poach, point,

ower, press, shove, stick, stuck,
enor, theme, wedge **06** burden,
mpose, motive, muscle, muzzle,
ierce, plunge, potche, propel, saddle,
hirst **07** aventre, essence, impetus,
mpulse, inflict, intrude, message,
hrutch **08** encumber, momentum,
ressure, protrude **09** have-at-him,
enetrate, substance **10** imbroccata
1 pertinacity **13** determination

**hrustplane**
4 sole

**hud**
4 bang, bash, beat, dump, plod,
vham **05** clonk, clump, clunk, crash,
lump, knock, smack, thump
6 bounce, wallop **07** thunder

**hug**
4 goon **05** rough, tough, yobbo
6 bandit, goonda, killer, mugger,
obber, thuggo, tsotsi **07** cosh boy,
orilla, hoodlum, ruffian, villain
8 assassin, gangster, hooligan,
nurderer, plug-ugly **09** cut-throat,
hansigar, roughneck

**huggery**
5 abuse **06** murder **07** killing
8 atrocity, butchery, foul play,
violence **09** brutality, vandalism
0 inhumanity **11** hooliganism,
viciousness

**hulium**
2 Tm

**humb**
4 inch **06** pollex
• **thumb through** **04** scan, skim
6 peruse **08** glance at **11** flip through,
eaf through **12** flick through **13** browse
hrough

**humbnail**
5 brief, pithy, quick, short, small
7 compact, concise **08** succinct
9 miniature

**humbs-down**
2 no **06** rebuff **07** refusal **08** negation,
urn down **09** rejection **11** disapproval

**humbs-up**
2 OK **03** yes **07** go-ahead **08** approval,
sanction **10** acceptance, green light
11 affirmation **13** encouragement

**hump**
3 box, cob, dad, dod, hit, rap **04** bang,
beat, blow, bonk, bump, cuff, daud,
dawd, ding, dong, dump, dunt, lamp,
paik, slap, thud, tund, whap, whop
5 clout, clunk, crash, knock, pound,
punch, smack, souse, throb, whack
6 batter, hammer, pummel, strike,
hrash, thwack, wallop **07** bethump,
pulsate, trounce **09** palpitate

**thumping**
3 big **04** huge, mega, very **05** great
6 highly, really, severe **07** extreme,
greatly, immense, intense, mammoth,
massive, titanic **08** colossal, enormous,
gigantic, severely, terrific, towering,
whopping **09** excessive, extremely,
intensely, seriously, swingeing,
unusually **10** exorbitant, gargantuan,
impressive, monumental, remarkably,

thundering, tremendous
**12** tremendously

**thunder**
**03** cry **04** bang, bawl, boom, clap,
howl, peal, roar, roll, yell **05** blast,
crack, crash, shout **06** bellow, holler,
rumble, scream, shriek **07** clamour,
foulder, resound **08** crashing, intonate,
outburst **09** explosion, fulminate,
upthunder **11** reverberate
**13** reverberation **14** raise your voice

**thundering**
**04** very **05** great **06** really, tonant
**07** greatly **08** enormous, severely
**09** excessive, extremely, intensely,
unusually **10** altitonant, foudroyant,
monumental, remarkable, tremendous
**11** unmitigated

**thunderous**
**04** loud **05** noisy **07** booming, roaring
**08** rumbling **09** deafening
**10** resounding, tumultuous **12** ear-
splitting **13** reverberating

**thunderstruck**
**05** agape, dazed **06** aghast, amazed
**07** floored, shocked, stunned
**09** astounded, flummoxed, paralysed,
petrified, staggered **10** astonished,
bowled over, nonplussed
**11** dumbfounded, open-mouthed
**12** wonder-struck **13** flabbergasted,
knocked for six **14** wonder-stricken

**Thursday**
**02** Th **03** Thu **04** Thur **05** Thurs

**thus**
**02** so **04** ergo, then **05** hence **08** like
this **09** as follows, in this way, therefore
**11** accordingly **12** consequently,
frankincense
• **thus far** **05** so far **07** up to now
**08** until now **09** up till now **13** up to this
point **14** up to the present

**thwack**
**03** hit **04** bash, beat, blow, cuff, flog,
slap **05** clout, smack, thump, whack
**06** buffet, strike, wallop

**thwart**
**03** pip **04** balk, foil, nark, stop **05** baulk,
block, check, crimp, cross, spite,
stimy, thraw **06** across, baffle, banjax,
defeat, hamper, hinder, hogtie,
impede, nobble, oppose, stimie,
stymie **07** adverse, athwart, pre-empt,
prevent, snooker, stonker **08** conflict,
obstruct, perverse, traverse
**09** crosswise, forestall, frustrate,
hindrance **10** transverse **11** frustration
**12** cross-grained **13** put the skids on

**tic**
**04** jerk **05** spasm **06** twitch **13** tic
douloureux

**tick**
**02** mo **03** dot, jar, pat, sec, tap **04** beat,
line, mark, tock, work, worm **05** check,
click, flash, jiffy, tally, trice, trust
**06** choose, credit, minute, moment,
second, select, stroke, whimsy
**07** instant **08** indicate, tick-tock
**09** twinkling **10** crib-biting
• **tick off** **04** mark, pick **05** check,

chide, prick, scold **06** bounce, carpet,
rebuke, see off, select **07** bawl out,
catch it, chew out, reprove, rollick,
rouse on, tell off, upbraid **08** call
down, check off, indicate, reproach
**09** dress down, go crook at, go crook
on, pull apart, reprimand, take apart
**10** go to town on **13** tear off a strip
**14** throw the book at **15** give someone
hell, put a tick against

**ticker**
**05** clock, heart, watch **08** examiner

**ticket**
**03** tag **04** card, chit, pass, slip, stub
**05** carte, check, label, token **06** ballot,
coupon, docket, permit, return
**07** licence, sticker, voucher, warrant
**09** pass-check **11** certificate,
counterfoil **12** lunch voucher
**13** authorization **15** luncheon voucher
• **ticket seller** **04** tout

**tickle**
**04** beat, nice **05** amuse, touch
**06** divert, excite, kittle, please, stroke,
thrill, tingle **07** delight, gratify, perplex
**08** insecure, interest, ticklish, unstable
**09** entertain, stimulate, titillate

**ticklish**
**04** nice **05** dodgy, risky **06** kittly,
knotty, subtle, thorny, touchy, tricky
**07** awkward, trickle **08** critical,
delicate, unchancy, unstable
**09** difficult, hazardous, sensitive
**10** precarious **11** problematic

**tiddly**
*see* **drunk**

**tide**
**03** ebb, ren, rin, run, sea **04** flow, flux,
neap, tied, time **05** drift, flood, tenor,
trend, water **06** course, happen,
season, spring, stream **07** current
**08** festival, movement, sea-water,
tendency **09** direction **10** rising tide
**11** opportunity
• **sudden rise of tide** **04** bore, eger
**05** eagre
• **tide over** **03** aid **04** help **06** assist
**07** help out, sustain **09** keep going
**10** see through **11** help through

**tidily**
**06** just so, neatly **07** in order, in place,
orderly, smartly **12** immaculately,
methodically **14** systematically

**tidings**
**03** gen **04** dope, news, word **06** advice,
report **07** message **08** bulletin
**09** greetings **11** information
**12** intelligence **13** communication

**tidy**
◇ *anagram indicator* **02** do **03** red **04** fair,
good, neat, redd, trim **05** ample, clean,
groom, kempt, large, order, plump,
primp, slick, smart, spick **06** comely,
fettle, neaten, redd up, spruce
**07** arrange, band-box, brush up, clean
up, clear up, in order, ordered,
orderly, shapely, sizable, smarten,
tiddley **08** clear out, generous,
sizeable, spruce up, well-kept
**09** declutter, efficient, organized,
shipshape **10** immaculate, methodical,

seasonable, square away, straighten, systematic **11** respectable, substantial, uncluttered, well-groomed, well-ordered **12** businesslike, considerable, spick-and-span, straighten up **13** clear the decks, straighten out

## tie

**03** fix **04** band, bind, bond, clip, curb, draw, duty, join, knot, lace, lash, link, moor, rope, tape **05** chain, cramp, limit, strap, unite **06** attach, be even, copula, couple, fasten, hamper, hinder, impede, oblige, ribbon, secure, tether **07** be equal, confine, confirm, connect, kinship, liaison, necktie, shackle **08** dead heat, deadlock, ligature, restrain, restrict **09** constrain, fastening, hindrance, restraint, stalemate **10** allegiance, commitment, connection, constraint, friendship, limitation, obligation **11** affiliation, be all square, restriction **12** relationship **13** be neck and neck

*Ties include:*

**03** bow
**04** bolo, neck
**05** ascot, dicky, stock
**06** clip-on, cravat, dickey, dickie, kipper, string
**07** overlay, owrelay, soubise
**08** bootlace, kerchief
**09** neckcloth, solitaire, steenkirk, waterfall
**10** tawdry lace
**11** neckerchief

- **tie down**   **03** fix **05** limit
**06** hamper, hinder **07** confine
**08** restrain, restrict **09** constrain
- **tied up**   **04** busy
- **tie in with**   **08** relate to **09** agree with, fit in with **13** correlate with **15** be connected with
- **tie together**   **04** knit **05** fagot **06** faggot
- **tie up**   **04** bind, do up, lash, moor, rope, seal **05** cable, chain, truss **06** attach, bail up, commit, engage, fasten, invest, ligate, occupy, secure, settle, string, tether, wind up, wrap up **07** connect, engross, Gordian, reserve **08** conclude, finalize, keep busy, restrain **09** terminate **11** spread-eagle **15** make unavailable

## tie-in

**04** link **05** tie-up **06** hook-up **07** liaison **08** relation **10** connection **11** affiliation, association **12** co-ordination, relationship

## tier

**03** row **04** band, bank, belt, deck, line, rank, tire, zone **05** floor, layer, level, stage, story **06** gradin, storey **07** echelon, gradine, stratum **09** bleachers

## tie-up

**04** bond, link **05** tie-in **07** analogy, mooring **08** alliance, parallel, relation **09** reference **10** connection, stand-still **11** association, correlation **12** entanglement, relationship **13** interrelation **14** correspondence

## tiff

**03** pet, row, sip **04** dram, huff, miff, sour, spat, sulk **05** dress, drink, lunch, scrap, set-to, stale, words **06** barney, dust-up, temper **07** dispute, quarrel, tantrum **08** squabble, trick out **09** ill-humour **10** difference, falling-out **12** disagreement

## tiger

**04** puma **06** jaguar **07** leopard, stripes **08** man-eater **11** Machaerodus, Machairodus

## tight

◇ *anagram indicator* **04** even, fast, firm, hard, mean, near, neat, pang, snug, taut, trig, trim **05** close, dodgy, drunk, fixed, harsh, merry, rigid, stiff, tense, tipsy, tough **06** at once, narrow, scanty, scarce, sealed, secure, severe, stingy, stoned, strict, tiddly, tricky **07** awkward, compact, concise, cramped, legless, limited, miserly, precise, sloshed, smashed, soundly, sozzled **06** airtight, clenched, delicate, hermetic, promptly, rigorous, strained, tanked up **09** competent, dangerous, difficult, niggardly, not enough, plastered, skin-tight, stretched, stringent, too little, well-oiled **10** compressed, hard-fought, impervious, inadequate, inflexible, restricted, soundproof, watertight **11** constricted, intoxicated, neck and neck, problematic, tight-fisted, well-matched **12** close-fitting, impenetrable, insufficient, parsimonious **13** evenly matched, figure-hugging, in short supply, penny-pinching

## tighten

**03** fix **04** swig **05** brace, cinch, close, cramp, crush, screw, swift, tense **06** beef up, fasten, firm up, narrow, pull up, secure, strait, take in, tauten, wind up **07** squeeze, stiffen, stretch **08** heighten, increase, make fast, restrain, rigidify, straiten **09** constrict, pull tight, toughen up **10** constringe, strengthen **12** make stricter

## tight-fisted

**04** mean **05** mingy, tight **06** stingy **07** miserly, sparing **08** grasping **09** niggardly **10** fast-handed **12** parsimonious **13** penny-pinching

## tight-lipped

**03** mum **04** mute **05** quiet **06** silent **08** reserved, reticent, taciturn **09** secretive **11** close-lipped **12** close-mouthed **13** unforthcoming **15** uncommunicative

## till

**02** to **03** dig, ear, ere, set **04** EPOS, farm, up to, work **05** peter, shale, until **06** plough **07** cash box, through, towards **08** checkout, rotavate, rotovate **09** cultivate **10** all through, cash drawer **11** boulder clay **12** cash register **13** up to the time of

## tilt

**03** hut, tip **04** bank, cant, cock, duel, heel, just, kant, lean, list, peak, ride, rock, rush, spar, tent, toss, trip

**05** angle, clash, cover, fight, joust, pitch, slant, slope **06** attack, awning, camber, careen, charge, combat, jostle, justle, thrust **07** contend, contest, dispute, incline **08** attitude, heel over, tilt yard **09** encounter, pas d'armes **10** tournament **11** inclination
- **at full tilt**   **06** all out **07** flat out **08** very fast **10** at full pelt, at top speed **11** at full blast, at full speed, very quickly **13** with full force

## timber

**03** log, rib **04** balk, beam, lath, pole, rung, spar, tree, wale, wood **05** baulk, board, build, karri, maple, plank, trees **06** forest, lumber, wooden **07** bunting, chesnut, templet **08** chestnut, stumpage, template, woodland **09** beechwood, sapodilla, unmusical **10** afrormosia, swing-stock **11** palmyra wood

*See also* **tree; wood**
- **measurement of timber**   *see* **measurement of wood** *under* **wood**
- **timber carrier**   **04** gill, jill

## timbre

**04** ring, tone **05** clang, color, klang, sound **06** colour, tamber **07** quality **08** tonality **09** resonance **10** klangfarbe, tone colour **12** voice quality

## time

**01** t **03** age, fix, set **04** aeon, beat, date, life, mora, peak, sith, span, term, tide **05** clock, count, meter, metre, point, space, spell, stage, tempo, while **06** adjust, heyday, rhythm **07** arrange, control, measure, session, stretch **08** duration, instance, interval, juncture, lifespan, occasion, regulate, schedule **09** calculate, programme, timetable **15** fourth dimension

*Times and periods of time include:*

**02** am, pm
**03** age, day, eon, era, min
**04** dawn, dusk, fall, hour, morn, noon, week, year
**05** epoch, month, night, sun-up, today
**06** autumn, decade, midday, minute, moment, morrow, period, season, second, spring, summer, sunset, winter
**07** bedtime, century, chiliad, daytime, evening, instant, midweek, morning, quarter, sunrise, teatime, tonight, weekday, weekend
**08** eternity, high noon, lifetime, tomorrow, twilight
**09** afternoon, decennium, fortnight, light-year, midsummer, nightfall, night-time
**10** generation, millennium, nanosecond, yesteryear
**11** long weekend, microsecond, millisecond
**12** quinquennium
**13** the early hours, wee small hours

*Time zones include:*

**02** AT, CT, ET, MT, PT
**03** AST, BST, CET, CST, EET, EST,

GMT, HST, MST, PST, WET **04** AKST, CYST, HAST, WAST, WEST **08** zulu time **10** Alaska Time **11** Central Time, Eastern Time, Pacific Time **12** Atlantic Time, Mountain Time **13** Greenwich Time

*See also* **geology**
• **after expected time** **04** late
• **ahead of time** **05** ahead, early **06** sooner **07** earlier, in front, up front **09** in advance **10** beforehand, previously
• **ahead of your time** **03** new **05** novel **07** radical **10** avant-garde, innovative **11** progressive **12** experimental **13** revolutionary
• **all the time** **05** among **06** always **07** forever, nonstop **08** all along **10** constantly **11** continually, incessantly, perpetually **12** continuously, interminably **15** twenty-four-seven
• **a long time** **03** eon, era **04** aeon, ages **05** years, yonks **07** decades, dog's age **08** eternity **09** centuries, millennia **11** generations **12** donkey's years **14** a week of Sundays **15** a month of Sundays
• **at all times** **03** e'er **04** ever **12** early and late
• **at any time** **03** e'er **04** ever, once, onst **07** anytime
• **at one time** **04** once **07** long ago **08** formerly **10** at one point, previously **11** in times past **14** simultaneously
• **at the proper time** **04** duly
• **at the right time** **03** pat
• **at the same time** **03** but, yet **04** then **05** still **06** anyway, at once, even so **07** however **08** meantime, together **09** meanwhile **10** for all that, in parallel **11** all together, nonetheless **12** concurrently, nevertheless **14** simultaneously **15** in the same breath, notwithstanding
• **at times** **06** whiles **08** off and on, on and off **09** sometimes **10** now and then **11** now and again, on occasions **12** every so often, occasionally **14** from time to time
• **behind the times** **03** old **04** past **05** dated **06** old hat **08** obsolete **09** out of date **10** fuddy-duddy, oldfangled **11** god-forsaken **12** god-forgotten, old-fashioned, out of fashion **13** unfashionable
• **behind time** **04** late **05** tardy **06** behind **07** delayed, overdue **10** unpunctual **14** behind schedule
• **brief space of time** **02** mo **03** bit, sec, wee
• **common time** **01** C
• **fit time** **03** tid
• **former times** **03** eld **04** yore
• **for the time being** **06** for now, pro tem **07** just now **08** meantime, right now **09** at present, meanwhile, presently **10** pro tempore **11** at the

moment, temporarily **12** for the moment **13** for the present, in the meantime
• **from time to time** **07** at times **09** sometimes **10** now and then, on occasion **11** ever and anon, now and again, still and end **12** every so often, occasionally, once in a while, periodically, sporadically, still and anon **13** spasmodically **14** intermittently **15** every now and then
• **in good time** **05** early **06** indeed, on time, timely, timous **07** betimes, timeous **08** timously **09** timeously **10** punctually **11** ahead of time **14** bright and early **15** ahead of schedule, with time to spare
• **in time** **06** on time **10** eventually, not too late, punctually **11** early enough
• **on time** **05** sharp **06** bang on, dead on, spot on, spot-on **07** exactly **08** on the dot, promptly, punctual **09** precisely **10** on schedule, punctually
• **opportune time** **04** seal, seel, siel, sele
• **play for time** **05** delay, stall **08** hang fire, hesitate **09** stonewall, temporize **10** filibuster **12** drag your feet **13** procrastinate
• **taking extra time** **04** lean
• **time after time** **05** often **09** many times **10** frequently, repeatedly **11** recurrently **12** time and again **13** again and again **15** on many occasions

**time-honoured**
**03** old **05** fixed, usual **06** age-old **07** ancient **08** historic **09** customary, venerable **10** accustomed **11** established, traditional **12** conventional **15** long-established

**timeless**
**07** abiding, ageless, endless, eternal, lasting **08** enduring, ill-timed, immortal, unending, untimely **09** deathless, immutable, permanent, premature **10** changeless, unchanging **11** everlasting **12** imperishable **14** indestructible

**timely**
**04** soon **05** early **06** prompt **08** punctual, suitable, temporal **09** opportune, well-timed **10** convenient, felicitous, propitious, seasonable, tempestive **11** appropriate **14** at the right time

**times**
**01** X

**timetable**
**03** fix, set **04** list, rota **05** diary, set up **06** agenda, roster **07** arrange, diarize, listing **08** calendar, schedule **09** programme **10** curriculum

**time-worn**
**03** old **04** aged, worn **05** dated, hoary, lined, passé, rusty, stale, stock, tired, trite **06** ragged, ruined, shabby

**07** ancient, cliché'd, outworn, rundown, worn out **08** bromidic, clichéed, decrepit, dog-eared, well-worn, wrinkled **09** hackneyed, out of date, weathered **10** broken-down, threadbare

**timid**
**03** shy **05** cissy, pavid, wimpy **06** afraid, modest, mousey, scared, yellow **07** bashful, chicken, fearful, gutless, nervous, wimpish **08** cowardly, retiring, timorous **09** shrinking, spineless **10** frightened, hen-hearted, irresolute, meticulous **11** lily-livered **12** apprehensive, faint-hearted **13** pigeon-hearted, pusillanimous **14** chicken-hearted, chicken-livered

**timidity**
**04** fear **07** shyness **09** cowardice **11** bashfulness, fearfulness **13** pusillanimity

**timorous**
**03** coy, shy **04** eery **05** aspen, eerie, mousy, scary, timid **06** afraid, aspine, modest, mousey, scared, scarey **07** bashful, fearful, meacock, nervous **08** cowardly, retiring **09** diffident, shrinking, tentative, trembling, tremulous **10** frightened, irresolute **12** apprehensive, faint-hearted **13** pusillanimous, unadventurous

**tin**
**02** Sn **03** can **05** money **06** paltry **09** argentine, Dutch oven
*See also* **money**

**tincture**
**02** or **03** dye, fur, hue, Sol **04** bufo, dash, hint, tint **05** aroma, imbue, metal, scent, shade, smack, spice, stain, tinge, touch, trace **06** arnica, colour, elixir, infuse, season, smatch **07** flavour, sericon, suffuse **08** laudanum, permeate **09** seasoning **10** suggestion **12** friar's balsam

**tine**
**03** bay, bez **04** lose, shut, snag, tare, teen, tiny, tray, trey, trez **05** point, prong, royal, spike, spire **06** kindle, perish **07** bay-tine, enclose **08** brow-tine, surroyal, trey-tine **09** bay-antler **10** affliction, brow-antler, trey-antler **11** crown antler

**tinge**
**03** bit, dye, eye **04** cast, dash, drop, hint, tang, tint, wash **05** imbue, pinch, shade, smack, stain, taint, tinct, touch, trace **06** colour **07** flavour, suffuse **08** encolour, tincture **09** encrimson **10** smattering, sprinkling, suggestion

**tingle**
**04** glow, itch, ring **05** prick, sting, thirl, throb **06** dindle, dinnle, quiver, shiver, thrill, tickle, tinkle, tremor **07** itching, prickle, tremble, vibrate **08** stinging, tickling **09** prickling **10** gooseflesh **12** goosepimples **14** pins and needles

**tingling**
**04** dirl **05** sting **06** dindle, dinnle **07** prickly

## tinker
**03** toy **04** play, prig, tink **05** caird, fixer **06** dabble, fiddle, hawker, meddle, mender, pedlar, potter, rascal, repair, tamper, trifle **07** botcher, bungler, didakai, didakei, didicoi, didicoy, tinkler **08** diddicoy **09** fool about, itinerant, mess about **10** fool around, mess around

## tinkle
**04** bell, buzz, call, ding, peal, ring **05** chime, chink, clink **06** jangle, jingle, tingle **07** urinate **09** phone call

## tinny
**04** thin **05** cheap, harsh, lucky **06** flimsy, jingly **07** jarring **08** jangling, metallic **09** cheapjack **11** high-pitched, poor-quality **13** insubstantial

## tinpot
**03** bad **04** poor, ropy **05** awful, ropey **06** crummy, paltry, shoddy **07** useless **08** inferior, mediocre, pathetic, rubbishy, slipshod **09** defective, imperfect **10** low-quality, second-rate **11** incompetent, substandard **13** insignificant **14** unsatisfactory

## tinsel
**04** loss, sham, show **05** cheap, gaudy, showy **06** flashy, tawdry, trashy **07** display, glitter, spangle **08** frippery, gimcrack, specious **09** clinquant, gaudiness **10** garishness, pretension, triviality **11** flamboyance, ostentation, superficial **12** meretricious, ostentatious **13** artificiality, worthlessness **14** insignificance **15** meaninglessness

## tint
**03** dye, hew, hue **04** cast, tone, wash **05** color, rinse, shade, stain, taint, tinct, tinge, touch, trace **06** affect, colour, streak **08** tincture

## tinware
**04** tole

## tiny
**03** wee **04** mini **05** diddy, small, teeny, weeny **06** little, midget, minute, petite, pocket, slight, teensy **08** dwarfish, trifling **09** itsy-bitsy, itty-bitty, miniature, minuscule, pint-sized **10** diminutive, fractional, negligible, teeny-weeny **11** Lilliputian, microscopic **12** teensy-weensy **13** infinitesimal, insignificant **14** circumstantial

## tip
◇ *head selection indicator* **03** cap, end, nap, nib, tap, top **04** acme, apex, bung, cant, clue, dump, gift, give, hand, head, hint, horn, lean, list, noop, pass, peak, perk, pour, tell, tilt, toom, toss, vail, warn **05** bonus, crown, dodge, empty, point, pouch, shoot, slant, spill, upset, vales **06** advice, advise, convey, gryfon, inform, midden, reward, summit, tip off, tip-off, topple, unload **07** capsize, caution, cumshaw, douceur, griffin, griffon, gryphon, incline, pointer, pour out, present, propine, slender, staithe, suggest, warning, wrinkle **08** bonamano,

forecast, forewarn, gratuity, overturn, pinnacle, slag heap, surmount **09** backshish, bakhshish, baksheesh, buonamano, extremity, pourboire **10** backsheesh, perquisite, refuse-heap, remunerate, suggestion, topple over **11** information, rubbish-heap **13** gratification **14** recommendation

## tip-off
◇ *head deletion indicator* **04** clue, hint, wire **07** pointer, warning **10** suggestion **11** information

## tipple
**03** bib, pot **04** down, dram, swig **05** booze, drink, paint, quaff, usual **06** imbibe, liquor, poison **07** alcohol, indulge **09** knock back **12** regular drink **14** favourite drink

## tippler
**03** sot **04** lush, soak, wino **05** alkie, dipso, drunk, toper **06** bibber, boozer, sponge **07** drinker, tosspot, winebag **08** drunkard, maltworm **09** inebriate **11** dipsomaniac, hard drinker

## tipsy
◇ *anagram indicator* **03** wet **04** awry **05** askew, bosky, drunk, happy, lushy, merry, moony, muzzy, nappy, oiled, rocky, tight, totty, woozy **06** mellow, screwy, slewed, sprung, squiff, tiddly **07** a pip out, screwed, squiffy, tiddled **08** cockeyed, glorious, pleasant, top-heavy **09** a peepe out, well-oiled **10** a peg too low **15** the worse for wear

## tirade
**04** rant **05** abuse **06** laisse **07** lecture **08** diatribe, harangue, outburst **09** invective, monorhyme, philippic **11** fulmination **12** admonishment, denunciation

## tire
**03** tax **04** bore, cook, drop, flag, tyre **05** drain, dress, sew up, train, use up, weary **06** attire, bejade, strain, tucker, volley **07** apparel, breathe, exhaust, fatigue, tire out, wear out **08** enervate, outweary, pinafore **09** broadside, equipment, furniture, headdress

## tired
**03** old **04** beat, jack, sick **05** all in, blown, bored, corny, fed up, jaded, rough, stale, trite, weary **06** bushed, drowsy, pooped, sleepy, wabbit, zonked **07** cliché'd, drained, shagged, wappend, wearied, whacked, worn-out **08** clichéed, dead-beat, dog-tired, dog-weary, fatigate, fatigued, flagging, outspent **09** enervated, exhausted, fagged out, forjaskit, forjeskit, hackneyed, knackered, pooped out, shattered, washed-out **10** clapped-out, shagged out, war-wearied, world-weary **11** ready to drop, tuckered out **12** sick and tired, world-wearied

## tireless
**08** diligent, resolute, untiring, vigorous **09** energetic, unwearied **10** determined, unflagging **11** industrious **13** indefatigable, inexhaustible

## tirelessly
**10** diligently, resolutely, untiringly, vigorously **13** energetically, indefatigably

## tiresome
**04** dull **05** weary **06** boring, gallus, tiring, trying **07** gallows, humdrum, irksome, routine, tedious **08** annoying **09** fatiguing, laborious, vexatious, wearisome **10** irritating, monotonous, prolixious, unexciting **11** troublesome **12** exasperating **13** uninteresting

## tiring
**04** hard **05** stiff, tough **06** taxing **07** arduous **08** draining, exacting, wearying **09** demanding, difficult, fatiguing, laborious, strenuous, wearisome **10** enervating, exhausting

## tiro, tyro
**05** pupil **06** novice **07** learner, starter, student, trainee **08** beginner, freshman, initiate, neophyte **09** greenhorn, novitiate **10** apprentice, catechumen, tenderfoot

## tissue
**03** web **04** mesh, suet, tela **05** gauze, stuff, weave **06** fabric, matter **07** Kleenex®, network, texture **08** gossamer, material **09** structure, substance, variegate **10** aerenchyma, interweave, mesenchyme **11** toilet paper **12** facial tissue, sclerenchyma, toilet tissue

## titan
**05** Atlas, giant **06** Helios **08** colossus, Hercules, Hyperion, superman **09** leviathan **10** Prometheus

## titanic
**04** huge, vast **05** giant, jumbo **06** mighty **07** immense, mammoth, massive **08** colossal, enormous, gigantic, towering **09** cyclopean, herculean, monstrous **10** monumental, prodigious, stupendous **11** mountainous

## titanium
**02** Ti

## titbit
**05** scrap, snack, treat **06** dainty, morsel **08** delicacy **09** appetizer **11** bonne-bouche

## tit for tat
**03** hat **06** in kind, titfer **07** revenge **08** reprisal, requital **10** quid pro quo **11** blow for blow, counterblow, counterbuff, lex talionis, like for like, retaliation **13** an eye for an eye, countercharge

## tithe
**03** pay, tax **04** duty, give, levy, rate, rent, toll **05** disme, teind, tenth **06** assess, charge, impost, take in, tariff **07** tribute **08** decimate, hand over **10** assessment

## titillate
**05** tease **06** arouse, excite, thrill, tickle, turn on **07** provoke **08** interest, intrigue **09** stimulate, tantalize

## titillating

**04** lewd, sexy **05** lurid **06** erotic
**07** naughty, teasing **08** arousing,
exciting **09** seductive, thrilling
**10** intriguing, suggestive **11** captivating,
interesting, provocative, sensational,
stimulating

## titivate

**05** groom, preen, primp, prink **06** doll
up, make up, tart up **07** touch up
**09** refurbish, smarten up

## title

**03** dub, tag **04** book, call, game, head,
name, rank, term, work **05** claim,
crown, deeds, label, match, prize,
right, style **06** credit, eponym, handle,
legend, office, stakes, status, trophy
**07** caption, contest, credits, dukedom,
entitle, epithet, heading, laurels
**08** headline, monicker, nickname,
position, subtitle **09** designate,
honorific, ownership, privilege,
pseudonym, sobriquet **10** nom-de-
plume, soubriquet **11** appellation,
competition, designation, entitlement,
inscription, prerogative, publication
**12** championship, denomination
**13** form of address **14** proprietorship

*Titles include:*

**01** M, U
**02** Dr, Mr, Ms
**03** bey, Dan, Dom, Don, Don, Mrs, Pir,
Rav, Reb, Rex, san, Sir, Sri, Ven
**04** amir, Aunt, babu, bhai, Capt,
Dame, Devi, Doña, emir, Frau,
Herr, Imam, Lady, Lord, Ma'am,
Miss, Prof, sama, Sant, Shri, tuan
**05** baboo, begum, ghazi, hodja,
khoja, Madam, Mirza, molla,
padre, pasha, Rebbe, Señor,
Swami, Uncle
**06** Doctor, Father, khodja, kumari,
Madame, Master, Mister, mollah,
moolah, Mother, mullah, Regina,
Señora, Signor, Sister, Tuanku
**07** Bahadur, Brother, Captain,
Colonel, effendi, esquire, Signior,
Signora, Signore
**08** Fräulein, Highness, memsahib,
Mistress, Monsieur, Señorita,
Viscount
**09** Monsignor, Professor, Signorina,
Signorino, Your Grace
**10** burra sahib
**11** Monseigneur, Your Majesty, Your
Worship
**12** Mademoiselle
**15** Right Honourable

## titter

**04** mock, sway **05** laugh, te-hee
**06** cackle, giggle, tee-hee, totter
**07** chortle, chuckle, snicker, snigger,
whicker

## tittle-tattle

**03** jaw, yak **04** chat, idle, yack
**06** babble, cackle, gossip, natter,
rumour, witter **07** blather, blether,
chatter, hearsay, prattle, twaddle
**08** chitchat, rabbit on, yack-yack
**09** tell tales **10** yackety-yak

## titular

**05** token **06** formal, puppet **07** nominal
**08** honorary, official, putative, so-
called **10** in name only, self-styled

## to

**01** t' **02** at, au, of, on **03** à la, aux, for,
tae **04** near, till, unto **05** until **06** before,
beside **07** against, as far as, forward,
towards

## toad

**04** bufo, pipa **07** paddock, puddock
**10** natterjack

## toadstool

*see* **mushroom**

## toady

**04** fawn, sook, zany **05** crawl, creep
**06** cringe, fawner, grovel, jackal,
kowtow, lackey, minion, sucker, suck
up, yes-man **07** crawler, flatter,
flunkey, Jenkins, truckle **08** bootlick,
butter up, hanger-on, parasite, suck-
hole, toadfish, truckler **09** flatterer,
groveller, sycophant **10** bootlicker,
tuft-hunter **11** curry favour, kiss the
feet, lick-platter, lickspittle **12** bow and
scrape

## to and fro

◇ *palindrome indicator*

## toast

**04** bake, heat, warm **05** brown, crisp,
drink, grill, roast **06** birsle, heat up,
honour, pledge, salute, scorch, warm
up **07** drink to, tribute **08** barbecue,
brindisi, scouther **09** sentiment **10** best
wishes, compliment, salutation
**11** compliments
*See also* **cheers**

## tobacco

**04** burn, chaw, chew, pipe, plug, quid,
weed **05** bacco, baccy **07** the weed

*Tobacco and tobacco preparations
include:*

**04** capa, shag
**05** régie, snout, snuff, snush, twist
**06** burley, dottle, rappee, return,
shisha, sneesh
**07** caporal, chewing, Latakia, nail-
rod, perique, pigtail, sheesha
**08** bird's-eye, canaster, honeydew,
short-cut, Virginia
**09** broad-leaf, cavendish, flue-cured,
mundungus, strip-leaf

*Tobacco pipes include:*

**03** cob
**04** bong, clay
**05** briar, brier, cutty, hooka, peace,
water
**06** dudeen, hookah, kalian, shisha
**07** calumet, chibouk, chillum,
corncob, dudheen, nargile,
nargily, sheesha
**08** calabash, narghile, narghily,
nargileh, nargilly
**09** chibouque, narghilly
**10** meerschaum
**12** churchwarden, hubble-bubble
**13** woodcock's-head

## toboggan

**04** dray, luge **05** pulka, slide, slipe,

train **06** Ski-doo®, sledge, sleigh
**07** bobsled, dogsled, kibitka, travois
**09** bobsleigh **11** hurly-hacket, skeleton
bob

## today

**02** AD **03** now **06** the day **07** just now,
this day **08** nowadays, right now
**09** these days **11** this evening, this
morning, this very day **12** at this
moment **13** the present day, this
afternoon **14** the present time

## toddle

**04** reel, rock, sway **05** lurch, shake,
waver **06** falter, teeter, totter, waddle,
wobble **07** saunter, stagger, stumble
**14** move unsteadily, walk unsteadily

## toddler

**04** trot

## to-do

**03** ado **04** flap, fuss, stew, stir **05** hoo-
ha **06** bother, bustle, flurry, furore,
rumpus, tumult, unrest, uproar
**07** quarrel, ruction, turmoil
**08** brouhaha, razmataz **09** agitation,
commotion **10** excitement, hullabaloo,
razzmatazz **11** disturbance,
performance, razzamatazz

## toe

**04** kick **05** digit **06** hallux, tootsy
**07** dewclaw, tootsie **09** prehallux
**12** tootsy-wootsy

## together

**03** cum **04** calm, cool **05** as one, atone,
on end **06** attone, in a row, stable,
united **07** as a team, jointly
**08** composed, in unison, mutually,
sensible **09** all at once, at one time, in
cahoots, in company, in concert, on
the trot, organized, pari passu **10** back
to back, hand in hand, side by side
**11** down-to-earth, level-headed,
unflappable **12** collectively,
concurrently, continuously, in
succession, successively, well-
adjusted, well-balanced **13** at the same
time, consecutively, in conjunction,
well-organized, without a break **14** as
a partnership, commonsensical,
simultaneously **15** in collaboration,
working together
• **come together** **03** gel **04** jell, meet
**05** close, rally **07** collect, convene
**10** amalgamate

## Togo

**02** TG **03** TGO

## toil

**03** net, tew, tug **04** grub, moil, slog,
trap, work **05** graft, grind, labor, slave,
snare, sweat, swink, yakka **06** drudge,
effort, labour, murder, strive, yacker,
yakker **07** fatigue, murther, slaving,
travail, turmoil **08** drudgery, drudgism,
exertion, hard work, industry, plug
away, struggle **09** persevere
**10** contention, donkey-work
**11** application, elbow grease **12** push
yourself **14** Hercules' choice **15** work
like a Trojan

## toiler

**05** navvy, slave **06** drudge, menial,

**toilet**

worker **07** grafter, slogger **08** labourer **09** struggler, workhorse **10** workaholic

**toilet**

**02** WC **03** APC, bog, can, lat, lav, loo **04** dike, head, john, kazi, toot, tout **05** dunny, Elsan®, heads, jacks, lavvy, potty **06** lavabo, throne, urinal **07** cludgie, cottage, crapper, latrine **08** bathroom, lavatory, outhouse, Portaloo®, rest room, superloo, the gents', washroom **09** cloakroom, necessary, the ladies' **10** facilities, powder room, reredorter, throne room, thunderbox **11** convenience, earth-closet, water closet **12** dressing-room, smallest room **14** comfort station, little boys' room, necessary house, necessary place **15** Parliament House

**toilsome**

**04** hard **05** tough **06** severe, taxing, uphill **07** arduous, painful, tedious, toiling, toylsom **08** tiresome **09** difficult, fatiguing, herculean, laborious, strenuous, toylesome, wearisome **10** burdensome **12** backbreaking

**token**

**04** clue, disc, mark, seal, sign, slug **05** check, index, jeton, proof, scrip, staff **06** coupon, emblem, hollow, jetton, pledge, signal, slight, symbol **07** counter, memento, minimal, nominal, portent, tessera, voucher, warning **08** cosmetic, evidence, keepsake, memorial, moniment, monument, reminder, souvenir, symbolic **09** insincere, precedent, sacrament, triumphal **10** abbey-piece, emblematic, expression, indication, plague-spot **11** perfunctory, recognition, remembrance, superficial **12** abbey-counter, recognizance **13** demonstration, manifestation **14** representation

**told**

◇ *homophone indicator*

**tolerable**

**02** OK **04** fair, so-so **06** not bad **07** average **08** adequate, all right, bearable, mediocre, middling, ordinary, passable **09** endurable, tol-lolish **10** acceptable, fairly good, not much cop, reasonable, sufferable **11** indifferent **12** run-of-the-mill, satisfactory **13** no great shakes, unexceptional

**tolerably**

**06** enough, fairly **08** bearably **10** acceptably, adequately, ordinarily, reasonably **12** sufficiently **13** indifferently

**tolerance**

**04** give, play **05** swing **06** lenity **07** laxness, stamina **08** leniency, patience, sympathy **09** allowance, clearance, endurance, fortitude, toughness, variation **10** good-humour, indulgence, liberalism, resilience, resistance, toleration **11** fluctuation, forbearance, magnanimity **13** understanding **14** open-

mindedness, permissiveness **15** broad-mindedness

**tolerant**

**03** lax **04** fair, soft **06** decent **07** lenient, liberal, patient **08** catholic, enduring, mellowed **09** compliant, easy-going, forgiving, indulgent **10** charitable, forbearing, open-minded, permissive **11** broad-minded, free and easy, kind-hearted, magnanimous, sympathetic **12** unprejudiced **13** long-suffering, understanding

**tolerate**

**04** bear, have, take, wear **05** abear, abide, admit, allow, brook, stand, thole **06** accept, endure, pardon, permit, suffer **07** condone, indulge, receive, stomach, swallow, warrant **08** sanction **09** put up with **11** countenance

**toleration**

**06** lenity **07** laxness, stamina **08** leniency, patience, sanction, sympathy **09** allowance, endurance, fortitude, toughness **10** acceptance, indulgence, liberalism, resilience, resistance, sufferance **11** forbearance, magnanimity **13** understanding **14** open-mindedness, permissiveness **15** broad-mindedness

**toll**

**03** bar, due, fee, jow, tax **04** call, cost, duty, harm, jole, joll, jowl, levy, loss, lure, peal, pike, rate, ring, warn **05** chime, clang, death, decoy, joule, knell, price, sound **06** charge, damage, demand, herald, injury, octroi, signal, strike, tariff **07** payment, penalty, pierage, pontage, scavage, tallage, tollage **08** announce, hardship **09** streetage, suffering **13** adverse effect

**tomb**

**04** bury, cist **05** crypt, death, grave, speos, vault **06** burial, dolmen, entomb, heroon, marble, shrine, tholus **07** funeral, mastaba, reposit **08** catacomb, cenotaph, hypogeum, monument, sacellum **09** hypogaeum, mausoleum, sepulcher, sepulchre, sepulture **10** repository **11** burial-place, sarcophagus **13** Holy Sepulchre

**tomboy**

**04** ramp, romp **05** hempy **06** hoiden, hoyden

**tombstone**

**05** stone **06** marble **08** memorial, monument **09** headstone **10** gravestone **12** through-stane, through-stone **13** memorial stone

**tomcat**

**03** gib

**tome**

**03** tom **04** book, opus, work **06** volume

**tomfoolery**

**03** tom **05** hooey, larks **06** idiocy **07** inanity, rubbish, trifles **08** clowning, mischief, nonsense **09** horseplay, jewellery, ornaments, silliness, stupidity **10** buffoonery, carrying on, skylarking **11** foolishness, shenanigans

**12** childishness, larking about, messing about

**ton**

**01** t **03** tun **07** fashion

**tone**

**03** air, hue **04** cast, feel, mood, note, suit, tint, tune, vein **05** blend, drift, force, match, pitch, shade, sound, style, tenor, tinge, twang **06** accent, colour, effect, go with, humour, manner, spirit, stress, temper, timbre, volume **07** quality **08** attitude, emphasis, strength, tincture, tonality **09** character, harmonize **10** co-ordinate, expression, go well with, inflection, intonation, modulation **12** accentuation
• **high tone 03** alt
• **tone down 03** dim **06** dampen, reduce, soften, subdew, subdue, temper **07** assuage, lighten **08** mitigate, moderate, play down, restrain **09** alleviate, soft-pedal
• **tone up 04** buck, trim **05** brace **06** buck up, tune up **07** freshen, shape up, touch up **08** brighten, limber up **09** sharpen up **10** invigorate

**toneless**

**03** dim **04** dull, grey **05** faded **07** neutral, relaxed **08** listless, tuneless **09** soundless, unmusical **10** colourless **11** unmelodious **12** unexpressive **14** expressionless

**Tonga**

**03** TON

**tongue**

**04** cant, doab, lick, rasp, spit, talk, vote **05** argot, clack, idiom, lingo, slang, utter, voice **06** glossa, jargon, lingua, patois, radula, red rag, speech **07** clapper, dialect **08** language, parlance **09** discourse, pronounce, utterance **10** articulate, vernacular **12** articulation
*See also* **language**

**tongue-tied**

**04** dumb, mute **06** silent **08** wordless **09** voiceless **10** dumbstruck, speechless **11** mush-mouthed **12** inarticulate, lost for words, tongue-tacked

**tonic**

**01** t **05** boost, final **06** bracer, fillip, saloop **07** cordial, home key, keynote **08** pick-me-up, roborant **09** analeptic, refresher, stimulant **11** restorative **12** shot in the arm **15** fundamental note
*See also* **note**

**too**

**03** tae **04** also, over, very **06** as well, overly, unduly **07** besides **08** likewise, moreover **09** extremely **10** in addition **11** excessively, furthermore **12** inordinately, ridiculously, unreasonably

**tool**

**03** cut **04** dupe, over, pawn, work, yoke **05** agent, chase, gismo, means, shape, tanto **06** agency, device, gadget, medium, minion, puppet, stooge, troppo, weapon **07** cat's-paw, fashion, flunkey, machine, utensil, vehicle **08** artefact, decorate, hireling, ornament **09** apparatus, appliance, implement **10** instrument, over-the-top **11** contraption, contrivance **12** intermediary

*Tools include:*

**02** ax
**03** awl, axe, gad, hod, hoe, loy, saw, sax, van
**04** adze, burr, card, celt, file, fork, froe, goad, hawk, jack, mace, mall, maul, peel, pick, plow, prod, prog, rake, rasp, risp, rule, snap, spud, vice
**05** auger, bevel, clamp, dolly, drill, level, plane, punch, snips, spade, steel, tongs
**06** bodkin, chaser, chisel, dibber, dibble, fuller, gimlet, hammer, jig-saw, mallet, mortar, needle, pestle, pliers, plough, sander, scutch, scythe, shears, shovel, sickle, trowel, wrench
**07** bolster, bradawl, chopper, cleaver, crowbar, forceps, fretsaw, hacksaw, handsaw, hay fork, jointer, mattock, nail gun, pick-axe, pincers, scalpel, scriber, spanner, stapler, swingle, T-square
**08** billhook, chainsaw, dividers, penknife, scissors, spraygun, tenon-saw, thresher, tommy bar, tweezers
**09** box cutter, grass-rake, jack-plane, pitchfork, plumb-line, secateurs, set-square
**10** jackhammer, paper-knife, protractor
**11** brace and bit, crochet hook, paper-cutter, pocket-knife, screwdriver, spirit level
**12** angle grinder, caulking-iron, digging stick, pruning-knife, sledgehammer, socket-wrench, wirestripper
**13** pinking-shears, pruning-shears, soldering-iron

*See also* **gardening; saw**

## tooth

**03** cog, jag **05** crena, prong, taste **06** dentil, joggle, relish **07** gnasher **08** appetite, denticle **09** interlock, serration **10** serrations **13** denticulation
*See also* **teeth**

## toothsome

**04** nice **05** sweet, tasty, yummy **06** dainty, morish **07** moreish, savoury, scrummy **08** luscious, pleasant, tempting **09** agreeable, delicious, palatable **10** appetizing, attractive, delectable **11** flavoursome, scrumptious **13** mouthwatering

## top

◇ *head selection indicator* **02** up **03** cap, cop, lid, nun, tip **04** acme, apex, beat, best, comb, cork, head, kill, lead, main, peak, roof, rule, tuft **05** chief, cover, crest, crown, excel, first, outdo, prime, ridge, shirt, smock, upper

**06** apogee, better, blouse, climax, coppin, exceed, finest, finish, height, jersey, jumper, ruling, summit, T-shirt, upmost, upward, utmost, vertex, zenith **07** cacumen, command, eclipse, garnish, highest, leading, maximum, premier, premium, spinner, stopper, supreme, surpass, sweater, tank top, topmost, topsail, topspin **08** crowning, decorate, dominant, foremost, greatest, outshine, outstrip, pinnacle, pullover, superior, surmount, tee shirt, very good **09** be first in, finish off, paramount, principal, sovereign, transcend, uppermost **10** pre-eminent, sweatshirt **11** culminating, culmination **12** highest point
*See also* **cut**
• **over the top 03** OTT **05** undue **06** lavish **07** extreme, too much **08** a bit much **09** excessive **10** exorbitant, immoderate, inordinate **11** extravagant, uncalled-for **12** unreasonable
• **top and tail** ◇ *ends deletion indicator*
• **top off** ◇ *head deletion indicator*
• **top up 05** add to, boost **06** fill up, refill, reload **07** augment **08** increase, recharge **09** replenish **10** supplement

## topi

**03** hat **04** sola **05** solah **07** sola hat **10** sola helmet

## topic

**04** head, text **05** issue, place, point, theme, topos **06** matter, thesis **07** subject **08** argument, question **09** hot button **10** hobby-horse, touch-me-not **11** commonplace, hardy annual, old chestnut **12** talking point **13** subject matter

## topical

**05** local **06** recent **07** current, popular **08** familiar, relevant, up-to-date **10** newsworthy **12** contemporary **13** up-to-the-minute

## topless

◇ *head deletion indicator*

## topmost

**03** top **05** first, upper **06** apical **07** highest, leading, maximum, supreme **08** dominant, foremost, loftiest, supernal **09** paramount, principal, uppermost

## top-notch

**02** A1 **03** ace, top **04** cool, fine, mega **05** crack, prime, super **06** superb, way-out, wicked **07** leading, premier, radical, supreme **08** peerless, splendid, superior **09** admirable, excellent, first-rate, matchless, top-flight **10** first-class **11** exceptional, outstanding, superlative **12** second-to-none **14** out of this world

## topping

◇ *juxtaposition down indicator* **05** crust **07** tipping **08** arrogant **09** excellent, wonderful

## topple

◇ *anagram indicator* **03** tip **04** fall, oust

**05** upset **06** totter, tumble, unseat **07** capsize, dismast, tip over **08** collapse, dethrone, displace, fall over, keel over, overturn **09** bring down, knock down, knock over, overthrow **11** overbalance

## top-secret

**06** secret **07** private **08** hush-hush, intimate, personal **09** sensitive **10** classified, restricted **12** confidential, off-the-record

## topsy-turvy

◇ *anagram indicator* **05** messy **06** untidy **07** chaotic, jumbled, mixed-up **08** confused **09** confusion, inside out **10** disorderly, in disorder, upside down **11** disarranged, in confusion **12** disorganized, looking-glass, tapsalteerie, tapsieteerie

## torch

**04** burn, link, tead, wisp **05** brand, flare, light, teade **06** ignite, lampad **07** cresset, roughie **08** arsonist, flambeau, splinter **09** firebrand, set alight, set fire to, set on fire **10** flashlight **11** put a match to

## torment

◇ *anagram indicator* **03** vex **04** bane, pain, pest, pine **05** agony, annoy, curse, grill, hound, tease, worry, wrack **06** badger, bother, harass, harrow, misery, ordeal, pester, plague **07** afflict, agitate, anguish, bedevil, crucify, furnace, Gehenna, provoke, scourge, torture, trouble **08** distress, irritate, nuisance, vexation **09** annoyance, martyrdom, persecute, suffering, tantalize **10** affliction, harassment, irritation **11** persecution, provocation **13** pain in the neck **15** thorn in the flesh

## torn

◇ *anagram indicator* **03** cut **04** rent, slit **05** split **06** ragged, ribbon, ripped, unsure **07** divided, enriven **08** lacerate, wavering **09** dithering, lacerated, uncertain, undecided **10** conflicted, in two minds, irresolute **11** vacillating

## tornado

**04** gale **05** storm **06** squall **07** cyclone, monsoon, tempest, twister, typhoon **09** hurricane, whirlwind **10** waterspout

## torpedo

**03** ray **05** wreck **07** tin fish **09** cramp-fish **11** electric ray

## torpid

**04** dead, dull, lazy, numb, slow **05** inert **06** drowsy, sleepy, supine **07** dormant, passive **08** deadened, inactive, indolent, lifeless, listless, sluggish **09** apathetic, lethargic, nerveless, somnolent **10** insensible, languorous **11** lethargical

## torpor

**05** sloth **06** acedia, apathy, stupor **07** inertia, languor **08** dullness, hebetude, laziness, lethargy, numbness, slowness **09** indolence, inertness, passivity, stupidity, torpidity **10** drowsiness, inactivity, sleepiness,

**torrent**

somnolence **12** lifelessness, listlessness, sluggishness

**torrent**
**04** gush, rush **05** flood, spate, storm **06** deluge, stream, volley **07** barrage, blatter, cascade **08** downpour, outburst **10** inundation

**torrential**
**05** heavy **07** driving, pelting, teeming **10** inundating, persistent **11** pouring down **13** bucketing down

**torrid**
**03** hot **04** arid, sexy **06** desert, erotic, red-hot, steamy **07** amorous, blazing, boiling, parched **08** scorched, sizzling, stifling, tropical **09** scorching, waterless **10** blistering, passionate, sweltering

**torsk**
**04** cusk

**tortoise**
**06** gopher **07** hicatee, testudo **08** galapago, hiccatee, terrapin

**tortuous**
◊ *anagram indicator* **06** zigzag **07** curving, devious, sinuous, winding **08** indirect, involved, twisting **09** ambagious, Byzantine **10** circuitous, convoluted, meandering, roundabout, serpentine **11** complicated

**torture**
◊ *anagram indicator* **03** fry, gip, gyp **04** pain, pine **05** abuse, agony, worry, wrack **06** harrow, martyr, misery, murder, plague, punish **07** afflict, agonize, anguish, crucify, murther, trouble **08** distress, ill-treat, mistreat **09** martyrdom, persecute, suffering, tantalize **10** affliction, excruciate, punishment **11** forcipation, persecution **12** excruciation, ill-treatment, mistreatment

---

*Torture forms and instruments include:*

---

**03** gin, saw
**04** boot, cage, pear, rack
**05** brank, gadge, irons, jougs, screw, wheel
**06** carcan, engine, harrow, picana, shabeh, spider, stocks, turcas
**07** bilboes, boiling, cat's paw, hooding, picquet, pillory, pincers, scourge, stoning, torment
**08** bootikin, branding, garrotte, knotting, pendulum, pressing, shin vice, trip-hook
**09** bastinado, gauntlets, gridirons, picketing, scarpines, strappado, treadmill
**10** brazen bull, cattle prod, impalement, iron collar, iron maiden, Judas scale, pilliwinks, spiked hare, starvation, suspension, thumbscrew, treadwheel
**11** cave of roses, forcipation, German chair, head crusher, Judas cradle, keelhauling, knee-capping, squassation, thumbscrews, wooden horse
**12** ball and chain, ducking-stool,

flesh tearers, scold's bridle, shrew's fiddle, skull crusher, Spanish chair, water torture
**13** cat-o'-nine-tails, electric shock, heretic's forks, Spanish mantle
**14** Austrian ladder, devil-on-the-neck, disembowelment, drunkard's cloak
**15** confession chair

---

**Tory**
**01** C **03** Con **04** blue **07** tantivy **08** Abhorrer **12** Conservative

**toss**
◊ *anagram indicator* **03** bum, lob, shy, tip **04** birl, cant, cast, flip, hurl, jerk, jolt, loft, perk, puck, rock, roll, sway **05** bandy, brank, chuck, drink, fling, heave, lurch, pitch, shake, sling, throw **06** bridle, dandle, slight, sprawl, squirm, thrash, tumble, welter, writhe **07** agitate, blanket, canvass, flutter, wriggle **09** commotion, confusion

**tot**
**03** dop, nip, sum **04** baby, dram, mite, shot, slug, swig **05** bairn, child **06** finger, infant **07** measure, swallow, toddler
*See also* **add; baby; drink**
• **tot up** **03** add, sum **05** add up, count, mount, tally, total **06** reckon **07** compute, count up, mount up **09** calculate

**total**
**03** add, all, lot, sum, tot **04** full, make, mass, rank **05** add up, count, gross, reach, sheer, sum up, tot up, utter, whole **06** all-out, amount, come to, entire, reckon **07** count up, full-out, perfect, pur sang **08** absolute, amount to, complete, entirety, integral, outright, subtotal, thorough, totality **09** aggregate, downright, out-and-out **10** consummate, grand total, undisputed **11** unmitigated, unqualified **13** comprehensive, thoroughgoing, unconditional

**totalitarian**
**08** despotic, one-party **09** tyrannous **10** monocratic, monolithic, omnipotent, oppressive **11** dictatorial **12** undemocratic **13** authoritarian

**totality**
**03** all, sum **05** total, whole **06** cosmos **07** pleroma **08** entirety, fullness, universe **09** aggregate, wholeness **10** entireness, everything **12** completeness

**totally**
**05** fully, quite **06** wholly **07** utterly **08** entirely, outright **09** perfectly **10** absolutely, completely, thoroughly **11** boots and all, undividedly **12** consummately, undisputedly **13** unmitigatedly **14** wholeheartedly **15** comprehensively, unconditionally

**totter**
◊ *anagram indicator* **04** reel, rock, roll, sway **05** lurch, shake, waver **06** daddle, dodder, falter, hotter, quiver, teeter, titter, topple, waddle, wobble **07** be shaky, stagger, stumble, tremble **10** be

insecure, be unstable, be unsteady **12** be precarious **14** move unsteadily

**touch**
**03** art, bit, dab, eat, hit, jot, nie, pat, pet, tap, tat, tig, use, way **04** abut, blow, dash, draw, feel, hand, harm, hint, hold, kiss, make, meet, move, nigh, nose, palm, palp, skim, spot, stir, take **05** bribe, brush, cheat, cover, drink, equal, flair, grain, graze, knack, match, pinch, point, reach, rival, skiff, skill, smack, speck, spice, stamp, style, taste, theft, tinge, trace, trait, upset, verge, weave, whiff, wound **06** adjoin, affect, aspect, attain, better, border, broach, caress, come to, detail, devour, finger, finish, fondle, handle, injure, little, manner, method, molest, muzzle, nicety, pierce, pocket, regard, sadden, smatch, strike, stroke, tickle **07** ability, concern, consume, contact, disturb, feature, impinge, impress, inspire, involve, knuckle, mention, minutia, rapport, receive, refer to, soupçon, speak of, surface, taction, texture, touch up **08** addition, allude to, approach, come near, deal with, fineness, remark on **09** dexterity, direction, influence, suspicion, tactility, technique **10** connection, suggestion, touchstone **11** association **12** lay a finger on, put a finger on **13** communication, craftsmanship, hold a candle to **14** be contiguous to, correspondence, have an effect on, have an impact on **15** come into contact
• **touch down** **04** land **05** rouge **06** come in **11** come to earth **12** come in to land
• **touch off** **04** fire **05** begin, cause, light **06** arouse, foment, ignite, set off **07** actuate, inflame, provoke, trigger **08** detonate, initiate, spark off **10** trigger off
• **touch up** **03** tat **04** tatt **06** revamp **07** brush up, enhance, improve, patch up, perfect, retouch **08** polish up, renovate, round off **09** finish off

**touch-and-go**
**04** dire, near **05** close, dodgy, hairy, risky **06** sticky, tricky **07** offhand, parlous **08** critical, perilous **09** dangerous, hazardous, uncertain **10** precarious **12** nerve-racking

**touchdown**
**07** arrival, landing **08** coming in **14** coming in to land

**touched**
**03** mad **04** daft **05** barmy, batty, crazy, dotty, loopy, moved, nutty, upset **06** insane **07** bonkers, stirred **08** affected, deranged, inspired **09** disturbed, eccentric, impressed **10** influenced, unbalanced

**touchiness**
**09** bad temper, petulance, surliness, testiness **10** grumpiness, tetchiness **11** crabbedness, grouchiness, peevishness, pettishness **12** captiousness, irascibility, irritability

## touching

**03** sad **05** hongi **06** libant, moving, tender **07** attaint, darshan, piteous, pitiful, tangent **08** handball, pathetic, pitiable, poignant, stirring, tangency **09** affecting, emotional, fingering, upsetting **10** concerning, contiguous, disturbing, impressive **11** cloud-topped **12** cloud-kissing, heart-rending **13** heartbreaking

## touchstone

**04** norm, test **05** gauge, guide, model, proof **07** measure, pattern **08** standard, template **09** benchmark, criterion, yardstick **11** Lydian stone

## touchwood

**04** funk, monk, punk **05** spunk **09** matchwood

## touchy

**04** edgy, sore **05** cross, huffy, miffy, mifty, ratty, risky **06** badass, chippy, feisty, grumpy, ornery, snuffy, tricky **07** awkward, crabbed, grouchy, huffish, peevish, prickly **08** badassed, captious, delicate **09** difficult, irascible, irritable, sensitive **11** bad-tempered, problematic, thin-skinned **13** controversial, over-sensitive, quick-tempered

## tough

**03** fit, nut, yob **04** firm, grim, hard, lout, thug **05** brute, bully, burly, butch, chewy, hardy, harsh, rigid, rough, rowdy, solid, stern, stiff, teuch, teugh, yobbo **06** badass, ballsy, keelie, knotty, robust, rugged, severe, sticky, strict, strong, sturdy, taxing, thorny, uphill **07** adamant, arduous, callous, durable, fibrous, gristly, rubbery, ruffian, unlucky, vicious, violent, viscous **08** badassed, baffling, criminal, exacting, hardened, hooligan, leathery, muscular, plug-ugly, puzzling, resolute, stalwart, vigorous **09** bovver boy, cut-throat, difficult, hard-faced, hardnosed, laborious, lager lout, obstinate, resilient, resistant, roughneck, strenuous, tenacious, violently, well-built **10** determined, disorderly, inflexible, perplexing, refractory, unpleasant, unyielding **11** distressing, intractable, troublesome, unfortunate **12** aggressively **13** uncomfortable **14** tough as leather, uncompromising

## toughen

**04** neal **05** brace **06** anneal, harden **07** fortify, stiffen **09** reinforce **10** strengthen **12** make stricter, substantiate

## toughness

**04** grit, guts **08** firmness, obduracy, strength, tenacity **09** hardiness **10** resilience, resistance, ruggedness, sturdiness **13** determination, inflexibility

## toupee

**03** jiz, rug, wig **04** gizz **05** caxon, jasey, major **06** bagwig, bobwig, Brutus, peruke, tie-wig **07** buzz-wig, periwig, Ramilie, spencer **08** postiche

**09** hairpiece **10** scratch-wig **14** transformation

## tour

◇ *anagram indicator* **02** do **03** van **04** hike, ride, road, rode, trip **05** drive, jaunt, round, tramp, visit **06** course, outing **07** circuit, explore, go round, journey **08** roadshow, sightsee **09** barnstorm, excursion, walkabout **10** expedition, inspection **11** travel round **12** drive through **13** peregrination **14** journey through

## tourist

**05** emmet **06** tourer **07** grockle, tripper, visitor, voyager **09** sightseer, sojourner, traveller **10** day-tripper, rubberneck **12** excursionist, globetrotter, holidaymaker

• **tourist attraction** *see* **Africa; America; Asia; Australia; Canada; Europe; London; Middle East; New York; New Zealand; Paris**

## tournament

**04** meet, seed **05** basho, event, jerid, joust, match **06** jereed, series **07** contest, meeting, tourney **08** carousel **09** carrousel **10** round robin **11** bridge-drive, competition **12** championship

## tousled

**06** untidy **07** ruffled, rumpled, tangled, tumbled, unkempt **08** messed up **10** disordered, in disarray **11** disarranged, dishevelled

## tout

**03** all, ask, pet **04** hawk, hype, plug, pout, push, seek, sell **05** blast, every, plier, trade, watch, whole **06** appeal, barker, inhale, market, peddle, praise, runner, toilet **07** commend, endorse, promote, solicit **08** petition **09** advertise **11** workwatcher

## tow

**03** lug, tug **04** drag, draw, haul, pull, rope **05** track, trail **09** transport
• **in tow 08** in convoy **10** by your side **12** accompanying

## towards

**02** to **03** for **04** near **05** about, anent, -wards **06** almost, nearly **07** close to, nearing **09** regarding **10** concerning, on the way to **11** approaching **12** to help pay for, with regard to **13** with respect to

## tower

**03** cap, top **04** loom, rear, rise, sail, soar **05** excel, mount, shoot **06** ascend, exceed **07** eclipse, surpass **08** dominate, overlook **09** transcend **10** overshadow
*See also* **tug**

---

*Tower types include:*

**04** bell, fort, gate, keep, mill, peel, rood, shot
**05** block, broch, clock, ivory, minar, pagod, round, spire, Texas, watch, water
**06** belfry, castle, church, column, donjon, gopura, nurhag, pagoda, turret

**07** bastion, citadel, conning, control, cooling, lookout, minaret, mirador, nuraghe, steeple
**08** barbican, bastille, brattice, fortress, hill-fort, martello, scaffold
**09** belvedere, campanile, peel-tower, smock mill, tower mill
**10** skyscraper, stronghold, watchtower
**11** demi-bastion
**13** fortification

---

*Towers include:*

**02** CN
**03** AMP, Sky
**04** Pisa
**05** Babel, Clock, Macau, Sears, Seoul, Tokyo
**06** Big Ben, Dragon, Eiffel, Kiev TV, London, Riga TV, Tahoto
**07** Alma-Ata, Leaning, Olympic, Praha TV, Yueyang
**08** Tallin TV, Tashkent, Tengwang
**09** Blackpool, Donauturm, Ostankino, Tianjin TV
**10** Collserola, Liberation
**11** Fernsehturm, The Euromast, Yellow Crane
**12** Petronas Twin, Stratosphere
**15** Oriental Pearl TV

---

• **tower of strength 04** prop **06** pillar **07** support **08** mainstay **09** supporter **12** friend in need

## towering

**04** high, tall **05** great, lofty **07** extreme, soaring, sublime, supreme **08** colossal, elevated, gigantic, imposing **10** impressive, inordinate, monumental, surpassing, unrivalled **11** magnificent, outstanding **12** incomparable, overpowering **13** extraordinary

## town

**04** burg, city, dorp, toun **05** borgo, bourg, burgh, urban **06** favela, Podunk, pueblo **07** borough, new town, suburbs, village **08** township **09** enclosure, outskirts, urban area **10** county town, market town, metropolis, settlement **11** conurbation **12** municipality **13** urban district

---

*County towns include:*

**03** Ayr
**04** Mold, Wick, York
**05** Banff, Cupar, Derry, Elgin, Lewes, Nairn, Omagh, Perth, Truro
**06** Armagh, Brecon, Durham, Exeter, Forfar, Lanark, London, Oakham, Oxford
**07** Appleby, Bedford, Belfast, Bristol, Cardiff, Chester, Denbigh, Dornoch, Ipswich, Kinross, Lerwick, Lincoln, Matlock, Morpeth, Newport, Norwich, Peebles, Preston, Reading, Renfrew, Selkirk, Taunton, Warwick, Wigtown
**08** Aberdeen, Barnsley, Beverley, Cardigan, Carlisle, Cromarty, Dingwall, Dumfries, Greenlaw, Hereford, Hertford, Jedburgh,

Kingston, Kirkwall, Monmouth, Pembroke, Rothesay, Stafford, Stirling
09 Aylesbury, Beaumaris, Cambridge, Dolgellau, Dumbarton, Newcastle
10 Haddington, Huntingdon, Linlithgow, Manchester, Montgomery, Nottingham, Presteigne, Shrewsbury, Stonehaven, Trowbridge, Winchester
11 Clackmannan, Downpatrick, Enniskillen, Northampton
12 Kircudbright
13 Middlesbrough, Northallerton

---

*English towns include:*

03 Ely
04 Bath, Bury, Hove, Hull, York
05 Ascot, Corby, Cowes, Crewe, Derby, Dover, Epsom, Ewell, Hythe, Leeds, Lewes, Luton, Otley, Poole, Ripon, Rugby, Truro, Wells, Wigan
06 Barnet, Bexley, Bodmin, Bolton, Bootle, Boston, Buxton, Darwen, Dudley, Durham, Exeter, Harlow, Harrow, Ilkley, Jarrow, Kendal, London, Ludlow, Oakham, Oldham, Oundle, Oxford, Slough, St Ives, Stroud, Torbay, Warley, Whitby, Widnes, Wirral, Woking, Yeovil
07 Andover, Arundel, Ashford, Bedford, Berwick, Bristol, Brixham, Burnley, Chatham, Cheddar, Chester, Crawley, Croydon, Dorking, Evesham, Exmouth, Gosport, Grimsby, Halifax, Harwich, Haworth, Helston, Horsham, Ipswich, Keswick, Lincoln, Malvern, Margate, Matlock, Morpeth, Newport, Norwich, Padstow, Preston, Reading, Redruth, Reigate, Royston, Runcorn, Salford, Stilton, Sudbury, Swindon, Taunton, Telford, Tilbury, Torquay, Ventnor, Walsall, Wantage, Warwick, Watford, Windsor
08 Abingdon, Barnsley, Basildon, Beverley, Bradford, Brighton, Carlisle, Coventry, Dartford, Falmouth, Grantham, Hastings, Hatfield, Hereford, Hertford, Kingston, Knowsley, Minehead, Newhaven, Nuneaton, Penzance, Plymouth, Ramsgate, Redditch, Richmond, Rochdale, Sandwell, Solihull, Spalding, Stafford, St Albans, Stamford, St Helens, Thetford, Westbury, Weymouth, Worthing
09 Aldeburgh, Aldershot, Ambleside, Ashbourne, Axminster, Aylesbury, Blackburn, Blackpool, Bletchley, Bracknell, Cambridge, Dartmouth, Doncaster, Gateshead, Gravesend, Greenwich, Guildford, Harrogate, King's Lynn, Lancaster, Leicester, Lichfield, Liverpool, Lowestoft,

Lyme Regis, Maidstone, Morecambe, Newcastle, Newmarket, Rochester, Rotherham, Salisbury, Sheerness, Sheffield, Sherborne, Southport, Southwold, St Austell, Stevenage, Stockport, Stratford, Wakefield, Worcester
10 Birkenhead, Birmingham, Bridgwater, Bromsgrove, Buckingham, Canterbury, Chelmsford, Cheltenham, Chichester, Colchester, Darlington, Dorchester, Eastbourne, Felixstowe, Folkestone, Gillingham, Gloucester, Hartlepool, Huntingdon, Kenilworth, Kensington, Launceston, Letchworth, Maidenhead, Manchester, Nottingham, Pontefract, Portsmouth, Scunthorpe, Shrewsbury, Sunderland, Tewkesbury, Warrington, Washington, Whitehaven, Winchester
11 Bognor Regis, Bournemouth, Cirencester, Cleethorpes, Farnborough, Glastonbury, High Wycombe, Northampton, Scarborough, Shaftesbury, Southampton
12 Chesterfield, Clacton-on-Sea, Great Malvern, Huddersfield, Loughborough, Macclesfield, Milton Keynes, North Shields, Peterborough, South Shields, Stoke-on-Trent, West Bromwich
13 Bury St Edmunds, Ellesmere Port, Great Yarmouth, Kidderminster, Leamington Spa, Littlehampton, Lytham St Anne's, Middlesbrough, Saffron Walden, Southend-on-Sea, West Bridgford, Wolverhampton
14 Ashby-de-la-Zouch, Bishop Auckland, Chipping Norton, Hemel Hempstead, Henley-on-Thames, Stockton-on-Tees, Tunbridge Wells
15 Ashton-under-Lyne, Barrow-in-Furness, Burton upon Trent, Sutton Coldfield, Weston-super-Mare

---

*Northern Irish towns include:*

05 Derry, Larne, Newry, Omagh
06 Antrim, Armagh, Bangor, Lurgan
07 Belfast, Lifford, Lisburn
08 Limavady, Portrush, Strabane
09 Ballymena, Banbridge, Coleraine, Cookstown, Dungannon, Portadown
10 Ballyclare, Ballymoney
11 Downpatrick, Enniskillen, Londonderry, Magherafelt, Newtownards, Portstewart
13 Carrickfergus

---

*Scottish towns include:*

03 Ayr
04 Oban, Tain, Wick
05 Alloa, Banff, Elgin, Keith, Kelso, Nairn, Perth, Scone, Troon

06 Alness, Dunbar, Dundee, Dunoon, Forfar, Girvan, Glamis, Hawick, Huntly, Irvine, Lanark, Thurso
07 Airdrie, Alloway, Braemar, Dornoch, Falkirk, Glasgow, Golspie, Gourock, Lerwick, Mallaig, Paisley, Peebles, Portree, Selkirk
08 Aberdeen, Arbroath, Banchory, Dalkeith, Dingwall, Dumfries, Dunblane, Fortrose, Giffnock, Greenock, Hamilton, Jedburgh, Kirkwall, Montrose, Stirling, Ullapool
09 Ardrossan, Callander, Clydebank, Dumbarton, Edinburgh, Inverness, Inverurie, Kingussie, Kirkcaldy, Lockerbie, Peterhead, Pitlochry, Prestwick, St Andrews, Stornoway, Stranraer
10 Coatbridge, Dalbeattie, Galashiels, Glenrothes, Kilmarnock, Kincardine, Linlithgow, Livingston, Motherwell, Newtonmore, Stonehaven
11 Blairgowrie, Campbeltown, Cowdenbeath, Crianlarich, Cumbernauld, Dunfermline, Fort William, Fraserburgh, Grangemouth, Gretna Green, Invergordon, John o'Groats, Port Glasgow
12 Auchterarder, East Kilbride, Lochgilphead
13 Castle Douglas, Kirkcudbright, Kirkintilloch
14 Grantown-on-Spey

---

*Welsh towns include:*

04 Bala, Mold, Rhyl
05 Barry, Conwy, Tenby, Tywyn
06 Bangor, Brecon, Ruthin
07 Cardiff, Cwmbrân, Denbigh, Harlech, Newport, Newtown, Swansea, Wrexham
08 Aberdare, Barmouth, Bridgend, Cardigan, Chepstow, Ebbw Vale, Hay-on-Wye, Holyhead, Lampeter, Llanelli, Monmouth, Pembroke, Pwllheli, Rhayader, St David's, Treorchy
09 Aberaeron, Carnarvon, Colwyn Bay, Dolgellau, Fishguard, Llandudno, Llangefni, Pontypool, Prestatyn, Welshpool
10 Caernarfon, Caerphilly, Carmarthen, Llandovery, Llangollen, Pontypridd, Porthmadog, Port Talbot
11 Abergavenny, Abertillery, Aberystwyth, Builth Wells, Machynlleth
12 Milford Haven
13 Haverfordwest, Merthyr Tydfil

---

*See also* **city; United Kingdom**
• **mushroom town** 04 camp
• **open space in town** 04 lung

**town-dweller**
03 cit 05 towny 07 burgher, citizen, oppidan 08 townsman, urbanite
10 townswoman

## township

**02** tp **04** deme, vill **06** parish **07** village **09** community

## toxic

**06** deadly, lethal **07** baneful, harmful, noxious **08** poisoned **09** dangerous, poisonous, unhealthy
*See also* **poison**

## toy

**04** jest, play, whim **05** dally, flirt, knack, model, sport, trick **06** bauble, beaker, fiddle, gewgaw, paddle, tinker, trifle **07** reduced, replica, trinket **08** crotchet **09** automaton, mess about, miniature, plaything **10** knick-knack, mess around, small-scale **12** reproduction

*Toys include:*

**03** ark, gun, top
**04** ball, bike, dart, doll, farm, fort, game, gonk, kite, Lego®, Sega®, XBox®, yo-yo
**05** coral, Dinky®, slide, swing, teddy, trike
**06** cap-gun, garage, go-kart, guitar, paints, pop-gun, puzzle, rattle, rocker, seesaw, tea set
**07** balloon, bicycle, box-kite, crayons, Digimon®, dreidel, drum set, Frisbee®, Game Boy®, marbles, Meccano®, ocarina, Play-Doh®, Pokémon®, rag doll, sandpit, scooter, shoofly, soft-toy, tumbler, Turtles®
**08** catapult, doll's cot, football, GameCube®, golliwog, hula-hoop, Matchbox®, mirliton, model car, model kit, Nintendo®, Noah's ark, pedal-car, pinwheel, skipjack, squeaker, Subbuteo®, train set, tricycle, windmill
**09** Action Man®, aeroplane, bandalore, Care Bears, doll's pram, gyroscope, playhouse, pogo stick, Sindy doll®, swingball, teddy bear, video game, whirligig
**10** baby-walker, Barbie doll®, doll's buggy, doll's house, fivestones, hobby-horse, kewpie doll, musical box, pantograph, peashooter, Plasticene®, Rubik's Cube®, Scalextric®, skateboard, Steiff bear, Super Mario®, tin soldier, toy soldier, trampoline, typewriter, weather box, Wendy house
**11** baby-bouncer, glove puppet, PlayStation®, shape-sorter, silly string, spacehopper, spinning top, stroboscope, Tantalus cup, thaumatrope, tiddly winks, water pistol, wheel of life
**12** action figure, boxing-gloves, computer game, executive toy, jack-in-the-box, jigsaw puzzle, kaleidoscope, model railway, mountain bike, My Little Pony, paddling-pool, Power Rangers®, praxinoscope, rocking-horse, skipping-rope, walkie-talkie, weather house
**13** Bob the Builder®, building block,

climbing-frame, modelling clay, Newton's cradle, sewing machine, Space Invaders®, Tiny-Tears doll®
**14** activity centre, bucket and spade, building-blocks, building-bricks, Cartesian devil, Cartesian diver, electronic game, Paddington Bear, Powerpuff Girls®

## trace

**03** bit, dog, jot, map, way **04** calk, copy, dash, draw, dreg, drop, find, hint, hunt, mark, move, plan, scar, seek, show, sign, spot, walk **05** chart, dig up, draft, pinch, relic, savor, scent, smack, spoor, stalk, tinge, token, touch, track, tract, trail, whiff, write **06** course, depict, derive, detect, engram, follow, fossil, pursue, record, savour, shadow, sketch **07** analyse, mark out, outline, proceed, remains, remnant, run down, smidgen, smidgin, soupçon, thought, uncover, unearth, vestige **08** chalk out, describe, discover, engramma, evidence, footmark, generate, moniment, monument, smidgeon, traverse **09** delineate, footprint, scintilla, suspicion, track down **10** hide or hair, impression, indication, suggestion **11** counterdraw, hide nor hair

## track

**03** dog, pug, ren, rin, run, way **04** beat, hunt, line, loke, mark, path, race, rack, rail, rake, road, sent, sign, slot, tail, tram, trod, wake **05** chase, drift, orbit, piste, route, scent, spoor, stalk, trace, tract, trade, trail, tread, troad, trode **06** course, follow, groove, ground, inside, pursue, riding, runway, shadow, sleuth, troade **07** circuit, footing, monitor, portage, tramway **08** argument, cycleway, footmark, footstep, sequence, sideline, speedway, traverse **09** cyclepath, footprint **10** serpentine, trajectory
*See also* **athletics**
• **keep track of** **04** plot **05** check, grasp, trace, watch **06** follow, record **07** monitor, observe, oversee **10** keep up with, understand **11** keep an eye on
• **lose track of** **04** miss **06** forget **08** misplace **13** lose touch with **15** lose contact with
• **make tracks** **02** go **04** dash **05** leave, scram **06** beat it, depart **07** dash off, make off **09** disappear **10** hit the road **15** leave footprints
• **off the beaten track** **06** remote **07** private **08** isolated, outlying, secluded **11** god-forsaken, in the sticks, out-of-the-way **12** unfrequented
• **on track** **06** on time **08** on course, on target **10** on schedule
• **track down** **04** find **05** catch, dig up, trace **06** detect, expose, turn up **07** capture, nose out, run down, uncover, unearth **08** discover, hunt down, sniff out **09** ferret out **10** run to earth **11** run to ground
• **tracks** **02** Ry

## tract

**03** lot **04** area, dene, plot, vast, zone **05** block, clime, essay, monte, trace, track **06** desert, extent, homily, region, sermon **07** booklet, expanse, leaflet, quarter, stretch, terrain **08** brochure, district, pamphlet, tractate, treatise **09** discourse, monograph, territory **12** disquisition, dissertation

## tractable

**04** tame **05** tawie **06** docile, pliant **07** pliable, willing **08** amenable, biddable, obedient, towardly, tractile, workable, yielding **09** compliant, malleable, treatable **10** governable, manageable, submissive **11** complaisant, persuadable **12** controllable

## traction

**04** drag, grip, pull **07** draught, drawing, haulage, pulling **08** adhesion, friction **09** telferage **10** propulsion, telpherage

## tractor

**03** cat **07** backhoe, pedrail, skidder **09** bulldozer **13** backhoe loader **14** traction engine

## trade

**02** go **03** art, buy, job, ply, ren, rin, run, way **04** deal, line, mart, sell, swap, work **05** craft, skill, track, trail, tread **06** barter, buying, career, course, custom, market, métier, mister, occupy, peddle, resort, switch **07** bargain, calling, dealing, rubbish, selling, traffic **08** business, commerce, exchange, medicine, merchant, peddling, practice, sideline, transact, treading, vocation **09** carpentry, clientele, customers, marketing **10** contraband, do business, employment, line of work, occupation, profession **11** commodities, merchandize, shopkeeping, trafficking **12** transactions

## trademark

**04** logo, mark, name, sign **05** badge, brand, crest, label, quirk, stamp **06** emblem, symbol **07** feature **08** hallmark, insignia **09** attribute, brand name, idiograph, tradename **10** brand label, speciality **11** peculiarity **12** idiosyncrasy **14** characteristic, typical quality **15** proprietary name

## tradename

**02** TN **05** brand, label

## trader

**05** bania, buyer, plier **06** banian, banyan, broker, coster, dealer, seller, vendor **07** higgler, peddler **08** marketer, merchant, pitchman, retailer, supplier **09** barrow boy, marketeer, tradesman **10** easterling, shopkeeper, trafficker, wholesaler **11** tradeswoman **12** costermonger

## tradesman, tradeswoman

**05** buyer **06** dealer, seller, trader, vendor, worker **07** artisan **08** mechanic, merchant, retailer **09** craftsman **10** journeyman, shopkeeper **11** craftswoman

## tradition

**03** way **04** rite **05** habit, usage **06** belief, cabala, custom, kabala, legend, praxis, ritual **07** cabbala, kabbala, qabalah, routine **08** ceremony, folklore, kabbalah, practice **10** convention, observance **11** institution

## traditional

**03** old, set **04** folk, oral **05** fixed, usual **06** age-old **07** old-line, pompier, routine **08** habitual, historic **09** customary, traditive, unwritten **10** accustomed, ceremonial **11** established **12** conservative, conventional, time-honoured, tralaticious, tralatitious **15** long-established

## traditionalist

**07** diehard **08** old fogey, old guard, old-liner **09** formalist **11** reactionary **12** conservative **13** stick-in-the-mud **15** conventionalist

## traduce

**04** slag **05** abuse, decry, knock, smear **06** defame, insult, malign, revile, vilify **07** asperse, blacken, detract, run down, slag off, slander **08** transmit **09** denigrate, deprecate, disparage, propagate, translate **10** calumniate, depreciate **12** misrepresent

## traducer

**06** abuser **07** defamer, knocker, smearer **08** asperser, vilifier **09** detractor, slanderer **10** denigrator, deprecator, disparager, mud-slinger **11** calumniator

## traffic

**03** buy **04** cars, deal, sell **05** queue, trade, truck **06** barter, hold-up, peddle **07** bargain, contact, dealing, freight, trade in, trading **08** business, commerce, dealings, exchange, gridlock, intrigue, peddling, shipping, tailback, vehicles **09** negotiate, relations, transport **10** congestion, do business, passengers, traffic jam **11** commodities, intercourse, trafficking **13** communication **14** transportation

## trafficker

**05** agent **06** broker, dealer, monger, seller, trader **07** peddler **08** marketer, merchant, supplier **11** distributor **12** merchandizer

## tragedy

**04** blow **06** buskin **08** calamity, disaster **09** adversity **10** affliction, misfortune **11** catastrophe, unhappiness

## tragic

◇ *anagram indicator* **03** sad **04** dire **05** awful, fatal **06** deadly **07** unhappy, unlucky **08** buskined, dreadful, ill-fated, pathetic, pitiable, shocking, terrible, Thespian, wretched **09** appalling, miserable, sorrowful **10** calamitous, deplorable, disastrous **11** unfortunate **12** catastrophic **13** heartbreaking

## tragically

**07** awfully **08** terribly **10** dreadfully, shockingly, wretchedly **11** appallingly

## trail

◇ *juxtaposition indicator* **03** dog, lag, tow, way **04** drag, draw, fall, hang, haul, hunt, path, pull, road, sign, tail, wake **05** chase, droop, marks, piste, reach, route, scent, spoor, stalk, sweep, trace, track, trade, train **06** dangle, dawdle, extend, follow, linger, loiter, pursue, ramble, runway, shadow, sleuth, stream, streel, trapes **07** abature, draggle, traipse **08** footpath, straggle, tag along, trauchle **09** footmarks **10** footprints
• **destroy trail** **04** foil
• **trail away** **04** fade, sink **06** lessen, shrink, weaken **07** die away, dwindle, subside, tail off **08** decrease, diminish, fade away, fall away, melt away, peter out, taper off, trail off **09** disappear

## trailblazer

**06** leader **07** founder, pioneer **09** developer, innovator **10** discoverer, pathfinder **13** ground-breaker

## train

◇ *anagram indicator* **03** aim, set **04** drag, file, line, lure, path, sack, tail, tire **05** breed, chain, coach, court, drill, flier, flyer, focus, groom, learn, level, local, longe, lunge, order, point, staff, study, suite, teach, track, trail, tutor **06** allure, cafila, column, convoy, direct, ground, kafila, lesson, nuzzle, school, series, sledge, stream, string **07** bring up, caffila, caravan, cortège, educate, improve, prepare, process, reskill, retinue, work out **08** be taught, choo-choo, exercise, instruct, practise, puff-puff, rehearse, sequence **09** be trained, entourage, followers, following, household, inculcate **10** attendants, be prepared, discipline, procession, succession **11** progression **12** indoctrinate **13** concatenation

---

*Train types include:*

---

**01** Q
**02** up
**03** APT, HST, owl, TGV, way
**04** boat, down, loco, mail, milk
**05** goods, hover, mixed, paddy, steam
**06** bullet, diesel, Maglev
**07** baggage, express, freight, through, tilting
**08** cable-car, corridor, monorail, push-pull
**09** aerotrain, excursion, high-speed, Intercity®, manriding, Pendolino®
**10** locomotive
**12** Freightliner®
**13** accommodation
**14** shuttle service
**15** steam locomotive

---

*Trains include:*

---

**04** Ivor
**06** Rocket, Thomas
**07** Mallard, The Ghan
**09** The A-Train

**13** Indian Pacific, Orient Express, Trans-Siberian
**14** Flying Scotsman
**15** Hogwarts Express

---

## trained

**03** fit **08** schooled **10** discerning **11** experienced

## trainee

**01** L **02** AT, ET **04** tiro **05** cadet, pupil **06** intern, novice **07** interne, learner, student **08** beginner **10** apprentice **11** probationer

## trainer

**02** PT **05** coach, tutor **06** mentor **07** handler, teacher **08** educator **10** instructor
*See also* **footwear; horseman, horsewoman**

## training

◇ *anagram indicator* **02** PT **03** CAT, CBT **05** drill **07** lessons, nurture, tuition, workout **08** coaching, exercise, learning, pedagogy, practice, teaching, tutoring **09** education, grounding, schooling **10** bringing up, discipline, tirocinium, upbringing, working-out **11** instruction, preparation **14** apprenticeship
• **out of training** **04** soft
• **youth in training** **04** page

## traipse

**03** gad **04** plod, slog, trek **05** trail, tramp, trape **06** slouch, trudge **08** slattern

## trait

**04** thew **05** quirk, touch, trick **06** stroke **07** feature, quality **08** property **09** attribute **11** peculiarity **12** idiosyncrasy **14** characteristic

## traitor

**03** dog, rat **05** Judas, kulak **07** nithing **08** betrayer, deceiver, defector, deserter, informer, proditor, quisling, renegade, traditor, treacher, turncoat, two-timer **09** traitress, treachour **11** backstabber, treachetour **12** collaborator, double-dealer **13** double-crosser **14** fifth columnist

## traitorous

**05** false **06** untrue **08** apostate, disloyal, renegade **09** faithless, seditious **10** perfidious, unfaithful **11** treacherous, treasonable **13** dishonourable, double-dealing **14** double-crossing

## trajectory

**04** line, path **05** orbit, route, track, trail **06** course, flight **10** flight path

## trammel

◇ *anagram indicator* **03** bar, net, tie **04** bond, clog, curb, rein **05** block, catch, chain, check **06** enmesh, entrap, fetter, hamper, hinder, hobble, impede **07** capture, confine, ensnare, inhibit, shackle **08** entangle, handicap, obstacle, restrain, restrict **09** hindrance, restraint **10** impediment **14** stumbling-block

## tramp

**03** bum **04** hike, hobo, plod, roam, rove, slag, slut, step, tart, trek, walk **05** caird, jakey, march, piker, rogue, stamp, stomp, stump, trail, tread, tromp, wench, whore **06** dosser, hooker, ramble, sloven, toerag, truant, trudge, vagrom, walker, whaler **07** dingbat, floater, floozie, gangrel, swagger, swagman, tinkler, traipse, trample, trollop, vagrant **08** clochard, cursitor, derelict, footslog, scrubber, slattern, straggle, stroller, vagabond **09** landloper, sundowner, toeragger **10** down-and-out, loose woman, prostitute **11** rinthereout, scatterling, Weary Willie **12** hallan-shaker **15** knight of the road

## trample

**04** foil **05** crush, poach, potch, stamp, tramp, tread, tromp **06** insult, squash, stramp **07** flatten, hobnail **08** override, ride down

## trance

**04** daze **05** dream, spell **06** stupor, transe **07** ecstasy, rapture, reverie **08** entrance **09** catalepsy **12** somnambulism **15** unconsciousness

## tranche

**03** cut **04** part **05** block, piece, slice, wedge **06** length **07** portion, section, segment **10** instalment

## tranquil

**04** calm, cool, easy **05** quiet, still **06** hushed, placid, sedate, serene, silent **07** pacific, relaxed, restful **08** composed, laid-back, peaceful **09** reposeful, unexcited **10** untroubled **11** undisturbed, unflappable **12** even-tempered **13** imperturbable, unimpassioned **14** disimpassioned

## tranquillity

**03** lee **04** calm, hush, rest **05** peace, quiet **06** repose **07** ataraxy, silence **08** ataraxia, calmness, coolness, quietism, quietude, serenity **09** composure, placidity, quietness, stillness **10** equanimity, sedateness **11** restfulness **12** peacefulness

## tranquillize

**04** calm, lull **05** quell, quiet, relax **06** opiate, pacify, sedate, serene, soothe **07** compose **09** narcotize

## tranquillizer

**06** downer, opiate **07** bromide **08** narcotic, quietive, sedative **09** calmative **10** depressant **11** barbiturate **12** sleeping pill *See also* **sedative**

## transact

**02** do **05** enact **06** handle, manage, settle **07** carry on, conduct, execute, perform **08** carry out, conclude, despatch, dispatch **09** discharge, negotiate, prosecute **10** accomplish

## transaction

**03** job **04** deal, deed **06** action, affair, annals, doings, gamble, matter, record **07** affairs, bargain, minutes, passage, reports **08** business, concerns, debt swap, goings-on, handling, straddle

**09** agreement, discharge, enactment, execution **10** enterprise, proceeding, put-through, settlement, swap option **11** arrangement, negotiation, proceedings, undertaking **12** control event, part-exchange, publications

## transactions

**02** tr **07** affairs, dealing, journal, memoirs

## transcend

**04** beat **05** excel, outdo **06** exceed **07** eclipse, surpass **08** go beyond, outshine, outstrip, overstep, surmount **09** rise above **11** leave behind

## transcendence

**09** greatness, sublimity, supremacy **10** ascendancy, excellence, paramouncy **11** paramountcy, pre-eminence, superiority **12** predominance **13** matchlessness, transcendency **15** incomparability

## transcendent

**07** sublime, supreme **08** numinous, peerless **09** excellent, excelling, ineffable, matchless, spiritual **10** superhuman, surpassing **11** magnificent, superlative **12** incomparable, supernatural, transcending, unparalleled **13** unsurpassable

## transcendental

**05** vague **08** mystical **09** excelling, spiritual **10** mysterious **12** metaphysical, otherworldly, supereminent, supernatural, transcending **13** preternatural

## transcribe

**04** copy, note **06** copy up, record, render **07** Braille, copy out, rewrite, write up **08** take down, write out **09** reproduce, translate **13** transliterate

## transcript

**04** copy, note **05** tenor **06** record, tenour **07** version **09** duplicate **10** manuscript **11** translation **12** reproduction **13** transcription **15** exemplification, transliteration

## transcription

**07** version **10** writing-out **11** translation **12** reproduction, transumption **15** transliteration

## transfer

◇ *anagram indicator* **02** ET **03** EFT, PET, PMT **04** deed, flit, GIFT, hand, move, pass, take, turn, ZIFT **05** carry, grant, ladle, remit, shift **06** assign, change, convey, pounce, remove **07** consign, pipette, removal **08** alienate, give over, hand over, handover, movement, relocate, sign away, sign over, transmit **09** negotiate, transhume, transport, transpose **10** assignment, changeover, conveyance, relocation, transplant **12** displacement, transduction, transference, transmission **13** transposition

## transfigure

◇ *anagram indicator* **05** alter, exalt, morph **06** change **07** convert, glorify **08** idealize **09** transform, translate,

**transmute 11** apotheosize **12** metamorphose

## transfix

**04** hold, spit, stun **05** rivet, spear, spike, stick **06** empale, impale, pierce, skewer **07** bestick, engross, petrify **08** paralyse **09** fascinate, hypnotize, mesmerize, spellbind **10** run through

## transform

◇ *anagram indicator* **04** turn **05** adapt, alter, morph, renew **06** absorb, change, mutate, reform **07** commute, convert, lithify, rebuild, receive, remodel, resolve **08** disclose **09** sovietize, translate, transmute, transpose **10** trans-shape, transverse **11** reconstruct, transfigure **12** decentralize, metamorphose, transmogrify **13** revolutionize **15** unprotestantize

## transformation

◇ *anagram indicator* **03** wig **06** change, reform **07** turning **08** dilation, mutation, petalody, phyllody, reaction, rotation, sepalody **09** reflexion, sea change, variation **10** alteration, conversion, dilatation, metaplasia, metastasis, reflection, revolution **11** reformation, translation **13** metamorphosis, transmutation **15** theriomorphosis, transfiguration

## transfuse

**05** imbue **06** instil **07** pervade, suffuse **08** permeate, transfer

## transgress

**03** err, sin **04** defy **05** break, lapse **06** breach, exceed, offend **07** disobey, violate **08** encroach, infringe, overstep, trespass **09** misbehave **10** contravene **11** prevaricate

## transgression

**03** sin **04** debt, slip **05** crime, error, fault, lapse, scape, wrong **06** breach, escape **07** misdeed, offence, offense **08** iniquity, peccancy, trespass **09** overgoing, violation **10** infraction, peccadillo, wrongdoing **12** disobedience, encroachment, infringement, misbehaviour, misdemeanour, overstepping **13** contravention

## transgressor

**05** felon **06** debtor, sinner **07** culprit, villain **08** criminal, evil-doer, offender **09** miscreant, wrongdoer **10** delinquent, lawbreaker, malefactor, trespasser

## transience

**07** brevity **08** caducity, fugacity **09** briefness, shortness **11** evanescence **12** ephemerality, fleetingness, fugitiveness, impermanence **13** deciduousness, temporariness **14** transitoriness

## transient

**05** brief, fleet, short **06** bubble, flying **07** passing **08** fleeting, volatile **09** ephemeral, fugacious, momentary, short-term, temporary **10** evanescent, short-lived, transitory **11** impermanent **13** summer-seeming

**transistor**
03 FET

**transit**
05 route 06 travel 07 haulage, journey, passage, reverse 08 carriage, crossing, movement, shipment, transfer 10 conveyance, journeying, pass across 11 culmination 14 transportation
• **in transit** 05 by air, by sea 06 by rail, by road 07 en route 08 on the way 10 travelling

**transition**
04 flux, leap, move 05 shift 06 change, switch 07 passage, passing 08 movement, progress 09 evolution, metabasis 10 alteration, changeover, conversion, metastasis, unbecoming 11 composition, development, progression 12 transitional 13 metamorphosis, rite of passage, transmutation 14 transformation

**transitional**
05 fluid 07 interim, passing 08 changing, twilight 09 temporary, unsettled 11 provisional 12 evolutionary, intermediate 13 developmental

**transitory**
05 brief, fleet, short 06 flying 07 passing 08 fleeting 09 deciduous, ephemeral, fugacious, momentary, short-term, temporary, transient 10 evanescent, fly-by-night, short-lived 11 impermanent

**translate**
◇ anagram indicator ◇ foreign word indicator 03 put 04 move, turn 05 alter, shift 06 change, decode, encode, reduce, render, reword 07 conster, convert, English, explain, improve, traduce 08 construe, decipher, relocate, renovate, simplify, transfer 09 enrapture, interpret, transform, transmute, transport 10 metaphrase, paraphrase, transcribe 12 transmogrify 13 transliterate

**translation**
◇ anagram indicator 03 key 04 crib, move, pony 05 gloss, horse, shift 06 change, motion 07 version 08 transfer 09 rendering, rendition, rewording 10 alteration, conversion, metaphrase, paraphrase, rephrasing, traduction 11 explanation, metaphrasis 12 transumption 13 metamorphosis, transcription, transmutation 14 interpretation, simplification, transformation 15 transliteration

**translator**
02 tr 03 CLT 07 exegete, glosser, Rhemist 08 dragoman, linguist, polyglot 09 Englisher, exegetist, glossator 10 glossarist, metaphrast, paraphrast 11 interpreter, paraphraser

**translucent**
05 clear 06 limpid 08 lancelet, pellucid 10 diaphanous, membranous, see-through, translucid 11 membraneous, transparent 13 membranaceous

**transmigration**
07 rebirth 13 reincarnation

14 metempsychosis, Pythagoreanism, transformation

**transmission**
04 show 06 entail, signal, spread 07 beaming, episode, message, passage, sending 08 carriage, despatch, dispatch, relaying, shipment, transfer 09 broadcast, diffusion, imparting, programme, simulcast, transport 10 convection, conveyance, production, trajection 11 consignment, performance 12 broadcasting, presentation, transference 13 communication, dissemination, transmittance
• **end of transmission** 04 over 10 over and out

**transmit**
03 fax 04 beam, bear, buzz, pass, pipe, send 05 carry, modem, radio, relay, remit 06 convey, hand on, impart, pass on, report, send on, spread 07 conduct, consign, diffuse, forward, mediate, message, network, radiate, send out, traduce, traject 08 despatch, dispatch, hand down, telecast, televise, transfer 09 broadcast, propagate, satellite, transport 11 communicate, disseminate, interrogate

**transmute**
◇ anagram indicator 05 alter 06 change, remake 07 convert, permute, sublime 08 transmew 09 alchemize, permutate, sublimate, transform, translate, transmove 10 transverse 11 transfigure 12 metamorphose, transmogrify

**transparency**
05 photo, slide, water 07 clarity, picture 08 openness, overhead 09 clearness, filminess, frankness, gauziness, limpidity, plainness, sheerness 10 candidness, directness, limpidness, patentness, photograph 11 obviousness, pellucidity 12 apparentness, distinctness, explicitness, pellucidness, translucence, translucency 13 translucidity 14 diaphanousness, forthrightness 15 perspicuousness, unambiguousness

**transparent**
04 open 05 clear, filmy, gauzy, lucid, plain, sheer, white 06 candid, direct, limpid, patent, watery 07 evident, hyaline, hyaloid, obvious, tiffany, visible 08 apparent, distinct, explicit, manifest, pellucid 10 colourless, diaphanous, forthright, noticeable, see-through 11 discernible, perceptible, translucent, unambiguous, undisguised, unequivocal 12 semipellucid, transpicuous, unmistakable 15 straightforward

**transparently**
07 clearly, plainly 08 patently 09 evidently, obviously 10 distinctly, explicitly, noticeably 11 discernibly, perceptibly 12 unmistakably 13 unambiguously, unequivocally

**transpire**
05 arise, ensue, occur, prove 06 appear, befall, exhale, happen 07 come out, turn out 09 come about, take place 10 come to pass 11 become known, be disclosed, come to light 14 become apparent

**transplant**
04 move 05 graft, repot, shift 06 remove, uproot 07 replant 08 displace, plant out, relocate, resettle, transfer 12 cluster graft

**transport**
◇ anagram indicator 02 MT 03 AST, fit, lag, put, ren, rin, run, SST 04 bear, haul, move, rail, rape, rush, ship, take, waft 05 bliss, bring, carry, cycle, exile, fetch, shift, witch 06 convey, deport, frenzy, ravish, remove, thrill 07 delight, ecstasy, elation, freight, haulage, medevac, overjoy, rapture, removal, traject, transit, vehicle 08 carriage, entrance, euphoria, shipment, shipping, transfer 09 captivate, carry away, electrify, enrapture, spellbind, translate 10 conveyance 11 mass transit 12 exhilaration 13 seventh heaven, transportance 14 transportation
*See also* **travel; vehicle**

*Public transport includes:*

03 bus, cab
04 taxi, tram, tube
05 ferry, metro, train
07 omnibus, railway, trolley
10 stagecoach, trolleybus
11 park-and-ride, underground
12 cable railway, light railway

**transportation**
07 airlift, freight, haulage, railage, removal, traffic, transit, waftage 08 carriage, shipment, shipping, transfer 09 fishyback 10 conveyance

**transported**
◇ anagram indicator 04 rapt 05 piped 08 traveled 09 rhapsodic, travelled

**transpose**
◇ anagram indicator 02 tr 04 move, swap, turn 05 alter, shift 06 change, invert, switch 07 convert, reorder 08 exchange, flip-flop, transfer 09 rearrange, transform 10 substitute 11 interchange, metathesize 13 anagrammatize

**transverse**
05 cross 06 thwart 07 oblique, reverse 08 diagonal 09 crossways, crosswise, transform 10 overthwart 11 transversal

**trap**
◇ containment indicator 03 gin, gob, net, pit, pot 04 drop, dupe, fall, grin, hook, lime, lock, lure, mesh, ploy, ruse, take, toil, weel, wile 05 bazoo, catch, creel, decoy, fault, mouth, noose, plant, snare, spell, sting, toils, trick 06 ambush, bunker, corner, danger, device, enmesh, entrap, hazard, tangle 07 beguile, capture, confine, deceive, ensnare, flytrap, gin trap, mantrap, mist-net, pin down, pitfall, putcher,

rat-trap, springe **08** artifice, cakehole, catch-pit, dead-fall, fall-trap, inveigle, putcheon, trapdoor, traphole, trickery **09** booby-trap, deception, mouse-trap, oubliette, snaphance, stratagem **10** catch-basin, dig a pit for, potato trap, snaphaunce, snaphaunch, subterfuge
*See also* **carriage**

### trapped
◊ *insertion indicator* **05** duped, stuck **06** caught, netted, snared **07** tricked **08** ambushed, beguiled, cornered, deceived, ensnared **09** inveigled **10** surrounded **11** in by the week

### trapper
**06** hunter **08** covering, huntsman, voyageur **12** backwoodsman, frontiersman

### trappings
**04** gear **05** dress **06** finery, livery, things **07** clothes, panoply, raiment **08** fittings, fixtures, housings **09** equipment, furniture, ornaments, trimmings **10** adornments, fripperies **11** accessories, decorations, furnishings **13** accoutrements, paraphernalia **14** accompaniments

### trash
◊ *anagram indicator* **03** mar, pan, rot **04** blah, bosh, bull, bunk, carp, dust, guff, junk, ruin, scum, sink, slam **05** balls, blame, break, check, decry, dreck, dregs, hooey, knock, leash, slate, smash, snipe, spoil, tripe, waste, wreck **06** attack, drivel, grunge, harass, kitsch, litter, rabble, ravage, refuse, scraps, trudge **07** baloney, censure, condemn, destroy, eyewash, garbage, hogwash, rhubarb, rubbish, run down, shatter, torpedo, wear out **08** badmouth, canaille, demolish, denounce, malarkey, nonsense, riff-raff, trashery, write off **09** criticize, denigrate, devastate, disparage, excoriate, gibberish, moonshine, sweepings, trashtrie, vandalize **10** balderdash, come down on, go to town on, vituperate **11** pick holes in **12** disapprove of, gobbledygook, offscourings, pull to pieces, put the boot in, tear to shreds, undesirables **13** find fault with, play havoc with, tear a strip off **15** do a hatchet job on, pass judgement on

### trashy
**04** naff **05** cheap **06** crappy, flimsy, kitsch, paltry, shabby, shoddy, tawdry, tinsel **07** kitschy **08** inferior, rubbishy **09** cheap-jack, third-rate, worthless **12** meretricious

### trauma
**04** hurt, jolt, pain **05** agony, grief, shock, upset, wound **06** damage, injury, lesion, ordeal, strain, stress **07** anguish, torture **08** disorder, distress, upheaval **09** suffering **11** disturbance

### traumatic
**07** harmful, hurtful, painful **08** shocking, wounding **09** agonizing, injurious, stressful, upsetting

**10** disturbing, unpleasant **11** distressing, frightening

### traumatize
**04** daze, hurt, numb, stun **05** amaze, appal, shock, upset **06** dismay, grieve, offend **07** astound, horrify, outrage, stagger, startle, stupefy **08** distress, paralyse

### travail
**04** slog, toil **05** grind, sweat, tears **06** effort, labour, strain, stress, throes, travel **07** travois, trouble **08** distress, drudgery, exertion, hardship **09** suffering **10** birth-pangs, childbirth **11** labour pains, tribulation

### travel
**02** go **03** ren, rin, run **04** meve, move, pass, ride, roam, rove, tour, trip, tube, walk, wend, wing **05** cover, cross, vroom, wagon, wheel **06** ramble, troupe, voyage, waggon, wander **07** advance, conduct, explore, impetus, journey, passage, proceed, touring, tourism, travail, trolley, wayfare **08** go abroad, progress, traverse **09** excursion, make a trip **10** expedition, go overseas, journeying, travelling, wanderings **11** go walkabout, make your way, see the world, sightseeing **13** globetrotting
*See also* **space**

---

*Travel methods and forms include:*

**03** bus, fly, row, ski
**04** bike, hike, punt, ride, sail, tour, trek, trip, walk
**05** cycle, drive, jaunt, march, motor, pilot, skate, steam, visit
**06** aviate, cruise, flight, outing, paddle, ramble, safari, voyage
**07** commute, holiday, journey, mission, shuttle
**09** excursion, freewheel, hitch-hike, migration, orienteer
**10** expedition, pilgrimage
**11** exploration

---

### traveller
**03** rep **05** agent, Gypsy, hiker, nomad, rider, tramp **06** bagman, spacer, tinker, tourer, viator **07** aviator, bushman, drifter, drummer, migrant, rambler, tourist, tripper, vagrant, voyager **08** aviatrix, commuter, explorer, roadster, salesman, seafarer, spaceman, wanderer, wayfarer **09** itinerant, passenger, peregrine, sightseer **10** commercial, saleswoman, spacewoman **11** salesperson **12** excursionist, globetrotter, holidaymaker **14** representative **15** knight of the road

### travelling
◊ *anagram indicator* **04** road, rode **06** mobile, moving, roving **07** migrant, nomadic, roaming, sailing, touring, vagrant **08** homeless **09** itinerant, itinerary, migrating, migratory, on the move, on the road, unsettled, wandering, wayfaring **11** peripatetic

### travel-worn
**05** tired, weary **07** seasick, waygone,

wayworn **08** footsore **09** jet-lagged **10** saddle-sore **11** travel-weary

### traverse
**03** lap, ply, ren, rin, run **04** deny, ford, pace, plod, race, ride, roam, span, walk, wear, wind, wing **05** cover, cross, motor, range, stump, trace, track, tramp **06** bridge, denial, oppose, overgo, parade, screen, thwart, voyage, wander **07** barrier, curtain, descend, dispute, examine, measure, oblique, parapet **08** consider, crossing, go across, pass over, progress, walk over **09** adversity, go through, negotiate, partition **10** contradict, crosspiece **11** obstruction, pass through, peregrinate **12** travel across **13** contradiction, travel through

### travesty
**04** sham **05** farce, spoof **06** parody, send-up, wind-up **07** apology, charade, mockery, take-off **08** disguise **09** black mass, burlesque, tall story **10** caricature, corruption, distortion, perversion

### trawl
**04** comb, hunt, sift, wade **06** search **07** look for **11** investigate

### treacherous
**03** icy **05** dirty, false, Punic, risky, snaky **06** guiled, trappy, unsafe, untrue **08** disloyal, perilous, slippery **09** dangerous, deceitful, faithless, hazardous, two-timing **10** perfidious, precarious, traitorous, unfaithful, unreliable **11** duplicitous **12** backstabbing, false-hearted **13** double-hearted, hollow-hearted, untrustworthy **14** double-crossing

### treacherously
**07** falsely **08** mala fide **10** disloyally **11** deceitfully, faithlessly **12** perfidiously

### treachery
**07** treason **08** bad faith, betrayal, sabotage, trahison **09** duplicity, falseness, Judas kiss, perfidy, two-timing **10** disloyalty, hollowness, infidelity, Punic faith **11** fides Punica, traitorhood **12** backstabbing **13** deceitfulness, double-dealing, faithlessness **14** double-crossing, unfaithfulness

### tread
**02** go **04** beat, form, gait, hike, pace, plod, step, trek, walk **05** clamp, clump, crush, dance, march, press, spurn, stamp, stomp, trace, track, trade, tramp **06** squash, stramp, stride, trudge, walk on **07** chalaza, flatten, footing, oppress, trample **08** business, copulate, footfall, footmark, footstep **09** footprint, press down **11** cicatricula
• **tread on someone's toes 03** irk, vex **04** hurt **05** annoy, upset **06** bruise, injure, offend **07** affront **08** infringe **10** discommode, disgruntle **13** inconvenience

### treason
**06** mutiny **07** perfidy **08** sedition, trahison **09** duplicity, rebellion,

**treasonable**

treachery **10** disloyalty, subversion **11** lese-majesty, leze-majesté, leze-majesty, perduellion, traitorhood **12** disaffection **14** traitorousness

**treasonable**
**05** false **08** disloyal, mutinous **09** faithless, seditious **10** perfidious, rebellious, subversive, traitorous, unfaithful

**treasure**
**03** gem **04** cash, gems, gold, love **05** adore, cache, guard, hoard, money, prize, value **06** dote on, esteem, jewels, revere, riches, taonga, wealth **07** cherish, darling, fortune, idolize, worship **08** hold dear, preserve **09** valuables **11** masterpiece, pride and joy **13** think highly of **14** crème de la crème

**treasurer**
**06** bursar, fiscal, purser **07** cashier, steward **08** quaestor **10** camerlengo, camerlingo, cash-keeper **11** purse-bearer

**treasury**
**04** bank, fisc, fisk **05** cache, chest, funds, hoard, money, store, vault **06** assets, camera, corpus **07** bursary, capital, coffers **08** finances, revenues **09** exchequer, resources, thesaurus **10** repository, storehouse

**treat**
◇ *anagram indicator* **02** do **03** buy, fun, rub, tar, tub, use, vat, vet, wax **04** cure, gift, give, heal, tend, view, wine, worm **05** amuse, apply, besee, cover, dress, feast, lay on, nurse, paint, party, prime, put on, serve, smear, stand, study, waste, wheel **06** doctor, handle, manage, outing, parley, pay for, regale, regard, review, thrill **07** banquet, care for, delight, discuss, present, provide, take out **08** attend to, consider, deal with, medicate, pleasure, spread on, surprise **09** amusement, cover with, enjoyment, entertain, excursion, look after, negotiate, poeticize, tartarize **10** indulgence, minister to, pay the bill **11** celebration, foot the bill, negotiation **13** behave towards, entertainment, gratification

**treatable**
**07** curable **08** moderate, operable **09** medicable, reparable, tractable **10** reformable, remediable **11** rectifiable

**treatise**
**05** essay, ethic, paper, study, summa, tract **06** Cybele, system, thesis **07** pandect **08** Almagest, lapidary, pamphlet, prodrome, tractate **09** cosmology, discourse, festilogy, festology, monograph **10** arithmetic, dendrology, exposition, halieutics **11** gnomonology **12** disquisition, dissertation

**treatment**
◇ *anagram indicator* **03** EST, use **04** care, cure, deal **05** doing, usage **06** action, demean, notice, reason, remedy

**07** affront, conduct, dealing, demaine, demayne, demeane, healing, measure, nursing, quarter, regimen, surgery, therapy **08** cosmesis, coverage, dealings, handling **09** behaviour, discursus, going-over **10** asepticism, discussion, management, medicament, medication, observance **12** manipulation, therapeutics **13** antisepticism **14** discountenance

**treaty**
**04** bond, deal, pact **05** peace **06** pledge **07** bargain, compact, concord **08** alliance, assiento, contract, covenant, entreaty, protocol **09** agreement, concordat **10** convention, engagement **11** negotiation **12** pacification

*Treaties and agreements include:*

**03** Edo (Treaty of)
**04** Jay's (Treaty), Rome (Treaty of), SALT
**05** Baden, Dover (Treaty of), Ghent (Treaty of), Kyoto (accord), Lyons (Treaty of), Paris (Treaties of), Union
**06** Amiens (Treaty of), Berlin (Treaty of), London (Treaties of), Madrid (Treaty of), Passau (Treaty of), Poland (Partitions of), Tilsit (Treaties of), Vienna (Treaties of)
**07** Barrier (Treaties), Dresden (Treaty of), Nanjing (Treaty of), Nystadt (Treaty of), Tianjin (Treaty of), Utrecht (Peace of)
**08** Brussels (Treaty of), Kanagawa (Treaty of), Lausanne (Treaty of), Pyrenees (Treaty of the), Tientsin (Treaty of)
**09** Bucharest (Treaties of), Hay-Herrán (Treaty), Karlowitz (Treaty of), Pressburg (Treaty of), St Germain (Treaty of)
**10** Adrianople (Treaty of), Anglo-Iraqi (Treaty), Maastricht (Treaty), Magna Carta, Paris Pacts, San Stefano (Treaty of), Versailles (Treaty of), Warsaw Pact, Washington (Treaty of), Westphalia (Peace of)
**11** Fort Stanwix (Treaties of), Locarno Pact, Vereeniging (Peace of), Westminster (Treaty of)
**12** Brest-Litovsk (Treaty of), Lateran Pacts
**13** North Atlantic (Treaty), Social Chapter, Triple Entente
**14** Hague Agreement, Hoare-Laval Pact
**15** Entente Cordiale, Munich Agreement

**treble**
**04** high **05** sharp **06** piping, shrill, triple **07** soprano **09** threefold **11** high-pitched

**tree**
**04** bush, limb, spar **05** shrub **06** corner, wooden **07** gallows **08** pedigree
*See also* **palm; pine; rubber**

*Tree types include:*

**03** nut
**04** palm

**05** covin, fruit
**06** bonsai, citron, citrus, forest, timber
**07** conifer, dwarfed
**08** hardwood, softwood
**09** broad-leaf, Christmas, deciduous, evergreen
**10** ornamental

*Trees include:*

**02** bo, ti
**03** ash, asp, bay, bel, box, elm, fig, fir, gum, ita, jak, koa, may, nim, oak, sal, tea, ule, yew
**04** acer, akee, arar, atap, bito, coco, cola, dali, dhak, dika, dita, eugh, gean, holm, hule, ilex, jack, kola, lime, lind, mate, mowa, neem, nipa, olea, ombu, palm, pear, pine, plum, poon, rata, rimu, shea, sorb, teak, teil, toon, upas, yang
**05** ackee, afara, alder, apple, aspen, assai, balsa, beech, birch, bodhi, cacao, carob, cedar, china, ebony, elder, fruit, guava, hazel, holly, karri, kauri, larch, lemon, lilac, lotus, mango, maple, morus, olive, papaw, peach, pecan, piñon, pipal, plane, rowan, salix, thorn, tulip, yucca
**06** acacia, almond, bamboo, banana, banyan, baobab, bonsai, cashew, cassia, cherry, damson, gingko, jarrah, laurel, linden, papaya, pawpaw, poplar, prunus, quince, rubber, sapele, spruce, walnut, willow
**07** apricot, Banksia, blue gum, conifer, cork oak, cypress, dogwood, hickory, quassia, redwood, sequoia, wych elm
**08** chestnut, date palm, Dutch elm, eucalypt, ghost gum, hardwood, hawthorn, hornbeam, mahogany, mandarin, mangrove, mulberry, oleaster, softwood, sycamore, tamarisk
**09** araucaria, blackwood, Chile pine, crab apple, deciduous, evergreen, jacaranda, kauri-pine, leylandii, matagouri, melaleuca, paperbark, persimmon, sassafras, Scots pine, stone pine, whitebeam, wych-hazel
**10** blackthorn, breadfruit, cottonwood, Douglas fir, eucalyptus, ornamental, sandalwood, witch hazel
**11** bottle brush, bristlecone, coconut palm, copper beech, false acacia, golden larch, London plane, mountain ash, Norfolk pine, pussy willow, silver birch, silver maple, slippery elm
**12** monkey puzzle, Monterey pine, Wellingtonia
**13** angel's trumpet, horse chestnut, Japanese maple, sweet chestnut, weeping willow
**14** cedar of Lebanon, Lombardy poplar
**15** bristlecone pine

• **abounding in trees** **04** elmy, oaky, piny

- **clump of trees** 03 mot 04 mott
05 bluff, copse, motte, plump
06 spinny 07 spinney
- **embedded tree** 04 snag
- **isolated tree** 04 ombu
- **tree stump** 04 runt
- **tree trunk** 03 log 04 bole, butt,
stud 06 ricker

**tree-planted walk**
04 xyst 06 xystos, xystus

**trek**
04 drag, hike, plod, roam, rove, slog,
trip, walk, yomp 05 march, stage,
tramp 06 ramble, safari, trudge
07 journey, migrate, odyssey, traipse
09 migration 10 expedition

**trellis**
03 net 04 grid, mesh 05 grate 06 grille
07 grating, lattice, network, treille
08 espalier 09 framework
11 latticework 12 reticulation

**tremble**
◇ *anagram indicator* 04 rock 05 quake,
shake 06 dither, dodder, hotter, judder,
quaver, quiver, shiver, tremor, wobble,
wuther 07 shudder, vibrate, whither
09 vibration 10 tremulousness

**trembling**
◇ *anagram indicator* 04 yips 06 quaver,
shakes 07 quaking, rocking, shaking
09 juddering, quavering, quivering,
shivering, tremulous, vibration
10 heart-quake, shuddering
11 oscillation, trepidation

**tremendous**
04 huge, vast 05 great 06 wicked
07 amazing, corking, howling,
immense, massive 08 colossal,
dreadful, enormous, gigantic,
smashing, terrific, towering
09 wonderful 10 formidable,
impressive, incredible, marvellous,
prodigious, remarkable, stupendous,
thundering 11 elephantine,
exceptional, sensational, spectacular
13 extraordinary 14 out of this world

**tremendously**
04 very 06 highly, really 07 acutely,
awfully, greatly, utterly 08 severely
09 decidedly, extremely, intensely,
unusually 10 remarkably, thoroughly,
uncommonly 11 exceedingly,
excessively, frightfully
12 immoderately, inordinately,
terrifically, unreasonably
13 exceptionally 15 extraordinarily

**tremor**
05 quake, shake, shock 06 dindle,
dinnle, quaver, quiver, shiver, thrill,
wobble 07 shudder, temblor, tremble
09 agitation, foreshock, marsquake,
moonquake, quavering, trembling,
vibration 10 earthquake, titubation

**tremulous**
◇ *anagram indicator* 05 aspen, jumpy,
shaky, timid 06 afraid, aspine, scared
07 anxious, excited, fearful, jittery,
nervous, quivery, shaking, trembly
08 agitated, timorous, unsteady,
wavering 09 quavering, quivering,

shivering, trembling, vibrating
10 frightened

**trench**
03 cut, fur, pit, sap 04 dike, dyke, foss,
furr, grip, leat, leet, line, moat, rill
05 boyau, ditch, drain, fosse, gripe,
verge 06 border, furrow, gullet, gutter,
trough 07 channel, cunette, slidder
08 encroach, entrench, parallel,
waterway 09 earthwork 10 excavation
12 entrenchment
*See also* **ocean**

**trenchant**
05 acute, blunt, clear, sharp, terse
06 astute, biting 07 acerbic, caustic,
cutting, mordant, pungent 08 clear-cut,
distinct, emphatic, forceful, incisive,
scathing, vigorous 09 effective
10 forthright, no-nonsense, perceptive
11 penetrating, unequivocal
13 perspicacious

**trend**
03 fad 04 bend, bent, flow, look, mode,
rage, tide, turn, wind 05 craze, drift,
style, vogue 06 course, downer, latest
07 bearing, current, fashion, leaning
08 downturn, tendency
09 bandwagon, consensus, direction,
downswing 10 mainstream, rising tide
11 inclination, radical chic 13 name of
the game

**trendsetter**
05 model 06 leader, new man
07 pioneer 08 new woman
09 innovator, modernist, modern man
11 modern woman, trailblazer
12 avant-gardist 13 avant-gardiste,
groundbreaker

**trendy**
02 in 03 hip, now 04 cool 05 funky,
natty 06 groovy, latest, modish,
snazzy, with it 07 right-on, stylish,
voguish 10 all the rage 11 fashionable
13 up-to-the-minute 14 fashion-
forward

**trepidation**
04 fear 05 alarm, dread, worry
06 dismay, fright, nerves, qualms,
tremor, unease 07 anxiety, emotion,
jitters, shaking 08 disquiet 09 agitation,
cold sweat, quivering, trembling
10 excitement, misgivings, uneasiness
11 butterflies, nervousness, palpitation
12 apprehension, perturbation
13 consternation

**trespass**
03 sin 05 poach, wrong 06 invade,
offend 07 impinge, intrude, offence,
violate 08 encroach, infringe, invasion,
obdurate, poaching 09 intrusion
violation 10 transgress, wrongdoing
12 encroachment, infringement,
misdemeanour 13 contravention,
transgression

**trespasser**
06 sinner 07 burglar, poacher
08 criminal, evil-doer, intruder,
offender 10 delinquent, encroacher
12 transgressor

**tress**
04 curl, hair, lock, tail 05 braid, bunch,

plait, swits 06 strand, switch 07 pigtail,
ringlet 08 trammels

**trial**
03 try 04 bane, case, exam, pest, test
05 assay, check, cross, dummy, grief,
pilot, probe, study 06 appeal, assess,
assize, bother, burden, dry run, hassle,
misery, ordeal, sample, screen, trinal,
try out, try-out 07 analyse, approof,
attempt, contest, examine, hearing,
inquiry, lawsuit, retrial, scratch,
testing, test run, trouble 08 appraise,
audition, distress, dummy run,
endeavor, evaluate, hardship,
nuisance, practice, tribunal, vexation
09 adventure, adversity, annoyance,
endeavour, probation, rehearsal,
selection, suffering, threefold
10 affliction, experiment, litigation,
temptation 11 approbation,
competition, cross to bear,
examination, exploratory, investigate,
provisional, tribulation 12 cause
célèbre, experimental, probationary
13 pain in the neck 14 experiment with
15 thorn in the flesh

**triangle**

*Triangles include:*

05 right
07 Bermuda, eternal, Pascal's,
scalene, similar, warning
09 cocked hat, congruent, isosceles,
spherical
11 acute-angled, equilateral, right-
angled
12 obtuse-angled

**triangular**
08 trigonal, trigonic 09 trigonous
10 three-sided, trilateral, triquetral
11 triquetrous 13 three-cornered
14 triangle-shaped
- **triangular piece** 04 gair, gare, gore
05 fichu, godet

**tribal**
05 class, group 06 ethnic, family,
native 08 gentilic 09 sectional
10 indigenous

**tribe**
03 iwi, rod 04 clan, hapu, race, sept
05 blood, breed, caste, class, group,
house, ngati, stock 06 branch, family,
nation, people 07 dynasty 08 division
11 ethnic group

*Tribes of Israel:*

03 Dan, Gad
05 Asher, Judah
06 Reuben, Simeon
07 Ephraim, Zebulun
08 Benjamin, Issachar, Manasseh,
Naphtali

*See also* **aboriginal; African;
American; Asian; European**

**tribulation**
03 woe 04 blow, care, pain 05 curse,
grief, trial, worry 06 burden, misery,
ordeal, sorrow 07 anxiety, reverse,
travail, trouble 08 distress, hardship,
vexation 09 adversity, heartache,

suffering **10** affliction, misfortune
**11** unhappiness **12** wretchedness

**tribunal**
**03** bar, EAT **04** rota **05** bench, court,
trial **07** hearing **09** Areopagus,
committee **11** examination, inquisition
**12** confessional **13** kangaroo court

**tribune**
**04** bema

**tributary**
**04** fork **05** bogan, river **06** branch,
feeder, stream **08** influent **09** confluent
**10** head-stream **12** contributing

**tribute**
**03** due, fee, tax **04** cain, duty, gift, kain,
levy, scat, skat, toll **05** gavel, paean,
proof, scatt **06** charge, credit, eulogy,
homage, honour, praise, tariff
**07** payment, pension, present, respect
**08** accolade, applause, encomium,
evidence, good word, offering, Rome-
scot **09** drift-land, gratitude, panegyric,
Rome-penny **10** compliment,
dedication **11** good opinion, high
opinion, Peter's pence, recognition,
testimonial **12** commendation,
contribution **15** acknowledgement

**trice**
**02** mo **03** sec **04** haul, tick **05** flash,
jiffy, shake **06** minute, moment, pulley,
second **07** instant **09** twinkling

**trichosanthin**
**01** Q

**trick**
◇ *anagram indicator* **02** do **03** art, con,
fix, fob, fun, gag, kid, rig, tip, toy
**04** dupe, fake, feat, flam, fool, gift, gull,
hang, have, hoax, jape, joke, mock,
pass, pawk, ploy, rook, ruse, scam,
sell, sham, trap, trim, turn, vice, wile
**05** antic, bluff, bogus, caper, cheat,
cozen, dodge, false, flair, fraud, glaik,
gleek, knack, plant, prank, quirk, skill,
skite, skyte, spell, stall, stunt, watch
**06** adroit, antick, begunk, chouse,
deceit, delude, device, diddle, double,
ersatz, forged, frolic, genius, have on,
illude, juggle, lead on, mirage, outwit,
palter, rip-off, secret, shavie, take in,
talent **07** ability, anticke, antique,
beguile, chicane, deceive, defraud,
faculty, fantasy, fast one, feigned,
frame-up, knowhow, leg-pull, mislead,
pliskie, roughie, skylark, slinter,
swindle, trinket, wrinkle **08** artifice,
capacity, doubling, facility, flimflam,
gimcrack, hoodwink, illusion,
jimcrack, prestige, skin game, subtlety
**09** curveball, deception, defective,
expedient, gold brick, imitation,
manoeuvre, mousetrap, stratagem,
technique, underplot **10** apparition,
artificial, capability, hocus-pocus,
pleasantry, subterfuge, subtleness,
under-craft, unreliable **11** conjuration,
counter-cast, counterfeit, galliardise,
hornswoggle, legerdemain, monkey
shine, pull one over, trompe d'oeil
**12** starting hole, take for a ride, trick of
light **13** double-shuffle, practical joke,
sleight of hand **14** pull a fast one on,
three-card monte

• **number of tricks** **03** nap **04** book,
slam
• **trick out** **04** do up, fard, tiff
**05** adorn, array **06** attire, bedeck, doll
up, tart up **07** dress up, trick up
**08** decorate, ornament, spruce up

**trickery**
**04** trap **05** fraud, guile **06** deceit,
ropery, slight **07** cantrip, cunning,
dodgery, jookery, joukery, sleight
**08** artifice, cheating, illusion, jugglery,
practice, pretence, wiliness
**09** chicanery, deception, duplicity,
imposture, stratagem, swindling
**10** conveyance, dishonesty, hanky-
panky, hocus-pocus, imposition,
shenanigan, subterfuge
**11** contrivance, legerdemain,
shenanigans, skulduggery
**12** skullduggery **13** double-dealing,
funny business, jiggery-pokery, sleight
of hand **14** joukery-pawkery, monkey
business **15** smoke and mirrors

**trickle**
**03** ren, rin, run **04** drib, drip, drop,
leak, ooze, seep **05** exude **06** filter,
gutter **07** dribble, driblet, drizzle,
dropple, seepage **08** dribblet, ticklish
**09** percolate **10** flow slowly, precarious

**trickster**
**04** hood, rook **05** cheat, fraud, joker,
rogue, shark **06** con man, dodger,
hoaxer, rascal **07** cozener, diddler,
hoodlum, hustler, tricker **08** con
woman, deceiver, impostor, swindler
**09** artificer, charlatan, con artist,
fraudster, pretender, tregetour
**10** dissembler, mountebank **11** illy
whacker

**tricky**
◇ *anagram indicator* **03** sly **04** foxy, wily
**05** dicey, dodgy, elvan, elven, nasty
**06** artful, crafty, elfish, elvish, knotty,
pretty, shifty, subtle, thorny
**07** awkward, cunning, devious, finicky
**08** delicate, scheming, slippery,
ticklish **09** deceitful, difficult, sensitive
**11** complicated, legerdemain,
problematic

**tried**
**06** proved, proven, tested **07** trusted
**08** reliable **10** dependable
**11** established, trustworthy

**trifle**
**03** bit, fig, toy **04** dash, doit, drop, fool,
iota, play, song, spot **05** dally, flirt,
sport, straw, touch, trace, wally
**06** bauble, dabble, daidle, faddle,
fiddle, fisgig, fizgig, frivol, geegaw,
gewgaw, little, meddle, niggle, paddle,
palter, peddle, piffle, pingle, potter,
tiddle, trivia, wanton **07** flamfew,
fribble, nothing, old song, quiddle,
trinket **08** falderal, fal de rol, flea-bite,
folderol, niffnaff, pittance, whim-
wham **09** bagatelle, mess about,
plaything **10** dilly-dally, knick-knack,
mess around, triviality **11** fiddlestick,
inessential, small amount **12** fiddle-
faddle **13** play the wanton

**trifling**
**04** idle **05** empty, minor, petty, potty,
seely, silly, small **06** faddle, fallal,
futile, paltry, slight **07** fooling, foolish,
puerile, shallow, trivial **08** baubling,
boy's play, childish, fiddling, frippery,
immoment, nonsense, nugatory,
piddling, piffling **09** dalliance,
desipient, fribbling, fribblish, frivolous,
whifflery, worthless **10** negligible
**11** superficial, unimportant **12** fiddle-
faddle **13** insignificant
**14** inconsiderable **15** inconsequential

**trigger**
**04** spur **05** catch, cause, lever, start
**06** elicit, prompt, set off, switch
**07** produce, provoke **08** activate,
generate, initiate, spark off, stimulus,
touch off **09** day-length **10** bring about
**11** set in action, set in motion

**trill**
**04** lilt, pipe, roll, sing **05** flute, shake,
twirl **06** quaver, warble **07** trundle

**trim**
◇ *head deletion indicator* ◇ *tail deletion
indicator* **03** cut, dub, fit, fur, lop, net,
way **04** barb, chop, clip, cool, crop,
dink, dock, edge, face, form, lace,
neat, nett, pare, slim, snip, snod, tidy,
tosh, trig **05** adorn, array, braid, cheat,
dress, frill, guard, natty, order, prune,
roach, ruche, shape, shave, shear,
slick, smart, smirk, state, tight, trick
**06** adjust, border, dapper, donsie,
edging, fettle, fit out, fringe, health,
humour, neaten, plight, reduce,
smooth, snazzy, spruce, svelte,
temper, thrash, tidy up, trimly
**07** arrange, balance, compact, curtail,
cut down, festoon, fitness, garnish,
orderly, slender **08** clean-cut, contract,
decorate, decrease, diminish, fittings,
ornament, trimming, well-kept
**09** condition, cut back on, embellish,
scale down, shipshape, underbear
**10** decoration **11** clean-limbed,
disposition, in good order,
presentable, streamlined, well-
dressed, well-groomed **12** spick-and-
span **13** well-turned-out

**trimming**
**03** end **04** gimp, gymp, trim **05** braid,
extra, frill, guard, guimp, robin
**06** border, edging, fringe, paring,
piping, robing **07** cascade, cutting,
falbala, garnish, macramé, macrami,
marabou **08** clipping, frou-frou,
furbelow, marabout **09** accessory,
adornment, balancing, garniture,
passement **10** decoration
**11** fimbriation **13** accompaniment,
embellishment, ornamentation,
passementerie

**Trinidad and Tobago**
**02** TT **03** TTO

**trinket**
**04** seal **05** bijou, charm, jewel, trick
**06** bauble, doodad, doodah, geegaw,
gewgaw, trifle **07** flamfew, trankum
**08** delicacy, gimcrack, kickshaw,
ornament, whim-wham **09** bagatelle,

kickshaws **10** knick-knack
**11** whigmaleery **12** whigmaleerie

## trio
**05** triad **06** triune, troika **07** musette,
trilogy, trinity, triplet **08** terzetto,
triunity **09** threesome **10** triplicity
**11** triumvirate
*See also* **three; threesome**

## trip
◇ *anagram indicator* **03** hop, ren, rin, run
**04** buzz, fall, flip, high, hurl, kilt, link,
ride, sail, skip, slip, spin, tilt, tour
**05** caper, dance, dream, drive, error,
flock, foray, gaffe, jaunt, jolly, lapse,
slide, spurn, waltz, whirl **06** booboo,
bummer, gambol, howler, outing,
sortie, spring, tiptoe, tootle, totter,
tumble, vision, voyage **07** bloomer,
blunder, clanger, fantasy, faux pas,
journey, mistake, stagger, stumble
**08** freak-out, illusion **09** excursion,
false step **10** apparition, expedition,
experience, inaccuracy
**13** hallucination **15** lose your footing
• **trip up** **04** trap **05** catch, snare, trick
**06** ambush, outwit, waylay **07** ensnare
**08** catch out, fall over, outsmart,
surprise **09** wrongfoot **10** disconcert
**15** throw off balance

## tripe
**03** rot **04** blah, bosh, guff, tosh **05** balls,
hooey, trash **06** bunkum, drivel
**07** baloney, eyewash, garbage,
hogwash, inanity, rhubarb, rubbish,
twaddle **08** claptrap, entrails,
malarkey, nonsense, tommyrot
**09** bullswool, moonshine, poppycock
**10** balderdash

## triple
**04** trio **05** third, triad **06** treble, triune,
troika **07** perfect, trilogy, trinity, triplet
**08** three-ply, three-way, triunity
**09** threefold, threesome **10** sdrucciola,
three times, tripartite, triplicate,
triplicity **11** triumvirate

## tripod
**03** cat, pod **06** trivet **08** triangle
**09** brand-iron

## tripper
**07** grockle, tourist, voyager
**09** sightseer, traveller **12** excursionist,
holidaymaker

## trite
**04** dull, worn **05** banal, corny, stale,
stock, tired **06** beaten, common
**07** cliché'd, routine, worn-out
**08** clichéed, cornball, ordinary,
overdone, overused, overworn, tritical,
truistic, well-worn **09** hackneyed,
rinky-dink **10** threadbare, uninspired,
unoriginal **11** commonplace, Mickey
Mouse, novelettish, predictable,
stereotyped, well-trodden **12** run-of-
the-mill **13** platitudinous

## tritium
**01** T **13** heavy hydrogen

## triton
**03** eft **04** evet, newt

## triumph
**03** hit, joy, win **04** beat, coup, crow,

feat, pomp **05** exult, gloat, glory,
paean, revel, trump **06** defeat, insult
**07** conquer, elation, mastery, pageant,
prevail, prosper, rejoice, succeed,
success, swagger, victory **08** conquest,
dominate, jubilate, overcome,
overcrow, vanquish, walkover
**09** celebrate, exultance, exultancy,
festivity, happiness, overwhelm,
rejoicing, sensation, win the day
**10** attainment, exultation, jubilation,
observance **11** achievement,
celebration, gain mastery
**12** masterstroke **13** flying colours
**14** accomplishment
• **expression of triumph** **02** ha, ho,
io **03** aha, hah, hey, hoa, hoh, Jai, oho,
olé **04** ha-ha **05** heigh, there **06** yippee
**07** so there

## triumphant
**05** proud **06** elated, joyful **07** crowing,
winning **08** boastful, exultant, gloating,
glorious, jubilant **09** cock-a-hoop,
rejoicing, triumphal **10** conquering,
successful, swaggering, victorious
**11** celebratory **12** prize-winning

## trivia
**03** pap **06** Hecate **07** details, trifles
**08** minutiae **12** trivialities
**13** irrelevancies **14** technicalities

## trivial
**04** bald **05** banal, dinky, minor, petty,
small, trite **06** flimsy, frothy, little,
measly, paltry **08** everyday, gimcrack,
piddling, piffling, snippety, trifling
**09** frivolous, quibbling, rinky-dink,
small beer, worthless **10** incidental,
negligible, peppercorn, vernacular
**11** commonplace, meaningless,
unimportant **12** cutting no ice,
pettifogging **13** insignificant, no great
shakes **14** inconsiderable
**15** inconsequential, of no
consequence

## triviality
**06** detail, trifle **07** nothing **08** banality,
frippery, nonsense, pretence
**09** frivolity, pettiness, puerility,
smallness **10** nothingism **11** foolishness
**12** technicality, unimportance
**13** worthlessness **14** insignificance
**15** meaninglessness

## trivialize
**07** devalue, scoff at **08** belittle,
minimize, play down **09** underplay
**10** depreciate, undervalue
**12** Hollywoodize **13** underestimate

## troglodyte
**04** wren **11** cave-dweller

## troll
**03** elf **04** drow, harl, jinn, roll, rove,
spin, trow **05** dwarf, gnome, pooka
**06** allure, goblin, ramble, stroll
**07** trundle **08** trolling **09** circulate
**10** repetition

## trolley
**04** corf **05** bogey, bogie, brute, dolly,
truck **06** gurney **07** tramcar **09** caddie
car **10** caddie cart, traymobile
**11** dinner-wagon

## trollop
**03** pro, pug, tom **04** bawd, dell, drab,
moll, punk, road, stew, tart **05** brass,
broad, quail, quiff, stale, tramp, trull,
wench, whore **06** bulker, callet,
geisha, harlot, hooker, mutton, plover
**07** cocotte, floozie, hetaera, hostess,
hustler, lorette, polecat, rent-boy,
venture **08** bona-roba, callgirl, dolly-
mop, magdalen, strumpet
**09** courtesan, hierodule, loose fish
**10** cockatrice, convertite, fancy
woman, loose woman, prostitute,
rough trade, vizard-mask **11** fallen
woman, fille de joie, laced mutton,
night-walker, poule de luxe, public
woman, working girl **12** fille des rues,
painted woman, scarlet woman, street-
walker **13** grande cocotte **14** lady of
the night, woman of the town

## troop
**02** go, tp **03** mob **04** army, band, body,
crew, gang, herd, kern, pack, team,
turm, unit, walk **05** bunch, crowd,
flock, group, horde, kerne, march,
squad, swarm, turme **06** parade,
school, stream, throng, troupe, trudge
**07** cavalry, company, consort,
convoys, gunners, militia, traipse
**08** assemble, brigades, division,
fighters, military, platoons, soldiers,
squadron **09** commandos, fusiliers,
gathering, multitude, regiments,
squadrons **10** assemblage, contingent,
paratroops, servicemen **11** armed
forces, infantrymen **12** paratroopers,
servicewomen

## trophy
**03** cup, pot **05** award, prize **06** spoils
**07** laurels, memento **08** souvenir
**10** silverware

*Trophies include:*

**02** TT
**05** FA Cup
**06** Fed Cup
**07** Auld Mug, Gold Cup, Grey Cup,
Uber Cup
**08** Davis Cup, Ryder Cup, The
Ashes, World Cup
**09** Aresti Cup, Claret Jug, Curtis Cup,
Thomas Cup, Walker Cup
**10** Masters Cup, Solheim Cup,
Stanley Cup, Winston Cup
**11** Admiral's Cup, America's Cup,
Calcutta Cup, Eschborn Cup,
Kinnaird Cup, McCarthy Cup,
Scottish Cup
**12** Camanachd Cup, Lugano Trophy,
Webb Ellis Cup
**13** Heisman trophy, Leonard Trophy,
Sam Maguire Cup
**14** Continental Cup, Jesters' Club
Cup
**15** Champions Trophy, Lilienthal
Medal, Louis Vuitton Cup, Nascar
Nextel Cup, Scotch Whisky Cup

*See also* **award**

## tropical
**03** hot **05** humid **06** steamy, sultry,
torrid **07** boiling, very hot **08** stifling
**09** luxuriant **10** boiling hot, figurative,
sweltering

## trot
**03** jog, ren, rin, run **04** crib, pace
**05** crone **06** bustle, canter, scurry
**07** dogtrot, heigh-ho, jogtrot, passage,
scamper, scuttle, tripple **08** heich-how
• **on the trot 04** busy **06** in a row, in
turn **10** back to back **12** continuously,
sequentially, successively
**13** consecutively **15** uninterruptedly
• **trot out 06** adduce, drag up, recite,
relate, repeat **07** bring up, exhibit
**08** bring out, rehearse **09** reiterate
**12** bring forward

## troubadour
**04** poet **06** singer **08** jongleur,
mariachi, minstrel, trouvère, trouveur
**09** balladeer, cantabank
**11** Minnesinger

## trouble
◇ *anagram indicator* **03** ado, ail, dog, fix,
jam, noy, vex, woe **04** care, fash, fuss,
gram, heat, mess, moil, pain, rile, work
**05** annoy, grame, grief, kaugh, muddy,
pains, sturt, trial, upset, visit, weigh,
worry **06** barrat, bother, burden,
corner, cumber, defect, effort, harass,
hassle, hatter, kiaugh, molest, pickle,
put out, sadden, scrape, shadow,
shtook, shtuck, strife, tsuris, tumult,
unease, unrest **07** afflict, agitate,
ailment, anxiety, concern, disease,
disturb, failure, illness, mismake,
perplex, perturb, problem, schtook,
schtuck, thought, torment, travail,
tsouris **08** disorder, disquiet, distress,
exercise, exertion, fighting, hardship,
headache, hot water, irritate,
nuisance, problems, shutdown,
stalling, stopping, struggle, upheaval,
vexation **09** adversity, agitation,
annoyance, attention, breakdown,
commotion, complaint, heartache,
packing-up, suffering, tight spot, weigh
down **10** affliction, conking-out,
cutting-out, difficulty, disability,
discommode, disconcert, irritation,
misfortune, solicitude, uneasiness
**11** botheration, disturbance,
malfunction, tribulation
**13** inconvenience, make the effort
**14** solicitousness, thoughtfulness

## troubled
◇ *anagram indicator* **05** tense, upset
**06** afraid, on edge, uneasy **07** anxious,
fearful, fretful, nervous, uptight,
worried **08** agonized, bothered,
dismayed, strained **09** concerned,
disturbed, ill at ease, perturbed
**10** disquieted, distracted, distraught,
distressed, frightened **11** overwrought
**12** apprehensive **14** hot and bothered

## troublemaker
**03** Ted **05** mixer **07** inciter, stirrer
**08** agitator, Teddy boy **09** bovver boy,
firebrand **10** incendiary, instigator,
ringleader **12** rabble-rouser
**13** mischief-maker

## troublesome
◇ *anagram indicator* **04** hard **05** pesky,
rowdy, spiny **06** infest, plaguy, taxing,
thorny, tricky, trying, unruly
**07** awkward, brickle, irksome,

plaguey, testing **08** annoying, exacting,
fashious, tiresome **09** demanding,
difficult, laborious, turbulent,
vexatious, wearisome, worrisome
**10** bothersome, disturbing, irritating,
perturbing, plaguesome, rebellious
**11** importunate, mischievous
**12** incommodious, inconvenient
**13** insubordinate, unco-operative

## trough
**03** gum, hod, tie, tye **04** crib, duct
**05** chute, ditch, drain, flame, gully,
hutch, shoot, shute, stock, trunk
**06** backet, feeder, furrow, groove,
gutter, hollow, hopper, manger, sluice,
straik, strake, trench, valley
**07** channel, conduit, launder **08** sheep-
dip **09** sand table **10** depression
**12** seasoning-tub **13** feeding trough
**14** watering-trough

## trounce
**04** beat, best, drub, lick, rout **05** crush,
paste, thump **06** defeat, hammer,
harass, indict, punish, rebuke, thrash,
wallop **07** clobber, shellac
**09** overwhelm, slaughter

## troupe
**03** set **04** band, cast **05** group, troop
**06** ballet **07** company

## trouper
**05** actor **06** player **07** artiste, old hand,
veteran **08** thespian **09** performer
**10** theatrical **11** entertainer

## trousers
**04** bags, daks, keks **05** cords, jeans,
kecks, Levis®, longs, pants, trews
**06** breeks, Capris, chinos, denims,
shorts, slacks, trouse **07** gauchos,
nankins, trouses **08** bloomers,
breeches, bumsters, flannels, jodhpurs,
nankeens, overalls, trossers, trowsers
**09** corduroys, dungarees, moleskins,
strossers **10** Capri pants, cargo pants,
drainpipes, Oxford bags, spongebags
**12** innominables, reach-me-downs
**14** indescribables, inexpressibles
• **part of trousers 03** fly

## trout
**04** peal, peel **05** sewen, sewin
**06** finnac **07** finnack, finnock, herling,
hirling, rainbow **08** gillaroo, whitling
**09** steelhead **10** fingerling, squeteague

## Troy
**01** t **05** Ilium

## truancy
**07** absence, jigging, skiving, wagging
**08** shirking **11** absenteeism, French
leave, malingering

## truant
**03** jig, kip, wag **04** bunk **05** dodge,
hooky, idler, miche, mitch, mooch,
shirk, skive **06** absent, desert, dodger,
hookey, skiver **07** goof off, missing,
runaway, shirker, vagrant **08** absentee,
deserter, malinger, skive off **09** play
hooky **10** malingerer, play the wag,
play truant

## truce
**03** bar, pax **04** lull, rest, stay **05** break,
fains, let-up, peace **06** barley, fains I

**07** barleys, respite, treague **08** fainites,
interval **09** armistice, ceasefire,
cessation **10** moratorium, suspension
**12** intermission, pacification

## truck
**02** PU **03** HGV, ute, van **04** skip, tram
**05** bogey, bogie, chore, dolly, float,
lorry, trade, wagon **06** bakkie, barter,
crummy, dumper, pick-up, tipper,
waggon **07** bargain, contact, rubbish,
traffic, trolley, trundle, utility
**08** business, commerce, dealings,
exchange **09** honey-cart, persevere,
relations **10** connection, honey-
wagon, juggernaut **11** association,
honey-waggon, intercourse **12** curtain-
sider, utility truck **13** communication
**14** utility vehicle

## truculence
**08** defiance, rudeness, violence
**09** hostility, pugnacity **11** bellicosity
**12** belligerence, disobedience
**14** aggressiveness **15** bad-
temperedness, quarrelsomeness

## truculent
**04** rude **05** cross, cruel **06** fierce,
savage, sullen **07** defiant, hostile,
violent **09** bellicose, combative
**10** aggressive, pugnacious **11** bad-
tempered, belligerent, contentious,
disobedient, ill-tempered, quarrelsome
**12** antagonistic, discourteous,
obstreperous **13** argumentative,
disrespectful

## trudge
**03** pad **04** haul, hike, plod, slog, toil,
trek, vamp, walk **05** clump, march,
stump, tramp, trash **06** labour, lumber,
stodge, taigle, trapes **07** shuffle,
splodge, splotch, traipse, trudger
**10** pad the hoof

## true
◇ *anagram indicator* **04** fast, firm, flat,
just, leal, real, trew, very **05** close,
exact, loyal, plumb, right, sooth, truly,
truth, valid **06** actual, dinkum, honest,
proper, trusty, truthy **07** correct,
devoted, dinki-di, exactly, factual,
genuine, precise, rightly, sincere,
staunch, typical **08** absolute, accurate,
constant, faithful, honestly, properly,
reliable, rightful, straight, truthful,
unerring **09** authentic, corrected,
correctly, dedicated, perfectly,
precisely, steadfast, veracious,
veritable, veritably **10** accurately,
dependable, fair dinkum, faithfully,
honourable, legitimate, truthfully,
undeniable, unerringly
**11** conformable, true-hearted,
trustworthy, veraciously
• **hold true 02** go

## true-blue
**04** true **05** loyal **06** trusty **07** devoted,
diehard, staunch **08** constant, faithful,
orthodox **09** committed, confirmed,
dedicated **10** unwavering **12** card-
carrying **13** dyed-in-the-wool
**14** uncompromising

## truism
**05** axiom, truth **06** cliché **07** bromide
**09** platitude **11** commonplace

## truly
**04** fegs, full, real, true, very **05** quite **06** certes, indeed, in fact, really, simply, surely, verily **07** exactly, greatly, in truth, rightly, soothly **08** actually, honestly, of a truth, on my word, properly **09** certainly, correctly, extremely, genuinely, in reality, precisely, sincerely, soothlich, veritable **10** constantly, definitely, on my honour, truthfully, undeniably **11** indubitably, steadfastly, undoubtedly **13** exceptionally, o' my conscience, without a doubt **14** upon conscience

## trump
**03** cap, top **04** ruff **05** blast, outdo **06** allege **07** deceive, eclipse, surpass, triumph, trumpet, upstage **08** Jew's-harp, outshine **13** knock spots off
• **trump up** **04** fake **06** cook up, create, devise, invent, make up **07** concoct, falsify **08** contrive **09** fabricate

## trumped-up
**04** fake **05** bogus, faked, false **06** made-up, phoney, untrue **08** cooked-up, invented, spurious **09** concocted, contrived, falsified **10** fabricated

## trumpery
**05** cheap, nasty, showy **06** flashy, shabby, shoddy, tawdry, trashy **07** mockado, rubbish, useless **08** rubbishy, trifling **09** valueless, worthless **10** pasteboard **12** meretricious

## trumpet
**03** bay, cry, lur **04** call, horn, lure, parp, roar, toot, tuba **05** blare, blast, bugle, chide, clang, conch, shell, shout, sound, trump, vaunt **06** bellow, cornet, corona, herald, lituus, sennet, summon, tucket **07** alchemy, alchymy, buccina, clarino, clarion, corolla, salpinx, tantara **08** announce, denounce, proclaim, ram's horn, trombone **09** advertise, broadcast, celebrate, last trump **11** taratantara **12** watering-call
• **blow your own trumpet** **04** brag, crow **05** boast, skite, swank **07** show off, talk big **09** loudmouth **15** blow your own horn

## trumps
• **ace of trumps** **03** tib
• **no trumps** **02** NT

## truncate
**03** cut, lop **04** clip, crop, dock, maim, pare, trim **05** prune **06** reduce **07** curtail, shorten **08** cut short, diminish **10** abbreviate

## truncheon
**04** club, cosh **05** baton, billy, carve, staff, stick **06** batoon, billie, cudgel **09** shillalah **10** billystick, knobkerrie, nightstick, shillelagh

## trundle
**04** bowl, chug, hoop, roll, spin **05** trill, troll, truck, twirl **06** castor, cruise, roller **07** trindle **09** freewheel

## trunk
**03** box, leg, log **04** body, bole, bulk, butt, case, nose, runt, stem, tube **05** chest, crate, frame, shaft, snout, stalk, stick, stock, torso **06** coffer **08** Saratoga, sea chest, suitcase **09** proboscis, telescope **10** pea-shooter **11** portmanteau

## truss
**03** pad, tie **04** bind, hang, pack, prop, stay, wrap **05** brace, joist, shore, strap, strut **06** bundle, corbel, fasten, lace up, pack up, pinion, secure, tether, tuck up **07** bandage, binding, dorlach, make off, support **08** bundle up, buttress, muffle up, string up **09** principal

## trust
**03** EZT, VCT **04** affy, care, duty, give, hope, tick, trow **05** faith **06** assign, assume, bank on, belief, charge, commit, credit, expect, rely on **07** believe, combine, confide, consign, count on, custody, entrust, imagine, presume, suppose, surmise, swear by **08** be sure of, credence, delegate, depend on, fidelity, reliance, turn over **09** assurance, believe in, certainty **10** commitment, confidence, conviction, dependance, dependence, obligation, protection, street cred **11** expectation, safekeeping, trusteeship **12** guardianship **14** put your trust in, responsibility

## trustee
**02** tr **05** agent **06** keeper **08** assignee, executor, guardian **09** custodian, executrix, fiduciary **10** depositary **13** administrator

## trusting
**05** naive **06** unwary **08** gullible, innocent, trustful **09** confiding, credulous, ingenuous, unguarded **12** unsuspecting **13** unquestioning

## trustworthiness
**05** steel **07** honesty, loyalty **08** devotion **09** integrity, stability **10** commitment **11** reliability **12** faithfulness, sensibleness **13** dependability, steadfastness **14** honourableness, responsibility **15** faithworthiness, level-headedness

## trustworthy
**04** safe, true **05** loyal, sound **06** honest, stable, trusty **07** devoted, ethical, staunch, upright **08** faithful, reliable, sensible **09** authentic, committed, steadfast **10** creditable, dependable, honourable, principled **11** level-headed, responsible **14** good as your word

## trusty
**04** firm, true **05** loyal, solid **06** honest, stanch, steady, strong **07** staunch, upright **08** faithful, reliable **09** greatcoat **10** dependable, supportive **11** responsible, trustworthy **15** straightforward

## truth
**04** fact, true **05** axiom, facts, maxim, right, sooth **06** gospel, honour, truism, verity **07** candour, honesty, loyalty, realism, reality **08** accuracy, fidelity, validity, veracity **09** actualité, actuality, constancy, exactness, frankness, home truth, integrity, knowledge, precision, principle, rightness, sincerity **10** cold turkey, legitimacy **11** correctness, genuineness, historicity, uprightness **12** authenticity, faithfulness, truthfulness **14** honourableness, the gospel truth
• **in truth** **05** sooth, troth, truly **06** indeed, in fact, really, surely, troggs **07** insooth, soothly **08** actually, en vérité, forsooth, honestly, in effect **09** assuredly, in reality, soothlich **10** to be honest **11** truth to tell **12** in actual fact **13** if truth be told, in point of fact **15** as a matter of fact

## truthful
**04** open, true **05** exact, frank, right, sooth, valid **06** candid, honest **07** correct, factual, precise, sincere **08** accurate, faithful, reliable, soothful, straight **09** realistic, soothfast, veracious, veridical, veritable **10** forthright, veridicous **11** trustworthy

## truthfully
**05** truly **06** openly **08** honestly, reliably **09** correctly, factually, precisely, sincerely **10** accurately, faithfully

## truthfulness
**06** verity **07** candour, honesty **08** openness, veracity **09** frankness, sincerity **11** uprightness **12** straightness **13** righteousness

## try
**02** go **03** aim, sap, tax **04** bash, burl, fand, fond, hear, pree, pull, seek, shot, sift, stab, test, tire **05** annoy, assay, crack, drain, essay, fling, judge, prove, taste, tempt, trial, weary, whirl **06** choice, effort, purify, refine, render, sample, strain, stress, strive, try out, weaken **07** afflict, attempt, examine, exhaust, extract, have a go, inspect, stretch, turn out, undergo, venture, wear out **08** appraise, evaluate, irritate, purified **09** appraisal, endeavour, give it a go, have a bash, have a lash, have a shot, have a stab, undertake **10** evaluation, experience, experiment, have a crack **11** give it a burl, have a lash at, investigate **13** make demands on
• **try out** **04** test **05** taste, try on **06** sample **07** inspect **08** appraise, check out, evaluate **10** have a pop at, take a pop at

## trying
**04** hard **05** tough, trial **06** severe, taxing **07** arduous, testing **08** annoying, tiresome **09** demanding, difficult, searching, stressful, vexatious, wearisome **10** bothersome, irritating **11** aggravating, distressing, troublesome **12** exasperating
• **trying situation** **03** cow

## tub
**03** dan, keg, kid, kit, tun, vat **04** back, bath, butt, cask, cowl, kier **05** basin,

## tubby

keeve, kieve, stand **06** barrel, bucket, pulpit **07** bathtub, bran-pie, bran tub, salt-fat, washtub **08** ash-leach, hogshead, lucky dip, salt-foot, swill-tub **09** container

## tubby

**03** fat **05** buxom, obese, plump, podgy, pudgy, stout **06** chubby, portly, rotund **07** paunchy **08** roly-poly **09** corpulent **10** overweight **15** well-upholstered

## tube

**03** CRT, vas **04** duct, hose, pipe, vein **05** inlet, shaft, spout, trunk **06** outlet, tubing **07** channel, conduit, snorkel **08** aircraft, cylinder **09** capillary **13** television set, umbilical cord
*See also* **London**

## tuber

**03** set **04** coco, eddo **05** cocco **06** jicama, mashua, potato, yautia **08** earth-nut **10** seed potato **11** sweet potato **13** water chestnut

## tuberculosis

**02** TB **05** lupus **08** phthisis, scrofula **11** consumption **12** pearl disease

## tubular

**04** pipy **05** piped, tubal, tubar **06** tubate **07** quilled **08** pipelike, tubelike, tubiform, tubulate, tubulous, vasiform

## tuck

**03** tap **04** beat, chow, cram, ease, eats, fold, food, grub, kilt, nosh, push **05** meals, pleat, scoff, scrab, snack, stuff **06** crease, gather, hamper, insert, pucker, rapier, ruffle, snacks, stroke, thrust **08** eatables **11** comestibles **12** gird yourself
• **tuck away** **04** hide, save **05** hoard, store **06** save up **07** conceal **09** stash away
• **tuck in, tuck into** ◇ *insertion indicator* **03** eat, sup **04** dine **05** eat up, feast, gorge, scoff **06** devour, gobble **08** wolf down **11** eat heartily
• **tuck in, tuck up** **04** kilt **05** truss **06** fold in, wrap up **07** cover up **08** make snug, put to bed **09** fold under **15** make comfortable

## Tuesday

**02** Tu **03** Tue **04** Tues

## tuft

**03** dag, top **04** coma, hank, knop, knot, lock, tait, tate, tuzz, wisp **05** beard, brush, bunch, clump, crest, flock, plume, quiff, scopa, swits, truss, tuffe, whisk **06** dallop, dollop, goatee, pencil, pompom, pompon, switch, tassel, toorie, tourie, tuffet **07** cluster, cowlick, daglock, fetlock, flaught, floccus, hassock, pompoon, scopula, topknot, tussock **08** aigrette, corn silk, dislodge, fascicle, imperial, plumelet **09** fascicule, flocculus, scalp lock **10** fasciculus **12** witches' broom

## tug

**03** lug, pug, rug, tit, tow **04** drag, draw, haul, jerk, pull, rive, tire, toil, yank **05** heave, pluck **06** jigger, strain, strive, wrench **07** saccade, tow boat, tracker

## tuition

**05** grind **07** lessons **08** coaching, guidance, teaching, training, tutelage **09** education, schooling **11** instruction **12** guardianship

## tumble

◇ *anagram indicator* **04** dive, drop, fall, flop, reel, roll, sway, toss, trip **05** heave, lurch, pitch, slide, touse, touze, towse, towze **06** jumble, plunge, rumple, topple, tousle, touzle, trip up, unseat, welter **07** decline, plummet, stumble **08** collapse, decrease, dishevel, disorder, fall over, nosedive **09** knock down, overthrow, tumble-dry **10** disarrange, somersault, throw about **12** fall headlong
• **tumble to** **03** get **04** suss, twig **05** grasp, savvy **07** realize **08** perceive **09** latch on to **10** comprehend, cotton on to, understand **13** become aware of, get the picture

## tumbledown

◇ *anagram indicator* **05** shaky **06** ruined, unsafe **07** crumbly, rickety, ruinous **08** decrepit, unstable, unsteady **09** crumbling, tottering **10** broken-down, ramshackle **11** dilapidated **14** disintegrating

## tumbler

**03** cup, mug **05** glass **06** beaker, goblet **07** acrobat, gymnast, tumbrel **10** water glass **13** contortionist, drinking-glass **15** jerry-come-tumble

## tumid

**06** turgid **07** bloated, bulbous, bulging, flowery, fulsome, pompous, stilted, swollen **08** affected, enlarged, inflated, puffed up **09** bombastic, distended, grandiose, high-flown, overblown, tumescent **10** euphuistic **11** pretentious, protuberant **12** magniloquent **13** grandiloquent

## tummy

**03** gut **05** belly **06** inside, paunch **07** abdomen, insides, stomach **08** pot-belly **11** bread basket, corporation

## tumour

**03** -oma **04** lump, onco- **06** cancer, growth **08** neoplasm, swelling **09** turgidity **10** malignancy

*Tumours include:*

**05** gumma, myoma, Wilm's
**06** epulis, glioma, lipoma, myxoma
**07** adenoma, angioma, fibroma, myeloma, sarcoma
**08** lymphoma, melanoma, teratoma, xanthoma
**09** carcinoma, papilloma, syphiloma
**10** meningioma
**11** astrocytoma, rodent ulcer
**12** glioblastoma, mesothelioma, osteosarcoma
**13** neuroblastoma
**14** retinoblastoma

## tumult

◇ *anagram indicator* **03** din, row **04** coil, riot, rore, rout, stir **05** babel, brawl, chaos, deray, hurly, noise, stoor, stour, surge, whirl **06** affray, bedlam, bustle,

fracas, hubbub, mutiny, racket, romage, ruffle, rumpus, stowre, strife, unrest, uproar **07** brattle, clamour, ferment, turmoil **08** disarray, disorder, shouting, stramash, upheaval, williwaw **09** agitation, commotion, confusion, hurricane **10** hullabaloo, hurly-burly, rabblement **11** disturbance, pandemonium **12** pandaemonium

## tumultuous

**04** loud, wild **05** noisy, rowdy **06** fierce, hectic, raging, stormy, unruly **07** excited, fervent, riotous, violent **08** agitated, frenzied, restless, troubled, vehement **09** clamorous, deafening, disturbed, troublous, turbulent **10** boisterous, disorderly, hurly-burly, tumultuary **12** uncontrolled

## tumulus

**03** how, low **04** howe, mote **05** motte **06** barrow

## tune

**03** air, set, toy **04** ayre, dump, lilt, note, port, rant, song, tone, toon **05** adapt, dance, ditty, loure, motif, pitch, round, theme, utter **06** adjust, attune, choral, chorus, jingle, maggot, melody, spring, strain, temper **07** express, hunt's-up, melisma, ragtime **08** folk-tune, regulate, saraband, serenade **09** harmonize, sarabande, siciliano, signature, theme song, theme tune **10** light-o'-love **11** schottische, synchronize **13** melodiousness, signature tune
• **change your tune** **08** do a U-turn **14** change your mind
• **in tune with** **04** true **07** d'accord **12** agreeing with, in accord with **13** in harmony with **14** in sympathy with **15** in agreement with
• **out of tune** **04** ajar **05** false **06** at odds, off-key **07** jarring, untuned **08** distuned, mistuned, out of key, scordato **11** disagreeing

## tuneful

**04** tuny **06** catchy, mellow **07** melodic, musical, tunable **08** pleasant, sonorous, tuneable **09** agreeable, melodious **10** euphonious, harmonious **11** mellifluous

## tuneless

**05** harsh **06** atonal, silent **08** clashing **09** dissonant, unmelodic, unmusical **10** discordant, unpleasant **11** cacophonous, horrisonant, unmelodious **12** disagreeable

## tungsten

**01** W

## tunic

**05** ao dai, kurta **06** blouse, camese, camise, chiton, kabaya, kameez, khurta, kirtle, tabard, taberd **07** choroid, tunicle **08** chorioid **09** laticlave **12** chorioid coat

## tuning device

**03** peg **08** magic eye

## Tunisia

**02** TN **03** TUN

## tunnel

**tunnel**
03 dig, sap 04 bore, flue, head, hole, mine 05 cundy, drift, qanat, shaft 06 burrow, condie, subway, syrinx 07 chimney, gallery, incline, passage 08 excavate, wormhole 09 penetrate, undermine, underpass 10 passageway

*Tunnels include:*

03 Aki, Box
05 Keijo, Rokko
06 FATIMA, Fréjus, Fucino, Haruna, Hoosac, Kanmon, Mersey, Moffat, Seikan, Thames
07 Arlberg, Cascade, Channel, Chunnel, Holland, Laerdal, Øresund, Simplon, Vereina
08 Apennine, Flathead, Hokuriku, Hyperion, Lierasen, Nakayama, Posilipo, Tronquoy
09 Dayaoshan, Eupalinus, Furka Base, Mont Blanc
10 Chesbrough, Dai-shimizu, Gorigamine, Lotschberg, Qinling I-II, Rogers Pass, St Gotthard
11 Kilsby Ridge, Mt MacDonald, Shin-shimizu, Tower Subway
12 Detroit River, Moscow subway
13 Great Apennine, Iwate Ichinohe, Severomuyskiy
14 NEAT St Gotthard, Romeriksporten
15 Monte Santomarco, Orange-Fish River

**tunny**
04 tuna 13 horse mackerel

**turban**
05 mitre, pagri, toque 06 tulban 07 puggery, puggree, turband, turbant, turbond 08 puggaree, tulipant 09 turribant

**turbid**
03 dim 04 foul, hazy 05 dense, foggy, fuzzy, muddy, murky, riley, roily, thick 06 cloudy, drumly, impure, opaque 07 clouded, muddled, unclear 08 confused, feculent 09 turbulent, unsettled 10 disordered, incoherent

**turbulence**
◊ *anagram indicator* 05 chaos, storm 06 buller, tumult, unrest 07 boiling, turmoil 08 disorder, upheaval 09 agitation, commotion, confusion, roughness 10 disruption 11 instability, pandemonium

**turbulent**
◊ *anagram indicator* 04 wild 05 noisy, rough, rowdy 06 choppy, raging, stormy, unruly 07 foaming, furious, riotous, violent 08 agitated, blustery, confused, factious, mutinous, unstable 09 in turmoil, unbridled, unsettled 10 boisterous, disordered, disorderly, outrageous, rebellious, tumultuous 11 combustious, tempestuous 12 obstreperous 13 insubordinate, undisciplined

**turf**
03 sod 04 clod, fail, feal, lawn, terf 05 divot, gazon, glebe, grass, green, patch, scraw, sward, terfe 06 gazoon 07 flaught 09 territory 12 putting green

• **turf out** 04 fire, oust, sack 05 eject, elbow, evict, expel 06 banish, remove 07 dismiss, kick out, turn out 08 chuck out, fling out, throw out 09 discharge 10 dispossess 14 give the elbow to

**turgid**
07 dilated, flowery, fulsome, pompous, stilted, swollen, turgent 08 affected, inflated 09 bombastic, grandiose, high-flown, overblown 11 extravagant, pretentious 12 magniloquent, ostentatious 13 grandiloquent

**Turkey**
02 TR 03 TUR

**Turkmenistan**
02 TM 03 TKM

**Turks and Caicos Islands**
03 TCA

**turmoil**
◊ *anagram indicator* 03 din, row 04 dust, moil, stir, toil 05 chaos, noise, stoor, stour 06 bedlam, bustle, flurry, hubbub, pother, pudder, stowre, tumult, uproar 07 ferment, trouble 08 disarray, disorder, disquiet, upheaval 09 agitation, commotion, confusion 10 turbulence 11 disturbance, appearance, difference, tracasserie 12 pandemonium 13 Sturm und Drang 14 the devil and all

• **place of turmoil** 04 hell 11 Pandemonium 12 Pandaemonium

**turn**
◊ *anagram indicator* ◊ *reversal indicator* 01 U 02 go 03 act, aim, fit, jar, lot, rev, say, set, U-ey, U-ie 04 bash, bend, bent, bias, bout, cast, form, grow, loop, make, move, pass, reel, roll, send, shot, slew, slue, sour, spin, stab, time, veer, wind 05 adapt, alter, apply, crack, curve, cycle, drift, drive, focus, go bad, go off, hinge, issue, mould, pivot, point, round, scare, shape, shift, shock, spell, spoil, start, stint, swing, trend, trick, twirl, twist, U-turn, whirl 06 adjust, appeal, attend, become, chance, change, circle, corner, crisis, curdle, depend, direct, divert, do a U-ey, do a U-ie, favour, fright, gyrate, invert, manner, modify, mutate, period, render, resort, return, rotate, spiral, swerve, swivel, take up 07 benefit, convert, deflect, develop, deviate, fashion, go round, heading, illness, leaning, remodel, reverse, revolve, routine, service, winding 08 aptitude, come to be, courtesy, exigency, give back, good deed, gyration, hand over, kindness, nauseate, occasion, reversal, rotation, round off, surprise, tendency, transfer 09 chuck a U-ey, chuck a U-ie, deviation, direction, faintness, infatuate, performer, transform, translate, transmute, variation 10 alteration, appearance, difference, divergence, make rancid, propensity, revolution 11 culmination, inclination, nervousness, opportunity, performance, vicissitude 12 become rancid, have recourse, metamorphose

13 act of kindness 15 go round and round

• **to a turn** 07 exactly 09 correctly, perfectly, precisely 12 to perfection

• **turn against** 07 dislike 08 distrust 12 disapprove of 13 make hostile to 15 become hostile to

• **turn aside** 04 daff 05 avert, parry, swits, twist 06 depart, divert, put off, swerve, switch 07 askance, deflect, deviate, diverge, diverse, fend off, reverse, ward off 08 withdraw 09 sidetrack

• **turn away** 05 avert 06 depart, refuse, reject, return 07 decline, deflect, deviate 08 move away, send away 09 discharge 12 cold shoulder, cold-shoulder

• **turn back** ◊ *reversal indicator* 05 clock, repel 06 go back, return, revert, revolt 07 reflect, retreat 09 drive back, force back, retrovert

• **turn down** 04 bend, mute, veto 05 lower, spurn 06 double, invert, lessen, muffle, rebuff, reduce, refuse, reject, soften 07 decline, quieten 08 decrease 09 knock back, repudiate 11 make quieter

• **turn in** 04 sell, shop 05 dob in, enter, grass, rat on 06 betray, give in, give up, hand in, invert, retire, return, rumble, submit, tell on, tender 07 deliver, go to bed, let down, sack out, sell out, split on 08 denounce, give back, go back on, hand over, inform on, register, renege on, squeal on 09 hit the hay, surrender, walk out on 10 hit the sack 11 double-cross, turn traitor 12 be disloyal to 13 stab in the back 14 be unfaithful to, break faith with

• **turn of events** 06 affair, result 07 outcome 08 incident 09 happening 10 occurrence, phenomenon

• **turn off** 04 bore, hang, kill, quit, stop 05 leave, repel 06 divert, offend, put off, sicken, unplug 07 deviate, disgust, dismiss, pull off, shut off, turn out 08 alienate, complete, nauseate, shut down 09 branch off, displease, switch off 10 depart from, disconnect, discourage, disenchant 11 turn against

• **turn of phrase** 05 idiom, style 06 saying 07 diction 08 locution, metaphor 10 expression, foreignism 11 phraseology

• **turn on** 04 plug 05 put on, start 06 arouse, attack, excite, fall on, hang on, please, plug in, rest on, ride on, thrill 07 attract, connect, hinge on, lay into, round on, set upon, start on, start up 08 activate, depend on, switch on 09 start in on, stimulate 14 be contingent on

• **turn out** 02 go 03 try 04 come, fire, make, rout, sack, sort, trie 05 clear, dress, eject, empty, end up, ensue, evict, expel, fadge, issue, prove 06 appear, arrive, attend, banish, become, bounce, clothe, deport, emerge, happen, muster, pan out, result, show up, turn up, unplug

**07** develop, dismiss, drum out, fall out, kick out, present, produce, succeed, turf out, turn off **08** assemble, chuck out, churn out, clean out, clear out, throw out **09** be present, come about, discharge, eventuate, fabricate, switch off, transpire **10** disconnect **11** manufacture

• **turn over** ◇ *reversal down indicator* **02** TO **03** rob **04** flip, mill, mull, roll **05** upend, upset, volve **06** assign, invert, pass on, ponder, tumble **07** capsize, consign, deliver, examine, reverse, start up **08** consider, hand over, keel over, meditate, mull over, overturn, roll over, ruminate, transfer **09** reflect on, surrender, think over **10** deliberate, think about, turn turtle **11** contemplate

• **turn up** ◇ *reversal down indicator* **02** go **03** act, dig **04** bash, bend, bias, cock, come, find, loop, plow, root, rout, shew, show, spin, stab, time **05** crack, curve, cycle, dig up, drift, raise, round, scare, shift, shock, spell, stint, trend, twirl, twist, whirl, wroot **06** appear, arrive, attend, cast up, chance, change, circle, corner, expose, fright, grub up, invert, look up, period, plough, reveal, show up, swivel **07** amplify, disgust, disturb, illness, leaning, routine, subsoil, turn out, uncover, unearth **08** disclose, discover, gyration, increase, occasion, reversal, rotation, tendency **09** be present, deviation, direction, faintness, intensify, performer, variation **10** alteration, appearance, difference, divergence, make louder, propensity, revolution, strengthen **11** inclination, materialize, nervousness, opportunity, performance **12** bring to light

## turncoat
**03** rat **04** fink, scab **07** seceder, traitor **08** apostate, blackleg, defector, deserter, renegade, renegate **10** backslider **11** Vicar of Bray **13** tergiversator

## turned
◇ *anagram indicator* ◇ *reversal indicator* **03** off **04** sour **06** soured **08** reversed **09** fashioned **10** upside down

## turning
◇ *anagram indicator* ◇ *reversal indicator* **04** bend, fork, turn **05** curve **07** shaping, turn-off, winding **08** junction, reversal, rotation **09** deviation **10** conversion, crossroads **14** transformation

## turning-point
**04** crux, turn **06** crisis, moment, tropic **08** solstice **09** watershed **10** crossroads **13** moment of truth **14** critical moment, decisive moment

## turnip
**04** neep **05** navew, swede **07** tumshie **09** breadroot **10** dunderhead

## turnout
**04** gate, gear, team, togs **05** array, crowd, dress, get-up **06** attire, muster, number, outfit, output, siding, strike,

things **07** clobber, clothes, display, striker **08** assembly, audience **09** gathering **10** appearance, assemblage, attendance **12** congregation

## turnover
◇ *reversal indicator* **04** flow **05** yield **06** bridie, change, income, output, volume **07** outturn, profits, revenue **08** business, movement **10** production **11** replacement **12** productivity, transference

## turpitude
**04** evil **07** badness **08** baseness, foulness, iniquity, vileness, villainy **09** depravity **10** corruption, degeneracy, immorality, sinfulness, wickedness **11** corruptness, criminality, viciousness **13** nefariousness **14** flagitiousness

## tusk
**03** gam **04** tush **05** torsk

## tussle
**03** vie **04** bout, fray **05** brawl, fight, mêlée, scrap, scrum, set-to, touse, touze, towse, towze **06** battle, dust-up, fracas, tousle, touzle **07** compete, contend, contest, grapple, punch-up, scuffle, tuilyie, tuilzie, wrestle **08** conflict, scramble, struggle **09** scrimmage **10** contention **11** competition

## tutelage
**03** eye **04** care **05** aegis **06** charge **07** custody, tuition **08** guidance, teaching, wardship **09** education, patronage, schooling, vigilance **10** protection **11** instruction, preparation **12** guardianship

## tutor
**04** abbé, guru **05** coach, drill, guide, teach, train **06** direct, mentor, school **07** control, dominie, educate, lecture, teacher **08** educator, governor, guardian, instruct, lecturer **09** governess, preceptor, supervise **10** discipline, instructor, répétiteur, supervisor **11** preceptress **12** schoolmaster

## tutorial
**05** class **06** lesson **07** guiding, seminar, teach-in **08** coaching, didactic, teaching **09** educative, educatory **13** instructional

## Tuvalu
**03** TUV

## TV
*see* **television**

## twaddle
**03** rot **04** blah, bosh, bunk, guff, tosh **05** balls, hooey, stuff, trash **06** bunkum, drivel, gabble, gossip, hot air, piffle, tattle, waffle **07** baloney, eyewash, fadaise, garbage, hogwash, inanity, rhubarb, rubbish, twattle **08** blathers, blethers, claptrap, malarkey, nonsense, slipslop, tommyrot **09** bullswool, moonshine, poppycock **10** balderdash **12** gobbledygook

## tweak
◇ *anagram indicator* **03** fit, nip, tug **04** jerk, pull, suit **05** adapt, pinch, twist **06** adjust, change, modify, tuning, twinge, twitch **07** fitting, shaping, squeeze **08** fine-tune, revision **09** agitation, amendment, arranging **10** adaptation, adjustment, alteration, conversion, fine-tuning, perplexity **11** accommodate, rearranging, remodelling **12** modification **13** accommodation, rearrangement **15** make adjustments

## twee
**04** cute **05** sweet **06** cutesy, dainty, pretty, quaint **08** affected, precious **11** sentimental

## twelve
**02** dz **03** doz, XII **05** dozen **06** zodiac

## Twelve Days of Christmas
*see* **Christmas**

## twenty
**02** XX

## twice
◇ *repetition indicator* **02** bi-, di- **03** bin-, bis **06** doubly

## twiddle
◇ *anagram indicator* **04** turn **05** twirl, twist **06** adjust, fiddle, finger, rotate, swivel, wiggle **07** twitter **08** ornament

• **twiddle your thumbs** **08** kill time **13** kick your heels **15** have nothing to do

## twig
**03** get, see **04** reis, rice, whip, with **05** birch, grasp, shoot, spray, sprig, stick, swits, twist, withe, withy **06** branch, fathom, fettle, rumble, switch, wattle, wicker **07** catch on, fashion, observe, ramulus, realize, sarment **08** cotton on, offshoot, perceive, tumble to **10** comprehend, understand

*See also* **understand**

## twilight
**03** dim, ebb **04** dusk, last **05** dying, final, gloom **06** ebbing, sunset **07** decline, dimness, evening, obscure, partial, shadowy **08** cockshut, demi-jour, evenfall, gloaming, glooming, owl-light **09** crepuscle, darkening, declining, half-light **10** crepuscule, indefinite **11** crepuscular **12** transitional **15** Götterdämmerung

## twin
**04** dual, join, link, mate, pair, part, yoke **05** clone, gemel, match **06** couple, double, fellow, paired, ringer **07** combine, couplet, deprive, matched, twofold **08** didymous, likeness, matching, parallel, separate **09** corollary, duplicate, identical, lookalike **10** complement, dead ringer, equivalent **11** counterpart, symmetrical **13** corresponding

*Twins include:*

**04** Esau, Gibb (Maurice), Gibb (Robin), Kray (Reggie), Kray (Ronnie)
**05** Diana, Jacob, Remus, Viola,

Waugh (Mark), **Waugh** (Steve)
**06** Apollo, **Bunker** (Chang), **Bunker**
(Eng), **Castor**, **Dromio** (of Ephesus),
**Dromio** (of Syracuse), **Pollux**
**07** Artemis, **Piccard** (Auguste),
**Piccard** (Jean-Felix), **Romulus**,
**Stanley** (Francis), **Stanley** (Freelon),
**Weasley** (Fred), **Weasley** (George)
**08** Hercules, **Iphicles**, **Louis XIV**,
**Philippe**
**09** O'Sullivan (Isabel), **O'Sullivan** (Pat),
**Sebastian**
**10** Antipholus (of Ephesus),
**Antipholus** (of Syracuse),
**Tweedledee**, **Tweedledum**

## twine
**04** bend, coil, cord, curl, knit, loop,
part, wind, wrap, yarn **05** braid, plait,
twist, weave **06** spiral, string, tangle,
thread **07** deprive, entwine, wreathe,
wriggle **08** encircle, separate,
surround, whipping **09** intorsion,
intortion **10** intertwine

## twinge
**04** ache, grip, pain, pang, stab
**05** cramp, pinch, prick, spasm, throb,
throe, twang, tweak **06** stitch, twitch
**08** shooting

## twinkle
◇ *anagram indicator* **04** wink **05** blink,
flash, gleam, glint, light, shine, twink
**06** quiver **07** flicker, glimmer, glisten,
glitter, shimmer, shining, sparkle,
vibrate **09** coruscate, twinkling
**11** coruscation, scintillate
**13** scintillation

## twinkling
◇ *anagram indicator* **02** mo **03** sec **04** jiff,
tick, wink **05** flash, jiffy, nitid, shake,
trice, twink **06** bright, minute, moment,
no time, second **07** instant, shining,
winking **08** blinking, flashing,
gleaming, polished **09** short time,
sparkling **10** flickering, glimmering,
glistening, glittering, shimmering
**11** coruscating **13** scintillating,
scintillation

## twirl
◇ *anagram indicator* **04** coil, curl, spin,
turn, wind **05** pivot, trill, twist, wheel,
whirl, whorl **06** gyrate, rotate, spiral,
swivel **07** revolve, trundle, twiddle,
twizzle **08** gyration, rotation
**09** pirouette **10** revolution
**11** convolution **12** tirlie-wirlie

## twirling
◇ *anagram indicator* **05** gyral **07** pivotal
**08** gyratory, pivoting, rotating, rotatory,
spinning, whirling **09** revolving
**10** swivelling **11** pirouetting

## twist
◇ *anagram indicator* **03** arc, cue
**04** bend, coil, cord, curl, flaw, kink,
loop, rick, roll, rove, skew, slew, slue,
spin, turn, twig, warp, whim, wind
**05** alter, angle, braid, break, curve,
freak, plait, quirk, screw, slant, twine,
twirl, weave, wrest, wrick, wring
**06** change, defect, deform, foible,
garble, oddity, rotate, spiral, sprain,
squirm, strain, strand, swivel, tangle,

thread, wamble, wigwag, wimple,
wreath, wrench, writhe, zigzag
**07** contort, distort, entwine, falsify,
pervert, revolve, swindle, torsion,
twizzle, whimple, wreathe, wriggle
**08** entangle, misquote, misshape,
squiggle, surprise, wresting
**09** misreport, turnabout, variation
**10** aberration, contortion, distortion,
intertwine, perversion **11** convolution,
peculiarity **12** idiosyncrasy,
imperfection, misrepresent
• **twist someone's arm** **05** bully,
force **06** coerce, lean on **07** dragoon
**08** bulldoze, persuade **10** intimidate,
pressurize **14** put the screws on

## twisted
◇ *anagram indicator* **03** odd **04** wavy
**05** kinky, thraw **06** thrawn, thrown,
warped **07** deviant, sinuous, strange,
tortile, winding **08** peculiar, squiggly
**09** contorted, perverted, unnatural

## twister
**04** gale **05** cheat, crook, fraud, rogue,
storm **06** con man, phoney, squall
**07** cyclone, monsoon, tempest,
tornado, typhoon **08** con woman,
deceiver, swindler **09** con artist,
hurricane, scoundrel, trickster,
whirlwind **10** blackguard

## twisty
**06** zigzag **07** curving, sinuous, winding
**08** indirect, tortuous **10** circuitous,
meandering, roundabout, serpentine

## twit
**03** ass, git **04** berk, clot, dope, dork,
fool, geek, goop, nerd, nerk, prat
**05** chump, clown, dweeb, idiot, ninny,
twerp **06** nitwit **07** airhead, halfwit,
pinhead, plonker, saphead, twitter
**08** imbecile **09** blockhead, simpleton
**10** nincompoop **11** knuckle-head
**13** proper Charlie

## twitch
◇ *anagram indicator* **03** tic, tig, tit, tug
**04** jerk, jump, pull, yips **05** blink,
pluck, shake, spasm, start, tweak
**06** quiver, shiver, snatch, tremor
**07** flutter, the yips, tremble **09** vellicate
**10** convulsion

## twitchy
**04** edgy **05** het up, jerky, jumpy, nervy,
shaky, tense **06** on edge, uneasy
**07** anxious, fidgety, in a stew, jittery,
keyed up, nervous, panicky, restive,
uptight, wound up **08** agitated, in a
sweat, in a tizzy **12** apprehensive

## twitter
**03** cry, gab **04** chat, sing, song
**05** cheep, chirp, tweet **06** babble,
gabble, gossip, jabber, jargon, warble,
witter **07** blather, blether, chatter,
chirrup, chitter, prattle, twaddle,
whistle **08** chirping, tweeting
**09** palpitate **10** chirruping

## two
**02** ll **04** pair **05** deuce, twain **06** couple
• **the two** **04** both

## two-faced
**05** false, lying **07** devious **09** deceitful,
insincere **10** Janus-faced, perfidious

**11** dissembling, duplicitous,
treacherous **12** hypocritical **13** double-
dealing, untrustworthy

## twofold
**04** dual, twin **05** duple **06** bifold,
binary, double, duplex **07** twafald,
twifold, twyfold **09** duplicate

## two-master
**04** buss

## twosome
**03** duo **04** duet, pair **06** couple **09** tête-
à-tête

## two-up
**03** swy **05** swy-up **07** swy game

## two-wheeler
**04** cart

## Tyche
**07** Fortuna

## tycoon
**05** baron, mogul **06** fat cat **07** magnate,
supremo **08** big noise **09** big cheese,
financier, moneybags **10** capitalist
**12** entrepreneur, moneyspinner
**13** industrialist

## Tyler
**03** Wat

## Tyneside
**02** NE

## type
◇ *anagram indicator* **03** ilk, key, set
**04** face, font, form, hair, kind, make,
mark, norm, sort **05** brand, breed,
class, fount, genre, genus, group,
model, order, print, stamp, style
**06** emblem, letter, number, strain,
symbol **07** epitome, example, letters,
numbers, pattern, species, symbols,
variety **08** category, exemplar,
insignia, original, printing, specimen,
standard, typeface **09** archetype,
character, exemplify, lettering,
prefigure, prototype, symbolize,
typewrite **10** characters, embodiment,
foreshadow **11** description,
designation, subdivision
**12** anticipation, quintessence
**13** foreshadowing **14** classification
• **confused type** **02** pi **03** pie, pye
• **type size** **03** gem **04** body, pica
**05** canon **06** minion **07** brevier, English
**09** bourgeois, Columbian, nonpareil
**10** longprimer **11** emerald type, Great
Primer

## typeface
*Typefaces include:*

**05** Arial
**06** Bell MT, Impact, Lucida, Modern,
Tahoma
**07** Courier, Curlz MT, Marlett, MS
Serif, Verdana
**08** Garamond, Jokerman, MS
Gothic, MS Mincho, Playbill,
Rockwell, Webdings
**09** Colonna MT, Wide Latin,
Wingdings
**10** Arial Black, Courier New, Lucida
Sans
**11** Baskerville, Book Antiqua, Comic
Sans MS, MS Sans Serif, Poor

Richard, Trebuchet MS
13 Century Gothic, Lucida Console,
Times New Roman
14 Franklin Gothic
15 Bookman Old Style

## typhoon
05 storm 06 squall, typhon 07 cyclone,
tempest, tornado, twister 09 hurricane,
whirlwind

## typical
04 trew, true 05 model, stock, typal,
typic, usual 06 normal, Podunk
07 average, classic 08 ordinary,
orthodox, standard, true-bred
10 archetypal, emblematic, figurative,
indicative, stereotype 11 distinctive
12 conventional, illustrative, run-of-
the-mill 13 typographical
14 characteristic, quintessential,
representative

## typically
07 as a rule, usually 08 normally

09 routinely 10 habitually, ordinarily
11 classically, customarily

## typify
05 image 06 embody, imbody, shadow
08 indicate 09 epitomize, exemplify,
personify, represent, symbolize
10 foreshadow, illustrate
11 encapsulate, foresignify
12 characterize

## tyrannical
05 cruel, harsh 06 lordly, severe, strict,
unjust 08 absolute, despotic,
Neronian, ruthless, satrapal, tyrannic
09 arbitrary, imperious 10 autocratic,
despotical, high-handed, oppressive,
peremptory, repressive 11 dictatorial,
domineering, magisterial, overbearing
12 overpowering, totalitarian,
unreasonable 13 authoritarian

## tyrannize
04 lord 05 bully, crush 06 coerce
07 dictate, enslave, oppress, repress

08 browbeat, domineer, suppress
09 subjugate, terrorize 10 intimidate,
lord it over

## tyranny
07 cruelty, liberty 08 severity
09 autocracy, despotism, harshness,
injustice 10 absolutism, domination,
oppression, strictness 12 dictatorship,
ruthlessness 13 imperiousness 14 high-
handedness

## tyrant
05 bully, pewee 06 despot, peewee
08 autocrat, dictator, martinet
09 oppressor, tyranness 10 absolutist,
taskmaster 11 slave-driver
13 authoritarian

*See also* **despot**

## tyro
*see* **tiro, tyro**

# U

**U**
07 uniform 10 upper-class

**ubiquitous**
06 common, global 08 frequent
09 pervasive, universal 10 everywhere,
ubiquarian, wall-to-wall 11 ever-
present, omnipresent

**ubiquity**
09 frequency 10 commonness,
popularity, prevalence
12 omnipresence, universality
13 pervasiveness

**Uganda**
03 EAU, UGA

**ugliness**
04 evil 06 danger, horror, menace
08 disgrace, enormity, vileness
09 deformity, nastiness, plainness
10 homeliness, horridness
11 heinousness, hideousness,
monstrosity 12 unloveliness
13 frightfulness, offensiveness,
repulsiveness, unsightliness
14 unpleasantness

**ugly**
◇ anagram indicator 04 evil, foul, loth,
vile 05 grave, loath, nasty, plain
06 gorgon, grotty, homely, horrid,
oughly, ouglie, unfair 07 hideous,
hostile, ogreish 08 alarming, butt-ugly,
deformed, horrible, ill-faced, ill-faste,
ill-faurd, plug-ugly, shocking, sinister,
terrible, unlovely 09 dangerous,
frightful, grotesque, loathsome,
misshapen, monstrous, obnoxious,
offensive, repulsive, revolting, ugly as
sin, unsightly 10 disgusting, ill-looking,
ill-natured, unpleasant 11 disquieting,
ill-favoured, threatening
12 disagreeable, evil-favoured,
unattractive 13 objectionable
15 unprepossessing

**UK**
see **United Kingdom**

**Ukraine**
02 UA 03 UKR

**ulcer**
04 boil, noma, sore 05 issue, rupia
06 aphtha, canker, fester 07 abscess,
bedsore, fistula, sycosis 08 open sore
09 impostume 10 plague-sore,
ulceration 11 peptic ulcer 13 varicose
ulcer 14 decubitus ulcer

**ulster**
02 NI 04 coat

**ulterior**
06 covert, hidden, secret 07 private,
remoter, selfish 08 personal

09 concealed, secondary
10 underlying, unrevealed
11 undisclosed, unexpressed

**ultimate**
◇ tail selection indicator 03 end, ult
04 best, last, peak 05 basic, final, ideal
06 height, summit, utmost 07 closing,
epitome, extreme, highest, maximum,
perfect, primary, radical, supreme,
topmost 08 eventual, furthest, greatest,
last word, limiting, remotest, terminal
09 elemental 10 concluding,
perfection, the mostest 11 chef
d'oeuvre, culmination, fundamental,
masterpiece, summum bonum,
superlative 12 consummation
14 daddy of them all

**ultimately**
◇ tail selection indicator 03 ult 06 at last
07 finally 08 after all, in the end
09 basically, primarily 10 eventually
13 fundamentally, sooner or later 15 in
the last resort

**ultra-**
05 extra 09 extremely, unusually
10 especially, remarkably
11 excessively 13 exceptionally
15 extraordinarily

**ultraviolet**
02 UV

**ululate**
03 cry, sob 04 hoot, howl, keen, moan,
wail, weep 05 mourn 06 holler,
lament, scream 07 screech

**umbrage**
• take umbrage 06 be hurt, resent
07 be angry, be upset 08 be miffed, be
put out, get huffy 09 be annoyed 10 be
insulted, be offended, feel put out
11 take offence 13 be exasperated, take
exception 14 take personally

**umbrella**
05 aegis, cover 06 agency 08 auspices
09 en tout cas 10 protection

---

*Umbrellas and parasols include:*

04 gamp, mush
05 dumpy
06 brolly, chatta
07 gingham
08 marquise, mushroom, ombrella,
sunshade, umbrello
09 en tout cas
11 bumbershoot

---

**umpire**
03 ref, ump 05 judge 06 odd-man
07 arbiter, control, daysman, mediate,
oddsman, referee 08 linesman,
mediator, moderate, oversman,
stickler 09 arbitrate, birlieman, byrlaw-
man, moderator 10 adjudicate,
arbitrator 11 adjudicator
*See also* **cricket**

**umpteen**
06 oodles, plenty 08 millions,
numerous, very many 09 a good many,
countless, thousands 11 innumerable

**UN**
see **United Nations**

**unabashed**
04 bold 06 brazen 07 blatant
09 abashless, confident, unashamed,
undaunted 10 undismayed 11 bold as
brass, unconcerned 13 in
countenance, unembarrassed

**unable**
04 weak 05 unfit 06 cannot 08 impotent
09 incapable, powerless
10 inadequate, unequipped
11 incompetent, ineffectual,
unqualified

**unabridged**
04 full 05 uncut, whole 06 entire
08 complete 10 full-length
11 uncondensed, unshortened
12 unexpurgated

**unacceptable**
04 non-U 05 wrong 07 a bit off
09 obnoxious, offensive, unwelcome
10 unpleasant, unsuitable
11 intolerable, undesirable
12 disagreeable, inadmissible
13 beyond the pale, disappointing,
objectionable 14 unsatisfactory

**unaccommodating**
05 rigid 08 perverse, stubborn
09 obstinate, unbending 10 inflexible,
unyielding 11 disobliging
12 intransigent 13 uncomplaisant,
unco-operative 14 uncompromising

**unaccompanied**
04 lone, solo 05 alone, secco 06 lonely,
silent, single 09 on your own 10 by
yourself, unattended, unescorted
12 single-handed

**unaccountable**
03 odd 04 free 05 queer 06 immune
07 bizarre, curious, strange, unusual
08 baffling, peculiar, puzzling,
singular, uncommon 09 insoluble,
unheard-of 10 mysterious
11 astonishing 12 impenetrable,
inexplicable, unfathomable
13 extraordinary, not answerable,
unexplainable 14 not responsible

**unaccountably**
09 strangely 10 bafflingly, incredibly,
puzzlingly 12 inexplicably,
miraculously, mysteriously,
mystifyingly 13 unexplainably

**unaccustomed**
03 new 06 unused, unwont 07 strange,
unusual 08 uncommon, unwonted,
wontless 09 different, insuitate
10 remarkable, surprising, unexpected,
unfamiliar 11 unpractised
12 unacquainted 13 extraordinary,
inexperienced, unprecedented

**unacquainted**
06 unused 07 strange, unknown,
unusual 08 ignorant 10 unfamiliar,
uninformed 12 unaccustomed
13 inexperienced

**unadorned**
04 bald, bare 05 plain, stark 06 severe,
simple 07 undight 08 homespun
10 restrained 11 undecorated,
unvarnished 12 unornamented
13 unembellished 15 straightforward

## unadulterated

**04** neat, pure, real, true **05** sheer, solid, total, utter **06** simple **07** genuine, natural, perfect, sincere, unmixed **08** absolute, complete, flawless, straight, thorough **09** authentic, downright, unalloyed, undiluted **11** unmitigated, unqualified **14** unsophisticate **15** unsophisticated

## unaffected

**04** real, true **05** naive, plain **06** candid, honest, immune, simple **07** artless, genuine, natural, sincere, unmoved **08** unspoilt **09** guileless, ingenuous, unaltered, unchanged, untouched **10** impervious, unassuming **11** indifferent, unconcerned **13** unpretentious **15** straightforward, unsophisticated

## unafraid

**05** brave **06** daring **08** fearless, intrepid, unfeared **09** confident, dauntless, undaunted **10** courageous, unshakable **11** unshakeable **13** imperturbable

## unalterable

**05** final, fixed, rigid **09** immovable, immutable, permanent **10** inflexible, invariable, unchanging, unyielding **11** hard and fast, reverseless **12** unchangeable

## unaltered

**04** as is **09** invariant

## unanimity

**05** unity **06** accord, unison **07** concert, concord, harmony **09** agreement, consensus **10** congruence **11** concurrence, consistency **14** like-mindedness

## unanimous

**05** as one, joint, solid **06** common, united **08** in accord **09** concerted **10** concordant, consistent, harmonious, like-minded **11** in agreement **12** single-minded

## unanimously

**05** as one **06** nem con **08** as one man **09** in concert, of one mind, unopposed **10** conjointly **12** with one voice **15** by common consent

## unannounced

**06** abrupt, chance, sudden **07** amazing, unusual **09** startling **10** accidental, fortuitous, surprising, unexpected, unforeseen **11** astonishing, unlooked-for **13** unanticipated, unpredictable

## unanswerable

**05** final **08** absolute **10** conclusive, unarguable, undeniable **11** irrefutable **12** indisputable, irrefragable **13** incontestable

## unanswered

**04** open **05** vexed **07** in doubt **09** undecided, unsettled **10** unrequited, unresolved, up in the air

## unappetizing

**07** insipid **09** tasteless, unsavoury **10** off-putting, unexciting, uninviting, unpleasant **11** distasteful, unappealing,

unpalatable **12** disagreeable, unattractive **13** uninteresting

## unapproachable

**04** cold, cool **05** aloof **06** remote **07** distant **08** reserved **09** withdrawn **10** forbidding, unfriendly, unsociable **11** standoffish **12** inaccessible, unresponsive **15** uncommunicative

## unapt

**04** slow **05** inapt, unfit **08** unfitted, unsuited, untimely **10** inapposite, malapropos, unsuitable **12** inapplicable, unseasonable **13** inappropriate

## unarmed

**04** bare, open, weak **05** inerm, naked **07** exposed **08** helpless **10** unweaponed, vulnerable **11** defenceless, unprotected

## unashamed

**04** open **06** direct, honest **07** blatant **08** bashless **09** shameless, unabashed **10** impenitent **11** unconcealed, undisguised, unrepentant

## unasked

**08** unbidden, unsought, unwanted **09** uninvited, voluntary **10** unrequired **11** spontaneous, unannounced, unrequested, unsolicited

## unassailable

**05** sound **06** proven, secure **08** absolute, positive **09** well-armed **10** conclusive, invincible, inviolable, undeniable **11** impregnable, irrefutable **12** indisputable, inexpugnable, invulnerable **13** incontestable, well-fortified

## unassertive

**03** shy **04** meek **05** mousy, quiet, timid **06** mousey **07** bashful **08** backward, retiring, timorous **09** diffident **10** unassuming **12** self-effacing

## unassuming

**03** shy **04** meek **05** quiet **06** demure, humble, modest, simple **07** natural **08** reticent, retiring **10** restrained **11** unassertive, unobtrusive **12** self-effacing, underbearing **13** unpretentious

## unattached

**04** free **05** loose **06** single **08** detached **09** available, fancy-free, footloose, on your own, unengaged, unmarried **10** by yourself, with no ties **11** independent, uncommitted **12** unaffiliated

## unattended

**05** alone **07** ignored **08** forsaken **09** abandoned, forgotten, neglected, unguarded, unwatched **10** unescorted **11** disregarded **12** unsupervised **13** unaccompanied

## unattractive

**04** ugly **05** gross, plain, warby **06** grungy, homely, scungy, skanky, unsexy **08** butt-ugly, ill-faurd, uncomely, unlovely **09** offensive, repellent, unsavoury, unsightly, unwelcome **10** disgusting, off-putting, unexciting, uninviting, unpleasant

**11** distasteful, ill-favoured, unappealing, undesirable, unpalatable **12** disagreeable, unappetizing **13** no oil painting, objectionable **15** not much to look at, unprepossessing

## unauthorized

**07** illegal, illicit **08** unlawful **09** forbidden, irregular **10** prohibited, unapproved, unlicensed, unofficial **11** unchartered, unwarranted **12** illegitimate, unsanctioned

## unavailing

**04** vain **06** beaten, failed, futile, losing **07** sterile, unlucky, useless **08** abortive, defeated, luckless, nugatory, thwarted **09** fruitless **10** frustrated **11** ineffective, unfortunate **12** unprevailing, unproductive, unprofitable, unsuccessful

## unavoidable

**04** sure **05** fatal, fated **07** certain **08** destined, required **09** mandatory, necessary **10** compulsory, inevitable, inexorable, obligatory **11** ineluctable, inescapable, predestined

## unaware

**04** deaf **05** blind **07** witless **08** heedless, ignorant, wareless **09** in the dark, oblivious, unknowing, unmindful, unwitting **10** insentient, uninformed, with no idea **11** incognizant, unconscious **12** unsuspecting **13** unenlightened

## unawares

**05** aback **07** unwares **08** abruptly, off guard, on the hop, suddenly **09** in the dark, red-handed **10** by surprise, mistakenly, unprepared **11** insidiously, unknowingly, unwittingly **12** accidentally, à l'improviste, unexpectedly, unthinkingly **13** inadvertently, unconsciously **15** unintentionally

## unbalanced

◇ *anagram indicator* **03** mad **05** barmy, crazy **06** biased, insane, mental, uneven, unfair, unjust **07** erratic, lunatic, unequal, unsound **08** crackers, demented, deranged, doolally, lopsided, one-sided, partisan, unstable, unsteady **09** disturbed, stir-crazy **10** irrational, prejudiced **11** dysharmonic, inequitable, mentally ill **12** asymmetrical, round the bend **13** round the twist **14** wrong in the head

## unbearable

**06** too bad **07** too much **08** the limit **10** importable **11** intolerable, unendurable **12** excruciating, insufferable, the last straw, unacceptable **13** insupportable

## unbeatable

**04** best **07** supreme **09** excellent, matchless, rock-solid **10** invincible **11** indomitable, unstoppable **12** second to none **13** unconquerable, unsurpassable

## unbeaten

**07** supreme, unbowed, winning **09** unsubdued **10** triumphant,

## unbecoming

undefeated, victorious
**11** unconquered, unsurpassed
**12** unvanquished

## unbecoming

**08** improper, indecent, infra dig,
unseemly, unworthy **09** unfitting,
unseeming, unsightly **10** indecorous,
indelicate, misseeming, unladylike,
unsuitable **11** unbefitting **12** ill-
beseeming, unattractive
**13** inappropriate, ungentlemanly
**15** infra dignitatem

## unbeknown

• **unbeknown to 07** unknown
**09** unheard of **10** unrealized
**11** unperceived **13** unbeknownst to

## unbelief

**05** doubt **07** atheism **09** disbelief
**10** scepticism **11** agnosticism,
incredulity

## unbelievable

**06** unreal **07** amazing **08** unlikely
**10** far-fetched, impossible,
improbable, incredible, outlandish,
remarkable, staggering **11** astonishing,
implausible, incredulous, unthinkable
**12** preposterous, unconvincing,
unimaginable **13** extraordinary,
inconceivable

## unbelievably

**09** amazingly **10** incredibly
**12** outlandishly, unimaginably
**13** inconceivably **15** extraordinarily

## unbeliever

**06** zendik **07** atheist, doubter, infidel,
sceptic **08** agnostic **11** disbeliever,
nullifidian **14** doubting Thomas

## unbelieving

**07** dubious, infidel **08** doubtful,
doubting **09** miscreant, sceptical
**10** suspicious **11** distrustful,
incredulous, nullifidian, unconvinced,
unpersuaded **12** disbelieving

## unbend

**04** thaw, undo **05** relax **06** uncoil,
uncurl **08** loosen up, unbuckle,
unbutton, unfasten, unfreeze
**10** straighten

## unbending

**04** firm **05** aloof, rigid, stern, stiff, tough
**06** formal, severe, strict **07** distant
**08** Catonian, hardline, relaxing,
reserved, resolute, stubborn
**10** forbidding, formidable, inflexible,
unyielding **12** intransigent
**14** uncompromising

## unbiased

**04** fair, just **06** candid **07** neutral
**08** balanced **09** equitable, impartial,
objective **10** even-handed, fair-
minded, open-minded, uncoloured
**11** independent **12** uninfluenced,
unprejudiced **13** disinterested,
dispassionate

## unbidden

**04** free **07** unasked, willing
**08** unforced, unwanted **09** uninvited,
unwelcome, voluntary **10** unprompted
**11** spontaneous, unsolicited

## unbind

**04** free, undo **05** loose, solve, untie
**06** loosen, unyoke **07** release, set free,
unchain, unloose **08** liberate, unfasten,
unfetter, unloosen **09** unshackle

## unblemished

**04** pure **05** clear, white **07** perfect
**08** flawless, spotless, unflawed
**09** unspotted, unstained, unsullied,
untainted **10** immaculate
**11** untarnished **13** unimpeachable
**14** irreproachable

## unblinking

**04** calm, cool **06** steady **07** assured
**08** composed, fearless, unafraid
**09** impassive **10** unwavering
**11** emotionless, unemotional,
unfaltering, unflinching, unshrinking
**13** imperturbable

## unblushing

**04** bold **06** amoral, brazen **07** blatant
**08** immodest, impudent **09** shameless,
unabashed, unashamed
**13** unembarrassed **15** conscience-proof

## unborn

**06** coming, future, to-come **07** awaited,
in utero **08** expected, unyeaned
**09** embryonic **10** subsequent,
succeeding **11** non-existent

## unbosom

**04** bare, tell **05** admit **06** let out, reveal
**07** confess, confide, divulge, lay bare,
pour out, tell all, uncover **08** disclose,
unburden

## unbounded

**04** vast **07** endless **08** infinite
**09** boundless, limitless, unbridled,
unchecked, unlimited
**12** immeasurable, unconfinable,
uncontrolled, unrestrained,
unrestricted

## unbreakable

**05** solid, tough **06** rugged, strong
**07** durable **09** resistant, toughened
**10** adamantine **11** infrangible
**12** shatterproof **14** indestructible

## unbridled

**04** wild **07** rampant, riotous
**08** unbitted, uncurbed **09** excessive,
unchecked **10** immoderate, licentious,
profligate, ungoverned **11** intemperate
**12** uncontrolled, unrestrained
**13** unconstrained

## unbroken

**04** wild **05** rough, sheer, solid, whole
**06** entire, in a row, intact, single
**07** endless, non-stop, unbroke,
untamed **08** complete, constant,
seamless, unbeaten **09** ceaseless,
incessant, perpetual, unceasing,
undivided, unmatched **10** continuate,
continuous, successive, unequalled,
unrivalled **11** progressive, unremitting,
unsurpassed **13** uninterrupted
**14** undomesticated

## unburden

**04** bare, tell **05** admit **06** let out, reveal
**07** cast off, confess, confide, divulge,
lay bare, offload, pour out, tell all,
uncover **08** disclose **09** discharge

## unbutton

**04** undo

## uncalled-for

**07** unasked **08** needless, unsought
**09** unwelcome **10** gratuitous,
undeserved, unprompted, unprovoked
**11** unjustified, unnecessary,
unsolicited, unwarranted

## uncannily

**05** oddly **08** spookily **09** bizarrely,
strangely **10** incredibly, remarkably
**11** unnaturally **12** mysteriously
**14** supernaturally **15** extraordinarily

## uncanny

**03** odd **05** eerie, queer, weird
**06** creepy, spooky, unsafe **07** bizarre,
strange **08** eldritch, pokerish
**09** fantastic, unearthly, unnatural,
wanchancy **10** incredible, mysterious,
remarkable, wanchancie
**11** exceptional **12** supernatural
**13** extraordinary, preternatural,
unaccountable

## uncared-for

**07** run-down, squalid **08** derelict,
deserted, forsaken, stranded,
untended, untilled, unweeded
**09** abandoned, neglected, overgrown
**11** dilapidated, disregarded,
undervalued, unhusbanded
**12** uncultivated, unmaintained
**13** unappreciated

## uncaring

**04** cold **07** callous, unmoved
**09** unfeeling **11** indifferent,
unconcerned **12** uninterested
**13** inconsiderate, marble-hearted,
unsympathetic **14** marble-breasted

## unceasing

**07** endless, non-stop, undying
**08** constant, unbroken, unending
**09** ceaseless, continual, continued,
incessant, perpetual **10** continuous,
persistent, relentless **11** everlasting,
never-ending, unrelenting, unremitting

## unceremonious

**04** rude **06** abrupt, casual, direct,
sudden **07** off-hand, relaxed
**08** familiar, impolite, informal, laid-
back, sans gêne **09** easy-going
**10** unofficial **11** undignified
**12** discourteous **13** disrespectful

## uncertain

◇ *anagram indicator* **04** iffy, open
**05** dicey, dodgy, risky, shaky, vague
**06** chancy, fitful, slippy, unsure
**07** chancey, dubious, erratic, unclear,
unknown, vagrant, various
**08** doubtful, hesitant, insecure,
slippery, unsteady, variable, wavering
**09** hazardous, irregular, undecided,
unsettled **10** ambivalent, changeable,
conflicted, inconstant, indefinite, in
two minds, of two minds, precarious,
touch-and-go, unreliable, unresolved,
up in the air **11** speculative,
unconfirmed, unconvinced,
vacillating **12** equivocating, in the
balance, questionable, undetermined
**13** indeterminate, unforeseeable,
unpredictable

## uncertainly
**05** shyly **06** warily **07** timidly
**09** dubiously, haltingly **10** delayingly,
doubtfully, hesitantly, in two minds,
waveringly **11** reluctantly, sceptically,
tentatively, unwillingly
**12** indecisively, irresolutely,
stammeringly, stutteringly **13** half-
heartedly, vacillatingly

## uncertainty
**02** if **05** doubt, qualm **06** qualms
**07** dilemma **09** ambiguity, confusion,
misgiving, riskiness, vagueness
**10** hesitation, insecurity, perplexity,
puzzlement, scepticism, uneasiness
**11** ambivalence, contingency
**12** bewilderment, irresolution,
peradventure **13** unreliability

## unchallengeable
**05** final **07** sacless **08** absolute
**10** conclusive **11** impregnable,
irrefutable **12** inappellable,
indisputable, irrefragable
**13** incontestable

## unchangeable
**05** final, fixed **07** eternal **08** constant
**09** immutable, permanent
**10** changeless, invariable, unchanging
**11** stereotyped **12** irreversible
**14** intransmutable

## unchanging
**04** same **06** steady **07** abiding, eternal,
lasting **08** constant, enduring
**09** permanent, perpetual, phaseless,
steadfast, unvarying **10** changeless,
invariable

## uncharitable
**04** hard, mean **05** cruel, harsh, stern
**06** severe, unkind **07** callous
**09** unfeeling **10** unfriendly, ungenerous
**11** hard-hearted, insensitive,
unchristian, unforgiving
**13** unsympathetic **15** uncompassionate

## uncharted
**03** new **05** alien **06** virgin **07** foreign,
strange, unknown **09** unplumbed
**10** unexplored, unfamiliar, unsurveyed
**12** undiscovered

## unchaste
**04** lewd **05** frail, light, loose **06** fallen,
impure, wanton **07** defiled, immoral,
wappend **08** depraved, immodest
**09** dishonest, dissolute **10** licentious
**11** light-heeled, promiscuous

## unchecked
**03** raw **04** wild **06** unruly **07** rampant,
riotous, violent **08** uncurbed, unreined
**09** unbridled **10** boisterous,
unhindered **12** uncontrolled,
unrestrained **13** undisciplined

## uncivil
**04** curt, rude **05** gruff, surly **06** abrupt,
coarse **07** bearish, boorish, brusque,
ill-bred, uncouth **08** churlish, impolite,
unseemly **09** menseless **10** ungracious,
unmannerly **11** bad-mannered, ill-
mannered **12** discourteous
**13** disrespectful

## uncivilized
**04** wild **05** rough **06** savage **07** boorish,

brutish, heathen, salvage, uncouth,
untamed **08** barbaric, impolite
**09** barbarian, barbarous, primitive,
unrefined **10** antisocial, heathenish,
illiterate, tramontane, uncultured,
uneducated **13** unenlightened
**15** unsophisticated

## unclassifiable
**05** vague **07** elusive **08** doubtful
**09** uncertain **10** ill-defined, indefinite,
indistinct **11** indefinable, undefinable
**13** indescribable, indeterminate
**14** unidentifiable

## unclassified
**05** basic, known **06** lowest, public
**07** general, minimal, minimum
**08** official, revealed, ungraded
**09** disclosed, published **11** on the
record **12** unrestricted **14** for
publication

## uncle
**03** eme, oom **10** pawnbroker

---
*Uncles include:*

| | | |
|---|---|---|
| **03** | Bob, Joe, Pio, Sam, Tom | |
| **05** | Henry, Lynch (Andrew), Remus, Silas, Vanya | |
| **06** | Domkin (George), Fester, Jasper (John), Julius, Shandy (Toby), Wilson (Arthur) | |
| **07** | Flowers (Philip), Forsyte (Old Jolyon), Trotter (Albert) | |
| **08** | Bulgaria, Claudius, McCaslin (Buck), McCaslin (Buddy) | |
| **09** | Cobbleigh (Tom), Old Jolyon | |
| **10** | Richard III | |
| **11** | Pumblechook | |
| **15** | Richard the Third | |
---

## unclean
**03** bad **04** evil, foul, lewd **05** dirty,
grimy **06** filthy, grubby, impure, soiled,
wicked **07** corrupt, defiled, profane,
sullied, tainted **08** ordurous, polluted
**10** unhygienic **11** adulterated,
unwholesome **12** contaminated

## unclear
**03** dim **04** hazy, iffy **05** foggy, vague
**06** unsure **07** dubious, obscure
**08** doubtful **09** ambiguous, equivocal,
non liquet, uncertain, unsettled
**10** convoluted, indefinite, indistinct
**12** undetermined

## unclothed
**04** bare, nude **05** naked **06** unclad
**08** disrobed, in the raw, starkers,
stripped **09** in the buff, undressed
**10** stark-naked **15** in the altogether

## uncomfortable
**04** cold, hard, mean **05** tense, unked,
unket, unkid **06** on edge, uneasy
**07** anxious, awkward, cramped,
nervous, painful, worried **08** troubled
**09** disturbed, ill at ease **10** disquieted,
distressed, ill-fitting, irritating
**11** discomfited, embarrassed
**12** disagreeable **13** self-conscious

## uncommitted
**04** free **07** neutral **08** floating
**09** available, fancy-free, footloose,
undecided **10** non-aligned,

unattached, uninvolved **11** non-
partisan **12** free-floating

## uncommon
◇ *anagram indicator* **03** odd **04** rare,
seld, very **05** queer **06** scarce
**07** bizarre, curious, notable, special,
strange, unusual **08** abnormal,
atypical, peculiar, singular, striking
**10** infrequent, remarkable, remarkably,
unfamiliar **11** distinctive, exceptional,
out of the way, outstanding **12** like
gold dust **13** extraordinary **15** thin on
the ground

## uncommonly
◇ *anagram indicator* **04** seld, very
**06** rarely, seldom **09** extremely,
strangely, unusually **10** abnormally,
peculiarly, remarkably, singularly
**12** infrequently, occasionally,
particularly **13** exceptionally,
outstandingly

## uncommunicative
**03** shy **04** curt **05** aloof, brief, close,
quiet **06** silent **08** reserved, reticent,
retiring, taciturn **09** diffident, secretive,
withdrawn **10** buttoned-up, unsociable
**11** tight-lipped **12** unresponsive
**13** unforthcoming

## uncomplicated
◇ *anagram indicator* **04** easy **05** clear
**06** direct, simple **10** uninvolved
**11** undemanding **15** straightforward

## uncompromising
**04** firm **05** rigid, stiff, tough **06** gritty,
strict **07** diehard **08** hardline, obdurate,
stubborn **09** hard-faced, hardshell,
immovable, obstinate, out-and-out,
unbending **10** inexorable, inflexible,
unyielding **12** intransigent
**15** unaccommodating

## unconcealable
**05** clear, plain **07** obvious **08** manifest
**09** insistent **13** irrepressible
**14** insuppressible, uncontrollable

## unconcealed
**04** open, pert **05** frank, naked, overt
**06** patent, public **07** blatant, evident,
obvious, visible **08** admitted, apparent,
manifest, unveiled **09** unashamed
**10** noticeable **11** conspicuous **12** ill-
concealed, undissembled **13** self-
confessed **15** undistinguished

## unconcern
**06** apathy **09** aloofness **10** detachment,
negligence, remoteness
**11** callousness, disinterest,
insouciance, nonchalance
**12** indifference **13** pococurantism

## unconcerned
**04** cool **05** aloof, sober **06** casual,
remote **07** callous, distant, relaxed,
unmoved **08** carefree, careless,
composed, detached, not fussy,
uncaring **09** apathetic, impartial, not
fussed, oblivious, unruffled, unworried
**10** complacent, insouciant,
nonchalant, uninvolved, untroubled
**11** indifferent, pococurante,
unperturbed **12** uninterested
**13** disinterested, dispassionate,
unsympathetic

## unconditional
04 full, pure 05 total, utter 06 entire
07 plenary 08 absolute, complete,
definite, outright, positive, termless
09 categoric, downright, out-and-out,
unlimited 10 conclusive, unreserved
11 categorical, unequivocal,
unqualified 12 thoroughgoing
wholehearted 13 thoroughgoing

## unconditionally
05 fully 06 purely 07 totally 08 entirely
10 absolutely, completely
11 simpliciter 12 unreservedly
13 categorically, unequivocally
14 wholeheartedly

## unconfirmed
08 ignorant, unproved, unproven
10 unratified, unverified
14 uncorroborated 15 unauthenticated,
unsubstantiated

## unconformity
12 irregularity 13 disconformity,
discontinuity

## uncongenial
08 unsuited 09 unsavoury
10 discordant, unfriendly, uninviting,
unpleasant 11 displeasing, distasteful,
unappealing 12 antagonistic,
antipathetic, disagreeable,
incompatible, unattractive
13 unsympathetic

## unconnected
07 foreign 08 confused, detached,
separate 09 illogical, unrelated
10 disjointed, incoherent, irrational,
irrelevant, unattached 11 independent,
off the point 12 disconnected
13 inappropriate, unco-ordinated
14 beside the point

## unconquerable
08 enduring 09 ingrained 10 inveterate,
invincible, unbeatable, unyielding
11 indomitable, insuperable
12 irresistible, overpowering,
undefeatable 13 irrepressible
14 insurmountable

## unconscionable
06 amoral, unholy 07 extreme,
ungodly 08 criminal 09 excessive,
unearthly, unethical 10 exorbitant,
immoderate, inordinate, outrageous
11 extravagant 12 preposterous,
unpardonable, unprincipled,
unreasonable, unscrupulous
13 unjustifiable, unwarrantable

## unconscious
03 out 04 deaf 05 blind, dazed
06 asleep, innate, latent, put out,
reflex, zonked 07 drugged, fainted, in a
coma, out cold, stunned, unaware,
witless 08 comatose, heedless,
ignorant, knee-jerk, lifeless
09 automatic, collapsed, concussed,
impulsive, oblivious, passed out,
repressed, senseless, unmindful,
unwitting 10 accidental, blacked out,
insensible, knocked out, subliminal,
suppressed, unthinking 11 inadvertent,
incognizant, inconscient, inconscious,
instinctive, involuntary
12 subconscious 13 unintentional

14 dead to the world, out for the count
• **render unconscious** 04 stun 06 lay
out, put out 07 garotte, garrote
08 garrotte, knock out

## unconsciously
10 heedlessly, insensibly
11 impulsively, obliviously,
unmindfully, unwittingly
12 accidentally, subliminally,
unthinkingly 13 automatically,
inadvertently, instinctively,
involuntarily 15 unintentionally

## unconsciousness
04 coma, doze 05 faint, sleep
06 snooze, torpor, trance 08 blackout,
daydream, narcosis, numbness
12 inconscience, stupefaction
13 insensibility

## unconstraint
07 abandon, freedom 08 openness
09 unreserve 10 liberality, relaxation
11 unrestraint 12 laissez-faire

## uncontrollable
03 mad 04 wild 06 strong, unruly
07 furious, violent 08 absolute
10 disorderly 11 intractable
12 indisputable, out of control,
ungovernable, unmanageable
13 irrepressible

## uncontrolled
◇ *anagram indicator* 04 wild 06 random,
randon, unruly 07 rampant, riotous,
runaway, violent 08 uncurbed
09 unbridled, unchecked
10 boisterous, unhindered, unmastered
12 unrestrained 13 undisciplined

## unconventional
◇ *anagram indicator* 03 odd 04 rare,
zany 05 gipsy, gypsy, outré, spacy,
wacky, weird 06 far-out, freaky, fringe,
spacey, way-out 07 bizarre, oddball,
offbeat, radical, unusual 08 abnormal,
bohemian, freakish, original, out there,
uncommon 09 different, eccentric,
irregular, left-field 10 avant-garde,
individual, long-haired, unorthodox
11 alternative, uncustomary
12 experimental 13 idiosyncratic

## unconvincing
04 lame, weak 05 fishy 06 farfet, feeble,
flimsy 07 dubious, suspect 08 doubtful,
unlikely 10 far-fetched, improbable
11 implausible 12 questionable

## uncooked
03 raw 09 au naturel

## unco-operative
04 rude 07 awkward, cubbish, stroppy
08 stubborn 09 obstinate, unhelpful
10 unpleasant 12 bloody-minded

## unco-ordinated
◇ *anagram indicator* 05 inept 06 clumsy
07 awkward 08 bumbling, bungling,
ungainly 09 maladroit 10 disjointed,
ungraceful 11 clodhopping

## uncork
04 open, undo 05 clear, crack
06 broach, expose, unseal 07 uncover
08 push open 09 break open, burst
open, force open, prise open, slide
open

## uncouth
◇ *anagram indicator* 04 rude 05 crude,
rough 06 clumsy, coarse, gauche,
rugged, rustic, unrude, vulgar
07 awkward, boorish, loutish,
unknown 08 impolite, improper,
ungainly, unseemly 09 graceless,
rough-hewn, unrefined 10 uncultured,
unfamiliar, ungraceful 11 bad-
mannered, ill-mannered, rough as
bags, uncivilized 12 uncultivated
15 unsophisticated

## uncover
04 bare, leak, open, peel, rake, show
05 dig up, strip, unlid 06 detect,
exhume, expose, reveal, unheal,
unhele, unmask, unrake, unveil,
unwrap 07 dismask, divulge, lay bare,
lay open, unearth 08 disclose,
discover, unbonnet, unshroud
09 make known, unsheathe 12 bring to
light 13 blow the lid off, lift the lid off,
take the lid off

## uncritical
05 naive 07 unfussy 08 gullible, trusting
09 accepting, credulous, incurious
11 superficial, unselective
12 undiscerning 13 unquestioning
14 non-judgemental

## unctuous
04 glib, oily 05 slick, suave 06 creamy,
greasy, smarmy, smooth 07 fawning,
gushing, servile 09 insincere, pietistic,
plausible 10 obsequious
11 sycophantic 12 ingratiating
13 sanctimonious

## uncultivated
03 new 04 wild 05 feral, rough, waste
06 desert, fallow, incult 07 natural,
wilding 11 unhusbanded

## uncultured
04 hick, rude 05 crude, ocker, rough
06 coarse, incult, rustic 07 boorish, ill-
bred, uncouth 09 barbarous, unrefined
10 philistine 11 uncivilized
12 uncultivated 14 unintellectual
15 unsophisticated

## undaunted
04 bold 05 brave 07 impavid, unbowed
08 fearless, intrepid, resolute, unafraid
09 dauntless, steadfast, unalarmed
10 courageous, undeterred,
undismayed, unflagging
11 indomitable 13 undiscouraged

## undecided
04 moot, open 05 vague 06 unsure
07 dubious, in doubt, unknown
08 doubtful, hesitant, wavering
09 debatable, dithering, uncertain,
unsettled 10 ambivalent, indecisive,
indefinite, in two minds, irresolute, of
two minds, unresolved, up in the air
11 uncommitted 12 equivocating, in
the balance 13 unestablished

## undecorated
05 plain, stark 06 severe, simple
07 austere 08 inornate 09 classical,
unadorned 10 functional
12 unornamented 13 unembellished

## undefeated
07 supreme, unbowed, winning

## undefended

08 unbeaten 09 unsubdued
10 triumphant, victorious
11 unconquered, unsurpassed
12 unvanquished

## undefended

04 open 05 naked 07 exposed,
unarmed 09 pregnable, unguarded
10 vulnerable 11 defenceless,
unfortified, unprotected

## undefiled

04 pure 05 clean, clear 06 chaste,
intact, virgin 08 sinless 08 flawless,
spotless, unsoiled, virginal
09 inviolate, unspotted, unstained,
unsullied 10 immaculate, intemerate
11 unblemished

## undefined

04 hazy 05 vague 06 woolly 07 inexact,
shadowy, tenuous, unclear
08 formless, nebulous 09 imprecise
10 ill-defined, indefinite, indistinct
11 unexplained, unspecified
13 indeterminate

## undemonstrative

04 cold, cool 05 aloof, stiff 06 formal,
remote 07 distant 08 reserved, reticent
09 impassive, withdrawn
10 phlegmatic, restrained
11 unemotional 12 unresponsive
15 uncommunicative

## undeniable

04 sure 05 clear 06 patent, proven
07 certain, evident, obvious
08 definite, manifest, positive
09 excellent, hard facts, undoubted
11 beyond doubt, indubitable,
irrefutable 12 disputable,
unmistakable 13 incontestable
14 beyond question, unquestionable
15 unexceptionable

## undeniably

09 certainly 10 definitely, positively
11 beyond doubt, indubitably,
undoubtedly 12 indisputably,
unmistakably 14 beyond question,
unquestionably

## undependable

06 fickle 07 erratic 08 unstable,
variable 09 mercurial, uncertain
10 capricious, changeable, inconstant,
unreliable 11 fair-weather, treacherous
12 inconsistent 13 irresponsible,
unpredictable, untrustworthy

## under

◇ *juxtaposition down indicator* 04 down,
less 05 below, lower 06 within
07 beneath 08 downward, junior to,
less than, under par 09 lower than
10 inferior to, underneath 11 secondary
to, subordinate 13 subordinate to,
subservient to

## underclothes

*see* **underwear**

## undercover

03 sly 06 covert, hidden, secret
07 furtive, private 08 hush-hush,
stealthy 09 concealed 11 clandestine,
underground 12 confidential,
intelligence 13 surreptitious

## undercurrent

04 aura, hint 05 drift, sense, tinge, trend
07 feeling, flavour 08 movement,
overtone, tendency, underset,
undertow 09 underflow, undertone
10 atmosphere, suggestion

## undercut

04 mine 05 filet 08 excavate, gouge
out, scoop out, underbid 09 hollow
out, undermine, undersell
10 tenderloin, underprice
11 undercharge 14 charge less than

## underdog

04 prey 05 loser 06 victim 07 outcast
08 outsider 09 little man
11 unfortunate, weaker party 12 the
exploited

## underdone

04 rare 09 half-baked

## underestimate

07 dismiss 08 belittle, minimize,
misjudge, play down 09 disparage, sell
short, underrate 10 look down on,
trivialize, undervalue 12 miscalculate

## undergarment

*see* **underwear**

## undergo

04 bear 05 enjoy, stand 06 endure,
suffer 07 sustain, weather 08 submit to,
tolerate, underlie 09 go through, put up
with, withstand 10 experience 11 pass
through

## underground

04 tube 05 metro 06 buried, covert,
hidden, secret, subway, sunken
07 covered, furtive, illegal, radical
08 secretly 09 concealed, hypogeous
10 avant-garde, hypogaeous,
subversive, undercover, unofficial,
unorthodox 11 alternative, below
ground, clandestine 12 experimental,
subterranean 13 revolutionary,
surreptitious 15 below the surface

---

*Underground and metro transport
systems include:*

01 T
03 DLR
04 BART, DART
07 the Tube
09 Chicago El, Rome Metro
10 City Circle, Paris Métro
11 Berlin S-Bahn, Berlin U-Bahn,
Madrid Metro, Munich S-Bahn,
Munich U-Bahn
13 New York Subway
15 Clockwork Orange, Washington
Metro

*See also* **London**

---

## undergrowth

05 brush, scrub 06 briars, bushes,
shrubs, spring 07 bracken, thicket
08 brambles 09 brushwood, shrubbery,
underwood 10 vegetation 11 ground
cover

## underhand

03 sly 05 shady 06 crafty, secret,
shonky, sneaky 07 crooked, devious,
furtive, immoral, oblique 08 improper,
scheming, sinister, sneaking, stealthy

09 deceitful, deceptive, dishonest,
unethical 10 backstairs, fraudulent
11 clandestine, unobtrusive
12 unscrupulous 13 hole-and-corner,
surreptitious

## underline

04 mark 06 stress 07 point up
09 emphasize, highlight, italicize
10 accentuate, foreground, underscore
15 draw attention to

## underling

05 slave 06 lackey, menial, minion,
nobody 07 flunkey, servant 08 hireling,
inferior, munchkin, weakling
09 nonentity 11 subordinate

## underlying

04 root 05 basal, basic 06 hidden,
latent, veiled 07 lurking, primary,
subject 08 inherent 09 concealed,
essential, intrinsic, subjacent
10 elementary 11 fundamental,
subordinate

## undermine

03 dig, mar, sap 04 mine 05 erode
06 damage, impair, injure, tunnel,
weaken 07 cripple, destroy, handbag,
subvert, vitiate 08 excavate, sabotage,
undercut, wear away 09 underwork
14 make less secure

## undernourished

06 hungry 07 starved 08 anorexic,
underfed 09 anorectic
12 malnourished

## underprivileged

04 poor 05 needy 06 in need, in want
08 deprived 09 destitute, oppressed
10 in distress 11 impecunious
12 impoverished 13 disadvantaged

## underrate

07 dismiss 08 belittle, inferior
09 disparage, downgrade, extenuate,
sell short 10 depreciate, look down on,
undervalue 13 underestimate

## under-secretary

02 US

## undersell

03 cut 05 slash 06 reduce 08 mark
down, play down, undercut
09 disparage, sell short 10 depreciate,
understate 11 undercharge

## undershirt

04 vest 06 semmit 07 singlet, surcoat

## undersized

03 wee 04 puny, tiny 05 dwarf, pygmy,
scrub, small, teeny 06 little, minute,
teensy 07 runtish, stunted 08 pint-size
09 atrophied, miniature, pint-sized
11 underweight 14 underdeveloped
15 achondroplastic

## understand

03 dig, get, see 04 gaum, gorm, grok,
hear, know, read, take, twig 05 catch,
click, get it, grasp, imply, learn, savey,
savvy, think 06 accept, assume,
fathom, follow, gather, make of,
rumble, savvey, take in 07 believe,
comfort, discern, elusive, feel for, get
wise, make out, presume, realize,
support, suppose, suss out

**08** conceive, conclude, contrive, cotton on, perceive, tumble to **09** apprehend, empathize, enter into, figure out, interpret, latch onto, penetrate, recognize **10** appreciate, comprehend, sympathize **11** commiserate, get the drift, make sense of **12** feel sorry for, get a handle on, get the hang of, identify with, know the ropes **13** get the drift of, get the message, get the picture, the penny drops
• **failure to understand** **04** anan, anon

## understandable
**05** clear, lucid, plain **06** direct **07** natural **08** expected **10** acceptable, accessible, admissible, penetrable, reasonable **11** transparent, unambiguous **12** intelligible, unsurprising **14** comprehensible, self-explaining **15** self-explanatory, straightforward

## understanding
**03** ken **04** gaum, gorm, head, idea, kind, pact, view, with **05** grasp, sense, trust **06** accord, belief, loving, notion, tender, uptake, wisdom **07** bargain, comfort, command, compact, conceit, empathy, entente, feeling, harmony, insight, lenient, opinion, patient, support **08** sympathy, tolerant **09** agreement, awareness, forgiving, hindsight, intellect, judgement, knowledge, sensitive **10** compassion, discerning, forbearing, impression, perception, supportive, thoughtful **11** arrangement, considerate, consolation, discernment, intelligent, sympathetic **12** appreciation, apprehension, intelligence **13** commiseration, compassionate, comprehension **14** interpretation

## understate
**07** dismiss **08** belittle, minimize, play down **09** soft-pedal, underplay **11** make light of

## understated
**04** mild **05** faint **06** low-key, subtle **07** implied **08** indirect **09** toned-down **10** indefinite, indistinct

## understatement
**07** litotes, meiosis **09** dismissal, restraint **12** minimization, underplaying

## understood
**05** tacit **07** assumed, implied **08** accepted, familiar, implicit, inferred, presumed, unspoken, unstated **09** unwritten **11** transparent

## understudy
**05** locum **06** deputy, double, fill-in, relief **07** reserve, stand-in **10** substitute **11** replacement

## undersurface
**03** pad **04** sole **05** belly **08** intrados, pavilion **09** gastraeum

## undertake
**03** try **05** agree, begin **06** accept, assume, pledge, tackle, take on **07** attempt, promise, receive

**08** commence, contract, covenant, deal with, embark on, perceive, set about, shoulder **09** endeavour, get down to, guarantee, set in hand, underfong **10** enterprise, take in hand **13** put your hand to, set your hand to **14** commit yourself, get to grips with, grasp the nettle, turn your hand to **15** apply yourself to

## undertaker
**06** editor, surety **07** sponsor **08** compiler, upholder **09** mortician, projector, publisher **10** contractor **12** entrepreneur **15** funeral director

## undertaking
**03** job, vow **04** call, plan, task, word **06** affair, effort, pledge, scheme **07** attempt, emprise, project, promise, venture, warrant **08** business, campaign, contract, warranty **09** assurance, challenge, endeavour, guarantee, operation **10** commitment, enterprise **12** enterprising

## undertone
**04** aura, hint **05** tinge, touch, trace **06** murmur **07** feeling, flavour, whisper **09** undernote, undersong **10** atmosphere, intimation, suggestion **11** connotation **12** undercurrent

## undervalue
**07** disable, dismiss **08** disprize, minimize, misjudge, misprise, misprize **09** disparage, sell short, underrate **10** depreciate, look down on **13** underestimate

## underwater
**06** sunken **08** demersal, demersed, immersed, undersea, undertow **09** submarine, submerged **10** subaquatic, subaqueous

## underwear
**06** smalls, undies **08** grundies, lingerie, scanties, skivvies, underset **09** innerwear **10** underlinen **11** underthings **12** underclothes **13** underclothing, undergarments **14** unmentionables

---

*Underwear includes:*

**03** bra
**04** body, coms, jump, slip, vest
**05** bania, cimar, combs, cymar, jupon, pants, shift, tanga, teddy, thong, tunic
**06** banian, banyan, basque, briefs, corset, garter, girdle, knicks, semmit, skivvy, teddie, trunks
**07** chemise, drawers, G-string, hosiery, linings, panties, singlet, spencer, Y-fronts
**08** bloomers, camisole, chuddies, frillies, knickers, subucula, thermals
**09** brassière, crinoline, jockstrap, long johns, petticoat, stockings, union suit, wyliecoat
**10** suspenders, underdress, underpants, undershirt, underskirt
**11** boxer shorts, directoires, undershorts
**12** body stocking, camiknickers, combinations

**13** liberty bodice, suspender-belt
**14** French knickers

## underweight
**04** thin **08** underfed **10** undersized **11** half-starved **14** undernourished

## underworld
**03** Dis, pit **04** Ades, fire, hell **05** abyss, below, Hades, Sheol **06** Erebus, the mob, Tophet **07** Abaddon, Acheron, Gehenna, inferno **08** gangland, Tartarus **09** down there, Malebolge, perdition **10** other place, subterrene **11** nether world, underground **12** lower regions **13** bottomless pit, criminal world **14** organized crime **15** abode of the devil, infernal regions

## underwrite
**04** back, fund, sign **05** write **06** insure **07** approve, confirm, endorse, finance, initial, sponsor, support **08** sanction **09** authorize, guarantee, subscribe, subsidize **11** countersign

## undesirable
**04** foul **05** nasty **08** disliked, riff-raff, unwanted **09** obnoxious, offensive, repugnant, unwelcome **10** unpleasant, unsuitable **11** distasteful, unwished-for **12** disagreeable, unacceptable **13** objectionable

## undeveloped
**04** rude **06** latent, neuter **07** dwarfed, stunted **08** immature, inchoate, unformed **09** embryonic, infantile, potential, unfledged **10** developing, primordial, Third World **12** less advanced **14** underdeveloped

## undignified
**06** clumsy **07** foolish **08** improper, ungainly, unseemly **09** inelegant **10** indecorous, unbecoming, unsuitable **13** inappropriate

## undiluted
**04** neat, pure **05** heady, sheer, utter **06** strong **07** unmixed **08** straight, unspoilt **09** unalloyed, unblended **11** unmitigated, unqualified **12** concentrated

## undisciplined
◇ *anagram indicator* **04** wild **06** unruly, wanton, wilful **07** wayward **08** unsteady **09** untrained **10** unreliable, unschooled **11** disobedient **12** disorganized, obstreperous, uncontrolled, unrestrained, unsystematic **13** unpredictable

## undisguised
**04** bald, open **05** frank, naked, overt, stark, utter **06** patent **07** blatant, evident, genuine, obvious **08** apparent, explicit, manifest, outright, unmasked, unveiled **09** unadorned **11** transparent, unconcealed **12** undissembled **13** thoroughgoing

## undisguisedly
**06** openly **07** frankly, overtly **08** outright, patently **09** blatantly, obviously **12** unreservedly **13** transparently

### undisputed
**04** fact, sure **07** certain **08** accepted, unargued **09** undoubted **10** conclusive, recognized, undeniable **11** indubitable, irrefutable, uncontested **12** acknowledged, indisputable, unchallenged, unquestioned

### undistinguished
**04** so-so **05** banal, plain **06** common **07** ordinar, plebean **08** everyday, inferior, mediocre, nameless, ordinary, plebeian **10** not much cop, pedestrian **11** indifferent, not up to much **12** run-of-the-mill, unimpressive, unremarkable **13** no great shakes, unexceptional

### undisturbed
**04** calm, even **05** quiet **06** placid, serene **07** equable **08** composed, tranquil, wakeless **09** collected, quietsome, unruffled, untouched **10** motionless, unaffected, untroubled **11** unconcerned, unperturbed **13** uninterrupted

### undivided
**03** one **04** full **05** solid, total, whole **06** entire, intact, single, united **07** serious, sincere **08** combined, complete, unbroken **09** dedicated, exclusive, unanimous **10** individual, unreserved **11** individuate, pro indiviso, unqualified **12** concentrated, wholehearted

### undo
◇ *anagram indicator* **03** dup, mar **04** free, open, poop, ruin **05** annul, crush, loose, poupe, quash, solve, spoil, untie, unzip, upset, wreck **06** cancel, defeat, loosen, offset, repeal, revoke, seduce, unbend, unclew, unhook, unlace, unlock, unwind, unwork, unwrap **07** destroy, nullify, release, retract, reverse, shatter, subvert, undight, unravel, unshape **08** overturn, separate, set aside, unbuckle, unbutton, unfasten **09** disanoint, undermine **10** invalidate, neutralize, obliterate **11** disentangle

### undoing
◇ *anagram indicator* **04** ruin **05** shame **06** defeat **07** opening **08** collapse, disgrace, downfall, reversal, weakness **09** defeature, overthrow, ruination **10** defeasance **11** destruction, unfastening

### undomesticated
**04** wild **05** feral **06** savage **07** natural, untamed **11** uncivilized **12** ferae naturae

### undone
◇ *anagram indicator* **04** left, lost, open **05** loose **06** adrift, opened, ruined, untied **07** ignored, omitted, seduced, unlaced **08** annulled, betrayed, unlocked **09** destroyed, forgotten, neglected, unwrought **10** incomplete, passed over, unbuttoned, unfastened, unfinished **11** outstanding, uncompleted, unfulfilled **14** unaccomplished
• **come undone** **03** run

### undoubted
**04** sure **06** patent **07** certain, obvious **08** definite **10** undisputed **11** indubitable, irrefutable, uncontested, undesirable **12** acknowledged, indisputable, unchallenged, unquestioned **14** unquestionable

### undoubtedly
**04** sure **06** surely **07** no doubt **08** of course **09** assuredly, certainly, doubtless **10** definitely, manifestly, no question, undeniably **11** beyond doubt, indubitably **12** unmistakably, without doubt **14** unquestionably

### undreamed-of
**07** amazing **08** undreamt **09** unheard-of **10** incredible, miraculous, unexpected, unforeseen, unhoped-for, unimagined **11** astonishing, unsuspected **13** inconceivable

### undress
**04** peel, shed **05** strip **06** devest, divest, nudity, remove, streak, uncase, unrobe **07** discase, disrobe, peel off, take off **08** disarray, unclothe **09** disattire, nakedness **10** déshabillé, dishabille **11** make unready **13** get your kit off

### undressed
**04** nude **05** naked **08** disrobed, en cuerpo, in the raw, starkers, stripped, untented **09** in the buff, self-faced, unclothed **10** stark-naked **12** not a stitch on **15** in the altogether

### undue
**07** extreme **08** improper, needless **09** excessive, obtrusive **10** immoderate, inordinate, undeserved **11** exaggerated, extravagant, superfluous, uncalled-for, unjustified, unnecessary, unwarranted **12** unreasonable **13** inappropriate

### undulate
**04** roll, wave, wavy **05** heave, surge, swell **06** billow, ripple **07** vibrate **11** rise and fall

### undulating
**04** wavy **05** waved **06** undate **07** rolling, sinuous **08** flexuose, flexuous, rippling, undulant, undulose, undulous **09** billowing, up-and-down **10** undulatory

### unduly
◇ *anagram indicator* **03** too **04** over **08** overmuch **10** wrongfully **11** excessively, obtrusively **12** immoderately, inordinately, unreasonably **13** exaggeratedly, unjustifiably, unnecessarily

### undutiful
**05** slack **06** remiss **08** careless, disloyal, unfilial **09** negligent **10** defaulting, delinquent, neglectful

### undying
**07** abiding, eternal, lasting **08** constant, immortal, infinite, unending, unfading **09** deathless, perennial, permanent, perpetual, unceasing **10** continuing **11** everlasting, sempiternal

### undoubted *(column 2 continued)*

**12** imperishable, undiminished **14** indestructible

### unearth
**04** find **05** dig up **06** detect, dig out, exhume, expose, reveal **07** uncover **08** discover, disinter, excavate **12** brin to light

### unearthly
**05** eerie, weird **06** absurd, creepy, unholy **07** ghostly, phantom, strange, uncanny, ungodly **08** eldritch **09** appalling, celestial, unheard-of **10** horrendous, outrageous **12** otherworldly, preposterous, supernatural, unreasonable **13** preternatural, spine-chilling **14** unconscionable

### unease
**05** alarm, doubt, worry **06** qualms **07** anxiety, dis-ease **08** disquiet **09** agitation, misgiving, suspicion **10** discomfort, inquietude, uneasiness **11** nervousness **12** apprehension, perturbation

### uneasily
**04** hard

### uneasiness
**05** alarm, doubt, qualm, worry **06** qualms, unease **07** anxiety, disease malaise, misease, trouble **08** disquiet **09** agitation, dysphoria, misgiving, suspicion **10** discomfort, inquietude, solicitude **11** nervousness **12** apprehension, perturbation **14** distemperature, solicitousness **15** dissatisfaction

### uneasy
◇ *anagram indicator* **04** edgy **05** nervy, shaky, tense, upset **06** on edge, queasy, queazy, unsure **07** alarmed, anxious, fidgety, jittery, keyed up, nervous, restive, twitchy, unquiet, worried, wound up **08** agitated, disquiet, insecure, restless, strained, troubled, worrying **09** disturbed, ill at ease, impatient, perturbed, troubling, unnerving, unrestful, unsettled **10** disquieted, disturbing, perturbing, unsettling **11** disquieting **12** apprehensive **13** disconcerting, uncomfortable

### uneconomic
**10** loss-making **12** uncommercial, unprofitable **15** non-profit-making

### unedifying
**04** idle

### uneducated
**06** unread **08** ignorant, untaught **09** benighted, lack-Latin, unlearned **10** illiterate, philistine, uncultured, uninformed, unschooled **12** uncultivated

### unemotional
**04** cold, cool **05** bland **06** stolid **08** detached, reserved **09** apathetic, bloodless, impassive, objective, unfeeling **10** phlegmatic **11** indifferent, passionless, unexcitable **12** phlegmatical, unresponsive **13** dispassionate **15** undemonstrative

## unemphatic
**08** downbeat **10** played-down
**11** underplayed, understated,
unobtrusive **12** soft-pedalled
**14** unostentatious

## unemployed
**04** idle **07** jobless, laid off, unwaged
**08** workless **09** on the dole, out of
work, redundant **10** unoccupied

## unending
**07** endless, eternal, undated, undying
**08** constant **09** ceaseless, continual,
incessant, perpetual, unceasing
**10** continuous **11** everlasting, never-
ending, unremitting **12** interminable
**13** thorough-going, uninterrupted

## unendurable
**10** shattering, unbearable
**11** intolerable **12** insufferable,
overwhelming **13** insupportable

## unenthusiastic
**04** cool, damp **05** blasé, bored
**07** neutral, unmoved **08** lukewarm
**09** apathetic, Laodicean, reluctant
**10** nonchalant **11** half-hearted,
indifferent, unimpressed
**12** uninterested, unresponsive

## unenviable
**09** dangerous, difficult, thankless
**10** unpleasant **11** uncongenial,
undesirable **12** disagreeable
**13** uncomfortable

## unequal
**06** biased, uneven, unfair, unjust,
unlike **07** not up to, varying
**08** lopsided, unfitted, unsuited
**09** different, disparate, excessive,
incapable, irregular, unmatched
**10** dissimilar, inadequate, unbalanced
**11** incompetent, inequitable,
unqualified **12** asymmetrical, not cut
out for **14** discriminatory

## unequalled
**06** unique **07** supreme **08** peerless,
unbeaten, unpeered **09** matchless,
nonpareil, paramount, unmatched
**10** inimitable, pre-eminent, surpassing,
unrivalled **11** exceptional,
unpatterned, unsurpassed
**12** incomparable, transcendent,
unparalleled

## unequivocal
**05** clear, plain **06** direct, square
**07** evident, express **08** absolute,
definite, distinct, explicit, outright,
positive, straight **10** unreserved
**11** categorical, unambiguous,
unqualified **12** unmistakable
**15** straightforward

## unequivocally
**06** firmly **07** clearly **08** directly
**10** definitely, distinctly, explicitly,
positively **12** unmistakably
**13** unambiguously **14** unquestionably

## unerring
**04** dead, sure **05** clean, exact
**07** certain, perfect, uncanny
**08** accurate, inerrant **09** faultless,
unfailing **10** impeccable, infallible

## unerringly
**04** bang, dead **10** accurately, infallibly
**11** unfailingly

## unethical
**04** evil **05** shady, wrong **06** wicked
**07** illegal, illicit, immoral **08** improper
**09** dishonest, underhand
**12** disreputable, unprincipled,
unscrupulous **13** dishonourable
**14** unprofessional

## uneven
◇ *anagram indicator* **03** odd **05** bumpy,
jerky, lumpy, rough, ruggy, stony
**06** coarse, craggy, fitful, jagged,
patchy, rugged, spotty, unfair
**07** crooked, erratic, ruffled, rumpled,
streaky, unequal **08** lopsided, one-
sided, scratchy, unsteady, variable,
wrinkled **09** inequable, irregular,
spasmodic **10** accidented, changeable,
ill-matched, unbalanced
**11** fluctuating, inequitable
**12** asymmetrical, inconsistent,
intermittent

## uneventful
**04** dull **05** quiet **06** boring **07** humdrum,
routine, tedious **08** everyday, ordinary,
unvaried **10** monotonous, unexciting
**11** commonplace, unmemorable
**12** run-of-the-mill, unremarkable
**13** unexceptional, uninteresting

## unexampled
**05** novel **06** unique **09** unheard-of,
unmatched **10** unequalled
**11** unpatterned **12** incomparable,
unparalleled **13** unprecedented
**15** never before seen

## unexceptionable
**04** mild, safe **05** bland **08** harmless,
innocent **09** excellent, innocuous,
peaceable **10** undeniable
**11** inoffensive **15** unobjectionable

## unexceptional
**04** so-so **05** usual **06** common, normal
**07** average, typical **08** everyday,
mediocre, ordinary **10** not much cop
**11** indifferent, not up to much,
unmemorable **12** run-of-the-mill,
unimpressive, unremarkable **13** no
great shakes **15** undistinguished

## unexcitable
**04** calm, cool **06** serene **07** relaxed
**08** composed, laid-back **09** contained,
easy-going, impassive **10** phlegmatic
**11** passionless **13** dispassionate,
imperturbable, self-possessed,
unimpassioned

## unexpected
◇ *anagram indicator* **04** snap **05** shock
**06** abrupt, chance, sudden, unware,
unwary, wonder **07** amazing,
unhoped, unusual, unwarie
**08** emergent, unweened **09** inopinate,
startling **10** accidental, fortuitous,
surprising, unforeseen **11** astonishing,
unlooked-for **12** out of the blue
**13** unanticipated, unpredictable

## unexpectedly
◇ *anagram indicator* **06** unware
**08** abruptly, by chance, suddenly,
unawares, unwarely **11** ex improviso

**12** accidentally, à l'improviste,
fortuitously, out of the blue,
phenomenally, refreshingly,
surprisingly **13** unpredictably
**14** without warning

## unexpressive
**05** blank **06** vacant **07** deadpan
**08** immobile **09** impassive
**11** emotionless, inscrutable
**12** inexpressive **13** inexpressible
**14** expressionless

## unfading
**04** fast **07** abiding, durable, lasting,
undying **08** constant, enduring,
fadeless **09** evergreen, unfailing
**12** imperishable **13** immarcescible

## unfailing
**04** sure, true **05** loyal **06** steady
**07** certain, staunch, undying
**08** constant, faithful, reliable, unerring,
unfading **09** steadfast **10** dependable,
infallible **12** indefectible, inexhaustive
**13** inexhaustible

## unfair
◇ *anagram indicator* **04** bent, foul, ugly
**05** crook, shady, thick **06** biased,
unjust **07** a bit off, bigoted, crooked,
partial, slanted **08** one-sided, partisan,
weighted, wrongful **09** arbitrary,
deceitful, dishonest, unethical,
unmerited **10** prejudiced, unbalanced,
undeserved **11** inequitable, uncalled-
for, unwarranted **12** below the belt,
over the score, unprincipled,
unreasonable, unscrupulous
**14** discriminatory

## unfairly
◇ *anagram indicator* **04** foul **07** wrongly
**08** biasedly, unjustly **09** illegally,
partially **10** improperly, unlawfully
**11** dishonestly, inequitably
**12** unreasonably

## unfairness
**04** bias **05** cross **07** bigotry, unright
**08** inequity, misusage **09** injustice,
prejudice **10** partiality **12** one-
sidedness, partisanship
**14** discrimination **15** inequitableness

## unfaithful
**05** false **06** fickle, unleal, untrue
**07** godless **08** cheating, disloyal
**09** deceitful, dishonest, faithless,
insincere, two-timing **10** adulterous,
inconstant, perfidious, unreliable
**11** duplicitous, treacherous,
unbelieving **13** double-dealing,
untrustworthy

## unfaltering
**04** firm **05** fixed **06** steady **08** constant,
resolute, tireless, untiring **09** steadfast,
unfailing **10** unflagging, unswerving,
unwavering, unyielding **11** unflinching
**12** pertinacious **13** indefatigable

## unfamiliar
◇ *anagram indicator* **03** new **05** alien,
novel **07** curious, foreign, strange,
uncouth, unknown, unusual
**08** selcouth, uncommon, unversed
**09** different, uncharted, unskilled
**10** unexplored, uninformed
**11** unpractised **12** unaccustomed,

unacquainted, unconversant
**13** inexperienced

## unfashionable
**03** out **04** lame **05** daggy, dated, dowdy, passé **06** démodé, old hat, square **08** obsolete, outmoded, unmodish **09** out of date, shapeless, unpopular **10** antiquated **12** old-fashioned, out of fashion

## unfasten
**04** open, undo **05** loose, unbar, unfix, unpin, untie, unzip **06** detach, loosen, unbend, unhasp, unlock, unwrap **07** unclasp, unloose, untruss **08** separate, unbuckle, uncouple, unloosen **10** disconnect

## unfathomable
**04** deep **06** hidden **07** abysmal **08** abstruse, baffling, esoteric, profound **09** unplumbed, unsounded **10** bottomless, fathomless, mysterious, unknowable **11** inscrutable, unsoundable **12** immeasurable, impenetrable, inexplicable **14** indecipherable

## unfavourable
**03** bad, ill **04** foul, poor **07** adverse, hostile, ominous, unlucky **08** contrary, critical, inimical, negative, untimely, untoward **09** ill-suited **10** prejudiced, unfriendly **11** in a bad light, inopportune, threatening, unfortunate, unpromising **12** discouraging, inauspicious, unseasonable **15** disadvantageous, uncomplimentary

## unfavourably
**03** ill **05** badly **06** poorly **09** adversely, in bad part, in ill part, unhappily **10** negatively **13** unfortunately, unpromisingly

## unfeeling
**04** cold, hard **05** cruel, harsh, stony **06** brutal **07** callous, inhuman **08** hardened, pitiless, uncaring **09** heartless, merciless **10** impassible, iron-headed, iron-witted **11** hard-hearted, insensitive, iron-hearted **13** unsympathetic

## unfeigned
**04** pure, real **05** frank **07** genuine, natural, sincere **08** unforced **09** heartfelt **10** unaffected **11** spontaneous **12** undissembled, wholehearted

## unfettered
**04** free **09** chainless, unbridled, unchecked **10** unconfined, unhampered, unhindered, unshackled **11** uninhibited **12** unrestrained, untrammelled **13** unconstrained

## unfinished
◊ *tail deletion indicator* **05** crude, rough **06** undone **07** lacking, sketchy, wanting **08** half-done, inchoate **09** deficient, imperfect, incondite **10** incomplete **11** uncompleted, unfulfilled **14** unaccomplished

## unfit
◊ *anagram indicator* **03** ill **04** weak **05** inapt **06** feeble, flabby, impair,

unable, unmeet **07** unequal, useless **08** decrepit, disabled, improper, unsuited **09** condemned, incapable, unhealthy, untrained **10** inadequate, ineligible, out of shape, unprepared, unsuitable **11** debilitated, ill-equipped, incompetent, ineffective, unqualified **12** disqualified **13** inappropriate, incapacitated **14** out of condition

## unflagging
**05** fixed **06** steady **07** staunch **08** constant, tireless, untiring **09** assiduous, unceasing, unfailing **10** persistent, unswerving **11** persevering, undeviating, unfaltering, unremitting **12** never-failing, single-minded **13** indefatigable

## unflappable
**04** calm, cool **07** equable **08** composed, laid-back **09** collected, easy-going, impassive, supercool, unruffled, unworried **10** phlegmatic **11** level-headed, unexcitable **13** imperturbable, self-possessed

## unflattering
**05** blunt **06** candid, honest **08** critical **09** outspoken **10** unbecoming **12** unattractive, unfavourable **15** uncomplimentary, unprepossessing

## unflinching
**04** bold, firm, sure **05** fixed **06** steady **07** staunch **08** constant, resolute, stalwart, unshaken **09** steadfast **10** determined, unblenched, unblinking, unswerving, unwavering **11** unblenching, unfaltering, unshrinking

## unflinchingly
**04** fast **06** boldly, firmly **08** steadily **09** staunchly **10** resolutely **11** steadfastly **12** unswervingly, unwaveringly **13** unfalteringly, unshrinkingly

## unfold
**04** grow, open, show, tell, undo **06** deploy, emerge, evolve, extend, relate, result, reveal, spread, unclew, uncoil, unfurl, unroll, untuck, unwrap **07** clarify, develop, display, explain, flatten, narrate, open out, present, uncover, unravel, work out **08** describe, disclose, shake out, undouble **09** come about, elaborate, explicate, interpret, make known, spread out **10** disenvelop, disinvolve, illustrate, straighten, stretch out **13** straighten out

## unforeseen
**06** casual, sudden **07** amazing, unusual **09** startling **10** surprising, unexpected **11** astonishing, unavoidable, unlooked-for, unpredicted **13** unanticipated, unpredictable

## unforgettable
**07** notable, special **08** historic, striking **09** important, indelible, memorable, momentous **10** impressive, noteworthy, remarkable **11** distinctive, exceptional, significant **13** extraordinary

## unforgivable
**08** shameful **10** deplorable, outrageous **11** disgraceful, inexcusable, intolerable **12** contemptible, indefensible, unpardonable **13** reprehensible, unjustifiable

## unforgiven
**10** unabsolved, unredeemed **11** unrepentant **12** unregenerate

## unfortunate
◊ *anagram indicator* **03** ill **04** evil, poor **05** tough **06** doomed **07** adverse, hapless, ruinous, unhappy, unlucky **08** hopeless, ill-fated, ill-timed, luckless, untimely, untoward, wretched **09** ill-omened **10** calamitous, deplorable, disastrous, ill-advised, lamentable, unpleasant, unsuitable **11** evil-starred, injudicious, inopportune, misfortuned, regrettable **12** disaventrous, unfavourable, unsuccessful **13** inappropriate, misadventured **14** disadventurous **15** disadvantageous

## unfortunately
◊ *anagram indicator* **04** alas **05** sadly **08** sad to say **09** unhappily, unluckily, worse luck **11** regrettably, sad to relate **13** I am sorry to say

## unfounded
**04** idle **05** false **08** baseless, spurious, unproven **09** trumped-up **10** bottomless, fabricated, groundless **11** conjectural, unjustified, unsupported **14** uncorroborated **15** unsubstantiated

## unfrequented
**04** lone **06** lonely, remote, untrod **08** deserted, desolate, isolated, secluded, solitary, untraded, wasteful **09** untrodden, unvisited **11** god-forsaken, sequestered, uninhabited

## unfriendly
**04** cold, cool, sour **05** aloof, chill, fraim, fremd, surly **06** chilly, fremit, frosty, frozen, unkind, wintry **07** distant, hostile, wintery **08** inimical, strained, unkindly **10** aggressive, unpleasant, unsociable **11** ill-disposed, quarrelsome, standoffish, uncongenial, unwelcoming **12** antagonistic, disagreeable, inauspicious, inhospitable, inimicitious **13** unneighbourly **14** unapproachable

## unfrock
**06** demote, depose, ungown **07** degrade, dismiss, suspend

## unfruitful
**04** arid **06** barren **07** sterile **08** infecund **09** exhausted, fruitless, infertile **10** unprolific **11** infructuous, unrewarding **12** impoverished, unproductive, unprofitable

## unfurl
**04** grow, open, undo **05** break **06** emerge, evolve, extend, result, spread, uncoil, unfold, unroll, unwrap **07** develop, display, flatten, open out, uncover, unravel, work out **09** come about, spread out **10** straighten, stretch out **13** straighten out

## ungainly

◇ *anagram indicator* **05** gawky
**06** clumsy, gauche, ungain
**07** awkward, loutish, uncouth
**08** gangling, unwieldy **09** awkwardly, inelegant, lumbering, maladroit
**10** ungraceful **13** unco-ordinated

## ungodly

**05** world **06** sinful, wicked **07** corrupt, godless, immoral, impious, profane
**08** depraved, unsocial **09** unearthly
**10** horrendous, iniquitous, outrageous
**11** blasphemous, intolerable, irreligious **12** preposterous, unreasonable **14** unconscionable

## ungovernable

**04** wild **06** unruly **10** disorderly, masterless, rebellious, refractory, ungoverned **12** unmanageable
**14** uncontrollable, unrestrainable

## ungracious

**04** rude **07** boorish, ill-bred, mesquin, offhand, uncivil **08** churlish, impolite, mesquine **09** graceless **10** ungraceful, unhandsome, unmannerly **11** bad-mannered, disgracious **12** discourteous
**13** disrespectful

## ungrateful

**04** rude **07** ingrate, irksome, selfish, uncivil **08** heedless, impolite
**09** thankless **10** ungracious, unthankful
**11** ill-mannered **12** disagreeable
**14** unappreciative

## unguarded

**04** rash **06** unwary **07** exposed, foolish
**08** careless, heedless, off guard
**09** foolhardy, impolitic, imprudent, lippening, unweighed **10** incautious, indiscreet, undefended, unscreened, unthinking, vulnerable **11** defenceless, inadvertent, inattentive, thoughtless, unpatrolled, unprotected
**12** undiplomatic **13** ill-considered, uncircumspect

## ungulate

**03** cow **04** deer **05** horse, takin, tapir
**06** hoofed **09** Dinoceras
**10** Deinoceras, mesohippus, rhinoceros, rhinocerot **11** rhinocerote
**12** hippopotamus, Uintatherium
**13** Palaeotherium, Titanotherium

## unhappily

◇ *anagram indicator* **04** alas **05** sadly
**08** sad to say, shrewdly **09** unluckily, worse luck **11** maliciously, regrettably, sad to relate **12** unfavourably
**13** unfortunately **14** unsuccessfully

## unhappy

◇ *anagram indicator* **03** low, sad **04** blue, down, glum **05** fed up, inapt, upset
**06** clumsy, gloomy **07** awkward, doleful, hapless, unlucky **08** dejected, dolorous, downcast, ill-fated, luckless, mournful, tactless **09** depressed, ill-chosen, long-faced, miserable, sorrowful, woebegone **10** despondent, dispirited, ill-advised, ill-starred, melancholy, unsuitable **11** crestfallen, injudicious, mischievous, unfortunate
**12** disconsolate, infelicitous

**13** inappropriate **14** down in the dumps

## unharmed

**04** safe **05** sound, whole **06** intact, unhurt **09** undamaged, uninjured, unscathed, untouched

## unhealthy

**03** ill **04** sick, weak **05** crook, frail, pasty **06** ailing, feeble, infirm, morbid, poorly, sickly, unwell **07** harmful, invalid, noxious, unsound **08** diseased, epinosic **09** dangerous, injurious, unnatural **10** indisposed, insalutary, insanitary, unhygienic, unsanitary
**11** debilitated, detrimental, unwholesome **12** insalubrious

## unheard-of

**03** new **06** unsung **07** obscure, unknown, unusual **08** shocking
**09** offensive **10** outrageous, unfamiliar, unheralded **11** exceptional, undreamed-of, unthinkable
**12** preposterous, unacceptable, unbelievable, undiscovered, unimaginable **13** extraordinary, inconceivable, unprecedented

## unheeded

**07** ignored, unnoted **08** unminded, untented **09** disobeyed, forgotten, neglected, unnoticed **10** overlooked, unobserved, unremarked
**11** disregarded

## unhelpful

**04** rude **06** rustic, touchy **07** awkward, boorish, cubbish, loutish, prickly, stroppy **08** stubborn **09** irritable, obstinate **10** unpleasant **11** disobliging, obstructive, troublesome **12** bloody-minded **13** oversensitive, unco-operative **15** unaccommodating

## unheralded

**06** unsung **08** surprise **09** unnoticed
**10** unexpected, unforeseen
**11** unannounced **12** unadvertised, unproclaimed, unpublicized, unrecognized

## unhesitating

**05** ready **06** prompt **07** instant
**08** implicit **09** automatic, confident, immediate **10** unwavering
**11** spontaneous, unfaltering
**12** wholehearted **13** instantaneous, unquestioning

## unhinge

**05** craze, upset **06** madden **07** confuse, derange, unnerve **08** disorder, distract, drive mad, unsettle **09** unbalance

## unhinged

**03** mad **04** nuts **05** barmy, crazy, loony, loopy, nutty, potty **06** insane
**07** berserk, bonkers, frantic, lunatic
**08** confused, demented, deranged
**09** delirious, disturbed, unsettled
**10** disordered, distraught, irrational, out to lunch, unbalanced **11** not all there **12** round the bend **13** off your rocker, of unsound mind, out of your mind, round the twist **15** non compos mentis

## unholy

◇ *anagram indicator* **04** evil **06** sinful, wicked **07** corrupt, godless, immoral, impious, ungodly **08** depraved, dreadful, shocking, terrible
**09** unearthly, unnatural **10** horrendous, iniquitous, outrageous
**11** blasphemous, irreligious
**12** unreasonable **14** unconscionable

## unhook

**04** free, undo **05** loose, untie **06** loosen
**07** release **08** unfasten

## unhoped-for

**10** incredible, surprising, unexpected, unforeseen **11** undreamed-of, unlooked-for **12** unbelievable, unimaginable **13** unanticipated

## unhurried

**04** calm, easy, slow **06** sedate
**07** relaxed **08** laid-back **09** easy-going, leisurely **10** deliberate

## unhurt

**02** OK **04** okay, safe **05** sound, whole
**06** intact **08** all right, unharmed
**09** uninjured, unscathed, untouched
**12** whole-skinned

## unhygienic

**04** foul **05** dirty **06** filthy, impure
**07** dirtied, noisome, noxious, unclean
**08** feculent, infected, infested, polluted
**09** unhealthy **10** insanitary
**11** unhealthful, unsanitized
**12** contaminated, insalubrious
**13** disease-ridden

## unidentified

**06** secret **07** obscure, strange, unknown, unnamed **08** nameless, unmarked **09** anonymous, incognito
**10** mysterious, unfamiliar
**12** unclassified, unrecognized

## unification

**05** union **06** enosis, fusion, merger
**07** uniting **08** alliance **09** coalition
**10** federation **11** coalescence, combination, integration
**12** amalgamation **13** confederation, incorporation

## uniform

**01** U **03** rig **04** even, flat, garb, like, same, sole, suit **05** alike, dress, equal, habit, level, robes **06** livery, outfit, smooth, stable, steady **07** costume, equable, regalia, regular, similar
**08** constant, insignia, of a piece, unbroken **09** identical, unvarying
**10** consistent, invariable, monotonous, throughout, unchanging
**11** homogeneous, regimentals, undeviating

## uniformity

**06** tedium **08** drabness, dullness, evenness, flatness, monotony, sameness **09** constancy **10** regularity, similarity, similitude **11** homogeneity
**12** homomorphism **13** invariability

## unify

**03** mix **04** bind, fuse, join, weld
**05** blend, merge, unite **07** combine
**08** coalesce **09** integrate

**unifying**
**10** amalgamate **11** consolidate **12** come together **13** bring together

**unifying**
**06** unific **07** henotic, uniting **11** combinatory, esemplastic, reconciling **13** consolidative

**unimaginable**
**07** amazing **08** unlikely **09** fantastic, unheard-of **10** far-fetched, impossible, incredible, outlandish, staggering **11** astonishing, implausible, undreamed-of, unthinkable **12** mind-boggling, preposterous, unbelievable, unconvincing **13** extraordinary, inconceivable

**unimaginative**
**03** dry **04** dull, tame **05** banal, samey, stale, usual **06** barren, boring **07** mundane, prosaic, routine **08** lifeless, ordinary **09** hackneyed **10** flat-footed, pedestrian, unexciting, uninspired, unoriginal **11** predictable **12** matter-of-fact

**unimpaired**
**05** sound **06** entire, intact **08** integral
• **remain unimpaired 04** last

**unimpeachable**
**07** perfect **08** reliable, spotless **09** blameless, faultless **10** dependable, immaculate, impeccable **11** unblemished **12** unassailable **14** irreproachable, unquestionable **15** unchallengeable

**unimpeded**
**04** free, open **05** clear **08** all-round **09** unblocked, unchecked **10** unhampered, unhindered **11** uninhibited **12** unrestrained, untrammelled **13** unconstrained

**unimportant**
**04** idle **05** light, minor, petty **06** slight **07** trivial **08** marginal, nugatory, peddling, trifling **09** minuscule, no big deal, secondary, small-time, worthless **10** immaterial, incidental, irrelevant, negligible, peripheral **11** down-the-line, Mickey Mouse **12** inconsequent **13** insignificant, insubstantial, no great shakes **14** inconsiderable **15** inconsequential, of no consequence

**unimpressive**
**04** dull **06** common **07** average **08** mediocre, ordinary **10** unexciting, unimposing **11** commonplace, indifferent **12** unremarkable **13** unexceptional, uninteresting, unspectacular **15** undistinguished

**uninhabited**
**04** lone **05** empty **06** desert, lonely, vacant **08** deserted, desolate, wasteful **09** abandoned, unpeopled, unsettled **10** unoccupied **11** unpopulated

**uninhibited**
**04** free, open **05** frank **06** candid, rave-up **07** natural, relaxed **08** informal **09** abandoned, liberated, outspoken **10** unreserved **11** spontaneous **12** uncontrolled, unrestrained, unrestricted **13** unconstrained **15** unself-conscious

**uninspired**
**04** dull **05** samey, stale, stock, trite **06** boring **07** humdrum, pompier, prosaic **08** ordinary **10** flat-footed, pedestrian, unexciting, unoriginal **11** commonplace, indifferent, uninspiring **13** unexceptional, unimaginative, uninteresting **15** undistinguished

**uninspiring**
**03** dry **04** dull, flat, tame **05** ho-hum, samey, stale, trite **06** boring, dreary, jejune, tiring **07** humdrum, insipid, prosaic, routine, tedious **08** tiresome, unvaried **10** long-winded, monotonous, uneventful, unexciting **11** commonplace, repetitious, stultifying **13** institutional, unimaginative, uninteresting **14** soul-destroying

**unintelligent**
**04** dull, dumb, slow **05** dense, silly, thick **06** obtuse, stupid **07** fatuous, foolish, witless **08** gormless **09** brainless **10** half-witted, unthinking **11** empty-headed, unreasoning

**unintelligible**
**07** complex, garbled, jumbled, muddled, obscure **08** involved, puzzling **09** illegible, scrambled **10** incoherent, mysterious, unreadable **11** complicated, double Dutch **12** impenetrable, inarticulate, unfathomable **14** indecipherable

**unintentional**
**08** careless **09** unplanned, unwilling, unwitting **10** accidental, fortuitous, unintended **11** inadvertent, involuntary, unconscious **12** uncalculated **14** unpremeditated

**uninterested**
**05** blasé, bored **07** distant **08** listless **09** apathetic, impassive, incurious **10** uninvolved **11** indifferent, pococurante, unconcerned **12** unresponsive **14** not giving a damn, not giving a hoot, not giving a toss, unenthusiastic

**uninteresting**
**03** dry **04** drab, dull, flat, tame **05** samey, stale **06** boring, dreary **07** humdrum, prosaic, tedious **08** tiresome **09** incurious, wearisome **10** monotonous, pedestrian, uneventful, unexciting **11** indifferent, uninspiring **12** unimpressive

**uninterrupted**
**06** steady **07** endless, non-stop **08** constant, peaceful, straight, unbroken, unending **09** ceaseless, continual, continued, incessant, sustained, unceasing **10** continuous **11** undisturbed, unremitting

**uninvited**
**07** unasked **08** unbidden, unsought, unwanted **09** unwelcome **11** unsolicited

**uninviting**
**09** offensive, repellent, repulsive, unsavoury **10** forbidding, off-putting, unpleasant **11** distasteful, unappealing,

undesirable, unwelcoming **12** disagreeable, unappetizing, unattractive

**uninvolved**
**04** free **06** dégagé **09** fancy-free, footloose, unengaged **10** unattached, unhampered, unhindered **11** independent, uncommitted **12** untrammelled

**union**
**01** U **04** club, yoke **05** blend, close, unity **06** accord, cement, fusion, league, merger **07** harmony, joining, mixture, uniting, wedding, wedlock **08** alliance, juncture, marriage, nuptials, spousage **09** agreement, coalition, espousals, matrimony, synthesis, unanimity **10** consortium, couplement, federation, trade union, Zollverein **11** association, cementation, coadunation, coalescence, combination, concurrence, confederacy, conjugation, conjunction, unification **12** amalgamation **13** confederation, consolidation **14** conglutination
*See also* **rugby**

*Unions include:*

**02** AU, CU, EU
**03** AUT, CDU, CGT, CWU, EIS, EMU, FBU, GMB, ITU, NFU, NUJ, NUM, NUS, NUT, RFU, RMT
**04** BIFU, CCCP, TGWU, UEFA, USSR, ZANU, ZAPU
**05** BECTU, T and G
**06** Amicus, NUMAST, Soviet, UNISON
**07** African
**08** European

**unionist**
**01** U **02** UU

**unique**
**03** one **04** lone, only, sole **05** alone **06** one-off, single **07** unusual **08** peerless, singular, solitary **09** matchless, nonpareil, unmatched **10** inimitable, one and only, one of a kind, pre-eminent, sui generis, unequalled, unrivalled **11** idiographic **12** incomparable, unparalleled **13** unprecedented

**uniquely**
**04** only **06** singly, solely **08** by itself, markedly **09** specially **10** inimitably, peculiarly, peerlessly, remarkably, singularly **11** in its own way, matchlessly **12** incomparably **13** distinctively

**unison**
**05** unity **06** accord **07** concert, concord, harmony **09** agreement, unanimity **11** co-operation
• **in unison 08** in chorus **09** in harmony **10** homophonic **11** in agreement **13** at the same time, in co-operation **14** simultaneously **15** at the same moment

**unit**
**03** ace, one **04** flat, item, part **05** corps,

## unite

force, piece, squad, train, whole
**06** entity, module, patrol, system
**07** brigade, element, portion, section, segment **08** assembly
**09** component, task force
**10** detachment, individual
**11** constituent

*See also* **measurement; measurement of pressure** *under* **pressure; military; unit of weight** *under* **weight**

## unite

**03** fay, lap, tie, wad, wed **04** ally, band, fuse, join, knit, knot, link, lock, meng, ming, pool, weld **05** blend, clasp, close, joint, marry, menge, merge, twist, unify **06** cement, cleave, couple, embody, imbody, splice **07** accrete, combine, conjoin, connect, consort **08** coalesce, copulate, federate **09** associate, coadunate, conjugate, co-operate, synoecize **10** amalgamate, close ranks, join forces **11** confederate, consolidate, incorporate
**12** concorporate, conglutinate, pull together **15** consubstantiate, make common cause

## united

**01** U **03** one **04** ment **05** meint, meynt **06** agreed, allied, menged, minged, pooled **07** unified
**08** combined, conjoint, in accord
**09** concerted, conjoined, corporate, unanimous **10** affiliated, collective, like-minded **11** amalgamated, conjunctive, co-operative, in agreement **12** incorporated
**13** concorporated

## United Arab Emirates

**03** ARE, UAE

## United Kingdom

**02** UK

*See also* **prime minister**

UK cities include:

**03** Ely
**04** Bath, York
**05** Derby, Leeds, Newry, Ripon, Truro, Wells
**06** Armagh, Bangor, Dundee, Durham, Exeter, London, Oxford
**07** Belfast, Bristol, Cardiff, Chester, Glasgow, Lincoln, Lisburn, Newport, Norwich, Preston, Salford, Swansea
**08** Aberdeen, Bradford, Brighton, Carlisle, Coventry, Hereford, Kingston, Plymouth, St Albans, St Davids, Stirling
**09** Cambridge, Edinburgh, Inverness, Lancaster, Leicester, Lichfield, Liverpool, Newcastle, Salisbury, Sheffield, Wakefield, Worcester
**10** Birmingham, Canterbury, Chichester, Gloucester, Manchester, Nottingham, Portsmouth, Sunderland, Winchester
**11** Londonderry, Southampton, Westminster
**13** Wolverhampton

UK landmarks include:

**04** Fens, Tyne
**06** Big Ben, Exmoor, Mersey, Severn, Thames
**07** Avebury, Glencoe, Needles, Snowdon
**08** Balmoral, Bass Rock, Ben Nevis, Dartmoor, Land's End, Loch Ness
**09** Cape Wrath, Chilterns, Cotswolds, Helvellyn, London Eye, New Forest, Offa's Dyke, Royal Mile, Snowdonia, Tay Bridge
**10** Beachy Head, Cader Idris, Holy Island, Ironbridge, Kew Gardens, Loch Lomond, Lough Earne, Lough Neagh, Stonehenge, The Gherkin, Windermere
**11** Arthur's Seat, Canary Wharf, Forth Bridge, Hever Castle, Isle of Wight, John O'Groats, Leeds Castle, Lizard Point, Menai Bridge, Old Man of Hoy, Scafell Pike, York Minster
**12** Antonine Wall, Brighton Pier, Castle Howard, Cheddar Gorge, Forest of Dean, Hadrian's Wall, Hampton Court, Humber Bridge, Lake District, Peak District, Seven Sisters, Severn Bridge
**13** Arundel Castle, Blue John Caves, Brecon Beacons, Bridge of Sighs, Hatfield House, Liver Building, Norfolk Broads, Robin Hood's Bay, Royal Pavilion, Tower of London, Warwick Castle, Windsor Castle
**14** Blackpool Tower, Blenheim Palace, Giant's Causeway, Holyrood Palace, Inverary Castle, Isle of Anglesey, Sherwood Forest, Stirling Castle, Wells Cathedral
**15** Angel of the North, Bodleian Library, Caledonian Canal, Cerne Abbas Giant, Chatsworth House, Edinburgh Castle, Flamborough Head, Grand Union Canal, Post Office Tower, St Michael's Mount

*See also* **town**

## United Nations

United Nations members:

**04** Chad, Cuba, Fiji, Iran, Iraq, Laos, Mali, Oman, Peru, Togo
**05** Benin, Chile, China, Congo, Egypt, Gabon, Ghana, Haiti, India, Italy, Japan, Kenya, Libya, Malta, Nauru, Nepal, Niger, Palau, Qatar, Samoa, Spain, Sudan, Syria, Tonga, Yemen
**06** Angola, Belize, Bhutan, Brazil, Canada, Cyprus, France, Greece, Guinea, Guyana, Israel, Jordan, Kuwait, Latvia, Malawi, Mexico, Monaco, Norway, Panama, Poland, Russia, Rwanda, Serbia, Sweden, Turkey, Tuvalu, Uganda, Zambia
**07** Albania, Algeria, Andorra, Armenia, Austria, Bahrain, Belarus, Belgium, Bolivia, Burundi, Comoros, Croatia, Denmark, Ecuador, Eritrea, Estonia, Finland, Georgia, Germany, Grenada, Hungary, Iceland, Ireland, Jamaica, Lebanon, Lesotho, Liberia, Moldova, Morocco, Myanmar, Namibia, Nigeria, Romania, Senegal, Somalia, St Lucia, Tunisia, Ukraine, Uruguay, Vanuatu, Vietnam
**08** Barbados, Botswana, Bulgaria, Cambodia, Cameroon, Colombia, Djibouti, Dominica, Ethiopia, Honduras, Kiribati, Malaysia, Maldives, Mongolia, Pakistan, Paraguay, Portugal, Slovakia, Slovenia, Sri Lanka, Suriname, Tanzania, Thailand, Zimbabwe
**09** Argentina, Australia, Cape Verde, Costa Rica, East Timor, Guatemala, Indonesia, Lithuania, Macedonia, Mauritius, Nicaragua, San Marino, Singapore, Swaziland, The Gambia, Venezuela
**10** Azerbaijan, Bangladesh, El Salvador, Kazakhstan, Kyrgyzstan, Luxembourg, Madagascar, Mauritania, Montenegro, Mozambique, New Zealand, North Korea, Seychelles, South Korea, Tajikistan, The Bahamas, Uzbekistan
**11** Afghanistan, Burkina Faso, Côte d'Ivoire, Philippines, Saudi Arabia, Sierra Leone, South Africa, Switzerland
**12** Guinea-Bissau, Turkmenistan
**13** Czech Republic, Liechtenstein, United Kingdom
**14** Papua New Guinea, Solomon Islands, The Netherlands
**15** Marshall Islands, St Kitts and Nevis
**16** Brunei Darussalam, Equatorial Guinea
**17** Antigua and Barbuda, Dominican Republic, Trinidad and Tobago
**18** São Tomé and Príncipe, United Arab Emirates
**19** Serbia and Montenegro
**20** Bosnia and Herzegovina
**21** United States of America
**22** Central African Republic
**25** St Vincent and the Grenadines
**27** Federated States of Micronesia
**28** Democratic Republic of the Congo

## United States of America

**02** US **03** USA **08** Uncle Sam

*See also* **president; state**

US cities include:

**02** LA, NY
**03** NYC
**05** Boise, Dover, Miami, Salem
**06** Albany, Austin, Boston, Dallas, Denver, Helena, Juneau, Pierre, St Paul, Topeka
**07** Atlanta, Augusta, Chicago, Concord, Detroit, Houston,

Jackson, Lansing, Lincoln, Madison, Memphis, New York, Olympia, Phoenix, Raleigh, Santa Fe, Seattle, Trenton
**08** Bismarck, Cheyenne, Columbia, Columbus, Hartford, Honolulu, Las Vegas, Portland, Richmond, San Diego
**09** Annapolis, Baltimore, Des Moines, Frankfort, Milwaukee, Nashville
**10** Baton Rouge, Carson City, Charleston, Harrisburg, Little Rock, Los Angeles, Montgomery, Montpelier, New Orleans, Pittsburgh, Providence, Sacramento, San Antonio, Washington
**11** New York City, Springfield, Tallahassee
**12** Indianapolis, Oklahoma City, Philadelphia, Salt Lake City, San Francisco, Washington DC
**13** Jefferson City

*US landmarks include:*

**05** Yukon
**07** Capitol, Rockies
**08** Colorado, Lake Erie, Missouri, Mt Elbert, Mt Vernon, Pentagon, Yosemite
**09** Graceland, Hollywood, Hoover Dam, Lake Huron, Milwaukee, Mt Rainier
**10** Everglades, Great Lakes, Joshua Tree, Mt McKinley, Mt Rushmore, Mt St Helens, Sears Tower, White House
**11** Grand Canyon, Lake Ontario, Liberty Bell, Mississippi, Pearl Harbor, Space Needle, Yellowstone
**12** Appalachians, Carnegie Hall, Lake Michigan, Lake Superior, Niagara Falls
**13** Great Salt Lake
**14** Brooklyn Bridge, Monument Valley, Rocky Mountains
**15** Lincoln Memorial, Statue of Liberty

**unity**
**03** one **05** peace, union **06** accord **07** concert, concord, harmony, oneness **09** agreement, consensus, integrity, unanimity, wholeness **10** solidarity **11** unification **12** amalgamation, togetherness

**universal**
**01** U **03** all **05** total, whole **06** common, cosmic, entire, global, varsal, versal **07** general **08** all-round, catholic, ecumenic **09** unlimited, worldwide **10** ecumenical, ubiquitous **11** omnipresent **12** all-embracing, all-inclusive **13** comprehensive **14** across-the-board

**universality**
**08** entirety, totality, ubiquity **10** commonness, generality, prevalence **11** catholicity **12** completeness, predominance **14** generalization

**universally**
**06** always **09** uniformly **10** everywhere, invariably **12** ubiquitously

**universe**
**03** all **05** world **06** cosmos, nature **07** heavens **08** creation, everyone **09** firmament, macrocosm **14** the sum of things

**university**
**01** U **03** uni **07** academy, college, varsity **08** academia **09** institute **11** polytechnic

*Ivy League universities:*

**04** Yale
**05** Brown
**07** Cornell, Harvard
**08** Columbia
**09** Dartmouth, Princeton
**12** Pennsylvania

*Seven Sisters colleges:*

**05** Smith
**06** Vassar
**07** Barnard
**08** Bryn Mawr
**09** Radcliffe, Wellesley
**12** Mount Holyoke

*Universities include:*

**02** OU
**03** LSE, MIT, UCL
**04** City, Open, UCLA
**05** Aston, Keele, UMIST
**06** Brunel, Durham, Leiden, Napier, Oxford
**07** Caltech, Warwick
**08** Ann Arbor, Berkeley, Sorbonne, Stanford
**09** Cambridge, St Andrews
**10** De Montfort, Heriot-Watt
**12** Robert Gordon, Thames Valley
**13** Royal Holloway
**14** Trinity College
**15** California State, Imperial College, Juilliard School

*See also* **college**
• **at university 02** up

**unjust**
**05** wrong **06** biased, unfair, wanton **07** partial, unequal **08** one-sided, partisan, wrongful, wrongous **10** iniquitous, prejudiced, undeserved **11** inequitable, unjustified, unrighteous **12** unreasonable

**unjustifiable**
**05** undue **09** excessive **10** immoderate, outrageous **11** inexcusable, uncalled-for, unwarranted **12** indefensible, unacceptable, unforgivable, unpardonable, unreasonable

**unkempt**
◇ *anagram indicator* **05** messy, ratty, rough, tousy, touzy, towsy, towzy **06** frowsy, frowzy, scungy, shabby, sloppy, untidy **07** rumpled, scraggy, scruffy, squalid, tousled **08** scraggly, slobbish, slovenly, uncombed **09** mal soigné, shambolic, ungroomed **10** disordered, scraggling, unpolished **11** dishevelled

**unkind**
**04** mean **05** cruel, harsh, nasty, snide **06** bitchy, shabby **07** callous, inhuman, vicious **08** inhumane, pitiless, ruthless, spiteful, uncaring, unkindly **09** heartless, malicious, unfeeling **10** malevolent, unfriendly **11** cold-hearted, disobliging, hard-hearted, insensitive, thoughtless **12** uncharitable **13** inconsiderate, unsympathetic

**unkindness**
**05** spite **07** cruelty **08** meanness **09** harshness **10** ill-feeling, inhumanity **11** callousness **13** insensitivity, maliciousness **14** unfriendliness **15** hard-heartedness

**unknowable**
**06** untold **08** infinite **12** incalculable, unfathomable, unimaginable **13** unconditioned, unforeseeable, unpredictable **15** unascertainable

**unknowing**
**06** chance, unwist **07** unaware **08** ignorant **09** unplanned, unwitting **10** accidental, unintended, unthinking **11** inadvertent, involuntary, unconscious **12** unsuspecting **13** unintentional

**unknown**
**01** X, Y, Z **03** ign, new **04** dark **05** alien **06** hidden, occult, secret, unkent, untold **07** foreign, obscure, strange, unnamed **08** nameless, unkenned **09** anonymous, concealed, incognito, uncharted, unheard-of **10** mysterious, substance x, undivulged, unexplored, unfamiliar, unrevealed **11** undisclosed **12** undiscovered, unidentified

**unlawful**
**06** banned **07** illegal, illicit, vicious **08** criminal, non licet, outlawed, wrongful **09** forbidden **10** prohibited, unlicensed **12** illegitimate, unauthorized, unsanctioned **13** against the law

**unleash**
**04** free **05** let go, loose, untie **07** deliver, release, set free, unloose **08** let loose, untether

**unless**
**03** but **04** less, nisi, save **06** except **07** without

**unlettered**
**08** ignorant, untaught **09** unlearned, untutored **10** illiterate, uneducated, unlessoned, unschooled

**unlike**
**06** unlich **07** difform, diverse, opposed, unequal, various **08** distinct, opposite **09** as against, different, disparate, divergent, unconform, unrelated **10** contrasted, dissimilar, ill-matched **11** as opposed to **12** dissimilar to, incompatible, in contrast to **13** different from, heterogeneous **14** out of character

**unlikely**
◇ *anagram indicator* **04** last, slim **05** faint, fishy, small **06** farfet, remote,

slight, unlike **07** distant, dubious, outside, suspect **08** doubtful **09** fictional **10** far-fetched, improbable, improbably, incredible, suspicious, unexpected, unsuitable **11** implausible, unpromising **12** questionable, unbelievable, unconvincing, unimaginable **13** inconceivable **14** inconsiderable **15** unprepossessing

## unlimited

◇ *ends deletion indicator* **04** full, vast **05** great, total **06** untold **07** endless, immense **08** absolute, complete, infinite **09** boundless, countless, extensive, limitless, shoreless, unbounded, unchecked, unimpeded, universal **10** indefinite, unconfined, unhampered **11** confineless, illimitable, measureless, unqualified **12** immeasurable, incalculable, uncontrolled, unrestricted **13** inexhaustible, unconditional, unconstrained **15** all-encompassing

## unload

**04** dump **05** empty, strip **06** remove, unlade, unpack, unship, vacate **07** disload, offload, relieve **08** unburden, uncharge **09** disburden, discharge, unfraught **10** disburthen

## unlock

**04** free, open, undo **05** unbar **06** unbolt **07** release, unlatch **08** disclose, unfasten

## unlooked-for

**05** lucky **06** chance **08** surprise **09** fortunate **10** fortuitous, surprising, unexpected, unforeseen, unhoped-for **11** undreamed-of, unpredicted, unthought-of **13** unanticipated

## unloved

**05** hated **06** dumped **07** spurned **08** detested, disliked, forsaken, loveless, rejected, unwanted **09** neglected, unpopular **10** uncared-for

## unluckily

**04** alas **05** sadly **08** sad to say **09** unhappily, worse luck **11** regrettably, sad to relate **13** I am sorry to say, unfortunately

## unlucky

**04** poor **05** black, stiff, tough **06** cursed, donsie, doomed, jinxed, wicked **07** adverse, hapless, infaust, ominous, unhappy **08** ill-fated, luckless, sinister, unchancy, untoward, wretched **09** ill-omened, mischancy, miserable, wanchancy **10** calamitous, disastrous, ill-starred, left-handed, unpleasant, wanchancie **11** star-crossed, unfortunate, unpromising **12** catastrophic, inauspicious, unfavourable, unpropitious, unsuccessful **14** down on your luck **15** disadvantageous

## unmanageable

**04** wild **05** bulky **06** gallus, unruly, wanton **07** awkward, gallows, ropable, unhandy, unweldy **08** ropeable, unwieldy **09** difficult, wieldless

**10** cumbersome, disorderly, refractary, refractory, weeldlesse **11** intractable, troublesome **12** incommodious, inconvenient, obstreperous, recalcitrant, ungovernable **13** impracticable **14** uncontrollable

## unmanly

**03** wet **04** base, soft, weak **05** cissy, weedy, wussy **06** craven, effete, feeble, yellow **07** wimpish **08** cowardly, womanish **09** weak-kneed **10** effeminate, namby-pamby **11** lily-livered **13** dishonourable **14** chicken-hearted

## unmannerly

**04** rude **07** boorish, ill-bred, low-bred, uncivil, uncouth **08** impolite **09** graceless, misleared **10** ungracious **11** bad-mannered, ill-mannered **12** badly-behaved, discourteous **13** disrespectful

## unmarried

**04** free, lone **05** unwed **06** maiden, single **08** celibate, divorced **09** available, on your own, separated **10** unattached **11** partnerless

## unmask

**04** bare, show **06** detect, expose, reveal, show up, unveil **07** uncloak, uncover, unvisor **08** disclose, discover, unvizard

## unmatched

**03** odd **04** orra **06** unique **07** supreme **08** peerless **09** matchless, nonpareil, paramount **10** consummate, unequalled, unexampled, unfellowed, unrivalled **11** unparagoned, unsurpassed **12** incomparable, unparalleled **13** beyond compare

## unmentionable

**05** taboo **08** immodest, indecent, shameful, shocking **09** forbidden **10** abominable, scandalous, unpleasant **11** disgraceful, unspeakable, unutterable **12** embarrassing

## unmerciful

**04** hard **05** cruel **06** brutal **07** callous **08** pitiless, ruthless, sadistic, uncaring **09** heartless, merciless, spareless, unfeeling, unsparing **10** implacable, relentless **11** remorseless, unrelenting

## unmethodical

**06** random **07** muddled **08** confused **09** desultory, haphazard, illogical, irregular **10** disorderly **11** unorganized **12** unsystematic **13** unco-ordinated

## unmindful

**03** lax **04** deaf **05** blind, slack **06** remiss **07** unaware **08** careless, heedless **09** forgetful, negligent, oblivious, unheeding **10** neglectful, regardless **11** inattentive, indifferent, unconscious

## unmistakable

**04** sure **05** clear, frank, plain **06** patent **07** blatant, certain, decided, evident, glaring, obvious **08** clear-cut, definite, distinct, explicit, manifest, positive, striking, univocal **10** pronounced, undeniable **11** conspicuous,

indubitable, unambiguous, unequivocal, well-defined **12** indisputable **14** beyond question, unquestionable

## unmistakably

**06** surely **07** clearly, plainly **08** proclaim **09** blatantly, certainly, evidently, obviously **10** definitely, distinctly, manifestly, undeniably **11** doubtlessly, indubitably **12** indisputably, without doubt **13** conspicuously, unambiguously, unequivocally **14** unquestionably **15** without question

## unmitigated

**04** grim, pure, rank **05** harsh, sheer, utter **06** arrant **07** intense, perfect **08** absolute, complete, outright, thorough, unabated, unbroken **09** downright, out-and-out **10** consummate, persistent, relentless, unmodified, unredeemed, unrelieved **11** unqualified, unrelenting, unremitting **12** unalleviated, undiminished **13** thoroughgoing

## unmixed

**03** net, raw **04** mere, neat, nett, pure **07** sincere **09** unallayed **12** unadulterate, uncompounded **13** unadulterated

## unmoved

**04** calm, cold, firm **06** steady **07** adamant, dry-eyed **08** resolute, resolved, unshaken **09** impassive, unbending, unchanged, unfeeling, unstirred, untouched **10** determined, inflexible, unaffected, unwavering **11** indifferent, unconcerned, undeviating, unimpressed **12** unresponsive **13** dispassionate

## unnamed

**04** anon **05** house **09** anonymous

## unnatural

◇ *anagram indicator* **03** odd **05** false, queer, stiff **06** farfet, forced, formal, staged, unholy, wooden **07** bizarre, feigned, fustian, heinous, inhuman, pompous, stilted, strange, uncanny, unusual **08** abnormal, absonant, affected, freakish, kindless, laboured, peculiar, strained, uncommon, unkindly **09** anomalous, contrived, insincere, irregular, monstrous, perverted **10** artificial, disnatured, far-fetched, forcedness, monstruous **11** constrained, stiff-necked **12** cataphysical, supernatural **13** against nature, extraordinary, self-conscious, unspontaneous

## unnaturally

◇ *anagram indicator* **05** oddly **08** unkindly **09** strangely, unusually **10** abnormally, peculiarly, uncommonly **11** irregularly **15** extraordinarily

## unnecessarily

**10** needlessly **11** excessively **12** immoderately **13** superfluously

## unnecessary

**06** wasted **08** needless, unneeded, unwanted **09** excessive, redundant

**unnerve**

**10** expendable, gratuitous, unrequired **11** dispensable, inessential, superfluous, uncalled-for **12** non-essential, tautological

**unnerve**

**05** alarm, daunt, scare, shake, unman, upset, worry **06** deject, dismay, put out, rattle, weaken **07** fluster, perturb, shake up **08** confound, disquiet, frighten, unsettle **10** demoralize, disconcert, discourage, dishearten, intimidate

**unnoticed**

**06** unseen **07** ignored **08** unheeded **09** neglected **10** overlooked, unobserved, unremarked **11** disregarded **12** undiscovered, unrecognized

**unobstructed**

**04** fair, open **05** plain

**unobtrusive**

**05** quiet **06** humble, low-key, modest **07** subdued **08** retiring **09** underhand **10** restrained, unassuming **11** unassertive **12** self-effacing, unaggressive, unnoticeable **13** inconspicuous, unpretentious **14** unostentatious

**unobtrusively**

**06** humbly **07** on the QT, quietly **08** modestly **10** on the quiet **15** inconspicuously, surreptitiously, unpretentiously

**unoccupied**

**04** free, idle, room, void **05** empty, waste **06** otiose, vacant **07** jobless **08** deserted, forsaken, inactive, workless **09** at liberty, désoeuvré **10** disengaged, unemployed **11** uninhabited, unpopulated

**unofficial**

**04** curb, kerb **05** black **06** fringe **07** illegal, private **08** informal, personal **10** undeclared, unratified **11** alternative, unconfirmed **12** confidential, off-the-record, unauthorized **15** unauthenticated

**unoriginal**

**05** stale, trite **06** copied **07** copycat, cribbed, derived, slavish **09** hackneyed, ready-made **10** derivative, second-hand, uninspired **11** predictable **12** cliché-ridden **13** unimaginative

**unorthodox**

◇ *anagram indicator* **03** new **04** cult, zany **05** fresh, novel **06** fringe, way-out **07** unusual **08** abnormal, creative **09** eccentric, heterodox, irregular, left-field **10** innovative, off the wall **11** alternative **13** nonconformist **14** unconventional

**unpaid**

**03** due **04** free **05** owing **06** unfeed **07** overdue, payable, pending, pro bono, unwaged **08** honorary **09** remaining, unsettled, voluntary **10** unsalaried **11** outstanding, uncollected **14** pro bono publico, unremunerative

**unpalatable**

**05** nasty **06** bitter **07** insipid **08** inedible **09** offensive, repellent, repugnant, uneatable, unsavoury **10** disgusting, unpleasant **11** distasteful **12** disagreeable, unappetizing, unattractive

**unparalleled**

**04** rare **06** unique **07** supreme **08** peerless **09** matchless, unmatched **10** unequalled, unrivalled **11** exceptional, superlative, unsurpassed **12** incomparable, without equal **13** beyond compare, unprecedented

**unpardonable**

**08** shameful, shocking **10** deplorable, outrageous, scandalous **11** disgraceful, inexcusable **12** indefensible, irremissible, unforgivable **13** reprehensible, unjustifiable **14** unconscionable

**unperturbed**

**04** calm, cool **06** placid, poised, serene **08** composed, tranquil **09** collected, impassive, unexcited, unruffled, unworried **10** untroubled **11** undisturbed, unflappable, unflinching, unflustered **13** self-possessed

**unpleasant**

**03** bad **04** foul, grim, mean, rude, sour **05** awful, crook, nasty, surly **06** filthy, mingin', stinky, thorny, ungain, unkind **07** drastic, hostile, minging, noisome **08** impolite **09** offensive, repugnant, repulsive, traumatic **10** aggressive, disgusting, ill-natured, unfriendly **11** bad-tempered, distasteful, quarrelsome, troublesome, undesirable, unpalatable **12** disagreeable, discourteous, unappetizing, unattractive **13** objectionable

**unpleasantness**

**04** fuss **05** upset **06** bother, furore **07** scandal, trouble **08** bad blood **09** annoyance, esclandre, nastiness **10** bad feeling, ill-feeling **13** embarrassment

**unpolished**

**04** bare, rude **05** crude, rough **06** coarse, vulgar **07** sketchy, uncouth, unfiled, unkempt **08** agrestic, home-bred, unpolite, unworked **09** unrefined **10** provincial, uncultured, unfinished **11** uncivilized, unfashioned **12** uncultivated **13** rough and ready, wild and woolly **15** unsophisticated

**unpopular**

**05** hated **07** avoided, ignored, shunned, unloved **08** detested, disliked, rejected, unwanted **09** neglected, unwelcome **10** friendless **11** undesirable **12** unattractive **13** unfashionable, unsought-after

**unprecedented**

**03** new **07** unheard, unknown, unusual **08** abnormal, freakish, original, uncommon **09** unheard-of **10** remarkable, unequalled,

unexampled, unrivalled **11** exceptional **12** unparalleled **13** extraordinary, revolutionary

**unpredictable**

◇ *anagram indicator* **06** chance, fickle, random, slippy **07** erratic **08** slippery, unstable, variable, volatile **09** mercurial **10** capricious, changeable, inconstant, unexpected, unreliable **12** incalculable **13** unforeseeable

**unprejudiced**

**04** fair, just **08** balanced, detached, unbiased **09** impartial, objective **10** even-handed, fair-minded, open-minded, uncoloured **11** enlightened, non-partisan, unpossessed **12** cosmopolitan **13** dispassionate

**unpremeditated**

**07** offhand **09** extempore, impromptu, impulsive, unplanned **10** fortuitous, off-the-cuff, unprepared **11** spontaneous, unmeditated, unrehearsed **13** unintentional **15** spur-of-the-moment

**unprepared**

**03** raw **05** ad-lib, crude **07** napping, unready **09** half-baked, surprised, unplanned, unwilling **10** flat-footed, improvised, incomplete, off-the-cuff, unfinished, unpurvaide, unpurveyed **11** ill-equipped, spontaneous, unrehearsed **12** unsuspecting **14** on the wrong foot

**unprepossessing**

**04** ugly **05** plain **06** homely **08** ordinary, unlikely, unlovely **10** forbidding, unexciting, unpleasing **11** indifferent, unappealing **12** unattractive, unremarkable **13** unexceptional, uninteresting **15** undistinguished

**unpretentious**

**05** plain **06** homely, honest, humble, modest, simple **07** natural **08** discreet, ordinary **10** penny-plain, unaffected, unassuming **11** unobtrusive **14** unostentatious **15** straightforward

**unprincipled**

**07** corrupt, crooked, devious, immoral **09** deceitful, dishonest, reprobate, underhand, unethical **10** profligate **12** uninstructed, unscrupulous **13** discreditable, dishonourable **14** unprofessional

**unproductive**

**03** dry, shy **04** arid, dead, idle, lean, poor, vain, yeld, yell **05** blank, waste **06** barren, futile, otiose **07** sterile, useless **09** fruitless, infertile, worthless **10** unfruitful **11** ineffective, unrewarding **12** unprofitable **13** inefficacious **14** unremunerative

**unprofessional**

**03** lax **06** casual, sloppy **08** improper, inexpert, unseemly **09** negligent, unethical, unskilled, untrained **10** amateurish, indecorous **11** incompetent, inefficient **12** inadmissible, unacceptable, unprincipled, unscrupulous **13** inexperienced

## unprofitable
**04** lean **08** bootless

## unpromising
**06** gloomy **07** adverse, ominous
**08** doubtful, unlikely **10** depressing
**11** dispiriting **12** discouraging,
inauspicious, unfavourable,
unpropitious

## unprotected
**04** open, soft **05** naked **06** liable
**07** exposed, unarmed **08** helpless
**09** uncovered, unguarded
**10** unattended, undefended,
unshielded, vulnerable **11** defenceless,
unfortified, unsheltered

## unprovable
**12** unverifiable **14** indemonstrable,
indeterminable, undemonstrable
**15** unascertainable

## unqualified
**05** inapt, round, total, unfit, utter
**07** amateur, perfect, plenary
**08** absolute, complete, outright,
positive, thorough **09** downright,
incapable, out-and-out, unallayed,
untrained **10** consummate, ineligible,
unlicensed, unprepared, unreserved,
unsuitable **11** categorical, ill-equipped,
incompetent, unequivocal,
unmitigated **12** unrestricted,
wholehearted **13** inexperienced,
unconditional

## unquestionable
**04** sure **05** clear **06** patent **07** certain,
obvious **08** absolute, definite, flawless,
manifest **09** faultless **10** conclusive,
undeniable **11** indubitable, irrefutable,
self-evident, unequivocal
**12** indisputable, unchallenged,
unmistakable **13** incontestable
**14** beyond question

## unquestionably
**06** firmly **07** clearly **08** directly
**09** certainly **10** definitely, distinctly,
explicitly, manifestly, positively
**11** indubitably, irrefutably
**12** unmistakably **13** unambiguously,
unequivocally

## unquestioning
**08** implicit **11** unqualified
**12** questionless, unhesitating,
wholehearted **13** unconditional

## unravel
◇ *anagram indicator* **04** fray, free, undo
**05** solve **06** evolve, unknit, unknot,
unwind **07** clear up, explain, resolve,
sort out, work out **08** separate,
untangle **09** extricate, figure out,
interpret, penetrate, puzzle out
**11** disentangle **13** straighten out

## unreadable
**07** complex, garbled, jumbled,
muddled, obscure **08** involved,
puzzling **09** illegible, scrambled
**10** incoherent, mysterious
**11** complicated, double Dutch
**12** impenetrable, inarticulate,
unfathomable **14** indecipherable,
unintelligible

## unreal
**04** fake, faux, mock, sham **05** false,
phony **06** aerial, ersatz, hollow, made-
up, phoney, shadow, untrue
**07** amazing, bizarre, phantom, pretend
**08** aeriform, fanciful, illusive, illusory,
mythical, nebulous, notional
**09** fairytale, fantastic, imaginary,
legendary, moonshiny, phantosme,
storybook, synthetic, visionary,
whimsical **10** artificial, chimerical,
fictitious, immaterial, incredible,
ungrounded **11** Disneyesque, make-
believe, non-existent **12** hypothetical,
unbelievable **13** insubstantial

## unrealistic
**08** quixotic, romantic, wild-eyed
**10** idealistic, impossible, unworkable
**11** impractical, theoretical
**12** unreasonable **13** impracticable
**14** over-optimistic

## unreality
**09** irreality, phoniness **10** hollowness,
phoneyness **11** bizarreness, make-
believe **12** fancifulness, illusoriness,
nebulousness, non-existence
**13** artificiality, imaginariness

## unreasonable
**03** mad, OTT **05** silly, steep, undue
**06** absurd, biased, stupid, unfair,
unjust **07** foolish, froward, obscene
**08** a bit much, exacting, perverse
**09** arbitrary, excessive, expensive,
illogical, ludicrous, senseless
**10** exorbitant, far-fetched, headstrong,
immoderate, iniquitous, irrational,
outrageous, over the top, scandalous
**11** extravagant, nonsensical,
opinionated, uncalled-for, unchristian,
unjustified, unrealistic, unwarranted
**12** extortionate, inconsistent,
preposterous, unacceptable **13** unco-
operative, unjustifiable

## unreasoning
**04** wild **05** brute, crazy, silly **06** absurd,
unwise **07** brutish, foolish, invalid,
unsound **09** arbitrary, beastlike,
illogical, senseless **10** groundless,
irrational, ridiculous **11** implausible,
nonsensical **12** inconsistent,
unreasonable **14** beside yourself

## unrecognizable
**07** altered, changed **09** disguised,
incognito **10** unknowable
**12** incognizable **14** unidentifiable

## unrecognized
**06** unseen **07** ignored **08** unheeded
**09** neglected, unnoticed
**10** overlooked, unobserved,
unremarked **11** disregarded
**12** undiscovered

## unrefined
**03** raw **05** blunt, crude, rough
**06** coarse, earthy, rustic, vulgar
**07** bestial **09** rough-hewn, untreated
**10** uncultured, unfinished, unpolished,
unpurified **11** unprocessed
**12** uncultivated **15** unsophisticated

## unregenerate
**06** sinful, wicked **07** natural
**08** hardened, obdurate, stubborn

**09** abandoned, obstinate, shameless
**10** impenitent, persistent, refractory,
unreformed **11** intractable,
unconverted, unrepentant
**12** incorrigible, recalcitrant

## unrelated
**06** unlike **07** foreign **08** distinct,
separate **09** different, disparate
**10** dissimilar, extraneous, irrelevant
**11** independent, off the point,
unconnected **12** inconsequent,
relationless, unassociated **14** beside
the point

## unrelenting
**05** cruel, stern **06** steady **07** endless
**08** constant, pitiless, ruthless,
unabated, unbroken **09** ceaseless,
continual, incessant, merciless,
perpetual, unceasing, unsparing
**10** continuous, implacable,
inexorable, relentless, unmerciful
**11** remorseless, unforgiving,
unremitting **12** intransigent
**14** uncompromising

## unreliable
◇ *anagram indicator* **04** iffy **05** dodgy,
false, trick **06** fickle, shonky
**07** unsound **08** doubtful, fallible, in-
and-out, mistaken, slippery, unstable
**09** deceptive, erroneous, sieve-like,
uncertain **10** fly-by-night, inaccurate
**11** implausible **12** disreputable,
questionable, unconvincing,
undependable **13** irresponsible,
temperamental, untrustworthy

## unremitting
**08** constant, tireless, unabated,
unbroken **09** assiduous, ceaseless,
continual, continued, incessant,
intensive, perpetual, unceasing
**10** continuous, relentless
**11** irremissive, remorseless,
unrelenting **13** indefatigable

## unrepentant
**07** callous **08** hardened, obdurate
**09** confirmed, shameless, unabashed,
unashamed **10** impenitent
**12** incorrigible, unapologetic,
unregenerate

## unrequited
**07** ignored, snubbed, spurned
**08** rejected **09** discarded, neglected
**10** unanswered **11** not returned
**12** unrecognized **14** unacknowledged,
unreciprocated

## unreserved
**04** free, full, open **05** frank, total
**06** candid, direct, entire **08** absolute,
complete, explicit, outgoing,
unbooked **09** extrovert, outspoken,
talkative, unlimited **10** forthright
**11** uninhibited, unqualified, whole-
footed **12** heart-to-heart, unhesitating,
unrestrained, unrestricted,
wholehearted **13** communicative,
demonstrative, unconditional

## unreservedly
**03** out **05** fully **07** totally, utterly
**08** entirely, outright **09** out-and-out
**10** absolutely, completely

14 unhesitatingly, wholeheartedly
15 unconditionally

**unresisting**
04 meek 06 docile 07 passive
08 obedient 09 unsisting 10 submissive

**unresolved**
04 moot 05 vague, vexed 07 pending
08 doubtful, unsolved 09 undecided,
unsettled 10 indefinite, irresolute,
unanswered, up in the air
12 undetermined 13 problematical

**unresponsive**
04 cool 05 aloof 06 frigid 07 unmoved
08 echoless 09 apathetic, withdrawn
10 unaffected 11 indifferent
12 uninterested 13 unsympathetic

**unrest**
◊ anagram indicator 05 worry 06 unease
07 discord, protest, turmoil 08 disorder,
disquiet 09 agitation, commotion,
rebellion 10 discontent, dissension,
uneasiness 11 disturbance
12 disaffection, perturbation,
restlessness 15 dissatisfaction

**unrestrained**
◊ anagram indicator 04 free, wild
05 frank, loose 06 hearty, lavish,
wanton 07 natural, rampant, unyoked
08 impotent 09 abandoned, libertine,
unbounded, unbridled, unchecked
10 boisterous, immoderate, inordinate,
unbuttoned, unfettered, unhindered,
unlaboured, unreserved
11 extravagant, full-frontal,
intemperate, uninhibited, unrepressed
12 uncontrolled 13 irrepressible,
unconstrained, wild and woolly

**unrestricted**
◊ anagram indicator 04 free, open
05 clear 06 public 08 absolute, open
door 09 chainless, unbounded,
unimpeded, unlimited, unopposed
10 free-for-all, unhindered, unreserved
12 discretional, unobstructed
13 discretionary, unconditional

**unripe**
05 green 07 unready 08 immature
09 unripened 11 out of season,
undeveloped

**unrivalled**
07 supreme 08 peerless 09 matchless,
nonpareil, unmatched, untouched
10 inimitable, unequalled
11 superlative, unsurpassed
12 incomparable, unparalleled,
without equal 13 beyond compare

**unruffled**
04 calm, cool, even 05 level 06 serene,
smooth 08 composed, peaceful,
tranquil 09 collected 10 untroubled
11 undisturbed, unperturbed
13 imperturbable

**unruly**
◊ anagram indicator 04 rag'd, wild
05 ragde, rowdy 06 stormy, wanton,
wilful 07 lawless, riotous, rulesse,
wayward 08 mutinous, ruleless, torn-
down 09 camstairy, camsteary,
turbulent 10 camsteerie, disorderly,
disruptive, headstrong, rebellious,

refractary, refractory 11 disobedient,
intractable 12 obstreperous,
recalcitrant, ungovernable,
unmanageable 13 insubordinate,
undisciplined 14 uncontrollable

**unsafe**
05 dicey, fishy, hairy, risky 06 chancy
07 exposed, rickety, uncanny,
unsound 08 high-risk, insecure,
perilous, unstable 09 dangerous,
hazardous, uncertain 10 precarious,
unreliable, vulnerable 11 defenceless,
treacherous

**unsaid**
08 unspoken, unstated, unvoiced
09 unuttered 10 undeclared
11 unexpressed, unmentioned
12 unpronounced

**unsatisfactory**
04 lame, poor, ropy, tame, weak
05 empty, lousy, rocky, ropey, wrong
06 faulty 08 inferior, mediocre
09 defective, deficient, imperfect, off-
colour 10 inadequate, sub-optimal,
unsuitable 11 displeasing, frustrating
12 insufficient, unacceptable,
unsatisfying 13 disappointing,
dissatisfying

**unsavoury**
05 nasty 06 sordid 07 squalid
09 obnoxious, offensive, on the nose,
repellent, repugnant, repulsive,
revolting, sickening, tasteless
10 disgusting, nauseating, unpleasant
11 distasteful, undesirable, unpalatable
12 disagreeable, disreputable,
unappetizing, unattractive
13 objectionable

**unscathed**
04 safe 05 sound, whole 06 intact,
unhurt 08 unharmed 09 undamaged,
uninjured, untouched 13 with whole
skin

**unscramble**
◊ anagram indicator 06 decode
08 decipher

**unscrupulous**
07 corrupt, crooked, immoral
08 improper, ruthless 09 dishonest,
shameless, unethical 10 Rottweiler,
unscrupled, villainous 12 unprincipled
13 dishonourable 14 unconscionable

**unseasonable**
08 ill-timed, mistimed, untimely
10 malapropos, out of place,
seasonable, unsuitable 11 inopportune
12 intempestive 13 inappropriate

**unseasoned**
05 green 08 unprimed 09 unmatured,
untreated 10 unprepared, untempered

**unseat**
04 oust 05 throw 06 depose, remove,
topple, unship 07 dismiss, unhorse
08 dethrone, dishorse, dismount,
displace, unsaddle 09 discharge,
overthrow

**unseemly**
◊ anagram indicator 05 undue 06 indign
07 uncivil 08 improper, uncomely,
unhonest 09 unrefined 10 ill-looking,

indecorous, indelicate, unbecoming,
unhandsome, unsuitable
11 unbefitting, undignified
12 disreputable 13 discreditable,
inappropriate

**unseen**
06 hidden, uneyed, veiled 07 cryptic,
lurking, obscure 09 concealed,
invisible, unnoticed 10 unbeholden,
undetected, unobserved
11 unobtrusive 13 inexperienced

**unselfish**
04 kind 05 noble 07 liberal
08 generous, selfless 10 altruistic,
charitable, open-handed, single-eyed
11 magnanimous, self-denying
12 humanitarian 13 disinterested,
philanthropic 14 public-spirited, self-
forgetting 15 self-sacrificing

**unsentimental**
05 tough 09 hard-faced, hardnosed,
practical, pragmatic, realistic,
unfeeling 10 hard-headed, iron-
headed, unromantic 11 hard as nails,
level-headed, unemotional

**unserviceable**
02 U/S

**unsettle**
◊ anagram indicator 04 faze 05 feese,
feeze, phase, phese, shake, throw,
unfix, upset 06 bother, pheese,
pheeze, rattle, ruffle 07 agitate,
confuse, disturb, fluster, perturb,
trouble 09 discomfit, unbalance
10 discompose, disconcert
11 destabilize

**unsettled**
◊ anagram indicator 04 edgy, open
05 fazed, owing, shaky, tense, upset
06 futile, on edge, queasy, queazy,
roving, shaken, uneasy, unpaid
07 aimless, anxious, fidgety, lawless,
overdue, payable, vagrant 08 agitated,
confused, deserted, desolate, doubtful,
drifting, goalless, insecure, rambling,
restless, troubled, unguided,
unnerved, unstable, unsteady,
vagabond, variable 09 abandoned,
disturbed, flustered, in arrears,
pointless, turbulent, uncertain,
undecided, unpeopled, wandering
10 changeable, inconstant, irresolute,
undirected, unoccupied, unresolved,
up in the air 11 disoriented,
outstanding, purposeless, to be
decided, undiscussed, uninhabited,
unmotivated, unpopulated
12 indetermined, in the balance,
undetermined 13 directionless,
unpredictable 14 in a state of flux

**unshakable, unshakeable**
04 firm, sure 05 fixed 06 stable
07 staunch 08 constant, resolute
09 immovable, steadfast
10 determined, unswerving,
unwavering 11 well-founded
12 unassailable

**unsightly**
04 ugly 07 hideous 09 repugnant,
repulsive, revolting 10 off-putting,
unpleasant 11 carbuncular

**12** disagreeable, unattractive **15** unprepossessing

**unskilful**
**03** bad **05** inept **06** clumsy, gauche **07** awkward **08** bungling, fumbling, inexpert, unartful, untaught **09** maladroit, unskilled, untrained **10** amateurish, uneducated, unhandsome, untalented **11** incompetent, unpractised, unqualified **13** inexperienced **14** unprofessional

**unskilled**
**04** rude **06** simple, ungain **07** unwitty **08** inexpert **09** unperfect, untrained **10** amateurish **11** incompetent, unpractised, unqualified **13** inexperienced **14** unprofessional

**unsociable**
**04** cold, cool **05** aloof **06** chilly **07** distant, hostile **08** reserved, retiring, solitary, taciturn **09** reclusive, withdrawn **10** insociable, unfriendly **11** introverted, standoffish, uncongenial **12** inhospitable **13** unforthcoming, unneighbourly **15** uncommunicative, uncompanionable

**unsoiled**
*see* **unsullied**

**unsolicited**
**07** unasked **08** unsought, unwanted **09** sponte sua, uninvited, unwelcome, voluntary **10** gratuitous, unasked-for **11** spontaneous, uncalled-for, unrequested

**unsophisticated**
**03** jay **04** naif **05** basic, crude, naive, plain **06** direct, native, simple **07** artless, genuine, natural, verdant **08** cornball, corn-pone, innocent **09** childlike, guileless, ingenuous, small-town, unrefined, unworldly **10** provincial, unaffected, uninvolved **11** rudimentary, undeveloped **13** inexperienced, unadulterated, uncomplicated, unpretentious **15** straightforward

**unsound**
◇ *anagram indicator* **03** ill **04** weak **05** false, frail, shaky, wonky **06** ailing, broken, faulty, flawed, hollow, rotten, unsafe, unwell, wobbly **07** damaged, injured, invalid, rickety **08** delicate, deranged, diseased, insecure, unhinged, unstable, unsteady **09** dangerous, defective, erroneous, illogical, unfounded, unhealthy, untenable **10** disordered, fallacious, ill-founded, unbalanced, unreliable **11** unwholesome

**unsparing**
**04** hard **05** harsh, round, stern **06** lavish, severe **07** drastic, liberal, profuse **08** abundant, generous, rigorous, ruthless, slashing **09** bountiful, merciless, plenteous **10** implacable, munificent, open-handed, relentless, ungrudging, unmerciful, unstinting **11** unforgiving **14** uncompromising

**unspeakable**
**05** awful **08** dreadful, horrible, nameless, shocking, terrible **09** appalling, execrable, frightful, monstrous, nefandous **10** horrendous **11** unthinkable, unutterable **12** unbelievable, unimaginable **13** inconceivable, indescribable, inexpressible, unmentionable

**unspeakably**
**07** awfully **08** terribly **11** appallingly, frightfully, unthinkably, unutterably **12** horrendously, unbelievably, unimaginably **13** inconceivably, indescribably, inexpressibly

**unspecified**
**05** vague **07** obscure, unknown, unnamed **09** uncertain, undecided, undefined **10** indefinite, mysterious **12** undetermined, unidentified

**unspectacular**
**04** dull **06** boring, common **07** average **08** mediocre, ordinary, plodding **10** unexciting **12** unimpressive, unremarkable **13** uninteresting

**unspoilt**
**07** natural, perfect **08** pristine, unharmed **09** preserved, unchanged, undamaged, untouched **10** unaffected, unimpaired **11** unblemished **15** unsophisticated

**unspoken**
**04** mute **05** tacit **06** silent, unsaid **07** assumed, implied **08** implicit, inferred, unstated, wordless **09** unuttered, voiceless **10** undeclared, understood **11** unexpressed

**unstable**
◇ *anagram indicator* **03** mad **04** nuts, weak **05** barmy, batty, crazy, daffy, dippy, dodgy, loony, loopy, moody, nutty, risky, shaky, wonky **06** fitful, infirm, insane, labile, mental, slippy, tickle, unsafe, wankle, wobbly **07** bananas, bonkers, brittle, bruckle, erratic, flighty, meshuga, rickety, unsound **08** crackers, deranged, insecure, instable, ricketty, shifting, slippery, ticklish, unhinged, unstayed, unsteady, variable, volatile, wavering **09** disturbed, mercurial, tottering, unsettled **10** capricious, changeable, inconstant, off balance, off the wall, out to lunch, precarious, unbalanced, unreliable **11** fluctuating, light-minded, off your head, unballasted, vacillating **12** inconsistent, round the bend **13** off your rocker, round the twist, unpredictable, untrustworthy **14** off your trolley, wrong in the head

**unsteady**
◇ *anagram indicator* **05** dotty, giddy, shaky, totty, warby, wonky **06** cranky, groggy, titupy, unsafe, wambly, wavery, wobbly **07** doddery, rickety, tittupy **08** insecure, skittish, unstable, variable, waverous **09** irregular, tottering, versatile **10** flickering, inconstant, precarious, unreliable **11** light-headed, treacherous, unballasted

**• be unsteady 04** flit **05** waver **06** coggle, wobble **09** vacillate

**unstinting**
**04** full **05** ample, large **06** lavish **07** liberal, profuse **08** abundant, generous, prodigal **09** abounding, bountiful, plentiful, unsparing **10** munificent, ungrudging

**unstoppable**
**07** undying **08** unending **09** unceasing **10** inevitable **11** unavoidable, unrelenting, unremitting **13** without a let-up

**unsubstantial**
**04** airy **07** shadowy **10** cloud-built

**unsubstantiated**
**07** dubious **08** unproved, unproven **09** debatable **10** disputable, unattested, unverified **11** unconfirmed, unsupported **12** questionable **13** unestablished **14** uncorroborated

**unsuccessful**
**04** lost, sour, vain **06** beaten, failed, futile, losing **07** bungled, fumbled, sterile, unlucky, useless **08** abortive, defeated, luckless, thwarted, washed-up **09** fruitless **10** frustrated, miscarried, trade-falne, unavailing **11** ineffective, ineffectual, trade-fallen, unfortunate **12** unproductive, unprofitable

**unsuitable**
**05** amiss, inapt, inept, unapt, unfit **08** improper, unlikely, unseemly, unsorted, unsuited **09** unfitting **10** inapposite, ineligible, malapropos, out of place, unbecoming **11** incongruent, incongruous **12** incompatible, inconvenient, infelicitous, unacceptable **13** inappropriate

**unsullied**
**04** pure **05** clean **06** intact **07** perfect **08** pristine, spotless, unsoiled **09** stainless, undefiled, unspoiled, unspotted, unstained, untainted, untouched **10** immaculate **11** unblackened, unblemished, uncorrupted, untarnished

**unsung**
**07** obscure, unknown **08** unhailed **09** anonymous, forgotten, neglected, unpraised **10** overlooked, unhonoured **11** disregarded, unacclaimed **12** uncelebrated, unrecognized **14** unacknowledged

**unsure**
**04** iffy **05** vague **07** dubious, unknown **08** doubtful, hesitant, insecure, wavering **09** dithering, sceptical, tentative, uncertain, undecided **10** ambivalent, indefinite, in two minds, irresolute, precarious, suspicious **11** uncommitted, unconvinced, unpersuaded **12** equivocating **13** untrustworthy

**unsurpassed**
**07** supreme **08** unbeaten **09** matchless, unmatched **10** surpassing, unequalled, unexcelled, unrivalled **11** exceptional, superlative **12** incomparable, second-

to-none, transcendent, unparalleled **13** state-of-the-art

## unsurprising
**08** expected, forecast, foreseen, hoped-for, promised **09** looked-for, predicted, wished-for **10** forseeable **11** anticipated, predictable

## unsuspecting
**05** naive **06** simple, unwary **07** unaware **08** gullible, innocent, off guard, trustful, trusting **09** credulous, ingenuous **11** unconscious **12** unsuspicious

## unswerving
**04** firm, sure, true **05** fixed **06** direct, steady **07** devoted, staunch **08** constant, resolute, untiring **09** dedicated, immovable, steadfast **10** unflagging, unwavering **11** undeviating, unfaltering **12** single-minded

## unsympathetic
**04** cold, hard **05** cruel, harsh, stony **06** unkind **07** callous, hostile, inhuman, unmoved **08** pitiless, soulless, uncaring **09** hard-faced, heartless, unfeeling, unpitying **11** hard as nails, hard-hearted, ill-disposed, indifferent, insensitive, unconcerned **12** antagonistic, unresponsive

## unsystematic
**06** random, sloppy, untidy **07** chaotic, jumbled, muddled **08** confused, slapdash **09** haphazard, illogical, irregular, shambolic, unplanned **10** disorderly **11** unorganized **12** disorganized, unmethodical, unstructured **13** unco-ordinated **14** indiscriminate

## untamed
**04** wild **05** feral **06** fierce, savage **07** haggard, salvage **08** unmanned **09** barbarous **10** unmellowed, untameable **14** undomesticated

## untangle
**04** undo **05** solve **07** resolve, unravel, work out **08** detangle **09** extricate **11** disentangle **13** straighten out

## untarnished
**04** pure **05** clean **06** bright, intact **07** glowing, shining **08** polished, pristine, spotless, unsoiled, unspoilt **09** burnished, stainless, unbraided, unspotted, unstained, unsullied **10** immaculate, impeccable **11** unblemished **13** unimpeachable

## untenable
**05** rocky, shaky **06** flawed **07** unsound **09** illogical, intenable **10** fallacious **11** inexcusable **12** indefensible, unreasonable **13** insupportable, unjustifiable, unsustainable **14** unmaintainable

## unthinkable
**06** absurd **08** shocking, unlikely **09** illogical, unheard-of **10** impossible, improbable, incredible, outrageous, staggering **11** implausible, incogitable **12** preposterous, unbelievable,

unimaginable, unreasonable **13** inconceivable

## unthinking
**04** rash, rude **06** unkind, vacant **08** careless, heedless, impolite, knee-jerk, tactless **09** automatic, impulsive, negligent, Pavlovian **10** incogitant, indiscreet, mechanical **11** insensitive, instinctive, involuntary, thoughtless, unconscious **12** undiplomatic, unrespective **13** inconsiderate

## unthinkingly
**06** rashly, rudely **08** stupidly **09** foolishly **10** carelessly, impolitely, recklessly, tactlessly **11** unfeelingly **12** indiscreetly **13** inattentively, insensitively, thoughtlessly **15** inconsiderately

## untidily
**07** dirtily, messily **08** sloppily **09** scruffily **10** disorderly, sluttishly **11** chaotically **12** topsy-turvily **13** shambolically **15** like a dog's dinner

## untidy
◊ *anagram indicator* **04** foul **05** dirty, messy, ratty, tatty **06** sloppy **07** chaotic, haywire, jumbled, muddled, raunchy, rumpled, scruffy, unkempt **08** slipshod, slovenly, sluttish **09** cluttered, shambolic **10** bedraggled, disorderly, slatternly, topsy-turvy **11** dishevelled **12** disorganized, unsystematic

## untie
**04** free, undo **05** loose, solve **06** loosen, unbind, unknit, unknot, unwrap **07** release, resolve, unhitch, untruss **08** unfasten

## until
**02** to **04** till, unto, up to **05** hasta, prior, while **06** before, up till **07** prior to **08** as late as **11** earlier than, up to the time

## untimely
**05** early **07** awkward **08** ill-timed, immature, timeless **09** importune, premature **10** malapropos, unsuitable **11** inopportune, prematurely, unfortunate **12** inauspicious, inconvenient, infelicitous, intempestive, unseasonable, unseasonably **13** inappropriate, inopportunely

## untiring
**06** dogged, steady **07** devoted, staunch **08** constant, resolute, tireless **09** dedicated, incessant, tenacious, unceasing, unfailing **10** determined, persistent, unflagging **11** persevering, unfaltering, unremitting **13** indefatigable

## untold
**08** infinite **09** boundless, countless, uncounted **10** unnumbered, unreckoned **11** innumerable, measureless, uncountable, undreamed-of, unutterable **12** immeasurable, incalculable, unimaginable **13** inconceivable, indescribable, inexhaustible, inexpressible

## untouched
**04** safe **06** intact, unhurt, virgin **08** pristine, unharmed **09** unaltered, unchanged, undamaged, uninjured, unscathed, unstirred **10** unaffected, unimpaired, unrivalled **11** unimpressed

## untoward
**05** amiss **07** adverse, awkward, froward, ominous, unlucky **08** annoying, contrary, ill-timed, improper, unseemly, untimely, worrying **09** unfitting, vexatious **10** disastrous, indecorous, irritating, unbecoming, unexpected, unsuitable **11** inopportune, troublesome, unfortunate **12** inauspicious, inconvenient, unfavourable, unpropitious **13** inappropriate

## untrained
**03** raw **06** unbred **07** amateur **08** inexpert, untaught **09** unskilled **10** uneducated, unschooled **11** incompetent, unpractised, unqualified **13** inexperienced, undisciplined **14** unprofessional

## untried
**03** new **05** novel **08** unproved, untested **10** innovative, innovatory **11** exploratory **12** experimental **13** unestablished

## untroubled
**04** calm, cool **06** placid, serene, steady **08** composed, peaceful, tranquil **09** impassive, unexcited, unruffled, unstirred, unworried **11** unconcerned, undisturbed, unflappable, unflustered, unperturbed **14** inapprehensive

## untrue
◊ *anagram indicator* **05** false, wrong **06** made-up, mythic **07** inexact, untruly **08** disloyal, mistaken, mythical, two-faced **09** deceitful, deceptive, dishonest, erroneous, incorrect, legendary, trumped-up, two-timing **10** fabricated, fallacious, fraudulent, inaccurate, misleading, perfidious, unfaithful, unofficial, untruthful **11** inauthentic **12** untruthfully **13** untrustworthy

## untrustworthy
**05** false **06** fickle, sleeky, slippy, unsure, untrue **08** disloyal, slippery, two-faced, untrusty **09** deceitful, dishonest, faithless **10** capricious, fly-by-night, unfaithful, unreliable, untruthful **11** duplicitous, treacherous **12** disreputable **13** dishonourable

## untruth
**03** fib, lie **04** tale **05** false, lying, porky, story **06** deceit **07** falsity, fiction, perjury, whopper **09** falsehood, falseness, invention, tall story **10** inveracity **11** fabrication, made-up story **14** unfaithfulness, untruthfulness

## untruthful
**05** false, lying **06** untrue **07** crooked **08** invented, two-faced **09** deceitful, dishonest, erroneous, fictional, insincere **10** fabricated, fallacious,

mendacious **11** unveracious
**12** hypocritical

## untutored
**06** simple **07** artless **08** ignorant,
inexpert, unversed **09** unlearned,
unrefined, untrained **10** illiterate,
uneducated, unlessoned, unschooled
**11** unpractised **12** uninstructed
**13** inexperienced **15** unsophisticated

## untwine
**06** uncoil, unwind **07** unravel, untwist
**10** disentwine

## untwist
**05** ravel, unlay **06** detort, uncoil,
unwind **07** unravel, untwine

## unused
**03** new **04** idle **05** blank, clean, extra,
fresh, spare **06** maiden **07** surplus,
unusual **08** left over, pristine,
untapped, unwonted **09** available,
remaining, untouched **10** unemployed,
unfamiliar **11** unexploited, unpractised
**12** unaccustomed, unacquainted
**13** inexperienced

## unusual
◇ *anagram indicator* **03** odd **04** rare,
unco **05** freak, kinky, queer, weird
**06** exotic, freaky, unwont **07** bizarre,
curious, offbeat, special, strange
**08** abnormal, atypical, freakish,
peculiar, singular, uncommon,
unwonted **09** anomalous, different,
eccentric, irregular **10** phenomenal,
remarkable, surprising, unexpected,
unfamiliar, unorthodox **11** exceptional,
out of the way **12** unacquainted
**13** extraordinary, unprecedented
**14** unconventional
*See also* **strange**

## unusually
◇ *anagram indicator* **04** very **05** oddly
**08** devilish **09** bizarrely, curiously,
extremely **10** especially, peculiarly,
remarkably, singularly **11** exceedingly
**12** particularly, prodigiously,
tremendously **13** exceptionally
**15** extraordinarily

## unutterable
**07** extreme **09** egregious, ineffable,
nefandous **11** unspeakable
**12** overwhelming, unimaginable
**13** indescribable, inexpressible

## unvarnished
**04** bare, pure **05** frank, naked, plain,
sheer, stark **06** candid, honest, simple
**07** sincere **09** unadorned
**11** undisguised **13** unembellished
**15** straightforward

## unveil
**04** bare **06** betray, expose, reveal,
unmask **07** divulge, lay bare, lay open,
uncover **08** disclose, discover **09** make
known **11** disenshroud **12** bring to light
**13** take the lid off

## unwanted
**05** extra **06** otiose **07** outcast, surplus,
useless **08** rejected, unneeded
**09** discarded, redundant, undesired,
uninvited, unwelcome **10** unrequired

**11** superfluous, unnecessary,
unsolicited

## unwarranted
**05** wrong **06** unjust **10** gratuitous,
groundless, undeserved, unprovoked
**11** inexcusable, uncalled-for,
unjustified, unnecessary
**12** indefensible, unreasonable
**13** unjustifiable

## unwary
**04** rash **05** hasty **08** careless, heedless,
off guard, reckless **09** imprudent,
unguarded **10** incautious, indiscreet,
unthinking **11** thoughtless

## unwashed
**04** dark, dull, foul, miry **05** black, dirty,
dusty, grimy, manky, messy, mucky,
muddy, slimy, sooty, yucky **06** chatty,
clarty, cloudy, cruddy, filthy, greasy,
grotty, grubby, grungy, scungy,
shabby, soiled **07** clouded, defiled,
grufted, scruffy, squalid, stained,
sullied, unclean **08** polluted, unsoaped
**09** tarnished **10** flea-bitten, insanitary,
unhygienic
**• the great unwashed 05** plebs
**06** the mob **07** the herd **08** riff-raff, the
crowd **09** the crowds, the masses, the
rabble **12** the hoi polloi **13** the lower
class **14** the proletariat, the rank and
file **15** the common people, the lower
classes, the working class

## unwavering
**06** steady, sturdy **07** staunch
**08** resolute, unshaken, untiring
**09** dedicated, rock-solid, steadfast,
tenacious **10** consistent, determined,
unflagging, unshakable, unswerving
**11** down-the-line, undeviating,
unfaltering, unshakeable **12** single-
minded **13** unquestioning

## unwelcome
**08** excluded, rejected, unwanted,
worrying **09** uninvited, unpopular,
upsetting **10** unpleasant **11** distasteful,
undesirable, unpalatable
**12** disagreeable, unacceptable

## unwell
**03** bad, ill **04** ropy, sick **05** badly,
crook, dicky, queer, ropey, rough,
seedy, unfit, warby **06** ailing, groggy,
poorly, sickly **07** run down **09** in a bad
way, off-colour, unhealthy
**10** indisposed, out of sorts **15** under the
weather

## unwholesome
**03** bad, wan **04** evil, junk, pale **05** pasty
**06** morbid, pallid, rotten, sickly,
wicked **07** anaemic, harmful, immoral,
noxious, rotting, tainted, unsound
**08** decaying, epinosic **09** degrading,
depraving, poisonous, unhealthy
**10** corrupting, insalutary, insanitary,
perverting, unhygienic
**12** demoralizing, innutritious,
insalubrious

## unwieldy
**05** bulky, hefty **06** clumsy **07** awkward,
hulking, massive, weighty
**08** cumbrous, ungainly **09** ponderous

**10** cumbersome **12** incommodious,
inconvenient, unmanageable

## unwilling
**04** loth, slow **05** loath **06** averse
**07** opposed **08** backward, grudging,
hesitant, loathful **09** reluctant,
repugnant, resistant **10** indisposed
**11** disinclined **13** unintentional **14** not
having any of, unenthusiastic

## unwillingness
**08** nolition, slowness **09** hesitancy,
objection **10** reluctance
**12** backwardness, loathfulness
**13** indisposition **14** disinclination

## unwind
◇ *anagram indicator* **03** veg **04** undo
**05** chill, relax **06** cool it, unclew,
uncoil, unreel, unroll, unwrap, veg out
**07** slacken, unravel, unreave, untwist
**08** calm down, chill out, wind down
**09** hang loose **10** take it easy
**11** disentangle **13** let yourself go, put
your feet up **14** take things easy **15** let
your hair down

## unwise
◇ *anagram indicator* **04** rash **05** silly
**06** insane, stupid, unredy **07** foolish,
unready **08** reckless **09** foolhardy, ill-
judged, impolitic, imprudent,
senseless **10** ill-advised, indiscreet
**11** improvident, inadvisable,
inexpedient, injudicious, thoughtless
**12** short-sighted **13** ill-considered,
irresponsible

## unwitting
**06** chance **07** unaware **09** unknowing,
unplanned, unweeting **10** accidental,
unintended, unthinking **11** inadvertent,
involuntary, unconscious
**12** unsuspecting **13** unintentional

## unwonted
**04** rare **07** strange, unusual **08** atypical,
peculiar, singular, uncommon
**09** unheard-of **10** infrequent,
unexpected, unfamiliar **11** exceptional,
uncustomary **12** unaccustomed
**13** extraordinary

## unworldly
**05** green, naive **08** gullible, innocent
**09** ingenuous, spiritual, visionary
**10** idealistic **11** impractical
**12** metaphysical, otherworldly
**13** inexperienced **14** transcendental
**15** unsophisticated

## unworried
**08** composed, downbeat **09** collected,
unabashed, unruffled **10** undismayed,
untroubled **11** unperturbed

## unworthy
**04** base **06** indign, shabby **07** ignoble
**08** improper, inferior, shameful,
unseemly, wanwordy **09** unfitting,
worthless **10** despicable, ineligible,
unbecoming, undeserved, unsuitable
**11** disgraceful, incongruous,
unbefitting, undeserving
**12** contemptible, disreputable
**13** discreditable, dishonourable,
inappropriate **14** unprofessional

## unwritten

**04** oral **05** tacit **06** verbal **08** accepted, implicit, unpenned **09** customary **10** recognized, understood, unrecorded **11** traditional, word-of-mouth **12** conventional

## unwrought

**03** raw **04** live, rude

## unyielding

**04** firm, grim, hard **05** rigid, solid, stern, stiff, stout, tough **06** marble **07** adamant, granite, staunch **08** hardline, obdurate, resolute, stubborn **09** immovable, inelastic, iron-bound, obstinate, steadfast, unbending **10** determined, implacable, inexorable, inflexible, relentless, rock-ribbed, unwavering **11** intractable, unrelenting **12** intransigent, pertinacious **14** uncompromising

## unzip

**04** free, open, undo **06** detach, loosen, unhook, unpack, unwind **07** release **08** separate **10** decompress

## up

◇ *reversal down indicator*

## up-and-coming

**05** eager **07** pushing **09** ambitious, assertive, go-getting, promising **12** enterprising

## up and down

◇ *palindrome indicator*

## upbeat

**04** rosy **06** bright, cheery **07** bullish, buoyant, hopeful **08** cheerful, positive **09** promising **10** favourable, heartening, optimistic **11** encouraging **14** forward-looking

## upbraid

**04** twit **05** chide, scold, storm **06** berate, rebuke, upbray **07** censure, reproof, reprove, rouse on, shake up, tick off **08** admonish, reproach **09** castigate, criticize, go crook at, go crook on, reprimand **10** exprobrate

## upbringing

**04** care **07** nurture, raising, rearing, tending **08** breeding, teaching, training **09** education, parenting **10** bringing-up **11** cultivation, instruction

## upcoming

**04** near **05** close **06** at hand, coming **07** looming **08** imminent, in the air, on the way **09** impending **11** approaching, forthcoming, in the offing **12** on the horizon **13** about to happen, almost upon you **14** round the corner **15** fast approaching

## update

**05** amend, renew **06** revamp, revise **07** correct, upgrade **08** renovate **09** modernize

## up-front

**04** free, open **05** bluff, blunt, early, first, frank, plain **06** candid, direct, honest, sooner **07** advance, earlier, genuine, initial, primary, sincere **08** explicit, straight, truthful **09** downright, in advance, initially, outspoken

**10** beforehand, forthright **11** hard-hitting, plain-spoken **12** introductory **15** straightforward

## upgrade

**05** raise **06** better, uphill, uprate **07** advance, elevate, enhance, improve, promote **09** modernize **10** ameliorate, make better

## upheaval

**05** chaos, upset **06** romage, uplift, upturn **07** rummage, shake-up, turmoil, upthrow **08** disorder, shake-out **09** confusion, overthrow **10** disruption, earthquake, revolution **11** disturbance

## uphill

**04** hard **05** tough **06** ascent, taxing, tiring **07** arduous, onerous, upgrade **09** ascending, difficult, gruelling, laborious, punishing, strenuous, wearisome **10** burdensome, exhausting

## uphold

**04** back, keep **06** defend, hold to **07** confirm, endorse, fortify, justify, promote, stand by, stand to, support, sustain, warrant **08** advocate, champion, maintain **09** vindicate **10** strengthen **11** countenance

## upkeep

**04** care, keep **06** outlay, repair **07** oncosts, running, support **08** expenses **09** overheads **10** sustenance **11** expenditure, maintenance, subsistence **12** conservation, preservation, running costs **14** operating costs

## uplift

◇ *reversal down indicator* **04** draw, lift **05** boost, edify, elate, exalt, heave, hoist, raise **06** better, lift up, mark-up, refine **07** advance, collect, elevate, improve, inspire, raising, upgrade, upthrow **08** civilize, increase, upheaval **09** cultivate, elevation, enlighten **10** ameliorate, betterment, enrichment, refinement **11** advancement, cultivation, edification, enhancement, improvement **13** enlightenment

## upmarket

**04** fine, high **05** prime, prize **06** choice, de luxe, select **07** quality, upscale **08** prestige, superior, top-notch **09** admirable, excellent, exclusive, expensive, first-rate, high-class, reputable, top-flight **10** first-class, respectful, unrivalled **11** exceptional, good-quality, prestigious **13** distinguished, par excellence

## upper

**03** top **04** high, over **06** higher, senior **07** eminent, exalted, greater, loftier, topmost **08** elevated, superior **09** important, uppermost
• **upper hand** **04** edge, sway **07** control, mastery **08** dominion, eminence, forehand **09** advantage, dominance, supremacy **10** ascendancy, domination **11** superiority

## upper-class

**01** U **04** posh **05** élite, noble **06** plummy, swanky **07** toffish **08** cutglass, high-born, well-born, well-bred **09** exclusive, high-class, patrician, top-drawer **11** blue-blooded **12** aristocratic

## uppermost

**03** top **04** main **05** chief, first, major **07** highest, leading, primary, supreme, topmost **08** dominant, foremost, greatest, loftiest **09** paramount, principal **10** pre-eminent **11** predominant

## uppity

**05** cocky **06** swanky **07** stuck-up **08** affected, arrogant, assuming, snobbish **09** bigheaded, bumptious, conceited **10** hoity-toity **11** impertinent, overweening, toffee-nosed **12** presumptuous, supercilious **13** self-important

## upright

**04** good, just **05** erect, moral, noble, sheer, steep, white **06** decent, honest, supine, worthy **07** ethical **08** straight, vertical, virtuous **09** elevation, reputable, righteous **10** high-minded, honourable, principled, upstanding **11** respectable, trustworthy, verticality **13** at right angles, incorruptible, perpendicular
• **set upright** **04** cock, rear **05** erect **10** straighten

## uprising

◇ *reversal down indicator* **06** mutiny, putsch, revolt, rising **08** intifada **09** coup d'état, overthrow, rebellion **10** insurgence, revolution **12** insurrection

## uproar

**03** din **04** flaw, hell, riot **05** hoo-ha, noise, raird, rammy, reird **06** bedlam, clamor, dirdam, dirdum, émeute, fracas, furore, hoo-hah, hubbub, mayhem, outcry, racket, randan, rumpus, tumult **07** clamour, garboil, ruction, turmoil, whoobub **08** brouhaha, disorder, hubbuboo **09** commotion, confusion, imbroglio **10** hullabaloo, rough music, turbulence **11** pandemonium **12** insurrection, katzenjammer, Pandaemonium **13** collieshangie

## uproarious

**04** loud, wild **05** noisy, rowdy **07** killing, riotous **08** confused **09** clamorous, deafening, hilarious **10** boisterous, hysterical, rip-roaring, rollicking, rowdy-dowdy **11** rib-tickling **12** unrestrained **13** side-splitting

## uproot

**04** weed **05** rip up **06** pull up, remove **07** destroy, root out, weed out, wipe out **08** displace, supplant **09** eradicate **11** averruncate

## upset

◇ *anagram indicator* ◇ *reversal down indicator* **03** bug, eat, tip **04** coup, cowp, hurt, purl **05** het up, shake,

**upsetting**

shock, spill, worry **06** bother, chew up, choked, dismay, grieve, gutrot, gutted, jangle, malady, put out, ruffle, sadden, shaken, take on, tip out, topple, upcast **07** agitate, ailment, annoyed, anxious, break up, capsize, confuse, disrupt, disturb, fluster, grieved, illness, jealous, overset, perturb, reverse, shake up, shake-up, trouble, unhappy, unnerve, uptight, worried **08** agitated, bothered, confused, dismayed, disorder, disquiet, distress, in a state, irritate, overturn, renverse, sickness, surprise, troubled, unsteady, upheaval, worked up **09** aggrieved, agitation, complaint, disturbed, flustered, in a bad way, knock over, mess about, overthrow, perturbed, shattered, unsettled **10** discompose, disconcert, disruption, distressed, mess around, traumatize, tumble over **11** coup the cran, destabilize, discomposed, disorganize, disturbance **12** disconcerted, perturbation, play hell with **13** play havoc with **14** discomboberate, discombobulate

**upsetting**

◇ *anagram indicator* **08** alarming, assuming, worrying **09** conceited, overthrow, startling **10** disturbing, off-putting, perturbing, unsettling **11** distressing, frightening, overturning, presumption **13** disconcerting

**upshot**

**03** aim, end **05** issue, loose, proof **06** finish, pay-off, result, sequel **07** outcome, success **10** conclusion, dénouement **11** consequence, culmination

**upside down**

◇ *reversal down indicator* **05** upset **06** turned **07** chaotic, inverse, jumbled, muddled, up-ended **08** confused, inverted, messed up, upturned **10** disordered, in disarray, overturned, resupinate, topsy-turvy, wrong way up **11** wrong side up **13** heels o'er gowdy, heels over head

• **turn upside down 05** up-end, upset **06** invert, mess up **07** disturb, whemmle, whomble, whommle, whumble **08** demolish **09** overthrow **10** make untidy, topsy-turvy **11** disorganize **13** turn inside out

**upstage**

**03** top **04** beat, best **05** dwarf, excel, outdo **07** eclipse, outrank, surpass **08** outclass, outshine, outstrip, superior **09** transcend **10** overshadow, put to shame **11** stand-offish **13** put in the shade

**upstanding**

**04** firm, good, true **05** erect, moral **06** honest, strong **07** ethical, upright **08** virtuous **10** four-square, honourable, principled **11** trustworthy **13** incorruptible

**upstart**

**06** nobody **07** parvenu **08** jumped-up, mushroom **09** arriviste **10** new-fangled **12** nouveau riche **13** social climber

**upsurge**

**04** gain, hike, rise **05** boost, surge **06** growth, spread, step-up, upturn **07** advance, build-up **08** addition, increase **09** expansion, extension, increment, rocketing **10** escalation **11** development, enlargement, heightening, mushrooming, snowballing **12** augmentation, skyrocketing **13** proliferation **15** intensification

**uptight**

**04** edgy **05** angry, nervy, tense **06** hung-up, on edge, uneasy **07** anxious, prickly **09** irritated **11** strait-laced **12** conventional

**up-to-date**

**02** in **03** hip, new, now, rad **04** cool, gear **06** groovy, latest, modern, recent, trendy, with it **07** à la page, current **08** space-age, swinging **09** in fashion, prevalent **10** all the rage, present-day **11** fashionable, in the groove **12** contemporary **13** state-of-the-art, up to the minute

• **bring up-to-date 09** modernize

**upturn**

◇ *anagram indicator* ◇ *reversal down indicator* **04** rise **05** boost **07** revival, upsurge, upswing **08** increase, recovery, upheaval **10** betterment **11** disturbance, improvement **12** amelioration

**upward, upwards**

◇ *reversal down indicator* **03** top **06** rising, uphill **07** going up **08** moving up **09** ascending

• **upwards of 04** over **05** above **08** more than **09** exceeding **10** higher than, in excess of

**uranium**

**01** U

**urban**

**04** city, town **05** civic **07** built-up, oppidan **09** inner-city, municipal **12** metropolitan **13** megalopolitan

**urbane**

**05** civil, suave **06** smooth **07** elegant, refined **08** cultured, debonair, mannerly, polished, well-bred **09** civilized, courteous **10** cultivated **12** well-mannered **13** sophisticated

**urbanity**

**04** ease **05** charm, grace **06** polish **07** culture, suavity **08** civility, courtesy, elegance **10** eutrapelia, refinement, smoothness **11** cultivation, worldliness **12** mannerliness **14** sophistication

**urchin**

**03** elf, imp, kid **04** brat, waif **05** child, gamin, rogue **06** rascal **07** mudlark **08** hedgehog, hurcheon, townskip **09** hunchback, street kid **10** ragamuffin **11** guttersnipe

**urge**

**03** beg, hie, nag, yen **04** goad, hist, itch, need, prod, push, spur, wish **05** chevy, chirp, chivy, drive, egg on, fancy, force, impel, plead, press **06** advise, appeal, chivvy, compel, desire, excite, exhort, hasten, incite, induce, libido, threap, threep **07** beseech, counsel, enforce, entreat, impetus, implore, impulse, incense, longing, procure **08** advocate, persuade, perswade, yearning **09** cacoethes, constrain, eagerness, encourage, instigate, prompting, recommend, stimulate **10** compulsion **11** inclination

• **urge on 02** ca' **03** caa', egg, hie **04** edge, mush, spur **05** whoop, yoick **06** compel, giddap, giddup, halloa, halloo, hoicks, whet on, yoicks **07** giddy-up **09** instigate **11** whet forward

**urgency**

**04** need **05** haste, hurry, press **06** preace, prease, stress **07** gravity, preasse **08** clamancy, exigency, instance, instancy, pressure, priority **09** extremity, necessity **10** importance **11** importunity, seriousness **14** imperativeness

**urgent**

**04** dire **05** acute, eager, grave, prior, vital **07** crucial, earnest, exigent, instant, serious **08** critical, emergent, pressing, strident **09** emergency, essential, immediate, important, importune, insistent, necessary, strenuous **10** compelling, imperative, persistent, persuasive **11** top-priority

**urinate**

**02** go **03** pee, wee, wet **04** leak, whiz **05** slash, stale, urine, whizz **06** pee-pee, piddle, tiddle, tinkle, wee-wee, widdle **07** relieve **09** make water, micturate, pass water, take a leak **11** spend a penny **12** be taken short, ease yourself **13** be caught short **15** relieve yourself

**urn**

**04** olla **07** kitchen, ossuary, samovar **08** the Ashes **09** ballot box

**Uruguay**

**01** U **03** ROU, Uru, URY

**US**

◇ *dialect word indicator* **08** Uncle Sam

**usable**

**05** valid **07** current, working **08** fit to use **09** available, practical **10** functional **11** exploitable, operational, serviceable

**usage**

**03** law, use, way **04** form, mode, rule **05** habit, idiom, style **06** custom, method, usance **07** control, meaning, practic, routine, running **08** handling, parlance, practice **09** etiquette, formalism, modernism, operation, procedure, tradition, treatment **10** consuetude, convention, employment, expression, management, regulation **11** application, institution, phraseology, terminology **12** way of writing **13** way of speaking

**use**

◇ *anagram indicator* **02** do **03** end, ply, try, ure **04** call, good, help, milk, need,

**used**

work **05** abuse, apply, avail, bleed, cause, enjoy, point, right, spend, treat, usage, value, waste, wield, worth **06** custom, demand, draw on, employ, expend, follow, handle, misuse, object, profit, resort **07** ability, benefit, consume, exhaust, exploit, observe, operate, purpose, service, utilize **08** accustom, cash in on, deal with, exercise, impose on, occasion, practise, put to use, resort to **09** advantage, go through, habituate, make use of, manoeuvre, necessity, operation, privilege, regularly **10** employment, get through, imposition, manipulate, permission, usefulness **11** application, utilization **12** exploitation, manipulation, mistreatment **13** bring into play **15** take advantage of
• **used to 06** wont to **07** given to, prone to **08** inured to **10** adjusted to, at home with **11** practised in **12** accustomed to, familiar with, habituated to, in the habit of, no stranger to **14** acclimatized to
• **use up** ◇ *reversal down indicator* **03** sap **04** burn, take **05** drain, spend, waste **06** absorb, devour, finish, peruse, work up **07** consume, deplete, eat into, exhaust, fritter, tire out **08** squander **09** go through

**used**

◇ *anagram indicator* **04** wont, worn **05** usual **06** expert, soiled **07** cast-off **08** dog-eared, pre-owned **09** customary, nearly-new **10** hand-me-down, second-hand **11** experienced

**useful**

**04** able **05** handy, nifty **06** expert **07** helpful, skilful, skilled **08** behovely, fruitful, valuable **09** competent, effective, practical, practised, rewarding **10** all-purpose, beneficial, convenient, functional, productive, proficient, profitable, worthwhile **11** experienced, serviceable **12** advantageous **14** general-purpose

**usefulness**

**03** use **04** good, help **05** avail, value, worth **06** profit **07** benefit, fitness, service, utility **08** efficacy **09** advantage **10** efficiency **11** convenience **12** practicality **13** functionality **15** serviceableness

**useless**

◇ *anagram indicator* **03** bad, dud **04** bung, idle, poor, ropy, vain, void, weak **05** awful, kaput, lousy, ropey **06** futile, grotty, no good, otiose **07** botched **08** bootless, frippery, hopeless, pathetic, terrible, unusable **09** fruitless, half-assed, incapable, pointless, to no avail, unhelpful, worthless **10** broken-down, clapped-out, effectless, unavailing, unworkable **11** impractical, incompetent, ineffective, ineffectual, inefficient **12** unproductive, unprofitable **13** inefficacious **14** a load of garbage, a load of rubbish, good-for-nothing

**uselessness**

**08** futility, idleness **09** inutility **10** ineptitude **12** hopelessness, incompetence **14** impracticality, ineffectuality **15** ineffectiveness

**usher**

**04** lead, show **05** guide, macer, pilot, steer **06** direct, escort **07** chobdar, conduct, marshal **08** Black Rod, huissier **09** accompany, assistant, attendant, introduce, usherette **10** doorkeeper
• **usher in 06** herald, launch, ring in **07** precede **08** announce, initiate **09** introduce **10** inaugurate **13** pave the way for **14** mark the start of

**usual**

**05** stock **06** common, normal, wonted **07** average, general, ordinar, regular, routine, typical **08** accepted, customed, everyday, expected, familiar, habitual, ordinary, orthodox, standard **09** customary **10** accustomed, exceptless, recognized, regulation **11** commonplace, established, predictable, traditional **12** conventional **13** unexceptional

**usually**

**03** usu **06** mainly, mostly **07** as a rule, chiefly **08** commonly, normally **09** generally, in the main, on average, regularly, routinely, typically **10** by and large, habitually, on the whole, ordinarily **13** traditionally **14** for the most part

**usurer**

**05** gripe **07** Shylock **09** loan-shark **10** gombeen-man, note-shaver **11** money-lender **12** extortionist

**usurp**

**04** take **05** annex, seize, steal **06** assume **08** arrogate, supplant, take over **10** commandeer **11** appropriate

**usury**

**06** excess **07** gombeen **08** interest **09** extortion **12** money-lending

**Utah**

**02** UT

**utensil**

**04** tool **06** device, gadget **09** apparatus, appliance, implement **10** instrument **11** contrivance

*Kitchen utensils include:*

**03** bin, pan, wok
**04** etna, fork
**05** corer, ladle, mouli, sieve, tongs, whisk
**06** baster, bun tin, grater, juicer, karahi, masher, mincer, peeler, shears, sifter, skewer, stoner, tureen, zester
**07** blender, cake tin, cleaver, cocotte, flan tin, griddle, grinder, loaf tin, milk pan, ramekin, skillet, skimmer, spatula, steamer, terrine
**08** blini pan, breadbin, colander, crêpe pan, cruet set, egg-timer, grill pan, ham stand, herb mill, mandolin, pie plate, saucepan, scissors, stockpot, strainer, tea

caddy, teaspoon, wine rack
**09** bain marie, blowtorch, brochette, can-opener, casserole, corkscrew, dough hook, egg slicer, fish slice, fondue set, frying pan, gravy boat, mezzaluna, muffin tin, paella pan, pie funnel, punch bowl, sharpener, spice rack, tin-opener, toast rack
**10** breadboard, bread knife, butter dish, cook's knife, egg coddler, egg poacher, fish kettle, jelly mould, knife block, liquidizer, mixing bowl, nutcracker, pasta ladle, pasta maker, pepper mill, quiche dish, rice cooker, rolling pin, slow cooker, steak knife, storage jar, table knife, tea infuser, waffle iron, wine cooler
**11** baking sheet, boning knife, butter knife, cheese board, cheese knife, cooling rack, garlic press, melon baller, omelette pan, oyster knife, pastry board, pastry brush, potato ricer, roasting pan, roasting tin, sandwich tin, soufflé dish, tea strainer, thermometer, wooden spoon
**12** bottle opener, butter curler, carving knife, cheese slicer, deep-fat fryer, dessert spoon, egg separator, flour dredger, icing syringe, measuring jug, nutmeg grater, palette knife, pastry cutter, potato masher, pudding basin, pudding mould, salad spinner, serving spoon, yoghurt maker
**13** butcher's block, chopping-board, draining spoon, food processor, ice-cream scoop, kitchen scales, lemon squeezer, preserving pan
**14** measuring spoon, pressure cooker, straining spoon, vegetable knife
**15** grapefruit knife, meat thermometer, mortar and pestle

**utilitarian**

**05** lowly **06** useful **08** sensible **09** effective, efficient, practical, pragmatic **10** convenient, functional **11** down-to-earth, serviceable **13** unpretentious

**utility**

**03** use, ute **04** good, help, tool **05** avail, value, worth **06** profit **07** benefit, fitness, service **08** efficacy **09** advantage **10** efficiency, usefulness **11** convenience **12** practicality **15** serviceableness

**utilize**

**03** use **05** adapt **06** employ **07** exploit **08** put to use, resort to **09** make use of **13** turn to account **15** take advantage of

**utmost**

**03** end, top **04** best, last, most, peak **05** final **07** extreme, hardest, highest, maximum, supreme **08** farthest, furthest, greatest, remotest, ultimate **09** outermost, paramount **11** furthermost

**Utopia**

**04** Eden **05** bliss **06** heaven **07** Elysium,

## Utopian

Erewhon **08** paradise **09** Shangri-la
**12** Garden of Eden **13** heaven on earth,
seventh heaven

### Utopian

**04** airy **05** dream, ideal **07** Elysian,
perfect, wishful **08** fanciful, illusory,
romantic **09** fantastic, imaginary,
visionary **10** chimerical, idealistic,
unworkable **11** impractical

### utter

◊ *homophone indicator* **03** say **04** dead,
emit, pass, pure, rank, talk, tell, vend,
vent **05** outer, plain, sheer, sound,
speak, stark, state, total, voice
**06** accent, arrant, entire, goddam, put
out, reveal, tongue **07** declaim,
declare, deliver, divulge, express,
extreme, goddamn, perfect
**08** absolute, announce, complete,
monotone, outright, positive,
proclaim, thorough, vocalize
**09** downright, enunciate, goddamned,
out-and-out, pronounce, verbalize
**10** articulate, consummate
**11** categorical, come out with,
unmitigated, unqualified **12** put into
words **13** thoroughgoing

### utterance

**03** cry **04** talk, word **05** drawl, mouth,
voice **06** remark, speech, tongue
**07** comment, inanity, opinion
**08** delivery, prophecy **09** outgiving,
prolation, speech act, statement
**10** expression, outpouring
**11** declaration, enunciation
**12** announcement, articulation,
proclamation **13** pronouncement

### utterly

**03** dog **04** dead, pure, rank **05** fully,
plumb, stark **06** goddam, wholly
**07** goddamn, totally **08** entirely
**09** downright, goddamned, perfectly,
to the wide **10** absolutely, completely,
thoroughly **13** categorically

### U-turn

**03** uey **07** wheelie **08** reversal **09** about-
turn, backtrack, volte-face

### Uzbekistan

**02** UZ **03** UZB

## V
03 vee 06 victor

### vacancy
03 gap, job 04 hole, post, room
05 blank, place 07 inanity, leisure,
opening, vacuity 08 idleness, position
09 blankness, emptiness, situation
10 inactivity 11 opportunity

### vacant
04 free, void 05 blank, empty, inane
06 absent, dreamy, unused
07 deadpan, vacuous 08 deserted,
gaumless, gormless, not in use,
unfilled 09 abandoned, available
10 unoccupied, unthinking
11 inattentive, uninhabited 12 absent-
minded 14 expressionless

### vacate
04 quit 05 annul, leave, waive
06 unload 07 abandon 08 evacuate,
withdraw

### vacated
03 red 04 redd

### vacation
03 vac 04 hols, long, rest, trip 05 break,
leave 06 recess 07 holiday, leisure,
non-term, time off, vacance, voiding
08 furlough, holidays 12 intermission

### vaccinate
03 jab, jag 07 protect, syringe
08 immunize 09 inoculate

### vaccination
03 jab 04 dose, shot 09 injection
11 inoculation 12 immunization

### vacillate
◇ *anagram indicator* 04 halt, sway, wave
05 haver, waver 06 didder, dither,
teeter, waffle, wobble 07 whiffle
08 hesitate 09 fluctuate, oscillate,
temporize 11 back and fill 12 shilly-
shally, tergiversate 14 blow hot and
cold, go back and forth

### vacillating
◇ *anagram indicator* 06 feeble
08 hesitant, waffling, wavering
09 spineless, uncertain 10 indecisive,
irresolute, unresolved, willy-nilly
11 oscillating 15 shilly-shallying

### vacillation
◇ *anagram indicator* 06 waffle
08 wavering, wobbling 09 dithering,
hesitancy 10 hesitation, indecision
11 fluctuation, inconstancy
12 irresolution, shilly-shally
13 temporization 14 indecisiveness,
tergiversation 15 shilly-shallying

### vacuity
04 void 05 space 06 apathy, hollow,

vacuum 07 inanity 08 idleness
09 blankness, emptiness
11 nothingness, vacuousness
12 listlessness

### vacuous
04 idle, void 05 blank, empty, inane
06 stupid, vacant 07 foolish 08 unfilled
09 apathetic 11 empty-headed
14 expressionless

### vacuum
03 gap, vac 04 void 05 chasm, space
06 Hoover®, lacuna 07 vacuity
09 emptiness 11 nothingness
• **vacuum flask** 05 dewar
07 Thermos®

### vagabond
03 bum 04 hobo 05 caird, nomad,
piker, rogue, rover, scamp, tramp
06 beggar, dosser, rascal, roving
07 dingbat, floater, gadling, gangrel,
migrant, outcast, vagrant 08 clochard,
cursitor, palliard, runabout, runagate,
straggle, wanderer 09 itinerant,
landloper, sundowner, unsettled
10 down-and-out, land-louper
11 rinthereout, scatterling, Weary
Willie 12 hallan-shaker 15 knight of the
road

### vagary
04 whim 05 fancy, prank, quirk
06 fegary, humour, megrim, whimsy
07 caprice 08 crotchet, rambling
10 digression

### vagrancy
08 nomadism 09 wandering
10 itinerancy, travelling
12 homelessness, rootlessness

### vagrant
◇ *anagram indicator* 03 bum 04 hobo
05 caird, derro, rogue, scamp, tramp
06 beggar, dosser, rascal, roving,
truant, vagrom, walker 07 drifter,
erratic, floater, gangrel, nomadic,
roaming, tinkler 08 cursitor, homeless,
rootless, straggle, stroller, vagabond,
wanderer 09 itinerant, landloper,
shiftless, uncertain, unsettled,
wandering 10 inconstant, land-louper,
travelling 11 rinthereout, scatterling
12 gang-there-out, hallan-shaker,
rolling stone 14 circumforanean
15 circumforaneous

### vague
◇ *anagram indicator* 03 dim, lax 04 hazy
05 faint, foggy, fuzzy, loose, misty,
rough, woozy 06 unsure, wander,
woolly 07 blurred, evasive, general,
inexact, obscure, of a sort, of sorts,
shadowy, sketchy, unclear
08 nebulous, yonderly 09 ambiguous,
amorphous, imprecise, uncertain,
undefined, unfocused 10 ill-defined,
indefinite, indistinct, out of focus,
unspecific 11 approximate,
generalized 12 undetermined, woolly-
minded 13 indeterminate
14 transcendental

### vaguely
◇ *anagram indicator* 05 dimly 07 faintly
08 slightly, vacantly 09 distantly,

inexactly, obscurely 11 imprecisely
14 absent-mindedly

### vagueness
07 dimness 08 haziness 09 ambiguity,
faintness, fuzziness, looseness,
obscurity 10 generality, impression,
woolliness 11 imprecision, uncertainty
12 inexactitude

### vain
04 idle 05 empty, proud, vogie, waste
06 devoid, futile, hollow, snooty
07 foppish, haughty, stuck-up, useless
08 abortive, affected, arrogant,
nugatory, vaporous, wasteful
09 bigheaded, conceited, coxcombic,
fruitless, pointless, worthless
10 coxcomical, groundless,
peacockish, sleeveless, swaggering,
unavailing 11 coxcombical, egotistical,
empty-headed, pretentious, swell-
headed, thoughtless 12 narcissistic,
ostentatious, unproductive,
unprofitable 13 high and mighty, self-
important, swollen-headed
• **in vain** 04 no go 06 vainly 07 in
waste 09 fruitless, to no avail, uselessly
10 for nothing 11 fruitlessly
13 ineffectually 14 unsuccessfully

### vainglorious
04 vain 05 cocky, proud 06 swanky
07 crowing 08 arrogant, boastful,
bragging, puffed up 09 bigheaded,
conceited 10 swaggering 11 egotistical
13 swollen-headed 14 self-flattering

### vainly
04 no go 07 for vain, to no end 09 to no
avail, uselessly 10 for nothing
11 fruitlessly 13 ineffectually
14 unsuccessfully

### vale
*see* **farewell; valley**

### valediction
05 adieu, aloha 06 shalom, so long
07 goodbye, send-off 08 farewell
11 leave-taking 14 shalom aleichem

### valedictory
04 last 05 final 07 parting 08 farewell
10 apopemptic

### valet
03 man 06 Jeeves, lackey 07 lacquey
10 manservant 11 body servant 14 valet
de chambre

### valetudinarian
04 weak 05 frail 06 feeble, infirm,
sickly, weakly 07 invalid 08 delicate,
neurotic 13 hypochondriac

### valiant
04 bold, prow 05 brave 06 heroic,
mighty, plucky, strong 07 gallant,
staunch 08 fearless, intrepid, valorous
09 audacious, dauntless
10 courageous, determined
11 indomitable, lion-hearted,
redoubtable 12 stout-hearted

### valiantly
06 boldly 07 bravely 08 pluckily
09 gallantly, staunchly 10 fearlessly,
heroically, intrepidly 11 audaciously,
dauntlessly, indomitably
12 courageously 14 stout-heartedly

## valid

04 good, just 05 legal, sound 06 cogent, lawful, proper, strong 07 binding, genuine, logical, weighty 08 bona fide, credible, licensed, official 09 authentic, available, effectual 10 accredited, applicable, approbated, legitimate, meaningful, reasonable 11 justifiable, substantial, well-founded 12 acknowledged, well-grounded

## validate

06 attest, ratify, verify 07 certify, confirm, endorse 08 accredit, legalize 09 authorize, formalize 10 underwrite 11 corroborate 12 authenticate, substantiate

## validation

11 attestation, endorsement 12 confirmation, ratification 13 accreditation, authorization, corroboration, formalization 14 authentication

## validity

05 force, logic, point, vigor 06 vigour, weight 07 cogency, grounds 08 legality, strength 09 authority, soundness, substance 10 lawfulness, legitimacy 14 justifiability

## valley

03 cwm, den, ria 04 comb, dale, dean, dell, dene, gill, glen, park, vale, wadi, wady 05 combe, coomb, griff, grike, gryke, gulch, heuch, heugh, slade, Tempe, water 06 clough, coombe, dingle, graben, griffe, hollow, strath, Tophet, trough 07 Gehenna, wind gap 09 re-entrant

## valorous

04 bold 05 brave 06 heroic, plucky 07 doughty, gallant, valiant 08 fearless, intrepid, stalwart 09 dauntless 10 courageous, mettlesome 11 lion-hearted 12 stout-hearted

## valour

05 value, worth 06 mettle, spirit, virtue 07 bravery, courage, heroism, prowess 08 boldness, valiance, valiancy, war-proof 09 fortitude, gallantry 11 doughtiness, intrepidity 12 fearlessness 15 lion-heartedness

## valuable

04 dear 05 noble 06 costly, golden, prized, useful, valued, worthy 07 helpful 08 fruitful, precious 09 cherished, deserving, expensive, important, priceless, treasured 10 beneficial, invaluable, profitable, worthwhile 12 advantageous, constructive

## valuation

05 price, prise, prize, stent, value 06 extent, survey 08 estimate 09 appraisal, expertise 10 assessment, evaluation 11 stocktaking 12 appraisement

## value

03 use 04 cost, gain, good, prys, rate 05 merit, price, prize, worth 06 admire, assess, esteem, ethics, morals, profit, revere, survey 07 benefit, cherish, respect, utility 08 appraise, efficacy, estimate, evaluate, hold dear, treasure 09 advantage, standards 10 appreciate, excellence, importance, principles, usefulness 11 put a price on 12 desirability, significance 15 set great store by

• **of little value**   03 low 05 cheap 06 common

• **something of little value**   04 damn 06 button, trifle 10 boondoggle

## valued

04 dear 05 loved 06 priced, prized 07 beloved 08 esteemed 09 cherished, respected, treasured 14 highly regarded

## valueless

04 naff, poor 05 cheap 06 futile, paltry, trashy 07 trivial, useless 08 nugatory, rubbishy, trifling, unusable 09 pointless, worthless 10 unavailing 11 ineffectual, meaningless, unimportant 13 insignificant

## valve

*Valves include:*

04 ball, blow, gate, side, tube 05 bleed, choke, clack, diode, heart, slide 06 escape, mitral, mixing, needle, poppet, puppet, safety, triode, ventil 07 exhaust, petcock, seacock, snifter, tetrode 08 bicuspid, bistable, cylinder, dynatron, snifting, throttle, turncock 09 air-intake, butterfly, induction, injection, magnetron, non-return, semilunar, thyratron 10 Eustachian, thermionic

## vamp

05 Circe, flirt, siren 06 trudge 07 charmer, Delilah, Lorelei, patch up 08 coquette 09 temptress 10 seductress 11 enchantress, femme fatale

## van

02 RV 03 ute 04 wing 05 lorry, truck, wagon 06 camper, pick-up, waggon 07 caravan, minivan, trailer, utility 08 carriage, vanguard 09 advantage, Dormobile®, meat wagon, motor home, Winnebago® 10 baggage-car, black Maria, freight-car, mobile home, panel truck 11 patrol-wagon, railroad car 12 pantechnicon, utility truck 14 utility vehicle

## vanadium

01 V

## vandal

03 yob 04 lout, thug 05 rough, rowdy, tough 06 locust, mugger 07 hoodlum, mobster, ravager, ruffian, wrecker 08 hooligan 09 bovver boy, desolater, despoiler, ransacker 10 delinquent, demolisher 11 annihilator

## vandalize

◇ *anagram indicator* 04 ruin, sink 05 break, smash, trash, wreck 06 ravage 07 destroy, shatter, torpedo 08 demolish, write off 09 devastate

## vane

03 fan, web 04 fane, wing 05 blade, plume 07 dogvane 08 windsail 11 weathercock

## vanguard

03 van 04 fore, lead 05 front 09 forefront, front line, spearhead 10 firing line

## vanish

04 exit, fade 05 faint, ghost, leave 06 depart, die out, exhale 07 emanate, evanish, fade out 08 disperse, dissolve, evanesce, fade away, melt away, peter out 09 disappear, evaporate, fizzle out 11 go up in smoke 12 end up in smoke 13 dematerialize

## vanity

04 airs, pomp 05 folly, pride 07 conceit, egotism, foppery 08 futility, idleness, self-love, vainesse, vainness 09 arrogance 10 narcissism, pretension, snootiness, triviality 11 affectation, haughtiness, ostentation, self-conceit 12 extravagance 13 bigheadedness, conceitedness, dressing-table

## vanquish

04 beat, drub, lick, rout 05 crush, paste, quell, smash, thump 06 defeat, hammer, humble, master, subdue, thrash 07 clobber, conquer, repress, trounce 08 confound, overcome 09 overpower, overwhelm, subjugate 10 annihilate 11 triumph over 15 make mincemeat of

## Vanuatu

03 VUT

## vapid

04 dull, flat, limp, weak 05 banal, bland, stale, trite 06 boring, flashy, jejune, watery 07 insipid, tedious, vacuous 08 lifeless, tiresome 10 colourless, wishy-washy 11 uninspiring

## vaporous

04 fumy, vain 05 foggy, misty 06 flimsy, fumous, steamy 07 gaseous 08 fanciful, halitous 10 chimerical 13 insubstantial

## vapour

03 fog 04 brag, damp, fume, haze, mist, reek, roke 05 boast, fumes, smoke, steam 06 breath 07 halitus, show off, swagger 09 evaporate 10 exhalation

## variable

01 X, Y, Z 03 var 04 Mira 05 Algol 06 factor, fickle, fitful, uneven 07 moonish, mutable, Protean 08 flexible, shifting, unstable, unsteady, wavering 09 fluxional, irregular, parameter 10 changeable, fluxionary, inconstant 11 chameleonic, fluctuating, vacillating 13 pulsating star, temperamental, unpredictable

## variance

04 odds 06 strife 07 discord, dispute, dissent 08 conflict, division 09 deviation, dichotomy, variation 10 alteration, difference, dissension, divergence 11 discrepancy

**variant**

12 disagreement 13 inconsistency
• **at variance** 03 odd 06 at odds, at
outs 07 arguing 08 clashing
09 differing, out of step 10 in conflict
11 conflicting, disagreeing, quarrelling
13 at loggerheads 14 in disagreement

**variant**

◇ *anagram indicator* 03 var 05 rogue
07 derived, deviant, variate, varying,
version 08 modified 09 changeful,
character, different, divergent,
variation 11 alternative, diversified

**variation**

◇ *anagram indicator* 05 pulse 06 change
07 fluxion, novelty, variant, variety,
varying 08 variance 09 departure,
deviation, diversity, saltation
10 alteration, alternance, difference,
inflection, modulation 11 discrepancy,
fluctuation 12 orthogenesis

**varied**

◇ *anagram indicator* 05 dedal, mixed
06 daedal, motley, sundry 07 diverse,
various 08 assorted 09 different
10 accidented 11 wide-ranging
12 multifarious 13 heterogeneous,
miscellaneous

**variegated**

◇ *anagram indicator* 04 pied 05 jaspe,
paned, vairé 06 broken, motley,
veined 07 brocked, brockit, clouded,
dappled, marbled, mottled, various
08 distinct, speckled, streaked
09 checkered, chequered, dapple-bay,
harlequin, proud-pied 10 poikilitic
12 varicoloured 13 multicoloured,
parti-coloured, party-coloured

**variety**

◇ *anagram indicator* 03 var 04 brew,
kind, make, sort, type 05 brand, breed,
class, color, range 06 change, colour,
medley, strain 07 mixture, species
08 category 09 diversity, pot-pourri,
variation 10 assortment, collection,
difference, miscellany, subspecies
11 versatility 12 multiplicity
13 dissimilarity 14 classification

**various**

◇ *anagram indicator* 04 many 05 mixed
06 motley, sundry, unlike, varied
07 diverse, several, varying
08 assorted, distinct 09 different,
differing, disparate, uncertain
10 changeable, dissimilar, variegated
11 diversified 13 heterogeneous,
miscellaneous

**varnish**

03 lac 04 coat, dope 05 glair, glaze,
gloss, japan, resin 06 dammar,
dammer, enamel, lacker, mastic,
polish, veneer 07 coating, lacquer,
mastich, shellac 08 kauri gum, shell-
lac 10 lacquering, nail enamel, nail
polish 12 French polish, Japan lacquer,
polyurethane, vernis martin 13 etching
ground

**vary**

◇ *anagram indicator* 04 hunt 05 alter,
clash, range, spice, waver 06 change,
depart, differ, modify 07 deviate,
diverge, inflect, qualify, variate 08 be
at odds, disagree, modulate
09 alternate, diversify, embellish,
fluctuate, oscillate, permutate,
transform 12 metamorphose

**vase**

03 jar, jug, urn 04 ewer 05 diota, flask
06 hydria, luster, lustre, vessel
07 amphora, Canopus, pitcher, potiche
09 moon flask 10 Canopic jar, Canopic
urn, cornucopia

**vassal**

03 man 04 serf 05 liege, slave 06 client,
thrall 07 bondman, servile, subject,
villein 08 bondsman, liegeman,
retainer 09 dependant 11 bondservant,
subordinate

**vassalage**

03 fee 04 fief 07 bondage, prowess,
serfdom, slavery 08 thraldom
09 servitude 10 dependence,
subjection, villeinage 11 subjugation

**vast**

04 huge 05 great 07 immense, massive
08 colossal, cyclopic, enormous, far-
flung, gigantic, infinite, sweeping
09 boundless, cyclopean, cyclopian,
extensive, limitless, monstrous,
unlimited 10 monumental, tremendous
11 appreciable, never-ending
12 considerable, immeasurable

**vastly**

06 hugely 07 greatly 09 immensely,
massively 10 enormously, infinitely
11 boundlessly, extensively, limitlessly
12 immeasurably 13 without limits

**vat**

03 fat, tub 04 back, case, keir, kier,
tank 05 cuvée, keeve, stand 06 barrel,
girnel, tan-pit 07 wine fat 08 pressfat

**Vatican City**

01 V 03 VAT

**vault**

◇ *anagram indicator* 04 arch, dome,
jump, leap, over, roof, span, tomb,
vaut 05 bound, clear, crypt, embow,
vaute, vawte 06 cavern, cellar, cupola,
heaven, hurdle, spring 07 concave
08 leap-frog 09 cul-de-four,
mausoleum, wagon roof 10 depository,
repository, strongroom, undercroft,
wine-cellar 11 safe-deposit 13 safety-
deposit

**vaunt**

03 gab 04 brag, crow 05 boast, swank
06 flaunt, parade 07 exult in, show off,
trumpet 08 vanguard 15 blow your
own horn

**veer**

04 cast, tack, turn, wind 05 sheer, shift,
slack, swing, wheel 06 broach,
change, pay out, swerve, wester
07 box-haul, deviate, diverge, norther,
peel off, souther, whiffle 09 come
round

**vegetable**

*Vegetables include:*

03 oca, pea, rua, yam
04 bean, cole, eddo, kale, leek,
neep, okra, sium, spud, taro, wort
05 chard, choko, cress, gumbo,
laver, mooli, onion, swede
06 bhindi, carrot, celery, chives,
chocho, daikon, endive, fennel,
garlic, kumara, lentil, manioc,
marrow, mibuna, mizuna,
pepper, potato, radish, rocket,
sorrel, squash, tomato, turnip
07 avocado, bok choy, cabbage,
cardoon, cassava, chayote,
chicory, gherkin, lettuce, pak
choi, parsnip, pumpkin, salsify,
shallot, skirret, snow pea,
spinach, tapioca
08 baby corn, beetroot, borecole,
broccoli, capsicum, celeriac,
cucumber, eggplant, finochio,
kohlrabi, leaf beet, mushroom,
red onion, soya bean, zucchini
09 artichoke, asparagus, aubergine,
bean shoot, broad bean,
butternut, calabrese, courgette,
finocchio, mange-tout, petit pois,
red pepper, Romanesco,
sweetcorn
10 bean sprout, butter bean, cavolo
nero, French bean, lollo rosso,
red cabbage, runner bean, swiss
chard, Tuscan kale, watercress
11 bamboo shoot, cauliflower,
Chinese leaf, green pepper,
horseradish, lady's finger, spring
onion, sweet potato
12 black cabbage, marrow-squash,
savoy cabbage, summer squash,
turnip greens, winter squash,
yellow pepper
13 ladies' fingers
14 Brussels sprout, Chinese cabbage,
globe artichoke
15 vegetable marrow

*See also* **bean**

**vegetarian**

05 vegan, vegie 06 veggie 08 ovo-lacto
09 lactarian 11 Pythagorean

**vegetate**

04 idle 07 moulder 08 go to seed,
languish, stagnate 09 do nothing,
rusticate 10 degenerate 11 deteriorate

**vegetation**

04 sudd 05 flora, plant, trees 06 plants
07 flowers, herbage, verdure, vesture
08 greenery, savagery

**vehemence**

04 fire, heat, zeal 05 force, power,
verve 06 ardour, energy, fervor, vigour,
warmth 07 fervour, passion, urgency
08 emphasis, fervency, strength,
violence 09 animation, intensity
10 enthusiasm 12 forcefulness

**vehement**

03 hot 04 keen, warm 05 eager
06 ardent, fervid, fierce, heated, strong,
urgent 07 earnest, fervent, intense,
violent, zealous 08 animated,
emphatic, forceful, forcible, powerful,
spirited, vigorous 10 passionate,
thunderous 11 impassioned
12 enthusiastic

**vehicle**

05 means, organ 06 agency, medium

**07** channel **09** mechanism, transport **10** conveyance, instrument

*Vehicles include:*

**03** bus, cab, car, cat, fly, gig, HGV, HOV, tip, ute, van
**04** arba, biga, bike, boat, cart, drag, dray, duck, ekka, hack, Jeep®, kago, kart, scow, ship, sled, solo, tank, taxi, tram, trap, tube, wain
**05** araba, coach, cycle, lorry, plane, stage, sulky, train, truck, Vespa®, wagon
**06** bakkie, camper, go-cart, hansom, hearse, Humvee®, jalopy, jinker, landau, litter, Maglev, matatu, sledge, sleigh, surrey, tandem, troika, tuk tuk
**07** bicycle, blokart, caravan, crew cab, dog-cart, minibus, minivan, omnibus, phaeton, Pullman, ricksha, scooter, sidecar, sleeper, tractor, trailer, Transit®, trishaw, utility
**08** barouche, brougham, Cape cart, carriage, golf cart, minimoto, monorail, rickshaw, toboggan, tricycle, wagon-lit
**09** bobsleigh, buck-wagon, campervan, charabanc, estate car, milk float, motorbike, Winnebago®
**10** boneshaker, four-in-hand, jinricksha, jinrikisha, juggernaut, motorcycle, pocket bike, post-chaise, Scotch cart, sedan-chair, service car, stagecoach, trolleybus
**11** caravanette, jinrickshaw, steam-roller
**12** double-decker, pantechnicon, station wagon
**13** fork-lift truck, penny-farthing, people carrier
**14** four-wheel drive
**15** hackney-carriage, recovery vehicle

*See also* **aircraft; bicycle; car; carriage; ship**

*International Vehicle Registration codes include:*

**01** **A** (Austria), **B** (Belgium), **C** (Cuba), **D** (Germany), **E** (Spain), **F** (France), **G** (Gabon), **H** (Hungary), **I** (Italy), **J** (Japan), **K** (Cambodia), **L** (Luxembourg), **M** (Malta), **N** (Norway), **P** (Portugal), **Q** (Qatar), **S** (Sweden), **T** (Thailand), **V** (Vatican City), **Z** (Zambia)
**02** **AL** (Albania), **AM** (Armenia), **AZ** (Azerbaijan), **BD** (Bangladesh), **BF** (Burkina Faso), **BG** (Bulgaria), **BH** (Belize), **BR** (Brazil), **BS** (The Bahamas), **BW** (Botswana), **BY** (Belarus), **BZ** (Belize), **CH** (Switzerland), **CI** (Côte d'Ivoire), **CL** (Sri Lanka), **CO** (Colombia), **CR** (Costa Rica), **CU** (Cuba), **CY** (Cyprus), **CZ** (Czech Republic), **DK** (Denmark), **DY** (Benin), **DZ** (Algeria), **EC** (Ecuador), **ES** (El Salvador), **ET** (Egypt), **FL** (Liechtenstein), **FO** (Faroe Islands),

**GB** (Great Britain), **GE** (Georgia), **GH** (Ghana), **GR** (Greece), **HK** (Hong Kong), **HR** (Croatia), **IL** (Israel), **IR** (Iran), **IS** (Iceland), **JA** (Jamaica), **KS** (Kyrgyzstan), **KZ** (Kazakhstan), **LB** (Liberia), **LS** (Lesotho), **LT** (Lithuania), **LV** (Latvia), **MA** (Morocco), **MC** (Monaco), **MD** (Moldova), **MK** (Macedonia), **MS** (Mauritius), **MW** (Malawi), **NA** (Netherlands Antilles), **NL** (Netherlands), **NZ** (New Zealand), **PA** (Panama), **PE** (Peru), **PK** (Pakistan), **PL** (Poland), **PY** (Paraguay), **QA** (Qatar), **RA** (Argentina), **RB** (Benin), **RC** (Taiwan), **RG** (Guinea), **RH** (Haiti), **RI** (Indonesia), **RL** (Lebanon), **RM** (Madagascar), **RN** (Niger), **RO** (Romania), **RP** (Philippines), **RU** (Burundi), **SA** (Saudi Arabia), **SD** (Swaziland), **SK** (Slovakia), **SN** (Senegal), **SO** (Somalia), **SU** (Belarus), **SY** (Seychelles), **TG** (Togo), **TJ** (Tajikistan), **TM** (Turkmenistan), **TN** (Tunisia), **TR** (Turkey), **TT** (Trinidad and Tobago), **UA** (Ukraine), **UZ** (Uzbekistan), **VN** (Vietnam), **WD** (Dominica), **WG** (Grenada), **WL** (St Lucia), **WS** (Samoa), **WV** (St Vincent and the Grenadines), **YV** (Venezuela), **ZA** (South Africa), **ZW** (Zimbabwe)
**03** **AFG** (Afghanistan), **AND** (Andorra), **ARM** (Armenia), **AUS** (Australia), **BDS** (Barbados), **BIH** (Bosnia and Herzegovina), **BOL** (Bolivia), **BRN** (Bahrain), **BRU** (Brunei), **CAM** (Cameroon), **CDN** (Canada), **DOM** (Dominican Republic), **EAK** (Kenya), **EAT** (Tanzania), **EAU** (Uganda), **EAZ** (Tanzania), **EST** (Estonia), **ETH** (Ethiopia), **FIN** (Finland), **FJI** (Fiji), **GAB** (Gabon), **GBA** (Alderney), **GBG** (Guernsey), **GBJ** (Jersey), **GBM** (Isle of Man), **GBZ** (Gibraltar), **GCA** (Guatemala), **GUY** (Guyana), **HKJ** (Jordan), **IND** (India), **IRL** (Ireland), **IRQ** (Iraq), **KWT** (Kuwait), **LAO** (Laos), **LAR** (Libya), **MAL** (Malaysia), **MEX** (Mexico), **MGL** (Mongolia), **MNE** (Montenegro), **MOC** (Mozambique), **MYA** (Myanmar), **NAM** (Namibia), **NAU** (Nauru), **NEP** (Nepal), **NGR** (Nigeria), **NIC** (Nicaragua), **PNG** (Papua New Guinea), **RCA** (Central African Republic), **RCB** (Republic of Congo), **RCH** (Chile), **RGB** (Guinea-Bissau), **RIM** (Mauritania), **RMM** (Mali), **ROK** (South Korea), **ROU** (Uruguay), **RSM** (San Marino), **RUS** (Russia), **RWA** (Rwanda), **SGP** (Singapore), **SLO** (Slovenia), **SME** (Suriname), **SRB** (Serbia), **SUD** (Sudan), **SVN** (Slovenia), **SYR** (Syria), **TCH** (Chad), **USA** (United States of America), **WAG** (The Gambia), **WAL** (Sierra Leone), **WAN** (Nigeria), **YAR** (Yemen), **ZRE** (Democratic Republic of the Congo)

## veil

**04** caul, film, hide, mask, mist, vail, vele **05** blind, burka, burqa, cloak, cover, scarf, scene, shade, veale, velum, volet **06** boorka, canopy, chadar, chador, kiss-me, mantle, purdah, shroud, sudary, weeper, wimple **07** bourkha, chaddar, chaddor, chuddah, chuddar, conceal, cover up, curtain, humeral, modesty, obscure, veiling, whimple, yashmak **08** chrismal, covering, disguise, kalyptra, mantilla, sudarium **09** encurtain **10** camouflage, lambrequin **11** concealment, kiss-me-quick
*See also* **scarf**

## veiled

**06** covert, hidden, masked, secret **07** cloaked, covered, obscure **08** indirect, shrouded **09** concealed, disguised **13** surreptitious

## vein

**03** rib **04** lode, mode, mood, seam, tone, vena **05** costa, nerve, style, tenor, varix **06** cavity, humour, marble, strain, streak, stripe **07** fissure, nervure, stratum **08** stringer **11** blood vessel, disposition, inclination, temperament

*Veins and arteries include:*

**05** aorta, iliac, renal, ulnar **06** portal, radial, thread, tibial **07** basilic, carotid, coeliac, femoral, frontal, gastric, hepatic, jugular, organic, precava, saphena, splenic **08** axillary, brachial, coronary, postcava, praecava, superior, temporal, varicose, vena cava **09** popliteal, pulmonary, spermatic **10** innominate, mesenteric, subclavian **11** common iliac **14** anterior tibial **15** brachiocephalic, posterior tibial

## veined

**05** jaspe **06** venose, venous **07** marbled **08** streaked **10** reticulate, variegated

## velocity

**01** v **04** pace, rate **05** speed **08** celerity, rapidity **09** fleetness, quickness, swiftness
• **velocity constant** **01** k

## velvet

**05** gains, panne **06** dévoré, vellet, velour, velure **07** mockado, velours **08** chenille, suedette, winnings **09** three-pile

## venal

**04** bent **06** venous **07** buyable, corrupt **08** bribable, grafting **09** mercenary **10** simoniacal **11** corruptible

## vendetta

**04** feud **06** enmity **07** quarrel, rivalry **08** bad blood **09** blood-feud

## vendor

**06** seller, trader **07** butcher, camelot **08** merchant, salesman, stockist, supplier

**veneer**
04 mask, show 05 front, gloss, guise, layer 06 façade, fineer, finish 07 coating, display, surface 08 covering, pretence 09 grass-moth 10 appearance, lamination

**venerable**
03 Ven 04 aged, Bede, wise 06 august 07 revered 08 esteemed, honoured 09 dignified, respected, venerated 10 worshipped

**venerate**
04 fear 05 adore 06 esteem, honour, revere 07 iconize, respect, worship 09 reverence

**veneration**
03 awe 05 dulia, honor 06 esteem, honour, latria 07 douleia, respect, worship 08 devotion 09 adoration, aniconism, reverence, sublimity 10 hyperdulia, Mariolatry, Maryolatry 12 symbololatry

**Venezuela**
02 YV 03 VEN

**vengeance**
03 utu 04 harm 05 curse, wrack, wreak 07 revenge 08 mischief, reprisal, requital 09 extremely, vengement 10 avengement 11 exceedingly, retaliation, retribution
• **with a vengeance** 05 fully 07 flat out, greatly 09 furiously, like crazy, to the full, violently 10 forcefully, powerfully, thoroughly, vigorously 11 exceedingly, to the utmost, with a wanion 12 with a witness 13 energetically 14 to a great degree, to a great extent 15 with a wild wanion

**vengeful**
08 avenging, punitive, spiteful 09 rancorous 10 implacable, revengeful, vindictive 11 retaliatory, retributive

**venial**
05 minor 06 slight 07 trivial 08 trifling 09 excusable 10 forgivable, negligible, pardonable 11 permissible 13 insignificant

**venom**
04 hate 05 spite, toxin, virus 06 enmity, malice, poison 07 envenom, ill-will, rancour, swelter 08 acrimony 09 animosity, hostility, poisonous, virulence 11 malevolence

**venomous**
05 fatal, toxic 06 bitter, deadly, lethal 07 baleful, baneful, noxious, vicious 08 spiteful, viperish, viperous, virulent 09 malicious, malignant, poisonous, rancorous 10 malevolent, vindictive

**vent**
03 air, gap 04 duct, emit, flue, hole, pipe, sale 05 salse, scent, sniff, snuff, utter, voice, wreak 06 crenel, escape, let out, market, outlet, smoker 07 airhole, chimney, express, opening, orifice, passage, pour out, publish, release 08 aperture, blowhole, breather, emission, spiracle, vomitory 09 discharge, solfatara 10 mud volcano 11 black smoker, let off steam, take it out on 14 counter-opening

**ventilate**
03 air, fan 04 cool 06 aerate, debate, winnow 07 discuss, express, freshen

**ventilation**
06 airing 07 cooling 08 aeration 10 freshening

**venture**
03 put 04 dare, jump, luck, mint, risk, sink 05 assay, fling, foray, stake, throw, wager 06 chance, gamble, hazard, venter, ventre 07 advance, exploit, imperil, presume, pretend, project, suggest 08 be so bold, endanger, make bold 09 adventure, endeavour, operation, promotion, speculate, volunteer 10 enterprise, prostitute, put forward 11 speculation, undertaking 14 take the liberty

**venturesome**
04 bold 05 brave, risky 06 daring, plucky 07 doughty 08 fearless, intrepid, spirited 09 audacious, daredevil, dauntless 10 courageous 11 adventurous 12 enterprising

**venue**
see **stadium**

**venus**
04 clam 05 cohog 06 copper, Hesper, quahog, venery, vesper 07 Lucifer, quahaug 08 Hesperus 09 Aphrodite, round clam 11 evening star, morning star

**veracious**
04 true 05 exact, frank 06 honest 07 factual, genuine 08 accurate, credible, faithful, truthful

**veracity**
05 truth 07 candour, honesty, probity 08 accuracy 09 frankness, integrity, rectitude 10 exactitude 12 truthfulness

**veranda**
05 lanai, porch, stoep, stoop 06 piazza 07 decking, gallery, terrace, viranda, virando

**verbal**
◊ *homophone indicator* 04 oral, said 05 abuse, vocal 06 insult, spoken 07 literal, uttered, voluble 09 invective 10 articulate, linguistic 11 word-of-mouth

**verbalize**
03 say 04 tell, word 05 speak, state, utter, voice 06 assert, convey, report 07 declare, get over, put over 08 announce, point out 09 enunciate, formulate, pronounce, put across 10 articulate, put in words 11 communicate, give voice to 12 put into words

**verbatim**
07 closely, exactly 09 literally, precisely 11 to the letter, word for word

**verbiage**
06 waffle 07 wordage, wording 08 pleonasm 09 prolixity, verbosity

**verbose**
05 gassy, windy, wordy 06 prolix 07 diffuse, voluble, wordish 09 garrulous 10 long-winded, loquacious, pleonastic 12 periphrastic 14 circumlocutory

**verbosity**
08 verbiage 09 garrulity, loquacity, prolixity, windiness, wordiness 10 logorrhoea, multiloquy 14 long-windedness, loquaciousness

**verdant**
04 lush 05 fresh, green, leafy, virid 06 virent 11 viridescent

**verdict**
05 vardy 06 ruling, verdit 07 finding, opinion 08 decision, judgment, recovery, sentence 09 judgement 10 assessment, conclusion 12 adjudication, rough justice

**verdure**
05 grass 07 foliage, greenth, herbage, leafage 08 greenery, verdancy, viridity 09 freshness, greenness 12 viridescence

**verge**
03 rim, rod 04 berm, brim, edge, pale, tend 05 brink, limit, merge, point, range, scope, slope, touch, virge 06 border, edging, margin, trench 07 horizon, incline 08 boundary, precinct, road-edge, roadside 09 threshold 11 long paddock, nature strip 12 jurisdiction
• **verge on** 04 near 08 approach, border on 11 come close to, tend towards

**verification**
05 audit, proof 08 checking 10 validation 11 attestation 12 ascertaining, confirmation, constatation 13 corroboration 14 authentication, substantiation

**verify**
05 audit, check, prove 06 attest 07 bear out, confirm, support 08 accredit, validate 09 ascertain 11 corroborate 12 authenticate, substantiate

**verisimilitude**
07 realism 09 semblance 10 likeliness 11 credibility, resemblance, ring of truth 12 authenticity, plausibility 13 vraisemblance

**veritable**
04 fair, rank, real, true 05 right, sheer, utter 06 actual 07 genuine, perfect, regular 08 absolute, complete, outright, positive, thorough 09 out-and-out 10 consummate 11 unmitigated

**verity**
05 sooth, truth 07 reality 08 validity, veracity 09 actuality, soundness 12 authenticity, truthfulness

**vermin**

*Vermin include:*

03 rat
04 lice, mice, moth

**Vermont**
05 louse, mouse
06 pigeon, weevil
09 cockroach

*See also* **rodent**

**Vermont**
02 VT

**vermouth**
02 It 06 French 07 Cinzano®, Martini®

**vernacular**
05 idiom, lingo, local 06 common,
argon, native, speech, tongue, vulgar
07 dialect, endemic, popular, trivial
08 informal, language, parlance
09 idioticon 10 colloquial, indigenous
12 vulgar tongue

**Veronica**
04 Hebe 09 speedwell

**versatile**
◇ anagram indicator 05 handy
07 Protean 08 all-round, flexible,
unsteady, variable 09 adaptable,
many-sided 10 adjustable, all-purpose,
changeable 12 multifaceted,
multipurpose

**verse**
01 v 04 line, rime, sijo, vers 05 haiku,
onic, meter, metre, rhyme 06 heroic,
ingle, poetry, riddle, stanza
07 doggrel, elegiac, iambics, Leonine,
pennill, stichos, strophe, versify
08 doggerel, elegiacs, glyconic,
singsong, trochaic, versicle
09 amphigory, vers libre 11 acatalectic,
septenarius 12 Archilochian, nursery
rhyme 13 vers de société, vers
d'occasion, versification
*See also* **poem**

**versed**
02 up 04 deep, read 06 strong, traded,
turned 07 learned, perfect, skilled,
studied, versant 08 deep-read, familiar,
overseen, reversed, scienced,
seasoned 09 competent, practised
10 conversant, proficient
11 experienced 13 knowledgeable

**versifier**
04 poet 06 rhymer, verser 07 poetess,
rhymist 09 metrifier, poetaster,
poeticule, rhymester 10 verse-maker,
verse-smith 11 verse-monger
12 versificator

**version**
◇ anagram indicator 02 EV, NV, RV
04 form, kind, sort, type 05 cover, Itala,
model, style 06 design, report, Rev Ver,
Targum, update 07 account, edition,
reading, turning, variant 08 rough cut
09 microcosm, portrayal, rendering
10 adaptation, paraphrase
11 translation 14 interpretation, King
James Bible

**versus**
01 v 02 vs 06 facing 07 against, playing
08 opposing 09 as against, instead of
10 rather than 11 as opposed to 12 in
contrast to 14 in opposition to

**vertex**
03 top 04 acme, apex, peak 05 crown
06 apogee, height, summit, zenith

08 pinnacle 09 extremity 12 highest
point

**vertical**
05 apeak, apeek, erect, on end, plumb,
sheer 07 upright 10 straight up,
upstanding 13 perpendicular

**vertigo**
06 megrim 09 dizziness, giddiness,
wooziness 15 light-headedness

**verve**
03 zip 04 brio, dash, élan, life 05 force,
gusto 06 energy, relish, spirit, vigour,
whammo 07 fervour, passion, pizzazz,
sparkle 08 vitality, vivacity
09 animation 10 enthusiasm, liveliness

**very**
01 v 02 ae 03 e'er, way 04 ever, fell,
mega, mere, pure, real, same, self, très,
true, unco 05 assai, awful, dooms,
exact, hefty, ideal, jolly, molto, plain,
quite, sheer, stiff, truly, utter 06 actual,
as hell, bloody, damned, deeply,
dogged, ever so, highly, mighty, pretty,
proper, really, simple 07 acutely, all
that, awfully, genuine, good and,
gradely, greatly, hell of a, hellova,
helluva, majorly, only too, passing,
perfect, precise 08 bitching, devilish,
graithly, selfsame, spanking, stinking,
suitable, terribly, uncommon
09 eminently, extremely, identical,
unusually 10 absolutely, abundantly,
incredibly, not a little, remarkably,
uncommonly 11 exceedingly,
excessively 12 particularly,
unbelievably

**vessel**
03 ark, jar, jug, pot, tun, urn, vat
04 boat, bowl, ewer, ship 05 billy,
craft, peter, plate 06 barque, flagon,
holder 07 airship, pitcher, vassail,
vessail 09 container 10 receptacle
*See also* **container; ship**

**vest**
03 bib 04 garb, robe 05 drape, dress,
endow, grant, lodge 06 bestow, clothe,
confer, invest, semmit, supply
07 descend, devolve, empower,
entrust, garment, singlet 08 sanction,
vestment 09 authorize, waistcoat
10 undershirt 11 sequestrate

**Vesta**
06 Hestia

**vestibule**
04 hall 05 entry, foyer, lobby, porch
06 atrium, exedra 07 exhedra, hallway,
narthex, portico, pronaos, tambour
08 anteroom, entrance 09 forecourt
11 oeil-de-boeuf 12 entrance hall

**vestige**
04 hint, mark, sign 05 print, scrap,
shred, token, touch, trace, track, whiff
06 relics 07 glimmer, inkling, remains,
remnant, residue 09 footprint,
remainder, suspicion 10 impression,
indication

**vestigial**
07 reduced 09 remaining, surviving
10 incomplete 11 rudimentary,
undeveloped

**vestment**
04 vest 09 vestiment

*Clerical vestments include:*

03 alb
04 cope, cowl, hood
05 amice, cotta, ephod, frock, habit,
mitre, scarf, stole
06 mantle, rochet, saccos, sakkos,
tippet, wimple
07 biretta, cassock, chimere,
humeral, maniple, pallium,
soutane, tallith, tunicle
08 chasuble, dalmatic, mozzetta,
rational, scapular, skullcap,
surplice, yarmulka
09 dog-collar, phelonion
10 Geneva gown, omophorion,
phaelonion, sticharion
11 Geneva bands, humeral veil
12 superhumeral
14 clerical collar

**vet**
04 scan 05 audit, check 06 review,
screen, survey 07 examine, inspect
08 appraise, check out 10 scrutinize
11 investigate

**vetch**
03 ers 04 tare, tine 05 fitch

**veteran**
03 old, pro 05 adept 06 expert, master
07 old hand, warrior 08 old-timer,
seasoned 09 old stager, practised
10 campaigner, pastmaster, proficient
11 experienced, long-serving 13 battle-
scarred, old campaigner

**veto**
03 ban, nix 05 block 06 forbid, negate,
reject 07 embargo, rule out
08 disallow, negative, prohibit, turn
down 09 blackball, interdict, proscribe
10 thumbs-down 11 prohibition
12 proscription

**vex**
03 bug, noy 04 fret, haze, hump, rile
05 annoy, grief, spite, upset, worry
06 bother, enrage, excess, grieve,
harass, hassle, molest, needle, pester,
put out, rankle, wind up 07 afflict,
agitate, chagrin, discuss, disturb, hack
off, perturb, provoke, tick off, torment,
trouble 08 bepester, brass off, distress,
irritate 09 aggravate, cheese off
10 exasperate

**vexation**
03 noy 04 bind, bore, fury, pain
05 anger, pique, upset, worry
06 bother, plague 07 chagrin
08 headache, irritant, nuisance
09 annoyance 11 aggravation,
frustration 12 exasperation
14 disappointment
*See also* **annoyance**

**vexatious**
05 pesky 06 noyous, plaguy, trying,
vexing 07 irksome, nagging, nimious,
peevish, plaguey, teasing 08 annoying,
fashious, worrying 09 pestilent,
provoking, upsetting, worrisome
10 bothersome, burdensome, irritating,
tormenting 11 aggravating, infuriating,

**vexed**
pestiferous, troublesome
12 exasperating

**vexed**
04 moot, sore 05 irate, riled, tough, upset 06 knotty, miffed, narked, peeved, put out, tricky 07 annoyed, awkward, debated, hassled, nettled, ruffled, worried 08 agitated, bothered, confused, disputed, harassed, provoked, troubled 09 contested, difficult, disturbed, flustered, in dispute, irritated, perplexed 10 aggravated, displeased, infuriated 11 exasperated

**viability**
10 expedience 11 feasibility, possibility, workability 12 practicality 13 achievability 14 practicability, reasonableness

**viable**
05 sound 08 feasible, operable, possible, workable 10 achievable, commercial 11 practicable, sustainable

**vibes**
04 aura, feel 08 ambience, emotions, feelings 10 atmosphere, vibrations

**vibrancy**
02 go 04 life, zest 05 oomph 06 energy, spirit, vigour 07 pizzazz, sparkle, stamina 08 strength, vitality, vivacity 09 animation 10 exuberance, get-up-and-go, liveliness

**vibrant**
05 vivid 06 bright, lively 07 dynamic 08 animated, electric, resonant, spirited, striking, vigorous 09 brilliant, colourful, energetic, sparkling, thrilling, vibrating, vivacious 12 electrifying

**vibrate**
◇ *anagram indicator* 03 jar 04 dirl, ring, sway 05 quake, shake, swing, thirl 06 dindle, dinnle, hotter, judder, quiver, shimmy, shiver, thrill, tingle 07 flutter, pulsate, resound, shudder, tremble, twinkle 08 brandish, resonate, undulate 09 oscillate, pendulate 11 reverberate

**vibration**
03 jar 04 dirl 05 pulse, quake, throb 06 dindle, dinnle, hotter, judder, quiver, shimmy, thrill, tremor 07 diadrom, flutter, frisson, shaking 08 fremitus 09 juddering, pulsation, resonance, trembling 10 resounding 11 oscillation, seismic wave 12 seismic shock 13 reverberation, tremulousness

**vicar**
03 Rev, Vic 06 cleric, curate, deputy, parson, pastor, priest, rector 08 chaplain, minister, preacher, reverend 09 clergyman 10 arch-priest, substitute 11 clergywoman 15 perpetual curate

**vicarious**
06 acting 08 indirect 09 surrogate 10 empathetic, second-hand 11 substituted

**vice**
03 sin 04 evil, flaw, grip, tool 05 fault,

screw 06 defect, foible 07 blemish, buffoon, failing 08 bad habit, iniquity, weakness 09 depravity, evil-doing 10 bestiality, degeneracy, immorality, profligacy, wickedness, wrongdoing 12 besetting sin, imperfection 13 transgression

**vice versa**
02 vv 09 inversely 10 conversely, oppositely 12 contrariwise, reciprocally

**vicinity**
04 area 08 district, environs, locality, nearness 09 precincts, proximity 11 propinquity 12 surroundings 13 neighbourhood

**vicious**
03 bad 04 foul, mean, vile 05 catty, cruel, nasty 06 bitchy, brutal, faulty, fierce, impure, lethal, morbid, savage, wicked 07 heinous, immoral, violent 08 depraved, impaired, mistaken, spiteful, unlawful, venomous, virulent 09 barbarous, dangerous, ferocious, malicious, malignant 10 malevolent, vindictive 11 bad-tempered

**viciously**
06 wildly 07 cruelly 08 brutally, fiercely, lethally, savagely 09 violently

**viciousness**
05 spite, venom 06 malice 07 cruelty, rancour 08 ferocity, savagery 09 brutality, depravity, viciosity, virulence, vitiosity 10 bitchiness, wickedness 11 malevolence 12 spitefulness

**vicissitude**
04 turn 05 shift, twist 06 change 07 weather 08 mutation 09 deviation, variation 10 alteration, revolution 11 alternation, fluctuation

**victim**
04 butt, dupe, fool, host, mark, prey 05 patsy 06 martyr, muggee, nebish, quarry, sucker, target 07 fall guy, nebbich, nebbish 08 casualty, fatality, murderee, paranoic, soft mark, sufferer 09 paranoeic, paranoiac, sacrifice, scapegoat 11 sitting duck 13 sitting target
• **fall victim to** 05 catch 07 develop, fall for 08 contract 09 succumb to 10 fall prey to 11 be taken in by 12 be attacked by, be deceived by, be overcome by 14 be stricken with 15 become a target of

**victimize**
03 con 04 dupe, fool, rook 05 bully, cheat, frame, shaft, sting, trick 06 fleece, pick on, prey on, rip off 07 deceive, defraud, exploit, swindle 08 hoodwink, stitch up 09 bamboozle, persecute 11 have it in for

**victor**
01 V 05 champ, first 06 top dog, winner 08 bangster, champion 09 conqueror 10 vanquisher 11 pancratiast, prize-winner 13 victor ludorum

**Victoria**
02 VR 03 Vic 04 Nike

**victorious**
03 top 05 first 07 winning 08 champion unbeaten 09 prevalent 10 conquering, successful, triumphant 11 vanquishing 12 prize-winning

**victory**
01 V 02 VE, VJ 03 Jai, win 04 gree, Nike 07 mastery, success, triumph, winning 08 conquest, squeaker, walk-away, walkover 09 checkmate, landslide 11 subjugation, superiority, triple crown
• **sign of victory** 01 V

**victuals**
04 chow, eats, food, grub, nosh, tuck 05 bread, scran 06 stores, viands 07 aliment, edibles, rations, vittles 08 eatables, supplies 10 provisions, sustenance 11 comestibles

**vie**
03 bid 05 fight, rival, stake 06 strive 07 compare, compete, contend, contest, declare 08 corrival, struggle 09 challenge

**Vietnam**
02 VN 03 VNM

**view**
02 Vw 03 see 04 espy, idea, look, scan 05 angle, judge, range, scene, sight, study, vista, watch 06 aspect, belief, descry, gaze at, look at, notion, regard review, sketch, survey, vision 07 account, examine, feeling, glimpse inspect, observe, opinion, outlook, picture, purpose, thought, witness 08 attitude, consider, eyesight, panorama, perceive, portrait, prospect scrutiny 09 intention, judgement, landscape, portrayal, sentiment, spectacle 10 appearance, assessment, conviction, estimation, impression, inspection, perception, scrutinize 11 contemplate, examination, expectation, observation, perspective 13 contemplation, range of vision
• **in view of** 07 whereas 11 considering 13 bearing in mind
• **on view** 05 shown 06 on show 07 showing 09 displayed, exhibited, on display, presented 10 made public

**viewer**
07 goggler, watcher 08 observer, onlooker 09 inspector, spectator

**viewpoint**
05 angle, slant 06 stance 07 feeling, opinion 08 attitude, position, prospect 10 standpoint, watchpoint 11 observatory, perspective, point of view

**vigil**
04 wake 05 watch 07 lookout 08 stake-out, watching 10 deathwatch 11 wakefulness 12 pernoctation

**vigilance**
05 guard, watch 07 caution 09 alertness 11 carefulness, guardedness, observation, wakefulness 12 watch and ward, watchfulness 13 attentiveness 14 circumspection

## vigilant

05 alert, awake, aware 07 careful, zealous, wakeful 08 cautious, wakerife, watchful 09 Argus-eyed, attentive, observant, wide-awake 10 on the watch, unsleeping 11 circumspect, on your guard 12 on the lookout, on the qui vive

## vigilante

05 guard, watch 07 lookout 08 sentinel, watchman 10 armed guard 11 watchperson 13 Guardian Angel, security guard

## vignette

03 act 04 plan, turn 05 cameo, draft, scene 06 design, sketch 07 diagram, drawing, outline 08 abstract, skeleton 14 representation

## vigorous

◇ anagram indicator 04 go-go, hard, rank 05 alive, brisk, green, hefty, lusty, round, sound, stout, tough, vital, vivid, young 06 active, bouncy, lively, manful, punchy, raucle, robust, rugged, sprack, strong, vegete 07 dynamic, healthy, intense, lustick, nervous 08 animated, athletic, forceful, forcible, lustique, muscular, powerful, spirited, swanking, youthful 09 energetic, gymnastic, strenuous 11 flourishing, full-blooded, gymnastical

## vigorously

◇ anagram indicator 04 hard 06 lively 07 briskly, eagerly, lustily 08 heartily, strongly 09 in a big way 10 forcefully, like billy-o, powerfully 11 like billy-oh, strenuously 12 like old boots 13 energetically

## vigour

03 pep, vim, zip 04 bant, birr, brio, dash, élan, fire, pith 05 flush, force, gusto, heart, might, moxie, oomph, power, verve 06 energy, health, spirit, stingo 07 pizzazz, potency, stamina 08 activity, dynamism, strength, virility, vitality, vivacity 09 animation, toughness 10 liveliness, robustness 12 forcefulness 13 vivaciousness

## vile

◇ anagram indicator 03 bad, low 04 base, evil, foul, mean, vild 05 nasty, vilde 06 horrid, impure, paltry, scurvy, sinful, wicked 07 beastly, corrupt, debased, earthly, noxious, scabbed, vicious 08 depraved, horrible, infamous, wretched 09 appalling, degrading, loathsome, miserable, obnoxious, offensive, repugnant, repulsive, revolting, sickening, villanous, worthless 10 degenerate, despicable, detestable, disgusting, iniquitous, nauseating, scandalous, unpleasant, villainous 11 disgraceful, distasteful 12 contemptible, disagreeable

## vileness

06 evil 06 infamy 07 outrage 08 baseness, foulness, meanness, ugliness 09 depravity, nastiness, profanity, turpitude 10 corruption,

degeneracy, wickedness 11 noxiousness 13 offensiveness

## vilification

03 mud 05 abuse 07 calumny 09 aspersion, contumely, criticism, invective 10 defamation, revilement, scurrility 11 denigration, mud-slinging 12 calumniation, vituperation 13 disparagement

## vilify

04 slag, slam 05 abuse, decry, knock, slate, smear, snipe 06 berate, debase, defame, malign, revile 07 asperse, rubbish, run down, slag off, slander, traduce 08 badmouth, denounce, vilipend 09 denigrate, disparage 10 calumniate, stigmatize, vituperate

## village

02 pa 03 pah, vil 04 dorp, duar, gram, vill, wick 05 aldea, douar, dowar, kraal, thorp 06 hamlet, kainga, thorpe 07 clachan, endship, kampong, kirkton, outport 08 kirk town, township 09 borghetto, community, rancheria 10 Chautauqua, settlement 14 shopping centre

## villain

04 base 05 baddy, bravo, devil, heavy, knave, rogue 06 baddie, rascal, wretch 07 low-born, villein 08 criminal, escapado, evildoer, scelerat 09 miscreant, reprobate, scelerate, scoundrel, wrongdoer 10 malefactor

*Villains include:*

04 **Case**, **Cass** (Dunstan), **Hyde** (Mr), **Iago**
05 **Bates** (Norman), **Doone** (Carver), **Queeg** (Captain), **Regan**
06 **Lecter** (Dr Hannibal), **Oswald**, **Silver** (Long John)
07 **Antonio**, **Bateman** (Patrick), **Blofeld** (Ernst), **Goneril**
08 **Cornwall** (Duke of), **Injun Joe**
09 **Voldemort** (Lord)
10 **Darth Vader**, **Goldfinger** (Auric), **Richard III**
12 **Aaron the Moor**
14 **Bonnie and Clyde**, **Sauron the Great**

## villainous

03 bad 04 evil, vile 05 cruel 06 gallus, sinful, wicked 07 debased, gallows, heinous, inhuman, roguish, vicious 08 criminal, depraved, fiendish, terrible 09 miscreant, nefarious, notorious 10 degenerate, detestable, iniquitous 11 disgraceful, opprobrious

## villainy

03 sin 04 vice 05 crime 07 badness, knavery, roguery 08 atrocity, baseness, disgrace, iniquity 09 depravity, rascality, turpitude 10 wickedness 11 criminality, delinquency

## vindicate

04 free 05 clear, right, salve 06 acquit, assert, avenge, uphold, verify 07 absolve, darrain, darrayn, deraign, justify, warrant 08 advocate, champion, darraign, darraine,

maintain 09 darraigne, exculpate, exonerate 11 corroborate

## vindication

07 apology, defence, defense, support 08 apologia, theodicy 09 assertion 10 apologetic 11 exculpation, exoneration, extenuation 12 compurgation, verification 13 justification 14 substantiation

## vindictive

08 punitive, spiteful, vengeful, venomous 09 malicious, rancorous 10 implacable, malevolent, revengeful 11 retributive, unforgiving, vindicative

## vine

06 muscat 08 grape ivy, heartpea, muscadel, muscatel 09 ayahuasco, heartseed 10 wonga-wonga 12 winter cherry

## vinegar

05 eisel 06 alegar, eisell, energy, vigour 07 souring 08 wood acid 10 acetic acid

## vintage

03 cru, era, old 04 best, crop, fine, ripe, time, wine, year 05 epoch, prime 06 choice, gather, mature, origin, period, select 07 classic, harvest, quality, supreme, veteran 08 enduring, superior 09 gathering 11 high-quality

## viol

02 gu 03 gju, gue 05 quint, rebec 06 quinte, rebeck

## viola

04 alto 05 gamba, pance, pansy 06 paunce, pawnce, violet

## violate

◇ anagram indicator 04 rape 05 abuse, break, flout, fract, wreck 06 breach, defile, invade, molest, offend, ravish 07 debauch, defiled, despoil, disobey, disrupt, disturb, infract, outrage, profane, vitiate 08 infringe, stuprate 09 desecrate, dishonour 10 contravene, transgress 13 interfere with

## violation

◇ anagram indicator 04 rape 05 abuse, crime 06 breach, mopery 07 offence, outrage 08 invasion, trespass 09 injustice, sacrilege, vitiation 10 defilement, disruption, infraction, spoliation, stupration 11 desecration, profanation 12 infringement, private wrong 13 breach of trust, contravention, transgression

## violence

04 fury, rage, rape 05 force, might, power, wrath 06 frenzy, injury, stoush, tumult 07 cruelty, outrage, passion 08 ferocity, fighting, foul play, savagery, severity, strength, wildness 09 bloodshed, brutality, intensity, roughness, vehemence 10 aggression, fierceness, turbulence 11 hostilities, profanation 12 forcefulness

## violent

◇ anagram indicator 03 het, hot 04 high, rage, rank, rude, wild 05 acute, cruel, fiery, force, great, harsh, heady, hefty, rough, sharp, tough 06 brutal, fierce, savage, severe, stormy, strong, sturdy

**07** drastic, extreme, flaming, furious, intense, riotous, rousing, ruffian, vicious **08** dramatic, forceful, forcible, maddened, powerful, slap-bang, towering, vehement **09** ferocious, hot-headed, impetuous, murderous, turbulent **10** aggressive, headstrong, outrageous, passionate, tumultuous **11** destructive, devastating **12** bloodthirsty, excruciating, ungovernable, unrestrained **15** blood-and-thunder

**violently**
◇ *anagram indicator* **04** rank, slap **05** amain, tough **06** wildly **07** cruelly, greatly, sharply **08** brutally, fiercely, savagely, severely, slap-bang, strongly **09** extremely, intensely, viciously **10** powerfully **11** ferociously, hot-headedly, impetuously **12** aggressively, dramatically **14** uncontrollably, with a vengeance

**violin**
**02** gu **03** gju, gue, kit **05** Amati, strad **06** catgut, fiddle, leader **07** chikara **10** Stradivari **12** Stradivarius
• **violin part 03** nut, rib **04** back, neck, soul **05** belly, f-hole, table **06** bridge, button **07** bass-bar **08** purfling **09** sound post **11** fingerboard

**VIP**
**03** nib, pot **04** lion, star **06** bigwig, top dog **07** big name, big shot, magnate, notable **08** big noise, luminary, somebody **09** big cheese, celebrity, dignitary, personage **11** heavyweight

**viper**
**03** asp **05** adder **08** cerastes, mocassin, moccasin **09** berg-adder, river-jack **10** fer-de-lance **11** rattlesnake

**virago**
**04** fury **05** randy, scold, shrew, vixen **06** amazon, dragon, gorgon, randie, tartar **08** harridan **09** battle-axe, brimstone, termagant, Xanthippe

**virgin**
**03** new **04** girl, maid, pure **05** fresh, Virgo **06** chaste, intact, maiden, modest, vestal **07** Madonna, pucelle **08** celibate, maidenly, spotless, unspoilt, virginal **09** stainless, undefiled, unsullied, untainted, untouched **10** immaculate, unattained **11** unblemished, unexploited

**virginal**
**04** pure **05** fresh, snowy, white **06** chaste, vestal, virgin **08** celibate, maidenly, pristine, spotless **09** inviolate, stainless, undefiled, untouched **10** immaculate **11** uncorrupted, undisturbed **15** parthenogenetic

**Virginia**
**02** VA

**Virgin Islands**
**02** VI **03** BVI, VGB, VIR

**virginity**
**05** honor **06** cherry, honour, purity, virtue **08** chastity, pucelage

**09** innocence **10** chasteness, maidenhead, maidenhood

**virile**
**05** lusty, macho, manly **06** potent, robust, rugged, strong **08** forceful, muscular, vigorous **09** masculine, strapping **10** red-blooded

**virility**
**06** energy, vigour **07** manhood, potency **08** machismo **09** manliness **10** ruggedness **11** masculinity

**virtual**
**07** implied **08** implicit, in effect, virtuous **09** effective, essential, potential, practical **11** prospective **12** in all but name

**virtually**
**06** almost, nearly **08** as good as, in effect **09** in essence **10** more or less **11** effectively, practically **12** in all but name, to all intents

**virtue**
**04** good, plus **05** asset, merit, vertu, worth **06** credit, dharma, honour, valour, vertue **07** benefit, honesty, probity, quality **08** efficacy, goodness, morality, strength **09** advantage, attribute, rectitude, virginity **10** excellence, worthiness **11** saving grace **14** accomplishment, high-mindedness

*The seven virtues:*

**04** hope
**05** faith
**07** charity, justice
**08** prudence
**09** fortitude
**10** temperance

• **by virtue of 07** by way of, owing to **08** by dint of, thanks to **09** because of, by means of **11** on account of **13** with the help of

**virtuosity**
**05** éclat, flair, skill **06** finish, polish **07** bravura, finesse, mastery, panache **08** artistry, wizardry **09** expertise **10** brilliance

**virtuoso**
**06** expert, genius, master **07** maestro, prodigy, skilful **08** dazzling, masterly **09** brilliant, excellent

**virtuous**
**04** good **05** moral **06** chaste, decent, graced, honest, worthy **07** angelic, ethical, upright, virtual **08** innocent **09** blameless, continent, exemplary, righteous **10** honourable, upstanding **11** clean-living, respectable **12** squeaky-clean **13** incorruptible, unimpeachable **14** above suspicion, high-principled, irreproachable **15** beyond suspicion

**virulence**
**05** spite, venom **06** hatred, malice, poison, rancor, spleen **07** rancour, vitriol **08** acrimony, toxicity **09** hostility, malignity **10** antagonism, bitterness, malignancy

**11** malevolence, viciousness **14** vindictiveness

**virulent**
**05** fatal, toxic **06** bitter, deadly, lethal, severe **07** extreme, hostile, intense, vicious, waspish **08** spiteful, venomous **09** injurious, malicious, malignant, poisonous, rancorous, vitriolic **10** blistering, malevolent, pernicious, vindictive **11** acrimonious

**virus**

*Viruses include:*

**03** CDV, DNA, EBV, flu, FLV, HIV, HPV, pox, pro, RNA
**04** arbo, cold, ECHO, filo, HTLV, myxo, rota
**05** Ebola, flavi, hanta, irido, lenti, parvo, phage, retro, rhino
**06** baculo, calici, cowpox, herpes, papova
**07** oncorna, picorna, polyoma, variola
**08** morbilli, Vaccinia, West Nile
**09** Coxsackie, influenza, mimivirus, norovirus, papilloma
**10** hepatitis A, hepatitis B, hepatitis C, Lassa fever, leaf mosaic
**11** chikungunya, coronavirus, Epstein-Barr
**13** bacteriophage, parainfluenza
**14** human papilloma
**15** canine distemper

**visa**
**04** pass, visé **06** carnet, docket, permit **07** licence, warrant **08** passport, sanction **09** green card **10** permission **11** endorsement, safe-conduct **13** authorization, laissez-passer **14** permis de séjour

**vis-à-vis**
**06** facing **08** opposite **09** as regards **10** face-to-face **11** over against **12** in relation to

**viscera**
**04** guts **06** bowels, vitals **07** giblets, innards, insides **08** entrails, gralloch, harigals **09** harigalds **10** intestines

**viscous**
**04** slab **05** gluey, gooey, gummy, stiff, tacky, thick, tough **06** glairy, mucous, sticky, viscid **07** treacly, viscose **08** glareous **09** glaireous, glutinous, resistant **10** gelatinous **12** mucilaginous

**Vishnu**
*see* **incarnation**

**visible**
**04** open **05** clear, overt, plain **06** patent, visual **07** evident, exposed, in sight, obvious, showing **08** apparent, manifest, palpable **10** aspectable, in evidence, noticeable, observable **11** conspicuous, discernible, perceivable, perceptible, unconcealed, undisguised **12** recognizable **15** distinguishable

**visibly**
**06** openly **07** clearly, overtly, plainly **08** patently **09** evidently, obviously

**10** manifestly, noticeably
**11** perceptibly **13** conspicuously

**vision**
**04** idea, look, view **05** dream, ghost,
ideal, image, sight **06** glance, mirage,
seeing, wraith **07** aisling, chimera,
fantasy, imagine, insight, phantom,
picture, spectre **08** daydream,
delusion, eyesight, illusion, phantasm
**09** foresight, intuition, phantosme
**10** apparition, conception, perception,
revelation **11** fata Morgana,
imagination, mental image
**13** hallucination, mental picture **14** far-
sightedness **15** optical illusion

**visionary**
**04** aery, seer **05** aerie **06** dreamy,
mystic, unreal **07** dreamer, prophet,
utopian **08** airdrawn, fanciful, idealist,
illusory, quixotic, romantic, theorist
**09** fantasist, imaginary, moonshiny,
prophetic **10** daydreamer, Don
Quixote, far-sighted, idealistic,
ideologist, ivory-tower, perceptive
**11** impractical, translunary,
unpractical, unrealistic
**13** impracticable, rainbow-chaser

**visit**
**03** gam, see **04** call, chat, mump, stay,
stop, take **05** curse, haunt, pop in,
smite **06** call by, call in, call on, come
by, drop by, look in, look up, plague,
punish, stop by, stop in, take in, wait
on **07** afflict, examine, inflict, inspect,
sojourn, stop off, trouble **08** call in on,
drop in on, frequent, go and see, go
over to, stay with, stop in at, stop over,
wait upon **09** call round, come round,
excursion, first-foot, go round to,
house call, stop off at **10** salutation,
stop over at **13** spend time with

**visitation**
**05** trial, visit **06** blight, ordeal
**08** calamity, disaster, haunting
**10** appearance, infliction, inspection,
punishment **11** catastrophe,
examination **13** manifestation

**visitor**
**05** guest **06** caller **07** company, tourist
**08** manuhiri, stranger **09** traveller
**12** holidaymaker **13** bird of passage

**visor**
**05** sight **06** mesail, mezail, umbrel,
umbril **07** umbrere **08** umbriere

**vista**
**04** view **05** scene **06** avenue, vision
**07** outlook **08** enfilade, panorama,
prospect **11** perspective

**visual**
**05** optic **06** ocular, visive **07** optical,
visible **08** specular **10** observable

**visualize**
**03** see **07** imagine, picture **08** conceive,
envisage, envision

**vital**
**03** key **05** alive, basic **06** lively, living,
urgent, zoetic **07** animate, crucial,
dynamic, vibrant **08** animated, critical,
decisive, forceful, spirited, vigorous
**09** energetic, essential, important,

necessary, requisite, vivacious
**10** imperative, life-giving, quickening
**11** fundamental, significant
**12** invigorating, life-and-death
**13** indispensable

**vitality**
**02** go **03** sap, zap **04** life, zest, zing
**05** juice, oomph **06** bounce, energy,
fizzen, foison, spirit, vigour **07** fusion,
pizzazz, sparkle, stamina, vivency
**08** strength, vivacity **09** animation
**10** exuberance, get-up-and-go,
liveliness **13** vivaciousness

**vitally**
**08** urgently **09** crucially **10** critically,
decisively **11** essentially, importantly
**13** fundamentally, significantly

**vitamin**

*Vitamins include:*

**01** A, B, C, D, E, G, H, K, P
**06** biotin, citrin, niacin
**07** adermin, aneurin, retinol, thiamin
**08** carotene, thiamine
**09** folic acid, menadione
**10** calciferol, pyridoxine, riboflavin,
tocopherol
**11** menaquinone, pteroic acid
**12** ascorbic acid, bioflavonoid,
linoleic acid
**13** linolenic acid, nicotinic acid,
phylloquinone
**14** cyanocobalamin, dehydroretinol,
ergocalciferol, phytomenadione
**15** cholecalciferol, pantothenic acid,
vitamin B complex

**vitiate**
**03** mar **04** harm, rape, ruin **05** blend,
spoil, sully, taint **06** blight, debase,
defile, impair, injure, mucker, weaken
**07** blemish, corrupt, debauch,
deprave, devalue, nullify, pervert,
pollute, violate **09** undermine
**10** adulterate, invalidate
**11** contaminate

**vitriolic**
**06** biting, bitter **07** abusive, acerbic,
caustic, mordant, vicious **08** sardonic,
scathing, venomous, virulent
**09** malicious, trenchant
**11** acrimonious, destructive
**12** vituperative

**vituperate**
**03** nag **04** slag, slam **05** abuse, blame,
knock, slang, slate **06** berate, rebuke,
revile, vilify **07** censure, rubbish, run
down, slag off, upbraid **08** denounce,
reproach **09** castigate **10** blackguard

**vituperation**
**04** flak **05** abuse, blame, stick
**07** censure, obloquy **08** diatribe,
knocking, reproach **09** contumely,
invective, philippic, reprimand
**10** revilement, rubbishing, scurrility
**11** castigation, objurgation, slagging-
off **12** vilification

**vituperative**
**05** harsh **07** abusive **08** sardonic,
scornful **09** insulting, withering
**10** belittling, censorious, derogatory,

scurrilous **11** fulminatory, opprobrious
**12** calumniatory, denunciatory

**vivacious**
**05** jolly, merry, smart **06** bright,
bubbly, chirpy, lively **08** animated,
cheerful, spirited, sportive **09** ebullient,
in spirits, long-lived, sparkling,
sprightly **12** effervescent, high-spirited,
light-hearted

**vivacity**
**02** go **03** fiz, zap **04** brio, élan, fizz, life,
zing **05** oomph **06** energy, spirit, vigour
**07** pizzazz, sparkle, spirits **08** activity,
dynamism, vitality **09** animation,
merriness **10** ebullience, liveliness
**13** effervescence

**vivid**
**04** live, rich, vive **05** clear, lurid, sharp
**06** bright, lively, strong **07** dynamic,
eidetic, glaring, glowing, graphic,
intense, vibrant **08** animated, dazzling,
distinct, dramatic, lifelike, powerful,
spirited, striking, vigorous **09** brilliant,
colourful, graphical, memorable,
pictorial, realistic **11** picturesque

**vividly**
**06** richly **07** clearly **08** brightly, strongly
**09** intensely, memorably, vibrantly
**10** distinctly, powerfully **11** brilliantly,
graphically **12** dramatically,
flamboyantly

**vividness**
**04** glow, life **05** color **06** colour
**07** clarity, realism **08** lucidity,
radiance, strength **09** intensity,
sharpness **10** brightness, brilliancy,
refulgence

**viz**
**02** ie, sc **04** scil, sciz **05** to wit
**06** namely, that is **08** scilicet
**09** videlicet **11** that is to say **12** in other
words, specifically

**vocabulary**
**04** cant **05** idiom, lexis, vocab, words
**07** lexicon **08** glossary, language,
wordbook **09** idioticon, thesaurus
**10** dictionary **11** nomenclator **12** Basic
English, nomenclature

**vocal**
◇ *homophone indicator* **04** oral, said,
sung **05** blunt, frank, noisy **06** phonal,
shrill, spoken, voiced **07** uttered
**08** eloquent, strident **09** expressed,
outspoken, talkative **10** articulate,
expressive, forthright, resounding,
vociferous

**vocalize**
**03** air, say **04** sing, tell, vent, word
**05** speak, state, utter, voice **06** assert,
convey, report **07** declare, express, get
over, put over **08** announce, intimate,
point out **09** enunciate, formulate,
pronounce, put across, ventilate,
verbalize **10** articulate
**11** communicate, give voice to **12** put
into words

**vocally**
**10** eloquently, stridently
**12** articulately, expressively,
forthrightly

## vocation

03 job 04 line, post, role, work 05 craft, trade 06 career, métier, office 07 calling, mission, pursuit 08 business 10 employment, occupation, profession

## vociferous

04 loud 05 blunt, frank, noisy, vocal 08 shouting, strident, vehement 09 clamorous, outspoken 10 forthright, thundering 12 obstreperous

## vociferously

06 loudly 07 bluntly, frankly, noisily, vocally 10 stridently, vehemently 11 outspokenly

## vogue

03 fad 04 mode, rage 05 craze, style, taste, trend 06 custom 07 fashion, the rage 08 the thing 09 the latest 10 popularity 11 fashionable
• in vogue 02 in 06 modish, trendy, with it 07 current, popular, stylish, voguish 09 prevalent 11 fashionable 13 up-to-the-minute

## voice

03 air, say, vox 04 alto, bass, cast, pipe, tone, view, vote, will, wish 05 elect, mezzo, mouth, organ, sound, taish, tenor, utter, words 06 airing, assert, convey, medium, report, rumour, singer, speech, taisch, talk of, throat, tongue, treble 07 acclaim, appoint, declare, divulge, express, mention, opinion, soprano, speak of 08 approval, baritone, castrato, decision, disclose, falsetto, language, nominate 09 contralto, enunciate, utterance, verbalize 10 articulate, expression, give tongue, inflection, instrument, intonation, mouthpiece, reputation 11 contra-tenor, Heldentenor 12 articulation, counter-tenor, mezzo-soprano 13 basso profundo

## void

03 gap 04 emit, lack, null, vain, want 05 abyss, annul, avoid, belch, blank, chasm, clear, drain, eject, empty, inane, inept, space 06 cancel, cavity, devoid, hollow, lacuna, remove, vacant, vacuum 07 dismiss, drained, emptied, invalid, lacking, nullify, opening, rescind, send out, useless, vacuity 08 abnegate, annulled, defecate, deserted, evacuate, nugatory, send away, unfilled 09 blankness, cancelled, clear away, discharge, emptiness, nullified, worthless 10 invalidate, unoccupied, unutilized 11 ineffectual

## volatile

◇ anagram indicator 05 giddy, Latin 06 fickle, fitful, lively 07 erratic, flighty 08 fleeting, restless, skittish, unstable, unsteady, variable, volcanic 09 explosive, irregular, mercurial, transient, unsettled, up and down 10 capricious, changeable, inconstant, short-lived 11 light-winged 13 temperamental, unpredictable

## volatility

09 shakiness 10 fickleness, fitfulness, insecurity 11 flightiness, fluctuation, inconstancy, instability, uncertainty, variability 12 irresolution, unsteadiness 13 unreliability 14 capriciousness, changeableness, precariousness

## volcano

05 salse 08 spitfire 15 burning mountain

*Volcanoes include:*

03 Apo, Awu, Usu
04 Etna, Fuji, Laki, Taal
05 Hekla, Kenya, Mayon, Pelée, Thera, Thira, Unzen
06 Ararat, Erebus, Hudson, Katmai, Sangay
07 Jurullo, Kilauea, Rainier, Ruapehu, Surtsey, Tambora, Vulcano
08 Cotopaxi, Krakatoa, Mauna Kea, Mauna Loa, Pinatubo, St Helens, Tarawera, Vesuvius
09 Aconcagua, Coseguina, El Chichon, Helgafell, Karisimbi, Lamington, Paricutín, Pichincha, Santorini, Stromboli, Tongariro
10 Bezymianny, Chimborazo, Galunggung, La Soufrire, Lassen Peak, Tungurahua
11 Kilimanjaro, Nyamuragira
12 Citlaltépetl, Ixtaccihuatl, Klyuchevskoy, Popocatèpetl
13 Nevado del Ruiz, Ojos del Salado, Soufrire Hills, Volcán El Misti
14 Cerro Incahuasi
15 Haleakala Crater

## vole

08 Arvicola, water dog, water rat 10 water mouse 11 meadow mouse

## volition

04 will 06 choice, option 07 purpose 08 choosing, election, free will, velleity 10 preference, resolution 13 determination
• of your own volition 06 freely 08 by choice 09 purposely, willingly 11 consciously, voluntarily 12 deliberately 13 intentionally, spontaneously 15 of your own accord

## volley

04 hail, tire 05 blast, burst, round, salvo 06 flight, shower 07 barrage, platoon 08 cannonry 09 cannonade, discharge, fusillade 11 bombardment

## volte-face

◇ reversal indicator 05 U-turn 08 reversal 09 about-face, about-turn, turnabout 13 enantiodromia

## voluble

06 chatty, fluent, verbal 07 twining, verbose 09 garrulous, talkative 10 articulate, changeable, loquacious 11 forthcoming

## volume

01 v 03 tom, vol 04 body, book, bulk, code, mass, rise, roll, size, tome 05 codex, noise, sound, space, swell 06 amount, scroll 07 omnibus 08 capacity, decibels, loudness, quantity, solidity 09 aggregate, amplitude 10 dimensions 11 publication

## voluminous

03 big 04 full, huge, vast 05 ample, baggy, bulky, large, roomy 08 spacious 09 billowing, capacious

## voluntarily

06 freely 08 by choice, by my will 09 purposely, willingly 12 deliberately 13 intentionally 15 of your own accord

## voluntary

03 vol 04 free 06 unpaid, votive, willed 07 willing 08 designed, free-will, optional, postlude, unforced 09 volunteer 10 deliberate, gratuitous, purposeful, ultroneous, unsalaried, without pay 11 intentional, spontaneous, unsolicited

## volunteer

03 vol 05 offer 06 tender 07 advance, proffer, propose, suggest 08 activist, do-gooder, fencible 09 home guard, reformado, voluntary 10 put forward 11 come forward, helping hand, step forward 15 voluntary worker
• volunteers 02 TA 03 AVR, CDV, UVF, VAD 04 RNVR

## voluptuary

07 playboy 08 hedonist, sybarite 09 bon vivant, bon viveur, debauchee, epicurean, libertine 10 profligate, sensualist 14 pleasure-seeker

## voluptuous

05 buxom 06 sultry 07 opulent, sensual, shapely 08 enticing, luscious, sensuous 09 luxurious, seductive 10 curvaceous, effeminate, goloptious, goluptious, hedonistic 11 full-figured 13 self-indulgent

## vomit

03 cat 04 barf, boak, bock, boke, honk, puke, sick, spew, spue 05 chuck, heave, retch 06 be sick, emetic, sick up 07 bring up, chuck up, chunder, fetch up, throw up, upchuck 08 disgorge, parbreak 10 egurgitate 11 rainbow yawn, regurgitate

## vomiting

04 puke, sick 06 emesis, puking 07 barfing, spewing 08 chucking, ejection, parbreak, retching, sickness 10 chundering, sick as a dog 11 hyperemesis 12 anacatharsis, haematemesis 13 regurgitation 15 morning sickness

## voracious

04 avid 06 greedy, hungry 07 swinish 08 edacious, gourmand, ravening, ravenous 09 devouring, rapacious 10 gluttonous, insatiable, omnivorous, prodigious, voraginous

## voracity

05 greed 06 hunger 07 avidity, edacity 08 rapacity 12 ravenousness

## vortex

04 eddy 05 whirl 09 maelstrom, whirlpool, whirlwind 10 tourbillon 11 tourbillion

## votary

**06** addict **07** devotee, Paphian, sectary **08** adherent, bacchant, believer, disciple, follower **10** worshipper

## vote

**01** X **02** no **03** aye, nay, yea, yes **04** poll **05** elect, go for, put in, voice **06** ballot, choose, opt for, return **07** declare, propose, re-elect, suggest, write-in **08** division, election, plump for, suffrage **09** franchise **10** plebiscite, referendum **11** ballot paper, show of hands **12** go to the polls **15** enfranchisement
• **vote in** **04** pick **05** adopt, co-opt, elect, voice **06** choose, opt for, prefer, return, select **07** appoint, vote for **08** decide on, plump for **09** designate, determine
• **vote out** **04** oust **06** demote, remove, topple, unseat **07** boot out, dismiss, turf out **08** dethrone, displace **09** overthrow

## voter

**02** no **03** nay, yea, yes **04** vote **05** fagot **06** faggot **07** burgher, citizen **08** balloter, colonist, outvoter **10** franchiser, free person, ten-pounder **11** constituent **13** floating voter

## vouch

• **vouch for** **04** back **06** affirm, assert, assure, avouch, uphold, verify **07** certify, confirm, endorse, support, swear to, warrant **08** attest to, speak for **09** answer for, guarantee **10** asseverate

## voucher

**02** LV **04** chit, note **05** paper, token **06** chitty, coupon, docket, ticket **07** warrant **08** document **09** book token, gift token **11** youth credit

## vouchsafe

**04** cede, give **05** deign, grant, vouch, yield **06** accord, bestow, beteem, confer, impart **07** beteeme **09** guarantee **10** condescend

## vow

**03** vum **04** avow, hest, hete, oath **05** heast, hecht, hight, swear **06** affirm, behote, bename, devote, heaste, pledge **07** behight, profess, promise, protest **08** dedicate **09** nuncupate, undertake **11** nuncupation **12** give your word

## vowel

**01** a, e, i, o, u
• **vowel sound** **05** schwa

## voyage

**04** sail, tour, trip **06** course, cruise, safari, travel **07** journey, odyssey, passage, traffic, travels **08** crossing, put to sea, shipping, traverse **10** enterprise, expedition, navigation **12** rough passage **13** middle passage

## Vulcan

**10** Hephaestus

## vulgar

**03** low **04** lewd, loud, naff, rude, vulg **05** bawdy, broad, cheap, crude, dirty, flash, gaudy, rough, showy, tacky, tarty, usual **06** coarse, common, filthy, flashy, garish, glitzy, kitsch, public, ribald, risqué, tawdry **07** boorish, general, ill-bred, obscene, plebean, popular, uncouth, upstart **08** banausic, gorblimy, impolite, improper, indecent, low-lived, ordinary, plebeian **09** customary, gorblimey, hoi polloi, low-minded, off-colour, offensive, pandemian, prevalent, tasteless, unrefined **10** indecorous, indelicate, suggestive, threepenny, uncultured, vernacular **11** commonplace, distasteful, near the bone, picturesque **12** ostentatious **13** cheap and nasty **15** unsophisticated

## vulgarian

**04** pleb, snob **05** tiger **07** plebean, tigress **08** plebeian

## vulgarity

**07** crudity **08** ribaldry, rudeness **09** crudeness, gaudiness, indecency **10** coarseness, garishness, tawdriness **11** ostentation

## vulnerable

◇ *anagram indicator* **04** open, weak **06** tender **07** exposed **08** helpless, high-risk, in danger, insecure, wide open **09** powerless, pregnable, sensitive, unguarded **11** defenceless, susceptible, unprotected **12** open to attack **15** exposed to danger

## vulture

**05** gripe, grype, urubu **06** condor **08** aasvogel, zopilote **09** gallinazo, gier-eagle, ossifrage **11** carrion crow, lammergeier, lammergeyer **13** turkey buzzard

# W

**W**
07 double-u, whiskey 09 double-you

**wacky**
◇ *anagram indicator* 03 odd 04 daft,
wild, zany 05 crazy, goofy, loony,
loopy, nutty, silly 06 screwy
07 bonkers, erratic, offbeat
09 eccentric 10 irrational
13 unpredictable

**wad**
03 bun, pad 04 ball, cake, hunk, lump,
mass, plug, roll 05 block, chunk,
marry, wodge 06 bundle, dossil,
pledge 07 pledget 08 sandwich,
security

**wadding**
06 filler, lining 07 batting, filling,
packing, padding 08 stuffing 10 cotton
wool 14 quilting-cotton

**waddle**
04 rock, sway 06 clumsy, daidle,
hoddle, toddle, totter, wobble
07 shuffle

**wade**
02 go 04 ford, roll 05 cross, lurch
06 paddle, splash, wallow, welter
08 flounder, traverse
• **wade in**  05 set to 06 tear in 07 pitch
in 08 launch in 10 get stuck in 11 wade
through 12 trawl through 13 plough
through

**wader, wading bird**
*see* **bird**

**wafer**
04 host, seal 05 matza, matzo
06 matzah, matzoh

**waffle**
04 guff, wave 05 gofer, waver
06 babble, gaufer, gaufre, gopher, hot
air, jabber 07 blather, blether, padding,
prattle 08 blathers, blethers, nonsense,
rabbit on, witter on 09 vacillate,
verbosity, wittering, wordiness
10 cotton wool 11 vacillation
12 gobbledygook

**waft**
04 blow, puff, turn, wave, wing
05 carry, drift, float, glide, scent, whiff
06 beckon, breath, breeze, winnow
07 current, draught 08 transmit
09 transport

**wag**
◇ *anagram indicator* 03 bob, jig, nod,
wit 04 bunk, fool, lick, move, rock, stir,
sway, walk, wave 05 clown, comic,
droll, joker, shake, swing, troll
06 fellow, gagman, jester, quiver,
truant, waggle, wiggle, wobble

07 flutter, vibrate 08 banterer,
brandish, comedian, humorist
09 oscillate, play hooky 10 play truant

**wage**
03 fee, pay, war 04 gage, hire, levy,
meed 05 bribe, screw 06 battle,
hazard, pledge, pursue, reward, salary
07 carry on, conduct, contend,
execute, imprest, payment, pension,
returns, stipend 08 earnings, engage in,
penny-fee, pittance, practise
09 allowance, emolument, undertake
10 recompense, wage-packet
12 compensation, remuneration

**wager**
03 bet, lay, wad, wed 04 gage, punt,
risk 05 put on, sport, stake 06 chance,
gamble, hazard, pledge 07 flutter, lay
odds, venture 09 speculate
11 speculation 14 gaming contract

**waggish**
04 arch 05 droll, funny, merry, witty
06 facete, impish, jocose 07 amusing,
comical, jesting, jocular, playful,
puckish, risible, roguish 08 humorous,
sportive 09 bantering, facetious
10 frolicsome 11 mischievous

**waggle**
◇ *anagram indicator* 03 wag 04 wave
05 shake 06 bobble, jiggle, wiggle,
wobble 07 flutter 09 oscillate
12 niddle-noddle

**wagon**
03 car, van 04 cart, corf, drag, dray,
wain 05 buggy, float, gambo, hutch,
lorry, train, truck 06 boxcar, camion,
hopper, telega 07 caisson, chariot,
cocopan, flatcar, fourgon, gondola,
kibitka, tank car, tartana 08 carriage,
democrat, schooner 09 low-loader
10 freight-car, luggage-van 15 prairie
schooner
• **on the wagon**  02 TT 06 tee-tee
08 teetotal

**waif**
04 puff, weft 05 stray, wefte 06 orphan,
streak, urchin 07 wasting 09 foundling,
neglected, wandering 10 ragamuffin

**wail**
02 io 03 cry, sob 04 bawl, howl, keen,
moan, weep, yowl 05 groan
06 bemoan, lament, yammer
07 ululate, vagitus, weeping
08 complain 09 complaint, ululation

**waistcoat**
04 vest 05 gilet 06 bodice, bolero,
jerkin 07 surcoat

**wait**
03 spy 04 bide, halt, hold, rest, stay,
tend 05 abide, await, delay, lurch,
pause, stand, tarry, watch 06 ambush,
attend, escort, expect, hang in, hang
on, hold-up, linger, remain, sit out,
taihoa 07 stand by 08 hang fire,
hesitate, hold back, interval, sentinel,
watchman 09 bide tryst, hang about
10 hang around, hesitation 12 bide
your time 13 lick your chops
• **wait on**  03 see 04 tend 05 serve
06 attend 07 work for 08 attend to
09 look after 10 minister to, take care of

**waiter, waitress**
04 host, tray 05 Nippy 06 busboy,
butler, carhop, commis, garçon,
mousmé, Nippie, salver, server
07 busgirl, hostess, maître d',
mousmee, pannier, steward, waitron
08 watchman 09 attendant, sommelier
10 stewardess 12 maître d'hôtel

**waive**
04 cede 05 avoid, defer, evade, forgo,
yield 06 forego, give up, ignore, reject,
resign, vacate 07 abandon, forsake, put
away 08 postpone, renounce, set aside
09 do without, surrender 10 relinquish
12 dispense with, strain a point

**waiver**
08 deferral 09 remission, surrender
10 abdication, disclaimer
11 abandonment, resignation
12 postponement, renunciation
14 relinquishment

**wake**
04 fire, goad, path, prod, rear, rise, stir,
warn, wash, whet 05 alert, arise,
awake, egg on, get up, rouse, track,
trail, train, vigil, waken, watch, waves
06 arouse, awaken, come to, excite,
notify, revive, signal, stir up
07 animate, funeral 08 activate,
backwash, festival, lichwake,
lykewake, serenade 09 aftermath,
galvanize, reanimate, stimulate
10 bring round, death-watch 11 make
aware of 13 become aware of 15 make
conscious of

**wakeful**
04 wary 05 alert 06 waking 07 heedful,
rousing 08 restless, vigilant, wakerife,
watchful, waukrife 09 attentive,
awakening, insomniac, observant,
sleepless 10 unsleeping

**wakefulness**
05 vigil 08 insomnia 09 vigilance
12 restlessness, watchfulness
13 attentiveness, sleeplessness

**waken**
04 fire, rise, stir, wake, whet 05 awake,
evoke, get up, rouse 06 arouse,
awaken, excite, ignite, kindle, stir up,
waking 07 animate, enliven, quicken
08 activate 09 galvanize, stimulate

**Wales**
*see* **council; town**

**walk**
03 lag, leg, pad, wag, way 04 beat,
foot, gait, hike, hump, lane, lead, limp,
mall, move, pace, path, pawn, plod,
step, trek, trog, turn, xyst, yomp
05 allée, alley, amble, drive, flock,
guide, march, paseo, round, route,
steps, stump, track, trail, tramp, tread,
usher 06 avenue, behave, depart,
escort, foot it, hoof it, pasear, ramble,
rounds, sashay, spread, stride, stroll,
trapes, trudge, xystos, xystus
07 alameda, berceau, circuit, conduct,
gallery, passage, pathway, saunter,
terrace, traipse, walkway 08 ambulate,
carriage, footpath, frescade, go on
foot, pavement, shepherd, sidewalk,
traverse, withdraw 09 accompany,

boulevard, circulate, disappear, esplanade, promenade **10** ambulatory, pad the hoof, pipe-opener **11** perambulate **13** hunting-ground, pedestrianize **15** stretch your legs
• **walk off with, walk away with 03** bag, nip **04** lift, nick, whip **05** filch, pinch, steal, swipe **06** nobble, pocket **07** knock up, snaffle **08** knock off, liberate, souvenir **09** duckshove, go off with, relieve of **10** run off with **11** make off with **14** help yourself to
• **walk of life 04** area, line **05** arena, field, trade **06** career, course, métier, sphere **07** calling, pursuit **08** activity, vocation **10** background, occupation, profession
• **walk out 05** leave **06** mutiny, revolt, strike **07** protest **08** stop work **09** down tools **10** go on strike
• **walk out on 04** dump, jilt **06** desert **07** abandon, forsake **08** run out on **15** leave high and dry, leave in the lurch
• **walk over 05** abuse, cross **06** misuse **07** oppress **08** ill-treat, impose on, traverse **09** profiteer, trample on **10** manipulate **12** take for a ride **13** take liberties **14** play off against, pull a fast one on **15** take advantage of
• **walk unsteadily 04** halt, stot **06** daddle, hobble, paddle, totter **07** shamble, stumble

### walker
**03** ped **05** hiker **06** fuller, ganger **07** rambler, vagrant **08** forester **09** ambulator **10** colporteur, pedestrian **11** stick insect

### walking-stick
**04** cane **05** waddy **06** kebbie, waddie **07** hickory **08** ash-plant **10** blackthorn **11** Malacca-cane **12** Penang-lawyer
*See also* **stick**

### walk-out
**06** revolt, strike **07** protest **08** stoppage **09** rebellion

### walkover
**02** WO **05** cinch **06** doddle **07** easy win, laugher **08** cakewalk, pushover **10** child's play **11** easy victory, piece of cake

### walkway
**04** lane, path, road **05** track **07** passage, pathway **08** footpath, pavement, sidewalk **09** bush track, esplanade, promenade

### wall
**02** wa' **04** mure

*Wall types include:*

**03** dam, sea
**04** dike, dyke
**05** block, brick, death, fence, hedge, inner, mural, party
**06** bailey, cavity, garden, paling, screen, shield
**07** barrier, bulwark, curtain, divider, parapet, rampart, sea-wall
**08** abutment, bulkhead, buttress, dry-stone, obstacle,

palisade, stockade
**09** barricade, enclosure, partition, retaining
**10** embankment
**11** breeze-block, load-bearing, outer bailey
**13** fortification, stud partition
**14** flying buttress

*Walls include:*

**05** Great
**06** Berlin
**07** Wailing, Western
**08** Antonine, Hadrian's

• **go to the wall 04** fail, flop, fold **05** slump **06** finish, go bust **07** founder, go under **08** collapse **09** break down **11** come to an end, fall through **12** disintegrate **13** come to nothing
• **wall in 03** pen **04** cage, hold, ring, wrap **05** bound, fence, frame, hedge, hem in **06** circle, corral, shut in **07** close in, confine, enclose, envelop **08** encircle, surround **09** encompass **10** circummure **12** circumscribe

### wallaby
**06** quokka, tammar **13** brush kangaroo

### wallet
**04** case **05** pouch, purse **06** folder, holder **08** bill-fold, notecase, pochette **10** pocketbook

### wallop
**03** hit, lam **04** bash, beat, beer, belt, blow, bonk, drub, kick, lick, rout, swat, whop **05** clout, crush, paste, pound, punch, smack, swipe, thump, whack **06** batter, buffet, defeat, gallop, hammer, pummel, strike, thrash, thwack **07** clobber, heavily, noisily, trounce **08** flounder, vanquish
*See also* **beer; blow**

### wallow
**03** lie **04** bask, blow, loll, roll, wade **05** enjoy, glory, heave, lurch, revel, surge **06** muddle, relish, splash, tumble, well up, welter **07** delight, indulge, slubber **08** flounder **09** luxuriate

### walrus
**05** morse **06** sea cow **08** seahorse **09** rosmarine

### wan
**04** dark, pale, took, weak **05** ashen, bleak, faint, lurid, pasty, waxen, weary, white **06** feeble, gained, gloomy, pallid, sickly **07** anaemic, ghastly **08** mournful **09** washed out, whey-faced **10** colourless **11** discoloured

### wand
**03** rod **04** mace, twig, vare **05** baton, sprig, staff, stick **06** batoon **07** sceptre, thyrsus **08** caduceus **09** goldstick

### wander
◇ *anagram indicator* **03** err, gad **04** moon, rave, roam, roll, rove, veer, wend **05** amble, drift, mooch, mouch, prowl, range, ratch, stray, taver, vague,

wheel **06** babble, cruise, depart, gibber, maraud, mither, moider, ramble, streel, stroam, stroll, swerve, taiver, wilder **07** deviate, digress, diverge, maunder, meander, moither, pilgrim, saunter, swan off, traipse **08** aberrate, bewilder, divagate, go astray, squander, straggle, stravaig, traverse, turn away **09** bat around, excursion, expatiate, forwander, kick about, moon about **10** kick around, moon around, pilgrimage, ratch about **11** extravagate, lose your way, peregrinate, vagabondize **12** stooge around, talk nonsense **14** walk the streets

### wanderer
**04** waif **05** Gypsy, nomad, rover, stray **06** nomade, ranger **07** drifter, erratic, pilgrim, rambler, vagrant, voyager **08** prodigal, stroller, vagabond, wayfarer **09** itinerant, straggler, traveller **12** rolling stone

### wandering
**03** gad **04** roam, rove, waff, waif **05** drift, error **06** errant, erring, flight, roving **07** erratic, journey, meander, nomadic, odyssey, strayed, travels, vagrant **08** aberrant, drifting, errantry, homeless, rambling, rootless, vagabond, voyaging **09** departure, deviation, erroneous, evagation, excursion, itinerant, migratory, strolling, unsettled, walkabout, wayfaring **10** aberration, digression, divergence, journeying, meandering, solivagant, travelling **11** extravagant, noctivagant, peripatetic **13** peregrination, peregrinatory **14** circumforanean **15** circumforaneous

### wane
**03** dim, ebb **04** drop, fade, fail, fall, sink, welk **05** abate, decay, droop, welke **06** fading, lessen, shrink, vanish, weaken, wither **07** atrophy, decline, dwindle, failure, sinking, subside **08** contract, decrease, diminish, fade away, peter out, taper off **09** abatement, dwindling, lessening, weakening **10** diminution, subsidence **11** contraction, tapering off **12** degeneration
• **on the wane 06** ebbing, fading **08** dropping, moribund **09** declining, dwindling, lessening, subsiding, weakening, withering **11** obsolescent, on the way out, tapering off **12** degenerating, on the decline **13** deteriorating, on its last legs

### wangle
**03** fix **04** work **06** fiddle, manage, scheme **07** arrange, falsify, finagle, pull off **08** contrive, engineer **09** manoeuvre **10** manipulate **12** wheel and deal

### want
**04** lack, like, lust, miss, mole, need, pine, will, wish **05** covet, crave, fancy **06** besoin, dearth, defect, demand, desire, hunger, penury, pining, thirst **07** absence, blemish, call for, craving, hope for, long for, longing, paucity,

pine for, poverty, require **08** appetite, coveting, feel like, scarcity, shortage, yearn for, yearning **09** be without, hunger for, indigence, privation, thirst for **10** deficiency, desiderate, feebleness, inadequacy, scantiness **11** destitution, requirement **13** be deficient in, insufficiency

**wanting**

**03** for **04** less, poor **05** needy, short **06** absent, faulty **07** lacking, missing, without **08** amissing, desirous **09** defective, deficient, imperfect **10** inadequate **11** substandard **12** insufficient, unacceptable **13** disappointing **14** not up to scratch, unsatisfactory

**wanton**

◇ *anagram indicator* **03** gay, rig **04** idle, lewd, nice, rake, rash, roué, slut, tart, wild **05** cadgy, whore **06** frisky, frolic, harlot, impure, jovial, kidgie, lecher, toyish, trifle, unfair, unjust, unruly **07** amorous, Don Juan, immoral, riggish, smicker, toysome, trifler, trollop, twigger **08** arrogant, Casanova, immodest, insolent, petulant, prodigal, reckless, skittish, sportive, strumpet **09** abandoned, arbitrary, debauchee, dissipate, dissolute, lecherous, libertine, malicious, merciless, pointless, shameless **10** capricious, cork-heeled, dissipated, gratuitous, groundless, lascivious, malevolent, prostitute, unprovoked, voluptuary **11** extravagant, promiscuous **12** unmanageable, unrestrained **13** self-indulgent, undisciplined, unjustifiable

**war**

**04** army **05** clash, excel, fight, worse, worst **06** combat, defeat, enmity, stoush, strife, strive **07** contend, contest, ill-will, make war, wage war, warfare **08** campaign, conflict, fighting **09** bloodshed **10** antagonism, contention, take up arms **11** cross swords, hostilities **13** confrontation

*War types include:*

**03** hot
**04** cold, germ, holy
**05** blitz, civil, jihad, total, trade, world
**06** ambush, attack, battle, jungle, nerves, trench
**07** assault, limited, nuclear, private
**08** chemical, intifada, invasion, skirmish, struggle
**09** attrition, guerrilla
**10** asymmetric, biological, biowarfare, blitzkrieg, engagement, manoeuvres, resistance
**11** bombardment
**12** asymmetrical, state of siege
**13** armed conflict, counter-attack

*Wars include:*

**03** Cod
**04** 1812, Boer, Gulf, Iraq, Sikh, Zulu
**05** Chaco, Dutch, Great, Maori, Opium, Punic, Roses, World
**06** Afghan, Balkan, Barons', Gallic,

Indian, Korean, Six-Day, Trojan, Vendée, Winter
**07** Bishops', Crimean, Italian, Mexican, Pacific, Persian, Servile, Vietnam
**08** Crusades, Football, Iran-Iraq, Peasants', Religion, Ten Years'
**09** Black Hawk, Falklands, Yom Kippur
**10** Devolution, Jenkins' Ear, Napoleonic, Peninsular, Queen Anne's, Seven Years', Suez Crisis
**11** Arab-Israeli, Eighty Years', Indian Civil, King Philip's, Thirty Years'
**12** English Civil, Hundred Years', Independence, King William's, Russian Civil, Russo-Finnish, Russo-Turkish, Spanish Civil
**13** American Civil, Grand Alliance, Russo-Japanese
**14** Boxer Rebellion, Franco-Prussian, Indian Uprising, July Revolution, Triple Alliance
**15** Easter Rebellion

See also **battle**
• **war cry** **04** hoop, word **05** havoc, whoop **06** banzai, slogan **07** war song **08** Geronimo **09** alalagmos, battle-cry, watchword **11** rallying-cry
• **war god** **03** Tiu, Tiw, Tyr **04** Mars **08** Quirinus

**warble**

**03** cry **04** call, sing, song **05** carol, chirl, chirp, trill, yodel **06** quaver, record, relish **07** chirrup, rellish, twitter

**ward**

**04** area, care, fend, room, unit, zone **05** guard, minor, parry, pupil, spike, watch **06** charge **07** cubicle, custody, lookout, protégé, quarter **08** district, division, precinct, protégée **09** apartment, dependant, maternity **10** protection, sanatorium, sanitarium **11** compartment **12** guardianship
• **ward off** **04** fend, wear, weir **05** avert, avoid, block, dodge, evade, parry, repel **06** defend, shield, thwart **07** beat off, deflect, fend off, forfend **08** stave off, turn away **09** drive back, forestall, turn aside **11** averruncate

**warden**

**06** keeper, ranger, regent, warder **07** curator, janitor, steward **08** bearward, guardian, meter man, overseer, sentinel, watchman **09** caretaker, concierge, constable, custodian, meter maid, protector **10** gatekeeper, supervisor **11** housekeeper, lollipop man **12** lollipop lady **13** administrator, lollipop woman **14** superintendent

**warder**

**05** guard, screw **06** jailer, keeper, warden **08** wardress **09** beefeater, custodian **13** prison officer

**wardrobe**

**04** robe **06** attire, closet, locker, outfit **07** almirah, apparel, armoire, cabinet, clothes **08** cupboard, garments **09** garderobe

**warehouse**

**04** hong, shed **05** depot, store **06** bodega, godown, lock-up **07** store up **08** entrepot **09** goods shed, stockroom **10** depository, repository, storehouse **11** freight shed

**wares**

**05** goods, stock, stuff **07** brokery, pedlary, produce **08** ironware, products **11** charcuterie, commodities, merchandise

**warfare**

**03** war **04** arms **05** blows **06** battle, combat, strife **07** contest, discord, feuding **08** campaign, conflict, fighting, struggle **10** contention **11** hostilities **13** confrontation, passage of arms

**warily**

**06** cagily **07** charily **08** gingerly, uneasily, with care **09** carefully, guardedly **10** cautiously, hesitantly, vigilantly, watchfully **12** suspiciously **13** circumspectly, distrustfully **14** apprehensively

**wariness**

**04** care **06** cautel, unease **07** caution **08** caginess, distrust, prudence, wariment **09** alertness, attention, foresight, hesitancy, suspicion, vigilance **10** discretion **11** carefulness, heedfulness, mindfulness **12** apprehension, watchfulness **13** defensiveness **14** circumspection

**warlike**

**07** hawkish, hostile, martial **08** cavalier, militant, military **09** bellicose, combative **10** aggressive, battailous, pugnacious, unfriendly **11** belligerent **12** antagonistic, bloodthirsty, militaristic, warmongering

**warlock**

**05** demon, witch **06** wizard **08** conjurer, magician, sorcerer **09** enchanter **11** necromancer

**warm**

**03** het, hot, lew, sun **04** beat, fine, heat, kind, luke, melt, rich, stir, thaw **05** angry, balmy, calid, close, eager, fresh, rouse, sunny, tepid, toast **06** ardent, caring, excite, genial, hearty, heated, heat up, kindly, lively, loving, mellow, please, reheat, tender, toasty **07** affable, amiable, amorous, animate, beating, cheer up, cordial, delight, earnest, enliven, excited, fervent, glowing, intense, liven up, sincere, thermal, zealous **08** cheerful, friendly, interest, lukewarm, make warm, relaxing, vehement, well-to-do **09** harassing, heartfelt, stimulate, strenuous, temperate **10** hospitable, indelicate, passionate **11** comfortable, kind-hearted, sympathetic **12** affectionate, enthusiastic **15** put some life into
• **warm to** **11** begin to like
• **warm up** **04** heat **07** prepare **08** exercise, limber up, loosen up

## warm-blooded
**04** rash **06** ardent, lively **07** earnest, fervent **08** spirited **09** emotional, excitable, impetuous, vivacious **10** hot-blooded, passionate **11** endothermic, homothermal, homothermic **12** enthusiastic, homothermous, idiothermous

## warm-hearted
**04** kind **06** ardent, genial, hearty, kindly, loving, tender **07** cordial **08** generous **11** kind-hearted, sympathetic **12** affectionate **13** compassionate, tender-hearted

## warmonger
**04** hawk **09** aggressor **10** militarist **12** sabre-rattler

## warmth
**04** care, fire, glow, heat, love, zeal **05** ardor, flame **06** ardour **07** fervour, hotness, passion, unction **08** fervency, kindness, sympathy, warmness **09** affection, eagerness, intensity, sincerity, vehemence **10** compassion, cordiality, enthusiasm, kindliness, tenderness **11** hospitality **12** friendliness

## warn
**03** vor **04** tell, urge **05** alert, awarn, shore **06** advise, exhort, forbid, inform, notify, rebuke, summon, tip off **07** caution, command, counsel, let know, portend, presage, reprove, warrant **08** admonish, forewarn, instruct **09** factorize, premonish, reprimand **10** give notice **13** sound the alarm **14** put on your guard

## warning
**04** call, hint, omen, sign, wire **05** alarm, alert **06** advice, augury, caveat, lesson, notice, signal, threat, tip-off **07** caution, counsel, example, ominous, portent, presage, summons **08** monition, monitory **10** admonition, admonitory, cautionary, wake-up call, yellow card **11** information, premonition, premonitory, threatening **12** notification **13** advance notice
*See also* **alarm; signal**
• **expression of warning** **03** nix, now **04** cave, fore, gang, mind **06** timber **07** Achtung, you wait! **08** gardyloo **09** scaldings

## warp
◊ *anagram indicator* **04** bend, bent, bias, cast, kink, turn **05** kedge, quirk, throw, twist **06** buckle, defect, deform, spring, swerve **07** contort, corrupt, deviate, distort, entwine, pervert **08** miscarry, misshape **09** deviation **10** contortion, distortion, perversion **11** deformation **12** irregularity

## warrant
**04** able, back, fiat, keep, warn **05** allow, proof, sepad, swear **06** affirm, assure, avouch, behote, defend, excuse, pardon, permit, pledge, uphaud, uphold **07** approve, behight, call for, caption, certify, consent, declare, defence, deserve, empower, endorse, entitle, justify, licence, license, precept, predict, presage, promise, protect, require, support, voucher **08** defender, detainer, guaranty, mittimus, sanction, security, transire, vouch for, warranty **09** answer for, assurance, authority, authorize, consent to, diligence, execution, guarantee, underclay, vouchsafe **10** commission, permission, underwrite, validation **11** necessitate **12** bench-warrant, death warrant, fugie-warrant, peace-warrant **13** authorization, justification, search warrant **14** lettre de cachet
• **warrant officer** **02** WO **03** CSM, RSM **04** bos'n **05** bosun **09** boatswain

## warrantable
**05** legal, right **06** lawful, proper **09** allowable, estimable, excusable, necessary **10** defensible, reasonable **11** accountable, justifiable, permissible

## warranty
**04** bond **06** pledge **08** contract, covenant, evidence **09** assurance, guarantee **11** certificate **13** authorization, justification

## warring
◊ *anagram indicator* **05** at war **07** hostile, opposed **08** fighting, opposing **09** combatant, embattled **10** contending **11** belligerent, conflicting **14** at daggers drawn

## warrior
**05** brave, ghazi **06** Amazon, haiduk, wardog, warman **07** berserk, fighter, heyduck, soldier, warlock, warwolf **08** champion, warhorse **09** berserker, combatant **11** fighting man

## warship
**03** cog, ram **06** galley **07** cruiser, man-o'-war **08** man-of-war **09** blockship, destroyer, first-rate **10** battleship, turret ship **11** capital ship, dreadnaught, dreadnought, torpedo boat **13** battle-cruiser

## wart
**03** wen **04** lump **06** anbury, growth **07** verruca **09** keratosis, papilloma **10** angleberry **11** excrescence **12** protuberance

## wary
**04** cagy, ware **05** alert, aware, cagey, chary, leery, tenty **06** tentie **07** careful, guarded, heedful, prudent, thrifty **08** cautious, vigilant, watchful **09** attentive, wide-awake **10** on the alert, suspicious **11** circumspect, distrustful, on your guard **12** on the lookout **14** circumspective

## wash
**03** fen, lap, lip, mop, wet **04** bath, beat, coat, dash, flow, hold, lave, lick, roll, sind, slop, soak, synd, wave, wipe **05** bathe, clean, layer, marsh, rinse, scrub, souse, stain, stick, sujee, surge, sweep, swell, swill **06** douche, lotion, shower, sloosh, soogee, soogie, soojey, splash, sponge, stream **07** cleanse, coating, launder, laundry, moisten, shampoo, stand up, washing **08** cleaning, swab down **09** cleansing, freshen up, have a bath, have a wash, hold water **10** be accepted, laundering, pass muster **11** be plausible, carry weight, have a shower **12** bear scrutiny, be believable, be convincing, get cleaned up **15** bear examination
• **wash your hands of** **07** abandon **08** give up on

## washed-out
**03** wan **04** flat, pale **05** all in, ashen, drawn, faded, spent, weary **06** pallid **07** anaemic, drained, haggard, worn-out **08** blanched, bleached, dog-tired, fatigued, tired-out **09** exhausted, knackered **10** colourless, lacklustre **14** dead on your feet

## Washington
**02** WA **04** Wash

## washout
**04** flop, mess **06** fiasco **07** debacle, failure, no-hoper **08** disaster **11** lead balloon **14** disappointment

## wasp
**05** vespa **06** hornet **07** gallfly **08** ruby-tail **09** cuckoo fly, mud dauber, velvet ant **12** yellow jacket

## waspish
**05** cross, testy **06** bitchy, crabby, grumpy, touchy **07** crabbed, grouchy, peevish, prickly **08** captious, critical, petulant, snappish, spiteful, virulent **09** crotchety, irascible, irritable **11** bad-tempered, ill-tempered **12** cantankerous

## wastage
**04** loss **05** decay **07** atrophy **08** draining, marasmus **10** emaciation, exhausting **11** dissipation, squandering **12** degeneration **14** frittering away

## waste
◊ *anagram indicator* **03** nub **04** bare, blow, crud, gash, kill, knub, lose, loss, pass, pine, rape, raze, ruin, sack, slag, vain, wild **05** abuse, bleak, drain, dregs, dross, empty, erode, extra, husks, offal, scrap, slops, spend, spill, spoil, trash **06** barren, debris, desert, dismal, dreary, expend, injure, lavish, litter, misuse, ravage, refuse, shrink, slurry, unused, wither **07** atrophy, consume, despoil, destroy, exhaust, garbage, neglect, pillage, rubbish, ruinous, shrivel, splurge, useless **08** cast away, desolate, effluent, emaciate, lay waste, left-over, misspend, rejected, squander, unwanted **09** depredate, devastate, dissipate, go through, leftovers, profusion, recrement, throw away, worthless **10** desolation, devastated, dilapidate, get through, impoverish, unoccupied **11** consumption, destruction, dissipation, expenditure, fritter away, offscouring, prodigality, prodigalize, squandering, superfluous, uninhabited **12** extravagance, offscourings, uncultivated, unproductive, unprofitable, wastefulness **13** supernumerary **14** misapplication **15** become emaciated
*See also* **kill**

## wasted

◇ *anagram indicator* **04** high, lost, weak **05** drunk, gaunt, spent **07** useless, war-worn, worn-out **08** ill-spent, needless, shrunken, weakened, withered **09** atrophied, emaciated, exhausted, washed-out **10** shrivelled, squandered, unrequired **11** unexploited, unnecessary **12** down the drain

## wasteful

**04** vain **06** lavish **07** ruinous **08** desolate, prodigal, wastfull, wastrife **09** unthrifty, wasterife **10** profitless, profligate, thriftless **11** extravagant, improvident, spendthrift, uninhabited **12** uneconomical, unfrequented

## wasteland

**04** fell, void, wild **05** waste, wilds **06** desert, tundra **07** thwaite **08** badlands **09** emptiness **10** barrenness, wilderness

## wasting

**05** tabes **07** atrophy **08** marasmic, marasmus, phthisis, syntexis **09** cirrhosis, consuming, symptosis **10** colliquant, destroying, emaciating, enfeebling, tabescence **11** colliquable, consumption, consumptive, devastating, tabefaction **12** colliquative, contabescent

## wastrel

**04** waif **05** idler, waste **06** feeble, loafer, refuse, skiver **07** goof-off, lounger, shirker **08** layabout **09** lazybones **10** malingerer, ne'er-do-well, profligate **11** spendthrift **14** good-for-nothing

## watch

**03** eye, nit, see, spy **04** espy, heed, keep, mark, mind, nark, note, scan, tend, tout, view, wait, wake, ward **05** await, clock, flock, guard, scout, spial, vigil **06** follow, gape, gaze at, look at, look on, look to, notice, peer at, perv at, regard, shadow, survey, ticker **07** inspect, look out, lookout, monitor, observe, outlook, overeye, protect, stare at **08** repeater, sentinel, take care, take heed, tick-tick **09** alertness, attention, be careful, look after, timepiece, vigilance **10** inspection, keep tabs on, stemwinder, take care of, wristwatch **11** chronometer, contemplate, keep an eye on, observation, superintend, supervision **12** pay attention, pernoctation, surveillance, watchfulness
*See also* **clock**
• **watch out 04** mind **06** notice **07** keep nit, look out **08** cockatoo, keep cave, stand nit **10** be vigilant **12** keep a lookout **13** stand cockatoo
• **watch over 04** mind, tend, ward **05** guard **06** defend, shield **07** protect, shelter **08** preserve, sentinel, shepherd **09** look after, supervise **10** take care of **11** keep an eye on **14** stand guard over

## watchdog

**07** monitor **08** guard dog, guardian, house-dog **09** custodian, inspector, ombudsman, protector, regulator, vigilante **10** scrutineer **11** housekeeper

## watcher

**03** spy **05** Argus **06** viewer **07** lookout, witness **08** audience, looker-on, observer, onlooker **09** spectator **10** eyewitness, televiewer

## watchful

**04** wary **05** alert, chary **07** guarded, heedful **08** cautious, open-eyed, vigilant, wakerife, waukrife **09** adviceful, attentive, avizefull, observant, wide awake **10** suspicious **11** circumspect, on your guard **12** on the lookout, on the qui vive

## watchfulness

**07** caution **08** wariness **09** alertness, attention, dragonism, suspicion, vigilance **10** observance **11** heedfulness **12** cautiousness **13** attentiveness **14** circumspection, suspiciousness

## watchman

**03** nit **04** wait **05** guard **06** waiter **07** Charley, Charlie, rug gown, wakeman **08** chokidar, cockatoo, night-man, sentinel **09** caretaker, chowkidar, custodian, nitkeeper **10** speculator **13** security guard

## watchword

**03** cry **05** maxim, motto **06** byword, signal, slogan **07** nayword, tag line **08** buzz word, password **09** battle-cry, catchword, magic word, principle **10** shibboleth **11** catchphrase, rallying-cry

## water

**02** aq, ea **03** eau, sea, wet **04** aqua, hose, lake, rain, soak **05** class, douse, drink, flood, oasis, ocean, river, spray **06** dampen, drench, lustre, saliva, stream **07** current, moisten, quality, torrent **08** flooding, irrigate, moisture, saturate, sprinkle, surround **09** Adam's wine, waterhole **10** excellence **12** transparency
*See also* **lake; river; sea**

*Mineral water brands include:*

**05** Evian®
**06** Buxton®, Ty Nant®, Vittel®, Volvic®
**07** Perrier®
**08** Aqua Pura®
**10** Strathmore®
**13** Pennine Spring®, San Pellegrino®
**14** Highland Spring®

• **hold water 04** hold, wash, work **05** stand, stick **06** cohere, hold up **07** stand up **08** convince, ring true **09** make sense **10** be accepted **11** be plausible, carry weight, pass the test, remain valid **12** bear scrutiny, be believable, be convincing **15** bear examination
• **water carrier 06** bhisti **07** bheesty, bhistee **08** Aquarius, bheestie
• **water down 03** mix **04** thin **06** dilute, soften, weaken **07** qualify **08** mitigate, moderate, play down, tone down **09** attenuate, soft-pedal **10** adulterate

## watercourse

**04** burn, khor, lead, nala, rean, reen, wadi **05** brook, canal, ditch, donga, drain, nalla, nulla, rhine, rhyne, river, shott, whelm **06** arroyo, nallah, nullah, spruit, stream **07** channel, pughole **09** sunk fence **12** water-channel
*See also* **river**

## waterfall

**03** lin **04** drop, fall, foss, linn, salt **05** chute, falls, force, rapid, sault, shoot, shute, spout **06** lasher, rapids **07** cascade, chignon, necktie, torrent **08** cataract, overfall **10** salmon leap

*Waterfalls include:*

**04** Huka
**05** Angel, Della, Glass, Pilao, Tysse
**06** Boyoma, Iguaçu, Krimml, Ormeli, Ribbon, Tugela
**07** Mtarazi, Niagara, Stanley, Thukela
**08** Cuquenán, Gavarnie, Gullfoss, Itatinga, Kaieteur, Takkakaw, Victoria, Wallaman, Yosemite
**09** Churchill, Dettifoss, Giessbach, Multnomah, Staubbach
**10** Cleve-Garth, Sutherland, Wollomombi
**11** Reichenbach, Trummelbach
**12** Cusiana River, Paulo Alfonso, Silver Strand
**13** Mardalsfossen, Tyssetrengane, Upper Yosemite, Vestre Mardola

## waterproof, waterproof material

**03** mac **04** mack **05** loden **06** anorak, arctic, cagoul, camlet, coated, kagool, kagoul, poncho **07** Barbour®, cagoule, camelot, jaconet, kagoule, oilskin, proofed, slicker, tanking **09** damp-proof, macintosh, sou'wester, tarpaulin **10** impervious, mackintosh, rubberized, tarpauling, trench coat, watertight **11** Barbour® coat, gutta-percha, impermeable **12** antigropelos **13** antigropeloes, Barbour® jacket **14** water-repellent, water-resistant

## watertight

**04** firm **05** sound **06** sealed, stanch **07** staunch **08** airtight, flawless, hermetic **09** foolproof **10** waterproof **11** impregnable **12** indisputable, unassailable

## watery

**03** wet **04** damp, thin, weak **05** blear, eager, fluid, moist, runny, soggy, vapid, washy **06** bleary, liquid, serous, sloppy **07** aqueous, diluted, hydrous, insipid, shilpit **08** hydatoid, skinking, squelchy **09** tasteless **10** wishy-washy **11** adulterated, flavourless, transparent, watered-down

## wave

◇ *anagram indicator* **03** sea, waw **04** curl, flap, flow, foam, rash, rush, sign, stir, surf, sway, waff, waft, wawe **05** crimp, drift, float, flood, flote, froth, hover, shake, surge, sweep, swell, swing, trend, waver **06** beckon, billow,

comber, direct, quiver, ripple, roller, signal, stream, waffle **07** breaker, current, decuman, feather, flutter, gesture, impulse, soliton, tide rip, upsurge, wavelet **08** backwash, brandish, flourish, increase, indicate, movement, outbreak, tendency, undulate, whitecap **09** tidal wave, vacillate **10** crispation, supersonic, undulation, white horse **11** beachcomber, gesticulate, ground swell
• **make waves** **12** cause trouble **13** disturb things, stir up trouble
• **wave aside** **05** spurn **06** reject, shelve **07** dismiss **08** set aside **09** disregard **10** brush aside **15** pour cold water on
• **wave down** **06** summon **08** flag down **12** signal to stop

**waver**
◇ anagram indicator **04** reel, rock, sway, vary, wave **05** haver, shake **06** change, didder, dither, falter, seesaw, teeter, totter, waffle, wobble **07** give way, stagger, tremble **08** hesitate **09** fluctuate, hum and haw, oscillate, vacillate **10** equivocate **11** be undecided **12** shilly-shally

**waverer**
**07** doubter, haverer, wobbler **08** ditherer **14** shilly-shallier

**wavering**
◇ anagram indicator **04** wavy **05** shaky **07** dithery, stagger **08** doubtful, doubting, firmless, havering, hesitant **09** ambiguous, dithering, hesitance, hesitancy **10** hesitation, indecision, in two minds, of two minds **11** vacillatory **12** double-minded **15** shilly-shallying

**wavy**
**04** undé **05** curly, curvy, oundy, undee **06** nebulé, nebuly, repand, ridged, undate, wiggly, zigzag **07** curling, curving, rippled, sinuate, sinuous, undated, winding **08** sinuated, undulate, wavering **09** snow goose **10** flamboyant, undulating, undulatory **11** fluctuating

**wax**
**03** say **04** cere, grow, kiss, pela, rise, seal, talk, tell **05** mount, speak, state, swell, utter, voice, widen **06** become, expand, extend, spread **07** address, broaden, cerumen, declaim, declare, develop, enlarge, express, fill out, magnify, passion **08** converse, increase, paraffin **09** enunciate, get bigger, hold forth, pronounce **10** articulate **11** communicate

**waxen**
**03** wan **04** pale **05** ashen, livid, white **06** pallid **07** anaemic, ghastly, whitish **09** bloodless **10** colourless

**waxy**
**04** soft **05** irate, pasty, waxen **06** pallid **07** cereous **08** incensed **09** ceraceous **11** impressible **14** impressionable

**way**
◇ anagram indicator **01** E, N, S, W **02** Rd, St, Wy **03** far, via **04** gate, lane, mode,

path, plan, road, rode, room, tool, very, will, wise, wont **05** habit, lines, means, route, scope, state, style, track, trait, usage, weigh **06** access, avenue, course, custom, esteem, manner, method, nature, really, street, system, temper **07** channel, conduct, fashion, highway, journey, passage, pathway, process, respect, roadway **08** approach, district, position, practice, progress, strategy **09** behaviour, condition, direction, mannerism, procedure, technique **10** instrument **11** disposition, peculiarity, personality, temperament **12** idiosyncrasy, thoroughfare **14** characteristic, course of action **15** instrumentality
• **all the way** **02** up **04** thro, thru **07** through **08** straight
• **by the way** **02** ob **03** BTW **06** obiter **07** apropos **09** en passant, in passing **11** secondarily **12** incidentally **14** by the same token **15** à propos de bottes, parenthetically
• **either way** ◇ palindrome indicator
• **give way** **02** go **03** sag **04** bend, cede, sink **05** break, burst, crack, yield **06** cave in, fall in, give in, relent, shrink, spring, submit, swerve **07** concede, subside, succumb **08** collapse, fall back, withdraw **09** give place, surrender **10** capitulate, give ground **12** disintegrate
• **make your way** **04** wend **06** travel **07** journey
• **on the way** **07** en route **09** in transit
• **quickest way** **07** beeline
• **under way** **05** afoot, begun, going **06** moving **07** started **08** in motion **10** in progress **11** in operation, progressing **12** off the ground
• **way of life** **04** life **05** world **08** position **09** lifestyle, situation **12** modus vivendi
• **ways and means** **04** cash **05** funds, tools **07** capital, methods **08** capacity, reserves **09** procedure, resources **10** capability **11** wherewithal
• **whichever way you look at it** ◇ palindrome indicator

**wayfarer**
**05** Gypsy, nomad, rover **06** viator, walker **07** pilgrim, swagger, swagman, trekker, voyager **08** traveler, wanderer **09** itinerant, journeyer, piepowder, traveller **12** globetrotter

**wayfaring**
**06** roving **07** nomadic, walking **08** drifting, rambling, voyaging **09** itinerant, wandering **10** journeying, travelling **11** peripatetic

**waylay**
**03** lay **05** belay, catch, seize **06** accost, ambush, attack, hold up **07** set upon, stick up **08** obstruct, surprise **09** intercept **10** buttonhole **12** lie in wait for

**way-out**
**04** lost, rapt, wild **05** crazy, wacky, weird **06** exotic, far-out, freaky **07** bizarre, off-beat, unusual

**09** eccentric, excellent, fantastic, left-field **10** avant-garde, outlandish, unorthodox **11** exceptional, progressive **12** experimental **14** unconventional

**wayward**
**06** fickle, unruly, wilful **07** peevish **08** contrary, obdurate, perverse, stubborn **09** irregular, obstinate **10** capricious, changeable, headstrong, rebellious, refractory, self-willed **11** disobedient, intractable, loup-the-dyke **12** contumacious, incorrigible, ungovernable, unmanageable **13** insubordinate, unpredictable

**waywardness**
**08** obduracy **09** contumacy, obstinacy **10** perversity, unruliness, wilfulness **12** contrariness, disobedience, perverseness, stubbornness **14** rebelliousness **15** insubordination

**weak**
**01** W **03** dim, low **04** dull, fade, gone, lame, poor, puny, soft, thin **05** cissy, faint, frail, milky, runny, shaky, weedy **06** debile, facile, faulty, feeble, flimsy, infirm, meagre, pallid, sickly, single, slight, unable, watery **07** brickle, diluted, exposed, fragile, insipid, lacking, muffled, stifled, unsound, useless, worn out **08** cowardly, delicate, fatigued, impotent **09** defective, deficient, enervated, exhausted, forceless, imperfect, powerless, spineless, strung out, tasteless, unguarded, unhealthy, untenable **10** effeminate, fizzenless, foisonless, fusionless, inadequate, indecisive, indistinct, irresolute, unstressed, vulnerable **11** adulterated, debilitated, defenceless, fushionless, impressible, ineffectual, unprotected **12** inconclusive, invertebrate, unconvincing **13** imperceptible, pusillanimous **14** inconsiderable, valetudinarian

**weaken**
**03** sap **04** fade, fail, flag, kill, pall, thin, tire **05** abate, appal, craze, delay, droop, lower, taint **06** deduct, dilute, ease up, impair, lessen, reduce, soften, temper **07** cripple, disable, dwindle, exhaust, give way, unnerve **08** diminish, enervate, enfeeble, entender, intender, mitigate, moderate, paralyse, soften up **09** extenuate, undermine, water down **10** debilitate, disconcert, effeminate, effeminize **12** incapacitate **13** disinvigorate **14** take the edge off

**weakening**
**06** easing, fading, waning **07** failing **08** dilution, flagging, lowering **09** abatement, dwindling, lessening, reduction **10** enervation, impairment, moderation **11** extenuation, frontolysis, undermining **12** debilitation, diminishment, enfeeblement

**weakling**
**03** wet **04** drip, tonk, weed, wimp, wuss **05** cissy, mouse, wally **06** coward

## weakly

07 dilling, doormat, milksop
08 softling, underdog 09 underling
10 namby-pamby

## weakly

06 feebly, lamely 07 faintly, frailly
08 slightly 09 tenuously 10 helplessly
11 implausibly, powerlessly
12 dispiritedly, indecisively,
pathetically 13 ineffectively

## weak-minded

04 daft 07 pliable 09 compliant,
spineless, weak-kneed 10 irresolute,
submissive 11 complaisant,
persuadable, persuasible 12 faint-
hearted 13 pusillanimous

## weakness

04 flaw 05 doubt, fault, folly 06 defect,
dotage, foible, liking 07 acrasia,
apepsia, blemish, cachexy, failing,
frailty, languor, passion 08 azoturia,
cachexia, debility, delicacy, fondness,
frailtee, penchant, soft spot, trembles
09 frailness, impotence, infirmity,
lassitude, weak point 10 deficiency,
effeminacy, enervation, feebleness,
flimsiness, incapacity, myasthenia,
proclivity 11 dubiousness, inclination,
paraparesis, shortcoming,
tenuousness, uncertainty,
unsoundness 12 Achilles' heel,
delicateness, doubtfulness,
enfeeblement, imperfection,
phonasthenia, predilection,
unlikelihood, unlikeliness
13 improbability, powerlessness,
vulnerability 14 far-fetchedness,
implausibility, predisposition
15 ineffectiveness, second
childhood

## weal

04 mark, scar, wale, welt 05 bends,
ridge, wheal, wound 06 streak, stripe
07 welfare 08 cicatrix 09 cicatrice,
contusion 12 commonwealth 14 the
sum of things

## wealth

04 cash, ease, mass, pelf 05 bling,
funds, goods, lucre, means, money,
store 06 assets, bounty, estate,
mammon, plenty, riches 07 capital,
finance, fortune, fulness, tallent,
warison 08 fullness, opulence,
property, richesse, treasure, treasury,
warrison 09 abundance, affluence,
plenitude, profusion, resources,
substance, wellbeing 10 cornucopia,
prosperity 11 copiousness,
loadsamoney, possessions

## wealthy

04 oofy, posh, rich 05 flush, pluty, solid
06 fat-cat, loaded 07 moneyed,
opulent, well-off 08 affluent, well-to-
do 10 filthy rich, prosperous, well-
heeled 11 comfortable, made of
money, rolling in it, substantial
12 stinking rich

## weapon

03 arm

---

*Weapons include:*

03 bow, gas, gun, IED, Uzi, WMD
04 bomb, Colt®, cosh, dirk, épée,
foil, ICBM, Mace®, mine, pike,
Scud
05 arrow, BB gun, billy, bolas, CS
gas, H-bomb, knife, lance,
Luger®, panga, rifle, sabre, sling,
spear, sword, Taser®, vouge
06 airgun, cannon, cudgel, dagger,
Exocet®, glaive, jambok,
magnum, Mauser, mortar,
musket, pistol, rapier, rocket, six-
gun, taiaha, tomboc
07 assegai, balista, bayonet,
bazooka, bomblet, Bren gun,
caltrop, halberd, handgun,
harpoon, longbow, machete,
poleaxe, poniard, sjambok, sten
gun, stun gun, tear-gas, torpedo,
woomera
08 air rifle, atom bomb, ballista,
blowpipe, calthrop, catapult,
chemical, claymore, crossbow,
field gun, howitzer, landmine,
nail bomb, nerve gas, nunchaku,
oerlikon, partisan, revolver,
scimitar, shuriken, stiletto,
threshel, time-bomb, tomahawk,
tommy gun
09 automatic, battleaxe, boomerang,
Mills bomb, smart bomb,
trebuchet, truncheon, turret-gun
10 bowie knife, broadsword, flick-
knife, gatling gun, machine-gun,
mustard gas, napalm bomb,
nulla-nulla, peashooter,
shillelagh, six-shooter
11 Agent Orange, blunderbuss, bow
and arrow, cluster-bomb, daisy-
cutter, depth-charge, hand
grenade, kalashnikov, neutron
bomb, submunition, water pistol
12 bunker buster, flame-thrower,
hydrogen bomb, quarterstaff
13 Cruise missile, knuckleduster,
submachine-gun
14 incendiary bomb, rocket-
launcher
15 thermobaric bomb, Winchester®
rifle

---

*See also* **dagger; gun; knife; missile;
sword**

## wear

◇ *insertion indicator* 03 air, don, fly, rub,
use 04 bear, edge, fray, have, pack,
pass, show, stub 05 carry, dress, erode,
grind, guide, mount, put on, spend,
sport, waste, weary 06 abrade, accept,
affect, assume, attire, become, damage,
endure, have on, outfit 07 believe,
clothes, conduct, consume, corrode,
costume, display, dress in, erosion,
exhaust, exhibit, fashion, service, utility
08 abrasion, clothing, friction,
garments, tolerate, traverse 09 corrosion
10 durability, employment, usefulness
11 be clothed in, be dressed in,
deteriorate, wear and tear 12 become
weaker 13 become thinner,
deterioration 14 fray at the edges
• **wear down** 05 erode, grind
06 abrade, impair, lessen, reduce
07 attrite, consume, corrode, degrade,
rub away 08 diminish, macerate,
overcome, soften up 09 grind down,
undermine 10 chip away at

• **wear off** 03 ebb 04 fade, fray, wan
05 abate 06 lessen, weaken 07 dwindle
subside 08 decrease, diminish, peter
out 09 disappear
• **wear on** 04 go by, go on, pass
06 elapse
• **wear out** 03 sap 04 fray, mush, tire
05 break, drain, erode, trash, use up,
waste 06 harass, impair, peruse, strain,
stress 07 consume, exhaust, fatigue,
frazzle, knacker, knock up, tire out
08 enervate, forspend, overteem
09 forspend 11 deteriorate, wear
through

## wearily

07 tiredly 08 drowsily, sleepily
10 listlessly 11 unexcitedly
13 lethargically

## weariness

05 ennui 07 fatigue, languor
08 lethargy 09 lassitude, tiredness
10 drowsiness, enervation, exhaustion
sleepiness 11 prostration, Weltschmerz
12 listlessness, taedium vitae
• **expression of weariness** 04 hech
07 heigh-ho

## wearing

◇ *containment indicator* 02 in 06 taxing,
tiring, trying 07 erosive, irksome
08 tiresome 09 consuming, fatiguing,
wearisome 10 durability, exhausting,
oppressive 12 exasperating

## wearisome

04 dull 06 boring, dreary, trying
07 humdrum, irksome, tedious,
wearing 08 annoying, tiresome,
weariful 09 fatiguing, vexatious
10 bothersome, burdensome,
exhausting, monotonous
11 troublesome 12 exasperating

## weary

03 bug, fag, irk, sap, tax 04 bore, cloy,
fade, fail, jade, puny, tire 05 all in,
annoy, bored, drain, ennui, jaded,
tired 06 aweary, betoil, burden,
bushed, done in, drowsy, harass,
pooped, sicken, sleepy, zonked
07 drained, exhaust, fatigue, tedious,
tire out, wear out, whacked, worn out
08 awearied, dead beat, dog-tired,
dog-weary, enervate, fatigued,
forweary, half-dead, irritate, tiresome,
toil-worn, trauchle, wiped out
09 exhausted, fagged out, knackered,
overweary, pooped out, ramfeezle,
think long, unexcited 10 brassed off,
browned off, cheesed off, debilitate,
exasperate 11 tuckered out 12 bored to
tears, sick and tired, uninterested
14 unenthusiastic

## wearying

06 taxing, tiring, trying 07 wearing
08 draining 09 fatiguing, wearisome
10 exhausting

## weasel

04 mink 05 stoat, taira, tayra 06 grison,
marten 07 whitret 08 whittret
09 delundung, wolverene, wolverine
10 whitterick

## weather

03 dry, set, sky 04 gain, pass 05 brave,

slope, stand **06** endure, expose, harden, resist, season, suffer **07** climate, dryness, outlook, ride out, survive, toughen **08** forecast, humidity, overcome, stick out, surmount, windward **09** rise above, sunniness, windiness, withstand **10** cloudiness, conditions, get through **11** come through, live through, pull through, temperature

*Weather phenomena include:*

**03** fog, ice
**04** gale, hail, haze, mist, rain, smog, snow, thaw, wind
**05** cloud, frost, sleet, slush, storm
**06** breeze, deluge, shower, squall
**07** chinook, cyclone, drizzle, drought, mistral, monsoon, rainbow, tempest, thunder, tornado, twister, typhoon
**08** black ice, downpour, heatwave, sunshine
**09** hoar frost, hurricane, lightning, snowstorm, whirlwind

*See also* **cloud; ice; precipitation; snow; storm; wind**
• **under the weather** **03** ill **04** ropy, sick **05** crook, drunk, lousy, queer, ropey, rough, seedy **06** ailing, groggy, grotty, poorly **08** below par, hung over, nauseous **09** off-colour, squeamish **10** indisposed, out of sorts **15** the worse for wear

**weave**
◊ *anagram indicator* **03** rya, web **04** cane, fuse, knit, lace, spin, wind **05** braid, merge, plait, tweel, twill, twist, unite **06** create, damask, make up, plight, tissue, zigzag **07** compose, entwine, inweave, texture **08** contrive **09** construct, fabricate, interlace, interwork **10** criss-cross, intercross, intertwine, interweave **11** put together

**weaver**
**04** loom

**weaver bird**
**04** taha **06** bishop, ox-bird, quelea **09** grenadier **10** zebra finch **11** Java sparrow

**web**
**03** mat, net **04** knot, mesh, plot, tela, trap, vane, weft **05** skein, snare **06** tangle **07** complex, lattice, netting, network, texture, webbing **08** intrigue, lacework, mesh-work, vexillum **11** fabrication, interlacing, latticework

**wed**
**03** wad **04** ally, fuse, join, link, yoke **05** blend, marry, merge, unify, unite, wager **06** pledge, splice **07** combine, espouse **08** coalesce, security **09** commingle **10** get hitched, get married, get spliced, interweave, take to wife, tie the knot **13** take the plunge **14** lead to the altar, lead up the aisle

**wedded**
**06** joined, wifely **07** marital, married, nuptial, spousal **08** conjugal **09** connubial, husbandly **11** matrimonial

**wedding**
**05** union **06** bridal, huppah, mating **07** chuppah, nuptial, wedlock **08** espousal, hymeneal, hymenean, marriage, nuptials, spousage **09** espousals, matrimony **11** epithalamic, matrimonial **15** marriage service
*See also* **anniversary; marriage**

**wedge**
**03** fit, gad, gib, jam, key, ram **04** cram, lump, pack, push, trig **05** block, chock, chunk, cleat, crowd, force, lodge, piece, quoin, stuff, wodge **06** cotter, scotch, thrust **07** blaster, feather, squeeze **08** doorstop, triangle **09** space band, whipstock

**wedlock**
**05** union **08** marriage **09** matrimony **13** holy matrimony

**Wednesday**
**03** Wed **04** Weds

**wee**
**03** pee, sma **04** leak, tiny **05** small, teeny, urine, weeny **06** little, midget, minute, teensy **07** urinate **09** itsy-bitsy, miniature, minuscule **10** diminutive, negligible, teeny-weeny **11** Lilliputian, microscopic **13** insignificant

**weed**
**03** hoe **04** tare

*Weeds include:*

**03** ers
**04** dock, moss
**05** daisy, vetch
**06** fat hen, nettle, oxalis, spurge, yarrow
**07** bracken, ragweed, ribwort
**08** bindweed, duckweed, knapweed, plantain, self-heal
**09** chickweed, coltsfoot, dandelion, ground ivy, groundsel, horsetail, knotgrass, liverwort, pearlwort, snakeweed, speedwell, sun spurge
**10** cinquefoil, common reed, couch grass, curled dock, deadnettle, sow thistle, thale cress
**11** ground elder, meadow grass, petty spurge, salad burnet, St John's wort, white clover
**12** annual nettle, rough hawkbit, sheep's sorrel
**13** common burdock, field wood rush, large bindweed, pineapple weed, small bindweed
**14** common plantain, shepherd's purse
**15** broad-leaved dock, burnet saxifrage, common chickweed, creeping thistle, greater plantain, lesser celandine, perennial nettle, stemless thistle

*See also* **cannabis; seaweed; tobacco**
• **weed out** **05** purge **06** remove **07** isolate, root out **08** get rid of **09** eliminate, eradicate, extirpate

**weedkiller**
**06** diquat **08** atrazine, Paraquat®, simazine **09** herbicide, weedicide

**10** glyphosate **11** glufosinate, graminicide **14** sodium chlorate

**weedy**
**03** wet **04** puny, thin, weak **05** frail, lanky, wussy **06** feeble, skinny **07** insipid, scrawny, wimpish **08** gangling **09** weak-kneed **10** undersized

**week**
**01** w **03** ouk **04** oulk

**weekly**
**09** by the week, every week, once a week **10** hebdomadal **11** hebdomadary **12** hebdomadally

**weep**
**03** cry, sob **04** bawl, blub, drip, leak, moan, ooze, pipe, rain, seep, wail **05** droop, exude, greet, mourn, whine **06** beweep, boo-hoo, greete, grieve, lament, snivel **07** blubber, outweep, whimper **09** be in tears, shed tears **11** pipe your eye

**weepy**
**04** oozy **05** teary **06** crying, labile **07** sobbing, tearful, weeping **08** greeting, sob-stuff **09** melodrama **10** blubbering, lachrymose, tear-jerker **11** sentimental

**weigh**
**03** sit, way **04** ride **05** loose, poise, raise, scale, worry **06** burden, ponder **07** afflict, balance, depress, examine, get down, oppress, perpend, trouble **08** bear down, consider, evaluate, mull over, unanchor **09** disanchor, ponderate, reflect on, think over **10** deliberate, meditate on **11** contemplate **13** have a weight of **14** tip the scales at
• **weigh down** **04** load **05** pease, peaze, peise, peize, peyse, poise, worry **06** burden **07** afflict, depress, get down, oppress, trouble **08** bear down, outweigh, overload **09** press down, weigh upon
• **weigh up** **05** scale **06** assess, ponder, size up **07** balance, compare, discuss, examine **08** chew over, consider, evaluate, mull over **09** think over **10** deliberate **11** contemplate

**weighing machine**
**04** tron **05** trone **06** bismar **09** steelyard

**weight**
**01** w **02** wt **03** agw, gvw **04** bias, bulk, duty, gr wt, last, lead, load, mark, mass, nt wt, onus, pith, sway, tare **05** angle, clout, flesh, force, pease, peaze, peise, peize, peyse, poise, power, slang, slant, twist, value, wecht, worry **06** burden, impact, moment, scales, slight, strain **07** ballast, gravity, oppress, plummet, tonnage, trouble **08** gravitas, handicap, live load, poundage, pressure, quantity **09** authority, heaviness, influence, prejudice, substance, unbalance, weigh down **10** importance, importancy, ponderance, ponderancy **11** avoirdupois, consequence, encumbrance **12** significance

**13** consideration, preponderance
**14** impressiveness, responsibility
*See also* **boxing**
• **unit of weight** **01** g, k, l, t **02** as, cg, ct, dg, gm, gr, hg, kg, lb, mg, oz, st **03** cwt, grt, kat, kin, kip, mna, oke, tod, ton, wey **04** boll, gram, kati, khat, kilo, mina, obol, pood, rotl, seer, tola, unce **05** candy, carat, catty, kandy, katti, liang, maneh, maund, ounce, picul, pikul, pound, stone, tical, todde, tonne **06** candie, carrat, cental, denier, dirhem, fother, gramme, kantar, shekel, talent **07** centner, lispund, scruple **08** decigram, lispound **09** centigram, milligram **10** decigramme **11** centigramme, milligramme

**weightless**
**04** airy **05** light **11** imponderous **13** insubstantial

**weighty**
**05** bulky, grave, great, heavy, hefty, solid, vital **06** severe, solemn, taxing **07** crucial, massive, onerous, pesante, serious **08** critical, exacting, pregnant, worrying **09** demanding, difficult, important, momentous, ponderous **10** burdensome **11** influential, significant, substantial **13** authoritative, consequential

**weir**
**03** pen **04** wear **05** cauld, garth, guard **06** lasher **07** ward off **09** fish-garth

**weird**
◊ *anagram indicator* **03** odd, rum **04** doom, eery, fate **05** charm, eerie, queer, spell, witch **06** creepy, far-out, spooky, way-out, weyard **07** bizarre, destine, ghostly, strange, uncanny, weyward **08** eldritch, forewarn, freakish, peculiar, witching **09** grotesque, happening, left-field, unearthly, unnatural **10** mysterious **12** supernatural **13** preternatural

**weirdly**
**06** eerily **08** spookily **09** bizarrely, strangely **11** unnaturally **12** mysteriously **14** supernaturally

**weirdo**
**03** dag, nut **04** card, case, cure, geek, kook, loon, wack **05** crank, flake, freak, loony **06** nutter **07** cupcake, dingbat, nutcase, oddball, odd fish **08** crackpot **09** character, eccentric, fruitcake, queer fish **14** fish out of water

**welcome**
◊ *containment indicator* **04** free, hail, meet **05** greet **06** accept, salute **07** acclaim, embrace, karanga, popular, powhiri, proface, receive **08** glad hand, greeting, haeremai, pleasant, pleasing **09** agreeable, approve of, ben venuto, desirable, gratulate, reception, red carpet **10** acceptable, acceptance, delightful, gratifying, refreshing, salutation, salutary **11** acclamation, appreciated, hospitality **13** be pleased with **15** be satisfied with

**welcoming**
**04** cosy, warm **06** genial, hearty **07** affable, cordial, earnest **08** amicable, cheerful, friendly, homelike, pleasant, relaxing, sociable **09** agreeable, gemütlich, heartfelt, open-armed **10** hospitable **11** comfortable, stimulating, warm-hearted **12** affectionate, invigorating, wholehearted

**weld**
**04** bind, bond, fuse, join, link, pile, seal, seam, wald **05** braze, joint, seize, unite, wield **06** cement, solder **07** connect **09** dyer's-weed **10** mignonette, yellow-weed **11** dyer's rocket **15** dyer's-yellowweed

**welfare**
**04** good, heal, weal **05** hayle, state **06** health, income, profit **07** benefit, comfort, fortune, payment, pension, sick pay, success **08** interest, security **09** advantage, allowance, happiness, soundness, wellbeing **10** commonweal, prosperity **14** social security

**well**
**02** my, OK, so **03** eye, far, fit, jet, lor, sae, spa **04** ably, bien, eddy, fine, flow, font, good, gush, ooze, pool, pour, rise, rush, seep, weel **05** aweel, fitly, flood, fount, fully, good-o, issue, lucky, right, sound, spout, spurt, surge, swell, wally **06** atweel, cavity, deeply, easily, fairly, geyser, good-oh, hearty, highly, kindly, proper, robust, source, spring, stream, strong, supply, warmly **07** adeptly, clearly, closely, cockpit, fortune, greatly, happily, healthy, luckily, Mickery, rightly, spouter, trickle **08** all right, brim over, decently, expertly, fountain, genially, pleasing, probably, properly, suitably, thriving, very much, wellhead **09** advisable, agreeable, agreeably, carefully, certainly, correctly, fittingly, fortunate, glowingly, in the pink, reservoir, skilfully, to a wonder, water hole **10** able-bodied, abundantly, adequately, admiringly, completely, favourably, generously, hospitably, intimately, pleasantly, profoundly, rigorously, splendidly, thoroughly, very likely, wellspring **11** approvingly, comfortable, comfortably, competently, conceivably, effectively, efficiently, excellently, flourishing, fortunately, intensively **12** considerably, conveniently, in good health, proficiently, prosperously, satisfactory, successfully, sufficiently, watering hole **13** hale and hearty, industriously, quite possibly, substantially, weeping spring **14** satisfactorily, to a great extent **15** comprehensively
• **as well** **03** als, and, tae, too **04** also, both **06** to boot **07** besides **08** moreover **10** in addition **11** furthermore **14** into the bargain
• **as well as** **09** along with, including **12** in addition to, not to mention, over

and above, together with **14** to say nothing of
• **well done** **04** euge **05** bravo **06** encore, hurrah **08** congrats, good show **13** à la bonne heure **15** congratulations

**well-advised**
**04** wise **05** sound **06** shrewd **07** politic, prudent **08** sensible **09** judicious, sagacious **10** far-sighted, reasonable **11** circumspect, long-sighted

**well-balanced**
**04** even, sane **05** level, sober, sound **06** sorted, stable **08** balanced, rational, sensible, together **10** harmonious, reasonable **11** level-headed, symmetrical, well-ordered **12** well-adjusted

**well-behaved**
**04** good **06** polite **07** orderly **08** mannerly, obedient **09** compliant **10** good as gold, respectful **11** considerate, co-operative **12** under control, well-mannered

**wellbeing**
**04** good **06** health, wealth **07** comfort, welfare **09** eudaemony, happiness **10** eudaemonia, good health

**well-bred**
**05** civil **06** polite, urbane **07** gallant, genteel, refined **08** cultured, ladylike, mannerly **09** courteous **10** cultivated, upper-crust **11** blue-blooded, comme il faut, gentlemanly **12** aristocratic, well-mannered **13** well-brought-up

**well-built**
**05** beefy, burly, stout **06** brawny, strong, sturdy **08** muscular **09** strapping

**well-deserved**
**03** due **04** just, meet **07** condign, merited **08** deserved, rightful **09** justified **11** appropriate

**well-disposed**
**06** toward **07** healthy **08** amicable, friendly, towardly **09** agreeable, well-aimed **10** benevolent, favourable, well-minded, well-placed **11** sympathetic **12** well-arranged

**well-dressed**
**04** chic, neat, tidy, trim **05** natty, smart **06** dapper, spruce **07** elegant, stylish **11** fashionable, well-groomed

**well-founded**
**03** fit **05** right, sound, valid **06** proper **08** sensible **09** plausible, warranted **10** acceptable, reasonable **11** justifiable, sustainable

**well-groomed**
**04** neat, tidy, trim **05** smart **06** dapper, soigné, spruce **07** soignée **11** well-dressed **13** well-turned-out

**well-heeled**
**04** oofy, posh, rich **05** flush, solid **06** fat-cat, loaded **07** moneyed, opulent, wealthy, well-off **08** affluent, well-to-do **10** filthy rich, prosperous **11** comfortable, made of money, rolling in it, substantial **12** stinking rich

## well-informed
**02** up **06** au fait, sussed **07** clued-up **09** au courant

## well-known
**04** name **05** famed, noted, usual **06** common, famous, notour, of note **07** eminent, notable **08** familiar, renowned **09** notorious **10** celebrated, proverbial **11** illustrious, widely-known

## well-mannered
**05** civil **06** polite, urbane **07** gallant, genteel, refined **08** cultured, ladylike, mannerly, well-bred **09** bien élevé, courteous **10** cultivated, upper-crust **11** blue-blooded, gentlemanly **12** aristocratic, house-trained **13** well-brought-up

## well-nigh
**05** welly **06** all but, almost, nearly **09** just about, virtually **11** practically

## well-off
**04** bein, bien, rich **05** flush, lucky **06** loaded, monied **07** moneyed, wealthy **08** affluent, thriving, well-to-do **09** fortunate **10** filthy rich, forehanded, in the money, prosperous, successful, well-heeled **11** comfortable, made of money, rolling in it **12** stinking rich **15** with money to burn

## well-read
**07** studied **08** cultured, educated, lettered, literate **12** well-informed **13** knowledgeable

## Wells
**02** HG

## well-spoken
**05** clear **06** fluent **08** coherent, eloquent **10** articulate **13** well-expressed

## well-thought-of
**07** admired, revered **08** esteemed, honoured **09** respected, venerated **10** looked up to **14** highly regarded

## well-to-do
**04** oofy, posh, rich, warm **05** flush **06** fat-cat, loaded **07** moneyed, wealthy, well-off **08** affluent **10** filthy rich, prosperous **11** comfortable, made of money, rolling in it, substantial **12** stinking rich

## well-versed
**02** up **06** au fait **07** trained **08** deep-read, familiar **10** acquainted, conversant **11** experienced **13** knowledgeable

## well-wisher
**03** fan **06** friend **09** supporter **10** well-willer **11** sympathizer

## well-worn
**04** worn **05** corny, stale, stock, tired, trite **06** frayed, ragged, shabby **07** cliché'd, scruffy, worn-out **08** clichéd, overused, timeworn **09** hackneyed **10** threadbare, unoriginal **11** commonplace, stereotyped **13** battle-scarred

## welsh
**01** W **02** do **05** cheat **06** diddle **07** defraud, swindle

*Welsh first names include:*

**03** Dai, Huw, Nye, Wyn
**04** Aled, Alun, Ceri, Dewi, Enid, Eryl, Evan, Glyn, Gwen, Gwyn, Ifor, Ioan, Owen, Rees, Rhys, Siôn
**05** Carys, Cerys, Dilys, Dylan, Elwyn, Emlyn, Emrys, Ffion, Gavin, Haydn, Howel, Hywel, Idris, Ieuan, Lloyd, Madoc, Megan, Nerys, Olwen, Olwin, Olwyn, Rhian, Tudor
**06** Dafydd, Delyth, Dilwyn, Eirian, Eirlys, Eluned, Gareth, Gaynor, Gladys, Glenda, Glenys, Glynis, Gwenda, Gwilym, Howell, Mervyn, Morgan, Olwyne
**07** Aneirin, Aneurin, Bronwen, Brynmor, Eiluned, Geraint, Gwenyth, Gwillym, Gwyneth, Myfanwy, Myrddin, Peredur, Vaughan
**08** Angharad, Llewelyn, Meredith, Morwenna, Rhiannon
**09** Gwendolen, Gwenllian

*See also* **county; town**

## welt
**03** dry **04** beat, blow, lash, mark, scar, weal **05** ridge, world, wound **06** streak, stripe, wither **08** cicatrix **09** cicatrice, contusion

## welter
**03** web **04** mess, roll, toss, wade **05** heave, lurch, pitch **06** jumble, muddle, splash, tangle, wallow **07** smother **08** flounder, mish-mash **09** confusion **10** hotchpotch

## wend
*see* **Slav**
• **wend your way** **02** go **04** hike, move, plod, walk **05** amble **06** travel, trudge, wander **07** meander, proceed **08** progress **11** make your way

## west
**01** W **03** Mae **08** New World, Occident **10** Occidental
• **go west** ◇ *reversal indicator* **03** die **06** perish **11** be destroyed **12** be dissipated

## western
**01** W **06** ponent **07** westlin **10** occidental

## Western Sahara
**03** ESH

## West Virginia
**02** WV **03** W Va

## wet
**03** dip, wat **04** damp, dank, dram, drip, fool, jerk, moil, nerd, rain, soak, soft, sour, wash, weak, weed, weet, wimp, wuss **05** bewet, cissy, douse, flood, humid, idiot, imbue, madid, moist, muggy, rainy, softy, soggy, soppy, spray, steep, swamp, sweat, tipsy, wally, water, weedy **06** beweep, clammy, daggle, dampen, drench, drippy, effete, embrue, feeble, imbrue, liquid, madefy, slippy, sloppy, sluice,

soaked, sodden, soused, splash, spongy, watery **07** debauch, draggle, drizzle, embrewe, milksop, moisten, pouring, raining, showery, soaking, sopping, squidgy, tearful, teeming, wetness, wimpish **08** bedabble, bedrench, dampness, drenched, dripping, humidity, irrigate, moisture, pathetic, saturate, slippery, sprinkle, timorous, weakling, wringing **09** drizzling, irriguous, moistness, saturated, spineless **10** clamminess, imbruement, irresolute, namby-pamby, sopping wet **11** ineffective, ineffectual, madefaction, waterlogged **12** condensation
• **wet behind the ears** **03** new, raw **05** green, naive **06** callow **08** gullible, immature, innocent **09** untrained **13** inexperienced
• **wet patch** *see* **sea**

## wetness
**03** wet **04** damp **05** water **06** liquid **08** dampness, dankness, humidity, moisture **09** sogginess **10** clamminess, rising damp, soddenness **12** condensation

## whack
**03** box, cut, hit, lot, rap **04** bang, bash, beat, belt, biff, blow, cuff, part, slap, sock **05** clout, quota, share, smack, stint, thump **06** buffet, murder, strike, stroke, thrash, wallop **07** attempt, clobber, portion, rake-off **08** division **09** allowance, parcel out **10** allocation, percentage, proportion **14** slice of the cake

## whacking
**04** huge, mega, vast **05** giant, gross, jumbo **07** beating, immense, mammoth, massive, socking, Titanic, whaling **08** almighty, colossal, enormous, gigantic, great big, plonking, whopping **09** ginormous, humongous, monstrous, thrashing, walloping **10** astronomic, gargantuan, large-scale, prodigious, stupendous, tremendous **11** God-almighty **12** considerable

## whale
**05** Cetus **06** thrash

*Whales include:*

**03** fin, orc, sei
**04** blue, grey, orca
**05** black, minke, pigmy, piked, pilot, right, sperm, white
**06** baleen, beaked, beluga, caa'ing, finner, killer
**07** bowhead, dolphin, finback, grampus, Layard's, narwhal, rorqual, toothed
**08** cachalot, humpback, porpoise
**09** Greenland, grindhval, razorback, whalebone
**10** bottlenose, humpbacked
**11** bottle-nosed, false killer
**12** river dolphin, strap-toothed
**13** common rorqual, Risso's dolphin, sulphur-bottom
**15** gangetic dolphin, harbour porpoise

# wharf

## wharf
**03** kay, key **04** dock, pier, quay **05** jetty **06** marina, staith **07** staithe **08** dockyard, quayside **12** landing-stage

## what
**02** eh, my

## what's-its-name
**05** gismo, thing **06** doings, doodad, doodah, doofus, jigger, thingy **07** doobrey, doobrie, whatnot, whatsit **08** thingamy **09** doohickey, jigamaree, jiggumbob, thingummy, timenoguy **12** thingummybob, thingummyjig **14** what-d'you-call-it **15** whatchamacallit

## wheat
**04** corn **05** durum, emmer, fitch, rivet, spelt **06** bulgur, sharps **07** bulghur, einkorn **08** amelcorn, semolina, Triticum

## wheedle
**03** cog **04** blag, coax, draw **05** carny, charm, court **06** cajole, carney, cozy up, cuiter, entice, induce, phrase, whilly **07** beguile, flatter, tweedle, win over **08** butter up, inveigle, persuade, soft-soap, talk into **09** sweet-talk, whillywha **10** whillywhaw

## wheel
◇ *reversal indicator* **04** disc, hoop, reel, ring, roam, roll, spin, turn **05** dolly, orbit, pivot, ratch, rhomb, snail, swing, truck, twirl, whirl **06** circle, dollar, gyrate, roller, rotate, sheave, swivel, wander **07** bicycle, go round, refrain, revolve, trindle, trochus, trolley, truckle **08** encircle, gyration, rotation, tricycle **10** revolution

*Wheels include:*

**03** big, cog, fly
**04** buff, cart, gear, idle, mill, worm
**05** bedel, bevel, crown, drive, idler, sakia, wagon, water
**06** castor, charka, escape, Ferris, paddle, prayer, sakieh
**07** balance, driving, fortune, potter's, ratchet, sakiyeh
**08** roulette, spinning, sprocket, spur gear, steering
**09** Catherine
**13** spinning jenny, throwing table, whirling-table

• **at the wheel** **07** driving, turning **08** in charge, steering **09** at the helm, directing, heading up, in command, in control **11** responsible **14** behind the wheel

## wheeze
**03** gag **04** gasp, hiss, idea, joke, pant, plan, ploy, rasp, ruse **05** antic, cough, crack, prank, story, stunt, trick, whiss **06** scheme **07** whaisle, whaizle, whistle, wrinkle **08** anecdote, chestnut, one-liner **11** catchphrase **13** practical joke

## whelp
**03** cub, pup **05** puppy **07** brachet **08** bratchet

## whereabouts
**04** site **05** place **08** location, position, vicinity **09** situation

## wherewithal
**04** cash, dosh, loot **05** brass, bread, dough, funds, gravy, lolly, means, money, ready, smash **06** greens, moolah, stumpy **07** capital, readies, scratch, shekels **08** greenies, supplies **09** megabucks, necessary, resources **11** spondulicks

## whet
**04** edge, file, hone, stir **05** grind, preen, rouse **06** arouse, awaken, excite, incite, kindle, stroke **07** provoke, quicken, sharpen **08** appetize, increase **09** stimulate, titillate **11** scythe-stone

## whiff
**04** gust, hint, puff, reek **05** aroma, blast, cigar, jiffy, odour, scent, smell, sniff, stink, touch, trace **06** breath, inhale, stench **07** draught, glimpse, soupçon **09** cigarette, suspicion **10** suggestion

## while
**02** as **04** span, time, when **05** spell, throw, until **06** period, season **07** stretch, whereas **08** although, interval **09** the whilst **13** in the middle of

• **while away** **03** use **04** pass **05** spend, use up **06** devote, occupy

## whim
**03** fad, toy **04** flam, idea, kink, swim, urge **05** crank, craze, fancy, flisk, freak, quirk **06** humour, maggot, megrim, notion, vagary, whimsy **07** caprice, conceit, impulse, passion, whimsey **08** crotchet **11** whigmaleery **12** whigmaleerie

## whimper
**03** cry, sob **04** mewl, moan, pule, weep **05** groan, whine **06** snivel, whinge **07** grizzle, sniffle

## whimsical
**03** fay, fey, fie, odd **05** dotty, droll, fairy, funny, queer, weird **06** quaint, quirky, whimsy **07** baroque, curious, playful, toysome, unusual **08** fanciful, peculiar **09** crotchety, eccentric, fantastic, impulsive **10** capricious, crotcheted **11** Disneyesque, fantastical, mischievous **13** unpredictable

## whimsy
**03** odd **04** tick, whim **05** droll, funny, weird **06** fisgig, fizgig, quaint, quirky **07** curious, playful, unusual **08** fanciful, peculiar **09** eccentric, whimsical **10** changeable **13** unpredictable

## whine
**03** cry, sob **04** beef, carp, moan, pule, wail **05** bleat, gripe, groan **06** grouch, grouse, kvetch, peenge, whinge, yammer **07** grizzle, grumble, wheenge, whimper **08** complain **09** bellyache, complaint

## whinge
**04** beef, carp, moan **05** greet, gripe, groan, winge **06** grouse, peenge

**07** grumble, wheenge **08** complain **09** bellyache, complaint

## whip
◇ *anagram indicator* **03** cat, fly, mix, tan, tat, taw **04** beat, belt, cane, crop, dart, dash, firk, flay, flit, flog, goad, hide, jerk, lash, prod, pull, push, rush, spur, stir, tear, urge, whap, whop, yank **05** birch, braid, drive, flash, knout, outdo, quirt, rouse, steal, strap, swish, thong, whack, whang, whisk **06** beat up, breech, defeat, driver, feague, incite, larrup, prompt, punish, snatch, switch, thrash, wallop **07** agitate, chabouk, cowhide, instant, kurbash, overlay, provoke, rawhide, scourge, sjambok **08** ash-plant, bullwhip, chastise, coachman, kourbash, overcast, vapulate **09** bullwhack, castigate, coachwhip, flagellum, horsewhip, instigate, longe whip, lunge whip, stock whip **10** black snake, discipline, flagellate, riding-crop **11** hunting-crop, hunting-whip, lunging whip, overcasting **13** cat-o'-nine-tails

• **whip up** ◇ *anagram indicator* **04** beat **06** arouse, excite, foment, incite, kindle, stir up, work up **07** agitate, inflame, provoke, psych up **09** instigate, stimulate

## whippersnapper
**03** imp **05** scamp **06** nipper, rascal **07** upstart, whiffet **08** whipster **09** pipsqueak, scallywag **11** hobbledehoy **14** snipper-snapper

## whipping
**05** knout **06** caning, defeat, hiding, laldie **07** beating, belting, lashing, tanning **08** birching, flogging, spanking **09** scourging, thrashing, walloping **10** punishment **11** castigation, overcasting **12** flagellation

## whirl
◇ *anagram indicator* **04** daze, eddy, reel, roll, spin, tirl, turn **05** pivot, round, swing, swirl, twirl, twist, waltz, wheel **06** bustle, circle, flurry, gyrate, hubbub, jumble, muddle, rotate, series, swivel, tumult, uproar **07** revolve **08** gyration, rotation **09** agitation, commotion, confusion, giddiness, pirouette, turn round **10** hurly-burly, revolution, succession **12** circumgyrate, merry-go-round

• **give something a whirl** **03** try **06** strive **07** attempt, have a go, venture **09** endeavour, have a bash, have a lash, have a shot, have a stab **10** have a crack **11** give it a burl

## whirlpool
**04** eddy, gulf, weal, weel, weil, wiel **05** gurge **06** vortex **08** sea purse, swelchie **09** Charybdis, maelstrom

## whirlwind
**04** eddy, rash **05** babel, chaos, hasty, noise, quick, rapid, swift **06** bedlam, furore, hubbub, speedy, tumult, typhon, uproar, vortex **07** anarchy, clamour, cyclone, tornado, turmoil, typhoon **08** headlong, madhouse **09** commotion, confusion, impetuous,

## whisk

impulsive, lightning, sand-devil **10** cockeye bob, hullabaloo, tourbillon **11** pandemonium, tourbillion, white squall

## whisk

◊ *anagram indicator* **03** fly, mix, zip **04** beat, belt, bolt, bomb, dart, dash, dive, lash, pelt, race, rush, stir, tear, tuft, whid, whip, wipe **05** brush, flick, hurry, scoot, shoot, speed, sweep, swish, whist **06** beater, chowri, chowry, hasten, switch, twitch **07** panicle **09** egg beater **12** swizzle-stick

## whiskey

**01** W

## whisky

**04** dram, half **05** hooch **06** double, hootch **08** the grain **09** aqua vitae, good stuff, the cratur **10** barley-bree, barley-broo, usquebaugh **11** barley-broth, mountain dew, the Auld Kirk, water of life

*Whiskies include:*

**03** rye
**04** malt
**06** poteen, red-eye, Scotch
**07** blended, Bourbon, potheen, spunkie
**08** peat-reek, sour mash
**09** moonshine
**10** cornbrandy, corn whisky, single malt, tanglefoot
**12** the real McCoy
**13** the real Mackay
**14** chain lightning, tarantula juice

## whisper

**03** bur **04** burr, buzz, hark, hint, hiss, sigh **05** round, sough, tinge, trace, whiff **06** breath, gossip, mumble, murmur, mutter, report, rumour, rustle, tittle, whisht **07** breathe, divulge, soupçon, wheesht **08** innuendo, intimate, low voice, susurrus **09** insinuate, soft voice, suspicion, susurrate, undertone **10** quiet voice, say quietly, suggestion **11** insinuation, pig's whisper **12** speak quietly, stage whisper **14** whittie-whattie

## whistle

**04** call, ping, pipe, sing, song, sowf **05** cheep, chirp, siren, sowff, sowth, whiss **06** hooter, siffle, throat, warble **07** catcall, summons, tweedle, warbler, wheeple **09** quail-call, quail-pipe

## whit

**03** bit, jot, rap **04** atom, dash, drop, fico, haet, ha'it, hate, hoot, iota, mite, snap, spot **05** aught, crumb, grain, piece, pinch, point, scrap, shred, speck, straw, trace **06** little **07** modicum, red cent **08** fragment, particle

## white

**03** wan **04** hoar, leuc-, leuk-, pale, pure **05** ashen, hoary, leuco-, leuko-, light, moral, pasty, waxen **06** albino, bright, honest, Pakeha, palagi, pallid **07** albumen, anaemic, niveous, upright

**08** innocent, reliable, spotless, virtuous **09** blameless, bloodless, burnished, stainless, undefiled **10** auspicious, colourless, favourable, honourable, immaculate **11** transparent, unblemished, unburnished **12** light-skinned

*Whites include:*

**04** ecru, grey, lily, opal, whey
**05** cream, ivory, milky, snowy
**06** argent, creamy, pearly, silver
**08** magnolia
**09** champagne, lily-white, snow-white
**11** silver-white

## white-collar

**06** office **08** clerical, salaried **09** executive, non-manual **12** professional

## whiten

**03** cam **04** calm, caum, fade, pale, snow **06** blanch, bleach **08** dealbate, etiolate, pipeclay **09** whitewash

## whitewash

**04** beat, best, drub, -gate, hide, lick **05** crush, paste **06** granny, hammer, thrash **07** clobber, conceal, cover up, cover-up, grannie, trounce **08** suppress **09** calcimine, deception, gloss over, Kalsomine® **10** camouflage **11** concealment, make light of **13** defeat utterly

## whittle

**03** cut, hew, use **04** fret, pare, trim **05** carve, erode, peach, shape, shave, use up **06** reduce, scrape **07** blanket, consume, eat away **08** diminish, wear away **09** undermine

## whole

**03** all, fit, lot, sum **04** full, hale, mint, unit, well **05** piece, sound, total, uncut **06** entire, entity, healed, intact, strong, unhurt **07** healthy, perfect **08** complete, ensemble, entirety, fullness, integral, sum total, totality, unbroken, unedited, unharmed **09** aggregate, inviolate, undamaged, undivided, uninjured **10** altogether, completely, everything, in one piece, unabridged **11** full-blooded
• **on the whole 06** mostly **07** as a rule **08** all in all **09** generally, in general, in the main **10** by and large **13** predominantly **14** for the most part

## wholehearted

**04** real, true, warm **06** hearty **07** devoted, earnest, genuine, sincere, zealous **08** complete, emphatic **09** committed, dedicated, heartfelt, unfeigned **10** passionate, unreserved, unstinting **11** boots and all, unqualified **12** enthusiastic

## wholeheartedly

**06** warmly **08** heartily **09** genuinely, sincerely **10** completely **12** emphatically, passionately, unreservedly

## wholesale

**04** mass **05** broad, great, total **06** en bloc **07** in gross, massive, totally

**08** outright, sweeping **09** extensive, massively **11** extensively, far-reaching, wide-ranging **12** all-inclusive **13** comprehensive **14** indiscriminate **15** comprehensively

## wholesome

**04** good, pure **05** clean, moral, sound, sweet **06** decent, proper **07** bracing, ethical, healthy, helpful, holesom **08** edifying, healsome, holesome, hygienic, physical, remedial, salutary, sanitary, sensible, virtuous **09** healthful, improving, righteous, uplifting **10** beneficial, healthsome, honourable, nourishing, nutritious, propitious, reasonable, refreshing, salubrious **11** respectable **12** invigorating, squeaky-clean

## wholly

**03** all **04** only **05** clear, fully, quite **06** in toto, purely **07** sheerly, totally, utterly **08** entirely **09** perfectly, tout à fait **10** absolutely, altogether, completely, thoroughly **11** exclusively **14** in every respect **15** comprehensively

## whoop

**02** ho! **03** cry **04** hoop, hoot, roar, yell **05** cheer, shout **06** holler, hurrah, scream, shriek

## whopper

**03** fib, lie **05** fable, giant, whale **07** cracker, mammoth, monster, plumper, slapper, stonker, swapper, swinger, swopper, untruth **08** colossus, scrouger **09** falsehood, leviathan, tall story **10** fairy story, socdolager, sogdolager **11** fabrication, sockdolager, sockdoliger, sockdologer **12** hippopotamus, slockdolager
*See also* **lie**

## whopping

**03** big **04** huge, mega, vast **05** giant, great, jumbo, large **07** immense, mammoth, massive, whaling **08** almighty, enormous, gigantic, great big, plonking, slapping, whacking **09** ginormous, humongous, thrashing, walloping **10** monumental, prodigious, staggering, tremendous **11** God-almighty **13** extraordinary

## whore

**03** pro, pug, tom **04** bawd, dell, drab, hoor, moll, punk, road, stew, tart **05** brass, broad, quail, quiff, stale, tramp, trull, wench **06** bulker, callet, geisha, harlot, hooker, mutton, plover **07** cocotte, floozie, hetaera, hostess, hustler, lorette, Paphian, pinnace, polecat, rent-boy, trollop, venture **08** bona-roba, callgirl, dolly-mop, magdalen, strumpet **09** courtesan, hierodule, loose fish **10** cockatrice, convertite, fancy woman, loose woman, prostitute, rough trade, vizard-mask **11** fallen woman, fille de joie, laced mutton, night-walker, poule de luxe, public woman, working girl **12** fille des rues, scarlet woman, street-walker **13** grande cocotte **14** lady of the night, woman of the town
*See also* **prostitute**

## whorehouse
**03** kip **04** crib, stew **06** bagnio, bordel **07** brothel, Corinth **08** bordello, cathouse, hothouse, red light **10** bawdy-house, flash-house **12** knocking-shop, leaping-house **13** sporting house, vaulting-house **14** house of ill fame, massage parlour **15** disorderly house

## whorl
**04** coil, loop, turn **05** helix, twirl, twist **06** spiral, volute, vortex **07** calicle, calycle, corolla **08** calycule, gyration, verticil, volution **09** corkscrew **11** convolution

## wicked
◇ *anagram indicator* **03** ace, bad, def, fab, ill, rad **04** cool, evil, foul, mean, mega, neat, vile, wick **05** awful, boffo, brill, cruel, felon, nasty, wrong **06** divine, fierce, groovy, guilty, impish, severe, sinful, unholy, unkind, way-out **07** amazing, corrupt, crucial, debased, harmful, heinous, immoral, intense, naughty, radical, roguish, ungodly, unlucky, vicious **08** clinking, depraved, devilish, dreadful, fabulous, heavenly, perverse, rascally, shameful, spiteful, stonking, terrible, terrific **09** abandoned, admirable, atrocious, brilliant, difficult, dissolute, egregious, excellent, fantastic, felonious, high-viced, injurious, miscreant, nefarious, offensive, scelerate, worthless **10** abominable, evil-minded, facinorous, flagitious, iniquitous, not half bad, scandalous, unpleasant, villainous **11** distressing, facinerious, mischievous, sensational, the business, troublesome, unrighteous **12** black-hearted, second to none, unprincipled **14** out of this world

## wickedness
**03** ill, sin **04** evil **06** naught **07** impiety, pravity, villany **08** atrocity, enormity, evilness, foulness, iniquity, vileness, villainy **09** amorality, depravity, reprobacy **10** corruption, immorality, sinfulness **11** abomination, corruptness, heinousness **12** devilishness, fiendishness, shamefulness **13** dissoluteness **15** unrighteousness

## wickerwork
**05** ratan **06** rattan, wattle, wicker **10** basket-work, wattle-work

## wide
**01** w **04** full, vast, wily **05** ample, baggy, broad, fully, great, loose, roomy **06** astray, astute, remote **07** dilated, distant, general, immense **08** expanded, extended, spacious **09** all the way, capacious, extensive, off course, off target **10** completely, off the mark **11** far-reaching, wide-ranging **12** latitudinous **13** comprehensive **15** to the full extent

## wide-awake
**04** keen, wary **05** alert, aware, sharp **06** astute, roused **07** heedful, wakened **08** vigilant, watchful **09** conscious, observant, on the ball **10** fully awake, on the alert, on your toes **11** quick-witted **12** on the qui vive

## wide-eyed
**04** open **05** dazed, frank, fresh, naive **06** amazed, simple **07** angelic, artless, natural, shocked, stunned **08** dewy-eyed, gullible, innocent, open-eyed, startled, trustful, trusting **09** astounded, childlike, credulous, guileless, ingenuous, staggered, surprised, unworldly **10** astonished, bewildered, bowled over, confounded, gobsmacked, taken aback **11** dumbfounded, open-mouthed **12** lost for words, unsuspecting **13** flabbergasted, inexperienced, knocked for six, thunderstruck **15** unsophisticated

## widely
**07** broadly **09** generally **11** extensively **15** comprehensively

## widen
**06** dilate, expand, extend, flanch, let out, spread **07** broaden, distend, enlarge, flaunch, stretch **08** increase

## wide-open
**04** open, wide **06** gaping, spread **07** exposed **09** outspread **10** vulnerable **11** defenceless, susceptible, unfortified, unprotected **12** outstretched

## wide-ranging
**05** broad **08** sweeping, thorough **09** extensive, important, momentous, universal **10** widespread **11** far-reaching, scattershot, significant **13** comprehensive, thoroughgoing

## widespread
**04** rife **05** broad **06** common, global **07** general, prolate **08** far-flung, sweeping **09** extensive, pervasive, prevalent, universal, unlimited, wholesale **10** wall-to-wall **11** far-reaching

## widow
**04** sati **05** widdy **06** relict, suttee **07** bereave, dowager **08** feme sole, war widow **10** grass widow **11** hempen widow **12** queen dowager

## width
**01** w **04** beam, span **05** girth, range, reach, scope **06** extent **07** breadth, compass, measure **08** diameter, latitude, wideness **09** amplitude, broadness, largeness, thickness **13** extensiveness

## wield
**03** ply, use **04** gain, have, hold, play, rule, sway, wave, weld, wild, wind **05** apply, enjoy, exert, shake, sownd, swing **06** employ, handle, manage **07** command, control, possess, utilize **08** brandish, exercise, flourish, maintain **10** manipulate

## wife
**01** w **02** ux **03** rib **04** dame, frau, lady, mate **05** bride, dutch, femme, queen, woman **06** missis, missus, spouse, vahine, wahine **07** consort, hostess, old lady, partner **08** helpmate,

helpmeet, princess **09** child-wife, companion, concubine, first lady, other half **10** better half, her indoors, stepmother **11** little woman, sister-in-law **12** kickie-wickie, married woman **13** daughter-in-law **14** the little woman

## wig
**03** jiz, tie **04** gizz, jasy, jazy **05** caxon, Irish, jasey, major, scold, syrup **06** bagwig, bobwig, Brutus, peruke, rebuke, tie-wig, toupee, toupet **07** buzz-wig, periwig, Ramilie, scratch, spencer **08** perruque, postiche, Ramilies, Ramillie **09** hairpiece, Ramillies **10** full-bottom, scratch-wig **14** transformation

## wiggle
**03** wag **04** jerk **05** shake, twist **06** jiggle, squirm, twitch, waggle, writhe **07** wriggle

## wild
◇ *anagram indicator* **03** mad, shy **04** bush, daft, keen, nuts, rash **05** angry, crazy, feral, livid, messy, myall, nutty, potty, rough, rowdy, waste, weald, wield **06** absurd, barren, casual, chance, choppy, desert, ferine, fierce, fuming, gallus, raging, random, rugged, savage, stormy, unruly, untame, untidy, unwise **07** agitato, aimless, bananas, berserk, blazing, bonkers, brutish, enraged, excited, fervent, foolish, frantic, furious, gallows, lawless, natural, rampant, riotous, ropable, salvage, tousled, uncouth, unkempt, untamed, violent, wayward **08** agitated, agrestal, blustery, chimeric, demented, desolate, fanciful, forsaken, frenzied, incensed, reckless, romantic, ropeable, terrific, unbroken, uncombed, vehement, warragal, warragle, warragul, warrigal **09** agrestial, arbitrary, barbarous, enjoyable, fanatical, fantastic, ferocious, foolhardy, haphazard, hit-or-miss, imprudent, impulsive, irregular, primitive, turbulent, unsettled **10** accidental, boisterous, chimerical, disordered, disorderly, distracted, distraught, fortuitous, hopping mad, incidental, infuriated, irrational, licentious, outrageous, passionate, ridiculous **11** approximate, dishevelled, extravagant, fantastical, impractical, purposeless, tempestuous, uncivilized, uninhabited, unpopulated **12** enthusiastic, ferae naturae, inhospitable, out of control, preposterous, unconsidered, uncontrolled, uncultivated, ungovernable, unmanageable, unrestrained **13** impracticable, serendipitous, undisciplined, uninhabitable **14** beside yourself, indiscriminate, skimble-skamble, uncontrollable, undomesticated
• **run wild** ◇ *anagram indicator* **04** lamp, riot **05** feral **07** rampage

## wild animal
*see* **animal**

## wilderness
05 waste, wilds 06 desert, jungle
09 wasteland

## wild flower
*see* **flower**

## wildlife
05 fauna 07 animals

## wildly
◇ *anagram indicator* 07 angrily, noisily
08 absurdly, casually 09 aimlessly,
defiantly, foolishly, furiously, riotously
10 recklessly 11 arbitrarily, chaotically,
haphazardly 12 anarchically,
boisterously, outrageously,
rebelliously, ridiculously
13 extravagantly, fantastically,
irresponsibly 14 preposterously,
uncontrollably, unmethodically,
unrestrainedly

## wilds
04 wops 06 desert 07 outback, the
bush, wop-wops 08 the scrub 09 the
mallee, the sticks, wasteland
10 backblocks, the boonies, wilderness
11 remote areas 12 back of Bourke, the
boondocks 15 the back of beyond

## wiles
05 fraud, guile, ploys, ruses 06 deceit,
dodges, tricks 07 cunning, devices
08 cheating, trickery 09 chicanery,
deception 10 artfulness, craftiness,
manoeuvres, stratagems, subterfuge
12 contrivances

## wilful
06 dogged, mulish 07 planned,
wayward, willing 08 contrary,
obdurate, perverse, stubborn, willyard,
willyart 09 conscious, obstinate, pig-
headed, voluntary 10 calculated,
deliberate, determined, headstrong,
inflexible, refractory, self-willed,
unyielding 11 intentional, intractable
12 intransigent, premeditated
14 uncompromising

## will
02 'll 03 aim, way 04 lust, mind, Self,
want, wish 05 fancy, leave, order
06 astray, choice, choose, compel,
confer, decree, desire, devise, direct,
intend, option, ordain, pass on 07 at a
loss, command, feeling, purpose,
require, resolve 08 attitude, bequeath,
decision, hand down, pass down,
pleasure, transfer, volition 09 dispose
of, intention, testament, willpower
10 bewildered, discretion, preference,
resolution 11 disposition, inclination,
prerogative 13 determination
14 purposefulness

## William
02 Wm 04 Bill, Will 05 Billy, Willy

## willing
02 on 04 game, glad, keen 05 eager,
happy, prone, ready 06 chosen
07 content, pleased, up for it
08 amenable, biddable, disposed,
inclined, prepared, so-minded
09 agreeable, compliant, volitient,
voluntary 10 consenting, favourable
11 co-operative, intentional
12 enthusiastic, well-disposed

## willingly
04 leve, lief, soon 05 lieve 06 freely,
gladly 07 eagerly, happily, readily
08 by choice, in a hurry 09 like a shot
10 cheerfully 11 voluntarily 12 nothing
loath 14 unhesitatingly

## willingness
04 will, wish 06 desire, favour
07 consent 08 volition 09 agreement,
readiness 10 compliance, enthusiasm
11 disposition, inclination
12 complaisance 13 agreeableness

## will-o'-the-wisp
06 min min 07 fen-fire, spunkie
08 wildfire 09 nightfire 11 fatuous fire,
ignis fatuus 12 Jack-o'-lantern 13 friar's
lantern

## willow
04 sale, seal 05 osier, salix, sauch,
saugh, withy 06 sallow

## willowy
04 slim, tall 05 lithe 06 limber, lissom,
supple, svelte 07 slender 08 flexible,
graceful 09 lithesome, sylph-like

## willpower
04 grit, will 05 drive 07 resolve
10 commitment, doggedness,
resolution 11 persistence, self-
command, self-control, self-mastery
13 determination 14 self-discipline,
strength of will

## willy-nilly
08 by chance, perforce, randomly
10 carelessly 11 arbitrarily,
haphazardly, irregularly, necessarily,
of necessity 12 compulsorily, nolens
volens 14 unmethodically

## wilt
03 ebb, sag, wot 04 fade, fail, flag, flop,
sink, wane, woot 05 droop, faint, taint
06 lessen, weaken, wither 07 dwindle,
shrivel 08 diminish, grow less, languish

## wily
03 fly, sly 04 foxy, wide 05 sharp
06 artful, astute, crafty, shifty, shrewd,
tricky 07 crooked, cunning, versute
08 cheating, guileful, scheming
09 deceitful, deceptive, designing,
underhand 10 intriguing, streetwise

## wimp
03 wet 04 clot, drip, fool, jerk, nerd,
sook, tonk, weed, wuss 05 clown,
softy, wally 07 milksop 10 namby-
pamby

## wimpish
03 wet 04 soft, weak 05 cissy, weedy,
wussy 06 drippy, effete, feeble
08 pathetic, timorous 09 spineless
10 irresolute, namby-pamby
11 ineffective, ineffectual

## win
03 get, net, pot 04 earn, gain, mine
05 carry, catch, penny, reach 06 allure,
attain, effect, obtain, open up, result,
secure 07 achieve, acquire, collect,
conquer, mastery, prevail, procure,
receive, succeed, success, triumph,
victory 08 atchieve, carry off,
conquest, overcome, persuade
09 come first, win the day

10 accomplish, strike gold 11 come in
first, finish first, squeeze home 12 be
victorious, come out on top, turn up
trumps, win hands down 13 hit the
jackpot, squeak through 14 achieve
success
• **win over** 04 sway 05 bribe, charm
06 allure, engage, nobble 07 attract,
buy over, convert 08 convince,
persuade, win round 09 influence, talk
round 10 bring round, conciliate
11 prevail upon

## wince
04 jerk, jump, kick, reel 05 cower,
quail, start 06 blench, cringe, flinch,
recoil, roller, shrink 08 draw back
09 pull a face

## wind
◇ *anagram indicator* 02 go 03 air
04 bend, burp, coil, curl, furl, gale,
gust, haul, hint, loop, puff, reel, roll,
turn, veer, wrap 05 blast, curve, hoist,
snake, twine, twist, weave, wield
06 breath, breeze, enfold, ramble,
spiral, writhe, zigzag 07 bluster,
conceit, current, deviate, draught,
meander, turning, wreathe, wriggle
08 encircle 10 air-current, flatulence,
suggestion 12 twist and turn

*Winds include:*

04 berg, bise, bora, east, föhn, helm
05 Eurus, north, Notus, trade, zonda
06 Auster, Boreas, breeze, buster,
   doctor, El Niño, La Niña, levant,
   samiel, simoom, zephyr
07 Aquilon, austral, chinook,
   cyclone, etesian, gregale,
   khamsin, meltemi, mistral,
   monsoon, pampero, sirocco,
   tornado, twister
08 Argestes, Favonian, Favonius,
   libeccio, westerly, williwaw
09 harmattan, hurricane, nor'wester,
   snow eater, southerly, whirlwind
10 Cape doctor, Euroclydon,
   prevailing, tramontana, wet
   chinook, willy-willy
11 anticyclone
15 southerly buster

• **get wind of** 07 learn of 08 discover
09 hear about 12 find out about
13 become aware of
• **in the wind** 07 likely 08 expected,
probable 10 on the cards 13 about to
happen
• **put the wind up** 05 alarm, daunt,
panic, scare, spook 06 boggle, rattle
07 agitate, perturb, startle, unnerve
08 frighten 10 discourage 13 sound
the alarm
• **wind down** 04 slow, stop 05 chill,
relax 06 cool it, ease up, lessen,
reduce, unwind 07 decline, dwindle,
subside 08 calm down, chill out, de-
stress, diminish, slow down 09 hang
loose, lighten up 10 slacken off, take
it easy 11 come to an end, quieten
down 12 bring to an end 13 let
yourself go, put your feet up 14 take
things easy 15 let your hair down
• **wind up** 03 end, kid, rib 04 fool,
furl, goof, span, stop 05 anger,

## windbag

annoy, close, end up, hoist, tease, trick, uptie **06** excite, finish, settle **07** agitate, tighten **08** conclude, finalize, finish up, irritate **09** close down, liquidate, make fun of, terminate **10** disconcert **12** bring to an end, find yourself **13** bring to a close **15** pull someone's leg

## windbag

**04** bore **06** gasbag, gossip **07** blether, boaster **08** bigmouth, braggart

## winded

**06** puffed **07** panting **09** out of puff, puffed out **10** breathless **11** out of breath

## windfall

**04** find **05** manna, motza **06** caduac, motser, motzer **07** bonanza, godsend, jackpot **12** stroke of luck **13** treasure-trove

## winding

◇ *anagram indicator* **04** mazy, turn **06** creeky, spiral **07** bending, coiling, crankle, crooked, curving, devious, sinuate, sinuous, turning, twining **08** flexuose, flexuous, indirect, sinuated, tortuous, twisting **09** meandrian, meandrous **10** circuitous, convoluted, meandering, roundabout, serpentine **11** anfractuous **12** serpentinous **14** crinkle-crankle

## window

**05** light **07** opening

*Windows include:*

**03** bay, bow
**04** pane, rose, sash, shop
**05** oriel, Velux®
**06** dormer, French, lancet, louvre, Norman, screen, ticket
**07** compass, lucarne, sliding
**08** astragal, bull's eye, casement, fanlight, porthole, skylight
**09** decorated, mullioned, patio door
**10** windscreen
**11** oeil-de-boeuf
**12** double-glazed, early English, quarterlight, stained glass
**13** double-glazing, perpendicular
**14** Catherine wheel
**15** secondary-glazed

## windpipe

**05** pipes **06** larynx, throat **07** pharynx, trachea, weasand **08** thrapple, thropple, throttle **11** weasand-pipe

## windswept

**04** open **05** bleak, blowy, messy, windy **06** barren, untidy **07** exposed, in a mess, ruffled, tousled, unkempt **08** desolate **09** windblown **10** disordered **11** dishevelled, unprotected, unsheltered

## windward

**04** luff **07** weather
• **beat to windward** **04** turn, work **06** laveer
• **to windward** **02** up **05** aloof **08** a-weather

## windy

**04** wild **05** blowy, gusty, nervy, timid, wordy **06** afraid, breezy, on edge, prolix, scared, stormy, turgid, uneasy **07** anxious, chicken, nervous, pompous, squally, ventose, verbose **08** blustery, rambling, stressed **09** bombastic, garrulous, windswept **10** frightened, long-winded **11** tempestuous

## wine

**02** en- **03** eno-, oen-, oin-, vin **04** oeno-, oino-, vino **05** plonk

*Wines include:*

**03** Dão, dry, red, sec
**04** Asti, brut, cask, Cava, fino, hock, port, rosé, sack, Sekt, Tent
**05** blush, bombo, Douro, Fitou, Gamay, house, Mâcon, Médoc, plonk, Rioja, Soave, straw, sweet, Syrah, table, Tavel, Tokay, tonic, white
**06** Alsace, Barolo, Barsac, Beaune, canary, claret, grappa, Graves, Malaga, Malbec, Merlot, mulled, Muscat, Pontac, sherry, Shiraz
**07** alicant, Amarone, Auslese, Barbera, Bunyuls, Chablis, Chianti, Cinsaut, demi-sec, Madeira, Margaux, Marsala, moselle, oloroso, Orvieto, Pomerol, retsina, sangria, vintage, Vouvray
**08** Alicante, Bordeaux, Brunello, bucellas, Burgundy, Carignan, Cinsault, Dolcetto, Frascati, Garnacha, Glühwein, Grenache, house red, jerepigo, Kabinett, Malvasia, Marsanne, Montilla, Muscadet, muscatel, Nebbiolo, New World, Palomino, Pauillac, Pinotage, prosecco, Riesling, Rousanne, ruby port, Sancerre, Sauterne, Sémillon, Spätlese, Spumante, St Julien, Vermouth, vin santo
**09** Bardolino, Carignane, champagne, Colombard, dry sherry, fortified, Frizzante, Hermitage, Lambrusco, Langue d'Oc, Minervois, Pinot Gris, Pinot Noir, Sauternes, sparkling, St-Émilion, Tarragona, tawny port, Trebbiano, Ugni Blanc, white port, Zinfandel
**10** Barbaresco, Beaujolais, Chambertin, Chardonnay, Constantia, Grignolino, house white, Manzanilla, Mateus Rosé, Monastrell, Muscadelle, Piesporter, Pinot Blanc, Sangiovese, Verdicchio, vinho verde
**11** alcohol-free, amontillado, Chenin Blanc, Niersteiner, Pinot Grigio, Pouilly-Fumé, Rüdesheimer, Steinberger, sweet sherry, Tempranillo, vintage port
**12** Blanc de Noirs, Côtes du Rhône, Johannisberg, medium sherry, Pedro Ximénez, Ruby Cabernet, Tinta Barroca, Valpolicella
**13** Blanc de Blancs, Cabernet Franc,
Château Lafite, Liebfraumilch, Montepulciano, Pouilly-Fuissé
**14** Crémant d'Alsace, Crémant de Loire, Lacrima Christi, Sauvignon Blanc
**15** Crozes-Hermitage, Gewürztraminer, lachryma Christi

*Wine-bottle sizes include:*

**06** flagon, magnum
**08** jeroboam, rehoboam
**09** balthazar
**10** methuselah, salmanazar
**11** Marie-Jeanne
**14** nebuchadnezzar

*See also* **bottle**
• **wine-grower** **05** viner **08** vigneron

## wine glass

**05** flute, glass **06** goblet **07** balloon **08** schooner **09** straw-stem

## wing

**02** el **03** ala, arm, fan, fly, set, van **04** flit, move, part, pass, race, sail, side, soar, vane, waft, zoom **05** alula, flank, flock, glide, group, hurry, penny, pinna, right, speed **06** annexe, branch, circle, flight, hasten, pinion, travel **07** adjunct, coterie, faction, section, segment **08** grouping **09** extension, liverwing **10** attachment **11** parascenium
• **wing it** **04** vamp **05** ad-lib **06** busk it **09** play by ear **11** extemporize **15** speak off the cuff

## wingless

◇ *ends deletion indicator*

## wink

**04** pink **05** blink, eliad, flash, gleam, glint **06** eyliad, illiad, moment, second **07** connive, eyeliad, flicker, flutter, glimmer, glitter, instant, nictate, sparkle, twinkle **08** oeillade **09** nictation, nictitate **10** glimmering **11** nictitation, split second
• **wink at** **06** ignore **07** condone, neglect **08** overlook, pass over **09** disregard **14** take no notice of **15** turn a blind eye to

## winkle

**04** pupu, worm **05** flush, force, prise **07** draw out, extract **09** extricate

## winner

**03** ace, dux **05** champ **06** top dog, victor **08** champion, prizeman **09** conqueror, medallist **10** prizewoman, vanquisher **11** prizewinner, title-holder, world-beater **13** Nobel laureate

## winning

**02** up **05** sweet **06** lovely **07** amiable, winsome **08** alluring, charming, engaging, fetching, pleasing, unbeaten **09** beguiling, endearing **10** attractive, bewitching, conquering, delightful, enchanting, persuasive, successful, triumphant, undefeated, victorious **11** captivating, vanquishing **13** prepossessing

## winnings
**05** booty, gains, prize **06** prizes, spoils, velvet **07** jackpot, profits, takings **08** proceeds **10** prize money

## winnow
**03** fan, fly, van **04** comb, cull, flap, part, sift, sort, waft **06** divide, screen, select **07** diffuse, flutter **08** separate **09** ventilate

## winsome
**05** sweet **06** comely, lovely, pretty **07** amiable **08** alluring, charming, cheerful, engaging, fetching, pleasant, pleasing **09** appealing, beguiling, endearing **10** attractive, bewitching, delectable, delightful, enchanting **11** captivating **13** prepossessing

## wintry
**03** icy, raw **04** cold, cool **05** bleak, harsh, snowy **06** arctic, biting, chilly, dismal, frosty, frozen, hiemal, stormy **07** brumous, glacial, hostile **08** desolate, freezing, hibernal, piercing **09** cheerless **10** Decemberly, unfriendly **11** Decemberish

## wipe
**03** dab, dry, mop, rub **04** blow, dust, jibe, null, scar, swab **05** brand, brush, clean, clear, dicht, dight, erase, purge, scrub, sweep, swipe **06** cancel, forget, reject, remove, sponge, strike **07** cleanse, deterge, expunct, expunge, sarcasm, take off **08** absterge, get rid of, take away **09** eliminate, eradicate **12** handkerchief
• **wipe out 03** zap **04** kill, null, raze **05** erase, purge, sweep, waste **06** efface, murder, rub out, sponge **07** abolish, blot out, destroy, expunct, expunge **08** blow away, decimate, demolish, massacre **09** eliminate, eradicate, extirpate, liquidate, polish off **10** annihilate, obliterate **11** exterminate

## wire
**04** bind, coil **05** cable, snare **06** aerial, needle, tip-off **07** connect, protect, support, warning **08** telegram **09** telegraph, telephone **10** pickpocket **11** information **13** finishing line

## wire-pulling
**04** pull **05** clout **08** intrigue, plotting, scheming **09** influence **10** conspiring **12** manipulation

## wiry
**04** lean, wavy **05** rough, tough **06** coarse, sinewy, strong **08** muscular

## Wisconsin
**02** WI **03** Wis

## wisdom
**05** sense **06** genius, reason, sanity **07** insight **08** learning, prudence, sagacity, sapience **09** erudition, foresight, judgement, knowledge **10** astuteness, experience **11** common sense, discernment, penetration, skilfulness, speculation **12** intelligence **13** comprehension, enlightenment, judiciousness, understanding **14** circumspection

## wise
**03** way **04** sage, wice **05** aware, godly, pious, sound, weise, weize, witty **06** astute, clever, manner, owlish, shrewd **07** erudite, knowing, learned, politic, prudent, sapient, skilful **08** discreet, educated, informed, rational, sensible **09** judicious, sagacious **10** discerning, far-sighted, perceptive, proficient, reasonable **11** circumspect, common-sense, enlightened, experienced, intelligent, long-sighted, well-advised **12** well-informed **13** knowledgeable, sophisticated, understanding
• **put wise 04** tell, warn **05** alert **06** clue in, fill in, inform, notify, tip off, wise up **08** apprise **10** intimate to **15** put in the picture
• **wise man**

*The Three Wise Men:*

**06** Caspar
**08** Melchior
**09** Balthasar

*See also* **sage**

## wiseacre
**03** owl **05** Solon **07** wise guy **08** wiseling **09** Gothamite, smart alec **10** clever dick **11** smartypants

## wisecrack
**03** gag, pun **04** barb, gibe, jest, joke, quip **05** funny **06** in-joke **08** one-liner **09** witticism

## wisely
**06** sagely **07** clearly, soundly **08** sensibly, shrewdly **09** advisedly, knowingly **10** rationally **11** sagaciously **12** perceptively **13** intelligently

## wish
**03** ask, bid, wis, yen **04** hope, know, long, lust, need, pine, urge, want, whim, will, wist **05** covet, crave, fancy, order, yearn **06** aspire, desire, direct, hanker, hunger, liking, prefer, thirst **07** believe, bewitch, bidding, command, craving, longing, request, require **08** fondness, instruct, yearning **09** hankering, recommend **10** aspiration, preference **11** inclination, instruction, malediction
• **best wishes 04** best **08** mazeltov, well-wish **09** good-speed

## wishy-washy
**04** flat, pale, thin, weak **05** bland, vapid **06** feeble, sloppy, watery **07** diluted, insipid, vanilla **09** tasteless **10** namby-pamby **11** ineffective, ineffectual, watered-down **12** milk-and-water

## wisp
**04** lock, tuft, wase **05** flock, piece, plume, shred, twist **06** strand, thread

## wispy
**04** fine, thin **05** faint, frail, light **06** flimsy, slight **07** fragile **08** delicate, ethereal, gossamer, straggly **10** attenuated **13** insubstantial

## wistful
**03** sad **06** dreamy, intent, musing **07** earnest, forlorn, longing, pensive, wishful **08** dreaming, mournful, yearning **09** regretful **10** meditative, melancholy, reflective, thoughtful **12** disconsolate **13** contemplative

## wistfully
**05** sadly **09** forlornly, longingly, pensively **10** mournfully **11** plaintively **12** thoughtfully

## wit
**03** wag **04** know, mind, nous, salt **05** comic, joker, sense **06** banter, brains, esprit, gagman, humour, levity, reason, wisdom **07** discern, insight, marbles, sparkle **08** badinage, comedian, concetto, drollery, gumption, humorist, merum sal, repartee, sagacity, satirist **09** Attic salt, bel esprit, eutrapely, faculties, funniness, ingenuity, intellect, invention, judgement, mother wit, recognize, wittiness **10** astuteness, cleverness, eutrapelia, jocularity, liveliness, shrewdness **11** common sense, imagination, information, waggishness **12** homme d'esprit, intelligence **13** facetiousness, understanding

## witch
**04** mage, wich, wych **05** crone, magus **08** magician

*Witches, witch doctors and wizards include:*

**03** hag, hex
**05** Hecat, lamia, sibyl, weird
**06** Hecate, magian, mganga, shaman, voodoo, wisard, zendik
**07** angekok, carline, sangoma, warlock, wise man
**08** angekkok, conjurer, marabout, night-hag
**09** enchanter, galdragon, occultist, pythoness, sorceress, wise woman, witch-wife
**10** besom-rider, craigfluke, reim-kennar
**11** enchantress, gyre-carline, medicine man, necromancer, thaumaturge
**12** Weird Sisters
**13** thaumaturgist

*Witch- and wizard-related terms include:*

**03** hex
**04** mojo, muti, wart
**05** charm, coven, goety, magic, spell, wicca
**06** cackle, potion, Sabbat, voodoo, voudou
**07** cantrip, gramary, hag-seed, pricker, Sabbath, sorcery
**08** black art, black cat, cauldron, diablery, familiar, gramarye, pishogue, wizardry
**09** diablerie, enchanted, occultism, the occult, witch's hat
**10** black magic, broomstick, divination, necromancy, witchcraft
**11** apotropaism, conjuration, enchantment, incantation,

thaumaturgy, the black art, witch-finder
**12** witching hour
**14** Walpurgis night

### witchcraft
**03** obi **04** obia **05** magic, obeah, spell, wicca **06** makatu, voodoo **07** myalism, sorcery **08** wizardry **09** occultism, the occult **10** black magic, divination, necromancy **11** conjuration, enchantment, incantation, the black art

### witch doctor
**06** mganga, shaman **07** angekok, sangoma **08** magician, marabout **11** medicine man **13** medicine woman

### witch hunt
**08** hounding **09** hue and cry **11** McCarthyism

### with
◊ *juxtaposition indicator* **01** w **02** by, in, of **03** cum, mit **04** avec **05** among, using **06** beside, having **08** together **09** including **10** containing, possessing **13** accompanied by **14** in the company of

### withdraw
◊ *deletion indicator* **02** go **04** pull, walk **05** annul, leave, unsay **06** abjure, call in, cancel, cry off, depart, detach, go away, opt out, recall, recant, recede, recoil, remove, repair, retire, revoke, secede, shrink **07** abolish, back out, call off, deflect, draw out, drop out, extract, give way, go aside, inshell, nullify, pull out, rescind, retract, retreat, scratch, subduce, subduct, take out **08** disclaim, draw back, evacuate, fall back, pull away, pull back, separate, step down, subtract, take away, take back **09** turn aside **10** declare off, shrink back **11** contract out, discontinue **14** absent yourself

### withdrawal
**03** tap **04** exit **06** exodus, recall, shrink **07** Dunkirk, removal, retiral, retreat **08** backword, delivery, pullback, recourse **09** breakaway, departure, disavowal, recession, revulsion, secession **10** abjuration, disclaimer, drawing out, evacuation, extraction, retirement, revocation, subduction, taking away **11** abstraction, drawing back, falling back, pulling back, recantation, repudiation, subtraction **13** disengagement

### withdrawn
**03** shy **05** aloof, quiet **06** hidden, remote, silent **07** distant, private, retired **08** alienate, detached, isolated, reserved, retiring, secluded, solitary, taciturn **09** introvert, shrinking **10** unsociable **11** introverted, out-of-the-way **12** unresponsive **13** unforthcoming **15** uncommunicative

### wither
**03** die, dry **04** fade, sear, sere, wane, welk, welt, wilt **05** arefy, blast, decay, droop, dry up, taint, waste **06** blight, die off, gizzen, perish, scorch, shrink,

weaken **07** decline, destroy, dwindle, miff off, mortify, shrivel **08** fade away, languish **09** disappear, humiliate **12** disintegrate

### withering
**06** deadly, fading **08** autumnal, blasting, scathing, scornful, snubbing, wounding **09** blighting, scorching **10** marcescent, mortifying **11** destructive, devastating, humiliating **12** contemptuous, death-dealing

### withhold
◊ *deletion indicator* **04** curb, hide, keep, stop **05** check **06** deduct, detain, refuse, retain **07** conceal, control, decline, forbear, repress, reserve **08** hold back, keep back, postpone, restrain, subtract, suppress **11** keep in check

### within
◊ *hidden indicator* ◊ *insertion indicator* **02** in **04** into **05** intra **06** entire, herein, inside **07** indoors, not over **08** inside of, inwardly **09** in reach of **10** enclosed by **12** surrounded by

### with it
**02** in **03** hep, hip **04** cool **05** funky, natty, ritzy, vogue **06** glitzy, groovy, modern, modish, snazzy, trendy **08** up-to-date **10** all the rage **11** fashionable, progressive **12** contemporary **13** up-to-the-minute **14** fashion-forward

### without
◊ *containment indicator* ◊ *deletion indicator* **01** a-, x **02** an-, ex, w/o **03** sen **04** less, sans, sine **06** beyond, except, unless **07** lacking, needing, outside, wanting **08** free from, in need of **09** not having, outwardly **10** deprived of

### withstand
**04** bear, defy, face **05** brave, fight, stand **06** endure, hinder, oppose, resist, take on, thwart **07** hold off, hold out, last out, survive, weather **08** confront, cope with, tolerate, tough out **09** put up with, stand fast, stand firm, stand up to **10** tough it out **14** hold your ground **15** stand your ground

### witless
**04** daft, dull, nuts **05** barmy, crazy, inane, loony, loopy, nutty, potty, silly **06** cuckoo, mental, raving, stupid **07** bonkers, foolish, idiotic, moronic, unaware **08** doolally, gaumless, gormless, mindless **09** cretinous, imbecilic, senseless, up the wall **10** half-witted **11** empty-headed, off the rails, unconscious **12** mad as a hatter, off your chump **13** off your rocker, unintelligent **14** wrong in the head

### witness
**03** see **04** mark, note, show, sign, view **05** prove, see in, teste, watch **06** affirm, attest, depose, evince, expert, look on, notice, obtest, record, verify, viewer **07** bear out, confirm, endorse, observe, support, testify, vouchee, watcher **08** deponent, evidence, looker-on, observer, onlooker, perceive, speak for, validate **09** attestant, authority, bystander, spectator, testifier,

testimony **10** eyewitness, man of skill **11** bear witness, compurgator, corroborate, countersign **12** be evidence of, give evidence
• **bear witness 04** aver, show **05** prove **06** adjure, affirm, assert, attest, evince, record, verify **07** certify, confirm, declare, display, endorse, testify **08** evidence, manifest, vouch for **10** asseverate **11** corroborate, demonstrate

### witter
**04** chat **06** babble, drivel, gabble, gossip, jabber, patter, rattle **07** blather, blether, chatter, twaddle, twattle, twitter

### witticism
**03** hit, pun **04** jibe, joke, quip **06** bon mot **07** epigram, riposte **08** one-liner, repartee **09** impromptu, wisecrack **10** jeu d'esprit, pleasantry **11** play on words
*See also* **joke**

### wittingly
**08** by design, wilfully **09** knowingly, on purpose, purposely, studiedly, willingly **10** designedly **11** consciously **12** calculatedly, deliberately **13** intentionally

### witty
**04** wise **05** comic, droll, funny, light, salty, smart **06** clever, lively **07** amusing, jocular, lambent, waggish **08** discreet, fanciful, humorous, original, pregnant, sensible **09** brilliant, conceited, facetious, ingenious, sarcastic, sparkling, spiritual, spirituel, whimsical **11** coruscating, sharp-witted, spirituelle

### wizard
**03** ace, hex **04** good, star, whiz **05** adept, great, super, witch **06** expert, genius, master, superb, wisard **07** hotshot, maestro, prodigy, warlock, wise man **08** conjurer, magician, smashing, sorcerer, terrific, virtuoso **09** brilliant, enchanter, enjoyable, fantastic, occultist, wonderful **10** delightful, marvellous, tremendous **11** necromancer, sensational, thaumaturge
*See also* **witch**

### wizened
**04** thin, worn **05** lined **07** dried up, gnarled **08** shrunken, withered, wrinkled **10** shrivelled

### wobble
◊ *anagram indicator* **04** rock, sway **05** quake, shake, waver **06** coggle, dither, dodder, quaver, quiver, seesaw, teeter, totter, tremor, wabble **07** precess, quaking, shoggle, stagger, tremble, vibrate **08** hesitate **09** fluctuate, oscillate, vacillate, vibration **11** oscillation **12** shilly-shally, unsteadiness, wibble-wobble

### wobbly
◊ *anagram indicator* **05** shaky, wonky **06** uneven, unsafe **07** doddery, rickety **08** unstable, unsteady **09** doddering,

quavering, teetering, tottering, trembling **10** unbalanced

## Wodehouse
**02** PG

## woe
**02** wo **03** sad, wae **04** bale, dool, dule, pain **05** agony, curse, doole, gloom, grief, sorry, tears, trial **06** burden, misery, sorrow, tsuris **07** anguish, sadness, trouble, tsouris **08** calamity, disaster, distress, hardship, wretched **09** adversity, dejection, heartache, suffering **10** affliction, depression, heartbreak, melancholy, misfortune **11** tribulation, unhappiness **12** wretchedness

## woebegone
**03** sad **04** blue **06** gloomy **07** doleful, forlorn, tearful **08** dejected, downcast, mournful, troubled, wretched **09** long-faced, miserable, sorrowful **10** dispirited, lugubrious **11** crestfallen, downhearted, tear-stained **12** disconsolate **13** grief-stricken **14** down in the mouth

## woeful
◇ *anagram indicator* **03** bad, sad **04** mean, poor **05** awful, cruel, lousy, sorry, waefu' **06** feeble, gloomy, paltry, rotten, tragic, waeful **07** doleful, unhappy, waesome **08** dreadful, grieving, grievous, hopeless, mournful, pathetic, pitiable, shocking, terrible, wretched **09** afflicted, appalling, miserable, sorrowful **10** calamitous, deplorable, disastrous, inadequate, lamentable **11** disgraceful, distressing **12** catastrophic, disconsolate, heart-rending **13** disappointing, heartbreaking

## woefully
**05** sadly **07** awfully, lousily **08** gloomily, pitiably, terribly **09** dolefully, forlornly, miserably, unhappily **10** deplorably, dreadfully, hopelessly, lamentably, mournfully, shockingly, tragically, wretchedly **11** appallingly **12** disastrously, pathetically **13** disgracefully **14** disconsolately

## wolf
**04** lobo **05** Romeo **06** coyote, lecher **07** Don Juan, Isegrim, seducer **08** Casanova, Isengrim **09** ladies' man, thylacine, womanizer **10** lady-killer **11** philanderer
• **wolf down** **04** bolt, cram, gulp **05** gorge, scoff, stuff **06** devour, gobble **07** put away **08** pack away

## woman
**01** w **03** bit, chi, gin, hag, hen, her, she, Tib **04** baby, bint, bird, chai, doll, fair, feme, frau, girl, jane, Judy, lady, lass, maid, Mary, minx, mort, peat, puss, sort, wife **05** belle, biddy, broad, chick, cutie, cutty, dolly, femme, fille, filly, flirt, hussy, lover, madam, peach, popsy, quean, randy, wench **06** au pair, blowze, cummer, damsel, female, geisha, gillet, jillet, kimmer, lassie, maiden, moppet, number, ogress, sheila, shiksa, tomboy, tottie,

wahine **07** bag lady, fiancée, mystery, nymphet, partner, reverse **08** mistress, princess **09** charwoman, dolly bird, plain Jane **10** bit of stuff, Cinderella, girlfriend, sweetheart **11** beauty queen **12** bachelorette, bobby-dazzler
*See also* **girl**
• **first woman** **03** Eve **07** Pandora
• **good woman** **01** S **02** St **04** sant **05** Saint

## womanhood
**05** woman **08** maturity **09** adulthood, womankind, womenfolk, womenkind **10** muliebrity, womenfolks

## womanizer
*Womanizers and libertines include:*

**04** goat, lech, rake, roué, wolf **05** letch, Romeo **06** gay dog, lecher **07** Don Juan, seducer, wastrel **08** Casanova, Lothario, Lovelace, palliard, rakehell **09** debauchee, ladies' man, libertine, reprobate, voluptary **10** Corinthian, lady-killer, profligate, sensualist **11** gay deceiver, philanderer

## womanly
**04** kind, warm **06** female, tender **07** shapely **08** feminine, ladylike, motherly, womanish **10** effeminate, well-formed

## women
• **excluding women** **04** stag
• **Women's Institute** **02** WI
*See also* **woman**

## wonder
**03** awe **04** gape, marl, muse **05** doubt, ferly, marle, query, sight, think **06** admire, marvel, ponder, puzzle, rarity **07** cruller, inquire, miracle, prodigy, reflect **08** be amazed, meditate, pleasure, question, surprise **09** amazement, curiosity, nonpareil, spectacle, speculate **10** admiration, conjecture, phenomenon, stand in awe, wonderment **11** ask yourself, be astounded, be surprised, fascination **12** astonishment, be astonished, bewilderment **13** be dumbfounded **14** be lost for words

*The Seven Wonders of the World:*

**15** Pyramids of Egypt **16** Colossus of Rhodes **18** Pharos of Alexandria **21** Statue of Zeus at Olympia **23** Hanging Gardens of Babylon **24** Mausoleum of Halicarnassus, Temple of Artemis at Ephesus

• **expression of wonder** **01** O **02** oh **03** god, wow **04** gosh, whew **05** wowee **06** heyday, wheugh **07** good-now **08** gracious **09** Jesus wept **13** stone the crows

## wonderful
**03** ace, def, fab, old, rad **04** boss, cool, keen, mean, mega, neat **05** beaut, boffo, brill, bully, crack, dicty, dilly, great, hunky, jammy, lummy, socko,

super, triff **06** castor, divine, famous, far-out, geason, groovy, mighty, peachy, superb, way-out, wicked, wizard **07** amazing, awesome, capital, classic, crucial, elegant, épatant, magical, mirable, radical, ripping, stellar, strange, tipping, topping, triffic, trimmer **08** champion, clinking, fabulous, glorious, heavenly, jim-dandy, knockout, smashing, spiffing, splendid, stonking, stunning, terrific, top-notch **09** admirable, brilliant, copacetic, excellent, fantastic, righteous, startling **10** astounding, delightful, incredible, marvellous, not half bad, phenomenal, remarkable, staggering, stupendous, surprising, tremendous **11** astonishing, fantabulous, magnificent, outstanding, sensational **12** second to none **13** extraordinary **14** out of this world

## wonderfully
**06** purely **09** amazingly, extremely **10** incredibly **12** phenomenally, terrifically, tremendously, unbelievably **13** fantastically

## wonky
**04** awry, weak **05** amiss, askew, shaky, wrong **06** wobbly **07** crooked, unsound **08** unsteady **09** skew-whiff

## wont
**03** use, way **04** fain, rule, used **05** given, habit **06** custom **07** routine **08** inclined, practice **10** accustomed, habituated

## wonted
**04** tame **05** daily, usual **06** common, normal **07** regular, routine **08** familiar, frequent, habitual **09** customary **10** accustomed, habituated **12** conventional

## woo
**03** wow **04** seek **05** chase, court **06** pursue **07** address, attract, look for, romance **09** cultivate, encourage **10** make love to, pay court to **13** seek the hand of

## wood
**03** mad, wud **04** bowl, hyle, shaw, tree **05** copse, cross, grove, hurst, trees, woods, xylem **06** fierce, forest, planks, pulpit **07** coppice, furious, spinney, thicket **08** woodland **10** plantation
*See also* **forest; golf club; timber**

*Woods include:*

**03** ash, box, cam, elm, fir, nut, oak, ply, red, sap, yew **04** bass, cord, cork, deal, ebon, fire, hard, iron, lana, lime, pine, pink, pulp, rimu, rose, sasa, soft, teak **05** alder, apple, balsa, beech, black, brush, cedar, drift, ebony, green, hazel, heart, larch, maple, match, olive, peach, plane, ramin, satin, tiger, torch, tulip, utile, white, zebra **06** acacia, bamboo, bitter, brazil, candle, cherry, cotton, jarrah, linden, lumber, obeche, orange, padauk, pedauk, poplar, rubber, sandal, sapele, spruce, timber,

veneer, walnut, willow
**07** Amboina, bubinga, hickory, palmyra, quassia
**08** amaranth, chestnut, cocobolo, hornbeam, Huon pine, kindling, mahogany, red lauan, seasoned, silky oak, sycamore
**09** chipboard, fruitwood, hardboard, jacaranda, quebracho
**10** afrormosia, Douglas fir, paper birch
**11** black cherry, lignum vitae, purple heart, radiata pine, tulip poplar, white walnut, yellow birch
**13** sweet chestnut

• **measurement of wood** **04** cord
**05** stere **06** fathom, square
**08** standard **09** board-foot, decastere, decisltere **10** hoppus foot **15** hoppus cubic foot
• **out of the woods** **04** safe
**06** secure **10** home and dry, in the clear **11** out of danger **12** safe and sound **15** out of difficulty
• **piece of wood** **03** cat, log
**04** beam, chip, lath, slat **05** block, board, dwang, plank, split, staff, wedge **06** batten, billet, fillet, flitch, loggat, planch, timber, tipcat
**07** bunting **08** splinter **09** four-by-two, scantling, two-by-four

**wooded**
**05** woody **06** sylvan **08** forested, nemorous, timbered **09** arboreous
**11** arboraceous, bush-covered, tree-covered

**wooden**
**04** dull, hard, slow, tree **05** blank, empty, heavy, rigid, stiff, treen, woody **06** clumsy, leaden, stodgy, stupid, timber, vacant **07** awkward, deadpan, stilted, vacuous **08** lifeless, ligneous **09** graceless, impassive, inhibited, unnatural **10** insensible, spiritless
**11** emotionless, unemotional
**12** unresponsive **14** expressionless

**woodland**
**04** bush, wood **05** copse, grove, trees, woods **06** forest, miombo, timber
**07** boscage, boskage, coppice, spinney, thicket **10** plantation

**woodpecker**
**05** Picus **06** yaffle, yucker **07** awlbird, flicker, piculet, witwall **08** hickwall, rainbird **10** yaffingale

**wood sorrel**
**03** oca **06** oxalis **08** shamrock

**woody**
**05** bosky **06** sylvan, wooded, wooden, xyloid **08** forested, ligneous **11** tree-covered

**wool**
**02** oo **03** ket **04** coat, down, hair, kemp, noil, yarn **05** flock, llama, noils
**06** Angora, botany, fleece, jersey, pelage, staple, two-ply, vicuña
**07** floccus, morling **08** cashmere, mortling, shatoosh **09** shahtoosh, strouding **13** linsey-woolsey
• **pull the wool over someone's eyes** **03** con **04** dupe, fool **05** trick

**06** delude, take in **07** deceive
**08** hoodwink **09** bamboozle **12** pull a swiftie, put one over on **14** pull a fast one on

**wool-gathering**
**06** dreamy **11** day-dreaming, distraction, inattention **12** absent-minded **13** forgetfulness, preoccupation

**woollen fabric**
*see* **fabric**

**woolly**
**04** hazy **05** downy, foggy, fuzzy, hairy, sheep, vague, woozy **06** cloudy, fleecy, fluffy, frizzy, jersey, jumper, lanate, lanose, shaggy **07** blurred, muddled, sweater, unclear, woollen **08** cardigan, confused, floccose, nebulous, pullover **10** flocculent, ill-defined, indefinite, indistinct
**12** woolly-haired

**woozy**
**05** dazed, dizzy, rocky, tipsy, vague
**06** wobbly, woolly **07** bemused, blurred, fuddled **08** confused, unsteady
**09** befuddled, nauseated **11** light-headed

**word**
**03** gen, mot, put, say, vow **04** book, chat, dope, hint, info, name, news, oath, sign, talk, term, text, will
**05** couch, order, speak, state, write
**06** advice, decree, gossip, honour, lyrics, notice, phrase, pledge, remark, report, rumour, saying, script, signal, war cry **07** account, command, comment, explain, express, flatter, go-ahead, hearsay, low-down, mandate, message, palabra, promise, scandal, tidings, vocable, warning, whisper
**08** bulletin, dispatch, libretto, password, thumbs-up **09** assertion, assurance, guarantee, statement, tête-à-tête, utterance, watchword
**10** communiqué, discussion, expression, green light
**11** commandment, declaration, designation, information, instruction, speculation, undertaking
**12** consultation, conversation, intelligence **13** communication
*See also* **speech**
• **have words** **03** row **05** argue
**06** bicker **07** dispute, quarrel
**08** disagree, squabble
• **in a word** **07** briefly, in brief, in short, to sum up **09** concisely, to be brief **10** succinctly **11** in a nutshell, summarizing **14** to put it briefly
• **in other words** **02** ie **05** id est
**06** that is
• **word for word** **06** verbal
**07** closely, exactly, literal **08** ad verbum, verbatim **09** literally, precisely **10** accurately

**wordiness**
**06** waffle **07** wordage **08** verbiage
**09** garrulity, loquacity, prolixity, verbosity **10** logorrhoea **11** diffuseness, perissology, verboseness
**13** garrulousness **14** long-windedness
**15** verbal diarrhoea

**wording**
**04** text **05** style, tenor, words
**07** diction, wordage **08** language, phrasing, speaking, verbiage
**09** subtitles, utterance, verbalism
**10** expression **11** phraseology, terminology **13** choice of words

**word-perfect**
**05** exact **06** spot-on **08** accurate, faithful, verbatim **13** letter-perfect

**wordplay**
**03** pun, wit **04** puns **07** punning
**08** repartee **10** witticisms
**11** paronomasia

**wordy**
**05** windy **06** phrasy, prolix **07** diffuse, verbose **08** rambling **09** garrulous
**10** discursive, long-winded, loquacious

**work**
◊ *anagram indicator* **02** do, go, op **03** art, dig, fag, fix, hat, job, ply, ren, rin, run, sew, tut, use **04** ache, acts, book, char, deed, duty, edge, farm, form, fuss, guts, line, make, mill, move, opus, plan, play, poem, shop, slog, take, task, tick, till, toil **05** cause, chore, craft, drive, field, graft, guide, knead, model, mould, parts, piece, plant, purge, shape, shift, skill, slave, study, trade, trick, yakka **06** action, cajole, career, charge, create, doings, drudge, effect, effort, fiddle, go well, handle, labour, manage, métier, oeuvre, strain, wangle, yacker **07** achieve, actions, arrange, calling, control, execute, factory, fashion, ferment, foundry, innards, mission, operate, peg away, perform, process, prosper, pull off, pursuit, squeeze, succeed, travail, trouble, writing **08** business, contrive, creation, drudgery, engineer, exercise, exertion, function, have a job, industry, movement, painting, plug away, treatise, vocation, workings, workshop **09** cultivate, embroider, hard yakka, influence, machinery, manoeuvre, mechanism, penetrate
**10** accomplish, assignment, be employed, bring about, commission, embroidery, employment, livelihood, manipulate, occupation, production, profession **11** achievement, be effective, composition, elbow grease, pull strings, undertaking, workmanship
**12** be successful, working parts
**13** exert yourself, installations
**14** accomplishment, be satisfactory, earn your living, line of business, responsibility **15** slog your guts out
• **bit of work** **01** J **03** erg **05** joule
**08** therblig
• **day's work** **04** darg **05** stent, stint
**06** man-day **07** journey
• **the works** **06** the lot **10** everything
**11** the whole lot **15** the whole shebang
• **work out** **04** dope, plan, toil **05** drill, serve, solve, total, train **06** come to, deduce, devise, evolve, finish, go well, invent, pan out, warm up **07** add up to, arrange, clear up, come out, develop, dope out, exhaust, expiate, keep fit,

## workable

prosper, resolve, sort out, succeed, turn out **08** amount to, contrive, exercise, organize, practise **09** calculate, construct, elaborate, figure out, formulate, puzzle out **10** understand **11** be effective, put together
• **work up** **03** tew **04** meng, ming, move, spur, whet **05** menge, reach, rouse, use up **06** arouse, excite, expand, incite, kindle, stir up, subact **07** achieve, agitate, animate, build up, ferment, inflame **08** generate, summon up **09** elaborate, instigate, stimulate

## workable

**06** doable, viable **08** feasible, possible **09** practical, realistic **11** practicable

## workaday

**04** dull **06** common **07** average, humdrum, mundane, prosaic, routine, toiling, work-day, working **08** everyday, familiar, ordinary **09** labouring, practical **11** commonplace **12** run-of-the-mill

## worker

**03** ant, bee **04** hand, peon, temp **06** coater, Indian, key man, legger, toiler **07** artisan, battler, grinder, ouvrier, workman **08** employee, grisette, labourer, mechanic, ouvrière, strapper, stuccoer **09** craftsman, hired hand, hired help, midinette, operative, salaryman, tradesman, workhorse, workwoman **10** mechanical, painstaker, railroader, rouseabout, wage-earner, workaholic, working man **11** breadwinner, craftswoman, proletarian, tradeswoman **12** Gastarbeiter, willing horse, working woman **13** member of staff

## workforce

**03** men **05** hands, staff **06** labour **07** workers **08** manpower, skeleton **09** employees, personnel, shop floor **10** workpeople **11** labour force **14** human resources

## working

◇ *anagram indicator* **02** on **03** pit **04** guts, live, mine **05** going, parts, shaft, waste, works **06** action, active, in a job, in work, manner, method, quarry, system **07** innards, process, routine, running **08** diggings, employed, movement **09** endeavour, labouring, machinery, mechanism, operating, operation, operative **10** in business **11** excavations, functioning, operational **12** up and running, working parts **13** installations **14** in working order

## workman, workwoman

**04** hand, hobo **05** hunky, navvy **06** beamer, glazer, master, worker **07** artisan, seagull, wharfie **08** apron-man, employee, gunsmith, labourer, mechanic **09** artificer, craftsman, operative, prud'homme, stage hand **10** journeyman, rouseabout, surfaceman **11** craftswoman **12** manual worker, tradesperson

## workmanlike

**05** adept **06** expert **07** careful, skilful, skilled **08** masterly, thorough **09** competent, efficient **10** proficient **11** painstaking **12** businesslike, professional, satisfactory

## workmanship

**03** art **04** work **05** craft, skill **06** finish **07** facture, tooling **08** artifice, artistry **09** execution, expertise, handiwork, technique **10** handicraft **11** manufacture **13** craftsmanship

## workmate

**03** lad **08** co-worker **09** associate, colleague **10** work-fellow, yoke-fellow **12** fellow-worker

## workout

**05** drill **06** warm-up **08** aerobics, exercise, practice, training **10** gymnastics, isometrics **11** eurhythmics, limbering up **13** callisthenics

## workshop

**03** lab **04** mill, shop **05** class, forge, plant, works **06** garage, smithy, studio **07** atelier, factory, seminar **08** plumbery, smithery, workroom **09** cooperage, symposium **10** laboratory, study group **11** machine-shop, rigging-loft **15** discussion group

## work-shy

**04** idle, lazy, lusk, slow **05** inert, slack, tardy **06** laesie, lither, torpid **07** languid, luskish **08** bone-idle, fainéant, inactive, indolent, slothful, sluggish **09** lethargic **10** languorous, slow-moving **14** good-for-nothing

## workwoman

*see* **workman, workwoman**

## world

**03** age, era, man, orb **04** area, days, life, star, vale **05** class, earth, epoch, field, globe, group, realm, times **06** cosmos, domain, nature, people, period, planet, public, sphere, system **07** kingdom, mankind, reality, section, society **08** creation, division, everyone, humanity, province, universe **09** everybody, existence, humankind, human race, situation, way of life **10** department, experience, population **11** environment **12** heavenly body

*World heritage sites include:*

**03** Bam, Omo, Taï
**04** Agra, Bath, Graz, Lima, Manú, Pisa, Riga, San'a, Troy, Tyre
**05** Aksum, Awash, Berne, Bosra, Copán, Cuzco, Delos, Galle, Hatra, Kandy, Lyons, Ohrid, Paris, Petra, Quito, Siena, Sucre, Uluru
**06** Abomey, Aleppo, Amazon, Assisi, Bassae, Byblos, Cyrene, Darién, Delphi, Durham, Göreme, Kakadu, Naples, Oporto, Orkney, Paphos, Potosí, Puebla, Sangay, Sousse, Thebes, Toledo, Treves, Venice, Verona, Vienna, Warsaw
**07** Abu Mena, Avebury, Avignon, Baalbek, Caracas, Djemila,

Garamba, Gwynedd, Holy See, Olympia, San Juan, Segovia, St Kilda, Vicenza, Virunga
**08** Agra Fort, Alhambra, Altamira, Carthage, Chartres, Damascus, Durmitor, Florence, Ghadamès, Hattusas, Mount Tai, Palenque, Pyramids, Pyrénées, Sabratha, Salvador, Salzburg, Shark Bay, Sigiriya, Stari Ras, Taj Mahal, Timbuktu, Valletta, Würzburg
**09** Abu Simbel, Auschwitz, Ayutthaya, Dubrovnik, Edinburgh, Epidaurus, Greenwich, Gros Morne, Huascarán, Jerusalem, Mesa Verde, Nemrut Dag, Parthenon, Serengeti
**10** El Escorial, Everglades, Generalife, Hierapolis, Hildesheim, Ironbridge, Monte Albán, Monticello, Persepolis, Pont du Gard, Stonehenge, Versailles
**11** Ajanta caves, Danube Delta, Ellora caves, Gorée Island, Hagia Sophia, Leptis Magna, Machu Picchu, Madara Rider, Mohenjo-daro, Quedlinburg, Teotihuacán, Vatican City, Western Wall, Westminster, Yellowstone
**12** Altamira Cave, Ancient Kyoto, Fraser Island, Hadrian's Wall, Koguryo Tombs, Mont-St-Michel, Santo Domingo, The Great Wall
**13** Blue Mountains, Fontainebleau, Fontenay Abbey, Great Zimbabwe, Rila Monastery, Tower of London
**14** Aldabra Islands, Blenheim Palace, Elephanta caves, Fountains Abbey, Giant's Causeway, Heraion of Samos, Imperial Palace, Uluru-Kata Tjuta
**15** Aachen Cathedral, Amiens Cathedral, Ironbridge Gorge, Kasbah of Algiers, Kathmandu Valley, Nubian monuments, Speyer Cathedral, Statue of Liberty

• **on top of the world** **05** happy **06** elated, joyful **08** ecstatic, euphoric, exultant, jubilant, thrilled **09** delighted, exuberant, overjoyed, rapturous **10** enraptured, in raptures **11** exhilarated, high as a kite, on cloud nine, over the moon, tickled pink **14** pleased as Punch **15** in seventh heaven
• **out of this world** **02** ET **03** ace, rad **04** cool, mean, mega, neat **05** brill, great **06** divine, superb, way-out, wicked **07** crucial, radical **08** fabulous, heavenly, smashing, stonking, stunning, terrific **09** excellent, fantastic, wonderful **10** delightful, incredible, marvellous, phenomenal, remarkable **11** sensational **12** second to none, unbelievable **13** indescribable

## worldly

**06** carnal, greedy, mortal, urbane **07** earthly, knowing, mondain, mundane, outward, profane, secular, selfish, terrene **08** covetous, grasping, material, mondaine, physical, temporal **09** ambitious, corporeal **10** avaricious, streetwise **11** experienced, terrestrial, unspiritual, worldly-wise **12** cosmopolitan **13** materialistic, sophisticated

**worldly-wise**
**06** shrewd, urbane **07** cynical, knowing, worldly **10** cultivated, perceptive, streetwise **11** experienced **12** cosmopolitan **13** sophisticated

**worldwide**
**06** global **07** general, mondial **08** catholic **09** universal **10** ubiquitous **11** transglobal **13** international

**worm**
**04** grub **05** snake **06** dragon, maggot, squirm **07** remorse

*Worms include:*

**03** eel, lug, pin, rag
**04** flat, hook, tape
**05** arrow, earth, fluke, leech, round
**06** peanut, ribbon, thread
**07** annelid, bristle
**08** sea mouse
**09** hairy Mary
**10** blood fluke, liver fluke

**worn**
**03** old **04** bare, used **05** all in, drawn, jaded, spent, tatty, tired, trite, weary **06** bushed, done in, frayed, ragged, shabby **07** haggard, thumbed, worn-out **08** careworn, dog-tired, fatigued, strained, tattered **09** exhausted, hackneyed, in tatters, knackered **10** threadbare **13** weather-bitten
• **worn out 03** old **04** beat, gone, past, used **05** all in, banal, corny, rough, seedy, stale, stock, tacky, tatty, tired, trite, warby, weary **06** bushed, common, done in, épuisé, failed, frayed, pooped, ragged, shabby, wasted, zonked **07** cliché'd, épuisée, to-worke, traikit, useless, wearied, whacked **08** clichéed, dead-beat, decrepit, dog-tired, dog-weary, forfairn, overused, tattered, time-worn, tired out **09** bedridden, disjaskit, exhausted, geriatric, hackneyed, knackered, moth-eaten, pooped out, shattered, washed-out, worm-eaten **10** broken-down, clapped-out, overworked, pedestrian, shagged out, threadbare, uninspired, unoriginal, yawn-making **11** commonplace, ready to drop, stereotyped, tuckered out, wearing thin **12** cliché-ridden, journey-bated, overscutched, run-of-the-mill **13** on its last legs, platitudinous, unimaginative

**worried**
◊ *anagram indicator* **04** worn **05** het up, tense, upset, wired **06** afraid, on edge, uneasy **07** anxious, fearful, fretful, haunted, in a stew, jittery, nervous, uptight **08** agonized, bothered, dismayed, in a tizzy, strained, troubled **09** concerned, disturbed, ill at ease, perturbed **10** disquieted, distracted,

distraught, distressed, frightened **11** overwrought **12** apprehensive **14** beside yourself, hot and bothered **15** a bundle of nerves

**worrisome**
**05** hairy, scary **06** vexing **07** irksome **08** insecure, worrying **09** agonizing, upsetting, vexatious **10** bothersome, disturbing, nail-biting, perturbing **11** disquieting, distressing, frightening, troublesome

**worry**
◊ *anagram indicator* **03** bug, dog, eat, nag, tew, tiz, vex **04** bite, care, faze, fear, frab, fret, gnaw, pest, stew **05** annoy, choke, deave, deeve, devil, eat up, feese, feeze, go for, harry, phase, phese, sweat, tease, tizzy, touse, touze, towse, towze, trial, upset **06** attack, badger, bother, burden, hang-up, harass, hassle, misery, niggle, pester, pheese, pheeze, pingle, plague, savage, strain, stress, tear at, unease, worrit **07** agitate, agonize, anguish, anxiety, concern, disturb, perturb, problem, tension, torment, trouble **08** disquiet, distress, headache, irritate, nuisance, unsettle, vexation **09** aggravate, agitation, annoyance, be anxious, misgiving **10** be troubled, irritation, perplexity **11** disturbance, fearfulness **12** apprehension, be distressed, perturbation **13** climb the walls, consternation **14** responsibility
• **expression of worry 04** uh-oh, yike **05** yikes **06** cripes

**worrying**
**05** hairy, scary **06** trying, uneasy **07** anxious, weighty **08** alarming, niggling **09** agonizing, harassing, upsetting, worrisome **10** disturbing, nail-biting, perturbing, unsettling **11** disquieting, distressing, troublesome

**worsen**
**04** sink, slip **06** weaken **07** decline, go to pot **08** get worse, heighten, increase **09** aggravate, intensify **10** degenerate, exacerbate, go downhill **11** deteriorate **13** go down the tube **14** go down the tubes

**worsening**
**05** decay **07** decline **10** pejoration **12** degeneration, exacerbation **13** deterioration, retrogression

**worship**
**02** Wp **04** laud, love, puja **05** adore, deify, exalt, extol, glory **06** admire, homage, honour, Ibadat, praise, prayer, pray to, regard, revere **07** adulate, dignity, glorify, idolize, opus Dei, prayers, respect **08** adultery, devotion, geolatry, idolatry, naturism, religion, satanism, venerate **09** adoration, adulation, aniconism, devotions, diabolism, laudation, pyrolatry, reverence, snake cult **10** astrolatry, bardolatry, exaltation, eye-service, heliolatry, iconolatry, litholatry, ophiolatry, reputation, veneration **11** angelolatry, be devoted to, deification, idolization, physiolatry,

theriolatry **13** anthropolatry, glorification, thaumatolatry

*Places of worship include:*

**03** wat
**04** fane, kirk, shul
**05** abbey, gompa
**06** bethel, chapel, church, mandir, masjid, mosque, pagoda, shrine, temple, vihara
**07** chantry, convent, minster
**08** gurdwara
**09** cathedral, monastery, synagogue
**10** tabernacle
**12** meeting-house

*See also* **abbey; religious**

**worshipful**
**02** Wp **04** awed, Wpfl **05** pious **06** devout, humble, loving, solemn **07** adoring, devoted, dutiful **08** admiring, obeisant **10** respectful **11** deferential, reverential

**worshipper**
*see* **believer**

**worst**
**03** war **04** beat, best, drub, lick **05** crush, paste, smash, thump **06** damage, defeat, hammer, master, subdue, thrash **07** clobber, conquer, trounce **08** overcome, pessimal, pessimum, vanquish **09** devastate, overpower, overthrow, slaughter, subjugate, whitewash **10** annihilate **13** run rings round **14** get the better of **15** make mincemeat of

**worth**
**02** be **03** use **04** cost, gain, good, help, rate **05** avail, carat, merit, price, value, virtu **06** become, carrat, credit, desert, happen, profit, virtue **07** benefit, deserts, quality, service, utility **08** eminence, meriting, repaying, valuable **09** advantage, deserving, substance **10** assistance, excellence, excellency, importance, justifying, usefulness, warranting, worthiness **11** possessions **12** significance

**worthily**
**04** well **08** laudably, reliably, valuably **09** admirably **10** creditably, honourably **11** commendably

**worthless**
**03** bad, bum, low **04** base, junk, naff, orra, poor, punk, raca, vile, waff **05** blown, cheap, junky, light, sorry, tripy **06** abject, cruddy, crummy, draffy, drossy, futile, naught, no good, ornery, paltry, trashy, tripey **07** corrupt, drunken, ignoble, mauvais, nothing, shotten, trivial, useless **08** beggarly, castaway, draffish, gimcrack, jimcrack, mauvaise, nugatory, rubbishy, sixpenny, trifling, trumpery, twopenny, unusable, unworthy, wanwordy, wretched **09** brummagem, cheap-jack, no-account, pointless, valueless **10** despicable, unavailing, unprizable **11** ineffectual, littleworth, meaningless, stramineous, unimportant **12** contemptible **13** insignificant **14** good-for-nothing, not worth shucks

**worthless thing** 03 mud 04 dirt, grot
05 nyaff 06 fag end 10 catchpenny

**worthlessness**
07 ambs-ace, ames-ace 08 futility
09 cheapness 11 lack of worth,
nothingness, unusability, uselessness
13 pointlessness 15 ineffectualness,
meaninglessness

**worthwhile**
04 good 05 tanti 06 useful, worthy
07 gainful, helpful, of value
08 valuable 09 estimable, rewarding
10 beneficial, productive, profitable
11 justifiable 12 advantageous,
constructive

**worthy**
03 fit, VIP 04 good, name 05 moral,
noble 06 big gun, bigwig, decent,
honest, honour, top dog 07 big shot,
notable, upright 08 big noise, laudable,
luminary, reliable, somebody, top
brass, valuable, virtuous 09 admirable,
big cheese, deserving, dignitary,
estimable, excellent, personage,
reputable, righteous 10 creditable,
excellence, honourable, notability,
worthwhile 11 appropriate,
commendable, meritorious,
respectable, trustworthy
12 praiseworthy

**would**
01 'd

**would-be**
04 keen 05 eager 07 budding, hopeful,
longing, wannabe, wishful 08 aspiring,
striving 09 ambitious, soi-disant
10 optimistic 12 endeavouring,
enterprising

**wound**
◇ anagram indicator 03 cut, hit, pip
04 ache, bite, blow, dunt, gash, harm,
hurt, pain, scar, sore, stab, tear, vuln,
win't 05 bless, graze, grief, saber,
sabre, shock, shoot, slash, touch, upset
06 damage, grieve, injure, injury,
insult, lesion, offend, pierce, slight,
trauma 07 anguish, mortify, scratch,
torment 08 distress, lacerate, puncture,
sword-cut 09 vulnerate 10 heartbreak,
laceration, traumatism, traumatize

**wow**
03 boy, cor

**wrack**
◇ anagram indicator 05 wreck
07 remnant, seaweed, torment, torture
08 wreckage 09 vengeance
10 punishment 11 destruction,
devastation

**wraith**
05 ghost, shade, spook 06 double,
spirit 07 phantom, spectre 08 revenant
10 apparition, astral body
12 doppelgänger

**wrangle**
03 rag, row 04 herd, spar, spat, tiff
05 argue, clash, fight, scrap, set-to
06 argufy, barney, bicker, cample,
cangle, debate, dust-up, hassle, jangle,
tussle 07 brabble, brangle, contend,
contest, dispute, fall out, punch-up,

quarrel, wrestle 08 argument, disagree,
ergotize, squabble 09 altercate, argy-
bargy, bickering, have it out, have
words 10 digladiate 11 altercation,
controversy, cross swords
12 disagreement 13 have it out with,
slanging match 15 be at loggerheads,
have a bone to pick

**wrap**
◇ containment indicator 03 hap, lap, rug,
wap 04 bind, cape, fold, hide, mail,
pack, robe, roll, snug, wind 05 amice,
boost, cloak, cover, scarf, shawl,
sheet, stole, throw 06 clothe, cocoon,
emboss, encase, enfold, mantle,
muffle, parcel, roll up, shroud, swathe,
wimple 07 commend, embrace,
enclose, envelop, flannel, immerse,
involve, obscure, package, snuggle,
swaddle, whimple 08 bemuffle, bundle
up, enswathe, entangle, gift-wrap,
inswathe, parcel up, surround
09 clingfilm, night-rail 11 acclamation
**wrap up** 03 end, hap 04 mail 05 dry
up 06 belt up, bundle, enfold, infold,
pack up, parcel, shut up, wind up
07 be quiet, package 08 complete,
conclude, gift-wrap, muffle up, parcel
up, pipe down, round off 09 finish off,
terminate 11 dress warmly, give it a
rest 12 put a sock in it 13 bring to a
close, shut your mouth 14 close the
book on, hold your tongue 15 wear
warm clothes

**wrapper**
04 case 05 cover, folio, paper
06 casing, jacket, sheath, sleeve
08 covering, envelope, Jiffy bag®,
wrapping 09 packaging 10 dust jacket

**wrapping**
04 case, foil 05 paper 06 carton, swathe
07 tinfoil, wrapper 08 envelope, Jiffy
bag® 09 packaging 10 bubble pack,
Cellophane® 11 blister card, blister
pack, envelopment, silver paper

**wrapt**
see **rapt**

**wrath**
03 ire 04 fury, rage 05 anger, angry
06 ardour, choler, spleen, temper
07 passion 09 annoyance 10 bitterness,
irritation, resentment 11 displeasure,
indignation 12 exasperation

**wrathful**
03 mad 05 angry, cross, irate, ratty,
spewy, wroth 06 bitter, choked, ireful,
raging 07 crooked, enraged, furious,
ropable, stroppy, uptight 08 burned up,
furibund, hairless, in a paddy,
incensed, up in arms 09 in a lather,
indignant, raving mad, seeing red,
ticked off 10 aggravated, displeased,
hopping mad, infuriated
11 disgruntled, fit to be tied 12 on the
warpath

**wreak**
04 harm, vent 05 cause 06 avenge,
bestow, create, damage, effect, punish
07 execute, express, inflict, unleash
08 carry out, drive out, exercise
09 vengeance 10 bring about,
perpetrate, punishment

**wreath**
03 lei 04 band, loop, ring 05 crown,
torse 06 anadem, circle 07 chaplet,
circlet, coronet, festoon, garland
09 snowdrift 10 civic crown

**wreathe**
04 coil, turn, wind, wrap 05 adorn,
crown, twine, twist, wring 06 enfold,
enwrap, shroud 07 contort, entwine,
envelop, festoon 08 decorate, encircle,
surround 10 intertwine, interweave

**wreck**
◇ anagram indicator 03 gum, mar
04 crab, loss, mess, ruin, sink 05 break,
gum up, mouse, smash, split, spoil,
trash, wrack 06 cast up, debris, pieces,
ravage, rubble 07 chicken, destroy,
disable, flotsam, handbag, remains,
shatter, torpedo, undoing 08 breaking,
cast away, demolish, derelict, disaster,
neurotic, smashing, stramash, write
off, write-off 09 devastate, fragments,
ruination, shipwreck 10 basket-case,
demolition, disruption, shattering
11 bag of nerves, destruction,
devastation 13 play havoc with
14 bundle of nerves

**wreckage**
◇ anagram indicator 04 ruin 05 lagan,
ligan, wrack 06 debris, pieces, rubble
07 flotsam, remains 08 detritus
09 fragments

**wrench**
03 fit, rip, tug 04 ache, blow, jerk, pain,
pang, pull, rick, tear, yank 05 force,
shock, twist, wrest, wring 06 sorrow,
sprain, strain 07 distort, sadness,
spanner 08 upheaval 09 uprooting

**wrest**
03 win 04 pull, rack, take, turn
05 force, screw, seize, thraw, twist,
wring 06 sprain, strain, wrench
07 distort, extract, pervert 10 distortion
12 misinterpret

**wrestle**
03 vie 05 argue, fight 06 battle, combat,
debate, strive, tussle, wraxle, writhe
07 bulldog, contend, contest, dispute,
grapple, scuffle, wrangle, wriggle
08 struggle

**wrestling**
◇ anagram indicator

Wrestling holds and throws include:

03 hug
04 lock
06 grovet, nelson, souple, suplex
07 bear hug, buttock, hip-lock
08 arm throw, body lock, headlock,
scissors
09 ankle lace, body throw
10 Boston crab, full nelson,
hammerlock
11 backbreaker, scissor hold
12 cross-buttock, scissors hold,
stranglehold
14 grand amplitude

Wrestling-related terms include:

03 mat, pin
04 bout, fall, hold, open, sumo

**05** judge
**06** action, bridge
**07** default, referee
**08** chairman, exposing, reversal, takedown
**09** bridge out, freestyle, grapevine, gut wrench, passivity
**10** arm control, Greco-Roman
**13** central circle, cross-body ride, passivity zone
**14** danger position, protection area
**15** double-leg tackle, single leg tackle, technical points

## wretch
**03** rat **04** worm **05** being, devil, exile, miser, rogue, snake, swine **06** insect, rascal, vassal **07** cullion, outcast, ruffian, scroyle, villain **08** blighter, creature, recreant, vagabond **09** miscreant, miserable, rakeshame, scoundrel **10** peelgarlic, pilgarlick, rascallion **11** rapscallion **14** good-for-nothing

## wretched
◇ *anagram indicator* **02** wo **03** bad, low, sad, woe **04** base, mean, poor, vile **05** awful, ratty, seely, sorry, woful **06** abject, bloody, cursed, damned, darned, dashed, effing, gloomy, odious, paltry, rascal, woeful, wretch **07** blasted, doleful, flaming, forlorn, hapless, hateful, piteous, pitiful, unhappy, unlucky **08** annoying, blinking, blooming, dejected, downcast, dratting, dreadful, fiendish, flipping, hopeless, horrible, inferior, infernal, pathetic, pitiable, shameful, shocking, terrible **09** appalling, atrocious, depressed, life-weary, loathsome, miserable, worthless **10** confounded, deplorable, despicable, detestable, distraught, distressed, melancholy, outrageous, unpleasant **11** crestfallen, unfortunate **12** contemptible, disconsolate **13** broken-hearted

## wretchedly
**05** sadly **07** awfully, lousily **08** gloomily, pitiably, terribly, woefully **09** dolefully, forlornly, miserably, unhappily **10** deplorably, dreadfully, hopelessly, lamentably, mournfully, shockingly, tragically **11** appallingly **12** disastrously, pathetically **13** disgracefully **14** disconsolately

## wriggle
**04** bend, duck, edge, jerk, shun, turn, wind, worm **05** crawl, dodge, elude, evade, hedge, shirk, sidle, slink, snake, twine, twist **06** escape, eschew, jiggle, squirm, twitch, waggle, wamble, wiggle, writhe, zigzag **07** forbear, wrestle **08** get out of, get round, scriggle, sidestep, squiggle **09** extricate, give a miss, manoeuvre **10** body-swerve, circumvent **11** abstain from, refrain from, run away from **12** keep away from, stay away from, steer clear of

## wring
**04** coil, hurt, pain, rack, rend, stab, tear **05** exact, force, pinch, screw, thraw,

twist, wound, wrest **06** coerce, extort, harrow, injure, mangle, pierce, wrench, writhe **07** distort, extract, squeeze, torture, wreathe **08** distress, lacerate

## wrinkle
**03** tip **04** fold, idea, line, lirk, plow, ruck, seam **05** frown, ridge, rivel, whelk **06** crease, furrow, gather, notion, plough, pucker, ruckle, ruck up, ruffle, rumple, runkle, trench, wimple **07** crankle, crimple, crinkle, crumple, frounce, frumple, shrivel, whimple **09** unsmooth **10** corrugate, crow's-foot **10** suggestion, unevenness **11** corrugation

## wrinkled
**04** ropy **05** crêpy, ropey **06** crepey, crimpy, ridged, rucked, rugate, rugose, rugous **07** creased, crinkly, furrowy, puckery, ruffled, rumpled, wizened, wrinkly, wrizled **08** crankled, crinkled, crumpled, frounced, furrowed, puckered, rivelled, writhled **09** chamfered **10** corrugated

## wrist
**06** carpus **11** shackle-bone

## writ
**04** tolt **05** brief, sci fa **06** capias, decree, elegit, extent, venire **07** dedimus, latitat, precept, process, summons, warrant **08** mandamus, mittimus, noverint, replevin, subpoena **09** nisi prius **10** certiorari, court order, devastavit, distringas, inhibition, injunction, law-burrows, praemunire **11** fieri facias, jury-process, quo warranto, scire facias, supersedeas, supplicavit **12** habeas corpus, quare impedit, venire facias **13** ad inquirendum, audita querela

## write
**03** pen **04** copy, note **05** carve, chalk, draft, print, trace **06** create, decree, draw up, indite, pencil, record, scrawl, scribe, scrive **07** compose, dash off, engrave, jot down, put down, screeve, scrieve, set down **08** inscribe, note down, register, scribble, sling ink, take down **09** character, poeticize, transpose **10** correspond, transcribe, underwrite **11** communicate, make a note of
• **write off** **05** annul, crash, smash, wreck **06** cancel, delete **07** destroy, nullify, smash up, wipe out **08** amortize, cross out, demolish **09** disregard **11** forget about

## writer
**03** pen **06** author **12** man of letters **14** woman of letters

*Writers include:*

**04** bard, hack, poet
**05** clerk
**06** author, editor, fabler, penman, pen-pal, rhymer, scribe
**07** blogger, copyist, diarist
**08** annalist, composer, essayist, lyricist, novelist, penwoman, reporter, satirist
**09** columnist, dramatist, historian,

pen-friend, penpusher, scribbler, sonneteer, web author
**10** biographer, chronicler, copywriter, journalist, librettist, playwright
**11** contributor, ghost writer, storyteller
**12** leader-writer, poet laureate, scriptwriter, stenographer
**13** calligraphist, correspondent, court reporter, fiction writer, lexicographer
**14** autobiographer
**15** technical author, technical writer

*See also* **author; biography; chef; diary; essay; fable; historian; journalist; lexicographer; literary; playwright; poet; satirist**
• **the writer** **02** me
• **this writer** **01** I

## write-up
**05** study **06** rating, report, review, survey **08** analysis, critique, scrutiny **09** appraisal, criticism, judgement, recension, summing-up **10** assessment, commentary, evaluation **11** examination

## writhe
◇ *anagram indicator* **03** wry **04** coil, curl, jerk, toss, wind **05** thraw, twist, wring **06** squirm, thrash, thresh, wiggle **07** contort, distort, wrestle, wriggle **08** scriggle, struggle **10** intertwine **12** twist and turn

## writing
**02** MS **03** pen **04** dite, fist, hand, opus, text, work **05** entry, print, prose, words **06** scrawl, script, volume **08** document, scribble **10** manuscript, penmanship **11** calligraphy, composition, handwriting, publication

*Writing instruments include:*

**03** nib, pen
**04** Biro®, reed
**05** quill
**06** crayon, dip pen, pencil, stylus
**07** cane pen
**08** brailler, CD marker, steel pen
**09** ballpoint, eraser pen, ink pencil, marker pen
**10** felt-tip pen, lead-pencil, rollerball, typewriter
**11** board marker, fountain pen, highlighter
**12** cartridge pen, writing brush
**13** laundry marker, Roman metal pen, word-processor
**14** calligraphy pen, coloured pencil
**15** permanent marker

*Writings include:*

**04** blog, book, news, poem, tale
**05** diary, drama, essay, lyric, paper, story, study
**06** annals, fanfic, letter, memoir, record, report, review, satire, script, sketch, sonnet, thesis, weblog
**07** account, apology, article, epistle, feature, history, journal, parable, profile
**08** apologia, critique, tip sheet,

treatise, yearbook
**09** biography, chronicle, criticism, discourse, editorial, life story, monograph, narrative, statement, technical
**10** commentary, literature, propaganda, scientific, travelogue
**11** confessions, copywriting, documentary
**12** dissertation
**13** autobiography, legal document
**14** correspondence
**15** advertising copy, curriculum vitae, newspaper column

*See also* **alphabet; scripture**

**written**
**06** penned **07** drawn up, set down
**08** recorded **09** pen-and-ink
**10** documental, documented
**11** documentary, transcribed

**wrong**
◇ *anagram indicator* **01** X **03** bad, bum, sin **04** awry, back, bent, evil, harm, hurt, tort **05** abuse, amiss, badly, cheat, crime, crook, error, false, inapt, spoil **06** astray, curved, damage, delict, faulty, guilty, ill-use, impair, injure, injury, inside, malign, seduce, sinful, unfair, unjust, wicked **07** abusion, abusive, crooked, defraud, illegal, illicit, immoral, in error, inverse, misdeed, off base, off beam, offence, oppress, reverse, to blame, twisted, unright, wrongly **08** contrary, criminal, faultily, ill-treat, improper, inequity, iniquity, inverted, maltreat, mistaken, mistreat, opposite, trespass, unlawful, unseemly **09** defective, discredit, dishonest, dishonour, erroneous, felonious, grievance, imprecise, incorrect, inexactly, injustice, off target, unethical, unfitting
**10** fallacious, immorality, improperly, inaccurate, inapposite, indecorous, iniquitous, malapropos, mistakenly, out of order, sinfulness, unfairness, unsuitable, up the spout, wickedness, wrongdoing **11** blameworthy, erroneously, imprecisely, incongruous, incorrectly, misinformed, unjustified
**12** inaccurately, infelicitous, infringement, misrepresent, unlawfulness **13** dishonourable, hardly the time, inappropriate, reprehensible, transgression, wide of the mark
**14** hardly the place, unconventional, unsatisfactory
• **go wrong** **04** fail, miss **05** stray **06** go phut, pack up **07** conk out, pervert, seize up **08** backfire, collapse, go astray, walk awry **09** break down, not make it **11** come to grief, come unglued, come unstuck, malfunction, stop working **12** come a cropper, go on the blink, go on the fritz **13** become unstuck, come to nothing **14** be unsuccessful
• **in the wrong** **06** guilty **07** at fault, in error, to blame **08** mistaken **11** blameworthy

**wrongdoer**
**05** felon **06** sinner **07** culprit
**08** criminal, evildoer, offender
**09** miscreant **10** delinquent, lawbreaker, malefactor, trespasser
**12** transgressor

**wrongdoing**
**03** sin **04** evil, miss **05** crime, error, fault
**06** felony **07** misdeed, offence
**08** iniquity, mischief **09** misfaring
**10** immorality, maleficent, maleficial, sinfulness, wickedness
**11** delinquency, lawbreaking, maleficence, malfeasance
**13** transgression

**wrongful**
**04** evil **05** wrong **06** unfair, unjust, wicked **07** illegal, illicit, immoral
**08** criminal, improper, tortious, unlawful **09** dishonest, injurious, unethical **11** blameworthy, unjustified, unwarranted **12** illegitimate
**13** dishonourable, reprehensible

**wrongfully**
**03** ill **06** unduly **08** unfairly, unjustly
**09** illegally, illicitly, immorally
**10** criminally, improperly
**11** dishonestly, unethically **13** against the law **14** illegitimately

**wrongly**
◇ *anagram indicator* **05** amiss, badly
**07** athwart, in error **09** by mistake
**10** mistakenly **11** erroneously, incorrectly **12** inaccurately

**wrought**
◇ *anagram indicator* **04** made **06** beaten, formed, ornate, shaped **08** hammered
**09** decorated, fashioned **10** decorative, ornamental, ornamented
**12** manufactured
• **wrought up** **05** upset **07** anxious, nervous, ruffled, worried **08** agitated, in a tizzy, troubled, unnerved
**09** disturbed, flustered, in a lather, unsettled **10** distraught **12** disconcerted

**wry**
**03** dry **05** askew, canny, cross, droll, pawky, thraw, witty **06** bitter, ironic, swerve, thrawn, uneven, warped, writhe **07** contort, crooked, mocking, pervert, twisted **08** deformed, perverse, sardonic, scoffing **09** contorted, distorted, sarcastic **10** distortion, ill-natured

**Wyoming**
**02** WY **03** Wyo

# X

**X**
02 ex 03 chi, ten 04 xray

**xenon**
02 Xe

## xenophobia
06 racism 09 racialism, xenophoby
13 ethnocentrism
15 ethnocentricity

## xenophobic
06 racist 09 parochial, racialist
12 ethnocentric 13 ethnocentrist

## Xerox®
04 copy 05 print 06 run off
09 duplicate, facsimile, photocopy,
Photostat®, reproduce

## Xmas
02 Xm 04 Noel, Yule 05 Nowel
06 Crimbo, Nowell 08 Chrissie,
Nativity, Yuletide 09 Christmas
13 Christmas-tide, Christmas-time

## X-ray, xray
01 X 08 skiagram 09 angiogram,
mammogram, pyelogram, radiogram,
sialogram, skiagraph, X-ray image
10 mammograph, radiograph, röntgen
ray 11 shadowgraph
13 encephalogram 14 encephalograph,
X-ray photograph

## xylophone
07 gamelan, marimba 08 sticcado,
sticcato 09 xylorimba
12 metallophone

# Y

**Y**
03 wye 06 yankee

**yacht**
02 MY 04 maxi, scow 06 dragon
07 cruiser 08 keelboat 10 knockabout

**yack**
03 gab, jaw, yap 04 blah, chat, rant
06 babble, confab, gossip, harp on, hot
air, jabber, tattle 07 blather, chatter,
chinwag, prattle, twattle 08 witter on,
yack-yack 11 yackety-yack

**yam**
06 camote 09 breadroot, Dioscorea
11 sweet potato

**yank**
◊ anagram indicator 03 tug 04 blow,
haul, jerk, pull, slap 05 heave
06 snatch, wrench

**yankee**
01 y

**yap**
03 cur, gab, jaw 04 bark, fool, yelp
05 mouth, nyaff, scold 06 babble,
jabber, natter, yatter 07 bumpkin,
chatter, prattle 08 witter on

**yard**
01 y 02 yd 03 Hof, ree 04 mews, quad,
reed 05 court, garth, meuse 06 garden
08 knackery 09 courtyard
10 quadrangle, rick-barton 13 barrack
square, cloister-garth

**yardstick**
05 gauge, scale 07 measure 08 standard
09 benchmark, criterion, guideline
10 comparison, touchstone

**yarn**
03 abb 04 chat, gimp, gymp, line, tale,
talk, tram, wool 05 fable, fibre, guimp,
lisle, story, twist 06 Angora, bouclé,
cotton, crewel, mohair, saxony,
strand, thread, two-ply, zephyr 07 four-
ply, genappe, textile, worsted
08 anecdote, chenille, wheeling
09 Crimplene®, fibroline, fingering,
organzine, tall story 10 tell a story,
water twist 11 fabrication

**yawn**
04 gant, gape 08 oscitate

**yawning**
04 huge, vast, wide 06 drowsy, gaping
08 wide-open 09 cavernous, oscitancy
10 oscitation

**yaws**
04 boba, buba 10 framboesia 12 button
scurvy

**yea**
see **yes**

**year**
01 a, y 02 yr 03 sun 11 twelvemonth
12 calendar year

*Years include:*

03 gap
04 leap
05 great, lunar, solar
06 fiscal, Hebrew, Julian, Sothic
07 natural, perfect, tropica
08 academic, Platonic, sidereal
09 canicular, financial
10 sabbatical
11 anomalistic, equinoctial
12 astronomical
14 ecclesiastical

*See also* **animal**
• **in the year** 01 a 02 an 04 anno
• **in this year** 02 ha 07 hoc anno
• **many years** 03 age, eon, era
04 aeon 05 calpa, decad, kalpa,
yonks 06 decade, lustre, pentad
07 century, chiliad, lustrum
08 triennia 09 centenary, decennary,
decennium, great year, millenary,
millennia, septennia, triennial,
triennium 10 centennial, millennium,
quadrennia, septennium
11 bimillenary, quadrennium,
quinquennia 12 donkey's years,
quinquennium
• **year in, year out** 09 endlessly,
regularly 10 repeatedly
11 continually 12 monotonously,
persistently, time and again 13 again
and again

**yearbook**
06 annual

**yearling**
03 hog 05 stirk

**yearly**
02 pa 05 per an 06 annual 07 per year
08 annually, per annum 09 every year,
once a year, perennial 11 perennially

**yearn**
03 yen 04 ache, earn, erne, itch, long,
pant, pine, sigh, want, wish 05 covet,
crave, fancy, green, grein 06 desire,
hanker, hunger, thirst 08 languish
09 think long

**yearning**
◊ anagram indicator 03 yen 04 wish
05 fancy 06 desire, hanker, hunger,
pining, rennet, thirst 07 craving,
longing, panting, wistful 09 hankering
11 nympholepsy

**yeast**
04 barm, bees, cell, yest 06 leaven,
torula 13 Saccharomyces

**yell**
03 cry 04 bawl, howl, roar, yeld, yelp,
yowl 05 shout, tiger, whoop 06 barren,
bellow, cry out, holler, scream, shriek,
squall, squeal 07 screech, yelloch
08 skelloch 12 unproductive

**yellow**
04 nesh, soft, weak, yolk 05 faint,
mangy, timid 06 coward, cowish,
craven, flaxen, fulvid, sallow, scared
07 chicken, citrine, fearful, fulvous,
gutless, jittery, luteous, meacock,
nithing, unmanly, wimpish, xanthic
08 clay-bank, cowardly, icterine,
timorous, unheroic, xanthous
09 dastardly, spineless, vitellary,
vitelline, weak-kneed 10 flavescent,
spiritless 11 icteritious, lily-livered,
milk-livered, sensational, sulphureous
12 faint-hearted, weak-spirited, white-
livered, xanthochroic
13 pusillanimous, yellow-bellied
14 chicken-hearted, chicken-livered

*Yellows include:*

02 or
04 buff, gold, sand
05 amber, khaki, lemon, maize,
ochre, peach, tawny, topaz
06 auburn, canary, fallow, golden,
sienna, sulfur
07 mustard, saffron, sulphur
08 daffodil, primrose
10 chartreuse, light-brown
11 straw-colour

**yellowhammer**
04 yite 08 yeldring, yeldrock, yoldring

**yelp**
03 bay, cry, yap, yip 04 bark, yawp,
yell, yowl 05 boast, nyaff, quest
06 squeal

**Yemen**
03 YAR, YEM

**yen**
01 Y 02 Yn 04 itch, lust, urge 05 thing,
yearn 06 desire, hunger 07 craving,
longing, passion 08 yearning
09 hankering

**yeoman**
04 exon 07 goodman 09 beefeater

**yes**
01 I 02 ay, OK 03 aye, yah, yea, yep
04 okay, ou ay, sure, yeah 05 jokol,
quite, right, uh-huh, yokul 06 agreed,
and how, indeed, ja wohl, rather
07 quite so 08 all right, of course, very
well 09 certainly 10 absolutely, by all
means, definitely 11 affirmative

**yes-man**
05 toady 06 lackey, minion 07 crawler
09 sycophant, toad-eater 10 bootlicker

**yet**
03 but, now, too 04 also, even 05 as
yet, by now, howbe, so far, still
06 anyway, by then, even so
07 already, besides, further, howbeit,
however, thus far 08 hitherto,
moreover, until now 09 up till now
10 all the same, for all that, heretofore,
in addition, up till then 11 furthermore,
just the same, nonetheless
12 nevertheless, up to this time 14 into
the bargain 15 notwithstanding
• **as yet** 05 so far 07 thus far, till now,
up to now 08 hitherto 13 up to this
point

**yield**
◊ anagram indicator 03 bow, net, pan,
pay, sag 04 bear, bend, cede, crop,
duck, earn, fall, give, haul, meal, vail
05 admit, agree, allow, defer, fetch,

## yielding

forgo, grant, gross, repay **06** accede, accord, afford, cave in, comply, forego, give in, give up, income, output, permit, profit, render, resign, return, reward, submit, supply **07** abandon, bring in, concede, consent, deliver, furnish, give out, give way, harvest, produce, product, provide, revenue, succumb, takings **08** abdicate, earnings, fructify, generate, give over, part with, proceeds, renounce **09** acquiesce, fructuate, give place, surrender **10** bring forth, capitulate, give ground, knock under, relinquish **11** admit defeat, go along with **12** knuckle under **14** resign yourself **15** throw in the towel

## yielding

◇ *anagram indicator* **04** easy, give, soft **05** buxom **06** facile, flabby, pliant, quaggy, spongy, supple **07** ductile, elastic, pliable, springy **08** amenable, biddable, flexible, obedient, obliging **09** compliant, complying, resilient, tractable **10** compliance, submissive **11** acquiescent, complaisant, unresisting **13** accommodating

## yob, yobbo

**03** hob, lob, oaf, oik **04** boor, calf, clod, coof, cuif, dolt, gawk, hick, hoon, jake, lout, slob, swad **05** yahoo, yobbo **06** lubber **07** bumpkin, hallion, lumpkin **08** bull-calf, loblolly **09** barbarian, lager lout, roughneck **10** clodhopper **11** chuckle-head, hobbledehoy

## yobbish

**04** rude **05** crude, gawky, gruff, rough **06** coarse, oafish, rustic, vulgar **07** boorish, doltish, ill-bred, loutish, uncouth **08** bungling, churlish, ignorant, impolite **09** unrefined **10** uneducated, unmannerly **11** clodhopping, ill-mannered, uncivilized

## yobbo

*see* yob, yobbo

## yoke

**03** bow, tie **04** bond, join, link, span, team, tool **05** hitch, thing, union, unite **06** burden, couple, halter, inspan, object, square **07** bondage, bracket, connect, enslave, harness, slavery, tyranny **08** coupling **09** servility, servitude **10** oppression **11** enslavement, subjugation

## yokel

**04** boor, hick, jake, Jock, rube **06** joskin, rustic **07** bucolic, hayseed, peasant **09** hillbilly **10** clodhopper **13** country cousin **14** country bumpkin

## you

**01** U **02** du, tu **03** Sie **04** thee, vous
• **you and me** **02** us, we

## young

**03** fry, kid, new **04** baby **05** brood, early, green, issue, jeune, small **06** babies, family, infant, junior, litter, little, recent, youthy **07** ageless, growing, progeny, teenage, youthly **08** childish, children, immature, juvenile, under age, vigorous, youthful **09** beardless, childlike, fledgling, miniature, offspring, unfledged **10** adolescent, fledgeling, little ones **11** undeveloped **13** inexperienced **15** in the first flush
*See also* **animal**

## younger

**02** yr **04** less **05** chota **06** junior **10** latter-born

## youngster

**03** boy, cub, kid, lad, tot **04** brat, girl, gyte, lass, teen, tyke, wean **05** bairn, bimbo, child, smoutsprig, sprog, youth **06** nipper, rug rat, shaver **07** hellion, protegé, subteen, tiny tot, toddler, young 'un **08** teenager, young man **10** adolescent, ankle-biter, knave-bairn, young adult, young woman **11** young person

## your

**02** yr **03** thy
• **yours** **05** thine
• **yours truly** **02** me **06** myself **09** tout à vous

## youth

**03** boy, kid, lad **04** colt, lout, lowt, page, teen, yoof **05** child, prime, teens **06** Adonis, childe, chylde, gunsel, infant, keelie, kipper, spring **07** boyhood, homeboy, juvenal, May-lord **08** calf-time, girlhood, homegirl, juvenile, springal, teenager, the young, young man **09** childhood, freshness, greenhorn, hot-rodder, lager lout, salad days, springald, stripling, youngster **10** adolescent, immaturity, recentness, young adult **11** adolescence, hobbledehoy, leaping-time, teeny-bopper, young people **12** inexperience, teenage years

## youthful

**04** spry **05** fresh, young **06** active, boyish, lively, tender, vernal **07** buoyant, girlish **08** blooming, childish, immature, juvenile, vigorous **09** sprightly, youngling, youngthly **13** inexperienced, well-preserved **14** bread-and-butter **15** in the first flush

## youthfulness

**06** vigour **08** spryness, vivacity **09** freshness **10** juvenility, liveliness **12** juvenileness **13** sprightliness, vivaciousness

## yowl

**03** bay, cry **04** bawl, howl, wail, yawl, yell, yelp **06** squall **07** screech, ululate **09** caterwaul

## ytterbium

**02** Yb

## yttrium

**01** Y

## yuck

**02** fy **03** yuk **04** itch, yech

## yucky

**04** foul **05** dirty, gross, itchy, messy, mucky **06** filthy, grotty, grungy, sickly **08** horrible **09** revolting **10** disgusting, unpleasant

## Yukon Territory

**02** YT

# Z

**Z**
03 zed, zee 04 Zulu 06 izzard

**Zambia**
01 Z 03 RNR, ZMB

**zany**
◇ *anagram indicator* 03 odd 04 daft
05 crazy, droll, funny, kooky, toady,
wacky 06 absurd 07 amusing, bizarre,
comical 08 clownish, merryman
09 eccentric, screwball, simpleton
10 ridiculous

**Zanzibar**
03 EAZ

**zap**
03 hit 04 do in, kill 05 erase, force,
shoot 06 rub out, strike 07 bump off,
correct, destroy, wipe out 08 vitality
09 finish off

**zeal**
04 fire, zest 05 gusto, study, verve
06 ardour, energy, fervor, spirit, vigour,
warmth 07 bigotry, fervour, passion
08 devotion, keenness 09 eagerness,
intensity, vehemence, zelotypia
10 commitment, dedication,
enthusiasm, fanaticism 11 earnestness
12 propagandism

**zealot**
05 bigot 07 fanatic, radical, zealant
08 militant, partisan 09 extremist
10 enthusiast 11 eager beaver

**zealous**
04 keen, warm 05 eager, fiery
06 ardent, fervid, gung-ho, stanch
07 bigoted, burning, devoted, diehard,
earnest, fervent, intense, staunch
08 militant, spirited 09 committed,
dedicated, fanatical, strenuous
10 passionate 11 impassioned, true-
devoted 12 enthusiastic, wholehearted
14 enthusiastical

**zealously**
06 keenly 07 eagerly 08 ardently
09 earnestly, fervently, instantly,
staunchly 11 fanatically
12 passionately

**zenith**
01 z 03 top 04 acme, apex, peak
06 apogee, climax, height, summit,
vertex 07 optimum 08 meridian,
pinnacle 09 high point 11 culmination
12 highest point

**zero**
01 O, z 03 nil, zip 04 blob, duck, love,
null 05 nadir, zilch, zippo 06 bottom,

cipher, cypher, naught, nought
07 nothing 08 duck's egg, goose-egg
11 diddly-squat 12 absolute zero
• **zero in on**   05 fix on 06 aim for
07 focus on, head for, level at, train on
08 centre on, direct at, home in on,
pinpoint 10 converge on
13 concentrate on

**zest**
04 husk, peel, rind, rine, skin, tang,
zeal, zing 05 crust, gusto, shell, spice,
taste 06 relish, savour, vigour
07 epicarp, flavour 08 appetite,
interest, keenness, piquancy
09 eagerness, enjoyment
10 enthusiasm, exuberance,
integument, liveliness 11 joie de vivre

**Zeus**
07 Jupiter

**zigzag**
03 yaw 04 path, tack, wind 05 curve,
snake, twist 07 crooked, meander,
sinuous, vandyke, winding
08 indented, traverse, twisting
10 meandering, serpentine 14 crinkle-
crankle

**Zimbabwe**
02 ZW 03 ZWE

**zinc**
02 Zn

**zing**
02 go 03 pep, zip 04 brio, dash, élan,
life, zest 05 oomph, punch, scorn
06 energy, spirit, vigour 07 pizzazz,
sparkle 08 vitality 09 animation,
criticize 10 enthusiasm, get-up-and-go,
liveliness 11 joie de vivre

**zip**
01 O 02 go 03 fly, pep 04 belt, dash,
élan, life, pelt, race, rush, tear, whiz,
zero, zest, zing, zoom 05 drive, flash,
gusto, hurry, oomph, punch, scoot,
shoot, speed, verve, vroom, whisk,
whizz 06 energy, spirit, vigour,
whoosh 07 nothing, pizzazz, sparkle
08 vitality 10 enthusiasm, get-up-and-
go, liveliness 13 slide fastener
*See also* **United States of America**

**zirconium**
02 Zr

**zither**
06 cither 07 cithern, cittern, kantela,
kantele 08 autoharp

**zodiac**
04 year 07 baldric 08 baldrick
09 baudricke

---

*Zodiac signs:*

---

03 Leo, Ram
04 Bull, Crab, Fish, Goat, Lion
05 Aries, Libra, Twins, Virgo
06 Archer, Cancer, Gemini, Pisces,
Scales, Taurus, Virgin
07 Balance, Scorpio
08 Aquarius, Scorpion
09 Capricorn

11 Sagittarius, Water-bearer
12 Water-carrier

**zone**
01 z 04 area, belt, zona 05 tract
06 girdle, region, sector, sphere
07 section, stratum 08 district, province
09 territory

**zoo**
06 aviary 08 aquarium 09 menagerie
10 animal park, safari park
14 zoological park

**zoology**

---

*Branches of zoology include:*

---

07 ecology, zoonomy, zootaxy
08 cetology, oecology
09 acarology, hippology,
   mammalogy, ophiology,
   therology
10 autecology, conchology,
   embryology, entomology,
   limacology, malacology,
   morphology, nematology
11 arachnology, herpetology,
   ichthyology, insectology,
   myrmecology, ornithology
12 gnotobiology, parasitology,
   protozoology, zoopathology
13 helminthology, neuroethology,
   palaeozoology, zoophysiology
14 archaeozoology
15 lepidopterology

---

*Zoologists include:*

---

03 **Pye** (John David)
04 **Beer** (Sir Gavin Rylands de), **Mayr**
   (Ernst Walter), **Owen** (Sir Richard)
05 **Fabre** (Jean Henri), **Hubel** (David
   Hunter), **Krebs** (Sir John), **Krogh**
   (August), **Kühne** (Wilhelm)
06 **Darwin** (Charles), **Flower** (Sir
   William Henry), **Frisch** (Karl von),
   **Kinsey** (Alfred), **Lorenz** (Konrad
   Zacharias), **Morris** (Desmond John),
   **Müller** (Johannes Peter), **Newton**
   (Alfred), **Pavlov** (Ivan)
07 **Agassiz** (Louis), **Audubon** (John
   James), **Dawkins** (Richard), **Durrell**
   (Gerald), **Galvani** (Luigi), **Hodgkin**
   (Sir Alan Lloyd), **Mantell** (Gideon
   Algernon), **Medawar** (Sir Peter
   Brian), **Wallace** (Alfred Russel)
08 **Hamilton** (William Donald),
   **Linnaeus** (Carolus)
09 **Aristotle**, **Schaudinn** (Fritz
   Richard), **Tinbergen** (Nikolaas)
10 **Kettlewell** (Henry Bernard David)
11 **Sherrington** (Sir Charles Scott)
12 **Wigglesworth** (Sir Vincent Brian),
   **Wynne-Edwards** (Vero Copner)

**zoom**
03 fly, zap, zip 04 belt, buzz, dash,
dive, pelt, race, rush, soar, tear, whiz
05 flash, shoot, speed, vroom, whirl
06 hurtle, streak 08 go all out

**zulu**
01 Z
• **Zulu warriors**  04 impi